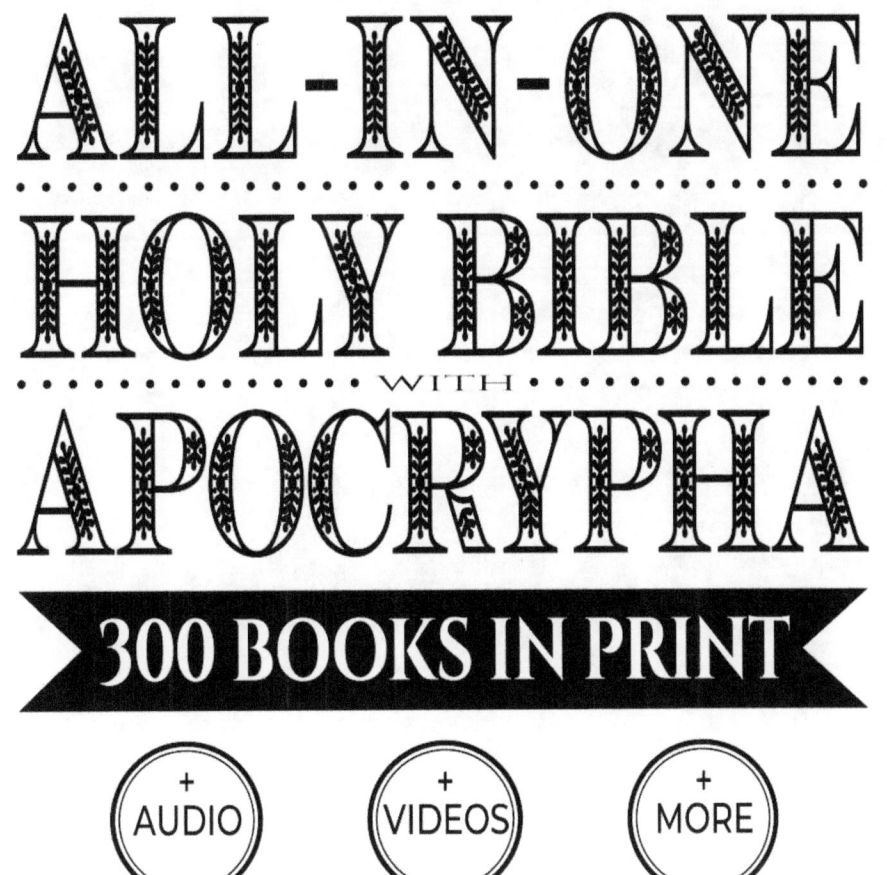

PLUS AUDIOBOOK, VIDEOS, AND THOUSANDS OF DIGITAL BOOKS

Features the complete Old and New Testaments, thousands of books of apocrypha, pseudepigrapha, and Judeo-Christian history, and much more in easy-to-read English

Dunatos Publishing in partnership with Covenant Press of the
COVENANT CHRISTIAN COALITION
www.ccc.one | www.lsvbible.com

PRESENTED TO
BY

ALL-IN-ONE HOLY BIBLE WITH APOCRYPHA

300 BOOKS IN PRINT

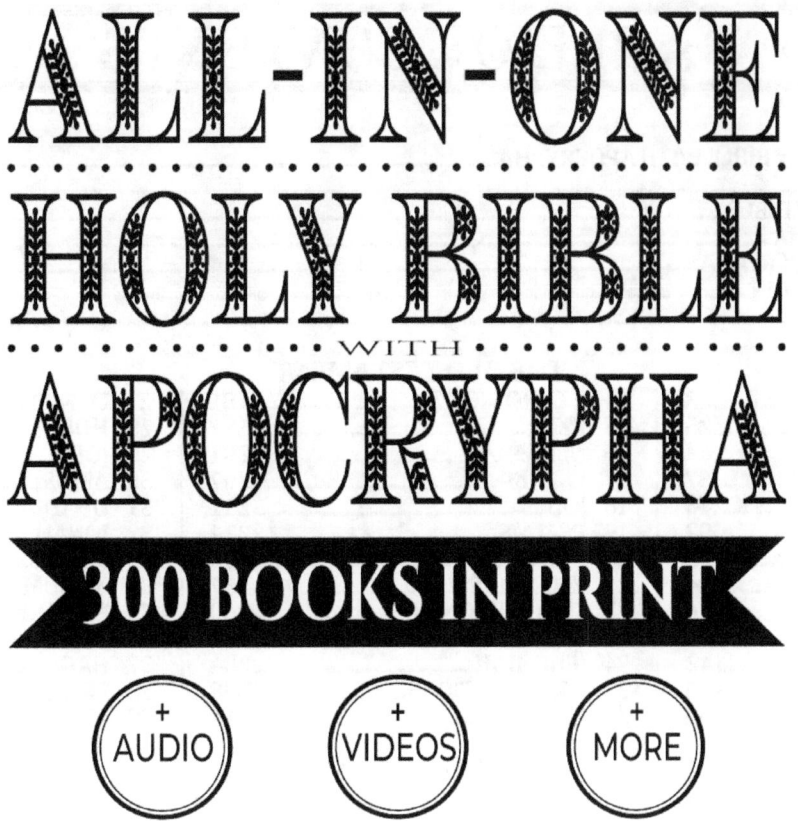

PLUS AUDIOBOOK, VIDEOS, AND THOUSANDS OF DIGITAL BOOKS

Features the complete Old and New Testaments, thousands of books of apocrypha, pseudepigrapha, and Judeo-Christian history, and much more in easy-to-read English

Dunatos Publishing in partnership with Covenant Press of the
COVENANT CHRISTIAN COALITION
www.ccc.one | www.lsvbible.com
ISBN: 978-1-954419-49-0

The Literal Standard Version of The Holy Bible is a registered copyright of Covenant Press and the Covenant Christian Coalition (© 2020) but has been subsequently released under the Creative Commons Attribution-ShareAlike license (CC BY-SA) per our desire to provide God's word freely. CC BY-SA extends *only* to the 66 books of the Holy Bible. Covenant Press requests that the text remain unaltered in the English language and that translations based on the LSV maintain the same spirit of faithfulness to the original Hebrew, Aramaic, and Greek text. Attribution of minor citations for personal or non-commercial use can be provided as simply "LSV" or "Literal Standard Version." Citations for commercial use, or distribution of the entire LSV Bible or entire book(s) of the LSV Bible, must be fully attributed and include both "Literal Standard Version (LSV)" and the name of our organization. The purpose behind the LSV is to provide readers with a modern, easy-to-read, literal, and accurate translation of the Bible that is free to read, distribute, and translate from. We pray that God will use the LSV to illuminate the hearts and minds of multitudes with the good news that His Son Jesus Christ came in the flesh, died for our sins as a substitutionary sacrifice, rose bodily from the dead, and is coming back again.

The Complete Apocrypha®, *Ancient Historia*™, and all books of the *All-In-One Holy Bible with Apocrypha*™ in print contained herein, outside of the 66 books of the Holy Bible, are registered copyrights of Covenant Press (© 2022, 2024, 2025). They may be shared, copied, and transmitted for non-commercial personal use only, up to 1,000 verses, so long as the name of the translation is included either as "Literal Standard Version" or "LSV." This permission does *not* extend to the use of any file sharing service or posting of links to the copyrighted material on non-approved websites, email servers, or through other digital means. Any commercial use up to and including 500 verses, not to constitute the entirety of any of these books or more than twenty-five percent of the work in which the LSV is cited, does not require permission from Covenant Press. Any commercial use in excess of these requirements must be approved by Covenant Press. Note that the copyrighted 2022, 2024, and 2025 editions are distinct from the non-copyrighted 2018 edition. *The Complete Apocrypha®* is a U.S. registered trademark; commercial use in any form requires permission from Covenant Press. Covenant Press actively protects its registered and unregistered marks.

TABLE OF CONTENTS

ABOUT THE ALL-IN-ONE HOLY BIBLE WITH APOCRYPHA IV
PREFACE TO THE LSV BIBLE V
INTRODUCTION TO THE LSV BIBLE VI
PREFACE TO THE APOCRYPHA VIII
INTRODUCTION TO THE APOCRYPHA IX
THE GOOD NEWS OF SALVATION X
KEY SCRIPTURES XI

THE OLD TESTAMENT

1	GENESIS	3	14	2 CHRONICLES	181	27	DANIEL	333
2	EXODUS	25	15	EZRA	197	28	HOSEA	340
3	LEVITICUS	44	16	NEHEMIAH	201	29	JOEL	344
4	NUMBERS	57	17	ESTHER	207	30	AMOS	345
5	DEUTERONOMY	76	18	JOB	211	31	OBADIAH	348
6	JOSHUA	92	19	PSALMS	221	32	JONAH	348
7	JUDGES	103	20	PROVERBS	248	33	MICAH	349
8	RUTH	114	21	ECCLESIASTES	257	34	NAHUM	351
9	1 SAMUEL	116	22	SONG OF SONGS	260	35	HABAKKUK	352
10	2 SAMUEL	130	23	ISAIAH	262	36	ZEPHANIAH	353
11	1 KINGS	142	24	JEREMIAH	284	37	HAGGAI	354
12	2 KINGS	156	25	LAMENTATIONS	308	38	ZECHARIAH	355
13	1 CHRONICLES	169	26	EZEKIEL	311	39	MALACHI	358

THE NEW TESTAMENT

40	MATTHEW	363	49	EPHESIANS	446	58	HEBREWS	456
41	MARK	377	50	PHILIPPIANS	448	59	JAMES	461
42	LUKE	386	51	COLOSSIANS	449	60	1 PETER	462
43	JOHN	401	52	1 THESSALONIANS	451	61	2 PETER	464
44	ACTS	413	53	2 THESSALONIANS	452	62	1 JOHN	465
45	ROMANS	428	54	1 TIMOTHY	453	63	2 JOHN	467
46	1 CORINTHIANS	434	55	2 TIMOTHY	454	64	3 JOHN	467
47	2 CORINTHIANS	440	56	TITUS	455	65	JUDE	467
48	GALATIANS	444	57	PHILEMON	456	66	REVELATION	468

ADDITIONS TO THE BIBLE

67 APOCRYPHAL ESTHER 479
68 APOCRYPHAL PSALMS 480
APOCRYPHAL DANIEL 482
   69 THE PRAYER OF AZARIAH AND SONG OF THE THREE HOLY CHILDREN 482
   70 SUSANNA AND THE ELDERS 483
   71 BEL AND THE DRAGON 484
72 ACTS 29 485

UNIVERSAL DEUTEROCANON

73	TOBIT	486	77	1 BARUCH	520
74	JUDITH	490	78	EPISTLE OF JEREMIAH	522
75	WISDOM	496	79	1 MACCABEES	523
76	SIRACH	503	80	2 MACCABEES	537

ORTHODOX DEUTEROCANON

81	1 ESDRAS	548	93	THE TESTAMENT OF NAPHTALI	591
82	2 ESDRAS	555	94	THE TESTAMENT OF GAD	592
83	3 MACCABEES	569	95	THE TESTAMENT OF ASHER	593
84	4 MACCABEES	573	96	THE TESTAMENT OF JOSEPH	594
85	PRAYER OF MANASSEH	580	97	THE TESTAMENT OF BENJAMIN	596

TESTAMENTS OF THE TWELVE PATRIARCHS 581
   86 THE TESTAMENT OF REUBEN 581
   87 THE TESTAMENT OF SIMEON 582
   88 THE TESTAMENT OF LEVI 583
   89 THE TESTAMENT OF JUDAH 585
   90 THE TESTAMENT OF ISSACHAR 588
   91 THE TESTAMENT OF ZEBULUN 589
   92 THE TESTAMENT OF DAN 590

98 JUBILEES 598
1 ENOCH 627
   99 THE BOOK OF THE WATCHERS 627
   100 THE BOOK OF ALLEGORIES OF ENOCH 632
   101 THE ASTRONOMICAL BOOK 639
   102 THE BOOK OF DREAM VISIONS 642
   103 THE EPISTLE OF ENOCH 645

JUDEO-CHRISTIAN LEGENDS AND PSEUDEPIGRAPHA

- 104 **2 ENOCH** 649
- 105 **3 ENOCH** 657
- 106 **BOOK OF GIANTS** 669
- 107 **LIFE OF ADAM AND EVE** 670
- 108 **BOOK OF CREATION** 674
- 109 **TESTAMENT OF ABRAHAM** 676
- 110 **TESTAMENT OF ISAAC** 681
- 111 **TESTAMENT OF JACOB** 683
- 112 **LADDER OF JACOB** 685
- 113 **JOSEPH AND ASENATH** 687
- 114 **TESTAMENT OF JOB** 695
- 115 **TESTAMENT OF MOSES** 700
- 116 **TESTAMENT OF SOLOMON** 702
- 117 **PSALMS OF SOLOMON** 710
- 118 **LIVES OF THE PROPHETS** 714
- 119 **WORDS OF GAD THE SEER** 717
- 120 **ASCENSION OF ISAIAH** 722
- 121 **2 BARUCH** 727
- 122 **3 BARUCH** 739
- 123 **4 BARUCH** 742
- 124 **APOCRYPHON OF JANNES AND JAMBRES** 745
- 125 **APOCRYPHON OF EZEKIEL** 746
- 126 **EPISTLE OF ARISTEAS** 747

NEW TESTAMENT APOCRYPHA AND THE APOSTOLIC FATHERS

- 127 **DIDACHE** 759
- **EPISTLES OF KING ABGAR AND JESUS** 761
  - 128 EPISTLE OF KING ABGAR TO JESUS 761
  - 129 EPISTLE OF JESUS TO KING ABGAR 761
- 130 **EPISTLE OF THE APOSTLES** 761
- 131 **APOSTOLIC CHURCH ORDER** 767
- 132 **EPISTLE OF BARNABAS** 768
- 133 **EPISTLE TO THE LAODICEANS** 774
- **CORRESPONDENCE OF PAUL AND SENECA** 774
  - 134 FIRST EPISTLE OF SENECA TO PAUL 774
  - 135 FIRST EPISTLE OF PAUL TO SENECA 774
  - 136 SECOND EPISTLE OF SENECA TO PAUL 775
  - 137 SECOND EPISTLE OF PAUL TO SENECA 775
  - 138 THIRD EPISTLE OF SENECA TO PAUL 775
  - 139 THIRD EPISTLE OF PAUL TO SENECA 775
  - 140 FOURTH EPISTLE OF SENECA TO PAUL 775
  - 141 FOURTH EPISTLE OF PAUL TO SENECA 775
  - 142 FIFTH EPISTLE OF SENECA TO PAUL 775
  - 143 FIFTH EPISTLE OF PAUL TO SENECA 775
  - 144 SIXTH EPISTLE OF SENECA TO PAUL 775
  - 145 SEVENTH EPISTLE OF SENECA TO PAUL 775
  - 146 EIGHTH EPISTLE OF SENECA TO PAUL 775
  - 147 SIXTH EPISTLE OF PAUL TO SENECA 776
- 148 **TRADITIONS OF MATTHIAS** 776
- 149 **EPISTLE OF LENTULUS** 776
- 150 **1 CLEMENT** 776
- 151 **2 CLEMENT** 785
- **SEVEN EPISTLES OF IGNATIUS** 788
  - 152 TO THE EPHESIANS 788
  - 153 TO THE MAGNESIANS 790
  - 154 TO THE TRALLIANS 791
  - 155 TO THE ROMANS 792
  - 156 TO THE PHILADELPHIANS 793
  - 157 TO THE SMYRNAEANS 794
  - 158 TO POLYCARP 795
- 159 **EPISTLE OF POLYCARP TO THE PHILIPPIANS** 796
- 160 **MARTYRDOM OF POLYCARP** 797
- 161 **EPISTLE OF MATHETES TO DIOGNETUS** 800
- 162 **THE SHEPHERD OF HERMAS** 802
  - VISIONS 802
  - COMMANDMENTS 807
  - SIMILITUDES 812
- 163 **ODES OF PEACE** 825
- 164 **EXPOSITION OF THE ORACLES OF THE LORD** 830
- 165 **APOLOGY OF ARISTIDES** 831
- 166 **APOLOGY FOR CHRISTIANITY** 835

APOCRYPHAL AND PSEUDEPIGRAPHAL GOSPELS

- 167 **INFANCY GOSPEL OF JAMES** 836
- 168 **INFANCY GOSPEL OF THOMAS** 839
- 169 **ARABIC INFANCY GOSPEL** 841
- 170 **GOSPEL OF THE NATIVITY OF MARY** 848
- 171 **HISTORY OF JOSEPH THE CARPENTER** 850
- 172 **LIFE OF JOHN THE BAPTIST** 853
- 173 **GOSPEL OF PETER** 858
- 174 **GOSPEL OF THOMAS** 859
- 175 **GOSPEL OF THE TWELVE HOLY APOSTLES** 864
  - 176 REVELATION OF SIMEON KEPHA 865
  - 177 REVELATION OF JAMES THE APOSTLE 866
  - 178 REVELATION OF JOHN THE LITTLE 866
- **FRAGMENTARY GOSPELS** 868
  - 179 GOSPEL OF THE HEBREWS 868
  - 180 GOSPEL OF THE NAZARENES 868
  - 181 GOSPEL OF THE EGYPTIANS 868
  - 182 THE OXYRHYNCUS GOSPEL 868
  - 183 THE UNKNOWN GOSPEL 869

THE PILATE CYCLE

- **ACTS OF PILATE** 869
  - 184 THE PASSION AND RESURRECTION 869
  - 185 THE DESCENT INTO HADES 875
  - 186 EPISTLE OF PILATE TO CLAUDIUS 878
- **NARRATIVE OF JOSEPH OF ARIMATHEA** 878
- **CORRESPONDENCE OF PILATE** 880
  - 188 EPISTLE OF HEROD TO PILATE 880
  - 189 EPISTLE OF PILATE TO HEROD 881
  - 190 ANAPHORA PILATI 881
- 191 **PARADOSIS PILATI** 881
- 192 **VINDICTA SALVATORIS** 882
- 193 **MORS PILATI** 884

APOCRYPHAL AND PSEUDEPIGRAPHAL ACTS

ACTS OF PAUL 885
   194 THE FIRST ACT 885
   195 THE SECOND ACT (ACTS OF PAUL AND THECLA) 886
   196 THE THIRD ACT 888
   197 THE FOURTH ACT 889
   198 THE FIFTH ACT 889
   199 THE SIXTH ACT 890
   200 THE SEVENTH ACT (3 CORINTHIANS) 890
   201 THE EIGHTH ACT 891
   202 THE NINTH ACT 891
   203 THE MARTYRDOM OF PAUL 891
204 ACTS OF PETER 892
   205 THE MARTYRDOM OF PETER 901
206 ACTS OF JOHN 903
   207 THE DEATH OF JOHN 912
208 ACTS OF ANDREW 913
   209 THE MARTYRDOM OF ANDREW 915
ACTS OF THOMAS 917
   210 THE FIRST ACT 917
   211 THE SECOND ACT 919
   212 THE THIRD ACT 921
   213 THE FOURTH ACT 922
   214 THE FIFTH ACT 923
   215 THE SIXTH ACT 924
   216 THE SEVENTH ACT 925
   217 THE EIGHTH ACT 926
   218 THE NINTH ACT 928
   219 THE TENTH ACT 932
   220 THE ELEVENTH ACT 934
   221 THE TWELFTH ACT 935
   222 THE THIRTEENTH ACT 936
   223 THE MARTYRDOM OF THOMAS 937
224 ACTS OF PETER AND THE TWELVE APOSTLES 939
225 ACTS OF PETER AND PAUL 940
226 ACTS OF ANDREW AND MATTHIAS 945
227 ACTS OF PETER AND ANDREW 947
228 ACTS OF BARNABAS 948
ACTS OF XANTHIPPE, POLYXENA, AND REBECCA 950
   229 ACT OF XANTHIPPE 950
   230 ACT OF POLYXENA 954
   231 ACT OF REBECCA 955
232 ACTS OF PERPETUA AND FELICITAS 957

APOCRYPHAL AND PSEUDEPIGRAPHAL APOCALYPSES

233 REVELATION OF ABRAHAM 961
234 REVELATION OF ELIJAH 966
235 REVELATION OF ZEPHANIAH 968
236 REVELATION OF PETER 970
237 REVELATION OF THOMAS 972
238 REVELATION OF STEPHEN 973
239 REVELATION OF THE VIRGIN 974

NOTABLE WRITINGS AND CREEDS OF THE EARLY CHURCH AND KEY EXTRABIBLICAL REFERENCES

THE SIBYLLINE ORACLES 978
   240 BOOK I 979
   241 BOOK II 982
   242 BOOK III 984
   243 BOOK IV 990
   244 BOOK V 992
   245 BOOK VI 996
   246 BOOK VII 996
   247 BOOK VIII 997
   248 BOOK XI 1001
   249 BOOK XII 1004
   250 BOOK XIII 1006
   251 BOOK XIV 1007
   252 ORACLE FRAGMENTS 1010
253 FIRST APOLOGY 1011
254 SECOND APOLOGY 1024
255 APOLOGY TO MARCUS AURELIUS 1027
256 DISCOURSES OF MELITO 1030

257 A PLEA FOR THE CHRISTIANS	**1033**
APOLOGY TO AUTOLYCUS	**1043**
258 BOOK I	1043
259 BOOK II	1046
260 BOOK III	1055
261 DISCOURSE CONCERNING HADES	**1061**
262 THE MURATORIAN CANON	**1063**
263 GELASIAN DECREE	**1063**
THE EARLIEST CREEDS	**1066**
264 RULE OF FAITH	1066
265 OLD ROMAN SYMBOL	1066
266 CREED OF CYPRIAN OF CARTHAGE	1067
267 DEIR BALYZEH CREED	1067
268 CREED OF ANTIOCH	1067
269 NICENE CREED	1067
270 APOSTLES' CREED	1067
271 FIRST CREED OF ANTIOCH	1067
272 SECOND CREED OF ANTIOCH	1068
273 THIRD CREED OF ANTIOCH	1068
274 FOURTH CREED OF ANTIOCH	1068
275 CREED OF THE WESTERN SERDICAN COUNCIL	1068
276 CREED OF THE EASTERN SERDICAN COUNCIL	1069
277 THE LONG-LINED CREED	1069
278 CREED OF JERUSALEM	1070
279 FIRST CREED OF SIRMIUM	1070
280 SECOND CREED OF SIRMIUM	1071
281 FOURTH CREED OF SIRMIUM	1072
282 NICENO-THRACIAN CREED	1072
283 NINTH CONFESSION OF SELEUCIA	1072
284 HOMOIAN CREED	1072
285 NICENO-CONSTANTINOPOLITAN CREED	1073
286 CREED OF THE FIRST COUNCIL OF TOLEDO	1073
287 CHALCEDONIAN CREED	1074
288 ATHANASIAN CREED	1074
KEY EXTRABIBLICAL REFERENCES	**1075**
289 FAMINE STELE	1075
290 ADMONITIONS OF IPUWER	1076
291 TEL DAN STELE	1079
292 MERNEPTAH STELE	1079
293 MESHA STELE	1079
294 KURKH MONOLITHS	1080
295 MARA BAR SERAPION ON JESUS	1080
296 PLINY THE YOUNGER ON CHRISTIANS	1080
297 TRAJAN'S REPLY TO PLINY	1081
298 TACITUS ON CHRISTIANS	1081
299 SUETONIUS ON CHRISTIANS	1081
300 PHLEGON OF TRALLES	1081
📖 301–1,000+ THE EXPANDED DIGITAL LIBRARY	**1083**

APPENDIX

ABOUT THE BIBLE	**1087**
LANGUAGES OF THE BIBLE	**1088**
BEFORE THERE WAS TIME	**1089**
CREATION	**1095**
GENESIS CHRONOLOGIES	**1101**
TIMELINE OF HISTORY	**1102**
TABLE OF NATIONS	**1104**
MAP OF ISRAEL	**1105**
JERUSALEM IN THE 1ST CENTURY	**1106**
GLOSSARY	**1107**
THE FAITH ONCE DELIVERED	**1111**
FALSE TEACHINGS REJECTED BY THE CHURCH (HERESIES)	**1112**
COVENANT OF THE CCC	**1113**
CONVICTIONS OF THE CCC	**1114**
POSITIONS OF THE CCC	**1115**

ALL-IN-ONE HOLY BIBLE WITH APOCRYPHA

In the annals of biblical scholarship, few projects rival the ambition and scope of the *All-In-One Holy Bible with Apocrypha*. This monumental collection stands as the largest assemblage of early Judeo-Christian and apocryphal texts ever compiled, encompassing 300 complete and unabridged books and ancient works in its printed form—including the Holy Bible—and thousands of additional works accessible through the Expanded Digital Library, including fresh English revisions of the ancient works of Josephus and Eusebius. Rooted in the Literal Standard Version (LSV), a modern translation celebrated for its fidelity to the original languages, the *All-In-One Holy Bible with Apocrypha* preserves the integrity of these ancient writings while making them accessible to contemporary readers. Beyond its scholarly significance, this collection has been submitted to the Guinness Book of World Records as the longest single-volume published book in the world, a distinction that underscores its unprecedented scale and the dedication of its editors. With its 300 printed books bound into a single volume, the collection is nearly two million words in print and countless millions of words when including the digital material.

The Literal Standard Version as a Foundation

At the heart of the *All-In-One Holy Bible with Apocrypha* (the 300 print books as well as the digital works) lies its reliance on the Literal Standard Version, a translation first published in 2020. The LSV is renowned for its commitment to formal equivalence, a methodology that prioritizes word-for-word accuracy over interpretive paraphrase. By adhering closely to the Hebrew, Aramaic, and Greek manuscripts (and in the case of apocryphal texts, additionally Latin, Ethiopic, Coptic, Syriac, and Slavonic), the LSV ensures that the nuances of the original texts—whether canonical or apocryphal—are faithfully conveyed. This approach is particularly significant for apocryphal writings, many of which have suffered from inconsistent translations or editorial liberties over time. The use of the LSV provides a consistent and reliable framework, enabling readers to engage with these texts in a manner that balances scholarly precision with modern readability.

Defining the Apocrypha and the Scope of the Collection

The term "apocrypha," from the Greek ἀπόκρυφος (apókruphos), meaning "hidden," refers to religious texts that were excluded from the canonical Scriptures of the Hebrew Bible and the New Testament. Composed primarily (but not exclusively) between 200 BC and AD 200, these writings encompass a diverse array of genres—narratives, wisdom literature, apocalyptic visions, and pseudepigrapha—that illuminate the religious, cultural, and historical contexts of their time. While not universally accepted as authoritative, apocryphal texts have been preserved and studied for centuries, offering scholars and readers alike a broader lens through which to view the development of Judeo-Christian thought. This all-in-one collection, based on and greatly expanding the *LSV Master Collection*, distinguishes itself through its extraordinary comprehensiveness. It includes not only familiar apocryphal books such as Tobit and the Maccabees—long valued for their historical and theological insights—but also a vast array of lesser-known works, such as the Testament of Abraham, the Apocalypse of Elijah, and the Lives of the Prophets, as well as historic gnostic books, creeds and key writings of the Early Church, and secular references that validate the biblical account. With 300 books bound in a single printed volume, including the complete text of the Holy Bible as rendered in the LSV, the collection surpasses all previous compilations in scale and ambition. The Expanded Digital Library, increasing the total to literally thousands of works, further enhances its scope, making it an unparalleled resource for exploring the full spectrum of biblical and parabiblical literature.

The Significance of Apocryphal Texts

Apocryphal texts hold immense value for biblical studies, offering insights that enrich our understanding of the canonical Scriptures. The books of the Maccabees, for example, provide a detailed chronicle of the Jewish revolt against Hellenistic rule in the second century BC, a pivotal event that shapes the historical backdrop of the New Testament. Similarly, works like the Wisdom of Solomon and Sirach explore themes of ethics, divine wisdom, and human conduct that echo the canonical wisdom literature. Even texts excluded from mainstream traditions, such as the apocalyptic Book of Enoch or the pseudepigraphal Testaments of the Twelve Patriarchs, reveal the diversity of beliefs and practices within early Jewish and Christian communities. The all-in-one collection challenges their marginalization by presenting them alongside the Holy Bible, inviting readers to reconsider their significance as historical, literary, and spiritual artifacts, while also recognizing that their canonical rejection is a legitimate and Spirit-led decision of the Church based on their (1) lack of apostolic authorship and acceptance in the Church, (2) late dates of composition in comparison to the authentic biblical texts, (3) often incompatible or even heretical doctrines, and (4) frequent use of pseudepigraphy. These works are not God-breathed Scripture, but they do inform our understanding of Scripture and the cultural and religious contexts in which Scripture was written.

A Landmark Achievement in Modern Scholarship

Translated into contemporary, easy-to-read English using highly-precise formal equivalence, the *All-In-One Holy Bible with Apocrypha* is more than a collection; it is a transformative tool for religious scholarship. By assembling the largest array of apocryphal texts ever published, it provides an unprecedented opportunity to study the interplay between canonical and non-canonical writings. Its dual-format accessibility—print for traditional engagement and digital for advanced research—ensures its utility for both personal and academic study. The searchable digital text, in particular, facilitates detailed analysis, enabling scholars to trace themes, linguistic patterns, and historical influences with ease. This collection also reflects the evolving nature of biblical studies in the digital age. While the print volume stands as a testament to the enduring power of the written word, the digital edition embraces technological advancements, broadening access and fostering new avenues of exploration. Together, they position this collection as a bridge between past and present, preserving ancient texts while making them relevant to modern audiences. The *All-In-One Holy Bible with Apocrypha* represents a landmark achievement in biblical scholarship and publishing. Its inclusion of 300 books in print—encompassing the Holy Bible and an extensive array of apocryphal texts—and thousands of works via digital access establishes it as the most comprehensive collection of its kind. Grounded in the Literal Standard Version, it offers a faithful and accessible rendition of these writings, illuminating the rich tapestry of Judeo-Christian thought beyond the traditional canon. Its submission to the Guinness Book of World Records as the largest single-volume published book in print underscores its physical and intellectual magnitude, but its true legacy lies in its potential to deepen our understanding of the biblical world. For scholars, theologians, and casual readers alike, this collection is an indispensable resource, poised to reshape the study of religious history for generations to come.

PREFACE TO THE LSV BIBLE

Many have undertaken translation of the sacred Hebrew, Aramaic, and Greek writings—known collectively as *The Holy Bible*—into English, with varying degrees of success. The word *Bible* comes from the Greek βιβλία, the plural form of βιβλίον ("book" or "scroll"). Thus, the Holy Books or Holy Scrolls are the protocanonical collection of God-breathed writings central to Judeo-Christian belief. Christians regard the original autographic manuscripts to be directly inspired by God, inerrant ("without error"), and infallible ("without fault"; i.e., incapable of fallacy). The absolute truth of God revealed therein is the basis for the Protestant/Evangelical doctrine of Sola Scriptura ("by Scripture alone")—the fundamental belief that God's word stands alone as the ultimate arbiter of religious, spiritual, and historical truth because that knowledge which is directly revealed by God to mankind is perfect and without flaw. All beliefs and theories regarding origins and religion are only true insofar as they agree with Scripture, and are false inasmuch as they disagree.

While Christians recognize the infallibility of the autographs, there is also necessary recognition that the original writings have been lost to history. What we now possess are manuscript copies or copies of copies of the originals. Some of these copies were made shortly after the originals and others were written many decades later. To complicate matters, there are distinct manuscript versions and text-types of the Old and New Testaments with minor discrepancies. For the Old Testament we must consider the distinctives between various manuscript versions such as the Masoretic Text (MT), Septuagint (LXX), Samaritan Pentateuch (SP), and Dead Sea Scrolls (DSS). And for the New Testament, translators compare the Alexandrian, Western, and Byzantine text-types.

The goal of any good translation is to produce a readable text that preserves the original autographic meaning and comes as close as possible to translating, word-for-word, manuscripts that accurately represent the original writings. It's with this goal in mind that the Literal Standard Version (LSV) was written—a modern, yet literal English translation based upon the most prolific texts: the Masoretic Text (MT) for the Old Testament and the Textus Receptus (TR) and Majority Text (M) for the New. However, in certain, specific instances other manuscript versions and text-types are used where the evidence seems incontrovertible (e.g., the LXX and DSS in the Hebrew and Aramaic; the Alexandrian in the Greek).

While many may at first feel disoriented by the cacophony of textual questions, it should be stated with utmost certainty that one of the *many* things that sets The Holy Bible apart as the unique and divinely inspired word of God is that the manuscript evidence for it is simply overwhelming. No other ancient text, religious or otherwise, has as much manuscript support as The Holy Bible. There are literally tens of thousands of papyri fragments, external citations, and complete copies of ancient manuscripts in the original languages and though there are minor variations, the texts, across all versions, are largely identical. Recent discoveries, such as the Dead Sea Scrolls, add further weight to the authenticity of the Scriptures and the accuracy of the translation-base from which we translate to English.

Distinctive features of the Literal Standard Version of The Holy Bible:

- A modern, literal, word-for-word (formal equivalence) English translation of the Holy Scriptures utilizing English word rearrangement when necessitated for readability. The LSV is the most literal translation of The Holy Bible, with significant improvement over previous literal translations, including Robert Young's excellent Young's Literal Translation.

- Preservation of verb tenses wherever possible.

- Utilization of the transliterated Tetragrammaton in the Old Testament. All uppercase LORD is used in the New Testament when a reference to YHWH is likely.

- Generally consistent approach to formal equivalence translation; most English translations use a broad set of words when translating a single Greek or Hebrew word based on context. We are striving to only use varying words when the context demands it.

- Removal of many Hebrew and Greek transliterations; remember, *transliterations* are generally not *translations*.

- Unlike most translations, justified typographic alignment consistent with the style of the original Hebrew, Aramaic, and Greek biblical autographs. The ancient caesura mark is used for easy readability of poetic literature such as the Psalms.

- Inclusion of the verses found in older English translations such as the King James Version (KJV) that are not found in many modern translations; and inclusion of the alternative LXX Genesis chronology set next to the MT. These are contained within bolded double brackets for distinction.

- Capitalized pronouns and other nounal forms when referring to God, Christ, or the Holy Spirit. References to the Messenger of the LORD are also capitalized when the subject appears to be a clear reference to God or the Messiah (as found in translations such as the NKJV).

Note: As you read, you will occasionally come across video content related to what you're reading: **scan a QR code to watch.**

INTRODUCTION TO THE LSV BIBLE

The Literal Standard Version of The Holy Bible is a major revision of Young's Literal Translation (YLT). It maintains many of Robert Young's great contributions to the field of Bible translation and research. The relationship of the LSV to Young's Literal Translation is similar to that of the English Standard Version (ESV) to the Revised Standard Version or the New King James Version (NKJV) and Modern English Version (MEV) to the KJV. Young's Literal Translation was the most literal translation of The Holy Bible ever made into English up to this point for three key reasons: 1. Preservation of verb tenses, 2. Consistent word-for-word translation, and 3. General preservation of word order.

The LSV maintains the first two rules while having more flexibility with the third, which actually results in a more literal end-result. To understand why, you must first understand the nature of language. Language is a series of written and/or spoken words that convey meaning. Words *and* meaning are inherent to the definition of language. Furthermore, words have meaning by themselves, but also when structured together. A word by itself contains meaning but has no context. As grand an undertaking as the YLT was, it suffered from overdependence on word order at the expense of readability. This begs the question: if word order is maintained, but a sentence is unreadable, is a translation truly made? Languages not only differ in alphabet, but also in word order and sentence structure. For instance, in the Latin languages "I love you" would be structured "You I love." In the Germanic family it would be the former. In more complicated sentences, the differing word order can result in unintelligible translation if the word order is maintained. Since context and sentence structure are as vital to translation as capturing the proper meaning of each word, the translators of the LSV have used these three key principles in translation:

1. Preservation of verb tenses
2. Consistent word-for-word translation
3. Preservation of word order when readability is unimpacted, but revised word order when necessary for readability.

The use of these three principles in combination with other LSV peculiarities *discussed on the next page* has resulted in the most literal translation of The Holy Bible into modern English, as well as the most distinctive.

Another translation, *why?*

There have been a slew of new English translations in the past half-century, which may cause some to wonder why the need for another. The translators agree with the premise that different translations can serve different demographics and different reading levels to maximize exposure to God's word. In this sense, the LSV is not a competitor to other excellent translations, but is complimentary. As the most literal modern English translation, the LSV is an excellent resource for deep and thoughtful Bible study and research, essentially an interlinear in terms of word-for-word translation, but arranged with English sentence structure. At the same time, some newer translations and revisions are twisting the Holy Scriptures in order to appease a postmodern, progressive, and secular readership. The LSV is a line in the sand against such perversion. Let God's word speak on its own terms. The LSV has been translated to improve upon what has come before and to ensure that God's word in English is passed along to the next generation.

The Name of God

One of the first things a reader may notice about the LSV is the use of the transliterated Tetragrammaton ("YHWH") instead of "LORD." This decision was made on the premise that God did in fact reveal His Name as YHWH to the Israelites of antiquity and many Scriptures emphasize the importance and sacredness of His Name. Replacing His actual Name with an English title does disservice to the Name and to the many Scriptures that emphasize the Name. At the same time, an impersonal title such as "LORD" may cause the reader to view an ever-present and very personal God impersonally. We want the reader to recognize that God has indeed given us His Name and we must respect His decision. Moreover, while a handful of translations use a pronounceable name, we thought it best to recognize that none of these names are universally accepted in scholarship and the original unpointed Hebrew did not provide us with the vowels. *Yahweh, Yehovah*, and others, are mere suggestions based on differing bodies of research. While "Yahweh" or something of very similar pronunciation seems the most likely, or at least as close as we may come at the present time, we have chosen to use the transliterated Tetragrammaton because it is more than likely accurate, represents the original unpointed Name, and leaves it to the reader to respectfully and thoughtfully pronounce the Name according to the research they are more personally persuaded by. At the same time, we have opted to retain many Anglicized names, including the Name of God's Son, *Jesus*. Our reasons are threefold: *first*, it is already a name and not a title; *second*, the Name is in near-universal use in the English-speaking world; and *third*, it is a close transliteration of the original Greek *Iesous*.

Justified typographic alignment, the caesura mark, and other formatting peculiarities

The LSV may be the only English translation of The Holy Bible entirely formatted with justified typographic alignment throughout. This same format is maintained in poetic literature. While some readers may prefer paragraph breaks in narrative and line breaks in poetic portions for the purpose of readability, it was the decision of the translators to mimic the style of the original Hebrew, Aramaic, and Greek autographs in presenting God's word as a continuous text block. This decision wasn't arbitrary. In formatting the text this way, the LSV sets itself against the modern push for more and more formatting within the text, in favor of simplicity. Furthermore, the modern trend even extended to differentiating the words of Christ in red letters, as if God's word should be divided in such a way. The LSV is the polar opposite, regarding the entirety of Scripture as God-breathed, with its different genres of literature resting on a level playing field.

In summary, this formatting decision was made to mimic the style of the original autographs, elevate the entirety of Scripture as God-breathed, exclude the possibility of formatting passages in a way contrary to the author's intended delivery, and finally: it was made for ease of sharing in an era where digital reading is as common as reading from paper. Whether it be a printed copy, an eBook, an app, or some other format, the LSV is the easiest translation to copy and share ever made. In addition, justified typographic alignment throughout reduces the overall length of the printed and digital editions by a substantial margin, offering considerable cost savings to publishers and distributors seeking to get God's word into as many hands as possible.

Like alignment, the LSV adopts a more ancient approach to handle quotations. Recent translations continue the trend of deeply-nested quotation marks, which many readers find confusing. The original biblical autographs contained no punctuation denoting the opening or closing of a quotation, whereas many modern translations use alternating double quotes (" ") and single quotes (' ') to nest quotes two, three, or even four levels deep. The LSV utilizes a middle approach between modern translations and the older English translations like the KJV, which didn't use quotation marks at all. The LSV uses double quotes to denote the outermost quotation within a single chapter (similar to recent translations), and a capitalized opening word of a nested quote (similar to the King James Version). This lends itself to a simpler, more elegant, and easier-to-follow text.

For ease of readability, the LSV includes the double pipe ("||") *caesura mark* to separate phrases within poetic portions of Scripture. The caesura mark was extensively used this way in ancient Greek, Latin, and English poetry. Verse numbers, periods, colons, semicolons, question marks, exclamation marks, and em dashes generally stand in for caesura marks in these passages if they are followed by a capital letter.

Finally, clarifying, interpolated words are placed in unbolded brackets ("[ ]") to make clear that they do not form part of the original Hebrew, Aramaic, and Greek text. Bolded double brackets ("**[[ ]]**") are reserved for identifying words, phrases, and passages whose inclusion in the original text is disputed.

Definite articles and prepositions

The greatest flexibility in translation can be found in regard to definite articles and prepositions. The LSV is generally more literal with definite articles than the YLT. Definite articles are often surrounded by brackets when they are missing from the original text (although not always—when the use of the definite article in English is demanded). When the definite article's usage is flexible, the LSV generally defers to the original text in its absence or inclusion.

While the LSV doesn't use a single word to consistently translate each preposition, the LSV does strive to maintain consistency in semantic range (in other words, a certain set of English prepositions are matched to each Bible language preposition, and the consistency is maintained wherever possible). This consistency results in the LSV being equally literal and readable.

Church, repentance, baptism, **and** *age*

The LSV chooses a literal translation even for "theologically loaded" words like ἐκκλησία (LSV: "assembly"), μετάνοια (LSV: "conversion"), βάπτισμα (LSV: "immersion"), and עוֹלָם and αἰών (LSV: "age" or "continuous," depending on the context). These decisions were not made to disparage the common translations and were not made lightly. They were made to give the reader the best sense of what the original words mean in English, without the use of words that are the result of centuries of theological tradition. The frequent translation of metanoia as "repentance" has been particularly troubling to scholars who emphasize the fundamental differences in their etymology and meaning, with the original Greek word referring to persuasion, conversion, or a change of mind or belief.

You can read and search the LSV Bible for free online by scanning the QR code here:

PREFACE TO THE APOCRYPHA

The *All-In-One Holy Bible with Apocrypha* includes the entire 2024 edition of *The Complete Apocrypha*®, with brand new and freshly revised translations of the Sibylline Oracles (13 books), Epistles of King Abgar and Jesus, Epistle of the Apostles, both of Justin Martyr's Apologies, Melito's Apology to Marcus Aurelius and a book of his other extant writings, Athenagoras' A Plea for the Christians, the three books of Theophilus' Apology to Autolycus, Hippolytus' Discourse on Hades, and additional Psalms found among the Dead Sea Scrolls, making the 2024 edition by far the largest single-volume collection of apocryphal and early, extra-biblical Judeo-Christian writings ever assembled (most of which originates from before AD 200). But the collection is now massively expanded, to include literally thousands of additional works, including all the contemporary-English translations of the works of Josephus and Eusebius that comprise *Ancient Historia*™, and thousands of apocryphal epistles, gospels, and Acts, as well as gnostic works, epistles, and more, including material up through the Middle Ages. This library of apocryphal works is not Scripture but is the definitive collection of very early extra-biblical writings in the Judeo-Christian tradition.

    The Complete Apocrypha®, *Ancient Historia*™, and the additional printed works of the *All-In-One Holy Bible with Apocrypha* follow many of the same translation principles and formatting practices as the *Literal Standard Version of The Holy Bible* (LSV), published in 2020. You can consult the preface and introduction to the LSV for more information about the translation and formatting style of this edition. In general, this collection is a highly literal, word-for-word (formal equivalence) translation, formatted with justified text blocks in the manner of the original manuscripts. The caesura mark is used in lieu of line breaks in poetic portions of the text, except in the Oracles which were written in hexameter and here in English have every fifth line numbered. Unlike the LSV Bible, the Tetragrammaton is not used (except in a handful of specific cases that demand its use), but where a reference to the Divine Name is likely, the all-uppercase title *LORD* can be found for distinction.

    Opinions of the apocryphal works vary, but they generally fall into either of two extremes: the first is the view that these works are inherently heretical because of their absence from the Protocanon and must be censored and condemned at all costs; the second is the view that traditional religious authorities, Jewish and Christian alike, are responsible for a massive coverup of divine revelation by excluding many of these texts from the canon, and that these works should be regarded as hidden Scripture. Both views are a sort of knee-jerk reaction to a more nuanced reality. On the one hand, we can have total confidence in the protocanonical 66 books of the Bible, and the deuterocanonical books have always held a sort of secondary or "limbo" status. The Muratorian Canon of the 2nd century demonstrates as much, and early collators and translators like Jerome fought against the full inclusion of the Deuterocanon. Even in the early years of the Reformation we see a hesitancy toward these texts—Luther did not consider these works equal to Scripture (although he did consider them worthy of study); likewise, the 1611 King James Version consigned the intertestamental Deuterocanon to an essentially appendix status, demoted with the title *Apocrypha* ("hidden" or "obscure" writings).

    There are good reasons not to consider these texts equal to Scripture: first, they are scarcely if ever quoted in the protocanonical books, and the handful of possible quotations and allusions are highly controversial. Second, the Old Testament and intertestamental apocryphal texts appear to have been written much later than the 39 protocanonical books (and often in Greek rather than Hebrew); likewise, the apocryphal New Testament texts and Apostolic Fathers are generally thought to have been written decades, even many decades, after the core 27 books of the New Testament. Third, manuscripts are scarcer and show much greater historical redaction than the protocanonical books. Fourth, a number of the supposed pseudepigraphical works show a tendency toward perfectionist soteriology (i.e., an aversion or ignorance toward the Old and New Testament system of atoning, substitutionary sacrifice and the imputation of righteousness). And fifth, some of the narratives describe very fanciful and exaggerated descriptions that generally seem out-of-sync with the biblical tradition—Abraham conversing with death personified, Jacob's sons utilizing superpowers to conquer Canaan, Solomon binding demons to build the Temple, Isaiah flying through and describing each level of Heaven, and so forth.

    On the other hand, there is little doubt the biblical writers had at least some familiarity with these texts or perhaps the oral traditions on which they were based: Jude seemingly quotes from Enoch; Paul mentions names found only in some of the apocryphal literature; Jesus celebrated the Feast of Dedication (Hanukkah), a festival established according to the accounts found in 1 and 2 Maccabees. The debate over the Apocrypha often belies simpler conclusions: some apocryphal texts are simply historical accounts (e.g., Maccabees); other apocryphal texts were not necessarily written to add to Scripture, but rather as entertaining stories—*fictions even*—in a similar vein to what contemporary Jewish and Christian writers do; still others may contain kernels of primordial oral traditions harkening back to real sayings and accounts between God and man. The apocryphal books are not to be revered as Scripture, but they do help us understand the history, traditions, and thinking at the time much of the Bible was written.

    This edition is based on and greatly expands the bestselling 2018, 2022, and 2024 editions (© 2022 and 2024), featuring, in addition to the complete Holy Bible, thousands of apocryphal and ancient Judeo-Christian books, creeds, and early secular writings that attest to the Bible's authenticity. This is the largest Apocrypha collection ever published; it includes all of the deuterocanonical books, the Apostolic Fathers, many of the key early Christian writings, the Oracles, and most known pseudepigraphal works. Introductions are included with all apocryphal works, containing useful information on narrative, context, date of composition, and theological relevance.

LANGUAGES AND DATES OF COMPOSITION: Like the Bible, which was originally composed in Hebrew, Aramaic, and Greek, the apocryphal works were also likely written in those languages. However, there are not always extant manuscripts in those languages remaining, so the translation-base, in addition to Hebrew, Aramaic, and Greek, also includes Syriac (a dialect of Aramaic), Coptic, Ethiopic, Latin, and Slavonic. Secular scholarship generally assigns most of the works in this collection to the 3rd century BC through the 3rd century AD, although some works likely underwent considerable medieval redaction, including the Testament of Solomon and the Book of Jasher. The *All-In-One Holy Bible with Apocrypha* also includes many works from the Early Middle Ages.

LONGEST AND SHORTEST BOOKS: The Book of Jasher, also called Sefer haYashar, while containing fewer chapters than 1 Enoch (91 vs. 108), is the longest book in this complete collection by far (available via access key). It is a midrash exploring biblical history in great detail, from the creation of mankind all the way to the death of Joshua and the conquest of Canaan. A contemporary translation of the Merneptah Stele (circa 1208 BC), which positively identifies Israel as existing during the period of the Judges, is the shortest work in this collection.

Compare Catholic, Orthodox, Ethiopian, and LSV collections and learn more about the different books of the Bible and apocrypha by scanning the QR code to the right:

INTRODUCTION TO THE APOCRYPHA

The Deuterocanon, more commonly known as *Apocrypha*, is the collection of writings often sandwiched between the Old and New Testaments. These books are considered by some Christian denominations to be canonical or semi-canonical. While Protestants largely reject the books as spurious or even heretical, and the Roman and Orthodox churches accept them as canonical, it may be wise to recognize that historic Christianity has held to more of a middle ground, including by Reformers such as Martin Luther and early Catholic writers like Jerome. There has always been a distinction between protocanonical books of the Bible and the deuterocanonical books—the former being near-universally attested to as God-breathed by the Church and the latter often questioned for their canonicity. At the same time, the deuterocanonical books are held in higher regard than the truly heretical Gnostic works that were written after the advent of Christianity. While it is unwise to hold the apocryphal Deuterocanon to the same God-breathed standard as the 66 books of the Bible, we hold, as Martin Luther did, to their value as possibly true and good to read, but unverified:

"Apocrypha, that are books which are not considered equal to the Holy Scriptures, but are useful and good to read."

Because certain books of the Roman Catholic Deuterocanon do not rise to the level of Holy Scripture, we must reject their canonicity, but that rejection does not exclude their profitability for reading as enlightening works that closely mirror Scripture and inform us about ancient, biblical history. They are lower than Scripture, but not spurious or inherently heretical. The Constitution of the CCC states:

> "The Bible is the final authority for all matters of life, faith, and doctrine and in its original Hebrew, Greek, and Aramaic form is completely infallible. The Bible says that the heart is deceitful above all else (Jer. 17:9) and the understanding of mankind corrupted (1 Cor. 1:20; 3:19), so God's word must inform and ultimately decide all questions of truth and doctrine. The CCC rejects the deuterocanonical books, otherwise known as Apocrypha, because the ancient Jewish canons excluded them, Jesus excludes the time period in which they were written in Luke 11:50–51, no references can be found to them in the New Testament, and early Christians like Jerome fought against their inclusion. However, the Bible mentions and makes allusion to several books that are not in the current Protestant canon such as Jasher, Enoch, and the Wars of the Lord. The true canon begins with Genesis, ends with Revelation, excludes the Apocrypha, and likely includes several of these other referenced books, although it is not clear that the current translations of Jasher, Enoch, and others are accurate translations of the original writings and therefore their authority is in dispute. For this reason, only the sixty-six books of the Protestant canon are considered authoritative and divinely inspired, although the study of Jasher, Enoch, and other books that are explicitly mentioned or referenced in Scripture is not precluded, so long as the studier recognizes their current unverifiable state."

With this basic foundation laid, we can now appreciate the deuterocanonical books for what they are: valuable historical and biblical commentaries with perhaps bits of real Scripture intertwined, but not works on which to formulate doctrine. Lastly, it should be noted that the book transliterated "Jasher" is the one most in question in this collection. It was written no later than the mid-16th century AD, but there is debate regarding whether this is in fact the original *Jasher* referenced in the Bible, or, if it is a later, spurious work.

THE GOOD NEWS OF SALVATION

In accordance with the Scriptures, Christ the Messiah, the Son of the living God, became human, incarnate in the person of Jesus of Nazareth, lived a morally perfect and sinless life, died for our sins on the Cross as a substitutionary sacrifice, was buried in a tomb, and was raised bodily from the dead on the third day. Everyone who hears and accepts this message of salvation, believing in their heart that God raised the Christ from the dead, will be pardoned of all their sins, given the gift of the Holy Spirit, and granted everlasting life in perpetual union with God. Salvation is found in Christ alone by grace alone through faith alone and not by works.

LEGALISM
*attacks the Good News by **ADDING** works and impossible standards, making the Good News bad news to be feared.*

OUTCOME:
Self-righteousness, hypocrisy, pride, mercilessness, Pharisaism, lack of assurance, and works done for the wrong reasons.

FAITH IN JESUS ALONE

OUTCOME:
Assurance, rest, eternal life, and the fruits of the Spirit: love, joy, peace, patience, kindness, goodness, faithfulness, gentleness, and self-control.

LAWLESSNESS
*attacks the Good News by **REMOVING** faith, teaching that faith in Jesus is unnecessary for salvation.*

OUTCOME:
Moral relativism, immorality, hedonism, universalism, paganism, polytheism, atheism, agnosticism, rebelliousness, and lawless living.

Questions about the Good News?
Learn more by scanning the QR code to the right:

⸎ x ⸎

KEY SCRIPTURES

God, Creator and source of all things	Gen. 1:1
Man created in the image of God	Gen. 1:27
Man given dominion over the earth	Gen. 1:28
God completes creation in six days	Gen. 1:31–2:1 (cf. Ex. 20:11)
The seventh day is the Sabbath	Gen. 2:2
Marriage, the union of one man and one woman	Gen. 2:24
Man disobeys God's single commandment and falls into sin	Gen. 3 (cf. Rom. 5:12)
God promises a human Redeemer	Gen. 3:15
God destroys the ancient, evil world with a flood	Gen. 6–7
The earth is replenished through Noah and his family	Gen. 8–10
God scatters mankind and creates different languages	Gen. 11
Abraham, the father of Israel	Gen. 12:1–4
Abraham's faith counted as righteousness	Gen. 15:6
God's covenant established with Isaac and not Ishmael	Gen. 17:18–19
Isaac's son Jacob becomes Israel	Gen. 32:27–28
God reveals that His Name is Y$_{HWH}$	Ex. 3:13–15
The Israelites escape slavery in Egypt and receive the Law	Ex. 12:31–42; 19–24
God gives the Holy Land to the Israelites	Josh. 1:1–6
God's own Son to rule all nations from Zion	Ps. 2
The coming Redeemer will die as an atoning sacrifice for our sins	Isa. 53
Jesus the Messiah, the Son of God, born of a virgin, is revealed	Mt. 1:1–2:6; Lk. 1:26–2:52
Jesus reveals that salvation is only found in Him	Jn. 14:6 (cf. Acts 4:12)
Jesus gives His life as an atoning sacrifice for our sins	Mt. 27:11–56; Jn. 18:28–37
Jesus is buried in a rich man's tomb	Mt. 27:57–61; Jn. 19:38–42
Jesus is resurrected from the dead and appears to many	Mt. 28:1–15; Lk. 24:1–49; Jn. 20
Jesus reveals the Trinity	Mt. 28:19 (cf. Lk. 3:22; Jn. 14:26; 15:26; Acts 2:33; 2 Cor. 13:14)
Jesus ascends into Heaven	Mk. 16:19; Lk. 24:50–53; Acts 1:6–9
Jesus will return to the same place He left	Acts 1:10–11 (cf. Zech. 14:1–5)
The Holy Spirit is given to the Church on Pentecost	Acts 2:1–4 (cf. Acts 1:1–5)
The Early Church is filled with zeal and love for one another	Acts 2:42–47
The Church is the mystical Body of Christ, made of many members	1 Cor. 12:12–27
The Gospel explicitly defined	1 Cor. 15:1–8
Believers will be resurrected to inherit eternal life	1 Cor. 15:50–58 (cf. Jn. 3:1–18, 3:36; 5:24)
Everyone is wicked and in need of Jesus	Rom. 3:9–20, 23; Isa. 64:6; Jas. 3:2
Salvation is through faith alone	Rom. 3:21–5:21; Gal. 2:15–5:6; Eph. 2:8–9
Believers called to live holy lives	1 Thess. 4:1–12
Believers will be taken to Heaven by Jesus	Jn. 14:1–4; 1 Thess. 4:16–18
Jesus defeats the Devil and rules all nations	Rev. 12:7–10; 19:11–16
Jesus judges all men and unbelievers are destroyed	Rev. 20:11–15
A new heaven, new earth, and New Jerusalem	Rev. 21:1–27 (cf. Isa. 65:17; 2 Pet. 3:13)
Jesus is coming soon, invitation to believe	Rev. 22

xii

THE OLD TESTAMENT
Also known as the Tanakh (תָּנָ״ךְ) and originally written in Hebrew and Aramaic

GENESIS

CHAPTER 1

¹In [the] beginning God created the heavens and the earth, ²and the earth was formless and void, and darkness [was] on the face of the deep, and the Spirit of God [was] fluttering on the face of the waters, ³and God says, "Let light be"; and light is. ⁴And God sees that the light [is] good, and God separates between the light and the darkness, ⁵and God calls the light "Day," and the darkness He has called "Night"; and there is an evening, and there is a morning—day one. ⁶And God says, "Let an expanse be in the midst of the waters, and let it be separating between waters and waters." ⁷And God makes the expanse, and it separates between the waters which [are] under the expanse, and the waters which [are] above the expanse: and it is so. ⁸And God calls the expanse "Heavens"; and there is an evening, and there is a morning—[the] second day. ⁹And God says, "Let the waters under the heavens be collected to one place, and let the dry land be seen": and it is so. ¹⁰And God calls the dry land "Earth," and the collection of the waters He has called "Seas"; and God sees that [it is] good. ¹¹And God says, "Let the earth yield tender grass, herb sowing seed, fruit-tree (whose seed [is] in itself) making fruit after its kind, on the earth": and it is so. ¹²And the earth brings forth tender grass, herb sowing seed after its kind, and tree making fruit (whose seed [is] in itself) after its kind; and God sees that [it is] good; ¹³and there is an evening, and there is a morning—[the] third day. ¹⁴And God says, "Let luminaries be in the expanse of the heavens, to make a separation between the day and the night, then they have been for signs, and for appointed times, and for days and years, ¹⁵and they have been for luminaries in the expanse of the heavens to give light on the earth": and it is so. ¹⁶And God makes the two great luminaries, the great luminary for the rule of the day, and the small luminary—and the stars—for the rule of the night; ¹⁷and God gives them in the expanse of the heavens to give light on the earth, ¹⁸and to rule over day and over night, and to make a separation between the light and the darkness; and God sees that [it is] good; ¹⁹and there is an evening, and there is a morning—[the] fourth day. ²⁰And God says, "Let the waters teem with the teeming living creature, and let [the] bird fly above the earth on the face of the expanse of the heavens." ²¹And God creates the great dragons, and every living creature that is creeping, which the waters have teemed with, after their kind, and every bird with wing, after its kind, and God sees that [it is] good. ²²And God blesses them, saying, "Be fruitful, and multiply, and fill the waters in the seas, and let the bird multiply in the earth": ²³and there is an evening, and there is a morning—[the] fifth day. ²⁴And God says, "Let the earth bring forth the living creature after its kind, livestock and creeping thing, and beast of the earth after its kind": and it is so. ²⁵And God makes the beast of the earth after its kind, and the livestock after their kind, and every creeping thing of the ground after its kind, and God sees that [it is] good. ²⁶And God says, "Let Us make man in Our image, according to Our likeness, and let them rule over [the] fish of the sea, and over [the] bird of the heavens, and over livestock, and over all the earth, and over every creeping thing that is creeping on the earth." ²⁷And God creates the man in His image; in the image of God He created him, a male and a female He created them. ²⁸And God blesses them, and God says to them, "Be fruitful, and multiply, and fill the earth, and subdue it, and rule over [the] fish of the sea, and over [the] bird of the heavens, and over every living thing that is creeping on the earth." ²⁹And God says, "Behold, I have given to you every herb sowing seed, which [is] on the face of all the earth, and every tree in which [is] the fruit of a tree sowing seed, to you it is for food; ³⁰and to every beast of the earth, and to every bird of the heavens, and to every creeping thing on the earth, in which [is] breath of life, every green herb [is] for food": and it is so. ³¹And God sees all that He has done, and behold, [it is] very good; and there is an evening, and there is a morning—the sixth day.

CHAPTER 2

¹And the heavens and the earth are completed, and all their host; ²and God completes by the seventh day His work which He has made, and ceases by the seventh day from all His work which He has made. ³And God blesses the seventh day, and sanctifies it, for in it He has ceased from all His work which God had created for making. ⁴These [are] the generations of the heavens and of the earth in their being created, in the day of YHWH God's making the earth and the heavens; ⁵and no shrub of the field is yet in the earth, and no herb of the field yet sprouts, for YHWH God has not rained on the earth, and there is not a man to serve the ground, ⁶and a mist goes up from the earth, and has watered the whole face of the ground. ⁷And YHWH God forms the man—dust from the ground, and breathes into his nostrils breath of life, and the man becomes a living creature. ⁸And YHWH God plants a garden in Eden, at the east, and He sets there the man whom He has formed; ⁹and YHWH God causes to sprout from the ground every tree desirable for appearance, and good for food, and the Tree of Life in the midst of the garden, and the Tree of the Knowledge of Good and Evil. ¹⁰And a river is going out from Eden to water the garden, and from there it is parted, and has become four chief [rivers]; ¹¹the name of the first [is] Pison, it [is] that which is surrounding the whole land of Havilah where the gold [is], ¹²and the gold of that land [is] good; the bdellium and the shoham stone [are] there; ¹³and the name of the second river [is] Gihon, it [is] that which is surrounding the whole land of Cush; ¹⁴and the name of the third river [is] Hiddekel, it [is] that which is going east of Asshur; and the fourth river is the Euphrates. ¹⁵And YHWH God takes the man, and causes him to rest in the Garden of Eden, to serve it and to keep it. ¹⁶And YHWH God lays a charge on the man, saying, "From every tree of the garden eating you eat; ¹⁷but from the Tree of the Knowledge of Good and Evil, you do not eat from it, for in the day of your eating from it—dying you die." ¹⁸And YHWH God says, "[It is] not good for the man to be alone; I make him a helper as his counterpart." ¹⁹And YHWH God forms from the ground every beast of the field, and every bird of the heavens, and brings [them] to the man, to see what he calls it; and whatever the man calls a living creature, that [is] its name. ²⁰And the man calls names to all the livestock, and to bird of the heavens, and to every beast of the field; but for man a helper has not been found as his counterpart. ²¹And YHWH God causes a deep sleep to fall on the man, and he sleeps, and He takes one of his ribs, and closes up flesh in its stead. ²²And YHWH God builds up the rib which He has taken out of the man into a woman, and brings her to the man; ²³and the man says, "This at last! Bone of my bone, and flesh of my flesh!" For this is called Woman, for this has been taken from Man; ²⁴therefore a man leaves his father and his mother, and has cleaved to his wife, and they have become one flesh. ²⁵And both of them are naked, the man and his wife, and they are not ashamed of themselves.

CHAPTER 3

¹And the serpent has been cunning above every beast of the field which YHWH God has made, and he says to the woman, "Is it true that God has said, You do not eat from every tree of the garden?" ²And the woman says to the serpent, "From the fruit of the trees of the garden we eat, ³but from the fruit of the tree which [is] in the midst of the garden, God has said, You do not eat of it, nor touch it, lest you die." ⁴And the serpent says to the woman, "Dying, you do not die, ⁵for God knows that in the day of your eating of it—your eyes have been opened, and you have been as God, knowing good and evil." ⁶And the woman sees that the tree [is] good for food, and that it [is] pleasant to the eyes, and the tree is desirable to make [one] wise, and she takes from its fruit and eats, and also gives [some] to her husband with her, and he eats; ⁷and the eyes of them both are opened, and they know that they [are] naked, and they sew fig-leaves, and

make girdles for themselves. ⁸And they hear the sound of Y𝐻WH God walking up and down in the garden at the breeze of the day, and the man and his wife hide themselves from the face of Y𝐻WH God in the midst of the trees of the garden. ⁹And Y𝐻WH God calls to the man and says to him, "Where [are] you?" ¹⁰And he says, "I have heard Your sound in the garden, and I am afraid, for I am naked, and I hide myself." ¹¹And He says, "Who has declared to you that you [are] naked? Have you eaten from the tree of which I have commanded you not to eat?" ¹²And the man says, "The woman whom You placed with me—she has given to me from the tree, and I eat." ¹³And Y𝐻WH God says to the woman, "What [is] this you have done?" And the woman says, "The serpent has caused me to forget, and I eat." ¹⁴And Y𝐻WH God says to the serpent, "Because you have done this, cursed [are] you above all the livestock, and above every beast of the field: on your belly you go, and dust you eat, [for] all days of your life; ¹⁵and I put enmity between you and the woman, and between your seed and her Seed; He bruises your head, and you bruise His heel." ¹⁶To the woman He said, "Multiplying I multiply your sorrow and your conception; you will bear children in sorrow, and your desire [is] toward your Man [[or husband]], and He [[or he]] will rule over you." ¹⁷And to the man He said, "Because you have listened to the voice of your wife, and eat from the tree concerning which I have charged you, saying, You do not eat of it, cursed [is] the ground on your account; in sorrow you eat of it [for] all days of your life, ¹⁸and it brings forth thorn and bramble for you, and you have eaten the herb of the field; ¹⁹by the sweat of your face you eat bread until your return to the ground, for you have been taken out of it, for dust you [are], and to dust you return." ²⁰And the man calls his wife's name Eve, for she has been mother of all living. ²¹And Y𝐻WH God makes coats of skin [for] the man and his wife, and clothes them. ²²And Y𝐻WH God says, "Behold, the man was as one of Us, as to the knowledge of good and evil; and now, lest he send forth his hand, and has also taken from the Tree of Life, and eaten, and lived for all time." ²³Y𝐻WH God sends him forth from the Garden of Eden to serve the ground from which he has been taken; ²⁴indeed, He casts out the man, and causes the cherubim to dwell at the east of the Garden of Eden with the sword of flame whirling around to guard the way of the Tree of Life.

CHAPTER 4

¹And the man knew his wife Eve, and she conceives and bears Cain, and says, "I have acquired a man by Y𝐻WH"; ²and she adds to bear his brother, even Abel. And Abel is feeding a flock, and Cain has been servant of the ground. ³And it comes to pass at the end of days that Cain brings from the fruit of the ground a present to Y𝐻WH; ⁴and Abel, he has brought, he also, from the female firstlings of his flock, and from their fat ones; and Y𝐻WH looks to Abel and to his present, ⁵and to Cain and to his present He has not looked; and it is very displeasing to Cain, and his countenance is fallen. ⁶And Y𝐻WH says to Cain, "Why do you have displeasure? And why has your countenance fallen? ⁷Is there not, if you do well, acceptance? And if you do not do well, sin [[or a sin-offering]] is lying at the opening, and its [[or His]] desire [is] for you, and you rule over it [[or by Him]]." ⁸And Cain says to his brother Abel, [["Let us go into the field";]] and it comes to pass in their being in the field, that Cain rises up against his brother Abel, and slays him. ⁹And Y𝐻WH says to Cain, "Where [is] your brother Abel?" And he says, "I have not known; am I my brother's keeper?" ¹⁰And He says, "What have you done? The voice of your brother's blood is crying to Me from the ground; ¹¹and now, cursed [are] you from the ground, which has opened her mouth to receive the blood of your brother from your hand; ¹²when you till the ground, it will not add to give its strength to you—a wanderer, even a trembling one, you are in the earth." ¹³And Cain says to Y𝐻WH, "My punishment is too great than to bear; ¹⁴behold, You have driven me today from off the face of the ground, and from Your face I am hid; and I have been a wanderer, even a trembling one, in the earth, and it has been—everyone finding me will slay me." ¹⁵And Y𝐻WH says to him, "Therefore, of any slayer of Cain it is required sevenfold"; and Y𝐻WH sets to Cain a token that none finding him will slay him. ¹⁶And Cain goes out from before Y𝐻WH, and dwells in the land, moving about east of Eden; ¹⁷and Cain knows his wife, and she conceives, and bears Enoch; and he is building a city, and he calls the name of the city, according to the name of his son—Enoch. ¹⁸And born to Enoch is Irad; and Irad has begotten Mehujael; and Mehujael has begotten Methusael; and Methusael has begotten Lamech. ¹⁹And Lamech takes to himself two wives, the name of the first Adah, and the name of the second Zillah. ²⁰And Adah bears Jabal, he has been father of those inhabiting tents and [having] purchased livestock; ²¹and the name of his brother [is] Jubal, he has been father of everyone handling harp and pipe. ²²And Zillah, she also bears Tubal-Cain, an instructor of every craftsman in bronze and iron; and a sister of Tubal-Cain [is] Naamah. ²³And Lamech says to his wives: "Adah and Zillah, hear my voice; Wives of Lamech, give ear [to] my saying: For I have slain a man for my wound, || Even a young man for my hurt; ²⁴For sevenfold is required for Cain, || And for Lamech seventy-sevenfold." ²⁵And Adam again knows his wife, and she bears a son, and calls his name Seth, "for God has appointed for me another seed instead of Abel": for Cain had slain him. ²⁶And to Seth, to him also a son has been born, and he calls his name Enos; then a beginning was made of preaching in the Name of Y𝐻WH.

CHAPTER 5

¹This [is] an account of the generations of Adam. In the day of God's creating man, in the likeness of God He has made him; ²a male and a female He has created them, and He blesses them, and calls their name Man, in the day of their being created. ³And Adam lives one hundred and thirty years [[or two hundred and thirty years]], and begets [a son] in his likeness, according to his image, and calls his name Seth. ⁴And the days of Adam after his begetting Seth are eight hundred years [[or seven hundred years]], and he begets sons and daughters. ⁵And all the days of Adam which he lived are nine hundred and thirty years, and he dies. ⁶And Seth lives one hundred and five years [[or two hundred and five years]], and begets Enos. ⁷And Seth lives after his begetting Enos eight hundred and seven years [[or seven hundred and seven years]], and begets sons and daughters. ⁸And all the days of Seth are nine hundred and twelve years, and he dies. ⁹And Enos lives ninety years [[or one hundred and ninety years]], and begets Cainan. ¹⁰And Enos lives after his begetting Cainan eight hundred and fifteen years [[or seven hundred and fifteen years]], and begets sons and daughters. ¹¹And all the days of Enos are nine hundred and five years, and he dies. ¹²And Cainan lives seventy years [[or one hundred and seventy years]], and begets Mahalaleel. ¹³And Cainan lives after his begetting Mahalaleel eight hundred and forty years [[or seven hundred and forty years]], and begets sons and daughters. ¹⁴And all the days of Cainan are nine hundred and ten years, and he dies. ¹⁵And Mahalaleel lives sixty-five years [[or one hundred and sixty-five years]], and begets Jared. ¹⁶And Mahalaleel lives after his begetting Jared eight hundred and thirty years [[or seven hundred and thirty years]], and begets sons and daughters. ¹⁷And all the days of Mahalaleel are eight hundred and ninety-five years, and he dies. ¹⁸And Jared lives one hundred and sixty-two years, and begets Enoch. ¹⁹And Jared lives after his begetting Enoch eight hundred years, and begets sons and daughters. ²⁰And all the days of Jared are nine hundred and sixty-two years, and he dies. ²¹And Enoch lives sixty-five years [[or one hundred and sixty-five years]], and begets Methuselah. ²²And Enoch habitually walks with God after his begetting Methuselah three hundred years [[or two hundred years]], and begets sons and daughters. ²³And all the days of Enoch are three hundred and sixty-five years. ²⁴And Enoch habitually walks with God, and he is not, for God has taken him. ²⁵And Methuselah lives one hundred and eighty-seven years, and begets Lamech. ²⁶And Methuselah lives after his begetting Lamech seven hundred and eighty-two years, and begets sons and daughters. ²⁷And all the days of Methuselah are nine hundred and sixty-nine years, and he dies. ²⁸And Lamech lives one hundred and eighty-two years [[or one hundred and

eighty-eight years]], and begets a son, ²⁹and calls his name Noah, saying, "This [one] comforts us concerning our work, and concerning the labor of our hands, because of the ground which YHWH has cursed." ³⁰And Lamech lives after his begetting Noah five hundred and ninety-five years [[or five hundred and sixty-five years]], and begets sons and daughters. ³¹And all the days of Lamech are seven hundred and seventy-seven years [[or seven hundred and fifty-three years]], and he dies. ³²And Noah is a son of five hundred years, and Noah begets Shem, Ham, and Japheth.

CHAPTER 6

¹And it comes to pass that mankind has begun to multiply on the face of the ground, and daughters have been born to them, ²and the sons of God see that they, the daughters of men, [are] beautiful, and they take women for themselves of all whom they have chosen. ³And YHWH says, "My Spirit does not strive in man for all time, for indeed, he [is] flesh, but his days have been one hundred and twenty years." ⁴The giants were in the earth in those days, and even afterward, when sons of God come in to the daughters of men, and they have borne to them those who [were] the mighty from of old, the men of renown. ⁵And YHWH sees that the wickedness of man [is] abundant in the earth, and every imagination of the thoughts of his heart [is] only evil every day; ⁶and YHWH regrets that He has made man in the earth, and He grieves Himself—to His heart. ⁷And YHWH says, "I wipe away man whom I have created from off the face of the ground, from man to beast, to creeping thing, and to bird of the heavens, for I have regretted that I have made them." ⁸And Noah found grace in the eyes of YHWH. ⁹These [are] the generations of Noah: Noah [is] a righteous man; he has been perfect among his generations; Noah has habitually walked with God. ¹⁰And Noah begets three sons: Shem, Ham, and Japheth. ¹¹And the earth is corrupt before God, and the earth is filled [with] violence. ¹²And God sees the earth, and behold, it has been corrupted, for all flesh has corrupted its way on the earth. ¹³And God said to Noah, "An end of all flesh has come before Me, for the earth has been full of violence from their presence; and behold, I am destroying them with the earth. ¹⁴Make an ark of gopher-wood for yourself; you make rooms within the Ark, and you have covered it from inside and from outside with pitch; ¹⁵and this [is] how you do it: three hundred cubits [is] the length of the Ark, fifty cubits its breadth, and thirty cubits its height; ¹⁶you make a window for the Ark, and you finish it to a cubit from above; and you put the opening of the Ark in its side; you make it [with] lower, second, and third [stories]. ¹⁷And I, behold, I am bringing in the flood of waters on the earth, to destroy from under the heavens all flesh in which [is] a living spirit; all that [is] in the earth expires. ¹⁸And I have established My covenant with you, and you have come into the Ark—you, and your sons, and your wife, and your son's wives with you; ¹⁹and of all that lives, of all flesh, you bring two from every [kind] into the Ark, to keep alive with you; they are male and female. ²⁰From the bird after its kind, and from the livestock after its kind, [and] from every creeping thing of the ground after its kind, two of every [kind] they come to you, to keep alive. ²¹And you, take for yourself from all food that is eaten; and you have gathered [it] to yourself, and it has been for you and for them for food." ²²And Noah does according to all that God has commanded him; so he has done.

CHAPTER 7

¹And YHWH says to Noah, "Come, you and all your house, into the Ark, for I have seen you [are] righteous before Me in this generation; ²you take seven pairs from all the clean beasts to yourself, a male and its female; and of the beasts which are not clean—two, a male and its female; ³also, seven pairs from [each] bird of the heavens, a male and a female, to keep alive seed on the face of all the earth; ⁴for after seven more days I am sending rain on the earth [for] forty days and forty nights, and have wiped away all the substance that I have made from off the face of the ground." ⁵And Noah does according to all that YHWH has commanded him. ⁶And Noah [is] a son of six hundred years, and the flood of waters has been on the earth. ⁷And Noah goes—and his sons, and his wife, and his sons' wives with him—into the Ark, out of the presence of the waters of the flood; ⁸from the clean beast, and from the beast that [is] not clean, and from the bird, and of everything that is creeping on the ground, ⁹they have come to Noah two by two into the Ark, a male and a female, as God has commanded Noah. ¹⁰And it comes to pass, after seven days, that waters of the flood have been on the earth. ¹¹In the six hundredth year of the life of Noah, in the second month, on the seventeenth day of the month, on this day all [the] fountains of the great deep have been broken up, and the network of the heavens has been opened, ¹²and the shower is on the earth [for] forty days and forty nights. ¹³On this very same day Noah, and Shem, and Ham, and Japheth, sons of Noah, and Noah's wife, and the three wives of his sons with them, went into the Ark— ¹⁴they, and every living creature after its kind, and every beast after its kind, and every creeping thing that is creeping on the earth after its kind, and every bird after its kind (every bird, every wing). ¹⁵And they come to Noah, into the Ark, two by two of all the flesh in which [is] a living spirit; ¹⁶and they that are coming in, male and female of all flesh, have come in as God has commanded him, and YHWH closes [it] for him. ¹⁷And the flood is on the earth [for] forty days, and the waters multiply and lift up the Ark, and it is raised up from off the earth; ¹⁸and the waters are mighty and multiply exceedingly on the earth; and the Ark goes on the face of the waters. ¹⁹And the waters have been very, very mighty on the earth, and all the high mountains are covered which [are] under the whole heavens; ²⁰the waters prevailed from above the mountains, and cover [them] fifteen cubits; ²¹and all flesh expires that is moving on the earth, among bird, and among livestock, and among beast, and among every teeming thing which is teeming on the earth, and all mankind; ²²all in whose nostrils [is] breath of a living spirit—of all that [is] in the dry land—have died. ²³And all the substance that is on the face of the ground is wiped away—from man to beast, to creeping thing, and to bird of the heavens; indeed, they are wiped away from the earth, and only Noah is left, and those who [are] with him in the Ark; ²⁴and the waters are mighty on the earth [for] one hundred and fifty days.

CHAPTER 8

¹And God remembers Noah, and every living thing, and all the livestock which [are] with him in the Ark, and God causes a wind to pass over the earth, and the waters subside, ²and the fountains of the deep and the network of the heavens are closed, and the shower is restrained from the heavens. ³And the waters return from off the earth, going on and returning; and the waters are lacking at the end of one hundred and fifty days. ⁴And the Ark rests, in the seventh month, on the seventeenth day of the month, on mountains of Ararat; ⁵and the waters have been going on and decreasing until the tenth month; in the tenth [month], on the first of the month, the heads of the mountains appeared. ⁶And it comes to pass, at the end of forty days, that Noah opens the window of the Ark which he made, ⁷and he sends forth the raven, and it goes out, going out and turning back until the drying of the waters from off the earth. ⁸And he sends forth the dove from him to see whether the waters have been lightened from off the face of the ground, ⁹and the dove has not found rest for the sole of her foot, and she turns back to him, to the Ark, for waters [are] on the face of all the earth, and he puts out his hand, and takes her, and brings her in to him, into the Ark. ¹⁰And he stays yet seven more days, and adds to send forth the dove from the Ark; ¹¹and the dove comes to him at evening, and behold, an olive leaf [is] torn off in her mouth; and Noah knows that the waters have been lightened from off the earth. ¹²And he stays yet seven more days, and sends forth the dove, and it did not add to return to him anymore. ¹³And it comes to pass in the six hundredth and first year, in the first [month], on the first of the month, the waters have been dried from off the earth; and Noah turns aside the covering of the Ark, and looks, and behold, the face of the ground has been dried. ¹⁴And in the second month, on the twenty-seventh day of the month, the earth has become dry. ¹⁵And God speaks to Noah, saying, "Go out from the Ark, you, and your wife, and your sons, and your sons' wives with you; ¹⁶every living thing that [is] with you, of all flesh, among bird, and among livestock, and among every creeping thing which is creeping on the earth, bring out with you; ¹⁷and they have teemed in the earth, and been fruitful, and have multiplied on the earth." ¹⁸And Noah goes out, and his sons, and his wife, and his sons' wives with him; ¹⁹every beast, every creeping thing, and every bird;

every creeping thing on the earth, after their families, have gone out from the Ark. ²⁰And Noah builds an altar to YHWH, and takes from every clean beast and from every clean bird, and causes burnt-offerings to ascend on the altar; ²¹and YHWH smells the refreshing fragrance, and YHWH says to His heart, "I do not continue to disfavor the ground because of man anymore, though the imagination of the heart of man [is] evil from his youth; and I do not continue to strike all living anymore, as I have done; ²²during all [the] days of the earth, seed-time and harvest, and cold and heat, and summer and winter, and day and night never cease."

CHAPTER 9

¹And God blesses Noah and his sons, and says to them, "Be fruitful, and multiply, and fill the earth; ²and your fear and your dread is on every beast of the earth, and on every bird of the heavens, on all that creeps on the ground, and on all fishes of the sea—into your hand they have been given. ³Every creeping thing that is alive, to you it is for food; as the green herb I have given to you the whole; ⁴only flesh in its life—its blood—you do not eat. ⁵And only your blood for your lives do I require; from the hand of every living thing I require it, and from the hand of man, from the hand of every man's brother I require the life of man; ⁶whoever sheds man's blood, by man is his blood shed: for in the image of God has He made man. ⁷And you, be fruitful and multiply, teem in the earth, and multiply in it." ⁸And God speaks to Noah, and to his sons with him, saying, ⁹"And I, behold, I am establishing My covenant with you, and with your seed after you, ¹⁰and with every living creature which [is] with you, among bird, among livestock, and among every beast of the earth with you, from all who are going out of the Ark—to every beast of the earth. ¹¹And I have established My covenant with you, and all flesh is not cut off anymore by waters of a flood, and there is not a flood to destroy the earth anymore." ¹²And God says, "This is a token of the covenant which I am giving between Me and you, and every living creature that [is] with you, to continuous generations; ¹³My bow I have given in the cloud, and it has been for a token of a covenant between Me and the earth; ¹⁴and it has come to pass (in My sending a cloud over the earth) that the bow has been seen in the cloud, ¹⁵and I have remembered My covenant which is between Me and you, and every living creature among all flesh, and the waters no longer become a flood to destroy all flesh; ¹⁶and the bow has been in the cloud, and I have seen it—to remember the perpetual covenant between God and every living creature among all flesh which [is] on the earth." ¹⁷And God says to Noah, "This [is] a token of the covenant which I have established between Me and all flesh that [is] on the earth." ¹⁸And the sons of Noah who are going out of the Ark are Shem, and Ham, and Japheth; and Ham is father of Canaan. ¹⁹These three [are] sons of Noah, and from these has all the earth been overspread. ²⁰And Noah remains a man of the ground, and plants a vineyard, ²¹and drinks of the wine, and is drunken, and uncovers himself in the midst of the tent. ²²And Ham, father of Canaan, sees the nakedness of his father, and declares to his two brothers outside. ²³And Shem takes—Japheth also—the garment, and they place on the shoulder of them both, and go backward, and cover the nakedness of their father; and their faces [are] backward, and their father's nakedness they have not seen. ²⁴And Noah awakens from his wine, and knows that which his young son has done to him, ²⁵and says: "Cursed [is] Canaan, || Servant of servants he is to his brothers." ²⁶And he says: "Blessed of my God YHWH [is] Shem, || And Canaan is servant to him. ²⁷God gives beauty to Japheth, || And he dwells in tents of Shem, || And Canaan is servant to him." ²⁸And Noah lives after the flood three hundred and fifty years; ²⁹and all the days of Noah are nine hundred and fifty years, and he dies.

CHAPTER 10

¹And these [are] the generations of the sons of Noah, Shem, Ham, and Japheth: and sons are born to them after the flood. ²Sons of Japheth [are] Gomer, and Magog, and Madai, and Javan, and Tubal, and Meshech, and Tiras. ³And sons of Gomer [are] Ashkenaz, and Riphath, and Togarmah. ⁴And sons of Javan [are] Elishah, and Tarshish, Kittim, and Dodanim. ⁵By these the islands of the nations have been parted in their lands, each by his tongue, by their families, in their nations. ⁶And sons of Ham [are] Cush, and Mitzraim, and Phut, and Canaan. ⁷And sons of Cush [are] Seba, and Havilah, and Sabtah, and Raamah, and Sabtechah; and sons of Raamah [are] Sheba and Dedan. ⁸And Cush has begotten Nimrod; ⁹he has begun to be a hero in the land; he has been a hero in hunting before YHWH; therefore it is said, "As Nimrod the hero [in] hunting before YHWH." ¹⁰And the first part of his kingdom is Babel, and Erech, and Accad, and Calneh, in the land of Shinar; ¹¹from that land he has gone out to Asshur, and builds Nineveh, even the broad places of the city, and Calah, ¹²and Resen, between Nineveh and Calah; it [is] the great city. ¹³And Mitzraim has begotten the Ludim, and the Anamim, and the Lehabim, and the Naphtuhim, ¹⁴and the Pathrusim, and the Casluhim (from where have come out Philistim), and the Caphtorim. ¹⁵And Canaan has begotten Sidon his firstborn, and Heth, ¹⁶and the Jebusite, and the Amorite, and the Girgashite, ¹⁷and the Hivite, and the Arkite, and the Sinite, ¹⁸and the Arvadite, and the Zemarite, and the Hamathite; and afterward the families of the Canaanite have been scattered. ¹⁹And the border of the Canaanite is from Sidon, [in] your coming toward Gerar, to Gaza; [in] your coming toward Sodom, and Gomorrah, and Admah, and Zeboim, to Lasha. ²⁰These [are] sons of Ham, by their families, by their tongues, in their lands, in their nations. ²¹As for Shem, father of all sons of Eber, the older brother of Japheth, he has also begotten. ²²Sons of Shem [are] Elam, and Asshur, and Arphaxad, and Lud, and Aram. ²³And sons of Aram [are] Uz, and Hul, and Gether, and Mash. ²⁴And Arphaxad has begotten Salah, and Salah has begotten Eber. ²⁵And two sons have been born to Eber; the name of the first [is] Peleg (for in his days the earth has been divided), and his brother's name [is] Joktan. ²⁶And Joktan has begotten Almodad, and Sheleph, and Hazarmaveth, and Jerah, ²⁷and Hadoram, and Uzal, and Diklah, ²⁸and Obal, and Abimael, and Sheba, ²⁹and Ophir, and Havilah, and Jobab; all these [are] sons of Joktan; ³⁰and their dwelling is from Mesha, [in] your coming toward Sephar, a mountain of the east. ³¹These [are] sons of Shem, by their families, by their tongues, in their lands, by their nations. ³²These [are] families of the sons of Noah, by their generations, in their nations, and by these the nations have been parted in the earth after the flood.

CHAPTER 11

¹And the whole earth is of one language, and of the same words, ²and it comes to pass, in their journeying from the east, that they find a valley in the land of Shinar and dwell there; ³and they each say to his neighbor, "Give help, let us make bricks, and burn [them] thoroughly": and the brick is to them for stone, and the bitumen has been to them for mortar. ⁴And they say, "Give help, let us build for ourselves a city and tower with its head in the heavens, and make for ourselves a name, lest we be scattered over the face of all the earth." ⁵And YHWH comes down to see the city and the tower which the sons of men have built; ⁶and YHWH says, "Behold, the people [is] one, and one language [is] to them all, and this it has dreamed of doing; and now, nothing is restrained from them of that which they have purposed to do. ⁷Give help, let us go down there and confuse their language, so that a man will not understand the language of his companion." ⁸And YHWH scatters them from there over the face of all the earth, and they cease to build the city; ⁹therefore [one] has called its name Babel, for there YHWH has confused the language of all the earth, and from there YHWH has scattered them over the face of all the earth. ¹⁰These [are] the generations of Shem: Shem [is] a son of one hundred years, and begets Arphaxad two years after the flood. ¹¹And Shem lives after his begetting Arphaxad five hundred years, and begets sons and daughters. ¹²And Arphaxad has lived thirty-five years [[or one hundred and thirty-five years]], and begets Salah. ¹³And Arphaxad lives after his begetting Salah four hundred and three years [[or four hundred and thirty years]], and begets sons and daughters. ¹⁴And Salah has lived thirty years [[or one hundred and thirty years]], and

GENESIS

begets Eber. ¹⁵And Salah lives after his begetting Eber four hundred and three years [[*or* three hundred and thirty years]], and begets sons and daughters. ¹⁶And Eber lives thirty-four years [[*or* one hundred and thirty-four years]], and begets Peleg. ¹⁷And Eber lives after his begetting Peleg four hundred and thirty years [[*or* three hundred and seventy years]], and begets sons and daughters. ¹⁸And Peleg lives thirty years [[*or* one hundred and thirty years]], and begets Reu. ¹⁹And Peleg lives after his begetting Reu two hundred and nine years, and begets sons and daughters. ²⁰And Reu lives thirty-two years [[*or* one hundred and thirty-two years]], and begets Serug. ²¹And Reu lives after his begetting Serug two hundred and seven years, and begets sons and daughters. ²²And Serug lives thirty years [[*or* one hundred and thirty years]], and begets Nahor. ²³And Serug lives after his begetting Nahor two hundred years, and begets sons and daughters. ²⁴And Nahor lives twenty-nine years [[*or* seventy-nine years]], and begets Terah. ²⁵And Nahor lives after his begetting Terah one hundred and nineteen years [[*or* one hundred and twenty-nine years]], and begets sons and daughters. ²⁶And Terah lives seventy years, and begets Abram, Nahor, and Haran. ²⁷And these [are] the generations of Terah: Terah has begotten Abram, Nahor, and Haran; and Haran has begotten Lot; ²⁸and Haran dies in the presence of Terah his father, in the land of his birth, in Ur of the Chaldees. ²⁹And Abram and Nahor take to themselves wives; the name of Abram's wife [is] Sarai, and the name of Nahor's wife [is] Milcah, daughter of Haran, father of Milcah, and father of Iscah. ³⁰And Sarai is barren—she has no child. ³¹And Terah takes his son Abram, and Lot, son of Haran, his son's son, and his daughter-in-law Sarai, wife of his son Abram, and they go out with them from Ur of the Chaldees, to go toward the land of Canaan; and they come to Haran, and dwell there. ³²And the days of Terah are two hundred and five years, and Terah dies in Haran.

CHAPTER 12

¹And YHWH says to Abram, "Go for yourself, from your land, and from your family, and from the house of your father, to the land which I show you. ²And I make you become a great nation, and bless you, and make your name great; and be a blessing. ³And I bless those blessing you, and I curse him who is cursing you, and all families of the ground have been blessed in you." ⁴And Abram goes on, as YHWH has spoken to him, and Lot goes with him, and Abram [is] a son of seventy-five years in his going out from Haran. ⁵And Abram takes his wife Sarai, and his brother's son Lot, and all their substance that they have gained, and the persons that they have obtained in Haran; and they go out to go toward the land of Canaan; and they come to the land of Canaan. ⁶And Abram passes over into the land, to the place of Shechem, to the oak of Moreh; and the Canaanite [is] then in the land. ⁷And YHWH appears to Abram and says, "To your seed I give this land"; and there he builds an altar to YHWH, who has appeared to him. ⁸And he removes from there toward a mountain at the east of Beth-El, and stretches out the tent (Beth-El at the west, and Hai at the east), and he builds an altar to YHWH there, and preaches in the Name of YHWH. ⁹And Abram journeys, going on and journeying toward the south. ¹⁰And there is a famine in the land, and Abram goes down toward Egypt to sojourn there, for the famine [is] grievous in the land; ¹¹and it comes to pass as he has drawn near to enter Egypt, that he says to his wife Sarai, "Now behold, I have known that you [are] a woman of beautiful appearance; ¹²and it has come to pass that the Egyptians see you, and they have said, This [is] his wife; and they have slain me, and you they keep alive: ¹³please say you [are] my sister, so that it is well with me because of you, and my soul has lived for your sake." ¹⁴And it comes to pass, at the entering of Abram into Egypt, that the Egyptians see the woman that she [is] exceedingly beautiful; ¹⁵and princes of Pharaoh see her, and praise her to Pharaoh, and the woman is taken [to] Pharaoh's house; ¹⁶and to Abram he has done good because of her, and he has sheep and oxen, and male donkeys, and menservants, and handmaids, and female donkeys, and camels. ¹⁷And YHWH plagues Pharaoh and his house—great plagues—for the matter of Sarai, Abram's wife. ¹⁸And Pharaoh calls for Abram and says, "What [is] this you have done to me? Why have you not declared to me that she [is] your wife? ¹⁹Why have you said, She [is] my sister, and I take her to myself for a wife? And now, behold, your wife, take and go." ²⁰And Pharaoh charges men concerning him, and they send him away, and his wife, and all that he has.

CHAPTER 13

¹And Abram goes up from Egypt (he and his wife, and all that he has, and Lot with him) toward the south; ²and Abram [is] exceedingly wealthy in livestock, in silver, and in gold. ³And he goes on his journeys from the south, even to Bethel, to the place where his tent had been at the commencement, between Bethel and Hai— ⁴to the place of the altar which he made there at the first, and there Abram preaches in the Name of YHWH. ⁵And also to Lot, who is going with Abram, there has been sheep and oxen and tents; ⁶and the land has not permitted them to dwell together, for their substance has been much, and they have not been able to dwell together; ⁷and there is a strife between those feeding Abram's livestock and those feeding Lot's livestock; and the Canaanite and the Perizzite [are] then dwelling in the land. ⁸And Abram says to Lot, "Please let there not be strife between me and you, and between my shepherds and your shepherds, for we [are] men—brothers. ⁹Is not all the land before you? Please be parted from me; if to the left, then I to the right; and if to the right, then I to the left." ¹⁰And Lot lifts up his eyes, and sees the whole circuit of the Jordan that it [is] all a watered country (before YHWH's destroying Sodom and Gomorrah, as YHWH's garden, as the land of Egypt), in your coming toward Zoar, ¹¹and Lot chooses for himself the whole circuit of the Jordan; and Lot journeys from the east, and they are parted—a man from his companion; ¹²Abram has dwelt in the land of Canaan, and Lot has dwelt in the cities of the circuit, and moves [his] tent to Sodom; ¹³and the men of Sodom [are] evil, and sinners before YHWH exceedingly. ¹⁴And YHWH said to Abram, after Lot's being parted from him, "Now lift up your eyes and look from the place where you [are], northward, and southward, and eastward, and westward; ¹⁵for the whole of the land which you are seeing, I give it to you and to your Seed for all time. ¹⁶And I have set your seed as dust of the earth, so that, if one is able to number the dust of the earth, even your seed is numbered; ¹⁷rise, go up and down through the land, to its length, and to its breadth, for to you I give it." ¹⁸And Abram moves [his] tent, and comes, and dwells among the oaks of Mamre, which [are] in Hebron, and builds there an altar to YHWH.

CHAPTER 14

¹And it comes to pass in the days of Amraphel king of Shinar, Arioch king of Ellasar, Chedorlaomer king of Elam, and Tidal king of nations, ²they have made war with Bera king of Sodom, and with Birsha king of Gomorrah, Shinab king of Admah, and Shemeber king of Zeboim, and the king of Bela, which [is] Zoar. ³All these have been joined together to the Valley of Siddim, which [is] the Salt Sea; ⁴[for] twelve years they served Chedorlaomer, and the thirteenth year they rebelled. ⁵And in the fourteenth year came Chedorlaomer, and the kings who [are] with him, and they strike the Rephaim in Ashteroth Karnaim, and the Zuzim in Ham, and the Emim in Shaveh Kiriathaim, ⁶and the Horites in their Mount Seir, to El-Paran, which [is] by the wilderness; ⁷and they turn back and come to En-Mishpat, which [is] Kadesh, and strike the whole field of the Amalekite, and also the Amorite who is dwelling in Hazezon-Tamar. ⁸And the king of Sodom goes out, and the king of Gomorrah, and the king of Admah, and the king of Zeboim, and the king of Bela, which [is] Zoar; and they set in array [for] battle with them in the Valley of Siddim, ⁹with Chedorlaomer king of Elam, and Tidal king of nations, and Amraphel king of Shinar, and Arioch king of Ellasar; four kings with the five. ¹⁰And the Valley of Siddim [is] full of bitumen-pits; and the kings of Sodom and Gomorrah flee, and fall there, and those left have fled to the mountain. ¹¹And they take the whole substance of Sodom and Gomorrah, and the whole of their food, and go away; ¹²and they take Lot, Abram's brother's son (seeing he is

GENESIS

dwelling in Sodom), and his substance, and go away. ¹³And one who is escaping comes and declares to Abram the Hebrew, and he is dwelling among the oaks of Mamre the Amorite, brother of Eshcol, and brother of Aner, and they [are] Abram's allies. ¹⁴And Abram hears that his brother has been taken captive, and he draws out his trained servants, three hundred and eighteen, and pursues to Dan. ¹⁵And he divides himself against them by night, he and his servants, and strikes them, and pursues them to Hobah, which [is] at the left of Damascus; ¹⁶and he brings back the whole of the substance, and he has also brought back his brother Lot and his substance, and also the women and the people. ¹⁷And the king of Sodom goes out to meet him (after his turning back from the striking of Chedorlaomer, and of the kings who [are] with him), to the Valley of Shaveh, which [is] the king's valley. ¹⁸And Melchizedek king of Salem has brought out bread and wine, and he [is] priest of God Most High; ¹⁹and he blesses him and says, "Blessed [is] Abram to God Most High, possessing the heavens and earth; ²⁰and blessed [is] God Most High, who has delivered your adversaries into your hand"; and he gives to him a tenth of all. ²¹And the king of Sodom says to Abram, "Give to me the persons, and take the substance to yourself," ²²and Abram says to the king of Sodom, "I have lifted up my hand to YHWH, God Most High, possessing the heavens and earth— ²³from a thread even to a shoe-strap I do not take of anything which you have, that you do not say, I have made Abram rich; ²⁴save only that which the young men have eaten, and the portion of the men who have gone with me—Aner, Eshcol, and Mamre—they take their portion."

CHAPTER 15

¹After these things the word of YHWH has been to Abram in a vision, saying, "Do not fear, Abram, I [am] a shield to you, your reward [is] exceedingly great." ²And Abram says, "Lord YHWH, what do You give to me, and I am going childless? And an acquired son in my house is Demmesek Eliezer." ³And Abram says, "Behold, to me You have not given seed, and behold, a servant will be my heir." ⁴And behold, the word of YHWH [is] to him, saying, "This [one] will not be your heir; but he who comes out from your bowels, he will be your heir"; ⁵and He brings him out outside and says, "Now look attentively toward the heavens and count the stars, if you are able to count them"; and He says to him, "Thus is your seed." ⁶And he has believed in YHWH, and He reckons it to him—righteousness. ⁷And He says to him, "I [am] YHWH who brought you out from Ur of the Chaldees, to give to you this land to possess it"; ⁸and he says, "Lord YHWH, whereby do I know that I possess it?" ⁹And He says to him, "Take for Me a heifer of three years, and a female goat of three years, and a ram of three years, and a turtle-dove, and a young bird"; ¹⁰and he takes all these to Him, and separates them in the midst, and puts each piece opposite its fellow, but the bird he has not divided; ¹¹and the ravenous birds come down on the carcasses, and Abram causes them to turn back. ¹²And the sun is about to go in, and deep sleep has fallen on Abram, and behold, a terror of great darkness is falling on him; ¹³and He says to Abram, "knowing—know that your seed is a sojourner in a land not theirs, and they have served them, and they have afflicted them four hundred years, ¹⁴and the nation also whom they serve I judge, and after this they go out with great substance; ¹⁵and you come to your fathers in peace; you are buried in a good old age; ¹⁶and the fourth generation turns back here, for the iniquity of the Amorite is not yet complete." ¹⁷And it comes to pass—the sun has gone in, and thick darkness has been and behold, a furnace of smoke, and a lamp of fire, which has passed over between those pieces. ¹⁸In that day has YHWH made with Abram a covenant, saying, "To your seed I have given this land, from the River of Egypt to the great river, the Euphrates River, ¹⁹with the Kenite, and the Kenizzite, and the Kadmonite, ²⁰and the Hittite, and the Perizzite, and the Rephaim, ²¹and the Amorite, and the Canaanite, and the Girgashite, and the Jebusite."

CHAPTER 16

¹And Sarai, Abram's wife, has not borne to him, and she has a handmaid, an Egyptian, and her name [is] Hagar; ²and Sarai says to Abram, "Now behold, YHWH has restrained me from bearing, please go in to my handmaid; perhaps I am built up from her"; and Abram listens to the voice of Sarai. ³And Sarai, Abram's wife, takes Hagar the Egyptian, her handmaid, at the end of the tenth year of Abram's dwelling in the land of Canaan, and gives her to her husband Abram—to him for a wife, ⁴and he goes in to Hagar, and she conceives, and she sees that she has conceived, and her mistress is lightly esteemed in her eyes. ⁵And Sarai says to Abram, "My violence [is] for you; I have given my handmaid into your bosom, and she sees that she has conceived, and I am lightly esteemed in her eyes; YHWH judges between me and you." ⁶And Abram says to Sarai, "Behold, your handmaid [is] in your hand, do to her that which is good in your eyes"; and Sarai afflicted her, and she flees from her presence. ⁷And the Messenger of YHWH finds her by the fountain of water in the wilderness, by the fountain in the way [to] Shur, ⁸and He says, "Hagar, Sarai's handmaid, from where have you come, and to where do you go?" And she says, "From the presence of Sarai, my mistress, I am fleeing." ⁹And the Messenger of YHWH says to her, "Return to your mistress, and humble yourself under her hands"; ¹⁰and the Messenger of YHWH says to her, "Multiplying I multiply your seed, and it is not numbered from multitude"; ¹¹and the Messenger of YHWH says to her, "Behold you [are] conceiving, and bearing a son, and have called his name Ishmael, for YHWH has listened to your affliction; ¹²and he is a wild-donkey man, his hand against everyone, and everyone's hand against him—and before the face of all his brothers he dwells." ¹³And she calls the Name of YHWH who is speaking to her, "You [are], O God, my beholder"; for she said, "Even here have I looked behind my beholder?" ¹⁴Therefore has one called the well, "The well of the Living One, my beholder"; behold, between Kadesh and Bered. ¹⁵And Hagar bears a son to Abram; and Abram calls the name of his son, whom Hagar has borne, Ishmael; ¹⁶and Abram [is] a son of eighty-six years in Hagar's bearing Ishmael to Abram.

CHAPTER 17

¹And Abram is a son of ninety-nine years, and YHWH appears to Abram, and says to him, "I [am] God Almighty, habitually walk before Me, and be perfect; ²and I give My covenant between Me and you, and multiply you very exceedingly." ³And Abram falls on his face, and God speaks with him, saying, ⁴"I—behold, My covenant [is] with you, and you have become father of a multitude of nations; ⁵and your name is no longer called Abram, but your name has been Abraham, for father of a multitude of nations have I made you; ⁶and I have made you exceedingly fruitful, and made you become nations, and kings go out from you. ⁷And I have established My covenant between Me and you, and your seed after you, throughout their generations, for a perpetual covenant, to become God to you, and to your seed after you; ⁸and I have given to you, and to your seed after you, the land of your sojournings, the whole land of Canaan, for a continuous possession, and I have become their God." ⁹And God says to Abraham, "And you keep My covenant, you and your seed after you, throughout their generations; ¹⁰this [is] My covenant which you keep between Me and you, and your seed after you: every male of you [is] to be circumcised; ¹¹and you have circumcised the flesh of your foreskin, and it has become a token of a covenant between Me and you. ¹²And a son of eight days is circumcised by you; every male throughout your generations, born in the house, or bought with money from any son of a stranger, who is not of your seed; ¹³he is certainly circumcised who [is] born in your house, or bought with your money; and My covenant has become in your flesh a perpetual covenant; ¹⁴and an uncircumcised one, a male, the flesh of whose foreskin is not circumcised, indeed, that person has been cut off from his people; My covenant he has broken." ¹⁵And God says to Abraham, "Sarai your wife—you do not call her name Sarai, for Sarah [is] her name; ¹⁶and I have blessed her, and have also given to you a son from her; and I have blessed her, and she has become nations—kings of peoples are from her." ¹⁷And Abraham falls on his face, and laughs, and says in his heart, "Is one born to the son of one hundred years? Or does Sarah—daughter of ninety years—bear?" ¹⁸And Abraham says to God, "O that Ishmael may live before You"; ¹⁹and God says, "Your wife Sarah is certainly bearing a son to you, and you have called his name Isaac, and I have established My covenant with him, for a perpetual covenant, to his seed after him. ²⁰As

for Ishmael, I have heard you; behold, I have blessed him, and made him fruitful, and multiplied him, very exceedingly; twelve princes does he beget, and I have made him become a great nation; ²¹and My covenant I establish with Isaac, whom Sarah does bear to you at this appointed time in the next year"; ²²and He finishes speaking with him, and God goes up from Abraham. ²³And Abraham takes his son Ishmael, and all those born in his house, and all those bought with his money—every male among the men of Abraham's house and circumcises the flesh of their foreskin, in this very same day, as God has spoken with him. ²⁴And Abraham [is] a son of ninety-nine years in the flesh of his foreskin being circumcised; ²⁵and his son Ishmael [is] a son of thirteen years in the flesh of his foreskin being circumcised; ²⁶in this very same day Abraham has been circumcised, and his son Ishmael; ²⁷and all the men of his house—born in the house, and bought with money from the son of a stranger—have been circumcised with him.

CHAPTER 18

¹And YHWH appears to him among the oaks of Mamre, and he is sitting at the opening of the tent, about the heat of the day; ²and he lifts up his eyes and looks, and behold, three men standing by him, and he sees, and runs to meet them from the opening of the tent, and bows himself toward the earth, ³and he says, "My Lord, if now I have found grace in Your eyes, please do not pass on from Your servant; ⁴please let a little water be accepted, and wash Your feet, and recline under the tree; ⁵and I bring a piece of bread, and support Your heart; afterward pass on, for therefore You have passed over to Your servant"; and they say, "So may you do as you have spoken." ⁶And Abraham hurries toward the tent, to Sarah, and says, "Hurry three measures of flour-meal, knead, and make cakes"; ⁷and Abraham ran to the herd, and takes a son of the herd, tender and good, and gives to the young man, and he hurries to prepare it; ⁸and he takes butter and milk, and the son of the herd which he has prepared, and sets before them; and he is standing by them under the tree, and they eat. ⁹And they say to him, "Where [is] Sarah your wife?" And he says, "Behold—in the tent"; ¹⁰and He says, "Returning I return to you, about the time of life, and behold, to Sarah your wife a son." And Sarah is listening at the opening of the tent, which is behind him; ¹¹and Abraham and Sarah [are] aged, entering into days—the way of women has ceased to be to Sarah; ¹²and Sarah laughs in her heart, saying, "After I have waxed old have I had pleasure? My lord [is] also old!" ¹³And YHWH says to Abraham, "Why [is] this? Sarah has laughed, saying, Is it really true—I bear—and I am aged? ¹⁴Is anything too wonderful for YHWH? At the appointed time I return to you, about the time of life, and Sarah has a son." ¹⁵And Sarah denies, saying, "I did not laugh"; for she has been afraid; and He says, "No, but you did laugh." ¹⁶And the men rise from there, and look on the face of Sodom, and Abraham is going with them to send them away; ¹⁷and YHWH said, "Am I concealing from Abraham that which I am doing, ¹⁸and Abraham certainly becomes a great and mighty nation, and blessed in him have been all nations of the earth? ¹⁹For I have known him, that he commands his children, and his house after him (and they have kept the way of YHWH), to do righteousness and judgment, that YHWH may bring on Abraham that which He has spoken concerning him." ²⁰And YHWH says, "The cry of Sodom and Gomorrah—because great; and their sin—because exceedingly grievous: ²¹I go down now, and see whether according to its cry which is coming to Me they have done completely—and if not—I know"; ²²and the men turn from there, and go toward Sodom; and Abraham is yet standing before YHWH. ²³And Abraham draws near and says, "Do You also consume righteous with wicked? ²⁴Perhaps there are fifty righteous in the midst of the city; do You also consume, and not bear with the place for the sake of the fifty righteous who [are] in its midst? ²⁵Far be it from You to do according to this thing, to put to death the righteous with the wicked; that it has been—as the righteous so the wicked—far be it from You; does the Judge of all the earth not do justice?" ²⁶And YHWH says, "If I find in Sodom fifty righteous in the midst of the city, then have I borne with all the place for their sake." ²⁷And Abraham answers and says, "Now behold, I have willed to speak to the Lord, and I [am] dust and ashes; ²⁸perhaps there are lacking five of the fifty righteous—do You destroy for five the whole of the city?" And He says, "I do not destroy [it], if I find there forty-five." ²⁹And he adds again to speak to Him and says, "Perhaps there are found there forty?" And He says, "I do not do [it], because of the forty." ³⁰And he says, "Please let it not be displeasing to the Lord, and I speak: perhaps there are found there thirty?" And He says, "I do not do [it], if I find there thirty." ³¹And he says, "Now behold, I have willed to speak to the Lord: perhaps there are found there twenty?" And He says, "I do not destroy [it], because of the twenty." ³²And he says, "Please let it not be displeasing to the Lord, and I speak only this time: perhaps there are found there ten?" And He says, "I do not destroy [it], because of the ten." ³³And YHWH goes on, when He has finished speaking to Abraham, and Abraham has turned back to his place.

CHAPTER 19

¹And two of the messengers come toward Sodom at evening, and Lot is sitting at the gate of Sodom, and Lot sees, and rises to meet them, and bows himself—face to the earth, ²and he says, "Now behold, my lords, please turn aside to the house of your servant, and lodge, and wash your feet—then you have risen early and gone on your way"; and they say, "No, but we lodge in the broad place." ³And he presses on them greatly, and they turn aside to him, and come into his house; and he makes a banquet for them, and has baked unleavened things; and they eat. ⁴Before they lie down, the men of the city—men of Sodom—have surrounded the house, from young even to aged, all the people from the extremity; ⁵and they call to Lot and say to him, "Where [are] the men who have come to you tonight? Bring them out to us, and we know them." ⁶And Lot goes out to them, to the opening, and the door has shut behind him, ⁷and says, "Please, my brothers, do not do evil; ⁸now behold, I have two daughters who have not known anyone; please let me bring them out to you, and do to them as [is] good in your eyes; only do nothing to these men, for therefore they have come in within the shadow of my roof." ⁹And they say, "Come near here"; they also say, "This one has come to sojourn, and he certainly judges! Now, we do evil to you more than [to] them"; and they press against the man, against Lot greatly, and come near to break the door. ¹⁰And the men put forth their hand, and bring in Lot to them, into the house, and have shut the door; ¹¹and the men who [are] at the opening of the house they have struck with blindness, from small even to great, and they weary themselves to find the opening. ¹²And the men say to Lot, "Whom have you here still? Son-in-law, your sons also, and your daughters, and all whom you have in the city, bring out from this place; ¹³for we are destroying this place, for their cry has been great [before] the face of YHWH, and YHWH does send us to destroy it." ¹⁴And Lot goes out and speaks to his sons-in-law, those taking his daughters, and says, "Rise, go out from this place, for YHWH is destroying the city"; and he is as [one] mocking in the eyes of his sons-in-law. ¹⁵And when the dawn has ascended, then the messengers press on Lot, saying, "Rise, take your wife, and your two daughters who are found present, lest you are consumed in the iniquity of the city." ¹⁶And he lingers, and the men lay hold on his hand, and on the hand of his wife, and on the hand of his two daughters, through the mercy of YHWH to him, and they bring him out, and cause him to rest outside the city. ¹⁷And it comes to pass, when he has brought them outside, that he says, "Escape for your life; do not look behind you, nor stand in all the circuit; escape to the mountain, lest you are consumed." ¹⁸And Lot says to them, "Oh not [so], my lord; ¹⁹now behold, your servant has found grace in your eyes, and you make great your kindness which you have done with me by saving my life, and I am unable to escape to the mountain, lest the evil cleave [to] me and I have died; ²⁰now behold, this city [is] near to flee there, and it [is] little; please let me escape there (is it not little?) that my soul may live." ²¹And he says to him, "Behold, I have also accepted your face for this thing, without overthrowing the city [for] which you have spoken; ²²hurry, escape there, for I am not able

to do anything until your entering there"; therefore he calls the name of the city Zoar. ²³The sun has gone out on the earth, and Lot has entered into Zoar, ²⁴and YHWH has rained on Sodom and on Gomorrah brimstone and fire from YHWH, from the heavens; ²⁵and He overthrows these cities, and all the circuit, and all the inhabitants of the cities, and that which is shooting up from the ground. ²⁶And his wife looks from behind him, and she becomes a pillar of salt! ²⁷And Abraham rises early in the morning to the place where he has stood [before] the face of YHWH, ²⁸and he looks on the face of Sodom and Gomorrah, and on all the face of the land of the circuit, and sees, and behold, the smoke of the land went up as smoke of the furnace. ²⁹And it comes to pass, in God's destroying the cities of the circuit, that God remembers Abraham, and sends Lot out of the midst of the overthrow in the overthrowing of the cities in which Lot dwelt. ³⁰And Lot goes up out of Zoar, and dwells in the mountain, and his two daughters with him, for he has been afraid of dwelling in Zoar, and he dwells in a cave, he and his two daughters. ³¹And the firstborn says to the younger, "Our father [is] old, and there is not a man in the earth to come in to us, as [is] the way of all the earth; ³²come, we cause our father to drink wine, and lie with him, and preserve a seed from our father." ³³And they cause their father to drink wine on that night; and the firstborn goes in and lies with her father, and he has not known in her lying down or in her rising up. ³⁴And it comes to pass, on the next day, that the firstborn says to the younger, "Behold, I have lain with my father last night: we also cause him to drink wine tonight, then go in, lie with him, and we preserve a seed from our father." ³⁵And they cause their father to drink wine on that night also, and the younger rises and lies with him, and he has not known in her lying down or in her rising up. ³⁶And the two daughters of Lot conceive from their father, ³⁷and the firstborn bears a son and calls his name Moab: he [is] father of Moab to this day. ³⁸As for the younger, she has also born a son and calls his name Ben-Ammi: he [is] father of the sons of Ammon to this day.

CHAPTER 20

¹And Abraham journeys from there toward the land of the south, and dwells between Kadesh and Shur, and sojourns in Gerar; ²and Abraham says concerning his wife Sarah, "She is my sister"; and Abimelech king of Gerar sends and takes Sarah. ³And God comes to Abimelech in a dream of the night and says to him, "Behold, you [are] a dead man, because of the woman whom you have taken—and she married to a husband." ⁴And Abimelech has not drawn near to her, and he says, "Lord, do you also slay a righteous nation? ⁵Has he not himself said to me, She [is] my sister! And she, even she herself, said, He [is] my brother; in the integrity of my heart, and in the innocence of my hands, I have done this." ⁶And God says to him in the dream, "Indeed, I have known that in the integrity of your heart you have done this, and I withhold you, even I, from sinning against Me, therefore I have not permitted you to come against her; ⁷and now send back the man's wife, for he [is] inspired, and he prays for you, and you live; and if you do not send back, know that dying you die, you and all that you have." ⁸And Abimelech rises early in the morning, and calls for all his servants, and speaks all these words in their ears; and the men fear exceedingly; ⁹and Abimelech calls for Abraham and says to him, "What have you done to us? And what have I sinned against you, that you have brought on me, and on my kingdom, a great sin? Works which are not done you have done with me." ¹⁰Abimelech also says to Abraham, "What have you seen that you have done this thing?" ¹¹And Abraham says, "Because I said, Surely the fear of God is not in this place, and they have slain me for the sake of my wife; ¹²and also, she is truly my sister, daughter of my father, only not daughter of my mother, and she becomes my wife; ¹³and it comes to pass, when God has caused me to wander from my father's house, that I say to her, This [is] your kindness which you do with me: at every place to where we come, say of me, He [is] my brother." ¹⁴And Abimelech takes sheep and oxen, and servants and handmaids, and gives to Abraham, and sends back his wife Sarah to him; ¹⁵and Abimelech says, "Behold, my land [is] before you, where it is good in your eyes, dwell"; ¹⁶and to Sarah he has said, "Behold, I have given one thousand pieces of silver to your brother; behold, it is to you a covering of eyes, to all who are with you"; and by all this she is reasoned with. ¹⁷And Abraham prays to God, and God heals Abimelech and his wife, and his handmaids, and they bear: ¹⁸for YHWH restraining had restrained every womb of the house of Abimelech, because of Sarah, Abraham's wife.

CHAPTER 21

¹And YHWH has looked after Sarah as He has said, and YHWH does to Sarah as He has spoken; ²and Sarah conceives, and bears a son to Abraham, to his old age, at the appointed time that God has spoken of with him; ³and Abraham calls the name of his son who is born to him, whom Sarah has borne to him—Isaac; ⁴and Abraham circumcises his son Isaac, [being] a son of eight days, as God has commanded him. ⁵And Abraham [is] a son of one hundred years in his son Isaac being born to him, ⁶and Sarah says, "God has made laughter for me; everyone who is hearing laughs for me." ⁷She also says, "Who has said to Abraham, Sarah has suckled sons, that I have born a son for his old age?" ⁸And the boy grows, and is weaned, and Abraham makes a great banquet in the day of Isaac's being weaned; ⁹and Sarah sees the son of Hagar the Egyptian, whom she has borne to Abraham, mocking, ¹⁰and she says to Abraham, "Cast out this handmaid and her son; for the son of this handmaid has no possession with my son—with Isaac." ¹¹And the thing is very wrong in the eyes of Abraham, for his son's sake; ¹²and God says to Abraham, "Let it not be wrong in your eyes because of the youth, and because of your handmaid: all that Sarah says to you—listen to her voice, for in Isaac is a seed called to you. ¹³As for the son of the handmaid also, for a nation I set him, because he [is] your seed." ¹⁴And Abraham rises early in the morning, and takes bread, and a bottle of water, and gives to Hagar (placing [it] on her shoulder), also the boy, and sends her out; and she goes on, and goes astray in the wilderness of Beer-Sheba; ¹⁵and the water is consumed from the bottle, and she places the boy under one of the shrubs. ¹⁶And she goes and sits by herself opposite [him], far off, about a bow-shot, for she said, "Do not let me look on the death of the boy"; and she sits opposite [him], and lifts up her voice, and weeps. ¹⁷And God hears the voice of the youth; and the messenger of God calls to Hagar from the heavens and says to her, "What to you, Hagar? Do not fear; for God has listened to the voice of the youth where he [is]; ¹⁸rise, lift up the youth, and lay hold on him with your hand, for I set him for a great nation." ¹⁹And God opens her eyes, and she sees a well of water, and she goes and fills the bottle [with] water, and causes the youth to drink; ²⁰and God is with the youth, and he grows, and dwells in the wilderness, and is an archer; ²¹and he dwells in the wilderness of Paran, and his mother takes for him a wife from the land of Egypt. ²²And it comes to pass at that time that Abimelech speaks—Phichol also, head of his host—to Abraham, saying, "God [is] with you in all that you are doing; ²³and now, swear to me by God here: you do not lie to me, or to my continuator, or to my successor; according to the kindness which I have done with you—do with me, and with the land in which you have sojourned." ²⁴And Abraham says, "I swear." ²⁵And Abraham reasoned with Abimelech concerning the matter of a well of water which Abimelech's servants have violently taken away, ²⁶and Abimelech says, "I have not known who has done this thing, and even you did not declare to me, and I also, I have not heard except today." ²⁷And Abraham takes sheep and oxen, and gives to Abimelech, and they make, both of them, a covenant; ²⁸and Abraham sets seven lambs of the flock by themselves. ²⁹And Abimelech says to Abraham, "What [are] they—these seven lambs which you have set by themselves?" ³⁰And he says, "For—the seven lambs you accept from my hand, so that it becomes a witness for me that I have dug this well"; ³¹therefore he has called that place "Beer-Sheba," for both of them have sworn there. ³²And they make a covenant in Beer-Sheba, and Abimelech rises—Phichol also, head of his host—and they return to the land of the Philistines; ³³and [Abraham] plants a tamarisk in Beer-Sheba, and preaches there in the Name of YHWH, the perpetual God; ³⁴and Abraham sojourns in the land of the Philistines many days.

CHAPTER 22

¹And it comes to pass after these things that God has tried Abraham and says to him, "Abraham"; and he says, "Here I [am]." ²And He says, "Now take your son, your only one, whom you have loved, even Isaac, and go for yourself to the land of Moriah, and cause him to ascend there for a burnt-offering on one of the mountains of which I speak to you." ³And Abraham rises early in the morning, and saddles his donkey, and takes two of his young men with him, and his son Isaac, and he cleaves the wood of the burnt-offering, and rises and goes to the place of which God has spoken to him. ⁴On the third day—Abraham lifts up his eyes, and sees the place from afar; ⁵and Abraham says to his young men, "Remain by yourselves here with the donkey, and I and the youth go over there and worship, and return to you." ⁶And Abraham takes the wood of the burnt-offering, and places on his son Isaac, and he takes in his hand the fire, and the knife; and they go on both of them together. ⁷And Isaac speaks to his father Abraham and says, "My father," and he says, "Here I [am], my son." And he says, "Behold, the fire and the wood, and where the lamb for a burnt-offering?" ⁸And Abraham says, "God provides for Himself the lamb for a burnt-offering, my son"; and they go on both of them together. ⁹And they come to the place of which God has spoken to him, and there Abraham builds the altar, and arranges the wood, and binds his son Isaac, and places him on the altar above the wood; ¹⁰and Abraham puts forth his hand, and takes the knife—to slaughter his son. ¹¹And the Messenger of YHWH calls to him from the heavens and says, "Abraham, Abraham"; and he says, "Here I [am]"; ¹²and He says, "Do not put forth your hand to the youth, nor do anything to him, for now I have known that you are fearing God, and have not withheld your son, your only one, from Me." ¹³And Abraham lifts up his eyes, and looks, and behold, a ram behind, seized in a thicket by its horns; and Abraham goes, and takes the ram, and causes it to ascend for a burnt-offering instead of his son; ¹⁴and Abraham calls the name of that place "YHWH-Jireh," because it is said this day in the mountain, "YHWH provides." ¹⁵And the Messenger of YHWH calls to Abraham a second time from the heavens, ¹⁶and says, "I have sworn by Myself—a declaration of YHWH—that because you have done this thing, and have not withheld your son, your only one, ¹⁷that blessing I bless you, and multiplying I multiply your seed as stars of the heavens, and as sand which [is] on the seashore; and your Seed possesses the gate of His enemies; ¹⁸and all nations of the earth have blessed themselves in your Seed, because you have listened to My voice." ¹⁹And Abraham turns back to his young men, and they rise and go together to Beer-Sheba; and Abraham dwells in Beer-Sheba. ²⁰And it comes to pass after these things that it is declared to Abraham, saying, "Behold, Milcah has borne, even she, sons to your brother Nahor: ²¹his firstborn Huz, and his brother Buz; and Kemuel father of Aram, ²²and Chesed, and Hazo, and Pildash, and Jidlaph, and Bethuel; ²³and Bethuel has begotten Rebekah"; Milcah has borne these eight to Nahor, Abraham's brother; ²⁴and his concubine, whose name [is] Reumah, she also has borne Tebah, and Gaham, and Tahash, and Maachah.

CHAPTER 23

¹And the life of Sarah is one hundred and twenty-seven years—years of the life of Sarah; ²and Sarah dies in Kirjath-Arba, which [is] Hebron, in the land of Canaan, and Abraham goes to mourn for Sarah, and to lament her. ³And Abraham rises up from the presence of his dead, and speaks to the sons of Heth, saying, ⁴"A sojourner and a settler I [am] with you; give to me a possession of a burying-place with you, and I bury my dead from before me." ⁵And the sons of Heth answer Abraham, saying to him, ⁶"Hear us, my lord; a prince of God [are] you in our midst; in the choice of our burying-places bury your dead: none of our burying-places do we withhold from you, from burying your dead." ⁷And Abraham rises and bows himself to the people of the land, to the sons of Heth, ⁸and he speaks with them, saying, "If it is your desire to bury my dead from before me, hear me, and meet for me with Ephron, son of Zoar; ⁹and he gives to me the cave of Machpelah, which he has, which [is] in the extremity of his field; for full money does he give it to me, in your midst, for a possession of a burying-place." ¹⁰And Ephron is sitting in the midst of the sons of Heth, and Ephron the Hittite answers Abraham in the ears of the sons of Heth, of all those entering the gate of his city, saying, ¹¹"No, my lord, hear me: the field I have given to you, and the cave that [is] in it, to you I have given it; before the eyes of the sons of my people I have given it to you—bury your dead." ¹²And Abraham bows himself before the people of the land, ¹³and speaks to Ephron in the ears of the people of the land, saying, "Only—if you would hear me—I have given the money of the field—accept from me, and I bury my dead there." ¹⁴And Ephron answers Abraham, saying to him, ¹⁵"My lord, hear me: the land—four hundred shekels of silver; between me and you, what [is] it? Bury your dead." ¹⁶And Abraham listens to Ephron, and Abraham weighs to Ephron the silver which he has spoken of in the ears of the sons of Heth, four hundred silver shekels, passing with the merchant. ¹⁷And established are the field of Ephron, which [is] in Machpelah, which [is] before Mamre, the field and the cave which [is] in it, and all the trees which [are] in the field, which [are] around all its border, ¹⁸to Abraham by purchase, before the eyes of the sons of Heth, among all entering the gate of his city. ¹⁹And after this Abraham has buried his wife Sarah at the cave of the field of Machpelah before Mamre (which [is] Hebron), in the land of Canaan; ²⁰and established are the field, and the cave which [is] in it, to Abraham for a possession of a burying-place, from the sons of Heth.

CHAPTER 24

¹And Abraham [is] old, he has entered into days, and YHWH has blessed Abraham in all [things]; ²and Abraham says to his servant, the eldest of his house, who is ruling over all that he has, "Please put your hand under my thigh, ³and I cause you to swear by YHWH, God of the heavens and God of the earth, that you do not take a wife for my son from the daughters of the Canaanite, in the midst of whom I am dwelling; ⁴but to my land and to my family you go, and have taken a wife for my son, for Isaac." ⁵And the servant says to him, "It may be the woman is not willing to come after me to this land; do I at all cause your son to return to the land from where you came out?" ⁶And Abraham says to him, "Take heed to yourself lest you cause my son to return there; ⁷YHWH, God of the heavens, who has taken me from the house of my father, and from the land of my birth, and who has spoken to me, and who has sworn to me, saying, To your seed I give this land, He sends His messenger before you, and you have taken a wife for my son from there; ⁸and if the woman is not willing to come after you, then you have been acquitted from this my oath: only you do not cause my son to return there." ⁹And the servant puts his hand under the thigh of Abraham his lord, and swears to him concerning this matter. ¹⁰And the servant takes ten camels of the camels of his lord and goes, also of all the goods of his lord in his hand, and he rises, and goes to Aram-Naharaim, to the city of Nahor; ¹¹and he causes the camels to kneel at the outside of the city, at the well of water, at evening, at the time of the coming out of the women who draw water. ¹²And he says, "YHWH, God of my lord Abraham, please cause to meet before me this day—(and do kindness with my lord Abraham; ¹³behold, I am standing by the fountain of water, and daughters of the men of the city are coming out to draw water; ¹⁴and it has been, the young person to whom I say, Please incline your pitcher and I drink, and she has said, Drink, and I also water your camels)—her [whom] You have decided for Your servant, for Isaac; and by it I know that You have done kindness with my lord." ¹⁵And it comes to pass, before he has finished speaking, that behold, Rebekah (who was born to Bethuel, son of Milcah, wife of Nahor, brother of Abraham) is coming out, and her pitcher on her shoulder; ¹⁶and the young person [is] of very good appearance, a virgin, and a man has not known her; and she goes down to the fountain, and fills her pitcher, and comes up. ¹⁷And the servant runs to meet her and says, "Please let me swallow a little water from your pitcher"; ¹⁸and she says, "Drink, my lord"; and she hurries, and lets down her

pitcher on her hand, and gives him drink. ¹⁹And she finishes giving him drink and says, "Also for your camels I draw until they have finished drinking"; ²⁰and she hurries, and empties her pitcher into the drinking-trough, and runs again to the well to draw, and draws for all his camels. ²¹And the man, wondering at her, remains silent, to know whether YHWH has made his way prosperous or not. ²²And it comes to pass, when the camels have finished drinking, that the man takes a golden ring (whose weight [is] a bekah), and two bracelets for her hands (whose weight [is] ten [bekahs] of gold), ²³and says, "Whose daughter [are] you? Please declare to me, is the house of your father a place for us to lodge in?" ²⁴And she says to him, "I [am] daughter of Bethuel, son of Milcah, whom she has borne to Nahor." ²⁵She also says to him, "Both straw and provender [are] abundant with us, also a place to lodge in." ²⁶And the man bows, and pays respect to YHWH, ²⁷and says, "Blessed [is] YHWH, God of my lord Abraham, who has not left off His kindness and His truth with my lord—I [being] in the way, YHWH has led me to the house of my lord's brothers." ²⁸And the young person runs, and declares to the house of her mother according to these words. ²⁹And Rebekah has a brother, and his name [is] Laban, and Laban runs to the man who [is] outside, to the fountain; ³⁰indeed, it comes to pass, when he sees the ring, and the bracelets on the hands of his sister, and when he hears the words of his sister Rebekah, saying, "Thus has the man spoken to me," that he comes to the man, and behold, he is standing by the camels by the fountain. ³¹And he says, "Come in, O blessed one of YHWH! Why do you stand outside—and I have prepared the house and place for the camels?" ³²And he brings in the man into the house, and looses the camels, and gives straw and provender for the camels, and water to wash his feet, and the feet of the men who [are] with him: ³³and sets before him to eat; but he says, "I do not eat until I have spoken my word"; and he says, "Speak." ³⁴And he says, "I [am] Abraham's servant; ³⁵and YHWH has blessed my lord exceedingly, and he is great; and He gives to him flock, and herd, and silver, and gold, and menservants, and maidservants, and camels, and donkeys; ³⁶and Sarah, my lord's wife, bears a son to my lord, after she has been aged, and he gives to him all that he has. ³⁷And my lord causes me to swear, saying, You do not take a wife to my son from the daughters of the Canaanite, in whose land I am dwelling. ³⁸If not—to the house of my father you go, and to my family, and you have taken a wife for my son. ³⁹And I say to my lord, It may be the woman does not come after me; ⁴⁰and he says to me, YHWH, before whom I have habitually walked, sends His messenger with you, and has prospered your way, and you have taken a wife for my son from my family, and from the house of my father; ⁴¹then you are acquitted from my oath, when you come to my family; and if they do not give [one] to you, then you have been acquitted from my oath. ⁴²And I come to the fountain today, and I say, YHWH, God of my lord Abraham, now if You are making prosperous my way in which I am going— ⁴³(behold, I am standing by the fountain of water), then the virgin is coming out to draw, and I have said to her, Please let me drink a little water from your pitcher, ⁴⁴and she has said to me, Both drink, and I also draw for your camels—she is the woman whom YHWH has decided for my lord's son. ⁴⁵Before I finish speaking to my heart, then behold, Rebekah is coming out, and her pitcher [is] on her shoulder, and she goes down to the fountain and draws; and I say to her, Please let me drink, ⁴⁶and she hurries and lets down her pitcher from off her and says, Drink, and I also water your camels; and I drink, and she has also watered the camels. ⁴⁷And I ask her, and say, Whose daughter [are] you? And she says, Daughter of Bethuel, son of Nahor, whom Milcah has borne to him, and I put the ring on her nose, and the bracelets on her hands, ⁴⁸and I bow, and pay respect before YHWH, and I bless YHWH, God of my lord Abraham, who has led me in the true way to receive the daughter of my lord's brother for his son. ⁴⁹And now, if you are dealing kindly and truly with my lord, declare to me; and if not, declare to me; and I turn to the right or to the left." ⁵⁰And Laban answers—Bethuel also—and they say, "The thing has gone out from YHWH; we are not able to speak to you bad or good; ⁵¹behold, Rebekah [is] before you, take and go, and she is a wife to your lord's son, as YHWH has spoken." ⁵²And it comes to pass, when the servant of Abraham has heard their words, that he bows himself toward the earth before YHWH; ⁵³and the servant takes out vessels of silver, and vessels of gold, and garments, and gives to Rebekah; precious things also he has given to her brother and to her mother. ⁵⁴And they eat and drink, he and the men who [are] with him, and lodge all night; and they rise in the morning, and he says, "Send me to my lord"; ⁵⁵and her brother says—her mother also, "Let the young person abide with us a week or ten days, afterward she goes." ⁵⁶And he says to them, "Do not delay me, seeing YHWH has prospered my way; send me away, and I go to my lord"; ⁵⁷and they say, "Let us call for the young person, and inquire of her mouth"; ⁵⁸and they call for Rebekah, and say to her, "Do you go with this man?" And she says, "I go." ⁵⁹And they send away their sister Rebekah, and her nurse, and Abraham's servant, and his men; ⁶⁰and they bless Rebekah, and say to her, "You [are] our sister; become thousands of myriads, and your seed possesses the gate of those hating it." ⁶¹And Rebekah and her young women arise, and ride on the camels, and go after the man; and the servant takes Rebekah and goes. ⁶²And Isaac has come in from the entrance of the Well of the Living One, my Beholder; and he is dwelling in the land of the south, ⁶³and Isaac goes out to meditate in the field, at the turning of the evening, and he lifts up his eyes, and looks, and behold, camels are coming. ⁶⁴And Rebekah lifts up her eyes, and sees Isaac, and comes down off the camel; ⁶⁵and she says to the servant, "Who [is] this man who is walking in the field to meet us?" And the servant says, "It [is] my lord"; and she takes the veil, and covers herself. ⁶⁶And the servant recounts to Isaac all the things that he has done, ⁶⁷and Isaac brings her into the tent of his mother Sarah, and he takes Rebekah, and she becomes his wife, and he loves her, and Isaac is comforted after [the death of] his mother.

CHAPTER 25

¹And Abraham adds and takes a wife, and her name [is] Keturah; ²and she bears to him Zimran, and Jokshan, and Medan, and Midian, and Ishbak, and Shuah. ³And Jokshan has begotten Sheba and Dedan; and the sons of Dedan were Asshurim, and Letushim, and Leummim; ⁴and the sons of Midian [are] Ephah, and Epher, and Enoch, and Abidah, and Eldaah: all these [are] sons of Keturah. ⁵And Abraham gives all that he has to Isaac; ⁶and to the sons of the concubines whom Abraham has, Abraham has given gifts, and sends them away from his son Isaac (in his being yet alive) eastward, to the east country. ⁷And these [are] the days of the years of the life of Abraham, which he lived, one hundred and seventy-five years; ⁸and Abraham expires, and dies in a good old age, aged and satisfied, and is gathered to his people. ⁹And his sons Isaac and Ishmael bury him at the cave of Machpelah, at the field of Ephron, son of Zoar the Hittite, which [is] before Mamre— ¹⁰the field which Abraham bought from the sons of Heth—there Abraham has been buried, and his wife Sarah. ¹¹And it comes to pass after the death of Abraham, that God blesses his son Isaac; and Isaac dwells by the Well of the Living One, my Beholder. ¹²And these [are] the generations of Ishmael, Abraham's son, whom Hagar the Egyptian, Sarah's handmaid, has borne to Abraham; ¹³and these [are] the names of the sons of Ishmael, by their names, according to their births: firstborn of Ishmael, Nebajoth; and Kedar, and Adbeel, and Mibsam, ¹⁴and Mishma, and Dumah, and Massa, ¹⁵Hadar, and Tema, Jetur, Naphish, and Kedemah: ¹⁶these are sons of Ishmael, and these [are] their names, by their villages, and by their towers; twelve princes according to their peoples. ¹⁷And these [are] the years of the life of Ishmael, one hundred and thirty-seven years; and he expires, and dies, and is gathered to his people; ¹⁸and they dwell from Havilah to Shur, which [is] before Egypt, in [your] going toward Asshur; in the presence of all his brothers has he fallen. ¹⁹And these [are] the generations of Isaac, Abraham's son: Abraham has begotten Isaac; ²⁰and Isaac is a son of forty years in his taking Rebekah, daughter of Bethuel the Aramean, from Padan-Aram, sister of Laban the Aramean, to him for a wife. ²¹And Isaac makes plea to YHWH before his wife, for she [is] barren: and YHWH accepts his plea, and his wife Rebekah conceives, ²²and the children struggle together within her, and she says, "If [it is] right—why [am] I thus?" And she goes to seek YHWH. ²³And YHWH says to her, "Two nations [are] in your womb, and two peoples from your bowels are parted; and the [one] people is stronger than

the [other] people; and the older serves the younger." ²⁴And her days to bear are fulfilled, and behold, twins [are] in her womb; ²⁵and the first comes out all red as a hairy robe, and they call his name Esau; ²⁶and afterward his brother has come out, and his hand is taking hold on Esau's heel, and one calls his name Jacob; and Isaac [is] a son of sixty years in her bearing them. ²⁷And the youths grew, and Esau is a man acquainted [with] hunting, a man of the field; and Jacob [is] a plain man, inhabiting tents; ²⁸and Isaac loves Esau, for [his] game [is] in his mouth; and Rebekah is loving Jacob. ²⁹And Jacob boils stew, and Esau comes in from the field, and he [is] weary; ³⁰and Esau says to Jacob, "Please let me eat some of this red-red thing, for I [am] weary"; therefore [one] has called his name Edom; ³¹and Jacob says, "Sell your birthright to me today." ³²And Esau says, "Behold, I am going to die, and what is this to me—a birthright?" ³³And Jacob says, "Swear to me today": and he swears to him, and sells his birthright to Jacob; ³⁴and Jacob has given bread and stew of lentils to Esau, and he eats, and drinks, and rises, and goes; and Esau despises the birthright.

CHAPTER 26

¹And there is a famine in the land, besides the first famine which was in the days of Abraham, and Isaac goes to Abimelech king of the Philistines, to Gerar. ²And YHWH appears to him and says, "Do not go down toward Egypt, dwell in the land concerning which I speak to you, ³sojourn in this land, and I am with you, and bless you, for to you and to your seed I give all these lands, and I have established the oath which I have sworn to your father Abraham; ⁴and I have multiplied your seed as stars of the heavens, and I have given to your seed all these lands; and all nations of the earth have blessed themselves in your Seed; ⁵because that Abraham has listened to My voice, and keeps My charge, My commands, My statutes, and My laws." ⁶And Isaac dwells in Gerar; ⁷and men of the place ask him of his wife, and he says, "She [is] my sister": for he has been afraid to say, "My wife—lest the men of the place kill me for Rebekah, for she [is] of good appearance." ⁸And it comes to pass, when the days have been prolonged to him there, that Abimelech king of the Philistines looks through the window, and sees, and behold, Isaac is playing with his wife Rebekah. ⁹And Abimelech calls for Isaac and says, "Behold, she [is] surely your wife; and how could you have said, She [is] my sister?" And Isaac says to him, "Because I said, Lest I die for her." ¹⁰And Abimelech says, "What [is] this you have done to us? As a little thing one of the people had lain with your wife, and you had brought on us guilt"; ¹¹and Abimelech commands all the people, saying, "He who comes against this man or against his wife, dying does die." ¹²And Isaac sows in that land, and finds in that year a hundredfold, and YHWH blesses him; ¹³and the man is great, and goes on, going on and becoming great, until he has been very great, ¹⁴and he has possession of a flock, and possession of a herd, and an abundant service; and the Philistines envy him, ¹⁵and all the wells which his father's servants dug in the days of his father Abraham, the Philistines have stopped them, and fill them with dust. ¹⁶And Abimelech says to Isaac, "Go from us; for you have become much mightier than we"; ¹⁷and Isaac goes from there, and encamps in the Valley of Gerar, and dwells there; ¹⁸and Isaac turns back, and digs the wells of water which they dug in the days of his father Abraham, which the Philistines have stopped after the death of Abraham, and he calls to them names according to the names which his father called them. ¹⁹And Isaac's servants dig in the valley, and find there a well of living water, ²⁰and shepherds of Gerar strive with shepherds of Isaac, saying, "The water [is] ours"; and he calls the name of the well "Strife," because they have striven habitually with him; ²¹and they dig another well, and they strive also for it, and he calls its name "Hatred." ²²And he removes from there, and digs another well, and they have not striven for it, and he calls its name "Enlargements," and says, "For—now has YHWH given enlargement to us, and we have been fruitful in the land." ²³And he goes up from there [to] Beer-Sheba, ²⁴and YHWH appears to him during that night and says, "I [am] the God of your father Abraham, do not fear, for I [am] with you, and have blessed you, and have multiplied your seed, because of My servant Abraham"; ²⁵and he builds there an altar, and preaches in the Name of YHWH, and stretches out there his tent, and there Isaac's servants dig a well. ²⁶And Abimelech has gone to him from Gerar, and Ahuzzath his friend, and Phichol head of his host; ²⁷and Isaac says to them, "Why have you come to me, and you have hated me, and you send me away from you?" ²⁸And they say, "We have certainly seen that YHWH has been with you, and we say, Now let there be an oath between us, between us and you, and let us make a covenant with you; ²⁹do no evil with us, as we have not touched you, and as we have only done good with you, and send you away in peace; you [are] now blessed of YHWH." ³⁰And he makes a banquet for them, and they eat and drink, ³¹and rise early in the morning, and swear to one another, and Isaac sends them away, and they go from him in peace. ³²And it comes to pass during that day that Isaac's servants come and declare to him concerning the circumstances of the well which they have dug, and say to him, "We have found water"; ³³and he calls it Shebah, [oath,] therefore the name of the city [is] Beer-Sheba, [Well of the Oath,] to this day. ³⁴And Esau is a son of forty years, and he takes a wife, Judith, daughter of Beeri the Hittite, and Bashemath, daughter of Elon the Hittite, ³⁵and they are a bitterness of spirit to Isaac and to Rebekah.

CHAPTER 27

¹And it comes to pass that Isaac [is] aged, and his eyes are too dim for seeing, and he calls [for] his older son Esau and says to him, "My son"; and he says to him, "Here I [am]." ²And he says, "Now behold, I have become aged, I have not known the day of my death; ³and now, please take up your instruments, your quiver, and your bow, and go out to the field, and hunt provision for me, ⁴and make tasteful things for me, [such] as I have loved, and bring [them] to me, and I eat, so that my soul blesses you before I die." ⁵And Rebekah is listening while Isaac is speaking to his son Esau; and Esau goes to the field to hunt game—to bring in; ⁶and Rebekah has spoken to her son Jacob, saying, "Behold, I have heard your father speaking to your brother Esau, saying, ⁷Bring game for me, and make tasteful things for me, and I eat, and bless you before YHWH before my death. ⁸And now, my son, listen to my voice, to that which I am commanding you: ⁹Now go to the flock, and take for me two good kids of the goats from there, and I make them tasteful things for your father, [such] as he has loved; ¹⁰and you have taken [them] to your father, and he has eaten, so that his soul blesses you before his death." ¹¹And Jacob says to his mother Rebekah, "Behold, my brother Esau [is] a hairy man, and I [am] a smooth man, ¹²it may be my father feels me, and I have been in his eyes as a deceiver, and have brought on me disapproval, and not a blessing"; ¹³and his mother says to him, "On me your disapproval, my son; only listen to my voice, and go, take for me." ¹⁴And he goes, and takes, and brings to his mother, and his mother makes tasteful things, [such] as his father has loved; ¹⁵and Rebekah takes the desirable garments of Esau her older son, which [are] with her in the house, and puts them on Jacob her younger son; ¹⁶and she has put the skins of the kids of the goats on his hands, and on the smooth of his neck, ¹⁷and she gives the tasteful things, and the bread which she has made, into the hand of her son Jacob. ¹⁸And he comes to his father and says, "My father"; and he says, "Here I [am]; who [are] you, my son?" ¹⁹And Jacob says to his father, "I [am] Esau your firstborn; I have done as you have spoken to me; please rise, sit and eat of my game, so that your soul blesses me." ²⁰And Isaac says to his son, "What [is] this you have hurried to find, my son?" And he says, "That which your God YHWH has caused to come before me." ²¹And Isaac says to Jacob, "Please come near, and I feel you, my son, whether you [are] he, my son Esau, or not." ²²And Jacob comes near to his father Isaac, and he feels him, and says, "The voice [is] the voice of Jacob, and the hands hands of Esau." ²³And he has not discerned him, for his hands have been hairy, as the hands of his brother Esau, and he blesses him, ²⁴and says, "You are he—my son Esau?" And he says, "I [am]." ²⁵And he says, "Bring [it] near to me, and I eat of my son's game, so that my soul blesses you"; and he brings [it] near to him, and he eats; and he brings wine to him, and he drinks. ²⁶And his father Isaac says to him, "Please come near and kiss me, my son"; ²⁷and he comes near, and kisses him, and he smells the fragrance of his garments, and blesses him, and says, "See, the fragrance of my son [is] as the fragrance of a field which YHWH has blessed; ²⁸and God gives to you of the dew of the heavens, and of

the fatness of the earth, and abundance of grain and wine; ²⁹peoples serve you, and nations bow themselves to you, be mighty over your brothers, and the sons of your mother bow themselves to you; those who curse you [are] cursed, and those who bless you [are] blessed." ³⁰And it comes to pass, as Isaac has finished blessing Jacob, and Jacob is only just going out from the presence of his father Isaac, that his brother Esau has come in from his hunting; ³¹and he also makes tasteful things, and brings to his father, and says to his father, "Let my father arise, and eat of his son's game, so that your soul blesses me." ³²And his father Isaac says to him, "Who [are] you?" And he says, "I [am] your son, your firstborn, Esau"; ³³and Isaac trembles a very great trembling and says, "Who, now, [is] he who has provided game, and brings to me, and I eat of all before you come in, and I bless him? Indeed, he is blessed." ³⁴When Esau hears the words of his father, then he cries a very great and bitter cry, and says to his father, "Bless me, me also, O my father"; ³⁵and he says, "Your brother has come with subtlety, and takes your blessing." ³⁶And he says, "Is it because he whose name is called Jacob takes me by the heel these two times? He has taken my birthright; and behold, now he has taken my blessing"; he also says, "Have you not kept back a blessing for me?" ³⁷And Isaac answers and says to Esau, "Behold, a mighty one have I set him over you, and all his brothers have I given to him for servants, and [with] grain and wine have I sustained him; and for you now, what will I do, my son?" ³⁸And Esau says to his father, "One blessing have you my father? Bless me, me also, O my father"; and Esau lifts up his voice, and weeps. ³⁹And his father Isaac answers and says to him, "Behold, of the fatness of the earth is your dwelling, and of the dew of the heavens from above; ⁴⁰and by your sword you live, and your brother serves you; and it has come to pass, when you rule, that you have broken his yoke from off your neck." ⁴¹And Esau hates Jacob, because of the blessing with which his father blessed him, and Esau says in his heart, "The days of mourning [for] my father draw near, and I slay my brother Jacob." ⁴²And the words of Esau her older son are declared to Rebekah, and she sends and calls for Jacob her younger son, and says to him, "Behold, your brother Esau is comforting himself in regard to you—to slay you; ⁴³and now, my son, listen to my voice, and rise, flee for yourself to my brother Laban, to Haran, ⁴⁴and you have dwelt with him some days, until your brother's fury turns back, ⁴⁵until your brother's anger turns back from you, and he has forgotten that which you have done to him, and I have sent and taken you from there; why am I bereaved even of you both the same day?" ⁴⁶And Rebekah says to Isaac, "I have been disgusted with my life because of the presence of the daughters of Heth; if Jacob takes a wife of the daughters of Heth, like these—from the daughters of the land—why do I live?"

CHAPTER 28

¹And Isaac calls to Jacob, and blesses him, and commands him, and says to him, "You must not take a wife of the daughters of Canaan; ²rise, go to Padan-Aram, to the house of your mother's father Bethuel, and take for yourself a wife from there, from the daughters of your mother's brother Laban; ³and God Almighty bless you, and make you fruitful, and multiply you, and you have become an assembly of peoples; ⁴and He gives to you the blessing of Abraham, to you and to your seed with you, to cause you to possess the land of your sojournings, which God gave to Abraham." ⁵And Isaac sends Jacob away, and he goes to Padan-Aram, to Laban, son of Bethuel the Aramean, brother of Rebekah, mother of Jacob and Esau. ⁶And Esau sees that Isaac has blessed Jacob, and has sent him to Padan-Aram to take to himself from there a wife—in his blessing him that he lays a charge on him, saying, You must not take a wife from the daughters of Canaan— ⁷that Jacob listens to his father and to his mother, and goes to Padan-Aram— ⁸and Esau sees that the daughters of Canaan are evil in the eyes of his father Isaac, ⁹and Esau goes to Ishmael, and takes Mahalath, daughter of Ishmael, Abraham's son, sister of Nebajoth, to his wives, to himself, for a wife. ¹⁰And Jacob goes out from Beer-Sheba, and goes toward Haran, ¹¹and he touches at a [certain] place, and lodges there, for the sun has gone in, and he takes of the stones of the place, and makes [them] his pillows, and lies down in that place. ¹²And he dreams, and behold, a ladder set up on the earth, and its head is touching the heavens; and behold, messengers of God are going up and coming down by it; ¹³and behold, YHWH is standing on it, and He says, "I [am] YHWH, God of your father Abraham, and God of Isaac; the land on which you are lying, to you I give it, and to your seed; ¹⁴and your seed has been as the dust of the land, and you have broken forth westward, and eastward, and northward, and southward, and all families of the ground have been blessed in you and in your seed. ¹⁵And behold, I [am] with you, and have kept you wherever you go, and have caused you to return to this ground; for I do not leave you until I have surely done that which I have spoken to you." ¹⁶And Jacob awakens out of his sleep and says, "Surely YHWH is in this place, and I did not know"; ¹⁷and he fears and says, "How fearful [is] this place; this is nothing but a house of God, and this a gate of the heavens." ¹⁸And Jacob rises early in the morning, and takes the stone which he has made his pillows, and makes it a standing pillar, and pours oil on its top, ¹⁹and he calls the name of that place Bethel, [house of God,] and yet, Luz [is] the name of the city at the first. ²⁰And Jacob vows a vow, saying, "Seeing God is with me, and has kept me in this way which I am going, and has given to me bread to eat, and a garment to put on— ²¹when I have turned back in peace to the house of my father, and YHWH has become my God, ²²then this stone which I have made a standing pillar is a house of God, and all that You give to me—tithing I tithe to You."

CHAPTER 29

¹And Jacob lifts up his feet, and goes toward the land of the sons of the east; ²and he looks, and behold, a well in the field, and behold, there [are] three droves of a flock crouching by it, for they water the droves from that well, and the great stone [is] on the mouth of the well. ³(When all the droves have been gathered there, and they have rolled the stone from off the mouth of the well, and have watered the flock, then they have turned back the stone on the mouth of the well to its place.) ⁴And Jacob says to them, "My brothers, where [are] you from?" And they say, "We [are] from Haran." ⁵And he says to them, "Have you known Laban, son of Nahor?" And they say, "We have known." ⁶And he says to them, "Does he have peace?" And they say, "Peace; and behold, his daughter Rachel is coming with the flock." ⁷And he says, "Behold, the day [is] still great, [it is] not time for the livestock to be gathered; water the flock, and go, delight yourselves." ⁸And they say, "We are not able, until all the droves be gathered together, and they have rolled away the stone from the mouth of the well, and we have watered the flock." ⁹He is yet speaking with them, and Rachel has come with the flock which her father has, for she [is] shepherdess; ¹⁰and it comes to pass, when Jacob has seen Rachel, daughter of his mother's brother Laban, and the flock of his mother's brother Laban, that Jacob comes near and rolls the stone from off the mouth of the well, and waters the flock of his mother's brother Laban. ¹¹And Jacob kisses Rachel, and lifts up his voice, and weeps, ¹²and Jacob declares to Rachel that he [is] her father's brother, and that he [is] Rebekah's son, and she runs and declares [it] to her father. ¹³And it comes to pass, when Laban hears the report of his sister's son Jacob, that he runs to meet him, and embraces him, and kisses him, and brings him into his house; and he recounts to Laban all these things, ¹⁴and Laban says to him, "You [are] surely my bone and my flesh"; and he dwells with him a month of days. ¹⁵And Laban says to Jacob, "Is it because you [are] my brother that you have served me for nothing? Declare to me what your hire [is]." ¹⁶And Laban has two daughters, the name of the older [is] Leah, and the name of the younger Rachel, ¹⁷and the eyes of Leah [are] tender, and Rachel has been beautiful of form and beautiful of appearance. ¹⁸And Jacob loves Rachel and says, "I serve you seven years for Rachel your younger daughter": ¹⁹and Laban says, "It is better for me to give her to you than to give her to another man; dwell with me"; ²⁰and Jacob serves for Rachel seven years; and they are in his eyes as some days, because of his loving her. ²¹And Jacob says to Laban, "Give up my wife, for my days have been fulfilled, and I go in to her"; ²²and Laban gathers all the men of the place, and makes a banquet. ²³And it comes to pass in the evening, that he takes his daughter Leah, and brings her to him, and he goes in to her; ²⁴and Laban

gives his maidservant Zilpah to her, to his daughter Leah, [for] a maidservant. ²⁵And it comes to pass in the morning, that behold, it [is] Leah; and he says to Laban, "What [is] this you have done to me? Have I not served with you for Rachel? And why have you deceived me?" ²⁶And Laban says, "It is not done so in our place, to give the younger before the firstborn; ²⁷fulfill the period of seven [for] this one, and we also give to you this one, for the service which you serve with me yet seven other years." ²⁸And Jacob does so, and fulfills the period of seven [for] this one, and he gives his daughter Rachel to him for a wife for him; ²⁹and Laban gives his maidservant Bilhah to his daughter Rachel for a maidservant for her. ³⁰And he also goes in to Rachel, and he also loves Rachel more than Leah; and he serves with him yet seven other years. ³¹And YHWH sees that Leah [is] the hated one, and He opens her womb, and Rachel [is] barren; ³²and Leah conceives, and bears a son, and calls his name Reuben, for she said, "Because YHWH has looked on my affliction; because now does my husband love me." ³³And she conceives again, and bears a son, and says, "Because YHWH has heard that I [am] the hated one, He also gives to me even this [one]"; and she calls his name Simeon. ³⁴And she conceives again and bears a son, and says, "Now [is] the time, my husband is joined to me, because I have born to him three sons," therefore has [one] called his name Levi. ³⁵And she conceives again and bears a son, and this time says, "I praise YHWH"; therefore has she called his name Judah; and she ceases from bearing.

CHAPTER 30

¹And Rachel sees that she has not borne to Jacob, and Rachel is envious of her sister, and says to Jacob, "Give me sons, and if there is none—I die." ²And Jacob's anger burns against Rachel, and he says, "Am I in stead of God who has withheld from you the fruit of the womb?" ³And she says, "Behold, my handmaid Bilhah, go in to her, and she bears on my knees, and I am built up, even I, from her"; ⁴and she gives Bilhah her maidservant to him for a wife, and Jacob goes in to her; ⁵and Bilhah conceives, and bears a son to Jacob, ⁶and Rachel says, "God has decided for me, and has also listened to my voice, and gives a son to me"; therefore she has called his name Dan. ⁷And Bilhah, Rachel's maidservant, conceives again, and bears a second son to Jacob, ⁸and Rachel says, "With wrestlings of God I have wrestled with my sister, indeed, I have prevailed"; and she calls his name Napthali. ⁹And Leah sees that she has ceased from bearing, and she takes Zilpah her maidservant, and gives her to Jacob for a wife; ¹⁰and Zilpah, Leah's maidservant, bears a son to Jacob, ¹¹and Leah says, "A troop is coming"; and she calls his name Gad. ¹²And Zilpah, Leah's maidservant, bears a second son to Jacob, ¹³and Leah says, "Because of my happiness, for daughters have pronounced me blessed"; and she calls his name Asher. ¹⁴And Reuben goes in the days of wheat-harvest, and finds love-apples in the field, and brings them to his mother Leah, and Rachel says to Leah, "Please give to me of the love-apples of your son." ¹⁵And she says to her, "Is your taking my husband a little thing, that you have also taken the love-apples of my son?" And Rachel says, "He therefore lies with you tonight, for your son's love-apples." ¹⁶And Jacob comes in from the field at evening; and Leah goes to meet him and says, "You come in to me, for [in] hiring I have hired you with my son's love-apples"; and he lies with her during that night. ¹⁷And God listens to Leah, and she conceives, and bears a son to Jacob, a fifth, ¹⁸and Leah says, "God has given my hire, because I have given my maidservant to my husband"; and she calls his name Issachar. ¹⁹And Leah conceives again, and she bears a sixth son to Jacob, ²⁰and Leah says, "God has endowed me—a good dowry; this time my husband dwells with me, for I have borne six sons to him"; and she calls his name Zebulun; ²¹and afterward she has borne a daughter, and calls her name Dinah. ²²And God remembers Rachel, and God listens to her, and opens her womb, ²³and she conceives and bears a son, and says, "God has gathered up my reproach"; ²⁴and she calls his name Joseph, saying, "YHWH is adding to me another son." ²⁵And it comes to pass, when Rachel has borne Joseph, that Jacob says to Laban, "Send me away, and I go to my place, and to my land; ²⁶give up my wives and my children, for whom I have served you, and I go; for you have known my service which I have served you." ²⁷And Laban says to him, "Now if I have found grace in your eyes—I have observed diligently that YHWH blesses me for your sake." ²⁸He also says, "Define your hire to me, and I give." ²⁹And he says to him, "You have known that which I have served you [in], and that which your substance was with me; ³⁰for [it is] little which you have had at my appearance, and it breaks forth into a multitude, and YHWH blesses you at my coming; and now, when do I make, I also, for my own house?" ³¹And he says, "What do I give to you?" And Jacob says, "You do not give me anything; if you do this thing for me, I turn back; I have delight; I watch your flock; ³²I pass through all your flock today to turn aside every speckled and spotted sheep from there, and every brown sheep among the lambs, and speckled and spotted among the goats—and it has been my hire; ³³and my righteousness has answered for me in the day to come, when it comes in for my hire before your face—everyone which is not speckled and spotted among [my] goats, and brown among [my] lambs—it is stolen with me." ³⁴And Laban says, "Behold, O that it were according to your word"; ³⁵and he turns aside during that day the striped and the spotted male goats, and all the speckled and the spotted female goats, everyone that [has] white in it, and every brown one among the lambs, and he gives into the hand of his sons, ³⁶and sets a journey of three days between himself and Jacob; and Jacob is feeding the rest of the flock of Laban. ³⁷And Jacob takes to himself a rod of fresh poplar and almond and plane-tree, and peels in them white peelings, making bare the white that [is] on the rods, ³⁸and sets up the rods which he has peeled in the gutters in the watering troughs (where the flock comes to drink), in front of the flock, that they may conceive in their coming to drink; ³⁹and the flocks conceive at the rods, and the flock bears striped, speckled, and spotted ones. ⁴⁰And Jacob has parted the lambs, and he puts the face of the flock toward the striped, also all the brown in the flock of Laban, and he sets his own droves by themselves, and has not set them near Laban's flock. ⁴¹And it has come to pass, whenever the strong ones of the flock conceive, that Jacob sets the rods before the eyes of the flock in the gutters, to cause them to conceive by the rods, ⁴²and when the flock is feeble, he does not set [them]; and the feeble ones have been Laban's, and the strong ones Jacob's. ⁴³And the man increases very exceedingly, and has many flocks, and maidservants, and menservants, and camels, and donkeys.

CHAPTER 31

¹And he hears the words of Laban's sons, saying, "Jacob has taken all that our father has; indeed, from that which our father has, he has made all this glory"; ²and Jacob sees the face of Laban, and behold, it is not with him as before. ³And YHWH says to Jacob, "Return to the land of your fathers, and to your family, and I am with you." ⁴And Jacob sends and calls for Rachel and for Leah to the field to his flock; ⁵and says to them, "I am beholding your father's face—that it is not toward me as before, and the God of my father has been with me, ⁶and you have known that with all my power I have served your father, ⁷and your father has played on me, and has changed my hire ten times; and God has not permitted him to do evil with me. ⁸If he says thus: The speckled are your hire, then all the flock bore speckled ones; and if he says thus: The striped are your hire, then all the flock bore striped; ⁹and God takes away the substance of your father, and gives to me. ¹⁰And it comes to pass at the time of the flock conceiving, that I lift up my eyes and see in a dream, and behold, the male goats, which are going up on the flock, [are] striped, speckled, and spotted; ¹¹and the Messenger of God says to me in the dream, Jacob, and I say, Here I [am]. ¹²And He says, Now lift up your eyes and see [that] all the male goats which are going up on the flock [are] striped, speckled, and spotted, for I have seen all that Laban is doing to you; ¹³I [am] the God of Bethel where you have anointed a standing pillar, where you have vowed a vow to me; now, arise, go out from this land, and return to the land of your birth." ¹⁴And Rachel answers—Leah also—and says to him, "Have we yet a portion and inheritance in the house of our father? ¹⁵Have we not been reckoned strangers to him? For he has sold us, and he also utterly consumes our money; ¹⁶for all the wealth which God has taken away from our father, it [is] ours, and our children's; and now, all that God has said to you—do." ¹⁷And Jacob rises, and lifts up his sons and his wives on the camels, ¹⁸and leads all his livestock, and all his

GENESIS

substance which he has acquired, the livestock of his getting, which he has acquired in Padan-Aram, to go to his father Isaac, to the land of Canaan. ¹⁹And Laban has gone to shear his flock, and Rachel steals the teraphim which her father has; ²⁰and Jacob deceives the heart of Laban the Aramean, because he has not declared to him that he is fleeing; ²¹and he flees, he and all that he has, and rises, and passes over the River, and sets his face [toward] the Mount of Gilead. ²²And it is told to Laban on the third day that Jacob has fled, ²³and he takes his brothers with him, and pursues after him a journey of seven days, and overtakes him in the Mount of Gilead. ²⁴And God comes to Laban the Aramean in a dream of the night and says to him, "Take heed to yourself lest you speak with Jacob from good to evil." ²⁵And Laban overtakes Jacob; and Jacob has fixed his tent in the mountain; and Laban with his brothers have fixed [theirs] in the Mount of Gilead. ²⁶And Laban says to Jacob, "What have you done that you deceive my heart, and lead away my daughters as captives of the sword? ²⁷Why have you hidden yourself to flee, and deceive me, and have not declared to me, and I send you away with joy and with songs, with tambourine and with harp, ²⁸and have not permitted me to kiss my sons and my daughters? Now you have acted foolishly in doing [so]; ²⁹my hand is to God to do evil with you, but the God of your father last night has spoken to me, saying, Take heed to yourself from speaking with Jacob from good to evil. ³⁰And now, you have certainly gone, because you have been very desirous for the house of your father; why have you stolen my gods?" ³¹And Jacob answers and says to Laban, "Because I was afraid, for I said, Lest you violently take away your daughters from me; ³²with whomsoever you find your gods—he must not live; before our brothers discern for yourself what [is] with me, and take to yourself": and Jacob has not known that Rachel has stolen them. ³³And Laban goes into the tent of Jacob, and into the tent of Leah, and into the tent of the two handmaidens, and has not found; and he goes out from the tent of Leah, and goes into the tent of Rachel. ³⁴And Rachel has taken the teraphim, and puts them in the furniture of the camel, and sits on them; and Laban feels all the tent, and has not found; ³⁵and she says to her father, "Let it not be displeasing in the eyes of my lord that I am not able to rise at your presence, for the way of women [is] on me"; and he searches, and has not found the teraphim. ³⁶And it is displeasing to Jacob, and he strives with Laban; and Jacob answers and says to Laban, "What [is] my transgression? What my sin, that you have burned after me? ³⁷For you have felt all my vessels: what have you found of all the vessels of your house? Set here before my brothers, and your brothers, and they decide between us both. ³⁸These twenty years I [am] with you: your ewes and your female goats have not miscarried, and the rams of your flock I have not eaten; ³⁹the torn I have not brought to you—I repay it—from my hand you seek it; I have been deceived by day, and I have been deceived by night; ⁴⁰I have been [thus]: drought has consumed me in the day, and frost by night, and my sleep wanders from my eyes. ⁴¹This [is] to me twenty years in your house: I have served you fourteen years for your two daughters, and six years for your flock; and you change my hire ten times; ⁴²unless the God of my father, the God of Abraham, and the Fear of Isaac, had been for me, surely now you had sent me away empty; God has seen my affliction and the labor of my hands, and reproves last night." ⁴³And Laban answers and says to Jacob, "The daughters [are] my daughters, and the sons my sons, and the flock my flock, and all that you are seeing [is] mine; and to my daughters—what do I to these today, or to their sons whom they have born? ⁴⁴And now, come, let us make a covenant, I and you, and it has been for a witness between me and you." ⁴⁵And Jacob takes a stone, and lifts it up [for] a standing pillar; ⁴⁶and Jacob says to his brothers, "Gather stones," and they take stones, and make a heap; and they eat there on the heap; ⁴⁷and Laban calls it Jegar-Sahadutha; and Jacob has called it Galeed. ⁴⁸And Laban says, "This heap [is] witness between me and you today"; therefore has he called its name Galeed; ⁴⁹Mizpah also, for he said, "YHWH watches between me and you, for we are hidden from one another; ⁵⁰if you afflict my daughters, or take wives beside my daughters—there is no man with us—see, God [is] witness between me and you." ⁵¹And Laban says to Jacob, "Behold, this heap, and behold, the standing pillar which I have cast between me and you; ⁵²this heap [is] witness, and the standing pillar [is] witness, that I do not pass over this heap to you, and that you do not pass over this heap and this standing pillar to me—for evil; ⁵³the God of Abraham and the God of Nahor, judges between us—the God of their father," and Jacob swears by the Fear of his father Isaac. ⁵⁴And Jacob sacrifices a sacrifice on the mountain, and calls to his brothers to eat bread, and they eat bread, and lodge on the mountain; ⁵⁵and Laban rises early in the morning, and kisses his sons and his daughters, and blesses them; and Laban goes on, and turns back to his place.

CHAPTER 32

¹And Jacob has gone on his way, and messengers of God come on him; ²and Jacob says, when he has seen them, "This [is] the camp of God"; and he calls the name of that place "Two Camps." ³And Jacob sends messengers before him to his brother Esau, toward the land of Seir, the field of Edom, ⁴and commands them, saying, "Thus you say to my lord, to Esau, Thus said your servant Jacob: I have sojourned with Laban, and I linger until now; ⁵and I have ox, and donkey, flock, and manservant, and maidservant, and I send to declare to my lord, to find grace in his eyes." ⁶And the messengers return to Jacob, saying, "We came to your brother, to Esau, and he is also coming to meet you, and four hundred men with him"; ⁷and Jacob fears exceedingly, and is distressed, and he divides the people who [are] with him, and the flock, and the herd, and the camels, into two camps, ⁸and says, "If Esau comes to one camp, and has struck it—then the camp which is left has been for an escape." ⁹And Jacob says, "God of my father Abraham and God of my father Isaac, YHWH who says to me, Return to your land and to your family, and I do good with you: ¹⁰I have been unworthy of all the kind acts and of all the truth which You have done with your servant—for with my staff I passed over this Jordan, and now I have become two camps. ¹¹Please deliver me from the hand of my brother, from the hand of Esau: for I am fearing him, lest he come and has struck me—mother beside sons; ¹²and You have said, I certainly do good with you, and have set your seed as the sand of the sea, which is not numbered because of the multitude." ¹³And he lodges there during that night, and takes from that which is coming into his hand, a present for his brother Esau: ¹⁴female goats two hundred, and male goats twenty, ewes two hundred, and rams twenty, ¹⁵suckling camels and their young ones thirty, cows forty, and bullocks ten, female donkeys twenty, and foals ten; ¹⁶and he gives into the hand of his servants every drove by itself, and says to his servants, "Pass over before me, and a space you put between drove and drove." ¹⁷And he commands the first, saying, "When my brother Esau meets you, and has asked you, saying, Whose [are] you? And to where do you go? And whose [are] these before you? ¹⁸Then you have said, Your servant Jacob's: it [is] a present sent to my lord, to Esau; and behold, he also [is] behind us." ¹⁹And he commands also the second, also the third, also all who are going after the droves, saying, "According to this manner do you speak to Esau in your finding him, ²⁰and you have also said, Behold, your servant Jacob [is] behind us"; for he said, "I pacify his face with the present which is going before me, and afterward I see his face; it may be he lifts up my face"; ²¹and the present passes over before his face, and he has lodged during that night in the camp. ²²And he rises in that night, and takes his two wives, and his two maidservants, and his eleven children, and passes over the passage of Jabbok; ²³and he takes them, and causes them to pass over the brook, and he causes that which he has to pass over. ²⁴And Jacob is left alone, and One wrestles with him until the ascending of the dawn; ²⁵and He sees that He is not able for him, and He comes against the hollow of his thigh, and the hollow of Jacob's thigh is disjointed in his wrestling with Him; ²⁶and He says, "Send Me away, for the dawn has ascended": and he says, "I do not send You away, except You have blessed me." ²⁷And He says to him, "What [is] your name?" And he says, "Jacob." ²⁸And He says, "Your name is no longer called Jacob, but Israel; for you have reigned with God and with men, and prevail." ²⁹And Jacob asks and says, "Please declare Your Name"; and He says, "Why [is] this, you ask for My Name?" And He blesses him there. ³⁰And Jacob calls the name of the place Peniel: "For I have seen God face to face, and my life is delivered"; ³¹and the sun

rises on him when he has passed over Penuel, and he is halting on his thigh; ³²therefore the sons of Israel do not eat the sinew which shrank, which [is] on the hollow of the thigh, to this day, because He came against the hollow of Jacob's thigh, against the sinew which shrank.

CHAPTER 33

¹And Jacob lifts up his eyes, and looks, and behold, Esau is coming, and with him four hundred men; and he divides the children to Leah, and to Rachel, and to the two maidservants; ²and he sets the maidservants and their children first, and Leah and her children behind, and Rachel and Joseph last. ³And he himself passed over before them, and bows himself to the earth seven times, until his drawing near to his brother, ⁴and Esau runs to meet him, and embraces him, and falls on his neck, and kisses him, and they weep; ⁵and he lifts up his eyes, and sees the women and the children, and says, "What [are] these to you?" And he says, "The children with whom God has favored your servant." ⁶And the maidservants draw near, they and their children, and bow themselves; ⁷and Leah also draws near, and her children, and they bow themselves; and afterward Joseph has drawn near with Rachel, and they bow themselves. ⁸And he says, "What to you [is] all this camp which I have met?" And he says, "To find grace in the eyes of my lord." ⁹And Esau says, "I have abundance, my brother, that which you have, let it be for yourself." ¹⁰And Jacob says, "No, please, now if I have found grace in your eyes, then you have received my present from my hand, because that I have seen your face, as the seeing of the face of God, and you are pleased with me; ¹¹please receive my blessing which is brought to you, because God has favored me, and because I have all [things]"; and he presses on him, and he receives [it], ¹²and says, "Let us journey and go on, and I go on before you." ¹³And he says to him, "My lord knows that the children [are] tender, and the suckling flock and the herd [are] with me; when they have beaten them one day, then all the flock has died. ¹⁴Please let my lord pass over before his servant, and I lead on gently, according to the foot of the work which [is] before me, and to the foot of the children, until I come to my lord, to Seir." ¹⁵And Esau says, "Please let me place with you some of the people who [are] with me"; and he said, "Why [is] this? I find grace in the eyes of my lord." ¹⁶And Esau turns back on that day on his way to Seir; ¹⁷and Jacob has journeyed to Succoth, and builds a house for himself, and has made shelters for his livestock, therefore he has called the name of the place Succoth. ¹⁸And Jacob comes safe [to the] city of Shechem, which [is] in the land of Canaan, in his coming from Padan-Aram, and encamps before the city, ¹⁹and he buys the portion of the field where he has stretched out his tent, from the hand of the sons of Hamor, father of Shechem, for one hundred kesitah; ²⁰and he sets up there an altar, and proclaims at it God—the God of Israel.

CHAPTER 34

¹And Dinah, daughter of Leah, whom she has borne to Jacob, goes out to look on the daughters of the land, ²and Shechem, son of Hamor the Hivite, a prince of the land, sees her, and takes her, and lies with her, and humbles her; ³and his soul cleaves to Dinah, daughter of Jacob, and he loves the young person, and speaks to the heart of the young person. ⁴And Shechem speaks to his father Hamor, saying, "Take for me this girl for a wife." ⁵And Jacob has heard that he has defiled his daughter Dinah, and his sons were with his livestock in the field, and Jacob kept silent until their coming. ⁶And Hamor, father of Shechem, goes out to Jacob to speak with him; ⁷and the sons of Jacob came in from the field when they heard, and the men grieve themselves, and it [is] very displeasing to them, for folly he has done against Israel, to lie with the daughter of Jacob—and so it is not done. ⁸And Hamor speaks with them, saying, "Shechem, my son, his soul has cleaved to your daughter; please give her to him for a wife, ⁹and join in marriage with us; you give your daughters to us, and you take our daughters for yourselves, ¹⁰and you dwell with us, and the land is before you; dwell and trade [in] it, and have possessions in it." ¹¹And Shechem says to her father and to her brothers, "Let me find grace in your eyes, and that which you say to me, I give; ¹²multiply on me dowry and gift exceedingly, and I give as you say to me, and give to me the young person for a wife." ¹³And the sons of Jacob answer Shechem and his father Hamor deceitfully, and they speak (because he defiled their sister Dinah), ¹⁴and say to them, "We are not able to do this thing, to give our sister to one who has a foreskin, for it [is] a reproach to us. ¹⁵Only for this we consent to you: if you are as we, to have every male of you circumcised, ¹⁶then we have given our daughters to you, and we take your daughters for ourselves, and we have dwelt with you, and have become one people; ¹⁷and if you do not listen to us to be circumcised, then we have taken our daughter, and have gone." ¹⁸And their words are good in the eyes of Hamor, and in the eyes of Shechem, Hamor's son; ¹⁹and the young man did not delay to do the thing, for he had delight in Jacob's daughter, and he is honorable above all the house of his father. ²⁰And Hamor comes—his son Shechem also—to the gate of their city, and they speak to the men of their city, saying, ²¹"These men are peaceable with us; then let them dwell in the land, and trade [in] it; and the land, behold, [is] wide before them; their daughters let us take to ourselves for wives, and our daughters give to them. ²²Only for this do the men consent to us, to dwell with us, to become one people, in every male of us being circumcised, as they are circumcised; ²³their livestock, and their substance, and all their beasts—are they not ours? Only let us consent to them, and they dwell with us." ²⁴And to Hamor, and to his son Shechem, do all those going out of the gate of his city listen, and every male is circumcised, all those going out of the gate of his city. ²⁵And it comes to pass, on the third day, in their being pained, that two of the sons of Jacob, Simeon and Levi, Dinah's brothers, take each his sword, and come in against the city confidently, and slay every male; ²⁶and Hamor, and his son Shechem, they have slain by the mouth of the sword, and they take Dinah out of Shechem's house, and go out. ²⁷Jacob's sons have come in on the wounded, and they spoil the city, because they had defiled their sister; ²⁸their flock and their herd, and their donkeys, and that which [is] in the city, and that which [is] in the field, have they taken; ²⁹and all their wealth, and all their infants, and their wives they have taken captive, and they spoil also all that [is] in the house. ³⁰And Jacob says to Simeon and to Levi, "You have troubled me, by causing me to stink among the inhabitants of the land, among the Canaanite, and among the Perizzite: and I [am] few in number, and they have been gathered against me, and have struck me, and I have been destroyed, I and my house." ³¹And they say, "Does he make our sister as a harlot?"

CHAPTER 35

¹And God says to Jacob, "Rise, go up to Bethel, and dwell there, and make there an altar to God, who appeared to you in your fleeing from the face of your brother Esau." ²And Jacob says to his household, and to all who [are] with him, "Turn aside the gods of the stranger which [are] in your midst, and cleanse yourselves, and change your garments; ³and we rise, and go up to Bethel, and I make there an altar to God, who is answering me in the day of my tribulation, and is with me in the way that I have gone." ⁴And they give to Jacob all the gods of the stranger that [are] in their hand, and the rings that [are] in their ears, and Jacob hides them under the oak which [is] by Shechem; ⁵and they journey, and the terror of God is on the cities which [are] around them, and they have not pursued after the sons of Jacob. ⁶And Jacob comes to Luz which [is] in the land of Canaan (it [is] Bethel), he and all the people who [are] with him, ⁷and he builds there an altar, and proclaims at the place the God of Bethel: for there had God been revealed to him, in his fleeing from the face of his brother. ⁸And Deborah, Rebekah's nurse, dies, and she is buried at the lower part of Bethel, under the oak, and he calls its name "Oak of Weeping." ⁹And God appears to Jacob again, in his coming from Padan-Aram, and blesses him; ¹⁰and God says to him, "Your name [is] Jacob: your name is no longer called Jacob, but Israel is your name"; and He calls his name Israel. ¹¹And God says to him, "I [am] God Almighty; be fruitful and multiply, a nation and an assembly of nations is from you, and kings

from your loins go out; ¹²and the land which I have given to Abraham and to Isaac—to you I give it, indeed to your seed after you I give the land." ¹³And God goes up from him, in the place where He has spoken with him. ¹⁴And Jacob sets up a standing pillar in the place where He has spoken with him, a standing pillar of stone, and he pours on it an oblation, and he pours on it oil; ¹⁵and Jacob calls the name of the place where God spoke with him Bethel. ¹⁶And they journey from Bethel, and there is yet a distance of land before entering Ephratha, and Rachel bears, and is sharply pained in her bearing; ¹⁷and it comes to pass, in her being sharply pained in her bearing, that the midwife says to her, "Do not fear, for this also [is] a son for you." ¹⁸And it comes to pass in the going out of her soul (for she died), that she calls his name Ben-Oni; and his father called him Benjamin; ¹⁹and Rachel dies, and is buried in the way to Ephratha, which [is] Beth-Lehem, ²⁰and Jacob sets up a standing pillar over her grave; which [is] the standing pillar of Rachel's grave to this day. ²¹And Israel journeys, and stretches out his tent beyond the Tower of Edar; ²²and it comes to pass in Israel's dwelling in that land, that Reuben goes, and lies with his father's concubine Bilhah; and Israel hears. ²³And the sons of Jacob are twelve. Sons of Leah: Jacob's firstborn Reuben, and Simeon, and Levi, and Judah, and Issachar, and Zebulun. ²⁴Sons of Rachel: Joseph and Benjamin. ²⁵And sons of Bilhah, Rachel's maidservant: Dan and Naphtali. ²⁶And sons of Zilpah, Leah's maidservant: Gad and Asher. These [are] sons of Jacob, who have been born to him in Padan-Aram. ²⁷And Jacob comes to his father Isaac, at Mamre, the city of Arba (which [is] Hebron), where Abraham and Isaac have sojourned. ²⁸And the days of Isaac are one hundred and eighty years, ²⁹and Isaac expires, and dies, and is gathered to his people, aged and satisfied with days; and his sons Esau and Jacob bury him.

CHAPTER 36

¹And these [are] the generations of Esau, who [is] Edom. ²Esau has taken his wives from the daughters of Canaan: Adah daughter of Elon the Hittite, and Aholibamah daughter of Anah, daughter of Zibeon the Hivite, ³and Bashemath daughter of Ishmael, sister of Nebajoth. ⁴And Adah bears to Esau, Eliphaz; and Bashemath has borne Reuel; ⁵and Aholibamah has borne Jeush, and Jaalam, and Korah. These [are] sons of Esau, who were born to him in the land of Canaan. ⁶And Esau takes his wives, and his sons, and his daughters, and all the persons of his house, and his livestock, and all his beasts, and all his substance which he has acquired in the land of Canaan, and goes into the country from the face of his brother Jacob; ⁷for their substance was more abundant than to dwell together, and the land of their sojournings was not able to bear them because of their livestock; ⁸and Esau dwells in Mount Seir: Esau is Edom. ⁹And these [are] the generations of Esau, father of Edom, in Mount Seir. ¹⁰These [are] the names of the sons of Esau: Eliphaz son of Adah, wife of Esau; Reuel son of Bashemath, wife of Esau. ¹¹And the sons of Eliphaz are Teman, Omar, Zepho, and Gatam, and Kenaz; ¹²and Timnah has been concubine to Eliphaz son of Esau, and she bears to Eliphaz, Amalek; these [are] sons of Adah wife of Esau. ¹³And these [are] sons of Reuel: Nahath and Zerah, Shammah and Mizzah; these were sons of Bashemath wife of Esau. ¹⁴And these have been the sons of Aholibamah daughter of Anah, daughter of Zibeon, wife of Esau; and she bears to Esau, Jeush and Jaalam and Korah. ¹⁵These [are] chiefs of the sons of Esau: sons of Eliphaz, firstborn of Esau: Chief Teman, Chief Omar, Chief Zepho, Chief Kenaz, ¹⁶Chief Korah, Chief Gatam, Chief Amalek; these [are] chiefs of Eliphaz, in the land of Edom; these [are] sons of Adah. ¹⁷And these [are] sons of Reuel son of Esau: Chief Nahath, Chief Zerah, Chief Shammah, Chief Mizzah; these [are] chiefs of Reuel, in the land of Edom; these [are] sons of Bashemath wife of Esau. ¹⁸And these [are] sons of Aholibamah wife of Esau: Chief Jeush, Chief Jaalam, Chief Korah; these [are] chiefs of Aholibamah daughter of Anah, wife of Esau. ¹⁹These [are] sons of Esau (who [is] Edom), and these their chiefs. ²⁰These [are] sons of Seir the Horite, the inhabitants of the land: Lotan, and Shobal, and Zibeon, and Anah, ²¹and Dishon, and Ezer, and Dishan; these [are] chiefs of the Horites, sons of Seir, in the land of Edom. ²²And the sons of Lotan are Hori and Heman; and a sister of Lotan [is] Timna. ²³And these [are] sons of Shobal: Alvan and Manahath, and Ebal, Shepho and Onam. ²⁴And these [are] sons of Zibeon, both Ajah and Anah: it [is] Anah that has found the Imim in the wilderness, in his feeding the donkeys of his father Zibeon. ²⁵And these [are] sons of Anah: Dishon, and Aholibamah daughter of Anah. ²⁶And these [are] sons of Dishon: Hemdan, and Eshban, and Ithran, and Cheran. ²⁷These [are] sons of Ezer: Bilhan, and Zaavan, and Akan. ²⁸These [are] sons of Dishan: Uz and Aran. ²⁹These [are] chiefs of the Horite: Chief Lotan, Chief Shobal, Chief Zibeon, Chief Anah, ³⁰Chief Dishon, Chief Ezer, Chief Dishan: these [are] chiefs of the Horite in reference to their chiefs in the land of Seir. ³¹And these [are] the kings who have reigned in the land of Edom before the reigning of a king over the sons of Israel. ³²And Bela son of Beor reigns in Edom, and the name of his city [is] Dinhabah; ³³and Bela dies, and Jobab son of Zerah from Bozrah reigns in his stead; ³⁴and Jobab dies, and Husham from the land of the Temanite reigns in his stead. ³⁵And Husham dies, and Hadad son of Bedad reigns in his stead (who strikes Midian in the field of Moab), and the name of his city [is] Avith; ³⁶and Hadad dies, and Samlah of Masrekah reigns in his stead; ³⁷and Samlah dies, and Saul from Rehoboth of the River reigns in his stead; ³⁸and Saul dies, and Ba'al-hanan son of Achbor reigns in his stead; ³⁹and Ba'al-hanan son of Achbor dies, and Hadar reigns in his stead, and the name of his city [is] Pau; and his wife's name [is] Mehetabel daughter of Matred, daughter of Me-zahab. ⁴⁰And these [are] the names of the chiefs of Esau, according to their families, according to their places, by their names: Chief Timnah, Chief Alvah, Chief Jetheth, ⁴¹Chief Aholibamah, Chief Elah, Chief Pinon, ⁴²Chief Kenaz, Chief Teman, Chief Mibzar, ⁴³Chief Magdiel, Chief Iram: these [are] chiefs of Edom, in reference to their dwellings, in the land of their possession; he [is] Esau father of Edom.

CHAPTER 37

¹And Jacob dwells in the land of his father's sojournings—in the land of Canaan. ²These [are] the generations of Jacob: Joseph, a son of seventeen years, has been enjoying himself with his brothers among the flock (and he [is] a youth), with the sons of Bilhah, and with the sons of Zilpah, his father's wives, and Joseph brings in an account of their evil to their father. ³And Israel has loved Joseph more than any of his sons, for he [is] a son of his old age, and has made for him a long coat; ⁴and his brothers see that their father has loved him more than any of his brothers, and they hate him, and have not been able to speak [to] him peaceably. ⁵And Joseph dreams a dream, and declares to his brothers, and they add still more to hate him. ⁶And he says to them, "Please hear this dream which I have dreamed: ⁷that, behold, we are binding bundles in the midst of the field, and behold, my bundle has arisen, and has also stood up, and behold, your bundles are all around, and they bow themselves to my bundle." ⁸And his brothers say to him, "Do you certainly reign over us? Do you certainly rule over us?" And they add still more to hate him, for his dreams, and for his words. ⁹And he dreams yet another dream, and recounts it to his brothers, and says, "Behold, I have dreamed a dream again, and behold, the sun and the moon, and eleven stars, are bowing themselves to me." ¹⁰And he recounts to his father, and to his brothers; and his father pushes against him, and says to him, "What [is] this dream which you have dreamed? Do we certainly come, I, and your mother, and your brothers—to bow ourselves to you, to the earth?" ¹¹And his brothers are zealous against him, and his father has watched the matter. ¹²And his brothers go to feed the flock of their father in Shechem, ¹³and Israel says to Joseph, "Are your brothers not feeding in Shechem? Come, and I send you to them"; and he says to him, "Here I [am]"; ¹⁴and he says to him, "Now go see the peace of your brothers, and the peace of the flock, and bring me back word"; and he sends him from the Valley of Hebron, and he comes to Shechem. ¹⁵And a man finds him, and behold, he is wandering in the field, and the man asks him, saying, "What do you seek?" ¹⁶And he says, "I am seeking my brothers, please declare to me where they are feeding." ¹⁷And the man says, "They have journeyed from this, for I have heard some saying, Let us go to Dothan," and Joseph goes after his brothers, and finds them in Dothan. ¹⁸And they see him from afar, even before he draws near to them, and they conspire against him to put him to death. ¹⁹And they say to one another,

"Behold, this man of the dreams comes; ²⁰and now, come, and we slay him, and cast him into one of the pits, and have said, An evil beast has devoured him; and we see what his dreams are." ²¹And Reuben hears, and delivers him out of their hand, and says, "Let us not strike the life"; ²²and Reuben says to them, "Shed no blood; cast him into this pit which [is] in the wilderness, and do not put forth a hand on him," in order to deliver him out of their hand, to bring him back to his father. ²³And it comes to pass, when Joseph has come to his brothers, that they strip Joseph of his coat, the long coat which [is] on him, ²⁴and take him and cast him into the pit, and the pit [is] empty, there is no water in it. ²⁵And they sit down to eat bread, and they lift up their eyes, and look, and behold, a caravan of Ishmaelites coming from Gilead, and their camels carrying spices, and balm, and myrrh, going to take [them] down to Egypt. ²⁶And Judah says to his brothers, "What gain when we slay our brother, and have concealed his blood? ²⁷Come, and we sell him to the Ishmaelites, and our hands are not on him, for he [is] our brother—our flesh"; and his brothers listen. ²⁸And Midianite merchantmen pass by and they draw out and bring up Joseph out of the pit, and sell Joseph to the Ishmaelites for twenty pieces of silver, and they bring Joseph into Egypt. ²⁹And Reuben returns to the pit, and behold, Joseph is not in the pit, and he tears his garments, ³⁰and he returns to his brothers and says, "The boy is not, and I—to where am I going?" ³¹And they take the coat of Joseph, and slaughter a kid of the goats, and dip the coat in the blood, ³²and send the long coat, and they bring [it] to their father, and say, "We have found this; please discern whether it [is] your son's coat or not." ³³And he discerns it and says, "My son's coat! An evil beast has devoured him; torn—Joseph is torn!" ³⁴And Jacob tears his raiment, and puts sackcloth on his loins, and becomes a mourner for his son many days, ³⁵and all his sons and all his daughters rise to comfort him, and he refuses to comfort himself, and says, "For I go down to my son mourning, to Sheol," and his father weeps for him. ³⁶And the Midianites have sold him to Egypt, to Potiphar, a eunuch of Pharaoh, head of the executioners.

CHAPTER 38

¹And it comes to pass, at that time, that Judah goes down from his brothers, and turns aside to a man, an Adullamite, whose name [is] Hirah; ²and Judah sees there the daughter of a man, a Canaanite, whose name [is] Shuah, and takes her, and goes in to her. ³And she conceives, and bears a son, and he calls his name Er; ⁴and she conceives again, and bears a son, and calls his name Onan; ⁵and she adds again, and bears a son, and calls his name Shelah; and he was in Chezib in her bearing him. ⁶And Judah takes a wife for Er, his firstborn, and her name [is] Tamar; ⁷and Er, Judah's firstborn, is evil in the eyes of YHWH, and YHWH puts him to death. ⁸And Judah says to Onan, "Go in to the wife of your brother, and marry her, and raise up seed to your brother"; ⁹and Onan knows that the seed is not [reckoned] his; and it has come to pass, if he has gone in to his brother's wife, that he has destroyed [it] to the earth, so as not to give seed to his brother; ¹⁰and that which he has done is evil in the eyes of YHWH, and He puts him also to death. ¹¹And Judah says to his daughter-in-law Tamar, "Abide [as] a widow at your father's house, until my son Shelah grows up"; for he said, "Lest he die—even he—like his brothers"; and Tamar goes and dwells at her father's house. ¹²And the days are multiplied, and the daughter of Shuah, Judah's wife, dies; and Judah is comforted, and goes up to his sheep-shearers, he and Hirah his friend the Adullamite, to Timnath. ¹³And it is declared to Tamar, saying, "Behold, your husband's father is going up to Timnath to shear his flock"; ¹⁴and she turns aside the garments of her widowhood from off her, and covers herself with a veil, and wraps herself up, and sits in the opening of Enayim, which [is] by the way to Timnath, for she has seen that Shelah has grown up, and she has not been given to him for a wife. ¹⁵And Judah sees her, and reckons her for a harlot, for she has covered her face, ¹⁶and he turns aside to her by the way and says, "Please come, let me come in to you," for he has not known that she [is] his daughter-in-law; and she says, "What do you give to me, that you may come in to me?" ¹⁷And he says, "I send a kid of the goats from the flock." And she says, "Do you give a pledge until you send [it]?" ¹⁸And he says, "What [is] the pledge that I give to you?" And she says, "Your seal, and your ribbon, and your staff which [is] in your hand"; and he gives to her, and goes in to her, and she conceives to him; ¹⁹and she rises, and goes, and turns aside her veil from off her, and puts on the garments of her widowhood. ²⁰And Judah sends the kid of the goats by the hand of his friend the Adullamite, to receive the pledge from the hand of the woman, and he has not found her. ²¹And he asks the men of her place, saying, "Where [is] the separated one—she in Enayim, by the way?" And they say, "There has not been in this [place] a separated one." ²²And he turns back to Judah and says, "I have not found her; and the men of the place also have said, There has not been in this [place] a separated one," ²³and Judah says, "Let her take to herself, lest we become despised; behold, I sent this kid, and you have not found her." ²⁴And it comes to pass about three months [after], that it is declared to Judah, saying, "Your daughter-in-law Tamar has committed fornication; and also, behold, she has conceived by fornication": and Judah says, "Bring her out—and she is burned." ²⁵She is brought out, and she has sent to her husband's father, saying, "To a man whose these [are], I [am] pregnant"; and she says, "Please discern whose these [are]—the seal, and the ribbons, and the staff." ²⁶And Judah discerns and says, "She has been more righteous than I, because that I did not give her to my son Shelah"; and he has not added to know her again. ²⁷And it comes to pass in the time of her bearing, that behold, twins [are] in her womb; ²⁸and it comes to pass in her bearing, that [one] gives out a hand, and the midwife takes and binds on his hand a scarlet thread, saying, "This has come out first." ²⁹And it comes to pass as he draws back his hand, that behold, his brother has come out, and she says, "What! You have broken forth—the breach [is] on you"; and he calls his name Perez; ³⁰and afterward his brother has come out, on whose hand [is] the scarlet thread, and he calls his name Zerah.

CHAPTER 39

¹And Joseph has been brought down to Egypt, and Potiphar, a eunuch of Pharaoh, head of the executioners, an Egyptian man, buys him out of the hands of the Ishmaelites who have brought him there. ²And YHWH is with Joseph, and he is a prosperous man, and he is in the house of his lord the Egyptian, ³and his lord sees that YHWH is with him, and all that he is doing YHWH is causing to prosper in his hand, ⁴and Joseph finds grace in his eyes and serves him, and he appoints him over his house, and all that he has he has given into his hand. ⁵And it comes to pass from the time that he has appointed him over his house, and over all that he has, that YHWH blesses the house of the Egyptian for Joseph's sake, and the blessing of YHWH is on all that he has, in the house, and in the field; ⁶and he leaves all that he has in the hand of Joseph, and he has not known anything that he has, except the bread which he is eating. And Joseph is of a handsome form, and of a handsome appearance. ⁷And it comes to pass after these things, that his lord's wife lifts up her eyes to Joseph and says, "Lie with me"; ⁸and he refuses and says to his lord's wife, "Behold, my lord has not known what [is] with me in the house, and all that he has he has given into my hand; ⁹none is greater in this house than I, and he has not withheld from me anything, except you, because you [are] his wife; and how will I do this great evil? Then I have sinned against God." ¹⁰And it comes to pass at her speaking to Joseph day [by] day, that he has not listened to her, to lie near her, to be with her; ¹¹and it comes to pass about this day, that he goes into the house to do his work, and there is none of the men of the house there in the house, ¹²and she catches him by his garment, saying, "Lie with me"; and he leaves his garment in her hand, and flees, and goes outside. ¹³And it comes to pass, when she sees that he has left his garment in her hand, and flees outside, ¹⁴that she calls for the men of her house, and speaks to them, saying, "See, he has brought a man to us, a Hebrew, to play with us; he has come in to me, to lie with me, and I call with a loud voice, ¹⁵and it comes to pass, when he hears that I have lifted up my voice and call, that he leaves his garment near me, and flees, and goes outside." ¹⁶And she places his garment near her, until the coming in of his lord to his house. ¹⁷And she speaks to him according to these words, saying, "The Hebrew servant whom you have brought to us, has come in to me to play with me; ¹⁸and it comes to pass, when I lift my voice and call, that he leaves his garment near me, and flees outside." ¹⁹And it comes to pass, when his lord

hears the words of his wife, which she has spoken to him, saying, "According to these things has your servant done to me," that his anger burns; ²⁰and Joseph's lord takes him, and puts him to the round-house, a place where the king's prisoners [are] bound; and he is there in the round-house. ²¹And YHWH is with Joseph, and stretches out kindness to him, and puts his grace in the eyes of the chief of the round-house; ²²and the chief of the round-house gives into the hand of Joseph all the prisoners who [are] in the round-house, and of all that they are doing there, he has been doer; ²³the chief of the round-house does not see anything under his hand, because YHWH [is] with him, and that which he is doing YHWH is causing to prosper.

CHAPTER 40

¹And it comes to pass, after these things—the butler of the king of Egypt and the baker have sinned against their lord, against the king of Egypt; ²and Pharaoh is angry against his two eunuchs, against the chief of the butlers, and against the chief of the bakers, ³and puts them in confinement in the house of the chief of the executioners, into the round-house, the place where Joseph [is] a prisoner, ⁴and the chief of the executioners charges Joseph with them, and he serves them; and they are in confinement [for some] days. ⁵And they dream a dream both of them, each his dream in one night, each according to the interpretation of his dream, the butler and the baker whom the king of Egypt has, who [are] prisoners in the round-house. ⁶And Joseph comes to them in the morning, and sees them, and behold, they [are] morose; ⁷and he asks Pharaoh's eunuchs who [are] with him in confinement in the house of his lord, saying, "Why [are] your faces sad today?" ⁸And they say to him, "We have dreamed a dream, and there is no interpreter of it"; and Joseph says to them, "Are interpretations not with God? Please recount to me." ⁹And the chief of the butlers recounts his dream to Joseph and says to him, "In my dream, then behold, a vine [is] before me! ¹⁰And in the vine [are] three branches, and it [is] as it were flourishing; gone up has its blossom, its clusters have ripened grapes; ¹¹and Pharaoh's cup [is] in my hand, and I take the grapes and press them into the cup of Pharaoh, and I give the cup into the hand of Pharaoh." ¹²And Joseph says to him, "This [is] its interpretation: the three branches are three days; ¹³yet, within three days Pharaoh lifts up your head, and has put you back on your station, and you have given the cup of Pharaoh into his hand, according to the former custom when you were his butler. ¹⁴Surely if you have remembered me with you, when it is well with you, and have please done kindness with me, and have made mention of me to Pharaoh, then you have brought me out from this house, ¹⁵for I was really stolen from the land of the Hebrews; and here also I have done nothing that they have put me in the pit [for]." ¹⁶And the chief of the bakers sees that he has interpreted good, and he says to Joseph, "I also [am] in a dream, and behold, three baskets of white bread [are] on my head, ¹⁷and in the highest basket [are] of all [kinds] of Pharaoh's food, work of a baker; and the birds are eating them out of the basket, from off my head." ¹⁸And Joseph answers and says, "This [is] its interpretation: the three baskets are three days; ¹⁹yet, within three days Pharaoh lifts up your head from off you, and has hanged you on a tree, and the birds have eaten your flesh from off you." ²⁰And it comes to pass, on the third day, Pharaoh's birthday, that he makes a banquet to all his servants, and lifts up the head of the chief of the butlers, and the head of the chief of the bakers among his servants, ²¹and he puts back the chief of the butlers to his butlership, and he gives the cup into the hand of Pharaoh; ²²and the chief of the bakers he has hanged, as Joseph has interpreted to them; ²³and the chief of the butlers has not remembered Joseph, but forgets him.

CHAPTER 41

¹And it comes to pass, at the end of two years of days that Pharaoh is dreaming, and behold, he is standing by the River, ²and behold, from the River coming up are seven cows, of beautiful appearance, and fat [in] flesh, and they feed among the reeds; ³and behold, seven other cows are coming up after them out of the River, of bad appearance, and lean [in] flesh, and they stand near the cows on the edge of the River, ⁴and the cows of bad appearance and lean [in] flesh eat up the seven cows of beautiful appearance, and fat—and Pharaoh awakens. ⁵And he sleeps, and dreams a second time, and behold, seven ears are coming up on one stalk, fat and good, ⁶and behold, seven ears, thin, and blasted with an east wind, are springing up after them; ⁷and the thin ears swallow the seven fat and full ears—and Pharaoh awakens, and behold, a dream. ⁸And it comes to pass in the morning, that his spirit is moved, and he sends and calls all the enchanters of Egypt, and all its wise men, and Pharaoh recounts to them his dream, and there is no interpreter of them to Pharaoh. ⁹And the chief of the butlers speaks with Pharaoh, saying, "I mention my sin this day: ¹⁰Pharaoh has been angry against his servants, and puts me in confinement in the house of the chief of the executioners, me and the chief of the bakers; ¹¹and we dream a dream in one night, I and he, each according to the interpretation of his dream we have dreamed. ¹²And there [is] with us a youth, a Hebrew, servant to the chief of the executioners, and we recount to him, and he interprets to us our dreams, [to] each according to his dream has he interpreted, ¹³and it comes to pass, as he has interpreted to us so it has been, me he put back on my station, and him he hanged." ¹⁴And Pharaoh sends and calls Joseph, and they cause him to run out of the pit, and he shaves, and changes his garments, and comes to Pharaoh. ¹⁵And Pharaoh says to Joseph, "I have dreamed a dream, and there is no interpreter of it, and I have heard concerning you, saying, You understand a dream to interpret it," ¹⁶and Joseph answers Pharaoh, saying, "Without me—God answers Pharaoh with peace." ¹⁷And Pharaoh speaks to Joseph: "In my dream, behold, I am standing by the edge of the River, ¹⁸and behold, out of the River coming up are seven cows, fat [in] flesh, and of beautiful form, and they feed among the reeds; ¹⁹and behold, seven other cows are coming up after them, thin, and of very bad form, and lean [in] flesh; I have not seen like these in all the land of Egypt for badness. ²⁰And the lean and the bad cows eat up the first seven fat cows, ²¹and they come in to their midst, and it has not been known that they have come in to their midst, and their appearance [is] bad as at the commencement; and I awake. ²²And I see in my dream, and behold, seven ears are coming up on one stalk, full and good; ²³and behold, seven ears, withered, thin, blasted with an east wind, are springing up after them; ²⁴and the thin ears swallow the seven good ears; and I tell [it] to the enchanters, and there is none declaring [it] to me." ²⁵And Joseph says to Pharaoh, "The dream of Pharaoh is one: that which God is doing he has declared to Pharaoh; ²⁶the seven good cows are seven years, and the seven good ears are seven years, the dream is one; ²⁷and the seven thin and bad cows which are coming up after them are seven years, and the seven empty ears, blasted with an east wind, are seven years of famine; ²⁸this [is] the thing which I have spoken to Pharaoh: God has shown Pharaoh what He is doing. ²⁹Behold, seven years are coming of great abundance in all the land of Egypt, ³⁰and seven years of famine have arisen after them, and all the plenty is forgotten in the land of Egypt, and the famine has finished the land, ³¹and the plenty is not known in the land because of that famine afterward, for it [is] very grievous. ³²And because of the repeating of the dream to Pharaoh twice, surely the thing is established by God, and God is hurrying to do it. ³³And now, let Pharaoh provide a man, intelligent and wise, and set him over the land of Egypt; ³⁴let Pharaoh make and appoint overseers over the land, and receive a fifth of the land of Egypt in the seven years of plenty, ³⁵and they gather all the food of these good years that are coming, and heap up grain under the hand of Pharaoh—food in the cities; and they have kept [it], ³⁶and the food has been for a store for the land, for the seven years of famine which are in the land of Egypt; and the land is cut off by the famine." ³⁷And the thing is good in the eyes of Pharaoh, and in the eyes of all his servants, ³⁸and Pharaoh says to his servants, "Do we find like this, a man in whom the Spirit of God [is]?" ³⁹And Pharaoh says to Joseph, "After God's causing you to know all this, there is none intelligent and wise as you; ⁴⁰you are over my house, and at your mouth do all my people kiss; only in the throne I am greater than you." ⁴¹And Pharaoh says to Joseph, "See, I have put you over all the land of Egypt." ⁴²And Pharaoh turns aside his seal-ring from off his hand, and puts it on the hand of Joseph, and clothes him [with] garments of fine linen, and places a chain of gold on his neck, ⁴³and causes

him to ride in the second chariot which he has, and they proclaim before him, "Bow the knee!" And [he] set him over all the land of Egypt. ⁴⁴And Pharaoh says to Joseph, "I [am] Pharaoh, and without you a man does not lift up his hand and his foot in all the land of Egypt"; ⁴⁵and Pharaoh calls Joseph's name Zaphnath-Paaneah, and he gives to him Asenath daughter of Poti-Pherah, priest of On, for a wife, and Joseph goes out over the land of Egypt. ⁴⁶And Joseph [is] a son of thirty years in his standing before Pharaoh king of Egypt, and Joseph goes out from the presence of Pharaoh, and passes over through all the land of Egypt; ⁴⁷and the land makes in the seven years of plenty by handfuls. ⁴⁸And he gathers all the food of the seven years which have been in the land of Egypt, and puts food in the cities; the food of the field which [is] around [each] city has he put in its midst; ⁴⁹and Joseph gathers grain as sand of the sea, multiplying exceedingly, until he has ceased to number, for there is no number. ⁵⁰And to Joseph were born two sons before the year of famine comes, whom Asenath daughter of Poti-Pherah, priest of On, has borne to him, ⁵¹and Joseph calls the name of the firstborn Manasseh: "For God has made me to forget all my labor, and all the house of my father"; ⁵²and the name of the second he has called Ephraim: "For God has caused me to be fruitful in the land of my affliction." ⁵³And the seven years of plenty are completed which have been in the land of Egypt, ⁵⁴and the seven years of famine begin to come, as Joseph said, and famine is in all the lands, but in all the land of Egypt has been bread; ⁵⁵and all the land of Egypt is famished, and the people cry to Pharaoh for bread, and Pharaoh says to all the Egyptians, "Go to Joseph; that which he says to you—do." ⁵⁶And the famine has been over all the face of the land, and Joseph opens all [places] which have [grain] in them, and sells to the Egyptians; and the famine is severe in the land of Egypt, ⁵⁷and all the earth has come to Egypt, to buy, to Joseph, for the famine was severe in all the earth.

CHAPTER 42

¹And Jacob sees that there is grain in Egypt, and Jacob says to his sons, "Why do you look at each other?" ²He also says, "Behold, I have heard that there is grain in Egypt, go down there, and buy for us from there, and we live and do not die"; ³and the ten brothers of Joseph go down to buy grain in Egypt, ⁴and Benjamin, Joseph's brother, Jacob has not sent with his brothers, for he said, "Lest harm meet him." ⁵And the sons of Israel come to buy in the midst of those coming, for the famine has been in the land of Canaan, ⁶and Joseph is the ruler over the land, he who is selling to all the people of the land, and Joseph's brothers come and bow themselves to him—face to the earth. ⁷And Joseph sees his brothers, and discerns them, and makes himself strange to them, and speaks sharp things with them, and says to them, "From where have you come?" And they say, "From the land of Canaan—to buy food." ⁸And Joseph discerns his brothers, but they have not discerned him, ⁹and Joseph remembers the dreams which he dreamed of them and says to them, "You [are] spies; you have come to see the nakedness of the land." ¹⁰And they say to him, "No, my lord, but your servants have come to buy food; ¹¹we [are] all of us sons of one man, we [are] right men; your servants have not been spies"; ¹²and he says to them, "No, but you have come to see the nakedness of the land"; ¹³and they say, "Your servants [are] twelve brothers; we [are] sons of one man in the land of Canaan, and behold, the young one [is] with our father today, and one is not." ¹⁴And Joseph says to them, "This [is] that which I have spoken to you, saying, You [are] spies, ¹⁵by this you are proved: [as] Pharaoh lives, if you go out from this—except by your young brother coming here; ¹⁶send one of you, and let him bring your brother, and you, remain bound, and let your words be proved, whether truth be with you: and if not, [as] Pharaoh lives, surely you [are] spies"; ¹⁷and he gathers them into confinement [for] three days. ¹⁸And Joseph says to them on the third day, "Do this and live; I fear God! ¹⁹If you [are] right men, let one of your brothers be bound in the house of your confinement, and you, go, carry in grain [for] the famine of your houses, ²⁰and you bring your young brother to me, and your words are established, and you do not die"; and they do so. ²¹And they say to one another, "Truly we [are] guilty concerning our brother, because we saw the distress of his soul, in his making supplication to us, and we did not listen: therefore this distress has come on us." ²²And Reuben answers them, saying, "Did I not speak to you, saying, Do not sin against the boy? And you did not listen; and his blood also, behold, it is required." ²³And they have not known that Joseph understands, for the interpreter [is] between them; ²⁴and he turns around from them, and weeps, and turns back to them, and speaks to them, and takes Simeon from them, and binds him before their eyes. ²⁵And Joseph commands, and they fill their vessels [with] grain, also to put back the money of each of them into his sack, and to give to them provision for the way; and one does to them so. ²⁶And they lift up their grain on their donkeys, and go from there, ²⁷and the one opens his sack to give provender to his donkey at a lodging-place, and he sees his money, and behold, it [is] in the mouth of his bag, ²⁸and he says to his brothers, "My money has been put back, and also, behold, in my bag": and their heart goes out, and they tremble, to one another saying, "What [is] this God has done to us!" ²⁹And they come to their father Jacob, to the land of Canaan, and they declare to him all the things meeting them, saying, ³⁰"The man, the lord of the land, has spoken with us sharp things, and makes us as spies of the land; ³¹and we say to him, We [are] right men, we have not been spies, ³²we [are] twelve brothers, sons of our father, one is not, and the young one [is] today with our father in the land of Canaan. ³³And the man, the lord of the land, says to us, By this I know that you [are] right men—leave one of your brothers with me, and take [for] the famine of your houses and go, ³⁴and bring your young brother to me, and I know that you [are] not spies, but you [are] right men; I give your brother to you, and you trade with the land." ³⁵And it comes to pass, they are emptying their sacks, and behold, the bundle of each man's silver [is] in his sack, and they see their bundles of silver, they and their father, and are afraid; ³⁶and their father Jacob says to them, "You have bereaved me; Joseph is not, and Simeon is not, and Benjamin you take—all these [things] have been against me." ³⁷And Reuben speaks to his father, saying, "You put to death my two sons, if I do not bring him to you; give him into my hand, and I bring him back to you"; ³⁸and he says, "My son does not go down with you, for his brother [is] dead, and he by himself is left; when harm has met him in the way in which you go, then you have brought down my grey hairs in sorrow to Sheol."

CHAPTER 43

¹And the famine [is] severe in the land; ²and it comes to pass, when they have finished eating the grain which they brought from Egypt, that their father says to them, "Return, buy for us a little food." ³And Judah speaks to him, saying, "The man protesting protested to us, saying, You do not see my face without your brother [being] with you; ⁴if you are sending our brother with us, we go down, and buy for you food, ⁵and if you are not sending—we do not go down, for the man said to us, You do not see my face without your brother [being] with you." ⁶And Israel says, "Why did you do evil to me, by declaring to the man that you had yet a brother?" ⁷And they say, "The man asked diligently concerning us, and concerning our family, saying, Is your father yet alive? Have you a brother? And we declare to him according to the tenor of these things; do we certainly know that he will say, Bring down your brother?" ⁸And Judah says to his father Israel, "Send the youth with me, and we arise, and go, and live, and do not die, both we, and you, and our infants. ⁹I am guarantor [for] him, from my hand you require him; if I have not brought him to you, and set him before you—then I have sinned against you all the days; ¹⁰for if we had not lingered, surely now we had returned these two times." ¹¹And their father Israel says to them, "If so, now, do this: take of the praised thing of the land in your vessels, and take down to the man a present, a little balm, and a little honey, spices and myrrh, nuts and almonds; ¹²and double money take in your hand, even the money which is brought back in the mouth of your bags, you take back in your hand, it may be it [is] an oversight. ¹³And take your brother, and rise, return to the man; ¹⁴and God Almighty give to you mercies before the man, so that he has sent to you your other brother and Benjamin; and I, when I am bereaved—I am bereaved." ¹⁵And the men take this present, double money also they have taken in their hand, and Benjamin; and they rise, and go down to Egypt, and stand before Joseph; ¹⁶and Joseph sees Benjamin with them and says to him who [is] over his

house, "Bring the men into the house, and slaughter an animal, and make ready, for the men eat with me at noon." ¹⁷And the man does as Joseph has said, and the man brings in the men into the house of Joseph, ¹⁸and the men are afraid because they have been brought into the house of Joseph, and they say, "For the matter of the money which was put back in our bags at the commencement are we brought in—to roll himself on us, and to throw himself on us, and to take us for servants—our donkeys also." ¹⁹And they come near to the man who [is] over the house of Joseph, and speak to him at the opening of the house, ²⁰and say, "O my lord, we really come down at the commencement to buy food; ²¹and it comes to pass, when we have come to the lodging-place, and open our bags, that behold, each one's money [is] in the mouth of his bag, our money in its weight, and we bring it back in our hand; ²²and other money have we brought down in our hand to buy food; we have not known who put our money in our bags." ²³And he says, "Peace to you, do not fear: your God and the God of your father has given to you hidden treasure in your bags, your money came to me"; and he brings out Simeon to them. ²⁴And the man brings in the men into Joseph's house, and gives water, and they wash their feet; and he gives provender for their donkeys, ²⁵and they prepare the present until the coming of Joseph at noon, for they have heard that there they eat bread. ²⁶And Joseph comes into the house, and they bring to him the present which [is] in their hand, into the house, and bow themselves to him, to the earth; ²⁷and he asks of them of peace and says, "Is your father well? The aged man of whom you have spoken, is he yet alive?" ²⁸And they say, "Your servant our father [is] well, he is yet alive"; and they bow, and pay respect. ²⁹And he lifts up his eyes and sees his brother Benjamin, his mother's son, and says, "Is this your young brother, of whom you have spoken to me?" And he says, "God favor you, my son." ³⁰And Joseph hurries, for his bowels have been moved for his brother, and he seeks to weep, and enters the inner chamber, and weeps there; ³¹and he washes his face, and goes out, and refrains himself, and says, "Place bread." ³²And they place for him by himself, and for them by themselves, and for the Egyptians who are eating with him by themselves: for the Egyptians are unable to eat bread with the Hebrews, for it [is] an abomination to the Egyptians. ³³And they sit before him, the firstborn according to his birthright, and the young one according to his youth, and the men wonder one at another; ³⁴and he lifts up gifts from before him to them, and the gift of Benjamin is five hands more than the gifts of all of them; and they drink, indeed, they drink abundantly with him.

CHAPTER 44

¹And he commands him who [is] over his house, saying, "Fill the bags of the men [with] food, as they are able to carry, and put the money of each in the mouth of his bag; ²and my cup, the silver cup, you put in the mouth of the bag of the young one, and his grain-money"; and he does according to the word of Joseph which he has spoken. ³The morning is bright, and the men have been sent away, they and their donkeys— ⁴they have gone out of the city—they have not gone far off—and Joseph has said to him who [is] over his house, "Rise, pursue after the men; and you have overtaken them, and you have said to them: Why have you repaid evil for good? ⁵Is this not that with which my lord drinks? And he observes diligently with it; you have done evil [in] that which you have done." ⁶And he overtakes them, and speaks to them these words, ⁷and they say to him, "Why does my lord speak according to these words? Far be it from your servants to do according to this word; ⁸behold, the money which we found in the mouth of our bags we brought back to you from the land of Canaan, and how do we steal from the house of your lord silver or gold? ⁹With whomsoever of your servants it is found, he has died, and we also are to my lord for servants." ¹⁰And he says, "Now also, according to your words, so it [is]; he with whom it is found becomes my servant, and you are acquitted"; ¹¹and they hurry and take down each his bag to the earth, and each opens his bag; ¹²and he searches—at the eldest he has begun, and at the youngest he has completed—and the cup is found in the bag of Benjamin; ¹³and they tear their garments, and each loads his donkey, and they return to the city. ¹⁴And Judah and his brothers come to the house of Joseph, and he is yet there, and they fall to the earth before him; ¹⁵and Joseph says to them, "What [is] this deed that you have done? Have you not known that a man like me diligently observes?" ¹⁶And Judah says, "What do we say to my lord? What do we speak? And how do we justify ourselves? God has found out the iniquity of your servants; behold, we [are] servants to my lord, both we, and he in whose hand the cup has been found"; ¹⁷and he says, "Far be it from me to do this; the man in whose hand the cup has been found, he becomes my servant; and you, go up in peace to your father." ¹⁸And Judah comes near to him and says, "O my lord, please let your servant speak a word in the ears of my lord, and do not let your anger burn against your servant—for you are as Pharaoh. ¹⁹My lord has asked his servants, saying, Do you have a father or brother? ²⁰And we say to my lord, We have a father, an aged one, and a child of old age, a little one; and his brother died, and he is left alone of his mother, and his father has loved him. ²¹And you say to your servants, Bring him down to me, and I set my eye on him; ²²and we say to my lord, The youth is not able to leave his father, when he has left his father, then he has died; ²³and you say to your servants, If your young brother does not come down with you, you do not add to see my face. ²⁴And it comes to pass, that we have come up to your servant my father, that we declare to him the words of my lord; ²⁵and our father says, Return, buy for us a little food, ²⁶and we say, We are not able to go down; if our young brother is with us, then we have gone down; for we are not able to see the man's face, and our young brother not with us. ²⁷And your servant my father says to us, You have known that my wife bore two to me, ²⁸and one goes out from me, and I say, Surely he is torn—torn! And I have not seen him since; ²⁹when you have taken also this from my presence, and harm has met him, then you have brought down my grey hairs with evil to Sheol. ³⁰And now, at my coming to your servant my father, and the youth not with us (and his soul is bound up in his soul), ³¹then it has come to pass, when he sees that the youth is not, that he has died, and your servants have brought down the grey hairs of your servant our father with sorrow to Sheol; ³²for your servant obtained the youth by guarantee to my father, saying, If I do not bring him to you—then I have sinned against my father all the days. ³³And now, please let your servant abide instead of the youth [as] a servant to my lord, and the youth goes up with his brothers, ³⁴for how do I go up to my father, and the youth not with me? Lest I look on the evil which finds my father."

CHAPTER 45

¹And Joseph has not been able to refrain himself before all those standing by him, and he calls, "Put out every man from me"; and no man has stood with him when Joseph makes himself known to his brothers, ²and he gives forth his voice in weeping, and the Egyptians hear, and the house of Pharaoh hears. ³And Joseph says to his brothers, "I [am] Joseph, is my father yet alive?" And his brothers have not been able to answer him, for they have been troubled at his presence. ⁴And Joseph says to his brothers, "Please come near to me," and they come near; and he says, "I [am] your brother Joseph, whom you sold into Egypt; ⁵and now, do not be grieved, nor let it be displeasing in your eyes that you sold me here, for God has sent me before you to preserve life. ⁶Because these two years the famine [is] in the heart of the land, and yet five years [remain in] which there is neither plowing nor harvest; ⁷and God sends me before you, to place a remnant of you in the land, and to give life to you by a great escape; ⁸and now, you have not sent me here, but God, and He sets me for a father to Pharaoh, and for lord to all his house, and ruler over all the land of Egypt. ⁹Hurry, and go up to my father, then you have said to him, Thus said your son Joseph: God has set me for lord to all Egypt; come down to me, do not stay, ¹⁰and you have dwelt in the land of Goshen, and been near to me, you and your sons, and your son's sons, and your flock, and your herd, and all that you have, ¹¹and I have nourished you there—for yet [are] five years of famine—lest you become poor, you

and your household, and all that you have. ¹²And behold, your eyes are seeing, and the eyes of my brother Benjamin, that [it is] my mouth which is speaking to you; ¹³and you have declared to my father all my glory in Egypt, and all that you have seen, and you have hurried, and have brought down my father here." ¹⁴And he falls on the neck of his brother Benjamin, and weeps, and Benjamin has wept on his neck; ¹⁵and he kisses all his brothers, and weeps over them; and afterward his brothers have spoken with him. ¹⁶And the sound has been heard in the house of Pharaoh, saying, "The brothers of Joseph have come"; and it is good in the eyes of Pharaoh, and in the eyes of his servants, ¹⁷and Pharaoh says to Joseph, "Say to your brothers, This you do: load your beasts, and go, enter the land of Canaan, ¹⁸and take your father, and your households, and come to me, and I give to you the good of the land of Egypt, and you eat the fat of the land. ¹⁹Indeed, you have been commanded: this you do, take for yourselves out of the land of Egypt, wagons for your infants, and for your wives, and you have brought your father, and come; ²⁰and your eye has no pity on your vessels, for the good of all the land of Egypt [is] yours." ²¹And the sons of Israel do so, and Joseph gives wagons to them by the command of Pharaoh, and he gives to them provision for the way; ²²to all of them has he given—to each changes of garments, and to Benjamin he has given three hundred pieces of silver, and five changes of garments; ²³and to his father he has sent thus: ten donkeys carrying of the good things of Egypt, and ten female donkeys carrying grain and bread, even food for his father for the way. ²⁴And he sends his brothers away, and they go; and he says to them, "Do not be angry in the way." ²⁵And they go up out of Egypt, and come to the land of Canaan, to their father Jacob, ²⁶and they declare to him, saying, "Joseph [is] yet alive," and that he [is] ruler over all the land of Egypt; and his heart ceases, for he has not given credence to them. ²⁷And they speak to him all the words of Joseph, which he has spoken to them, and he sees the wagons which Joseph has sent to carry him away, and the spirit of their father Jacob lives; ²⁸and Israel says, "Enough! My son Joseph [is] yet alive; I go and see him before I die."

CHAPTER 46

¹And Israel journeys, and all that he has, and comes to Beer-Sheba, and sacrifices sacrifices to the God of his father Isaac; ²and God speaks to Israel in visions of the night and says, "Jacob, Jacob"; and he says, "Here I [am]." ³And He says, "I [am] God, God of your father, do not be afraid of going down to Egypt, for I set you there for a great nation; ⁴I go down with you to Egypt, and I also certainly bring you up, and Joseph puts his hand on your eyes." ⁵And Jacob rises from Beer-Sheba, and the sons of Israel carry away their father Jacob, and their infants, and their wives, in the wagons which Pharaoh has sent to carry him, ⁶and they take their livestock, and their goods which they have acquired in the land of Canaan, and come into Egypt—Jacob, and all his seed with him, ⁷his sons, and his sons' sons with him, his daughters, and his sons' daughters, indeed, all his seed he brought with him into Egypt. ⁸And these [are] the names of the sons of Israel who are coming into Egypt: Jacob and his sons, Jacob's firstborn, Reuben. ⁹And sons of Reuben: Enoch, and Phallu, and Hezron, and Carmi. ¹⁰And sons of Simeon: Jemuel, and Jamin, and Ohad, and Jachin, and Zohar, and Shaul son of the Canaanite. ¹¹And sons of Levi: Gershon, Kohath, and Merari. ¹²And sons of Judah: Er, and Onan, and Shelah, and Perez, and Zerah (and Er and Onan die in the land of Canaan). And sons of Perez are Hezron and Hamul. ¹³And sons of Issachar: Tola, and Phuvah, and Job, and Shimron. ¹⁴And sons of Zebulun: Sered, and Elon, and Jahleel. ¹⁵These [are] sons of Leah whom she bore to Jacob in Padan-Aram, and his daughter Dinah; all the persons of his sons and his daughters [are] thirty-three. ¹⁶And sons of Gad: Ziphion, and Haggi, Shuni, and Ezbon, Eri, and Arodi, and Areli. ¹⁷And sons of Asher: Jimnah, and Ishuah, and Isui, and Beriah, and their sister Serah. And sons of Beriah: Heber and Malchiel. ¹⁸These [are] sons of Zilpah, whom Laban gave to his daughter Leah, and she bears these to Jacob—sixteen persons. ¹⁹Sons of Rachel, Jacob's wife: Joseph and Benjamin. ²⁰And born to Joseph in the land of Egypt (whom Asenath daughter of Poti-Pherah, priest of On, has borne to him) [are] Manasseh and Ephraim. ²¹And sons of Benjamin: Belah, and Becher, and Ashbel, Gera, and Naaman, Ehi, and Rosh, Muppim, and Huppim, and Ard. ²²These [are] sons of Rachel, who were born to Jacob; all the persons [are] fourteen. ²³And sons of Dan: Hushim. ²⁴And sons of Naphtali: Jahzeel, and Guni, and Jezer, and Shillem. ²⁵These [are] sons of Bilhah, whom Laban gave to his daughter Rachel; and she bears these to Jacob—all the persons [are] seven. ²⁶All the persons who are coming to Jacob to Egypt, coming out of his thigh, apart from the wives of Jacob's sons, all the persons [are] sixty-six. ²⁷And the sons of Joseph who have been born to him in Egypt [are] two persons. All the persons of the house of Jacob who are coming into Egypt [are] seventy. ²⁸And Judah he has sent before him to Joseph, to direct before him to Goshen, and they come into the land of Goshen; ²⁹and Joseph harnesses his chariot, and goes up to meet his father Israel, to Goshen, and appears to him, and falls on his neck, and weeps on his neck again; ³⁰and Israel says to Joseph, "Let me die this time, after my seeing your face, for you [are] yet alive." ³¹And Joseph says to his brothers, and to the house of his father, "I go up, and declare to Pharaoh, and say to him, My brothers, and the house of my father who [are] in the land of Canaan have come to me; ³²and the men [are] feeders of a flock, for they have been men of livestock; and their flock, and their herd, and all that they have, they have brought. ³³And it has come to pass, when Pharaoh calls for you and has said, What [are] your works? ³⁴That you have said, Your servants have been men of livestock from our youth, even until now, both we and our fathers, in order that you may dwell in the land of Goshen, for the abomination of the Egyptians is everyone feeding a flock."

CHAPTER 47

¹And Joseph comes and declares [it] to Pharaoh, and says, "My father, and my brothers, and their flock, and their herd, and all they have, have come from the land of Canaan, and behold, they [are] in the land of Goshen." ²And out of his brothers he has taken five men, and sets them before Pharaoh; ³and Pharaoh says to his brothers, "What [are] your works?" And they say to Pharaoh, "Your servants [are] feeders of a flock, both we and our fathers"; ⁴and they say to Pharaoh, "We have come to sojourn in the land, for there is no pasture for the flock which your servants have, for the famine in the land of Canaan [is] grievous; and now, please let your servants dwell in the land of Goshen." ⁵And Pharaoh speaks to Joseph, saying, "Your father and your brothers have come to you: ⁶the land of Egypt is before you; cause your father and your brothers to dwell in the best of the land—they dwell in the land of Goshen, and if you have known, and there are among them men of ability, then you have set them [as] heads over the livestock I have." ⁷And Joseph brings in his father Jacob, and causes him to stand before Pharaoh; and Jacob blesses Pharaoh. ⁸And Pharaoh says to Jacob, "How many [are] the days of the years of your life?" ⁹And Jacob says to Pharaoh, "The days of the years of my sojournings [are] one hundred and thirty years; few and evil have been the days of the years of my life, and they have not reached the days of the years of the life of my fathers, in the days of their sojournings." ¹⁰And Jacob blesses Pharaoh, and goes out from before Pharaoh. ¹¹And Joseph settles his father and his brothers, and gives a possession to them in the land of Egypt, in the best of the land, in the land of Rameses, as Pharaoh commanded; ¹²and Joseph nourishes his father, and his brothers, and all the house of his father [with] bread, according to the mouth of the infants. ¹³And there is no bread in all the land, for the famine [is] very grievous, and the land of Egypt and the land of Canaan are feeble because of the famine; ¹⁴and Joseph gathers all the silver that is found in the land of Egypt and in the land of Canaan, for the grain that they are buying, and Joseph brings the silver into the house of Pharaoh. ¹⁵And the silver is consumed out of the land of Egypt and out of the land of Canaan, and all the Egyptians come to Joseph, saying, "Give bread to us—why do we die before you, though the money has ceased?" ¹⁶And Joseph says, "Give your livestock; and I give to you for your livestock, if the money has ceased." ¹⁷And they bring in their livestock to Joseph, and Joseph gives to them bread, for the horses, and for the livestock of the flock, and for the livestock of the herd, and for the donkeys; and he tends them with bread, for all their livestock, during that year. ¹⁸And that year is finished, and they come to him on the second year, and say to him, "We do not hide from my lord, that since

the money has been finished, and possession of the livestock [is] to my lord, there has not been left before my lord except our bodies, and our ground; ¹⁹why do we die before your eyes, both we and our ground? Buy us and our ground for bread, and we and our ground are servants to Pharaoh; and give seed, and we live, and do not die, and the ground is not desolate." ²⁰And Joseph buys all the ground of Egypt for Pharaoh, for the Egyptians have each sold his field, for the famine has been severe on them, and the land becomes Pharaoh's; ²¹as for the people, he has removed them to cities from the [one] end of the border of Egypt even to its [other] end. ²²Only the ground of the priests he has not bought, for the priests have a portion from Pharaoh, and they have eaten their portion which Pharaoh has given to them, therefore they have not sold their ground. ²³And Joseph says to the people, "Behold, I have bought you today and your ground for Pharaoh; behold, seed for you, and you have sown the ground, ²⁴and it has come to pass in the increases, that you have given a fifth to Pharaoh, and four of the parts are for yourselves, for seed of the field, and for your food, and for those who [are] in your houses, and for food for your infants." ²⁵And they say, "You have revived us; we find grace in the eyes of my lord, and have been servants to Pharaoh"; ²⁶and Joseph sets it for a statute to this day, concerning the ground of Egypt, [that] Pharaoh has a fifth; only the ground of the priests alone has not become Pharaoh's. ²⁷And Israel dwells in the land of Egypt, in the land of Goshen, and they have possession in it, and are fruitful, and multiply exceedingly; ²⁸and Jacob lives in the land of Egypt seventeen years, and the days of Jacob, the years of his life, are one hundred and forty-seven years. ²⁹And the days of Israel are near to die, and he calls for his son, for Joseph, and says to him, "Now if I have found grace in your eyes, please put your hand under my thigh, and you have done kindness and truth with me; please do not bury me in Egypt, ³⁰and I have lain with my fathers, and you have carried me out of Egypt, and buried me in their burying-place." And he says, "I do according to your word"; ³¹and he says, "Swear to me"; and he swears to him, and Israel bows himself on the head of the bed.

CHAPTER 48

¹And it comes to pass, after these things, that [one] says to Joseph, "Behold, your father is sick"; and he takes his two sons with him, Manasseh and Ephraim. ²And [one] declares [it] to Jacob and says, "Behold, your son Joseph is coming to you"; and Israel strengthens himself, and sits on the bed. ³And Jacob says to Joseph, "God Almighty has appeared to me, in Luz, in the land of Canaan, and blesses me, ⁴and says to me, Behold, I am making you fruitful, and have multiplied you, and given you for an assembly of peoples, and given this land to your seed after you, a continuous possession. ⁵And now, your two sons, who are born to you in the land of Egypt, before my coming to you to Egypt, they [are] mine; Ephraim and Manasseh, as Reuben and Simeon, they are mine; ⁶and your family which you have begotten after them are yours; by the name of their brothers they are called in their inheritance. ⁷And I—in my coming in from Padan-[Aram] Rachel has died by me in the land of Canaan, in the way, while yet a distance of land to enter Ephrata, and I bury her there in the way of Ephrata, which [is] Beth-Lehem." ⁸And Israel sees the sons of Joseph and says, "Who [are] these?" ⁹And Joseph says to his father, "They [are] my sons, whom God has given to me in this [place]"; and he says, "Please bring them to me, and I bless them." ¹⁰And the eyes of Israel have been heavy from age—he is unable to see; and he brings them near to him, and he kisses them and cleaves to them; ¹¹and Israel says to Joseph, "I had not thought [possible] to see your face, and behold, God has also showed me your seed." ¹²And Joseph brings them out from between his knees, and bows himself on his face to the earth; ¹³and Joseph takes them both, Ephraim in his right hand toward Israel's left, and Manasseh in his left toward Israel's right, and brings [them] near to him. ¹⁴And Israel puts out his right hand and places [it] on the head of Ephraim, who [is] the younger, and his left hand on the head of Manasseh; he has guided his hands wisely, for Manasseh [is] the firstborn. ¹⁵And he blesses Joseph and says, "God, before whom my fathers Abraham and Isaac habitually walked: God who is feeding me from my being to this day: ¹⁶the Messenger who is redeeming me from all evil blesses the youths, and my name is called on them, and the name of my fathers Abraham and Isaac; and they increase into a multitude in the midst of the land." ¹⁷And Joseph sees that his father sets his right hand on the head of Ephraim, and it is wrong in his eyes, and he supports the hand of his father to turn it aside from off the head of Ephraim to the head of Manasseh; ¹⁸and Joseph says to his father, "Not so, my father, for this [is] the firstborn; set your right hand on his head." ¹⁹And his father refuses and says, "I have known, my son, I have known; he also becomes a people, and he also is great, and yet, his young brother is greater than he, and his seed is the fullness of the nations"; ²⁰and he blesses them in that day, saying, "By you does Israel bless, saying, God set you as Ephraim and as Manasseh"; and he sets Ephraim before Manasseh. ²¹And Israel says to Joseph, "Behold, I am dying, and God has been with you, and has brought you back to the land of your fathers; ²²and I have given to you one portion above your brothers, which I have taken out of the hand of the Amorite by my sword and by my bow."

CHAPTER 49

¹And Jacob calls to his sons and says, "Be gathered together, and I declare to you that which happens with you in the latter end of the days. ²Be assembled, and hear, sons of Jacob, || And listen to your father Israel. ³Reuben! You [are] my firstborn, || My power, and beginning of my strength, || The abundance of exaltation, || And the abundance of strength; ⁴Unstable as water, you are not abundant; For you have gone up your father's bed; Then you have defiled [it]: He went up my couch! ⁵Simeon and Levi [are] brothers! Instruments of violence—their espousals! ⁶Into their secret, do not come, O my soul! Do not be united to their assembly, O my glory; For in their anger they slew a man, || And in their self-will eradicated a prince. ⁷Cursed [is] their anger, for [it is] fierce, || And their wrath, for [it is] sharp; I divide them in Jacob, || And I scatter them in Israel. ⁸Judah! Your brothers praise you! Your hand [is] on the neck of your enemies, || Sons of your father bow themselves to you. ⁹A lion's whelp [is] Judah, || For prey, my son, you have gone up; He has bent, he has crouched as a lion, || And as a lioness; who causes him to arise? ¹⁰The scepter does not turn aside from Judah, || And a lawgiver from between his feet, || Until his Seed comes; And His [is] the obedience of peoples. ¹¹Binding to the vine his donkey, || And to the choice vine the colt of his donkey, || He has washed in wine his clothing, || And in the blood of grapes his covering; ¹²Red [are] eyes with wine, || And white [are] teeth with milk! ¹³Zebulun dwells at a haven of the seas, || And he [is] for a haven of ships; And his side [is] to Sidon. ¹⁴Issachar [is] a strong donkey, || Crouching between the two folds; ¹⁵And he sees rest, that [it is] good, || And the land, that [it is] pleasant, || And he inclines his shoulder to bear, || And is a servant for tribute. ¹⁶Dan judges his people, || As one of the tribes of Israel; ¹⁷Dan is a serpent by the way, a viper by the path, || Which is biting the horse's heels, || And its rider falls backward. ¹⁸For Your salvation I have waited, YHWH! ¹⁹Gad! A troop assaults him, || But he assaults last. ²⁰Out of Asher his bread [is] fat; And he gives delicacies of a king. ²¹Naphtali [is] a doe sent away, || Who is giving beautiful young ones. ²²Joseph [is] a fruitful son; A fruitful son by a fountain, || Daughters step over the wall; ²³And embitter him indeed, they have striven, || Indeed, archers hate him; ²⁴And his bow abides in strength, || And strengthened are the arms of his hands || By the hands of the Mighty One of Jacob, || From where is a shepherd, a son of Israel. ²⁵By the God of your father who helps you, || And the Mighty One who blesses you, || Blessings of the heavens from above, || Blessings of the deep lying under, || Blessings of breasts and womb— ²⁶Your father's blessings have been mighty || Above the blessings of my progenitors, || To the limit of the perpetual heights || They are for the head of Joseph, || And for the crown of the one || Separate [from] his brothers. ²⁷Benjamin! A wolf tears; In the morning he eats prey, || And at evening he apportions spoil." ²⁸All these [are] the twelve tribes of Israel, and this [is] that which their father has spoken to them, and he blesses them; each according to his blessing he has blessed them. ²⁹And he commands them and says to them, "I am being gathered to my people; bury me by my fathers, at the cave which [is] in the field of Ephron the Hittite; ³⁰in the cave which [is] in

the field of Machpelah, which [is] on the front of Mamre, in the land of Canaan, which Abraham bought with the field from Ephron the Hittite for a possession of a burying-place; ³¹(there they buried Abraham and his wife Sarah; there they buried Isaac and his wife Rebekah; and there I buried Leah); ³²the purchase of the field and of the cave which [is] in it, [is] from sons of Heth." ³³And Jacob finishes commanding his sons, and gathers up his feet to the bed, and expires, and is gathered to his people.

CHAPTER 50

¹And Joseph falls on his father's face, and weeps over him, and kisses him; ²and Joseph commands his servants, the physicians, to embalm his father, and the physicians embalm Israel; ³and they fulfill for him forty days, for so they fulfill the days of the embalmed, and the Egyptians weep for him seventy days. ⁴And the days of his weeping pass away, and Joseph speaks to the house of Pharaoh, saying, "Now if I have found grace in your eyes, please speak in the ears of Pharaoh, saying, ⁵My father caused me to swear, saying, Behold, I am dying; in my burying-place which I have prepared for myself in the land of Canaan, there you bury me; and now, please let me go up and bury my father, then I return"; ⁶and Pharaoh says, "Go up and bury your father, as he caused you to swear." ⁷And Joseph goes up to bury his father, and all [the] servants of Pharaoh go up with him, [the] elderly of his house, and all [the] elderly of the land of Egypt, ⁸and all the house of Joseph, and his brothers, and the house of his father; only their infants, and their flock, and their herd, have they left in the land of Goshen; ⁹and there go up with him both chariot and horsemen, and the camp is very great. ¹⁰And they come to the threshing-floor of Atad, which [is] beyond the Jordan, and they lament there, a lamentation great and very grievous; and he makes for his father a mourning seven days, ¹¹and the inhabitant of the land, the Canaanite, sees the mourning in the threshing-floor of Atad and says, "A grievous mourning [is] this to the Egyptians"; therefore [one] has called its name "The mourning of the Egyptians," which [is] beyond the Jordan. ¹²And his sons do to him so as he commanded them, ¹³and his sons carry him away to the land of Canaan, and bury him in the cave of the field of Machpelah, which Abraham bought with the field for a possession of a burying-place, from Ephron the Hittite, on the front of Mamre. ¹⁴And Joseph turns back to Egypt, he and his brothers, and all who are going up with him to bury his father, after his burying his father. ¹⁵And the brothers of Joseph see that their father is dead, and say, "Perhaps Joseph hates us, and certainly returns to us all the evil which we did with him." ¹⁶And they give a charge for Joseph, saying, "Your father commanded before his death, saying, ¹⁷Thus you say to Joseph: Ah, now, please bear with the transgression of your brothers and their sin, for they have done you evil; and now, please bear with the transgression of the servants of the God of your father"; and Joseph weeps in their speaking to him. ¹⁸And his brothers also go and fall before him, and say, "Behold, we [are] to you for servants." ¹⁹And Joseph says to them, "Do not fear, for [am] I in the place of God? ²⁰As for you, you devised evil against me, [but] God devised it for good, in order to do as [at] this day, to keep alive a numerous people; ²¹and now, do not fear: I nourish you and your infants"; and he comforts them, and speaks to their heart. ²²And Joseph dwells in Egypt, he and the house of his father, and Joseph lives one hundred and ten years, ²³and Joseph looks on Ephraim's sons of a third [generation]; sons also of Machir, son of Manasseh, have been born on the knees of Joseph. ²⁴And Joseph says to his brothers, "I am dying, and God certainly inspects you, and has caused you to go up from this land, to the land which He has sworn to Abraham, to Isaac, and to Jacob." ²⁵And Joseph causes the sons of Israel to swear, saying, "God certainly inspects you, and you have brought up my bones from this [place]." ²⁶And Joseph dies, a son of one hundred and ten years, and they embalm him, and he is put into a coffin in Egypt.

EXODUS

CHAPTER 1

¹And these [are] the names of the sons of Israel who are coming into Egypt; each man and his household have come with Jacob: ²Reuben, Simeon, Levi, and Judah, ³Issachar, Zebulun, and Benjamin, ⁴Dan, and Naphtali, Gad, and Asher. ⁵And all the persons coming out of the thigh of Jacob are seventy persons; as for Joseph, he was in Egypt. ⁶And Joseph dies, and all his brothers, and all that generation; ⁷and the sons of Israel have been fruitful, and they teem, and multiply, and are very, very mighty, and the land is filled with them. ⁸And there rises a new king over Egypt, who has not known Joseph, ⁹and he says to his people, "Behold, the people of the sons of Israel [are] more numerous and mighty than we. ¹⁰Give help! Let us act wisely concerning it, lest it multiply, and it has come to pass, when war happens, that it has been joined, even it, to those hating us, and has fought against us, and has gone up out of the land." ¹¹And they set princes of tribute over it, so as to afflict it with their burdens, and it builds the store-cities of Pithom and Rameses for Pharaoh; ¹²and as they afflict it, so it multiplies, and so it breaks forth, and they are distressed because of the sons of Israel; ¹³and the Egyptians cause the sons of Israel to serve with rigor, ¹⁴and make their lives bitter in hard service, in clay, and in brick, and in every [kind] of service in the field; all their service in which they have served [is] with rigor. ¹⁵And the king of Egypt speaks to the midwives, the Hebrewesses (of whom the name of the first [is] Shiphrah, and the name of the second Puah), ¹⁶and says, "When you cause the Hebrew women to bear, and have looked on the children, if it [is] a son, then you have put him to death; and if it [is] a daughter, then she has lived." ¹⁷And the midwives fear God, and have not done as the king of Egypt has spoken to them, and they keep the boys alive; ¹⁸and the king of Egypt calls for the midwives and says to them, "Why have you done this thing, and keep the boys alive?" ¹⁹And the midwives say to Pharaoh, "Because the Hebrew women [are] not as the Egyptian women, for they [are] lively; before the midwife comes to them—they have borne!" ²⁰And God does good to the midwives, and the people multiply, and are very mighty; ²¹and it comes to pass, because the midwives have feared God, that He makes households for them; ²²and Pharaoh lays a charge on all his people, saying, "Every son who is born—you cast him into the River, and every daughter you keep alive."

CHAPTER 2

¹And there goes a man of the house of Levi, and he takes the daughter of Levi, ²and the woman conceives, and bears a son, and she sees him, that he [is] beautiful, and she hides him [for] three months, ³and she has not been able to hide him anymore, and she takes an ark of rushes for him, and covers it with bitumen and with pitch, and puts the boy in it, and puts [it] in the weeds by the edge of the River; ⁴and his sister stations herself far off, to know what is done to him. ⁵And a daughter of Pharaoh comes down to bathe at the River, and her girls are walking by the side of the River, and she sees the ark in the midst of the weeds, and sends her handmaid, and she takes it, ⁶and opens, and sees him—the boy, and behold, a child weeping! And she has pity on him and says, "This is [one] of the Hebrews' children." ⁷And his sister says to the daughter of Pharaoh, "Do I go? When I have called a suckling woman of the Hebrews for you, then she suckles the boy for you"; ⁸and the daughter of Pharaoh says to her, "Go"; and the virgin goes, and calls the mother of the boy, ⁹and the daughter of Pharaoh says to her, "Take this boy away, and suckle him for me, and I give your hire"; and the woman takes the boy, and suckles him. ¹⁰And the boy grows, and she brings him to the daughter of Pharaoh, and he is to her for a son, and she calls his name Moses, and says, "Because I have drawn him from the water." ¹¹And it comes to pass, in those days, that Moses is grown, and he goes out to his brothers, and

looks on their burdens, and sees a man, an Egyptian, striking a man, a Hebrew, [one] of his brothers, ¹²and he turns here and there, and sees that there is no man, and strikes the Egyptian, and hides him in the sand. ¹³And he goes out on the second day, and behold, two men, Hebrews, are striving, and he says to the wrongdoer, "Why do you strike your neighbor?" ¹⁴And he says, "Who set you for a head and judge over us? Are you saying [it] to slay me as you have slain the Egyptian?" And Moses fears and says, "Surely the thing has been known." ¹⁵And Pharaoh hears of this thing, and seeks to slay Moses, and Moses flees from the face of Pharaoh, and dwells in the land of Midian, and dwells by the well. ¹⁶And to a priest of Midian [are] seven daughters, and they come and draw, and fill the troughs to water the flock of their father, ¹⁷and the shepherds come and drive them away, and Moses arises, and saves them, and waters their flock. ¹⁸And they come to their father Reuel, and he says, "Why have you hurried to come in today?" ¹⁹And they say, "A man, an Egyptian, has delivered us out of the hand of the shepherds, and has also diligently drawn for us, and waters the flock"; ²⁰and he says to his daughters, "And where [is] he? Why [is] this [that] you left the man? Call for him, and he eats bread." ²¹And Moses is willing to dwell with the man, and he gives his daughter Zipporah to Moses, ²²and she bears a son, and he calls his name Gershom, for he said, "I have been a sojourner in a strange land." ²³And it comes to pass during these many days, that the king of Egypt dies, and the sons of Israel sigh because of the service, and cry, and their cry goes up to God, because of the service; ²⁴and God hears their groaning, and God remembers His covenant with Abraham, with Isaac, and with Jacob; ²⁵and God sees the sons of Israel, and God knows.

CHAPTER 3

¹And Moses has been feeding the flock of his father-in-law Jethro, priest of Midian, and he leads the flock behind the wilderness, and comes to the mountain of God, to Horeb; ²and the Messenger of YHWH appears to him in a flame of fire, out of the midst of the bush, and he sees, and behold, the bush is burning with fire, and the bush is not consumed. ³And Moses says, "Now I turn aside and see this great appearance. Why is the bush not burned?" ⁴And YHWH sees that he has turned aside to see, and God calls to him out of the midst of the bush and says, "Moses! Moses!" And he says, "Here I [am]." ⁵And He says, "Do not come near here. Cast your shoes from off your feet, for the place on which you are standing is holy ground." ⁶He also says, "I [am] the God of your father, God of Abraham, God of Isaac, and God of Jacob"; and Moses hides his face, for he is afraid to look toward God. ⁷And YHWH says, "I have certainly seen the affliction of My people who [are] in Egypt, and I have heard their cry because of its exactors, for I have known its pains; ⁸and I go down to deliver it out of the hand of the Egyptians, and to cause it to go up out of the land to a land good and broad, to a land flowing with milk and honey—to the place of the Canaanite, and the Hittite, and the Amorite, and the Perizzite, and the Hivite, and the Jebusite. ⁹And now, behold, the cry of the sons of Israel has come to Me, and I have also seen the oppression with which the Egyptians are oppressing them, ¹⁰and now, come, and I send you to Pharaoh; and bring out My people, the sons of Israel, from Egypt." ¹¹And Moses says to God, "Who [am] I, that I go to Pharaoh, and that I bring out the sons of Israel from Egypt?" ¹²And He says, "Because I am with you, and this [is] the sign to you that I have sent you: in your bringing out the people from Egypt—you serve God on this mountain." ¹³And Moses says to God, "Behold, I am coming to the sons of Israel, and have said to them, The God of your fathers has sent me to you, and they have said to me, What [is] His Name? What do I say to them?" ¹⁴And God says to Moses, "I AM THAT WHICH I AM." He also says, "Thus you say to the sons of Israel: I AM has sent me to you." ¹⁵And God says again to Moses, "Thus you say to the sons of Israel: YHWH, God of your fathers, God of Abraham, God of Isaac, and God of Jacob, has sent me to you; this [is] My Name for all time, and this [is] My memorial, to generation [and] generation. ¹⁶Go, and you have gathered the elderly of Israel, and have said to them: YHWH, God of your fathers, has appeared to me, God of Abraham, Isaac, and Jacob, saying, I have certainly inspected you, and that which is done to you in Egypt; ¹⁷and I say [that] I bring you up out of the affliction of Egypt to the land of the Canaanite, and the Hittite, and the Amorite, and the Perizzite, and the Hivite, and the Jebusite, to a land flowing [with] milk and honey. ¹⁸And they have listened to your voice, and you have entered, you and [the] elderly of Israel, to the king of Egypt, and you have said to him: YHWH, God of the Hebrews, has met with us; and now, please let us go a journey of three days into the wilderness, and we sacrifice to our God YHWH. ¹⁹And I have known that the king of Egypt does not permit you to go, unless by a strong hand, ²⁰and I have put forth My hand, and have struck Egypt with all My wonders, which I do in its midst—and afterward he sends you away. ²¹And I have given the grace of this people in the eyes of the Egyptians, and it has come to pass, when you go, you do not go empty; ²²and [every] woman has asked from her neighbor, and from her who is sojourning in her house, [for] vessels of silver, and vessels of gold, and garments, and you have put [them] on your sons and on your daughters, and have spoiled the Egyptians."

CHAPTER 4

¹And Moses answers and says, "And if they do not give credence to me, nor listen to my voice, and say, YHWH has not appeared to you?" ²And YHWH says to him, "What [is] this in your hand?" And he says, "A rod"; ³and He says, "Cast it to the earth"; and he casts it to the earth, and it becomes a serpent—and Moses flees from its presence. ⁴And YHWH says to Moses, "Put forth your hand, and lay hold on the tail of it"; and he puts forth his hand, and lays hold on it, and it becomes a rod in his hand— ⁵"so that they believe that YHWH, God of their fathers, has appeared to you, God of Abraham, God of Isaac, and God of Jacob." ⁶And YHWH says to him again, "Now put your hand into your bosom"; and he puts his hand into his bosom, and he brings it out, and behold, his hand [is] leprous as snow; ⁷and He says, "Put your hand back into your bosom"; and he puts his hand back into his bosom, and he brings it out from his bosom, and behold, it has turned back as his flesh— ⁸"and it has come to pass, if they do not give credence to you, and do not listen to the voice of the first sign, that they have given credence to the voice of the latter sign. ⁹And it has come to pass, if they do not give credence even to these two signs, nor listen to your voice, that you have taken of the waters of the River, and have poured [it] on the dry land, and the waters which you take from the River have been, indeed, they have become blood on the dry land." ¹⁰And Moses says to YHWH, "O my Lord, I [am] not a man of words, either yesterday, or before, or since Your speaking to Your servant, for I [am] slow of mouth, and slow of tongue." ¹¹And YHWH says to him, "Who appointed a mouth for man? Or who appoints the mute, or deaf, or open, or blind? Is it not I, YHWH? ¹²And now, go, and I am with your mouth, and have directed you that which you speak"; ¹³and he says, "O my Lord, please send by the hand [of another that] You send." ¹⁴And the anger of YHWH burns against Moses, and He says, "Is Aaron the Levite not your brother? I have known that he speaks well, and also, behold, he is coming out to meet you; when he has seen you, then he has rejoiced in his heart, ¹⁵and you have spoken to him, and have set the words in his mouth, and I am with your mouth, and with his mouth, and have directed you that which you do; ¹⁶and he, he has spoken to the people for you, and it has come to pass, he is to you for a mouth, and you are to him for God; ¹⁷and you take this rod in your hand, with which you do the signs." ¹⁸And Moses goes and turns back to his father-in-law Jethro, and says to him, "Please let me go, and I return to my brothers who [are] in Egypt, and I see whether they are yet alive." And Jethro says to Moses, "Go in peace." ¹⁹And YHWH says to Moses in Midian, "Go, return to Egypt, for all the men who seek your life have died"; ²⁰and Moses takes his wife, and his sons, and causes them to ride on the donkey, and turns back to the land of Egypt, and Moses takes the rod of God in his hand. ²¹And YHWH says to Moses, "In your going to return to Egypt, see—all the wonders which I have put in your hand—that you have done them before Pharaoh, and I strengthen his heart, and he does not send the people away; ²²and you have said to Pharaoh,

Thus said YHWH: My son, My firstborn [is] Israel, ²³and I say to you, send My son away, and he serves Me; and [if] you refuse to send him away, behold, I am slaying your son, your firstborn." ²⁴And it comes to pass in the way, in a lodging place, that YHWH meets him, and seeks to put him to death; ²⁵and Zipporah takes a flint, and cuts off the foreskin of her son, and causes [it] to touch his feet, and says, "You [are] surely a bridegroom of blood to me"; ²⁶and He desists from him. Then she said, "A bridegroom of blood," in reference to the circumcision. ²⁷And YHWH says to Aaron, "Go into the wilderness to meet Moses"; and he goes, and meets him on the mountain of God, and kisses him, ²⁸and Moses declares to Aaron all the words of YHWH with which He has sent him, and all the signs with which He has charged him. ²⁹And Moses goes—Aaron also—and they gather all the elderly of the sons of Israel, ³⁰and Aaron speaks all the words which YHWH has spoken to Moses, and does the signs before the eyes of the people; ³¹and the people believe when they hear that YHWH has looked after the sons of Israel, and that He has seen their affliction; and they bow and pay respect.

CHAPTER 5

¹And afterward Moses and Aaron have entered, and they say to Pharaoh, "Thus said YHWH, God of Israel: Send My people away, and they keep a celebration for Me in the wilderness"; ²and Pharaoh says, "Who [is] YHWH, that I listen to His voice to send Israel away? I have not known YHWH, and I also do not send Israel away." ³And they say, "The God of the Hebrews has met with us; please let us go a journey of three days into the wilderness, and we sacrifice to our God YHWH, lest He meet us with pestilence or with sword." ⁴And the king of Egypt says to them, "Why, Moses and Aaron, do you free the people from its works? Go to your burdens." ⁵Pharaoh also says, "Behold, the people of the land [are] numerous now, and you have caused them to cease from their burdens!" ⁶And on that day Pharaoh commands the exactors among the people and its authorities, saying, ⁷"You do not add to give straw to the people for the making of the bricks as before—they go and have gathered straw for themselves; ⁸and you put on them the proper quantity of the bricks which they are making before, you do not diminish from it, for they are remiss, therefore they are crying, saying, Let us go, let us sacrifice to our God; ⁹let the service be heavy on the men, and let them work at it, and not be dazzled by lying words." ¹⁰And the exactors of the people, and its authorities, go out, and speak to the people, saying, "Thus said Pharaoh: I do not give you straw, ¹¹you—go, take straw for yourselves where you can find [it], for there is nothing diminished of your service." ¹²And the people are scattered over all the land of Egypt, to gather stubble for straw, ¹³and the exactors are making haste, saying, "Complete your works, the matter of a day in its day, as when there is straw." ¹⁴And the authorities of the sons of Israel, whom the exactors of Pharaoh have placed over them, are beaten, saying, "Why have you not completed your portion in making brick as before, both yesterday and today?" ¹⁵And the authorities of the sons of Israel come in and cry to Pharaoh, saying, "Why do you do thus to your servants? ¹⁶Straw is not given to your servants, and they are saying to us, Make bricks, and behold, your servants are struck—and your people have sinned." ¹⁷And he says, "Remiss—you are remiss, therefore you are saying, Let us go, let us sacrifice to YHWH; ¹⁸and now, go, serve; and straw is not given to you, and you give the [required] measure of bricks." ¹⁹And the authorities of the sons of Israel see them in affliction, saying, "You do not diminish from your bricks; the matter of a day in its day." ²⁰And they meet Moses and Aaron standing to meet them in their coming out from Pharaoh, ²¹and say to them, "YHWH look on you, and judge, because you have caused our fragrance to stink in the eyes of Pharaoh, and in the eyes of his servants—to give a sword into their hand to slay us." ²²And Moses turns back to YHWH and says, "Lord, why have You done evil to this people? Why [is] this [that] You have sent me? ²³And since I have come to Pharaoh to speak in Your Name, he has done evil to this people, and You have not delivered Your people at all."

CHAPTER 6

¹And YHWH says to Moses, "Now you see that which I do to Pharaoh, for with a strong hand he sends them away, indeed, with a strong hand he casts them out of his land." ²And God speaks to Moses and says to him, "I [am] YHWH, ³and I appear to Abraham, to Isaac, and to Jacob, as God Almighty; as for My Name YHWH, I have not been known to them; ⁴and I have also established My covenant with them, to give the land of Canaan to them, the land of their sojournings, wherein they have sojourned; ⁵and I have also heard the groaning of the sons of Israel, whom the Egyptians are causing to serve, and I remember My covenant. ⁶Therefore say to the sons of Israel: I [am] YHWH, and I have brought you out from under the burdens of the Egyptians, and have delivered you from their service, and have redeemed you by an outstretched arm, and by great judgments, ⁷and have taken you to Myself for a people, and I have been to you for God, and you have known that I [am] your God YHWH, who is bringing you out from under the burdens of the Egyptians; ⁸and I have brought you to the land which I have lifted up My hand to give it to Abraham, to Isaac, and to Jacob, and have given it to you—a possession; I [am] YHWH." ⁹And Moses speaks so to the sons of Israel, and they did not listen to Moses, for anguish of spirit, and for harsh service. ¹⁰And YHWH speaks to Moses, saying, ¹¹"Go in, speak to Pharaoh king of Egypt, and he sends the sons of Israel out of his land"; ¹²and Moses speaks before YHWH, saying, "Behold, the sons of Israel have not listened to me, and how does Pharaoh hear me, and I of uncircumcised lips?" ¹³And YHWH speaks to Moses and to Aaron, and charges them for the sons of Israel, and for Pharaoh king of Egypt, to bring out the sons of Israel from the land of Egypt. ¹⁴These [are] heads of the house of their fathers. Sons of Reuben firstborn of Israel: Enoch, and Phallu, Hezron, and Carmi; these [are] families of Reuben. ¹⁵And sons of Simeon: Jemuel, and Jamin, and Ohad, and Jachin, and Zohar, and Shaul, son of the Canaanite; these [are] families of Simeon. ¹⁶And these [are] the names of the sons of Levi, as to their births: Gershon, and Kohath, and Merari; and the years of the life of Levi [are] one hundred and thirty-seven years. ¹⁷The sons of Gershon: Libni and Shimi, as to their families. ¹⁸And the sons of Kohath: Amram, and Izhar, and Hebron, and Uzziel; and the years of the life of Kohath [are] one hundred and thirty-three years. ¹⁹And the sons of Merari: Mahli and Mushi; these [are] families of Levi, as to their births. ²⁰And Amram takes his aunt Jochebed to himself for a wife, and she bears Aaron and Moses to him; and the years of the life of Amram [are] one hundred and thirty-seven years. ²¹And sons of Izhar: Korah, and Nepheg, and Zichri. ²²And sons of Uzziel: Mishael, and Elzaphan, and Sithri. ²³And Aaron takes Elisheba daughter of Amminadab, sister of Naashon, to himself for a wife, and she bears to him Nadab, and Abihu, Eleazar, and Ithamar. ²⁴And sons of Korah: Assir, and Elkanah, and Abiasaph; these [are] families of the Korahite. ²⁵And Eleazar, Aaron's son, has taken to himself [one] of the daughters of Putiel for a wife for himself, and she bears Phinehas to him; these [are] heads of the fathers of the Levites, as to their families. ²⁶This [is] Aaron—and Moses—to whom YHWH said, "Bring out the sons of Israel from the land of Egypt, by their hosts"; ²⁷these are they who are speaking to Pharaoh king of Egypt, to bring out the sons of Israel from Egypt, this [is] Moses—and Aaron. ²⁸And it comes to pass in the day of YHWH's speaking to Moses in the land of Egypt, ²⁹that YHWH speaks to Moses, saying, "I [am] YHWH, speak to Pharaoh king of Egypt all that I am speaking to you." ³⁰And Moses says before YHWH, "Behold, I [am] of uncircumcised lips, and how does Pharaoh listen to me?"

CHAPTER 7

¹And YHWH says to Moses, "See, I have given you [as] a god to Pharaoh, and your brother Aaron is your prophet; ²you speak all that I command you, and your brother Aaron speaks to Pharaoh, and he has sent the sons of Israel out of his land. ³And I harden the heart of Pharaoh, and have multiplied My signs and My wonders in the land of Egypt, ⁴and Pharaoh does not listen, and I have put My hand on Egypt, and have brought out My hosts, My people, the sons of Israel, from the land of Egypt by great judgments; ⁵and the Egyptians have known that I [am] YHWH, in My stretching out My hand against Egypt; and I have brought out the sons of Israel from their midst." ⁶And Moses does—Aaron also—as YHWH commanded them; so have they done; ⁷and Moses [is] a son of eighty years, and

Aaron [is] a son of eighty-three years, in their speaking to Pharaoh. ⁸And YHWH speaks to Moses and to Aaron, saying, ⁹"When Pharaoh speaks to you, saying, Give a wonder for yourselves; then you have said to Aaron, Take your rod and cast [it] before Pharaoh—it becomes a dragon." ¹⁰And Moses goes in—Aaron also—to Pharaoh, and they do so as YHWH has commanded; and Aaron casts his rod before Pharaoh and before his servants, and it becomes a dragon. ¹¹And Pharaoh also calls for wise men and for sorcerers; and the enchanters of Egypt, they also, with their [enchanting] flames, do so, ¹²and they each cast down his rod, and they become dragons, and the rod of Aaron swallows their rods; ¹³and the heart of Pharaoh is strong, and he has not listened to them, as YHWH has spoken. ¹⁴And YHWH says to Moses, "The heart of Pharaoh has been hard, he has refused to send the people away; ¹⁵go to Pharaoh in the morning, behold, he is going out to the water, and you have stood to meet him by the edge of the River, and the rod which was turned to a serpent you take in your hand, ¹⁶and you have said to him: YHWH, God of the Hebrews, has sent me to you, saying, Send My people away, and they serve Me in the wilderness; and behold, you have not listened until now. ¹⁷Thus said YHWH: By this you know that I [am] YHWH; behold, I am striking with the rod which [is] in my hand, on the waters which [are] in the River, and they have been turned to blood, ¹⁸and the fish that [are] in the River die, and the River has stunk, and the Egyptians have been wearied of drinking waters from the River." ¹⁹And YHWH says to Moses, "Say to Aaron, Take your rod, and stretch out your hand against the waters of Egypt, against their streams, against their rivers, and against their ponds, and against all their collections of waters; and they are blood—and there has been blood in all the land of Egypt, both in [vessels of] wood, and in [those of] stone." ²⁰And Moses and Aaron do so, as YHWH has commanded, and he lifts up [his hand] with the rod, and strikes the waters which [are] in the River, before the eyes of Pharaoh and before the eyes of his servants, and all the waters which [are] in the River are turned to blood, ²¹and the fish which [is] in the River has died, and the River stinks, and the Egyptians have not been able to drink water from the River; and the blood is in all the land of Egypt. ²²And the enchanters of Egypt do so with their secrets, and the heart of Pharaoh is strong, and he has not listened to them, as YHWH has spoken, ²³and Pharaoh turns and goes into his house, and has not set his heart even to this; ²⁴and all the Egyptians seek water all around the River to drink, for they have not been able to drink of the waters of the River. ²⁵And seven days are completed after YHWH's striking the River.

CHAPTER 8

¹And YHWH says to Moses, "Go to Pharaoh, and you have said to him, Thus said YHWH: Send My people away, and they serve Me; ²and if you are refusing to send [them] away, behold, I am striking all your border with frogs; ³and the River has teemed [with] frogs, and they have gone up and gone into your house, and into the inner-chamber of your bed, and on your couch, and into the house of your servants, and among your people, and into your ovens, and into your kneading-troughs; ⁴indeed, on you, and on your people, and on all your servants the frogs go up." ⁵And YHWH says to Moses, "Say to Aaron, Stretch out your hand, with your rod, against the streams, against the rivers, and against the ponds, and cause the frogs to come up against the land of Egypt." ⁶And Aaron stretches out his hand against the waters of Egypt, and the frog comes up, and covers the land of Egypt; ⁷and the enchanters do so with their secrets, and cause the frogs to come up against the land of Egypt. ⁸And Pharaoh calls for Moses and for Aaron and says, "Make supplication to YHWH, that he may turn aside the frogs from me, and from my people, and I send the people away, and they sacrifice to YHWH." ⁹And Moses says to Pharaoh, "Beautify yourself over me; when do I make supplication for you, and for your servants, and for your people, to cut off the frogs from you and from your houses—only in the River they remain?" ¹⁰And he says, "Tomorrow." And he says, "According to your word [it is], so that you know that there is none like our God YHWH, ¹¹and the frogs have turned aside from you, and from your houses, and from your servants, and from your people; only in the River they remain." ¹²And Moses—Aaron also—goes out from Pharaoh, and Moses cries to YHWH concerning the matter of the frogs which He has set on Pharaoh; ¹³and YHWH does according to the word of Moses, and the frogs die out of the houses, out of the courts, and out of the fields, ¹⁴and they heap them up together, and the land stinks. ¹⁵And Pharaoh sees that there has been a respite, and he has hardened his heart, and has not listened to them, as YHWH has spoken. ¹⁶And YHWH says to Moses, "Say to Aaron, Stretch out your rod, and strike the dust of the land, and it has become gnats in all the land of Egypt." ¹⁷And they do so, and Aaron stretches out his hand with his rod, and strikes the dust of the land, and the gnats are on man and on beast; all the dust of the land has been gnats in all the land of Egypt. ¹⁸And the enchanters do so with their secrets, to bring out the gnats, and they have not been able, and the gnats are on man and on beast; ¹⁹and the enchanters say to Pharaoh, "It [is] the finger of God"; and the heart of Pharaoh is strong, and he has not listened to them, as YHWH has spoken. ²⁰And YHWH says to Moses, "Rise early in the morning, and station yourself before Pharaoh, behold, he is going out to the waters, and you have said to him, Thus said YHWH: Send My people away, and they serve Me; ²¹for if you are not sending My people away, behold, I am sending against you, and against your servants, and against your people, and against your houses, the beetle, and the houses of the Egyptians have been full of the beetle, and also the ground on which they are. ²²And I have separated in that day the land of Goshen, in which My people are staying, that the beetle is not there, so that you know that I [am] YHWH in the midst of the land, ²³and I have put a division between My people and your people; this sign is tomorrow." ²⁴And YHWH does so, and the grievous beetle enters the house of Pharaoh, and the house of his servants, and in all the land of Egypt the land is corrupted from the presence of the beetle. ²⁵And Pharaoh calls to Moses and to Aaron and says, "Go, sacrifice to your God in the land"; ²⁶and Moses says, "[It is] not right to do so—for us to sacrifice the abomination of the Egyptians to our God YHWH; behold, we sacrifice the abomination of the Egyptians before their eyes—and they do not stone us! ²⁷We go a journey of three days into the wilderness and have sacrificed to our God YHWH as He says to us." ²⁸And Pharaoh says, "I send you away, and you have sacrificed to your God YHWH in the wilderness, only do not go very far off; make supplication for me"; ²⁹and Moses says, "Behold, I am going out from you, and have made supplication to YHWH, and tomorrow the beetle has turned aside from Pharaoh, from his servants, and from his people; only, do not let Pharaoh add to deceive in not sending the people away to sacrifice to YHWH." ³⁰And Moses goes out from Pharaoh, and makes supplication to YHWH, ³¹and YHWH does according to the word of Moses, and turns aside the beetle from Pharaoh, from his servants, and from his people—there has not been one left; ³²and Pharaoh also hardens his heart at this time, and has not sent the people away.

CHAPTER 9

¹And YHWH says to Moses, "Go to Pharaoh, and you have spoken to him, Thus said YHWH, God of the Hebrews: Send My people away, and they serve Me; ²for if you are refusing to send [them] away, and are still keeping hold on them, ³behold, the hand of YHWH is on your livestock which [are] in the field, on horses, on donkeys, on camels, on herd, and on flock—a very grievous pestilence. ⁴And YHWH has separated between the livestock of Israel and the livestock of Egypt, and there does not die a thing of all the sons of Israel; ⁵and YHWH sets an appointed time, saying, Tomorrow YHWH does this thing in the land." ⁶And YHWH does this thing on the next day, and all the livestock of Egypt die, and of the livestock of the sons of Israel not one has died; ⁷and Pharaoh sends, and behold, not even one of the livestock of Israel has died, and the heart of Pharaoh is hard, and he has not sent the people away. ⁸And YHWH says to Moses and to Aaron, "Take for yourselves the fullness of your handfuls—soot of a furnace, and Moses has sprinkled it toward the heavens, before the eyes of Pharaoh, ⁹and it has become small dust over all the land of Egypt, and it has become on man and on livestock a boil breaking forth [with] blisters in all the land of Egypt." ¹⁰And they take the soot of the furnace, and stand before Pharaoh, and Moses sprinkles it toward the heavens, and it is a boil [with] blisters breaking forth on man and on beast; ¹¹and the

enchanters have not been able to stand before Moses because of the boil, for the boil has been on the enchanters, and on all the Egyptians. ¹²And YHWH strengthens the heart of Pharaoh, and he has not listened to them, as YHWH has spoken to Moses. ¹³And YHWH says to Moses, "Rise early in the morning, and station yourself before Pharaoh, and you have said to him, Thus said YHWH, God of the Hebrews: Send My people away, and they serve Me, ¹⁴for at this time I am sending all My plagues to your heart, and on your servants, and on your people, so that you know that there is none like Me in all the earth, ¹⁵for now I have put forth My hand, and I strike you, and your people, with pestilence, and you are hidden from the earth. ¹⁶And yet for this I have caused you to stand, so as to show you My power, and for the sake of declaring My Name in all the earth; ¹⁷still you are exalting yourself against My people—so as not to send them away; ¹⁸behold, I am raining very grievous hail about [this] time tomorrow, such as has not been in Egypt from the day of its founding and until now. ¹⁹And now, send, strengthen your livestock and all that you have in the field; every man and beast which is found in the field, and is not gathered into the house—the hail has come down on them, and they have died." ²⁰He who is fearing the word of YHWH among the servants of Pharaoh has caused his servants and his livestock to flee to the houses; ²¹and he who has not set his heart to the word of YHWH leaves his servants and his livestock in the field. ²²And YHWH says to Moses, "Stretch forth your hand toward the heavens, and there is hail in all the land of Egypt, on man, and on beast, and on every herb of the field in the land of Egypt." ²³And Moses stretches out his rod toward the heavens, and YHWH has given voices and hail, and fire goes toward the earth, and YHWH rains hail on the land of Egypt, ²⁴and there is hail, and fire catching itself in the midst of the hail, very grievous, such as has not been in all the land of Egypt since it has become a nation. ²⁵And the hail strikes all that [is] in the field in all the land of Egypt, from man even to beast, and the hail has struck every herb of the field, and it has broken every tree of the field; ²⁶only in the land of Goshen, where the sons of Israel [are], there has been no hail. ²⁷And Pharaoh sends, and calls for Moses and for Aaron, and says to them, "I have sinned this time—YHWH [is] the righteous, and I and my people [are] the wicked, ²⁸make supplication to YHWH, and plead that there be no voices of God and hail, and I send you away, and you do not add to remain." ²⁹And Moses says to him, "At my going out of the city, I spread my palms to YHWH—the voices cease, and there is no more hail, so that you know that the earth [is] YHWH's; ³⁰but you and your servants—I have known that you are not yet afraid of the face of YHWH God." ³¹And the flax and the barley have been struck, for the barley [is] budding, and the flax forming flowers, ³²and the wheat and the rye have not been struck, for they are late. ³³And Moses goes out from Pharaoh, [from] the city, and spreads his hands to YHWH, and the voices and the hail cease, and rain has not been poured out to the earth; ³⁴and Pharaoh sees that the rain has ceased, and the hail and the voices, and he continues to sin, and hardens his heart, he and his servants; ³⁵and the heart of Pharaoh is strong, and he has not sent the sons of Israel away, as YHWH has spoken by the hand of Moses.

CHAPTER 10

¹And YHWH says to Moses, "Go to Pharaoh, for I have declared his heart hard, and the heart of his servants, so that I set these signs of Mine in their midst, ²and so that you recount in the ears of your son, and of your son's son, that which I have done in Egypt, and My signs which I have set among them, and you have known that I [am] YHWH." ³And Moses comes in—Aaron also—to Pharaoh, and they say to him, "Thus said YHWH, God of the Hebrews: Until when have you refused to be humbled at My presence? Send My people away, and they serve Me, ⁴for if you are refusing to send My people away, behold, tomorrow I am bringing in the locust into your border, ⁵and it has covered the eye of the land, and none is able to see the land, and it has eaten the remnant of that which is escaped, which is left to you from the hail, and it has eaten every tree which is springing out of the field for you; ⁶and they have filled your houses, and the houses of all your servants, and the houses of all the Egyptians, which neither your fathers nor your father's fathers have seen, since the day of their being on the ground to this day." And he turns and goes out from Pharaoh. ⁷And the servants of Pharaoh say to him, "Until when does this [one] become a snare to us? Send the men away, and they serve their God YHWH; do you not yet know that Egypt has perished?" ⁸And Moses is brought back—Aaron also—to Pharaoh, and he says to them, "Go, serve your God YHWH, but who—who [are] those going?" ⁹And Moses says, "With our young ones, and with our aged ones, we go, with our sons, and with our daughters, with our flock, and our herd, we go, for we have a festival to YHWH." ¹⁰And he says to them, "Be it so, YHWH [is] with you when I send you and your infants away; see—for evil [is] before your faces. ¹¹Not so! Go now, you who [are] men, and serve YHWH, for that you are seeking"; and [one] casts them out from the presence of Pharaoh. ¹²And YHWH says to Moses, "Stretch out your hand against the land of Egypt for the locust, and it goes up against the land of Egypt, and eats every herb of the land—all that the hail has left." ¹³And Moses stretches out his rod against the land of Egypt, and YHWH has led an east wind over the land all that day, and all the night; the morning has been, and the east wind has lifted up the locust. ¹⁴And the locust goes up against all the land of Egypt, and rests in all the border of Egypt—very grievous: before it there has not been such a locust as it, and after it there is none such; ¹⁵and it covers the eye of all the land, and the land is darkened; and it eats every herb of the land, and all the fruit of the trees which the hail has left, and there has not been left any green thing in the trees, or in the herb of the field, in all the land of Egypt. ¹⁶And Pharaoh hurries to call for Moses and for Aaron and says, "I have sinned against your God YHWH, and against you, ¹⁷and now, please bear with my sin, only this time, and make supplication to your God YHWH, that He may turn aside from off me only this death." ¹⁸And he goes out from Pharaoh, and makes supplication to YHWH, ¹⁹and YHWH turns a very strong sea wind, and it lifts up the locust, and blows it into the Red Sea—there has not been left one locust in all the border of Egypt; ²⁰and YHWH strengthens the heart of Pharaoh, and he has not sent the sons of Israel away. ²¹And YHWH says to Moses, "Stretch out your hand toward the heavens, and there is darkness over the land of Egypt, and the darkness is felt." ²²And Moses stretches out his hand toward the heavens, and there is darkness—thick darkness in all the land of Egypt [for] three days; ²³they have not seen one another, and none has risen from his place [for] three days; but there has been light for all the sons of Israel in their dwellings. ²⁴And Pharaoh calls to Moses and says, "Go, serve YHWH, only your flock and your herd are stayed, your infants also go with you"; ²⁵and Moses says, "You also give sacrifices and burnt-offerings in our hand, and we have prepared for our God YHWH; ²⁶and also our livestock go with us—there is not left a hoof, for we take from it to serve our God YHWH; and we do not know how we serve YHWH until our going there." ²⁷And YHWH strengthens the heart of Pharaoh, and he has not been willing to send them away; ²⁸and Pharaoh says to him, "Go from me, take heed to yourself, do not add to see my face, for in the day you see my face you die"; ²⁹and Moses says, "You have spoken correctly, I do not add to see your face anymore."

CHAPTER 11

¹And YHWH says to Moses, "One more plague I bring in on Pharaoh and on Egypt, afterward he sends you away from this; when he is sending you away, he surely casts you out from this [place] altogether; ²now speak in the ears of the people, and they ask—each man from his neighbor, and each woman from her neighbor—[for] vessels of silver and vessels of gold." ³And YHWH gives the grace of the people in the eyes of the Egyptians; also the man Moses [is] very great in the land of Egypt, in the eyes of the servants of Pharaoh, and in the eyes of the people. ⁴And Moses says, "Thus said YHWH: About midnight I am going out into the midst of Egypt, ⁵and every firstborn in the land of Egypt has died, from the firstborn of Pharaoh who is sitting on his throne, to the firstborn of the maidservant who [is] behind the millstones, and all the firstborn of beasts; ⁶and there has been a great cry in all the land

of Egypt, such as there has not been, and such as there is not again; ⁷and against all the sons of Israel a dog does not sharpen its tongue, from man even to beast, so that you know that YHWH makes a separation between the Egyptians and Israel. ⁸And all these servants of yours have come down to me, and bowed themselves to me, saying, Go out, you and all the people who [are] at your feet; and afterward I go out"; and he goes out from Pharaoh in the heat of anger. ⁹And YHWH says to Moses, "Pharaoh does not listen to you, so as to multiply My wonders in the land of Egypt"; ¹⁰and Moses and Aaron have done all these wonders before Pharaoh, and YHWH strengthens Pharaoh's heart, and he has not sent the sons of Israel out of his land.

CHAPTER 12

¹And YHWH speaks to Moses and to Aaron in the land of Egypt, saying, ²"This month [is] the chief of months to you—it [is] the first of the months of the year to you; ³speak to all the congregation of Israel, saying, In the tenth of this month they take to themselves, each man, a lamb for the house of the fathers, a lamb for a house. ⁴And if the household is too few for a lamb, then he has taken, he and his neighbor who is near to his house, for the number of persons, each according to his eating you count for the lamb. ⁵A lamb, a perfect one, a male, a son of a year, let [it] be to you; you take [it] from the sheep or from the goats. ⁶And it has become a charge to you, until the fourteenth day of this month, and the whole assembly of the congregation of Israel has slaughtered it between the evenings; ⁷and they have taken of the blood, and have put [it] on the two doorposts, and on the lintel over the houses in which they eat it. ⁸And they have eaten the flesh in this night, a roast with fire; they eat it with unleavened things and bitters; ⁹you do not eat of it raw, or boiled in water at all, but a roast with fire, its head with its legs, and with its innards; ¹⁰and you do not leave of it until morning, and that which is remaining of it until morning you burn with fire. ¹¹And thus you eat it: your loins girded, your sandals on your feet, and your staff in your hand, and you have eaten it in haste; it is YHWH's Passover, ¹²and I have passed over through the land of Egypt during this night, and have struck every firstborn in the land of Egypt, from man even to beast, and I do judgments on all the gods of Egypt; I [am] YHWH. ¹³And the blood has become a sign for you on the houses where you [are], and I have seen the blood, and have passed over you, and a plague is not on you for destruction in My striking in the land of Egypt. ¹⁴And this day has become a memorial to you, and you have kept it [for] a celebration to YHWH throughout your generations—a continuous statute; you keep it [for] a celebration. ¹⁵Seven days you eat unleavened things; only—in the first day you cause leaven to cease out of your houses; for anyone eating anything fermented from the first day until the seventh day, indeed, that person has been cut off from Israel. ¹⁶And in the first day [is] a holy convocation, and in the seventh day you have a holy convocation; any work is not done in them, only that which is eaten by any person—it alone is done by you, ¹⁷and you have observed the Unleavened Things, for in this very day I have brought out your hosts from the land of Egypt, and you have observed this day throughout your generations—a continuous statute. ¹⁸In the first [month], on the fourteenth day of the month, in the evening, you eat unleavened things until the twenty-first day of the month, at evening; ¹⁹seven days leaven is not found in your houses, for anyone eating anything fermented—that person has been cut off from the congregation of Israel, among the sojourners or among the natives of the land; ²⁰you do not eat anything fermented—in all your dwellings you eat [only] unleavened things." ²¹And Moses calls for all [the] elderly of Israel and says to them, "Draw out and take for yourselves [from] the flock, for your families, and slaughter the Passover-sacrifice; ²²and you have taken a bunch of hyssop, and have dipped [it] in the blood which [is] in the basin, and have struck [it] on the lintel, and on the two doorposts, from the blood which [is] in the basin, and you, you do not go out—each from the opening of his house—until morning. ²³And YHWH has passed on to strike the Egyptians, and has seen the blood on the lintel, and on the two doorposts, and YHWH has passed over the opening, and does not permit the destruction to come into your houses to strike. ²⁴And you have observed this thing for a statute to you and to your sons for all time; ²⁵and it has been, when you come to the land which YHWH gives to you as He has spoken, that you have kept this service; ²⁶and it has come to pass, when your sons say to you, What [is] this service you have? ²⁷That you have said, It [is] a sacrifice of Passover to YHWH, who passed over the houses of the sons of Israel in Egypt, in His striking the Egyptians, and our houses He delivered." ²⁸And the people bow and pay respect, and the sons of Israel go and do as YHWH commanded Moses and Aaron; so they have done. ²⁹And it comes to pass, at midnight, that YHWH has struck every firstborn in the land of Egypt, from the firstborn of Pharaoh who is sitting on his throne, to the firstborn of the captive who [is] in the prison-house, and every firstborn of beasts. ³⁰And Pharaoh rises by night, he and all his servants, and all the Egyptians, and there is a great cry in Egypt, for there is not a house where there is not [one] dead, ³¹and he calls for Moses and for Aaron by night and says, "Rise, go out from the midst of my people, both you and the sons of Israel, and go, serve YHWH according to your word; ³²take both your flock and your herd as you have spoken, and go; then you have also blessed me." ³³And the Egyptians are urgent on the people, hastening to send them away out of the land, for they said, "We are all dead"; ³⁴and the people take up their dough before it is fermented, their kneading-troughs [are] bound up in their garments on their shoulder. ³⁵And the sons of Israel have done according to the word of Moses, and they ask for vessels of silver and vessels of gold, and garments, from the Egyptians; ³⁶and YHWH has given the grace of the people in the eyes of the Egyptians, and they cause them to ask, and they spoil the Egyptians. ³⁷And the sons of Israel journey from Rameses to Succoth, about six hundred thousand men on foot, apart from infants; ³⁸and a great rabble has also gone up with them, and flock and herd—very much livestock. ³⁹And they bake unleavened cakes with the dough which they have brought out from Egypt, for it has not fermented; for they have been cast out of Egypt, and have not been able to delay, and also they have not made provision for themselves. ⁴⁰And the dwelling of the sons of Israel [in] which they have dwelt in Egypt [is] four hundred and thirty years; ⁴¹and it comes to pass, at the end of four hundred and thirty years—indeed, it comes to pass on this very same day—all the hosts of YHWH have gone out from the land of Egypt. ⁴²It [is] a night of watchings to YHWH, to bring them out from the land of Egypt; it [is] this night of watchings to YHWH to all the sons of Israel throughout their generations. ⁴³And YHWH says to Moses and Aaron, "This [is] a statute of the Passover; any son of a stranger does not eat of it; ⁴⁴and any man's servant, the purchase of money, when you have circumcised him—then he eats of it; ⁴⁵a settler or hired servant does not eat of it; ⁴⁶it is eaten in one house, you do not carry out of the house [any] of the flesh outside, and you do not break a bone of it; ⁴⁷all the congregation of Israel keeps it. ⁴⁸And when a sojourner sojourns with you, and has made a Passover to YHWH, every male of his [is] to be circumcised, and then he comes near to keep it, and he has been as a native of the land, but any uncircumcised one does not eat of it; ⁴⁹one law is to a native, and to a sojourner who is sojourning in your midst." ⁵⁰And all the sons of Israel do as YHWH commanded Moses and Aaron; so they have done. ⁵¹And it comes to pass on this very same day, YHWH has brought out the sons of Israel from the land of Egypt by their hosts.

CHAPTER 13

¹And YHWH speaks to Moses, saying, ²"Sanctify to Me every firstborn, opening any womb among the sons of Israel, among man and among beast; it [is] Mine." ³And Moses says to the people, "Remember this day [in] which you have gone out from Egypt, from the house of servants, for by strength of hand YHWH has brought you out from this, and anything fermented is not eaten; ⁴you are going out today, in the month of Abib. ⁵And it has been, when YHWH brings you to the land of the Canaanite, and of the Hittite, and of the Amorite, and of the Hivite, and of the Jebusite, which He has sworn to your fathers to give to you, a land flowing with milk and honey, that you have done this service in this month. ⁶Seven days you eat unleavened things, and in the seventh day [is] a celebration to YHWH; ⁷unleavened things are eaten the seven days, and anything fermented is not seen with you; indeed, leaven is not seen with you in all your

border. ⁸And you have declared to your son in that day, saying, [It is] because of what YHWH did to me, in my going out from Egypt, ⁹and it has been to you for a sign on your hand, and for a memorial between your eyes, so that the Law of YHWH is in your mouth, for by a strong hand YHWH has brought you out from Egypt; ¹⁰and you have kept this statute at its appointed time from days to days. ¹¹And it has been, when YHWH brings you to the land of the Canaanite as He has sworn to you and to your fathers, and has given it to you, ¹²that you have caused everyone opening a womb to pass over to YHWH, and every firstling—the increase of beasts which you have: the males [are] YHWH's. ¹³And every firstling of a donkey you ransom with a lamb, and if you do not ransom [it], then you have beheaded it; and you ransom every firstborn of man among your sons. ¹⁴And it has been, when your son asks you hereafter, saying, What [is] this? That you have said to him, By strength of hand YHWH has brought us out from Egypt, from a house of servants; ¹⁵indeed, it comes to pass, when Pharaoh has been pained to send us away, that YHWH slays every firstborn in the land of Egypt, from the firstborn of man even to the firstborn of beast; therefore I am sacrificing to YHWH all opening a womb who [are] males, and I ransom every firstborn of my sons; ¹⁶and it has been for a token on your hand, and for frontlets between your eyes, for by strength of hand YHWH has brought us out of Egypt." ¹⁷And it comes to pass in Pharaoh's sending the people away, that God has not led them the way of the land of the Philistines, for it [is] near; for God said, "Lest the people sigh in their seeing war, and have turned back toward Egypt"; ¹⁸and God turns around the people the way of the wilderness of the Red Sea, and the sons of Israel have gone up by fifties from the land of Egypt. ¹⁹And Moses takes the bones of Joseph with him, for he certainly caused the sons of Israel to swear, saying, "God certainly inspects you, and you have brought up my bones from this [place] with you." ²⁰And they journey from Succoth, and encamp in Etham at the extremity of the wilderness, ²¹and YHWH is going before them by day in a pillar of a cloud, to lead them in the way, and by night in a pillar of fire, to give light to them, to go by day and by night; ²²He does not remove the pillar of the cloud by day, and the pillar of the fire by night, [from] before the people.

CHAPTER 14

¹And YHWH speaks to Moses, saying, ²"Speak to the sons of Israel, and they turn back and encamp before Pi-Hahiroth, between Migdol and the sea, before Ba'al-Zephon; you encamp in front of it by the sea, ³and Pharaoh has said of the sons of Israel, They are entangled in the land, the wilderness has shut on them; ⁴and I have strengthened the heart of Pharaoh, and he has pursued after them, and I am honored by Pharaoh, and by all his force, and the Egyptians have known that I [am] YHWH"; and they do so. ⁵And it is declared to the king of Egypt that the people have fled, and the heart of Pharaoh and of his servants is turned against the people, and they say, "What [is] this we have done, that we have sent Israel away from our service?" ⁶And he harnesses his chariot, and he has taken his people with him, ⁷and he takes six hundred chosen chariots, even all the chariots of Egypt, and captains over them all; ⁸and YHWH strengthens the heart of Pharaoh king of Egypt, and he pursues after the sons of Israel, and the sons of Israel are going out with a high hand, ⁹and the Egyptians pursue after them, and all the chariot horses of Pharaoh, and his horsemen, and his force, overtake them, encamping by the sea, by Pi-Hahiroth, before Ba'al-Zephon. ¹⁰And Pharaoh has drawn near, and the sons of Israel lift up their eyes, and behold, the Egyptians are journeying after them, and they fear exceedingly, and the sons of Israel cry to YHWH. ¹¹And they say to Moses, "Because there are no graves in Egypt, have you taken us away to die in a wilderness? What is this you have done to us—to bring us out from Egypt? ¹²Is this not the word which we spoke to you in Egypt, saying, Cease from us, and we serve the Egyptians; for [it is] better for us to serve the Egyptians than to die in a wilderness?" ¹³And Moses says to the people, "Do not fear, station yourselves, and see the salvation of YHWH, which He does for you today; for as you have seen the Egyptians today, you add no more to see them for all time; ¹⁴YHWH fights for you, and you keep silent." ¹⁵And YHWH says to Moses, "Why do you cry to Me? Speak to the sons of Israel, and they journey; ¹⁶and you, lift up your rod, and stretch out your hand toward the sea, and cleave it, and the sons of Israel go into the midst of the sea on dry land. ¹⁷And I—behold, I am strengthening the heart of the Egyptians, and they go in after them, and I am honored by Pharaoh, and by all his force, by his chariots, and by his horsemen; ¹⁸and the Egyptians have known that I [am] YHWH, in My being honored by Pharaoh, by his chariots, and by his horsemen." ¹⁹And the Messenger of God, who is going before the camp of Israel, journeys and goes at their rear; and the pillar of the cloud journeys from their front, and stands at their rear; ²⁰and comes in between the camp of the Egyptians and the camp of Israel, and the cloud and the darkness are, and he enlightens the night, and the one has not drawn near to the other all the night. ²¹And Moses stretches out his hand toward the sea, and YHWH causes the sea to go on by a strong east wind all the night, and makes the sea become dry ground, and the waters are cleaved, ²²and the sons of Israel go into the midst of the sea on dry land, and the waters [are] a wall to them, on their right and on their left. ²³And the Egyptians pursue, and go in after them (all the horses of Pharaoh, his chariots, and his horsemen) into the midst of the sea, ²⁴and it comes to pass, in the morning watch, that YHWH looks to the camp of the Egyptians through the pillar of fire and of the cloud, and troubles the camp of the Egyptians, ²⁵and turns aside the wheels of their chariots, and they lead them with difficulty, and the Egyptians say, "Let us flee from the face of Israel, for YHWH is fighting for them against the Egyptians." ²⁶And YHWH says to Moses, "Stretch out your hand toward the sea, and the waters turn back on the Egyptians, on their chariots, and on their horsemen." ²⁷And Moses stretches out his hand toward the sea, and the sea turns back, at the turning of the morning, to its perennial flow, and the Egyptians are fleeing at its coming, and YHWH shakes off the Egyptians in the midst of the sea, ²⁸and the waters turn back, and cover the chariots and the horsemen, even all the force of Pharaoh, who are coming in after them into the sea—there has not been left even one of them. ²⁹And the sons of Israel have gone on dry land in the midst of the sea, and the waters [are] a wall to them, on their right and on their left; ³⁰and YHWH saves Israel out of the hand of the Egyptians in that day, and Israel sees the Egyptians dead on the seashore, ³¹and Israel sees the great hand with which YHWH has worked against the Egyptians, and the people fear YHWH, and remain steadfast in YHWH, and in His servant Moses.

CHAPTER 15

¹Then Moses sings—and the sons of Israel—this song to YHWH, and they speak, saying, "I sing to YHWH, || For triumphing He has triumphed; The horse and its rider He has thrown into the sea. ²My strength and song is YAH, || And He is become my salvation: This [is] my God, and I glorify Him; God of my father, and I exalt Him. ³YHWH [is] a man of battle; YHWH [is] His Name. ⁴Chariots of Pharaoh and his force || He has cast into the sea; And the choice of his captains || Have sunk in the Red Sea! ⁵The depths cover them; They went down into the depths as a stone. ⁶Your right hand, O YHWH, || Has become honorable in power; Your right hand, O YHWH, || Crushes an enemy. ⁷And in the abundance of Your excellence || You throw down Your withstanders, || You send forth Your wrath—It consumes them as stubble. ⁸And by the wind of Your anger || Waters have been heaped together; Flowings have stood as a heap; Depths have been congealed || In the heart of a sea. ⁹The enemy said, I pursue, I overtake; I apportion spoil; My soul is filled with them; I draw out my sword; My hand destroys them— ¹⁰You have blown with Your wind || The sea has covered them; They sank as lead in mighty waters. ¹¹Who [is] like You among the gods, O YHWH? Who [is] like You—honorable in holiness—Fearful in praises—doing wonders? ¹²You have stretched out Your right hand—Earth swallows them! ¹³You have led forth in Your kindness || The people whom You have redeemed. You have led on in Your strength || To Your holy habitation.

[14] Peoples have heard, they are troubled; Pain has seized inhabitants of Philistia. [15] Then chiefs of Edom have been troubled; Mighty ones of Moab—Trembling seizes them! All inhabitants of Canaan have melted! [16] Terror and dread fall on them; By the greatness of Your arm || They are still as a stone, || Until Your people pass over, O YHWH; Until the people pass over || Whom You have purchased. [17] You bring them in, and plant them || In a mountain of Your inheritance, || A fixed place for Your dwelling You have made, O YHWH; A sanctuary, O Lord, Your hands have established; [18] YHWH reigns—[for] all time and forever!" [19] For the horse of Pharaoh has gone in with his chariots and with his horsemen into the sea, and YHWH turns back the waters of the sea on them, and the sons of Israel have gone on dry land in the midst of the sea. [20] And Miriam the inspired one, sister of Aaron, takes the timbrel in her hand, and all the women go out after her, with timbrels and with choruses; [21] and Miriam answers to them: "Sing to YHWH, || For triumphing He has triumphed; The horse and its rider He has thrown into the sea!" [22] And Moses causes Israel to journey from the Red Sea, and they go out to the wilderness of Shur, and they go three days in the wilderness, and have not found water, [23] and they come to Marah, and have not been able to drink the waters of Marah, for they [are] bitter; therefore [one] has called its name Marah. [24] And the people murmur against Moses, saying, "What do we drink?" [25] And he cries to YHWH, and YHWH shows him a tree, and he casts [it] into the waters, and the waters become sweet. He has made a statute for them there, and an ordinance, and He has tried them there, [26] and He says, "If you really listen to the voice of your God YHWH, and do that which is right in His eyes, and have listened to His commands, and kept all His statutes, none of the sickness which I laid on the Egyptians do I lay on you, for I, YHWH, am healing you." [27] And they come to Elim, and there [are] twelve fountains of water, and seventy palm trees; and they encamp there by the waters.

CHAPTER 16

[1] And they journey from Elim, and all the congregation of the sons of Israel come to the wilderness of Sin, which [is] between Elim and Sinai, on the fifteenth day of the second month of their going out from the land of Egypt. [2] And all the congregation of the sons of Israel murmur against Moses and against Aaron in the wilderness; [3] and the sons of Israel say to them, "Oh that we had died by the hand of YHWH in the land of Egypt, in our sitting by the flesh-pot, in our eating bread to satiety—for you have brought us out to this wilderness to put all this assembly to death with hunger." [4] And YHWH says to Moses, "Behold, I am raining bread from the heavens for you—and the people have gone out and gathered the matter of a day in its day—so that I try them whether they walk in My law or not; [5] and it has been on the sixth day, that they have prepared that which they bring in, and it has been double above that which they gather day [by] day." [6] And Moses says—Aaron also—to all the sons of Israel, "Evening—and you have known that YHWH has brought you out from the land of Egypt; [7] and morning—and you have seen the glory of YHWH, in His hearing your murmurings against YHWH, and what [are] we, that you murmur against us?" [8] And Moses says, "In YHWH's giving to you flesh to eat in the evening, and bread in the morning to satiety—in YHWH's hearing your murmurings, which you are murmuring against Him, and what [are] we? Your murmurings [are] not against us, but against YHWH." [9] And Moses says to Aaron, "Say to all the congregation of the sons of Israel, Come near before YHWH, for He has heard your murmurings"; [10] and it comes to pass, when Aaron is speaking to all the congregation of the sons of Israel, that they turn toward the wilderness, and behold, the glory of YHWH is seen in the cloud. [11] And YHWH speaks to Moses, saying, [12] "I have heard the murmurings of the sons of Israel; speak to them, saying, Between the evenings you eat flesh, and in the morning you are satisfied [with] bread, and you have known that I [am] your God YHWH." [13] And it comes to pass in the evening, that the quail comes up, and covers the camp, and in the morning there has been the lying of dew around the camp, [14] and the lying of the dew goes up, and behold, on the face of the wilderness [is] a thin, bare thing, thin as hoarfrost on the earth. [15] And the sons of Israel see, and say to one another, "What [is] it?" For they have not known what it [is]; and Moses says to them, "It [is] the bread which YHWH has given to you for food. [16] This [is] the thing which YHWH has commanded: Gather of it, each according to his eating, an omer for the counted head; and the number of your persons, take, each, for those in his tent." [17] And the sons of Israel do so, and they gather, he who is [gathering] much, and he who is [gathering] little; [18] and they measure with an omer, and he who is [gathering] much has nothing over, and he who is [gathering] little has no lack, each according to his eating they have gathered. [19] And Moses says to them, "Let no man leave of it until morning"; [20] and they have not listened to Moses, and some of them leave of it until morning, and it brings up worms and stinks; and Moses is angry with them. [21] And they gather it morning by morning, each according to his eating; when the sun has been warm, then it has melted. [22] And it comes to pass on the sixth day, they have gathered a second bread, two omers for one, and all the princes of the congregation come in, and declare [it] to Moses. [23] And he says to them, "It [is] that which YHWH has spoken: A rest—a holy Sabbath to YHWH—[is] tomorrow; that which you bake, bake; and that which you boil, boil; and all that is remaining, let [it] rest for yourselves for preservation until the morning." [24] And they let it rest until the morning, as Moses has commanded, and it has not stunk, and a worm has not been in it. [25] And Moses says, "Eat it today, for today [is] a Sabbath to YHWH; today you do not find it in the field: [26] six days you gather it, and in the seventh day—the Sabbath—there is none in it." [27] And it comes to pass on the seventh day, some of the people have gone out to gather, and have not found. [28] And YHWH says to Moses, "How long have you refused to keep My commands and My laws? [29] See, because YHWH has given the Sabbath to you, therefore He is giving to you on the sixth day bread of two days; each abide [in] his place, no one goes out from his place on the seventh day." [30] And the people rest on the seventh day, [31] and the house of Israel calls its name Manna, and it [is] as white coriander seed; and its taste [is] as a cake with honey. [32] And Moses says, "This [is] the thing which YHWH has commanded: Fill the omer with it, for a charge for your generations, so that they see the bread which I have caused you to eat in the wilderness, in My bringing you out from the land of Egypt." [33] And Moses says to Aaron, "Take one pot, and put the fullness of the omer of manna [in] there, and let it rest before YHWH, for a charge for your generations"; [34] as YHWH has given command to Moses, so Aaron lets it rest before the Testimony, for a charge. [35] And the sons of Israel have eaten the manna [for] forty years, until their coming to the land to be inhabited; they have eaten the manna until their coming to the extremity of the land of Canaan. [36] And the omer is a tenth of the ephah.

CHAPTER 17

[1] And all the congregation of the sons of Israel journey from the wilderness of Sin, on their journeys, by the command of YHWH, and encamp in Rephidim, and there is no water for the people to drink; [2] and the people strive with Moses, and say, "Give us water, and we drink." And Moses says to them, "Why do you strive with me? Why do you try YHWH?" [3] And the people thirst for water there, and the people murmur against Moses, and say, "Why [is] this [that] you have brought us up out of Egypt to put us to death, also our sons and our livestock, with thirst?" [4] And Moses cries to YHWH, saying, "What do I do to this people? Yet a little, and they have stoned me." [5] And YHWH says to Moses, "Pass over before the people, and take with you from [the] elderly of Israel, and take your rod in your hand, with which you have struck the River, and you have gone. [6] Behold, I am standing before you there on the rock in Horeb, and you have struck on the rock, and waters have come out from it, and the people have drunk." And Moses does so before the eyes of [the] elderly of Israel, [7] and he calls the name of the place Massah, and Meribah, because of the strife of the sons of Israel, and because of their trying YHWH, saying, "Is YHWH in our midst or not?" [8] And

Amalek comes, and fights with Israel in Rephidim, ⁹and Moses says to Joshua, "Choose men for us, and go out, fight with Amalek: tomorrow I am standing on the top of the hill, and the rod of God in my hand." ¹⁰And Joshua does as Moses has said to him, to fight with Amalek, and Moses, Aaron, and Hur have gone up [to] the top of the height; ¹¹and it has come to pass, when Moses lifts up his hand, that Israel has been mighty, and when he lets his hands rest, that Amalek has been mighty. ¹²And the hands of Moses [are] heavy, and they take a stone and set [it] under him, and he sits on it, and Aaron and Hur have taken hold on his hands, one on this [side] and one on that [side]; and his hands are steadfast until the going in of the sun; ¹³and Joshua weakens Amalek and his people by the mouth of the sword. ¹⁴And YHWH says to Moses, "Write this, a memorial in a Scroll, and set [it] in the ears of Joshua, that I utterly wipe away the remembrance of Amalek from under the heavens"; ¹⁵and Moses builds an altar, and calls its name YHWH-Nissi, ¹⁶and says, "Because a hand [is] on the throne of YAH, war [is] to YHWH with Amalek from generation [to] generation."

CHAPTER 18

¹And Jethro priest of Midian, father-in-law of Moses, hears all that God has done for Moses and for His people Israel, that YHWH has brought out Israel from Egypt, ²and Jethro, father-in-law of Moses, takes Zipporah, wife of Moses, after her parting, ³and her two sons, of whom the name of one [is] Gershom, for he said, "I have been a sojourner in a strange land"; ⁴and the name of the other [is] Eliezer, for, "The God of my father [is] for my help, and He delivers me from the sword of Pharaoh." ⁵And Jethro, father-in-law of Moses, comes, and his sons, and his wife, to Moses, to the wilderness where he is encamping—the mountain of God; ⁶and he says to Moses, "I, your father-in-law Jethro, am coming to you, and your wife, and her two sons with her." ⁷And Moses goes out to meet his father-in-law, and bows himself, and kisses him, and they ask of one another of welfare, and come into the tent; ⁸and Moses recounts to his father-in-law all that YHWH has done to Pharaoh, and to the Egyptians, on account of Israel, all the travail which has found them in the way, and [how] YHWH delivers them. ⁹And Jethro rejoices for all the good which YHWH has done to Israel, whom He has delivered from the hand of the Egyptians; ¹⁰and Jethro says, "Blessed [is] YHWH, who has delivered you from the hand of the Egyptians, and from the hand of Pharaoh—who has delivered this people from under the hand of the Egyptians; ¹¹now I have known that YHWH [is] greater than all the gods, for in the thing they have acted proudly—[He is] above them!" ¹²And Jethro, father-in-law of Moses, takes a burnt-offering and sacrifices [it] for God; and Aaron comes in, and all [the] elderly of Israel, to eat bread with the father-in-law of Moses, before God. ¹³And it comes to pass on the next day, that Moses sits to judge the people, and the people stand before Moses from the morning to the evening; ¹⁴and the father-in-law of Moses sees all that he is doing for the people and says, "What [is] this thing which you are doing for the people? Why are you sitting by yourself, and all the people standing by you from morning until evening?" ¹⁵And Moses says to his father-in-law, "Because the people come to me to seek God; ¹⁶when they have a matter, it has come to me, and I have judged between a man and his neighbor, and made known the statutes of God, and His laws." ¹⁷And the father-in-law of Moses says to him, "The thing which you are doing [is] not good; ¹⁸you surely wear away, both you, and this people which [is] with you, for the thing is too heavy for you, you are not able to do it by yourself. ¹⁹Now listen to my voice, I counsel you, and God is with you: be for the people before God, and you have brought in the things to God; ²⁰and you have warned them [concerning] the statutes and the laws, and have made known to them the way in which they go, and the work which they do. ²¹And you provide out of all the people men of ability, fearing God, men of truth, hating dishonest gain, and have placed [these] over them [for] heads of thousands, heads of hundreds, heads of fifties, and heads of tens, ²²and they have judged the people at all times; and it has come to pass, they bring every great matter to you, and they judge every small matter themselves; and lighten it from off yourself, and they have borne with you. ²³If you do this thing, and God has commanded you, then you have been able to stand, and all this people also goes to its place in peace." ²⁴And Moses listens to the voice of his father-in-law, and does all that he said, ²⁵and Moses chooses men of ability out of all Israel, and makes them chiefs over the people [for] heads of thousands, heads of hundreds, heads of fifties, and heads of tens, ²⁶and they have judged the people at all times; they bring the hard matter to Moses, and they judge every small matter themselves. ²⁷And Moses sends his father-in-law away, and he goes away to his own land.

CHAPTER 19

¹In the third month of the going out of the sons of Israel from the land of Egypt, in this day they have come into the wilderness of Sinai, ²and they journey from Rephidim, and enter the wilderness of Sinai, and encamp in the wilderness; and Israel encamps there before the mountain. ³And Moses has gone up to God, and YHWH calls to him out of the mountain, saying, "Thus you say to the house of Jacob, and declare to the sons of Israel: ⁴You have seen that which I have done to the Egyptians, and [how] I carry you on eagles' wings and bring you to Myself. ⁵And now, if you really listen to My voice, then you have kept My covenant, and have been a special treasure to Me more than all the peoples, for all the earth [is] Mine; ⁶and you are to Me a kingdom of priests and a holy nation: these [are] the words which you speak to the sons of Israel." ⁷And Moses comes, and calls for [the] elderly of the people, and sets before them all these words which YHWH has commanded him; ⁸and all the people answer together and say, "All that YHWH has spoken we do"; and Moses returns the words of the people to YHWH. ⁹And YHWH says to Moses, "Behold, I am coming to you in the thickness of the cloud, so that the people hear in My speaking with you, and also believe in you for all time"; and Moses declares the words of the people to YHWH. ¹⁰And YHWH says to Moses, "Go to the people and you have sanctified them today and tomorrow, and they have washed their garments, ¹¹and have been prepared for the third day; for on the third day YHWH comes down on Mount Sinai before the eyes of all the people. ¹²And you have made a border [for] the people all around, saying, Take heed to yourselves, going up into the mountain or coming against its extremity; whoever is coming against the mountain is certainly put to death; ¹³a hand does not come against him, for he is certainly stoned or shot through, whether beast or man—it does not live; in the prolonging of the ram's horn they go up into the mountain." ¹⁴And Moses comes down from the mountain to the people, and sanctifies the people, and they wash their garments; ¹⁵and he says to the people, "Be prepared for the third day, do not come near to a woman." ¹⁶And it comes to pass, on the third day, while it is morning, that there are voices, and lightnings, and a heavy cloud on the mountain, and the sound of a very strong horn; and all the people who [are] in the camp tremble. ¹⁷And Moses brings out the people from the camp to meet God, and they station themselves at the lower part of the mountain, ¹⁸and Mount Sinai [is] wholly [in] smoke from the presence of YHWH, who has come down on it in fire, and its smoke goes up as smoke of the furnace, and the whole mountain trembles exceedingly; ¹⁹and the sound of the horn is going on, and [is] very strong; Moses speaks, and God answers him with a voice. ²⁰And YHWH comes down on Mount Sinai, to the top of the mountain, and YHWH calls for Moses to the top of the mountain, and Moses goes up. ²¹And YHWH says to Moses, "Go down, protest to the people, lest they break through to YHWH to see, and many of them have fallen; ²²and also the priests who are coming near to YHWH sanctify themselves, lest YHWH break forth on them." ²³And Moses says to YHWH, "The people [are] unable to come up to Mount Sinai, for You have protested to us, saying, Make a border [for] the mountain, then you have sanctified it." ²⁴And YHWH says to him, "Go, descend, then you have come up, you and Aaron with you; and the priests and the people do not break through to come up to YHWH, lest He break forth on them." ²⁵And Moses goes down to the people and speaks to them.

CHAPTER 20

¹And God speaks all these words, saying, ²"I [am] your God YHWH, who has brought you out of the land of Egypt, out of a house of servants. ³You have no other Gods before Me. ⁴You do not make a carved image for yourself, or any likeness which [is] in the heavens above, or which [is] in the earth beneath, or which [is] in the waters under the earth. ⁵You do not bow yourself to them, nor serve them: for I, your God YHWH, [am] a zealous God, charging iniquity of fathers on sons, on a third and on a fourth [generation] of those hating Me, ⁶and doing kindness to thousands, of those loving Me and keeping My commands. ⁷You do not take up the Name of your God YHWH for a vain thing, for YHWH does not acquit him who takes up His Name for a vain thing. ⁸Remember the Sabbath day to sanctify it; ⁹six days you labor and have done all your work, ¹⁰and the seventh day [is] a Sabbath to your God YHWH; you do not do any work, you, and your son, and your daughter, your manservant, and your handmaid, and your livestock, and your sojourner who is within your gates— ¹¹for [in] six days YHWH has made the heavens and the earth, the sea, and all that [is] in them, and rests in the seventh day; therefore YHWH has blessed the Sabbath day and sanctifies it. ¹²Honor your father and your mother, so that your days are prolonged on the ground which your God YHWH is giving to you. ¹³You do not murder. ¹⁴You do not commit adultery. ¹⁵You do not steal. ¹⁶You do not answer [with] a false testimony against your neighbor. ¹⁷You do not desire the house of your neighbor, you do not desire the wife of your neighbor, or his manservant, or his handmaid, or his ox, or his donkey, or anything which [is] your neighbor's." ¹⁸And all the people are seeing the voices, and the flames, and the sound of the horn, and the mountain smoking; and the people see, and move, and stand far off, ¹⁹and say to Moses, "Speak with us, and we hear, and do not let God speak with us, lest we die." ²⁰And Moses says to the people, "Do not fear, for God has come to try you, and in order that His fear may be before your faces—that you do not sin." ²¹And the people stand far off, and Moses has drawn near to the thick darkness where God [is]. ²²And YHWH says to Moses, "Thus you say to the sons of Israel: You have seen that I have spoken with you from the heavens; ²³you do not make gods of silver and gods of gold [to be] with Me—you do not make [any idol] for yourselves. ²⁴You make an altar of earth for Me, and you have sacrificed on it your burnt-offerings and your peace-offerings, your flock and your herd; in every place where I cause My Name to be remembered I come to you, and have blessed you. ²⁵And if you make an altar of stones for Me, you do not build them of hewn work; when you have waved your tool over it, then you defile it; ²⁶neither do you go up by steps on My altar, that your nakedness is not revealed on it.

CHAPTER 21

¹And these [are] the judgments which you set before them: ²When you buy a Hebrew servant, he serves [for] six years, and in the seventh he goes out as a freeman for nothing; ³if he comes in by himself, he goes out by himself; if he [is] owner of a wife, then his wife has gone out with him; ⁴if his lord gives a wife to him, and she has borne sons or daughters to him—the wife and her children are her lord's, and he goes out by himself. ⁵And if the servant really says: I have loved my lord, my wife, and my sons—I do not go out free, ⁶then his lord has brought him near to God, and has brought him near to the door, or to the doorpost, and his lord has bored his ear with an awl, and he has served him for all time. ⁷And when a man sells his daughter for a handmaid, she does not go out according to the going out of the menservants; ⁸if [it is] evil in the eyes of her lord, so that he has not betrothed her, then he has let her be ransomed; he has no power to sell her to a strange people, in his dealing treacherously with her. ⁹And if he betroths her to his son, he does to her according to the right of daughters. ¹⁰If he takes another [woman] for him, he does not withdraw her food, her covering, and her habitation; ¹¹and if he does not do these three for her, then she has gone out for nothing, without money. ¹²He who strikes a man so that he has died is certainly put to death; ¹³as for him who has not laid wait, but God has brought [him] to his hand, I have even set a place for you to where he flees. ¹⁴And when a man presumes against his neighbor to slay him with subtlety, you take him from My altar to die. ¹⁵And he who strikes his father or his mother is certainly put to death. ¹⁶And he who steals a man, and has sold him, and he has been found in his hand, is certainly put to death. ¹⁷And he who is reviling his father or his mother is certainly put to death. ¹⁸And when men contend, and a man has struck his neighbor with a stone, or with the fist, and he does not die, but has fallen on the bed; ¹⁹if he rises, and has gone up and down outside on his staff, then the striker has been acquitted; he only gives [for] his cessation, and he is thoroughly healed. ²⁰And when a man strikes his manservant or his handmaid with a rod, and he has died under his hand—he is certainly avenged; ²¹only if he remains a day, or two days, he is not avenged, for he [is] his money. ²²And when men strive, and have struck a pregnant woman, and her children have come out, and there is no harm [to them], he is certainly fined as the husband of the woman lays on him, and he has given through the judges; ²³and if there is harm [to them], then you have given life for life, ²⁴eye for eye, tooth for tooth, hand for hand, foot for foot, ²⁵burning for burning, wound for wound, stripe for stripe. ²⁶And when a man strikes the eye of his manservant, or the eye of his handmaid, and has destroyed it, he sends him away as a freeman for his eye; ²⁷and if he knocks out a tooth of his manservant or a tooth of his handmaid, he sends him away as a freeman for his tooth. ²⁸And when an ox gores man or woman, and they have died, the ox is certainly stoned, and his flesh is not eaten, and the owner of the ox [is] acquitted; ²⁹and if the ox is [one] accustomed to gore before, and it has been testified to its owner, and he does not watch it, and it has put to death a man or woman, the ox is stoned, and its owner is also put to death. ³⁰If atonement is laid on him, then he has given the ransom of his life, according to all that is laid on him; ³¹whether it gores a son or gores a daughter, according to this judgment it is done to him. ³²If the ox gores a manservant or a handmaid, he gives thirty silver shekels to their lord, and the ox is stoned. ³³And when a man opens a pit, or when a man digs a pit, and does not cover it, and an ox or donkey has fallen [in] there— ³⁴the owner of the pit repays, he gives back money to its owner, and the dead is his. ³⁵And when a man's ox strikes the ox of his neighbor and it has died, then they have sold the living ox, and halved its money, and they also halve the dead one; ³⁶or, [if] it has been known that the ox is [one] accustomed to gore before, and its owner does not watch it, he certainly repays ox for ox, and the dead is his.

CHAPTER 22

¹When a man steals an ox or sheep, and has slaughtered it or sold it, he repays [with] five of the herd for the ox, and four of the flock for the sheep. ²If in the breaking through, the thief is found, and he has been struck and has died, there is no blood for him; ³if the sun has risen on him, blood [is] for him, he certainly repays; if he has nothing, then he has been sold for his theft; ⁴if the theft is certainly found alive in his hand, whether ox, or donkey, or sheep—he repays double. ⁵When a man depastures a field or vineyard, and has sent out his beast, and it has pastured in the field of another, he repays [with] the best of his field, and the best of his vineyard. ⁶When fire goes forth and has found thorns, and a stack, or the standing grain, or the field has been consumed, he who causes the burning certainly repays. ⁷When a man gives silver or vessels to his neighbor to keep, and it has been stolen out of the man's house; if the thief is found, he repays double. ⁸If the thief is not found, then the master of the house has been brought near to God [to see] whether he has not put forth his hand against the work of his neighbor. ⁹For every matter of transgression, for ox, for donkey, for sheep, for raiment, for any lost thing of which it is said that it is his, the matter of them both comes to God; he whom God condemns repays double to his neighbor. ¹⁰When a man gives to his neighbor a donkey, or ox, or sheep, or any beast to keep, and it has died, or has been hurt, or taken captive, [with] none seeing— ¹¹an oath of YHWH is between them both, that he has not put forth his hand against the work of

his neighbor, and its owner has accepted, and he does not repay; ¹²but if it is certainly stolen from him, he repays to its owner; ¹³if it is certainly torn, he brings it in [as] a witness; he does not repay the torn thing. ¹⁴And when a man asks for [anything] from his neighbor, and it has been hurt or has died—its owner not being with it—he certainly repays; ¹⁵if its owner [is] with it, he does not repay—if it [is] a hired thing, it has come for its hire. ¹⁶And when a man entices a virgin who [is] not betrothed, and has lain with her, he certainly endows her to himself for a wife; ¹⁷if her father utterly refuses to give her to him, he weighs out money according to the dowry of virgins. ¹⁸You do not keep a witch alive. ¹⁹Whoever lies with a beast is certainly put to death. ²⁰He who is sacrificing to a god, except to YHWH alone, is devoted. ²¹And you do not oppress a sojourner, nor crush him, for you have been sojourners in the land of Egypt. ²²You do not afflict any widow or orphan; ²³if you really afflict him, surely if he cries to Me at all, I certainly hear his cry; ²⁴and My anger has burned, and I have slain you by the sword, and your wives have been widows, and your sons orphans. ²⁵If you lend money [to] My poor people [who are] with you, you are not as a usurer to him; you do not lay usury on him; ²⁶if you take the garment of your neighbor in pledge at all, you return it to him during the going in of the sun: ²⁷for it is his only covering, it [is] his garment for his skin; wherein does he lie down? And it has come to pass, when he cries to Me, that I have heard, for I [am] gracious. ²⁸You do not revile God, and you do not curse a prince among your people. ²⁹You do not delay your fullness and your liquids; you give the firstborn of your sons to Me; ³⁰so you do to your ox [and] to your sheep; it is with its mother [for] seven days, on the eighth day you give it to Me. ³¹And you are holy men to Me, and you do not eat flesh torn in the field, you cast it to a dog.

CHAPTER 23

¹You do not lift up a vain report; you do not put your hand with a wicked man to be a violent witness. ²You are not after many to [do] evil, nor do you testify concerning a strife, to turn aside after many to cause [others] to turn aside; ³and you do not honor a poor man in his strife. ⁴When you meet your enemy's ox or his donkey going astray, you certainly turn it back to him; ⁵when you see the donkey of him who is hating you crouching under its burden, then you have ceased from leaving [it] to it—you certainly leave [it] with him. ⁶You do not turn aside the judgment of your poor in his strife; ⁷you keep far off from a false matter, and you do not slay an innocent and righteous man; for I do not justify a wicked man. ⁸And you do not take a bribe, for the bribe binds the open-[eyed] and perverts the words of the righteous. ⁹And you do not oppress a sojourner, since you have known the soul of the sojourner, for you have been sojourners in the land of Egypt. ¹⁰And [for] six years you sow your land and have gathered its increase; ¹¹and [in] the seventh you release it, and have left it, and the needy of your people have eaten, and the beast of the field eats their remainder; so you do to your vineyard [and] to your olive-yard. ¹²Six days you do your work, and on the seventh day you rest, so that your ox and your donkey rest, and the son of your handmaid and the sojourner is refreshed; ¹³and in all that which I have said to you—take heed; and you do not mention the name of other gods; it is not heard on your mouth. ¹⁴You keep a celebration to Me three times in a year: ¹⁵you keep the Celebration of Unleavened Things (you eat unleavened things [for] seven days as I have commanded you, at the time appointed [in] the month of Abib; for in it you have come forth out of Egypt, and you do not appear [in] My presence empty); ¹⁶and the Celebration of Harvest, the first-fruits of your works which you sow in the field; and the Celebration of the Ingathering in the outgoing of the year, in your gathering your works out of the field. ¹⁷Three times in a year all your males appear before [the] face of the Lord YHWH. ¹⁸You do not sacrifice the blood of My sacrifice on a fermented thing, and the fat of My festival does not remain until morning; ¹⁹the beginning of the first-fruits of your ground you bring into the house of your God YHWH; you do not boil a kid in its mother's milk. ²⁰Behold, I am sending a Messenger before you to keep you in the way, and to bring you to the place which I have prepared; ²¹be watchful because of His presence, and listen to His voice, do not rebel against Him, for He does not bear with your transgression, for My Name [is] in His heart; ²²for if you listen diligently to His voice, and have done all that which I speak, then I have been at enmity with your enemies, and have distressed those distressing you. ²³For My Messenger goes before you, and has brought you to the Amorite, and the Hittite, and the Perizzite, and the Canaanite, the Hivite, and the Jebusite, and I have cut them off. ²⁴You do not bow yourself to their gods, nor serve them, nor do according to their doings, but utterly devote them, and thoroughly break their standing pillars. ²⁵And you have served your God YHWH, and He has blessed your bread and your water, and I have turned aside sickness from your heart; ²⁶there is not a miscarrying and barren one in your land; I fulfill the number of your days. ²⁷I send My terror before you, and I have put to death all the people among whom you come, and I have given the neck of all your enemies to you. ²⁸And I have sent the hornet before you, and it has cast out the Hivite, the Canaanite, and the Hittite from before you; ²⁹I do not cast them out from before you in one year, lest the land be a desolation, and the beast of the field has multiplied against you; ³⁰I cast them out little [by] little from before you, until you are fruitful, and have inherited the land. ³¹And I have set your border from the Red Sea, even to the sea of the Philistines, and from the wilderness to the River; for I give the inhabitants of the land into your hand, and you have cast them out from before you. ³²You do not make a covenant with them and with their gods; ³³they do not dwell in your land, lest they cause you to sin against Me when you serve their gods, when it becomes a snare to you."

CHAPTER 24

¹And He said to Moses, "Come up to YHWH, you, and Aaron, Nadab, and Abihu, and seventy from [the] elderly of Israel, and you have bowed yourselves far off"; ²and Moses has drawn near to YHWH by himself; and they do not draw near, and the people do not go up with him. ³And Moses comes in, and recounts to the people all the words of YHWH, and all the judgments, and all the people answer [with] one voice, and say, "All the words which YHWH has spoken we do." ⁴And Moses writes all the words of YHWH, and rises early in the morning, and builds an altar under the hill, and twelve standing pillars for the twelve tribes of Israel; ⁵and he sends the youths of the sons of Israel, and they cause burnt-offerings to ascend, and sacrifice sacrifices of peace-offerings to YHWH—calves. ⁶And Moses takes half of the blood and puts [it] in basins, and he has sprinkled half of the blood on the altar; ⁷and he takes the Scroll of the Covenant, and proclaims [it] in the ears of the people, and they say, "All that which YHWH has spoken we do, and we obey." ⁸And Moses takes the blood and sprinkles [it] on the people, and says, "Behold, the blood of the covenant which YHWH has made with you, concerning all these things." ⁹And Moses goes up, Aaron also, Nadab and Abihu, and seventy from [the] elderly of Israel, ¹⁰and they see the God of Israel, and under His feet [is] as the work of a pavement of sapphire, and as the substance of the heavens for purity; ¹¹and He has not put forth His hand to those of the sons of Israel who are near, and they see God, and eat and drink. ¹²And YHWH says to Moses, "Come up to Me [on] the mountain and be there, and I give to you the tablets of stone, and the Law, and the command, which I have written to direct them." ¹³And Moses rises—his minister Joshua also—and Moses goes up to the mountain of God; ¹⁴and he has said to the elderly, "Abide for us in this [place] until we return to you, and behold, Aaron and Hur [are] with you—he who has matters comes near to them." ¹⁵And Moses goes up to the mountain, and the cloud covers the mountain; ¹⁶and the glory of YHWH dwells on Mount Sinai, and the cloud covers it [for] six days, and He calls to Moses on the seventh day from the midst of the cloud. ¹⁷And the appearance of the glory of YHWH [is] as a consuming fire on the top of the mountain, before the eyes of the sons of Israel; ¹⁸and Moses goes into the midst of the cloud, and goes up to the mountain, and Moses is on the mountain forty days and forty nights.

CHAPTER 25

¹And YHWH speaks to Moses, saying, ²"Speak to the sons of Israel, and they take a raised-offering for Me; you take My raised-offering from every man whose heart impels him. ³And this [is] the raised-offering which you

take from them: gold, and silver, and bronze, ⁴and blue, and purple, and scarlet, and linen, and goats' [hair], ⁵and rams' skins made red, and tachashim skins, and shittim wood, ⁶oil for the light, spices for the anointing oil, and for the incense of the spices, ⁷shoham stones, and stones for setting for an ephod, and for a breastplate. ⁸And they have made a sanctuary for Me, and I have dwelt in their midst; ⁹according to all that which I am showing you, the pattern of the Dwelling Place, and the pattern of all its vessels, even so you make [it]. ¹⁰And they have made an ark of shittim wood; two cubits and a half its length, and a cubit and a half its breadth, and a cubit and a half its height; ¹¹and you have overlaid it [with] pure gold, you overlay it inside and outside, and you have made a ring of gold on it all around. ¹²And you have cast four rings of gold for it, and have put [them] on its four feet, even two rings on its one side, and two rings on its second side; ¹³and you have made poles of shittim wood, and have overlaid them [with] gold, ¹⁴and have brought the poles into the rings on the sides of the Ark, to carry the Ark by them; ¹⁵the poles are in the rings of the Ark, they are not turned aside from it; ¹⁶and you have put the Testimony which I give to you into the Ark. ¹⁷And you have made a propitiatory covering of pure gold, two cubits and a half its length, and a cubit and a half its breadth; ¹⁸and you have made two cherubim of gold; you make them beaten work at the two ends of the propitiatory covering; ¹⁹and make one cherub at the end on this [side] and one cherub at the end on that [side]; at the propitiatory covering you make the cherubim on its two ends. ²⁰And the cherubim have been spreading out wings on high, covering over the propitiatory covering with their wings, and their faces [are] toward one another—the faces of the cherubim are toward the propitiatory covering. ²¹And you have put the propitiatory covering on the Ark above, and you put the Testimony which I give to you into the Ark; ²²and I have met with you there, and have spoken with you from off the propitiatory covering (from between the two cherubim, which [are] on the Ark of the Testimony) all that which I command you concerning the sons of Israel. ²³And you have made a table of shittim wood, two cubits its length, and a cubit its breadth, and a cubit and a half its height, ²⁴and have overlaid it [with] pure gold, and have made a crown of gold for it all around, ²⁵and have made a border of a handbreadth for it all around, and have made a crown of gold for its border all around. ²⁶And you have made four rings of gold for it, and have put the rings on the four corners, which [are] at its four feet; ²⁷close by the border are the rings for places for poles to carry the table; ²⁸and you have made the poles of shittim wood, and have overlaid them with gold, and the table has been carried with them; ²⁹and you have made its dishes, and its bowls, and its covers, and its cups, with which they pour out; you make them of pure gold; ³⁰and you have put Bread of the Presentation on the table before Me continually. ³¹And you have made a lampstand of pure gold; the lampstand is made of beaten work; its base, and its branch, its calyxes, its knobs, and its flowers are of the same; ³²and six branches are coming out of its sides, three branches of the lampstand out of the first side, and three branches of the lampstand out of the second side; ³³three calyxes made like almonds in one branch, a knob and a flower, and three calyxes made like almonds in one branch, a knob and a flower—so for the six branches which are coming out from the lampstand. ³⁴And in the lampstand [are] four calyxes made like almonds, its knobs and its flowers; ³⁵and a knob under two branches of the same, and a knob under two branches of the same, and a knob under two branches of the same, for the six branches which are coming out of the lampstand; ³⁶their knobs and their branches are of the same, all of it one beaten work of pure gold; ³⁷and you have made its seven lamps, and [one] has caused its lamps to go up, and it has given light over [and] beyond its front. ³⁸And its snuffers and its snuff dishes [are] of pure gold; ³⁹he makes it of a talent of pure gold, with all these vessels. ⁴⁰Now see and make [them] by their pattern which you are shown on the mountain."

CHAPTER 26

¹"And you make the Dwelling Place [with] ten curtains of twined linen, and blue, and purple, and scarlet; [with] cherubim, the work of a designer, you make them; ²the length of the one curtain [is] twenty-eight by the cubit, and the breadth of the one curtain [is] four by the cubit, one measure [is] for all the curtains; ³five of the curtains are joining to one another, and five curtains are joining to one another. ⁴And you have made loops of blue on the edge of the first curtain, at the end in the joining; and so you make in the edge of the outermost curtain, in the joining of the second. ⁵You make fifty loops in the first curtain, and you make fifty loops in the edge of the curtain which [is] in the joining of the second, causing the loops to take hold to one another; ⁶and you have made fifty hooks of gold, and have joined the curtains to one another by the hooks, and the Dwelling Place has been one. ⁷And you have made curtains of goats' [hair] for a tent over the Dwelling Place; you make eleven curtains: ⁸the length of one curtain [is] thirty by the cubit, and the breadth of one curtain [is] four by the cubit; one measure [is] for the eleven curtains; ⁹and you have joined the five curtains apart, and the six curtains apart, and have doubled the six curtains at the front of the tent. ¹⁰And you have made fifty loops on the edge of the first curtain, the outermost in the joining, and fifty loops on the edge of the curtain which is joining the second; ¹¹and you have made fifty hooks of bronze, and have brought in the hooks into the loops, and have joined the tent, and it has been one. ¹²And the excess remaining in the curtains of the tent—the half of the curtain which is remaining—has spread over the back part of the Dwelling Place; ¹³and the cubit on this [side], and the cubit on that [side], in the remaining [part] of the length of the curtains of the tent, is spread out over the sides of the Dwelling Place, on this [side] and on that [side], to cover it; ¹⁴and you have made a covering for the tent of rams' skins made red, and a covering of tachashim skins above. ¹⁵And you have made the boards for the Dwelling Place of shittim wood, standing up; ¹⁶ten cubits [is] the length of the board, and a cubit and a half the breadth of one board; ¹⁷two handles [are] to one board, joined to one another; so you make for all the boards of the Dwelling Place; ¹⁸and you have made the boards of the Dwelling Place—twenty boards for the south side southward; ¹⁹and you make forty sockets of silver under the twenty boards, two sockets under one board for its two handles, and two sockets under the other board for its two handles. ²⁰And for the second side of the Dwelling Place, for the north side, [are] twenty boards, ²¹and their forty sockets of silver, two sockets under one board, and two sockets under another board. ²²And for the sides of the Dwelling Place westward, you make six boards. ²³And you make two boards for the corners of the Dwelling Place in the two sides. ²⁴And they are pairs beneath, and together they are pairs above its head to one ring; so is it for them both, they are for the two corners. ²⁵And they have been eight boards, and their sockets of silver [are] sixteen sockets, two sockets under one board, and two sockets under another board. ²⁶And you have made bars of shittim wood: five for the boards of the first side of the Dwelling Place, ²⁷and five bars for the boards of the second side of the Dwelling Place, and five bars for the boards of the side of the Dwelling Place at the two sides, westward; ²⁸and one has caused the middle bar in the midst of the boards to reach from end to end; ²⁹and you overlay the boards [with] gold, and you make their rings of gold [for] places for bars, and have overlaid their bars with gold; ³⁰and you have raised up the Dwelling Place according to its fashion which you have been shown on the mountain. ³¹And you have made a veil of blue, and purple, and scarlet, and twined linen, the work of a designer; he makes it [with] cherubim; ³²and you have put it on four pillars of shittim wood, overlaid [with] gold, their pegs [are] of gold, on four sockets of silver. ³³And you have put the veil under the hooks, and have brought in the Ark of the Testimony there within the veil; and the veil has made a separation for you between the holy and the Holy of Holies. ³⁴And you have put the propitiatory covering on the Ark of the Testimony in the Holy of Holies. ³⁵And you have set the table at the outside of the veil, and the lampstand opposite the table on the side of the Dwelling Place southward, and you put the table on the north side. ³⁶And you have made a covering for the opening of the tent of blue, and purple, and scarlet, and twined linen, the work of an embroiderer; ³⁷and you have made five pillars of shittim [wood] for the covering, and have overlaid them [with] gold, their pegs [are] of gold, and you have cast five sockets of bronze for them."

EXODUS

CHAPTER 27

¹"And you have made the altar of shittim wood, five cubits the length, and five cubits the breadth—the altar is square—and three cubits [is] its height. ²And you have made its horns on its four corners, its horns are of the same, and you have overlaid it [with] bronze. ³And you have made its pots to remove its ashes, and its shovels, and its bowls, and its forks, and its fire-pans, even all its vessels you make of bronze. ⁴And you have made a grate of network of bronze for it, and have made four rings of bronze on the net on its four extremities, ⁵and have put it under the rim of the altar beneath, and the net has been up to the middle of the altar. ⁶And you have made poles for the altar, poles of shittim wood, and have overlaid them [with] bronze. ⁷And the poles have been brought into the rings, and the poles have been on the two sides of the altar in carrying it. ⁸You make it hollow [with] boards; as it has been showed [to] you on the mountain, so do they make [it]. ⁹And you have made the court of the Dwelling Place: for the south side southward, hangings for the court of twined linen, the length of the first side [is] one hundred by the cubit, ¹⁰and its twenty pillars and their twenty sockets [are] of bronze, the pegs of the pillars and their fillets [are] of silver; ¹¹and so for the north side in length, hangings of one hundred [cubits] in length, and its twenty pillars and their twenty sockets [are] of bronze, the pegs of the pillars and their fillets [are] of silver. ¹²And [for] the breadth of the court at the west side [are] hangings of fifty cubits, their pillars ten, and their sockets ten. ¹³And the breadth of the court at the east side, eastward, [is] fifty cubits. ¹⁴And the hangings at the side [are] fifteen cubits, their pillars three, and their sockets three. ¹⁵And at the second side [are] hangings of fifteen [cubits], their pillars three, and their sockets three. ¹⁶And for the gate of the court [is] a covering of twenty cubits of blue, and purple, and scarlet, and twined linen, the work of an embroiderer; their pillars four, their sockets four. ¹⁷All the pillars of the court all around [are] filleted [with] silver, their pegs [are] silver, and their sockets bronze. ¹⁸The length of the court [is] one hundred by the cubit, and the breadth fifty by fifty, and the height five cubits, of twined linen, and their sockets [are] bronze; ¹⁹for all the vessels of the Dwelling Place, in all its service, and all its pins, and all the pins of the court, [are] bronze. ²⁰And you command the sons of Israel, and they bring pure oil of beaten olive to you for the light, to cause the lamp to go up continually. ²¹In the Tent of Meeting, at the outside of the veil, which [is] over the Testimony, Aaron—his sons also—arrange it from evening until morning before YHWH. [It is] a continuous statute for their generations, from the sons of Israel."

CHAPTER 28

¹"And you, bring your brother Aaron near to you, and his sons with him, from the midst of the sons of Israel, for his being priest to Me, [even] Aaron, Nadab, and Abihu, Eleazar, and Ithamar, sons of Aaron; ²and you have made holy garments for your brother Aaron, for glory and for beauty; ³and you speak to all the wise of heart, whom I have filled [with] a spirit of wisdom, and they have made the garments of Aaron to sanctify him for his being priest to Me. ⁴And these [are] the garments which they make: a breastplate, and an ephod, and an upper robe, and an embroidered coat, a turban, and a girdle; indeed, they have made holy garments for your brother Aaron, and for his sons, for his being priest to Me. ⁵And they take the gold, and the blue, and the purple, and the scarlet, and the linen, ⁶and have made the ephod of gold, blue, and purple, and scarlet, and twined linen, the work of a designer; ⁷it has two shoulders joining at its two ends, and it is joined. ⁸And the girdle of his ephod which [is] on him, according to its work, is of the same, of gold, blue, and purple, and scarlet, and twined linen. ⁹And you have taken the two shoham stones, and have engraved the names of the sons of Israel on them; ¹⁰six of their names on the first stone, and the names of the remaining six on the second stone, according to their births; ¹¹the work of an engraver of stone, [as] engravings of a signet—you engrave the names of the sons of Israel on the two stones; encompassing, you make them [with] filigrees of gold. ¹²And you have set the two stones on the shoulders of the ephod—stones of memorial to the sons of Israel—and Aaron has borne their names before YHWH, on his two shoulders, for a memorial. ¹³And you have made filigrees of gold, ¹⁴and you make them [with] two chains of pure gold [as] wreathed work, work of thick bands, and you have put the thick chains on the filigrees. ¹⁵And you have made a breastplate of judgment, the work of a designer; you make it according to the work of the ephod; you make it of gold, blue, and purple, and scarlet, and twined linen; ¹⁶it is square, doubled, a span its length, and a span its breadth. ¹⁷And you have set settings of stone in it, four rows of stone: a row of sardius, topaz, and carbuncle [is] the first row; ¹⁸and the second row [is] emerald, sapphire, and diamond; ¹⁹and the third row [is] opal, agate, and amethyst; ²⁰and the fourth row [is] beryl, and onyx, and jasper; they are embroidered with gold in their settings, ²¹and the stones are according to the names of the sons of Israel, twelve according to their names, [as] engravings of a signet, each with his name; they are for the twelve tribes. ²²And you have made wreathed chains on the breastplate, [the] work of thick bands of pure gold; ²³and you have made two rings of gold on the breastplate, and have put the two rings on the two ends of the breastplate; ²⁴and you have put the two thick bands of gold on the two rings at the ends of the breastplate; ²⁵and you put the two ends of the two thick bands on the two filigrees, and you have put [them] on the shoulders of the ephod toward the front of its face. ²⁶And you have made two rings of gold, and have set them on the two ends of the breastplate, on its border, which [is] toward the side of the ephod within it; ²⁷and you have made two rings of gold, and have put them on the two shoulders of the ephod, from beneath, in front of its face, close by its joining, above the girdle of the ephod, ²⁸and they bind the breastplate by its rings to the rings of the ephod with a ribbon of blue, to be above the girdle of the ephod, and the breastplate is not loosed from the ephod. ²⁹And Aaron has borne the names of the sons of Israel in the breastplate of judgment, on his heart, in his going into the holy place, for a memorial before YHWH continually. ³⁰And you have put the Lights and the Perfections into the breastplate of judgment, and they have been on the heart of Aaron, in his going in before YHWH, and Aaron has borne the judgment of the sons of Israel on his heart before YHWH continually. ³¹And you have made the upper robe of the ephod completely of blue, ³²and the opening for his head has been in its midst; there is a border for its opening all around—the work of a weaver—[and] there is as the opening of a [linen] habergeon for it; it is not torn. ³³And you have made on its hem pomegranates of blue, and purple, and scarlet, on its hem all around, and bells of gold in their midst all around; ³⁴a bell of gold and a pomegranate [and] a bell of gold and a pomegranate [are] on the hems of the upper robe all around. ³⁵And it has been on Aaron to minister in, and its sound has been heard in his coming into the holy place before YHWH, and in his going out, and he does not die. ³⁶And you have made a flower of pure gold, and have engraved engravings of a signet on it: Holy to YHWH; ³⁷and you have put it on a blue ribbon, and it has been on the turban—it is toward the front of the face of the turban; ³⁸and it has been on the forehead of Aaron, and Aaron has borne the iniquity of the holy things which the sons of Israel hallow, even all their holy gifts; and it has been on his forehead continually for a pleasing thing for them before YHWH. ³⁹And you have embroidered the coat of linen, and have made a turban of linen, and you make a girdle—the work of an embroiderer. ⁴⁰And you make coats for the sons of Aaron, and you have made girdles for them, and you make caps for them, for glory and for beauty; ⁴¹and you have clothed your brother Aaron with them, and his sons with him, and have anointed them, and have consecrated their hand, and have sanctified them, and they have been priests to Me. ⁴²And make linen trousers for them to cover the naked flesh; they are from the loins even to the thighs; ⁴³and they have been on Aaron and on his sons in their going into the Tent of Meeting, or in their drawing near to the altar to minister in the holy place, and they do not bear iniquity nor have they died; [it is] a continuous statute to him and to his seed after him."

CHAPTER 29

¹"And this [is] the thing which you do to them, to hallow them, for being priests to Me: take one bullock, a son of the herd, and two rams, perfect ones, ²and unleavened bread, and unleavened cakes anointed with oil; you make them of fine wheat flour, ³and you have put

them on one basket, and have brought them near in the basket, also the bullock and the two rams. ⁴And you bring Aaron and his sons near to the opening of the Tent of Meeting, and have bathed them with water; ⁵and you have taken the garments, and have clothed Aaron with the coat, and the upper robe of the ephod, and the ephod, and the breastplate, and have girded him with the girdle of the ephod, ⁶and have set the turban on his head, and have put the holy crown on the turban, ⁷and have taken the anointing oil, and have poured [it] on his head, and have anointed him. ⁸And you bring his sons near, and have clothed them [with] coats, ⁹and have girded them [with] a girdle (Aaron and his sons), and have bound caps on them; and the priesthood has been theirs by a continuous statute, and you have consecrated the hand of Aaron, and the hand of his sons, ¹⁰and have brought the bullock near before the Tent of Meeting, and Aaron has laid—his sons also—their hands on the head of the bullock. ¹¹And you have slaughtered the bullock before YHWH, at the opening of the Tent of Meeting, ¹²and have taken of the blood of the bullock, and have put [it] on the horns of the altar with your finger, and you pour out all the blood at the foundation of the altar; ¹³and you have taken all the fat which is covering the innards, and the redundance on the liver, and the two kidneys, and the fat which [is] on them, and have made incense on the altar; ¹⁴and the flesh of the bullock, and his skin, and his dung, you burn with fire at the outside of the camp; it [is] a sin-offering. ¹⁵And you take the first ram, and Aaron and his sons have laid their hands on the head of the ram, ¹⁶and you have slaughtered the ram, and have taken its blood, and have sprinkled [it] around the altar, ¹⁷and you cut the ram into its pieces, and have washed its innards, and its legs, and have put [them] on its pieces, and on its head; ¹⁸and you have made incense with the whole ram on the altar. It [is] a burnt-offering to YHWH, a refreshing fragrance; it [is] a fire-offering to YHWH. ¹⁹And you have taken the second ram, and Aaron has laid—his sons also—their hands on the head of the ram, ²⁰and you have slaughtered the ram, and have taken of its blood, and have put [it] on the tip of the right ear of Aaron, and on the tip of the right ear of his sons, and on the thumb of their right hand, and on the great toe of their right foot, and have sprinkled the blood around the altar; ²¹and you have taken of the blood which [is] on the altar, and of the anointing oil, and have sprinkled [it] on Aaron, and on his garments, and on his sons, and on the garments of his sons with him, and he has been hallowed, he and his garments, and his sons, and the garments of his sons with him. ²²And you have taken from the ram the fat, and the fat tail, and the fat which is covering the innards, and the redundance on the liver, and the two kidneys, and the fat which [is] on them, and the right leg, for it [is] a ram of consecration, ²³and one round cake of bread, and one cake of oiled bread, and one thin cake out of the basket of the unleavened things which [is] before YHWH; ²⁴and you have set the whole on the hands of Aaron, and on the hands of his sons, and have waved them [for] a wave-offering before YHWH, ²⁵and you have taken them out of their hand, and have made incense on the altar beside the burnt-offering, for refreshing fragrance before YHWH; it [is] a fire-offering to YHWH. ²⁶And you have taken the breast from the ram of the consecration which [is] for Aaron, and have waved it [for] a wave-offering before YHWH, and it has become your portion; ²⁷and you have sanctified the breast of the wave-offering, and the leg of the raised-offering, which has been waved, and which has been lifted up from the ram of the consecration, of that which [is] for Aaron, and of that which [is] for his sons; ²⁸and it has been for Aaron and for his sons, by a continuous statute from the sons of Israel, for it [is] a raised-offering; and it is a raised-offering from the sons of Israel, from the sacrifices of their peace-offerings—their raised-offering to YHWH. ²⁹And the holy garments which are Aaron's are for his sons after him, to be anointed in them and to consecrate their hand in them; ³⁰[for] seven days the priest in his stead (of his sons) puts them on when he goes into the Tent of Meeting to minister in the holy place. ³¹And you take the ram of the consecration and have boiled its flesh in the holy place; ³²and Aaron has eaten—his sons also—the flesh of the ram, and the bread which [is] in the basket, at the opening of the Tent of Meeting; ³³and they have eaten those things by which there is atonement to consecrate their hand, to sanctify them; and a stranger does not eat [them], for they [are] holy; ³⁴and if there is left of the flesh of the consecration or of the bread until the morning, then you have burned that which is left with fire; it is not eaten, for it [is] holy. ³⁵And you have done thus to Aaron and to his sons, according to all that I have commanded you; [for] seven days you consecrate their hand; ³⁶and a bullock, a sin-offering, you prepare daily for the atonements, and you have atoned for the altar in your making atonement on it, and have anointed it to sanctify it; ³⁷[for] seven days you make atonement for the altar, and have sanctified it, and the altar has been most holy; all that is coming against the altar is holy. ³⁸And this [is] that which you prepare on the altar: two lambs, sons of a year, daily continually; ³⁹you prepare the first lamb in the morning, and you prepare the second lamb between the evenings; ⁴⁰and a tenth part of fine flour mixed with a fourth part of a hin of beaten oil, and a fourth part of a hin of wine [for] a drink-offering, [is] for the first lamb. ⁴¹And you prepare the second lamb between the evenings; according to the present of the morning, and according to its drink-offering, you prepare for it, for refreshing fragrance, a fire-offering to YHWH— ⁴²a continual burnt-offering for your generations [at] the opening of the Tent of Meeting before YHWH, to where I meet with you to speak to you there, ⁴³and I have met with the sons of Israel there, and it has been sanctified by My glory. ⁴⁴And I have sanctified the Tent of Meeting and the altar, and I sanctify Aaron and his sons for being priests to Me, ⁴⁵and I have dwelt in the midst of the sons of Israel, and have become their God, ⁴⁶and they have known that I [am] their God YHWH, who has brought them out of the land of Egypt, that I may dwell in their midst; I [am] their God YHWH."

CHAPTER 30

¹"And you have made an altar [for] making incense; you make it of shittim wood; ²a cubit its length and a cubit its breadth (it is square), and two cubits its height; its horns [are] of the same. ³And you have overlaid it with pure gold—its top, and around its sides, and its horns; and you have made a crown of gold for it all around; ⁴and you make two rings of gold for it, under its crown on its two ribs; you make [them] on its two sides, and they have become places for poles to carry it with them. ⁵And you have made the poles of shittim wood, and have overlaid them with gold; ⁶and you have put it before the veil, which [is] by the Ark of the Testimony, before the propitiatory covering which [is] over the Testimony, where I meet with you. ⁷And Aaron has made incense on it, incense of spices, morning by morning; in his making the lamps right, he makes incense [on] it, ⁸and in Aaron's causing the lamps to go up between the evenings, he makes incense [on] it; [it is] a continual incense before YHWH throughout your generations. ⁹You do not cause strange incense to go up on it—and burnt-offering and present; and you do not pour out a drink-offering on it; ¹⁰and Aaron has made atonement on its horns once in a year, by the blood of the sin-offering of atonements; once in a year he makes atonement for it, throughout your generations; it [is] most holy to YHWH." ¹¹And YHWH speaks to Moses, saying, ¹²"When you take up the census of the sons of Israel for their numbers, then they have each given an atonement [for] his soul to YHWH in their being numbered, and there is no plague among them in their being numbered. ¹³This they give, everyone passing over to those numbered, half a shekel, by the shekel of the holy place (the shekel [is] twenty gerahs); half a shekel [is] the raised-offering to YHWH; ¹⁴everyone passing over to those numbered, from a son of twenty years and upwards, gives the raised-offering of YHWH; ¹⁵the rich do not multiply, and the poor do not diminish from the half-shekel, to give the raised-offering of YHWH, to make atonement for your souls. ¹⁶And you have taken the atonement-money from the sons of Israel, and have given it for the service of the Tent of Meeting; and it has been to the sons of Israel for a memorial before YHWH, to make atonement for your souls." ¹⁷And YHWH speaks to Moses, saying, ¹⁸"And you have made a laver of bronze (and its base of bronze), for washing; and you have put it between the Tent of Meeting and the altar, and have put water [in] there, ¹⁹and Aaron and his sons have washed their hands and their feet from it; ²⁰they wash [with] water in their going into the Tent of Meeting, and do not die; or in their drawing near to the altar to minister, to make incense [as] a fire-offering

to YHWH, ²¹then they have washed their hands and their feet, and they do not die, and it has been a continuous statute to them, to him and to his seed, throughout their generations." ²²And YHWH speaks to Moses, saying, ²³"And you, take [these] principal spices for yourself: five hundred [shekels] of liquid myrrh, and the half of that—two hundred and fifty [shekels]—of spice-cinnamon, and two hundred and fifty [shekels] of spice-cane, ²⁴and five hundred [shekels] of cassia, by the shekel of the holy place, and a hin of olive oil; ²⁵and you have made it a holy anointing oil, a compound mixture, work of a compounder; it is a holy anointing oil. ²⁶And with it you have anointed the Tent of Meeting, and the Ark of the Testimony, ²⁷and the table and all its vessels, and the lampstand and its vessels, and the altar of incense, ²⁸and the altar of burnt-offering and all its vessels, and the laver and its base; ²⁹and you have sanctified them, and they have been most holy; all that is coming against them is holy; ³⁰and you anoint Aaron and his sons, and have sanctified them for being priests to Me. ³¹And you speak to the sons of Israel, saying, This is a holy anointing oil to Me, throughout your generations; ³²it is not poured on [the] flesh of man, and you make nothing [else] like it in its proportion; it [is] holy—it is holy to you; ³³a man who compounds [any] like it, or who puts of it on a stranger, has even been cut off from his people." ³⁴And YHWH says to Moses, "Take to yourself spices—stacte, and onycha, and galbanum—spices and pure frankincense; they are part for part; ³⁵and you have made it an incense, a compound, work of a compounder, salted, pure, holy; ³⁶and you have beaten [some] of it small, and have put of it before the Testimony in the Tent of Meeting, to where I meet with you; it is most holy to you. ³⁷As for the incense which you make, you do not make [any] for yourselves in its proportion; it is holy to you for YHWH; ³⁸a man who makes [any] like it—to be refreshed by it—has even been cut off from his people."

CHAPTER 31

¹And YHWH speaks to Moses, saying, ²"See, I have called by name Bezaleel, son of Uri, son of Hur, of the tribe of Judah, ³and I fill him [with] the Spirit of God, in wisdom, and in understanding, and in knowledge, and in all work, ⁴to devise inventions to work in gold, and in silver, and in bronze, ⁵and in a carving of stone for settings, and in a carving of wood to work in all work. ⁶And I, behold, have given with him Aholiab, son of Ahisamach, of the tribe of Dan, and I have given wisdom in the heart of every wise-hearted one, and they have made all that which I have commanded you. ⁷The Tent of Meeting, and the Ark of Testimony, and the propitiatory covering which [is] on it, and all the vessels of the tent, ⁸and the table and its vessels, and the pure lampstand and all its vessels, and the altar of the incense, ⁹and the altar of the burnt-offering and all its vessels, and the laver and its base, ¹⁰and the colored garments, and the holy garments for Aaron the priest, and the garments of his sons, for acting as priests in; ¹¹and the anointing oil, and the incense of the spices for the holy place; according to all that I have commanded you—they do." ¹²And YHWH speaks to Moses, saying, ¹³"And you, speak to the sons of Israel, saying, Surely you keep My Sabbaths, for it [is] a sign between Me and you throughout your generations, to know that I, YHWH, am sanctifying you; ¹⁴and you have kept the Sabbath, for it [is] holy to you, he who is defiling it is certainly put to death—for any who does work in it—that person has even been cut off from the midst of his people. ¹⁵[For] six days work is done, and in the seventh day [is] a Sabbath of holy rest to YHWH; any who does work in the Sabbath day is certainly put to death, ¹⁶and the sons of Israel have observed the Sabbath; to keep the Sabbath throughout their generations [is] a perpetual covenant— ¹⁷it [is] a sign between Me and the sons of Israel for all time; for [in] six days YHWH made the heavens and the earth, and in the seventh day He has ceased and is refreshed." ¹⁸And He gives to Moses, when He finishes speaking with him in Mount Sinai, two tablets of the Testimony, tablets of stone, written by the finger of God.

CHAPTER 32

¹And the people see that Moses is delaying to come down from the mountain, and the people assemble against Aaron, and say to him, "Rise, make gods for us, who go before us, for this Moses—the man who brought us up out of the land of Egypt—we have not known what has happened to him." ²And Aaron says to them, "Break off the rings of gold which [are] in the ears of your wives, your sons, and your daughters, and bring [them] to me"; ³and all the people break off the rings of gold which [are] in their ears, and bring [them] to Aaron, ⁴and he receives [it] from their hand, and fashions it with an engraving tool, and makes it [into] a molten calf, and they say, "These [are] your gods, O Israel, who brought you up out of the land of Egypt!" ⁵And Aaron sees, and builds an altar before it, and Aaron calls, and says, "A festival to YHWH—tomorrow"; ⁶and they rise early on the next day, and cause burnt-offerings to ascend, and bring peace-offerings near; and the people sit down to eat and to drink, and rise up to play. ⁷And YHWH says to Moses, "Go, descend, for your people whom you have brought up out of the land of Egypt have done corruptly, ⁸they have quickly turned aside from the way that I have commanded them; they have made a molten calf for themselves, and bow themselves to it, and sacrifice to it, and say, These [are] your gods, O Israel, who brought you up out of the land of Egypt!" ⁹And YHWH says to Moses, "I have seen this people, and behold, it [is] a stiff-necked people; ¹⁰and now, leave Me alone, and My anger burns against them, and I consume them, and I make you become a great nation." ¹¹And Moses appeases the face of his God YHWH and says, "Why, O YHWH, does Your anger burn against Your people, whom You have brought forth out of the land of Egypt with great power and with a strong hand? ¹²Why do the Egyptians speak, saying, He brought them out in calamity to slay them among mountains, and to consume them from off the face of the ground? Turn back from the heat of Your anger, and relent from this calamity against Your people. ¹³Be mindful of Abraham, of Isaac, and of Israel, Your servants, to whom You have sworn by Yourself, and to whom You speak: I multiply your seed as stars of the heavens, and all this land, as I have said, I give to your seed, and they have inherited [it] for all time"; ¹⁴and YHWH relents from the evil which He has spoken of doing to His people. ¹⁵And Moses turns, and goes down from the mountain, and the two tablets of the Testimony [are] in his hand, tablets written on both their sides; they [are] written on this [side] and on that [side]; ¹⁶and the tablets are the work of God, and the writing is the writing of God, engraved on the tablets. ¹⁷And Joshua hears the voice of the people in their shouting and says to Moses, "A noise of battle in the camp!" ¹⁸And he says, "It is not the voice of the crying of might, nor is it the voice of the crying of weakness—I am hearing a voice of singing." ¹⁹And it comes to pass, when he has drawn near to the camp, that he sees the calf, and the dancing, and the anger of Moses burns, and he casts the tablets out of his hands, and breaks them below the mountain; ²⁰and he takes the calf which they have made, and burns [it] with fire, and grinds [it] until [it is] small, and scatters [it] on the face of the waters, and causes the sons of Israel to drink. ²¹And Moses says to Aaron, "What has this people done to you, that you have brought in a great sin on it?" ²²And Aaron says, "Do not let the anger of my lord burn; you have known the people, that it [is beset] with evil; ²³and they say to me, Make gods for us, who go before us, for this Moses—the man who brought us up out of the land of Egypt we have not known what has happened to him; ²⁴and I say to them, Whoever has gold, let them break [it] off, and they give [it] to me, and I cast it into the fire, and this calf comes out." ²⁵And Moses sees the people, that it [is] unbridled, for Aaron has made it unbridled for contempt among its withstanders, ²⁶and Moses stands in the gate of the camp and says, "Who [is] for YHWH? [Come] to me!" And all the sons of Levi are gathered to him; ²⁷and he says to them, "Thus said YHWH, God of Israel: Each put his sword by his thigh, pass over and turn back from gate to gate through the camp, and each slay his brother, and each his friend, and each his relation." ²⁸And the sons of Levi do according to the word of Moses, and there falls of the people on that day about three thousand men, ²⁹and Moses says, "Consecrate your hand to YHWH today, for a man [is] against his son, and against his brother, so as to bring a blessing on you today." ³⁰And it comes to pass, on the next day, that Moses says to the people, "You have sinned a great sin, and now I go up to YHWH, perhaps I can atone for your sin." ³¹And Moses turns back to YHWH and says, "Ah, now this people has sinned a great sin, that they make a god of gold for themselves; ³²and now, if You take away

their sin—and if not—please blot me out of Your scroll which You have written." ³³And YHWH says to Moses, "Whoever has sinned against Me—I blot him out of My scroll; ³⁴and now, go, lead the people wherever I have spoken to you of; behold, My Messenger goes before you, and in the day of my charging—then I have charged their sin on them." ³⁵And YHWH plagues the people because they made the calf which Aaron made.

CHAPTER 33

¹And YHWH speaks to Moses, "Go, ascend from this [place], you and the people, whom you have brought up out of the land of Egypt, to the land which I have sworn to Abraham, to Isaac, and to Jacob, saying, I give it to your seed. ²And I have sent a Messenger before you, and have cast out the Canaanite, the Amorite, and the Hittite, and the Perizzite, the Hivite, and the Jebusite. ³[Go up] to a land flowing with milk and honey, for I do not go up in your midst, for you [are] a stiff-necked people—lest I consume you in the way." ⁴And the people hear this sad thing, and mourn; and none puts his ornaments on him. ⁵And YHWH says to Moses, "Say to the sons of Israel: You [are] a stiff-necked people; [in] one moment I could come up into your midst and could have consumed you; and now, put down your ornaments from off you, and I know what I do to you"; ⁶and the sons of Israel take off their ornaments at Mount Horeb. ⁷And Moses takes the tent, and has stretched it out at the outside of the camp, far off from the camp, and has called it, "Tent of Meeting"; and it has come to pass, everyone seeking YHWH goes out to the Tent of Meeting, which [is] at the outside of the camp. ⁸And it has come to pass, at the going out of Moses to the tent, all the people rise, and have stood, each at the opening of his tent, and have looked expectantly after Moses, until his going into the tent. ⁹And it has come to pass, at the going in of Moses to the tent, the pillar of the cloud comes down, and has stood at the opening of the tent, and He has spoken with Moses; ¹⁰and all the people have seen the pillar of the cloud standing at the opening of the tent, and all the people have risen and bowed themselves, each at the opening of his tent. ¹¹And YHWH has spoken to Moses face to face, as a man speaks to his friend; and he has turned back to the camp, and his minister Joshua, son of Nun, a youth, does not depart out of the tent. ¹²And Moses says to YHWH, "See, You are saying to me, Bring up this people, and You have not caused me to know whom You send with me; and You have said, I have known you by name, and you have also found grace in My eyes. ¹³And now, if, please, I have found grace in Your eyes, please cause me to know Your way, and I know You, so that I find grace in Your eyes, and consider that this nation [is] Your people"; ¹⁴and He says, "My presence goes, and I have given rest to you." ¹⁵And he says to Him, "If Your presence is not going—do not take us up from this [place]; ¹⁶and in what is it known now, that I have found grace in Your eyes—I and Your people—is it not in Your going with us? And we have been distinguished—I and Your people—from all the people who [are] on the face of the ground." ¹⁷And YHWH says to Moses, "Even this thing which you have spoken I do; for you have found grace in My eyes, and I know you by name." ¹⁸And he says, "Please show me Your glory"; ¹⁹and He says, "I cause all My goodness to pass before your face, and have called concerning the Name of YHWH before you, and favored him whom I favor, and loved him whom I love." ²⁰He also says, "You are unable to see My face, for man does not see Me and live"; ²¹YHWH also says, "Behold, a place [is] by Me, and you have stood on the rock, ²²and it has come to pass, in the passing by of My glory, that I have set you in a cleft of the rock, and spread out My hands over you until My passing by, ²³and I have turned aside My hands, and you have seen My back parts, and My face is not seen."

CHAPTER 34

¹And YHWH says to Moses, "Hew for yourself two tablets of stone like the first, and I have written on the tablets the words which were on the first tablets which you have broken; ²and be prepared at morning, and you have come up in the morning to Mount Sinai, and have stood before Me there, on the top of the mountain, ³and no man comes up with you, and also no man is seen in all the mountain, also the flock and the herd do not feed toward the front of that mountain." ⁴And he hews two tablets of stone like the first, and Moses rises early in the morning, and goes up to Mount Sinai as YHWH commanded him, and takes [the] two tablets of stone in his hand. ⁵And YHWH comes down in a cloud, and stations Himself with him there, and calls in the Name of YHWH, ⁶and YHWH passes over before his face, and calls: "YHWH, YHWH God, merciful and gracious, slow to anger, and abundant in kindness and truth, ⁷keeping kindness for thousands, taking away iniquity, and transgression, and sin, and not entirely acquitting, charging iniquity of fathers on sons and on sons' sons, on a third and on a fourth [generation]." ⁸And Moses hurries, and bows to the earth, and pays respect, ⁹and says, "Now if I have found grace in Your eyes, O my Lord, please let my Lord go in our midst (for it [is] a stiff-necked people), and you have forgiven our iniquity and our sin, and have inherited us." ¹⁰And He says, "Behold, I am making a covenant. I do wonders before all your people, which have not been done in all the earth, or in any nation, and all the people in whose midst you [are in] have seen the work of YHWH, for it [is] fearful—that which I am doing with you. ¹¹Observe for yourself that which I am commanding you today. Behold, I am casting out from before you the Amorite, and the Canaanite, and the Hittite, and the Perizzite, and the Hivite, and the Jebusite; ¹²take heed to yourself lest you make a covenant with the inhabitant of the land into which you are going, lest it become a snare in your midst; ¹³for you break down their altars, and you shatter their standing pillars, and you cut down its Asherim; ¹⁴for you do not bow yourselves to another god—for YHWH, whose Name [is] Zealous, is a zealous God. ¹⁵Lest you make a covenant with the inhabitant of the land, and they have gone whoring after their gods, and have sacrificed to their gods, and [one] has called to you, and you have eaten of his sacrifice, ¹⁶and you have taken of their daughters for your sons, and their daughters have gone whoring after their gods, and have caused your sons to go whoring after their gods; ¹⁷you do not make a molten god for yourself. ¹⁸You keep the Celebration of Unleavened Things; [for] seven days you eat unleavened things, as I have commanded you, at an appointed time, [in] the month of Abib: for in the month of Abib you came out from Egypt. ¹⁹All opening a womb [are] Mine, and every firstling of your livestock born a male, [whether] ox or sheep; ²⁰and you ransom the firstling of a donkey with a lamb; and if you do not ransom, then you have beheaded it; you ransom every firstborn of your sons, and they do not appear before Me empty. ²¹[For] six days you work, and on the seventh day you rest; in plowing-time and in harvest you rest. ²²And you observe [the] Celebration of Weeks for yourself, of [the] first-fruits of wheat-harvest; and the Celebration of Ingathering at the revolution of the year. ²³Three times in a year all your males appear before the Lord YHWH, God of Israel; ²⁴for I dispossess nations from before you, and have enlarged your border, and no man desires your land in your going up to appear before your God YHWH three times in a year. ²⁵You do not slaughter the blood of My sacrifice with a fermented thing; and the sacrifice of the Celebration of the Passover does not remain until morning. ²⁶You bring the first of the first-fruits of the land into the house of your God YHWH. You do not boil a kid in its mother's milk." ²⁷And YHWH says to Moses, "Write these words for yourself, for I have made a covenant with you and with Israel according to the tenor of these words." ²⁸And he is there with YHWH forty days and forty nights; he has not eaten bread, and he has not drunk water; and he writes on the tablets the matters of the covenant—the Ten Commandments. ²⁹And it comes to pass, when Moses is coming down from Mount Sinai (and the two tablets of the Testimony [are] in the hand of Moses in his coming down from the mountain), that Moses has not known that the skin of his face has shone in His speaking with him, ³⁰and Aaron sees—all the sons of Israel also—Moses, and behold, the skin of his face has shone, and they are afraid of coming near to him. ³¹And Moses calls to them, and Aaron and all the princes in the congregation return to him, and Moses speaks to them; ³²and afterward all the sons of Israel have come near, and he charges them with all that YHWH has spoken with him in Mount Sinai. ³³And Moses finishes speaking with them, and puts a veil on his face; ³⁴and in the going in of Moses before YHWH to speak with Him, he turns aside the veil until his coming out; and he has come out and has spoken to the sons of Israel that which he is commanded; ³⁵and the sons of Israel have seen the face of Moses, that the

skin of the face of Moses has shone, and Moses has put back the veil on his face until his going in to speak with Him.

CHAPTER 35

¹And Moses assembles all the congregation of the sons of Israel and says to them, "These [are] the things which YHWH has commanded—to do them: ²[For] six days work is done, and on the seventh day there is a holy [day] for you, a Sabbath of rest to YHWH; any who does work in it is put to death; ³you do not burn a fire in any of your dwellings on the Sabbath day." ⁴And Moses speaks to all the congregation of the sons of Israel, saying, "This [is] the thing which YHWH has commanded, saying, ⁵Take a raised-offering for YHWH from among you; everyone whose heart [is] willing brings it [as] the raised-offering of YHWH: gold, and silver, and bronze, ⁶and blue, and purple, and scarlet, and linen, and goats' [hair], ⁷and rams' skins made red, and tachashim skins, and shittim wood, ⁸and oil for the light, and spices for the anointing oil, and for the spice-incense, ⁹and shoham stones, and stones for settings, for an ephod, and for a breastplate. ¹⁰And all the wise-hearted among you come in, and make all that YHWH has commanded: ¹¹the Dwelling Place, its tent, and its covering, its hooks, and its boards, its bars, its pillars, and its sockets, ¹²the Ark and its poles, the propitiatory covering, and the veil of the covering, ¹³the table and its poles, and all its vessels, and the Bread of the Presentation, ¹⁴and the lampstand for the light, and its vessels, and its lamps, and the oil for the light, ¹⁵and the altar of incense, and its poles, and the anointing oil, and the spice-incense, and the covering of the opening at the opening of the Dwelling Place, ¹⁶the altar of burnt-offering and the bronze grate which it has, its poles, and all its vessels, the laver and its base, ¹⁷the hangings of the court, its pillars, and their sockets, and the covering of the gate of the court, ¹⁸the pins of the Dwelling Place, and the pins of the court, and their cords, ¹⁹the colored garments, to do service in the holy place, the holy garments for Aaron the priest, and the garments of his sons to act as priest in." ²⁰And all the congregation of the sons of Israel go out from the presence of Moses, ²¹and they come in—every man whom his heart has lifted up, and everyone whom his spirit has made willing—they have brought in the raised-offering of YHWH for the work of the Tent of Meeting, and for all its service, and for the holy garments. ²²And they come in—the men with the women—every willing-hearted one—they have brought in nose-ring, and earring, and seal-ring, and necklace, all golden goods, even everyone who has waved a wave-offering of gold to YHWH. ²³And every man with whom has been found blue, and purple, and scarlet, and linen, and goats' [hair], and rams' skins made red, and tachashim skins, have brought [them] in; ²⁴everyone lifting up a raised-offering of silver and bronze has brought in the raised-offering of YHWH; and everyone with whom has been found shittim wood for any work of the service brought [it] in. ²⁵And every wise-hearted woman has spun with her hands, and they bring in yarn—of the blue, and the purple, [and] the scarlet—and the linen; ²⁶and all the women whose heart has lifted them up in wisdom, have spun the goats' [hair]. ²⁷And the princes have brought in the shoham stones, and the stones for settings, for the ephod, and for the breastplate, ²⁸and the spices, and the oil for the light, and for the anointing oil, and for the spice-incense; ²⁹every man and woman of the sons of Israel (whom their heart has made willing to bring in for all the work which YHWH commanded to be done by the hand of Moses) brought in a willing-offering to YHWH. ³⁰And Moses says to the sons of Israel, "See, YHWH has called Bezaleel, son of Uri, son of Hur, of the tribe of Judah, by name, ³¹and He fills him [with] the Spirit of God, in wisdom, in understanding, and in knowledge, and in all work, ³²even to devise inventions to work in gold, and in silver, and in bronze, ³³and in a carving of stones for settings, and in a carving of wood to work in any work of design. ³⁴And He has put [it] in his heart to direct, he and Aholiab, son of Ahisamach, of the tribe of Dan; ³⁵He has filled them with wisdom of heart to do every work, of engraver, and designer, and embroiderer (in blue, and in purple, in scarlet, and in linen), and weaver, who does any work, and of designers of designs."

CHAPTER 36

¹And Bezaleel, and Aholiab, and every wise-hearted man, in whom YHWH has given wisdom and understanding to know to do every work of the service of the holy place, have done according to all that YHWH commanded. ²And Moses calls to Bezaleel, and to Aholiab, and to every wise-hearted man in whose heart YHWH has given wisdom, everyone whom his heart lifted up, to come near to the work to do it. ³And they take from before Moses all the raised-offering which the sons of Israel have brought in for the work of the service of the holy place to do it; and still they have brought to him a willing-offering morning by morning. ⁴And all the wise men, who are doing all the work of the holy place, each come from his work which they are doing, ⁵and speak to Moses, saying, "The people are multiplying to bring in more than sufficient for the service of the work which YHWH commanded [us] to do." ⁶And Moses commands, and they cause a voice to pass over through the camp, saying, "Do not let man or woman make anymore work for the raised-offering of the holy place"; and the people are restrained from bringing, ⁷and the work has been sufficient for them, for all the work, to do it, and to leave. ⁸And all the wise-hearted ones among the doers of the work make the Dwelling Place; he has made them [with] ten curtains of twined linen, and blue, and purple, and scarlet, [with] cherubim, the work of a designer. ⁹The length of one curtain [is] twenty-eight by the cubit, and the breadth of one curtain [is] four by the cubit; one measure [is] for all the curtains. ¹⁰And he joins the five curtains to one another, and the [other] five curtains he has joined to one another; ¹¹and he makes loops of blue on the edge of one curtain, at the end, in the joining; so he has made in the edge of the outmost curtain, in the joining of the second; ¹²he has made fifty loops in the first curtain, and he has made fifty loops in the end of the curtain which [is] in the joining of the second; the loops are taking hold on one another. ¹³And he makes fifty hooks of gold, and joins the curtains to one another by the hooks, and the Dwelling Place is one. ¹⁴And he makes curtains of goats' [hair] for a tent over the Dwelling Place; eleven curtains he has made them; ¹⁵the length of one curtain [is] thirty by the cubit, and the breadth of one curtain [is] four cubits; one measure [is] for the eleven curtains; ¹⁶and he joins the five curtains apart, and the six curtains apart. ¹⁷And he makes fifty loops on the outer edge of the curtain, in the joining; and he has made fifty loops on the edge of the curtain which is joining the second; ¹⁸and he makes fifty hooks of bronze to join the tent—to be one; ¹⁹and he makes a covering for the tent of rams' skins made red, and a covering of tachashim skins above. ²⁰And he makes the boards for the Dwelling Place of shittim wood, standing up; ²¹ten cubits [is] the length of the [one] board, and a cubit and a half the breadth of the [one] board; ²²two handles [are] to one board, joined to one another; so he has made for all the boards of the Dwelling Place. ²³And he makes the boards for the Dwelling Place; twenty boards for the south side southward; ²⁴and he has made forty sockets of silver under the twenty boards: two sockets under one board for its two handles, and two sockets under the other board for its two handles. ²⁵And for the second side of the Dwelling Place, for the north side, he has made twenty boards, ²⁶and their forty sockets of silver: two sockets under one board, and two sockets under the other board; ²⁷and for the sides of the Dwelling Place westward, he has made six boards; ²⁸and he has made two boards for the corners of the Dwelling Place, in the two sides; ²⁹and they have been twins below, and together they are twins at its head, at one ring; so he has done to both of them at the two corners; ³⁰and there have been eight boards; and their sockets of silver [are] sixteen sockets, two sockets under one board. ³¹And he makes bars of shittim wood: five for the boards of the first side of the Dwelling Place, ³²and five bars for the boards of the second side of the Dwelling Place, and five bars for the boards of the Dwelling Place, for the sides westward; ³³and he makes the middle bar to enter into the midst of the boards from end to end; ³⁴and he has overlaid the boards with gold, and he has made their rings of gold, places for bars, and he overlays the bars with gold. ³⁵And he makes the veil of blue, and purple, and scarlet, and twined linen; he has made it [with] cherubim—the work of a designer; ³⁶and he makes four pillars of shittim [wood] for it, and overlays them with gold; their pegs [are] of gold; and he casts four sockets of silver for them. ³⁷And he makes a covering for the opening of the tent, of blue, and purple, and scarlet, and twined linen, the

work of an embroiderer, ³⁸also its five pillars, and their pegs; and he overlaid their tops and their fillets [with] gold, and their five sockets [are] bronze.

CHAPTER 37

¹And Bezaleel makes the Ark of shittim wood; two cubits and a half its length, and a cubit and a half its breadth, and a cubit and a half its height; ²and he overlays it with pure gold inside and outside, and makes a wreath of gold for it all around; ³and he casts four rings of gold for it on its four feet, even two rings on its one side, and two rings on its second side; ⁴and he makes poles of shittim wood, and overlays them with gold, ⁵and he brings in the poles into the rings, by the sides of the Ark, to carry the Ark. ⁶And he makes a propitiatory covering of pure gold, two cubits and a half its length, and a cubit and a half its breadth; ⁷and he makes two cherubim of gold; he has made them of beaten work at the two ends of the propitiatory covering— ⁸one cherub at the end on this [side] and one cherub at the end on that [side]; he has made the cherubim from [above] the propitiatory covering, at its two ends; ⁹and the cherubim are spreading out wings on high, covering over the propitiatory covering with their wings, and their faces [are] toward one another; the faces of the cherubim have been toward the propitiatory covering. ¹⁰And he makes the table of shittim wood; two cubits its length, and a cubit its breadth, and a cubit and a half its height, ¹¹and overlays it with pure gold, and makes a wreath of gold for it all around. ¹²And he makes a border for it of a handbreadth around, and makes a wreath of gold around for its border; ¹³and he casts four rings of gold for it, and puts the rings on the four corners which [are] at its four feet; ¹⁴the rings have been close by the border, places for poles to carry the table. ¹⁵And he makes the poles of shittim wood, and overlays them with gold, to carry the table; ¹⁶and he makes the vessels which [are] on the table, its dishes, and its bowls, and its cups, and the cups by which they pour out, of pure gold. ¹⁷And he makes the lampstand of pure gold; he has made the lampstand of beaten work, its base, and its branch, its calyxes, its knobs, and its flowers, have been of the same; ¹⁸and six branches are coming out of its sides, three branches of the lampstand out of its one side, and three branches of the lampstand out of its second side; ¹⁹three calyxes, made like almonds, in one branch, a knob and a flower; and three calyxes, made like almonds, in another branch, a knob and a flower; so for the six branches which are coming out of the lampstand. ²⁰And in the lampstand [are] four calyxes, made like almonds, its knobs, and its flowers, ²¹and a knob under the two branches of the same, and a knob under the two branches of the same, and a knob under the two branches of the same, [are] for the six branches which are coming out of it; ²²their knobs and their branches have been of the same; all of it one beaten work of pure gold. ²³And he makes its seven lamps, and its snuffers, and its snuff-dishes, of pure gold; ²⁴he has made it of a talent of pure gold, and with all its vessels. ²⁵And he makes the incense-altar of shittim wood; a cubit its length, and a cubit its breadth (square), and two cubits its height; its horns have been of the same; ²⁶and he overlays it with pure gold, around its top and its sides, and its horns; and he makes a wreath of gold for it all around; ²⁷and he has made two rings of gold for it under its wreath, at its two corners, at its two sides, for places for poles to carry it with them. ²⁸And he makes the poles of shittim wood, and overlays them with gold; ²⁹and he makes the holy anointing oil, and the pure spice-incense—work of a compounder.

CHAPTER 38

¹And he makes the altar of burnt-offering of shittim wood; five cubits its length, and five cubits its breadth (square), and three cubits its height; ²and he makes its horns on its four corners; its horns have been of the same; and he overlays it with bronze; ³and he makes all the vessels of the altar, the pots, and the shovels, and the sprinkling-pans, the forks, and the fire-pans; he has made all its vessels of bronze. ⁴And he makes a bronze grate of network for the altar, under its rim beneath, to its midst; ⁵and he casts four rings for the four ends of the bronze grate—places for bars; ⁶and he makes the poles of shittim wood, and overlays them with bronze; ⁷and he brings in the poles into the rings on the sides of the altar, to carry it with them; he made it hollow [with] boards. ⁸And he makes the laver of bronze, and its base of bronze, with the mirrors of the women assembling, who have assembled at the opening of the Tent of Meeting. ⁹And he makes the court: at the south side southward, the hangings of the court of twined linen, one hundred by the cubit, ¹⁰their pillars [are] twenty, and their bronze sockets twenty, the pegs of the pillars and their fillets [are] silver; ¹¹and at the north side, one hundred by the cubit, their pillars [are] twenty, and their sockets of bronze twenty; the pegs of the pillars and their fillets [are] silver; ¹²and at the west side [are] hangings, fifty by the cubit; their pillars [are] ten, and their sockets ten; the pegs of the pillars and their fillets [are] silver; ¹³and at the east side eastward, fifty cubits. ¹⁴The hangings on the side [are] fifteen cubits, their pillars three, and their sockets three, ¹⁵and at the second side at the gate of the court, on this [side] and on that [side]— hangings of fifteen cubits, their pillars three, and their sockets three; ¹⁶all the hangings of the court around [are] of twined linen, ¹⁷and the sockets for the pillars of bronze, the pegs of the pillars and their fillets of silver, and the overlaying of their tops of silver, and all the pillars of the court are filleted with silver. ¹⁸And the covering of the gate of the court [is] the work of an embroiderer, of blue, and purple, and scarlet, and twined linen; and twenty cubits [is] the length, and the height with the breadth [is] five cubits, corresponding to the hangings of the court; ¹⁹and their pillars [are] four, and their sockets of bronze four, their pegs [are] of silver, and the overlaying of their tops and their fillets [are] of silver; ²⁰and all the pins for the Dwelling Place, and for the court all around, [are] of bronze. ²¹These are the numberings of the Dwelling Place (the Dwelling Place of Testimony), which has been numbered by the command of Moses, the service of the Levites, by the hand of Ithamar son of Aaron the priest. ²²And Bezaleel son of Uri, son of Hur, of the tribe of Judah, has made all that YHWH commanded Moses; ²³and with him [is] Aholiab son of Ahisamach, of the tribe of Dan, an engraver, and designer and embroiderer in blue, and in purple, and in scarlet, and in linen. ²⁴All the gold which is prepared for the work in all the work of the holy place (and it is the gold of the wave-offering) [is] twenty-nine talents, and seven hundred and thirty shekels, by the shekel of the holy place. ²⁵And the silver of those numbered of the congregation [is] one hundred talents, and one thousand and seven hundred and seventy-five shekels, by the shekel of the holy place; ²⁶a bekah for the counted head (half a shekel, by the shekel of the holy place), for everyone who is passing over to those numbered, from a son of twenty years and upwards, for six hundred thousand and three thousand and five hundred and fifty. ²⁷And one hundred talents of silver are for casting the sockets of the holy place, and the sockets of the veil; one hundred sockets for the hundred talents, a talent for a socket; ²⁸and [from] the one thousand and seven hundred and seventy-five [shekels] he has made pegs for the pillars, and overlaid their tops, and filleted them. ²⁹And the bronze of the wave-offering [is] seventy talents, and two thousand and four hundred shekels; ³⁰and he makes with it the sockets of the opening of the Tent of Meeting, and the bronze altar, and the bronze grate which it has, and all the vessels of the altar, ³¹and the sockets of the court all around, and the sockets of the gate of the court, and all the pins of the Dwelling Place, and all the pins of the court all around.

CHAPTER 39

¹And of the blue, and the purple, and the scarlet, they made colored garments, to minister in the holy place; and they make the holy garments which [are] for Aaron, as YHWH has commanded Moses. ²And he makes the ephod, of gold, blue, and purple, and scarlet, and twined linen, ³and they expand the plates of gold, and have cut off wires to work in the midst of the blue, and in the midst of the purple, and in the midst of the scarlet, and in the midst of the linen—the work of a designer; ⁴they have made shoulder-pieces for it, joining; it is joined at its two ends. ⁵And the girdle of his ephod which [is] on it is of the same, according to its work, of gold, blue, and purple, and scarlet, and twined linen, as YHWH has commanded Moses. ⁶And they prepare the shoham stones, set [with] filigrees of gold, engraved with engravings of a signet—the names of the sons of Israel on [them]; ⁷and he sets them on the shoulders of the ephod— stones of memorial for the sons of Israel, as YHWH has commanded Moses. ⁸And he makes

the breastplate, the work of a designer, like the work of the ephod, of gold, blue, and purple, and scarlet, and twined linen; ⁹it has been square; they have made the breastplate double, a span its length, and a span its breadth, doubled. ¹⁰And they fill four rows of stones in it: a row of a sardius, a topaz, and a carbuncle [is] the first row; ¹¹and the second row an emerald, a sapphire, and a diamond; ¹²and the third row an opal, an agate, and an amethyst; ¹³and the fourth row a beryl, an onyx, and a jasper—set [with] filigrees of gold in their settings. ¹⁴And the stones, according to the names of the sons of Israel, are twelve, according to their names, engravings of a signet, each according to his name, for the twelve tribes. ¹⁵And they make wreathed chains on the breastplate, [the] work of thick bands of pure gold; ¹⁶and they make two filigrees of gold, and two rings of gold, and put the two rings on the two ends of the breastplate, ¹⁷and they put the two thick bands of gold on the two rings on the ends of the breastplate, ¹⁸and they have put the two ends of the two thick bands on the two filigrees, and they put them on the shoulders of the ephod, toward the front of its face. ¹⁹And they make two rings of gold, and set [them] on the two ends of the breastplate, on its border, which [is] on the side of the ephod within; ²⁰and they make two rings of gold, and put them on the two shoulders of the ephod below, in front of its front, close by its joining, above the girdle of the ephod; ²¹and they bind the breastplate by its rings to the rings of the ephod, with a ribbon of blue, to be above the girdle of the ephod, and the breastplate is not loosed from off the ephod, as YHWH has commanded Moses. ²²And he makes the upper robe of the ephod, the work of a weaver, completely of blue; ²³and the opening of the upper robe [is] in its midst, as the opening of a [linen] habergeon, [with] a border for its opening all around; it is not torn; ²⁴and they make on the hems of the upper robe pomegranates of blue, and purple, and scarlet, twined. ²⁵And they make bells of pure gold, and put the bells in the midst of the pomegranates, on the hems of the upper robe, all around, in the midst of the pomegranates; ²⁶a bell and a pomegranate [and] a bell and a pomegranate [are] on the hems of the upper robe all around, to minister in, as YHWH has commanded Moses. ²⁷And they make the coats of linen, the work of a weaver, for Aaron and for his sons, ²⁸and the turban of linen, and the beautiful caps of linen, and the linen trousers, of twined linen, ²⁹and the girdle of twined linen, and blue, and purple, and scarlet, the work of an embroiderer, as YHWH has commanded Moses. ³⁰And they make the flower of the holy crown of pure gold, and write a writing on it, engravings of a signet: "Holy to YHWH"; ³¹and they put a ribbon of blue on it, to put [it] on the turban above, as YHWH has commanded Moses. ³²And all the service of the Dwelling Place of the Tent of Meeting is completed; and the sons of Israel do according to all that YHWH has commanded Moses; so they have done. ³³And they bring in the Dwelling Place to Moses, the tent, and all its vessels, its hooks, its boards, its bars, and its pillars, and its sockets; ³⁴and the covering of rams' skins, which are made red, and the covering of tachashim skins, and the veil of the covering; ³⁵the Ark of the Testimony and its poles, and the propitiatory covering; ³⁶the table, all its vessels, and the Bread of the Presentation; ³⁷the pure lampstand, its lamps, the lamps of arrangement, and all its vessels, and the oil for the light. ³⁸And the golden altar, and the anointing oil, and the spice-incense, and the covering of the opening of the tent; ³⁹the bronze altar and the bronze grate which it has, its poles, and all its vessels, the laver and its base; ⁴⁰the hangings of the court, its pillars, and its sockets; and the covering for the gate of the court, its cords, and its pins; and all the vessels of the service of the Dwelling Place, for the Tent of Meeting; ⁴¹the colored clothes to minister in the holy place, the holy garments for Aaron the priest, and the garments of his sons, to act as priest in. ⁴²According to all that YHWH has commanded Moses, so the sons of Israel have done all the service; ⁴³and Moses sees all the work, and behold, they have done it as YHWH has commanded; so they have done. And Moses blesses them.

CHAPTER 40

¹And YHWH speaks to Moses, saying, ²"On the first day of the month, in the first month, you raise up the Dwelling Place of the Tent of Meeting, ³and have set the Ark of the Testimony [in] there, and have covered over the Ark with the veil, ⁴and have brought in the table, and set its arrangement in order, and have brought in the lampstand, and caused its lamps to go up. ⁵And you have put the golden altar for incense before the Ark of the Testimony, and have put the covering of the opening to the Dwelling Place, ⁶and have put the altar of the burnt-offering before the opening of the Dwelling Place of the Tent of Meeting, ⁷and have put the laver between the Tent of Meeting and the altar, and have put water [in] there. ⁸And you have set the court all around, and have placed the covering of the gate of the court, ⁹and have taken the anointing oil, and anointed the Dwelling Place, and all that [is] in it, and hallowed it, and all its vessels, and it has been holy; ¹⁰and you have anointed the altar of the burnt-offering, and all its vessels, and sanctified the altar, and the altar has been most holy; ¹¹and you have anointed the laver and its base, and sanctified it. ¹²And you have brought Aaron and his sons near to the opening of the Tent of Meeting, and have bathed them with water; ¹³and you have clothed Aaron with the holy garments, and anointed him, and sanctified him, and he has acted as priest to Me. ¹⁴And you bring his sons near, and have clothed them with coats, ¹⁵and anointed them as you have anointed their father, and they have acted as priests to Me, and their anointing has been to them for a continuous priesthood throughout their generations." ¹⁶And Moses does according to all that YHWH has commanded him; so he has done. ¹⁷And it comes to pass, in the first month, in the second year, on the first of the month, the Dwelling Place has been raised up; ¹⁸and Moses raises up the Dwelling Place, and sets its sockets, and places its boards, and places its bars, and raises its pillars, ¹⁹and spreads the tent over the Dwelling Place, and puts the covering of the tent on it above, as YHWH has commanded Moses. ²⁰And he takes and puts the Testimony into the Ark, and sets the poles on the Ark, and puts the propitiatory covering on the Ark above; ²¹and brings the Ark into the Dwelling Place, and places the veil of the covering, and covers over the Ark of the Testimony, as YHWH has commanded Moses. ²²And he puts the table in the Tent of Meeting, on the side of the Dwelling Place northward, at the outside of the veil, ²³and sets in order the arrangement of bread on it, before YHWH, as YHWH has commanded Moses. ²⁴And he puts the lampstand in the Tent of Meeting, opposite the table, on the side of the Dwelling Place southward, ²⁵and causes the lamps to go up before YHWH, as YHWH has commanded Moses. ²⁶And he sets the golden altar in the Tent of Meeting, before the veil, ²⁷and makes incense on it—spice-incense—as YHWH has commanded Moses. ²⁸And he sets the covering [at] the opening of the Dwelling Place, ²⁹and he has set the altar of the burnt-offering [at] the opening of the Dwelling Place of the Tent of Meeting, and causes the burnt-offering to go up on it, and the present, as YHWH has commanded Moses. ³⁰And he puts the laver between the Tent of Meeting and the altar, and puts water [in] there for washing, ³¹and Moses and Aaron and his sons have washed their hands and their feet at the same; ³²in their going into the Tent of Meeting, and in their drawing near to the altar, they wash, as YHWH has commanded Moses. ³³And he raises up the court all around the Dwelling Place, and around the altar, and places the covering of the gate of the court; and Moses completes the work. ³⁴And the cloud covers the Tent of Meeting, and the glory of YHWH has filled the Dwelling Place; ³⁵and Moses has not been able to go into the Tent of Meeting, for the cloud has dwelt on it, and the glory of YHWH has filled the Dwelling Place. ³⁶And in the going up of the cloud from off the Dwelling Place the sons of Israel journey in all their journeys; ³⁷and if the cloud does not go up then they do not journey, until the day of its going up. ³⁸For the cloud of YHWH [is] on the Dwelling Place by day, and fire is in it by night, before the eyes of all the house of Israel in all their journeys.

LEVITICUS

CHAPTER 1

¹And Yhwh calls to Moses, and speaks to him out of the Tent of Meeting, saying, ²"Speak to the sons of Israel, and you have said to them: Any man of you, when he brings an offering near to Yhwh out of the livestock—out of the herd or out of the flock—you bring your offering near. ³If his offering [is] a burnt-offering out of the herd, he brings a male near, a perfect one, to the opening of the Tent of Meeting; he brings it near at his pleasure before Yhwh; ⁴and he has laid his hand on the head of the burnt-offering, and it has been accepted for him to make atonement for him; ⁵and he has slaughtered the son of the herd before Yhwh; and sons of Aaron, the priests, have brought the blood near, and sprinkled the blood around the altar, which [is] at the opening of the Tent of Meeting. ⁶And he has stripped the burnt-offering, and has cut it into its pieces; ⁷and the sons of Aaron the priest have put fire on the altar, and arranged wood on the fire; ⁸and sons of Aaron, the priests, have arranged the pieces, with the head and the fat, on the wood, which [is] on the fire, which [is] on the altar; ⁹and he washes its innards and its legs with water; and the priest has made incense with the whole on the altar, a burnt-offering, a fire-offering of refreshing fragrance to Yhwh. ¹⁰And if his offering [is] out of the flock—out of the sheep or out of the goats—he brings a male near, a perfect one, for a burnt-offering, ¹¹and he has slaughtered it by the side of the altar northward, before Yhwh; and sons of Aaron, the priests, have sprinkled its blood around the altar; ¹²and he has cut it into its pieces, and its head and its fat, and the priest has arranged them on the wood, which [is] on the fire, which [is] on the altar; ¹³and he washes the innards and the legs with water, and the priest has brought the whole near, and has made incense on the altar; it [is] a burnt-offering, a fire-offering of refreshing fragrance to Yhwh. ¹⁴And if his offering [is] a burnt-offering out of the bird to Yhwh, then he has brought his offering near out of the turtle-doves or out of the young pigeons, ¹⁵and the priest has brought it near to the altar, and has wrung off its head, and has made incense on the altar, and its blood has been wrung out by the side of the altar; ¹⁶and he has turned aside its crop with its feathers, and has cast it near the altar, eastward, to the place of ashes; ¹⁷and he has cleaved it with its wings (he does not separate [it]), and the priest has made it an incense on the altar, on the wood, which [is] on the fire; it [is] a burnt-offering, a fire-offering of refreshing fragrance to Yhwh."

CHAPTER 2

¹"And when a person brings an offering near, a present to Yhwh, [and] his offering is of flour, then he has poured oil on it, and has put frankincense on it; ²and he has brought it to the sons of Aaron, the priests, and one [of the priests] has taken from there the fullness of his hand of its flour and of its oil, besides all its frankincense, and the priest has made incense with its memorial on the altar, a fire-offering of refreshing fragrance to Yhwh; ³and the remnant of the present [is] for Aaron and for his sons, most holy, of the fire-offerings of Yhwh. ⁴And when you bring an offering near, a present baked in an oven, [it is of] unleavened cakes of flour mixed with oil, or thin unleavened cakes anointed with oil. ⁵And if your offering [is] a present [made] on the griddle, it is of flour, mixed with oil, unleavened; ⁶divide it into parts, and you have poured oil on it; it [is] a present. ⁷And if your offering [is] a present [made] on the frying-pan, it is made of flour with oil, ⁸and you have brought in the present which is made of these to Yhwh, and [one] has brought it near to the priest, and he has brought it near to the altar, ⁹and the priest has lifted up from the present its memorial, and has made incense on the altar, a fire-offering of refreshing fragrance to Yhwh; ¹⁰and the remnant of the present [is] for Aaron and for his sons, most holy, of the fire-offerings of Yhwh. ¹¹No present which you bring near to Yhwh is made fermented, for you do not make incense [as] a fire-offering to Yhwh with any leaven or any honey. ¹²An offering of first-[fruits]—you bring them near to Yhwh, but they do not go up on the altar for refreshing fragrance. ¹³And every offering—your present—you season with salt, and you do not let the salt of the covenant of your God cease from your present; you bring salt near with all your offerings. ¹⁴And if you bring a present of first-fruits near to Yhwh, you bring the present of your first-fruits near of green ears, roasted with fire, beaten out [grain] of a fruitful field, ¹⁵and you have put oil on it, and laid frankincense on it, [for] it [is] a present; ¹⁶and the priest has made incense with its memorial from its beaten out [grain], and from its oil, besides all its frankincense, [as] a fire-offering to Yhwh."

CHAPTER 3

¹"And if his offering [is] a sacrifice of peace-offerings, if he is bringing near out of the herd, whether male or female, he brings a perfect one near before Yhwh, ²and he has laid his hand on the head of his offering, and has slaughtered it at the opening of the Tent of Meeting, and sons of Aaron, the priests, have sprinkled the blood around the altar. ³And he has brought near from the sacrifice of the peace-offerings a fire-offering to Yhwh, the fat which is covering the innards, and all the fat which [is] on the innards, ⁴and the two kidneys, and the fat which [is] on them, which [is] on the flanks, and the redundance on the liver above the kidneys—he turns it aside, ⁵and sons of Aaron have made it an incense on the altar, on the burnt-offering which [is] on the wood, which [is] on the fire, [as] a fire-offering of refreshing fragrance to Yhwh. ⁶And if his offering [is] out of the flock for a sacrifice of peace-offerings to Yhwh, male or female, he brings a perfect one near; ⁷if he is bringing a sheep near [for] his offering, then he has brought it near before Yhwh, ⁸and has laid his hand on the head of his offering, and has slaughtered it before the Tent of Meeting, and sons of Aaron have sprinkled its blood around the altar. ⁹And he has brought near from the sacrifice of the peace-offerings a fire-offering to Yhwh, its fat, the whole fat tail close by the bone—he turns it aside, and the fat which is covering the innards, and all the fat which [is] on the innards, ¹⁰and the two kidneys, and the fat which [is] on them, which [is] on the flanks, and the redundance on the liver above the kidneys—he turns it aside, ¹¹and the priest has made it an incense on the altar [as] bread of a fire-offering to Yhwh. ¹²And if his offering [is] a goat, then he has brought it near before Yhwh, ¹³and has laid his hand on its head, and has slaughtered it before the Tent of Meeting, and sons of Aaron have sprinkled its blood around the altar; ¹⁴and he has brought his offering near from it, a fire-offering to Yhwh, the fat which is covering the innards, and all the fat which [is] on the innards, ¹⁵and the two kidneys, and the fat which [is] on them, which [is] on the flanks, and the redundance on the liver above the kidneys—he turns it aside, ¹⁶and the priest has made them an incense on the altar [as] bread of a fire-offering, for refreshing fragrance; all the fat [is] Yhwh's. ¹⁷[This is] a continuous statute throughout your generations in all your dwellings: you do not eat any fat or any blood."

CHAPTER 4

¹And Yhwh speaks to Moses, saying, ²"Speak to the sons of Israel, saying, When a person sins through ignorance against any of the commands of Yhwh [regarding things] which are not to be done, and has done [something] against one of these— ³if the priest who is anointed sins according to the guilt of the people, then he has brought near for his sin which he has sinned a bullock, a son of the herd, a perfect one, to Yhwh, for a sin-offering, ⁴and he has brought in the bullock to the opening of the Tent of Meeting before Yhwh, and has laid his hand on the head of the bullock, and has slaughtered the bullock before Yhwh. ⁵And the priest who is anointed has taken of the blood of the bullock, and has brought it into the Tent of Meeting, ⁶and the priest has dipped his finger in the blood, and sprinkled of the blood seven times before

YHWH, at the front of the veil of the holy place; ⁷and the priest has put of the blood on the horns of the altar of spice-incense before YHWH, which [is] in the Tent of Meeting, and he pours out all the blood of the bullock at the foundation of the altar of the burnt-offering, which [is] at the opening of the Tent of Meeting. ⁸And he lifts up from it all the fat of the bullock of the sin-offering, the fat which is covering over the innards, and all the fat which [is] on the innards, ⁹and the two kidneys, and the fat which [is] on them, which [is] on the flanks, and the redundance on the liver above the kidneys—he turns it aside, ¹⁰as it is lifted up from the ox of the sacrifice of the peace-offerings; and the priest has made them an incense on the altar of the burnt-offering. ¹¹And the skin of the bullock, and all its flesh, with its head, and with its legs, and its innards, and its dung— ¹²he has even brought out the whole bullock to the outside of the camp, to a clean place, to the place of the pouring out of the ashes, and he has burned it on the wood with fire; it is burned beside the place of the pouring out of the ashes. ¹³And if all the congregation of Israel errs ignorantly, and the thing has been hidden from the eyes of the assembly, and they have done [something against] one of all the commands of YHWH [regarding things] which are not to be done, and have been guilty; ¹⁴when the sin which they have sinned concerning it has been known, then the assembly has brought a bullock near, a son of the herd, for a sin-offering, and they have brought it in before the Tent of Meeting; ¹⁵and the elderly of the congregation have laid their hands on the head of the bullock, before YHWH, and [one] has slaughtered the bullock before YHWH. ¹⁶And the priest who is anointed has brought in of the blood of the bullock to the Tent of Meeting, ¹⁷and the priest has dipped his finger in the blood, and has sprinkled seven times before YHWH at the front of the veil, ¹⁸and he puts [some] of the blood on the horns of the altar which [is] before YHWH, which [is] in the Tent of Meeting; and he pours out all the blood at the foundation of the altar of the burnt-offering, which [is] at the opening of the Tent of Meeting; ¹⁹and he lifts up all its fat from it, and has made incense on the altar. ²⁰And he has done to the bullock as he has done to the bullock of the sin-offering, so he does to it; and the priest has made atonement for them, and it has been forgiven them; ²¹and he has brought out the bullock to the outside of the camp, and has burned it as he has burned the first bullock; it [is] a sin-offering of the assembly. ²²When a prince sins, and has done [something against] one of all the commands of his God YHWH [regarding things] which are not to be done, through ignorance, and has been guilty, ²³or his sin wherein he has sinned has been made known to him, then he has brought in his offering, a kid of the goats, a male, a perfect one, ²⁴and he has laid his hand on the head of the goat, and has slaughtered it in the place where he slaughters the burnt-offering before YHWH; it [is] a sin-offering. ²⁵And the priest has taken of the blood of the sin-offering with his finger, and has put [it] on the horns of the altar of the burnt-offering, and he pours out its blood at the foundation of the altar of the burnt-offering, ²⁶and he makes incense on the altar with all its fat, as the fat of the sacrifice of the peace-offerings; and the priest has made atonement for him because of his sin, and it has been forgiven him. ²⁷And if any person of the people of the land sins through ignorance, by his doing [something against] one of the commands of YHWH [regarding things] which are not to be done, and has been guilty, ²⁸or his sin which he has sinned has been made known to him, then he has brought in his offering, a kid of the goats, a perfect one, a female, for his sin which he has sinned, ²⁹and he has laid his hand on the head of the sin-offering, and has slaughtered the sin-offering in the place of the burnt-offering. ³⁰And the priest has taken of its blood with his finger, and has put [it] on the horns of the altar of the burnt-offering, and he pours out all its blood at the foundation of the altar, ³¹and he turns aside all its fat, as the fat has been turned aside from off the sacrifice of the peace-offerings, and the priest has made incense on the altar for refreshing fragrance to YHWH; and the priest has made atonement for him, and it has been forgiven him. ³²And if he brings in a sheep [for] his offering, a female for a sin-offering, he brings in a perfect one, ³³and he has laid his hand on the head of the sin-offering, and has slaughtered it for a sin-offering in the place where he slaughters the burnt-offering. ³⁴And the priest has taken of the blood of the sin-offering with his finger, and has put [it] on the horns of the altar of the burnt-offering, and he pours out all its blood at the foundation of the altar, ³⁵and he turns aside all its fat, as the fat of the sheep is turned aside from the sacrifice of the peace-offerings, and the priest has made them an incense on the altar, according to the fire-offerings of YHWH, and the priest has made atonement for him, for his sin which he has sinned, and it has been forgiven him."

CHAPTER 5
¹"And when a person sins, and has heard the voice of an oath, and he [is] witness, or has seen, or has known—if he does not declare [it], then he has borne his iniquity. ²Or when a person comes against anything unclean, or against a carcass of an unclean beast, or against a carcass of unclean livestock, or against a carcass of an unclean teeming creature, and it has been hidden from him, then he [is] unclean and guilty; ³or when he comes against [the] uncleanness of man, even any of his uncleanness whereby he is unclean, and it has been hidden from him, and he has known, then he has been guilty. ⁴Or when a person swears, speaking wrongfully with the lips to do evil, or to do good, even anything which man speaks wrongfully with an oath, and it has been hid from him—when he has known then he has been guilty of one of these; ⁵and it has been when he is guilty of one of these, that he has confessed concerning that which he has sinned, ⁶and has brought in his guilt-offering to YHWH for his sin which he has sinned, a female out of the flock, a lamb, or a kid of the goats, for a sin-offering, and the priest has made atonement for him because of his sin. ⁷And if his hand does not reach to the sufficiency of a lamb, then he has brought in his guilt-offering—he who has sinned—two turtle-doves or two young pigeons to YHWH, one for a sin-offering and one for a burnt-offering; ⁸and he has brought them to the priest, and has brought near that which [is] for a sin-offering first, and has wrung off its head from its neck, and does not separate [it], ⁹and he has sprinkled of the blood of the sin-offering on the side of the altar, and that which is left of the blood is wrung out at the foundation of the altar; it [is] a sin-offering. ¹⁰And he makes the second a burnt-offering, according to the ordinance, and the priest has made atonement for him because of his sin which he has sinned, and it has been forgiven him. ¹¹And if his hand does not reach to two turtle-doves, or to two young pigeons, then he has brought in his offering—he who has sinned—a tenth of an ephah of flour for a sin-offering; he puts no oil on it, nor does he put frankincense on it, for it [is] a sin-offering, ¹²and he has brought it to the priest, and the priest has taken a handful from it of the fullness of his hand—its memorial—and has made incense on the altar, according to the fire-offerings of YHWH; it [is] a sin-offering. ¹³And the priest has made atonement for him, for his sin which he has sinned against one of these, and it has been forgiven him, and [the remnant] has been for the priest, like the present." ¹⁴And YHWH speaks to Moses, saying, ¹⁵"When a person commits a trespass, and has sinned through ignorance against the holy things of YHWH, then he has brought in his guilt-offering to YHWH, a ram, a perfect one, out of the flock, at your valuation [in] silver—shekels by the shekel of the holy place—for a guilt-offering. ¹⁶And that which he has sinned against the holy thing he repays, and is adding to it its fifth, and has given it to the priest, and the priest makes atonement for him with the ram of the guilt-offering, and it has been forgiven him. ¹⁷And when any person sins, and has done [something against] one of all the commands of YHWH [regarding things] which are not to be done, and has not known, then he has been guilty, and has borne his iniquity. ¹⁸Then he has brought in a ram, a perfect one, out of the flock, at your valuation, for a guilt-offering, to the priest; and the priest has made atonement for him, for his ignorance in which he has erred and he has not known, and it has been forgiven him; ¹⁹it [is] a guilt-offering; he has certainly been guilty before YHWH."

CHAPTER 6
¹And YHWH speaks to Moses, saying, ²"When any person sins, and has committed a trespass against YHWH, and has lied to his fellow concerning a deposit, or concerning fellowship, or concerning violent robbery, or has oppressed his fellow; ³or has found a lost thing, and has lied concerning it, and has sworn to a falsehood, concerning one of all

[these] which man does, sinning in them: ⁴then it has been, when he sins and has been guilty, that he has returned the plunder which he has violently taken away, or the thing which he has gotten by oppression, or the deposit which has been deposited with him, or the lost thing which he has found; ⁵or all that concerning which he swears falsely, he has even repaid it in its principal, and he is adding to it its fifth; he gives it to him whose it [is] in the day of his guilt-offering. ⁶And he brings his guilt-offering to YHWH, a ram, a perfect one, out of the flock, at your valuation, for a guilt-offering, to the priest, ⁷and the priest has made atonement for him before YHWH, and it has been forgiven him, concerning one thing of all that he does, by being guilty therein." ⁸And YHWH speaks to Moses, saying, ⁹"Command Aaron and his sons, saying, This [is] a law of the burnt-offering: the burnt-offering on [the] burning pile [remains] on the altar all the night until the morning, and the fire of the altar is burning on it. ¹⁰And the priest has put on his long robe of fine linen, and he puts his fine linen trousers on his flesh, and has lifted up the ashes which the fire consumes with the burnt-offering on the altar, and has put them near the altar; ¹¹and he has stripped off his garments, and has put on other garments, and has brought out the ashes to the outside of the camp, to a clean place. ¹²And the fire on the altar is burning on it, it is not quenched, and the priest has burned wood on it morning by morning, and has arranged the burnt-offering on it, and has made incense on it [with] the fat of the peace-offerings; ¹³fire is continually burning on the altar, it is not quenched. ¹⁴And this [is] a law of the present: sons of Aaron have brought it near before YHWH to the front of the altar, ¹⁵and [one] has lifted up of it with his hand from the flour of the present, and from its oil, and all the frankincense which [is] on the present, and has made incense on the altar of refreshing fragrance—its memorial to YHWH. ¹⁶And Aaron and his sons eat the remnant of it; it is eaten [with] unleavened things in a holy place—they eat it in the court of the Tent of Meeting. ¹⁷It is not baked [with] anything fermented; I have given it [for] their portion out of My fire-offerings; it [is] most holy, like the sin-offering, and like the guilt-offering. ¹⁸Every male among the sons of Aaron eats it—a continuous statute throughout your generations, out of the fire-offerings of YHWH. All that comes against them is holy." ¹⁹And YHWH speaks to Moses, saying, ²⁰"This [is] an offering of Aaron and of his sons, which they bring near to YHWH in the day of his being anointed: a tenth of the ephah of flour [for] a continual present, half of it in the morning, and half of it in the evening; ²¹it is made on a griddle with oil—you bring it in stirred; you bring baked pieces of the present near [for] a refreshing fragrance to YHWH. ²²And the priest who is anointed in his stead, from among his sons, makes it; [it is] a continuous statute of YHWH; it is completely burned as incense; ²³and every present of a priest is a whole burnt-offering; it is not eaten." ²⁴And YHWH speaks to Moses, saying, ²⁵"Speak to Aaron and to his sons, saying, This [is] a law of the sin-offering: in the place where the burnt-offering is slaughtered, the sin-offering is slaughtered before YHWH; it [is] most holy. ²⁶The priest who is making atonement with it eats it; it is eaten in a holy place, in the court of the Tent of Meeting. ²⁷all that comes against its flesh is holy, and when [any] of its blood is sprinkled on the garment, that on which it is sprinkled you wash in the holy place; ²⁸and an earthen vessel in which it is boiled is broken, and if it is boiled in a bronze vessel, then it is scoured and rinsed with water. ²⁹Every male among the priests eats it—it [is] most holy; ³⁰and no sin-offering, [any] of whose blood is brought into the Tent of Meeting to make atonement in the holy place, is eaten; it is burned with fire."

CHAPTER 7

¹"And this [is] a law of the guilt-offering: it [is] most holy; ²in the place where they slaughter the burnt-offering they slaughter the guilt-offering, and he sprinkles its blood on the altar all around, ³and he brings near all its fat from it, the fat tail, and the fat which is covering the innards, ⁴and the two kidneys, and the fat which [is] on them, which [is] on the flanks, and the redundance on the liver above the kidneys—he turns it aside; ⁵and the priest has made them an incense on the altar, a fire-offering to YHWH; it [is] a guilt-offering. ⁶Every male among the priests eats it; it is eaten in a holy place—it [is] most holy; ⁷as [is] a sin-offering, so [is] a guilt-offering; one law [is] for them; the priest who makes atonement by it—it is his. ⁸And the priest who is bringing any man's burnt-offering near, the skin of the burnt-offering which he has brought near, it is the priest's, his own; ⁹and every present which is baked in an oven, and all done in a frying-pan, and on a griddle, [is] the priest's who is bringing it near; it is his; ¹⁰and every present, mixed with oil or dry, is for all the sons of Aaron—one as another. ¹¹And this [is] a law of the sacrifice of the peace-offerings which [one] brings near to YHWH: ¹²if he brings it near for a thank-offering, then he has brought near with the sacrifice of thank-offering unleavened cakes mixed with oil, and thin unleavened cakes anointed with oil, and of stirred flour cakes mixed with oil; ¹³besides the cakes, he brings fermented bread near [with] his offering, besides the sacrifice of thank-offering of his peace-offerings; ¹⁴and he has brought near from it one [cake] from every offering [as] a raised-offering to YHWH for the priest who is sprinkling the blood of the peace-offerings; it is for him; ¹⁵as for the flesh of the sacrifice of the thank-offering of his peace-offerings, it is eaten in the day of his offering; he does not leave of it until morning. ¹⁶And if the sacrifice of his offering [is] a vow or free-will offering, it is eaten in the day of his bringing his sacrifice near; and on the next day the remnant of it is also eaten; ¹⁷and the remnant of the flesh of the sacrifice is burned with fire on the third day; ¹⁸and if any of the flesh of the sacrifice of his peace-offerings is eaten at all on the third day, it is not pleasing; it is not reckoned for him who is bringing it near; it is an abomination, and the person who is eating of it bears his iniquity. ¹⁹And the flesh which comes against any unclean thing is not eaten; it is burned with fire; as for the flesh, every clean one eats of the flesh; ²⁰and the person who eats of the flesh of the sacrifice of the peace-offerings which [are] YHWH's, and his uncleanness [is] on him, indeed, that person has been cut off from his people. ²¹And when a person comes against anything unclean, of the uncleanness of man, or of the uncleanness of beasts, or of any unclean teeming creature, and has eaten of the flesh of the sacrifice of the peace-offerings which [are] YHWH's, indeed, that person has been cut off from his people." ²²And YHWH speaks to Moses, saying, ²³"Speak to the sons of Israel, saying, You do not eat any fat of ox, and sheep, and goat; ²⁴and the fat of a carcass, and the fat of a torn thing, is prepared for any work, but you certainly do not eat it; ²⁵for whoever eats the fat of the beast, of which [one] brings near [as] a fire-offering to YHWH, indeed, the person who eats [it] has been cut off from his people. ²⁶And you do not eat any blood in all your dwellings, of bird, or of beast; ²⁷any person who eats any blood, indeed, that person has been cut off from his people." ²⁸And YHWH speaks to Moses, saying, ²⁹"Speak to the sons of Israel, saying, He who is bringing the sacrifice of his peace-offerings near to YHWH brings in his offering to YHWH from the sacrifice of his peace-offerings; ³⁰his own hands bring in the fire-offerings of YHWH; the fat beside the breast—he brings it in with the breast to wave it [as] a wave-offering before YHWH. ³¹And the priest has made incense with the fat on the altar, and the breast has been Aaron's and his sons; ³²and you give the right leg to the priest [as] a raised-offering of the sacrifices of your peace-offerings; ³³he from the sons of Aaron who is bringing the blood of the peace-offerings and the fat near—the right leg is for a portion for him. ³⁴For I have taken the breast of the wave-offering and the leg of the raised-offering from the sons of Israel, from the sacrifices of their peace-offerings, and I give them to Aaron the priest, and to his sons, by a continuous statute, from the sons of Israel." ³⁵This [is] an anointed portion [for] Aaron, and an anointed portion [for] his sons out of the fire-offerings of YHWH, in the day he has brought them near to act as priest of YHWH, ³⁶which YHWH has commanded to give to them from the sons of Israel, in the day of His anointing them—a continuous statute throughout their generations. ³⁷This [is] the law for burnt-offering, for present, and for sin-offering, and for guilt-offering, and for consecrations, and for a sacrifice of the peace-offerings, ³⁸which YHWH has commanded Moses in Mount Sinai, in the day of His commanding the sons of Israel to bring their offerings near to YHWH, in the wilderness of Sinai.

CHAPTER 8

¹And YHWH speaks to Moses, saying, ²"Take Aaron and his sons with him, and the

garments, and the anointing oil, and the bullock of the sin-offering, and the two rams, and the basket of unleavened things, ³and assemble all the congregation to the opening of the Tent of Meeting." ⁴And Moses does as YHWH has commanded him, and the congregation is assembled to the opening of the Tent of Meeting, ⁵and Moses says to the congregation, "This [is] the thing which YHWH has commanded to do." ⁶And Moses brings Aaron and his sons near, and bathes them with water, ⁷and puts the coat on him, and girds him with the girdle, and clothes him with the upper robe, and puts the ephod on him, and girds him with the girdle of the ephod, and binds [it] to him with it, ⁸and puts the breastplate on him, and puts the Lights and the Perfections into the breastplate, ⁹and puts the turban on his head, and puts the golden flower of the holy crown on the turban, toward the front of its face, as YHWH has commanded Moses. ¹⁰And Moses takes the anointing oil, and anoints the Dwelling Place, and all that [is] in it, and sanctifies them; ¹¹and he sprinkles of it on the altar seven times, and anoints the altar, and all its vessels, and the laver, and its base, to sanctify them; ¹²and he pours of the anointing oil on the head of Aaron, and anoints him to sanctify him. ¹³And Moses brings the sons of Aaron near, and clothes them [with] coats, and girds them [with] girdles, and binds caps to them, as YHWH has commanded Moses. ¹⁴And he brings the bullock of the sin-offering near, and Aaron lays—his sons also—their hands on the head of the bullock of the sin-offering, ¹⁵and [one] slaughters, and Moses takes the blood, and puts [it] around the horns of the altar with his finger, and cleanses the altar, and he has poured out the blood at the foundation of the altar, and sanctifies it, to make atonement on it. ¹⁶And he takes all the fat that [is] on the innards, and the redundance on the liver, and the two kidneys, and their fat, and Moses makes incense on the altar, ¹⁷and the bullock, and its skin, and its flesh, and its dung, he has burned with fire, at the outside of the camp, as YHWH has commanded Moses. ¹⁸And he brings the ram of the burnt-offering near, and Aaron and his sons lay their hands on the head of the ram, ¹⁹and [one] slaughters, and Moses sprinkles the blood around the altar; ²⁰and he has cut the ram into its pieces, and Moses makes incense with the head, and the pieces, and the fat, ²¹and he has washed the innards and the legs with water, and Moses makes incense with the whole ram on the altar; it [is] a burnt-offering for refreshing fragrance; it [is] a fire-offering to YHWH, as YHWH has commanded Moses. ²²And he brings the second ram near, a ram of the consecrations, and Aaron and his sons lay their hands on the head of the ram, ²³and [one] slaughters, and Moses takes of its blood, and puts [it] on the tip of the right ear of Aaron, and on the thumb of his right hand, and on the great toe of his right foot; ²⁴and he brings the sons of Aaron near, and Moses puts of the blood on the tip of their right ear, and on the thumb of their right hand, and on the great toe of their right foot. And Moses sprinkles the blood around the altar, ²⁵and takes the fat, and the fat tail, and all the fat that [is] on the innards, and the redundance on the liver, and the two kidneys, and their fat, and the right leg; ²⁶and out of the basket of unleavened things, which [is] before YHWH, he has taken one unleavened cake, and one cake of oiled bread, and one thin cake, and puts [them] on the fat, and on the right leg; ²⁷and he puts the whole on the hands of Aaron, and on the hands of his sons, and waves them [as] a wave-offering before YHWH. ²⁸And Moses takes them from off their hands, and makes incense on the altar, on the burnt-offering—they [are] consecrations for refreshing fragrance; it [is] a fire-offering to YHWH; ²⁹and Moses takes the breast, and waves it [as] a wave-offering before YHWH; it has been for Moses for a portion of the ram of the consecrations, as YHWH has commanded Moses. ³⁰And Moses takes of the anointing oil, and of the blood which [is] on the altar, and sprinkles [them] on Aaron, on his garments, and on his sons, and on the garments of his sons with him, and he sanctifies Aaron, his garments, and his sons, and the garments of his sons with him. ³¹And Moses says to Aaron and to his sons, "Boil the flesh at the opening of the Tent of Meeting, and there you eat it and the bread which [is] in the basket of the consecrations, as I have commanded, saying, Aaron and his sons eat it. ³²And the remnant of the flesh and of the bread you burn with fire; ³³and you do not go out from the opening of the Tent of Meeting [for] seven days, until the day of the fullness, the days of your consecration—for seven days he consecrates your hand; ³⁴as he has done on this day, YHWH has commanded to do, to make atonement for you; ³⁵and you abide at the opening of the Tent of Meeting by day and by night [for] seven days, and you have kept the charge of YHWH, and do not die, for so I have been commanded." ³⁶And Aaron does—his sons also—all the things which YHWH has commanded by the hand of Moses.

CHAPTER 9

¹And it comes to pass on the eighth day, Moses has called for Aaron and for his sons, and for [the] elderly of Israel, ²and he says to Aaron, "Take a calf for yourself, a son of the herd, for a sin-offering, and a ram for a burnt-offering, perfect ones, and bring [them] near before YHWH. ³And you speak to the sons of Israel, saying, Take a kid of the goats for a sin-offering, and a calf, and a lamb, sons of a year, perfect ones, for a burnt-offering, ⁴and a bullock and a ram for peace-offerings, to sacrifice before YHWH, and a present mixed with oil; for today YHWH has appeared to you." ⁵And they take that which Moses has commanded to the front of the Tent of Meeting, and all the congregation draws near and stands before YHWH; ⁶and Moses says, "This [is] the thing which YHWH has commanded; do [it], and the glory of YHWH appears to you." ⁷And Moses says to Aaron, "Draw near to the altar, and make your sin-offering, and your burnt-offering, and make atonement for yourself, and for the people, and make the offering of the people, and make atonement for them, as YHWH has commanded." ⁸And Aaron draws near to the altar, and slaughters the calf of the sin-offering, which [is] for himself; ⁹and the sons of Aaron bring the blood near to him, and he dips his finger in the blood, and puts [it] on the horns of the altar, and he has poured out the blood at the foundation of the altar; ¹⁰and the fat, and the kidneys, and the redundance of the liver, of the sin-offering, he has made incense on the altar, as YHWH has commanded Moses; ¹¹and he has burned the flesh and the skin with fire, at the outside of the camp. ¹²And he slaughters the burnt-offering, and the sons of Aaron have presented the blood to him, and he sprinkles it around the altar; ¹³and they have presented the burnt-offering to him, by its pieces, and the head, and he makes incense on the altar; ¹⁴and he washes the innards and the legs, and makes incense for the burnt-offering on the altar. ¹⁵And he brings the offering of the people near, and takes the goat of the sin-offering which [is] for the people, and slaughters it, and makes it a sin-offering, like the first; ¹⁶and he brings the burnt-offering near, and makes it, according to the ordinance; ¹⁷and he brings the present near, and fills his palm with it, and makes incense on the altar, apart from the burnt-offering of the morning. ¹⁸And he slaughters the bullock and the ram, a sacrifice of the peace-offerings, which [are] for the people, and sons of Aaron present the blood to him (and he sprinkles it around the altar), ¹⁹and the fat of the bullock, and of the ram, the fat tail, and the covering [of the innards], and the kidneys, and the redundance on the liver, ²⁰and they set the fat on the breasts, and he makes incense with the fat on the altar; ²¹and Aaron has waved the breasts and the right leg [as] a wave-offering before YHWH, as He has commanded Moses. ²²And Aaron lifts up his hand toward the people, and blesses them, and comes down from making the sin-offering, and the burnt-offering, and the peace-offerings. ²³And Moses goes in—Aaron also—to the Tent of Meeting, and they come out, and bless the people, and the glory of YHWH appears to all the people; ²⁴and fire comes out from before YHWH, and consumes the burnt-offering and the fat on the altar; and all the people see, and cry aloud, and fall on their faces.

CHAPTER 10

¹And the sons of Aaron, Nadab and Abihu, each take his censer, and put fire in them, and put incense on it, and bring strange fire near before YHWH, which He has not commanded them; ²and fire goes out from before YHWH and consumes them, and they die before YHWH. ³And Moses says to Aaron, "It [is] that which YHWH has spoken, saying, By those drawing near to Me I am sanctified, and in the face of all the people I am honored"; and Aaron is silent. ⁴And Moses calls to Mishael and to Elzaphan, sons of Uzziel, uncle of Aaron, and says to them, "Come near, carry your brothers from the front of the holy place to the

outside of the camp"; ⁵and they come near, and carry them in their coats to the outside of the camp, as Moses has spoken. ⁶And Moses says to Aaron and his sons, to Eleazar and to Ithamar, "You do not uncover your heads, and you do not tear your garments, that you do not die, and He is angry on all the congregation; as for your brothers, the whole house of Israel, they lament the burning which YHWH has kindled; ⁷and you do not go out from the opening of the Tent of Meeting, lest you die, for the anointing oil of YHWH [is] on you"; and they do according to the word of Moses. ⁸And YHWH speaks to Aaron, saying, ⁹"You do not drink wine and strong drink, you and your sons with you, in your going into the Tent of Meeting, and you do not die—a continuous statute throughout your generations, ¹⁰so as to make a separation between the holy and the common, and between the unclean and the pure; ¹¹and to teach the sons of Israel all the statutes which YHWH has spoken to them by the hand of Moses." ¹²And Moses speaks to Aaron and his sons, to Eleazar and to Ithamar, who are left, "Take the present that is left from the fire-offerings of YHWH, and eat it unleavened near the altar, for it [is] most holy, ¹³and you have eaten it in the holy place, for it [is] your portion, and the portion of your sons, from the fire-offerings of YHWH; for so I have been commanded. ¹⁴And you eat the breast of the wave-offering and the leg of the raised-offering in a clean place, you, and your sons, and your daughters with you; they have been given for your portion and the portion of your sons, out of the sacrifices of peace-offerings of the sons of Israel; ¹⁵the leg of the raised-offering, and breast of the wave-offering, besides fire-offerings of the fat, they bring in to wave [as] a wave-offering before YHWH, and it has been to you, and to your sons with you, by a continuous statute, as YHWH has commanded." ¹⁶And Moses has diligently sought the goat of the sin-offering, and behold, it is burned, and he is angry against Eleazar and against Ithamar, sons of Aaron, who are left, saying, ¹⁷"Why have you not eaten the sin-offering in the holy place, for it [is] most holy—and He has given it to you to take away the iniquity of the congregation, to make atonement for them before YHWH? ¹⁸Behold, its blood has not been brought into the holy place within; eating you eat it in the holy place, as I have commanded." ¹⁹And Aaron speaks to Moses, "Behold, today they have brought their sin-offering and their burnt-offering near before YHWH; and [things] like these meet me, yet I have eaten a sin-offering today; is it good in the eyes of YHWH?" ²⁰And Moses listens, and it is good in his eyes.

CHAPTER 11

¹And YHWH speaks to Moses and to Aaron, saying to them, ²"Speak to the sons of Israel, saying, This [is] the beast which you eat out of all the beasts which [are] on the earth: ³any dividing a hoof, and cleaving the cleft of the hooves, bringing up the cud, among the beasts—you eat it. ⁴Only, this you do not eat, of those bringing up the cud, and of those dividing the hoof: the camel, though it is bringing up the cud, yet the hoof is not dividing—it [is] unclean to you; ⁵and the hyrax, though it is bringing up the cud, yet the hoof is not divided—it [is] unclean to you; ⁶and the hare, though it is bringing up the cud, yet the hoof has not divided—it [is] unclean to you; ⁷and the sow, though it is dividing the hoof, and cleaving the cleft of the hoof, yet it does not bring up the cud—it [is] unclean to you. ⁸You do not eat of their flesh, and you do not come against their carcass—they [are] unclean to you. ⁹This you eat of all which [are] in the waters: anything that has fins and scales in the waters, in the seas, and in the brooks, them you eat; ¹⁰and anything that does not have fins and scales in the seas, and in the brooks, of any teeming creature of the waters, and of any creature which lives, which [is] in the waters—they [are] an abomination to you; ¹¹indeed, they are an abomination to you; you do not eat of their flesh, and you detest their carcass. ¹²Anything that does not have fins and scales in the waters—it [is] an abomination to you. ¹³And these you detest of the bird—they are not eaten, they [are] an abomination: the eagle, and the bearded vulture, and the osprey, ¹⁴and the kite, and the falcon after its kind, ¹⁵every raven after its kind, ¹⁶and the ostrich, and the nightjar [[or male ostrich]], and the seagull, and the hawk after its kind, ¹⁷and the little owl, and the cormorant, and the great owl, ¹⁸and the waterhen, and the pelican, and the Egyptian vulture, ¹⁹and the stork, the heron after its kind, and the hoopoe, and the bat. ²⁰Every teeming creature which is flying, which is going on four [legs]—it [is] an abomination to you. ²¹Only, this you eat of any teeming thing which is flying, which is going on four, which has legs above its feet, to move with them on the earth; ²²these of them you eat: the locust after its kind, and the bald locust after its kind, and the cricket after its kind, and the grasshopper after its kind; ²³and every teeming thing which is flying, which has four feet—it [is] an abomination to you. ²⁴And you are made unclean by these; anyone who is coming against their carcass is unclean until the evening; ²⁵and anyone who is lifting up of their carcass washes his garments, and has been unclean until the evening— ²⁶even every beast which is dividing the hoof, and is not cloven-footed, and is not bringing up the cud—they [are] unclean to you; anyone who is coming against them is unclean. ²⁷And anything going on its paws, among all the beasts which are going on four—they [are] unclean to you; anyone who is coming against their carcass is unclean until the evening; ²⁸and he who is lifting up their carcass washes his garments, and has been unclean until the evening—they [are] unclean to you. ²⁹And this [is] the unclean to you among the teeming things which are teeming on the earth: the weasel, and the muroid, and the tortoise [[or large lizard]] after its kind, ³⁰and the gecko [[or ferret]], and the chameleon, and the lizard, and the snail, and the mole; ³¹these [are] the unclean to you among all which are teeming; anyone who is coming against them in their death is unclean until the evening. ³²And anything on which anyone of them falls, in their death, is unclean, of any vessel of wood or garment or skin or sack, any vessel in which work is done is brought into water, and has been unclean until the evening, then it has been clean; ³³and any earthen vessel, into the midst of which [any] one of them falls, all that [is] in its midst is unclean, and you break it. ³⁴Of all the food which is eaten, that on which comes [such] water, is unclean, and all drink which is drunk in any [such] vessel is unclean; ³⁵and anything on which [any] of their carcass falls is unclean; oven or double pots, it is broken down, they [are] unclean, indeed, they are unclean to you. ³⁶Only, a fountain or pit, a collection of water, is clean, but that which is coming against their carcass is unclean; ³⁷and when [any] of their carcass falls on any sown seed which is sown—it [is] clean; ³⁸and when water is put on the seed, and [any] of its carcass has fallen on it—it [is] unclean to you. ³⁹And when any of the beasts which are for food for you dies, he who is coming against its carcass is unclean until the evening; ⁴⁰and he who is eating of its carcass washes his garments, and has been unclean until the evening; and he who is lifting up its carcass washes his garments, and has been unclean until the evening. ⁴¹And every teeming thing which is teeming on the earth is an abomination, it is not eaten; ⁴²anything going on the belly, and any going on four, to every multiplier of feet, to every teeming thing which is teeming on the earth—you do not eat them, for they [are] an abomination; ⁴³you do not make yourselves abominable with any teeming thing which is teeming, nor do you make yourselves unclean with them, so that you have been unclean with them. ⁴⁴For I [am] your God YHWH, and you have sanctified yourselves, and you have been holy, for I [am] holy; and you do not defile your persons with any teeming thing which is creeping on the earth; ⁴⁵for I [am] YHWH who am bringing you up out of the land of Egypt to become your God; and you have been holy, for I [am] holy. ⁴⁶This [is] a law of the beasts, and of the bird, and of every living creature which is moving in the waters, and of every creature which is teeming on the earth, ⁴⁷to make separation between the unclean and the pure, and between the beast that is eaten, and the beast that is not eaten."

CHAPTER 12

¹And YHWH speaks to Moses, saying, ²"Speak to the sons of Israel, saying, A woman when she gives seed, and has borne a male, then she has been unclean [for] seven days; she is unclean according to the days of separation for her sickness; ³and in the eighth day the flesh of his foreskin is circumcised; ⁴and she abides in the blood of her cleansing [for] thirty-three days; she does not come against any holy thing, and she does not go into the sanctuary, until the fullness of the days of her cleansing. ⁵And if she bears a female, then she has been unclean [for] two weeks, as in her

separation; and she abides by the blood of her cleansing [for] sixty-six days. ⁶And in the fullness of the days of her cleansing for son or for daughter she brings in a lamb, a son of a year, for a burnt-offering, and a young pigeon or a turtle-dove for a sin-offering, to the opening of the Tent of Meeting, to the priest; ⁷and he has brought it near before YHWH, and has made atonement for her, and she has been cleansed from the fountain of her blood; this [is] the law of her who is bearing, in regard to a male or to a female. ⁸And if her hand does not find the sufficiency of a sheep, then she has taken two turtle-doves or two young pigeons, one for a burnt-offering and one for a sin-offering, and the priest has made atonement for her, and she has been cleansed."

CHAPTER 13

¹And YHWH speaks to Moses and to Aaron, saying, ²"When a man has a rising, or scab, or bright spot in the skin of his flesh, and it has become a leprous plague in the skin of his flesh, then he has been brought to Aaron the priest, or to one of his sons the priests; ³and the priest has seen the plague in the skin of the flesh, and the hair in the plague has turned white, and the appearance of the plague [is] deeper than the skin of his flesh—it [is] a plague of leprosy, and the priest has seen him, and has pronounced him unclean. ⁴And if the bright spot is white in the skin of his flesh, and its appearance is not deeper than the skin, and its hair has not turned white, then the priest has shut up [him who has] the plague [for] seven days. ⁵And the priest has seen him on the seventh day, and behold, the plague has stood in his eyes, the plague has not spread in the skin, and the priest has shut him up [for] a second seven days. ⁶And the priest has seen him on the second seventh day, and behold, the plague has faded, and the plague has not spread in the skin, and the priest has pronounced him clean; it [is] a scab, and he has washed his garments, and has been clean. ⁷And if the scab spreads greatly in the skin, after his being seen by the priest for his cleansing, then he has been seen a second time by the priest; ⁸and the priest has seen, and behold, the scab has spread in the skin, and the priest has pronounced him unclean; it [is] leprosy. ⁹When a plague of leprosy is in a man, then he has been brought to the priest, ¹⁰and the priest has seen, and behold, a white rising in the skin, and it has turned the hair white, and a quickening of raw flesh [is] in the rising— ¹¹it [is] an old leprosy in the skin of his flesh, and the priest has pronounced him unclean; he does not shut him up, for he [is] unclean. ¹²And if the leprosy breaks out greatly in the skin, and the leprosy has covered all the skin of [him who has] the plague, from his head even to his feet, to all that appears to the eyes of the priest, ¹³then the priest has seen, and behold, the leprosy has covered all his flesh, and he has pronounced [him who has] the plague clean; it has all turned white; he [is] clean. ¹⁴And in the day of raw flesh being seen in him, he is unclean; ¹⁵and the priest has seen the raw flesh, and has pronounced him unclean; the raw flesh is unclean—it [is] leprosy. ¹⁶Or when the raw flesh turns back, and has been turned to white, then he has come to the priest, ¹⁷and the priest has seen him, and behold, the plague has been turned to white, and the priest has pronounced clean [him who has] the plague; he [is] clean. ¹⁸And when flesh has in it, in its skin, an ulcer, and it has been healed, ¹⁹and there has been in the place of the ulcer a white rising, or a bright white spot, reddish, then it has been seen by the priest, ²⁰and the priest has seen, and behold, its appearance [is] lower than the skin, and its hair has turned white, and the priest has pronounced him unclean; it [is] a plague of leprosy—it has broken out in an ulcer. ²¹And if the priest sees it, and behold, there is no white hair in it, and it is not lower than the skin, and has faded, then the priest has shut him up [for] seven days; ²²and if it spreads greatly in the skin, then the priest has pronounced him unclean—it [is] a plague; ²³and if the bright spot stays in its place—it has not spread—it [is] an inflammation of the ulcer; and the priest has pronounced him clean. ²⁴Or when flesh has a fiery burning in its skin, and the quickening of the burning, the bright white spot, has been reddish or white, ²⁵and the priest has seen it, and behold, the hair has turned white in the bright spot, and its appearance [is] deeper than the skin, it [is] leprosy; it has broken out in the burning, and the priest has pronounced him unclean; it [is] a plague of leprosy. ²⁶And if the priest sees it, and behold, there is no white hair on the bright spot, and it is not lower than the skin, and it has faded, then the priest has shut him up [for] seven days; ²⁷and the priest has seen him on the seventh day, [and] if it spreads greatly in the skin, then the priest has pronounced him unclean; it [is] a plague of leprosy. ²⁸And if the bright spot stays in its place, it has not spread in the skin, and has faded; it [is] a rising of the burning, and the priest has pronounced him clean; for it [is] inflammation of the burning. ²⁹And when a man (or a woman) has a plague in him, in the head or in the beard, ³⁰then the priest has seen the plague, and behold, its appearance is deeper than the skin, and a thin, shining hair [is] in it, and the priest has pronounced him unclean; it [is] a scale—it [is] a leprosy of the head or of the beard. ³¹And when the priest sees the scaly plague, and behold, its appearance is not deeper than the skin, and there is no black hair in it, then the priest has shut up [him who has] the scaly plague [for] seven days. ³²And the priest has seen the plague on the seventh day, and behold, the scale has not spread, and a shining hair has not been in it, and the appearance of the scale is not deeper than the skin, ³³then he has shaved himself, but he does not shave the scale; and the priest has shut up [him who has] the scale [for] a second seven days. ³⁴And the priest has seen the scale on the seventh day, and behold, the scale has not spread in the skin, and its appearance is not deeper than the skin, and the priest has pronounced him clean, and he has washed his garments, and has been clean. ³⁵And if the scale spreads greatly in the skin after his cleansing, ³⁶and the priest has seen him, and behold, the scale has spread in the skin, the priest does not seek for the shining hair—he is unclean; ³⁷and if in his eyes the scale has stayed, and black hair has sprung up in it, the scale has been healed—he [is] clean—and the priest has pronounced him clean. ³⁸And when a man or woman has bright spots in the skin of their flesh, white bright spots, ³⁹and the priest has seen, and behold, white [and] faded bright spots [are] in the skin of their flesh—it [is] a freckled spot broken out in the skin; he [is] clean. ⁴⁰And when a man's head [is] polished, he [is] bald; he [is] clean; ⁴¹and if his head is polished from the corner of his face, he [is] bald of the forehead; he [is] clean. ⁴²And when there is in the bald back of the head, or in the bald forehead, a reddish-white plague, it [is] a leprosy breaking out in the bald back of the head, or in the bald forehead; ⁴³and the priest has seen him, and behold, the rising of the reddish-white plague in the bald back of the head, or in the bald forehead, [is] as the appearance of leprosy, in the skin of the flesh, ⁴⁴he [is] a leprous man—he [is] unclean; the priest pronounces him utterly unclean; his plague [is] in his head. ⁴⁵As for the leper in whom [is] the plague, his garments are torn, and his head is uncovered, and he covers over the upper lip, and he calls, Unclean! Unclean! ⁴⁶He is unclean all the days that the plague [is] in him; he [is] unclean. He dwells alone; his dwelling [is] at the outside of the camp. ⁴⁷And when there is a plague of leprosy in any garment—in a garment of wool, or in a garment of linen, ⁴⁸or in the warp, or in the woof, of linen or of wool, or in a skin, or in any work of skin— ⁴⁹and the plague has been greenish or reddish in the garment, or in the skin, or in the warp, or in the woof, or in any vessel of skin, it [is] a plague of leprosy, and it has been shown [to] the priest. ⁵⁰And the priest has seen the plague, and has shut up [that which has] the plague [for] seven days; ⁵¹and he has seen the plague on the seventh day, and the plague has spread in the garment, or in the warp, or in the woof, or in the skin, of all that is made of skin for work, the plague [is] a fretting leprosy; it [is] unclean. ⁵²And he has burned the garment, or the warp, or the woof, in wool or in linen, or any vessel of skin in which the plague is; for it [is] a fretting leprosy; it is burned with fire. ⁵³And if the priest sees, and behold, the plague has not spread in the garment, or in the warp, or in the woof, or in any vessel of skin, ⁵⁴then the priest has commanded, and they have washed that in which the plague [is], and he has shut it up [for] a second seven days. ⁵⁵And the priest has seen [that which has] the plague after it has been washed, and behold, the plague has not changed its aspect, and the plague has not spread—it [is] unclean; you burn it with fire; it [is] a fretting in its back-part or in its front-part. ⁵⁶And if the priest has seen, and behold, the plague has faded after it has been washed, then he has torn it out of the garment, or out of the skin, or out of the warp, or out of the woof;

⁵⁷and if it is still seen in the garment, or in the warp, or in the woof, or in any vessel of skin, it [is] a fretting; you burn it with fire—that in which the plague [is]. ⁵⁸And the garment, or the warp, or the woof, or any vessel of skin which you wash when the plague has turned aside from them, then it has been washed a second time, and has been clean. ⁵⁹This [is] the law of a plague of leprosy [in] a garment of wool or of linen, or of the warp or of the woof, or of any vessel of skin, to pronounce it clean or to pronounce it unclean."

CHAPTER 14

¹And YHWH speaks to Moses, saying, ²"This is a law of the leper, in the day of his cleansing, that he has been brought to the priest, ³and the priest has gone out to the outside of the camp, and the priest has seen, and behold, the plague of leprosy has ceased from the leper, ⁴and the priest has commanded, and he has taken for him who is to be cleansed, two clean living birds, and cedar wood, and scarlet, and hyssop. ⁵And the priest has commanded, and he has slaughtered one bird on an earthen vessel, over running water; ⁶[as for] the living bird, he takes it, and the cedar wood, and the scarlet, and the hyssop, and has dipped them and the living bird in the blood of the slaughtered bird, over the running water, ⁷and he has sprinkled on him who is to be cleansed from the leprosy seven times, and has pronounced him clean, and has sent out the living bird over the face of the field. ⁸And he who is to be cleansed has washed his garments, and has shaved all his hair, and has bathed with water, and has been clean, and afterward he comes into the camp, and has dwelt at the outside of his tent [for] seven days. ⁹And it has been, on the seventh day—he shaves all his hair, his head, and his beard, and his eyebrows, even all his hair he shaves, and he has washed his garments, and has bathed his flesh with water, and has been clean. ¹⁰And on the eighth day he takes two lambs, perfect ones, and one ewe-lamb, daughter of a year, a perfect one, and three-tenth parts of flour [for] a present, mixed with oil, and one log of oil. ¹¹And the priest who is cleansing has caused the man who is to be cleansed to stand with them before YHWH, at the opening of the Tent of Meeting, ¹²and the priest has taken one male lamb, and has brought it near for a guilt-offering, also the log of oil, and has waved them [as] a wave-offering before YHWH. ¹³And he has slaughtered the lamb in the place where he slaughters the sin-offering and the burnt-offering, in the holy place; for like the sin-offering, the guilt-offering is for the priest; it [is] most holy. ¹⁴And the priest has taken of the blood of the guilt-offering, and the priest has put [it] on the tip of the right ear of him who is to be cleansed, and on the thumb of his right hand, and on the great toe of his right foot; ¹⁵and the priest has taken of the log of oil, and has poured [it] on the left palm of the priest, ¹⁶and the priest has dipped his right finger in the oil which [is] on his left palm, and has sprinkled of the oil with his finger seven times before YHWH. ¹⁷And of the remainder of the oil which [is] on his palm, the priest puts [it] on the tip of the right ear of him who is to be cleansed, and on the thumb of his right hand, and on the great toe of his right foot, on the blood of the guilt-offering; ¹⁸and the remnant of the oil which [is] on the palm of the priest, he puts [it] on the head of him who is to be cleansed, and the priest has made atonement for him before YHWH. ¹⁹And the priest has made the sin-offering, and has made atonement for him who is to be cleansed from his uncleanness, and afterward he slaughters the burnt-offering; ²⁰and the priest has caused the burnt-offering to ascend, also the present, on the altar, and the priest has made atonement for him, and he has been clean. ²¹And if he [is] poor, and his hand is not reaching [these things], then he has taken one lamb [for] a guilt-offering, for a wave-offering, to make atonement for him, and one-tenth part of flour mixed with oil for a present, and a log of oil, ²²and two turtle-doves, or two young pigeons, which his hand reaches to, and one has been a sin-offering and one a burnt-offering; ²³and he has brought them in on the eighth day for his cleansing to the priest, to the opening of the Tent of Meeting, before YHWH. ²⁴And the priest has taken the lamb of the guilt-offering, and the log of oil, and the priest has waved them [as] a wave-offering before YHWH; ²⁵and he has slaughtered the lamb of the guilt-offering, and the priest has taken of the blood of the guilt-offering, and has put [it] on the tip of the right ear of him who is to be cleansed, and on the thumb of his right hand, and on the great toe of his right foot; ²⁶and the priest pours of the oil on the left palm of the priest; ²⁷and the priest has sprinkled with his right finger of the oil which [is] on his left palm, seven times before YHWH. ²⁸And the priest has put of the oil which [is] on his palm, on the tip of the right ear of him who is to be cleansed, and on the thumb of his right hand, and on the great toe of his right foot, on the place of the blood of the guilt-offering; ²⁹and he puts the remnant of the oil which [is] on the palm of the priest on the head of him who is to be cleansed, to make atonement for him, before YHWH. ³⁰And he has made one of the turtle-doves or of the young pigeons (from that which his hand reaches to, ³¹[even] that which his hand reaches to), one a sin-offering and one a burnt-offering, besides the present, and the priest has made atonement for him who is to be cleansed before YHWH. ³²This [is] a law of him in whom [is] a plague of leprosy, whose hand does not reach to his cleansing." ³³And YHWH speaks to Moses and to Aaron, saying, ³⁴"When you come into the land of Canaan, which I am giving to you for a possession, and I have put a plague of leprosy in a house [in] the land of your possession, ³⁵then he whose the house [is] has come in and declared [it] to the priest, saying, Some plague has appeared to me in the house; ³⁶and the priest has commanded, and they have prepared the house before the priest comes in to see the plague (that all which [is] in the house is not unclean), and afterward the priest comes in to see the house; ³⁷and he has seen the plague, and behold, the plague [is] in the walls of the house, hollow streaks, greenish or reddish, and their appearance [is] lower than the wall, ³⁸and the priest has gone out of the house to the opening of the house, and has shut up the house [for] seven days. ³⁹And the priest has turned back on the seventh day, and has seen, and behold, the plague has spread in the walls of the house, ⁴⁰and the priest has commanded, and they have drawn out the stones in which the plague [is], and have cast them to the outside of the city, to an unclean place; ⁴¹and he causes the house to be scraped all around inside, and they have poured out the clay which they have scraped off, at the outside of the city, at an unclean place; ⁴²and they have taken other stones, and brought [them] to the place of the stones, and he takes other clay and has coated the house. ⁴³And if the plague returns, and has broken out in the house, after he has drawn out the stones, and after the scraping of the house, and after the coating, ⁴⁴then the priest has come in and seen, and behold, the plague has spread in the house; it [is] a fretting leprosy in the house; it [is] unclean. ⁴⁵And he has broken down the house, its stones, and its wood, and all the clay of the house, and he has brought [them] forth to the outside of the city, to an unclean place. ⁴⁶And he who is going into the house all the days he has shut it up, is unclean until the evening; ⁴⁷and he who is lying in the house washes his garments; and he who is eating in the house washes his garments. ⁴⁸And if the priest certainly comes in, and has seen, and behold, the plague has not spread in the house after the coating of the house, then the priest has pronounced the house clean, for the plague has been healed. ⁴⁹And he has taken two birds, and cedar wood, and scarlet, and hyssop for the cleansing of the house; ⁵⁰and he has slaughtered one bird on an earthen vessel, over running water; ⁵¹and he has taken the cedar wood, and the hyssop, and the scarlet, and the living bird, and has dipped them in the blood of the slaughtered bird, and in the running water, and has sprinkled against the house seven times. ⁵²And he has cleansed the house with the blood of the bird, and with the running water, and with the living bird, and with the cedar wood, and with the hyssop, and with the scarlet; ⁵³and he has sent the living bird away to the outside of the city to the face of the field, and has made atonement for the house, and it has been clean. ⁵⁴This [is] the law for every plague of the leprosy and for scale, ⁵⁵and for leprosy of a garment, and of a house, ⁵⁶and for a rising, and for a scab, and for a bright spot— ⁵⁷to direct in the day of being unclean, and in the day of being clean; this [is] the law of the leprosy."

CHAPTER 15

¹And YHWH speaks to Moses and to Aaron, saying, ²"Speak to the sons of Israel, and you have said to them: When there is discharging out of the flesh of any man, he [is] unclean [from] his discharge; ³and this is his uncleanness in his discharge—his flesh has

run with his discharge, or his flesh has stopped from his discharge; it [is] his uncleanness. ⁴Every bed on which he who has the discharging lies is unclean, and every vessel on which he sits is unclean; ⁵and anyone who comes against his bed washes his garments, and has bathed with water, and been unclean until the evening. ⁶And he who is sitting on the vessel on which he sits who has the discharging, washes his garments, and has bathed with water, and been unclean until the evening. ⁷And he who is coming against the flesh of him who has the discharging, washes his garments, and has bathed with water, and been unclean until the evening. ⁸And when he who has the discharging spits on him who is clean, then he has washed his garments, and has bathed with water, and been unclean until the evening. ⁹And all the saddle on which he who has the discharging rides is unclean; ¹⁰and anyone who is coming against anything which is under him is unclean until the evening, and he who is carrying them washes his garments, and has bathed with water, and been unclean until the evening. ¹¹And anyone against whom he who has the discharging comes (and has not rinsed his hands with water) has even washed his garments, and bathed with water, and been unclean until the evening. ¹²And the earthen vessel which he who has the discharging comes against is broken; and every wooden vessel is rinsed with water. ¹³And when he who has the discharging is clean from his discharge, then he has numbered seven days for himself for his cleansing, and has washed his garments, and has bathed his flesh with running water, and been clean. ¹⁴And on the eighth day he takes two turtle-doves or two young pigeons for himself, and has come in before YHWH to the opening of the Tent of Meeting, and has given them to the priest; ¹⁵and the priest has made them, one a sin-offering and one a burnt-offering; and the priest has made atonement for him before YHWH, because of his discharge. ¹⁶And when a man's seed [from] intercourse goes out from him, then he has bathed all his flesh with water, and been unclean until the evening. ¹⁷And any garment, or any skin on which there is seed [from] intercourse, has also been washed with water, and been unclean until the evening. ¹⁸And a woman with whom a man lies with seed [from] intercourse, they also have bathed with water, and been unclean until the evening. ¹⁹And when a woman has discharging—blood is her discharge in her flesh—she is in her separation [for] seven days, and anyone who is coming against her is unclean until the evening. ²⁰And anything on which she lies in her separation is unclean, and anything on which she sits is unclean; ²¹and anyone who is coming against her bed washes his garments, and has bathed with water, and been unclean until the evening. ²²And anyone who is coming against any vessel on which she sits washes his garments, and has washed with water, and been unclean until the evening. ²³And if it [is] on the bed, or on the vessel on which she is sitting, in his coming against it, he is unclean until the evening. ²⁴And if a man really lies with her, and her separation is on him, then he has been unclean [for] seven days, and all the bed on which he lies is unclean. ²⁵And when a woman's discharge of blood flows many days within the time of her separation, or when it flows over her separation—all the days of the discharge of her uncleanness are as the days of her separation; she [is] unclean. ²⁶Every bed on which she lies all the days of her discharge is as the bed of her separation to her, and every vessel on which she sits is unclean as the uncleanness of her separation; ²⁷and anyone who is coming against them is unclean, and has washed his garments, and has bathed with water, and been unclean until the evening. ²⁸And if she has been clean from her discharge, then she has numbered seven days for herself, and afterward she is clean; ²⁹and on the eighth day she takes two turtle-doves or two young pigeons for herself, and has brought them to the priest, to the opening of the Tent of Meeting; ³⁰and the priest has made one a sin-offering and one a burnt-offering, and the priest has made atonement for her before YHWH, because of the discharge of her uncleanness. ³¹And you have separated the sons of Israel from their uncleanness, and they do not die in their uncleanness, in their defiling My Dwelling Place which [is] in their midst. ³²This [is] the law of him who has the discharging, and of him whose seed [from] intercourse goes out from him, to become unclean with it, ³³and of her who is sick in her separation, and of him who has the discharging (his discharge, of the male or of the female), and of a man who lies with an unclean woman."

CHAPTER 16
¹And YHWH speaks to Moses after the death of the two sons of Aaron, in their drawing near before YHWH, and they die; ²indeed, YHWH says to Moses, "Speak to your brother Aaron, and he does not come in at all times to the holy place within the veil, to the front of the propitiatory covering, which [is] on the Ark, and he does not die, for I am seen in a cloud on the propitiatory covering. ³With this Aaron comes into the holy place: with a bullock, a son of the herd, for a sin-offering, and a ram for a burnt-offering; ⁴he puts on a holy linen coat, and linen trousers are on his flesh, and he girds himself with a linen girdle, and he wraps himself up with a linen turban; they [are] holy garments; and he has bathed his flesh with water and put them on. ⁵And from the congregation of the sons of Israel he takes two kids of the goats for a sin-offering and one ram for a burnt-offering; ⁶and Aaron has brought the bullock of the sin-offering near, which is his own, and has made atonement for himself and for his house; ⁷and he has taken the two goats, and has caused them to stand before YHWH, at the opening of the Tent of Meeting. ⁸And Aaron has given lots over the two goats, one lot for YHWH and one lot for a goat of departure; ⁹and Aaron has brought the goat near, on which the lot for YHWH has gone up, and has made it a sin-offering. ¹⁰And the goat on which the lot for a goat of departure has gone up is caused to stand living before YHWH to make atonement by it, to send it away for a goat of departure into the wilderness. ¹¹And Aaron has brought the bullock of the sin-offering near, which is his own, and has made atonement for himself and for his house, and has slaughtered the bullock of the sin-offering which [is] his own, ¹²and has taken the fullness of the censer of burning coals of fire from off the altar, from before YHWH, and the fullness of his hands of thin spice-incense, and has brought [it] within the veil, ¹³and he has put the incense on the fire before YHWH, and the cloud of the incense has covered the propitiatory covering which [is] on the Testimony, and he does not die. ¹⁴And he has taken of the blood of the bullock, and has sprinkled with his finger on the front of the propitiatory covering eastward; even at the front of the propitiatory covering he sprinkles seven times of the blood with his finger. ¹⁵And he has slaughtered the goat of the sin-offering which [is] the people's, and has brought in its blood to the inside of the veil, and has done with its blood as he has done with the blood of the bullock, and has sprinkled it on the propitiatory covering, and at the front of the propitiatory covering, ¹⁶and he has made atonement for the holy place because of the uncleanness of the sons of Israel, and because of their transgressions in all their sins; and so he does for the Tent of Meeting which is dwelling with them in the midst of their uncleannesses. ¹⁷And no man is in the Tent of Meeting in his going in to make atonement in the holy place, until his coming out; and he has made atonement for himself, and for his house, and for all the assembly of Israel. ¹⁸And he has gone out to the altar which [is] before YHWH, and has made atonement for it; and he has taken of the blood of the bullock and of the blood of the goat, and has put [it] around the horns of the altar; ¹⁹and he has sprinkled on it of the blood with his finger seven times, and has cleansed it, and has hallowed it from the uncleannesses of the sons of Israel. ²⁰And he has ceased from making atonement [for] the holy place, and the Tent of Meeting, and the altar, and has brought the living goat near; ²¹and Aaron has laid his two hands on the head of the living goat, and has confessed over it all the iniquities of the sons of Israel, and all their transgressions in all their sins, and has put them on the head of the goat, and has sent [it] away by the hand of a ready man into the wilderness; ²²and the goat has borne on himself all their iniquities to a land of separation. And he has sent the goat away into the wilderness, ²³and Aaron has come into the Tent of Meeting, and has stripped off the linen garments which he had put on in his going into the holy place, and has placed them there; ²⁴and he has bathed his flesh with water in the holy place, and has put on his garments, and has come out, and has made his burnt-offering, and the burnt-offering of the people, and has made atonement for himself and for the people; ²⁵and with the fat of the sin-

offering he makes incense on the altar. ²⁶And he who is sending the goat away for a goat of departure washes his garments, and has bathed his flesh with water, and afterward he comes into the camp. ²⁷And the bullock of the sin-offering and the goat of the sin-offering, whose blood has been brought in to make atonement in the holy place, [one] brings out to the outside of the camp, and they have burned their skins, and their flesh, and their dung with fire; ²⁸and he who is burning them washes his garments, and has bathed his flesh with water, and afterward he comes into the camp. ²⁹And it has been for a continuous statute to you, in the seventh month, on the tenth of the month, you humble yourselves, and do no work—the native and the sojourner who is sojourning in your midst; ³⁰for on this day he makes atonement for you, to cleanse you; you are clean from all your sins before YHWH; ³¹it [is] a Sabbath of rest for you, and you have humbled yourselves—a continuous statute. ³²And the priest whom he anoints, and whose hand he consecrates to act as priest instead of his father, has made atonement, and has put on the linen garments, the holy garments; ³³and he has made atonement [for] the holy sanctuary; and [for] the Tent of Meeting, even [for] the altar he makes atonement; indeed, he makes atonement for the priests and for all the people of the assembly. ³⁴And this has been for a continuous statute to you, to make atonement for the sons of Israel, because of all their sins, once in a year"; and he does as YHWH has commanded Moses.

CHAPTER 17

¹And YHWH speaks to Moses, saying, ²"Speak to Aaron and to his sons, and to all the sons of Israel; and you have said to them: This [is] the thing which YHWH has commanded, saying, ³Any man of the house of Israel who slaughters ox, or lamb, or goat in the camp, or who slaughters [it] at the outside of the camp, ⁴and has not brought it in to the opening of the Tent of Meeting to bring an offering near to YHWH before the Dwelling Place of YHWH, blood is reckoned to that man—he has shed blood—and that man has been cut off from the midst of his people; ⁵so that the sons of Israel bring in their sacrifices which they are sacrificing on the face of the field, indeed, they have brought them to YHWH, to the opening of the Tent of Meeting, to the priest, and they have sacrificed sacrifices of peace-offerings to YHWH with them. ⁶And the priest has sprinkled the blood on the altar of YHWH, at the opening of the Tent of Meeting, and has made incense with the fat for refreshing fragrance to YHWH; ⁷and they do not sacrifice their sacrifices anymore to the goat [idols] after which they are going whoring; this is a continuous statute to them, throughout their generations. ⁸And you say to them: Any man of the house of Israel, or of the sojourners who sojourns in your midst, who causes burnt-offering or sacrifice to ascend, ⁹and does not bring it in to the opening of the Tent of Meeting to make it to YHWH—that man has been cut off from his people. ¹⁰And any man of the house of Israel, or of the sojourners who is sojourning in your midst, who eats any blood, I have even set My face against the person who is eating the blood, and have cut him off from the midst of his people; ¹¹for the life of the flesh is in the blood, and I have given it to you on the altar, to make atonement for your souls; for it [is] the blood which makes atonement for the soul. ¹²Therefore I have said to the sons of Israel: No person among you eats blood, and the sojourner who is sojourning in your midst does not eat blood; ¹³and any man of the sons of Israel, or of the sojourners who is sojourning in your midst, who hunts game, beast or bird, which is eaten—has even poured out its blood and covered it with dust; ¹⁴for [it is] the life of all flesh, its blood is for its life; and I say to the sons of Israel: You do not eat [the] blood of any flesh, for the life of all flesh is its blood; anyone eating it is cut off. ¹⁵And any person who eats a carcass or torn thing, among natives or among sojourners, has washed his garments and bathed with water, and been unclean until the evening—then he has been clean; ¹⁶and if he does not wash, and does not bathe his flesh—then he has borne his iniquity."

CHAPTER 18

¹And YHWH speaks to Moses, saying, ²"Speak to the sons of Israel, and you have said to them: I [am] your God YHWH; ³you do not do according to the work of the land of Egypt in which you have dwelt, and you do not do according to the work of the land of Canaan to where I am bringing you in, and you do not walk in their statutes. ⁴You do My judgments and you keep My statutes, to walk in them; I [am] your God YHWH. ⁵And you have kept My statutes and My judgments which man does and lives in them; I [am] YHWH. ⁶None of you draws near to any relation of his flesh to uncover nakedness; I [am] YHWH. ⁷You do not uncover the nakedness of your father and the nakedness of your mother, she [is] your mother; you do not uncover her nakedness. ⁸You do not uncover the nakedness of the wife of your father; it [is] the nakedness of your father. ⁹The nakedness of your sister, daughter of your father, or daughter of your mother, born at home or born outside—you do not uncover their nakedness. ¹⁰The nakedness of your son's daughter, or of your daughter's daughter—you do not uncover their nakedness; for theirs [is] your nakedness. ¹¹The nakedness of a daughter of your father's wife, begotten of your father, she [is] your sister—you do not uncover her nakedness. ¹²You do not uncover the nakedness of a sister of your father; she [is] a relation of your father. ¹³You do not uncover the nakedness of your mother's sister, for she [is] your mother's relation. ¹⁴You do not uncover the nakedness of your father's brother; you do not draw near to his wife; she [is] your aunt. ¹⁵You do not uncover the nakedness of your daughter-in-law; she [is] your son's wife; you do not uncover her nakedness. ¹⁶You do not uncover the nakedness of your brother's wife; it [is] your brother's nakedness. ¹⁷You do not uncover the nakedness of a woman and her daughter, nor do you take her son's daughter and her daughter's daughter, to uncover her nakedness; they [are] her relations; it [is] wickedness. ¹⁸And you do not take a woman [in addition] to her sister, to be an adversary, to uncover her nakedness beside her, in her life. ¹⁹And you do not draw near to a woman in the separation of her uncleanness to uncover her nakedness. ²⁰And you do not give your seed [from] intercourse to the wife of your fellow, to become unclean with her. ²¹And you do not give from your seed to pass over to the Molech, nor do you defile the Name of your God; I [am] YHWH. ²²And you do not lie with a male as one lies with a woman; it [is] an abomination. ²³And you do not commit your intercourse with any beast, to become unclean with it; and a woman does not stand before a beast to mate with it; it [is] perversion. ²⁴Do not defile yourselves with all these, for with all these the nations have been defiled which I am sending away from before you; ²⁵and the land is defiled, and I charge its iniquity on it, and the land vomits out its inhabitants. ²⁶And you have kept My statutes and My judgments, and do not do [any] of all these abominations, the native and the sojourner who is sojourning in your midst, ²⁷for the men of the land who [are] before you have done all these abominations and the land is defiled, ²⁸and the land does not vomit you out in your defiling it, as it has vomited out the nation which [is] before you; ²⁹for anyone who does [any] of all these abominations—even the persons who are doing [so]—have been cut off from the midst of their people; ³⁰and you have kept My charge, so as not to do [any] of the abominable statutes which have been done before you, and you do not defile yourselves with them; I [am] your God YHWH."

CHAPTER 19

¹And YHWH speaks to Moses, saying, ²"Speak to all the congregation of the sons of Israel, and you have said to them: You are holy, because I, your God YHWH, [am] holy. ³You each fear his mother and his father, and you keep My Sabbaths; I [am] your God YHWH. ⁴You do not turn to the idols, and you do not make a molten god for yourselves; I [am] your God YHWH. ⁵And when you sacrifice a sacrifice of peace-offerings to YHWH, you sacrifice it at your pleasure; ⁶it is eaten in the day of your sacrificing [it], and on the next day, and that which is left to the third day is burned with fire, ⁷and if it is really eaten on the third day, it [is] an abomination, it is not pleasing, ⁸and he who is eating it bears his iniquity, for he has defiled the holy thing of YHWH, and that person has been cut off from his people. ⁹And in your reaping the harvest of your land you do not completely reap the corner of your field, and you do not gather the gleaning of your harvest, ¹⁰and you do not glean your vineyard, even the omitted part of your vineyard you do not gather, you leave them for the poor and for the sojourner; I [am] your God YHWH. ¹¹You do

LEVITICUS

not steal, nor feign, nor lie—each against his fellow. ¹²And you do not swear by My Name for falsehood, or you have defiled the Name of your God; I [am] YHWH. ¹³You do not oppress your neighbor, nor take plunder; the wages of the hired worker do not remain with you until morning. ¹⁴You do not revile the deaf; and you do not put a stumbling block before the blind; and you have been afraid of your God; I [am] YHWH. ¹⁵You do not do perversity in judgment; you do not lift up the face of the poor, nor honor the face of the great; you judge your fellow in righteousness. ¹⁶You do not go slandering among your people; you do not stand against the blood of your neighbor; I [am] YHWH. ¹⁷You do not hate your brother in your heart; you certainly reprove your fellow, and do not permit sin on him. ¹⁸You do not take vengeance, nor watch the sons of your people; and you have had love for your neighbor as yourself; I [am] YHWH. ¹⁹You keep My statutes. You do not cause your livestock to mate [with] two kinds; you do not sow your field with two kinds; and a garment of two kinds, mixed material, does not go up on you. ²⁰And when a man lies with a woman with seed [from] intercourse, and she [is] a maidservant, betrothed to a man, and not really ransomed, or freedom has not been given to her, there is an investigation; they are not put to death, for she [is] not free. ²¹And he has brought in his guilt-offering to YHWH, to the opening of the Tent of Meeting, a ram [for] a guilt-offering, ²²and the priest has made atonement for him with the ram of the guilt-offering before YHWH, for his sin which he has sinned, and it has been forgiven him because of his sin which he has sinned. ²³And when you come into the land and have planted all [kinds] of trees [for] food, then you have reckoned its fruit as uncircumcised, it is uncircumcised to you [for] three years, it is not eaten, ²⁴and in the fourth year all its fruit is holy—praises for YHWH. ²⁵And in the fifth year you eat its fruit—to add to you its increase; I [am] your God YHWH. ²⁶You do not eat with the blood. You do not enchant, nor observe clouds. ²⁷You do not round the corner of your head, nor destroy the corner of your beard. ²⁸And you do not put a cutting for the soul in your flesh; and a writing, a cross-mark, you do not put on yourself; I [am] YHWH. ²⁹You do not defile your daughter to cause her to go whoring, that the land does not go whoring, and the land has been full of wickedness. ³⁰You keep My Sabbaths and you revere My sanctuary; I [am] YHWH. ³¹You do not turn to those having familiar spirits, and you do not seek for wizards, to become unclean by them; I [am] your God YHWH. ³²You rise up at the presence of grey hairs, and you have honored the presence of an old man, and have been afraid of your God; I [am] YHWH. ³³And when a sojourner sojourns with you in your land, you do not oppress him; ³⁴the sojourner who is sojourning with you is to you as a native among you, and you have had love for him as for yourself, for you have been sojourners in the land of Egypt; I [am] your God YHWH. ³⁵You do not do perversity in the judgment, in the measure, in the weight, and in the liquid measure; ³⁶you have righteous balances, righteous weights, a righteous ephah, and a righteous hin; I [am] your God YHWH, who has brought you out from the land of Egypt; ³⁷and you have observed all my statutes, and all my judgments, and have done them; I [am] YHWH."

CHAPTER 20

¹And YHWH speaks to Moses, saying, ²"And you say to the sons of Israel: Any man of the sons of Israel, and of the sojourners who is sojourning in Israel, who gives to the Molech from his seed, is certainly put to death; the people of the land stone him with stone; ³and I set My face against that man, and have cut him off from the midst of his people, for he has given to the Molech from his seed, so as to defile My sanctuary, and to defile My holy Name. ⁴And if the people of the land really hide their eyes from that man, in his giving to the Molech from his seed, so as not to put him to death, ⁵then I have set My face against that man and against his family, and have cut him off, and all who are going whoring after him, even going whoring after the Molech, from the midst of their people. ⁶And the person who turns to those having familiar spirits, and to the wizards, to go whoring after them, I have even set My face against that person, and cut him off from the midst of his people. ⁷And you have sanctified yourselves, and you have been holy, for I [am] your God YHWH; ⁸and you have kept My statutes and have done them; I [am] YHWH, sanctifying you. ⁹For any man who reviles his father and his mother is certainly put to death; he has reviled his father and his mother: his blood [is] on him. ¹⁰And a man who commits adultery with a man's wife—who commits adultery with the wife of his neighbor—the adulterer and the adulteress are surely put to death. ¹¹And a man who lies with his father's wife—he has uncovered the nakedness of his father—both of them are certainly put to death; their blood [is] on them. ¹²And a man who lies with his daughter-in-law—both of them are certainly put to death; they have done perversion; their blood [is] on them. ¹³And a man who lies with a male as one lies with a woman—both of them have done an abomination; they are certainly put to death; their blood [is] on them. ¹⁴And a man who takes the woman and her mother—it [is] wickedness; they burn him and them with fire, and there is no wickedness in your midst. ¹⁵And a man who commits his intercourse with a beast is certainly put to death, and you slay the beast. ¹⁶And a woman who draws near to any beast to mate with it—you have even slain the woman and the beast; they are certainly put to death; their blood [is] on them. ¹⁷And a man who takes his sister, a daughter of his father or daughter of his mother, and he has seen her nakedness, and she sees his nakedness—it is a shame; and they have been cut off before the eyes of the sons of their people; he has uncovered the nakedness of his sister; he bears his iniquity. ¹⁸And a man who lies with a sick woman and has uncovered her nakedness, her fountain he has made bare, and she has uncovered the fountain of her blood—even both of them have been cut off from the midst of their people. ¹⁹And you do not uncover the nakedness of your mother's sister and your father's sister, because his relation he has made bare; they bear their iniquity. ²⁰And a man who lies with his aunt, he has uncovered the nakedness of his uncle; they bear their sin; they die childless. ²¹And a man who takes his brother's wife—it [is] impurity; he has uncovered the nakedness of his brother; they are childless. ²²And you have kept all My statutes and all My judgments, and have done them, and the land does not vomit you out to where I am bringing you in to dwell in it; ²³and you do not walk in the statutes of the nation which I am sending away from before you, for they have done all these, and I am wearied with them. ²⁴And I say to you, You possess their ground, and I give it to you to possess it—a land flowing with milk and honey. I [am] your God YHWH, who has separated you from the peoples. ²⁵And you have made separation between the pure beasts and the unclean, and between the unclean bird and the pure, and you do not make yourselves abominable by beast or by bird, or by anything which creeps [on] the ground which I have separated to you for unclean. ²⁶And you have been holy to Me, for I, YHWH, [am] holy; and I separate you from the peoples to become Mine. ²⁷And a man or woman, when there is a familiar spirit in them, or who [are] wizards, are certainly put to death; they stone them with stone; their blood [is] on them."

CHAPTER 21

¹And YHWH says to Moses, "Speak to the priests, sons of Aaron, and you have said to them: No one defiles himself for a [dead] person among his people, ²except for his relation who [is] near to him: for his mother, and for his father, and for his son, and for his daughter, and for his brother, ³and for his sister, the virgin, who is near to him, who has not been to a man; he is defiled for her. ⁴A master [priest] does not defile himself among his people—to defile himself; ⁵they do not make baldness on their head, and they do not shave the corner of their beard, and they do not make a cutting in their flesh; ⁶they are holy to their God, and they do not defile the Name of their God, for the fire-offerings of YHWH, bread of their God, they are bringing near, and have been holy. ⁷They do not take a woman of harlotry, or defiled, and they do not take a woman cast out from her husband, for he [is] holy to his God; ⁸and you have sanctified him, for he is bringing the bread of your God near. He is holy to you, for I, YHWH, sanctifying you, [am] holy. ⁹And when a daughter of any priest defiles herself by going whoring—she is defiling her father; she is burned with fire. ¹⁰And the high priest of his brothers, on whose head the anointing oil is poured, and who has consecrated his hand to put on the garments, does not uncover his head, nor tear his garments, ¹¹nor does he come beside any dead

person; he does not defile himself for his father and for his mother; ¹²nor does he go out from the sanctuary, nor does he defile the sanctuary of his God, for the separation of the anointing oil of his God [is] on him; I [am] YHWH. ¹³And he takes a wife in her virginity; ¹⁴a widow, or cast out, or defiled, [or] a harlot—these he does not take, but he takes a virgin of his own people [for] a wife, ¹⁵and he does not defile his seed among his people; for I [am] YHWH, sanctifying him." ¹⁶And YHWH speaks to Moses, saying, ¹⁷"Speak to Aaron, saying, No man of your seed throughout their generations in whom there is blemish draws near to bring the bread of his God near, ¹⁸for no man in whom [is] a blemish draws near: a man blind, or lame, or disfigured, or deformed, ¹⁹or a man in whom there is a breach in the foot, or a breach in the hand, ²⁰or hunchbacked, or a dwarf, or [with] a defect in his eye, or [with] an itch, or [with] a scab, or [with] a broken testicle. ²¹No man in whom is blemish (of the seed of Aaron the priest) comes near to bring the fire-offerings of YHWH near; blemish [is] in him; he does not come near to bring the bread of his God near. ²²Bread of his God—from the most holy things and from the holy things—he eats; ²³only, he does not come toward the veil, and he does not draw near to the altar; for blemish [is] in him; and he does not defile My sanctuaries; for I [am] YHWH, sanctifying them." ²⁴And Moses speaks to Aaron, and to his sons, and to all the sons of Israel.

CHAPTER 22

¹And YHWH speaks to Moses, saying, ²"Speak to Aaron and to his sons, and they are separated from the holy things of the sons of Israel, and they do not defile My holy Name in what they are hallowing to Me; I [am] YHWH. ³Say to them: Throughout your generations, any man who draws near, out of all your seed, to the holy things which the sons of Israel sanctify to YHWH, and his uncleanness [is] on him—indeed, that person has been cut off from before My face; I [am] YHWH. ⁴Any man of the seed of Aaron, and he is leprous or has discharging—he does not eat of the holy things until he is clean; and he who is coming against any uncleanness of a person, or a man whose seed [from] intercourse goes out from him, ⁵or a man who comes against any teeming thing which is unclean to him, or against a man who is unclean to him, even any of his uncleanness— ⁶the person who comes against it has even been unclean until the evening, and does not eat of the holy things, but has bathed his flesh with water, ⁷and the sun has gone in, and he has been clean, and afterward he eats of the holy things, for it [is] his food; ⁸he does not eat a carcass or torn thing, to become unclean with it; I [am] YHWH. ⁹And they have kept My charge, and bear no sin for it, that they have died for it when they defile it; I [am] YHWH sanctifying them. ¹⁰And no stranger eats of the holy thing; a settler [with] a priest and a hired worker does not eat of the holy thing; ¹¹but when a priest buys a person, the purchase of his money, he eats of it, also one born in his house; they eat of his bread. ¹²And a priest's daughter, when she is a strange man's, she does not eat of the raised-offering of the holy things; ¹³but a priest's daughter, when she is a widow, or cast out, and has no seed, and has turned back to the house of her father, as [in] her youth, she eats of her father's bread; but no stranger eats of it. ¹⁴And when a man eats of a holy thing through ignorance, then he has added its fifth part to it, and has given [it] to the priest, with the holy thing; ¹⁵and they do not defile the holy things of the sons of Israel—that which they lift up to YHWH, ¹⁶or have caused them to bear the iniquity of the guilt-offering in their eating their holy things; for I [am] YHWH, sanctifying them." ¹⁷And YHWH speaks to Moses, saying, ¹⁸"Speak to Aaron, and to his sons, and to all the sons of Israel, and you have said to them: Any man of the house of Israel, or of the sojourners in Israel, who brings his offering near, of all his vows, or of all his willing offerings which they bring near to YHWH for a burnt-offering— ¹⁹[you bring near] at your pleasure a perfect one, a male of the herd, of the sheep or of the goats; ²⁰nothing in which [is] blemish do you bring near, for it is not for a pleasing thing for you. ²¹And when a man brings a sacrifice of peace-offerings near to YHWH, to complete a special vow, or for a willing-offering, of the herd or of the flock, it is perfect for a pleasing thing: no blemish is in it. ²²Blind, or broken, or maimed, or [having] an oozing sore [[or a defect of the eye]], or itch, or scab—you do not bring these near to YHWH, and you do not make a fire-offering from them on the altar to YHWH. ²³As for an ox or sheep [that] is deformed or stunted—you make it a willing-offering, but it is not pleasing for a vow. ²⁴As for bruised, or beaten, or torn, or cut—you do not bring [it] near to YHWH; and in your land you do not do it. ²⁵And you do not bring the bread of your God near from the hand of a son of a stranger, from any of these, for their corruption [is] in them; blemish [is] in them; they are not pleasing for you." ²⁶And YHWH speaks to Moses, saying, ²⁷"When ox, or lamb, or goat is born, and it has been under its mother [for] seven days, then from the eighth day and from now on, it is pleasing for an offering, a fire-offering to YHWH; ²⁸but an ox or sheep—you do not slaughter it and its young one in one day. ²⁹And when you sacrifice a sacrifice of thanksgiving to YHWH, you sacrifice at your pleasure; ³⁰it is eaten on that day—you do not leave of it until morning; I [am] YHWH. ³¹And you have kept my commands and have done them; I [am] YHWH, ³²and you do not defile My holy Name, and I have been hallowed in the midst of the sons of Israel; I [am] YHWH, sanctifying you, ³³who am bringing you up out of the land of Egypt, to become your God; I [am] YHWH."

CHAPTER 23

¹And YHWH speaks to Moses, saying, ²"Speak to the sons of Israel, and you have said to them: Appointed times of YHWH, which you proclaim [as] holy convocations, these [are] My appointed times. ³[For] six days work is done, and in the seventh day [is] a Sabbath of rest, a holy convocation; you do no work; it [is] a Sabbath to YHWH in all your dwellings. ⁴These [are] appointed times of YHWH, holy convocations, which you proclaim in their appointed times: ⁵in the first month, on the fourteenth of the month, between the evenings, [is] the Passover to YHWH; ⁶and on the fifteenth day of this month [is] the Celebration of Unleavened Things to YHWH; [for] seven days you eat unleavened things; ⁷on the first day you have a holy convocation, you do no servile work; ⁸and you have brought a fire-offering near to YHWH [for] seven days; in the seventh day [is] a holy convocation; you do no servile work." ⁹And YHWH speaks to Moses, saying, ¹⁰"Speak to the sons of Israel, and you have said to them: When you come into the land which I am giving to you, and have reaped its harvest, and have brought in the sheaf, the beginning of your harvest to the priest, ¹¹then he has waved the sheaf before YHWH for your acceptance; on the next day of the Sabbath the priest waves it. ¹²And you have prepared a lamb, a perfect one, a son of a year, in the day of your waving the sheaf for a burnt-offering to YHWH, ¹³and its present [is] two-tenth parts of flour mixed with oil, a fire-offering to YHWH, a refreshing fragrance, and its drink-offering [is] a fourth of the hin of wine. ¹⁴And you do not eat bread and roasted grain and full ears until this very day, until your bringing in the offering of your God—a continuous statute throughout your generations, in all your dwellings. ¹⁵And you have numbered for yourselves from the day after the Sabbath, from the day of your bringing in the sheaf of the wave-offering: they are seven perfect Sabbaths; ¹⁶you number fifty days to the day after the seventh Sabbath, and you have brought a new present near to YHWH; ¹⁷you bring in two [loaves] of bread out of your dwellings [for] a wave-offering; they are of two-tenth parts of flour; they are baked [with] yeast—first-[fruits] to YHWH. ¹⁸And you have brought near, besides the bread, seven lambs, perfect ones, sons of a year, and one bullock, a son of the herd, and two rams; they are a burnt-offering to YHWH, with their present and their drink-offerings, a fire-offering of refreshing fragrance to YHWH. ¹⁹And you have prepared one kid of the goats for a sin-offering, and two lambs, sons of a year, for a sacrifice of peace-offerings, ²⁰and the priest has waved them, besides the bread of the first-[fruits], [as] a wave-offering before YHWH, besides the two lambs; they are holy to YHWH for the priest; ²¹and you have proclaimed in this very day [that] it is a holy convocation for yourselves, you do no servile work—a continuous statute in all your dwellings, throughout your generations. ²²And in your reaping the harvest of your land you do not complete the corner of your field in your reaping, and you do not gather the gleaning of your harvest, you leave them for the poor and for the sojourner; I [am] your God YHWH." ²³And YHWH speaks to Moses, saying, ²⁴"Speak to the sons of Israel, saying, In the seventh month, on the first of the month,

you have a Sabbath, a memorial of shouting, a holy convocation; ²⁵you do no servile work, and you have brought a fire-offering near to YHWH." ²⁶And YHWH speaks to Moses, saying, ²⁷"Only—on the tenth of this seventh month is the Day of Atonements; you have a holy convocation, and you have humbled yourselves, and have brought a fire-offering near to YHWH; ²⁸and you do no work in this very day, for it is a day of atonements, to make atonement for you, before your God YHWH. ²⁹For any person who is not humbled in this very day has even been cut off from his people; ³⁰and any person who does any work in this very day, I have even destroyed that person from the midst of his people; ³¹you do no work—a continuous statute throughout your generations in all your dwellings. ³²It [is] a Sabbath of rest for yourselves, and you have humbled yourselves in the ninth of the month at evening; you keep your Sabbath from evening until evening." ³³And YHWH speaks to Moses, saying, ³⁴"Speak to the sons of Israel, saying, In the fifteenth day of this seventh month [is the] Celebration of Shelters [for] seven days to YHWH; ³⁵the first day [is] a holy convocation, you do no servile work; ³⁶[for] seven days you bring a fire-offering near to YHWH, on the eighth day you have a holy convocation, and you have brought a fire-offering near to YHWH; it [is] a restraint, you do no servile work. ³⁷These [are] appointed times of YHWH, which you proclaim [as] holy convocations, to bring a fire-offering near to YHWH, a burnt-offering, and a present, a sacrifice, and drink-offerings, a thing of a day in its day, ³⁸apart from the Sabbaths of YHWH, and apart from your gifts, and apart from all your vows, and apart from all your willing-offerings, which you give to YHWH. ³⁹Only—on the fifteenth day of the seventh month, in your gathering the increase of the land, you keep the celebration of YHWH [for] seven days; on the first day [is] a Sabbath, and on the eighth day a Sabbath; ⁴⁰and you have taken for yourselves on the first day the fruit of beautiful trees, branches of palms, and boughs of thick trees, and willows of a brook, and have rejoiced before your God YHWH [for] seven days. ⁴¹And you have kept it [as] a celebration to YHWH, seven days in a year—a continuous statute throughout your generations; in the seventh month you keep it [as] a celebration. ⁴²You dwell in shelters [for] seven days; all who are natives in Israel dwell in shelters, ⁴³so that your generations know that I caused the sons of Israel to dwell in shelters in My bringing them out of the land of Egypt; I [am] your God YHWH." ⁴⁴And Moses speaks to the sons of Israel [concerning] the appointed times of YHWH.

CHAPTER 24

¹And YHWH speaks to Moses, saying, ²"Command the sons of Israel, and they bring pure oil of beaten olive to you for the lamp, to cause a light to go up continually; ³Aaron arranges it at the outside of the veil of the Testimony, in the Tent of Meeting, from evening until morning before YHWH continually—a continuous statute throughout your generations; ⁴he arranges the lights on the pure lampstand before YHWH continually. ⁵And you have taken flour, and have baked twelve cakes with it, two-tenth parts are in one cake, ⁶and you have set them [in] two rows (six in the row) on the pure table before YHWH, ⁷and you have put pure frankincense on the row, and it has been with the bread for a memorial, a fire-offering to YHWH. ⁸On each Sabbath day he arranges it before YHWH continually, from the sons of Israel—a perpetual covenant; ⁹and it has been for Aaron and for his sons, and they have eaten it in the holy place, for it [is] most holy to him, from the fire-offerings of YHWH—a continuous statute." ¹⁰And a son of an Israeli woman goes out (and he [is] son of an Egyptian man) in the midst of the sons of Israel, and the son of the Israeli woman and a man of Israel strive in the camp, ¹¹and the son of the Israeli woman execrates the Name and reviles; and they bring him to Moses; and his mother's name [is] Shelomith daughter of Dibri, of the tribe of Dan; ¹²and he causes him to rest in confinement—to explain to them by the mouth of YHWH. ¹³And YHWH speaks to Moses, saying, ¹⁴"Bring out the reviler to the outside of the camp; and all those hearing have laid their hands on his head, and all the congregation has stoned him. ¹⁵And you speak to the sons of Israel, saying, When any man reviles his God—then he has borne his sin; ¹⁶and he who is execrating the Name of YHWH is certainly put to death; all the congregation certainly casts stones at him; as a sojourner so a native, in his execrating the Name, he is put to death. ¹⁷And when a man strikes any soul of man, he is certainly put to death. ¹⁸And he who strikes a beast repays it, body for body. ¹⁹And when a man puts a blemish in his fellow, as he has done so it is done to him; ²⁰breach for breach, eye for eye, tooth for tooth; as he puts a blemish in a man so it is done in him. ²¹And he who strikes a beast repays it, and he who strikes [the life of] man is put to death. ²²One judgment is for you; as a sojourner so is a native; for I [am] your God YHWH." ²³And Moses speaks to the sons of Israel, and they bring out the reviler to the outside of the camp, and stone him [with] stone; and the sons of Israel have done as YHWH has commanded Moses.

CHAPTER 25

¹And YHWH speaks to Moses, in Mount Sinai, saying, ²"Speak to the sons of Israel, and you have said to them: When you come into the land which I am giving to you, then the land has kept a Sabbath to YHWH. ³[For] six years you sow your field, and [for] six years you prune your vineyard, and have gathered its increase, ⁴and in the seventh year is a Sabbath of rest for the land, a Sabbath to YHWH; you do not sow your field, and you do not prune your vineyard; ⁵you do not reap the spontaneous growth of your harvest, and you do not gather the grapes of your separated thing; it is a year of rest for the land. ⁶And the Sabbath [increase] of the land has been for you for food, to you, and to your manservant, and to your handmaid, and to your hired worker, and to your settler, who are sojourning with you; ⁷and for your livestock, and for the beast which [is] in your land, is all its increase for [them] to eat. ⁸And you have numbered seven Sabbaths of years for yourself, seven times seven years, and the days of the seven Sabbaths of years have been forty-nine years for you, ⁹and you have caused a horn of shouting to pass over in the seventh month, on the tenth of the month; in the Day of Atonements you cause a horn to pass over through all your land; ¹⁰and you have hallowed the year, the fiftieth year; and you have proclaimed liberty in the land to all its inhabitants; it is a Jubilee for you; and you have turned back each to his possession; indeed, you return each to his family. ¹¹It [is] a Jubilee, the fiftieth year, it is a year for you; you do not sow, nor reap its spontaneous growth, nor gather its separated things; ¹²for it [is] a Jubilee—it is holy to you; you eat its increase from the field; ¹³you return each to his possession in this Year of the Jubilee. ¹⁴And when you sell anything to your fellow, or buy from the hand of your fellow, you do not oppress one another; ¹⁵you buy from your fellow by the number of years after the Jubilee; he sells to you by the number of the years of increase; ¹⁶you multiply its price according to the multitude of the years, and you diminish its price according to the fewness of the years; for [it is] a number of increases [that] he is selling to you; ¹⁷and you do not oppress one another, and you have been afraid of your God; for I [am] your God YHWH. ¹⁸And you have done My statutes, and you keep My judgments, and have done them, and you have dwelt on the land confidently, ¹⁹and the land has given its fruit, and you have eaten to satiety, and have dwelt confidently on it. ²⁰And when you say, What do we eat in the seventh year, behold, do we not sow, nor gather our increase? ²¹Then I have commanded My blessing on you in the sixth year, and it has made the increase for three years; ²²and you have sown [in] the eighth year, and have eaten of the old increase; you eat the old until the ninth year, until the coming in of its increase. ²³And the land is not sold—to extinction, for the land [is] Mine, for you [are] sojourners and settlers with Me; ²⁴and in all the land of your possession you give a redemption for the land. ²⁵When your brother becomes poor, and has sold his possession, then his redeemer who is near to him has come, and he has redeemed the sold thing of his brother; ²⁶and when a man has no redeemer, and his own hand has attained [means], and he has found [it] as sufficient [for] its redemption, ²⁷then he has reckoned the years of its sale, and has given back that which is over to the man to whom he sold [it], and he has returned to his possession. ²⁸And if his hand has not found sufficiency to give back to him, then his sold thing has been in the hand of him who buys it until the Year of Jubilee; and it has gone out in the Jubilee, and he has returned to his possession. ²⁹And when

a man sells a dwelling-house [in] a walled city, then his right of redemption has been until the completion of a year from its selling; his right of redemption is [during these] days; ³⁰and if it is not redeemed to him until the fullness of a perfect year, then the house which [is] in a walled city has been established to extinction to him buying it, throughout his generations; it does not go out in the Jubilee. ³¹And a house of the villages which have no surrounding wall is reckoned on the field of the country; there is redemption for it, and it goes out in the Jubilee. ³²As for cities of the Levites—houses of the cities of their possession—continuous redemption is for the Levites; ³³as for him who redeems from the Levites, then the sale of a house (and [in] the city of his possession) has gone out in the Jubilee, for the houses of the cities of the Levites are their possession in the midst of the sons of Israel. ³⁴And a field, a outskirt of their cities, is not sold; for it [is] a continuous possession for them. ³⁵And when your brother has become poor, and his hand has failed with you, then you have kept hold on him, sojourner and settler, and he has lived with you; ³⁶you take no usury or increase from him; and you have been afraid of your God; and your brother has lived with you; ³⁷you do not give your money to him in usury, and you do not give your food for increase. ³⁸I [am] your God YHWH, who has brought you out of the land of Egypt to give the land of Canaan to you, to become your God. ³⁹And when your brother becomes poor with you, and he has been sold to you, you do not lay servile service on him; ⁴⁰he is as a hired worker [and] as a settler with you; he serves with you until the Year of the Jubilee— ⁴¹then he has gone out from you, he and his sons with him, and has turned back to his family; and he turns back to the possession of his fathers. ⁴²For they [are] My servants, whom I have brought out from the land of Egypt: they are not sold [with] the sale of a servant; ⁴³you do not rule over him with rigor, and you have been afraid of your God. ⁴⁴And your manservant and your handmaid whom you have [are] from the nations who [are] around you; you buy manservant and handmaid from them, ⁴⁵and also from the sons of the settlers who are sojourning with you, you buy from them, and from their families who [are] with you, which they have begotten in your land, and they have been to you for a possession; ⁴⁶and you have taken them for an inheritance for your sons after you, to inherit [for] a possession; you lay service on them for all time, but on your brothers, the sons of Israel, each with his brother—you do not rule over him with rigor. ⁴⁷And when the hand of a sojourner or settler with you attains [riches], and your brother with him has become poor, and he has been sold to a sojourner, a settler with you, or to the root of the family of a sojourner, ⁴⁸after he has been sold, there is a right of redemption for him; one of his brothers redeems him, ⁴⁹or his uncle or a son of his uncle redeems him, or any of the relations of his flesh, of his family, redeems him, or [if] his own hand has attained [means] then he has been redeemed. ⁵⁰And he has reckoned with his buyer from the year of his being sold to him until the Year of Jubilee, and the money of his sale has been by the number of years; it is with him as the days of a hired worker. ⁵¹If many years still [remain], he gives back his redemption [money] according to them, from the money of his purchase. ⁵²And if few are left of the years until the Year of Jubilee, then he has reckoned with him [and] he gives back his redemption [money] according to his years; ⁵³as a hired worker, year by year, he is with him, and he does not rule him with rigor before your eyes. ⁵⁴And if he is not redeemed in these [years], then he has gone out in the Year of Jubilee, he and his sons with him. ⁵⁵For the sons of Israel [are] servants to Me; they [are] My servants whom I have brought out of the land of Egypt; I [am] your God YHWH."

CHAPTER 26

¹"You do not make idols for yourselves; and you do not set up carved image or standing image for yourselves; and you do not put a stone of imagery in your land, to bow yourselves to it; for I [am] your God YHWH. ²You keep My Sabbaths and you revere My sanctuary; I [am] YHWH. ³If you walk in My statutes, and you keep My commands, and have done them, ⁴then I have given your rains in their season, and the land has given her produce, and the tree of the field gives its fruit; ⁵and the threshing has reached to you, [and] the gathering, and the gathering reaches the sowing-[time]; and you have eaten your bread to satiety, and have dwelt confidently in your land. ⁶And I have given peace in the land, and you have lain down, and there is none causing trembling; and I have caused evil beasts to cease out of the land, and the sword does not pass over into your land. ⁷And you have pursued your enemies, and they have fallen before you by the sword; ⁸and five of you have pursued one hundred, and one hundred of you pursue a myriad; and your enemies have fallen before you by the sword. ⁹And I have turned to you, and have made you fruitful, and have multiplied you, and have established My covenant with you; ¹⁰and you have eaten old [store], and you bring out the old because of the new. ¹¹And I have given My Dwelling Place in your midst, and My soul does not loathe you; ¹²and I have habitually walked in your midst, and have become your God, and you become My people; ¹³I [am] your God YHWH, who has brought you out of the land of the Egyptians, from being their servants; and I break the bars of your yoke and cause you to go erect. ¹⁴And if you do not listen to Me and do not do all these commands, ¹⁵and if you kick at My statutes, and if your soul loathes My judgments, so as not to do all My commands—to your breaking My covenant— ¹⁶I also do this to you: I have even appointed trouble over you, the consumption, and the burning fever, consuming eyes, and causing pain of soul; and you have sowed your seed in vain, and your enemies have eaten it; ¹⁷and I have set My face against you, and you have been struck before your enemies; and those hating you have ruled over you, and you have fled when there is none pursuing you. ¹⁸And if up to these you [still] do not listen to Me—then I have added to discipline you sevenfold for your sins; ¹⁹and I have broken the pride of your strength, and have made your heavens as iron, and your earth as bronze; ²⁰and your strength has been consumed in vain, and your land does not give her produce, and the tree of the land does not give its fruit. ²¹And if you walk with Me [in] opposition, and are not willing to listen to Me, then I have added to you a plague sevenfold, according to your sins, ²²and sent the beast of the field against you, and it has bereaved you; and I have cut off your livestock, and have made you few, and your ways have been desolate. ²³And if by these you are not instructed by Me, and have walked with Me [in] opposition, ²⁴then I have walked—I also—with you in opposition, and have struck you, even I, sevenfold for your sins; ²⁵and I have brought in a sword on you, executing the vengeance of a covenant; and you have been gathered to your cities, and I have sent pestilence into your midst, and you have been given into the hand of an enemy. ²⁶In My breaking your staff of bread, then ten women have baked your bread in one oven, and have given back your bread by weight; and you have eaten and are not satisfied. ²⁷And if for this you do not listen to Me, and have walked with Me in opposition, ²⁸then I have walked with you in the fury of opposition, and have disciplined you, even I, sevenfold for your sins. ²⁹And you have eaten [the] flesh of your sons; and you eat [the] flesh of your daughters. ³⁰And I have destroyed your high places, and cut down your images, and have put your carcasses on the carcasses of your idols, and My soul has loathed you; ³¹and I have made your cities a ruin, and have made your sanctuaries desolate, and I do not smell your refreshing fragrance; ³²and I have made the land desolate, and your enemies who are dwelling in it have been astonished at it. ³³And I scatter you among nations, and have drawn out a sword after you, and your land has been a desolation, and your cities are a ruin. ³⁴Then the land enjoys its Sabbaths all the days of the desolation—and you [are] in the land of your enemies; then the land rests, and has enjoyed its Sabbaths; ³⁵it rests all the days of the desolation [for] that which it has not rested in your Sabbaths, in your dwelling on it. ³⁶And those who are left of you—I have also brought a faintness into their heart in the lands of their enemies, and the sound of a leaf driven away has pursued them, and they have fled [as in] flight from a sword—and they have fallen, and there is none pursuing. ³⁷And they have stumbled on one another, as from the face of a sword, and there is none pursuing, and you have no standing before your enemies, ³⁸and you have perished among the nations, and the land of your enemies has consumed you. ³⁹And those who are left of you—they consume away in their iniquity, in the lands of your enemies; and also in the iniquities of their fathers, they consume away with them.

⁴⁰And [if] they have confessed their iniquity and the iniquity of their fathers, in their trespass which they have trespassed against Me, and also that they have walked with Me in opposition, ⁴¹when I also walk in opposition to them, and have brought them into the land of their enemies—if then their uncircumcised heart is humbled, and then they accept the punishment of their iniquity— ⁴²then I have remembered My covenant [with] Jacob, and also My covenant [with] Isaac, and also My covenant [with] Abraham I remember, and I remember the land. ⁴³And the land is left by them, and enjoys its Sabbaths, in the desolation without them, and they accept the punishment of their iniquity, because, even because, they have kicked against My judgments, and their soul has loathed My statutes, ⁴⁴and also even this, in their being in the land of their enemies, I have not rejected them, nor have I loathed them, to consume them, to break My covenant with them; for I [am] their God YHWH— ⁴⁵then I have remembered for them the covenant of the ancestors, whom I brought forth out of the land of Egypt before the eyes of the nations to become their God; I [am] YHWH." ⁴⁶These [are] the statutes, and the judgments, and the laws, which YHWH has given between Him and the sons of Israel in Mount Sinai, by the hand of Moses.

CHAPTER 27

¹And YHWH speaks to Moses, saying, ²"Speak to the sons of Israel, and you have said to them: When a man makes a special vow in your valuation of persons to YHWH, ³then your valuation has been of the male from a son of twenty years even to a son of sixty years, and your valuation has been fifty shekels of silver by the shekel of the holy place. ⁴And if it [is] a female, then your valuation has been thirty shekels; ⁵and if from a son of five years even to a son of twenty years, then your valuation of the male has been twenty shekels, and for the female, ten shekels; ⁶and if from a son of a month even to a son of five years, then your valuation of the male has been five shekels of silver, and for the female your valuation [is] three shekels of silver; ⁷and if from a son of sixty years and above, if a male, then your valuation has been fifteen shekels, and for a female, ten shekels. ⁸And if he is poorer than your valuation, then he has presented himself before the priest, and the priest has valued him; according to that which the hand of him who is vowing reaches, the priest values him. ⁹And if [it is] a beast of which they bring near [as] an offering to YHWH, all that [one] gives of it to YHWH is holy; ¹⁰he does not change it nor exchange it, a good for a bad, or a bad for a good; and if he really exchanges beast for beast, then it has been [holy] and its exchange is holy. ¹¹And if [it is] any unclean beast of which they do not bring near [as] an offering to YHWH, then he has presented the beast before the priest, ¹²and the priest has valued it, whether good or bad; according to your valuation, O priest, so it is; ¹³and if he really redeems it, then he has added its fifth to your valuation. ¹⁴And when a man sanctifies his house [as] a holy thing to YHWH, then the priest has valued it, whether good or bad; as the priest values it so it stands; ¹⁵and if he who is sanctifying redeems his house, then he has added a fifth of the money of your valuation to it, and it has become his. ¹⁶And if a man sanctifies to YHWH from a field of his possession, then your valuation has been according to its seed—a homer of barley-seed at fifty shekels of silver; ¹⁷if he sanctifies his field from the Year of the Jubilee, according to your valuation it stands; ¹⁸and if he sanctifies his field after the Jubilee, then the priest has reckoned the money to him according to the years which are left, to the Year of the Jubilee, and it has been diminished from your valuation. ¹⁹And if he really redeems the field—he who is sanctifying it—then he has added a fifth of the money of your valuation to it, and it has been established to him; ²⁰and if he does not redeem the field, or if he has sold the field to another man, it is not redeemed anymore; ²¹and the field has been, in its going out in the Jubilee, holy to YHWH as a field which is devoted; his possession is for the priest. ²²And if he sanctifies a field of his purchase to YHWH, which [is] not of the fields of his possession, ²³then the priest has reckoned to him the amount of your valuation up to the Year of Jubilee, and he has given your valuation in that day [as] a holy thing to YHWH; ²⁴in the Year of the Jubilee the field returns to him from whom he bought it, to him who [has] the possession of the land. ²⁵And all your valuation is by the shekel of the holy place: the shekel is twenty gerahs. ²⁶Only, a firstling which is YHWH's firstling among beasts—no man sanctifies it, whether ox or sheep; it [is] YHWH's. ²⁷And if [from] among the unclean beast, then he has ransomed [it] at your valuation, and he has added its fifth to it; and if it is not redeemed, then it has been sold at your valuation. ²⁸Only, no devoted thing which a man devotes to YHWH of all that he has, of man, and beast, and of the field of his possession, is sold or redeemed; every devoted thing is most holy to YHWH. ²⁹No devoted thing, which is devoted of man, is ransomed, it is surely put to death. ³⁰And all tithe of the land, of the seed of the land, of the fruit of the tree, is YHWH's; [it is] holy to YHWH. ³¹And if a man really redeems [any] of his tithe, he adds its fifth to it. ³²And all the tithe of the herd and of the flock—all that passes by under the rod—the tenth is holy to YHWH; ³³he does not inquire between good and bad, nor does he exchange it; and if he really exchanges it, then it has been [holy] and its exchange is holy; it is not redeemed." ³⁴These [are] the commands which YHWH has commanded Moses for the sons of Israel in Mount Sinai.

NUMBERS

CHAPTER 1

¹And YHWH speaks to Moses in the wilderness of Sinai, in the Tent of Meeting, on the first of the second month, in the second year of their going out of the land of Egypt, saying, ²"Take a census of all the congregation of the sons of Israel by their families, by the house of their fathers, in the number of names—every male by their counted heads; ³from a son of twenty years and upward, everyone going out to the host in Israel, you number them by their hosts, you and Aaron; ⁴and with you there is a man for a tribe, each is a head of the house of his fathers. ⁵And these [are] the names of the men who stand with you: for Reuben, Elizur son of Shedeur; ⁶for Simeon, Shelumiel son of Zurishaddai; ⁷for Judah, Nahshon son of Amminadab; ⁸for Issachar, Nathaneel son of Zuar; ⁹for Zebulun, Eliab son of Helon; ¹⁰for the sons of Joseph: for Ephraim, Elishama son of Ammihud; for Manasseh, Gamaliel son of Pedahzur; ¹¹for Benjamin, Abidan son of Gideoni; ¹²for Dan, Ahiezer son of Ammishaddai; ¹³for Asher, Pagiel son of Ocran; ¹⁴for Gad, Eliasaph son of Deuel; ¹⁵for Naphtali, Ahira son of Enan." ¹⁶These [are] those called of the congregation, princes of the tribes of their fathers; they [are] heads of the thousands of Israel. ¹⁷And Moses takes—Aaron also—these men, who were defined by name, ¹⁸and they assembled all the congregation on the first of the second month, and they declare their births, by their families, by the house of their fathers, in the number of names from a son of twenty years and upward, by their counted heads, ¹⁹as YHWH has commanded Moses; and he numbers them in the wilderness of Sinai. ²⁰And the sons of Reuben, Israel's firstborn—their births, by their families, by the house of their fathers, in the number of names, by their counted heads, every male from a son of twenty years and upward, everyone going out to the host— ²¹their numbered ones, for the tribe of Reuben, are forty-six thousand and five hundred. ²²Of the sons of Simeon—their births, by their families, by the house of their fathers, its numbered ones in the number of names, by their counted heads, every male from a son of

twenty years and upward, everyone going out to the host— ²³their numbered ones, for the tribe of Simeon, [are] fifty-nine thousand and three hundred. ²⁴Of the sons of Gad—their births, by their families, by the house of their fathers, in the number of names, from a son of twenty years and upward, everyone going out to the host— ²⁵their numbered ones, for the tribe of Gad, [are] forty-five thousand and six hundred and fifty. ²⁶Of the sons of Judah—their births, by their families, by the house of their fathers, in the number of names, from a son of twenty years and upward, everyone going out to the host— ²⁷their numbered ones, for the tribe of Judah, [are] seventy-four thousand and six hundred. ²⁸Of the sons of Issachar—their births, by their families, by the house of their fathers, in the number of names, from a son of twenty years and upward, everyone going out to the host— ²⁹their numbered ones, for the tribe of Issachar, [are] fifty-four thousand and four hundred. ³⁰Of the sons of Zebulun—their births, by their families, by the house of their fathers, in the number of names, from a son of twenty years and upward, everyone going out to the host— ³¹their numbered ones, for the tribe of Zebulun, [are] fifty-seven thousand and four hundred. ³²Of the sons of Joseph: of the sons of Ephraim—their births, by their families, by the house of their fathers, in the number of names, from a son of twenty years and upward, everyone going out to the host— ³³their numbered ones, for the tribe of Ephraim, [are] forty thousand and five hundred. ³⁴Of the sons of Manasseh—their births, by their families, by the house of their fathers, in the number of names, from a son of twenty years and upward, everyone going out to the host— ³⁵their numbered ones, for the tribe of Manasseh, [are] thirty-two thousand and two hundred. ³⁶Of the sons of Benjamin—their births, by their families, by the house of their fathers, in the number of names, from a son of twenty years and upward, everyone going out to the host— ³⁷their numbered ones, for the tribe of Benjamin, [are] thirty-five thousand and four hundred. ³⁸Of the sons of Dan—their births, by their families, by the house of their fathers, in the number of names, from a son of twenty years and upward, everyone going out to the host— ³⁹their numbered ones, for the tribe of Dan, [are] sixty-two thousand and seven hundred. ⁴⁰Of the sons of Asher—their births, by their families, by the house of their fathers, in the number of names, from a son of twenty years and upward, everyone going out to the host— ⁴¹their numbered ones, for the tribe of Asher, [are] forty-one thousand and five hundred. ⁴²Of the sons of Naphtali—their births, by their families, by the house of their fathers, in the number of names, from a son of twenty years and upward, everyone going out to the host— ⁴³their numbered ones, for the tribe of Naphtali, [are] fifty-three thousand and four hundred. ⁴⁴These [are] those numbered, whom Moses numbered—Aaron also—and the princes of Israel, twelve men, each one has been [the representative] for the house of his fathers. ⁴⁵And they are, all those numbered of the sons of Israel, by the house of their fathers, from a son of twenty years and upward, everyone going out to the host in Israel, ⁴⁶indeed, all those numbered are six hundred thousand and three thousand and five hundred and fifty. ⁴⁷And the Levites, for the tribe of their fathers, have not numbered themselves in their midst, ⁴⁸seeing YHWH speaks to Moses, saying, ⁴⁹"Only the tribe of Levi you do not number, and you do not take up their census in the midst of the sons of Israel; ⁵⁰and you, appoint the Levites over the Dwelling Place of the Testimony, and over all its vessels, and over all that it has; they carry the Dwelling Place, and all its vessels, and they serve it; and they encamp around the Dwelling Place. ⁵¹And in the journeying of the Dwelling Place, the Levites take it down, and in the encamping of the Dwelling Place, the Levites raise it up; and the stranger who is coming near is put to death." ⁵²And the sons of Israel have encamped, each by his camp, and each by his standard, by their hosts; ⁵³and the Levites encamp around the Dwelling Place of the Testimony; and there is no wrath on the congregation of the sons of Israel, and the Levites have kept the charge of the Dwelling Place of the Testimony. ⁵⁴And the sons of Israel do according to all that YHWH has commanded Moses; so they have done.

CHAPTER 2

¹And YHWH speaks to Moses and to Aaron, saying, ²"The sons of Israel encamp, each by his standard, with ensigns of the house of their fathers; they encamp around, from in sight of the Tent of Meeting." ³And those encamping eastward toward the sun-rising [are] of the standard of the camp of Judah, by their hosts; and the prince of the sons of Judah [is] Nahshon, son of Amminadab; ⁴and his host, and their numbered ones, [are] seventy-four thousand and six hundred. ⁵And those encamping by him [are] of the tribe of Issachar; and the prince of the sons of Issachar [is] Nethaneel son of Zuar; ⁶and his host, and its numbered ones, [are] fifty-four thousand and four hundred. ⁷The tribe of Zebulun [is with them]; and the prince of the sons of Zebulun [is] Eliab son of Helon; ⁸and his host, and its numbered ones, [are] fifty-seven thousand and four hundred. ⁹All those numbered of the camp of Judah [are] one hundred thousand and eighty thousand and six thousand and four hundred, by their hosts; they journey first. ¹⁰The standard of the camp of Reuben [is] southward, by their hosts; and the prince of the sons of Reuben [is] Elizur son of Shedeur; ¹¹and his host, and its numbered ones, [are] forty-six thousand and five hundred. ¹²And those encamping by him [are of] the tribe of Simeon; and the prince of the sons of Simeon [is] Shelumiel son of Zurishaddai; ¹³and his host, and their numbered ones, [are] fifty-nine thousand and three hundred. ¹⁴And the tribe of Gad [is with him]; and the prince of the sons of Gad [is] Eliasaph son of Reuel; ¹⁵and his host, and their numbered ones, [are] forty-five thousand and six hundred and fifty. ¹⁶All those numbered of the camp of Reuben [are] one hundred thousand and fifty-one thousand and four hundred and fifty, by their hosts; and they journey second. ¹⁷And the Tent of Meeting has journeyed [with] the camp of the Levites in the middle of the camps; as they encamp so they journey, each at his station by their standards. ¹⁸The standard of the camp of Ephraim, by their hosts, [is] westward; and the prince of the sons of Ephraim [is] Elishama son of Ammihud; ¹⁹and his host, and their numbered ones, [are] forty thousand and five hundred. ²⁰And by him [is] the tribe of Manasseh; and the prince of the sons of Manasseh [is] Gamaliel son of Pedahzur; ²¹and his host, and their numbered ones, [are] thirty-two thousand and two hundred. ²²And the tribe of Benjamin [is with them]; and the prince of the sons of Benjamin [is] Abidan son of Gideoni; ²³and his host, and their numbered ones, [are] thirty-five thousand and four hundred. ²⁴All those numbered of the camp of Ephraim [are] one hundred thousand and eight thousand and one hundred, by their hosts; and they journey third. ²⁵The standard of the camp of Dan [is] northward, by their hosts; and the prince of the sons of Dan [is] Ahiezer son of Ammishaddai; ²⁶and his host, and their numbered ones, [are] sixty-two thousand and seven hundred. ²⁷And those encamping by him [are of] the tribe of Asher; and the prince of the sons of Asher [is] Pagiel son of Ocran; ²⁸and his host, and their numbered ones, [are] forty-one thousand and five hundred. ²⁹And the tribe of Naphtali [is with them]; and the prince of the sons of Naphtali [is] Ahira son of Enan; ³⁰and his host, and their numbered ones, [are] fifty-three thousand and four hundred. ³¹All those numbered of the camp of Dan [are] one hundred thousand and fifty-seven thousand and six hundred; they journey at the rear by their standards. ³²These [are] those numbered of the sons of Israel by the house of their fathers; all those numbered of the camps by their hosts [are] six hundred thousand and three thousand and five hundred and fifty. ³³And the Levites have not numbered themselves in the midst of the sons of Israel, as YHWH has commanded Moses. ³⁴And the sons of Israel do according to all that YHWH has commanded Moses; so they have encamped by their standards, and so they have journeyed, each by his families, by the house of his fathers.

CHAPTER 3

¹And these [are] the generations of Aaron and Moses, in the day of YHWH's speaking with Moses in Mount Sinai. ²And these [are] the names of the sons of Aaron: the firstborn Nadab, and Abihu, Eleazar, and Ithamar; ³these [are] the names of the sons of Aaron, the anointed priests, whose hand he has consecrated for acting as priest. ⁴And Nadab dies—Abihu also—before YHWH, in their bringing strange fire near before YHWH, in the wilderness of Sinai, and they did not have sons; and Eleazar—Ithamar also—acts as

NUMBERS

priest in the presence of their father Aaron. ⁵And YHWH speaks to Moses, saying, ⁶"Bring the tribe of Levi near, and you have caused it to stand before Aaron the priest, and they have served him, ⁷and kept his charge, and the charge of all the congregation before the Tent of Meeting, to do the service of the Dwelling Place; ⁸and they have kept all the vessels of the Tent of Meeting, and the charge of the sons of Israel, to do the service of the Dwelling Place; ⁹and you have given the Levites to Aaron and to his sons; they are surely given to him out of the sons of Israel. ¹⁰And you appoint Aaron and his sons, and they have kept their priesthood, and the stranger who comes near is put to death." ¹¹And YHWH speaks to Moses, saying, ¹²"And I, behold, have taken the Levites from the midst of the sons of Israel instead of every firstborn opening a womb among the sons of Israel, and the Levites have been Mine; ¹³for every firstborn [is] Mine, in the day of My striking every firstborn in the land of Egypt I have sanctified to Myself every firstborn in Israel, from man to beast; they are Mine; I [am] YHWH." ¹⁴And YHWH speaks to Moses in the wilderness of Sinai, saying, ¹⁵"Number the sons of Levi by the house of their fathers, by their families; every male from a son of a month and upward—you number them." ¹⁶And Moses numbers them according to the command of YHWH, as he has been commanded. ¹⁷And these are the sons of Levi by their names: Gershon, and Kohath, and Merari. ¹⁸And these [are] the names of the sons of Gershon by their families: Libni and Shimei. ¹⁹And the sons of Kohath by their families: Amram, and Izhar, Hebron, and Uzziel. ²⁰And the sons of Merari by their families: Mahli and Mushi; these are the families of the Levites, by the house of their fathers. ²¹Of Gershon—the family of the Libnite and the family of the Shimite; these are the families of the Gershonite. ²²Their numbered ones, in number, every male from a son of a month and upward, their numbered ones [are] seven thousand and five hundred. ²³The families of the Gershonite encamp westward behind the Dwelling Place. ²⁴And the prince of a father's house for the Gershonite [is] Eliasaph son of Lael. ²⁵And the charge of the sons of Gershon in the Tent of Meeting [is] the Dwelling Place, and the tent, its covering, and the veil at the opening of the Tent of Meeting, ²⁶and the hangings of the court, and the veil at the opening of the court, which [is] by the Dwelling Place and by the altar all around, and its cords, to all its service. ²⁷And of Kohath—the family of the Amramite, and the family of the Izharite, and the family of the Hebronite, and the family of the Uzzielite; these are families of the Kohathite. ²⁸In number, all the males, from a son of a month and upward, [are] eight thousand and six hundred, keeping the charge of the holy place. ²⁹The families of the sons of Kohath encamp southward by the side of the Dwelling Place. ³⁰And the prince of a father's house for the families of the Kohathite [is] Elizaphan son of Uzziel. ³¹And their charge [is] the Ark, and the table, and the lampstand, and the altars, and the vessels of the holy place with which they serve, and the veil, and all its service. ³²And Eleazar son of Aaron the priest [is] the prince of the princes of the Levites, [with] the oversight of the keepers of the charge of the holy place. ³³Of Merari—the family of the Mahlite and the family of the Mushite; these [are] the families of Merari. ³⁴And their numbered ones, in number, all the males from a son of a month and upward, [are] six thousand and two hundred. ³⁵And the prince of a father's house for the families of Merari [is] Zuriel son of Abihail; they encamp northward by the side of the Dwelling Place. ³⁶And the oversight [and] charge of the sons of Merari [are] the boards of the Dwelling Place, and its bars, and its pillars, and its sockets, and all its vessels, and all its service, ³⁷and the pillars of the court all around, and their sockets, and their pins, and their cords. ³⁸And those encamping before the Dwelling Place eastward, before the Tent of Meeting, at the east, [are] Moses and Aaron, and his sons, keeping the charge of the sanctuary for the charge of the sons of Israel, and the stranger who comes near is put to death. ³⁹All those numbered of the Levites whom Moses numbered—Aaron also—by the command of YHWH, by their families, every male from a son of a month and upward, [are] twenty-two thousand. ⁴⁰And YHWH says to Moses, "Number every firstborn male of the sons of Israel from a son of a month and upward, and take up the number of their names; ⁴¹and you have taken the Levites for Me (I [am] YHWH), instead of every firstborn among the sons of Israel, and the livestock of the Levites instead of every firstling among the livestock of the sons of Israel." ⁴²And Moses numbers, as YHWH has commanded him, all the firstborn among the sons of Israel. ⁴³And every firstborn male, by the number of names, from a son of a month and upward, of their numbered ones, are twenty-two thousand two hundred and seventy-three. ⁴⁴And YHWH speaks to Moses, saying, ⁴⁵"Take the Levites instead of every firstborn among the sons of Israel, and the livestock of the Levites instead of their livestock; and the Levites have been Mine; I [am] YHWH. ⁴⁶And [from] those ransomed of the two hundred and seventy-three of the firstborn of the sons of Israel, who are more than the Levites, ⁴⁷you have even taken five shekels apiece by the counted head—you take by the shekel of the holy place; the shekel [is] twenty gerahs; ⁴⁸and you have given the money to Aaron and to his sons, whereby those over and above are ransomed." ⁴⁹And Moses takes the ransom money from those over and above those ransomed by the Levites; ⁵⁰he has taken the money from the firstborn of the sons of Israel—one thousand and three hundred and sixty-five, by the shekel of the holy place; ⁵¹and Moses gives the money of those ransomed to Aaron and to his sons, according to the command of YHWH, as YHWH has commanded Moses.

CHAPTER 4

¹And YHWH speaks to Moses and to Aaron, saying, ²"Take a census of the sons of Kohath from the midst of the sons of Levi, by their families, by the house of their fathers; ³from a son of thirty years and upward, even until a son of fifty years, everyone going in to the host, to do work in the Tent of Meeting. ⁴This [is] the service of the sons of Kohath in the Tent of Meeting [for] the most holy things: ⁵when Aaron and his sons have come in, in the journeying of the camp, and have taken down the veil of the hanging, and have covered the Ark of the Testimony with it, ⁶then they have put a covering of tachash skin on it, and have spread a garment completely of blue above, and have placed its poles. ⁷And they spread a garment of blue over the table of the presence, and have put the dishes, and the spoons, and the bowls, and the cups of the drink-offering on it, and the bread of continuity is on it, ⁸and they have spread a garment of scarlet over them, and have covered it with a covering of tachash skin, and have placed its poles, ⁹and have taken a garment of blue, and have covered the lampstand of the lamp, and its lights, and its snuffers, and its snuff-dishes, and all its oil vessels with which they minister to it; ¹⁰and they have put it and all its vessels into a covering of tachash skin, and have put [it] on the bar. ¹¹And they spread a garment of blue over the golden altar, and have covered it with a covering of tachash skin, and have placed its poles, ¹²and have taken all the vessels of ministry with which they minister in the holy place, and have put [them] into a garment of blue, and have covered them with a covering of tachash skin, and have put [them] on the bar, ¹³and have removed the ashes of the altar, and have spread a garment of purple over it, ¹⁴and have put on it all its vessels with which they minister on it—the censers, the hooks, and the shovels, and the bowls, all the vessels of the altar—and have spread a covering of tachash skin on it, and have placed its poles. ¹⁵And Aaron has finished—his sons also—covering the holy place, and all the vessels of the holy place, in the journeying of the camp, and afterward the sons of Kohath come in to carry [it], and they do not come to the holy thing, lest they have died; these [things are] the burden of the sons of Kohath in the Tent of Meeting. ¹⁶And the oversight of Eleazar, son of Aaron the priest, [is] the oil of the lamp, and the spice-incense, and the present of continuity, and the anointing oil, the oversight of all the Dwelling Place and of all that [is] in it, in the sanctuary and in its vessels." ¹⁷And YHWH speaks to Moses and to Aaron, saying, ¹⁸"You do not cut off the tribe of the families of the Kohathite from the midst of the Levites; ¹⁹but do this for them, and they have lived and do not die in their drawing near [to] the Holy of Holies: Aaron and his sons go in, and have set them, each man to his service, and to his burden, ²⁰and they do not go in to see when the holy thing is swallowed, lest they have died." ²¹And YHWH speaks to Moses, saying, ²²"Also take a census of the sons of Gershon by the house of

their fathers, by their families; ²³from a son of thirty years and upward, until a son of fifty years, you number them—everyone who is going in to serve the host, to do the service in the Tent of Meeting. ²⁴This [is] the service of the families of the Gershonite, to serve and for burden: ²⁵and they have carried the curtains of the Dwelling Place, and the Tent of Meeting, its covering, and the covering of the tachash [skin] which [is] on it above, and the veil at the opening of the Tent of Meeting, ²⁶and the hangings of the court, and the veil at the opening of the gate of the court which [is] by the Dwelling Place, and by the altar all around, and their cords, and all the vessels of their service, and all that is made for them—and they have served. ²⁷By the command of Aaron and his sons is all the service of the sons of the Gershonite, in all their burden and in all their service; and you have laid a charge on them concerning the charge of all their burden. ²⁸This [is] the service of the families of the sons of the Gershonite in the Tent of Meeting; and their charge [is] under the hand of Ithamar son of Aaron the priest. ²⁹The sons of Merari, by their families, by the house of their fathers—you number them; ³⁰from a son of thirty years and upward even to a son of fifty years, you number them—everyone who is going in to the host, to do the service of the Tent of Meeting. ³¹And this [is] the charge of their burden, of all their service in the Tent of Meeting: the boards of the Dwelling Place, and its bars, and its pillars, and its sockets, ³²and the pillars of the court all around, and their sockets, and their pins, and their cords, of all their vessels, and of all their service; and you number the vessels of the charge of their burden by name. ³³This [is] the service of the families of the sons of Merari, for all their service, in the Tent of Meeting, by the hand of Ithamar son of Aaron the priest." ³⁴And Moses numbers—Aaron also, and the princes of the congregation—the sons of the Kohathite, by their families, and by the house of their fathers, ³⁵from a son of thirty years and upward even to a son of fifty years, everyone who is going in to the host, for service in the Tent of Meeting, ³⁶and their numbered ones, by their families, are two thousand seven hundred and fifty. ³⁷These [are] those numbered of the families of the Kohathite, everyone who is serving in the Tent of Meeting, whom Moses and Aaron numbered by the command of Yhwh, by the hand of Moses. ³⁸And those numbered of the sons of Gershon, by their families, and by the house of their fathers, ³⁹from a son of thirty years and upward even to a son of fifty years, everyone who is going in to the host, for service in the Tent of Meeting, ⁴⁰even their numbered ones, by their families, by the house of their fathers, are two thousand and six hundred and thirty. ⁴¹These [are] those numbered of the families of the sons of Gershon, everyone who is serving in the Tent of Meeting, whom Moses and Aaron numbered by the command of Yhwh. ⁴²And those numbered of the families of the sons of Merari, by their families, by the house of their fathers, ⁴³from a son of thirty years and upward even to a son of fifty years, everyone who is going in to the host, for service in the Tent of Meeting, ⁴⁴even their numbered ones, by their families, are three thousand and two hundred. ⁴⁵These [are] those numbered of the families of the sons of Merari, whom Moses and Aaron numbered by the command of Yhwh, by the hand of Moses. ⁴⁶All those numbered, whom Moses numbered—Aaron also, and the princes of Israel—of the Levites, by their families, and by the house of their fathers, ⁴⁷from a son of thirty years and upward even to a son of fifty years, everyone who is going in to do the work of the service, even the service of burden in the Tent of Meeting, ⁴⁸even their numbered ones are eight thousand and five hundred and eighty; ⁴⁹he has numbered them by the command of Yhwh, by the hand of Moses, each man by his service, and by his burden, with his numbered ones, as Yhwh has commanded Moses.

CHAPTER 5

¹And Yhwh speaks to Moses, saying, ²"Command the sons of Israel, and they send out of the camp every leper, and everyone with discharging, and everyone defiled by a body; ³you send out from male even to female; you send them to the outside of the camp and they do not defile their camps in the midst of which I dwell." ⁴And the sons of Israel do so, and they send them out to the outside of the camp; as Yhwh has spoken to Moses so the sons of Israel have done. ⁵And Yhwh speaks to Moses, saying, ⁶"Speak to the sons of Israel: Man or woman, when they do any of the sins of man, by committing a trespass against Yhwh, and that person [is] guilty, ⁷and they have confessed their sin which they have done, then he has restored his guilt in its principal, and is adding its fifth to it, and has given [it] to him in reference to whom he has been guilty. ⁸And if the man has no redeemer to restore the guilt to, the guilt which is restored [is] to Yhwh for the priest, apart from the ram of the atonements, whereby he makes atonement for him. ⁹And every raised-offering of all the holy things of the sons of Israel, which they bring near to the priest, becomes his; ¹⁰and any man's hallowed things become his; that which any man gives to the priest becomes his." ¹¹And Yhwh speaks to Moses, saying, ¹²"Speak to the sons of Israel, and you have said to them: When any man's wife turns aside, and has committed a trespass against him, ¹³and a man has lain with her [with] the seed [from] intercourse, and it has been hid from the eyes of her husband, and concealed, and she has been defiled, and there is no witness against her, and she has not been caught, ¹⁴and a spirit of jealousy has passed over him, and he has been jealous [for] his wife, and she has been defiled—or a spirit of jealousy has passed over him, and he has been jealous [for] his wife, and she has not been defiled— ¹⁵then the man has brought in his wife to the priest, and he has brought in her offering for her—a tenth of the ephah of barley meal; he does not pour oil on it, nor does he put frankincense on it, for it [is] a present of jealousy, a present of memorial, causing remembrance of iniquity. ¹⁶And the priest has brought her near, and has caused her to stand before Yhwh, ¹⁷and the priest has taken holy water in an earthen vessel, and the priest takes of the dust which is on the floor of the Dwelling Place, and has put [it] into the water, ¹⁸and the priest has caused the woman to stand before Yhwh, and has uncovered the woman's head, and has given the present of the memorial into her hands (it [is] a present of jealousy), and the bitter waters which cause the curse are in the hand of the priest. ¹⁹And the priest has caused her to swear, and has said to the woman, If no man has lain with you, and if you have not turned aside [to] uncleanness under your husband, be free from these bitter waters which cause the curse; ²⁰and you, if you have turned aside under your husband, and if you have been defiled, and a man commits his intercourse with you besides your husband— ²¹then the priest has caused the woman to swear with an oath of execration, and the priest has said to the woman—Yhwh gives you for an execration and for a curse in the midst of your people, in Yhwh's giving your thigh to fall and your belly to swell, ²²and these waters which cause the curse have gone into your bowels to cause the belly to swell and the thigh to fall; and the woman has said, Amen, Amen. ²³And the priest has written these execrations in a scroll, and has blotted [them] out with the bitter waters, ²⁴and has caused the woman to drink the bitter waters which cause the curse, and the waters which cause the curse have entered into her for bitter things. ²⁵And the priest has taken the present of jealousy out of the hand of the woman, and has waved the present before Yhwh, and has brought it near to the altar; ²⁶and the priest has taken a handful of the present, its memorial, and has made incense on the altar, and afterward causes the woman to drink the water; ²⁷indeed, he has caused her to drink the water, and it has come to pass, if she has been defiled and commits a trespass against her husband, that the waters which cause the curse have gone into her for bitter things, and her belly has swelled, and her thigh has fallen, and the woman has become an execration in the midst of her people. ²⁸And if the woman has not been defiled, and is clean, then she has been acquitted, and has been sown [with] seed. ²⁹This [is] the law of jealousies when a wife turns aside under her husband and has been defiled, ³⁰or when a spirit of jealousy passes over a man and he has been jealous of his wife, then he has caused the woman to stand before Yhwh, and the priest has done to her all this law, ³¹and the man has been acquitted from iniquity, and that woman bears her iniquity."

CHAPTER 6

¹And Yhwh speaks to Moses, saying, ²"Speak to the sons of Israel, and you have said to them: When a man or woman does extraordinarily by vowing a vow of a Nazarite, to be separate to Yhwh, ³he keeps separate

NUMBERS

from wine and strong drink; he does not drink vinegar of wine and vinegar of strong drink, and he does not drink any juice of grapes, and he does not eat moist or dry grapes; ⁴all [the] days of his separation he does not eat of anything which is made of the wine-vine, from kernels even to husk. ⁵All [the] days of the vow of his separation a razor does not pass over his head; he is holy until the fullness of the days [in] which he separates himself to YHWH; the upper part of the hair of his head has grown up. ⁶All [the] days of his keeping separate to YHWH, he does not go near a dead person; ⁷for his father, or for his mother, for his brother, or for his sister—he does not become unclean for them at their death, for the separation of his God [is] on his head; ⁸all [the] days of his separation he [is] holy to YHWH. ⁹And when the dead dies beside him in an instant, suddenly, and he has defiled the head of his separation, then he has shaved his head in the day of his cleansing; on the seventh day he shaves it, ¹⁰and on the eighth day he brings in two turtle-doves or two young pigeons to the priest, to the opening of the Tent of Meeting, ¹¹and the priest has prepared one for a sin-offering and one for a burnt-offering, and has made atonement for him because of that which he has sinned by the body, and he has hallowed his head on that day; ¹²and he has separated to YHWH the days of his separation, and he has brought in a lamb, a son of a year, for a guilt-offering, and the former days are fallen, for his separation has been defiled. ¹³And this [is] the law of the Nazarite: in the day of the fullness of the days of his separation, he is brought to the opening of the Tent of Meeting, ¹⁴and he has brought his offering near to YHWH—one male lamb, a son of a year, a perfect one, for a burnt-offering, and one female lamb, a daughter of a year, a perfect one, for a sin-offering, and one ram, a perfect one, for peace-offerings, ¹⁵and a basket of unleavened things of flour, cakes mixed with oil, and thin cakes of unleavened things anointed with oil, and their present, and their drink-offerings. ¹⁶And the priest has brought [them] near before YHWH, and has made his sin-offering and his burnt-offering; ¹⁷and he makes the ram [as] a sacrifice of peace-offerings to YHWH, besides the basket of unleavened things; and the priest has made its present and its drink-offering. ¹⁸And the Nazarite has shaved (at the opening of the Tent of Meeting) the head of his separation, and has taken the hair of the head of his separation, and has put [it] on the fire which [is] under the sacrifice of the peace-offerings. ¹⁹And the priest has taken the boiled shoulder from the ram, and one unleavened cake out of the basket, and one thin unleavened cake, and has put [them] on the palms of the Nazarite after his shaving [the hair of] his separation; ²⁰and the priest has waved them [as] a wave-offering before YHWH; it [is] holy to the priest, besides the breast of the wave-offering, and besides the leg of the raised-offering; and afterward the Nazarite drinks wine. ²¹This [is] the law of the Nazarite who vows his offering to YHWH for his separation, apart from that which his hand attains; according to his vow which he vows so he does by the law of his separation." ²²And YHWH speaks to Moses, saying, ²³"Speak to Aaron and to his sons, saying, Thus you bless the sons of Israel, saying to them: ²⁴YHWH bless you and keep you; ²⁵YHWH cause His face to shine on you, || And favor you; ²⁶YHWH lift up His countenance on you, || And appoint for you—peace. ²⁷And they have put My Name on the sons of Israel, and I bless them."

CHAPTER 7

¹And it comes to pass on the day [when] Moses [was] finishing to set up the Dwelling Place, that he anoints it, and sanctifies it, and all its vessels, and the altar, and all its vessels, and he anoints them, and sanctifies them, ²and the princes of Israel (heads of the house of their fathers, they [are] princes of the tribes, they who are standing over those numbered) bring near, ³indeed, they bring their offering before YHWH of six covered wagons and twelve oxen—a wagon for two of the princes, and an ox for one—and they bring them near before the Dwelling Place. ⁴And YHWH speaks to Moses, saying, ⁵"Receive [these] from them, and they have been [used] for doing the service of the Tent of Meeting, and you have given them to the Levites, each according to his service." ⁶And Moses takes the wagons and the oxen, and gives them to the Levites. ⁷He has given the two wagons and the four oxen to the sons of Gershon, according to their service, ⁸and he has given the four wagons and the eight oxen to the sons of Merari, according to their service, by the hand of Ithamar son of Aaron the priest, ⁹but he has not given [any] to the sons of Kohath, for the service of the holy place [is] on them, [which] they carry on the shoulder. ¹⁰And the princes bring the dedication of the altar near in the day of its being anointed, indeed, the princes bring their offering near before the altar. ¹¹And YHWH says to Moses, "One prince a day, one prince a day—they bring their offering near for the dedication of the altar." ¹²And he who is bringing his offering near on the first day is Nahshon son of Amminadab, of the tribe of Judah. ¹³And his offering [is] one silver dish, its weight one hundred and thirty [shekels], [and] one silver bowl of seventy shekels, by the shekel of the holy place, both of them full of flour mixed with oil for a present; ¹⁴one golden spoon of ten [shekels], full of incense; ¹⁵one bullock, a son of the herd, one ram, one lamb, a son of a year, for a burnt-offering; ¹⁶one kid of the goats for a sin-offering; ¹⁷and for a sacrifice of the peace-offerings: two oxen, five rams, five male goats, five lambs, sons of a year; this [is] the offering of Nahshon son of Amminadab. ¹⁸On the second day Nethaneel son of Zuar, prince of Issachar, has brought [an offering] near. ¹⁹He has brought his offering near: one silver dish, its weight one hundred and thirty [shekels], [and] one silver bowl of seventy shekels, by the shekel of the holy place, both of them full of flour mixed with oil for a present; ²⁰one golden spoon of ten [shekels], full of incense; ²¹one bullock, a son of the herd, one ram, one lamb, a son of a year, for a burnt-offering; ²²one kid of the goats for a sin-offering; ²³and for a sacrifice of the peace-offerings: two oxen, five rams, five male goats, five lambs, sons of a year; this [is] the offering of Nethaneel son of Zuar. ²⁴On the third day, Eliab son of Helon, prince of the sons of Zebulun— ²⁵his offering [is] one silver dish, its weight one hundred and thirty [shekels], [and] one silver bowl of seventy shekels, by the shekel of the holy place, both of them full of flour mixed with oil for a present; ²⁶one golden spoon of ten [shekels], full of incense; ²⁷one bullock, a son of the herd, one ram, one lamb, a son of a year, for a burnt-offering; ²⁸one kid of the goats for a sin-offering; ²⁹and for a sacrifice of the peace-offerings: two oxen, five rams, five male goats, five lambs, sons of a year; this [is] the offering of Eliab son of Helon. ³⁰On the fourth day, Elizur son of Shedeur, prince of the sons of Reuben— ³¹his offering [is] one silver dish, its weight one hundred and thirty [shekels], [and] one silver bowl of seventy shekels, by the shekel of the holy place, both of them full of flour mixed with oil for a present; ³²one golden spoon of ten [shekels], full of incense; ³³one bullock, a son of the herd, one ram, one lamb, a son of a year, for a burnt-offering; ³⁴one kid of the goats for a sin-offering; ³⁵and for a sacrifice of the peace-offerings: two oxen, five rams, five male goats, five lambs, sons of a year; this [is] the offering of Elizur son of Shedeur. ³⁶On the fifth day, Shelumiel son of Zurishaddai, prince of the sons of Simeon— ³⁷his offering [is] one silver dish, its weight one hundred and thirty [shekels], [and] one silver bowl of seventy shekels, by the shekel of the holy place, both of them full of flour mixed with oil for a present; ³⁸one golden spoon of ten [shekels], full of incense; ³⁹one bullock, a son of the herd, one ram, one lamb, a son of a year, for a burnt-offering; ⁴⁰one kid of the goats for a sin-offering; ⁴¹and for a sacrifice of the peace-offerings: two oxen, five rams, five male goats, five lambs, sons of a year; this [is] the offering of Shelumiel son of Zurishaddai. ⁴²On the sixth day, Eliasaph son of Deuel, prince of the sons of Gad— ⁴³his offering [is] one silver dish, its weight one hundred and thirty [shekels], [and] one silver bowl of seventy shekels, by the shekel of the holy place, both of them full of flour mixed with oil for a present; ⁴⁴one golden spoon of ten [shekels], full of incense; ⁴⁵one bullock, a son of the herd, one ram, one lamb, a son of a year, for a burnt-offering; ⁴⁶one kid of the goats for a sin-offering; ⁴⁷and for a sacrifice of the peace-offerings: two oxen, five rams, five male goats, five lambs, sons of a year; this [is] the offering of Eliasaph son of Deuel. ⁴⁸On the seventh day, Elishama son of Ammihud, prince of the sons of Ephraim— ⁴⁹his offering [is] one silver dish, its weight one hundred and thirty [shekels], [and] one silver bowl of seventy shekels, by the shekel of the holy place, both of them full of flour mixed with oil for a present; ⁵⁰one golden spoon of ten [shekels], full of incense; ⁵¹one bullock, a son of the herd, one ram, one lamb, a son of a year, for a burnt-offering; ⁵²one kid of the goats

for a sin-offering; ⁵³and for a sacrifice of the peace-offerings: two oxen, five rams, five male goats, five lambs, sons of a year; this [is] the offering of Elishama son of Ammihud. ⁵⁴On the eighth day, Gamaliel son of Pedahzur, prince of the sons of Manasseh— ⁵⁵his offering [is] one silver dish, its weight one hundred and thirty [shekels], [and] one silver bowl of seventy shekels, by the shekel of the holy place, both of them full of flour mixed with oil for a present; ⁵⁶one golden spoon of ten [shekels], full of incense; ⁵⁷one bullock, a son of the herd, one ram, one lamb, a son of a year, for a burnt-offering; ⁵⁸one kid of the goats for a sin-offering; ⁵⁹and for a sacrifice of the peace-offerings: two oxen, five rams, five male goats, five lambs, sons of a year; this [is] the offering of Gamaliel son of Pedahzur. ⁶⁰On the ninth day, Abidan son of Gideoni, prince of the sons of Benjamin— ⁶¹his offering [is] one silver dish, its weight one hundred and thirty [shekels], [and] one silver bowl of seventy shekels, by the shekel of the holy place, both of them full of flour mixed with oil for a present; ⁶²one golden spoon of ten [shekels], full of incense; ⁶³one bullock, a son of the herd, one ram, one lamb, a son of a year, for a burnt-offering; ⁶⁴one kid of the goats for a sin-offering: ⁶⁵and for a sacrifice of the peace-offerings: two oxen, five rams, five male goats, five lambs, sons of a year; this [is] the offering of Abidan son of Gideoni. ⁶⁶On the tenth day, Ahiezer son of Ammishaddai, prince of the sons of Dan— ⁶⁷his offering [is] one silver dish, its weight one hundred and thirty [shekels], [and] one silver bowl of seventy shekels, by the shekel of the holy place, both of them full of flour mixed with oil for a present; ⁶⁸one golden spoon of ten [shekels], full of incense; ⁶⁹one bullock, a son of the herd, one ram, one lamb, a son of a year, for a burnt-offering; ⁷⁰one kid of the goats for a sin-offering; ⁷¹and for a sacrifice of the peace-offerings: two oxen, five rams, five male goats, five lambs, sons of a year; this [is] the offering of Ahiezer son of Ammishaddai. ⁷²On the eleventh day, Pagiel son of Ocran, prince of the sons of Asher— ⁷³his offering [is] one silver dish, its weight one hundred and thirty [shekels], [and] one silver bowl of seventy shekels, by the shekel of the holy place, both of them full of flour mixed with oil for a present; ⁷⁴one golden spoon of ten [shekels], full of incense; ⁷⁵one bullock, a son of the herd, one ram, one lamb, a son of a year, for a burnt-offering; ⁷⁶one kid of the goats for a sin-offering; ⁷⁷and for a sacrifice of the peace-offerings: two oxen, five rams, five male goats, five lambs, sons of a year; this [is] the offering of Pagiel son of Ocran. ⁷⁸On the twelfth day, Ahira son of Enan, prince of the sons of Naphtali— ⁷⁹his offering [is] one silver dish, its weight one hundred and thirty [shekels], [and] one silver bowl of seventy shekels, by the shekel of the holy place, both of them full of flour mixed with oil for a present; ⁸⁰one golden spoon of ten [shekels], full of incense; ⁸¹one bullock, a son of the herd, one ram, one lamb, a son of a year, for a burnt-offering; ⁸²one kid of the goats for a sin-offering; ⁸³and for a sacrifice of the peace-offerings: two oxen, five rams, five male goats, five lambs, sons of a year; this [is] the offering of Ahira son of Enan. ⁸⁴This [is] the dedication of the altar, in the day of its being anointed by the princes of Israel: twelve silver dishes, twelve silver bowls, twelve golden spoons; ⁸⁵each silver dish [is] one hundred and thirty [shekels], and each bowl seventy; all the silver of the vessels [is] two thousand and four hundred [shekels], by the shekel of the holy place; ⁸⁶twelve golden spoons full of incense, ten [shekels] each spoon, by the shekel of the holy place; all the gold of the spoons [is] one hundred and twenty [shekels]; ⁸⁷all the oxen for burnt-offering [are] twelve bullocks; twelve rams, twelve lambs, sons of a year, and their present, and twelve kids of the goats for sin-offering; ⁸⁸and all the oxen for the sacrifice of the peace-offerings [are] twenty-four bullocks; sixty rams, sixty male goats, sixty lambs, sons of a year; this is the dedication of the altar in the day of its being anointed. ⁸⁹And in the entering of Moses into the Tent of Meeting to speak with Him, indeed, he hears the voice speaking to him from off the propitiatory covering which [is] on the Ark of the Testimony, from between the two cherubim; and He speaks to him.

CHAPTER 8

¹And YHWH speaks to Moses, saying, ²"Speak to Aaron, and you have said to him: In your causing the lights to go up, the seven lights give light toward the front of the face of the lampstand." ³And Aaron does so; he has caused its lights to go up toward the front of the face of the lampstand, as YHWH has commanded Moses. ⁴And this [is] the work of the lampstand: beaten work of gold; from its thigh to its flower it [is] beaten work; as the appearance which YHWH showed Moses, so he has made the lampstand. ⁵And YHWH speaks to Moses, saying, ⁶"Take the Levites from the midst of the sons of Israel, and you have cleansed them. ⁷And thus you do to them to cleanse them: sprinkle waters of atonement on them, and they have caused a razor to pass over all their flesh, and have washed their garments, and cleansed themselves, ⁸and have taken a bullock, a son of the herd, and its present, flour mixed with oil, and you take a second bullock, a son of the herd, for a sin-offering; ⁹and you have brought the Levites near before the Tent of Meeting, and you have assembled all the congregation of the sons of Israel, ¹⁰and you have brought the Levites near before YHWH, and the sons of Israel have laid their hands on the Levites, ¹¹and Aaron has waved the Levites [as] a wave-offering before YHWH, from the sons of Israel, and they have been [consecrated] for doing the service of YHWH. ¹²And the Levites lay their hands on the head of the bullocks, and make one a sin-offering and one a burnt-offering to YHWH, to atone for the Levites. ¹³And you have caused the Levites to stand before Aaron, and before his sons, and have waved them [as] a wave-offering to YHWH; ¹⁴and you have separated the Levites from the midst of the sons of Israel, and the Levites have become Mine; ¹⁵and afterward the Levites come in to serve the Tent of Meeting, and you have cleansed them, and have waved them [as] a wave-offering. ¹⁶For they are certainly given to Me out of the midst of the sons of Israel, instead of him who opens any womb—the firstborn of all; I have taken them for Myself from the sons of Israel; ¹⁷for every firstborn among the sons of Israel [is] Mine, among man and among beast; in the day of My striking every firstborn in the land of Egypt I sanctified them for Myself; ¹⁸and I take the Levites instead of every firstborn among the sons of Israel. ¹⁹And I give the Levites [as] gifts to Aaron and to his sons, from the midst of the sons of Israel, to do the service of the sons of Israel in the Tent of Meeting, and to make atonement for the sons of Israel, and there is no plague among the sons of Israel in the sons of Israel drawing near to the holy place." ²⁰And Moses does—Aaron also, and all the congregation of the sons of Israel—to the Levites according to all that YHWH has commanded Moses concerning the Levites; so the sons of Israel have done to them. ²¹And the Levites cleanse themselves, and wash their garments, and Aaron waves them [as] a wave-offering before YHWH, and Aaron makes atonement for them to cleanse them, ²²and afterward the Levites have gone in to do their service in the Tent of Meeting, before Aaron and before his sons; as YHWH has commanded Moses concerning the Levites, so they have done to them. ²³And YHWH speaks to Moses, saying, ²⁴"This [is] who [is] for the Levites: from a son of twenty-five years and upward he goes in to serve the host in the service of the Tent of Meeting, ²⁵and from a son of fifty years he returns from the host of the service, and does not serve anymore, ²⁶and he has ministered with his brothers in the Tent of Meeting, to keep the charge, and does not do service; thus you do to the Levites concerning their charge."

CHAPTER 9

¹And YHWH speaks to Moses, in the wilderness of Sinai, in the second year of their going out of the land of Egypt, in the first month, saying, ²"Also, the sons of Israel prepare the Passover in its appointed time; ³in the fourteenth day of this month between the evenings you prepare it in its appointed time; you prepare it according to all its statutes and according to all its ordinances." ⁴And Moses speaks to the sons of Israel to prepare the Passover, ⁵and they prepare the Passover in the first [month], on the fourteenth day of the month, between the evenings, in the wilderness of Sinai; according to all that YHWH has commanded Moses, so the sons of Israel have done. ⁶And there are men who have been defiled by the body of a man, and they have not been able to prepare the Passover on that day, and they come near before Moses and before Aaron on that day, ⁷and those men say to him, "We are defiled by the body of a man; why are we withheld so as not to bring the offering of YHWH near in its appointed time, in the midst of the sons of Israel?" ⁸And Moses says to them, "Stand, and

I hear what YHWH has commanded concerning you." ⁹And YHWH speaks to Moses, saying, ¹⁰"Speak to the sons of Israel, saying, Though any man is unclean by a body or in a distant journey (of you or of your generations), he has still prepared a Passover to YHWH, ¹¹they prepare it in the second month, on the fourteenth day, between the evenings; they eat it with unleavened and bitter things; ¹²they do not leave of [it] until morning; and they do not break a bone in it; they prepare it according to all the statute of the Passover. ¹³And the man who is clean, and has not been on a journey, and has ceased to prepare the Passover, indeed, that person has been cut off from his people; because he has not brought the offering of YHWH near in its appointed time, that man bears his sin. ¹⁴And when a sojourner sojourns with you, then he has prepared a Passover to YHWH—according to the statute of the Passover and according to its ordinance, so he does; one statute is for you, indeed, for a sojourner and for a native of the land." ¹⁵And in the day of the raising up of the Dwelling Place, the cloud has covered the Dwelling Place, even the Tent of the Testimony; and in the evening there is as an appearance of fire on the Dwelling Place until morning; ¹⁶so it is continually; the cloud covers it, also the appearance of fire by night. ¹⁷And according to the going up of the cloud from off the tent, then afterward the sons of Israel journey; and in the place where the cloud dwells, there the sons of Israel encamp; ¹⁸by the command of YHWH the sons of Israel journey, and by the command of YHWH they encamp; all the days that the cloud dwells over the Dwelling Place they encamp. ¹⁹And in the cloud prolonging itself over the Dwelling Place many days, then the sons of Israel have kept the charge of YHWH, and do not journey. ²⁰And so when the cloud is over the Dwelling Place [for] a number of days: by the command of YHWH they encamp, and by the command of YHWH they journey. ²¹And so when the cloud is from evening until morning, when the cloud has gone up in the morning, then they have journeyed; whether by day or by night, when the cloud has gone up, then they have journeyed. ²²Whether two days, or a month, or days, in the cloud prolonging itself over the Dwelling Place, to dwell over it, the sons of Israel encamp and do not journey; and in its being lifted up they journey. ²³By the command of YHWH they encamp, and by the command of YHWH they journey; they have kept the charge of YHWH, by the command of YHWH in the hand of Moses.

CHAPTER 10

¹And YHWH speaks to Moses, saying, ²"Make two trumpets of silver for yourself; you make them of beaten work, and they have been for you for the convocation of the congregation, and for the journeying of the camps; ³and they have blown with them, and all the congregation has assembled to you at the opening of the Tent of Meeting. ⁴And if they blow with one, then the princes, heads of the thousands of Israel, have assembled to you; ⁵and you have blown—a shout, and the camps which are encamping eastward have journeyed. ⁶And you have blown—a second shout, and the camps which are encamping southward have journeyed; they blow a shout for their journeys. ⁷And in the assembling of the assembly you blow, and do not shout; ⁸and sons of Aaron, the priests, blow with the trumpets; and they have been for a continuous statute to you throughout your generations. ⁹And when you go into battle in your land against the adversary who is distressing you, then you have shouted with the trumpets, and you have been remembered before your God YHWH, and you have been saved from your enemies. ¹⁰And in the day of your gladness, and in your appointed times, and in the beginnings of your months, you have also blown with the trumpets over your burnt-offerings, and over the sacrifices of your peace-offerings, and they have been for a memorial to you before your God; I [am] your God YHWH." ¹¹And it comes to pass, in the second year, in the second month, on the twentieth of the month, the cloud has gone up from off the Dwelling Place of the Testimony, ¹²and the sons of Israel journey in their journeys from the wilderness of Sinai, and the cloud dwells in the wilderness of Paran; ¹³and they journey at first by the command of YHWH in the hand of Moses. ¹⁴And the standard of the camp of the sons of Judah journeys in the first [place], by their hosts, and over its host [is] Nahshon son of Amminadab. ¹⁵And over the host of the tribe of the sons of Issachar [is] Nathaneel son of Zuar. ¹⁶And over the host of the tribe of the sons of Zebulun [is] Eliab son of Helon. ¹⁷And the Dwelling Place has been taken down, and the sons of Gershon and the sons of Merari have journeyed, carrying the Dwelling Place. ¹⁸And the standard of the camp of Reuben has journeyed, by their hosts, and over its host [is] Elizur son of Shedeur. ¹⁹And over the host of the tribe of the sons of Simeon [is] Shelumiel son of Zurishaddai. ²⁰And over the host of the tribe of the sons of Gad [is] Eliasaph son of Deuel. ²¹And the Kohathites have journeyed, carrying the Dwelling Place, and the [others] have raised up the Dwelling Place until their coming in. ²²And the standard of the camp of the sons of Ephraim has journeyed, by their hosts, and over its host [is] Elishama son of Ammihud. ²³And over the host of the tribe of the sons of Manasseh [is] Gamaliel son of Pedahzur. ²⁴And over the host of the tribe of the sons of Benjamin [is] Abidan son of Gideoni. ²⁵And the standard of the camp of the sons of Dan has journeyed (rearward to all the camps), by their hosts, and over its host [is] Ahiezer son of Ammishaddai. ²⁶And over the host of the tribe of the sons of Asher [is] Pagiel son of Ocran. ²⁷And over the host of the tribe of the sons of Naphtali [is] Ahira son of Enan. ²⁸These [are] the journeys of the sons of Israel by their hosts when they journey. ²⁹And Moses says to Hobab son of Raguel the Midianite, father-in-law of Moses, "We are journeying to the place of which YHWH has said, I give it to you; go with us, and we have done good to you, for YHWH has spoken good concerning Israel." ³⁰And he says to him, "I do not go; but I go to my land and to my family." ³¹And he says, "Please do not forsake us, because you have known our encamping in the wilderness, and you have been to us for eyes; ³²and it has come to pass, when you go with us—indeed, it has come to pass—that good which YHWH does kindly with us, we have done it kindly to you." ³³And they journey from the mountain of YHWH a journey of three days; and the Ark of the Covenant of YHWH is journeying before them [for] the journey of three days, to spy out a resting place for them; ³⁴and the cloud of YHWH [is] on them by day, in their journeying from the camp. ³⁵And it comes to pass in the journeying of the Ark, that Moses says, "Rise, O YHWH, and Your enemies are scattered, and those hating You flee from Your presence." ³⁶And in its resting he says, "Return, O YHWH, [to] the myriads, the thousands of Israel."

CHAPTER 11

¹And the people are evil, as those sighing habitually in the ears of YHWH, and YHWH hears, and His anger burns, and the fire of YHWH burns among them, and consumes in the extremity of the camp. ²And the people cry to Moses, and Moses prays to YHWH, and the fire is quenched; ³and he calls the name of that place Taberah, for the fire of YHWH has "burned" among them. ⁴And the rabble who [are] in its midst have lusted greatly, and the sons of Israel also turn back and weep, and say, "Who gives us flesh? ⁵We have remembered the fish which we eat in Egypt for nothing, the cucumbers, and the melons, and the leeks, and the onions, and the garlic; ⁶and now our soul [is] dry, there is not anything, except the manna, before our eyes." ⁷And the manna is as coriander seed, and its aspect as the aspect of bdellium; ⁸the people have turned aside and gathered [it], and ground [it] with millstones, or beat [it] in a mortar, and boiled [it] in a pan, and made it cakes, and its taste has been as the taste of the moisture of oil. ⁹And in the descending of the dew on the camp by night, the manna descends on it. ¹⁰And Moses hears the people weeping by its families, each at the opening of his tent, and the anger of YHWH burns exceedingly, and in the eyes of Moses [it is] evil. ¹¹And Moses says to YHWH, "Why have You done evil to Your servant? And why have I not found grace in Your eyes—to put the burden of all this people on me? ¹²I—have I conceived all this people? I—have I begotten it, that You say to me, Carry it in your bosom, as the one supporting carries the nursing suckling, to the ground which You have sworn to its fathers? ¹³From where do I have flesh to give to all this people? For they weep to me, saying, Give flesh to us, and we eat. ¹⁴I am not able—I alone—to bear all this people, for [it is] too heavy for me; ¹⁵and if thus You are doing to me—please slay me; slay, if I have found grace in your eyes, and do not let me look on my affliction." ¹⁶And YHWH says to Moses, "Gather to Me seventy men from [the] elderly of Israel, whom you have known that

they are [the] elderly of the people, and its authorities; and you have taken them to the Tent of Meeting, and they have stationed themselves there with you, ¹⁷and I have come down and spoken with you there, and have kept back of the Spirit which [is] on you, and have put [that One] on them, and they have borne some of the burden of the people with you, and you do not bear [it] alone. ¹⁸And you say to the people: Sanctify yourselves for tomorrow, and you have eaten flesh, for you have wept in the ears of YHWH, saying, Who gives us flesh? For we [had] good in Egypt; and YHWH has given flesh to you, and you have eaten. ¹⁹You do not eat one day, nor two days, nor five days, nor ten days, nor twenty days, ²⁰[but] even to a month of days, until it comes out from your nostrils, and it has become an abomination to you, because that you have loathed YHWH, who [is] in your midst, and weep before Him, saying, Why is this [that] we have come out of Egypt!" ²¹And Moses says, "Six hundred thousand footmen [are] the people in whose midst I [dwell]; and You, You have said, I give flesh to them, and they have eaten [for] a month of days! ²²Is flock and herd slaughtered for them, that one has found [enough] for them? Are all the fishes of the sea gathered for them, that one has found [enough] for them?" ²³And YHWH says to Moses, "Has the hand of YHWH become short? Now you see whether My word meets you or not." ²⁴And Moses goes out, and speaks the words of YHWH to the people, and gathers seventy men from [the] elderly of the people, and causes them to stand around the tent, ²⁵and YHWH comes down in the cloud, and speaks to him, and keeps back of the Spirit which [is] on him, and puts [that One] on the seventy elderly men; and it comes to pass at the resting of the Spirit on them, that they prophesy, and they have never done [so] again. ²⁶And two of the men are left in the camp, the name of the first [is] Eldad and the name of the second Medad, and the spirit rests on them (and they are among those written, but they have not gone out to the tent), and they prophesy in the camp; ²⁷and the young man runs, and declares [it] to Moses, and says, "Eldad and Medad are prophesying in the camp." ²⁸And Joshua son of Nun, minister of Moses, [one] of his young men, answers and says, "My lord Moses, restrain them." ²⁹And Moses says to him, "Are you zealous for me? O that all YHWH's people were prophets! That YHWH would put His Spirit on them!" ³⁰And Moses is gathered to the camp, he and [the] elderly of Israel. ³¹And a spirit has journeyed from YHWH, and cuts off quails from the sea, and leaves [them] by the camp, as a day's journey here and as a day's journey there, around the camp, and about two cubits above the face of the land. ³²And the people rise all that day, and all the night, and all the day after, and gather the quails—he who has least has gathered ten homers—and they spread them out for themselves around the camp. ³³The flesh is yet between their teeth—it is not yet cut off—and the anger of YHWH has burned among the people, and YHWH strikes [with] a very great striking among the people; ³⁴and [one] calls the name of that place Kibroth-Hattaavah, for there they have buried the people who lust. ³⁵From Kibroth-Hattaavah the people have journeyed to Hazeroth, and they are in Hazeroth.

CHAPTER 12

¹And Miriam speaks—Aaron also—against Moses concerning the circumstance of the Cushite woman whom he had taken, for he had taken a Cushite woman; ²and they say, "Has YHWH only spoken by Moses? Has he not also spoken by us?" And YHWH hears. ³And the man Moses [is] very humble, more than any of the men who [are] on the face of the ground. ⁴And YHWH suddenly says to Moses, and to Aaron, and to Miriam, "Come out, you three, to the Tent of Meeting"; and those three come out. ⁵And YHWH comes down in the pillar of the cloud, and stands at the opening of the tent, and calls Aaron and Miriam, and both of them come out. ⁶And He says, "Now hear My words: If your prophet is of YHWH, || I make Myself known to him in a vision; I speak with him in a dream. ⁷Not so My servant Moses; He [is] steadfast in all My house. ⁸I speak with him mouth to mouth, || Even [by] an appearance, and not in riddles; And he beholds the form of YHWH attentively. Now why have you not been afraid || To speak against My servant—against Moses?" ⁹And the anger of YHWH burns against them, and He goes on, ¹⁰and the cloud has turned aside from off the tent, and behold, Miriam [is] leprous as snow; and Aaron turns to Miriam, and behold, leprous! ¹¹And Aaron says to Moses, "O my lord, please do not lay [this] sin on us [in] which we have been foolish, and [in] which we have sinned; ¹²please do not let her be as [one] dead, when in his coming out from the womb of his mother—the half of his flesh is consumed." ¹³And Moses cries to YHWH, saying, "O God, please give healing to her! Please!" ¹⁴And YHWH says to Moses, "But [if] her father had but spat in her face—is she not ashamed [for] seven days? She is shut out [for] seven days at the outside of the camp, and afterward she is gathered." ¹⁵And Miriam is shut out at the outside of the camp [for] seven days, and the people have not journeyed until Miriam is gathered; ¹⁶and afterward the people have journeyed from Hazeroth, and they encamp in the wilderness of Paran.

CHAPTER 13

¹And YHWH speaks to Moses, saying, ²"Send men for yourself, and they spy out the land of Canaan, which I am giving to the sons of Israel; one man—you send one man for the tribe of his fathers, everyone a prince among them." ³And Moses sends them from the wilderness of Paran by the command of YHWH; all of them [are] men, [and] they are heads of the sons of Israel, ⁴and these [are] their names: for the tribe of Reuben, Shammua son of Zaccur; ⁵for the tribe of Simeon, Shaphat son of Hori; ⁶for the tribe of Judah, Caleb son of Jephunneh; ⁷for the tribe of Issachar, Igal son of Joseph; ⁸for the tribe of Ephraim, Oshea son of Nun; ⁹for the tribe of Benjamin, Palti son of Raphu; ¹⁰for the tribe of Zebulun, Gaddiel son of Sodi; ¹¹for the tribe of Joseph (for the tribe of Manasseh), Gaddi son of Susi; ¹²for the tribe of Dan, Ammiel son of Gemalli; ¹³for the tribe of Asher, Sethur son of Michael; ¹⁴for the tribe of Naphtali, Nahbi son of Vopshi; ¹⁵for the tribe of Gad, Geuel son of Machi. ¹⁶These [are] the names of the men whom Moses has sent to spy out the land; and Moses calls Hoshea son of Nun, Joshua. ¹⁷And Moses sends them to spy out the land of Canaan and says to them, "Go up this [way] into the south, and you have gone up the mountain, ¹⁸and have seen the land, what it [is], and the people which is dwelling on it, whether it [is] strong or feeble, [and] whether it [is] few or many; ¹⁹and what the land [is] in which it is dwelling, whether it [is] good or bad; and what [are] the cities in which it is dwelling, whether in camps or in fortresses. ²⁰And what the land [is], whether it [is] fat or lean; whether there is wood in it or not; and you have strengthened yourselves, and have taken of the fruit of the land"; now the days [are] days of the first-fruits of grapes. ²¹And they go up and spy out the land, from the wilderness of Zin to Rehob at the going in to Hamath; ²²and they go up by the south, and come to Hebron, and there [are] Ahiman, Sheshai, and Talmai, children of Anak (and Hebron was built seven years before Zoan in Egypt), ²³and they come to the Brook of Eshcol, and cut down a branch and one cluster of grapes there, and they carry it on a staff by two, also [some] of the pomegranates, and of the figs. ²⁴That place has been called the Brook of Eshcol, because of the cluster which the sons of Israel cut from there. ²⁵And they return from spying out the land at the end of forty days. ²⁶And they go and come to Moses, and to Aaron, and to all the congregation of the sons of Israel, to the wilderness of Paran, to Kadesh; and they bring them and all the congregation back word, and show them the fruit of the land. ²⁷And they recount to him, and say, "We came to the land to where you have sent us, and it is indeed flowing with milk and honey—and this [is] its fruit; ²⁸only, surely the people which is dwelling in the land [is] strong; and the cities are fortified [and] very great; and we have also seen children of Anak there. ²⁹Amalek is dwelling in the land of the south, and the Hittite, and the Jebusite, and the Amorite are dwelling in the hill country, and the Canaanite is dwelling by the sea, and by the side of the Jordan." ³⁰And Caleb stills the people concerning Moses and says, "Let us certainly go up—and we have possessed it; for we are thoroughly able to [do] it." ³¹And the men who have gone up with him said, "We are not able to go up against the people, for it [is] stronger than we"; ³²and they bring out an evil account of the land which they have spied out to the sons of Israel, saying, "The land into which we passed over to spy it out is a land eating up its inhabitants; and all the people whom we saw in its midst [are] men of stature; ³³and there we saw the giants, sons of Anak, of the giants; and we are as

grasshoppers in our own eyes—and so we were in their eyes."

CHAPTER 14

¹And all the congregation lifts up, and they give forth their voice, and the people weep during that night; ²and all the sons of Israel murmur against Moses and against Aaron, and all the congregation says to them, "O that we had died in the land of Egypt, or in this wilderness, O that we had died! ³And why is YHWH bringing us to this land to fall by the sword, [that] our wives and our infants become a prey? Is it not good for us to return to Egypt?" ⁴And they say to one another, "Let us appoint a head and return to Egypt." ⁵And Moses falls—Aaron also—on their faces, before all the assembly of the congregation of the sons of Israel. ⁶And Joshua son of Nun and Caleb son of Jephunneh, of those spying out the land, have torn their garments, ⁷and they speak to all the congregation of the sons of Israel, saying, "The land into which we have passed over to spy it out [is] a very, very good land; ⁸if YHWH has delighted in us, then He has brought us into this land, and has given it to us, a land which is flowing with milk and honey; ⁹only, do not rebel against YHWH: and you, do not fear the people of the land, for they [are] our bread; their defense has turned aside from off them, and YHWH [is] with us; do not fear them." ¹⁰And all the congregation says to stone them with stones, and the glory of YHWH has appeared in the Tent of Meeting to all the sons of Israel. ¹¹And YHWH says to Moses, "Until when does this people despise Me? And until when do they not believe in Me, for all the signs which I have done in its midst? ¹²I strike it with pestilence, and dispossess it, and make you become a nation greater and mightier than it." ¹³And Moses says to YHWH, "Then the Egyptians have heard! For with Your power You have brought up this people out of their midst, ¹⁴and they have said [it] to the inhabitant of this land, they have heard that You, YHWH, [are] in the midst of this people, that You are seen eye to eye—O YHWH, and Your cloud is standing over them—and in a pillar of cloud You are going before them by day, and in a pillar of fire by night. ¹⁵And You have put to death this people as one man, and the nations who have heard Your fame have spoken, saying, ¹⁶From YHWH's want of ability to bring in this people to the land which He has sworn to them, He slaughters them in the wilderness. ¹⁷And now, please let the power of my Lord be great, as You have spoken, saying, ¹⁸YHWH [is] slow to anger and of great kindness, bearing away iniquity and transgression, and not entirely acquitting, charging iniquity of fathers on sons, on a third and on a fourth [generation]— ¹⁹please forgive the iniquity of this people, according to the greatness of Your kindness, and as You have borne with this people from Egypt, even until now." ²⁰And YHWH says, "I have forgiven according to your word, ²¹but nevertheless, as I live, indeed, the whole earth is filled [with] the glory of YHWH, ²²for all the men who are seeing My glory and My signs which I have done in Egypt and in the wilderness, and try Me these ten times, and have not listened to My voice— ²³they do not see the land which I have sworn to their fathers, indeed, none of those despising Me see it; ²⁴but My servant Caleb, because there has been another spirit with him, and he is fully after Me—I have brought him into the land to where he has entered, and his seed possesses it. ²⁵And the Amalekite and the Canaanite are dwelling in the valley; tomorrow turn and journey for yourselves into the wilderness—the way of the Red Sea." ²⁶And YHWH speaks to Moses and to Aaron, saying, ²⁷"Until when [do I bear] with this evil congregation—they who are murmuring against Me? The murmurings of the sons of Israel, which they are murmuring against Me, I have heard; ²⁸say to them: As I live—a declaration of YHWH—if, as you have spoken in My ears, do I not do so to you? ²⁹Your carcasses fall in this wilderness, even all your numbered ones, to all your number, from a son of twenty years and upward, who have murmured against Me; ³⁰you do not come into the land [for] which I have lifted up My hand to cause you to dwell in it, except Caleb son of Jephunneh and Joshua son of Nun. ³¹As for your infants—of whom you have said, They become a spoil—I have even brought them in, and they have known the land which you have kicked against; ³²as for you—your carcasses fall in this wilderness, ³³and your sons are shepherding in the wilderness [for] forty years, and have borne your whoredoms until your carcasses are consumed in the wilderness; ³⁴by the number of the days [in] which you spied out the land, forty days—a day for a year, a day for a year— you bear your iniquities [for] forty years, and you have known My opposition; ³⁵I, YHWH, have spoken; if, nonetheless, I do this to all this evil congregation who are meeting against Me—they are consumed in this wilderness, and there they die." ³⁶Then the men whom Moses has sent to spy out the land, [who] then return and cause all the congregation to murmur against him by bringing out an evil account concerning the land, ³⁷even the men bringing out an evil account of the land, they die by the plague before YHWH; ³⁸and Joshua son of Nun and Caleb son of Jephunneh have lived, of those men who go to spy out the land. ³⁹And Moses speaks these words to all the sons of Israel, and the people mourn exceedingly, ⁴⁰and they rise early in the morning, and go up to the top of the mountain, saying, "Here we [are], and we have come up to the place which YHWH has spoken of, for we have sinned." ⁴¹And Moses says, "Why [is] this [that] you are transgressing the command of YHWH? For it does not prosper; ⁴²do not go up, for YHWH is not in your midst, and you are not struck before your enemies; ⁴³for the Amalekite and the Canaanite [are] there before you, and you have fallen by the sword, because that you have turned back from after YHWH, and YHWH is not with you." ⁴⁴And they presume to go up to the top of the mountain, but the Ark of the Covenant of YHWH, and Moses, have not departed out of the midst of the camp. ⁴⁵And the Amalekite and the Canaanite who are dwelling in that mountain come down and strike them, and beat them down to Hormah.

CHAPTER 15

¹And YHWH speaks to Moses, saying, ²"Speak to the sons of Israel, and you have said to them: When you come into the land of your dwellings, which I am giving to you, ³then you have prepared a fire-offering to YHWH, a burnt-offering or a sacrifice, for separating a vow or free-will offering, or in your appointed things, to make a refreshing fragrance to YHWH, out of the herd or out of the flock. ⁴And he who is bringing his offering near to YHWH has brought a present near of a tenth part of flour mixed with a fourth of the hin of oil; ⁵and you prepare a fourth of the hin of wine for a drink-offering, with the burnt-offering or for the sacrifice, for one lamb; ⁶or for a ram you prepare a present of two-tenth parts of flour mixed with a third of the hin of oil; ⁷and you bring a third part of the hin of wine near for a drink-offering—a refreshing fragrance to YHWH. ⁸And when you make a son of the herd a burnt-offering, or a sacrifice for separating a vow, or peace-offerings to YHWH, ⁹then he has brought near for the son of the herd a present of three-tenth parts of flour mixed with a half of the hin of oil; ¹⁰and you bring a half of the hin of wine near for a drink-offering, [for] a fire-offering of refreshing fragrance to YHWH; ¹¹thus it is done for one ox, or for one ram, or for a lamb of the sheep or of the goats. ¹²According to the number that you prepare, so you do to each, according to their number; ¹³every native does thus with these, for bringing a fire-offering near of refreshing fragrance to YHWH; ¹⁴and when a sojourner sojourns with you, or whoever [is] in your midst throughout your generations, and he has made a fire-offering of refreshing fragrance to YHWH, as you do so he does. ¹⁵One statute is for you of the congregation and for the sojourner who is sojourning, a continuous statute throughout your generations: as you [are] so is the sojourner before YHWH; ¹⁶one law and one ordinance is for you and for the sojourner who is sojourning with you." ¹⁷And YHWH speaks to Moses, saying, ¹⁸"Speak to the sons of Israel, and you have said to them: In your coming into the land to where I am bringing you in, ¹⁹then it has been, in your eating of the bread of the land, you raise up a raised-offering to YHWH; ²⁰you raise up a cake of the first of your dough [as] a raised-offering; as the raised-offering of a threshing-floor, so you raise it up. ²¹You give to YHWH from the first of your dough [as] a raised-offering throughout your generations. ²²And when you err, and do not do all these commands which YHWH has spoken to Moses— ²³the whole that YHWH has charged on you by the hand of Moses, from the day that YHWH has commanded and from now on, throughout your generations— ²⁴then it has been, if from the eyes of the congregation it has been done through ignorance, that all the congregation has prepared one bullock, a son of the herd,

for a burnt-offering, for refreshing fragrance to YHWH, and its present, and its drink-offering, according to the ordinance, and one kid of the goats for a sin-offering. ²⁵And the priest has made atonement for all the congregation of the sons of Israel, and it has been forgiven them, for it [is] ignorance, and they have brought in their offering, a fire-offering to YHWH, and their sin-offering before YHWH for their ignorance; ²⁶and it has been forgiven to all the congregation of the sons of Israel and to the sojourner who is sojourning in their midst, for that all the people [did it] through ignorance. ²⁷And if one person sins through ignorance, then he has brought a female goat near, daughter of a year, for a sin-offering; ²⁸and the priest has made atonement for the person who is erring, in his sinning through ignorance before YHWH, by making atonement for him, and it has been forgiven him; ²⁹one law is for yourselves—for the native among the sons of Israel and for the sojourner who is sojourning in their midst—for him who is doing [anything] through ignorance. ³⁰And the person who does [evil] with a high hand—of the native or of the sojourner—he is reviling YHWH, and that person has been cut off from the midst of his people; ³¹because he despised the word of YHWH and has broken His command, that person is certainly cut off; his iniquity [is] on him." ³²And the sons of Israel are in the wilderness, and they find a man gathering wood on the Sabbath day, ³³and those finding him gathering wood bring him near to Moses, and to Aaron, and to all the congregation, ³⁴and they place him in confinement, for it [is] not explained what is [to be] done to him. ³⁵And YHWH says to Moses, "The man is certainly put to death [by] all the congregation stoning him with stones at the outside of the camp." ³⁶And all the congregation brings him out to the outside of the camp and stone him with stones, and he dies, as YHWH has commanded Moses. ³⁷And YHWH speaks to Moses, saying, ³⁸"Speak to the sons of Israel, and you have commanded to them, and they have made fringes on the skirts of their garments for themselves, throughout their generations, and they have put a ribbon of blue on the fringe of the skirt, ³⁹and it has been to you for a fringe, and you have seen it, and have remembered all the commands of YHWH, and have done them, and you do not search after your heart and after your eyes, after which you are going whoring, ⁴⁰so that you remember and have done all My commands, and you have been holy to your God. ⁴¹I [am] your God YHWH, who has brought you out from the land of Egypt to become your God; I [am] your God YHWH."

CHAPTER 16

¹And Korah, son of Izhar, son of Kohath, son of Levi, takes both Dathan and Abiram sons of Eliab, and On son of Peleth, sons of Reuben, ²and they rise up before Moses with men of the sons of Israel, two hundred and fifty princes of the congregation, called of the convention, men of renown, ³and they are assembled against Moses and against Aaron, and say to them, "Enough of you! For all the congregation—all of them [are] holy, and YHWH [is] in their midst; and why do you lift yourselves up above the assembly of YHWH?" ⁴And Moses hears, and falls on his face, ⁵and he speaks to Korah and to all his congregation, saying, "Indeed, [in the] morning YHWH may cause [you] to know those who are His and him who is holy, and has brought [him] near to Him; even him whom He fixes on He brings near to Him. ⁶Do this: take censers for yourselves—Korah and all his company—⁷and put fire in them and put incense on them before YHWH tomorrow, and it has been, the man whom YHWH chooses, he [is] the holy one—enough of you, sons of Levi!" ⁸And Moses says to Korah, "Now hear, sons of Levi; ⁹is it little to you that the God of Israel has separated you from the congregation of Israel to bring you near to Himself, to do the service of the Dwelling Place of YHWH, and to stand before the congregation to serve them? ¹⁰Indeed, He brings you near, and all your brothers, the sons of Levi, with you—and you have also sought the priesthood! ¹¹Therefore, you and all your congregation are meeting against YHWH; and Aaron, what [is] he, that you murmur against him?" ¹²And Moses sends to call for Dathan and for Abiram, sons of Eliab, and they say, "We do not come up! ¹³Is it little that you have brought us up out of a land flowing with milk and honey, to put us to death in a wilderness, that you also certainly make yourself prince over us? ¹⁴Indeed, you have not brought us into a land flowing with milk and honey, nor do you give an inheritance of field and vineyard to us; do you pick out the eyes of these men? We do not come up!" ¹⁵And it is very displeasing to Moses, and he says to YHWH, "Do not turn to their present; I have not taken one donkey from them, nor have I afflicted one of them." ¹⁶And Moses says to Korah, "You and all your congregation, be [present] before YHWH—you, and they, and Aaron—tomorrow; ¹⁷and let each take his censer and you have put incense on them, and each has brought his censer near before YHWH—two hundred and fifty censers; indeed, you and Aaron, each [with] his censer." ¹⁸And they each take his censer, and put fire on them, and lay incense on them, and they stand at the opening of the Tent of Meeting with Moses and Aaron. ¹⁹And Korah assembles all the congregation against them at the opening of the Tent of Meeting, and the glory of YHWH is seen by all the congregation. ²⁰And YHWH speaks to Moses and to Aaron, saying, ²¹"Be separated from the midst of this congregation, and I consume them in a moment"; ²²and they fall on their faces, and say, "God, God of the spirits of all flesh—one man sins, and are You angry against all the congregation?" ²³And YHWH speaks to Moses, saying, ²⁴"Speak to the congregation, saying, Go up from around the dwelling place of Korah, Dathan, and Abiram." ²⁵And Moses rises, and goes to Dathan and Abiram, and [the] elderly of Israel go after him, ²⁶and he speaks to the congregation, saying, "Now turn aside from the tents of these wicked men, and do not come against anything that they have, lest you are consumed in all their sins." ²⁷And they go up from the dwelling place of Korah, Dathan, and Abiram, from all around, and Dathan and Abiram have come out, standing at the opening of their tents, with their wives, and their sons, and their infants. ²⁸And Moses says, "By this you know that YHWH has sent me to do all these works, that [they are] not from my own heart; ²⁹if these die according to the death of all men, or the charge of all men is charged on them, YHWH has not sent me; ³⁰but if YHWH does a strange thing, and the ground has opened her mouth and swallowed them and all that they have, and they have gone down alive to Sheol, then you have known that these men have despised YHWH." ³¹And it comes to pass at his finishing speaking all these words, that the ground which [is] under them cleaves, ³²and the earth opens her mouth and swallows them, and their houses, and all the men who [are] for Korah, and all the goods, ³³and they go down—they and all that they have—alive to Sheol, and the earth closes over them, and they perish from the midst of the assembly; ³⁴and all Israel who [are] around them have fled at their voice, for they said, "Lest the earth swallow us"; ³⁵and fire has come out from YHWH and consumes the two hundred and fifty men bringing the incense near. ³⁶And YHWH speaks to Moses, saying, ³⁷"Say to Eleazar son of Aaron the priest to lift up the censers from the midst of the burning and scatter the fire away, for they have been hallowed. ³⁸[As for] the censers of these sinners against their own souls, indeed, they have made them [into] spread-out plates [for] a covering for the altar, for they have brought them near before YHWH, and they are hallowed; and they become a sign to the sons of Israel." ³⁹And Eleazar the priest takes the bronze censers which they who are burned had brought near, and they spread them out [for] a covering for the altar— ⁴⁰a memorial to the sons of Israel, so that a stranger who is not of the seed of Aaron does not draw near to make incense before YHWH, and is not as Korah and as his congregation, as YHWH has spoken by the hand of Moses to him. ⁴¹And on the next day all the congregation of the sons of Israel murmurs against Moses and against Aaron, saying, "You have put the people of YHWH to death." ⁴²And it comes to pass, in the congregation being assembled against Moses and against Aaron, that they turn toward the Tent of Meeting, and behold, the cloud has covered it and the glory of YHWH is seen; ⁴³and Moses comes—Aaron also—to the front of the Tent of Meeting. ⁴⁴And YHWH speaks to Moses, saying, ⁴⁵"Get up from the midst of this congregation, and I consume them in a moment"; and they fall on their faces, ⁴⁶and Moses says to Aaron, "Take the censer and put fire on it from off the altar, and place incense, and go quickly to the congregation and make atonement for them, for the wrath has gone out from the presence of YHWH—the plague has begun." ⁴⁷And Aaron takes [it] as Moses

has spoken, and runs to the midst of the assembly, and behold, the plague has begun among the people; and he gives the incense, and makes atonement for the people, ⁴⁸and stands between the dead and the living, and the plague is restrained; ⁴⁹and those who die by the plague are fourteen thousand and seven hundred, apart from those who die for the matter of Korah; ⁵⁰and Aaron turns back to Moses, to the opening of the Tent of Meeting, and the plague has been restrained.

CHAPTER 17

¹And YHWH speaks to Moses, saying, ²"Speak to the sons of Israel, and take a rod from each of them, for a father's house, from all their princes, for the house of their fathers—twelve rods; you write the name of each on his rod, ³and you write Aaron's name on the tribe of Levi; for one rod [is] for the head of their fathers' house. ⁴And you have placed them in the Tent of Meeting before the Testimony, where I meet with you. ⁵And it has come to pass, the man's rod on whom I fix flourishes, and I have caused the murmurings of the sons of Israel, which they are murmuring against you, to cease from off Me." ⁶And Moses speaks to the sons of Israel, and all their princes give to him one rod for a prince, one rod for a prince, for their fathers' house—twelve rods; and the rod of Aaron [is] in the midst of their rods; ⁷and Moses places the rods before YHWH in the Tent of the Testimony. ⁸And it comes to pass, on the next day, that Moses goes into the Tent of the Testimony, and behold, the rod of Aaron has flourished for the house of Levi, and brings out a bud, and blossoms [with] a blossom, and produces almonds; ⁹and Moses brings out all the rods from before YHWH to all the sons of Israel, and they look, and each takes his rod. ¹⁰And YHWH says to Moses, "Put back the rod of Aaron before the Testimony, for a charge, for a sign to the sons of rebellion, and you remove their murmurings from off Me, and they do not die"; ¹¹and Moses does as YHWH has commanded him; so he has done. ¹²And the sons of Israel speak to Moses, saying, "Behold, we have expired, we have perished, all of us have perished! ¹³Any who is at all drawing near to the Dwelling Place of YHWH dies; have we not been consumed—to expire?"

CHAPTER 18

¹And YHWH says to Aaron, "You, and your sons, and the house of your father with you, bear the iniquity of the sanctuary; and you and your sons with you bear the iniquity of your priesthood; ²and also your brothers, the tribe of Levi, the tribe of your father, bring near with you, and they are joined to you, and serve you, even you and your sons with you, before the Tent of the Testimony. ³And they have kept your charge, and the charge of all the tent; only, they do not come near to the vessels of the holy place and to the altar, and they do not die, either they or you; ⁴and they have been joined to you and have kept the charge of the Tent of Meeting for all the service of the tent; and a stranger does not come near to you; ⁵and you have kept the charge of the holy place and the charge of the altar, and there is no more wrath against the sons of Israel. ⁶And I, behold, have taken your brothers the Levites from the midst of the sons of Israel; they are a gift given to you by YHWH to do the service of the Tent of Meeting; ⁷and you and your sons with you keep your priesthood for everything of the altar and within the veil, and you have served; I make your priesthood a gift [for] service; and the stranger who is coming near is put to death." ⁸And YHWH speaks to Aaron: "And I, behold, have given to you the charge of My raised-offerings, of all the hallowed things of the sons of Israel—I have given them to you and to your sons for the anointing, by a continuous statute. ⁹This is yours from the most holy things, from the fire: all their offering, of all their present, and of all their sin-offering, and of all their guilt-offering, which they give back to Me, is most holy to you and to your sons; ¹⁰you eat it among the most holy things; every male eats it; it is holy to you. ¹¹And this [is] yours: the raised-offering of their gift, with all the wave-offerings of the sons of Israel; I have given them to you, and to your sons, and to your daughters with you, by a continuous statute; every clean one in your house eats it; ¹²all the best of the oil, and all the best of the new wine, and wheat—their first-[fruits] which they give to YHWH—I have given them to you. ¹³The first-fruits of all that [is] in their land, which they bring to YHWH, are yours; every clean one in your house eats it; ¹⁴every devoted thing in Israel is yours; ¹⁵everyone opening a womb of all flesh which they bring near to YHWH, among man and among beast, is yours; only, you certainly ransom the firstborn of man, and you ransom the firstling of the unclean beast. ¹⁶And their ransomed ones from a son of a month, you ransom with your valuation [for] five shekels of silver, by the shekel of the holy place; it [is] twenty gerahs. ¹⁷Only, the firstling of a cow, or the firstling of a sheep, or the firstling of a goat, you do not ransom, they [are] holy: you sprinkle their blood on the altar, and you make incense of their fat [as] a fire-offering of refreshing fragrance to YHWH; ¹⁸and their flesh is yours, as the breast of the wave-offering and as the right leg are yours. ¹⁹All the raised-offerings of the holy things, which the sons of Israel lift up to YHWH, I have given to you, and to your sons, and to your daughters with you, by a continuous statute—a covenant of salt; it [is] continuous before YHWH to you and to your seed with you." ²⁰And YHWH says to Aaron, "You do not inherit in their land, and you do not have a portion in their midst: I [am] your portion and your inheritance in the midst of the sons of Israel; ²¹and to the sons of Levi, behold, have given all the tenth in Israel for inheritance in exchange for their service which they are serving—the service of the Tent of Meeting. ²²And the sons of Israel no longer come near to the Tent of Meeting, to bear sin, to die, ²³and the Levites have done the service of the Tent of Meeting, and they bear their iniquity; [it is] a continuous statute throughout your generations that they have no inheritance in the midst of the sons of Israel; ²⁴but the tithe of the sons of Israel which they lift up to YHWH, a raised-offering, I have given to the Levites for inheritance; therefore I have said of them, They have no inheritance in the midst of the sons of Israel." ²⁵And YHWH speaks to Moses, saying, ²⁶"And you speak to the Levites, and you have said to them: When you take the tithe from the sons of Israel which I have given to you from them for your inheritance, then you have lifted up the raised-offering of YHWH from it, a tithe of the tithe; ²⁷and your raised-offering has been reckoned to you as grain from the threshing-floor and as the fullness from the wine-vat; ²⁸so you lift up—you also—the raised-offering of YHWH from all your tithes which you receive from the sons of Israel; and you have given the raised-offering of YHWH from it to Aaron the priest; ²⁹out of all your gifts you lift up every raised-offering of YHWH, out of all its fat—its hallowed part—out of it. ³⁰And you have said to them: In your lifting up its fat out of it, then it has been reckoned to the Levites as increase of a threshing-floor and as increase of a wine-vat; ³¹and you have eaten it in every place, you and your households, for it [is] your hire in exchange for your service in the Tent of Meeting; ³²and you bear no sin for it in your lifting up its fat out of it, but you do not defile the holy things of the sons of Israel, and you do not die."

CHAPTER 19

¹And YHWH speaks to Moses and to Aaron, saying, ²"This [is] a statute of the law which YHWH has commanded, saying, Speak to the sons of Israel, and they bring a red cow to you, a perfect one, in which there is no blemish, on which no yoke has gone up; ³and you have given it to Eleazar the priest, and he has brought it out to the outside of the camp, and has slaughtered it before him. ⁴And Eleazar the priest has taken of its blood with his finger, and has sprinkled [it] toward the front of the face of the Tent of Meeting from its blood seven times; ⁵and [one] has burned the cow before his eyes; her skin, and her flesh, and her blood, besides her dung, he burns; ⁶and the priest has taken cedar wood, and hyssop, and scarlet, and has cast [them] into the midst of the burning of the cow; ⁷and the priest has washed his garments, and has bathed his flesh with water, and afterward comes into the camp, and the priest is unclean until the evening; ⁸and he who is burning it washes his garments with water, and has bathed his flesh with water, and is unclean until the evening. ⁹And a clean man has gathered the ashes of the cow, and has placed [them] at the outside of the camp in a clean place, and it has become a charge for the congregation of the sons of Israel for waters of separation—it [is for] sin; ¹⁰and he who is gathering the ashes of the heifer has washed his garments and is unclean until the evening; and it has been to the sons of Israel and to the sojourner who is sojourning in their midst for a continuous statute. ¹¹He who is coming against the dead body of any man is unclean [for] seven days;

¹²he cleanses himself for it on the third day and on the seventh day, [and] he is clean; and if he does not cleanse himself on the third day and on the seventh day, he is not clean. ¹³Anyone who is coming against the dead, against the body of man who dies, and does not cleanse himself, he has defiled the Dwelling Place of YHWH, and that person has been cut off from Israel, for water of separation is not sprinkled on him; he is unclean; his uncleanness [is] still on him. ¹⁴This [is] the law when a man dies in a tent: everyone who is coming into the tent and all that [is] in the tent are unclean [for] seven days; ¹⁵and every open vessel which has no covering of thread on it is unclean. ¹⁶And everyone on the face of the field who comes against the pierced of a sword, or against the dead, or against a bone of man, or against a grave, is unclean [for] seven days; ¹⁷and for the unclean person they have taken from the ashes of the burning of the [cow], and he has put running water over it into a vessel; ¹⁸and a clean person has taken hyssop, and has dipped [it] in water, and has sprinkled [it] on the tent, and on all the vessels, and on the persons who have been there, and on him who is coming against a bone, or against one pierced, or against the dead, or against a grave. ¹⁹And the clean has sprinkled [it] on the unclean on the third day and on the seventh day, and has cleansed him on the seventh day, and he has washed his garments, and has bathed with water, and has been clean in the evening. ²⁰And the man who is unclean and does not cleanse himself, indeed, that person has been cut off from the midst of the assembly; for he has defiled the sanctuary of YHWH; water of separation is not sprinkled on him; he [is] unclean. ²¹And it has been for a continuous statute to them, that he who is sprinkling the water of separation washes his garments, and he who is coming against the water of separation is unclean until the evening, ²²and all against which the unclean person comes is unclean, and the person who is coming against [it] is unclean until the evening."

CHAPTER 20

¹And the sons of Israel, all the congregation, come [into] the wilderness of Zin in the first month, and the people abide in Kadesh; and Miriam dies there and is buried there. ²And there has been no water for the congregation, and they are assembled against Moses and against Aaron, ³and the people strive with Moses and speak, saying, "And oh that we had expired when our brothers expired before YHWH! ⁴And why have you brought in the assembly of YHWH to this wilderness to die there, we and our beasts? ⁵And why have you brought us up out of Egypt to bring us to this evil place? [It is] not a place of seed, and fig, and vine, and pomegranate; and there is no water to drink." ⁶And Moses and Aaron go in from the presence of the assembly to the opening of the Tent of Meeting and fall on their faces, and the glory of YHWH is seen by them. ⁷And YHWH speaks to Moses, saying, ⁸"Take the rod and assemble the congregation—you and your brother Aaron—and you have spoken to the rock before their eyes, and it has given its water, and you have brought out water to them from the rock, and have watered the congregation and their beasts." ⁹And Moses takes the rod from before YHWH as He has commanded him, ¹⁰and Moses and Aaron assemble the assembly to the front of the rock, and he says to them, "Now hear, O rebels, do we bring out water to you from this rock?" ¹¹And Moses lifts up his hand and strikes the rock with his rod twice; and much water comes out, and the congregation drinks, and their beasts [drink]. ¹²And YHWH says to Moses and to Aaron, "Because you have not believed in Me to sanctify Me before the eyes of the sons of Israel, therefore you do not bring in this assembly to the land which I have given to them." ¹³These [are] the waters of Meribah, because the sons of Israel have "striven" with YHWH, and He is sanctified among them. ¹⁴And Moses sends messengers from Kadesh to the king of Edom, "Thus said your brother Israel: You have known all the travail which has found us, ¹⁵that our fathers go down to Egypt, and we dwell in Egypt [for] many days, and the Egyptians do evil to us and to our fathers; ¹⁶then we cry to YHWH, and He hears our voice, and sends a Messenger, and is bringing us out of Egypt; and behold, we [are] in Kadesh, a city [in] the extremity of your border. ¹⁷Please let us pass over through your land; we do not pass over through a field or through a vineyard, nor do we drink waters of a well; we go the way of the king, we do not turn aside [to] the right or left until we pass over your border." ¹⁸And Edom says to him, "You do not pass over through me, lest I come out to meet you with the sword." ¹⁹And the sons of Israel say to him, "We go in the highway, and if we drink of your waters—I and my livestock—then I have given their price; only, let me pass over on my feet, nothing [more]." ²⁰And he says, "You do not pass over"; and Edom comes out to meet him with many people and with a strong hand; ²¹and Edom refuses to permit Israel to pass over through his border, and Israel turns aside from off him. ²²And the sons of Israel, all the congregation, journey from Kadesh and come to Mount Hor, ²³and YHWH speaks to Moses and to Aaron in Mount Hor, on the border of the land of Edom, saying, ²⁴"Aaron is gathered to his people, for he does not go into the land which I have given to the sons of Israel, because that you provoked My mouth at the waters of Meribah. ²⁵Take Aaron and his son Eleazar, and cause them to go up Mount Hor, ²⁶and strip Aaron of his garments, and you have clothed his son Eleazar [with] them, and Aaron is gathered, and dies there." ²⁷And Moses does as YHWH has commanded, and they go up to Mount Hor before the eyes of all the congregation, ²⁸and Moses strips Aaron of his garments, and clothes his son Eleazar with them, and Aaron dies there on the top of the mountain; and Moses comes down—Eleazar also—from the mountain, ²⁹and all the congregation sees that Aaron has expired, and all the house of Israel laments Aaron [for] thirty days.

CHAPTER 21

¹And the Canaanite, king of Arad, dwelling in the south, hears that Israel has come the way of the Atharim, and he fights against Israel, and takes [some] of them captive. ²And Israel vows a vow to YHWH and says, "If You certainly give this people into my hand, then I have devoted their cities"; ³and YHWH listens to the voice of Israel and gives up the Canaanite, and he devotes them and their cities, and calls the name of the place Hormah. ⁴And they journey from Mount Hor, the way of the Red Sea, to go around the land of Edom, and the soul of the people is short in the way, ⁵and the people speak against God and against Moses, "Why have you brought us up out of Egypt to die in a wilderness? For there is no bread, and there is no water, and our soul has been weary of this light bread." ⁶And YHWH sends the burning serpents among the people, and they bite the people, and many people of Israel die; ⁷and the people come to Moses and say, "We have sinned, for we have spoken against YHWH and against you; pray to YHWH that He turns the serpent aside from us"; and Moses prays in behalf of the people. ⁸And YHWH says to Moses, "Make a burning [serpent] for yourself, and set it on an ensign; and it has been, everyone who is bitten and has seen it—he has lived." ⁹And Moses makes a serpent of bronze, and sets it on the ensign, and it has been, if the serpent has bitten any man, and he has looked expectantly to the serpent of bronze—he has lived. ¹⁰And the sons of Israel journey and encamp in Oboth. ¹¹And they journey from Oboth and encamp in Ije-Abarim, in the wilderness that [is] on the front of Moab, at the rising of the sun. ¹²From there they have journeyed and encamp in the Valley of Zared. ¹³From there they have journeyed and encamp beyond Arnon, which [is] in the wilderness which is coming out of the border of the Amorite, for Arnon [is] the border of Moab, between Moab and the Amorite; ¹⁴therefore it is said in [the] scroll of the Wars of YHWH: "Waheb in Suphah, || And the brooks of Arnon; ¹⁵And the spring of the brooks, || Which turned aside to the dwelling of Ar, || And has leaned to the border of Moab." ¹⁶And from there [they journeyed] to Beer; it [is] the well [concerning] which YHWH said to Moses, "Gather the people, and I give water to them." ¹⁷Then Israel sings this song: "Spring up, O well, || Let all answer to it! ¹⁸A well—princes have dug it, || Nobles of the people have prepared it, || With the lawgiver, with their staffs." And from the wilderness [they journeyed] to Mattanah, ¹⁹and from Mattanah to Nahaliel, and from Nahaliel to Bamoth, ²⁰and from Bamoth, in the valley which [is] in the field of Moab, [to] the top of Pisgah, which has looked on the front of the wilderness. ²¹And Israel sends messengers to Sihon king of the Amorite, saying, ²²"Let me pass through your land, we do not turn aside into a field or into a vineyard; we do not drink waters of a well; we go in the king's way until we pass

NUMBERS

over your border." ²³And Sihon has not permitted Israel to pass through his border, and Sihon gathers all his people, and comes out to meet Israel in the wilderness, and comes to Jahaz, and fights against Israel. ²⁴And Israel strikes him by the mouth of the sword, and possesses his land from Arnon to Jabbok—to the sons of Ammon; for the border of the sons of Ammon [is] strong. ²⁵And Israel takes all these cities, and Israel dwells in all the cities of the Amorite, in Heshbon and in all its villages; ²⁶for Heshbon is a city of Sihon king of the Amorite, and he has fought against the former king of Moab, and takes all his land out of his hand as far as Arnon; ²⁷therefore those using allegories say: "Enter Heshbon, || Let the city of Sihon be built and ready, ²⁸For fire has gone out from Heshbon, || A flame from the city of Sihon, || It has consumed Ar of Moab, || Owners of the high places of Arnon. ²⁹Woe to you, O Moab, || You have perished, O people of Chemosh! He has given his sons [as] fugitives, || And his daughters into captivity, || To Sihon king of the Amorite! ³⁰And we shoot them; Heshbon has perished as far as Dibon, || And we make desolate as far as Nophah, || Which [is] as far as Medeba." ³¹And Israel dwells in the land of the Amorite, ³²and Moses sends to spy out Jaazer, and they capture its villages, and dispossess the Amorite who [is] there, ³³and turn and go up the way of Bashan, and Og king of Bashan comes out to meet them, he and all his people, to battle [at] Edrei. ³⁴And YHWH says to Moses, "Do not fear him, for into your hand I have given him, and all his people, and his land, and you have done to him as you have done to Sihon king of the Amorite, who is dwelling in Heshbon." ³⁵And they strike him, and his sons, and all his people, until he has no remnant left to him, and they possess his land.

CHAPTER 22

¹And the sons of Israel journey and encamp in the plains of Moab beyond the Jordan, [by] Jericho. ²And Balak son of Zippor sees all that Israel has done to the Amorite, ³and Moab is exceedingly afraid of the presence of the people, for it [is] numerous; and Moab is distressed by the presence of the sons of Israel, ⁴and Moab says to [the] elderly of Midian, "Now the assembly licks up all that is around us, as the ox licks up the green thing of the field." And Balak son of Zippor [is] king of Moab at that time, ⁵and he sends messengers to Balaam son of Beor, to Pethor, which [is] by the River of the land of the sons of his people, to call for him, saying, "Behold, a people has come out of Egypt; behold, it has covered the eye of the land, and it is abiding in front of me; ⁶and now, come, please curse this people for me, for it [is] mightier than I. It may be I prevail, [and] we strike it, and I cast it out from the land; for I have known that which you bless is blessed, and that which you curse is cursed." ⁷And [the] elderly of Moab and [the] elderly of Midian go with divinations in their hand, and they come to Balaam and speak the words of Balak to him, ⁸and he says to them, "Lodge here tonight, and I have brought you back word, as YHWH speaks to me"; and the princes of Moab abide with Balaam. ⁹And God comes to Balaam and says, "Who [are] these men with you?" ¹⁰And Balaam says to God, "Balak, son of Zippor, king of Moab, has sent to me: ¹¹Behold, the people that is coming out from Egypt and covers the eye of the land—now come, pierce it for me; it may be I am able to fight against it and have cast it out"; ¹²and God says to Balaam, "You do not go with them; you do not curse the people, for it [is] blessed." ¹³And Balaam rises in the morning and says to the princes of Balak, "Go to your land, for YHWH is refusing to permit me to go with you"; ¹⁴and the princes of Moab rise, and come to Balak, and say, "Balaam is refusing to come with us." ¹⁵And Balak adds yet to send princes, more numerous and honored than these, ¹⁶and they come to Balaam and say to him, "Thus said Balak son of Zippor: Please do not be withheld from coming to me, ¹⁷for I honor you very greatly, and all that you say to me I do; and come, please pierce this people for me." ¹⁸And Balaam answers and says to the servants of Balak, "If Balak gives to me the fullness of his house of silver and gold, I am not able to pass over the command of my God YHWH, to do a little or a great thing; ¹⁹and now, please abide in this [place], you also, tonight, then I know what YHWH is adding to speak with me." ²⁰And God comes to Balaam by night and says to him, "If the men have come to call for you, rise, go with them, and only the thing which I speak to you—do it." ²¹And Balaam rises in the morning, and saddles his donkey, and goes with the princes of Moab, ²²and the anger of God burns because he is going, and the Messenger of YHWH stations Himself in the way for an adversary to him, and he is riding on his donkey, and two of his servants [are] with him, ²³and the donkey sees the Messenger of YHWH standing in the way with His drawn sword in His hand, and the donkey turns aside out of the way and goes into a field, and Balaam strikes the donkey to turn it aside into the way. ²⁴And the Messenger of YHWH stands in a narrow path of the vineyards, [with] a wall on this [side] and a wall on that [side], ²⁵and the donkey sees the Messenger of YHWH, and is pressed to the wall, and presses Balaam's foot to the wall, and he adds to strike her; ²⁶and the Messenger of YHWH adds to pass over, and stands in a narrow place where there is no way to turn aside [to] the right or left, ²⁷and the donkey sees the Messenger of YHWH, and crouches under Balaam, and the anger of Balaam burns, and he strikes the donkey with a staff. ²⁸And YHWH opens the mouth of the donkey, and she says to Balaam, "What have I done to you that you have struck me these three times?" ²⁹And Balaam says to the donkey, "Because you have rolled yourself against me; oh that there were a sword in my hand, for now I had slain you"; ³⁰and the donkey says to Balaam, "Am I not your donkey on which you have ridden since [I became] yours, even to this day? Have I at all been accustomed to do thus to you?" And he says, "No." ³¹And YHWH uncovers the eyes of Balaam, and he sees the Messenger of YHWH standing in the way with His drawn sword in His hand, and he bows and pays respect, to his face; ³²and the Messenger of YHWH says to him, "Why have you struck your donkey these three times? Behold, I have come out for an adversary, for [your] way has been perverse before Me, ³³and the donkey sees Me and turns aside at My presence these three times; unless she had turned aside from My presence, surely I had also slain you now, and kept her alive." ³⁴And Balaam says to the Messenger of YHWH, "I have sinned, for I did not know that You [are] standing to meet me in the way; and now, if [it is] evil in Your eyes, I turn back by myself." ³⁵And the Messenger of YHWH says to Balaam, "Go with the men; and only the word which I speak to you—it you speak"; and Balaam goes with the princes of Balak. ³⁶And Balak hears that Balaam has come, and goes out to meet him, to a city of Moab, which [is] on the border of Arnon, which [is] in the extremity of the border; ³⁷and Balak says to Balaam, "Did I not diligently send to you to call for you? Why did you not come to me? Am I not truly able to honor you?" ³⁸And Balaam says to Balak, "Behold, I have come to you; now, am I able to speak anything at all? The word which God sets in my mouth—it I speak." ³⁹And Balaam goes with Balak, and they come to Kirjath-Huzoth, ⁴⁰and Balak sacrifices oxen and sheep, and sends [some] to Balaam and to the princes who [are] with him; ⁴¹and it comes to pass in the morning, that Balak takes Balaam and causes him to go up [to] the high places of Ba'al, and he sees the extremity of the people from there.

CHAPTER 23

¹And Balaam says to Balak, "Build seven altars for me in this [place], and prepare seven bullocks and seven rams for me in this [place]." ²And Balak does as Balaam has spoken, and Balak—Balaam also—offers a bullock and a ram on the altar, ³and Balaam says to Balak, "Station yourself by your burnt-offering and I go on, it may be YHWH comes to meet me, and the thing which He shows me I have declared to you"; and he goes [to] a high place. ⁴And God comes to Balaam, and he says to Him, "I have arranged the seven altars, and I offer a bullock and a ram on the altar"; ⁵and YHWH puts a word in the mouth of Balaam and says, "Return to Balak, and thus you speak." ⁶And he returns to him, and behold, he is standing by his burnt-offering, he and all the princes of Moab. ⁷And he takes up his allegory and says: "Balak king of Moab leads me from Aram; From mountains of the east. Come—curse Jacob for me, || And come—be indignant [with] Israel. ⁸How do I pierce [when] God has not pierced? And how am I indignant [when] YHWH has not been indignant? ⁹For from the top of rocks I see him, || And from heights I behold him; Behold a people! He dwells alone, || And does not reckon himself among nations. ¹⁰Who has counted the dust of Jacob, || And the number of the fourth of Israel? Let me die the death of upright ones, || And let my last end be like his!" ¹¹And Balak says to Balaam, "What have you

done to me? I have taken you to pierce my enemies, and behold, you have certainly blessed"; ¹²and he answers and says, "That which YHWH puts in my mouth—do I not take heed to speak it?" ¹³And Balak says to him, "Come! Come to another place with me, from where you see it—you see only its extremity, and you do not see all of it, and pierce it for me there"; ¹⁴and he takes him [to] the field of Zophim, to the top of Pisgah, and builds seven altars, and offers a bullock and a ram on the altar. ¹⁵And he says to Balak, "Station yourself here by your burnt-offering, and I meet [Him] there"; ¹⁶and YHWH comes to Balaam, and sets a word in his mouth, and says, "Return to Balak, and thus you speak." ¹⁷And he comes to him, and behold, he is standing by his burnt-offering, and the princes of Moab [are] with him, and Balak says to him: "What has YHWH spoken?" ¹⁸And he takes up his allegory and says: "Rise, Balak, and hear; Give ear to me, son of Zippor. ¹⁹God [is] not a man—and lies, || And a son of man—and relents! Has He said—and He does not do [it]? And spoken—and He does not confirm it? ²⁰Behold, I have received [only] to bless; Indeed, He blesses, and I cannot reverse it. ²¹He has not beheld iniquity in Jacob, || Nor has He seen perverseness in Israel; His God YHWH [is] with him, || And a shout of a king [is] in him. ²²God is bringing them out from Egypt, || As the swiftness of a wild ox for him; ²³For no enchantment [is] against Jacob, || Nor divination against Israel; At the time it is said of Jacob and Israel, || O what God has worked! ²⁴Behold, the people rises as a lioness, || And he lifts himself up as a lion; He does not lie down until he eats prey, || And drinks blood of pierced ones." ²⁵And Balak says to Balaam, "Neither pierce it at all, nor bless it at all"; ²⁶and Balaam answers and says to Balak, "Have I not spoken to you, saying, All that YHWH speaks—I do it?" ²⁷And Balak says to Balaam, "Please come, I take you to another place; it may be it is right in the eyes of God to pierce it for me from there." ²⁸And Balak takes Balaam to the top of Peor, which is looking on the front of the wilderness, ²⁹and Balaam says to Balak, "Build seven altars for me in this [place], and prepare seven bullocks and seven rams for me in this [place]"; ³⁰and Balak does as Balaam said, and he offers a bullock and a ram on an altar.

CHAPTER 24

¹And Balaam sees that [it is] good in the eyes of YHWH to bless Israel, and he has not gone as time by time to seek enchantments, and he sets his face toward the wilderness; ²and Balaam lifts up his eyes, and sees Israel dwelling by its tribes, and the Spirit of God is on him, ³and he takes up his allegory and says: "An affirmation of Balaam son of Beor, || And an affirmation of the man whose eyes are shut, ⁴An affirmation of him who is hearing sayings of God, || Who sees a vision of the Almighty, || Falling—and eyes uncovered: ⁵How good have been your tents, O Jacob, || Your dwelling places, O Israel; ⁶They have been stretched out as valleys, || As gardens by a river; As aloes YHWH has planted, || As cedars by waters; ⁷He makes water flow from his buckets, || And his seed [is] in many waters; And his King [is] higher than Gog [[or Agag]], || And his kingdom is exalted. ⁸God is bringing him out of Egypt, || As the swiftness of a wild ox for him, || He eats up nations—his adversaries, || And he breaks their bones, || And he strikes [with] his arrows. ⁹He has bent, he has lain down as a lion, || And as a lioness, who raises him up? He who is blessing you [is] blessed, || And he who is cursing you [is] cursed." ¹⁰And the anger of Balak burns against Balaam, and he strikes his hands; and Balak says to Balaam, "I called you to pierce my enemies, and behold, you have certainly blessed these three times; ¹¹and now, flee for yourself to your place; I have said, I greatly honor you, and behold, YHWH has kept you back from honor." ¹²And Balaam says to Balak, "Did I not also speak to your messengers whom you have sent to me, saying, ¹³If Balak gives to me the fullness of his house of silver and gold, I am not able to pass over the command of YHWH, to do good or evil of my own heart; that which YHWH speaks—it I speak? ¹⁴And now, behold, I am going to my people; come, I counsel you [concerning] that which this people does to your people in the latter end of the days." ¹⁵And he takes up his allegory and says: "An affirmation of Balaam son of Beor, || And an affirmation of the man whose eyes [are] shut; ¹⁶An affirmation of him who is hearing sayings of God, || And knowing knowledge of the Most High; He sees a vision of the Almighty, || Falling—and eyes uncovered: ¹⁷I see Him, but not now; I behold Him, but not near; A star has proceeded from Jacob, || And a scepter has risen from Israel, || And has struck corners of Moab, || And has destroyed all sons of Seth. ¹⁸And Edom has been a possession, || And Seir has been a possession [for] his enemies, || And Israel is doing valiantly; ¹⁹And [One] rules out of Jacob, || And has destroyed a remnant from the city." ²⁰And he sees Amalek, and takes up his allegory, and says: "Amalek [is] first [among] nations, || But his latter end—destruction forever." ²¹And he sees the Kenite, and takes up his allegory, and says: "Your dwelling [is] enduring, || And your nest is being set in a rock, ²²But the Kenite is for a burning; Until when does Asshur keep you captive?" ²³And he takes up his allegory and says: "Woe! Who lives when God does this? ²⁴But ships [come] from the side of Chittim, || And they have humbled Asshur, || And they have humbled Eber, || But it is also perishing forever." ²⁵And Balaam rises, and goes, and turns back to his place, and Balak has also gone on his way.

CHAPTER 25

¹And Israel dwells in Shittim, and the people begin to go whoring to daughters of Moab, ²and they call for the people to the sacrifices of their gods, and the people eat and bow themselves to their gods, ³and Israel is joined to Ba'al-Peor, and the anger of YHWH burns against Israel. ⁴And YHWH says to Moses, "Take all the chiefs of the people and hang them before YHWH in sight of the sun; and the fierceness of the anger of YHWH turns back from Israel." ⁵And Moses says to [the] judges of Israel, "Each slays his men who are joined to Ba'al-Peor." ⁶And behold, a man of the sons of Israel has come, and brings a Midianitess to his brothers before the eyes of Moses and before the eyes of all the congregation of the sons of Israel, who are weeping at the opening of the Tent of Meeting; ⁷and Phinehas, son of Eleazar, son of Aaron the priest, sees, and rises from the midst of the congregation, and takes a javelin in his hand, ⁸and goes in after the man of Israel to the hollow place, and pierces them both, the man of Israel and the woman—to her belly, and the plague is restrained from the sons of Israel; ⁹and the dead by the plague are twenty-four thousand. ¹⁰And YHWH speaks to Moses, saying, ¹¹"Phinehas, son of Eleazar, son of Aaron the priest, has turned back My fury from the sons of Israel by his being zealous with My zeal in their midst, and I have not consumed the sons of Israel in My zeal. ¹²Therefore say, Behold, I am giving My covenant of peace to him, ¹³and it has been to him and to his seed after him [for] a covenant of a continuous priesthood, because that he has been zealous for his God, and makes atonement for the sons of Israel." ¹⁴And the name of the man of Israel who is struck, who has been struck with the Midianitess, [is] Zimri son of Salu, prince of the house of a father of the Simeonite; ¹⁵and the name of the woman who is struck, the Midianitess, [is] Cozbi daughter of Zur; he [is] head of peoples of a father's house in Midian. ¹⁶And YHWH speaks to Moses, saying, ¹⁷"Distress the Midianites, and you have struck them, ¹⁸for they are adversaries to you with their frauds, [with] which they have acted fraudulently to you, concerning the matter of Peor and concerning the matter of Cozbi, daughter of a prince of Midian, their sister, who is struck in the day of the plague for the matter of Peor."

CHAPTER 26

¹And it comes to pass, after the plague, that YHWH speaks to Moses and to Eleazar son of Aaron the priest, saying, ²"Take a census of all the congregation of the sons of Israel, from a son of twenty years and upward, by the house of their fathers, everyone going out to the host in Israel." ³And Moses speaks—Eleazar the priest also—with them in the plains of Moab by the Jordan, [near] Jericho, saying, ⁴"From a son of twenty years and upward," as YHWH has commanded Moses and the sons of Israel who are coming out from the land of Egypt. ⁵Reuben, firstborn of Israel—sons of Reuben: of Enoch [is] the family of the Enochite; of Pallu the family of the Palluite; ⁶of Hezron the family of the Hezronite; of Carmi the family of the Carmite. ⁷These [are] families of the Reubenite, and their numbered ones are forty-three thousand and seven hundred and thirty. ⁸And the son of Pallu [is] Eliab; ⁹and the sons of Eliab [are] Nemuel, and Dathan, and Abiram; this [is that] Dathan and Abiram, called ones of the congregation, who have striven against Moses and against Aaron in the congregation of Korah, in their striving

against YHWH, ¹⁰and the earth opens her mouth, and swallows them and Korah, in the death of the congregation, in the fire consuming the two hundred and fifty men, and they become a sign; ¹¹but the sons of Korah did not die. ¹²Sons of Simeon by their families: of Nemuel [is] the family of the Nemuelite; of Jamin the family of the Jaminite; of Jachin the family of the Jachinite; ¹³of Zerah the family of the Zerahite; of Shaul the family of the Shaulite. ¹⁴These [are] families of the Simeonite—twenty-two thousand and two hundred. ¹⁵Sons of Gad by their families: of Zephon [is] the family of the Zephonite; of Haggi the family of the Haggite; of Shuni the family of the Shunite; ¹⁶of Ozni the family of the Oznite; of Eri the family of the Erite: ¹⁷of Arod the family of the Arodite; of Areli the family of the Arelite. ¹⁸These [are] families of the sons of Gad by their numbered ones—forty thousand and five hundred. ¹⁹Sons of Judah [are] Er and Onan; and Er dies—Onan also—in the land of Canaan. ²⁰And sons of Judah by their families are: of Shelah the family of the Shelanite; of Perez the family of the Perezite; of Zerah the family of the Zerahite; ²¹and sons of Perez are: of Hezron the family of the Hezronite; of Hamul the family of the Hamulite. ²²These [are] families of Judah by their numbered ones—seventy-six thousand and five hundred. ²³Sons of Issachar by their families: of Tola [is] the family of the Tolaite; of Pua the family of the Punite; ²⁴of Jashub the family of the Jashubite; of Shimron the family of the Shimronite. ²⁵These [are] families of Issachar by their numbered ones—sixty-four thousand and three hundred. ²⁶Sons of Zebulun by their families: of Sered [is] the family of the Sardite; of Elon the family of the Elonite; of Jahleel the family of the Jahleelite. ²⁷These [are] families of the Zebulunite by their numbered ones—sixty thousand and five hundred. ²⁸Sons of Joseph by their families [are] Manasseh and Ephraim. ²⁹Sons of Manasseh: of Machir [is] the family of the Machirite; and Machir has begotten Gilead; of Gilead [is] the family of the Gileadite. ³⁰These [are] sons of Gilead: of Jeezer [is] the family of the Jeezerite; of Helek the family of the Helekite; ³¹and of Asriel the family of the Asrielite; and of Shechem the family of the Shechemite; ³²and of Shemida the family of the Shemidaite; and of Hepher the family of the Hepherite. ³³And Zelophehad son of Hepher had no sons, but [only] daughters, and the names of the daughters of Zelophehad [are] Mahlah, and Noah, Hoglah, Milcah, and Tirzah. ³⁴These [are] families of Manasseh, and their numbered ones [are] fifty-two thousand and seven hundred. ³⁵These [are] sons of Ephraim by their families: of Shuthelah [is] the family of the Shuthelhite; of Becher the family of the Bachrite; of Tahan the family of the Tahanite. ³⁶And these [are] sons of Shuthelah: of Eran the family of the Eranite. ³⁷These [are] families of the sons of Ephraim by their numbered ones—thirty-two thousand and five hundred. These [are] sons of Joseph by their families. ³⁸Sons of Benjamin by their families: of Bela [is] the family of the Belaite; of Ashbel the family of the Ashbelite; of Ahiram the family of the Ahiramite; ³⁹of Shupham the family of the Shuphamite; of Hupham the family of the Huphamite. ⁴⁰And sons of Bela are Ard and Naaman: [of Ard is] the family of the Ardite; of Naaman the family of the Naamite. ⁴¹These [are] sons of Benjamin by their families, and their numbered ones [are] forty-five thousand and six hundred. ⁴²These [are] sons of Dan by their families: of Shuham [is] the family of the Shuhamite; these [are] families of Dan by their families; ⁴³all the families of the Shuhamite by their numbered ones—sixty-four thousand and four hundred. ⁴⁴Sons of Asher by their families: of Jimna [is] the family of the Jimnite; of Jesui the family of the Jesuite; of Beriah the family of the Beriite. ⁴⁵Of sons of Beriah: of Heber [is] the family of the Heberite; of Malchiel the family of the Malchielite. ⁴⁶And the name of the daughter of Asher [is] Sarah. ⁴⁷These [are] families of the sons of Asher by their numbered ones—fifty-three thousand and four hundred. ⁴⁸Sons of Naphtali by their families: of Jahzeel [is] the family of the Jahzeelite; of Guni the family of the Gunite; ⁴⁹of Jezer the family of the Jezerite; of Shillem the family of the Shillemite. ⁵⁰These [are] families of Naphtali by their families, and their numbered ones [are] forty-five thousand and four hundred. ⁵¹These [are] numbered ones of the sons of Israel—six hundred thousand and one thousand seven hundred and thirty. ⁵²And YHWH speaks to Moses, saying, ⁵³"The land is apportioned to these by inheritance, by the number of names; ⁵⁴to the many you increase their inheritance, and to the few you diminish their inheritance; each is given his inheritance according to his numbered ones. ⁵⁵Surely the land is apportioned by lot; they inherit by the names of the tribes of their fathers; ⁵⁶their inheritance is apportioned according to the lot between many and few." ⁵⁷And these [are] numbered ones of the Levite by their families: of Gershon [is] the family of the Gershonite; of Kohath the family of the Kohathite; of Merari the family of the Merarite. ⁵⁸These [are] families of the Levite: the family of the Libnite, the family of the Hebronite, the family of the Mahlite, the family of the Mushite, the family of the Korathite. And Kohath has begotten Amram, ⁵⁹and the name of Amram's wife is Jochebed, daughter of Levi, whom has been born to Levi in Egypt; and she bears to Amram Aaron, and Moses, and their sister Miriam. ⁶⁰And born to Aaron [are] Nadab, and Abihu, Eleazar, and Ithamar; ⁶¹and Nadab dies—Abihu also—in their bringing strange fire near before YHWH. ⁶²And their numbered ones are twenty-three thousand, every male from a son of a month and upwards, for they have not numbered themselves in the midst of the sons of Israel, because an inheritance has not been given to them in the midst of the sons of Israel. ⁶³These [are] those numbered by Moses and Eleazar the priest, who have numbered the sons of Israel in the plains of Moab by the Jordan, [near] Jericho; ⁶⁴and among these there has not been a man of those numbered by Moses and Aaron the priest, who numbered the sons of Israel in the wilderness of Sinai, ⁶⁵for YHWH said of them, "They certainly die in the wilderness"; and there has not been left a man of them, except Caleb son of Jephunneh and Joshua son of Nun.

CHAPTER 27

¹And daughters of Zelophehad son of Hepher, son of Gilead, son of Machir, son of Manasseh, of the families of Manasseh son of Joseph, draw near—and these [are] the names of his daughters: Mahlah, Noah, and Hoglah, and Milcah, and Tirzah— ²and stand before Moses, and before Eleazar the priest, and before the princes, and all the congregation, at the opening of the Tent of Meeting, saying, ³"Our father died in the wilderness, and he was not in the midst of the congregation who were gathered together against YHWH in the congregation of Korah, but he died for his own sin, and had no sons; ⁴why is the name of our father withdrawn from the midst of his family because he has no son? Give a possession to us in the midst of the brothers of our father"; ⁵and Moses brings their cause near before YHWH. ⁶And YHWH speaks to Moses, saying, ⁷"The daughters of Zelophehad are speaking correctly; you certainly give to them a possession of an inheritance in the midst of their father's brothers, and have caused the inheritance of their father to pass over to them. ⁸And you speak to the sons of Israel, saying, When a man dies and has no son, then you have caused his inheritance to pass over to his daughter; ⁹and if he has no daughter, then you have given his inheritance to his brothers; ¹⁰and if he has no brothers, then you have given his inheritance to his father's brothers; ¹¹and if his father has no brothers, then you have given his inheritance to his relation who is near to him of his family, and he has possessed it"; and it has been to the sons of Israel for a statute of judgment, as YHWH has commanded Moses. ¹²And YHWH says to Moses, "Go up to this Mount Abarim, and see the land which I have given to the sons of Israel; ¹³and you have seen it, and you have been gathered to your people, also you, as your brother Aaron has been gathered, ¹⁴because you provoked My mouth in the wilderness of Zin, in the strife of the congregation—to sanctify Me at the waters before their eyes"; they [are] the waters of Meribah, in Kadesh, in the wilderness of Zin. ¹⁵And Moses speaks to YHWH, saying, ¹⁶"YHWH, God of the spirits of all flesh, appoint a man over the congregation, ¹⁷who goes out before them, and who comes in before them, and who takes them out, and who brings them in, and the congregation of YHWH is not as sheep which have no shepherd." ¹⁸And YHWH says to Moses, "Take Joshua son of Nun to yourself, a man in whom [is] the Spirit, and you have laid your hand on him, ¹⁹and have caused him to stand before Eleazar the priest and before all the congregation, and have charged him before their eyes, ²⁰and have put of your splendor on him, so that all the congregation of the sons of Israel listens. ²¹And he stands before Eleazar the priest, and he has inquired before YHWH for him by the judgment of the

Lights; at his word they go out, and at his word they come in, he and all the sons of Israel with him—even all the congregation." ²²And Moses does as Yʜᴡʜ has commanded him, and takes Joshua and causes him to stand before Eleazar the priest and before all the congregation, ²³and lays his hands on him and charges him, as Yʜᴡʜ has spoken by the hand of Moses.

CHAPTER 28

¹And Yʜᴡʜ speaks to Moses, saying, ²"Command the sons of Israel, and you have said to them: My offering, My bread for My fire-offerings, My refreshing fragrance, you take heed to bring near to Me in its appointed time. ³And you have said to them: This [is] the fire-offering which you bring near to Yʜᴡʜ: two lambs, sons of a year, perfect ones, daily, [for] a continual burnt-offering; ⁴you prepare the first lamb in the morning, and you prepare the second lamb between the evenings; ⁵and a tenth of the ephah of flour for a present mixed with a fourth of the hin of beaten oil; ⁶[it is] a continual burnt-offering, which was made in Mount Sinai for refreshing fragrance, [for] a fire-offering to Yʜᴡʜ. ⁷And its drink-offering [is] a fourth of the hin for one lamb; pour out a drink-offering of strong drink to Yʜᴡʜ in the holy place. ⁸And you prepare the second lamb between the evenings; as the present of the morning and as its drink-offering, you prepare [it as] a fire-offering of refreshing fragrance to Yʜᴡʜ. ⁹And on the Sabbath day, two lambs, sons of a year, perfect ones, and two-tenth parts of flour, a present mixed with oil, and its drink-offering— ¹⁰the burnt-offering of the Sabbath in its Sabbath, besides the continual burnt-offering and its drink-offering. ¹¹And in the beginnings of your months you bring a burnt-offering near to Yʜᴡʜ: two bullocks, sons of the herd, and one ram, seven lambs, sons of a year, perfect ones; ¹²and three-tenth parts of flour, a present mixed with oil, for one bullock, and two-tenth parts of flour, a present mixed with oil, for one ram; ¹³and a tenth—a tenth part of flour, a present mixed with oil, for one lamb, [for] a burnt-offering, a refreshing fragrance, a fire-offering to Yʜᴡʜ; ¹⁴and their drink-offerings are a half of the hin for a bullock, and a third of the hin for a ram, and a fourth of the hin for a lamb, of wine; this [is] the burnt-offering of every month for the months of the year. ¹⁵And one kid of the goats is prepared for a sin-offering to Yʜᴡʜ, besides the continual burnt-offering and its drink-offering. ¹⁶And in the first month, on the fourteenth day of the month, [is] the Passover to Yʜᴡʜ; ¹⁷and in the fifteenth day of this month [is] a festival; [for] seven days unleavened bread is eaten. ¹⁸In the first day [is] a holy convocation; you do no servile work; ¹⁹and you have brought a fire-offering near, a burnt-offering to Yʜᴡʜ: two bullocks, sons of the herd, and one ram, and seven lambs, sons of a year, they are perfect ones for you; ²⁰and their present of flour mixed with oil—you prepare three-tenth parts for a bullock and two-tenth parts for a ram; ²¹you prepare a tenth—a tenth part for one lamb, for the seven lambs, ²²and one goat [for] a sin-offering, to make atonement for you. ²³Apart from the burnt-offering of the morning, which [is] for the continual burnt-offering, you prepare these; ²⁴like these you prepare bread of a fire-offering daily [for] seven days, a refreshing fragrance to Yʜᴡʜ; it is prepared besides the continual burnt-offering and its drink-offering. ²⁵And on the seventh day you have a holy convocation; you do no servile work. ²⁶And on the day of the first-fruits, in your bringing a new present near to Yʜᴡʜ, in your weeks, you have a holy convocation; you do no servile work. ²⁷And you have brought a burnt-offering near for refreshing fragrance to Yʜᴡʜ: two bullocks, sons of the herd, one ram, seven lambs, sons of a year, ²⁸and their present, flour mixed with oil, three-tenth parts for one bullock, two-tenth parts for one ram, ²⁹a tenth—a tenth part for one lamb, for the seven lambs, ³⁰one kid of the goats to make atonement for you; ³¹apart from the continual burnt-offering and its present, you prepare [them] and their drink-offerings; they are perfect ones for you."

CHAPTER 29

¹"And in the seventh month, on the first of the month, you have a holy convocation; you do no servile work; it is a day of shouting to you; ²and you have prepared a burnt-offering for refreshing fragrance to Yʜᴡʜ: one bullock, a son of the herd, one ram, seven lambs, sons of a year, perfect ones; ³and their present of flour mixed with oil: three-tenth parts for the bullock, two-tenth parts for the ram, ⁴and one-tenth part for one lamb, for the seven lambs; ⁵and one kid of the goats [for] a sin-offering, to make atonement for you; ⁶apart from the burnt-offering of the month and its present, and the continual burnt-offering and its present, and their drink-offerings, according to their ordinance, for refreshing fragrance, a fire-offering to Yʜᴡʜ. ⁷And on the tenth of this seventh month you have a holy convocation, and you have humbled your souls; you do no work; ⁸and you have brought a burnt-offering near to Yʜᴡʜ, a refreshing fragrance: one bullock, a son of the herd, one ram, seven lambs, sons of a year; they are perfect ones for you; ⁹and their present of flour mixed with oil: three-tenth parts for the bullock, two-tenth parts for one ram, ¹⁰a tenth—a tenth part for one lamb, for the seven lambs, ¹¹one kid of the goats [for] a sin-offering, apart from the sin-offering of the atonements, and the continual burnt-offering and its present, and their drink-offerings. ¹²And on the fifteenth day of the seventh month you have a holy convocation; you do no servile work; and you have celebrated a festival to Yʜᴡʜ [for] seven days, ¹³and have brought a burnt-offering near, a fire-offering of refreshing fragrance, to Yʜᴡʜ: thirteen bullocks, sons of the herd, two rams, fourteen lambs, sons of a year; they are perfect ones; ¹⁴and their present of flour mixed with oil: three-tenth parts for one bullock, for the thirteen bullocks, two-tenth parts for one ram, for the two rams, ¹⁵and a tenth—a tenth part for one lamb, for the fourteen lambs; ¹⁶and one kid of the goats [for] a sin-offering, apart from the continual burnt-offering, its present, and its drink-offering. ¹⁷And on the second day: twelve bullocks, sons of the herd, two rams, fourteen lambs, sons of a year, perfect ones; ¹⁸and their present and their drink-offerings for the bullocks, for the rams, and for the sheep, in their number, according to the ordinance; ¹⁹and one kid of the goats [for] a sin-offering, apart from the continual burnt-offering, and its present, and their drink-offerings. ²⁰And on the third day: eleven bullocks, two rams, fourteen lambs, sons of a year, perfect ones; ²¹and their present and their drink-offerings for the bullocks, for the rams, and for the lambs, in their number, according to the ordinance; ²²and one goat [for] a sin-offering, apart from the continual burnt-offering, and its present, and its drink-offering. ²³And on the fourth day: ten bullocks, two rams, fourteen lambs, sons of a year, perfect ones; ²⁴their present and their drink-offerings for the bullocks, for the rams, and for the lambs, in their number, according to the ordinance; ²⁵and one kid of the goats [for] a sin-offering, apart from the continual burnt-offering, its present, and its drink-offering. ²⁶And on the fifth day: nine bullocks, two rams, fourteen lambs, sons of a year, perfect ones; ²⁷and their present and their drink-offerings for the bullocks, for the rams, and for the lambs, in their number, according to the ordinance; ²⁸and one goat [for] a sin-offering, apart from the continual burnt-offering, and its present, and its drink-offering. ²⁹And on the sixth day: eight bullocks, two rams, fourteen lambs, sons of a year, perfect ones; ³⁰and their present and their drink-offerings for the bullocks, for the rams, and for the lambs, in their number, according to the ordinance; ³¹and one goat [for] a sin-offering, apart from the continual burnt-offering, its present, and its drink-offering. ³²And on the seventh day: seven bullocks, two rams, fourteen lambs, sons of a year, perfect ones; ³³and their present and their drink-offerings for the bullocks, for the rams, and for the lambs, in their number, according to the ordinance; ³⁴and one goat [for] a sin-offering, apart from the continual burnt-offering, its present, and its drink-offering. ³⁵On the eighth day you have a restraint; you do no servile work; ³⁶and you have brought a burnt-offering near, a fire-offering of refreshing fragrance, to Yʜᴡʜ: one bullock, one ram, seven lambs, sons of a year, perfect ones; ³⁷their present and their drink-offerings for the bullock, for the ram, and for the lambs, in their number, according to the ordinance; ³⁸and one goat [for] a sin-offering, apart from the continual burnt-offering, and its present, and its drink-offering. ³⁹You prepare these to Yʜᴡʜ in your appointed times—apart from your vows and your free-will offerings—for your burnt-offerings, and for your presents, and for your drink-offerings, and for your peace-offerings." ⁴⁰And Moses speaks to the sons of Israel according to all that Yʜᴡʜ has commanded Moses.

CHAPTER 30

¹And Moses speaks to the heads of the tribes of the sons of Israel, saying, "This [is] the thing which YHWH has commanded: ²When a man vows a vow to YHWH, or has sworn an oath to bind a bond on his soul, he does not defile his word; he does according to all that is going out from his mouth. ³And when a woman vows a vow to YHWH, and has bound a bond in the house of her father in her youth, ⁴and her father has heard her vow and her bond which she has bound on her soul, and her father has kept silent to her, then all her vows have been established, and every bond which she has bound on her soul is established. ⁵And if her father has disallowed her in the day of his hearing, none of her vows and her bonds which she has bound on her soul are established, and YHWH is propitious to her, for her father has disallowed her. ⁶And if she is having a husband, and her vows [are] on her, or a wrongful utterance [on] her lips which she has bound on her soul, ⁷and her husband has heard, and in the day of his hearing he has kept silent to her, then her vows have been established, and her bonds which she has bound on her soul are established. ⁸And if in the day of her husband's hearing he disallows her, then he has broken her vow which [is] on her, and the wrongful utterance of her lips which she has bound on her soul, and YHWH is propitious to her. ⁹As for the vow of a widow or cast-out woman, all that she has bound on her soul is established on her. ¹⁰And if she has vowed [in] the house of her husband, or has bound a bond on her soul with an oath, ¹¹and her husband has heard, and has kept silent to her—he has not disallowed her—then all her vows have been established, and every bond which she has bound on her soul is established. ¹²And if her husband certainly breaks them in the day of his hearing, none of the outgoing of her lips concerning her vows, or concerning the bond of her soul, is established—her husband has broken them—and YHWH is propitious to her. ¹³Every vow and every oath—a bond to humble a soul—her husband establishes it, or her husband breaks it; ¹⁴and if her husband certainly keeps silent to her from day to day, then he has established all her vows or all her bonds which [are] on her; he has established them, for he has kept silent to her in the day of his hearing; ¹⁵and if he indeed breaks them after his hearing, then he has borne her iniquity." ¹⁶These [are] the statutes which YHWH has commanded Moses between a man and his wife, between a father and his daughter, in her youth, [in] the house of her father.

CHAPTER 31

¹And YHWH speaks to Moses, saying, ²"Execute the vengeance of the sons of Israel against the Midianites—afterward you are gathered to your people." ³And Moses speaks to the people, saying, "Arm men from [among] you for the war, and they are against Midian, to put the vengeance of YHWH on Midian; ⁴one thousand for a tribe—you send one thousand for a tribe, of all the tribes of Israel, to the war." ⁵And there are given out of the thousands of Israel one thousand for a tribe—twelve thousand armed ones [for] war; ⁶and Moses sends them, one thousand for a tribe, to the war; [he sent] them and Phinehas son of Eleazar the priest to the war, with the holy vessels and the trumpets of shouting in his hand. ⁷And they war against Midian, as YHWH has commanded Moses, and slay every male; ⁸and they have slain the kings of Midian besides their pierced ones: Evi, and Rekem, and Zur, and Hur, and Reba—five kings of Midian; and they have slain Balaam son of Beor with the sword. ⁹And the sons of Israel take the women of Midian and their infants captive; and they have plundered all their livestock, and all their substance, and all their wealth; ¹⁰and they have burned all their cities, with their habitations, and all their towers, with fire. ¹¹And they take all the spoil and all the prey, among man and among beast; ¹²and they bring in the captives, and the prey, and the spoil to Moses, and to Eleazar the priest, and to the congregation of the sons of Israel, to the camp, to the plains of Moab, which [are] by the Jordan, [near] Jericho. ¹³And Moses, and Eleazar the priest, and all the princes of the congregation, go out to meet them, to the outside of the camp, ¹⁴and Moses is angry against the inspectors of the force, chiefs of the thousands, and chiefs of the hundreds, who are coming in from the warfare of battle. ¹⁵And Moses says to them, "Have you kept every female alive? ¹⁶Behold, they have been to the sons of Israel, through the word of Balaam, to cause a trespass against YHWH in the matter of Peor, and the plague is in the congregation of YHWH. ¹⁷And now, slay every male among the infants, indeed, slay every woman knowing a man by the lying of a male; ¹⁸and all the infants among the women who have not known the lying of a male you have kept alive for yourselves. ¹⁹And you, encamp at the outside of the camp [for] seven days; any who has slain a person, and any who has come against a pierced one, cleanse yourselves on the third day and on the seventh day—you and your captives; ²⁰and every garment, and every skin vessel, and every work of goats' [hair], and every wooden vessel, you yourselves cleanse." ²¹And Eleazar the priest says to the men of war who go to battle, "This [is] the statute of the law which YHWH has commanded Moses: ²²only the gold, and the silver, the bronze, the iron, the tin, and the lead, ²³everything which may go into fire, you cause to pass over through fire, and it has been clean; it is surely cleansed with the water of separation; and all that may not go into fire, you cause to pass over through water; ²⁴and you have washed your garments on the seventh day and have been clean, and afterward you come into the camp." ²⁵And YHWH speaks to Moses, saying, ²⁶"Take up the sum of the prey of the captives, among man and among beast, you, and Eleazar the priest, and the heads of the fathers of the congregation; ²⁷and you have halved the prey between those handling the battle, who go out to the war, and all the congregation; ²⁸and you have raised a tribute to YHWH from the men of battle, who go out to the war, one body out of five hundred, of man, and of the herd, and of the donkeys, and of the flock; ²⁹you take from their half and have given [it] to Eleazar the priest [as] a raised-offering of YHWH. ³⁰And from the sons of Israel's half you take one possession out of fifty, of man, of the herd, of the donkeys, and of the flock, of all the livestock, and you have given them to the Levites keeping the charge of the Dwelling Place of YHWH." ³¹And Moses does—Eleazar the priest also—as YHWH has commanded Moses. ³²And the prey, the remainder of the spoil which the people of the host have spoiled, is six hundred thousand and seventy thousand and five thousand of the flock; ³³and seventy-two thousand of the herd; ³⁴and sixty-one thousand donkeys; ³⁵and of mankind—of the women who have not known the lying of a male—all the persons [are] thirty-two thousand. ³⁶And the half, the portion of those who go out into the war, is [in] number three hundred thousand and thirty thousand and seven thousand and five hundred of the flock. ³⁷And the tribute to YHWH of the sheep is six hundred seventy-five; ³⁸and the herd [is] thirty-six thousand, and their tribute to YHWH [is] seventy-two; ³⁹and the donkeys [are] thirty thousand and five hundred, and their tribute to YHWH [is] sixty-one; ⁴⁰and of mankind [are] sixteen thousand, and their tribute to YHWH [is] thirty-two persons. ⁴¹And Moses gives the tribute—YHWH's raised-offering—to Eleazar the priest, as YHWH has commanded Moses. ⁴²And of the sons of Israel's half, which Moses halved from the men who war— ⁴³and the congregation's half is three hundred thousand and thirty thousand [and] seven thousand and five hundred of the flock; ⁴⁴and thirty-six thousand of the herd; ⁴⁵and thirty thousand and five hundred donkeys; ⁴⁶and sixteen thousand of mankind— ⁴⁷Moses takes from the sons of Israel's half one possession from the fifty, of man and of beast, and gives them to the Levites keeping the charge of the Dwelling Place of YHWH, as YHWH has commanded Moses. ⁴⁸And the inspectors whom the thousands of the host have (heads of the thousands and heads of the hundreds), draw near to Moses, ⁴⁹and they say to Moses, "Your servants have taken up the sum of the men of war who [are] with us, and not a man of us has been missed; ⁵⁰and we bring YHWH's offering near, each of that which he has found of vessels of gold—chain, and bracelet, seal-ring, [ear]-ring, and bead—to make atonement for ourselves before YHWH." ⁵¹And Moses receives—Eleazar the priest also—the gold from them, every vessel of workmanship; ⁵²and all the gold of the raised-offering which they have lifted up to YHWH is sixteen thousand seven hundred and fifty shekels, from heads of the thousands and from heads of the hundreds; ⁵³(the men of the host have each taken spoil for himself); ⁵⁴and Moses takes—Eleazar the priest also—the gold from the heads of the thousands and of the

NUMBERS

hundreds, and they bring it into the Tent of Meeting [as] a memorial for the sons of Israel before YHWH.

CHAPTER 32

¹And much livestock has [belonged] to the sons of Reuben and to the sons of Gad—very many; and they see the land of Jazer and the land of Gilead, and behold, the place [is] a place [for] livestock; ²and the sons of Gad and the sons of Reuben come in and speak to Moses, and to Eleazar the priest, and to the princes of the congregation, saying, ³"Ataroth, and Dibon, and Jazer, and Nimrah, and Heshbon, and Elealeh, and Shebam, and Nebo, and Beon, ⁴the land which YHWH has struck before the congregation of Israel, is a land for livestock, and your servants have livestock." ⁵And they say, "If we have found grace in your eyes, let this land be given to your servants for a possession; cause us not to pass over the Jordan." ⁶And Moses says to the sons of Gad and to the sons of Reuben, "Do your brothers go to the battle, and you—do you sit here? ⁷And why discourage the heart of the sons of Israel from passing over to the land which YHWH has given to them? ⁸Thus your fathers did in my sending them from Kadesh-Barnea to see the land; ⁹and they go up to the Valley of Eshcol, and see the land, and discourage the heart of the sons of Israel so as not to go into the land which YHWH has given to them; ¹⁰and the anger of YHWH burns in that day, and He swears, saying, ¹¹They do not see—the men who are coming up out of Egypt from a son of twenty years and upward—the ground which I have sworn to Abraham, to Isaac, and to Jacob, for they have not been fully after Me, ¹²except Caleb son of Jephunneh the Kenezite and Joshua son of Nun, for they have been fully after YHWH; ¹³and the anger of YHWH burns against Israel, and He causes them to wander in the wilderness [for] forty years, until the consumption of all the generation which is doing evil in the eyes of YHWH. ¹⁴And behold, you have risen in the stead of your fathers, an increase of sinful men, to add yet to the fury of the anger of YHWH toward Israel; ¹⁵when you turn back from after Him, then He has added yet to leave him in the wilderness, and you have done corruptly to all this people." ¹⁶And they come near to him and say, "We build folds for the flock here for our livestock, and cities for our infants; ¹⁷but we are armed, hastening before the sons of Israel until we have brought them to their place; and our infants have dwelt in the cities of defense because of the inhabitants of the land; ¹⁸we do not return to our houses until the sons of Israel have each inherited his inheritance, ¹⁹for we do not inherit with them across the Jordan and beyond, for our inheritance has come to us beyond the Jordan at the [sun]-rising." ²⁰And Moses says to them, "If you do this thing, if you are armed before YHWH for battle, ²¹and every armed one of you has passed over the Jordan before YHWH, until His dispossessing His enemies from before Him, ²²and the land has been subdued before YHWH, then afterward you return, and have been acquitted by YHWH and by Israel, and this land has been to you for a possession before YHWH. ²³And if you do not do so, behold, you have sinned against YHWH, and know that your sin finds you; ²⁴build for yourselves cities for your infants and folds for your flock, and that which is going out from your mouth you do." ²⁵And the sons of Gad and the sons of Reuben speak to Moses, saying, "Your servants do as my lord is commanding; ²⁶our infants, our wives, our livestock, and all our beasts, are there in cities of Gilead, ²⁷and your servants pass over, every armed one of the host, before YHWH, to battle, as my lord is saying." ²⁸And Moses commands Eleazar the priest, and Joshua son of Nun, and the heads of the fathers of the tribes of the sons of Israel concerning them; ²⁹and Moses says to them, "If the sons of Gad and the sons of Reuben pass over the Jordan with you, everyone armed for battle, before YHWH, and the land has been subdued before you, then you have given the land of Gilead to them for a possession; ³⁰and if they do not pass over armed with you, then they have possessions in your midst in the land of Canaan." ³¹And the sons of Gad and the sons of Reuben answer, saying, "That which YHWH has spoken to your servants, so we do; ³²we pass over armed before YHWH [to] the land of Canaan, and with us [is] the possession of our inheritance beyond the Jordan." ³³And Moses gives to them—to the sons of Gad, and to the sons of Reuben, and to the half of the tribe of Manasseh son of Joseph—the kingdom of Sihon king of the Amorite and the kingdom of Og king of Bashan, the land by its cities, in the borders, the cities of the surrounding land. ³⁴And the sons of Gad build Dibon, and Ataroth, and Aroer, ³⁵and Atroth, Shophan, and Jaazer, and Jogbehah, ³⁶and Beth-Nimrah, and Beth-Haran, cities of defense, and sheepfolds. ³⁷And the sons of Reuben have built Heshbon, and Elealeh, and Kirjathaim, ³⁸and Nebo, and Ba'al-Meon (changed in name), and Shibmah, and they call the names of the cities which they have built by [these] names. ³⁹And sons of Machir son of Manasseh go to Gilead, and capture it, and dispossess the Amorite who [is] in it; ⁴⁰and Moses gives Gilead to Machir son of Manasseh, and he dwells in it. ⁴¹And Jair son of Manasseh has gone and captures their towns, and calls them "Towns of Jair"; ⁴²and Nobah has gone and captures Kenath and its villages, and calls it Nobah, by his own name.

CHAPTER 33

¹These [are] the journeys of the sons of Israel who have come out of the land of Egypt, by their hosts, by the hand of Moses and Aaron; ²and Moses writes their outgoings, by their journeys, by the command of YHWH; and these [are] their journeys, by their outgoings: ³And they journey from Rameses in the first month, on the fifteenth day of the first month; from the day after the Passover the sons of Israel have gone out with a high hand before the eyes of all the Egyptians— ⁴and the Egyptians are burying those whom YHWH has struck among them, every firstborn, and YHWH has done judgments on their gods. ⁵And the sons of Israel journey from Rameses and encamp in Succoth. ⁶And they journey from Succoth and encamp in Etham, which [is] in the extremity of the wilderness. ⁷And they journey from Etham and turn back over Pi-Hahiroth, which [is] on the front of Ba'al-Zephon, and they encamp before Migdol. ⁸And they journey from Pi-Hahiroth, and pass over through the midst of the sea into the wilderness, and go a journey of three days in the wilderness of Etham, and encamp in Marah. ⁹And they journey from Marah and come to Elim, and twelve fountains of waters and seventy palm trees [are] in Elim, and they encamp there. ¹⁰And they journey from Elim and encamp by the Red Sea. ¹¹And they journey from the Red Sea and encamp in the wilderness of Sin. ¹²And they journey from the wilderness of Sin and encamp in Dophkah. ¹³And they journey from Dophkah and encamp in Alush. ¹⁴And they journey from Alush and encamp in Rephidim; and there was no water there for the people to drink. ¹⁵And they journey from Rephidim and encamp in the wilderness of Sinai. ¹⁶And they journey from the wilderness of Sinai and encamp in Kibroth-Hattaavah. ¹⁷And they journey from Kibroth-Hattaavah and encamp in Hazeroth. ¹⁸And they journey from Hazeroth and encamp in Rithmah. ¹⁹And they journey from Rithmah and encamp in Rimmon-Parez. ²⁰And they journey from Rimmon-Parez and encamp in Libnah. ²¹And they journey from Libnah and encamp in Rissah. ²²And they journey from Rissah and encamp in Kehelathah. ²³And they journey from Kehelathah and encamp in Mount Shapher. ²⁴And they journey from Mount Shapher and encamp in Haradah. ²⁵And they journey from Haradah and encamp in Makheloth. ²⁶And they journey from Makheloth and encamp in Tahath. ²⁷And they journey from Tahath and encamp in Tarah. ²⁸And they journey from Tarah and encamp in Mithcah. ²⁹And they journey from Mithcah and encamp in Hashmonah. ³⁰And they journey from Hashmonah and encamp in Moseroth. ³¹And they journey from Moseroth and encamp in Bene-Jaakan. ³²And they journey from Bene-Jaakan and encamp at Hor-Hagidgad. ³³And they journey from Hor-Hagidgad and encamp in Jotbathah. ³⁴And they journey from Jotbathah and encamp in Ebronah. ³⁵And they journey from Ebronah and encamp in Ezion-Gaber. ³⁶And they journey from Ezion-Gaber and encamp in the wilderness of Zin, which [is] Kadesh. ³⁷And they journey from Kadesh and encamp in Mount Hor, in the extremity of the land of Edom. ³⁸And Aaron the priest goes up to Mount Hor by the command of YHWH, and dies there in the fortieth year of the going out of the sons of Israel from the land of Egypt, in the fifth month, on the first of the month; ³⁹and Aaron [is] a son of one hundred and twenty-three years in his dying on Mount Hor. ⁴⁰And the Canaanite, king of Arad, who is dwelling in the south in the land of Canaan, hears of the coming of the sons of Israel. ⁴¹And they

journey from Mount Hor and encamp in Zalmonah. ⁴²And they journey from Zalmonah and encamp in Punon. ⁴³And they journey from Punon and encamp in Oboth. ⁴⁴And they journey from Oboth and encamp in Ije-Abarim, in the border of Moab. ⁴⁵And they journey from Iim and encamp in Dibon-Gad. ⁴⁶And they journey from Dibon-Gad and encamp in Almon-Diblathaim. ⁴⁷And they journey from Almon-Diblathaim and encamp in the mountains of Abarim, before Nebo. ⁴⁸And they journey from the mountains of Abarim and encamp in the plains of Moab by the Jordan, [near] Jericho. ⁴⁹And they encamp by the Jordan, from Beth-Jeshimoth as far as Abel-Shittim in the plains of Moab. ⁵⁰And YHWH speaks to Moses in the plains of Moab by the Jordan, [near] Jericho, saying, ⁵¹"Speak to the sons of Israel, and you have said to them: When you are passing over the Jordan to the land of Canaan, ⁵²then you have dispossessed all the inhabitants of the land from before you, and have destroyed all their imagery, indeed, you destroy all their molten images, and you lay waste [to] all their high places, ⁵³and you have possessed the land and dwelt in it, for I have given the land to you to possess it. ⁵⁴And you have inherited the land by lot, by your families; to the many you increase their inheritance, and to the few you diminish their inheritance; to where the lot goes out to him, it is his; you inherit by the tribes of your fathers. ⁵⁵And if you do not dispossess the inhabitants of the land from before you, then it has been [that] those whom you let remain of them [are] for pricks in your eyes and for thorns in your sides, and they have distressed you on the land in which you are dwelling, ⁵⁶and it has come to pass, as I thought to do to them, I do to you."

CHAPTER 34

¹And YHWH speaks to Moses, saying, ²"Command the sons of Israel, and you have said to them: When you are coming into the land of Canaan—this [is] the land which falls to you by inheritance, the land of Canaan, by its borders— ³then the south quarter has been to you from the wilderness of Zin, by the sides of Edom, indeed, the south border has been to you from the extremity of the Salt Sea eastward; ⁴and the border has turned around to you from the south to the ascent of Akrabbim, and has passed on to Zin, and its outgoings have been from the south to Kadesh-Barnea, and it has gone out at Hazar-Addar, and has passed on to Azmon; ⁵and the border has turned around from Azmon to the Brook of Egypt, and its outgoings have been at the sea. ⁶As for the west border, even the Great Sea has been a border to you; this is the west border to you. ⁷And this is the north border to you: from the Great Sea you mark out for yourselves Mount Hor; ⁸from Mount Hor you mark out to go to Hamath, and the outgoings of the border have been to Zedad, ⁹and the border has gone out to Ziphron, and its outgoings have been at Hazar-Enan; this is the north border to you. ¹⁰And you have marked out for yourselves for the border eastward, from Hazar-Enan to Shepham; ¹¹and the border has gone down from Shepham to Riblah, on the east of Ain, and the border has gone down, and has struck against the shoulder of the Sea of Chinnereth eastward; ¹²and the border has gone down to the Jordan, and its outgoings have been at the Salt Sea; this is the land for you by its borders all around." ¹³And Moses commands the sons of Israel, saying, "This [is] the land which you inherit by lot, which YHWH has commanded to give to the nine tribes and the half of the tribe; ¹⁴for the tribe of the sons of Reuben, by the house of their fathers, and the tribe of the children of Gad, by the house of their fathers, have received [their inheritance]; and [those of] the half of the tribe of Manasseh have received their inheritance; ¹⁵the two tribes and the half of the tribe have received their inheritance beyond the Jordan, [near] Jericho, eastward, at the [sun]-rising." ¹⁶And YHWH speaks to Moses, saying, ¹⁷"These [are] the names of the men who give the inheritance of the land to you: Eleazar the priest and Joshua son of Nun. ¹⁸And one prince—you take one prince from a tribe to give the land by inheritance. ¹⁹And these [are] the names of the men: of the tribe of Judah, Caleb son of Jephunneh; ²⁰and of the tribe of the sons of Simeon, Shemuel son of Aminihud; ²¹of the tribe of Benjamin, Elidad son of Chislon; ²²and a prince of the tribe of the sons of Dan, Bukki son of Jogli; ²³of the sons of Joseph, a prince of the tribe of the sons of Manasseh, Hanniel son of Ephod; ²⁴and a prince of the tribe of the sons of Ephraim, Kemuel son of Shiphtan; ²⁵and a prince of the tribe of the sons of Zebulun, Elizaphan son of Parnach; ²⁶and a prince of the tribe of the sons of Issachar, Paltiel son of Azzan; ²⁷and a prince of the tribe of the sons of Asher, Ahihud son of Shelomi; ²⁸and a prince of the tribe of the sons of Naphtali, Pedahel son of Ammihud." ²⁹These [are] those whom YHWH has commanded to give the sons of Israel inheritance in the land of Canaan.

CHAPTER 35

¹And YHWH speaks to Moses in the plains of Moab by the Jordan, [near] Jericho, saying, ²"Command the sons of Israel, and they have given to the Levites cities to inhabit from the inheritance of their possession; you also give [the] outskirt around them, of the cities, to the Levites. ³And the cities have been for them to inhabit, and their outskirts are for their livestock, and for their goods, and for all their beasts. ⁴And the outskirts of the cities which you give to the Levites [are], from the wall of the city and outside, one thousand cubits around. ⁵And you have measured from the outside of the city: the east quarter—two thousand by the cubit, and the south quarter—two thousand by the cubit, and the west quarter—two thousand by the cubit, and the north quarter—two thousand by the cubit; and the city [is] in the midst; this is the outskirts of the cities to them. ⁶And the cities which you give to the Levites [are] the six cities of refuge, which you give for the fleeing there of the manslayer, and besides them you give forty-two cities; ⁷all the cities which you give to the Levites [are] forty-eight cities, them and their outskirts. ⁸And the cities which you give [are] from the possession of the sons of Israel; from the many you multiply, and from the few you diminish; each, according to his inheritance which they inherit, gives to the Levites from his cities." ⁹And YHWH speaks to Moses, saying, ¹⁰"Speak to the sons of Israel, and you have said to them: When you are passing over the Jordan to the land of Canaan, ¹¹and have prepared cities for yourselves—they are cities of refuge to you—then a manslayer, striking a person through ignorance, has fled there, ¹²and the cities have been for a refuge to you from the redeemer, and the manslayer does not die until his standing before the congregation for judgment. ¹³As for the cities which you give, six [are] cities of refuge to you; ¹⁴three of the cities you give from beyond the Jordan, and three of the cities you give in the land of Canaan; they are cities of refuge. ¹⁵For sons of Israel, and for a sojourner, and for a settler in their midst, are these six cities for a refuge, for the fleeing there of anyone striking a person through ignorance. ¹⁶And if he has struck him with an instrument of iron, and he dies, he [is] a murderer: the murderer is certainly put to death. ¹⁷And if he has struck him with a stone [in] the hand, with which he could die, and he dies, he [is] a murderer: the murderer is certainly put to death. ¹⁸Or [if] he has struck him with a wooden instrument [in] the hand, with which he could die, and he dies, he [is] a murderer: the murderer is certainly put to death. ¹⁹The redeemer of blood puts the murderer to death himself; in his coming against him he puts him to death. ²⁰And if he pushes him in hatred, or has cast [anything] at him by lying in wait, and he dies, ²¹or he has struck him with his hand in enmity, and he dies, the striker is certainly put to death; he [is] a murderer; the redeemer of blood puts the murderer to death in his coming against him. ²²And if, in an instant, without enmity, he has pushed him, or has cast any instrument at him without lying in wait, ²³or with any stone with which he could die, without seeing, indeed, causes [it] to fall on him, and he dies, and he [is] not his enemy, nor seeking his evil, ²⁴then the congregation has judged between the striker and the redeemer of blood by these judgments. ²⁵And the congregation has delivered the manslayer out of the hand of the redeemer of blood, and the congregation has caused him to return to the city of his refuge, to where he has fled, and he has dwelt in it until the death of the chief priest who has been anointed with the holy oil. ²⁶And if the manslayer indeed goes out [from] the border of the city of his refuge to where he flees, ²⁷and the redeemer of blood has found him at the outside of the border of the city of his refuge, and the redeemer of blood has slain the manslayer, blood [is] not [reckoned] to him; ²⁸for he dwells in the city of his refuge until the death of the chief priest; and after the death of the chief priest the manslayer turns back to the city of his possession. ²⁹And these things

NUMBERS

have been for a statute of judgment to you throughout your generations, in all your dwellings. ³⁰Whoever strikes a person, by the mouth of witnesses [one] slays the murderer; and one witness does not testify against a person to cause [him] to die. ³¹And you take no atonement for the life of a murderer who [is] condemned to die, for he is certainly put to death; ³²and you take no atonement for him [who had] to flee to the city of his refuge, to return to dwell in the land, until the death of the priest. ³³And you do not profane the land which you [are] in, for blood profanes the land; as for the land, it is not pardoned for blood which is shed in it except by the blood of him who sheds it; ³⁴and you do not defile the land in which you are dwelling, in the midst of which I dwell, for I, YHWH, dwell in the midst of the sons of Israel."

CHAPTER 36

¹And the heads of the fathers of the families of the sons of Gilead, son of Machir, son of Manasseh, of the families of the sons of Joseph, come near and speak before Moses and before the princes, heads of the fathers of the sons of Israel, ²and say, "YHWH commanded my lord to give the land for inheritance by lot to the sons of Israel, and my lord has been commanded by YHWH to give the inheritance of our brother Zelophehad to his daughters. ³Now [if] they have been [given] to one from the sons of the [other] tribes of the sons of Israel for wives, and their inheritance has been withdrawn from the inheritance of our fathers, and has been added to the inheritance of the tribe which is theirs, and it is withdrawn from the lot of our inheritance, ⁴and if it is the Jubilee of the sons of Israel, then their inheritance has been added to the inheritance of the tribe which is theirs, and their inheritance is withdrawn from the inheritance of the tribe of our fathers." ⁵And Moses commands the sons of Israel by the command of YHWH, saying, "The tribe of the sons of Joseph is speaking correctly; ⁶this [is] the thing which YHWH has commanded concerning the daughters of Zelophehad, saying, To those good in their eyes let them be for wives; only, let them be for wives to a family of the tribe of their fathers; ⁷and the inheritance of the sons of Israel does not turn around from tribe to tribe; for each of the sons of Israel cleaves to the inheritance of the tribe of his fathers. ⁸And every daughter possessing an inheritance from the tribes of the sons of Israel is for a wife to one from the family of the tribe of her father, so that the sons of Israel each possess the inheritance of his fathers, ⁹and the inheritance does not turn around from [one] tribe to another tribe; for each of the tribes of the sons of Israel cleaves to his inheritance." ¹⁰As YHWH has commanded Moses, so the daughters of Zelophehad have done, ¹¹and Mahlah, Tirzah, and Hoglah, and Milcah, and Noah, daughters of Zelophehad, are for wives to the sons of their fathers' brothers; ¹²they have been for wives [to men] from the families of the sons of Manasseh, son of Joseph, and their inheritance is with the tribe of the family of their father. ¹³These [are] the commands and the judgments which YHWH has commanded by the hand of Moses concerning the sons of Israel, in the plains of Moab by the Jordan, [near] Jericho.

DEUTERONOMY

CHAPTER 1

¹These [are] the words which Moses has spoken to all Israel beyond the Jordan in the wilderness, in the plain opposite Suph, between Paran, and Tophel, and Laban, and Hazeroth, and Di-Zahab. ²[It takes] eleven days [to go] from Horeb, the way of Mount Seir, to Kadesh-Barnea. ³And it comes to pass in the fortieth year, in the eleventh month, on the first of the month, Moses has spoken to the sons of Israel according to all that YHWH has commanded him concerning them, ⁴after his striking Sihon king of the Amorite who is dwelling in Heshbon, and Og king of Bashan who is dwelling in Ashtaroth in Edrei. ⁵Beyond the Jordan, in the land of Moab, Moses has begun to explain this law, saying, ⁶"Our God YHWH has spoken to us in Horeb, saying, For you dwell at this mountain long enough; ⁷turn and journey for yourselves, and go to the mountain of the Amorite, and to all its neighboring places in the plain, in the hill-country, and in the low country, and in the south, and in the haven of the sea, the land of the Canaanite, and of Lebanon, as far as the great river, the Euphrates River; ⁸see, I have set the land before you; go in and possess the land which YHWH has sworn to your fathers, to Abraham, to Isaac, and to Jacob, to give to them and to their seed after them. ⁹And I speak to you at that time, saying, I am not able to bear you by myself; ¹⁰your God YHWH has multiplied you, and behold, today you [are] as the stars of the heavens for multitude; ¹¹YHWH, God of your fathers, is adding to you, as you [are], one thousand times, and blesses you as He has spoken to you. ¹²How do I bear your pressure, and your burden, and your strife by myself? ¹³Provide wise and understanding men for yourselves that are known to your tribes, and I set them for your heads; ¹⁴and you answer me and say, The thing which you have spoken [is] good to do. ¹⁵And I take the heads of your tribes, wise men that are known, and I appoint them [as] heads over you, princes of thousands, and princes of hundreds, and princes of fifties, and princes of tens, and authorities for your tribes. ¹⁶And I command your judges at that time, saying, Listen between your brothers—then you have judged [in] righteousness between a man, and his brother, and his sojourner; ¹⁷you do not discern faces in judgment; you hear the little as well as the great; you are not afraid of the face of any, for the judgment is God's, and the thing which is too hard for you, you bring near to me, and I have heard it. ¹⁸And I command you at that time all the things which you do. ¹⁹And we journey from Horeb, and go [through] all that great and fearful wilderness which you have seen, the way of the hill-country of the Amorite, as our God YHWH has commanded us, and we come to Kadesh-Barnea. ²⁰And I say to you, You have come to the hill-country of the Amorite, which our God YHWH is giving to us; ²¹see, your God YHWH has set the land before you; go up, possess, as YHWH, God of your fathers, has spoken to you; do not fear, nor be frightened. ²²And you come near to me, all of you, and say, Let us send men before us, and they search the land for us, and they bring us back word [concerning] the way in which we go up into it, and the cities to which we come in; ²³and the thing is good in my eyes, and I take twelve men from you, one man for the tribe. ²⁴And they turn and go up to the hill-country, and come to the Valley of Eshcol, and spy it out, ²⁵and they take in their hand from the fruit of the land, and bring [it] down to us, and bring us back word, and say, The land is good which our God YHWH is giving to us. ²⁶And you have not been willing to go up, and you provoke the mouth of your God YHWH, ²⁷and murmur in your tents, and say, In YHWH's hating us He has brought us out of the land of Egypt, to give us into the hand of the Amorite—to destroy us; ²⁸to where are we going up? Our brothers have melted our heart, saying, [The] people [are] greater and taller than we; [the] cities [are] great and fortified up to the heavens, and we have also seen sons of Anakim there. ²⁹And I say to you, Do not be terrified, nor be afraid of them; ³⁰your God YHWH, who is going before you—He fights for you, according to all that He has done with you in Egypt before your eyes, ³¹and in the wilderness where you have seen that your God YHWH has carried you, as a man carries his son, in all the way which you have gone until your coming to this place. ³²And in this thing you are not steadfast in your God YHWH, ³³who is going before you in the way to search out for you a place for your encamping, in fire by night, to show you in the way in which you go, and in a cloud by day. ³⁴And YHWH hears the voice of your words, and is angry, and swears,

saying, ³⁵Not one of these men of this evil generation sees the good land which I have sworn to give to your fathers, ³⁶except Caleb son of Jephunneh—he sees it, and to him I give the land on which he has trodden, and to his sons, because that he has been fully after YHWH. ³⁷Moreover, YHWH has been angry with me for your sake, saying, Indeed, you do not go in there; ³⁸Joshua son of Nun, who is standing before you, he goes in there; strengthen him, for he causes Israel to inherit [it]. ³⁹And your infants, of whom you have said, They are for a prey, and your sons who today have not known good and evil, they go in there, and I give it to them, and they possess it; ⁴⁰but you, turn and journey for yourselves toward the wilderness, the way of the Red Sea. ⁴¹And you answer and say to me, We have sinned against YHWH; we go up and we have fought, according to all that which our God YHWH has commanded us; and you each gird on his weapons of war, and you are ready to go up into the hill-country; ⁴²and YHWH says to me, Say to them, You do not go up, nor fight, for I am not in your midst, and you are not struck before your enemies. ⁴³And I speak to you, and you have not listened, and provoke the mouth of YHWH, and act proudly, and go up into the hill-country; ⁴⁴and the Amorite who is dwelling in that hill-country comes out to meet you, and they pursue you as the bees do, and strike you in Seir, even to Hormah. ⁴⁵And you return and weep before YHWH, and YHWH has not listened to your voice, nor has He given ear to you; ⁴⁶and you dwell in Kadesh [for] many days, according to the days which you had dwelt."

CHAPTER 2

¹"And we turn and journey into the wilderness, the way of the Red Sea, as YHWH has spoken to me, and we go around Mount Seir [for] many days. ²And YHWH speaks to me, saying, ³For you go around this mountain long enough; turn for yourselves northward. ⁴And the people command you, saying, You are passing over into the border of your brothers, sons of Esau, who are dwelling in Seir, and they are afraid of you; and you have been very watchful; ⁵you do not strive with them, for I do not give [any] of their land to you—even the treading of the sole of a foot; I have given Mount Seir to Esau for a possession. ⁶You buy food from them with money, and have eaten; and you also buy water from them with money, and have drunk. ⁷For your God YHWH has blessed you in all the work of your hands; He has known your walking in this great wilderness these forty years; your God YHWH [is] with you; you have not lacked anything. ⁸And we pass by from our brothers, sons of Esau, who are dwelling in Seir, by the way of the plain, by Elath and by Ezion-Gaber, and we turn and pass over the way of the wilderness of Moab; ⁹and YHWH says to me, Do not distress Moab, nor stir yourself up against them [in] battle, for I do not give [any] of their land to you [for] a possession; for I have given Ar to the sons of Lot [for] a possession. ¹⁰The Emim have formerly dwelt in it, a people great, and numerous, and tall as the Anakim; ¹¹they are reckoned [as] Rephaim, they also, as the Anakim; and the Moabites call them Emim. ¹²And the Horim have formerly dwelt in Seir, but the sons of Esau dispossess them, and destroy them from before them, and dwell in their stead, as Israel has done to the land of his possession which YHWH has given to them. ¹³Now rise and pass over the Brook of Zered for yourselves; and we pass over the Brook of Zered. ¹⁴And the days which we have walked from Kadesh-Barnea until we have passed over the Brook of Zered [are] thirty-eight years, until the consumption of all the generation of the men of battle from the midst of the camp, as YHWH has sworn to them; ¹⁵and indeed the hand of YHWH has been against them, to destroy them from the midst of the camp until they are consumed. ¹⁶And it comes to pass, when all the men of battle have finished dying from the midst of the people, ¹⁷that YHWH speaks to me, saying, ¹⁸Today you are passing over the border of Moab, even Ar, ¹⁹and [when] you have come near the sons of Ammon, you do not distress them, nor stir yourself up against them, for I do not give [any] of the land of the sons of Ammon to you [for] a possession; for I have given it to the sons of Lot [for] a possession. ²⁰It is reckoned [as] a land of Rephaim, even it; Rephaim formerly dwelt in it, and the Ammonites call them Zamzummim, ²¹a people great, and numerous, and tall as the Anakim, and YHWH destroys them before them, and they dispossess them, and dwell in their stead, ²²as He has done for the sons of Esau who are dwelling in Seir, when He destroyed the Horim from before them, and they dispossess them, and dwell in their stead to this day. ²³As for the Avim who are dwelling in villages as far as Gaza, the Caphtorim—who are coming out from Caphtor—have destroyed them, and dwell in their stead. ²⁴Rise, journey, and pass over the Brook of Arnon; see, I have given into your hand Sihon king of Heshbon, the Amorite, and his land; begin to possess [it], and stir yourself up against him [in] battle. ²⁵This [is] the day I begin to put your dread and your fear on the face of the peoples under the whole heavens, who hear your fame, and have trembled and been pained because of you. ²⁶And I send messengers from the wilderness of Kedemoth to Sihon king of Heshbon, [with] words of peace, saying, ²⁷Let me pass over through your land; in the way—in the way I go, I do not turn aside [to the] right or left. ²⁸You sell me food for money, and I have eaten; and you give to me water for money, and I have drunk; only, let me pass over on my feet, ²⁹as the sons of Esau who are dwelling in Seir and the Moabites who are dwelling in Ar have done for me, until I pass over the Jordan to the land which our God YHWH is giving to us. ³⁰And Sihon king of Heshbon has not been willing to let us pass over by him, for your God YHWH has hardened his spirit and strengthened his heart, so as to give him into your hand as at this day. ³¹And YHWH says to me, See, I have begun to give Sihon and his land before your faces; begin to possess—to possess his land. ³²And Sihon comes out to meet us, he and all his people, to the battle at Jahaz; ³³and our God YHWH gives him before our faces, and we strike him, and his sons, and all his people; ³⁴and we capture all his cities at that time, and devote the whole city—men, and the women, and the infants; we have not left a remnant; ³⁵only, we have spoiled the livestock for ourselves, and the spoil of the cities which we have captured. ³⁶From Aroer, which [is] by the edge of the Brook of Arnon, and the city which [is] by the brook, even to Gilead, there has not been a city which [is] too high for us; our God YHWH has given the whole before our faces. ³⁷Only, you have not drawn near to the land of the sons of Ammon—any part of the Brook of Jabbok, and cities of the hill-country, and anything which our God YHWH has [not] commanded."

CHAPTER 3

¹"And we turn and go up the way to Bashan, and Og king of Bashan comes out to meet us, he and all his people, to the battle [at] Edrei. ²And YHWH says to me, Do not fear him, for I have given him, and all his people, and his land into your hand, and you have done to him as you have done to Sihon king of the Amorite who is dwelling in Heshbon. ³And our God YHWH indeed gives Og king of Bashan and all his people into our hands, and we strike him until there has been no remnant left to him; ⁴and we capture all his cities at that time; there has not been a city which we have not taken from them—sixty cities, all the region of Argob, the kingdom of Og in Bashan. ⁵All these [are] cities fortified with high walls, double gates, and bar, apart from very many cities of the open place; ⁶and we devote them, as we have done to Sihon king of Heshbon, devoting [the] men, the women, and the infants of every city; ⁷and all the livestock, and the spoil of the cities, we have spoiled for ourselves. ⁸And at that time we take the land out of the hand of the two kings of the Amorite, which is beyond the Jordan, from the Brook of Arnon to Mount Hermon ⁹(Sidonians call Hermon Sirion, and the Amorites call it Senir), ¹⁰all the cities of the plain, and all Gilead, and all Bashan, as far as Salchah and Edrei, cities of the kingdom of Og in Bashan. ¹¹For only Og king of Bashan had been left of the remnant of the Rephaim; behold, his bedstead [is] a bedstead of iron. Is it not in Rabbath of the sons of Ammon? Its length [is] nine cubits and its breadth [is] four cubits, by the cubit of a man. ¹²And this land, [which] we had possessed at that time, from Aroer, which [is] by the Brook of Arnon, and the half of Mount Gilead and its cities, I have given to the Reubenite and to the Gadite; ¹³and the rest of Gilead and all Bashan, the kingdom of Og, I have given to the half tribe of Manasseh; all the region of Argob, with all Bashan—it is called the land of [the] Rephaim. ¹⁴Jair son of Manasseh has taken all the region of Argob, as far as the border of Geshuri and Maachathi ([namely] Bashan), and calls them by his own name, Havoth-Jair, to this day. ¹⁵And I have given Gilead to Machir. ¹⁶And to the Reubenite

and to the Gadite I have given from Gilead even to the Brook of Arnon, the middle of the valley and the border, even to the Brook of Jabbok, the border of the sons of Ammon, ¹⁷and the plain, and the Jordan, and the border, from Chinnereth even to the Sea of the Plain (the Salt Sea), under the Springs of Pisgah, at the [sun]-rising. ¹⁸And at that time I command you, saying, Your God YHWH has given this land to you to possess it; you pass over armed before your brothers the sons of Israel, all the sons of might. ¹⁹Only your wives, and your infants, and your livestock—I have known that you have much livestock—dwell in your cities which I have given to you, ²⁰until YHWH gives rest to your brothers like yourselves, and they also have possessed the land which your God YHWH is giving to them beyond the Jordan; then you have each turned back to his possession which I have given to you. ²¹And I have commanded Joshua at that time, saying, Your eyes are seeing all that which your God YHWH has done to these two kings—so YHWH does to all the kingdoms to where you are passing over; ²²do not fear them, for your God YHWH—He is fighting for you. ²³And to YHWH I beg for grace at that time, saying, ²⁴Lord YHWH, You have begun to show Your servant Your greatness and Your strong hand; for who [is] a god in the heavens or in earth who does according to Your works and according to Your might? ²⁵Please let me pass over and see the good land which [is] beyond the Jordan, this good hill-country, and Lebanon. ²⁶And YHWH shows Himself angry with me for your sake, and has not listened to me, and YHWH says to me, Enough of you; do not add to speak to Me about this thing anymore; ²⁷go up [to] the top of Pisgah, and lift up your eyes westward, and northward, and southward, and eastward, and see with your eyes, for you do not pass over this Jordan; ²⁸and charge Joshua, and strengthen him, and harden him, for he passes over before this people, and he causes them to inherit the land which you see. ²⁹And we dwell in a valley opposite Beth-Peor."

CHAPTER 4

¹"And now, O Israel, listen to the statutes and to the judgments which I am teaching you to do, so that you live, and have gone in, and possessed the land which YHWH God of your fathers is giving to you. ²You do not add to the word which I am commanding you, nor diminish from it, to keep the commands of your God YHWH which I am commanding you. ³Your eyes are seeing that which YHWH has done in Ba'al-Peor, for every man who has gone after Ba'al-Peor, your God YHWH has destroyed him from your midst; ⁴and you who are cleaving to your God YHWH [are] alive today—all of you. ⁵See, I have taught you statutes and judgments, as my God YHWH has commanded me, to do so in the midst of the land to where you are going in to possess it; ⁶and you have kept and done [them] (for it [is] your wisdom and your understanding) before the eyes of the peoples who hear all these statutes, and they have said, Surely a people wise and understanding [is] this great nation. ⁷For which [is] the great nation that has God [so] near to it, as our God YHWH, in all we have called to Him? ⁸And which [is] the great nation which has righteous statutes and judgments according to all this law which I am setting before you today? ⁹Only, take heed to yourself, and watch your soul exceedingly, lest you forget the things which your eyes have seen, and lest they turn aside from your heart all [the] days of your life; and you have made them known to your sons and to your sons' sons. ¹⁰[Never forget] the day when you have stood before your God YHWH in Horeb, in YHWH's saying to me, Assemble the people to Me, and I cause them to hear My words, so that they learn to fear Me all the days that they are alive on the ground, and they teach their sons; ¹¹and you draw near and stand under the mountain, and the mountain is burning with fire to the heart of the heavens, [with] darkness, cloud, and thick darkness, ¹²and YHWH speaks to you out of the midst of the fire; you are hearing a voice of words, but you are seeing no likeness, only a voice; ¹³and He declares His covenant to you, which He has commanded you to do, the Ten Commandments, and He writes them on two tablets of stone. ¹⁴And YHWH has commanded me at that time to teach you statutes and judgments, for your doing them in the land to where you are passing over to possess it. ¹⁵And you have been very watchful of your souls, for you have not seen any likeness in the day of YHWH's speaking to you in Horeb out of the midst of the fire, ¹⁶lest you do corruptly, and have made for yourselves a carved image, a likeness of any figure: a form of male or female, ¹⁷a form of any beast which [is] in the earth, a form of any winged bird which flies in the heavens, ¹⁸a form of any creeping thing on the ground, a form of any fish which [is] in the waters below the earth. ¹⁹And lest you lift up your eyes to the heavens, and have seen the sun, and the moon, and the stars, all the host of the heavens, and have been drawn away, and have bowed yourself to them and served them, which your God YHWH has apportioned to all the peoples under all the heavens. ²⁰And YHWH has taken you, and He is bringing you out from the iron furnace, from Egypt, to be to Him for a people, an inheritance, as [at] this day. ²¹And YHWH has showed Himself angry with me because of your words, and swears to my not passing over the Jordan, and to my not going into the good land which your God YHWH is giving to you [for] an inheritance; ²²for I am dying in this land; I am not passing over the Jordan, but you are passing over and have possessed this good land. ²³Take heed to yourselves lest you forget the covenant of your God YHWH which He has made with you, and have made a carved image for yourselves, a likeness of anything [concerning] which your God YHWH has charged you; ²⁴for your God YHWH is a consuming fire—a zealous God. ²⁵When you beget sons and sons' sons, and you have become old in the land, and have done corruptly, and have made a carved image, a likeness of anything, and have done evil in the eyes of YHWH to provoke Him to anger, ²⁶I have caused the heavens and the earth to testify against you this day, that you perish utterly quickly from off the land to where you are passing over the Jordan to possess it; you do not prolong days on it, but are utterly destroyed; ²⁷and YHWH has scattered you among the peoples, and you have been left few in number among the nations to where YHWH leads you, ²⁸and you have served gods there, work of man's hands, wood and stone, which do not see, nor hear, nor eat, nor smell. ²⁹And you have sought your God YHWH from there, and have found [Him] when you seek Him with all your heart and with all your soul. ³⁰In the distress of yours, when all these things have found you in the latter end of the days, and you have turned back to your God YHWH and have listened to His voice—³¹for your God YHWH [is] a merciful God—He does not fail you, nor destroy you, nor forget the covenant of your fathers which He has sworn to them. ³²For ask now of the former days which have been before you, from the day that God created man on the earth, and from the [one] end of the heavens even to the [other] end of the heavens, whether there has been as this great thing, or [if anything] has been heard like it. ³³Has a people heard the voice of God speaking out of the midst of the fire, as you have heard, you—and live? ³⁴Or has God tried to go in to take a nation for Himself from the midst of a nation, by trials, by signs, and by wonders, and by war, and by a strong hand, and by an outstretched arm, and by great terrors, according to all that your God YHWH has done to you in Egypt before your eyes? ³⁵You—you have been shown [it], to know that He, YHWH, [is] God; there is none else besides Him. ³⁶He has caused you to hear His voice from the heavens, to instruct you; and on earth He has showed you His great fire, and you have heard His words out of the midst of the fire. ³⁷And because that He has loved your fathers, He also fixes on their seed after them, and brings you out in His presence, by His great power, from Egypt, ³⁸to dispossess nations greater and stronger than you from your presence, to bring you in to give their land to you [for] an inheritance, as [at] this day. ³⁹And you have known today, and have turned [it] back to your heart, that He, YHWH, [is] God in the heavens above and on the earth below—there is none else; ⁴⁰and you have kept His statutes and His commands which I am commanding you today, so that it is well for you, and for your sons after you, and so that you prolong days on the ground which your God YHWH is giving to you—all the days." ⁴¹Then Moses separates three cities beyond the Jordan, toward the sun-rising, ⁴²for the fleeing there of the manslayer who slays his neighbor unknowingly, and he is not hating him before, and he has fled to one of these cities and he has lived: ⁴³Bezer in the wilderness, in the land of the plain, for the Reubenite; and Ramoth in Gilead for the Gadite; and Golan in Bashan for the Manassite. ⁴⁴And this [is] the law which Moses has set

before the sons of Israel; ⁴⁵these [are] the testimonies, and the statutes, and the judgments, which Moses has spoken to the sons of Israel in their coming out of Egypt, ⁴⁶beyond the Jordan, in the valley opposite Beth-Peor, in the land of Sihon, king of the Amorite, who is dwelling in Heshbon, whom Moses and the sons of Israel have struck in their coming out of Egypt; ⁴⁷and they possess his land and the land of Og king of Bashan, two kings of the Amorite who [are] beyond the Jordan, [toward] the sun-rising, ⁴⁸from Aroer, which [is] by the edge of the Brook of Arnon, even to Mount Zion, which [is] Hermon— ⁴⁹and all the plain beyond the Jordan eastward, even to the Sea of the Plain, below the Springs of Pisgah.

CHAPTER 5

¹And Moses calls to all Israel and says to them, "Hear, O Israel, the statutes and the judgments which I am speaking in your ears today, and you have learned them and have observed to do them. ²Our God YHWH made a covenant with us in Horeb; ³YHWH has not made this covenant with our fathers, but with us, we—these here—all of us living today. ⁴YHWH has spoken with you face to face on the mountain, out of the midst of the fire; ⁵I am standing between YHWH and you, at that time, to declare the word of YHWH to you, for you have been afraid from the presence of the fire, and you have not gone up into the mountain; for [He] says: ⁶I, YHWH, [am] your God who has brought you out from the land of Egypt, from a house of servants. ⁷You have no other gods in My presence. ⁸You do not make a carved image for yourself, any likeness which [is] in the heavens above, or which [is] in the earth beneath, or which [is] in the waters under the earth. ⁹You do not bow yourself to them, nor serve them: for I, your God YHWH, [am] a zealous God, charging iniquity of fathers on sons, and on a third and on a fourth [generation] of those hating Me, ¹⁰and doing kindness to thousands, of those loving Me and of those keeping My commands. ¹¹You do not take up the Name of your God YHWH for a vain thing, for YHWH does not acquit him who takes up His Name for a vain thing. ¹²Observe the Sabbath day to sanctify it, as your God YHWH has commanded you; ¹³six days you labor and have done all your work, ¹⁴and the seventh day [is] a Sabbath to your God YHWH; you do not do any work, you, and your son, and your daughter, and your manservant, and your handmaid, and your ox, and your donkey, and all your livestock, and your sojourner who [is] within your gates, so that your manservant and your handmaid rest like yourself. ¹⁵And you have remembered that you have been a servant in the land of Egypt, and your God YHWH brings you out from there by a strong hand and by an outstretched arm; therefore your God YHWH has commanded you to keep the Sabbath day. ¹⁶Honor your father and your mother, as your God YHWH has commanded you, so that your days are prolonged, and so that it is well with you on the ground which your God YHWH is giving to you. ¹⁷You do not murder. ¹⁸You do not commit adultery. ¹⁹You do not steal. ²⁰You do not answer [with] a false testimony against your neighbor. ²¹You do not desire your neighbor's wife, nor do you covet your neighbor's house, his field, and his manservant, and his handmaid, his ox, and his donkey, and anything which [is] your neighbor's. ²²YHWH has spoken these words to all your assembly in the mountain, out of the midst of the fire, [and] of the cloud, and of the thick darkness, [with] a great voice; and He has not added; and He writes them on two tablets of stone and gives them to me. ²³And it comes to pass, as you hear the voice out of the midst of the darkness and of the mountain burning with fire, that you come near to me, all [the] heads of your tribes and your elderly, ²⁴and say, Behold, our God YHWH has showed us His glory and His greatness; and we have heard His voice out of the midst of the fire; this day we have seen that God speaks with man—and he has lived. ²⁵And now, why do we die? For this great fire consumes us if we add to hear the voice of our God YHWH anymore—then we have died. ²⁶For who of all flesh [is] he who has heard the voice of the living God speaking out of the midst of the fire like us, and lives? ²⁷Draw near and hear all that which our God YHWH says, and you, you speak to us all that which our God YHWH speaks to you, and we have listened and done it. ²⁸And YHWH hears the voice of your words in your speaking to me, and YHWH says to me, I have heard the voice of the words of this people which they have spoken to you; they have done well [in] all that they have spoken. ²⁹O that their heart had been thus to them, to fear Me and to keep My commands [for] all the days, that it may be well with them and with their sons for all time! ³⁰Go, say to them, Return for yourselves, to your tents; ³¹and you, stand here with Me, and let Me speak to you all the command, and the statutes, and the judgments which you teach them, and they have done [them] in the land which I am giving to them to possess it. ³²And you have observed to do as your God YHWH has commanded you, you do not turn aside [to] the right or left; ³³in all the way which your God YHWH has commanded you—walk, so that you live, and [it is] well with you, and you have prolonged days in the land which you possess."

CHAPTER 6

¹"And this [is] the command, the statutes and the judgments which your God YHWH has commanded to teach you to do in the land which you are passing over there to possess it, ²so that you fear your God YHWH, to keep all His statutes and His commands which I am commanding you, you, and your son, and your son's son, all [the] days of your life, and so that your days are prolonged. ³And you have heard, O Israel, and observed to do [them], that it may be well with you, and that you may multiply exceedingly, as YHWH, God of your fathers, has spoken to you, [in] the land flowing with milk and honey. ⁴Hear, O Israel: Our God YHWH—YHWH [is] one! ⁵And you have loved your God YHWH with all your heart, and with all your soul, and with all your might. ⁶And these words which I am commanding you today have been on your heart, ⁷and you have repeated them to your sons, and spoken of them in your sitting in your house, and in your walking in the way, and in your lying down, and in your rising up, ⁸and have bound them for a sign on your hand, and they have been for frontlets between your eyes, ⁹and you have written them on doorposts of your house and on your gates. ¹⁰And it has been, when your God YHWH brings you into the land which He has sworn to your fathers, to Abraham, to Isaac, and to Jacob, to give to you great and good cities which you have not built, ¹¹and houses full of all good things which you have not filled, and wells dug which you have not dug, vineyards and olive-yards which you have not planted, that you have eaten and been satisfied. ¹²Take heed to yourself lest you forget YHWH who has brought you out of the land of Egypt, out of a house of servants. ¹³You fear your God YHWH, and you serve Him, and you swear by His Name. ¹⁴You do not go after other gods, of the gods of the peoples who [are] around you, ¹⁵for your God YHWH [is] a zealous God in your midst—lest the anger of your God YHWH burns against you, and He has destroyed you from off the face of the ground. ¹⁶You do not try your God YHWH as you tried [Him] in Massah. ¹⁷You diligently keep the commands of your God YHWH, and His testimonies and His statutes which He has commanded you, ¹⁸and you have done that which is right and good in the eyes of YHWH, so that it is well with you, and you have gone in and possessed the good land which YHWH has sworn to your fathers, ¹⁹to drive away all your enemies from your presence, as YHWH has spoken. ²⁰When your son asks you hereafter, saying, What [are] the testimonies, and the statutes, and the judgments which our God YHWH has commanded you? ²¹Then you have said to your son, We have been servants of Pharaoh in Egypt, and YHWH brings us out of Egypt by a high hand; ²²and YHWH gives signs and wonders, great and severe, on Egypt, on Pharaoh, and on all his house, before our eyes; ²³and He has brought us out from there, in order to bring us in, to give to us the land which He had sworn to our fathers. ²⁴And YHWH commands us to do all these statutes, to fear our God YHWH, for good to ourselves [for] all the days, to keep us alive, as [at] this day; ²⁵and it is righteousness for us when we observe to do all this command before our God YHWH, as He has commanded us."

CHAPTER 7

¹"When your God YHWH brings you into the land to where you are going in to possess it, and He has cast out many nations from your presence, the Hittite, and the Girgashite, and the Amorite, and the Canaanite, and the Perizzite, and the Hivite, and the Jebusite, seven nations more numerous and mighty than you, ²and your God YHWH has given them before you, then you have struck them—you utterly devote them—you do not make a

DEUTERONOMY

covenant with them, nor do you favor them. ³And you do not join in marriage with them; you do not give your daughter to his son, and you do not take his daughter to your son, ⁴for he turns aside your son from after Me, and they have served other gods; and the anger of YHWH has burned against you and has destroyed you quickly. ⁵But thus you do to them: you break down their altars, and you shatter their standing pillars, and you cut down their Asherim, and you burn their carved images with fire. ⁶For you [are] a holy people to your God YHWH; your God YHWH has fixed on you, to be to Him for a peculiar people, out of all the peoples who [are] on the face of the ground. ⁷YHWH has delighted in you and fixes on you, not because of your being more numerous than any of the peoples, for you [are] the least of all the peoples, ⁸but because of YHWH's loving you, and because of His keeping the oath which He has sworn to your fathers; YHWH has brought you out by a strong hand, and ransoms you from a house of servants, from the hand of Pharaoh king of Egypt. ⁹And you have known that He, your God YHWH, [is] God, the faithful God keeping the covenant and the kindness with those loving Him and with those keeping His commands, for one thousand generations, ¹⁰and repaying to those hating Him to their face, to destroy them; He does not delay to him who is hating Him, He repays [it] to him to his face. ¹¹And you have kept the command, and the statutes, and the judgments, which I am commanding you today to do them. ¹²And it has been, because you hear these judgments, and have kept and done them, that your God YHWH has kept the covenant and the kindness with you which He has sworn to your fathers, ¹³and has loved you, and blessed you, and multiplied you, and has blessed the fruit of your womb, and the fruit of your ground, your grain, and your new wine, and your oil, the increase of your oxen, and the wealth of your flock, on the ground which He has sworn to your fathers to give to you. ¹⁴Blessed are you above all the peoples; there is not a barren man or a barren woman in you—nor among your livestock; ¹⁵and YHWH has turned aside every sickness from you, and none of the evil diseases of Egypt (which you have known) does He put on you, and He has put them on all hating you. ¹⁶And you have consumed all the peoples whom your God YHWH is giving to you; your eye has no pity on them, and you do not serve their gods, for it [is] a snare to you. ¹⁷When you say in your heart, These nations [are] more numerous than I, how am I able to dispossess them? ¹⁸You are not afraid of them; you surely remember that which your God YHWH has done to Pharaoh and to all of Egypt, ¹⁹the great trials which your eyes have seen, and the signs, and the wonders, and the strong hand, and the outstretched arm, with which your God YHWH has brought you out; so does your God YHWH do to all the peoples of whose presence you are afraid. ²⁰And your God YHWH also sends the locust among them, until the destruction of those who are left, even those who are hidden from your presence; ²¹you are not terrified by their presence, for your God YHWH [is] in your midst, a God great and fearful. ²²And your God YHWH has cast out these nations from your presence little [by] little (you are not able to consume them quickly, lest the beast of the field multiplies against you), ²³and your God YHWH has given them before you, and confused them [with] a great destruction until their being destroyed; ²⁴and He has given their kings into your hand, and you have destroyed their name from under the heavens; no man stations himself in your presence until you have destroyed them. ²⁵You burn the carved images of their gods with fire; you do not desire the silver and gold on them, nor have you taken [it] for yourself, lest you are snared by it, for it [is] an abomination [to] your God YHWH; ²⁶and you do not bring in an abomination to your house, or you have been devoted like it—you utterly detest it and you utterly abhor it; for it [is] devoted."

CHAPTER 8

¹"All the command which I am commanding you today you observe to do, so that you live, and have multiplied, and gone in, and possessed the land which YHWH has sworn to your fathers; ²and you have remembered all the way which your God YHWH has caused you to go these forty years in the wilderness, in order to humble you to try you, to know that which [is] in your heart, whether you keep His commands or not. ³And He humbles you, and causes you to hunger, and causes you to eat the manna (which you have not known, even your fathers have not known), in order to cause you to know that man does not live by bread alone, but man lives by everything proceeding [from] the mouth of YHWH. ⁴Your raiment has not worn out from off you, and your foot has not swelled these forty years, ⁵and you have known with your heart that as a man disciplines his son, your God YHWH is disciplining you, ⁶and you have kept the commands of your God YHWH, to walk in His ways and to fear Him. ⁷For your God YHWH is bringing you into a good land, a land of brooks of waters, of fountains, and of depths coming out in valley and in mountain; ⁸a land of wheat, and barley, and vine, and fig, and pomegranate; a land of oil olive and honey; ⁹a land in which you eat bread without scarcity—you do not lack anything in it; a land whose stones [are] iron, and you dig bronze out of its mountains. ¹⁰And you have eaten and been satisfied, and have blessed your God YHWH on the good land which he has given to you. ¹¹Take heed to yourself lest you forget your God YHWH so as not to keep His commands, and His judgments, and His statutes which I am commanding you today; ¹²lest you eat and have been satisfied, and build good houses and have inhabited [them], ¹³and your herd and your flock are multiplied, and silver and gold are multiplied to you, and all that is yours is multiplied, ¹⁴and your heart has been high, and you have forgotten your God YHWH who is bringing you out of the land of Egypt, out of a house of servants; ¹⁵who is causing you to go in the great and the terrible wilderness [with] burning serpent, and scorpion, and thirst—where there is no water; who is bringing out waters to you from the flinty rock; ¹⁶who is causing you to eat manna in the wilderness, which your fathers have not known, in order to humble you, and in order to try you, to do you good in your latter end; ¹⁷and you have said in your heart, My power and the might of my hand have made this wealth for me. ¹⁸And you have remembered your God YHWH, for it [is] He who is giving power to you to make wealth, in order to establish His covenant which He has sworn to your fathers, as [at] this day. ¹⁹And it has been, if you really forget your God YHWH, and have gone after other gods, and served them, and bowed yourself to them, I have testified against you today that you utterly perish. ²⁰As the nations whom YHWH is destroying from your presence, so you perish, because you do not listen to the voice of your God YHWH."

CHAPTER 9

¹"Hear, O Israel: You are passing over the Jordan today to go in to possess nations greater and mightier than yourself, cities great and fortified up to the heavens, ²a people great and tall, sons of Anakim, whom you have known, and [of whom] you have heard: Who stations himself before sons of Anak? ³And you have known today that your God YHWH [is] He who is passing over before you [as] a consuming fire; He destroys them, and He humbles them before you, and you have dispossessed them, and destroyed them quickly, as YHWH has spoken to you. ⁴You do not speak in your heart (in your God YHWH's driving them away from before you), saying, In my righteousness YHWH has brought me in to possess this land; but in YHWH dispossessing these nations from your presence, [it is because of] their being wicked. ⁵[It is] not in your righteousness and in the uprightness of your heart [that] you are going in to possess their land, but in YHWH dispossessing these nations from your presence, [it is because of] their being wicked, and in order to establish the word which YHWH has sworn to your fathers, to Abraham, to Isaac, and to Jacob; ⁶and you have known that [it is] not in your righteousness [that] your God YHWH is giving this good land to you to possess it, for you [are] a people stiff of neck. ⁷Remember [and] do not forget that [with] which you have made your God YHWH angry in the wilderness; from the day that you have come out of the land of Egypt until your coming to this place, you have been rebellious against YHWH; ⁸even in Horeb you have made YHWH angry, and YHWH shows Himself angry against you—to destroy you. ⁹In my going up into the mountain to receive the tablets of stone (tablets of the covenant which YHWH has made with you), then I abide on the mountain forty days and forty nights; I have not eaten bread and I have not drunk water; ¹⁰and YHWH gives to me the two tablets of

stone written with the finger of God, and on them [is] according to all the words which YHWH has spoken with you on the mountain, out of the midst of the fire, in the day of the assembly. ⁱⁱAnd it comes to pass, at the end of forty days and forty nights, YHWH has given the two tablets of stone to me—tablets of the covenant. ¹²Then YHWH says to me, Rise, go down, hurry from here, for your people whom you have brought out of Egypt have done corruptly; they have quickly turned aside from the way which I have commanded them—they have made a molten thing for themselves! ¹³And YHWH speaks to me, saying, I have seen this people, and behold, it [is] a people stiff of neck. ¹⁴Desist from Me, and I destroy them, and blot out their name from under the heavens, and I make you become a nation more mighty and numerous than it. ¹⁵And I turn and come down from the mountain, and the mountain is burning with fire, and the two tablets of the covenant [are] on my two hands, ¹⁶and I see, and behold, you have sinned against your God YHWH; you have made a molten calf for yourselves; you have quickly turned aside from the way which YHWH has commanded you. ¹⁷And I lay hold on the two tablets, and cast them out of my two hands, and break them before your eyes, ¹⁸and I throw myself before YHWH, as at first, [for] forty days and forty nights; I have not eaten bread and I have not drunk water, because of all your sins which you have sinned by doing evil in the eyes of YHWH, to make Him angry. ¹⁹For I have been afraid because of the anger and the fury with which YHWH has been angry against you, to destroy you; and YHWH also listens to me at this time. ²⁰And YHWH has showed Himself very angry with Aaron, to destroy him, and I also pray for Aaron at that time. ²¹And I have taken your sin, the calf which you have made, and I burn it with fire, and beat it, grinding well until it [is] small as dust, and I cast its dust into the brook which is going down out of the mountain. ²²And in Taberah, and in Massah, and in Kibroth-Hattaavah, you have been making YHWH angry; ²³also in YHWH's sending you from Kadesh-Barnea, saying, Go up and possess the land which I have given to you; then you provoke the mouth of your God YHWH, and have not given credence to Him, nor listened to His voice. ²⁴You have been rebellious against YHWH from the day of my knowing you. ²⁵And I throw myself before YHWH—the forty days and the forty nights when I had thrown myself—because YHWH has commanded to destroy you; ²⁶and I pray to YHWH, and say, Lord YHWH, do not destroy Your people and Your inheritance whom You have ransomed in Your greatness, whom You have brought out of Egypt with a strong hand; ²⁷be mindful of Your servants, of Abraham, of Isaac, and of Jacob; do not turn to the stiffness of this people, and to its wickedness, and to its sin, ²⁸lest the land from which You have brought us out says, Because of YHWH's want of ability to bring them into the land of which He has spoken to them, and because of His hating them, He brought them out to put them to death in the wilderness. ²⁹And they [are] Your people and Your inheritance, whom You have brought out by Your great power and by Your outstretched arm!"

CHAPTER 10

¹"At that time YHWH has said to me, Hew two tablets of stone for yourself like the first, and come up to Me into the mountain, and you have made an ark of wood for yourself, ²and I write on the tablets the words which were on the first tablets, which you have broken, and you have placed them in the Ark. ³And I make an ark of shittim wood, and hew two tablets of stone like the first, and go up to the mountain with the two tablets in my hand. ⁴And He writes on the tablets according to the first writing, the Ten Commandments, which YHWH has spoken to you in the mountain, out of the midst of the fire, in the day of the assembly, and YHWH gives them to me, ⁵and I turn and come down from the mountain, and put the tablets in the Ark which I had made, and they are there, as YHWH commanded me. ⁶And the sons of Israel have journeyed from Beeroth of the sons of Jaakan to Mosera; Aaron died there, and he is buried there, and his son Eleazar acts as priest in his stead. ⁷From there they journeyed to Gudgodah, and from Gudgodah to Jotbathah, a land of brooks of water. ⁸At that time YHWH has separated the tribe of Levi to carry the Ark of the Covenant of YHWH, to stand before YHWH, to serve Him, and to bless in His Name to this day; ⁹therefore there has not been a portion and inheritance for Levi with his brothers; YHWH Himself [is] his inheritance, as your God YHWH has spoken to him. ¹⁰And I have stood in the mountain, as the former days, [for] forty days and forty nights, and YHWH also listens to me at that time; YHWH has not willed to destroy you. ¹¹And YHWH says to me, Rise, go to journey before the people, and they go in and possess the land which I have sworn to their fathers to give to them. ¹²And now, O Israel, what is your God YHWH asking from you, except to fear your God YHWH, to walk in all His ways, and to love Him, and to serve your God YHWH with all your heart and with all your soul, ¹³to keep the commands of YHWH, and His statutes which I am commanding you today, for good for you? ¹⁴Behold, the heavens, even the heavens of the heavens, [belong] to your God YHWH, [as does] the earth and all that [is] in it. ¹⁵Only, YHWH has delighted in your fathers, to love them, and He fixes on their seed after them—on you, out of all the peoples, as [at] this day. ¹⁶And you have circumcised the foreskin of your heart, and you do not harden your neck anymore. ¹⁷For He, your God YHWH, [is] God of the gods and Lord of the lords—the great, the mighty, and the fearful God, who does not accept by appearances, nor takes a bribe; ¹⁸He is doing the judgment of fatherless and widow, and loving the sojourner, to give bread and raiment to him. ¹⁹And you have loved the sojourner, for you were sojourners in the land of Egypt. ²⁰You fear your God YHWH, you serve Him, and you cleave to Him, and you swear by His Name. ²¹He [is] your praise, and He [is] your God, who has done these great and fearful [things] with you which your eyes have seen. ²²Your fathers went down to Egypt with seventy persons, and now your God YHWH has made you as [the] stars of the heavens for multitude."

CHAPTER 11

¹"And you have loved your God YHWH, and kept His charge, and His statutes, and His judgments, and His commands, [for] all the days; ²and you have known today—for it is not your sons who have not known and who have not seen the discipline of your God YHWH, His greatness, His strong hand, and His outstretched arm; ³and His signs and His doings which He has done in the midst of Egypt, to Pharaoh king of Egypt and to all his land; ⁴and that which He has done to the force of Egypt, to its horses, and to its chariot, when He has caused the waters of the Red Sea to flow against their faces in their pursuing after them, and YHWH destroys them, to this day; ⁵and that which He has done to you in the wilderness until your coming to this place; ⁶and that which He has done to Dathan and to Abiram, sons of Eliab, sons of Reuben, when the earth has opened her mouth and swallows them, and their houses, and their tents, and all that lives which is at their feet, in the midst of all Israel— ⁷but [it is] your eyes which are seeing all the great work of YHWH which He has done. ⁸And you have kept all the command which I am commanding you today, so that you are strong, and have gone in, and possessed the land to where you are passing over to possess it, ⁹and so that you prolong days on the ground which YHWH has sworn to your fathers to give to them and to their seed—a land flowing with milk and honey. ¹⁰For the land to where you are going in to possess it is not as the land of Egypt from where you have come out, where you sow your seed and have watered with your foot, as a garden of the green herb; ¹¹but the land to where you are passing over to possess it [is] a land of hills and valleys—it drinks water of the rain of the heavens— ¹²a land which your God YHWH is searching; the eyes of your God YHWH [are] continually on it, from the beginning of the year even to the latter end of the year. ¹³And it has been, if you listen diligently to My commands which I am commanding you today, to love your God YHWH, and to serve Him with all your heart and with all your soul, ¹⁴then I have given the rain of your land in its season—autumn rain and spring rain—and you have gathered your grain, and your new wine, and your oil, ¹⁵and I have given herbs in your field for your livestock, and you have eaten and been satisfied. ¹⁶Take heed to yourselves lest your heart be enticed, and you have turned aside, and served other gods, and bowed yourselves to them, ¹⁷and the anger of YHWH has burned against you, and He has restrained the heavens and there is no rain, and the ground does not give her increase, and you have perished quickly from off the good land which YHWH is giving to you. ¹⁸And you have placed these words of mine on your

DEUTERONOMY

heart and on your soul, and have bound them for a sign on your hand, and they have been for frontlets between your eyes; ¹⁹and you have taught them to your sons by speaking of them in your sitting in your house, and in your going in the way, and in your lying down, and in your rising up, ²⁰and have written them on the doorposts of your house and on your gates, ²¹so that your days are multiplied, and the days of your sons, on the ground which YHWH has sworn to your fathers to give to them, as the days of the heavens above the earth. ²²For if you diligently keep all this command which I am commanding you to do—to love your God YHWH, to walk in all His ways, and to cleave to Him— ²³then YHWH has dispossessed all these nations from before you, and you have possessed nations greater and mightier than you. ²⁴Every place on which the sole of your foot treads is yours: from the wilderness and Lebanon, from the river, the Euphrates River, even to the Western Sea, is your border. ²⁵No man stations himself in your presence; your God YHWH puts your dread and your fear on the face of all the land on which you tread, as He has spoken to you. ²⁶See, today I am setting before you a blessing and a reviling: ²⁷the blessing when you listen to the commands of your God YHWH which I am commanding you today; ²⁸and the reviling if you do not listen to the commands of your God YHWH, and have turned aside from the way which I am commanding you today, to go after other gods which you have not known. ²⁹And it has been, when your God YHWH brings you into the land to where you are going in to possess it, that you have given the blessing on Mount Gerizim and the reviling on Mount Ebal; ³⁰are they not beyond the Jordan, behind the way of the going in of the sun, in the land of the Canaanite who is dwelling in the plain opposite Gilgal, near the oaks of Moreh? ³¹For you are passing over the Jordan to go in to possess the land which your God YHWH is giving to you; and you have possessed it, and dwelt in it, ³²and observed to do all the statutes and the judgments which I am setting before you today."

CHAPTER 12

¹"These [are] the statutes and the judgments which you observe to do in the land which YHWH, God of your fathers, has given to you to possess it, all the days that you are living on the ground. ²You utterly destroy all the places where the nations which you are dispossessing served their gods, on the high mountains, and on the heights, and under every green tree; ³and you have broken down their altars, and shattered their standing pillars, and you burn their Asherim with fire, and you cut down carved images of their gods, and have destroyed their name out of that place. ⁴You do not do so to your God YHWH; ⁵rather—that you seek after the place which your God YHWH chooses out of all your tribes to put His Name there, for His Dwelling Place, and you have entered there, ⁶and have brought in there your burnt-offerings, and your sacrifices, and your tithes, and the raised-offering of your hand, and your vows, and your free-will offerings, and the firstlings of your herd and of your flock; ⁷and you have eaten there before your God YHWH, and have rejoiced in every putting forth of your hand, you and your households, with which your God YHWH has blessed you. ⁸You do not do according to all that we are doing here today—each [doing] anything that is right in his own eyes— ⁹for until now you have not come to the rest and to the inheritance which your God YHWH is giving to you. ¹⁰When you have passed over the Jordan, and have dwelt in the land which your God YHWH is causing you to inherit, and He has given rest to you from all your surrounding enemies, and you have dwelt confidently, ¹¹then it has been, the place on which your God YHWH fixes to cause His Name to dwell there, there you bring in all that which I am commanding you: your burnt-offerings, and your sacrifices, your tithes, and the raised-offering of your hand, and all the choice of your vows which you vow to YHWH. ¹²And you have rejoiced before your God YHWH, you, and your sons, and your daughters, and your menservants, and your handmaids, and the Levite who [is] within your gates, for he has no part and inheritance with you. ¹³Take heed to yourself lest you cause your burnt-offerings to ascend in any place which you see; ¹⁴rather—that in the place which YHWH chooses in one of your tribes, there you cause your burnt-offerings to ascend, and there you do all that which I am commanding you. ¹⁵Nevertheless, you slaughter anything of the desire of your soul, and have eaten [its] flesh according to the blessing of your God YHWH which He has given to you in all your gates; the unclean and the clean eat it, as [if] the roe and as [if] the deer. ¹⁶Only, you do not eat the blood—you pour it on the earth as water; ¹⁷you are not able to eat within your gates the tithe of your grain, and of your new wine, and your oil, and the firstlings of your herd and of your flock, and any of your vows which you vow, and your free-will offerings, and a raised-offering of your hand; ¹⁸but you eat it before your God YHWH in the place which your God YHWH fixes on, you, and your son, and your daughter, and your manservant, and your handmaid, and the Levite who [is] within your gates, and you have rejoiced before your God YHWH in every putting forth of your hand; ¹⁹take heed to yourself lest you forsake the Levite [for] all your days on your ground. ²⁰When your God YHWH enlarges your border, as He has spoken to you, and you have said, Let me eat flesh—for your soul desires to eat flesh—you eat flesh of all the desire of your soul. ²¹When the place is far from you [in] which your God YHWH chooses to put His Name there, then you have sacrificed from your herd and from your flock which YHWH has given to you, as I have commanded you, and have eaten within your gates, of all the desire of your soul; ²²only, as the roe and the deer is eaten, so do you eat it; the unclean and the clean alike eat it. ²³Only, be sure not to eat the blood, for the blood [is] the life, and you do not eat the life with the flesh; ²⁴you do not eat it—you pour it on the earth as water; ²⁵you do not eat it, in order that it may be well with you and with your sons after you when you do that which [is] right in the eyes of YHWH. ²⁶Only, your holy things which you have, and your vows, you take up, and have gone to the place which YHWH chooses, ²⁷and you have made your burnt-offerings—the flesh and the blood—on the altar of your God YHWH; and the blood of your sacrifices is poured out by the altar of your God YHWH, and you eat the flesh. ²⁸Observe, and you have obeyed all these words which I am commanding you, in order that it may be well with you and with your sons after you for all time, when you do that which [is] good and right in the eyes of your God YHWH. ²⁹When your God YHWH cuts off the nations—to where you are going in to possess them—from your presence, and you have possessed them, and have dwelt in their land— ³⁰take heed to yourself lest you are ensnared after them, after their being destroyed out of your presence, and lest you inquire about their gods, saying, How do these nations serve their gods, that I also do so? ³¹You do not do so to your God YHWH; for every abomination that YHWH has hated they have done for their gods, for they even burn their sons and their daughters with fire for their gods. ³²The whole thing which I am commanding you, you observe to do it; you do not add to it, nor diminish from it."

CHAPTER 13

¹"When a prophet or a dreamer of a dream arises in your midst, and he has given a sign or wonder to you, ²and the sign and the wonder has come to pass, which he has spoken of to you, saying, Let us go after other gods (which you have not known) and serve them, ³you do not listen to the words of that prophet or to that dreamer of the dream, for your God YHWH is trying you to know whether you are loving your God YHWH with all your heart and with all your soul; ⁴you walk after your God YHWH, and you fear Him, and you keep His commands, and you listen to His voice, and you serve Him, and you cleave to Him. ⁵And that prophet or that dreamer of the dream is put to death, for he has spoken apostasy against your God YHWH (who is bringing you out of the land of Egypt, and has ransomed you out of a house of servants), to drive you out of the way in which your God YHWH has commanded you to walk, and you have put away evil from your midst. ⁶When your brother, son of your mother, or your son, or your daughter, or the wife of your bosom, or your friend who [is] as your own soul, moves you in secret, saying, Let us go and serve other gods (which you have not known, you and your fathers, ⁷of the gods of the peoples who [are] around you, who are near to you, or who are far off from you, from the end of the earth even to the [other] end of the earth), ⁸you do not consent to him, nor listen to him, nor does your eye have pity on him, nor do you spare, nor do you cover him over. ⁹But you surely kill him; your hand is on him in the first place to

put him to death, and the hand of all the people last; ¹⁰and you have stoned him with stones and he has died, for he has sought to drive you away from your God YHWH, who is bringing you out of the land of Egypt, out of a house of servants; ¹¹and all Israel hears and fears, and does not add to do like this evil thing in your midst. ¹²When you hear [someone] in one of your cities, which your God YHWH is giving to you to dwell there, saying, ¹³Men, sons of worthlessness, have gone out of your midst, and they force away the inhabitants of their city, saying, Let us go and serve other gods (which you have not known), ¹⁴then you have inquired, and searched, and asked diligently, and behold, [if] truth, the thing is established; this abomination has been done in your midst— ¹⁵you surely strike the inhabitants of that city by the mouth of the sword, devoting it and all that [is] in it, even its livestock, by the mouth of the sword. ¹⁶And you gather all its spoil into the midst of its broad place, and have completely burned the city and all its spoil with fire for your God YHWH, and it has been a continuous heap, it is not built anymore; ¹⁷and nothing from any of that [which is] devoted stays in your hand, so that YHWH turns back from the fierceness of His anger, and has given mercies to you, and loved you, and multiplied you, as He has sworn to your fathers, ¹⁸because you listen to the voice of your God YHWH, to keep all his commands which I am commanding you today, to do that which [is] right in the eyes of your God YHWH."

CHAPTER 14

¹"You [are] sons of your God YHWH; you do not cut yourselves, nor make baldness between your eyes for the dead; ²for you [are] a holy people to your God YHWH, and YHWH has fixed on you to be to Him for a people, a peculiar treasure, out of all the peoples who [are] on the face of the ground. ³You do not eat any abomination; ⁴this [is] the beast which you eat: ox, lamb of the sheep, or kid of the goats, ⁵deer, and roe, and fallow deer, and wild goat, and ibex, and antelope, and zemer; ⁶and every beast dividing the hoof, and cleaving the cleft into two hooves, bringing up the cud, among the beasts—you eat it. ⁷Only, this you do not eat, of those bringing up the cud, and of those dividing the cloven hoof: the camel, and the hare, and the hyrax, for they are bringing up the cud, but the hoof has not divided—they [are] unclean to you; ⁸and the sow, for it is dividing the hoof, and not [bringing] up the cud—it [is] unclean to you; you do not eat of their flesh, and you do not come against their carcass. ⁹This you eat of all which [are] in the waters: anything that has fins and scales you eat; ¹⁰and anything which does not have fins and scales you do not eat—it [is] unclean to you. ¹¹Any clean bird you eat; ¹²and these [are] they of which you do not eat: the eagle, and the bearded vulture, and the osprey, ¹³and the kite, and the falcon, and the vulture after its kind; ¹⁴and every raven after its kind; ¹⁵and the ostrich, and the nightjar [[*or* male ostrich]], and the seagull, and the hawk after its kind; ¹⁶the little owl, and the great owl, and the waterhen, ¹⁷and the pelican, and the Egyptian vulture, and the cormorant, ¹⁸and the stork, and the heron after its kind, and the hoopoe, and the bat. ¹⁹And every teeming thing which is flying—it [is] unclean to you; they are not eaten; ²⁰any clean bird you eat. ²¹You do not eat of any carcass; you give it to the sojourner who [is] within your gates, and he has eaten it; or sell [it] to a stranger; for you [are] a holy people to your God YHWH. You do not boil a kid in its mother's milk. ²²You certainly tithe all the increase of your seed which the field is bringing forth year by year; ²³and you have eaten before your God YHWH, in the place where He chooses to cause His Name to dwell, the tithe of your grain, of your new wine, and of your oil, and the firstlings of your herd, and of your flock, so that you learn to fear your God YHWH [for] all the days. ²⁴And when the way is too much for you, that you are not able to carry it—when the place is too far off from you which your God YHWH chooses to put His Name there, when your God YHWH blesses you—²⁵then you have given [it] in money, and have bound up the money in your hand, and gone to the place on which your God YHWH fixes; ²⁶and you have given the money for anything which your soul desires, for oxen, and for sheep, and for wine, and for strong drink, and for anything which your soul asks for, and you have eaten before your God YHWH there, and you have rejoiced, you and your house. ²⁷As for the Levite who [is] within your gates, you do not forsake him, for he has no portion and inheritance with you. ²⁸At the end of three years you bring out all the tithe of your increase in that year, and have placed [it] within your gates; ²⁹and the Levite has come in—for he has no part and inheritance with you—and the sojourner, and the fatherless, and the widow, who [are] within your gates, and they have eaten, and been satisfied, so that your God YHWH blesses you in all the work of your hand which you do."

CHAPTER 15

¹"At the end of seven years you make a release, ²and this [is] the matter of the release: every owner of a loan [is] to release his hand which he lifts up against his neighbor, he does not exact of his neighbor and of his brother, but has proclaimed a release to YHWH; ³of the stranger you may exact, but that which is yours with your brother your hand releases, ⁴except there is an end [when] no poor [are] with you; for YHWH greatly blesses you in the land which your God YHWH is giving to you [for] an inheritance to possess it, ⁵only if you listen diligently to the voice of your God YHWH, to observe to do all this command which I am commanding you today. ⁶For your God YHWH has blessed you as He has spoken to you; and you have lent [to] many nations, but you have not borrowed; and you have ruled over many nations, but they do not rule over you. ⁷When there is with you any poor of one of your brothers, in one of your cities, in your land which your God YHWH is giving to you, you do not harden your heart, nor shut your hand from your needy brother; ⁸for you certainly open your hand to him, and certainly lend him sufficiency for his lack which he lacks. ⁹Take heed to yourself lest there be a worthless word in your heart, saying, The seventh year [is] near, the year of release; and your eye is evil against your needy brother, and he does not give to him, and he has called to YHWH concerning you, and it has been sin in you; ¹⁰you certainly give to him, and your heart is not sad in your giving to him, for because of this thing your God YHWH blesses you in all your works and in every putting forth of your hand; ¹¹because the poor does not cease out of the land, therefore I am commanding you, saying, You certainly open your hand to your brother, to your poor and to your needy one in your land. ¹²When your brother is sold to you, a Hebrew or a Hebrewess, and he has served you [for] six years, then in the seventh year you send him away free from you. ¹³And when you send him away free from you, you do not send him away empty; ¹⁴you certainly adorn him from your flock, and from your threshing-floor, and from your wine-vat; you give to him [from] that which your God YHWH has blessed you [with], ¹⁵and you have remembered that you have been a servant in the land of Egypt, and your God YHWH ransoms you; therefore I am commanding you this thing today. ¹⁶And it has been, when he says to you, I do not go out from you, because he has loved you and your house, because [it is] good for him with you, ¹⁷then you have taken the awl, and have put [it] through his ear, and through the door, and he has been a perpetual servant to you; and you also do so to your handmaid. ¹⁸It is not hard in your eyes in your sending him away free from you; for [his worth has been] double the hire of a hired worker [when] he has served you six years; and your God YHWH has blessed you in all that you do. ¹⁹Every firstling that is born in your herd and in your flock—you sanctify the male to your God YHWH; you do not work with the firstling of your ox, nor shear the firstling of your flock; ²⁰you eat it before your God YHWH year by year, in the place which YHWH chooses, you and your house. ²¹And when there is a blemish in it, [or it is] lame or blind, [or has] any evil blemish, you do not sacrifice it to your God YHWH; ²²you eat it within your gates, the unclean and the clean alike, as the roe and as the deer. ²³Only, you do not eat its blood—you pour it on the earth as water."

CHAPTER 16

¹"Observe the month of Abib, and you have made a Passover to your God YHWH, for in the month of Abib your God YHWH has brought you out of Egypt by night; ²and you have sacrificed a Passover to your God YHWH, of the flock and of the herd, in the place which YHWH chooses to cause His Name to dwell there. ³You do not eat any fermented thing with it; [for] seven days you eat unleavened things with it, bread of affliction (for you have come out of the land of Egypt in haste), so that you remember the day of your coming out of the

land of Egypt all [the] days of your life; ⁴and leaven is not seen with you in all your border [for] seven days, and there does not remain [any] of the flesh which you sacrifice at evening on the first day until morning. ⁵You are not able to sacrifice the Passover within any of your gates which your God YHWH is giving to you, ⁶except at the place which your God YHWH chooses to cause His Name to dwell—there you sacrifice the Passover in the evening, at the going in of the sun, the season of your coming out of Egypt; ⁷and you have cooked and eaten in the place on which your God YHWH fixes, and have turned in the morning and gone to your tents; ⁸[for] six days you eat unleavened things, and on the seventh day [is] a restraint to your God YHWH; you do no work. ⁹You number seven weeks for yourself; you begin to number seven weeks from the beginning of the sickle among the standing grain, ¹⁰and you have observed the Celebration of Weeks to your God YHWH, a tribute of a free-will offering of your hand, which you give as your God YHWH blesses you. ¹¹And you have rejoiced before your God YHWH, you, and your son, and your daughter, and your manservant, and your handmaid, and the Levite who [is] within your gates, and the sojourner, and the fatherless, and the widow, who [are] in your midst, in the place which your God YHWH chooses to cause His Name to dwell there, ¹²and you have remembered that you have been a servant in Egypt, and have observed and done these statutes. ¹³You observe the Celebration of Shelters for yourself [for] seven days, in your ingathering of your threshing-floor and of your wine-vat; ¹⁴and you have rejoiced in your celebration, you, and your son, and your daughter, and your manservant, and your handmaid, and the Levite, and the sojourner, and the fatherless, and the widow, who [are] within your gates. ¹⁵[For] seven days you celebrate before your God YHWH in the place which YHWH chooses, for your God YHWH blesses you in all your increase and in every work of your hands, and you have been only rejoicing. ¹⁶Three times in a year all of your males appear before your God YHWH in the place which He chooses: in the Celebration of Unleavened Things, and in the Celebration of Weeks, and in the Celebration of Shelters; and they do not appear before YHWH empty; ¹⁷each [gives] according to the gift of his hand, according to the blessing of your God YHWH, which He has given to you. ¹⁸You set for yourself judges and authorities within all your gates which your God YHWH is giving to you, for your tribes; and they have judged the people [with] a righteous judgment. ¹⁹You do not turn aside judgment; you do not discern faces, nor take a bribe, for the bribe blinds the eyes of the wise and perverts the words of the righteous. ²⁰Righteousness—you pursue righteousness, so that you live and have possessed the land which your God YHWH is giving to you. ²¹You do not plant an Asherah of any trees for yourself near the altar of your God YHWH, which you make for yourself, ²²and you do not raise up any standing image for yourself which your God YHWH is hating."

CHAPTER 17

¹"You do not sacrifice to your God YHWH ox or sheep in which there is a blemish—any bad thing; for it [is] an abomination [to] your God YHWH. ²When there is found in your midst, in one of your cities which your God YHWH is giving to you, a man or a woman who does evil in the eyes of your God YHWH by transgressing His covenant, ³and he goes and serves other gods, and bows himself to them, and to the sun, or to the moon, or to any of the host of the heavens, which I have not commanded, ⁴and it has been declared to you, and you have heard, and have searched diligently, and behold, [if] truth, the thing is established; this abomination has been done in Israel— ⁵then you have brought out that man or that woman who has done this evil thing, to your gates—the man or the woman—and you have stoned them with stones, and they have died. ⁶By the mouth of two witnesses or three witnesses is he who is being put to death put to death; he is not put to death by the mouth of one witness; ⁷the hand of the witnesses is on him in the first place to put him to death, and the hand of all the people last; and you have put away evil out of your midst. ⁸When anything is too hard for you for judgment, between blood and blood, between plea and plea, and between stroke and stroke—matters of strife within your gates—then you have risen and gone up to the place on which your God YHWH fixes, ⁹and have come to the priests, the Levites, and to the judge who is in those days, and have inquired, and they have declared the word of judgment to you, ¹⁰and you have done according to the tenor of the word which they declare to you ([they] of that place which YHWH chooses); and you have observed to do according to all that they direct you. ¹¹According to the tenor of the law which they direct you, and according to the judgment which they say to you, you do; you do not turn aside from the word which they declare to you [to] the right or left. ¹²And the man who acts with presumption, so as not to listen to the priest (who is standing to serve your God YHWH there), or to the judge, even that man has died, and you have put away evil from Israel, ¹³and all the people hear and fear, and do not presume anymore. ¹⁴When you come into the land which your God YHWH is giving to you, and have possessed it, and dwelt in it, and you have said, Let me set a king over me like all the nations which [are] around me— ¹⁵you certainly set a king over you on whom YHWH fixes; you set a king over you from the midst of your brothers; you are not able to set a stranger over you, who is not your brother. ¹⁶Only, he does not multiply horses for himself, nor cause the people to return to Egypt, so as to multiply horses, seeing YHWH has said to you, You do not add to return in this way anymore. ¹⁷And he does not multiply wives for himself, and his heart does not turn aside, and he does not exceedingly multiply silver and gold for himself. ¹⁸And it has been, when he sits on the throne of his kingdom, that he has written a copy of this law for himself, on a scroll, from [that] before the priests, the Levites, ¹⁹and it has been with him, and he has read in it all [the] days of his life, so that he learns to fear his God YHWH, to keep all the words of this law and these statutes—to do them, ²⁰so that his heart is not high above his brothers, and so as not to turn aside from the command [to] the right or left, so that he prolongs days over his kingdom, he and his sons in the midst of Israel."

CHAPTER 18

¹"There is not for the priests, the Levites—all the tribe of Levi—a portion and inheritance with Israel; they eat fire-offerings of YHWH, even His inheritance, ²and he has no inheritance in the midst of his brothers; YHWH Himself [is] his inheritance, as He has spoken to him. ³And this is the priest's right from the people, from those sacrificing a sacrifice, whether ox or sheep, he has even given to the priest the leg, and the two cheeks, and the stomach; ⁴you give to him the first of your grain, of your new wine, and of your oil, and the first of the fleece of your flock; ⁵for your God YHWH has fixed on him, out of all your tribes, to stand to serve in the Name of YHWH—him and his sons continually. ⁶And when the Levite comes from one of your cities, out of all Israel where he has sojourned, and has come with all the desire of his soul to the place which YHWH chooses, ⁷then he has ministered in the Name of his God YHWH like all his brothers, the Levites, who are standing there before YHWH. ⁸They eat portion like portion, apart from his sold things from the fathers. ⁹When you are coming into the land which your God YHWH is giving to you, you do not learn to do according to the abominations of those nations. ¹⁰There is not found in you one causing his son and his daughter to pass over into fire, a user of divinations, an observer of clouds, and an enchanter, and a sorcerer, ¹¹and a charmer, and one inquiring from a familiar spirit, and a wizard, and one seeking to the dead. ¹²For everyone doing these [is] an abomination [to] YHWH, and because of these abominations your God YHWH is dispossessing them from your presence. ¹³You must be perfect with your God YHWH, ¹⁴for these nations whom you are possessing listen to observers of clouds and to diviners; but you—your God YHWH has not permitted you so. ¹⁵Your God YHWH raises up for you a Prophet like me out of your brothers, out of your brothers—you must listen to Him, ¹⁶according to all that you asked from your God YHWH in Horeb, in the day of the assembly, saying, Do not let me add to hear the voice of my God YHWH, and do not let me see this great fire anymore, and I do not die; ¹⁷and YHWH says to me, They have done well [in] what they have spoken; ¹⁸I raise up for them a Prophet like you out of the midst of their brothers, and I have given My words in His mouth, and He has spoken to them all that which I command Him; ¹⁹and it has been [that] the man who does not listen to My words

DEUTERONOMY

which He speaks in My Name, I require [it] of him. ²⁰Only, the prophet who presumes to speak a word in My Name, which I have not commanded him to speak, and who speaks in the name of other gods, indeed, that prophet has died. ²¹And when you say in your heart, How do we know the word which YHWH has not spoken? ²²That which the prophet speaks in the Name of YHWH, and the thing is not, and does not come—it [is] the word which YHWH has not spoken; the prophet has spoken it in presumption; you are not afraid of him."

CHAPTER 19

¹"When your God YHWH cuts off the nations whose land your God YHWH is giving to you, and you have dispossessed them, and dwelt in their cities and in their houses, ²you separate three cities for yourself in the midst of your land which your God YHWH is giving to you to possess it. ³You prepare the way for yourself, and have divided into three parts the border of your land which your God YHWH causes you to inherit, and it has been for the fleeing there of every manslayer. ⁴And this [is] the matter of the manslayer who flees there, and has lived: he who strikes his neighbor unknowingly, and is not hating him before— ⁵even he who comes into a forest with his neighbor to hew wood, and his hand has driven with an axe to cut the tree, and the iron has slipped from the wood, and has met his neighbor, and he has died—he flees to one of these cities, and has lived, ⁶lest the redeemer of blood pursue after the manslayer when his heart is hot and has overtaken him, because the way is great, and has struck his life, and he has no sentence of death, for he is not hating him before; ⁷therefore I am commanding you, saying, You separate three cities for yourself. ⁸And if your God YHWH enlarges your border, as He has sworn to your fathers, and has given to you all the land which He has spoken to give to your fathers— ⁹when you keep all this command to do it, which I am commanding you today, to love your God YHWH and to walk in His ways [for] all the days—then you have added three more cities for yourself to these three; ¹⁰and [do this] lest innocent blood is shed in the midst of your land which your God YHWH is giving to you [for] an inheritance, and there has been blood on you. ¹¹And when a man is hating his neighbor, and has lain in wait for him, and risen against him, and struck his life, and he has died, then he has fled to one of these cities, ¹²and [the] elderly of his city have sent and taken him from there, and given him into the hand of the redeemer of blood, and he has died; ¹³your eye has no pity on him, and you have put away the innocent blood from Israel, and it is well with you. ¹⁴You do not remove a border of your neighbor, which they of former times have made, in your inheritance, which you inherit in the land which your God YHWH is giving to you to possess it. ¹⁵One witness does not rise against a man for any iniquity and for any sin, in any sin which he sins; by the mouth of two witnesses or by the mouth of three witnesses is a thing established. ¹⁶When a violent witness rises against a man to testify against him apostasy, ¹⁷then both of the men who have the strife have stood before YHWH, before the priests and the judges who are in those days, ¹⁸and the judges have searched diligently, and behold, the witness [is] a false witness who has testified a falsehood against his brother, ¹⁹then you have done to him as he devised to do to his brother, and you have put away evil out of your midst, ²⁰and those who are left hear and fear, and do not add to do according to this evil thing in your midst anymore. ²¹And your eye does not pity—life for life, eye for eye, tooth for tooth, hand for hand, foot for foot."

CHAPTER 20

¹"When you go out to battle against your enemy, and have seen horse and chariot—a people more numerous than you—you are not afraid of them, for your God YHWH [is] with you, who is bringing you up out of the land of Egypt; ²and it has been, in your drawing near to the battle, that the priest has come near, and spoken to the people, ³and said to them, Hear, O Israel: You are drawing near today to battle against your enemies, do not let your hearts be tender, do not fear, nor make haste, nor be terrified at their presence, ⁴for your God YHWH [is] He who is going with you, to fight for you with your enemies—to save you. ⁵And the authorities have spoken to the people, saying, Who [is] the man that has built a new house and has not dedicated it? Let him go and return to his house, lest he die in battle and another man dedicate it. ⁶And who [is] the man that has planted a vineyard and has not made it common? Let him go and return to his house, lest he die in battle, and another man make it common. ⁷And who [is] the man that has betrothed a woman and has not taken her? Let him go and return to his house, lest he die in battle, and another man take her. ⁸And the authorities have added to speak to the people and said, Who [is] the man that is afraid and tender of heart? Let him go and return to his house, and the heart of his brothers does not melt like his heart. ⁹And it has come to pass, as the authorities finish to speak to the people, that they have appointed princes of the hosts at the head of the people. ¹⁰When you draw near to a city to fight against it, then you have called to it for peace, ¹¹and it has been, if it answers you [with] peace, and has opened to you, then it has come to pass, all the people who are found in it are for tributaries to you, and have served you. ¹²And if it does not make peace with you, and has made war with you, then you have laid siege against it, ¹³and your God YHWH has given it into your hand, and you have struck every male of it by the mouth of the sword. ¹⁴Only, the women, and the infants, and the livestock, and all that is in the city, all its spoil, you seize for yourself, and you have eaten the spoil of your enemies which your God YHWH has given to you. ¹⁵So you do to all the cities which are very far off from you, which are not of the cities of these nations. ¹⁶Only, of the cities of these peoples which your God YHWH is giving to you [for] an inheritance, you do not keep alive any [that are] breathing; ¹⁷for you certainly devote the Hittite, and the Amorite, the Canaanite, and the Perizzite, the Hivite, and the Jebusite, as your God YHWH has commanded you, ¹⁸so that they do not teach you to do according to all their abominations which they have done for their gods, and you have sinned against your God YHWH. ¹⁹When you lay siege to a city [for] many days to fight against it, to capture it, you do not destroy its trees to force an axe against them, for you eat of them, and you do not cut them down—for the tree of the field [is] man's—to go in at your presence in the siege. ²⁰Only, the tree of which you know that it [is] not a fruit-tree, you destroy it, and have cut [it] down, and have built a bulwark against the city which is making war with you until you have subdued it."

CHAPTER 21

¹"When one is found slain, fallen in a field on the ground which your God YHWH is giving to you to possess it, [and] it is not known who has struck him, ²then your elderly and yours [of those] judging have gone out and measured to the cities which [are] around the slain one, ³and it has been, the city which [is] near to the slain one, even [the] elderly of that city have taken a heifer of the herd, which has not been worked with, which has not drawn in a yoke, ⁴and [the] elderly of that city have brought down the heifer to a hard valley, which is not tilled nor sown, and have beheaded the heifer there in the valley. ⁵And the priests, sons of Levi, have come near—for your God YHWH has fixed on them to serve Him and to bless in the Name of YHWH, and by their mouth is every strife and every stroke— ⁶and all [the] elderly of that city, who are near to the slain one, wash their hands over the heifer which is beheaded in the valley, ⁷and they have answered and said, Our hands have not shed this blood, and our eyes have not seen— ⁸receive atonement for Your people Israel, whom You have ransomed, O YHWH, and do not permit innocent blood in the midst of Your people Israel; and the blood has been pardoned to them, ⁹and you put away the innocent blood out of your midst, for you do that which [is] right in the eyes of YHWH. ¹⁰When you go out to battle against your enemies, and your God YHWH has given them into your hand, and you have taken captive its captivity, ¹¹and have seen a woman of beautiful form in the captivity, and have delighted in her, and have taken [her] to yourself for a wife, ¹²then you have brought her into the midst of your household, and she has shaved her head, and prepared her nails, ¹³and turned aside the raiment of her captivity from off her, and has dwelt in your house, and lamented her father and her mother [for] a month of days, and afterward you go in to her and have married her, and she has been to you for a wife. ¹⁴And it has been, if you have not delighted in her, that you have sent her away at her desire, and surely you do not sell her for money; you do not tyrannize over her,

because that you have humbled her. ¹⁵When a man has two wives, one loved and the other hated, and they have borne sons to him (the loved one and the hated one), and the firstborn son has been to the hated one, ¹⁶then it has been, in the day of his causing his sons to inherit that which he has, he is not able to declare firstborn the son of the loved one, in the face of the son of the hated one—the firstborn. ¹⁷But the firstborn, son of the hated one, he acknowledges, to give to him a double portion of all that is found with him, for he [is] the beginning of his strength; to him [is] the right of the firstborn. ¹⁸When a man has a son apostatizing and being rebellious—he is not listening to the voice of his father and to the voice of his mother, and they have disciplined him, and he does not listen to them— ¹⁹then his father and his mother have laid hold on him, and they have brought him out to [the] elderly of his city, and to the gate of his place, ²⁰and have said to [the] elderly of his city, Our son—this one—is apostatizing and being rebellious; he is not listening to our voice—a glutton and drunkard. ²¹Then all the men of his city have stoned him with stones and he has died, and you have put away the evil out of your midst, and all Israel hears and fears. ²²And when there is a sin in a man [with] a judgment of death, and he has been put to death, and you have hanged him on a tree, ²³his corpse does not remain on the tree, for you certainly bury him in the day—for he who is hanged [becomes] a curse of God—and you do not defile your ground which your God YHWH is giving to you [for] an inheritance."

CHAPTER 22

¹"You do not see the ox of your brother or his sheep driven away, and have hidden yourself from them, you certainly turn them back to your brother; ²and if your brother [is] not near to you, and you have not known him, then you have removed it to the midst of your house, and it has been with you until your brother seeks it, and you have given it back to him; ³and so you do to his donkey, and so you do to his garment, and so you do to any lost thing of your brother's, which is lost by him, and you have found it; you are not able to hide yourself. ⁴You do not see the donkey of your brother, or his ox, falling in the way, and have hid yourself from them; you certainly raise [them] up for him. ⁵Anything of a man is not on a woman, nor does a man put on the garment of a woman, for anyone doing these [is] an abomination [to] your God YHWH. ⁶When a bird's nest comes before you in the way, in any tree, or on the earth, [with] brood or eggs, and the mother is sitting on the brood or on the eggs, you do not take the mother with the young ones; ⁷you certainly send the mother away, and take the young ones for yourself, so that it is well with you and you have prolonged days. ⁸When you build a new house, then you have made a parapet for your roof, and you do not put blood on your house when one falls from it. ⁹You do not sow your vineyard [with] two kinds [of seed], lest the fullness of the seed which you sow and the increase of the vineyard be separated. ¹⁰You do not plow with an ox and with a donkey together. ¹¹You do not put on mixed material, wool and linens together. ¹²You make fringes for yourself on the four skirts of your covering with which you cover [yourself]. ¹³When a man takes a wife, and has gone in to her, and hated her, ¹⁴and laid evil deeds of words against her, and brought out an evil name against her, and said, I have taken this woman, and I draw near to her, and I have not found proofs of virginity in her; ¹⁵then the father of the girl, and her mother, have taken and brought out the girl's proofs of virginity to [the] elderly of the city in the gate, ¹⁶and the father of the girl has said to the elderly, I have given my daughter to this man for a wife, and he hates her; ¹⁷and behold, he has laid evil deeds of words, saying, I have not found proofs of virginity for your daughter—and these [are] the proofs of virginity of my daughter! And they have spread out the garment before [the] elderly of the city. ¹⁸And [the] elderly of that city have taken the man, and discipline him, ¹⁹and fined him one hundred pieces of silver, and given [them] to the father of the girl, because he has brought out an evil name on a virgin of Israel; and she is to him for a wife—he is not able to send her away [for] all his days. ²⁰And if this thing has been truth—proofs of virginity have not been found for the girl— ²¹then they have brought out the girl to the opening of her father's house, and the men of her city have stoned her with stones and she has died, for she has done folly in Israel, to go whoring [in] her father's house; and you have put away evil out of your midst. ²²When a man is found lying with a woman married to a husband, then both of them have died—the man who is lying with the woman, and the woman; and you have put away evil out of Israel. ²³When there is a girl, a virgin, betrothed to a man, and a man has found her in a city and lain with her, ²⁴then you have brought them both out to the gate of that city, and stoned them with stones, and they have died: the girl, because that she has not cried in a city; and the man, because that he has humbled his neighbor's wife; and you have put away evil out of your midst. ²⁵And if the man finds the girl who is betrothed in a field, and the man has laid hold on her, and lain with her, then the man who has lain with her has died alone; ²⁶and you do not do anything to the girl—the girl has no deadly sin; for as a man rises against his neighbor and has murdered him, [taking] a life, so [is] this thing; ²⁷for he found her in a field, [and when] she has cried—the girl who is betrothed—then she has no savior. ²⁸When a man finds a girl, a virgin who is not betrothed, and has caught her, and lain with her, and they have been found, ²⁹then the man who is lying with her has given fifty pieces of silver to the father of the girl, and she is to him for a wife; because that he has humbled her, he is not able to send her away [for] all his days. ³⁰A man does not take his father's wife, nor uncover his father's skirt."

CHAPTER 23

¹"No one wounded, bruised, or cut in the genitals enters into the assembly of YHWH; ²a bastard does not enter into the assembly of YHWH; even a tenth generation of him does not enter into the assembly of YHWH. ³An Ammonite and a Moabite do not enter into the assembly of YHWH; even a tenth generation of them do not enter into the assembly of YHWH—for all time, ⁴because that they have not come before you with bread and with water in the way, in your coming out from Egypt, and because he has hired against you Balaam son of Beor, of Pethor of Aram-Naharaim, to revile you; ⁵and your God YHWH has not been willing to listen to Balaam, and your God YHWH turns the reviling to a blessing for you, because your God YHWH has loved you; ⁶you do not seek their peace and their good all your days—for all time. ⁷You do not detest an Edomite, for he [is] your brother; you do not detest an Egyptian, for you have been a sojourner in his land; ⁸sons who are begotten of them, a third generation of them, enter into the assembly of YHWH. ⁹When a camp goes out against your enemies, then you have kept from every evil thing. ¹⁰When there is a man who is not clean in you, from an accident at night, then he has gone out to the outside of the camp; he does not come into the midst of the camp; ¹¹and it has been, at the turning of the evening, he bathes with water, and at the going in of the sun he comes into the midst of the camp. ¹²And you have a station at the outside of the camp, and you have gone out there outside; ¹³and you have a peg on your staff, and it has been, in your sitting outside, that you have dug with it, and turned back, and covered your filth. ¹⁴For your God YHWH is walking up and down in the midst of your camp, to deliver you and to give your enemies before you, and your camp has been holy, and He does not see the nakedness of anything in you, and has turned back from after you. ¹⁵You do not shut up a servant to his lord, who escapes to you from his lord; ¹⁶he dwells with you in your midst, in the place which he chooses within one of your gates, where it is pleasing to him; you do not oppress him. ¹⁷There is not a whore among the daughters of Israel, nor is there a whoremonger among the sons of Israel; ¹⁸you do not bring the wage of a whore or the price of a dog into the house of your God YHWH for any vow; for even both of them [are] an abomination [to] your God YHWH. ¹⁹You do not lend in usury to your brother—usury of money, usury of food, usury of anything which is lent on usury. ²⁰You may lend in usury to a stranger, but you do not lend in usury to your brother, so that your God YHWH blesses you in every putting forth of your hand on the land to where you go in to possess it. ²¹When you vow a vow to your God YHWH, you do not delay to complete it; for your God YHWH certainly requires it from you, lest it has been sin in you. ²²And when you refrain to vow, it is not sin in you. ²³You keep and have done the utterance of your lips, as you have vowed to your God YHWH, a free-will offering which you have

DEUTERONOMY

spoken with your mouth. ²⁴When you come into the vineyard of your neighbor, then you have eaten grapes according to your desire, your sufficiency, but you do not put [any] into your vessel. ²⁵When you come in among the standing grain of your neighbor, then you have plucked the ears with your hand, but you do not wave a sickle over the standing grain of your neighbor."

CHAPTER 24

¹"When a man takes a wife and has married her, and it has been, if she does not find grace in his eyes (for he has found nakedness in her of anything), then he has written a writing of divorce for her, and given [it] into her hand, and sent her out of his house; ²when she has gone out of his house, and has gone and been another man's, ³and the latter man has hated her, and written a writing of divorce for her, and given [it] into her hand, and sent her out of his house, or when the latter man dies, who has taken her to himself for a wife, ⁴her former husband who sent her away is not able to return to take her to be to him for a wife, after that she has become defiled; for it [is] an abomination before YHWH, and you do not cause the land to sin which your God YHWH is giving to you [for] an inheritance. ⁵When a man takes a new wife, he does not go out into the host, and [one] does not pass over to him for anything; he is free at his own house [for] one year, and his wife, whom he has taken, he has made glad. ⁶No one takes millstones and rider in pledge, for it [is one's] life he is taking in pledge. ⁷When a man is found stealing a person from his brothers, from the sons of Israel, and has tyrannized over him and sold him, then that thief has died, and you have put away evil out of your midst. ⁸Take heed in the plague of leprosy, to watch greatly, and to do according to all that the priests, the Levites, teach you; you observe to do as I have commanded them; ⁹remember that which your God YHWH has done to Miriam in the way, in your coming out of Egypt. ¹⁰When you lift up a debt of anything on your brother, you do not go into his house to obtain his pledge; ¹¹you stand at the outside, and the man on whom you are lifting [it] up is bringing out the pledge to you at the outside. ¹²And if he is a poor man, you do not lie down with his pledge; ¹³you certainly give back the pledge to him at the going in of the sun, and he has lain down in his own raiment and has blessed you; and it is righteousness to you before your God YHWH. ¹⁴You do not oppress a hired worker, poor and needy, of your brothers or of your sojourner who is in your land within your gates; ¹⁵you give him his hire in his day, and the sun does not go in on it, for he [is] poor, and he is supporting his life on it, lest he cries against you to YHWH, and it has been sin in you. ¹⁶Fathers are not put to death for sons, and sons are not put to death for fathers—they are each put to death for his own sin. ¹⁷You do not turn aside the judgment of a fatherless sojourner, nor take the garment of a widow in pledge; ¹⁸and you have remembered that you have been a servant in Egypt, and your God YHWH ransoms you from there; therefore I am commanding you to do this thing. ¹⁹When you reap your harvest in your field, and have forgotten a sheaf in a field, you do not return to take it; it is for the sojourner, for the fatherless, and for the widow, so that your God YHWH blesses you in all the work of your hands. ²⁰When you beat your olive, you do not examine the branch behind you; it is for the sojourner, for the fatherless, and for the widow. ²¹When you cut your vineyard, you do not glean behind you; it is for the sojourner, for the fatherless, and for the widow; ²²and you have remembered that you have been a servant in the land of Egypt; therefore I am commanding you to do this thing."

CHAPTER 25

¹"When there is a strife between men, and they have come near to the judgment, and they have judged, and declared righteous the righteous, and declared wrong the wrongdoer, ²then it has come to pass, if the wrongdoer is to be struck, that the judge has caused him to fall down, and [one] has struck him in his presence, according to the sufficiency of his wrongdoing, by number; ³he strikes him forty [times]; he is not adding, lest he is adding to strike him above these many stripes, and your brother be lightly esteemed in your eyes. ⁴You do not muzzle an ox in its threshing. ⁵When brothers dwell together, and one of them has died and has no son, the wife of the dead is not given to a strange man; her husband's brother goes in to her, and has taken her to him for a wife, and performs the duty of her husband's brother; ⁶and it has been, the firstborn which she bears rises for the name of his dead brother, and his name is not wiped away out of Israel. ⁷And if the man does not delight to take his brother's wife, then his brother's wife has gone up to the gate, to the elderly, and said, My husband's brother is refusing to raise up a name for his brother in Israel; he has not been willing to perform the duty of my husband's brother; ⁸and [the] elderly of his city have called for him, and spoken to him, and he has stood and said, I have no desire to take her. ⁹Then his brother's wife has drawn near to him before the eyes of the elderly, and drawn his shoe from off his foot, and spat in his face, and answered and said, Thus it is done to the man who does not build up the house of his brother; ¹⁰and his name has been called in Israel, The house of him whose shoe is drawn off. ¹¹When men strive together with one another, and the wife of one has drawn near to deliver her husband out of the hand of his striker, and has put forth her hand, and laid hold on his private parts, ¹²then you have cut off her hand; your eye does not spare. ¹³You do not have [both] a great stone and a small stone in your bag. ¹⁴You do not have a great ephah and a small ephah in your house. ¹⁵You have a complete and just stone, [and] you have a complete and just ephah, so that they prolong your days on the ground which your God YHWH is giving to you; ¹⁶for anyone doing these things, anyone doing iniquity, [is] an abomination [to] your God YHWH. ¹⁷Remember that which Amalek has done to you in the way in your going out from Egypt, ¹⁸that he has met you in the way, and strikes among you all those feeble behind you (when you [were] weary and fatigued), and is not fearing God. ¹⁹And it has been, in your God YHWH giving rest to you from all your surrounding enemies, in the land which your God YHWH is giving to you [for] an inheritance to possess it, you blot out the remembrance of Amalek from under the heavens—you do not forget."

CHAPTER 26

¹"And it has been, when you come into the land which your God YHWH is giving to you [for] an inheritance, and you have possessed it and dwelt in it, ²that you have taken from the first of all the fruits of the ground, which you bring in out of your land which your God YHWH is giving to you, and have put [it] in a basket, and gone to the place which your God YHWH chooses to cause His Name to dwell there. ³And you have come to the priest who is in those days, and have said to him, I have declared to your God YHWH today that I have come into the land which YHWH has sworn to our fathers to give to us; ⁴and the priest has taken the basket out of your hand and placed it before the altar of your God YHWH. ⁵And you have answered and said before your God YHWH, My father [is] a perishing Aramean! And he goes down to Egypt, and sojourns there with few men, and becomes a great, mighty, and populous nation there; ⁶and the Egyptians do us evil, and afflict us, and put hard service on us; ⁷and we cry to YHWH, God of our fathers, and YHWH hears our voice, and sees our affliction, and our labor, and our oppression; ⁸and YHWH brings us out from Egypt by a strong hand, and by an outstretched arm, and by great fear, and by signs, and by wonders, ⁹and He brings us to this place, and gives this land to us—a land flowing with milk and honey. ¹⁰And now, behold, I have brought in the first of the fruits of the ground which you have given to me, O YHWH. (And you have placed it before your God YHWH, and bowed yourself before your God YHWH, ¹¹and rejoiced in all the good which your God YHWH has given to you and to your house—you, and the Levite, and the sojourner who [is] in your midst.) ¹²When you complete to tithe all the tithe of your increase in the third year, the year of the tithe, then you have given to the Levite, to the sojourner, to the fatherless, and to the widow, and they have eaten within your gates and been satisfied, ¹³and you have said before your God YHWH, I have put away the separated thing out of the house, and have also given it to the Levite, and to the sojourner, and to the orphan, and to the widow, according to all Your command which You have commanded me; I have not passed over from Your commands, nor have I forgotten. ¹⁴I have not eaten of it in my affliction, nor have I put away of it for uncleanness, nor have I given of it for the dead; I have listened to the voice of my God YHWH; I have done according to all that You

DEUTERONOMY

have commanded me; ¹⁵look from Your holy habitation, from the heavens, and bless Your people Israel and the ground which You have given to us, as You have sworn to our fathers—a land flowing [with] milk and honey. ¹⁶This day your God YHWH is commanding you to do these statutes and judgments; and you have listened and done them with all your heart and with all your soul. ¹⁷Today you have proclaimed YHWH to be to you for God, that [you are] to walk in His ways, and to keep His statutes, and His commands, and His judgments, and to listen to His voice. ¹⁸And today YHWH has proclaimed you to be to Him for a people, a peculiar treasure, as He has spoken to you, that [you are] to keep all His commands, ¹⁹so as to make you highest above all the nations whom He has made for a praise, and for a name, and for beauty, and for your being a holy people to your God YHWH, as He has spoken."

CHAPTER 27

¹And Moses and [the] elderly of Israel command the people, saying, "Keep all the command which I am commanding you today; ²and it has been, in the day that you pass over the Jordan to the land which your God YHWH is giving to you, that you have raised up great stones for yourself, and plastered them with plaster, ³and written on them all the words of this law in your passing over, so that you go into the land which your God YHWH is giving to you—a land flowing with milk and honey, as YHWH, God of your fathers, has spoken to you. ⁴And it has been, in your passing over the Jordan, you raise up these stones which I am commanding you today, in Mount Ebal, and you have plastered them with plaster, ⁵and built an altar there to your God YHWH, an altar of stones; you do not wave iron over them. ⁶You build the altar of your God YHWH [with] complete stones, and have caused burnt-offerings to ascend on it to your God YHWH, ⁷and sacrificed peace-offerings, and eaten there, and rejoiced before your God YHWH, ⁸and written on the stones all the words of this law, well engraved." ⁹And Moses speaks—the priests, the Levites, also—to all Israel, saying, "Keep silent and hear, O Israel: This day you have become a people for your God YHWH; ¹⁰and you have listened to the voice of your God YHWH, and done His commands and His statutes which I am commanding you today." ¹¹And Moses commands the people on that day, saying, ¹²"These stand on Mount Gerizzim to bless the people, in your passing over the Jordan: Simeon, and Levi, and Judah, and Issachar, and Joseph, and Benjamin. ¹³And these stand, for the reviling, on Mount Ebal: Reuben, Gad, and Asher, and Zebulun, Dan, and Naphtali." ¹⁴And the Levites have answered and said to every man of Israel [with] a loud voice: ¹⁵"Cursed [is] the man who makes a carved and molten image, an abomination [to] YHWH, work of the hands of a craftsman, and has put [it] in a secret place." And all the people have answered and said, "Amen." ¹⁶"Cursed [is] he who is making light of his father and his mother." And all the people have said, "Amen." ¹⁷"Cursed [is] he who is removing his neighbor's border." And all the people have said, "Amen." ¹⁸"Cursed [is] he who is causing the blind to err in the way." And all the people have said, "Amen." ¹⁹"Cursed [is] he who is turning aside the judgment of fatherless, sojourner, and widow." And all the people have said, "Amen." ²⁰"Cursed [is] he who is lying with his father's wife, for he has uncovered his father's skirt." And all the people have said, "Amen." ²¹"Cursed [is] he who is lying with any beast." And all the people have said, "Amen." ²²"Cursed [is] he who is lying with his sister, daughter of his father or daughter of his mother." And all the people have said, "Amen." ²³"Cursed [is] he who is lying with his mother-in-law." And all the people have said, "Amen." ²⁴"Cursed [is] he who is striking his neighbor in secret." And all the people have said, "Amen." ²⁵"Cursed [is] he who is taking a bribe to strike a person, innocent blood." And all the people have said, "Amen." ²⁶"Cursed [is] he who does not establish the words of this law, to do them." And all the people have said, "Amen."

CHAPTER 28

¹"And it has been, if you listen diligently to the voice of your God YHWH, to observe to do all His commands which I am commanding you today, that your God YHWH has made you highest above all the nations of the earth, ²and all these blessings have come on you and overtaken you, because you listen to the voice of your God YHWH: ³Blessed [are] you in the city, and blessed [are] you in the field. ⁴Blessed [is] the fruit of your womb, and the fruit of your ground, and the fruit of your livestock, the increase of your oxen, and the wealth of your flock. ⁵Blessed [is] your basket and your kneading-trough. ⁶Blessed [are] you in your coming in, and blessed [are] you in your going out. ⁷YHWH makes your enemies, who are rising up against you, to be struck before your face; in one way they come out to you, and in seven ways they flee before you. ⁸YHWH commands the blessing with you in your storehouses, and in every putting forth of your hand, and has blessed you in the land which your God YHWH is giving to you. ⁹YHWH establishes you to Himself for a holy people, as He has sworn to you, when you keep the commands of your God YHWH and have walked in His ways; ¹⁰and all the peoples of the land have seen that the Name of YHWH is called by you, and they have been afraid of you. ¹¹And YHWH has made you abundant in good, in the fruit of the womb, and in the fruit of your livestock, and in the fruit of your ground, on the ground which YHWH has sworn to your fathers to give to you. ¹²YHWH opens his good treasure to you—the heavens—to give the rain of your land in its season, and to bless all the work of your hand, and you have lent to many nations, and you do not borrow. ¹³And YHWH has set you for head and not for tail; and you have been only above, and are not beneath, for you listen to the commands of your God YHWH, which I am commanding you today, to keep and to do, ¹⁴and you do not turn aside from all the words which I am commanding you today [to] the right or left, to go after other gods, to serve them. ¹⁵And it has been, if you do not listen to the voice of your God YHWH, to observe to do all His commands and His statutes which I am commanding you today, that all these revilings have come on you and overtaken you: ¹⁶Cursed [are] you in the city, and cursed [are] you in the field. ¹⁷Cursed [is] your basket and your kneading-trough. ¹⁸Cursed [is] the fruit of your body, and the fruit of your land, the increase of your oxen, and the wealth of your flock. ¹⁹Cursed [are] you in your coming in, and cursed [are] you in your going out. ²⁰YHWH sends the curse, the trouble, and the rebuke on you, in every putting forth of your hand which you do, until you are destroyed, and until you perish quickly, because of the evil of your doings [by] which you have forsaken Me. ²¹YHWH causes the pestilence to cleave to you until He consumes you from off the ground to where you are going in to possess it. ²²YHWH strikes you with consumption, and with fever, and with inflammation, and with extreme burning, and with sword, and with blasting, and with mildew, and they have pursued you until you perish ²³And your heavens which [are] over your head have been bronze, and the earth which [is] under you iron; ²⁴YHWH gives dust and ashes [for] the rain of your land; it comes down on you from the heavens until you are destroyed. ²⁵YHWH makes you struck before your enemies; in one way you go out to them, and in seven ways you flee before them, and you have been for a trembling to all kingdoms of the earth; ²⁶and your carcass has been for food for every bird of the heavens and for the beast of the earth, and there is none causing [them] to tremble. ²⁷YHWH strikes you with the ulcer of Egypt, and with lumps, and with scurvy, and with itch, of which you are not able to be healed. ²⁸YHWH strikes you with madness, and with blindness, and with astonishment of heart; ²⁹and you have been groping at noon, as the blind gropes in darkness; and you do not cause your ways to prosper; and you have been only oppressed and plundered [for] all the days, and there is no savior. ³⁰You betroth a woman, and another man lies with her; you build a house, and do not dwell in it; you plant a vineyard, and do not make it common; ³¹your ox [is] slaughtered before your eyes, and you do not eat of it; your donkey [is] violently taken away from before you, and it is not given back to you; your sheep [are] given to your enemies, and there is no savior for you. ³²Your sons and your daughters [are] given to another people, and your eyes are looking and consumed for them all the day, but your hand is not to God! ³³A people whom you have not known eat the fruit of your ground and all your labor; and you have been only oppressed and bruised [for] all the days; ³⁴and you have been mad because of the sight of your eyes which you see. ³⁵YHWH strikes you with a severe ulcer on the knees and on the legs (of which you are not able to be healed), from the sole of your

foot even to your crown. ³⁶YHWH causes you and your king whom you raise up over you to go to a nation which you have not known, you and your fathers, and you have served other gods there—wood and stone; ³⁷and you have been for an astonishment, for an allegory, and for a byword among all the peoples to where YHWH leads you. ³⁸You take much seed out into the field, and you gather little in, for the locust consumes it; ³⁹you plant vineyards and have labored, but you do not drink wine, nor gather [grapes], for the worm consumes it; ⁴⁰olives are yours in all your border, but you do not pour out oil, for your olive falls off. ⁴¹You beget sons and daughters, but they are not with you, for they go into captivity; ⁴²the locust possesses all your trees and the fruit of your ground; ⁴³the sojourner who [is] in your midst goes up very high above you, and you go down very low; ⁴⁴he lends [to] you, and you do not lend [to] him; he is for head and you are for tail. ⁴⁵And all these curses have come on you, and pursued you, and overtaken you, until you are destroyed, because you have not listened to the voice of your God YHWH, to keep His commands and His statutes which he has commanded you; ⁴⁶and they have been on you for a sign and for a wonder, also on your seed—for all time. ⁴⁷Because that you have not served your God YHWH with joy and with gladness of heart, because of the abundance of all things— ⁴⁸you have served your enemies, whom YHWH sends against you, in hunger, and in thirst, and in nakedness, and in lack of all things; and He has put a yoke of iron on your neck until He has destroyed you. ⁴⁹YHWH lifts up a nation against you from afar, from the end of the earth—it flies as the eagle—a nation whose tongue you have not heard, ⁵⁰a nation of fierce countenance, which does not accept the face of the aged and does not favor the young; ⁵¹and it has eaten the fruit of your livestock and the fruit of your ground, until you are destroyed; which does not leave to you grain, new wine, and oil, the increase of your oxen, and the wealth of your flock, until it has destroyed you. ⁵²And it has laid siege to you in all your gates until your walls come down—the high and the fortified ones in which you are trusting, in all your land; indeed, it has laid siege to you in all your gates, in all your land which your God YHWH has given to you. ⁵³And you have eaten the fruit of your body, [the] flesh of your sons and your daughters (whom your God YHWH has given to you), in the siege and in the constriction with which your enemies constrict you. ⁵⁴The man who is tender in you, and who [is] very delicate—his eye is evil against his brother, and against the wife of his bosom, and against the remnant of his sons whom he leaves, ⁵⁵against giving to one of them of the flesh of his sons whom he eats, because he has nothing left for himself in the siege and in the constriction with which your enemy constricts you in all your gates. ⁵⁶The tender woman in you, and the delicate, who has not tried the sole of her foot to place on the ground because of delicateness and because of tenderness—her eye is evil against the husband of her bosom, and against her son, and against her daughter, ⁵⁷and against her seed which comes out from between her feet, even against her sons whom she bears, for she eats them in secret, in the lacking of everything, in the siege and in the constriction with which your enemy constricts you within your gates. ⁵⁸If you do not observe to do all the words of this law which are written in this scroll, to fear this honored and fearful Name—your God YHWH— ⁵⁹then YHWH has made your strokes extraordinary, and the strokes [against] your seed [are] great strokes that are persisting and severe sicknesses that are persisting. ⁶⁰And He has brought back all the diseases of Egypt on you, from the presence of which you have been afraid, and they have cleaved to you. ⁶¹Also every sickness and every stroke which is not written in the scroll of this law—YHWH causes them to go up on you until you are destroyed, ⁶²and you have been left with few men, whereas that you would have been as stars of the heavens for multitude, for you have not listened to the voice of your God YHWH. ⁶³And it has been, as YHWH has rejoiced over you to do you good and to multiply you, so YHWH rejoices over you to destroy you and to lay you waste; and you have been pulled away from off the ground to where you are going in to possess it; ⁶⁴and YHWH has scattered you among all the peoples, from the end of the earth even to the [other] end of the earth; and you have served other gods there which you have not known, you and your fathers—wood and stone. ⁶⁵And you do not rest among those nations, indeed, there is no resting place for the sole of your foot, and YHWH has given to you a trembling heart, and failing of eyes, and grief of soul there; ⁶⁶and your life has been hanging in suspense before you, and you have been afraid by night and by day, and you do not have assurance in your life; ⁶⁷in the morning you say, O that it were evening! And in the evening you say, O that it were morning! (From the fear of your heart, with which you are afraid, and from the sight of your eyes which you see.) ⁶⁸And YHWH has brought you back to Egypt in ships, by the way of which I said to you, You do not add to see it anymore; and you have sold yourselves to your enemies there, for menservants and for maidservants, and there is no buyer."

CHAPTER 29
¹These [are] the words of the covenant which YHWH has commanded Moses to make with the sons of Israel in the land of Moab, apart from the covenant which He made with them in Horeb. ²And Moses calls to all Israel and says to them, "You have seen all that which YHWH has done before your eyes in the land of Egypt, to Pharaoh, and to all his servants, and to all his land— ³the great trials which your eyes have seen, the signs, and those great wonders. ⁴And YHWH has not given to you a heart to know, and eyes to see, and ears to hear, until this day. ⁵And I cause you to go in a wilderness [for] forty years; your garments have not been consumed from off you, and your shoe has not worn away from off your foot; ⁶you have not eaten bread, and you have not drunk wine and strong drink, so that you know that I [am] your God YHWH. ⁷And you come to this place, and Sihon king of Heshbon—also Og king of Bashan—comes out to meet us to battle, and we strike them, ⁸and take their land, and give it for an inheritance to the Reubenite, and to the Gadite, and to the half of the tribe of the Manassite; ⁹and you have kept the words of this covenant and done them, so that you cause all that you do to prosper. ¹⁰You are standing today, all of you, before your God YHWH: your heads, your tribes, your elderly, and your authorities, every man of Israel, ¹¹your infants, your wives, and your sojourner who [is] in the midst of your camps, from the hewer of your wood to the drawer of your water, ¹²for your passing over into the covenant of your God YHWH, and into His oath which your God YHWH is making with you today, ¹³in order to establish you to Himself for a people today, and He Himself is your God, as He has spoken to you, and as He has sworn to your fathers, to Abraham, to Isaac, and to Jacob. ¹⁴And I am not making this covenant and this oath with you alone, ¹⁵but with him who is here with us, standing before our God YHWH today, and with him who is not here with us today, ¹⁶for you have known how you dwelt in the land of Egypt, and how we passed by through the midst of the nations which you have passed by; ¹⁷and you see their abominations, and their idols of wood and stone, silver and gold, which [are] with them, ¹⁸lest there be among you a man or woman, or family or tribe, whose heart is turning from our God YHWH today, to go to serve the gods of those nations, lest there be in you a root bearing the fruit of gall and wormwood; ¹⁹and it has been, in his hearing the words of this oath, that he has blessed himself in his heart, saying, I have peace, though I go on in the stubbornness of my heart—in order to sweep away the watered with the thirsty. ²⁰YHWH is not willing to be propitious to him, for then the anger of YHWH smokes, also His zeal, against that man, and all the oath which is written in this scroll has lain down on him, and YHWH has blotted out his name from under the heavens, ²¹and YHWH has separated him for calamity out of all the tribes of Israel, according to all the oaths of the covenant which is written in this Scroll of the Law. ²²And the latter generation of your sons who rise after you, and the stranger who comes in from a far-off land, have said, when they have seen the strokes of that land and its sicknesses which YHWH has sent into it: ²³The whole land is burned [with] brimstone and salt, it is not sown, nor does it shoot up, nor does any herb go up on it there, like the overthrow of Sodom and Gomorrah, Admah and Zeboim, which YHWH overturned in His anger and in His fury. ²⁴Indeed, all the nations have said, Why has YHWH done thus to this land? Why the heat of this great anger? ²⁵And they have said, Because that they have forsaken the covenant of YHWH, God of their fathers, which He made with them in His bringing them out of the land

of Egypt, ²⁶and they go and serve other gods, and bow themselves to them—gods which they have not known, and which He has not apportioned to them; ²⁷and the anger of YHWH burns against that land, to bring in on it all the reviling that is written in this scroll, ²⁸and YHWH plucks them from off their ground in anger, and in fury, and in great wrath, and casts them into another land, as [at] this day. ²⁹The things hidden [belong] to our God YHWH, and the things revealed [belong] to us and to our sons for all time, to do all the words of this law."

CHAPTER 30

¹"And it has been, when all these things come on you, the blessing and the reviling, which I have set before you, and you have brought [them] back to your heart among all the nations to where your God YHWH has driven you away, ²and have turned back to your God YHWH and listened to His voice, according to all that I am commanding you today, you and your sons, with all your heart and with all your soul— ³then your God YHWH has turned back [to] your captivity and pitied you, indeed, He has turned back and gathered you out of all the peoples to where your God YHWH has scattered you. ⁴If your outcast is in the extremity of the heavens, your God YHWH gathers you from there and He takes you from there; ⁵and your God YHWH has brought you into the land which your fathers have possessed, and you have inherited it, and He has done you good, and multiplied you above your fathers. ⁶And your God YHWH has circumcised your heart and the heart of your seed, to love your God YHWH with all your heart and with all your soul, for the sake of your life; ⁷and your God YHWH has put all this oath on your enemies and on those hating you, who have pursued you. ⁸And you turn back, and have listened to the voice of YHWH, and have done all His commands which I am commanding you today; ⁹and your God YHWH has made you abundant in every work of your hand, in the fruit of your body, and in the fruit of your livestock, and in the fruit of your ground, for good; for YHWH turns back to rejoice over you for good, as He rejoiced over your fathers, ¹⁰for you listen to the voice of your God YHWH, to keep His commands and His statutes which are written in the scroll of this law, for you turn back to your God YHWH with all your heart and with all your soul. ¹¹For this command which I am commanding you today, it is not too wonderful for you, nor [is] it far off. ¹²It is not in the heavens, saying, Who goes up into the heavens for us, and takes it for us, and causes us to hear it, that we may do it? ¹³And it [is] not beyond the sea, saying, Who passes over beyond the sea for us, and takes it for us, and causes us to hear it, that we may do it? ¹⁴For the word is very near to you, in your mouth, and in your heart—to do it. ¹⁵See, today I have set before you life and good, and death and evil, ¹⁶in that today I am commanding you to love your God YHWH, to walk in His ways, and to keep His commands, and His statutes, and His judgments; and you have lived and multiplied, and your God YHWH has blessed you in the land to where you are going in to possess it. ¹⁷And if your heart turns, and you do not listen, and have been drawn away, and have bowed yourself to other gods and served them, ¹⁸I have declared to you this day that you certainly perish, you do not prolong days on the ground which you are passing over the Jordan to go in there to possess it. ¹⁹I have caused the heavens and the earth to testify against you today—I have set before you life and death, the blessing and the reviling, and you have fixed on life, so that you live, you and your seed, ²⁰to love your God YHWH, to listen to His voice, and to cleave to Him (for He [is] your life and the length of your days), to dwell on the ground which YHWH has sworn to your fathers, to Abraham, to Isaac, and to Jacob, to give to them."

CHAPTER 31

¹And Moses goes and speaks these words to all Israel, ²and he says to them, "I [am] a son of one hundred and twenty years today; I am not able to go out and to come in anymore, and YHWH has said to me, You do not pass over this Jordan. ³Your God YHWH—He is passing over before you; He destroys these nations from before you, and you have possessed them; Joshua—he is passing over before you, as YHWH has spoken. ⁴And YHWH has done to them as he has done to Sihon and to Og, kings of the Amorite, and to their land, whom He destroyed. ⁵And YHWH has given them before your face, and you have done to them according to all the command which I have commanded you; ⁶be strong and courageous, do not fear, nor be terrified because of them, for your God YHWH [is] He who is going with you; He does not fail you nor forsake you." ⁷And Moses calls for Joshua and says to him before the eyes of all Israel, "Be strong and courageous, for you go in with this people to the land which YHWH has sworn to their fathers to give to them, and you cause them to inherit it; ⁸and YHWH [is] He who is going before you, He Himself is with you; He does not fail you nor forsake you; do not fear, nor be frightened." ⁹And Moses writes this law and gives it to the priests (sons of Levi, those carrying the Ark of the Covenant of YHWH), and to all [the] elderly of Israel, ¹⁰and Moses commands them, saying, "At the end of seven years, in the appointed time, the year of release, in the Celebration of Shelters, ¹¹in the coming in of all Israel to see the face of YHWH in the place which He chooses, you proclaim this law before all Israel in their ears. ¹²Assemble the people, the men, and the women, and the infants, and your sojourner who [is] within your gates, so that they hear, and so that they learn, and have feared your God YHWH, and observed to do all the words of this law; ¹³and their sons, who have not known, hear and have learned to fear your God YHWH [for] all the days which you are living on the ground to where you are passing over the Jordan to possess it." ¹⁴And YHWH says to Moses, "Behold, your days have drawn near to die; call Joshua, and station yourselves in the Tent of Meeting, and I charge him"; and Moses goes—Joshua also—and they station themselves in the Tent of Meeting, ¹⁵and YHWH is seen in the tent in a pillar of a cloud; and the pillar of the cloud stands at the opening of the tent. ¹⁶And YHWH says to Moses, "Behold, you are lying down with your fathers, and this people has risen and gone whoring after the gods of the stranger of the land, into the midst of which it has entered, and it has forsaken Me and broken My covenant which I made with it; ¹⁷and My anger has burned against it in that day, and I have forsaken them, and hidden My face from them, and it has been for consumption, and many evils and distresses have found it, and it has said in that day, [Is] it not because my God is not in my midst that these evils have found me? ¹⁸And I certainly hide My face in that day for all the evil which it has done, for it has turned to other gods. ¹⁹And now, write this song for yourselves, and teach it [to] the sons of Israel; put it in their mouths, so that this song is to Me for a witness against the sons of Israel. ²⁰When I bring them to the ground flowing with milk and honey, which I have sworn to their fathers, and they have eaten, and been satisfied, and been fat, and have turned to other gods, and they have served them, and despised Me, and broken My covenant, ²¹then it has been, when many evils and distresses meet it, that this song has testified to its face for a witness; for it is not forgotten out of the mouth of its seed, for I have known its imagining which it is doing today, before I bring them into the land of which I have sworn." ²²And Moses writes this song on that day, and teaches it [to] the sons of Israel. ²³Then He commands Joshua son of Nun, and says, "Be strong and courageous, for you bring in the sons of Israel to the land which I have sworn to them, and I am with you." ²⁴And it comes to pass, when Moses finishes to write the words of this law on a scroll, until their completion, ²⁵that Moses commands the Levites carrying the Ark of the Covenant of YHWH, saying, ²⁶"Take this Scroll of the Law, and you have set it on the side of the Ark of the Covenant of your God YHWH, and it has been against you for a witness there; ²⁷for I have known your rebellion and your stiff neck; behold, in my being yet alive with you today, you have been rebelling against YHWH, and surely also after my death. ²⁸Assemble to me all the elderly of your tribes, and your authorities, and I speak these words in their ears, and cause the heavens and the earth to testify against them, ²⁹for I have known that you act very corruptly after my death, and have turned aside from the way which I commanded you, and evil has met you in the latter end of the days, because you do evil in the eyes of YHWH, to make Him angry with the work of your hands." ³⁰And Moses speaks the words of this song in the ears of all the assembly of Israel, until their completion:

CHAPTER 32

¹"Give ear, O heavens, and I speak; And you hear, O earth, sayings of my mouth! ²My doctrine drops as rain; My sayings flow as

dew; As storms on the tender grass, || And as showers on the herb, ³For I proclaim the Name of YHWH; Ascribe greatness to our God! ⁴The Rock—His work [is] perfect, || For all His ways [are] just; God of steadfastness, and without iniquity; Righteous and upright [is] He. ⁵It has done corruptly to Him; Their blemish is not of His sons, || A generation perverse and crooked! ⁶Do you act thus to YHWH, || O people foolish and not wise? Is He not your Father—He who bought you? He made you, and establishes you. ⁷Remember days of old—Understand the years of many generations—Ask your father, and he tells you; Your elderly, and they say to you: ⁸In the Most High causing nations to inherit, || In His separating sons of Adam—He sets up the borders of the peoples || By the number of the sons of God [[*or* sons of Israel]]. ⁹For YHWH's portion [is] His people, || Jacob [is] the line of His inheritance. ¹⁰He finds him in a land—a desert, || And in a void—a howling wilderness, || He turns him around—He causes him to understand—He keeps him as the apple of His eye. ¹¹As an eagle wakes up its nest, || Flutters over its young ones, || Spreads its wings [and] takes them, || Carries them on its pinions— ¹²YHWH alone leads him, || And there is no strange god with him. ¹³He makes him ride on high places of earth, || And he eats increase of the fields, || And He makes him suck honey from a rock, || And oil out of the flint of a rock; ¹⁴Butter of the herd, and milk of the flock, || With fat of lambs, and rams of sons of Bashan, || And male goats, with fat of kidneys of wheat; And of the blood of the grape you drink wine! ¹⁵And Yeshurun waxes fat, and kicks; You have been fat, you have been thick, || You have been covered. And he leaves God who made him, || And dishonors the Rock of his salvation. ¹⁶They make Him zealous with strangers, || They make Him angry with abominations. ¹⁷They sacrifice to the demons, not God, || To gods they have not known, || New ones—they came from the vicinity; Your fathers have not feared them! ¹⁸You forget the Rock that begot you, || And neglect God who forms you. ¹⁹And YHWH sees and despises—For the provocation of His sons and His daughters. ²⁰And He says: I hide My face from them, || I see what their latter end [is]; For they [are] a contrary generation, || Sons in whom is no steadfastness. ²¹They have made Me jealous by [what is] not God, || They made Me angry by their vanities; And I make them jealous by [what is] not a people, || I make them angry by a foolish nation. ²²For a fire has been kindled in My anger, || And it burns to the lowest [part] of Sheol, || And consumes earth and its increase, || And sets on fire [the] foundations of mountains. ²³I heap calamities on them, || I consume My arrows on them. ²⁴Exhausted by famine, || And consumed by heat and bitter destruction—I also send the teeth of beasts on them, || With poison of fearful things of the dust. ²⁵The sword destroys from outside, || And out of the inner-chambers—terror, || Both youth and virgin, || Suckling with man of grey hair. ²⁶I have said: I blow them away, || I cause their remembrance to cease from man; ²⁷If I do not fear the anger of an enemy, || Lest their adversaries know—Lest they say, Our hand is high, || And YHWH has not worked all this. ²⁸For they [are] a nation lost to counsels, || And there is no understanding in them. ²⁹If only they were wise, || They would deal wisely [with] this, || They would attend to their latter end! ³⁰How does one pursue a thousand, || And two cause a myriad to flee, || If not that their Rock has sold them, || And YHWH has shut them up? ³¹For their rock [is] not as our Rock || (And our enemies [are] judges!) ³²For their vine [is] of the vine of Sodom, || And of the fields of Gomorrah; Their grapes [are] grapes of gall—They have bitter clusters; ³³The poison of dragons [is] their wine || And the fierce venom of cobras. ³⁴Is it not laid up with Me? Sealed among My treasures? ³⁵Vengeance and retribution [are] Mine, || At the due time—their foot slides; For near is a day of their calamity, || And things prepared for them have hastened. ³⁶For YHWH judges His people, || And gives comfort over His servants. For He sees the going away of power, || And none is restrained and left. ³⁷And He has said, Where [are] their gods—The rock in which they trusted? ³⁸Who eat the fat of their sacrifices, || [And] drink the wine of their drink-offering? Let them arise and help you, || Let it be a hiding place for you! ³⁹See, now, that I [am] He, || And there is no god besides Me; I put to death and I keep alive; I have struck and I heal; And there is not a deliverer from My hand, ⁴⁰For I lift up My hand to the heavens, || And have said, I live for all time! ⁴¹If I have sharpened the brightness of My sword, || And My hand lays hold on judgment, || I return vengeance to My adversaries, || And to those hating Me—I repay! ⁴²I make My arrows drunk with blood, || And My sword devours flesh, || From the blood of the pierced and captive, || From the head of the leaders of the enemy. ⁴³Sing, O nations, [with] His people, || For He avenges the blood of His servants, || And He turns back vengeance on His adversaries, || And has pardoned His land [and] His people." ⁴⁴And Moses comes and speaks all the words of this song in the ears of the people, he and Hoshea son of Nun; ⁴⁵and Moses finishes to speak all these words to all Israel, ⁴⁶and says to them, "Set your heart to all the words which I am testifying against you today, that you command your sons to observe to do all the words of this law, ⁴⁷for it [is] not a vain thing for you, for it [is] your life, and by this thing you prolong days on the ground to where you are passing over the Jordan to possess it." ⁴⁸And YHWH speaks to Moses on this very same day, saying, ⁴⁹"Go up to this Mount Abarim, Mount Nebo, which [is] in the land of Moab, which [is] on the front of Jericho, and see the land of Canaan which I am giving to the sons of Israel for a possession; ⁵⁰and die on the mountain to where you are going up, and be gathered to your people, as your brother Aaron has died on Mount Hor and is gathered to his people; ⁵¹because you trespassed against Me in the midst of the sons of Israel at the waters of Meribath-Kadesh, the wilderness of Zin, because you did not sanctify Me in the midst of the sons of Israel. ⁵²Indeed, you see the land before [you], but you do not go in there to the land which I am giving to the sons of Israel."

CHAPTER 33

¹And this [is] the blessing [with] which Moses the man of God blessed the sons of Israel before his death, ²and he says: "YHWH has come from Sinai, || And has risen from Seir for them; He has shone from Mount Paran, || And has come [with] myriads of holy ones; At His right hand [came] a fiery law [[*or* a flaming fire]] for them. ³Indeed, He [is] loving the peoples; All His holy ones [are] in Your hand, || And they sat down at Your foot, || [Each] lifts up Your words. ⁴Moses has commanded a law for us, || A possession of the assembly of Jacob. ⁵And He is King in Yeshurun, || In the heads of the people gathering together, || The tribes of Israel! ⁶Let Reuben live, and not die, || And let his men be an [incalculable] number. ⁷And this [is] for Judah, and he says: Hear, O YHWH, the voice of Judah, || And You bring him in to his people; His hand has striven for him, || And You are a help from his adversaries. ⁸And of Levi he said: Your Perfections and your Lights [are] for your pious one, || Whom You have tried in Massah, || You strive with him at the waters of Meribah; ⁹Who is saying of his father and his mother, || I have not seen him; And he has not discerned his brothers, || And he has not known his sons; For they have observed Your saying, || And they keep Your covenant. ¹⁰They teach Your judgments to Jacob, || And Your law to Israel; They put incense in Your nose, || And whole burnt-offering on Your altar. ¹¹Bless, O YHWH, his strength, || And accept the work of his hands, || Strike the loins of his withstanders, || And of those hating him—that they do not rise! ¹²Of Benjamin he said: The beloved of YHWH dwells confidently by Him, || Covering him over every day; Indeed, he dwells between His shoulders. ¹³And of Joseph he said: His land [is] blessed [by] YHWH, || By a precious thing of the heavens, || By dew, and by the deep crouching beneath, ¹⁴And by a precious thing—fruits of the sun, || And by a precious thing—cast forth by the months, ¹⁵And by a chief thing—of the ancient mountains, || And by a precious thing—of the continuous heights, ¹⁶And by a precious thing—of earth and its fullness, || And the good pleasure of Him who is dwelling in the bush; Let it come for the head of Joseph, || And for the crown of him [who is] separate from his brothers. ¹⁷His splendor [is] a firstling of his ox, || And his horns [are] horns of a wild ox; With them he pushes the peoples || Altogether to the ends of the earth; And they [are] the myriads of Ephraim, || And they [are] the thousands of Manasseh. ¹⁸And of Zebulun he said: Rejoice, O Zebulun, in your going out, || And, O Issachar, in your tents; ¹⁹They call peoples [to] the mountain, || There they sacrifice righteous sacrifices; For they suck up the abundance of the seas, || And hidden things hidden in the sand. ²⁰And of Gad he said:

DEUTERONOMY

Blessed is he who is enlarging Gad, || He dwells as a lioness, || And has torn the arm—also the crown! ²¹And he provides the first part for himself, || For there the portion of the lawgiver is covered, || And he comes [with] the heads of the people; He has done the righteousness of YHWH, || And His judgments with Israel. ²²And of Dan he said: Dan [is] a lion's whelp; He leaps from Bashan. ²³And of Naphtali he said: O Naphtali, satisfied with pleasure, || And full of the blessing of YHWH, || Possess [the] west and [the] south. ²⁴And of Asher he said: Asher [is] blessed with sons, || Let him be accepted by his brothers, || And dipping his foot in oil. ²⁵Iron and bronze [are] your shoes, || And as your days—your strength. ²⁶[There is] none like the God of Yeshurun, || Riding the heavens to your help, || And in His excellence the skies. ²⁷The eternal God [is] a habitation, || And beneath [are] continuous arms. And He casts out the enemy from your presence and says, Destroy! ²⁸And Israel dwells [in] confidence alone; The eye of Jacob [is] to a land of grain and wine; Also His heavens drop down dew. ²⁹O your blessedness, O Israel! Who is like you? A people saved by YHWH, || The shield of your help, || And He who [is] the sword of your excellence! And your enemies are subdued for you, || And you tread on their high places."

CHAPTER 34

¹And Moses goes up from the plains of Moab to Mount Nebo, the top of Pisgah, which [is] on the front of Jericho, and YHWH shows him all the land—Gilead to Dan, ²and all Naphtali, and the land of Ephraim, and Manasseh, and all the land of Judah to the Western Sea, ³and the south, and the circuit of the Valley of Jericho, the city of palms, to Zoar. ⁴And YHWH says to him, "This [is] the land which I have sworn to Abraham, to Isaac, and to Jacob, saying, I give it to your seed; I have caused you to see with your eyes, but you do not pass over there." ⁵And Moses, servant of the Lord, dies there in the land of Moab, according to the command of YHWH; ⁶and He buries him in a valley in the land of Moab, opposite Beth-Peor, and no man has known his burying place to this day. ⁷And Moses [is] a son of one hundred and twenty years when he dies; his eye has not become dim, nor has his moisture fled. ⁸And the sons of Israel lament Moses in the plains of Moab [for] thirty days; and the days of weeping [and] mourning for Moses are completed. ⁹And Joshua son of Nun is full of the spirit of wisdom, for Moses had laid his hands on him, and the sons of Israel listen to him, and do as YHWH commanded Moses. ¹⁰And there has not arisen a prophet in Israel like Moses anymore, whom YHWH has known face to face, ¹¹in reference to all the signs and the wonders which YHWH sent him to do in the land of Egypt, to Pharaoh, and to all his servants, and to all his land, ¹²and in reference to all the strong hand and to all the great fear which Moses did before the eyes of all Israel.

JOSHUA

CHAPTER 1

¹And it comes to pass after the death of Moses, servant of YHWH, that YHWH speaks to Joshua son of Nun, minister of Moses, saying, ²"My servant Moses is dead, and now, rise, pass over this Jordan, you and all this people, to the land which I am giving to them, to the sons of Israel. ³Every place on which the sole of your foot treads, I have given it to you, as I have spoken to Moses. ⁴From this wilderness and Lebanon, and to the great river, the Euphrates River, all the land of the Hittites, and to the Great Sea—the going in of the sun—is your border. ⁵No man stations himself before you all [the] days of your life; as I have been with Moses, I am with you, I do not fail you, nor forsake you; ⁶be strong and courageous, for you cause this people to inherit the land which I have sworn to their fathers to give to them. ⁷Only, be strong and very courageous, to observe to do according to all the Law which Moses My servant commanded you; you do not turn aside from it right or left, so that you act wisely in every [place] to where you go; ⁸the scroll of this Law does not depart out of your mouth, and you have meditated in it by day and by night, so that you observe to do according to all that is written in it, for then you cause your way to prosper, and then you act wisely. ⁹Have I not commanded you? Be strong and courageous; do not be terrified nor frightened, for your God YHWH [is] with you in every [place] to where you go." ¹⁰And Joshua commands the authorities of the people, saying, ¹¹"Pass over into the midst of the camp, and command the people, saying, Prepare provision for yourselves, for within three days you are passing over this Jordan, to go in to possess the land which your God YHWH is giving to you to possess it." ¹²And to the Reubenite, and to the Gadite, and to the half of the tribe of Manasseh, Joshua has spoken, saying, ¹³"Remember the word which Moses, servant of YHWH, commanded you, saying, Your God YHWH is giving rest to you, and He has given this land to you; ¹⁴your wives, your infants, and your substance, abide in the land which Moses has given to you beyond the Jordan, and you pass over by fifties, before your brothers, all the mighty men of valor, and have helped them, ¹⁵until YHWH gives rest to your brothers as to yourselves, and they have possessed, even they, the land which your God YHWH is giving to them; then you have turned back to the land of your possession, and have possessed it, which Moses, servant of YHWH, has given to you beyond the Jordan, [at] the sun-rising." ¹⁶And they answer Joshua, saying, "All that you have commanded us we do; and to every [place] to where you send us, we go; ¹⁷according to all that we listened to [from] Moses, so we listen to you; surely your God YHWH is with you as He has been with Moses. ¹⁸Any man who provokes your mouth, and does not hear your words, in all that you command him, is put to death; only, be strong and courageous."

CHAPTER 2

¹And Joshua son of Nun silently sends two men, spies, from Shittim, saying, "Go, see the land—and Jericho"; and they go and come into the house of a woman, a harlot, and her name [is] Rahab, and they lie down there. ²And it is told to the king of Jericho, saying, "Behold, men have come in here tonight, from the sons of Israel, to search the land." ³And the king of Jericho sends to Rahab, saying, "Bring out the men who are coming to you, who have come into your house, for they have come to search the entirety of the land." ⁴And the woman takes the two men, and hides them, and says thus: "The men came to me, and I have not known where they [are] from; ⁵and it comes to pass—the gate is to [be] shut—in the dark, and the men have gone out; I have not known to where the men have gone; pursue, hurry after them, for you overtake them"; ⁶and she has caused them to go up on the roof, and hides them with the flax wood, which is arranged for her on the roof. ⁷And the men have pursued after them the way of the Jordan, by the fords, and they have shut the gate afterward when the pursuers have gone out after them. ⁸And before they lie down, she has gone up to them on the roof, ⁹and she says to the men, "I have known that YHWH has given the land to you, and that your terror has fallen on us, and that all the inhabitants of the land have melted at your presence. ¹⁰For we have heard how YHWH dried up the waters of the Red Sea at your presence, in your going out of Egypt, and that which you have done to the two kings of the Amorite who [are] beyond the Jordan; to Sihon and to Og whom you devoted. ¹¹And we hear, and our heart melts, and there has not stood anymore spirit in [any] man from your presence, for He, your God YHWH, [is] God in the heavens above and on the earth below. ¹²And now, please swear to me by YHWH—because I have done kindness with you—that you have done, even you, kindness with the house of my father, and have given a true token to me, ¹³and have kept alive my father, and my mother, and my brothers, and my sisters, and all that they have, and have delivered our souls from death." ¹⁴And the men say to her, "Our soul to die for yours; if you do not declare this—our matter, then it has been, in YHWH's giving this land to us, that we have done kindness and truth with you." ¹⁵And she causes them to go down by a rope through the window, for her

JOSHUA

house [is] in the side of the wall, and she [is] dwelling in the wall; ¹⁶and she says to them, "Go to the mountain, lest the pursuers come on you; and you have been hidden there three days until the turning back of the pursuers, and afterward you go on your way." ¹⁷And the men say to her, "We are acquitted of this, your oath, which you have caused us to swear: ¹⁸behold, we are coming into the land, bind this line of scarlet thread to the window by which you have caused us to go down, and gather your father, and your mother, and your brothers, and all the house of your father to you, to the house; ¹⁹and it has been, anyone who goes out from the doors of your house outside, his blood [is] on his head, and we are innocent; and anyone who is with you in the house, his blood [is] on our head, if a hand is on him; ²⁰and if you declare this—our matter, then we have been acquitted from your oath which you have caused us to swear." ²¹And she says, "According to your words, so it [is]"; and she sends them away, and they go; and she binds the scarlet line to the window. ²²And they go, and come to the mountain, and abide there three days until the pursuers have turned back; and the pursuers seek in all the way, and have not found. ²³And the two men turn back, and come down from the hill, and pass over, and come to Joshua son of Nun, and recount to him all that has come on them; ²⁴and they say to Joshua, "Surely YHWH has given all the land into our hand; and also, all the inhabitants of the land have melted at our presence."

CHAPTER 3

¹And Joshua rises early in the morning, and they journey from Shittim, and come to the Jordan, he and all the sons of Israel, and they lodge there before they pass over. ²And it comes to pass, at the end of three days, that the authorities pass over into the midst of the camp, ³and command the people, saying, "When you see the Ark of the Covenant of your God YHWH, and the priests, the Levites, carrying it, then you journey from your place, and have gone after it; ⁴only, a distance is between you and it, about two thousand cubits by measure; you do not come near to it, so that you know the way in which you go, for you have not passed over in the way before." ⁵And Joshua says to the people, "Sanctify yourselves, for tomorrow YHWH does wonders in your midst." ⁶And Joshua speaks to the priests, saying, "Take up the Ark of the Covenant, and pass over before the people"; and they take up the Ark of the Covenant, and go before the people. ⁷And YHWH says to Joshua, "This day I begin to make you great in the eyes of all Israel, so that they know that as I was with Moses I am with you; ⁸and you, command the priests carrying the Ark of the Covenant, saying, When you come to the extremity of the waters of the Jordan, stand in the Jordan." ⁹And Joshua says to the sons of Israel, "Come near here, and hear the words of your God YHWH"; ¹⁰and Joshua says, "By this you know that the living God [is] in your midst, and He certainly dispossesses from before you the Canaanite, and the Hittite, and the Hivite, and the Perizzite, and the Girgashite, and the Amorite, and the Jebusite: ¹¹behold, the Ark of the Covenant of the Lord of all the earth is passing over before you into the Jordan; ¹²and now, take for yourselves twelve men out of the tribes of Israel, one man—one man for a tribe; ¹³and it has been, at the resting of the soles of the feet of the priests carrying the Ark of YHWH, Lord of all the earth, in the waters of the Jordan, the waters of the Jordan are cut off—the waters which are coming down from above—and they stand—one heap." ¹⁴And it comes to pass, in the journeying of the people from their tents to pass over the Jordan, and of the priests carrying the Ark of the Covenant before the people, ¹⁵and at those carrying the Ark coming to the Jordan, and the feet of the priests carrying the Ark have been dipped in the extremity of the waters (and the Jordan is full over all its banks all the days of harvest)— ¹⁶that the waters stand; those coming down from above have risen—one heap, very far above Adam, the city which [is] at the side of Zaretan; and those going down by the Sea of the Plain (the Salt Sea), have been completely cut off; and the people have passed through opposite Jericho; ¹⁷and the priests carrying the Ark of the Covenant of YHWH stand on dry ground in the midst of the Jordan— established, and all Israel are passing over on dry ground until all the nation has completed to pass over the Jordan.

CHAPTER 4

¹And it comes to pass, when all the nation has completed to pass over the Jordan, that YHWH speaks to Joshua, saying, ²"Take for yourselves twelve men out of the people, one man—one man out of a tribe; ³and command them, saying, Take up for yourselves from this [place], from the midst of the Jordan, from the established standing-place of the feet of the priests, twelve stones, and you have removed them over with you, and placed them in the lodging-place in which you lodge tonight." ⁴And Joshua calls to the twelve men whom he prepared out of the sons of Israel, one man— one man out of a tribe; ⁵and Joshua says to them, "Pass over before the Ark of your God YHWH into the midst of the Jordan, and each of you lift up one stone on his shoulder, according to the number of the tribes of the sons of Israel, ⁶so that this is a sign in your midst when your children ask hereafter, saying, What [are] these stones to you? ⁷That you have said to them, Because the waters of the Jordan were cut off, at the presence of the Ark of the Covenant of YHWH; in its passing over into the Jordan the waters of the Jordan were cut off; and these stones have been for a memorial to the sons of Israel for all time." ⁸And the sons of Israel do so as Joshua commanded, and take up twelve stones out of the midst of the Jordan, as YHWH has spoken to Joshua, according to the number of the tribes of the sons of Israel, and remove them over with them to the lodging-place, and place them there, ⁹even the twelve stones Joshua has raised up out of the midst of the Jordan, the place of the standing of the feet of the priests carrying the Ark of the Covenant, and they are there to this day. ¹⁰And the priests carrying the Ark are standing in the midst of the Jordan until the completion of the whole thing which YHWH commanded Joshua to speak to the people, according to all that Moses commanded Joshua, and the people hurry and pass over. ¹¹And it comes to pass, when all the people have completed to pass over, that the Ark of YHWH passes over, and the priests, in the presence of the people; ¹²and the sons of Reuben, and the sons of Gad, and the half of the tribe of Manasseh, pass over, by fifties, before the sons of Israel, as Moses had spoken to them; ¹³about forty thousand, armed ones of the host, passed over before YHWH for battle, to the plains of Jericho. ¹⁴On that day YHWH has made Joshua great in the eyes of all Israel, and they fear him, as they feared Moses, all [the] days of his life. ¹⁵And YHWH speaks to Joshua, saying, ¹⁶"Command the priests carrying the Ark of the Testimony, and they come up out of the Jordan." ¹⁷And Joshua commands the priests, saying, "Come up out of the Jordan." ¹⁸And it comes to pass, in the coming up of the priests carrying the Ark of the Covenant of YHWH out of the midst of the Jordan—the soles of the feet of the priests have been drawn up into the dry ground— and the waters of the Jordan return to their place, and go over all its banks as before. ¹⁹And the people have come up out of the Jordan on the tenth of the first month, and encamp in Gilgal, in the extremity east of Jericho; ²⁰and these twelve stones, which they have taken out of the Jordan, Joshua has raised up in Gilgal. ²¹And he speaks to the sons of Israel, saying, "When your sons ask their fathers hereafter, saying, What [are] these stones? ²²Then you have caused your sons to know, saying, Israel passed over this Jordan on dry land; ²³because your God YHWH dried up the waters of the Jordan at your presence, until your passing over, as your God YHWH did to the Red Sea which He dried up at our presence until our passing over; ²⁴so that all the people of the land know the hand of YHWH—that it [is] strong, so that you have feared your God YHWH [for] all the days."

CHAPTER 5

¹And it comes to pass, when all the kings of the Amorite which [are] beyond the Jordan, toward the sea, and all the kings of the Canaanite which [are] by the sea, hear how that YHWH has dried up the waters of the Jordan at the presence of the sons of Israel until their passing over, that their heart is melted, and there has not been anymore spirit in them because of the presence of the sons of Israel. ²At that time YHWH said to Joshua, "Make knives of flint for yourself, and return, circumcise the sons of Israel a second time"; ³and Joshua makes knives of flint for himself, and circumcises the sons of Israel at the height of the foreskins. ⁴And this [is] the thing [for] which Joshua circumcises [them]: all the people who are coming out of Egypt, who are

JOSHUA

males, all the men of war have died in the wilderness, in the way, in their coming out of Egypt, ⁵for all the people who are coming out were circumcised, and all the people who [are] born in the wilderness, in the way, in their coming out from Egypt, they have not circumcised; ⁶for forty years the sons of Israel have gone in the wilderness, until all the nation of the men of war who are coming out of Egypt, who did not listen to the voice of YHWH, to whom YHWH has sworn not to show them the land which YHWH swore to their fathers to give to us, a land flowing with milk and honey, are consumed; ⁷and He raised up their sons in their stead, Joshua has circumcised them, for they have been uncircumcised, for they have not circumcised them in the way. ⁸And it comes to pass, when all the nation has completed to be circumcised, that they abide in their places in the camp until their recovering; ⁹and YHWH says to Joshua, "Today I have rolled the reproach of Egypt from off you"; and [one] calls the name of that place Gilgal to this day. ¹⁰And the sons of Israel encamp in Gilgal, and make the Passover on the fourteenth day of the month, at evening, in the plains of Jericho; ¹¹and they eat of the old grain of the land on the next day of the Passover, unleavened things and roasted [grain], on this very same day; ¹²and the manna ceases on the next day in their eating of the old grain of the land, and there has been no more manna for [the] sons of Israel, and they eat of the increase of the land of Canaan in that year. ¹³And it comes to pass in Joshua's being by Jericho, that he lifts up his eyes, and looks, and behold, [there is] one standing in front of him, and his drawn sword [is] in his hand, and Joshua goes to him, and says to him, "Are you for us or for our adversaries?" ¹⁴And He says, "No, for I [am] Prince of YHWH's host; now I have come"; and Joshua falls on his face to the earth, and pays respect, and says to Him, "What is my Lord speaking to His servant?" ¹⁵And the Prince of YHWH's host says to Joshua, "Cast off your shoe from off your foot, for the place on which you are standing is holy"; and Joshua does so.

CHAPTER 6

¹And Jericho shuts itself up, and is shut up, because of the presence of the sons of Israel—none going out, and none coming in. ²And YHWH says to Joshua, "See, I have given Jericho and its king into your hand—mighty men of valor, ³and you have surrounded the city—all the men of battle—going around the city once; thus you do [for] six days; ⁴and seven priests carry seven horns of the rams before the Ark, and on the seventh day you go around the city seven times, and the priests blow with the horns, ⁵and it has been, in the prolonging of the horn of the ram, in your hearing the voice of the horn, all the people shout [with] a great shout, and the wall of the city has fallen under it, and the people have gone up, each straight before him." ⁶And Joshua son of Nun calls to the priests and says to them, "Carry the Ark of the Covenant, and seven priests carry seven horns of the rams before the Ark of YHWH"; ⁷and He said to the people, "Pass over, and go around the city, and he who is armed passes over before the Ark of YHWH." ⁸And it comes to pass, when Joshua speaks to the people, that the seven priests carrying seven horns of the rams before YHWH have passed over and blown with the horns, and the Ark of the Covenant of YHWH is going after them; ⁹and he who is armed is going before the priests blowing the horns, and he who is gathering up is going after the Ark, going on and blowing with the horns; ¹⁰and Joshua has commanded the people, saying, "Do not shout, nor cause your voice to be heard, nor does a word go out from your mouth, until the day of my saying to you, Shout! Then you have shouted." ¹¹And the Ark of YHWH goes around the city, going around once, and they come into the camp, and lodge in the camp. ¹²And Joshua rises early in the morning, and the priests carry the Ark of YHWH, ¹³and seven priests carrying seven horns of the rams before the Ark of YHWH are walking, going on, and they have blown with the horns—and he who is armed is going before them, and he who is gathering up is going behind the Ark of YHWH—going on and blowing with the horns. ¹⁴And they go around the city once on the second day, and return to the camp; thus they have done [for] six days. ¹⁵And it comes to pass, on the seventh day, that they rise early, at the ascending of the dawn, and go around the city, according to this manner, seven times; (only on that day have they gone around the city seven times); ¹⁶and it comes to pass, at the seventh time, the priests have blown with the horns, and Joshua says to the people, "Shout! For YHWH has given the city to you; ¹⁷and the city has been devoted, it and all that [is] in it, to YHWH; only Rahab the harlot lives, she and all who [are] with her in the house, for she hid the messengers whom we sent; ¹⁸and surely you have kept from the devoted thing, lest you devote [yourselves], and have taken from the devoted thing, and have made the camp of Israel become a devoted thing, and have troubled it; ¹⁹and all the silver and gold, and vessels of bronze and iron—it [is] holy to YHWH; it comes into the treasury of YHWH." ²⁰And the people shout, and blow with the horns, and it comes to pass, when the people hear the voice of the horn, that the people shout [with] a great shout, and the wall falls under it, and the people goes up into the city, each straight before him, and they capture the city; ²¹and they devote all that [is] in the city, from man even to woman, from young even to aged, even to ox, and sheep, and donkey, by the mouth of the sword. ²²And Joshua said to the two men who are spying out the land, "Go into the house of the woman, the harlot, and bring out the woman from there, and all whom she has, as you have sworn to her." ²³And the young men, those spying, go in and bring out Rahab, and her father, and her mother, and her brothers, and all whom she has; indeed, they have brought out all her relatives, and place them at the outside of the camp of Israel. ²⁴And they have burned the city with fire, and all that [is] in it; only, the silver and the gold, and the vessels of bronze, and of iron, they have given [to] the treasury of the house of YHWH; ²⁵and Rahab the harlot, and the house of her father, and all whom she has, Joshua has kept alive; and she dwells in the midst of Israel to this day, for she hid the messengers whom Joshua sent to spy out Jericho. ²⁶And Joshua adjures [them] at that time, saying, "Cursed [is] the man before YHWH who raises up and has built this city, [even] Jericho; he lays its foundation in his firstborn, and he sets up its doors in his youngest." ²⁷And YHWH is with Joshua, and his fame is in all the land.

CHAPTER 7

¹And the sons of Israel commit a trespass in the devoted thing, and Achan, son of Carmi, son of Zabdi, son of Zerah, of the tribe of Judah, takes from the devoted thing, and the anger of YHWH burns against the sons of Israel. ²And Joshua sends men from Jericho to Ai, which [is] near Beth-Aven, on the east of Bethel, and speaks to them, saying, "Go up and spy out the land"; and the men go up and spy Ai, ³and they return to Joshua, and say to him, "Do not let all the people go up; let about two thousand men, or about three thousand men, go up, and they strike Ai; do not cause all the people to labor there; for they [are] few." ⁴So about three thousand men of the people go up from there, and they flee before the men of Ai, ⁵and the men of Ai strike about thirty-six men from them, and pursue them before the gate to Shebarim, and they strike them in Morad; and the heart of the people is melted, and becomes water. ⁶And Joshua tears his garments, and falls on his face to the earth before the Ark of YHWH until the evening, he and [the] elderly of Israel, and they cause dust to go up on their head. ⁷And Joshua says, "Aah! Lord YHWH, why have You caused this people to pass over the Jordan at all, to give us into the hand of the Amorite to destroy us? And oh that we had been willing—and we dwell beyond the Jordan! ⁸Oh, Lord, what do I say, after that Israel has turned the neck before its enemies? ⁹And the Canaanite and all the inhabitants of the land hear, and have come around against us, and cut off our name from the earth; and what do You do for Your great Name?" ¹⁰And YHWH says to Joshua, "Rise, for you—why this—[that] you [are] falling on your face? ¹¹Israel has sinned, and they have also

JOSHUA

transgressed My covenant which I commanded them, and also taken of the devoted thing, and also stolen, and also deceived, and also put [it] among their vessels, ¹²and the sons of Israel have not been able to stand before their enemies; they turn the neck before their enemies, for they have become a devoted thing; I do not add to be with you—if you do not destroy the devoted thing from your midst. ¹³Rise, sanctify the people, and you have said, Sanctify yourselves for tomorrow; for thus said YHWH, God of Israel: A devoted thing [is] in your midst, O Israel, you are not able to stand before your enemies until your turning aside the devoted thing from your midst; ¹⁴and you have been brought near in the morning by your tribes, and it has been [that] the tribe which YHWH captures draws near by families, and the family which YHWH captures draws near by households, and the household which YHWH captures draws near by men; ¹⁵and it has been, he who is captured with the devoted thing is burned with fire, he and all that he has, because he has transgressed the covenant of YHWH, and because he has done folly in Israel." ¹⁶And Joshua rises early in the morning, and brings Israel near by its tribes, and the tribe of Judah is captured; ¹⁷and he brings the family of Judah near, and he captures the family of the Zerahite; and he brings the family of the Zerahite near by men, and Zabdi is captured; ¹⁸and he brings his household near by men, and Achan—son of Carmi, son of Zabdi, son of Zerah, of the tribe of Judah—is captured. ¹⁹And Joshua says to Achan, "My son, please give glory to YHWH, God of Israel, and give thanks to Him, and now declare to me what you have done—do not hide [it] from me." ²⁰And Achan answers Joshua and says, "Truly I have sinned against YHWH, God of Israel, and I have done thus and thus; ²¹and I see among the spoil a good robe of Shinar, and two hundred shekels of silver, and one wedge of gold, whose weight [is] fifty shekels, and I desire them, and take them; and behold, they [are] hid in the earth, in the midst of my tent, and the silver [is] under it." ²²And Joshua sends messengers, and they run to the tent, and behold, it is hidden in his tent, and the silver [is] under it; ²³and they take them out of the midst of the tent, and bring them to Joshua, and to all the sons of Israel, and pour them out before YHWH. ²⁴And Joshua takes Achan son of Zerah, and the silver, and the robe, and the wedge of gold, and his sons, and his daughters, and his ox, and his donkey, and his flock, and his tent, and all that he has, and all Israel with him, and they brought them up [to] the Valley of Achor. ²⁵And Joshua says, "Why have you troubled us? YHWH troubles you this day!" And all Israel cast stone at him, and they burn them with fire, and they stone them with stones, ²⁶and they raise up a great heap of stones over him to this day, and YHWH turns back from the heat of His anger, therefore [one] has called the name of that place "Valley of Achor" until this day.

CHAPTER 8

¹And YHWH says to Joshua, "Do not fear, nor be frightened, take with you all the people of war, and rise, go up to Ai; see, I have given into your hand the king of Ai, and his people, and his city, and his land, ²and you have done to Ai and to her king as you have done to Jericho and to her king; only spoil its spoil and its livestock for yourselves; for you set an ambush for the city at its rear." ³And Joshua rises, and all the people of war, to go up to Ai, and Joshua chooses thirty thousand men, mighty men of valor, and sends them away by night, ⁴and commands them, saying, "See, you are ones lying in wait against the city, at the rear of the city, you do not go very far off from the city, and all of you have been prepared, ⁵and I and all the people who [are] with me draw near to the city, and it has come to pass, when they come out to meet us as at the first, and we have fled before them, ⁶and they have come out after us until we have drawn them out of the city, for they say, They are fleeing before us as at the first, and we have fled before them, ⁷and you rise from the ambush, and have occupied the city, and your God YHWH has given it into your hand; ⁸and it has been, when you capture the city, you burn the city with fire, you do according to the word of YHWH, see, I have commanded you." ⁹And Joshua sends them away, and they go to the ambush, and abide between Bethel and Ai, on the west of Ai; and Joshua lodges on that night in the midst of the people. ¹⁰And Joshua rises early in the morning, and inspects the people, and goes up, he and [the] elderly of Israel, before the people to Ai; ¹¹and all the people of war who [are] with him have gone up, and draw near and come in before the city, and encamp on the north of Ai; and the valley [is] between him and Ai. ¹²And he takes about five thousand men, and sets them [for] an ambush between Bethel and Ai, on the west of the city; ¹³and they set the people, all the camp which [is] on the north of the city, and its rear on the west of the city, and that night Joshua goes on into the midst of the valley. ¹⁴And it comes to pass, when the king of Ai sees [it], that he hurries, and rises early, and the men of the city go out to meet Israel for battle, he and all his people, at the appointed time, at the front of the plain, and he has not known that an ambush [is] against him, on the rear of the city. ¹⁵And Joshua and all Israel [seem] struck before them, and flee the way of the wilderness, ¹⁶and all the people who [are] in the city are called to pursue after them, and they pursue after Joshua, and are drawn away out of the city, ¹⁷and there has not been a man left in Ai and Bethel who has not gone out after Israel, and they leave the city open, and pursue after Israel. ¹⁸And YHWH says to Joshua, "Stretch out with the javelin which [is] in your hand toward Ai, for I give it into your hand"; and Joshua stretches out with the javelin which [is] in his hand toward the city, ¹⁹and the ambush has risen [with] haste, out of its place, and they run at the stretching out of his hand, and go into the city, and capture it, and hurry, and burn the city with fire. ²⁰And the men of Ai look behind them, and see, and behold, the smoke of the city has gone up to the heavens, and there has not been power in them to flee here and there—and the people who are fleeing to the wilderness have turned against the pursuer— ²¹and Joshua and all Israel have seen that the ambush has captured the city, and that the smoke of the city has gone up, and they turn back and strike the men of Ai; ²²and these have come out from the city to meet them, and they are in the midst of Israel, some on this [side], and some on that [side], and they strike them until he has not left a remnant and escaped one to them; ²³and they have caught the king of Ai alive, and bring him near to Joshua. ²⁴And it comes to pass, at Israel's finishing to slay all the inhabitants of Ai in the field, in the wilderness in which they pursued them (and all of them fall by the mouth of the sword until their consumption), that all of Israel turns back to Ai, and strikes it by the mouth of the sword; ²⁵and all who fall during the day, of men and of women, are twelve thousand—all men of Ai. ²⁶And Joshua has not brought back his hand which he stretched out with the javelin until he has devoted all the inhabitants of Ai; ²⁷only the livestock and the spoil of that city has Israel spoiled for themselves, according to the word of YHWH which He commanded Joshua. ²⁸And Joshua burns Ai, and makes it a continuous heap—a desolation to this day; ²⁹and he has hanged the king of Ai on the tree until evening, and at the going in of the sun Joshua has commanded, and they take down his carcass from the tree, and cast it to the opening of the gate of the city, and raise a great heap of stones over it until this day. ³⁰Then Joshua builds an altar to YHWH, God of Israel, in Mount Ebal, ³¹as Moses, servant of YHWH, commanded the sons of Israel, as it is written in the Scroll of the Law of Moses—an altar of whole stones, over which he has not waved iron—and they cause burnt-offerings to go up on it to YHWH, and sacrifice peace-offerings; ³²and he writes there on the stones a copy of the Law of Moses, which he has written in the presence of the sons of Israel. ³³And all Israel, and its elderly, and authorities, and his judges, are standing on this [side] and on that [side] of the Ark, before the priests, the Levites, carrying the Ark of the Covenant of YHWH, the sojourner as well as the native, half of them in front of Mount Gerizim, and the half of them in front of Mount Ebal, as Moses servant of YHWH had commanded to bless the people of Israel at the first. ³⁴And afterward he has proclaimed all the words of the Law, the blessing and the reviling, according to all that is written in the Scroll of the Law; ³⁵there has not been a thing of all that Moses commanded which Joshua has not proclaimed before all the assembly of Israel, and the women, and the infants, and the sojourner who is going in their midst.

CHAPTER 9

¹And it comes to pass, when all the kings who [are] beyond the Jordan, in the hill-country, and in the low-country, and in every haven of the Great Sea, toward Lebanon, the Hittite,

JOSHUA

and the Amorite, the Canaanite, the Perizzite, the Hivite, and the Jebusite, hear— ²that they gather themselves together to fight with Joshua, and with Israel—[with] one mouth. ³And the inhabitants of Gibeon have heard that which Joshua has done to Jericho and to Ai, ⁴and they work, even they, with subtlety, and go, and feign to be ambassadors, and take old sacks for their donkeys, and wine-bottles, old, and split, and bound up, ⁵and sandals, old and patched, on their feet, and old garments on them, and all the bread of their provision is dry—it was crumbs. ⁶And they go to Joshua, to the camp at Gilgal, and say to him, and to the men of Israel, "We have come from a far-off land, and now, make a covenant with us"; ⁷and the men of Israel say to the Hivite, "It may be [that] you are dwelling in our midst, so how do we make a covenant with you?" ⁸And they say to Joshua, "We [are] your servants." And Joshua says to them, "Who [are] you? And where do you come from?" ⁹And they say to him, "Your servants have come from a very far-off land, for the Name of your God YHWH, for we have heard His fame, and all that He has done in Egypt, ¹⁰and all that He has done to the two kings of the Amorite who [are] beyond the Jordan, to Sihon king of Heshbon, and to Og king of Bashan, who [is] in Ashtaroth. ¹¹And our elderly, and all the inhabitants of our land speak to us, saying, Take provision in your hand for the way, and go to meet them, and you have said to them: We [are] your servants, and now, make a covenant with us; ¹²this bread of ours—we provided ourselves with it hot out of our houses, on the day of our coming out to go to you, and now, behold, it is dry, and has been crumbs; ¹³and these [are] the wine-bottles which we filled, new, and behold, they have split; and these, our garments and our sandals, have become old, from the exceeding greatness of the way." ¹⁴And the men take of their provision, and have not asked the mouth of YHWH; ¹⁵and Joshua makes peace with them, and makes a covenant with them, to keep them alive; and the princes of the congregation swear to them. ¹⁶And it comes to pass, that at the end of three days after they have made a covenant with them, that they hear that they [are] their neighbors—that they are dwelling in their midst. ¹⁷And the sons of Israel journey and come to their cities on the third day—and their cities [are] Gibeon, and Chephirah, and Beeroth, and Kirjath-Jearim— ¹⁸and the sons of Israel have not struck them, for the princes of the congregation have sworn to them by YHWH, God of Israel, and all the congregation murmur against the princes. ¹⁹And all the princes say to all the congregation, "We have sworn to them by YHWH, God of Israel; and now, we are not able to come against them; ²⁰we do this to them, and have kept them alive, and wrath is not on us, because of the oath which we have sworn to them." ²¹And the princes say to them, "They live, and are hewers of wood and drawers of water for all the congregation, as the princes spoke to them." ²²And Joshua calls for them, and speaks to them, saying, "Why have you deceived us, saying, We are very far from you, yet you [are] dwelling in our midst? ²³And now you are cursed, and none of you is cut off [from being] a servant, even hewers of wood and drawers of water, for the house of my God." ²⁴And they answer Joshua and say, "Because it was certainly declared to your servants that your God YHWH commanded His servant Moses to give all the land to you, and to destroy all the inhabitants of the land from before you; and we fear greatly for ourselves because of you, and we do this thing; ²⁵and now, behold, we [are] in your hand, as [it is] good, and as [it is] right in your eyes to do to us—do." ²⁶And he does to them so, and delivers them from the hand of the sons of Israel, and they have not slain them; ²⁷and on that day Joshua makes them hewers of wood and drawers of water for the congregation, and for the altar of YHWH, to this day, at the place which He chooses.

CHAPTER 10

¹And it comes to pass, when Adoni-Zedek king of Jerusalem hears that Joshua has captured Ai, and devotes it (as he had done to Jericho and to her king so he has done to Ai and to her king), and that the inhabitants of Gibeon have made peace with Israel, and are in their midst— ²that they are greatly afraid, because Gibeon [is] a great city, as one of the royal cities, and because it [is] greater than Ai, and all its men [are] heroes. ³And Adoni-Zedek king of Jerusalem sends to Hoham king of Hebron, and to Piram king of Jarmuth, and to Japhia king of Lachish, and to Debir king of Eglon, saying, ⁴"Come up to me, and help me, and we strike Gibeon, for it has made peace with Joshua, and with the sons of Israel." ⁵And five kings of the Amorite (the king of Jerusalem, the king of Hebron, the king of Jarmuth, the king of Lachish, the king of Eglon) are gathered together, and go up, they and all their camps, and encamp against Gibeon, and fight against it. ⁶And the men of Gibeon send to Joshua, to the camp at Gilgal, saying, "Do not let your hand cease from your servants; come up to us [with] haste, and give safety to us, and help us; for all the kings of the Amorite, dwelling in the hill-country, have been assembled against us." ⁷And Joshua goes up from Gilgal, he, and all the people of war with him, even all the mighty men of valor. ⁸And YHWH says to Joshua, "Do not be afraid of them, for I have given them into your hand, there does not stand a man of them in your presence." ⁹And Joshua comes to them suddenly (all the night he has gone up from Gilgal), ¹⁰and YHWH crushes them before Israel, and strikes them [with] a great striking at Gibeon, and pursues them the way of the ascent of Beth-Horon, and strikes them to Azekah, and to Makkedah. ¹¹And it comes to pass, in their fleeing from the face of Israel—they [are] in the descent of Beth-Horon—and YHWH has cast great stones on them out of the heavens, to Azekah, and they die; more are they who have died by the hailstones than they whom the sons of Israel have slain by the sword. ¹²Then Joshua speaks to YHWH in the day of YHWH's giving up the Amorites before the sons of Israel, and he says before the eyes of Israel, "Sun—stand still in Gibeon; and moon—in the Valley of Ajalon"; ¹³and the sun stands still, and the moon has stood—until the nation takes vengeance [on] its enemies; is it not written on the Scroll of the Upright, "and the sun stands in the midst of the heavens, and has not hurried to go in—as a perfect day?" ¹⁴And there has not been like that day before it or after it, for YHWH's listening to the voice of a man; for YHWH is fighting for Israel. ¹⁵And Joshua turns back, and all Israel with him, to the camp at Gilgal. ¹⁶And these five kings flee, and are hidden in a cave at Makkedah, ¹⁷and it is declared to Joshua, saying, "The five kings have been found hidden in a cave at Makkedah." ¹⁸And Joshua says, "Roll great stones to the mouth of the cave, and appoint men over it to watch them; ¹⁹and you, do not stand, pursue after your enemies, and you have struck them from the rear; do not permit them to go into their cities, for your God YHWH has given them into your hand." ²⁰And it comes to pass, when Joshua and the sons of Israel finish to strike them [with] a very great striking until they are consumed, and the remnant who have remained of them go into the fortified cities, ²¹that all the people return to the camp, to Joshua, [at] Makkedah, in peace; none moved his tongue sharply against the sons of Israel. ²²And Joshua says, "Open the mouth of the cave, and bring out to me these five kings from the cave"; ²³and they do so, and bring out to him these five kings from the cave: the king of Jerusalem, the king of Hebron, the king of Jarmuth, the king of Lachish, the king of Eglon. ²⁴And it comes to pass, when they bring out these kings to Joshua, that Joshua calls to every man of Israel, and says to the captains of the men of war, who have gone with him, "Draw near, set your feet on the necks of these kings"; and they draw near, and set their feet on their necks. ²⁵And Joshua says to them, "Do not fear, nor be frightened; be strong and courageous; for thus does YHWH do to all your enemies with whom you are fighting"; ²⁶and Joshua strikes them afterward, and puts them to death, and hangs them on five trees; and they are hanging on the trees until the evening. ²⁷And it comes to pass, at the time of the going in of the sun, Joshua has commanded, and they take them down from off the trees, and cast them into the cave where they had been hid, and put great stones on the mouth of the cave until this very day. ²⁸And Joshua has captured Makkedah on that day, and he strikes it by the mouth of the sword, and he has devoted its king, them and every person who [is] in it—he has not left a remnant; and he does to the king of Makkedah as he did to the king of Jericho. ²⁹And Joshua passes over, and all Israel with him, from Makkedah [to] Libnah, and fights with Libnah; ³⁰and YHWH also gives it into the hand of Israel, and its king, and [Joshua] strikes it by the mouth of the sword, and every person who [is] in it—he does not leave a remnant in it; and he does to its king as he did to the king of Jericho. ³¹And Joshua passes over, and all Israel with him, from Libnah to

Lachish, and encamps against it, and fights against it. ³²And YHWH gives Lachish into the hand of Israel, and [Joshua] captures it on the second day, and strikes it by the mouth of the sword, and every person who [is] in it, according to all that he did to Libnah. ³³Then Horam king of Gezer has come up to help Lachish, and Joshua strikes him and his people, until he has not left a remnant to him. ³⁴And Joshua passes over, and all Israel with him, from Lachish to Eglon, and they encamp against it, and fight against it, ³⁵and capture it on that day, and strike it by the mouth of the sword, and every person who [is] in it he has devoted on that day, according to all that he did to Lachish. ³⁶And Joshua goes up, and all Israel with him, from Eglon to Hebron, and they fight against it, ³⁷and capture it, and strike it by the mouth of the sword, and its king, and all its cities, and every person who [is] in it—he has not left a remnant—according to all that he did to Eglon—and devotes it, and every person who [is] in it. ³⁸And Joshua turns back, and all Israel with him, to Debir, and fights against it, ³⁹and captures it, and its king, and all its cities, and they strike them by the mouth of the sword, and devote every person who [is] in it—he has not left a remnant; as he did to Hebron so he did to Debir, and to its king, and as he did to Libnah, and to its king. ⁴⁰And Joshua strikes all the land of the hill-country, and of the south, and of the low-country, and of the springs, and all their kings—he has not left a remnant, and he has devoted all that breathe, as YHWH, God of Israel, commanded. ⁴¹And Joshua strikes them from Kadesh-Barnea, even to Gaza, and all the land of Goshen, even to Gibeon; ⁴²and Joshua has captured all these kings and their land [at] one time, for YHWH, God of Israel, is fighting for Israel. ⁴³And Joshua turns back, and all Israel with him, to the camp at Gilgal.

CHAPTER 11

¹And it comes to pass, when Jabin king of Hazor hears, that he sends to Jobab king of Madon, and to the king of Shimron, and to the king of Achshaph, ²and to the kings who [are] on the north in the hill-country, and in the plain south of Chinneroth, and in the low country, and in the elevations of Dor, on the west, ³[to] the Canaanite on the east, and on the west, and the Amorite, and the Hittite, and the Perizzite, and the Jebusite in the hill-country, and the Hivite under Hermon, in the land of Mizpeh— ⁴and they go out, they and all their camps with them, a people numerous, as the sand which [is] on the seashore for multitude, and [with] very many horse and charioteer; ⁵and all these kings are met together, and they come and encamp together at the waters of Merom, to fight with Israel. ⁶And YHWH says to Joshua, "Do not be afraid of their presence, for about this time tomorrow I am giving all of them slain before Israel; hamstring their horses, and burn their chariots with fire." ⁷And Joshua comes, and all the people of war with him, against them by the waters of Merom, and they suddenly fall on them; ⁸and YHWH gives them into the hand of Israel, and they strike them and pursue them to the great Sidon, and to Misrephoth-Maim, and to the Valley of Mizpeh eastward, and they strike them, until he has not left a remnant to them; ⁹and Joshua does to them as YHWH commanded to him; he has hamstrung their horses, and burned their chariots with fire. ¹⁰And Joshua turns back at that time, and captures Hazor, and he has struck its king by the sword; for Hazor [was] formerly head of all these kingdoms; ¹¹and they strike every person who [is] in it by the mouth of the sword; he has devoted—he has not left anyone breathing, and he has burned Hazor with fire; ¹²and all the cities of these kings, and all their kings, Joshua has captured, and he strikes them by the mouth of the sword; he devoted them, as Moses, servant of YHWH, commanded. ¹³Only, all the cities which are standing by their hill, Israel has not burned them—except Joshua has burned Hazor, only; ¹⁴and all the spoil of these cities, and the livestock, the sons of Israel have spoiled for themselves; only, they have struck every man by the mouth of the sword, until their destroying them; they have not left anyone breathing. ¹⁵As YHWH commanded His servant Moses, so Moses commanded Joshua, and so Joshua has done; he has not turned aside a thing of all that YHWH commanded Moses. ¹⁶And Joshua takes all this land: the hill-country, and all the south, and all the land of Goshen, and the low country, and the plain, even the hill-country of Israel and its low lands, ¹⁷from the Mount of Halak, which is going up [to] Seir, and to Ba'al-Gad, in the Valley of Lebanon, under Mount Hermon; and he has captured all their kings, and he strikes them, and puts them to death. ¹⁸Joshua has made war with all these kings [for] many days; ¹⁹there has not been a city which made peace with the sons of Israel except the Hivite, inhabitants of Gibeon; they have taken the whole in battle; ²⁰for it has been from YHWH to strengthen their heart, to meet in battle with Israel, in order to devote them, so that they have no grace, but in order to destroy them, as YHWH commanded Moses. ²¹And Joshua comes at that time, and cuts off the Anakim from the hill-country, from Hebron, from Debir, from Anab, and from all the hill-country of Judah, and from all the hill-country of Israel; Joshua has devoted them with their cities. ²²There has not been Anakim left in the land of the sons of Israel; only in Gaza, in Gath, and in Ashdod, were they left. ²³And Joshua takes the whole of the land, according to all that YHWH has spoken to Moses, and Joshua gives it for an inheritance to Israel according to their divisions, by their tribes; and the land has rest from war.

CHAPTER 12

¹And these [are] kings of the land whom the sons of Israel have struck, and possess their land beyond the Jordan, at the sun-rising, from the Brook of Arnon to Mount Hermon, and all the plain eastward: ²Sihon, king of the Amorite, who is dwelling in Heshbon, ruling from Aroer which [is] on the border of the Brook of Arnon, and the middle of the brook, and half of Gilead, and to the Brook of Jabok, the border of the sons of Ammon; ³and the plain to the Sea of Chinneroth eastward, and to the Sea of the Plain (the Salt Sea) eastward, the way to Beth-Jeshimoth, and from the south under the Springs of Pisgah. ⁴And the border of Og king of Bashan (of the remnant of the Rephaim), who is dwelling in Ashtaroth and in Edrei, ⁵and ruling in Mount Hermon, and in Salcah, and in all Bashan, to the border of the Geshurite, and the Maachathite, and half of Gilead, the border of Sihon king of Heshbon. ⁶Moses, servant of YHWH, and the sons of Israel have struck them, and Moses, servant of YHWH, gives it—a possession to the Reubenite, and to the Gadite, and to the half of the tribe of Manasseh. ⁷And these [are] kings of the land whom Joshua and the sons of Israel have struck beyond the Jordan westward, from Ba'al-Gad, in the Valley of Lebanon, and to the Mount of Halak, which is going up to Seir; and Joshua gives it to the tribes of Israel—a possession according to their divisions; ⁸in the hill-country, and in the low country, and in the plain, and in the springs, and in the wilderness, and in the south; the Hittite, the Amorite, and the Canaanite, the Perizzite, the Hivite, and the Jebusite: ⁹the king of Jericho, one; the king of Ai, which [is] beside Bethel, one; ¹⁰the king of Jerusalem, one; the king of Hebron, one; ¹¹the king of Jarmuth, one; the king of Lachish, one; ¹²the king of Eglon, one; the king of Gezer, one; ¹³the king of Debir, one; the king of Geder, one; ¹⁴the king of Hormah, one; the king of Arad, one; ¹⁵the king of Libnah, one; the king of Adullam, one; ¹⁶the king of Mekkedah, one; the king of Beth-El, one; ¹⁷the king of Tappuah, one; the king of Hepher, one; ¹⁸the king of Aphek, one; the king of Lasharon, one; ¹⁹the king of Madon, one; the king of Hazor, one; ²⁰the king of Shimron-Meron, one; the king of Achshaph, one; ²¹the king of Taanach, one; the king of Megiddo, one; ²²the king of Kedesh, one; the king of Jokneam of Carmel, one; ²³the king of Dor, at the elevation of Dor, one; the king of the nations of Gilgal, one; ²⁴the king of Tirzah, one; all the kings [are] thirty-one.

CHAPTER 13

¹And Joshua is old, entering into days, and YHWH says to him, "You have become aged, you have entered into days; as for the land, very much has been left to possess. ²This [is] the land that is left: all the circuits of the Philistines, and all Geshuri, ³from Sihor which [is] on the front of Egypt, and to the border of Ekron northward (it is reckoned to the Canaanite), five princes of the Philistines, the Gazathite, and the Ashdothite, the Eshkalonite, the Gittite, and the Ekronite, also the Avim; ⁴from the south, all the land of the Canaanite, and Mearah, which [is] to the Sidonians, to Aphek, to the border of the Amorite; ⁵and the land of the Giblite, and all Lebanon, at the sun-rising, from Ba'al-Gad under Mount Hermon, to the going in to Hamath: ⁶all the inhabitants of the hill-country, from Lebanon to Misrephoth-Maim,

all the Sidonians: I dispossess them before the sons of Israel; only, cause it to fall to Israel for an inheritance, as I have commanded you. ⁷And now, apportion this land for an inheritance to the nine tribes, and half of the tribe of Manasseh." ⁸With [the other half], the Reubenite and the Gadite have received their inheritance, which Moses has given to them beyond the Jordan eastward, as Moses servant of YHWH has given to them; ⁹from Aroer, which [is] on the edge of the Brook of Arnon, and the city which [is] in the midst of the brook, and all the plain of Medeba to Dibon, ¹⁰and all the cities of Sihon king of the Amorite, who reigned in Heshbon, to the border of the sons of Ammon, ¹¹and Gilead, and the border of the Geshurite, and of the Maachathite, and all Mount Hermon, and all Bashan to Salcah; ¹²all the kingdom of Og in Bashan, who reigned in Ashtaroth and in Edrei; he was left of the remnant of the Rephaim, and Moses strikes them, and dispossesses them; ¹³and the sons of Israel did not dispossess the Geshurite, and the Maachathite; and Geshur and Maachath dwell in the midst of Israel to this day. ¹⁴Only, he has not given an inheritance to the tribe of Levi; fire-offerings of YHWH, God of Israel, [are] its inheritance, as He has spoken to it. ¹⁵And Moses gives to the tribe of the sons of Reuben, for their families; ¹⁶and the border is to them from Aroer, which [is] on the edge of the Brook of Arnon, and the city which [is] in the midst of the brook, and all the plain by Medeba, ¹⁷Heshbon, and all its cities which [are] in the plain, Dibon, and Bamoth-Ba'al, and Beth-Ba'al-Meon, ¹⁸and Jahazah, and Kedemoth, and Mephaath, ¹⁹and Kirjathaim, and Sibmah, and Zareth-Shahar, on the mountain of the valley, ²⁰and Beth-Peor, and the Springs of Pisgah, and Beth-Jeshimoth, ²¹and all the cities of the plain, and all the kingdom of Sihon king of the Amorite, who reigned in Heshbon, whom Moses struck, with the princes of Midian, Evi, and Rekem, and Zur, and Hur, and Reba, princes of Sihon, inhabitants of the land. ²²And the sons of Israel have slain Balaam, son of Beor, the diviner, with the sword, among their wounded ones. ²³And the border of the sons of Reuben is the Jordan, and [its] border; this [is] the inheritance of the sons of Reuben, for their families, the cities and their villages. ²⁴And Moses gives to the tribe of Gad, to the sons of Gad, for their families; ²⁵and the border to them is Jazer, and all the cities of Gilead, and half of the land of the sons of Ammon, to Aroer which [is] on the front of Rabbah, ²⁶and from Heshbon to Ramath-Mispeh, and Betonim, and from Mahanaim to the border of Debir, ²⁷and in the valley, Beth-Aram, and Beth-Nimrah, and Succoth, and Zaphon, the rest of the kingdom of Sihon king of Heshbon, the Jordan and [its] border, to the extremity of the Sea of Chinnereth, beyond the Jordan eastward. ²⁸This [is] the inheritance of the sons of Gad, for their families, the cities and their villages. ²⁹And Moses gives to the half-tribe of Manasseh; and it is to the half-tribe of the sons of Manasseh, for their families. ³⁰And their border is from Mahanaim, all Bashan, all the kingdom of Og king of Bashan, and all the small towns of Jair, which [are] in Bashan—sixty cities; ³¹and half of Gilead, and Ashteroth, and Edrei, cities of the kingdom of Og in Bashan, [are] to the sons of Machir, son of Manasseh, to the half of the sons of Machir, for their families. ³²These [are] they whom Moses caused to inherit in the plains of Moab beyond the Jordan, [by] Jericho, eastward; ³³and Moses did not give an inheritance to the tribe of Levi; YHWH, God of Israel, Himself, [is] their inheritance, as He has spoken to them.

CHAPTER 14

¹And these [are] they of the sons of Israel who inherited in the land of Canaan, whom Eleazar the priest, and Joshua son of Nun, and the heads of the fathers of the tribes of the sons of Israel, caused to inherit; ²their inheritance [is] by lot, as YHWH commanded by the hand of Moses, for the nine tribes and the half-tribe; ³for Moses has given the inheritance of two of the tribes, and of half of the tribe, beyond the Jordan, and he has not given an inheritance to the Levites in their midst; ⁴for the sons of Joseph have been two tribes, Manasseh and Ephraim, and they have not given a portion to the Levites in the land, except cities to dwell in, and their outskirts for their livestock, and for their possessions; ⁵as YHWH commanded Moses, so the sons of Israel have done, and they apportion the land. ⁶And the sons of Judah come near to Joshua in Gilgal, and Caleb son of Jephunneh the Kenezzite says to him, "You have known the word that YHWH has spoken to Moses, the man of God, concerning me and concerning you in Kadesh-Barnea: ⁷I [was] a son of forty years in Moses, servant of YHWH, sending me from Kadesh-Barnea, to spy out the land, and I bring him back word as with my heart; ⁸and my brothers who have gone up with me have caused the heart of the people to melt, and I have been fully after my God YHWH; ⁹and Moses swears in that day, saying, Nevertheless—the land on which your foot has trodden, it is to you for an inheritance, and to your sons—for all time, for you have been fully after my God YHWH. ¹⁰And now, behold, YHWH has kept me alive, as He has spoken, these forty-five years, since YHWH spoke this word to Moses when Israel went in the wilderness; and now, behold, I [am] a son of eighty-five years today; ¹¹yet today I [am] strong as in the day of Moses' sending me; as my power [was] then, so [is] my power now, for battle, and to go out, and to come in. ¹²And now, give this hill-country to me, of which YHWH spoke in that day, for you heard in that day, for Anakim [are] there, and great, fortified cities; if [it] so be [that] YHWH [is] with me, then I have dispossessed them, as YHWH has spoken." ¹³And Joshua blesses him, and gives Hebron to Caleb son of Jephunneh for an inheritance, ¹⁴therefore Hebron has been to Caleb son of Jephunneh the Kenezzite for an inheritance to this day, because that he was fully after YHWH, God of Israel; ¹⁵and the name of Hebron [was] formerly Kirjath-Arba (the man [was] the greatest among the Anakim); and the land has rest from war.

CHAPTER 15

¹And the lot for the tribe of the sons of Judah, for their families, is to the border of Edom; the wilderness of Zin southward, at the extremity of the south; ²and to them the south border is at the extremity of the Salt Sea, from the bay which is looking southward; ³and it has gone out to the south to Maaleh-Akrabbim, and passed over to Zin, and gone up on the south to Kadesh-Barnea, and passed over [to] Hezron, and gone up to Adar, and turned around to Karkaa, ⁴and passed over [to] Azmon, and gone out [at] the Brook of Egypt, and the outgoings of the border have been at the sea; this is the south border to you. ⁵And the east border [is] the Salt Sea, to the extremity of the Jordan, and the border at the north quarter [is] from the bay of the sea, at the extremity of the Jordan; ⁶and the border has gone up [to] Beth-Hoglah, and passed over on the north of Beth-Arabah, and the border has gone up [to] the stone of Bohan son of Reuben; ⁷and the border has gone up toward Debir from the Valley of Achor, and northward looking to Gilgal, which [is] opposite the ascent of Adummim, which [is] on the south of the brook, and the border has passed over to the waters of En-Shemesh, and its outgoings have been to En-Rogel; ⁸and the border has gone up the Valley of the Son of Hinnom, to the side of the Jebusite on the south (it [is] Jerusalem), and the border has gone up to the top of the hill-country which [is] on the front of the Valley of Hinnom westward, which [is] in the extremity of the Valley of the Rephaim northward; ⁹and the border has been marked out, from the top of the hill-country to the fountain of the waters of Nephtoah, and has gone out to the cities of Mount Ephron, and the border has been marked out [to] Ba'alah (it [is] Kirjath-Jearim); ¹⁰and the border has gone around from Ba'alah westward, to Mount Seir, and passed over to the side of Mount Jearim (it [is] Chesalon), on the north, and gone down [to] Beth-Shemesh, and passed over to Timnah; ¹¹and the border has gone out to the side of Ekron northward, and the border has been marked out [to] Shicron, and has passed over to Mount Ba'alah, and gone out [to] Jabneel; and the outgoings of the border have been at the sea. ¹²And the west border [is] to the Great Sea, and [its] border; this [is] the border of the sons of Judah all around for their families. ¹³And to Caleb son of Jephunneh he has given a portion in the midst of the sons of Judah, according to the command of YHWH to Joshua, [even] the city of Arba, father of Anak—it [is] Hebron. ¹⁴And Caleb is dispossessing there the three sons of Anak: Sheshai, and Ahiman, and Talmai, children of Anak, ¹⁵and he goes up there to the inhabitants of Debir; and the name of Debir [was] formerly Kirjath-Sepher. ¹⁶And Caleb says, "He who strikes Kirjath-Sephar, and has captured it—I have given my daughter Achsah to him for a wife." ¹⁷And Othniel son of Kenaz, brother of Caleb,

captures it, and he gives his daughter Achsah to him for a wife. ⁱ⁸And it comes to pass, in her coming in, that she persuades him to ask [for] a field from her father, and she comes down off the donkey, and Caleb says to her, "What do you [want]?" ¹⁹And she says, "Give a blessing to me; when you have given me the land of the south, then you have given springs of waters to me"; and he gives the upper springs and the lower springs to her. ²⁰This [is] the inheritance of the tribe of the sons of Judah, for their families. ²¹And the cities at the extremity of the tribe of the sons of Judah are to the border of Edom in the south, Kabzeel, and Eder, and Jagur, ²²and Kinah, and Dimonah, and Adadah, ²³and Kedesh, and Hazor, and Ithnan, ²⁴Ziph, and Telem, and Bealoth, ²⁵and Hazor, Hadattah, and Kerioth, Hezron (it [is] Hazor), ²⁶Amam, and Shema, and Moladah, ²⁷and Hazar-Gaddah, and Heshmon, and Beth-Palet, ²⁸and Hazar-Shual, and Beer-Sheba, and Bizjothjah, ²⁹Ba'alah, and Iim, and Azem, ³⁰and Eltolad, and Chesil, and Hormah, ³¹and Ziklag, and Madmannah, and Sansannah, ³²and Lebaoth, and Shilhim, and Ain, and Rimmon; all the cities [are] twenty-nine, and their villages. ³³In the low country: Eshtaol, and Zoreah, and Ashnah, ³⁴and Zanoah, and En-Gannim, Tappuah, and Enam, ³⁵Jarmuth, and Adullam, Socoh, and Azekah, ³⁶and Sharaim, and Adithaim, and Gederah, and Gederothaim; fourteen cities and their villages. ³⁷Zenan, and Hadashah, and Migdal-Gad, ³⁸and Dilean, and Mizpeh, and Joktheel, ³⁹Lachish, and Bozkath, and Eglon, ⁴⁰and Cabbon, and Lahmam, and Kithlish, ⁴¹and Gederoth, Beth-Dagon, and Naamah, and Makkedah; sixteen cities and their villages. ⁴²Libnah, and Ether, and Ashan, ⁴³and Jiphtah, and Ashnah, and Nezib, ⁴⁴and Keilah, and Achzib, and Mareshah; nine cities and their villages. ⁴⁵Ekron and its towns and its villages, ⁴⁶from Ekron and westward, all that [are] by the side of Ashdod, and their villages. ⁴⁷Ashdod, its towns and its villages, Gaza, its towns and its villages, to the Brook of Egypt, and the Great Sea, and [its] border. ⁴⁸And in the hill-country: Shamir, and Jattir, and Socoh, ⁴⁹and Dannah, and Kirjath-Sannah (it [is] Debir), ⁵⁰and Anab, and Eshtemoh, and Anim, ⁵¹and Goshen, and Holon, and Giloh; eleven cities and their villages. ⁵²Arab, and Dumah, and Eshean, ⁵³and Janum, and Beth-Tappuah, and Aphekah, ⁵⁴and Humtah, and Kirjath-Arba (it [is] Hebron), and Zior; nine cities and their villages. ⁵⁵Maon, Carmel, and Ziph, and Juttah, ⁵⁶and Jezreel, and Jokdeam, and Zanoah, ⁵⁷Cain, Gibeah, and Timnah; ten cities and their villages. ⁵⁸Halhul, Beth-Zur, and Gedor, ⁵⁹and Maarath, and Beth-Anoth, and Eltekon; six cities and their villages. ⁶⁰Kirjath-Ba'al (it [is] Kirjath-Jearim), and Rabbah; two cities and their villages. ⁶¹In the wilderness: Beth-Arabah, Middin, and Secacah, ⁶²and Nibshan, and the City of Salt, and En-Gedi; six cities and their villages. ⁶³As for the Jebusites, inhabitants of Jerusalem, the sons of Judah have not been able to dispossess them, and the Jebusite dwells with the sons of Judah in Jerusalem to this day.

CHAPTER 16

¹And the lot for the sons of Joseph goes out from Jordan [by] Jericho, to the waters of Jericho on the east, to the wilderness going up from Jericho in the hill-country of Beth-El, ²and has gone out from Beth-El to Luz, and passed over to the border of Archi [to] Ataroth, ³and gone down westward to the border of Japhleti, to the border of the lower Beth-Horon, and to Gezer, and its outgoings have been at the sea. ⁴And the sons of Joseph—Manasseh and Ephraim—inherit. ⁵And the border of the sons of Ephraim is by their families; and the border of their inheritance is on the east, Atroth-Addar to the upper Beth-Horon; ⁶and the border has gone out at the sea, to Michmethah on the north, and the border has gone around eastward [to] Taanath-Shiloh, and passed over it eastward to Janohah, ⁷and gone down from Janohah [to] Ataroth, and to Naarath, and touched against Jericho, and gone out at the Jordan. ⁸From Tappuah the border goes westward to the Brook of Kanah, and its outgoings have been at the sea: this [is] the inheritance of the tribe of the sons of Ephraim, for their families. ⁹And the separate cities of the sons of Ephraim [are] in the midst of the inheritance of the sons of Manasseh, all the cities and their villages; ¹⁰and they have not dispossessed the Canaanite who is dwelling in Gezer, and the Canaanite dwells in the midst of Ephraim to this day, and is for forced labor—serving.

CHAPTER 17

¹And the lot is for the tribe of Manasseh (for he [is] firstborn of Joseph), for Machir firstborn of Manasseh, father of Gilead, for he has been a man of war, and his are Gilead and Bashan. ²And there is [a lot] for the sons of Manasseh who are left, for their families; for the sons of Abiezer, and for the sons of Helek, and for the sons of Asriel, and for the sons of Shechem, and for the sons of Hepher, and for the sons of Shemida; these [are] the children of Manasseh son of Joseph—the males—by their families. ³As for Zelophehad, son of Hepher, son of Gilead, son of Machir, son of Manasseh, he has no children except daughters, and these [are] the names of his daughters: Mahlah, and Noah, Hoglah, Milcah, and Tirzah, ⁴and they draw near before Eleazar the priest, and before Joshua son of Nun, and before the princes, saying, "YHWH commanded Moses to give an inheritance to us in the midst of our brothers"; and he gives to them, at the command of YHWH, an inheritance in the midst of the brothers of their father. ⁵And ten portions fall [to] Manasseh, apart from the land of Gilead and Bashan, which [are] beyond the Jordan; ⁶for the daughters of Manasseh have inherited an inheritance in the midst of his sons, and the land of Gilead has been for the sons of Manasseh who are left. ⁷And the border of Manasseh is from Asher to Michmethah, which [is] on the front of Shechem, and the border has gone on to the right, to the inhabitants of En-Tappuah. ⁸The land of Tappuah has been for Manasseh, and Tappuah to the border of Manasseh for the sons of Ephraim. ⁹And the border has come down [to] the Brook of Kanah, southward of the brook; these cities of Ephraim [are] in the midst of the cities of Manasseh, and the border of Manasseh [is] on the north of the brook, and its outgoings are at the sea. ¹⁰Southward [is] for Ephraim and northward for Manasseh, and the sea is his border, and in Asher they meet on the north, and in Issachar on the east. ¹¹And in Issachar and in Asher, Manasseh has Beth-Shean and its towns, and Ibleam and its towns, and the inhabitants of Dor and its towns, and the inhabitants of En-Dor and its towns, and the inhabitants of Taanach and its towns, and the inhabitants of Megiddo and its towns—three counties. ¹²And the sons of Manasseh have not been able to occupy these cities, and the Canaanite is desirous to dwell in this land, ¹³and it comes to pass, when the sons of Israel have been strong, that they put the Canaanite to forced labor, and have not utterly dispossessed him. ¹⁴And the sons of Joseph speak with Joshua, saying, "Why have you given an inheritance to me—one lot and one portion, and I [am] a numerous people? YHWH has blessed me until now." ¹⁵And Joshua says to them, "If you [are] a numerous people, go up to the forest for yourself, then you have created [a place] for yourself there in the land of the Perizzite and of the Rephaim, when Mount Ephraim has been narrow for you." ¹⁶And the sons of Joseph say, "The mountain is not enough for us, and a chariot of iron [is] with every Canaanite who is dwelling in the land of the valley—to him who [is] in Beth-Shean and its towns, and to him who [is] in the Valley of Jezreel." ¹⁷And Joshua speaks to the house of Joseph, to Ephraim and to Manasseh, saying, "You [are] a numerous people, and have great power; you do not have [only] one lot, ¹⁸because the mountain is yours; because it [is] a forest—you have created it, and its outgoings have been yours; because you dispossess the Canaanite, though it has chariots of iron—though it [is] strong."

CHAPTER 18

¹And all the congregation of the sons of Israel is assembled [at] Shiloh, and they cause the Tent of Meeting to dwell there, and the land has been subdued before them. ²And there are seven tribes left among the sons of Israel who have not shared their inheritance, ³and Joshua says to the sons of Israel, "Until when are you remiss to go in to possess the land which He, YHWH, God of your fathers, has given to you? ⁴Give three men from you for [each] tribe, and I send them, and they rise and go up and down through the land, and describe it according to their inheritance, and come to me, ⁵and they have divided it into seven portions—Judah stays by its border on the south, and the house of Joseph stays by their border on the north— ⁶and you describe the land [in] seven portions, and have brought [it] to me here, and I have cast a lot for you here before our God YHWH; ⁷for there is no portion for the Levites in your midst, for the priesthood of YHWH [is] their inheritance, and Gad, and Reuben, and half of the tribe of Manasseh received their

inheritance beyond the Jordan eastward, which Moses, servant of YHWH, gave to them." ⁸And the men rise and go; and Joshua commands those who are going to describe the land, saying, "Go, and walk up and down through the land, and describe it, and return to me, and here I cast a lot for you before YHWH in Shiloh." ⁹And the men go, and pass over through the land, and describe it by cities, in seven portions, on a scroll, and they come to Joshua, to the camp [at] Shiloh. ¹⁰And Joshua casts a lot for them in Shiloh before YHWH, and there Joshua apportions the land to the sons of Israel, according to their divisions. ¹¹And a lot goes up [for] the tribe of the sons of Benjamin, for their families; and the border of their lot goes out between the sons of Judah and the sons of Joseph. ¹²And the border is for them at the north side from the Jordan, and the border has gone up to the side of Jericho on the north, and gone up through the hill-country westward, and its outgoings have been at the wilderness of Beth-Aven; ¹³and the border has gone over there to Luz, to the side of Luz (it [is] Beth-El) southward, and the border has gone down [to] Atroth-Addar, by the hill that [is] on the south of the lower Beth-Horon; ¹⁴and the border has been marked out, and has gone around to the corner of the sea southward, from the hill which [is] at the front of Beth-Horon southward, and its outgoings have been to Kirjath-Ba'al (it [is] Kirjath-Jearim), a city of the sons of Judah: this [is] the west quarter. ¹⁵And the south quarter [is] from the end of Kirjath-Jearim, and the border has gone out westward, and has gone out to the fountain of the waters of Nephtoah; ¹⁶and the border has come down to the extremity of the hill which [is] on the front of the Valley of the Son of Hinnom, which [is] in the Valley of the Rephaim northward, and has gone down the Valley of Hinnom to the side of Jebusi southward, and gone down [to] En-Rogel, ¹⁷and has been marked out on the north, and gone out to En-Shemesh, and gone out to Geliloth, which [is] opposite the ascent of Adummim, and gone down [to] the stone of Bohan son of Reuben, ¹⁸and passed over to the side in front of the Arabah northward, and gone down to Arabah; ¹⁹and the border has passed over to the side of Beth-Hoglah northward, and the outgoings of the border have been to the north bay of the Salt Sea, to the south extremity of the Jordan; this [is] the south border; ²⁰and the Jordan borders it at the east quarter; this [is] the inheritance of the sons of Benjamin, by its borders all around, for their families. ²¹And the cities for the tribe of the sons of Benjamin, for their families, have been Jericho, and Beth-Hoglah, and the Valley of Keziz, ²²and Beth-Arabah, Zemaraim, and Beth-El, ²³and Avim, and Parah, and Ophrah, ²⁴and Chephar-Haammonai, and Ophni, and Gaba; twelve cities and their villages. ²⁵Gibeon, and Ramah, and Beeroth, ²⁶and Mizpeh, and Chephirah, and Mozah, ²⁷and Rekem, and Irpeel, and Taralah, ²⁸and Zelah, Eleph, and Jebusi (it [is] Jerusalem), Gibeath, Kirjath; fourteen cities and their villages. This [is] the inheritance of the sons of Benjamin, for their families.

CHAPTER 19

¹And the second lot goes out for Simeon, for the tribe of the sons of Simeon, for their families; and their inheritance is in the midst of the inheritance of the sons of Judah, ²and they have in their inheritance Beer-Sheba, and Sheba, and Moladah, ³and Hazar-Shual, and Balah, and Azem, ⁴and Eltolad, and Bethul, and Hormah, ⁵and Ziklag, and Beth-Marcaboth, and Hazar-Susah, ⁶and Beth-Lebaoth, and Sharuhen; thirteen cities and their villages. ⁷Ain, Remmon, and Ether, and Ashan; four cities and their villages; ⁸also all the villages which [are] around these cities, to Ba'alath-Beer, Ramoth of the south. This [is] the inheritance of the tribe of the sons of Simeon, for their families; ⁹out of the portion of the sons of Judah [is] the inheritance of the sons of Simeon, for the portion of the sons of Judah has been too much for them, and the sons of Simeon inherit in the midst of their inheritance. ¹⁰And the third lot goes up for the sons of Zebulun, for their families; and the border of their inheritance is to Sarid, ¹¹and their border has gone up toward the sea, and Maralah, and come against Dabbasheth, and come to the brook which [is] on the front of Jokneam, ¹²and turned back from Sarid eastward, at the sun-rising, by the border of Chisloth-Tabor, and gone out to Daberath, and gone up to Japhia, ¹³and there it has passed over eastward, to the east, to Gittah-Hepher, [to] Ittah-Kazin, and gone out [to] Rimmon-Methoar to Neah; ¹⁴and the border has gone around it, from the north to Hannathon; and its outgoings have been [in] the Valley of Jiphthah-El, ¹⁵and Kattath, and Nahallal, and Shimron, and Idalah, and Beth-Lehem; twelve cities and their villages. ¹⁶This [is] the inheritance of the sons of Zebulun, for their families, these cities and their villages. ¹⁷The fourth lot has gone out for Issachar, for the sons of Issachar, for their families; ¹⁸and their border is [at] Jezreel, and Chesulloth, and Shunem, ¹⁹and Haphraim, and Shihon, and Anaharath, ²⁰and Rabbith, and Kishion, and Abez, ²¹and Remeth, and En-Gannim, and En-Haddah, and Beth-Pazzez; ²²and the border has touched against Tabor, and Shahazimah, and Beth-Shemesh, and the outgoings of their border have been [at] the Jordan; sixteen cities and their villages. ²³This [is] the inheritance of the tribe of the sons of Issachar, for their families, the cities and their villages. ²⁴And the fifth lot goes out for the tribe of the sons of Asher, for their families; ²⁵and their border is Helkath, and Hali, and Beten, and Achshaph, ²⁶and Alammelech, and Amad, and Misheal; and it touches against Carmel westward, and against Shihor-Libnath; ²⁷and has turned back, at the sun-rising, [to] Beth-Dagon, and come against Zebulun, and against the Valley of Jiphthah-El toward the north of Beth-Emek, and Neiel, and has gone out to Cabul on the left, ²⁸and Hebron, and Rehob, and Hammon, and Kanah, to great Sidon; ²⁹and the border has turned back to Ramah, and to the fortified city Tyre; and the border has turned back to Hosah, and its outgoings are at the sea, from the coast to Achzib, ³⁰and Ummah, and Aphek, and Rehob; twenty-two cities and their villages. ³¹This [is] the inheritance of the tribe of the sons of Asher, for their families, these cities and their villages. ³²The sixth lot has gone out for the sons of Naphtali—for the sons of Naphtali, for their families; ³³and their border is from Heleph, from Allon in Zaanannim, and Adami, Nekeb, and Jabneel, to Lakkum, and its outgoings are [at] the Jordan; ³⁴and the border has turned back westward [to] Aznoth-Tabor, and gone out there to Hukkok, and touched against Zebulun on the south, and it has touched against Asher on the west, and against Judah [at] the Jordan, at the sun-rising; ³⁵and the cities of defense [are] Ziddim, Zer, and Hammath, Rakkath, and Chinnereth, ³⁶and Adamah, and Ramah, and Hazor, ³⁷and Kedesh, and Edrei, and En-Hazor, ³⁸and Iron, and Migdal-El, Horem, and Beth-Anath, and Beth-Shemesh; nineteen cities and their villages. ³⁹This [is] the inheritance of the tribe of the sons of Naphtali, for their families, the cities and their villages. ⁴⁰The seventh lot has gone out for the tribe of the sons of Dan, for their families; ⁴¹and the border of their inheritance is Zorah, and Eshtaol, and Ir-Shemesh, ⁴²and Shalabbin, and Aijalon, and Jethlah, ⁴³and Elon, and Thimnathah, and Ekron, ⁴⁴and Eltekeh, and Gibbethon, and Ba'alath, ⁴⁵and Jehud, and Bene-Barak, and Gath-Rimmon, ⁴⁶and Me-Jarkon, and Rakkon, with the border in front of Joppa. ⁴⁷And the border of the sons of Dan goes out from them, and the sons of Dan go up and fight with Leshem, and capture it, and strike it by the mouth of the sword, and possess it, and dwell in it, and call Leshem, Dan, according to the name of their father Dan. ⁴⁸This [is] the inheritance of the tribe of the sons of Dan, for their families, these cities and their villages. ⁴⁹And they finish to give the land in inheritance, by its borders, and the sons of Israel give an inheritance to Joshua son of Nun in their midst; ⁵⁰by the command of YHWH they have given to him the city which he asked for, Timnath-Serah, in the hill-country of Ephraim, and he builds the city and dwells in it. ⁵¹These [are] the inheritances which Eleazar the priest, and Joshua son of Nun, and the heads of the fathers of the tribes of the sons of Israel, have caused to inherit by lot, in Shiloh, before YHWH, at the opening of the Tent of Meeting; and they finish to apportion the land.

CHAPTER 20

¹And YHWH speaks to Joshua, saying, ²"Speak to the sons of Israel, saying, Give cities of refuge for yourselves, as I have spoken to you by the hand of Moses, ³for the fleeing there of a manslayer striking life through ignorance, without knowledge; and they have been for a refuge to you from the redeemer of blood. ⁴When [one] has fled to one of these cities, and has stood [at] the opening of the gate of the city, and has spoken his matter in the ears of [the] elderly of that city, then they have

gathered him into the city to them, and have given a place to him, and he has dwelt with them. ⁵And when the redeemer of blood pursues after him, then they do not shut up the manslayer into his hand, for he has struck his neighbor without knowledge, and is not hating him until now; ⁶and he has dwelt in that city until his standing before the congregation for judgment, until the death of the chief priest who is in those days—then the manslayer turns back and has come to his city, and to his house, to the city from where he fled." ⁷And they sanctify Kedesh in Galilee, in the hill-country of Naphtali, and Shechem in the hill-country of Ephraim, and Kirjath-Arba (it [is] Hebron), in the hill-country of Judah; ⁸and beyond the Jordan, [at] Jericho eastward, they have given Bezer in the wilderness, in the plain, out of the tribe of Reuben, and Ramoth in Gilead out of the tribe of Gad, and Golan in Bashan out of the tribe of Manasseh. ⁹These have been cities of meeting for all the sons of Israel, and for a sojourner who is sojourning in their midst, for the fleeing there of anyone striking life through ignorance, and he does not die by the hand of the redeemer of blood until his standing before the congregation.

CHAPTER 21

¹And the heads of the fathers of the Levites draw near to Eleazar the priest, and to Joshua son of Nun, and to the heads of the fathers of the tribes of the sons of Israel, ²and they speak to them in Shiloh, in the land of Canaan, saying, "YHWH commanded by the hand of Moses to give to us cities to dwell in, and their outskirts for our livestock." ³And the sons of Israel give to the Levites, out of their inheritance, at the command of YHWH, these cities and their outskirts: ⁴and the lot goes out for the families of the Kohathite, and there are for the sons of Aaron the priest (of the Levites), out of the tribe of Judah, and out of the tribe of Simeon, and out of the tribe of Benjamin, thirteen cities by lot, ⁵and for the sons of Kohath who are left, out of the families of the tribe of Ephraim, and out of the tribe of Dan, and out of the half-tribe of Manasseh, ten cities by lot. ⁶And for the sons of Gershon, out of the families of the tribe of Issachar, and out of the tribe of Asher, and out of the tribe of Naphtali, and out of the half-tribe of Manasseh in Bashan, [are] thirteen cities by lot. ⁷For the sons of Merari, for their families, out of the tribe of Reuben, and out of the tribe of Gad, and out of the tribe of Zebulun, [are] twelve cities. ⁸And the sons of Israel give these cities and their outskirts to the Levites, as YHWH commanded by the hand of Moses, by lot. ⁹And they give out of the tribe of the sons of Judah, and out of the tribe of the sons of Simeon, these cities which are called by name; ¹⁰and they are for the sons of Aaron, of the families of the Kohathite, of the sons of Levi, for the first lot has been theirs; ¹¹and they give to them the city of Arba father of Anak (it [is] Hebron), in the hill-country of Judah, and its outskirts around it; ¹²and they have given the field of the city and its villages to Caleb son of Jephunneh for his possession. ¹³And to the sons of Aaron the priest they have given the city of refuge [for] the manslayer, Hebron and its outskirts, and Libnah and its outskirts, ¹⁴and Jattir and its outskirts, and Eshtemoa and its outskirts, ¹⁵and Holon and its outskirts, and Debir and its outskirts, ¹⁶and Ain and its outskirts, and Juttah and its outskirts, Beth-Shemesh and its outskirts; nine cities out of these two tribes. ¹⁷And out of the tribe of Benjamin, Gibeon and its outskirts, Geba and its outskirts, ¹⁸Anathoth and its outskirts, and Almon and its outskirts—four cities; ¹⁹all the cities of the sons of Aaron the priests, [are] thirteen cities and their outskirts. ²⁰And for the families of the sons of Kohath, the Levites, who are left of the sons of Kohath, even the cities of their lot are of the tribe of Ephraim; ²¹and they give to them the city of refuge [for] the manslayer, Shechem and its outskirts, in the hill-country of Ephraim, and Gezer and its outskirts, ²²and Kibzaim and its outskirts, and Beth-Horon and its outskirts—four cities. ²³And out of the tribe of Dan, Eltekeh and its outskirts, Gibbethon and its outskirts, ²⁴Aijalon and its outskirts, Gath-Rimmon and its outskirts—four cities. ²⁵And out of the half-tribe of Manasseh, Taanach and its outskirts, and Gath-Rimmon and its outskirts—two cities; ²⁶all the cities [are] ten and their outskirts, for the families of the sons of Kohath who are left. ²⁷And for the sons of Gershon, of the families of the Levites, out of the half-tribe of Manasseh, the city of refuge [for] the manslayer, Golan in Bashan and its outskirts, and Beeshterah and its outskirts—two cities. ²⁸And out of the tribe of Issachar, Kishon and its outskirts, Dabarath and its outskirts, ²⁹Jarmuth and its outskirts, En-Gannim and its outskirts—four cities. ³⁰And out of the tribe of Asher, Mishal and its outskirts, Abdon and its outskirts, ³¹Helkath and its outskirts, and Rehob and its outskirts—four cities. ³²And out of the tribe of Naphtali, the city of refuge [for] the manslayer, Kedesh in Galilee and its outskirts, and Hammoth-Dor and its outskirts, and Kartan and its outskirts—three cities; ³³all the cities of the Gershonite, for their families, [are] thirteen cities and their outskirts. ³⁴And for the families of the sons of Merari, the Levites, who are left, [are,] out of the tribe of Zebulun, Jokneam and its outskirts, Kartah and its outskirts, ³⁵Dimnah and its outskirts, Nahalal and its outskirts—four cities. ³⁶And out of the tribe of Reuben, Bezer and its outskirts, and Jahazah and its outskirts, ³⁷Kedemoth and its outskirts, and Mephaath and its outskirts—four cities. ³⁸And out of the tribe of Gad, the city of refuge [for] the manslayer, Ramoth in Gilead and its outskirts, and Mahanaim and its outskirts, ³⁹Heshbon and its outskirts, Jazer and its outskirts—four cities [in] all. ⁴⁰All the cities for the sons of Merari, for their families, who are left of the families of the Levites—their lot is twelve cities. ⁴¹All the cities of the Levites in the midst of the possession of the sons of Israel [are] forty-eight cities, and their outskirts. ⁴²These cities are each city and its outskirts around it; so to all these cities. ⁴³And YHWH gives to Israel the whole of the land which He has sworn to give to their fathers, and they possess it, and dwell in it; ⁴⁴and YHWH gives rest to them all around, according to all that which He has sworn to their fathers, and there has not stood a man in their presence of all their enemies, YHWH has given the whole of their enemies into their hand; ⁴⁵there has not fallen a thing of all the good thing which YHWH spoke to the house of Israel—the whole has come.

CHAPTER 22

¹Then Joshua calls for the Reubenite, and for the Gadite, and for the half-tribe of Manasseh, ²and says to them, "You have kept the whole of that which Moses, servant of YHWH, commanded you, and you listen to my voice, to all that I have commanded you; ³you have not left your brothers these many days to this day, and have kept the charge—the command of your God YHWH. ⁴And now, your God YHWH has given rest to your brothers, as He spoke to them; and now, turn, and go for yourselves to your tents, to the land of your possession, which Moses, servant of YHWH, has given to you beyond the Jordan. ⁵Only, be very watchful to do the command and the Law which Moses, servant of YHWH, commanded you, to love your God YHWH, and to walk in all His ways, and to keep His commands, and to cleave to Him, and to serve Him, with all your heart, and with all your soul." ⁶And Joshua blesses them, and sends them away, and they go to their tents. ⁷And to the half-tribe of Manasseh Moses has given, in Bashan, and to its [other] half Joshua has given with their brothers beyond the Jordan westward; and also when Joshua has sent them away to their tents, then he blesses them, ⁸and speaks to them, saying, "Turn back to your tents with great riches, and with very much livestock, with silver, and with gold, and with bronze, and with iron, and with very much raiment; divide the spoil of your enemies with your brothers." ⁹And the sons of Reuben, and the sons of Gad, and the half-tribe of Manasseh, turn back and go from the sons of Israel out of Shiloh, which [is] in the land of Canaan, to go to the land of Gilead, to the land of their possession, in which they have possession, according to the command of YHWH, by the hand of Moses; ¹⁰and they come to the districts of the Jordan, which [are] in the land of Canaan, and the sons of Reuben, and the sons of Gad, and the half-tribe of Manasseh, build an altar there by the Jordan—a great altar in appearance. ¹¹And the sons of Israel hear, saying, "Behold, the sons of Reuben, and the sons of Gad, and the half-tribe of Manasseh, have built the altar at the frontier of the land of Canaan, in the districts of the Jordan, at the passage of the sons of Israel." ¹²And the sons of Israel hear, and all the congregation of the sons of Israel is assembled at Shiloh, to go up against them to war; ¹³and the sons of Israel send to the sons of Reuben, and to the sons of Gad, and to the half-tribe of Manasseh—to the land of Gilead—Phinehas son of Eleazar the priest, ¹⁴and ten princes with him, one prince—one prince for a house of a father, for all the tribes of Israel, and each of them a head of a house of their fathers, for the thousands of

JOSHUA

Israel. ¹⁵And they come to the sons of Reuben, and to the sons of Gad, and to the half-tribe of Manasseh, to the land of Gilead, and speak with them, saying, ¹⁶"Thus said all the congregation of YHWH: What [is] this trespass which you have trespassed against the God of Israel, to turn back today from after YHWH, by your building an altar for yourselves, for your rebelling today against YHWH? ¹⁷Is the iniquity of Peor little to us, from which we have not been cleansed until this day—and the plague is in the congregation of YHWH, ¹⁸that you turn back today from after YHWH? And it has been [that] you rebel against YHWH today, and tomorrow He is angry against all the congregation of Israel. ¹⁹And surely, if the land of your possession is unclean, pass over for yourselves to the land of the possession of YHWH, where the Dwelling Place of YHWH has dwelt, and have possession in our midst; and do not rebel against YHWH, and do not rebel against us, by your building an altar for yourselves, besides the altar of our God YHWH. ²⁰Did Achan son of Zerah not commit a trespass in the devoted thing, and there was wrath on all the congregation of Israel? And he alone did not expire in his iniquity." ²¹And the sons of Reuben, and the sons of Gad, and the half-tribe of Manasseh, answer and speak with the heads of the thousands of Israel: ²²"The God of gods—YHWH, the God of gods—YHWH, He is knowing, and Israel—he knows, if [we are] in rebellion, and if in trespass against YHWH, do not save us this day! ²³[If we] are building an altar for ourselves to turn back from after YHWH, and if to cause burnt-offering and present to go up on it, and if to make peace-offerings on it—YHWH Himself requires [it]. ²⁴And nevertheless, we have done it from fear of [this] thing, saying, Hereafter your sons speak to our sons, saying, And what have you to [do with] YHWH God of Israel? ²⁵For YHWH has put a border between us and you, O sons of Reuben, and sons of Gad—Jordan; you have no portion in YHWH—and your sons have caused our sons to cease, not to fear YHWH. ²⁶And we say, Now let us prepare to build the altar for ourselves—not for burnt-offering, nor for sacrifice— ²⁷but it [is] a witness between us and you, and between our generations after us, to do the service of YHWH before Him with our burnt-offerings, and with our sacrifices, and with our peace-offerings, and your sons do not say hereafter to our sons, You have no portion in YHWH. ²⁸And we say, And it has been, when they say [so] to us, and to our generations hereafter, that we have said, See the pattern of the altar of YHWH, which our fathers made—not for burnt-offering nor for sacrifice—but it [is] a witness between us and you. ²⁹Far be it from us to rebel against YHWH, and to turn back from after YHWH today, to build an altar for burnt-offering, for present, and for sacrifice, apart from the altar of our God YHWH, which [is] before His Dwelling Place." ³⁰And Phinehas the priest, and the princes of the congregation, and the heads of the thousands of Israel, who [are] with him, hear the words which the sons of Reuben, and the sons of Gad, and the sons of Manasseh have spoken, and it is good in their eyes. ³¹And Phinehas son of Eleazar the priest says to the sons of Reuben, and to the sons of Gad, and to the sons of Manasseh, "Today we have known that YHWH [is] in our midst, because you have not committed this trespass against YHWH—then you have delivered the sons of Israel out of the hand of YHWH." ³²And Phinehas son of Eleazar the priest, and the princes, turn back from the sons of Reuben, and from the sons of Gad, out of the land of Gilead, to the land of Canaan, to the sons of Israel, and bring them back word; ³³and the thing is good in the eyes of the sons of Israel, and the sons of Israel bless God, and have not spoken to go up against them to war, to destroy the land which the sons of Reuben, and the sons of Gad, are dwelling in. ³⁴And the sons of Reuben and the sons of Gad proclaim concerning the altar, that, "[It is] a witness between us that YHWH [is] God."

CHAPTER 23

¹And it comes to pass, many days after that YHWH has given rest to Israel from all their surrounding enemies, that Joshua is old, entering into days, ²and Joshua calls for all Israel, for his elderly, and for his heads, and for his judges, and for his authorities, and says to them, "I have become old; I have entered into days; ³and you have seen all that your God YHWH has done to all these nations because of you, for your God YHWH [is] He who is fighting for you; ⁴see, I have caused these nations who are left to fall to you for an inheritance to your tribes, from the Jordan (and all the nations which I cut off), and the Great Sea [at] the [setting] sun. ⁵As for your God YHWH, He thrusts them from your presence, and has dispossessed them from before you, and you have possessed their land, as your God YHWH has spoken to you, ⁶and you have been very strong to keep and to do the whole that is written in the Scroll of the Law of Moses, so as not to turn aside from it right or left, ⁷so as not to go in among these nations, these who are left with you; and you do not make mention of the name of their gods, nor do you swear, nor do you serve them, nor do you bow yourselves to them; ⁸but you cleave to your God YHWH, as you have done until this day. ⁹And YHWH is dispossessing great and mighty nations from before you; as for you, none has stood in your presence until this day; ¹⁰one man of you pursues a thousand, for your God YHWH [is] He who is fighting for you, as He has spoken to you; ¹¹and you have been very watchful for yourselves to love your God YHWH. ¹²But—if you turn back at all and have cleaved to the remnant of these nations, these who are left with you, and intermarried with them, and gone in to them, and they to you, ¹³certainly know that your God YHWH is not continuing to dispossess these nations from before you, and they have been to you for a trap, and for a snare, and for a scourge, in your sides, and for thorns in your eyes, until you perish from off this good ground which your God YHWH has given to you. ¹⁴And behold, I am going, today, in the way of all the earth, and you have known—with all your heart, and with all your soul—that there has not fallen one thing of all the good things which your God YHWH has spoken concerning you; the whole have come to you; there has not failed of it one thing. ¹⁵And it has been, as there has come on you all the good thing which your God YHWH has spoken to you, so YHWH brings on you the whole of the evil thing, until His destroying you from off this good ground which your God YHWH has given to you; ¹⁶in your transgressing the covenant of your God YHWH which He commanded you, and you have gone and served other gods, and bowed yourselves to them, then the anger of YHWH has burned against you, and you have perished quickly from off the good land which He has given to you."

CHAPTER 24

¹And Joshua gathers all the tribes of Israel to Shechem, and calls for [the] elderly of Israel, and for his heads, and for his judges, and for his authorities, and they station themselves before God. ²And Joshua says to all the people, "Thus said YHWH, God of Israel: Beyond the River your fathers have dwelt of old—Terah father of Abraham and father of Nachor—and they serve other gods; ³and I take your father Abraham from beyond the River, and cause him to go through all the land of Canaan, and multiply his seed, and give Isaac to him. ⁴And I give Jacob and Esau to Isaac; and I give Mount Seir to Esau, to possess it; and Jacob and his sons have gone down to Egypt. ⁵And I send Moses and Aaron, and plague Egypt, as I have done in its midst, and afterward I have brought you out. ⁶And I bring out your fathers from Egypt, and you go to the sea, and the Egyptians pursue after your fathers, with chariot and with horsemen, to the Red Sea; ⁷and they cry to YHWH, and He sets thick darkness between you and the Egyptians, and brings the sea over him, and covers them, and your eyes see that which I have done in Egypt; and you dwell in a wilderness [for] many days. ⁸And I bring you into the land of the Amorite who is dwelling beyond the Jordan, and they fight with you, and I give them into your hand, and you possess their land, and I destroy them out of your presence. ⁹And Balak son of Zippor, king of Moab, rises and fights against Israel, and sends and calls for Balaam son of Beor, to revile you, ¹⁰and I have not been willing to listen to Balaam, and he greatly blesses you, and I deliver you out of his hand. ¹¹And you pass over the Jordan, and come to Jericho, and the possessors of Jericho fight against you—the Amorite, and the Perizzite, and the Canaanite, and the Hittite, and the Girgashite, the Hivite, and the Jebusite—and I give them into your hand. ¹²And I send the hornet before you, and it casts them out from your presence—two kings of the Amorite—not by your sword, nor by your bow. ¹³And I give a land to you for which you have not labored, and cities which you have not built, and you dwell in them; you are eating of vineyards and olive-yards which you have not planted. ¹⁴And now, fear YHWH, and serve Him,

JOSHUA

in perfection and in truth, and turn aside the gods which your fathers served beyond the River, and in Egypt, and serve YHWH; ¹⁵and if [it is] wrong in your eyes to serve YHWH—choose for yourselves today whom you serve—whether the gods whom your fathers served, which [are] beyond the River, or the gods of the Amorite in whose land you are dwelling; but me and my house—we serve YHWH." ¹⁶And the people answer and say, "Far be it from us to forsake YHWH, to serve other gods; ¹⁷for our God YHWH [is] He who is bringing us and our fathers up out of the land of Egypt, out of a house of servants, and who has done these great signs before our eyes, and keeps us in all the way in which we have gone, and among all the peoples through whose midst we passed; ¹⁸and YHWH casts out the whole of the peoples, even the Amorite inhabiting the land, from our presence; we also serve YHWH, for He [is] our God." ¹⁹And Joshua says to the people, "You are not able to serve YHWH, for He [is] a most holy God; He [is] a zealous God; He does not bear with your transgression and with your sins. ²⁰When you forsake YHWH, and have served gods of a stranger, then He has turned back and done harm to you, and consumed you, after that He has done good to you." ²¹And the people say to Joshua, "No, but we serve YHWH!" ²²And Joshua says to the people, "You are witnesses against yourselves, that you have chosen YHWH for yourselves, to serve Him," and they say, "Witnesses!" ²³"And now, turn aside the gods of the stranger which [are] in your midst, and incline your heart to YHWH, God of Israel." ²⁴And the people say to Joshua, "We serve our God YHWH, and we listen to His voice." ²⁵And Joshua makes a covenant with the people on that day, and lays a statute and an ordinance on it, in Shechem. ²⁶And Joshua writes these words in the Scroll of the Law of God, and takes a great stone, and raises it up there under the oak which [is] in the sanctuary of YHWH. ²⁷And Joshua says to all the people, "Behold, this stone is for a witness against us, for it has heard all the sayings of YHWH which He has spoken with us, and it has been for a witness against you, lest you lie against your God." ²⁸And Joshua sends the people away, each to his inheritance. ²⁹And it comes to pass, after these things, that Joshua son of Nun, servant of YHWH, dies, a son of one hundred and ten years, ³⁰and they bury him in the border of his inheritance, in Timnath-Serah, which [is] in the hill-country of Ephraim, on the north of the hill of Gaash. ³¹And Israel serves YHWH all [the] days of Joshua, and all [the] days of the elderly who prolonged days after Joshua, and who knew all the work of YHWH which He did to Israel. ³²And the bones of Joseph, which the sons of Israel brought up out of Egypt, they buried in Shechem, in the portion of the field which Jacob bought from the sons of Hamor father of Shechem, with one hundred kesitah; and they are for an inheritance to the sons of Joseph. ³³And Eleazar son of Aaron died, and they bury him in a hill of his son Phinehas, which was given to him in the hill-country of Ephraim.

JUDGES

CHAPTER 1

¹And it comes to pass after the death of Joshua, that the sons of Israel ask of YHWH, saying, "Who goes up for us to the Canaanite, at the commencement, to fight against it?" ²And YHWH says, "Judah goes up; behold, I have given the land into his hand." ³And Judah says to his brother Simeon, "Go up with me into my lot, and we fight against the Canaanite—and I have gone, even I, with you into your lot"; and Simeon goes with him. ⁴And Judah goes up, and YHWH gives the Canaanite and the Perizzite into their hand, and they strike them in Bezek—ten thousand men; ⁵and they find Adoni-Bezek in Bezek, and fight against him, and strike the Canaanite and the Perizzite. ⁶And Adoni-Bezek flees, and they pursue after him, and seize him, and cut off his thumbs and his great toes, ⁷and Adoni-Bezek says, "Seventy kings—their thumbs and their great toes cut off—have been gathering under my table; as I have done so God has repaid to me"; and they bring him to Jerusalem, and he dies there. ⁸And the sons of Judah fight against Jerusalem, and capture it, and strike it by the mouth of the sword, and they have sent the city into fire; ⁹and afterward the sons of Judah have gone down to fight against the Canaanite inhabiting the hill-country, and the south, and the low country; ¹⁰and Judah goes to the Canaanite who is dwelling in Hebron (and the name of Hebron [was] formerly Kirjath-Arba), and they strike Sheshai, and Ahiman, and Talmai. ¹¹And he goes there to the inhabitants of Debir (and the name of Debir [was] formerly Kirjath-Sepher), ¹²and Caleb says, "He who strikes Kirjath-Sepher and has captured it—then I have given my daughter Achsah to him for a wife." ¹³And Othniel son of Kenaz, younger brother of Caleb, captures it, and he gives his daughter Achsah to him for a wife. ¹⁴And it comes to pass in her coming in, that she persuades him to ask from her father the field, and she comes down off the donkey, and Caleb says to her, "What do you [want]?" ¹⁵And she says to him, "Give a blessing to me; when you have given me the south land—then you have given springs of water to me"; and Caleb gives the upper springs and the lower springs to her. ¹⁶And the sons of the Kenite, father-in-law of Moses, have gone up out of the city of palms with the sons of Judah [to] the wilderness of Judah, which [is] in the south of Arad, and they go and dwell with the people. ¹⁷And Judah goes with his brother Simeon, and they strike the Canaanite inhabiting Zephath, and devote it; and [one] calls the name of the city Hormah. ¹⁸And Judah captures Gaza and its border, and Askelon and its border, and Ekron and its border; ¹⁹and YHWH is with Judah, and he occupies the hill-country, but not to dispossess the inhabitants of the valley, for they have chariots of iron. ²⁰And they give Hebron to Caleb, as Moses has spoken, and he dispossesses the three sons of Anak there. ²¹And the sons of Benjamin have not dispossessed the Jebusite inhabiting Jerusalem; and the Jebusite dwells with the sons of Benjamin, in Jerusalem, until this day. ²²And the house of Joseph goes up—even they—to Beth-El, and YHWH [is] with them; ²³and the house of Joseph causes [men] to spy out Beth-El (and the name of the city [was] formerly Luz), ²⁴and the watchers see a man coming out from the city, and say to him, "Please show us the entrance of the city, and we have done kindness with you." ²⁵And he shows them the entrance of the city, and they strike the city by the mouth of the sword, and they have sent the man and all his family away; ²⁶and the man goes to the land of the Hittites, and builds a city, and calls its name Luz—it [is] its name to this day. ²⁷And Manasseh has not occupied Beth-Shean and its towns, and Taanach and its towns, and the inhabitants of Dor and its towns, and the inhabitants of Iblaim and its towns, and the inhabitants of Megiddo and its towns, and the Canaanite is desirous to dwell in that land; ²⁸and it comes to pass, when Israel has been strong, that he sets the Canaanite to forced labor, and has not utterly dispossessed it. ²⁹And Ephraim has not dispossessed the Canaanite who is dwelling in Gezer, and the Canaanite dwells in its midst, in Gezer. ³⁰Zebulun has not dispossessed the inhabitants of Kitron, and the inhabitants of Nahalol, and the Canaanite dwells in its midst, and they become forced labor. ³¹Asher has not dispossessed the inhabitants of Accho, and the inhabitants of Sidon, and Ahlab, and Achzib, and Helbah, and Aphik, and Rehob; ³²and the Asherite dwells in the midst of the Canaanite, the inhabitants of the land, for it has not dispossessed them. ³³Naphtali has not dispossessed the inhabitants of Beth-Shemesh, and the inhabitants of Beth-Anath, and he dwells in the midst of the Canaanite, the inhabitants of the land; and the inhabitants of Beth-Shemesh and of Beth-Anath were for forced labor for them. ³⁴And the Amorites press the sons of Dan to the mountain, for they have not permitted them to go down to the valley; ³⁵and the Amorite is desirous to dwell in Mount Heres, in Aijalon, and in Shaalbim, and the hand of the house of Joseph is heavy, and they are for forced labor; ³⁶and the border of the Amorite [is] from the ascent of Akrabbim, from the rock and upward.

JUDGES

CHAPTER 2

¹And the Messenger of YHWH goes up from Gilgal to Bochim, ²and says, "I cause you to come up out of Egypt, and bring you into the land which I have sworn to your fathers, and say, I do not break My covenant with you for all time; and you make no covenant with the inhabitants of this land—you break down their altars; and you have not listened to My voice—what [is] this you have done? ³And I have also said, I do not cast them out from your presence, and they have been for adversaries to you, and their gods are for a snare to you." ⁴And it comes to pass, when the Messenger of YHWH speaks these words to all the sons of Israel, that the people lift up their voice and weep, ⁵and they call the name of that place Bochim, and sacrifice to YHWH there. ⁶And Joshua sends the people away, and the sons of Israel go, each to his inheritance, to possess the land; ⁷and the people serve YHWH all [the] days of Joshua, and all [the] days of [the] elderly who prolonged days after Joshua, who saw all the great work of YHWH which He did to Israel. ⁸And Joshua son of Nun, servant of YHWH, dies, a son of one hundred and ten years, ⁹and they bury him in the border of his inheritance, in Timnath-Heres, in the hill-country of Ephraim, on the north of Mount Gaash; ¹⁰and all that generation have also been gathered to their fathers, and another generation rises after them who have not known YHWH, and even the work which He has done to Israel. ¹¹And the sons of Israel do evil in the eyes of YHWH, and serve the Ba'alim, ¹²and forsake YHWH, God of their fathers, who brings them out from the land of Egypt, and go after other gods (of the gods of the peoples who [are] around them), and bow themselves to them, and provoke YHWH, ¹³indeed, they forsake YHWH, and do service to Ba'al and to Ashtaroth. ¹⁴And the anger of YHWH burns against Israel, and He gives them into the hand of spoilers, and they spoil them, and He sells them into the hand of their surrounding enemies, and they have not been able to stand before their enemies anymore; ¹⁵in every [place] where they have gone out, the hand of YHWH has been against them for calamity, as YHWH has spoken, and as YHWH has sworn to them, and they are greatly distressed. ¹⁶And YHWH raises up judges, and they save them from the hand of their spoilers; ¹⁷and they have also not listened to their judges, but have gone whoring after other gods, and bow themselves to them; they have turned aside [with] haste out of the way [in] which their fathers walked to obey the commands of YHWH—they have not done so. ¹⁸And when YHWH raised up judges for them—then YHWH was with the judge, and saved them out of the hand of their enemies all [the] days of the judge; for YHWH sighs, because of their groaning from the presence of their oppressors, and of those thrusting them away. ¹⁹And it has come to pass, when the judge dies—they turn back and have done corruptly above their fathers, to go after other gods, to serve them, and to bow themselves to them; they have not fallen from their doings, and from their stiff way. ²⁰And the anger of YHWH burns against Israel, and He says, "Because that this nation has transgressed My covenant which I commanded their fathers, and have not listened to My voice— ²¹I also do not continue to dispossess any from before them of the nations which Joshua has left when he dies, ²²in order to try Israel by them, whether they are keeping the way of YHWH, to go in it, as their fathers kept [it], or not." ²³And YHWH leaves these nations, so as not to dispossess them quickly, and did not give them into the hand of Joshua.

CHAPTER 3

¹And these [are] the nations which YHWH left, to try Israel by them, all who have not known all the wars of Canaan; ²(only for the sake of the generations of the sons of Israel knowing, to teach them war, only those who formerly have not known them)— ³five princes of the Philistines, and all the Canaanite, and the Zidonian, and the Hivite inhabiting Mount Lebanon, from Mount Ba'al-Hermon to the entering in of Hamath; ⁴and they are to prove Israel by them, to know whether they obey the commands of YHWH that He commanded their fathers by the hand of Moses. ⁵And the sons of Israel have dwelt in the midst of the Canaanite, the Hittite, and the Amorite, and the Perizzite, and the Hivite, and the Jebusite, ⁶and take their daughters to them for wives, and have given their daughters to their sons, and they serve their gods; ⁷and the sons of Israel do evil in the eyes of YHWH, and forget their God YHWH, and serve the Ba'alim and the Asheroth. ⁸And the anger of YHWH burns against Israel, and He sells them into the hand of Chushan-Rishathaim king of Aram-Naharaim, and the sons of Israel serve Chushan-Rishathaim eight years; ⁹and the sons of Israel cry to YHWH, and YHWH raises a savior to the sons of Israel, and he saves them—Othniel son of Kenaz, Caleb's younger brother; ¹⁰and the Spirit of YHWH is on him, and he judges Israel, and goes out to battle, and YHWH gives Chushan-Rishathaim king of Aram into his hand, and his hand is strong against Chushan-Rishathaim; ¹¹and the land rests forty years. And Othniel son of Kenaz dies, ¹²and the sons of Israel add to do evil in the eyes of YHWH; and YHWH strengthens Eglon king of Moab against Israel, because that they have done evil in the eyes of YHWH; ¹³and he gathers the sons of Ammon and Amalek to himself, and goes and strikes Israel, and they possess the city of palms; ¹⁴and the sons of Israel serve Eglon king of Moab eighteen years. ¹⁵And the sons of Israel cry to YHWH, and YHWH raises a savior to them, Ehud son of Gera, a Benjamite (a man [with] his right hand bound), and the sons of Israel send a present by his hand to Eglon king of Moab; ¹⁶and Ehud makes a sword for himself, and it has two mouths (its length [is] a cubit), and he girds it under his long robe on his right thigh; ¹⁷and he brings the present near to Eglon king of Moab, and Eglon [is] a very fat man. ¹⁸And it comes to pass, when he has finished to bring the present near, that he sends the people carrying the present away, ¹⁹and he himself has turned back from the carved images which [are] at Gilgal and says, "I have a secret word for you, O king"; and he says, "Hush!" And all those standing by him go out from him. ²⁰And Ehud has come to him, and he is sitting in the cool upper chamber which he has for himself, and Ehud says, "I have a word of God for you"; and he rises from off the throne; ²¹and Ehud puts forth his left hand, and takes the sword from off his right thigh, and thrusts it into his belly; ²²and the hilt also goes in after the blade, and the fat shuts on the blade, that he has not drawn the sword out of his belly, and he goes out [through] the antechamber [[or and the dung came out]]. ²³And Ehud goes out at the porch, and shuts the doors of the upper chamber on him, and has bolted [it]; ²⁴and he has gone out, and his servants have come in, and look, and behold, the doors of the upper chamber are bolted, and they say, "He is surely covering his feet, [relieving himself,] in the cool inner chamber." ²⁵And they stay until confounded, and behold, he is not opening the doors of the upper chamber, and they take the key, and open, and behold, their lord is fallen to the earth—dead. ²⁶And Ehud escaped during their lingering, and has passed by the images, and escapes to Seirath. ²⁷And it comes to pass, in his coming in, that he blows with a horn in the hill-country of Ephraim, and the sons of Israel go down with him from the hill-country, and he before them; ²⁸and he says to them, "Pursue after me, for YHWH has given your enemies, the Moabites, into your hand"; and they go down after him, and capture the passages of the Jordan toward Moab, and have not permitted a man to pass over. ²⁹And they strike Moab at that time, about ten thousand men, all robust, and everyone a man of valor, and no man has escaped, ³⁰and Moab is humbled in that day under the hand of Israel; and the land rests [for] eighty years. ³¹And after him has been Shamgar son of Anath, and he strikes the Philistines—six hundred men—with an ox-goad, and he also saves Israel.

CHAPTER 4

¹And the sons of Israel add to do evil in the eyes of YHWH when Ehud is dead, ²and YHWH sells them into the hand of Jabin king of Canaan, who has reigned in Hazor, and Sisera [is] the head of his host, and he is dwelling in Harosheth of the nations; ³and the sons of Israel cry to YHWH, for he has nine hundred chariots of iron, and he has oppressed the sons of Israel mightily [for] twenty years. ⁴And Deborah, a woman, a prophetess, wife of Lapidoth, she is judging Israel at that time, ⁵and she is dwelling under the palm-tree of Deborah, between Ramah and Beth-El, in the hill-country of Ephraim, and the sons of Israel go up to her for judgment. ⁶And she sends and calls for Barak son of Abinoam, out of Kedesh-Naphtali, and says to him, "Has YHWH, God of Israel, not commanded? Go, and you have drawn toward Mount Tabor, and have taken with you ten thousand men, out of the sons of

Naphtali, and out of the sons of Zebulun, ⁷and I have drawn to you, to the Brook of Kishon, Sisera, head of the host of Jabin, and his chariot, and his multitude, and have given him into your hand." ⁸And Barak says to her, "If you go with me, then I have gone; and if you do not go with me, I do not go"; ⁹and she says, "I certainly go with you; only, surely your glory is not on the way which you are going, for YHWH sells Sisera into the hand of a woman"; and Deborah rises and goes with Barak to Kedesh. ¹⁰And Barak calls Zebulun and Naphtali to Kedesh, and he goes up—ten thousand men [are] at his feet—and Deborah goes up with him. ¹¹And Heber the Kenite has been separated from the Kenite, from the sons of Hobab father-in-law of Moses, and he stretches out his tent to the oak in Zaanaim, which [is] by Kedesh. ¹²And they declare to Sisera that Barak son of Abinoam has gone up to Mount Tabor, ¹³and Sisera calls all his chariots, nine hundred chariots of iron, and all the people who [are] with him, from Harosheth of the nations, to the Brook of Kishon. ¹⁴And Deborah says to Barak, "Rise, for this [is] the day in which YHWH has given Sisera into your hand; has YHWH not gone out before you?" And Barak goes down from Mount Tabor, and ten thousand men after him. ¹⁵And YHWH destroys Sisera, and all the chariots, and all the camp, by the mouth of the sword, before Barak, and Sisera comes down from off the chariot, and flees on his feet. ¹⁶And Barak has pursued after the chariots and after the camp, to Harosheth of the nations, and all the camp of Sisera falls by the mouth of the sword—there has not been left even one. ¹⁷And Sisera has fled on his feet to the tent of Jael wife of Heber the Kenite, for [there is] peace between Jabin king of Hazor and the house of Heber the Kenite; ¹⁸and Jael goes out to meet Sisera and says to him, "Turn aside, my lord, turn aside to me, do not fear"; and he turns aside to her, into the tent, and she covers him with a mantle. ¹⁹And he says to her, "Please give me a little water to drink, for I am thirsty"; and she opens the bottle of milk, and gives him to drink, and covers him. ²⁰And he says to her, "Stand at the opening of the tent, and it has been, if any comes in, and has asked you and said, Is there a man here? That you have said, There is not." ²¹And Jael wife of Heber takes the pin of the tent, and takes the hammer in her hand, and goes to him gently, and strikes the pin into his temples, and it fastens in the earth—and he has been fast asleep, and is weary—and he dies. ²²And behold, Barak is pursuing Sisera, and Jael comes out to meet him, and says to him, "Come, and I show you the man whom you are seeking"; and he comes to her, and behold, Sisera is fallen—dead, and the pin [is] in his temples. ²³And God humbles Jabin king of Canaan before the sons of Israel on that day, ²⁴and the hand of the sons of Israel goes, going on and becoming hard on Jabin king of Canaan, until they have cut off Jabin king of Canaan.

JUDGES

CHAPTER 5

¹And Deborah sings—also Barak son of Abinoam—on that day, saying, ²"For freeing leaders in Israel, || For a people willingly offering themselves, || Bless YHWH. ³Hear, you kings; give ear, you princes, || I sing to YHWH, || I sing praise to YHWH, God of Israel. ⁴YHWH, in Your going forth out of Seir, || In Your stepping out of the field of Edom, || The earth trembled and the heavens dropped, || And thick clouds dropped water. ⁵Hills flowed from the face of YHWH, || This one—Sinai—From the face of YHWH, God of Israel. ⁶In the days of Shamgar son of Anath—In the days of Jael—The ways have ceased, || And those going in the paths go [in] crooked ways. ⁷Villages ceased in Israel—they ceased, || Until I arose—Deborah, || That I arose, a mother in Israel. ⁸He chooses new gods, || Then war [is] at the gates! A shield is not seen—and a spear || Among forty thousand in Israel. ⁹My heart [is] to the lawgivers of Israel, || Who are offering themselves willingly among the people, || Bless YHWH! ¹⁰Riders on white donkeys—Sitters on a long robe—And walkers by the way—meditate! ¹¹By the voice of shouters || Between the places of drawing water, || There they give out righteous acts of YHWH, || Righteous acts of His villages in Israel, || Then the people of YHWH have gone down to the gates. ¹²Awake, awake, Deborah; Awake, awake, utter a song; Rise, Barak, and take your captivity captive, || Son of Abinoam. ¹³Then him who is left of the majestic ones He caused to rule the people of YHWH, || He caused me to rule among the mighty. ¹⁴From Ephraim [are] those whose root [is] in Amalek, || After you, Benjamin, among your peoples, || From Machir lawgivers came down, || And from Zebulun those drawing with the reed of a writer. ¹⁵And princes in Issachar [are] with Deborah, || Indeed, Issachar [is] right with Barak, || Into the valley he was sent on his feet. In the divisions of Reuben, || The decrees of heart [are] great! ¹⁶Why have you abided between the boundaries, || To hear lowings of herds? For the divisions of Reuben, || The searchings of heart [are] great! ¹⁷Gilead dwelt beyond the Jordan, || And why does Dan sojourn [in] ships? Asher has abided at the haven of the seas, || And dwells by his creeks. ¹⁸Zebulun [is] a people who exposed its soul to death, || Naphtali also—on high places of the field. ¹⁹Kings came—they fought; Then kings of Canaan fought, || In Taanach, by the waters of Megiddo; They did not take gain of money! ²⁰They fought from the heavens: The stars fought with Sisera from their highways. ²¹The Brook of Kishon swept them away, || The most ancient brook—the Brook of Kishon. You tread down strength, O my soul! ²²Then the horse-heels were broken, || By gallopings—gallopings of its mighty ones. ²³Curse Meroz, said a messenger of YHWH, || Cursing, curse its inhabitants! For they did not come to the help of YHWH, || To the help of YHWH among the mighty! ²⁴Above women is Jael, || The wife of Heber the Kenite, || She is blessed above women in the tent. ²⁵He asked for water—she gave milk; She brought butter near in a lordly dish. ²⁶She sends forth her hand to the pin, || And her right hand to the laborers' hammer, || And she hammered Sisera—she struck his head, || Indeed, she struck, and it passed through his temple. ²⁷He bowed between her feet—He fell, he lay down; He bowed between her feet, he fell; Where he bowed, there he fell—destroyed. ²⁸She has looked out through the window—Indeed, she cries out—the mother of Sisera, || Through the lattice: Why is his chariot delaying to come? Why have the steps of his chariot tarried? ²⁹The wise ones, her princesses, answer her, || Indeed, she returns her sayings to herself: ³⁰Do they not find? They apportion spoil, || A female—two females—for every head, || Spoil of finger-work for Sisera, || Spoil of embroidered finger-work, || Finger-work—a pair of embroidered things, || For the necks of the spoil! ³¹So do all Your enemies perish, O YHWH, || And those loving Him [are] || As the going out of the sun in its might!" And the land rests [for] forty years.

CHAPTER 6

¹And the sons of Israel do evil in the eyes of YHWH, and YHWH gives them into the hand of Midian [for] seven years, ²and the hand of Midian is strong against Israel, [so] the sons of Israel have made for themselves the nooks which [are] in the mountains, and the caves, and the strongholds [to hide] from the presence of Midian. ³And it has been, if Israel has sowed, that Midian has come up, and Amalek, and the sons of the east, indeed, they have come up against him, ⁴and encamp against them, and destroy the increase of the land until your entering Gaza; and they leave no sustenance in Israel, either sheep, or ox, or donkey; ⁵for they and their livestock come up, with their tents; they come in as the fullness of the locust for multitude, and of them and of their livestock there is no number, and they come into the land to destroy it. ⁶And Israel is very weak from the presence of Midian, and the sons of Israel cry to YHWH. ⁷And it comes to pass, when the sons of Israel have cried to YHWH concerning Midian, ⁸that YHWH sends a man, a prophet, to the sons of Israel, and he says to them, "Thus said YHWH, God of Israel: I have brought you up out of Egypt, and I bring you out from a house of servants, ⁹and I deliver you out of the hand of the Egyptians, and out of the hand of all your oppressors, and I cast them out from your presence, and I give their land to you, ¹⁰and I say to you, I [am] your God YHWH, you do not fear the gods of the Amorite in whose land you are dwelling—and you have not listened to My voice." ¹¹And the Messenger of YHWH comes and sits under the oak which [is] in Ophrah, which [is] to Joash the Abi-Ezrite, and his son Gideon is beating out wheat in the winepress, to remove [it] from the presence of the Midianites; ¹²and the Messenger of YHWH appears to him and says to him, "YHWH [is] with you, O mighty man of valor." ¹³And Gideon says to Him, "O my Lord, [if] YHWH is indeed with us, then why has all this found us? And where [are] all His wonders which our

JUDGES

fathers recounted to us, saying, Has YHWH not brought us up out of Egypt? And now YHWH has left us, and gives us into the hand of Midian." ¹⁴And YHWH turns to him and says, "Go in this—your power; and you have saved Israel out of the hand of Midian—have I not sent you?" ¹⁵And he says to Him, "O my Lord, with what do I save Israel? Behold, my chief [is] weak in Manasseh, and I [am] the least in the house of my father." ¹⁶And YHWH says to him, "Because I am with you—you have struck the Midianites as one man." ¹⁷And he says to Him, "Now if I have found grace in Your eyes, then You have done a sign for me that You are speaking with me. ¹⁸Please do not move from here until my coming to You, and I have brought out my present, and put it before You"; and He says, "I abide until your return." ¹⁹And Gideon has gone in, and prepares a kid of the goats, and an ephah of flour [worth] of unleavened things; he has put the flesh in a basket, and he has put the broth in a pot, and he brings [them] out to Him, to the place of the oak, and brings [them] near. ²⁰And the Messenger of God says to him, "Take the flesh and the unleavened things, and place [them] on this rock—and pour out the broth"; and he does so. ²¹And the Messenger of YHWH puts forth the end of the staff which [is] in His hand, and comes against the flesh, and against the unleavened things, and the fire goes up out of the rock and consumes the flesh and the unleavened things—and the Messenger of YHWH has gone from his eyes. ²²And Gideon sees that He [is] the Messenger of YHWH, and Gideon says, "Aah, Lord YHWH! For so I have looked on the Messenger of YHWH face to face!" ²³And YHWH says to him, "Peace to you; do not fear; you do not die." ²⁴And Gideon builds an altar to YHWH there, and calls it YHWH-Shalom, it [is] yet in Ophrah of the Abi-Ezrites to this day. ²⁵And it comes to pass, on that night, that YHWH says to him, "Take the young ox which your father has, and the second bullock of seven years, and you have thrown down the altar of Ba'al which your father has, and cut down the Asherah which [is] by it, ²⁶and you have built an altar to your God YHWH on the top of this stronghold, by the arrangement, and have taken the second bullock, and caused a burnt-offering to ascend with the wood of the Asherah which you cut down." ²⁷And Gideon takes ten men of his servants, and does as YHWH has spoken to him, and it comes to pass, because he has been afraid of the house of his father, and the men of the city, to do [it] by day, that he does [it] by night. ²⁸And the men of the city rise early in the morning, and behold, the altar of Ba'al has been broken down, and the Asherah which is by it has been cut down, and the second bullock has been offered on the altar which is built. ²⁹And they say to one another, "Who has done this thing?" And they inquire and seek, and they say, "Gideon son of Joash has done this thing." ³⁰And the men of the city say to Joash, "Bring out your son, and he dies, because he has broken down the altar of Ba'al, and because he has cut down the Asherah which [is] by it." ³¹And Joash says to all who have stood against him, "You, do you plead for Ba'al? You—do you save him? He who pleads for him is put to death during the morning; if he [is] a god he pleads against him himself, because he has broken down his altar." ³²And he calls him, on that day, Jerubba'al, saying, "The Ba'al pleads against him, because he has broken down his altar." ³³And all Midian and Amalek and the sons of the east have been gathered together, and pass over, and encamp in the Valley of Jezreel, ³⁴and the Spirit of YHWH has clothed Gideon, and he blows with a horn, and Abi-Ezer is called after him; ³⁵and he has sent messengers into all Manasseh, and it is also called after him; and he has sent messengers into Asher, and into Zebulun, and into Naphtali, and they come up to meet them. ³⁶And Gideon says to God, "If You are Savior of Israel by my hand, as You have spoken, ³⁷behold, I am placing the fleece of wool in the threshing-floor: if dew is only on the fleece, and dryness on all the earth—then I have known that You save Israel by my hand, as You have spoken"; ³⁸and it is so, and he rises early on the next day, and presses the fleece, and wrings dew out of the fleece—the fullness of the bowl of waters. ³⁹And Gideon says to God, "Do not let Your anger burn against me, and I only speak this time; please let me try only this time with the fleece—please let there be only dryness on the fleece, and let there be dew on all the earth." ⁴⁰And God does so on that night, and there is only dryness on the fleece, and there has been dew on all the earth.

CHAPTER 7

¹And Jerubba'al (he [is] Gideon) rises early, and all the people who [are] with him, and they encamp by the well of Harod, and the camp of Midian has been on the south of him, on the height of Moreh, in the valley. ²And YHWH says to Gideon, "The people who [are] with you [are] too many for My giving Midian into their hand, lest Israel beautify itself against Me, saying, My hand has given salvation to me; ³and now, please call in the ears of the people, saying, Whoever [is] afraid and trembling, let him turn back and go early from Mount Gilead"; and there return twenty-two thousand of the people, and ten thousand have been left. ⁴And YHWH says to Gideon, "The people [are] yet too many; bring them down to the water, and I refine him for you there; and it has been, he of whom I say to you, This goes with you—he goes with you; and any of whom I say to you, This does not go with you—he does not go." ⁵And he brings the people down to the water, and YHWH says to Gideon, "Everyone who laps of the water with his tongue as the dog laps—you set him apart; also everyone who bows on his knees to drink." ⁶And the number of those lapping with their hand to their mouth is three hundred men, and all the rest of the people have bowed down on their knees to drink water. ⁷And YHWH says to Gideon, "I save you by the three hundred men who are lapping, and have given Midian into your hand, and all the people go, each to his place." ⁸And the people take the provision in their hand, and their horns, and he has sent every man of Israel away, each to his tents; and he has kept hold on the three hundred men, and the camp of Midian has been by him at the lower part of the valley. ⁹And it comes to pass, on that night, that YHWH says to him, "Rise, go down into the camp, for I have given it into your hand; ¹⁰and if you are afraid to go down—go down, you and your young man Phurah, to the camp, ¹¹and you have heard what they speak, and afterward your hands are strengthened, and you have gone down against the camp." And he goes down, he and his young man Phurah, to the extremity of the fifties who [are] in the camp; ¹²and Midian, and Amalek, and all the sons of the east are lying in the valley, as the locust for multitude, and of their camels there is no number, as sand which [is] on the seashore for multitude. ¹³And Gideon comes in, and behold, a man is recounting a dream to his companion, and says, "Behold, I have dreamed a dream, and behold, a cake of barley-bread is turning itself over into the camp of Midian, and it comes to the tent, and strikes it, and it falls, and turns it upwards, and the tent has fallen." ¹⁴And his companion answers and says, "This is nothing except the sword of Gideon son of Joash, a man of Israel; God has given Midian and all the camp into his hand." ¹⁵And it comes to pass, when Gideon hears the narration of the dream and its interpretation, that he bows himself, and turns back to the camp of Israel, and says, "Rise, for YHWH has given the camp of Midian into your hand." ¹⁶And he divides the three hundred men [into] three detachments, and puts horns into the hand of all of them, and empty pitchers, and lamps within the pitchers. ¹⁷And he says to them, "Look at me, and thus do; and behold, I am coming into the extremity of the camp—and it has been—as I do so you do; ¹⁸and I have blown with a horn—I and all who [are] with me, and you have blown with horns, even you, around all the camp, and have said, For YHWH and for Gideon!" ¹⁹And Gideon comes—and the hundred men who [are] with him—into the extremity of the camp, [at] the beginning of the middle watch (they had just posted watchmen), and they blow with horns—also dashing in pieces the pitchers which [are] in their hand; ²⁰and the three detachments blow with horns, and break the pitchers, and keep hold with their left hand on the lamps, and with their right hand on the horns to blow, and they cry, "The sword of YHWH and of Gideon!" ²¹And they each stand in his place, around the camp, and all the camp runs, and they shout, and flee; ²²and the three hundred blow the horns, and YHWH sets the sword of each against his companion, even through all the camp; and the camp flees to Beth-Shittah, at Zererath, to the border of Abel-Meholah, by Tabbath. ²³And the men of Israel are called from Naphtali, and from Asher, and from all Manasseh, and pursue after Midian. ²⁴And Gideon has sent messengers into all the hill-country of Ephraim, saying, "Come down to meet Midian, and capture the waters from them as far as Beth-Barah, and the Jordan";

and every man of Ephraim is called, and they capture the waters as far as Beth-Barah, and the Jordan, ²⁵and they capture two of the heads of Midian, Oreb and Zeeb, and slay Oreb at the rock of Oreb, and they have slain Zeeb at the wine-vat of Zeeb, and they pursue into Midian; and they have brought the heads of Oreb and Zeeb to Gideon beyond the Jordan.

CHAPTER 8

¹And the men of Ephraim say to him, "What [is] this thing you have done to us—not to call for us when you went to fight with Midian?" And they strive with him severely; ²and he says to them, "What have I now done like you? Are the gleanings of Ephraim not better than the harvest of Abi-Ezer? ³God has given the heads of Midian, Oreb and Zeeb, into your hand; and what have I been able to do like you?" Then their temper desisted from off him in his speaking this thing. ⁴And Gideon comes to the Jordan, passing over, he and the three hundred men who [are] with him—wearied, yet pursuing— ⁵and he says to the men of Succoth, "Please give cakes of bread to the people who [are] at my feet, for they [are] wearied, and I am pursuing after Zebah and Zalmunna, kings of Midian." ⁶And the heads of Succoth say, "Is the hand of Zebah and Zalmunna now in your hand, that we give bread to your host?" ⁷And Gideon says, "Therefore—in YHWH's giving Zebah and Zalmunna into my hand—I have threshed your flesh with the thorns of the wilderness, and with the threshing instruments." ⁸And he goes up there [to] Penuel, and speaks to them thus; and the men of Penuel answer him as the men of Succoth answered. ⁹And he also speaks to the men of Penuel, saying, "In my turning back in peace, I break down this tower." ¹⁰And Zebah and Zalmunna [are] in Karkor, and their camps with them, about fifteen thousand, all who are left of all the camp of the sons of the east; and those falling [are] one hundred and twenty thousand men, drawing sword. ¹¹And Gideon goes up the way of those who dwell in tents, on the east of Nobah and Jogbehah, and strikes the camp, and the camp was confident; ¹²and Zebah and Zalmunna flee, and he pursues after them, and captures the two kings of Midian, Zebah and Zalmunna, and he has caused all the camp to tremble. ¹³And Gideon son of Joash turns back from the battle, at the going up of the sun, ¹⁴and captures a young man of the men of Succoth, and asks him, and he describes to him the heads of Succoth, and its elderly—seventy-seven men. ¹⁵And he comes to the men of Succoth and says, "Behold Zebah and Zalmunna, with whom you reproached me, saying, Is the hand of Zebah and Zalmunna now in your hand that we give bread to your men who [are] wearied?" ¹⁶And he takes the elderly of the city, and [the] thorns of the wilderness, and the threshing instruments, and teaches the men of Succoth by them, ¹⁷and he has broken down the Tower of Penuel, and slays the men of the city. ¹⁸And he says to Zebah and to Zalmunna, "What manner of men [were they] whom you slew in Tabor?" And they say, "As you—so they, [each] one as the form of the king's sons." ¹⁹And he says, "They [were] my brothers—sons of my mother; YHWH lives, if you had kept them alive—I would not kill you." ²⁰And he says to his firstborn Jether, "Rise, slay them"; and the young man has not drawn his sword, for he has been afraid, for he [is] yet a youth. ²¹And Zebah and Zalmunna say, "Rise and fall on us; for as the man—his might"; and Gideon rises, and slays Zebah and Zalmunna, and takes the crescents which [are] on the necks of their camels. ²²And the men of Israel say to Gideon, "Rule over us, both you, and your son, and your son's son, for you have saved us from the hand of Midian." ²³And Gideon says to them, "I do not rule over you, nor does my son rule over you; YHWH rules over you." ²⁴And Gideon says to them, "Let me ask a petition of you, and each give to me the ring of his prey, for they have rings of gold, for they [are] Ishmaelites." ²⁵And they say, "We certainly give"; and they spread out the garment, and each casts the ring of his prey there; ²⁶and the weight of the rings of gold which he asked for is one thousand and seven hundred [shekels] of gold, apart from the crescents, and the pendants, and the purple garments, which [are] on the kings of Midian, and apart from the chains which [are] on the necks of their camels, ²⁷and Gideon makes it into an ephod, and sets it up in his city, in Ophrah, and all Israel go whoring after it there, and it is for a snare to Gideon and to his house. ²⁸And Midian is humbled before the sons of Israel, and have not added to lift up their head; and the land rests [for] forty years in the days of Gideon. ²⁹And Jerubba'al son of Joash goes and dwells in his own house, ³⁰and there have been seventy sons of Gideon, coming out of his loin, for he had many wives; ³¹and his concubine, who [is] in Shechem, has borne to him—even she—a son, and he appoints his name Abimelech. ³²And Gideon son of Joash dies, in a good old age, and is buried in the burying-place of his father Joash, in Ophrah of the Abi-Ezrite. ³³And it comes to pass, when Gideon [is] dead, that the sons of Israel turn back and go whoring after the Ba'alim, and set Ba'al-Berith over them for a god; ³⁴and the sons of Israel have not remembered their God YHWH, who is delivering them out of the hand of all their surrounding enemies, ³⁵neither have they done kindness with the house of Jerubba'al—Gideon—according to all the good which he did with Israel.

CHAPTER 9

¹And Abimelech son of Jerubba'al goes to Shechem, to his mother's brothers, and speaks to them, and to all the family of the house of his mother's father, saying, ²"Now speak in the ears of all the masters of Shechem, Which [is] good for you—seventy men ruling over you (all the sons of Jerubba'al), or one man ruling over you? And you have remembered that I [am] your bone and your flesh." ³And his mother's brothers speak concerning him, in the ears of all the masters of Shechem, all these words, and their heart inclines after Abimelech, for they said, "He [is] our brother"; ⁴and they give seventy [pieces] of silver out of the house of Ba'al-Berith to him, and Abimelech hires vain and unstable men with them, and they go after him; ⁵and he goes into the house of his father at Ophrah, and slays his brothers, sons of Jerubba'al, seventy men, on one stone; and Jotham, youngest son of Jerubba'al, is left, for he was hidden. ⁶And all the masters of Shechem are gathered together, and all the house of Millo, and come and cause Abimelech to reign for king at the oak of the camp which [is] in Shechem; ⁷and they declare [it] to Jotham, and he goes and stands on the top of Mount Gerizim, and lifts up his voice, and calls, and says to them, "Listen to me, O masters of Shechem, and God listens to you: ⁸The trees have diligently gone to anoint a king over them, and they say to the olive, Reign over us. ⁹And the olive says to them, Have I ceased from my fatness, by which they honor gods and men, that I have gone to stagger over the trees? ¹⁰And the trees say to the fig, Come, reign over us. ¹¹And the fig says to them, Have I ceased from my sweetness, and my good increase, that I have gone to stagger over the trees? ¹²And the trees say to the vine, Come, reign over us. ¹³And the vine says to them, Have I ceased from my new wine, which is making gods and men glad, that I have gone to stagger over the trees? ¹⁴And all the trees say to the bramble, Come, reign over us. ¹⁵And the bramble says to the trees, If in truth you are anointing me for king over you, come, take refuge in my shadow; and if not—fire comes out from the bramble, and devours the cedars of Lebanon. ¹⁶And now, if you have acted in truth and in sincerity when you make Abimelech king; and if you have done good with Jerubba'al, and with his house; and if you have done to him according to the deed of his hands— ¹⁷because my father has fought for you, and casts his life away from [him], and delivers you from the hand of Midian; ¹⁸and you have risen against the house of my father today, and slay his sons, seventy men, on one stone, and cause Abimelech son of his handmaid to reign over the masters of Shechem, because he [is] your brother— ¹⁹indeed, if in truth and in sincerity you have acted with Jerubba'al and with his house this day, rejoice in Abimelech, and he rejoices—even he—in you; ²⁰and if not—fire comes out from Abimelech and devours the masters of Shechem and the house of Millo, and fire comes out from the masters of Shechem and from the house of Millo, and devours Abimelech." ²¹And Jotham hurries, and flees, and goes to Beer, and dwells there, from the face of his brother Abimelech. ²²And Abimelech is prince over Israel [for] three years, ²³and God sends an evil spirit between Abimelech and the masters of Shechem, and the masters of Shechem deal treacherously with Abimelech, ²⁴for [the] coming in of [the] violence [against] seventy sons of Jerubba'al, and to place their blood on their brother Abimelech, who slew them, and on the masters of Shechem, who strengthened his

hands to slay his brothers. ²⁵And the masters of Shechem set ambushes for him on the top of the hills, and rob everyone who passes over by them in the way, and it is declared to Abimelech. ²⁶And Gaal son of Ebed comes—also his brothers—and they pass over into Shechem, and the masters of Shechem trust in him, ²⁷and go out into the field, and gather their vineyards, and tread, and make praises, and go into the house of their god, and eat and drink, and revile Abimelech. ²⁸And Gaal son of Ebed says, "Who [is] Abimelech, and who [is] Shechem, that we serve him? Is [he] not son of Jerubba'al? And his commander Zebul? The men of Hamor father of Shechem serve you, and why do we serve him—we? ²⁹And oh that this people were in my hand—then I turn Abimelech aside"; and he says to Abimelech, "Increase your host, and come out." ³⁰And Zebul, prince of the city, hears the words of Gaal son of Ebed, and his anger burns, ³¹and he sends messengers to Abimelech deceitfully, saying, "Behold, Gaal son of Ebed and his brothers are coming into Shechem, and behold, they are fortifying the city against you; ³²and now, rise by night, you and the people who [are] with you, and lay wait in the field, ³³and it has been, in the morning, about the rising of the sun, you rise early, and have pushed against the city; and behold, he and the people who [are] with him are going out to you—and you have done to him as your hand finds." ³⁴And Abimelech rises, and all the people who [are] with him, by night, and they lay wait against Shechem—four detachments; ³⁵and Gaal son of Ebed goes out, and stands at the opening of the gate of the city, and Abimelech rises—also the people who [are] with him—from the ambush, ³⁶and Gaal sees the people and says to Zebul, "Behold, people are coming down from the top of the hills"; and Zebul says to him, "You are seeing the shadow of the hills like men." ³⁷And Gaal adds yet to speak and says, "Behold, people are coming down from the high part of the land, and another detachment is coming by the way of the oak of Meonenim." ³⁸And Zebul says to him, "Where [is] your mouth now, in that you say, Who [is] Abimelech that we serve him? Is this not the people against which you have kicked? Please go out now and fight against it." ³⁹And Gaal goes out before the masters of Shechem, and fights against Abimelech, ⁴⁰and Abimelech pursues him, and he flees from his presence, and many fall wounded—to the opening of the gate. ⁴¹And Abimelech abides in Arumah, and Zebul casts out Gaal and his brothers from dwelling in Shechem. ⁴²And it comes to pass, on the next day, that the people go out to the field, and they declare [it] to Abimelech, ⁴³and he takes the people, and divides them into three detachments, and lays wait in a field, and looks, and behold, the people are coming out from the city, and he rises against them, and strikes them. ⁴⁴And Abimelech and the detachments who [are] with him have pushed on, and stand at the opening of the gate of the city, and the two detachments have pushed against all who are in the field, and strike them, ⁴⁵and Abimelech has fought against the city all that day, and captures the city, and has slain the people who [are] in it, and he breaks down the city, and sows it [with] salt. ⁴⁶And all the masters of the Tower of Shechem hear, and go into the high place of the house of the god Berith, ⁴⁷and it is declared to Abimelech that all the masters of the Tower of Shechem have gathered themselves together, ⁴⁸and Abimelech goes up to Mount Zalmon, he and all the people who [are] with him, and Abimelech takes the great axe in his hand, and cuts off a bough of the trees, and lifts it up, and sets [it] on his shoulder, and says to the people who [are] with him, "What you have seen me do—hurry, do as I [have done]." ⁴⁹And every one of the people cuts down his bough and goes after Abimelech, and sets [them] at the high place, and burns the high place with fire by these, and also all the men of the Tower of Shechem die—about one thousand men and women. ⁵⁰And Abimelech goes to Thebez, and encamps against Thebez, and captures it, ⁵¹and a strong tower has been in the midst of the city, and all the men and the women flee there, and all the masters of the city, and they shut [it] behind them, and go up on the roof of the tower. ⁵²And Abimelech comes to the tower, and fights against it, and draws near to the opening of the tower to burn it with fire, ⁵³and a certain woman casts a piece of a millstone on the head of Abimelech, and breaks his skull, ⁵⁴and he calls quickly to the young man carrying his weapons and says to him, "Draw your sword, and you have put me to death, lest they say of me—A woman slew him"; and his young man pierced him through, and he dies. ⁵⁵And the men of Israel see that Abimelech [is] dead, and each one goes to his place; ⁵⁶and God turns back the evil of Abimelech which he did to his father to slay his seventy brothers; ⁵⁷and God has returned all the evil of the men of Shechem on their [own] head, and the cursing of Jotham son of Jerubba'al comes to them.

CHAPTER 10

¹And there rises after Abimelech, to save Israel, Tola son of Puah, son of Dodo, a man of Issachar, and he is dwelling in Shamir, in the hill-country of Ephraim, ²and he judges Israel [for] twenty-three years, and he dies, and is buried in Shamir. ³And there rises Jair the Gileadite after him, and he judges Israel [for] twenty-two years, ⁴and he has thirty sons riding on thirty donkey-colts, and they have thirty cities (they call them Havoth-Jair to this day), which [are] in the land of Gilead; ⁵and Jair dies, and is buried in Kamon. ⁶And the sons of Israel add to do evil in the eyes of YHWH, and serve the Ba'alim, and Ashtaroth, and the gods of Aram, and the gods of Sidon, and the gods of Moab, and the gods of the sons of Ammon, and the gods of the Philistines, and forsake YHWH, and have not served Him; ⁷and the anger of YHWH burns against Israel, and He sells them into the hand of the Philistines, and into the hand of the sons of Ammon, ⁸and they crush and oppress the sons of Israel in that year; [and for] eighteen years—all the sons of Israel [who] are beyond the Jordan, in the land of the Amorite, which [is] in Gilead. ⁹And the sons of Ammon pass over the Jordan to also fight against Judah, and against Benjamin, and against the house of Ephraim, and Israel has great distress. ¹⁰And the sons of Israel cry to YHWH, saying, "We have sinned against You, because we have even forsaken our God, and serve the Ba'alim." ¹¹And YHWH says to the sons of Israel, "[Have I] not [saved you] from the Egyptians, and from the Amorite, from the sons of Ammon, and from the Philistines? ¹²And the Zidonians, and Amalek, and Maon have oppressed you, and you cry to Me, and I save you out of their hand; ¹³and you have forsaken Me, and serve other gods, therefore I do not add to save you. ¹⁴Go and cry to the gods on which you have fixed; they save you in the time of your tribulation." ¹⁵And the sons of Israel say to YHWH, "We have sinned, do to us according to all that is good in Your eyes; only please deliver us this day." ¹⁶And they turn aside the gods of the stranger out of their midst, and serve YHWH, and His soul is grieved with the misery of Israel. ¹⁷And the sons of Ammon are called together, and encamp in Gilead, and the sons of Israel are gathered together, and encamp in Mizpah. ¹⁸And the people—heads of Gilead—say to one another, "Who [is] the man that begins to fight against the sons of Ammon? He is for head to all inhabitants of Gilead."

CHAPTER 11

¹And Jephthah the Gileadite has been a mighty man of valor, and he [is the] son of a harlot woman; and Gilead begets Jephthah, ²and the wife of Gilead bears sons to him, and the wife's sons grow up and cast Jephthah out, and say to him, "You do not inherit in the house of our father; for you [are the] son of another woman." ³And Jephthah flees from the face of his brothers, and dwells in the land of Tob; and vain men gather themselves together to Jephthah, and they go out with him. ⁴And it comes to pass, after a time, that the sons of Ammon fight with Israel, ⁵and it comes to pass, when the sons of Ammon have fought with Israel, that [the] elderly of Gilead go to take Jephthah from the land of Tob; ⁶and they say to Jephthah, "Come, and you have been for a captain to us, and we fight against the sons of Ammon." ⁷And Jephthah says to [the] elderly of Gilead, "Have you not hated me? And you cast me out from the house of my father, and why have you come to me now when you are in distress?" ⁸And [the] elderly of Gilead say to Jephthah, "Therefore, now, we have turned back to you; and you have gone with us, and have fought against the sons of Ammon, and you have been for head to us—to all the inhabitants of Gilead." ⁹And Jephthah says to [the] elderly of Gilead, "If you are taking me back to fight against the sons of Ammon, and YHWH has given them before me—am I for a head to you?" ¹⁰And [the] elderly of Gilead say to Jephthah, "YHWH is listening between us—if we do not do so according to your word." ¹¹And Jephthah goes with [the] elderly of Gilead, and the people set him over them for

head and for captain, and Jephthah speaks all his words before YHWH in Mizpeh. ¹²And Jephthah sends messengers to the king of the sons of Ammon, saying, "What [is this] to me and to you, that you have come to me, to fight in my land?" ¹³And the king of the sons of Ammon says to the messengers of Jephthah, "Because Israel took my land in his coming up out of Egypt, from Arnon, and to the Jabbok, and to the Jordan; and now, restore them in peace." ¹⁴And Jephthah adds yet and sends messengers to the king of the sons of Ammon, ¹⁵and says to him, "Thus said Jephthah: Israel did not take the land of Moab, and the land of the sons of Ammon, ¹⁶for in their coming up out of Egypt, Israel goes in the wilderness to the Red Sea, and comes to Kadesh, ¹⁷and Israel sends messengers to the king of Edom, saying, Please let me pass over through your land, and the king of Edom did not listen; and [Israel] has also sent to the king of Moab, and he has not been willing; and Israel abides in Kadesh, ¹⁸and he goes through the wilderness, and goes around the land of Edom and the land of Moab, and comes in at the rising of the sun of the land of Moab, and they encamp beyond Arnon, and have not come into the border of Moab, for Arnon [is] the border of Moab. ¹⁹And Israel sends messengers to Sihon, king of the Amorite, king of Heshbon, and Israel says to him, Please let us pass over through your land, to my place, ²⁰and Sihon has not trusted Israel to pass over through his border, and Sihon gathers all his people, and they encamp in Jahaz, and fight with Israel; ²¹and YHWH, God of Israel, gives Sihon and all his people into the hand of Israel, and they strike them, and Israel possesses all the land of the Amorite, the inhabitant of that land, ²²and they possess all the border of the Amorite from Arnon, and to the Jabbok, and from the wilderness, and to the Jordan. ²³And now, YHWH, God of Israel, has dispossessed the Amorite from the presence of His people Israel, and you would possess it! ²⁴That which your god Chemosh causes you to possess—do you not possess it? And all that which our God YHWH has dispossessed from our presence—we possess it. ²⁵And now, [are] you at all better than Balak son of Zippor, king of Moab? Did he strive with Israel at all? Did he fight against them at all? ²⁶In Israel's dwelling in Heshbon and in its towns, and in Aroer and in its towns, and in all the cities which [are] by the sides of Arnon [for] three hundred years—and why have you not delivered them in that time? ²⁷And I have not sinned against you, and you are doing evil with me—to fight against me. YHWH, the Judge, judges between the sons of Israel and the sons of Ammon today." ²⁸And the king of the sons of Ammon has not listened to the words of Jephthah which he sent to him, ²⁹and the Spirit of YHWH is on Jephthah, and he passes over Gilead and Manasseh, and passes over Mizpeh of Gilead, and he has passed over from Mizpeh of Gilead to the sons of Ammon. ³⁰And Jephthah vows a vow to YHWH and says, "If You give the sons of Ammon into my hand at all— ³¹then it has been, that which comes out from the doors of my house at all to meet me in my turning back in peace from the sons of Ammon—it has been for YHWH, or I have offered up a burnt-offering for it." ³²And Jephthah passes over to the sons of Ammon to fight against them, and YHWH gives them into his hand, ³³and he strikes them from Aroer, and to [where] you are going in to Minnith—twenty cities—and to the meadow of the vineyards, [with] a very great striking; and the sons of Ammon are humbled at the presence of the sons of Israel. ³⁴And Jephthah comes into Mizpeh, to his house, and behold, his daughter is coming out to meet him with timbrels, and with choruses, and except her alone, he has no son or daughter. ³⁵And it comes to pass, when he sees her, that he tears his garments and says, "Aah! My daughter, you have caused me to bend greatly, and you have been among those troubling me; and I have opened my mouth to YHWH, and I am not able to turn back." ³⁶And she says to him, "My father, you have opened your mouth to YHWH, do to me as it has gone out from your mouth, after that YHWH has done vengeance for you on your enemies, on the sons of Ammon." ³⁷And she says to her father, "Let this thing be done to me; desist from me [for] two months, and I go on, and have gone down on the hills, and I weep for my virginity—I and my friends." ³⁸And he says, "Go"; and he sends her away [for] two months, and she goes, she and her friends, and she weeps for her virginity on the hills; ³⁹and it comes to pass at the end of two months that she turns back to her father, and he does to her his vow which he has vowed, and she did not know a man; and it is a statute in Israel: ⁴⁰from time to time the daughters of Israel go to talk to the daughter of Jephthah the Gileadite, four days in a year.

CHAPTER 12

¹And the men of Ephraim are called together, and pass over northward, and say to Jephthah, "Why have you passed over to fight against the sons of Ammon, and have not called on us to go with you? We burn your house with fire over you." ²And Jephthah says to them, "I have been a man of great strife (I and my people) with the sons of Ammon, and I call you, and you have not saved me out of their hand, ³and I see that you are not a savior, and I put my life in my hand, and pass over to the sons of Ammon, and YHWH gives them into my hand—and why have you come up to me this day to fight against me?" ⁴And Jephthah gathered all the men of Gilead, and fights with Ephraim, and the men of Gilead strike Ephraim, because they said, "You Gileadites [are] fugitives of Ephraim, in the midst of Ephraim—in the midst of Manasseh." ⁵And Gilead captures the passages of the Jordan to Ephraim, and it has been, when [any of] the fugitives of Ephraim say, "Let me pass over," and the men of Gilead say to him, "[Are] you an Ephraimite?" And he says, "No"; ⁶that they say to him, "Now say, Shibboleth"; and he says, "Sibboleth," and is not prepared to speak right—and they seize him, and slaughter him at the passages of the Jordan, and there fall at that time, of Ephraim, forty-two chiefs. ⁷And Jephthah judged Israel [for] six years, and Jephthah the Gileadite dies, and is buried in [one of] the cities of Gilead. ⁸And after him Ibzan of Beth-Lehem judges Israel, ⁹and he has thirty sons, and thirty daughters he gave away [in marriage], and thirty daughters he brought in from outside for his sons; and he judges Israel [for] seven years. ¹⁰And Ibzan dies, and is buried in Beth-Lehem. ¹¹And after him Elon the Zebulunite judges Israel, and he judges Israel [for] ten years, ¹²and Elon the Zebulunite dies, and is buried in Aijalon, in the land of Zebulun. ¹³And after him, Abdon son of Hillel, the Pirathonite, judges Israel, ¹⁴and he has forty sons, and thirty grandsons, riding on seventy donkey-colts, and he judges Israel [for] eight years. ¹⁵And Abdon son of Hillel, the Pirathonite, dies, and is buried in Pirathon, in the land of Ephraim, in the hill-country of the Amalekite.

CHAPTER 13

¹And the sons of Israel add to do evil in the eyes of YHWH, and YHWH gives them into the hand of the Philistines [for] forty years. ²And there is a certain man of Zorah, of the family of the Danite, and his name [is] Manoah, his wife [is] barren, and has not borne; ³and the Messenger of YHWH appears to the woman and says to her, "Now behold, you [are] barren and have not borne; when you have conceived, then you have borne a son. ⁴And now, please take heed and do not drink wine and strong drink, and do not eat any unclean thing, ⁵for behold, you are conceiving and bearing a son, and a razor does not go up on his head, for the youth is a Nazarite to God from the womb, and he begins to save Israel out of the hand of the Philistines." ⁶And the woman comes and speaks to her husband, saying, "A Man of God has come to me, and His appearance [is] as the appearance of the Messenger of God, very fearful, and I have not asked Him where He [is] from, and he has not declared His Name to me; ⁷and He says to me, Behold, you are pregnant, and bearing a son, and now do not drink wine and strong drink, and do not eat any unclean thing, for the youth is a Nazarite to God from the womb until the day of his death." ⁸And Manoah makes plea to YHWH and says, "O my Lord, the Man of God whom You sent, please let Him come in again to us, and direct us what we do to the youth who is born." ⁹And God listens to the voice of Manoah, and the Messenger of God comes again to the woman, and she [is] sitting in a field, and her husband Manoah is not with her, ¹⁰and the woman hurries, and runs, and declares [it] to her husband, and says to him, "Behold, He has appeared to me—the Man who came on [that] day to me." ¹¹And Manoah rises, and goes after his wife, and comes to the Man, and says to Him, "Are you the Man who spoke to the woman?" And He says, "I [am]." ¹²And Manoah says, "Now let Your words come to pass; what is the custom of the youth—and his work?" ¹³And the Messenger of YHWH says to Manoah, "Of all that I said to the woman let her take heed; ¹⁴she does not

eat of anything which comes out from the wine-vine, and she does not drink wine and strong drink, and she does not eat any unclean thing; she observes all that I have commanded her." ¹⁵And Manoah says to the Messenger of YHWH, "Please let us detain You, and we prepare a kid of the goats before You." ¹⁶And the Messenger of YHWH says to Manoah, "If you detain Me—I do not eat of your bread; and if you prepare a burnt-offering—offer it to YHWH"; for Manoah has not known that He [is] the Messenger of YHWH. ¹⁷And Manoah says to the Messenger of YHWH, "What [is] Your Name? When Your words come to pass, then we have honored You." ¹⁸And the Messenger of YHWH says to him, "Why do you ask this, My Name, since it [is] incomprehensible?" ¹⁹And Manoah takes the kid of the goats, and the present, and offers on the rock to YHWH, and He is doing wonderfully, and Manoah and his wife are looking on, ²⁰and it comes to pass, in the going up of the flame from off the altar toward the heavens, that the Messenger of YHWH goes up in the flame of the altar, and Manoah and his wife are looking on, and they fall on their faces to the earth, ²¹and the Messenger of YHWH has not added again to appear to Manoah, and to his wife, then Manoah has known that He [is] the Messenger of YHWH. ²²And Manoah says to his wife, "We certainly die, for we have seen God." ²³And his wife says to him, "If YHWH were desirous to put us to death, He had not received burnt-offering and present from our hands, nor showed us all these things, nor caused us to hear [anything] like this as [at this] time." ²⁴And the woman bears a son, and calls his name Samson, and the youth grows, and YHWH blesses him, ²⁵and the Spirit of YHWH begins to move him in the camp of Dan, between Zorah and Eshtaol.

CHAPTER 14

¹And Samson goes down to Timnath, and sees a woman in Timnath of the daughters of the Philistines, ²and comes up and declares [it] to his father and to his mother, and says, "I have seen a woman in Timnath, of the daughters of the Philistines; and now, take her for me for a wife." ³And his father says to him—also his mother, "Is there no woman among the daughters of your brothers, and among all my people, that you are going to take a woman from the uncircumcised Philistines?" And Samson says to his father, "Take her for me, for she is right in my eyes." ⁴And his father and his mother have not known that it [is] from YHWH, that He is seeking a meeting of the Philistines; and the Philistines are ruling over Israel at that time. ⁵And Samson goes down—also his father and his mother, to Timnath, and they come to the vineyards of Timnath, and behold, a lion's whelp roars at meeting him, ⁶and the Spirit of YHWH prospers over him, and he tears it as the tearing of a kid, and there is nothing in his hand, and he has not declared to his father and to his mother that which he has done. ⁷And he goes down and speaks to the woman, and she is right in the eyes of Samson; ⁸and he turns back after [some] days to take her, and turns aside to see the carcass of the lion, and behold, a swarm of bees [are] in the body of the lion—and honey. ⁹And he takes it down on to his hands, and goes on, going and eating; and he goes to his father, and to his mother, and gives to them, and they eat, and he has not declared to them that he took down the honey from the body of the lion. ¹⁰And his father goes down to the woman, and Samson makes a banquet there, for so the young men does; ¹¹and it comes to pass, when they see him, that they take thirty companions, and they are with him. ¹²And Samson says to them, "Now let me put forth a riddle to you; if you certainly declare it to me [in] the seven days of the banquet, and have found [it] out, then I have given thirty linen shirts and thirty changes of garments to you; ¹³and if you are not able to declare [it] to me, then you have given thirty linen shirts and thirty changes of garments to me." And they say to him, "Put forth your riddle, and we hear it!" ¹⁴And he says to them: "Out of the eater came forth something to eat, || And out of the strong came forth [something] sweet"; and they were not able to declare the riddle [in] three days. ¹⁵And it comes to pass, on the seventh day, that they say to Samson's wife, "Entice your husband, that he declare the riddle to us, lest we burn you and the house of your father with fire; have you not called for us [here] to rob us?" ¹⁶And Samson's wife weeps for it and says, "You have only hated me, and have not loved me; you have put forth the riddle to the sons of my people, but have not declared it to me"; and he says to her, "Behold, I have not declared [it] to my father and to my mother—and I declare [it] to you?" ¹⁷And she weeps for it the seven days [in] which their banquet has been, and it comes to pass on the seventh day that he declares [it] to her, for she has distressed him; and she declares the riddle to the sons of her people. ¹⁸And the men of the city say to him on the seventh day, before the sun goes in: "What [is] sweeter than honey? And what [is] stronger than a lion?" And he says to them: "Unless you had plowed with my heifer, || You had not found out my riddle." ¹⁹And the Spirit of YHWH prospers over him, and he goes down to Ashkelon, and strikes down thirty of their men, and takes their armor, and gives the changes to those declaring the riddle; and his anger burns, and he goes up to the house of his father; ²⁰and Samson's wife becomes his companion's, who had attended to him.

CHAPTER 15

¹And it comes to pass after [some] days, in the days of wheat-harvest, that Samson looks after his wife, with a kid of the goats, and says, "I go in to my wife, to the inner chamber"; and her father has not permitted him to go in, ²and her father says, "I certainly said that you surely hated her, and I give her to your companion; is her younger sister not better than she? Please let her be to you instead of her." ³And Samson says of them, "I am more innocent this time than the Philistines, though I am doing evil with them." ⁴And Samson goes and catches three hundred foxes, and takes torches, and turns tail to tail, and puts a torch between the two tails, in the midst, ⁵and kindles fire in the torches, and sends [them] out into the standing grain of the Philistines, and burns [it] from heap even to standing grain, even to vineyard [and] olive-yard. ⁶And the Philistines say, "Who has done this?" And they say, "Samson, son-in-law of the Timnite, because he has taken away his wife, and gives her to his companion"; and the Philistines go up, and burn her and her father with fire. ⁷And Samson says to them, "Though you do thus, nevertheless I am avenged on you, and afterward I cease!" ⁸And he strikes them hip and thigh [with] a great striking, and goes down and dwells in the cleft of the rock of Etam. ⁹And the Philistines go up, and encamp in Judah, and are spread out in Lehi, ¹⁰and the men of Judah say, "Why have you come up against us?" And they say, "We have come up to bind Samson, to do to him as he has done to us." ¹¹And three thousand men of Judah go down to the cleft of the rock of Etam, and say to Samson, "Have you now known that the Philistines are rulers over us? And what [is] this you have done to us?" And he says to them, "As they did to me, so I did to them." ¹²And they say to him, "We have come down to bind you—to give you into the hand of the Philistines." And Samson says to them, "Swear to me, lest you fall on me yourselves." ¹³And they speak to him, saying, "No, but we certainly bind you, and have given you into their hand, and we certainly do not put you to death"; and they bind him with two thick bands, new ones, and bring him up from the rock. ¹⁴He has come to Lehi—and the Philistines have shouted at meeting him—and the Spirit of YHWH prospers over him, and the thick bands which [are] on his arms are as flax which they burn with fire, and his bands are melted from off his hands, ¹⁵and he finds a fresh jawbone of a donkey, and puts forth his hand and takes it, and strikes down one thousand men with it. ¹⁶And Samson says, "With the jawbone of a donkey, heap on heaps—I have struck down one thousand men with the jawbone of a donkey!" ¹⁷And it comes to pass, when he finishes speaking, that he casts away the jawbone out of his hand, and calls that place Ramath-Lehi; ¹⁸and he thirsts exceedingly, and calls to YHWH, and says, "You have given this great salvation by the hand of Your servant; and now, I die with thirst, and have fallen into the hand of the uncircumcised." ¹⁹And God cleaves the hollow place which [is] in Lehi, and waters come out of it, and he drinks, and his spirit comes back, and he revives; therefore [one] has called its name "The fountain of him who is calling," which [is] in Lehi to this day. ²⁰And he judges Israel in the days of the Philistines [for] twenty years.

CHAPTER 16

¹And Samson goes to Gaza, and sees a woman there, a harlot, and goes in to her; ²[it is told] to the Gazathites, saying, "Samson has come in here"; and they go around and lay wait for him all the night at the gate of the city, and keep themselves silent all the night, saying, "Until the morning light—then we have slain him." ³And Samson lies down until the middle of the night, and rises in the middle of the night, and lays hold on the doors of the gate of the city, and on the two side-posts, and removes them with the bar, and puts [them] on his shoulders, and takes them up to the top of the hill, which [is] on the front of Hebron. ⁴And it comes to pass afterward that he loves a woman in the Valley of Sorek, and her name [is] Delilah, ⁵and the princes of the Philistines come up to her, and say to her, "Entice him, and see wherein his great power [is], and wherein we are able for him—and we have bound him to afflict him, and each one of us gives eleven hundred pieces of silver to you." ⁶And Delilah says to Samson, "Please declare to me wherein your great power [is], and with what you are bound, to afflict you." ⁷And Samson says to her, "If they bind me with seven green cords which have not been dried, then I have been weak, and have been as one of mankind." ⁸And the princes of the Philistines bring up to her seven green cords which have not been dried, and she binds him with them. ⁹And the ambush is abiding with her in an inner chamber, and she says to him, "Philistines [are] on you, Samson!" And he breaks the cords as a thread of tow is broken in its touching fire, and his power has not been known. ¹⁰And Delilah says to Samson, "Behold, you have played on me, and speak lies to me; now, please declare to me with what you are bound." ¹¹And he says to her, "If they certainly bind me with thick bands, new ones, by which work has not been done, then I have been weak, and have been as one of mankind." ¹²And Delilah takes thick bands, new ones, and binds him with them, and says to him, "Philistines [are] on you, Samson!" And the ambush is abiding in an inner chamber, and he breaks them from off his arms as a thread. ¹³And Delilah says to Samson, "Until now you have played on me, and speak lies to me; declare to me with what you are bound." And he says to her, "If you weave the seven locks of my head with the web." ¹⁴And she fixes [it] with the pin and says to him, "Philistines [are] on you, Samson!" And he awakens out of his sleep, and pulls out the pin of the loom, and with the web. ¹⁵And she says to him, "How do you say, I have loved you, and your heart is not with me? These three times you have played on me, and have not declared to me wherein your great power [is]." ¹⁶And it comes to pass, because she distressed him with her words all the days, and urges him, and his soul is grieved to death, ¹⁷that he declares all his heart to her, and says to her, "A razor has not gone up on my head, for I [am] a Nazarite to God from the womb of my mother; if I have been shaven, then my power has turned aside from me, and I have been weak, and have been as all of mankind." ¹⁸And Delilah sees that he has declared all his heart to her, and she sends and calls for the princes of the Philistines, saying, "Come up this time, for he has declared all his heart to me"; and the princes of the Philistines have come up to her, and bring up the money in their hand. ¹⁹And she makes him sleep on her knees, and calls for a man, and shaves the seven locks of his head, and begins to afflict him, and his power turns aside from off him; ²⁰and she says, "Philistines [are] on you, Samson!" And he awakens out of his sleep and says, "I go out as time by time, and shake free"; but he has not known that YHWH has turned aside from off him. ²¹And the Philistines seize him, and pick out his eyes, and bring him down to Gaza, and bind him with two bronze chains; and he is grinding in the prison-house. ²²And the hair of his head begins to shoot up when he has been shaven, ²³and the princes of the Philistines have been gathered together to sacrifice a great sacrifice to their god Dagon, and to rejoice; and they say, "Our god has given our enemy Samson into our hand." ²⁴And the people see him, and praise their god, for they said, "Our god has given into our hand our enemy, and he who is laying waste to our land, and who multiplied our wounded." ²⁵And it comes to pass, when their heart [is] glad, that they say, "Call for Samson, and he entertains for us"; and they call for Samson out of the prison-house, and he entertains their faces, and they cause him to stand between the pillars. ²⁶And Samson says to the young man who is keeping hold on his hand, "Let me also feel the pillars on which the house is established, and I lean on them." ²⁷And the house has been full of the men and the women, and all the princes of the Philistines [are] there, and about three thousand men and women [are] on the roof, who are watching Samson entertain. ²⁸And Samson calls to YHWH and says, "Lord YHWH, please remember me and please strengthen me only this time, O God; and I am avenged—vengeance at once—because of my two eyes, on the Philistines." ²⁹And Samson turns aside [to] the two middle pillars, on which the house is established, and on which it is supported, [to] one with his right hand and one with his left; ³⁰and Samson says, "Let me die with the Philistines," and he inclines himself powerfully, and the house falls on the princes, and on all the people who [are] in it, and the dead whom he has put to death in his death are more than those whom he put to death in his life. ³¹And his brothers come down, and all the house of his father, and lift him up, and bring him up, and bury him between Zorah and Eshtaol, in the burying-place of his father Manoah; and he has judged Israel [for] twenty years.

CHAPTER 17

¹And there is a man of the hill-country of Ephraim, and his name [is] Micah, ²and he says to his mother, "The eleven hundred pieces of silver which have been taken of yours, and [of which] you have sworn, and also spoken in my ears; behold, the silver [is] with me, I have taken it"; and his mother says, "Blessed [is] my son of YHWH." ³And he gives back the eleven hundred pieces of silver to his mother, and his mother says, "I had certainly sanctified the silver to YHWH, from my hand, for my son, to make a carved image, and a molten image; and now, I give it back to you." ⁴And he gives back the money to his mother, and his mother takes two hundred pieces of silver, and gives them to a refiner, and he makes them a carved image, and a molten image, and it is in the house of Micah. ⁵As for the man Micah, he has a house of gods, and he makes an ephod, and teraphim, and consecrates the hand of one of his sons, and he is for a priest to him; ⁶in those days there is no king in Israel, each does that which is right in his own eyes. ⁷And there is a young man of Beth-Lehem-Judah, of the family of Judah, and he [is] a Levite, and he [is] a sojourner there. ⁸And the man goes out of the city, out of Beth-Lehem-Judah, to sojourn where he finds, and comes to the hill-country of Ephraim, to the house of Micah, to work his way. ⁹And Micah says to him, "Where do you come from?" And he says to him, "I [am] a Levite of Beth-Lehem-Judah, and I am going to sojourn where I find." ¹⁰And Micah says to him, "Dwell with me, and be for a father and for a priest to me, and I give ten pieces of silver to you for the days, and a suit of garments, and your sustenance"; and the Levite goes [in]. ¹¹And the Levite is willing to dwell with the man, and the young man is to him as one of his sons. ¹²And Micah consecrates the hand of the Levite, and the young man is for a priest to him, and he is in the house of Micah, ¹³and Micah says, "Now I have known that YHWH does good to me, for the Levite has been for a priest to me."

CHAPTER 18

¹In those days there is no king in Israel, and in those days the tribe of the Danite is seeking an inheritance to inhabit for itself, for [that] has not fallen to it to that day in the midst of the tribes of Israel by inheritance. ²And the sons of Dan send, out of their family, five of their men—men, sons of valor—from Zorah, and from Eshtaol, to traverse the land, and to search it, and they say to them, "Go, search the land"; and they come into the hill-country of Ephraim, to the house of Micah, and lodge

there. ³They [are] with the household of Micah, and they have discerned the voice of the young man, the Levite, and turn aside there, and say to him, "Who has brought you here? And what are you doing in this [place]? And why are you here?" ⁴And he says to them, "Thus and thus has Micah done to me; and he hires me, and I am for a priest to him." ⁵And they say to him, "Please ask of God, and we know whether our way on which we are going is prosperous." ⁶And the priest says to them, "Go in peace; before YHWH [is] your way in which you go." ⁷And the five men go, and come to Laish, and see the people which [is] in its midst, dwelling confidently, according to the custom of Zidonians, quiet and confident; and there is none putting to shame in the land in [any] thing, possessing restraint, and they [are] far off from the Zidonians, and have no word with [any] man. ⁸And they come to their brothers at Zorah and Eshtaol, and their brothers say to them, "What [did] you [find]?" ⁹And they say, "Rise, and we go up against them, for we have seen the land, and behold—very good; and you are keeping silent! Do not be slothful to go—to enter to possess the land. ¹⁰When you go, you come to a confident people, and the land [is] large on both hands, for God has given it into your hand, a place where there is no lack of anything which [is] in the land." ¹¹And there journey there, of the family of the Danite, from Zorah, and from Eshtaol, six hundred men girded with weapons of war. ¹²And they go up and encamp in Kirjath-Jearim, in Judah, therefore they have called that place, "Camp of Dan," until this day; behold, behind Kirjath-Jearim. ¹³And they pass over there [to] the hill-country of Ephraim, and come to the house of Micah. ¹⁴And the five men, those going to traverse the land of Laish, answer and say to their brothers, "Have you known that in these houses there is an ephod, and teraphim, and carved image, and molten image? And now, know what you do." ¹⁵And they turn aside there, and come to the house of the young man, the Levite, the house of Micah, and ask of him of welfare— ¹⁶(and the six hundred men girded with their weapons of war, who [are] of the sons of Dan, are standing at the opening of the gate)— ¹⁷indeed, the five men, those going to traverse the land, go up—they have come in there—they have taken the carved image, and the ephod, and the teraphim, and the molten image—and the priest is standing at the opening of the gate, and the six hundred men who are girded with weapons of war— ¹⁸indeed, these have entered the house of Micah, and take the carved image, the ephod, and the teraphim, and the molten image; and the priest says to them, "What are you doing?" ¹⁹And they say to him, "Keep silent, lay your hand on your mouth, and go with us, and be for a father and for a priest to us: is it better your being a priest for the house of one man, or your being priest for a tribe and for a family in Israel?" ²⁰And the heart of the priest is glad, and he takes the ephod, and the teraphim, and the carved image, and goes into the midst of the people, ²¹and they turn and go, and put the infants, and the livestock, and the baggage, before them. ²²They have been far off from the house of Micah—and the men who [are] in the houses which [are] near the house of Micah have been called together, and overtake the sons of Dan, ²³and call to the sons of Dan, and they turn their faces around, and say to Micah, "What [is this] to you that you have been called together?" ²⁴And he says, "You have taken my gods which I made, and the priest, and you go; and what more do I [have]? And what [is] this you say to me, What [is this] to you?" ²⁵And the sons of Dan say to him, "Do not let your voice be heard with us, lest men bitter in soul fall on you, and you have gathered your life, and the life of your household"; ²⁶and the sons of Dan go on their way, and Micah sees that they are stronger than he, and turns, and goes back to his house. ²⁷And they have taken that which Micah had made, and the priest whom he had, and come in against Laish, against a people quiet and confident, and strike them by the mouth of the sword, and have burned the city with fire, ²⁸and there is no deliverer, for it [is] far off from Sidon, and they have no word with [any] man, and it [is] in the valley which [is] by Beth-Rehob; and they build the city, and dwell in it, ²⁹and call the name of the city Dan, by the name of their father Dan, who was born to Israel; and yet Laish [is] the name of the city at the first. ³⁰And the sons of Dan raise up the carved image for themselves, and Jonathan son of Gershom, son of Manasseh, he and his sons have been priests for the tribe of the Danite, until the day of the expulsion of [the people] of the land. ³¹And they appoint for themselves the carved image of Micah, which he had made, all the days of the house of God being in Shiloh.

CHAPTER 19

¹And it comes to pass in those days, when there is no king in Israel, that there is a man, a Levite, a sojourner in the sides of the hill-country of Ephraim, and he takes a wife for himself, a concubine, out of Beth-Lehem-Judah; ²and his concubine commits whoredom against him, and she goes from him to the house of her father, to Beth-Lehem-Judah, and is there four months of days. ³And her husband rises and goes after her, to speak to her heart, to bring her back, and his young man [is] with him, and a couple of donkeys; and she brings him into the house of her father, and the father of the young woman sees him, and rejoices to meet him. ⁴And his father-in-law keeps hold on him, father of the young woman, and he abides with him three days, and they eat and drink, and lodge there. ⁵And it comes to pass, on the fourth day, that they rise early in the morning, and he rises to go, and the father of the young woman says to his son-in-law, "Support your heart with a morsel of bread, and afterward you go on." ⁶And both of them sit, and eat and drink together, and the father of the young woman says to the man, "Please be willing and lodge all night, and let your heart be glad." ⁷And the man rises to go, and his father-in-law presses on him, and he turns back and lodges there. ⁸And he rises early in the morning, on the fifth day, to go, and the father of the young woman says, "Please support your heart"; and they have tarried until the turning of the day, and both of them eat. ⁹And the man rises to go, he, and his concubine, and his young man, but his father-in-law, father of the young woman, says to him, "Now behold, the day has fallen toward evening, please lodge all night; behold, the declining of the day! Lodge here and let your heart be glad—and you have risen early tomorrow for your journey, and you have gone to your tent." ¹⁰And the man has not been willing to lodge all night, and he rises, and goes, and comes in until [he is] opposite Jebus (it [is] Jerusalem), and a couple of saddled donkeys [are] with him; and his concubine [is] with him. ¹¹They [are] near Jebus, and the day has greatly gone down, and the young man says to his lord, "Please come, and we turn aside to this city of the Jebusite and lodge in it." ¹²And his lord says to him, "Let us not turn aside to the city of a stranger, that is not of the sons of Israel there, but we have passed over to Gibeah." ¹³And he says to his young man, "Come, and we draw near to one of the places, and have lodged in Gibeah, or in Ramah." ¹⁴And they pass over, and go on, and the sun goes in on them near Gibeah, which is of Benjamin; ¹⁵and they turn aside there to go in to lodge in Gibeah, and he goes in and sits in a broad place of the city, and there is no man gathering them into the house to lodge. ¹⁶And behold, an old man has come from his work from the field in the evening, and the man [is] of the hill-country of Ephraim, and he [is] a sojourner in Gibeah, and the men of the place [are] Benjamites. ¹⁷And he lifts up his eyes, and sees the man, the traveler, in a broad place of the city, and the old man says, "To where do you go? And where do you come from?" ¹⁸And he says to him, "We are passing over from Beth-Lehem-Judah to the sides of the hill-country of Ephraim—I [am] from there, and I go to Beth-Lehem-Judah; and I am going to the house of YHWH, and there is no man gathering me into the house, ¹⁹and there is both straw and provender for our donkeys, and there is also bread and wine for me, and for your handmaid, and for the young man with your servants; there is no lack of anything." ²⁰And the old man says, "Peace to you; only, all your lack [is] on me, but do not lodge in the broad place." ²¹And he brings him into his house, and mixes [food] for the donkeys, and they wash their feet, and eat and drink. ²²They are making their heart glad, and behold, men of the city, men—sons of worthlessness—have gone around the house, beating on the door, and they speak to the old man, the master of the house, saying, "Bring out the man who has come into your house, and we know him." ²³And the man, the master of the house, goes out to them and says to them, "No, my brothers, please do not do evil after that this man has come into my house; do not do this folly; ²⁴behold, my daughter, the virgin, and his concubine, please let me bring them out and you humble them, and do that which is good

in your eyes to them, and do not do this foolish thing to this man." ²⁵And the men have not been willing to listen to him, and the man takes hold on his concubine and brings [her] out to them outside, and they know her and roll themselves on her all the night until the morning, and they send her away in the ascending of the dawn; ²⁶and the woman comes in at the turning of the morning, and falls at the opening of the man's house where her lord [is], until the light. ²⁷And her lord rises in the morning, and opens the doors of the house, and goes out to go on his way, and behold, the woman, his concubine, is fallen at the opening of the house, and her hands [are] on the threshold, ²⁸and he says to her, "Rise, and we go"; but there is no answering, and he takes her on the donkey, and the man rises and goes to his place, ²⁹and comes into his house, and takes the knife, and lays hold on his concubine, and cuts her in pieces to her bones—into twelve pieces, and sends her into all the border of Israel. ³⁰And it has come to pass, everyone who sees has said, "There has not been—indeed, there has not been seen [anything] like this, from the day of the coming up of the sons of Israel out of the land of Egypt until this day; set your [heart] on it, take counsel, and speak."

CHAPTER 20

¹And all the sons of Israel go out, and the congregation is assembled as one man, from Dan even to Beer-Sheba, and the land of Gilead, to YHWH, at Mizpeh. ²And the chiefs of all the people, of all the tribes of Israel, station themselves in the assembly of the people of God, four hundred thousand footmen drawing sword. ³And the sons of Benjamin hear that the sons of Israel have gone up to Mizpeh. And the sons of Israel say, "Speak! How has this evil been?" ⁴And the man, the Levite, husband of the woman who has been murdered, answers and says, "My concubine and I went into Gibeah, which [is] of Benjamin, to lodge; ⁵and the masters of Gibeah rise against me—and they go around the house against me by night—they thought to slay me, and they have humbled my concubine, and she dies; ⁶and I lay hold on my concubine, and cut her in pieces, and send her into all the country of the inheritance of Israel; for they have done wickedness and folly in Israel; ⁷behold, you [are] all sons of Israel; give for yourselves a word and counsel here." ⁸And all the people rise as one man, saying, "None of us goes to his tent, and none of us turns aside to his house; ⁹and now, this [is] the thing which we do to Gibeah: [we go up] against it by lot! ¹⁰And we have taken ten men of one hundred, of all the tribes of Israel, and one hundred of a thousand, and a thousand of a myriad, to receive provision for the people, to do, at their coming to Gibeah of Benjamin, according to all the folly which it has done in Israel." ¹¹And every man of Israel is gathered to the city, as one man—companions. ¹²And the tribes of Israel send men among all the tribes of Benjamin, saying, "What [is] this evil which has been among you? ¹³And now, give up the men—sons of worthlessness—which [are] in Gibeah, and we put them to death, and we put away evil from Israel." And [the sons of] Benjamin have not been willing to listen to the voice of their brothers, the sons of Israel; ¹⁴and the sons of Benjamin are gathered out of the cities to Gibeah, to go out to battle with the sons of Israel. ¹⁵And the sons of Benjamin number themselves on that day; out of the cities [are] twenty-six thousand men drawing sword, apart from the inhabitants of Gibeah, [who] numbered themselves, seven hundred chosen men; ¹⁶among all this people [are] seven hundred chosen men, their right hand bound, each of these slinging with a stone at the hair, and he does not err. ¹⁷And the men of Israel numbered themselves, apart from Benjamin, four hundred thousand men, drawing sword, each of these a man of war. ¹⁸And they rise and go up to Beth-El, and ask of God, and the sons of Israel say, "Who goes up for us at the commencement to battle with the sons of Benjamin?" And YHWH says, "Judah—at the commencement." ¹⁹And the sons of Israel rise in the morning, and encamp against Gibeah, ²⁰and the men of Israel go out to battle with Benjamin, and the men of Israel set themselves in array [for] battle with them, against Gibeah, ²¹and the sons of Benjamin come out from Gibeah, and destroy twenty-two thousand men in Israel on that day—to the earth. ²²And the people, the men of Israel, strengthen themselves, and add to set in array [for] battle in the place where they arranged themselves on the first day. ²³And the sons of Israel go up and weep before YHWH until the evening, and ask of YHWH, saying, "Do I add to draw near to battle with the sons of my brother Benjamin?" And YHWH says, "Go up against him." ²⁴And the sons of Israel draw near to the sons of Benjamin on the second day, ²⁵and Benjamin comes out to meet them from Gibeah on the second day, and destroy eighteen thousand men among the sons of Israel again—to the earth; all these are drawing sword. ²⁶And all the sons of Israel go up, even all the people, and come to Beth-El, and weep, and sit there before YHWH, and fast on that day until the evening, and cause burnt-offerings and peace-offerings to ascend before YHWH. ²⁷And the sons of Israel ask of YHWH—and the Ark of the Covenant of God [is] there in those days, ²⁸and Phinehas son of Eleazar, son of Aaron, is standing before it in those days, saying, "Do I add to go out to battle again with the sons of my brother Benjamin, or do I cease?" And YHWH says, "Go up, for tomorrow I give him into your hand." ²⁹And Israel sets ones lying in wait against Gibeah, all around, ³⁰and the sons of Israel go up against the sons of Benjamin on the third day, and arrange themselves against Gibeah, as time by time. ³¹And the sons of Benjamin come out to meet the people; they have been drawn away out of the city, and begin to strike [some] of the people—wounded as time by time—in the highways (of which one is going up to Beth-El, and the other to Gibeah in the field), [are] about thirty men of Israel. ³²And the sons of Benjamin say, "They are struck before us as at the beginning"; but the sons of Israel said, "Let us flee, and draw them away out of the city, to the highways." ³³And all the men of Israel have risen from their place, and arrange themselves at Ba'al-Tamar, and the ambush of Israel is coming forth out of its place, out of the meadow of Gibeah. ³⁴And they come in from the front against Gibeah—ten thousand chosen men out of all Israel—and the battle [is] grievous, and they have not known that the calamity is reaching toward them. ³⁵And YHWH strikes Benjamin before Israel, and the sons of Israel destroy in Benjamin, on that day, twenty-five thousand and one hundred men; all these [are] drawing sword. ³⁶And the sons of Benjamin see that they have been struck—and the men of Israel give place to Benjamin, for they have trusted in the ambush which they had set against Gibeah, ³⁷and the ambush has hurried, and pushes against Gibeah, and the ambush draws itself out, and strikes the whole of the city by the mouth of the sword. ³⁸And the appointed sign of the men of Israel with the ambush was their causing a great volume of smoke to go up from the city. ³⁹And the men of Israel turn in battle, and Benjamin has begun to strike the wounded among the men of Israel, about thirty men, for they said, "Surely they are utterly struck before us, as [at] the first battle"; ⁴⁰but the volume has begun to go up from the city—a pillar of smoke—and Benjamin turns behind, and behold, the perfection of the city has gone up toward the heavens. ⁴¹And the men of Israel have turned, and the men of Benjamin are troubled, for they have seen that the calamity has struck against them— ⁴²and they turn before the men of Israel to the way of the wilderness, and the battle has followed them; and those who [are] from the cities are destroying them in their midst; ⁴³they have surrounded the Benjamites—they have pursued them—they have trodden them down with ease as far as the front of Gibeah, at the sun-rising. ⁴⁴And eighteen thousand men of Benjamin fall—all these [were] men of valor; ⁴⁵and they turn and flee toward the wilderness, to the rock of Rimmon; and they glean five thousand of their men in the highways, and follow after them to Gidom, and strike two thousand [more] of their men. ⁴⁶And all those falling of Benjamin are twenty-five thousand men drawing sword, on that day—all these [were] men of valor; ⁴⁷but six hundred men turn and flee into the wilderness, to the rock of Rimmon, and they dwell in the rock of Rimmon four months. ⁴⁸And the men of Israel have turned back to the sons of Benjamin, and strike them by the mouth of the sword out of the city—men even to livestock, even to all that is found; they have also sent all the cities which are found into the fire.

CHAPTER 21

¹And the men of Israel have sworn in Mizpeh, saying, "None of us gives his daughter to Benjamin for a wife." ²And the people come to Beth-El, and sit there until the evening before God, and lift up their voice, and weep [with] a

great weeping, ³and say, "Why, O YHWH, God of Israel, has this been in Israel—to be lacking one tribe from Israel today?" ⁴And it comes to pass on the next day, that the people rise early, and build an altar there, and cause burnt-offerings and peace-offerings to ascend. ⁵And the sons of Israel say, "Who [is] he that has not come up in the assembly to YHWH out of all the tribes of Israel?" For the great oath has been concerning him who has not come up to YHWH to Mizpeh, saying, "He is surely put to death." ⁶And the sons of Israel sigh concerning their brother Benjamin, and say, "Today there has been one tribe cut off from Israel, ⁷what do we do for them—for those who are left—for wives, since we have sworn by YHWH not to give to them from our daughters for wives?" ⁸And they say, "Who is [that] one out of the tribes of Israel who has not come up to YHWH to Mizpeh?" And behold, none has come to the camp from Jabesh-Gilead—to the assembly. ⁹And the people numbered themselves, and behold, there is no man from the inhabitants of Jabesh-Gilead. ¹⁰And the congregation sends twelve thousand men of the sons of valor there, and commands them, saying, "Go—and you have struck the inhabitants of Jabesh-Gilead by the mouth of the sword, even the women and the infants. ¹¹And this [is] the thing which you do; every male, and every woman knowing the lying of a male, you devote." ¹²And they find four hundred young women, virgins, out of the inhabitants of Jabesh-Gilead, who have not known man by the lying of a male, and they bring them to the camp at Shiloh, which [is] in the land of Canaan. ¹³And all the congregation sends [word] and speaks to the sons of Benjamin who [are] in the rock of Rimmon, and proclaims peace to them; ¹⁴and Benjamin turns back at that time, and they give to them the women whom they have kept alive of the women of Jabesh-Gilead, and they have not found for [all of] them so. ¹⁵And the people sighed concerning Benjamin, for YHWH had made a breach among the tribes of Israel. ¹⁶And [the] elderly of the congregation say, "What do we do to the remnant for wives—for the women have been destroyed out of Benjamin?" ¹⁷And they say, "A possession of an escaped party [is] to Benjamin, and a tribe is not blotted out from Israel; ¹⁸and we are not able to give wives to them out of our daughters, for the sons of Israel have sworn, saying, Cursed [is] he who is giving a wife to Benjamin." ¹⁹And they say, "Behold, a festival of YHWH [is] in Shiloh, from time to time, which [is] on the north of Beth-El, at the rising of the sun, by the highway which is going up from Beth-El to Shechem, and on the south of Lebonah." ²⁰And they command the sons of Benjamin, saying, "Go—and you have laid wait in the vineyards, ²¹and have seen, and behold, if the daughters of Shiloh come out to dance in dances—then you have gone out from the vineyards, and each caught his wife out of the daughters of Shiloh for yourselves, and have gone to the land of Benjamin; ²²and it has been, when their fathers or their brothers come in to plead to us, that we have said to them, Favor us [by] them, for we have not each taken his wife in battle, for you have not given [wives] to them at this time, [so] you are [not] guilty." ²³And the sons of Benjamin do so, and take women according to their number, out of the dancers whom they have seized; and they go, and return to their inheritance, and build the cities, and dwell in them. ²⁴And the sons of Israel go up and down there at that time, each to his tribe, and to his family; and they each go out there to his inheritance. ²⁵In those days there is no king in Israel; each does that which is right in his own eyes.

RUTH

CHAPTER 1

¹And it comes to pass, in [the] days [when] the ones judging judge, that there is a famine in the land, and there goes a man from Beth-Lehem-Judah to sojourn in the fields of Moab, he, and his wife, and his two sons. ²And the name of the man [is] Elimelech, and the name of his wife Naomi, and the name of his two sons Mahlon and Chilion, Ephraimites from Beth-Lehem-Judah; and they come into the fields of Moab, and are there. ³And Elimelech husband of Naomi dies, and she is left, she and her two sons; ⁴and they take to them wives, Moabitesses: the name of the first [is] Orpah, and the name of the second Ruth; and they dwell there about ten years. ⁵And they die also, both of them—Mahlon and Chilion—and the woman is left of her two children and of her husband. ⁶And she rises, she and her daughters-in-law, and turns back from the fields of Moab, for she has heard in the fields of Moab that God has looked after His people—to give to them bread. ⁷And she goes out from the place where she has been, and her two daughters-in-law with her, and they go in the way to return to the land of Judah. ⁸And Naomi says to her two daughters-in-law, "Go, return, each to the house of her mother; YHWH does with you kindness as you have done with the dead, and with me; ⁹YHWH grants to you, and you find rest each in the house of her husband"; and she kisses them, and they lift up their voice and weep. ¹⁰And they say to her, "Surely with you we go back to your people." ¹¹And Naomi says, "Turn back, my daughters; why do you go with me? Are there yet to me sons in my bowels that they have been to you for husbands? ¹²Turn back, my daughters, go, for I am too aged to be to a husband; though I had said, There is for me hope, also, I have been tonight to a husband, and also I have borne sons: ¹³do you wait for them until they grow up? Do you shut yourselves up for them, not to be to a husband? No, my daughters, for more bitter to me than to you, for the hand of YHWH has gone out against me." ¹⁴And they lift up their voice, and weep again, and Orpah kisses her mother-in-law, and Ruth has cleaved to her. ¹⁵And she says, "Behold, your sister-in-law has turned back to her people, and to her god, turn back after your sister-in-law." ¹⁶And Ruth says, "Do not urge me to leave you—to turn back from after you; for to where you go I go, and where you lodge I lodge; your people [is] my people, and your God my God. ¹⁷Where you die I die, and there I am buried; thus does YHWH to me, and thus He adds—for death itself parts between me and you." ¹⁸And she sees that she is strengthening herself to go with her, and she ceases to speak to her; ¹⁹and the two of them go until their coming to Beth-Lehem; and it comes to pass at their coming to Beth-Lehem, that all the city is moved at them, and they say, "Is this Naomi?" ²⁰And she says to them, "Do not call me Naomi; call me Mara, for the Almighty has dealt very bitterly to me, ²¹I went out full, and YHWH has brought me back empty, why do you call me Naomi, and YHWH has testified against me, and the Almighty has done evil to me?" ²²And Naomi turns back, and Ruth the Moabitess, her daughter-in-law, with her, who has turned back from the fields of Moab, and they have come to Beth-Lehem at the commencement of barley-harvest.

CHAPTER 2

¹And Naomi has an acquaintance of her husband's, a man mighty in wealth, of the family of Elimelech, and his name [is] Boaz. ²And Ruth the Moabitess says to Naomi, "Please let me go into the field, and I gather among the ears of grain after him in whose eyes I find grace"; and she says to her, "Go, my daughter." ³And she goes and comes and gathers in a field after the reapers, and her chance happens—the portion of the field is Boaz's who [is] of the family of Elimelech. ⁴And behold, Boaz has come from Beth-Lehem, and says to the reapers, "YHWH [is] with you"; and they say to him, "YHWH blesses you." ⁵And Boaz says to his young man who is set over the reapers, "Whose [is] this young person?" ⁶And the young man who is set over the reapers answers and says, "A young woman—Moabitess—she [is], who came back with Naomi from the fields of Moab, ⁷and she says, Please let me glean and I have gathered among the sheaves after the reapers; and she comes and remains since the

RUTH

morning and until now; she sat in the house a little [while]." ⁸And Boaz says to Ruth, "Have you not heard, my daughter? Do not go to glean in another field, and also, do not pass over from here, and thus you cleave to my young women: ⁹your eyes [are] on the field which they reap, and you have gone after them; have I not charged the young men not to touch you? When you are thirsty then you have gone to the vessels, and have drunk from that which the young men draw." ¹⁰And she falls on her face, and bows herself to the earth, and says to him, "Why have I found grace in your eyes, to discern me, and I a stranger?" ¹¹And Boaz answers and says to her, "It has been thoroughly declared to me all that you have done with your mother-in-law, after the death of your husband, and you leave your father, and your mother, and the land of your birth, and come to a people which you have not known before. ¹²YHWH repays your work, and your reward is complete from YHWH, God of Israel, under whose wings you have come to take refuge." ¹³And she says, "Let me find grace in your eyes, my lord, because you have comforted me, and because you have spoken to the heart of your maidservant, and I am not as one of your maidservants." ¹⁴And Boaz says to her, "At meal-time come near here, and you have eaten of the bread, and dipped your morsel in the vinegar." And she sits at the side of the reapers, and he reaches to her roasted grain, and she eats, and is satisfied, and leaves. ¹⁵And she rises to glean, and Boaz charges his young men, saying, "Even between the sheaves she gleans, and you do not cause her to blush; ¹⁶and also you surely cast to her of the handfuls—and have left, and she has gleaned, and you do not push against her." ¹⁷And she gleans in the field until the evening, and beats out that which she has gleaned, and it is about an ephah of barley; ¹⁸and she takes [it] up, and goes into the city, and her mother-in-law sees that which she has gleaned, and she brings out and gives to her that which she left from her satiety. ¹⁹And her mother-in-law says to her, "Where have you gleaned today? And where have you worked? May he who is discerning you be blessed." And she declares to her mother-in-law with whom she has worked, and says, "The name of the man with whom I have worked today [is] Boaz." ²⁰And Naomi says to her daughter-in-law, "Blessed [is] he of YHWH who has not forsaken His kindness with the living and with the dead"; and Naomi says to her, "The man is a relation of ours; he [is] of our redeemers." ²¹And Ruth the Moabitess says, "Also he surely said to me, Near the young people whom I have you cleave until they have completed the whole of the harvest which I have." ²²And Naomi says to her daughter-in-law Ruth, "Good, my daughter, that you go out with his young women, and they do not come against you in another field." ²³And she cleaves to the young women of Boaz to glean, until the completion of the barley-harvest, and of the wheat-harvest, and she dwells with her mother-in-law.

CHAPTER 3

¹And her mother-in-law Naomi says to her, "My daughter, do I not seek rest for you, that it may be well with you? ²And now, is not Boaz of our acquaintance, with whose young women you have been? Behold, he is winnowing the threshing-floor of barley tonight, ³and you have bathed, and anointed yourself, and put your garments on you, and gone down to the threshing-floor; do not let yourself be known to the man until he completes to eat and to drink; ⁴and it comes to pass, when he lies down, that you have known the place where he lies down, and have gone in, and uncovered his feet, and lain down—and he declares to you that which you do." ⁵And she says to her, "All that you say—I do." ⁶And she goes down [to] the threshing-floor, and does according to all that her mother-in-law commanded her. ⁷And Boaz eats and drinks, and his heart is glad; and he goes in to lie down at the end of the heap; and she comes in gently, and uncovers his feet, and lies down. ⁸And it comes to pass, at the middle of the night, that the man trembles, and turns himself, and behold, a woman is lying at his feet. ⁹And he says, "Who [are] you?" And she says, "I [am] Ruth your handmaid, and you have spread your skirt over your handmaid, for you [are] a redeemer." ¹⁰And he says, "Blessed [are] you of YHWH, my daughter; you have dealt more kindly at the latter end than at the beginning—not to go after the young men, either poor or rich. ¹¹And now, my daughter, do not fear, all that you say I do to you, for all the gate of my people knows that you [are] a virtuous woman. ¹²And now, surely, true, that I [am] a redeemer, but also there is a redeemer nearer than I. ¹³Lodge tonight, and it has been in the morning, if he redeems you, well: he redeems; and if he does not delight to redeem you, then I have redeemed you—I; YHWH lives! Lie down until the morning." ¹⁴And she lies down at his feet until the morning, and rises before one discerns another; and he says, "Let it not be known that the woman has come into the floor." ¹⁵And he says, "Give the covering which [is] on you, and keep hold on it"; and she keeps hold on it, and he measures six [measures] of barley, and lays [it] on her; and he goes into the city. ¹⁶And she comes to her mother-in-law, and she says, "Who [are] you, my daughter?" And she declares to her all that the man has done to her. ¹⁷And she says, "These six [measures] of barley he has given to me, for he said, You do not go in empty to your mother-in-law." ¹⁸And she says, "Sit still, my daughter, until you know how the matter falls, for the man does not rest except he has completed the matter today."

CHAPTER 4

¹And Boaz has gone up to the gate, and sits there, and behold, the redeemer is passing by of whom Boaz had spoken, and he says, "Turn aside, sit down here, such a one, such a one"; and he turns aside and sits down. ²And he takes ten men from [the] elderly of the city, and says, "Sit down here"; and they sit down. ³And he says to the redeemer, "A portion of the field which [is] to our brother, to Elimelech, has Naomi sold, who has come back from the fields of Moab; ⁴and I said, I uncover your ear, saying, Buy before the inhabitants and before [the] elderly of my people; if you redeem—redeem, and if none redeems—declare [it] to me and I know, for there is none except you to redeem, and I after you." And he says, "I redeem [it]." ⁵And Boaz says, "In the day of your buying the field from the hand of Naomi, then from Ruth the Moabitess, wife of the dead, you have bought [it], to raise up the name of the dead over his inheritance." ⁶And the redeemer says, "I am not able to redeem [it] for myself, lest I destroy my inheritance; redeem for yourself—you—my right of redemption, for I am not able to redeem." ⁷And this [is] formerly in Israel for redemption and for exchanging, to establish anything: a man has drawn off his sandal, and given [it] to his neighbor, and this [is] the Testimony in Israel. ⁸And the redeemer says to Boaz, "Buy [it] for yourself," and draws off his sandal. ⁹And Boaz says to the elderly, and [to] all the people, "You [are] witnesses today that I have bought all that [belonged] to Elimelech, and all that [belonged] to Chilion and Mahlon, from the hand of Naomi; ¹⁰and also Ruth the Moabitess, wife of Mahlon, I have bought to myself for a wife, to raise up the name of the dead over his inheritance; and the name of the dead is not cut off from among his brothers, and from the gate of his place; witnesses you [are] today." ¹¹And all the people who [are] in the gate say—also the elderly, "Witnesses! YHWH makes the woman who is coming to your house as Rachel and as Leah, both of whom built the house of Israel; and you do virtuously in Ephrathah, and proclaim the name in Beth-Lehem; ¹²and let your house be as the house of Perez (whom Tamar bore to Judah), of the seed which YHWH gives to you of this young woman." ¹³And Boaz takes Ruth, and she becomes his wife, and he goes in to her, and YHWH gives conception to her, and she bears a son. ¹⁴And the women say to Naomi, "Blessed [is] YHWH who has not let a redeemer cease to you today, and his name is proclaimed in Israel, ¹⁵and he has been to you for a restorer of life, and for a nourisher of your old age, for your daughter-in-law who has loved you—who is better to you than seven sons—has borne him." ¹⁶And Naomi takes the boy, and lays him in her bosom, and is to him for a nurse; ¹⁷and the neighboring women give a name to him, saying, "There has been a son born to Naomi," and they call his name Obed; he [is] father of Jesse, father of David. ¹⁸And these are generations of Perez: Perez begot Hezron, ¹⁹and Hezron begot Ram, and Ram begot Amminidab, ²⁰and Amminidab begot Nahshon, and Nahshon begot Salmon, ²¹and Salmon begot Boaz, and Boaz begot Obed, ²²and Obed begot Jesse, and Jesse begot David.

1 SAMUEL

CHAPTER 1

¹And there is a certain man of Ramathaim-Zophim, of the hill-country of Ephraim, and his name [is] Elkanah, son of Jeroham, son of Elihu, son of Tohu, son of Zuph, an Ephraimite, ²and he has two wives, the name of the first [is] Hannah, and the name of the second Peninnah, and Peninnah has children, and Hannah has no children. ³And that man has gone up out of his city from time to time, to bow himself, and to sacrifice, before YHWH of Hosts, in Shiloh, and there [are] two sons of Eli, Hophni and Phinehas, priests of YHWH. ⁴And the day comes, and Elkanah sacrifices, and he has given portions to his wife Peninnah, and to all her sons and her daughters, ⁵and he gives a certain portion to Hannah—double, for he has loved Hannah, and YHWH has shut her womb; ⁶and her rival has also provoked her greatly, so as to make her tremble, for YHWH has shut up her womb. ⁷And so is done year by year, from the time of her going up into the house of YHWH, so she provokes her, and she weeps, and does not eat. ⁸And her husband Elkanah says to her, "Hannah, why do you weep? And why do you not eat? And why is your heart afflicted? Am I not better to you than ten sons?" ⁹And Hannah rises after eating in Shiloh, and after drinking, and Eli the priest is sitting on the throne by the doorpost of the temple of YHWH. ¹⁰And she is bitter in soul, and prays to YHWH, and weeps greatly, ¹¹and vows a vow, and says, "YHWH of Hosts, if You certainly look on the affliction of Your handmaid, and have remembered me, and do not forget Your handmaid, and have given to Your handmaid seed of men—then I have given him to YHWH all [the] days of his life, and a razor does not go up on his head." ¹²And it has been, when she multiplied praying before YHWH, that Eli is watching her mouth, ¹³and Hannah, she is speaking over her heart—only her lips are moving, and her voice is not heard, and Eli reckons her to be drunken. ¹⁴And Eli says to her, "Until when are you drunken? Turn aside your wine from you." ¹⁵And Hannah answers and says, "No, my lord, I [am] a woman sharply pained in spirit, and I have not drunk wine and strong drink, and I pour out my soul before YHWH; ¹⁶do not put your handmaid before a daughter of worthlessness, for from the abundance of my meditation, and of my provocation, I have spoken until now." ¹⁷And Eli answers and says, "Go in peace, and the God of Israel gives your petition which you have asked of Him." ¹⁸And she says, "Let your handmaid find grace in your eyes"; and the woman goes on her way, and eats, and her face has not been [downcast] for herself anymore. ¹⁹And they rise early in the morning, and bow themselves before YHWH, and turn back, and come to their house in Ramah, and Elkanah knows his wife Hannah, and YHWH remembers her; ²⁰and it comes to pass, at the revolution of the days, that Hannah conceives, and bears a son, and calls his name Samuel, for, "I have asked for him from YHWH." ²¹And the man Elkanah goes up, and all his house, to sacrifice to YHWH the sacrifice of the days, and his vow. ²²And Hannah has not gone up, for she said to her husband, "Until the youth is weaned—then I have brought him in, and he has appeared before the face of YHWH, and dwelt there for all time." ²³And her husband Elkanah says to her, "Do that which is good in your eyes; abide until your weaning him; only, let YHWH establish His word"; and the woman abides and suckles her son until she has weaned him, ²⁴and she causes him to go up with her when she has weaned him, with three bullocks, and one ephah of flour, and a bottle of wine, and she brings him into the house of YHWH at Shiloh, and the youth [is but] a youth. ²⁵And they slaughter the bullock, and bring in the youth to Eli, ²⁶and she says, "O my lord, your soul lives! My lord, I [am] the woman who stood with you in this [place], to pray to YHWH; ²⁷I prayed for this youth, and YHWH gives to me my petition which I asked of Him; ²⁸and I also have called him to YHWH, all the days that he has lived—he is called to YHWH"; and he bows himself there before YHWH.

CHAPTER 2

¹And Hannah prays and says: "My heart has exulted in YHWH, ‖ My horn has been high in YHWH, ‖ My mouth has been large over my enemies, ‖ For I have rejoiced in Your salvation. ²There is none holy like YHWH, ‖ For there is none except You, ‖ And there is no rock like our God. ³You do not multiply—you speak haughtily—The old saying goes out from your mouth, ‖ For YHWH [is] a God of knowledge, ‖ And actions are weighed by Him. ⁴Bows of the mighty are broken, ‖ And the stumbling have girded on strength. ⁵The satiated hired themselves for bread, ‖ And the hungry have ceased. While the barren has borne seven, ‖ And she abounding with sons has languished. ⁶YHWH puts to death, and keeps alive, ‖ He brings down to Sheol, and brings up. ⁷YHWH dispossesses, and He makes rich, ‖ He makes low, indeed, He makes high. ⁸He raises the poor from the dust, ‖ He lifts up the needy from a dunghill, ‖ To cause [them] to sit with nobles, ‖ Indeed, He causes them to inherit a throne of glory, ‖ For the fixtures of earth [are] of YHWH, ‖ And He sets the habitable world on them. ⁹He keeps the feet of His saints, ‖ And the wicked are silent in darkness, ‖ For man does not become mighty by power. ¹⁰YHWH—His adversaries are broken down, ‖ He thunders against them in the heavens: YHWH judges the ends of the earth, ‖ And gives strength to His king, ‖ And exalts the horn of His anointed." ¹¹And Elkanah goes to Ramath, to his house, and the youth has been serving YHWH [in] the presence of Eli the priest; ¹²and the sons of Eli [are] sons of worthlessness, they have not known YHWH. ¹³And the custom of the priests with the people [is that when] any man is sacrificing a sacrifice, then the servant of the priest has come in when the flesh is boiling, and [with] the hook of three teeth in his hand, ¹⁴and has struck [it] into the pan, or kettle, or cauldron, or pot; all that the hook brings up the priest takes for himself; thus they do to all Israel who are coming in there in Shiloh. ¹⁵Also, before they make incense with the fat, then the priest's servant has come in and said to the man who is sacrificing, "Give flesh to roast for the priest, and he does not take boiled flesh from you, but raw"; ¹⁶and the man says to him, "Let them surely make incense with the fat according to the [custom] today, then take to yourself as your soul desires"; and he has said to him, "Surely you give now; and if not—I have taken by strength." ¹⁷And the sin of the young men is very great [in] the presence of YHWH, for the men have despised the offering of YHWH. ¹⁸And Samuel is ministering [in] the presence of YHWH, a youth girt [with] an ephod of linen; ¹⁹and his mother makes a small upper coat for him, and she has brought it up to him from time to time, in her coming up with her husband to sacrifice the sacrifice of the time. ²⁰And Eli blessed Elkanah and his wife, and said, "YHWH appoints seed of this woman for you, for the petition which she asked for YHWH"; and they have gone to their place. ²¹When YHWH has looked after Hannah, then she conceives and bears three sons and two daughters; and the youth Samuel grows up with YHWH. ²²And Eli [is] very old, and has heard all that his sons do to all Israel, and how that they lie with the women who are assembling [at] the opening of the Tent of Meeting, ²³and he says to them, "Why do you do things like these? For I am hearing of your evil words from all the people—these! ²⁴No, my sons; for the report which I am hearing is not good, causing the people of YHWH to transgress. ²⁵If a man sins against a man, then God has judged him; but if a man sins against YHWH, who prays for him?" And they do not listen to the voice of their father, though YHWH has delighted to put them to death. ²⁶And the youth Samuel is going on and growing up, and [is] good with both YHWH, and also with men. ²⁷And a man of God comes to Eli and says to him, "Thus said YHWH: Was I really revealed to the house of your father in their being in Egypt, before Pharaoh's house, ²⁸even to choose him out of all the tribes of Israel for a priest for Myself, to go up on My altar, to make incense, to bear an ephod before Me, and I give to the house of your father all the fire-offerings of the sons of Israel? ²⁹Why do you kick at My sacrifice and at My offering, which I commanded [in] My habitation, and honor your sons above Me, to make yourselves fat from the first part of every offering of Israel, of My people? ³⁰Therefore—a declaration of YHWH, God of Israel—I certainly said, Your house and the house of your father walk up and down before Me for all time; and now—a

declaration of YHWH—Far be it from Me! For he who is honoring Me, I honor, and those despising Me, are lightly esteemed. ³¹Behold, days [are] coming, and I have cut off your arm, and the arm of the house of your father, that an old man is not in your house; ³²and you have beheld an adversary [in My] habitation, in all that He does good with Israel, and there is not an old man in your house all the days. ³³And the man of yours I do not cut off from My altar—[My purpose is] to consume your eyes, and to grieve your soul; and all the increase of men [in] your house die; ³⁴and this [is] the sign to you that comes to your two sons, to Hophni and Phinehas—in one day both of them die; ³⁵and I have raised up a steadfast priest for Myself; he does as in My heart and in My soul; and I have built a steadfast house for him, and he has walked up and down before My anointed all the days; ³⁶and it has been, everyone who is left in your house comes to bow himself to him for a wage of silver and a cake of bread, and has said, Please admit me to one of the priest's offices, to eat a morsel of bread."

CHAPTER 3

¹And the youth Samuel is serving YHWH before Eli, and the word of YHWH has been precious in those days—there is no vision breaking forth. ²And it comes to pass, at that time, that Eli is lying down in his place, and his eyes have begun [to be] faded—he is not able to see. ³And the lamp of God is not yet extinguished, and Samuel is lying down in the temple of YHWH, where the Ark of God [is], ⁴and YHWH calls to Samuel, and he says, "Here I [am]." ⁵And he runs to Eli and says, "Here I [am], for you have called for me"; and he says, "I did not call; turn back, lie down"; and he goes and lies down. ⁶And YHWH adds to call Samuel again, and Samuel rises and goes to Eli, and says, "Here I [am], for you have called for me"; and he says, "I have not called, my son, turn back, lie down." ⁷And Samuel has not yet known YHWH, and the word of YHWH is not yet revealed to him. ⁸And YHWH adds to call Samuel the third time, and he rises and goes to Eli, and says, "Here I [am], for you have called for me"; and Eli understands that YHWH is calling to the youth. ⁹And Eli says to Samuel, "Go, lie down, and it has been, if He calls to you, that you have said, Speak, YHWH, for Your servant is hearing"; and Samuel goes and lies down in his place. ¹⁰And YHWH comes, and stations Himself, and calls as time by time, "Samuel, Samuel"; and Samuel says, "Speak, for Your servant is hearing." ¹¹And YHWH says to Samuel, "Behold, I am doing a thing in Israel, at which the two ears of everyone hearing it tingle. ¹²In that day I establish to Eli all that I have spoken to his house, beginning and completing; ¹³and I have declared to him that I am judging his house for all time, for the iniquity which he has known, for his sons are making themselves vile, and he has not restrained them, ¹⁴and therefore I have sworn to the house of Eli: the iniquity of the house of Eli is not atoned for, by sacrifice, and by offering—for all time." ¹⁵And Samuel lies until the morning, and opens the doors of the house of YHWH, and Samuel is afraid of declaring the vision to Eli. ¹⁶And Eli calls Samuel and says, "Samuel, my son"; and he says, "Here I [am]." ¹⁷And he says, "What [is] the word which He has spoken to you? Please do not hide it from me; so God does to you, and so does He add, if you hide from me a word of all the words that He has spoken to you." ¹⁸And Samuel declares to him the whole of the words, and has not hid from him; and he says, "It [is] YHWH; that which is good in His eyes He does." ¹⁹And Samuel grows up, and YHWH has been with him, and has not let any of his words fall to the earth; ²⁰and all Israel knows, from Dan even to Beer-Sheba, that Samuel is established for a prophet to YHWH. ²¹And YHWH adds to appear in Shiloh, for YHWH has been revealed to Samuel, in Shiloh, by the word of YHWH.

CHAPTER 4

¹And the word of Samuel is to all Israel, and Israel goes out to meet the Philistines for battle, and they encamp by Eben-Ezer, and the Philistines have encamped in Aphek, ²and the Philistines set themselves in array to meet Israel, and the battle spreads itself, and Israel is struck before the Philistines, and they strike among the ranks in the field about four thousand men. ³And the people come into the camp, and [the] elderly of Israel say, "Why has YHWH struck us today before the Philistines? We take the Ark of the Covenant of YHWH from Shiloh to ourselves, and it comes into our midst, and He saves us out of the hand of our enemies." ⁴And the people send to Shiloh, and they take from there the Ark of the Covenant of YHWH of Hosts, inhabiting the cherubim, and there [are] two sons of Eli with the Ark of the Covenant of God, Hophni and Phinehas. ⁵And it comes to pass, at the coming in of the Ark of the Covenant of YHWH to the camp, that all Israel shouts [with] a great shout, and the earth is moved. ⁶And the Philistines hear the noise of the shouting, and say, "What [is] the noise of this great shout in the camp of the Hebrews?" And they perceive that the Ark of YHWH has come into the camp. ⁷And the Philistines are afraid, for they said, "God has come into the camp"; and they say, "Woe to us, for there has been nothing like this before. ⁸Woe to us, who delivers us out of the hand of these majestic gods? These [are] the gods who are striking the Egyptians with every plague in the wilderness. ⁹Strengthen yourselves, and become men, O Philistines, lest you do service to Hebrews, as they have done to you—then you have become men, and have fought." ¹⁰And the Philistines fight, and Israel is struck, and they each flee to his tents, and the slaughter is very great, and thirty thousand footmen of Israel fall; ¹¹and the Ark of God has been taken, and the two sons of Eli, Hophni and Phinehas, have died. ¹²And a man of Benjamin runs out of the ranks, and comes into Shiloh, on that day, and his long robes [are] torn, and earth [is] on his head; ¹³and he comes in, and behold, Eli is sitting on the throne by the side of the way, watching, for his heart has been trembling for the Ark of God, and the man has come into the city and declares [it], and all the city cries out. ¹⁴And Eli hears the noise of the cry and says, "What [is] the noise of this tumult?" And the man hurried, and comes in, and tells Eli. ¹⁵And Eli is a son of ninety-eight years, and his eyes have stood, and he has not been able to see. ¹⁶And the man says to Eli, "I [am] he who has come out of the ranks, and I have fled out of the ranks today"; and he says, "What has been the matter, my son?" ¹⁷And he who is bearing tidings answers and says, "Israel has fled before the Philistines, and also a great slaughter has been among the people, and also your two sons have died—Hophni and Phinehas—and the Ark of God has been captured." ¹⁸And it comes to pass, at his mentioning the Ark of God, that he falls backward from off the throne, by the side of the gate, and his neck is broken, and he dies, for the man [is] old and heavy, and he has judged Israel [for] forty years. ¹⁹And his daughter-in-law, wife of Phinehas, [is] pregnant, about to bear, and she hears the report of the taking of the Ark of God, that her father-in-law and her husband have died, and she bows, and bears, for her pains have turned on her. ²⁰And at the time of her death, the women who are standing by her say, "Do not fear, for you have borne a son," she has not answered, nor set her heart [to it]; ²¹and she calls the youth Ichabod, saying, "Glory has removed from Israel," because of the taking of the Ark of God, and because of her father-in-law and her husband. ²²And she says, "Glory has removed from Israel, for the Ark of God has been taken."

CHAPTER 5

¹And the Philistines have taken the Ark of God, and bring it in from Eben-Ezer to Ashdod, ²and the Philistines take the Ark of God and bring it into the house of Dagon, and set it near Dagon. ³And the Ashdodites rise early on the next day, and behold, Dagon is fallen on its face to the earth, before the Ark of YHWH; and they take Dagon, and put it back in its place. ⁴And they rise early in the morning on the next day, and behold, Dagon is fallen on its face to the earth, before the Ark of YHWH, and the head of Dagon, and the two palms of its hands are cut off at the threshold, only Dagon's [body] has been left of him; ⁵therefore the priests of Dagon, and all those coming into the house of Dagon, do not tread on the threshold of Dagon, in Ashdod, until this day. ⁶And the hand of YHWH is heavy on the Ashdodites, and He makes them desolate, and strikes them with lumps, Ashdod and its borders. ⁷And the men of Ashdod see that [it is] so, and have said, "The Ark of the God of Israel does not abide with us, for His hand has been hard on us, and on our god Dagon." ⁸And they send and gather all the princes of the Philistines to them, and say, "What do we do to the Ark of the God of Israel?" And they say, "Let the Ark of the God of Israel be brought around to Gath"; and they bring around the Ark of the God of Israel; ⁹and it comes to pass after they have brought it around, that the hand of YHWH is against the

city—a very great destruction; and He strikes the men of the city, from small and to great; and lumps break forth on them. ¹⁰And they send the Ark of God to Ekron, and it comes to pass, at the coming in of the Ark of God to Ekron, that the Ekronites cry out, saying, "They have brought around the Ark of the God of Israel to us, to put us and our people to death." ¹¹And they send and gather all the princes of the Philistines, and say, "Send the Ark of the God of Israel away, and it turns back to its place, and it does not put us and our people to death"; for there has been a deadly destruction throughout all the city, the hand of God has been very heavy there, ¹²and the men who have not died have been struck with lumps, and the cry of the city goes up into the heavens.

CHAPTER 6

¹And the Ark of YHWH is in the field of the Philistines [for] seven months, ²and the Philistines call for priests and for diviners, saying, "What do we do to the Ark of YHWH? Let us know with what we send it to its place." ³And they say, "If you are sending the Ark of the God of Israel away, you do not send it away empty; for you certainly send back a guilt-offering to Him; then you are healed, and it has been known to you why His hand does not turn aside from you." ⁴And they say, "What [is] the guilt-offering which we send back to Him?" And they say, "The number of the princes of the Philistines—five golden lumps, and five golden muroids—for one plague [is] to you all, and to your princes, ⁵and you have made images of your lumps, and images of your muroids that are corrupting the land, and have given glory to the God of Israel; it may be [that] He lightens His hand from off you, and from off your gods, and from off your land; ⁶and why do you harden your heart as the Egyptians and Pharaoh hardened their heart? Do they not—when He has rolled Himself on them—send them away, and they go? ⁷And now, take and make one new cart, and two suckling cows, on which a yoke has not gone up, and you have bound the cows in the cart, and caused their young ones to turn back from after them to the house, ⁸and you have taken the Ark of YHWH, and put it on the cart, and the vessels of gold which you have returned to Him—a guilt-offering—you put in a coffer on its side, and have sent it away, and it has gone; ⁹and you have seen if it goes up the way of its own border, to Beth-Shemesh—He has done this great evil to us; and if not, then we have known that His hand has not come against us; it has been an accident to us." ¹⁰And the men do so, and take two suckling cows, and bind them in the cart, and they shut up their young ones in the house; ¹¹and they place the Ark of YHWH on the cart, and the coffer, and the golden muroids, and the images of their lumps. ¹²And the cows go straight in the way, on the way to Beth-Shemesh, they have gone in one highway, going and lowing, and have not turned aside right or left; and the princes of the Philistines are going after them to the border of Beth-Shemesh. ¹³And the Beth-Shemeshites are reaping their wheat-harvest in the valley, and they lift up their eyes, and see the Ark, and rejoice to see [it]. ¹⁴And the cart has come into the field of Joshua the Beth-Shemeshite, and stands there, and there [is] a great stone, and they cleave the wood of the cart, and they have caused the cows to ascend [as] a burnt-offering to YHWH. ¹⁵And the Levites have taken down the Ark of YHWH, and the coffer which [is] with it, in which [are] the vessels of gold, and place [them] on the great stone; and the men of Beth-Shemesh have caused burnt-offerings to ascend and sacrifice sacrifices in that day to YHWH; ¹⁶and the five princes of the Philistines have seen [it], and return [to] Ekron, on that day. ¹⁷And these [are] the golden lumps which the Philistines have sent back—a guilt-offering to YHWH: one for Ashdod, one for Gaza, one for Ashkelon, one for Gath, one for Ekron; ¹⁸and the golden muroids—the number of all the cities of the Philistines, for the five princes, from the fortified city even to a village of the open place, and to the great stone [[or great meadow]] on which they placed the Ark of YHWH—[are] in the field of Joshua the Beth-Shemeshite to this day. ¹⁹And He strikes among the men of Beth-Shemesh, for they looked into the Ark of YHWH, indeed, He strikes seventy men [out] of fifty thousand men [[or fifty thousand and seventy men]] among the people; and the people mourn, because YHWH struck among the people [with] a great striking. ²⁰And the men of Beth-Shemesh say, "Who is able to stand before YHWH, this holy God? And to whom does He go up from us?" ²¹And they send messengers to the inhabitants of Kirjath-Jearim, saying, "The Philistines have sent back the Ark of YHWH; come down, take it up with you."

CHAPTER 7

¹And the men of Kirjath-Jearim come and bring up the Ark of YHWH, and bring it into the house of Abinadab, in the height, and they have sanctified his son Eleazar to keep the Ark of YHWH. ²And it comes to pass, from the day of the dwelling of the Ark in Kirjath-Jearim, that the days are multiplied—indeed, they are twenty years—and all the house of Israel wails after YHWH. ³And Samuel speaks to all the house of Israel, saying, "If you are turning back to YHWH with all your heart—turn aside the gods of the stranger from your midst, and Ashtaroth; and prepare your heart for YHWH, and serve Him only, and He delivers you out of the hand of the Philistines." ⁴And the sons of Israel turn aside the Ba'alim and Ashtaroth, and serve YHWH alone; ⁵and Samuel says, "Gather all Israel to Mizpeh, and I pray to YHWH for you." ⁶And they are gathered to Mizpeh, and draw water, and pour out before YHWH, and fast on that day, and say there, "We have sinned against YHWH"; and Samuel judges the sons of Israel in Mizpeh. ⁷And the Philistines hear that the sons of Israel have gathered themselves to Mizpeh; and the princes of the Philistines go up against Israel, and the sons of Israel hear, and are afraid of the presence of the Philistines. ⁸And the sons of Israel say to Samuel, "Do not keep silent for us from crying to our God YHWH, and He saves us out of the hand of the Philistines." ⁹And Samuel takes a fat lamb, and causes it to go up—a whole burnt-offering to YHWH; and Samuel cries to YHWH for Israel, and YHWH answers him; ¹⁰and Samuel is causing the burnt-offering to go up—and the Philistines have drawn near to battle against Israel—and YHWH thunders with a great noise, on that day, on the Philistines, and troubles them, and they are struck before Israel. ¹¹And the men of Israel go out from Mizpeh, and pursue the Philistines, and strike them to the place of Beth-Car. ¹²And Samuel takes a stone, and sets [it] between Mizpeh and Shen, and calls its name Eben-Ezer, saying, "Until now YHWH has helped us." ¹³And the Philistines are humbled, and have not added anymore to come into the border of Israel, and the hand of YHWH is on the Philistines all the days of Samuel. ¹⁴And the cities which the Philistines have taken from Israel are restored to Israel—from Ekron even to Gath—and Israel has delivered their border out of the hand of the Philistines; and there is peace between Israel and the Amorite. ¹⁵And Samuel judges Israel all the days of his life, ¹⁶and he has gone from year to year, and gone around Beth-El, and Gilgal, and Mizpeh, and judged Israel [in] all these places; ¹⁷and his returning [is] to Ramath, for his house [is] there, and he has judged Israel there, and he builds an altar to YHWH there.

CHAPTER 8

¹And it comes to pass, when Samuel [is] aged, that he makes his sons judges over Israel. ²And the name of his firstborn son is Joel, and the name of his second Abiah, judges in Beer-Sheba: ³and his sons have not walked in his ways, and turn aside after the dishonest gain, and take a bribe, and turn aside judgment. ⁴And all [the] elderly of Israel gather themselves together, and come to Samuel at Ramath, ⁵and say to him, "Behold, you have become aged, and your sons have not walked in your ways; now, appoint a king to us, to judge us, like all the nations." ⁶And the thing is evil in the eyes of Samuel when they have said, "Give a king to us, to judge us"; and Samuel prays to YHWH. ⁷And YHWH says to Samuel, "Listen to the voice of the people, to all that they say to you, for they have not rejected you, but they have rejected Me from reigning over them. ⁸According to all the works that they have done from the day of My bringing them up out of Egypt, even to this day, when they forsake Me, and serve other gods—so they are also doing to you. ⁹And now, listen to their voice; only, surely you certainly protest to them, and have declared to them the custom of the king who reigns over them." ¹⁰And Samuel speaks all the words of YHWH to the people who are asking [for] a king from him, ¹¹and says, "This is the custom of the king who reigns over you: he takes your sons, and has appointed for himself among his chariots, and among his horsemen, and they have run before his chariots; ¹²also to appoint for himself heads of thousands, and heads of

fifties; also to plow his plowing, and to reap his reaping; and to make instruments of his war, and instruments of his charioteer. ¹³And he takes your daughters for perfumers, and for cooks, and for bakers; ¹⁴and your fields, and your vineyards, and your olive-yards—he takes the best, and has given to his servants. ¹⁵And he tithes your seed and your vineyards, and has given to his eunuchs, and to his servants. ¹⁶And your menservants and your maidservants, and the best of your young men and your donkeys, he takes, and has prepared for his own work; ¹⁷he tithes your flock, and you are for servants to him. ¹⁸And you have cried out in that day because of the king whom you have chosen for yourselves, and YHWH does not answer you in that day." ¹⁹And the people refuse to listen to the voice of Samuel, and say, "No, but a king is over us, ²⁰and we have been, even we, like all the nations; and our king has judged us, and gone out before us, and fought our battles." ²¹And Samuel hears all the words of the people, and speaks them in the ears of YHWH; ²²and YHWH says to Samuel, "Listen to their voice, and you have caused a king to reign over them." And Samuel says to the men of Israel, "Go, each man, to his city."

CHAPTER 9

¹And there is a man of Benjamin, and his name [is] Kish, son of Abiel, son of Zeror, son of Bechorath, son of Aphiah, a Benjamite, a mighty man of valor, ²and he has a son, and his name [is] Saul, a choice youth and handsome, and there is not a man among the sons of Israel more handsome than he—from his shoulder and upward, higher than any of the people. ³And the donkeys of Kish, father of Saul, are lost, and Kish says to his son Saul, "Now take one of the young men with you, and rise, go, seek the donkeys." ⁴And he passes over through the hill-country of Ephraim, and passes over through the land of Shalisha, and they have not found [them]; and they pass over through the land of Shaalim, and they are not; and he passes over through the land of Benjamin, and they have not found [them]. ⁵They have come to the land of Zuph, and Saul has said to his young man who [is] with him, "Come, and we return, lest my father leave off from the donkeys, and has been sorrowful for us." ⁶And he says to him, "Now behold, a man of God [is] in this city, and the man is honored; all that he speaks certainly comes; now, we go there, it may be he declares to us our way on which we have gone." ⁷And Saul says to his young man, "And behold, we go, and what do we bring to the man? For the bread has gone from our vessels, and there is no present to bring to the man of God—what [is] with us?" ⁸And the young man adds to answer Saul and says, "Behold, there is found a fourth of a shekel of silver with me: and I have given to the man of God, and he has declared our way to us." ⁹Formerly in Israel, thus said the man in his going to seek God: "Come and we go to the seer." For the "prophet" of today is formerly called "the seer." ¹⁰And Saul says to his young man, "Your word [is] good; come, we go"; and they go to the city where the man of God [is]. ¹¹They are going up in the ascent of the city, and have found young women going out to draw water, and say to them, "Is the seer in this [place]?" ¹²And they answer them and say, "He is; behold, before you! Hurry, now, for he has come to the city today, for the people [have] a sacrifice today in a high place. ¹³At your going into the city so you find him, before he goes up to the high place to eat; for the people do not eat until his coming, for he blesses the sacrifice; afterward, they who are called eat, and now, go up, for you should find him at this time." ¹⁴And they go up to the city; they are coming into the midst of the city, and behold, Samuel is coming out to meet them, to go up to the high place; ¹⁵and YHWH had uncovered the ear of Samuel one day before the coming of Saul, saying, ¹⁶"At this time tomorrow, I send to you a man out of the land of Benjamin—and you have anointed him for leader over My people Israel, and he has saved My people out of the hand of the Philistines; for I have seen My people, for its cry has come to Me." ¹⁷When Samuel has seen Saul, then YHWH has answered him, "Behold, the man of whom I have spoken to you; this [one] restrains My people." ¹⁸And Saul draws near to Samuel in the midst of the gate and says, "Please declare to me where this seer's house [is]." ¹⁹And Samuel answers Saul and says, "I [am] the seer; go up before me into the high place, and you have eaten with me today, and I have sent you away in the morning, and all that [is] in your heart I declare to you. ²⁰And as for the donkeys which are lost from you [for] three days as of today, do not set your heart to them, for they have been found; and to whom [is] all the desire of Israel? Is it not to you and to all your father's house?" ²¹And Saul answers and says, "Am I not a Benjamite—of the smallest of the tribes of Israel? And my family the least of all the families of the tribe of Benjamin? And why have you spoken to me according to this word?" ²²And Samuel takes Saul, and his young man, and brings them into the chamber, and gives a place to them at the head of those called; and they [are] about thirty men. ²³And Samuel says to the cook, "Give the portion which I gave to you, of which I said to you, Set it by you." ²⁴(And the cook lifts up the leg, and that which [is] on it, and sets [it] before Saul), and he says, "Behold, that which is left; [it] is set before your face—eat, for it is kept for you for this appointed time, [at my] saying, I have called the people"; and Saul eats with Samuel on that day. ²⁵And they come down from the high place to the city, and he speaks with Saul on the roof. ²⁶And they rise early, and it comes to pass, at the ascending of the dawn, that Samuel calls to Saul, on the roof, saying, "Rise, and I send you away"; and Saul rises, and they go out, both of them—he and Samuel, outside. ²⁷They are going down in the extremity of the city, and Samuel has said to Saul, "Say to the young man that he should pass on before us (and he passes on), and you, stand at this time, and I cause you to hear the word of God."

CHAPTER 10

¹And Samuel takes the vial of the oil, and pours [it] on his head, and kisses him, and says, "Is it not because YHWH has appointed you over His inheritance for leader? ²In your going from me today—then you have found two men by the grave of Rachel, in the border of Benjamin, at Zelzah, and they have said to you, The donkeys have been found which you have gone to seek; and behold, your father has left the matter of the donkeys, and has sorrowed for you, saying, What do I do for my son? ³And you have passed on there, and beyond, and have come to the oak of Tabor, and three men going up to God to Beth-El have found you there, one carrying three kids, and one carrying three cakes of bread, and one carrying a bottle of wine, ⁴and they have asked of your welfare, and given two loaves to you, and you have received from their hand. ⁵Afterward you come to the hill of God, where the garrison of the Philistines [is], and it comes to pass, at your coming in there to the city, that you have met a band of prophets coming down from the high place, and before them stringed instrument, and tambourine, and pipe, and harp, and they are prophesying; ⁶and the Spirit of YHWH has prospered over you, and you have prophesied with them, and have turned into a [new] man; ⁷and it has been, when these signs come to you—do for yourself as your hand finds, for God [is] with you. ⁸And you have gone down before me to Gilgal, and behold, I am going down to you, to cause burnt-offerings to ascend, to sacrifice sacrifices of peace-offerings; you wait [for] seven days until my coming to you, and I have made known to you that which you do." ⁹And it has been, at his turning his shoulder to go from Samuel, that God turns to him another heart, and all these signs come on that day, ¹⁰and they come in there to the height, and behold, a band of prophets [is there] to meet him, and the Spirit of God prospers over him, and he prophesies in their midst. ¹¹And it comes to pass, all knowing him before, see, and behold, he has prophesied with prophets, and the people say to one another, "What [is] this [that] has happened to the son of Kish? Is Saul also among the prophets?" ¹²And a man there answers and says, "And who [is] their father?" Therefore it has been for an allegory, "Is Saul also among the prophets?" ¹³And he ceases from prophesying, and comes to the high place, ¹⁴and the uncle of Saul says to him, and to his young man, "To where did you go?" And he says, "To seek the donkeys; and we see that they are not, and we come to Samuel." ¹⁵And the uncle of Saul says, "Please declare to me what Samuel said to you." ¹⁶And Saul says to his uncle, "He certainly declared to us that the donkeys were found"; and of the matter of the kingdom he has not declared to him that which Samuel said. ¹⁷And Samuel calls the people to YHWH to Mizpeh, ¹⁸and says to the sons of Israel, "Thus said YHWH, God of Israel: I have brought up Israel out of Egypt, and I deliver you out of the hand of the Egyptians, and out of the hand of all the kingdoms who are oppressing you; ¹⁹and you have rejected

1 SAMUEL

your God today, who [is] Himself your Savior out of all your evils and your distresses, and you say, No, but you set a king over us; and now, station yourselves before Yhwh, by your tribes, and by your thousands." ²⁰And Samuel brings all the tribes of Israel near, and the tribe of Benjamin is captured, ²¹and he brings the tribe of Benjamin near by its families, and the family of Matri is captured, and Saul son of Kish is captured, and they seek him, and he has not been found. ²²And they ask again of Yhwh, "Has the man come here yet?" And Yhwh says, "Behold, he has been hidden near the vessels." ²³And they run and bring him there, and he stationed himself in the midst of the people, and he is higher than any of the people from his shoulder and upward. ²⁴And Samuel says to all the people, "Have you seen him on whom Yhwh has fixed, for there is none like him among all the people?" And all the people shout, and say, "Let the king live!" ²⁵And Samuel speaks to the people the right of the kingdom, and writes in a scroll, and places [it] before Yhwh; and Samuel sends all the people away, each to his house. ²⁶And Saul has also gone to his house, to Gibeah, and the force goes with him whose heart God has touched; ²⁷and the sons of worthlessness have said, "How can this one save us?" And they despise him, and have not brought a present to him; and he is as one being deaf.

CHAPTER 11

¹And Nahash the Ammonite comes up, and encamps against Jabesh-Gilead, and all the men of Jabesh say to Nahash, "Make a covenant with us, and we serve you." ²And Nahash the Ammonite says to them, "For this I cut [a covenant] with you, in picking out every right eye of yours—and I have set it [for] a reproach on all Israel." ³And [the] elderly of Jabesh say to him, "Leave us alone [for] seven days, and we send messengers into all the border of Israel: and if there is none saving us—then we have come out to you." ⁴And the messengers come to Gibeah of Saul, and speak the words in the ears of the people, and all the people lift up their voice and weep; ⁵and behold, Saul has come out of the field after the herd, and Saul says, "What [is that] to the people, that they weep?" And they recount the words of the men of Jabesh to him. ⁶And the Spirit of God prospers over Saul, in his hearing these words, and his anger burns greatly, ⁷and he takes a couple of oxen, and cuts them in pieces, and sends [them] through all the border of Israel, by the hand of the messengers, saying, "He who is not coming out after Saul and after Samuel—thus it is done to his oxen"; and the fear of Yhwh falls on the people, and they come out as one man. ⁸And he inspects them in Bezek, and the sons of Israel are three hundred thousand, and the men of Judah thirty thousand. ⁹And they say to the messengers who are coming, "Thus you say to the men of Jabesh-Gilead: Tomorrow you have safety—by the heat of the sun"; and the messengers come and declare [it] to the men of Jabesh, and they rejoice; ¹⁰and the men of Jabesh say [to the Ammonites], "Tomorrow we come out to you, and you have done to us according to all that [is] good in your eyes." ¹¹And it comes to pass, on the next day, that Saul puts the people in three detachments, and they come into the midst of the camp in the morning-watch, and strike Ammon until the heat of the day; and it comes to pass that those left are scattered, and there have not been left two of them together. ¹²And the people say to Samuel, "Who is he that says, Saul reigns over us? Give up the men, and we put them to death." ¹³And Saul says, "There is no man put to death on this day, for today Yhwh has worked salvation in Israel." ¹⁴And Samuel says to the people, "Come and we go to Gilgal, and renew the kingdom there"; ¹⁵and all the people go to Gilgal, and cause Saul to reign there before Yhwh in Gilgal, and sacrifice sacrifices of peace-offerings there before Yhwh, and Saul rejoices there—and all the men of Israel—very greatly.

CHAPTER 12

¹And Samuel says to all Israel, "Behold, I have listened to your voice, to all that you said to me, and I cause a king to reign over you, ²and now, behold, the king is habitually walking before you, and I have become aged and gray-headed, and my sons, behold, they [are] with you, and I have habitually walked before you from my youth until this day. ³Behold, here I [am]; testify against me before Yhwh, and before His anointed; whose ox have I taken, and whose donkey have I taken, and whom have I oppressed; whom have I bruised, and of whose hand have I taken a ransom, and hide my eyes with it? And I restore [it] to you." ⁴And they say, "You have not oppressed us, nor have you crushed us, nor have you taken anything from the hand of anyone." ⁵And he says to them, "Yhwh [is] a witness against you, and His anointed [is] a witness this day, that you have not found anything in my hand"; and they say, "A witness." ⁶And Samuel says to the people, "Yhwh [is] He who made Moses and Aaron, and who brought up your fathers out of the land of Egypt! ⁷And now, station yourselves, and I judge you before Yhwh, with all the righteous acts of Yhwh, which He did with you, and with your fathers. ⁸When Jacob has come to Egypt, and your fathers cry to Yhwh, then Yhwh sends Moses and Aaron, and they bring out your fathers from Egypt, and cause them to dwell in this place, ⁹and they forget their God Yhwh, and He sells them into the hand of Sisera, head of the host of Hazor, and into the hand of the Philistines, and into the hand of the king of Moab, and they fight against them, ¹⁰and they cry to Yhwh, and say, We have sinned, because we have forsaken Yhwh, and serve the Ba'alim, and Ashtaroth, and now, deliver us out of the hand of our enemies, and we serve You. ¹¹And Yhwh sends Jerubba'al, and Bedan, and Jephthah, and Samuel, and delivers you out of the hand of your surrounding enemies, and you dwell confidently. ¹²And you see that Nahash king of the sons of Ammon has come against you, and you say to me, No, but a king reigns over us; and your God Yhwh [is] your king! ¹³And now, behold the king whom you have chosen—whom you have asked for! And behold, Yhwh has placed a king over you. ¹⁴If you fear Yhwh, and have served Him, and listened to His voice, then you do not provoke the mouth of Yhwh, and you have been—both you and the king who has reigned over you—after your God Yhwh. ¹⁵And if you do not listen to the voice of Yhwh—then you have provoked the mouth of Yhwh, and the hand of Yhwh has been against you, and against your fathers. ¹⁶Also now, station yourselves and see this great thing which Yhwh is doing before your eyes; ¹⁷is it not wheat-harvest today? I call to Yhwh, and He gives voices and rain; and know and see that your evil is great which you have done in the eyes of Yhwh, to ask [for] a king for yourselves." ¹⁸And Samuel calls to Yhwh, and Yhwh gives voices and rain on that day, and all the people greatly fear Yhwh and Samuel; ¹⁹and all the people say to Samuel, "Pray for your servants to your God Yhwh, and we do not die, for we have added evil to all our sins to ask [for] a king for ourselves." ²⁰And Samuel says to the people, "Do not fear; you have done all this evil; only, do not turn aside from after Yhwh—and you have served Yhwh with all your heart, ²¹and you do not turn aside after the vain things which do not profit nor deliver, for they [are] vain, ²²for Yhwh does not leave His people, on account of His great Name; for Yhwh has been pleased to make you for a people to Him. ²³I, also, far be it from me to sin against Yhwh, by ceasing to pray for you, and I have directed you in the good and upright way; ²⁴only, fear Yhwh, and you have served Him in truth with all your heart, for see that which He has made great with you; ²⁵and if you really do evil, both you and your king are consumed."

CHAPTER 13

¹Saul [is] a son of [[thirty]] years in his reigning, and he has reigned over Israel [forty]-two years, ²then Saul chooses for himself three thousand [men] out of Israel; and two thousand are with Saul in Michmash, and in the hill-country of Beth-El; and one thousand have been with Jonathan in Gibeah of Benjamin; and he has sent each one of the remnant of the people to his tents. ³And Jonathan strikes the garrison of the Philistines which [is] in Geba, and the Philistines hear, and Saul has blown with a horn through all the land, saying, "Let the Hebrews hear." ⁴And all Israel have heard, saying, "Saul has struck the garrison of the Philistines," and also, "Israel has been abhorred by the Philistines"; and the people are called after Saul to Gilgal. ⁵And the Philistines have been gathered to fight with Israel; thirty thousand chariots, and six thousand horsemen, and a people as the sand which [is] on the seashore for multitude; and they come up and encamp in Michmash, east of Beth-Aven. ⁶And the men of Israel have seen that they are distressed, that the people have been oppressed, and the people hide themselves in caves, and in thickets, and in rocks, and in high places, and in pits. ⁷And Hebrews have passed over the Jordan to the

land of Gad and Gilead; and Saul [is] yet in Gilgal, and all the people have trembled after him. ⁸And he waits seven days, according to the appointment with Samuel, and Samuel has not come to Gilgal, and the people are scattered from off him. ⁹And Saul says, "Bring the burnt-offering and the peace-offerings near to me"; and he causes the burnt-offering to ascend. ¹⁰And it comes to pass at his completing to cause the burnt-offering to ascend, that behold, Samuel has come, and Saul goes out to meet him, to bless him; ¹¹and Samuel says, "What have you done?" And Saul says, "Because I saw that the people were scattered from off me, and you had not come at the appointment of the days, and the Philistines are gathered to Michmash, ¹²and I say, Now the Philistines come down to me to Gilgal, and I have not appeased the face of YHWH; and I force myself, and cause the burnt-offering to ascend." ¹³And Samuel says to Saul, "You have been foolish; you have not kept the command of your God YHWH, which He commanded you, for now YHWH had established your kingdom over Israel for all time; ¹⁴and now, your kingdom does not stand, YHWH has sought [for] a man for Himself according to His own heart, and YHWH charges him for leader over His people, for you have not kept that which YHWH commanded you." ¹⁵And Samuel rises, and goes up from Gilgal to Gibeah of Benjamin; and Saul inspects the people who are found with him, about six hundred men, ¹⁶and Saul, and his son Jonathan, and the people who are found with them, are abiding in Gibeah of Benjamin, and the Philistines have encamped in Michmash. ¹⁷And the destroyer goes out from the camp of the Philistines—three detachments: one detachment turns to the way of Ophrah, to the land of Shual, ¹⁸and one detachment turns the way of Beth-Horon, and one detachment turns the way of the border which is looking on the Valley of the Zeboim, toward the wilderness. ¹⁹And a craftsman is not found in all the land of Israel, for the Philistines said, "Lest the Hebrews make sword or spear"; ²⁰and all Israel goes down to the Philistines, to each sharpen his plowshare, and his coulter, and his axe, and his mattock; ²¹and there has been the file for mattocks, and for coulters, and for three-pronged rakes, and for the axes, and to set up the goads. ²²And it has been, in the day of battle, that there has not been found a sword and spear in the hand of any of the people who [are] with Saul and with Jonathan—but it is found with Saul and with his son Jonathan. ²³And the station of the Philistines goes out to the passage of Michmash.

CHAPTER 14

¹And the day comes that Jonathan son of Saul says to the young man carrying his weapons, "Come, and we pass over to the station of the Philistines, which [is] on the other side of this"; and he has not declared [it] to his father. ²And Saul is abiding at the extremity of Gibeah, under the pomegranate which [is] in Migron, and the people who [are] with him [are] about six hundred men, ³and Ahiah, son of Ahitub, brother of Ichabod, son of Phinehas son of Eli priest of YHWH in Shiloh, [was] bearing an ephod; and the people did not know that Jonathan has gone. ⁴And between the passages where Jonathan sought to pass over to the station of the Philistines [is] the edge of a rock on one side, and the edge of a rock on the other side, and the name of one is Bozez, and the name of the other Seneh. ⁵One edge [is] fixed on the north in front of Michmash, and the one on the south in front of Gibeah. ⁶And Jonathan says to the young man carrying his weapons, "Come, and we pass over to the station of these uncircumcised; it may be YHWH works for us, for there is no restraint to YHWH to save by many or by few." ⁷And the bearer of his weapons says to him, "Do all that [is] in your heart; turn for yourself; behold, I [am] with you, as your own heart." ⁸And Jonathan says, "Behold, we are passing over to the men, and are revealed to them; ⁹if they thus say to us, Stand still until we have come to you, then we have stood in our place, and do not go up to them; ¹⁰and if they thus say, Come up against us, then we have gone up, for YHWH has given them into our hand, and this [is] the sign to us." ¹¹And both of them are revealed to the station of the Philistines, and the Philistines say, "Behold, Hebrews are coming out of the holes where they have hid themselves." ¹²And the men of the station answer Jonathan, and the bearer of his weapons, and say, "Come up to us, and we cause you to know something." And Jonathan says to the bearer of his weapons, "Come up after me, for YHWH has given them into the hand of Israel." ¹³And Jonathan goes up on his hands, and on his feet, and the bearer of his weapons after him; and they fall before Jonathan, and the bearer of his weapons is putting [them] to death after him. ¹⁴And the first striking which Jonathan and the bearer of his weapons have struck is of about twenty men, in about half a furrow of a yoke of a field, ¹⁵and there is a trembling in the camp, in the field, and among all the people, the station and the destroyers have trembled—even they, and the earth shakes, and it becomes a trembling of God. ¹⁶And the watchmen of Saul in Gibeah of Benjamin see, and behold, the multitude has melted away, and it goes on, and is beaten down. ¹⁷And Saul says to the people who [are] with him, "Now inspect and see; who has gone from us?" And they inspect, and behold, Jonathan and the bearer of his weapons are not. ¹⁸And Saul says to Ahiah, "Bring the Ark of God near"; for the Ark of God has been with the sons of Israel on that day. ¹⁹And it comes to pass, while Saul spoke to the priest, that the noise which [is] in the camp of the Philistines goes on, going on and becoming great, and Saul says to the priest, "Remove your hand." ²⁰And Saul is called, and all the people who [are] with him, and they come to the battle, and behold, the sword of each has been against his neighbor—a very great destruction. ²¹And the Hebrews [who] have been with the Philistines before the day prior, who had gone up with them into the camp, have turned around, even they, to be with Israel who [are] with Saul and Jonathan, ²²and all the men of Israel, who are hiding themselves in the hill-country of Ephraim, have heard that the Philistines have fled, and they pursue—even they—after them in battle. ²³And YHWH saves Israel on that day, and the battle has passed over to Beth-Aven. ²⁴And the men of Israel have been distressed on that day, and Saul adjures the people, saying, "Cursed [is] the man who eats food until the evening, and I have been avenged of my enemies"; and none of the people have tasted food. ²⁵And all [those of] the land have come into a forest, and there is honey on the face of the field; ²⁶and the people come into the forest, and behold, the honey dropped, and none is moving his hand to his mouth, for the people feared the oath. ²⁷And Jonathan has not heard of his father's adjuring the people, and puts forth the end of the rod, which [is] in his hand, and dips it in the honeycomb, and brings back his hand to his mouth—and his eyes see! ²⁸And a man of the people answers and says, "Your father certainly adjured the people, saying, Cursed [is] the man who eats food today; and the people are weary." ²⁹And Jonathan says, "My father has troubled the land; now see that my eyes have become bright because I tasted a little of this honey. ³⁰How much more if the people had well eaten today of the spoil of its enemies which it has found, for now the striking has not been great among the Philistines." ³¹And they strike on that day among the Philistines from Michmash to Aijalon, and the people are very weary, ³²and the people make toward the spoil, and take sheep, and oxen, and sons of the herd, and slaughter on the earth, and the people eat with the blood. ³³And they declare to Saul, saying, "Behold, the people are sinning against YHWH, to eat with the blood." And he says, "You have dealt treacherously, roll a great stone to me today." ³⁴And Saul says, "Be scattered among the people, and you have said to them: Each bring his ox to me, and each his sheep; and you have slain [them] in this place, and eaten, and you do not sin against YHWH to eat with the blood." And all the people bring [them]—each one [with] his ox in his hand, that night—and slaughter [them] there. ³⁵And Saul builds an altar to YHWH; with it he has begun to build altars to YHWH. ³⁶And Saul says, "Let us go down after the Philistines by night, and we prey on them until the morning light, and do not leave a man of them." And they say, "Do all that is good in your eyes." And the priest says, "Let us draw near to God here." ³⁷And Saul asks of God, "Do I go down after the Philistines? Do You give them into the hand of Israel?" And He has not answered him on that day. ³⁸And Saul says, "Everyone draw near here, the chiefs of the people, and know and see in what this sin has been today; ³⁹for YHWH lives, who is saving Israel: surely if it is in my son Jonathan, surely he certainly dies"; and none is answering him out of all the people. ⁴⁰And he says to all Israel, "You are on one side, and I and my son Jonathan are on another side"; and the people

1 SAMUEL

say to Saul, "Do that which is good in your eyes." ⁴¹And Saul says to YHWH, God of Israel, "Give perfection"; and Jonathan and Saul are captured, and the people went out. ⁴²And Saul says, "Cast between me and my son Jonathan"; and Jonathan is captured. ⁴³And Saul says to Jonathan, "Declare to me, what have you done?" And Jonathan declares to him and says, "I certainly tasted a little honey with the end of the rod that [is] in my hand; behold, I die!" ⁴⁴And Saul says, "Thus God does, and thus does He add, for you certainly die, Jonathan." ⁴⁵And the people say to Saul, "Does Jonathan die who worked this great salvation in Israel? Certainly not! YHWH lives, if there falls to the earth [even one] hair from his head, for with God he has worked this day"; and the people rescue Jonathan, and he has not died. ⁴⁶And Saul goes up from after the Philistines, and the Philistines have gone to their place; ⁴⁷and Saul captured the kingdom over Israel, and he fights all around against all his enemies, against Moab, and against the sons of Ammon, and against Edom, and against the kings of Zobah, and against the Philistines, and wherever he turns he distresses [them]. ⁴⁸And he makes a force, and strikes Amalek, and delivers Israel out of the hand of its spoiler. ⁴⁹And the sons of Saul are Jonathan, and Ishui, and Melchi-Shua; as for the name of his two daughters, the name of the firstborn [is] Merab, and the name of the younger Michal; ⁵⁰and the name of the wife of Saul [is] Ahinoam, daughter of Ahimaaz; and the name of the head of his host [is] Abner son of Ner, uncle of Saul; ⁵¹and Kish [is] the father of Saul, and Ner, the father of Abner, [is] the son of Ahiel. ⁵²And the war is severe against the Philistines all the days of Saul; when Saul has seen any mighty man, and any son of valor, then he gathers him to himself.

CHAPTER 15

¹And Samuel says to Saul, "YHWH sent me to anoint you for king over His people, over Israel; and now, listen to the voice of the words of YHWH. ²Thus said YHWH of Hosts: I have looked after that which Amalek did to Israel, that which he laid for him in the way in his going up out of Egypt. ³Now go, and you have struck Amalek, and devoted all that he has, and you have no pity on him, and have put to death from man to woman, from infant to suckling, from ox to sheep, from camel to donkey." ⁴And Saul summons the people, and inspects them in Telaim, two hundred thousand footmen, and ten thousand [are] men of Judah. ⁵And Saul comes to a city of Amalek, and lays wait in a valley; ⁶and Saul says to the Kenite, "Go, turn aside, go down from the midst of Amalek, lest I consume you with it, and you did kindness with all the sons of Israel, in their going up out of Egypt"; and the Kenite turns aside from the midst of Amalek. ⁷And Saul strikes Amalek from Havilah [to] your going to Shur, which [is] on the front of Egypt, ⁸and he catches Agag king of Amalek alive, and he has devoted all the people by the mouth of the sword; ⁹and Saul has pity—also the people—on Agag, and on the best of the flock, and of the herd, of the seconds, and on the lambs, and on all that [is] good, and have not been willing to devote them; and all the work, despised and wasted—it they devoted. ¹⁰And the word of YHWH is to Samuel, saying, ¹¹"I have regretted that I caused Saul to reign for king, for he has turned back from after Me, and he has not performed My words"; and it is displeasing to Samuel, and he cries to YHWH all the night. ¹²And Samuel rises early to meet Saul in the morning, and it is declared to Samuel, saying, "Saul has come to Carmel, and behold, he is setting up a monument to himself, and goes around, and passes over, and goes down to Gilgal." ¹³And Samuel comes to Saul, and Saul says to him, "Blessed [are] you of YHWH; I have performed the word of YHWH." ¹⁴And Samuel says, "And what [is] the noise of this flock in my ears—and the noise of the herd which I am hearing?" ¹⁵And Saul says, "They have brought them from Amalek, because the people had pity on the best of the flock, and of the herd, in order to sacrifice to your God YHWH, and we have devoted the remnant." ¹⁶And Samuel says to Saul, "Desist, and I declare to you that which YHWH has spoken to me tonight"; and he says to him, "Speak." ¹⁷And Samuel says, "Are you not, if you [are] little in your own eyes, head of the tribes of Israel? And YHWH anoints you for king over Israel, ¹⁸and YHWH sends you in the way, and says, Go, and you have devoted the sinners, the Amalekite, and fought against them until they are consumed; ¹⁹and why have you not listened to the voice of YHWH—and fly to the spoil, and do evil in the eyes of YHWH?" ²⁰And Saul says to Samuel, "Because—I have listened to the voice of YHWH, and I go in the way which YHWH has sent me, and bring in Agag king of Amalek, and I have devoted Amalek; ²¹and the people take of the spoil of the flock and herd, the first part of the devoted thing, for sacrifice to your God YHWH in Gilgal." ²²And Samuel says, "Has YHWH had delight in burnt-offerings and sacrifices as [in] listening to the voice of YHWH? Behold, listening is better than sacrifice; to give attention than fat of rams; ²³for rebellion [is as] a sin of divination, and stubbornness [is as] iniquity and teraphim; because you have rejected the word of YHWH, He also rejects you from [being] king." ²⁴And Saul says to Samuel, "I have sinned, for I passed over the command of YHWH, and your words; because I have feared the people, I also listen to their voice; ²⁵and now, please bear with my sin, and return with me, and I bow myself to YHWH." ²⁶And Samuel says to Saul, "I do not return with you; for you have rejected the word of YHWH, and YHWH rejects you from being king over Israel." ²⁷And Samuel turns around to go, and he lays hold on the skirt of his upper robe—and it is torn! ²⁸And Samuel says to him, "YHWH has torn the kingdom of Israel from you today, and given it to your neighbor who is better than you; ²⁹and also, the Preeminence of Israel does not lie nor relent, for He [is] not a man that He should relent." ³⁰And he says, "I have sinned; now please honor me before [the] elderly of my people and before Israel, and return with me; and I have bowed myself to your God YHWH." ³¹And Samuel turns back after Saul, and Saul bows himself to YHWH; ³²and Samuel says, "Bring Agag king of Amalek to me," and Agag comes to him daintily, and Agag says, "Surely the bitterness of death has turned aside." ³³And Samuel says, "As your sword bereaved women—so is your mother bereaved above women"; and Samuel hews Agag in pieces before YHWH in Gilgal. ³⁴And Samuel goes to Ramath, and Saul has gone to his house—to Gibeah of Saul. ³⁵And Samuel has not added to see Saul until the day of his death, for Samuel mourned for Saul, and YHWH regretted that He had caused Saul to reign over Israel.

CHAPTER 16

¹And YHWH says to Samuel, "Until when are you mourning for Saul, and I have rejected him from reigning over Israel? Fill your horn with oil and go, I send you to Jesse the Beth-Lehemite, for I have seen among his sons a king for Myself." ²And Samuel says, "How do I go? When Saul has heard, then he has slain me." And YHWH says, "You take a heifer of the herd in your hand, and have said, I have come to sacrifice to YHWH; ³and you have called for Jesse in the sacrifice, and I cause you to know that which you do, and you have anointed for Me him of whom I speak to you." ⁴And Samuel does that which YHWH has spoken, and comes to Beth-Lehem, and [the] elderly of the city tremble to meet him, and [one] says, "Is your coming peace?" ⁵And he says, "Peace; I have come to sacrifice to YHWH, sanctify yourselves, and you have come in with me to the sacrifice"; and he sanctifies Jesse and his sons, and calls them to the sacrifice. ⁶And it comes to pass, in their coming in, that he sees Eliab and says, "Surely His anointed [is] here before YHWH." ⁷And YHWH says to Samuel, "Do not look at his appearance, and at the height of his stature, for I have rejected him; for [it is] not as man sees—for man looks at the eyes, and YHWH looks at the heart." ⁸And Jesse calls to Abinadab, and causes him to pass by before Samuel; and he says, "Indeed, YHWH has not fixed on this [one]." ⁹And Jesse causes Shammah to pass by, and he says, "Indeed, YHWH has not fixed on this [one]." ¹⁰And Jesse causes seven of his sons to pass by before Samuel, and Samuel says to Jesse, "YHWH has not fixed on these." ¹¹And Samuel says to Jesse, "Are the young men finished?" And he says, "Yet the youngest has been left; and behold, he delights himself among the flock"; and Samuel says to Jesse, "Send and take him, for we do not turn around until his coming in here." ¹²And he sends, and brings him in, and he [is] ruddy, with beautiful eyes, and of good appearance; and YHWH says, "Rise, anoint him, for this [is] he." ¹³And Samuel takes the horn of oil, and anoints him in the midst of his brothers, and the Spirit of YHWH prospers over David from that day and onward; and Samuel rises and goes to Ramath. ¹⁴And the Spirit of YHWH turned aside from Saul, and a spirit of sadness from YHWH terrified him; ¹⁵and the servants of Saul say to him, "Now behold, a

spirit of sadness [from] God is terrifying you; ¹⁶now let our lord command your servants before you [that] they seek a skillful man playing on a harp, and it has come to pass, in the spirit of sadness [from] God being on you, that he has played with his hand and [it is] well with you." ¹⁷And Saul says to his servants, "Now provide for me a man playing well—then you have brought [him] to me." ¹⁸And one of the servants answers and says, "Behold, I have seen a son of Jesse the Beth-Lehemite, skillful in playing, and a mighty, virtuous man, and a man of battle, and intelligent in word, and a man of form, and YHWH [is] with him." ¹⁹And Saul sends messengers to Jesse and says, "Send to me your son David, who [is] with the flock." ²⁰And Jesse takes a donkey, bread, and a bottle of wine, and one kid of the goats, and sends [them] by the hand of his son David to Saul. ²¹And David comes to Saul, and stands before him, and he loves him greatly; and he is a bearer of his weapons. ²²And Saul sends to Jesse, saying, "Please let David stand before me, for he has found grace in my eyes." ²³And it has come to pass, in the spirit of [sadness from] God being on Saul, that David has taken the harp, and played with his hand, and Saul has refreshment and gladness, and the spirit of sadness has turned aside from off him.

CHAPTER 17

¹And the Philistines gather their camps to battle, and are gathered to Shochoh, which [is] to Judah, and encamp between Shochoh and Azekah, in Ephes-Dammim; ²and Saul and the men of Israel have been gathered, and encamp by the Valley of Elah, and set in array [for] battle to meet the Philistines. ³And the Philistines are standing on the mountain on this [side], and Israel is standing on the mountain on that [side], and the valley [is] between them. ⁴And a man goes out, the champion from the camps of the Philistines, his name [is] Goliath, from Gath; his height [is] six cubits and a span [[or four cubits and a span]], ⁵and a helmet of bronze [is] on his head, and he is clothed [with] a scaled coat of mail, and the weight of the coat of mail [is] five thousand shekels of bronze, ⁶and a frontlet of bronze [is] on his feet, and a javelin of bronze between his shoulders, ⁷and the wood of his spear [is] like a weavers' beam, and the flame of his spear [is] six hundred shekels of iron, and the bearer of the buckler is going before him. ⁸And he stands and calls to the ranks of Israel, and says to them, "Why do you come out to set in array for battle? [Am] I not the Philistine, and you the servants of Saul? Choose a man for yourselves, and let him come down to me; ⁹if he is able to fight with me, and has struck me, then we have been for servants to you; and if I prevail against him, and have struck him, then you have been for servants to us, and have served us." ¹⁰And the Philistine says, "I have reproached the ranks of Israel this day; give a man to me and we fight together!" ¹¹And Saul hears—and all Israel—these words of the Philistine, and they are broken down and greatly afraid. ¹²And David [is] son of this Ephraimite of Beth-Lehem-Judah, whose name [is] Jesse, and he has eight sons, and the man has become aged among men in the days of Saul; ¹³and the three eldest sons of Jesse go, they have gone after Saul to battle; and the name of his three sons who have gone into battle [are] Eliab the firstborn, and his second Abinadab, and the third Shammah. ¹⁴And David is the youngest, and the three eldest have gone after Saul, ¹⁵and David is going and returning from Saul, to feed the flock of his father at Beth-Lehem. ¹⁶And the Philistine draws near, morning and evening, and stations himself [for] forty days. ¹⁷And Jesse says to his son David, "Now take an ephah of this roasted [grain] and these ten loaves for your brothers, and run to the camp to your brothers; ¹⁸and take these ten cuttings of the cheese to the head of the one thousand, and inspect your brothers for welfare, and receive their pledge." ¹⁹And Saul, and they, and all the men of Israel, [are] in the Valley of Elah, fighting with the Philistines. ²⁰And David rises early in the morning, and leaves the flock to a keeper, and lifts up, and goes, as Jesse commanded him, and he comes to the path, and to the force which is going out to the rank, and they have shouted for battle; ²¹and Israel and the Philistines set in array rank to meet rank. ²²And David lets down the goods from off him on the hand of a keeper of the goods, and runs into the rank, and comes and asks of his brothers of [their] welfare. ²³And he is speaking with them, and behold, a man, the champion, is coming up, his name [is] Goliath the Philistine, from Gath, out of the ranks of the Philistines, and he speaks according to those words, and David hears; ²⁴and all the men of Israel, when they see the man, flee from his presence, and are greatly afraid. ²⁵And the men of Israel say, "Have you seen this man who is coming up? For he is coming up to reproach Israel, and it has been—the man who strikes him, the king enriches him with great riches, and he gives his daughter to him, and makes his father's house free in Israel." ²⁶And David speaks to the men who are standing by him, saying, "What is done to the man who strikes this Philistine, and has turned aside reproach from Israel? For who [is] this uncircumcised Philistine that he has reproached the ranks of the living God?" ²⁷And the people speak to him according to this word, saying, "Thus it is done to the man who strikes him." ²⁸And Eliab, his eldest brother, hears when he speaks to the men, and the anger of Eliab burns against David, and he says, "Why [is] this—[that] you have come down? And to whom have you left those few sheep in the wilderness? I have known your pride, and the evil of your heart—for you have come down to see the battle." ²⁹And David says, "What have I done now? Is it not a word?" ³⁰And he turns around from him to another, and says according to this word, and the people return him word as the first word. ³¹And the words which David has spoken are heard, and they declare [them] before Saul, and he receives him; ³²and David says to Saul, "Let no man's heart fall because of him, your servant goes, and has fought with this Philistine." ³³And Saul says to David, "You are not able to go to this Philistine, to fight with him, for you [are] a youth, and he [has been] a man of war from his youth." ³⁴And David says to Saul, "Your servant has been a shepherd among the sheep for his father, and the lion has come—and the bear—and has taken away a sheep out of the drove, ³⁵and I have gone out after him, and struck him, and delivered [it] out of his mouth, and he rises against me, and I have taken hold on his beard, and struck him, and put him to death. ³⁶Your servant has struck both the lion and the bear, and this uncircumcised Philistine has been as one of them, for he has reproached the ranks of the living God." ³⁷And David says, "YHWH, who delivered me out of the paw of the lion, and out of the paw of the bear, He delivers me from the hand of this Philistine." And Saul says to David, "Go, and YHWH is with you." ³⁸And Saul clothes David with his long robe, and has put a helmet of bronze on his head, and clothes him with a coat of mail. ³⁹And David girded his sword above his long robe, and begins to go, for he has not tried [it]; and David says to Saul, "I am not able to go with these, for I had not tried"; and David turns them aside from off him. ⁴⁰And he takes his staff in his hand, and chooses five smooth stones for himself from the brook, and puts them in the shepherds' vessel that he has, even in the leather pouch, and his sling [is] in his hand, and he draws near to the Philistine. ⁴¹And the Philistine goes on, going and drawing near to David, and the man carrying the buckler [is] before him, ⁴²and the Philistine looks attentively, and sees David, and despises him, for he was a youth, and ruddy, with a handsome appearance. ⁴³And the Philistine says to David, "Am I a dog that you are coming to me with sticks?" And the Philistine reviles David by his gods, ⁴⁴and the Philistine says to David, "Come to me, and I give your flesh to the bird of the heavens, and to the beast of the field." ⁴⁵And David says to the Philistine, "You are coming to me with sword, and with spear, and with buckler, and I am coming to you in the Name of YHWH of Hosts, God of the ranks of Israel, which you have reproached! ⁴⁶This day YHWH shuts you up into my hand—and I have struck you, and turned aside your head from off you, and given the carcass of the camp of the Philistines this day to the bird of the heavens, and to the beast of the earth, and all the earth knows that God is for Israel! ⁴⁷And all this assembly knows that YHWH does not save by sword and by spear, for the battle [is] YHWH's, and He has given you into our hand." ⁴⁸And it has come to pass, that the Philistine has risen, and goes, and draws near to meet David, and David hurries and runs to the rank to meet the Philistine, ⁴⁹and David puts forth his hand into the vessel, and takes a stone from there, and slings, and strikes the Philistine on his forehead, and the stone sinks into his forehead, and he falls on his face to the earth. ⁵⁰And David is stronger than the Philistine with a sling and with a stone, and strikes the Philistine, and puts him to death,

and there is no sword in the hand of David, ⁵¹and David runs and stands over the Philistine, and takes his sword, and draws it out of its sheath, and puts him to death, and cuts off his head with it; and the Philistines see that their hero [is] dead, and flee. ⁵²And the men of Israel rise—also Judah—and shout, and pursue the Philistines until you enter the valley, and to the gates of Ekron, and the wounded of the Philistines fall in the way of Shaaraim, even to Gath, and to Ekron, ⁵³and the sons of Israel return from burning after the Philistines, and spoil their camps. ⁵⁴And David takes the head of the Philistine, and brings it to Jerusalem, and he has put his weapons in his own tent. ⁵⁵And when Saul sees David going out to meet the Philistine, he has said to Abner, head of the host, "Whose son [is] this—the youth, Abner?" And Abner says, "Your soul lives, O king, I have not known." ⁵⁶And the king says, "Ask whose son this [is]—the young man." ⁵⁷And when David turns back from striking the Philistine, then Abner takes him and brings him in before Saul, and the head of the Philistine [is] in his hand; ⁵⁸and Saul says to him, "Whose son [are] you, O youth?" And David says, "Son of your servant Jesse, the Beth-Lehemite."

CHAPTER 18

¹And it comes to pass, when he finishes to speak to Saul, that the soul of Jonathan has been bound to the soul of David, and Jonathan loves him as his own soul. ²And Saul takes him on that day, and has not permitted him to return to the house of his father. ³And Jonathan makes—David also—a covenant, because he loves him as his own soul, ⁴and Jonathan strips himself of the upper robe which [is] on him, and gives it to David, and his long robe, even to his sword, and to his bow, and to his girdle. ⁵And David goes out wherever Saul sends him; he acted wisely, and Saul sets him over the men of war, and it is good in the eyes of all the people, and also in the eyes of the servants of Saul. ⁶And it comes to pass, in their coming in, in David's returning from striking the Philistine, that the women come out from all the cities of Israel to sing—also the dancers—to meet Saul the king, with tambourines, with joy, and with three-stringed instruments; ⁷and the women answer—those playing, and say, "Saul has struck among his thousands, || And David among his myriads." ⁸And it is exceedingly displeasing to Saul, and this thing is evil in his eyes, and he says, "They have given myriads to David, and they have given the thousands to me, and what more [is there] for him but the kingdom?" ⁹And Saul is eyeing David from that day and from then on. ¹⁰And it comes to pass, on the next day, that the spirit of sadness [from] God prospers over Saul, and he prophesies in the midst of the house, and David is playing with his hand, as [he did] day by day, and the javelin [is] in the hand of Saul, ¹¹and Saul casts the javelin and says, "I strike through David, even through the wall"; and David turns around out of his presence twice. ¹²And Saul is afraid of the presence of David, for YHWH has been with him, and He has turned aside from Saul; ¹³and Saul turns him aside from him, and appoints him to himself [for] head of one thousand, and he goes out and comes in, before the people. ¹⁴And David is acting wisely in all his ways, and YHWH [is] with him, ¹⁵and Saul sees that he is acting very wisely, and is afraid of him, ¹⁶and all Israel and Judah love David when he is going out and coming in before them. ¹⁷And Saul says to David, "Behold, my elder daughter Merab—I give her to you for a wife; only, be for a son of valor to me, and fight the battles of YHWH"; and Saul said, "Do not let my hand be on him, but let the hand of the Philistines be on him." ¹⁸And David says to Saul, "Who [am] I? And what [is] my life—the family of my father in Israel—that I am son-in-law of the king?" ¹⁹And it comes to pass, at the time of the giving of Merab daughter of Saul to David, that she has been given to Adriel the Meholathite for a wife. ²⁰And Michal daughter of Saul loves David, and they declare [it] to Saul, and the thing is right in his eyes, ²¹and Saul says, "I give her to him, and she is for a snare to him, and the hand of the Philistines is on him"; and Saul says to David, "By the second—you become my son-in-law today." ²²And Saul commands his servants, "Speak to David gently, saying, Behold, the king has delighted in you, and all his servants have loved you, and now, be son-in-law of the king." ²³And the servants of Saul speak these words in the ears of David, and David says, "Is it a light thing in your eyes to be son-in-law of the king—and I a poor man, and lightly esteemed?" ²⁴And the servants of Saul declare [it] to him, saying, "David has spoken according to these words." ²⁵And Saul says, "Thus you say to David, There is no delight for the king in dowry, but in one hundred foreskins of the Philistines—to be avenged on the enemies of the king"; and Saul thought to cause David to fall by the hand of the Philistines. ²⁶And his servants declare these words to David, and the thing is right in the eyes of David, to be son-in-law of the king; and the days have not been full, ²⁷and David rises and goes, he and his men, and strikes two hundred men among the Philistines, and David brings in their foreskins, and they set them before the king, to be son-in-law of the king; and Saul gives his daughter Michal to him for a wife. ²⁸And Saul sees and knows that YHWH [is] with David, and Michal daughter of Saul has loved him, ²⁹and Saul adds to be afraid of the presence of David still; and Saul is an enemy of David [for] all the days. ³⁰And the princes of the Philistines come out, and it comes to pass from the time of their coming out, David has acted more wisely than any of the servants of Saul, and his name is very precious.

CHAPTER 19

¹And Saul speaks to his son Jonathan, and to all his servants, to put David to death, ²and Jonathan son of Saul delighted in David exceedingly, and Jonathan declares [it] to David, saying, "My father Saul is seeking to put you to death, and now, please take heed in the morning, and you have abided in a secret place and been hidden, ³and I go out, and have stood by the side of my father in the field where you [are], and I speak of you to my father, and have seen what [is coming], and have declared [it] to you." ⁴And Jonathan speaks good of David to his father Saul and says to him, "Do not let the king sin against his servant, against David, because he has not sinned against you, and because his works [are] very good for you; ⁵indeed, he puts his life in his hand, and strikes the Philistine, and YHWH works a great salvation for all Israel; you have seen, and rejoice, and why do you sin against innocent blood, to put David to death for nothing?" ⁶And Saul listens to the voice of Jonathan, and Saul swears, "YHWH lives—he does not die." ⁷And Jonathan calls for David, and Jonathan declares all these words to him, and Jonathan brings in David to Saul, and he is before him as before. ⁸And there adds to be war, and David goes out and fights against the Philistines, and strikes among them [with] a great striking, and they flee from his face. ⁹And a spirit of sadness [from] YHWH is to Saul, and he is sitting in his house, and his javelin [is] in his hand, and David is playing with the hand, ¹⁰and Saul seeks to strike with the javelin through David, and through the wall, and he frees himself from the presence of Saul, and he strikes the javelin through the wall; and David has fled and escapes during that night. ¹¹And Saul sends messengers to the house of David to watch him, and to put him to death in the morning; and his wife Michal declares [it] to David, saying, "If you are not delivering your life tonight—tomorrow you are put to death." ¹²And Michal causes David to go down through the window, and he goes on, and flees, and escapes; ¹³and Michal takes the teraphim, and lays [it] on the bed, and she has put the mattress of goats' [hair for] his pillows, and covers [it] with a garment. ¹⁴And Saul sends messengers to take David, and she says, "He [is] sick." ¹⁵And Saul sends the messengers to see David, saying, "Bring him up in the bed to me in order to put him to death." ¹⁶And the messengers come in, and behold, the teraphim [are] on the bed, and the mattress of goats' [hair for] his pillows. ¹⁷And Saul says to Michal, "Why have you thus deceived me—that you send my enemy away, and he escapes?" And Michal says to Saul, "He said to me, Send me away. Why do I put you to death?" ¹⁸And David has fled, and escapes, and comes to Samuel at Ramath, and declares to him all that Saul has done to him, and he goes, he and Samuel, and they dwell in Naioth. ¹⁹And it is declared to Saul, saying, "Behold, David [is] in Naioth in Ramah." ²⁰And Saul sends messengers to take David, and they see the assembly of the prophets prophesying, and Samuel standing, set over them, and the Spirit

of God is on Saul's messengers, and they prophesy—they also. ²¹And they declare [it] to Saul, and he sends other messengers, and they prophesy—they also; and Saul adds and sends messengers a third time, and they prophesy—they also. ²²And he goes—he also—to Ramath, and comes to the great well which [is] in Sechu, and asks and says, "Where [are] Samuel and David?" And [one] says, "Behold, in Naioth in Ramah." ²³And he goes there—to Naioth in Ramah, and the Spirit of God is on him also; and he goes, going on, and he prophesies until his coming to Naioth in Ramah, ²⁴and he strips off—he also—his garments, and prophesies—he also—before Samuel, and falls down naked all that day and all the night; therefore they say, "Is Saul also among the prophets?"

CHAPTER 20

¹And David flees from Naioth in Ramah, and comes, and says before Jonathan, "What have I done? What [is] my iniquity? And what [is] my sin before your father, that he is seeking my life?" ²And he says to him, "Far be it! You do not die; behold, my father does not do anything great or small and does not uncover my ear; and why does my father hide this thing from me? This [thing] is not." ³And David swears again and says, "Your father has certainly known that I have found grace in your eyes, and he says, Do not let Jonathan know this, lest he is grieved; and yet, YHWH lives, and your soul lives, but—as a step between me and death." ⁴And Jonathan says to David, "What does your soul [desire]? Command and I do it for you." ⁵And David says to Jonathan, "Behold, the new moon [is] tomorrow; and I certainly sit with the king to eat; and you have sent me away, and I have been hidden in a field until the third evening; ⁶if your father looks after me at all, then you have said, David earnestly asked of me to run to his city of Beth-Lehem, for there [is] a sacrifice of the days for all the family. ⁷If thus he says: Good; [there is] peace for your servant; and if it is very displeasing to him—know that the evil has been determined by him; ⁸and you have done kindness to your servant, for you have brought your servant into a covenant of YHWH with you—and if there is iniquity in me, put me to death yourself; for why [is] this [that] you bring me to your father?" ⁹And Jonathan says, "Far be it from you! For I certainly do not know that the evil has been determined by my father to come on you, and I do not declare it to you." ¹⁰And David says to Jonathan, "Who declares [it] to me? Or what [if] your father answers you sharply?" ¹¹And Jonathan says to David, "Come, and we go out into the field"; and both of them go out into the field. ¹²And Jonathan says to David, "YHWH, God of Israel, [is my witness]—when I search out my father about [this] time tomorrow [or] the third [day], and behold, [there is] good toward David, and I do not then send to you, and have uncovered your ear—¹³thus YHWH does to Jonathan, and thus He adds; when the evil concerning you is good to my father, then I have uncovered your ear, and sent you away, and you have gone in peace, and YHWH is with you, as he was with my father; ¹⁴and not only while I am alive do you do the kindness of YHWH with me, and I do not die, ¹⁵but you do not cut off your kindness from my house for all time, nor in YHWH's cutting off the enemies of David, each one from off the face of the ground." ¹⁶So Jonathan cuts [a covenant] with the house of David, and YHWH has sought [it] from the hand of the enemies of David; ¹⁷and Jonathan adds to cause David to swear, because he loves him, for he has loved him [as] the love [for] his own soul. ¹⁸And Jonathan says to him, "Tomorrow [is] the new moon, and you have been looked after, for your seat is looked after; ¹⁹and on the third day you certainly come down, and have come to the place where you were hidden in the day of the work, and have remained near the stone of Ezel. ²⁰And I shoot three of the arrows at the side, sending out at a mark for myself; ²¹and behold, I send the youth, [saying], Go, find the arrows. If I say to the youth at all, Behold, the arrows [are] on this side of you—take them and come, for [there is] peace for you, and there is no [adverse] word—[as] YHWH lives. ²²And if thus I say to the young man, Behold, the arrows [are] beyond you—go, for YHWH has sent you away; ²³as for the thing which you and I have spoken, behold, YHWH [is] between me and you for all time." ²⁴And David is hidden in the field, and it is the new moon, and the king sits down by the food to eat, ²⁵and the king sits on his seat, as time by time, on a seat by the wall, and Jonathan rises, and Abner sits at the side of Saul, and David's place is looked after. ²⁶And Saul has not spoken anything on that day, for he said, "It [is] an accident; he is not clean—surely not clean." ²⁷And it comes to pass on the second day of the new moon, that David's place is looked after, and Saul says to his son Jonathan, "Why has the son of Jesse not come in, either yesterday or today, to the food?" ²⁸And Jonathan answers Saul, "David has earnestly asked [permission] from me [to go] to Beth-Lehem, ²⁹and he says, Please send me away, for we have a family sacrifice in the city, and my brother has given command to me himself, and now, if I have found grace in your eyes, please let me go away and see my brothers; therefore he has not come to the table of the king." ³⁰And the anger of Saul burns against Jonathan, and he says to him, "Son of a perverse [woman] of rebellion! Have I not known that you are fixing on the son of Jesse to your own shame, and to the shame of the nakedness of your mother? ³¹For all the days that the son of Jesse lives on the ground you are not established, you and your kingdom; and now, send and bring him to me, for he [is] a son of death." ³²And Jonathan answers his father Saul and says to him, "Why is he put to death? What has he done?" ³³And Saul casts the javelin at him to strike him, and Jonathan knows that it has been determined by his father to put David to death. ³⁴And Jonathan rises from the table in the heat of anger, and has not eaten food on the second day of the new moon, for he has been grieved for David, for his father put him to shame. ³⁵And it comes to pass in the morning, that Jonathan goes out into the field for the appointment with David, and a little youth [is] with him. ³⁶And he says to his youth, "Now run, find the arrows which I am shooting"; the youth is running, and he has shot the arrow, causing [it] to pass over him. ³⁷And the youth comes to the place of the arrow which Jonathan has shot, and Jonathan calls after the youth, and says, "Is the arrow not beyond you?" ³⁸And Jonathan calls after the youth, "Speed, hurry, do not stand"; and Jonathan's youth gathers the arrows, and comes to his lord. ³⁹And the youth has not known anything, only Jonathan and David knew the word. ⁴⁰And Jonathan gives his weapons to the youth whom he has and says to him, "Go, carry into the city." ⁴¹The youth has gone, and David has risen from Ezel, at the south, and falls on his face to the earth, and bows himself three times, and they kiss one another, and they weep with one another, until David exerted himself; ⁴²and Jonathan says to David, "Go in peace, in that we have sworn—the two of us—in the Name of YHWH, saying, YHWH is between me and you, and between my seed and your seed—for all time"; and he rises and goes; and Jonathan has gone into the city.

CHAPTER 21

¹And David comes to Nob, to Ahimelech the priest, and Ahimelech trembles at meeting David and says to him, "Why [are] you alone, and no man [is] with you?" ²And David says to Ahimelech the priest, "The king has commanded me [on] a matter, and he says to me, Let no man know anything of the matter about which I send you, and which I have commanded you; and [my] young men know [to go] to such and such a place. ³And now, what is there under your hand? Give five loaves into my hand, or that which is found." ⁴And the priest answers David and says, "There is no common bread under my hand, but there is holy bread; if only the youths have been kept from women." ⁵And David answers the priest and says to him, "Surely, if women have been restrained from us as before in my going out, then the vessels of the young men are holy, and it [is] a common way; and also, surely it is sanctified today in the vessel." ⁶And the priest gives the holy thing to him, for there was no bread there except the Bread of the Presentation, which is turned aside from the presence of YHWH to put hot bread [there] in the day of its being taken away. ⁷And there [is] a man of the servants of Saul detained before YHWH on that day, and his name [is] Doeg the Edomite, chief of the shepherds whom Saul has. ⁸And David says to Ahimelech, "And is there not spear or sword here under your hand? For I have taken neither my sword nor my vessels in my hand, for the matter of the king was urgent." ⁹And the priest says, "The sword of Goliath the Philistine, whom you struck in the Valley of Elah, behold, it is wrapped in a garment behind the ephod, if you take it to yourself, take; for there is none other except it in this [place]." And David says,

1 SAMUEL

"There is none like it—give it to me." ¹⁰And David rises and flees on that day from the face of Saul, and comes to Achish king of Gath; ¹¹and the servants of Achish say to him, "Is this not David, the king of the land? Is it not of this one [that] they sing in dances, saying, Saul struck among his thousands, and David among his myriads?" ¹²And David lays these words in his heart, and is exceedingly afraid of the face of Achish king of Gath, ¹³and changes his behavior before their eyes, and feigns himself mad in their hand, and scribbles on the doors of the gate, and lets down his spittle to his beard. ¹⁴And Achish says to his servants, "Behold, you see a man acting as a madman; why do you bring him to me? ¹⁵Am I lacking madmen, that you have brought in this one to act as a madman before me? Does this one come into my house?"

CHAPTER 22

¹And David goes from there, and escapes to the cave of Adullam, and his brothers hear, and all the house of his father, and they go down to him there; ²and every man in distress gathers themselves to him, and every man who has an exactor, and every man bitter in soul, and he is for head over them, and there are about four hundred men with him. ³And David goes from there to Mizpeh of Moab and says to the king of Moab, "Please let my father and my mother come out with you, until I know what God does for me"; ⁴and he leads them before the king of Moab, and they dwell with him all the days of David's being in the fortress. ⁵And the prophet Gad says to David, "You do not abide in a fortress, go, and you have entered the land of Judah for yourself"; and David goes and enters the forest of Hareth. ⁶And Saul hears that David has become known, and the men who [are] with him, and Saul is abiding in Gibeah, under the grove in Ramah, and his spear [is] in his hand, and all his servants [are] standing by him. ⁷And Saul says to his servants who are standing by him, "Now hear, sons of Benjamin; does the son of Jesse also give fields and vineyards to all of you? Does he appoint all of you [to be] heads of thousands and heads of hundreds? ⁸For all of you have conspired against me, and there is none uncovering my ear about my son's cutting [a covenant] with the son of Jesse, and there is none of you grieving for me, and uncovering my ear, that my son has raised up my servant against me, to lie in wait as [at] this day." ⁹And Doeg the Edomite answers, who is set over the servants of Saul, and says, "I have seen the son of Jesse coming to Nob, to Ahimelech son of Ahitub, ¹⁰and he inquires of YHWH for him, and has given provision to him, and has given the sword of Goliath the Philistine to him." ¹¹And the king sends to call Ahimelech son of Ahitub, the priest, and all the house of his father, the priests, who [are] in Nob, and all of them come to the king; ¹²and Saul says, "Now hear, son of Ahitub"; and he says, "Here I [am], my lord." ¹³And Saul says to him, "Why have you conspired against me, you and the son of Jesse, by your giving bread and a sword to him, and to inquire of God for him, to rise against me, to lie in wait, as [at] this day?" ¹⁴And Ahimelech answers the king and says, "And who among all your servants [is] as David—faithful, and son-in-law of the king, and has turned aside to your council, and is honored in your house? ¹⁵Today have I begun to inquire of God for him? Far be it from me! Do not let the king lay anything against his servant, against any of the house of my father, for your servant has known nothing of all this, little or much." ¹⁶And the king says, "You surely die, Ahimelech, you and all the house of your father." ¹⁷And the king says to the runners, those standing by him, "Turn around, and put the priests of YHWH to death, because their hand [is] also with David, and because they have known that he is fleeing, and have not uncovered my ear"; and the servants of the king have not been willing to put forth their hand to come against the priests of YHWH. ¹⁸And the king says to Doeg, "Turn around, and come against the priests"; and Doeg the Edomite turns around, and comes against the priests himself, and in that day puts to death eighty-five men bearing a linen ephod, ¹⁹and Nob, the city of the priests, he has struck by the mouth of the sword, from man and to woman, from infant and to suckling, and ox, and donkey, and sheep, by the mouth of the sword. ²⁰And one son of Ahimelech, son of Ahitub, escapes, and his name [is] Abiathar, and he flees after David, ²¹and Abiathar declares to David that Saul has slain the priests of YHWH. ²²And David says to Abiathar, "I have known on that day when Doeg the Edomite [is] there, that he certainly declares [it] to Saul; I have brought [it] around to every person of the house of your father; ²³dwell with me; do not fear; for he who seeks my life seeks your life; for you [are my] charge with me."

CHAPTER 23

¹And they declare to David, saying, "Behold, the Philistines are fighting against Keilah, and they are spoiling the threshing-floors." ²And David inquires of YHWH, saying, "Do I go? And have I struck among these Philistines?" And YHWH says to David, "Go, and you have struck among the Philistines, and saved Keilah." ³And David's men say to him, "Behold, we here in Judah are afraid; and how much more when we go to Keilah, to the ranks of the Philistines?" ⁴And David adds again to inquire of YHWH, and YHWH answers him and says, "Rise, go down to Keilah, for I am giving the Philistines into your hand." ⁵And David goes, and his men, to Keilah, and fights with the Philistines, and leads away their livestock, and strikes among them [with] a great striking, and David saves the inhabitants of Keilah. ⁶And it comes to pass, in the fleeing of Abiathar son of Ahimelech to David, to Keilah, an ephod came down in his hand. ⁷And it is declared to Saul that David has come to Keilah, and Saul says, "God has made him known for my hand, for he has been shut in, to enter into a city of doors and bar." ⁸And Saul summons all the people to the battle, to go down to Keilah, to lay siege to David and to his men. ⁹And David knows that Saul is devising the evil against him and says to Abiathar the priest, "Bring the ephod near." ¹⁰And David says, "YHWH, God of Israel, Your servant has certainly heard that Saul is seeking to come to Keilah, to destroy the city on my account. ¹¹Do the possessors of Keilah shut me up into his hand? Does Saul come down as Your servant has heard? YHWH, God of Israel, please declare [it] to Your servant." And YHWH says, "He comes down." ¹²And David says, "Do the possessors of Keilah shut up me and my men into the hand of Saul?" And YHWH says, "They shut [you] up." ¹³And David rises—and his men—about six hundred men, and they go out from Keilah, and go up and down where they go up and down; and it has been declared to Saul that David has escaped from Keilah, and he ceases to go out. ¹⁴And David abides in the wilderness, in fortresses, and abides in the hill-country, in the wilderness of Ziph; and Saul seeks him [for] all the days, and God has not given him into his hand. ¹⁵And David sees that Saul has come out to seek his life, and David [is] in the wilderness of Ziph, in a forest. ¹⁶And Jonathan son of Saul rises, and goes to David [in the] forest, and strengthens his hand in God, ¹⁷and says to him, "Do not fear, for the hand of my father Saul does not find you, and you reign over Israel, and I am to you for second, and also so knows my father Saul." ¹⁸And both of them make a covenant before YHWH; and David abides in the forest, and Jonathan has gone to his house. ¹⁹And the Ziphites go up to Saul at Gibeah, saying, "Is David not hiding himself with us in fortresses, in the forest, in the height of Hachilah, which [is] on the south of the desolate place? ²⁰And now, by all the desire of your soul, O king, to come down, come down, and ours [is] to shut him up into the hand of the king." ²¹And Saul says, "Blessed [are] you of YHWH, for you have pity on me; ²²now go prepare yet, and know and see his place where his foot is; who has seen him there? For [one] has said to me, He is very cunning. ²³And see and know of all the hiding places where he hides himself, and you have turned back prepared to me, and I have gone with you, and it has been, if he is in the land, that I have searched him out through all the thousands of Judah." ²⁴And they rise and go to Ziph before Saul, and David and his men [are] in the wilderness of Maon, in the plain, at the south of the desolate place. ²⁵And Saul and his men go to seek, and they declare [it] to David, and he goes down the rock, and abides in the wilderness of Maon; and Saul hears, and pursues after David [to] the wilderness of Maon. ²⁶And Saul goes on this side of the mountain, and David and his men on that side of the mountain, and David is hurried to go from the face of Saul, and Saul and his men are surrounding David and his men, to catch them. ²⁷And a messenger has come to Saul, saying, "Hurry, and come, for the Philistines have pushed against the land." ²⁸And Saul turns back from pursuing after David, and goes to meet the Philistines, therefore they have called that place "The Rock of Divisions."

1 SAMUEL

²⁹And David goes up there, and abides in fortresses [at] En-gedi.

CHAPTER 24

¹And it comes to pass, when Saul has turned back from after the Philistines, that they declare to him, saying, "Behold, David [is] in the wilderness of En-gedi." ²And Saul takes three thousand chosen men out of all Israel, and goes to seek David and his men, on the front of the rocks of the wild goats, ³and he comes to folds of the flock, on the way, and there [is] a cave, and Saul goes in to cover his feet; and David and his men are abiding in the sides of the cave. ⁴And the men of David say to him, "Behold, the day of which YHWH said to you, Behold, I am giving your enemy into your hand, and you have done to him as it is good in your eyes"; and David rises and cuts off the skirt of the upper robe which [is] on Saul with stealth. ⁵And it comes to pass afterward that the heart of David strikes him, because that he has cut off the skirt which [is] on Saul, ⁶and he says to his men, "Far be it from me, by YHWH; I do not do this thing to my lord—to the anointed of YHWH—to put forth my hand against him, for he [is] the anointed of YHWH." ⁷And David subdues his men by words, and has not permitted them to rise against Saul; and Saul has risen from the cave, and goes on the way; ⁸and David rises afterward, and goes out from the cave, and calls after Saul, saying, "My lord, O king!" And Saul looks attentively behind him, and David bows—face to the earth—and pays respect. ⁹And David says to Saul, "Why do you hear the words of man, saying, Behold, David is seeking your calamity? ¹⁰Behold, this day your eyes have seen how that YHWH has given you into my hand today in the cave; and [one] said to slay you, and [my eye] has pity on you, and I say, I do not put forth my hand against my lord, for he [is] the anointed of YHWH. ¹¹And my father, see, indeed see the skirt of your upper robe in my hand; for by cutting off the skirt of your upper robe, and I have not slain you, know and see that there is not evil and transgression in my hand, and I have not sinned against you, and you are hunting my soul to take it! ¹²YHWH judges between me and you, and YHWH has avenged me of you, and my hand is not on you; ¹³as the allegory of the ancients says, Wickedness goes out from the wicked, and my hand is not on you. ¹⁴After whom has the king of Israel come out? After whom are you pursuing? After a dead dog! After one flea! ¹⁵And YHWH has been for judge, and has judged between me and you, indeed, He sees and pleads my cause, and delivers me out of your hand." ¹⁶And it comes to pass, when David completes to speak these words to Saul, that Saul says, "Is this your voice, my son David?" And Saul lifts up his voice, and weeps. ¹⁷And he says to David, "You [are] more righteous than I; for you have done me good, and I have done you evil; ¹⁸and you have declared today how that you have done good with me, how that YHWH shut me up into your hand, and you did not slay me, ¹⁹and that a man finds his enemy, and has sent him away in a good manner; and YHWH repays you good for that which you did to me this day. ²⁰And now, behold, I have known that you certainly reign, and the kingdom of Israel has stood in your hand; ²¹and now, swear to me by YHWH [that] you do not cut off my seed after me, nor do you destroy my name from the house of my father." ²²And David swears to Saul, and Saul goes to his house, and David and his men have gone up to the fortress.

CHAPTER 25

¹And Samuel dies, and all Israel is gathered, and mourns for him, and buries him in his house, in Ramah; and David rises and goes down to the wilderness of Paran. ²And [there is] a man in Maon, and his work [is] in Carmel; and the man [is] very great, and he has three thousand sheep and one thousand goats; and he is shearing his flock in Carmel. ³And the name of the man [is] Nabal, and the name of his wife [is] Abigail, and the woman [is] of good understanding, and of beautiful form, and the man [is] hard and evil [in his] doings; and he [is] a Calebite. ⁴And David hears in the wilderness that Nabal is shearing his flock, ⁵and David sends ten young men, and David says to the young men, "Go up to Carmel, and you have come to Nabal, and asked of him in my name of welfare, ⁶and said thus to the living: And peace to you, and peace to your house, and peace to all that you have! ⁷And now, I have heard that you have shearers; now, the shepherds whom you have have been with us, we have not put them to shame, nor has anything been looked after by them, all the days of their being in Carmel. ⁸Ask your young men, and they declare [it] to you, and the young men find grace in your eyes, for we have come on a good day; please give that which your hand finds to your servants and to your son, to David." ⁹And the young men of David come in, and speak to Nabal according to all these words, in the name of David—and rest. ¹⁰And Nabal answers the servants of David and says, "Who [is] David, and who [is] the son of Jesse? Have servants been multiplied today who are each breaking away from his master? ¹¹And have I taken my bread, and my water, and my flesh, which I slaughtered for my shearers, and have given [it] to men whom I have not known where they [are] from?" ¹²And the young men of David turn on their way, and turn back, and come in, and declare to him according to all these words. ¹³And David says to his men, "Each gird on his sword"; and they each gird on his sword, and David also girds on his sword, and about four hundred men go up after David, and two hundred have remained by the vessels. ¹⁴And one young man of the youths has declared [it] to Abigail wife of Nabal, saying, "Behold, David has sent messengers out of the wilderness to bless our lord, and he flies on them; ¹⁵and the men [are] very good to us, and have not put us to shame, and we have not looked after anything all the days we have gone up and down with them, in our being in the field; ¹⁶they have been a wall to us both by night and by day, all the days of our being with them, feeding the flock. ¹⁷And now, know and consider what you do; for evil has been determined against our lord, and against all his house, and he [is] too much a son of worthlessness to be spoken to." ¹⁸And Abigail hurries, and takes two hundred loaves, and two bottles of wine, and five sheep, prepared, and five measures of roasted grain, and one hundred bunches of raisins, and two hundred bunches of figs, and sets [them] on the donkeys. ¹⁹And she says to her young men, "Pass over before me; behold, I am coming after you"; and she has not declared [it] to her husband Nabal; ²⁰and it has come to pass, she is riding on the donkey and is coming down in the secret part of the hill-country, and behold, David and his men are coming down to meet her, and she meets them. ²¹And David said, "Surely in vain I have kept all that this [one] has in the wilderness, and nothing has been looked after of all that he has, and he turns back to me evil for good; ²²thus God does to the enemies of David, and thus He adds, if I leave of all that he has until the morning light—of those sitting on the wall." ²³And Abigail sees David, and hurries and comes down from off the donkey, and falls on her face before David, and bows herself to the earth, ²⁴and falls at his feet and says, "On me, my lord, the iniquity; and please let your handmaid speak in your ear, and hear the words of your handmaid. ²⁵Please do not let my lord set his heart to this man of worthlessness, on Nabal, for as his name [is] so [is] he; Nabal [is] his name, and folly [is] with him; and I, your handmaid, did not see the young men of my lord whom you sent; ²⁶and now, my lord, YHWH lives, and your soul lives, in that YHWH has withheld you from coming in with blood, and to save your hand from yourself—now let your enemies be as Nabal, even those seeking evil toward my lord. ²⁷And now, this blessing which your maidservant has brought to my lord—it has been given to the young men who are going up and down at the feet of my lord. ²⁸Please bear with the transgression of your handmaid, for YHWH certainly makes a steadfast house for my lord; for my lord has fought the battles of YHWH, and evil is not found in you [all] your days. ²⁹And man rises to pursue you and to seek your soul, and the soul of my lord has been bound in the bundle of life with your God YHWH; as for the soul of your enemies, He slings them out in the midst of the hollow of the sling. ³⁰And it has been, when YHWH does to my lord according to all the good which He has spoken concerning you, and appointed you for leader over Israel, ³¹that this is not to you for a stumbling-block, and for an offense of heart to my lord—either to shed blood for nothing, or my lord's restraining himself; and YHWH has done good to my lord, and you have remembered your handmaid." ³²And David says to Abigail, "Blessed [is] YHWH, God of Israel, who has sent you to meet me this day, ³³and blessed [is] your discretion, and blessed [are] you in that you have restrained me this day from coming in with blood, and to restrain my hand to myself. ³⁴And yet, YHWH lives, God of Israel, who has

kept me back from doing evil with you, for unless you had hurried, and come to meet me, surely there had not been left to Nabal until the morning light, of those sitting on the wall." ³⁵And David receives from her hand that which she has brought to him, and he has said to her, "Go up in peace to your house; see, I have listened to your voice, and accept your face." ³⁶And Abigail comes to Nabal, and behold, he has a banquet in his house, like a banquet of the king, and the heart of Nabal [is] glad within him, and he [is] drunk to excess, and she has not declared anything to him, little or much, until the morning light. ³⁷And it comes to pass in the morning, when the wine is gone out from Nabal, that his wife declares these things to him, and his heart dies within him, and he has been as a stone. ³⁸And it comes to pass [in] about ten days, that YHWH strikes Nabal and he dies, ³⁹and David hears that Nabal [is] dead and says, "Blessed [is] YHWH who has pleaded the cause of my reproach from the hand of Nabal, and His servant has kept back from evil, and YHWH has turned back the wickedness of Nabal on his own head"; and David sends and speaks with Abigail, to take her to himself for a wife. ⁴⁰And the servants of David come to Abigail at Carmel, and speak to her, saying, "David has sent us to you to take you to himself for a wife." ⁴¹And she rises and bows herself—face to the earth—and says, "Behold, your handmaid [is] for a maidservant to wash the feet of the servants of my lord." ⁴²And Abigail hurries and rises, and rides on the donkey; and [there are] five of her young women who are going at her feet; and she goes after the messengers of David, and is to him for a wife. ⁴³And David has taken Ahinoam from Jezreel, and they are—even both of them—for wives to him; ⁴⁴and Saul gave his daughter Michal, David's wife, to Phalti son of Laish, who [is] of Gallim.

CHAPTER 26

¹And the Ziphites come to Saul at Gibeah, saying, "Is David not hiding himself in the height of Hachilah, on the front of the desert?" ²And Saul rises, and goes down to the wilderness of Ziph, and with him [are] three thousand men, chosen ones of Israel, to seek David in the wilderness of Ziph. ³And Saul encamps in the height of Hachilah, which [is] on the front of the desert, by the way, and David is abiding in the wilderness, and he sees that Saul has come into the wilderness after him; ⁴and David sends spies, and knows that Saul has come to Nachon, ⁵and David rises, and comes to the place where Saul has encamped, and David sees the place where Saul has lain, and Abner son of Ner, head of his host, and Saul is lying in the path, and the people are encamping around him. ⁶And David answers and says to Ahimelech the Hittite, and to Abishai son of Zeruiah, brother of Joab, saying, "Who goes down with me to Saul, to the camp?" And Abishai says, "I go down with you." ⁷And David comes—and Abishai—by night to the people, and behold, Saul is lying sleeping in the path, and his spear is pressed into the earth by his pillow, and Abner and the people are lying around him. ⁸And Abishai says to David, "God has shut up your enemy into your hand today; and now, please let me strike him with [the] spear, even into the earth, at once—and not repeat [it] to him." ⁹And David says to Abishai, "Do not destroy him; for who has put forth his hand against the anointed of YHWH and been acquitted?" ¹⁰And David says, "YHWH lives; except YHWH strikes him, or his day comes that he has died, or he goes down into battle and has been consumed— ¹¹far be it from me, by YHWH, from putting forth my hand against the anointed of YHWH; and now, please take the spear which [is] by his pillow, and the jug of water, and we go away." ¹²And David takes the spear, and the jug of water by the pillow of Saul, and they go away, and there is none seeing, and there is none knowing, and there is none awaking, for all of them are sleeping, for a deep sleep [from] YHWH has fallen on them. ¹³And David passes over to the other side, and stands on the top of the hill far off—great [is] the place between them; ¹⁴and David calls to the people, and to Abner son of Ner, saying, "Do you not answer, Abner?" And Abner answers and says, "Who [are] you [who] have called to the king?" ¹⁵And David says to Abner, "Are you not a man? And who [is] like you in Israel? But why have you not watched over your lord the king? For one of the people had come in to destroy the king, your lord. ¹⁶This thing which you have done is not good; YHWH lives, but you [are] sons of death, in that you have not watched over your lord, over the anointed of YHWH; and now, see where the king's spear [is], and the jug of water which [is] by his pillow." ¹⁷And Saul discerns the voice of David and says, "Is this your voice, my son David?" And David says, "My voice, my lord, O king!" ¹⁸And he says, "Why [is] this—my lord is pursuing after his servant? For what have I done, and what evil [is] in my hand? ¹⁹And now, please let my lord the king hear the words of his servant: if YHWH has moved you against me, let Him accept a present; but if [merely] the sons of men, they [are] cursed before YHWH, for today they have cast me out from being admitted into the inheritance of YHWH, saying, Go, serve other gods. ²⁰And now, do not let my blood fall to the earth before the face of YHWH, for the king of Israel has come out to seek one flea, as [one] pursues the partridge in mountains." ²¹And Saul says, "I have sinned; return, my son David, for I do evil to you no more, because that my soul has been precious in your eyes this day; behold, I have acted foolishly, and err very greatly." ²²And David answers and says, "Behold, the king's spear; and let one of the young men pass over, and receive it; ²³and YHWH turns each back to his righteousness and his faithfulness, in that YHWH has given you into [my] hand today, and I have not been willing to put forth my hand against the anointed of YHWH, ²⁴and behold, as your soul has been great in my eyes this day, so is my soul great in the eyes of YHWH, and He delivers me out of all distress." ²⁵And Saul says to David, "Blessed [are] you, my son David, also working you work, and also prevailing you prevail." And David goes on his way, and Saul has turned back to his place.

CHAPTER 27

¹And David says to his heart, "Now I am consumed by the hand of Saul one day; there is nothing better for me than that I diligently escape to the land of the Philistines, and Saul has been despairing of me—of seeking me anymore in all the border of Israel, and I have escaped out of his hand." ²And David rises, and passes over, he and six hundred men who [are] with him, to Achish son of Maoch king of Gath; ³and David dwells with Achish in Gath, he and his men, each one with his household, [even] David and his two wives, Ahinoam the Jezreelitess, and Abigail wife of Nabal the Carmelitess. ⁴And it is declared to Saul that David has fled to Gath, and he has not added to seek him anymore. ⁵And David says to Achish, "Now if I have found grace in your eyes, they give a place to me in one of the cities of the field, and I dwell there, indeed, why does your servant dwell in the royal city with you?" ⁶And Achish gives Ziklag to him in that day, therefore Ziklag has been for the kings of Judah until this day. ⁷And the number of the days which David has dwelt in the field of the Philistines [is one year] of days and four months; ⁸and David and his men go up, and they push toward the Geshurite, and the Gerizite, and the Amalekite (for they are inhabitants of the land from of old), as you come to Shur and to the land of Egypt, ⁹and David has struck the land, and does not keep alive man and woman, and has taken sheep, and oxen, and donkeys, and camels, and garments, and turns back, and comes to Achish. ¹⁰And Achish says, "To where have you pushed today?" And David says, "Against the south of Judah, and against the south of the Jerahmeelite, and to the south of the Kenite." ¹¹David keeps alive neither man nor woman, to bring in [word] to Gath, saying, "Lest they declare [it] against us, saying, Thus David has done, and thus [is] his custom all the days that he has dwelt in the fields of the Philistines." ¹²And Achish believes in David, saying, "He has made himself utterly abhorred among his people in Israel, and has been for a perpetual servant to me."

CHAPTER 28

¹And it comes to pass in those days, that the Philistines gather their camps for the war, to fight against Israel, and Achish says to David, "You certainly know that you go out with me into the camp, you and your men." ²And David says to Achish, "Therefore you know that which your servant does." And Achish says to David, "Therefore I appoint you keeper of my head [for] all the days." ³And Samuel has died, and all Israel mourns for him, and buries him in Ramah, even in his city, and Saul has turned aside those having familiar spirits, and the wizards, out of the land. ⁴And the Philistines are gathered, and come in, and encamp in Shunem, and Saul gathers all Israel, and they encamp in Gilboa, ⁵and Saul sees the camp of

1 SAMUEL

the Philistines, and fears, and his heart trembles greatly, ⁶and Saul inquires of YHWH, and YHWH has not answered him, either by the dreams, or by the Lights, or by the prophets. ⁷And Saul says to his servants, "Seek a woman for me possessing a familiar spirit, and I go to her, and inquire of her"; and his servants say to him, "Behold, a woman possessing a familiar spirit [is] in En-dor." ⁸And Saul disguises himself and puts on other garments, and goes, he and two of the men with him, and they come to the woman by night, and he says, "Please divine to me by the familiar spirit, and cause him whom I say to you to come up to me." ⁹And the woman says to him, "Behold, you have known that which Saul has done, that he has cut off those having familiar spirits, and the wizards, out of the land; and why are you laying a snare for my soul—to put me to death?" ¹⁰And Saul swears to her by YHWH, saying, "YHWH lives, punishment does not meet you for this thing." ¹¹And the woman says, "Whom do I bring up to you?" And he says, "Bring up Samuel to me." ¹²And the woman sees Samuel, and cries with a loud voice, and the woman speaks to Saul, saying, "Why have you deceived me? For you [are] Saul!" ¹³And the king says to her, "Do not fear; for what have you seen?" And the woman says to Saul, "I have seen gods coming up out of the earth." ¹⁴And he says to her, "What [is] his form?" And she says, "An aged man is coming up, and he [is] covered with an upper robe"; and Saul knows that he [is] Samuel, and bows—face to the earth—and pays respect. ¹⁵And Samuel says to Saul, "Why have you troubled me, to bring me up?" And Saul says, "I have great distress, and the Philistines are fighting against me, God has turned aside from me, and has not answered me anymore, either by the hand of the prophets, or by dreams; and I call for you to let me know what I [should] do." ¹⁶And Samuel says, "And why do you ask me, and YHWH has turned aside from you, and is your enemy? ¹⁷And YHWH does for Himself as He has spoken by my hand, and YHWH tears the kingdom out of your hand, and gives it to your neighbor—to David. ¹⁸Because you have not listened to the voice of YHWH, nor did the fierceness of His anger on Amalek—therefore YHWH has done this thing to you this day; ¹⁹indeed, YHWH also gives Israel into the hand of the Philistines with you, and tomorrow you and your sons [are] with me; YHWH also gives the camp of Israel into the hand of the Philistines." ²⁰And Saul hurries and falls—the fullness of his stature—to the earth, and fears greatly because of the words of Samuel; also power was not in him, for he had not eaten bread all the day, and all the night. ²¹And the woman comes to Saul, and sees that he has been greatly troubled, and says to him, "Behold, your maidservant has listened to your voice, and I put my soul in my hand, and I obey your words which you have spoken to me; ²²and now, please listen, you also, to the voice of your maidservant, and I set a morsel of bread before you; and eat, and there is power in you when you go in the way." ²³And he refuses and says, "I do not eat"; and his servants urge him on, and also the woman, and he listens to their voice, and rises from the earth, and sits on the bed. ²⁴And the woman has a calf of the stall in the house, and she hurries and slaughters it, and takes flour, and kneads, and bakes it [into] unleavened things, ²⁵and brings [them] near before Saul, and before his servants, and they eat, and rise, and go on during that night.

CHAPTER 29

¹And the Philistines gather all their camps to Aphek, and Israel is encamping at a fountain which [is] in Jezreel, ²and the princes of the Philistines are passing on by hundreds, and by thousands, and David and his men are passing on in the rear with Achish. ³And the heads of the Philistines say, "What [are] these Hebrews?" And Achish says to the heads of the Philistines, "Is this not David, servant of Saul king of Israel, who has been with me these days or these years, and I have not found anything in him [wrong] from the day of his falling away until this day?" ⁴And the heads of the Philistines are angry against him, and the heads of the Philistines say to him, "Send back the man, and he turns back to his place to where you have appointed him, and does not go down with us into battle, and is not for an adversary to us in battle; and with what does this one reconcile himself to his lord—is it not with the heads of those men? ⁵Is this not David, of whom they answer in choruses, saying, Saul has struck among his thousands, and David among his myriads?" ⁶And Achish calls to David and says to him, "YHWH lives, surely you [are] upright, and good in my eyes is your going out, and your coming in with me in the camp, for I have not found evil in you from the day of your coming to me until this day; but you are not good in the eyes of the princes; ⁷and now, return, and go in peace, and you do no evil in the eyes of the princes of the Philistines." ⁸And David says to Achish, "But what have I done? And what have you found in your servant from the day that I have been before you until this day—that I do not go in and have fought against the enemies of my lord the king?" ⁹And Achish answers and says to David, "I have known that you [are] good in my eyes as a messenger of God; only, the princes of the Philistines have said, He does not go up with us into battle; ¹⁰and now, rise early in the morning—and the servants of your lord who have come with you. When you have risen early in the morning, and have light, then go." ¹¹And David rises early, he and his men, to go in the morning, to return to the land of the Philistines, and the Philistines have gone up to Jezreel.

CHAPTER 30

¹And it comes to pass, in the coming in of David and his men to Ziklag on the third day, that the Amalekites have pushed toward the south, and to Ziklag, and strike Ziklag, and burn it with fire, ²and they take the women who [are] in it captive; they have not put anyone to death from small to great, and they lead [them] away, and go on their way. ³And David comes in—and his men—to the city, and behold, [it is] burned with fire, and their wives, and their sons, and their daughters have been taken captive. ⁴And David lifts up—and the people who [are] with him—their voice and weep, until they have no power to weep. ⁵And the two wives of David have been taken captive, Ahinoam the Jezreelitess, and Abigail wife of Nabal the Carmelite; ⁶and David has great distress, for the people have said to stone him, for the soul of all the people has been bitter, each for his sons and for his daughters; and David strengthens himself in his God YHWH. ⁷And David says to Abiathar the priest, son of Ahimelech, "Please bring the ephod near to me"; and Abiathar brings the ephod near to David, ⁸and David inquires of YHWH, saying, "I pursue after this troop—do I overtake it?" And He says to him, "Pursue, for you certainly overtake, and certainly deliver." ⁹And David goes on, he and six hundred men who [are] with him, and they come to the Brook of Besor, and those left have stood still, ¹⁰and David pursues, he and four hundred men (and two hundred men stand still who have been too faint to pass over the Brook of Besor), ¹¹and they find a man, an Egyptian, in the field, and take him to David, and give bread to him, and he eats, and they cause him to drink water, ¹²and give to him a piece of a bunch of dried figs, and two bunches of raisins, and he eats, and his spirit returns to him, for he has not eaten bread nor drunk water [for] three days and three nights. ¹³And David says to him, "Whose [are] you? And where [are] you from?" And he says, "I [am] an Egyptian youth, servant to a man, an Amalekite, and my lord forsakes me, for I have been sick [for] three days, ¹⁴we pushed [to] the south of the Cherethite, and against that which [is] to Judah, and against the south of Caleb, and we burned Ziklag with fire." ¹⁵And David says to him, "Do you bring me down to this troop?" And he says, "Swear to me by God [that] you do not put me to death, nor do you shut me up into the hand of my lord, and I bring you down to this troop." ¹⁶And he brings him down, and behold, they are spread out over the face of all the earth, eating, and drinking, and celebrating, with all the great spoil which they have taken out of the land of the Philistines, and out of the land of Judah. ¹⁷And David strikes them from the twilight even to the evening of the next day, and there has not escaped of them a man, except four hundred young men who have ridden on the camels and flee. ¹⁸And David delivers all that the Amalekites have taken; David has also delivered his two wives. ¹⁹And nothing of theirs has lacked, from small to great, and to sons and daughters, and from the spoil, even to all that they had taken to themselves, David has brought back the whole, ²⁰and David takes the whole of the flock and of the herd [that] they have led on before these livestock, and they say, "This [is] David's spoil." ²¹And David comes to the two hundred men who were too faint to go after David, and whom they cause to abide at the Brook of Besor, and they go out to meet David, and to meet the people who

1 SAMUEL

[are] with him, and David approaches the people, and asks of them of welfare. ²²And every bad and worthless man, of the men who have gone with David, answers, indeed, they say, "Because that they have not gone with us we do not give to them of the spoil which we have delivered, except each his wife and his children, and they lead away and go." ²³And David says, "You do not do so, my brothers, with that which YHWH has given to us, and He preserves us, and gives the troop which comes against us into our hand; ²⁴and who listens to you in this thing? For as the portion of him who was brought down into battle, so also [is] the portion of him who is abiding by the vessels—they share alike." ²⁵And it comes to pass from that day and forward, that he appoints it for a statute and for an ordinance for Israel to this day. ²⁶And David comes to Ziklag, and sends of the spoil to [the] elderly of Judah, to his friends, saying, "Behold, a blessing for you of the spoil of the enemies of YHWH," ²⁷to those in Beth-El, and to those in South Ramoth, and to those in Jattir, ²⁸and to those in Aroer, and to those in Siphmoth, and to those in Eshtemoa, ²⁹and to those in Rachal, and to those in the cities of the Jerahmeelites, and to those in the cities of the Kenites, ³⁰and to those in Hormah, and to those in Chor-Ashan, and to those in Athach, ³¹and to those in Hebron, and to all the places where David—he and his men—had gone up and down.

CHAPTER 31

¹And the Philistines are fighting against Israel, and the men of Israel flee from the face of the Philistines, and fall wounded in Mount Gilboa, ²and the Philistines follow Saul and his sons, and the Philistines strike Jonathan, and Abinadab, and Malchishua, the sons of Saul. ³And the battle is hard against Saul, and the archers find him—men with bow—and he is greatly pained by the archers; ⁴and Saul says to the bearer of his weapons, "Draw your sword, and pierce me with it, lest they come—these uncircumcised—and have pierced me, and rolled themselves on me"; and the bearer of his weapons has not been willing, for he is greatly afraid, and Saul takes the sword, and falls on it. ⁵And the bearer of his weapons sees that Saul [is] dead, and he falls—he also—on his sword, and dies with him; ⁶and Saul dies, and three of his sons, and the bearer of his weapons, also all his men, together on that day. ⁷And they see—the men of Israel, who [are] beyond the valley, and who [are] beyond the Jordan—that the men of Israel have fled, and that Saul and his sons have died, and they forsake the cities and flee, and Philistines come in, and dwell in them. ⁸And it comes to pass on the next day, that the Philistines come to strip the wounded, and they find Saul and his three sons fallen on Mount Gilboa, ⁹and they cut off his head, and strip off his weapons, and send [them] into the land of the surrounding Philistines, to proclaim tidings [in] the house of their idols, and [among] the people; ¹⁰and they place his weapons [in] the house of Ashtaroth, and they have fixed his body on the wall of Beth-Shan. ¹¹And they hear regarding it—the inhabitants of Jabesh-Gilead—that which the Philistines have done to Saul, ¹²and all the men of valor arise, and go all the night, and take the body of Saul, and the bodies of his sons, from the wall of Beth-Shan, and come to Jabesh, and burn them there, ¹³and they take their bones, and bury [them] under the tamarisk in Jabesh, and fast seven days.

2 SAMUEL

CHAPTER 1

¹And it comes to pass after the death of Saul, that David has returned from striking the Amalekite, and David dwells in Ziklag [for] two days, ²and it comes to pass, on the third day, that behold, a man has come in out of the camp from Saul, and his garments [are] torn, and earth [is] on his head; and it comes to pass in his coming to David, that he falls to the earth and pays respect. ³And David says to him, "Where do you come from?" And he says to him, "I have escaped out of the camp of Israel." ⁴And David says to him, "What has been the matter? Please declare [it] to me." And he says, "That the people have fled from the battle, and also a multitude of the people have fallen, and they die; and also Saul and his son Jonathan have died." ⁵And David says to the youth who is declaring [it] to him, "How have you known that Saul and his son Jonathan [are] dead?" ⁶And the youth who is declaring [it] to him says, "I happened to meet in Mount Gilboa, and behold, Saul is leaning on his spear; and behold, the chariots and those possessing horses have followed him; ⁷and he turns behind him, and sees me, and calls to me, and I say, Here I [am]. ⁸And he says to me, Who [are] you? And I say to him, I [am] an Amalekite. ⁹And he says to me, Please stand over me and put me to death, for the arrow has seized me, for all my soul [is] still in me. ¹⁰And I stand over him, and put him to death, for I knew that he does not live after his falling, and I take the crown which [is] on his head, and the bracelet which [is] on his arm, and bring them to my lord here." ¹¹And David takes hold on his garments, and tears them, and also all the men who [are] with him, ¹²and they mourn, and weep, and fast until the evening, for Saul, and for his son Jonathan, and for the people of YHWH, and for the house of Israel, because they have fallen by the sword. ¹³And David says to the youth who is declaring [it] to him, "Where [are] you from?" And he says, "I [am] the son of a sojourner, an Amalekite." ¹⁴And David says to him, "How were you not afraid to put forth your hand to destroy the anointed of YHWH?" ¹⁵And David calls to one of the youths and says, "Draw near—fall on him"; and he strikes him, and he dies; ¹⁶and David says to him, "Your blood [is] on your own head, for your mouth has testified against you, saying, I put to death the anointed of YHWH." ¹⁷And David laments with this lamentation over Saul, and over his son Jonathan; ¹⁸and he says to teach the sons of Judah "The Bow"; behold, it is written on the Scroll of the Upright: ¹⁹"The beauty of Israel || [Is] wounded on your high places; How the mighty have fallen! ²⁰Do not declare [it] in Gath, || Do not proclaim the tidings in the streets of Ashkelon, || Lest they rejoice—The daughters of the Philistines, || Lest they exult—The daughters of the uncircumcised! ²¹Mountains of Gilboa! No dew nor rain be on you, || And fields of raised-offerings! For there has become loathsome || The shield of the mighty, || The shield of Saul—without the anointed with oil. ²²From the blood of the wounded, || From the fat of the mighty, || The bow of Jonathan || Has not turned backward; And the sword of Saul does not return empty. ²³Saul and Jonathan! They are loved and pleasant in their lives, || And in their death they have not been parted. They have been lighter than eagles, || They have been mightier than lions! ²⁴Daughters of Israel! Weep for Saul, || Who is clothing you [in] scarlet with delights. Who is lifting up ornaments of gold on your clothing. ²⁵How the mighty have fallen || In the midst of the battle! Jonathan [was] wounded on your high places! ²⁶I am in distress for you, my brother Jonathan, || You were very pleasant to me; Your love was wonderful to me, || Above the love of women! ²⁷How the mighty have fallen, || Indeed, the weapons of war perish!"

CHAPTER 2

¹And it comes to pass afterward, that David inquires of YHWH, saying, "Do I go up into one of the cities of Judah?" And YHWH says to him, "Go up." And David says, "To where do I go up?" And He says, "To Hebron." ²And David goes up there, and also his two wives, Ahinoam the Jezreelitess, and Abigail wife of Nabal the Carmelite; ³and David has brought up his men who [are] with him—a man and his household—and they dwell in the cities of Hebron. ⁴And the men of Judah come, and anoint David there for king over the house of Judah; and they declare to David, saying, "The men of Jabesh-Gilead [are] they who buried Saul." ⁵And David sends messengers to the men of Jabesh-Gilead and says to them, "Blessed [are] you of YHWH, in that you have done this kindness with your lord, with Saul, that you bury him. ⁶And now YHWH does kindness and truth with you, and I also do this good with you because you have done this thing; ⁷and now your hands are strong, and be

for sons of valor, for your lord Saul [is] dead, and the house of Judah has also anointed me for king over them." ⁸And Abner, son of Ner, head of the host which Saul has, has taken Ish-Bosheth, son of Saul, and causes him to pass over to Mahanaim, ⁹and causes him to reign over Gilead, and over the Ashurite, and over Jezreel, and over Ephraim, and over Benjamin, and over Israel—all of it. ¹⁰Ish-Bosheth son of Saul [is] a son of forty years in his reigning over Israel, and he has reigned [for] two years; only the house of Judah has been after David. ¹¹And the number of the days that David has been king in Hebron, over the house of Judah, is seven years and six months. ¹²And Abner son of Ner goes out, and servants of Ish-Bosheth son of Saul, from Mahanaim to Gibeon. ¹³And Joab son of Zeruiah, and servants of David, have gone out, and they meet by the pool of Gibeon together, and sit down, these by the pool on this [side], and these by the pool on that [side]. ¹⁴And Abner says to Joab, "Now let the youths rise and they play before us"; and Joab says, "Let them rise." ¹⁵And they rise and pass over, in number twelve of Benjamin, even of Ish-Bosheth son of Saul, and twelve of the servants of David. ¹⁶And they each lay hold on the head of his companion, and his sword [is] in the side of his companion, and they fall together, and [one] calls that place Helkath-Hazzurim, which [is] in Gibeon, ¹⁷and the battle is very hard on that day, and Abner is struck, and the men of Israel, before the servants of David. ¹⁸And there are three sons of Zeruiah there: Joab, and Abishai, and Asahel; and Asahel [is] light on his feet, as one of the roes which [are] in the field, ¹⁹and Asahel pursues after Abner, and has not turned aside to go to the right or to the left, from after Abner. ²⁰And Abner looks behind him and says, "Are you he—Asahel?" And he says, "I [am]." ²¹And Abner says to him, "Turn aside to your right hand or to your left, and seize one of the youths for yourself, and take his armor for yourself"; and Asahel has not been willing to turn aside from after him. ²²And Abner adds again, saying to Asahel, "Turn aside from after me, why do I strike you to the earth? And how do I lift up my face to your brother Joab?" ²³And he refuses to turn aside, and Abner strikes him with the back part of the spear to the fifth [rib], and the spear comes out from behind him, and he falls there, and dies under it; and it comes to pass, everyone who has come to the place where Asahel has fallen and dies—they stand still. ²⁴And Joab and Abishai pursue after Abner, and the sun has gone in, and they have come to the height of Ammah, which [is] on the front of Giah, the way of the wilderness of Gibeon. ²⁵And the sons of Benjamin gather themselves together after Abner, and become one troop, and stand on the top of a certain height, ²⁶and Abner calls to Joab and says, "Does the sword consume forever? Have you not known that it is bitterness in the latter end? And until when do you not say to the people to turn back from after their brothers?" ²⁷And Joab says, "God lives! For unless you had spoken, surely then from the morning each of the people had gone up from after his brother." ²⁸And Joab blows with a horn, and all the people stand still, and no longer pursue after Israel, nor have they added to fight anymore. ²⁹And Abner and his men have gone through the plain all that night, and pass over the Jordan, and go on [through] all Bithron, and come to Mahanaim. ³⁰And Joab has turned back from after Abner, and gathers all the people, and there are lacking of the servants of David nineteen men, and Asahel; ³¹and the servants of David have struck of Benjamin, even among the men of Abner, three hundred and sixty men—they died. ³²And they lift up Asahel, and bury him in the burying-place of his father, which [is] in Beth-Lehem, and they go all the night—Joab and his men—and [dawn's light] shines on them in Hebron.

CHAPTER 3

¹And the war is long between the house of Saul and the house of David, and David is going on and [is] strong, and the house of Saul is going on and [is] weak. ²And there are sons born to David in Hebron, and his firstborn is Amnon, of Ahinoam the Jezreelitess, ³and his second [is] Chileab, of Abigail wife of Nabal the Carmelite, and the third [is] Absalom son of Maacah daughter of Talmai king of Geshur, ⁴and the fourth [is] Adonijah son of Haggith, and the fifth [is] Shephatiah son of Abital, ⁵and the sixth [is] Ithream, of Eglah wife of David; these have been born to David in Hebron. ⁶And it comes to pass, in the war being between the house of Saul and the house of David, that Abner has been strengthening himself in the house of Saul, ⁷and Saul has a concubine, and her name [is] Rizpah daughter of Aiah, and [Ish-Bosheth] says to Abner, "Why have you gone in to the concubine of my father?" ⁸And it is exceedingly displeasing to Abner, because of the words of Ish-Bosheth, and he says, "[Am] I the head of a dog—that in reference to Judah, today I do kindness with the house of your father Saul, to his brothers, and to his friends, and have not delivered you into the hand of David—that you charge against me iniquity concerning the woman today? ⁹Thus God does to Abner, and thus He adds to him, surely as YHWH has sworn to David—surely so I do to him: ¹⁰to cause the kingdom to pass over from the house of Saul, and to raise up the throne of David over Israel, and over Judah, from Dan even to Beer-Sheba." ¹¹And he is not able to return a word [to] Abner anymore, because of his fearing him. ¹²And Abner sends messengers to David for himself, saying, "Whose [is] the land?" [And] saying, "Make your covenant with me, and behold, my hand [is] with you, to bring around all Israel to you." ¹³And [David] says, "Good—I make a covenant with you; only, one thing I am asking of you, that is, you do not see my face, except [that] you first bring in Michal daughter of Saul in your coming in to see my face." ¹⁴And David sends messengers to Ish-Bosheth son of Saul, saying, "Give up my wife Michal, whom I betrothed to myself with one hundred foreskins of the Philistines." ¹⁵And Ish-Bosheth sends, and takes her from a man, from Phaltiel son of Laish, ¹⁶and her husband goes with her, going on and weeping behind her, to Bahurim, and Abner says to him, "Go, return"; and he turns back. ¹⁷And the word of Abner was with [the] elderly of Israel, saying, "Thus far you have been seeking David for king over you, ¹⁸and now, do [it], for YHWH has spoken of David saying, [It is] by the hand of my servant David to save My people Israel out of the hand of the Philistines, and out of the hand of all their enemies." ¹⁹And Abner also speaks in the ears of Benjamin, and Abner also goes to speak in the ears of David in Hebron all that [is] good in the eyes of Israel, and in the eyes of all the house of Benjamin, ²⁰and Abner comes to David, to Hebron, and twenty men [are] with him, and David makes a banquet for Abner and for the men who [are] with him. ²¹And Abner says to David, "I arise, and go, and gather the whole of Israel to my lord the king, and they make a covenant with you, and you have reigned over all that your soul desires"; and David sends Abner away, and he goes in peace. ²²And behold, the servants of David, and Joab, have come from the troop, and have brought much spoil with them, and Abner is not with David in Hebron, for he has sent him away, and he goes in peace; ²³and Joab and all the host that [were] with him have come, and they declare to Joab, saying, "Abner son of Ner has come to the king, and he sends him away, and he goes in peace." ²⁴And Joab comes to the king and says, "What have you done? Behold, Abner has come to you! Why [is] this—you have sent him away, and he is really gone? ²⁵You have known Abner son of Ner, that he came to deceive you, and to know your going out and your coming in, and to know all that you are doing." ²⁶And Joab goes out from David, and sends messengers after Abner, and they bring him back from the well of Sirah, and David did not know. ²⁷And Abner turns back to Hebron, and Joab turns him aside to the midst of the gate to speak with him quietly, and strikes him there in the fifth [rib]—and he dies—for the blood of his brother Asahel. ²⁸And David hears afterward and says, "My kingdom and I [are] acquitted by YHWH for all time, from the blood of Abner son of Ner; ²⁹it stays on the head of Joab, and on all the house of his father, and there is not cut off from the house of Joab one who has discharging, and leprous, and laying hold on a staff, and falling by a sword, and lacking bread." ³⁰And Joab and his brother Abishai slew Abner because that he put their brother Asahel to death in Gibeon, in battle. ³¹And David says to Joab, and to all the people who [are] with him, "Tear your garments, and gird on sackcloth, and mourn before Abner"; and King David is going after the bier. ³²And they bury Abner in Hebron, and the king lifts up his voice, and weeps at the grave of Abner, and all the people weep; ³³and the king laments for Abner and says, "Does Abner die as the death of a fool? ³⁴Your hands not bound, || And your feet not brought near to chains! You have fallen as one falling before sons of evil!" And all the people add to weep over him. ³⁵And all the people come to cause David to eat bread while yet day, and David

swears, saying, "Thus God does to me, and thus He adds, for—before the going in of the sun, I taste no bread or any other thing." ³⁶And all the people have discerned [it], and it is good in their eyes, as all that the king has done is good in the eyes of all the people; ³⁷and all the people know, even all Israel, in that day, that it has not been from the king—to put Abner son of Ner to death. ³⁸And the king says to his servants, "Do you not know that a prince and a great one has fallen this day in Israel? ³⁹And today I [am] tender, and an anointed king: and these men, sons of Zeruiah, [are] too hard for me; YHWH repays to the doer of the evil according to his evil."

CHAPTER 4

¹And the son of Saul hears that Abner [is] dead in Hebron, and his hands are feeble, and all of Israel has been troubled. ²And two men, heads of troops, have been [to] the son of Saul, the name of the first [is] Baanah, and the name of the second Rechab, sons of Rimmon the Beerothite, of the sons of Benjamin, for Beeroth is also reckoned to Benjamin, ³and the Beerothites flee to Gittaim, and are sojourners there to this day. ⁴And to Jonathan son of Saul [is] a son—lame; he was a son of five years at the coming in of the rumor of [the death of] Saul and Jonathan, out of Jezreel, and his nurse lifts him up, and flees, and it comes to pass in her hastening to flee, that he falls, and becomes lame, and his name [is] Mephibosheth. ⁵And the sons of Rimmon the Beerothite, Rechab and Baanah, go, and come in at the heat of the day to the house of Ish-Bosheth, and he is lying down—the lying down of noon; ⁶and they have come there, to the midst of the house, taking wheat, and they strike him to the fifth [rib], and Rechab and his brother Baanah have escaped; ⁷indeed, they come into the house, and he is lying on his bed, in the inner part of his bed-chamber, and they strike him, and put him to death, and turn his head aside, and they take his head, and go the way of the plain all the night, ⁸and bring in the head of Ish-Bosheth to David in Hebron, and say to the king, "Behold, the head of Ish-Bosheth, son of Saul, your enemy, who sought your life; and YHWH gives vengeance to my lord the king this day, of Saul and of his seed." ⁹And David answers Rechab and his brother Baanah, sons of Rimmon the Beerothite, and says to them, "YHWH lives, who has redeemed my soul out of all adversity, ¹⁰when one is declaring to me, saying, Behold, Saul is dead, and he was as a bearer of tidings in his own eyes, then I take hold on him, and slay him in Ziklag, instead of my giving to him [for] the tidings. ¹¹Also—when wicked men have slain the righteous man in his own house, on his bed; and now, do I not require his blood from your hand, and have taken you away from the earth?" ¹²And David commands the young men, and they slay them, and cut off their hands and their feet, and hang [them] over the pool in Hebron, and they have taken the head of Ish-Bosheth, and bury [it] in the burying-place of Abner in Hebron.

CHAPTER 5

¹And all the tribes of Israel come to David, to Hebron, and speak, saying, "Behold, we [are] your bone and your flesh; ²also thus far, in Saul's being king over us, you have been he who is bringing out and bringing in Israel, and YHWH says to you, You feed My people Israel, and you are for leader over Israel." ³And all [the] elderly of Israel come to the king, to Hebron, and King David makes a covenant with them in Hebron before YHWH, and they anoint David for king over Israel. ⁴A son of thirty years [is] David in his being king; he has reigned [for] forty years; ⁵he reigned over Judah in Hebron [for] seven years and six months, and in Jerusalem he reigned [for] thirty-three years, over all Israel and Judah. ⁶And the king goes, and his men, to Jerusalem, to the Jebusite, the inhabitant of the land, and they speak to David, saying, "You do not come in here, except [that] you turn aside the blind and the lame," saying, "David does not come in here." ⁷And David captures the fortress of Zion, it [is] the City of David. ⁸And on that day David says, "Anyone striking the Jebusite, let him go up by the watercourse (and the lame and the blind—the hated of David's soul)." Therefore they say, "The blind and lame—he does not come into the house." ⁹And David dwells in the fortress, and calls it the City of David, and David builds all around, from Millo and inward, ¹⁰and David goes, going on and becoming great, and YHWH, God of Hosts, [is] with him. ¹¹And Hiram king of Tyre sends messengers to David, and cedar-trees, and craftsmen of wood, and craftsmen of stone, for walls, and they build a house for David, ¹²and David knows that YHWH has established him for king over Israel, and that He has lifted up his kingdom, because of His people Israel. ¹³And again David takes concubines and wives out of Jerusalem, after his coming from Hebron, and again there are born to David sons and daughters. ¹⁴And these [are] the names of those born to him in Jerusalem: Shammuah, and Shobab, and Nathan, and Solomon, ¹⁵and Ibhar, and Elishua, and Nepheg, and Japhia, ¹⁶and Elishama, and Eliada, and Eliphalet. ¹⁷And the Philistines hear that they have anointed David for king over Israel, and all the Philistines come up to seek David, and David hears, and goes down to the fortress, ¹⁸and the Philistines have come, and are spread out in the Valley of Rephaim. ¹⁹And David asks of YHWH, saying, "Do I go up to the Philistines? Do You give them into my hand?" And YHWH says to David, "Go up, for I certainly give the Philistines into your hand." ²⁰And David comes to Ba'al-Perazim, and David strikes them there, and says, "YHWH has broken forth [on] my enemies before me, as the breaking forth of waters"; therefore he has called the name of that place Ba'al-Perazim. ²¹And they forsake their idols there, and David and his men lift them up. ²²And the Philistines add again to come up, and are spread out in the Valley of Rephaim, ²³and David asks of YHWH, and He says, "You do not go up, turn around to their rear, and you have come to them from the front [[or in front]] of the mulberries, ²⁴and it comes to pass, in your hearing the sound of a stepping in the tops of the mulberries, then you move sharply, for then YHWH has gone out before you to strike in the camp of the Philistines." ²⁵And David does so, as YHWH commanded him, and strikes the Philistines from Geba to your coming to Gazer.

CHAPTER 6

¹And again David gathered every chosen one in Israel—thirty thousand, ²and David rises and goes, and all the people who [are] with him, from Ba'ale-Judah, to bring up the Ark of God from there, whose name has been called—the Name of YHWH of Hosts, inhabiting the cherubim—on it. ³And they cause the Ark of God to ride on a new cart, and lift it up from the house of Abinadab, which [is] in the height, and Uzzah and Ahio sons of Abinadab are leading the new cart; ⁴and they lift it up from the house of Abinadab, which [is] in the height, with the Ark of God, and Ahio is going before the Ark, ⁵and David and all the house of Israel are playing before YHWH, with all kinds of [instruments] of fir-wood, even with harps, and with psalteries, and with timbrels, and with horns, and with cymbals. ⁶And they come to the threshing-floor of Nachon, and Uzzah puts forth [his hand] to the Ark of God, and lays hold on it, for they released the oxen; ⁷and the anger of YHWH burns against Uzzah, and God strikes him there for the error, and he dies there by the Ark of God. ⁸And it is displeasing to David, because that YHWH has broken forth a breach on Uzzah, and [one] calls that place Perez-Uzzah to this day; ⁹and David fears YHWH on that day and says, "How does the Ark of YHWH come to me?" ¹⁰And David has not been willing to turn aside the Ark of YHWH to himself, to the City of David, and David turns it aside to the house of Obed-Edom the Gittite, ¹¹and the Ark of YHWH inhabits the house of Obed-Edom the Gittite [for] three months, and YHWH blesses Obed-Edom and all his house. ¹²And it is declared to King David, saying, "YHWH has blessed the house of Obed-Edom, and all that he has, because of the Ark of God"; and David goes and brings up the Ark of God from the house of Obed-Edom to the City of David with joy. ¹³And it comes to pass, when those carrying the Ark of YHWH have stepped six steps, that he sacrifices an ox and a fatling. ¹⁴And David is dancing with all [his] strength before YHWH, and David is girded with a linen ephod, ¹⁵and David and all the house of Israel are bringing up the Ark of YHWH with shouting, and with the voice of a horn, ¹⁶and it has come to pass, the Ark of YHWH has come into the City of David, and Michal daughter of Saul has looked through the window and sees King David moving and dancing before YHWH, and she despises him in her heart. ¹⁷And they bring in the Ark of YHWH, and set it up in its place, in the midst of the tent which David has spread out for it, and David causes burnt-offerings and peace-offerings to ascend before YHWH. ¹⁸And David finishes from causing the burnt-offering and the peace-offerings to ascend, and blesses the people in the Name of

YHWH of Hosts, ¹⁹and he apportions to all the people, to all the multitude of Israel, from man and to woman, to each, one cake of bread, and one eshpar, and one ashisha, and all the people go, each to his house. ²⁰And David turns back to bless his house, and Michal daughter of Saul goes out to meet David and says, "How honorable was the king of Israel today, who was uncovered today before the eyes of the handmaids of his servants, as one of the vain ones is openly uncovered!" ²¹And David says to Michal, "Before YHWH, who fixed on me above your father, and above all his house, to appoint me leader over the people of YHWH, and over Israel—indeed, I played before YHWH; ²²and I have been more vile than this, and have been low in my eyes, and with the handmaids whom you have spoken of, I am honored with them." ²³As for Michal daughter of Saul, she had no child until the day of her death.

CHAPTER 7

¹And it comes to pass, when the king sat in his house, and YHWH has given rest to him all around, from all his enemies, ²that the king says to Nathan the prophet, "Now see, I am dwelling in a house of cedars, but the Ark of God is dwelling in the midst of the curtain." ³And Nathan says to the king, "All that [is] in your heart—go, do, for YHWH [is] with you." ⁴And it comes to pass in that night, that the word of YHWH is to Nathan, saying, ⁵"Go, and you have said to My servant, to David, Thus said YHWH: Do you build for Me a house for My dwelling in? ⁶For I have not dwelt in a house even from the day of My bringing up the sons of Israel out of Egypt, even to this day, and am walking up and down in a tent and in a dwelling place. ⁷During all [the time] that I have walked up and down among all the sons of Israel, have I spoken a word with one of the tribes of Israel, which I commanded to feed my people Israel, saying, Why have you not built a house of cedars for Me? ⁸And now, thus you say to My servant, to David, Thus said YHWH of Hosts: I have taken you from the pasture, from after the flock, to be leader over My people, over Israel; ⁹and I am with you wherever you have gone, and I cut off all your enemies from your presence, and have made a great name for you, as the name of the great ones who [are] in the earth, ¹⁰and I have appointed a place for My people, for Israel, and have planted it, and it has dwelt in its place, and it is not troubled anymore, and the sons of perverseness do not add to afflict it anymore, as in the beginning, ¹¹even from the day that I appointed judges over My people Israel; and I have given rest to you from all your enemies, and YHWH has declared to you that YHWH makes a house for you. ¹²When your days are full, and you have lain with your fathers, then I have raised up your seed after you which goes out from your bowels, and have established his kingdom; ¹³he builds a house for My Name, and I have established the throne of his kingdom for all time. ¹⁴I am to him for a father, and he is to Me for a son; whom in his dealing perversely I have even reproved with a rod of men, and with strokes of the sons of Adam, ¹⁵and My kindness does not turn aside from him, as I turned it aside from Saul, whom I turned aside from before you, ¹⁶and your house and your kingdom [are] steadfast before you for all time, your throne is established for all time." ¹⁷According to all these words, and according to all this vision, so spoke Nathan to David. ¹⁸And King David comes in and sits before YHWH, and says, "Who [am] I, Lord YHWH? And what [is] my house, that You have brought me here? ¹⁹And yet this [is] little in Your eyes, Lord YHWH, and You also speak concerning the house of Your servant far off; and this [is] the law of the man, Lord YHWH. ²⁰And what does David add more to speak to You? And You, You have known Your servant, Lord YHWH. ²¹Because of Your word, and according to Your heart, You have done all this greatness, to cause Your servant to know [it]. ²²Therefore You have been great, YHWH God, for there is none like You, and there is no God except You, according to all that we have heard with our ears. ²³And who [is] as Your people, as Israel—one nation in the earth, whom God has gone to redeem for a people for Himself, and to make for Himself a name—and to do for Yourself the greatness—even fearful things for Your land, at the presence of Your people, whom You have redeemed for Yourself out of Egypt—[among the] nations and their gods? ²⁴Indeed, You establish Your people Israel for Yourself, for a people for Yourself for all time, and You, YHWH, have been to them for God. ²⁵And now, YHWH God, the word which You have spoken concerning Your servant, and concerning his house, establish for all time, and do as You have spoken. ²⁶And Your Name is great for all time, saying, YHWH of Hosts [is] God over Israel, and the house of Your servant David is established before You, ²⁷for You, YHWH of Hosts, God of Israel, have uncovered the ear of Your servant, saying, I build a house for you, therefore Your servant has found his heart to pray this prayer to You. ²⁸And now, Lord YHWH, You [are] God Himself, and Your words are truth, and You speak this goodness to Your servant, ²⁹and now, begin and bless the house of Your servant, to be before You for all time, for You, Lord YHWH, have spoken, and by Your blessing the house of Your servant is blessed for all time."

CHAPTER 8

¹And it comes to pass afterward that David strikes the Philistines, and humbles them, and David takes the bridle of the metropolis out of the hand of the Philistines. ²And he strikes Moab, and measures them with a line, causing them to lie down on the earth, and he measures two lines to put to death, and the fullness of the line to keep alive, and the Moabites are for servants to David, bearers of a present. ³And David strikes Hadadezer son of Rehob, king of Zobah, in his going to bring back his power by the River [Euphrates]; ⁴and David captures from him one thousand and seven hundred horsemen, and twenty thousand footmen, and David utterly destroys the whole of the chariateers; he leaves only one hundred of their chariateers. ⁵And Aram of Damascus comes to give help to Hadadezer king of Zobah, and David strikes twenty-two thousand men of Aram; ⁶and David puts garrisons in Aram of Damascus, and Aram is for a servant to David, carrying a present; and YHWH saves David wherever he has gone; ⁷and David takes the shields of gold which were on the servants of Hadadezer, and brings them to Jerusalem; ⁸and from Betah, and from Berothai, cities of Hadadezer, King David has taken very much bronze. ⁹And Toi king of Hamath hears that David has struck all the force of Hadadezer, ¹⁰and Toi sends his son Joram to King David to ask of him of welfare, and to bless him (because that he has fought against Hadadezer, and strikes him, for Hadadezer had been a man of wars [with] Toi), and in his hand have been vessels of silver, and vessels of gold, and vessels of bronze, ¹¹also King David sanctified them to YHWH, with the silver and the gold which he sanctified of all the nations which he subdued: ¹²of Aram, and of Moab, and of the sons of Ammon, and of the Philistines, and of Amalek, and of the spoil of Hadadezer son of Rehob king of Zobah. ¹³And David makes a name in his turning back from his striking Aram in the Valley of Salt—eighteen thousand; ¹⁴and he puts garrisons in Edom—he has put garrisons in all of Edom, and all Edom are servants to David; and YHWH saves David wherever he has gone. ¹⁵And David reigns over all Israel, and David is doing judgment and righteousness to all his people, ¹⁶and Joab son of Zeruiah [is] over the host, and Jehoshaphat son of Ahilud [is] remembrancer, ¹⁷and Zadok son of Ahitub, and Ahimelech son of Abiathar, [are] priests, and Seraiah [is] scribe, ¹⁸and Benaiah son of Jehoiada [is over] both the Cherethite and the Pelethite, and the sons of David have been ministers.

CHAPTER 9

¹And David says, "Is there yet any left of the house of Saul, and I do with him kindness because of Jonathan?" ²And the house of Saul has a servant, and his name [is] Ziba, and they call for him to David; and the king says to him, "Are you Ziba?" And he says, "Your servant." ³And the king says, "Is there not yet a man of the house of Saul, and I do with him the kindness of God?" And Ziba says to the king, "Jonathan has yet a son—lame." ⁴And the king says to him, "Where [is] he?" And Ziba says to the king, "Behold, he [is] in the house of Machir, son of Ammiel, in Behold-Debar." ⁵And King David sends, and takes him out of the house of Machir son of Ammiel, of Behold-Debar, ⁶and Mephibosheth son of Jonathan, son of Saul, comes to David, and falls on his face, and pays respect, and David says, "Mephibosheth"; and he says, "Behold, your servant." ⁷And David says to him, "Do not be afraid; for I certainly do with you kindness because of your father Jonathan, and have given back to you all the field of your father Saul, and you continually eat bread at my table." ⁸And he bows himself and says, "What

2 SAMUEL

[is] your servant, that you have turned to the dead dog—such as I?" ⁹And the king calls to Ziba servant of Saul and says to him, "All that was of Saul and of all his house, I have given to the son of your lord, ¹⁰and you have served the land for him, you and your sons, and your servants, and have brought in, and there has been bread for the son of your lord, and he has eaten it; and Mephibosheth, son of your lord, continually eats bread at my table"; and Ziba has fifteen sons and twenty servants. ¹¹And Ziba says to the king, "According to all that my lord the king commands his servant, so your servant does." "As for Mephibosheth," [says the king,] "he is eating at my table as one of the sons of the king." ¹²And Mephibosheth has a young son, and his name [is] Micha, and everyone dwelling in the house of Ziba [are] servants to Mephibosheth. ¹³And Mephibosheth is dwelling in Jerusalem, for he is continually eating at the table of the king, and he [is] lame [in] his two feet.

CHAPTER 10

¹And it comes to pass afterward, that the king of the sons of Ammon dies, and his son Hanun reigns in his stead, ²and David says, "I do kindness with Hanun son of Nahash, as his father did kindness with me"; and David sends to comfort him by the hand of his servants concerning his father, and the servants of David come into the land of the sons of Ammon. ³And the heads of the sons of Ammon say to their lord Hanun, "Is David honoring your father in your eyes because he has sent comforters to you? For has David not sent his servants to you to search the city, and to spy it, and to overthrow it?" ⁴And Hanun takes the servants of David, and shaves off the half of their beard, and cuts off their long robes in the midst—to their buttocks, and sends them away; ⁵and they declare [it] to David, and he sends to meet them, for the men have been greatly ashamed, and the king says, "Abide in Jericho until your beard springs up—then you have returned." ⁶And the sons of Ammon see that they have been abhorred by David, and the sons of Ammon send and hire Aram of Beth-Rehob, and Aram of Zoba, twenty thousand footmen, and the king of Maacah [with] one thousand men, and Ish-Tob [with] twelve thousand men; ⁷and David hears, and sends Joab, and all the host—the mighty men. ⁸And the sons of Ammon come out, and set in array [for] battle, at the opening of the gate, and Aram of Zoba, and Rehob, and Ish-Tob, and Maacah, [are] by themselves in the field; ⁹and Joab sees that the front of the battle has been to him before and behind, and he chooses [out] of all the chosen in Israel, and sets in array to meet Aram, ¹⁰and he has given the rest of the people into the hand of his brother Abishai, and sets in array to meet the sons of Ammon. ¹¹And he says, "If Aram is stronger than I, then you have been for salvation to me, and if the sons of Ammon are stronger than you, then I have come to give salvation to you; ¹²be strong and strengthen yourself for our people, and for the cities of our God, and YHWH does that which is good in His eyes." ¹³And Joab draws near, and the people who [are] with him, to battle against Aram, and they flee from his presence; ¹⁴and the sons of Ammon have seen that Aram has fled, and they flee from the presence of Abishai, and go into the city; and Joab turns back from the sons of Ammon, and comes to Jerusalem. ¹⁵And Aram sees that it is struck before Israel, and they are gathered together; ¹⁶and Hadadezer sends, and brings out Aram which [is] beyond the River, and they come to Helam, and Shobach, head of the host of Hadadezer, [is] before them. ¹⁷And it is declared to David, and he gathers all Israel, and passes over the Jordan, and comes to Helam, and Aram sets itself in array to meet David, and they fight with him; ¹⁸and Aram flees from the presence of Israel, and David slays seven hundred charioteers and forty thousand horsemen of Aram, and he has struck Shobach, [the] head of its host, and he dies there. ¹⁹And all the kings—servants of Hadadezer—see that they have been struck before Israel, and make peace with Israel, and serve them; and Aram is afraid to help the sons of Ammon anymore.

CHAPTER 11

¹And it comes to pass, at the revolution of the year—at the time of the going out of the messengers—that David sends Joab, and his servants with him, and all Israel, and they destroy the sons of Ammon, and lay siege against Rabbah, but David is dwelling in Jerusalem. ²And it comes to pass, at evening-time, that David rises from off his bed, and walks up and down on the roof of the king's house, and sees a woman bathing from the roof, and the woman [is] of very good appearance, ³and David sends and inquires about the woman, and [someone] says, "Is this not Bathsheba, daughter of Eliam, wife of Uriah the Hittite?" ⁴And David sends messengers, and takes her, and she comes to him, and he lies with her—and she is purifying herself from her uncleanness—and she turns back to her house; ⁵and the woman conceives, and sends, and declares [it] to David, and says, "I [am] conceiving." ⁶And David sends to Joab, [saying], "Send Uriah the Hittite to me," and Joab sends Uriah to David; ⁷and Uriah comes to him, and David asks of the prosperity of Joab, and of the prosperity of the people, and of the prosperity of the war. ⁸And David says to Uriah, "Go down to your house, and wash your feet"; and Uriah goes out of the king's house, and there goes out a gift from the king after him, ⁹and Uriah lies down at the opening of the king's house, with all the servants of his lord, and has not gone down to his house. ¹⁰And they declare [it] to David, saying, "Uriah has not gone down to his house"; and David says to Uriah, "Have you not come from a journey? Why have you not gone down to your house?" ¹¹And Uriah says to David, "The ark, and Israel, and Judah, are abiding in shelters, and my lord Joab, and the servants of my lord, are encamping on the face of the field; and should I go to my house to eat and to drink, and to lie with my wife? [By] your life and the life of your soul—if I do this thing." ¹²And David says to Uriah, "Also abide in this [place] today, and tomorrow I send you away"; and Uriah abides in Jerusalem on that day and on the next day, ¹³and David calls for him, and he eats before him, and drinks, and he causes him to drink, and he goes out in the evening to lie on his bed with the servants of his lord, and he has not gone down to his house. ¹⁴And it comes to pass in the morning that David writes a letter to Joab and sends [it] by the hand of Uriah; ¹⁵and he writes in the letter, saying, "Place Uriah in front of the face of the most severe battle, and you have turned back from after him, and he has been struck, and has died." ¹⁶And it comes to pass in Joab's watching of the city, that he appoints Uriah to the place where he knew that valiant men [were]; ¹⁷and the men of the city go out and fight with Joab, and [some] of the people, from the servants of David, fall; and Uriah the Hittite also dies. ¹⁸And Joab sends and declares to David all the matters of the war, ¹⁹and commands the messenger, saying, "At your finishing all the matters of the war to speak to the king, ²⁰then, it has been, if the king's fury ascends, and he has said to you, Why did you draw near to the city to fight? Did you not know that they shoot from off the wall? ²¹Who struck Abimelech son of Jerubbesheth? Did a woman not cast a piece of a rider from the wall on him, and he dies in Thebez? Why did you draw near to the wall? That you have said, Also—your servant Uriah the Hittite is dead." ²²And the messenger goes, and comes in, and declares to David all that with which Joab sent him, ²³and the messenger says to David, "Surely the men have been mighty against us, and come out to us into the field, and we are on them to the opening of the gate, ²⁴and those shooting shoot at your servants from off the wall, and [some] of the servants of the king are dead, and also, your servant Uriah the Hittite is dead." ²⁵And David says to the messenger, "Thus you say to Joab, Do not let this thing be evil in your eyes; for thus and thus the sword devours; strengthen your warfare against the city, and throw it down; so you strengthen him." ²⁶And the wife of Uriah hears that her husband Uriah [is] dead, and laments for her lord; ²⁷and the mourning passes by, and David sends and gathers her to his house, and she is to him for a wife, and bears a son to him; and the thing which David has done is evil in the eyes of YHWH.

CHAPTER 12

¹And YHWH sends Nathan to David, and he comes to him, and says to him: "Two men have been in one city, one rich and one poor. ²The rich has very many flocks and herds, ³but the poor one has nothing, except one little ewe-lamb which he has bought and keeps alive. And it grows up together with him and with his sons. It eats of his morsel, and it drinks from his cup, and it lies in his bosom, and it is as a daughter to him. ⁴And a traveler comes to the rich man, and he spares to take from his own flock, and from his own herd, to prepare for the traveling [man] who has come

to him; and he takes the ewe-lamb of the poor man and prepares it for the man who has come to him." ⁵And the anger of David burns against the man exceedingly, and he says to Nathan, "YHWH lives, surely the man who is doing this [is] a son of death, ⁶and [for] the ewe-lamb he repays fourfold, because that he has done this thing, and because that he had no pity." ⁷And Nathan says to David, "You [are] the man! Thus said YHWH, God of Israel: I anointed you for king over Israel, and I delivered you out of the hand of Saul; ⁸and I give to you the house of your lord, and the wives of your lord, into your bosom, and I give the house of Israel and Judah to you; and if [that is] too little, then I add such and such [things] to you. ⁹Why have you despised the word of YHWH, to do evil in His eyes? You have struck Uriah the Hittite by the sword, and you have taken his wife for a wife for yourself, and you have slain him by the sword of the sons of Ammon. ¹⁰And now, the sword does not turn aside from your house for all time, because you have despised Me, and take the wife of Uriah the Hittite to be for a wife for yourself; ¹¹thus said YHWH: Behold, I am raising up calamity against you, out of your [own] house, and have taken your wives before your eyes, and given [them] to your neighbor, and he has lain with your wives before the eyes of this sun; ¹²for you have done [it] in secret, and I do this thing before all Israel, and before the sun." ¹³And David says to Nathan, "I have sinned against YHWH." And Nathan says to David, "Also—YHWH has caused your sin to pass away; you do not die; ¹⁴only, because you have caused the enemies of YHWH to greatly despise by this thing, also—the son who is born to you surely dies." ¹⁵And Nathan goes to his house, and YHWH strikes the boy, whom the wife of Uriah has borne to David, and it is incurable; ¹⁶and David seeks God for the youth, and David keeps a fast, and has gone in and lodged, and lain on the earth. ¹⁷And [the] elderly of his house rise against him, to raise him up from the earth, and he has not been willing, nor has he eaten bread with them; ¹⁸and it comes to pass on the seventh day, that the boy dies, and the servants of David fear to declare to him that the boy is dead, for they said, "Behold, in the boy being alive we spoke to him, and he did not listen to our voice; and how do we say to him, The boy is dead? Then he has done evil." ¹⁹And David sees that his servants are whispering, and David understands that the boy is dead, and David says to his servants, "Is the boy dead?" And they say, "Dead." ²⁰And David rises from the earth, and bathes and anoints [himself], and changes his raiment, and comes into the house of YHWH, and bows himself, and comes to his house, and asks and they place bread for him, and he eats. ²¹And his servants say to him, "What [is] this thing you have done? Because of the living boy you have fasted and you weep, and when the boy is dead you have risen and eat bread." ²²And he says, "While the boy is alive I have fasted and I weep, for I said, Who knows [if] YHWH pities me and the boy has lived? ²³And now, he has died, why [is] this—I fast? Am I able to bring him back again? I am going to him, and he does not return to me." ²⁴And David comforts his wife Bathsheba, and goes in to her, and lies with her, and she bears a son, and he calls his name Solomon; and YHWH has loved him, ²⁵and sends by the hand of Nathan the prophet, and calls his name Jedidiah, because of YHWH. ²⁶And Joab fights against Rabbah of the sons of Ammon, and captures the royal city, ²⁷and Joab sends messengers to David and says, "I have fought against Rabbah—I have also captured the city of waters; ²⁸and now, gather the rest of the people, and encamp against the city, and capture it, lest I capture the city, and my name has been called on it." ²⁹And David gathers all the people, and goes to Rabbah, and fights against it, and captures it; ³⁰and he takes the crown of their king from off his head, and its weight [is] a talent of gold, and precious stones, and it is on the head of David; and he has brought out the spoil of the city—very much; ³¹and he has brought out the people who [are] in it, and sets [them] to the saw, and to cutting instruments of iron, and to axes of iron, and has caused them to pass over into the brick-kiln; and so he does to all the cities of the sons of Ammon; and David turns back, and all the people, to Jerusalem.

CHAPTER 13

¹And it comes to pass afterward that Absalom son of David has a beautiful sister, and her name [is] Tamar, and Amnon son of David loves her. ²And Amnon has distress—even to become sick, because of his sister Tamar, for she [is] a virgin, and it is hard in the eyes of Amnon to do anything to her. ³And Amnon has a friend, and his name [is] Jonadab, son of Shimeah, David's brother, and Jonadab [is] a very wise man, ⁴and says to him, "Why [are] you thus lean, O king's son, morning by morning? Do you not declare [it] to me?" And Amnon says to him, "Tamar—sister of my brother Absalom—I am loving." ⁵And Jonadab says to him, "Lie down on your bed, and feign yourself sick, and your father has come in to see you, and you have said to him: Please let my sister Tamar come in and give me bread to eat; and she has made the food before my eyes so that I see [it], and have eaten from her hand." ⁶And Amnon lies down, and feigns himself sick, and the king comes in to see him, and Amnon says to the king, "Please let my sister Tamar come, and she makes two cakes before my eyes, and I eat from her hand." ⁷And David sends to Tamar, to the house, saying, "Now go to the house of your brother Amnon and make food for him." ⁸And Tamar goes to the house of her brother Amnon, and he is lying down, and she takes the dough, and kneads, and makes cakes before his eyes, and cooks the cakes, ⁹and takes the frying-pan, and pours out before him, and he refuses to eat, and Amnon says, "Have everyone go out from me"; and everyone goes out from him. ¹⁰And Amnon says to Tamar, "Bring the food into the inner chamber, and I eat from your hand"; and Tamar takes the cakes that she has made and brings [them] to her brother Amnon [in] the inner chamber, ¹¹and she brings [them] near to him to eat, and he lays hold on her, and says to her, "Come, lie with me, my sister." ¹²And she says to him, "No, my brother, do not humble me, for it is not done so in Israel; do not do this folly. ¹³And I—to where do I cause my reproach to go? And you are as one of the fools in Israel; and now, please speak to the king; for he does not withhold me from you." ¹⁴And he has not been willing to listen to her voice, and is stronger than she, and humbles her, and lies with her. ¹⁵And Amnon hates her—a very great hatred—that greater [is] the hatred with which he has hated her than the love with which he loved her, and Amnon says to her, "Rise, go." ¹⁶And she says to him, "Because of the circumstances this evil is greater than the other that you have done with me—to send me away"; and he has not been willing to listen to her, ¹⁷and calls his young man, his servant, and says, "Now send this one away from me outside, and bolt the door after her." ¹⁸And a long coat [is] on her, for such upper robes daughters of the king who [are] virgins put on—and his servant takes her outside, and has bolted the door after her. ¹⁹And Tamar takes ashes for her head, and has torn the long coat that [is] on her, and puts her hand on her head, and goes, going on and crying; ²⁰and her brother Absalom says to her, "Has your brother Amnon been with you? And now, my sister, keep silent, he [is] your brother; do not set your heart to this thing"; and Tamar dwells—but desolate—in the house of her brother Absalom. ²¹And King David has heard all these things, and it is very displeasing to him; ²²and Absalom has not spoken with Amnon either evil or good, for Absalom is hating Amnon, because that he humbled his sister Tamar. ²³And it comes to pass, after two years of days, that Absalom has shearers in Ba'al-Hazor, which [is] near Ephraim, and Absalom calls for all the sons of the king. ²⁴And Absalom comes to the king and says, "Now behold, your servant has shearers, please let the king go—and his servants—with your servant." ²⁵And the king says to Absalom, "No, my son, please let us not all go, and we are not too heavy on you"; and he presses on him, and he has not been willing to go, and he blesses him. ²⁶And Absalom says, "If not, please let my brother Amnon go with us"; and the king says to him, "Why does he go with you?" ²⁷And Absalom urges for him, and he sends Amnon and all the sons of the king with him. ²⁸And Absalom commands his young men, saying, "Now see, when the heart of Amnon [is] glad with wine, and I have said to you, Strike Amnon, that you have put him to death; do not fear; is it not because I have commanded you? Be strong, indeed, become sons of valor." ²⁹And the young men of Absalom do to Amnon as Absalom commanded, and all the sons of the king rise, and they ride, each on his mule, and flee. ³⁰And it comes to pass—they [are] in the way—and the report has come to David, saying, "Absalom has struck all the sons of the king, and there is not left [even] one of them"; ³¹and the king rises, and tears his garments, and lies

on the earth, and all his servants are standing by [with] torn garments. ³²And Jonadab son of Shimeah, David's brother, answers and says, "Do not let my lord say, The whole of the young men, the sons of the king, they have put to death; for Amnon alone [is] dead, for it has been appointed by the command of Absalom from the day of his humbling his sister Tamar; ³³and now, do not let my lord the king lay the word to his heart, saying, All the sons of the king have died, for Amnon alone [is] dead." ³⁴And Absalom flees, and the young man who is watching lifts up his eyes and looks, and behold, many people are coming by the way behind him, on the side of the hill. ³⁵And Jonadab says to the king, "Behold, the sons of the king have come; as the word of your servant, so it has been." ³⁶And it comes to pass at his finishing to speak, that behold, the sons of the king have come, and they lift up their voice, and weep, and also the king and all his servants have wept—a very great weeping. ³⁷And Absalom has fled, and goes to Talmai, son of Ammihud, king of Geshur, and [David] mourns for his son all the days. ³⁸And Absalom has fled, and goes to Geshur, and is there [for] three years; ³⁹and King David determines to go out to Absalom, for he has been comforted for Amnon, for [he is] dead.

CHAPTER 14

¹And Joab son of Zeruiah knows that the heart of the king [is] on Absalom, ²and Joab sends to Tekoah, and takes a wise woman from there, and says to her, "Please feign yourself a mourner, and now put on garments of mourning, and do not anoint yourself with oil, and you have been as a woman mourning for the dead [for] these many days, ³and you have gone to the king, and spoken to him, according to this word"; and Joab puts the words into her mouth. ⁴And the woman of Tekoah speaks to the king, and falls on her face to the earth, and pays respect, and says, "Save, O king." ⁵And the king says to her, "What do you [want]?" And she says, "I [am] truly a widow woman, and my husband dies, ⁶and your maidservant has two sons; and both of them strive in a field, and there is no deliverer between them, and one strikes the other, and puts him to death; ⁷and behold, the whole family has risen against your maidservant, and say, Give up him who strikes his brother, and we put him to death for the life of his brother whom he has slain, and we also destroy the heir; and they have quenched my coal which is left—so as not to set a name and remnant on the face of the ground for my husband." ⁸And the king says to the woman, "Go to your house, and I give charge concerning you." ⁹And the woman of Tekoah says to the king, "On me, my lord, O king, [is] the iniquity, and on the house of my father; and the king and his throne [are] innocent." ¹⁰And the king says, "He who speaks to you, and you have brought him to me, then he does not add to come against you anymore." ¹¹And she says, "Please let the king remember by your God YHWH, that the redeemer of blood does not add to destroy, and they do not destroy my son"; and he says, "YHWH lives; if there falls [even one] hair of your son to the earth." ¹²And the woman says, "Please let your maidservant speak a word to my lord the king"; and he says, "Speak." ¹³And the woman says, "And why have you thought thus concerning the people of God? Indeed, the king is speaking this thing as a guilty one, in that the king has not brought back his outcast; ¹⁴for we surely die, and [are] as water which is running down to the earth, which is not gathered, and God does not accept a person, and has devised plans in that the outcast is not outcast by Him. ¹⁵And now that I have come to speak this word to my lord the king, [it is] because the people made me afraid, and your maidservant says, Please let me speak to the king; it may be the king does the word of his handmaid, ¹⁶for the king listens to deliver his handmaid out of the paw of the man [seeking] to destroy me and my son together out of the inheritance of God, ¹⁷and your maidservant says, Please let the word of my lord the king be for ease; for as a messenger of God so [is] my lord, the king, to understand the good and the evil; and your God YHWH is with you." ¹⁸And the king answers and says to the woman, "Please do not hide from me the thing that I am asking you"; and the woman says, "Please let my lord the king speak." ¹⁹And the king says, "Is the hand of Joab with you in all this?" And the woman answers and says, "Your soul lives, my lord, O king, none [turn] to the right or to the left from all that my lord the king has spoken; for your servant Joab commanded me, and he put all these words in the mouth of your maidservant. ²⁰Your servant Joab has done this thing in order to bring around the appearance of the thing, and my lord [is] wise, according to the wisdom of a messenger of God, to know all that [is] in the land." ²¹And the king says to Joab, "Now behold, you have done this thing; and go, bring back the young man Absalom." ²²And Joab falls on his face to the earth, and pays respect, and blesses the king, and Joab says, "Today your servant has known that I have found grace in your eyes, my lord, O king, in that the king has done the word of his servant." ²³And Joab rises and goes to Geshur, and brings in Absalom to Jerusalem, ²⁴and the king says, "Let him turn around to his house, and he does not see my face." And Absalom turns around to his house, and he has not seen the face of the king. ²⁵And there was no man [so] beautiful in all Israel like Absalom, to praise greatly; from the sole of his foot even to his crown there was no blemish in him; ²⁶and in his shaving his head—and it has been at the end of year by year that he shaves [it], for it [is] heavy on him, and he has shaved it—he has even weighed out the hair of his head—two hundred shekels by the king's weight. ²⁷And there are born to Absalom three sons and one daughter, and her name [is] Tamar; she was a woman of beautiful appearance. ²⁸And Absalom dwells in Jerusalem [for] two years of days, and he has not seen the face of the king; ²⁹and Absalom sends to Joab, to send him to the king, and he has not been willing to come to him; and he sends again a second time, and he has not been willing to come. ³⁰And he says to his servants, "See, the portion of Joab [is] by the side of mine, and he has barley there; go and burn it with fire"; and the servants of Absalom burn the portion with fire. ³¹And Joab rises and comes to Absalom in the house, and says to him, "Why have your servants burned the portion that I have with fire?" ³²And Absalom says to Joab, "Behold, I sent to you, saying, Come here, and I send you to the king to say, Why have I come in from Geshur? [It was] good for me while I [was] there—and now, let me see the king's face, and if there is iniquity in me then you have put me to death." ³³And Joab comes to the king, and declares [it] to him, and he calls to Absalom, and he comes to the king, and bows himself to him, on his face, to the earth, before the king, and the king gives a kiss to Absalom.

CHAPTER 15

¹And it comes to pass afterward that Absalom prepares a chariot and horses for himself, and fifty men are running before him; ²and Absalom has risen early, and stood by the side of the way of the gate, and it comes to pass, every man who has a pleading to come to the king for judgment, that Absalom calls to him and says, "Of what city [are] you?" And he says, "Your servant [is] of one of the tribes of Israel." ³And Absalom says to him, "See, your matters [are] good and straightforward—and there is none listening to you from the king." ⁴And Absalom says, "Who makes me judge in the land, that every man who has a plea and judgment comes to me? Then I have declared him righteous." ⁵And it has come to pass, in the drawing near of anyone to bow himself to him, that he has put forth his hand, and laid hold on him, and given a kiss to him; ⁶and Absalom does according to this thing to all Israel who come in for judgment to the king, and Absalom steals the heart of the men of Israel. ⁷And it comes to pass, at the end of forty years, that Absalom says to the king, "Please let me go, and I complete my vow that I vowed to YHWH in Hebron, ⁸for your servant has vowed a vow in my dwelling in Geshur, in Aram, saying, If YHWH certainly brings me back to Jerusalem, then I have served YHWH." ⁹And the king says to him, "Go in peace"; and he rises and goes to Hebron, ¹⁰and Absalom sends spies through all the tribes of Israel, saying, "At your hearing the voice of the horn, then you have said, Absalom has reigned in Hebron." ¹¹And two hundred men have gone with Absalom out of Jerusalem, invited ones, and they are going in their simplicity, and have not known anything; ¹²and Absalom sends Ahithophel the Gilonite, a counselor of David, out of his city, out of Gilo, in his sacrificing sacrifices; and the conspiracy is strong, and the people are going and increasing with Absalom. ¹³And he who is declaring tidings comes to David, saying, "The heart of the men of Israel has been after Absalom." ¹⁴And David says to all his servants who [are] with him in Jerusalem, "Rise, and we flee, for we have no escape from the face of Absalom; hurry to go,

2 SAMUEL

lest he hurries, and has overtaken us, and forced evil on us, and struck the city by the mouth of the sword." ¹⁵And the servants of the king say to the king, "According to all that my lord the king chooses—behold, your servants do." ¹⁶And the king goes out, and all his household at his feet, and the king leaves ten women—concubines—to keep the house. ¹⁷And the king goes out, and all the people at his feet, and they stand still at the farthest off house. ¹⁸And all his servants are passing on at his side, and all the Cherethite, and all the Pelethite, and all the Gittites, six hundred men who came at his feet from Gath, are passing on at the front of the king. ¹⁹And the king says to Ittai the Gittite, "Why do you go—you also—with us? Return and abide with the king, for you [are] a stranger, and also an exile, you—to your place. ²⁰Your coming in [was only] yesterday, and should I move you to go with us today, since I am going over [to] where [I do not know where] I am going? Return, and take your brothers back. Kindness and truth [be] with you." ²¹And Ittai answers the king and says, "YHWH lives, and my lord the king lives, surely in the place where my lord the king is—if for death, if for life, surely your servant is there." ²²And David says to Ittai, "Go and pass over"; and Ittai the Gittite passes over, and all his men, and all the infants who [are] with him. ²³And all the land is weeping [with] a great voice, and all the people are passing over; and the king is passing over through the Brook of Kidron, and all the people are passing over on the front of the way of the wilderness; ²⁴and behold, also Zadok, and all the Levites with him, are carrying the Ark of the Covenant of God, and they make the Ark of God firm, and Abiathar goes up, until the completion of all the people to pass over out of the city. ²⁵And the king says to Zadok, "Take back the Ark of God to the city; if I find grace in the eyes of YHWH, then He has brought me back, and shown me it and His habitation; ²⁶and if thus He says, I have not delighted in you; here I [am], He does to me as [is] good in His eyes." ²⁷And the king says to Zadok the priest, "Are you a seer? Return to the city in peace, and your son Ahimaaz, and Jonathan son of Abiathar, your two sons with you; ²⁸see, I am lingering in the plains of the wilderness until the coming in of a word from you to declare to me." ²⁹And Zadok takes back—and Abiathar—the Ark of God to Jerusalem, and they abide there. ³⁰And David is going up in the ascent of the [Mount of] Olives, going up and weeping, and he has the head covered, and he is going barefooted, and all the people who [are] with him have each covered his head, and have gone up, going up and weeping; ³¹and David declared, saying, "Ahithophel [is] among the conspirators with Absalom"; and David says, "Please make the counsel of Ahithophel foolish, O YHWH." ³²And it comes to pass, David has come to the top, where he bows himself to God, and behold, Hushai the Archite [is there] to meet him, [with] his coat torn, and earth on his head; ³³and David says to him, "If you have passed on with me then you have been for a burden on me, ³⁴and if you return to the city and have said to Absalom, I am your servant, O king; I [am] also servant of your father until now, and presently, I [am] also your servant; then you have made void the counsel of Ahithophel for me; ³⁵and are Zadok and Abiathar the priests not with you there? And it has been, the whole of the matter that you hear from the house of the king you declare to Zadok and to Abiathar the priests. ³⁶Behold, their two sons [are] there with them: Ahimaaz to Zadok, and Jonathan to Abiathar, and you have sent to me by their hand anything that you hear." ³⁷And Hushai, David's friend, comes to the city, and Absalom comes to Jerusalem.

CHAPTER 16

¹And David has passed on a little from the top, and behold, Ziba, servant of Mephibosheth, [is there] to meet him, and a couple of donkeys [are] saddled, and on them [are] two hundred loaves, and one hundred bunches of raisins, and one hundred of summer-fruit, and a bottle of wine. ²And the king says to Ziba, "What [are] these to you?" And Ziba says, "The donkeys for the household of the king to ride on, and the bread and the summer-fruit for the young men to eat, and the wine for the wearied to drink in the wilderness." ³And the king says, "And where [is] the son of your lord?" And Ziba says to the king, "Behold, he is abiding in Jerusalem, for he said, Today the house of Israel gives back the kingdom of my father to me." ⁴And the king says to Ziba, "Behold, all that Mephibosheth has [is] for you"; and Ziba says, "I have bowed myself—I find grace in your eyes, my lord, O king." ⁵And King David has come to Bahurim, and behold, a man there is coming out, of the family of the house of Saul, and his name [is] Shimei, son of Gera, he comes out, coming out and reviling; ⁶and he stones David with stones, and all the servants of King David, and all the people, and all the mighty men on his right and on his left. ⁷And thus said Shimei in his reviling: "Go out, go out, O man of blood, and man of worthlessness! ⁸YHWH has turned back on you all the blood of the house of Saul, in whose stead you have reigned, and YHWH gives the kingdom into the hand of your son Absalom; and behold, you [are] in your evil, for you [are] a man of blood." ⁹And Abishai son of Zeruiah says to the king, "Why does this dead dog revile my lord the king? Please let me pass over and I turn aside his head." ¹⁰And the king says, "And what do I [have to do] with you, O sons of Zeruiah? For let him revile; even because YHWH has said to him, Revile David; and who says, Why have You done so?" ¹¹And David says to Abishai, and to all his servants, "Behold, my son who came out of my bowels is seeking my life, and also surely now the Benjamite; leave him alone, and let him revile, for YHWH has commanded [so] to him; ¹²it may be YHWH looks on my affliction, and YHWH has turned back good to me for his reviling this day." ¹³And David goes with his men in the way, and Shimei is going at the side of the hill opposite him, going on, and he reviles, and stones with stones close by him, and has dusted with dust. ¹⁴And the king comes in, and all the people who [are] with him, wearied, and they are refreshed there. ¹⁵And Absalom and all the people, the men of Israel, have come to Jerusalem, and Ahithophel with him, ¹⁶and it comes to pass, when Hushai the Archite, David's friend, has come to Absalom, that Hushai says to Absalom, "Let the king live! Let the king live!" ¹⁷And Absalom says to Hushai, "[Is] this your kindness with your friend? Why have you not gone with your friend?" ¹⁸And Hushai says to Absalom, "No, for he whom YHWH has chosen, and this people, even all the men of Israel, I am his, and I abide with him; ¹⁹and secondly, for whom do I labor? Is it not before his son? As I served before your father, so I am before you." ²⁰And Absalom says to Ahithophel, "Give counsel for yourself [for] what we do." ²¹And Ahithophel says to Absalom, "Go in to the concubines of your father, whom he left to keep the house, and all Israel has heard that you have been abhorred by your father, and the hands of all who [are] with you have been strong." ²²And they spread out the tent for Absalom on the roof, and Absalom goes in to the concubines of his father before the eyes of all Israel. ²³And the counsel of Ahithophel which he counseled in those days [is] as [when] one inquires at the word of God; so [is] all the counsel of Ahithophel both to David and to Absalom.

CHAPTER 17

¹And Ahithophel said to Absalom, "Please let me choose twelve thousand men, and I arise and pursue after David tonight, ²and come on him, and he [will be] weary and feeble-handed, and I have caused him to tremble, and all the people who [are] with him have fled, and I have struck the king by himself, ³and I bring back all the people to you—as the turning back of the whole [except] the man whom you are seeking—[then] all the people are [at] peace." ⁴And the word is right in the eyes of Absalom, and in the eyes of all [the] elderly of Israel. ⁵And Absalom says, "Now call for Hushai the Archite also, and we hear what [is] in his mouth—even he." ⁶And Hushai comes to Absalom, and Absalom speaks to him, saying, "According to this word Ahithophel has spoken; do we do his word? If not, you—speak." ⁷And Hushai says to Absalom, "The counsel that Ahithophel has counseled [is] not good at this time." ⁸And Hushai says, "You have known your father and his men, that they [are] heroes, and they are bitter in soul as a bereaved bear in a field, and your father [is] a man of war, and does not lodge with the people; ⁹behold, now, he is hidden in one of the pits, or in one of the places, and it has been at the falling among them at the commencement, that the hearer has heard and said, There has been a slaughter among the people who [are] after Absalom; ¹⁰and he also, the son of valor, whose heart [is] as the heart of the lion, utterly melts, for all Israel knows that your father is a hero, and those with him [are] sons of valor. ¹¹So that I have counseled: let all Israel be diligently gathered to you, from Dan even to Beer-

Sheba, as the sand that [is] by the sea for multitude, and you yourself are going in the midst; ¹²and we have come to him in one of the places where he is found, and we [are] on him as the dew falls on the ground, and there has not been left of him and of all the men who [are] with him even one. ¹³And if he is gathered to a city, then they have caused all Israel to carry ropes to that city, and we have drawn it to the brook until there has not even been found a stone there." ¹⁴And Absalom says—and all the men of Israel, "The counsel of Hushai the Archite [is] better than the counsel of Ahithophel"; and YHWH willed to make void the good counsel of Ahithophel for the sake of YHWH's bringing the calamity to Absalom. ¹⁵And Hushai says to Zadok and to Abiathar the priests, "Thus and thus Ahithophel has counseled Absalom and the elderly of Israel, and thus and thus I have counseled; ¹⁶and now, send quickly, and declare [it] to David, saying, Do not lodge in the plains of the wilderness tonight, and also, certainly pass over, lest there is a swallowing up of the king and of all the people who are with him." ¹⁷And Jonathan and Ahimaaz are standing at En-Rogel, and the maidservant has gone and declared [it] to them—and they go and have declared [it] to King David—for they are not able to be seen to go into the city. ¹⁸And a youth sees them, and declares [it] to Absalom; and both of them go on quickly, and come to the house of a man in Bahurim, and he has a well in his court, and they go down there, ¹⁹and the woman takes and spreads the covering over the face of the well, and spreads the ground grain on it, and the thing has not been known. ²⁰And the servants of Absalom come to the woman at the house, and say, "Where [are] Ahimaaz and Jonathan?" And the woman says to them, "They passed over the brook of water"; and they seek, and have not found, and return to Jerusalem. ²¹And it comes to pass, after their going on, that they come up out of the well, and go and declare [it] to King David, and say to David, "Rise, and pass over the waters quickly, for thus has Ahithophel counseled against you." ²²And David rises, and all the people who [are] with him, and they pass over the Jordan, until the morning light, until not one has been lacking who has not passed over the Jordan. ²³And Ahithophel has seen that his counsel was not done, and he saddles the donkey, and rises and goes to his house, to his city, and gives charge to his household, and strangles himself, and dies, and he is buried in the burying-place of his father. ²⁴And David came to Mahanaim, and Absalom passed over the Jordan, he and all the men of Israel with him; ²⁵and Absalom has set Amasa over the host instead of Joab, and Amasa [is] a man's son whose name is Ithra the Israeli who has gone in to Abigail, daughter of Nahash, sister of Zeruiah, mother of Joab; ²⁶and Israel encamps with Absalom [in] the land of Gilead. ²⁷And it comes to pass at the coming in of David to Mahanaim, that Shobi son of Nahash, from Rabbah of the sons of Ammon, and Machir son of Ammiel, from Behold-Debar, and Barzillai the Gileadite, from Rogelim, ²⁸[have brought] bed, and basin, and earthen vessel, and wheat, and barley, and flour, and roasted [grain], and beans, and lentiles, and roasted [pulse], ²⁹and honey, and butter, and sheep, and cheese of cows; they have brought [these] near for David, and for the people who [are] with him to eat, for they said, "Your people [are] hungry, and weary, and thirsty, in the wilderness."

CHAPTER 18

¹And David inspects the people who [are] with him, and sets over them heads of thousands and heads of hundreds, ²and David sends the third of the people by the hand of Joab, and the third by the hand of Abishai, son of Zeruiah, brother of Joab, and the third by the hand of Ittai the Gittite, and the king says to the people, "I certainly go out—I also—with you." ³And the people say, "You do not go out, for if we utterly flee, they do not set [their] heart on us; and if half of us die, they do not set [their] heart to us—for [you are] now like ten thousand of us; and now, [it is] better that you are for a helper to us from the city." ⁴And the king says to them, "That which is good in your eyes I do"; and the king stands at the side of the gate, and all the people have gone out by hundreds and by thousands, ⁵and the king charges Joab, and Abishai, and Ittai, saying, "[Deal] gently—for me, for the youth, for Absalom"; and all the people heard in the king's charging all the heads concerning Absalom. ⁶And the people go out into the field to meet Israel, and the battle is in a forest of Ephraim; ⁷and the people of Israel are struck there before the servants of David, and the striking there is great on that day—twenty thousand; ⁸and the battle there is scattered over the face of all the land, and the forest multiplies to devour among the people more than those whom the sword has devoured in that day. ⁹And Absalom meets before the servants of David, and Absalom is riding on the mule, and the mule comes in under an entangled bough of the great oak, and his head takes hold on the oak, and he is placed between the heavens and the earth, and the mule that [is] under him has passed on. ¹⁰And one man sees, and declares [it] to Joab, and says, "Behold, I saw Absalom hanging in an oak." ¹¹And Joab says to the man who is declaring [it] to him, "And behold, you have seen—and why did you not strike him there to the earth—and [it would be] on me to give to you ten pieces of silver and one girdle?" ¹²And the man says to Joab, "Indeed, though I am weighing on my hand one thousand pieces of silver, I do not put forth my hand to the son of the king; for in our ears the king has charged you, and Abishai, and Ittai, saying, Observe who [is] against the youth—against Absalom; ¹³or I had done a vain thing against my soul, and no matter is hid from the king, and you would station yourself opposite from [me]." ¹⁴And Joab says, "[It is] not right [that] I linger before you"; and he takes three darts in his hand, and strikes them into the heart of Absalom, while he [is] alive, in the midst of the oak. ¹⁵And they go around—ten youths carrying weapons of Joab—and strike Absalom, and put him to death. ¹⁶And Joab blows with a horn, and the people turn back from pursuing after Israel, for Joab has kept back the people; ¹⁷and they take Absalom and cast him into the great pit in the forest, and set up a very great heap of stones over him, and all Israel has fled—each to his tent. ¹⁸And Absalom has taken, and sets up for himself in his life, the standing-pillar that [is] in the king's valley, for he said, "I have no son to cause my name to be remembered"; and he calls the standing-pillar by his own name, and it is called "The Monument of Absalom" to this day. ¹⁹And Ahimaaz son of Zadok said, "Please let me run, and I bear the king tidings, for YHWH has delivered him out of the hand of his enemies"; ²⁰and Joab says to him, "You are not a man of tidings this day, but you have borne tidings on another day, and this day you do not bear tidings, because the king's son [is] dead." ²¹And Joab says to Cushi, "Go, declare to the king that which you have seen"; and Cushi bows himself to Joab, and runs. ²²And Ahimaaz son of Zadok adds again and says to Joab, "And whatever it is, please let me run, I also, after the Cushite." And Joab says, "Why [is] this—you are running, my son, and [there are] no tidings found from you?" ²³"And whatever happens," he said, "let me run." And he says to him, "Run"; and Ahimaaz runs the way of the circuit, and passes by the Cushite. ²⁴And David is sitting between the two gates, and the watchman goes to the roof of the gate, to the wall, and lifts up his eyes, and looks, and behold, a man running by himself. ²⁵And the watchman calls, and declares [it] to the king, and the king says, "If [he is] by himself, tidings [are] in his mouth"; and he comes, coming on and drawing near. ²⁶And the watchman sees another man running, and the watchman calls to the gatekeeper, and says, "Behold, a man running by himself"; and the king says, "This one is also bearing tidings." ²⁷And the watchman says, "I see the running of the first as the running of Ahimaaz son of Zadok." And the king says, "This [is] a good man, and he comes with good tidings." ²⁸And Ahimaaz calls and says to the king, "Peace"; and he bows himself to the king, on his face, to the earth, and says, "Blessed [is] your God YHWH who has shut up the men who lifted up their hand against my lord the king." ²⁹And the king says, "Peace to the youth—for Absalom?" And Ahimaaz says, "I saw the great multitude, at the sending away of the servant of the king, even your servant [by] Joab, and I have not known what [it is]." ³⁰And the king says, "Turn around, station yourself here"; and he turns around and stands still. ³¹And behold, the Cushite has come, and the Cushite says, "Let tidings be proclaimed, my lord, O king; for today YHWH has delivered you out of the hand of all those rising up against you." ³²And the king says to the Cushite, "Peace to the youth—for Absalom?" And the Cushite says, "Let them be—as the youth—the enemies of my lord the king, and all who have risen up against you for evil." ³³And the king trembles, and goes up on the upper chamber of the gate, and weeps,

and thus he has said in his going, "My son Absalom! My son! My son Absalom! Oh that I had died for you, Absalom, my son, my son!"

CHAPTER 19

¹And it is declared to Joab, "Behold, the king is weeping and mourning for Absalom"; ²and the salvation on that day becomes mourning to all the people, for the people have heard on that day, saying, "The king has been grieved for his son." ³And the people steals away, on that day, to go into the city, as the people steal away, who are ashamed, in their fleeing in battle; ⁴and the king has covered his face, indeed, the king cries [with] a loud voice, "My son Absalom! Absalom, my son, my son!" ⁵And Joab comes into the house to the king and says, "Today you have put to shame the faces of all your servants, those delivering your life today, and the life of your sons, and of your daughters, and the life of your wives, and the life of your concubines, ⁶to love your enemies, and to hate those loving you, for today you have declared that you have no princes and servants, for today I have known that if Absalom [were] alive, and all of us dead today, that then it were right in your eyes. ⁷And now, rise, go out and speak to the heart of your servants, for I have sworn by YHWH, that [if] you are not going out—there does not lodge a man with you tonight; and this [is] worse for you than all the evil that has come on you from your youth until now." ⁸And the king rises, and sits in the gate, and they have declared to all the people, saying, "Behold, the king is sitting in the gate"; and all the people come in before the king, and Israel has fled, each to his tents. ⁹And it comes to pass, all the people are contending through all the tribes of Israel, saying, "The king delivered us out of the hand of our enemies, indeed, he himself delivered us out of the hand of the Philistines, and now he has fled out of the land because of Absalom, ¹⁰and Absalom whom we anointed over us [is] dead in battle, and now, why are you silent—to bring back the king?" ¹¹And King David sent to Zadok and to Abiathar the priests, saying, "Speak to [the] elderly of Judah, saying, Why are you last to bring back the king to his house, since the word of all Israel has come to the king, to his house; ¹²you [are] my brothers, you [are] my bone and my flesh, and why are you last to bring back the king? ¹³And say to Amasa, Are you not my bone and my flesh? Thus God does to me, and thus He adds, if you are not head of the host before me instead of Joab [for] all the days." ¹⁴And he inclines the heart of all the men of Judah as one man, and they send to the king, "Return, you and all your servants." ¹⁵And the king turns back, and comes to the Jordan, and Judah has come to Gilgal, to go to meet the king, to bring the king over the Jordan, ¹⁶and Shimei son of Gera, the Benjamite, who [is] from Bahurim, hurries, and comes down with the men of Judah, to meet King David, ¹⁷and one thousand men [are] with him from Benjamin, and Ziba servant of the house of Saul, and his fifteen sons and his twenty servants with him, and they have gone prosperously over the Jordan before the king. ¹⁸And the ferry-boat has passed over to carry over the household of the king, and to do that which [is] good in his eyes, and Shimei son of Gera has fallen before the king in his passing over into the Jordan, ¹⁹and he says to the king, "Do not let my lord impute iniquity to me; neither remember that which your servant did perversely in the day that my lord the king went out from Jerusalem—for the king to set [it] to his heart; ²⁰for your servant has known that I have sinned; and behold, I have come today, first of all the house of Joseph, to go down to meet my lord the king." ²¹And Abishai son of Zeruiah answers and says, "Is Shimei not put to death for this—because he reviled the anointed of YHWH?" ²²And David says, "And what do I [have to do] with you, O sons of Zeruiah, that today you are for an adversary to me? Is any man put to death in Israel today? For have I not known that today I [am] king over Israel?" ²³And the king says to Shimei, "You do not die"; and the king swears to him. ²⁴And Mephibosheth son of Saul has come down to meet the king—and he did not prepare his feet, nor did he prepare his upper lip, indeed, he did not wash his garments, even from the day of the going away of the king, until the day that he came in peace— ²⁵and it comes to pass, when he has come to Jerusalem to meet the king, that the king says to him, "Why did you not go with me, Mephibosheth?" ²⁶And he says, "My lord, O king, my servant deceived me, for your servant said, I saddle the donkey for myself, and ride on it, and go with the king, for your servant [is] lame; ²⁷and he utters slander against your servant to my lord the king, and my lord the king [is] as a messenger of God; and do that which is good in your eyes, ²⁸for all the house of my father have been nothing except men of death before my lord the king, and you set your servant among those eating at your table, and what right do I have anymore—even to cry anymore to the king?" ²⁹And the king says to him, "Why do you speak anymore of your matters? I have said, You and Ziba—share the field." ³⁰And Mephibosheth says to the king, "Indeed, let him take the whole, after that my lord the king has come in peace to his house." ³¹And Barzillai the Gileadite has gone down from Rogelim, and passes over the Jordan with the king, to send him away over the Jordan; ³²and Barzillai [is] very aged, a son of eighty years, and he has sustained the king in his abiding in Mahanaim, for he [is] a very great man; ³³and the king says to Barzillai, "Pass over with me, and I have sustained you in Jerusalem with me." ³⁴And Barzillai says to the king, "How many [are] the days of the years of my life, that I go up with the king to Jerusalem? ³⁵I [am] a son of eighty years today; do I know between good and evil? Does your servant taste that which I am eating, and that which I drink? Do I listen anymore to the voice of male and female singers? And why is your servant for a burden to my lord the king anymore? ³⁶As a little thing, your servant passes over the Jordan with the king, and why does the king repay me this repayment? ³⁷Please let your servant turn back again, and I die in my own city, near the burying-place of my father and of my mother—and behold, your servant Chimham, let him pass over with my lord the king, and do to him that which [is] good in your eyes." ³⁸And the king says, "Chimham goes over with me, and I do to him that which [is] good in your eyes, indeed, all that you fix on me I do to you." ³⁹And all the people pass over the Jordan, and the king has passed over, and the king gives a kiss to Barzillai, and blesses him, and he turns back to his place. ⁴⁰And the king passes over to Gilgal, and Chimham has passed over with him, and all the people of Judah, and they bring over the king, and also the half of the people of Israel. ⁴¹And behold, all the men of Israel are coming to the king, and they say to the king, "Why have our brothers, the men of Judah, stolen you—and they bring the king and his household over the Jordan, and all the men of David with him?" ⁴²And all the men of Judah answer against the men of Israel, "Because the king [is] near to us, and why [is] this [that] you are displeased about this matter? Have we eaten of the king's [substance] at all? Has he lifted up a gift to us?" ⁴³And the men of Israel answer the men of Judah, and say, "We have ten parts in the king, and also more than you in David; and why have you lightly esteemed us, that our word has not been first to bring back our king?" And the word of the men of Judah is sharper than the word of the men of Israel.

CHAPTER 20

¹And there happened to be a man of worthlessness there, and his name [is] Sheba, son of Bichri, a Benjamite, and he blows with a horn and says, "We have no portion in David, and we have no inheritance in the son of Jesse; each [goes] to his tents, O Israel." ²And every man of Israel goes up from after David, after Sheba son of Bichri, and the men of Judah have cleaved to their king, from the Jordan even to Jerusalem. ³And David comes to his house at Jerusalem. And the king takes the ten women-concubines whom he had left to keep the house, and puts them in a house of ward and sustains them, and he has not gone in to them, and they are shut up to the day of their death, living in widowhood. ⁴And the king says to Amasa, "Call the men of Judah for me [within] three days, and you, stand here," ⁵and Amasa goes to call Judah, and tarries beyond the appointed time that he had appointed him; ⁶and David says to Abishai, "Now Sheba son of Bichri does evil to us more than Absalom; you, take the servants of your lord, and pursue after him, lest he has found fortified cities for himself, and delivered himself [from] our eye." ⁷And the men of Joab go out after him, and the Cherethite, and the Pelethite, and all the mighty men, and they go out from Jerusalem to pursue after Sheba son of Bichri; ⁸they [are] near the great stone that [is] in Gibeon, and Amasa has gone before them, and Joab [is] girded; he has put his long robe on him, and on it a girdle—a sword [is] fastened on his loins in its sheath; and he has gone out, and it falls. ⁹And Joab says to Amasa, "Are you [in] peace,

my brother?" And the right hand of Joab lays hold on the beard of Amasa to give a kiss to him; ¹⁰and Amasa has not been watchful of the sword that [is] in the hand of Joab, and he strikes him with it to the fifth [rib], and sheds out his bowels to the earth, and he has not repeated [it] to him, and he dies; and Joab and his brother Abishai have pursued after Sheba son of Bichri. ¹¹And a man has stood by him, of the young men of Joab, and says, "He who has delight in Joab, and he who [is] for David—after Joab!" ¹²And Amasa is rolling himself in blood, in the midst of the highway, and the man sees that all the people have stood still, and he brings around Amasa out of the highway to the field, and casts a garment over him when he has seen that everyone who has come by him has stood still. ¹³When he has been removed out of the highway, every man has passed on after Joab, to pursue after Sheba son of Bichri. ¹⁴And he passes over through all the tribes of Israel to Abel, and to Beth-Maachah, and to all the Berites, and they are assembled, and also go in after him, ¹⁵and they go in and lay siege against him, in Abel of Beth-Maachah, and cast up a mound against the city, and it stands in a trench, and all the people who are [are] with Joab are destroying, to cause the wall to fall. ¹⁶And a wise woman calls out of the city, "Hear! Hear! Please say to Joab, Come near here, and I speak to you." ¹⁷And he comes near to her, and the woman says, "Are you Joab?" And he says, "I [am]." And she says to him, "Hear the words of your handmaid"; and he says, "I am hearing." ¹⁸And she speaks, saying, "They spoke often in former times, saying, Let them diligently inquire at Abel, and so they finished. ¹⁹I [am] of the peaceable, faithful ones of Israel; you are seeking to destroy a city and mother in Israel; why do you swallow up the inheritance of YHWH?" ²⁰And Joab answers and says, "Far be it—far be it from me; I do not swallow up nor destroy. ²¹The matter [is] not so; for a man of the hill-country of Ephraim—Sheba son of Bichri [is] his name—has lifted up his hand against the king, against David; give him up by himself, and I go away from the city." And the woman says to Joab, "Behold, his head is cast to you over the wall." ²²And the woman comes to all the people in her wisdom, and they cut off the head of Sheba son of Bichri, and cast [it] to Joab, and he blows with a horn, and they are scattered from the city, each [goes] to his tents, and Joab has turned back to Jerusalem to the king. ²³And Joab [is] over all the host of Israel, and Benaiah son of Jehoiada [is] over the Cherethite, and over the Pelethite, ²⁴and Adoram [is] over the tribute, and Jehoshaphat son of Ahilud [is] the remembrancer, ²⁵and Sheva [is] scribe, and Zadok and Abiathar [are] priests, ²⁶and also, Ira the Jairite has been minister to David.

CHAPTER 21

¹And there is a famine in the days of David [for] three years, year after year, and David seeks the face of YHWH, and YHWH says, "[This is] for Saul and for the bloody house, because that he put the Gibeonites to death." ²And the king calls for the Gibeonites and says to them—as for the Gibeonites, they [are] not of the sons of Israel, but of the remnant of the Amorite, and the sons of Israel had sworn to them, and Saul seeks to strike them in his zeal for the sons of Israel and Judah— ³indeed, David says to the Gibeonites, "What do I do for you? And with what do I make atonement? And bless the inheritance of YHWH." ⁴And the Gibeonites say to him, "We have no silver and gold by Saul and by his house, and we have no man to put to death in Israel"; and he says, "What you are saying I do to you." ⁵And they say to the king, "The man who consumed us, and who devised against us—we have been destroyed from stationing ourselves in all the border of Israel— ⁶let there be given to us seven men of his sons, and we have hanged them before YHWH, in the height of Saul, the chosen of YHWH." And the king says, "I give"; ⁷and the king has pity on Mephibosheth son of Jonathan, son of Saul, because of the oath of YHWH that [is] between them, between David and Jonathan son of Saul; ⁸and the king takes the two sons of Rizpah daughter of Aiah, whom she bore to Saul, Armoni and Mephibosheth, and the five sons of Michal daughter of Saul whom she bore to Adriel son of Barzillai the Meholathite, ⁹and gives them into the hand of the Gibeonites, and they hang them in the hill before YHWH; and the seven fall together, and they have been put to death in the days of harvest, in the first [days], the commencement of barley-harvest. ¹⁰And Rizpah daughter of Aiah takes the sackcloth, and stretches it out for herself on the rock, from the commencement of harvest until water has been poured out on them from the heavens, and has not permitted a bird of the heavens to rest on them by day, or the beast of the field by night. ¹¹And it is declared to David that which Rizpah daughter of Aiah, concubine of Saul, has done, ¹²and David goes and takes the bones of Saul, and the bones of his son Jonathan, from the possessors of Jabesh-Gilead, who had stolen them from the broad place of Beth-Shan, where the Philistines hanged them, in the day of the Philistines striking Saul in Gilboa; ¹³and he brings up there the bones of Saul, and the bones of his son Jonathan, and they gather the bones of those hanged, ¹⁴and bury the bones of Saul and of his son Jonathan in the land of Benjamin, in Zelah, in the burying-place of his father Kish, and do all that the king commanded, and God accepts the plea for the land afterward. ¹⁵And again the Philistines have war with Israel, and David goes down, and his servants with him, and they fight with the Philistines; and David is weary, ¹⁶and Ishbi-Benob, who [is] among the children of the giant—the weight of his spear [is] three hundred [shekels in] weight of bronze, and he is girded with a new one—speaks of striking David, ¹⁷and Abishai son of Zeruiah gives help to him, and strikes the Philistine, and puts him to death; then the men of David swear to him, saying, "You do not go out with us to battle again, nor quench the lamp of Israel." ¹⁸And it comes to pass afterward that the battle is again in Gob with the Philistines. Then Sibbechai the Hushathite has struck Saph, who [is] among the children of the giant. ¹⁹And the battle is again in Gob with the Philistines, and Elhanan son of Jaare-Oregim, the Beth-Lehemite, strikes [a brother of] Goliath the Gittite, and the wood of his spear [is] like a weavers' beam. ²⁰And the battle is again in Gath, and there is a man of [great] stature, and the fingers of his hands [are] six, and the toes of his feet [are] six—twenty-four in number, and he has also been born to the giant, ²¹and he reproaches Israel, and Jonathan son of Shimeah, David's brother, strikes him; ²²these four have been born to the giant in Gath, and they fall by the hand of David, and by the hand of his servants.

CHAPTER 22

¹And David speaks the words of this song to YHWH in the day YHWH has delivered him out of the hand of all his enemies, and out of the hand of Saul, ²and he says: "YHWH [is] my rock, || And my bulwark, and a deliverer to me, ³My God [is] my rock—I take refuge in Him; My shield, and the horn of my salvation, || My high tower, and my refuge! My Savior, You save me from violence! ⁴I call on YHWH, [who is worthy] to be praised: And I am saved from my enemies. ⁵When the breakers of death surrounded me, || The streams of the worthless terrify me, ⁶The cords of Sheol have surrounded me, || The snares of death have been before me. ⁷In my adversity I call on YHWH, || And I call to my God, || And He hears my voice from His temple, || And my cry [is] in His ears, ⁸And the earth shakes and trembles, || Foundations of the heavens are troubled, || And are shaken, for He has wrath! ⁹Smoke has gone up by His nostrils, || And fire devours from His mouth; Brands have been kindled by it. ¹⁰And He inclines the heavens and comes down, || And thick darkness [is] under His feet. ¹¹And He rides on a cherub and flies, || And is seen on the wings of the wind. ¹²And He sets darkness around Him [for His] dwelling places, || Darkness of waters [and] thick clouds of the skies. ¹³From the brightness before Him || Brands of fire were kindled! ¹⁴YHWH thunders from the heavens, || And the Most High gives forth His voice. ¹⁵And He sends forth arrows, and scatters them; Lightning, and troubles them; ¹⁶And the streams of the sea are seen, || [The] foundations of the world are revealed, || By the rebuke of YHWH, || From the breath of the spirit of His anger. ¹⁷He sends from above—He takes me, || He draws me out of many waters. ¹⁸He delivers me from my strong enemy, || From those hating me, || For they were stronger than me. ¹⁹They are before me in a day of my calamity, || And YHWH is my support, ²⁰And He brings me out to a large place, || He draws me out for He delighted in me. ²¹YHWH repays me, || According to my righteousness, || According to the cleanness of my hands, He returns to me. ²²For I have kept the ways of YHWH, || And have not done wickedly against my God. ²³For all His judgments [are] before me, || As for His

statutes, I do not turn from them. ²⁴And I am perfect before Him, ‖ And I keep myself from my iniquity. ²⁵And YHWH returns to me, ‖ According to my righteousness, ‖ According to my cleanness before His eyes. ²⁶With the kind You show Yourself kind, ‖ With the perfect man You show Yourself perfect, ²⁷With the pure You show Yourself pure, ‖ And with the perverse You show Yourself a wrestler. ²⁸And You save the poor people, ‖ But Your eyes on the high cause [them] to fall. ²⁹For You [are] my lamp, O YHWH, ‖ And YHWH lightens my darkness. ³⁰For by You I run [against] a troop, ‖ By my God I leap a wall. ³¹God—His way [is] perfect, ‖ The saying of YHWH is tried, ‖ He [is] a shield to all those trusting in Him. ³²For who is God except YHWH? And who [is the] Rock except our God? ³³God—my bulwark, [my] strength, ‖ And He makes my way perfect; ³⁴Making my feet like does, ‖ And causes me to stand on my high places, ³⁵Teaching my hands for battle, ‖ And a bow of bronze was brought down by my arms, ³⁶And You give the shield of Your salvation to me, ‖ And Your lowliness makes me great. ³⁷You enlarge my step under me, ‖ And my ankles have not slipped. ³⁸I pursue my enemies and destroy them, ‖ And I do not turn until they are consumed. ³⁹And I consume them, and strike them, ‖ And they do not rise, and fall under my feet. ⁴⁰And You gird me [with] strength for battle, ‖ You cause my withstanders to bow under me. ⁴¹And my enemies—You give to me the neck, ‖ Those hating me—and I cut them off. ⁴²They look, and there is no savior; To YHWH, and He has not answered them. ⁴³And I beat them as dust of the earth, ‖ As mire of the streets I beat them small—I spread them out! ⁴⁴And You deliver me ‖ From the strivings of my people, ‖ You place me for a head of nations; A people I have not known serve me. ⁴⁵Sons of a stranger feign obedience to me, ‖ At the hearing of the ear they listen to me. ⁴⁶Sons of a stranger fade away, ‖ And gird themselves by their close places. ⁴⁷YHWH lives, and blessed [is] my Rock, ‖ And exalted is my God—The Rock of my salvation. ⁴⁸God—who is giving vengeance to me, ‖ And bringing down peoples under me, ⁴⁹And bringing me forth from my enemies, ‖ Indeed, You raise me up above my withstanders. You deliver me from a man of violence. ⁵⁰Therefore I confess You, O YHWH, among nations, ‖ And I sing praise to Your Name. ⁵¹Magnifying the salvations of His king, ‖ And doing loving-kindness to His anointed, ‖ To David, and to his seed—for all time!"

CHAPTER 23

¹And these [are] the last words of David: "A declaration of David son of Jesse, ‖ And a declaration of the man raised up— Concerning the anointed of the God of Jacob, ‖ And the sweetness of the songs of Israel: ²The Spirit of YHWH has spoken by me, ‖ And His word [is] on my tongue. ³He said—the God of Israel—to me, ‖ He spoke—the Rock of Israel: He who is ruling over man [is] righteous, ‖ He is ruling in the fear of God. ⁴And he rises as the light of morning, ‖ A morning sun [with] no clouds! By the shining, by the rain, ‖ Tender grass of the earth! ⁵For though my house [is] not so with God; So He made a perpetual covenant with me, ‖ Arranged in all things, and kept; For all my salvation, and all desire, ‖ For He has not caused [it] to spring up. ⁶As for the worthless—All of them [are] driven away as a thorn, ‖ For they are not taken away by hand; ⁷And the man who comes against them ‖ Is filled with iron and the staff of a spear, ‖ And they are utterly burned with fire ‖ In the cessation." ⁸These [are] the names of the mighty ones whom David has: sitting in the seat [is] the Tachmonite, head of the captains—he [is] Adino, who hardened himself against eight hundred—wounded at one time. ⁹And after him [is] Eleazar son of Dodo, son of Ahohi, of the three mighty men with David; in their exposing themselves among the Philistines—they have been gathered there to battle, and the men of Israel go up— ¹⁰he has arisen, and strikes among the Philistines until his hand has been weary, and his hand cleaves to the sword, and YHWH works a great salvation on that day, and the people turn back after him only to strip off. ¹¹And after him [is] Shammah son of Agee the Hararite, and the Philistines are gathered into a company, and there is a portion of the field full of lentils there, and the people have fled from the presence of the Philistines, ¹²and he stations himself in the midst of the portion, and delivers it, and strikes the Philistines, and YHWH works a great salvation. ¹³And three of the thirty heads go down and come to the harvest, to David, to the cave of Adullam, and the company of the Philistines are encamping in the Valley of Rephaim, ¹⁴and David [is] then in a fortress, and the station of the Philistines [is] then in Beth-Lehem, ¹⁵and David longs and says, "Who gives me a drink of the water of the well of Beth-Lehem, which [is] by the gate?" ¹⁶And the three mighty ones cleave through the camp of the Philistines, and draw water out of the well of Beth-Lehem, which [is] by the gate, and take [it] up, and bring [it] to David; and he was not willing to drink it, and pours it out to YHWH, ¹⁷and says, "Far be it from me, O YHWH, to do this; is it the blood of the men who are going with their lives?" And he was not willing to drink it; the three mighty ones did these [things]. ¹⁸And Abishai brother of Joab, son of Zeruiah, he [is] head of three, and he is lifting up his spear against three hundred—wounded, and he has a name among three. ¹⁹Is he not the honored of the three? And he becomes their head; and he has not come to the [first] three. ²⁰And Benaiah son of Jehoiada (son of a man of valor, great in deeds from Kabzeel), has struck two lion-like men of Moab, and he has gone down and struck the lion in the midst of the pit in a day of snow. ²¹And he has struck the Egyptian man, a man of appearance, and a spear [is] in the hand of the Egyptian, and he goes down to him with a rod, and takes the spear violently away out of the hand of the Egyptian, and slays him with his own spear. ²²Benaiah son of Jehoiada has done these [things], and has a name among the three mighty ones. ²³He is honored more than the thirty, but he did not come to the three; and David sets him over his guard. ²⁴Asahel brother of Joab [is] of the thirty; Elhanan son of Dodo of Beth-Lehem, ²⁵Shammah the Harodite, Elika the Harodite, ²⁶Helez the Paltite, Ira son of Ikkesh the Tekoite, ²⁷Abiezer the Annethothite, Mebunnai the Hushathite, ²⁸Zalmon the Ahohite, Maharai the Netophathite, ²⁹Heleb son of Baanah the Netophathite, Ittai son of Ribai from Gibeah of the sons of Benjamin, ³⁰Benaiah the Pirathonite, Hiddai of the brooks of Gaash, ³¹Abi-Albon the Arbathite, Azmaveth the Barhumite, ³²Eliahba the Shaalbonite, of the sons of Jashen, Jonathan, ³³Shammah the Hararite, Ahiam son of Sharar the Hararite, ³⁴Eliphelet son of Ahasbai, son of the Maachathite, Eliam son of Ahithophel the Gilonite, ³⁵Hezrai the Carmelite, Paarai the Arbite, ³⁶Igal son of Nathan from Zobah, Bani the Gadite, ³⁷Zelek the Ammonite, Naharai the Beerothite, bearer of the weapons of Joab son of Zeruiah, ³⁸Ira the Ithrite, Gareb the Ithrite, ³⁹Uriah the Hittite: thirty-seven in all.

CHAPTER 24

¹And the anger of YHWH adds to burn against Israel, and [an adversary] moves David about them, saying, "Go, number Israel and Judah." ²And the king says to Joab, head of the host that [is] with him, "Now go to and fro through all the tribes of Israel, from Dan even to Beer-Sheba, and inspect the people; then I have known the number of the people." ³And Joab says to the king, "Indeed, your God YHWH adds to the people, as they are, one hundred times, and the eyes of my lord the king are seeing; and my lord the king, why is he desirous of this thing?" ⁴And the word of the king is severe toward Joab, and against the heads of the force, and Joab goes out, and the heads of the force, [from] before the king to inspect the people, even Israel; ⁵and they pass over the Jordan, and encamp in Aroer, on the right of the city that [is] in the midst of the Brook of Gad, and to Jazer, ⁶and they come to Gilead, and to the land of Tahtim-Hodshi, and they come to Dan-Jaan, and around to Sidon, ⁷and they come to the fortress of Tyre, and all the cities of the Hivite, and of the Canaanite, and go out to the south of Judah, to Beer-Sheba. ⁸And they go to and fro through all the land, and come in to Jerusalem at the end of nine months and twenty days, ⁹and Joab gives the account of the inspection of the people to the king, and Israel is eight hundred thousand men of valor, drawing sword, and the men of Judah five hundred thousand men. ¹⁰And the heart of David strikes him, after that he has numbered the people, and David says to YHWH, "I have greatly sinned in that which I have done, and now, O YHWH, please cause the iniquity of Your servant to pass away, for I have acted very foolishly." ¹¹And David rises in the morning, and the word of YHWH has been to Gad the prophet, seer of David, saying, ¹²"Go, and you have spoken to David, Thus said YHWH: I am lifting up three [choices] for you, choose one of them, and I do [it] to you." ¹³And

Gad comes to David, and declares [it] to him, and says to him, "Does seven years of famine come to you in your land? Or are you fleeing before your adversary [for] three months—and he is pursuing you? Or is there pestilence [for] three days in your land? Now, know and see what word I take back to Him sending me." ¹⁴And David says to Gad, "I have great distress; please let us fall into the hand of YHWH, for His mercies [are] many, but do not let me fall into the hand of man." ¹⁵And YHWH gives a pestilence on Israel from the morning even to the time appointed, and there dies of the people, from Dan even to Beer-Sheba, seventy thousand men, ¹⁶and the messenger puts forth his hand to Jerusalem to destroy it, and YHWH sighs concerning the calamity, and says to the messenger who is destroying among the people, "Enough, now, cease your hand"; and the messenger of YHWH was near the threshing-floor of Araunah the Jebusite. ¹⁷And David speaks to YHWH when he sees the messenger who is striking among the people, and says, "Behold, I have sinned, indeed, I have done perversely; and these—the flock—what have they done? Please let Your hand be on me and on the house of my father." ¹⁸And Gad comes to David on that day and says to him, "Go up, raise an altar to YHWH in the threshing-floor of Araunah the Jebusite"; ¹⁹and David goes up, according to the word of Gad, as YHWH commanded. ²⁰And Araunah looks, and sees the king and his servants passing over to him, and Araunah goes out and bows himself to the king [with] his face to the earth. ²¹And Araunah says, "Why has my lord the king come to his servant?" And David says, "To buy the threshing-floor from you, to build an altar to YHWH, and the plague is restrained from the people." ²²And Araunah says to David, "Let my lord the king take [it] and cause that which is good in his eyes to ascend; see, [here are] the oxen for a burnt-offering, and the threshing instruments, and the instruments of the oxen, for wood"; ²³Araunah has given the whole [as] a king to a king; and Araunah says to the king, "Your God YHWH accepts you." ²⁴And the king says to Araunah, "No, for I surely buy from you for a price, and I do not cause burnt-offerings to ascend to my God YHWH for nothing"; and David buys the threshing-floor and the oxen for fifty shekels of silver, ²⁵and David builds an altar to YHWH there, and causes burnt-offerings and peace-offerings to ascend, and YHWH accepts the plea for the land, and the plague is restrained from Israel.

1 KINGS

CHAPTER 1
¹And King David [is] old, entering into days, and they cover him with garments, and he has no heat, ²and his servants say to him, "Let them seek [for] a young woman, a virgin, for my lord the king, and she has stood before the king, and is a companion to him, and has lain in your bosom, and my lord the king has heat." ³And they seek [for] a beautiful young woman in all the border of Israel, and find Abishag the Shunammite, and bring her to the king, ⁴and the young woman [is] very, very beautiful, and she is a companion to the king, and serves him, and the king has not known her. ⁵And Adonijah son of Haggith is lifting himself up, saying, "I reign"; and he prepares for himself a chariot and horsemen, and fifty men running before him, ⁶and his father has not grieved him [all] his days, saying, "Why have you done this?" And he also [is] of a very good form, and [his mother] bore him after Absalom. ⁷And his words are with Joab son of Zeruiah, and with Abiathar the priest, and they help after Adonijah; ⁸and Zadok the priest, and Benaiah son of Jehoiada, and Nathan the prophet, and Shimei, and Rei, and the mighty ones whom David has, have not been with Adonijah. ⁹And Adonijah sacrifices sheep and oxen and fatlings near the stone of Zoheleth that [is] by En-Rogel, and calls all his brothers, sons of the king, and for all the men of Judah, servants of the king; ¹⁰and he has not called Nathan the prophet, and Benaiah, and the mighty ones, and his brother Solomon. ¹¹And Nathan speaks to Bathsheba, mother of Solomon, saying, "Have you not heard that Adonijah son of Haggith has reigned, and our lord David has not known? ¹²And now, come, please let me counsel you, and deliver your life and the life of your son Solomon; ¹³go and enter in to King David, and you have said to him: Have you not, my lord, O king, sworn to your handmaid, saying, Surely your son Solomon reigns after me, and he sits on my throne? And why has Adonijah reigned? ¹⁴Behold, you are yet speaking there with the king, and I come in after you, and have completed your words." ¹⁵And Bathsheba comes in to the king, [into] the inner chamber, and the king [is] very aged, and Abishag the Shunammite is serving the king; ¹⁶and Bathsheba bows and pays respect to the king, and the king says, "What do you [want]?" ¹⁷And she says to him, "My lord, you have sworn by your God YHWH to your handmaid, [saying], Surely your son Solomon reigns after me, and he sits on my throne; ¹⁸and now, behold, Adonijah has reigned, and now, my lord, O king, you have not known; ¹⁹and he sacrifices ox, and fatling, and sheep in abundance, and calls for all the sons of the king, and for Abiathar the priest, and for Joab head of the host—and he has not called for your servant Solomon. ²⁰And you, my lord, O king, the eyes of all Israel [are] on you, to declare to them who sit on the throne of my lord the king after him; ²¹and it has been, when my lord the king lies with his fathers, that I have been, I and my son Solomon—[reckoned] sinners." ²²And behold, she is yet speaking with the king, and Nathan the prophet has come in; ²³and they declare to the king, saying, "Behold, Nathan the prophet"; and he comes in before the king, and bows himself to the king, on his face to the earth. ²⁴And Nathan says, "My lord, O king, you have said, Adonijah reigns after me, and he sits on my throne; ²⁵for he has gone down today, and sacrifices ox, and fatling, and sheep, in abundance, and calls for all the sons of the king, and for the heads of the host, and for Abiathar the priest, and behold, they are eating and drinking before him, and they say, Let King Adonijah live! ²⁶But he has not called for me, your servant, and for Zadok the priest, and for Benaiah, son of Jehoiada, and for your servant Solomon. ²⁷if this thing has been from my lord the king, then you have not caused your servant to know who sits on the throne of my lord the king after him." ²⁸And King David answers and says, "Call for Bathsheba for me"; and she comes in before the king, and stands before the king. ²⁹And the king swears and says, "YHWH lives, who has redeemed my soul out of all adversity; ³⁰surely as I swore to you by YHWH, God of Israel, saying, Surely your son Solomon reigns after me, and he sits on my throne in my stead; surely so I do this day." ³¹And Bathsheba bows—face to the earth—and pays respect to the king, and says, "Let my lord, King David, live for all time." ³²And King David says, "Call for Zadok the priest, and for Nathan the prophet, and for Benaiah son of Jehoiada for me"; and they come in before the king. ³³And the king says to them, "Take the servants of your lord with you, and you have caused my son Solomon to ride on my own mule, and caused him to go down to Gihon, ³⁴and Zadok the priest has anointed him there—and Nathan the prophet—for king over Israel, and you have blown with a horn and said, Let King Solomon live; ³⁵and you have come up after him, and he has come in and has sat on my throne, and he reigns in my stead, and I have appointed him to be leader over Israel, and over Judah." ³⁶And Benaiah son of Jehoiada answers the king and says, "Amen! So does YHWH, God of my lord the king, say; ³⁷as YHWH has been with my lord the king, so is He with Solomon, and makes his throne greater than the throne of my lord King David." ³⁸And Zadok the priest goes down, and Nathan the prophet, and Benaiah son of Jehoiada, and the Cherethite, and the Pelethite, and they cause Solomon to ride on the mule of King David, and cause him to go to Gihon, ³⁹and Zadok the priest takes the horn of oil out of the tent, and anoints Solomon, and they blow with a horn, and all the people say, "Let King Solomon live." ⁴⁰And all the people come up after him, and the people are piping with pipes, and rejoicing [with] great joy, and the earth splits with their voice. ⁴¹And Adonijah hears, and all those called who [are] with him, and they have finished to eat, and Joab hears the noise of the horn and says,

"Why [is] the noise of the city roaring?" ⁴²He is yet speaking, and behold, Jonathan son of Abiathar the priest has come in, and Adonijah says, "Come in, for you [are] a man of valor, and you bear good tidings." ⁴³And Jonathan answers and says to Adonijah, "Truly our lord King David has caused Solomon to reign, ⁴⁴and the king sends with him Zadok the priest, and Nathan the prophet, and Benaiah son of Jehoiada, and the Cherethite, and the Pelethite, and they cause him to ride on the king's mule, ⁴⁵and they anoint him—Zadok the priest and Nathan the prophet—for king in Gihon, and have come up there rejoicing, and the city is moved; it [is] the noise that you have heard. ⁴⁶And also Solomon has sat on the throne of the kingdom, ⁴⁷and also the servants of the king have come into bless our lord King David, saying, Your God makes the name of Solomon better than your name, and his throne greater than your throne; and the king bows himself on the bed, ⁴⁸and also thus the king has said, Blessed [is] YHWH, God of Israel, who has given [one] sitting on my throne today, and my eyes are seeing." ⁴⁹And they tremble, and rise—all those called who [are] for Adonijah—and go, each on his way; ⁵⁰and Adonijah fears because of Solomon, and rises, and goes, and lays hold on the horns of the altar. ⁵¹And it is declared to Solomon, saying, "Behold, Adonijah fears King Solomon, and behold, he has laid hold on the horns of the altar, saying, Let King Solomon swear to me as today—he does not put his servant to death by the sword." ⁵²And Solomon says, "If he becomes a virtuous man—there does not fall [even one] hair of his to the earth, and if evil is found in him—then he has died." ⁵³And King Solomon sends, and they bring him down from off the altar, and he comes in and bows himself to King Solomon, and Solomon says to him, "Go to your house."

CHAPTER 2

¹And the days of David to die draw near, and he charges his son Solomon, saying, ²"I am going in the way of all the earth, and you have been strong, and become a man, ³and you have kept the charge of your God YHWH, to walk in His ways, to keep His statutes, His commands, and His judgments, and His testimonies, as it is written in the Law of Moses, so that you do wisely [in] all that you do, and wherever you turn, ⁴so that YHWH establishes His word which He spoke to me, saying, If your sons observe their way to walk before Me in truth, with all their heart, and with all their soul; saying, A man of yours is never cut off from the throne of Israel. ⁵And also, you have known that which he did to me—Joab son of Zeruiah—that which he did to two heads of the hosts of Israel, to Abner son of Ner, and to Amasa son of Jether—that he slays them, and makes the blood of war in peace, and puts the blood of war in his girdle, that [is] on his loins, and in his sandals that [are] on his feet; ⁶and you have done according to your wisdom, and do not let his old age go down in peace to Sheol. ⁷And you do kindness to the sons of Barzillai the Gileadite, and they have been among those eating at your table, for so they drew near to me in my fleeing from the face of your brother Absalom. ⁸And behold, Shimei son of Gera, the Benjamite of Bahurim, [is] with you, and he reviled me—a grievous reviling—in the day of my going to Mahanaim; and he has come down to meet me at the Jordan, and I swear to him by YHWH, saying, I do not put you to death by the sword; ⁹and now, do not acquit him, for you [are] a wise man, and you have known that which you do to him, and have brought down his old age with blood to Sheol." ¹⁰And David lies down with his fathers, and is buried in the City of David, ¹¹and the days that David has reigned over Israel [are] forty years; he has reigned seven years in Hebron, and he has reigned thirty-three years in Jerusalem. ¹²And Solomon has sat on the throne of his father David, and his kingdom is established greatly, ¹³and Adonijah son of Haggith comes to Bathsheba, mother of Solomon, and she says, "Is your coming peace?" And he says, "Peace." ¹⁴And he says, "I have a word for you," and she says, "Speak." ¹⁵And he says, "You have known that the kingdom was mine, and all Israel had set their faces toward me for reigning, and the kingdom is turned around, and is my brother's, for it was his from YHWH; ¹⁶and now, I am asking one petition of you—do not turn back my face"; and she says to him, "Speak." ¹⁷And he says, "Please speak to Solomon the king, for he does not turn back your face, and he gives Abishag the Shunammite to me for a wife." ¹⁸And Bathsheba says, "Good; I speak to the king for you." ¹⁹And Bathsheba comes to King Solomon to speak to him for Adonijah, and the king rises to meet her, and bows himself to her, and sits on his throne, and places a throne for the mother of the king, and she sits at his right hand. ²⁰And she says, "I ask one small petition of you, do not turn back my face"; and the king says to her, "Ask, my mother, for I do not turn back your face." ²¹And she says, "Let Abishag the Shunammite be given to your brother Adonijah for a wife." ²²And King Solomon answers and says to his mother, "And why are you asking [for] Abishag the Shunammite for Adonijah? Also ask [for] the kingdom for him—for he [is] my elder brother—even for him, and for Abiathar the priest, and for Joab son of Zeruiah." ²³And King Solomon swears by YHWH, saying, "Thus God does to me, and thus He adds—surely Adonijah has spoken this word against his [own] soul; ²⁴and now, YHWH lives, who has established me, and causes me to sit on the throne of my father David, and who has made a house for me as He spoke—surely Adonijah is put to death today." ²⁵And King Solomon sends by the hand of Benaiah son of Jehoiada, and he falls on him, and he dies. ²⁶And the king said to Abiathar the priest, "Go to Anathoth, to your fields; for you [are] a man of death, but I do not put you to death in this day, because you have carried the Ark of Lord YHWH before my father David, and because you were afflicted in all that my father was afflicted in." ²⁷And Solomon casts out Abiathar from being priest of YHWH, to fulfill the word of YHWH which He spoke concerning the house of Eli in Shiloh. ²⁸And the report has come to Joab—for Joab has turned aside after Adonijah, though he did not turn aside after Absalom—and Joab flees to the tent of YHWH, and lays hold on the horns of the altar. ²⁹And it is declared to King Solomon that Joab has fled to the tent of YHWH, and behold, [is] near the altar; and Solomon sends Benaiah son of Jehoiada, saying, "Go, fall on him." ³⁰And Benaiah comes into the tent of YHWH and says to him, "Thus said the king: Come out"; and he says, "No, but I die here." And Benaiah brings back word [to] the king, saying, "Thus spoke Joab, indeed, thus he answered me." ³¹And the king says to him, "Do as he has spoken, and fall on him, and you have buried him, and turned aside the causeless blood which Joab shed from off me, and from off the house of my father; ³²and YHWH has turned back his blood on his own head, [on him] who has fallen on two men more righteous and better than he, and slays them with the sword—and my father David did not know—Abner son of Ner, head of the host of Israel, and Amasa son of Jether, head of the host of Judah; ³³indeed, their blood has turned back on the head of Joab, and on the head of his seed for all time; and for David, and for his seed, and for his house, and for his throne, there is peace for all time, from YHWH." ³⁴And Benaiah son of Jehoiada goes up and falls on him, and puts him to death, and he is buried in his own house in the wilderness, ³⁵and the king puts Benaiah son of Jehoiada over the host in his stead, and the king has put Zadok the priest in the stead of Abiathar. ³⁶And the king sends and calls for Shimei, and says to him, "Build a house for yourself in Jerusalem, and you have dwelt there, and do not go out [from] there anywhere; ³⁷and it has been, in the day of your going out, and you have passed over the Brook of Kidron, you certainly know that you surely die—your blood is on your head." ³⁸And Shimei says to the king, "The word [is] good; as my lord the king has spoken so your servant does"; and Shimei dwells in Jerusalem many days. ³⁹And it comes to pass, at the end of three years, that two of the servants of Shimei flee to Achish son of Maachah, king of Gath, and they declare to Shimei, saying, "Behold, your servants [are] in Gath"; ⁴⁰and Shimei rises, and saddles his donkey, and goes to Gath, to Achish, to seek his servants, and Shimei goes and brings his servants from Gath. ⁴¹And it is declared to Solomon that Shimei has gone from Jerusalem to Gath, and returns, ⁴²and the king sends and calls for Shimei, and says to him, "Have I not caused you to swear by YHWH—and I testify against you, saying, In the day of your going out, and you have gone anywhere, you certainly know that you surely die; and you say to me, The word I have heard [is] good? ⁴³And why have you not kept the oath of YHWH, and the charge that I charged on you?" ⁴⁴And the king says to Shimei, "You have known all the evil that your heart has known, which you did to my father David, and YHWH has turned back your evil on your head, ⁴⁵and King Solomon [is] blessed, and the throne of David

is established before YHWH for all time." ⁴⁶And the king charges Benaiah son of Jehoiada, and he goes out and falls on him, and he dies, and the kingdom is established in the hand of Solomon.

CHAPTER 3

¹And Solomon joins in marriage with Pharaoh king of Egypt, and takes the daughter of Pharaoh, and brings her to the City of David, until he completes to build his own house, and the house of YHWH, and the wall of Jerusalem all around. ²Only, the people are sacrificing in high places, for there has not been built a house for the Name of YHWH until those days. ³And Solomon loves YHWH, to walk in the statutes of his father David—only, he is sacrificing and making incense in high places— ⁴and the king goes to Gibeon, to sacrifice there, for it [is] the great high place; Solomon causes one thousand burnt-offerings to ascend on that altar. ⁵YHWH has appeared to Solomon in Gibeon, in a dream of the night, and God says, "Ask—what do I give to you?" ⁶And Solomon says, "You have done with Your servant, my father David, great kindness, as he walked before You in truth and in righteousness, and in uprightness of heart with You, and You keep this great kindness for him, and give to him a son sitting on his throne, as [at] this day. ⁷And now, O YHWH my God, You have caused Your servant to reign instead of my father David; and I [am] a little child, I do not know [how] to go out and to come in; ⁸and Your servant [is] in the midst of your people, whom You have chosen, a people numerous, that is not numbered nor counted for multitude, ⁹and You have given an understanding heart to Your servant, to judge Your people, to discern between good and evil; for who is able to judge this great people of Yours?" ¹⁰And the thing is good in the eyes of the Lord, that Solomon has asked this thing, ¹¹and God says to him, "Because that you have asked for this thing, and have not asked for many days for yourself, nor asked for riches for yourself, nor asked for the life of your enemies, and have asked for discernment for yourself to understand judgment, ¹²behold, I have done according to your words; behold, I have given a wise and understanding heart to you, that there has not been [one] like you before you, and after you there does not arise [one] like you; ¹³and also, that which you have not asked for I have given to you, both riches and honor, that there has not been a man like you among the kings [for] all your days; ¹⁴and if you walk in My ways to keep My statutes, and My commands, as your father David walked, then I have prolonged your days." ¹⁵And Solomon awakens, and behold, [it was] a dream; and he comes to Jerusalem, and stands before the Ark of the Covenant of YHWH, and causes burnt-offerings to ascend, and makes peace-offerings, and he makes a banquet for all his servants. ¹⁶Then two women, harlots, come to the king, and they stand before him, ¹⁷and the first woman says, "O my lord, this woman and I are dwelling in one house, and I bring forth with her, in the house; ¹⁸and it comes to pass on the third day of my bringing forth, that this woman also brings forth, and we [are] together, there is no stranger with us in the house, except the two of us, in the house. ¹⁹And the son of this woman dies at night, because she has lain on him, ²⁰and she rises in the middle of the night, and takes my son from beside me—and your handmaid is asleep—and lays him in her bosom, and she has laid her dead son in my bosom; ²¹and I rise in the morning to suckle my son, and behold, [he is] dead; and I consider in the morning concerning it, and behold, it was not my son whom I bore." ²²And the other woman says, "No, but my son [is] the living, and your son the dead"; and this [one] says, "No, but your son [is] the dead, and my son the living." And they speak before the king. ²³And the king says, "This [one] says, This [is] my son, the living, and your son [is] the dead; and that [one] says, No, but your son [is] the dead, and my son the living." ²⁴And the king says, "Take a sword for me"; and they bring the sword before the king, ²⁵and the king says, "Cut the living child into two, and give half to one, and half to the other." ²⁶And the woman whose son [is] the living one says to the king (for her bowels yearned over her son), indeed, she says, "O my lord, give the living child to her, and do not put him to death at all"; and this [one] says, "Let him be neither mine or yours—cut [him]." ²⁷And the king answers and says, "Give the living child to her [who wants him], and do not put him to death at all; she [is] his mother." ²⁸And all [in] Israel hear of the judgment that the king has judged, and fear because of the king, for they have seen that the wisdom of God [is] in his heart to do judgment.

CHAPTER 4

¹And King Solomon is king over all Israel, ²and these [are] the heads whom he has: Azariah son of Zadok [is] the priest; ³Elihoreph and Ahiah sons of Shisha [are] scribes; Jehoshaphat son of Ahilud [is] remembrancer; ⁴and Benaiah son of Jehoiada [is] over the host; and Zadok and Abiathar [are] priests; ⁵and Azariah son of Nathan [is] over the officers; and Zabud son of Nathan [is] minister, friend of the king; ⁶and Ahishar [is] over the household, and Adoniram son of Abda [is] over the tribute. ⁷And Solomon has twelve officers over all Israel, and they have sustained the king and his household—a month in the year is on each one for sustenance; ⁸and these [are] their names: Ben-Hur in the hill-country of Ephraim; ⁹Ben-Dekar in Makaz, and Shaalbim, and Beth-Shemesh, and Elon-Beth-Hanan; ¹⁰Ben-Hesed, in Aruboth, has Sochoh and all the land of Hepher; ¹¹Ben-Abinadab [has] all the elevation of Dor; Taphath daughter of Solomon became his wife; ¹²Baana Ben-Ahilud [has] Taanach and Megiddo, and all Beth-Shean, which [is] by Zartanah beneath Jezreel, from Beth-Shean to Abel-Meholah, to beyond Jokneam; ¹³Ben-Geber, in Ramoth-Gilead, has the small towns of Jair son of Manasseh, which [are] in Gilead; he has a portion of Argob that [is] in Bashan—sixty great cities [with] wall and bronze bar; ¹⁴Ahinadab son of Iddo [has] Mahanaim; ¹⁵Ahimaaz [is] in Naphtali; he also has taken Basemath daughter of Solomon for a wife; ¹⁶Baanah Ben-Hushai [is] in Asher, and in Aloth; ¹⁷Jehoshaphat Ben-Paruah [is] in Issachar; ¹⁸Shimei Ben-Elah [is] in Benjamin; ¹⁹Geber Ben-Uri [is] in the land of Gilead, the land of Sihon king of the Amorite, and of Og king of Bashan: and [he is] the one officer who [is] in the land. ²⁰Judah and Israel [are] many, as the sand that [is] by the sea for multitude, eating and drinking and rejoicing. ²¹And Solomon has been ruling over all the kingdoms, from the River [to] the land of the Philistines and to the border of Egypt: they are bringing a present near, and serving Solomon, all [the] days of his life. ²²And the provision of Solomon for one day is thirty cors of flour, and sixty cors of meal, ²³ten fat oxen, and twenty feeding oxen, and one hundred sheep, apart from deer, and roe, and fallow-deer, and fatted beasts of the stalls, ²⁴for he is ruling over all beyond the river, from Tiphsah and to Gaza, over all the kings beyond the River, and he has peace from all his surrounding servants. ²⁵And Judah dwells—and Israel—in confidence, each under his vine, and under his fig tree, from Dan even to Beer-Sheba, all the days of Solomon. ²⁶And Solomon has forty thousand stalls of horses for his chariots, and twelve thousand horsemen. ²⁷And these officers have sustained King Solomon and everyone drawing near to the table of King Solomon, each [in] his month; they let nothing be lacking. ²⁸And the barley and the straw, for horses and for dromedaries, they bring to the place where they are, each according to his ordinance. ²⁹And God gives very much wisdom and understanding to Solomon, and breadth of heart, as the sand that [is] on the edge of the sea; ³⁰and the wisdom of Solomon is greater than the wisdom of any of the sons of the east, and [greater] than all the wisdom of Egypt; ³¹and he is wiser than all men, [wiser] than Ethan the Ezrahite, and Heman, and Chalcol, and Darda, sons of Mahol, and his name is in all the surrounding nations. ³²And he speaks three thousand allegories, and his songs [are] one thousand and five; ³³and he speaks concerning the trees, from the cedar that [is] in Lebanon, even to the hyssop that is coming out in the wall, and he speaks concerning the livestock, and concerning the bird, and concerning the creeping things, and concerning the fishes, ³⁴and there come out [those] of all the peoples to hear the wisdom of Solomon, from all kings of the earth who have heard of his wisdom.

CHAPTER 5

¹And Hiram king of Tyre sends his servants to Solomon, for he heard that they had anointed him for king instead of his father, for Hiram was loving toward David all the days; ²and Solomon sends to Hiram, saying, ³"You have known my father David, that he has not been able to build a house for the Name of his God YHWH, because of the wars that have been all around him, until YHWH's putting them under

the soles of his feet. ⁴And now, my God YHWH has given rest to me all around, there is no adversary nor evil occurrence, ⁵and behold, I am saying to build a house for the Name of my God YHWH, as YHWH spoke to my father David, saying, Your son whom I appoint in your stead on your throne, he builds the house for My Name. ⁶And now, command, and they cut down cedars for me out of Lebanon, and my servants are with your servants, and I give the hire of your servants to you according to all that you say, for you have known that there is not a man among us acquainted with cutting wood, like the Sidonians." ⁷And it comes to pass at Hiram's hearing the words of Solomon, that he rejoices exceedingly and says, "Blessed [is] YHWH today, who has given to David a wise son over this numerous people." ⁸And Hiram sends to Solomon, saying, "I have heard that which you have sent to me, I do all your desire concerning cedar-wood and fir-wood; ⁹my servants bring [them] down from Lebanon to the sea, and I make them floats in the sea to the place that you send to me, and I have spread them out there; and you take [them] up, and you execute my desire, to give the food [for] my house." ¹⁰And Hiram is giving cedar-trees and fir-trees to Solomon—all his desire, ¹¹and Solomon has given twenty thousand cors of wheat to Hiram, [the] food for his house, and twenty cors of beaten oil; thus Solomon gives to Hiram year by year. ¹²And YHWH has given wisdom to Solomon as He spoke to him, and there is peace between Hiram and Solomon, and both of them make a covenant. ¹³And King Solomon lifts up a tribute out of all Israel, and the tribute is thirty thousand men, ¹⁴and he sends them to Lebanon, ten thousand a month, by changes; they are in Lebanon [for] a month [and] two months in their own house; and Adoniram [is] over the tribute. ¹⁵And King Solomon has seventy thousand bearing burdens, and eighty thousand hewing in the mountain, ¹⁶apart from the three thousand and three hundred heads of the officers of Solomon who [are] over the work—those ruling over the people who are working in the business. ¹⁷And the king commands, and they bring great stones, precious stones, [and] hewn stones, to lay the foundation of the house; ¹⁸and the builders of Solomon, and the builders of Hiram, and the Giblites hew [them], and prepare the wood and the stones to build the house.

CHAPTER 6

¹And it comes to pass, in the four hundred and eightieth year of the going out of the sons of Israel from the land of Egypt, in the fourth year—in the month of Ziv, it [is] the second month—of the reigning of Solomon over Israel, that he builds the house for YHWH. ²As for the house that King Solomon has built for YHWH, its length [is] sixty cubits, and its breadth twenty, and its height thirty cubits. ³As for the porch on the front of the temple of the house, its length [is] twenty cubits on the front of the breadth of the house; its breadth [is] ten by the cubit on the front of the house; ⁴and he makes frames of narrowing windows for the house. ⁵And he builds a couch against the wall of the house all around, [even] the walls of the house all around, of the temple and of the oracle, and makes sides all around. ⁶The lowest couch, its breadth [is] five by the cubit; and the middle, its breadth [is] six by the cubit; and the third, its breadth [is] seven by the cubit, for he has put withdrawings of the house all around outside—not to lay hold on the walls of the house. ⁷And the house, in its being built, has been built of perfect stone [that was] brought; and hammer and the axe—any instrument of iron—was not heard in the house in its being built. ⁸The opening of the middle side [is] at the right shoulder of the house, and with windings they go up on the middle one, and from the middle one to the third. ⁹And he builds the house, and completes it, and covers the house [with] beams and rows of cedars. ¹⁰And he builds the couch against all the house, its breadth [is] five cubits, and it takes hold of the house by cedar-wood. ¹¹And the word of YHWH is to Solomon, saying, ¹²"This house that you are building—if you walk in My statutes, and do My judgments, indeed, have done all My commands, to walk in them, then I have established My word with you, which I spoke to your father David, ¹³and have dwelt in the midst of the sons of Israel, and do not forsake My people Israel." ¹⁴And Solomon builds the house and completes it; ¹⁵and he builds the walls of the house within with beams of cedar, from the floor of the house to the walls of the ceiling; he has overlaid the inside with wood, and covers the floor of the house with ribs of fir. ¹⁶And he builds the twenty cubits on the sides of the house with ribs of cedar, from the floor to the walls; and he builds for it within, for the oracle, for the Holy of Holies. ¹⁷And [this area of] the house was forty by the cubit; it [is the area of] the temple before My face. ¹⁸And the cedar for the house within [is] carvings of knobs and openings of flowers; the whole [is] cedar, there is not a stone seen. ¹⁹And he has prepared the oracle in the midst of the house within, to put the Ark of the Covenant of YHWH there. ²⁰And before the oracle [is] twenty cubits in length, and twenty cubits in breadth, and its height [is] twenty cubits; and he overlays it with gold refined, and overlays the altar with cedar. ²¹And Solomon overlays the house within with gold refined, and causes [it] to pass over in chains of gold before the oracle, and overlays it with gold. ²²And he has overlaid the whole of the house with gold, until the completion of all the house; and the whole of the altar that the oracle has, he has overlaid with gold. ²³And he makes two cherubim of the oil-tree within the oracle; their height [is] ten cubits; ²⁴and the first wing of the cherub [is] five cubits, and the second wing of the cherub five cubits—ten cubits from the ends of his wings even to the ends of his wings; ²⁵and the second cherub [is] ten by the cubit; one measure and one form [are] of the two cherubim, ²⁶the height of the first cherub [is] ten by the cubit, and so [is] the second cherub; ²⁷and he sets the cherubim in the midst of the inner house, and they spread out the wings of the cherubim, and a wing of the first comes against the wall, and a wing of the second cherub is coming against the second wall, and their wings [stretched] into the midst of the house, coming wing against wing; ²⁸and he overlays the cherubim with gold, ²⁹and he has carved all around the walls of the house with engravings of carvings, cherubim, and palm trees, and openings of flowers, inside and outside. ³⁰And he has overlaid the floor of the house with gold, inside and outside; ³¹as for the opening of the oracle, he made doors of the oil-tree; the lintel [and] doorposts [are] a fifth [of the wall]. ³²And the two doors [are] of the oil-tree, and he has carved on them carvings of cherubim, and palm-trees, and openings of flowers, and overlaid with gold, and he causes the gold to go down on the cherubim and on the palm-trees. ³³And so he has made for the opening of the temple, doorposts of the oil-tree, from the fourth [of the wall]. ³⁴And the two doors [are] of fir-tree, the two sides of the first door are revolving, and the two hangings of the second door are revolving. ³⁵And he has carved cherubim, and palms, and openings of flowers, and overlaid the carved work with straightened gold. ³⁶And he builds the inner court, three rows of hewn work, and a row of beams of cedar. ³⁷In the fourth year the house of YHWH has been founded, in the month of Ziv, ³⁸and in the eleventh year, in the month of Bul (the eighth month), the house has been finished in all its matters, and in all its ordinances, and he builds it [in] seven years.

CHAPTER 7

¹And Solomon has built his own house [in] thirteen years, and he finishes all his house. ²And he builds the House of the Forest of Lebanon; its length [is] one hundred cubits, and its breadth fifty cubits, and its height thirty cubits, on four rows of cedar pillars, and cedar-beams on the pillars; ³and [it is] covered with cedar above, on the sides that [are] on the forty-five pillars, fifteen in the row. ⁴And frames [are] in three rows, and window [is] toward window three times. ⁵And all the openings and the doorposts [are of] square frame; and window [is] toward window three times. ⁶And he has made the porch of the pillars; its length fifty cubits, and its breadth thirty cubits, and the porch [is] before them, and pillars and a thick place [are] before them. ⁷And the porch of the throne where he judges—the porch of judgment—he has made, and [it is] covered with cedar from the floor to the floor. ⁸As for his house where he dwells, the other court [is] within the porch—it has been as this work; and he makes a house for the daughter of Pharaoh—whom Solomon has taken—like this porch. ⁹All these [are] of precious stones, according to the measures of hewn work, sawn with a saw, inside and outside, even from the foundation to the coping, and at the outside, to the great court. ¹⁰And the foundation [is] of precious stones, great stones, stones of ten cubits, and stones of eight cubits; ¹¹and precious stones

1 KINGS

[are] above, according to the measures of hewn work, and cedar; ¹²and the great court around [is] three rows of hewn work, and a row of cedar-beams, even for the inner court of the house of YHWH, and for the porch of the house. ¹³And King Solomon sends and takes Hiram out of Tyre— ¹⁴he [is the] son of a woman, a widow, of the tribe of Naphtali, and his father [is] a man of Tyre, a worker in bronze, and he is filled with the wisdom and the understanding, and the knowledge to do all work in bronze—and he comes to King Solomon, and does all his work. ¹⁵And he forms the two pillars of bronze; eighteen cubits [is] the height of the first pillar, and a cord of twelve cubits goes around the second pillar. ¹⁶And he has made two chapiters to put on the tops of the pillars, cast in bronze; five cubits the height of the first capital, and five cubits the height of the second capital. ¹⁷Nets of network, wreaths of chain-work [are] for the chapiters that [are] on the top of the pillars, seven for the first capital, and seven for the second capital. ¹⁸And he makes the pillars, and two rows around on the one network, to cover the chapiters that [are] on the top, with the pomegranates, and so he has made for the second capital. ¹⁹And the chapiters that [are] on the top of the pillars [are] of lily-work in the porch, four cubits; ²⁰and the chapiters on the two pillars also [have pomegranates] above, close by the protuberance that [is] beside the net; and the pomegranates [are] two hundred, in rows around on the second capital. ²¹And he raises up the pillars for the porch of the temple, and he raises up the right pillar, and calls its name Jachin, and he raises up the left pillar, and calls its name Boaz; ²²and on the top of the pillars [is] lily-work; and the work of the pillars [is] completed. ²³And he makes the molten sea, ten by the cubit from its edge to its edge; [it is] round all about, and its height [is] five by the cubit, and a line of thirty by the cubit surrounds it around; ²⁴and knobs beneath its brim around are going around it, ten by the cubit, going around the sea; the knobs [are] in two rows, cast in its being cast. ²⁵It is standing on twelve oxen, three facing the north, and three facing the west, and three facing the south, and three facing the east, and the sea [is] on them above, and all their back parts [are] inward. ²⁶And its thickness [is] a handbreadth, and its edge [is] as the work of the edge of a cup, [as] flowers of lilies; it contains two thousand baths. ²⁷And he makes the ten bases of bronze; the length of the one base [is] four by the cubit, and its breadth [is] four by the cubit, and its height [is] three by the cubit. ²⁸And this [is] the work of the base: they have borders, and the borders [are] between the joinings; ²⁹and on the borders that [are] between the joinings [are] lions, oxen, and cherubim, and on the joinings a base above, and beneath the lions and the oxen [are] additions—sloping work. ³⁰And four wheels of bronze [are] for the one base, and axles of bronze; and its four corners have shoulders—the molten shoulders [are] under the laver, beside each addition. ³¹And its mouth within the capital and above [is] by the cubit, and its mouth [is] round, the work of the base, a cubit and half a cubit; and also on its mouth [are] carvings and their borders, square, not round. ³²And the four wheels [are] under the borders, and the spokes of the wheels [are] in the base, and the height of the one wheel [is] a cubit and half a cubit. ³³And the work of the wheels [is] as the work of the wheel of a chariot, their spokes, and their axles, and their felloes, and their naves; the whole [is] molten. ³⁴And four shoulders [are] for the four corners of the one base; its shoulders [are] out of the base. ³⁵And in the top of the base [is] the half of a cubit in the height all around; and on the top of the base its spokes and its borders [are] of the same. ³⁶And he engraves on the tablets of its spokes, and on its borders, cherubim, lions, and palm-trees, according to the void space of each, and additions all around. ³⁷Thus he has made the ten bases; they all have one casting, one measure, one form. ³⁸And he makes ten lavers of bronze; the one laver contains forty baths [and] the one laver [is] four by the cubit; one laver on the one base [is] for [each of] the ten bases; ³⁹and he puts the five bases on the right side of the house, and five on the left side of the house, and he has put the sea on the right side of the house eastward—from toward the south. ⁴⁰And Hiram makes the lavers, and the shovels, and the bowls; and Hiram completes to do all the work that he made for King Solomon, [for] the house of YHWH: ⁴¹two pillars, and bowls of the chapiters that [are] on the top of the two pillars, and the two nets to cover the two bowls of the chapiters that [are] on the top of the pillars; ⁴²and the four hundred pomegranates for the two nets (two rows of pomegranates for the one net to cover the two bowls of the chapiters that [are] on the front of the pillars); ⁴³and the ten bases, and the ten lavers on the bases; ⁴⁴and the one sea, the twelve oxen under the sea, ⁴⁵and the pots, and the shovels, and the bowls; and all these vessels, that Hiram has made for King Solomon [for] the house of YHWH, [are] of polished bronze. ⁴⁶The king has cast them in the circuit of the Jordan, in the thick soil of the ground, between Succoth and Zarthan. ⁴⁷And Solomon places the whole of the vessels; because of the very great abundance, the weight of the bronze has not been searched out. ⁴⁸And Solomon makes all the vessels that [are] in the house of YHWH: the altar of gold, and the table of gold (on which [is] the Bread of the Presentation), ⁴⁹and the lampstands, five on the right, and five on the left, before the oracle, of refined gold, and the flowers, and the lamps, and the tongs, of gold, ⁵⁰and the basins, and the snuffers, and the bowls, and the spoons, and the censers, of refined gold, and the hinges for the doors of the inner-house, for the Holy of Holies, for the doors of the house of the temple, of gold. ⁵¹And it is complete—all the work that King Solomon has made [for] the house of YHWH, and Solomon brings in the sanctified things of his father David; he has put the silver, and the gold, and the vessels in the treasuries of the house of YHWH.

CHAPTER 8

¹Then Solomon assembles the elderly of Israel, and all the heads of the tribes, princes of the fathers of the sons of Israel, to King Solomon, to Jerusalem, to bring up the Ark of the Covenant of YHWH from the City of David—it [is] Zion; ²and all the men of Israel are assembled to King Solomon, in the month of Ethanim, in the festival (the seventh month). ³And all [the] elderly of Israel come in, and the priests lift up the Ark, ⁴and bring up the Ark of YHWH, and the Tent of Meeting, and all the holy vessels that [are] in the tent, indeed, the priests and the Levites bring them up. ⁵And King Solomon and all the congregation of Israel who are assembled to him [are] with him before the Ark, sacrificing sheep and oxen, that are not counted nor numbered for multitude. ⁶And the priests bring in the Ark of the Covenant of YHWH to its place, to the oracle of the house, to the Holy of Holies, to the place of the wings of the cherubim; ⁷for the cherubim are spreading forth two wings to the place of the Ark, and the cherubim cover over the Ark, and over its poles from above; ⁸and they lengthen the poles, and the heads of the poles are seen from the holy [place] on the front of the oracle, and are not seen outside, and they are there to this day. ⁹There is nothing in the Ark, only the two tablets of stone which Moses put there in Horeb when YHWH covenanted with the sons of Israel in their going out of the land of Egypt. ¹⁰And it comes to pass, in the going out of the priests from the holy [place], that the cloud has filled the house of YHWH, ¹¹and the priests have not been able to stand to minister because of the cloud, for the glory of YHWH has filled the house of YHWH. ¹²Then Solomon said, "YHWH has said [He is] to dwell in thick darkness; ¹³I have surely built a house of habitation for You; a fixed place for Your abiding for all ages." ¹⁴And the king turns his face around, and blesses the whole assembly of Israel; and all the assembly of Israel is standing. ¹⁵And he says, "Blessed [is] YHWH, God of Israel, who spoke by His mouth with my father David, and by His hand has fulfilled [it], saying, ¹⁶From the day that I brought out My people, even Israel, from Egypt, I have not fixed on a city out of all the tribes of Israel, to build a house for My Name being there; and I fix on David to be over My people Israel. ¹⁷And it is with the heart of my father David to build a house for the Name of YHWH, God of Israel, ¹⁸and YHWH says to my father David, Because that it has been with your heart to build a house for My Name, you have done well that it has been with your heart; ¹⁹only, you do not build the house, but your son who is coming out from your loins, he builds the house for My Name. ²⁰And YHWH establishes His word which He spoke, and I am risen up instead of my father David, and I sit on the throne of Israel, as YHWH spoke, and build the house for the Name of YHWH, God of Israel, ²¹and I set a place for the Ark there, where the covenant of YHWH [is], which He made with our fathers in His bringing them out from the land of Egypt." ²²And Solomon stands before the altar of

YHWH, in front of all the assembly of Israel, and spreads his hands toward the heavens, ²³and says, "YHWH, God of Israel, there is not a God like You, in the heavens above and on the earth below, keeping the covenant and the kindness for Your servants, those walking before You with all their heart, ²⁴which You have kept for Your servant, my father David, that which You spoke to him; indeed, You speak with Your mouth, and with Your hand have fulfilled [it], as [at] this day. ²⁵And now, YHWH, God of Israel, keep for Your servant, my father David, that which You spoke to him, saying, A man of yours is never cut off from before My face, sitting on the throne of Israel—only, if your sons watch their way, to walk before Me as you have walked before Me. ²⁶And now, O God of Israel, please let Your word be established which You have spoken to Your servant, my father David. ²⁷But is it true [that] God dwells on the earth? Behold, the heavens and the heavens of the heavens cannot contain You, how much less this house which I have built! ²⁸Then You have turned to the prayer of Your servant, and to his supplication, O YHWH my God, to listen to the cry and to the prayer which Your servant is praying before You today, ²⁹for Your eyes being open toward this house night and day, toward the place of which You have said, My Name is there; to listen to the prayer which Your servant prays toward this place. ³⁰Then You have listened to the supplication of Your servant, and of Your people Israel, which they pray toward this place; indeed, You listen in the place of Your dwelling, in the heavens—and You have listened, and have forgiven, ³¹that which a man sins against his neighbor, and he has lifted up an oath on him to cause him to swear, and the oath has come in before Your altar in this house, ³²then You hear in the heavens, and have done, and have judged Your servants, to declare wicked the wicked, to put his way on his [own] head, and to declare righteous the righteous, to give him according to his righteousness. ³³In Your people Israel being struck before an enemy, because they sin against You, and they have turned back to You, and have confessed Your Name, and prayed, and made supplication to You in this house, ³⁴then you hear in the heavens, and have forgiven the sin of Your people Israel, and brought them back to the ground that You gave to their fathers. ³⁵In the heavens being restrained, and there is no rain, because they sin against You, and they have prayed toward this place, and confessed Your Name, and turn back from their sin, for You afflict them, ³⁶then You hear in the heavens, and have forgiven the sin of Your servants, and of Your people Israel, for You direct them [to] the good way in which they go, and have given rain on Your land which You have given to Your people for inheritance. ³⁷Famine—when it is in the land; pestilence—when it is [in the land]; blasting, mildew, locust; caterpillar—when it is [in the land]; when its enemy has distressed it in the land [in] its gates, any plague, any sickness—³⁸any prayer, any supplication that [is] of any man of all Your people Israel, each who knows the plague of his own heart, and has spread his hands toward this house, ³⁹then You hear in the heavens, the settled place of Your dwelling, and have forgiven, and have done, and have given to each according to all his ways, whose heart You know (for You have known—You alone—the heart of all the sons of man), ⁴⁰so that they fear You all the days that they are living on the face of the ground that You have given to our fathers. ⁴¹And also, to the stranger who is not of Your people Israel, and has come from a far-off land for Your Name's sake— ⁴²for they hear of Your great Name, and of Your strong hand, and of Your outstretched arm—and he has come in and prayed toward this house, ⁴³You hear in the heavens, the settled place of Your dwelling, and have done according to all that the stranger calls to You for, in order that all the peoples of the earth may know Your Name, to fear You like Your people Israel, and to know that Your Name has been called on this house which I have built. ⁴⁴When Your people go out to battle against its enemy, in the way that You send them, and they have prayed to YHWH [in] the way of the city which you have fixed on, and of the house which I have built for Your Name, ⁴⁵then You have heard their prayer and their supplication in the heavens, and have maintained their cause. ⁴⁶When they sin against You (for there is not a man who does not sin), and You have been angry with them, and have given them up before an enemy, and they have taken captive their captivity to the land of the enemy far off or near; ⁴⁷and they have turned [it] back to their heart in the land to where they have been taken captive, and have turned back, and made supplication to You in the land of their captors, saying, We have sinned and done perversely—we have done wickedly; ⁴⁸indeed, they have turned back to You with all their heart and with all their soul, in the land of their enemies who have taken them captive, and have prayed to You [in] the way of their land, which You gave to their fathers, the city which You have chosen, and the house which I have built for Your Name: ⁴⁹then You have heard in the heavens, the settled place of Your dwelling, their prayer and their supplication, and have maintained their cause, ⁵⁰and have forgiven Your people who have sinned against You, even all their transgressions which they have transgressed against You, and have given them mercies before their captors, and they have had mercy [on] them— ⁵¹for they [are] Your people and Your inheritance, whom You brought out of Egypt, out of the midst of the furnace of iron— ⁵²for Your eyes being open to the supplication of Your servant, and to the supplication of Your people Israel, to listen to them in all they call to You for; ⁵³for You have separated them to Yourself for an inheritance, out of all the peoples of the earth, as You spoke by the hand of Your servant Moses, in Your bringing out our fathers from Egypt, O Lord YHWH." ⁵⁴And it comes to pass, at Solomon's finishing to pray to YHWH all this prayer and supplication, he has risen from before the altar of YHWH, from bending on his knees and [having] his hands spread out to the heavens, ⁵⁵and he stands and blesses all the assembly of Israel [with] a loud voice, saying, ⁵⁶"Blessed [is] YHWH who has given rest to His people Israel, according to all that He has spoken; not [even] one word has fallen of all His good word, which He spoke by the hand of His servant Moses. ⁵⁷Our God YHWH is with us as He has been with our fathers; He does not forsake us nor leave us; ⁵⁸to incline our heart to Himself, to walk in all His ways, and to keep His commands, and His statutes, and His judgments, which He commanded our fathers; ⁵⁹and these, my words, with which I have made supplication before YHWH, are near to our God YHWH by day and by night, to maintain the cause of His servant, and the cause of His people Israel, the matter of a day in its day, ⁶⁰that all the peoples of the earth may know that He, YHWH, [is] God; there is none else; ⁶¹and your heart has been perfect with our God YHWH, to walk in His statutes, and to keep His commands, as [at] this day." ⁶²And the king and all Israel with him are sacrificing a sacrifice before YHWH; ⁶³and Solomon sacrifices the sacrifice of peace-offerings, which he has sacrificed to YHWH: twenty-two thousand oxen and one hundred and twenty thousand sheep; and the king and all the sons of Israel dedicate the house of YHWH. ⁶⁴On that day the king has sanctified the middle of the court that [is] before the house of YHWH, for he has made the burnt-offering, and the present, and the fat of the peace-offerings there; for the altar of bronze that [is] before YHWH [is] too small to contain the burnt-offering, and the present, and the fat of the peace-offerings. ⁶⁵And Solomon makes, at that time, the festival—and all Israel with him, a great assembly from the entering in of Hamath to the Brook of Egypt—before our God YHWH, [for] seven days and seven [more] days—fourteen days. ⁶⁶On the eighth day he has sent the people away, and they bless the king, and go to their tents, rejoicing and glad of heart for all the good that YHWH has done to His servant David, and to His people Israel.

CHAPTER 9

¹And it comes to pass, at Solomon's finishing to build the house of YHWH, and the house of the king, and all the desire of Solomon that he delighted to do, ²that YHWH appears to Solomon a second time, as He appeared to him in Gibeon, ³and YHWH says to him, "I have heard your prayer and your supplication with which you have made supplication before Me; I have hallowed this house that you have built to put My Name there for all time, and My eyes and My heart have been there [for] all the days. ⁴And you—if you walk before Me as your father David walked, in simplicity of heart, and in uprightness, to do according to all that I have commanded you, [and] you keep My statutes and My judgments, ⁵then I have established the throne of your kingdom over Israel for all time, as I spoke to your father David, saying, A man of yours is never cut off from [being] on the throne of Israel. ⁶If

you at all turn back—you and your sons—from after Me, and do not keep My commands [and] My statutes that I have set before you, and have gone and served other gods, and bowed yourselves to them, ⁷then I have cut off Israel from the face of the ground that I have given to them, and the house that I have hallowed for My Name I send away from My presence, and Israel has been for an allegory and for a byword among all the peoples; ⁸as for this house [that] is high, everyone passing by it is astonished, and has hissed, and they have said, Why has YHWH done this to this land and to this house? ⁹And they have said, Because that they have forsaken their God YHWH, who brought out their fathers from the land of Egypt, and they lay hold on other gods, and bow themselves to them and serve them; therefore YHWH has brought all this calamity on them." ¹⁰And it comes to pass, at the end of twenty years, that Solomon has built the two houses, the house of YHWH, and the house of the king. ¹¹Hiram king of Tyre has assisted Solomon with cedar-trees, and with fir-trees, and with gold, according to all his desire; then King Solomon gives to Hiram twenty cities in the land of Galilee. ¹²And Hiram comes out from Tyre to see the cities that Solomon has given to him, and they have not been right in his eyes, ¹³and he says, "What [are] these cities that you have given to me, my brother?" And one calls them the land of Cabul to this day. ¹⁴And Hiram sends one hundred and twenty talents of gold to the king. ¹⁵And this [is] the matter of the tribute that King Solomon has lifted up, to build the house of YHWH, and his own house, and Millo, and the wall of Jerusalem, and Hazor, and Megiddo, and Gezer ¹⁶(Pharaoh king of Egypt has gone up and captures Gezer, and burns it with fire, and he has slain the Canaanite who is dwelling in the city, and gives it [as] presents to his daughter, wife of Solomon). ¹⁷And Solomon builds Gezer, and the lower Beth-Horon, ¹⁸and Ba'alath, and Tadmor in the wilderness, in the land, ¹⁹and all the cities of stores that King Solomon has, and the cities of the chariots, and the cities of the horsemen, and the desire of Solomon that he desired to build in Jerusalem, and in Lebanon, and in all the land of his dominion. ²⁰The whole of the people that is left of the Amorite, the Hittite, the Perizzite, the Hivite, and the Jebusite, who [are] not of the sons of Israel— ²¹their sons who are left behind them in the land, whom the sons of Israel have not been able to devote—he has even lifted up a tribute of service [on] them to this day. ²²And Solomon has not appointed a servant out of the sons of Israel, for they [are] the men of war, and his servants, and his heads, and his captains, and the heads of his chariots, and his horsemen. ²³These [are] the five hundred and fifty heads of the officers who [are] over the work of Solomon, those ruling among the people who are laboring in the work. ²⁴Only, the daughter of Pharaoh went up out of the City of David to her house that [Solomon] built for her; then he built Millo. ²⁵And Solomon caused burnt-offerings and peace-offerings to ascend three times in a year on the altar that he built for YHWH, and he burned it as incense with that which [is] before YHWH, and finished the house. ²⁶And King Solomon has made a navy in Ezion-Geber, that is beside Eloth, on the edge of the Sea of Suph, in the land of Edom. ²⁷And Hiram sends his servants in the navy, shipmen knowing the sea, with servants of Solomon, ²⁸and they come to Ophir, and take four hundred and twenty talents of gold from there, and bring [it] to King Solomon.

CHAPTER 10

¹And the queen of Sheba is hearing of the fame of Solomon concerning the Name of YHWH, and comes to try him with enigmas, ²and she comes to Jerusalem, with a very great company, camels carrying spices, and very much gold, and precious stone, and she comes to Solomon, and speaks to him all that has been with her heart. ³And Solomon declares to her all her matters—there has not been a thing hid from the king that he has not declared to her. ⁴And the queen of Sheba sees all the wisdom of Solomon, and the house that he built, ⁵and the food of his table, and the sitting of his servants, and the standing of his ministers, and their clothing, and his butlers, and his burnt-offering that he causes to ascend in the house of YHWH, and there has not been anymore spirit in her. ⁶And she says to the king, "The word that I heard in my land has been true concerning your matters and your wisdom; ⁷and I gave no credence to the words until I have come, and my eyes see, and behold, not [even] half was declared to me; you have added wisdom and goodness to the report that I heard. ⁸O the blessedness of your men, O the blessedness of your servants—these—who are standing before you continually, who are hearing your wisdom! ⁹Your God YHWH is blessed, who delighted in you, to put you on the throne of Israel; in YHWH's loving Israel for all time He sets you for king, to do judgment and righteousness." ¹⁰And she gives to the king one hundred and twenty talents of gold, and very many spices, and precious stone; there never again came in abundance like that spice that the queen of Sheba gave to King Solomon. ¹¹And also, the navy of Hiram that bore gold from Ophir, brought in very much almug-trees and precious stone from Ophir; ¹²and the king makes the almug-trees a support for the house of YHWH, and for the house of the king, and harps and psalteries for singers; there have not come such almug-trees, nor have there been seen [such] to this day. ¹³And King Solomon gave to the queen of Sheba all her desire that she asked, apart from that which he gave to her as a memorial of King Solomon, and she turns and goes to her land, she and her servants. ¹⁴And the weight of the gold that has come to Solomon in one year is six hundred sixty-six talents of gold, ¹⁵apart from [that of] the tourists, and of the traffic of the merchants, and of all the kings of Arabia, and of the governors of the land. ¹⁶And King Solomon makes two hundred bucklers of alloyed gold—six hundred [shekels] of gold go up on the one buckler; ¹⁷and three hundred shields of alloyed gold—three pounds of gold go up on the one shield; and the king puts them [in] the House of the Forest of Lebanon. ¹⁸And the king makes a great throne of ivory, and overlays it with refined gold; ¹⁹the throne has six steps, and a round top [is] to the throne behind it, and hands [are] on this [side] and on that, to the place of the sitting, and two lions are standing near the hands, ²⁰and twelve lions are standing there on the six steps, on this [side] and on that; it has not been made so for any kingdom. ²¹And all the drinking vessels of King Solomon [are] of gold, and all the vessels of the House of the Forest of Lebanon [are] of refined gold—there are none of silver; it was not reckoned in the days of Solomon for anything, ²²for the king has a navy of Tarshish at sea with a navy of Hiram; once in three years the navy of Tarshish comes, carrying gold, and silver, ivory, and apes, and peacocks [[*or* monkeys]]. ²³And King Solomon is greater than any of the kings of the earth for riches and for wisdom, ²⁴and all the earth is seeking the presence of Solomon, to hear his wisdom that God has put into his heart, ²⁵and they are each bringing his present, vessels of silver, and vessels of gold, and garments, and armor, and spices, horses, and mules, the matter of a year in a year. ²⁶And Solomon gathers chariots, and horsemen, and he has one thousand and four hundred chariots, and twelve thousand horsemen, and he places them in the cities of the chariot, and with the king in Jerusalem. ²⁷And the king makes the silver in Jerusalem as stones, and he has made the cedars as the sycamores that [are] in the low country, for abundance. ²⁸And the outgoing of the horses that King Solomon has [is] from Egypt, and from Keveh; merchants of the king take from Keveh at a price; ²⁹and a chariot comes up and comes out of Egypt for six hundred pieces of silver, and a horse for one hundred and fifty, and so for all the kings of the Hittites, and for the kings of Aram; they bring out by their hand.

CHAPTER 11

¹And King Solomon has loved many strange women, and the daughter of Pharaoh, females of Moab, Ammon, Edom, Sidon, [and] of the Hittites, ²of the nations of which YHWH said to the sons of Israel, "You do not go in to them, and they do not go in to you; surely they turn aside your heart after their gods"; Solomon has cleaved to them for love. ³And he has seven hundred wives, princesses, and three hundred concubines; and his wives turn aside his heart. ⁴And it comes to pass, at the time of Solomon's old age, his wives have turned aside his heart after other gods, and his heart has not been perfect with his God YHWH, like the heart of his father David. ⁵And Solomon goes after Ashtoreth goddess of the Zidonians, and after Milcom the abomination of the Ammonites; ⁶and Solomon does evil in the eyes of YHWH, and has not been fully after YHWH, like his father David. ⁷Then Solomon builds a high place for Chemosh the abomination of Moab, in the hill that [is] on the

front of Jerusalem, and for Molech the abomination of the sons of Ammon; ⁸and so he has done for all his strange women, who are perfuming and sacrificing to their gods. ⁹And YHWH shows Himself angry with Solomon, for his heart has turned aside from YHWH, God of Israel, who had appeared to him twice, ¹⁰and given a charge to him concerning this thing, not to go after other gods; and he has not kept that which YHWH commanded, ¹¹and YHWH says to Solomon, "Because that this has been with you, and you have not kept My covenant and My statutes that I charged on you, I surely tear the kingdom from you, and have given it to your servant. ¹²Only, I do not do it in your days, for the sake of your father David; I tear it out of the hand of your son; ¹³only, I do not tear away all of the kingdom; I give one tribe to your son, for the sake of My servant David, and for the sake of Jerusalem that I have chosen." ¹⁴And YHWH raises up an adversary against Solomon, Hadad the Edomite; he [is] of the seed of the king in Edom; ¹⁵and it comes to pass, in David's being with Edom, in the going up of Joab head of the host to bury the slain, that he strikes every male in Edom— ¹⁶for six months Joab abided there, and all Israel, until the cutting off of every male in Edom— ¹⁷and Hadad flees, he and certain Edomites, of the servants of his father, with him, to go to Egypt, and Hadad [is] a little youth, ¹⁸and they rise out of Midian, and come into Paran, and take men with them out of Paran, and come into Egypt, to Pharaoh king of Egypt, and he gives a house to him, and has commanded bread for him, and has given land to him. ¹⁹And Hadad finds grace in the eyes of Pharaoh exceedingly, and he gives to him a wife, the sister of his own wife, sister of Tahpenes the mistress; ²⁰and the sister of Tahpenes bears to him his son Genubath, and Tahpenes weans him within the house of Pharaoh, and Genubath is in the house of Pharaoh in the midst of the sons of Pharaoh. ²¹And Hadad has heard in Egypt that David has lain with his fathers, and that Joab head of the host is dead, and Hadad says to Pharaoh, "Send me away, and I go to my land." ²²And Pharaoh says to him, "But what are you lacking with me, that behold, you are seeking to go to your own land?" And he says, "Nothing, but you certainly send me away." ²³And God raises an adversary against him, Rezon son of Eliadah, who has fled from Hadadezer king of Zobah, his lord, ²⁴and gathers men to himself, and is head of a troop in David's slaying them, and they go to Damascus, and dwell in it, and reign in Damascus; ²⁵and he is an adversary against Israel all the days of Solomon (besides the evil that Hadad [did]), and he cuts off in Israel, and reigns over Aram. ²⁶And Jeroboam son of Nebat, an Ephraimite of Zereda—the name of whose mother [is] Zeruah, a widow woman—servant to Solomon, he also lifts up a hand against the king; ²⁷and this [is] the thing [for] which he lifted up a hand against the king: Solomon built Millo—he shut up the breach of the city of his father David, ²⁸and the man Jeroboam [is] mighty in valor, and Solomon sees that the young man is doing business, and appoints him over all the burden of the house of Joseph. ²⁹And it comes to pass, at that time, that Jeroboam has gone out from Jerusalem, and Ahijah the Shilonite, the prophet, finds him in the way, and he is covering himself with a new garment; and both of them [are] by themselves in a field, ³⁰and Ahijah lays hold on the new garment that [is] on him, and tears it [into] twelve pieces, ³¹and says to Jeroboam, "Take ten pieces for yourself, for thus said YHWH, God of Israel: Behold, I am tearing the kingdom out of the hand of Solomon, and have given the ten tribes to you, ³²but he has the one tribe for My servant David's sake, and for Jerusalem's sake, the city which I have fixed on, out of all the tribes of Israel, ³³because they have forsaken Me, and bow themselves to Ashtoreth, goddess of the Zidonians, to Chemosh god of Moab, and to Milcom god of the sons of Ammon, and have not walked in My ways, to do that which [is] right in My eyes, and My statutes and My judgments, like his father David. ³⁴And I do not take the whole of the kingdom out of his hand, for I make him prince all [the] days of his life, for the sake of My servant David whom I chose, who kept My commands and My statutes; ³⁵and I have taken the kingdom out of the hand of his son, and given it to you—the ten tribes; ³⁶and to his son I give one tribe, for there being a lamp before Me for My servant David in Jerusalem [for] all the days, the city that I have chosen for Myself to put My Name there. ³⁷And I take you, and you have reigned over all that your soul desires, and you have been king over Israel; ³⁸and it has been, if you hear all that I command you, and have walked in My ways, and done that which is right in My eyes, to keep My statutes and My commands, as My servant David did, that I have been with you, and have built a steadfast house for you, as I built for David, and have given Israel to you, ³⁹and I humble the seed of David for this; only, not [for] all the days." ⁴⁰And Solomon seeks to put Jeroboam to death, and Jeroboam rises and flees to Egypt, to Shishak king of Egypt, and he is in Egypt until the death of Solomon. ⁴¹And the rest of the matters of Solomon, and all that he did, and his wisdom, are they not written on the scroll of the matters of Solomon? ⁴²And the days that Solomon has reigned in Jerusalem over all Israel [are] forty years, ⁴³and Solomon lies with his fathers, and is buried in the city of his father David, and his son Rehoboam reigns in his stead.

CHAPTER 12

¹And Rehoboam goes to Shechem, for all Israel has come to Shechem to make him king. ²And it comes to pass, at Jeroboam son of Nebat's hearing (and he [is] yet in Egypt where he has fled from the presence of Solomon the king, and Jeroboam dwells in Egypt), ³that they send and call for him; and they come—Jeroboam and all the assembly of Israel—and speak to Rehoboam, saying, ⁴"Your father hardened our yoke, and you, now, lighten [some] of the hard service of your father, and his heavy yoke that he put on us, and we serve you." ⁵And he says to them, "Yet go [for] three days, and come back to me"; and the people go. ⁶And King Rehoboam consults with the elderly who have been standing in the presence of his father Solomon, in his being alive, saying, "How are you counseling to answer this people?" ⁷And they speak to him, saying, "If, today, you are a servant of this people, and have served them, and answered them, and spoken good words to them, then they have been servants to you [for] all the days." ⁸And he forsakes the counsel of the elderly which they counseled him, and consults with the boys who have grown up with him, who are standing before him; ⁹and he says to them, "What are you counseling, and we answer this people, who have spoken to me, saying, Lighten [some] of the yoke that your father put on us?" ¹⁰And they speak to him—the boys who had grown up with him—saying, "Thus you say to this people who have spoken to you, saying, Your father made our yoke heavy, and you, make [it] light on us; thus you speak to them, My little [finger] is thicker than the loins of my father; ¹¹and now, my father laid a heavy yoke on you, and I add to your yoke; my father disciplined you with whips, and I discipline you with scorpions." ¹²And they come—Jeroboam and all the people—to Rehoboam, on the third day, as the king had spoken, saying, "Come back to me on the third day." ¹³And the king answers the people sharply, and forsakes the counsel of the elderly which they counseled him, ¹⁴and speaks to them, according to the counsel of the boys, saying, "My father made your yoke heavy, and I add to your yoke; my father disciplined you with whips, and I discipline you with scorpions"; ¹⁵and the king did not listen to the people, for the revolution was from YHWH, in order to establish His word that YHWH spoke by the hand of Ahijah the Shilonite to Jeroboam son of Nebat. ¹⁶And all Israel sees that the king has not listened to them, and the people send the king back word, saying, "What portion do we have in David? Indeed, there is no inheritance in the son of Jesse; [return] to your tents, O Israel; now see your house, O David!" And Israel goes to its tents. ¹⁷As for the sons of Israel, those dwelling in the cities of Judah—Rehoboam reigns over them. ¹⁸And King Rehoboam sends Adoram who [is] over the tribute, and all Israel casts stones at him, and he dies; and King Rehoboam has strengthened himself to go up into a chariot to flee to Jerusalem; ¹⁹and Israel transgresses against the house of David to this day. ²⁰And it comes to pass, at all Israel hearing that Jeroboam has returned, that they send and call him to the congregation, and cause him to reign over all Israel; none has been after the house of David except the tribe of Judah alone. ²¹And Rehoboam comes to Jerusalem, and assembles all the house of Judah and the tribe of Benjamin, one hundred and eighty thousand chosen warriors, to fight with the house of Israel, to bring back the kingdom to Rehoboam son of Solomon. ²²And the word of God is to Shemaiah a man of God,

saying, ²³"Speak to Rehoboam son of Solomon, king of Judah, and to all the house of Judah and Benjamin, and the rest of the people, saying, ²⁴Thus said YHWH: You do not go up nor fight with your brothers the sons of Israel; let each return to his house, for this thing has been from Me"; and they hear the word of YHWH, and turn back to go according to the word of YHWH. ²⁵And Jeroboam builds Shechem in the hill-country of Ephraim, and dwells in it, and goes out there, and builds Penuel; ²⁶and Jeroboam says in his heart, "Now the kingdom turns back to the house of David— ²⁷if this people goes up to make sacrifices in the house of YHWH in Jerusalem, then the heart of this people has turned back to their lord, to Rehoboam king of Judah, and they have slain me, and turned back to Rehoboam king of Judah." ²⁸And the king takes counsel, and makes two calves of gold, and says to them, "Enough of you from going up to Jerusalem; behold, your gods, O Israel, which brought you up out of the land of Egypt." ²⁹And he sets the one in Beth-El, and the other he has put in Dan, ³⁰and this thing becomes a sin, and the people go before the one—to Dan. ³¹And he makes the house of high places, and makes priests from the extremities of the people, who were not of the sons of Levi; ³²and Jeroboam makes a festival in the eighth month, on the fifteenth day of the month, like the festival that [is] in Judah, and he offers on the altar—so he did in Beth-El—to sacrifice to the calves which he made, and he has appointed in Beth-El the priests of the high places that he made. ³³And he offers up on the altar that he made in Beth-El, on the fifteenth day of the eighth month, in the month that he devised from his own heart, and he makes a festival for the sons of Israel, and offers on the altar—to make incense.

CHAPTER 13

¹And behold, a man of God has come from Judah, by the word of YHWH, to Beth-El, and Jeroboam is standing by the altar—to make incense; ²and he calls against the altar, by the word of YHWH, and says, "Altar! Altar! Thus said YHWH: Behold, a son is born to the house of David—Josiah [is] his name—and he has sacrificed on you the priests of the high places who are making incense on you, and bones of man are burned on you." ³And he has given a sign on that day, saying, "This [is] the sign that YHWH has spoken, Behold, the altar is torn, and the ashes that [are] on it [are] poured forth." ⁴And it comes to pass, at the king's hearing the word of the man of God that he calls against the altar in Beth-El, that Jeroboam puts forth his hand from off the altar, saying, "Catch him"; and his hand that he has put forth against him is dried up, and he is not able to bring it back to himself, ⁵and the altar is torn, and the ashes [are] poured forth from the altar, according to the sign that the man of God had given by the word of YHWH. ⁶And the king answers and says to the man of God, "Please appease the face of your God YHWH, and pray for me, and my hand comes back to me"; and the man of God appeases the face of YHWH, and the hand of the king comes back to him, and it is as at the beginning. ⁷And the king speaks to the man of God, "Come in with me to the house, and refresh yourself, and I give a gift to you." ⁸And the man of God says to the king, "If you give to me the half of your house, I do not go in with you, nor do I eat bread, nor do I drink water, in this place; ⁹for so He commanded me by the word of YHWH, saying, You do not eat bread nor drink water, nor return in the way that you have come." ¹⁰And he goes on in another way, and has not turned back in the way in which he came in to Beth-El. ¹¹And a certain aged prophet is dwelling in Beth-El, and his son comes and recounts to him every deed that the man of God has done today in Beth-El, the words that he has spoken to the king—indeed, they recount them to their father. ¹²And their father says to them, "Where [is] this—the way he has gone?" And his sons see the way that the man of God who came from Judah has gone. ¹³And he says to his sons, "Saddle the donkey for me," and they saddle the donkey for him, and he rides on it, ¹⁴and goes after the man of God, and finds him sitting under the oak, and says to him, "Are you the man of God who has come from Judah?" And he says, "I [am]." ¹⁵And he says to him, "Come with me to the house and eat bread." ¹⁶And he says, "I am not able to return with you, and to go in with you, nor do I eat bread or drink water with you in this place, ¹⁷for [there is] a word to me by the word of YHWH, You do not eat bread nor drink water there [and] you do not return to go in the way in which you came." ¹⁸And he says to him, "I [am] also a prophet like you, and a messenger spoke to me by the word of YHWH, saying, Bring him back with you to your house, and he eats bread and drinks water." He has lied to him. ¹⁹And he turns back with him, and eats bread in his house, and drinks water. ²⁰And it comes to pass—they are sitting at the table—and [there] is a word of YHWH to the prophet who brought him back, ²¹and he calls to the man of God who came from Judah, saying, "Thus said YHWH: Because that you have provoked the mouth of YHWH, and have not kept the command that your God YHWH charged you, ²²and turn back and eat bread and drink water in the place of which He said to you, You do not eat bread nor drink water—your carcass does not come into the burying-place of your fathers." ²³And it comes to pass, after his eating bread, and after his drinking, that he saddles the donkey for him, for the prophet whom he had brought back, ²⁴and he goes, and a lion finds him in the way, and puts him to death, and his carcass is cast in the way, and the donkey is standing near it, and the lion is standing near the carcass. ²⁵And behold, men are passing by, and see the carcass cast in the way, and the lion standing near the carcass, and they come and speak [of it] in the city in which the old prophet is dwelling. ²⁶And the prophet who brought him back out of the way hears and says, "It [is] the man of God who provoked the mouth of YHWH, and YHWH gives him to the lion, and it destroys him, and puts him to death, according to the word of YHWH that he spoke to him." ²⁷And he speaks to his sons saying, "Saddle the donkey for me," and they saddle [it]. ²⁸And he goes and finds his carcass cast in the way, and the donkey and the lion are standing near the carcass—the lion has not eaten the carcass nor destroyed the donkey. ²⁹And the prophet takes up the carcass of the man of God, and places it on the donkey, and brings it back, and the old prophet comes to the city to mourn and to bury him, ³⁰and he places his carcass in his own grave, and they mourn for him, "Oh, my brother!" ³¹And it comes to pass, after his burying him, that he speaks to his sons, saying, "At my death—you have buried me in the burying-place in which the man of God is buried; place my bones near his bones; ³²for the word certainly comes to pass that he called by the word of YHWH concerning the altar which [is in] Beth-El, and concerning all the houses of the high places that [are] in cities of Samaria." ³³After this thing Jeroboam has not turned from his evil way, and turns back, and makes priests of high places from the extremities of the people; he who is desirous—he consecrates his hand, and he is of the priests of the high places. ³⁴And in this thing is the sin of the house of Jeroboam, even to cut [it] off, and to destroy [it] from off the face of the ground.

CHAPTER 14

¹At that time Abijah son of Jeroboam was sick, ²and Jeroboam says to his wife, "Now rise and change yourself, and they do not know that you [are the] wife of Jeroboam, and you have gone to Shiloh; behold, Ahijah the prophet [is] there; he spoke to me of [being] king over this people; ³and you have taken in your hand ten loaves, and crumbs, and a bottle of honey, and have gone to him; he declares to you what becomes of the youth." ⁴And the wife of Jeroboam does so, and rises, and goes to Shiloh, and enters the house of Ahijah, and Ahijah is not able to see, for his eyes have stood because of his age. ⁵And YHWH said to Ahijah, "Behold, the wife of Jeroboam is coming to seek a word from you concerning her son, for he is sick; thus and thus you speak to her, and it comes to pass at her coming in, that she is making herself strange." ⁶And it comes to pass, at Ahijah's hearing the sound of her feet [as] she came to the opening, that he says, "Come in, wife of Jeroboam, why is this [that] you are making yourself strange? And I am sent to you [with] a sharp thing. ⁷Go, say to Jeroboam, Thus said YHWH, God of Israel: Because that I have made you high out of the midst of the people, and appoint you leader over my people Israel, ⁸and tear the kingdom from the house of David, and give it to you—and you have not been as My servant David who kept My commands, and who walked after Me with all his heart, to only do that which [is] right in My eyes, ⁹and you do evil above all who have been before you, and go, and make other gods and molten images for yourself to provoke Me to anger, and you have cast Me behind your back— ¹⁰therefore, behold, I am bringing calamity to the house of Jeroboam, and have cut off to Jeroboam those

1 KINGS

sitting on the wall—shut up and left—in Israel, and have put away the posterity of the house of Jeroboam, as one puts away the dung until its consumption; ¹¹the dogs eat him who dies of Jeroboam in a city, and birds of the heavens eat him who dies in a field, for YHWH has spoken. ¹²And you, rise, go to your house; in the going in of your feet to the city, the boy has died; ¹³and all Israel has mourned for him, and buried him, for this one—by himself—of Jeroboam comes to a grave, because there has been found in him a good thing toward YHWH, God of Israel, in the house of Jeroboam. ¹⁴And YHWH has raised up for Himself a king over Israel who cuts off the house of Jeroboam this day—and what? Even now! ¹⁵And YHWH has struck Israel as the reed is moved by the waters, and has plucked Israel from off this good ground that He gave to their fathers, and scattered them beyond the River, because that they made their Asherim, provoking YHWH to anger; ¹⁶and He gives up Israel because of the sins of Jeroboam that he sinned, and that he caused Israel to sin." ¹⁷And the wife of Jeroboam rises, and goes, and comes to Tirzah; she has come to the threshold of the house, and the youth dies; ¹⁸and they bury him, and all Israel mourns for him, according to the word of YHWH that he spoke by the hand of His servant Ahijah the prophet. ¹⁹And the rest of the matters of Jeroboam, how he fought, and how he reigned, behold, they are written on the scroll of the Chronicles of the Kings of Israel. ²⁰And the days that Jeroboam reigned [are] twenty-two years, and he lies with his fathers, and his son Nadab reigns in his stead. ²¹And Rehoboam son of Solomon has reigned in Judah; Rehoboam [is] a son of forty-one years in his reigning, and he has reigned seventeen years in Jerusalem, the city that YHWH chose to set His Name there, out of all the tribes of Israel, and the name of his mother [is] Naamah the Ammonitess. ²²And Judah does evil in the eyes of YHWH, and they make Him zealous above all that their fathers did by their sins that they have sinned. ²³And they build—they also—for themselves high places, and standing-pillars, and Asherim, on every high height, and under every green tree; ²⁴and a whoremonger has also been in the land; they have done according to all the abominations of the nations that YHWH dispossessed from the presence of the sons of Israel. ²⁵And it comes to pass, in the fifth year of King Rehoboam, Shishak king of Egypt has gone up against Jerusalem, ²⁶and he takes the treasures of the house of YHWH, and the treasures of the house of the king, indeed, he has taken the whole; and he takes all the shields of gold that Solomon made. ²⁷And King Rehoboam makes shields of bronze in their stead, and has made [them] a charge on the hand of the heads of the runners, those keeping the opening of the house of the king, ²⁸and it comes to pass, from the going in of the king to the house of YHWH, the runners carry them, and have brought them back to the chamber of the runners. ²⁹And the rest of the matters of Rehoboam and all that he did, are they not written on the scroll of the Chronicles of the Kings of Judah? ³⁰And there has been war between Rehoboam and Jeroboam [for] all the days; ³¹and Rehoboam lies with his fathers, and is buried with his fathers in the City of David, and the name of his mother [is] Naamah the Ammonitess, and his son Abijam reigns in his stead.

CHAPTER 15

¹And in the eighteenth year of King Jeroboam son of Nebat, Abijam has reigned over Judah; ²he has reigned three years in Jerusalem, and the name of his mother [is] Maachah daughter of Abishalom; ³and he walks in all the sins of his father that he did before him, and his heart has not been perfect with his God YHWH, as the heart of his father David; ⁴but for David's sake his God YHWH has given to him a lamp in Jerusalem, to raise up his son after him, and to establish Jerusalem, ⁵in that David did that which [is] right in the eyes of YHWH, and did not turn aside from all that He commanded him all [the] days of his life—except in the matter of Uriah the Hittite; ⁶and there has been war between Rehoboam and Jeroboam all the days of his life. ⁷And the rest of the matters of Abijam and all that he did, are they not written on the scroll of the Chronicles of the Kings of Judah? And there has been war between Abijam and Jeroboam; ⁸and Abijam lies with his fathers, and they bury him in the City of David, and his son Asa reigns in his stead. ⁹And in the twentieth year of Jeroboam king of Israel, Asa has reigned over Judah, ¹⁰and he has reigned forty-one years in Jerusalem, and the name of his mother [is] Maachah daughter of Abishalom. ¹¹And Asa does that which [is] right in the eyes of YHWH, like his father David, ¹²and removes the whoremongers out of the land, and turns aside all the idols that his fathers made; ¹³and also his mother Maachah—he turns her aside from being mistress, in that she made a horrible thing for an Asherah, and Asa cuts down her horrible thing, and burns [it] by the Brook of Kidron; ¹⁴but the high places have not been removed; only, the heart of Asa has been perfect with YHWH [for] all his days, ¹⁵and he brings in the sanctified things of his father, and his own sanctified things, to the house of YHWH: silver, and gold, and vessels. ¹⁶And there has been war between Asa and Baasha king of Israel [for] all their days, ¹⁷and Baasha king of Israel goes up against Judah, and builds Ramah, not to permit anyone going out and coming in to Asa king of Judah. ¹⁸And Asa takes all the silver and the gold that are left in the treasures of the house of YHWH, and the treasures of the house of the king, and gives them into the hand of his servants, and King Asa sends them to Ben-Hadad, son of Tabrimmon, son of Hezion king of Aram, who is dwelling in Damascus, saying, ¹⁹"A covenant [is] between me and you, between my father and your father; behold, I have sent a reward of silver and gold to you; go, break your covenant with Baasha king of Israel, and he goes up from off me." ²⁰And Ben-Hadad listens to King Asa, and sends the heads of the forces that he has against cities of Israel, and strikes Ijon, and Dan, and Abel-Beth-Maachah, and all Chinneroth, besides all the land of Naphtali; ²¹and it comes to pass at Baasha's hearing, that he ceases from building Ramah, and dwells in Tirzah. ²²And King Asa has summoned all Judah—there is none exempt—and they lift up the stones of Ramah, and its wood, that Baasha has built, and King Asa builds with them Geba of Benjamin, and Mizpah. ²³And the rest of all the matters of Asa, and all his might, and all that he did, and the cities that he built, are they not written on the scroll of the Chronicles of the Kings of Judah? Only, at the time of his old age he was diseased in his feet; ²⁴and Asa lies with his fathers, and is buried with his fathers in the city of his father David, and his son Jehoshaphat reigns in his stead. ²⁵And Nadab son of Jeroboam has reigned over Israel, in the second year of Asa king of Judah, and he reigns over Israel two years, ²⁶and does evil in the eyes of YHWH, and goes in the way of his father, and in his sin that he made Israel to sin. ²⁷And Baasha son of Ahijah, of the house of Issachar, conspires against him, and Baasha strikes him in Gibbethon, which [belonged] to the Philistines—and Nadab and all Israel are laying siege against Gibbethon— ²⁸indeed, Baasha puts him to death in the third year of Asa king of Judah, and reigns in his stead. ²⁹And it comes to pass, at his reigning, he has struck the whole house of Jeroboam, he has not left any breathing to Jeroboam until his destroying him, according to the word of YHWH, that He spoke by the hand of His servant Ahijah the Shilonite, ³⁰because of the sins of Jeroboam that he sinned, and that he caused Israel to sin, by his provocation with which he provoked YHWH, God of Israel, to anger. ³¹And the rest of the matters of Nadab and all that he did, are they not written on the scroll of the Chronicles of the Kings of Israel? ³²And there has been war between Asa and Baasha king of Israel [for] all their days. ³³In the third year of Asa king of Judah, Baasha son of Ahijah has reigned over all Israel in Tirzah, twenty-four years, ³⁴and he does evil in the eyes of YHWH, and walks in the way of Jeroboam, and in his sin that he caused Israel to sin.

CHAPTER 16

¹And a word of YHWH is to Jehu son of Hanani, against Baasha, saying, ²"Because that I have raised you up out of the dust, and appoint you leader over My people Israel, and you walk in the way of Jeroboam, and cause My people Israel to sin—to provoke Me to anger with their sins; ³behold, I am putting away the posterity of Baasha, even the posterity of his house, and have given up your house as the house of Jeroboam son of Nebat; ⁴the dogs eat him who dies of Baasha in a city, and [the] bird of the heavens eats him who dies of his in a field." ⁵And the rest of the matters of Baasha, and that which he did, and his might, are they not written on the scroll of the Chronicles of the Kings of Israel? ⁶And Baasha lies with his fathers, and is buried in Tirzah, and his son Elah reigns in his stead. ⁷And also by the hand

1 KINGS

of Jehu son of Hanani the prophet a word of YHWH has been concerning Baasha, and concerning his house, and concerning all the evil that he did in the eyes of YHWH to provoke Him to anger with the work of his hands, to be like the house of Jeroboam, and concerning that for which he struck him. ⁸In the twenty-sixth year of Asa king of Judah, Elah son of Baasha has reigned over Israel in Tirzah, two years; ⁹and his servant Zimri conspires against him (head of the half of the chariots) and he [is] in Tirzah drinking—a drunkard in the house of Arza, who [is] over the house in Tirzah. ¹⁰And Zimri comes in and strikes him, and puts him to death, in the twenty-seventh year of Asa king of Judah, and reigns in his stead; ¹¹and it comes to pass in his reigning, at his sitting on his throne, he has struck the whole house of Baasha; he has not left to him any sitting on the wall, and of his redeemers, and of his friends. ¹²And Zimri destroys the whole house of Baasha, according to the word of YHWH that He spoke concerning Baasha, by the hand of Jehu the prophet, ¹³concerning all the sins of Baasha, and the sins of his son Elah, that they sinned, and that they caused Israel to sin to provoke YHWH, God of Israel, with their vanities. ¹⁴And the rest of the matters of Elah and all that he did, are they not written on the scroll of the Chronicles of the Kings of Israel? ¹⁵In the twenty-seventh year of Asa king of Judah, Zimri has reigned seven days in Tirzah; and the people are encamping against Gibbethon, which [belonged] to the Philistines; ¹⁶and the people who are encamping hear, saying, "Zimri has conspired, and also has struck the king"; and all Israel causes Omri head of the host to reign over Israel on that day in the camp. ¹⁷And Omri goes up, and all Israel with him, from Gibbethon, and they lay siege to Tirzah. ¹⁸And it comes to pass, at Zimri's seeing that the city has been captured, that he comes into a high place of the house of the king, and burns the house of the king over himself with fire, and he dies, ¹⁹for his sins that he sinned, to do evil in the eyes of YHWH, to walk in the way of Jeroboam, and in his sin that he did, to cause Israel to sin; ²⁰and the rest of the matters of Zimri and his conspiracy that he made, are they not written on the scroll of the Chronicles of the Kings of Israel? ²¹Then the sons of Israel are parted into halves; half of the people have been after Tibni son of Ginath to cause him to reign, and the [other] half after Omri; ²²and the people that are after Omri are stronger than the people that are after Tibni son of Ginath, and Tibni dies, and Omri reigns. ²³In the thirty-first year of Asa king of Judah, Omri has reigned over Israel twelve years; he has reigned in Tirzah six years, ²⁴and he buys the Mount of Samaria from Shemer with two talents of silver, and builds [on] the mountain, and calls the name of the city that he has built by the name of Shemer, lord of the hill—Samaria. ²⁵And Omri does evil in the eyes of YHWH, and does evil above all who [are] before him, ²⁶and walks in all the way of Jeroboam son of Nebat, and in his sin that he caused Israel to sin, to provoke YHWH, God of Israel, with their vanities. ²⁷And the rest of the matters of Omri that he did and his might that he exercised, are they not written on the scroll of the Chronicles of the Kings of Israel? ²⁸And Omri lies with his fathers, and is buried in Samaria, and his son Ahab reigns in his stead. ²⁹And Ahab son of Omri has reigned over Israel in the thirty-eighth year of Asa king of Judah, and Ahab son of Omri reigns over Israel in Samaria twenty-two years, ³⁰and Ahab son of Omri does evil in the eyes of YHWH above all who [are] before him. ³¹And it comes to pass, as if it had been trivial—his walking in the sins of Jeroboam son of Nebat—that he takes a wife, Jezebel daughter of Ethba'al, king of the Zidonians, and goes and serves Ba'al, and bows himself to it, ³²and raises up an altar for Ba'al in the house of the Ba'al, which he built in Samaria; ³³and Ahab makes the Asherah, and Ahab adds to do so as to provoke YHWH, God of Israel, above all the kings of Israel who have been before him. ³⁴In his days Hiel the Beth-Elite has built Jericho; he laid its foundation with Abiram his firstborn, and he set up its doors with Segub his youngest, according to the word of YHWH that He spoke by the hand of Joshua son of Nun.

CHAPTER 17

¹And Elijah the Tishbite, of the inhabitants of Gilead, says to Ahab, "YHWH, God of Israel, lives, before whom I have stood, there is not dew and rain these years, except according to my word." ²And the word of YHWH is to him, saying, ³"Go from this [place]; and you have turned for yourself eastward, and been hidden by the Brook of Cherith that [is] on the front of the Jordan, ⁴and it has been [that] you drink from the brook, and I have commanded the ravens to sustain you there." ⁵And he goes and does according to the word of YHWH, indeed, he goes and dwells by the Brook of Cherith, that [is] on the front of the Jordan, ⁶and the ravens are bringing bread and flesh to him in the morning, and bread and flesh in the evening, and he drinks from the brook. ⁷And it comes to pass, at the end of [the] days, that the brook dries up, for there has been no rain in the land, ⁸and the word of YHWH is to him, saying, ⁹"Rise, go to Zarephath, that [belongs] to Sidon, and you have dwelt there; behold, I have commanded a widow woman to sustain you there." ¹⁰And he rises, and goes to Zarephath, and comes to the opening of the city, and behold, there [is] a widow woman gathering sticks, and he calls to her and says, "Please bring a little water to me in a vessel, and I drink." ¹¹And she goes to bring [it], and he calls to her and says, "Please bring a morsel of bread to me in your hand." ¹²And she says, "Your God YHWH lives, I do not have a cake, but the fullness of the hand of meal in a pitcher, and a little oil in a dish; and behold, I am gathering two sticks, and have gone in and prepared it for myself, and for my son, and we have eaten it—and died." ¹³And Elijah says to her, "Do not fear, go, do according to your word, only make a little cake for me there, in the first place, and you have brought [it] out to me; and for you and for your son make [it] last; ¹⁴for thus said YHWH, God of Israel: The pitcher of meal is not consumed, and the dish of oil is not lacking, until the day of YHWH's giving a shower on the face of the ground." ¹⁵And she goes, and does according to the word of Elijah, and she eats, she and he and her household [for many] days; ¹⁶the pitcher of meal was not consumed, and the dish of oil did not lack, according to the word of YHWH that He spoke by the hand of Elijah. ¹⁷And it comes to pass, after these things, the son of the woman, mistress of the house, has been sick, and his sickness is very severe until no breath has been left in him. ¹⁸And she says to Elijah, "What [is this] to me and to you, O man of God? You have come to me to cause my iniquity to be remembered, and to put my son to death!" ¹⁹And he says to her, "Give your son to me"; and he takes him out of her bosom, and takes him up to the upper chamber where he is abiding, and lays him on his own bed, ²⁰and cries to YHWH and says, "My God YHWH, have You also brought calamity on the widow with whom I am sojourning, to put her son to death?" ²¹And he stretches himself out on the boy three times, and calls to YHWH and says, "O YHWH my God, please let the soul of this boy return into his midst"; ²²and YHWH listens to the voice of Elijah, and the soul of the boy turns back into his midst, and he lives. ²³And Elijah takes the boy, and brings him down from the upper chamber of the house, and gives him to his mother, and Elijah says, "See, your son lives!" ²⁴And the woman says to Elijah, "Now [by] this I have known that you [are] a man of God, and the word of YHWH in your mouth [is] truth."

CHAPTER 18

¹And the days are many, and the word of YHWH has been to Elijah in the third year, saying, "Go, appear to Ahab, and I give rain on the face of the ground"; ²and Elijah goes to appear to Ahab. And the famine is severe in Samaria, ³and Ahab calls to Obadiah, who [is] over the house—and Obadiah has been fearing YHWH greatly, ⁴and it comes to pass, in Jezebel's cutting off the prophets of YHWH, that Obadiah takes one hundred prophets, and hides them, fifty men in a cave, and has sustained them with bread and water— ⁵and Ahab says to Obadiah, "Go through the land, to all fountains of waters, and to all the brooks, perhaps we find hay, and keep alive horse and mule, and do not cut off any of the livestock." ⁶And they apportion the land to themselves, to pass over into it; Ahab has gone in one way by himself, and Obadiah has gone in another way by himself; ⁷and Obadiah [is] in the way, and behold, Elijah [is there] to meet him; and he discerns him, and falls on his face and says, "Are you he—my lord Elijah?" ⁸And he says to him, "I [am]; go, say to your lord, Behold, Elijah." ⁹And he says, "What have I sinned, that you are giving your servant into the hand of Ahab—to put me to death? ¹⁰Your God YHWH lives, if there is a nation and kingdom to where my lord has not sent to seek [for] you; and they said, He is not, then he caused the kingdom and the nation to swear, that it does

not find you; ¹¹and now, you are saying, Go, say to your lord, Behold, Elijah; ¹²and it has been, I go from you, and the Spirit of YHWH lifts you up to where I do not know, and I have come to declare to Ahab, and he does not find you, and he has slain me; and your servant is fearing YHWH from my youth. ¹³Has it not been declared to my lord that which I have done in Jezebel's slaying the prophets of YHWH, that I hide one hundred men of the prophets of YHWH, fifty by fifty in a cave, and sustained them with bread and water? ¹⁴And now you are saying, Go, say to my lord, Behold, Elijah—and he has slain me!" ¹⁵And Elijah says, "YHWH of Hosts lives, before whom I have stood, surely I appear to him today." ¹⁶Obadiah goes to meet Ahab, and declares [it] to him, and Ahab goes to meet Elijah. ¹⁷[And it] comes to pass at Ahab's seeing Elijah that Ahab says to him, "Are you he—the troubler of Israel?" ¹⁸And he says, "I have not troubled Israel, but you and the house of your father, in your forsaking the commands of YHWH, and you go after the Ba'alim; ¹⁹and now, send, gather all Israel to me, to the Mount of Carmel, and the four hundred and fifty prophets of Ba'al, and the four hundred prophets of Asherah who are eating at the table of Jezebel." ²⁰And Ahab sends among all the sons of Israel, and gathers the prophets to the Mount of Carmel; ²¹and Elijah comes near to all the people and says, "Until when are you leaping on the two branches? If YHWH [is] God, go after Him; and if Ba'al, go after him"; and the people have not answered him a word. ²²And Elijah says to the people, "I have been left, by myself, a prophet of YHWH; and the prophets of Ba'al [are] four hundred and fifty men; ²³and let them give two bullocks to us, and they choose one bullock for themselves, and cut it in pieces, and place [it] on the wood, and place no fire; and I prepare the other bullock, and have put [it] on the wood, and I do not place fire— ²⁴and you have called in the name of your god, and I call in the Name of YHWH, and it has been, the god who answers by fire—He [is] the God." And all the people answer and say, "The word [is] good." ²⁵And Elijah says to the prophets of Ba'al, "Choose one bullock for yourselves, and prepare [it] first, for you [are] the multitude, and call in the name of your god, and place no fire." ²⁶And they take the bullock that [one] gave to them, and prepare [it], and call in the name of Ba'al from the morning even until the noon, saying, "O Ba'al, answer us!" And there is no voice, and there is none answering; and they leap on the altar that one had made. ²⁷And it comes to pass, at noon, that Elijah mocks at them and says, "Call with a loud voice, for he [is] a god, for he is meditating, or pursuing, or on a journey; it may be he is asleep, and awakes." ²⁸And they call with a loud voice, and cut themselves, according to their ordinance, with swords and with spears, until a flowing of blood [is] on them; ²⁹and it comes to pass, at the passing by of the noon, that they feign themselves prophets until the going up of the present, and there is no voice, and there is none answering, and there is none attending. ³⁰And Elijah says to all the people, "Come near to me"; and all the people come near to him, and he repairs the altar of YHWH that is broken down; ³¹and Elijah takes twelve stones, according to the number of the tribes of the sons of Jacob, to whom the word of YHWH was, saying, "Israel is your name"; ³²and he builds an altar with the stones, in the Name of YHWH, and makes a trench, as about the space of two measures of seed, around the altar. ³³And he arranges the wood, and cuts the bullock in pieces, and places [it] on the wood, and says, "Fill four pitchers of water, and pour [them] on the burnt-offering, and on the wood"; ³⁴and he says, "Do [it] a second time"; and they do [it] a second time; and he says, "Do [it] a third time"; and they do [it] a third time; ³⁵and the water goes around the altar, and he has also filled the trench with water. ³⁶And it comes to pass, at the going up of the [evening] present, that Elijah the prophet comes near and says, "YHWH, God of Abraham, Isaac, and Israel, let it be known today that You [are] God in Israel, and that I, Your servant, have done the whole of these things by Your word; ³⁷answer me, O YHWH, answer me, and this people [then] knows that You [are] YHWH God; and You have turned their heart backward." ³⁸And a fire falls [from] YHWH, and consumes the burnt-offering, and the wood, and the stones, and the dust, and it has licked up the water that [is] in the trench. ³⁹And all the people see, and fall on their faces, and say, "YHWH, He [is] the God! YHWH, He [is] the God!" ⁴⁰And Elijah says to them, "Catch the prophets of Ba'al; do not let a man escape from them"; and they catch them, and Elijah brings them down to the Brook of Kishon, and slaughters them there. ⁴¹And Elijah says to Ahab, "Go up, eat and drink, because of the sound of the noise of the shower." ⁴²And Ahab goes up to eat, and to drink, and Elijah has gone up to the top of Carmel, and he stretches himself out on the earth, and he places his face between his knees, ⁴³and says to his young man, "Now go up, look attentively [toward] the way of the sea"; and he goes up and looks attentively, and says, "There is nothing"; and he says, "Turn back," seven times. ⁴⁴And it comes to pass, at the seventh, that he says, "Behold, a little thickness as the palm of a man is coming up out of the sea." And he says, "Go up, say to Ahab, Bind and go down, and the shower does not restrain you." ⁴⁵And it comes to pass, in the meantime, that the heavens have become black—thick clouds and wind—and the shower is great; and Ahab rides, and goes to Jezreel, ⁴⁶and the hand of YHWH has been on Elijah, and he girds up his loins, and runs before Ahab, until your entering Jezreel.

CHAPTER 19

¹And Ahab declares to Jezebel all that Elijah did, and all of how he slew all the prophets by the sword, ²and Jezebel sends a messenger to Elijah, saying, "Thus the gods do, and thus do they add—surely about this time tomorrow, I make your life as the life of one of them." ³And he fears, and rises, and goes for his life, and comes to Beer-Sheba, that [is] Judah's, and leaves his young man there, ⁴and he himself has gone a day's journey into the wilderness, and comes and sits under a certain broom tree, and desires his soul to die, and says, "Enough, now, O YHWH, take my soul, for I [am] not better than my fathers." ⁵And he lies down and sleeps under a certain broom tree, and behold, a messenger is reaching toward him and says to him, "Rise, eat"; ⁶and he looks attentively, and behold, at his bolster [is] a cake [on] burning stones, and a dish of water, and he eats, and drinks, and turns, and lies down. ⁷And the messenger of YHWH turns back a second time, and is reaching toward him, and says, "Rise, eat, for the way is too great for you"; ⁸and he rises, and eats, and drinks, and goes in the power of that food [for] forty days and forty nights, to the mountain of God—Horeb. ⁹And he comes in there, to the cave, and lodges there, and behold, the word of YHWH [is] to him, and says to him, "What are you [doing] here, Elijah?" ¹⁰And he says, "I have been very zealous for YHWH, God of Hosts, for the sons of Israel have forsaken Your covenant—they have thrown down Your altars, and they have slain Your prophets by the sword, and I am left, I, by myself, and they seek my life—to take it." ¹¹And He says, "Go out, and you have stood on the mountain before YHWH." And behold, YHWH is passing by, and a wind—great and strong—is tearing mountains, and shattering rocks before YHWH, [but] YHWH [is] not in the wind; and after the wind [is] a shaking, [but] YHWH [is] not in the shaking; ¹²and after the shaking [is] a fire, [but] YHWH [is] not in the fire; and after the fire [is] a voice [like] a small whisper; ¹³and it comes to pass, at Elijah's hearing [it], that he wraps his face in his robe, and goes out, and stands at the opening of the cave, and behold, a voice [speaks] to him, and it says, "What are you [doing] here, Elijah?" ¹⁴And he says, "I have been very zealous for YHWH, God of Hosts; for the sons of Israel have forsaken Your covenant, they have thrown down Your altars, and they have slain Your prophets by the sword, and I am left, I, by myself, and they seek my life—to take it." ¹⁵And YHWH says to him, "Go, return on your way to the wilderness of Damascus, and you have gone in, and anointed Hazael for king over Aram, ¹⁶and you anoint Jehu son of Nimshi for king over Israel, and you anoint Elisha son of Shaphat, of Abel-Meholah, for prophet in your stead. ¹⁷And it has been, he who has escaped from the sword of Hazael, Jehu puts to death, and he who has escaped from the sword of Jehu, Elisha puts to death; ¹⁸and I have left in Israel seven thousand—all the knees that have not bowed to Ba'al, and every mouth that has not kissed him." ¹⁹And he goes there, and finds Elisha son of Shaphat, and he is plowing; twelve yoke [are] before him, and he [is] with the twelfth; and Elijah passes over to him, and casts his robe at him, ²⁰and he forsakes the ox, and runs after Elijah, and says, "Please let me give a kiss to my father and to my mother, and I go after you." And he says to him, "Go, turn back, for what have I done to you?" ²¹And he turns back from after him, and takes the yoke of the ox, and sacrifices it, and with [the] instruments of

the ox he has boiled its flesh, and gives to the people, and they eat, and he rises, and goes after Elijah, and serves him.

CHAPTER 20

¹And Ben-Hadad king of Aram has gathered all his force, and thirty-two kings [are] with him, and horse and chariot, and he goes up and lays siege against Samaria, and fights with it, ²and sends messengers to Ahab king of Israel, to the city, ³and says to him, "Thus said Ben-Hadad: Your silver and your gold are mine, and your wives and your sons—the best—are mine." ⁴And the king of Israel answers and says, "According to your word, my lord, O king: I [am] yours, and all that I have." ⁵And the messengers turn back and say, "Thus spoke Ben-Hadad, saying, Surely I sent to you, saying, Your silver, and your gold, and your wives, and your sons, you give to me; ⁶for if, at this time tomorrow, I send my servants to you, then they have searched your house, and the houses of your servants, and it has been [that] every desirable thing of your eyes they place in their hand, and have taken [them] away." ⁷And the king of Israel calls to all [the] elderly of the land and says, "Please know and see that this [one] is seeking evil, for he sent to me for my wives, and for my sons, and for my silver, and for my gold, and I did not withhold from him." ⁸And all the elderly and all the people say to him, "Do not listen, nor consent." ⁹And he says to the messengers of Ben-Hadad, "Say to my lord the king, All that you sent to your servant for at the first I do, and this thing I am not able to do"; and the messengers go and take him back word. ¹⁰And Ben-Hadad sends to him and says, "Thus the gods do to me, and thus do they add, if the dust of Samaria suffice for handfuls for all the people who [are] at my feet." ¹¹And the king of Israel answers and says, "Speak: Do not let him who is girding on boast himself as him who is loosing [his armor]." ¹²And it comes to pass at the hearing of this word—and he is drinking, he and the kings, in the shelters—that he says to his servants, "Set yourselves"; and they set themselves against the city. ¹³And behold, a certain prophet has come near to Ahab king of Israel and says, "Thus said YHWH: Have you seen all this great multitude? Behold, I am giving it into your hand today, and you have known that I [am] YHWH." ¹⁴And Ahab says, "By whom?" And he says, "Thus said YHWH: By the young men of the heads of the provinces"; and he says, "Who directs the battle?" And he says, "You." ¹⁵And he inspects the young men of the heads of the provinces, and they are two hundred and thirty-two, and after them he has mustered all the people, all the sons of Israel—seven thousand, ¹⁶and they go out at noon, and Ben-Hadad is drinking—drunk in the shelters, he and the kings, the thirty-two kings helping him. ¹⁷And the young men of the heads of the provinces go out at the first, and Ben-Hadad sends, and they declare to him, saying, "Men have come out of Samaria." ¹⁸And he says, "If they have come out for peace, catch them alive; and if they have come out for battle, catch them alive." ¹⁹And these have gone out of the city—the young men of the heads of the provinces—and the force that [is] after them, ²⁰and each strikes his man, and Aram flees, and Israel pursues them, and Ben-Hadad king of Aram escapes on a horse—and the horsemen; ²¹and the king of Israel goes out, and strikes the horses, and the charioteers, and has struck among the Arameans a great striking. ²²And the prophet comes near to the king of Israel and says to him, "Go, strengthen yourself, and know and see that which you do, for at the turn of the year the king of Aram is coming up against you." ²³And the servants of the king of Aram said to him, "Their gods [are] gods of hills, therefore they were stronger than us; and yet, we fight with them in the plain—are we not stronger than they? ²⁴And this thing you do: turn aside each of the kings out of his place, and set captains in their stead; ²⁵and you, number for yourself a force as the force that is fallen from you, and horse for horse, and chariot for chariot, and we fight with them in the plain; are we not stronger than they?" And he listens to their voice, and does so. ²⁶And it comes to pass at the turn of the year, that Ben-Hadad inspects the Arameans, and goes up to Aphek, to battle with Israel, ²⁷and the sons of Israel have been inspected, and supported, and go to meet them, and the sons of Israel encamp before them, like two flocks of goats, and the Arameans have filled the land. ²⁸And a man of God comes near, and speaks to the king of Israel and says, "Thus said YHWH: Because that the Arameans have said, YHWH [is] God of [the] hills, but He [is] not God of [the] valleys—I have given the whole of this great multitude into your hand, and you have known that I [am] YHWH." ²⁹And they encamp opposite one another [for] seven days, and it comes to pass on the seventh day, that the battle draws near, and the sons of Israel strike one hundred thousand footmen of Aram in one day. ³⁰And those left flee to Aphek, into the city, and the wall falls on twenty-seven chief men who are left, and Ben-Hadad has fled, and comes into the city, into the innermost part. ³¹And his servants say to him, "Now behold, we have heard that the kings of the house of Israel—that they are kind kings; please let us put sackcloth on our loins and ropes on our heads, and we go out to the king of Israel; it may be he keeps you alive." ³²And they gird sackcloth on their loins, and ropes [are] on their heads, and they come to the king of Israel, and say, "Your servant Ben-Hadad has said, Please let me live"; and he says, "Is he still alive? He [is] my brother." ³³And the men observe diligently, and hurry, and catch [the word] from him, and say, "Your brother Ben-Hadad"; and he says, "Go in, bring him"; and Ben-Hadad comes out to him, and he causes him to come up on the chariot. ³⁴And he says to him, "The cities that my father took from your father, I give back, and you make streets for yourself in Damascus, as my father did in Samaria; and I, with a covenant, send you away"; and he makes a covenant with him, and sends him away. ³⁵And a certain man of the sons of the prophets said to his neighbor by the word of YHWH, "Please strike me"; and the man refuses to strike him, ³⁶and he says to him, "Because that you have not listened to the voice of YHWH, behold, you are going from me, and the lion has struck you"; and he goes from him, and the lion finds him, and strikes him. ³⁷And he finds another man and says, "Please strike me"; and the man strikes him, striking and wounding, ³⁸and the prophet goes and stands for the king on the way, and disguises himself with ashes on his eyes. ³⁹And it comes to pass—the king is passing by—that he has cried to the king and says, "Your servant went out into the midst of the battle, and behold, a man has turned aside and brings a man to me, and says, Keep this man; if he is at all missing, then your life has been for his life, or you weigh out a talent of silver; ⁴⁰and it comes to pass, your servant is working here and there, and he is not!" And the king of Israel says to him, "Your judgment [is] right; you have determined [it]." ⁴¹And he hurries and turns aside the ashes from off his eyes, and the king of Israel discerns him, that he [is] of the prophets, ⁴²and he says to him, "Thus said YHWH: Because you have sent away the man I devoted, out of [your] hand, even your life has been for his life, and your people for his people"; ⁴³and the king of Israel goes to his house, sulky and angry, and comes to Samaria.

CHAPTER 21

¹And it comes to pass after these things, a vineyard has been to Naboth the Jezreelite, that [is] in Jezreel, near the palace of Ahab king of Samaria, ²and Ahab speaks to Naboth, saying, "Give your vineyard to me, and it is for a garden of green herbs for me, for it [is] near by my house, and I give to you a better vineyard than it in its stead; if [this is] good in your eyes, I give to you its price [in] silver." ³And Naboth says to Ahab, "Far be it from me, by YHWH, my giving the inheritance of my fathers to you"; ⁴and Ahab comes to his house, sulky and angry, because of the word that Naboth the Jezreelite has spoken to him when he says, "I do not give the inheritance of my fathers to you," and he lies down on his bed, and turns around his face, and has not eaten bread. ⁵And his wife Jezebel comes to him, and speaks to him, "Why [is] this [that] your spirit [is] sulky, and you are not eating bread?" ⁶And he says to her, "Because I speak to Naboth the Jezreelite, and say to him, Give your vineyard to me for money, or if you desire, I give a vineyard to you in its stead; and he says, I do not give my vineyard to you." ⁷And his wife Jezebel says to him, "You now execute rule over Israel! Rise, eat bread, and let your heart be glad—I give the vineyard of Naboth the Jezreelite to you." ⁸And she writes letters in the name of Ahab, and seals with his seal, and sends the letters to the elderly and to the nobles who are in his city, those dwelling with Naboth, ⁹and she writes in the letters, saying, "Proclaim a fast, and cause Naboth to sit at the head of the people, ¹⁰and cause two men—sons of worthlessness—to sit opposite him, and they testify of him, saying, You have blessed [[or cursed]] God and [the] king; and

they have brought him out, and stoned him, and he dies." ¹¹And the men of his city, the elderly and the nobles who are dwelling in his city, do as Jezebel has sent to them, as written in the letters that she sent to them, ¹²they have proclaimed a fast, and caused Naboth to sit at the head of the people, ¹³and two men—sons of worthlessness—come in, and sit opposite him, and the men of worthlessness testify of him, even Naboth, before the people, saying, "Naboth blessed [[*or* cursed]] God and [the] king"; and they take him out to the outside of the city, and stone him with stones, and he dies; ¹⁴and they send to Jezebel, saying, "Naboth was stoned, and is dead." ¹⁵And it comes to pass, at Jezebel's hearing that Naboth has been stoned, and is dead, that Jezebel says to Ahab, "Rise, possess the vineyard of Naboth the Jezreelite, that he refused to give to you for money, for Naboth is not alive but dead." ¹⁶And it comes to pass, at Ahab's hearing that Naboth is dead, that Ahab rises to go down to the vineyard of Naboth the Jezreelite, to possess it. ¹⁷And the word of YHWH is to Elijah the Tishbite, saying, ¹⁸"Rise, go down to meet Ahab king of Israel, who [is] in Samaria—behold, in the vineyard of Naboth, to where he has gone down to possess it, ¹⁹and you have spoken to him, saying, Thus said YHWH: Have you murdered, and also possessed? And you have spoken to him, saying, Thus said YHWH: In the place where the dogs licked the blood of Naboth, the dogs lick your blood, even yours." ²⁰And Ahab says to Elijah, "Have you found me, O my enemy?" And he says, "I have found—because of your selling yourself to do evil in the eyes of YHWH; ²¹behold, I am bringing calamity on you, and have taken away your posterity, and cut off from Ahab those sitting on the wall, and restrained, and left, in Israel, ²²and given up your house like the house of Jeroboam son of Nebat, and like the house of Baasha son of Ahijah, for the provocation with which you have provoked [Me], and cause Israel to sin. ²³And YHWH has also spoken of Jezebel, saying, The dogs eat Jezebel in the bulwark of Jezreel; ²⁴the dogs eat him who dies of Ahab in a city, and [the] bird of the heavens eats him who dies in a field; ²⁵surely there has been none like Ahab, who sold himself to do evil in the eyes of YHWH, whom his wife Jezebel has moved, ²⁶and he does very abominably to go after the idols, according to all that the Amorite did whom YHWH dispossessed from the presence of the sons of Israel." ²⁷And it comes to pass, at Ahab's hearing these words, that he tears his garments, and puts sackcloth on his flesh, and fasts, and lies in sackcloth, and goes gently. ²⁸And the word of YHWH is to Elijah the Tishbite, saying, ²⁹"Have you seen that Ahab has been humbled before Me? Because that he has been humbled before Me, I do not bring in the calamity in his days; I bring in the calamity on his house in the days of his son."

CHAPTER 22

¹And they sit still three years; there is no war between Aram and Israel. ²And it comes to pass in the third year, that Jehoshaphat king of Judah comes down to the king of Israel, ³and the king of Israel says to his servants, "Have you not known that Ramoth-Gilead [is] ours? And we are keeping silent from taking it out of the hand of the king of Aram!" ⁴And he says to Jehoshaphat, "Do you go with me to battle [against] Ramoth-Gilead?" And Jehoshaphat says to the king of Israel, "As I am, so [are] you; as my people, so your people; as my horses, so your horses." ⁵And Jehoshaphat says to the king of Israel, "Please seek the word of YHWH today"; ⁶and the king of Israel gathers the prophets, about four hundred men, and says to them, "Do I go to battle against Ramoth-Gilead, or do I refrain?" And they say, "Go up, and the Lord gives [it] into the hand of the king." ⁷And Jehoshaphat says, "[Is there] not a prophet of YHWH still here that we may seek from him?" ⁸And the king of Israel says to Jehoshaphat, "Yet one man [remains] to seek YHWH from him, and I have hated him, for he does not prophesy good concerning me, but evil—Micaiah son of Imlah"; and Jehoshaphat says, "Do not let the king say so." ⁹And the king of Israel calls to a certain eunuch and says, "Hurry along Micaiah son of Imlah." ¹⁰And the king of Israel and Jehoshaphat king of Judah are sitting, each on his throne, clothed with garments, in a threshing-floor, at the opening of the Gate of Samaria, and all the prophets are prophesying before them. ¹¹And Zedekiah son of Chenaanah makes horns of iron for himself and says, "Thus said YHWH: By these you push the Arameans until they are consumed"; ¹²and all the prophets are prophesying so, saying, "Go up to Ramoth-Gilead, and prosper, and YHWH has given [it] into the hand of the king." ¹³And the messenger who has gone to call Micaiah has spoken to him, saying, "Now behold, the words of the prophets, with one mouth, [are] good toward the king; please let your word be as the word of one of them—and you have spoken good." ¹⁴And Micaiah says, "YHWH lives; surely that which YHWH says to me—it I speak." ¹⁵And he comes to the king, and the king says to him, "Micaiah, do we go to Ramoth-Gilead, to battle, or do we refrain?" And he says to him, "Go up, and prosper, and YHWH has given [it] into the hand of the king." ¹⁶And the king says to him, "How many times am I adjuring you that you speak nothing to me but truth in the Name of YHWH?" ¹⁷And he says, "I have seen all Israel scattered on the hills as sheep that have no shepherd, and YHWH says, These have no master; let them return—each to his house in peace." ¹⁸And the king of Israel says to Jehoshaphat, "Have I not said to you, He does not prophesy of me good, but evil?" ¹⁹And he says, "Therefore, hear a word of YHWH! I have seen YHWH sitting on His throne, and all the host of the heavens standing by Him, on His right and on His left; ²⁰and YHWH says, Who entices Ahab, and he goes up and falls in Ramoth-Gilead? And this one says thus, and that one is saying thus. ²¹And the spirit goes out and stands before YHWH, and says, I entice him; and YHWH says to him, By what? ²²And he says, I go out, and have been a spirit of falsehood in the mouth of all his prophets; and He says, You entice, and also you are able; go out and do so. ²³And now, behold, YHWH has put a spirit of falsehood in the mouth of all these prophets of yours, and YHWH has spoken calamity concerning you." ²⁴And Zedekiah son of Chenaanah draws near and strikes Micaiah on the cheek, and says, "Where [is] this [that] the spirit [from] YHWH has passed over from me to speak with you?" ²⁵And Micaiah says, "Behold, you are seeing on that day when you go into the innermost chamber to be hidden." ²⁶And the king of Israel says, "Take Micaiah, and turn him back to Amon head of the city, and to Joash son of the king, ²⁷and you have said, Thus said the king: Place this one in the house of restraint, and cause him to eat bread of oppression, and water of oppression, until my coming in peace." ²⁸And Micaiah says, "If you return in peace at all, YHWH has not spoken by me"; and he says, "Hear, O peoples, all of them." ²⁹And the king of Israel goes up—and Jehoshaphat king of Judah—to Ramoth-Gilead. ³⁰And the king of Israel says to Jehoshaphat to disguise himself, and to go into battle, "And you, put on your garments." And the king of Israel disguises himself, and goes into battle. ³¹And the king of Aram commanded the thirty-two heads of the charioteers whom he has, saying, "You do not fight with small or with great, but with the king of Israel by himself." ³²And it comes to pass, at the heads of the charioteers seeing Jehoshaphat, that they said, "He [is] surely the king of Israel!" And they turn aside to him to fight, and Jehoshaphat cries out, ³³and it comes to pass, at the heads of the charioteers seeing that he [is] not the king of Israel, that they turn back from after him. ³⁴And a man has drawn with a bow in his simplicity, and strikes the king of Israel between the joinings and the coat of mail, and he says to his charioteer, "Turn your hand, and take me out from the camp, for I have become sick." ³⁵And the battle increases on that day, and the king has been caused to stand in the chariot, in front of Aram, and he dies in the evening, and the blood of the wound runs out to the midst of the chariot, ³⁶and he causes the cry to pass over through the camp, at the going in of the sun, saying, "Each to his city, and each to his land!" ³⁷And the king dies, and comes into Samaria, and they bury the king in Samaria; ³⁸and [one] rinses the chariot by the pool of Samaria, and the dogs lick his blood when they had washed the armor, according to the word of YHWH that He spoke. ³⁹And the rest of the matters of Ahab, and all that he did, and the house of ivory that he built, and all the cities that he built, are they not written on the scroll of the Chronicles of the Kings of Israel? ⁴⁰And Ahab lies with his fathers, and his son Ahaziah reigns in his stead. ⁴¹And Jehoshaphat son of Asa has reigned over Judah in the fourth year of Ahab king of Israel, ⁴²Jehoshaphat [is] a son of thirty-five years in his reigning, and he has reigned twenty-five years in Jerusalem, and the name of his mother [is] Azubah daughter of Shilhi. ⁴³And he walks in all the way of his father Asa, he has not turned aside from it, to do that which [is] right in the eyes of

YHWH; only, the high places have not been removed—the people are still sacrificing and making incense in high places. ⁴⁴And Jehoshaphat makes peace with the king of Israel; ⁴⁵and the rest of the matters of Jehoshaphat, and his might that he exercised, and with which he fought, are they not written on the scroll of the Chronicles of the Kings of Judah? ⁴⁶And the remnant of the whoremongers who were left in the days of his father Asa he took away out of the land; ⁴⁷and there is no king in Edom; he set up a king. ⁴⁸Jehoshaphat made ships of Tarshish to go to Ophir for gold, and they did not go, for the ships were broken in Ezion-Geber. ⁴⁹Then Ahaziah son of Ahab said to Jehoshaphat, "Let my servants go with your servants in the ships"; and Jehoshaphat was not willing. ⁵⁰And Jehoshaphat lies with his fathers, and is buried with his fathers in the city of his father David, and his son Jehoram reigns in his stead. ⁵¹Ahaziah son of Ahab has reigned over Israel in Samaria in the seventeenth year of Jehoshaphat king of Judah, and reigns over Israel two years, ⁵²and does evil in the eyes of YHWH, and walks in the way of his father, and in the way of his mother, and in the way of Jeroboam son of Nebat who caused Israel to sin, ⁵³and serves the Ba'al, and bows himself to it, and provokes YHWH, God of Israel, according to all that his father had done.

2 KINGS

CHAPTER 1

¹And Moab transgresses against Israel after the death of Ahab, ²and Ahaziah falls through the lattice in his upper chamber that [is] in Samaria, and is sick, and sends messengers, and says to them, "Go, inquire of Ba'al-Zebub god of Ekron if I recover from this sickness." ³And a messenger of YHWH has spoken to Elijah the Tishbite, "Rise, go up to meet the messengers of the king of Samaria, and speak to them, Is it because there is not a God in Israel—you are going to inquire of Ba'al-Zebub god of Ekron? ⁴And therefore, thus said YHWH: The bed to where you have gone up, you do not come down from it, for you certainly die"; and Elijah goes on. ⁵And the messengers return to him, and he says to them, "What [is] this—you have turned back!" ⁶And they say to him, "A man has come up to meet us and says to us, Go, return to the king who sent you, and you have said to him, Thus said YHWH: Is it because there is not a God in Israel—you are sending to inquire of Ba'al-Zebub god of Ekron? Therefore, the bed to where you have gone up, you do not come down from it, for you certainly die." ⁷And he says to them, "What [is] the fashion of the man who has come up to meet you, and speaks these words to you?" ⁸And they say to him, "A hairy man, and a girdle of skin girt around his loins"; and he says, "He [is] Elijah the Tishbite." ⁹And he sends to him a head of fifty and his fifty, and he goes up to him (and behold, he is sitting on the top of the hill), and he speaks to him, "O man of God, the king has spoken, Come down." ¹⁰And Elijah answers and speaks to the head of the fifty, "And if I [am] a man of God, fire comes down from the heavens and consumes you and your fifty"; and fire comes down from the heavens and consumes him and his fifty. ¹¹And he turns and sends to him another head of fifty and his fifty, and he answers and speaks to him, "O man of God, thus said the king: Hurry, come down." ¹²And Elijah answers and speaks to them, "If I [am] a man of God, fire comes down from the heavens and consumes you and your fifty"; and fire of God comes down from the heavens and consumes him and his fifty. ¹³And he turns and sends a third head of fifty and his fifty, and the third head of fifty goes up, and comes in, and bows on his knees before Elijah, and makes supplication to him, and speaks to him, "O man of God, please let my soul and the soul of your servants—these fifty—be precious in your eyes. ¹⁴Behold, fire has come down from the heavens and consumes the two heads of the former fifties and their fifties; and now, let my soul be precious in your eyes." ¹⁵And a messenger of YHWH speaks to Elijah, "Go down with him, do not be afraid of him"; and he rises and goes down with him to the king, ¹⁶and speaks to him, "Thus said YHWH: Because that you have sent messengers to inquire of Ba'al-Zebub god of Ekron—is it because there is not a God in Israel to inquire of His word? Therefore, the bed to where you have gone up—you do not come down from it, for you certainly die." ¹⁷And he dies, according to the word of YHWH that Elijah spoke, and Jehoram reigns in his stead, in the second year of Jehoram son of Jehoshaphat king of Judah, for he had no son. ¹⁸And the rest of the matters of Ahaziah that he did, are they not written on the scroll of the Chronicles of the Kings of Israel?

CHAPTER 2

¹And it comes to pass, at YHWH's taking up Elijah to the heavens in a whirlwind, that Elijah goes, and Elisha, from Gilgal, ²and Elijah says to Elisha, "Please abide here, for YHWH has sent me to Beth-El"; and Elisha says, "YHWH lives, and your soul lives, if I leave you"; and they go down to Beth-El. ³And sons of the prophets who [are] in Beth-El come out to Elisha, and say to him, "Have you known that today YHWH is taking your lord from your head?" And he says, "I also have known—keep silent." ⁴And Elijah says to him, "Elisha, please abide here, for YHWH has sent me to Jericho"; and he says, "YHWH lives, and your soul lives, if I leave you"; and they come to Jericho. ⁵And sons of the prophets who [are] in Jericho come near to Elisha, and say to him, "Have you known that today YHWH is taking your lord from your head?" And he says, "I also have known—keep silent." ⁶And Elijah says to him, "Please abide here, for YHWH has sent me to the Jordan"; and he says, "YHWH lives, and your soul lives, if I leave you"; and both of them go on— ⁷and fifty men of the sons of the prophets have gone on, and stand opposite [them] far off—and both of them have stood by the Jordan. ⁸And Elijah takes his robe, and wraps [it] together, and strikes the waters, and they are halved, here and there, and both of them pass over on dry land. ⁹And it comes to pass, at their passing over, that Elijah has said to Elisha, "Ask what I do for you before I am taken from you." And Elisha says, "Indeed, please let there be a double portion of your spirit to me"; ¹⁰and he says, "You have asked a hard thing; if you see me taken from you, it is to you so; and if not, it is not." ¹¹And it comes to pass, they are going, going on and speaking, and behold, a chariot of fire and horses of fire [appear], and they separate between them both, and Elijah goes up to the heavens in a whirlwind. ¹²And Elisha is seeing, and he is crying, "My father! My father! The chariot of Israel and its horsemen!" And he has not seen him again; and he takes hold on his garments and tears them into two pieces. ¹³And he takes up the robe of Elijah that fell from off him, and turns back and stands on the edge of the Jordan, ¹⁴and he takes the robe of Elijah that fell from off him, and strikes the waters, and says, "Where [is] YHWH, God of Elijah—even He?" And he strikes the waters, and they are halved, here and there, and Elisha passes over. ¹⁵And they see him—the sons of the prophets who [are] in Jericho—from opposite [them], and they say, "The spirit of Elijah has rested on Elisha"; and they come to meet him, and bow themselves to him to the earth, ¹⁶and say to him, "Now behold, there are fifty men with your servants, sons of valor: please let them go, and they seek your lord, lest the Spirit of YHWH has taken him up, and casts him on one of the hills or into one of the valleys"; and he says, "You do not send." ¹⁷And they press on him, until he is ashamed, and he says, "Send"; and they send fifty men, and they seek three days, and have not found him; ¹⁸and they return to him—and he is abiding in Jericho—and he says to them, "Did I not say to you, Do not go?" ¹⁹And the men of the city say to Elisha, "Now behold, the site of the city [is] good, as my lord sees, and the waters [are] bad, and the earth sterile." ²⁰And he says, "Bring a new dish to me, and place salt there"; and they bring [it] to him, ²¹and he goes out to the source of the waters, and casts salt there, and says, "Thus said YHWH: I have given healing to these waters; there is not anymore death and sterility there." ²²And the waters are healed to this day, according to the word of Elisha that he spoke.

²³And he goes up from there to Beth-El, and he is going up in the way, and little youths have come out from the city, and scoff at him, and say to him, "Go up, bald-head! Go up, bald-head!" ²⁴And he looks behind him, and sees them, and declares them vile in the Name of YHWH, and two bears come out of the forest and ripped apart forty-two of the boys. ²⁵And he goes from there to the hill of Carmel, and from there he has turned back to Samaria.

CHAPTER 3

¹And Jehoram son of Ahab has reigned over Israel, in Samaria, in the eighteenth year of Jehoshaphat king of Judah, and he reigns twelve years, ²and does evil in the eyes of YHWH, only not like his father, and like his mother, and he turns aside the standing-pillar of Ba'al that his father made; ³surely he has cleaved to the sins of Jeroboam son of Nebat that he caused Israel to sin; he has not turned aside from it. ⁴And Mesha king of Moab was a sheep-master, and he rendered to the king of Israel one hundred thousand lambs and one hundred thousand rams, [with] wool, ⁵and it comes to pass at the death of Ahab, that the king of Moab transgresses against the king of Israel. ⁶And King Jehoram goes out from Samaria in that day, and inspects all Israel, ⁷and goes and sends to Jehoshaphat king of Judah, saying, "The king of Moab has transgressed against me; do you go with me to Moab for battle?" And he says, "I go up, as I, so you; as my people, so your people; as my horses, so your horses." ⁸And he says, "Where [is] this—the way we go up?" And he says, "The way of the wilderness of Edom." ⁹And the king of Israel goes, and the king of Judah, and the king of Edom, and they turn around the way seven days, and there has been no water for the camp, and for the livestock that [are] at their feet, ¹⁰and the king of Israel says, "Aah! For YHWH has called for these three kings to give them into the hand of Moab." ¹¹And Jehoshaphat says, "Is there not a prophet of YHWH here, and we seek YHWH by him?" And one of the servants of the king of Israel answers and says, "Here [is] Elisha son of Shaphat, who poured water on the hands of Elijah." ¹²And Jehoshaphat says, "The word of YHWH is with him"; and the king of Israel goes down to him, and Jehoshaphat, and the king of Edom. ¹³And Elisha says to the king of Israel, "And what do I [have to do] with you? Go to the prophets of your father, and to the prophets of your mother"; and the king of Israel says to him, "No, for YHWH has called for these three kings to give them into the hand of Moab." ¹⁴And Elisha says, "YHWH of Hosts lives, before whom I have stood; for unless I am lifting up the face of Jehoshaphat king of Judah, I do not look to you, nor see you; ¹⁵and now, bring a musician to me"; and it has been, at the playing of the musician, that the hand of YHWH is on him, ¹⁶and he says, "Thus said YHWH: Make this valley ditches—ditches; ¹⁷for thus said YHWH: You do not see wind, nor do you see rain, and that valley is full of water, and you have drunk—you, and your livestock, and your beasts. ¹⁸And this has been light in the eyes of YHWH, and he has given Moab into your hand, ¹⁹and you have struck every fortified city, and every choice city, and you cause every good tree to fall, and you stop all fountains of waters, and you mar every good portion with stones." ²⁰And it comes to pass in the morning, at the ascending of the [morning] present, that behold, waters are coming in from the way of Edom, and the land is filled with the waters, ²¹and all of Moab has heard that the kings have come up to fight against them, and they are called together, from everyone girding on a girdle and upward, and they stand by the border. ²²And they rise early in the morning, and the sun has shone on the waters, and the Moabites see, from opposite [them], [that] the waters [are] red as blood, ²³and say, "This [is] blood; the kings have been surely destroyed, and they each strike his neighbor; and now for spoil, Moab!" ²⁴And they come to the camp of Israel, and Israel rises, and strikes the Moabites, and they flee from their face; and they enter into Moab, so as to strike Moab, ²⁵and they break down the cities, and they each cast his stone [on] every good portion, and have filled it, and they stop every fountain of water, and they cause every good tree to fall—until one had left its stones in Kir-Haraseth, and the slingers go around and strike it. ²⁶And the king of Moab sees that the battle has been too strong for him, and he takes with him seven hundred men drawing sword, to cleave through to the king of Edom, and they have not been able, ²⁷and he takes his son, the firstborn who reigns in his stead, and causes him to ascend [as] a burnt-offering on the wall, and there is great wrath against Israel, and they journey from off him, and return to the land.

CHAPTER 4

¹And a certain woman of the wives of the sons of the prophets has cried to Elisha, saying, "Your servant, my husband, is dead, and you have known that your servant was fearing YHWH, and the lender has come to take my two children to himself for servants." ²And Elisha says to her, "What do I do for you? Declare to me, what do you have in the house?" And she says, "Your maidservant has nothing in the house except a pot of oil." ³And he says, "Go, ask [for] vessels for yourself from outside, from all your neighbors—empty vessels—let [them] not be few; ⁴and you have entered, and have shut the door on you, and on your sons, and have poured it into all these vessels, and the full ones you remove." ⁵And she goes from him, and shuts the door on her, and on her sons; they are bringing [them] near to her, and she is pouring [it] out, ⁶and it comes to pass, at the filling of the vessels, that she says to her son, "Bring another vessel near to me," and he says to her, "There is not another vessel"; and the oil stays. ⁷And she comes and declares [it] to the man of God, and he says, "Go, sell the oil, and repay your loan; and you [and] your sons live off the rest." ⁸And the day comes that Elisha passes over to Shunem, and there [is] a great woman, and she lays hold on him to eat bread, and it comes to pass, at the time of his passing over, he turns aside there to eat bread, ⁹and she says to her husband, "Now behold, I have known that he is a holy man of God, passing over by us continually; ¹⁰please let us make a little upper chamber of the wall, and we set for him there a bed, and a table, and a high seat, and a lampstand; and it has been, in his coming to us, he turns aside there." ¹¹And the day comes that he comes in there, and turns aside to the upper chamber, and lies there, ¹²and he says to his young man Gehazi, "Call for this Shunammite"; and he calls for her, and she stands before him. ¹³And he says to him, "Now say to her, Behold, you have troubled yourself concerning us with all this trouble; what can [I] do for you? Is it to speak for you to the king, or to the head of the host?" And she says, "I am dwelling in the midst of my people." ¹⁴And he says, "And what can [I] do for her?" And Gehazi says, "Truly she has no son, and her husband [is] aged." ¹⁵And he says, "Call for her"; and he calls for her, and she stands at the opening, ¹⁶and he says, "At this season, according to the time of life, you are embracing a son"; and she says, "No, my lord, O man of God, do not lie to your maidservant." ¹⁷And the woman conceives and bears a son, at this season, according to the time of life that Elisha spoke of to her. ¹⁸And the boy grows, and the day comes that he goes out to his father, to the reapers, ¹⁹and he says to his father, "My head, my head"; and he says to the young man, "Carry him to his mother"; ²⁰and he carries him, and brings him to his mother, and he sits on her knees until the noon, and dies. ²¹And she goes up, and lays him on the bed of the man of God, and shuts [the door] on him, and goes out, ²²and calls to her husband and says, "Please send one of the young men and one of the donkeys to me, and I run to the man of God, and return." ²³And he says, "Why are you going to him today? [It is] neither new moon nor Sabbath!" And she says, "Peace [to you]!" ²⁴And she saddles the donkey and says to her young man, "Lead, and go, do not restrain riding for me, except I have commanded [so] to you." ²⁵And she goes, and comes to the man of God, to the hill of Carmel, and it comes to pass, at the man of God's seeing her from within view, that he says to his young man Gehazi, "Behold, this Shunammite; ²⁶now please run to meet her, and say to her, Is there peace to you? Is there peace to your husband? Is there peace to the boy?" And she says, "Peace." ²⁷And she comes to the man of God, to the hill, and lays hold on his feet, and Gehazi comes near to thrust her away, and the man of God says, "Leave her alone, for her soul [is] bitter to her, and YHWH has hidden [it] from me, and has not declared [it] to me." ²⁸And she says, "Did I ask for a son from my lord? Did I not say, Do not deceive me?" ²⁹And he says to Gehazi, "Gird up your loins, and take my staff in your hand, and go; when you meet a man, you do not greet him; and when a man greets you, you do not answer him; and you have laid my staff on the face of the youth." ³⁰And the mother of the youth says, "YHWH lives, and your soul lives—

2 KINGS

if I leave you"; and he rises and goes after her. ³¹And Gehazi has passed on before them, and lays the staff on the face of the youth, and there is no voice, and there is no attention, and he turns back to meet him, and declares to him, saying, "The youth has not awoken." ³²And Elisha comes into the house, and behold, the youth is dead, laid on his bed, ³³and he goes in and shuts the door on them both, and prays to YHWH. ³⁴And he goes up, and lies down on the boy, and puts his mouth on his mouth, and his eyes on his eyes, and his hands on his hands, and stretches himself on him, and the flesh of the boy becomes warm; ³⁵and he turns back and walks in the house, once here and once there, and goes up and stretches himself on him, and the youth sneezes until seven times, and the youth opens his eyes. ³⁶And he calls to Gehazi and says, "Call to this Shunammite"; and he calls her, and she comes to him, and he says, "Lift up your son." ³⁷And she goes in, and falls at his feet, and bows herself to the earth, and lifts up her son, and goes out. ³⁸And Elisha has turned back to Gilgal, and the famine [is] in the land, and the sons of the prophets are sitting before him, and he says to his young man, "Set on the great pot, and boil stew for the sons of the prophets." ³⁹And one goes out to the field to gather herbs, and finds a vine of the field, and gathers gourds of the field from it—the fullness of his garment—and comes in and splits [them] into the pot of stew, for they did not know [them]; ⁴⁰and they pour out for the men to eat, and it comes to pass at their eating of the stew, that they have cried out, and say, "Death [is] in the pot, O man of God!" And they have not been able to eat. ⁴¹And he says, "Then bring a meal"; and he casts into the pot and says, "Pour out for the people, and they eat"; and there was no bad thing in the pot. ⁴²And a man has come from Ba'al-Shalishah, and brings to the man of God bread of first-fruits, twenty loaves of barley, and full ears of grain in its husk, and he says, "Give to the people, and they eat." ⁴³And his minister says, "How do I give this before one hundred men?" And he says, "Give to the people, and they eat, for thus said YHWH: Eat and leave"; ⁴⁴and he gives before them, and they eat and leave, according to the word of YHWH.

CHAPTER 5

¹And Naaman, head of the host of the king of Aram, was a great man before his lord, and accepted of face, for YHWH had given salvation to Aram by him, and the man was mighty in valor, [but] leprous. ²And the Arameans have gone out [by] troops, and they take a little girl captive out of the land of Israel, and she is before the wife of Naaman, ³and she says to her mistress, "O that my lord [were] before the prophet who [is] in Samaria; then he recovers him from his leprosy." ⁴And [one] goes in and declares [it] to his lord, saying, "Thus and thus the girl who [is] from the land of Israel has spoken." ⁵And the king of Aram says, "Go, enter, and I send a letter to the king of Israel"; and he goes and takes in his hand ten talents of silver, and six thousand [pieces] of gold, and ten changes of garments. ⁶And he brings in the letter to the king of Israel, saying, "And now, at the coming in of this letter to you, behold, I have sent my servant Naaman to you, and you have recovered him from his leprosy." ⁷And it comes to pass, at the king of Israel's reading the letter, that he tears his garments and says, "Am I God, to put to death and to keep alive, that this [one] is sending to me to recover a man from his leprosy? For surely know now, and see, for he is presenting himself to me." ⁸And it comes to pass, at Elisha the man of God's hearing that the king of Israel has torn his garments, that he sends to the king, saying, "Why have you torn your garments? Please let him come to me, and he knows that there is a prophet in Israel." ⁹And Naaman comes, with his horses and with his chariot, and stands at the opening of the house for Elisha; ¹⁰and Elisha sends a messenger to him, saying, "Go, and you have washed seven times in the Jordan, and your flesh turns back to you—and be clean." ¹¹And Naaman is angry, and goes on and says, "Behold, I said, He certainly comes out to me, and has stood and called in the Name of his God YHWH, and waved his hand over the place, and recovered the leper. ¹²Are not Abana and Pharpar, rivers of Damascus, better than all the waters of Israel? Do I not wash in them and I have been clean?" And he turns and goes on in fury. ¹³And his servants come near, and speak to him, and say, "My father, the prophet had spoken a great thing to you—do you not do [it]? And surely, when he has said to you, Wash, and be clean." ¹⁴And he goes down and dips in the Jordan seven times, according to the word of the man of God, and his flesh turns back as the flesh of a little youth, and is clean. ¹⁵And he turns back to the man of God, he and all his camp, and comes in, and stands before him, and says, "Now behold, I have known that there is not a God in all the earth except in Israel; and now, please take a blessing from your servant." ¹⁶And he says, "YHWH lives, before whom I have stood—if I take [it]"; and he presses on him to take, and he refuses. ¹⁷And Naaman says, "If not, please let a couple of mules' burden of earth be given to your servant, for your servant makes no more burnt-offering and sacrifice to other gods, but [only sacrifices] to YHWH. ¹⁸For in this thing may YHWH be propitious to your servant, in the coming in of my lord into the house of Rimmon to bow himself there, and he was supported by my hand, and I bowed myself [in] the house of Rimmon; for my bowing myself in the house of Rimmon, may YHWH now be propitious to your servant in this thing." ¹⁹And he says to him, "Go in peace." And he goes from him a distance of land, ²⁰and Gehazi, servant of Elisha the man of God, says, "Behold, my lord has spared this Aramean Naaman, not to receive from his hand that which he brought; for YHWH lives; if I have run after him, then I have taken something from him." ²¹And Gehazi pursues after Naaman, and Naaman sees one running after him, and comes down off the chariot to meet him, and says, "Is there peace?" ²²And he says, "Peace; my lord has sent me, saying, Behold, now, this, two young men of the sons of the prophets have come to me from the hill-country of Ephraim; please give a talent of silver and two changes of garments to them." ²³And Naaman says, "Be pleased, take two talents"; and he urges him, and binds two talents of silver in two purses, and two changes of garments, and gives [them] to two of his young men, and they carry [them] before him; ²⁴and he comes to the high place, and takes [them] out of their hand, and lays [them] up in the house, and sends the men away, and they go. ²⁵And he has come in, and stands by his lord, and Elisha says to him, "From where—Gehazi?" And he says, "Your servant did not go here or there." ²⁶And he says to him, "My heart did not go when the man turned from off his chariot to meet you; is it a time to take silver, and to take garments, and olives, and vines, and flock, and herd, and menservants, and maidservants? ²⁷Indeed, the leprosy of Naaman cleaves to you and to your seed for all time"; and he goes out from before him—leprous as snow.

CHAPTER 6

¹And sons of the prophet say to Elisha, "Now behold, the place where we are dwelling before you is too narrow for us; ²please let us go to the Jordan, and we each take one beam from there, and we make a place there for ourselves to dwell there"; and he says, "Go." ³And the one says, "Please be willing, and go with your servants"; and he says, "I go." ⁴And he goes with them, and they come to the Jordan, and cut down the trees, ⁵and it comes to pass, the one is felling the beam, and the iron [ax head] has fallen into the water, and he cries and says, "Aah! My lord, for it was borrowed!" ⁶And the man of God says, "To where has it fallen?" And he shows him the place, and he cuts a stick, and casts [it] there, and causes the iron to swim, ⁷and says, "Raise [it] up for yourself"; and he puts forth his hand and takes it. ⁸And the king of Aram has been fighting against Israel, and takes counsel with his servants, saying, "At such and such a place [is] my encamping." ⁹And the man of God sends to the king of Israel, saying, "Take heed of passing by this place, for the Arameans are coming down there"; ¹⁰and the king of Israel sends to the place of which the man of God spoke to him, and warned him, and he is preserved there not [just] once and not [just] twice. ¹¹And the heart of the king of Aram is tossed about concerning this thing, and he calls to his servants and says to them, "Do you not declare to me who of us [is] for the king of Israel?" ¹²And one of his servants says, "No, my lord, O king, for Elisha the prophet, who [is] in Israel, declares to the king of Israel the words that you speak in the inner part of your bedchamber." ¹³And he says, "Go and see where he [is], and I send and take him"; and it is declared to him, saying, "Behold—in Dothan." ¹⁴And he sends horses and chariot, and a heavy force there, and they come in by night, and go around against the city. ¹⁵And the servant of the man of God rises early, and goes out, and behold, a force is surrounding the city, and horse and chariot, and his young man

says to him, "Aah! My lord, how do we do?" ¹⁶And he says, "Do not fear, for more [are] they who [are] with us than they who [are] with them." ¹⁷And Elisha prays and says, "YHWH, please open his eyes, and he sees"; and YHWH opens the eyes of the young man, and he sees, and behold, the hill is full of horses and chariots of fire around Elisha. ¹⁸And they come down to it, and Elisha prays to YHWH and says, "Please strike this nation with blindness"; and He strikes them with blindness, according to the word of Elisha. ¹⁹And Elisha says to them, "This [is] not the way, nor [is] this the city; come after me, and I lead you to the man whom you seek"; and he leads them to Samaria. ²⁰And it comes to pass, at their coming to Samaria, that Elisha says, "YHWH, open the eyes of these, and they see"; and YHWH opens their eyes, and they see, and behold, [they are] in the midst of Samaria! ²¹And the king of Israel says to Elisha at his seeing them, "My father, do I strike, do I strike?" ²²And he says, "You do not strike; are you striking those whom you have taken captive with your sword and with your bow? Set bread and water before them, and they eat, and drink, and go to their lord." ²³And he prepares great provision for them, and they eat and drink, and he sends them away, and they go to their lord: and troops of Aram have not added to come into the land of Israel anymore. ²⁴And it comes to pass afterward, that Ben-Hadad king of Aram gathers all his camp, and goes up, and lays siege to Samaria, ²⁵and there is a great famine in Samaria, and behold, they are laying siege to it, until the head of a donkey is at eighty pieces of silver, and a forth of the cab of dove's dung at five pieces of silver. ²⁶And it comes to pass, the king of Israel is passing by on the wall, and a woman has cried to him, saying, "Save, my lord, O king." ²⁷And he says, "YHWH does not save you—from where do I save you? Out of the threshing-floor or out of the wine-vat?" ²⁸And the king says to her, "What is [troubling] you?" And she says, "This woman said to me, Give your son, and we eat him today, and we eat my son tomorrow; ²⁹and we boil my son and eat him, and I say to her on the next day, Give your son, and we eat him; and she hides her son." ³⁰And it comes to pass, at the king's hearing the words of the woman, that he tears his garments, and he is passing by on the wall, and the people see, and behold, the sackcloth [is] within on his flesh. ³¹And he says, "Thus God does to me and thus He adds, if the head of Elisha son of Shaphat remains on him this day." ³²And Elisha is sitting in his house, and the elderly are sitting with him, and [the king] sends a man from before him; before the messenger comes to him, even he himself said to the elderly, "Have you seen that this son of the murderer has sent [him] to turn aside my head? See, at the coming in of the messenger, shut the door, and you have held him fast at the door, is not the sound of the feet of his lord behind him?" ³³He is yet speaking with them, and behold, the messenger is coming down to him, and he says, "Behold, this [is] the calamity from YHWH; why do I wait for YHWH anymore?"

CHAPTER 7

¹And Elisha says, "Hear a word of YHWH! Thus said YHWH: About this time tomorrow, a measure of fine flour [is] at a shekel, and two measures of barley at a shekel, in the Gate of Samaria." ²And the captain whom the king has, by whose hand he has been supported, answers the man of God and says, "Behold, YHWH is making windows in the heavens—will this thing be?" And he says, "Behold, you are seeing it with your eyes, and you do not eat thereof." ³And four men have been leprous at the opening of the gate, and they say to one another, "Why are we sitting here until we have died? ⁴If we have said, We go into the city, then the famine [is] in the city and we have died there; and if we have sat here, then we have died; and now, come and we go down to the camp of Aram; if they keep us alive, we live, and if they put us to death—we have died." ⁵And they rise in the twilight, to go to the camp of Aram, and they come to the extremity of the camp of Aram, and behold, there is not a man there, ⁶seeing YHWH has caused the camp of Aram to hear a noise of chariot and a noise of horse—a noise of great force, and they say to one another, "Behold, the king of Israel has hired against us the kings of the Hittites, and the kings of Egypt, to come against us." ⁷And they rise and flee in the twilight, and forsake their tents, and their horses, and their donkeys—the camp as it [is]—and flee for their life. ⁸And these lepers come to the extremity of the camp, and come into one tent, and eat, and drink, and lift up silver, and gold, and garments from there, and go and hide; and they turn back and go into another tent, and lift up from there, and go and hide. ⁹And they say to one another, "We are not doing right this day; it [is] a day of tidings, and we are keeping silent; and we have waited until the morning light, then punishment has found us; and now, come and we go in and declare [it] to the house of the king." ¹⁰And they come in, and call to the gatekeeper of the city, and declare for themselves, saying, "We have come to the camp of Aram, and behold, there is no man or sound of man there, but the bound horse, and the bound donkey, and tents as they [are]." ¹¹And he calls the gatekeepers, and they declare [it] to the house of the king within. ¹²And the king rises by night and says to his servants, "Now let me declare to you that which the Arameans have done to us; they have known that we are famished, and they go out from the camp to be hidden in the field, saying, When they come out from the city, then we catch them alive, and we enter into the city." ¹³And one of his servants answers and says, "Then please let them take five of the horses that are left, that have been left in it—behold, they [are] as all the multitude of Israel who have been left in it; behold, they are as all the multitude of Israel who have been consumed—and we send and see." ¹⁴And they take two chariot-horses, and the king sends [them] after the camp of Aram, saying, "Go, and see." ¹⁵And they go after them to the Jordan, and behold, all the way is full of garments and vessels that the Arameans have cast away in their haste, and the messengers return and declare [it] to the king. ¹⁶And the people go out and spoil the camp of Aram, and there is a measure of fine flour at a shekel, and two measures of barley at a shekel, according to the word of YHWH. ¹⁷And the king has appointed the captain, by whose hand he is supported, over the gate, and the people tread him down in the gate, and he dies, as the man of God spoke, which he spoke in the coming down of the king to him, ¹⁸indeed, it comes to pass, according to the speaking of the man of God to the king, saying, "Two measures of barley at a shekel, and a measure of fine flour at a shekel are, at this time tomorrow, in the Gate of Samaria"; ¹⁹and the captain answers the man of God and says, "And behold, YHWH is making windows in the heavens—will this thing be?" And he says, "Behold, you are seeing it with your eyes, and you do not eat thereof"; ²⁰and it comes to him so, and the people tread him down in the gate, and he dies.

CHAPTER 8

¹And Elisha spoke to the woman whose son he had revived, saying, "Rise and go, you and your household, and sojourn where you sojourn, for YHWH has called for a famine, and also, it is coming to the land [for] seven years." ²And the woman rises, and does according to the word of the man of God, and goes, she and her household, and sojourns in the land of the Philistines [for] seven years. ³And it comes to pass, at the end of seven years, that the woman turns back from the land of the Philistines, and goes out to cry to the king for her house and for her field. ⁴And the king is speaking to Gehazi, servant of the man of God, saying, "Please recount to me the whole of the great things that Elisha has done." ⁵And it comes to pass, he is recounting to the king how he had revived the dead, and behold, the woman whose son he had revived is crying to the king for her house and for her field, and Gehazi says, "My lord, O king, this [is] the woman, and this [is] her son, whom Elisha revived." ⁶And the king inquires of the woman, and she recounts to him, and the king appoints a certain eunuch to her, saying, "Give back all that she has, and all the increase of the field from the day of her leaving the land even until now." ⁷And Elisha comes to Damascus, and Ben-Hadad king of Aram is sick, and it is declared to him, saying, "The man of God has come here." ⁸And the king says to Hazael, "Take a present in your hand, and go to meet the man of God, and you have sought YHWH by him, saying, Do I revive from this sickness?" ⁹And Hazael goes to meet him, and takes a present in his hand, even of every good thing of Damascus, a burden of forty camels, and he comes in and stands before him, and says, "Your son Ben-Hadad, king of Aram, has sent me to you, saying, Do I revive from this sickness?" ¹⁰And Elisha says to him, "Go, say,

You certainly do not revive, seeing [that] YHWH has showed me that he surely dies." ¹¹And he sets his face, indeed, he sets [it] until he is ashamed, and the man of God weeps. ¹²And Hazael says, "Why is my lord weeping?" And he says, "Because I have known the evil that you do to the sons of Israel—you send their fortifications into fire, and you slay their young men with sword, and you dash their sucklings to pieces, and you rip up their pregnant women." ¹³And Hazael says, "But what [is] your servant—the dog, that he does this great thing?" And Elisha says, "YHWH has showed me you—king of Aram." ¹⁴And he goes from Elisha, and comes to his lord, and he says to him, "What did Elisha say to you?" And he says, "He said to me, You certainly recover." ¹⁵And it comes to pass on the next day, that he takes the coarse cloth, and dips [it] in water, and spreads [it] on his face, and he dies, and Hazael reigns in his stead. ¹⁶And in the fifth year of Joram son of Ahab, king of Israel—and Jehoshaphat [is] king of Judah—Jehoram son of Jehoshaphat, king of Judah, has reigned; ¹⁷he was a son of thirty-two years in his reigning, and he has reigned eight years in Jerusalem. ¹⁸And he walks in the way of the kings of Israel, as the house of Ahab did, for a daughter of Ahab was to him for a wife, and he does evil in the eyes of YHWH, ¹⁹and YHWH was not willing to destroy Judah, for the sake of His servant David, as He said to him, to give a lamp to him—to his sons [for] all the days. ²⁰In his days Edom has revolted from under the hand of Judah, and they cause a king to reign over them, ²¹and Joram passes over to Zair, and all the chariots with him, and he himself has risen by night, and strikes Edom that is coming around to him, and the heads of the chariots, and the people flee to their tents; ²²and Edom revolts from under the hand of Judah until this day; then Libnah revolts at that time. ²³And the rest of the matters of Joram and all that he did, are they not written on the scroll of the Chronicles of the Kings of Judah? ²⁴And Joram lies with his fathers, and is buried with his fathers in the City of David, and his son Ahaziah reigns in his stead. ²⁵In the twelfth year of Joram son of Ahab, king of Israel, Ahaziah son of Jehoram, king of Judah, has reigned; ²⁶Ahaziah [is] a son of twenty-two years in his reigning, and he has reigned one year in Jerusalem, and the name of his mother [is] Athaliah daughter of Omri, king of Israel, ²⁷and he walks in the way of the house of Ahab, and does evil in the eyes of YHWH, like the house of Ahab, for he [is] son-in-law of the house of Ahab. ²⁸And he goes with Joram son of Ahab to battle with Hazael king of Aram in Ramoth-Gilead, and the Arameans strike Joram, ²⁹and Joram the king turns back to be healed in Jezreel of the wounds with which the Arameans strike him in Ramah, in his fighting with Hazael king of Aram, and Ahaziah son of Jehoram, king of Judah, has gone down to see Joram son of Ahab in Jezreel, for he is sick.

CHAPTER 9

¹And Elisha the prophet has called to one of the sons of the prophets and says to him, "Gird up your loins, and take this vial of oil in your hand, and go to Ramoth-Gilead, ²and you have gone in there, and see Jehu son of Jehoshaphat, son of Nimshi, there, and you have gone in, and caused him to rise out of the midst of his brothers, and brought him into the inner part of an inner-chamber, ³and taken the vial of oil, and poured [it] on his head, and said, Thus said YHWH: I have anointed you for king to Israel; and you have opened the door, and fled, and do not wait." ⁴And the young man goes—the young man the prophet—to Ramoth-Gilead, ⁵and comes in, and behold, chiefs of the force are sitting, and he says, "I have a word for you, O chief!" And Jehu says, "To which of all of us?" And he says, "To you, O chief." ⁶And he rises and comes into the house, and he pours the oil on his head, and says to him, "Thus said YHWH, God of Israel: I have anointed you for king to the people of YHWH, to Israel, ⁷and you have struck the house of your lord Ahab, and I have required the blood of My servants the prophets, and the blood of all the servants of YHWH, from the hand of Jezebel; ⁸and all the house of Ahab has perished, and I have cut off from Ahab those sitting on the wall, and restrained, and left, in Israel, ⁹and I have given up the house of Ahab like the house of Jeroboam son of Nebat, and as the house of Baasha son of Ahijah, ¹⁰and dogs eat Jezebel in the portion of Jezreel, and there is none burying"; and he opens the door and flees. ¹¹And Jehu has gone out to the servants of his lord, and [one] says to him, "Is there peace? Why did this madman come to you?" And he says to them, "You have known the man and his talk." ¹²And they say, "False! Declare to us now"; and he says, "He spoke thus and thus to me, saying, Thus said YHWH: I have anointed you for king to Israel." ¹³And they hurry—each [one]—and take his garment, and put [it] under him at the top of the stairs, and blow with a horn, and say, "Jehu has reigned!" ¹⁴And Jehu son of Jehoshaphat, son of Nimshi, conspires against Joram. And Joram was keeping in Ramoth-Gilead, he and all Israel, from the presence of Hazael king of Aram, ¹⁵and King Joram turns back to be healed in Jezreel, of the wounds with which the Arameans strike him in his fighting with Hazael king of Aram. And Jehu says, "If it is your mind, do not let an escaped one go out from the city, to go to declare [it] in Jezreel." ¹⁶And Jehu rides, and goes to Jezreel, for Joram is lying there, and Ahaziah king of Judah has gone down to see Joram. ¹⁷And the watchman is standing on the tower in Jezreel, and sees the company of Jehu in his coming and says, "I see a company"; and Joram says, "Take a rider and send [him] to meet them, and let him say, Is there peace?" ¹⁸And the rider on the horse goes to meet him and says, "Thus said the king: Is there peace?" And Jehu says, "And what is peace to you? Turn around behind me." And the watchman declares, saying, "The messenger came to them, and he has not returned." ¹⁹And he sends a second rider on a horse, and he comes to them and says, "Thus said the king: Is there peace?" And Jehu says, "And what is peace to you? Turn around behind me." ²⁰And the watchman declares, saying, "He came to them, and he has not returned, and the driving [is] like the driving of Jehu son of Nimshi, for he drives with madness." ²¹And Jehoram says, "Harness"; and his chariot is harnessed, and Jehoram king of Israel goes out, and Ahaziah king of Judah, each in his chariot, and they go out to meet Jehu, and find him in the portion of Naboth the Jezreelite. ²²And it comes to pass, at Jehoram's seeing Jehu, that he says, "Is there peace, Jehu?" And he says, "What [is] the peace, while the whoredoms of your mother Jezebel, and her witchcrafts, are many?" ²³And Jehoram turns his hands and flees, and says to Ahaziah, "Deceit, O Ahaziah!" ²⁴And Jehu has filled his hand with a bow, and strikes Jehoram between his arms, and the arrow goes out from his heart, and he bows down in his chariot. ²⁵And [Jehu] says to his captain Bidkar, "Lift up, cast him into the portion of the field of Naboth the Jezreelite—for remember, you and I were riding together after his father Ahab, and YHWH lifted this burden on him: ²⁶Have I not seen the blood of Naboth and the blood of his sons last night—a declaration of YHWH—indeed, I have repaid to you in this portion—a declaration of YHWH—and now, lift up, cast him into the portion, according to the word of YHWH." ²⁷And Ahaziah king of Judah has seen, and flees the way of the garden-house, and Jehu pursues after him, and says, "Strike him—also him—in the chariot," in the going up to Gur, that [is] Ibleam, and he flees to Megiddo, and dies there, ²⁸and his servants carry him to Jerusalem in a chariot, and bury him in his burying-place with his fathers in the City of David. ²⁹And in the eleventh year of Joram son of Ahab, Ahaziah reigned over Judah. ³⁰And Jehu comes to Jezreel, and Jezebel has heard, and puts her eyes in paint and beautifies her head, and looks out through the window. ³¹And Jehu has come into the gate, and she says, "Was there peace [for] Zimri—slayer of his lord?" ³²And he lifts up his face to the window and says, "Who [is] with me? Who?" And two [or] three eunuchs look out to him; ³³and he says, "Let her go"; and they let her go, and [some] of her blood is sprinkled on the wall, and on the horses, and he treads her down. ³⁴And he comes in, and eats, and drinks, and says, "Now look after this cursed one and bury her, for she [is] a king's daughter." ³⁵And they go to bury her, and have not found [anything] of her except the skull, and the feet, and the palms of the hands. ³⁶And they turn back, and declare [it] to him, and he says, "It [is] the word of YHWH that He spoke by the hand of this servant, Elijah the Tishbite, saying, In the portion of Jezreel the dogs eat the flesh of Jezebel, ³⁷and the carcass of Jezebel has been as dung on the face of the field in the portion of Jezreel, that they do not say, This [is] Jezebel."

2 KINGS

CHAPTER 10

¹And Ahab has seventy sons in Samaria, and Jehu writes letters, and sends [them] to Samaria, to the heads of Jezreel, the elderly, and to those supporting Ahab, saying, ²"And now, at the coming in of this letter to you, and sons of your lord [are] with you, and the chariots and the horses, and a fortified city, and the armor, [are] with you, ³that you have seen the best and the most upright of the sons of your lord, and have set [him] on the throne of his father, and fight for the house of your lord." ⁴And they fear very greatly, and say, "Behold, the two kings have not stood before him, and how do we stand—we?" ⁵And he who [is] over the house, and he who [is] over the city, and the elderly, and those supporting, send to Jehu, saying, "We [are] your servants, and all that you say to us we do; we do not make anyone king—do that which [is] good in your eyes." ⁶And he writes a letter to them a second time, saying, "If you [are] for me, and are listening to my voice, take the heads of the men—the sons of your lord, and come to me about this time tomorrow, to Jezreel"; and the sons of the king [are] seventy men, with the great ones of the city—those bringing them up. ⁷And it comes to pass, at the coming in of the letter to them, that they take the sons of the king, and slaughter seventy men, and put their heads in baskets, and send [them] to him at Jezreel, ⁸and the messenger comes in, and declares [it] to him, saying, "They have brought in the heads of the sons of the king," and he says, "Make them two heaps at the opening of the gate until the morning." ⁹And it comes to pass in the morning, that he goes out, and stands, and says to all the people, "You are righteous; behold, I have conspired against my lord, and slay him—and who struck all these? ¹⁰Now you know that nothing falls of the word of YHWH to the earth that YHWH spoke against the house of Ahab, and YHWH has done that which He spoke by the hand of His servant Elijah." ¹¹And Jehu strikes all those left to the house of Ahab in Jezreel, and all his great men, and his acquaintances, and his priests, until he has not left a remnant to him. ¹²And he rises, and comes in and goes to Samaria; he [is] at the shepherds' shearing-house in the way, ¹³and Jehu has found the brothers of Ahaziah king of Judah and says, "Who [are] you?" And they say, "We [are] brothers of Ahaziah, and we go down to greet the sons of the king and the sons of the mistress." ¹⁴And he says, "Catch them alive"; and they catch them alive, and slaughter them at the pit of the shearing-house, forty-two men, and he has not left [even one] man of them. ¹⁵And he goes there, and finds Jehonadab son of Rechab to meet him, and blesses him, and says to him, "Is your heart right, as my heart [is] with your heart?" And Jehonadab says, "It is." "Then it is; give your hand"; and he gives his hand, and he causes him to come up into the chariot to him, ¹⁶and says, "Come with me, and look on my zeal for YHWH"; and they cause him to ride in his chariot. ¹⁷And he comes to Samaria, and strikes all those left to Ahab in Samaria, until his destroying him, according to the word of YHWH that He spoke to Elisha. ¹⁸And Jehu gathers the whole of the people and says to them, "Ahab served Ba'al a little—Jehu serves him much: ¹⁹and now, all the prophets of Ba'al, all his servants, and all his priests, call to me; do not let a man be lacking, for I have a great sacrifice for Ba'al; everyone who is lacking—he does not live"; and Jehu has done [it] in subtlety, in order to destroy the servants of Ba'al. ²⁰And Jehu says, "Sanctify a restraint for Ba'al"; and they proclaim [it]. ²¹And Jehu sends into all Israel, and all the servants of Ba'al come in, and there has not been left a man who has not come in; and they come into the house of Ba'al, and the house of Ba'al is full—mouth to mouth. ²²And he says to him who [is] over the wardrobe, "Bring out clothing for all those serving Ba'al"; and he brings out the clothing to them. ²³And Jehu goes in—and Jehonadab son of Rechab—to the house of Ba'al, and says to the servants of Ba'al, "Search and see, lest there be [any] from the servants of YHWH here with you—but [only] the servants of Ba'al by themselves." ²⁴And they come in to make sacrifices and burnt-offerings, and Jehu has set eighty men for himself in an out-place, and says, "The man who lets [any] of the men whom I am bringing into your hand escape—his soul for his soul." ²⁵And it comes to pass, at his finishing to make the burnt-offering, that Jehu says to the runners and to the captains, "Go in, strike them, let none come out"; and they strike them by the mouth of the sword, and the runners and the captains cast [them] out; and they go to the city, to the house of Ba'al, ²⁶and bring out the standing-pillars of the house of Ba'al, and burn them, ²⁷and break down the standing-pillar of Ba'al, and break down the house of Ba'al, and appoint it for a latrine to this day. ²⁸And Jehu destroys Ba'al out of Israel, ²⁹only [not]—the sins of Jeroboam son of Nebat, that he caused Israel to sin, Jehu has not turned aside from after them—the calves of gold that [are] at Beth-El and in Dan. ³⁰And YHWH says to Jehu, "Because that you have done well, to do that which [is] right in My eyes—according to all that [is] in My heart you have done to the house of Ahab—the sons of the fourth [generation] sit on the throne of Israel for you." ³¹And Jehu has not taken heed to walk in the Law of YHWH, God of Israel, with all his heart; he has not turned aside from the sins of Jeroboam that he caused Israel to sin. ³²In those days YHWH has begun to cut off [some] in Israel, and Hazael strikes them in all the border of Israel, ³³from the Jordan, at the sun-rising: the whole land of Gilead, of the Gadite, and the Reubenite, and the Manassite (from Aroer, that [is] by the Brook of Arnon), even Gilead and Bashan. ³⁴And the rest of the matters of Jehu, and all that he did, and all his might, are they not written on the scroll of the Chronicles of the Kings of Israel? ³⁵And Jehu lies with his fathers, and they bury him in Samaria, and his son Jehoahaz reigns in his stead. ³⁶And the days that Jehu has reigned over Israel in Samaria [are] twenty-eight years.

CHAPTER 11

¹And Athaliah [is] mother of Ahaziah, and she has seen that her son [is] dead, and she rises, and destroys all the seed of the kingdom; ²and Jehosheba daughter of king Joram, sister of Ahaziah, takes Joash son of Ahaziah, and steals him out of the midst of the sons of the king who are put to death, him and his nurse, in the inner part of the bed-chambers, and they hide him from the presence of Athaliah, and he has not been put to death, ³and he is with her, in the house of YHWH, hiding himself, six years, and Athaliah is reigning over the land. ⁴And in the seventh year Jehoiada has sent and takes the heads of the hundreds, of the executioners and of the runners, and brings them to him, into the house of YHWH, and makes a covenant with them, and causes them to swear in the house of YHWH, and shows them the son of the king, ⁵and commands them, saying, "This [is] the thing that you do; the third of you [are] going in on the Sabbath, and keepers of the charge of the house of the king, ⁶and the third [is] at the Gate of Sur, and the third at the gate behind the runners, and you have kept the charge of the house pulled down; ⁷and two parts of you, all going out on the Sabbath—they have kept the charge of the house of YHWH about the king, ⁸and you have surrounded the king all around, each with his weapons in his hand, and he who is coming to the ranges is put to death; and be with the king in his going out and in his coming in." ⁹And the heads of the hundreds do according to all that Jehoiada the priest commanded, and take—each [one]—his men going in on the Sabbath, with those going out on the Sabbath, and come to Jehoiada the priest, ¹⁰and the priest gives to the heads of the hundreds the spears and the shields that King David had, that [are] in the house of YHWH. ¹¹And the runners stand, each with his weapons in his hand, from the right shoulder of the house to the left shoulder of the house, by the altar and by the house, by the king all around; ¹²and he brings out the son of the king, and puts the crown on him, and the Testimony, and they make him king, and anoint him, and strike the hand, and say, "Let the king live." ¹³And Athaliah hears the voice of the runners [and] of the people, and she comes to the people [in] the house of YHWH, ¹⁴and looks, and behold, the king is standing by the pillar, according to the ordinance, and the heads and the trumpets [are] by the king, and all the people of the land are rejoicing and blowing with trumpets, and Athaliah tears her garments, and calls, "Conspiracy! Conspiracy!" ¹⁵And Jehoiada the priest commands the heads of the hundreds, inspectors of the force, and says to them, "Bring her out to the outside of the ranges, and him who is going after her, put to death by the sword": for the priest had said, "Do not let her be put to death in the house of YHWH." ¹⁶And they make sides for her, and she enters the way of the entering in of the horses to the house of the king, and is put to death there. ¹⁷And Jehoiada makes the covenant between YHWH and the king and the people, to be for a people to YHWH, and between the king and the

2 KINGS

people. ¹⁸And all the people of the land go to the house of Ba'al, and break it down; they have thoroughly broken its altars and its images, and they have slain Mattan priest of Ba'al before the altars; and the priest sets inspectors over the house of YHWH, ¹⁹and takes the heads of the hundreds, and the executioners, and the runners, and all the people of the land, and they bring down the king from the house of YHWH, and come by the way of the gate of the runners, to the house of the king, and he sits on the throne of the kings. ²⁰And all the people of the land rejoice, and the city [is] quiet, and they have put Athaliah to death by the sword in the house of the king; ²¹Jehoash is a son of seven years in his reigning.

CHAPTER 12

¹In the seventh year of Jehu, Jehoash has reigned, and he has reigned forty years in Jerusalem, and the name of his mother [is] Zibiah of Beer-Sheba, ²and Jehoash does that which is right in the eyes of YHWH all his days in which Jehoiada the priest directed him, ³only, the high places have not been removed—the people are still sacrificing and making incense in high places. ⁴And Jehoash says to the priests, "All the money of the sanctified things that is brought into the house of YHWH, the money of him who is passing over, the money of each of the souls—his valuation, all the money that goes up on the heart of a man to bring into the house of YHWH, ⁵the priests take to themselves, each from his acquaintance, and they strengthen the breach of the house in all [places] there where a breach is found." ⁶And it comes to pass, in the twenty-third year of King Jehoash, the priests have not strengthened the breach of the house, ⁷and King Jehoash calls to Jehoiada the priest, and to the priests, and says to them, "Why are you not strengthening the breach of the house? And now, receive no money from your acquaintances, but give it for the breach of the house." ⁸And the priests do not consent to receive money from the people, nor to strengthen the breach of the house, ⁹and Jehoiada the priest takes a chest, and pierces a hole in its lid, and puts it near the altar, on the right side, as one comes into the house of YHWH, and the priests keeping the threshold have put all the money there that is brought into the house of YHWH. ¹⁰And it comes to pass, at their seeing that the money [is] abundant in the chest, that there goes up a scribe of the king, and of the high priest, and they bind [it] up, and count the money that is found [in] the house of YHWH, ¹¹and have given the weighed money into the hands of those doing the work, those inspecting the house of YHWH, and they bring it out to those working in the wood, and to builders who are working in the house of YHWH, ¹²and to those [repairing] the wall, and to hewers of stone, and to buy wood and hewn stones to strengthen the breach of the house of YHWH, and for all that goes out on the house, to strengthen it. ¹³Only, there is not made for the house of YHWH basins of silver, snuffers, bowls, trumpets, any vessel of gold, and vessel of silver, out of the money that is brought into the house of YHWH; ¹⁴for they give it to those doing the work, and they have strengthened the house of YHWH with it, ¹⁵and they do not reckon with the men into whose hand they give the money to give to those doing the work, for they are dealing in faithfulness. ¹⁶The money of a trespass-offering and the money of sin-offerings is not brought into the house of YHWH—it is for the priests. ¹⁷Then Hazael king of Aram goes up and fights against Gath, and captures it, and Hazael sets his face to go up against Jerusalem; ¹⁸and Jehoash king of Judah takes all the sanctified things that Jehoshaphat, and Jehoram, and Ahaziah, his fathers, kings of Judah, had sanctified, and his own sanctified things, and all the gold that is found in the treasures of the house of YHWH and of the house of the king, and sends [them] to Hazael king of Aram, and he goes up from off Jerusalem. ¹⁹And the rest of the matters of Joash and all that he did, are they not written on the scroll of the Chronicles of the Kings of Judah? ²⁰And his servants rise, and make a conspiracy, and strike Joash in the house of Millo, that is going down to Silla. ²¹Indeed, Jozachar son of Shimeath, and Jehozabad son of Shemer, his servants, have struck him, and he dies, and they bury him with his fathers in the City of David, and his son Amaziah reigns in his stead.

CHAPTER 13

¹In the twenty-third year of Joash son of Ahaziah, king of Judah, Jehoahaz son of Jehu has reigned over Israel in Samaria, seventeen years, ²and he does evil in the eyes of YHWH, and goes after the sins of Jeroboam son of Nebat, that he caused Israel to sin—he did not turn aside from it, ³and the anger of YHWH burns against Israel, and He gives them into the hand of Hazael king of Aram, and into the hand of Ben-Hadad son of Hazael, all the days. ⁴And Jehoahaz appeases the face of YHWH, and YHWH listens to him, for He has seen the oppression of Israel, for the king of Aram has oppressed them— ⁵and YHWH gives a savior to Israel, and they go out from under the hand of Aram, and the sons of Israel dwell in their tents as before; ⁶only, they have not turned aside from the sins of the house of Jeroboam that he caused Israel to sin, therein they walked, and also, the Asherah has remained in Samaria— ⁷for he did not leave to Jehoahaz of the people except fifty horsemen, and ten chariots, and ten thousand footmen, for the king of Aram has destroyed them, and makes them as dust for threshing. ⁸And the rest of the matters of Jehoahaz, and all that he did, and his might, are they not written on the scroll of the Chronicles of the Kings of Israel? ⁹And Jehoahaz lies with his fathers, and they bury him in Samaria, and his son Joash reigns in his stead. ¹⁰In the thirty-seventh year of Joash king of Judah, Jehoash son of Jehoahaz has reigned over Israel in Samaria, sixteen years, ¹¹and he does evil in the eyes of YHWH, he has not turned aside from all the sins of Jeroboam son of Nebat that he caused Israel to sin, therein he walked. ¹²And the rest of the matters of Joash, and all that he did, and his might with which he fought with Amaziah king of Judah, are they not written on the scroll of the Chronicles of the Kings of Israel? ¹³And Joash lies with his fathers, and Jeroboam has sat on his throne, and Joash is buried in Samaria with the kings of Israel. ¹⁴And Elisha has been sick with his sickness in which he dies, and Joash king of Israel comes down to him and weeps on his face, and says, "My father, my father, the chariot of Israel, and its horsemen." ¹⁵And Elisha says to him, "Take bow and arrows": and he takes bow and arrows for himself. ¹⁶And he says to the king of Israel, "Place your hand on the bow"; and he places his hand, and Elisha puts his hands on the hands of the king, ¹⁷and says, "Open the window eastward"; and he opens, and Elisha says, "Shoot," and he shoots; and he says, "An arrow of salvation from YHWH, and an arrow of salvation against Aram, and you have struck Aram, in Aphek, until consuming." ¹⁸And he says, "Take the arrows," and he takes; and he says to the king of Israel, "Strike to the earth"; and he strikes three times, and stays. ¹⁹And the man of God is angry against him and says, "By striking five or six times then you had struck Aram until consuming; but now you [only] strike Aram three times." ²⁰And Elisha dies, and they bury him, and troops of Moab come into the land at the coming in of the year, ²¹and it comes to pass, they are burying a man, and behold, they have seen the troop, and cast the man into the grave of Elisha, and the man goes and comes against the bones of Elisha, and lives, and rises on his feet. ²²And Hazael king of Aram has oppressed Israel all the days of Jehoahaz, ²³and YHWH favors them, and pities them, and turns to them for the sake of His covenant with Abraham, Isaac, and Jacob, and has not been willing to destroy them, nor to cast them from His presence as yet. ²⁴And Hazael king of Aram dies, and his son Ben-Hadad reigns in his stead, ²⁵and Jehoash son of Jehoahaz turns and takes the cities out of the hand of Ben-Hadad son of Hazael that he had taken out of the hand of his father Jehoahaz in war; Joash has struck him three times, and he brings back the cities of Israel.

CHAPTER 14

¹In the second year of Joash son of Jehoahaz, king of Israel, Amaziah son of Joash, king of Judah, has reigned; ²he was a son of twenty-five years in his reigning, and he has reigned twenty-nine years in Jerusalem, and the name of his mother [is] Jehoaddan of Jerusalem, ³and he does that which [is] right in the eyes of YHWH, only not like his father David; he has done according to all that his father Joash did, ⁴only, the high places have not been removed—the people are still sacrificing and making incense in high places. ⁵And it comes to pass, when the kingdom has been strong in his hand, that he strikes his servants, those striking his father the king, ⁶and the sons of those striking [him] he has not put to death, as it is written in the Scroll of the Law of Moses that YHWH commanded, saying, "Fathers are

2 KINGS

not put to death for sons, and sons are not put to death for fathers, but each is put to death for his own sin." ⁷He has struck ten thousand of Edom in the Valley of Salt, and seized Selah in war, and [one] calls its name Joktheel to this day, ⁸then Amaziah has sent messengers to Jehoash son of Jehoahaz, son of Jehu, king of Israel, saying, "Come, we look one another in the face." ⁹And Jehoash king of Israel sends to Amaziah king of Judah, saying, "The thorn that [is] in Lebanon has sent to the cedar that [is] in Lebanon, saying, Give your daughter to my son for a wife; and a beast of the field that [is] in Lebanon passes by, and treads down the thorn. ¹⁰You have certainly struck Edom, and your heart has lifted you up; be honored, and abide in your house; and why do you stir yourself up in evil, that you have fallen, you and Judah with you?" ¹¹And Amaziah has not listened, and Jehoash king of Israel goes up, and they look one another in the face, he and Amaziah king of Judah, in Beth-Shemesh, that [is] Judah's, ¹²and Judah is struck before Israel, and they each flee to his tent. ¹³And Jehoash king of Israel caught Amaziah king of Judah, son of Jehoash, son of Ahaziah, in Beth-Shemesh, and they come to Jerusalem, and he bursts through the wall of Jerusalem, at the Gate of Ephraim to the Corner Gate, four hundred cubits, ¹⁴and has taken all the gold and the silver, and all the vessels that are found in the house of YHWH, and in the treasures of the house of the king, and the sons of the pledges, and turns back to Samaria. ¹⁵And the rest of the matters of Jehoash that he did, and his might, and how he fought with Amaziah king of Judah, are they not written on the scroll of the Chronicles of the Kings of Israel? ¹⁶And Jehoash lies with his fathers, and is buried in Samaria with the kings of Israel, and his son Jeroboam reigns in his stead. ¹⁷And Amaziah son of Joash, king of Judah, lives after the death of Jehoash son of Jehoahaz, king of Israel, fifteen years, ¹⁸and the rest of the matters of Amaziah, are they not written on the scroll of the Chronicles of the Kings of Judah? ¹⁹And they make a conspiracy against him in Jerusalem, and he flees to Lachish, and they send after him to Lachish, and put him to death there, ²⁰and lift him up on the horses, and he is buried in Jerusalem with his fathers in the City of David. ²¹And all the people of Judah take Azariah, and he [is] a son of sixteen years, and cause him to reign instead of his father Amaziah; ²²he has built Elath, and brings it back to Judah, after the lying of the king with his fathers. ²³In the fifteenth year of Amaziah son of Joash, king of Judah, Jeroboam son of Joash, king of Israel, has reigned in Samaria, forty-one years, ²⁴and he does evil in the eyes of YHWH; he has not turned aside from all the sins of Jeroboam son of Nebat that he caused Israel to sin. ²⁵He has brought back the border of Israel, from the entering in of Hamath to the sea of the desert, according to the word of YHWH, God of Israel, that He spoke by the hand of His servant Jonah son of Amittai the prophet, who [is] of Gath-Hepher, ²⁶for YHWH has seen the very bitter affliction of Israel, and there is none restrained, and there is none left, and there is no helper for Israel; ²⁷and YHWH has not spoken to blot out the name of Israel from under the heavens, and saves them by the hand of Jeroboam son of Joash. ²⁸And the rest of the matters of Jeroboam, and all that he did, and his might with which he fought, and with which he brought back Damascus, and Hamath of Judah, into Israel, are they not written on the scroll of the Chronicles of the Kings of Israel? ²⁹And Jeroboam lies with his fathers, with the kings of Israel, and his son Zechariah reigns in his stead.

CHAPTER 15

¹In the twenty-seventh year of Jeroboam king of Israel, Azariah son of Amaziah, king of Judah, has reigned; ²he was a son of sixteen years in his reigning, and he has reigned fifty-two years in Jerusalem, and the name of his mother [is] Jecholiah of Jerusalem, ³and he does that which [is] right in the eyes of YHWH, according to all that his father Amaziah did, ⁴only, the high places have not been removed—the people are still sacrificing and making incense in high places. ⁵And YHWH strikes the king, and he is a leper to the day of his death, and he dwells in a separate house, and Jotham son of the king [is] over the house, judging the people of the land. ⁶And the rest of the matters of Azariah and all that he did, are they not written on the scroll of the Chronicles of the Kings of Judah? ⁷And Azariah lies with his fathers, and they bury him with his fathers in the city of David, and his son Jotham reigns in his stead. ⁸In the thirty-eighth year of Azariah king of Judah, Zechariah son of Jeroboam has reigned over Israel in Samaria, six months, ⁹and he does evil in the eyes of YHWH as his fathers did; he has not turned aside from the sins of Jeroboam son of Nebat that he caused Israel to sin. ¹⁰And Shallum son of Jabesh conspires against him, and strikes him before the people, and puts him to death, and reigns in his stead. ¹¹And the rest of the matters of Zechariah, behold, they are written on the scroll of the Chronicles of the Kings of Israel. ¹²It [is] the word of YHWH that He spoke to Jehu, saying, "Sons of the fourth [generation] sit on the throne of Israel for you"; and it is so. ¹³Shallum son of Jabesh has reigned in the thirty-ninth year of Uzziah king of Judah, and he reigns a month of days in Samaria; ¹⁴and Menahem son of Gadi goes up from Tirzah and comes to Samaria, and strikes Shallum son of Jabesh in Samaria, and puts him to death, and reigns in his stead. ¹⁵And the rest of the matters of Shallum and his conspiracy that he made, behold, they are written on the scroll of the Chronicles of the Kings of Israel. ¹⁶Then Menahem strikes Tiphsah, and all who [are] in it, and its borders from Tirzah, for it did not open [to him], and he strikes [it], [and] he has ripped up all its pregnant women. ¹⁷In the thirty-ninth year of Azariah king of Judah, Menahem son of Gadi has reigned over Israel in Samaria, ten years. ¹⁸And he does evil in the eyes of YHWH; he has not turned aside from the sins of Jeroboam son of Nebat that caused Israel to sin, all his days. ¹⁹Pul king of Asshur has come against the land, and Menahem gives one thousand talents of silver to Pul, for his hand being with him to strengthen the kingdom in his hand. ²⁰And Menahem brings out the silver [from] Israel, [from] all the mighty men of wealth, to give to the king of Asshur, fifty shekels of silver for each one, and the king of Asshur turns back and has not stayed there in the land. ²¹And the rest of the matters of Menahem and all that he did, are they not written on the scroll of the Chronicles of the Kings of Israel? ²²And Menahem lies with his fathers, and his son Pekahiah reigns in his stead. ²³In the fiftieth year of Azariah king of Judah, Pekahiah son of Menahem has reigned over Israel in Samaria, two years, ²⁴and he does evil in the eyes of YHWH; he has not turned aside from the sins of Jeroboam son of Nebat that he caused Israel to sin. ²⁵And Pekah son of Remaliah, his captain, conspires against him, and strikes him in Samaria, in the high place of the house of the king with Argob and Arieh; and fifty men of the sons of the Gileadites [were] with him, and he puts him to death, and reigns in his stead. ²⁶And the rest of the matters of Pekahiah and all that he did, behold, they are written on the scroll of the Chronicles of the Kings of Israel. ²⁷In the fifty-second year of Azariah king of Judah, Pekah son of Remaliah has reigned over Israel in Samaria, twenty years, ²⁸and he does evil in the eyes of YHWH, he has not turned aside from the sins of Jeroboam son of Nebat that he caused Israel to sin. ²⁹In the days of Pekah king of Israel, Tiglath-Pileser king of Asshur has come, and takes Ijon, and Abel-Beth-Maachah, and Janoah, and Kedesh, and Hazor, and Gilead, and Galilee, all the land of Naphtali, and removes them to Asshur. ³⁰And Hoshea son of Elah makes a conspiracy against Pekah son of Remaliah, and strikes him, and puts him to death, and reigns in his stead, in the twentieth year of Jotham son of Uzziah. ³¹And the rest of the matters of Pekah and all that he did, behold, they are written on the scroll of the Chronicles of the Kings of Israel. ³²In the second year of Pekah son of Remaliah, king of Israel, Jotham son of Uzziah, king of Judah, has reigned. ³³He was a son of twenty-five years in his reigning, and he has reigned sixteen years in Jerusalem, and the name of his mother [is] Jerusha daughter of Zadok, ³⁴and he does that which [is] right in the eyes of YHWH; he has done according to all that his father Uzziah did. ³⁵Only, the high places have not been removed—the people are still sacrificing and making incense in high places; he has built the high gate of the house of YHWH. ³⁶And the rest of the matters of Jotham and all that he did, are they not written on the scroll of the Chronicles of the Kings of Judah? ³⁷In those days YHWH has begun to send Rezin king of Amram and Pekah son of Remaliah against Judah. ³⁸And Jotham lies with his fathers, and is buried with his fathers in the city of his father David, and his son Ahaz reigns in his stead.

CHAPTER 16

¹In the seventeenth year of Pekah son of Remaliah, Ahaz son of Jotham, king of Judah, has reigned. ²Ahaz [is] a son of twenty years in his reigning, and he has reigned sixteen years in Jerusalem, and he has not done that which [is] right in the eyes of his God YHWH, like his father David, ³and he walks in the way of the kings of Israel, and he has also caused his son to pass over into fire, according to the abominations of the nations that YHWH dispossessed from the presence of the sons of Israel, ⁴and he sacrifices and makes incense in high places, and on the heights, and under every green tree. ⁵Then Rezin king of Aram, and Pekah son of Remaliah, king of Israel, go up to Jerusalem, to battle, and they lay siege to Ahaz, and they have not been able to fight. ⁶At that time Rezin king of Aram has brought back Elath to Aram, and casts out the Jews from Elath, and the Arameans have come to Elath, and dwell there to this day. ⁷And Ahaz sends messengers to Tiglath-Pileser king of Asshur, saying, "I [am] your servant and your son; come up and save me out of the hand of the king of Aram, and out of the hand of the king of Israel, who are rising up against me." ⁸And Ahaz takes the silver and the gold that is found in the house of YHWH, and in the treasures of the house of the king, and sends to the king of Asshur [as] a bribe. ⁹And the king of Asshur listens to him, and the king of Asshur goes up to Damascus, and seizes it, and removes [the people of] it to Kir, and he has put Rezin to death. ¹⁰And King Ahaz goes to meet Tiglath-Pileser king of Asshur [at] Damascus, and sees the altar that [is] in Damascus, and King Ahaz sends to Urijah the priest the likeness of the altar, and its pattern, according to all its work, ¹¹and Urijah the priest builds the altar according to all that King Ahaz has sent from Damascus; so Urijah the priest did until the coming in of King Ahaz from Damascus. ¹²And the king comes in from Damascus, and the king sees the altar, and the king draws near on the altar, and offers on it, ¹³and burns his burnt-offering and his present as incense, and pours out his drink-offering, and sprinkles the blood of the peace-offerings that he has, on the altar. ¹⁴As for the altar of bronze that [is] before YHWH—he brings [it] near from the front of the house, from between the altar and the house of YHWH, and puts it on the side of the altar, northward. ¹⁵And King Ahaz commands him—Urijah the priest—saying, "On the great altar burn as incense the burnt-offering of the morning, and the present of the evening, and the burnt-offering of the king, and his present, and the burnt-offering of all the people of the land, and their present, and their drink-offerings; and all the blood of the burnt-offering, and all the blood of the sacrifice, you sprinkle on it, and the altar of bronze is for me to inquire [by]." ¹⁶And Urijah the priest does according to all that King Ahaz commanded. ¹⁷And King Ahaz cuts off the borders of the bases, and turns aside the laver from off them, and he has taken down the sea from off the bronze oxen that [are] under it, and puts it on a pavement of stones. ¹⁸And the covered place for the Sabbath that they built in the house, and the entrance of the king outside, he turned [from] the house of YHWH, because of the king of Asshur. ¹⁹And the rest of the matters of Ahaz that he did, are they not written on the scroll of the Chronicles of the Kings of Judah? ²⁰And Ahaz lies with his fathers, and is buried with his fathers in the City of David, and his son Hezekiah reigns in his stead.

CHAPTER 17

¹In the twelfth year of Ahaz king of Judah, Hoshea son of Elah has reigned over Israel in Samaria, nine years, ²and he does evil in the eyes of YHWH, only, not as the kings of Israel who were before him; ³Shalmaneser king of Asshur came up against him, and Hoshea is a servant to him, and renders a present to him. ⁴And the king of Asshur finds in Hoshea a conspiracy, in that he has sent messengers to So king of Egypt, and has not caused a present to go up to the king of Asshur, as year by year, and the king of Asshur restrains him, and binds him in a house of restraint. ⁵And the king of Asshur goes up into all the land, and he goes up to Samaria, and lays siege against it [for] three years; ⁶in the ninth year of Hoshea, the king of Asshur has captured Samaria, and removes Israel to Asshur, and causes them to dwell in Halah, and in Habor, [by] the river Gozan, and [in] the cities of the Medes. ⁷And it comes to pass, because the sons of Israel have sinned against their God YHWH—who brings them up out of the land of Egypt, from under the hand of Pharaoh king of Egypt—and fear other gods, ⁸and walk in the statutes of the nations that YHWH dispossessed from the presence of the sons of Israel, and of the kings of Israel that they made; ⁹and the sons of Israel covertly do things that [are] not right against their God YHWH, and build high places for themselves in all their cities, from a tower of the watchers to the fortified city, ¹⁰and set up standing-pillars and Asherim for themselves on every high height, and under every green tree, ¹¹and make incense there in all high places, like the nations that YHWH removed from their presence, and do evil things to provoke YHWH, ¹²and serve the idols, of which YHWH said to them, "You do not do this thing." ¹³And YHWH testifies against Israel, and against Judah, by the hand of every prophet, and every seer, saying, "Turn back from your evil ways, and keep My commands, My statutes, according to all the Law that I commanded your fathers, and that I sent to you by the hand of My servants the prophets"; ¹⁴and they have not listened, and harden their neck, like the neck of their fathers, who did not remain steadfast in their God YHWH, ¹⁵and reject His statutes and His covenant that He made with their fathers, and His testimonies that He testified against them, and go after the vain thing, and become vain, and after the nations that are around them, of whom YHWH commanded them not to do like them. ¹⁶And they forsake all the commands of their God YHWH, and make a molten image for themselves—two calves, and make an Asherah, and bow themselves to all the host of the heavens, and serve Ba'al, ¹⁷and cause their sons and their daughters to pass over through fire, and divine divinations, and use enchantments, and sell themselves to do evil in the eyes of YHWH, to provoke Him. ¹⁸And YHWH shows Himself very angry against Israel, and turns them aside from His presence; none has been left, only the tribe of Judah by itself. ¹⁹Also Judah has not kept the commands of their God YHWH, and they walk in the statutes of Israel that they had made. ²⁰And YHWH kicks against all the seed of Israel, and afflicts them, and gives them into the hand of spoilers, until He has cast them out of His presence, ²¹for He has torn Israel from the house of David, and they make Jeroboam son of Nebat king, and Jeroboam drives Israel from after YHWH, and has caused them to sin a great sin, ²²and the sons of Israel walk in all the sins of Jeroboam that he did, they have not turned aside from them, ²³until YHWH has turned Israel aside from His presence, as He spoke by the hand of all His servants the prophets, and Israel is removed from off its land to Asshur, to this day. ²⁴And the king of Asshur brings in [people] from Babylon and from Cutha, and from Ava, and from Hamath, and Sepharvaim, and causes [them] to dwell in the cities of Samaria instead of the sons of Israel, and they possess Samaria, and dwell in its cities; ²⁵and it comes to pass, at the commencement of their dwelling there, they have not feared YHWH, and YHWH sends the lions among them, and they are destroying among them. ²⁶And they speak to the king of Asshur, saying, "The nations that you have removed and place in the cities of Samaria have not known the custom of the God of the land, and He sends the lions among them, and behold, they are destroying them, as they do not know the custom of the God of the land." ²⁷And the king of Asshur commands, saying, "Cause one of the priests to go there whom you removed from there, and they go and dwell there, and he teaches them the custom of the God of the land." ²⁸And one of the priests whom they removed from Samaria comes in, and dwells in Beth-El, and he is teaching them how they fear YHWH, ²⁹and each nation is making its gods, and they place [them] in the houses of the high places that the Samaritans have made—each nation in their cities where they are dwelling. ³⁰And the men of Babylon have made Succoth-Benoth, and the men of Cuth have made Nergal, and the men of Hamath have made Ashima, ³¹and the Avites have made Nibhaz and Tartak, and the Sepharvites are burning their sons with fire to Adrammelech and Anammelech, gods of Sepharvim. ³²And they are fearing YHWH, and make for themselves from their extremities priests of high places, and they are working for them in the house of the high places. ³³They are fearing YHWH, and they are serving their gods, according to the custom of the nations from where they removed them. ³⁴To this day they are doing according to the former customs—they are not fearing YHWH, and are not doing according to their statutes, and

according to their ordinances, and according to the Law, and according to the command, that YHWH commanded the sons of Jacob whose name He made Israel, ³⁵and YHWH makes a covenant with them and charges them, saying, "You do not fear other gods, nor bow yourselves to them, nor serve them, nor sacrifice to them, ³⁶but YHWH who brought you up out of the land of Egypt with great power, and with an outstretched arm, Him you fear, and to Him you bow yourselves, and to Him you sacrifice; ³⁷and the statutes, and the judgments, and the Law, and the command, that He wrote for you, you observe to do all the days, and you do not fear other gods; ³⁸and you do not forget the covenant that I have made with you, and you do not fear other gods; ³⁹but you fear your God YHWH, and He delivers you out of the hand of all your enemies"; ⁴⁰and they have not listened, but they are doing according to their former custom, ⁴¹and these nations are fearing YHWH, and they have served their carved images, both their sons and their sons' sons; as their fathers did, they are doing to this day.

CHAPTER 18

¹And it comes to pass, in the third year of Hoshea son of Elah, king of Israel, Hezekiah son of Ahaz, king of Judah, has reigned; ²he was a son of twenty-five years in his reigning, and he has reigned twenty-nine years in Jerusalem, and the name of his mother [is] Abi daughter of Zechariah. ³And he does that which [is] right in the eyes of YHWH, according to all that his father David did, ⁴he has turned aside the high places, and broken in pieces the standing-pillars, and cut down the Asherah, and beaten down the bronze serpent that Moses made, for up to these days the sons of Israel were making incense to it, and he calls it "a piece of bronze." ⁵In YHWH, God of Israel, he has trusted, and after him there has not been like him among all the kings of Judah, nor [among any] who were before him; ⁶and he cleaves to YHWH, he has not turned aside from after Him, and keeps His commands that YHWH commanded Moses. ⁷And YHWH has been with him; in every place where he goes out he acts wisely, and he rebels against the king of Asshur, and has not served him; ⁸he has struck the Philistines, even to Gaza and its borders, from a tower of watchers to the fortified city. ⁹And it comes to pass, in the fourth year of King Hezekiah—it [is] the seventh year of Hoshea son of Elah, king of Israel—Shalmaneser king of Asshur has come up against Samaria and lays siege to it, ¹⁰and they capture it at the end of three years; in the sixth year of Hezekiah—it [is] the ninth year of Hoshea king of Israel—Samaria has been captured, ¹¹and the king of Asshur removes Israel to Asshur, and placed them in Halah, and in Habor [by] the river Gozan, and [in] cities of the Medes, ¹²because that they have not listened to the voice of their God YHWH, and transgress His covenant—all that He commanded Moses, servant of YHWH—indeed, they have not listened nor done [it]. ¹³And in the fourteenth year of King Hezekiah, Sennacherib king of Asshur has come up against all the fortified cities of Judah, and seizes them, ¹⁴and Hezekiah king of Judah sends to the king of Asshur at Lachish, saying, "I have sinned, turn back from off me; that which you put on me I bear"; and the king of Asshur lays on Hezekiah king of Judah three hundred talents of silver and thirty talents of gold, ¹⁵and Hezekiah gives all the silver that is found in the house of YHWH and in the treasures of the house of the king; ¹⁶at that time Hezekiah has cut off the doors of the temple of YHWH, and the pillars that Hezekiah king of Judah had overlaid, and gives them to the king of Asshur. ¹⁷And the king of Asshur sends Tartan, and the chief of the eunuchs, and the chief of the butlers, from Lachish, to King Hezekiah, with a heavy force, to Jerusalem, and they go up and come to Jerusalem, and they go up, and come in and stand by the conduit of the upper pool that [is] in the highway of the fuller's field. ¹⁸And they call to the king, and Eliakim son of Hilkiah, who [is] over the house, and Shebna the scribe, and Joah son of Asaph, the remembrancer, go out to them. ¹⁹And the chief of the butlers says to them, "Now say to Hezekiah, Thus said the great king, the king of Asshur: What [is] this confidence in which you have confided? ²⁰You have said: Only a word of the lips! Counsel and might [are] for battle; now, on whom have you trusted that you have rebelled against me? ²¹Now behold, you have trusted for yourself on the staff of this broken reed, on Egypt; which a man leans on, and it has gone into his hand and pierced it! So [is] Pharaoh king of Egypt to all those trusting on him. ²²And when you say to me, We have trusted in our God YHWH, is it not He whose high places and whose altars Hezekiah has turned aside, and says to Judah and to Jerusalem, You bow yourselves before this altar in Jerusalem? ²³And now, please give a pledge for yourself to my lord the king of Asshur, and I give two thousand horses to you, if you are able to give riders for yourself on them. ²⁴And how do you turn back the face of one captain of the least of the servants of my lord, that you trust for yourself on Egypt for chariot and for horsemen? ²⁵Have I now come up without YHWH against this place to destroy it? YHWH said to me, Go up against this land, and you have destroyed it." ²⁶And Eliakim son of Hilkiah says—and Shebna and Joah—to the chief of the butlers, "Please speak to your servants [in] Aramaic, for we are understanding, but do not speak with us [in] Jewish, in the ears of the people who [are] on the wall." ²⁷And the chief of the butlers says to them, "For your lord, and to you, has my lord sent me to speak these words? Is it not for the men—those sitting on the wall—to eat their own dung and to drink their own water, with you?" ²⁸And the chief of the butlers stands and calls with a great voice [in] Jewish, and speaks and says, "Hear a word of the great king, the king of Asshur— ²⁹thus said the king: Do not let Hezekiah lift you up, for he is not able to deliver you out of his hand; ³⁰and do not let Hezekiah make you trust in YHWH, saying, YHWH certainly delivers us, and this city is not given into the hand of the king of Asshur. ³¹Do not listen to Hezekiah, for thus said the king of Asshur: Make a blessing with me, and come out to me, and each eat of his vine, and each [eat] of his fig tree, and each drink the waters of his own well, ³²until my coming in, and I have taken you to a land like your own land, a land of grain and new wine, a land of bread and vineyards, a land of olive oil, and honey; and live, and do not die; and do not listen to Hezekiah when he persuades you, saying, YHWH delivers us. ³³Have each of the gods of the nations ever delivered his land out of the hand of the king of Asshur? ³⁴Where [are] the gods of Hamath and Arpad? Where [are] the gods of Sepharvaim, Hena, and Ivvah, that they have delivered Samaria out of my hand? ³⁵Who [are they] among all the gods of the lands that have delivered their land out of my hand, that YHWH delivers Jerusalem out of my hand?" ³⁶And the people have kept silent, and have not answered him a word, for the command of the king is, saying, "Do not answer him." ³⁷And Eliakim son of Hilkiah, who [is] over the house, comes in, and Shebna the scribe, and Joah son of Asaph, the remembrancer, to Hezekiah, with torn garments, and they declare to him the words of the chief of the butlers.

CHAPTER 19

¹And it comes to pass, at King Hezekiah's hearing, that he tears his garments, and covers himself with sackcloth, and enters the house of YHWH, ²and sends Eliakim, who [is] over the house, and Shebna the scribe, and the elderly of the priests, covering themselves with sackcloth, to Isaiah the prophet, son of Amoz, ³and they say to him, "Thus said Hezekiah: This day [is] a day of distress, and rebuke, and despising; for sons have come to the birth, and there is not power to bring forth. ⁴It may be your God YHWH hears all the words of the chief of the butlers with which the king of Asshur his lord has sent him to reproach the living God, and has decided concerning the words that your God YHWH has heard, and you have lifted up prayer for the remnant that is found." ⁵And the servants of King Hezekiah come to Isaiah, ⁶and Isaiah says to them, "Thus you say to your lord, Thus said YHWH: Do not be afraid because of the words that you have heard, with which the servants of the king of Asshur have reviled Me. ⁷Behold, I am giving a spirit in him, and he has heard a report, and has turned back to his land, and I have caused him to fall by the sword in his land." ⁸And the chief of the butlers turns back and finds the king of Asshur fighting against Libnah, for he has heard that he has journeyed from Lachish. ⁹And he hears concerning Tirhakah king of Cush, saying, "Behold, he has come out to fight with you"; and he turns and sends messengers to Hezekiah, saying, ¹⁰"Thus you speak to Hezekiah king of Judah, saying, Do not let your God in whom you are trusting lift you up, saying, Jerusalem is not given into the hand of the king of Asshur. ¹¹Behold, you have heard that which the kings of Asshur have done to all

the lands—to devote them; and are you delivered? ¹²Did the gods of the nations deliver them whom my fathers destroyed—Gozan, and Haran, and Rezeph, and the sons of Eden, who [are] in Thelassar? ¹³Where [is] the king of Hamath, and the king of Arpad, and the king of the city of Sepharvaim, Hena, and Ivvah?" ¹⁴And Hezekiah takes the letters out of the hand of the messengers and reads them, and goes up to the house of YHWH, and Hezekiah spreads it before YHWH. ¹⁵And Hezekiah prays before YHWH and says, "O YHWH, God of Israel, inhabiting the cherubim, You [are] God Himself—You alone—to all the kingdoms of the earth: You have made the heavens and the earth. ¹⁶Incline, O YHWH, Your ear, and hear; open, O YHWH, Your eyes, and see; and hear the words of Sennacherib with which he has sent him to reproach the living God. ¹⁷Truly, O YHWH, kings of Asshur have laid waste the nations and their land, ¹⁸and have put their gods into fire, for they [are] no gods, but work of the hands of man, wood and stone, and destroy them. ¹⁹And now, O our God YHWH, please save us out of his hand, and all kingdoms of the earth know that You [are] YHWH God—You alone." ²⁰And Isaiah son of Amoz sends to Hezekiah, saying, "Thus said YHWH, God of Israel: That which you have prayed to Me concerning Sennacherib king of Asshur I have heard; ²¹this [is] the word that YHWH spoke concerning him: Trampled on you—laughed at you || Has the virgin daughter of Zion; Shaken the head behind you || Has the daughter of Jerusalem! ²²Whom have you reproached and reviled? And against whom lifted up a voice? Indeed, you lift up your eyes on high—Against the Holy One of Israel! ²³By the hand of your messengers || You have reproached the Lord, and say, || In the multitude of my chariots I have come up to a high place of mountains—The sides of Lebanon, || And I cut down the height of its cedars, || The choice of its firs, || And I enter the lodging of its extremity, || The forest of its Carmel. ²⁴I have dug, and drunk strange waters, || And I dry up with the sole of my steps || All floods of a bulwark. ²⁵Have you not heard from afar [that] I made it, || From days of old that I formed it? Now I have brought it in, || And it becomes a desolation, || Ruinous heaps [are] fortified cities, ²⁶And their inhabitants [are] feeble-handed, || They were broken down, and are dried up, || They have been the herb of the field, || And the greenness of the tender grass, || Grass of the roofs, || And blasted grain—before it has risen up! ²⁷And your sitting down, and your going out, || And your coming in, I have known, || And your anger toward Me; ²⁸Because of your anger toward Me, || And your noise—it came up into My ears, || I have put My hook in your nose, || And My bridle in your lips, || And have caused you to turn back || In the way in which you came. ²⁹And this [is] the sign to you, || Food of the year [is] the spontaneous growth, || And in the second year the self-produced, || And in the third year you sow, and reap, || And plant vineyards, and eat their fruits. ³⁰And it has continued—The escaped of the house of Judah || That has been left—to take root beneath, || And has made fruit upward. ³¹For a remnant goes out from Jerusalem, || And an escape from Mount Zion; The zeal of YHWH [of Hosts] does this. ³²Therefore, thus said YHWH, || Concerning the king of Asshur: He does not come into this city, || Nor does he shoot an arrow there, || Nor does he come before it with shield, || Nor does he pour out a mound against it. ³³In the way that he comes in—In it he turns back, || And to this city he does not come in, || A declaration of YHWH— ³⁴And I have covered over this city, || To save it for My own sake, || And for the sake of My servant David." ³⁵And it comes to pass, in that night, that a messenger of YHWH goes out, and strikes one hundred eighty-five thousand in the camp of Asshur, and they rise early in the morning, and behold, all of them [are] dead corpses. ³⁶And Sennacherib king of Asshur journeys, and goes, and turns back, and dwells in Nineveh; ³⁷and it comes to pass, he is bowing himself in the house of his god Nisroch, and [his sons] Adramelech and Sharezar have struck him with the sword, and they have escaped to the land of Ararat, and his son Esar-Haddon reigns in his stead.

CHAPTER 20

¹In those days Hezekiah has been sick to death, and Isaiah son of Amoz the prophet comes to him and says to him, "Thus said YHWH: Give a charge to your house, for you are dying, and do not live." ²And he turns around his face to the wall, and prays to YHWH, saying, ³"Ah, now, O YHWH, please remember how I have habitually walked before You in truth and with a perfect heart, and I have done that which [is] good in Your eyes"; and Hezekiah weeps [with] a great weeping. ⁴And it comes to pass, [when] Isaiah has not [yet] gone out to the middle court, that the word of YHWH has been to him, saying, ⁵"Return, and you have said to Hezekiah, leader of My people, Thus said YHWH, God of your father David: I have heard your prayer, I have seen your tear, behold, I give healing to you. On the third day you go up to the house of YHWH; ⁶and I have added fifteen years to your days, and I deliver you and this city out of the hand of the king of Asshur, and have covered over this city for My own sake, and for the sake of My servant David." ⁷And Isaiah says, "Take a cake of figs"; and they take and lay [it] on the boil, and he revives. ⁸And Hezekiah says to Isaiah, "What [is] the sign that YHWH gives healing to me, that I have gone up to the house of YHWH on the third day?" ⁹And Isaiah says, "This [is] the sign to you from YHWH, that YHWH does the thing that He has spoken—[will] the shadow have gone on ten degrees, or does it turn back ten degrees?" ¹⁰And Hezekiah says, "It has been light for the shadow to incline ten degrees; no, but let the shadow turn backward ten degrees." ¹¹And Isaiah the prophet calls to YHWH, and He brings back the shadow by the degrees that it had gone down in the degrees of Ahaz—backward ten degrees. ¹²At that time Berodach-Baladan son of Baladan, king of Babylon, has sent letters and a present to Hezekiah, for he heard that Hezekiah had been sick; ¹³and Hezekiah listens to them, and shows them all the house of his treasury, the silver, and the gold, and the spices, and the good ointment, and all the house of his vessels, and all that has been found in his treasuries; there has not been a thing that Hezekiah has not showed them in his house and in all his dominion. ¹⁴And Isaiah the prophet comes to King Hezekiah and says to him, "What did these men say? And from where do they come to you?" And Hezekiah says, "They have come from a far-off land—from Babylon." ¹⁵And he says, "What did they see in your house?" And Hezekiah says, "They saw all that [is] in my house; there has not been a thing that I have not showed them among my treasures." ¹⁶And Isaiah says to Hezekiah, "Hear a word of YHWH: ¹⁷Behold, days are coming, and all that [is] in your house, and [all] that your father has treasured up until this day, has been carried to Babylon; there is not a thing left, said YHWH; ¹⁸and of your sons who go out from you, whom you beget, they take away, and they have been eunuchs in the palace of the king of Babylon." ¹⁹And Hezekiah says to Isaiah, "The word of YHWH that you have spoken [is] good"; and he says, "Why not, if there is peace and truth in my days?" ²⁰And the rest of the matters of Hezekiah, and all his might, and how he made the pool, and the conduit, and brings in the waters to the city, are they not written on the scroll of the Chronicles of the Kings of Judah? ²¹And Hezekiah lies with his fathers, and his son Manasseh reigns in his stead.

CHAPTER 21

¹Manasseh [is] a son of twelve years in his reigning, and he has reigned fifty-five years in Jerusalem, and the name of his mother [is] Hephzi-Bah; ²and he does evil in the eyes of YHWH, according to the abominations of the nations that YHWH dispossessed from the presence of the sons of Israel, ³and he turns and builds the high places that his father Hezekiah destroyed, and raises altars for Ba'al, and makes an Asherah, as Ahab king of Israel did, and bows himself to all the host of the heavens, and serves them. ⁴And he has built altars in the house of YHWH, of which YHWH said, "In Jerusalem I put My Name." ⁵And he builds altars to all the host of the heavens in the two courts of the house of YHWH; ⁶and he has caused his son to pass through fire, and observed clouds, and used enchantment, and dealt with a familiar spirit and wizards; he has multiplied to do evil in the eyes of YHWH—to provoke to anger. ⁷And he sets the carved image of the Asherah that he made in the house of which YHWH said to David and to his son Solomon, "In this house, and in Jerusalem, that I have chosen out of all the tribes of Israel, I put My Name for all time; ⁸and I do not add to cause the foot of Israel to move from the ground that I gave to their fathers, only, if they observe to do according to all that I commanded them, and to all the Law that My servant Moses commanded them." ⁹And they have not listened, and Manasseh

causes them to err, to do evil above the nations that YHWH destroyed from the presence of the sons of Israel. ¹⁰And YHWH speaks by the hand of his servants the prophets, saying, ¹¹"Because that Manasseh king of Judah has done these abominations—he has done evil above all that the Amorites have done who [are] before him, and also causes Judah to sin by his idols— ¹²therefore, thus said YHWH, God of Israel: Behold, I am bringing in calamity on Jerusalem and Judah, that whoever hears of it, his two ears tingle. ¹³And I have stretched out the line of Samaria over Jerusalem, and the plummet of the house of Ahab, and wiped Jerusalem as one wipes the dish—he has wiped, and has turned [it] on its face. ¹⁴And I have left the remnant of My inheritance, and given them into the hand of their enemies, and they have been for a prey and for a spoil to all their enemies, ¹⁵because that they have done evil in My eyes, and are provoking Me to anger from the day that their fathers came out of Egypt, even to this day." ¹⁶And also, Manasseh has shed very much innocent blood, until he has filled Jerusalem mouth to mouth, apart from his sin that he has caused Judah to sin, to do evil in the eyes of YHWH. ¹⁷And the rest of the matters of Manasseh, and all that he did, and his sin that he sinned, are they not written on the scroll of the Chronicles of the Kings of Judah? ¹⁸And Manasseh lies with his fathers, and is buried in the garden of his house, in the garden of Uzza, and his son Amon reigns in his stead. ¹⁹Amon [is] a son of twenty-two years in his reigning, and he has reigned two years in Jerusalem, and the name of his mother [is] Meshullemeth daughter of Haruz of Jotbah, ²⁰and he does evil in the eyes of YHWH, as his father Manasseh did, ²¹and walks in all the way that his father walked in, and serves the idols that his father served, and bows himself to them, ²²and forsakes YHWH, God of his fathers, and has not walked in the way of YHWH. ²³And the servants of Amon conspire against him, and put the king to death in his own house, ²⁴and the people of the land strike all those conspiring against King Amon, and the people of the land cause his son Josiah to reign in his stead. ²⁵And the rest of the matters of Amon that he did, are they not written on the scroll of the Chronicles of the Kings of Judah? ²⁶And [one] buries him in his burying-place in the garden of Uzza, and his son Josiah reigns in his stead.

CHAPTER 22

¹Josiah [is] a son of eight years in his reigning, and he has reigned thirty-one years in Jerusalem, and the name of his mother [is] Jedidah daughter of Adaiah of Boskath, ²and he does that which is right in the eyes of YHWH, and walks in all the way of his father David, and has not turned aside [to] the right or left. ³And it comes to pass, in the eighteenth year of King Josiah, the king has sent Shaphan son of Azaliah, son of Meshullam, the scribe, to the house of YHWH, saying, ⁴"Go up to Hilkiah the high priest, and he completes the silver that is brought into the house of YHWH, that the keepers of the threshold have gathered from the people, ⁵and they give it into the hand of those doing the work, the overseers, in the house of YHWH, and they give it to those doing the work, that [are] in the house of YHWH, to strengthen the breach of the house, ⁶to craftsmen, and to builders, and [to repairers of] the wall, and to buy wood and hewn stones to strengthen the house; ⁷only, the silver that is given into their hand is not reckoned with them, for they are dealing in faithfulness." ⁸And Hilkiah the high priest says to Shaphan the scribe, "I have found [the] Scroll of the Law in the house of YHWH"; and Hilkiah gives the scroll to Shaphan, and he reads it. ⁹And Shaphan the scribe comes to the king, and brings the king back word, and says, "Your servants have poured out the silver that has been found in the house, and give it into the hand of those doing the work, the inspectors, in the house of YHWH." ¹⁰And Shaphan the scribe declares to the king, saying, "Hilkiah the priest has given a scroll to me"; and Shaphan reads it before the king. ¹¹And it comes to pass, at the king's hearing the words of the Scroll of the Law, that he tears his garments, ¹²and the king commands Hilkiah the priest, and Ahikam son of Shaphan, and Achbor son of Michaiah, and Shaphan the scribe, and Asahiah servant of the king, saying, ¹³"Go, seek YHWH for me, and for the people, and for all Judah, concerning the words of this scroll that is found, for great [is] the fury of YHWH that is kindled against us, because that our fathers have not listened to the words of this scroll, to do according to all that is written for us." ¹⁴And Hilkiah the priest goes, and Ahikam, and Achbor, and Shaphan, and Asahiah, to Huldah the prophetess, wife of Shallum, son of Tikvah, son of Harhas, keeper of the garments, and she is dwelling in Jerusalem in the second [quarter], and they speak to her. ¹⁵And she says to them, "Thus said YHWH, God of Israel: Say to the man who has sent you to me, ¹⁶Thus said YHWH: Behold, I am bringing in calamity to this place and on its inhabitants, all the words of the scroll that the king of Judah has read, ¹⁷because that they have forsaken Me, and make incense to other gods, so as to provoke Me to anger with every work of their hands, and My wrath has been kindled against this place, and it is not quenched. ¹⁸And to the king of Judah, who is sending you to seek YHWH, thus you say to him, Thus said YHWH, God of Israel: The words that you have heard— ¹⁹because your heart [is] tender, and you are humbled because of YHWH, in your hearing that which I have spoken against this place, and against its inhabitants, to be for a desolation, and for a reviling, and you tear your garments and weep before Me—I also have heard—a declaration of YHWH— ²⁰therefore, behold, I am gathering you to your fathers, and you have been gathered to your grave in peace, and your eyes do not look on any of the calamity that I am bringing in on this place"; and they bring the king back word.

CHAPTER 23

¹And the king sends, and they gather all [the] elderly of Judah and Jerusalem to him, ²and the king goes up to the house of YHWH, and every man of Judah, and all the inhabitants of Jerusalem, with him, and the priests, and the prophets, and all the people, from small to great, and he reads in their ears all the words of the Scroll of the Covenant that is found in the house of YHWH. ³And the king stands by the pillar, and makes the covenant before YHWH, to walk after YHWH, and to keep His commands, and His testimonies, and His statutes, with all the heart, and with all the soul, to establish the words of this covenant that are written on this scroll, and all the people stand in the covenant. ⁴And the king commands Hilkiah the high priest, and the priests of the second order, and the keepers of the threshold, to bring out from the temple of YHWH all the vessels that are made for Ba'al, and for the Asherah, and for all the host of the heavens, and he burns them at the outside of Jerusalem, in the fields of Kidron, and has carried their ashes to Beth-El. ⁵And he has caused to cease the idolatrous priests whom the kings of Judah have appointed (and they make incense in high places, in cities of Judah and outskirts of Jerusalem), and those making incense to Ba'al, to the sun, and to the moon, and to the twelve signs, and to all the host of the heavens. ⁶And he brings out the Asherah from the house of YHWH to the outside of Jerusalem, to the Brook of Kidron, and burns it at the Brook of Kidron, and beats it small to dust, and casts its dust on the grave of the sons of the people. ⁷And he breaks down the houses of the whoremongers that [are] in the house of YHWH, where the women are weaving houses for the Asherah. ⁸And he brings in all the priests out of the cities of Judah, and defiles the high places where the priests have made incense, from Geba to Beer-Sheba, and has broken down the high places of the gates that [are] at the opening of the Gate of Joshua, head of the city, that [is] on a man's left hand at the gate of the city; ⁹only, the priests of the high places do not come up to the altar of YHWH in Jerusalem, but they have eaten unleavened things in the midst of their brothers. ¹⁰And he has defiled Topheth that [is] in the Valley of the Son of Hinnom, so that no man causes his son and his daughter to pass over through fire to Molech. ¹¹And he causes to cease the horses that the kings of Judah have given to the sun from the entering in of the house of YHWH, by the chamber of Nathan-Melech the eunuch, that [is] in the outskirts; and he has burned the chariots of the sun with fire. ¹²And the altars that [are] on the top of the upper chamber of Ahaz, that the kings of Judah made, and the altars that Manasseh made in the two courts of the house of YHWH, the king has broken down, and removes from there, and has cast their dust into the Brook of Kidron. ¹³And the high places that [are] on the front of Jerusalem, that [are] on the right of the Mount of Corruption, that Solomon king of Israel had built to Ashtoreth, abomination of the Zidonians, and Chemosh, abomination of Moab, and to Milcom, abomination of the sons of Ammon, the king has defiled. ¹⁴And he has broken the standing-

pillars in pieces, and cuts down the Asherim, and fills their place with bones of men; ¹⁵and also the altar that [is] in Beth-El, the high place that Jeroboam son of Nebat made, by which he made Israel sin, both that altar and the high place he has broken down, and burns the high place—he has beat it small to dust, and has burned the Asherah. ¹⁶And Josiah turns, and sees the graves that [are] there on the mountain, and sends and takes the bones out of the graves, and burns [them] on the altar, and defiles it, according to the word of YHWH that the man of God proclaimed, who proclaimed these things. ¹⁷And he says, "What [is] this sign that I see?" And the men of the city say to him, "The grave of the man of God who has come from Judah, and proclaims these things that you have done concerning the altar of Beth-El." ¹⁸And he says, "Leave him alone, let no man touch his bones"; and they let his bones escape with the bones of the prophet who came out of Samaria. ¹⁹And also all the houses of the high places that [are] in the cities of Samaria, that the kings of Israel made to provoke to anger, Josiah has turned aside, and does to them according to all the deeds that he did in Beth-El. ²⁰And he slays all the priests of the high places who [are] there by the altars, and burns the bones of man on them, and turns back to Jerusalem. ²¹And the king commands the whole of the people, saying, "Make a Passover to your God YHWH, as it is written on this scroll of the covenant." ²²Surely there has not been made like this Passover from the days of the ones judging who judged Israel, even all the days of the kings of Israel, and of the kings of Judah; ²³but in the eighteenth year of King Josiah, this Passover has been made to YHWH in Jerusalem. ²⁴And also, those having familiar spirits, and the wizards, and the teraphim, and the idols, and all the abominations that were seen in the land of Judah, and in Jerusalem, Josiah has put away, in order to establish the words of the Law that are written on the scroll that Hilkiah the priest has found in the house of YHWH. ²⁵And like him there has not been before him a king who turned back to YHWH with all his heart, and with all his soul, and with all his might, according to all the Law of Moses, and after him there has none risen like him. ²⁶Only, YHWH has not turned back from the fierceness of His great anger with which His anger burned against Judah, because of all the provocations with which Manasseh provoked him, ²⁷and YHWH says, "I also turn Judah aside from my presence, as I turned Israel aside, and I have rejected this city that I have chosen—Jerusalem, and the house of which I said, My Name is there." ²⁸And the rest of the matters of Josiah and all that he did, are they not written on the scroll of the Chronicles of the Kings of Judah? ²⁹In his days Pharaoh Necho king of Egypt has come up against the king of Asshur, by the Euphrates River, and King Josiah goes out to meet him, and [Pharaoh Necho] puts him to death in Megiddo when he sees him. ³⁰And his servants cause him to ride dying from Megiddo, and bring him to Jerusalem, and bury him in his own grave, and the people of the land take Jehoahaz son of Josiah, and anoint him, and cause him to reign instead of his father. ³¹Jehoahaz [is] a son of twenty-three years in his reigning, and he has reigned three months in Jerusalem, and the name of his mother [is] Hamutal daughter of Jeremiah of Libnah, ³²and he does evil in the eyes of YHWH, according to all that his fathers did, ³³and Pharaoh Necho binds him in Riblah, in the land of Hamath, from reigning in Jerusalem, and he puts a fine on the land—one hundred talents of silver, and a talent of gold. ³⁴And Pharaoh Necho causes Eliakim son of Josiah to reign instead of his father Josiah, and turns his name to Jehoiakim, and he has taken Jehoahaz away, and he comes to Egypt, and dies there. ³⁵And Jehoiakim has given the silver and the gold to Pharaoh; only he valued the land to give the silver by the command of Pharaoh; from each, according to his valuation, he exacted the silver and the gold, from the people of the land, to give to Pharaoh Necho. ³⁶Jehoiakim [is] a son of twenty-five years in his reigning, and he has reigned eleven years in Jerusalem, and the name of his mother [is] Zebudah daughter of Pedaiah of Rumah, ³⁷and he does evil in the eyes of YHWH, according to all that his fathers did.

CHAPTER 24

¹In his days Nebuchadnezzar king of Babylon has come up, and Jehoiakim is a servant to him [for] three years; and he turns and rebels against him, ²and YHWH sends against him the troops of the Chaldeans, and the troops of Aram, and the troops of Moab, and the troops of the sons of Ammon, and He sends them against Judah to destroy it, according to the word of YHWH that He spoke by the hand of His servants the prophets; ³only, by the command of YHWH it has been against Judah to turn [them] aside from His presence, for the sins of Manasseh, according to all that he did, ⁴and also the innocent blood that he has shed, and he fills Jerusalem with innocent blood, and YHWH was not willing to forgive. ⁵And the rest of the matters of Jehoiakim and all that he did, are they not written on the scroll of the Chronicles of the Kings of Judah? ⁶And Jehoiakim lies with his fathers, and his son Jehoiachin reigns in his stead. ⁷And the king of Egypt has not added anymore to go out from his own land, for the king of Babylon has taken, from the Brook of Egypt to the Euphrates River, all that had been to the king of Egypt. ⁸Jehoiachin [is] a son of eighteen years in his reigning, and he has reigned three months in Jerusalem, and the name of his mother [is] Nehushta daughter of Elnathan of Jerusalem, ⁹and he does evil in the eyes of YHWH, according to all that his fathers did. ¹⁰At that time servants of Nebuchadnezzar king of Babylon have come up to Jerusalem, and the city goes into siege, ¹¹and Nebuchadnezzar king of Babylon comes against the city, and his servants are laying siege to it, ¹²and Jehoiachin king of Judah goes out to the king of Babylon, he, and his mother, and his servants, and his chiefs, and his eunuchs, and the king of Babylon takes him in the eighth year of his reign, ¹³and brings out from there all the treasures of the house of YHWH, and the treasures of the house of the king, and cuts in pieces all the vessels of gold that Solomon king of Israel made in the temple of YHWH, as YHWH had spoken. ¹⁴And he has removed all Jerusalem, and all the chiefs, and all the mighty men of valor—ten thousand [is] the expulsion—and every craftsman and smith; none has been left except the poor of the people of the land. ¹⁵And he removes Jehoiachin to Babylon, and the mother of the king, and the wives of the king, and his eunuchs, and the mighty ones of the land—he has caused a removal to go from Jerusalem to Babylon, ¹⁶and all the men of valor, seven thousand, and the craftsmen and the smiths, one thousand, the whole [are] mighty men, warriors; and the king of Babylon brings them in a captivity to Babylon. ¹⁷And the king of Babylon causes his father's brother Mattaniah to reign in his stead, and turns his name to Zedekiah. ¹⁸Zedekiah [is] a son of twenty-one years in his reigning, and he has reigned eleven years in Jerusalem, and the name of his mother [is] Hamutal daughter of Jeremiah of Libnah, ¹⁹and he does evil in the eyes of YHWH according to all that Jehoiakim did, ²⁰for by the anger of YHWH it has been against Jerusalem and against Judah, until He [finally] cast them out from His presence. And Zedekiah rebels against the king of Babylon.

CHAPTER 25

¹And it comes to pass, in the ninth year of his reign, in the tenth month, on the tenth of the month, Nebuchadnezzar king of Babylon has come, he and all his force, against Jerusalem, and encamps against it, and builds a surrounding fortification against it. ²And the city enters into siege until the eleventh year of King Zedekiah. ³On the ninth of the month, when the famine is severe in the city, then there has not been bread for the people of the land. ⁴And the city is broken up, and all the men of war [go] by night the way of the gate, between the two walls that [are] by the garden of the king, and the Chaldeans [are] against the city all around, and [the king] goes the way of the plain. ⁵And the force of the Chaldeans pursue after the king, and overtake him in the plains of Jericho, and all his force have been scattered from him; ⁶and they seize the king, and bring him up to the king of Babylon, to Riblah, and they speak judgment with him. ⁷And they have slaughtered the sons of Zedekiah before his eyes, and he has blinded the eyes of Zedekiah, and binds him with bronze chains, and they bring him to Babylon. ⁸And in the fifth month, on the seventh of the month (it [is] the nineteenth year of King Nebuchadnezzar king of Babylon), Nebuzaradan chief of the executioners, servant of the king of Babylon, has come to Jerusalem, ⁹and he burns the house of YHWH, and the house of the king, and all the houses of Jerusalem, indeed, he has burned every great house with fire; ¹⁰and all the forces of the Chaldeans, who [are] with the chief of the executioners, have broken down

the walls of Jerusalem all around. ¹¹And the rest of the people, those left in the city, and those falling who have fallen to the king of Babylon, and the rest of the multitude, Nebuzaradan chief of the executioners has removed; ¹²and of the poor of the land the chief of the executioners has left for vinedressers and for farmers. ¹³And the pillars of bronze that [are] in the house of YHWH, and the bases, and the sea of bronze, that [is] in the house of YHWH, the Chaldeans have broken in pieces, and carry away their bronze to Babylon. ¹⁴And the pots, and the shovels, and the snuffers, and the spoons, and all the vessels of bronze with which they minister, they have taken; ¹⁵and the fire-pans, and the bowls that [are] wholly of silver, the chief of the executioners has taken. ¹⁶The two pillars, the one sea, and the bases that Solomon made for the house of YHWH, there was no weighing of the bronze of all these vessels; ¹⁷eighteen cubits [is] the height of the one pillar, and the capital on it [is] of bronze, and the height of the capital [is] three cubits, and the net and the pomegranates [are] on the capital all around—the whole [is] of bronze; and the second pillar has like these, with the net. ¹⁸And the chief of the executioners takes Seraiah the head priest, and Zephaniah the second priest, and the three keepers of the threshold; ¹⁹and he has taken out of the city a certain eunuch who is appointed over the men of war, and five men of those seeing the king's face who have been found in the city, and the head scribe of the host who musters the people of the land, and sixty men of the people of the land who are found in the city; ²⁰and Nebuzaradan chief of the executioners takes them, and causes them to go to the king of Babylon, to Libnah, ²¹and the king of Babylon strikes them, and puts them to death in Riblah, in the land of Hamath, and he removes Judah from off its land. ²²And the people that are left in the land of Judah whom Nebuchadnezzar king of Babylon has left—he appoints Gedaliah son of Ahikam, son of Shaphan, over them. ²³And all the heads of the forces hear—they and the men—that the king of Babylon has appointed Gedaliah, and they come to Gedaliah, to Mizpah, even Ishmael son of Nethaniah, and Johanan son of Kareah, and Seraiah son of Tanhumeth the Netophathite, and Jaazaniah son of the Maachathite—they and their men; ²⁴and Gedaliah swears to them and to their men, and says to them, "Do not be afraid of the servants of the Chaldeans, dwell in the land and serve the king of Babylon, and it is good for you." ²⁵And it comes to pass, in the seventh month, Ishmael son of Nathaniah has come, son of Elishama of the seed of the kingdom, and ten men with him, and they strike Gedaliah, and he dies, and the Jews and the Chaldeans who have been with him in Mizpah. ²⁶And all the people rise, from small even to great, and the heads of the forces, and come to Egypt, for they have been afraid of the presence of the Chaldeans. ²⁷And it comes to pass, in the thirty-seventh year of the expulsion of Jehoiachin king of Judah, in the twelfth month, on the twenty-seventh of the month, Evil-Merodach king of Babylon has lifted up, in the year of his reigning, the head of Jehoiachin king of Judah, out of the house of restraint, ²⁸and speaks good things with him and puts his throne above the throne of the kings who [are] with him in Babylon, ²⁹and has changed the garments of his restraint, and he has eaten bread continually before him all [the] days of his life, ³⁰and his allowance—a continual allowance—has been given to him from the king, the matter of a day in its day, all [the] days of his life.

1 CHRONICLES

CHAPTER 1

¹Adam, Seth, Enosh, ²Kenan, Mahalaleel, Jered, ³Enoch, Methuselah, Lamech, ⁴Noah, Shem, Ham, and Japheth. ⁵Sons of Japheth: Gomer and Magog, and Madai, and Javan, and Tubal, and Meshech, and Tiras. ⁶And sons of Gomer: Ashchenaz, and Riphath, and Togarmah. ⁷And sons of Javan: Elisha, and Tarshishah, Kittim, and Dodanim. ⁸Sons of Ham: Cush, and Mizraim, Put, and Canaan. ⁹And sons of Cush: Seba and Havilah, and Sabta, and Raamah, and Sabtecka. And sons of Raamah: Sheba and Dedan. ¹⁰And Cush begot Nimrod: he began to be a mighty one in the land. ¹¹And Mizraim begot the Ludim, and the Anamim, and the Lehabim, and the Naphtuhim, ¹²and the Pathrusim, and the Casluhim (from whom the Philistim came out), and the Caphtorim. ¹³And Canaan begot Sidon his firstborn, and Heth, ¹⁴and the Jebusite, and the Amorite, and the Girgashite, ¹⁵and the Hivite, and the Arkite, and the Sinite, ¹⁶and the Arvadite, and the Zemarite, and the Hamathite. ¹⁷Sons of Shem: Elam and Asshur, and Arphaxad, and Lud, and Aram, and Uz, and Hul, and Gether, and Meshech. ¹⁸And Arphaxad begot Shelah, and Shelah begot Eber. ¹⁹And two sons have been born to Eber, the name of the first [is] Peleg, for in his days the earth has been divided, and the name of his brother is Joktan. ²⁰And Joktan begot Almodad, and Sheleph, and Hazarmaveth, and Jerah, ²¹and Hadoram, and Uzal, and Diklah, ²²and Ebal, and Abimael, and Sheba, ²³and Ophir, and Havilah, and Jobab; all these [are] sons of Joktan. ²⁴Shem, Arphaxad, Shelah, ²⁵Eber, Peleg, Reu, ²⁶Serug, Nahor, Terah, ²⁷Abram—he [is] Abraham. ²⁸Sons of Abraham: Isaac and Ishmael. ²⁹These [are] their generations: [the] firstborn of Ishmael [was] Nebaioth, then Kedar, and Adheel, and Mibsam, ³⁰Mishma, and Dumah, Massa, Hadad, and Tema, ³¹Jetur, Naphish, and Kedema. These are sons of Ishmael. ³²And sons of Keturah, Abraham's concubine: she bore Zimran, and Jokshan, and Medan, and Midian, and Ishbak, and Shuah. And sons of Jokshan: Sheba and Dedan. ³³And sons of Midian: Ephah and Epher, and Enoch, and Abida, and Eldaah; all these [are] sons of Keturah. ³⁴And Abraham begets Isaac. Sons of Isaac: Esau and Israel. ³⁵Sons of Esau: Eliphaz, Reuel, and Jeush, and Jaalam, and Korah. ³⁶Sons of Eliphaz: Teman, and Omar, Zephi, and Gatam, Kenaz, and Timna, and Amalek. ³⁷Sons of Reuel: Nahath, Zerah, Shammah, and Mizzah. ³⁸And sons of Seir: Lotan, and Shobal, and Zibeon, and Anah, and Dishon, and Ezar, and Dishan. ³⁹And sons of Lotan: Hori and Homam, and sister of Lotan [is] Timna. ⁴⁰Sons of Shobal: Alian, and Manahath, and Ebal, Shephi, and Onam. And sons of Zideon: Aiah and Anah. ⁴¹The sons of Anah: Dishon. And sons of Dishon: Amram, and Eshban, and Ithran, and Cheran. ⁴²Sons of Ezer: Bilhan, and Zavan, Jakan. Sons of Dishan: Uz and Aran. ⁴³And these [are] the kings who reigned in the land of Edom before the reigning of a king of the sons of Israel: Bela son of Beor, and the name of his city [is] Dinhabah. ⁴⁴And Bela dies, and Jobab son of Zerah from Bozrah reigns in his stead; ⁴⁵and Jobab dies, and Husham from the land of the Temanite reigns in his stead; ⁴⁶and Husham dies, and Hadad son of Bedad reigns in his stead (who strikes Midian in the field of Moab) and the name of his city [is] Avith; ⁴⁷and Hadad dies, and Samlah from Masrekah reigns in his stead; ⁴⁸and Samlah dies, and Shaul from Rehoboth of the River reigns in his stead; ⁴⁹and Shaul dies, and Ba'al-Hanan son of Achbor reigns in his stead; ⁵⁰and Ba'al-Hanan dies, and Hadad reigns in his stead, and the name of his city [is] Pai, and the name of his wife [is] Mehetabel daughter of Matred, daughter of Me-Zahab; Hadad also dies. ⁵¹And chiefs of Edom are: Chief Timnah, Chief Aliah, Chief Jetheth, ⁵²Chief Aholibamah, Chief Elah, Chief Pinon, ⁵³Chief Kenaz, Chief Teman, Chief Mibzar, ⁵⁴Chief Magdiel, Chief Iram. These [are] chiefs of Edom.

CHAPTER 2

¹These [are] sons of Israel: Reuben, Simeon, Levi, and Judah, Issachar, and Zebulun, ²Dan, Joseph, and Benjamin, Naphtali, Gad, and Asher. ³Sons of Judah: Er, and Onan, and Shelah, three have been born to him of a daughter of Shua the Canaanitess. And Er, firstborn of Judah, is evil in the eyes of YHWH, and He puts him to death. ⁴And his daughter-in-law Tamar has borne Perez and Zerah to him. All the sons of Judah [are] five. ⁵Sons of Perez: Hezron, and Hamul. ⁶And sons of Zerah: Zimri, and Ethan, and Heman, and Calcol, and Dara; all of them five. ⁷And sons of Carmi: Achar, troubler of Israel, who trespassed in the devoted thing. ⁸And sons of Ethan: Azariah. ⁹And sons of Hezron who were born to him: Jerahmeel, and Ram, and

1 CHRONICLES

Chelubai. ¹⁰And Ram begot Amminadab, and Amminadab begot Nahshon, prince of the sons of Judah; ¹¹and Nahshon begot Salma, and Salma begot Boaz, ¹²and Boaz begot Obed, and Obed begot Jesse; ¹³and Jesse begot his firstborn Eliab, and Abinadab the second, and Shimea the third, ¹⁴Nethaneel the fourth, Raddai the fifth, ¹⁵Ozem the sixth, David the seventh, ¹⁶and their sisters Zeruiah and Abigail. And sons of Zeruiah: Abishai, and Joab, and Asah-El—three. ¹⁷And Abigail has borne Amasa, and the father of Amasa [is] Jether the Ishmaelite. ¹⁸And Caleb son of Hezron has begotten Azubah, Issheh, and Jerioth; and these [are] her sons: Jesher, and Shobab, and Ardon. ¹⁹And Azubah dies, and Caleb takes Ephrath to himself, and she bears Hur to him. ²⁰And Hur begot Uri, and Uri begot Bezaleel. ²¹And afterward Hezron has gone in to a daughter of Machir father of Gilead, and he has taken her, and he [is] a son of sixty years, and she bears Segub to him. ²²And Segub begot Jair, and he has twenty-three cities in the land of Gilead, ²³and he takes Geshur and Aram, the small villages of Jair, from them, with Kenath and its small towns, sixty cities—all these [belonged to] the sons of Machir father of Gilead. ²⁴And after the death of Hezron in Caleb-Ephratah, then the wife of Hezron, Abijah, even bears to him Asshur, father of Tekoa. ²⁵And sons of Jerahmeel, firstborn of Hezron, are: the firstborn Ram, and Bunah, and Oren, and Ozem, Ahijah. ²⁶And Jerahmeel has another wife, and her name [is] Atarah, she [is] mother of Onam. ²⁷And sons of Ram, firstborn of Jerahmeel, are Maaz, and Jamin, and Eker. ²⁸And sons of Onam are Shammai and Jada. And sons of Shammai: Nadab and Abishur. ²⁹And the name of the wife of Abishur [is] Abihail, and she bears Ahban and Molid to him. ³⁰And sons of Nadab: Seled and Appaim; and Seled dies without sons. ³¹And sons of Appaim: Ishi. And sons of Ishi: Sheshan. And sons of Sheshan: Ahlai. ³²And sons of Jada, brother of Shammai: Jether and Jonathan; and Jether dies without sons. ³³And sons of Jonathan: Peleth and Zaza. These were sons of Jerahmeel. ³⁴And Sheshan had no sons, but daughters, and Sheshan has a servant, an Egyptian, and his name [is] Jarha, ³⁵and Sheshan gives his daughter to his servant Jarha for a wife, and she bears Attai to him; ³⁶and Attai begot Nathan, and Nathan begot Zabad, ³⁷and Zabad begot Ephlal, and Ephlal begot Obed, ³⁸and Obed begot Jehu, ³⁹and Jehu begot Azariah, and Azariah begot Helez, and Helez begot Eleasah, ⁴⁰and Eleasah begot Sismai, and Sismai begot Shallum, ⁴¹and Shallum begot Jekamiah, and Jekamiah begot Elishama. ⁴²And sons of Caleb brother of Jerahmeel: Mesha his firstborn, he [is] father of Ziph; and sons of Mareshah: Abi-Hebron. ⁴³And sons of Hebron: Korah, and Tappuah, and Rekem, and Shema. ⁴⁴And Shema begot Raham father of Jorkoam, and Rekem begot Shammai. ⁴⁵And a son of Shammai [is] Maon, and Maon [is] father of Beth-Zur. ⁴⁶And Ephah concubine of Caleb bore Haran, and Moza, and Gazez; and Haran begot Gazez. ⁴⁷And sons of Jahdai: Regem, and Jotham, and Geshem, and Pelet, and Ephah, and Shaaph. ⁴⁸The concubine of Caleb, Maachah, bore Sheber and Tirhanah; ⁴⁹and she bears Shaaph father of Madmannah, Sheva father of Machbenah, and father of Gibea; and a daughter of Caleb [is] Achsa. ⁵⁰These were sons of Caleb son of Hur, firstborn of Ephrathah: Shobal father of Kirjath-Jearim, ⁵¹Salma father of Beth-Lehem, Hareph father of Beth-Gader. ⁵²And there are sons to Shobal father of Kirjath-Jearim: Haroeh, half of the Menuhothite, ⁵³and the families of Kirjath-Jearim: the Ithrite, and the Puhite, and the Shumathite, and the Mishraite. The Zorathite and the Eshtaolite went out from these. ⁵⁴Sons of Salma: Beth-Lehem, and the Netophathite, Atroth, Beth-Joab, and half of the Menuhothite, the Zorite; ⁵⁵and the families of the scribes, the inhabitants of Jabez: Tirathites, Shimeathites, Suchathites. They [are] the Kenites, those coming of Hammath father of the house of Rechab.

CHAPTER 3

¹And these were sons of David, who were born to him in Hebron: the firstborn Amnon, of Ahinoam the Jezreelitess; second Daniel, of Abigail the Carmelitess; ²the third Absalom, son of Maachah daughter of Talmai king of Geshur; the fourth Adonijah, son of Haggith; ³the fifth Shephatiah, of Abital; the sixth Ithream, of his wife Eglah. ⁴Six have been borne to him in Hebron, and he reigns seven years and six months there, and he has reigned thirty-three years in Jerusalem. ⁵And these were born to him in Jerusalem: Shimea, and Shobab, and Nathan, and Solomon—four, of Bathsheba daughter of Ammiel. ⁶Also Ibhar, and Elishama, and Eliphelet, ⁷and Nogah, and Nepheg, and Japhia, ⁸and Elishama, and Eliada, and Eliphelet—nine. ⁹All [are] sons of David, apart from sons of the concubines, and their sister Tamar. ¹⁰And the son of Solomon [is] Rehoboam, Abijah his son, Asa his son, Jehoshaphat his son, ¹¹Joram his son, Ahaziah his son, Joash his son, ¹²Amaziah his son, Azariah his son, Jotham his son, ¹³Ahaz his son, Hezekiah his son, Manasseh his son, ¹⁴Amon his son, Josiah his son. ¹⁵And sons of Josiah: the firstborn Johanan, the second Jehoiakim, the third Zedekiah, the fourth Shallum. ¹⁶And sons of Jehoiakim: Jeconiah his son, Zedekiah his son. ¹⁷And sons of Jeconiah: Assir; Salathiel his son; ¹⁸also Malchiram and Pedaiah, and Shenazzar, Jecamiah, Hoshama, and Nedabiah. ¹⁹And sons of Pedaiah: Zerubbabel and Shimei. And sons of Zerubbabel: Meshullam, and Hananiah, and their sister Shelomith, ²⁰and Hashubah, and Ohel, and Berechiah, and Hasadiah, Jushab-Hesed—five. ²¹And sons of Hananiah: Pelatiah, and Jesaiah, sons of Rephaiah, sons of Arnan, sons of Obadiah, sons of Shechaniah. ²²And sons of Shechaniah: Shemaiah; and sons of Shemaiah: Hattush, and Igeal, and Bariah, and Neariah, and Shaphat—six. ²³And sons of Neariah: Elioenai, and Hezekiah, and Azrikam—three. ²⁴And sons of Elioenai: Hodaiah, and Eliashib, and Pelaiah, and Akkub, and Johanan, and Delaiah, and Anani—seven.

CHAPTER 4

¹Sons of Judah: Perez, Hezron, and Carmi, and Hur, and Shobal. ²And Reaiah son of Shobal begot Jahath, and Jahath begot Ahumai and Lahad; these [are] families of the Zorathite. ³And these [are] of the father of Etam: Jezreel, and Ishma, and Idbash; and the name of their sister [is] Hazzelelponi; ⁴and Penuel [is] father of Gedor, and Ezer father of Hushah. These [are] sons of Hur, firstborn of Ephratah, father of Beth-Lehem. ⁵And to Ashhur father of Tekoa were two wives, Helah and Naarah; ⁶and Naarah bears to him Ahuzzam, and Hepher, and Temeni, and Haahashtari: these [are] sons of Naarah. ⁷And sons of Helah: Zereth, and Zohar, and Ethnan. ⁸And Coz begot Anub, and Zobebah, and the families of Aharhel son of Harum. ⁹And Jabez is honored above his brothers, and his mother called his name Jabez, saying, "Because I have brought forth with grief." ¹⁰And Jabez calls to the God of Israel, saying, "If blessing You bless me, then You have made my border great, and Your hand has been with me, and You have kept [me] from evil—not to grieve me"; and God brings in that which he asked. ¹¹And Chelub brother of Shuah begot Mehir; he [is] father of Eshton. ¹²And Eshton begot Beth-Rapha, and Paseah, and Tehinnah father of Ir-Nahash; these [are] men of Rechah. ¹³And sons of Kenaz: Othniel and Seraiah; and sons of Othniel: Hathath. ¹⁴And Meonothai begot Ophrah, and Seraiah begot Joab father of the Valley of the Craftsmen, for they were craftsmen. ¹⁵And sons of Caleb son of Jephunneh: Iru, Elah, and Naam; and sons of Elah: even Kenaz. ¹⁶And sons of Jehaleleel: Ziph and Ziphah, Tiria, and Asareel. ¹⁷And sons of Ezra: Jether, and Mered, and Epher, and Jalon. And she bears Miriam, and Shammai, and Ishbah father of Eshtemoa. ¹⁸And his wife Jehudijah bore Jered father of Gedor, and Heber father of Socho, and Jekuthiel father of Zanoah. And these [are] sons of Bithiah daughter of Pharaoh, whom Mered took, ¹⁹and sons of the wife of Hodiah sister of Nahom: Abi-Keilah the Garmite, and Eshtemoa the Maachathite. ²⁰And sons of Shimon: Amnon, and Rinnah, Ben-Hanon, and Tilon; and sons of Ishi: Zoheth, and Ben-Zoheth. ²¹Sons of Shelah son of Judah: Er father of Lecah, and Laadah father of Mareshah, and the families of the house of the service of fine linen, of the house of Ashbea; ²²and Jokim, and the men of Chozeba, and Joash, and Saraph, who ruled over Moab and Jashubi-Lehem; and these things [are] ancient. ²³They [are] the potters and inhabitants of Netaim and Gedera; they dwelt there with the king in his work. ²⁴Sons of Simeon: Nemuel, and Jamin, Jarib, Zerah, Shaul; ²⁵Shallum his son, Mibsam his son, Mishma his son. ²⁶And sons of Mishma: Hammuel his son, Zacchur his son, Shimei his son. ²⁷And to Shimei [are] sixteen sons and six daughters, and to his brothers there are not many sons, and none of their families have multiplied as much as the sons of Judah. ²⁸And they dwell in Beer-Sheba, and Moladah, and Hazar-Shaul, ²⁹and in Bilhah, and in Ezem, and in Tolad, ³⁰and in Bethuel, and in Hormah, and

in Ziklag, ³¹and in Beth-Marcaboth, and in Hazar-Susim, and in Beth-Birei, and in Shaarim; these [are] their cities until the reigning of David. ³²And their villages [are] Etam, and Ain, Rimmon, and Tochen, and Ashan—five cities, ³³and all their villages that [are] around these cities to Ba'al; these [are] their dwellings, and they have their genealogy: ³⁴even Meshobab, and Jamlech, and Joshah son of Amaziah, ³⁵and Joel, and Jehu son of Josibiah, son of Seraiah, son of Asiel, ³⁶and Elioenai, and Jaakobah, and Jeshohaiah, and Asaiah, and Adiel, and Jesimiel, and Benaiah, ³⁷and Ziza son of Shiphi, son of Allon, son of Jedaiah, son of Shimri, son of Shemaiah. ³⁸These who are coming in by name [are] princes in their families, and the house of their fathers has broken forth into a multitude; ³⁹and they go to the entrance of Gedor, to the east of the valley, to seek pasture for their flock, ⁴⁰and they find pasture, fat and good, and the land broad of sides, and quiet, and safe, for those dwelling there before are of Ham. ⁴¹And these who are written by name come in the days of Hezekiah king of Judah, and strike their tents, and the habitations that have been found there, and devote them to destruction to this day, and dwell in their stead, because pasture for their flock [is] there. ⁴²And of them, of the sons of Simeon, five hundred men have gone to Mount Seir, and Pelatiah, and Neariah, and Rephaiah, and Uzziel, sons of Ishi, at their head, ⁴³and they strike the remnant of those escaped of Amalek, and dwell there to this day.

CHAPTER 5

¹As for sons of Reuben, firstborn of Israel—for he [is] the firstborn, and on account of his profaning the bed of his father his birthright has been given to the sons of Joseph son of Israel, and [he is] not to be reckoned by genealogy for the birthright, ²for Judah has been mighty over his brother, and for leader above him, and the birthright [is] to Joseph— ³sons of Reuben, firstborn of Israel: Enoch, and Pallu, Hezron, and Carmi. ⁴Sons of Joel: Shemaiah his son, Gog his son, Shimei his son, ⁵Micah his son, Reaiah his son, Ba'al his son, ⁶Beerah his son, whom Tilgath-Pilneser king of Asshur removed; he [is] prince of the Reubenite. ⁷And his brothers, by their families, in the genealogy of their generations, [are] heads: Jeiel, and Zechariah, ⁸and Bela son of Azaz, son of Shema, son of Joel—he is dwelling in Aroer, even to Nebo and Ba'al-Meon; ⁹and he dwelt at the east even to the entering in of the wilderness, even from the Euphrates River, for their livestock were multiplied in the land of Gilead. ¹⁰And they have made war with the Hagarites in the days of Saul, who fall by their hand, and they dwell in their tents over all the face of the east of Gilead. ¹¹And the sons of Gad have dwelt opposite them in the land of Bashan to Salcah: ¹²Joel the head, and Shapham the second, and Jaanai and Shaphat in Bashan; ¹³and their brothers of the house of their fathers [are] Michael, and Meshullam, and Sheba, and Jorai, and Jachan, and Zia, and Heber—seven. ¹⁴These [are] sons of Abihail son of Huri, son of Jaroah, son of Gilead, son of Michael, son of Jeshishai, son of Jahdo, son of Buz; ¹⁵Ahi son of Abdiel, son of Guni, [is] head of the house of their fathers; ¹⁶and they dwell in Gilead in Bashan, and in her small towns, and in all outskirts of Sharon, on their outskirts; ¹⁷all of them reckoned themselves by genealogy in the days of Jotham king of Judah, and in the days of Jeroboam king of Israel. ¹⁸Sons of Reuben, and the Gadite, and the half of the tribe of Manasseh, of sons of valor, men carrying shield and sword, and treading bow, and taught in battle, [are] forty-four thousand and seven hundred and sixty, going out to the host. ¹⁹And they make war with the Hagarites, and Jetur, and Naphish, and Nodab, ²⁰and they are helped against them, and the Hagarites are given into their hand, and all who [are] with them, for they cried to God in battle, and He received their plea, because they trusted in Him. ²¹And they take their livestock captive—fifty thousand of their camels, and two hundred and fifty thousand sheep, and two thousand donkeys, and one hundred thousand of mankind; ²²for many have fallen pierced, for the battle [is] of God; and they dwell in their stead until the expulsion. ²³And the sons of the half of the tribe of Manasseh dwelt in the land, from Bashan to Ba'al-Hermon, and Senir, and Mount Hermon; they have multiplied. ²⁴And these [are] heads of the house of their fathers: even Epher, and Ishi, and Eliel, and Azriel, and Jeremiah, and Hodaviah, and Jahdiel, men mighty in valor, men of renown, heads of the house of their fathers. ²⁵And they trespass against the God of their fathers, and go whoring after the gods of the peoples of the land whom God destroyed from their presence; ²⁶and the God of Israel stirs up the spirit of Pul king of Asshur, and the spirit of Tilgath-Pilneser king of Asshur, and he removes them—even the Reubenite, and the Gadite, and the half of the tribe of Manasseh—and brings them to Halah, and Habor, and Hara, and the River of Gozan to this day.

CHAPTER 6

¹Sons of Levi: Gershon, Kohath, and Merari. ²And the sons of Kohath: Amram, Izhar, and Hebron, and Uzziel. ³And sons of Amram: Aaron, and Moses, and [his daughter] Miriam. And sons of Aaron: Nadab, and Abihu, Eleazar, and Ithamar. ⁴Eleazar begot Phinehas, Phinehas begot Abishua, ⁵and Abishua begot Bukki, and Bukki begot Uzzi, ⁶and Uzzi begot Zerahiah, and Zerahiah begot Meraioth, ⁷Meraioth begot Amariah, and Amariah begot Ahitub, ⁸and Ahitub begot Zadok, and Zadok begot Ahimaaz, ⁹and Ahimaaz begot Azariah, and Azariah begot Johanan, ¹⁰and Johanan begot Azariah—him who acted as priest in the house that Solomon built in Jerusalem. ¹¹And Azariah begets Amariah, and Amariah begot Ahitub, ¹²and Ahitub begot Zadok, and Zadok begot Shallum, ¹³and Shallum begot Hilkiah, and Hilkiah begot Azariah, ¹⁴and Azariah begot Seraiah, and Seraiah begot Jehozadak; ¹⁵and Jehozadak has gone in YHWH's removing Judah and Jerusalem by the hand of Nebuchadnezzar. ¹⁶Sons of Levi: Gershom, Kohath, and Merari. ¹⁷And these [are] names of sons of Gershom: Libni and Shimei. ¹⁸And sons of Kohath: Amram, and Izhar, and Hebron, and Uzziel. ¹⁹Sons of Merari; Mahli and Mushi. And these [are] families of the Levite according to their fathers; ²⁰of Gershom: Libni his son, Jahath his son, Zimmah his son, ²¹Joah his son, Iddo his son, Zerah his son, Jeaterai his son. ²²Sons of Kohath: Amminadab his son, Korah his son, Assir his son, ²³Elkanah his son, and Ebiasaph his son, and Assir his son, ²⁴Tahath his son, Uriel his son, Uzziah his son, and Shaul his son. ²⁵And sons of Elkanah: Amasai and Ahimoth. ²⁶Elkanah—sons of Elkanah: Zophai his son, and Nahath his son, ²⁷Eliab his son, Jeroham his son, Elkanah his son. ²⁸And sons of Samuel: the firstborn Vashni, and the second Abijah. ²⁹Sons of Merari: Mahli, Libni his son, Shimei his son, Uzzah his son, ³⁰Shimea his son, Haggiah his son, Asaiah his son. ³¹And these [are] they whom David stationed over the parts of the song of the house of YHWH, from the resting of the Ark, ³²and they are ministering before the Dwelling Place of the Tent of Meeting, in song, until the building by Solomon of the house of YHWH in Jerusalem; and they stand according to their ordinance over their service. ³³And these [are] those standing, and their sons, of the sons of the Kohathite: Heman the singer, son of Joel, son of Shemuel, ³⁴son of Elkanah, son of Jeroham, son of Eliel, son of Toah, ³⁵son of Zuph, son of Elkanah, son of Mahath, son of Amasai, ³⁶son of Elkanah, son of Joel, son of Azariah, son of Zephaniah, ³⁷son of Tahath, son of Assir, son of Ebiasaph, son of Korah, ³⁸son of Izhar, son of Kohath, son of Levi, son of Israel. ³⁹And his brother Asaph, who is standing on his right—Asaph, son of Berachiah, son of Shimea, ⁴⁰son of Michael, son of Baaseiah, son of Malchiah, ⁴¹son of Ethni, son of Zerah, son of Adaiah, ⁴²son of Ethan, son of Zimmah, son of Shimei, ⁴³son of Jahath, son of Gershom, son of Levi. ⁴⁴And sons of Merari, their brothers, on the left: Ethan son of Kishi, son of Abdi, son of Malluch, ⁴⁵son of Hashabiah, son of Amaziah, son of Hilkiah, ⁴⁶son of Amzi, son of Bani, son of Shamer, ⁴⁷son of Mahli, son of Mushi, son of Merari, son of Levi. ⁴⁸And their brothers the Levites are put to all the service of the Dwelling Place of the house of God. ⁴⁹And Aaron and his sons are making incense on the altar of the burnt-offering, and on the altar of the incense, for all the work of the Holy of Holies, and to make atonement for Israel, according to all that Moses servant of God commanded. ⁵⁰And these [are] sons of Aaron: Eleazar his son, Phinehas his son, Abishua his son, ⁵¹Bukki his son, Uzzi his son, Zerahiah his son, ⁵²Meraioth his son, Amariah his son, Ahitub his son, ⁵³Zadok his son, Ahimaaz his son. ⁵⁴And these [are] their dwellings, throughout their towers, in their borders, of the sons of Aaron, of the family of the Kohathite, for the lot was theirs; ⁵⁵and they give to them Hebron in the land of Judah and its outskirts around it; ⁵⁶and they gave the field of the city and its villages to Caleb son of

1 CHRONICLES

Jephunneh. ⁵⁷And they gave the cities of refuge to the sons of Aaron: Hebron, and Libnah and its outskirts, and Jattir, and Eshtemoa and its outskirts, ⁵⁸and Hilen and its outskirts, Debir and its outskirts, ⁵⁹and Ashan and its outskirts, and Beth-Shemesh and its outskirts. ⁶⁰And from the tribe of Benjamin: Geba and its outskirts, and Allemeth and its outskirts, and Anathoth and its outskirts. All their cities [are] thirteen cities among their families. ⁶¹And to the sons of Kohath, those left of the family of the tribe, from the half of the tribe, the half of Manasseh, by lot, [are] ten cities. ⁶²And to the sons of Gershom, for their families, from the tribe of Issachar, and from the tribe of Asher, and from the tribe of Naphtali, and from the tribe of Manasseh in Bashan, [are] thirteen cities. ⁶³To the sons of Merari, for their families, from the tribe of Reuben, and from the tribe of Gad, and from the tribe of Zebulun, by lot, [are] twelve cities. ⁶⁴And the sons of Israel give the cities and their outskirts to the Levites. ⁶⁵And they give by lot from the tribe of the sons of Judah, and from the tribe of the sons of Simeon, and from the tribe of the sons of Benjamin, these cities which they call by name; ⁶⁶and some of the families of the sons of Kohath have cities of their border from the tribe of Ephraim; ⁶⁷and they give the cities of refuge to them: Shechem and its outskirts in the hill-country of Ephraim, and Gezer and its outskirts, ⁶⁸and Jokmeam and its outskirts, and Beth-Horan and its outskirts, ⁶⁹and Aijalon and its outskirts, and Gath-Rimmon and its outskirts; ⁷⁰and from the half tribe of Manasseh: Aner and its outskirts, and Bileam and its outskirts, for the family of the sons of Kohath who are left. ⁷¹To the sons of Gershom from the family of the half of the tribe of Manasseh: Golan in Bashan and its outskirts, and Ashtaroth and its outskirts; ⁷²and from the tribe of Issachar: Kedesh and its outskirts, Daberath and its outskirts, ⁷³and Ramoth and its outskirts, and Anem and its outskirts; ⁷⁴and from the tribe of Asher: Mashal and its outskirts, and Abdon and its outskirts, ⁷⁵and Hukok and its outskirts, and Rehob and its outskirts; ⁷⁶and from the tribe of Naphtali: Kedesh in Galilee and its outskirts, and Hammon and its outskirts, and Kirjathaim and its outskirts. ⁷⁷To the sons of Merari who are left, from the tribe of Zebulun: Rimmon and its outskirts, Tabor and its outskirts; ⁷⁸and from beyond the Jordan by Jericho, at the east of the Jordan, from the tribe of Reuben: Bezer in the wilderness and its outskirts, and Jahzah and its outskirts, ⁷⁹and Kedemoth and its outskirts, and Mephaath and its outskirts; ⁸⁰and from the tribe of Gad: Ramoth in Gilead and its outskirts, and Mahanaim and its outskirts, ⁸¹and Heshbon and its outskirts, and Jazer and its outskirts.

CHAPTER 7

¹And sons of Issachar: Tola, and Puah, Jashub, and Shimron—four. ²And sons of Tola: Uzzi, and Rephaiah, and Jeriel, and Jahmai, and Jibsam, and Shemuel, heads of the house of their fathers, [even] of Tola, mighty men of valor in their generations; their number in the days of David [is] twenty-two thousand and six hundred. ³And sons of Uzzi: Izrahiah; and sons of Izrahiah: Michael, and Obadiah, and Joel, Ishiah, Hamishah—all of them heads. ⁴And beside them, by their generations, of the house of their fathers, [are] thirty-six thousand troops of the host of battle, for they multiplied wives and sons; ⁵and their brothers of all the families of Issachar, mighty men of valor, listed by their genealogy, [are] eighty-seven thousand for the whole. ⁶Of Benjamin: Bela, and Becher, and Jediael—three. ⁷And sons of Bela: Ezbon, and Uzzi, and Uzziel, and Jerimoth, and Iri—five; heads of a house of fathers, mighty men of valor, with their genealogy, twenty-two thousand and thirty-four. ⁸And sons of Becher: Zemirah, and Joash, and Eliezar, and Elioenai, and Omri, and Jerimoth, and Abijah, and Anathoth, and Alameth. All these [are] sons of Becher, ⁹with their genealogy, after their generations, heads of a house of their fathers, mighty men of valor, twenty thousand and two hundred. ¹⁰And sons of Jediael: Bilhan; and sons of Bilhan: Jeush, and Benjamin, and Ehud, and Chenaanah, and Zethan, and Tarshish, and Ahishahar. ¹¹All these [are] sons of Jediael, even heads of the fathers, mighty in valor, seventeen thousand and two hundred going out to the host for battle. ¹²And Shuppim and Huppim [are] sons of Ir, [and] Hushim [is] the son of Aher. ¹³Sons of Naphtali: Jahziel, and Guni, and Jezer, and Shallum, sons of Bilhah. ¹⁴Sons of Manasseh: Ashriel, whom Jaladah his Aramean concubine bore, with Machir father of Gilead. ¹⁵And Machir took wives for Huppim and for Shuppim, and the name of the first [is] Maachah, and the name of the second Zelophehad, and Zelophehad has daughters. ¹⁶And Maachah wife of Machir bears a son and calls his name Peresh, and the name of his brother [is] Sheresh, and his sons [are] Ulam and Rakem. ¹⁷And son of Ulam: Bedan. These [are] sons of Gilead son of Machir, son of Manasseh. ¹⁸And his sister Hammolecheth bore Ishhod, and Abiezer, and Mahalah. ¹⁹And the sons of Shemida are Ahian, and Shechem, and Likhi, and Aniam. ²⁰And sons of Ephraim: Shuthelah, and Bered his son, and Tahath his son, and Eladah his son, and Tahath his son, ²¹and Zabad his son, and Shuthelah his son, and Ezer, and Elead; and men of Gath who are born in the land have slain them because they came down to take their livestock. ²²And their father Ephraim mourns many days, and his brothers come to comfort him, ²³and he goes in to his wife, and she conceives and bears a son, and he calls his name Beriah, because his house had been in calamity— ²⁴and his daughter [is] Sherah, and she builds Beth-Horon, the lower and the upper, and Uzzen-Sherah— ²⁵Rephah [is] his son, and Resheph, and Telah his son, and Tahan his son, ²⁶Laadan his son, Ammihud his son, Elishama his son, ²⁷Nun his son, Joshua his son. ²⁸And their possession and their dwellings [are] Beth-El and its small towns, and Naaran to the east, and Gezer and its small towns to the west, and Shechem and its small towns, as far as Gaza and its small towns; ²⁹and by the parts of the sons of Manasseh [are] Beth-Shean and its small towns, Taanach and its small towns, Megiddo and its small towns, Dor and its small towns; the sons of Joseph, son of Israel, dwelt in these. ³⁰Son of Asher: Imnah, and Ishve, and Ishvi, and Beriah, and their sister Serah. ³¹And sons of Beriah: Heber and Malchiel—he [is] father of Birzavith. ³²And Heber begot Japhlet, and Shomer, and Hotham, and their sister Shua. ³³And sons of Japhlet: Pasach, and Bimhal, and Ashvath; these [are] sons of Japhlet. ³⁴And sons of Shamer: Ahi, and Rohgah, Jehubbah, and Aram. ³⁵And [each] son of his brother Helem: Zophah, and Imna, and Shelesh, and Amal. ³⁶Sons of Zophah: Suah, and Harnepher, and Shual, and Beri, and Imrah, ³⁷Bezer, and Hod, and Shamma, and Shilshah, and Ithran, and Beera. ³⁸And sons of Jether: Jephunneh, and Pispah, and Ara. ³⁹And sons of Ulla: Arah, and Hanniel, and Rezia. ⁴⁰All these [are] sons of Asher, heads of the house of the fathers, chosen ones, mighty in valor, heads of the princes, with their genealogy, for the host, for battle, their number [is] twenty-six thousand men.

CHAPTER 8

¹And Benjamin begot Bela his firstborn, Ashbel the second, and Aharah the third, ²Nohah the fourth, and Rapha the fifth. ³And there are sons to Bela: Addar, and Gera, ⁴and Abihud, and Abishua, and Naaman, and Ahoah, ⁵and Gera, and Shephuphan, and Huram. ⁶And these [are] sons of Ehud—they are heads of fathers to the inhabitants of Geba, and they remove them to Manahath: ⁷even Naaman, and Ahiah, and Gera, who removed them and begot Uzza and Ahihud. ⁸And Shaharaim begot in the field of Moab after his sending them away; Hushim and Baara [are] his wives. ⁹And he begets of his wife Hodesh: Jobab, and Zibia, and Mesha, and Malcham, ¹⁰and Jeuz, and Shachiah, and Mirmah. These [are] his sons, heads of fathers. ¹¹And of Hushim he begot Ahitub and Elpaal. ¹²And sons of Elpaal: Eber, and Misheam, and Shamer (he built Ono and Lod and its small towns), ¹³and Beriah and Shema (they [are] the heads of fathers to the inhabitants of Aijalon—they caused the inhabitants of Gath to flee), ¹⁴and Ahio, Shashak, and Jeremoth, ¹⁵and Zebadiah, and Arad, and Ader, ¹⁶and Michael, and Ispah, and Joha, sons of Beriah, ¹⁷and Zebadiah, and Meshullam, and Hezeki, and Heber, ¹⁸and Ishmerai, and Jezliah, and Jobab, sons of Elpaal; ¹⁹and Jakim, and Zichri, and Zabdi, ²⁰and Elienai, and Zillethai, and Eliel, ²¹and Adaiah, and Beraiah, and Shimrath, sons of Shimei; ²²and Ishpan, and Heber, and Eliel, ²³and Abdon, and Zichri, and Hanan, ²⁴and Hananiah, and Elam, and Antothijah, ²⁵and Iphedeiah, and Penuel, sons of Shashak; ²⁶and Shamsherai, and Shehariah, and Athaliah, ²⁷and Jaareshiah, and Eliah, and Zichri, sons of Jeroham. ²⁸These [are] heads of fathers, by their generations, [the] heads. These dwelt in Jerusalem. ²⁹And the father of Gibeon has dwelt in Gibeon, and the name of his wife [is] Maachah; ³⁰and his son, the firstborn, [is] Abdon, and Zur, and Kish, and Ba'al, and

Nadab, ³¹and Gedor, and Ahio, and Zacher; ³²and Mikloth begot Shimeah. And they also dwelt opposite their brothers—with their brothers in Jerusalem. ³³And Ner begot Kish, and Kish begot Saul, and Saul begot Jonathan, and Malchi-Shua, and Abinadab, and Esh-Ba'al. ³⁴And a son of Jonathan [is] Merib-Ba'al, and Merib-Ba'al begot Micah; ³⁵and sons of Micah: Pithon, and Melech, and Tarea, and Ahaz: ³⁶and Ahaz begot Jehoadah, and Jehoadah begot Alemeth, and Azmaveth, and Zimri; and Zimri begot Moza, ³⁷and Moza begot Binea, Raphah his son, Eleasah his son, Azel his son. ³⁸And to Azel [are] six sons, and these [are] their names: Azrikam, Bocheru, and Ishmael, and Sheariah, and Obadiah, and Hanan. All these [are] sons of Azel. ³⁹And sons of his brother Eshek: Ulam his firstborn, Jehush the second, and Eliphelet the third. ⁴⁰And the sons of Ulam are men mighty in valor, treading bow, and multiplying sons and son's sons—one hundred and fifty. All these [are] of the sons of Benjamin.

CHAPTER 9

¹And all [those of] Israel have reckoned themselves by genealogy, and behold, they are written on the scroll of the kings of Israel and Judah—they were removed to Babylon for their trespass. ²And the first inhabitants, who [are] in their possession, in their cities, of Israel, [are] the priests, the Levites, and the Nethinim. ³And those who dwelt in Jerusalem of the sons of Judah, and of the sons of Benjamin, and of the sons of Ephraim and Manasseh: ⁴Uthai son of Ammihud, son of Omri, son of Imri, son of Bani, of the sons of Perez, son of Judah. ⁵And of the Shilonite: Asaiah the firstborn, and his sons. ⁶And of the sons of Zerah: Jeuel, and their brothers—six hundred and ninety. ⁷And of the sons of Benjamin: Sallu son of Meshullam, son of Hodaviah, son of Hassenuah, ⁸and Ibneiah son of Jeroham, and Elah son of Uzzi, son of Michri, and Meshullam son of Shephatiah, son of Reuel, son of Ibnijah. ⁹And their brothers, according to their generations, [are] nine hundred and fifty-six. All these [are] men, heads of fathers, according to the house of their fathers. ¹⁰And of the priests: Jedaiah, and Jehoiarib, and Jachin, ¹¹and Azariah son of Hilkiah, son of Meshullam, son of Zadok, son of Meraioth, son of Ahitub, leader in the house of God; ¹²and Adaiah son of Jeroham, son of Pashhur, son of Malchijah, and Maasai son of Adiel, son of Jahzerah, son of Meshullam, son of Meshillemith, son of Immer. ¹³And their brothers, heads of the house of their fathers, [are] one thousand and seven hundred and sixty, mighty in valor, for the work of the service of the house of God. ¹⁴And of the Levites: Shemaiah son of Hashshub, son of Azrikam, son of Hashabiah, of the sons of Merari; ¹⁵and Bakbakkar, Heresh, and Galal, and Mattaniah son of Micah, son of Zichri, son of Asaph; ¹⁶and Obadiah son of Shemariah, son of Galal, son of Jeduthun, and Berechiah, son of Asa, son of Elkanah, who is dwelling in the villages of the Netophathite. ¹⁷And the gatekeepers [are] Shallum, and Akkub, and Talmon, and Ahiman, and their brothers—Shallum [is] the head; ¹⁸and until now they [are] at the gate of the king eastward; they [are] the gatekeepers for the companies of the sons of Levi. ¹⁹And Shallum son of Kore, son of Ebiasaph, son of Korah, and his brothers, of the house of his father, the Korahites, [are] over the work of the service, keepers of the thresholds of the tent, and their fathers [are] over the camp of YHWH, keepers of the entrance; ²⁰and Phinehas son of Eleazar has been leader over them formerly; YHWH [is] with him. ²¹Zechariah son of Meshelemiah [is] gatekeeper at the opening of the Tent of Meeting. ²²All of those who are chosen for gatekeepers at the thresholds [are] two hundred and twelve; they [are] in their villages, by their genealogy; they whom David and Samuel the seer appointed in their office. ²³And they and their sons [are] over the gates of the house of YHWH, even of the house of the tent, by watches. ²⁴The gatekeepers are at [the] four sides: east, west, north, and south. ²⁵And their brothers in their villages [are] to come in with these for seven days from time to time. ²⁶For the four chiefs of the gatekeepers in office, they are Levites, and they have been over the chambers, and over the treasuries of the house of God, ²⁷and they lodge around the house of God, for the watch [is] on them, and they [are] over the opening, even morning by morning. ²⁸And [some] of them [are] over the vessels of service, for they bring them in by number, and by number they take them out. ²⁹And [some] of them are appointed over the vessels, even over all the vessels of the holy place, and over the fine flour, and the wine, and the oil, and the frankincense, and the spices. ³⁰And [some] of the sons of the priests are mixing the mixture for spices. ³¹And Mattithiah of the Levites (he [is] the firstborn to Shallum the Korahite), [is] in office over the work of the pans. ³²And of the sons of the Kohathite, [some] of their brothers [are] over the bread of the arrangement, to prepare [it] Sabbath by Sabbath. ³³And these who sing, heads of fathers of the Levites, in the chambers, [are] free, for [they are] over them in the work by day and by night. ³⁴These heads of the fathers of the Levites [are] heads throughout their generations. These have dwelt in Jerusalem. ³⁵And the father of Gibeon, Jehiel, has dwelt in Gibeon, and the name of his wife [is] Maachah; ³⁶and his son, the firstborn, [is] Abdon, and Zur, and Kish, and Ba'al, and Ner, and Nadab, ³⁷and Gedor, and Ahio, and Zechariah, and Mikloth. ³⁸And Mikloth begot Shimeam, and they have also dwelt opposite their brothers—with their brothers in Jerusalem. ³⁹And Ner begot Kish, and Kish begot Saul, and Saul begot Jonathan, and Malchi-Shua, and Abinadab, and Esh-Ba'al. ⁴⁰And a son of Jonathan [is] Merib-Ba'al, and Merib-Ba'al begot Micah. ⁴¹And sons of Micah: Pithon, and Melech, and Tahrea, ⁴²and Ahaz—he begot Jaarah, and Jaarah begot Alemeth, and Azmaveth, and Zimri, and Zimri begot Moza, ⁴³and Moza begot Binea, and Rephaiah his son, Eleasah his son, Azel his son. ⁴⁴And to Azel [are] six sons, and these [are] their names: Azrikam, Bocheru, and Ishmael, and Sheariah, and Obadiah, and Hanan; these [are] sons of Azel.

CHAPTER 10

¹And the Philistines have fought with Israel, and the men of Israel flee from the face of the Philistines, and fall wounded in Mount Gilboa, ²and the Philistines pursue after Saul, and after his sons, and the Philistines strike Jonathan, and Abinadab, and Malchi-Shua, sons of Saul. ³And the battle [is] heavy on Saul, and those shooting with the bow find him, and he is wounded by those shooting, ⁴and Saul says to the bearer of his weapons, "Draw your sword and pierce me with it, lest these uncircumcised come and have abused me." And the bearer of his weapons has not been willing, for he fears exceedingly, and Saul takes the sword, and falls on it; ⁵and the bearer of his weapons sees that Saul [is] dead, and falls, he also, on the sword, and dies; ⁶and Saul dies, and his three sons, and all his house—they died together. ⁷And all the men of Israel who [are] in the valley see that they have fled and that Saul and his sons have died, and they forsake their cities and flee, and the Philistines come and dwell in them. ⁸And it comes to pass, on the next day, that the Philistines come to strip the wounded, and find Saul and his sons fallen in Mount Gilboa, ⁹and strip him, and carry away his head and his weapons, and send [them] into the land of the surrounding Philistines to proclaim tidings [to] their idols and the people; ¹⁰and they put his weapons in the house of their gods, and have fixed his skull in the house of Dagon. ¹¹And all Jabesh-Gilead hears of all that the Philistines have done to Saul, ¹²and all the men of valor rise and carry away the body of Saul, and the bodies of his sons, and bring them to Jabesh, and bury their bones under the oak in Jabesh, and fast seven days. ¹³And Saul dies because of his trespass that he trespassed against YHWH, against the word of YHWH that he did not keep, and also for asking to inquire of a familiar spirit; ¹⁴and he did not inquire of YHWH, and He puts him to death, and turns around the kingdom to David son of Jesse.

CHAPTER 11

¹And all Israel is gathered to David at Hebron, saying, "Behold, we [are] your bone and your flesh; ²even in time past, even in Saul's being king, it is you who are taking out and bringing in Israel, and your God YHWH says to you: You feed My people Israel, and you are leader over My people Israel." ³And all [the] elderly of Israel come to the king at Hebron, and David makes a covenant with them in Hebron before YHWH, and they anoint David for king over Israel, according to the word of YHWH by the hand of Samuel. ⁴And David goes, and all Israel, to Jerusalem—it [is] Jebus—and the Jebusite [is] there, the inhabitants of the land. ⁵And the inhabitants of Jebus say to David, "You do not come in here"; and David captures the fortress of Zion—it [is] the City of David. ⁶And David says, "Whoever strikes the Jebusite first becomes head and prince"; and

1 CHRONICLES

Joab son of Zeruiah goes up first and becomes head. ⁷And David dwells in the fortress, therefore they have called it the City of David; ⁸and he builds the city all around, from Millo, and to the circumference, and Joab restores the rest of the city. ⁹And David goes, going on and becoming great, and YHWH of Hosts [is] with him. ¹⁰And these [are] heads of the mighty ones whom David has, who are strengthening themselves with him in his kingdom, with all Israel, to cause him to reign, according to the word of YHWH, over Israel. ¹¹And this [is] an account of the mighty ones whom David has: Jashobeam son of a Hachmonite [is] head of the thirty; he is lifting up his spear against three hundred—wounded, at one time. ¹²And after him [is] Eleazar son of Dodo the Ahohite, he [is] among the three mighty; ¹³he has been with David in Pas-Dammim, and the Philistines have been gathered there to battle, and a portion of the field is full of barley, and the people have fled from the face of the Philistines, ¹⁴and they station themselves in the midst of the portion, and deliver it, and strike the Philistines, and YHWH saves [with] a great salvation. ¹⁵And three of the thirty heads go down on the rock to David, to the cave of Adullam, and the host of the Philistines is encamping in the Valley of Rephaim, ¹⁶and David [is] then in the fortress, and the station of the Philistines [is] then in Beth-Lehem, ¹⁷and David longs and says, "Who gives me water to drink from the well of Beth-Lehem that [is] at the gate!" ¹⁸And the three break through the camp of the Philistines, and draw water from the well of Beth-Lehem that [is] at the gate, and carry and bring [it] to David, and David has not been willing to drink it, and pours it out to YHWH, ¹⁹and says, "Far be it from me, by my God, to do this; do I drink the blood of these men with their lives? For with their lives they have brought it"; and he was not willing to drink it; these [things] the three mighty ones did. ²⁰And Abishai brother of Joab, he has been head of the three: and he is lifting up his spear against three hundred—wounded, and has a name among three. ²¹Of the three he is more honored than the [other] two, and becomes their head; but he has not come to the [first] three. ²²Benaiah son of Jehoiada, son of a man of valor, of great deeds, from Kabzeel: he has struck the two lion-like Moabites, and he has gone down and struck the lion in the midst of the pit, in the day of snow. ²³And he has struck the man, the Egyptian, a man of [great] measure—five by the cubit—and in the hand of the Egyptian [is] a spear like a weavers' beam, and he goes down to him with a rod, and violently takes away the spear out of the hand of the Egyptian, and slays him with his own spear. ²⁴These [things] Benaiah son of Jehoiada has done, and has a name among the three mighty ones. ²⁵Of the thirty, behold, he [is] honored, but he has not come to the [first] three, and David sets him over his guard. ²⁶And the mighty ones of the forces [are] Asahel brother of Joab, Elhanan son of Dodo of Beth-Lehem, ²⁷Shammoth the Harorite, Helez the Pelonite, ²⁸Ira son of Ikkesh the Tekoite, Abi-Ezer the Annethothite, ²⁹Sibbecai the Hushathite, Ilai the Ahohite, ³⁰Maharai the Netophathite, Heled son of Baanah the Netophathite, ³¹Ithai son of Ribai of Gibeah, of the sons of Benjamin, Benaiah the Pirathonite, ³²Hurai of the brooks of Gaash, Abiel the Arbathite, ³³Azmaveth the Baharumite, Eliahba the Shaalbonite, ³⁴the sons of Hashem the Gizonite, Jonathan son of Shage the Hararite, ³⁵Ahiam son of Sacar the Hararite, Eliphal son of Ur, ³⁶Hepher the Mecherathite, Ahijah the Pelonite, ³⁷Hezor the Carmelite, Naarai son of Ezbai, ³⁸Joel brother of Nathan, Mibhar son of Haggeri, ³⁹Zelek the Ammonite, Naharai the Berothite, bearer of the weapons of Joab son of Zeruiah, ⁴⁰Ira the Ithrite, Gareb the Ithrite, ⁴¹Uriah the Hittite, Zabad son of Ahlai, ⁴²Adina son of Shiza the Reubenite, head of the Reubenites, and thirty by him, ⁴³Hanan son of Maachah, and Joshaphat the Mithnite, ⁴⁴Uzzia the Ashterathite, Shama and Jehiel sons of Hothan the Aroerite, ⁴⁵Jediael son of Shimri, and his brother Joha the Tizite, ⁴⁶Eliel the Mahavite, and Jeribai, and Joshaviah, sons of Elnaam, and Ithmah the Moabite, ⁴⁷Eliel, and Obed, and Jaasiel the Mesobaite.

CHAPTER 12

¹And these [are] those coming to David at Ziklag, while shut up because of Saul son of Kish, and they [are] among the mighty ones, helping the battle, ²armed with bow, right and left handed, with stones, and with arrows, with bows, of the brothers of Saul, of Benjamin. ³The head [is] Ahiezer, and Joash, sons of Shemaab the Gibeathite, and Jeziel, and Pelet, sons of Azmaveth, and Berachah, and Jehu the Antothite, ⁴and Ishmaiah the Gibeonite, a mighty one among the thirty, and over the thirty, and Jeremiah, and Jahaziel, and Johanan, and Josabad the Gederathite. ⁵Eluzai, and Jerimoth, and Bealiah, and Shemariah, and Shephatiah the Haruphite; ⁶Elkanah, and Jesiah, and Azareel, and Joezer, and Jashobeam the Korahites, ⁷and Joelah, and Zebadiah, sons of Jeroham of Gedor. ⁸And of the Gadite there have been separated to David, to the fortress, to the wilderness, mighty men of valor, men of the host for battle, setting in array buckler and spear, and their faces [are as] the face of the lion, and as roes on the mountains for speed: ⁹Ezer the head, Obadiah the second, Eliab the third, ¹⁰Mishmannah the fourth, Jeremiah the fifth, ¹¹Attai the sixth, Eliel the seventh, ¹²Johanan the eighth, Elzabad the ninth, ¹³Jeremiah the tenth, Machbannai the eleventh. ¹⁴These [are] of the sons of Gad, heads of the host; the least [is] one of one hundred, and the greatest, of one thousand; ¹⁵these [are] they who have passed over the Jordan in the first month—and it is full over all its banks—and cause all [those in] the valley to flee to the east and to the west. ¹⁶And [some] from the sons of Benjamin and Judah came to David at the stronghold, ¹⁷and David goes out before them, and answers and says to them, "If you have come to me for peace, to help me, I have a heart to unite with you; and if to betray me to my adversaries—without violence in my hands—the God of our fathers sees and reproves." ¹⁸And the Spirit has clothed Amasai, head of the captains: "To you, O David, and with you, O son of Jesse—peace! Peace to you, and peace to your helper, for your God has helped you"; and David receives them, and puts them among the heads of the troop. ¹⁹And [some] from Manasseh have defected to David in his coming with the Philistines against Israel to battle—and they did not help them, for by counsel the princes of the Philistines sent him away, saying, "He defects with our heads to his master Saul." ²⁰In his going to Ziglag there have fallen to him from Manasseh: Adnah, and Jozabad, and Jediael, and Michael, and Jozabad, and Elihu, and Zillthai, heads of the thousands who [are] of Manasseh; ²¹and they have helped with David over the troop, for all of them [are] mighty men of valor, and they are captains in the host, ²²for at that time, day by day, they come to David to help him, until it is a great camp, like a camp of God. ²³And these [are] the numbers of the head, of the armed men of the host; they have come to David at Hebron to turn around the kingdom of Saul to him, according to the mouth of YHWH. ²⁴The sons of Judah, carrying buckler and spear, [are] six thousand and eight hundred, armed ones of the host. ²⁵Of the sons of Simeon, mighty men of valor for the host, [are] seven thousand and one hundred. ²⁶Of the sons of Levi [are] four thousand and six hundred; ²⁷and Jehoiada [is] the leader of the Aaronite, and with him [are] three thousand and seven hundred, ²⁸and Zadok, a young man, a mighty man of valor, and of the house of his father [are] twenty-two heads. ²⁹And of the sons of Benjamin, brothers of Saul, [are] three thousand, and until now their greater part are keeping the charge of the house of Saul. ³⁰And of the sons of Ephraim [are] twenty thousand and eight hundred, mighty men of valor, men of renown, according to the house of their fathers. ³¹And of the half of the tribe of Manasseh [are] eighteen thousand, who have been defined by name, to come to cause David to reign. ³²And of the sons of Issachar, having understanding for the times, to know what Israel should do; their heads [are] two hundred, and all their brothers [are] at their command. ³³Of Zebulun, going forth to the host, arranging battle with all instruments of battle, [are] fifty thousand, and keeping rank without a double heart. ³⁴And of Naphtali, one thousand heads, and with them, with buckler and spear, [are] thirty-seven thousand. ³⁵And of the Danite, arranging battle, [are] twenty-eight thousand and six hundred. ³⁶And of Asher, going forth to the host, to arrange battle, [are] forty thousand. ³⁷And from beyond the Jordan, of the Reubenite, and of the Gadite, and of the half of the tribe of Manasseh, with all instruments of the host for battle, [are] one hundred and twenty thousand. ³⁸All these [are] men of war, keeping rank—they have come to Hebron with a perfect heart, to cause David to reign over all Israel, and also all the rest of Israel [are] of one heart, to cause David

to reign, ³⁹and they are there, with David, three days, eating and drinking, for their brothers have prepared for them. ⁴⁰And also those near to them—to Issachar, and Zebulun, and Naphtali—are bringing in bread on donkeys, and on camels, and on mules, and on oxen—food of fine flour, fig-cakes and grape-cakes, and wine, and oil, and oxen, and sheep, in abundance, for joy [is] in Israel.

CHAPTER 13

¹And David consults with the heads of the thousands and of the hundreds, [and] with every leader, ²and David says to all the assembly of Israel, "If it is good to you, and it has broken forth from our God YHWH—we send to our brothers, those left in all the lands of Israel, and the priests and the Levites with them in the cities of their outskirts, and they are gathered to us, ³and we bring around the Ark of our God to us, for we did not seek Him in the days of Saul." ⁴And all the assembly says to do so, for the thing is right in the eyes of all the people. ⁵And David assembles all Israel from Shihor of Egypt even to the entering in of Hamath, to bring in the Ark of God from Kirjath-Jearim, ⁶and David goes up, and all Israel, to Ba'alah, to Kirjath-Jearim that [belongs] to Judah, to bring up from there the Ark of God, YHWH, inhabiting the cherubim, where the Name is called on. ⁷And they place the Ark of God on a new cart from the house of Abinadab, and Uzza and Ahio are leading the cart, ⁸and David and all Israel are playing before God, with all strength, and with songs, and with harps, and with psalteries, and with timbrels, and with cymbals, and with trumpets. ⁹And they come to the threshing-floor of Chidon, and Uzza puts forth his hand to seize the Ark, for the oxen were released, ¹⁰and the anger of YHWH is kindled against Uzza, and He strikes him, because that he has put forth his hand on the Ark, and he dies there before God. ¹¹And it is displeasing to David, because YHWH has made a breach on Uzza, and one calls that place "Breach of Uzza" to this day. ¹²And David fears God on that day, saying, "How do I bring the Ark of God to me?" ¹³And David has not turned aside the Ark to himself, to the City of David, and turns it aside to the house of Obed-Edom the Gittite. ¹⁴And the Ark of God dwells with the household of Obed-Edom, in his house, three months, and YHWH blesses the house of Obed-Edom, and all that he has.

CHAPTER 14

¹And Huram king of Tyre sends messengers to David, and cedar-wood, and craftsmen of walls, and craftsmen of wood, to build a house for him. ²And David knows that YHWH has established him for king over Israel, because of the lifting up on high of his kingdom, for the sake of His people Israel. ³And David takes wives again in Jerusalem, and David begets sons and daughters again; ⁴and these [are] the names of the children whom he has in Jerusalem: Shammua, and Shobab, Nathan, and Solomon, ⁵and Ibhar, and Elishua, and Elpalet, ⁶and Nogah, and Nepheg, and Japhia, ⁷and Elishama, and Beeliada, and Eliphalet. ⁸And the Philistines hear that David has been anointed for king over all Israel, and all the Philistines go up to seek David, and David hears, and goes out before them. ⁹And the Philistines have come, and rush into the Valley of Rephaim, ¹⁰and David asks of God, saying, "Do I go up against the Philistines—and have You given them into my hand?" And YHWH says to him, "Go up, and I have given them into your hand." ¹¹And they go up into Ba'al-Perazim, and David strikes them there, and David says, "God has broken up my enemies by my hand, like the breaking up of waters"; therefore they have called the name of that place Ba'al-Perazim. ¹²And they leave their gods there, and David commands, and they are burned with fire. ¹³And the Philistines add again, and rush into the valley, ¹⁴and David asks again of God, and God says to him, "Do not go up after them, turn around from them, and you have come to them from the front [[or in front]] of the mulberries; ¹⁵and it comes to pass, when you hear the sound of the stepping at the heads of the mulberries, then you go out into battle, for God has gone out before you to strike the camp of the Philistines." ¹⁶And David does as God commanded him, and they strike the camp of the Philistines from Gibeon even to Gazer; ¹⁷and the name of David goes out into all the lands, and YHWH has put his fear on all the nations.

CHAPTER 15

¹And he makes houses for himself in the City of David, and prepares a place for the Ark of God, and stretches out a tent for it. ²Then David said, "None [are] to carry the Ark of God, except the Levites, for YHWH has fixed on them to carry the Ark of God and to serve Him for all time." ³And David assembles all Israel to Jerusalem, to bring up the Ark of YHWH to its place that he had prepared for it. ⁴And David gathers the sons of Aaron and the Levites— ⁵of sons of Kohath: Uriel the chief and one hundred and twenty of his brothers; ⁶of sons of Merari: Asaiah the chief and two hundred and twenty of his brothers; ⁷of sons of Gershom: Joel the chief and one hundred and thirty of his brothers; ⁸of sons of Elizaphan: Shemaiah the chief and two hundred of his brothers; ⁹of sons of Hebron: Eliel the chief and eighty of his brothers; ¹⁰of sons of Uzziel: Amminadab the chief and one hundred and twelve of his brothers. ¹¹And David calls to Zadok and to Abiathar the priests, and to the Levites, to Uriel, Asaiah, and Joel, Shemaiah, and Eliel, and Amminadab, ¹²and says to them, "You [are] heads of the fathers of the Levites; sanctify yourselves, you and your brothers, and you have brought up the Ark of YHWH, God of Israel, to [the place] I have prepared for it; ¹³because you [did] not [do it] at the first, our God YHWH made a breach on us, because we did not seek Him according to the ordinance." ¹⁴And the priests and the Levites sanctify themselves to bring up the Ark of YHWH, God of Israel; ¹⁵and sons of the Levites carry the Ark of God, as Moses commanded, according to the word of YHWH, above them with poles on their shoulder. ¹⁶And David says to the heads of the Levites to appoint their brothers the singers, with instruments of song, psalteries, and harps, and cymbals, sounding, to lift up with the voice for joy. ¹⁷And the Levites appoint Heman son of Joel, and of his brothers, Asaph son of Berechiah, and of the sons of Merari their brothers, Ethan son of Kushaiah; ¹⁸and with them their brothers, the seconds [in rank]: Zechariah, Ben, and Jaaziel, and Shemiramoth, and Jehiel, and Unni, Eliab, and Benaiah, and Maaseiah, and Mattithiah, and Elipheleh, and Mikneiah; and Obed-Edom and Jeiel the gatekeepers; ¹⁹and the singers, Heman, Asaph, and Ethan, [are] to sound with cymbals of bronze; ²⁰and Zechariah, and Aziel, and Shemiramoth, and Jeheil, and Unni, and Eliab, and Maaseiah, and Benaiah, with psalteries over the girls' [voices], ²¹and Mattithiah, and Elipheleh, and Mikneiah, and Obed-Edom, and Jeiel, and Azaziah, to oversee with harps on the eighth. ²²And Chenaniah, head of the Levites, [is] over the burden; he instructs about the burden, for he [is] intelligent. ²³And Berechiah and Elkanah [are] gatekeepers for the Ark. ²⁴And Shebaniah, and Joshaphat, and Nethaneel, and Amasai, and Zechariah, and Benaiah, and Eliezer the priests, are blowing with trumpets before the Ark of God; and Obed-Edom and Jehiah [are] gatekeepers for the Ark. ²⁵And it is David, and [the] elderly of Israel, and the heads of the thousands, who are going to bring up the Ark of the Covenant of YHWH from the house of Obed-Edom with joy; ²⁶and it comes to pass, in God's helping the Levites carrying the Ark of the Covenant of YHWH, that they sacrifice seven bullocks and seven rams. ²⁷And David is wrapped in an upper robe of fine linen, and all the Levites who are carrying the Ark, and the singers, and Chenaniah head of the burden of the singers; and an Ephod of linen [is] on David. ²⁸And all of Israel is bringing up the Ark of the Covenant of YHWH with shouting, and with the sound of a horn, and with trumpets, and with cymbals, sounding with psalteries and harps, ²⁹and it comes to pass, the Ark of the Covenant of YHWH is entering into the City of David, and Michal daughter of Saul is looking through the window, and sees King David dancing and playing, and despises him in her heart.

CHAPTER 16

¹And they bring in the Ark of God, and set it up in the midst of the tent that David has stretched out for it, and they bring burnt-offerings and peace-offerings near before God; ²and David ceases from offering the burnt-offering and the peace-offerings, and blesses the people in the Name of YHWH, ³and gives a portion to every man of Israel, both man and woman: to each a cake of bread, and a measure of wine, and a grape-cake. ⁴And he puts before the Ark of YHWH, those ministering from the Levites, even to make mention of, and to thank, and to give praise to YHWH, God of Israel: ⁵Asaph the head, and his second Zechariah; Jeiel, and Shemiramoth, and Jehiel, and Mattithiah, and Eliab, and

Benaiah, and Obed-Edom, and Jeiel, with instruments of psalteries, and with harps; and Asaph is sounding with cymbals; ⁶and Benaiah and Jahaziel the priests [are] continually [sounding] with trumpets before the Ark of the Covenant of God. ⁷On that day, at that time, David has given at the beginning to give thanks to YHWH by the hand of Asaph and his brothers: ⁸"Give thanks to YHWH, call on His Name, || Make His doings known among the peoples. ⁹Sing to Him, sing psalms to Him, || Meditate on all His wonders. ¹⁰Boast yourselves in His Holy Name, || The heart of those seeking YHWH rejoices. ¹¹Seek YHWH and His strength, || Seek His face continually. ¹²Remember His wonders that He did, || His signs, and the judgments of His mouth, ¹³O seed of Israel, His servant, || O sons of Jacob, His chosen ones! ¹⁴He [is] our God YHWH, || His judgments [are] in all the earth. ¹⁵Remember His covenant for all time, || The word He commanded—To one thousand generations, ¹⁶Which He has made with Abraham, || And His oath—to Isaac, ¹⁷And He establishes it to Jacob for a statute, || To Israel [for] a perpetual covenant, ¹⁸Saying, To you I give the land of Canaan, || The portion of your inheritance, ¹⁹When you were few in number, || As a little thing, and sojourners in it. ²⁰And they go up and down, || From nation to nation, || And from a kingdom to another people. ²¹He has not permitted any to oppress them, || And reproves kings on their account: ²²Do not come against My anointed ones, || And do no evil against My prophets. ²³Sing to YHWH, all the earth, || Proclaim His salvation from day to day. ²⁴Recount His glory among nations, || His wonders among all the peoples. ²⁵For great [is] YHWH, and greatly praised, || And He [is] fearful above all gods. ²⁶For all gods of the peoples [are] nothing, || And YHWH has made the heavens. ²⁷Splendor and majesty [are] before Him, || Strength and joy [are] in His place. ²⁸Ascribe to YHWH, you families of peoples, || Ascribe to YHWH glory and strength. ²⁹Ascribe to YHWH the glory of His Name, || Lift up a present, and come before Him. Bow yourselves to YHWH, || In the beauty of holiness. ³⁰Be pained before Him, all the earth; Also, the world is established, || It is not moved! ³¹The heavens rejoice, and the earth is glad, || And they say among nations, YHWH has reigned! ³²The sea roars, and its fullness, || The field exults, and all that [is] in it, ³³Then trees of the forest sing, || From the presence of YHWH, || For He has come to judge the earth! ³⁴Give thanks to YHWH, for [He is] good, || For His kindness [is] for all time, ³⁵And say, Save us, O God of our salvation, || And gather us, and deliver us from the nations, || To give thanks to Your Holy Name, || To triumph in Your praise. ³⁶Blessed [is] YHWH, God of Israel, || From age to age"; And all the people say, "Amen," and have given praise to YHWH. ³⁷And he leaves there [those] of Asaph and of his brothers, before the Ark of the Covenant of YHWH, to minister before the Ark continually, according to the matter of a day in its day; ³⁸both Obed-Edom and their sixty-eight brothers, and Obed-Edom son of Jeduthun, and Hosah, for gatekeepers; ³⁹and Zadok the priest, and his brothers the priests, before the Dwelling Place of YHWH, in a high place that [is] in Gibeon, ⁴⁰to cause burnt-offerings to ascend continually to YHWH on the altar of burnt-offering, morning and evening, and for all that is written in the Law of YHWH that He charged on Israel. ⁴¹And with them [are] Heman and Jeduthun, and the rest of those chosen, who were defined by name, to give thanks to YHWH, for His kindness [is] for all time; ⁴²and with them—Heman and Jeduthun—[are] trumpets and cymbals for those sounding, and instruments of the song of God, and the sons of Jeduthun [are] at the gate. ⁴³And all the people go, each to his house, and David turns around to bless his house.

CHAPTER 17

¹And it comes to pass as David sat in his house, that David says to Nathan the prophet, "Behold, I am dwelling in a house of cedars, and the Ark of the Covenant of YHWH [is] under curtains"; ²and Nathan says to David, "All that [is] in your heart do, for God [is] with you." ³And it comes to pass on that night that a word of God is to Nathan, saying, ⁴"Go, and you have said to My servant David, Thus said YHWH: You do not build for Me the house to dwell in. ⁵For I have not dwelt in a house from the day that I brought up Israel until this day, and I am [going] from tent to tent, and from the Dwelling Place. ⁶Wherever I have walked up and down among all Israel, have I spoken a word with one of [the] judges of Israel, whom I commanded to feed My people, saying, Why have you not built a house of cedars for Me? ⁷And now, thus you say to My servant, to David, Thus said YHWH of Hosts: I have taken you from the habitation, from after the sheep, to be leader over My people Israel, ⁸and I am with you wherever you have walked, and I cut off all your enemies from your presence, and have made a name for you like the name of the great ones who [are] in the earth. ⁹And I have prepared a place for My people Israel, and planted it, and it has dwelt in its place, and is not troubled anymore, and the sons of perverseness do not add to wear it out as at first, ¹⁰indeed, even from the days that I appointed judges over My people Israel. And I have humbled all your enemies, and I declare to you that YHWH builds a house for you. ¹¹And it has come to pass, when your days have been fulfilled to go with your fathers, that I have raised up your seed after you, who is of your sons, and I have established his kingdom; ¹²he builds a house for Me, and I have established his throne for all time; ¹³I am to him for a father, and he is to Me for a son, and I do not turn aside My kindness from him as I turned it aside from him who was before you, ¹⁴and I have established him in My house, and in My kingdom for all time, and his throne is established for all time." ¹⁵According to all these words, and according to all this vision, so spoke Nathan to David. ¹⁶And David the king comes in and sits before YHWH, and says, "Who [am] I, O YHWH God, and what [is] my house, that You have brought me here? ¹⁷And this is small in Your eyes, O God, and You speak concerning the house of Your servant far off, and have seen me as a type of the man who is on high, O YHWH God! ¹⁸What more does David add to You for the honor of Your servant; and You have known Your servant. ¹⁹O YHWH, for Your servant's sake, and according to Your own heart You have done all this greatness, to make known all these great things. ²⁰O YHWH, there is none like You, and there is no god except You, according to all that we have heard with our ears. ²¹And who [is] as Your people Israel, one nation in the earth whom God has gone to ransom to Himself for a people, to make a great and fearful name for Yourself, to cast out nations from the presence of Your people whom You have ransomed out of Egypt? ²²Indeed, You appoint Your people Israel to Yourself for a people for all time, and You, O YHWH, have been to them for God. ²³And now, O YHWH, let the word that You have spoken concerning Your servant, and concerning his house, be steadfast for all time, and do as You have spoken; ²⁴and let it be steadfast, and Your Name is great for all time, saying, YHWH of Hosts, God of Israel, [is] God to Israel, and the house of Your servant David is established before You; ²⁵for You, O my God, have uncovered the ear of Your servant—to build a house for him, therefore Your servant has found [desire] to pray before You. ²⁶And now, YHWH, You [are] God Himself, and You speak this goodness concerning Your servant; ²⁷and now, You have been pleased to bless the house of Your servant, to be before You for all time; for You, O YHWH, have blessed, and it is blessed for all time."

CHAPTER 18

¹And it comes to pass after this, that David strikes the Philistines, and humbles them, and takes Gath and its small towns out of the hand of the Philistines; ²and he strikes Moab, and the Moabites are servants to David, bringing a present. ³And David strikes Hadarezer king of Zobah, at Hamath, in his going to establish his power by the Euphrates River, ⁴and David captures from him one thousand chariots, and seven thousand horsemen, and twenty thousand footmen, and David utterly destroys all the chariots, and leaves of them [only] one hundred chariots. ⁵And Aram of Damascus comes to give help to Hadarezer king of Zobah, and David strikes twenty-two thousand men in Aram, ⁶and David puts [garrisons] in Aram of Damascus, and the Arameans are for servants to David, carrying a present, and YHWH gives salvation to David wherever he has gone. ⁷And David takes the shields of gold that have been on the servants of Hadarezer, and brings them to Jerusalem; ⁸and from Tibhath, and from Chun, cities of Hadarezer, David has taken very much bronze; with it Solomon has made the bronze sea, and the pillars, and the vessels of bronze. ⁹And Tou king of Hamath hears that David has struck the whole force of Hadarezer king of Zobah, ¹⁰and he sends his son Hadoram to King David, to ask of him of peace, and to bless

him, because that he has fought against Hadarezer and strikes him (for Hadarezer had been a man of wars with Tou); and [with him were] all kinds of vessels, of gold, and silver, and bronze; ¹¹King David has also sanctified them to YHWH with the silver and the gold that he has taken from all the nations, from Edom, and from Moab, and from the sons of Ammon, and from the Philistines, and from Amalek. ¹²And Abishai son of Zeruiah has struck Edom in the Valley of Salt—eighteen thousand, ¹³and he puts garrisons in Edom, and all the Edomites are servants to David; and YHWH saves David wherever he has gone. ¹⁴And David reigns over all Israel, and he is doing judgment and righteousness to all his people, ¹⁵and Joab son of Zeruiah [is] over the host, and Jehoshaphat son of Ahilud [is] remembrancer, ¹⁶and Zadok son of Ahitub and Abimelech son of Abiathar [are] priests, and Shavsha [is] scribe, ¹⁷and Benaiah son of Jehoiada [is] over the Cherethite and the Pelethite, and the chief sons of David [are] at the hand of the king.

CHAPTER 19

¹And it comes to pass after this, that Nahash king of the sons of Ammon dies, and his son reigns in his stead, ²and David says, "I do kindness with Hanun son of Nahash, for his father did kindness with me"; and David sends messengers to comfort him concerning his father. And the servants of David come to the land of the sons of Ammon, to Hanun, to comfort him, ³and the heads of the sons of Ammon say to Hanun, "Is David honoring your father in your eyes because he has sent comforters to you? Have his servants not come to you in order to search, and to overthrow, and to spy out the land?" ⁴And Hanun takes the servants of David and shaves them, and cuts their long robes in the midst, to the buttocks, and sends them away. ⁵And [some] go and declare to David concerning the men, and he sends to meet them—for the men have been greatly ashamed—and the king says, "Dwell in Jericho until your beard is grown, then you have returned." ⁶And the sons of Ammon see that they have made themselves abhorred by David, and Hanun and the sons of Ammon send one thousand talents of silver, to hire for themselves, from Aram-Naharaim, and from Aram-Maachah, and from Zobah, chariots and horsemen; ⁷and they hire for themselves thirty-two thousand chariots, and the king of Maachah and his people, and they come in and encamp before Medeba, and the sons of Ammon have been gathered out of their cities, and come to the battle. ⁸And David hears, and sends Joab, and all the host of the mighty men, ⁹and the sons of Ammon come out and set in array [for] battle at the opening of the city, and the kings who have come [are] by themselves in the field. ¹⁰And Joab sees that the front of the battle has been to him, before and behind, and he chooses out of all the choice in Israel, and sets in array to meet Aram, ¹¹and he has given the remnant of the people into the hand of his brother Abishai, and they set in array to meet the sons of Ammon. ¹²And he says, "If Aram is stronger than me, then you have been for salvation to me; and if the sons of Ammon are stronger than you, then I have saved you; ¹³be strong, and we strengthen ourselves, for our people, and for the cities of our God, and YHWH does that which is good in His eyes." ¹⁴And Joab draws near, and the people who [are] with him, before Aram to battle, and they flee from his face; ¹⁵and the sons of Ammon have seen that Aram has fled, and they flee—they also—from the face of his brother Abishai, and go into the city. And Joab comes to Jerusalem. ¹⁶And Aram sees that they have been struck before Israel, and send messengers, and bring out Aram that [is] beyond the River, and Shophach head of the host of Hadarezer [is] before them. ¹⁷And it is declared to David, and he gathers all Israel, and passes over the Jordan, and comes to them, and sets in array against them; indeed, David sets in array [for] battle to meet Aram, and they fight with him; ¹⁸and Aram flees from the face of Israel, and David slays seven thousand charioteers and forty thousand footmen of Aram, and he has put Shophach head of the host to death. ¹⁹And the servants of Hadarezer see that they have been struck before Israel, and they make peace with David and serve him, and Aram has not been willing to help the sons of Ammon anymore.

CHAPTER 20

¹And it comes to pass, at the time of the turn of the year—at the time of the going out of the messengers—that Joab leads out the force of the host, and destroys the land of the sons of Ammon, and comes in and besieges Rabbah—David is abiding in Jerusalem—and Joab strikes Rabbah, and breaks it down. ²And David takes the crown of their king from off his head, and finds it [to be] a talent of gold [in] weight, and [with] precious stone in it, and it is on the head of David; and he has brought out very much spoil of the city, ³and he has brought out the people who [are] in it, and sets [them] to the saw, and to cutting instruments of iron, and to axes; and thus David does to all cities of the sons of Ammon, and David turns back—and all the people—to Jerusalem. ⁴And it comes to pass after this, that war remains in Gezer with the Philistines; then Sibbechai the Hushathite has struck Sippai, of the children of the giant, and they are humbled. ⁵And there is war with the Philistines again, and Elhanan son of Jair strikes Lahmi, brother of Goliath the Gittite, the wood of whose spear [is] like a weavers' beam. ⁶And there is war in Gath again, and there is a man of [great] measure, and his fingers and his toes [are] six and six—twenty-four [total], and he has also been born to the giant. ⁷And he reproaches Israel, and Jonathan son of Shimea, brother of David, strikes him. ⁸These were born to the giant in Gath, and they fall by the hand of David, and by the hand of his servants.

CHAPTER 21

¹Then Satan stands up against Israel, and persuades David to number Israel, ²and David says to Joab and to the heads of the people, "Go, number Israel from Beer-Sheba even to Dan, and bring [the account] to me, and I know their number." ³And Joab says, "YHWH adds to His people as they are one hundred times; are they not, my lord, O king, all of them for servants to my lord? Why does my lord seek this? Why is he for a cause of guilt to Israel?" ⁴And the word of the king [is] severe against Joab, and Joab goes out, and goes up and down in all Israel, and comes to Jerusalem. ⁵And Joab gives the account of the numbering of the people to David, and all Israel is one million and one hundred thousand, each drawing sword, and Judah [is] four hundred and seventy thousand, each drawing sword. ⁶And he has not numbered Levi and Benjamin in their midst, for the word of the king was abominable with Joab. ⁷And it is evil in the eyes of God concerning this thing, and He strikes Israel, ⁸and David says to God, "I have sinned exceedingly in that I have done this thing; and now, please cause the iniquity of Your servant to pass away, for I have acted very foolishly." ⁹And YHWH speaks to Gad, seer of David, saying, ¹⁰"Go, and you have spoken to David, saying, Thus said YHWH: I am extending three [choices] to you; choose one of these for yourself, and I do [it] to you." ¹¹And Gad comes to David and says to him, "Thus said YHWH: Take for yourself— ¹²either famine for three years, or three months to be consumed from the face of your adversaries (even [for] the sword of your enemies to overtake), or three days of the sword of YHWH (even pestilence in the land, and a messenger of YHWH destroying in all the border of Israel); and now, see; what word do I return to Him who is sending me?" ¹³And David says to Gad, "I am greatly distressed, please let me fall into the hand of YHWH, for His mercies [are] very many, and do not let me fall into the hand of man." ¹⁴And YHWH gives a pestilence in Israel, and there falls from Israel seventy thousand men, ¹⁵and God sends a messenger to Jerusalem to destroy it, and as he is destroying, YHWH has seen, and is comforted concerning the calamity, and says to the messenger who [is] destroying, "Enough now, cease your hand." And the messenger of YHWH is standing by the threshing-floor of Ornan the Jebusite, ¹⁶and David lifts up his eyes, and sees the messenger of YHWH standing between the earth and the heavens, and his sword [is] drawn in his hand, stretched out over Jerusalem, and David falls, and the elderly, covered with sackcloth, on their faces. ¹⁷And David says to God, "Did I not command to number the people? Indeed, it [is] I who have sinned, and done great evil: and these, the flock, what did they do? O YHWH, my God, please let Your hand be on me, and on the house of my father, and not on Your people—to be plagued." ¹⁸And the messenger of YHWH commanded to Gad to say to David, "Surely David goes up to raise an altar to YHWH in the threshing-floor of Ornan the Jebusite." ¹⁹And David goes up by the word of Gad, that

1 CHRONICLES

he spoke in the Name of YHWH. ²⁰And Ornan turns back and sees the messenger, and his four sons [are] with him hiding themselves, and Ornan is threshing wheat. ²¹And David comes to Ornan, and Ornan looks attentively and sees David, and goes out from the threshing-floor, and bows himself to David—face to the earth. ²²And David says to Ornan, "Give the place of the threshing-floor to me, and I build an altar to YHWH in it; give it to me for full price, and the plague is restrained from the people." ²³And Ornan says to David, "Take [it] to yourself, and my lord the king does that which is good in his eyes; see, I have given the oxen for burnt-offerings, and the threshing instruments for wood, and the wheat for a present; I have given the whole." ²⁴And King David says to Ornan, "No, for I surely buy [it] for full price; for I do not lift up that which is yours to YHWH, so as to offer a burnt-offering without cost." ²⁵And David gives to Ornan six hundred shekels of gold [in] weight for the place; ²⁶and David builds an altar to YHWH there, and offers burnt-offerings and peace-offerings, and calls to YHWH, and He answers him from the heavens with fire on the altar of the burnt-offering. ²⁷And YHWH speaks to the messenger, and he turns back his sword to its sheath. ²⁸At that time, when David sees that YHWH has answered him in the threshing-floor of Ornan the Jebusite, then he sacrifices there; ²⁹and the Dwelling Place of YHWH that Moses made in the wilderness, and the altar of the burnt-offering, [are] at that time at a high place in Gibeon; ³⁰and David is not able to go before it to seek God, for he has been afraid because of the sword of the messenger of YHWH.

CHAPTER 22

¹And David says, "This is the house of YHWH God, and this [is] the altar for burnt-offering for Israel." ²And David says to gather the sojourners who [are] in the land of Israel, and appoints hewers to hew hewn-stones to build a house of God. ³And David has prepared iron in abundance for nails for leaves of the gates and for couplings, and bronze in abundance—there is no weighing, ⁴and cedar-trees without number, for the Zidonians and the Tyrians brought in cedar-trees in abundance to David. ⁵And David says, "My son Solomon [is] a youth and tender, and the house to be built for YHWH [is] to be made exceedingly great, for renown and for beauty to all the lands; now let me prepare for it"; and David prepares in abundance before his death. ⁶And he calls for his son Solomon, and charges him to build a house for YHWH, God of Israel, ⁷and David says to his son Solomon, "As for me, it has been with my heart to build a house for the Name of my God YHWH, ⁸and the word of YHWH [is] against me, saying, You have shed blood in abundance, and you have made great wars; you do not build a house for My Name, for you have shed much blood to the earth before Me. ⁹Behold, a son is born to you; he is a man of rest, and I have given rest to him from all his surrounding enemies, for Solomon is his name, and I give peace and quietness to Israel in his days; ¹⁰he builds a house for My Name, and he is to Me for a son, and I [am] to him for a father, and I have established the throne of his kingdom over Israel for all time. ¹¹Now my son, YHWH is with you, and you have prospered, and have built the house of your God YHWH, as He spoke concerning you. ¹²Only, may YHWH give wisdom and understanding to you, and charge you concerning Israel, even to keep the Law of your God YHWH, ¹³then you prosper, if you observe to do the statutes and the judgments that YHWH charged Moses with concerning Israel; be strong and courageous; do not fear, nor be cast down. ¹⁴And behold, in my affliction I have prepared for the house of YHWH one hundred thousand talents of gold, and one million talents of silver; and of bronze and of iron there is no weighing, for it has been in abundance; and I have prepared wood and stones, and you add to them. ¹⁵And with you in abundance [are] workmen, hewers and craftsmen of stone and of wood, and every skillful man for every work. ¹⁶Of the gold, of the silver, and of the bronze, and of the iron, there is no number; arise and do, and YHWH is with you." ¹⁷And David gives charge to all heads of Israel to give help to his son Solomon, [saying], ¹⁸"Is your God YHWH not with you? Indeed, He has given rest to you all around, for He has given the inhabitants of the land into my hand, and the land has been subdued before His people. ¹⁹Now give your heart and your soul to seek for your God YHWH, and rise and build the sanctuary of YHWH God, to bring in the Ark of the Covenant of YHWH, and the holy vessels of God, to the house that is built for the Name of YHWH."

CHAPTER 23

¹And David was old and satisfied with days, and he causes his son Solomon to reign over Israel, ²and gathers all the heads of Israel, and the priests, and the Levites; ³and the Levites are numbered from a son of thirty years and upward, and their number, for their counted heads, is of thirty-eight thousand mighty men. ⁴Of these, twenty-four thousand [are] to preside over the work of the house of YHWH, and six thousand officers and judges, ⁵and four thousand gatekeepers, and four thousand giving praise to YHWH, "with instruments that I made for praising," [says David.] ⁶And David distributes them into divisions of the sons of Levi—of Gershon, Kohath, and Merari. ⁷Of the Gershonite: Laadan and Shimei. ⁸Sons of Laadan: the head [is] Jehiel, and Zetham, and Joel—three. ⁹Sons of Shimei: Shelomith, and Haziel, and Haran—three; these [are] heads of the fathers of Laadan. ¹⁰And sons of Shimei: Jahath, Zina, and Jeush, and Beriah; these [are] the four sons of Shimei. ¹¹And Jahath is the head, and Zizah the second, and Jeush and Beriah have not multiplied sons, and they become the house of a father by one numbering. ¹²Sons of Kohath: Amram, Izhar, Hebron, and Uzziel—four. ¹³Sons of Amram: Aaron and Moses; and Aaron is separated for his sanctifying the Holy of Holies, he and his sons, for all time, to make incense before YHWH, to serve Him, and to bless in His Name for all time. ¹⁴As for Moses, the man of God, his sons are called after the tribe of Levi. ¹⁵Sons of Moses: Gershom and Eliezer. ¹⁶Sons of Gershom: Shebuel the head. ¹⁷And sons of Eliezer are Rehabiah the head, and Eliezer had no other sons, and the sons of Rehabiah have multiplied exceedingly. ¹⁸Sons of Izhar: Shelomith the head. ¹⁹Sons of Hebron: Jeriah the head, Amariah the second, Jahaziel the third, and Jekameam the fourth. ²⁰Sons of Uzziel: Micah the head, and Ishshiah the second. ²¹Sons of Merari: Mahli and Mushi; sons of Mahli: Eleazar and Kish. ²²And Eleazar dies, and he had no sons, but daughters, and their brothers, sons of Kish, take them. ²³Sons of Mushi: Mahli, and Eder, and Jerimoth—three. ²⁴These [are] sons of Levi, by the house of their fathers, heads of the fathers, by their appointments, in the number of names, by their counted heads, doing the work for the service of the house of YHWH, from a son of twenty years and upward, ²⁵for David said, "YHWH, God of Israel, has given rest to His people, and He dwells in Jerusalem for all time"; ²⁶and also of the Levites, "None [are] to carry the Dwelling Place and all its vessels for its service"; ²⁷for by the last words of David they [took] the number of the sons of Levi from a son of twenty years and upward, ²⁸for their station [is] at the side of the sons of Aaron, for the service of the house of YHWH, over the courts, and over the chambers, and over the cleansing of every holy thing, and the work of the service of the house of God, ²⁹and for the bread of the arrangement, and for fine flour for present, and for the thin unleavened cakes, and for [the work of] the pan, and for that which is stirred, and for all [liquid] measure and [solid] measure; ³⁰and to stand, morning by morning, to give thanks, and to give praise to YHWH, and so at evening; ³¹and for all the burnt-offerings—burnt-offerings to YHWH for Sabbaths, for new moons, and for appointed times, by number, according to the ordinance on them continually, before YHWH. ³²And they have kept the charge of the Tent of Meeting, and the charge of the holy place, and the charge of their brothers, the sons of Aaron, for the service of the house of YHWH.

CHAPTER 24

¹And [these are] their divisions, of the sons of Aaron. [The] sons of Aaron [are] Nadab, and Abihu, Eleazar, and Ithamar. ²And Nadab dies—and Abihu—in the presence of their father, and they had no sons, and Eleazar and Ithamar act as priests. ³And David distributes them—and Zadok of the sons of Eleazar, and Ahimelech of the sons of Ithamar—according to their office in their service; ⁴and there are found of the sons of Eleazar more for heads of the mighty men than of the sons of Ithamar; and they distribute them. Of the sons of Eleazar, heads for [each] house of [their] fathers—sixteen; and of the sons of Ithamar, for [each] house of their fathers—eight. ⁵And they distribute them by lots, with one another, for they have been princes of the holy place and princes of God, from the sons of Eleazar

# 1 CHRONICLES

and from the sons of Ithamar. ⁶And Shemaiah son of Nethaneel the scribe, of the Levites, writes them before the king, and the princes, and Zadok the priest, and Ahimelech son of Abiathar, and heads of the fathers for priests and for Levites, one house of a father being taken possession of for Eleazar and one being taken possession of for Ithamar. ⁷And the first lot goes out for Jehoiarib, for Jedaiah the second, ⁸for Harim the third, for Seorim the fourth, ⁹for Malchijah the fifth, for Mijamin the sixth, ¹⁰for Hakkoz the seventh, for Abijah the eighth, ¹¹for Jeshuah the ninth, for Shecaniah the tenth, ¹²for Eliashib the eleventh, for Jakim the twelfth, ¹³for Huppah the thirteenth, for Jeshebeab the fourteenth, ¹⁴for Bilgah the fifteenth, for Immer the sixteenth, ¹⁵for Hezir the seventeenth, for Aphses the eighteenth, ¹⁶for Pethahiah the nineteenth, for Jehezekel the twentieth, ¹⁷for Jachin the twenty-first, for Gamul the twenty-second, ¹⁸for Delaiah the twenty-third, for Maaziah the twenty-fourth. ¹⁹These [are] their appointments for their service, to come into the house of YHWH, according to their ordinance by the hand of their father Aaron, as YHWH God of Israel commanded them. ²⁰And of the sons of Levi who are left—of sons of Amram: Shubael; of sons of Shubael: Jehdeiah. ²¹Of Rehabiah, of sons of Rehabiah: the head Ishshiah. ²²Of the Izharite: Shelomoth; of sons of Shelomoth: Jahath. ²³And sons of Jeriah: Amariah the second, Jahaziel the third, Jekameam the fourth. ²⁴Sons of Uzziel: Michah; of sons of Michah: Shamir. ²⁵Ishshiah [is] a brother of Michah; of sons of Ishshiah: Zechariah; ²⁶sons of Merari: Mahli and Mushi; sons of Jaaziah: Beno; ²⁷sons of Merari, of Jaaziah: Beno, and Shoham, and Zaccur, and Ibri. ²⁸Of Mahli: Eleazar, who had no sons; ²⁹of Kish, sons of Kish: Jerahmeel. ³⁰And sons of Mushi [are] Mahli, and Eder, and Jerimoth; these [are] sons of the Levites, for the house of their fathers, ³¹and they also cast lots just as their brothers, the sons of Aaron, before David the king, and Zadok, and Ahimelech, and heads of the fathers for priests and for Levites; the chief father just as his younger brother.

CHAPTER 25

¹And David and the heads of the host separate for service, of the sons of Asaph, and Heman, and Jeduthun, who are prophesying with harps, with psalteries, and with cymbals; and the number of the workmen is according to their service. ²Of sons of Asaph: Zaccur, and Joseph, and Nethaniah, and Asharelah; sons of Asaph [are] by the side of Asaph, who is prophesying by the side of the king. ³Of Jeduthun, sons of Jeduthun: Gedaliah, and Zeri, and Jeshaiah, [and Shimei, and] Hashabiah, and Mattithiah, six, by the side of their father Jeduthun; he is prophesying with a harp, for giving of thanks and of praise for YHWH. ⁴Of Heman, sons of Heman: Bukkiah, Mattaniah, Uzziel, Shebuel, and Jerimoth, Hananiah, Hanani, Eliathah, Giddalti, and Romamti-Ezer, Joshbekashah, Mallothi, Hothir, Mahazioth; ⁵all these [are] sons of Heman, seer of the king in the things of God, to lift up a horn; and God gives fourteen sons and three daughters to Heman. ⁶All these [are] by the side of their father in the song of the house of YHWH, with cymbals, psalteries, and harps, for the service of the house of God; by the side of the king [are] Asaph, and Jeduthun, and Heman. ⁷And their number, with their brothers taught in the song of YHWH—all who are intelligent—[is] two hundred and eighty-eight. ⁸And they cause lots to fall, charge next to [charge], the small as well as the great, the intelligent with the learner. ⁹And the first lot goes out for Asaph to Joseph; the second, Gedaliah—him, and his brothers and his sons—twelve; ¹⁰the third, Zaccur, his sons and his brothers—twelve; ¹¹the fourth to Izri, his sons and his brothers—twelve; ¹²the fifth, Nethaniah, his sons and his brothers—twelve; ¹³the sixth, Bukkiah, his sons and his brothers—twelve; ¹⁴the seventh, Jesharelah, his sons and his brothers—twelve; ¹⁵the eighth, Jeshaiah, his sons and his brothers—twelve; ¹⁶the ninth, Mattaniah, his sons and his brothers—twelve; ¹⁷the tenth, Shimei, his sons and his brothers—twelve; ¹⁸eleventh, Azareel, his sons and his brothers—twelve; ¹⁹the twelfth to Hashabiah, his sons and his brothers—twelve; ²⁰for the thirteenth, Shubael, his sons and his brothers—twelve; ²¹for the fourteenth, Mattithiah, his sons and his brothers—twelve; ²²for the fifteenth to Jeremoth, his sons and his brothers—twelve; ²³the sixteenth to Hananiah, his sons and his brothers—twelve; ²⁴the seventeenth to Joshbekashah, his sons and his brothers—twelve; ²⁵the eighteenth to Hanani, his sons and his brothers—twelve; ²⁶the nineteenth to Mallothi, his sons and his brothers—twelve; ²⁷the twentieth to Eliathah, his sons and his brothers—twelve; ²⁸the twenty-first to Hothir, his sons and his brothers—twelve; ²⁹the twenty-second to Giddalti, his sons and his brothers—twelve; ³⁰the twenty-third to Mahazioth, his sons and his brothers—twelve; ³¹the twenty-fourth to Romamti-Ezer, his sons and his brothers—twelve.

CHAPTER 26

¹For the divisions of the gatekeepers, of the Korahites: Meshelemiah son of Kore, of the sons of Asaph; ²and sons of Meshelemiah: Zechariah the firstborn, Jediael the second, Zebadiah the third, Jathniel the fourth, ³Elam the fifth, Jehohanan the sixth, Elioenai the seventh. ⁴And moreover, sons of Obed-Edom: Shemaiah the firstborn, Jehozabad the second, Joah the third, and Sacar the fourth, and Nethaneel the fifth, ⁵Ammiel the sixth, Issachar the seventh, Peullethai the eighth, for God has blessed him. ⁶And sons have been born to his son Shemaiah, who are ruling throughout the house of their father, for they [are] mighty men of valor. ⁷Sons of Shemaiah: Othni, and Rephael, and Obed, [and] Elzabad; his brothers Elihu and Semachiah [are] sons of valor. ⁸All these [are] of the sons of Obed-Edom; they, and their sons, and their brothers, men of valor with might for service—sixty-two of Obed-Edom. ⁹And sons and brothers of Meshelemiah, sons of valor—eighteen; ¹⁰and of Hosah, of the sons of Merari, [are these] sons: Shimri the head (though he was not firstborn, yet his father sets him for head), ¹¹Hilkiah the second, Tebaliah the third, Zechariah the fourth; all the sons and brothers of Hosah—thirteen. ¹²For these [are] the divisions of the gatekeepers, of the heads of the mighty ones, [with] charges just as their brothers, to minister in the house of YHWH, ¹³and they cause lots to fall, the small as well as the great, according to the house of their fathers, for every gate. ¹⁴And the lot falls eastward to Shelemiah; and [for] his son Zechariah, a counselor with understanding, they cause lots to fall, and his lot goes out northward; ¹⁵to Obed-Edom southward, and to his sons, the house of the gatherings; ¹⁶to Shuppim and to Hosah to the west, with Shallecheth Gate, in the highway, the ascent, watch next to watch; ¹⁷to the east [are] six Levites, to the north [are] four each day, to the south [are] four each day, and for the gatherings, two by two; ¹⁸at Parbar, to the west, [are] four at the highway, two at Parbar. ¹⁹These are the divisions of the gatekeepers, of the sons of the Korahite, and of the sons of Merari. ²⁰And of the Levites, Ahijah [is] over the treasures of the house of God, even for the treasures of the holy things. ²¹Sons of Laadan, sons of the Gershonite, of Laadan, heads of the fathers of Laadan the Gershonite: Jehieli. ²²Sons of Jehieli: Zetham and his brother Joel, over the treasures of the house of YHWH. ²³Of the Amramite, of the Izharite, of the Hebronite, of [the] Uzzielite— ²⁴and Shebuel son of Gershom, son of Moses, [is] president over the treasures. ²⁵And his brothers, of Eliezer: Rehabiah his son, and Jeshaiah his son, and Joram his son, and Zichri his son, and Shelomith his son. ²⁶This Shelomith and his brothers [are] over all the treasures of the holy things that David the king, and heads of the fathers, even heads of thousands, and of hundreds, and heads of the host, sanctified; ²⁷from the battles and from the spoil, they sanctified to strengthen the house of YHWH; ²⁸and all that Samuel the seer, and Saul son of Kish, and Abner son of Ner, and Joab son of Zeruiah sanctified, everyone sanctifying [anything—it is] by the side of Shelomith and his brothers. ²⁹Of the Izharite, Chenaniah and his sons [are] for the outward work over Israel, for officers and for judges. ³⁰Of the Hebronite, Hashabiah and his brothers, one thousand and seven hundred sons of valor, [are] over the inspection of Israel, beyond the Jordan westward, for all the work of YHWH, and for the service of the king. ³¹Of the Hebronite, Jerijah [is] the head of the Hebronite, according to the generations of his fathers. In the fortieth year of the reign of David they have been sought out, and there are found among them mighty men of valor, in Jazer of Gilead— ³²and his brothers, two thousand and seven hundred sons of valor, [are] heads of the fathers, and King David appoints them over the Reubenite, and the Gadite, and the half of the tribe of the Manassite, for every matter of God and matter of the king.

CHAPTER 27

¹ And the sons of Israel, after their number, heads of the fathers, and princes of the thousands and of the hundreds, and their officers, those serving the king in any matter of the divisions, that are coming in and going out month by month throughout all months of the year, [are] twenty-four thousand in each division. ² Over the first division for the first month [is] Jashobeam son of Zabdiel, and twenty-four thousand [are] on his division; ³ [he was] of the sons of Perez, [and] the head of all princes of the hosts for the first month. ⁴ And over the division of the second month [is] Dodai the Ahohite, and Mikloth [is] also president of his division, and twenty-four thousand [are] on his division. ⁵ Head of the third host, for the third month, [is] Benaiah son of Jehoiada, the head priest, and twenty-four thousand [are] on his division. ⁶ This Benaiah [is] a mighty one of the thirty, and over the thirty, and his son Ammizabad [is in] his division. ⁷ The fourth, for the fourth month, [is] Asahel brother of Joab, and his son Zebadiah after him, and twenty-four thousand [are] on his division. ⁸ The fifth, for the fifth month, [is] the prince Shamhuth the Izrahite, and twenty-four thousand [are] on his division. ⁹ The sixth, for the sixth month, [is] Ira son of Ikkesh the Tekoite, and twenty-four thousand [are] on his division. ¹⁰ The seventh, for the seventh month, [is] Helez the Pelonite, of the sons of Ephraim, and twenty-four thousand [are] on his division. ¹¹ The eighth, for the eighth month, [is] Sibbecai the Hushathite, of the Zerahite, and twenty-four thousand [are] on his division. ¹² The ninth, for the ninth month, [is] Abiezer the Antothite, of the Benjamite, and twenty-four thousand [are] on his division. ¹³ The tenth, for the tenth month, [is] Maharai the Netophathite, of the Zerahite, and twenty-four thousand [are] on his division. ¹⁴ Eleventh, for the eleventh month, [is] Benaiah the Pirathonite, of the sons of Ephraim, and twenty-four thousand [are] on his division. ¹⁵ The twelfth, for the twelfth month, [is] Heldai the Netophathite, of Othniel, and twenty-four thousand [are] on his division. ¹⁶ And over the tribes of Israel: the leader of the Reubenite [is] Eliezer son of Zichri; of the Simeonite, Shephatiah son of Maachah; ¹⁷ of the Levite, Hashabiah son of Kemuel; of the Aaronite, Zadok; ¹⁸ of Judah, Elihu, of the brothers of David; of Issachar, Omri son of Michael; ¹⁹ of Zebulun, Ishmaiah son of Obadiah; of Naphtali, Jerimoth son of Azriel; ²⁰ of the sons of Ephraim, Hoshea son of Azaziah; of the half of the tribe of Manasseh, Joel son of Pedaiah; ²¹ of the half of Manasseh in Gilead, Iddo son of Zechariah; of Benjamin, Jaasiel son of Abner; of Dan, Azareel son of Jeroham. ²² These [are the] heads of the tribes of Israel. ²³ But David has not taken up their number from a son of twenty years and under, for YHWH had said [He would] multiply Israel as the stars of the heavens. ²⁴ Joab son of Zeruiah has begun to number, but has not finished; and there is wrath against Israel for this, and the number has not gone up in the account of the Chronicles of King David. ²⁵ And Azmaveth son of Adiel [is] over the treasures of the king; and Jonathan son of Uzziah [is] over the treasures in the field, in the cities, and in the villages, and in the towers; ²⁶ and Ezri son of Chelub [is] over workmen of the field for the service of the ground; ²⁷ and Shimei the Ramathite [is] over the vineyards; and Zabdi the Shiphmite [is] over what [is] in the vineyards for the treasures of wine; ²⁸ and Ba'al-Hanan the Gederite [is] over the olives and the sycamores that [are] in the low country; and Joash [is] over the treasures of oil; ²⁹ and Shitrai the Sharonite [is] over the herds that are feeding in Sharon; and Shaphat son of Adlai [is] over the herds in the valleys; ³⁰ and Obil the Ishmaelite [is] over the camels; and Jehdeiah the Meronothite [is] over the donkeys; ³¹ and Jaziz the Hagerite [is] over the flock; all these [are] heads of the substance that King David has. ³² And Jonathan, David's uncle, [is] counselor, a man of understanding, [and] he is also a scribe; and Jehiel son of Hachmoni [is] with the sons of the king; ³³ and Ahithophel [is] counselor to the king; and Hushai the Archite [is] the friend of the king; ³⁴ and after Ahithophel [is] Jehoiada son of Benaiah, and Abiathar; and the head of the host of the king [is] Joab.

CHAPTER 28

¹ And David assembles all the heads of Israel, heads of the tribes, and heads of the divisions who are serving the king, and heads of the thousands, and heads of the hundreds, and heads of all the substance and possessions of the king, and of his sons, with the officers and the mighty ones, and of every mighty man of valor—to Jerusalem. ² And David the king rises on his feet and says, "Hear me, my brothers and my people, I [had it] with my heart to build a house of rest for the Ark of the Covenant of YHWH, and for the footstool of our God, and I prepared to build, ³ and God has said to me, You do not build a house for My Name, for you [are] a man of wars, and you have shed blood. ⁴ And YHWH, God of Israel, fixes on me out of all the house of my father to be for king over Israel for all time, for He has fixed on Judah for a leader, and in the house of Judah, the house of my father, and among the sons of my father, He has been pleased with me to make [me] king over all Israel; ⁵ and out of all my sons—for YHWH has given many sons to me—He also fixes on my son Solomon, to sit on the throne of the kingdom of YHWH over Israel, ⁶ and says to me, Your son Solomon builds My house and My courts, for I have fixed on him [to be] to Me for a son, and I am to him for a father. ⁷ And I have established his kingdom for all time, if he is strong to do My commands and My judgments, as at this day. ⁸ And now, before the eyes of all Israel, the assembly of YHWH, and in the ears of our God, keep and seek all the commands of your God YHWH, so that you possess this good land, and have caused your sons to inherit after you for all time. ⁹ And you, my son Solomon, know the God of your father, and serve Him with a perfect heart and with a willing mind, for YHWH is seeking all hearts, and He is understanding every imagination of the thoughts; if you seek Him, He is found by you, and if you forsake Him, He casts you off forever. ¹⁰ See, now, for YHWH has fixed on you to build a house for a sanctuary; be strong, and do." ¹¹ And David gives to his son Solomon the pattern of the porch, and of its houses, and of its treasures, and of its upper chambers, and of its innermost chambers, and of the house of the atonement; ¹² and the pattern of all that has been with him by the Spirit, for the courts of the house of YHWH, and for all the surrounding chambers, for the treasures of the house of God, and for the treasures of the things sacrificed; ¹³ and for the divisions of the priests and of the Levites, and for all the work of the service of the house of YHWH, and for all vessels of service of the house of YHWH, ¹⁴ even gold by weight, for [things of] gold, for all instruments of every service; for all instruments of silver by weight, for all instruments of every service; ¹⁵ and [by] weight for the lampstands of gold, and their lamps of gold, by weight [for] lampstand and lampstand, and its lamps; and for the lampstands of silver, by weight for a lampstand and its lamps, according to the service of lampstand and lampstand; ¹⁶ and the gold [by] weight for tables of the arrangement, for table and table, and silver for the tables of silver; ¹⁷ and the forks, and the bowls, and the cups of pure gold, and for the basins of gold, by weight for basin and basin, and for the basins of silver, by weight for basin and basin, ¹⁸ and for the altar of incense, refined gold by weight, and for the pattern of the chariot of the cherubim of gold, spreading and covering over the Ark of the Covenant of YHWH. ¹⁹ The whole [is] in writing from the hand of YHWH, "He caused me to understand all the work of the pattern," [said David.] ²⁰ And David says to his son Solomon, "Be strong and courageous, and do; do not fear nor be frightened, for YHWH God, my God, [is] with you; He does not fail you, nor forsake you, to the completion of all the work of the service of the house of YHWH. ²¹ And behold, divisions of the priests and of the Levites [are] for all the service of the house of God; and with you in all work [is] every willing one with wisdom, for every service; and the heads and all the people [are] according to all your words."

CHAPTER 29

¹ And David the king says to all the assembly, "My son Solomon—the one on whom God has fixed—[is] young and tender, and the work [is] great, for the palace is not for man, but for YHWH God; ² and with all my power I have prepared for the house of my God, the gold for [things of] gold, and the silver for [things of] silver, and the bronze for [things of] bronze, the iron for [things of] iron, and the wood for [things of] wood, shoham stones, and settings, and stones of painting and of diverse colors, and all [kinds of] precious stone, and stones of white marble, in abundance. ³ And again, because of my delighting in the house of my God, the substance I have—a peculiar treasure of gold and silver—I have given for

the house of my God, even over and above all I have prepared for the holy house: ⁴three thousand talents of gold, of the gold of Ophir, and seven thousand talents of refined silver, to overlay the walls of the houses, ⁵even gold for [things of] gold, and silver for [things of] silver, and for all the work by the hand of craftsmen; and who [is] he that is offering to willingly consecrate his hand to YHWH today?" ⁶And the heads of the fathers, and the heads of the tribes of Israel, and the heads of the thousands, and of the hundreds, and the heads of the work of the king, offer willingly. ⁷And they give for the service of the house of God five thousand talents and ten thousand drams of gold, and ten thousand talents of silver, and eighteen thousand talents of bronze, and one hundred thousand talents of iron; ⁸and he with whom stones are found has given [them] to the treasury of the house of YHWH, by the hand of Jehiel the Gershonite. ⁹And the people rejoice because of their offering willingly, for with a perfect heart they have offered willingly to YHWH; and David the king has also rejoiced [with] great joy. ¹⁰And David blesses YHWH before the eyes of all the assembly, and David says, "Blessed [are] You, YHWH, God of Israel, our Father, from age even to age. ¹¹To You, O YHWH, [is] the greatness, and the might, and the beauty, and the victory, and the splendor, because of all in the heavens and in the earth; to You, O YHWH, [is] the kingdom, and He who is lifting up Himself over all for head; ¹²and the riches, and the honor [are] from before You, and You are ruling over all, and in Your hand [is] power and might, and [it is] in Your hand to make great and to give strength to all. ¹³And now, our God, we are giving thanks to You, and giving praise to Your beautiful Name; ¹⁴indeed, because who [am] I, and who [are] my people, that we retain power to offer thus willingly? But the whole [is] from You, and we have given to You out of Your [own] hand; ¹⁵for we [are] sojourners and settlers before You, like all our fathers; our days on the land [are] as a shadow, and there is none abiding. ¹⁶O our God YHWH, all this store [with] which we have prepared to build a house for You, for Your Holy Name, [is] out of Your [own] hand, and the whole [is] of You. ¹⁷And I have known, my God, that You are trying the heart, and desire uprightness; I, in the uprightness of my heart, have willingly offered all these; and now, I have seen Your people who are found here with joy to offer willingly to You. ¹⁸O YHWH, God of Abraham, Isaac, and Israel, our fathers, keep this for all time for the imagination of the thoughts of the heart of Your people, and prepare their heart for You; ¹⁹and give a perfect heart to my son Solomon, to keep Your commands, Your testimonies, and Your statutes, and to do the whole, even to build the palace [for] which I have prepared." ²⁰And David says to all the assembly, "Now bless your God YHWH"; and all the assembly blesses YHWH, God of their fathers, and bows and pays respect to YHWH and to the king. ²¹And they sacrifice sacrifices to YHWH, and cause burnt-offerings to ascend to YHWH on that next day: one thousand bullocks, one thousand rams, one thousand lambs, and their oblations, and sacrifices in abundance for all Israel. ²²And they eat and drink before YHWH on that day with great joy, and cause Solomon son of David to reign a second time, and anoint [him] before YHWH for leader, and Zadok for priest. ²³And Solomon sits on the throne of YHWH for king instead of his father David, and prospers, and all of Israel listens to him, ²⁴and all the heads, and the mighty men, and also all the sons of King David have given a hand under Solomon the king; ²⁵and YHWH makes Solomon exceedingly great before the eyes of all Israel, and puts on him the splendor of the kingdom that has not been on any king over Israel before him. ²⁶And David son of Jesse has reigned over all Israel, ²⁷and the days that he has reigned over Israel [are] forty years; he reigned in Hebron seven years, and he reigned in Jerusalem thirty-three; ²⁸and he dies in a good old age, satisfied with days, riches, and honor, and his son Solomon reigns in his stead. ²⁹And the matters of David the king, the first and the last, behold, they are written beside the matters of Samuel the seer, and beside the matters of Nathan the prophet, and beside the matters of Gad the seer, ³⁰with all his reign, and his might, and the times that went over him, and over Israel, and over all kingdoms of the lands.

2 CHRONICLES

CHAPTER 1

¹And Solomon son of David strengthens himself over his kingdom, and his God YHWH [is] with him, and makes him exceedingly great. ²And Solomon says to all Israel, to heads of the thousands, and of the hundreds, and to the ones judging, and to every honorable one of all Israel, heads of the fathers, ³and they go—Solomon, and all the assembly with him—to the high place that [is] in Gibeon, for God's Tent of Meeting has been there, that Moses, servant of YHWH, made in the wilderness, ⁴but David had the Ark of God brought up from Kirjath-Jearim to the [place] David had prepared for it, for he stretched out a tent for it in Jerusalem; ⁵and the altar of bronze that Bezaleel son of Uri, son of Hur made, he put before the Dwelling Place of YHWH; and Solomon and the assembly seek Him [there]. ⁶And Solomon goes up there, on the altar of bronze, before YHWH, that [is] at the Tent of Meeting, and causes one thousand burnt-offerings to ascend on it. ⁷In that night God has appeared to Solomon and says to him, "Ask—what do I give to you?" ⁸And Solomon says to God, "You have done great kindness with my father David, and have caused me to reign in his stead. ⁹Now, O YHWH God, Your word with my father David is steadfast, for You have caused me to reign over a people [as] numerous as the dust of the earth; ¹⁰now, give wisdom and knowledge to me, and I go out before this people, and I come in, for who judges this—Your great people?" ¹¹And God says to Solomon, "Because that this has been with your heart, and you have not asked for riches, wealth, and honor, and the life of those hating you, and also have not asked for many days, and ask for wisdom and knowledge for yourself, so that you judge My people over which I have caused you to reign— ¹²the wisdom and the knowledge is given to you, and riches and wealth and honor I [also] give to you, that there has not been so to the kings who [are] before you, and after you it is not so." ¹³And Solomon comes in to Jerusalem [from] the high place that [is] in Gibeon, from before the Tent of Meeting, and reigns over Israel, ¹⁴and Solomon gathers chariots and horsemen, and he has one thousand and four hundred chariots, and twelve thousand horsemen, and he places them in the cities of the chariots, and with the king in Jerusalem. ¹⁵And the king makes the silver and the gold in Jerusalem as stones, and the cedars he made as sycamores that [are] in the low country, for abundance. ¹⁶And the source of the horses that [are] for Solomon [is] from Egypt and from Keva; merchants of the king take [them] from Keva at a price, ¹⁷and they come up, and bring out a chariot from Egypt for six hundred pieces of silver, and a horse for one hundred and fifty, and so for all the kings of the Hittites and the kings of Aram—they bring [them] out by their hand.

CHAPTER 2

¹And Solomon says to build a house for the Name of YHWH, and a house for his kingdom, ²and Solomon numbers seventy thousand men bearing burden, and eighty thousand men hewing in the mountain, and three thousand and six hundred overseers over them. ³And Solomon sends to Huram king of Tyre, saying, "When you have dealt with my father David, then you send cedars to him to build a house for him to dwell in; ⁴behold, I am building a house for the Name of my God YHWH, to sanctify [it] to Him, to make incense before Him, incense of spices, and a continual arrangement, and burnt-offerings at morning and at evening, at Sabbaths, and at new moons, and at appointed times of our God YHWH; this [is] on Israel for all time. ⁵And the house that I am building [is] great, for our God [is] greater than all gods; ⁶and who retains strength to build a house for Him, since the heavens, even the heavens of the heavens, do not contain Him? And who [am] I that I build a house for Him, except to make incense before

Him? ⁷And now, send a wise man to me to work in gold, and in silver, and in bronze, and in iron, and in purple, and crimson, and blue, and knowing to engrave engravings with the wise men who [are] with me in Judah and in Jerusalem, whom my father David prepared; ⁸and send to me cedar-trees, firs, and algums from Lebanon, for I have known that your servants know to cut down trees of Lebanon, and behold, my servants [are] with your servants, ⁹even to prepare trees in abundance for me, for the house that I am building [is] great and wonderful. ¹⁰And behold, I have given to your servants, to hewers, to those cutting the trees, twenty thousand cors of beaten wheat, and twenty thousand cors of barley, and twenty thousand baths of wine, and twenty thousand baths of oil." ¹¹And Huram king of Tyre answers in writing, and sends [it] to Solomon: "In the love of YHWH for His people, He has set you [as] king over them." ¹²And Huram says, "Blessed [is] YHWH, God of Israel, who made the heavens and the earth, who has given a wise son to David the king, knowing wisdom and understanding, who builds a house for YHWH, and a house for his kingdom. ¹³And now, I have sent a wise man having understanding, of [my] father Huram ¹⁴(son of a woman of the daughters of Dan, and his father a man of Tyre), knowing to work in gold, and in silver, in bronze, in iron, in stones, and in wood, in purple, in blue, and in fine linen, and in crimson, and to engrave any engraving, and to devise any invention that is given to him, with your wise men, and the wise men of my lord, your father David. ¹⁵And now, the wheat, and the barley, the oil, and the wine, as my lord said, let him send to his servants, ¹⁶and we cut trees out of Lebanon, according to all your need, and bring them to you—floats by sea, to Joppa, and you take them up to Jerusalem." ¹⁷And Solomon numbers all the men, the sojourners who [are] in the land of Israel, after the numbering with which his father David numbered them, and they are found [to be] one hundred and fifty thousand and three thousand and six hundred; ¹⁸and he makes from them seventy thousand burden-bearers, and eighty thousand hewers in the mountain, and three thousand and six hundred overseers, to cause the people to work.

CHAPTER 3

¹And Solomon begins to build the house of YHWH in Jerusalem, on the mount of Moriah where He appeared to his father David, in the place that David had prepared, in the threshing-floor of Ornan the Jebusite, ²and he begins to build in the second [day], in the second month, in the fourth year of his reign. ³And [in] these Solomon has been instructed to build the house of God: the length [in] cubits by the former measure [is] sixty cubits, and the breadth twenty cubits. ⁴As for the porch that [is] on the front, the length [is] by the front of the breadth of the house—twenty cubits, and the height one hundred and twenty [[or twenty]], and he overlays it within with pure gold. ⁵And he has covered the large house with fir-trees, and he covers it with fine gold, and causes palms and chains to ascend on it, ⁶and he overlays the house with precious stone for beauty, and the gold [is] gold of Parvaim, ⁷and he covers the house, the beams, the thresholds, and its walls, and its doors, with gold, and has engraved cherubim on the walls. ⁸And he makes the most holy house: its length by the front of the breadth of the house—twenty cubits, and its breadth twenty cubits, and he covers it with six hundred talents of fine gold; ⁹and the weight of the nails [is] fifty shekels of gold, and he has covered the upper chambers with gold. ¹⁰And he makes two cherubim in the most holy house, image work, and he overlays them with gold; ¹¹as for the wings of the cherubim, their length [is] twenty cubits, the wing of the one [is] five cubits, touching the wall of the house, and the other wing [is] five cubits, touching the wing of the other cherub. ¹²And the wing of the other cherub [is] five cubits touching the wall of the house, and the other wing [is] five cubits, adhering to the wing of the other cherub. ¹³The wings of these cherubim are spreading forth twenty cubits, and they are standing on their feet and their faces [are] inward. ¹⁴And he makes the veil of blue, and purple, and crimson, and fine linen, and causes cherubim to go up on it. ¹⁵And he makes two pillars at the front of the house, thirty-five cubits in length, and the ornament that [is] on their heads [is] five cubits. ¹⁶And he makes chains in the oracle, and puts [them] on the heads of the pillars, and makes one hundred pomegranates, and puts [them] on the chains. ¹⁷And he raises up the pillars on the front of the temple, one on the right and one on the left, and calls the name of that on the right Jachin, and the name of that on the left Boaz.

CHAPTER 4

¹And he makes an altar of bronze: twenty cubits its length, and twenty cubits its breadth, and ten cubits its height. ²And he makes the molten sea; ten by the cubit, from its edge to its edge, round in encompassment, and its height [is] five by the cubit, and a line of thirty by the cubit surrounds it around. ³And the likeness of oxen [is] under it, encompassing it all around, ten to the cubit, surrounding the sea around; two rows of oxen are cast in its being cast. ⁴It is standing on twelve oxen, three facing the north, and three facing the west, and three facing the south, and three facing the east, and the sea [is] on them above, and all their back parts [are] within. ⁵And its thickness [is] a handbreadth, and its lip as the work of the lip of a cup flowered with lilies; holding [within]—it contains three thousand baths. ⁶And he makes ten lavers, and puts five on the right, and five on the left, to wash with them; they purge the work of the burnt-offering with them; and the sea [is] for priests to wash with. ⁷And he makes the ten lampstands of gold, according to their ordinance, and places [them] in the temple, five on the right, and five on the left. ⁸And he makes ten tables, and places [them] in the temple, five on the right, and five on the left; and he makes one hundred bowls of gold. ⁹And he makes the court of the priests, and the great court, and doors for the court, and he has overlaid their doors with bronze. ¹⁰And he has placed the sea on the right shoulder eastward, from toward the south. ¹¹And Huram makes the pots, and the shovels, and the bowls, and Huram finishes to make the work that he made for King Solomon in the house of God; ¹²two pillars, and the bowls, and the crowns on the heads of the two pillars, and the two networks to cover the two bowls of the crowns that [are] on the heads of the pillars; ¹³and the four hundred pomegranates for the two networks, two rows of pomegranates for the one network, to cover the two bowls of the crowns that [are] on the front of the pillars. ¹⁴And he has made the bases; and he has made the lavers on the bases; ¹⁵the one sea, and the twelve oxen under it, ¹⁶and the pots, and the shovels, and the forks, and all their vessels, his father Huram has made for King Solomon, for the house of YHWH, of bronze purified. ¹⁷The king has cast them in the circuit of the Jordan, in the thick soil of the ground, between Succoth and Zeredathah. ¹⁸And Solomon makes all these vessels in great abundance, that the weight of the bronze has not been searched out. ¹⁹And Solomon makes all the vessels that [are for] the house of God, and the altar of gold, and the tables, and on them [is] Bread of the Presentation; ²⁰and the lampstands, and their lamps, for their burning according to the ordinance, before the oracle, of gold refined; ²¹and the flowers, and the lamps, and the tongs of gold—it [is] the perfection of gold; ²²and the snuffers, and the bowls, and the spoons, and the censers, of gold refined, and the opening of the house, its innermost doors to the Holy of Holies, and the doors of the house to the temple, of gold.

CHAPTER 5

¹And all the work that Solomon made for the house of YHWH is finished, and Solomon brings in the sanctified things of his father David, and the silver, and the gold, and all the vessels he has put among the treasures of the house of God. ²Then Solomon assembles the elderly of Israel, and all the heads of the tribes, princes of the fathers of the sons of Israel, to Jerusalem, to bring up the Ark of the Covenant of YHWH from the City of David—it [is] Zion. ³And all the men of Israel are assembled to the king in the celebration—it [is] the seventh month; ⁴and all [the] elderly of Israel come in, and the Levites lift up the Ark, ⁵and they bring up the Ark, and the Tent of Meeting, and all the holy vessels that [are] in the tent; the priests, the Levites, have brought them up; ⁶and King Solomon and all the congregation of Israel who are convened to him before the Ark are sacrificing sheep and oxen that are not counted nor numbered from multitude. ⁷And the priests bring in the Ark of the Covenant of YHWH to its place, to the oracle of the house, to the Holy of Holies, to the place of the wings of the cherubim; ⁸and the cherubim are spreading out wings over the place of the Ark, and the cherubim cover over the Ark, and

over its poles, from above; ⁹and they lengthen the poles, and the heads of the poles are seen out of the Ark on the front of the oracle, and they are not seen outside; and it is there to this day. ¹⁰There is nothing in the Ark but the two tablets that Moses gave in Horeb, where YHWH covenanted with the sons of Israel, in their going out from Egypt. ¹¹And it comes to pass, in the going out of the priests from the holy place—for all the priests who are present have sanctified themselves, there is none to watch by divisions, ¹²and the Levites, the singers, to all of them, to Asaph, to Heman, to Jeduthun, and to their sons, and to their brothers, clothed in white linen, with cymbals, and with psalteries, and harps, are standing on the east of the altar, and with them one hundred and twenty priests blowing with trumpets— ¹³indeed, it comes to pass, trumpeters and singers [are] as one, to sound [with] one voice—to praise and to give thanks to YHWH, and at the lifting up of the sound with trumpets, and with cymbals, and with instruments of song, and at giving praise to YHWH, [saying], "For [He is] good, for His kindness [is] for all time," that the house is filled with a cloud—the house of YHWH, ¹⁴and the priests have not been able to stand to minister from the presence of the cloud, for the glory of YHWH has filled the house of God.

CHAPTER 6

¹Then Solomon said, "YHWH said [He would] dwell in thick darkness, ²and I have built a house of habitation for You, and a fixed place for Your dwelling for all ages." ³And the king turns around his face, and blesses the whole assembly of Israel, and the whole assembly of Israel is standing, ⁴and he says, "Blessed [is] YHWH, God of Israel, who has spoken with His mouth with my father David, and with His hands has fulfilled [it], saying, ⁵From the day that I brought out My people from the land of Egypt, I have not fixed on a city out of any of the tribes of Israel to build a house for my name being there, and I have not fixed on a man to be leader over My people Israel; ⁶and I fix on Jerusalem for My Name being there, and I fix on David to be over My people Israel. ⁷And it is with the heart of my father David to build a house for the Name of YHWH God of Israel, ⁸and YHWH says to my father David, Because that it has been with your heart to build a house for My Name, you have done well that it has been with your heart, ⁹but you do not build the house, for your son who comes forth out from your loins, he builds the house for My Name. ¹⁰And YHWH establishes His word that He spoke, and I rise up in the stead of my father David, and sit on the throne of Israel, as YHWH spoke, and I build the house for the Name of YHWH, God of Israel, ¹¹and I place the Ark there, where the covenant of YHWH [is] that He made with the sons of Israel." ¹²And he stands before the altar of YHWH, in front of all the assembly of Israel, and spreads out his hand— ¹³for Solomon has made a scaffold of bronze, and puts it in the midst of the court, five cubits its length, and five cubits its breadth, and three cubits its height, and he stands on it, and kneels on his knees in front of all the assembly of Israel, and spreads forth his hands toward the heavens— ¹⁴and says, "O YHWH God of Israel, there is not like You a god in the heavens and in the earth, keeping the covenant and the kindness for Your servants who are walking before You with all their heart; ¹⁵who has kept for Your servant, my father David, that which You spoke to him; indeed, You speak with Your mouth, and with Your hand have fulfilled [it], as at this day. ¹⁶And now, O YHWH, God of Israel, keep for Your servant, my father David, that which You spoke to him, saying, A man of yours is never cut off from before My face, sitting on the throne of Israel—only, if your sons watch their way to walk in My law, as you have walked before Me. ¹⁷And now, O YHWH, God of Israel, let Your word be steadfast that You have spoken to Your servant, to David. ¹⁸For is it true [that] God dwells with man on the earth? Behold, the heavens, and the heavens of the heavens, do not contain You, how much less this house that I have built? ¹⁹And You have turned to the prayer of Your servant, and to his supplication, O YHWH my God, to listen to the cry and to the prayer that Your servant is praying before You, ²⁰for Your eyes being open toward this house by day and by night, toward the place that You have said to put Your Name there, to listen to the prayer that Your servant prays toward this place. ²¹And You have listened to the supplications of Your servant, and of Your people Israel, that they pray toward this place, and You hear from the place of Your dwelling, from the heavens, and have listened, and forgiven. ²²If a man sins against his neighbor, and he has lifted up an oath on him to cause him to swear, and the oath has come in before Your altar in this house— ²³then You hear from the heavens, and have done, and have judged Your servants, to give back to the wicked, to put his way on his head, and to declare righteous the righteous, to give to him according to his righteousness. ²⁴And if Your people Israel is struck before an enemy because they sin against You, and they have turned back and confessed Your Name, and prayed and made supplication before You in this house— ²⁵then You hear from the heavens and have forgiven the sin of Your people Israel, and caused them to return to the ground that You have given to them, and to their fathers. ²⁶In the heavens being restrained and there is no rain because they sin against You, and they have prayed toward this place and confessed Your Name, [and] they turn back from their sin because You afflict them— ²⁷then You hear in the heavens, and have forgiven the sin of Your servants, and of Your people Israel, because You direct them to the good way in which they walk, and have given rain on Your land that You have given to Your people for an inheritance. ²⁸Famine, when it is in the land, [and] pestilence, when it is [in the land], blasting and mildew, locust and caterpillar, when they are [in the land], when its enemies have distressed it in the land—its gates, any plague and any sickness; ²⁹any prayer, any supplication that is for any man, and for all Your people Israel, when they each know his own plague, and his own pain, and he has spread out his hands toward this house— ³⁰then You hear from the heavens, the settled place of Your dwelling, and have forgiven, and have given to each according to all his ways (because You know his heart, for You alone have known the heart of the sons of men), ³¹so that they fear You, to walk in Your ways, all the days that they are living on the face of the ground that You have given to our fathers. ³²And also, to the stranger who is not of Your people Israel, and he has come from a far-off land for the sake of Your great Name, and Your strong hand, and Your outstretched arm, and they have come in and prayed toward this house— ³³then You hear from the heavens, from the settled place of Your dwelling, and have done according to all that the stranger calls to You for, so that all the peoples of the earth know Your Name, so as to fear You, as Your people Israel, and to know that Your Name is called on this house that I have built. ³⁴When Your people go out to battle against its enemies in the way that You send them, and they have prayed to You [in] the way of this city that You have fixed on, and the house that I have built for Your Name— ³⁵then You have heard their prayer and their supplication from the heavens, and have maintained their cause. ³⁶When they sin against You—for there is not a man who does not sin—and You have been angry with them, and have given them before an enemy, and their captors have taken them captive to a land far off or near; ³⁷and they have turned [it] back to their heart in the land to where they have been taken captive, and have turned back and made supplication to You in the land of their captivity, saying, We have sinned, we have done perversely, and have done wickedly; ³⁸indeed, they have turned back to You with all their heart, and with all their soul, in the land of their captivity, to where they have taken them captive, and they have prayed [in] the way of their land that You have given to their fathers, and of the city that You have chosen, and of the house that I have built for Your Name— ³⁹then You have heard from the heavens, from the settled place of Your dwelling, their prayer and their supplications, and have maintained their cause, and forgiven Your people who have sinned against You. ⁴⁰Now my God, I implore You, let Your eyes be open and Your ears attentive to the prayer of this place. ⁴¹And now, rise, O YHWH God, to Your rest, You and the Ark of Your strength; Your priests, O YHWH God, are clothed with salvation, and Your saints rejoice in the goodness. ⁴²O YHWH God, do not turn back the face of Your anointed, be mindful of the kind acts of Your servant David."

CHAPTER 7

¹And at Solomon's finishing to pray, then the fire has come down from the heavens and consumes the burnt-offering and the sacrifices, and the glory of YHWH has filled the house, ²and the priests have not been able to

go into the house of YHWH, because the glory of YHWH has filled the house of YHWH. ³And all the sons of Israel are looking on the descending of the fire, and the glory of YHWH on the house, and they bow—faces to the earth—on the pavement, and pay respect, and give thanks to YHWH, [saying], "For [He is] good, for His kindness [is] for all time!" ⁴And the king and all the people are sacrificing a sacrifice before YHWH, ⁵and King Solomon sacrifices the sacrifice: twenty-two thousand of the herd and one hundred and twenty thousand of the flock; and the king and all the people dedicate the house of God. ⁶And the priests are standing over their charges, and the Levites with instruments of the song of YHWH that David the king made, to give thanks to YHWH, for His kindness [is] for all time, in David's praising by their hand—and the priests are blowing trumpets opposite them, and all of Israel is standing. ⁷And Solomon sanctifies the middle of the court that [is] before the house of YHWH, for he has made the burnt-offerings and the fat of the peace-offerings there, for the altar of bronze that Solomon made has not been able to contain the burnt-offering, and the present, and the fat. ⁸And Solomon makes the celebration at that time [for] seven days, and all Israel with him—a very great assembly—from the entering in of Hamath to the Brook of Egypt. ⁹And they make a restraint on the eighth day, because they have made the dedication of the altar [for] seven days, and the celebration [for] seven days. ¹⁰And on the twenty-third day of the seventh month he has sent the people to their tents, rejoicing, and glad in heart, for the goodness that YHWH has done to David, and to Solomon, and to His people Israel. ¹¹And Solomon finishes the house of YHWH, and the house of the king; and all that has come on the heart of Solomon to do in the house of YHWH, and in his own house, he has caused to prosper. ¹²And YHWH appears to Solomon by night and says to him, "I have heard your prayer, and have fixed on this place for Myself for a house of sacrifice. ¹³If I restrain the heavens and there is no rain, and if I lay charge on the locust to consume the land, and if I send pestilence among My people— ¹⁴and My people on whom My Name is called are humbled, and pray, and seek My face, and turn back from their evil ways, then I hear from the heavens, and forgive their sin, and heal their land. ¹⁵Now My eyes are open and My ears attentive to the prayer of this place; ¹⁶and now, I have chosen and sanctified this house for My Name being there for all time; indeed, My eyes and My heart have been there [for] all the days. ¹⁷And you, if you walk before Me as your father David walked, even to do according to all that I have commanded you, and keep My statutes and My judgments— ¹⁸then I have established the throne of your kingdom, as I covenanted with your father David, saying, A man of yours is never cut off [from] ruling in Israel; ¹⁹and if you turn back—you—and have forsaken My statutes and My commands that I have placed before you, and have gone and served other gods, and bowed yourselves to them—then I have plucked them from off My ground that I have given to them, ²⁰and this house that I have sanctified for My Name, I cast from before My face, and make it for a proverb and for a byword among all the peoples. ²¹And this house that has been high is an astonishment to everyone passing by it, and he has said, Why has YHWH done thus to this land and to this house? ²²And they have said, Because that they have forsaken YHWH, God of their fathers, who brought them out from the land of Egypt, and lay hold on other gods, and bow themselves to them, and serve them, therefore He has brought all this calamity on them."

CHAPTER 8

¹And it comes to pass at the end of twenty years that Solomon has built the house of YHWH and his own house. ²As for the cities that Huram has given to Solomon, Solomon has built them, and he causes the sons of Israel to dwell there. ³And Solomon goes to Hamath-Zobah, and lays hold on it; ⁴and he builds Tadmor in the wilderness, and all the cities of store that he has built in Hamath. ⁵And he builds Beth-Horon the upper, and Beth-Horon the lower—cities of defense, with walls, double gates, and bar— ⁶and Ba'alath, and all the cities of store that Solomon had, and all the cities of the chariot, and the cities of the horsemen, and all the desire of Solomon that he desired to build in Jerusalem, and in Lebanon, and in all the land of his dominion. ⁷All the people who are left of the Hittite, and the Amorite, and the Perizzite, and the Hivite, and the Jebusite, who are not of Israel— ⁸of their sons who have been left after them in the land, whom the sons of Israel did not consume—Solomon lifts up a tribute to this day. ⁹And Solomon has made none of the sons of Israel servants for his work, but they [are] men of war, and heads of his captains, and heads of his charioteers, and of his horsemen; ¹⁰and these [are] heads of the officers whom King Solomon has, two hundred and fifty who are rulers among the people. ¹¹And Solomon has brought up the daughter of Pharaoh from the City of David to the house that he built for her, for he said, "My wife does not dwell in the house of David king of Israel, for they are holy to whom the Ark of YHWH has come." ¹²Then Solomon has caused burnt-offerings to ascend to YHWH on the altar of YHWH that he built before the porch, ¹³even by the matter of a day in its day, to cause to ascend according to the command of Moses, on Sabbaths, and on new moons, and on appointed times, three times in a year—in the Celebration of Unleavened Things, and in the Celebration of Weeks, and in the Celebration of Shelters. ¹⁴And he establishes, according to the ordinance of his father David, the divisions of the priests over their service, and of the Levites over their charges, to praise and to minister before the priests, according to the matter of a day in its day, and the gatekeepers in their divisions at every gate, for so [is] the command of David the man of God. ¹⁵And they have not turned aside [from] the command of the king concerning the priests and the Levites, in reference to any matter, and to the treasures. ¹⁶And all the work of Solomon is prepared until the day of the foundation of the house of YHWH, and until its completion; the house of YHWH is perfect. ¹⁷Then Solomon has gone to Ezion-Geber, and to Elath, on the border of the sea, in the land of Edom; ¹⁸and Huram sends to him, by the hand of his servants, ships and servants knowing the sea, and they go with servants of Solomon to Ophir, and take four hundred and fifty talents of gold from there, and bring it to King Solomon.

CHAPTER 9

¹And the queen of Sheba has heard of the fame of Solomon, and comes to Jerusalem to try Solomon with acute sayings, with a very great company, and camels carrying spices and gold in abundance, and precious stone; and she comes to Solomon, and speaks with him all that has been with her heart, ²and Solomon declares all her matters to her, and there has not been hid a thing from Solomon that he has not declared to her. ³And the queen of Sheba sees the wisdom of Solomon, and the house that he has built, ⁴and the food of his table, and the sitting of his servants, and the standing of his ministers, and their clothing, and his stewards, and their clothing, and his burnt-offering that he offered up in the house of YHWH, and there has not been anymore spirit in her. ⁵And she says to the king, "The word [is] true that I heard in my land concerning your matters and concerning your wisdom, ⁶and I have given no credence to their words until I have come and my eyes see, and behold, there has not been declared to me the half of the abundance of your wisdom—you have added to the report that I heard. ⁷O the blessedness of your men, and the blessedness of your servants—these—who are standing before you continually, and hearing your wisdom. ⁸Let your God YHWH be blessed who has delighted in you to put you on His throne for king for your God YHWH; in the love of your God to Israel, to establish it for all time, He has put you over them for king, to do judgment and righteousness." ⁹And she gives to the king one hundred and twenty talents of gold, and spices in great abundance, and precious stone; and there has not been any such spice as the queen of Sheba has given to King Solomon. ¹⁰And also, servants of Huram, and servants of Solomon, who brought in gold from Ophir, have brought in algum-trees and precious stone. ¹¹And the king makes the algum-trees [into] staircases for the house of YHWH, and for the house of the king, and harps and psalteries for singers; and there have been none seen like these before in the land of Judah. ¹²And King Solomon has given to the queen of Sheba all her desire that she asked, apart from that which she had brought to the king, and she turns and goes to her land, she and her servants. ¹³And the weight of the gold that is coming to Solomon in one year is six hundred and sixty-six talents of gold, ¹⁴apart from [what] the tourists and the merchants

are bringing in; and all the kings of Arabia, and the governors of the land, are bringing in gold and silver to Solomon. ¹⁵And King Solomon makes two hundred bucklers of alloyed gold—he causes six hundred [shekels] of alloyed gold to go up on the one buckler; ¹⁶and three hundred shields of alloyed gold—he causes three hundred [shekels] of gold to go up on the one shield, and the king puts them in the House of the Forest of Lebanon. ¹⁷And the king makes a great throne of ivory, and overlays it with pure gold; ¹⁸and six steps [are] to the throne, and a footstool of gold, [and] they are fastened to the throne; and [places for] hands [are] on this [side] and on that [side] on the place of the sitting, and two lions are standing near the hands, ¹⁹and twelve lions are standing there on the six steps on this [side] and on that [side]: it has not been made so for any kingdom. ²⁰And all the drinking vessels of King Solomon [are] of gold, and all the vessels of the House of the Forest of Lebanon [are] of refined gold—silver is not reckoned in the days of Solomon for anything; ²¹for ships of the king are going to Tarshish with servants of Huram: once in three years the ships of Tarshish come carrying gold, and silver, ivory, apes, and peacocks [[or monkeys]]. ²²And King Solomon becomes greater than any of the kings of the earth for riches and wisdom; ²³and all the kings of the earth are seeking the presence of Solomon to hear his wisdom that God has put in his heart, ²⁴and they are each bringing in his present, vessels of silver, and vessels of gold, and garments, harness, and spices, horses, and mules, a rate year by year. ²⁵And there are four thousand stalls for horses and chariots, and twelve thousand horsemen for Solomon, and he placed them in cities of the chariot, and with the king in Jerusalem. ²⁶And he is ruling over all the kings from the River even to the land of the Philistines, and to the border of Egypt. ²⁷And the king makes the silver in Jerusalem as stones, and he has made the cedars as sycamores that [are] in the low country, for abundance, ²⁸and they are bringing out horses from Egypt to Solomon, and from all the lands. ²⁹And the rest of the matters of Solomon, the first and the last, are they not written beside the matters of Nathan the prophet, and beside the prophecy of Ahijah the Shilonite, and with the visions of Iddo the seer concerning Jeroboam son of Nebat? ³⁰And Solomon reigns in Jerusalem over all Israel [for] forty years, ³¹and Solomon lies with his fathers, and they bury him in the city of his father David, and his son Rehoboam reigns in his stead.

CHAPTER 10

¹And Rehoboam goes to Shechem, for all of Israel has come [to] Shechem to cause him to reign. ²And it comes to pass, at Jeroboam son of Nebat—who [is] in Egypt because he has fled from the face of Solomon the king—hearing, that Jeroboam turns back out of Egypt; ³and they send and call for him, and Jeroboam comes in, and all of Israel, and they speak to Rehoboam, saying, ⁴"Your father made our yoke sharp, and now, make light [some] of the sharp service of your father, and [some] of his heavy yoke that he put on us, and we serve you." ⁵And he says to them, "Yet three days—then return to me"; and the people go. ⁶And King Rehoboam consults with the aged men who have been standing before his father Solomon in his being alive, saying, "How are you counseling to answer this people?" ⁷And they speak to him, saying, "If you become good to this people, and have been pleased with them, and spoken to them good words, then they have been servants to you [for] all the days." ⁸And he forsakes the counsel of the aged men that they counseled him, and consults with the boys who have grown up with him, those standing before him, ⁹and he says to them, "What are you counseling, and we answer this people that have spoken to me, saying, Make light [some] of the yoke that your father put on us?" ¹⁰And the boys who have grown up with him speak with him, saying, "Thus you say to the people who have spoken to you, saying, Your father made our yoke heavy, and you, make light [some] of our yoke; thus you say to them, My little finger is thicker than the loins of my father; ¹¹and now, my father laid a heavy yoke on you, and I add to your yoke; my father disciplined you with whips, and I—with scorpions." ¹²And Jeroboam comes in, and all the people, to Rehoboam on the third day, as the king spoke, saying, "Return to me on the third day." ¹³And the king answers them sharply, and King Rehoboam forsakes the counsel of the aged men, ¹⁴and speaks to them according to the counsel of the boys, saying, "My father made your yoke heavy, and I add to it; my father disciplined you with whips, and I—with scorpions." ¹⁵And the king has not listened to the people, for the revolution has been from God, for the sake of YHWH's establishing His word that He spoke by the hand of Abijah the Shilonite to Jeroboam son of Nebat. ¹⁶And all Israel have seen that the king has not listened to them, and the people send back [word to] the king, saying, "What portion do we have in David? Indeed, there is no inheritance in a son of Jesse; [go], each to your tents, O Israel! Now see your house, O David!" And all [in] Israel go to their tents. ¹⁷As for the sons of Israel who are dwelling in the cities of Judah—Rehoboam reigns over them. ¹⁸And King Rehoboam sends Hadoram, who [is] over the tribute, and the sons of Israel cast stones at him, and he dies; and King Rehoboam has strengthened himself to go up into a chariot to flee to Jerusalem; ¹⁹and Israel transgresses against the house of David to this day.

CHAPTER 11

¹And Rehoboam comes to Jerusalem, and assembles the house of Judah and Benjamin—one hundred and eighty thousand chosen warriors—to fight with Israel, to bring back the kingdom to Rehoboam. ²And a word of YHWH is to Shemaiah, a man of God, saying, ³"Speak to Rehoboam son of Solomon king of Judah, and to all Israel in Judah and Benjamin, saying, ⁴Thus said YHWH: You do not go up nor fight with your brothers! Let each return to his house, for this thing has been from Me"; and they hear the words of YHWH, and turn back from going against Jeroboam. ⁵And Rehoboam dwells in Jerusalem, and builds cities for a bulwark in Judah, ⁶indeed, he builds Beth-Lehem, and Etam, and Tekoa, ⁷and Beth-Zur, and Shocho, and Adullam, ⁸and Gath, and Mareshah, and Ziph, ⁹and Adoraim, and Lachish, and Azekah, ¹⁰and Zorah, and Aijalon, and Hebron, that [are] in Judah and in Benjamin, cities of bulwarks. ¹¹And he strengthens the bulwarks, and puts leaders in them, and treasures of food, and oil, and wine, ¹²and in each and every city [he puts] bucklers and spears, and strengthens them very greatly; and he has Judah and Benjamin. ¹³And the priests and the Levites that [are] in all Israel have stationed themselves by him, out of all their border, ¹⁴for the Levites have left their outskirts and their possession, and they come to Judah and to Jerusalem, for Jeroboam and his sons have cast them off from acting as priests for YHWH, ¹⁵and he establishes for himself priests for high places, and for goat [idols] and for calf [idols] that he made. ¹⁶And after them, out of all the tribes of Israel, those giving their heart to seek YHWH, God of Israel, have come to Jerusalem to sacrifice to YHWH, God of their father. ¹⁷And they strengthen the kingdom of Judah, and strengthen Rehoboam son of Solomon, for three years, because they walked in the way of David and Solomon for three years. ¹⁸And Rehoboam takes a wife for himself, Mahalath, child of Jerimoth son of David, [and of] Abigail daughter of Eliab son of Jesse. ¹⁹And she bears sons to him: Jeush, and Shamaria, and Zaham. ²⁰And after her he has taken Maachah daughter of Absalom, and she bears to him Abijah, and Attai, and Ziza, and Shelomith. ²¹And Rehoboam loves Maachah daughter of Absalom above all his wives and his concubines—for he has taken eighteen wives and sixty concubines—and he begets twenty-eight sons and sixty daughters. ²²And Rehoboam appoints Abijah son of Maachah for head, for leader among his brothers, for to cause him to reign. ²³And he has understanding, and disperses from all his sons to all lands of Judah and Benjamin, to all cities of the bulwarks, and gives provision in abundance to them; and he asks for a multitude of wives [for them].

CHAPTER 12

¹And it comes to pass, at the establishing of the kingdom of Rehoboam, and at his strengthening himself, he has forsaken the Law of YHWH, and all Israel with him. ²And it comes to pass, in the fifth year of King Rehoboam, Shishak king of Egypt has come up against Jerusalem—because they trespassed against YHWH— ³with one thousand and two hundred chariots, and with sixty thousand horsemen, and there is no number to the people who have come with him out of Egypt—Lubim, Sukkiim, and Cushim— ⁴and he captures the cities of the

bulwarks that [are] of Judah, and comes to Jerusalem. ⁵And Shemaiah the prophet has come to Rehoboam and the heads of Judah who have been gathered to Jerusalem [to escape] from the presence of Shishak, and says to them, "Thus said YHWH: You have forsaken Me, and also, I have left you in the hand of Shishak"; ⁶and the heads of Israel are humbled—and the king—and they say, "YHWH [is] righteous." ⁷And when YHWH sees that they have been humbled, a word of YHWH has been [sent] to Shemaiah, saying, "They have been humbled; I do not destroy them, and I have given to them as a little thing for an escape, and I do not pour out My fury in Jerusalem by the hand of Shishak; ⁸but they become servants to him, and they know My service, and the service of the kingdoms of the lands." ⁹And Shishak king of Egypt comes up against Jerusalem, and takes the treasures of the house of YHWH and the treasures of the house of the king—he has taken the whole—and he takes the shields of gold that Solomon had made; ¹⁰and King Rehoboam makes shields of bronze in their stead, and has given [them] a charge on the hand of the heads of the runners who are keeping the opening of the house of the king; ¹¹and it comes to pass, from the time of the going in of the king to the house of YHWH, the runners have come in and lifted them up, and brought them back to the chamber of the runners. ¹²And in his being humbled, the wrath of YHWH has turned back from him, so as not to destroy to completion; and also, there have been good things in Judah. ¹³And King Rehoboam strengthens himself in Jerusalem and reigns; for Rehoboam [is] a son of forty-two years in his reigning, and he has reigned seventeen years in Jerusalem, the city that YHWH has chosen to put His Name there, out of all the tribes of Israel, and the name of his mother [is] Naamah the Ammonitess, ¹⁴and he does evil, for he has not prepared his heart to seek YHWH. ¹⁵And the matters of Rehoboam, the first and the last, are they not written among the matters of Shemaiah the prophet, and of Iddo the seer, concerning genealogy? And the wars of Rehoboam and Jeroboam [are for] all the days; ¹⁶and Rehoboam lies with his fathers, and is buried in the City of David, and his son Abijah reigns in his stead.

CHAPTER 13

¹In the eighteenth year of King Jeroboam, Abijah reigns over Judah; ²he has reigned three years in Jerusalem (and the name of his mother [is] Michaiah daughter of Uriel, from Gibeah), and there has been war between Abijah and Jeroboam. ³And Abijah directs the war with a force of mighty men of war, four hundred thousand chosen men, and Jeroboam has set in array [for] battle with him, with eight hundred thousand chosen men, mighty men of valor. ⁴And Abijah rises up on the hill of Zemaraim that [is] in the hill-country of Ephraim, and says, "Hear me, Jeroboam and all Israel! ⁵Is it not for you to know that YHWH, God of Israel, has given the kingdom over Israel to David for all time, to him and to his sons—a covenant of salt? ⁶And Jeroboam, son of Nebat, servant of Solomon son of David, rises up and rebels against his lord! ⁷And vain men are gathered to him, sons of worthlessness, and they strengthen themselves against Rehoboam son of Solomon, and Rehoboam was a youth, and tender of heart, and has not strengthened himself against them. ⁸And now you are saying to strengthen yourselves before the kingdom of YHWH in the hand of the sons of David, and you [are] a numerous multitude, and calves of gold [are] with you that Jeroboam has made for you for gods. ⁹Have you not cast out the priests of YHWH, the sons of Aaron, and the Levites, and make priests for yourselves like the peoples of the lands? Everyone who has come to fill his hand with a bullock, a son of the herd, and seven rams, even he has been a priest for [those which are] not gods! ¹⁰As for us, YHWH [is] our God, and we have not forsaken Him, and priests are ministering to YHWH, sons of Aaron and the Levites, in the work, ¹¹and are making incense to YHWH, burnt-offerings morning by morning, and evening by evening, and incense of spices, and the arrangement of bread [is] on the pure table, and the lampstand of gold, and its lamps, to burn evening by evening, for we are keeping the charge of our God YHWH, and you have forsaken Him. ¹²And behold, with us—at [our] head—[is] God, and His priests and trumpets of shouting to shout against you; O sons of Israel, do not fight with YHWH, God of your fathers, for you do not prosper." ¹³And Jeroboam has brought around the ambush to come in from behind them, and they are before Judah, and the ambush [is] behind them. ¹⁴And Judah turns, and behold, the battle [is] against them, before and behind, and they cry to YHWH, and the priests are blowing with trumpets, ¹⁵and the men of Judah shout; and it comes to pass, at the shouting of the men of Judah, that God has struck Jeroboam and all Israel before Abijah and Judah. ¹⁶And the sons of Israel flee from the face of Judah, and God gives them into their hand, ¹⁷and Abijah and his people strike among them a great striking, and five hundred thousand chosen men of Israel fall wounded. ¹⁸And the sons of Israel are humbled at that time, and the sons of Judah are strong, for they have leaned on YHWH, God of their fathers. ¹⁹And Abijah pursues after Jeroboam and captures cities from him: Beth-El and its small towns, and Jeshanah and its small towns, and Ephraim and its small towns. ²⁰And Jeroboam has not retained power anymore in the days of Abijah, and YHWH strikes him, and he dies. ²¹And Abijah strengthens himself, and takes fourteen wives for himself, and begets twenty-two sons and sixteen daughters; ²²and the rest of the matters of Abijah, and his ways, and his words, are written in the commentary of the prophet Iddo.

CHAPTER 14

¹And Abijah lies with his fathers, and they bury him in the City of David, and his son Asa reigns in his stead. In his days the land was quiet [for] ten years. ²And Asa does that which is good and that which is right in the eyes of his God YHWH, ³and turns aside the altars of the stranger, and the high places, and breaks the standing-pillars, and cuts down the Asherim, ⁴and commands to Judah to seek YHWH, God of their fathers, and to do the Law and the command; ⁵and he turns aside the high places and the images out of all cities of Judah, and the kingdom is quiet before him. ⁶And he builds cities of bulwarks in Judah, for the land has quiet; and there is no war with him in these years, because YHWH has given rest to him. ⁷And he says to Judah, "Let us build these cities, and surround [them] with wall, and towers, double gates, and bars, while the land [is] before us, because we have sought our God YHWH, we have sought, and He gives rest to us all around"; and they build and prosper. ⁸And Asa has a force of three hundred thousand from Judah carrying buckler and spear, and two hundred and eighty thousand from Benjamin carrying shield and treading bow; all these [are] mighty men of valor. ⁹And Zerah the Cushite comes out to them with a force of one million [men] and three hundred chariots, and he comes to Mareshah. ¹⁰and Asa goes out before him, and they set in array [for] battle in the Valley of Zephathah at Mareshah. ¹¹And Asa calls to his God YHWH and says, "YHWH, it is nothing for You to help, between the mighty and those who have no power; help us, O YHWH, our God, for we have leaned on You, and in Your Name we have come against this multitude; O YHWH, You [are] our God; do not let mortal man prevail against You!" ¹²And YHWH strikes the Cushim before Asa and before Judah, and the Cushim flee, ¹³and Asa and the people who [are] with him pursue them even to Gerar, and there falls [many] from the Cushim, for they have no preserving, because they have been broken before YHWH and before His camp; and [those of Judah] carry away very much spoil, ¹⁴and strike all the cities around Gerar, for a fear of YHWH has been on them, and they spoil all the cities, for abundant spoil has been in them; ¹⁵and they have also struck tents of livestock, and they capture sheep in abundance, and camels, and return to Jerusalem.

CHAPTER 15

¹And the Spirit of God has been on Azariah son of Oded, ²and he goes out before Asa and says to him, "Hear me, Asa, and all Judah and Benjamin; YHWH [is] with you—in your being with Him, and if you seek Him, He is found by you, and if you forsake Him, He forsakes you; ³and many days [are] to Israel without [the] true God, and without a teaching priest, and without law, ⁴and it turns back in its distress to YHWH, God of Israel, and they seek Him, and He is found by them, ⁵and in those times there is no peace for him who is going out, and for him who is coming in, for many troubles [are] on all the inhabitants of the lands, ⁶and they have been beaten down, nation by nation, and city by city, for God has troubled them with every adversity; ⁷and you, be strong, and do not let your hands be feeble, for there is a

reward for your work." ⁸And at Asa's hearing these words, and the prophecy of Oded the prophet, he has strengthened himself, and causes the abominations to pass away out of all the land of Judah and Benjamin, and out of the cities that he has captured from the hill-country of Ephraim, and renews the altar of YHWH that [is] before the porch of YHWH, ⁹and gathers all Judah and Benjamin, and the sojourners with them out of Ephraim, and Manasseh, and out of Simeon—for they have defected to him from Israel in abundance, in their seeing that his God YHWH [is] with him. ¹⁰And they are gathered to Jerusalem in the third month of the fifteenth year of the reign of Asa, ¹¹and sacrifice to YHWH on that day from the spoil they have brought in—seven hundred oxen and seven thousand sheep, ¹²and they enter into a covenant to seek YHWH, God of their fathers, with all their heart and with all their soul, ¹³and everyone who does not seek for YHWH, God of Israel, is put to death, from small to great, from man to woman. ¹⁴And they swear to YHWH with a loud voice, and with shouting, and with trumpets, and with horns, ¹⁵and all Judah rejoices concerning the oath, for they have sworn with all their heart, and they have sought Him with all their goodwill, and He is found by them, and YHWH gives rest to them all around. ¹⁶And also Maachah, mother of Asa the king—he has removed her from [being] mistress, in that she has made for an Asherah a horrible thing, and Asa cuts down her horrible thing, and beats [it] small, and burns [it] by the Brook of Kidron: ¹⁷yet the high places have not been removed from Israel; only, the heart of Asa has been perfect all his days. ¹⁸And he brings in the sanctified things of his father, and his own sanctified things, to the house of God: silver, and gold, and vessels. ¹⁹And war has not been until the thirty-fifth year of the reign of Asa.

CHAPTER 16

¹In the thirty-sixth year of the reign of Asa, Baasha king of Israel has come up against Judah, and builds Ramah, so as not to permit any going out and coming in to Asa king of Judah. ²And Asa brings out silver and gold from the treasures of the house of YHWH and of the house of the king, and sends [them] to Ben-Hadad king of Aram, who is dwelling in Damascus, saying, ³"A covenant [is] between me and you, and between my father and your father, behold, I have sent silver and gold to you; go, break your covenant with Baasha king of Israel, and he goes up from off me." ⁴And Ben-Hadad listens to King Asa, and sends the heads of the forces that he has to cities of Israel, and they strike Ijon, and Dan, and Abel-Maim, and all the stores, cities of Naphtali. ⁵And it comes to pass, at Baasha's hearing, that he ceases from building Ramah, and lets his work rest; ⁶and Asa the king has taken all Judah, and they carry away the stones of Ramah and its wood that Baasha has built [with], and he builds Geba and Mizpah with them. ⁷And at that time Hanani the seer has come to Asa king of Judah and says to him, "Because of your leaning on the king of Aram, and you have not leaned on your God YHWH, therefore the force of the king of Aram has escaped from your hand. ⁸Did the Cushim and the Lubim not become a very great force for multitude, for chariot, and for horsemen? And in your leaning on YHWH He gave them into your hand, ⁹for YHWH—His eyes go to and fro in all the earth, to show Himself strong [for] a people whose heart [is] perfect toward Him; you have been foolish concerning this, because from now on there are wars with you." ¹⁰And Asa is angry at the seer, and puts him [in] the house of stocks, for [he is] in a rage with him for this; and Asa oppresses [some] of the people at that time. ¹¹And behold, the matters of Asa, the first and the last, behold, they are written on the scroll of the kings of Judah and Israel. ¹²And Asa is diseased—in the thirty-ninth year of his reign—in his feet, until his disease is excessive; and also in his disease he has not sought YHWH, but among physicians. ¹³And Asa lies with his fathers, and dies in the forty-first year of his reign, ¹⁴and they bury him in [one of] his graves that he had prepared for himself in the City of David, and they cause him to lie on a bed that [one] has filled [with] spices, and various kinds of mixtures, with perfumed work; and they burn a very great burning for him.

CHAPTER 17

¹And his son Jehoshaphat reigns in his stead, and he strengthens himself against Israel, ²and puts a force in all the fortified cities of Judah, and puts garrisons in the land of Judah, and in the cities of Ephraim that his father Asa had captured. ³And YHWH is with Jehoshaphat, for he has walked in the first ways of his father David, and has not sought for the Ba'alim, ⁴for he has sought for the God of his father, and he has walked in His commands, and not according to the work of Israel. ⁵And YHWH establishes the kingdom in his hand, and all Judah gives a present to Jehoshaphat, and he has riches and honor in abundance, ⁶and his heart is high in the ways of YHWH, and again he has turned aside the high places and the Asherim out of Judah. ⁷And in the third year of his reign he has sent for his heads, for Ben-Hail, and for Obadiah, and for Zechariah, and for Nethaneel, and for Michaiah, to teach in cities of Judah; ⁸and with them the Levites: Shemaiah, and Nethaniah, and Zebadiah, and Asahel, and Shemiramoth, and Jonathan, and Adonijah, and Tobijath, and Tob-Adonijah—the Levites; and with them Elishama and Jehoram, the priests. ⁹And they teach in Judah, and the Scroll of the Law of YHWH [is] with them, and they go around into all cities of Judah, and teach among the people. ¹⁰And there is a fear of YHWH on all kingdoms of the lands that [are] around Judah, and they have not fought with Jehoshaphat; ¹¹and [some] from the Philistines are bringing a present to Jehoshaphat, and silver [as] tribute; also, the Arabians are bringing to him a flock of seven thousand and seven hundred rams, and seven thousand and seven hundred male goats. ¹²And Jehoshaphat is going on and becoming very great, and he builds palaces and cities of store in Judah, ¹³and he has much work in cities of Judah; and men of war, mighty men of valor, [are] in Jerusalem. ¹⁴And these [are] their numbers, for the house of their fathers—of Judah, heads of thousands: Adnah the head, and with him three hundred thousand mighty men of valor; ¹⁵and at his hand [is] Jehohanan the head, and with him two hundred and eighty thousand; ¹⁶and at his hand [is] Amasiah son of Zichri, who is willingly offering himself to YHWH, and with him two hundred thousand mighty men of valor. ¹⁷And of Benjamin, mighty men of valor: Eliada, and with him two hundred thousand armed with bow and shield; ¹⁸and at his hand [is] Jehozabad, and with him one hundred and eighty thousand armed ones of the host. ¹⁹These [are] those serving the king, apart from those whom the king put in the fortress cities in all of Judah.

CHAPTER 18

¹And Jehoshaphat has riches and honor in abundance, and joins affinity to Ahab, ²and goes down at the end of [certain] years to Samaria to [visit] Ahab, and Ahab sacrifices sheep and oxen in abundance for him and for the people who [are] with him, and persuades him to go up to Ramoth-Gilead. ³And Ahab king of Israel says to Jehoshaphat king of Judah, "Do you go with me [to] Ramoth-Gilead?" And he says to him, "As I—so you, and as your people—my people, and [we go] with you into the battle." ⁴And Jehoshaphat says to the king of Israel, "Please seek the word of YHWH this day." ⁵And the king of Israel gathers the prophets, four hundred men, and says to them, "Do we go to Ramoth-Gilead to battle, or do I refrain?" And they say, "Go up, and God gives [it] into the hand of the king." ⁶And Jehoshaphat says, "[Is there] not still a prophet of YHWH here, and we seek from him?" ⁷And the king of Israel says to Jehoshaphat, "[There is] still one man to seek YHWH from him, and I have hated him, for he is not prophesying of good concerning me, but of evil [for] all his days, he [is] Micaiah son of Imlah"; and Jehoshaphat says, "Do not let the king say so." ⁸And the king of Israel calls to a certain officer and says, "Hurry Micaiah son of Imlah." ⁹And the king of Israel and Jehoshaphat king of Judah are sitting, each on his throne, clothed with garments, and they are sitting in a threshing-floor at the opening of the Gate of Samaria, and all the prophets are prophesying before them. ¹⁰And Zedekiah son of Chenaanah makes horns of iron for himself and says, "Thus said YHWH: ¹¹With these you push Aram until you have consumed them." And all the prophets are prophesying so, saying, "Go up [to] Ramath-Gilead and prosper, and YHWH has given [it] into the hand of the king." ¹²And the messenger who has gone to call for Micaiah has spoken to him, saying, "Behold, the words of the prophets [as] one mouth [are] good toward the king, and please let your word be like one of theirs: and you have spoken good." ¹³And Micaiah says "YHWH lives, surely that which my God says, I speak it." ¹⁴And he comes to the king,

and the king says to him, "Micaiah, do we go to Ramoth-Gilead to battle, or do I refrain?" And he says, "Go up, and prosper, and they are given into your hand." ¹⁵And the king says to him, "How many times am I adjuring you that you speak to me only truth in the Name of YHWH?" ¹⁶And he says, "I have seen all Israel scattered on the mountains, as sheep that have no shepherd, and YHWH says, There are no masters for these, they each return to his house in peace." ¹⁷And the king of Israel says to Jehoshaphat, "Did I not say to you [that] he does not prophesy good concerning me, but rather of evil?" ¹⁸And [Micaiah] says, "Therefore, hear a word of YHWH: I have seen YHWH sitting on His throne, and all the host of the heavens standing on His right and His left; ¹⁹and YHWH says, Who entices Ahab king of Israel, and he goes up and falls in Ramoth-Gilead? And this speaker says thus, and that speaker thus. ²⁰And the spirit goes out, and stands before YHWH, and says, I entice him; and YHWH says to him, With what? ²¹And he says, I go out, and have become a spirit of falsehood in the mouth of all his prophets. And He says, You entice, and also, you are able; go out and do so. ²²And now, behold, YHWH has put a spirit of falsehood in the mouth of these prophets of yours, and YHWH has spoken calamity concerning you." ²³And Zedekiah son of Chenaanah comes near and strikes Micaiah on the cheek, and says, "Where [is] this—the way the spirit [from] YHWH passed over from me to speak with you?" ²⁴And Micaiah says, "Behold, you see in that day that you enter into the innermost chamber to be hidden." ²⁵And the king of Israel says, "Take Micaiah, and turn him back to Amon head of the city, and to Joash son of the king, ²⁶and you have said, Thus said the king: Put this [one] in the house of restraint, and cause him to eat bread of oppression, and water of oppression, until my return in peace." ²⁷And Micaiah says, "If you certainly return in peace, YHWH has not spoken by me"; and he says, "Hear, O peoples, all of them!" ²⁸And the king of Israel goes up—and Jehoshaphat king of Judah—to Ramoth-Gilead; ²⁹and the king of Israel says to Jehoshaphat to disguise himself, and to go into battle, "And you, put on your garments." And the king of Israel disguises himself, and they go into battle. ³⁰And the king of Aram has commanded the heads of the charioteers whom he has, saying, "You do not fight with small or with great, except with the king of Israel by himself." ³¹And it comes to pass at the heads of the charioteers seeing Jehoshaphat, that they have said, "He is the king of Israel," and they turn around against him to fight, and Jehoshaphat cries out, and YHWH has helped him, and God entices them from him; ³²indeed, it comes to pass, at the heads of the charioteers seeing that it has not been the king of Israel—they turn back from after him. ³³And a man has drawn with a bow in his simplicity, and strikes the king of Israel between the joinings and the coat of mail, and he says to the charioteer, "Turn your hand, and you have brought me out of the camp, for I have become [gravely] sick." ³⁴And the battle increases on that day, and the king of Israel has been propped up in the chariot in front of Aram until the evening, and he dies at the time of the going in of the sun.

CHAPTER 19

¹And Jehoshaphat king of Judah turns back to his house in peace, to Jerusalem, ²and Jehu son of Hanani the seer goes out to his presence and says to King Jehoshaphat, "Do you love to give help to the wicked and to those hating YHWH? And for this, wrath [is] against you from before YHWH, ³but good things have been found with you, for you have put away the Asheroth out of the land, and have prepared your heart to seek God." ⁴And Jehoshaphat dwells in Jerusalem, and he turns back and goes out among the people from Beer-Sheba to the hill-country of Ephraim, and brings them back to YHWH, God of their fathers. ⁵And he establishes judges in the land, in all the fortified cities of Judah, for every city, ⁶and says to the ones judging, "See what you are doing—for you do not judge for man, but for YHWH, who [is] with you in the matter of judgment; ⁷and now, let fear of YHWH be on you, observe and do, for there is not perverseness with our God YHWH, and favoring by appearance, and taking of a bribe." ⁸And also in Jerusalem, Jehoshaphat has appointed of the Levites, and of the priests, and of the heads of the fathers of Israel, for the judgment of YHWH, and for strife; and they return to Jerusalem, ⁹and he lays a charge on them, saying, "Thus do you do in the fear of YHWH, in faithfulness, and with a perfect heart, ¹⁰and any strife that comes to you of your brothers who are dwelling in their cities, between blood and blood, between law and command, statutes, and judgments, then you have warned them and they do not become guilty before YHWH, and wrath has not been on you and on your brothers; thus do you do, and you are not guilty. ¹¹And behold, Amariah the head priest [is] over you for every matter of YHWH, and Zebadiah son of Ishmael, the leader of the house of Judah, [is] for every matter of the king, and the Levites [are] officers before you; be strong and do, and YHWH is with the good."

CHAPTER 20

¹And it comes to pass after this, the sons of Moab have come in, and the sons of Ammon, and with them of the peoples, to battle against Jehoshaphat. ²And [some] come in and declare [it] to Jehoshaphat, saying, "A great multitude has come against you from beyond the sea, from Aram, and behold, they [are] in Hazezon-Tamar—it [is] En-Gedi." ³And Jehoshaphat fears, and sets his face to seek for YHWH, and proclaims a fast over all Judah; ⁴and Judah is gathered to inquire of YHWH; also, from all the cities of Judah they have come to seek YHWH. ⁵And Jehoshaphat stands in the assembly of Judah and Jerusalem, in the house of YHWH, at the front of the new court, ⁶and says, "O YHWH, God of our fathers, are You not God in the heavens? Indeed, You are ruling over all kingdoms of the nations, and power and might [are] in Your hand, and there is none with You to station himself. ⁷Are You not our God? You have dispossessed the inhabitants of this land from before Your people Israel, and give it to the seed of Your friend Abraham for all time, ⁸and they dwell in it, and build a sanctuary in it for You, for Your Name, saying, ⁹If evil comes on us—sword, judgment, and pestilence, and famine—we stand before this house, and before You, for Your Name [is] in this house, and cry to You out of our distress, and You hear and save. ¹⁰And now, behold, sons of Ammon, and Moab, and Mount Seir, whom You did not grant to Israel to go in against in their coming out of the land of Egypt, for they turned aside from off them and did not destroy them, ¹¹and behold, they are repaying to us—to come to drive us out of Your possession that You have caused us to possess. ¹²O our God, do You not execute judgment on them? For there is no power in us before this great multitude that has come against us, and we do not know what we do, but our eyes [are] on You." ¹³And all Judah is standing before YHWH, also their infants, their wives, and their sons. ¹⁴And the Spirit of YHWH has been on Jahaziel, son of Zechariah, son of Benaiah, son of Jeiel, son of Mattaniah, the Levite, of the sons of Asaph, in the midst of the assembly, ¹⁵and he says, "Attend, all Judah, and you inhabitants of Jerusalem, and O King Jehoshaphat, Thus said YHWH to you: You do not fear, nor be afraid of the face of this great multitude, for the battle [is] not for you, but for God. ¹⁶Tomorrow, go down against them, behold, they are coming up by the ascent of Ziz, and you have found them in the end of the valley, the front of the wilderness of Jeruel. ¹⁷[It is] not for you to fight in this; station yourselves, stand, and see the salvation of YHWH with you, O Judah and Jerusalem—do not be afraid nor fear—tomorrow go out before them, and YHWH [is] with you." ¹⁸And Jehoshaphat bows—face to the earth—and all Judah and the inhabitants of Jerusalem have fallen before YHWH, to bow themselves to YHWH. ¹⁹And the Levites, of the sons of the Kohathites, and of the sons of the Korahites, rise to give praise to YHWH, God of Israel, with a loud voice on high. ²⁰And they rise early in the morning, and go out to the wilderness of Tekoa, and in their going out Jehoshaphat has stood and says, "Hear me, O Judah and inhabitants of Jerusalem, remain steadfast in your God YHWH, and be steadfast; remain steadfast in His prophets and prosper." ²¹And he takes counsel with the people, and appoints singers for YHWH, and those giving praise for the honor of holiness, in the going out before the armed [men], and saying, "Give thanks to YHWH, for His kindness [is] for all time." ²²And at the time they have begun with singing and praise, YHWH has put ambushes against the sons of Ammon, Moab, and Mount Seir, who are coming in to Judah, and they are struck, ²³and the sons of Ammon stand up, and Moab, against the inhabitants of Mount Seir, to devote and to destroy, and at their finishing with the inhabitants of Seir, they helped, a man against his neighbor, to destroy. ²⁴And

Judah has come to the watchtower in the wilderness, and they look toward the multitude, and behold, they [are] carcasses fallen to the earth, and none [had] an escape, ²⁵and Jehoshaphat comes in, and his people, to seize their spoil, and they find among them, in abundance, both goods and carcasses, and desirable vessels, and they take spoil for themselves without prohibition, and they are seizing the spoil [for] three days, for it [is] abundant. ²⁶And on the fourth day they have been assembled at the Valley of Blessing, for there they blessed YHWH: therefore they have called the name of that place, "Valley of Blessing," to this day. ²⁷And they return, every man of Judah and Jerusalem, and Jehoshaphat at their head, to go back to Jerusalem with joy, for YHWH has made them rejoice over their enemies. ²⁸And they come to Jerusalem with psalteries, and with harps, and with trumpets, to the house of YHWH. ²⁹And there is a fear of God on all kingdoms of the lands in their hearing that YHWH has fought with the enemies of Israel, ³⁰and the kingdom of Jehoshaphat is quiet, and his God gives rest to him all around. ³¹And Jehoshaphat reigns over Judah, a son of thirty-five years in his reigning, and he has reigned twenty-five years in Jerusalem, and the name of his mother [is] Azubah daughter of Shilhi. ³²And he walks in the way of his father Asa, and has not turned aside from it, to do that which is right in the eyes of YHWH. ³³Only, the high places have not been removed, and still the people have not prepared their heart for the God of their fathers. ³⁴And the rest of the matters of Jehoshaphat, the first and the last, behold, they are written among the matters of Jehu son of Hanani, who has been mentioned on the scroll of the kings of Israel. ³⁵And after this Jehoshaphat king of Judah has joined himself with Ahaziah king of Israel (he did wickedly in doing [this]), ³⁶and he joins him with himself to make ships to go to Tarshish, and they make ships in Ezion-Geber, ³⁷and Eliezer son of Dodavah, of Mareshah, prophesies against Jehoshaphat, saying, "For your joining yourself with Ahaziah, YHWH has broken up your works"; and the ships are broken, and have not retained [power] to go to Tarshish.

CHAPTER 21

¹And Jehoshaphat lies with his fathers, and is buried with his fathers in the City of David, and his son Jehoram reigns in his stead. ²And he has brothers, sons of Jehoshaphat: Azariah, and Jehiel, and Zechariah, and Azariah, and Michael, and Shephatiah; all these [are] sons of Jehoshaphat king of Israel, ³and their father gives to them many gifts of silver and of gold, and of precious things, with fortified cities in Judah, and he has given the kingdom to Jehoram, for he [is] the firstborn. ⁴And Jehoram rises up over the kingdom of his father, and strengthens himself, and slays all his brothers with the sword, and also of the heads of Israel. ⁵Jehoram [is] a son of thirty-two years in his reigning, and he has reigned eight years in Jerusalem, ⁶and he walks in the way of the kings of Israel, as the house of Ahab did, for a daughter of Ahab has been to him for a wife, and he does evil in the eyes of YHWH, ⁷and YHWH has not been willing to destroy the house of David, for the sake of the covenant that He made with David, and as He had said to give a lamp to him and to his sons [for] all the days. ⁸In his days Edom has revolted from under the hand of Judah, and they cause a king to reign over them; ⁹and Jehoram passes over with his heads, and all the chariots with him, and it comes to pass, he has risen by night and strikes the Edomites who are coming around against him, and the princes of the chariots, ¹⁰and Edom revolts from under the hand of Judah to this day; then Libnah revolts at that time from under his hand, because he has forsaken YHWH, God of his fathers; ¹¹also, he has made high places on the mountains of Judah, and causes the inhabitants of Jerusalem to commit whoredom, and compels Judah. ¹²And a writing from Elijah the prophet comes to him, saying, "Thus said YHWH, God of your father David: Because that you have not walked in the ways of your father Jehoshaphat, and in the ways of Asa king of Judah, ¹³and you walk in the way of the kings of Israel, and cause Judah and the inhabitants of Jerusalem to commit whoredom like the whoredoms of the house of Ahab, and also your brothers, the house of your father, who are better than yourself, you have slain; ¹⁴behold, YHWH is striking [with] a great striking among your people, and among your sons, and among your wives, and among all your goods— ¹⁵and you, with many sicknesses, with disease of your bowels, until your bowels come out by the sickness, day by day." ¹⁶And YHWH wakes up against Jehoram the spirit of the Philistines and of the Arabians, who [are] beside the Cushim, ¹⁷and they come up into Judah, and break into it, and take captive all the substance that is found at the house of the king, and also his sons, and his wives, and there has not been left to him a son except Jehoahaz the youngest of his sons. ¹⁸And after all this YHWH has plagued him in his bowels by a disease for which there is no healing, ¹⁹and it comes to pass, from days to days, and at the time of the going out of the end of two years, his bowels have gone out with his sickness, and he dies of severe diseases, and his people have not made for him a burning like the burning of his fathers. ²⁰He was a son of thirty-two [years] in his reigning, and he has reigned eight years in Jerusalem, and he goes without desire, and they bury him in the City of David, and not in the graves of the kings.

CHAPTER 22

¹And the inhabitants of Jerusalem cause his youngest son Ahaziah to reign in his stead (for the troop had slain all the chiefly that came in with the Arabians to the camp), and Ahaziah son of Jehoram, king of Judah, reigns. ²Ahaziah [is] a son of twenty-two years in his reigning, and he has reigned one year in Jerusalem, and the name of his mother [is] Athaliah daughter of Omri; ³he has also walked in the ways of the house of Ahab, for his mother has been his counselor to do wickedly. ⁴And he does evil in the eyes of YHWH, like the house of Ahab, for they have been his counselors, after the death of his father, for destruction to him. ⁵Also, he has walked in their counsel, and goes with Jehoram son of Ahab, king of Israel, to battle against Hazael king of Aram in Ramoth-Gilead, and they of Ramah strike Joram; ⁶and he turns back to be healed in Jezreel because of the wounds with which they had struck him in Ramah, in his fighting with Hazael king of Aram. And Azariah son of Jehoram, king of Judah, has gone down to see Jehoram son of Ahab in Jezreel, for he [is] sick; ⁷and to come to Joram has been from God [for] the destruction of Ahaziah; and in his coming he has gone out with Jehoram to Jehu son of Nimshi, whom YHWH anointed to cut off the house of Ahab. ⁸And it comes to pass, in Jehu's executing judgment with the house of Ahab, that he finds the heads of Judah and sons of the brothers of Ahaziah, ministers of Ahaziah, and slays them. ⁹And he seeks Ahaziah, and they capture him (and he is hiding himself in Samaria), and bring him to Jehu, and put him to death, and bury him, for they said, "He [is] son of Jehoshaphat, who sought YHWH with all his heart"; and there is none of the house of Ahaziah to retain power for the kingdom. ¹⁰And Athaliah mother of Ahaziah has seen that her son is dead, and she rises and destroys the whole seed of the kingdom of the house of Judah. ¹¹And Jehoshabeath daughter of the king takes Joash son of Ahaziah, and steals him from the midst of the sons of the king who are put to death, and puts him and his nurse into the inner part of the bed-chambers, and Jehoshabeath daughter of King Jehoram, wife of Jehoiada the priest, because she has been sister of Ahaziah, hides him from the face of Athaliah, and she has not put him to death. ¹²And he is with them in the house of God hiding himself [for] six years, and Athaliah is reigning over the land.

CHAPTER 23

¹And in the seventh year Jehoiada has strengthened himself, and takes the heads of the hundreds, even Azariah son of Jeroham, and Ishmael son of Jehohanan, and Azariah son of Obed, and Maaseiah son of Adaiah, and Elishaphat son of Zichri, into the covenant with him. ²And they go around in Judah, and gather the Levites out of all the cities of Judah, and heads of the fathers of Israel, and come to Jerusalem, ³and all the assembly make a covenant in the house of God with the king, and he says to them, "Behold, the son of the king reigns, as YHWH spoke concerning the sons of David. ⁴This [is] the thing that you do: the third of you, going in on the Sabbath, of the priests, and of the Levites, [are] for gatekeepers of the thresholds, ⁵and the third [are] at the house of the king, and the third at the Foundation Gate, and all the people [are] in the courts of the house of YHWH. ⁶And none enter the house of YHWH except the priests, and those ministering of the Levites (they go in for they [are] holy), and all the people keep the watch of YHWH; ⁷and the Levites have

surrounded the king all around, each with his weapon in his hand, and he who has gone into the house is put to death; and be with the king in his coming in and in his going out." ⁸And the Levites and all Judah do according to all that Jehoiada the priest has commanded, and each takes his men going in on the Sabbath, with those going out on the Sabbath, for Jehoiada the priest has not let away the divisions. ⁹And Jehoiada the priest gives to the heads of the hundreds the spears, and the shields, and the bucklers that [are] King David's, that [are] in the house of God; ¹⁰and he stations the whole of the people, and each [with] his dart in his hand, from the right shoulder of the house to the left shoulder of the house, at the altar, and at the house, by the king, all around. ¹¹And they bring out the son of the king, and put the crown on him, and [give him] the Testimony, and cause him to reign; and Jehoiada and his sons anoint him, and say, "Let the king live!" ¹²And Athaliah hears the voice of the people who are running, and who are praising the king, and she comes to the people [in] the house of YHWH, ¹³and sees, and behold, the king is standing by his pillar in the entrance, and the heads, and the trumpets [are] by the king, and all the people of the land rejoicing and shouting with trumpets, and the singers with instruments of song, and the teachers, to praise, and Athaliah tears her garments and says, "Conspiracy! Conspiracy!" ¹⁴And Jehoiada the priest brings out the heads of the hundreds, inspectors of the force, and says to them, "Take her out from within the rows, and he who has gone after her is put to death by the sword"; for the priest said, "Do not put her to death [in] the house of YHWH." ¹⁵And they make sides for her, and she comes to the entrance of the Horse Gate at the house of the king, and they put her to death there. ¹⁶And Jehoiada makes a covenant between him, and between all the people, and between the king, to be for a people to YHWH; ¹⁷and all the people enter the house of Ba'al, and break it down, indeed, they have broken his altars and his images, and they have slain Mattan priest of Ba'al before the altars. ¹⁸And Jehoiada puts the offices of the house of YHWH into the hand of the priests, the Levites, whom David had apportioned over the house of YHWH, to cause the burnt-offerings of YHWH to ascend, as written in the Law of Moses, with joy, and with singing, by the hands of David; ¹⁹and he stations the gatekeepers over the gates of the house of YHWH, and the unclean in anything do not go in. ²⁰And he takes the heads of the hundreds, and the majestic ones, and the rulers among the people, and all the people of the land, and brings down the king from the house of YHWH, and they come in through the high gate to the house of the king, and cause the king to sit on the throne of the kingdom. ²¹And all the people of the land rejoice, and the city has been quiet, and they have put Athaliah to death by the sword.

CHAPTER 24

¹Joash [is] a son of seven years in his reigning, and he has reigned forty years in Jerusalem, and the name of his mother [is] Zibiah of Beer-Sheba. ²And Joash does that which is right in the eyes of YHWH all the days of Jehoiada the priest. ³And Jehoiada takes two wives for him, and he begets sons and daughters. ⁴And it comes to pass after this, it has been with the heart of Joash to renew the house of YHWH, ⁵and he gathers the priests and the Levites, and says to them, "Go out to the cities of Judah, and gather money from all Israel to strengthen the house of your God sufficiently year by year, and you, hurry to the matter"; and the Levites have not hurried. ⁶And the king calls for Jehoiada the head and says to him, "Why have you not required of the Levites to bring in out of Judah and out of Jerusalem the tribute of Moses, servant of YHWH, and of the assembly of Israel, for the Tent of the Testimony? ⁷For sons of Athaliah, the wicked one, have broken up the house of God, and also, they have prepared all the holy things of the house of YHWH for Ba'alim." ⁸And the king commands, and they make one chest, and put it at the gate of the house of YHWH outside, ⁹and give an intimation in Judah and in Jerusalem to bring to YHWH the tribute of Moses, servant of God, [laid] on Israel in the wilderness. ¹⁰And all the heads, and all the people rejoice, and they bring in, and cast into the chest, to completion. ¹¹And it comes to pass, at the time one brings in the chest for the inspection of the king by the hand of the Levites, and at their seeing that the money [is] abundant, that a scribe of the king has come in, and an officer of the head-priest, and they empty the chest, and take it up and turn it back to its place; thus they have done day by day, and gather money in abundance. ¹²And the king and Jehoiada give it to the doers of the work of the service of the house of YHWH, and they are hiring hewers and craftsmen to renew the house of YHWH, and also—to craftsmen in iron and bronze to strengthen the house of YHWH. ¹³And those doing the business work, and there goes up lengthening to the work by their hand, and they establish the house of God by its proper measure, and strengthen it. ¹⁴And at their completing [it], they have brought in the rest of the money before the king and Jehoiada, and they make [with] it vessels for the house of YHWH, vessels of serving, and of offering up, and spoons, even vessels of gold and silver; and they are causing burnt-offerings to ascend in the house of YHWH continually, all the days of Jehoiada. ¹⁵And Jehoiada is aged and satisfied with days, and dies—a son of one hundred and thirty years in his death, ¹⁶and they bury him in the City of David with the kings, for he has done good in Israel, and with God and his house. ¹⁷And after the death of Jehoiada, heads of Judah have come in, and bow themselves to the king; then the king has listened to them, ¹⁸and they forsake the house of YHWH, God of their fathers, and serve the Asherim and the idols, and there is wrath on Judah and Jerusalem for this guilt of theirs. ¹⁹And He sends among them prophets, to bring them back to YHWH, and they testify against them, and they have not given ear; ²⁰and the Spirit of God has clothed Zechariah son of Jehoiada the priest, and he stands above the people, and says to them, "Thus said God: Why are you transgressing the commands of YHWH, and do not prosper? Because you have forsaken YHWH, He forsakes you." ²¹And they conspire against him, and stone him [with] stone by the command of the king, in the court of the house of YHWH, ²²and Joash the king has not remembered the kindness that his father Jehoiada did with him, and slays his son, and in his death he said, "YHWH sees and requires." ²³And it comes to pass, at the turn of the year, the force of Aram has come up against him, and they come to Judah and Jerusalem, and destroy all the heads of the people from the people, and they have sent all their spoil to the king of Damascus, ²⁴for with few men the force of Aram has come in, and YHWH has given into their hand a mighty force for multitude, because they have forsaken YHWH, God of their fathers; and they have executed judgments with Joash. ²⁵And in their going from him—for they left him with many diseases—his servants themselves have conspired against him for the blood of the sons of Jehoiada the priest, and slay him on his bed, and he dies; and they bury him in the City of David, and have not buried him in the graves of the kings. ²⁶And these [are] those conspiring against him: Zabad son of Shimeath the Ammonitess, and Jehozabad son of Shimrith the Moabitess. ²⁷As for his sons, and the greatness of the burden on him, and the foundation of the house of God, behold, they are written on the commentary of the scroll of the Kings; and his son Amaziah reigns in his stead.

CHAPTER 25

¹Amaziah [was] a son of twenty-five years [when] he has reigned, and he has reigned twenty-nine years in Jerusalem, and the name of his mother [is] Jehoaddan of Jerusalem, ²and he does that which is right in the eyes of YHWH—only, not with a perfect heart. ³And it comes to pass, when the kingdom has been strong on him, that he slays his servants, those striking his father the king, ⁴and he has not put their sons to death, but [did] as is written in the Law, in the Scroll of Moses, whom YHWH commanded, saying, "Fathers do not die for sons, and sons do not die for fathers, but they each die for his own sin." ⁵And Amaziah gathers Judah and appoints them according to the house of the fathers, for heads of the thousands and for heads of the hundreds, for all Judah and Benjamin; and he inspects them from a son of twenty years and upward, and finds them [to be] three hundred thousand chosen ones, going forth to the host, holding spear and buckler. ⁶And he hires out of Israel one hundred thousand mighty men of valor, with one hundred talents of silver; ⁷and a man of God has come to him, saying, "O king, the host of Israel does not go with you; for YHWH is not with Israel—all the sons of Ephraim; ⁸but if you are going, do [it], be strong for battle, God causes you to stumble before an enemy, for there is power in God to help, and

to cause to stumble." ⁹And Amaziah says to the man of God, "But what to do about the hundred talents that I have given to the troop of Israel?" And the man of God says, "YHWH has more to give to you than this." ¹⁰And Amaziah separates them, of the troop that has come to him from Ephraim, to go to their own place; and their anger burns mightily against Judah, and they return to their place in the heat of anger. ¹¹And Amaziah has strengthened himself, and leads his people, and goes to the Valley of Salt, and strikes ten thousand of the sons of Seir, ¹²And the sons of Judah have taken captive ten thousand alive, and they bring them to the top of the rock, and cast them from the top of the rock, and all of them have been broken. ¹³And the sons of the troop that Amaziah has sent back from going with him to battle—they rush against cities of Judah, from Samaria even to Beth-Horon, and strike three thousand of them, and seize much prey. ¹⁴And it comes to pass after the coming in of Amaziah from striking the Edomites, that he brings in the gods of the sons of Seir, and establishes them for gods for himself, and bows himself before them, and he makes incense to them. ¹⁵And the anger of YHWH burns against Amaziah, and He sends a prophet to him, and he says to him, "Why have you sought the gods of the people that have not delivered their people out of your hand?" ¹⁶And it comes to pass, in his speaking to him, that he says to him, "Have we appointed you for a counselor to the king? For you [must] cease; why do they strike you?" And the prophet ceases and says, "I have known that God has counseled to destroy you, because you have done this and have not listened to my counsel." ¹⁷And Amaziah king of Judah takes counsel, and sends to Joash son of Jehoahaz, son of Jehu, king of Israel, saying, ¹⁸"Come, we look one another in the face." And Joash king of Israel sends to Amaziah king of Judah, saying, "The thorn that [is] in Lebanon has sent to the cedar that [is] in Lebanon, saying, Give your daughter to my son for a wife; and a beast of the field that [is] in Lebanon passes by and treads down the thorn. ¹⁹You have said, Behold, I have struck Edom; and your heart has lifted you up to boast; now, abide in your house, why do you stir yourself up in evil, that you have fallen, you and Judah with you?" ²⁰And Amaziah has not listened, for it [is] from God in order to give them into [their] hand, because they have sought the gods of Edom; ²¹and Joash king of Israel goes up, and they look one another in the face, he and Amaziah king of Judah, in Beth-Shemesh, that [is] Judah's, ²²and Judah is struck before Israel, and they flee—each to his tents. ²³And Joash king of Israel has caught Amaziah king of Judah, son of Joash, son of Jehoahaz, in Beth-Shemesh, and brings him to Jerusalem, and breaks down in the wall of Jerusalem from the Gate of Ephraim to the Corner Gate—four hundred cubits, ²⁴and [takes] all the gold, and the silver, and all the vessels that are found in the house of God with Obed-Edom, and the treasures of the house of the king, and the sons of the pledges, and turns back to Samaria. ²⁵And Amaziah son of Joash, king of Judah, lives after the death of Joash son of Jehoahaz, king of Israel, fifteen years; ²⁶and the rest of the matters of Amaziah, the first and the last, behold, are they not written on the scrolls of the kings of Judah and Israel? ²⁷And from the time that Amaziah has turned aside from after YHWH—they make a conspiracy against him in Jerusalem, and he flees to Lachish, and they send after him to Lachish, and put him to death there, ²⁸and lift him up on the horses, and bury him with his fathers in the city of Judah.

CHAPTER 26

¹And all the people of Judah take Uzziah (and he [is] a son of sixteen years), and cause him to reign instead of his father Amaziah. ²He has built Eloth, and restores it to Judah after the king's lying with his fathers. ³Uzziah [is] a son of sixteen years in his reigning, and he has reigned fifty-two years in Jerusalem, and the name of his mother [is] Jecholiah of Jerusalem. ⁴And he does that which is right in the eyes of YHWH, according to all that his father Amaziah did, ⁵and he is as one seeking God in the days of Zechariah who has understanding in visions of God: and in the days of his seeking YHWH, God has caused him to prosper. ⁶And he goes forth and fights with the Philistines, and breaks down the wall of Gath, and the wall of Jabneh, and the wall of Ashdod, and builds cities [around] Ashdod, and among the Philistines. ⁷And God helps him against the Philistines, and against the Arabians who are dwelling in Gur-Ba'al and the Mehunim. ⁸And the Ammonites give a present to Uzziah, and his name goes to the entering in of Egypt, for he strengthened himself greatly. ⁹And Uzziah builds towers in Jerusalem, by the Corner Gate, and by the Valley Gate, and by the angle, and strengthens them; ¹⁰and he builds towers in the wilderness, and digs many wells, for he had much livestock, both in the low country and in the plain, farmers and vinedressers in the mountains, and in Carmel; for he was a lover of the ground. ¹¹And Uzziah has a force making war, going forth to the host, by troops, in the number of their reckoning by the hand of Jeiel the scribe and Masseiah the officer, by the hand of Hananiah [one] of the heads of the king. ¹²The whole number of heads of the fathers of the mighty men of valor [is] two thousand and six hundred; ¹³and by their hand [is] the force of the host—three hundred thousand and seven thousand and five hundred warriors, with mighty power to give help to the king against the enemy. ¹⁴And Uzziah prepares for them, for all the host, shields, and spears, and helmets, and coats of mail, and bows, even to stones of the slings. ¹⁵And he makes inventions in Jerusalem—a device of an inventor—to be on the towers, and on the corners, to shoot with arrows and with great stones, and his name goes out to a distance, for he has been wonderfully helped until he has been strong. ¹⁶And at his being strong his heart has been high to destruction, and he trespasses against his God YHWH, and goes into the temple of YHWH to make incense on the altar of incense. ¹⁷And Azariah the priest goes in after him, and with him eighty priests of YHWH, sons of valor, ¹⁸and they stand up against Uzziah the king, and say to him, "[It is] not for you, O Uzziah, to make incense to YHWH, but for priests, sons of Aaron, who are sanctified to make incense; go forth from the sanctuary, for you have trespassed, indeed, for you [will] not [have] honor from YHWH God." ¹⁹And Uzziah is angry, and in his hand [is] a censer to make incense, and in his being angry with the priests—the leprosy has risen in his forehead, before the priests, in the house of YHWH, from beside the altar of incense. ²⁰And Azariah the head priest looks toward him, and all the priests, and behold, he [is] leprous in his forehead, and they hurry him there, and also he himself has hurried to go out, for YHWH has plagued him. ²¹And Uzziah the king is a leper to the day of his death, and inhabits a separate house—a leper, for he has been cut off from the house of YHWH, and his son Jotham [is] over the house of the king, judging the people of the land. ²²And the rest of the matters of Uzziah, the first and the last, Isaiah son of Amoz the prophet has written; ²³and Uzziah lies with his fathers, and they bury him with his fathers in the field of the burying-place that the kings have, for they said, "He [is] a leper"; and his son Jotham reigns in his stead.

CHAPTER 27

¹Jotham [is] a son of twenty-five years in his reigning, and he has reigned sixteen years in Jerusalem, and the name of his mother [is] Jerushah daughter of Zadok. ²And he does that which is right in the eyes of YHWH, according to all that his father Uzziah did; only, he has not come into the temple of YHWH; and again the people are doing corruptly. ³He has built the Upper Gate of the house of YHWH, and in the wall of Ophel he has built abundantly; ⁴and he has built cities in the hill-country of Judah, and he has built palaces and towers in the forests. ⁵And he has fought with the king of the sons of Ammon, and prevails over them, and the sons of Ammon give to him in that year one hundred talents of silver, and ten thousand cors of wheat, and ten thousand of barley; the sons of Ammon have returned this to him both in the second year and in the third. ⁶And Jotham strengthens himself, for he has prepared his ways before his God YHWH. ⁷And the rest of the matters of Jotham, and all his battles, and his ways, behold, they are written on the scroll of the kings of Israel and Judah. ⁸He was a son of twenty-five years in his reigning, and he has reigned sixteen years in Jerusalem; ⁹and Jotham lies with his fathers, and they bury him in the City of David, and his son Ahaz reigns in his stead.

CHAPTER 28

¹Ahaz [is] a son of twenty years in his reigning, and he has reigned sixteen years in Jerusalem, and he has not done that which is right in the eyes of YHWH, as his father David, ²and walks in the ways of the kings of Israel, and has also made molten images for Ba'alim, ³and has made incense himself in the Valley of the Son

of Hinnom, and burns his sons with fire according to the abominations of the nations that YHWH dispossessed from the presence of the sons of Israel, ⁴and sacrifices and makes incense in high places, and on the heights, and under every green tree. ⁵And his God YHWH gives him into the hand of the king of Aram, and they strike him, and take captive a great captivity from him, and bring [them] to Damascus, and he has also been given into the hand of the king of Israel, and he strikes him [with] a great striking. ⁶And Pekah son of Remaliah slays one hundred and twenty thousand in Judah in one day (the whole [are] sons of valor), because of their forsaking YHWH, God of their fathers. ⁷And Zichri, a mighty one of Ephraim, slays Maaseiah son of the king, and Azrikam leader of the house, and Elkanah second to the king. ⁸And the sons of Israel take captive of their brothers: two hundred thousand wives, sons, and daughters; and they have also seized much spoil from them, and they bring in the spoil to Samaria. ⁹And there has been a prophet of YHWH there (Oded [is] his name), and he goes out before the host that has come to Samaria, and says to them, "Behold, in the fury of YHWH, God of your fathers, against Judah, He has given them into your hand, and you slay among them in rage—it has come to the heavens; ¹⁰and now you are saying to subdue sons of Judah and Jerusalem for menservants and for maidservants for yourselves; but are there not causes of guilt with you before your God YHWH? ¹¹And now, hear me, and send back the captives whom you have taken captive of your brothers, for the heat of the anger of YHWH [is] on you." ¹²And certain of the heads of the sons of Ephraim (Azariah son of Johanan, Berechiah son of Meshillemoth, and Jehizkiah son of Shallum, and Amasa son of Hadlai), rise up against those coming in from the host, ¹³and say to them, "You do not bring in the captives here, for guilt against YHWH [is already] on us, you are saying to add to our sin and to our guilt. For abundant [is] the guilt we have, and the fierceness of anger on Israel." ¹⁴And the armed men leave the captives and the prey before the heads and all the assembly; ¹⁵and the men who have been expressed by name rise and take hold on the captives, and they have clothed all their naked ones from the spoil, indeed, they clothe them, and shoe them, and cause them to eat and drink, and anoint them, and lead them on donkeys, even every feeble one, and bring them to Jericho, the city of palms, near their brothers, and return to Samaria. ¹⁶At that time King Ahaz has sent to the king of Asshur to give help to him; ¹⁷and again the Edomites have come, and strike in Judah, and take captive a captivity. ¹⁸And the Philistines have rushed against the cities of the low country, and of the south of Judah, and capture Beth-Shemesh, and Aijalon, and Gederoth, and Shocho and its villages, and Timnah and its villages, and Gimzo and its villages, and dwell there, ¹⁹for YHWH has humbled Judah because of Ahaz king of Israel, for he made free with Judah, even to commit a trespass against YHWH. ²⁰And Tilgath-Pilneser king of Asshur comes to him, and does distress him, and has not strengthened him, ²¹though Ahaz has taken a portion [out] of the house of YHWH, and [out] of the house of the king, and of the princes, and gives to the king of Asshur, yet it is no help to him. ²²And in the time of his distress—he adds to trespass against YHWH (this King Ahaz), ²³and he sacrifices to the gods of Damascus [which were] those striking him, and says, "Because the gods of the kings of Aram are helping them, I sacrifice to them, and they help me," and they have been to him to cause him to stumble, and to all Israel. ²⁴And Ahaz gathers the vessels of the house of God, and cuts in pieces the vessels of the house of God, and shuts the doors of the house of YHWH, and makes altars for himself in every corner in Jerusalem. ²⁵And in each and every city of Judah he has made high places to make incense to other gods, and provokes YHWH, God of his fathers. ²⁶And the rest of his matters, and all his ways, the first and the last, behold, they are written on the scroll of the kings of Judah and Israel. ²⁷And Ahaz lies with his fathers, and they bury him in the city, in Jerusalem, but have not brought him to the graves of the kings of Israel, and his son Hezekiah reigns in his stead.

CHAPTER 29

¹Hezekiah [was] a son of twenty-five years [when] he has reigned, and he has reigned twenty-nine years in Jerusalem, and the name of his mother [is] Abijah daughter of Zechariah; ²and he does that which is right in the eyes of YHWH, according to all that his father David did. ³He, in the first year of his reign, in the first month, has opened the doors of the house of YHWH, and strengthens them, ⁴and brings in the priests and the Levites, and gathers them to the broad place to the east. ⁵And he says to them, "Hear me, O Levites, now sanctify yourselves, and sanctify the house of YHWH, God of your fathers, and bring out the impurity from the holy place, ⁶for our fathers have trespassed, and done that which is evil in the eyes of our God YHWH, and forsake him, and turn around their faces from the Dwelling Place of YHWH, and give the neck. ⁷They have also shut the doors of the porch, and quench the lamps, and they have not made incense, and have not caused burnt-offering to ascend in the holy place to the God of Israel, ⁸and the wrath of YHWH is on Judah and Jerusalem, and He gives them for a trembling, for an astonishment, and for a hissing, as you are seeing with your eyes. ⁹And behold, our fathers have fallen by the sword, and our sons, and our daughters, and our wives [are] in captivity for this. ¹⁰Now [it is] with my heart to make a covenant before YHWH, God of Israel, and the fierceness of His anger turns back from us. ¹¹My sons, do not be at rest now, for YHWH has fixed on you to stand before Him, to serve Him, and to be ministering and making incense to Him." ¹²And the Levites rise—Mahath son of Amasai, and Joel son of Azariah, of the sons of the Kohathite; and of the sons of Merari: Kish son of Abdi, and Azariah son of Jehalelel; and of the Gershonite: Joah son of Zimmah, and Eden son of Joah; ¹³and of the sons of Elizaphan: Shimri and Jeiel; and of the sons of Asaph: Zechariah and Mattaniah; ¹⁴and of the sons of Heman: Jehiel and Shimei; and of the sons of Jeduthun: Shemaiah and Uzziel— ¹⁵and they gather their brothers, and sanctify themselves, and come in, according to the command of the king in the matters of YHWH, to cleanse the house of YHWH, ¹⁶and the priests come into the inner part of the house of YHWH to cleanse [it], and bring out all the uncleanness that they have found in the temple of YHWH to the court of the house of YHWH, and the Levites receive [it], to take [it] out to the Brook of Kidron outside. ¹⁷And they begin to sanctify on the first of the first month, and on the eighth day of the month they have come to the porch of YHWH, and they sanctify the house of YHWH in eight days, and on the sixteenth day of the first month they have finished. ¹⁸And they come in to Hezekiah the king within, and say, "We have cleansed all the house of YHWH, and the altar of the burnt-offering, and all its vessels, and the table of the arrangement, and all its vessels, ¹⁹and all the vessels that King Ahaz cast away in his reign—in his trespass—we have prepared and sanctified, and behold, they [are] before the altar of YHWH." ²⁰And Hezekiah the king rises early, and gathers the heads of the city, and goes up to the house of YHWH; ²¹and they bring in seven bullocks, and seven rams, and seven lambs, and seven young male goats, for a sin-offering for the kingdom, and for the sanctuary, and for Judah; and he commands to sons of Aaron, the priests, to cause [them] to ascend on the altar of YHWH. ²²And they slaughter the oxen, and the priests receive the blood, and sprinkle on the altar; and they slaughter the rams, and sprinkle the blood on the altar; and they slaughter the lambs, and sprinkle the blood on the altar; ²³and they bring the male goats of the sin-offering near before the king and the assembly, and they lay their hands on them; ²⁴and the priests slaughter them, and make a sin-offering with their blood on the altar, to make atonement for all Israel, that "For all Israel," said the king, "[is] the burnt-offering and the sin-offering." ²⁵And he appoints the Levites in the house of YHWH with cymbals, with psalteries, and with harps, by the command of David, and of Gad, seer of the king, and of Nathan the prophet, for the command [is] by the hand of YHWH, by the hand of His prophets; ²⁶and the Levites stand with the instruments of David, and the priests with the trumpets. ²⁷And Hezekiah commands to cause the burnt-offering to ascend on the altar; and at the time the burnt-offering began, the song of YHWH began, and the trumpets, and with [the] hands of [the] instruments of David king of Israel. ²⁸And all the assembly are worshiping, and the singers singing, and the trumpeters blowing; the whole [is] until the completion of the burnt-offering. ²⁹And at the completion of the offering up, the king and all those found with him have bowed, and pay respect. ³⁰And Hezekiah the king

commands—and the princes—to the Levites [to cause them] to give praise to YHWH in the words of David, and of Asaph the seer, and they praise—to joy, and they bow, and pay respect. ³¹And Hezekiah answers and says, "Now you have filled your hand for YHWH, come near, and bring in sacrifices and thank-offerings to the house of YHWH"; and the assembly brings in sacrifices and thank-offerings, and every willing-hearted one—burnt-offerings. ³²And the number of the burnt-offerings that the assembly has brought in is seventy oxen, one hundred rams, [and] two hundred lambs; for all these [are] a burnt-offering to YHWH. ³³And the sanctified things [are] six hundred oxen and three thousand sheep. ³⁴Only, the priests have become few, and have not been able to strip the whole of the burnt-offerings, and their brothers the Levites strengthen them until the completion of the work, and until the priests sanctify themselves, for the Levites [are] more upright of heart to sanctify themselves than the priests. ³⁵And also, burnt-offerings [are] in abundance, with fat of the peace-offerings, and with oblations for the burnt-offering; and the service of the house of YHWH is established, ³⁶and Hezekiah and all the people rejoice because of God's giving preparation to the people, for the thing has been suddenly.

CHAPTER 30

¹And Hezekiah sends to all Israel and Judah, and he has also written letters to Ephraim and Manasseh, [to cause them] to come to the house of YHWH in Jerusalem, to make a Passover to YHWH, God of Israel. ²And the king takes counsel, and his heads, and all the assembly in Jerusalem, to make the Passover in the second month, ³for they have not been able to make it at that time, for the priests have not sanctified themselves sufficiently, and the people have not been gathered to Jerusalem. ⁴And the thing is right in the eyes of the king, and in the eyes of all the assembly, ⁵and they establish the thing, to cause an intimation to pass over into all Israel, from Beer-Sheba even to Dan, to come to make a Passover to YHWH, God of Israel, in Jerusalem; for they had not done as it is written for a long time. ⁶And the runners go with letters from the hand of the king and his heads into all Israel and Judah, even according to the command of the king, saying, "O sons of Israel, turn back to YHWH, God of Abraham, Isaac, and Israel, and He turns back to the escaped part that is left of you from the hand of the kings of Asshur; ⁷and do not be like your fathers and like your brothers, who trespassed against YHWH, God of their fathers, and He gives them to desolation, as you see. ⁸Now do not harden your neck like your fathers, give a hand to YHWH, and come into His sanctuary that He has sanctified for all time, and serve your God YHWH, and the fierceness of His anger turns back from you; ⁹for in your turning back to YHWH, your brothers and your sons have mercies before their captors, even to return to this land, for your God YHWH [is] gracious and merciful, and He does not turn aside the face from you if you turn back to Him." ¹⁰And the runners are passing over from city to city in the land of Ephraim and Manasseh, even to Zebulun, but they are laughing at them and mocking at them, ¹¹only, certain from Asher, and Manasseh, and from Zebulun, have been humbled, and come to Jerusalem. ¹²Also, in Judah the hand of God has been to give one heart to them to do the command of the king and of the heads in the matter of YHWH; ¹³and many people are gathered to Jerusalem to make the Celebration of Unleavened Things in the second month—a mighty assembly for multitude. ¹⁴And they arise and turn aside the altars that [are] in Jerusalem, and they have turned aside all the incense altars, and cast [them] into the Brook of Kidron; ¹⁵and they slaughter the Passover-offering on the fourteenth of the second month, and the priests and the Levites have been ashamed, and sanctify themselves, and bring in burnt-offerings to the house of YHWH. ¹⁶And they stand on their station according to their ordinance, according to the Law of Moses the man of God; the priests are sprinkling the blood out of the hand of the Levites, ¹⁷for many [are] in the assembly who have not sanctified themselves, and the Levites [are] over the slaughtering of the Passover-offerings for everyone not clean, to sanctify [him] to YHWH: ¹⁸for a multitude of the people, many from Ephraim, and Manasseh, Issachar, and Zebulun, have not been cleansed, but have eaten the Passover otherwise than it is written; but Hezekiah prayed for them, saying, "YHWH, who [is] good, receives atonement for everyone ¹⁹who has prepared his heart to seek God—YHWH, God of his fathers—yet not according to the cleansing of the holy place"; ²⁰and YHWH listens to Hezekiah and heals the people. ²¹And the sons of Israel, those found in Jerusalem, make the Celebration of Unleavened Things [for] seven days with great joy; and the Levites and the priests are giving praise to YHWH day by day with instruments of praise before YHWH. ²²And Hezekiah speaks to the heart of all the Levites, those giving good understanding concerning YHWH, and they eat the appointed thing [for] seven days; sacrificing sacrifices of peace-offerings, and making confession to YHWH, God of their fathers. ²³And all the assembly take counsel to keep [it] another seven days, and they keep [it for] seven days [with] joy; ²⁴for Hezekiah king of Judah has presented one thousand bullocks and seven thousand sheep to the assembly; and the heads have presented one thousand bullocks and ten thousand sheep to the assembly; and priests sanctify themselves in abundance. ²⁵And all the assembly of Judah rejoices, and the priests, and the Levites, and all the assembly, those coming in from Israel, and the sojourners—those coming in from the land of Israel and those dwelling in Judah, ²⁶and there is great joy in Jerusalem; for from the days of Solomon son of David, king of Israel, there is not like this in Jerusalem, ²⁷and the priests, the Levites, rise and bless the people, and their voice is heard, and their prayer comes into His holy habitation in the heavens.

CHAPTER 31

¹And at the completion of all this, all [those of] Israel who are found present have gone out to the cities of Judah, and break the standing-pillars, and cut down the Asherim, and break down the high places and the altars, out of all Judah and Benjamin, and in Ephraim and Manasseh, even to completion, and all the sons of Israel return, each to his possession, to their cities. ²And Hezekiah appoints the divisions of the priests and of the Levites, by their divisions, each according to his service, of the priests and of the Levites, for burnt-offering and for peace-offerings, to minister and to give thanks, and to give praise in the gates of the camps of YHWH. ³And a portion of the king, from his substance, [is] for burnt-offerings, for burnt-offerings of the morning and of the evening, and the burnt-offerings of Sabbaths, and of new moons, and of appointed times, as it is written in the Law of YHWH. ⁴And he commands to the people, to the inhabitants of Jerusalem, to give the portion of the priests and of the Levites, so that they are strengthened in the Law of YHWH; ⁵and at the spreading forth of the thing, the sons of Israel have multiplied the first-fruit of grain, new wine, and oil, and honey, and of all the increase of the field, and they have brought in the tithe of the whole in abundance. ⁶And the sons of Israel and Judah, those dwelling in cities of Judah, have also brought in a tithe of herd and flock, and a tithe of the holy things that are sanctified to their God YHWH, and they set [them in] heaps of heaps. ⁷In the third month they have begun to lay the foundation of the heaps, and in the seventh month they have finished. ⁸And Hezekiah and the heads come in and see the heaps, and bless YHWH and His people Israel, ⁹and Hezekiah inquires at the priests and the Levites concerning the heaps, ¹⁰and Azariah the head priest, of the house of Zadok, speaks to him and says, "From the beginning of the bringing of the raised-offering to the house of YHWH, [there is enough] to eat, and to be satisfied, and to leave abundantly, for YHWH has blessed His people, and that left [is] this store." ¹¹And Hezekiah commands to prepare chambers in the house of YHWH, and they prepare, ¹²and they bring in the raised-offering, and the tithe, and the holy things faithfully; and over them is a leader, Conaniah the Levite, and his brother Shimei [is] second; ¹³and Jehiel, and Azaziah, and Nahath, and Asahel, and Jerimoth, and Jozabad, and Eliel, and Ismachiah, and Mahath, and Benaiah, [are] inspectors under the hand of Conaniah and his brother Shimei, by the appointment of Hezekiah the king, and Azariah leader of the house of God. ¹⁴And Kore son of Imnah the Levite, the gatekeeper at the east, [is] over the willing-offerings of God, to give the raised-offering of YHWH, and the most holy things. ¹⁵And by his hand [are] Eden, and Miniamin, and Jeshua, and Shemaiah, Amariah, and Shechaniah, in cities of the priests, faithfully to give to their brothers in

divisions, as the great so the small, ¹⁶apart from their genealogy, to males from a son of three years and upward, to everyone who has gone into the house of YHWH, by the matter of a day in its day, for their service in their charges, according to their divisions; ¹⁷and the genealogy of the priests by the house of their fathers, and of the Levites, from a son of twenty years and upward, in their charges, in their divisions; ¹⁸and to the genealogy among all their infants, their wives, and their sons, and their daughters to all the congregation, for in their faithfulness they sanctify themselves in holiness. ¹⁹And for sons of Aaron, the priests, in the fields of the outskirt of their cities, in each and every city, [are] men who have been defined by name, to give portions to every male among the priests, and to everyone who reckoned himself by genealogy among the Levites. ²⁰And Hezekiah does thus in all Judah, and does that which is good, and that which is right, and that which is true, before his God YHWH; ²¹and in every work that he has begun for the service of the house of God, and for the Law, and for the command, to seek for his God with all his heart, he has worked and prospered.

CHAPTER 32

¹After these things and this truth, Sennacherib king of Asshur has come, indeed, he comes to Judah, and encamps against the cities of the bulwarks, and says to break into them himself. ²And Hezekiah sees that Sennacherib has come, and his face [is] to the battle against Jerusalem, ³and he takes counsel with his heads and his mighty ones, to stop the waters of the fountains that [are] at the outside of the city—and they help him, ⁴and many people are gathered, and they stop all the fountains and the brook that is rushing into the midst of the land, saying, "Why do the kings of Asshur come, and have found much water?" ⁵And he strengthens himself, and builds the whole of the wall that is broken, and causes [it] to ascend to the towers, and at the outside of the wall [builds] another, and strengthens Millo [in] the City of David, and makes darts in abundance, and shields. ⁶And he puts heads of war over the people, and gathers them to him, to the broad place of a gate of the city, and speaks to their heart, saying, ⁷"Be strong and courageous, do not be afraid, nor be cast down from the face of the king of Asshur, and from the face of all the multitude that [is] with him, for with us [are] more than with him. ⁸With him [is] an arm of flesh, but with us [is] our God YHWH to help us and to fight our battles"; and the people are supported by the words of Hezekiah king of Judah. ⁹After this Sennacherib king of Asshur has sent his servants to Jerusalem—and he [is] by Lachish, and all his power with him—against Hezekiah king of Judah and against all Judah who [are] in Jerusalem, saying, ¹⁰"Thus said Sennacherib king of Asshur: On what are you trusting and abiding in the bulwark in Jerusalem? ¹¹Is Hezekiah not persuading you to give you up to die by famine and by thirst, saying, Our God YHWH delivers us from the hand of the king of Asshur? ¹²Has Hezekiah himself not turned aside His high places and His altars, and speaks to Judah and to Jerusalem, saying, You bow yourselves before one altar and you make incense on it? ¹³Do you not know what I have done—I and my fathers—to all peoples of the lands? Were the gods of the nations of the lands at all able to deliver their land out of my hand? ¹⁴Who among all the gods of these nations whom my fathers have devoted to destruction [is] he who has been able to deliver his people out of my hand, that your God is able to deliver you out of my hand? ¹⁵And now, do not let Hezekiah lift you up, nor persuade you thus, nor give credence to him, for no god of any nation and kingdom is able to deliver his people from my hand and from the hand of my fathers: also, surely your God does not deliver you from my hand!" ¹⁶And again his servants have spoken against YHWH God and against His servant Hezekiah, ¹⁷and he has written letters to give reproach to YHWH, God of Israel, and to speak against Him, saying, "As the gods of the nations of the lands that have not delivered their people from my hand, so the God of Hezekiah does not deliver His people from my hand." ¹⁸And they call with a great voice [in] Jewish against the people of Jerusalem who [are] on the wall, to frighten them and to trouble them, that they may capture the city, ¹⁹and they speak against the God of Jerusalem as against the gods of the peoples of the land—work of the hands of man. ²⁰And Hezekiah the king prays, and Isaiah son of Amoz the prophet, concerning this, and they cry to the heavens, ²¹and YHWH sends a messenger and cuts off every mighty man of valor—both leader and head—in the camp of the king of Asshur, and he turns back with shame of face to his land and enters the house of his god, and those coming out of his bowels have caused him to fall there by the sword. ²²And YHWH saves Hezekiah and the inhabitants of Jerusalem from the hand of Sennacherib king of Asshur and from the hand of all, and He leads them around; ²³and many are bringing in an offering to YHWH, to Jerusalem, and precious things to Hezekiah king of Judah, and he is lifted up before the eyes of all the nations after this. ²⁴In those days Hezekiah has been sick even to death, and he prays to YHWH, and He speaks to him and has appointed a wonder for him; ²⁵and Hezekiah has not returned according to the deed [done] to him, for his heart has been lofty, and there is wrath on him and on Judah and Jerusalem; ²⁶and Hezekiah is humbled for the loftiness of his heart, he and the inhabitants of Jerusalem, and the wrath of YHWH has not come on them in the days of Hezekiah. ²⁷And Hezekiah has very much riches and honor, and he has made treasures for himself of silver, and of gold, and of precious stone, and of spices, and of shields, and of all [kinds] of desirable vessels, ²⁸and storehouses for the increase of grain, and new wine, and oil, and stalls for all kinds of livestock, and herds for stalls; ²⁹and he has made cities for himself, and possessions of flocks and herds in abundance, for God has given very much substance to him. ³⁰And Hezekiah himself has stopped the upper source of the waters of Gihon, and directs them beneath to the west of the City of David, and Hezekiah prospers in all his work; ³¹and so with the ambassadors of the heads of Babylon, those sending to him to inquire of the wonder that has been in the land, God has left him to try him, to know all in his heart. ³²And the rest of the matters of Hezekiah and his kind acts, behold, they are written in the vision of Isaiah son of Amoz the prophet, on the scroll of the kings of Judah and Israel. ³³And Hezekiah lies with his fathers, and they bury him in the highest of the graves of the sons of David, and all Judah and the inhabitants of Jerusalem have done honor to him at his death, and his son Manasseh reigns in his stead.

CHAPTER 33

¹Manasseh is a son of twelve years in his reigning, and he has reigned fifty-five years in Jerusalem; ²and he does evil in the eyes of YHWH, like the abominations of the nations that YHWH dispossessed from the presence of the sons of Israel, ³and he turns and builds the high places that his father Hezekiah has broken down, and raises altars for Ba'alim, and makes Asherim, and bows himself to all the host of the heavens, and serves them. ⁴And he has built altars in the house of YHWH of which YHWH had said, "My Name is in Jerusalem for all time." ⁵And he builds altars for all the host of the heavens in the two courts of the house of YHWH. ⁶And he has caused his sons to pass over through fire in the Valley of the Son of Hinnom, and observed clouds and used enchantments and witchcraft, and dealt with a familiar spirit, and a wizard; he has multiplied to do evil in the eyes of YHWH, to provoke him to anger. ⁷And he places the carved image of the idol that he made in the house of God, of which God said to David, and to his son Solomon, "In this house, and in Jerusalem that I have chosen out of all the tribes of Israel, I put My Name for all time, ⁸and I do not add to turn aside the foot of Israel from off the ground that I appointed to your fathers, only, if they watch to do all that I have commanded them—to all the Law, and the statutes, and the ordinances by the hand of Moses." ⁹And Manasseh causes Judah and the inhabitants of Jerusalem to err, to do evil above the nations that YHWH destroyed from the presence of the sons of Israel. ¹⁰And YHWH speaks to Manasseh and to his people, and they have not attended, ¹¹and YHWH brings in against them the heads of the host that the king of Asshur has, and they capture Manasseh among the thickets, and bind him with bronze chains, and cause him to go to Babylon. ¹²And when he is in distress he has appeased the face of his God YHWH, and is exceedingly humbled before the God of his fathers, ¹³and prays to Him, and He accepts his plea, and hears his supplication, and brings him back to Jerusalem, to his kingdom, and Manasseh knows that He, YHWH, [is] God. ¹⁴And after this he has built an outer wall for

the City of David, on the west of Gihon, in the valley, and at the entering in at the Fish Gate, and it has gone around to the tower, and he makes it exceedingly high, and he puts heads of the force in all the cities of the bulwarks in Judah. ¹⁵And he turns aside the gods of the stranger, and the idol, out of the house of YHWH, and all the altars that he had built on the mountain of the house of YHWH and in Jerusalem, and casts [them] to the outside of the city. ¹⁶And he builds the altar of YHWH, and sacrifices on it sacrifices of peace-offerings and thank-offering, and commands to Judah to serve YHWH, God of Israel; ¹⁷but still the people are sacrificing in high places, only—to their God YHWH. ¹⁸And the rest of the matters of Manasseh, and his prayer to his God, and the matters of the seers, those speaking to him in the Name of YHWH, God of Israel, behold, they are [on the scroll of] the matters of the kings of Israel; ¹⁹and his prayer, and his plea, and all his sin, and his trespass, and the places in which he had built high places, and established the Asherim and the carved images before his being humbled, behold, they are written beside the matters of Hozai. ²⁰And Manasseh lies with his fathers, and they bury him in his own house, and his son Amon reigns in his stead. ²¹Amon [is] a son of twenty-two years in his reigning, and he has reigned two years in Jerusalem, ²²and he does evil in the eyes of YHWH, as his father Manasseh did, and Amon has sacrificed to all the carved images that his father Manasseh had made, and serves them, ²³and has not been humbled before YHWH, like the humbling of his father Manasseh, for Amon himself has multiplied guilt. ²⁴And his servants conspire against him and put him to death in his own house, ²⁵and the people of the land strike all those conspiring against King Amon, and the people of the land cause his son Josiah to reign in his stead.

CHAPTER 34

¹Josiah [is] a son of eight years in his reigning, and he has reigned thirty-one years in Jerusalem, ²and he does that which is right in the eyes of YHWH, and walks in the ways of his father David, and has not turned aside [to] the right or left. ³And in the eighth year of his reign (and he [is] yet a youth), he has begun to seek for the God of his father David, and in the twelfth year he has begun to cleanse Judah and Jerusalem from the high places, and the Asherim, and the carved images, and the molten images. ⁴And they break down the altars of the Ba'alim before him, and he has cut down the images that [are] on high above them, and the Asherim, and the carved images, and the molten images, he has broken and beaten small, and strews [them] on the surface of the graves of those sacrificing to them, ⁵and he has burned the bones of the priests on their altars, and cleanses Judah and Jerusalem, ⁶and in the cities of Manasseh, and Ephraim, and Simeon, even to Naphtali, with their tools, all around. ⁷And he breaks down the altars and the Asherim, and he has beaten down the carved images very small, and he has cut down all the images in all the land of Israel, and turns back to Jerusalem. ⁸And in the eighteenth year of his reign, to purify the land and the house, he has sent Shaphan son of Azaliah, and Maaseiah head of the city, and Joah son of Johaz the remembrancer, to strengthen the house of his God YHWH. ⁹And they come to Hilkiah the high priest, and they give the money that is brought into the house of God, that the Levites, keeping the threshold, have gathered from the hand of Manasseh, and Ephraim, and from all the remnant of Israel, and from all Judah, and Benjamin, and the inhabitants of Jerusalem, ¹⁰and they give [it] into the hand of the workmen, those appointed over the house of YHWH, and they give it [to] the workmen who are working in the house of YHWH, to repair and to strengthen the house; ¹¹and they give [it] to craftsmen and to builders to buy hewn stones, and wood for couplings and for beams [for] the houses that the kings of Judah had destroyed. ¹²And the men are working faithfully in the business, and over them are appointed Jahath and Obadiah, the Levites, of the sons of Merari, and Zechariah and Meshullam, of the sons of the Kohathite, to overlook; and of the Levites, everyone understanding about instruments of song, ¹³and over the burden-bearers, and overseers of everyone doing work for every service; and of the Levites [are] scribes, and officers, and gatekeepers. ¹⁴And in their bringing out the money that is brought into the house of YHWH, Hilkiah the priest has found the Scroll of the Law of YHWH by the hand of Moses, ¹⁵and Hilkiah answers and says to Shaphan the scribe, "I have found [the] Scroll of the Law in the house of YHWH"; and Hilkiah gives the scroll to Shaphan, ¹⁶and Shaphan brings in the scroll to the king, and brings the king back word again, saying, "All that has been given into the hand of your servants they are doing, ¹⁷and they pour out the money that is found in the house of YHWH, and give it into the hand of those appointed and into the hands of those doing the work." ¹⁸And Shaphan the scribe declares [it] to the king, saying, "Hilkiah the priest has given a scroll to me"; and Shaphan reads in it before the king. ¹⁹And it comes to pass, at the king's hearing the words of the Law, that he tears his garments, ²⁰and the king commands Hilkiah, and Ahikam son of Shaphan, and Abdon son of Micah, and Shaphan the scribe, and Asaiah, servant of the king, saying, ²¹"Go, seek YHWH for me, and for him who is left in Israel and in Judah, concerning the words of the scroll that is found, for great [is] the fury of YHWH that is poured on us, because that our fathers did not keep the word of YHWH to do according to all that is written on this scroll." ²²And Hilkiah goes, and they of the king, to Huldah the prophetess, wife of Shallum son of Tikvath, son of Hasrah, keeper of the garments, and she is dwelling in Jerusalem in the Second [Quarter], and they speak to her thus. ²³And she says to them, "Thus said YHWH, God of Israel: Say to the man who has sent you to me, ²⁴Thus said YHWH: Behold, I am bringing in calamity on this place and on its inhabitants, all the execrations that are written on the scroll that they read before the king of Judah, ²⁵because that they have forsaken Me, and make incense to other gods, so as to provoke Me with all the works of their hands, and My fury is poured out on this place, and it is not quenched. ²⁶And to the king of Judah who is sending you to inquire of YHWH, thus you say to him, Thus said YHWH God of Israel, whose words you have heard: ²⁷Because your heart [is] tender, and you are humbled before God in your hearing His words concerning this place and concerning its inhabitants, and are humbled before Me, and tear your garments, and weep before Me, indeed, I have also heard [you]—a declaration of YHWH. ²⁸Behold, I am gathering you to your fathers, and you have been gathered to your graves in peace, and your eyes do not look on all the calamity that I am bringing on this place and on its inhabitants"; and they bring the king back word. ²⁹And the king sends and gathers all the elderly of Judah and Jerusalem, ³⁰and the king goes up to the house of YHWH, and [to] every man of Judah, and the inhabitants of Jerusalem, and the priests, and the Levites, even all the people, from great even to small, and he reads in their ears all the words of the scroll of the covenant that is found in the house of YHWH. ³¹And the king stands on his station, and makes the covenant before YHWH to walk after YHWH, and to keep His commands, and His testimonies, and His statutes, with all his heart and with all his soul, to do the words of the covenant that are written on this scroll. ³²And he presents everyone who is found in Jerusalem and Benjamin, and the inhabitants of Jerusalem do according to the covenant of God, the God of their fathers. ³³And Josiah turns aside all the abominations out of all the lands that the sons of Israel have, and causes everyone who is found in Israel to serve, to serve their God YHWH; all his days they did not turn aside from after YHWH, God of their fathers.

CHAPTER 35

¹And Josiah makes a Passover to YHWH in Jerusalem, and they slaughter the Passover-offering on the fourteenth of the first month, ²and he stations the priests over their charges, and strengthens them for the service of the house of YHWH, ³and says to the Levites who are teaching all Israel, who are sanctified to YHWH, "Put the holy Ark in the house that Solomon son of David, king of Israel, built; it is not a burden on the shoulder to you. Now serve your God YHWH and His people Israel, ⁴and prepare, by the house of your fathers, according to your divisions, by the writing of David king of Israel, and by the writing of his son Solomon, ⁵and stand in the holy place, by the divisions of the house of the fathers of your brothers, sons of the people, and the portion of the house of a father of the Levites, ⁶and slaughter the Passover-offering and sanctify yourselves, and prepare for your brothers, to do according to the word of YHWH by the hand of Moses." ⁷And Josiah lifts up to the sons of the people a flock of lambs and young goats, the

whole for Passover-offerings, for everyone who is found, to the number of thirty thousand, and three thousand oxen: these [are] from the substance of the king. ⁸And his heads, for a willing-offering to the people, to the priests and to the Levites, have lifted up; Hilkiah, and Zechariah, and Jehiel, leaders in the house of God, have given two thousand and six hundred to the priests for Passover-offerings, and three hundred oxen; ⁹and Conaniah, and Shemaiah, and Nethaneel, his brothers, and Hashabiah, and Jeiel, and Jozabad, heads of the Levites, have lifted up five thousand to the Levites for Passover-offerings, and five hundred oxen. ¹⁰And the service is prepared, and the priests stand on their station, and the Levites on their divisions, according to the command of the king, ¹¹and they slaughter the Passover-offering, and the priests sprinkle out of their hand, and the Levites are stripping [them]; ¹²and they turn aside the burnt-offering to put them by the divisions of the house of the fathers of the sons of the people, to bring near to YHWH, as it is written in the scroll of Moses—and so for the oxen. ¹³And they cook the Passover with fire according to the ordinance, and they have cooked the sanctified things in pots, and in kettles, and in pans—for all the sons of the people. ¹⁴And afterward they have prepared for themselves and for the priests; for the priests, sons of Aaron, [are occupied] in the offering up of the burnt-offering and of the fat until night; and the Levites have prepared for themselves and for the priests, sons of Aaron. ¹⁵And the singers, sons of Asaph, [are] on their station according to the command of David, and Asaph, and Heman, and Jeduthun seer of the king, and the gatekeepers [are] at every gate; it is not for them to turn aside from off their service, for their brothers the Levites have prepared for them. ¹⁶And all the service of YHWH is prepared on that day to keep the Passover and to cause burnt-offering to ascend on the altar of YHWH, according to the command of King Josiah. ¹⁷And the sons of Israel who are found make the Passover at that time, and the Celebration of Unleavened Things, [for] seven days. ¹⁸And there has not been made a Passover like it in Israel from the days of Samuel the prophet, and none of the kings of Israel made such a Passover as Josiah has made, and the priests, and the Levites, and all Judah and Israel who are found, and the inhabitants of Jerusalem. ¹⁹In the eighteenth year of the reign of Josiah this Passover has been made. ²⁰After all this, when Josiah has prepared the house, Necho king of Egypt has come up to fight against Carchemish by the Euphrates, and Josiah goes forth to meet him; ²¹and he sends messengers to him, saying, "And what do I [have to do] with you, O king of Judah? I do not come against you today, but to the house with which I have war, and God commanded to hurry me; cease for yourself from God who [is] with me, and He does not destroy you." ²²And Josiah has not turned around his face from him, but has disguised himself to fight against him, and has not listened to the words of Necho, from the mouth of God, and comes to fight in the Valley of Megiddo; ²³and the archers shoot at King Josiah, and the king says to his servants, "Remove me, for I have become very sick." ²⁴And his servants remove him from the chariot, and cause him to ride on the second chariot that he has, and cause him to go to Jerusalem, and he dies, and is buried in the graves of his fathers, and all Judah and Jerusalem are mourning for Josiah, ²⁵and Jeremiah laments for Josiah, and all the male and female singers speak in their lamentations of Josiah to this day, and set them for a statute on Israel, and behold, they are written beside the Lamentations. ²⁶And the rest of the matters of Josiah and his kind acts, according as it is written in the Law of YHWH, ²⁷even his matters, the first and the last, behold, they are written on the scroll of the kings of Israel and Judah.

CHAPTER 36

¹And the people of the land take Jehoahaz son of Josiah and cause him to reign instead of his father in Jerusalem. ²Jehoahaz [is] a son of twenty-three years in his reigning, and he has reigned three months in Jerusalem, ³and the king of Egypt turns him aside in Jerusalem, and fines the land one hundred talents of silver, and a talent of gold; ⁴and the king of Egypt causes his brother Eliakim to reign over Judah and Jerusalem, and turns his name to Jehoiakim; and Necho has taken his brother Jehoahaz and brings him to Egypt. ⁵Jehoiakim [is] a son of twenty-five years in his reigning, and he has reigned eleven years in Jerusalem, and he does evil in the eyes of his God YHWH; ⁶Nebuchadnezzar king of Babylon has come up against him, and binds him in bronze chains to take him away to Babylon. ⁷And Nebuchadnezzar has brought from the vessels of the house of YHWH to Babylon, and puts them in his temple in Babylon. ⁸And the rest of the matters of Jehoiakim, and his abominations that he has done, and that which is found against him, behold, they are written on the scroll of the kings of Israel and Judah, and his son Jehoiachin reigns in his stead. ⁹Jehoiachin [is] a son of eight years in his reigning, and he has reigned three months and ten days in Jerusalem, and he does evil in the eyes of YHWH; ¹⁰and at the turn of the year King Nebuchadnezzar has sent and brings him to Babylon with the desirable vessels of the house of YHWH, and causes his brother Zedekiah to reign over Judah and Jerusalem. ¹¹Zedekiah [is] a son of twenty-one years in his reigning, and he has reigned eleven years in Jerusalem; ¹²and he does evil in the eyes of his God YHWH, he has not been humbled before Jeremiah the prophet [speaking] from the mouth of YHWH; ¹³and he has also rebelled against King Nebuchadnezzar who had caused him to swear by God, and he hardens his neck and strengthens his heart against turning back to YHWH, God of Israel. ¹⁴Also, all the heads of the priests and the people have multiplied to commit a trespass according to all the abominations of the nations, and they defile the house of YHWH that He has sanctified in Jerusalem. ¹⁵And YHWH, God of their fathers, sends to them by the hand of His messengers—rising early and sending—for He has had pity on His people and on His habitation, ¹⁶but they are mocking at the messengers of God, and despising His words, and acting deceitfully with His prophets, until the going up of the fury of YHWH against His people—until there is no healing. ¹⁷And He causes the king of the Chaldeans to go up against them, and he slays their chosen ones by the sword in the house of their sanctuary, and has had no pity on young man and virgin, old man and very aged—He has given the whole into his hand. ¹⁸And all the vessels of the house of God, the great and the small, and the treasures of the house of YHWH, and the treasures of the king and of his princes—he has brought the whole to Babylon. ¹⁹And they burn the house of God, and break down the wall of Jerusalem, and they have burned all its palaces with fire, and all its desirable vessels—to destruction. ²⁰And he removes those left of the sword to Babylon, and they are to him and to his sons for servants, until the reigning of the kingdom of Persia, ²¹to fulfill the word of YHWH in the mouth of Jeremiah, until the land has enjoyed its Sabbaths; all the days of the desolation it kept Sabbath—to the fullness of seventy years. ²²And in the first year of Cyrus king of Persia, at the completion of the word of YHWH in the mouth of Jeremiah, YHWH has awoken the spirit of Cyrus king of Persia, and he causes an intimation to pass over into all his kingdom, and also in writing, saying, ²³"Thus said Cyrus king of Persia: YHWH, God of the heavens, has given all kingdoms of the earth to me, and He has laid a charge on me to build a house for Him in Jerusalem which [is] in Judah; who is among you of all His people? His God YHWH [is] with him, and he goes up!"

EZRA

CHAPTER 1

¹And in the first year of Cyrus king of Persia, at the completion of the word of YHWH from the mouth of Jeremiah, has YHWH awoken the spirit of Cyrus king of Persia, and he causes an intimation to pass over into all his kingdom, and also in writing, saying, ²"Thus said Cyrus king of Persia: YHWH, God of the heavens, has given all kingdoms of the earth to me, and He has laid a charge on me to build a house for Him in Jerusalem, that [is] in Judah; ³who [is] among you of all His people? His God is with him, and he goes up to Jerusalem, that [is] in Judah, and builds the house of YHWH, God of Israel (He [alone is] God), that [is] in Jerusalem. ⁴And everyone who is left, of any of the places where he [is] a sojourner, the men of his place assist him with silver, and with gold, and with goods, and with beasts, along with a free-will offering for the house of God, that [is] in Jerusalem." ⁵And heads of the fathers of Judah and Benjamin rise, and the priests and the Levites, even everyone whose spirit God has awoken, to go up to build the house of YHWH, that [is] in Jerusalem; ⁶and all those around them have strengthened [them] with their hands, with vessels of silver, with gold, with goods, and with beasts, and with precious things, apart from all that has been offered willingly. ⁷And King Cyrus has brought out the vessels of the house of YHWH that Nebuchadnezzar has brought out of Jerusalem, and puts them in the house of his gods; ⁸indeed, Cyrus king of Persia brings them out by the hand of Mithredath the treasurer, and numbers them to Sheshbazzar the prince of Judah. ⁹And this [is] their number: dishes of gold thirty, dishes of silver one thousand, knives twenty-nine, ¹⁰basins of gold thirty, basins of silver (seconds) four hundred and ten, other vessels one thousand. ¹¹All the vessels of gold and of silver [are] five thousand and four hundred; the whole has Sheshbazzar brought up with the going up of the expulsion from Babylon to Jerusalem.

CHAPTER 2

¹And these [are] sons of the province who are going up—of the captives of the expulsion that Nebuchadnezzar king of Babylon removed to Babylon, and they return to Jerusalem and Judah, each to his city— ²who have come in with Zerubbabel, Jeshua, Nehemiah, Seraiah, Reelaiah, Mordecai, Bilshan, Mispar, Bigvai, Rehum, Baanah. The number of the men of the people of Israel: ³sons of Parosh, two thousand one hundred seventy-two; ⁴sons of Shephatiah, three hundred seventy-two; ⁵sons of Arah, seven hundred seventy-five; ⁶sons of Pahath-Moab, of the sons of Jeshua [and] Joab, two thousand eight hundred and twelve; ⁷sons of Elam, one thousand two hundred fifty-four; ⁸sons of Zattu, nine hundred and forty-five; ⁹sons of Zaccai, seven hundred and sixty; ¹⁰sons of Bani, six hundred forty-two; ¹¹sons of Bebai, six hundred twenty-three; ¹²sons of Azgad, one thousand two hundred twenty-two; ¹³sons of Adonikam, six hundred sixty-six; ¹⁴sons of Bigvai, two thousand fifty-six; ¹⁵sons of Adin, four hundred fifty-four; ¹⁶sons of Ater of Hezekiah, ninety-eight; ¹⁷sons of Bezai, three hundred twenty-three; ¹⁸sons of Jorah, one hundred and twelve; ¹⁹sons of Hashum, two hundred twenty-three; ²⁰sons of Gibbar, ninety-five; ²¹sons of Beth-Lehem, one hundred twenty-three; ²²men of Netophah, fifty-six; ²³men of Anathoth, one hundred twenty-eight; ²⁴sons of Azmaveth, forty-two; ²⁵sons of Kirjath-Arim, Chephirah, and Beeroth, seven hundred and forty-three; ²⁶sons of Ramah and Gaba, six hundred twenty-one; ²⁷men of Michmas, one hundred twenty-two; ²⁸men of Beth-El and Ai, two hundred twenty-three; ²⁹sons of Nebo, fifty-two; ³⁰sons of Magbish, one hundred fifty-six; ³¹sons of another Elam, one thousand two hundred fifty-four; ³²sons of Harim, three hundred and twenty; ³³sons of Lod, Hadid, and Ono, seven hundred twenty-five; ³⁴sons of Jericho, three hundred forty-five; ³⁵sons of Senaah, three thousand and six hundred and thirty. ³⁶The priests: sons of Jedaiah, of the house of Jeshua, nine hundred seventy-three; ³⁷sons of Immer, one thousand fifty-two; ³⁸sons of Pashhur, one thousand two hundred forty-seven; ³⁹sons of Harim, one thousand and seventeen. ⁴⁰The Levites: sons of Jeshua and Kadmiel, of the sons of Hodaviah, seventy-four. ⁴¹The singers: sons of Asaph, one hundred twenty-eight. ⁴²Sons of the gatekeepers: sons of Shallum, sons of Ater, sons of Talmon, sons of Akkub, sons of Hatita, sons of Shobai, the whole [are] one hundred thirty-nine. ⁴³The Nethinim: sons of Ziha, sons of Hasupha, sons of Tabbaoth, ⁴⁴sons of Keros, sons of Siaha, sons of Padon, ⁴⁵sons of Lebanah, sons of Hagabah, sons of Akkub, ⁴⁶sons of Hagab, sons of Shalmai, sons of Hanan, ⁴⁷sons of Giddel, sons of Gahar, sons of Reaiah, ⁴⁸sons of Rezin, sons of Nekoda, sons of Gazzam, ⁴⁹sons of Uzza, sons of Paseah, sons of Besai, ⁵⁰sons of Asnah, sons of Mehunim, sons of Nephusim, ⁵¹sons of Bakbuk, sons of Hakupha, sons of Harhur, ⁵²sons of Bazluth, sons of Mehida, sons of Harsha, ⁵³sons of Barkos, sons of Sisera, sons of Thamah, ⁵⁴sons of Neziah, sons of Hatipha. ⁵⁵Sons of the servants of Solomon: sons of Sotai, sons of Sophereth, sons of Peruda, ⁵⁶sons of Jaalah, sons of Darkon, sons of Giddel, ⁵⁷sons of Shephatiah, sons of Hattil, sons of Pochereth of Zebaim, sons of Ami. ⁵⁸All the Nethinim, and the sons of the servants of Solomon [are] three hundred ninety-two. ⁵⁹And these [are] those going up from Tel-Melah, Tel-Harsa, Cherub, Addan, Immer, and they have not been able to declare the house of their fathers, and their seed, whether they [are] of Israel: ⁶⁰sons of Delaiah, sons of Tobiah, sons of Nekoda, six hundred fifty-two. ⁶¹And of the sons of the priests: sons of Habaiah, sons of Koz, sons of Barzillai (who took a wife from the daughters of Barzillai the Gileadite, and is called by their name); ⁶²these have sought their register among those reckoning themselves by genealogy, and they have not been found, and they are redeemed from the priesthood, ⁶³and the Tirshatha says to them that they do not eat of the most holy things until the standing up of a priest with [the] Lights and with [the] Perfections. ⁶⁴All the assembly together [is] forty-two thousand three hundred sixty, ⁶⁵apart from their servants and their handmaids; these [are] seven thousand three hundred thirty-seven: and of them [are] two hundred male and female singers. ⁶⁶Their horses [are] seven hundred thirty-six, their mules, two hundred forty-five, ⁶⁷their camels, four hundred thirty-five, donkeys, six thousand seven hundred and twenty. ⁶⁸And some of the heads of the fathers in their coming to the house of YHWH that [is] in Jerusalem, have offered willingly for the house of God, to establish it on its base; ⁶⁹according to their power they have given to the treasure of the work; of gold, sixty-one thousand drams, and of silver, five thousand pounds, and of priests' coats, one hundred. ⁷⁰And the priests dwell, and the Levites, and of the people, and the singers, and the gatekeepers, and the Nethinim, in their cities; even all Israel in their cities.

CHAPTER 3

¹And the seventh month comes, and the sons of Israel [are] in the cities, and the people are gathered, as one man, to Jerusalem. ²And Jeshua son of Jozadak rises, and his brothers the priests, and Zerubbabel son of Shealtiel, and his brothers, and they build the altar of the God of Israel, to cause to ascend on it burnt-offerings, as it is written in the Law of Moses, the man of God. ³And they establish the altar on its bases, because of the fear on them of the peoples of the lands, and he causes burnt-offerings to ascend on it to YHWH, burnt-offerings for the morning and for the evening. ⁴And they make the Celebration of the Shelters as it is written, and the burnt-offering of the day daily in number according to the ordinance, the matter of a day in its day; ⁵and after this a continual burnt-offering, and for new moons, and for all appointed times of YHWH that are sanctified; and for everyone who is willingly offering a willing-offering to YHWH. ⁶From the first day of the seventh month they have begun to cause burnt-offerings to ascend to YHWH, and the temple of YHWH has not been founded, ⁷and they give

EZRA

money to hewers and to craftsmen, and food, and drink, and oil to Zidonians and to Tyrians, to bring in cedar-trees from Lebanon to the Sea of Joppa, according to the permission of Cyrus king of Persia concerning them. ⁸And in the second year of their coming to the house of God, to Jerusalem, in the second month, began Zerubbabel son of Shealtiel, and Jeshua son of Jozadak, and the remnant of their brothers the priests and the Levites, and all those coming from the captivity to Jerusalem, and they appoint the Levites from a son of twenty years and upward, to overlook the work of the house of YHWH. ⁹And Jeshua stands, [and] his sons, and his brothers, Kadmiel and his sons, sons of Judah together, to overlook those doing the work in the house of God; the sons of Henadad, [and] their sons and their brothers the Levites. ¹⁰And those building have founded the temple of YHWH, and they appoint the priests, clothed, with trumpets, and the Levites, sons of Asaph, with cymbals, to praise YHWH, by means of [the instruments of] David king of Israel. ¹¹And they respond in praising and in giving thanks to YHWH, "For [He is] good, for His kindness [is] for all time over Israel!" And all the people have shouted [with] a great shout in giving praise to YHWH, because the house of YHWH has been founded. ¹²And many of the priests, and the Levites, and the heads of the fathers, the aged men who had seen the first house— in this house being founded before their eyes—are weeping with a loud voice, and many with a shout, in joy, lifting up the voice; ¹³and the people are not discerning the noise of the shout of joy from the noise of the weeping of the people, for the people are shouting [with] a great shout, and the noise has been heard to a distance.

CHAPTER 4

¹And adversaries of Judah and Benjamin hear that the sons of the captivity are building a temple to YHWH, God of Israel, ²and they draw near to Zerubbabel, and to heads of the fathers, and say to them, "Let us build with you; for, like you, we seek to your God, and we are not sacrificing since the days of Esar-Haddon king of Asshur, who brought us up here." ³And Zerubbabel says to them, also Jeshua, and the rest of the heads of the fathers of Israel, "Not for you, and for us, to build a house to our God; but we ourselves together build to YHWH God of Israel, as King Cyrus, king of Persia, commanded us." ⁴And it comes to pass, the people of the land are making the hands of the people of Judah feeble, and troubling them in building, ⁵and are hiring against them counselors to make void their counsel all the days of Cyrus king of Persia, even until the reign of Darius king of Persia. ⁶And in the reign of Ahasuerus, in the commencement of his reign, they have written an accusation against the inhabitants of Judah and Jerusalem; ⁷and in the days of Artaxerxes have Bishlam, Mithredath, Tabeel, and the rest of his companions written to Artaxerxes king of Persia, and the writing of the letter is written in Aramaic, and interpreted in Aramaic. ⁸Rehum counselor, and Shimshai scribe have written a letter concerning Jerusalem to Artaxerxes the king, thus: ⁹Then Rehum counselor, and Shimshai scribe, and the rest of their companions, Dinaites, and Apharsathchites, Tarpelites, Apharsites, Archevites, Babylonians, Susanchites (who are Elamites), ¹⁰and the rest of the nations that the great and honorable Asnapper removed and set in the city of Samaria, and the rest beyond the river, and at such a time: ¹¹This [is] a copy of a letter that they have sent to him, to Artaxerxes the king: "Your servants, men beyond the river, and at such a time; ¹²be it known to the king, that the Jews who have come up from you to us, have come to Jerusalem, the rebellious and base city they are building, and the walls they have finished, and the foundations they join. ¹³Now let it be known to the king, that if this city is built and the walls finished, that they do not give toll, tribute, and custom; and at length it causes loss [to] the kings. ¹⁴Now because that the salt of the palace [is] our salt, and we have no patience to see the nakedness of the king, therefore we have sent and made known to the king; ¹⁵so that he seeks in the scroll of the records of your fathers, and you find in the scroll of the records, and know, that this city [is] a rebellious city, and causing loss [to] kings and provinces, and makers of sedition [are] in its midst from the days of old, therefore this city has been ruined. ¹⁶We are making known to the king that, if this city be built and the walls finished, by this means you have no portion beyond the river." ¹⁷The king has sent an answer to Rehum counselor, and Shimshai scribe, and the rest of their companions who are dwelling in Samaria, and the rest beyond the river, "Peace, and at such a time: ¹⁸The letter that you sent to us, explained, has been read before me, ¹⁹and by me a decree has been made, and they sought, and have found that this city is lifting up itself against kings from the days of old, and rebellion and sedition is made in it, ²⁰and mighty kings have been over Jerusalem, even rulers over all beyond the river, and toll, tribute, and custom is given to them. ²¹Now make a decree to cause these men to cease, and this city is not built, until a decree is made by me. ²²And beware of negligence in doing this; why does the hurt become great to the loss of the kings?" ²³Then from the time that a copy of the letter of King Artaxerxes is read before Rehum, and Shimshai the scribe, and their companions, they have gone in haste to Jerusalem, to the Jews, and caused them to cease by force and strength; ²⁴then ceased the service of the house of God that [is] in Jerusalem, and it ceased until the second year of the reign of Darius king of Persia.

CHAPTER 5

¹And the prophets have prophesied (Haggai the prophet, and Zechariah son of Iddo) to the Jews who [are] in Judah and in Jerusalem, in the Name of the God of Israel—to them. ²Then Zerubbabel son of Shealtiel, and Jeshua son of Jozadak, have risen, and begun to build the house of God, that [is] in Jerusalem, and with them are the prophets of God supporting them. ³At that time have come to them Tatnai, governor beyond the river, and Shethar-Boznai, and their companions, and thus they are saying to them, "Who has made for you a decree to build this house, and to finish this wall?" ⁴Then we have said thus to them, "What [are] the names of the men who are building this building?" ⁵And the eye of their God has been on [the] elders of [the] Jews, and they have not caused them to cease until [the] matter goes to Darius, and then they send back a letter concerning this thing. ⁶The copy of a letter that Tatnai, governor beyond the river, has sent, and Shethar-Boznai and his companions, the Apharsachites who [are] beyond the river, to Darius the king. ⁷A letter they have sent to him, and thus is it written in it: ⁸"To Darius the king, all peace! Be it known to the king that we have gone to the province of Judah, to the great house of God, and it is built [with] rolled stones, and wood is placed in the walls, and this work is done speedily, and prospering in their hand. ⁹Then we have asked of these elders, thus we have said to them, Who has made for you a decree to build this house, and to finish this wall? ¹⁰And also their names we have asked of them, to let you know, that we might write the names of the men who [are] at their head. ¹¹And thus they have returned us word, saying, We [are] servants of the God of the heavens and earth, and are building the house that was built many years before this, that a great king of Israel built and finished: ¹²but after that our fathers made the God of the heavens angry, he gave them into the hand of Nebuchadnezzar king of Babylon the Chaldean, and this house he destroyed, and the people he removed to Babylon; ¹³but in the first year of Cyrus king of Babylon, Cyrus the king made a decree to build this house of God, ¹⁴and also, the vessels of the house of God, of gold and silver, that Nebuchadnezzar had taken forth out of the temple that [is] in Jerusalem, and brought them to the temple of Babylon, them has Cyrus the king brought forth out of the temple of Babylon, and they have been given to [one], Sheshbazzar [is] his name, whom he made governor, ¹⁵and said to him, Lift up these vessels, go, put them down in the temple that [is] in Jerusalem, and the house of God is built on its place. ¹⁶Then this Sheshbazzar has come—he has laid the foundations of the house of God that [is] in Jerusalem, and from there even until now it has been building, and is not finished. ¹⁷And now, if it is good to the king, let a search be made in the treasure-house of the king, that [is] there in Babylon, whether it be that there was a decree made by Cyrus the king to build this house of God in Jerusalem, and the will of the king concerning this thing he sends to us."

CHAPTER 6

¹Then Darius the king made a decree, and they sought in the house of the scrolls of the treasuries placed there in Babylon, ²and there has been found at Achmetha, in a palace that

[is] in the province of Media, a scroll, and a record thus written within it [is]: ³"In the first year of Cyrus the king, Cyrus the king has made a decree concerning the house of God in Jerusalem: let the house be built in the place where they are sacrificing sacrifices, and its foundations strongly laid; its height sixty cubits, its breadth sixty cubits; ⁴three rows of rolled stones, and a row of new wood, and let the outlay be given out of the king's house. ⁵And also, the vessels of the house of God, of gold and silver, that Nebuchadnezzar took forth out of the temple that [is] in Jerusalem, and brought to Babylon, let be given back, and go to the temple that [is] in Jerusalem, [each] to its place, and put [them] down in the house of God. ⁶Now Tatnai, governor beyond the river, Shethar-Boznai, and their companions, the Apharsachites, who [are] beyond the river, be far from here; ⁷let alone the work of this house of God, let the governor of the Jews, and [the] elders of the Jews, build this house of God on its place. ⁸And a decree is made by me concerning that which you do with [the] elders of these Jews to build this house of God, that of [the] riches of [the] king, that [are] of [the] tribute beyond [the] river, let the outlay be given speedily to these men, that they do not cease; ⁹and what they are needing—both young bullocks, and rams, and lambs for burnt-offerings to the God of the heavens, wheat, salt, wine, and oil according to the saying of the priests who [are] in Jerusalem—let be given to them day by day without fail, ¹⁰that they are bringing sweet savors near to the God of the heavens, and praying for the life of the king, and of his sons. ¹¹And a decree is made by me, that anyone who changes this thing, let wood be pulled down from his house, and being raised up, let him be struck on it, and let his house be made a dunghill for this. ¹²And God, who caused His Name to dwell there, casts down any king and people that puts forth his hand to change, to destroy this house of God that [is] in Jerusalem; I Darius have made a decree; let it be done speedily." ¹³Then Tatnai, governor beyond the river, Shethar-Boznai, and their companions, according to that which Darius the king has sent, so they have done speedily; ¹⁴and [the] elders of [the] Jews are building and prospering through [the] prophecy of Haggai [the] prophet, and Zechariah son of Iddo, and they have built and finished by [the] decree of [the] God of Israel, and by [the] decree of Cyrus, and Darius, and Artaxerxes king of Persia. ¹⁵And this house has gone out until the third day of the month Adar, that is [in] the sixth year of the reign of Darius the king. ¹⁶And the sons of Israel have made, [and] the priests, and the Levites, and the rest of the sons of the captivity, a dedication of this house of God with joy, ¹⁷and have brought near for the dedication of this house of God: one hundred bullocks, two hundred rams, four hundred lambs; and twelve young male goats for a sin-offering for all Israel according to the number of the tribes of Israel; ¹⁸and they have established the priests in their divisions, and the Levites in their courses, over the service of God that [is] in Jerusalem, as it is written in the scroll of Moses. ¹⁹And the sons of the captivity make the Passover on the fourteenth of the first month, ²⁰for the priests and the Levites have been purified together—all of them [are] pure—and they slaughter the Passover for all the sons of the captivity, and for their brothers the priests, and for themselves. ²¹And the sons of Israel, those returning from the captivity, and everyone who is separated from the uncleanness of the nations of the land to them, to seek to Yʜᴡʜ, God of Israel, eat, ²²and they make the Celebration of Unleavened Things seven days with joy, for Yʜᴡʜ made them to rejoice, and turned around the heart of the king of Asshur to them, to strengthen their hands in the work of the house of God, the God of Israel.

CHAPTER 7

¹And after these things, in the reign of Artaxerxes king of Persia, Ezra son of Seraiah, son of Azariah, son of Hilkiah, ²son of Shallum, son of Zadok, son of Ahitub, ³son of Amariah, son of Azariah, son of Meraioth, ⁴son of Zerahiah, son of Uzzi, son of Bukki, ⁵son of Abishua, son of Phinehas, son of Eleazar, son of Aaron the head priest; ⁶Ezra himself has come up from Babylon, and he [is] a scribe ready in the Law of Moses, that Yʜᴡʜ God of Israel gave, and the king gives to him—according to the hand of his God Yʜᴡʜ on him—all his request. ⁷And there go up of the sons of Israel, and of the priests, and the Levites, and the singers, and the gatekeepers, and the Nethinim, to Jerusalem, in the seventh year of Artaxerxes the king. ⁸And he comes to Jerusalem in the fifth month, that [is in] the seventh year of the king, ⁹for on the first of the month he has founded the ascent from Babylon, and on the first of the fifth month he has come to Jerusalem, according to the good hand of his God on him, ¹⁰for Ezra has prepared his heart to seek the Law of Yʜᴡʜ, and to do, and to teach in Israel statute and judgment. ¹¹And this [is] a copy of the letter that King Artaxerxes gave to Ezra the priest, the scribe, a scribe of the words of the commands of Yʜᴡʜ, and of His statutes on Israel: ¹²"Artaxerxes, king of kings, to Ezra the priest, a perfect scribe of the Law of the God of the heavens, and at such a time: ¹³By me has been made a decree that everyone who is willing, in my kingdom, of the people of Israel and of its priests and Levites, to go to Jerusalem with you, go; ¹⁴because that from the king and his seven counselors you are sent, to inquire concerning Judah and concerning Jerusalem, with the Law of God that [is] in your hand, ¹⁵and to carry silver and gold that the king and his counselors willingly offered to the God of Israel, whose dwelling place [is] in Jerusalem, ¹⁶and all the silver and gold that you find in all the province of Babylon, with the free-will offerings of the people, and of the priests, offering willingly, for the house of their God that [is] in Jerusalem, ¹⁷therefore you speedily buy with this money, bullocks, rams, lambs, and their presents, and their drink-offerings, and bring them near to the altar of the house of your God that [is] in Jerusalem, ¹⁸and that which to you and to your brothers is good to do with the rest of the silver and gold, according to the will of your God you do. ¹⁹And the vessels that are given to you, for the service of the house of your God, make perfect before the God of Jerusalem; ²⁰and the rest of the necessary things of the house of your God, that it falls to you to give, you give from the treasure-house of the king. ²¹And by me—I Artaxerxes the king—is made a decree to all treasurers who [are] beyond the river, that all that Ezra the priest, scribe of the Law of the God of the heavens, asks of you, be done speedily: ²²To silver one hundred talents, and to wheat one hundred cors, and to wine one hundred baths, and to oil one hundred baths, and salt without reckoning; ²³all that [is] by the decree of the God of the heavens, let be done diligently for the house of the God of the heavens; for why is there wrath against the kingdom of the king and his sons? ²⁴And to you we are making known, that on any of the priests and Levites, singers, gatekeepers, Nethinim, and servants of the house of God, tribute and custom there is no authority to lift up. ²⁵And you, Ezra, according to the wisdom of your God, that [is] in your hand, appoint magistrates—even judges who may be judging—judging all the people who are beyond the river, to all knowing the Law of your God, and he who has not known, you cause to know; ²⁶and any who does not do the Law of your God, and the law of the king, judgment is done speedily on him, whether to death, or to banishment, or to confiscation of riches, and to bonds." ²⁷Blessed [is] Yʜᴡʜ, God of our fathers, who has given such a thing as this in the heart of the king, to beautify the house of Yʜᴡʜ that [is] in Jerusalem, ²⁸and to me has stretched out kindness before the king and his counselors, and before all the mighty heads of the king: and I have strengthened myself as the hand of my God Yʜᴡʜ [is] on me, and I gather out of Israel heads to go up with me.

CHAPTER 8

¹And these [are] heads of their fathers, and the genealogy of those going up with me, in the reign of Artaxerxes the king, from Babylon. ²From the sons of Phinehas: Gershom; from the sons of Ithamar: Daniel; from the sons of David: Hattush; ³from the sons of Shechaniah, from the sons of Pharosh: Zechariah, and with him, reckoning themselves by genealogy, of males one hundred and fifty. ⁴From the sons of Pahath-Moab: Elihoenai son of Zerahiah, and with him two hundred who are males. ⁵From the sons of Shechaniah: the son of Jahaziel, and with him three hundred who are males. ⁶And from the sons of Adin: Ebed son of Jonathan, and with him fifty who are males. ⁷And from the sons of Elam: Jeshaiah son of Athaliah, and with him seventy who are males. ⁸And from the sons of Shephatiah: Zebadiah son of Michael, and with him eighty who are males. ⁹From the sons of Joab: Obadiah son of Jehiel, and with him two hundred and eighteen who are males. ¹⁰And

EZRA

from the sons of Shelomith, the son of Josiphiah, and with him one hundred and sixty who are males. ¹¹And from the sons of Bebai: Zechariah son of Bebai, and with him twenty-eight who are males. ¹²And from the sons of Azgad: Johanan son of Hakkatan, and with him one hundred and ten who are males. ¹³And from the younger sons of Adonikam—and these [are] their names—Eliphelet, Jeiel, and Shemaiah, and with them sixty who are males. ¹⁴And from the sons of Bigvai, Uthai and Zabbud, and with them seventy who are males. ¹⁵And I gather them to the river that is going to Ahava, and we encamp there three days; and I consider about the people, and about the priests, and of the sons of Levi I have found none there; ¹⁶and I send for Eliezer, for Ariel, for Shemaiah, and for Elnathan, and for Jarib, and for Elnathan, and for Nathan, and for Zechariah, and for Meshullam, heads, and for Joiarib, and for Elnathan, men of understanding; ¹⁷and I charge them for Iddo the head, in the place Casiphia, and put in their mouth words to speak to Iddo, [and] his brothers the Nethinim, in the place Casiphia, to bring to us servants for the house of our God. ¹⁸And they bring to us, according to the good hand of our God on us, a man of understanding, of the sons of Mahli, son of Levi, son of Israel, and Sherebiah, and his sons, and his brothers, eighteen; ¹⁹and Hashabiah, and with him Jeshaiah, of the sons of Merari, his brothers, and their sons, twenty; ²⁰and from the Nethinim, whom David and the heads gave for the service of the Levites, two hundred and twenty Nethinim, all of them defined by name. ²¹And I proclaim there a fast, by the river Ahava, to afflict ourselves before our God, to seek from Him a right way for us, and for our infants, and for all our substance, ²²for I was ashamed to ask from the king a force and horsemen to help us because of the enemy in the way, for we spoke to the king, saying, "The hand of our God [is] on all seeking Him for good, and His strength and His wrath [is] on all forsaking Him." ²³And we fast, and seek from our God for this, and He accepts our plea. ²⁴And I separate from the heads of the priests, twelve, even Sherebiah, Hashabiah, and with them of their brothers ten, ²⁵and I weigh to them the silver, and the gold, and the vessels, a raised-offering of the house of our God, that the king, and his counselors, and his heads, and all Israel—those present—lifted up; ²⁶and I weigh to their hand six hundred and fifty talents of silver, and one hundred talents of vessels of silver, one hundred talents of gold, ²⁷and twenty basins of gold, of one thousand drams, and two vessels of good shining bronze, desirable as gold. ²⁸And I say to them, "You [are] holy to YHWH, and the vessels [are] holy, and the silver and the gold [are] a willing-offering to YHWH, God of your fathers; ²⁹watch, and keep, until you weigh before the heads of the priests, and of the Levites, and the heads of the fathers of Israel, in Jerusalem, in the chambers of the house of YHWH." ³⁰And the priests and the Levites took the weight of the silver, and of the gold, and of the vessels, to bring to Jerusalem to the house of our God. ³¹And we journey from the river Ahava, on the twelfth of the first month, to go to Jerusalem, and the hand of our God has been on us, and He delivers us from the hand of the enemy and the one lying in wait by the way; ³²and we come to Jerusalem, and dwell there three days. ³³And on the fourth day has been weighed the silver, and the gold, and the vessels, in the house of our God, to the hand of Meremoth son of Uriah the priest, and with him Eleazar son of Phinehas, and with them Jozabad son of Jeshua, and Noadiah son of Binnui, the Levites: ³⁴by number, by weight of everyone, and all the weight is written at that time. ³⁵Those coming in of the captives—sons of the expulsion—have brought burnt-offerings near to the God of Israel: twelve bullocks for all Israel, ninety-six rams, seventy-seven lambs, twelve young male goats for a sin-offering—the whole a burnt-offering to YHWH; ³⁶and they give the laws of the king to the lieutenants of the king and the governors beyond the river, and they have lifted up the people and the house of God.

CHAPTER 9

¹And at the completion of these things, the heads have drawn near to me, saying, "The people of Israel, and the priests, and the Levites, have not been separated from the peoples of the lands, as to their abominations, even the Canaanite, the Hittite, the Perizzite, the Jebusite, the Ammonite, the Moabite, the Egyptian, and the Amorite, ²for they have taken of their daughters to them, and to their sons, and the holy seed have mingled themselves among the peoples of the lands, and the hand of the heads and of the seconds have been first in this trespass." ³And at my hearing this word, I have torn my garment and my upper robe, and pluck out of the hair of my head, and of my beard, and sit astonished, ⁴and to me are gathered everyone trembling at the words of the God of Israel, because of the trespass of the expulsion, and I am sitting astonished until the present of the evening. ⁵And at the present of the evening I have risen from my affliction, and at my tearing my garment and my upper robe, then I bow down on my knees, and spread out my hands to my God YHWH, ⁶and say, "O my God, I have been ashamed, and have blushed to lift up, O my God, my face to You, for our iniquities have increased over the head, and our guilt has become great to the heavens. ⁷From the days of our fathers we [are] in great guilt to this day, and in our iniquities we have been given—we, our kings, our priests—into the hand of the kings of the lands, with sword, with captivity, and with spoiling, and with shame of face, as [at] this day. ⁸And now, as a small moment grace has been from our God YHWH, to leave an escape for us, and to give to us a nail in His holy place, by our God's enlightening our eyes, and by giving us a little quickening in our servitude; ⁹for we [are] servants, and in our servitude our God has not forsaken us, and stretches out to us kindness before the kings of Persia, to give to us a quickening to lift up the house of our God, and to cause its ruins to cease, and to give to us a wall in Judah and in Jerusalem. ¹⁰And now, what do we say, O our God, after this? For we have forsaken Your commands, ¹¹that You have commanded by the hands of Your servants the prophets, saying, The land into which you are going to possess it, [is] a land of impurity, by the impurity of the people of the lands, by their abominations with which they have filled it—from mouth to mouth—by their uncleanness; ¹²and now, your daughters you do not give to their sons, and their daughters you do not take to your sons, and you do not seek their peace, and their good—for all time, so that you are strong, and have eaten the good of the land, and given possession to your sons for all time. ¹³And after all that has come on us for our evil works, and for our great guilt (for You, O our God, have kept back of the rod from our iniquities, and have given to us an escape like this), ¹⁴do we turn back to break Your commands, and to join ourselves in marriage with the people of these abominations? Are You not angry against us—even to consumption—until there is no remnant and escaped part? ¹⁵O YHWH, God of Israel, You [are] righteous, for we have been left an escape, as [it is] this day; behold, we [are] before You in our guilt, for there is none to stand before You concerning this."

CHAPTER 10

¹And at Ezra's praying, and at his making confession, weeping and casting himself down before the house of God, there have been gathered to him out of Israel a very great assembly—men and women and children—for the people have wept, multiplying weeping. ²And Shechaniah son of Jehiel, of the sons of Elam, answers and says to Ezra, "We have trespassed against our God, and we settle strange women of the peoples of the land; and now there is hope for Israel concerning this, ³and now, let us make a covenant with our God, to cause all the women to go out, and that which is born of them, by the counsel of the Lord, and of those trembling at the command of our God, and according to law it is done; ⁴rise, for on you [is] the matter, and we [are] with you; be strong, and do." ⁵And Ezra rises, and causes the heads of the priests, the Levites, and all Israel, to swear to do according to this word—and they swear. ⁶And Ezra rises from before the house of God, and goes to the chamber of Jehohanan son of Eliashib; indeed, he goes there, bread he has not eaten, and water he has not drunk, for he is mourning because of the trespass of the expulsion. ⁷And they cause a voice to pass over into Judah and Jerusalem, to all sons of the expulsion, to be gathered to Jerusalem, ⁸and everyone who does not come in by the third day, according to the counsel of the heads and the elderly, all his substance is devoted, and himself separated from the assembly of the expulsion. ⁹And all the men of Judah and Benjamin are gathered to Jerusalem by the third day, it [is] the ninth month, on the twentieth of the month, and all the people sit

in the broad place of the house of God, trembling on account of the matter and of the showers. ¹⁰And Ezra the priest rises and says to them, "You have trespassed, and you settle strange women, to add to the guilt of Israel; ¹¹and now, make confession to YHWH, God of your fathers, and do His good pleasure, and be separated from the peoples of the land, and from the strange women." ¹²And all the assembly answers and says [with] a great voice, "Right; according to your word—on us to do; ¹³but the people [are] many, and [it is] the time of showers, and there is no power to stand outside, and the work [is] not for one day, nor for two, for we have multiplied to transgress in this thing. ¹⁴Please let our heads of all the assembly stand; and all who [are] in our cities, who have settled strange wives, come in at [the] appointed times, and with them [the] elderly of city and city, and judges in it, until the turning back of the fury of the wrath of our God from us, for this thing." ¹⁵Only Jonathan son of Asahel, and Jahaziah son of Tikvah, stood against this, and Meshullam, and Shabbethai the Levite, helped them. ¹⁶And the sons of the expulsion do so, and Ezra the priest, [and] men, heads of the fathers, for the house of their fathers, are separated, even all of them by name, and they sit on the first day of the tenth month, to examine the matter; ¹⁷and they finish with all the men who have settled strange women to the first day of the first month. ¹⁸And there are found of the sons of the priests that have settled strange women: of the sons of Jeshua son of Jozadak, and his brothers, Maaseiah, and Eliezer, and Jarib, and Gedaliah; ¹⁹and they give their hand to send out their wives, and being guilty, a ram of the flock for their guilt. ²⁰And of the sons of Immer: Hanani and Zebadiah; ²¹and of the sons of Harim: Maaseiah, and Elijah, and Shemaiah, and Jehiel, and Uzziah; ²²and of the sons of Pashhur: Elioenai, Maaseiah, Ishmael, Nethaneel, Jozabad, and Elasah. ²³And of the Levites: Jozabad, and Shimei, and Kelaiah (he [is] Kelita), Pethahiah, Judah, and Eliezer. ²⁴And of the singers: Eliashib. And of the gatekeepers: Shallum, and Telem, and Uri. ²⁵And of Israel: of the sons of Parosh: Ramiah, and Jeziah, and Malchijah, and Miamin, and Eleazar, and Malchijah, and Benaiah. ²⁶And of the sons of Elam: Mattaniah, Zechariah, and Jehiel, and Abdi, and Jeremoth, and Elijah. ²⁷And of the sons of Zattu: Elioenai, Eliashib, Mattaniah, and Jeremoth, and Zabad, and Aziza. ²⁸And of the sons of Bebai: Jehohanan, Hananiah, Zabbai, Athlai. ²⁹And of the sons of Bani: Meshullam, Malluch, and Adaiah, Jashub, and Sheal, and Ramoth. ³⁰And of the sons of Pahath-Moab: Adna, and Chelal, Benaiah, Maaseiah, Mattaniah, Bezaleel, and Binnui, and Manasseh. ³¹And of the sons of Harim: Eliezer, Ishijah, Malchiah, Shemaiah, Shimeon, ³²Benjamin, Malluch, Shemariah. ³³Of the sons of Hashum: Mattenai, Mattathah, Zabad, Eliphelet, Jeremai, Manasseh, Shimei. ³⁴Of the sons of Bani: Maadai, Amram, and Uel, ³⁵Benaiah, Bedeiah, Cheluhu, ³⁶Vaniah, Meremoth, Eliashib, ³⁷Mattaniah, Mattenai, and Jaasau, ³⁸and Bani, and Binnui, Shimei, ³⁹and Shelemiah, and Nathan, and Adaiah, ⁴⁰Machnadbai, Shashai, Sharai, ⁴¹Azareel, and Shelemiah, Shemariah, ⁴²Shallum, Amariah, Joseph. ⁴³Of the sons of Nebo: Jeiel, Mattithiah, Zabad, Zebina, Jadau, and Joel, Benaiah; ⁴⁴all these have taken strange women, and there are of them women who adopt sons.

NEHEMIAH

CHAPTER 1

¹Words of Nehemiah son of Hachaliah. And it comes to pass, in the month of Chisleu, the twentieth year, and I have been in Shushan the palace, ²and Hanani, one of my brothers, he and men of Judah come in, and I ask them concerning the Jews, the escaped part that have been left of the captivity, and concerning Jerusalem; ³and they say to me, "Those left, who have been left of the captivity there in the province, [are] in great evil, and in reproach, and the wall of Jerusalem is broken down, and its gates have been burned with fire." ⁴And it comes to pass, at my hearing these words, I have sat down, and I weep and mourn [for] days, and I am fasting and praying before the God of the heavens. ⁵And I say, "Ah, now, O YHWH, God of the heavens, God, the great and the fearful, keeping the covenant and kindness for those loving Him, and for those keeping His commands, ⁶please let Your ear be attentive and Your eyes open, to listen to the prayer of Your servant, that I am praying before You today, by day and by night, concerning the sons of Israel, Your servants, and confessing concerning the sins of the sons of Israel, that we have sinned against You; indeed, I and the house of my father have sinned; ⁷we have acted very corruptly against You, and have not kept the commands, and the statutes, and the judgments, that You commanded Your servant Moses. ⁸Please remember the word that You commanded Your servant Moses, saying, You trespass—I scatter you among peoples; ⁹and you have turned back to Me, and kept My commands, and done them—if your outcast is in the end of the heavens, there I gather them, and have brought them to the place that I have chosen to cause My Name to dwell there. ¹⁰And they [are] Your servants, and Your people, whom You have ransomed by Your great power, and by Your strong hand. ¹¹Ah, now, O Lord, please let Your ear be attentive to the prayer of Your servant, and to the prayer of Your servants, those delighting to fear Your Name; and please give prosperity to Your servant today, and give him for mercies before this man"; and I have been butler to the king.

CHAPTER 2

¹And it comes to pass, in the month of Nisan, the twentieth year of Artaxerxes the king, wine [is] before him, and I lift up the wine, and give to the king, and I had not been sad before him; ²and the king says to me, "Why [is] your face sad, and you not sick? This is nothing except sadness of heart"; and I fear very much, ³and say to the king, "Let the king live for all time! Why should my face not be sad, when the city, the place of the graves of my fathers, [is] a desolation, and its gates have been consumed with fire?" ⁴And the king says to me, "For what are you seeking?" And I pray to the God of the heavens, ⁵and say to the king, "If [it is] good to the king, and if your servant is pleasing before you, that you send me to Judah, to the city of the graves of my fathers, and I have built it." ⁶And the king says to me (and the queen is sitting near him), "How long is your journey? And when do you return?" And it is good before the king, and he sends me away, and I set to him a time. ⁷And I say to the king, "If [it is] good to the king, let letters be given to me for the governors beyond the River, that they let me pass over until I come to Judah: ⁸and a letter to Asaph, keeper of the paradise that the king has, that he give to me trees for beams [for] the gates of the palace that the house has, and for the wall of the city, and for the house into which I enter"; and the king gives to me, according to the good hand of my God on me. ⁹And I come to the governors beyond the River, and give to them the letters of the king; and the king sends with me heads of a force, and horsemen; ¹⁰and Sanballat the Horonite hears, and Tobiah the servant, the Ammonite, and it is evil to them—a great evil—that a man has come to seek good for the sons of Israel. ¹¹And I come to Jerusalem, and I am there three days, ¹²and I rise by night, I and a few men with me, and have not declared to a man what my God is giving to my heart to do for Jerusalem, and there is no beast with me except the beast on which I am riding. ¹³And I go out through the Valley Gate by night, and to the front of the Dragon Fountain, and to the Refuse Gate, and I am inspecting the walls of Jerusalem, that are broken down, and its gates consumed with fire. ¹⁴And I pass over to the Fountain Gate, and to the King's Pool, and there is no place for the beast under me to pass over, ¹⁵and I am going up through the brook by night, and am inspecting the wall, and turn back, and come in through the Valley Gate, and turn back. ¹⁶And the prefects have not known to where I have gone, and what I am doing; and to the Jews, and to the priests, and to the nobles, and to the prefects, and to the rest of those doing the work, until now I have not declared [it]; ¹⁷and I say to them, "You are seeing the evil that we are in, in that Jerusalem [is] desolate, and its gates have been burned with fire;

NEHEMIAH

come and we build the wall of Jerusalem, and we are not a reproach anymore." ¹⁸And I declare to them the hand of my God that is good on me, and also the words of the king that he said to me, and they say, "Let us rise, and we have built"; and they strengthen their hands for good. ¹⁹And Sanballat the Horonite hears, and Tobiah the servant, the Ammonite, and Geshem the Arabian, and they mock at us, and despise us, and say, "What [is] this thing that you are doing? Are you rebelling against the king?" ²⁰And I return them word, and say to them, "The God of the heavens—He gives prosperity to us, and we His servants rise and have built; and to you there is no portion, and right, and memorial in Jerusalem."

CHAPTER 3

¹And Eliashib the high priest rises, and his brothers the priests, and they build the Sheep Gate; they have sanctified it, and set up its doors, even to the Tower of Meah they have sanctified it, to the Tower of Hananeel; ²and by his hand men of Jericho have built; and by their hand Zaccur son of Imri has built; ³and sons of Hassenaah have built the Fish Gate; they have walled it, and set up its doors, its locks, and its bars. ⁴And by their hand Merimoth son of Urijah, son of Koz, has strengthened; and by his hand Meshullam son of Berechiah, son of Meshezabeel, has strengthened; and by his hand Zadok son of Baana has strengthened; ⁵and by his hand the Tekoites have strengthened, and their majestic ones have not brought in their neck to the service of their Lord. ⁶And Jehoiada son of Paseah and Meshullam son of Besodeiah have strengthened the Old Gate; they have walled it, and set up its doors, and its locks, and its bars. ⁷And by their hand Melatiah the Gibeonite has strengthened, and Jadon the Meronothite, men of Gibeon and of Mizpah, [belonging] to the throne of the governor beyond the River. ⁸By his hand Uzziel son of Harhaiah of the refiners has strengthened; and by his hand Hananiah son of [one of] the compounders has strengthened; and they leave Jerusalem to the broad wall. ⁹And by their hand Rephaiah son of Hur, head of the half of the district of Jerusalem, has strengthened. ¹⁰And by their hand Jedaiah son of Harumaph has strengthened, and opposite his own house; and by his hand Hattush son of Hashabniah has strengthened. ¹¹A second measure Malchijah son of Harim has strengthened, and Hashub son of Pahath-Moab, even the Tower of the Furnaces. ¹²And by his hand Shallum son of Halohesh, head of the half of the district of Jerusalem, has strengthened, he and his daughters. ¹³Hanun has strengthened the Valley Gate, and the inhabitants of Zanoah; they have built it, and set up its doors, its locks, and its bars, and one thousand cubits in the wall to the Refuse Gate. ¹⁴And Malchijah son of Rechab, head of the district of Beth-Haccerem, has strengthened the Refuse Gate; he builds it, and sets up its doors, its locks, and its bars. ¹⁵And Shallum son of Col-Hozeh, head of the district of Mizpah, has strengthened the Fountain Gate: he builds it, and covers it, and sets up its doors, its locks, and its bars, and the wall of the pool of Siloah, to the garden of the king, and to the steps that are going down from the City of David. ¹⁶After him Nehemiah son of Azbuk, head of the half of the district of Beth-Zur, has strengthened to opposite the graves of David, and to the pool that is made, and to the house of the mighty ones. ¹⁷After him the Levites have strengthened, [and] Rehum son of Bani; by his hand Hashabiah, head of the half of the district of Keilah, has strengthened for his district. ¹⁸After him their brothers have strengthened, [and] Bavvai son of Henadad, head of the half of the district of Keilah. ¹⁹And Ezer son of Jeshua, head of Mizpah, strengthens, by his hand, a second measure, from in front of the ascent of the armory at the angle. ²⁰After him Baruch son of Zabbai has hurried to strengthen a second measure from the angle to the opening of the house of Eliashib the high priest. ²¹After him Meremoth son of Urijah, son of Koz, has strengthened a second measure, from the opening of the house of Eliashib even to the completion of the house of Eliashib. ²²And after him the priests, men of the circuit, have strengthened. ²³After them Benjamin has strengthened, and Hashub, opposite their house; after him Azariah son of Maaseiah, son of Ananiah, has strengthened near his house. ²⁴After him Binnui son of Henadad has strengthened a second measure, from the house of Azariah to the angle, and to the corner. ²⁵Palal son of Uzai [strengthened] from opposite the angle, and the tower that is going out from the upper house of the king that [is] at the court of the prison; after him Pedaiah son of Parosh [strengthened]. ²⁶And the Nethinim have been dwelling in Ophel, to opposite the Water Gate at the east, and the tower that goes out. ²⁷After him the Tekoites have strengthened a second measure, from opposite the great tower that goes out, and to the wall of Ophel. ²⁸From above the Horse Gate the priests have strengthened, each opposite his house. ²⁹After them Zadok son of Immer has strengthened opposite his house; and after him Shemaiah son of Shechaniah, keeper of the East Gate, has strengthened. ³⁰After him Hananiah son of Shelemiah has strengthened, and Hanun the sixth son of Zalaph, a second measure; after him Meshullam son of Berechiah has strengthened opposite his chamber. ³¹After him Malchijah son of the refiner has strengthened, to the house of the Nethinim, and of the merchants, opposite the Miphkad Gate, and to the ascent of the corner. ³²And between the ascent of the corner and the Sheep Gate, the refiners and the merchants have strengthened.

CHAPTER 4

¹And it comes to pass, when Sanballat has heard that we are building the wall, that it is displeasing to him, and he is very angry and mocks at the Jews, ²and says before his brothers and the force of Samaria, indeed, he says, "What [are] the weak Jews doing? Are they left to themselves? Do they sacrifice? Do they complete in a day? Do they revive the stones out of the heaps of the rubbish—and they are burned?" ³And Tobiah the Ammonite [is] by him and says, "Also, that which they are building—if a fox goes up, then it has broken down their stone wall." ⁴"Hear, O our God, for we have been despised; and return their reproach on their own head, and give them for a spoil in a land of captivity; ⁵and do not cover over their iniquity, and do not let their sin be blotted out from before You, for they have provoked [You] to anger in front of those building. ⁶And we build the wall, and all the wall is joined—to its half, and the people have a heart to work. ⁷And it comes to pass, when Sanballat has heard, and Tobiah, and the Arabians, and the Ammonites, and the Ashdodites, that lengthening has gone up to the walls of Jerusalem, that the breeches have begun to be stopped, then it is very displeasing to them, ⁸and they conspire, all of them together, to come to fight against Jerusalem, and to do to it injury. ⁹And we pray to our God, and appoint a watch against them, by day and by night, because of them. ¹⁰And Judah says, "The power of the burden-bearers has become feeble, and the rubbish [is] abundant, and we are not able to build on the wall." ¹¹And our adversaries say, "They do not know, nor see, until we come into their midst, and have slain them, and caused the work to cease." ¹²And it comes to pass, when the Jews have come who are dwelling near them, that they say to us ten times from all the places to where you return—[they are] against us. ¹³And I appoint at the lowest of the places, at the back of the wall, in the clear places, indeed, I appoint the people, by their families, with their swords, their spears, and their bows. ¹⁴And I see, and rise up, and say to the nobles, and to the prefects, and to the rest of the people, "Do not be afraid of them; remember the Lord, the great and the fearful, and fight for your brothers, your sons, and your daughters, your wives, and your houses." ¹⁵And it comes to pass, when our enemies have heard that it has been known to us, and God frustrates their counsel, and we return, all of us, to the wall, each to his work; ¹⁶indeed, it comes to pass, from that day, half of my servants are working in the business, and half of them are keeping hold of both the spears, the shields, and the bows, and the coats of mail; and the heads [are] behind all the house of Judah. ¹⁷The builders on the wall, and the bearers of the burden, those loading, [each] with one of his hands is working in the business, and one is laying hold of the missile. ¹⁸And the builders [are] each with his sword, girded on his loins, and building, and he who is blowing with a horn [is] beside me. ¹⁹And I say to the nobles, and to the prefects, and to the rest of the people, "The work is abundant, and large, and we are separated on the wall, far off from one another; ²⁰in the place that you hear the voice of the horn there you are gathered to us; our God fights for us." ²¹And we are working in the business, and half of them are keeping hold of the spears, from the going up of the dawn until the coming forth of the stars. ²²Also, at that time I said to the people, "Let each lodge with

NEHEMIAH

his servant in the midst of Jerusalem, and they have been a watch for us by night, and [for] the work by day"; ²³and there are none—I, and my brothers, and my servants, and the men of the watch who [are] after me—there are none of us putting off our garments, each [has] his vessel of water.

CHAPTER 5

¹And there is a great cry of the people and their wives, concerning their brothers the Jews, ²indeed, there are [those] who are saying, "Our sons, and our daughters, we—are many, and we receive grain, and eat, and live." ³And there are [those] who are saying, "Our fields, and our vineyards, and our houses, we are pledging, and we receive grain for the famine." ⁴And there are [those] who are saying, "We have borrowed money for the tribute of the king, [on] our fields, and our vineyards; ⁵and now, as the flesh of our brothers [is] our flesh, as their sons [are] our sons, and behold, we are subduing our sons and our daughters for servants, and there are [those] of our daughters subdued, and our hand has no might, and our fields and our vineyards [are] to others." ⁶And it is very displeasing to me when I have heard their cry and these words, ⁷and my heart reigns over me, and I strive with the nobles, and with the prefects, and say to them, "You are exacting usury on one another"; and I set against them a great assembly, ⁸and say to them, "We have acquired our brothers the Jews, those sold to the nations, according to the ability that [is] in us, and you also sell your brothers, and they have been sold to us!" And they are silent, and have not found a word. ⁹And I say, "The thing that you are doing [is] not good; do you not walk in the fear of our God, because of the reproach of the nations our enemies? ¹⁰And also, I, my brothers, and my servants, are exacting silver and grain on them; please let us leave off this usury. ¹¹Please give back to them, as today, their fields, their vineyards, their olive-yards, and their houses, and the hundredth [part] of the money, and of the grain, of the new wine, and of the oil, that you are exacting of them." ¹²And they say, "We give back, and we seek nothing from them; so we do as you are saying." And I call the priests, and cause them to swear to do according to this thing; ¹³also, I have shaken my lap, and I say, "Thus God shakes out every man from his house and from his labor who does not perform this thing; indeed, thus is he shaken out and empty"; and all the assembly says, "Amen," and praises YHWH; and the people do according to this thing. ¹⁴Also, from the day that he appointed me to be their governor in the land of Judah, from the twentieth year even to the thirty-second year of Artaxerxes the king—twelve years—I, and my brothers, have not eaten the bread of the governor: ¹⁵the former governors who [are] before me have made themselves heavy on the people, and take of them in bread and wine, besides forty shekels in silver; also, their servants have ruled over the people—and I have not done so, because of the fear of God. ¹⁶And also, in the work of this wall I have done mightily, even a field we have not bought, and all my servants are gathered there for the work; ¹⁷and of the Jews, and of the prefects, one hundred and fifty men, and those coming to us of the nations that [are] around us, [are] at my table; ¹⁸and that which has been prepared for one day [is] one ox, six fat sheep, also birds have been prepared for me, and once in ten days of all wines abundantly, and with this, the bread of the governor I have not sought, for heavy is the service on this people. ¹⁹Remember for me, O my God, for good, all that I have done for this people.

CHAPTER 6

¹And it comes to pass, when it has been heard by Sanballat, and Tobiah, and by Geshem the Arabian, and by the rest of our enemies, that I have built the wall, and there has not been left in it a breach (also, until that time I had not set up the doors in the gates), ²that Sanballat sends, also Geshem, to me, saying, "Come and we meet together in the villages, in the Valley of Ono"; and they are thinking to do to me evil. ³And I send to them messengers, saying, "A great work I am doing, and I am not able to come down; why does the work cease when I let it alone, and have come down to you?" ⁴And they send to me, according to this word, four times, and I return them [word] according to this word. ⁵And Sanballat sends to me, according to this word, a fifth time, his servant, and an open letter in his hand; ⁶it is written in it, "Among the nations it has been heard, and Gashmu is saying: You and the Jews are thinking to rebel, therefore you are building the wall, and you have been to them for a king—according to these words! ⁷And also, you have appointed prophets to call for you in Jerusalem, saying, A king [is] in Judah, and now it is heard by the king according to these words; and now come, and we take counsel together." ⁸And I send to him, saying, "It has not been according to these words that you are saying, for from your own heart you are devising them"; ⁹for all of them are making us afraid, saying, "Their hands are too feeble for the work, and it is not done"; and now, strengthen my hands. ¹⁰And I have entered the house of Shemaiah son of Delaiah, son of Mehetabeel—and he is restrained—and he says, "Let us meet at the house of God, at the inside of the temple, and we shut the doors of the temple, for they are coming to slay you—indeed, by night they are coming to slay you." ¹¹And I say, "A man such as I—does he flee? And who as I, that goes into the temple, and lives? I do not go in." ¹²And I discern, and behold, God has not sent him, for in the prophecy he has spoken to me both Tobiah and Sanballat hired him, ¹³so that he [is] a hired worker, that I may fear and do so, and I had sinned, and it had been to them for an evil name that they may reproach me. ¹⁴Be mindful, O my God, of Tobiah, and of Sanballat, according to these his works, and also, of Noadiah the prophetess, and of the rest of the prophets who have been making me afraid. ¹⁵And the wall is completed in the twenty-fifth of Elul, on the fifty-second day; ¹⁶and it comes to pass, when all our enemies have heard, and all the nations who are all around us see, that they fall greatly in their own eyes, and know that by our God has this work been done. ¹⁷Also, in those days the nobles of Judah are multiplying their letters going to Tobiah, and those of Tobiah are coming to them; ¹⁸for many in Judah are sworn to him, for he [is] son-in-law to Shechaniah son of Arah, and his son Jehohanan has taken the daughter of Meshullam son of Berechiah; ¹⁹also, they have been speaking of his good deeds before me, and they have been taking my words out to him; Tobiah has sent letters to make me afraid.

CHAPTER 7

¹And it comes to pass, when the wall has been built, that I set up the doors, and the gatekeepers are appointed, and the singers, and the Levites, ²and I charge my brother Hanani, and Hananiah head of the palace, concerning Jerusalem—for he [is] as a man of truth, and fearing God above many— ³and I say to them, "Do not let the gates of Jerusalem be opened until the heat of the sun, and while they are standing by let them shut the doors, and fasten, and appoint guards of the inhabitants of Jerusalem, each at his watch, and each in front of his house." ⁴And the city [is] broad on both sides, and great, and the people [are] few in its midst, and there are no houses built; ⁵and my God puts it to my heart, and I gather the nobles, and the prefects, and the people, for the genealogy, and I find a scroll of the genealogy of those coming up at the beginning, and I find written in it: ⁶These [are] sons of the province, those coming up of the captives of the expulsion that Nebuchadnezzar king of Babylon removed—and they return to Jerusalem and to Judah, each to his city— ⁷who are coming in with Zerubbabel, Jeshua, Nehemiah, Azariah, Raamiah, Nahamani, Mordecai, Bilshan, Mispereth, Bigvai, Nehum, Baanah. The number of the men of the people of Israel: ⁸sons of Parosh, two thousand one hundred and seventy-two; ⁹sons of Shephatiah, three hundred seventy-two; ¹⁰sons of Arah, six hundred fifty-two; ¹¹sons of Pahath-Moab, of the sons of Jeshua and Joab, two thousand and eight hundred [and] eighteen; ¹²sons of Elam, one thousand two hundred fifty-four; ¹³sons of Zattu, eight hundred forty-five; ¹⁴sons of Zaccai, seven hundred and sixty; ¹⁵sons of Binnui, six hundred forty-eight; ¹⁶sons of Bebai, six hundred twenty-eight; ¹⁷sons of Azgad, two thousand three hundred twenty-two; ¹⁸sons of Adonikam, six hundred sixty-seven; ¹⁹sons of Bigvai, two thousand sixty-seven; ²⁰sons of Adin, six hundred fifty-five; ²¹sons of Ater of Hezekiah, ninety-eight; ²²sons of Hashum, three hundred twenty-eight; ²³sons of Bezai, three hundred twenty-four; ²⁴sons of Hariph, one hundred [and] twelve; ²⁵sons of Gibeon, ninety-five; ²⁶men of Beth-Lehem and Netophah, one hundred eighty-eight; ²⁷men of Anathoth, one hundred twenty-eight; ²⁸men of Beth-Azmaveth, forty-

NEHEMIAH

two; ²⁹men of Kirjath-Jearim, Chephirah, and Beeroth, seven hundred forty-three; ³⁰men of Ramah and Gaba, six hundred twenty-one; ³¹men of Michmas, one hundred and twenty-two; ³²men of Bethel and Ai, one hundred twenty-three; ³³men of the other Nebo, fifty-two; ³⁴sons of the other Elam, one thousand two hundred fifty-four; ³⁵sons of Harim, three hundred and twenty; ³⁶sons of Jericho, three hundred forty-five; ³⁷sons of Lod, Hadid, and Ono, seven hundred and twenty-one; ³⁸sons of Senaah, three thousand nine hundred and thirty. ³⁹The priests: sons of Jedaiah, of the house of Jeshua, nine hundred seventy-three; ⁴⁰sons of Immer, one thousand fifty-two; ⁴¹sons of Pashur, one thousand two hundred forty-seven; ⁴²sons of Harim, one thousand and seventeen. ⁴³The Levites: sons of Jeshua, of Kadmiel, of sons of Hodevah, seventy-four. ⁴⁴The singers: sons of Asaph, one hundred forty-eight. ⁴⁵The gatekeepers: sons of Shallum, sons of Ater, sons of Talmon, sons of Akkub, sons of Hatita, sons of Shobai: one hundred thirty-eight. ⁴⁶The Nethinim: sons of Ziha, sons of Hasupha, sons of Tabbaoth, ⁴⁷sons of Keros, sons of Sia, sons of Padon, ⁴⁸sons of Lebanah, sons of Hagaba, sons of Shalmai, ⁴⁹sons of Hanan, sons of Giddel, sons of Gahar, ⁵⁰sons of Reaiah, sons of Rezin, sons of Nekoda, ⁵¹sons of Gazzam, sons of Uzza, sons of Phaseah, ⁵²sons of Bezai, sons of Meunim, sons of Nephishesim, ⁵³sons of Bakbuk, sons of Hakupha, sons of Harhur, ⁵⁴sons of Bazlith, sons of Mehida, sons of Harsha, ⁵⁵sons of Barkos, sons of Sisera, sons of Tamah, ⁵⁶sons of Neziah, sons of Hatipha. ⁵⁷Sons of the servants of Solomon: sons of Sotai, sons of Sophereth, sons of Perida, ⁵⁸sons of Jaala, sons of Darkon, sons of Giddel, ⁵⁹sons of Shephatiah, sons of Hattil, sons of Pochereth of Zebaim, sons of Amon. ⁶⁰All the Nethinim and the sons of the servants of Solomon [are] three hundred ninety-two. ⁶¹And these [are] those coming up from Tel-Melah, Tel-Harsha, Cherub, Addon, and Immer—and they have not been able to declare the house of their fathers, and their seed, whether they [are] of Israel— ⁶²sons of Delaiah, sons of Tobiah, sons of Nekoda, six hundred forty-two. ⁶³And of the priests: sons of Habaiah, sons of Koz, sons of Barzillai (who has taken a wife from the daughters of Barzillai the Gileadite, and is called by their name). ⁶⁴These have sought their register among those reckoning themselves by genealogy, and it has not been found, and they are redeemed from the priesthood, ⁶⁵and the Tirshatha says to them that they do not eat of the most holy things until the standing up of the priest with [the] Lights and Perfections. ⁶⁶All the assembly together [is] forty-two thousand three hundred and sixty, ⁶⁷apart from their servants and their handmaids—these [are] seven thousand three hundred thirty-seven; and of them [are] male and female singers, two hundred forty-five. ⁶⁸Their horses [are] seven hundred thirty-six; their mules, two hundred [and] forty-five; ⁶⁹camels, four hundred thirty-five; donkeys, six thousand seven hundred and twenty. ⁷⁰And from the extremity of the heads of the fathers they have given to the work; the Tirshatha has given to the treasure, one thousand drams of gold, fifty bowls, five hundred and thirty priests' coats. ⁷¹And of the heads of the fathers they have given to the treasure of the work, twenty thousand drams of gold, and two thousand and two hundred pounds of silver. ⁷²And that which the rest of the people have given [is] twenty thousand drams of gold, and two thousand pounds of silver, and sixty-seven priests' coats. ⁷³And they dwell—the priests, and the Levites, and the gatekeepers, and the singers, and [some] of the people, and the Nethinim, and all Israel—in their cities, and the seventh month comes, and the sons of Israel [are] in their cities.

CHAPTER 8

¹And all the people are gathered as one man to the broad place that [is] before the Water Gate, and they say to Ezra the scribe to bring the Scroll of the Law of Moses, that YHWH commanded Israel. ²And Ezra the priest brings the Law before the assembly, both of men and women, and everyone intelligent to hear, on the first day of the seventh month, ³and he reads in it before the broad place that [is] before the Water Gate, from the light until the middle of the day, in front of the men, and the women, and those intelligent, and the ears of all the people [are] toward the Scroll of the Law. ⁴And Ezra the scribe stands on a tower of wood that they made for the purpose, and Mattithiah stands near him, and Shema, and Anaiah, and Urijah, and Hilkiah, and Maaseiah, on his right; and on his left Pedaiah, and Mishael, and Malchijah, and Hashum, and Hashbaddana, Zechariah, Meshullam. ⁵And Ezra opens the scroll before the eyes of all the people—for he has been above all the people—and at his opening [it] all the people have stood up, ⁶and Ezra blesses YHWH, the great God, and all the people answer, "Amen, Amen," with lifting up of their hands, and they bow and pay respect to YHWH—faces to the earth. ⁷And Jeshua, and Bani, and Sherebiah, Jamin, Akkub, Shabbethai, Hodijah, Maaseiah, Kelita, Azariah, Jozabad, Hanan, Pelaiah, and the Levites, giving the people understanding in the Law, and the people, [are] on their station, ⁸and they read in the Scroll, in the Law of God, explaining—so as to give the meaning, and they give understanding to the convocation. ⁹And Nehemiah—he [is] the Tirshatha—says (and Ezra the priest, the scribe, and the Levites who are instructing the people) to all the people, "Today is holy to your God YHWH, do not mourn, nor weep": for all the people are weeping at their hearing the words of the Law. ¹⁰And he says to them, "Go, eat fat things, and drink sweet things, and send portions to him for whom nothing is prepared, for today [is] holy to our Lord, and do not be grieved, for the joy of YHWH is your strength." ¹¹And the Levites are keeping all the people silent, saying, "Be silent, for today [is] holy, and do not be grieved." ¹²And all the people go to eat, and to drink, and to send portions, and to make great joy, because they have understood concerning the words that they made known to them. ¹³And on the second day have been gathered heads of the fathers of all the people, the priests, and the Levites, to Ezra the scribe, even to act wisely concerning the words of the Law. ¹⁴And they find written in the Law that YHWH commanded by the hand of Moses, that the sons of Israel dwell in shelters in the celebration, in the seventh month, ¹⁵and that they proclaim and cause to pass over all their cities (and in Jerusalem), saying, "Go out to the mountain, and bring leaves of the olive, and leaves of the oil tree, and leaves of the myrtle, and leaves of the palms, and leaves of thick trees, to make shelters as it is written." ¹⁶And the people go out, and bring in, and make for themselves shelters, each on his roof, and in their courts, and in the courts of the house of God, and in the broad place of the Water Gate, and in the broad place of the Gate of Ephraim. ¹⁷And they make—all the assembly of the captives of the captivity—shelters, and they sit in shelters; for the sons of Israel had not done, from the days of Jeshua son of Nun, so to that day, and there is very great joy. ¹⁸And he reads in the Scroll of the Law of God day by day, from the first day until the last day, and they make a celebration seven days, and on the eighth day a restraint, according to the ordinance.

CHAPTER 9

¹And in the twenty-fourth day of this month the sons of Israel have been gathered with fasting, and with sackcloth, and earth on them; ²and the seed of Israel are separated from all sons of a stranger, and stand and confess concerning their sins, and the iniquities of their fathers, ³and rise up on their station, and read in the Scroll of the Law of their God YHWH a fourth of the day, and a fourth they are confessing and bowing themselves to their God YHWH. ⁴And there stand up on the ascent, of the Levites, Jeshua, and Bani, Kadmiel, Shebaniah, Bunni, Sherebiah, Bani, Chenani, and they cry with a loud voice to their God YHWH. ⁵And the Levites say, [even] Jeshua, and Kadmiel, Bani, Hashabniah, Sherebiah, Hodijah, Shebaniah, Pethahiah, "Rise, bless your God YHWH, || From age to age, || And they bless the Name of Your glory || That [is] exalted above all blessing and praise. ⁶You [are] He, O YHWH—You have made the heavens, || The heavens of the heavens, and all their host, || The earth and all that [are] on it, || The seas and all that [are] in them, || And You are keeping all of them alive, || And the host of the heavens are bowing themselves to You. ⁷You [are] He, O YHWH God, || Who fixed on Abraham, || And brought him out from Ur of the Chaldeans, || And made his name Abraham, ⁸And found his heart steadfast before You, || So as to make with him the covenant, || To give the land of the Canaanite, || The Hittite, the Amorite, and the Perizzite, and the Jebusite, and the Girgashite, || To give [it] to his seed. And You establish Your words, || For You [are] righteous, ⁹And see the affliction of our fathers in Egypt, || And

NEHEMIAH

their cry have heard by the Sea of Suph, ¹⁰And give signs and wonders on Pharaoh, || And on all his servants, || And on all the people of his land, || For You have known that they have acted proudly against them, || And You make to Yourself a name as [at] this day. ¹¹And You have cleaved the sea before them, || And they pass over into the midst of the sea on the dry land, || And their pursuers You have cast into the depths, || As a stone, into the strong waters. ¹²And by a pillar of cloud You have led them by day, || And by a pillar of fire by night, || To lighten to them the way in which they go. ¹³And on Mount Sinai You have come down, || Even to speak with them from the heavens, || And You give to them right judgments, || And true laws, good statutes and commands. ¹⁴And Your holy Sabbath You have made known to them, || And commands, and statutes, and law, || You have commanded for them, || By the hand of Your servant Moses; ¹⁵And bread from the heavens You have given to them for their hunger, || And water from a rock have brought out to them for their thirst, || And say to them to go in to possess the land || That You have lifted up Your hand to give to them. ¹⁶And they and our fathers have acted proudly, || And harden their neck, || And have not listened to Your commands, ¹⁷Indeed, they refuse to listen, || And have not remembered Your wonders that You have done with them, || And harden their neck and appoint a head, || To turn back to their service, in their rebellion; And You [are] a God of pardons, || Gracious, and merciful, long-suffering, and abundant in kindness, || And have not forsaken them. ¹⁸Also, when they have made to themselves a molten calf, || And say, This [is] your god || That brought you up out of Egypt, || And do great despisings, ¹⁹And you, in Your abundant mercies, || Have not forsaken them in the wilderness—The pillar of the cloud has not turned aside from off them by day, || To lead them in the way, || And the pillar of the fire by night, || To give light to them and the way in which they go. ²⁰And Your good Spirit You have given, || To cause them to act wisely; And Your manna You have not withheld from their mouth, || And water You have given to them for their thirst, ²¹And forty years You have nourished them in a wilderness; They have not lacked; Their garments have not worn out, || And their feet have not swelled. ²²And You give to them kingdoms, and peoples, || And apportion them to the corner, || And they possess the land of Sihon, || And the land of the king of Heshbon, || And the land of Og king of Bashan. ²³And You have multiplied their sons as the stars of the heavens, || And bring them into the land || That You have said to their fathers to go in to possess. ²⁴And the sons come in, and possess the land, || And You humble the inhabitants of the land—the Canaanites—before them, || And give them into their hand, and their kings, || And the peoples of the land, || To do with them according to their pleasure. ²⁵And they capture fortified cities, and fat ground, || And possess houses full of all good, || Dug-wells, vineyards, and olive-yards, || And fruit-trees in abundance, || And they eat, and are satisfied, || And become fat, || And delight themselves in Your great goodness. ²⁶And they are disobedient, || And rebel against You, || And cast Your law behind their back, || And Your prophets they have slain, || Who testified against them, || To bring them back to You, || And they do great despisings, ²⁷And You give them into the hand of their adversaries, || And they distress them, || And in the time of their distress they cry to You, || And You, from the heavens, hear, || And according to Your abundant mercies, || Give saviors to them, || And they save them out of the hand of their adversaries. ²⁸And when they have rest, || They turn back to do evil before You, || And You leave them in the hand of their enemies, || And they rule over them; And they return, and call You, || And You hear from the heavens, || And deliver them many times, || According to Your mercies, ²⁹And testify against them, || To bring them back to Your law; And they have acted proudly, || And have not listened to Your commands, || And against Your judgments have sinned—Which man does and has lived in them—And they give a stubborn shoulder, || And have hardened their neck, || And have not listened. ³⁰And You draw over them many years, || And testify against them by Your Spirit, || By the hand of Your prophets, || And they have not given ear, || And You give them into the hand of peoples of the lands, ³¹and in Your abundant mercies || You have not made them a consumption, || Nor have forsaken them; For a God, gracious and merciful, [are] You. ³²And now, O our God—God, the great, the mighty, || And the fearful, || Keeping the covenant and the kindness—Do not let all the travail that has found us be little before You, || For our kings, for our heads, and for our priests, || And for our prophets, and for our fathers, || And for all Your people, || From the days of the kings of Asshur to this day; ³³And You [are] righteous concerning all that has come on us, || For You have done truth, || And we have done wickedly; ³⁴And our kings, our heads, || Our priests, and our fathers, || Have not done Your law, || Nor attended to Your commands, || And to Your testimonies, || That You have testified against them; ³⁵And they, in their kingdom, || And in Your abundant goodness, || That You have given to them, || And in the land, the large and the fat, || That You have set before them, || Have not served You, || Nor turned back from their evil doings. ³⁶Behold, we—today—[are] servants, || And the land that You have given to our fathers, || To eat its fruit and its good, || Behold, we [are] servants on it, ³⁷And its increase it is multiplying to the kings || Whom You have set over us || In our sins; And over our bodies they are ruling, || And over our livestock, || According to their pleasure, || And we [are] in great distress. ³⁸And for all this we are making a steadfast covenant, || And are writing, || And over him who is sealed || [Are] our heads, our Levites, [and] our priests."

CHAPTER 10

¹And over those sealed [are] Nehemiah the Tirshatha, son of Hachaliah, and Zidkijah, ²Seraiah, Azariah, Jeremiah, ³Pashhur, Amariah, Malchijah, ⁴Huttush, Shebaniah, Malluch, ⁵Harim, Meremoth, Obadiah, ⁶Daniel, Ginnethon, Baruch, ⁷Meshullam, Abijah, Mijamin, ⁸Maaziah, Bilgai, Shemaiah; these [are] the priests. ⁹And the Levites: both Jeshua son of Azaniah, Binnui of the sons of Henadad, Kadmiel; ¹⁰and their brothers: Shebaniah, Hodijah, Kelita, Pelaiah, Hanan, ¹¹Micha, Rehob, Hashabiah, ¹²Zaccur, Sherebiah, Shebaniah, ¹³Hodijah, Bani, Beninu. ¹⁴Heads of the people: Parosh, Pahath-Moab, Elam, Zatthu, Bani, ¹⁵Bunni, Azgad, Bebai, ¹⁶Adonijah, Bigvai, Adin, ¹⁷Ater, Hizkijah, Azzur, ¹⁸Hodijah, Hashum, Bezai, ¹⁹Hariph, Anathoth, Nebai, ²⁰Magpiash, Meshullam, Hezir, ²¹Meshezabeel, Zadok, Jaddua, ²²Pelatiah, Hanan, Anaiah, ²³Hoshea, Hananiah, Hashub, ²⁴Hallohesh, Pilha, Shobek, ²⁵Rehum, Hashabnah, Maaseiah, ²⁶and Ahijah, Hanan, Anan, ²⁷Malluch, Harim, Baanah. ²⁸And the rest of the people, the priests, the Levites, the gatekeepers, the singers, the Nethinim, and everyone who has been separated from the peoples of the lands to the Law of God, their wives, their sons, and their daughters, every knowing intelligent one, ²⁹are laying hold on their brothers, their majestic ones, and coming into an execration and an oath, to walk in the Law of God, that was given by the hand of Moses, servant of God, and to observe and to do all the commands of YHWH our Lord, and His judgments, and His statutes; ³⁰and that we do not give our daughters to the peoples of the land, and we do not take their daughters to our sons; ³¹and the peoples of the land who are bringing in the wares and any grain on the Sabbath day to sell, we do not receive of them on the Sabbath, and on a holy day, and we leave the seventh year, and usury on every hand. ³²And we have appointed for ourselves commands, to put on ourselves the third of a shekel in a year, for the service of the house of our God, ³³for bread of the arrangement, and the continual present, and the continual burnt-offering of the Sabbaths, of the new moons, for appointed times, and for holy things, and for sin-offerings, to make atonement for Israel, even all the work of the house of our God. ³⁴And we have caused the lots to fall for the offering of wood, [among] the priests, the Levites, and the people, to bring into the house of our God, by the house of our fathers, at times appointed, year by year, to burn on the altar of our God YHWH, as it is written in the Law, ³⁵and to bring in the first-fruits of our ground, and the first-fruits of all fruit of every tree, year by year, to the house of YHWH, ³⁶and the firstlings of our sons, and of our livestock, as it is written in the Law, and the firstlings of our herds and our flocks, to bring into the house of our God, to the priests who are ministering in the house of our God. ³⁷And the beginning of our dough, and our raised-offerings, and the fruit of every tree, of new wine, and of oil, we bring to the priests, into the chambers of the house of our God, and

NEHEMIAH

the tithe of our ground to the Levites; and they—the Levites—have the tithes in all the cities of our tillage; ³⁸and the priest, son of Aaron, has been with the Levites in the tithing of the Levites, and the Levites bring up the tithe of the tithe to the house of our God to the chambers, to the treasure-house; ³⁹for they bring to the chambers—the sons of Israel and the sons of Levi—the raised-offering of the grain, the new wine, and the oil, and there [are] vessels of the sanctuary, and the priests, those ministering, and the gatekeepers, and the singers, and we do not forsake the house of our God.

CHAPTER 11

¹And the heads of the people dwell in Jerusalem, and the rest of the people have caused lots to fall to bring in one out of ten to dwell in Jerusalem the holy city, and nine parts in the cities, ²and the people give a blessing to all the men who are offering themselves willingly to dwell in Jerusalem. ³And these [are] heads of the province who have dwelt in Jerusalem, and in cities of Judah, they have dwelt each in his possession in their cities; Israel, the priests, and the Levites, and the Nethinim, and the sons of the servants of Solomon. ⁴And in Jerusalem have dwelt of the sons of Judah, and of the sons of Benjamin. Of the sons of Judah: Athaiah son of Uzziah, son of Zechariah, son of Amariah, son of Shephatiah, son of Mahalaleel, of the sons of Perez; ⁵and Masseiah son of Baruch, son of Col-Hozeh, son of Hazaiah, son of Adaiah, son of Joiarib, son of Zechariah, son of Shiloni; ⁶all the sons of Perez who are dwelling in Jerusalem [are] four hundred sixty-eight, men of valor. ⁷And these [are] sons of Benjamin: Sallu son of Meshullam, son of Joed, son of Pedaiah, son of Kolaiah, son of Maaseiah, son of Ithiel, son of Jesaiah; ⁸and after him Gabbai, Sallai, nine hundred twenty-eight. ⁹And Joel son of Zichri [is] inspector over them, and Judah son of Senuah [is] over the city—second. ¹⁰Of the priests: Jedaiah son of Joiarib, Jachin, ¹¹Seraiah son of Hilkiah, son of Meshullam, son of Zadok, son of Meraioth, son of Ahitub, leader of the house of God, ¹²and their brothers doing the work of the house [are] eight hundred twenty-two; and Adaiah son of Jeroham, son of Pelaliah, son of Amzi, son of Zechariah, son of Pashhur, son of Malchiah, ¹³and his brothers, heads of fathers, two hundred forty-two; and Amashsai son of Azareel, son of Ahazai, son of Meshillemoth, son of Immer, ¹⁴and their brothers, one hundred twenty-eight mighty men of valor; and an inspector over them [is] Zabdiel, son of [one of] the great men. ¹⁵And of the Levites: Shemaiah son of Hashub, son of Azrikam, son of Hashabiah, son of Bunni, ¹⁶and Shabbethai, and Jozabad, [are] over the outward work of the house of God, of the heads of the Levites, ¹⁷and Mattaniah son of Micha, son of Zabdi, son of Asaph, [is] head—at the commencement he gives thanks in prayer; and Bakbukiah [is] second among his brothers, and Abda son of Shammua, son of Galal, son of Jeduthun. ¹⁸All the Levites, in the holy city, [are] two hundred eighty-four. ¹⁹And the gatekeepers, Akkub, Talmon, and their brothers, those watching at the gates, [are] one hundred seventy-two. ²⁰And the rest of Israel, of the priests, of the Levites, [are] in all cities of Judah, each in his inheritance; ²¹and the Nethinim are dwelling in Ophel, and Ziha and Gishpa [are] over the Nethinim. ²²And the overseer of the Levites in Jerusalem [is] Uzzi son of Bani, son of Hashabiah, son of Mattaniah, son of Micha—of the sons of Asaph, the singers [who are] for the front of the work of the house of God, ²³for the command of the king [is] on them, and support [is] for the singers, a matter of a day in its day. ²⁴And Pethahiah son of Meshezabeel, of the sons of Zerah, son of Judah, [is] by the hand of the king, for every matter of the people. ²⁵And at the villages with their fields, of the sons of Judah there have dwelt, in Kirjath-Arba and its small towns, and in Dibon and its small towns, and in Jekabzeel and its villages, ²⁶and in Jeshua, and in Moladah, and in Beth-Phelet, ²⁷and in Hazar-Shaul, and in Beer-Sheba and its small towns, ²⁸and in Ziklag, and in Mekonah and in its small towns, ²⁹and En-Rimmon, and in Zareah, and in Jarmuth, ³⁰Zanoah, Adullam, and their villages, Lachish and its fields, Azekah and its small towns; and they encamp from Beer-Sheba to the Valley of Hinnom. ³¹And sons of Benjamin [are] at Geba, Michmash, and Aija, and Beth-El, and its small towns, ³²Anathoth, Nob, Ananiah, ³³Hazor, Ramah, Gittaim, ³⁴Hadid, Zeboim, Neballat, ³⁵Lod, and Ono, the Valley of the Craftsmen. ³⁶And of the Levites, the divisions of Judah [are] for Benjamin.

CHAPTER 12

¹And these [are] the priests and the Levites who came up with Zerubbabel son of Shealtiel, and Jeshua: Seraiah, Jeremiah, Ezra, ²Amariah, Malluch, Hattush, ³Shechaniah, Rehum, Meremoth, ⁴Iddo, Ginnethoi, Abijah, ⁵Miamin, Maadiah, Bilgah, ⁶Shemaiah, and Joiarib, Jedaiah, ⁷Sallu, Amok, Hilkiah, Jedaiah; these [are] heads of the priests and of their brothers in the days of Jeshua. ⁸And the Levites: Jeshua, Binnui, Kadmiel, Sherebiah, Judah, Mattaniah, he [is] over the thanksgiving, and his brothers, ⁹and Bakbukiah and Unni, their brothers, [are] opposite them in charges. ¹⁰And Jeshua has begotten Joiakim, and Joiakim has begotten Eliashib, and Eliashib has begotten Joiada, ¹¹and Joiada has begotten Jonathan, and Jonathan has begotten Jaddua. ¹²And in the days of Joiakim have been priests, heads of the fathers: of Seraiah, Meraiah; of Jeremiah, Hananiah; ¹³of Ezra, Meshullam; of Amariah, Jehohanan; ¹⁴of Melicu, Jonathan; of Shebaniah, Joseph; ¹⁵of Harim, Adna; of Meraioth, Helkai; ¹⁶of Iddo, Zechariah; of Ginnethon, Meshullam; ¹⁷of Abijah, Zichri; of Miniamin; of Moadiah, Piltai; ¹⁸of Bilgah, Shammua; of Shemaiah, Jonathan; ¹⁹and of Joiarib, Mattenai; of Jedaiah, Uzzi; ²⁰of Sallai, Kallai; of Amok, Eber; ²¹of Hilkiah, Hashabiah; of Jedaiah, Nethaneel. ²²The Levites, in the days of Eliashib, Joiada, and Johanan, and Jaddua, are written, heads of fathers, and of the priests, in the kingdom of Darius the Persian. ²³Sons of Levi, heads of the fathers, are written on the scroll of the Chronicles even until the days of Johanan son of Eliashib; ²⁴and heads of the Levites: Hashabiah, Sherebiah, and Jeshua son of Kadmiel, and their brothers, [are] opposite them, to give praise, to give thanks, by command of David the man of God, charge close by charge. ²⁵Mattaniah, and Bakbukiah, Obadiah, Meshullam, Talmon, Akkub, [are] gatekeepers, keeping watch in the gatherings of the gates. ²⁶These [are] in the days of Joiakim son of Jeshua, son of Jozadak, and in the days of Nehemiah the governor, and of Ezra the priest, the scribe. ²⁷And at the dedication of the wall of Jerusalem they sought the Levites out of all their places, to bring them to Jerusalem, to make the dedication even with gladness, and with thanksgivings, and with singing, [with] cymbals, psalteries, and with harps; ²⁸and sons of the singers are gathered together even from the circuit around Jerusalem, and from the villages of Netophathi, ²⁹and from the house of Gilgal, and from fields of Geba and Azmaveth, the singers have built for villages for themselves around Jerusalem; ³⁰and the priests and the Levites are cleansed, and they cleanse the people, and the gates, and the wall. ³¹And I bring up the heads of Judah on the wall, and appoint two great thanksgiving companies and processions. At the right, on the wall, to the Refuse Gate; ³²and after them goes Hoshaiah, and half of the heads of Judah, ³³and Azariah, Ezra, and Meshullam, ³⁴Judah, and Benjamin, and Shemaiah, and Jeremiah; ³⁵and of the sons of the priests with trumpets, Zechariah son of Jonathan, son of Shemaiah, son of Mattaniah, son of Michaiah, son of Zaccur, son of Asaph, ³⁶and his brothers Shemaiah, and Azarael, Milalai, Gilalai, Maai, Nethaneel, and Judah, Hanani, with instruments of song of David the man of God, and Ezra the scribe [is] before them; ³⁷and by the Fountain Gate and in front of them, they have gone up by the steps of the City of David, at the going up of the wall beyond the house of David, and to the Water Gate eastward. ³⁸And the second thanksgiving company that is going opposite, and I after it, and half of the people on the wall from beyond the Tower of the Furnaces and to the broad wall, ³⁹and from beyond the Gate of Ephraim, and by the Old Gate, and by the Fish Gate, and the Tower of Hananeel, and the Tower of Meah, and to the Sheep Gate—and they have stood at the Prison Gate. ⁴⁰And the two thanksgiving companies stand in the house of God, and I and half of the prefects with me, ⁴¹and the priests, Eliakim, Maaseiah, Miniamin, Michaiah, Elioenai, Zechariah, Hananiah, with trumpets, ⁴²and Masseiah, and Shemaiah, and Eleazar, and Uzzi, and Jehohanan, and Malchijah, and Elam, and Ezer, and the singers sound, and Jezrahiah the inspector; ⁴³and they sacrifice on that day great sacrifices and rejoice, for God has made them rejoice [with] great joy, and also, the women and the children have rejoiced, and the joy of Jerusalem is heard—to a distance. ⁴⁴And

certain are appointed on that day over the chambers for treasures, for raised-offerings, for first-fruits, and for tithes, to gather into them out of the fields of the cities the portions of the law for priests, and for Levites, for the joy of Judah [is] over the priests, and over the Levites, who are standing up. ⁴⁵And the singers and the gatekeepers keep the charge of their God, even the charge of the cleansing—according to the command of David [and] his son Solomon, ⁴⁶for in the days of David and Asaph of old [were] heads of the singers, and a song of praise and thanksgiving to God. ⁴⁷And all Israel in the days of Zerubbabel, and in the days of Nehemiah, are giving the portions of the singers, and of the gatekeepers, the matter of a day in its day, and are sanctifying to the Levites, and the Levites are sanctifying to the sons of Aaron.

CHAPTER 13

¹On that day there was read in the scroll of Moses, in the ears of the people, and it has been found written in it that an Ammonite and Moabite does not come into the assembly of God for all time, ²because they have not come before the sons of Israel with bread and with water, and hire against them Balaam to revile them, and our God turns the reviling into a blessing. ³And it comes to pass, at their hearing the Law, that they separate all the mixed people from Israel. ⁴And before this Eliashib the priest, appointed over chambers of the house of our God, [is] a relation of Tobiah, ⁵and he makes for him a great chamber, and there they were formerly putting the present, the frankincense, and the vessels, and the tithe of the grain, the new wine, and the oil—the commanded thing of the Levites, and the singers, and the gatekeepers—and the raised-offering of the priests. ⁶And during all this I was not in Jerusalem, for in the thirty-second year of Artaxerxes king of Babylon I came to the king, and at the end of days I have asked of the king, ⁷and I come to Jerusalem, and understand concerning the evil that Eliashib has done for Tobiah, to make to him a chamber in the courts of the house of God, ⁸and it is very displeasing to me, and I cast all the vessels of the house of Tobiah outside, out of the chamber, ⁹and I command, and they cleanse the chambers, and I bring back there the vessels of the house of God with the present and the frankincense. ¹⁰And I know that the portions of the Levites have not been given, and they flee each to his field—the Levites and the singers, doing the work. ¹¹And I strive with the prefects, and say, "Why has the house of God been forsaken?" And I gather them, and set them on their station; ¹²and all Judah has brought in the tithe of the grain, and of the new wine, and of the oil, to the treasuries. ¹³And I appoint treasurers over the treasuries, Shelemiah the priest, and Zadok the scribe, and Pedaiah of the Levites; and by their hand [is] Hanan son of Zaccur, son of Mattaniah, for they have been reckoned steadfast, and on them [it is] to give a portion to their brothers. ¹⁴Be mindful of me, O my God, for this, and do not blot out my kind acts that I have done, for the house of my God, and for its charges. ¹⁵In those days I have seen in Judah those treading wine-vats on Sabbath, and bringing in the sheaves, and loading on the donkeys, and also, wine, grapes, and figs, and every burden, indeed, they are bringing into Jerusalem on the Sabbath day, and I testify in the day of their selling provision. ¹⁶And the Tyrians have dwelt in it, bringing in fish, and every ware, and selling on Sabbath to the sons of Judah and in Jerusalem. ¹⁷And I strive with the nobles of Judah, and say to them, "What [is] this evil thing that you are doing, and defiling the Sabbath day? ¹⁸Thus did not your fathers do? And our God brings in on us all this evil, and on this city, and you are adding fierceness on Israel, to defile the Sabbath." ¹⁹And it comes to pass, when the gates of Jerusalem have been dark before the Sabbath, that I command, and the doors are shut, and I command that they do not open them until after the Sabbath; and of my servants I have stationed at the gates; there does not come in a burden on the Sabbath day. ²⁰And they lodge—the merchants and sellers of all ware—at the outside of Jerusalem, once or twice, ²¹and I testify against them, and say to them, "Why are you lodging in front of the wall? If you repeat [it], I put forth a hand on you"; from that time they have not come in on the Sabbath. ²²And I command to the Levites that they be cleansed, and coming in, keeping the gates, to sanctify the Sabbath day. Also, this, remember for me, O my God, and have pity on me, according to the abundance of Your kindness. ²³Also, in those days, I have seen the Jews [who] have settled women of Ashdod, of Ammon, of Moab. ²⁴And of their sons, half are speaking Ashdoditish—and are not knowing to speak Jewish—and according to the language of people and people. ²⁵And I strive with them, and declare them vile, and strike certain of them, and pluck off their hair, and cause them to swear by God, "You do not give your daughters to their sons, nor do you take of their daughters to your sons, and to yourselves. ²⁶By these did not Solomon king of Israel sin? And among the many nations there was no king like him, and he was beloved by his God, and God makes him king over all Israel—even him [whom] the strange women caused to sin. ²⁷And do we listen to you to do all this great evil, to trespass against our God, to settle strange women?" ²⁸And [one] of the sons of Joiada son of Eliashib the high priest, [is] son-in-law to Sanballat the Horonite, and I cause him to flee from off me. ²⁹Be mindful of them, O my God, for the redeemed of the priesthood, and the covenant of the priesthood, and of the Levites. ³⁰And I have cleansed them from every stranger, and appoint charges to priests and to Levites, each in his work, ³¹and for the wood-offering at appointed times, and for first-fruits. Be mindful of me, O my God, for good.

ESTHER

CHAPTER 1

¹And it comes to pass, in the days of Ahasuerus—he [is] Ahasuerus who is reigning from Hodu even to Cush, one hundred twenty-seven provinces— ²in those days, at the sitting of King Ahasuerus on the throne of his kingdom, that [is] in Shushan the palace, ³in the third year of his reign, he has made a banquet to all his heads and his servants; of the force of Persia and Media, the chiefs and heads of the provinces [are] before him, ⁴in his showing the wealth of the glory of his kingdom, and the glory of the beauty of his greatness, many days—one hundred eighty days. ⁵And at the fullness of these days the king has made a banquet to all the people who are found in Shushan the palace, from great even to small, [for] seven days, in the court of the garden of the house of the king— ⁶white linen, white cotton, and blue, fastened with cords of fine linen and purple on rings of silver, and pillars of marble, couches of gold, and of silver, on a pavement of smaragdus, and white marble, and mother-of-pearl, and black marble— ⁷and the giving of drink in vessels of gold, and the vessels [are] various vessels, and the royal wine [is] abundant, as a memorial of the king. ⁸And the drinking [is] according to law, none is pressing, for so the king has appointed for every chief one of his house, to do according to the pleasure of man and man. ⁹Also Vashti the queen has made a banquet for women, in the royal house that King Ahasuerus has. ¹⁰On the seventh day, as the heart of the king is glad with wine, he has commanded to Mehuman, Biztha, Harbona, Bigtha, and Abagtha, Zethar, and Carcas, the seven eunuchs who are ministering in the presence of King Ahasuerus, ¹¹to bring in Vashti the queen before the king, with a royal crown, to show the peoples and the heads her beauty, for she [is] of good appearance, ¹²and the queen Vashti refuses to come in at the word of the king that [is] by the hand of the eunuchs, and the king is very angry, and his fury has burned in him. ¹³And the king says to

ESTHER

wise men, knowing the times—for so [is] the word of the king before all knowing law and judgment, ¹⁴and he who is near to him [is] Carshena, Shethar, Admatha, Tarshish, Meres, Marsena, Memucan, seven heads of Persia and Media seeing the face of the king, who are sitting first in the kingdom— ¹⁵"According to law, what should [I] do with Queen Vashti, because that she has not done the saying of King Ahasuerus by the hand of the eunuchs?" ¹⁶And Memucan says before the king and the heads, "Queen Vashti has not done perversely against the king by himself, but against all the heads, and against all the peoples that [are] in all provinces of King Ahasuerus; ¹⁷for the word of the queen goes forth to all the women, to render their husbands contemptible in their eyes, in their saying, King Ahasuerus commanded to bring in Vashti the queen before him, and she did not come; ¹⁸indeed, this day princesses of Persia and Media, who have heard the word of the queen, say [so] to all heads of the king, even according to the sufficiency of contempt and wrath. ¹⁹If to the king [it be] good, there goes forth a royal word from before him, and it is written with the laws of Persia and Media, and does not pass away, that Vashti does not come in before King Ahasuerus, and the king gives her royalty to her companion who [is] better than she; ²⁰and the sentence of the king that he makes has been heard in all his kingdom—for it [is] great—and all the wives give honor to their husbands, from great even to small." ²¹And the thing is good in the eyes of the king, and of the princes, and the king does according to the word of Memucan, ²²and sends letters to all provinces of the king, to province and province according to its writing, and to people and people according to its tongue, for every man being head in his own house—and speaking according to the language of his people.

CHAPTER 2

¹After these things, at the ceasing of the fury of King Ahasuerus, he has remembered Vashti, and that which she did, and that which has been decreed concerning her; ²and servants of the king, his ministers, say, "Let them seek for the king young women, virgins, of good appearance, ³and the king appoints inspectors in all provinces of his kingdom, and they gather every young woman—virgin, of good appearance—to Shushan the palace, to the house of the women, to the hand of Hegai eunuch of the king, keeper of the women, and to give their purifications, ⁴and the young woman who is good in the eyes of the king reigns instead of Vashti"; and the thing is good in the eyes of the king, and he does so. ⁵A man, a Jew, there has been in Shushan the palace, and his name [is] Mordecai son of Jair, son of Shimei, son of Kish, a Benjamite— ⁶who had been removed from Jerusalem with the expulsion that was removed with Jeconiah king of Judah, whom Nebuchadnezzar king of Babylon removed— ⁷and he is supporting Hadassah—she [is] Esther—daughter of his uncle, for she has neither father nor mother, and the young woman [is] of beautiful form, and of good appearance, and at the death of her father and her mother Mordecai has taken her to himself for a daughter. ⁸And it comes to pass, in the word of the king, even his law, being heard, and in many young women being gathered to Shushan the palace, to the hand of Hegai, that Esther is taken to the house of the king, to the hand of Hegai, keeper of the women, ⁹and the young woman is good in his eyes, and she receives kindness before him, and he hurries her purifications and her portions—to give to her, and the seven young women who are provided—to give to her, from the house of the king, and he changes her and her young women to a good [place in] the house of the women. ¹⁰Esther has not declared her people, and her family, for Mordecai has laid a charge on her that she does not declare [it]; ¹¹and during every day Mordecai is walking up and down before the court of the house of the women to know the welfare of Esther, and what is done with her. ¹²And in the drawing near of the turn of each young woman to come in to King Ahasuerus, at the end of there being to her—according to the law of the women—twelve months, for so they fulfill the days of their purifications; six months with oil of myrrh, and six months with perfumes, and with the purifications of women, ¹³and with this the young woman has come in to the king, all that she says is given to her to go in with her out of the house of the women to the house of the king; ¹⁴in the evening she has gone in, and in the morning she has turned back to the second house of the women, to the hand of Shaashgaz eunuch of the king, keeper of the concubines; she does not come in anymore to the king except the king has delighted in her, and she has been called by name. ¹⁵And in the drawing near of the turn of Esther—daughter of Abihail, uncle of Mordecai, whom he had taken to himself for a daughter—to come in to the king, she has not sought a thing except that which Hegai eunuch of the king, keeper of the women, says, and Esther is receiving grace in the eyes of all seeing her. ¹⁶And Esther is taken to King Ahasuerus, to his royal house, in the tenth month—it [is] the month of Tebeth—in the seventh year of his reign, ¹⁷and the king loves Esther above all the women, and she receives grace and kindness before him above all the virgins, and he sets a royal crown on her head, and causes her to reign instead of Vashti, ¹⁸and the king makes a great banquet to all his heads and his servants—the banquet of Esther—and has made a release to the provinces, and gives gifts as a memorial of the king. ¹⁹And in the virgins being gathered a second time, then Mordecai is sitting in the gate of the king; ²⁰Esther is not declaring her family and her people, as Mordecai has laid a charge on her, and the saying of Mordecai Esther is doing as when she was truly with him. ²¹In those days, when Mordecai is sitting in the gate of the king, has Bigthan been angry, and Teresh (two of the eunuchs of the king, the keepers of the threshold), and they seek to put forth a hand on King Ahasuerus, ²²and the thing is known to Mordecai, and he declares [it] to Esther the queen, and Esther speaks to the king in the name of Mordecai, ²³and the thing is sought out, and found, and both of them are hanged on a tree, and it is written in the scroll of the Chronicles before the king.

CHAPTER 3

¹After these things has King Ahasuerus exalted Haman son of Hammedatha the Agagite, and lifts him up, and sets his throne above all the heads who [are] with him, ²and all servants of the king, who [are] in the gate of the king, are bowing and doing homage to Haman, for so the king has commanded for him; and Mordecai does not bow nor pay respect. ³And the servants of the king, who [are] in the gate of the king, say to Mordecai, "Why [are] you transgressing the command of the king?" ⁴And it comes to pass, in their speaking to him, day by day, and he has not listened to them, that they declare [it] to Haman, to see whether the words of Mordecai stand, for he has declared to them that he [is] a Jew. ⁵And Haman sees that Mordecai is not bowing and doing homage to him, and Haman is full of fury, ⁶and it is contemptible in his eyes to put forth a hand on Mordecai by himself, for they have declared to him the people of Mordecai, and Haman seeks to destroy all the Jews who [are] in all the kingdom of Ahasuerus—the people of Mordecai. ⁷In the first month—it [is] the month of Nisan—in the twelfth year of King Ahasuerus, has one caused to fall Pur (that [is] the lot) before Haman, from day to day, and from month to month, [to] the twelfth, it [is] the month of Adar. ⁸And Haman says to King Ahasuerus, "There is one people scattered and separated among the peoples, in all provinces of your kingdom, and their laws [are] diverse from all people, and the laws of the king they are not doing, and for the king it is not profitable to permit them; ⁹if to the king [it be] good, let it be written to destroy them, and ten thousand talents of silver I weigh into the hands of those doing the work, to bring [it] into the treasuries of the king." ¹⁰And the king turns aside his signet from off his hand, and gives it to Haman son of Hammedatha the Agagite, adversary of the Jews; ¹¹and the king says to Haman, "The silver is given to you, and the people, to do with it as [it is] good in your eyes." ¹²And scribes of the king are called, on the first month, on the thirteenth day of it, and it is written according to all that Haman has commanded, to lieutenants of the king, and to the governors who [are] over province and province, and to the heads of people and people, province and province, according to its writing, and people and people according to its tongue, in the name of King Ahasuerus it has been written and sealed with the signet of the king, ¹³and letters to be sent by the hand of the runners to all provinces of the king, to cut off, to slay, and to destroy all the Jews, from young even to old, infant and women, on one day, on the thirteenth of the twelfth month—it [is] the month of Adar—and to seize their spoil, ¹⁴a copy of the writing to be made law in

each and every province is revealed to all the peoples, to be ready for this day. ¹⁵The runners have gone forth, hurried by the word of the king, and the law has been given in Shushan the palace, and the king and Haman have sat down to drink, and the city Shushan is perplexed.

CHAPTER 4

¹And Mordecai has known all that has been done, and Mordecai tears his garments, and puts on sackcloth and ashes, and goes forth into the midst of the city and cries—a cry loud and bitter, ²and he comes to the front of the gate of the king, but none is to come to the gate of the king with a sackcloth-garment. ³And in each and every province, the place where the word of the king, even his law, is coming, the Jews have a great mourning, and fasting, and weeping, and lamenting: sackcloth and ashes are spread for many. ⁴And young women of Esther come in and her eunuchs, and declare [it] to her, and the queen is exceedingly pained, and sends garments to clothe Mordecai, and to turn aside his sackcloth from off him, and he has not received [them]. ⁵And Esther calls to Hatach, of the eunuchs of the king, whom he has stationed before her, and gives him a charge for Mordecai, to know what this [is], and why this [is]. ⁶And Hatach goes out to Mordecai, to a broad place of the city, that [is] before the gate of the king, ⁷and Mordecai declares to him all that has met him, and the explanation of the money that Haman said to weigh to the treasuries of the king for the Jews, to destroy them, ⁸and the copy of the writing of the law that had been given in Shushan to destroy them he has given to him, to show Esther, and to declare [it] to her, and to lay a charge on her to go in to the king, to make supplication to him, and to seek from before him, for her people. ⁹And Hatach comes in and declares to Esther the words of Mordecai, ¹⁰and Esther speaks to Hatach, and charges him for Mordecai: ¹¹"All servants of the king, and people of the provinces of the king, know that any man and woman who comes to the king, into the inner court, who is not called—one law of his [is] to put [them] to death, apart from him to whom the king holds out the golden scepter, then he has lived; and I have not been called to come in to the king these thirty days." ¹²And they declare to Mordecai the words of Esther, ¹³and Mordecai commands to send back to Esther: "Do not think in your soul to be delivered [in] the house of the king, more than all the Jews, ¹⁴but if you keep entirely silent at this time, respite and deliverance remains to the Jews from another place, and you and the house of your fathers are destroyed; and who knows whether for a time like this you have come to the kingdom?" ¹⁵And Esther commands to send back to Mordecai: ¹⁶"Go, gather all the Jews who are found in Shushan, and fast for me, and do not eat nor drink three days, by night and by day; also I and my young women fast likewise, and so I go in to the king, that [is] not according to law, and when I have perished—I have perished." ¹⁷And Mordecai passes on, and does according to all that Esther has charged on him.

CHAPTER 5

¹And it comes to pass on the third day, that Esther puts on royalty, and stands in the inner-court of the house of the king in front of the house of the king, and the king is sitting on his royal throne, in the royal-house, opposite the opening of the house, ²and it comes to pass, at the king's seeing Esther the queen standing in the court, she has received grace in his eyes, and the king holds out to Esther the golden scepter that [is] in his hand, and Esther draws near, and touches the top of the scepter. ³And the king says to her, "What do you [want], Esther, O queen? And what [is] your request? To the half of the kingdom—and it is given to you." ⁴And Esther says, "If to the king [it be] good, the king comes in, and Haman, today, to the banquet that I have made for him"; ⁵and the king says, "Hurry Haman—to do the word of Esther"; and the king comes in, and Haman, to the banquet that Esther has made. ⁶And the king says to Esther, during the banquet of wine, "What [is] your petition? And it is given to you; and what [is] your request? To the half of the kingdom—and it is done." ⁷And Esther answers and says, "My petition and my request [is]: ⁸if I have found grace in the eyes of the king, and if to the king [it be] good, to give my petition, and to perform my request, the king comes, and Haman, to the banquet that I make for them, and tomorrow I do according to the word of the king." ⁹And Haman goes forth on that day rejoicing and glad in heart, and at Haman's seeing Mordecai in the gate of the king, and he has not risen nor moved for him, then is Haman full of fury against Mordecai. ¹⁰And Haman forces himself, and comes into his house, and sends, and brings in his friends, and his wife Zeresh, ¹¹and Haman recounts to them the glory of his wealth, and the abundance of his sons, and all that with which the king made him great, and with which he lifted him up above the heads and servants of the king. ¹²And Haman says, "Indeed, Esther the queen brought none in with the king, to the feast that she made, except myself, and also for tomorrow I am called to her, with the king, ¹³and all this is not profitable to me, during all the time that I am seeing Mordecai the Jew sitting in the gate of the king." ¹⁴And his wife Zeresh says to him, and all his friends, "Let them prepare a tree, in height fifty cubits, and in the morning speak to the king, and they hang Mordecai on it, and go in with the king to the banquet rejoicing"; and the thing is good before Haman, and he prepares the tree.

CHAPTER 6

¹On that night the sleep of the king has fled away, and he commands to bring in the scroll of memorials of the chronicles, and they are read before the king, ²and it is found written that Mordecai had declared concerning Bigthana and Teresh, two of the eunuchs of the king, of the keepers of the threshold, who sought to put forth a hand on King Ahasuerus. ³And the king says, "What honor and greatness has been done to Mordecai for this?" And the servants of the king, his ministers, say, "Nothing has been done with him." ⁴And the king says, "Who [is] in the court?" And Haman has come into the outer court of the house of the king, to say to the king to hang Mordecai on the tree that he had prepared for him. ⁵And the servants of the king say to him, "Behold, Haman is standing in the court"; and the king says, "Let him come in." ⁶And Haman comes in, and the king says to him, "What should [I] do with the man in whose honor the king has delighted?" And Haman says in his heart, "To whom does the king delight to do honor more than myself?" ⁷And Haman says to the king, "The man in whose honor the king has delighted, ⁸let them bring in royal clothing that the king has put on himself, and a horse on which the king has ridden, and that the royal crown be put on his head, ⁹and to give the clothing and the horse into the hand of a man of the heads of the king, the chiefs, and they have clothed the man in whose honor the king has delighted, and caused him to ride on the horse in a broad place of the city, and called before him: Thus it is done to the man in whose honor the king has delighted." ¹⁰And the king says to Haman, "Hurry, take the clothing and the horse, as you have spoken, and do so to Mordecai the Jew, who is sitting in the gate of the king; there does not fall a thing of all that you have spoken." ¹¹And Haman takes the clothing, and the horse, and clothed Mordecai, and causes him to ride in a broad place of the city, and calls before him, "Thus it is done to the man in whose glory the king has delighted." ¹²And Mordecai turns back to the gate of the king, and Haman has been hurried to his house mourning, and with covered head, ¹³and Haman recounts to his wife Zeresh, and to all his friends, all that has met him, and his wise men and his wife Zeresh say to him, "If Mordecai [is] of the seed of the Jews, before whom you have begun to fall, you are not able for him, but certainly fall before him." ¹⁴They are yet speaking with him, and eunuchs of the king have come, and hurry to bring in Haman to the banquet that Esther has made.

CHAPTER 7

¹And the king comes in, and Haman, to drink with Esther the queen, ²and the king says to Esther also on the second day, during the banquet of wine, "What [is] your petition, Esther, O queen? And it is given to you; and what [is] your request? To the half of the kingdom—and it is done." ³And Esther the queen answers and says, "If I have found grace in your eyes, O king, and if to the king [it be] good, let my life be given to me at my petition, and my people at my request; ⁴for we have been sold, I and my people, to cut off, to slay, and to destroy; and if for menservants and for maidservants we had been sold I had kept silent—but the adversity is not equal to the loss of the king." ⁵And King Ahasuerus says, indeed, he says to Esther the queen, "Who [is] he—this one? And where [is] this one whose

heart has filled him to do so?" ⁶And Esther says, "The man—adversary and enemy—[is] this wicked Haman"; and Haman has been afraid at the presence of the king and of the queen. ⁷And the king has risen, in his fury, from the banquet of wine, to the garden of the house, and Haman has remained to seek for his life from Esther the queen, for he has seen that evil has been determined against him by the king. ⁸And the king has turned back out of the garden of the house to the house of the banquet of wine, and Haman is falling on the couch on which Esther [is], and the king says, "Also to subdue the queen with me in the house?" The word has gone out from the mouth of the king, and the face of Haman they have covered. ⁹And Harbonah, one of the eunuchs, says before the king, "Also behold, the tree that Haman made for Mordecai, who spoke good for the king, is standing in the house of Haman, in height fifty cubits"; and the king says, "Hang him on it." ¹⁰And they hang Haman on the tree that he had prepared for Mordecai, and the fury of the king has lain down.

CHAPTER 8

¹On that day has King Ahasuerus given to Esther the queen the house of Haman, adversary of the Jews, and Mordecai has come in before the king, for Esther has declared what he [is] to her, ²and the king turns aside his signet, that he has caused to pass away from Haman, and gives it to Mordecai, and Esther sets Mordecai over the house of Haman. ³And Esther adds, and speaks before the king, and falls before his feet, and weeps, and makes supplication to him, to cause the evil of Haman the Agagite to pass away, and his scheme that he had devised against the Jews; ⁴and the king holds out to Esther the golden scepter, and Esther rises, and stands before the king, ⁵and says, "If to the king [it be] good, and if I have found grace before him, and the thing has been right before the king, and I [am] good in his eyes, let it be written to bring back the letters—a scheme of Haman son of Hammedatha the Agagite—that he wrote to destroy the Jews who [are] in all provinces of the king, ⁶for how do I endure when I have looked on the evil that finds my people? And how do I endure when I have looked on the destruction of my family?" ⁷And King Ahasuerus says to Esther the queen, and to Mordecai the Jew, "Behold, the house of Haman I have given to Esther, and him they have hanged on the tree, because that he put forth his hand on the Jews, ⁸and you, write for the Jews, as [it is] good in your eyes, in the name of the king, and seal with the signet of the king—for the writing that is written in the name of the king, and sealed with the signet of the king, there is none to turn back." ⁹And the scribes of the king are called, at that time, in the third month—it [is] the month of Sivan—in the twenty-third [day] of it, and it is written, according to all that Mordecai has commanded, to the Jews, and to the lieutenants, and the governors, and the heads of the provinces, that [are] from Hodu even to Cush, one hundred twenty-seven provinces—province and province according to its writing, and people and people according to its tongue, and to the Jews according to their writing, and according to their tongue. ¹⁰And he writes in the name of King Ahasuerus, and seals with the signet of the king, and sends letters by the hand of the runners with horses, riders of the dromedary, the mules, the young mares, ¹¹that the king has given to the Jews who [are] in each and every city, to be assembled, and to stand for their life, to cut off, to slay, and to destroy the whole force of the people and province who are distressing them, infants and women, and their spoil to seize. ¹²In one day, in all the provinces of King Ahasuerus, on the thirteenth of the twelfth month—it [is] the month of Adar— ¹³a copy of the writing to be made law in each and every province is revealed to all the peoples, and for the Jews being ready at this day to be avenged of their enemies. ¹⁴The runners, riding on the dromedary, [and] the mules, have gone out, hurried and pressed by the word of the king, and the law has been given in Shushan the palace. ¹⁵And Mordecai went out from before the king, in royal clothing of blue and white, and a great crown of gold, and a garment of fine linen and purple, and the city of Shushan has rejoiced and been glad; ¹⁶to the Jews has been light, and gladness, and joy, and honor, ¹⁷and in each and every province, and in each and every city, the place where the word of the king, even his law, is coming, gladness and joy [are] to the Jews, a banquet, and a good day; and many of the peoples of the land are becoming Jews, for a fear of the Jews has fallen on them.

CHAPTER 9

¹And in the twelfth month—it [is] the month of Adar—on the thirteenth day of it, in which the word of the king, even his law, has come to be done, in the day that the enemies of the Jews had hoped to rule over them, and it is turned that the Jews rule over those hating them— ²the Jews have been assembled in their cities, in all provinces of King Ahasuerus, to put forth a hand on those seeking their evil, and no man has stood in their presence, for their fear has fallen on all the peoples. ³And all heads of the provinces, and the lieutenants, and the governors, and those doing the work that the king has, are lifting up the Jews, for a fear of Mordecai has fallen on them; ⁴for great [is] Mordecai in the house of the king, and his fame is going into all the provinces, for the man Mordecai is going on and becoming great. ⁵And the Jews strike among all their enemies—a striking of the sword, and slaughter, and destruction—and do with those hating them according to their pleasure, ⁶and in Shushan the palace the Jews have slain and destroyed five hundred men; ⁷and Parshandatha, and Dalphon, and Aspatha, ⁸and Poratha, and Adalia, and Aridatha, ⁹and Parmashta, and Arisai, and Aridai, and Vajezatha, ¹⁰ten sons of Haman son of Hammedatha, adversary of the Jews, they have slain, and on the prey they have not put forth their hand. ¹¹On that day has come the number of the slain in Shushan the palace before the king, ¹²and the king says to Esther the queen, "In Shushan the palace the Jews have slain and destroyed five hundred men, and the ten sons of Haman; in the rest of the provinces of the king what have they done? And what [is] your petition? And it is given to you; and what your request again? And it is done." ¹³And Esther says, "If [it is] good to the king, let it also be given tomorrow, to the Jews who [are] in Shushan, to do according to the law of today; and the ten sons of Haman they hang on the tree." ¹⁴And the king commands [for it] to be done so; and a law is given in Shushan, and they have hanged the ten sons of Haman. ¹⁵And the Jews who [are] in Shushan are also assembled on the fourteenth day of the month of Adar, and they slay three hundred men in Shushan, and they have not put forth their hand on the prey. ¹⁶And the rest of the Jews, who [are] in the provinces of the king, have been assembled, even to stand for their life, and to rest from their enemies, and to slay seventy-five thousand among those hating them, and they have not put forth their hand on the prey; ¹⁷on the thirteenth day of the month of Adar, even to rest on the fourteenth of it, and to make it a day of banquet and of joy. ¹⁸And the Jews who [are] in Shushan have been assembled, on the thirteenth day of it, and on the fourteenth of it, even to rest on the fifteenth of it, and to make it a day of banquet and of joy. ¹⁹Therefore the Jews of the open places, who are dwelling in cities of the open places, are making the fourteenth day of the month of Adar—joy and banquet, and a good day, and of sending portions to one another. ²⁰And Mordecai writes these things, and sends letters to all the Jews who [are] in all provinces of King Ahasuerus, who are near and who are far off, ²¹to establish on them, to be keeping the fourteenth day of the month of Adar, and the fifteenth day of it, in every year and year, ²²as days on which the Jews have rested from their enemies, and the month that has been turned to them from sorrow to joy, and from mourning to a good day, to make them days of banquet and of joy, and of sending portions to one another, and gifts to the needy. ²³And the Jews have received that which they had begun to do, and that which Mordecai has written to them, ²⁴because Haman son of Hammedatha the Agagite, adversary of all the Jews, had devised concerning the Jews to destroy them, and had caused to fall Pur—that [is] the lot—to crush them and to destroy them; ²⁵and in her coming in before the king, he commanded with the letter, "Let his evil scheme that he devised against the Jews return on his own head," and they have hanged him and his sons on the tree, ²⁶therefore they have called these days Purim—by the name of the lot—therefore, because of all the words of this letter, and what they have seen concerning this, and what has come to them, ²⁷the Jews have established and received on them, and on their seed, and on all those joined to them, and it does not pass away, to be keeping these

ESTHER

two days according to their writing, and according to their season, in every year and year; ²⁸and these days are remembered and kept in every generation and generation, family and family, province and province, and city and city, and these days of Purim do not pass away from the midst of the Jews, and their memorial is not ended from their seed. ²⁹And Esther the queen, daughter of Abihail, writes, and Mordecai the Jew, with all might, to establish this second letter of Purim, ³⁰and he sends letters to all the Jews, to the one hundred twenty-seven provinces of the kingdom of Ahasuerus—words of peace and truth— ³¹to establish these days of Purim, in their seasons, as Mordecai the Jew has established on them, and Esther the queen, and as they had established on themselves, and on their seed—matters of the fastings, and of their cry. ³²And a saying of Esther has established these matters of Purim, and it is written in the Scroll.

CHAPTER 10

¹And King Ahasuerus sets a tribute on the land and the islands of the sea; ²and all the work of his strength, and his might, and the explanation of the greatness of Mordecai with which the king made him great, are they not written on the scroll of the Chronicles of Media and Persia? ³For Mordecai the Jew [is] second to King Ahasuerus, and a great man of the Jews, and accepted of the multitude of his brothers, seeking good for his people, and speaking peace to all his seed.

JOB

CHAPTER 1

¹There has been a man in the land of Uz—his name Job—and that man has been perfect and upright—both fearing God, and turning aside from evil. ²And seven sons and three daughters are borne to him, ³and his substance is seven thousand sheep, and three thousand camels, and five hundred pairs of oxen, and five hundred female donkeys, and a very abundant service; and that man is greater than any of the sons of the east. ⁴And his sons have gone and made a banquet—the house of each [in] his day—and have sent and called to their three sisters to eat and to drink with them; ⁵and it comes to pass, when they have gone around the days of the banquet, that Job sends and sanctifies them, and has risen early in the morning, and caused burnt-offerings to ascend—the number of them all—for Job said, "Perhaps my sons have sinned, yet blessed God in their heart." Thus Job does all the days. ⁶And the day is, that sons of God come to station themselves by YHWH, and there also comes Satan in their midst. ⁷And YHWH says to Satan, "Where do you come from?" And Satan answers YHWH and says, "From going to and fro in the land, and from walking up and down on it." ⁸And YHWH says to Satan, "Have you set your heart against My servant Job because there is none like him in the land, a man perfect and upright, fearing God, and turning aside from evil?" ⁹And Satan answers YHWH and says, "Is Job fearing God for nothing? ¹⁰Have You not made a hedge for him, and for his house, and for all that he has—all around? ¹¹You have blessed the work of his hands, and his substance has spread in the land, and yet, put forth Your hand now, and strike against anything that he has—if not, he blesses You to Your face!" ¹²And YHWH says to Satan, "Behold, all that he has [is] in your hand, only do not put forth your hand to him." And Satan goes out from the presence of YHWH. ¹³And the day is, that his sons and his daughters are eating and drinking wine in the house of their brother, the firstborn. ¹⁴And a messenger has come to Job and says, "The oxen have been plowing, and the female donkeys feeding by their sides, ¹⁵and Sheba falls, and takes them, and they have struck the young men by the mouth of the sword, and I have escaped—only I alone—to declare [it] to you." ¹⁶While this [one] is speaking another has also come and says, "Fire of God has fallen from the heavens, and burns among the flock, and among the young men, and consumes them, and I have escaped—only I alone—to declare [it] to you." ¹⁷While this [one] is speaking another also has come and says, "Chaldeans made three heads, and rush on the camels, and take them, and they have struck the young men by the mouth of the sword, and I have escaped—only I alone—to declare [it] to you." ¹⁸While this [one] is speaking another has also come and says, "Your sons and your daughters are eating, and drinking wine, in the house of their brother, the firstborn. ¹⁹And behold, a great wind has come from over the wilderness, and strikes against the four corners of the house, and it falls on the young men, and they are dead, and I have escaped—only I alone—to declare [it] to you." ²⁰And Job rises, and tears his robe, and shaves his head, and falls to the earth, and pays respect, ²¹and he says, "I came forth naked from the womb of my mother, || And naked I return there. YHWH has given and YHWH has taken; Let the Name of YHWH be blessed." ²²In all this Job has not sinned, nor given folly to God.

CHAPTER 2

¹And the day is, that sons of God come to station themselves by YHWH, and there also comes Satan in their midst to station himself by YHWH. ²And YHWH says to Satan, "From where have you come?" And Satan answers YHWH and says, "From going to and fro in the land, and from walking up and down in it." ³And YHWH says to Satan, "Have you set your heart to My servant Job because there is none like him in the land, a man perfect and upright, fearing God and turning aside from evil? And still he is keeping hold on his integrity, and you move Me against him to swallow him up for nothing!" ⁴And Satan answers YHWH and says, "A skin for a skin, and all that a man has he gives for his life. ⁵Yet, put forth Your hand now, and strike to his bone and to his flesh—if not, he blesses You to Your face!" ⁶And YHWH says to Satan, "Behold, he [is] in your hand; only take care of his life." ⁷And Satan goes forth from the presence of YHWH, and strikes Job with a severe ulcer from the sole of his foot to his crown. ⁸And he takes to him a potsherd to scrape himself with it, and he is sitting in the midst of the ashes. ⁹And his wife says to him, "You are still keeping hold on your integrity: bless God and die." ¹⁰And he says to her, "As one of the foolish women speaks, you speak; indeed, do we receive the good from God, and we do not receive the bad?" In all this Job has not sinned with his lips. ¹¹And three of the friends of Job hear of all this evil that has come on him, and they each come in from his place—Eliphaz the Temanite, and Bildad the Shuhite, and Zophar the Naamathite—and they have met together to come to bemoan him, and to comfort him; ¹²and they lift up their eyes from afar and have not discerned him, and they lift up their voice and weep, and each tears his robe, and sprinkle dust on their heads—heavenward. ¹³And they sit with him on the earth seven days and seven nights, and there is none speaking to him a word when they have seen that the pain has been very great.

CHAPTER 3

¹After this Job has opened his mouth, and reviles his day. ²And Job answers and says: ³"Let the day perish in which I am born, || And the night that has said: A man-child has been conceived. ⁴That day—let it be darkness, || Do not let God require it from above, || Nor let light shine on it. ⁵Let darkness and death-shade redeem it, || Let a cloud dwell on it, || Let them terrify it as the most bitter of days. ⁶That night—let thick darkness take it, || Let it not be united to days of the year, || Let it not come into the number of months. ⁷Behold! That night—let it be barren, || Let no singing come into it. ⁸Let the cursers of day mark it, || Who are ready to wake up Leviathan. ⁹Let the stars of its twilight be dark, || Let it wait for light, and there is none, || And let it not look on the eyelids of the dawn. ¹⁰Because it has not shut the doors || Of the womb that was mine! And

JOB

hide misery from my eyes. ¹¹Why do I not die from the womb? I have come forth from the belly and gasp! ¹²Why have knees been before me? And what [are] breasts, that I suck? ¹³For now, I have lain down, and am quiet, I have slept—then there is rest to me, ¹⁴With kings and counselors of earth, || These building ruins for themselves. ¹⁵Or with princes—they have gold, || They are filling their houses [with] silver. ¹⁶(Or I am not as a hidden abortion, || As infants—they have not seen light.) ¹⁷There the wicked have ceased troubling, || And there the wearied rest in power. ¹⁸Together prisoners have been at ease, || They have not heard the voice of an exactor, ¹⁹Small and great [are] the same there. And a servant [is] free from his lord. ²⁰Why does He give light to the miserable, and life to the bitter soul? ²¹Who are waiting for death, and it is not, || And they seek it above hid treasures. ²²Who are glad—to joy, || They rejoice when they find a grave. ²³To a man whose way has been hidden, || And whom God shuts up? ²⁴For before my food, my sighing comes, || And my roarings [are] poured out as waters. ²⁵For I feared a fear and it meets me, || And what I was afraid of comes to me. ²⁶I was not safe—nor was I quiet—Nor was I at rest—and trouble comes!"

CHAPTER 4

¹And Eliphaz the Temanite answers and says: ²"Has one tried a word with you? You are weary! And who is able to keep in words? ³Behold, you have instructed many, || And feeble hands you make strong. ⁴Your words raise up the stumbling one, || And you strengthen bowing knees. ⁵But now, it comes to you, || And you are weary; It strikes to you, and you are troubled. ⁶Is your reverence not your confidence? Your hope—the perfection of your ways? ⁷Now remember, || Who, being innocent, has perished? And where have the upright been cut off? ⁸As I have seen—plowers of iniquity, || And sowers of misery, reap it! ⁹From the breath of God they perish, || And from the spirit of His anger [are] consumed. ¹⁰The roaring of a lion, || And the voice of a fierce lion, || And teeth of young lions have been broken. ¹¹An old lion is perishing without prey, || And the whelps of the lioness separate. ¹²And a thing is secretly brought to me, || And my ear receives a little of it. ¹³In thoughts from visions of the night, || In the falling of deep sleep on men, ¹⁴Fear has met me, and trembling, || And the multitude of my bones caused to fear. ¹⁵And a spirit passes before my face, || The hair of my flesh stands up; ¹⁶It stands, and I do not discern its aspect, || A likeness [is] before my eyes, || Silence! And I hear a voice: ¹⁷Is mortal man more righteous than God? Is a man cleaner than his Maker? ¹⁸Behold, He puts no credence in His servants, || Nor sets praise in His messengers. ¹⁹Also—the inhabitants of houses of clay || (Whose foundation [is] in the dust, || They bruise them before a moth). ²⁰From morning to evening are beaten down, || Without any regarding, they perish forever. ²¹Has their excellence not been removed with them? They die, and not in wisdom!"

CHAPTER 5

¹"Pray, call, is there any to answer you? And to which of the holy ones do you turn? ²For provocation slays the perverse, || And envy puts to death the simple, ³I have seen the perverse taking root, || And I mark his habitation straight away, ⁴His sons are far from safety, || And they are bruised in the gate, || And there is no deliverer. ⁵Whose harvest the hungry eat, || And even take it from the thorns, || And the designing swallowed their wealth. ⁶For sorrow does not come forth from the dust, || Nor does misery spring up from the ground. ⁷For man is born to misery, || And the sparks go high to fly. ⁸Yet I inquire for God, || And for God I give my word, ⁹Doing great things, and there is no searching. Wonderful, until there is no numbering. ¹⁰Who is giving rain on the face of the land, || And is sending waters on the out-places. ¹¹To set the low on a high place, || And the mourners have been high [in] safety. ¹²Making void thoughts of the cunning, || And their hands do not execute wisdom. ¹³Capturing the wise in their subtlety, || And the counsel of wrestling ones was hurried, ¹⁴By day they meet darkness, || And as night—they grope at noon. ¹⁵He saves the needy from the sword in their mouth, || And from a strong hand, ¹⁶And there is hope for the poor, || And perverseness has shut her mouth. ¹⁷Behold, the blessedness of mortal man, || God reproves him: And do not despise the discipline of the Mighty, ¹⁸For He pains, and He binds up, || He strikes, and His hands heal. ¹⁹In six distresses He delivers you, || And in seven evil does not strike on you. ²⁰In famine He has redeemed you from death, || And in battle from the hands of the sword. ²¹When the tongue scourges you are hid, || And you are not afraid of destruction, || When it comes. ²²At destruction and at hunger you mock, || And of the beast of the earth, || You are not afraid. ²³(For with sons of the field [is] your covenant, || And the beast of the field || Has been at peace with you.) ²⁴And you have known that your tent [is] peace, || And inspected your habitation, and do not err, ²⁵And have known that your seed [is] numerous, || And your offspring as the herb of the earth; ²⁶You come in full age to the grave, || As the going up of a stalk in its season. ²⁷Behold, this—we searched it out—it [is] right, listen; And you, know for yourself!"

CHAPTER 6

¹And Job answers and says: ²"O that my provocation were thoroughly weighed, || And my calamity in balances || They would lift up together! ³For now it is heavier than the sands of the sea, || Therefore my words have been rash. ⁴For arrows of the Mighty [are] with me, || Whose poison is drinking up my spirit. Terrors of God array themselves [for] me! ⁵Does a wild donkey bray over tender grass? Does an ox low over his provender? ⁶Is an insipid thing eaten without salt? Is there sense in the drivel of dreams? ⁷My soul is refusing to touch! They [are] as my sickening food. ⁸O that my request may come, || That God may grant my hope! ⁹That God would please—and bruise me, || Loose His hand and cut me off! ¹⁰And yet it is my comfort || (And I exult in pain—He does not spare), || That I have not hidden || The sayings of the Holy One. ¹¹What [is] my power that I should hope? And what [is] my end that I should prolong my life? ¹²Is my strength the strength of stones? Is my flesh bronze? ¹³Is my help not with me, || And substance driven from me? ¹⁴To a despiser of his friends [is] shame, || And the fear of the Mighty he forsakes. ¹⁵My brothers have deceived as a brook, || As a stream of brooks they pass away. ¹⁶That are black because of ice, || By them snow hides itself. ¹⁷By the time they are warm they have been cut off, || By its being hot they have been || Extinguished from their place. ¹⁸The paths turn aside of their way, || They ascend into emptiness, and are lost. ¹⁹Passengers of Tema looked expectingly, || Travelers of Sheba hoped for them. ²⁰They were ashamed that one has trusted, || They have come to it and are confounded. ²¹Surely now you have become the same! You see a downfall, and are afraid. ²²Is it because I said, Give to me? And, By your power bribe for me? ²³And, Deliver me from the hand of an adversary? And, Ransom me from the hand of terrible ones? ²⁴Show me, and I keep silent, || And what I have erred, let me understand. ²⁵How powerful have been upright sayings, || And what reproof from you reproves? ²⁶For reproof—do you reckon words? And for wind—sayings of the desperate? ²⁷You cause anger to fall on the fatherless, || And are strange to your friend. ²⁸And now, please, look on me, || Even to your face do I lie? ²⁹Please turn back, let it not be perverseness, || Indeed, turn back again—my righteousness [is] in it. ³⁰Is there perverseness in my tongue? Does my palate not discern calamity?"

CHAPTER 7

¹"Is there not warfare to man on earth? And his days as the days of a hired worker? ²As a servant desires the shadow, || And as a hired worker expects his wage, ³So I have been caused to inherit months of vanity, || And they numbered nights of misery to me. ⁴If I lay down, then I have said, When do I rise, || And evening has been measured? And I have been full of tossings until dawn. ⁵My flesh has been clothed [with] worms, || And a clod of dust, || My skin has been shriveled and is loathsome, ⁶My days swifter than a loom, || And they are consumed without hope. ⁷Remember that my life [is] a breath, || My eye does not turn back to see good. ⁸The eye of my beholder does not behold me. Your eyes [are] on me—and I am not. ⁹A cloud has been consumed, and it goes, || So he who is going down to Sheol does not come up. ¹⁰He does not turn to his house again, || Nor does his place discern him again. ¹¹Also I do not withhold my mouth—I speak in the distress of my spirit, I talk in the bitterness of my soul. ¹²Am I a sea [monster], or a dragon, || That You set a watch over me? ¹³When I said, My bed comforts me, || In my talking He takes

away my couch. ¹⁴And You have frightened me with dreams, || And You terrify me from visions, ¹⁵And my soul chooses strangling, || Death rather than my bones. ¹⁶I have wasted away—I do not live for all time. Cease from me, for my days [are] vanity. ¹⁷What [is] man that You magnify him? And that You set Your heart to him? ¹⁸And inspect him in the mornings, || [And] in the evenings try him? ¹⁹How long do You not look from me? You do not desist until I swallow my spittle. ²⁰I have sinned, what do I do to You, || O watcher of man? Why have You set me for a mark to You, || And I am for a burden to myself—and what? ²¹You do not take away my transgression, || And [do not] cause my iniquity to pass away, || Because now, I lie down in dust, || And You have sought me—and I am not!"

CHAPTER 8

¹And Bildad the Shuhite answers and says: ²"Until when do you speak these things? And a strong wind—sayings of your mouth? ³Does God pervert judgment? And does the Mighty One pervert justice? ⁴If your sons have sinned before Him, || And He sends them away, || By the hand of their transgression, ⁵If you seek for God early, || And make supplication to the Mighty, ⁶If you [are] pure and upright, || Surely now He wakes for you, || And has completed || The habitation of your righteousness. ⁷And your beginning has been small, || And your latter end is very great. ⁸For inquire, please, of a former generation, || And prepare for a search of their fathers, ⁹For we [are] of yesterday, and we do not know, || For our days [are] a shadow on earth. ¹⁰Do they not show you—speak to you, || And from their heart bring forth words? ¹¹Does a rush rise without a marsh? A reed increase without water? ¹²While it [is] in its budding—uncropped, || Even before any herb it withers. ¹³So [are] the paths of all forgetting God, || And the hope of the profane perishes, ¹⁴Whose confidence is loathsome, || And the house of a spider his trust. ¹⁵He leans on his house—and it does not stand, || He takes hold on it—and it does not abide. ¹⁶He [is] green before the sun, || And over his garden his branch goes out. ¹⁷His roots are wrapped by a heap, || He looks for a house of stones. ¹⁸If [one] destroys him from his place, || Then it has feigned concerning him, || I have not seen you! ¹⁹Behold, this [is] the joy of His way, || And from the dust others spring up. ²⁰Behold, God does not reject the perfect, || Nor takes hold on the hand of evildoers. ²¹While He fills your mouth with laughter, || And your lips with shouting, ²²Those hating you put on shame, || And the tent of the wicked is not!"

CHAPTER 9

¹And Job answers and says: ²"Truly I have known that [it is] so, || But how is man righteous with God? ³If he delights to strive with Him—He does not answer him one of a thousand. ⁴Wise in heart and strong in power—Who has hardened toward Him and is at peace? ⁵Who is removing mountains, || And they have not known, || Who has overturned them in His anger. ⁶Who is shaking earth from its place, || And its pillars move themselves. ⁷Who is commanding to the sun, and it does not rise, || And the stars He seals up. ⁸Stretching out the heavens by Himself, || And treading on the heights of the sea, ⁹Making the Great Bear, Orion, and the Pleiades, || And the inner chambers of the south. ¹⁰Doing great things until there is no searching, || And wonderful, until there is no numbering. ¹¹Behold, He goes over by me, and I do not see, || And He passes on, and I do not attend to it. ¹²Behold, He snatches away, who brings it back? Who says to Him, What [are] You doing? ¹³God does not turn back His anger, || Proud helpers have bowed under Him. ¹⁴How much less do I answer Him? Choose out my words with Him? ¹⁵Whom, though I were righteous, I do not answer, || For my judgment I make supplication. ¹⁶Though I had called and He answers me, I do not believe that He gives ear [to] my voice. ¹⁷Because He bruises me with a storm, || And has multiplied my wounds for nothing. ¹⁸He does not permit me to refresh my spirit, || But fills me with bitter things. ¹⁹If of power, behold, the Strong One; And if of judgment—who convenes me? ²⁰If I am righteous, my mouth declares me wicked; [If] I am perfect, it declares me perverse. ²¹I am perfect; I do not know my soul, I despise my life. ²²It is the same thing, therefore I said, || He is consuming the perfect and the wicked. ²³If a scourge puts to death suddenly, He laughs at the trial of the innocent. ²⁴Earth has been given || Into the hand of the wicked. He covers the faces of her judges, || If not—where, who [is] he? ²⁵My days have been swifter than a runner, || They have fled, they have not seen good, ²⁶They have passed on with ships of reed, || As an eagle darts on food. ²⁷Though I say, I forget my talking, || I forsake my corner, and I brighten up! ²⁸I have been afraid of all my griefs, || I have known that You do not acquit me. ²⁹I become wicked; why [is] this? I labor [in] vain. ³⁰If I have washed myself with snow-water, || And purified my hands with soap, ³¹Then You dip me in corruption, || And my garments have detested me. ³²But if a man like myself—I answer Him, || We come together into judgment. ³³If there were a mediator between us, || He places his hand on us both. ³⁴He turns aside His rod from off me, || And His terror does not make me afraid, ³⁵I speak, and do not fear Him, but I am not right with myself."

CHAPTER 10

¹"My soul has been weary of my life, I leave off my talking to myself, I speak in the bitterness of my soul. ²I say to God, Do not condemn me, || Let me know why You strive [with] me. ³Is it good for You that You oppress? That You despise the labor of Your hands, || And shine on the counsel of the wicked? ⁴Do you have eyes of flesh? Do You see as man sees? ⁵[Are] Your days as the days of man? Your years as the days of a man? ⁶That You inquire for my iniquity, || And seek for my sin? ⁷For You know that I am not wicked, || And there is no deliverer from Your hand. ⁸Your hands have taken pains about me, || And they make me together all around, || And You swallow me up! ⁹Please remember || That You have made me as clay, || And You bring me back to dust. ¹⁰Do You not pour me out as milk? And curdle me as cheese? ¹¹Skin and flesh You put on me, || And fence me with bones and sinews. ¹²Life and kindness You have done with me. And Your inspection has preserved my spirit. ¹³And these You have laid up in Your heart, I have known that this [is] with You. ¹⁴If I sinned, then You have observed me, || And do not acquit me from my iniquity, ¹⁵If I have done wickedly—woe to me, || And righteously—I do not lift up my head, || Full of shame—then see my affliction, ¹⁶And it rises—as a lion You hunt me. And You turn back—You show Yourself wonderful in me. ¹⁷You renew Your witnesses against me, and multiply Your anger with me, || Changes and warfare [are] with me. ¹⁸And why from the womb || Have You brought me forth? I expire, and the eye does not see me. ¹⁹I am as [if] I had not been, || I am brought from the belly to the grave, ²⁰Are my days not few? Cease then, and put from me, || And I brighten up a little, ²¹Before I go, and do not return, || To a land of darkness and death-shade, ²²A land of obscurity as thick darkness, || Death-shade—and no order, || And the shining [is] as thick darkness."

CHAPTER 11

¹And Zophar the Naamathite answers and says: ²"Is a multitude of words not answered? And is a man of lips justified? ³Your boastings make men keep silent, || You scorn, and none is causing blushing! ⁴And you say, My discourse [is] pure, || And I have been clean in Your eyes. ⁵And yet, O that God had spoken! And opens His lips with you. ⁶And declares to you secrets of wisdom, for counsel has foldings. And know that God forgets of your iniquity for you. ⁷Do you find out God by searching? To perfection find out the Mighty One? ⁸Heights of the heavens—what [can] you do? Deeper than Sheol—what [can] you know? ⁹Its measure [is] longer than earth, and broader than the sea. ¹⁰If He passes on, and shuts up, and assembles, || Who then reverses it? ¹¹For He has known men of vanity, || And He sees iniquity, || And one does not consider [it]! ¹²And empty man is bold, || And man is born [as] the colt of a wild donkey. ¹³If you have prepared your heart, || And have spread out your hands to Him, ¹⁴If iniquity [is] in your hand, put it far off, || And do not let perverseness dwell in your tents. ¹⁵For then you lift up your face from blemish, || And you have been firm, and do not fear. ¹⁶For you forget misery, || As waters passed away you remember. ¹⁷And age rises above the noon, || You fly—you are as the morning. ¹⁸And you have trusted because there is hope, || And searched—in confidence you lie down, ¹⁹And you have rested, || And none is causing trembling, || And many have begged [at] your face; ²⁰And the eyes of the wicked are consumed, || And refuge has perished from them, || And their hope [is] a breathing out of soul!"

JOB

CHAPTER 12

¹And Job answers and says: ²"Truly—you [are] the people, and wisdom dies with you. ³I also have a heart like you, I am not fallen more than you, || And with whom is there not like these? ⁴I am a laughter to his friend: He calls to God, and He answers him, || A laughter [is] the perfect righteous one. ⁵A torch—despised in the thoughts of the secure || Is prepared for those sliding with the feet. ⁶The tents of spoilers are at peace, || And those provoking God have confidence, || Into whose hand God has brought. ⁷And yet, now ask [one of] the beasts, || And it shows you, || And a bird of the heavens, || And it declares to you. ⁸Or talk to the earth, and it shows you, || And fishes of the sea recount to you: ⁹Who has not known in all these, || That the hand of YHWH has done this? ¹⁰In whose hand [is] the breath of every living thing, || And the spirit of all flesh of man. ¹¹Does the ear not try words? And the palate taste food for itself? ¹²With the very aged [is] wisdom, || And [with] length of days [is] understanding. ¹³With Him [are] wisdom and might, || To Him [are] counsel and understanding. ¹⁴Behold, He breaks down, and it is not built up, || He shuts against a man, || And it is not opened. ¹⁵Behold, He keeps in the waters, and they are dried up, || And He sends them forth, || And they overturn the land. ¹⁶With Him [are] strength and wisdom, || His the deceived and deceiver. ¹⁷Causing counselors to go away [as] a spoil, || Indeed, He makes fools of judges. ¹⁸He has opened the bands of kings, || And He binds a girdle on their loins. ¹⁹Causing ministers to go away [as] a spoil || And strong ones He overthrows. ²⁰Turning aside the lip of the steadfast, || And the reason of the aged He takes away. ²¹Pouring contempt on princes, || And the girdle of the mighty He made feeble. ²²Removing deep things out of darkness, || And He brings out to light death-shade. ²³Magnifying the nations, and He destroys them, || Spreading out the nations, and He quiets them. ²⁴Turning aside the heart || Of the heads of the people of the land, || And He causes them to wander || In vacancy—no way! ²⁵They feel darkness, and not light, || He causes them to wander as a drunkard."

CHAPTER 13

¹"Behold, my eye has seen all, || My ear has heard, and it attends to it. ²According to your knowledge I have known—also I. I am not more fallen than you. ³Yet I speak for the Mighty One, || And I delight to argue for God. ⁴And yet, you [are] forgers of falsehood, || Physicians of nothing—all of you, ⁵O that you would keep perfectly silent, || And it would be to you for wisdom. ⁶Please hear my argument, || And attend to the pleadings of my lips, ⁷Do you speak perverseness for God? And do you speak deceit for Him? ⁸Do you accept His face, if you strive for God? ⁹Is [it] good that He searches you, || If, as one mocks at a man, you mock at Him? ¹⁰He surely reproves you, if you accept faces in secret. ¹¹Does His excellence not terrify you? And His dread fall on you? ¹²Your remembrances [are] allegories of ashes, || For high places of clay [are] your heights. ¹³Keep silent from me, and I speak, || And pass over me what will. ¹⁴Why do I take my flesh in my teeth? And my soul put in my hand? ¹⁵Behold, He slays me—I do not wait! Only, I argue my ways to His face. ¹⁶Also—He [is] to me for salvation, || For the profane do not come before Him. ¹⁷Hear my word diligently, || And my declaration with your ears. ¹⁸Now behold, I have set the cause in order, || I have known that I am righteous. ¹⁹Who [is] he that strives with me? For now I keep silent and gasp. ²⁰Only two things, O God, do with me, || Then I am not hidden from Your face: ²¹Put Your hand far off from me, || And do not let Your terror terrify me. ²²And You call, and I answer, || Or—I speak, and You answer me. ²³How many iniquities and sins do I have? Let me know my transgression and my sin. ²⁴Why do You hide Your face? And reckon me for an enemy to You? ²⁵Do You terrify a leaf driven away? And do You pursue the dry stubble? ²⁶For You write bitter things against me, || And cause me to possess iniquities of my youth, ²⁷And you put my feet in the stocks, || And observe all my paths—You set a print on the roots of my feet, ²⁸And he, as a rotten thing, wears away, || A moth has consumed him as a garment."

CHAPTER 14

¹"Man, born of woman! Of few days, and full of trouble! ²As a flower he has gone forth, and is cut off, || And he flees as a shadow and does not stand. ³Also—on this You have opened Your eyes, and bring me into judgment with You. ⁴Who gives a clean thing out of an unclean? Not one. ⁵If his days are determined, || The number of his months [are] with You, || You have made his limit, || And he does not pass over; ⁶Look away from off him that he may cease, || Until he enjoy as a hired worker his day. ⁷For there is hope for a tree, if it is cut down, || That it changes again, || That its tender branch does not cease. ⁸If its root becomes old in the earth, || And its stem dies in the dust, ⁹From the fragrance of water it flourishes, || And has made a crop as a plant. ¹⁰And a man dies, and becomes weak, || And man expires, and where [is] he? ¹¹Waters have gone away from a sea, || And a river becomes waste and dry. ¹²And man has lain down, and does not rise, || Until the wearing out of the heavens they do not awaken, || Nor are roused from their sleep. ¹³O that You would conceal me in Sheol, || Hide me until the turning of Your anger, || Set a limit for me, and remember me. ¹⁴If a man dies—does he revive? All [the] days of my warfare I wait, until my change comes. ¹⁵You call, and I answer You; To the work of Your hands You have desire. ¹⁶But now, You number my steps, || You do not watch over my sin. ¹⁷My transgression [is] sealed up in a bag, and You sew up my iniquity. ¹⁸And yet, a falling mountain wastes away, and a rock is removed from its place. ¹⁹Waters have worn away stones, || Their outpourings wash away the dust of earth, || And You have destroyed the hope of man. ²⁰You prevail [over] him forever, and he goes, || He is changing his countenance, || And You send him away. ²¹His sons are honored, and he does not know; And they are little, and he does not attend to them. ²²Only—his flesh is pained for him, || And his soul mourns for him."

CHAPTER 15

¹And Eliphaz the Temanite answers and says: ²"Does a wise man answer [with] vain knowledge? And fill his belly [with] an east wind? ³To reason with a word not useful? And speeches—no profit in them? ⁴Indeed, you make reverence void, and diminish meditation before God. ⁵For your mouth teaches your iniquity, || And you choose the tongue of the cunning. ⁶Your mouth declares you wicked, and not I, || And your lips testify against you. ⁷Are you the first man born? And were you formed before the heights? ⁸Do you hear of the secret counsel of God? And withdraw wisdom to you? ⁹What have you known, and we do not know? [What] do you understand, and it is not with us? ¹⁰Both the gray-headed || And the very aged [are] among us—Greater than your father [in] days. ¹¹Are the comforts of God too few for you? And a gentle word [is] with you, ¹²Why does your heart take you away? And why are your eyes high? ¹³Do you turn your spirit against God? And have brought out words from your mouth: ¹⁴What [is] man that he is pure, || And that he is righteous, one born of woman? ¹⁵Behold, He puts no credence in His holy ones, || And the heavens have not been pure in His eyes. ¹⁶Also—surely abominable and filthy || Is man drinking perverseness as water. ¹⁷I show you—listen to me—And this I have seen and declare, ¹⁸Which the wise declare—And have not hid—from their fathers. ¹⁹To them alone was the land given, || And a stranger did not pass over into their midst: ²⁰All [the] days of the wicked he is paining himself, || And few years have been laid up for the terrible one. ²¹A fearful voice [is] in his ears, || In peace a destroyer comes to him. ²²He does not believe to return from darkness, || And he watches for the sword. ²³He is wandering for bread: Where [is] it? He has known that ready at his hand || Is a day of darkness. ²⁴Adversity and distress terrify him, || They prevail over him as a king ready for a boaster. ²⁵For he stretched out his hand against God, || And against the Mighty he makes himself mighty. ²⁶He runs to Him with a neck, || With thick bosses of his shields. ²⁷For he has covered his face with his fat, || And makes vigor over [his] confidence. ²⁸And he inhabits cities cut off, houses not dwelt in, || That have been ready to become heaps. ²⁹He is not rich, nor does his wealth rise, || Nor does he stretch out their continuance on earth. ³⁰He does not turn aside from darkness, || A flame dries up his tender branch, || And he turns aside at the breath of His mouth! ³¹Do not let him put credence in vanity, || He has been deceived, || For vanity is his exchange. ³²It is not completed in his day, || And his bending branch is not green. ³³He shakes off his unripe fruit as a vine, || And casts off his blossom as an olive. ³⁴For the company of the profane [is]

barren, || And fire has consumed tents of bribery. ³⁵To conceive misery, and to bear iniquity, || Even their heart prepares deceit."

CHAPTER 16

¹And Job answers and says: ²"I have heard many such things, || Miserable comforters [are] you all. ³Is there an end to words of wind? Or what emboldens you that you answer? ⁴I also, like you, might speak, || If your soul were in my soul's stead. I might join against you with words, || And nod at you with my head. ⁵I might harden you with my mouth, || And the moving of my lips might be sparing. ⁶If I speak, my pain is not restrained, || And I cease—what goes from me? ⁷Only, now, it has wearied me; You have desolated all my company, ⁸And You loathe me, || For it has been a witness, || And my failure rises up against me, || It testifies in my face. ⁹His anger has torn, and He hates me, || He has gnashed at me with His teeth, || My adversary sharpens His eyes for me. ¹⁰They have gaped on me with their mouth, || In reproach they have struck my cheeks, || Together they set themselves against me. ¹¹God shuts me up to the perverse, || And turns me over to the hands of the wicked. ¹²I have been at ease, and He breaks me, || And He has laid hold on my neck, || And He breaks me in pieces, || And He raises me to Him for a mark. ¹³His archers go around against me. He split my reins, and does not spare, || He pours out my gall to the earth. ¹⁴He breaks me—breach on breach, || He runs on me as a mighty one. ¹⁵I have sewed sackcloth on my skin, || And have rolled my horn in the dust. ¹⁶My face is foul with weeping, || And on my eyelids [is] death-shade. ¹⁷Not for violence in my hands, || And my prayer [is] pure. ¹⁸O earth, do not cover my blood! And let there not be a place for my cry. ¹⁹Also, now, behold, my witness [is] in the heavens, || And my testifier in the high places. ²⁰My interpreter [is] my friend, || My eye has dropped to God; ²¹And He reasons for a man with God, || As a son of man for his friend. ²²When a few years come, || Then I go [on] the path of no return."

CHAPTER 17

¹"My spirit has been destroyed, || My days extinguished—graves [are] for me. ²If not—mockeries [are] with me. And my eye lodges in their provocations. ³Now place my pledge with You; Who is he that strikes hand with me? ⁴For You have hidden their heart from understanding, || Therefore You do not exalt them. ⁵For a portion he shows friendship, || And the eyes of his sons are consumed. ⁶And He set me up for a proverb of the peoples, || And I am a wonder before them. ⁷And my eye is dim from sorrow, || And my members—all of them—as a shadow. ⁸The upright are astonished at this, and the innocent stirs himself up against the profane. ⁹And the righteous lays hold [on] his way, || And the clean of hands adds strength. ¹⁰But please return and come in, all of you, || And I do not find a wise man among you. ¹¹My days have passed by, || My plans have been broken off, || The possessions of my heart! ¹²They appoint night for day, || Light [is] near because of darkness. ¹³If I wait—Sheol [is] my house, || In darkness I have spread out my bed. ¹⁴To corruption I have called: You [are] my father. To the worm: My mother and my sister. ¹⁵And where [is] my hope now? Indeed, my hope, who beholds it? ¹⁶You go down [to] the parts of Sheol, || If we may rest together on the dust."

CHAPTER 18

¹And Bildad the Shuhite answers and says: ²"When do you set an end to words? Consider, and afterward we speak. ³Why have we been reckoned as livestock? We have been defiled in your eyes! ⁴He is tearing himself in his anger. Is earth forsaken for your sake? And is a rock removed from its place? ⁵Also, the light of the wicked is extinguished. And there does not shine a spark of his fire. ⁶The light has been dark in his tent, || And his lamp over him is extinguished. ⁷The steps of his strength are restricted, || And his own counsel casts him down. ⁸For he is sent into a net by his own feet, || And he habitually walks on a snare. ⁹A trap seizes on the heel, || The designing prevails over him. ¹⁰His cord is hidden in the earth, || And his trap on the path. ¹¹Terrors have terrified him all around, || And they have scattered him—at his feet. ¹²His sorrow is hungry, || And calamity is ready at his side. ¹³It consumes the parts of his skin, || Death's firstborn consumes his parts. ¹⁴His confidence is drawn from his tent, || And it causes him to step to the king of terrors. ¹⁵It dwells in his tent—out of his provender, || Sulfur is scattered over his habitation. ¹⁶From beneath his roots are dried up, || And from above his crop is cut off. ¹⁷His memorial has perished from the land, || And he has no name on the street. ¹⁸They thrust him from light to darkness, || And cast him out from the habitable earth. ¹⁹He has no continuator, || Nor successor among his people, || And none is remaining in his dwellings. ²⁰At this day, those [in the] west have been astonished, || And those [in the] east have taken fright. ²¹Only these [are] dwelling places of the perverse, || And this [is] the place God has not known."

CHAPTER 19

¹And Job answers and says: ²"Until when do you afflict my soul, || And bruise me with words? ³These ten times you put me to shame, you do not blush. You make yourselves strange to me— ⁴And also—truly, I have erred, || My error remains with me. ⁵If, truly, you magnify yourselves over me, || And decide my reproach against me; ⁶Know now, that God turned me upside down, || And has set around His net against me, ⁷Behold, I cry out—violence, and am not answered, I cry aloud, and there is no judgment. ⁸He hedged up my way, and I do not pass over, || And He places darkness on my paths. ⁹He has stripped my honor from off me, || And He turns the crown from my head. ¹⁰He breaks me down all around, and I go, || And removes my hope like a tree. ¹¹And He kindles His anger against me, || And reckons me to Him as His adversaries. ¹²His troops come in together, || And they raise up their way against me, || And encamp around my tent. ¹³He has put my brothers far off from me, || And my acquaintances have surely been estranged from me. ¹⁴My neighbors have ceased || And my familiar friends have forgotten me, ¹⁵Sojourners of my house and my maids, || Reckon me for a stranger; I have been an alien in their eyes. ¹⁶I have called to my servant, || And he does not answer, || With my mouth I make supplication to him. ¹⁷My spirit is strange to my wife, || And my favors to the sons of my [mother's] womb. ¹⁸Also sucklings have despised me, I rise, and they speak against me. ¹⁹All the men of my counsel detest me, || And those I have loved, || Have been turned against me. ²⁰To my skin and to my flesh || My bone has cleaved, || And I deliver myself with the skin of my teeth. ²¹Pity me, pity me, you my friends, || For the hand of God has struck against me. ²²Why do you pursue me as God? And are not satisfied with my flesh? ²³Who grants now, that my words may be written? Who grants that they may be inscribed in a scroll? ²⁴With a pen of iron and lead—They may be hewn in a rock forever. ²⁵That—I have known my Redeemer, || The Living and the Last, || For He raises the dust. ²⁶And after my skin has surrounded this [body], || Then from my flesh I see God— ²⁷Whom I see on my side, || And my eyes have beheld, and not a stranger, || My reins have been consumed in my bosom. ²⁸But you say, Why do we pursue after him? And the root of the matter has been found in me. ²⁹Be afraid because of the sword, || For the punishments of the sword [are] furious, || That you may know that [there is] a judgment."

CHAPTER 20

¹And Zophar the Naamathite answers and says: ²"Therefore my thoughts cause me to answer, || And because of my sensations in me. ³I hear the discipline of my shame, || And the spirit of my understanding causes me to answer: ⁴Have you known this from antiquity? Since the placing of man on earth? ⁵That the singing of the wicked [is] short, || And the joy of the profane for a moment, ⁶Though his excellence goes up to the heavens, || He strikes his head against a cloud— ⁷He perishes as his own dung forever, || His beholders say, Where [is] he? ⁸He flees as a dream, and they do not find him, || And he is driven away as a vision of the night, ⁹The eye has not seen him, and does not add. And his place does not behold him again. ¹⁰His sons oppress the poor, || And his hands give back his wealth. ¹¹His bones have been full of his youth, and it lies down with him on the dust. ¹²Though he sweetens evil in his mouth, hides it under his tongue, ¹³has pity on it, and does not forsake it, and keeps it back in the midst of his palate, ¹⁴his food is turned in his bowels, the bitterness of cobras [is] in his heart. ¹⁵He has swallowed wealth, and vomits it. God drives it out from his belly. ¹⁶He sucks [the] gall of cobras, the tongue of a viper slays him. ¹⁷He does not look on streams, || Flowing of brooks of honey and butter. ¹⁸He is giving back [what]

he labored for, and does not consume [it]; As a bulwark [is] his exchange, and he does not exult. ¹⁹For he oppressed—he forsook the poor, || He has taken a house away violently, || And he does not build it. ²⁰For he has not known ease in his belly. With his desirable thing he does not deliver himself. ²¹There is not a remnant to his food, || Therefore his good does not stay. ²²In the fullness of his sufficiency he is constricted. Every perverse hand meets him. ²³It comes to pass, at the filling of his belly, || He sends forth against him || The fierceness of His anger, || Indeed, He rains on him in his eating. ²⁴He flees from an iron weapon, || A bow of bronze passes through him. ²⁵One has drawn, || And it comes out from the body, || And a glittering weapon proceeds from his gall. Terrors [are] on him. ²⁶All darkness is hid for his treasures, || A fire not blown consumes him, || The remnant is broken in his tent. ²⁷The heavens reveal his iniquity, || And earth is raising itself against him. ²⁸The increase of his house is removed, || Poured forth in a day of His anger. ²⁹This [is] the portion of a wicked man from God. And an inheritance appointed him by God."

CHAPTER 21

¹And Job answers and says: ²"Hear my word diligently, || And this is your consolation. ³Bear with me, and I speak, || And after my speaking—you may deride. ⁴[Is] my complaint [against] man? And if [so], why may my temper not become short? ⁵Turn to me, and be astonished, || And put hand to mouth. ⁶Indeed, if I have remembered, then I have been troubled. And my flesh has taken fright. ⁷Why do the wicked live? They have become old, || Indeed, they have been mighty in wealth. ⁸Their seed is established, || Before their face with them, || And their offspring before their eyes. ⁹Their houses [are] peace without fear, || Nor [is] a rod of God on them. ¹⁰His bullock breeds without fail. His cow brings forth safely, and does not miscarry. ¹¹They send forth their sucklings as a flock, || And their children skip, ¹²They lift [themselves] up at timbrel and harp, || And rejoice at the sound of a pipe. ¹³They wear out their days in good, || And in a moment go down [to] Sheol. ¹⁴And they say to God, Turn aside from us, || And the knowledge of Your ways || We have not desired. ¹⁵What [is] the Mighty One that we serve Him? And what do we profit when we meet with Him? ¹⁶Behold, their good [is] not in their hand || (The counsel of the wicked || Has been far from me). ¹⁷How often is the lamp of the wicked extinguished, || And their calamity comes on them? He apportions pangs in His anger. ¹⁸They are as straw before wind, || And as chaff a windstorm has stolen away, ¹⁹God lays up for his sons his sorrow, || He gives repayment to him—and he knows. ²⁰His own eyes see his destruction, || And he drinks of the wrath of the Mighty. ²¹For what [is] his delight in his house after him, || And the number of his months cut off? ²²Does [one] teach knowledge to God, || Since He judges [those] on high? ²³This [one] dies in his perfect strength, || Wholly at ease and quiet. ²⁴His breasts have been full of milk, || And marrow moistens his bones. ²⁵And this [one] dies with a bitter soul, || And has not eaten with gladness. ²⁶Together they lie down on the dust, || And the worm covers them over. ²⁷Behold, I have known your thoughts, || And the schemes against me you do wrongfully. ²⁸For you say, Where [is] the house of the noble? And where the tent—the dwelling places of the wicked? ²⁹Have you not asked those passing by the way? And do you not know their signs? ³⁰That the wicked is spared to a day of calamity. They are brought to a day of wrath. ³¹Who declares his way to his face? And [for] that which he has done, || Who gives repayment to him? ³²And he is brought to the graves, || And a watch is kept over the heap. ³³The clods of the valley have been sweet to him, || And he draws every man after him, || And there is no numbering before him. ³⁴And how do you comfort me [with] vanity, || And trespass has been left in your answers?"

CHAPTER 22

¹And Eliphaz the Temanite answers and says: ²"Is a man profitable to God, || Because a wise man is profitable to himself? ³Is it a delight to the Mighty One || That you are righteous? Is it gain, || That you make your ways perfect? ⁴Because of your reverence || Does He reason [with] you? He enters with you into judgment: ⁵Is your wickedness not abundant? And there is no end to your iniquities. ⁶For you take a pledge of your brother for nothing, || And you strip off the garments of the naked. ⁷You do not cause the weary to drink water, || And you withhold bread from the hungry. ⁸As for the man of arm—he has the earth, || And the accepted of face—he dwells in it. ⁹You have sent widows away empty, || And the arms of the fatherless are bruised. ¹⁰Therefore snares [are] all around you, || And sudden fear troubles you. ¹¹Or darkness—you do not see, || And abundance of waters covers you. ¹²Is God not high [in] the heavens? And see the summit of the stars, || That they are high. ¹³And you have said, How has God known? Does He judge through thickness? ¹⁴Thick clouds [are] a secret place to Him, || And He does not see, || And He habitually walks [above] the circle of the heavens. ¹⁵Do you observe the path of the age, || That men of iniquity have trodden, ¹⁶Who have been cut down unexpectedly? A flood is poured out on their foundation. ¹⁷Those saying to God, Turn aside from us, || And what does the Mighty One do to them? ¹⁸And He has filled their houses [with] good (And the counsel of the wicked || Has been far from me). ¹⁹The righteous see and they rejoice, || And the innocent mocks at them: ²⁰Surely our substance has not been cut off, || And fire has consumed their excellence. ²¹Now acquaint yourself with Him, and be at peace, || Thereby your increase [is] good. ²²Please receive a law from His mouth, || And set His sayings in your heart. ²³If you return to the Mighty you are built up, || You put iniquity far from your tents. ²⁴So as to set a defense on the dust, || And a covering on a rock of the valleys. ²⁵And the Mighty has been your defense, || And silver [is] strength to you. ²⁶For then you delight yourself on the Mighty, || And lift up your face to God, ²⁷You make supplication to Him, || And He hears you, || And you complete your vows. ²⁸And you decree a saying, || And it is established to you, || And light has shone on your ways. ²⁹For they have made low, || And you say, Lift up. And He saves the bowed down of eyes. ³⁰He delivers the one [who is] not innocent, || Indeed, he has been delivered || By the cleanness of your hands."

CHAPTER 23

¹And Job answers and says: ²"Also—today my complaint [is] bitter, || My hand has been heavy because of my sighing. ³O that I had known—and I find Him, || I come to His seat, ⁴I arrange the cause before Him, || And fill my mouth [with] arguments. ⁵I know the words He answers me, || And understand what He says to me. ⁶Does He strive with me in the abundance of power? No! Surely He puts [it] in me. ⁷There the upright reason with Him, || And I escape from mine who is judging—forever. ⁸Behold, I go forward—and He is not, || And backward—and I do not perceive Him. ⁹[To] the left in His working—and I do not see, || He is covered [on] the right, and I do not behold. ¹⁰For He has known the way with me, || He has tried me—I go forth as gold. ¹¹My foot has laid hold on His step, || I have kept His way, and do not turn aside, ¹²The command of His lips, and I do not depart. I have laid up above my allotted portion || The sayings of His mouth. ¹³And He [is] in one [mind], || And who turns Him back? And His soul has desired—and He does [it]. ¹⁴For He completes my portion, || And many such things [are] with Him. ¹⁵Therefore, I am troubled at His presence, I consider, and am afraid of Him. ¹⁶And God has made my heart soft, || And the Mighty has troubled me. ¹⁷For I have not been cut off before darkness, || And before me He covered thick darkness."

CHAPTER 24

¹"For this reason from the Mighty One || Times have not been hidden, || And those knowing Him have not seen His days. ²They reach the borders, || They have taken a drove away violently, || Indeed, they do evil. ³They lead away the donkey of the fatherless, || They take in pledge the ox of the widow, ⁴They turn aside the needy from the way, || Together have hid the poor of the earth. ⁵Behold, wild donkeys in a wilderness, || They have gone out about their work, || Seeking early for prey, || A mixture for himself—food for young ones. ⁶They reap his provender in a field, || And they glean the vineyard of the wicked. ⁷They cause the naked to lodge without clothing. And there is no covering in the cold. ⁸From the inundation of hills they are wet, || And without a refuge—have embraced a rock. ⁹They take away violently || The orphan from the breast, || And they lay a pledge on the poor. ¹⁰Naked, they have gone without clothing, || And hungry—have taken away a sheaf. ¹¹They make oil between their walls, || They have trodden winepresses, and thirst. ¹²Men groan

JOB

because of enmity, || And the soul of pierced ones cries, || And God does not give praise. ¹³They have been those rebelling against light, || They have not discerned His ways, || Nor abided in His paths. ¹⁴The murderer rises at the light, || He slays the poor and needy, || And in the night he is as a thief. ¹⁵And the eye of an adulterer || Has observed the twilight, || Saying, No eye beholds me. And he puts the face in secret. ¹⁶He has dug in the darkness—houses; By day they shut themselves up, || They have not known light. ¹⁷When together, morning [is] death-shade to them, || When he discerns the terrors of death-shade. ¹⁸He [is] light on the face of the waters, || Their portion is vilified in the earth, || He does not turn the way of vineyards. ¹⁹Drought—also heat—consume snow-waters, || Sheol—[those who] have sinned. ²⁰The womb forgets him, || The worm sweetens [on] him, || He is remembered no more, || And wickedness is broken as a tree. ²¹Treating evil the barren [who] does not bear, || And he does no good [to] the widow, ²²And [God] has drawn the mighty by His power, || He rises, and none believes in life. ²³He gives to him confidence, and he is supported, || And His eyes [are] on their ways. ²⁴They were high [for] a little, and they are not, || And they have been brought low. They are shut up as all [others], || And cut off as the head of an ear of grain. ²⁵And if not now, who proves me a liar, || And makes my word of nothing?"

CHAPTER 25

¹And Bildad the Shuhite answers and says: ²"The rule and fear [are] with Him, || Making peace in his high places. ³Is there [any] number to His troops? And on whom does His light not arise? ⁴And what? Is man righteous with God? And what? Is he pure—born of a woman? ⁵Behold—to the moon, and it does not shine, || And stars have not been pure in His eyes. ⁶How much less man—a grub, || And the son of man—a worm!"

CHAPTER 26

¹And Job answers and says: ²"How you have helped the powerless, || Saved an arm not strong! ³How you have given counsel to the unwise, || And made known wise plans in abundance. ⁴With whom have you declared words? And whose breath came forth from you? ⁵The Rephaim are formed, || Also their inhabitants beneath the waters. ⁶Sheol [is] naked before Him, || And there is no covering to destruction. ⁷Stretching out the north over desolation, || Hanging the earth on nothing, ⁸Binding up the waters in His thick clouds, || And the cloud is not burst under them. ⁹Taking hold of the face of the throne, || Spreading His cloud over it. ¹⁰He has placed a limit on the waters, || To the boundary of light with darkness. ¹¹Pillars of the heavens tremble, || And they wonder because of His rebuke. ¹²By His power He has quieted the sea, || And by His understanding struck the proud. ¹³He beautified the heavens by His Spirit, || His hand has formed the fleeing serpent. ¹⁴Behold, these [are] the borders of His way, and how little a matter is heard of Him, and who understands the thunder of His might?"

CHAPTER 27

¹And Job adds to lift up his allegory and says: ²"God lives! He turned aside my judgment, || And the Mighty—He made my soul bitter. ³For all the while my breath [is] in me, || And the wind of God in my nostrils. ⁴My lips do not speak perverseness, || And my tongue does not utter deceit. ⁵Defilement to me—if I justify you, || Until I expire I do not turn aside my integrity from me. ⁶On my righteousness I have laid hold, || And I do not let it go, || My heart does not reproach me while I live. ⁷My enemy is as the wicked, || And my withstander as the perverse. ⁸For what [is] the hope of the profane, || When He cuts off? When God casts off his soul? ⁹[Does] God hear his cry, || When distress comes on him? ¹⁰Does he delight himself on the Mighty? Call God at all times? ¹¹I show you by the hand of God, || That which [is] with the Mighty I do not hide. ¹²Behold, you—all of you—have seen, || And why [is] this—you are altogether vain? ¹³This [is] the portion of wicked man with God, || And the inheritance of terrible ones || They receive from the Mighty. ¹⁴If his sons multiply—a sword [is] for them. And his offspring [are] not satisfied [with] bread. ¹⁵His remnant are buried in death, || And his widows do not weep. ¹⁶If he heaps up silver as dust, || And prepares clothing as clay, ¹⁷He prepares—and the righteous puts [it] on, || And the innocent apportions the silver. ¹⁸He has built his house as a moth, || And as a shelter a watchman has made. ¹⁹He lies down rich, and he is not gathered, || He has opened his eyes, and he is not. ²⁰Terrors overtake him as waters, || By night a whirlwind has stolen him away. ²¹An east wind takes him up, and he goes, || And it frightens him from his place, ²²And it casts at him, and does not spare, || He diligently flees from its hand. ²³It claps its hands at him, || And it hisses at him from his place."

CHAPTER 28

¹"Surely there is a source for silver, || And a place for the gold they refine; ²Iron is taken from the dust, || And bronze [from] the firm stone. ³He has set an end to darkness, || And he is searching to all perfection, || A stone of darkness and death-shade. ⁴A stream has broken out from a sojourner, || Those forgotten of the foot, || They were low, they wandered from man. ⁵The earth! Bread comes forth from it, || And its under-part is turned like fire. ⁶A place of the sapphire [are] its stones, || And it has dust of gold. ⁷A path—a ravenous bird has not known it, || Nor has an eye of the falcon scorched it, ⁸Nor have the sons of pride trodden it, || The fierce lion has not passed over it. ⁹He sent forth his hand against the flint, || He overturned mountains from the root. ¹⁰Among rocks, he has cleaved brooks, || And his eye has seen every precious thing. ¹¹He has bound overflowing rivers, || And the hidden thing brings out [to] light. ¹²And the wisdom—from where is it found? And where [is] this, the place of understanding? ¹³Man has not known its arrangement, || Nor is it found in the land of the living. ¹⁴The deep has said, It [is] not in me, || And the sea has said, It is not with me. ¹⁵Gold is not given for it, || Nor is silver weighed—its price. ¹⁶It is not valued with pure gold of Ophir, || With precious onyx and sapphire, ¹⁷Gold and crystal do not equal it, || Nor [is] its exchange a vessel of fine gold. ¹⁸Corals and pearl are not remembered, || The acquisition of wisdom [is] above rubies. ¹⁹The topaz of Cush does not equal it, || It is not valued with pure gold. ²⁰And the wisdom—from where does it come? And where [is] this, the place of understanding? ²¹It has been hid from the eyes of all living. And from the bird of the heavens || It has been hidden. ²²Destruction and death have said: With our ears we have heard its fame. ²³God has understood its way, || And He has known its place. ²⁴For He looks to the ends of the earth, || He sees under the whole heavens, ²⁵To make a weight for the wind, || And He meted out the waters in measure. ²⁶In His making for the rain a limit, || And a way for the brightness of the voices, ²⁷Then He has seen and declares it, || He has prepared it, and also searched it out, ²⁸And He says to man: Behold, fear of the Lord, that [is] wisdom, || And to turn from evil [is] understanding."

CHAPTER 29

¹And Job adds to lift up his allegory and says: ²"Who makes me as [in] months past, || As [in] the days of God's preserving me? ³In His causing His lamp to shine on my head, || By His light I walk [through] darkness. ⁴As I have been in days of my maturity, || And the counsel of God on my tent. ⁵When yet the Mighty One [is] with me. Around me—my young ones, ⁶When washing my goings with butter, || And the firm rock [is] with me—streams of oil. ⁷When I go out to the gate by the city, || In a broad place I prepare my seat. ⁸Youths have seen me, and they have been hidden, || And the aged have risen—they stood up. ⁹Princes have kept in words, || And they place a hand on their mouth. ¹⁰The voice of leaders has been hidden, || And their tongue has cleaved to the palate. ¹¹For the ear heard, and declares me blessed, || And the eye has seen, and testifies [to] me. ¹²For I deliver the afflicted who is crying, || And the fatherless who has no helper. ¹³The blessing of the perishing comes on me, || And I cause the heart of the widow to sing. ¹⁴I have put on righteousness, and it clothes me, || My justice as a robe and a crown. ¹⁵I have been eyes to the blind, || And I [am] feet to the lame. ¹⁶I [am] a father to the needy, || And the cause I have not known I search out. ¹⁷And I break the jaw-teeth of the perverse, || And from his teeth I cast away prey. ¹⁸And I say, I expire with my nest, || And I multiply days as the sand. ¹⁹My root is open to the waters, || And dew lodges on my branch. ²⁰My glory [is] fresh with me, || And my bow is renewed in my hand. ²¹They have listened to me, || Indeed, they wait, and are silent for my counsel. ²²After my word they do not change, || And my speech drops on

them, ²³And they wait for me as [for] rain, || And they have opened wide their mouth || [As] for the spring rain. ²⁴I laugh at them—they give no credence, || And do not cause the light of my face to fall. ²⁵I choose their way, and sit [as] head, || And I dwell as a king in a troop, || When he comforts mourners."

CHAPTER 30

¹"And now, laughed at me, || Have the younger in days than I, || Whose fathers I have loathed to set || With the dogs of my flock. ²Also—the power of their hands, why [is it] to me? On them old age has perished. ³With want and with harsh famine, || They are gnawing a dry place [in] the recent night, || [In] desolation and ruin, ⁴Those cropping mallows near a shrub, || And their food [is] root of broom trees. ⁵They are cast out from the midst || (They shout against them as a thief), ⁶To dwell in a frightful place of valleys, || Holes of earth and clefts. ⁷They groan among shrubs, || They are gathered together under nettles. ⁸Sons of folly—even sons without name, || They have been struck from the land. ⁹And now, I have been their song, || And I am to them for a byword. ¹⁰They have detested me, || They have kept far from me, || And from before me have not spared to spit. ¹¹Because He loosed His cord and afflicts me, || And the bridle from before me, || They have cast away. ¹²A brood arises on the right hand, || They have cast away my feet, || And they raise up against me, || Their paths of calamity. ¹³They have broken down my path, || They profit by my calamity: He has no helper. ¹⁴They come as a wide breach, || Under the desolation have rolled themselves. ¹⁵He has turned terrors against me, || It pursues my abundance as the wind, || And as a thick cloud, || My safety has passed away. ¹⁶And now, in me my soul pours itself out, || Days of affliction seize me. ¹⁷[At] night my bone has been pierced in me, || And my gnawing [pain] does not lie down. ¹⁸By the abundance of power, || Is my clothing changed, || As the mouth of my coat it girds me. ¹⁹Casting me into mire, || And I have become like dust and ashes. ²⁰I cry to You, || And You do not answer me, I have stood, and You consider me. ²¹You are turned to be fierce to me, || With the strength of Your hand, || You oppress me. ²²You lift me up, || You cause me to ride on the wind, || And You melt—You level me. ²³For I have known You bring me back [to] death, || And [to] the house appointed for all living. ²⁴Surely not against the heap || Does He send forth the hand, || Though they have safety in its ruin. ²⁵Did I not weep for him whose day is hard? My soul has grieved for the needy. ²⁶When I expected good, then comes evil, || And I wait for light, and darkness comes. ²⁷My bowels have boiled, and have not ceased, || Days of affliction have gone before me. ²⁸I have gone mourning without the sun, || I have risen, I cry in an assembly. ²⁹I have been a brother to dragons, || And a companion to daughters of the ostrich. ³⁰My skin has been black on me, || And my bone has burned from heat, ³¹And my harp becomes mourning, || And my pipe the sound of weeping."

CHAPTER 31

¹"I made a covenant for my eyes, || And how do I attend to a virgin? ²And what [is] the portion of God from above? And the inheritance of the Mighty from the heights? ³Is not calamity to the perverse? And strangeness to workers of iniquity? ⁴Does He not see my ways, || And number all my steps? ⁵If I have walked with vanity, || And my foot hurries to deceit, ⁶He weighs me in righteous balances, || And God knows my integrity. ⁷If my step turns aside from the way, || And my heart has gone after my eyes, || And blemish has cleaved to my hands, ⁸Let me sow—and another eat, || And let my products be rooted out. ⁹If my heart has been enticed by a woman, || And I laid wait by the opening of my neighbor, ¹⁰Let my wife grind to another, || And let others bend over her. ¹¹For it [is] a wicked thing, and a judicial iniquity; ¹²For it [is] a fire, it consumes to destruction, || And takes root among all my increase, ¹³If I despise the cause of my manservant, || And of my handmaid, || In their contending with me, ¹⁴Then what do I do when God arises? And when He inspects, || What do I answer Him? ¹⁵Did He that made me in the womb not make him? Indeed, One prepares us in the womb. ¹⁶If I withhold the poor from pleasure, || And consume the eyes of the widow, ¹⁷And I eat my morsel by myself, || And the orphan has nothing [to] eat of it, ¹⁸(But from my youth || He grew up with me as [with] a father, || And from the belly of my mother I am led), ¹⁹If I see [any] perishing without clothing, || And there is no covering for the needy, ²⁰If his loins have not blessed me, || And from the fleece of my sheep || He does not warm himself, ²¹If I have waved my hand at the fatherless, || When I see [him] in the gate of my court, ²²Let my shoulder fall from its blade, || And the bone from my arm be broken. ²³For calamity [from] God [is] a dread to me, || And because of His excellence I am not able. ²⁴If I have made gold my confidence, || And to the pure gold have said, My trust; ²⁵If I rejoice because my wealth [is] great, || And because my hand has found abundance, ²⁶If I see the light when it shines, || And the precious moon walking, ²⁷And my heart is enticed in secret, || And my hand kisses my mouth, ²⁸It also [is] a judicial iniquity, || For I had lied to God above. ²⁹If I rejoice at the ruin of my hater, || And stirred up myself when evil found him, ³⁰Indeed, I have not permitted my mouth to sin, || To ask with an oath his life. ³¹If not, say, O men of my tent: O that we had of his flesh, we are not satisfied. ³²A stranger does not lodge in the street, || I open my doors to the traveler. ³³If I have covered my transgressions as Adam, || To hide my iniquity in my bosom, ³⁴Because I fear a great multitude, || And the contempt of families frightens me, || Then I am silent, I do not go out of the opening. ³⁵Who gives to me a hearing? Behold, my mark. The Mighty One answers me, || And my adversary has written a bill. ³⁶If not—on my shoulder I take it up, || I bind it [as] a crown on myself. ³⁷The number of my steps I tell Him, || As a leader I approach Him. ³⁸If my land cries out against me, || And together its furrows weep, ³⁹If I consumed its strength without money, || And the life of its possessors, I have caused to breathe out, ⁴⁰Instead of wheat let a thorn go forth, || And instead of barley a useless weed!" The words of Job are finished.

CHAPTER 32

¹And these three men cease from answering Job, for he [is] righteous in his own eyes, ²and the anger of Elihu son of Barachel the Buzite burns, of the family of Ram; his anger has burned against Job, because of his justifying himself more than God; ³and his anger has burned against his three friends, because that they have not found an answer, and condemn Job. ⁴And Elihu has waited earnestly beside Job with words, for they are older than he in days. ⁵And Elihu sees that there is no answer in the mouth of the three men, and his anger burns. ⁶And Elihu son of Barachel the Buzite answers and says: "I [am] young in days, and you [are] aged; Therefore I have feared, || And am afraid of showing you my opinion. ⁷I said, Days speak, || And a multitude of years teach wisdom. ⁸Surely a spirit is in man, || And the breath of the Mighty One || Causes them to understand. ⁹The multitude are not wise, || Nor do the aged understand judgment. ¹⁰Therefore I have said: Listen to me, I show my opinion—even I. ¹¹Behold, I have waited for your words, I give ear to your reasons, || Until you search out sayings. ¹²And to you I attend, || And behold, there is no reasoner for Job, || [Or] answerer of his sayings among you. ¹³Lest you say, We have found wisdom, || God thrusts him away, not man. ¹⁴And he has not set words in array for me, || And I do not answer him with your sayings. ¹⁵(They have broken down, || They have not answered again, || They removed words from themselves. ¹⁶And I have waited, but they do not speak, || For they have stood still, || They have not answered anymore.) ¹⁷I answer, even I—my share, || I show my opinion—even I. ¹⁸For I have been full of words, || The spirit of my breast has distressed me, ¹⁹Behold, my breast [is] as wine not opened, || It is broken up like new bottles. ²⁰I speak, and there is refreshment to me, || I open my lips and answer. ²¹Please do not let me accept the face of any, || Nor give flattering titles to man, ²²For I have not known to give flattering titles, || My Maker takes me away in a little."

CHAPTER 33

¹"And yet, please, O Job, || Hear my speech and give ear [to] all my words. ²Now behold, I have opened my mouth, || My tongue has spoken in the palate. ³Of the uprightness of my heart [are] my sayings, || And my lips have clearly spoken knowledge. ⁴The Spirit of God has made me, || And the breath of the Mighty quickens me. ⁵If you are able—answer me, || Set in array before me—station yourself. ⁶Behold, I [am], according to your word, for God, || I have also been formed from the clay. ⁷Behold, my terror does not frighten you, || And my burden on you is not heavy. ⁸Surely you have spoken in my ears, || And the sounds

of words I hear: ⁹I [am] pure, without transgression, || I [am] innocent, and I have no iniquity. ¹⁰Behold, He develops hindrances against me, || He reckons me for an enemy to Him, ¹¹He puts my feet in the stocks, || He watches all my paths. ¹²Behold, you have not been righteous [in] this, || I answer you, that God is greater than man. ¹³Why have you striven against Him, || When [for] all His matters He does not answer? ¹⁴For once God speaks, and twice (he does not behold it), ¹⁵In a dream—a vision of night, || In the falling of deep sleep on men, || In slumberings on a bed. ¹⁶Then He uncovers the ear of men, || And seals for their instruction, ¹⁷To turn aside man [from] doing, || And He conceals pride from man. ¹⁸He keeps back his soul from corruption, || And his life from passing away by a dart. ¹⁹And he has been reproved || With pain on his bed, || And the strife of his bones [is] enduring. ²⁰And his life has nauseated bread, || And his soul desirable food. ²¹His flesh is consumed from being seen, || And his bones are high, they were not seen! ²²And his soul draws near to the pit, || And his life to those causing death. ²³If there is a messenger by him, || An interpreter—one of a thousand, || To declare for man his uprightness, ²⁴Then He favors him and says, || Ransom him from going down to the pit, || I have found an atonement. ²⁵Fresher [is] his flesh than a child's, || He returns to the days of his youth. ²⁶He makes supplication to God, || And He accepts him. And he sees His face with shouting, || And He returns to man His righteousness. ²⁷[Then] he looks on men and says, || I sinned, and I have perverted uprightness, || And it has not been profitable to me. ²⁸He has ransomed my soul || From going over into the pit, || And my life looks on the light. ²⁹Behold, God works all these, || Twice, [even] three times with man, ³⁰To bring back his soul from the pit, || To be enlightened with the light of the living. ³¹Attend, O Job, listen to me, || Keep silent, and I speak. ³²If there are words—answer me, || Speak, for I have a desire to justify you. ³³If there are not—listen to me, || Keep silent, and I teach you wisdom."

CHAPTER 34

¹And Elihu answers and says: ²"Hear, O wise men, my words, || And, O knowing ones, give ear to me. ³For the ear tries words, || And the palate tastes to eat. ⁴Let us choose judgment for ourselves, || Let us know among ourselves what [is] good. ⁵For Job has said, I have been righteous, || And God has turned aside my right, ⁶Against my right do I lie? My arrow [is] mortal—without transgression. ⁷Who [is] a man like Job? He drinks scoffing like water, ⁸And he has traveled for company || With workers of iniquity, || So as to go with men of wickedness. ⁹For he has said, It does not profit a man || When he delights himself with God. ¹⁰Therefore, O men of heart, listen to me; Far be it from God to do wickedness, || And [from] the Mighty to do perverseness, ¹¹For He repays the work of man to him, || And according to the path of each He causes him to find. ¹²Indeed, truly, God does not do wickedly, || And the Mighty does not pervert judgment. ¹³Who has inspected for Himself the earth? And who has placed all the habitable world? ¹⁴If He sets His heart on him, || [If] He gathers His Spirit and His breath to Himself, ¹⁵All flesh expires together, || And man returns to dust. ¹⁶And if [there is] understanding, hear this, || Give ear to the voice of my words. ¹⁷Indeed, does one hating justice govern? Or do you condemn the Most Just? ¹⁸Who has said to a king, Worthless, || To princes, Wicked? ¹⁹That has not accepted the person of princes, || Nor has known the rich before the poor, || For all of them [are] a work of His hands. ²⁰[In] a moment they die, || And at midnight people shake, || And they pass away, || And they remove the mighty without hand. ²¹For His eyes [are] on the ways of each, || And He sees all his steps. ²²There is no darkness nor death-shade, || For workers of iniquity to be hidden there; ²³For He does not permit man anymore, || To go to God in judgment, ²⁴He breaks the mighty—no searching! And He appoints others in their stead. ²⁵Therefore He knows their works, || And He has overturned by night, || And they are bruised. ²⁶As wicked He has struck them, || In the place of beholders. ²⁷Because that against right || They have turned aside from after Him, || And have considered none of His ways, ²⁸To cause to come to Him || The cry of the poor, || And He hears the cry of the afflicted. ²⁹And He gives rest, and who makes wrong? And hides the face, and who beholds it? And in reference to a nation and to a man, || [It is] the same. ³⁰From the reigning of a profane man, || From the snares of a people; ³¹For has any said to God: I have taken away, || I do not do corruptly, ³²Besides [that which] I see, You show me, || If I have done iniquity—I do not add? ³³Does He repay by you, that you have refused—That you choose, and not I? And what you have known, speak. ³⁴Let men of heart say to me, || And a wise man is listening to me: ³⁵Job—he does not speak with knowledge, || And his words [are] not with wisdom. ³⁶My Father! Let Job be tried—to victory, || Because of answers for men of iniquity, ³⁷For he adds to his sin, || He vomits transgression among us, || And multiplies his sayings to God."

CHAPTER 35

¹And Elihu answers and says: ²"Have you reckoned this for judgment [when] you have said, || My righteousness [is] more than God's? ³For you say, What does it profit You? What do I profit from my sin? ⁴I return words, and your friends with you, ⁵Behold attentively the heavens—and see, || And behold the clouds, || They have been higher than you. ⁶If you have sinned, what do you do against Him? And your transgressions have been multiplied, || What do you do to Him? ⁷If you have been righteous, || What do you give to Him? Or what does He receive from your hand? ⁸For a man like yourself [is] your wickedness, || And for a son of man your righteousness. ⁹Because of the multitude of oppressions || They cause to cry out, || They cry because of the arm of the mighty. ¹⁰And none said, Where [is] God my Maker? Giving songs in the night, ¹¹Teaching us more than the beasts of the earth, || Indeed, He makes us wiser than the bird of the heavens. ¹²There they cry, and He does not answer, || Because of the pride of evildoers. ¹³Surely God does not hear vanity, || And the Mighty does not behold it. ¹⁴Indeed, though you say you do not behold Him, || Judgment [is] before Him, and stays for Him. ¹⁵And now, because there is not, || He has appointed His anger, || And He has not known in great extremity. ¹⁶And Job opens his mouth [with] vanity, || He multiplies words without knowledge."

CHAPTER 36

¹And Elihu adds and says: ²"Honor me a little, and I show you, || That yet for God [are] words. ³I lift up my knowledge from afar, || And I ascribe righteousness to my Maker. ⁴For my words [are] truly not false, || The perfect in knowledge [is] with you. ⁵Behold, God [is] mighty, and does not despise, || Mighty [in] power [and] heart. ⁶He does not revive the wicked, || And appoints the judgment of the poor; ⁷He does not withdraw His eyes from the righteous, || And [from] kings on the throne, || And causes them to sit forever, and they are high, ⁸And if prisoners in chains || They are captured with cords of affliction, ⁹Then He declares to them their work, || And their transgressions, || Because they have become mighty, ¹⁰And He uncovers their ear for instruction, || And commands that they turn back from iniquity. ¹¹If they hear and serve, || They complete their days in good, || And their years in pleasantness. ¹²And if they do not listen, || They pass away by the dart, || And expire without knowledge. ¹³And the profane in heart set the face, || They do not cry when He has bound them. ¹⁴Their soul dies in youth, || And their life among the defiled. ¹⁵He draws out the afflicted in his affliction, || And uncovers their ear in oppression. ¹⁶And He also moved you from a narrow place || [To] a broad place—no constriction under it, || And the sitting beyond of your table has been full of fatness. ¹⁷And you have fulfilled the judgment of the wicked, || Judgment and justice are upheld because of fury, ¹⁸Lest He move you with a stroke, || And the abundance of an atonement not turn you aside. ¹⁹Does He value your riches? He has gold, and all the forces of power. ²⁰Do not desire the night, || For the going up of peoples in their stead. ²¹Take heed—do not turn to iniquity, || For you have fixed on this || Rather than [on] affliction. ²²Behold, God sits on high by His power, || Who [is] like Him—a teacher? ²³Who has appointed to Him His way? And who said, You have done iniquity? ²⁴Remember that you magnify His work || That men have beheld. ²⁵All men have looked on it, || Man looks attentively from afar. ²⁶Behold, God [is] high, || And we do not know the number of His years, || Indeed, there [is] no searching. ²⁷When He diminishes droppings of the waters, || They refine rain according to its vapor, ²⁸Which clouds drop, || They distill on man abundantly. ²⁹Indeed, do [any] understand || The

JOB

spreadings out of a cloud? The noises of His dwelling place? ³⁰Behold, He has spread His light over it, || And He has covered the roots of the sea, ³¹For He judges peoples by them, || He gives food in abundance. ³²By two palms He has covered the light, || And lays a charge over it in meeting, ³³His shout shows it, || The livestock also, the rising [storm]."

CHAPTER 37

¹"Also, my heart trembles at this, || And it moves from its place. ²Listen diligently to the trembling of His voice, || Indeed, the sound goes forth from His mouth. ³He directs it under the whole heavens, || And its light [is] over the skirts of the earth. ⁴A voice roars after it—He thunders with the voice of His excellence, || And He does not hold them back, || When His voice is heard. ⁵God thunders with His voice wonderfully, || Doing great things and we do not know. ⁶For He says to snow: Be [on] the earth. And the small rain and great rain of His power. ⁷Into the hand of every man he seals, || For the knowledge by all men of His work. ⁸And the beast enters into [its] lair, || And it continues in its habitations. ⁹From the inner chamber comes a windstorm, || And from scatterings winds—cold, ¹⁰From the breath of God is frost given, || And the breadth of waters is constricted, ¹¹Indeed, by filling He presses out a cloud, [and] His light scatters a cloud. ¹²And it is turning itself around by His counsels, || For their doing all He commands them, || On the face of the habitable earth. ¹³Whether for a rod, or for His land, || Or for kindness—He causes it to come. ¹⁴Hear this, O Job, || Stand and consider the wonders of God. ¹⁵Do you know when God places them, || And caused the light of His cloud to shine? ¹⁶Do you know the balancings of a cloud? The wonders of the Perfect in knowledge? ¹⁷How your garments [are] warm, || In the quieting of the earth from the south? ¹⁸You have made an expanse with Him || For the clouds—strong as a hard mirror! ¹⁹Let us know what we say to Him, || We do not set in array because of darkness. ²⁰Is it declared to Him that I speak? If a man has spoken, surely he is swallowed up. ²¹And now, they have not seen the light, || It [is] bright in the clouds, || And the wind has passed by and cleanses them. ²²It comes from the golden north, || Fearful splendor [is] beside God. ²³The Mighty! We have not found Him out, || High in power and judgment, || He does not answer! And abundant in righteousness, ²⁴Therefore men fear Him, || He does not see any of the wise of heart."

CHAPTER 38

¹And YHWH answers Job out of the whirlwind and says: ²"Who [is] this—darkening counsel, || By words without knowledge? ³Now gird your loins as a man, || And I ask you, and you cause Me to know. ⁴Where were you when I founded the earth? Declare, if you have known understanding. ⁵Who placed its measures—if you know? Or who has stretched out a line on it? ⁶On what have its sockets been sunk? Or who has cast its cornerstone— ⁷In the singing together of [the] stars of morning, || When all [the] sons of God shout for joy? ⁸And He shuts up the sea with doors, || In its coming forth, it goes out from the womb. ⁹In My making a cloud its clothing, || And thick darkness its swaddling band, ¹⁰And I measure My statute over it, || And place bar and doors, ¹¹And say, To here you come, and no more, || And a command is placed || On the pride of your billows. ¹²Have you commanded morning since your days? Do you cause the dawn to know its place? ¹³To take hold on the skirts of the earth, || And the wicked are shaken out of it, ¹⁴It turns itself as clay of a seal || And they station themselves as clothed. ¹⁵And their light is withheld from the wicked, || And the arm lifted up is broken. ¹⁶Have you come to springs of the sea? And in searching the deep || Have you walked up and down? ¹⁷Were the gates of death revealed to you? And do you see the gates of death-shade? ¹⁸You have understanding, || Even to the broad places of earth! Declare—if you have known it all. ¹⁹Where [is] this—the way light dwells? And darkness, where [is] this—its place? ²⁰That you take it to its boundary, || And that you understand the paths of its house. ²¹You have known—for then you are born, || And the number of your days [are] many! ²²Have you come to the treasure of snow? Indeed, do you see the treasures of hail, ²³That I have kept back for a time of distress, || For a day of conflict and battle? ²⁴Where [is] this, the way light is apportioned? It scatters an east wind over the earth. ²⁵Who has divided a conduit for the flood? And a way for the lightning of the voices? ²⁶To cause [it] to rain on a land [with] no man, || A wilderness [with] no man in it. ²⁷To satisfy a desolate and ruined place, || And to cause to shoot up || The produce of the tender grass? ²⁸Does the rain have a father? Or who has begotten the drops of dew? ²⁹From whose belly came forth the ice? And the hoarfrost of the heavens, || Who has begotten it? ³⁰Waters are hidden as a stone, || And the face of the deep is captured. ³¹Do you bind the chains of the Pleiades? Or do you open the cords of Orion? ³²Do you bring out the twelve signs in [their] season? And do you comfort the Great Bear over her sons? ³³Have you known the statutes of the heavens? Or do you appoint || Its dominion in the earth? ³⁴Do you lift up your voice to the cloud, || And abundance of water covers you? ³⁵Do you send out lightnings, and they go || And say to you, Behold us? ³⁶Who has put wisdom in the inward parts? Or who has given understanding to the covered part? ³⁷Who numbers the clouds by wisdom? And the bottles of the heavens, || Who causes to lie down, ³⁸In the hardening of dust into hardness, || And clods cleave together? ³⁹Do you hunt prey for a lion? And fulfill the desire of young lions? ⁴⁰When they bow down in dens—Abide in a thicket for a covert? ⁴¹Who prepares for a raven his provision, || When his young ones cry to God? They wander without food."

CHAPTER 39

¹"Have you known the time of || The bearing of the wild goats of the rock? Do you mark the bringing forth of does? ²Do you number the months they fulfill? And have you known the time of their bringing forth? ³They bow down, || They bring forth their young ones safely, || They cast forth their pangs. ⁴Their young ones are safe, || They grow up in the field, they have gone out, || And have not returned to them. ⁵Who has sent forth the wild donkey free? Indeed, who opened the bands of the wild donkey? ⁶Whose house I have made the wilderness, || And his dwellings the barren land, ⁷He laughs at the multitude of a city, || He does not hear the cries of an exactor. ⁸The range of mountains [is] his pasture, || And he seeks after every green thing. ⁹Is a wild ox willing to serve you? Does he lodge by your crib? ¹⁰Do you bind a wild ox in a furrow [with] his thick band? Does he harrow valleys after you? ¹¹Do you trust in him because his power [is] great? And do you leave your labor to him? ¹²Do you trust in him || That he brings back your seed, || And gathers [it to] your threshing-floor? ¹³[The] wing of the crying ostriches exults, but as a pinion and feather of a stork? ¹⁴For she leaves her eggs on the earth, || And she warms them on the dust, ¹⁵And she forgets that a foot may press it, || And a beast of the field treads it down. ¹⁶It has hardened her young ones without her, || Her labor [is] in vain, without fear. ¹⁷For God has caused her to forget wisdom, || And He has not given a portion || To her in understanding; ¹⁸At the time she lifts herself up on high, || She laughs at the horse and his rider. ¹⁹Do you give might to the horse? Do you clothe his neck [with] a mane? ²⁰Do you cause him to rush as a locust? The splendor of his snorting [is] terrible. ²¹They dig in a valley, and he rejoices in power, || He goes forth to meet the armor. ²²He laughs at fear, and is not frightened, || And he does not turn back from the face of the sword. ²³Quiver rattles against him, || The flame of a spear, and a javelin. ²⁴He swallows the ground with trembling and rage, || And does not remain steadfast || Because of the sound of a horn. ²⁵Among the horns he says, Aha, || And from afar he smells battle, || Roaring of princes and shouting. ²⁶By your understanding does a hawk fly? Does he spread his wings to the south? ²⁷At your command does an eagle go up high? Or lift up his nest? ²⁸He inhabits a rock, || Indeed, he lodges on the tooth of a rock, and fortress. ²⁹From there he has sought food, || His eyes look attentively to a far-off place, ³⁰And his brood sucks up blood, || And where the pierced [are]—there [is] he!"

CHAPTER 40

¹And YHWH answers Job and says: ²"Is the striver with the Mighty instructed? The reprover of God, let him answer it." ³And Job answers YHWH and says: ⁴"Behold, I have been vile, || What do I return to You? I have placed my hand on my mouth. ⁵I have spoken once, and I do not answer, || And twice, and I do not add." ⁶And YHWH answers Job out of the whirlwind and says: ⁷"Now gird your loins as

JOB

a man, || I ask you, and you cause Me to know. ⁸Do you also make My judgment void? Do you condemn Me, || That you may be righteous? ⁹And do you have an arm like God? And do you thunder with a voice like His? ¹⁰Now put on excellence and loftiness, || Indeed, put on splendor and beauty. ¹¹Scatter abroad the wrath of your anger, || And see every proud one, and make him low. ¹²See every proud one—humble him, || And tread down the wicked in their place. ¹³Hide them in the dust together, || Bind their faces in secret. ¹⁴And even I praise you, || For your right hand gives salvation to you. ¹⁵Now behold, behemoth, || That I made with you: He eats grass as an ox. ¹⁶Now behold, his power [is] in his loins, || And his strength in the muscles of his belly. ¹⁷He bends his tail as a cedar, || The sinews of his thighs are wrapped together, ¹⁸His bones [are] tubes of bronze, || His bones [are] as a bar of iron. ¹⁹He [is] a beginning of the ways of God, || His Maker [alone] brings His sword near; ²⁰For mountains bear food for him, || And all the beasts of the field play there. ²¹He lies down under shades, || In a secret place of reed and marsh. ²²Shades cover him, [with] their shadow, || Willows of the brook cover him. ²³Behold, a flood oppresses—he does not hurry, || He is confident though Jordan || Comes forth to his mouth. ²⁴Does [one] take him by his eyes? || Does [one] pierce the nose with snares?"

CHAPTER 41
¹"Do you draw leviathan with a hook? And do you let down his tongue with a rope? ²Do you put a reed in his nose? And pierce his jaw with a thorn? ³Does he multiply supplications to you? Does he speak tender things to you? ⁴Does he make a covenant with you? Do you take him for a perpetual servant? ⁵Do you play with him as a bird? And do you bind him for your girls? ⁶(Companions feast on him, || They divide him among the merchants!) ⁷Do you fill his skin with barbed irons? And his head with fish-spears? ⁸Place your hand on him, || Remember the battle—do not add! ⁹Behold, the hope of him is found a liar, || Also, is one not cast down at his appearance? ¹⁰None so fierce that he awakes him, || And who [is] he [who] stations himself before Me? ¹¹Who has brought before Me and I repay? Under the whole heavens it [is] Mine. ¹²I do not keep silent concerning his parts, || And the matter of might, || And the grace of his arrangement. ¹³Who has uncovered the face of his clothing? Who enters within his double bridle? ¹⁴Who has opened the doors of his face? Around his teeth [are] terrible. ¹⁵A pride—strong ones of shields, || Shut up—a close seal. ¹⁶They draw near to one another, || And air does not enter between them. ¹⁷They adhere to one another, || They stick together and are not separated. ¹⁸His sneezings cause light to shine, || And his eyes [are] as the eyelids of the dawn. ¹⁹Flames go out of his mouth, sparks of fire escape. ²⁰Smoke goes forth out of his nostrils, || As a blown pot and reeds. ²¹His breath sets coals on fire, || And a flame goes forth from his mouth. ²²Strength lodges in his neck, || And grief exults before him. ²³The flakes of his flesh have adhered—Firm on him—it is not moved. ²⁴His heart [is] firm as a stone, || Indeed, firm as the lower piece. ²⁵The mighty are afraid at his rising, || From his breakings they keep themselves free. ²⁶The sword of his overtaker does not stand, || Spear, dart, and breastplate. ²⁷He reckons iron as straw, bronze as rotten wood. ²⁸The son of the bow does not cause him to flee, || Stones of the sling are turned into stubble by him. ²⁹Darts have been reckoned as stubble, || And he laughs at the shaking of a javelin. ³⁰Sharp points of clay [are] under him, || He spreads gold on the mire. ³¹He causes the deep to boil as a pot, || He makes the sea as a pot of ointment. ³²He causes a path to shine after him, || One thinks the deep to be hoary. ³³There is not on the earth his like, || That is made without terror. ³⁴He sees every high thing, || He [is] king over all sons of pride."

CHAPTER 42
¹And Job answers YHWH and says: ²"You have known that [for] all things You are able, || And no purpose is withheld from You. ³[You said], Who [is] this hiding counsel without knowledge? Therefore, I have declared, and do not understand, || Too wonderful for me, and I do not know. ⁴Please hear, and I speak; [You said], I ask you, and you cause Me to know. ⁵By the hearing of the ear I heard You, || And now my eye has seen You. ⁶Therefore I loathe [it], || And I have sighed on dust and ashes." ⁷And it comes to pass after YHWH's speaking these words to Job, that YHWH says to Eliphaz the Temanite, "My anger has burned against you and against your two friends, because you have not spoken correctly concerning Me, like My servant Job. ⁸And now, take seven bullocks and seven rams for yourselves, and go to My servant Job, and you have caused a burnt-offering to ascend for yourselves; and Job My servant prays for you, for surely I accept his face, so as not to do folly with you, because you have not spoken correctly concerning Me, like My servant Job." ⁹And they go—Eliphaz the Temanite, and Bildad the Shuhite, Zophar the Naamathite—and do as YHWH has spoken to them; and YHWH accepts the face of Job. ¹⁰And YHWH has turned [to] the captivity of Job in his praying for his friends, and YHWH adds [to] all that Job has—to double. ¹¹And all his brothers come to him, and all his sisters, and all his former acquaintances, and they eat bread with him in his house, and bemoan him, and comfort him concerning all the calamity that YHWH had brought on him, and they each gave to him one kesitah, and each one ring of gold. ¹²And YHWH has blessed the latter end of Job more than his beginning, and he has fourteen thousand of a flock, and six thousand camels, and one thousand pairs of oxen, and one thousand female donkeys. ¹³And he has seven sons and three daughters; ¹⁴and he calls the name of the first Jemima, and the name of the second Kezia, and the name of the third Keren-Happuch. ¹⁵And there have not been found women [as] beautiful as the daughters of Job in all the land, and their father gives to them an inheritance in the midst of their brothers. ¹⁶And Job lives after this one hundred and forty years, and sees his sons, and his sons' sons, four generations; ¹⁷and Job dies, aged and satisfied [with] days.

PSALMS

PSALM 1
¹O the blessedness of that one, || Who has not walked in the counsel of the wicked, || And has not stood in the way of sinners, || And has not sat in the seat of scorners; ²But his delight [is] in the Law of YHWH, || And in His law he meditates by day and by night: ³And he has been as a tree, || Planted by streams of water, || That gives its fruit in its season, || And its leaf does not wither, || And all that he does he causes to prosper. ⁴Not so the wicked: But [they are] as chaff that wind drives away! ⁵Therefore the wicked do not rise in judgment, || Nor sinners in the congregation of the righteous, ⁶For YHWH is knowing the way of the righteous, || And the way of the wicked is lost!

PSALM 2
¹Why have nations assembled tumultuously? And peoples meditate vanity? ²Kings of the earth station themselves, and princes have been united together, against YHWH, and against His Messiah: ³"Let us draw off Their cords, || And cast Their thick bands from us." ⁴He who is sitting in the heavens laughs, || The Lord mocks at them. ⁵Then He speaks to them in His anger, and in His wrath He troubles them: ⁶"And I have anointed My King, || On Zion—My holy hill." ⁷I declare concerning a statute: YHWH said to me, "You [are] My Son, today I have brought You forth. ⁸Ask of Me and I give nations [as] Your inheritance, || And the ends of the earth [for] Your possession. ⁹You rule them with a scepter of iron, || You crush them as a vessel of a potter." ¹⁰And now, O

kings, act wisely, || Be instructed, O judges of earth, ¹¹Serve YHWH with fear, || And rejoice with trembling. ¹²Kiss the Chosen One [[or Son]], lest He is angry, || And you perish [from] the way, || When His anger burns but a little, || O the blessedness of all trusting in Him!

PSALM 3

¹A PSALM OF DAVID, IN HIS FLEEING FROM THE FACE OF HIS SON ABSALOM. YHWH, how my distresses have multiplied! Many are rising up against me. ²Many are saying of my soul, "There is no salvation for him in God." Selah. ³And You, O YHWH, [are] a shield for me, || My glory, and lifter up of my head. ⁴My voice [is] to YHWH: I call and He answers me from His holy hill, Selah. ⁵I have lain down, and I sleep; || I have awoken, for YHWH sustains me. ⁶I am not afraid of myriads of people, || That they have set against me all around. ⁷Rise, O YHWH! Save me, my God! For You have struck all my enemies [on] the cheek. You have broken the teeth of the wicked. ⁸This salvation [is] of YHWH; Your blessing [is] on Your people! Selah.

PSALM 4

¹TO THE OVERSEER. WITH STRINGED INSTRUMENTS. A PSALM OF DAVID. In my calling answer me, || O God of my righteousness. In adversity You gave enlargement to me; Favor me, and hear my prayer. ²Sons of men! Until when [is] my glory for shame? You love a vain thing, you seek a lie. Selah. ³And know that YHWH || Has separated a saintly one to Himself. YHWH hears in my calling to Him. ⁴"Tremble, and do not sin"; Say [thus] in your heart on your bed, || And be silent. Selah. ⁵Sacrifice sacrifices of righteousness, || And trust in YHWH. ⁶Many are saying, "Who shows us good?" Lift on us the light of Your face, O YHWH, ⁷You have given joy in my heart, || From the time their grain and their wine || Have been multiplied. ⁸Together I lie down and sleep in peace, || For You, O YHWH, alone, || Cause me to dwell in confidence!

PSALM 5

¹TO THE OVERSEER. [BLOWN] INTO THE PIPES. A PSALM OF DAVID. Hear my sayings, O YHWH, || Consider my meditation. ²Be attentive to the voice of my cry, || My King and my God, || For I pray to You habitually. ³YHWH, [in] the morning You hear my voice, || [In] the morning I set in array for You, || And I look out [expectantly]. ⁴For You [are] not a God desiring wickedness, || Evil does not inhabit You. ⁵The boastful do not station themselves before Your eyes: You have hated all working iniquity, ⁶You destroy those speaking lies, || YHWH detests a man of blood and deceit. ⁷And I, in the abundance of Your kindness, || I enter Your house, || I bow myself toward Your holy temple in Your fear. ⁸O YHWH, lead me in Your righteousness, || Because of those observing me, || Make Your way straight before me, ⁹For there is no stability in their mouth. Their heart [is] mischiefs, || Their throat [is] an open grave, || They make their tongue smooth. ¹⁰Declare them guilty, O God, || Let them fall from their own counsels, || In the abundance of their transgressions || Drive them away, || Because they have been rebellious against You. ¹¹And all trusting in You rejoice, || They sing for all time, and You cover them over, || And those loving Your Name exult in You. ¹²For You bless the righteous, O YHWH, || Surrounding him with favor as a buckler!

PSALM 6

¹TO THE OVERSEER. WITH STRINGED INSTRUMENTS, ON THE EIGHTH. A PSALM OF DAVID. O YHWH, do not reprove me in Your anger, || Nor discipline me in Your fury. ²Favor me, O YHWH, for I [am] weak, || Heal me, O YHWH, || For my bones have been troubled, ³And my soul has been troubled greatly, || And You, O YHWH, until when? ⁴Turn back, O YHWH, draw out my soul, || Save me for Your kindness' sake. ⁵For in death there is no memorial of You, || In Sheol, who gives thanks to You? ⁶I have been weary with my sighing, || I meditate [on] my bed through all the night, || I dissolve my couch with my tear. ⁷My eye is old from provocation, || It is old because of all my adversaries, ⁸Turn from me all you workers of iniquity, || For YHWH heard the voice of my weeping, ⁹YHWH has heard my supplication, || YHWH receives my prayer. ¹⁰All my enemies are greatly ashamed and troubled, || They turn back—ashamed [in] a moment!

PSALM 7

¹A SHIGGAION OF DAVID, THAT HE SUNG TO YHWH CONCERNING THE WORDS OF CUSH, A BENJAMITE. O YHWH, my God, in You I have trusted, || Save me from all my pursuers, and deliver me. ²Lest he tear my soul as a lion, || Tearing, and there is no deliverer. ³O YHWH, my God, if I have done this, || If there is iniquity in my hands, ⁴If I have done my well-wisher evil, || And draw my adversary without cause, ⁵[Then] an enemy pursues my soul, and overtakes, || And treads down my life to the earth, || And places my glory in the dust. Selah. ⁶Rise, O YHWH, in Your anger, || Be lifted up at the wrath of my adversaries, || And awake Yourself for me. You have commanded judgment: ⁷And a congregation of peoples surround You, || And over it turn back on high. ⁸YHWH judges the peoples; Judge me, O YHWH, || According to my righteousness, || And according to my integrity [that is] on me. ⁹Please let the evil of the wicked be ended, || And establish the righteous, || And a trier of hearts and reins is the righteous God. ¹⁰My shield [is] on God, || Savior of the upright in heart! ¹¹God [is] judging right, || And He is not angry at all times. ¹²If [one] does not turn, || He sharpens His sword, || He has bent His bow [and] He prepares it, ¹³Indeed, He has prepared for Himself || Instruments of death, || He makes His arrows for burning pursuers. ¹⁴Behold, he travails [with] iniquity, || And he has conceived perverseness, || And has brought forth falsehood. ¹⁵He has prepared a pit, and he digs it, || And he falls into a ditch he makes. ¹⁶His perverseness returns on his head, || And his violence comes down on his crown. ¹⁷I thank YHWH, || According to His righteousness, || And I praise the Name of YHWH Most High!

PSALM 8

¹TO THE OVERSEER. ON THE GITTITH. A PSALM OF DAVID. YHWH, our Lord, || How majestic [is] Your Name in all the earth, || Who have set Your splendor on the heavens! ²From the mouths of infants and sucklings || You have founded strength, || Because of Your adversaries, || To still an enemy and a self-avenger. ³For I see Your heavens, a work of Your fingers, || [The] moon and stars that You established. ⁴What [is] man that You remember him? The son of man that You inspect him? ⁵You make him a little lower than the gods [[or God]], || And surround him with glory and majesty. ⁶You cause him to rule || Over the works of Your hands, || You have placed all under his feet. ⁷Sheep and oxen, all of them, || And also beasts of the field, ⁸Bird of the heavens, and fish of the sea, || Passing through the paths of the seas! ⁹YHWH, our Lord, || How majestic [is] Your Name in all the earth!

PSALM 9

¹TO THE OVERSEER. [SET] ON "DEATH OF THE SON." A PSALM OF DAVID. I confess, O YHWH, with all my heart, || I recount all Your wonders, ²I rejoice and exult in You, || I praise Your Name, O Most High. ³In my enemies turning backward, || They stumble and perish from Your face. ⁴For You have done my judgment and my right. You have sat on a throne, || Judging [with] righteousness. ⁵You have rebuked nations, || You have destroyed the wicked, || You have blotted out their name for all time and forever. ⁶The enemy—[your] destructions have been completed forever, || As for cities you have plucked up, || Their memorial has perished with them. ⁷And YHWH abides for all time, || He is preparing His throne for judgment. ⁸And He judges the world in righteousness, || He judges the peoples in uprightness. ⁹And YHWH is a tower for the bruised, || A tower for times of adversity. ¹⁰They trust in You who know Your Name, || For You have not forsaken those seeking You, O YHWH. ¹¹Sing praise to YHWH, inhabiting Zion, || Declare His acts among the peoples, ¹²For He who is seeking for blood || Has remembered them, || He has not forgotten the cry of the afflicted. ¹³Favor me, O

YHWH, || See my affliction by those hating me, || You who lift me up from the gates of death, ¹⁴So that I recount all Your praise, || In the gates of the daughter of Zion. I rejoice on Your salvation. ¹⁵Nations have sunk in a pit they made, || Their foot has been captured in a net that they hid. ¹⁶YHWH has been known, || He has done judgment; By a work of his hands || The wicked has been snared. Meditation. Selah. ¹⁷The wicked turn back to Sheol, || All nations forgetting God. ¹⁸For the needy is not forgotten forever, || [Nor] the hope of the humble lost for all time. ¹⁹Rise, O YHWH, do not let man be strong, || Let nations be judged before Your face. ²⁰Appoint them to fear, O YHWH, || Let nations know they [are] men! Selah.

PSALM 10

¹Why, YHWH, do You stand at a distance? Do You hide in times of adversity? ²Through the pride of the wicked, || Is the poor inflamed, || They are caught in schemes that they devised. ³Because the wicked has boasted || Of the desire of his soul, || And he has blessed a dishonest gainer, || He has despised YHWH. ⁴The wicked does not inquire according to the height of his face. "There is no God!" [are] all his schemes. ⁵His ways writhe at all times, || Your judgments [are] on high before him, || All his adversaries—he puffs at them. ⁶He has said in his heart, "I am not moved, || [And am] not in calamity to generation and generation." ⁷His mouth is full of oaths, || And deceits, and fraud: Under his tongue [is] perverseness and iniquity, ⁸He sits in an ambush of the villages, || He slays the innocent in secret places. His eyes secretly watch for the afflicted, ⁹He lies in wait in a secret place, as a lion in a covert. He lies in wait to catch the poor, || He catches the poor, drawing him into his net. ¹⁰He is bruised—he bows down, || The afflicted has fallen by his mighty ones. ¹¹He said in his heart, "God has forgotten, || He has hid His face, || He has never seen." ¹²Arise, O YHWH! O God, lift up Your hand! Do not forget the humble. ¹³Why has the wicked despised God? He has said in his heart, "It is not required." ¹⁴You have seen, || For You behold perverseness and anger; By giving into Your hand, || The afflicted leave [it] on You, || You have been a helper of the fatherless. ¹⁵Break the arm of the wicked and the evil, || Seek out his wickedness, find none; ¹⁶YHWH [is] King for all time and forever, || The nations have perished out of His land! ¹⁷You have heard the desire of the humble, O YHWH. You prepare their heart; You cause Your ear to attend, ¹⁸To judge the fatherless and bruised: He adds no more to oppress—man of the earth!

PSALM 11

¹TO THE OVERSEER. BY DAVID. In YHWH I trusted, how do you say to my soul, "They moved to your mountain [as] the bird?" ²For behold, the wicked bend a bow, || They have prepared their arrow on the string, || To shoot in darkness at the upright in heart. ³When the foundations are destroyed, || The righteous—what has he done? ⁴YHWH [is] in His holy temple: YHWH—His throne [is] in the heavens. His eyes see—His eyelids try the sons of men. ⁵YHWH tries the righteous. And the wicked and the lover of violence, || His soul has hated, ⁶He pours on the wicked snares, fire, and brimstone, || And a horrible wind [is] the portion of their cup. ⁷For YHWH [is] righteous, || He has loved righteousness, || His countenance sees the upright!

PSALM 12

¹TO THE OVERSEER. ON THE EIGHTH. A PSALM OF DAVID. Save, YHWH, for the saintly has failed, || For the steadfast have ceased || From the sons of men: ²They each speak vanity with his neighbor, || Lip of flattery! With heart and heart they speak. ³YHWH cuts off all lips of flattery, || A tongue speaking great things, ⁴Who said, "By our tongue we do mightily: Our lips [are] our own; who [is] lord over us?" ⁵Because of the spoiling of the poor, || Because of the groaning of the needy, || Now I arise, says YHWH, || I set in safety [him who] breathes for it. ⁶Sayings of YHWH [are] pure sayings—Silver tried in a furnace of earth, refined sevenfold. ⁷You, O YHWH, preserve them, || You keep us from this generation for all time. ⁸The wicked walk around continually, || According as vileness is exalted by sons of men!

PSALM 13

¹TO THE OVERSEER. A PSALM OF DAVID. Until when, O YHWH, || Do You forget me forever? Until when do You hide Your face from me? ²Until when do I set counsels in my soul, || [With] sorrow in my heart daily? Until when is my enemy exalted over me? ³Look attentively; Answer me, O YHWH, my God, || Enlighten my eyes, lest I sleep in death, ⁴Lest my enemy say, "I overcame him," || My adversaries rejoice when I am moved. ⁵And I have trusted in Your kindness, || My heart rejoices in Your salvation. ⁶I sing to YHWH, || For He has conferred benefits on me!

PSALM 14

¹TO THE OVERSEER. BY DAVID. A fool has said in his heart, "There is no God"; They have done corruptly, || They have done abominable actions, || There is not a doer of good. ²YHWH has looked from the heavens on the sons of men, || To see if there is a wise one—seeking God. ³The whole have turned aside, || Together they have been filthy: There is not a doer of good, not even one. ⁴Have all working iniquity not known? Those consuming my people have eaten bread, || They have not called YHWH. ⁵They have feared a fear there, || For God [is] in the generation of the righteous. ⁶You cause the counsel of the poor to stink, || Because YHWH [is] his refuge. ⁷"Who gives the salvation of Israel from Zion?" When YHWH turns back || [To] a captivity of His people, || Jacob rejoices—Israel is glad!

PSALM 15

¹A PSALM OF DAVID. YHWH, who sojourns in Your tent? Who dwells in Your holy hill? ²He who is walking uprightly, || And working righteousness, || And speaking truth in his heart. ³He has not slandered by his tongue, || He has not done evil to his friend; And he has not lifted up reproach || Against his neighbor. ⁴A rejected one [is] despised in his eyes, || And he honors those fearing YHWH. He has sworn to endure evil, and does not change; ⁵He has not given his silver in usury, || And has not taken a bribe against the innocent; Whoever is doing these is not moved for all time!

PSALM 16

¹A MIKTAM OF DAVID. Preserve me, O God, for I trusted in You. ²You have said to YHWH, "You [are] my Lord"; My goodness [is] not above You; ³For the holy ones who [are] in the land, || And the honorable, all my delight [is] in them. ⁴Their griefs are multiplied, [who] have hurried backward; I do not pour out their drink-offerings of blood, || Nor do I take up their names on my lips. ⁵YHWH [is] the portion of my share, and of my cup, || You uphold my lot. ⁶Lines have fallen to me in pleasant places, || Indeed, a beautiful inheritance [is] for me. ⁷I bless YHWH who has counseled me; Also [in] the nights my reins instruct me. ⁸I placed YHWH before me continually, || Because [He is] at my right hand I am not moved. ⁹Therefore my heart has been glad, || And my glory rejoices, || Also my flesh dwells confidently: ¹⁰For You do not leave my soul to Sheol, || Nor give your Holy One to see corruption. ¹¹You cause me to know the path of life; In Your presence [is] fullness of joys, || Pleasant things [are] by Your right hand forever!

PSALM 17

¹A PRAYER OF DAVID. Hear, O YHWH, righteousness, attend my cry, || Give ear [to] my prayer, without lips of deceit. ²My judgment goes out from before You; Your eyes see uprightly. ³You have proved my heart, || You have inspected by night, || You have tried me, You find nothing; My thoughts do not pass over my mouth. ⁴As for doings of man, || Through a word of Your lips I have observed || The paths of a destroyer; ⁵To uphold my goings in Your paths, || My steps have not slipped. ⁶I called You, for You answer me, || O God, incline Your ear to me, hear my speech. ⁷Separate Your kindness wonderfully, O Savior of the confiding, || By Your right hand, from withstanders. ⁸Keep me as the apple, the daughter of the eye; Hide me in the shadow of Your wings, ⁹From the face of the wicked who spoiled me, || [From] my enemies in soul who go around against me. ¹⁰They have closed up

their fat, || Their mouths have spoken with pride: ¹¹"Our steps have now surrounded [him]"; They set their eyes to turn aside in the land. ¹²His likeness as a lion desirous to tear, || As a young lion dwelling in secret places. ¹³Arise, O YHWH, go before his face, || Cause him to bend. Deliver my soul from the wicked, Your sword, ¹⁴From men, Your hand, O YHWH, || From men of the world, their portion [is] in life, || And [with] Your hidden things You fill their belly, || They are satisfied [with] sons, || And have left their abundance to their sucklings. ¹⁵I—in righteousness, || I see Your face; I am satisfied, in awaking, [with] Your form!

PSALM 18

¹To the Overseer. By a servant of YHWH, by David, who has spoken to YHWH the words of this song in the day YHWH delivered him from the hand of all his enemies, and from the hand of Saul, and he says: I love You, O YHWH, my strength. ²YHWH [is] my rock, and my bulwark, || And my deliverer, || My God [is] my rock, || I trust in Him: My shield, and the horn of my salvation, || My high tower. ³I call on YHWH, the Praised One, || And I am saved from my enemies. ⁴Cords of death have surrounded me, || And streams of the worthless make me afraid. ⁵Cords of Sheol have surrounded me, || Snares of death have been before me. ⁶In my adversity I call YHWH, || And I cry to my God. He hears my voice from His temple, || And My cry comes into His ears before Him. ⁷And the earth shakes and trembles, || And foundations of hills are troubled, || And they shake—because He has wrath. ⁸Smoke has gone up from His nostrils, || And fire from His mouth consumes, || Coals have been kindled by it. ⁹And He inclines the heavens, and comes down, || And thick darkness [is] under His feet. ¹⁰And He rides on a cherub, and flies, || And He flies on wings of wind. ¹¹He makes darkness His secret place, || Around Him His dwelling place, || Darkness of waters, thick clouds of the skies. ¹²From the brightness before Him His thick clouds have passed on, || Hail and coals of fire. ¹³And YHWH thunders in the heavens, || And the Most High gives forth His voice, || Hail and coals of fire. ¹⁴And He sends His arrows and scatters them, || And much lightning, and crushes them. ¹⁵And the streams of waters are seen, || And foundations of the earth are revealed, || From Your rebuke, O YHWH, || From the breath of the wind of Your anger. ¹⁶He sends from above—He takes me, || He draws me out of many waters. ¹⁷He delivers me from my strong enemy, || And from those hating me, || For they have been stronger than I. ¹⁸They go before me in a day of my calamity || And YHWH is for a support to me. ¹⁹And He brings me forth to a large place, || He draws me out, because He delighted in me. ²⁰YHWH repays me || According to my righteousness, || According to the cleanness of my hands, || He returns to me. ²¹For I have kept the ways of YHWH, || And have not done wickedly against my God. ²²For all His judgments [are] before me, || And I do not turn His statutes from me. ²³And I am perfect with Him, || And I keep myself from my iniquity. ²⁴And YHWH returns to me, || According to my righteousness, || According to the cleanness of my hands, || Before His eyes. ²⁵With the kind You show Yourself kind, || With a perfect man You show Yourself perfect. ²⁶With the pure You show Yourself pure, || And with the perverse You show Yourself a wrestler, ²⁷For You save a poor people, || And cause the eyes of the high to fall. ²⁸For You light my lamp, || My God YHWH enlightens my darkness. ²⁹For by You I run [against] a troop! And by my God I leap a wall. ³⁰God—perfect [is] His way, || The saying of YHWH is tried, || He [is] a shield to all those trusting in Him. ³¹For who [is] God besides YHWH? And who [is] a rock except our God? ³²God—who is girding me [with] strength, || And He makes my way perfect. ³³Making my feet like does, || And on my high places causes me to stand. ³⁴Teaching my hands for battle, || And a bow of bronze was brought down by my arms. ³⁵And You give to me the shield of Your salvation, || And Your right hand supports me, || And Your lowliness makes me great. ³⁶You enlarge my step under me, || And my ankles have not slipped. ³⁷I pursue my enemies, and overtake them, || And do not turn back until they are consumed. ³⁸I strike them, and they are not able to rise, || They fall under my feet, ³⁹And You gird me [with] strength for battle, || You cause my withstanders to bow under me. ⁴⁰As for my enemies—You have given to me the neck, || As for those hating me—I cut them off. ⁴¹They cry, and there is no savior, || On YHWH, and He does not answer them. ⁴²And I beat them as dust before wind, || I empty them out as mire of the streets. ⁴³You deliver me || From the strivings of the people, || You place me for a head of nations, || A people I have not known serve me. ⁴⁴At the hearing of the ear they listen to me, || Sons of a stranger feign obedience to me, ⁴⁵Sons of a stranger fade away, || And are slain out of their close places. ⁴⁶YHWH lives—and blessed [is] my rock, || And exalted is the God of my salvation. ⁴⁷God—who is giving vengeance to me, || And He subdues peoples under me, ⁴⁸My deliverer from my enemies, || You raise me above my withstanders, || Deliver me from a man of violence. ⁴⁹Therefore I confess You among nations, O YHWH, || And I sing praise to Your Name, ⁵⁰Magnifying the salvation of His king, || And doing kindness to His anointed, || To David, and to his seed—for all time!

PSALM 19

¹To the Overseer. A Psalm of David. The heavens [are] recounting the glory of God, || And the expanse [is] declaring the work of His hands. ²Day to day utters speech, || And night to night shows knowledge. ³There is no speech, and there are no words. Their voice has not been heard. ⁴Their line has gone forth into all the earth, || And their sayings to the end of the world, || In them He placed a tent for the sun, ⁵And he, as a bridegroom, goes out from his covering, || He rejoices as a mighty one || To run the path. ⁶From the end of the heavens [is] his going out, || And his revolution [is] to their ends, || And nothing is hid from his heat. ⁷The law of YHWH [is] perfect, refreshing the soul, || The testimonies of YHWH [are] steadfast, || Making the simple wise, ⁸The precepts of YHWH [are] upright, || Rejoicing the heart, || The command of YHWH [is] pure, enlightening the eyes, ⁹The fear of YHWH [is] clean, standing for all time, || The judgments of YHWH [are] true, || They have been righteous—together. ¹⁰They are more desirable than gold, || Indeed, than much fine gold; and sweeter than honey, || Even liquid honey of the comb. ¹¹Also—Your servant is warned by them, "In keeping them [is] a great reward." ¹²[His] errors—who understands? Declare me innocent from hidden ones, ¹³Also—keep back Your servant from presumptuous ones, || Do not let them rule over me, || Then I am perfect, || And declared innocent of much transgression. ¹⁴Let the sayings of my mouth, || And the meditation of my heart, || Be for a pleasing thing before You, || O YHWH, my rock, and my redeemer!

PSALM 20

¹To the Overseer. A Psalm of David. YHWH answers you, || In a day of adversity, || The Name of the God of Jacob sets you on high, ²He sends your help from the sanctuary, || And supports you from Zion, ³He remembers all your presents, || And reduces your burnt-offering to ashes. Selah. ⁴He gives to you according to your heart, || And fulfills all your counsel. ⁵We sing of Your salvation, || And in the Name of our God set up a banner. YHWH fulfills all your requests. ⁶Now I have known || That YHWH has saved His anointed, || He answers him from His holy heavens, || With the saving might of His right hand. ⁷Some of chariots, and some of horses, || And we of the Name of our God YHWH || Make mention. ⁸They have bowed and have fallen, || And we have risen and station ourselves upright. ⁹O YHWH, save the king, || He answers us in the day we call!

PSALM 21

¹To the Overseer. A Psalm of David. YHWH, the king is joyful in Your strength, || How greatly he rejoices in Your salvation. ²You gave the desire of his heart to him, || And You have not withheld the request of his lips. Selah. ³For You put blessings of goodness before him, || You set a crown of fine gold on his head. ⁴He has asked for life from You, || You have given length of days to him, || For all time and forever. ⁵Great [is] his glory in Your salvation, || You place splendor and majesty on him. ⁶For You make him blessings forever, || You cause him to rejoice with joy, || By Your countenance. ⁷For the king is trusting in YHWH, || And in the kindness of the Most High he is not moved. ⁸Your hand comes to all Your enemies, || Your right hand finds Your haters. ⁹You make them as a furnace of fire, || At the time of Your presence. YHWH swallows them in His anger, || And fire devours them. ¹⁰You destroy their fruit from earth, || And their seed from the sons of men. ¹¹For they stretched out evil against You, || They devised a wicked scheme, they do not prevail, ¹²For You make them turn their back, || When You prepare Your strings against their faces. ¹³Be exalted, O YHWH, in Your strength, || We sing and we praise Your might!

PSALM 22

¹To the Overseer. [Set] on "Doe of the Morning." A Psalm of David. My God, My God, why have You forsaken Me? Far from My salvation, || The words of My roaring? ²My God, I call by day, and You do not answer, || And by night, and am not silent. ³And You [are] holy, || Sitting—the Praise of Israel. ⁴In You our fathers trusted; They trusted, and You deliver them. ⁵To You they cried, and were delivered, || In You they trusted, and were not disappointed. ⁶And I [am] a worm, and no man, || A reproach of man, and despised of the people. ⁷All beholding Me mock at Me, || They make free with the lip—shake the head, ⁸"Roll to YHWH, He delivers Him, || He delivers Him, for He delighted in Him." ⁹For You [are] He bringing Me forth from the womb, || Causing Me to trust, || On the breasts of My mother. ¹⁰On You I have been cast from the womb, || From the belly of My mother You [are] My God. ¹¹Do not be far from Me, || For adversity is near, for there is no helper. ¹²Many bulls have surrounded Me, || Mighty ones of Bashan have surrounded Me, ¹³They have opened their mouth against Me, || A lion tearing and roaring. ¹⁴I have been poured out as waters, || And all my bones have separated themselves, || My heart has been like wax, || It is melted in the midst of My bowels. ¹⁵My power is dried up as an earthen vessel, || And My tongue is cleaving to My jaws. ¹⁶And You appoint Me to the dust of death, || For dogs have surrounded Me, || A company of evildoers has surrounded Me, || Piercing My hands and My feet. ¹⁷I count all My bones—they look expectingly, || They look on Me, ¹⁸They apportion My garments to themselves, || And they cause a lot to fall for My clothing. ¹⁹And You, O YHWH, do not be far off, || O My strength, hurry to help Me. ²⁰Deliver My soul from the sword, || My only one from the paw of a dog. ²¹Save Me from the mouth of a lion || And You have answered Me from the horns of the high places! ²²I declare Your Name to My brothers, || In the midst of the assembly I praise You. ²³You who fear YHWH, praise Him, || All the seed of Jacob, honor Him, || And be afraid of Him, all you seed of Israel. ²⁴For He has not despised, nor detested, || The affliction of the afflicted, || Nor has He hidden His face from Him, || And in His crying to Him He hears. ²⁵Of You My praise [is] in the great assembly. I complete My vows before His fearers. ²⁶The humble eat and are satisfied, || Those seeking Him praise YHWH, || Your heart lives forever. ²⁷Remember and return to YHWH, || Do all the ends of the earth, || And bow themselves before You, || Do all families of the nations, ²⁸For to YHWH [is] the kingdom, || And He is ruling among nations. ²⁹And the fat ones of earth have eaten, || And they bow themselves, || All going down to dust bow before Him, || And he [who] has not revived his soul. ³⁰A seed serves Him, || It is declared of the Lord to the generation. ³¹They come and declare His righteousness, || To a people that is born, that He has made!

PSALM 23

¹A Psalm of David. YHWH [is] my shepherd, I do not lack, ²He causes me to lie down in pastures of tender grass, || He leads me by quiet waters. ³He refreshes my soul, || He leads me in paths of righteousness || For His Name's sake; ⁴Also—when I walk in a valley of death-shade, || I fear no evil, for You [are] with me, || Your rod and Your staff—they comfort me. ⁵You arrange a table before me, || In front of my adversaries, || You have anointed my head with oil, || My cup is full! ⁶Surely goodness and kindness pursue me || All the days of my life, || And my dwelling [is] in the house of YHWH, || For [the] length of [my] days!

PSALM 24

¹A Psalm of David. To YHWH [is] the earth and its fullness, || The world and the inhabitants in it. ²For He has founded it on the seas, || And He establishes it on the floods. ³Who goes up into the hill of YHWH? And who rises up in His holy place? ⁴The clean of hands, and pure of heart, || Who has not lifted up his soul to vanity, || Nor has sworn to deceit. ⁵He carries away a blessing from YHWH, || Righteousness from the God of his salvation. ⁶This [is] a generation of those seeking Him. Seeking Your face, O Jacob! Selah. ⁷Lift up your heads, O gates! And be lifted up, O perpetual doors! And the King of Glory comes in! ⁸Who [is] this—"the King of Glory?" YHWH—strong and mighty, || YHWH, the mighty in battle. ⁹Lift up your heads, O gates! And be lifted up, O perpetual doors! And the King of Glory comes in! ¹⁰Who [is] He—this "King of Glory?" YHWH of hosts—He [is] the King of Glory! Selah.

PSALM 25

¹By David. [Aleph-Bet] To You, O YHWH, I lift up my soul. ²My God, in You I have trusted, || Do not let me be ashamed, || Do not let my enemies exult over me. ³Also let none waiting on You be ashamed, || Let the treacherous dealers without cause be ashamed. ⁴Your ways, O YHWH, cause me to know, || You teach me Your paths. ⁵Cause me to tread in Your truth, and teach me, || For You [are] the God of my salvation, || Near You I have waited all the day. ⁶Remember Your mercies, O YHWH, || And Your kindnesses, for they [are] from the age. ⁷Sins of my youth, and my transgressions, || Do not remember. According to Your kindness be mindful of me, || For Your goodness' sake, O YHWH. ⁸Good and upright [is] YHWH, || Therefore He directs sinners in the way. ⁹He causes the humble to tread in judgment, || And teaches the humble His way. ¹⁰All the paths of YHWH [are] kindness and truth, || To those keeping His covenant, || And His testimonies. ¹¹For Your Name's sake, O YHWH, || You have pardoned my iniquity, for it [is] great. ¹²Who [is] this—the man fearing YHWH? He directs him in the way He chooses. ¹³His soul remains in good, || And his seed possesses the land. ¹⁴The secret of YHWH [is] for those fearing Him, || And His covenant—to cause them to know. ¹⁵My eyes [are] continually to YHWH, || For He brings my feet out from a net. ¹⁶Turn to me, and favor me, || For I [am] lonely and afflicted. ¹⁷The distresses of my heart have enlarged themselves, || Bring me out from my distresses. ¹⁸See my affliction and my misery, || And bear with all my sins. ¹⁹See my enemies, for they have been many, || And they have hated me with violent hatred. ²⁰Keep my soul, and deliver me, || Do not let me be ashamed, for I trusted in You. ²¹Integrity and uprightness keep me, || For I have waited [on] You. ²²Redeem Israel, O God, from all his distresses!

PSALM 26

¹By David. Judge me, O YHWH, for I have walked in my integrity, || And I have trusted in YHWH, || I do not slide. ²Try me, O YHWH, and prove me, || My reins and my heart [are] purified, ³For Your kindness [is] before my eyes, || And I have habitually walked in Your truth. ⁴I have not sat with vain men, || And I do not enter with pretenders. ⁵I have hated the assembly of evildoers, || And I do not sit with the wicked. ⁶I wash my hands in innocence, || And I go around Your altar, O YHWH. ⁷To sound with a voice of confession, || And to recount all Your

wonders. ⁸YHWH, I have loved the habitation of Your house, || And the place of the Dwelling Place of Your glory. ⁹Do not gather my soul with sinners, || And my life with men of blood, ¹⁰In whose hand [is] a wicked scheme, || And their right hand [is] full of bribes. ¹¹And I walk in my integrity, || Redeem me, and favor me. ¹²My foot has stood in uprightness, || In assemblies I bless YHWH!

PSALM 27

¹BY DAVID. YHWH [is] my light and my salvation, || Whom do I fear? YHWH [is] the strength of my life, || Of whom am I afraid? ²When evildoers come near to me to eat my flesh, || My adversaries and my enemies to me, || They have stumbled and fallen. ³Though a host encamps against me, || My heart does not fear, || Though war rises up against me, || In this I [am] confident. ⁴One [thing] I asked of YHWH—it I seek: My dwelling in the house of YHWH, || All the days of my life, || To look on the pleasantness of YHWH, || And to inquire in His temple. ⁵For He hides me in a dwelling place in the day of evil, || He hides me in a secret place of His tent, || He raises me up on a rock. ⁶And now my head is lifted up, || Above my enemies—my surrounders, || And I sacrifice in His tent sacrifices of shouting, || I sing, indeed, I sing praise to YHWH. ⁷Hear, O YHWH, my voice—I call, || And favor me, and answer me. ⁸My heart said to You, "They sought my face, || Your face, O YHWH, I seek." ⁹Do not hide Your face from me, || Do not turn Your servant aside in anger, || You have been my help. Do not leave me, nor forsake me, || O God of my salvation. ¹⁰When my father and my mother || Have forsaken me, then YHWH gathers me. ¹¹Show me, O YHWH, Your way, || And lead me in a path of uprightness, || For the sake of my beholders. ¹²Do not give me to the will of my adversaries, || For false witnesses have risen against me, || And they breathe out violence to me. ¹³I had not believed to look on the goodness of YHWH || In the land of the living! ¹⁴Look to YHWH—be strong, || And He strengthens your heart, || Indeed, look to YHWH!

PSALM 28

¹BY DAVID. To You, O YHWH, I call, || My rock, do not be silent to me! Lest You are silent to me, || And I have been compared || With those going down to the pit. ²Hear the voice of my supplications, || In my crying to You, || In my lifting up my hands toward your holy oracle. ³Do not draw me with the wicked, || And with workers of iniquity, || Speaking peace with their neighbors, || And evil in their heart. ⁴Give to them according to their acting, || And according to the evil of their doings. Give to them according to the work of their hands. Return their deed to them. ⁵For they do not attend to the doing of YHWH, || And to the work of His hands. He throws them down, || And does not build them up. ⁶Blessed [is] YHWH, || For He has heard the voice of my supplications. ⁷YHWH [is] my strength, and my shield, || In Him my heart trusted, and I have been helped. And my heart exults, || And I thank Him with my song. ⁸YHWH [is] strength to him, || Indeed, the strength of the salvation of His anointed [is] He. ⁹Save Your people, and bless Your inheritance, || And feed them, and carry them for all time!

PSALM 29

¹A PSALM OF DAVID. Ascribe to YHWH, you sons of the mighty, || Ascribe to YHWH glory and strength. ²Ascribe to YHWH the glory of His Name, || Bow yourselves to YHWH, || In the beauty of holiness. ³The voice of YHWH [is] on the waters, || The God of glory has thundered, || YHWH [is] on many waters. ⁴The voice of YHWH [is] with power, || The voice of YHWH [is] with majesty, ⁵The voice of YHWH [is] shattering cedars, || Indeed, YHWH shatters the cedars of Lebanon. ⁶And He causes them to skip as a calf, || Lebanon and Sirion as a son of Reems, ⁷The voice of YHWH is hewing fiery flames, ⁸The voice of YHWH pains a wilderness, || YHWH pains the wilderness of Kadesh. ⁹The voice of YHWH pains the oaks, || And makes bare the forests, || And in His temple everyone says, "Glory!" ¹⁰YHWH has sat on the flood, || And YHWH sits [as] king for all time, ¹¹YHWH gives strength to His people, || YHWH blesses His people with peace!

PSALM 30

¹A PSALM. A SONG OF THE DEDICATION OF THE HOUSE OF DAVID. I exalt You, O YHWH, || For You have drawn me up, || And have not let my enemies rejoice over me. ²My God YHWH, I have cried to You, || And You heal me. ³YHWH, You have brought up my soul from Sheol, || You have kept me alive, || From going down [to] the pit. ⁴Sing praise to YHWH, you His saints, || And give thanks at the remembrance of His holiness, ⁵For—a moment [is] in His anger, || Life [is] in His goodwill, || At evening remains weeping, and at morning singing. ⁶And I have said in my ease, "I am not moved for all time." ⁷O YHWH, in Your good pleasure, || You have caused strength to remain for my mountain," || You have hidden Your face—I have been troubled. ⁸To You, O YHWH, I call, || And to YHWH I make supplication. ⁹"What gain [is] in my blood? In my going down to corruption? Does dust thank You? Does it declare Your truth? ¹⁰Hear, O YHWH, and favor me, O YHWH, be a helper to me." ¹¹You have turned my mourning to dancing for me, || You have loosed my sackcloth, || And gird me [with] joy. ¹²So that glory praises You, and is not silent, || O YHWH, my God, I thank You for all time!

PSALM 31

¹TO THE OVERSEER. A PSALM OF DAVID. In You, O YHWH, I have trusted, || Do not let me be ashamed for all time, || In Your righteousness deliver me. ²Incline Your ear to me quickly, deliver me, || Be to me for a strong rock, || For a house of bulwarks to save me. ³For You [are] my rock and my bulwark, || For Your Name's sake lead me and tend me. ⁴Bring me out from the net that they hid for me, || For You [are] my strength. ⁵Into Your hand I commit my spirit, || You have redeemed me, YHWH God of truth. ⁶I have hated the observers of lying vanities, || And I have been confident toward YHWH. ⁷I rejoice, and am glad in Your kindness, || In that You have seen my affliction, || You have known my soul in adversities. ⁸And You have not shut me up, || Into the hand of an enemy, || You have caused my feet to stand in a broad place. ⁹Favor me, O YHWH, for distress [is] to me, || My eye, my soul, and my body || Have become old by provocation. ¹⁰For my life has been consumed in sorrow || And my years in sighing. My strength has been feeble because of my iniquity, || And my bones have become old. ¹¹I have been a reproach among all my adversaries, || And to my neighbors exceedingly, || And a fear to my acquaintances, || Those seeing me without—fled from me. ¹²I have been forgotten as dead, out of mind, || I have been as a perishing vessel. ¹³For I have heard an evil account of many, || Fear [is] all around. In their being united against me, || They have devised to take my life, ¹⁴And I have trusted on You, || O YHWH, I have said, "You [are] my God." ¹⁵In Your hand [are] my times, || Deliver me from the hand of my enemies, || And from my pursuers. ¹⁶Cause Your face to shine on Your servant, || Save me in Your kindness. ¹⁷O YHWH, do not let me be ashamed, || For I have called You, let the wicked be ashamed, || Let them become silent to Sheol. ¹⁸Let lips of falsehood become mute, || That are speaking against the righteous, || Ancient sayings, in pride and contempt. ¹⁹How abundant is Your goodness, || That You have laid up for those fearing You, || You have worked for those trusting in You, || Before sons of men. ²⁰You hide them in the secret place of Your presence, || From schemes of man, || You conceal them in a dwelling place, || From the strife of tongues. ²¹Blessed [is] YHWH, || For He has made His kindness marvelous || To me in a city of bulwarks. ²²And I have said in my haste, "I have been cut off from before Your eyes," || But You have heard the voice of my supplications, || In my crying to You. ²³Love YHWH, all you His saints, || YHWH is keeping the faithful, || And repaying a proud doer abundantly. ²⁴Be strong, and He strengthens your heart, || All you who are waiting for YHWH!

PSALM 32

¹AN INSTRUCTION OF DAVID. O the blessedness of him whose transgression [is] forgiven, || Whose sin is covered. ²O the blessedness of a man, || To whom YHWH does not impute iniquity, || And in whose spirit there is no deceit. ³When I have kept silence, my bones have become old, || Through my roaring all the day. ⁴When by day and by night Your hand is heavy on me, || My moisture has been changed || Into the droughts of summer. Selah. ⁵I cause You to know my sin, || And I have not covered my iniquity. I have said, "I confess to YHWH concerning My transgressions," || And You have taken away the iniquity of my sin. Selah. ⁶For every saintly one prays this to You, || In the time to find [You]. Surely at an overflowing of many waters, || They do not come to him. ⁷You [are] a hiding place for me, || You keep me from

distress, || Surround me [with] songs of deliverance. Selah. ⁸I cause you to act wisely, || And direct you in the way that you go, || I cause My eye to take counsel concerning you. ⁹Do not be as a horse—as a mule, || Without understanding, || With bridle and bit, its ornaments, to curb, || Not to come near to you. ¹⁰Many [are] the pains of the wicked; As for him who is trusting in Yₕwₕ, || Kindness surrounds him. ¹¹Be glad in Yₕwₕ, and rejoice, you righteous, || And sing, all you upright of heart!

PSALM 33

¹Sing, you righteous, in Yₕwₕ, || [For] praise from upright ones [is] lovely. ²Give thanks to Yₕwₕ with a harp, || With stringed instrument of ten strings sing praise to Him, ³Sing to Him a new song, || Play skillfully with shouting. ⁴For the word of Yₕwₕ [is] upright, || And all His work [is] in faithfulness. ⁵Loving righteousness and judgment, || The earth is full of the kindness of Yₕwₕ. ⁶By the word of Yₕwₕ || The heavens have been made, || And all their host by the breath of His mouth. ⁷Gathering the waters of the sea as a heap, || Putting the depths in treasuries. ⁸All the earth is afraid of Yₕwₕ, || All the inhabitants of the world are afraid of Him. ⁹For He has spoken, and it is, || He has commanded, and it stands. ¹⁰Yₕwₕ made void the counsel of nations, || He disallowed the thoughts of the peoples. ¹¹The counsel of Yₕwₕ stands for all time, || The thoughts of His heart from generation to generation. ¹²O the blessedness of the nation whose God [is] Yₕwₕ, || Of the people He chose, || For an inheritance to Him. ¹³Yₕwₕ has looked from the heavens, || He has seen all the sons of men. ¹⁴From the fixed place of His dwelling, || He looked to all inhabitants of the earth; ¹⁵Who is forming their hearts together, || Who is attending to all their works. ¹⁶The king is not saved by the multitude of a force. A mighty man is not delivered, || By abundance of power. ¹⁷A false thing [is] the horse for safety, || And he does not deliver || By the abundance of his strength. ¹⁸Behold, the eye of Yₕwₕ [is] to those fearing Him, || To those waiting for His kindness, ¹⁹To deliver their soul from death, || And to keep them alive in famine. ²⁰Our soul has waited for Yₕwₕ, || He [is] our help and our shield, ²¹For our heart rejoices in Him, || For we have trusted in His Holy Name. ²²Let Your kindness, O Yₕwₕ, be on us, || As we have waited for You!

PSALM 34

¹By David, in his changing his behavior before Abimelech, and he drives him away, and he goes. [Aleph-Bet] I bless Yₕwₕ at all times, || His praise [is] continually in my mouth. ²In Yₕwₕ my soul boasts herself, || The humble hear and rejoice. ³Ascribe greatness to Yₕwₕ with me, || And we exalt His Name together. ⁴I sought Yₕwₕ, and He answered me, || And delivered me from all my fears. ⁵They looked expectantly to Him, || And they became bright, || And their faces are not ashamed. ⁶This poor [one] called, and Yₕwₕ heard, || And saved him from all his distresses. ⁷A messenger of Yₕwₕ is encamping, || Around those who fear Him, || And He arms them. ⁸Taste and see that Yₕwₕ [is] good, || O the blessedness of the man who trusts in Him. ⁹Fear Yₕwₕ, you His holy ones, || For there is no lack to those fearing Him. ¹⁰Young lions have lacked and been hungry, || And those seeking Yₕwₕ do not lack any good, ¹¹Come, children, listen to me, || I teach you the fear of Yₕwₕ. ¹²Who [is] the man that is desiring life? Loving days to see good? ¹³Keep your tongue from evil, || And your lips from speaking deceit. ¹⁴Turn aside from evil and do good, || Seek peace and pursue it. ¹⁵The eyes of Yₕwₕ [are] to the righteous, || And His ears to their cry. ¹⁶(The face of Yₕwₕ [is] on doers of evil, || To cut off their memorial from earth.) ¹⁷They cried, and Yₕwₕ heard, || And delivered them from all their distresses. ¹⁸Yₕwₕ [is] near to the broken of heart, || And He saves the bruised of spirit. ¹⁹Many [are] the afflictions of the righteous, || Yₕwₕ delivers him out of them all. ²⁰He is keeping all his bones, || Not one of them has been broken. ²¹Evil puts the wicked to death, || And those hating the righteous are desolate. ²²Yₕwₕ redeems the soul of His servants, || And none trusting in Him are desolate!

PSALM 35

¹By David. Strive, Yₕwₕ, with my strivers, fight with my fighters, ²Take hold of shield and buckler, and rise for my help, ³And draw out spear and lance, || To meet my pursuers. Say to my soul, "I [am] your salvation." ⁴They are ashamed and blush, those seeking my soul, || Turned backward and confounded, || Those devising my evil. ⁵They are as chaff before wind, || And a messenger of Yₕwₕ driving away. ⁶Their way is darkness and slipperiness, || And a messenger of Yₕwₕ—their pursuer. ⁷For without cause they hid their net [in] a pit for me, || Without cause they dug for my soul. ⁸Desolation meets him—he does not know, || And his net that he hid catches him, || He falls into it for desolation. ⁹And my soul is joyful in Yₕwₕ, || It rejoices in His salvation. ¹⁰All my bones say, "Yₕwₕ, who is like You, || Delivering the poor from the [one] stronger than he, || And the poor and needy from his plunderer." ¹¹Violent witnesses rise up, || That which I have not known they ask me. ¹²They pay me evil for good, bereaving my soul, ¹³And I—in their sickness my clothing [is] sackcloth, || I have humbled my soul with fastings, || And my prayer returns to my bosom. ¹⁴As [if] a friend, as [if] my brother, || I habitually walked, || As a mourner for a mother, || I have bowed down mourning. ¹⁵And they have rejoiced in my halting, || And have been gathered together, || The strikers were gathered against me, || And I have not known, || They have torn, and they have not ceased; ¹⁶With profane ones, mockers in feasts, || Gnashing their teeth against me. ¹⁷Lord, how long do You behold? Keep my soul back from their desolations, || My only one from young lions. ¹⁸I thank You in a great assembly, || I praise You among a mighty people. ¹⁹Do not let my enemies rejoice over me [with] falsehood, || Those hating me without cause wink the eye. ²⁰For they do not speak peace, || And against the quiet of the land, || They devise deceitful words, ²¹And they enlarge their mouth against me, || They said, "Aha, aha, our eye has seen." ²²You have seen, O Yₕwₕ, || Do not be silent, O Lord—do not be far from me, ²³Stir up, and wake to my judgment, || My God, and my Lord, to my plea. ²⁴Judge me according to Your righteousness, O Yₕwₕ my God, || And they do not rejoice over me. ²⁵They do not say in their heart, "Aha, our desire." They do not say, "We swallowed him up." ²⁶They are ashamed and confounded together, || Who are rejoicing at my evil. They put on shame and confusion, || Who are magnifying themselves against me. ²⁷They sing and rejoice, who are desiring my righteousness, || And they continually say, "Yₕwₕ is magnified, || Who is desiring the peace of His servant." ²⁸And my tongue utters Your righteousness, || All the day Your praise!

PSALM 36

¹To the Overseer. By a servant of Yₕwₕ, by David. The transgression of the wicked || Is affirming within my heart, "Fear of God is not before his eyes, ²For he made [it] smooth to himself in his eyes, || To find his iniquity to be hated. ³The words of his mouth [are] iniquity and deceit, || He ceased to act prudently—to do good. ⁴He devises iniquity on his bed, || He stations himself on a way not good, || He does not refuse evil." ⁵O Yₕwₕ, Your kindness [is] in the heavens, || Your faithfulness [is] to the clouds. ⁶Your righteousness [is] as mountains of God, || Your judgments [are] a great deep. You save man and beast, O Yₕwₕ. ⁷How precious [is] Your kindness, O God, || And the sons of men trust || In the shadow of Your wings. ⁸They are filled from the fatness of Your house, || And You cause them to drink the stream of Your delights. ⁹For a fountain of life [is] with You, || In Your light we see light. ¹⁰Draw out Your kindness to those knowing You, || And Your righteousness to the upright of heart. ¹¹Do not let a foot of pride meet me, || And do not let a hand of the wicked move me. ¹²Workers of iniquity have fallen there, || They have been overthrown, || And have not been able to arise!

PSALM 37

¹By David. [Aleph-Bet] Do not fret because of evildoers, || Do not be envious against doers of iniquity, ²For they are cut off speedily as grass, || And fade as the greenness of the tender grass. ³Trust in Yₕwₕ, and do good, || Dwell [in] the land, and enjoy faithfulness, ⁴And delight yourself on Yₕwₕ, || And He gives to you the petitions of your heart. ⁵Roll your way on Yₕwₕ, || And trust on Him, and He works, ⁶And has brought out your righteousness as light, || And your judgment as noon-day. ⁷Be silent for Yₕwₕ, and stay yourself for Him, || Do not fret because of him || Who is making his way prosperous, || Because of a man doing wicked schemes. ⁸Desist from anger, and forsake fury, || Do not fret yourself to only do evil. ⁹For evildoers are cut off, || As for those waiting on Yₕwₕ, they possess the land. ¹⁰And

yet a little [while], and the wicked is not, || And you have considered his place, and it is not. ¹¹And the humble possess the land, || And they have delighted themselves || In the abundance of peace. ¹²The wicked is devising against the righteous, || And gnashing his teeth against him. ¹³The Lord laughs at him, || For He has seen that his day comes. ¹⁴The wicked have opened a sword, || And they have bent their bow, || To cause the poor and needy to fall, || To slaughter the upright of the way. ¹⁵Their sword enters into their own heart, || And their bows are shattered. ¹⁶Better [is] the little of the righteous, || Than the store of many wicked. ¹⁷For the arms of the wicked are shattered, || And YHWH is sustaining the righteous. ¹⁸YHWH knows the days of the perfect, || And their inheritance is for all time. ¹⁹They are not ashamed in a time of evil, || And they are satisfied in days of famine. ²⁰But the wicked perish, and the enemies of YHWH, || Have been consumed as the preciousness of lambs, || They have been consumed in smoke. ²¹The wicked is borrowing and does not repay, || And the righteous is gracious and giving. ²²For His blessed ones possess the land, || And His reviled ones are cut off. ²³The steps of a man [are] from YHWH, || They have been prepared, || And He desires his way. ²⁴When he falls, he is not cast down, || For YHWH is sustaining his hand. ²⁵I have been young, || I have also become old, || And I have not seen the righteous forsaken, || And his seed seeking bread. ²⁶All the day he is gracious and lending, || And his seed [is] for a blessing. ²⁷Turn aside from evil, and do good, and dwell for all time. ²⁸For YHWH is loving judgment, || And He does not forsake His saintly ones, || They have been kept for all time, || And the seed of the wicked is cut off. ²⁹The righteous possess the land, || And they dwell on it forever. ³⁰The mouth of the righteous utters wisdom, || And his tongue speaks judgment. ³¹The law of his God [is] his heart, || His steps do not slide. ³²The wicked is watching for the righteous, || And is seeking to put him to death. ³³YHWH does not leave him in his hand, || Nor condemn him in his being judged. ³⁴Look to YHWH, and keep His way, || And He exalts you to possess the land, || In the wicked being cut off—you see! ³⁵I have seen the wicked terrible, || And spreading as a green native plant, ³⁶And he passes away, and behold, he is not, || And I seek him, and he is not found! ³⁷Observe the perfect, and see the upright, || For the latter end of each [is] peace. ³⁸And transgressors were destroyed together, || The latter end of the wicked was cut off. ³⁹And the salvation of the righteous [is] from YHWH, || Their strong place in a time of adversity. ⁴⁰And YHWH helps them and delivers them, || He delivers them from the wicked, || And saves them, || Because they trusted in Him!

PSALM 38

¹A PSALM OF DAVID. "TO CAUSE TO REMEMBER." YHWH, do not reprove me in Your wrath, || Nor discipline me in Your fury. ²For Your arrows have come down on me, || And You let down Your hand on me. ³Soundness is not in my flesh, || Because of Your indignation, || Peace is not in my bones, || Because of my sin. ⁴For my iniquities have passed over my head, || As a heavy burden—too heavy for me. ⁵Stunk— my wounds have become corrupt, || Because of my folly. ⁶I have been bent down, || I have been bowed down—to excess, || I have gone mourning all the day. ⁷For my flanks have been full of drought, || And soundness is not in my flesh. ⁸I have been feeble and struck—to excess, || I have roared from disquietude of heart. ⁹Lord, all my desire [is] before You, || And my sighing has not been hid from You. ¹⁰My heart [is] panting, my power has forsaken me, || And the light of my eyes, || Even they are not with me. ¹¹My lovers and my friends stand aloof from before my plague. And my neighbors have stood far off. ¹²And those seeking my soul lay a snare, || And those seeking my evil || Have spoken mischievous things, || And they meditate [on] deceits all the day. ¹³And I, as deaf, do not hear. And as a mute one who does not open his mouth. ¹⁴Indeed, I am as a man who does not hear, || And in his mouth are no reproofs. ¹⁵Because for You, O YHWH, I have waited, || You answer, O Lord my God. ¹⁶When I said, "Lest they rejoice over me, || In the slipping of my foot they magnified themselves against me." ¹⁷For I am ready to halt, || And my pain [is] continually before me. ¹⁸For I declare my iniquity, || I am sorry for my sin. ¹⁹And my enemies [are] lively, || They have been strong, and those hating me without cause, || Have been multiplied. ²⁰And those paying evil for good accuse me, || Because of my pursuing good. ²¹Do not forsake me, O YHWH, || My God, do not be far from me, ²²Hurry to help me, O Lord, my salvation!

PSALM 39

¹TO THE OVERSEER. FOR JEDUTHUN. A PSALM OF DAVID. I have said, "I observe my ways, || Against sinning with my tongue, || I keep a curb for my mouth, || While the wicked [is] before me." ²I was mute [with] silence, || I kept silent from good, and my pain is excited. ³My heart [is] hot within me, || In my meditating the fire burns, || I have spoken with my tongue. ⁴"Cause me to know, O YHWH, my end, || And the measure of my days—what it [is]," || I know how frail I [am]. ⁵Behold, You have made my days handbreadths, || And my age [is] as nothing before You, || Only, every man set up [is] all vanity. Selah. ⁶Only, each habitually walks in an image, || Only, [in] vain, they are disquieted, || He heaps up and does not know who gathers them. ⁷And now, what have I expected? O Lord, my hope—it [is] of You. ⁸Deliver me from all my transgressions, || Do not make me a reproach of the fool. ⁹I have been mute, I do not open my mouth, || Because You have done [it]. ¹⁰Turn aside Your stroke from off me, || From the striving of Your hand I have been consumed. ¹¹With reproofs against iniquity, || You have corrected man, || And dissolve his desirableness as a moth, || Only, every man [is] vanity. Selah. ¹²Hear my prayer, O YHWH, || And give ear [to] my cry, || Do not be silent to my tear, || For I [am] a sojourner with You, || A settler like all my fathers. ¹³Look from me, and I brighten up before I go and am not!

PSALM 40

¹TO THE OVERSEER. A PSALM OF DAVID. I have diligently expected YHWH, || And He inclines to me, and hears my cry, ²And He causes me to come up || From a pit of desolation—from mire of mud, || And He raises up my feet on a rock, || He is establishing my steps. ³And He puts a new song in my mouth, "Praise to our God." Many see and fear, and trust in YHWH. ⁴O the blessedness of the man || Who has made YHWH his trust, || And has not turned to the proud, || And those turning aside to lies. ⁵You have done much, my God YHWH; Your wonders and Your thoughts toward us, || There is none to arrange to You, || I declare and speak: They have been more than to be numbered. ⁶Sacrifice and present You have not desired, || But a body You have prepared for me, || Burnt and sin-offering You have not asked. ⁷Then I said, "Behold, I have come, || In the roll of the scroll it is written of me, ⁸I have delighted to do Your pleasure, my God, || And Your law [is] within my heart." ⁹I have proclaimed tidings of righteousness || In the great assembly, || Behold, I do not restrain my lips, || O YHWH, You have known. ¹⁰I have not concealed Your righteousness || In the midst of my heart, || I have told of Your faithfulness and Your salvation, || I have not hidden Your kindness and Your truth, || To the great assembly. ¹¹You, O YHWH, do not restrain Your mercies from me, || Your kindness and Your truth continually keep me. ¹²For innumerable evils have surrounded me, || My iniquities have overtaken me, || And I have not been able to see; They have been more than the hairs of my head, || And my heart has forsaken me. ¹³Be pleased, O YHWH, to deliver me, || O YHWH, make haste for my help. ¹⁴They are ashamed and confounded together, || Who are seeking my soul to destroy it, || They are turned backward, || And are ashamed, who are desiring my evil. ¹⁵They are desolate because of their shame, || Who are saying to me, "Aha, aha." ¹⁶All seeking You rejoice and are glad in You, || Those loving Your salvation continually say, "YHWH is magnified." ¹⁷And I [am] poor and needy, || The Lord devises for me. You [are] my help and my deliverer, O my God, do not linger.

PSALM 41

¹TO THE OVERSEER. A PSALM OF DAVID. O the blessedness of him || Who is acting wisely to the poor, || In a day of evil YHWH delivers him. ²YHWH preserves him and revives him, || He is blessed in the land, || And You do not give him into the will of his enemies. ³YHWH supports [him] on a bed of sickness, || You have turned his bed in his weakness. ⁴I said, "O YHWH, favor me, || Heal my soul, for I sinned against You," ⁵My enemies say evil of me: When he dies— his name has perished! ⁶And if he came to see—he speaks vanity, || His heart gathers iniquity to itself, || He goes out—at the street he speaks. ⁷All hating me whisper together against me, || Against me they devise evil to

me: ⁸A worthless thing is poured out on him, || And because he lay down he does not rise again. ⁹Even my ally, in whom I trusted, || One eating my bread, || Made the heel great against me, ¹⁰And You, YHWH, favor me, || And cause me to rise, || And I give repayment to them. ¹¹By this I have known, || That You have delighted in me, || Because my enemy does not shout over me. ¹²As for me, in my integrity, || You have taken hold on me, || And cause me to stand before You for all time. ¹³Blessed [is] YHWH, God of Israel, || From age to age. Amen and Amen.

PSALM 42

¹To the Overseer. An Instruction of the sons of Korah. As a deer pants for streams of water, || So my soul pants toward You, O God. ²My soul thirsted for God, for the living God, || When do I enter and see the face of God? ³My tear has been bread day and night to me, || In their saying to me all the day, "Where [is] your God?" ⁴These I remember, and pour out my soul in me, || For I pass over into the shelter, || I go softly with them to the house of God, || With the voice of singing and confession, || The multitude keeping celebration! ⁵Why bow yourself, O my soul? Indeed, are you troubled within me? Wait for God, for I still confess Him: The salvation of my countenance—my God! ⁶My soul bows itself in me, || Therefore I remember You from the land of Jordan, || And of the Hermons, from Mount Mizar. ⁷Deep is calling to deep || At the noise of Your waterspouts, || All Your breakers and Your billows passed over me. ⁸By day YHWH commands His kindness, || And by night a song [is] with me, || A prayer to the God of my life. ⁹I say to God my Rock, "Why have You forgotten me? Why do I go mourning in the oppression of an enemy?" ¹⁰With a sword in my bones || My adversaries have reproached me, || In their saying to me all the day, "Where [is] your God?" ¹¹Why bow yourself, O my soul? And why are you troubled within me? Wait for God, for I still confess Him, || The salvation of my countenance, and my God!

PSALM 43

¹Judge me, O God, || And plead my cause against a nation not pious, || You deliver me from a man of deceit and perverseness, ²For you [are] the God of my strength. Why have You cast me off? Why do I go up and down mourning, || In the oppression of an enemy? ³Send forth Your light and Your truth, || They lead me, they bring me in, || To Your holy hill, and to Your dwelling places. ⁴And I go to the altar of God, || To God, the joy of my rejoicing. And I thank You with a harp, O God, my God. ⁵Why bow yourself, O my soul? And why are you troubled within me? Wait for God, for I still confess Him, || The salvation of my countenance, and my God!

PSALM 44

¹To the Overseer. An Instruction of the sons of Korah. O God, we have heard with our ears, || Our fathers have recounted to us, || The work You worked in their days, || In the days of old. ²You, [with] Your hand, have dispossessed nations. And You plant them. You afflict peoples, and send them away. ³For they did not possess the land by their sword, || And their arm did not give salvation to them, || But Your right hand, and Your arm, || And the light of Your countenance, || Because You had accepted them. ⁴You [are] He, my King, O God, || Command the deliverances of Jacob. ⁵By You we push our adversaries, || By Your Name we tread down our withstanders, ⁶For I do not trust in my bow, || And my sword does not save me. ⁷For You have saved us from our adversaries, || And You have put to shame those hating us. ⁸In God we have boasted all the day, || And we thank Your Name for all time. Selah. ⁹In anger You have cast off and cause us to blush, || And do not go forth with our hosts. ¹⁰You cause us to turn backward from an adversary, || And those hating us, || Have spoiled for themselves. ¹¹You make us food like sheep, || And You have scattered us among nations. ¹²You sell Your people—without wealth, || And have not become great by their price. ¹³You make us a reproach to our neighbors, || A scorn and a reproach to our surrounders. ¹⁴You make us an allegory among nations, || A shaking of the head among peoples. ¹⁵All the day my confusion [is] before me, || And the shame of my face has covered me, ¹⁶Because of the voice of a reproacher and reviler, || Because of an enemy and a self-avenger. ¹⁷All this met us, and we did not forget You, || Nor have we dealt falsely in Your covenant. ¹⁸We do not turn our heart backward, || Nor turn aside our step from Your path. ¹⁹But You have struck us in a place of dragons, || And cover us over with death-shade. ²⁰If we have forgotten the Name of our God, || And spread our hands to a strange God, ²¹Does God not search this out? For He knows the secrets of the heart. ²²Surely, for Your sake we have been slain all the day, || Reckoned as sheep of the slaughter. ²³Stir up—why do You sleep, O Lord? Awake, do not cast us off forever. ²⁴Why do You hide Your face? You forget our afflictions and our oppression, ²⁵For our soul has bowed to the dust, || Our belly has cleaved to the earth. ²⁶Arise, a help to us, || And ransom us for your kindness' sake.

PSALM 45

¹To the Overseer. [Set] on "Lilies." An Instruction of the sons of Korah. A Song of Loves. My heart has stirred a good word, || I am telling my works to the King, || My tongue [is] the pen of a speedy writer. ²You have been beautified above the sons of men, || Grace has been poured into Your lips, || Therefore God has blessed You for all time. ³Gird Your sword on the thigh, O Mighty [One], || Your splendor and Your majesty! ⁴As for Your majesty—prosper [and] ride! Because of truth, meekness, [and] righteousness, || And Your right hand shows You fearful things. ⁵Your arrows [are] sharp—Peoples fall under You—In the heart of the enemies of the King. ⁶Your throne, O God, [is for] all time and forever, || A scepter of uprightness || [Is] the scepter of Your kingdom. ⁷You have loved righteousness and hate wickedness, || Therefore God, Your God, has anointed You || With oil of joy above Your companions. ⁸Myrrh, and aloes, [and] cassia || [Cover] all Your garments; Out of palaces of ivory, || Stringed instruments have made You glad. ⁹Daughters of kings [are] among Your precious ones, || A queen has stood at Your right hand, || In pure gold of Ophir. ¹⁰Listen, O daughter, and see, incline your ear, || And forget your people, and your father's house, ¹¹And the King desires your beauty, || Because He [is] your Lord—bow yourself to Him, ¹²And the daughter of Tyre with a present, || The rich of the people appease your face. ¹³All glory [is] the daughter of the king within, || Her clothing [is] with filigrees of gold. ¹⁴In various colors she is brought to the King; Afterward, virgins, her companions, || Are brought to You. ¹⁵They are brought with joy and gladness, || They come into the palace of the King. ¹⁶Instead of Your fathers are Your sons, || You appoint them for princes in all the earth. ¹⁷I make mention of Your Name in all generations, || Therefore peoples praise You, || For all time and forever!

PSALM 46

¹To the Overseer. By sons of Korah. For girls' [voices]. A Song. God [is] our refuge and strength, || A most sure help in adversities. ²Therefore we do not fear in the changing of earth, || And in the slipping of mountains || Into the heart of the seas. ³Roar—troubled are its waters, || Mountains shake in its pride. Selah. ⁴A river—its streams make glad the city of God, || Your holy place of the dwelling places of the Most High. ⁵God [is] in her midst—she is not moved, God helps her at the turn of the morning! ⁶Nations have been troubled, || Kingdoms have been moved, || He has given forth with His voice—earth melts. ⁷YHWH of Hosts [is] with us, || The God of Jacob [is] a tower for us. Selah. ⁸Come, see the works of YHWH, || Who has done astonishing things in the earth, ⁹Causing wars to cease, || To the end of the earth, He shatters the bow, || And He has cut apart the spear, || He burns chariots with fire. ¹⁰Desist, and know that I [am] God, || I am exalted among nations, || I am exalted in the earth. ¹¹YHWH of hosts [is] with us, || The God of Jacob [is] a tower for us! Selah.

PSALM 47

¹To the Overseer. A Psalm of the sons of Korah. All you peoples, clap the hand, || Shout to God with a voice of singing, ²For YHWH Most High [is] fearful, || A great King over all the earth. ³He leads peoples under us, and nations under our feet. ⁴He chooses for us our

inheritance, || The excellence of Jacob that He loves. Selah. ⁵God has gone up with a shout, || YHWH with the sound of a horn. ⁶Praise God—praise—give praise to our king, praise. ⁷For God [is] King of all the earth, || Give praise, O understanding one. ⁸God has reigned over nations, God has sat on His holy throne, ⁹Nobles of peoples have been gathered, || [With] the people of the God of Abraham, || For the shields of earth [are] to God, || Greatly has He been exalted!

PSALM 48

¹A SONG. A PSALM OF THE SONS OF KORAH. Great [is] YHWH, and greatly praised, || In the city of our God—His holy hill. ²Beautiful [for] elevation, || A joy of all the land, [is] Mount Zion, || The sides of the north, the city of [the] great King. ³God is known for a tower in her high places. ⁴For behold, the kings met, they passed by together, ⁵They have seen—so they have marveled, || They have been troubled, they were hurried away. ⁶Trembling has seized them there, || Pain, as of a travailing woman. ⁷By an east wind You shatter ships of Tarshish. ⁸As we have heard, so we have seen, || In the city of YHWH of hosts, || In the city of our God, God establishes her for all time. Selah. ⁹We have thought, O God, of Your kindness, || In the midst of Your temple, ¹⁰As [is] Your Name, O God, so [is] Your praise, || Over the ends of the earth, || Righteousness has filled Your right hand. ¹¹Mount Zion rejoices, || The daughters of Judah are joyful, || For the sake of Your judgments. ¹²Surround Zion, and go around her, count her towers, ¹³Set your heart to her bulwark, || Consider her high places, || So that you recount to a later generation, ¹⁴That this God [is] our God—For all time and forever, || He leads us over death!

PSALM 49

¹TO THE OVERSEER. A PSALM OF THE SONS OF KORAH. Hear this, all you peoples, || Give ear, all you inhabitants of the world. ²Both low and high, together rich and needy. ³My mouth speaks wise things, || And the meditations of my heart [are] things of understanding. ⁴I incline my ear to an allegory, || I open my riddle with a harp; ⁵Why do I fear in days of evil? The iniquity of my supplanters surrounds me. ⁶Those trusting on their wealth, || And in the multitude of their riches, || Show themselves foolish. ⁷A brother ransoms no one at all, || He does not give to God his atonement. ⁸And precious [is] the redemption of their soul, || And it has ceased for all time. ⁹And still he lives forever, || He does not see the pit. ¹⁰For he sees wise men die, || Together the foolish and brutish perish, || And have left their wealth to others. ¹¹Their heart [is that] their houses [are] for all time, || Their dwelling places from generation to generation. They proclaimed their names over the lands. ¹²And man does not remain in honor, || He has been like the beasts, they have been cut off. ¹³This their way [is] folly for them, || And their posterity are pleased with their sayings. Selah. ¹⁴They have set themselves as sheep for Sheol, || Death afflicts them, || And the upright rule over them in the morning, || And their form [is] for consumption. Sheol [is] a dwelling for him. ¹⁵Only, God ransoms my soul from the hand of Sheol, || For He receives me. Selah. ¹⁶Do not fear when one makes wealth, || When the glory of his house is abundant, ¹⁷For at his death he receives nothing, || His glory does not go down after him. ¹⁸For he blesses his soul in his life || (And they praise you when you do well for yourself.) ¹⁹It comes to the generation of his fathers, || They do not see the light forever. ²⁰Man in honor, who does not understand, || Has been like the beasts, they have been cut off!

PSALM 50

¹A PSALM OF ASAPH. The God of gods—YHWH—has spoken, || And He calls to the earth || From the rising of the sun to its going in. ²From Zion, the perfection of beauty, God shone. ³Our God comes, and is not silent, || Fire devours before Him, || And around Him it has been very tempestuous. ⁴He calls to the heavens from above, || And to the earth, to judge His people. ⁵Gather My saints to Me, || Making covenant with Me over a sacrifice. ⁶And the heavens declare His righteousness, || For God Himself is judging. Selah. ⁷Hear, O My people, and I speak, || O Israel, and I testify against you, || God—I [am] your God. ⁸I do not reprove you for your sacrifices, || Indeed, your burnt-offerings || [Are] continually before Me. ⁹I do not take a bullock from your house, || [Or] male goats from your folds. ¹⁰For every beast of the forest [is] Mine, || The livestock on the hills of oxen. ¹¹I have known every bird of the mountains, || And the wild beast of the field [is] with Me. ¹²If I am hungry I do not tell [it] to you, || For the world and its fullness [is] Mine. ¹³Do I eat the flesh of bulls, || And drink the blood of male goats? ¹⁴Sacrifice to God confession, || And complete your vows to the Most High. ¹⁵And call Me in a day of adversity, || I deliver you, and you honor Me. ¹⁶And to the wicked God has said: What to you—to recount My statutes? That you lift up My covenant on your mouth? ¹⁷Indeed, you have hated instruction, || And cast My words behind you. ¹⁸If you have seen a thief, || Then you are pleased with him, || And your portion [is] with adulterers. ¹⁹You have sent forth your mouth with evil, || And your tongue joins deceit together, ²⁰You sit, you speak against your brother, || You give slander against a son of your mother. ²¹These you did, and I kept silent, || You have thought that I am like you, || I reprove you, and set in array before your eyes. ²²Now understand this, || You who are forgetting God, || Lest I tear, and there is no deliverer. ²³He who is sacrificing praise honors Me, || As for him who makes a way, || I cause him to look on the salvation of God!

PSALM 51

¹TO THE OVERSEER. A PSALM OF DAVID, IN THE COMING OF NATHAN THE PROPHET TO HIM WHEN HE HAS GONE IN TO BATHSHEBA. Favor me, O God, according to Your kindness, || According to the abundance of Your mercies, || Blot out my transgressions. ²Thoroughly wash me from my iniquity, || And cleanse me from my sin, ³For I know my transgressions, || And my sin [is] continually before me. ⁴Against You, You only, I have sinned, || And done evil in Your eyes, || So that You are righteous in Your words, || You are pure in Your judging. ⁵Behold, I have been brought forth in iniquity, || And my mother conceives me in sin. ⁶Behold, You have desired truth in the inward parts, || And in the hidden part You cause me to know Wisdom. ⁷You cleanse me with hyssop and I am clean, || Wash me, and I am whiter than snow. ⁸You cause me to hear joy and gladness, || You make bones You have bruised joyful. ⁹Hide Your face from my sin. And blot out all my iniquities. ¹⁰Create for me a clean heart, O God, || And renew a right spirit within me. ¹¹Do not cast me forth from Your presence, || And do not take Your Holy Spirit from me. ¹²Restore to me the joy of Your salvation, || And a willing spirit sustains me. ¹³I teach transgressors Your ways, || And sinners return to You. ¹⁴Deliver me from blood, O God, God of my salvation, || My tongue sings of Your righteousness. ¹⁵O Lord, you open my lips, || And my mouth declares Your praise. ¹⁶For You do not desire sacrifice, or I give [it], || You do not accept burnt-offering. ¹⁷The sacrifices of God [are] a broken spirit, || A heart broken and bruised, O God, || You do not despise. ¹⁸Do good in Your good pleasure with Zion, || You build the walls of Jerusalem. ¹⁹Then You desire sacrifices of righteousness, || Burnt-offering, and whole burnt-offering, || Then they offer bullocks on your altar!

PSALM 52

¹TO THE OVERSEER. AN INSTRUCTION OF DAVID, IN THE COMING IN OF DOEG THE EDOMITE, AND HE DECLARES TO SAUL AND SAYS TO HIM, "DAVID CAME TO THE HOUSE OF AHIMELECH." Why do you boast in evil, O mighty one? The kindness of God [is] all the day. ²Your tongue devises mischiefs, || Like a sharp razor, working deceit. ³You have loved evil rather than good, || Lying, than speaking righteousness. Selah. ⁴You have loved all devouring words, || O you deceitful tongue. ⁵Also—God breaks you down forever, || Takes you, and pulls you out of the tent, || And He has uprooted you || Out of the land of the living. Selah. ⁶And the righteous see, || And fear, and laugh at him. ⁷"Behold, the man who does not make God his strong place, || And trusts in the abundance of his riches, || He is strong in his mischiefs." ⁸And I, as a green olive in the house of God, || I have trusted in the kindness of God, || For all time and forever, ⁹I thank You for all time, because You have done [it], || And I wait [on] Your Name for [it is] good before Your saints!

PSALM 53

¹To the Overseer. "On a disease." An Instruction of David. A fool said in his heart, "There is no God." They have done corruptly, || Indeed, they have done abominable iniquity, || There is none doing good. ²God looked on the sons of men from the heavens, || To see if there is an understanding one, || [One] seeking God. ³Everyone went back, together they became filthy, || There is none doing good—not even one. ⁴Workers of iniquity have not known, || Those eating my people have eaten bread, || They have not called God. ⁵There they feared a fear—there was no fear, || For God has scattered the bones of him || Who is encamping against you, || You have put to shame, || For God has despised them. ⁶Who gives the salvation of Israel from Zion? When God turns back [to] a captivity of His people, || Jacob rejoices—Israel is glad!

PSALM 54

¹To the Overseer. With stringed instruments. An Instruction of David, in the coming in of the Ziphim, and they say to Saul, "Is David not hiding himself with us?" O God, save me by Your Name, and judge me by Your might. ²O God, hear my prayer, || Give ear to the sayings of my mouth, ³For strangers have risen up against me || And terrible ones have sought my soul, || They have not set God before them. Selah. ⁴Behold, God [is] a helper to me, || The Lord [is] with those supporting my soul, ⁵Turn back the evil to my enemies, || Cut them off in Your truth. ⁶I sacrifice to You with a free-will offering, || I thank Your Name, O Yhwh, for [it is] good, ⁷For He delivered me from all adversity, || And my eye has looked on my enemies!

PSALM 55

¹To the Overseer. With stringed instruments. An Instruction of David. Give ear, O God, [to] my prayer, || And do not hide from my supplication. ²Attend to me, and answer me, || I mourn in my meditation, and make a noise, ³Because of the voice of an enemy, || Because of the oppression of the wicked, || For they cause sorrow to move against me, || And in anger they hate me. ⁴My heart is pained within me, || And terrors of death have fallen on me. ⁵Fear and trembling come to me, || And horror covers me. ⁶And I say, "Who gives to me a pinion as a dove?" I fly away and rest, ⁷Behold, I move far off, || I lodge in a wilderness. Selah. ⁸I hurry escape for myself, || From a rushing wind, from a whirlwind. ⁹Swallow up, O Lord, divide their tongue, || For I saw violence and strife in a city. ¹⁰By day and by night they go around it, on its walls. Both iniquity and perverseness [are] in its midst, ¹¹Mischiefs [are] in its midst. Fraud and deceit do not depart from its street. ¹²For an enemy does not reproach me, or I bear [it], || He who is hating me || Has not magnified himself against me, || Or I hide from him. ¹³But you, a man—as my equal, || My familiar friend, and my acquaintance. ¹⁴When together we sweeten counsel, || We walk into the house of God in company. ¹⁵Desolations [are] on them, || They go down [to] Sheol—alive, || For wickedness [is] in their dwelling, in their midst. ¹⁶I call to God, and Yhwh saves me. ¹⁷Evening, and morning, and noon, || I meditate, and make a noise, and He hears my voice, ¹⁸He has ransomed my soul in peace || From him who is near to me, || For with the multitude they were with me. ¹⁹God hears and afflicts them, || And He sits of old. Selah. Because they have no changes, and do not fear God, ²⁰He has sent forth his hands against his well-wishers, || He has defiled his covenant. ²¹His mouth has been sweeter than honey, || And his heart [is] war! His words have been softer than oil, || And they [are] drawn [swords]. ²²Cast on Yhwh that which He has given you, || And He sustains you, || He does not permit the moving of the righteous forever. ²³And You, O God, bring them down || To a pit of destruction, || Men of blood and deceit do not reach to half their days, || And I trust in You!

PSALM 56

¹To the Overseer. [Set] on "A Silent Dove Far Off." A Miktam of David, in the Philistines' taking hold of him in Gath. Favor me, O God, for man swallowed me up, || All the day fighting he oppresses me, ²My enemies have swallowed up all the day, || For many [are] fighting against me, O Most High, ³[In] the day I am afraid I am confident toward You. ⁴In God I praise His word, in God I have trusted, || I do not fear what flesh does to me. ⁵All the day they wrest my words, || All their thoughts [are] for evil concerning me, ⁶They assemble, they hide, they watch my heels, || When they have expected my soul. ⁷They escape by iniquity, || In anger put down the peoples, O God. ⁸You have counted my wandering, || You place my tear in Your bottle, || Are they not in Your scroll? ⁹Then turn back my enemies in the day I call. This I have known, that God [is] for me. ¹⁰In God I praise the word, || In Yhwh I praise the word. ¹¹In God I trusted, || I do not fear what man does to me, ¹²On me, O God, [are] Your vows, || I repay thank-offerings to You. ¹³For You have delivered my soul from death, || Do You not [keep] my feet from falling? To habitually walk before God in the light of the living!

PSALM 57

¹To the Overseer. "Do Not Destroy." A Miktam of David, in his fleeing from the face of Saul into a cave. Favor me, O God, favor me, || For my soul is trusting in You, || And I trust in the shadow of Your wings, || Until the calamities pass over. ²I call to God Most High, || To God [who] is perfecting for me. ³He sends from the heavens, and saves me, || He reproached [the one] who is panting after me. Selah. God sends forth His kindness and His truth. ⁴My soul [is] in the midst of lions, || I lie down [among] flames—sons of men, || Their teeth [are] a spear and arrows, || And their tongue a sharp sword. ⁵Be exalted above the heavens, O God, || Your glory above all the earth. ⁶They have prepared a net for my steps, || My soul has bowed down, || They have dug a pit before me, || They have fallen into its midst. Selah. ⁷My heart is prepared, O God, || My heart is prepared, || I sing and praise. ⁸Awake, my glory, awake, stringed instrument and harp, || I awake the morning dawn. ⁹I thank You among the peoples, O Lord, || I praise You among the nations. ¹⁰For Your kindness [is] great to the heavens, || And Your truth to the clouds. ¹¹Be exalted above the heavens, O God. Your glory above all the earth!

PSALM 58

¹To the Overseer. "Do Not Destroy." A Miktam of David. Is it true, O silent one, that you speak righteously? Do you judge uprightly, O sons of men? ²Even in heart you work iniquities, || In the land you ponder the violence of your hands. ³The wicked have been estranged from the womb, || They have erred from the belly, speaking lies. ⁴Their poison [is] as poison of a serpent, || As a deaf cobra shutting its ear, ⁵Which does not listen to the voice of whisperers, || A charmer of most skillful charms. ⁶O God, break their teeth in their mouth, || Break down the jaw-teeth of young lions, O Yhwh. ⁷They are melted as waters, || They go up and down for themselves, || His arrow proceeds as they cut themselves off. ⁸He goes on as a snail that melts, || [As] an untimely birth of a woman, || They have not seen the sun. ⁹Before your pots discern the bramble, || As living, He whirls away in His burning anger. ¹⁰The righteous rejoices that he has seen vengeance, || He washes his steps in the blood of the wicked. ¹¹And man says: "Surely fruit [is] for the righteous: Surely there is a God judging in the earth!"

PSALM 59

¹To the Overseer. "Do Not Destroy." A Miktam of David, in Saul's sending, and they watch the house to put him to death. Deliver me from my enemies, O my God, || Set me on high from my withstanders. ²Deliver me from workers of iniquity, || And save me from men of blood. ³For behold, they laid wait for my soul, || Strong ones are assembled against me, || Not my transgression nor my sin, O Yhwh. ⁴Without punishment they run and prepare themselves, || Stir up to meet me, and see. ⁵And You, Yhwh, God of Hosts, God of Israel, || Awake to inspect all the nations. Do not favor any treacherous dealers of iniquity. Selah. ⁶They return at evening, || They make a noise like a dog, || And go around the city. ⁷Behold, they belch out with their mouths, || Swords [are] in their lips, for "Who hears?" ⁸And You, O Yhwh, laugh at them, || You mock at all the nations. ⁹O my Strength, to You I take heed, || For God [is] my tower—the God of my kindness. ¹⁰God goes before me, || He causes me to look on my enemies. ¹¹Do not slay them, lest my people forget, || Shake them by Your strength, || And bring them down, O Lord our shield. ¹²The sin of their mouth [is] a word of their lips, || And they are captured in their pride, || And they recount from the curse and lying. ¹³Consume in fury, consume and they are not, || And they know that God is ruling in Jacob, || To the ends of the earth. Selah. ¹⁴And they return at evening, || They make a noise

like a dog, || And they go around the city. ¹⁵They wander for food, || If they are not satisfied—then they murmur. ¹⁶And I sing of Your strength, || And at morning I sing of Your kindness, || For You have been a tower to me, || And a refuge for me in a day of adversity. ¹⁷O my Strength, I sing praise to You, || For God [is] my tower, the God of my kindness!

PSALM 60

¹To the Overseer. [Set] on "Lily of Testimony." A Miktam of David, to teach, in his striving with Aram-Naharaim and with Aram-Zobah, when Joab turns back and strikes Edom in the Valley of Salt—twelve thousand. O God, You had cast us off, || You had broken us—had been angry! You turn back to us. ²You have caused the land to tremble, || You have broken it, || Heal its breaches, for it has moved. ³You have shown Your people a hard thing, || You have caused us to drink wine of trembling. ⁴You have given an ensign to those fearing You, || To be lifted up as an ensign || Because of truth. Selah. ⁵That Your beloved ones may be drawn out, || Save [with] Your right hand, and answer us. ⁶God has spoken in His holiness: I exult—I apportion Shechem, || And I measure the Valley of Succoth, ⁷Gilead [is] Mine, and Manasseh [is] Mine, || And Ephraim [is] the strength of My head, || Judah [is] My lawgiver, ⁸Moab [is] My pot for washing, || Over Edom I cast My shoe, || Shout, concerning Me, O Philistia. ⁹Who brings me [to] a city of bulwarks? Who has led me to Edom? ¹⁰Is it not You, O God? Have You cast us off? And do You not go forth, O God, with our hosts? ¹¹Give to us help from adversity, || And the deliverance of man [is] vain. ¹²We do mightily in God, || And He treads down our adversaries!

PSALM 61

¹To the Overseer. On stringed instruments. By David. Hear, O God, my loud cry, attend to my prayer. ²I call to You from the end of the land, || In the feebleness of my heart, || You lead me into a rock higher than I. ³For You have been a refuge for me, || A tower of strength because of the enemy. ⁴I sojourn in Your tent for all ages, || I trust in the secret place of Your wings. Selah. ⁵For You, O God, have listened to my vows, || You have appointed the inheritance || Of those fearing Your Name. ⁶You add days to the days of the king, || His years as generation and generation. ⁷He dwells before God for all time, || Appoint kindness and truth—they keep him. ⁸So I praise Your Name forever, || When I pay my vows day by day!

PSALM 62

¹To the Overseer. For Jeduthun. A Psalm of David. Toward God alone [is] my soul silent, || My salvation [is] from Him. ²He alone [is] my rock, and my salvation, || My tower, I am not much moved. ³Until when do you devise mischief against a man? All of you are destroyed, || As a wall inclined, a hedge that is cast down. ⁴Only—from his excellence || They have consulted to drive away, || They enjoy a lie, they bless with their mouth, || And revile with their heart. Selah. ⁵For God alone, be silent, O my soul, || For my hope [is] from Him. ⁶He alone [is] my rock and my salvation, || My tower, I am not moved. ⁷On God [is] my salvation, and my glory, || The rock of my strength, my refuge [is] in God. ⁸Trust in Him at all times, O people, || Pour forth your heart before Him, || God [is] a refuge for us. Selah. ⁹Surely vanity the low, a lie the high. In balances to go up || They [are] lighter than a breath. ¹⁰Do not trust in oppression, || And do not become vain in robbery, || Do not set the heart [on] wealth when it increases. ¹¹Once has God spoken, twice I heard this, || That "strength [is] with God." ¹²And with You, O Lord, [is] kindness, || For You repay to each, || According to his work!

PSALM 63

¹A Psalm of David, in his being in the wilderness of Judah. O God, You [are] my God, earnestly I seek You, || My soul has thirsted for You, || My flesh has longed for You, || In a dry and weary land, without waters. ²So I have seen You in the sanctuary, || To behold Your strength and Your glory. ³Because better [is] Your kindness than life, || My lips praise You. ⁴So I bless You in my life, || I lift up my hands in Your Name. ⁵As [with] milk and fatness is my soul satisfied, || And [with] singing lips my mouth praises. ⁶If I have remembered You on my bed, || I meditate on You in the watches. ⁷For You have been a help to me, || And I sing in the shadow of Your wings. ⁸My soul has cleaved after You, || Your right hand has taken hold on me. ⁹And they who seek my soul for desolation, || Go into the lower parts of the earth. ¹⁰They cause him to run on the edge of the sword, || They are a portion for foxes. ¹¹And the king rejoices in God, || Everyone swearing by Him boasts, || But the mouth of those speaking lies is stopped!

PSALM 64

¹To the Overseer. A Psalm of David. Hear, O God, my voice, in my meditation, || You keep my life from the fear of an enemy, ²Hide me from the secret counsel of evildoers, || From the tumult of workers of iniquity. ³Who sharpened their tongue as a sword, || They directed their arrow—a bitter word. ⁴To shoot the perfect in secret places, || Suddenly they shoot him, and do not fear. ⁵They strengthen an evil thing for themselves, || They recount of the hiding of snares, || They have said, "Who looks at it?" ⁶They search out perverse things, "We perfected a searching search," || And the inward part of man, and the heart, [are] deep. ⁷And God shoots them [with] an arrow, || Their wounds have been sudden, ⁸And they cause him to stumble, || Their own tongue [is] against them, || Every looker on them flees away. ⁹And all men fear, and declare the work of God, || And they have wisely considered His deed. ¹⁰The righteous rejoice in Yhwh, || And have trusted in Him, || And all the upright of heart boast!

PSALM 65

¹To the Overseer. A Psalm of David. A Song. To You, silence [and] praise, O God, in Zion, || And to You a vow is completed. ²Hearer of prayer, all flesh comes to You. ³Matters of iniquities were mightier than I, || Our transgressions—You cover them. ⁴O the blessedness of [him whom] You choose, || And draw near, he inhabits Your courts, || We are satisfied with the goodness of Your house, || Your holy temple. ⁵By fearful things in righteousness You answer us, || O God of our salvation, || The confidence of all far off || The ends of the earth and sea. ⁶Establishing mountains by His power, || He has been girded with might, ⁷Restraining the noise of seas, the noise of their billows, || And the multitude of the peoples. ⁸And the inhabitants of the uttermost parts || Are afraid from Your signs, || You cause the outgoings of morning and evening to sing. ⁹You have inspected the earth, and water it, || You make it very rich, the stream of God [is] full of water, || You prepare their grain, || When thus You prepare it, ¹⁰Its ridges have been filled, || Its furrow has been deepened, || You soften it with showers, || Its springing up You bless. ¹¹You have crowned the year of Your goodness, || And Your paths drop fatness. ¹²The pastures of a wilderness drop, || And You gird the hills with joy. ¹³The meadows are clothed with the flock, || And valleys are covered with grain, || They shout—indeed, they sing!

PSALM 66

¹To the Overseer. A Song. A Psalm. Shout to God, all the earth. ²Praise the glory of His Name, || Make honorable His praise. ³Say to God, "How fearful Your works—By the abundance of Your strength, || Your enemies feign obedience to You. ⁴All the earth bows to You, || They sing praise to You, they praise Your Name." Selah. ⁵Come, and see the works of God, || Fearful acts toward the sons of men. ⁶He has turned a sea to dry land, || Through a river they pass over on foot, || There we rejoice in Him. ⁷Ruling by His might for all time, || His eyes watch among the nations, || The stubborn do not exalt themselves. Selah. ⁸Bless our God you peoples, || And sound the voice of His praise, ⁹Who has placed our soul in life, || And has not permitted our feet to be moved. ¹⁰For You have tried us, O God, || You have refined us as the refining of silver. ¹¹You have brought us into a net, || You have placed pressure on our loins. ¹²You have caused man to ride at our head. We have entered into fire and into water, || And You bring us out to a watered place. ¹³I enter Your house with burnt-offerings, || I complete my vows to You, ¹⁴For my lips were opened, || And my mouth spoke in my distress: ¹⁵"I offer to You burnt-offerings of fatlings, || With incense of rams, I prepare a bullock with male goats." Selah. ¹⁶Come, hear, all you who fear God, || And I recount what He did for my soul. ¹⁷I have called to Him [with] my mouth, || And exaltation [is] under my tongue. ¹⁸Iniquity, if I have seen in my heart, || The Lord does not hear. ¹⁹But God has heard, || He has attended

to the voice of my prayer. ²⁰Blessed [is] God, || Who has not turned aside my prayer, || And His loving-kindness, from me!

PSALM 67

¹To the Overseer. With stringed instruments. A Psalm. A Song. God favors us and blesses us, || [And] causes His face to shine with us. Selah. ²For the knowledge of Your way in earth, || Your salvation among all nations. ³Peoples praise You, O God, || Peoples praise You, all of them. ⁴Nations rejoice and sing, || For You judge peoples uprightly, || And comfort peoples on earth. Selah. ⁵Peoples confess You, O God, || Peoples confess You—all of them. ⁶Earth has given her increase, God blesses us—our God, ⁷God blesses us, and all the ends of the earth fear Him!

PSALM 68

¹To the Overseer. A Psalm. A Song of David. God rises [and] His enemies are scattered! And those hating Him flee from His face. ²You drive them away as the driving away of smoke, || As the melting of wax before fire, || The wicked perish at the presence of God. ³And the righteous rejoice, they exult before God, || And they rejoice with gladness. ⁴Sing to God—praise His Name, || Raise up a highway for Him who is riding in deserts, || In Yah [is] His Name, and exult before Him. ⁵Father of the fatherless, and judge of the widows, || [Is] God in His holy habitation. ⁶God—causing the lonely to dwell at home, || Bringing out bound ones into prosperity, || Only—the stubborn have inhabited a dry place. ⁷O God, in Your going forth before Your people, || In Your stepping through the wilderness, Selah. ⁸The earth has shaken, || Indeed, the heavens have dropped before God, || This Sinai—before God, the God of Israel. ⁹You shake out a shower of free-will gifts, O God. Your inheritance, when it has been weary, || You have established it. ¹⁰Your creature has dwelt in it, || You prepare for the poor in Your goodness, O God. ¹¹The Lord gives the saying, || The female proclaimers [are] a numerous host. ¹²Kings of hosts utterly flee away, || And a female inhabitant of the house apportions spoil. ¹³Though you lie between two boundaries, || Wings of a dove covered with silver, || And her pinions with yellow gold. ¹⁴When the Mighty spreads kings in it, it snows in Salmon. ¹⁵A hill of God [is] the hill of Bashan, || A hill of heights [is] the hill of Bashan. ¹⁶Why do you envy, O high hills, || The hill God has desired for His seat? YHWH also dwells forever. ¹⁷The chariots of God [are] myriads, thousands of changes, || The Lord [is] among them, in Sinai, in the sanctuary. ¹⁸You have ascended on high, || You have taken captivity captive, || You have taken gifts for men, || That even the stubborn may rest, O Yah God. ¹⁹Blessed [is] the Lord, day by day He lays on us. God Himself [is] our salvation. Selah. ²⁰God Himself [is] to us a God for deliverances, || And YHWH Lord has the outgoings of death. ²¹Only—God strikes || The head of His enemies, || The hairy crown of a habitual walker in his guilt. ²²The Lord said: "From Bashan I bring back, || I bring back from the depths of the sea. ²³So that you dash your foot || In the blood of enemies—the tongue of Your dogs." ²⁴They have seen Your goings, O God, || Goings of my God, my king, in the sanctuary. ²⁵Singers have been before, || Behind [are] players on instruments, || Virgins playing with timbrels in the midst. ²⁶In assemblies bless God, || The Lord—from the fountain of Israel. ²⁷There [is] little Benjamin, their ruler, || Heads of Judah their defense, || Heads of Zebulun—heads of Naphtali. ²⁸Your God has commanded your strength, || Be strong, O God, You have worked this for us. ²⁹Because of Your temple at Jerusalem, || Kings bring a present to You. ³⁰Rebuke a beast of the reeds, a herd of bulls, || With calves of the peoples, || Each humbling himself with pieces of silver, || You scatter peoples delighting in conflicts. ³¹Fat ones come out of Egypt, || Cush causes her hands to run to God. ³²Kingdoms of the earth, sing to God, || Praise the Lord! Selah. ³³To Him who is riding on the heavens of the heavens of old, || Behold, He gives with His voice a strong voice. ³⁴Ascribe strength to God, || His excellence [is] over Israel, and His strength in the clouds. ³⁵Fearful, O God, out of Your sanctuaries, || The God of Israel Himself, || Giving strength and might to the people. Blessed [is] God!

PSALM 69

¹To the Overseer. [Set] on "Lilies." by David. Save me, O God, for waters have come to the soul. ²I have sunk in deep mire, || And there is no standing, || I have come into the depths of the waters, || And a flood has overflown me. ³I have been wearied with my calling, || My throat has been burned, || My eyes have been consumed, waiting for my God. ⁴Those hating me without cause || Have been more than the hairs of my head, || Mighty have been my destroyers, || My lying enemies, || That which I did not take away—I bring back. ⁵O God, You have known || Concerning my overturn, || And my desolations have not been hid from You. ⁶Do not let those waiting on You be ashamed because of me, || O Lord, YHWH of Hosts, || Do not let those seeking You || Blush because of me, || O God of Israel. ⁷For because of You I have borne reproach, || Shame has covered my face. ⁸I have been a stranger to my brother, || And a foreigner to sons of my mother. ⁹For [my] zeal for Your house has consumed me, || And the reproaches of Your reproachers || Have fallen on me. ¹⁰And I weep in the fasting of my soul, || And it is for a reproach to me. ¹¹And I make my clothing sackcloth, || And I am for an allegory to them. ¹²Those sitting at the gate meditate concerning me, || And those drinking strong drink, || Play on instruments. ¹³And my prayer [is] to You, O YHWH, || A time of good pleasure, O God, || In the abundance of Your kindness, || Answer me in the truth of Your salvation. ¹⁴Deliver me from the mire, and do not let me sink, || Let me be delivered from those hating me, || And from deep places of waters. ¹⁵Do not let a flood of waters overflow me, || Nor let the deep swallow me up, || Nor let the pit shut her mouth on me. ¹⁶Answer me, O YHWH, for Your kindness [is] good, || Turn to me according to the abundance of Your mercies, ¹⁷And do not hide Your face from Your servant, || For I am in distress—hurry, answer me. ¹⁸Be near to my soul—redeem it, || Ransom me because of my enemies. ¹⁹You have known my reproach, || And my shame, and my blushing, || All my adversaries [are] before You. ²⁰Reproach has broken my heart, and I am sick, || And I look for a bemoaner, and there is none, || And for comforters, and I have found none. ²¹And they give gall for my food, || And cause me to drink vinegar for my thirst. ²²Their table before them is for a snare, || And for a repayment—for a trap. ²³Their eyes are darkened from seeing, || And their loins continually shake You. ²⁴Pour Your indignation on them, || And the fierceness of Your anger seizes them. ²⁵Their tower is desolated, || There is no dweller in their tents. ²⁶For they have pursued him [whom] You have struck, || And recount of the pain of Your pierced ones. ²⁷Give punishment for their iniquity, || And they do not enter into Your righteousness. ²⁸They are blotted out of the scroll of life, || And are not written with the righteous. ²⁹And I [am] afflicted and pained, || Your salvation, O God, sets me on high. ³⁰I praise the Name of God with a song, || And I magnify Him with thanksgiving, ³¹And it is better to YHWH than an ox, || A bullock—horned [and] hoofed. ³²The humble have seen—they rejoice, || You who seek God—and your heart lives. ³³For YHWH listens to the needy, || And He has not despised His bound ones. ³⁴The heavens and earth praise Him, || Seas, and every moving thing in them. ³⁵For God saves Zion, || And builds the cities of Judah, || And they have dwelt there, and possess it. ³⁶And the seed of His servants inherit it, || And those loving His Name dwell in it!

PSALM 70

¹To the Overseer. By David. "To Cause to Remember." O God, [hurry] to deliver me, || O YHWH, hurry to help me. ²Let them be ashamed and confounded || Who are seeking my soul, || Let them be turned backward and blush || Who are desiring my evil. ³Let them turn back because of their shame, || Who are saying, "Aha, aha." ⁴Let all those seeking You rejoice and be glad in You, || And let those loving Your salvation || Continually say, "God is magnified." ⁵And I [am] poor and needy, O God, hurry to me, || You [are] my help and my deliverer, || O YHWH, do not linger!

PSALM 71

¹In You, O YHWH, I have trusted, || Do not let me be disappointed for all time. ²You deliver me in Your righteousness, || And cause me to escape, || Incline Your ear to me, and save me. ³Be a rock to me—a habitation, || To go in continually, || You have given command to save me, || For You [are] my rock and my bulwark. ⁴O my God, cause me to escape || From the hand of the wicked, || From the hand of the perverse and violent. ⁵For You [are] my hope, O Lord YHWH, || My trust from my youth. ⁶I have been supported from the womb by

You, ‖ You cut me out from my mother's bowels, ‖ My praise [is] continually in You. ⁷I have been as a wonder to many, ‖ And You [are] my strong refuge. ⁸My mouth is filled [with] Your praise, ‖ All the day [with] Your beauty. ⁹Do not cast me off at the time of old age, ‖ Do not forsake me according to the consumption of my power. ¹⁰For my enemies have spoken against me, ‖ And those watching my soul have taken counsel together, ¹¹Saying, "God has forsaken him, ‖ Pursue and catch him, for there is no deliverer." ¹²O God, do not be far from me, ‖ O my God, make haste for my help. ¹³They are ashamed, they are consumed, ‖ Who are opposing my soul, ‖ They are covered [with] reproach and blushing, ‖ Who are seeking my evil, ¹⁴And I continually wait with hope, ‖ And have added to all Your praise. ¹⁵My mouth recounts Your righteousness, ‖ All the day Your salvation, ‖ For I have not known the numbers. ¹⁶I come in [the] might of Lord YHWH, ‖ I mention Your righteousness—Yours alone. ¹⁷God, You have taught me from my youth, ‖ And until now I declare Your wonders. ¹⁸And also to old age and grey hairs, ‖ O God, do not forsake me, ‖ Until I declare Your strength to a generation, ‖ Your might to everyone that comes. ¹⁹And Your righteousness, O God, [is] to the heights, ‖ Because You have done great things, ‖ O God, who [is] like You? ²⁰Because You have showed me many and sad distresses, ‖ You turn back—You revive me, ‖ And from the depths of the earth, ‖ You turn back—You bring me up. ²¹You increase my greatness, ‖ And You surround—You comfort me, ²²I also thank You with a vessel of stringed instrument, ‖ Your truth, O my God, I sing to You with a harp, ‖ O Holy One of Israel, ²³My lips cry aloud when I sing praise to You, ‖ And my soul that You have redeemed, ²⁴My tongue also utters Your righteousness all the day, ‖ Because ashamed—because confounded, ‖ Have been those seeking my evil!

PSALM 72

¹BY SOLOMON. O God, give Your judgments to the king, ‖ And Your righteousness to the king's Son. ²He judges Your people with righteousness, ‖ And Your poor with judgment. ³The mountains bear peace to the people, ‖ And the heights by righteousness. ⁴He judges the poor of the people, ‖ Gives deliverance to the sons of the needy, ‖ And bruises the oppressor. ⁵They fear You with the sun, and before the moon, ‖ Generation—generations. ⁶He comes down as rain on mown grass, ‖ As showers—sprinkling the earth. ⁷The righteous flourish in His days, ‖ And abundance of peace until the moon is not. ⁸And He rules from sea to sea, ‖ And from the river to the ends of the earth. ⁹Desert-dwellers bow before Him, ‖ And His enemies lick the dust. ¹⁰Kings of Tarshish and of the islands send back a present. Kings of Sheba and Seba bring a reward near. ¹¹And all kings bow themselves to Him, ‖ All nations serve Him, ¹²For He delivers the needy who cries, ‖ And the poor when he has no helper, ¹³He has pity on the poor and needy, ‖ And He saves the souls of the needy, ¹⁴He redeems their soul from fraud and from violence, ‖ And their blood is precious in His eyes. ¹⁵And He lives, and the gold of Sheba [is] given to Him, ‖ And prayer is continually made for Him, ‖ All day He is continually blessed. ¹⁶There is a handful of grain in the earth, ‖ On the top of mountains, ‖ Its fruit shakes like Lebanon, ‖ And they flourish out of the city as the herb of the earth. ¹⁷His Name is for all time, ‖ Before the sun is His Name continued, ‖ And they bless themselves in Him, ‖ All nations pronounce Him blessed. ¹⁸Blessed is YHWH God, God of Israel, ‖ He alone is doing wonders, ¹⁹And blessed [is] the Name of His glory for all time, ‖ And the whole earth is filled [with] His glory. Amen and amen! ²⁰The prayers of David son of Jesse have been ended.

PSALM 73

¹A PSALM OF ASAPH. Surely God [is] good to Israel, to the clean of heart. And I—as a little thing, ‖ My feet have been turned aside, ²As nothing, my steps have slipped, ‖ For I have been envious of the boastful, ³I see the peace of the wicked, ‖ That there are no bands at their death, ⁴And their might [is] firm. ⁵They are not in the misery of mortals, ‖ And they are not plagued with common men. ⁶Therefore pride has encircled them, ‖ Violence covers them as a dress. ⁷Their eye has come out from fat. The imaginations of the heart transgressed; ⁸They do corruptly, ‖ And they speak in the wickedness of oppression, ‖ They speak from on high. ⁹They have set their mouth in the heavens, ‖ And their tongue walks in the earth. ¹⁰Therefore His people return here, ‖ And waters of fullness are wrung out to them. ¹¹And they have said, "How has God known? And is there knowledge in the Most High?" ¹²Behold, these [are] the wicked and easy ones of the age, ‖ They have increased strength. ¹³Only—a vain thing! I have purified my heart, ‖ And I wash my hands in innocence, ¹⁴And I am plagued all the day, ‖ And my reproof—every morning. ¹⁵If I have said, "I recount thus," ‖ Behold, I have deceived a generation of Your sons. ¹⁶And I think to know this, ‖ It [is] perverseness in my eyes, ¹⁷Until I come into the sanctuaries of God, ‖ I attend to their latter end. ¹⁸Surely You set them in slippery places, ‖ You have caused them to fall to desolations. ¹⁹How they have become a desolation as in a moment, ‖ They have been ended—consumed from terrors. ²⁰As a dream from awakening, O Lord, ‖ In awaking, You despise their image. ²¹For my heart shows itself violent, ‖ And my reins prick themselves, ²²And I am brutish, and do not know. I have been a beast with You. ²³And I [am] continually with You, ‖ You have laid hold on my right hand. ²⁴You lead me with Your counsel, ‖ And after, receive me [to] glory. ²⁵Whom do I have in the heavens? And none have I desired in earth [besides] You. ²⁶My flesh and my heart have been consumed, ‖ God [is] the rock of my heart and my portion for all time. ²⁷For behold, those far from You perish, ‖ You have cut off everyone, ‖ Who is going whoring from You. ²⁸And [the] nearness of God to me [is] good, ‖ I have placed my refuge in Lord YHWH, ‖ To recount all Your works!

PSALM 74

¹AN INSTRUCTION OF ASAPH. Why, O God, have You cast off forever? Your anger smokes against the flock of Your pasture. ²Remember Your congregation ‖ [That] You purchased of old, ‖ You redeemed the rod of Your inheritance, ‖ This Mount Zion—You dwelt in it. ³Lift up Your steps to the continuous desolations, ‖ Everything the enemy did wickedly in the sanctuary. ⁴Your adversaries have roared, ‖ In the midst of Your meeting-places, ‖ They have set their ensigns as ensigns. ⁵He is known as one bringing in on high ‖ Against a thicket of wood—axes. ⁶And now they break down its engravings, ‖ Together, with axe and hatchet, ⁷They have sent Your sanctuary into fire, ‖ They defiled the Dwelling Place of Your Name to the earth, ⁸They said in their hearts, "Let us oppress them together," ‖ They burned all the meeting-places of God in the land. ⁹We have not seen our ensigns, ‖ There is no longer a prophet, ‖ Nor with us is one knowing how long. ¹⁰Until when, O God, does an adversary reproach? Does an enemy despise Your Name forever? ¹¹Why do You turn back Your hand, ‖ Even Your right hand? Remove [it] from the midst of Your bosom. ¹²And God [is] my king of old, ‖ Working salvation in the midst of the earth. ¹³You have divided [the] sea by Your strength, ‖ You have shattered heads of dragons by the waters, ¹⁴You have broken the heads of leviathan, ‖ You make him food for the people of desert-dwellers. ¹⁵You have cleaved a fountain and a stream, ‖ You have dried up perennial flowings. ¹⁶The day [is] Yours, ‖ The night [is] also Yours, ‖ You have prepared a light-giver—the sun. ¹⁷You have set up all the borders of earth, ‖ Summer and winter—You have formed them. ¹⁸Remember this—an enemy reproached YHWH, ‖ And a foolish people have despised Your Name. ¹⁹Do not give up to a [wild] creature, ‖ The soul of Your turtle-dove, ‖ Do not forget the life of Your poor ones forever. ²⁰Look attentively to the covenant, ‖ For the dark places of earth, ‖ Have been full of habitations of violence. ²¹Do not let the oppressed turn back ashamed, ‖ Let the poor and needy praise Your Name, ²²Arise, O God, plead Your plea, ‖ Remember Your reproach from a fool all the day. ²³Do not forget the voice of Your adversaries, ‖ The noise of Your withstanders is going up continually!

PSALM 75

¹TO THE OVERSEER. "DO NOT DESTROY." A PSALM OF ASAPH. A SONG. We have given thanks to You, O God, ‖ We have given thanks, and Your Name [is] near, ‖ They have recounted Your wonders. ²When I receive an appointment, I judge uprightly. ³The earth and all its inhabitants are melted, ‖ I have pondered its pillars. Selah. ⁴I have said to the boastful, "Do not be boastful," ‖ And to the wicked, "Do not

raise up a horn." ⁵Do not raise up your horn on high || (You speak with a stiff neck). ⁶For not from the east, or from the west, || Nor from the wilderness—[is] elevation. ⁷But God [is] judging, || This He makes low—and this He lifts up. ⁸For a cup [is] in the hand of YHWH, || And the wine has foamed, || It is full of mixture, and He pours out of it, || Surely wring out its dregs, || And all the wicked of the earth drink, ⁹And I declare [it] for all time, || I sing praise to the God of Jacob, ¹⁰And I cut off all horns of the wicked, || The horns of the righteous are exalted!

PSALM 76

¹To the Overseer. With stringed instruments. A Psalm of Asaph. A Song. God [is] known in Judah, || His Name [is] great in Israel. ²And His dwelling place is in Salem, || And His habitation in Zion. ³There He has shattered arrows of a bow, || Shield, and sword, and battle. Selah. ⁴You [are] bright, majestic above hills of prey. ⁵The mighty of heart have spoiled themselves, || They have slept their sleep, || And none of the men of might found their hands. ⁶From Your rebuke, O God of Jacob, || Both rider and horse have been fast asleep. ⁷You, fearful [are] You, || And who stands before You, || Since You have been angry? ⁸You have sounded judgment from the heavens, || Earth has feared, and has been still, ⁹In the rising of God to judgment, || To save all the humble of earth. Selah. ¹⁰For the fierceness of man praises You, || You gird on the remnant of fierceness. ¹¹Vow and complete to your God YHWH, || All you surrounding Him, || They bring presents to the Fearful One. ¹²He gathers the spirit of leaders, || Fearful to the kings of earth!

PSALM 77

¹To the Overseer. For Jeduthun. A Psalm of Asaph. My voice [is] to God, and I cry, || My voice [is] to God, || And He has given ear to me. ²I sought the Lord in a day of my distress, || My hand has been spread out by night, || And it does not cease, || My soul has refused to be comforted. ³I remember God, and make a noise, || I meditate, and my spirit is feeble. Selah. ⁴You have taken hold of the watches of my eyes, || I have been moved, and I do not speak. ⁵I have reckoned the days of old, || The years of the ages. ⁶I remember my music in the night, || I meditate with my heart, and my spirit searches diligently: ⁷Does the Lord cast off for all ages? Does He add to be pleased no longer? ⁸Has His kindness ceased forever? The saying failed from generation to generation? ⁹Has God forgotten [His] favors? Has He shut up His mercies in anger? Selah. ¹⁰And I say: "My weakness is, || The changes of the right hand of the Most High." ¹¹I mention the doings of YAH, || For I remember Your wonders of old, ¹²And I have meditated on all Your working, || And I talk concerning Your doings. ¹³O God, Your way [is] in holiness, || Who [is] a great god like God? ¹⁴You [are] the God doing wonders. You have made Your strength known among the peoples, ¹⁵You have redeemed Your people with strength, || The sons of Jacob and Joseph. Selah. ¹⁶The waters have seen You, O God, || The waters have seen You, || They are afraid—also depths are troubled. ¹⁷Thick clouds have poured out waters, || The skies have given forth a noise, || Also—Your arrows go up and down. ¹⁸The voice of Your thunder [is] in the spheres, || Lightnings have lightened the world, || The earth has trembled, indeed, it shakes. ¹⁹Your way [is] in the sea, || And Your paths in many waters, || And Your tracks have not been known. ²⁰You have led Your people as a flock, || By the hand of Moses and Aaron!

PSALM 78

¹An Instruction of Asaph. Give ear, O my people, to my law, || Incline your ear to sayings of my mouth. ²I open my mouth with an allegory, || I bring forth hidden things of old, ³That we have heard and know, || And our fathers have recounted to us. ⁴We do not hide from their sons, || Recounting praises of YHWH to a later generation, || And His strength, and His wonders that He has done. ⁵And He raises up a testimony in Jacob, || And has placed a law in Israel, || That He commanded our fathers, || To make them known to their sons. ⁶So that a later generation knows, || Sons who are born, rise and recount to their sons, ⁷And place their confidence in God, || And do not forget the doings of God, || But keep His commands. ⁸And they are not like their fathers, || A generation apostatizing and being rebellious, || A generation—it has not prepared its heart, || Nor [is] its spirit steadfast with God. ⁹Sons of Ephraim—armed bearers of bow, || Have turned in a day of conflict. ¹⁰They have not kept the covenant of God, || And they have refused to walk in His law, ¹¹And they forget His doings, || And His wonders that He showed them. ¹²He has done wonders before their fathers, || In the land of Egypt—the field of Zoan. ¹³He cleft a sea, and causes them to pass over, || Indeed, He causes waters to stand as a heap. ¹⁴And leads them with a cloud by day, || And with a light of fire all the night. ¹⁵He cleaves rocks in a wilderness, || And gives drink—as the great deep. ¹⁶And brings out streams from a rock, || And causes waters to come down as rivers. ¹⁷And they still add to sin against Him, || To provoke the Most High in the dry place. ¹⁸And they try God in their heart, || To ask food for their lust. ¹⁹And they speak against God—they said: "Is God able to array a table in a wilderness?" ²⁰Behold, He has struck a rock, || And waters flow, indeed, streams overflow. "Also, [is] He able to give bread? Does He prepare flesh for His people?" ²¹Therefore YHWH has heard, || And He shows Himself angry, || And fire has been kindled against Jacob, || And anger has also gone up against Israel, ²²For they have not believed in God, || Nor have they trusted in His salvation. ²³And He commands clouds from above, || Indeed, He has opened doors of the heavens. ²⁴And He rains manna on them to eat, || Indeed, He has given grain of the heavens to them. ²⁵Each has eaten food of the mighty, || He sent provision to them to satiety. ²⁶He causes an east wind to journey in the heavens, || And leads a south wind by His strength, ²⁷And He rains on them flesh as dust, || And as sand of the seas—winged bird, ²⁸And causes [it] to fall in the midst of His camp, || Around His dwelling places. ²⁹And they eat, and are greatly satisfied, || And He brings their desire to them. ³⁰They have not been estranged from their desire, || Their food [is] yet in their mouth, ³¹And the anger of God has gone up against them, || And He slays among their fat ones, || And He caused youths of Israel to bend. ³²With all this they have sinned again, || And have not believed in His wonders. ³³And He consumes their days in vanity, || And their years in trouble. ³⁴If He slew them, then they sought Him, || And turned back, and earnestly sought God, ³⁵And they remember that God [is] their rock, || And God Most High their redeemer. ³⁶And they deceive Him with their mouth, || And lie to Him with their tongue, ³⁷And their heart has not been right with Him, || And they have not been steadfast in His covenant. ³⁸And He, the Merciful One, pardons iniquity, and does not destroy, || And has often turned back His anger, || And does not awaken all His fury. ³⁹And He remembers that they [are] flesh, || A wind going on—and it does not return. ⁴⁰How often do they provoke Him in the wilderness, || Grieve Him in the desolate place? ⁴¹Indeed, they turn back, and try God, || And have limited the Holy One of Israel. ⁴²They have not remembered His hand || The day He ransomed them from the adversary. ⁴³When He set His signs in Egypt, || And His wonders in the field of Zoan, ⁴⁴And He turns their streams to blood, || And they do not drink their floods. ⁴⁵He sends among them the beetle, and it consumes them, || And the frog, and it destroys them, ⁴⁶And gives their increase to the caterpillar, || And their labor to the locust. ⁴⁷He destroys their vine with hail, || And their sycamores with frost, ⁴⁸And delivers their beasts up to the hail, || And their livestock to the burning flames. ⁴⁹He sends on them the fury of His anger, || Wrath, and indignation, and distress—A discharge of evil messengers. ⁵⁰He ponders a path for His anger, || He did not keep back their soul from death, || Indeed, He delivered up their life to the pestilence. ⁵¹And He strikes every firstborn in Egypt, || The first-fruit of the strong in tents of Ham. ⁵²And causes His people to journey as a flock, || And guides them as a drove in a wilderness, ⁵³And He leads them confidently, || And they have not been afraid, || And the sea has covered their enemies. ⁵⁴And He brings them to the border of His sanctuary, || This mountain His right hand had acquired, ⁵⁵And casts out nations from before them, || And causes them to fall in the line of inheritance, || And causes the tribes of Israel to dwell in their tents, ⁵⁶And they tempt and provoke God Most High, || And have not kept His testimonies. ⁵⁷And they turn back, || And deal treacherously like their fathers, || They have been turned like a deceitful bow, ⁵⁸And make Him angry with their high places, || And make Him zealous with their carved images, ⁵⁹God has heard, and shows Himself angry. And kicks exceedingly against Israel. ⁶⁰And He

leaves the Dwelling Place of Shiloh, || The tent He had placed among men, ⁶¹And He gives His strength to captivity, || And His beauty into the hand of an adversary, ⁶²And delivers His people up to the sword, || And showed Himself angry with His inheritance. ⁶³Fire has consumed His young men, || And His virgins have not been praised. ⁶⁴His priests have fallen by the sword, || And their widows do not weep. ⁶⁵And the Lord wakes as a sleeper, || As a mighty one crying aloud from wine. ⁶⁶And He strikes His adversaries backward, || He has put a continuous reproach on them, ⁶⁷And He kicks against the tent of Joseph, || And has not fixed on the tribe of Ephraim. ⁶⁸And He chooses the tribe of Judah, || With Mount Zion that He loved, ⁶⁹And builds His sanctuary as a high place, || Like the earth, He founded it for all time. ⁷⁰And He fixes on His servant David, || And takes him from the folds of a flock, ⁷¹He has brought him in from behind suckling ones, || To rule over Jacob His people, || And over Israel His inheritance. ⁷²And he rules them according to the integrity of his heart, || And leads them by the skillfulness of his hands!

PSALM 79

¹A Psalm of Asaph. O God, nations have come into Your inheritance, || They have defiled Your holy temple, || They made Jerusalem become heaps, ²They gave the dead bodies of Your servants || [As] food for the birds of the heavens, || The flesh of Your saints || For the wild beast of the earth. ³They have shed their blood || As water around Jerusalem, || And there is none burying. ⁴We have been a reproach to our neighbors, || A scorn and a derision to our surrounders. ⁵Until when, O YHWH? Are You angry forever? Your jealousy burns as fire. ⁶Pour Your fury on the nations who have not known You, || And on kingdoms that have not called on Your Name. ⁷For [one] has devoured Jacob, || And they have made his habitation desolate. ⁸Do not remember for us the iniquities of forefathers, || Hurry, let Your mercies go before us, || For we have been very weak. ⁹Help us, O God of our salvation, || Because of the glory of Your Name, || And deliver us, and cover over our sins, || For Your Name's sake. ¹⁰Why do the nations say, "Where [is] their God?" Let [it] be known among the nations before our eyes, || The vengeance of the blood of Your servants that is shed. ¹¹Let the groaning of the prisoner come in before You, || According to the greatness of Your arm, || Leave the sons of death. ¹²And return to our neighbors, || Sevenfold to their bosom, their reproach, || With which they reproached You, O Lord. ¹³And we, Your people, and the flock of Your pasture, || We give thanks to You for all time, || We recount Your praise from generation to generation!

PSALM 80

¹To the Overseer. [Set] to "Lilies of Testimony." A Psalm of Asaph. Shepherd of Israel, give ear, || Leading Joseph as a flock, || Inhabiting the cherubim—shine forth, ²Before Ephraim, and Benjamin, and Manasseh, || Wake up Your might, and come for our salvation. ³O God, cause us to turn back, || And cause Your face to shine, and we are saved. ⁴YHWH, God of Hosts, until when? You have burned against the prayer of Your people. ⁵You have caused them to eat bread of tears, || And cause them to drink || With tears a third time. ⁶You make us a strife to our neighbors, || And our enemies mock at it. ⁷God of Hosts, turn us back, || And cause Your face to shine, and we are saved. ⁸You bring a vine out of Egypt, || You cast out nations, and plant it. ⁹You have looked before it, and root it, || And it fills the land, ¹⁰Hills have been covered [with] its shadow, || And its boughs [are] cedars of God. ¹¹It sends forth its branches to the sea, || And its shoots to the river. ¹²Why have You broken down its hedges, || And everyone passing by the way has plucked it? ¹³A boar out of the forest tears it, || And a wild beast of the fields grazes it. ¹⁴God of Hosts, turn back, we implore You, || Look from the heavens, and see, and inspect this vine, ¹⁵And the root that Your right hand planted, || And the branch You made strong for Yourself, ¹⁶Burned with fire—cut down, || They perish from the rebuke of Your face. ¹⁷Let Your hand be on the man of Your right hand || On the son of man You have strengthened for Yourself. ¹⁸And we do not go back from You, || You revive us, and in Your Name we call. ¹⁹O YHWH, God of Hosts, turn us back, || Cause Your face to shine, and we are saved!

PSALM 81

¹To the Overseer. On the Gittith. By Asaph. Cry aloud to God our strength, || Shout to the God of Jacob. ²Lift up a song, and give out a timbrel, || A pleasant harp with stringed instrument. ³Blow a horn in the month, || In the new moon, at the day of our festival, ⁴For it [is] a statute to Israel, || An ordinance of the God of Jacob. ⁵He has placed it—a testimony on Joseph, || In his going forth over the land of Egypt. A lip, I have not known—I hear. ⁶I turned aside his shoulder from the burden, || His hands pass over from the basket. ⁷In distress you have called and I deliver you, || I answer you in the secret place of thunder, || I try you by the waters of Meribah. Selah. ⁸Hear, O My people, and I testify to you, || O Israel, if you listen to me: ⁹There is not in you a strange god, || And you do not bow yourself to a strange god. ¹⁰I [am] your God YHWH, || Who brings you up out of the land of Egypt. Enlarge your mouth, and I fill it. ¹¹But My people did not listen to My voice, || And Israel has not consented to Me. ¹²And I send them away in the enmity of their heart, || They walk in their own counsels. ¹³O that My people were listening to Me, || Israel would walk in My ways. ¹⁴As a little thing I cause their enemies to bow, || And I turn back My hand against their adversaries, ¹⁵Those hating YHWH should have feigned [obedience] to Him, || And their time would last for all time. ¹⁶He causes him to eat of the fat of wheat, || And I satisfy you [with] honey from a rock!

PSALM 82

¹A Psalm of Asaph. God has stood in the congregation of God, || He judges among the gods. ²Until when do you judge perversely? And lift up the face of the wicked? Selah. ³Judge the weak and fatherless, || Declare the afflicted and the poor righteous. ⁴Let the weak and needy escape, || Deliver them from the hand of the wicked. ⁵They did not know, nor do they understand, || They habitually walk in darkness, || All the foundations of earth are moved. ⁶I have said, "You [are] gods, || And sons of the Most High—all of you, ⁷But you die as man, and you fall as one of the heads." ⁸Rise, O God, judge the earth, || For You have inheritance among all the nations!

PSALM 83

¹A Song. A Psalm of Asaph. O God, let there be no silence to You, || Do not be silent, nor be quiet, O God. ²For behold, Your enemies roar, || And those hating You have lifted up the head, ³They take crafty counsel against Your people, || And consult against Your hidden ones. ⁴They have said, "Come, and we cut them off from [being] a nation, || And the name of Israel is not remembered anymore." ⁵For they consulted in heart together, || They make a covenant against You, ⁶Tents of Edom, and Ishmaelites, Moab, and the Hagarenes, ⁷Gebal, and Ammon, and Amalek, Philistia with inhabitants of Tyre, ⁸Asshur is also joined with them, || They have been an arm to sons of Lot. Selah. ⁹Do to them as Midian, || As Sisera, as Jabin, at the Brook of Kishon. ¹⁰They were destroyed at Endor, || They were dung for the ground! ¹¹Make their nobles as Oreb and as Zeeb, || And as Zebah and Zalmunna—all their princes, ¹²Who have said, "Let us occupy the pastures of God for ourselves." ¹³O my God, make them as a rolling thing, || As stubble before wind. ¹⁴As a fire burns a forest, || And as a flame sets hills on fire, ¹⁵So You pursue them with Your whirlwind, || And trouble them with Your windstorm. ¹⁶Fill their faces [with] shame, || And they seek Your Name, O YHWH. ¹⁷They are ashamed and troubled forever, || Indeed, they are confounded and lost. ¹⁸And they know that You—Your Name [is] YHWH—By Yourself [are] the Most High over all the earth!

PSALM 84

¹To the Overseer. On the Gittith. A Psalm of the sons of Korah. How beloved Your dwelling places, YHWH of Hosts! ²My soul desired, indeed, it has also been consumed, || For the courts of YHWH, || My heart and my flesh cry aloud to the living God, ³Even a sparrow has found a house, || And a swallow a nest for herself, || Where she has placed her brood—Your altars, O YHWH of Hosts, || My king and my God. ⁴O the blessedness of those inhabiting Your house, || Yet they praise You. Selah. ⁵O the blessedness of a man whose strength is in You, || Highways [are] in their heart. ⁶Those passing through a valley of weeping make it a spring, || The early rain covers it with pools. ⁷They go from strength to strength, || He appears to God in Zion. ⁸O

PSALMS

YHWH, God of Hosts, hear my prayer, || Give ear, O God of Jacob. Selah. ⁹Our shield, see, O God, || And behold the face of Your anointed, ¹⁰For a day in Your courts [is] good, O Teacher! I have chosen rather to be at the threshold, || In the house of my God, || Than to dwell in tents of wickedness. ¹¹For YHWH God [is] a sun and a shield, || YHWH gives grace and glory. He does not withhold good || To those walking in uprightness. ¹²YHWH of Hosts! O the blessedness of a man trusting in You.

PSALM 85

¹To the Overseer. A Psalm of the sons of Korah. You have accepted, O YHWH, Your land, || You have turned [to] the captivity of Jacob. ²You have carried away the iniquity of Your people, || You have covered all their sin. Selah. ³You have gathered up all Your wrath, || You have turned back from the fierceness of Your anger. ⁴Turn back [to] us, O God of our salvation, || And make void Your anger with us. ⁵Are You angry against us for all time? Do You draw out Your anger || To generation and generation? ⁶Do You not turn back? You revive us, || And Your people rejoice in You. ⁷Show us, O YHWH, your kindness, || And You give to us Your salvation. ⁸I hear what God, YHWH, speaks, || For He speaks peace to His people, || And to His saints, and they do not turn back to folly. ⁹Surely His salvation [is] near to those fearing Him, || That glory may dwell in our land. ¹⁰Kindness and truth have met, || Righteousness and peace have kissed, ¹¹Truth springs up from the earth, || And righteousness looks out from the heavens, ¹²YHWH also gives that which is good, || And our land gives its increase. ¹³Righteousness goes before Him, || And makes a way for His footsteps!

PSALM 86

¹A Prayer of David. Incline, O YHWH, Your ear, || Answer me, for I [am] poor and needy. ²Keep my soul, for I [am] pious, || Save Your servant who is trusting to You, O You, my God. ³Favor me, O Lord, for I call to You all the day. ⁴Make glad the soul of Your servant, || For to You, O Lord, I lift up my soul. ⁵For You, Lord, [are] good and forgiving, || And abundant in kindness to all calling You. ⁶Hear, O YHWH, my prayer, || And attend to the voice of my supplications. ⁷In a day of my distress I call You, || For You answer me. ⁸There is none like You among the gods, O Lord, || And like Your works there are none. ⁹All nations that You have made || Come and bow themselves before You, O Lord, || And give honor to Your Name. ¹⁰For You [are] great, and doing wonders, || You [are] God alone. ¹¹Show me, O YHWH, Your way, || I walk in Your truth, || My heart rejoices to fear Your Name. ¹²I confess You, O Lord my God, with all my heart, || And I honor Your Name for all time. ¹³For Your kindness [is] great toward me, || And You have delivered my soul from the lowest Sheol. ¹⁴O God, the proud have risen up against me, || And a company of the terrible sought my soul, || And have not placed You before them, ¹⁵And You, O Lord, [are] God, merciful and gracious, || Slow to anger, and abundant in kindness and truth. ¹⁶Look to me, and favor me, || Give Your strength to Your servant, || And give salvation to a son of Your handmaid. ¹⁷Do with me a sign for good, || And those hating me see and are ashamed, || For You, O YHWH, have helped me, || Indeed, You have comforted me!

PSALM 87

¹A Psalm of the sons of Korah. A Song. His foundation [is] in holy mountains. ²YHWH is loving the gates of Zion || Above all the dwelling places of Jacob. ³Honorable things are spoken in You, || O city of God. Selah. ⁴I mention Rahab and Babel to those knowing Me, || Behold, Philistia, and Tyre, with Cush! This [one] was born there. ⁵And of Zion it is said: Each one was born in her, || And He, the Most High, establishes her. ⁶YHWH recounts in the describing of the peoples, "This [one] was born there." Selah. ⁷Also singers as players on instruments, || All my fountains [are] in You!

PSALM 88

¹A Song. A Psalm of the sons of Korah. To the Overseer. [Set] on "Sickness to Afflict." An Instruction of Heman the Ezrahite. O YHWH, God of my salvation, || Daily I have cried, nightly before You, ²My prayer comes in before You, || Incline Your ear to my loud cry, ³For my soul has been full of evils, || And my life has come to Sheol. ⁴I have been reckoned with those going down [to] the pit, || I have been as a man without strength. ⁵Among the dead—free, || As pierced ones lying in the grave, || Whom You have not remembered anymore, || Indeed, they have been cut off by Your hand. ⁶You have put me in the lowest pit, || In dark places, in depths. ⁷Your fury has lain on me, || And You have afflicted [with] all Your breakers. Selah. ⁸You have put my acquaintance far from me, || You have made me an abomination to them, || Shut up—I do not go forth. ⁹My eye has grieved because of affliction, || I called You, O YHWH, all the day, || I have spread out my hands to You. ¹⁰Do You do wonders to the dead? Does Rephaim rise? Do they thank You? Selah. ¹¹Is Your kindness recounted in the grave? Your faithfulness in destruction? ¹²Are Your wonders known in the darkness? And Your righteousness in the land of forgetfulness? ¹³And I, to You, O YHWH, I have cried, || And in the morning my prayer comes before You. ¹⁴Why, O YHWH, do You cast off my soul? You hide Your face from me. ¹⁵I [am] afflicted, and expiring from youth, || I have borne Your terrors—I pine away. ¹⁶Your wrath has passed over me, || Your terrors have cut me off, ¹⁷They have surrounded me as waters all the day, || They have gone around against me together, ¹⁸You have put lover and friend far from me, || My acquaintance [is] the place of darkness!

PSALM 89

¹An Instruction of Ethan the Ezrahite. Of the kind acts of YHWH, I sing for all time, || From generation to generation I make known Your faithfulness with my mouth, ²For I said, "Kindness is built for all time, || The heavens! You establish Your faithfulness in them." ³I have made a covenant for My chosen, || I have sworn to My servant David: ⁴"Even for all time I establish your seed, || And have built your throne to generation and generation." Selah. ⁵And the heavens confess Your wonders, O YHWH, || Your faithfulness [is] also in an assembly of holy ones. ⁶For who in the sky, compares himself to YHWH? [Who] is like to YHWH among sons of the mighty? ⁷God is very terrible, || In the secret counsel of His holy ones, || And fearful over all surrounding Him. ⁸O YHWH, God of Hosts, || Who [is] like You—a strong YAH? And Your faithfulness [is] around You. ⁹You [are] ruler over the pride of the sea, || In the lifting up of its billows You restrain them. ¹⁰You have bruised Rahab, as one wounded. You have scattered Your enemies with the arm of Your strength. ¹¹The heavens [are] Yours, || The earth [is] also Yours, || The habitable world and its fullness, || You have founded them. ¹²North and south You have appointed them, || Tabor and Hermon sing in Your Name. ¹³You have an arm with might, || Strong is Your hand—high Your right hand. ¹⁴Righteousness and judgment || [Are] the fixed place of Your throne, || Kindness and truth go before Your face. ¹⁵O the blessedness of the people knowing the shout, || O YHWH, they habitually walk in the light of Your face. ¹⁶They rejoice in Your Name all the day, || And they are exalted in Your righteousness, ¹⁷For You [are] the beauty of their strength, || And in Your good will is our horn exalted, ¹⁸For our shield [is] of YHWH, || And our king to the Holy One of Israel. ¹⁹Then You have spoken in vision, || To Your saint, indeed, || You say, I have placed help on a mighty one, || Exalted a chosen one out of the people, ²⁰I have found My servant David, || With My holy oil I have anointed him. ²¹With whom My hand is established, || My arm also strengthens him. ²²An enemy does not exact on him, || And a son of perverseness does not afflict him. ²³And I have beaten down his adversaries before him, || And I plague those hating him, ²⁴And My faithfulness and kindness [are] with him, || And in My Name is his horn exalted. ²⁵And I have set his hand on the sea, || And his right hand on the rivers. ²⁶He proclaims to Me: "You [are] my Father, || My God, and the rock of my salvation." ²⁷I also appoint him firstborn, || Highest of the kings of the earth. ²⁸For all time I keep for him My kindness, || And My covenant [is] steadfast with him. ²⁹And I have set his seed forever, || And his throne as the days of the heavens. ³⁰If his sons forsake My law, || And do not walk in My judgments; ³¹If they defile My statutes, || And do not keep My commands, ³²I have looked after their transgression with a rod, || And their iniquity

with strokes, ³³And I do not break My kindness from him, || Nor do I deal falsely in My faithfulness. ³⁴I do not profane My covenant, || And I do not change that which is going forth from My lips. ³⁵Once I have sworn by My holiness, || I do not lie to David, ³⁶His seed is for all time, || And his throne [is] as the sun before Me, ³⁷It is established as the moon for all time, || And the witness in the sky is steadfast. Selah. ³⁸And You, You have cast off, and reject, || You have shown Yourself angry with Your anointed, ³⁹Have rejected the covenant of Your servant, || You have defiled his crown to the earth, ⁴⁰You have broken down all his hedges, || You have made his fortifications a ruin. ⁴¹Everyone passing by the way has spoiled him, || He has been a reproach to his neighbors, ⁴²You have exalted the right hand of his adversaries, || You have caused all his enemies to rejoice. ⁴³Also—You turn back the sharpness of his sword, || And have not established him in battle, ⁴⁴Have caused [him] to cease from his brightness, || And have cast down his throne to the earth. ⁴⁵You have shortened the days of his youth, || Have covered him over [with] shame. Selah. ⁴⁶Until when, O YHWH, are You hidden? Does Your fury burn as fire forever? ⁴⁷Remember how [short] my lifetime [is]. Why have You created in vain || All the sons of men? ⁴⁸Who [is] the man that lives, and does not see death? He delivers his soul from the hand of Sheol. Selah. ⁴⁹Where [are] Your former kindnesses, O Lord, || [Which] You have sworn to David in Your faithfulness? ⁵⁰Remember, O Lord, the reproach of Your servants, || I have borne in my bosom all the strivings of the peoples, ⁵¹With which Your enemies reproached, O YHWH, || With which they have reproached || The steps of Your anointed. ⁵²Blessed [is] YHWH for all time. Amen and amen!

PSALM 90

¹A PRAYER OF MOSES, THE MAN OF GOD. Lord, You have been a habitation, || To us—in generation and generation, ²Before mountains were brought forth, || And You form the earth and the world, || Even from age to age You [are] God. ³You turn man to a bruised thing, || And say, Return, you sons of men. ⁴For one thousand years in Your eyes [are] as yesterday, || For it passes on, indeed, [as] a watch by night. ⁵You have inundated them, they are asleep, || In the morning he changes as grass. ⁶In the morning it flourishes, and has changed, || At evening it is cut down, and has withered. ⁷For we were consumed in Your anger, || And we have been troubled in Your fury. ⁸You have set our iniquities before You, || Our hidden things at the light of Your face, ⁹For all our days pined away in Your wrath, || We consumed our years as a meditation. ¹⁰The days of our years, in them [are] seventy years, || And if, by reason of might, eighty years, || Yet their enlargement [is] labor and vanity, || For it has been cut off quickly, and we fly away. ¹¹Who knows the power of Your anger? And according to Your fear—Your wrath? ¹²Let [us] know to number our days correctly, || And we bring the heart to wisdom. ¹³Turn back, O YHWH, until when? And regret concerning Your servants. ¹⁴Satisfy us at morning [with] Your kindness, || And we sing and rejoice all our days. ¹⁵Cause us to rejoice according to the days || Wherein You have afflicted us, || The years we have seen evil. ¹⁶Let Your work appear to Your servants, || And Your honor on their sons. ¹⁷And let the pleasantness of our God YHWH be on us, || And establish on us the work of our hands, || Indeed, establish the work of our hands!

PSALM 91

¹He who is dwelling || In the secret place of the Most High, || Habitually lodges in the shade of the Mighty, ²He is saying of YHWH, "My refuge, and my bulwark, my God, I trust in Him," ³For He delivers you from the snare of a fowler, || From a calamitous pestilence. ⁴He covers you over with His pinion, || And under His wings you trust, || His truth [is] a shield and buckler. ⁵You are not afraid of fear by night, || Of arrow that flies by day, ⁶Of pestilence that walks in thick darkness, || Of destruction that destroys at noon, ⁷One thousand fall at your side, || And a myriad at your right hand, || [But] it does not come near to you. ⁸But with your eyes you look, || And you see the reward of the wicked, ⁹(For You, O YHWH, [are] my refuge), || You made the Most High your habitation. ¹⁰Evil does not happen to you, || And a plague does not come near your tent, ¹¹For He charges His messengers for you, || To keep you in all your ways, ¹²On the hands they bear you up, || Lest you strike your foot against a stone. ¹³You tread on lion and cobra, || You trample young lion and dragon. ¹⁴Because he has delighted in Me, || I also deliver him—I set him on high, || Because he has known My Name. ¹⁵He calls Me, and I answer him, || I [am] with him in distress, || I deliver him, and honor him. ¹⁶I satisfy him with [the] length of [his] days, || And I cause him to look on My salvation!

PSALM 92

¹A PSALM. A SONG FOR THE SABBATH DAY. [It is] good to give thanks to YHWH, || And to sing praises to Your Name, O Most High, ²To declare Your kindness in the morning, || And Your faithfulness in the nights. ³On ten strings and on stringed instrument, || On higgaion, with harp. ⁴For You have caused me to rejoice, O YHWH, in Your work, || I sing concerning the works of Your hands. ⁵How great Your works have been, O YHWH, || Your thoughts have been very deep. ⁶A brutish man does not know, || And a fool does not understand this— ⁷When the wicked flourish as an herb, || And all workers of iniquity blossom—For their being destroyed forever and ever! ⁸And You [are] high for all time, O YHWH. ⁹For behold, Your enemies, O YHWH, || For behold, Your enemies perish, || All workers of iniquity separate themselves. ¹⁰And You exalt my horn as a wild ox, || I have been anointed with fresh oil. ¹¹And my eye looks on my enemies, || Of those rising up against me, || The evildoers, my ears hear. ¹²The righteous flourish as a palm-tree, || He grows as a cedar in Lebanon. ¹³Those planted in the house of YHWH, || In the courts of our God, flourish. ¹⁴Still they bring forth in old age, || They are fat and flourishing, ¹⁵To declare that YHWH my Rock [is] upright, || And there is no perverseness in Him!

PSALM 93

¹YHWH has reigned, || He has put on excellence, || YHWH put on strength, He girded Himself, || Also—the world is established, unmoved. ²Your throne is established since then, || You [are] from the age. ³Floods have lifted up, O YHWH, || Floods have lifted up their voice, || Floods lift up their breakers. ⁴Mightier than the voices of many mighty waters, breakers of a sea, || [Is] YHWH on high, ⁵Your testimonies have been very steadfast, || Holiness befits Your house, O YHWH, for [the] length of [Your] days!

PSALM 94

¹God of vengeance—YHWH! God of vengeance, shine forth. ²Be lifted up, judging the earth, || Send back a repayment on the proud. ³Until when do the wicked, O YHWH—Until when do the wicked exult? ⁴They utter—they speak arrogance, || All working iniquity boast [about] themselves. ⁵Your people, O YHWH, they bruise, || And they afflict Your inheritance. ⁶They slay widow and sojourner, || And they murder fatherless ones. ⁷And they say, "YAH does not see, || And the God of Jacob does not consider." ⁸Consider, you brutish among the people, || And you foolish, when do you act wisely? ⁹He who plants the ear, does He not hear? He who forms the eye, does He not see? ¹⁰He who is instructing nations, does He not reprove? He who is teaching man knowledge [is] YHWH. ¹¹He knows the thoughts of man, that they [are] vanity. ¹²O the blessedness of the man || Whom You instruct, O YAH, || And teach him out of Your law, ¹³To give rest to him from days of evil, || While a pit is dug for the wicked. ¹⁴For YHWH does not leave His people, || And does not forsake His inheritance. ¹⁵For judgment turns back to righteousness, || And after it all the upright of heart. ¹⁶Who rises up for me with evildoers? Who stations himself for me with workers of iniquity? ¹⁷Unless YHWH [were] a help to me, || My soul had almost inhabited silence. ¹⁸If I have said, "My foot has slipped," || Your kindness, O YHWH, supports me. ¹⁹In the abundance of my thoughts within me, || Your comforts delight my soul. ²⁰Is a throne of mischief joined [with] You? A framer of perverseness by statute? ²¹They decree against the soul of the righteous, || And declare innocent blood wicked. ²²And YHWH is for a high place to me, || And my God [is] for a rock—my refuge, ²³And He turns back their iniquity on them, || And in their wickedness cuts them off; Our God YHWH cuts them off!

PSALM 95

¹Come, we sing to Yhwh, || We shout to the rock of our salvation. ²We come before His face with thanksgiving, || We shout to Him with psalms. ³For Yhwh [is] a great God, || And a great King over all gods. ⁴In whose hand [are] the deep places of earth, || And the strong places of hills [are] His. ⁵Whose is the sea, and He made it, || And His hands formed the dry land. ⁶Come in, we bow ourselves, and we bend, || We kneel before Yhwh our Maker. ⁷For He [is] our God, and we the people of His pasture, || And the flock of His hand, || Today, if you listen to His voice, ⁸Do not harden your heart as [in] Meribah, || As [in] the day of Massah in the wilderness, ⁹Where your fathers have tried Me, || Have proved Me, indeed, have seen My work. ¹⁰Forty years I am weary of the generation, || And I say, "A people erring in heart—they! And they have not known My ways": ¹¹Where I swore in My anger, "If they come into My rest—!"

PSALM 96

¹Sing to Yhwh a new song, || Sing to Yhwh all the earth. ²Sing to Yhwh, bless His Name, || Proclaim His salvation from day to day. ³Declare His glory among nations, || His wonders among all the peoples. ⁴For Yhwh [is] great, and greatly praised, || He [is] fearful over all gods. ⁵For all the gods of the peoples [are] nothing, || And Yhwh made the heavens. ⁶Splendor and majesty [are] before Him, || Strength and beauty in His sanctuary. ⁷Ascribe to Yhwh, O families of the peoples, || Ascribe to Yhwh glory and strength. ⁸Ascribe to Yhwh the glory of His Name, || Lift up a present and come into His courts. ⁹Bow yourselves to Yhwh, || In the honor of holiness, || Be afraid of His presence, all the earth. ¹⁰Say among nations, "Yhwh has reigned, || Also—the world is established, unmoved, || He judges the peoples in uprightness." ¹¹The heavens rejoice, and the earth is joyful, || The sea and its fullness roar. ¹²The field exults, and all that [is] in it, || Then all trees of the forest sing, ¹³Before Yhwh, for He has come, || For He has come to judge the earth. He judges the world in righteousness, || And the peoples in His faithfulness!

PSALM 97

¹Yhwh has reigned, || The earth is joyful, many islands rejoice. ²Cloud and darkness [are] around Him, || Righteousness and judgment the basis of His throne. ³Fire goes before Him, || And burns around His adversaries. ⁴His lightnings have lightened the world, || The earth has seen, and is pained. ⁵Hills, like wax, melted before Yhwh, || Before the Lord of all the earth. ⁶The heavens declared His righteousness, || And all the peoples have seen His glory. ⁷All servants of a carved image are ashamed, || Those boasting themselves in idols, || Bow yourselves to Him, all you gods. ⁸Zion has heard and rejoices, || And daughters of Judah are joyful, || Because of Your judgments, O Yhwh. ⁹For You, Yhwh, [are] Most High over all the earth, || You have been exalted greatly over all gods. ¹⁰You who love Yhwh, hate evil, || He is keeping the souls of His saints, || He delivers them from the hand of the wicked. ¹¹Light [is] sown for the righteous, || And joy for the upright of heart. ¹²Rejoice, you righteous, in Yhwh, || And give thanks at the remembrance of His holiness!

PSALM 98

¹A Psalm. Sing to Yhwh a new song, || For He has done wonders, || His right hand and His holy arm have given salvation to Him. ²Yhwh has made His salvation known, || Before the eyes of the nations, || He has revealed His righteousness, ³He has remembered His kindness, || And His faithfulness to the house of Israel, || All the ends of the earth have seen the salvation of our God. ⁴Shout to Yhwh, all the earth, || Break forth, and cry aloud, and sing. ⁵Sing to Yhwh with harp, || With harp, and voice of praise, ⁶With trumpets, and voice of a horn, shout before the King, Yhwh. ⁷The sea and its fullness roar, || The world and the inhabitants in it. ⁸Floods clap hand, together hills cry aloud, ⁹Before Yhwh, || For He has come to judge the earth, || He judges the world in righteousness, || And the people in uprightness!

PSALM 99

¹Yhwh has reigned, peoples tremble, || The Inhabitant of the cherubim, the earth shakes. ²Yhwh [is] great in Zion, || And He [is] high over all the peoples. ³They praise Your Name, "Great, and fearful, [it] is holy!" ⁴And the strength of the king || Has loved judgment, || You have established uprightness; Judgment and righteousness in Jacob, || You have done. ⁵Exalt our God Yhwh, || And bow yourselves at His footstool, He [is] holy. ⁶Moses and Aaron among His priests, || And Samuel among those proclaiming His Name. They are calling to Yhwh, || And He answers them. ⁷He speaks to them in a pillar of cloud, || They have kept His testimonies, || And He has given the statute to them. ⁸O Yhwh, our God, || You have afflicted them, || You have been a forgiving God to them, || And taking vengeance on their actions. ⁹Exalt our God Yhwh, || And bow yourselves at His holy hill, || For our God Yhwh [is] holy!

PSALM 100

¹A Psalm of thanksgiving. Shout to Yhwh, all the earth! ²Serve Yhwh with joy, come before Him with singing. ³Know that Yhwh [is] God, || He made us, and we are His, || His people—and the flock of His pasture. ⁴Enter His gates with thanksgiving, || His courts with praise, || Give thanks to Him, bless His Name. ⁵For Yhwh [is] good, || His kindness [is] for all time, || And His faithfulness to generation and generation!

PSALM 101

¹A Psalm of David. I sing kindness and judgment, || To You, O Yhwh, I sing praise. ²I act wisely in a perfect way, || When do You come to me? I habitually walk in the integrity of my heart, || In the midst of my house. ³I do not set a worthless thing before my eyes, || I have hated the work of those turning aside, || It does not adhere to me. ⁴A perverse heart turns aside from me, || I do not know wickedness. ⁵Whoever slanders his neighbor in secret, || Him I cut off, || The high of eyes and proud of heart, || Him I do not endure. ⁶My eyes are on the faithful of the land, || To dwell with me, || Whoever is walking in a perfect way, he serves me. ⁷He who is working deceit does not dwell in my house, || Whoever is speaking lies is not established before my eyes. ⁸At morning I cut off all the wicked of the land, || To cut off from the city of Yhwh || All the workers of iniquity!

PSALM 102

¹A Prayer of the afflicted when he is feeble, and pours out his complaint before Yhwh. O Yhwh, hear my prayer, indeed, my cry comes to You. ²Do not hide Your face from me, || In a day of my adversity, || Incline Your ear to me, || In the day I call, hurry, answer me. ³For my days have been consumed in smoke, || And my bones have burned as a firebrand. ⁴Struck as the herb, and withered, is my heart, || For I have forgotten to eat my bread. ⁵From the voice of my sighing || My bone has cleaved to my flesh. ⁶I have been like to a pelican of the wilderness, || I have been as an owl of the dry places. ⁷I have watched, and I am || As a bird alone on the roof. ⁸All the day my enemies reproached me, || Those mad at me have sworn against me. ⁹Because I have eaten ashes as bread, || And have mingled my drink with weeping, ¹⁰From Your indignation and Your wrath, || For You have lifted me up, || And cast me down. ¹¹My days [are] stretched out as a shadow, || And I am withered as the herb. ¹²And You, O Yhwh, abide for all time, || And Your memorial from generation to generation. ¹³You rise—You pity Zion, || For the time to favor her, || For the appointed time has come. ¹⁴For Your servants have been pleased with her stones, || And they favor her dust. ¹⁵And nations fear the Name of Yhwh, || And all kings of the earth Your glory, ¹⁶For Yhwh has built Zion, || He has been seen in His glory, ¹⁷He turned to the prayer of the destitute, || And He has not despised their prayer. ¹⁸This is written for a later generation, || And the people created praise Yah. ¹⁹For He

has looked || From the high place of His sanctuary. YHWH looked attentively from the heavens to earth, ²⁰To hear the groan of the prisoner, || To loose sons of death, ²¹To declare in Zion the Name of YHWH, || And His praise in Jerusalem, ²²In the peoples being gathered together, || And the kingdoms—to serve YHWH. ²³He has humbled my power in the way, || He has shortened my days. ²⁴I say, "My God, do not take me up in the midst of my days," || Your years [are] through all generations. ²⁵You founded the earth before time, || And the heavens [are] the work of Your hands. ²⁶They perish, and You remain, || And all of them become old as a garment, || You change them as clothing, || And they are changed. ²⁷And You [are] the same, and Your years are not finished. ²⁸The sons of Your servants continue, || And their seed is established before You!

PSALM 103

¹BY DAVID. Bless, O my soul, YHWH, || And all my inward parts—His Holy Name. ²Bless, O my soul, YHWH, || And do not forget all His benefits, ³Who is forgiving all your iniquities, || Who is healing all your diseases, ⁴Who is redeeming your life from destruction, || Who is crowning you [with] kindness and mercies, ⁵Who is satisfying your desire with good, || Your youth renews itself as an eagle. ⁶YHWH is doing righteousness and judgments || For all the oppressed. ⁷He makes His ways known to Moses, || His acts to the sons of Israel. ⁸YHWH [is] merciful and gracious, || Slow to anger, and abundant in mercy. ⁹He does not strive forever, || Nor does He watch for all time. ¹⁰He has not done to us according to our sins, || Nor according to our iniquities || Has He conferred benefits on us. ¹¹For as the height of the heavens [is] above the earth, || His kindness has been mighty over those fearing Him. ¹²He has put our transgressions far from us—as the distance of east from west. ¹³As a father has mercy on sons, || YHWH has mercy on those fearing Him. ¹⁴For He has known our frame, || Remembering that we [are] dust. ¹⁵Mortal man! His days [are] as grass, || He flourishes as a flower of the field; ¹⁶For a wind has passed over it, and it is not, || And its place does not discern it anymore. ¹⁷And the kindness of YHWH || [Is] from age even to age on those fearing Him, || And His righteousness to sons' sons, ¹⁸To those keeping His covenant, || And to those remembering His precepts to do them. ¹⁹YHWH has established His throne in the heavens, || And His kingdom has ruled over all. ²⁰Bless YHWH, you His messengers, || Mighty in power—doing His word, || To listen to the voice of His word. ²¹Bless YHWH, all you His hosts, || His ministers—doing His pleasure. ²²Bless YHWH, all you His works, || In all places of His dominion. Bless, O my soul, YHWH!

PSALM 104

¹Bless, O my soul, YHWH! YHWH, my God, || You have been very great, || You have put on splendor and majesty. ²Covering Himself [with] light as a garment, || Stretching out the heavens as a curtain, ³Who is laying the beam of His upper chambers in the waters, || Who is making thick clouds His chariot, || Who is walking on wings of wind, ⁴Making His messengers—the winds, || His ministers— the flaming fire. ⁵He has founded earth on its bases, || It is not moved for all time and forever. ⁶The abyss! You have covered it as with clothing, || Waters stand above hills. ⁷They flee from Your rebuke, || They hurry away from the voice of Your thunder. ⁸They go up hills—they go down valleys, || To a place You have founded for them. ⁹You have set a border, they do not pass over, || They do not turn back to cover the earth. ¹⁰He is sending forth fountains in valleys, || They go on between hills. ¹¹They water every beast of the field, || Wild donkeys break their thirst. ¹²The bird of the heavens dwells by them, || From between the branches || They give forth the voice. ¹³Watering hills from His upper chambers, || The earth is satisfied from the fruit of Your works. ¹⁴Causing grass to spring up for livestock, || And herb for the service of man, || To bring forth bread from the earth, ¹⁵And wine—it makes the heart of man glad, || To cause the face to shine from oil, || And bread—it supports the heart of man. ¹⁶The trees of YHWH [are] satisfied, || Cedars of Lebanon that He has planted, ¹⁷Where birds make nests, || The stork—the firs [are] her house. ¹⁸The high hills [are] for wild goats, rocks [are] a refuge for hyraxes, ¹⁹He made the moon for seasons, || The sun has known his place of entrance. ²⁰You set darkness, and it is night, || Every beast of the forest creeps in it. ²¹The young lions are roaring for prey, || And to seek their food from God. ²²The sun rises, they are gathered, || And they crouch in their dens. ²³Man goes forth to his work, || And to his service—until evening. ²⁴How many have been Your works, O YHWH, || You have made all of them in wisdom, || The earth is full of your possessions. ²⁵This, the sea, great and broad of sides, || There [are] moving things— innumerable, || Living creatures—small with great. ²⁶There ships go—[and] leviathan, || That You have formed to play in it. ²⁷All of them look to You, || To give their food in its season. ²⁸You give to them—they gather, || You open Your hand—they [are] satisfied [with] good. ²⁹You hide Your face—they are troubled, || You gather their spirit—they expire, || And they return to their dust. ³⁰You send out Your Spirit, they are created, || And You renew the face of the ground. ³¹The glory of YHWH is for all time, || YHWH rejoices in His works, ³²Who is looking to earth, and it trembles, || He comes against hills, and they smoke. ³³I sing to YHWH during my life, || I sing praise to my God while I exist. ³⁴My meditation on Him is sweet, || I rejoice in YHWH. ³⁵Sinners are consumed from the earth, || And the wicked are no more. Bless, O my soul, YHWH. Praise YAH!

PSALM 105

¹Give thanks to YHWH—call on His Name, || Make His acts known among the peoples. ²Sing to Him—sing praise to Him, || Meditate on all His wonders. ³Boast yourselves in His Holy Name, || The heart of those seeking YHWH rejoices. ⁴Seek YHWH and His strength, || Seek His face continually. ⁵Remember His wonders that He did, || His signs and the judgments of His mouth. ⁶O seed of Abraham, His servant, || O sons of Jacob, His chosen ones. ⁷He [is] our God YHWH, || His judgments [are] in all the earth. ⁸He has remembered His covenant for all time, || The word He commanded to one thousand generations, ⁹That He has made with Abraham, || And His oath to Isaac, ¹⁰And establishes it to Jacob for a statute, || To Israel—a perpetual covenant, ¹¹Saying, "I give the land of Canaan to you, || The portion of your inheritance," ¹²In their being few in number, || But a few, and sojourners in it. ¹³And they go up and down, from nation to nation, || From a kingdom to another people. ¹⁴He has not permitted any to oppress them || And He reproves kings for their sakes. ¹⁵"Do not strike against My anointed, || And do no evil to My prophets." ¹⁶And He calls a famine on the land, || He has broken the whole staff of bread. ¹⁷He has sent a man before them, || Joseph has been sold for a servant. ¹⁸They have afflicted his feet with chains, || Iron has entered his soul, ¹⁹Until the time of the coming of His word || The saying of YHWH has tried him. ²⁰The king has sent, and looses him, || The ruler of the peoples, and draws him out. ²¹He has made him lord of his house, || And ruler over all his possessions. ²²To bind his chiefs at his pleasure, || And he makes his elderly wise. ²³And Israel comes into Egypt, || And Jacob has sojourned in the land of Ham. ²⁴And He makes His people very fruitful, || And makes it mightier than its adversaries. ²⁵He turned their heart to hate His people, || To conspire against His servants. ²⁶He has sent His servant Moses, || Aaron whom He had fixed on. ²⁷They have set among them the matters of His signs, || And wonders in the land of Ham. ²⁸He has sent darkness, and it is dark, || And they have not provoked His word. ²⁹He has turned their waters to blood, || And puts their fish to death. ³⁰Their land has teemed [with] frogs, || In the inner chambers of their kings. ³¹He has commanded, and the beetle comes, || Lice into all their border. ³²He has made their showers hail, || A flaming fire [is] in their land. ³³And He strikes their vine and their fig, || And shatters the trees of their border. ³⁴He has commanded, and the locust comes, || And the cankerworm— innumerable, ³⁵And it consumes every herb in their land, || And it consumes the fruit of their ground. ³⁶And He strikes every firstborn in their land, || The first-fruit of all their strength, ³⁷And brings them out with silver and gold, || And there is not a feeble one in its tribes. ³⁸Egypt has rejoiced in their going forth, || For their fear had fallen on them. ³⁹He has spread a cloud for a covering, || And fire to enlighten the night. ⁴⁰They have asked, and He brings quails, || And satisfies them [with] bread of the heavens. ⁴¹He has opened a rock, and waters flow, || They have gone on in dry places—a river. ⁴²For He has remembered His holy word, || With His servant Abraham, ⁴³And He brings forth His people with joy, || His chosen

ones with singing. ⁴⁴And He gives to them the lands of nations, || And they possess the labor of peoples, ⁴⁵That they may observe His statutes, || And may keep His laws. Praise YAH!

PSALM 106

¹Praise YAH, give thanks to YHWH, for [He is] good, for His kindness [is] for all time! ²Who utters the mighty acts of YHWH? Sounds all His praise? ³O the blessedness of those keeping judgment, || Doing righteousness at all times. ⁴Remember me, O YHWH, || With the favor of Your people, || Look after me in Your salvation. ⁵To look on the good of Your chosen ones, || To rejoice in the joy of Your nation, || To boast myself with Your inheritance. ⁶We have sinned with our fathers, || We have done perversely, we have done wickedly. ⁷Our fathers in Egypt, || Have not considered wisely Your wonders, || They have not remembered || The abundance of Your kind acts, || And provoke by the sea, at the Sea of Suph. ⁸And He saves them for His Name's sake, || To make His might known, ⁹And rebukes the Sea of Suph, and it is dried up, || And causes them to go || Through depths as a wilderness. ¹⁰And He saves them from the hand || Of him who is hating, || And redeems them from the hand of the enemy. ¹¹And waters cover their adversaries, || One of them has not been left. ¹²And they believe in His words, they sing His praise, ¹³They have hurried—forgotten His works, || They have not waited for His counsel. ¹⁴And they lust greatly in a wilderness, || And try God in a desert. ¹⁵And He gives to them their request, || And sends leanness into their soul. ¹⁶And they are envious of Moses in the camp, || Of Aaron, YHWH's holy one. ¹⁷Earth opens, and swallows up Dathan, || And covers over the company of Abiram. ¹⁸And fire burns among their company, || A flame sets the wicked on fire. ¹⁹They make a calf in Horeb, || And bow themselves to a molten image, ²⁰And change their glory || Into the form of an ox eating herbs. ²¹They have forgotten God their Savior, || The doer of great things in Egypt, ²²Of wonderful things in the land of Ham, || Of fearful things by the Sea of Suph. ²³And He commands to destroy them, || Unless Moses, His chosen one, || Had stood in the breach before Him, || To turn back His wrath from destroying. ²⁴And they kick against the desirable land, || They have not given credence to His word. ²⁵And they murmur in their tents, || They have not listened to the voice of YHWH. ²⁶And He lifts up His hand to them, || To cause them to fall in a wilderness, ²⁷And to cause their seed to fall among nations, || And to scatter them through lands. ²⁸And they are coupled to Ba'al-Peor, || And eat the sacrifices of the dead, ²⁹And they provoke to anger by their actions, || And a plague breaks forth on them, ³⁰And Phinehas stands, and executes judgment, || And the plague is restrained, ³¹And it is reckoned to him for righteousness, || From generation to generation—for all time. ³²And they cause wrath by the waters of Meribah, || And it is evil to Moses for their sakes, ³³For they have provoked his spirit, || And he speaks wrongfully with his lips. ³⁴They have not destroyed the peoples, || As YHWH had commanded to them, ³⁵And mix themselves among nations, and learn their works, ³⁶And serve their idols, || And they are for a snare to them. ³⁷And they sacrifice their sons and their daughters to the demons, ³⁸And they shed innocent blood—Blood of their sons and of their daughters, || Whom they have sacrificed to idols of Canaan, || And the land is profaned with blood. ³⁹And they are defiled with their works, || And commit whoredom in their habitual doings. ⁴⁰And the anger of YHWH || Is kindled against His people, || And He detests His inheritance. ⁴¹And gives them into the hand of nations, || And those hating them rule over them, ⁴²And their enemies oppress them, || And they are humbled under their hand. ⁴³He delivers them many times, || And they rebel in their counsel, || And they are brought low in their iniquity. ⁴⁴And He looks on their distress || When He hears their cry, ⁴⁵And remembers His covenant for them, || And is comforted, || According to the abundance of His kindness. ⁴⁶And He appoints them for mercies || Before all their captors. ⁴⁷Save us, O our God YHWH, and gather us from the nations, || To give thanks to Your Holy Name, || To glory in Your praise. ⁴⁸Blessed [is] YHWH, God of Israel, || From age until age. And all the people said, "Amen, praise YAH!"

PSALM 107

¹"Give thanks to YHWH, || For [He is] good, for His kindness [is] for all time": ²Let the redeemed of YHWH say [so], || Whom He redeemed from the hand of an adversary. ³And has gathered them from the lands, || From east and from west, || From north, and from the sea. ⁴They wandered in a wilderness, in a desert by the way, || They have not found a city of habitation. ⁵Hungry—indeed—thirsty, || Their soul becomes feeble in them, ⁶And they cry to YHWH in their adversity, || He delivers them from their distress, ⁷And causes them to tread in a right way, || To go to a city of habitation. ⁸They confess to YHWH His kindness, || And His wonders to the sons of men. ⁹For He has satisfied a longing soul, || And has filled a hungry soul [with] goodness. ¹⁰Inhabitants of dark places and death-shade, || Prisoners of affliction and of iron, ¹¹Because they changed the saying of God, || And despised the counsel of the Most High. ¹²And He humbles their heart with labor, || They have been feeble, and there is no helper. ¹³And they cry to YHWH in their adversity, || He saves them from their distresses. ¹⁴He brings them out from the dark place, || and death-shade, || And He draws away their bands. ¹⁵They confess to YHWH His kindness, || And His wonders to the sons of men. ¹⁶For He has broken doors of bronze, || And He has cut bars of iron. ¹⁷Fools, by means of their transgression, || And by their iniquities, afflict themselves. ¹⁸Their soul detests all food, || And they come near to the gates of death, ¹⁹And cry to YHWH in their adversity, || He saves them from their distresses, ²⁰He sends His word and heals them, || And delivers [them] from their destructions. ²¹They confess to YHWH His kindness, || And His wonders to the sons of men, ²²And they sacrifice sacrifices of thanksgiving, || And recount His works with singing. ²³Those going down [to] the sea in ships, || Doing business in many waters, ²⁴They have seen the works of YHWH, || And His wonders in the deep. ²⁵And He commands, and appoints a storm, || And it lifts up its billows, ²⁶They go up [to] the heavens, they go down [to] the depths, || Their soul is melted in evil. ²⁷They reel to and fro, and move as a drunkard, || And all their wisdom is swallowed up. ²⁸And they cry to YHWH in their adversity, || And He brings them out from their distresses. ²⁹He calms a whirlwind, || And their billows are hushed. ³⁰And they rejoice because they are quiet, || And He leads them to the haven of their desire. ³¹They confess to YHWH His kindness, || And His wonders to the sons of men, ³²And they exalt Him in [the] assembly of [the] people, || And praise Him in [the] seat of [the] elderly. ³³He makes rivers become a wilderness, || And fountains of waters become dry land. ³⁴A fruitful land becomes a barren place, || For the wickedness of its inhabitants. ³⁵He makes a wilderness become a pool of water, || And a dry land become fountains of waters. ³⁶And He causes the hungry to dwell there, || And they prepare a city of habitation. ³⁷And they sow fields, and plant vineyards, || And they make fruits of increase. ³⁸And He blesses them, and they multiply exceedingly, || And He does not diminish their livestock. ³⁹And they are diminished, and bow down, || By restraint, evil, and sorrow. ⁴⁰He is pouring contempt on nobles, || And causes them to wander in vacancy—no way. ⁴¹And sets the needy on high from affliction, || And places families as a flock. ⁴²The upright see and rejoice, || And all perversity has shut her mouth. ⁴³Who [is] wise, and observes these? They understand the kind acts of YHWH!

PSALM 108

¹A SONG. A PSALM OF DAVID. My heart is prepared, O God, || I sing, indeed, I sing praise, also my glory. ²Awake, stringed instrument and harp, || I awake the dawn. ³I thank You among peoples, O YHWH, || And I praise You among the nations. ⁴For Your kindness [is] great above the heavens, || And Your truth to the clouds. ⁵Be exalted above the heavens, O God, || And Your glory above all the earth. ⁶That Your beloved ones may be delivered, || Save [with] Your right hand, and answer us. ⁷God has spoken in His holiness: I exult, I apportion Shechem, || And I measure the Valley of Succoth, ⁸Gilead [is] Mine, Manasseh [is] Mine, || And Ephraim [is] the strength of My head, || Judah [is] My lawgiver, ⁹Moab [is] a pot for My washing, || On Edom I cast My shoe, || Over Philistia I habitually shout. ¹⁰Who brings me [into] the fortified city? Who has led me to Edom? ¹¹Have You not, O God, cast us off? And You do not go out, O God, with our hosts! ¹²Give to us help from adversity, || And the salvation of man is vain. ¹³We do mightily

PSALMS

in God, || And He treads down our adversaries!

PSALM 109

¹To the Overseer. A Psalm of David. O God of my praise, do not be silent, ²For the mouth of wickedness, and the mouth of deceit, || They have opened against me, || They have spoken with me—A tongue of falsehood, and words of hatred! ³They have surrounded me about, || And they fight me without cause. ⁴For my love they oppose me, and I—prayer! ⁵And they set against me evil for good, || And hatred for my love. ⁶Appoint the wicked over him, || And an adversary stands at his right hand. ⁷In his being judged, he goes forth wicked, || And his prayer is for sin. ⁸His days are few, another takes his oversight, ⁹His sons are fatherless, and his wife a widow. ¹⁰And his sons wander continually, || Indeed, they have begged, || And have sought out of their dry places. ¹¹An exactor lays a snare for all that he has, || And strangers spoil his labor. ¹²He has none to extend kindness, || Nor is there one showing favor to his orphans. ¹³His posterity is for cutting off, || Their name is blotted out in another generation. ¹⁴The iniquity of his fathers || Is remembered to YHWH, || And the sin of his mother is not blotted out. ¹⁵They are continually before YHWH, || And He cuts off their memorial from earth. ¹⁶Because that he has not remembered to do kindness, || And pursues the poor man and needy, || And the struck of heart—to slay, ¹⁷And he loves reviling, and it meets him, || And he has not delighted in blessing, || And it is far from him. ¹⁸And he puts on reviling as his robe, || And it comes in as water into his midst, || And as oil into his bones. ¹⁹It is to him as apparel—he covers himself, || And he girds it on for a continual girdle. ²⁰This [is] the wage of my accusers from YHWH, || And of those speaking evil against my soul. ²¹And You, O Lord YHWH, || Deal with me for Your Name's sake, || Because Your kindness [is] good, deliver me. ²²For I [am] poor and needy, || And my heart has been pierced in my midst. ²³I have gone as a shadow when it is stretched out, || I have been driven away as a locust. ²⁴My knees have been feeble from fasting, || And my flesh has failed of fatness. ²⁵And I have been a reproach to them, || They see me, they shake their head. ²⁶Help me, O YHWH my God, || Save me, according to Your kindness. ²⁷And they know that this [is] Your hand, || You, O YHWH, You have done it. ²⁸They revile, and You bless, || They have risen, and are ashamed, || And Your servant rejoices. ²⁹My accusers put on blushing, and are covered, || Their shame [is] as an upper robe. ³⁰I thank YHWH greatly with my mouth, || And I praise Him in the midst of many, ³¹For He stands at the right hand of the needy, || To save from those judging his soul.

PSALM 110

¹A Psalm of David. A declaration of YHWH to my Lord: "Sit at My right hand, || Until I make Your enemies Your footstool." ²YHWH sends the rod of Your strength from Zion, || Rule in the midst of Your enemies. ³Your people [are] free-will gifts in the day of Your strength, in the honors of holiness, || From the womb, from the morning, || You have the dew of Your youth. ⁴YHWH has sworn, and does not relent, "You [are] a priest for all time, || According to the order of Melchizedek." ⁵The Lord on Your right hand struck kings || In the day of His anger. ⁶He judges among the nations, || He has completed the carcasses, || Has struck the head over the mighty earth. ⁷He drinks from a brook in the way, || Therefore He lifts up the head!

PSALM 111

¹Praise YAH! [Aleph-Bet] I thank YHWH with the whole heart, || In the secret meeting of the upright, || And of the congregation. ²Great [are] the works of YHWH, || Sought out by all desiring them. ³Splendid and majestic is His work, || And His righteousness is standing forever. ⁴He has made a memorial of His wonders, || YHWH [is] gracious and merciful. ⁵He has given prey to those fearing Him, || He remembers His covenant for all time. ⁶He has declared the power of His works to His people, || To give to them the inheritance of nations. ⁷The works of His hands [are] true and just, || All His appointments [are] steadfast. ⁸They are sustained forever and for all time. They are made in truth and uprightness. ⁹He has sent redemption to His people, || He has appointed His covenant for all time, || His Name [is] holy and fearful. ¹⁰The fear of YHWH [is] the beginning of wisdom, || Good understanding have all doing them, || His praise [is] standing forever!

PSALM 112

¹Praise YAH! [Aleph-Bet] O the blessedness of one fearing YHWH, || He has greatly delighted in His commands. ²His seed is mighty in the earth, || The generation of the upright is blessed. ³Wealth and riches [are] in his house, || And his righteousness is standing forever. ⁴Light has risen in darkness to the upright, || Gracious, and merciful, and righteous. ⁵The man—good, gracious, and lending, || He sustains his matters in judgment. ⁶For he is not moved for all time; For the righteous is a continuous memorial. ⁷He is not afraid of an evil report, || His heart is prepared [and] confident in YHWH. ⁸His heart is sustained—he does not fear, || Until he looks on his adversaries. ⁹He has scattered—has given to the needy, || His righteousness is standing forever, || His horn is exalted with glory. ¹⁰The wicked sees, and has been angry, || He gnashes his teeth, and has melted, || The desire of the wicked perishes!

PSALM 113

¹Praise YAH! Praise, you servants of YHWH. Praise the Name of YHWH. ²The Name of YHWH is blessed, || From now on, and for all time. ³From the rising of the sun to its going in, || The Name of YHWH [is] praised. ⁴YHWH [is] high above all nations, || His glory [is] above the heavens. ⁵Who [is] as our God YHWH, || He is exalting [Himself] to sit? ⁶He is humbling [Himself] to look || On the heavens and on the earth. ⁷He is raising up the poor from the dust, || He exalts the needy from a dunghill. ⁸To cause [them] to sit with princes, || With the princes of His people. ⁹Causing the barren one of the house to sit, || A joyful mother of sons; praise YAH!

PSALM 114

¹In the going out of Israel from Egypt, || The house of Jacob from a strange people, ²Judah became His sanctuary, || Israel his dominion. ³The sea has seen, and flees, || The Jordan turns backward. ⁴The mountains have skipped as rams, || Heights as sons of a flock. ⁵What is [ailing] you, O sea, that you flee? O Jordan, you turn back! ⁶O mountains, you skip as rams! O heights, as sons of a flock! ⁷From before the Lord be afraid, O earth, || From before the God of Jacob, ⁸He is turning the rock to a pool of waters, || The flint to a fountain of waters!

PSALM 115

¹Not to us, O YHWH, not to us, || But to Your Name give glory, || For Your kindness, for Your truth. ²Why do the nations say, "Where, pray, [is] their God?" ³And our God [is] in the heavens, || All that He has pleased He has done. ⁴Their idols [are] silver and gold, work of man's hands, ⁵They have a mouth, and they do not speak, || They have eyes, and they do not see, ⁶They have ears, and they do not hear, || They have a nose, and they do not smell, ⁷Their hands, but they do not handle, || Their feet, and they do not walk; ⁸Nor do they mutter through their throat, || Their makers are like them, || Everyone who is trusting in them. ⁹O Israel, trust in YHWH, "He [is] their help and their shield." ¹⁰O house of Aaron, trust in YHWH, "He [is] their help and their shield." ¹¹You fearing YHWH, trust in YHWH, "He [is] their help and their shield." ¹²YHWH has remembered us, He blesses, || He blesses the house of Israel, || He blesses the house of Aaron, ¹³He blesses those fearing YHWH, || The small with the great. ¹⁴YHWH adds to you—to you and to your sons. ¹⁵Blessed [are] you of YHWH, || Maker of the heavens and earth, ¹⁶The heavens—the heavens [are] YHWH's, || And He has given the earth to sons of men; ¹⁷The dead do not praise YAH, || Nor any going down to silence. ¹⁸And we, we bless YAH, || From now on, and for all time. Praise YAH!

PSALM 116

¹I have loved, because YHWH hears My voice, my supplication, ²Because He has inclined His ear to me, || And during my days I call. ³Cords of death have surrounded me, || And straits of Sheol have found me, || I find distress and sorrow. ⁴And in the Name of YHWH I call: Ah, now, O YHWH, deliver my soul, ⁵YHWH [is] gracious, and righteous, || Indeed, our God [is] merciful, ⁶YHWH [is] a preserver of the simple, || I was low, and He gives salvation to me. ⁷Return, O my soul, to your rest, || For YHWH has conferred benefits on you. ⁸For You have delivered my soul from death, || My eyes from tears, my feet from overthrowing. ⁹I habitually walk before YHWH || In the lands of the living.

PSALMS

¹⁰I have believed, for I speak, || I have been greatly afflicted. ¹¹I said in my haste, "Every man [is] a liar." ¹²What do I return to YHWH? All His benefits [are] on me. ¹³I lift up the cup of salvation, || And in the Name of YHWH I call. ¹⁴Let me complete my vows to YHWH, || Now, before all His people. ¹⁵Precious in the eyes of YHWH [is] the death of His saints. ¹⁶Ah, now, O YHWH, for I [am] Your servant; I [am] Your servant, son of Your handmaid; You have opened my bonds. ¹⁷I sacrifice a sacrifice of thanks to You, || And in the Name of YHWH I call. ¹⁸Let me complete my vows to YHWH, || Now, before all His people, ¹⁹In the courts of the house of YHWH, || In your midst, O Jerusalem, praise YAH!

PSALM 117

¹Praise YHWH, all you nations, || Glorify Him, all you peoples! ²For His kindness has been mighty to us, || And the truth of YHWH [is] for all time. Praise YAH!

PSALM 118

¹Give thanks to YHWH, || For [He is] good, for His kindness [is] for all time. ²Now let Israel say, || His kindness [is] for all time. ³Now let the house of Aaron say, || His kindness [is] for all time. ⁴Now let those fearing YHWH say, || His kindness [is] for all time. ⁵I called YAH from the narrow place, || YAH answered me in a broad place. ⁶YHWH [is] for me, || I do not fear what man does to me. ⁷YHWH [is] for me among my helpers, || And I look on those hating me. ⁸Better to take refuge in YHWH, || Than to trust in man, ⁹Better to take refuge in YHWH, || Than to trust in princes. ¹⁰All nations have surrounded me, || In the Name of YHWH I surely cut them off. ¹¹They have surrounded me, || Indeed, they have surrounded me, || In the Name of YHWH I surely cut them off. ¹²They surrounded me as bees, || They have been extinguished as a fire of thorns, || In the Name of YHWH I surely cut them off. ¹³You have severely thrust me to fall, || And YHWH has helped me. ¹⁴YAH is my strength and song, || And He is to me for salvation. ¹⁵A voice of singing and salvation, || [Is] in the tents of the righteous, || The right hand of YHWH is doing valiantly. ¹⁶The right hand of YHWH is exalted, || The right hand of YHWH is doing valiantly. ¹⁷I do not die, but live, || And recount the works of YAH, ¹⁸YAH has severely disciplined me, || And has not given me up to death. ¹⁹Open gates of righteousness to me, || I enter into them—I thank YAH. ²⁰This [is] the gate to YHWH, || The righteous enter into it. ²¹I thank You, for You have answered me, || And are to me for salvation. ²²A stone the builders refused || Has become head of a corner. ²³This has been from YHWH, || It [is] wonderful in our eyes, ²⁴This [is] the day YHWH has made, || We rejoice and are glad in it. ²⁵Ah, now, O YHWH, please save, || Ah, now, O YHWH, please prosper. ²⁶Blessed [is] He who is coming || In the Name of YHWH, || We blessed you from the house of YHWH, ²⁷God [is] YHWH, and He gives light to us, || Direct the festal-sacrifice with cords, || To the horns of the altar. ²⁸You [are] my God, and I confess You, || My God, I exalt You. ²⁹Give thanks to YHWH, || For [He is] good, for His kindness [is] for all time!

PSALM 119

¹[ALEPH] O the blessedness of those perfect in the way, || They are walking in the Law of YHWH, ²O the blessedness of those keeping His testimonies, || They seek Him with the whole heart. ³Indeed, they have not done iniquity, || They have walked in His ways. ⁴You have commanded us to diligently keep Your precepts, ⁵O that my ways were prepared to keep Your statutes, ⁶Then I am not ashamed || In my looking to all Your commands. ⁷I confess You with uprightness of heart, || In my learning the judgments of Your righteousness. ⁸I keep Your statutes, do not utterly leave me! ⁹[BETH] With what does a young man purify his path? To observe—according to Your word. ¹⁰I have sought You with all my heart, || Do not let me err from Your commands. ¹¹I have hid Your saying in my heart, || That I do not sin before You. ¹²Blessed [are] You, O YHWH, teach me Your statutes. ¹³With my lips I have recounted || All the judgments of Your mouth. ¹⁴I have rejoiced in the way of Your testimonies, || As over all wealth. ¹⁵I meditate on Your precepts, || And I attentively behold Your paths. ¹⁶I delight myself in Your statutes, || I do not forget Your word. ¹⁷[GIMEL] Confer benefits on Your servant, || I live, and I keep Your word. ¹⁸Uncover my eyes, and I behold wonders out of Your law. ¹⁹I [am] a sojourner on earth, || Do not hide Your commands from me. ²⁰My soul has broken for desire || To Your judgments at all times. ²¹You have rebuked the cursed proud, || Who are erring from Your commands. ²²Remove reproach and contempt from me, || For I have kept Your testimonies. ²³Princes also sat—they spoke against me, || Your servant meditates on Your statutes, ²⁴Your testimonies [are] also my delight, || The men of my counsel! ²⁵[DALETH] My soul has cleaved to the dust, || Quicken me according to Your word. ²⁶I have recounted my ways, || And You answer me, teach me Your statutes, ²⁷Cause me to understand the way of Your precepts, || And I meditate on Your wonders. ²⁸My soul has dropped from affliction, || Establish me according to Your word. ²⁹Turn aside the way of falsehood from me || And favor me with Your law. ³⁰I have chosen the way of faithfulness, || I have compared Your judgments, ³¹I have adhered to Your testimonies, || O YHWH, do not put me to shame. ³²I run the way of Your commands, || For You enlarge my heart! ³³[HE] Show me, O YHWH, the way of Your statutes, || And I keep it—[to] the end. ³⁴Cause me to understand, and I keep Your law, || And observe it with the whole heart. ³⁵Cause me to tread in the path of Your commands, || For I have delighted in it. ³⁶Incline my heart to Your testimonies, || And not to dishonest gain. ³⁷Remove my eyes from seeing vanity, || Quicken me in Your way. ³⁸Establish Your saying to Your servant, || That [is] concerning Your fear. ³⁹Remove my reproach that I have feared, || For Your judgments [are] good. ⁴⁰Behold, I have longed for Your precepts, || Quicken me in Your righteousness. ⁴¹[WAW] And Your kindness meets me, O YHWH, || Your salvation according to Your saying. ⁴²And I answer him who is reproaching me a word, || For I have trusted in Your word. ⁴³And You do not utterly take away || The word of truth from my mouth, || Because I have hoped for Your judgment. ⁴⁴And I keep Your law continually, || For all time and forever. ⁴⁵And I habitually walk in a broad place, || For I have sought Your precepts. ⁴⁶And I speak of Your testimonies before kings, || And I am not ashamed. ⁴⁷And I delight myself in Your commands, || That I have loved, ⁴⁸And I lift up my hands to Your commands, || That I have loved, || And I meditate on Your statutes! ⁴⁹[ZAYIN] Remember the word to Your servant, || On which You have caused me to hope. ⁵⁰This [is] my comfort in my affliction, || That Your saying has quickened me. ⁵¹The proud have utterly scorned me, || I have not turned aside from Your law. ⁵²I remembered Your judgments of old, O YHWH, || And I comfort myself. ⁵³Horror has seized me, || Because of the wicked forsaking Your law. ⁵⁴Your statutes have been songs to me, || In the house of my sojournings. ⁵⁵I have remembered Your Name in the night, O YHWH, || And I keep Your law. ⁵⁶This has been to me, || That I have kept Your precepts! ⁵⁷[HETH] YHWH [is] my portion; I have said I would keep Your words, ⁵⁸I appeased Your face with the whole heart, || Favor me according to Your saying. ⁵⁹I have reckoned my ways, || And turn back my feet to Your testimonies. ⁶⁰I have made haste, || And did not delay, to keep Your commands. ⁶¹Cords of the wicked have surrounded me, || I have not forgotten Your law. ⁶²At midnight I rise to give thanks to You, || For the judgments of Your righteousness. ⁶³I [am] a companion to all who fear You, || And to those keeping Your precepts. ⁶⁴Of Your kindness, O YHWH, the earth is full, || Teach me Your statutes! ⁶⁵[TETH] You did good with Your servant, O YHWH, || According to Your word. ⁶⁶Teach me the goodness of reason and knowledge, || For I have believed in Your commands. ⁶⁷Before I am afflicted, I am erring, || And now I have kept Your saying. ⁶⁸You [are] good, and doing good, || Teach me Your statutes. ⁶⁹The proud have forged falsehood against me, || I keep Your precepts with the whole heart. ⁷⁰Their heart has been thick as fat, || I have delighted in Your law. ⁷¹[It is] good for me that I have been afflicted, || That I might learn Your statutes. ⁷²The Law of Your mouth [is] better to me || Than thousands of gold and silver! ⁷³[YOD] Your hands made me and establish me, || Cause me to understand, and I learn Your commands. ⁷⁴Those fearing You see me and rejoice, || Because I have hoped for Your word. ⁷⁵I have known, O YHWH, || That Your

judgments [are] righteous, || And [in] faithfulness You have afflicted me. ⁷⁶Please let Your kindness be to comfort me, || According to Your saying to Your servant. ⁷⁷Your mercies meet me, and I live, || For Your law [is] my delight. ⁷⁸The proud are ashamed, || For [with] falsehood they dealt perversely with me. I meditate on Your precepts. ⁷⁹Those fearing You turn back to me, || And those knowing Your testimonies. ⁸⁰My heart is perfect in Your statutes, || So that I am not ashamed. ⁸¹[KAPH] My soul has been consumed for Your salvation, || I have hoped for Your word. ⁸²My eyes have been consumed for Your word, || Saying, "When does it comfort me?" ⁸³For I have been as a bottle in smoke, || I have not forgotten Your statutes. ⁸⁴How many [are] the days of Your servant? When do You execute judgment || Against my pursuers? ⁸⁵The proud have dug pits for me, || That [are] not according to Your law. ⁸⁶All Your commands [are] faithfulness, || They have pursued me [with] falsehood, || Help me. ⁸⁷They have almost consumed me on earth, || And I have not forsaken Your precepts. ⁸⁸Quicken me according to Your kindness, || And I keep the Testimony of Your mouth! ⁸⁹[LAMED] For all time, O YHWH, Your word is set up in the heavens. ⁹⁰Your faithfulness from generation to generation, || You established earth, and it stands. ⁹¹According to Your ordinances || They have stood this day, for the whole—Your servants. ⁹²Unless Your law [were] my delights, || Then had I perished in my affliction. ⁹³I do not forget Your precepts for all time, || For You have quickened me by them. ⁹⁴I [am] Yours, save me, for I have sought Your precepts. ⁹⁵Your wicked waited for me to destroy me, || I understand Your testimonies. ⁹⁶I have seen an end of all perfection, || Your command [is] exceedingly broad! ⁹⁷[MEM] O how I have loved Your law! It [is] my meditation all the day. ⁹⁸Your command makes me wiser than my enemies, || For it [is] before me for all time. ⁹⁹I have acted wisely above all my teachers. For Your testimonies [are] my meditation. ¹⁰⁰Above elderly—I understand more, || For I have kept Your precepts. ¹⁰¹I restrained my feet from every evil path, || So that I keep Your word. ¹⁰²I did not turn aside from Your judgments, || For You have directed me. ¹⁰³How sweet Your saying has been to my palate, || Above honey to my mouth. ¹⁰⁴I have understanding from Your precepts, || Therefore I have hated every false path! ¹⁰⁵[NUN] Your word [is] a lamp to my foot, || And a light to my path. ¹⁰⁶I have sworn, and I confirm, || To keep the judgments of Your righteousness. ¹⁰⁷I have been afflicted very much, || O YHWH, quicken me, according to Your word. ¹⁰⁸Please accept [the] free-will offerings of my mouth, O YHWH, || And teach me Your judgments. ¹⁰⁹My soul [is] in my hand continually, || And I have not forgotten Your law. ¹¹⁰The wicked have laid a snare for me, || And I did not wander from your precepts. ¹¹¹I have inherited Your testimonies for all time, || For they [are] the joy of my heart. ¹¹²I have inclined my heart || To do Your statutes, for all time—[to] the end!

¹¹³[SAMEKH] I have hated doubting ones, || And I have loved Your law. ¹¹⁴You [are] my hiding place and my shield, || I have hoped for Your word. ¹¹⁵Turn aside from me, you evildoers, || And I keep the commands of my God. ¹¹⁶Sustain me according to Your saying, || And I live, and You do not put me to shame because of my hope. ¹¹⁷Support me, and I am saved, || And I look on Your statutes continually. ¹¹⁸You have trodden down || All going astray from Your statutes, || For their deceit [is] falsehood. ¹¹⁹Dross! You have caused to cease || All the wicked of the earth; Therefore I have loved Your testimonies. ¹²⁰My flesh has trembled from Your fear, || And I have been afraid from Your judgments! ¹²¹[AYIN] I have done judgment and righteousness, || Do not leave me to my oppressors. ¹²²Make Your servant sure for good, || Do not let the proud oppress me. ¹²³My eyes have been consumed for Your salvation. And for the saying of Your righteousness. ¹²⁴Do with Your servant according to Your kindness. And teach me Your statutes. ¹²⁵I [am] Your servant—cause me to understand, || And I know Your testimonies. ¹²⁶Time for YHWH to work! They have made Your law void. ¹²⁷Therefore I have loved Your commands || Above gold—even fine gold. ¹²⁸Therefore all my appointments I have declared wholly right, || I have hated every path of falsehood! ¹²⁹[PE] Your testimonies [are] wonderful, || Therefore my soul has kept them. ¹³⁰The opening of Your words enlightens, || Instructing the simple. ¹³¹I have opened my mouth, indeed, I pant, || For I have longed for Your commands. ¹³²Look to me, and favor me, || As customary to those loving Your Name. ¹³³Establish my steps by Your saying, || And any iniquity does not rule over me. ¹³⁴Ransom me from the oppression of man, || And I observe Your precepts, ¹³⁵Cause Your face to shine on Your servant, || And teach me Your statutes. ¹³⁶Streams of waters have come down my eyes, || Because they have not kept Your law! ¹³⁷[TSADE] You [are] righteous, O YHWH, || And Your judgments [are] upright. ¹³⁸You have appointed Your testimonies, || Righteous and exceedingly faithful, ¹³⁹My zeal has cut me off, || For my adversaries forgot Your words. ¹⁴⁰Your saying [is] tried exceedingly, || And Your servant has loved it. ¹⁴¹I [am] small, and despised, || I have not forgotten Your precepts. ¹⁴²Your righteousness [is] righteousness for all time, || And Your law [is] truth. ¹⁴³Adversity and distress have found me, || Your commands [are] my delights. ¹⁴⁴The righteousness of Your testimonies || [Is] to cause me to understand, and I live! ¹⁴⁵[QOF] I have called with the whole heart, || Answer me, O YHWH, I keep Your statutes, ¹⁴⁶I have called You, save me, || And I keep Your testimonies. ¹⁴⁷I have gone forward in the dawn, and I cry, || I have hoped for Your word. ¹⁴⁸My eyes have gone before the watches, || To meditate on Your saying. ¹⁴⁹Hear my voice, according to Your kindness, || YHWH, quicken me according to Your judgment. ¹⁵⁰My wicked pursuers have been near, || They have been far off from Your law. ¹⁵¹You [are] near, O YHWH, || And all Your commands [are] truth. ¹⁵²I have known Your testimonies of old, || That You have founded them for all time! ¹⁵³[RESH] See my affliction, and deliver me, || For I have not forgotten Your law. ¹⁵⁴Plead my plea, and redeem me, || Quicken me according to Your saying. ¹⁵⁵Salvation [is] far from the wicked, || For they have not sought Your statutes. ¹⁵⁶Your mercies [are] many, O YHWH, || Quicken me according to Your judgments. ¹⁵⁷My pursuers and adversaries are many, || I have not turned aside from Your testimonies. ¹⁵⁸I have seen treacherous ones, || And grieve myself, || Because they have not kept Your saying. ¹⁵⁹See, for I have loved Your precepts, || YHWH, quicken me according to Your kindness. ¹⁶⁰The sum of Your word [is] truth, || And every judgment of Your righteousness [is] for all time! ¹⁶¹[SHIN] Princes have pursued me without cause, || And my heart was afraid because of Your words. ¹⁶²I rejoice concerning Your saying, || As one finding abundant spoil. ¹⁶³I have hated falsehood, indeed I detest [it], || I have loved Your law. ¹⁶⁴Seven [times] in a day I have praised You, || Because of the judgments of Your righteousness. ¹⁶⁵Those loving Your law have abundant peace, || And they have no stumbling-block. ¹⁶⁶I have waited for Your salvation, O YHWH, || And I have done Your commands. ¹⁶⁷My soul has kept Your testimonies, || And I love them exceedingly. ¹⁶⁸I have kept Your precepts and Your testimonies, || For all my ways are before You! ¹⁶⁹[TAW] My loud cry comes near before You, O YHWH; Cause me to understand according to Your word. ¹⁷⁰My supplication comes in before You, || Deliver me according to Your saying. ¹⁷¹My lips utter praise, || For You teach me Your statutes. ¹⁷²My tongue sings of Your saying, || For all Your commands [are] righteous. ¹⁷³Your hand is for a help to me, || For I have chosen Your commands. ¹⁷⁴I have longed for Your salvation, O YHWH, || And Your law [is] my delight. ¹⁷⁵My soul lives, and it praises You, || And Your judgments help me. ¹⁷⁶I wandered as a lost sheep, [so] seek Your servant, || For I have not forgotten Your precepts!

PSALM 120

¹A SONG OF THE ASCENTS. I have called to YHWH in my distress, || And He answers me. ²O YHWH, deliver my soul from a lying lip, || From a deceitful tongue! ³What does He give to you? And what does He add to you? O deceitful tongue! ⁴Sharp arrows of a mighty one, with coals of broom trees. ⁵Woe to me, for I have inhabited Mesech, || I have dwelt with tents of Kedar. ⁶My soul has dwelt too much with him who is hating peace. ⁷I—peace, and when I speak they [are] for war!

PSALM 121

¹A SONG OF THE ASCENTS. I lift up my eyes to the hills, || From where does my help come? ²My help [is] from YHWH, || Maker of the heavens and earth, ³He does not permit your foot to be moved, || He who is preserving you does not slumber. ⁴Behold, He does not slumber, nor sleep, || He who is preserving Israel. ⁵YHWH [is] He who is preserving you, || YHWH [is] your

shade on your right hand, ⁶By day the sun does not strike you, || Nor the moon by night. ⁷YHWH preserves you from all evil, || He preserves your soul. ⁸YHWH preserves your going out and your coming in, || From now on—even for all time!

PSALM 122

¹A Song of the Ascents. By David. I have rejoiced in those saying to me, "We go to the house of YHWH." ²Our feet have been standing in your gates, O Jerusalem! ³Jerusalem—the built one—[Is] as a city that is joined to itself together. ⁴For there tribes have gone up, || Tribes of YAH, companies of Israel, || To give thanks to the Name of YHWH. ⁵For there thrones of judgment have sat, || Thrones of the house of David. ⁶Ask [for] the peace of Jerusalem, || Those loving you are at rest. ⁷Peace is in your bulwark, rest in your high places, ⁸For the sake of my brothers and my companions, || Please let me speak, "Peace [be] in you." ⁹For the sake of the house of our God YHWH, || I seek good for you!

PSALM 123

¹A Song of the Ascents. I have lifted up my eyes to You, || O dweller in the heavens. ²Behold, as eyes of menservants || [Are] to the hand of their masters, || As eyes of a maidservant || [Are] to the hand of her mistress, || So [are] our eyes to our God YHWH, || Until He favors us. ³Favor us, O YHWH, favor us, || For we have been greatly filled with contempt, ⁴Our soul has been greatly filled || With the scorning of the easy ones, || With the contempt of the arrogant!

PSALM 124

¹A Song of the Ascents. By David. If YHWH had not been for us || (Pray, let Israel say), ²If YHWH had not been for us, || In the rising up of man against us, ³Then they had swallowed us alive, || In the burning of their anger against us, ⁴Then the waters had overflowed us, || The stream passed over our soul, ⁵Then proud waters had passed over our soul. ⁶Blessed [is] YHWH who has not given us, || [As] prey to their teeth. ⁷Our soul has escaped as a bird from a snare of fowlers, || The snare was broken, and we have escaped. ⁸Our help [is] in the Name of YHWH, || Maker of the heavens and earth!

PSALM 125

¹A Song of the Ascents. Those trusting in YHWH [are] as Mount Zion, || It is not moved—it abides for all time. ²Jerusalem! Mountains [are] around her, || And YHWH [is] around His people, || From now on—even for all time. ³For the rod of wickedness does not rest on the lot of the righteous, || That the righteous do not put forth their hands on iniquity. ⁴Do good, O YHWH, to the good, || And to the upright in their hearts. ⁵As for those turning [to] their crooked ways, || YHWH causes them to go with workers of iniquity. Peace on Israel!

PSALM 126

¹A Song of the Ascents. In YHWH's turning back [to] the captivity of Zion, || We have been as dreamers. ²Then our mouth is filled [with] laughter, || And our tongue [with] singing, || Then they say among nations, "YHWH did great things with these." ³YHWH did great things with us, || We have been joyful. ⁴Turn again, O YHWH, [to] our captivity, || As streams in the south. ⁵Those sowing in tears, reap with singing, ⁶Whoever goes on and weeps, || Carrying the basket of seed, || Surely comes in with singing, carrying his sheaves!

PSALM 127

¹A Song of the Ascents. By Solomon. If YHWH does not build the house, || Its builders have labored at it in vain, || If YHWH does not watch a city, || A watchman has awoken in vain. ²Vain for you who are rising early, || Who delay sitting, eating the bread of griefs, || So He gives sleep to His beloved one. ³Behold, sons [are] an inheritance of YHWH, || The fruit of the womb [is] a reward. ⁴As arrows in the hand of a mighty one, || So [are] the sons of the young men. ⁵O the blessedness of the man || Who has filled his quiver with them, || They are not ashamed, || For they speak with enemies in the gate!

PSALM 128

¹A Song of the Ascents. O the blessedness of everyone fearing YHWH, || Who is walking in His ways. ²You surely eat the labor of your hands, || You [are] blessed, and good [is] to you. ³Your wife [is] as a fruitful vine in the sides of your house, || Your sons as olive plants around your table. ⁴Behold, surely thus is the man blessed who is fearing YHWH. ⁵YHWH blesses you out of Zion, || Look, then, on the good of Jerusalem, || All the days of your life, ⁶And see the sons of your sons! Peace on Israel!

PSALM 129

¹A Song of the Ascents. Often they distressed me from my youth, || Pray, let Israel say: ²Often they distressed me from my youth, || Yet they have not prevailed over me. ³Plowers have plowed over my back, || They have made their furrows long. ⁴YHWH [is] righteous, || He has cut apart cords of the wicked. ⁵All hating Zion [are] confounded and turn backward. ⁶They are as grass of the roofs, || That withers before it was drawn out, ⁷That has not filled the hand of a reaper, || And the bosom of a binder of sheaves. ⁸And the passers by have not said, "The blessing of YHWH [is] on you, || We blessed you in the Name of YHWH!"

PSALM 130

¹A Song of the Ascents. I have called You from the depths, YHWH. ²Lord, listen to my voice, || Your ears are attentive to the voice of my supplications. ³If You observe iniquities, Lord YAH, who stands? ⁴But forgiveness [is] with You, that You may be feared. ⁵I hoped [for] YHWH—my soul has hoped, || And I have waited for His word. ⁶My soul [is] for the Lord, || More than those watching for morning, || Watching for morning! ⁷Israel waits on YHWH, || For kindness [is] with YHWH, || And redemption [is] abundant with Him. ⁸And He redeems Israel from all his iniquities!

PSALM 131

¹A Song of the Ascents. By David. YHWH, my heart has not been haughty, || Nor have my eyes been high, || Nor have I walked in great things, || And in things too wonderful for me. ²Have I not compared, and kept my soul silent, || As a weaned one by its mother? As a weaned one by me [is] my soul. ³Israel waits on YHWH, || From now on, and for all time!

PSALM 132

¹A Song of the Ascents. Remember, YHWH, for David, all his afflictions; ²Who has sworn to YHWH, || He has vowed to the Mighty One of Jacob: ³"If I enter into the tent of my house, || If I go up on the couch of my bed, ⁴If I give sleep to my eyes, || To my eyelids—slumber, ⁵Until I find a place for YHWH, dwelling places for the Mighty One of Jacob." ⁶Behold, we have heard it in Ephratah, || We have found it in the fields of the forest. ⁷We come into His dwelling places, || We bow ourselves at His footstool. ⁸Arise, O YHWH, to Your rest, || You, and the Ark of Your strength, ⁹Your priests put on righteousness, || And Your pious ones cry aloud. ¹⁰For the sake of Your servant David, || Do not turn back the face of Your anointed. ¹¹YHWH has sworn truth to David, || He does not turn back from it: "Of the fruit of your body, || I set on the throne for you. ¹²If your sons keep My covenant, || And My testimonies that I teach them, || Their sons also forever and ever || Sit on the throne for you." ¹³For YHWH has fixed on Zion, || He has desired [it] for a seat to Himself, ¹⁴"This [is] My rest forever and ever, || Here I sit, for I have desired it. ¹⁵I greatly bless her provision, || I satisfy her poor [with] bread, ¹⁶And I clothe her priests [with] salvation, || And her pious ones sing aloud. ¹⁷There I cause a horn to spring up for David, || I have arranged a lamp for My Anointed. ¹⁸I clothe His enemies [with] shame, || And His crown flourishes on Him!"

PSALM 133

¹A Song of the Ascents. By David. Behold, how good and how pleasant || The dwelling of brothers—even together! ²As the good oil on the head, || Coming down on the beard, the beard of Aaron, || That comes down on the skirt of his robes, ³As dew of Hermon—That comes down on hills of Zion, || For there YHWH commanded the blessing—Life for all time!

PSALM 134

¹A Song of the Ascents. Behold, bless YHWH, all servants of YHWH, || Who are standing in the house of YHWH by night. ²Lift up your hands [in] the sanctuary, || And bless YHWH. ³YHWH

PSALMS

blesses you out of Zion, || The Maker of the heavens and earth!

PSALM 135

¹Praise YAH! Praise the Name of YHWH, || Praise, you servants of YHWH, ²Who are standing in the house of YHWH, || In the courts of the house of our God. ³Praise YAH! For YHWH [is] good, || Sing praise to His Name, for [it is] pleasant. ⁴For YAH has chosen Jacob for Himself, || Israel for His peculiar treasure. ⁵For I have known that YHWH [is] great, || Indeed, our Lord [is] above all gods. ⁶All that YHWH pleased He has done, || In the heavens and in earth, || In the seas and all deep places, ⁷Causing vapors to ascend from the end of the earth, || He has made lightnings for the rain, || Bringing forth wind from His treasures. ⁸Who struck the firstborn of Egypt, || From man to beast. ⁹He sent tokens and wonders into your midst, O Egypt, || On Pharaoh and on all his servants. ¹⁰Who struck many nations, and slew strong kings, ¹¹Even Sihon king of the Amorite, || And Og king of Bashan, || And all kingdoms of Canaan. ¹²And He gave their land an inheritance, || An inheritance to His people Israel, ¹³O YHWH, Your Name [is] for all time, || O YHWH, Your memorial from generation to generation. ¹⁴For YHWH judges His people, || And comforts Himself for His servants. ¹⁵The idols of the nations [are] silver and gold, || Work of the hands of man. ¹⁶They have a mouth, and they do not speak, || They have eyes, and they do not see, ¹⁷They have ears, and they do not give ear, || Nose—there is no breath in their mouth! ¹⁸Their makers are like them, || Everyone who is trusting in them. ¹⁹O house of Israel, bless YHWH, || O house of Aaron, bless YHWH, ²⁰O house of Levi, bless YHWH, || Those fearing YHWH, bless YHWH. ²¹Blessed [is] YHWH from Zion, || Inhabiting Jerusalem—praise YAH!

PSALM 136

¹Give thanks to YHWH, || For [He is] good, for His kindness [is] for all time. ²Give thanks to the God of gods, || For His kindness [is] for all time. ³Give thanks to the Lord of lords, || For His kindness [is] for all time. ⁴To Him doing great wonders by Himself alone, || For His kindness [is] for all time. ⁵To Him making the heavens by understanding, || For His kindness [is] for all time. ⁶To Him spreading the earth over the waters, || For His kindness [is] for all time. ⁷To Him making great lights, || For His kindness [is] for all time. ⁸The sun to rule by day, || For His kindness [is] for all time. ⁹The moon and stars to rule by night, || For His kindness [is] for all time. ¹⁰To Him striking Egypt in their firstborn, || For His kindness [is] for all time. ¹¹And bringing forth Israel from their midst, || For His kindness [is] for all time. ¹²By a strong hand and an outstretched-arm, || For His kindness [is] for all time. ¹³To Him cutting the Sea of Suph into parts, || For His kindness [is] for all time, ¹⁴And caused Israel to pass through its midst, || For His kindness [is] for all time, ¹⁵And shook out Pharaoh and his force in the Sea of Suph, || For His kindness [is] for all time. ¹⁶To Him leading His people in a wilderness, || For His kindness [is] for all time. ¹⁷To Him striking great kings, || For His kindness [is] for all time. ¹⁸Indeed, He slays majestic kings, || For His kindness [is] for all time. ¹⁹Even Sihon king of the Amorite, || For His kindness [is] for all time. ²⁰And Og king of Bashan, || For His kindness [is] for all time. ²¹And He gave their land for inheritance, || For His kindness [is] for all time. ²²An inheritance to Israel His servant, || For His kindness [is] for all time. ²³Who has remembered us in our lowliness, || For His kindness [is] for all time. ²⁴And He delivers us from our adversaries, || For His kindness [is] for all time. ²⁵Giving food to all flesh, || For His kindness [is] for all time. ²⁶Give thanks to the God of the heavens, || For His kindness [is] for all time!

PSALM 137

¹By rivers of Babylon—There we sat, || Indeed, we wept when we remembered Zion. ²We hung our harps on willows in its midst. ³For there our captors asked us the words of a song, || And our spoilers—joy: "Sing to us of a song of Zion." ⁴How do we sing the song of YHWH, || On the land of a stranger? ⁵If I forget you, O Jerusalem, my right hand forgets! ⁶My tongue cleaves to my palate, || If I do not remember you, || If I do not exalt Jerusalem above my chief joy. ⁷Remember, YHWH, for the sons of Edom, || The day of Jerusalem, || Those saying, "Raze, raze to its foundation!" ⁸O daughter of Babylon, O destroyed one, || O the blessedness of him who repays to you your deed, || That you have done to us. ⁹O the blessedness of him who seizes, and has dashed your sucklings on the rock!

PSALM 138

¹BY DAVID. I confess You with all my heart, || I praise You before the gods. ²I bow myself toward Your holy temple, || And I confess Your Name, || For Your kindness, and for Your truth, || For You have made Your saying great above all Your Name. ³In the day I called, when You answer me, || You strengthen me in my soul [with] strength. ⁴O YHWH, all kings of earth confess You, || When they have heard the sayings of Your mouth. ⁵And they sing in the ways of YHWH, || For the glory of YHWH [is] great. ⁶For YHWH [is] high, and He sees the lowly, || And He knows the haughty from afar. ⁷If I walk in the midst of distress You quicken me, || You send forth Your hand against the anger of my enemies, || And Your right hand saves me. ⁸YHWH perfects for me, || O YHWH, Your kindness [is] for all time, || Do not let the works of Your hands fall!

PSALM 139

¹TO THE OVERSEER. A PSALM OF DAVID. YHWH, You have searched me, and know. ²You have known my sitting down, || And my rising up, || You have attended to my thoughts from afar. ³You have fanned my path and my lying down, || And have been acquainted [with] all my ways. ⁴For there is not a word in my tongue, || Behold, O YHWH, You have known it all! ⁵You have besieged me behind and before, || And You place Your hand on me. ⁶Knowledge too wonderful for me, || It has been set on high, || I am not able for it. ⁷To where do I go from Your Spirit? And to where do I flee from Your face? ⁸If I ascend the heavens—You [are] there, || And spread out a bed in Sheol, behold, You! ⁹I take the wings of morning, || I dwell in the uttermost part of the sea, ¹⁰Also there Your hand leads me, || And Your right hand holds me. ¹¹And I say, "Surely darkness bruises me," || Then night [is] light to me. ¹²Also darkness does not hide from You, || And night shines as day, || As [is] darkness so [is] light. ¹³For You have possessed my reins, || You cover me in my mother's belly. ¹⁴I confess You, because I have been fearfully distinguished. Your works [are] wonderful, || And my soul is knowing [it] well. ¹⁵My substance was not hid from You, || When I was made in secret, || Curiously worked in the lower part of earth. ¹⁶Your eyes saw my unformed substance, || And all of them are written on Your scroll, || The days they were formed—And not one among them. ¹⁷And how precious Your thoughts have been to me, || O God, how great has been their sum! ¹⁸I recount them! They are more than the sand, || I have awoken, and I am still with You. ¹⁹Do You slay, O God, the wicked? Then, men of blood, turn aside from me! ²⁰Who exchange You for wickedness, || Your enemies [are] lifted up to vanity. ²¹Do I not hate, YHWH, those hating You? And grieve myself with Your withstanders? ²²I have hated them [with] perfect hatred, || They have become enemies to me. ²³Search me, O God, and know my heart, || Try me, and know my thoughts, ²⁴And see if a grievous way be in me, || And lead me in a perpetual way!

PSALM 140

¹TO THE OVERSEER. A PSALM OF DAVID. Deliver me, O YHWH, from an evil man, || Keep me from one of violence. ²Who have devised evils in the heart, || All the day they assemble [for] wars. ³They sharpened their tongue as a serpent, || Poison of a viper [is] under their lips. Selah. ⁴Preserve me, YHWH, from the hands of the wicked, || Keep me from one of violence, || Who have devised to overthrow my steps. ⁵The proud hid a snare for me—and cords, || They spread a net by the side of the path, || They have set snares for me. Selah. ⁶I have said to YHWH, "You [are] my God, || Hear, YHWH, the voice of my supplications." ⁷O YHWH, my Lord, strength of my salvation, || You have covered my head in the day of armor. ⁸Do not grant, O YHWH, the desires of the wicked, || Do not bring forth his wicked scheme, || They are high. Selah. ⁹The chief of my surrounders, || The perverseness of their lips covers them. ¹⁰They cause burning coals to fall on themselves, || He casts them into fire, || Into deep pits—they do not arise. ¹¹A talkative man is not established in the earth, || One of violence—evil hunts to overflowing. ¹²I have known that YHWH executes || The judgment of the afflicted, || The judgment of the needy. ¹³Surely the righteous give thanks to Your Name, || The upright dwell with Your presence!

PSALM 141

¹ A PSALM OF DAVID. O YHWH, I have called You, hurry to me, || Give ear [to] my voice when I call to You. ² My prayer is prepared—incense before You, || The lifting up of my hands—the evening present. ³ Set, O YHWH, a watch for my mouth, || Watch over the door of my lips. ⁴ Do not incline my heart to an evil thing, || To habitually do actions in wickedness, || Working iniquity with men, || Indeed, I do not eat of their pleasant things. ⁵ The righteous beat me [in] kindness. And reprove me, || My head does not disallow oil of the head, || For my prayer [is] still about their distress. ⁶ Their judges have been released by the sides of a rock, || And they have heard my sayings, || For they have been pleasant. ⁷ As one tilling and ripping up in the land, || Have our bones been scattered at the command of Saul. ⁸ But to You, O YHWH, my Lord, [are] my eyes, || In You I have trusted, || Do not make my soul bare. ⁹ Keep me from the trap they laid for me, || Even snares of workers of iniquity. ¹⁰ The wicked fall in their dragnets together, until I pass over!

PSALM 142

¹ AN INSTRUCTION OF DAVID. A PRAYER WHEN HE IS IN THE CAVE. My voice [is] to YHWH, I cry, || My voice [is] to YHWH, I beg [for] grace. ² I pour forth my meditation before Him, || I declare my distress before Him. ³ When my spirit has been feeble in me, || Then You have known my path; In the way [in] which I walk, || They have hid a snare for me. ⁴ Looking on the right hand—and seeing, || And I have none recognizing; Refuge has perished from me, || There is none inquiring for my soul. ⁵ I have cried to you, O YHWH, || I have said, "You [are] my refuge, || My portion in the land of the living." ⁶ Attend to my loud cry, || For I have become very low, || Deliver me from my pursuers, || For they have been stronger than I. ⁷ Bring forth my soul from prison to confess Your Name, || The righteous surround me about, || When You confer benefits on me!

PSALM 143

¹ A PSALM OF DAVID. O YHWH, hear my prayer, || Give ear to my supplications, || Answer me in Your faithfulness—in Your righteousness. ² And do not enter into judgment with Your servant, || For no one living is justified before You. ³ For an enemy has pursued my soul, || He has bruised my life to the earth, || He has caused me to dwell in dark places, || As the dead of old. ⁴ And my spirit has become feeble in me, || My heart has become desolate within me. ⁵ I have remembered days of old, || I have meditated on all Your acts, || I muse on the work of Your hand. ⁶ I have spread forth my hands to You, || My soul [is] as a weary land for You. Selah. ⁷ Hurry, answer me, O YHWH, || My spirit has been consumed, || Do not hide Your face from me, || Or I have been compared with those going down [to] the pit. ⁸ Cause me to hear Your kindness in the morning, || For I have trusted in You, || Cause me to know the way that I go, || For I have lifted up my soul to You. ⁹ Deliver me from my enemies, O YHWH, || Near You I am covered. ¹⁰ Teach me to do Your good pleasure, || For You [are] my God—Your Spirit [is] good, || Lead me into a land of uprightness. ¹¹ You quicken me for Your Name's sake, O YHWH, || In Your righteousness, You bring out my soul from distress, ¹² And in Your kindness cut off my enemies, || And have destroyed all the adversaries of my soul, || For I [am] Your servant!

PSALM 144

¹ BY DAVID. Blessed [is] YHWH my Rock, || Who is teaching My hands for war, || My fingers for battle. ² My kind one, and my bulwark, || My tower, and my deliverer, || My shield, and in whom I have trusted, || Who is subduing my people under me! ³ YHWH, what [is] man that You know him? The son of man, that You esteem him? ⁴ Man has been like a breath, || His days [are] as a shadow passing by. ⁵ YHWH, incline Your heavens and come down, || Strike against mountains, and they smoke. ⁶ Send forth lightning, and scatter them, || Send forth Your arrows, and trouble them, ⁷ Send forth Your hand from on high, || Free me, and deliver me from many waters, || From the hand of sons of a stranger, ⁸ Because their mouth has spoken vanity, || And their right hand [is] a right hand of falsehood. ⁹ O God, I sing to You a new song, || I sing praise to You on a stringed instrument of ten strings. ¹⁰ Who is giving deliverance to kings, || Who is freeing His servant David from the sword of evil. ¹¹ Free me, and deliver me || From the hand of sons of a stranger, || Because their mouth has spoken vanity, || And their right hand [is] a right hand of falsehood, ¹² Because our sons [are] as plants, || Becoming great in their youth, || Our daughters as hewn stones, || Polished—the likeness of a palace, ¹³ Our granaries [are] full, bringing out from kind to kind, || Our flocks are bringing forth thousands, || Ten thousands in our out-places, ¹⁴ Our oxen are carrying, there is no breach, || And there is no outgoing, || And there is no crying in our broad places. ¹⁵ O the blessedness of the people that is thus, || O the blessedness of the people whose God [is] YHWH!

PSALM 145

¹ A PRAISE [SONG] OF DAVID. [ALEPH-BET] I exalt You, my God, O king, || And bless Your Name for all time and forever. ² Every day I bless You, || And praise Your Name for all time and forever. ³ YHWH [is] great, and greatly praised, || And there is no searching of His greatness. ⁴ Generation to generation praises Your works, || And they declare Your mighty acts. ⁵ The majesty, the glory of Your splendor, || And the matters of Your wonders, I declare. ⁶ And they tell of the strength of Your fearful acts, || And I recount Your greatness. ⁷ They send forth the memorial of the abundance of Your goodness. And they sing of Your righteousness. ⁸ YHWH [is] gracious and merciful, || Slow to anger, and great in kindness. ⁹ YHWH [is] good to all, || And His mercies [are] over all His works. ¹⁰ O YHWH, all Your works confess You, || And Your saints bless You. ¹¹ They tell of the glory of Your kingdom, || And they speak of Your might, ¹² To make His mighty acts known to sons of men, || The glory of the majesty of His kingdom. ¹³ Your kingdom [is] a kingdom of all ages, || And Your dominion [is] in all generations. [[YHWH [is] faithful in all His words, || And kind in all His works.]] ¹⁴ YHWH is supporting all who are falling, || And raising up all who are bowed down. ¹⁵ The eyes of all look to You, || And You are giving their food to them in its season, ¹⁶ Opening Your hand, and satisfying || The desire of every living thing. ¹⁷ YHWH [is] righteous in all His ways, || And kind in all His works. ¹⁸ YHWH [is] near to all those calling Him, || To all who call Him in truth. ¹⁹ He does the desire of those fearing Him, || And He hears their cry, and saves them. ²⁰ YHWH preserves all those loving Him, || And He destroys all the wicked. ²¹ My mouth speaks the praise of YHWH, || And all flesh blesses His Holy Name, || For all time and forever!

PSALM 146

¹ Praise YAH! Praise, O my soul, YHWH. ² I praise YHWH during my life, || I sing praise to my God while I exist. ³ Do not trust in princes—in a son of man, || For he has no deliverance. ⁴ His spirit goes forth, he returns to his earth, || In that day his thoughts have perished. ⁵ O the blessedness of him || Who has the God of Jacob for his help, || His hope [is] on his God YHWH, ⁶ Making the heavens and earth, || The sea and all that [is] in them, || Who is keeping truth for all time, ⁷ Doing judgment for the oppressed, || Giving bread to the hungry. ⁸ YHWH is loosing the prisoners, || YHWH is opening (the eyes of) the blind, || YHWH is raising the bowed down, || YHWH is loving the righteous, ⁹ YHWH is preserving the strangers, || He causes the fatherless and widow to stand, || And He turns the way of the wicked upside down. ¹⁰ YHWH reigns for all time, || Your God, O Zion, to generation and generation, || Praise YAH!

PSALM 147

¹ Praise YAH! For [it is] good to praise our God, || For pleasant—lovely [is] praise. ² YHWH [is] building Jerusalem, || He gathers the driven away of Israel. ³ Who is giving healing to the broken of heart, || And is binding up their griefs. ⁴ Appointing the number of the stars, || He gives names to all of them. ⁵ Our Lord [is] great, and abundant in power, || There is no narration of His understanding. ⁶ YHWH is causing the meek to stand, || Making the wicked low to the earth. ⁷ Answer to YHWH with thanksgiving, || Sing to our God with a harp. ⁸ Who is covering the heavens with clouds, || Who is preparing rain for the earth, || Who is causing grass to spring up [on] mountains, ⁹ Giving to the beast its food, || To the young of the ravens that call. ¹⁰ He does not delight in the might of the horse, || He is not pleased in the legs of a man. ¹¹ YHWH is pleased with those fearing Him, || With those waiting for His kindness. ¹² Glorify, O Jerusalem, YHWH, || Praise your God, O Zion. ¹³ For He strengthened the bars of your gates, || He has

blessed your sons in your midst. ¹⁴Who is making your border peace, || He satisfies you [with] the fat of wheat. ¹⁵Who is sending forth His saying [on] earth, || His word runs very speedily. ¹⁶Who is giving snow like wool, || He scatters hoarfrost as ashes. ¹⁷Casting forth His ice like morsels, || Who stands before His cold? ¹⁸He sends forth His word and melts them, || He causes His wind to blow—the waters flow. ¹⁹Declaring His words to Jacob, || His statutes and His judgments to Israel. ²⁰He has not done so to any nation, || As for judgments, they have not known them. Praise YAH!

PSALM 148

¹Praise YAH! Praise YHWH from the heavens, || Praise Him in high places. ²Praise Him, all His messengers, || Praise Him, all His hosts. ³Praise Him, sun and moon, || Praise Him, all stars of light. ⁴Praise Him, heavens of heavens, || And you waters that are above the heavens. ⁵They praise the Name of YHWH, || For He commanded, and they were created. ⁶And He establishes them forever and for all time, || He gave a statute, and they do not pass over. ⁷Praise YHWH from the earth, || Dragons and all deeps, ⁸Fire and hail, snow and vapor, || Whirlwind doing His word; ⁹The mountains and all heights, || Fruit tree, and all cedars, ¹⁰The wild beast, and all livestock, || Creeping thing, and winged bird, ¹¹Kings of earth, and all peoples, || Chiefs, and all judges of earth, ¹²Young men, and also maidens, || Aged men, with youths, ¹³They praise the Name of YHWH, || For His Name alone has been set on high, || His splendor [is] above earth and heavens. ¹⁴And He exalts the horn of His people, || The praise of all His saints, || Of the sons of Israel, || A people near Him. Praise YAH!

PSALM 149

¹Praise YAH! Sing to YHWH a new song, || His praise in an assembly of saints. ²Israel rejoices in his Maker, || Sons of Zion rejoice in their king. ³They praise His Name in a dance, || Sing praise to Him with timbrel and harp. ⁴For YHWH is pleased with His people, || He beautifies the humble with salvation. ⁵Saints exult in glory, || They sing aloud on their beds. ⁶The exaltation of God [is] in their throat, || And a two-edged sword in their hand. ⁷To do vengeance among nations, || Punishments among the peoples. ⁸To bind their kings with chains, || And their honored ones with chains of iron, ⁹To do among them the judgment written, || It [is] an honor for all his saints. Praise YAH!

PSALM 150

¹Praise YAH! Praise God in His holy place, || Praise Him in the expanse of His strength. ²Praise Him in His mighty acts, || Praise Him according to the abundance of His greatness. ³Praise Him with blowing of horn, || Praise Him with stringed instrument and harp. ⁴Praise Him with timbrel and dance, || Praise Him with stringed instruments and pipe. ⁵Praise Him with cymbals of sounding, || Praise Him with cymbals of shouting. ⁶All that breathes praise YAH! Praise YAH!

PROVERBS

CHAPTER 1

¹Proverbs of Solomon, son of David, king of Israel: ²For knowing wisdom and instruction, || For understanding sayings of intelligence, ³For receiving the instruction of wisdom, || Righteousness, judgment, and uprightness, ⁴For giving to simple ones—prudence, || To a youth—knowledge and discretion. ⁵(The wise hear and increase learning, || And the intelligent obtain counsels.) ⁶For understanding a proverb and its sweetness, || Words of the wise and their acute sayings. ⁷Fear of YHWH [is the] beginning of knowledge, || Fools have despised wisdom and instruction! ⁸Hear, my son, the instruction of your father, || And do not leave the law of your mother, ⁹For they [are] a graceful wreath to your head, || And chains to your neck. ¹⁰My son, if sinners entice you, do not be willing. ¹¹If they say, "Come with us, we lay wait for blood, || We watch secretly for the innocent without cause, ¹²We swallow them as Sheol—alive, || And whole—as those going down [to] the pit, ¹³We find every precious substance, || We fill our houses [with] spoil, ¹⁴You cast your lot among us, || One purse is—to all of us." ¹⁵My son! Do not go in the way with them, || Withhold your foot from their path, ¹⁶For their feet run to evil, || And they hurry to shed blood. ¹⁷Surely in vain is the net spread out before the eyes of any bird. ¹⁸And they lay wait for their own blood, || They watch secretly for their own lives. ¹⁹So [are] the paths of every gainer of dishonest gain, || It takes the life of its owners. ²⁰Wisdom cries aloud in an out-place, || She gives forth her voice in broad places, ²¹She calls at the head of the multitudes, || In the openings of the gates, || In the city she says her sayings: ²²"Until when, you simple, do you love simplicity? And have scorners desired their scorning? And do fools hate knowledge? ²³Turn back at my reproof, behold, || I pour forth my spirit to you, || I make known my words with you. ²⁴Because I have called, and you refuse, || I stretched out my hand, and none is attending. ²⁵And you slight all my counsel, || And you have not desired my reproof. ²⁶I also laugh in your calamity, || I deride when your fear comes, ²⁷When your fear comes as destruction, || And your calamity comes as a windstorm, || When adversity and distress come on you. ²⁸Then they call me, and I do not answer, || They seek me earnestly, and do not find me. ²⁹Because that they have hated knowledge, || And have not chosen the fear of YHWH. ³⁰They have not consented to my counsel, || They have despised all my reproof, ³¹And they eat of the fruit of their way, || And they are filled from their own counsels. ³²For the turning of the simple slays them, || And the security of the foolish destroys them. ³³And whoever is listening to me dwells confidently, || And [is] quiet from fear of evil!"

CHAPTER 2

¹My son, if you accept my sayings, || And lay up my commands with you, ²To cause your ear to attend to wisdom, || You incline your heart to understanding, ³For if you call for intelligence, || [And] give forth your voice for intelligence, ⁴If you seek her as silver, || And search for her as hid treasures, ⁵Then you understand the fear of YHWH, || And you find the knowledge of God. ⁶For YHWH gives wisdom, || Knowledge and understanding from His mouth. ⁷Even to lay up substance for the upright, || A shield for those walking uprightly. ⁸To keep the paths of judgment, || And He preserves the way of His saints. ⁹Then you understand righteousness, || And judgment, and uprightness—every good path. ¹⁰For wisdom comes into your heart, || And knowledge is pleasant to your soul, ¹¹Thoughtfulness watches over you, || Understanding keeps you, ¹²To deliver you from an evil way, || From any speaking contrary things, ¹³Who are forsaking paths of uprightness, || To walk in ways of darkness, ¹⁴Who are rejoicing to do evil, || They delight in [the] contrariness of the wicked, ¹⁵Whose paths [are] crooked, || Indeed, they are perverted in their ways. ¹⁶To deliver you from the strange woman, || From the stranger who has made her sayings smooth, ¹⁷Who is forsaking the guide of her youth, || And has forgotten the covenant of her God. ¹⁸For her house has inclined to death, || And her paths to Rephaim. ¹⁹None going in to her return, || Nor do they reach the paths of life. ²⁰That you go in the way of the good, || And keep the paths of the righteous. ²¹For the upright inhabit the earth, || And the perfect are left in it, ²²And the wicked are cut off from the earth, || And treacherous dealers plucked out of it!

PROVERBS

CHAPTER 3

¹My son! Do not forget my law, || And let your heart keep my commands, ²For [the] length of [your] days and years, || Life and peace they add to you. ³Do not let kindness and truth forsake you, || Bind them on your neck, || Write them on the tablet of your heart, ⁴And find grace and good understanding || In the eyes of God and man. ⁵Trust to YHWH with all your heart, || And do not lean to your own understanding. ⁶In all your ways know Him, || And He makes your paths straight. ⁷Do not be wise in your own eyes, || Fear YHWH, and turn aside from evil. ⁸It is healing to your navel, || And moistening to your bones. ⁹Honor YHWH from your substance, || And from the beginning of all your increase; ¹⁰And your barns are filled [with] plenty, || And your presses break forth [with] new wine. ¹¹Discipline of YHWH, my son, do not despise, || And do not be distressed with His reproof, ¹²For whom YHWH loves He reproves, || Even as a father the son He is pleased with. ¹³O the blessedness of a man [who] has found wisdom, || And of a man [who] brings forth understanding. ¹⁴For better [is] her merchandise || Than the merchandise of silver, || And than gold—her increase. ¹⁵She [is] precious above rubies, || And all your pleasures are not comparable to her. ¹⁶Length of days [is] in her right hand, || In her left [are] wealth and honor. ¹⁷Her ways [are] ways of pleasantness, || And all her paths [are] peace. ¹⁸She [is] a tree of life to those laying hold on her, || And whoever is retaining her [is] blessed. ¹⁹YHWH founded the earth by wisdom, || He prepared the heavens by understanding. ²⁰By His knowledge depths have been broken, || And clouds drop dew. ²¹My son! Do not let them turn from your eyes, || Keep wisdom and thoughtfulness, ²²And they are life to your soul, and grace to your neck. ²³Then you go your way confidently, || And your foot does not stumble. ²⁴If you lie down, you are not afraid, || Indeed, you have lain down, || And your sleep has been sweet. ²⁵Do not be afraid of sudden fear, || And of the desolation of the wicked when it comes. ²⁶For YHWH is at your side, || And He has kept your foot from capture. ²⁷Do not withhold good from its owners, || When your hand [is] toward God to do [it]. ²⁸Do not say to your friend, || "Go, and return, and tomorrow I give," || When substance [is] with you. ²⁹Do not devise evil against your neighbor, || And he sitting confidently with you. ³⁰Do not strive with a man without cause, || If he has not done you evil. ³¹Do not be envious of a man of violence, || Nor fix on any of his ways. ³²For the perverted [is] an abomination to YHWH, || And His secret counsel [is] with the upright. ³³The curse of YHWH [is] in the house of the wicked. And He blesses the habitation of the righteous. ³⁴If He scorns the scorners, || Yet He gives grace to the humble. ³⁵The wise inherit glory, || And fools are bearing away shame!

CHAPTER 4

¹Hear, you sons, the instruction of a father, || And give attention to know understanding. ²For I have given to you good learning, do not forsake my law. ³For I have been a son to my father—tender, || And an only one before my mother. ⁴And he directs me, and he says to me: "Let your heart retain my words, || Keep my commands, and live. ⁵Get wisdom, get understanding, || Do not forget, nor turn away || From the sayings of my mouth. ⁶Do not forsake her, and she preserves you, || Love her, and she keeps you. ⁷The first thing [is] wisdom—get wisdom, || And with all your getting get understanding. ⁸Exalt her and she lifts you up, || She honors you when you embrace her. ⁹She gives a wreath of grace to your head, || She gives you a crown of beauty freely." ¹⁰Hear, my son, and receive my sayings, || And years of life [are] multiplied to you. ¹¹I have directed you in a way of wisdom, || I have caused you to tread in paths of uprightness. ¹²In your walking your step is not restricted, || And if you run, you do not stumble. ¹³Lay hold on instruction, do not desist, || Keep her, for she [is] your life. ¹⁴Do not enter into the path of the wicked, || And do not be blessed in a way of evildoers. ¹⁵Avoid it, do not pass over into it, || Turn aside from it, and pass on. ¹⁶For they do not sleep if they do no evil, || And their sleep has been taken away violently, || If they do not cause [some] to stumble. ¹⁷For they have eaten bread of wickedness, || And they drink wine of violence. ¹⁸And the path of the righteous [is] as a shining light, || Going and brightening until the day is established, ¹⁹The way of the wicked [is] as darkness, || They have not known at what they stumble. ²⁰My son, give attention to my words, || Incline your ear to my sayings, ²¹Do not let them turn aside from your eyes, || Preserve them in the midst of your heart. ²²For they [are] life to those finding them, || And healing to all their flesh. ²³Above every charge keep your heart, || For out of it [are] the outgoings of life. ²⁴Turn aside a contrary mouth from you, || And put perverse lips far from you, ²⁵Your eyes look straightforward, || And your eyelids look straight before you. ²⁶Ponder the path of your feet, || And all your ways [are] established. ²⁷Do not incline [to] the right or to the left, || Turn aside your foot from evil!

CHAPTER 5

¹My son! Give attention to my wisdom, || Incline your ear to my understanding, ²To observe thoughtfulness, || And your lips keep knowledge. ³For the lips of a strange woman drop honey, || And her mouth [is] smoother than oil, ⁴And her latter end [is] bitter as wormwood, || Sharp as a sword [with] mouths. ⁵Her feet are going down to death, || Her steps take hold of Sheol. ⁶The path of life—lest you ponder, || Her paths have moved—you do not know. ⁷And now, you sons, listen to me, || And do not turn from sayings of my mouth. ⁸Keep your way far from off her, || And do not come near to the opening of her house, ⁹Lest you give your splendor to others, || And your years to the fierce, ¹⁰Lest strangers be filled [with] your power, || And your labors in the house of a stranger, ¹¹And you have howled in your latter end, || In the consumption of your flesh and your food, ¹²And have said, "How I have hated instruction, || And my heart has despised reproof, ¹³And I have not listened to the voice of my teachers, || And have not inclined my ear to my teachers. ¹⁴As a little thing I have been all evil, || In the midst of an assembly and a congregation." ¹⁵Drink waters out of your own cistern, || Even flowing ones out of your own well. ¹⁶Let your fountains be scattered abroad, || In broad places streams of waters. ¹⁷Let them be to you for yourself, || And not to strangers with you. ¹⁸Let your fountain be blessed, || And rejoice because of the wife of your youth, ¹⁹A doe of loves, and a roe of grace! Let her loves satisfy you at all times, || Magnify yourself in her love continually. ²⁰And why do you magnify yourself, || My son, with a stranger? And embrace the bosom of a strange woman? ²¹For the ways of each are before the eyes of YHWH, || And He is pondering all his paths. ²²His own iniquities capture the wicked, || And he is holden with the ropes of his sin. ²³He dies without instruction, || And magnifies himself in the abundance of his folly!

CHAPTER 6

¹My son! If you have been guarantor for your friend, || Have struck your hand for a stranger, ²Have been snared with sayings of your mouth, || Have been captured with sayings of your mouth, ³Do this now, my son, and be delivered, || For you have come into the hand of your friend. Go, trample on yourself, and strengthen your friend, ⁴Do not give sleep to your eyes, || And slumber to your eyelids, ⁵Be delivered as a roe from the hand, || And as a bird from the hand of a fowler. ⁶Go to the ant, O slothful one, || See her ways and be wise; ⁷Which has no captain, overseer, and ruler, ⁸She prepares her bread in summer, || She gathered her food in harvest. ⁹Until when, O slothful one, do you lie? When do you arise from your sleep? ¹⁰A little sleep, a little slumber, || A little clasping of the hands to rest, ¹¹And your poverty has come as a traveler, || And your want as an armed man. ¹²A man of worthlessness, a man of iniquity, || Walking [with] perverseness of mouth, ¹³Winking with his eyes, speaking with his feet, || Directing with his fingers, ¹⁴Contrariness [is] in his heart, devising evil at all times, || He sends forth contentions. ¹⁵Therefore his calamity comes suddenly, || He is broken instantly—and no healing. ¹⁶These six has YHWH hated, || Indeed, seven [are] abominations to His soul: ¹⁷High eyes, || False tongues, || And hands shedding innocent blood, ¹⁸A heart devising thoughts of vanity, || Feet hastening to run to evil, ¹⁹A false witness [who] breathes out lies, || And one sending forth contentions between brothers. ²⁰Keep, my son, the command of your father, || And do not leave the law of your mother. ²¹Bind them on your heart continually, || Tie them on your neck. ²²In your going up and down, it leads you, || In your lying down, it watches over you, || And you have awoken—it talks [with] you. ²³For the command [is] a

lamp, || And the Law a light, || And a way of life [are] reproofs of instruction, ²⁴To preserve you from an evil woman, || From the flattery of the tongue of a strange woman. ²⁵Do not desire her beauty in your heart, || And do not let her take you with her eyelids. ²⁶For a harlot consumes to a cake of bread, || And an adulteress hunts the precious soul. ²⁷Does a man take fire into his bosom, || And are his garments not burned? ²⁸Does a man walk on the hot coals, || And are his feet not scorched? ²⁹So [is] he who has gone in to the wife of his neighbor, || None who touches her is innocent. ³⁰They do not despise the thief, || When he steals to fill his soul when he is hungry, ³¹And being found he repays sevenfold, || He gives all the substance of his house. ³²He who commits adultery [with] a woman lacks heart, || He who does it is destroying his soul. ³³He finds a stroke and shame, || And his reproach is not wiped away, ³⁴For jealousy [is] the fury of a man, || And he does not spare in a day of vengeance. ³⁵He does not accept the appearance of any atonement, || Indeed, he does not consent, || Though you multiply bribes!

CHAPTER 7

¹My son! Keep my sayings, || And lay up my commands with you. ²Keep my commands, and live, || And my law as the pupil of your eye. ³Bind them on your fingers, || Write them on the tablet of your heart. ⁴Say to wisdom, "You [are] my sister." And cry to understanding, "Relative!" ⁵To preserve you from a strange woman, || From a stranger who has made her sayings smooth. ⁶For at a window of my house, || I have looked out through my casement, ⁷And I see among the simple ones, || I discern among the sons, || A young man lacking understanding, ⁸Passing on in the street, near her corner, || And the way [to] her house he steps, ⁹In the twilight—in the evening of day, || In the darkness of night and blackness. ¹⁰And behold, a woman to meet him—(A harlot's dress, and watchful of heart, ¹¹She [is] noisy, and stubborn, her feet do not rest in her house. ¹²Now in an out-place, now in broad places, || And she lies in wait near every corner)— ¹³And she laid hold on him and kissed him, || She has hardened her face and says to him, ¹⁴"Sacrifices of peace-offerings [are] by me, || Today I have completed my vows. ¹⁵Therefore I have come forth to meet you, || To earnestly seek your face, and I find you. ¹⁶I decked my bed [with] ornamental coverings, || Carved works—cotton of Egypt. ¹⁷I sprinkled my bed [with] myrrh, aloes, and cinnamon. ¹⁸Come, we are filled [with] love until the morning, || We delight ourselves in loves. ¹⁹For the man is not in his house, || He has gone on a long journey. ²⁰He has taken a bag of money in his hand, || At the day of the new moon he comes to his house." ²¹She turns him aside with the abundance of her speech, || She forces him with the flattery of her lips. ²²He is going after her straight away, he comes as an ox to the slaughter, || And as a chain to the discipline of a fool, ²³Until an arrow splits his liver, || As a bird has hurried to a snare, || And has not known that it [is] for its life. ²⁴And now, you sons, listen to me, || And give attention to sayings of my mouth. ²⁵Do not let your heart turn to her ways, || Do not wander in her paths, ²⁶For many [are] the wounded she caused to fall, || And mighty [are] all her slain ones. ²⁷The ways of Sheol—her house, || Going down to inner chambers of death!

CHAPTER 8

¹Does wisdom not call? And understanding give forth her voice? ²At the head of high places by the way, || She has stood between the paths, ³At the side of the gates, at the mouth of the city, || The entrance of the openings, she cries aloud, ⁴"To you, O men, I call, || And my voice [is] to the sons of men. ⁵Understand, you simple ones, prudence, || And you fools, understand the heart, ⁶Listen, for I speak noble things, || And the opening of my lips [is] uprightness. ⁷For my mouth utters truth, || And wickedness [is] an abomination to my lips. ⁸All the sayings of my mouth [are] in righteousness, || Nothing in them is contrary and perverse. ⁹All of them [are] plain to the intelligent, || And upright to those finding knowledge. ¹⁰Receive my instruction, and not silver, || And knowledge rather than choice gold. ¹¹For wisdom [is] better than rubies, || Indeed, all delights are not comparable with it. ¹²I, wisdom, have dwelt with prudence, || And I find out a knowledge of purposes. ¹³The fear of YHWH [is] to hate evil; Pride, and arrogance, and an evil way, || And a contrary mouth, I have hated. ¹⁴Counsel and substance [are] mine, || I [am] understanding, I have might. ¹⁵By me kings reign, and princes decree righteousness, ¹⁶By me chiefs rule, and nobles, || All judges of earth. ¹⁷I love those loving me, || And those seeking me earnestly find me. ¹⁸Wealth and honor [are] with me, || Lasting substance and righteousness. ¹⁹My fruit [is] better than gold, even fine gold, || And my increase than choice silver. ²⁰I cause to walk in a path of righteousness, || In midst of paths of judgment, ²¹To cause my lovers to inherit substance, || Indeed, I fill their treasures. ²²YHWH possessed me—the beginning of His way, || Before His works since then. ²³I was anointed from the age, from the first, || From former states of the earth. ²⁴In there being no depths, I was brought forth, || In there being no fountains heavy [with] waters, ²⁵Before mountains were sunk, || Before heights, I was brought forth. ²⁶While He had not made the earth, and out-places, || And the top of the dusts of the world. ²⁷In His preparing the heavens I [am] there, || In His decreeing a circle on the face of the deep, ²⁸In His strengthening clouds above, || In His making strong fountains of the deep, ²⁹In His setting for the sea its limit, || And the waters do not transgress His command, || In His decreeing the foundations of earth, ³⁰Then I am near Him, a workman, || And I am a delight—day by day. Rejoicing before Him at all times, ³¹Rejoicing in the habitable part of His earth, || And my delights [are] with the sons of men. ³²And now, you sons, listen to me, || Indeed, blessed are they who keep my ways. ³³Hear instruction, and be wise, and do not slight. ³⁴O the blessedness of the man listening to me, || To watch at my doors day by day, || To watch at the doorposts of my entrance. ³⁵For whoever is finding me, has found life, || And brings out goodwill from YHWH. ³⁶And whoever is missing me, is wronging his soul, || All hating me have loved death!"

CHAPTER 9

¹Wisdom has built her house, || She has hewn out her pillars—seven. ²She has slaughtered her slaughter, || She has mingled her wine, || Indeed, she has arranged her table. ³She has sent forth her girls, || She cries on the tops of the high places of the city: ⁴"Who [is] simple? Let him turn aside here." Whoever lacks heart: she has said to him, ⁵"Come, eat of my bread, || And drink of the wine I have mingled. ⁶Forsake the simple and live, || And be blessed in the way of understanding." ⁷The instructor of a scorner || Is receiving for it—shame, || And a reprover of the wicked—his blemish. ⁸Do not reprove a scorner, lest he hate you, || Give reproof to the wise, and he loves you. ⁹Give to the wise, and he is wiser still, || Make known to the righteous, || And he increases learning. ¹⁰The commencement of wisdom [is] the fear of YHWH, || And a knowledge of the Holy Ones [is] understanding. ¹¹For by me your days multiply, || And years of life are added to you. ¹²If you have been wise, you have been wise for yourself, || And you have scorned—you bear [it] alone. ¹³A foolish woman [is] noisy, || Simple, and has not known what. ¹⁴And she has sat at the opening of her house, || On a throne—the high places of the city, ¹⁵To call to those passing by the way, || Who are going straight [on] their paths. ¹⁶"Who [is] simple? Let him turn aside here." And whoever lacks heart—she said to him, ¹⁷"Stolen waters are sweet, || And hidden bread is pleasant." ¹⁸And he has not known that Rephaim [are] there, || Her invited ones in deep places of Sheol!

CHAPTER 10

¹Proverbs of Solomon. A wise son causes a father to rejoice, || And a foolish son [is] an affliction to his mother. ²Treasures of wickedness do not profit, || And righteousness delivers from death. ³YHWH does not cause the soul of the righteous to hunger, || And He thrusts away the desire of the wicked. ⁴Poor [is] he who is working [with] a slothful hand, || And the hand of the diligent makes rich. ⁵Whoever is gathering in summer [is] a wise son, || Whoever is sleeping in harvest [is] a son causing shame. ⁶Blessings [are] for the head of the righteous, || And the mouth of the wicked covers violence. ⁷The remembrance of the righteous [is] for a blessing, || And the name of the wicked rots. ⁸The wise in heart accepts commands, || And a talkative fool kicks. ⁹Whoever is walking in integrity walks confidently, || And whoever is perverting his ways is known. ¹⁰Whoever is winking the eye gives grief, || And a talkative fool kicks. ¹¹A fountain of life [is] the mouth of

the righteous, || And the mouth of the wicked covers violence. ¹²Hatred awakens contentions, || And love covers over all transgressions. ¹³Wisdom is found in the lips of the intelligent, || And a rod [is] for the back of him who is lacking understanding. ¹⁴The wise lay up knowledge, and the mouth of a fool [is] near ruin. ¹⁵The wealth of the rich [is] his strong city, || The ruin of the poor [is] their poverty. ¹⁶The wage of the righteous [is] for life, || The increase of the wicked for sin. ¹⁷A traveler to life [is] he who is keeping instruction, || And whoever is forsaking rebuke is erring. ¹⁸Whoever is covering hatred with lying lips, || And whoever is bringing out an evil report is a fool. ¹⁹In the abundance of words transgression does not cease, || And whoever is restraining his lips [is] wise. ²⁰The tongue of the righteous [is] chosen silver, || The heart of the wicked—as a little thing. ²¹The lips of the righteous delight many, || And fools die for lack of heart. ²²The blessing of YHWH—it makes rich, || And He adds no grief with it. ²³To execute inventions [is] as play to a fool, || And wisdom to a man of understanding. ²⁴The feared thing of the wicked meets him, || And the desire of the righteous is given. ²⁵As the passing by of a windstorm, || So the wicked is not, || And the righteous is a perpetual foundation. ²⁶As vinegar to the teeth, || And as smoke to the eyes, || So [is] the slothful to those sending him. ²⁷The fear of YHWH adds days, || And the years of the wicked are shortened. ²⁸The hope of the righteous [is] joyful, || And the expectation of the wicked perishes. ²⁹The way of YHWH [is] strength to the perfect, || And ruin to workers of iniquity. ³⁰The righteous is not moved for all time, || And the wicked do not inhabit the earth. ³¹The mouth of the righteous utters wisdom, || And the tongue of contrariness is cut out. ³²The lips of the righteous know a pleasing thing, || And the mouth of the wicked perverseness!

CHAPTER 11

¹Balances of deceit [are] an abomination to YHWH, || And a perfect weight [is] His delight. ²Pride has come, and shame comes, || And wisdom [is] with the lowly. ³The integrity of the upright leads them, || And the perverseness of the treacherous destroys them. ⁴Wealth does not profit in a day of wrath, || And righteousness delivers from death. ⁵The righteousness of the perfect makes his way right, || And by his wickedness the wicked fall. ⁶The righteousness of the upright delivers them, || And in mischief the treacherous are captured. ⁷In the death of a wicked man, hope perishes, || And the expectation of the iniquitous has been lost. ⁸The righteous is drawn out from distress, || And the wicked goes in instead of him. ⁹A hypocrite corrupts his friend with the mouth, || And the righteous are drawn out by knowledge. ¹⁰A city exults in the good of the righteous, || And in the destruction of the wicked [is] singing. ¹¹By the blessing of the upright is a city exalted, || And by the mouth of the wicked thrown down. ¹²Whoever is despising his neighbor lacks heart, || And a man of understanding keeps silence. ¹³A busybody is revealing secret counsel, || And the faithful of spirit is covering the matter. ¹⁴Without counsels a people falls, || And deliverance [is] in a multitude of counselors. ¹⁵An evil [one] suffers when he has been guarantor [for] a stranger, || And whoever hates striking hands [in agreement] is confident. ¹⁶A gracious woman retains honor, || And terrible [men] retain riches. ¹⁷A kind man is rewarding his own soul, || And the fierce is troubling his own flesh. ¹⁸The wicked is getting a lying wage, || And whoever is sowing righteousness—a true reward. ¹⁹Correctly [is] righteousness for life, || And whoever is pursuing evil—for his own death. ²⁰The perverse of heart are an abomination to YHWH, || And the perfect of the way [are] His delight. ²¹Hand to hand, the wicked is not acquitted, || And the seed of the righteous has escaped. ²²A ring of gold in the nose of a sow— A beautiful woman and stubborn of behavior. ²³The desire of the righteous [is] only good, || The hope of the wicked [is] transgression. ²⁴There is [one] who is scattering, and yet is increased, || And [one] who is keeping back from uprightness, only to want. ²⁵A liberal soul is made fat, || And whoever is watering, he also is watered. ²⁶Whoever is withholding grain, the people execrate him, || And a blessing [is] for the head of him who is selling. ²⁷Whoever is earnestly seeking good || Seeks a pleasing thing, || And whoever is seeking evil—it meets him. ²⁸Whoever is confident in his wealth falls, || And as a leaf, the righteous flourish. ²⁹Whoever is troubling his own house inherits wind, || And the fool [is] a servant to the wise of heart. ³⁰The fruit of the righteous [is] a tree of life, || And whoever is taking souls [is] wise. ³¹Behold, the righteous is repaid in the earth, || Surely also the wicked and the sinner!

CHAPTER 12

¹Whoever is loving instruction, is loving knowledge, || And whoever is hating reproof [is] brutish. ²The good brings forth favor from YHWH, || And the man of wicked schemes He condemns. ³A man is not established by wickedness, || And the root of the righteous is not moved. ⁴A virtuous woman [is] a crown to her husband, || And as rottenness in his bones [is] one causing shame. ⁵The thoughts of the righteous [are] justice, || The counsels of the wicked—deceit. ⁶The words of the wicked [are]: "Lay [in] wait for blood," || And the mouth of the upright delivers them. ⁷Overthrow the wicked, and they are not, || And the house of the righteous stands. ⁸A man is praised according to his wisdom, || And the perverted of heart becomes despised. ⁹Better [is] the lightly esteemed who has a servant, || Than the self-honored who lacks bread. ¹⁰The righteous knows the life of his beast, || And the mercies of the wicked [are] cruel. ¹¹Whoever is tilling the ground is satisfied [with] bread, || And whoever is pursuing vanities is lacking heart. ¹²The wicked has desired the net of evildoers, || And the root of the righteous gives. ¹³The snare of the wicked [is] in transgression of the lips, || And the righteous goes out from distress. ¹⁴One [is] satisfied [with] good from the fruit of the mouth, || And the deed of man's hands returns to him. ¹⁵The way of a fool [is] right in his own eyes, || And whoever is listening to counsel [is] wise. ¹⁶The fool—his anger is known in a day, || And the prudent is covering shame. ¹⁷Whoever utters faithfulness declares righteousness, || And a false witness—deceit. ¹⁸A rash speaker is like piercings of a sword, || And the tongue of the wise is healing. ¹⁹The lip of truth is established forever, || And a tongue of falsehood for a moment. ²⁰Deceit [is] in the heart of those devising evil, || But for counselors of peace— joy. ²¹No iniquity is desired by the righteous, || And the wicked have been full of evil. ²²Lying lips [are] an abomination to YHWH, || And steadfast doers [are] his delight. ²³A prudent man is concealing knowledge, || And the heart of fools proclaims folly. ²⁴The hand of the diligent rules, || And slothfulness becomes tributary. ²⁵Sorrow in the heart of a man bows down, || And a good word makes him glad. ²⁶The righteous searches his companion, || And the way of the wicked causes them to err. ²⁷The slothful does not roast his game, || And the wealth of a diligent man is precious. ²⁸In the path of righteousness [is] life, || And in the way of [that] path [is] no death!

CHAPTER 13

¹A wise son—the instruction of a father, || And a scorner—he has not heard rebuke. ²A man eats good from the fruit of the mouth, || And the soul of the treacherous—violence. ³Whoever is keeping his mouth, is keeping his soul, || Whoever is opening wide his lips— ruin to him! ⁴The soul of the slothful is desiring, and does not have. And the soul of the diligent is made fat. ⁵The righteous hates a false word, || And the wicked causes abhorrence, and is confounded. ⁶Righteousness keeps him who is perfect in the way, || And wickedness overthrows a sin offering. ⁷There is [he] who is making himself rich, and has nothing, || Who is making himself poor, and wealth [is] abundant. ⁸The ransom of a man's life [are] his riches, || And the poor has not heard rebuke. ⁹The light of the righteous rejoices, || And the lamp of the wicked is extinguished. ¹⁰A vain man causes debate through pride, || And wisdom [is] with the counseled. ¹¹Wealth from vanity becomes little, || And whoever is gathering by the hand becomes great. ¹²Hope prolonged is making the heart sick, || And a tree of life [is] the coming desire. ¹³Whoever is despising the word is destroyed for it, || And whoever is fearing the command is repaid. ¹⁴The law of the wise [is] a fountain of life, || To turn aside from snares of death. ¹⁵Good understanding gives grace, || And the way of the treacherous [is] hard. ¹⁶Every prudent one deals with knowledge, || And a fool spreads out folly. ¹⁷A wicked messenger falls into evil, || And a faithful ambassador is healing. ¹⁸Whoever is refusing instruction—poverty and shame, || And whoever is observing reproof is honored.

PROVERBS

¹⁹A desire accomplished is sweet to the soul, || And an abomination to fools || [Is] to turn from evil. ²⁰Whoever is walking with wise men is wise, || And a companion of fools suffers evil. ²¹Evil pursues sinners, || And good repays the righteous. ²²A good man causes sons' sons to inherit, || And the sinner's wealth [is] laid up for the righteous. ²³Abundance of food—the tillage of the poor, || And substance is consumed without judgment. ²⁴Whoever is sparing his rod is hating his son, || And whoever is loving him has hurried his discipline. ²⁵The righteous is eating to the satiety of his soul, || And the belly of the wicked lacks!

CHAPTER 14

¹Every wise woman has built her house, || And the foolish breaks it down with her hands. ²Whoever is walking in his uprightness is fearing YHWH, || And the perverted is despising Him [in] his ways. ³A rod of pride [is] in the mouth of a fool, || And the lips of the wise preserve them. ⁴Without oxen a stall [is] clean, || And great [is] the increase by the power of the ox. ⁵A faithful witness does not lie, || And a false witness breathes out lies. ⁶A scorner has sought wisdom, and it is not, || And knowledge [is] easy to the intelligent. ⁷Go from before a foolish man, || Or you have not known the lips of knowledge. ⁸The wisdom of the prudent [is] to understand his way, || And the folly of fools [is] deceit. ⁹Fools mock at a guilt-offering, || And among the upright—a pleasing thing. ¹⁰The heart knows its own bitterness, || And a stranger does not interfere with its joy. ¹¹The house of the wicked is destroyed, || And the tent of the upright flourishes. ¹²There is a way—right before a man, || And its latter end [are] ways of death. ¹³Even in laughter is the heart pained, || And the latter end of joy [is] affliction. ¹⁴The backslider in heart is filled from his ways, || And a good man—from his fruits. ¹⁵The simple gives credence to everything, || And the prudent attends to his step. ¹⁶The wise is fearing and turning from evil, || And a fool is transgressing and is confident. ¹⁷Whoever is short of temper does folly, || And a man of wicked schemes is hated. ¹⁸The simple have inherited folly, || And the prudent are crowned [with] knowledge. ¹⁹The evil have bowed down before the good, || And the wicked at the gates of the righteous. ²⁰The poor is hated even of his neighbor, || And those loving the rich [are] many. ²¹Whoever is despising his neighbor sins, || Whoever is favoring the humble, || O his blessedness. ²²Do they who are devising evil not err? And kindness and truth [are] to those devising good, ²³In all labor there is advantage, || And a thing of the lips [is] only to want. ²⁴The crown of the wise is their wealth, || The folly of fools [is] folly. ²⁵A true witness is delivering souls, || And a deceitful one breathes out lies. ²⁶Strong confidence [is] in the fear of YHWH, || And there is a refuge to His sons. ²⁷The fear of YHWH [is] a fountain of life, || To turn aside from snares of death. ²⁸The honor of a king [is] in the multitude of a people, || And the ruin of a prince in lack of people. ²⁹Whoever is slow to anger [is] of great understanding, || And whoever is short in temper is exalting folly. ³⁰A healed heart [is] life to the flesh, || And rottenness to the bones [is] envy. ³¹An oppressor of the poor reproaches his Maker, || And whoever is honoring Him || Is favoring the needy. ³²The wicked is driven away in his wickedness, || And the righteous [is] trustful in his death. ³³Wisdom rests in the heart of the intelligent. And it is known in the midst of fools. ³⁴Righteousness exalts a nation, || And the righteousness of peoples [is] a sin-offering. ³⁵The favor of a king [is] to a wise servant, || And one causing shame is an object of his wrath!

CHAPTER 15

¹A soft answer turns back fury, || And a grievous word raises up anger. ²The tongue of the wise makes knowledge good, || And the mouth of fools utters folly. ³The eyes of YHWH are in every place, || Watching the evil and the good. ⁴A healed tongue [is] a tree of life, || And perverseness in it—a breach in the spirit. ⁵A fool despises the instruction of his father, || And whoever is regarding reproof is prudent. ⁶Abundant strength [is in] the house of the righteous, || And in the increase of the wicked—trouble. ⁷The lips of the wise scatter knowledge, || And the heart of fools [is] not right. ⁸The sacrifice of the wicked [is] an abomination to YHWH, || And the prayer of the upright [is] His delight. ⁹The way of the wicked [is] an abomination to YHWH, || And He loves whoever is pursuing righteousness. ¹⁰Discipline [is] grievous to him who is forsaking the path, || Whoever is hating reproof dies. ¹¹Sheol and destruction [are] before YHWH, || Surely also the hearts of the sons of men. ¹²A scorner does not love his reprover, || He does not go to the wise. ¹³A joyful heart makes the face glad, || And the spirit is struck by grief of heart. ¹⁴The heart of the intelligent seeks knowledge, || And the mouth of fools enjoys folly. ¹⁵All the days of the afflicted [are] evil, || And gladness of heart [is] a perpetual banquet. ¹⁶Better [is] a little with the fear of YHWH, || Than much treasure, and tumult with it. ¹⁷Better [is] an allowance of green herbs and love there, || Than a fatted ox, and hatred with it. ¹⁸A man of fury stirs up contention, || And the slow to anger appeases strife. ¹⁹The way of the slothful [is] as a hedge of briers, || And the path of the upright is raised up. ²⁰A wise son makes a father glad. And a foolish man is despising his mother. ²¹Folly is joy to one lacking heart, || And a man of intelligence directs [his] going. ²²The making void of purposes [is] without counsel, || And in a multitude of counselors it is established. ²³Joy [is] to a man in the answer of his mouth, || And a word in its season—how good! ²⁴A path of life [is] on high for the wise, || To turn aside from Sheol beneath. ²⁵YHWH pulls down the house of the proud, || And He sets up the border of the widow. ²⁶Thoughts of wickedness [are] an abomination to YHWH, || And sayings of pleasantness [are] pure. ²⁷A dishonest gainer is troubling his house, || And whoever is hating gifts lives. ²⁸The heart of the righteous meditates to answer, || And the mouth of the wicked utters evil things. ²⁹YHWH [is] far from the wicked, || And He hears the prayer of the righteous. ³⁰The light of the eyes makes the heart glad, || A good report makes the bone fat. ³¹An ear that is hearing the reproof of life || Lodges among the wise. ³²Whoever is refusing instruction is despising his soul, || And whoever is hearing reproof || Is getting understanding. ³³The fear of YHWH [is] the instruction of wisdom, || And humility [is] before honor!

CHAPTER 16

¹Arrangements of the heart [are] of man, || An answer of the tongue from YHWH. ²All the ways of a man are pure in his own eyes, || And YHWH is pondering the spirits. ³Roll your works to YHWH, || And your purposes are established, ⁴YHWH has worked all things for Himself, || And also the wicked—for a day of evil. ⁵Every proud one of heart [is] an abomination to YHWH, || Hand to hand—he is not acquitted. ⁶Iniquity is pardoned in kindness and truth, || And in the fear of YHWH || Turn aside from evil. ⁷When a man's ways please YHWH, even his enemies, || He causes to be at peace with him. ⁸Better [is] a little with righteousness, || Than abundance of increase without justice. ⁹The heart of man devises his way, || And YHWH establishes his step. ¹⁰An oath [is] on the lips of a king, || In judgment his mouth does not trespass. ¹¹A just beam and balances [are] YHWH's, || All the stones of the bag [are] His work. ¹²Doing wickedness [is] an abomination to kings, || For a throne is established by righteousness. ¹³Righteous lips [are] the delight of kings, || And he loves whoever is speaking uprightly, ¹⁴The fury of a king [is] messengers of death, || And a wise man pacifies it. ¹⁵In the light of a king's face [is] life, || And his goodwill [is] as a cloud of the spring rain. ¹⁶To get wisdom—how much better than gold, || And to get understanding—to be chosen [more] than silver! ¹⁷A highway of the upright [is] to turn from evil, || Whoever is preserving his soul is watching his way. ¹⁸Pride [is] before destruction, || And before stumbling—a haughty spirit. ¹⁹Better is humility of spirit with the poor, || Than to apportion spoil with the proud. ²⁰The wise in any matter finds good, || And whoever is trusting in YHWH, O his blessedness. ²¹For the wise in heart is called intelligent, || And sweetness of lips increases learning. ²²Understanding [is] a fountain of life to its possessors, || The instruction of fools is folly. ²³The heart of the wise causes his mouth to act wisely, || And he increases learning by his lips, ²⁴Sayings of pleasantness [are] a honeycomb, || Sweet to the soul, and healing to the bone. ²⁵There is a way right before a man, || And its latter end—ways of death. ²⁶A laboring man has labored for himself, || For his mouth has caused [him] to bend over it. ²⁷A worthless man is preparing evil, || And on his lips [is] as a burning fire. ²⁸A contrary man sends forth contention, || A tale-bearer is separating a familiar friend. ²⁹A violent man

entices his neighbor, || And causes him to go in a way [that is] not good. ³⁰Consulting his eyes to devise contrary things, || Moving his lips he has accomplished evil. ³¹Grey hairs [are] a crown of beauty, || It is found in the way of righteousness. ³²Better [is] the [one] slow to anger than the mighty, || And the ruler over his spirit than he who is taking a city. ³³The lot is cast into the center, || And all its judgment [is] from YHWH!

CHAPTER 17

¹Better [is] a dry morsel, and rest with it, || Than a house full of the sacrifices of strife. ²A wise servant rules over a son causing shame, || And he apportions an inheritance in the midst of brothers. ³A refining pot [is] for silver, and a furnace for gold, || And the trier of hearts [is] YHWH. ⁴An evildoer is attentive to lips of vanity, || Falsehood is giving ear to a mischievous tongue. ⁵Whoever is mocking at the poor || Has reproached his Maker, || Whoever is rejoicing at calamity is not acquitted. ⁶Sons' sons [are] the crown of old men, || And the glory of sons [are] their fathers. ⁷A lip of excellence is not fitting for a fool, much less a lip of falsehood for a noble. ⁸A stone of grace [is] the bribe in the eyes of its possessors, || Wherever it turns, it prospers. ⁹Whoever is covering transgression is seeking love, || And whoever is repeating a matter || Is separating a familiar friend. ¹⁰Rebuke comes down on the intelligent || More than one hundred stripes on a fool. ¹¹An evil man seeks only rebellion, || And a fierce messenger is sent against him. ¹²The meeting of a bereaved bear by a man, || And—not a fool in his folly. ¹³Whoever is returning evil for good, || Evil does not move from his house. ¹⁴The beginning of contention [is] a letting out of waters, || And leave the strife before it is meddled with. ¹⁵Whoever is justifying the wicked, || And condemning the righteous, || Even both of these [are] an abomination to YHWH. ¹⁶Why [is] this—a price in the hand of a fool to buy wisdom, || And a heart—there is none? ¹⁷The friend is loving at all times, || And a brother is born for adversity. ¹⁸A man lacking heart is striking hands, || He becomes a guarantor before his friend. ¹⁹Whoever is loving transgression is loving debate, || Whoever is making his entrance high is seeking destruction. ²⁰The perverse of heart does not find good, || And the [one] turned in his tongue falls into evil. ²¹Whoever is begetting a fool has affliction for it, || Indeed, the father of a fool does not rejoice. ²²A rejoicing heart does good to the body, || And a struck spirit dries the bone. ²³The wicked takes a bribe from the bosom, || To turn aside the paths of judgment. ²⁴The face of the intelligent [is] to wisdom, || And the eyes of a fool—at the end of the earth. ²⁵A foolish son [is] a provocation to his father, || And bitterness to her bearing him. ²⁶Also, [it] is not good to fine the righteous, || To strike nobles for uprightness. ²⁷One acquainted with knowledge is sparing his words, || And the cool of temper [is] a man of understanding. ²⁸Even a fool keeping silence is reckoned wise, || He who is shutting his lips [seems] intelligent!

CHAPTER 18

¹He who is separated seeks [his own] desire, || He interferes with all wisdom. ²A fool does not delight in understanding, || But in uncovering his heart. ³Contempt has also come with the coming of the wicked, || And with shame—reproach. ⁴The words of a man's mouth [are] deep waters, || The fountain of wisdom [is] a flowing brook. ⁵Favoring of the face of the wicked [is] not good, || To turn aside the righteous in judgment. ⁶The lips of a fool enter into strife, || And his mouth calls for stripes. ⁷The mouth of a fool [is] ruin to him, || And his lips [are] the snare of his soul. ⁸The words of a tale-bearer [are] as self-inflicted wounds, || And they have gone down [to] the inner parts of the heart. ⁹He also that is remiss in his work, || He [is] a brother to a destroyer. ¹⁰The Name of YHWH [is] a tower of strength, || The righteous runs into it, and is set on high. ¹¹The wealth of the rich [is] the city of his strength, || And as a wall set on high in his own imagination. ¹²The heart of man is high before destruction, || And humility [is] before honor. ¹³Whoever is answering a matter before he hears, || It is folly to him—and shame. ¹⁴The spirit of a man sustains his sickness, || And who bears a struck spirit? ¹⁵The heart of the intelligent gets knowledge, || And the ear of the wise seeks knowledge. ¹⁶The gift of a man makes room for him, || And it leads him before the great. ¹⁷The first in his own cause [seems] righteous, || [But] his neighbor comes and has searched him. ¹⁸The lot causes contentions to cease, || And it separates between the mighty. ¹⁹A brother transgressed against is as a strong city, || And contentions as the bar of a palace. ²⁰From the fruit of a man's mouth is his belly satisfied, || [From the] increase of his lips he is satisfied. ²¹Death and life [are] in the power of the tongue, || And those loving it eat its fruit. ²²[Whoever] has found a wife has found good, || And brings out goodwill from YHWH. ²³The poor speaks [with] supplications, || And the rich answers fierce things. ²⁴A man with friends—to show himself friendly, || And there is a lover adhering more than a brother!

CHAPTER 19

¹Better [is] the poor walking in his integrity, || Than the perverse [in] his lips—who [is] a fool. ²Also, without knowledge the soul [is] not good, || And the hasty in feet is sinning. ³The folly of man perverts his way, || And his heart is angry against YHWH. ⁴Wealth adds many friends, || And the poor is separated from his neighbor. ⁵A false witness is not acquitted, || Whoever breathes out lies is not delivered. ⁶Many beg the face of the noble, || And all have made friendship to a man of gifts. ⁷All the brothers of the poor have hated him, || Surely his friends have also been far from him, || He is pursuing words—they are not! ⁸Whoever is getting heart is loving his soul, || He is keeping understanding to find good. ⁹A false witness is not acquitted, || And whoever breathes out lies perishes. ¹⁰Luxury is not fitting for a fool, || Much less for a servant to rule among princes. ¹¹The wisdom of a man has deferred his anger, || And his glory [is] to pass over transgression. ¹²The wrath of a king [is] a growl as of a young lion, || And his goodwill as dew on the herb. ¹³A foolish son [is] a calamity to his father, || And the contentions of a wife [are] a continual dropping. ¹⁴House and wealth [are] the inheritance of fathers, || And an understanding wife [is] from YHWH. ¹⁵Sloth causes deep sleep to fall, || And an indolent soul hungers. ¹⁶Whoever is keeping the command is keeping his soul, || Whoever is despising His ways dies. ¹⁷Whoever is lending [to] YHWH is favoring the poor, || And He repays his deed to him. ¹⁸Discipline your son, for there is hope, || And do not lift up your soul to put him to death. ¹⁹A man of great wrath is bearing punishment, || For if you deliver, yet again you add. ²⁰Hear counsel and receive instruction, || So that you are wise in your latter end. ²¹The purposes in a man's heart [are] many, || And the counsel of YHWH—it stands. ²²The desirableness of a man [is] his kindness, || And the poor [is] better than a liar. ²³The fear of YHWH [is] to life, || And he remains satisfied—he is not charged with evil. ²⁴The slothful has hidden his hand in a dish, || Even to his mouth he does not bring it back. ²⁵Strike a scorner, and the simple acts prudently, || And give reproof to the intelligent, || He understands knowledge. ²⁶Whoever is spoiling a father causes a mother to flee, || A son causing shame, and bringing confusion. ²⁷Cease, my son, to hear instruction—To err from sayings of knowledge. ²⁸A worthless witness scorns judgment, || And the mouth of the wicked swallows iniquity. ²⁹Judgments have been prepared for scorners, || And stripes for the back of fools!

CHAPTER 20

¹Wine [is] a scorner—strong drink [is] noisy, || And any going astray in it is not wise. ²The fear of a king [is] a growl as of a young lion, || He who is causing him to be angry is wronging his soul. ³Cessation from strife is an honor to a man, || And every fool interferes. ⁴The slothful does not plow because of winter, || He asks in harvest, and there is nothing. ⁵Counsel in the heart of a man [is] deep water, || And a man of understanding draws it up. ⁶A multitude of men each proclaim his kindness, || And a man of steadfastness who finds? ⁷The righteous is habitually walking in his integrity, || O the blessedness of his sons after him! ⁸A king sitting on a throne of judgment, || Is scattering all evil with his eyes, ⁹Who says, "I have purified my heart, || I have been cleansed from my sin?" ¹⁰A stone and a stone, an ephah and an ephah, || Even both of them [are] an abomination to YHWH. ¹¹Even by his actions a youth makes himself known, || Whether his work is pure or upright. ¹²A hearing ear, and a seeing eye—YHWH has even made both of them. ¹³Do not love sleep, lest you become poor, || Open your eyes—be satisfied [with] bread. ¹⁴"Bad, bad," says the buyer, || And then he boasts himself going his way. ¹⁵Substance, gold, and a multitude of rubies, || Indeed, a

precious vessel, [are] lips of knowledge. ¹⁶When a stranger has been guarantor, take his garment, || And pledge it for strangers. ¹⁷The bread of falsehood [is] sweet to a man, || And afterward his mouth is filled [with] gravel. ¹⁸You establish purposes by counsel, || And with plans you make war. ¹⁹The busybody is a revealer of secret counsels, || And do not make yourself guarantor for a deceiver [with] his lips. ²⁰Whoever is vilifying his father and his mother, his lamp is extinguished in blackness of darkness. ²¹An inheritance gotten wrongly at first, || Even its latter end is not blessed. ²²Do not say, "I repay evil," || Wait for YHWH, and He delivers you. ²³A stone and a stone [are] an abomination to YHWH, || And balances of deceit [are] not good. ²⁴The steps of a man [are] from YHWH, || And man—how does he understand his way? ²⁵A snare to a man [that] he has swallowed a holy thing, || And to make inquiry after vows. ²⁶A wise king is scattering the wicked, || And turns the wheel back on them. ²⁷The breath of man [is] a lamp of YHWH, || Searching all the inner parts of the heart. ²⁸Kindness and truth keep a king, || And he has supported his throne by kindness. ²⁹The beauty of young men is their strength, || And the honor of old men is grey hairs. ³⁰Blows that wound cleanse away evil, || Also the scourges of the inner parts of the heart!

CHAPTER 21

¹The heart of a king [is] streams of waters in the hand of YHWH, || He inclines it wherever He pleases. ²Every way of a man [is] right in his own eyes, || And YHWH is pondering hearts. ³To do righteousness and judgment, || Is chosen of YHWH rather than sacrifice. ⁴Loftiness of eyes, and breadth of heart, || Tillage of the wicked [is] sin. ⁵The purposes of the diligent [are] only to advantage, || And of every hasty one, only to want. ⁶The making of treasures by a lying tongue, || [Is] a vanity driven away of those seeking death. ⁷The spoil of the wicked catches them, || Because they have refused to do judgment. ⁸The way of a man who is vile [is] contrary, || And the pure—his work [is] upright. ⁹Better to sit on a corner of the roof, || Than [with] a woman of contentions and a house of company. ¹⁰The soul of the wicked has desired evil, his neighbor is not gracious in his eyes. ¹¹When the scorner is punished, the simple becomes wise, || And in giving understanding to the wise He receives knowledge. ¹²The Righteous One is acting wisely || Toward the house of the wicked, || He is overthrowing the wicked for wickedness. ¹³Whoever is shutting his ear from the cry of the poor, || He also cries, and is not answered. ¹⁴A gift in secret pacifies anger, || And a bribe in the bosom—strong fury. ¹⁵To do justice [is] joy to the righteous, || But ruin to workers of iniquity. ¹⁶A man who is wandering from the way of understanding, || Rests in an assembly of Rephaim. ¹⁷Whoever [is] loving mirth [is] a poor man, || Whoever is loving wine and oil makes no wealth. ¹⁸The wicked [is] an atonement for the righteous, || And the treacherous dealer for the upright. ¹⁹Better to dwell in a wilderness land, || Than [with] a woman of contentions and anger. ²⁰A treasure to be desired, and oil, || [Is] in the habitation of the wise, || And a foolish man swallows it up. ²¹Whoever is pursuing righteousness and kindness, || Finds life, righteousness, and honor. ²²The wise has gone up a city of the mighty, || And brings down the strength of its confidence. ²³Whoever is keeping his mouth and his tongue, || Is keeping his soul from adversities. ²⁴Proud, haughty, scorner—his name, || Who is working in the wrath of pride. ²⁵The desire of the slothful slays him, || For his hands have refused to work. ²⁶All the day desiring he has desired, || And the righteous gives and does not withhold. ²⁷The sacrifice of the wicked [is] abomination, || Much more when he brings it in wickedness. ²⁸A false witness perishes, || And an attentive man speaks forever. ²⁹A wicked man has hardened by his face, || And the upright—he prepares his way. ³⁰There is no wisdom, nor understanding, || Nor counsel against YHWH. ³¹A horse is prepared for a day of battle, || And the deliverance [is] of YHWH!

CHAPTER 22

¹A name is chosen rather than much wealth, || Than silver and than gold—good grace. ²Rich and poor have met together, || YHWH [is] the Maker of them all. ³The prudent has seen the evil, and is hidden, || And the simple have passed on, and are punished. ⁴The end of humility [is] the fear of YHWH, riches, and honor, and life. ⁵Thorns [and] snares [are] in the way of the perverse, || Whoever is keeping his soul is far from them. ⁶Give instruction to a youth about his way, || Even when he is old he does not turn from it. ⁷The rich rules over the poor, || And a servant [is] the borrower to the lender. ⁸Whoever is sowing perverseness reaps sorrow, || And the rod of his anger wears out. ⁹The good of eye—he is blessed, || For he has given of his bread to the poor. ¹⁰Cast out a scorner—and contention goes out, || And strife and shame cease. ¹¹Whoever is loving cleanness of heart, || His lips [are] grace, || A king [is] his friend. ¹²The eyes of YHWH have kept knowledge, || And He overthrows the words of the treacherous. ¹³The slothful has said, "A lion [is] outside, || I am slain in the midst of the broad places." ¹⁴The mouth of strange women [is] a deep pit, || The abhorred of YHWH falls there. ¹⁵Folly is bound up in the heart of a youth, || The rod of discipline puts it far from him. ¹⁶He [who] is oppressing the poor to multiply his [riches], || Is giving to the rich—only to want. ¹⁷Incline your ear, and hear words of the wise, || And set your heart to my knowledge, ¹⁸For they are pleasant when you keep them in your heart, || They are prepared together for your lips. ¹⁹That your trust may be in YHWH, || I caused you to know today, even you. ²⁰Have I not written to you three times || With counsels and knowledge? ²¹To cause you to know the certainty of sayings of truth, || To return sayings of truth to those sending you. ²²Do not rob the poor because he [is] poor, || And do not bruise the afflicted in the gate. ²³For YHWH pleads their cause, || And has spoiled the soul of their spoilers. ²⁴Do not show yourself friendly with an angry man, || And do not go in with a man of fury, ²⁵Lest you learn his paths, || And have received a snare to your soul. ²⁶Do not be among those striking hands, || Among sureties [for] burdens. ²⁷If you have nothing to pay, || Why does he take your bed from under you? ²⁸Do not remove a border of ancient times, || That your fathers have made. ²⁹Have you seen a man speedy in his business? He stations himself before kings, || He does not station himself before obscure men!

CHAPTER 23

¹When you sit to eat with a ruler, || Diligently consider that which [is] before you, ²And you have put a knife to your throat, || If you [are] a man of appetite. ³Have no desire to his delicacies, seeing it [is] lying food. ⁴Do not labor to make wealth, || Cease from your own understanding, || Do you cause your eyes to fly on it? Then it is not. ⁵For wealth makes wings to itself, || It flies to the heavens as an eagle. ⁶Do not eat the bread of an evil eye, || And have no desire to his delicacies, ⁷For as he has thought in his soul, so he [is]. "Eat and drink," he says to you, || And his heart [is] not with you. ⁸You vomit up your morsel you have eaten, || And have marred your words that [are] sweet. ⁹Do not speak in the ears of a fool, || For he treads on the wisdom of your words. ¹⁰Do not remove a border of ancient times, || And do not enter into fields of the fatherless, ¹¹For their Redeemer [is] strong, || He pleads their cause with you. ¹²Bring your heart to instruction, || And your ear to sayings of knowledge. ¹³Do not withhold discipline from a youth, || When you strike him with a rod he does not die. ¹⁴You strike him with a rod, || And you deliver his soul from Sheol. ¹⁵My son, if your heart has been wise, || My heart rejoices, even mine, ¹⁶And my reins exult when your lips speak uprightly. ¹⁷Do not let your heart be envious at sinners, || But—in the fear of YHWH all the day. ¹⁸For is there a posterity? Then your hope is not cut off. ¹⁹Hear, my son, and be wise, || And make your heart blessed in the way, ²⁰Do not become drunk with wine, || Among gluttonous ones of flesh, ²¹For the drunkard and glutton become poor, || And drowsiness clothes with rags. ²²Listen to your father, who begot you, || And do not despise your mother when she has become old. ²³Buy truth, and do not sell, || Wisdom, and instruction, and understanding, ²⁴The father of the righteous rejoices greatly, || The begetter of the wise rejoices in him. ²⁵Your father and your mother rejoice, || Indeed, she bearing you is joyful. ²⁶Give, my son, your heart to me, || And let your eyes watch my ways. ²⁷For a harlot [is] a deep ditch, || And a strange woman [is] a narrow pit. ²⁸She also, as catching prey, lies in wait, || And she increases the treacherous among men. ²⁹Who has woe? Who has sorrow? Who has contentions? Who has complaint? Who has wounds without cause? Who has redness of eyes? ³⁰Those lingering by the wine, || Those going in to search out mixed wine. ³¹Do not see wine

when it shows itself red, || When it gives its color in the cup, || It goes up and down through the upright. ³²Its latter end—it bites as a serpent, || And it stings as a viper. ³³Your eyes see strange women, || And your heart speaks perverse things. ³⁴And you have been as one lying down in the heart of the sea, || And as one lying down on the top of a mast. ³⁵"They struck me, I have not been sick, || They beat me, I have not known. When I awake—I seek it yet again!"

CHAPTER 24

¹Do not be envious of evil men, || And do not desire to be with them. ²For their heart meditates [on] destruction, || And their lips speak perverseness. ³A house is built by wisdom, || And it establishes itself by understanding. ⁴And the inner parts are filled by knowledge, || [With] all precious and pleasant wealth. ⁵The wise [is] mighty in strength, || And a man of knowledge is strengthening power, ⁶For you make war for yourself by plans, || And deliverance [is] in a multitude of counselors. ⁷Wisdom [is] high for a fool, he does not open his mouth in the gate. ⁸Whoever is devising to do evil, || They call him a master of wicked thoughts. ⁹The thought of folly [is] sin, || And a scorner [is] an abomination to man. ¹⁰You have showed yourself weak in a day of adversity, || Your power is restricted, ¹¹If [from] delivering those taken to death, || And you take back those slipping to the slaughter. ¹²When you say, "Behold, we did not know this." Is the Ponderer of hearts not He who understands? And the Keeper of your soul He who knows? And He has rendered to man according to his work. ¹³My son, eat honey that [is] good, || And the honeycomb [is] sweet to your palate. ¹⁴So [is] the knowledge of wisdom to your soul, || If you have found that there is a posterity || And your hope is not cut off. ¹⁵Do not lay wait, O wicked one, || At the habitation of the righteous. Do not spoil his resting place. ¹⁶For the righteous fall and rise seven [times], || And the wicked stumble in evil. ¹⁷Do not rejoice in the falling of your enemy, || And do not let your heart be joyful in his stumbling, ¹⁸Lest YHWH see, and [it be] evil in His eyes, || And He has turned His anger from off him. ¹⁹Do not fret yourself at evildoers, do not be envious at the wicked, ²⁰For there is not a posterity to the evil, || The lamp of the wicked is extinguished. ²¹Fear YHWH, my son, and the king, || Do not mix yourself up with changers, ²²For their calamity rises suddenly, || And the ruin of them both—who knows! ²³These are also for the wise: [It] is not good to discern faces in judgment. ²⁴Whoever is saying to the wicked, "You [are] righteous," || Peoples execrate him—nations abhor him. ²⁵And it is pleasant to those reproving, || And a good blessing comes on them. ²⁶He who is returning straightforward words kisses lips. ²⁷Prepare your work in an out-place, || And make it ready in the field—go afterward, || Then you have built your house. ²⁸Do not be a witness against your neighbor for nothing, || Or you have enticed with your lips. ²⁹Do not say, "As he did to me, so I do to him, || I render to each according to his work." ³⁰I passed by near the field of a slothful man, || And near the vineyard of a man lacking heart. ³¹And behold, it has gone up—all of it—thorns! Nettles have covered its face, || And its stone wall has been broken down. ³²And I see—I set my heart, || I have seen—I have received instruction, ³³A little sleep—a little slumber—A little folding of the hands to lie down. ³⁴And your poverty has come [as] a traveler, || And your want as an armed man!

CHAPTER 25

¹These are also proverbs of Solomon, that men of Hezekiah king of Judah transcribed: ²The glory of God [is] to hide a thing, || And the glory of kings [is] to search out a matter. ³The heavens for height, and the earth for depth, || And the heart of kings—[are] unsearchable. ⁴Take away dross from silver, || And a vessel goes forth for the refiner, ⁵Take away the wicked before a king, || And his throne is established in righteousness. ⁶Do not honor yourself before a king, || And do not stand in the place of the great. ⁷For better [that] he has said to you, "Come up here," || Than [that] he humbles you before a noble, || Whom your eyes have seen. ⁸Do not go forth to strive, hurry, turn, || What do you do in its latter end, || When your neighbor causes you to blush? ⁹Plead your cause with your neighbor, || And do not reveal the secret counsel of another, ¹⁰Lest the hearer put you to shame, || And your evil report not turn back. ¹¹Apples of gold in imagery of silver, || [Is] the word spoken at its fit times. ¹²A ring of gold, and an ornament of pure gold, || [Is] the wise reprover to an attentive ear. ¹³As a vessel of snow in a day of harvest, || [So is] a faithful ambassador to those sending him, || And he refreshes the soul of his masters. ¹⁴Clouds and wind without rain, || [Is] a man boasting himself in a false gift. ¹⁵A ruler is persuaded by long-suffering, || And a soft tongue breaks a bone. ¹⁶You have found honey—eat your sufficiency, || Lest you are satiated [with] it, and have vomited it. ¹⁷Withdraw your foot from your neighbor's house, || Lest he is satiated [with] you, and has hated you. ¹⁸A maul, and a sword, and a sharp arrow, || [Is] the man testifying a false testimony against his neighbor. ¹⁹A bad tooth, and a tottering foot, || [Is] the confidence of the treacherous in a day of adversity. ²⁰Whoever is taking away a garment in a cold day, || [Is as] vinegar on natron, || And a singer of songs on a sad heart. ²¹If he who is hating you hungers, cause him to eat bread, || And if he thirsts, cause him to drink water. ²²For you are putting coals on his head, || And YHWH gives repayment to you. ²³A north wind brings forth rain, || And a secret tongue—indignant faces. ²⁴Better to sit on a corner of a roof, || Than [with] a woman of contentions, and a house of company. ²⁵[As] cold waters for a weary soul, || So [is] a good report from a far country. ²⁶A spring troubled, and a fountain corrupt, || [Is] the righteous falling before the wicked. ²⁷The eating of much honey is not good, || Nor a searching out of one's own honor—honor. ²⁸A city broken down without walls, || [Is] a man without restraint over his spirit!

CHAPTER 26

¹As snow in summer, and as rain in harvest, || So honor [is] not fitting for a fool. ²As a bird by wandering, as a swallow by flying, || So reviling without cause does not come. ³A whip is for a horse, a bridle for a donkey, || And a rod for the back of fools. ⁴Do not answer a fool according to his folly, || Lest you are like to him—even you. ⁵Answer a fool according to his folly, || Lest he is wise in his own eyes. ⁶He is cutting off feet, he is drinking injury, || Who is sending things by the hand of a fool. ⁷The two legs of the lame have been weak, || And an allegory in the mouth of fools. ⁸As one who is binding a stone in a sling, || So [is] he who is giving honor to a fool. ⁹A thorn has gone up into the hand of a drunkard, || And an allegory in the mouth of fools. ¹⁰The Former of all [is] great, || And He is rewarding a fool, || And is rewarding transgressors. ¹¹As a dog has returned to its vomit, || A fool is repeating his folly. ¹²You have seen a man wise in his own eyes, || More hope of a fool than of him! ¹³The slothful has said, || "A lion [is] in the way, || A lion [is] in the broad places." ¹⁴The door turns around on its hinge, || And the slothful on his bed. ¹⁵The slothful has hid his hand in a dish, || He is weary of bringing it back to his mouth. ¹⁶Wiser [is] the slothful in his own eyes, || Than seven [men] returning a reason. ¹⁷Laying hold on the ears of a dog, || [Is] a passer-by making himself wrath for strife [that is] not his own. ¹⁸As [one] pretending to be feeble, || Who is casting sparks, arrows, and death, ¹⁹So has a man deceived his neighbor, || And has said, "Am I not playing?" ²⁰Fire is going out without wood, || And contention ceases without a tale-bearer, ²¹Coal to burning coals, and wood to fire, || And a man of contentions to kindle strife. ²²The words of a tale-bearer [are] as self-inflicted wounds, || And they have gone down [to] the inner parts of the heart. ²³Silver of dross spread over potsherd, || [Are] burning lips and an evil heart. ²⁴A hater pretends by his lips, || And he places deceit in his heart, ²⁵When his voice is gracious do not trust in him, || For seven abominations [are] in his heart. ²⁶Hatred is covered by deceit, || Its wickedness is revealed in an assembly. ²⁷Whoever is digging a pit falls into it, || And the roller of a stone, it turns to him. ²⁸A lying tongue hates its bruised ones, || And a flattering mouth works an overthrow!

CHAPTER 27

¹Do not boast about tomorrow, || For you do not know what a day brings forth. ²Let another praise you, and not your own mouth, || A stranger, and not your own lips. ³A stone [is] heavy, and the sand [is] heavy, || And the anger of a fool || Is heavier than them both. ⁴Fury [is] fierce, and anger [is] overflowing, || And who stands before jealousy? ⁵Better [is] open reproof than hidden love. ⁶The wounds of a lover are faithful, || And the kisses of an enemy [are] abundant. ⁷A satiated soul treads down a honeycomb, || And every bitter thing

[is] sweet [to] a hungry soul. ⁸As a bird wandering from her nest, ‖ So [is] a man wandering from his place. ⁹Perfume and incense make the heart glad, ‖ And the sweetness of one's friend—from counsel of the soul. ¹⁰Do not forsake your own friend and the friend of your father, ‖ And do not enter the house of your brother in a day of your calamity, ‖ A near neighbor [is] better than a brother far off. ¹¹Be wise, my son, and make my heart glad, ‖ And I return a word [to] my reproacher. ¹²The prudent has seen the evil, he is hidden, ‖ The simple have passed on, they are punished. ¹³Take his garment when a stranger has been guarantor, ‖ And pledge it for a strange woman. ¹⁴Whoever is greeting his friend with a loud voice, ‖ Rising early in the morning, ‖ It is reckoned a light thing to him. ¹⁵A continual dropping in a day of rain, ‖ And a woman of contentions are alike, ¹⁶Whoever is hiding her has hidden the wind, ‖ And the ointment of his right hand calls out. ¹⁷Iron is sharpened by iron, ‖ And a man sharpens the face of his friend. ¹⁸The keeper of a fig tree eats its fruit, ‖ And the preserver of his master is honored. ¹⁹As [in] water the face [is] to face, ‖ So the heart of man to man. ²⁰Sheol and destruction are not satisfied, ‖ And the eyes of man are not satisfied. ²¹A refining pot [is] for silver, and a furnace for gold, ‖ And a man according to his praise. ²²If you beat the foolish in a mortar, ‖ Among washed things—with a pestle, ‖ His folly does not turn aside from off him. ²³Know the face of your flock well, ‖ Set your heart to the droves, ²⁴For riches [are] not for all time, ‖ Nor a crown to generation and generation. ²⁵The hay was revealed, and the tender grass seen, ‖ And the herbs of mountains gathered. ²⁶Lambs [are] for your clothing, ‖ And the price of the field [are] male goats, ²⁷And a sufficiency of goats' milk [is] for your bread, ‖ For bread to your house, and life to your girls!

CHAPTER 28

¹The wicked have fled and there is no pursuer, ‖ And the righteous is confident as a young lion. ²By the transgression of a land its heads are many, ‖ And by an understanding man, ‖ Who knows right—it is prolonged. ³A man—poor and oppressing the weak, ‖ [Is] a sweeping rain, and there is no bread. ⁴Those forsaking the Law praise the wicked, ‖ Those keeping the Law plead against them. ⁵Evil men do not understand judgment, ‖ And those seeking YHWH understand all. ⁶Better [is] the poor walking in his integrity, ‖ Than the perverse of ways who is rich. ⁷Whoever is keeping the Law is an intelligent son, ‖ And a friend of gluttons ‖ Causes his father to blush. ⁸Whoever is multiplying his wealth by biting and usury, ‖ Gathers it for one favoring the poor. ⁹Whoever is turning his ear from hearing the Law, ‖ Even his prayer [is] an abomination. ¹⁰Whoever is causing the upright to err in an evil way, ‖ He falls into his own pit, ‖ And the perfect inherits good. ¹¹A rich man is wise in his own eyes, ‖ And the intelligent poor searches him. ¹²In the exulting of the righteous the glory [is] abundant, ‖ And in the rising of the wicked man is apprehensive. ¹³Whoever is covering his transgressions does not prosper, ‖ And he who is confessing and forsaking has mercy. ¹⁴O the blessedness of a man fearing continually, ‖ And whoever is hardening his heart falls into evil. ¹⁵A growling lion, and a ranging bear, ‖ [Is] the wicked ruler over a poor people. ¹⁶A leader lacking understanding multiplies oppressions, ‖ Whoever is hating dishonest gain prolongs days. ¹⁷A man oppressed with the blood of a soul, ‖ Flees to the pit, [and] none takes hold on him [to help]. ¹⁸Whoever is walking uprightly is saved, ‖ And the perverted of ways falls at once. ¹⁹Whoever is tilling his ground is satisfied [with] bread, ‖ And whoever is pursuing vanity, ‖ Is filled [with] poverty. ²⁰A steadfast man has multiplied blessings, ‖ And whoever is hastening to be rich is not acquitted. ²¹[It] is not good to discern faces, ‖ And a man transgresses for a piece of bread. ²²The man [with] an evil eye [is] troubled for wealth, ‖ And he does not know that want meets him. ²³Whoever is reproving a man finds grace afterward, ‖ More than a flatterer with the tongue. ²⁴Whoever is robbing his father or his mother, ‖ And is saying, "It is not transgression," ‖ He is a companion to a destroyer. ²⁵Whoever is proud in soul stirs up contention, ‖ And whoever is trusting on YHWH is made fat. ²⁶Whoever is trusting in his heart is a fool, ‖ And whoever is walking in wisdom is delivered. ²⁷Whoever is giving to the poor has no lack, ‖ And whoever is hiding his eyes multiplied curses. ²⁸A man is hidden in the rising of the wicked, ‖ And the righteous multiply in their destruction!

CHAPTER 29

¹A man often reproved, hardening the neck, ‖ Is suddenly broken, and there is no healing. ²In the multiplying of the righteous the people rejoice, ‖ And in the ruling of the wicked the people sigh. ³A man loving wisdom makes his father glad, ‖ And a friend of harlots destroys wealth. ⁴A king establishes a land by judgment, ‖ And one receiving gifts throws it down. ⁵A man taking a portion above his neighbor, ‖ Spreads a net for his own steps. ⁶A snare [is] in the transgression of the evil, ‖ And the righteous sing and rejoice. ⁷The righteous knows the plea of the poor, ‖ The wicked does not understand knowledge. ⁸Men of scorning ensnare a city, ‖ And the wise turn back anger. ⁹A wise man is judged by the foolish man, ‖ And he has been angry, ‖ And he has laughed, and there is no rest. ¹⁰Men of blood hate the perfect, ‖ And the upright seek his soul. ¹¹A fool brings out all his mind, ‖ And the wise restrains it until afterward. ¹²A ruler who is attending to lying words, ‖ All his ministers [are] wicked. ¹³The poor and the man of frauds have met together, ‖ YHWH is enlightening the eyes of them both. ¹⁴A king that is judging the poor with truth, ‖ His throne is established forever. ¹⁵A rod and reproof give wisdom, ‖ And a youth let away is shaming his mother. ¹⁶In the multiplying of the wicked transgression multiplies, ‖ And the righteous look on their fall. ¹⁷Discipline your son, and he gives you comfort, ‖ Indeed, he gives delights to your soul. ¹⁸A people is made naked without a vision, ‖ And whoever is keeping the Law, O his blessedness! ¹⁹By words a servant is not instructed though he understand, ‖ And there is nothing answering. ²⁰You have seen a man hasty in his words! More hope of a fool than of him. ²¹Whoever is bringing up his servant delicately, from youth, ‖ [At] his latter end he is also continuator. ²²An angry man stirs up contention, ‖ And a furious man is multiplying transgression. ²³The pride of man humbles him, ‖ And humility of spirit upholds honor. ²⁴Whoever is sharing with a thief is hating his own soul, ‖ He hears execration, and does not tell. ²⁵Fear of man causes a snare, ‖ And the confident in YHWH is set on high. ²⁶Many are seeking the face of a ruler, ‖ And the judgment of each [is] from YHWH. ²⁷The perverse man [is] an abomination to the righteous, ‖ And the upright in the way [is] an abomination to the wicked!

CHAPTER 30

¹Words of Agur, son of Jakeh, the burden, a declaration of the man to Ithiel—to Ithiel and Ucal: I have wearied myself [for] God, ‖ I have wearied myself [for] God, and am consumed. ²For I am more brutish than anyone, ‖ And do not have the understanding of a man. ³Nor have I learned wisdom, ‖ Yet I know the knowledge of the Holy Ones. ⁴Who went up to the heavens, and comes down? Who has gathered the wind in His fists? Who has bound waters in a garment? Who established all ends of the earth? What [is] His Name? And what [is] His Son's Name? Surely you know! ⁵Every saying of God [is] tried, ‖ He [is] a shield to those trusting in Him. ⁶Do not add to His words, lest He reason with you, ‖ And you have been found false. ⁷Two things I have asked from You, ‖ Do not withhold from me before I die. ⁸Put vanity and a lying word far from me, ‖ Do not give poverty or wealth to me, ‖ Cause me to eat the bread of my portion, ⁹Lest I become satiated, and have denied, ‖ And have said, "Who [is] YHWH?" And lest I am poor, and have stolen, ‖ And have laid hold of the Name of my God. ¹⁰Do not accuse a servant to his lord, ‖ Lest he disapprove of you, and you are found guilty. ¹¹A generation lightly esteems their father, ‖ And does not bless their mother. ¹²A generation—pure in their own eyes, ‖ But not washed from their own filth. ¹³A generation—how high are their eyes, ‖ Indeed, their eyelids are lifted up. ¹⁴A generation—their teeth [are] swords, ‖ And their jaw-teeth [are] knives, ‖ To consume the poor from earth, ‖ And the needy from [among] men. ¹⁵To the leech [are] two daughters—Give! Give! Behold, three things are not satisfied, ‖ Four have not said "Sufficiency"; ¹⁶Sheol, and a restrained womb, ‖ Earth—it [is] not satisfied [with] water, ‖ And fire—it has not said, "Sufficiency," ¹⁷An eye that mocks at a father, ‖ And despises to obey a mother, ‖ Ravens of the valley dig it out, ‖ And young eagles eat it. ¹⁸Three things

have been too wonderful for me, || Indeed, four that I have not known: ⁱ⁹The way of the eagle in the heavens, || The way of a serpent on a rock, || The way of a ship in the heart of the sea, || And the way of a man in youth. ²⁰So—the way of an adulterous woman, || She has eaten and has wiped her mouth, || And has said, "I have not done iniquity." ²¹For three things has earth been troubled, || And for four—it is not able to bear: ²²For a servant when he reigns, || And a fool when he is satisfied with bread, ²³For a hated one when she rules, || And a maidservant when she succeeds her mistress. ²⁴Four [are] little ones of earth, || And they are made wiser than the wise: ²⁵The ants [are] a people not strong, || And they prepare their food in summer, ²⁶hyraxes [are] a people not strong, || And they place their house in a rock, ²⁷There is no king to the locust, || And it goes out—each one shouting, ²⁸A spider has two hands takes hold, || And is in the palaces of a king. ²⁹There are three going well, || Indeed, four are good in going: ³⁰An old lion—mighty among beasts, || That does not turn back from the face of any, ³¹A girt one of the loins, || Also a male goat, || And a king—troops with him. ³²If you have been foolish in lifting yourself up, || And if you have devised evil—hand to mouth! ³³For the churning of milk brings out butter, || And the wringing of the nose brings out blood, || And the forcing of anger brings out strife!

CHAPTER 31

¹Words of Lemuel, a king, a declaration that his mother taught him: ²"What, my son? And what, son of my womb? And what, son of my vows? ³Do not give your strength to women, || And your ways to wiping away of kings. ⁴[It is] not for kings, O Lemuel, || Not for kings, to drink wine, || And for princes—a desire of strong drink. ⁵Lest he drink, and forget the decree, || And change the judgment of any of the sons of affliction. ⁶Give strong drink to the perishing, || And wine to the bitter in soul, ⁷He drinks, and forgets his poverty, || And he does not remember his misery again. ⁸Open your mouth for the mute, || For the right of all sons of change. ⁹Open your mouth, judge righteously, || Both the cause of the poor and needy!" ¹⁰[ALEPH-BET] A woman of worth who finds? Indeed, her price [is] far above rubies. ¹¹The heart of her husband has trusted in her, || And he does not lack spoil. ¹²She has done him good, and not evil, || All [the] days of her life. ¹³She has sought wool and flax, || And with delight she works [with] her hands. ¹⁴She has been as ships of the merchant, || She brings in her bread from afar. ¹⁵Indeed, she rises while yet night, || And gives food to her household, || And a portion to her girls. ¹⁶She has considered a field, and takes it, || She has planted a vineyard from the fruit of her hands. ¹⁷She has girded her loins with might, || And strengthens her arms. ¹⁸She has perceived when her merchandise [is] good, || Her lamp is not extinguished in the night. ¹⁹She has sent forth her hands on a spindle, || And her hands have held a distaff. ²⁰She has spread forth her hand to the poor, || Indeed, she sent forth her hands to the needy. ²¹She is not afraid of her household from snow, || For all her household are clothed [with] scarlet. ²²She has made ornamental coverings for herself, || Silk and purple [are] her clothing. ²³Her husband is known in the gates, || In his sitting with [the] elderly of [the] land. ²⁴She has made linen garments, and sells, || And she has given a girdle to the merchant. ²⁵Strength and honor [are] her clothing, || And she rejoices at a latter day. ²⁶She has opened her mouth in wisdom, || And the law of kindness [is] on her tongue. ²⁷She [is] watching the ways of her household, || And she does not eat bread of sloth. ²⁸Her sons have risen up, and pronounce her blessed, || Her husband, and he praises her, ²⁹"The daughters who have done worthily [are] many, || You have gone up above them all." ³⁰Favor [is] deceitful, and beauty [is] vain, || A woman fearing YHWH, she may boast herself. ³¹Give to her of the fruit of her hands, || And her works praise her in the gates!

ECCLESIASTES

CHAPTER 1

¹Words of a preacher, son of David, king in Jerusalem: ²Vanity of vanities, said the Preacher, vanity of vanities: the whole [is] vanity. ³What advantage [is] to man by all his labor that he labors at under the sun? ⁴A generation is going, and a generation is coming, and the earth is standing for all time. ⁵Also, the sun has risen, and the sun has gone in, and to its place panting it is rising there. ⁶Going to the south, and turning around to the north, turning around, turning around, the wind is going, and by its circuits the wind has returned. ⁷All the streams are going to the sea, and the sea is not full; to a place to where the streams are going, there they are turning back to go. ⁸All these things are wearying; a man is not able to speak, the eye is not satisfied by seeing, nor is the ear filled from hearing. ⁹What [is] that which has been? It [is] that which is, and what [is] that which has been done? It [is] that which is done, and there is not an entirely new thing under the sun. ¹⁰There is a thing of which [one] says: "See this, it [is] new!" Already it has been in the ages that were before us! ¹¹There is not a remembrance of former [generations]; and also of the latter that are, there is no remembrance of them with those that are at the last. ¹²I, a preacher, have been king over Israel in Jerusalem. ¹³And I have given my heart to seek and to search out by wisdom concerning all that has been done under the heavens. It [is] a sad travail God has given to the sons of man to be humbled by it. ¹⁴I have seen all the works that have been done under the sun, and behold, the whole [is] vanity and distress of spirit! ¹⁵A crooked thing [one] is not able to make straight, and a lacking thing is not able to be numbered. ¹⁶I spoke with my heart, saying, "I, behold, have magnified and added wisdom above everyone who has been before me at Jerusalem, and my heart has seen wisdom and knowledge abundantly. ¹⁷And I give my heart to know wisdom, and to know madness and folly: I have known that even this [is] distress of spirit; ¹⁸for in abundance of wisdom [is] abundance of sadness, and he who adds knowledge adds pain."

CHAPTER 2

¹I said in my heart, "Pray, come, I try you with mirth, and look on gladness"; and behold, even it [is] vanity. ²Of laughter I said, "Foolish!" And of mirth, "What [is] this it is doing?" ³I have sought in my heart to draw out with wine my appetite (and my heart leading in wisdom), and to take hold on folly until I see where this [is]—the good to the sons of man of that which they do under the heavens, the number of the days of their lives. ⁴I made great my works, I built for myself houses, I planted for myself vineyards. ⁵I made for myself gardens and paradises, and I planted in them trees of every fruit. ⁶I made for myself pools of water, to water from them a forest shooting forth trees. ⁷I acquired menservants, and maidservants, and sons of the house were to me; also, I had much substance—herd and flock—above all who had been before me in Jerusalem. ⁸I also gathered for myself silver and gold, and the peculiar treasure of kings and of the provinces. I prepared for myself men-singers and women-singers, and the luxuries of the sons of man—a wife and wives. ⁹And I became great, and increased above everyone who had been before me in Jerusalem; also, my wisdom stood with me. ¹⁰And all that my eyes asked I did not keep back from them; I did not withhold my heart from any joy, for my heart rejoiced because of all my labor, and this has been my portion, from all my labor, ¹¹and I have looked on all my works that my hands have done, and on the labor that I have labored to do, and behold, the whole [is] vanity and distress of spirit, and there is no advantage under the sun! ¹²And I turned to see wisdom, and madness, and folly, but what [is] the man who comes after the king? That which [is] already—they have done it! ¹³And I saw that there is an advantage

to wisdom above folly, like the advantage of the light above the darkness. ¹⁴The wise—his eyes [are] in his head, and the fool is walking in darkness, and I also knew that one event happens with them all; ¹⁵and I said in my heart, "As it happens with the fool, it happens also with me, and why am I then more wise?" And I spoke in my heart, that also this [is] vanity: ¹⁶That there is no remembrance to the wise—with the fool—for all time, for that which [is] already, [in] the days that are coming is all forgotten, and how dies the wise? With the fool! ¹⁷And I have hated life, for sad to me [is] the work that has been done under the sun, for the whole [is] vanity and distress of spirit. ¹⁸And I have hated all my labor that I labor at under the sun, because I leave it to a man who is after me. ¹⁹And who knows whether he is wise or foolish? Yet he rules over all my labor that I have labored at, and that I have done wisely under the sun! This [is] also vanity. ²⁰And I turned around to cause my heart to despair concerning all the labor that I labored at under the sun. ²¹For there is a man whose labor [is] in wisdom, and in knowledge, and in equity, and to a man who has not labored therein he gives it—his portion! Even this [is] vanity and a great evil. ²²For what has been to a man by all his labor, and by the thought of his heart that he labored at under the sun? ²³For all his days are sorrows, and his travail sadness; even at night his heart has not lain down; this [is] also vanity. ²⁴There is nothing good in a man who eats, and has drunk, and has shown his soul good in his labor. This also I have seen that it [is] from the hand of God. ²⁵For who eats and who hurries out more than I? ²⁶For to a man who [is] good before Him, He has given wisdom, and knowledge, and joy; and to a sinner He has given travail, to gather and to heap up, to give to the good before God. Even this [is] vanity and distress of spirit.

CHAPTER 3

¹To everything—a season, and a time to every delight under the heavens: ²A time to bring forth, || And a time to die. A time to plant, || And a time to eradicate the planted. ³A time to slay, || And a time to heal, || A time to break down, || And a time to build up. ⁴A time to weep, || And a time to laugh. A time to mourn, || And a time to skip. ⁵A time to cast away stones, || And a time to heap up stones. A time to embrace, || And a time to be far from embracing. ⁶A time to seek, || And a time to destroy. A time to keep, || And a time to cast away. ⁷A time to tear, || And a time to sew. A time to be silent, || And a time to speak. ⁸A time to love, || And a time to hate. A time of war, || And a time of peace. ⁹What advantage does the doer have in that which he is laboring at? ¹⁰I have seen the travail that God has given to the sons of man to be humbled by it. ¹¹The whole He has made beautiful in its season; also, that knowledge He has put in their heart without which man does not find out the work that God has done from the beginning even to the end. ¹²I have known that there is no good for them except to rejoice and to do good during their life, ¹³indeed, even every man who eats and has drunk and seen good by all his labor, it [is] a gift of God. ¹⁴I have known that all that God does is for all time, to it nothing is to be added, and from it nothing is to be withdrawn; and God has worked that they fear before Him. ¹⁵What is that which has been? Already it is, and that which [is] to be has already been, and God requires that which is pursued. ¹⁶And again, I have seen under the sun the place of judgment—there [is] the wicked; and the place of righteousness—there [is] the wicked. ¹⁷I said in my heart, "The righteous and the wicked God judges, for a time [is] to every matter and for every work there." ¹⁸I said in my heart concerning the matter of the sons of man that God might cleanse them, so as to see that they themselves [are] beasts. ¹⁹For an event [is to] the sons of man, and an event [is to] the beasts, even one event [is] to them; as the death of this, so [is] the death of that; and one spirit [is] to all, and the advantage of man above the beast is nothing, for the whole [is] vanity. ²⁰The whole are going to one place, the whole have been from the dust, and the whole are turning back to the dust. ²¹Who knows the spirit of the sons of man that is going up on high, and the spirit of the beast that is going down below to the earth? ²²And I have seen that there is nothing better than that man rejoice in his works, for it [is] his portion; for who brings him to look on that which is after him?

CHAPTER 4

¹And I have turned, and I see all the oppressions that are done under the sun, and behold, the tear of the oppressed, and they have no comforter; and at the hand of their oppressors [is] power, and they have no comforter. ²And I am praising the dead who have already died above the living who are yet alive. ³And better than both of them [is] he who has not yet been, in that he has not seen the evil work that has been done under the sun. ⁴And I have seen all the labor, and all the benefit of the work, because for it a man is the envy of his neighbor. Even this [is] vanity and distress of spirit. ⁵The fool is clasping his hands, and eating his own flesh: ⁶"Better [is] a handful [with] quietness, than two handfuls [with] labor and distress of spirit." ⁷And I have turned, and I see a vain thing under the sun: ⁸There is one, and there is not a second; even son or brother he has not, and there is no end to all his labor! His eye also is not satisfied with riches, and [he does not say], "For whom am I laboring and bereaving my soul of good?" This also is vanity, it is a sad travail. ⁹The two [are] better than the one, in that they have a good reward by their labor. ¹⁰For if they fall, the one raises up his companion, but woe to the one who falls and there is not a second to raise him up! ¹¹Also, if two lie down, then they have heat, but how has one heat? ¹²And if the one strengthens himself, the two stand against him; and the threefold cord is not quickly broken. ¹³Better is a poor and wise youth than an old and foolish king, who has not known to be warned anymore. ¹⁴For from a house of prisoners he has come out to reign, for even in his own kingdom he has been poor. ¹⁵I have seen all the living, who are walking under the sun, with the second youth who stands in his place; ¹⁶there is no end to all the people, to all who were before them; also, the latter do not rejoice in him. Surely this also is vanity and distress of spirit.

CHAPTER 5

¹Keep your feet when you go to a house of God, and draw near to hear rather than to give of fools the sacrifice, for they do not know they do evil. ²Do not cause your mouth to hurry, and do not let your heart hurry to bring out a word before God, for God is in the heavens, and you on the earth, therefore let your words be few. ³For the dream has come by abundance of business, and the voice of a fool by abundance of words. ⁴When you vow a vow to God, do not delay to complete it, for there is no pleasure in fools; that which you vow—complete. ⁵Better that you do not vow, than that you vow and do not complete. ⁶Do not permit your mouth to cause your flesh to sin, nor say before the messenger that it [is] ignorance. Why is God angry because of your voice and has destroyed the work of your hands? ⁷For in the abundance of dreams both vanities and words abound; but fear God. ⁸If oppression of the poor, and violent taking away of judgment and righteousness you see in a province, do not marvel at the matter, for a higher than the high is observing, and high ones [are] over them. ⁹And the abundance of a land is for all. A king for a field is served. ¹⁰Whoever is loving silver is not satisfied [with] silver, nor he who is in love with stores [with] increase. Even this [is] vanity. ¹¹In the multiplying of good have its consumers been multiplied, and what benefit [is] to its possessor except the sight of his eyes? ¹²Sweet [is] the sleep of the laborer whether he eat little or much; and the sufficiency of the wealthy is not permitting him to sleep. ¹³There is a painful evil I have seen under the sun: wealth kept for its possessor, for his evil. ¹⁴And that wealth has been lost in an evil business, and he has begotten a son and there is nothing in his hand! ¹⁵As he came out from the belly of his mother, naked he turns back to go as he came, and he does not take away anything of his labor, that goes in his hand. ¹⁶And this also [is] a painful evil, just as he came, so he goes, and what advantage [is] to him who labors for wind? ¹⁷He also consumes all his days in darkness, and sadness, and wrath, and sickness abound. ¹⁸Behold, that which I have seen: [It is] good, because beautiful, to eat, and to drink, and to see good in all one's labor that he labors at under the sun, the number of the days of his life that God has given to him, for it [is] his portion. ¹⁹Every man also to whom God has given wealth and riches, and has given him power to eat of it, and to accept his portion, and to rejoice in his labor, this is a gift of God. ²⁰For he does not much remember the days of his life, for God is answering through the joy of his heart.

CHAPTER 6

¹There is an evil that I have seen under the sun, and it [is] great on man: ²A man to whom God gives wealth, and riches, and honor, and there is no lack to his soul of all that he desires, and God does not give him power to eat of it, but a stranger eats it; this [is] vanity, and it [is] an evil disease. ³If a man begets one hundred, and lives many years, and is great, because they are the days of his years, and his soul is not satisfied from the goodness, and also he has not had a grave, I have said, "Better than he [is] the untimely birth." ⁴For in vanity he came in, and in darkness he goes, and in darkness his name is covered, ⁵even the sun he has not seen nor known, more rest has this than that. ⁶And though he had lived one thousand years twice over, yet he has not seen good; does not everyone go to the same place? ⁷All the labor of man [is] for his mouth, || And yet the soul is not filled. ⁸For what advantage [is] to the wise above the fool? What to the poor who knows how to walk before the living? ⁹Better [is] the sight of the eyes than the going of the soul. This [is] also vanity and distress of spirit. ¹⁰What [is] that which has been? Already is its name called, and it is known that it [is] man, || And he is not able to contend with him who is stronger than he. ¹¹For there are many things multiplying vanity; What advantage [is] to man? ¹²For who knows what [is] good for a man in life, the number of the days of the life of his vanity, and he makes them as a shadow? For who declares to man what is after him under the sun?

CHAPTER 7

¹Better [is] a name than good perfume, || And the day of death than the day of birth. ²Better to go to a house of mourning, || Than to go to a house of banqueting, || For that is the end of all men, || And the living lays [it] to his heart. ³Better [is] sorrow than laughter, || For by the sadness of the face the heart becomes better. ⁴The heart of the wise [is] in a house of mourning, || And the heart of fools in a house of mirth. ⁵Better to hear a rebuke of a wise man, || Than [for] a man to hear a song of fools, ⁶For as the noise of thorns under the pot, || So [is] the laughter of a fool, even this [is] vanity. ⁷Surely oppression makes the wise mad, || And a gift destroys the heart. ⁸Better [is] the latter end of a thing than its beginning, || Better [is] the patient of spirit, than the haughty of spirit. ⁹Do not be hasty in your spirit to be angry, || For anger in the bosom of fools rests. ¹⁰Do not say, "What was it, || That the former days were better than these?" For you have not asked wisely of this. ¹¹Wisdom [is] good with an inheritance, || And an advantage [it is] to those beholding the sun. ¹²For wisdom [is] a defense, money [is] a defense, || And the advantage of the knowledge of wisdom [is], || She revives her possessors. ¹³See the work of God, || For who is able to make straight that which He made crooked? ¹⁴In a day of prosperity be in gladness, || And in a day of calamity consider: God has also made this alongside of that, || To the intent that man does not find anything after him. ¹⁵The whole I have considered in the days of my vanity. There is a righteous one perishing in his righteousness, and there is a wrongdoer prolonging [himself] in his wrong. ¹⁶Do not be over-righteous, nor show yourself too wise, why are you desolate? ¹⁷Do not do much wrong, neither be a fool, why do you die within your time? ¹⁸[It is] good that you lay hold on this, and also, do not withdraw your hand from that, for whoever is fearing God goes out with them all. ¹⁹The wisdom gives strength to a wise man, more than wealth the rulers who have been in a city. ²⁰Because there is not a righteous man on earth that does good and does not sin. ²¹Also to all the words that they speak do not give your heart, that you do not hear your servant reviling you. ²²For many times also has your heart known that you yourself have also reviled others. ²³All this I have tried by wisdom; I have said, "I am wise," and it [is] far from me. ²⁴Far off [is] that which has been, and deep, deep, who finds it? ²⁵I have turned around, also my heart, to know and to search, and to seek out wisdom, and reason, and to know the wrong of folly, and the madness of foolishness. ²⁶And I am finding more bitter than death, the woman whose heart [is] nets and snares, her hands [are] bands; the good before God escapes from her, but the sinner is captured by her. ²⁷See, this I have found, said the Preacher, one to one, to find out the reason ²⁸(that still my soul had sought, and I had not found), || One man, a teacher, I have found, and a woman among all these I have not found. ²⁹See, this alone I have found, that God made man upright, and they have sought out many inventions.

CHAPTER 8

¹Who [is] as the wise? And who knows the interpretation of a thing? The wisdom of man causes his face to shine, and the hardness of his face is changed. ²I [counsel]: keep the command of a king, even for the sake of an oath [to] God. ³Do not be troubled at his presence, you may go, do not stand in an evil thing, for all that he pleases he does. ⁴Where the word of a king [is] power [is], and who says to him, "What do you do?" ⁵Whoever is keeping a command knows no evil thing, and time and judgment the heart of the wise knows. ⁶For to every delight there is a time and a judgment, for the misfortune of man is great on him. ⁷For he does not know that which will be, for when it will be who declares to him? ⁸There is no man ruling over the spirit to restrain the spirit, and there is no authority over the day of death, and there is no discharge in battle, and wickedness does not deliver its possessors. ⁹All this I have seen so as to give my heart to every work that has been done under the sun; a time that man has ruled over man to his own evil. ¹⁰And so I have seen the wicked buried, and they went in, even from the Holy Place they go, and they are forgotten in the city whether they had so done. This [is] also vanity. ¹¹Because sentence has not been done [on] an evil work speedily, therefore the heart of the sons of man is full within them to do evil. ¹²Though a sinner is doing evil one hundred [times], and prolonging [himself] for it, surely also I know that there is good to those fearing God, who fear before Him. ¹³And good is not to the wicked, and he does not prolong days as a shadow, because he is not fearing before God. ¹⁴There is a vanity that has been done on the earth, that there are righteous ones to whom it is coming according to the work of the wicked, and there are wicked ones to whom it is coming according to the work of the righteous. I have said that this [is] also vanity. ¹⁵And I have praised mirth because there is no good to man under the sun except to eat and to drink, and to rejoice, and it remains with him of his labor the days of his life that God has given to him under the sun. ¹⁶When I gave my heart to know wisdom and to see the business that has been done on the earth (for there is also a spectator in whose eyes sleep is not by day and by night), ¹⁷then I considered all the work of God, that man is not able to find out the work that has been done under the sun, because though man labor to seek, yet he does not find; and even though the wise man speak of knowing he is not able to find.

CHAPTER 9

¹But all this I have laid to my heart, so as to clear up the whole of this, that the righteous and the wise, and their works, [are] in the hand of God, neither love nor hatred does man know, the whole [is] before them. ²The whole [is] as to the whole; one event is to the righteous and to the wicked, to the good, and to the clean, and to the unclean, and to him who is sacrificing, and to him who is not sacrificing; as [is] the good, so [is] the sinner, he who is swearing as he who is fearing an oath. ³This [is] an evil among all that has been done under the sun, that one event [is] to all, and also the heart of the sons of man is full of evil, and madness [is] in their heart during their life, and after it—to the dead. ⁴But [to] him who is joined to all the living there is confidence, for to a living dog it [is] better than to the dead lion. ⁵For the living know that they die, and the dead do not know anything, and there is no more reward to them, for their remembrance has been forgotten. ⁶Their love also, their hatred also, their envy also, has already perished, and they have no more portion for all time in all that has been done under the sun. ⁷Go, eat your bread with joy, and drink your wine with a glad heart, for already has God been pleased with your works. ⁸At all times let your garments be white, and do not let oil be lacking on your head. ⁹See life with the wife whom you have loved, all the days of the life of your vanity, that He has given to you under the sun, all the days of your vanity, for it [is] your portion in life, even of your labor that you are laboring at under the sun. ¹⁰All that your hand finds to do, with your power do, for there is no work, and plan, and knowledge, and wisdom in Sheol to where you are going. ¹¹I have turned so as to see under the sun, that not to the swift [is] the race, nor to the mighty the battle, nor even to the wise bread, nor even to the intelligent

ECCLESIASTES

wealth, nor even to the skillful grace, for time and chance happen with them all. ¹²For even man does not know his time; as fish that are taken hold of by an evil net, and as birds that are taken hold of by a snare, the sons of man are snared like these at an evil time when it falls on them suddenly. ¹³This also I have seen: wisdom under the sun, and it is great to me. ¹⁴A little city, and few men in it, and a great king has come to it, and has surrounded it, and has built against it great bulwarks; ¹⁵and there has been found in it a poor wise man, and he has delivered the city by his wisdom, and men have not remembered that poor man! ¹⁶And I said, "Better [is] wisdom than might, and the wisdom of the poor is despised, and his words are not heard." ¹⁷The words of the wise are heard in quiet, || More than the cry of a ruler over fools. ¹⁸Better [is] wisdom than weapons of conflict, || And one sinner destroys much good!

CHAPTER 10

¹Dead flies cause a perfumer's perfume || To send forth a stink; The precious by reason of wisdom—By reason of honor—a little folly! ²The heart of the wise [is] at his right hand, || And the heart of a fool at his left. ³And also, when he that is a fool || Is walking in the way, his heart is lacking, || And he has said to everyone, "He [is] a fool." ⁴If the spirit of the ruler goes up against you, do not leave your place, || For yielding quiets great sinners. ⁵There is an evil I have seen under the sun, || As ignorance that goes out from the ruler, ⁶He has set the fool in many high places, || And the rich sits in a low place. ⁷I have seen servants on horses, || And princes walking as servants on the earth. ⁸Whoever is digging a pit falls into it, || And whoever is breaking a hedge, a serpent bites him. ⁹Whoever is removing stones is grieved by them, || Whoever is cleaving trees endangered by them. ¹⁰If the iron has been blunt, || And he has not sharpened the face, || Then he increases strength, || And wisdom [is] advantageous to make right. ¹¹If the serpent bites without enchantment, || Then there is no advantage to a master of the tongue. ¹²Words of the mouth of the wise [are] gracious, || And the lips of a fool swallow him up. ¹³The beginning of the words of his mouth [is] folly, || And the latter end of his mouth || [Is] mischievous madness. ¹⁴And the fool multiplies words: "Man does not know that which is—And that which is after him, who declares to him?" ¹⁵The labor of the foolish wearies him, || In that he has not known to go to the city. ¹⁶Woe to you, O land, when your king [is] a youth, || And your princes eat in the morning. ¹⁷Blessed are you, O land, || When your king [is] a son of nobles, || And your princes eat in due season, || For might, and not for drunkenness. ¹⁸By slothfulness is the wall brought low, || And by idleness of the hands the house drops. ¹⁹For mirth they are making a feast, || And wine makes life joyful, || And the silver answers with all. ²⁰Even in your mind do not revile a king, || And in the inner parts of your bed-chamber do not revile the rich: For a bird of the heavens causes the voice to go, || And a possessor of wings declares the word.

CHAPTER 11

¹Send forth your bread on the face of the waters, || For in the multitude of the days you find it. ²Give a portion to seven, and even to eight, || For you do not know what evil is on the earth. ³If the thick clouds are full of rain, || On the earth they empty [themselves]; And if a tree falls in the south or to the north, || The place where the tree falls, there it is. ⁴Whoever is observing the wind does not sow, || And whoever is looking on the thick clouds does not reap. ⁵As you do not know what [is] the way of the spirit, || How—bones in the womb of the full one, || So you do not know the work of God who makes the whole. ⁶In the morning sow your seed, || And at evening do not withdraw your hand, || For you do not know which is right, this or that, || Or whether both of them alike [are] good. ⁷Sweet also [is] the light, || And good for the eyes to see the sun. ⁸But if man lives many years, || In all of them let him rejoice, || And remember the days of darkness, || For they are many! All that is coming [is] vanity. ⁹Rejoice, O young man, in your childhood, || And let your heart gladden you in days of your youth, || And walk in the ways of your heart, || And in the sight of your eyes, || And know that for all these, God brings you into judgment. ¹⁰And turn aside anger from your heart, || And cause evil to pass from your flesh, || For the childhood and the age [are] vanity!

CHAPTER 12

¹Remember also your Creator in days of your youth, || While that the evil days do not come, || Nor the years have arrived, that you say, || "I have no pleasure in them." ²While that the sun is not darkened, and the light, || And the moon, and the stars, || And the thick clouds returned after the rain. ³In the day that keepers of the house tremble, || And men of strength have bowed themselves, || And grinders have ceased, because they have become few. And those looking out at the windows have become dim, ⁴And doors have been shut in the street. When the noise of the grinding is low, || And [one] rises at the voice of the bird, || And all daughters of song are bowed down. ⁵Also of that which is high they are afraid, || And of the low places in the way, || And the almond-tree is despised, || And the grasshopper has become a burden, || And want is increased, || For man is going to his perpetual home, || And the mourners have gone around through the street. ⁶While that the silver cord is not removed, || And the golden bowl broken, || And the pitcher broken by the fountain, || And the wheel broken at the well. ⁷And the dust returns to the earth as it was, || And the spirit returns to God who gave it. ⁸Vanity of vanities, said the preacher, the whole [is] vanity. ⁹And further, because the preacher was wise, he still taught the people knowledge, and gave ear, and sought out—he made right many allegories. ¹⁰The preacher sought to find out pleasing words, and [that] written [by] the upright—words of truth. ¹¹Words of the wise [are] as the goads, and as nails planted [by] the masters of collections, they have been given by one Shepherd. ¹²And further, from these, my son, be warned; the making of many scrolls has no end, and much study [is] a weariness of the flesh. ¹³The end of the whole matter let us hear: "Fear God, and keep His commands, for this [is] the whole of man. ¹⁴For every work God brings into judgment, with every hidden thing, whether good or bad."

SONG OF SONGS

CHAPTER 1

¹The Song of Songs, that [is] of Solomon. ²Let him kiss me with kisses of his mouth, || For better [are] your loves than wine. ³For fragrance [are] your good perfumes. Perfume emptied out—your name, || Therefore have virgins loved you! ⁴Draw me: we run after you, || The king has brought me into his inner chambers, || We delight and rejoice in you, || We mention your loves more than wine, || Uprightly they have loved you! ⁵I [am] dark and lovely, daughters of Jerusalem, as tents of Kedar, as curtains of Solomon. ⁶Do not fear me, because I [am] very dark, || Because the sun has scorched me, || The sons of my mother were angry with me, || They made me keeper of the vineyards, || My vineyard—my own—I have not kept. ⁷Declare to me, you whom my soul has loved, || Where you delight, || Where you lie down at noon, || For why am I as one veiled, || By the ranks of your companions? ⁸If you do not know, || O beautiful among women, || Go forth by the traces of the flock, || And feed your kids by the shepherds' dwellings! ⁹To my joyous one in chariots of Pharaoh, I have compared you, my friend, ¹⁰Your cheeks have been lovely with garlands, your neck with chains. ¹¹We make garlands of gold for you, with studs of silver! ¹²While the king [is] in his circle, || My spikenard has given its fragrance. ¹³A bundle

of myrrh [is] my beloved to me, || Between my breasts it lodges. ¹⁴A cluster of cypress [is] my beloved to me, || In the vineyards of En-Gedi! ¹⁵Behold, you [are] beautiful, my friend, || Behold, you [are] beautiful, your eyes [are] doves. ¹⁶Behold, you [are] beautiful, my love, indeed, pleasant, || Indeed, our bed [is] green, ¹⁷The beams of our houses [are] cedars, || Our rafters [are] firs, I [am] a rose of Sharon, a lily of the valleys!

CHAPTER 2

¹As a lily among the thorns, ²So [is] my friend among the daughters! ³As a citron among trees of the forest, || So [is] my beloved among the sons, || In his shade I delighted, and sat down, || And his fruit [is] sweet to my palate. ⁴He has brought me to a house of wine, || And his banner over me [is] love, ⁵Sustain me with grape-cakes, || Support me with citrons, for I [am] sick with love. ⁶His left hand [is] under my head, || And his right embraces me. ⁷I have adjured you, daughters of Jerusalem, || By the roes or by the does of the field, || Do not stir up nor wake the love until she pleases! ⁸The voice of my beloved! Behold, this—he is coming, || Leaping on the mountains, skipping on the hills. ⁹My beloved [is] like to a roe, || Or to a young one of the harts. Behold, this—he is standing behind our wall, || Looking from the windows, || Blooming from the lattice. ¹⁰My beloved has answered and said to me, || "Rise up, my friend, my beautiful one, and come away, ¹¹For behold, the winter has passed by, || The rain has passed away—it has gone. ¹²The flowers have appeared in the earth, || The time of the singing has come, || And the voice of the turtle was heard in our land, ¹³The fig tree has ripened her green figs, || And the sweet-smelling vines have given forth fragrance, || Rise, come, my friend, my beautiful one, indeed, come away. ¹⁴My dove, in clefts of the rock, || In a secret place of the ascent, || Cause me to see your appearance, || Cause me to hear your voice, || For your voice [is] sweet, and your appearance lovely." ¹⁵Seize for us foxes, || Little foxes—destroyers of vineyards, || Even our sweet-smelling vineyards. ¹⁶My beloved [is] mine, and I [am] his, || Who is delighting among the lilies, ¹⁷Until the day breaks forth, || And the shadows have fled away, || Turn, be like, my beloved, || To a roe, or to a young one of the harts, || On the mountains of separation!

CHAPTER 3

¹On my bed by night, I sought him whom my soul has loved; I sought him, and I did not find him! ²Now let me rise, and go around the city, || In the streets and in the broad places, || I seek him whom my soul has loved! I sought him, and I did not find him. ³The watchmen have found me || (Who are going around the city), || "Have you seen him whom my soul has loved?" ⁴But I passed on a little from them, || Until I found him whom my soul has loved! I seized him, and did not let him go, || Until I brought him to the house of my mother—And the chamber of her that conceived me. ⁵I have adjured you, daughters of Jerusalem, || By the roes or by the does of the field, || Do not stir up nor wake the love until she pleases! ⁶Who [is] this coming up from the wilderness, || Like palm-trees of smoke, || Perfumed [with] myrrh and frankincense, || From every powder of the merchant? ⁷Behold, his couch, that [is] of Solomon, || Sixty mighty ones [are] around it, || Of the mighty of Israel, ⁸All of them holding sword, taught of battle, || Each his sword by his thigh, for fear at night. ⁹A palanquin King Solomon made for himself, || Of the wood of Lebanon, ¹⁰Its pillars he made of silver, || Its bottom of gold, its seat of purple, || Its midst lined [with] love, || By the daughters of Jerusalem. ¹¹Go forth, and look, you daughters of Zion, || On King Solomon, with the crown, || With which his mother crowned him, || In the day of his espousals, || And in the day of the joy of his heart!

CHAPTER 4

¹Behold, you [are] beautiful, my friend, behold, you [are] beautiful, || Your eyes [are] doves behind your veil, || Your hair as a row of the goats that have shone from Mount Gilead, ²Your teeth as a row of the shorn ones that have come up from the washing, || For all of them are forming twins, || And a bereaved one is not among them. ³As a thread of scarlet [are] your lips, || And your speech [is] lovely, || As the work of the pomegranate [is] your temple behind your veil, ⁴As the Tower of David [is] your neck, built for an armory, || The chief of the shields are hung on it, || All shields of the mighty. ⁵Your two breasts [are] as two fawns, || Twins of a roe, that are feeding among lilies. ⁶Until the day breaks forth, || And the shadows have fled away, || I go for myself to the mountain of myrrh, || And to the hill of frankincense. ⁷You [are] all beautiful, my friend, || And there is not a blemish in you. Come from Lebanon, O spouse, ⁸Come from Lebanon, come in. Look from the top of Amana, || From the top of Shenir and Hermon, || From the habitations of lions, || From the mountains of leopards. ⁹You have emboldened me, my sister-spouse, || Emboldened me with one of your eyes, || With one chain of your neck. ¹⁰How beautiful have been your loves, my sister-spouse, || How much better have been your loves than wine, || And the fragrance of your perfumes than all spices. ¹¹Your lips drop honey, O spouse, || Honey and milk [are] under your tongue, || And the fragrance of your garments || [Is] as the fragrance of Lebanon. ¹²A garden shut up [is] my sister-spouse, || A spring shut up—a fountain sealed. ¹³Your shoots a paradise of pomegranates, || With precious fruits, ¹⁴Cypresses with nard—nard and saffron, || Cane and cinnamon, || With all trees of frankincense, || Myrrh and aloes, with all chief spices. ¹⁵A fount of gardens, a well of living waters, || And flowings from Lebanon! ¹⁶Awake, O north wind, and come, O south, || Cause my garden to breathe forth, its spices let flow, || Let my beloved come to his garden, || And eat its pleasant fruits!

CHAPTER 5

¹I have come to my garden, my sister-spouse, || I have plucked my myrrh with my spice, || I have eaten my comb with my honey, || I have drunk my wine with my milk. Eat, O friends, drink, || Indeed, drink abundantly, O beloved ones! ²I am sleeping, but my heart wakes: The sound of my beloved knocking! "Open to me, my sister, my friend, || My dove, my perfect one, || For my head is filled [with] dew, || My locks [with] drops of the night." ³I have put off my coat, how do I put it on? I have washed my feet, how do I defile them? ⁴My beloved sent his hand from the network, || And my bowels were moved for him. ⁵I rose to open to my beloved, || And my hands dripped myrrh, || Indeed, my fingers were flowing [with] myrrh, || On the handles of the lock. ⁶I opened to my beloved, || But my beloved withdrew—he passed on, || My soul went forth when he spoke, I sought him, and did not find him. I called him, and he did not answer me. ⁷The watchmen who go around the city, || Found me, struck me, wounded me, || Keepers of the walls lifted up my veil from off me. ⁸I have adjured you, daughters of Jerusalem, || If you find my beloved—What do you tell him? That I [am] sick with love! ⁹What [is] your beloved above [any] beloved, || O beautiful among women? What [is] your beloved above [any] beloved, || That thus you have adjured us? ¹⁰My beloved [is] clear and ruddy, || Conspicuous above a myriad! ¹¹His head [is] pure gold—fine gold, || His locks flowing, dark as a raven, ¹²His eyes as doves by streams of water, || Washing in milk, sitting in fullness. ¹³His cheeks [are] as a bed of the spice, towers of perfumes, || His lips—lilies, dripping [and] flowing [with] myrrh, ¹⁴His hands rings of gold, set with beryl, || His heart bright ivory, covered with sapphires, ¹⁵His limbs pillars of marble, || Founded on sockets of fine gold, || His appearance as Lebanon, choice as the cedars. ¹⁶His mouth is sweetness—and all of him desirable, || This [is] my beloved, and this my friend, || O daughters of Jerusalem!

CHAPTER 6

¹To where has your beloved gone, || O beautiful among women? To where has your beloved turned, || And we seek him with you? ²My beloved went down to his garden, || To the beds of the spice, || To delight himself in the gardens, and to gather lilies. ³I [am] my beloved's, and my beloved [is] mine, || Who is delighting himself among the lilies. ⁴You [are] beautiful, my friend, as Tirzah, lovely as Jerusalem, || Awe-inspiring as bannered hosts. ⁵Turn around your eyes from before me, || Because they have made me proud. Your hair [is] as a row of the goats, || That have shone from Gilead, ⁶Your teeth as a row of the lambs, || That have come up from the washing, || Because all of them are forming twins, || And a bereaved one is not among them. ⁷As the work of the pomegranate [is] your temple behind your veil. ⁸Sixty are queens, and eighty concubines, || And virgins without number. ⁹One is my dove, my perfect one, || She [is] one of her mother, || She [is] the

choice one of her that bore her, || Daughters saw, and pronounce her blessed, || Queens and concubines, and they praise her. ¹⁰"Who [is] this that is looking forth as morning, || Beautiful as the moon—clear as the sun, || Awe-inspiring as bannered hosts?" ¹¹"To a garden of nuts I went down, || To look on the buds of the valley, || To see to where the vine had flourished, || The pomegranates had blossomed— ¹²I did not know my soul, || It made me—chariots of my people Nadib. ¹³Return, return, O Shulammith! Return, return, and we look on you. What do you see in Shulammith?

CHAPTER 7

¹As the chorus of "Mahanaim." How beautiful were your feet with sandals, O daughter of Nadib. The turnings of your sides [are] as ornaments, || Work of the hands of a craftsman. ²Your waist [is] a basin of roundness, || It does not lack the mixture, || Your body a heap of wheat, fenced with lilies, ³Your two breasts as two young ones, twins of a roe, ⁴Your neck as a tower of the ivory, || Your eyes pools in Heshbon, near the Gate of Bath-Rabbim, || Your face as a tower of Lebanon looking to Damascus, ⁵Your head on you as Carmel, || And the locks of your head as purple, || The king is bound with the flowings! ⁶How beautiful and how pleasant you have been, || O love, in delights. ⁷This your stature has been like to a palm, || And your breasts to clusters. ⁸I said, "Let me go up on the palm, || Let me lay hold on its boughs," || Indeed, let your breasts now be as clusters of the vine, || And the fragrance of your face as citrons, ⁹And your palate as the good wine—Flowing to my beloved in uprightness, || Strengthening the lips of the aged! ¹⁰I [am] my beloved's, and on me [is] his desire. ¹¹Come, my beloved, we go forth to the field, ¹²We lodge in the villages, we go early to the vineyards, || We see if the vine has flourished, || The sweet smelling-flower has opened. The pomegranates have blossomed, || There I give to you my loves; ¹³The mandrakes have given fragrance, || And at our openings all pleasant things, || New, indeed, old, my beloved, I laid up for you!

CHAPTER 8

¹Who makes you as a brother to me, || Suckling the breasts of my mother? I find you outside, I kiss you, || Indeed, they do not despise me, ²I lead you, I bring you into my mother's house, || She teaches me, I cause you to drink of the spiced wine, || Of the juice of my pomegranate, ³His left hand [is] under my head, || And his right embraces me. ⁴I have adjured you, daughters of Jerusalem, || How you stir up, || And how you wake the love until she pleases! ⁵Who [is] this coming from the wilderness, || Hastening herself for her beloved? Under the citron-tree I have awoken you, || There your mother pledged you, || There she [who] bore you gave a pledge. ⁶Set me as a seal on your heart, as a seal on your arm, || For strong as death is love, || Sharp as Sheol is jealousy, || Its burnings [are] burnings of fire, a flame of YAH! ⁷Many waters are not able to quench the love, || And floods do not wash it away. If one gives all the wealth of his house for love, || Treading down—they tread on it. ⁸We have a little sister, and she does not have breasts, || What do we do for our sister, || In the day that it is told of her? ⁹If she is a wall, we build by her a palace of silver. And if she is a door, || We fashion by her board-work of cedar. ¹⁰I [am] a wall, and my breasts as towers, || Then I have been in his eyes as one finding peace. ¹¹Solomon has a vineyard in Ba'al-Hamon, || He has given the vineyard to keepers, || Each brings for its fruit one thousand pieces of silver; ¹²My vineyard—my own—is before me, || The one thousand [is] for you, O Solomon. And the two hundred for those keeping its fruit. O dweller in gardens! ¹³The companions are attending to your voice, || Cause me to hear. Flee, my beloved, and be like to a roe, ¹⁴Or to a young one of the harts on mountains of spices!

ISAIAH

CHAPTER 1

¹The visions of Isaiah son of Amoz, that he has seen concerning Judah and Jerusalem, in the days of Uzziah, Jotham, Ahaz, Hezekiah, kings of Judah. ²Hear, O heavens, and give ear, O earth, || For YHWH has spoken: "I have nourished and brought up sons, || And they transgressed against Me. ³An ox has known its owner, || And a donkey the crib of its master, || Israel has not known, || My people have not understood." ⁴Oh, sinning nation, a people heavy [with] iniquity, || A seed of evildoers, sons—corrupters! They have forsaken YHWH, || They have despised the Holy One of Israel, || They have gone away backward. ⁵Why are you struck anymore? You add apostasy! Every head has become diseased, and every heart [is] sick. ⁶From the sole of the foot—to the head, || There is no soundness in it, || Wound, and bruise, and fresh striking! They have not been closed nor bound, || Nor have they softened with ointment. ⁷Your land [is] a desolation, your cities burned with fire, || Your ground—strangers are consuming it before you, || And a desolation as overthrown by strangers! ⁸And the daughter of Zion has been left, || As a shelter in a vineyard, || As a lodge in a place of cucumbers—as a city besieged. ⁹Unless YHWH of Hosts had left a remnant to us, || Shortly—we had been as Sodom, || We had been like to Gomorrah! ¹⁰Hear the word of YHWH, you rulers of Sodom, || Give ear to the Law of our God, you people of Gomorrah, ¹¹"Why the abundance of your sacrifices to Me?" says YHWH, || "I have been satiated [with] burnt-offerings of rams, || And fat of fatlings; And blood of bullocks, and lambs, || And I have not desired male goats. ¹²When you come to appear before Me, || Who has required this of your hand, || To trample My courts? ¹³Do not add to bring in a vain present, || Incense—it [is] an abomination to Me, || New moon, and Sabbath, calling of convocation! Do not render iniquity—and a restraint! ¹⁴My soul has hated your new moons and your set seasons, || They have been on Me for a burden, || I have been weary of bearing. ¹⁵And in your spreading forth your hands, I hide My eyes from you, || Also when you increase prayer, I do not hear, || Your hands have been full of blood. ¹⁶Wash yourselves, make yourselves pure, || Turn aside the evil of your doings, from before My eyes, || Cease to do evil, learn to do good. ¹⁷Seek judgment, make the oppressed blessed, || Judge the fatherless, strive [for] the widow. ¹⁸Now come, and we settle this," says YHWH, "If your sins are as scarlet, they will be white as snow, || If they are red as crimson, they will be as wool! ¹⁹If you are willing, and have listened, || The good of the land you consume, ²⁰And if you refuse, and have rebelled, || You are consumed [by] the sword," || For the mouth of YHWH has spoken. ²¹How has a faithful city become a harlot? I have filled it [with] judgment, || Righteousness lodges in it—now murderers. ²²Your silver has become dross, || Your drink defiled with water. ²³Your princes [are] apostates, and companions of thieves, || Everyone loving a bribe, and pursuing rewards, || They do not judge the fatherless, || And the plea of the widow does not come to them. ²⁴Therefore—a declaration of the Lord—YHWH of Hosts, the Mighty One of Israel: "Oh, I relieve Myself from My adversaries, || And avenge Myself against My enemies, ²⁵And I turn back My hand on you, || And I refine your dross as purity, || And I turn aside all your tin, ²⁶And I give back your judges as at the first, || And your counselors as in the beginning, || After this you are called, A city of righteousness—a faithful city." ²⁷Zion is redeemed in judgment, || And her captivity in righteousness. ²⁸And the destruction of transgressors and sinners [is] together, || And those forsaking YHWH are consumed. ²⁹For [men] are ashamed because of the oaks || That you have desired, || And you are confounded because of the gardens || That you have chosen. ³⁰For you are as an oak whose leaf is fading, || And as a garden that has no water. ³¹And the strong has been for tow, || And his

ISAIAH

work for a spark, || And both of them have burned together, || And there is none quenching!

CHAPTER 2

¹The thing that Isaiah son of Amoz has seen concerning Judah and Jerusalem: ²And it has come to pass, || In the latter end of the days, || The mountain of YHWH's house is established, || Above the top of the mountains, || And it has been lifted up above the heights, || And all the nations have flowed to it. ³And many peoples have gone and said, "Come, and we go up to the mountain of YHWH, || To the house of the God of Jacob, || And He teaches us of His ways, || And we walk in His paths, || For a law goes forth from Zion, || And a word of YHWH from Jerusalem. ⁴And He has judged between the nations, || And has given a decision to many peoples, || And they have beat their swords to plowshares, || And their spears to pruning-hooks, || Nation does not lift up sword to nation, || Nor do they learn anymore—war. ⁵O house of Jacob, come, || And we walk in the light of YHWH." ⁶For You have left Your people, the house of Jacob. For they have been filled from the east, || And [are] sorcerers like the Philistines, || And strike hands with the children of strangers. ⁷And its land is full of silver and gold, || And there is no end to its treasures, || And its land is full of horses, || And there is no end to its chariots, ⁸And its land is full of idols, || It bows itself to the work of its hands, || To that which its fingers have made, ⁹And the low bows down, and the high is humbled, || And You do not accept them. ¹⁰Enter into a rock, and be hidden in dust, || Because of the fear of YHWH, || And because of the honor of His excellence. ¹¹The haughty eyes of man have been humbled, || And the loftiness of men have been bowed down, || And YHWH alone has been set on high in that day. ¹²For a day [is] to YHWH of Hosts, || For every proud and high one, || And for every lifted up and low one, ¹³And for all cedars of Lebanon, || The high and the exalted ones, || And for all oaks of Bashan, ¹⁴And for all the high mountains, || And for all the exalted heights, ¹⁵And for every high tower, || And for every fortified wall, ¹⁶And for all ships of Tarshish, || And for all desirable pictures. ¹⁷And the haughtiness of man has been bowed down, || And the loftiness of men humbled, || And YHWH alone has been set on high in that day. ¹⁸And the idols—they completely pass away. ¹⁹And [men] have entered into caverns of rocks, || And into caves of dust, || Because of the fear of YHWH, || And because of the honor of His excellence, || In His rising to terrify the earth. ²⁰In that day man casts his idols of silver, || And his idols of gold, || That they have made for him to worship, || To moles, and to bats, ²¹To enter into cavities of the rocks, || And into clefts of the high places, || Because of the fear of YHWH, || And because of the honor of His excellence, || In His rising to terrify the earth. ²²Cease yourselves from man, || Whose breath [is] in his nostrils, || For—in what is he esteemed?

CHAPTER 3

¹For behold, the Lord, YHWH of Hosts, || Is turning aside from Jerusalem and from Judah || [Both] stay and staff: Every stay of bread and every stay of water; ²Mighty and man of war, judge and prophet, || And diviner and elderly, ³Head of fifty, and accepted of faces, || And counselor, and wise craftsmen, || And discerning charmer. ⁴And I have made youths their heads, || And sucklings rule over them. ⁵And the people has exacted—man on man, || Even a man on his neighbor, || The youths enlarge themselves against the aged, || And the lightly esteemed against the honored. ⁶When one lays hold on his brother, || Of the house of his father, [by] the garment, "Come, you are a ruler to us, || And this ruin [is] under your hand." ⁷He lifts up, in that day, saying, "I am not a binder up, || And in my house is neither bread nor garment, || You do not make me a ruler of the people." ⁸For Jerusalem has stumbled, and Judah has fallen, || For their tongue and their doings [are] against YHWH, || To provoke the eyes of His glory. ⁹The appearance of their faces witnessed against them, || And their sin, as Sodom, they declared, || They have not hidden! Woe to their soul, || For they have done evil to themselves. ¹⁰Say to the righteous that [it is] good, || Because they eat the fruit of their doings. ¹¹Woe to the wicked—evil, || Because the deed of his hand is done to him. ¹²My people—its exactors [are] sucklings, || And women have ruled over it. My people—your eulogists are causing to err, || And the way of your paths swallowed up. ¹³YHWH has stood up to plead, || And He is standing to judge the peoples. ¹⁴YHWH enters into judgment || With [the] elderly of His people, and its heads: "And you, you have consumed the vineyard, || Plunder of the poor [is] in your houses. ¹⁵Why? Why do you [do this]? You bruise My people, || And you grind the faces of the poor." A declaration of the Lord, YHWH of Hosts, || And YHWH says: ¹⁶"Because that daughters of Zion have been haughty, || And they walk stretching out the neck, || And deceiving [with] the eyes, || They go walking and mincing, || And they make a jingling with their feet, ¹⁷The Lord has also scabbed || The crown of the head of daughters of Zion, || And YHWH exposes their simplicity. ¹⁸In that day the Lord turns aside || The beauty of the jingling ornaments, || And of the embroidered works, || And of the crescents, ¹⁹Of the pendants, and the bracelets, and the veils, ²⁰Of the headdresses, and the ornaments of the legs, || And of the bands, || And of the perfume boxes, and the amulets, ²¹Of the seals, and of the nose-rings, ²²Of the costly apparel, and of the mantles, || And of the coverings, and of the purses, ²³Of the mirrors, and of the linen garments, || And of the hoods, and of the veils, ²⁴And it has been, instead of spice is muck, || And instead of a girdle, a rope, || And instead of curled work, baldness, || And instead of a stomacher a girdle of sackcloth. ²⁵For instead of glory, your men fall by sword, || And your might in battle. ²⁶And her openings have lamented and mourned, || Indeed, she has been emptied, she sits on the earth!"

CHAPTER 4

¹And seven women have taken hold on one man, || In that day, saying, "We eat our own bread, || And we put on our own raiment, || Only, let your name be called over us, || Remove our reproach." ²In that day is the Shoot of YHWH for desire and for glory, || And the fruit of the earth || For excellence and for beauty to the escaped of Israel. ³And it has been, he who is left in Zion, || And he who is remaining in Jerusalem, "Holy" is said of him, || Of everyone who is written for life in Jerusalem. ⁴If the Lord has washed away || The filth of daughters of Zion, || And purges the blood of Jerusalem from her midst, || By the spirit of judgment, and by the spirit of burning. ⁵Then YHWH has created || Over every fixed place of Mount Zion, || And over her convocations, || A cloud by day, and smoke, || And the shining of a flaming fire by night, || That over all glory—a safeguard, ⁶And a covering may be, || For a shadow from drought by day, || And for a refuge, and for a hiding place, || From inundation and from rain!

CHAPTER 5

¹Now let me sing for my Beloved, || A song of my Beloved as to His vineyard: My beloved has a vineyard in a fruitful hill, ²And He fences it, and casts out its stones, || And plants it [with] a choice vine, || And builds a tower in its midst, || And has also hewn out a winepress in it, || And He waits for the yielding of grapes, || And it yields bad ones! ³And now, O inhabitant of Jerusalem and man of Judah, || Please judge between Me and My vineyard. ⁴What [is there] to do still to My vineyard, || That I have not done in it? For what reason have I waited for the yielding of grapes, || And it yields [only] bad ones? ⁵And now, pray, let Me cause you to know, || That which I am doing to My vineyard, || To turn its hedge aside, || And it has been for consumption, || To break down its wall, || And it has been for a treading-place. ⁶And I make it a waste, || It is not pruned, nor arranged, || And brier and thorn have gone up, || And I lay a charge on the thick clouds, || From raining on it rain. ⁷Because the vineyard of YHWH of Hosts || [Is] the house of Israel, || And the man of Judah His pleasant plant, || And He waits for judgment, and behold, oppression, || For righteousness, and behold, a cry. ⁸Woe [to] those joining house to house, || They bring field near to field, || Until there is no place, || And you have been settled by yourselves || In the midst of the land! ⁹Do many houses not become a desolation by the weapons of YHWH of Hosts? Great and good without inhabitant! ¹⁰For ten acres of vineyard yield one bath, || And a homer of seed yields an ephah. ¹¹Woe [to] those rising early in the morning, || They pursue strong drink! Lingering in twilight, wine inflames them! ¹²And harp, and stringed instrument, tambourine, and pipe, || And wine, have been their banquets, || And they do not behold the work of YHWH, || Indeed, they have not seen the work of His hands. ¹³Therefore my people removed without knowledge, || And its

honorable ones are famished, || And its multitude dried up of thirst. ¹⁴Therefore Sheol has enlarged herself, || And has opened her mouth without limit. And its honor has gone down, and its multitude, || And its noise, and its exulting one—into her. ¹⁵And the low is bowed down, and the high humbled, || And the eyes of the haughty become low, ¹⁶And YHWH of Hosts is high in judgment, || And the Holy God sanctified in righteousness, ¹⁷And lambs have fed according to their leading, || And sojourners consume wastelands of the fat ones. ¹⁸Woe [to] those drawing out iniquity with cords of vanity, || And as [with] thick ropes of the cart—sin. ¹⁹Who are saying, "Let Him hurry, || Let Him hurry His work, that we may see, || And let the counsel of the Holy One of Israel || Draw near and come, and we know." ²⁰Woe [to] those saying to evil "good," and to good "evil," || Putting darkness for light, and light for darkness, || Putting bitter for sweet, and sweet for bitter. ²¹Woe [to] the wise in their own eyes, || And—before their own faces—intelligent! ²²Woe [to] the mighty to drink wine, || And men of strength to mingle strong drink. ²³Declaring righteous the wicked for a bribe, || And the righteousness of the righteous || They turn aside from him. ²⁴Therefore, as a tongue of fire devours stubble, || And flaming hay falls, || Their root is as muck, || And their flower goes up as dust. Because they have rejected the Law of YHWH of Hosts, || And despised the saying of the Holy One of Israel. ²⁵Therefore the anger of YHWH has burned among His people, || And He stretches out His hand against it, || And strikes it, and the mountains tremble, || And their carcass is as filth in the midst of the out-places. With all this His anger did not turn back, || And still His hand is stretched out! ²⁶And He lifted up an ensign to the far-off nations, || And hissed to it from the end of the earth, || And behold, with haste, it comes swiftly. ²⁷There is none weary, nor stumbling in it, || It does not slumber, nor sleep, || Nor has the girdle of its loins been opened, || Nor the strap of its sandals drawn away. ²⁸Whose arrows [are] sharp, and all its bows bent, || Hooves of its horses have been reckoned as flint, || And its wheels as a windstorm! ²⁹Its roaring [is] like a lioness, || It roars like young lions, || And it howls, and seizes prey, || And carries away safely, and there is none delivering. ³⁰And it howls against it in that day as the howling of a sea, || And it has looked attentively to the land, || And behold, darkness—distress, || And light has been darkened by its abundance!

CHAPTER 6

¹In the year of the death of King Uzziah—I see the Lord, sitting on a throne, high and lifted up, and His train is filling the temple. ²Seraphim are standing above it: each one has six wings; with two [each] covers its face, and with two [each] covers its feet, and with two [each] flies. ³And this one has called to that, and has said: "Holy, Holy, Holy, [is] YHWH of Hosts, || The fullness of all the earth [is] His glory!" ⁴And the posts of the thresholds are moved by the voice of him who is calling, and the house is full of smoke. ⁵And I say, "Woe to me, for I have been silent, || For I [am] a man of unclean lips, || And I am dwelling in [the] midst of a people of unclean lips, || Because the King, YHWH of Hosts, my eyes have seen." ⁶And one of the seraphim flees to me, and in his hand—a burning coal (with tongs he has taken [it] from off the altar), ⁷and he strikes against my mouth and says: "Behold, this has struck against your lips, || And your iniquity is turned aside, || And your sin is covered." ⁸And I hear the voice of the Lord, saying, "Whom do I send? And who goes for Us?" And I say, "Here I [am], send me." ⁹And He says, "Go, and you have said to this people, Hearing you hear, and you do not understand, || And seeing you see, and you do not know. ¹⁰Declare the heart of this people fat, || And declare its ears heavy, || And declare its eyes dazzled, || Lest it see with its eyes, || And hear with its ears, and consider with its heart, || And it has turned back, and has health." ¹¹And I say, "Until when, O Lord?" And He says, "Surely until cities have been ruined without inhabitant, || And houses without man, || And the ground is ruined—a desolation, ¹²And YHWH has put man far off, || And the forsaken part [is] great in the heart of the land. ¹³And yet a tenth in it, and it has turned, || And has been for a burning, || As a teil-tree, and as an oak, that in falling, || Has substance in them, || The holy seed [is] its substance!"

CHAPTER 7

¹And it comes to pass in the days of Ahaz, son of Jotham, son of Uzziah, king of Judah, [that] Rezin king of Aram, and Pekah, son of Remaliah, king of Israel, have gone up to Jerusalem, to battle against it, and he is not able to fight against it. ²And it is declared to the house of David, saying, "Aram has been led toward Ephraim," and his heart and the heart of his people is moved, like the moving of trees of a forest by the presence of wind. ³And YHWH says to Isaiah, "Now go forth to meet Ahaz, you and your son Shear-Jashub, to the end of the conduit of the upper pool, to the highway of the fuller's field, ⁴and you have said to him: Take heed, and be quiet, do not fear, || And do not let your heart be timid, || Because of these two tails of smoking brands, || For the fierceness of the anger of Rezin and Aram, || And the son of Remaliah. ⁵Because that Aram counseled evil against you, Ephraim and the son of Remaliah, saying, ⁶'We go up into Judah, and we distress it, || And we divide it to ourselves, || And we cause a king to reign in its midst—The son of Tabeal.' ⁷Thus said Lord YHWH: It does not stand, nor will it be! ⁸For the head of Aram [is] Damascus, || And the head of Damascus [is] Rezin, || And within sixty-five years || Is Ephraim broken from [being] a people. ⁹And the head of Ephraim [is] Samaria, || And the head of Samaria [is] the son of Remaliah. If you do not give credence, || Surely you are not steadfast." ¹⁰And YHWH adds to speak to Ahaz, saying, ¹¹"Ask for a sign from your God YHWH, || Make the request deep, or make [it] high upwards." ¹²And Ahaz says, "I do not ask nor try YHWH." ¹³And he says, "Now hear, O house of David, || Is it a little thing for you to weary men, || That you also weary my God? ¹⁴Therefore the Lord Himself gives a sign to you, || Behold, the virgin is conceiving, || And is bringing forth a Son, || And has called His Name Immanuel, ¹⁵He eats butter and honey, || When He knows to refuse evil, and to fix on good. ¹⁶For before the youth knows || To refuse evil, and to fix on good, || The land you are distressed with is forsaken, because of her two kings. ¹⁷YHWH brings on you, and on your people, || And on the house of your father, || Days that have not come, || Even from the day of the turning aside of Ephraim from Judah, || By the king of Asshur." ¹⁸And it has come to pass in that day, || YHWH hisses for a fly that [is] in the extremity of the brooks of Egypt, || And for a bee that [is] in the land of Asshur. ¹⁹And they have come, and all of them rested in the desolate valleys, || And in holes of the rocks, and on all the thorns, || And on all the commendable things. ²⁰In that day the Lord shaves, || By a razor that is hired beyond the river, || By the king of Asshur, || The head, and the hair of the feet, || Indeed, it also consumes the beard. ²¹And it has come to pass in that day, || A man keeps alive a heifer of the herd, || And two of the flock, ²²And it has come to pass, || He eats butter from the abundance of the yielding of milk, || For everyone who is left in the heart of the land eats butter and honey. ²³And it has come to pass in that day, || Every place where there are one thousand vines, || At one thousand pieces of silver, || Is for briers and for thorns. ²⁴He comes there with arrows and with bow, || Because all the land is brier and thorn. ²⁵And all the hills that are kept in order with a mattock, || There does not come [for] fear of brier and thorn, || And it has been for the sending forth of ox, || And for the treading of sheep!

CHAPTER 8

¹And YHWH says to me, "Take a great tablet to yourself, and write on it with an engraving tool of man, || To hurry spoil, enjoy prey." ²And I cause faithful witnesses to testify to me, Uriah the priest, and Zechariah son of Jeberechiah. ³And I draw near to the prophetess, and she conceives, and bears a son; and YHWH says to me, "Call his name Maher-shalal-hash-baz, ⁴for before the youth knows to cry, My father, and, My mother, one takes away the wealth of Damascus and the spoil of Samaria, before the king of Asshur." ⁵And YHWH adds to speak to me again, saying, ⁶"Because that this people has refused || The waters of Shiloah that go softly, || And is rejoicing with Rezin and the son of Remaliah, ⁷Therefore, behold, the Lord is bringing up on them, || The waters of the river, the mighty and the great || (The king of Asshur, and all his glory), || And it has gone up over all its streams, || And has gone on over all its banks. ⁸And it has passed on into Judah, || It has overflown and passed over, || It comes to the neck, || And the stretching out of its wings || Has been the fullness of the breadth of your land, O Immanuel! ⁹Be friends, O nations, and be broken, || And give ear, all you far-off ones

of earth, || Gird yourselves, and be broken, || Gird yourselves, and be broken. ¹⁰Take counsel, and it is broken, || Speak a word, and it does not stand, || Because of Immanuel!" ¹¹For thus has YHWH spoken to me with strength of hand, and instructs me against walking in the way of this people, saying, ¹²"You do not say, A confederacy, || To all to whom this people says, A confederacy, || And its fear you do not fear, || Nor declare fearful. ¹³YHWH of Hosts—Him you sanctify, || And He [is] your Fear, and He your Dread, ¹⁴And He has been for a sanctuary, || And for a stone of stumbling, and for a rock of falling, || To the two houses of Israel, || For a trap and for a snare to the inhabitants of Jerusalem. ¹⁵And many among them have stumbled and fallen, || And been broken, and snared, and captured." ¹⁶Bind up the testimony, || Seal the Law among My disciples. ¹⁷And I have waited for YHWH, || Who is hiding His face from the house of Jacob, || And I have looked for Him. ¹⁸Behold, I, and the children whom YHWH has given to me, || [Are] for signs and for wonders in Israel, || From YHWH of Hosts, who is dwelling in Mount Zion. ¹⁹And when they say to you, "Seek to those having familiar spirits, || And to wizards, who chatter and mutter," || Does a people not seek to its God? To the dead on behalf of the living? ²⁰To the Law and to the testimony! If not, let them say after this manner, "That there is no dawn to it." ²¹And it has passed over into it, hardened and hungry, || And it has come to pass, || That it is hungry, and has been angry, || And made light of its king, and of its God, || And has looked upwards. ²²And it looks attentively to the land, || And behold, adversity and darkness! Dimness, distress, and thick darkness are driven away, || But not the dimness for which she is in distress!

CHAPTER 9

¹For [there will be] no gloom on her who [is] distressed as at the former time. The land of Zebulun and the land of Naphtali, || So the latter has honored the way of the sea, || Beyond the Jordan, Galilee of the nations. ²The people who are walking in darkness || Have seen a great light, || Dwellers in a land of death-shade, || Light has shone on them. ³You have multiplied the nation, || You have made its joy great, || They have rejoiced before You as the joy in harvest, || As [men] rejoice in their apportioning spoil. ⁴Because the yoke of its burden, || And the staff of its shoulder, the rod of its exactor, || You have broken as [in] the day of Midian. ⁵For every battle of a warrior [is] with rushing, and raiment rolled in blood, || And it has been for burning—fuel of fire. ⁶For a Child has been born to us, || A Son has been given to us, || And the dominion is on His shoulder, || And He calls His Name || Wonderful, Counselor, Mighty God, || Father of Eternity, Prince of Peace. ⁷Of the increase of [His] dominion, || And of peace, there is no end, || On the throne of David, and on His kingdom, || To establish it, and to support it, || In judgment and in righteousness, || From now on, even for all time, || The zeal of YHWH of Hosts does this. ⁸The Lord has sent a word into Jacob, || And it has fallen in Israel. ⁹And the people have known—all of it, Ephraim, and the inhabitant of Samaria, || In pride and in greatness of heart, saying, ¹⁰"Bricks have fallen, and we build hewn work, || Sycamores have been cut down, and we renew cedars." ¹¹And YHWH sets the adversaries of Rezin on high above him, || And he joins his enemies together, ¹²Aram from before, and Philistia from behind, || And they devour Israel with the whole mouth. With all this His anger has not turned back, || And His hand is still stretched out. ¹³And the people has not turned back to Him who is striking it, || And they have not sought YHWH of Hosts. ¹⁴And YHWH cuts off head and tail from Israel, || Branch and reed—the same day. ¹⁵Elderly and accepted of faces—he [is] the head, || And prophet teaching falsehood—he [is] the tail. ¹⁶And the eulogists of this people are causing to err, || And its eulogized ones are consumed. ¹⁷Therefore, the Lord does not rejoice over its young men, || And He does not pity its orphans and its widows, || For everyone [is] profane, and an evildoer, || And every mouth is speaking folly. With all this His anger has not turned back, || And His hand is still stretched out. ¹⁸For wickedness has burned as a fire, || It devours brier and thorn, || And it kindles in thickets of the forest, || And they lift themselves up, an exaltation of smoke! ¹⁹In the wrath of YHWH of Hosts || The land has been consumed, || And the people is as fuel of fire; A man has no pity on his brother, ²⁰And cuts down on the right, and has been hungry, || And he devours on the left, || And they have not been satisfied, || They each devour the flesh of his own arm. ²¹Manasseh—Ephraim, and Ephraim—Manasseh, || Together they [are] against Judah, || With all this His anger has not turned back. And His hand is still stretched out!

CHAPTER 10

¹"Woe [to] those decreeing decrees of iniquity, || And writers who have prescribed perverseness, ²Of My people, || That widows may be their prey, || That they may spoil the fatherless. ³And what do you do at a day of inspection? And at desolation that comes from afar? Near whom do you flee for help? And where do you leave your glory? ⁴It has bowed down without Me || In the place of a bound one, || And they fall in the place of the slain." With all this His anger has not turned back, || And His hand is still stretched out. ⁵"Woe [to] Asshur, a rod of My anger, || And My indignation [is] a staff in their hand. ⁶I send him against a profane nation, || And concerning a people of My wrath || I charge him, || To spoil spoil, and to seize prey, || And to make it a treading-place as the clay of out places. ⁷And he does not think [it] so, || And his heart does not reckon [it] so, || For—to destroy [is] in his heart, || And to cut off nations—not a few. ⁸For he says, Are my princes not altogether kings? ⁹Is not Calno as Carchemish? Is not Hamath as Arpad? Is not Samaria as Damascus? ¹⁰As my hand has gotten to the kingdoms of a worthless thing, and their carved images, || [Greater] than Jerusalem and than Samaria, ¹¹Do I not—as I have done to Samaria, || And to her worthless things, || So do to Jerusalem and to her grievous things?" ¹²And it has come to pass, || When the Lord fulfills all His work || In Mount Zion and in Jerusalem, || I see concerning the fruit of the greatness || Of the heart of the king of Asshur, || And concerning the glory of the height of his eyes. ¹³For he has said, "I have worked by the power of my hand, || And by my wisdom, for I have been intelligent, || And I remove borders of the peoples, || And I have spoiled their chief ones, || And I put down the inhabitants as a mighty one, ¹⁴And my hand gets to the wealth of the peoples as to a nest, || And as a gathering of forsaken eggs || I have gathered all the earth, || And there has not been one moving wing, || Or opening mouth, or whispering." ¹⁵Does the axe glorify itself || Against him who is hewing with it? Does the saw magnify itself || Against him who is shaking it? As a rod waving those lifting it up! As a staff lifting up that which is not wood! ¹⁶Therefore the Lord, the Lord of Hosts, || Sends leanness among his fat ones, || And under his glory || He kindles a burning || As the burning of a fire. ¹⁷And the light of Israel has been for a fire, || And his Holy One for a flame, || And it has burned, and devoured his thorn || And his brier in one day. ¹⁸And the glory of his forest, and his fruitful field, || He consumes from soul even to flesh, || And it has been as the fainting of a standard-bearer. ¹⁹And the rest of the trees of his forest [are] few, || And a youth writes them. ²⁰And it has come to pass in that day, || The remnant of Israel, || And the escaped of the house of Jacob, || Do not add anymore to lean on its striker, || And have leaned on YHWH, || The Holy One of Israel, in truth. ²¹A remnant returns—a remnant of Jacob, || To the Mighty God. ²²For though your people Israel be as the sand of the sea, || A remnant of it returns, || A consumption determined, || Overflowing [with] righteousness. ²³For a consumption that is determined, || The Lord, YHWH of Hosts, || Is making in the midst of all the land. ²⁴Therefore, thus said the Lord, YHWH of Hosts: "Do not be afraid, My people, inhabiting Zion, because of Asshur, || He strikes you with a rod, || And his staff lifts up against you, in the way of Egypt. ²⁵For yet a very little [while], || And the indignation has been completed, || And My anger by their wearing out." ²⁶And YHWH of Hosts is awaking for him, || A scourge like the striking of Midian at the rock Oreb, || And his rod [is] over the sea, || And he has lifted it in the way of Egypt. ²⁷And it has come to pass in that day, || His burden is turned from off your shoulder, || And his yoke from off your neck, || And the yoke has been destroyed, because of prosperity. ²⁸He has come in against Aiath, || He has passed over into Migron, || At Michmash he looks after his vessels. ²⁹They have gone over the passage, || They have made Geba a lodging place, || Rama has trembled, || Gibeah of Saul fled. ³⁰Cry aloud [with] your voice, daughter of Gallim, || Give

ISAIAH

attention, Laish! Answer her, Anathoth. ³¹Madmenah has fled away, || The inhabitants of the high places have hardened themselves. ³²Yet today to remain in Nob, || The mountain of the daughter of Zion waves its hand, || The hill of Jerusalem. ³³Behold, the Lord, YHWH of Hosts, || Is lopping a branch with violence, || And the high of stature are cut down, || And the lofty have become low, ³⁴And He has gone around the thickets of the forest with iron, || And Lebanon falls by a mighty one!

CHAPTER 11

¹And a Rod has come out from the stock of Jesse, || And a Branch is fruitful from his roots. ²The Spirit of YHWH has rested on Him, || The Spirit of wisdom and understanding, || The Spirit of counsel and might, || The Spirit of knowledge and fear of YHWH. ³To refresh Him in the fear of YHWH, || And He does not judge by the sight of His eyes, || Nor decides by the hearing of His ears. ⁴And He has judged the poor in righteousness, || And decided for the humble of earth in uprightness, || And has struck earth with the rod of His mouth, || And He puts the wicked to death with the breath of His lips. ⁵And righteousness has been the girdle of His loins, || And faithfulness—the girdle of His reins. ⁶"And a wolf has sojourned with a lamb, || And a leopard lies down with a kid, || And calf, and young lion, and fatling [are] together, || And a little youth is leader over them. ⁷And cow and bear feed, || Together their young ones lie down, || And a lion eats straw as an ox. ⁸And a suckling has played by the hole of a cobra, || And on the den of a viper || The weaned one has put his hand. ⁹They do no evil, nor destroy in all My holy mountain, || For the earth has been full with the knowledge of YHWH, || As the waters are covering the sea." ¹⁰And there has been, in that day, || A Root of Jesse that is standing for an ensign of peoples, || Nations seek Him, || And His rest has been glorious! ¹¹And it has come to pass in that day, || The Lord adds His power a second time, || To get the remnant of His people that is left, || From Asshur, and from Egypt, || And from Pathros, and from Cush, || And from Elam, and from Shinar, || And from Hamath, and from islands of the sea, ¹²And He has lifted up an ensign to nations, || And gathers the driven away of Israel, || And He assembles the scattered of Judah, || From the four wings of the earth. ¹³And has turned aside the envy of Ephraim, || And the adversaries of Judah are cut off, || Ephraim does not envy Judah, || And Judah does not distress Ephraim. ¹⁴And they have flown on the shoulder of the Philistines westward, || Together they spoil the sons of the east, || Edom and Moab sending forth their hand, || And sons of Ammon obeying them. ¹⁵And YHWH has devoted to destruction || The tongue of the Sea of Egypt, || And has waved His hand over the river, || In the terror of His wind, || And has struck it at the seven streams, || And has caused [men] to tread [it] with shoes. ¹⁶And there has been a highway, || For the remnant of His people that is left, from Asshur, || As there was for Israel in the day of his coming up out of the land of Egypt!

CHAPTER 12

¹And you have said in that day: "I thank you, O YHWH, || Though You have been angry with me, || Your anger turns back, || And You comfort me. ²Behold, God [is] my salvation, I trust, and do not fear, || For my strength and song [is] YAH—YHWH, || And He is to me for salvation. ³And you have drawn waters with joy || Out of the fountains of salvation, ⁴And you have said in that day, || Give praise to YHWH, call on His Name. Make His acts known among the peoples. Make mention that His Name is set on high. ⁵Praise YHWH, for He has done excellence, || This is known in all the earth. ⁶Cry aloud, and sing, O inhabitant of Zion, || For the Holy One of Israel [is] great in your midst!"

CHAPTER 13

¹The burden of Babylon that Isaiah son of Amoz has seen: ²"Lift up an ensign on a high mountain, || Raise the voice to them, wave the hand, || And they go into the openings of nobles. ³I have given charge to My sanctified ones, || Also I have called My mighty ones for My anger, || Those rejoicing at My excellence." ⁴A voice of a multitude in the mountains, || A likeness of a numerous people, || A voice of noise from the kingdoms of nations who are gathered, || YHWH of Hosts inspecting a host of battle! ⁵They are coming in from a far-off land, || From the end of the heavens, || YHWH and the instruments of His indignation, || To destroy all the land. ⁶Howl, for the Day of YHWH [is] near, || It comes as destruction from the Mighty. ⁷Therefore, all hands fail, || And every heart of man melts. ⁸And they have been troubled, || Pains and pangs take them, || They are pained as a travailing woman, || A man marvels at his friend, || The appearance of flames—their faces! ⁹Behold, the Day of YHWH comes, || Fierce, with wrath, and heat of anger, || To make the land become a desolation, || Indeed, He destroys its sinning ones from it. ¹⁰For the stars of the heavens, and their constellations, || Do not cause their light to shine, || The sun has been darkened in its going out, || And the moon does not cause its light to come forth. ¹¹"And I have appointed evil on the world, || And on the wicked their iniquity, || And have caused the excellence of the proud to cease, || And I make the excellence of the terrible low. ¹²I make man more rare than fine gold, || And a common man than pure gold of Ophir. ¹³Therefore I cause the heavens to tremble, || And the earth shakes from its place, || In the wrath of YHWH of Hosts, || And in a day of the heat of His anger. ¹⁴And it has been, as a roe driven away, || And as a flock that has no gatherer, || Each to his people—they turn, || And each to his land—they flee. ¹⁵Everyone who is found is thrust through, || And everyone who is added falls by sword. ¹⁶And their sucklings are dashed to pieces before their eyes, || Their houses are spoiled, and their wives lain with. ¹⁷Behold, I am stirring up the Medes against them, || Who do not esteem silver, || And gold—they do not delight in it. ¹⁸And bows dash young men to pieces, || And they do not pity the fruit of the womb, || Their eye has no pity on sons. ¹⁹And Babylon, the beauty of kingdoms, || The glory, the excellence of the Chaldeans, || Has been as overthrown by God, || With Sodom and with Gomorrah. ²⁰She does not sit forever, || Nor continue to many generations, || Nor does Arab pitch tent there, || And shepherds do not lie down there. ²¹And desert-dwellers have lain down there, || And their houses have been full of howlers, || And daughters of an ostrich have dwelt there, || And goats skip there. ²²And howlers—he has responded in his forsaken habitations, || And dragons in palaces of delight, || And her time [is] near to come, || And her days are not drawn out!"

CHAPTER 14

¹For YHWH loves Jacob, || And has fixed again on Israel, || And given them rest on their own land, || And the sojourner has been joined to them, || And they have been admitted to the house of Jacob. ²And peoples have taken them, || And have brought them to their place, || And the house of Israel has inherited them, || On the land of YHWH, || For menservants and for maidservants, || And they have been captors of their captors, || And have ruled over their exactors. ³And it has come to pass, || In the day of YHWH's giving rest to you, || From your grief, and from your trouble, || And from the sharp bondage, || That has been served on you, ⁴That you have taken up this allegory || Concerning the king of Babylon, and said, "How the exactor has ceased, ⁵The golden one has ceased. YHWH has broken the staff of the wicked, || The scepter of rulers. ⁶He who is striking peoples in wrath, || A striking without intermission, || He who is ruling nations in anger, || Pursuing without restraint! ⁷At rest—all the earth has been quiet, || They have broken forth [into] singing. ⁸Even firs have rejoiced over you, || Cedars of Lebanon, [saying], Since you have lain down, || The hewer does not come up against us. ⁹Sheol beneath has been troubled at you, || To meet your coming in, || It is waking up Rephaim for you, || All chief ones of earth, || It has raised up from their thrones || All kings of nations. ¹⁰All of them answer and say to you, Even you have become weak like us! You have become like to us! ¹¹Your excellence has been brought down to Sheol, || The noise of your stringed instruments, || The worm has been spread out under you, || Indeed, the worm is covering you. ¹²How you have fallen from the heavens, || O shining one, son of the dawn! You have been cut down to earth, || O weakener of nations. ¹³And you said in your heart: I go up into the heavens, || I raise my throne above the stars of God, || And I sit on the mountain of meeting in the sides of the north. ¹⁴I go up above the heights of a thick cloud, I am like to the Most High. ¹⁵Only—you are brought down to Sheol, || To the sides of the pit. ¹⁶Your beholders look to you, they attend to you, || Is this the man causing the earth to tremble, ||

ISAIAH

Shaking kingdoms? ¹⁷He has made the world as a wilderness, || And he has broken down his cities, || He did not open the house of his bound ones. ¹⁸All kings of nations—all of them, || Have lain down in glory, each in his house, ¹⁹And you have been cast out of your grave, || As an abominable branch, raiment of the slain, || Thrust through ones of the sword, || Going down to the sons of the pit, || As a carcass trodden down. ²⁰You are not united with them in burial, || For you have destroyed your land, || You have slain your people, || The seed of evildoers is not named for all time. ²¹Prepare slaughter for his sons; Because of the iniquity of their fathers, || They do not rise, nor have possessed the land, || Nor filled the face of the world [with] cities. ²²And I have risen up against them," || A declaration of YHWH of Hosts, || "And have cut off, in reference to Babylon, || Name and remnant, and continuator and successor," || A declaration of YHWH. ²³"And have made it for a possession of a hedgehog, || And ponds of waters, || And swept it with the broom of destruction," || A declaration of YHWH of Hosts! ²⁴YHWH of Hosts has sworn, saying, "As I thought—so has it not been? And as I counseled—it stands; ²⁵To break Asshur in My land, || And I tread him down on My mountain, || And his yoke has turned from off them, || Indeed, his burden turns aside from off their shoulder. ²⁶This [is] the counsel that is counseled for all the earth, || And this [is] the hand that is stretched out for all the nations. ²⁷For YHWH of Hosts has purposed, || And who makes void? And His hand that is stretched out, || Who turns it back?" ²⁸In the year of the death of King Ahaz was this burden: ²⁹"Do not rejoice, Philistia, all of you, || That the rod of your striker has been broken, || For from the root of a serpent comes out a viper, || And its fruit [is] a flying, burning serpent. ³⁰And the firstborn of the poor have delighted, || And the needy lie down in confidence, || And I have put to death your root with famine, || And it slays your remnant. ³¹Howl, O gate; cry, O city, || You are melted, Philistia, all of you, || For smoke has come from the north, || And there is none alone in his set places." ³²And what does one answer the messengers of a nation? That YHWH has founded Zion, || And the poor of His people take refuge in it!

CHAPTER 15

¹The burden of Moab. Because in a night Ar of Moab was destroyed—It has been cut off, || Because in a night Kir of Moab was destroyed—It has been cut off. ²He has gone up to Bajith and Dibon, || The high places—to weep, || Moab howls on Nebo and on Medeba, || Baldness [is] on all its heads, every beard cut off. ³In its out-places they girded on sackcloth, || On its pinnacles, and in its broad places, || Everyone howls—going down with weeping. ⁴And Heshbon and Elealeh cry, || Their voice has been heard to Jahaz, || Therefore the armed ones of Moab shout, || His life has been grievous to him. ⁵My heart [is] toward Moab, || Her fugitives cry to Zoar, a heifer of the third [year], || For—the ascent of Luhith—He goes up in it with weeping, || For in the way of Horonaim, || They wake up a cry of destruction. ⁶For the waters of Nimrim are desolations, || For the hay has been withered, || The tender grass has been finished, || There has not been a green thing. ⁷Therefore the abundance he made, and their store, || They carry to the Brook of the Willows. ⁸For the cry has gone around the border of Moab, || Its howling [is] to Eglaim, || And its howling [is] to Beer-Elim. ⁹For the waters of Dimon have been full of blood, || For I set additions on Dimon, || A lion for the escaped of Moab, || And for the remnant of Adamah!

CHAPTER 16

¹Send a lamb [to] the ruler of the land, || From Selah in the wilderness, || To the mountain of the daughter of Zion. ²And it has come to pass, || As a wandering bird, cast out of a nest, || Are daughters of Moab, [at] fords of Arnon. ³Bring in counsel, do judgment, || Make your shadow as night in the midst of noon, || Hide outcasts, do not reveal the wanderer. ⁴My outcasts sojourn in you, O Moab, || Be a secret hiding place for them, || From the face of a destroyer, || For the extortioner has ceased, || Devastation has been finished, || The tramplers are consumed out of the land. ⁵And the throne is established in kindness, || And [One] has sat on it in truth, in the tent of David, || Judging and seeking judgment, and hastening righteousness. ⁶We have heard of the pride of Moab—very proud, || His pride, and his arrogance, and his wrath—his boastings [are] not right. ⁷Therefore Moab howls for Moab, all of it howls, || It meditates for the grape-cakes of Kir-Hareseth, || They are surely struck. ⁸Because fields of Heshbon languish, || The vine of Sibmah, || Lords of nations beat her choice vines, || They have come to Jazer, || They have wandered in a wilderness, || Her plants have spread themselves, || They have passed over a sea. ⁹Therefore I weep with the weeping of Jazer, || The vine of Sibmah, || I water you [with] my tear, || O Heshbon and Elealeh, || For—for your summer fruits, and for your harvest, || The shouting has fallen. ¹⁰And gladness and joy have been removed from the fruitful field, || And they do not sing in vineyards, nor shout, || The treader does not tread wine in the presses, || I have caused shouting to cease. ¹¹Therefore my bowels sound as a harp for Moab, || And my inward parts for Kir-Haresh. ¹²And it has come to pass, when it has been seen, || That Moab has been weary on the high place, || And he has come to his sanctuary to pray, || And is not able. ¹³This [is] the word that YHWH has spoken to Moab from that time, ¹⁴And now YHWH has spoken, saying, "In three years, as years of a hired worker, || The glory of Moab is lightly esteemed, || With all the great multitude, || And the remnant [is] little, small, not mighty!"

CHAPTER 17

¹The burden of Damascus. Behold, Damascus is taken away from [being] a city, || And it has been a heap—a ruin. ²The cities of Aroer are forsaken, || They are for droves, and they have lain down, || And there is none troubling. ³And the fortress has ceased from Ephraim, || And the kingdom from Damascus, || And the remnant of Aram are as the glory of the sons of Israel, || A declaration of YHWH of Hosts! ⁴And it has come to pass in that day, || The glory of Jacob waxes poor, || And the fatness of his flesh waxes lean. ⁵And it has come to pass, || As the gathering of the standing grain by the reaper, || And his arm reaps the ears, || And it has come to pass, || As the gathering of the ears in the Valley of Rephaim, ⁶And gleanings have been left in him, || As the surrounding of an olive, || Two—three berries on the top of a branch, || Four—five on the fruitful boughs, || A declaration of YHWH, God of Israel! ⁷In that day man looks to His Maker, || Indeed, his eyes look to the Holy One of Israel, ⁸And he does not look to the altars. The work of his own hands, || And that which his own fingers made, He does not see—the Asherim and the images. ⁹In that day the cities of his strength are || As the forsaken thing of the forest, || And the branch that they have left, || Because of the sons of Israel, || It has also been a desolation. ¹⁰Because you have forgotten the God of your salvation, || And have not remembered the Rock of your strength, || Therefore you plant plants of pleasantness, || And sow it with a strange shoot, ¹¹You cause your plant to become great in the day, || And make your seed to flourish in the morning, || The harvest [is] a heap in a day of overflowing, || And of mortal pain. ¹²Woe [to] the multitude of many peoples, || They sound as the sounding of seas; And the roaring of nations, || As the roaring of mighty waters [that] make a crashing. ¹³Nations crash as the roaring of many waters, || And He rebuked them, || And they fled far off, || And were pursued as chaff of hills before wind, || And as a rolling thing before a windstorm. ¹⁴At evening, behold, terror, before morning it is not, || This [is] the portion of our spoilers, || And the lot of our plunderers!

CHAPTER 18

¹Behold, land shadowed [with] wings, || That [is] beyond the rivers of Cush, ²That is sending ambassadors by sea, || Even with implements of reed on the face of the waters—Go, swift messengers, || To a nation drawn out and peeled, || To a people fearful from its beginning and onward, || A nation meeting out by line, and treading down, || Whose land floods have spoiled. ³All you inhabitants of the world, || And you dwellers of earth, || At the lifting up of an ensign on hills you look, || And at the blowing of a horn you hear. ⁴For thus said YHWH to me: "I rest, and I look on My settled place, || As a clear heat on an herb. As a thick cloud of dew in the heat of harvest. ⁵For before harvest, when the flower is perfect, || And the blossom is producing unripe fruit, || Then [One] has cut the sprigs with pruning hooks, || And the branches He has turned aside, cut down. ⁶They are left together to the ravenous bird of the mountains, || And to the beast of the earth, || And the ravenous bird has

summered on them, || And every beast of the earth winters on them. ⁷At that time a present is brought to Yʜᴡʜ of Hosts, || A nation drawn out and peeled. Even of a people fearful from the beginning until now, || A nation meting out by line, and treading down, || Whose land floods have spoiled, || To the place of the Name of Yʜᴡʜ of Hosts—Mount Zion!"

CHAPTER 19

¹The burden of Egypt. Behold, Yʜᴡʜ is riding on a swift thick cloud, || And He has entered Egypt, || And the idols of Egypt have been moved at His presence, || And the heart of Egypt melts in its midst. ²And I armed Egyptians against Egyptians, || And they fought, each against his brother, || And each against his neighbor, || City against city, kingdom against kingdom. ³And the spirit of Egypt has been emptied out in its midst. And I swallow up its counsel, || And they have sought to the idols, || And to the charmers, || And to those having familiar spirits, || And to the wizards. ⁴And I have delivered the Egyptians || Into the hand of a hard lord, || And a strong king rules over them, || A declaration of the Lord, Yʜᴡʜ of Hosts. ⁵And waters have failed from the sea, || And a river is desolated and dried up. ⁶And they have turned away the flowings, || Brooks of the bulwark have been weak and dried up, || Reed and flag have withered. ⁷Exposed things by the brook, by the edge of the brook, || And every sown thing of the brook, has withered, || It has been driven away, and is not. ⁸And the fishers have lamented, || And all casting a hook into the brook have mourned, || And those spreading dragnets on the face of the waters have languished. ⁹And makers of fine flax have been ashamed, || And weavers of networks. ¹⁰And its foundations have been struck, || All making wages [are] afflicted in soul. ¹¹Only, the princes of Zoan [are] fools, || The counsel of the wise ones of the counselors of Pharaoh has become brutish. How do you say to Pharaoh, "I am a son of the wise, a son of kings of antiquity?" ¹²Where [are] they now, your wise ones? Indeed, let them now tell [it] to you, || And they know what Yʜᴡʜ of Hosts has counseled against Egypt! ¹³Princes of Zoan have been foolish, || Princes of Noph have been lifted up, || And they have caused Egypt to err, || The chief of her tribes. ¹⁴Yʜᴡʜ has mingled in her midst || A spirit of perverseness, || And they have caused Egypt to err in all its work, || As a drunkard errs in his vomit. ¹⁵And there is no work to Egypt, || That head or tail, branch or reed, may do. ¹⁶In that day Egypt is like women, || And it has mourned, and been afraid, || Because of the waving of the hand of Yʜᴡʜ of Hosts, || That He is waving over it. ¹⁷And the land of Judah has been to Egypt for a cause of staggering, || Everyone who mentions it, fears for himself, || Because of the counsel of Yʜᴡʜ of Hosts, || That He is counseling against it. ¹⁸In that day there are five cities in the land of Egypt, || Speaking the lip of Canaan, || And swearing to Yʜᴡʜ of Hosts, || "The city of destruction," is said of one. ¹⁹In that day there is an altar to Yʜᴡʜ || In the midst of the land of Egypt, || And a standing pillar to Yʜᴡʜ near its border, ²⁰And it has been for a sign and for a testimony, || To Yʜᴡʜ of Hosts in the land of Egypt, || For they cry to Yʜᴡʜ from the face of oppressors, || And He sends a Savior to them, || Even a great one, and has delivered them. ²¹And Yʜᴡʜ has been known to Egypt, || And the Egyptians have known Yʜᴡʜ in that day, || And done sacrifice and present, || And vowed a vow to Yʜᴡʜ, and completed [it]. ²²And Yʜᴡʜ has struck Egypt, striking and healing, || And they have turned back to Yʜᴡʜ, || And He has accepted their plea, || And has healed them. ²³In that day a highway is out of Egypt to Asshur, || And the Assyrians have come into Egypt, || And the Egyptians into Asshur, || And the Egyptians have served with the Assyrians. ²⁴In that day Israel is third, || With Egypt, and with Asshur, || A blessing in the heart of the earth. ²⁵In that Yʜᴡʜ of Hosts blessed it, saying, "Blessed [is] My people—Egypt, || And the work of My hands—Asshur, || And My inheritance—Israel!"

CHAPTER 20

¹In the year of the coming in of Tartan to Ashdod, when Sargon king of Asshur sends him, and he fights against Ashdod and captures it, ²at that time Yʜᴡʜ spoke by the hand of Isaiah son of Amoz, saying, "Go, and you have loosed the sackcloth from off your loins, and you draw your sandal from off your foot," and he does so, going naked and barefoot. ³And Yʜᴡʜ says, "As My servant Isaiah has gone naked and barefoot three years, a sign and a wonder for Egypt and for Cush, ⁴so the king of Asshur leads the captivity of Egypt, and the expulsion of Cush, young and old, naked and barefoot, with seat uncovered—the nakedness of Egypt; ⁵and they have been frightened and ashamed of Cush their confidence, and of Egypt their beauty, ⁶and the inhabitant of this island has said in that day—Behold, thus [is] our trust, || To where we have fled for help, || To be delivered from the king of Asshur, || And how do we escape—we?"

CHAPTER 21

¹The burden of the wilderness of the sea. Like windstorms in the south for passing through, || It has come from the wilderness, || From a fearful land. ²A hard vision has been declared to me, || The treacherous dealer is dealing treacherously, || And the destroyer is destroying. Go up, O Elam, besiege, O Media, || I have caused all its sighing to cease. ³Therefore my loins have been filled [with] great pain, || Pangs have seized me as pangs of a travailing woman, || I have been bent down by hearing, || I have been troubled by seeing. ⁴My heart has wandered, trembling has terrified me, || He has made the twilight of my desire a fear to me, ⁵Arrange the table, watch in the watchtower, || Eat, drink, rise, you heads, anoint the shield, ⁶For thus said the Lord to me: "Go, station the watchman, || Let him declare that which he sees." ⁷And he has seen a chariot—a couple of horsemen, || The rider of a donkey, the rider of a camel, || And he has given attention—He has increased attention! ⁸And he cries, "A lion, my lord! I am continually standing on a watchtower by day, || And I am stationed on my ward whole nights. ⁹And behold, this, the chariot of a man is coming, || A couple of horsemen." And he answers and says: "Fallen, fallen has Babylon, || And He has broken all the carved images of her gods to the earth. ¹⁰O my threshing, and the son of my floor, || That which I heard from Yʜᴡʜ of Hosts, God of Israel, || I have declared to you!" ¹¹The burden of Dumah. [One] is calling to me from Seir, "Watchman, what of the night? Watchman, what of the night?" ¹²The watchman has said, "Morning has come, and also night, || If you inquire, inquire, return, come." ¹³The burden on Arabia. You lodge in a forest in Arabia, || O caravans of Dedanim. ¹⁴Inhabitants of the land of Tema || Have brought water to meet the thirsty, || With his bread they came before a fugitive. ¹⁵For they fled from the face of destructions, || From the face of an outstretched sword, || And from the face of a trodden bow, || And from the face of the grievousness of battle. ¹⁶For thus said the Lord to me: "Within a year, as years of a hired worker, || All the glory of Kedar has been consumed. ¹⁷And the remnant of the number of bow-men, || The mighty of the sons of Kedar, are few, || For Yʜᴡʜ, God of Israel, has spoken!"

CHAPTER 22

¹The burden of the Valley of Vision. What is [troubling] you now, that you have gone up, || All of you—to the roofs? ²Full of stirs—a noisy city—an exulting city, || Your pierced are not pierced of the sword, || Nor dead in battle. ³All your rulers fled from the bow together, || All found of you have been bound, || They have been kept bound together, || They have fled far off. ⁴Therefore I said, "Look [away] from me, || I am bitter in my weeping, do not hurry to comfort me, || For the destruction of the daughter of my people." ⁵For a day of noise, and of treading down, || And of perplexity, [is] to the Lord, Yʜᴡʜ of Hosts, || In the Valley of Vision, digging down a wall, || And crying to the mountain. ⁶And Elam has carried a quiver, || In a chariot of men—horsemen, || And Kir has exposed a shield. ⁷And it comes to pass, || The choice of your valleys have been full of chariots, || And the horsemen diligently place themselves at the gate. ⁸And one removes the covering of Judah, || And in that day you look || To the armor of the house of the forest, ⁹And you have seen the breaches of the City of David, || For they have become many, || And you gather the waters of the lower pool, ¹⁰And you numbered the houses of Jerusalem, || And you break down the houses to fortify the wall. ¹¹And you made a ditch between the two walls, || For the waters of the old pool, || And you have not looked to its Maker, || And you have not seen its Framer of old. ¹²And the Lord calls, Yʜᴡʜ of Hosts, || In that day, to weeping and to lamentation, || And to baldness and to girding on of sackcloth, ¹³And behold, joy and gladness, slaying of oxen, || And slaughtering

of sheep, || Eating of flesh, and drinking of wine, || Eat and drink, for tomorrow we die. ¹⁴And it has been revealed in my ears, || [By] YHWH of Hosts: This iniquity is not pardoned to you, || Until you die, said the Lord, YHWH of Hosts. ¹⁵Thus said the Lord, YHWH of Hosts: "Go forth, go to this steward, || To Shebna, who [is] over the house: ¹⁶What are you [doing] here? And who has [allowed] you here? That you have hewn out a tomb for yourself here? Hewing his tomb on high, || Carving a dwelling for himself in a rock. ¹⁷Behold, YHWH is casting you up and down, || A casting up and down, O mighty one, ¹⁸And your coverer covering, wrapping around, || Wraps you around, O babbler, || On a land of broad sides—there you die, || And there the chariots of your glory [are] the shame of the house of your lord. ¹⁹And I have thrust you from your station, || And he throws you down from your office. ²⁰And it has come to pass in that day, || That I have called to My servant, || To Eliakim son of Hilkiah. ²¹And I have clothed him with your coat, || And I strengthen him with your girdle, || And I give your garment into his hand, || And he has been for a father to the inhabitant of Jerusalem, || And to the house of Judah. ²²And I have placed the key || Of the house of David on his shoulder, || And he has opened, and none is shutting, || And has shut, and none is opening. ²³And I have fixed him [as] a nail in a steadfast place, || And he has been for a throne of glory || To the house of his father. ²⁴And they have hanged on him || All the glory of the house of his father, || The offspring and the issue, || All vessels of small quality, || From vessels of basins to all vessels of flagons. ²⁵In that day—a declaration of YHWH of Hosts, || The nail that is fixed is moved || In a steadfast place, || Indeed, it has been cut down, and has fallen, || And the burden that [is] on it has been cut off, || For YHWH has spoken!"

CHAPTER 23

¹The Burden of Tyre. Howl, you ships of Tarshish, || For it has been destroyed, || Without house, without entrance, || From the land of Chittim it was revealed to them. ²Be silent, you inhabitants of the island, || Trader of Sidon, passing the sea, they filled you. ³And the seed of Sihor [is] in many waters, || Her increase [is] the harvest of the brook, || And she is a market of nations. ⁴Be ashamed, O Sidon; for the sea spoke, || The strength of the sea, saying, "I have not been pained, nor have I brought forth, || Nor have I nourished young men, [nor] brought up virgins." ⁵As they are pained [at] the report of Egypt, || So [at] the report of Tyre. ⁶Pass over to Tarshish, howl, you inhabitants of the island, ⁷Is this your exulting one? Her antiquity [is] from the days of old, || Her own feet carry her far off to sojourn. ⁸Who has counseled this against Tyre, || The crowning one, whose traders [are] princes, || Her merchants—the honored of earth? ⁹YHWH of Hosts has counseled it, || To defile the excellence of all beauty, || To make light all the honored of earth. ¹⁰Pass through your land as a brook, || Daughter of Tarshish, || There is no longer a girdle. ¹¹He has stretched out His hand over the sea, || He has caused kingdoms to tremble, || YHWH has charged concerning the merchant one, || To destroy her strong places. ¹²And He says, "You do not add to exult anymore, || O oppressed one, virgin daughter of Sidon, || To Chittim arise, pass over, || Even there—there is no rest for you." ¹³Behold, the land of the Chaldeans—this people was not, || Asshur founded it for desert-dwellers, || They raised its watchtowers, || They lifted up her palaces—He has appointed her for a ruin! ¹⁴Howl, you ships of Tarshish, || For your strength has been destroyed. ¹⁵And it has come to pass in that day, || That Tyre is forgotten seventy years, || According to the days of one king. At the end of seventy years there is to Tyre as the song of the harlot. ¹⁶Take a harp, go around the city, O forgotten harlot, play well, || Multiply song that you may be remembered. ¹⁷And it has come to pass, || At the end of seventy years YHWH inspects Tyre, || And she has returned to her wage, || And she committed fornication || With all kingdoms of the earth on the face of the ground. ¹⁸And her merchandise and her wage have been holy to YHWH, || Not treasured up nor stored, || For her merchandise is to those sitting before YHWH, || To eat to satiety, and for a lasting covering!

CHAPTER 24

¹Behold, YHWH is emptying the earth, || And is making it desolate, || And has overturned [it on] its face, || And has scattered its inhabitants. ²And it has been—as a people so a priest, || As the servant so his master, || As the maidservant so her mistress, || As the buyer so the seller, || As the lender so the borrower, || As the usurer so he who is lifting [it] on himself. ³The earth is utterly emptied, and utterly spoiled, || For YHWH has spoken this word: ⁴The earth has mourned, faded, || The world has languished, faded, || They have languished—the high place of the people of the earth. ⁵And the earth has been defiled under its inhabitants, || Because they have transgressed laws, || They have changed a statute, || They have made void a perpetual covenant. ⁶Therefore a curse has consumed the earth, || And the inhabitants in it become desolate, || Therefore inhabitants of the earth have been consumed, || And few men have been left. ⁷The new wine has mourned, the vine languished, || All the joyful of heart have sighed. ⁸The joy of tambourines has ceased, || The noise of exulting ones has ceased, || The joy of a harp has ceased. ⁹They do not drink wine with a song, || Strong drink is bitter to those drinking it. ¹⁰It was broken down—a city of emptiness, || Every house has been shut from [its] entrance. ¹¹In out-places [is] a cry over the wine, || All joy has been darkened, || The joy of the land has been removed. ¹²Desolation [is] left in the city, || And the gate is struck [with] ruin. ¹³When thus it is in the heart of the land, || In the midst of the peoples, || As the surrounding of the olive, || As gleanings when harvest has been finished. ¹⁴They lift up their voice, || They sing of the excellence of YHWH, || They have cried aloud from the sea. ¹⁵Therefore honor YHWH in prosperity, || In islands of the sea, the Name of YHWH, God of Israel. ¹⁶From the skirt of the earth we heard songs, || The desire of the righteous. And I say, "Leanness [is] to me, || Leanness [is] to me, woe [is] to me." Treacherous dealers dealt treacherously, || Indeed, treachery, treacherous dealers dealt treacherously. ¹⁷Fear, and a snare, and a trap, || [Are] on you, O inhabitant of the earth. ¹⁸And it has come to pass, || He who is fleeing from the noise of the fear falls into the snare, || And he who is coming up from the midst of the snare, || Is captured by the trap, || For windows have been opened on high, || And foundations of the earth are shaken. ¹⁹The earth has been utterly broken down, || The earth has been utterly broken, || The earth has been utterly moved. ²⁰The earth staggers greatly as a drunkard, || And it has been moved as a lodge, || And its transgression has been heavy on it, || And it has fallen, and does not add to rise. ²¹And it has come to pass in that day, || YHWH lays a charge on the host of the high place in the high place, || And on the kings of the earth on the earth. ²²And they have been gathered—A gathering of bound ones in a pit, || And they have been shut up in a prison, || And after a multitude of days are inspected. ²³And the moon has been confounded, || And the sun has been ashamed, || For YHWH of Hosts has reigned || In Mount Zion, and in Jerusalem, || And before His elderly—glory!

CHAPTER 25

¹O YHWH, You [are] my God, I exalt You, I confess Your Name, || For You have done a wonderful thing, || Counsels of old, steadfastness, O steadfast One. ²For You made of a city a heap, || Of a fortified city a ruin, || A high place of strangers from [being] a city, || It is not built for all time. ³Therefore a strong people honors You, || A city of the terrible nations fears You. ⁴For You have been a stronghold for the poor, || A stronghold for the needy in his distress, || A refuge from storm, a shadow from heat, || When the spirit of the terrible [is] as a storm—a wall. ⁵As heat in a dry place, || You humble the noise of strangers, || [As] heat with the shadow of a thick cloud, || The singing of the terrible is humbled. ⁶And YHWH of Hosts has made, || For all the peoples in this mountain, || A banquet of fat things, || A banquet of preserved things, || Fat things full of marrow, || Preserved things—refined. ⁷And He has swallowed up in this mountain || The face of the wrapping that is wrapped over all the peoples, || And of the covering that is spread over all the nations. ⁸He has swallowed up death in victory, || And Lord YHWH has wiped [the] tear from off all faces, || And He turns aside the reproach of His people from off all the earth, || For YHWH has spoken. ⁹And [one] has said in that day, "Behold, this [is] our God, || We waited for Him, and He saves us, || This [is] YHWH, we have waited for Him, || We are glad and rejoice in His salvation!" ¹⁰For the hand of YHWH rests on this mountain, || And Moab is trodden down under Him, || As straw is trodden down

ISAIAH

on a dunghill. ¹¹And He spread out His hands in its midst, || As the swimmer spreads out to swim; And He has humbled his excellence || With the machinations of his hands. ¹²And the fortress of the high place of your walls || He has bowed down—He has made low, || He has caused [it] to come to the earth—to dust.

CHAPTER 26

¹In that day this song is sung in the land of Judah: "We have a strong city, || He makes salvation [for] walls and bulwark. ²Open the gates, || That a righteous nation may enter, || Preserving steadfastness. ³You keep [him] in peace [whose] imagination [is] stayed—peace! For he is confident in You. ⁴Trust in YHWH forever, || For in YAH—YHWH [is] a rock of ages, ⁵For He bowed down the dwellers on high, || A city set on high He makes low, || He makes it low to the earth, || He causes it to come to the dust, ⁶A foot treads it down, || Feet of the poor—steps of the weak. ⁷The path for the righteous [is] uprightness, || O upright One, || You ponder the path of the righteous. ⁸Also, [in] the path of Your judgments, || O YHWH, we have waited [for] You, || To Your Name and to Your remembrance || [Is] the desire of the soul. ⁹I desired You in the night [with] my soul, || Also, I seek You earnestly [with] my spirit within me, || For when Your judgments [are] on the earth, || The inhabitants of the world have learned righteousness. ¹⁰The wicked finds favor, || He has not learned righteousness, || He deals perversely in a land of straightforwardness, || And does not see the excellence of YHWH. ¹¹O YHWH, Your hand [is] high—they do not see, || They see the zeal of the people, and are ashamed, || Also, the fire consumes Your adversaries. ¹²O YHWH, You appoint peace to us, || For You have also worked all our works for us. ¹³O our God YHWH, lords have ruled us besides You, || Only, by You we make mention of Your Name. ¹⁴Dead—they do not live, || Rephaim, they do not rise, || Therefore You have inspected and destroy them, || Indeed, you destroy all their memory. ¹⁵You have added to the nation, O YHWH, || You have added to the nation, || You have been honored, || You have put all the ends of the earth far off. ¹⁶O YHWH, in distress they missed You, || They have poured out a whisper, || Your discipline [is] on them. ¹⁷When a pregnant woman comes near to the birth, || She is pained—she cries in her pangs, || So we have been from Your face, O YHWH. ¹⁸We have conceived, we have been pained. We have brought forth, as it were, wind, || We do not work salvation in the earth, || Nor do the inhabitants of the world fall. ¹⁹Your dead live—My dead body, they rise. Awake and sing, you dwellers in the dust, || For the dew of herbs [is] your dew, || And you cause the land of Rephaim to fall. ²⁰Come, My people, enter into your inner chambers, || And shut your doors behind you, || Hide yourself shortly [for] a moment until the indignation passes over. ²¹For behold, YHWH is coming out of His place, || To charge the iniquity of the inhabitant of the earth on him, || And the earth has revealed her blood, || Nor does she cover her slain anymore!"

CHAPTER 27

¹In that day YHWH lays a charge, || With His sword—the sharp, and the great, and the strong, || On leviathan—a fleeing serpent, || And on leviathan—a crooked serpent, || And He has slain the dragon that [is] in the sea. ²In that day respond to her, "A desirable vineyard, ³I, YHWH, am its keeper, || I water it every moment, || Lest any lay a charge against it, || Night and day I keep it! ⁴Fury is not in Me; Who gives Me a brier—a thorn in battle? I step into it, || I burn it at once. ⁵Or—he takes hold on My strength, || [That] he makes peace with Me, || [And] he makes peace with Me." ⁶He causes those coming in to take root, || Jacob blossoms, and Israel has flourished, || And they have filled the face of the world [with] increase. ⁷Has He struck him as the striking of his striker? Does He slay as the slaying of his slain? ⁸In measure, in sending it forth, you strive with it, || He has taken away by His sharp wind, || In the day of an east wind, ⁹Therefore the iniquity of Jacob is covered by this, || And this [is] all the fruit—To take away his sin, || In his setting all the stones of an altar, || As chalkstones beaten in pieces, || They do not rise—Asherim and images. ¹⁰For the fortified city [is] alone, || A habitation cast out and forsaken as a wilderness, || There the calf delights, || And there it lies down, || And has consumed its branches. ¹¹In the withering of its branch it is broken off, || Women are coming in [and] setting it on fire, || For it [is] not a people of understanding, || Therefore its Maker does not pity it, || And its Former does not favor it. ¹²And it has come to pass in that day, || YHWH beats out from the branch of the river, || To the stream of Egypt, || And you are gathered one by one, O sons of Israel. ¹³And it has come to pass in that day, || It is blown with a great horn, || And those perishing in the land of Asshur have come in, || And those cast out in the land of Egypt, || And have bowed themselves to YHWH, || In the holy mountain—in Jerusalem!

CHAPTER 28

¹Woe [to] the proud crown of the drunkards of Ephraim. And the fading flower of the beauty of his glory, || That [is] on the head of the fat valley of the broken down of wine. ²Behold, a mighty and strong one [is] to the Lord, || As a storm of hail—a destructive shower, || As an inundation of mighty waters overflowing, || He cast down to the earth with the hand. ³The proud crown of the drunkards of Ephraim is trodden down by feet, ⁴And the fading flower of the beauty of his glory || That [is] on the head of the fat valley, || Has been as its first-fruit before summer, || That its beholder sees; He swallows it while it [is] yet in his hand. ⁵In that day YHWH of Hosts is || For a crown of beauty, and for a circlet of glory, || To the remnant of His people. ⁶And for a spirit of judgment || To him who is sitting in the judgment, || And for might [to] those turning back the battle to the gate. ⁷And even these have erred through wine, || And have wandered through strong drink, || Priest and prophet erred through strong drink, || They have been swallowed up of the wine, || They wandered because of the strong drink, || They have erred in seeing, || They have stumbled judicially. ⁸For all tables have been full of vomit, || Filth—without place! ⁹By whom does He teach knowledge? And by whom does He cause to understand the report? The weaned from milk, the removed from breasts, ¹⁰For rule on rule, rule on rule, || Line on line, line on line, || A little here, a little there, ¹¹For by scorned lip, and by another tongue, || Does He speak to this people. ¹²To whom He has said, "This [is] the rest, give rest to the weary, || And this—the refreshing": And they have not been willing to hear, ¹³And to whom a word of YHWH has been, || Rule on rule, rule on rule, || Line on line, line on line, || A little here, a little there, || So that they go and have stumbled backward, || And been broken, and snared, and captured. ¹⁴Therefore, hear a word of YHWH, you men of scorning, || Ruling this people that [is] in Jerusalem. ¹⁵Because you have said: "We have made a covenant with death, || And we have made a provision with Sheol, || An overflowing scourge, when it passes over, || Does not meet us, || Though we have made a lie our refuge, || And have been hidden in falsehood." ¹⁶Therefore, thus said Lord YHWH: "Behold, I am laying a foundation in Zion, || A stone—a tried stone, a precious corner stone, a settled foundation, || He who is believing does not make haste. ¹⁷And I have put judgment for a line, || And righteousness for a plummet, || And hail sweeps away the refuge of lies, || And waters overflow the secret hiding place. ¹⁸And your covenant with death has been annulled, || And your provision with Sheol does not stand, || An overflowing scourge, when it passes over, || Then you have been to it for a treading-place. ¹⁹From the fullness of its passing over it takes you, || For it passes over morning by morning, || By day and by night, || And it has been only a trembling to consider the report." ²⁰For the bed has been shorter || Than to stretch one's self out in, || And the covering has been narrower || Than to wrap one's self up in. ²¹For as YHWH rises [at] Mount Perazim, || As He is troubled [at] the valley in Gibeon, || To do His work—strange [is] His work, || And to do His deed—strange [is] His deed." ²²And now, do not show yourselves scorners, || Lest your bands are strong, || For a consumption, that is determined, || I have heard, by the Lord, YHWH of Hosts, || [Is] for all the land. ²³Give ear, and hear my voice, || Attend, and hear my saying: ²⁴Does the plowman plow the whole day to sow? He opens and harrows his ground! ²⁵Has he not, if he has made its face level, || Then scattered fitches, and sprinkles cumin, || And has placed the principal wheat, || And the appointed barley, || And the rye [in] its own border? ²⁶And his God instructs him for judgment, || He directs him. ²⁷For fitches are not threshed with a sharp-pointed thing, || And the wheel of a cart turned around on cumin, || For fitches are beaten out with a staff,

ISAIAH

|| And cumin with a rod. ²⁸Bread-[grain] is beaten small, || For he does not severely thresh it forever, || Nor has a wheel of his cart crushed [it], || Nor do his hooves beat it small. ²⁹Even this from YHWH of Hosts has gone out, || He has made counsel wonderful, || He has made wisdom great!

CHAPTER 29

¹Woe [to] Ariel, Ariel, || The city of the encampment of David! Add year to year, let festivals go around. ²And I have sent distress to Ariel, || And it has been lamentation and mourning, || And it has been to me as Ariel. ³And I encamped, O babbler, against you, || And I laid siege against you—a camp. And I raised up bulwarks against you. ⁴And you have been low, || You speak from the earth, || And make your saying low from the dust, || And your voice has been from the earth, || As one having a familiar spirit, || And your saying whispers from the dust, ⁵And as small dust has been || The multitude of those scattering you, || And as chaff passing on the multitude of the terrible, || And it has been in an instant—suddenly. ⁶You are inspected by YHWH of Hosts, || With thunder, and with an earthquake, || And great noise, windstorm, and whirlwind, || And flame of devouring fire. ⁷And as a dream, a vision of night, || Has been the multitude of all the nations || Who are warring against Ariel, || And all its warriors, and its bulwark, || Even of those distressing her. ⁸And it has been, as when the hungry dreams, || And behold, he is eating, || And he has awoken, || And his soul [is] empty, || And as when the thirsty dreams, || And behold, he is drinking, || And he has awoken, || And behold, he is weary, || And his soul is longing, || So is the multitude of all the nations || Who are warring against Mount Zion. ⁹Linger and wonder, look, indeed, look, || Be drunk, and not with wine, || Stagger, and not with strong drink. ¹⁰For YHWH has poured out a spirit of deep sleep on you, || And He closes your eyes—the prophets, || And your heads—the seers—He covered. ¹¹And the vision of the whole is to you, || As words of the sealed scroll, || That they give to one knowing scrolls, || Saying, "Please read this," || And he has said, "I am not able, for it [is] sealed"; ¹²And the scroll is given to him who has not known scrolls, || Saying, "Please read this," || And he has said, "I have not known scrolls." ¹³And the Lord says: "Because this people has drawn near with its mouth, || And they have honored Me with its lips, || And it has put its heart far off from Me, || And their fear of Me is a precept taught by men! ¹⁴Therefore, behold, I am adding to do wonderfully with this people, || A wonder, and a marvel, || And the wisdom of its wise ones has perished, || And the understanding of its intelligent ones hides itself." ¹⁵Woe [to] those going deep from YHWH to hide counsel, || And whose works have been in darkness. And they say, "Who is seeing us? And who is knowing us?" ¹⁶Your perversion! Is the potter esteemed as clay, || That the work says of its maker, "He has not made me?" And the framed thing said of its framer, "He did not understand?" ¹⁷Is it not yet a very little [while], || And Lebanon has turned into a fruitful field, || And the fruitful field is reckoned for a forest? ¹⁸And the deaf have heard the words of a scroll in that day, || And out of thick darkness, and out of darkness, || The eyes of the blind see. ¹⁹And the humble have added joy in YHWH, || And the poor among men || Rejoice in the Holy One of Israel. ²⁰For the terrible one has ceased, || And the scorner has been consumed, || And all watching for iniquity have been cut off, ²¹Who cause men to sin in word, || And lay a snare for a reprover in the gate, || And turn aside the righteous into emptiness. ²²Therefore, thus said YHWH, || Who ransomed Abraham, || Concerning the house of Jacob: "Jacob is not ashamed now, || Nor does his face now become pale, ²³For in his seeing his children, || The work of My hand, in his midst, || They sanctify My Name, || And have sanctified the Holy One of Jacob, || And they declare the God of Israel fearful. ²⁴And the erring in spirit have known understanding, || And murmurers learn doctrine!"

CHAPTER 30

¹Woe [to] apostate sons, || A declaration of YHWH! To do counsel, and not from Me, || And to spread out a covering, and not of My Spirit, || So as to add sin to sin. ²Who are walking to go down to Egypt, || And have not asked My mouth, || To be strong in the strength of Pharaoh, || And to trust in the shadow of Egypt. ³And the strength of Pharaoh || Has been to you for shame, || And the trust in the shadow of Egypt confusion, ⁴For his princes were in Zoan, || And his messengers reach Hanes. ⁵He made all ashamed of a people that do not profit, || Not for help, and not for profit, || But for shame, and also for reproach! ⁶The burden of the beasts of the south. Into a land of adversity and distress, || Of young lion and of old lion, || From where [are] viper and flying, burning serpent, || They carry their wealth on the shoulder of donkeys, || And their treasures on the hump of camels, || To a people not profitable. ⁷Indeed, Egyptians [are] vanity, and help in vain, || Therefore I have cried concerning this: "Their strength [is] to sit still." ⁸No, go in, write it on a tablet with them, || And inscribe it on a scroll, || And it is for a latter day, for a witness for all time, ⁹That this [is] a people of rebellion, sons—liars, || Sons not willing to hear the Law of YHWH. ¹⁰Who have said to seers, "Do not see," || And to prophets, "Do not prophesy to us straightforward things, || Speak to us smooth things, prophesy deceits, ¹¹Turn aside from the way, || Decline from the path, || Cause the Holy One of Israel || To cease from before us." ¹²Therefore, thus said the Holy One of Israel: "Because of your kicking against this word, || And you trust in oppression, || And perverseness, and rely on it, ¹³Therefore this iniquity is to you as a breach falling, || Swelled out in a wall set on high, || Whose destruction comes suddenly, in an instant. ¹⁴And He has broken it || As the breaking of the potters' bottle, || Beaten down—He does not spare, || Nor is there found, in its beating down, || A potsherd to take fire from the burning, || And to draw out waters from a ditch." ¹⁵For thus said Lord YHWH, || The Holy One of Israel: "In returning and rest you are saved, || In keeping quiet and in confidence is your might," || And you have not been willing. ¹⁶And you say, "No, for we flee on a horse," || Therefore you flee, || And, "We ride on the swift!" Therefore your pursuers are swift. ¹⁷One thousand [flee] because of the rebuke of one, || Because of the rebuke of five you flee, || Until you have surely been left as a pole || On the top of the mountain, || And as an ensign on the height. ¹⁸And therefore YHWH waits to favor you, || And therefore He is exalted to pity you, || For YHWH [is] a God of judgment, || O the blessedness of all waiting for Him. ¹⁹For the people in Zion dwell in Jerusalem, || Do not weep—weeping, || Pitying, He pities you at the voice of your cry, || When He hears He answers you. ²⁰And the Lord has given to you bread of adversity, || And water of oppression. And your teachers remove no longer, || And your eyes have seen your teachers, ²¹And your ear hears a word behind you, saying, "This [is] the way, go in it," || When you turn to the right, || And when you turn to the left. ²²And you have defiled the covering of Your carved images of silver, || And the ephod of your molten image of gold, || You scatter them as a sickening thing, "Go out," you say to it. ²³And He has given rain [for] your seed, || With which you sow the ground, || And bread, the increase of the ground, || And it has been fat and plentiful, || Your livestock enjoy an enlarged pasture in that day. ²⁴And the oxen and the young donkeys serving the ground, || Eat fermented provender, || That one is winnowing with shovel and fan. ²⁵And there has been on every high mountain, || And on every exalted hill, || Streams—conduits of waters, || In a day of much slaughter, in the falling of towers. ²⁶And the light of the moon has been as the light of the sun, || And the light of the sun is sevenfold, || As the light of seven days, || In the day of YHWH's binding up the breach of His people, || When He heals the stroke of its wound. ²⁷Behold, the Name of YHWH is coming from far, || His anger is burning, and the flame [is] great, || His lips have been full of indignation, || And His tongue [is] as a devouring fire. ²⁸And His breath [is] as an overflowing stream, || It divides to the neck, || To sift nations with a sieve of vanity, || And a bridle causing to err, || [Is] on the jaws of the peoples. ²⁹Singing is to you as in a night sanctified for a festival, || And joy of heart as he who is going with a pipe, || To go to the mountain of YHWH, || To the rock of Israel. ³⁰And YHWH has caused || The splendor of His voice to be heard, || And the coming down of His arm || He shows with the raging of anger, || And the flame of a consuming fire, || Scattering, and inundation, and hailstone. ³¹For from the voice of YHWH Asshur [is] broken down, || He strikes with a rod. ³²And every passage of the settled staff, || That YHWH causes to rest on him, || Has been with tambourines and with harps, || And in battles of shaking He has fought with it. ³³For

Tophet is arranged from former time, || Even it is prepared for the king, || He has made deep, || He has made large, || Its pile [is] fire and much wood, || The breath of YHWH, || As a stream of brimstone, is burning in it!

CHAPTER 31

¹Woe [to] those going down to Egypt for help, || And [who] lean on horses, || And trust on chariots, because [they are] many, || And on horsemen, because [they are] very strong, || And have not looked on the Holy One of Israel, || And have not sought YHWH. ²And He [is] also wise, and brings in evil, || And He has not turned aside His words, || And He has risen against a house of evildoers, || And against the help of workers of iniquity. ³And the Egyptians [are men], and not God, || And their horses [are] flesh, and not spirit, || And YHWH stretches out His hand, || And the helper has stumbled, || And the helped one has fallen, || And together all of them are consumed. ⁴For thus said YHWH to me: "As the lion and the young lion growl over his prey, || Against whom a multitude of shepherds is called, || He is not frightened from their voice, || And he is not humbled from their noise; So YHWH of Hosts comes down || To war on Mount Zion, and on her height. ⁵As birds flying, so does YHWH of Hosts || Cover over Jerusalem, covering and delivering, || Passing over, and causing to escape." ⁶Turn back to Him from whom sons of Israel || Have deepened apostasy. ⁷For in that day each despises His idols of silver, and his idols of gold, || That your hands made to you—a sin. ⁸And Asshur has fallen by sword, not of the high, || Indeed, a sword—not of the low, consumes him, || And he has fled for himself from the face of a sword, || And his young men become tributary. ⁹And he passes on [to] his rock from fear, || And his princes have been frightened by the ensign—a declaration of YHWH, || Who has a light in Zion, || And who has a furnace in Jerusalem!

CHAPTER 32

¹Behold, a king reigns for righteousness, || As for princes, they rule for judgment. ²And each has been as a hiding place [from] wind, || And as a secret hiding place [from] inundation, || As streams of waters in a dry place, || As a shadow of a heavy rock in a weary land. ³And the eyes of beholders are not dazzled, || And the ears of hearers attend. ⁴And the heart of those hurried understands to know, || And the tongue of stammerers hurries to speak clearly. ⁵A fool is no more called "noble," || And to a miser it is not said, "rich"; ⁶For a fool speaks folly, || And his heart does iniquity, to do profanity, || And to speak error concerning YHWH, || To empty the soul of the hungry, || Indeed, he causes the thirsty to lack [their] drink. ⁷And the miser—his instruments [are] evil, || He has counseled wicked schemes, || To corrupt the poor with lying sayings, || Even when the needy speaks justly. ⁸And the noble counseled noble things, || And he rises up for noble things. ⁹Women, easy ones, rise, hear my voice, || Daughters, confident ones, give ear [to] my saying, ¹⁰In days and a year || You are troubled, O confident ones, || For harvest has been consumed, || The gathering does not come. ¹¹Tremble, you women, you easy ones, || Be troubled, you confident ones, || Strip and make bare, with a girdle on the loins, ¹²They are lamenting for breasts, || For fields of desire, for the fruitful vine. ¹³Over the ground of my people thorn [and] brier go up, || Surely over all houses of joy of the exulting city, ¹⁴The palace has been left, || The multitude of the city forsaken, || Fort and watchtower have been for dens for all time, || A joy of wild donkeys—a pasture of herds; ¹⁵Until the Spirit is emptied out on us from on high, || And a wilderness has become a fruitful field, || And the fruitful field is reckoned for a forest. ¹⁶And judgment has dwelt in the wilderness, || And righteousness remains in the fruitful field. ¹⁷And a work of the righteousness has been peace, || And a service of the righteousness—Keeping quiet and confidence for all time. ¹⁸And My people have dwelt in a peaceful habitation, || And in steadfast dwelling places, || And in quiet resting places. ¹⁹And it has hailed in the going down of the forest, || And the city is low in the valley. ²⁰Blessed [are] you sowing by all waters, || Sending forth the foot of the ox and the donkey!

CHAPTER 33

¹Woe, spoiler! And you not spoiled, || And treacherous! And they did not deal treacherously with you, || When you finish, O spoiler, you are spoiled, || When you finish dealing treacherously, || They deal treacherously with you. ²O YHWH, favor us, || We have waited for You, || Be their arm, in the mornings, || Indeed, our salvation in time of adversity. ³From the voice of a multitude peoples have fled, || From Your exaltation nations have been scattered. ⁴And Your spoil has been gathered, || A gathering of the caterpillar, || As a running to and fro of locusts || He is running on it. ⁵YHWH is set on high, for He is dwelling on high, || He filled Zion [with] judgment and righteousness, ⁶And has been the steadfastness of your times, || The strength of salvation, wisdom, and knowledge, || Fear of YHWH—it [is] His treasure. ⁷Behold, "Their Ariel," they have cried outside, || Messengers of peace weep bitterly. ⁸Highways have been desolated, || He who passes along the path has ceased, || He has broken covenant, || He has despised enemies, || He has not esteemed a man. ⁹The land has mourned, languished, || Lebanon has been confounded, || Sharon has been withered as a wilderness, || And Bashan and Carmel are shaking. ¹⁰Now I arise, says YHWH, || Now I am exalted, now I am lifted up. ¹¹You conceive chaff, you bear stubble; Your spirit—a fire [that] devours you. ¹²And peoples have been [as] burnings of lime, || Thorns, as sweepings, they burn with fire. ¹³Hear, you far off, that which I have done, || And know, you near ones, My might. ¹⁴Sinners have been afraid in Zion, || Trembling has seized the profane: Who dwells for us—consuming fire, || Who dwells for us—burnings of the age? ¹⁵Whoever is walking righteously, || And is speaking uprightly, || Kicking against gain of oppressions, || Shaking his hands from taking hold on a bribe, || Stopping his ear from hearing of blood, || And shutting his eyes from looking on evil, ¹⁶He inhabits high places, || Strongholds of rock [are] his high tower, || His bread has been given, his waters steadfast. ¹⁷Your eyes see a king in his beauty, || They see a far-off land. ¹⁸Your heart meditates [on] terror, || Where [is] he who is counting? Where [is] he who is weighing? Where [is] he who is counting the towers? ¹⁹You do not see the strong people, || A people deeper of lip than to be understood, || Of a scorned tongue, there is no understanding. ²⁰See Zion, the city of our meetings, || Your eyes see Jerusalem—a quiet habitation, || A tent not taken down, its pins are not removed forever, || And none of its cords are broken. ²¹But YHWH [is] mighty for us there, || A place of rivers—streams of broad sides, || No ship with oars goes into it, || And a mighty ship does not pass over it. ²²For YHWH, ours who is judging, || YHWH our lawgiver, || YHWH our King—He saves us. ²³Your ropes have been left, || They do not correctly strengthen their mast, || They have not spread out a sail, || Then a prey of much spoil has been apportioned, || The lame have taken spoil. ²⁴Nor does an inhabitant say, "I was sick"; The people dwelling in it [are] forgiven of [their] iniquity!

CHAPTER 34

¹Come near, you nations, to hear, || And you peoples, give attention, || The earth and its fullness hear, || The world, and all its productions. ²For to YHWH [is] wrath against all the nations, || And fury against all their host, || He has devoted them to destruction, || He has given them to slaughter. ³And their wounded are cast out, || And their carcasses cause their stench to ascend, || And mountains have been melted from their blood. ⁴And all the host of the heavens have been consumed, || And the heavens have been rolled together as a scroll, || And all their hosts fade, || As the fading of a leaf of a vine, || And as the fading one of a fig tree. ⁵For My sword was soaked in the heavens, || Behold, it comes down on Edom, || On the people of My curse for judgment. ⁶A sword [is] to YHWH—it has been full of blood, || It has been made fat with fatness, || With blood of lambs and male goats. With fat of kidneys of rams, || For to YHWH [is] a sacrifice in Bozrah, || And a great slaughter in the land of Edom. ⁷And reems have come down with them, || And bullocks with bulls, || And their land has been soaked from blood, || And their dust is made fat from fatness. ⁸(For a day of vengeance [is] to YHWH, || A year of recompenses for Zion's strife), ⁹And her streams have been turned to pitch, || And her dust to brimstone, || And her land has become burning pitch. ¹⁰She is not quenched by night and by day, || Her smoke goes up for all time, || She is desolate from generation to generation, || Forever and ever, none is passing into her. ¹¹And pelican and hedgehog possess her, || And owl and raven dwell in her,

|| And He has stretched out over her || A line of vacancy, and stones of emptiness. ¹²They call her nobles [to] the kingdom, || But there are none there, || And all her princes are at an end. ¹³And thorns have gone up her palaces, || Nettle and bramble [are] in her fortresses, || And it has been a habitation of dragons, || A court for daughters of an ostrich. ¹⁴And desert-dwellers have met with howlers, || And the goat calls for its companion, || Surely the night-owl has rested there, || And has found a place of rest for herself. ¹⁵The owl has made her nest there, || Indeed, she lays, and has hatched, || And has gathered under her shadow, || Surely vultures have been gathered there, || Each with its companion. ¹⁶Seek out of the scroll of YHWH, and read, || One of these has not been lacking, || None has missed its companion, || For My mouth—it has commanded, || And His Spirit—He has gathered them. ¹⁷And He has cast a lot for them, || And His hand has apportioned [it] to them by line, || They possess it for all time, || They dwell in it from generation to generation!

CHAPTER 35

¹They rejoice from the wilderness and dry place, || And the desert rejoices, || And flourishes as the rose, ²Flourishing it flourishes, and rejoices, || Indeed, [with] joy and singing, || The glory of Lebanon has been given to it, || The beauty of Carmel and Sharon, || They see the glory of YHWH, || The majesty of our God. ³Strengthen the feeble hands, || Indeed, strengthen the stumbling knees. ⁴Say to the hurried of heart, "Be strong, || Do not fear, behold, your God; vengeance comes, || The repayment of God, || He Himself comes and saves you." ⁵Then eyes of the blind are opened, || And ears of the deaf are unstopped, ⁶Then the lame leap as a deer, || And the tongue of the mute sings, || For waters have been broken up in a wilderness, || And streams in a desert. ⁷And the mirage has become a pond, || And the thirsty land—fountains of waters, || In the habitation of dragons, || Its place of lying down, || A court for reed and rush. ⁸And a highway has been there, and a way, || And it is called the "Way of Holiness." The unclean do not pass over it, || And He Himself [is] by them, || Whoever is going in the way—even fools do not err. ⁹No lion is there, || Indeed, a destructive beast does not ascend it, || It is not found there, || And the redeemed have walked, ¹⁰And the ransomed of YHWH return, || And have entered Zion with singing, || And [with] continuous joy on their head, || They attain joy and gladness, || And sorrow and sighing have fled away!

CHAPTER 36

¹And it comes to pass, in the fourteenth year of King Hezekiah, Sennacherib king of Asshur has come up against all the fortified cities of Judah, and seizes them. ²And the king of Asshur sends Rabshakeh from Lachish to Jerusalem, to King Hezekiah, with a heavy force, and he stands by the conduit of the upper pool, in the highway of the fuller's field, ³and Eliakim son of Hilkiah goes forth to him, who [is] over the house, and Shebna the scribe, and Joah son of Asaph, the remembrancer. ⁴And Rabshakeh says to them, "Now say to Hezekiah, Thus said the great king, the king of Asshur: What [is] this confidence in which you have confided? ⁵I have said, Only a word of the lips! Counsel and might [are] for battle. Now, on whom have you trusted, that you have rebelled against me? ⁶Behold, you have trusted on the staff of this broken reed—on Egypt—which a man leans on, and it has gone into his hand, and pierced it—so [is] Pharaoh king of Egypt to all those trusting on him. ⁷And do you say to me, We have trusted in our God YHWH? Is it not He whose high places and whose altars Hezekiah has turned aside, and says to Judah and to Jerusalem, Bow yourselves before this altar? ⁸And now, please negotiate with my lord the king of Asshur, and I give two thousand horses to you, if you are able to put riders on them for yourself. ⁹And how do you turn back the face of one captain of the least of the servants of my lord, and trust on Egypt for yourself, for chariot and for horsemen? ¹⁰And now, without YHWH have I come up against this land to destroy it? YHWH said to me, Go up to this land, and you have destroyed it." ¹¹And Eliakim says—and Shebna and Joah—to Rabshakeh, "Please speak to your servants [in] Aramaic, for we are understanding; and do not speak to us [in] Jewish, in the ears of the people who [are] on the wall." ¹²And Rabshakeh says, "To your lord, and to you, has my lord sent me to speak these words? Is it not for the men—those sitting on the wall to eat their own dung and to drink their own water with you?" ¹³And Rabshakeh stands and calls with a great voice [in] Jewish, and says, "Hear the words of the great king, the king of Asshur— ¹⁴thus said the king: Do not let Hezekiah lift you up, for he is not able to deliver you; ¹⁵and do not let Hezekiah make you trust to YHWH, saying, YHWH certainly delivers us, this city is not given into the hand of the king of Asshur. ¹⁶Do not listen to Hezekiah, for thus said the king of Asshur: Make a blessing with me, and come out to me, and each of you eat of his vine, and each of his fig tree, and each drink the waters of his own well, ¹⁷until my coming in, and I have taken you to a land like your own land, a land of grain and wine, a land of bread and vineyards, ¹⁸lest Hezekiah persuades you, saying, YHWH delivers us. Have the gods of the nations each delivered his land out of the hand of the king of Asshur? ¹⁹Where [are] the gods of Hamath and Arpad? Where [are] the gods of Sepharvaim, that they have delivered Samaria out of my hand? ²⁰Who among all the gods of these lands [are] they who have delivered their land out of my hand, that YHWH delivers Jerusalem out of my hand?" ²¹And they keep silent, and have not answered him a word, for a command of the king is, saying, "Do not answer him." ²²And Eliakim son of Hilkiah, who [is] over the house, comes in, and Shebna the scribe, and Joah son of Asaph, the remembrancer, to Hezekiah, with torn garments, and they declare to him the words of Rabshakeh.

CHAPTER 37

¹And it comes to pass, at King Hezekiah's hearing, that he tears his garments, and covers himself with sackcloth, and enters the house of YHWH, ²and sends Eliakim, who [is] over the house, and Shebna the scribe, and [the] elderly of the priests, covering themselves with sackcloth, to Isaiah son of Amoz the prophet, ³and they say to him, "Thus said Hezekiah: A day of distress, and rebuke, and despising, [is] this day; for sons have come to the birth, and there is not power to bear. ⁴It may be your God YHWH hears the words of Rabshakeh with which the king of Asshur his lord has sent him to reproach the living God, and has decided concerning the words that your God YHWH has heard, and you have lifted up prayer for the remnant that is found." ⁵And the servants of King Hezekiah come to Isaiah, ⁶and Isaiah says to them, "Thus you say to your lord, Thus said YHWH: Do not be afraid because of the words that you have heard, with which the servants of the king of Asshur have reviled Me. ⁷Behold, I am giving a spirit in him, and he has heard a report, and has turned back to his land, and I have caused him to fall by the sword in his land." ⁸And Rabshakeh turns back and finds the king of Asshur fighting against Libnah, for he has heard that he has journeyed from Lachish. ⁹And he hears concerning Tirhakah king of Cush, saying, "He has come out to fight with you"; and he hears, and sends messengers to Hezekiah, saying, ¹⁰"Thus you speak to Hezekiah king of Judah, saying, Do not let your God in whom you are trusting lift you up, saying, Jerusalem is not given into the hand of the king of Asshur. ¹¹Behold, you have heard that which the kings of Asshur have done to all the lands—to devote them—and you are delivered! ¹²Did the gods of the nations deliver them whom my fathers destroyed—Gozan, and Haran, and Rezeph, and the sons of Eden, who [are] in Telassar? ¹³Where [is] the king of Hamath, and the king of Arpad, and the king of the city of Sepharvaim, Hena, and Ivvah?" ¹⁴And Hezekiah takes the letters out of the hand of the messengers, and reads them, and Hezekiah goes up to the house of YHWH, and Hezekiah spreads it before YHWH. ¹⁵And Hezekiah prays to YHWH, saying, ¹⁶"YHWH of Hosts, God of Israel, inhabiting the cherubim, You [are] God Himself—You alone—to all kingdoms of the earth, You have made the heavens and the earth. ¹⁷Incline, O YHWH, Your ear, and hear; open, O YHWH, Your eyes and see; and hear all the words of Sennacherib that he has sent to reproach the living God. ¹⁸Truly, O YHWH, kings of Asshur have laid waste all the lands and their land, ¹⁹so as to put their gods into fire—for they [are] no gods, but work of the hands of man, wood and stone—and they destroy them. ²⁰And now, our God YHWH, save us from his hand, and all kingdoms of the earth know that You [are] YHWH, You alone." ²¹And Isaiah son of Amoz sends to Hezekiah, saying, "Thus said YHWH,

ISAIAH

God of Israel: That which you have prayed to Me concerning Sennacherib king of Asshur— ²²this [is] the word that YHWH spoke concerning him: Trampled on you, laughed at you, || Has the virgin daughter of Zion, || The daughter of Jerusalem has shaken the head behind you. ²³Whom have you reproached and reviled? And against whom—lifted up the voice? Indeed, you lift up your eyes on high || Against the Holy One of Israel. ²⁴By the hand of your servants || You have reviled the Lord, and say: In the multitude of my chariots || I have come up to a high place of hills, || The sides of Lebanon, || And I cut down the height of its cedars, || The choice of its firs, || And I enter the high place of its extremity, || The forest of its Carmel. ²⁵I have dug and drunk waters, || And I dry up with the sole of my steps || All floods of a bulwark. ²⁶Have you not heard from afar [that] I did it, || From days of old—that I formed it? Now I have brought it in, || And it is to make desolate, || Ruinous heaps—fortified cities, ²⁷And their inhabitants are feeble-handed, || They were broken down, and are dried up. They have been the herb of the field, || And the greenness of the tender grass, || Grass of the roofs, || And blasted grain, before it has risen up. ²⁸And your sitting down, and your going out, || And your coming in, I have known, || And your anger toward Me. ²⁹Because of your anger toward Me, || And your noise—it came up into My ears, || I have put My hook in your nose, || And My bridle in your lips, || And I have caused you to turn back || In the way in which you came. ³⁰And this [is] the sign to you, || Self-sown grain [is] food of the year, || And in the second year the spontaneous growth, || And in the third year, sow and reap, || And plant vineyards, and eat their fruit. ³¹And it has continued—The escaped of the house of Judah that has been left—To take root beneath, || And it has made fruit upward. ³²For a remnant goes forth from Jerusalem, || And an escape from Mount Zion, || The zeal of YHWH of Hosts does this. ³³Therefore, thus said YHWH, || Concerning the king of Asshur: He does not come into this city, || Nor does he shoot an arrow there, || Nor does he come before it [with] shield, || Nor does he pour out a mound against it. ³⁴In the way that he came, in it he turns back, || And to this city he does not come in, || A declaration of YHWH, ³⁵And I have covered over this city, || To save it, for My own sake, || And for the sake of My servant David. ³⁶And a messenger of YHWH goes out, and strikes in the camp of Asshur one hundred and eighty-five thousand; and [men] rise early in the morning, and behold, all of them [are] dead corpses. ³⁷And he journeys, and goes, and Sennacherib king of Asshur turns back, and dwells in Nineveh. ³⁸And it comes to pass, he is bowing himself in the house of his god Nisroch, and his sons Adrammelech and Sharezer have struck him with the sword, and they have escaped to the land of Ararat, and his son Esar-Haddon reigns in his stead.

CHAPTER 38

¹In those days has Hezekiah been sick to death, and Isaiah son of Amoz, the prophet, comes to him and says to him, "Thus said YHWH: Give a charge to your house, for you [are] dying, and do not live." ²And Hezekiah turns around his face to the wall, and prays to YHWH, ³and says, "Ah, now, O YHWH, please remember how I have habitually walked before You in truth, and with a perfect heart, and I have done that which [is] good in your eyes"; and Hezekiah weeps [with] a great weeping. ⁴And a word of YHWH is to Isaiah, saying, ⁵"Go, and you have said to Hezekiah, Thus said YHWH, God of your father David: I have heard your prayer, I have seen your tear, behold, I am adding fifteen years to your days, ⁶and out of the hand of the king of Asshur I deliver you and this city, and have covered over this city. ⁷And this [is] to you the sign from YHWH, that YHWH does this thing that He has spoken. ⁸Behold, I am bringing back the shadow of the degrees that it has gone down on the degrees of Ahaz, by the sun, backward ten degrees"; and the sun turns back ten degrees in the degrees that it had gone down. ⁹A writing of Hezekiah king of Judah concerning his being sick when he revives from his sickness: ¹⁰"I said in the cutting off of my days, || I go to the gates of Sheol, || I have numbered the remnant of my years. ¹¹I said, I do not see YAH—YAH! In the land of the living, || I do not behold man anymore, || With the inhabitants of the world. ¹²My sojourning has departed, || And been removed from me as a shepherd's tent, || I have drawn together, as a weaver, my life, || By weakness it cuts me off, || From day to night You end me. ¹³I have set [Him] as a lion until morning, || So He breaks all my bones, || From day to night You end me. ¹⁴As a crane—a swallow—so I chatter, || I mourn as a dove, || My eyes have been drawn up on high, || O YHWH, oppression [is] on me, be my guarantor. ¹⁵What do I say? Seeing He spoke to me, || And He Himself has worked, || I go softly all my years for the bitterness of my soul. ¹⁶Lord, [men] live by these, || And by all in them [is] the life of my spirit, || And You save me, make me to also live, ¹⁷Behold, He changed bitterness to peace for me, || And You have delighted in my soul without corruption, || For You have cast all my sins behind Your back. ¹⁸For Sheol does not confess You, || Death does not praise You, || Those going down to the pit do not hope for Your truth. ¹⁹The living, the living, he confesses You, || Like myself today; A father makes known to [his] sons of Your faithfulness, || O YHWH—to save me: And we sing my songs all [the] days of our lives || In the house of YHWH." ²¹And Isaiah says, "Let them take a bunch of figs, and plaster over the ulcer, and he lives." ²²And Hezekiah says, "What [is] the sign that I go up to the house of YHWH?"

CHAPTER 39

¹At that time, Merodach-Baladan, son of Baladan, king of Babylon, has sent letters and a present to Hezekiah when he hears that he has been sick and has become strong. ²And Hezekiah rejoices over them, and shows them the house of his spices, the silver, and the gold, and the spices, and the good ointment, and all the house of his vessels, and all that has been found in his treasures; there has not been a thing in his house, and in all his dominion, that Hezekiah has not showed them. ³And Isaiah the prophet comes to King Hezekiah and says to him, "What did these men say? And from where do they come to you?" And Hezekiah says, "They have come to me from a far-off land—from Babylon." ⁴And he says, "What did they see in your house?" And Hezekiah says, "They saw all that [is] in my house; there has not been a thing that I have not showed them among my treasures." ⁵And Isaiah says to Hezekiah, "Hear a word of YHWH of Hosts: ⁶Behold, days are coming, and all that [is] in your house, and that your fathers have treasured up until this day, has been carried to Babylon; there is not a thing left, said YHWH; ⁷and of your sons who come forth from you, whom you beget, they take, and they have been eunuchs in a palace of the king of Babylon." ⁸And Hezekiah says to Isaiah, "The word of YHWH that you have spoken [is] good"; and he says, "Because there is peace and truth in my days."

CHAPTER 40

¹"Comfort, comfort My people," says your God. ²Speak to the heart of Jerusalem, and call to her, || That her warfare has been completed, || That her punishment has been accepted, || That she has received from the hand of YHWH || Double for all her sins. ³A voice is crying in a wilderness: "Prepare the way of YHWH, || Make straight in a desert a highway for our God. ⁴Every valley is raised up, || And every mountain and hill become low, || And the crooked place has become a plain, || And the entangled places a valley. ⁵And the glory of YHWH has been revealed, || And all flesh have seen [it] together, || For the mouth of YHWH has spoken." ⁶A voice is saying, "Call," || And he said, "What do I call?" All flesh [is] grass, and all its goodness || [Is] as a flower of the field: ⁷Grass has withered, the flower faded, || For the Spirit of YHWH blew on it, || Surely the people [is] grass; ⁸Grass has withered, the flower faded, || But a word of our God rises forever. ⁹Get up on a high mountain, O Zion, || Proclaiming tidings, || Lift up your voice with power, O Jerusalem, proclaiming tidings, || Lift up, do not fear, say to cities of Judah, "Behold, your God." ¹⁰Behold, Lord YHWH comes with strength, || And His arm is ruling for Him, || Behold, His hire [is] with Him, and His wage before Him. ¹¹He feeds His flock as a shepherd, || He gathers lambs with His arm, || And He carries [them] in His bosom: He leads suckling ones. ¹²Who has measured the waters in the hollow of His hand, || And has meted out the heavens by a span, || And comprehended the dust of the earth in a measure, || And has weighed the mountains in scales, || And the hills in a balance? ¹³Who has meted out the Spirit of YHWH, || And [being] His counselor, teaches Him? ¹⁴With whom [did] He consult, || That he causes Him to understand? And

ISAIAH

teaches Him in the path of judgment, || And teaches Him knowledge? And causes Him to know the way of understanding? ¹⁵Behold, nations [are] as a drop from a bucket, || And have been reckoned as small dust of the balance, || Behold, He takes up islands as a small thing. ¹⁶And Lebanon is not sufficient to burn, || Nor its beasts sufficient for a burnt-offering. ¹⁷All the nations [are] as nothing before Him, || Less than nothing and emptiness, || They have been reckoned to Him. ¹⁸And to whom do you liken God, || And what likeness do you compare to Him? ¹⁹An artisan has poured out the carved image, || And a refiner spreads it over with gold, || And he is refining chains of silver. ²⁰He who is poor [by] raised-offerings, || Chooses a tree [that is] not rotten, || He seeks a skillful artisan for it, || To establish a carved image—not moved. ²¹Do you not know—do you not hear? Has it not been declared from the first to you? Have you not understood || [From] the foundations of the earth? ²²He who is sitting on the circle of the earth, || And its inhabitants [are] as grasshoppers, || He who is stretching out the heavens as a thin thing, || And spreads them as a tent to dwell in. ²³He who is making princes become nothing, || Has made judges of earth formless; ²⁴Indeed, they have not been planted, || Indeed, they have not been sown, || Indeed, their stock is not taking root in the earth, || And He has also blown on them, and they wither, || And a whirlwind takes them away as stubble. ²⁵And to whom do you liken Me, || And [to whom] I equal? Says the Holy One. ²⁶Lift up your eyes on high, || And see—who has created these? He who is bringing out their host by number, || He calls to all of them by name, || By the abundance of His strength || And mighty power, || Not one is lacking. ²⁷Why say, O Jacob, and speak, O Israel, "My way has been hid from YHWH, || And from my God my judgment passes over?" ²⁸Have you not known? Have you not heard? The God of the age—YHWH, || Preparer of the ends of the earth, || Is not wearied nor fatigued, || There is no searching of His understanding. ²⁹He is giving power to the weary, || And to those not strong He increases might. ³⁰Even youths are wearied and fatigued, || And young men utterly stumble, ³¹But those expecting YHWH pass [to] power, || They raise up the pinion as eagles, || They run and are not fatigued, || They go on and do not faint!

CHAPTER 41

¹Keep silent toward Me, O islands, || And the peoples pass on [to] power, || They come near, then they speak, "Together we draw near to judgment." ²Who stirred up a righteous one from the east? He calls him to His foot, || He gives nations before him, || And He causes him to rule kings, || He gives [them] as dust [to] his sword, || As driven stubble [to] his bow. ³He pursues them, he passes over in safety || A path he does not enter with his feet. ⁴Who has worked and done, || Calling the generations from the first? I, YHWH, the first, and with the last I [am] He. ⁵Islands have seen and fear, || The ends of the earth tremble, || They have drawn near, indeed, they come. ⁶They each help his neighbor, || And to his brother he says, "Be strong." ⁷And an artisan strengthens the refiner, || A smoother [with] a hammer, || Him who is beating [on] an anvil, saying, "For joining it [is] good," || And he strengthens it with nails, it is not moved! ⁸And you, O Israel, My servant, || Jacob, whom I have chosen, || Seed of Abraham, My lover, ⁹Whom I have taken hold of, from the ends of the earth, || And from its near places I have called you, || And I say to you, You [are] My servant, || I have chosen you, and not rejected you. ¹⁰Do not be afraid, for I [am] with you, do not look around, for I [am] your God, || I have strengthened you, || Indeed, I have helped you, indeed, I upheld you, || With the right hand of My righteousness. ¹¹Behold, all those displeased with you, || They are ashamed and blush, || They are as nothing, indeed, || The men who strive with you perish. ¹²You seek them, and do not find them, || The men who debate with you, || They are as nothing, indeed, as nothing, || The men who war with you. ¹³For I, your God YHWH, || Am strengthening your right hand, || He who is saying to you, "Do not fear, I have helped you." ¹⁴Do not fear, O worm Jacob, || You men of Israel, || I helped you, a declaration of YHWH, || Even your redeemer, the Holy One of Israel. ¹⁵Behold, I have set you for a new sharp threshing instrument, || Possessing teeth, you thresh mountains, || And beat small, and make hills as chaff. ¹⁶You winnow them, and a wind lifts them up, || And a whirlwind scatters them, || And you rejoice in YHWH, || [And] boast yourself in the Holy One of Israel. ¹⁷The poor and the needy are seeking water, || And there is none, || Their tongue has failed with thirst, || I, YHWH, answer them, || The God of Israel—I do not forsake them. ¹⁸I open rivers on high places, || And fountains in midst of valleys, || I make a wilderness become a pond of water, || And a dry land becomes springs of water. ¹⁹I give in a wilderness the cedar, || Shittah, and myrtle, and oil-tree, || I set in a desert the fir-pine and box-wood together. ²⁰So that they see, and know, || And regard, and act wisely together, || For the hand of YHWH has done this, || And the Holy One of Israel has created it. ²¹Bring your cause near, says YHWH, || Bring your mighty ones near, says the King of Jacob. ²²They bring [them] near, and declare to us that which happens, || Declare the first things—what they [are], || And we set our heart, and know their latter end, || Or cause us to hear the coming things. ²³Declare the things that are coming hereafter, || And we know that you [are] gods, || Indeed, you may do good or do evil, || And we look around and see [it] together. ²⁴Behold, you [are] of nothing, and your work of nothing, || An abomination—it fixes on you. ²⁵I have stirred up [one] from the north, || And he comes, || From the rising of the sun he calls in My Name, || And he comes in [on] prefects as [on] clay, || And as a potter treads down mire. ²⁶Who has declared from the first, and we know? And formerly, and we say, "Righteous?" Indeed, there is none declaring, || Indeed, there is none proclaiming, || Indeed, there is none hearing your sayings. ²⁷First to Zion, || Behold, behold them, || And to Jerusalem I give one proclaiming tidings, ²⁸And I see that there is no man, || Indeed, of these that there is no counselor, || And I ask them, and they return word: ²⁹"Behold, all of them [are] vanity, || Their works [are] nothing, || Their molten images [are] wind and emptiness!"

CHAPTER 42

¹Behold, My servant, I take hold on Him, || My Chosen One—My soul has accepted, I have put My Spirit on Him, || He brings forth judgment to nations. ²He does not cry, nor lift up, || Nor cause His voice to be heard in the street. ³A bruised reed He does not break, || And faded flax He does not quench, || He brings forth judgment to truth. ⁴He does not become weak nor bruised, || Until He sets judgment in the earth, || And islands wait with hope for His law. ⁵Thus said God, YHWH, || Creating the heavens, and stretching them out, || Spreading out the earth and its productions, || Giving breath to the people on it, || And spirit to those walking in it. ⁶I, YHWH, called you in righteousness, || And I lay hold on your hand, and keep you, || And I give you for a covenant of a people, || And a light of nations. ⁷To open the eyes of the blind, || To bring forth the bound one from prison, || Those sitting in darkness from the house of restraint. ⁸I [am] YHWH, this [is] My Name, || And I do not give My glory to another, || Nor My praise to carved images. ⁹The former things, behold, have come, || And I am declaring new things, || Before they spring up I cause you to hear. ¹⁰Sing a new song to YHWH, || His praise from the end of the earth, || You who are going down to the sea, and its fullness, || Islands, and their inhabitants. ¹¹The wilderness and its cities lift up [their voice], || Kedar inhabits the villages, || The inhabitants of Sela sing, || They cry from the top of mountains. ¹²They ascribe to YHWH glory, || And they declare His praise in the islands. ¹³YHWH goes forth as a mighty one. He stirs up zeal as a man of war, || He cries, indeed, He shrieks, || He shows Himself mighty against His enemies. ¹⁴I have kept silent from of old, || I keep silent, I refrain Myself, || I cry out as a travailing woman, || I desolate and swallow up together. ¹⁵I make desolate mountains and hills, || And I dry up all their herbs, || And I have made rivers become islands, || And I dry up ponds. ¹⁶And I have caused the blind to go, || In a way they have not known, || I cause them to tread in paths they have not known, || I make a dark place become light before them, || And unleveled places become a plain, || These [are] the things I have done to them, || And I have not forsaken them. ¹⁷Removed backward—utterly ashamed, || Are those trusting in a carved image, || Those saying to a molten image, "You [are] our gods." ¹⁸You deaf, hear; and you blind, look to see. ¹⁹Who [is] blind but My servant? And deaf as My messenger I send? Who [is] blind as he who is at peace, || Indeed, blind, as the servant of YHWH? ²⁰Seeing many things, and you do not

observe, || Opening ears, and he does not hear. ²¹YHWH has delight for the sake of His righteousness, || He magnifies law, and makes honorable. ²²And this [is] a people seized and spoiled, || Snared in holes—all of them, || And they were hidden in houses of restraint, || They have been for a prey, || And there is no deliverer, || A spoil, and none is saying, "Restore." ²³Who among you gives ear [to] this? Attends, and hears afterward? ²⁴Who has given Jacob for a spoil, || And Israel to the spoilers? Is it not YHWH—He against whom we sinned? Indeed, they have not been willing to walk in His ways, || Nor have they listened to His law. ²⁵And He pours fury on him, || His anger, and the strength of battle, || And it sets him on fire all around, || And he has not known, || And it burns against him, and he does not lay it to heart!

CHAPTER 43

¹And now, thus said YHWH, Your Creator, O Jacob, and your Fashioner, O Israel: Do not be afraid, for I have redeemed you, || I have called on your name—you [are] Mine. ²When you pass into waters, I [am] with you, || And into floods, they do not overflow you, || When you go into fire, you are not burned, || And a flame does not burn against you. ³For I—your God YHWH, || The Holy One of Israel, your Savior, || I have appointed Egypt your atonement, || Cush and Seba in your stead. ⁴Since you were precious in My eyes, || You were honored, and I have loved you, || And I appoint men in your stead, || And peoples instead of your life. ⁵Do not be afraid, for I [am] with you, || I bring in your seed from the east, || And I gather you from the west. ⁶I am saying to the north, "Give up," || And to the south, "Do not restrain." Bring in My sons from afar, || And My daughters from the end of the earth. ⁷Everyone who is called by My Name, || Even for My glory I have created him, || I have formed him, indeed, I have made him. ⁸He brought out a blind people who have eyes, || And deaf ones who have ears. ⁹All the nations have been gathered together, || And the peoples are assembled, || Who among them declares this, || And causes us to hear former things? They give their witnesses, || And they are declared righteous, || And they hear and say, "Truth." ¹⁰You [are] My witnesses, a declaration of YHWH, || And My servant whom I have chosen, || So that you know and give credence to Me, || And understand that I [am] He, || Before Me there was no God formed, || And after Me there is none. ¹¹I [am] YHWH, || And besides Me there is no savior. ¹²I declared, and saved, and proclaimed, || And there is no stranger with you, || And you [are] My witnesses, a declaration of YHWH, || And I [am] God. ¹³Even from the day I [am] He, || And there is no deliverer from My hand, || I work, and who turns it back? ¹⁴Thus said YHWH, your Redeemer, || The Holy One of Israel: "I have sent to Babylon for your sake, || And caused bars to descend—all of them, || And the Chaldeans, whose song [is] in the ships. ¹⁵I [am] YHWH, your Holy One, || Creator of Israel, your King." ¹⁶Thus said YHWH, || Who is giving a way in the sea, || And a path in the strong waters. ¹⁷Who is bringing forth chariot and horse, || A force, even a strong one: "They lie down together—they do not rise, || They have been extinguished, || They have been quenched as flax." ¹⁸Do not remember former things, || And do not consider ancient things. ¹⁹Behold, I am doing a new thing, now it springs up, || Do you not know it? Indeed, I put a way in a wilderness, || In a desolate place—floods. ²⁰The beast of the field honors Me, || Dragons and daughters of an ostrich, || For I have given waters in a wilderness, || Floods in a desolate place, || To give drink to My people—My chosen. ²¹I have formed this people for Myself, || They recount My praise. ²²And you have not called Me, O Jacob, || For you have been wearied of Me, O Israel, ²³You have not brought to Me, || The lamb of your burnt-offerings, || And [with] your sacrifices you have not honored Me, || I have not caused you to serve with a present, || Nor wearied you with frankincense. ²⁴You have not bought Me sweet cane with money, || And have not filled Me [with] the fat of your sacrifices, || Only—you have caused Me to serve with your sins, || You have wearied Me with your iniquities. ²⁵I [am] He who is blotting out Your transgressions for My own sake, || And I do not remember your sins. ²⁶Cause Me to remember—we are judged together, || Declare that you may be justified. ²⁷Your first father sinned, || And your interpreters transgressed against Me, ²⁸And I defile princes of the sanctuary, || And I give Jacob to destruction, and Israel to revilings!

CHAPTER 44

¹"And now, hear, O Jacob, My servant, || And Israel, whom I have fixed on— ²Thus said YHWH, your Maker, and your Former, || From the womb He helps you: Do not fear, My servant Jacob, || And Yeshurun, whom I have fixed on. ³For I pour waters on a thirsty one, || And floods on a dry land, || I pour My Spirit on your seed, || And My blessing on your offspring. ⁴And they have sprung up as among grass, || As willows by conduits of water. ⁵This [one] says, For I [am] YHWH's, || And this calls [himself] by the name of Jacob, || And this [one] writes [with] his hand, For YHWH, || And surnames himself by the name of Israel." ⁶Thus said YHWH, King of Israel, || And his Redeemer, YHWH of Hosts: "I [am] the first, and I [am] the last, || And besides Me there is no God. ⁷And who [is] as I, call and declare it, || And arrange it for Me, || Since My placing the people of antiquity, || And things that are coming, || And those that come, they declare to them. ⁸Do not fear, nor be afraid, || Have I not caused you to hear from that time, and declared? And you [are] My witnesses, || Is there a God besides Me? Indeed, there is none, || I have not known another Rock." ⁹Framers of a carved image, all of them [are] emptiness, || And their desirable things do not profit, || And they [are] their own witnesses, || They do not see, nor know, that they may be ashamed. ¹⁰Who has formed a god, || And poured out a molten image—not profitable? ¹¹Behold, all his companions are ashamed, || As for artisans—they [are] of men, || All of them gather together, they stand up, || They fear, they are ashamed together. ¹²He has worked iron [with] an axe, || And has worked with coals, || And forms it with hammers, || And works it by his powerful arm, || Indeed, he is hungry, and there is no power, || He does not drink water, and he is wearied. ¹³He has worked [with] wood, || He has stretched out a rule, || He marks it out with a line, || He makes it with carving tools, || And he marks it out with a compass, || And makes it according to the form of a man, || According to the beauty of a man, || To remain in the house. ¹⁴Cutting down cedars for himself, || He also takes a cypress, and an oak, || And he strengthens [it] for himself || Among the trees of a forest, || He has planted an ash, and the shower nourishes [it]. ¹⁵And it has been for man to burn, || And he takes of them, and becomes warm, || Indeed, he kindles [it], and has baked bread, || Indeed, he makes a god, and bows himself, || He has made it a carved image, || And he falls down to it. ¹⁶Half of it he has burned in the fire, || By [this] half of it he eats flesh, || He roasts a roasting and is satisfied, || Indeed, he is warm and says: "Aha, I have become warm, I have enjoyed the light." ¹⁷And he has made its remnant for a god—For his carved image, || He falls down to it, and worships, || And prays to it, and he says, "Deliver me, for you [are] my god." ¹⁸They have not known, nor do they understand, || For He has coated their eyes from seeing, || Their heart from acting wisely. ¹⁹And none turn [it] back to his heart, || Nor has knowledge nor understanding to say, "I have burned half of it in the fire, || Indeed, I have also baked bread over its coals, || I roast flesh and I eat, || And I make its remnant for an abomination, || I fall down to the stock of a tree." ²⁰Feeding on ashes, the heart is deceived, || It has turned him aside, || And he does not deliver his soul, nor says: "Is there not a lie in my right hand?" ²¹"Remember these, O Jacob, and Israel, || For you [are] My servant, || I formed you, you [are] a servant to Me, || O Israel, you do not forget Me. ²²I have blotted out, as [by] a thick cloud, || Your transgressions, || And as [by] a cloud, your sins, || Return to Me, for I have redeemed you." ²³Sing, O heavens, for YHWH has worked, || Shout, O lower parts of earth, || Break forth, O mountains, with singing, || Forest, and every tree in it, || For YHWH has redeemed Jacob, || And He beautifies Himself in Israel. ²⁴Thus said YHWH, your Redeemer, || And your Framer from the womb: "I [am] YHWH, doing all things, || Stretching out the heavens by Myself, || Spreading out the earth—who [is] with Me? ²⁵Making void the tokens of devisers, || And makes diviners mad, || Turning the wise backward, || And makes their knowledge foolish. ²⁶Confirming the word of His servant, || He perfects the counsel of His messengers, || Who is saying of Jerusalem, || She is inhabited, || And of cities of Judah, || They will be built, and her ruins I raise up, ²⁷Who is saying to the deep, || Be dry, and your rivers I cause to dry up, ²⁸Who is saying of Cyrus, My shepherd, ||

And he perfects all My delight, || So as to say of Jerusalem, You are built, || And of the temple, You are founded."

CHAPTER 45

¹Thus said YHWH, || To His anointed, to Cyrus, || Whose right hand I have laid hold on, || To subdue nations before him, || Indeed, I loose loins of kings, || To open double doors before him, || Indeed, gates are not shut: ²"I go before you, and make crooked places straight, || I shatter doors of bronze, || And I cut bars of iron apart, ³And have given to you treasures of darkness, || Even treasures of secret places, || So that you know that I, YHWH, || Who am calling on your name—[am] the God of Israel. ⁴For the sake of My servant Jacob, || And of Israel My chosen, || I also call you by your name, I surname you, || And you have not known Me. ⁵I [am] YHWH, and there is none else, || There is no God except Me, || I gird you, and you have not known Me. ⁶So that they know from the rising of the sun, || And from the west, that there is none besides Me, || I [am] YHWH, and there is none else, ⁷Forming light, and creating darkness, || Making peace, and creating calamity, || I [am] YHWH, doing all these things. ⁸Drop, you heavens, from above, || And clouds cause righteousness to flow, || Earth opens, and they are fruitful, || Salvation and righteousness spring up together, || I, YHWH, have created it. ⁹Woe [to] him who is striving with his Former || (A potsherd with potsherds of the ground!) Does clay say to its Framer, What [are] you doing? And your work, He has no hands? ¹⁰Woe [to] him who is saying to a father, What do you beget? Or to a wife, What do you bring forth?" ¹¹Thus said YHWH, The Holy One of Israel, and his Former: "Ask Me of the things coming concerning My sons, || Indeed, concerning the work of My hands, you command Me. ¹²I made earth, and created man on it, || My hands stretched out the heavens, || And I have commanded all their host. ¹³I have stirred him up in righteousness, || And I make all his ways straight, || He builds My city, and sends out My captivity, || Not for price, nor for bribe," said YHWH of Hosts. ¹⁴Thus said YHWH: "The labor of Egypt, || And the merchandise of Cush, || And of the Sebaim—men of measure, || Pass over to you, and they are yours, || They go after you, they pass over in chains, || And they bow themselves to you, || They pray to you: Surely God [is] in you, || And there is none else, no [other] God." ¹⁵Surely You [are] a God hiding Yourself, God of Israel—Savior! ¹⁶They have been ashamed, || And they have even blushed—all of them, || Those carving images have gone together in confusion. ¹⁷Israel has been saved in YHWH, || A perpetual salvation! You are not ashamed nor confounded || For all ages of eternity! ¹⁸For thus said YHWH, Creator of the heavens, || He is God, || Former of earth, and its Maker, || He established it—He did not create it empty, || For He formed it to be inhabited: "I [am] YHWH, and there is none else. ¹⁹I have not spoken in secret, in a dark place of the earth, || I have not said to the seed of Jacob, || Seek Me in vain, || I [am] YHWH, speaking righteousness, || Declaring uprightness. ²⁰Be gathered, and come in, || Come near together, you escaped of the nations, || They have not known, || Who are lifting up the wood of their carved image, || And praying to a god [that] does not save. ²¹Declare, and bring near, || Indeed, they take counsel together, || Who has proclaimed this from of old? [Who] has declared it from that time? Is it not I—YHWH? And there is no other god besides Me, || A God righteous and saving, there is none except Me. ²²Turn to Me, and be saved, all the ends of the earth, || For I [am] God, and there is none else. ²³I have sworn by Myself, || A word has gone out from My mouth in righteousness, || And it does not return, || That to Me, every knee bows, every tongue swears. ²⁴Only in YHWH, one has said, || Do I have righteousness and strength, || He comes to Him, || And all those displeased with Him are ashamed. ²⁵In YHWH are all the seed of Israel justified, || And they boast themselves."

CHAPTER 46

¹Bel has bowed down, Nebo is stooping, || Their idols have been for the beast and for livestock, || Your burdens are loaded, a burden to the weary. ²They have stooped, they have bowed together, || They have not been able to deliver the burden, || And have gone into captivity themselves. ³"Listen to Me, O house of Jacob, || And all the remnant of Israel, || Who are borne from the belly, || Who are carried from the womb, ⁴Even to old age, I [am] He, and to grey hairs I carry, || I made, and I bear, indeed, I carry and deliver. ⁵To whom do you liken Me, and make equal? And compare Me, that we may be like? ⁶They are pouring out gold from a bag, || And they weigh silver on the beam, || They hire a refiner, and he makes it a god, || They fall down, indeed, they bow themselves. ⁷They lift him up on the shoulder, || They carry him, and cause him to rest in his place, || And he stands, he does not move from his place, || Indeed, one cries to him, and he does not answer, || He does not save him from his adversity. ⁸Remember this, and show yourselves men, || Turn [it] back, O transgressors, to the heart. ⁹Remember former things of old, || For I [am] Mighty, and there is none else, || God—and there is none like Me. ¹⁰Declaring the latter end from the beginning, || And from of old that which has not been done, || Saying, My counsel stands, || And all My delight I do. ¹¹Calling a ravenous bird from the east, || The man of My counsel from a far land, || Indeed, I have spoken, indeed, I bring it in, || I have formed [it], indeed, I do it. ¹²Listen to Me, you mighty in heart, || Who are far from righteousness. ¹³I have brought My righteousness near, || It is not far off, || And My salvation—it does not linger, || And I have given salvation in Zion, || For Israel My glory!"

CHAPTER 47

¹"Come down, and sit on the dust, || O virgin daughter of Babylon, || Sit on the earth, there is no throne, || O daughter of the Chaldeans, || For they no longer cry to you, || O tender and delicate one. ²Take millstones, and grind flour, || Remove your veil, draw up the skirt, || Uncover the leg, pass over the floods. ³Your nakedness is revealed, indeed, your reproach is seen, || I take vengeance, and I do not meet a man." ⁴Our redeemer [is] YHWH of Hosts, || His Name [is] the Holy One of Israel. ⁵"Sit silent, and go into darkness, || O daughter of the Chaldeans, || For they no longer cry to you, Mistress of kingdoms. ⁶I have been angry against My people, I have defiled My inheritance || And I give them into your hand, || You have not appointed mercies for them, || You have made your yoke very heavy on the aged, ⁷And you say, I am mistress for all time, || While you have not laid these things to your heart, || You have not remembered the latter end of it. ⁸And now, hear this, O luxurious one, || Who is sitting confidently—Who is saying in her heart, I [am], and none else, || I do not sit [as] a widow, nor know bereavement. ⁹And these two things come to you, || In a moment, in one day: childlessness and widowhood, || They have come on you according to their perfection, || In the multitude of your sorceries, || In the exceeding might of your charms. ¹⁰And you are confident in your wickedness, || You have said, There is none seeing me, || Your wisdom and your knowledge, || It is turning you back, || And you say in your heart, I [am], and none else. ¹¹And evil has come in on you, || You do not know its rising, || And disaster falls on you, || You are not able to pacify it, || And desolation comes on you suddenly, || You do not know. ¹²Now stand in your charms, || And in the multitude of your sorceries, || In which you have labored from your youth, || It may be you are able to profit, || It may be you terrify! ¹³You have been wearied in the multitude of your counsels, || Now stand up and let them save you—The charmers of the heavens, || Those looking on the stars, || Those teaching concerning the months—From those things that come on you! ¹⁴Behold, they have been as stubble! Fire has burned them, || They do not deliver themselves from the power of the flame, || There is not a coal to warm them, a light to sit before it. ¹⁵So they have been to you with whom you have labored, || Your merchants from your youth, || They have each wandered to his passage, || None is saving you!"

CHAPTER 48

¹"Hear this, O house of Jacob, || Who are called by the name of Israel, || And from the waters of Judah came out, || Who are swearing by the Name of YHWH, || And make mention of the God of Israel, || Not in truth nor in righteousness. ²For they have been called from the Holy City, || And been supported on the God of Israel, || YHWH of Hosts [is] His Name. ³I declared the former things from that time, || And they have gone forth from My mouth, || And I proclaim them, || Suddenly I have done, and it comes. ⁴From My knowing that you are obstinate, || And your neck—a sinew of iron, || And your forehead—bronze, ⁵And from that time I declare [it] to you, || Before it comes I have caused you to hear, ||

Lest you say, My idol has done them, || And my carved image, || And my molten image commanded them. ⁶You have heard, see the whole of it, || And you, do you not declare? I have caused you to hear new things from this time, || And things reserved that you did not know. ⁷Now they have been produced and not from that time, || Indeed, before the day, and you have not heard them, || Lest you say, Behold, I have known them. ⁸Indeed, you have not heard, || Indeed, you have not known, || Indeed, your ear has not opened from that time, || For I have known you deal treacherously, || And [are] a transgressor from the belly, || One is crying to you. ⁹I defer My anger for My Name's sake, || And [for] My praise I restrain for you, || So as not to cut you off. ¹⁰Behold, I have refined you, and not with silver, || I have chosen you in a furnace of affliction. ¹¹For My sake, for My own sake, I do [it], || For how is it defiled? And I do not give My glory to another. ¹²Listen to me, O Jacob, and Israel, My called one, || I [am] He, || I [am] first, and I [am] last; ¹³Also, My hand has founded earth, || And My right hand stretched out the heavens, || I am calling to them, they stand together. ¹⁴Be gathered, all of you, and hear, || Who among them declared these things? YHWH has loved him, || He does His pleasure on Babylon, || And His arm [is on] the Chaldeans. ¹⁵I have spoken, indeed, I have called him, I have brought him in, || And he has made his way prosperous. ¹⁶Come near to Me, hear this, || I have not spoken in secret from the beginning, || From the time of its being, I [am] there, || And now Lord YHWH has sent Me, and His Spirit." ¹⁷Thus said YHWH, your Redeemer, || The Holy One of Israel: "I [am] your God YHWH, teaching you to profit, || Causing you to tread in the way you go. ¹⁸O that you had attended to My commands, || Then your peace is as a river, || And your righteousness as billows of the sea, ¹⁹And your seed is as sand, || And the offspring of your bowels as gravel, || His name would not be cut off nor destroyed before Me." ²⁰Go out from Babylon, flee from the Chaldeans, || Declare with a voice of singing, || Cause this to be heard, || Bring it forth to the end of the earth, || Say, "YHWH has redeemed His servant Jacob." ²¹And they have not thirsted in wastelands, || He has caused them to go on, || He has caused waters from a rock to flow to them, || Indeed, he cleaves a rock, and waters flow. ²²"There is no peace," said YHWH, "for the wicked!"

CHAPTER 49

¹Listen, O islands, to Me, || And attend, O peoples, from afar, || YHWH has called Me from the womb, || From the bowels of My mother || He has made mention of My Name. ²And He makes My mouth as a sharp sword, || He has hid Me in the shadow of His hand, || And He makes Me for a clear arrow, || He has hid Me in His quiver. ³And He says to me, "You are My servant, O Israel, || In whom I beautify Myself." ⁴And I said, "I labored in vain, || I consumed my power for emptiness and vanity, || But my judgment [is] with YHWH, || And my wage with my God." ⁵"And now," said YHWH, who is forming Me from the belly—His Servant, || To bring Jacob back to Him || (Though Israel is not gathered, || Yet I am honored in the eyes of YHWH, || And My God has been My strength). ⁶And He says, "It has been a light thing || That You are My Servant || To raise up the tribes of Jacob, || And to bring back the preserved of Israel, || And I have given You for a light to the nations, || To be My salvation to the end of the earth." ⁷Thus said YHWH, Redeemer of Israel, His Holy One, || To the despised in soul, || To the detested of a nation, || To the Servant of rulers: "Kings see, and have risen, princes, and worship, || For the sake of YHWH, who is faithful, || The Holy of Israel, and He chooses You." ⁸Thus said YHWH: "In a time of good pleasure I answered You, || And in a day of salvation I helped You, || And I keep You, and give You, || For a covenant of the people, || To establish the earth, || To cause to inherit desolate inheritances. ⁹To say to the bound, Go out, || To those in darkness, Be uncovered. They feed on the ways, || And their pasture is in all high places. ¹⁰They do not hunger, nor thirst, || Nor do mirage and sun strike them, || For He who is pitying them leads them, || And tends them by fountains of waters. ¹¹And I have made all My mountains for a way, || And My highways are lifted up. ¹²Behold, these come in from afar, || And behold, these from the north, and from the sea, || And these from the land of Sinim." ¹³Sing, O heavens, and rejoice, O earth, || And break forth, O mountains, with singing, || For YHWH has comforted His people, || And He pities His afflicted ones. ¹⁴And Zion says, "YHWH has forsaken me, || And my Lord has forgotten me." ¹⁵"Does a woman forget her suckling, || The loved one—the son of her womb? Indeed, these forget—but I do not forget you. ¹⁶Behold, I have carved you on the palms of the hand, || Your walls [are] continually before Me. ¹⁷Those building you have hurried, || Those destroying you, and laying you waste, go out from you. ¹⁸Lift up your eyes, [look] around and see, || All of them have been gathered, || They have come to you. [As] I live," a declaration of YHWH! "Surely you put on all of them as an ornament, || And you bind them on like a bride. ¹⁹Because your ruins, and your desolate places, || And the land of your ruins, || Are now surely restricted because of inhabitants, || And those consuming you have been far off. ²⁰Again the sons of your bereavement say in your ears: The place is too narrow for me, || Come near to me—and I dwell. ²¹And you have said in your heart: Who has begotten these for me? And I [am] bereaved and barren, || A captive, and turned aside, || And who has nourished these? Behold, I was left by myself, these—where [are] they from?" ²²Thus said Lord YHWH: "Behold, I lift up My hand to nations, || And I raise up My ensign to peoples, || And they have brought your sons in the bosom, || And your daughters are carried on the shoulder. ²³And kings have been your nursing fathers, || And their princesses—your nursing mothers; Face to the earth—they bow down to you, || And they lick up the dust of your feet, || And you have known that I [am] YHWH, || That those expecting Me are not ashamed." ²⁴Is prey taken from the mighty? And the captive of the righteous delivered? ²⁵For thus said YHWH: "Even the captive of the mighty is taken, || And the prey of the terrible is delivered, || And I strive with your striver, and I save your sons. ²⁶And I have caused your oppressors to eat their own flesh, || And they drink their own blood as new wine, || And all flesh has known that I, YHWH, || Your Savior, and your Redeemer, || [Am] the Mighty One of Jacob!"

CHAPTER 50

¹Thus said YHWH: "Where [is] this—the bill of your mother's divorce, || Whom I sent away? Or to which of My creditors have I sold you? Behold, you have been sold for your iniquities, || And for your transgressions || Your mother has been sent away. ²Why have I come, and there is no one? I called, and there is none answering, || Has My hand been at all short of redemption? And is there not power in Me to deliver? Behold, by My rebuke I dry up a sea, || I make rivers a wilderness, || Their fish stink, for there is no water, || And die with thirst. ³I clothe the heavens [with] blackness, || And I make their covering sackcloth." ⁴Lord YHWH has given to Me || The tongue of taught ones, || To know to aid the weary [by] a word, || He awakens [Me] morning by morning, || He awakens [My] ear to hear as taught ones. ⁵Lord YHWH opened My ear, || And I did not rebel—I did not move backward. ⁶I have given My back to those striking, || And My cheeks to those plucking out, || I did not hide My face from shame and spitting. ⁷And Lord YHWH gives help to Me, || Therefore I have not been ashamed, || Therefore I have set My face as a flint, || And I know that I am not ashamed. ⁸Near [is] He who is justifying Me, || Who contends with Me? We stand together, who [is] My opponent? Let him come near to Me. ⁹Behold, Lord YHWH gives help to Me, || Who [is] he that declares Me wicked? Behold, all of them wear out as a garment, || A moth eats them. ¹⁰"Who [is] among you, fearing YHWH, || Listening to the voice of His Servant, || That has walked in dark places, || And there is no brightness for him? Let him trust in the Name of YHWH, || And lean on his God. ¹¹Behold, all you kindling a fire, girding on sparks, || Walk in the light of your fire, || And in the sparks you have caused to burn, || This has been to you from My hand, || You lie down in grief!"

CHAPTER 51

¹"Listen to Me, you pursuing righteousness, || Seeking YHWH, || Look attentively to the rock—you have been hewn, || And to the hole of the pit—you have been dug. ²Look attentively to your father Abraham, || And to Sarah—she brings you forth, || For—one—I have called him, || And I bless him, and multiply him." ³For YHWH has comforted Zion, || He has comforted all her ruins, || And He sets her wilderness as Eden, || And her desert as a garden of YHWH, || Joy, indeed, gladness is found in her, || Confession, and the voice of

ISAIAH

song. ⁴"Attend to Me, O My people, || And, O My nation, give ear to Me. For a law goes out from Me, || And My judgment to the light, || I cause peoples to rest. ⁵My righteousness [is] near, || My salvation has gone out, || And My arms judge peoples, || Islands wait on Me, || Indeed, on My arm they wait with hope. ⁶Lift up your eyes to the heavens, || And look attentively to the earth beneath, || For the heavens have vanished as smoke, || And the earth wears out as a garment, || And its inhabitants die as gnats, || And My salvation is for all time, || And My righteousness is not broken. ⁷Listen to Me, you who know righteousness, || A people in whose heart [is] My law, || Do not fear the reproach of men, || And do not be frightened of their reviling, ⁸For a moth eats them as a garment, || And a worm eats them as wool, || And My righteousness is for all time, || And My salvation from generation to generation." ⁹Awake, awake, put on strength, O arm of YHWH, || Awake, as [in] days of old, generations of the ages, || Are You not it that is hewing down Rahab, || Piercing a dragon? ¹⁰Are You not it that is drying up a sea, || Waters of a great deep? That has made deep places of a sea || A way for the passing of the redeemed? ¹¹And the ransomed of YHWH return, || And they have come to Zion with singing, || And continuous joy [is] on their head, || They attain gladness and joy, || Sorrow and sighing have fled away, ¹²"I [am] He who comforts you, || Who [are] you—and you are afraid of man? He dies! And of the son of man—he is made [like] grass! ¹³And you forget YHWH your Maker, || Who is stretching out the heavens, and founding earth, || And you continually fear all the day, || Because of the fury of the oppressor, || As he has prepared to destroy. And where [is] the fury of the oppressor? ¹⁴A wanderer has hurried to be loosed, || And he does not die in the pit, || And his bread is not lacking. ¹⁵And I [am] your God YHWH, || Quieting the sea when its billows roar, || YHWH of Hosts [is] His Name. ¹⁶And I put My words in your mouth, || And have covered you with the shadow of My hand, || To plant the heavens, and to found earth, || And to say to Zion, You [are] My people." ¹⁷Stir yourself, stir yourself, rise, Jerusalem, || You who have drunk from the hand of YHWH || The cup of His fury, || The goblet, the cup of trembling, you have drunk, || You have wrung out. ¹⁸There is not a leader to her || Out of all the sons she has borne, || And there is none laying hold on her hand || Out of all the sons she has nourished. ¹⁹These two are meeting you, || Who is moved for you? Spoiling and destruction, famine and sword! By whom do I comfort you? ²⁰Your sons have been wrapped up, they have lain down, || At the head of all out places, as an antelope [in] a dragnet, || They are full of the fury of YHWH, || The rebuke of Your God. ²¹Therefore, please hear this, || O afflicted and drunken one, and not with wine, ²²Thus said your Lord YHWH, and your God, || He pleads [for] His people: "Behold, I have taken the cup of trembling out of your hand, || The goblet, the cup of My fury, || You do not add to drink it anymore. ²³And I have put it into the hand of those afflicting you, || Who have said to your soul, || Bow down, and we pass over, || And you make your body as the earth, || And as the street to those passing by!"

CHAPTER 52

¹Awake, awake, put on your strength, O Zion, || Put on the garments of your beauty, Jerusalem—the Holy City; For the uncircumcised and unclean no longer enter into you again. ²Shake yourself from dust, arise, sit, O Jerusalem, || Bands of your neck have loosed themselves, || O captive daughter of Zion. ³For thus said YHWH: "You have been sold for nothing, || And you are redeemed without money." ⁴For thus said Lord YHWH: "My people went down at first || To Egypt to sojourn there, || And Asshur—he has oppressed it for nothing. ⁵And now, what [have] I here," || A declaration of YHWH, || "That My people are taken for nothing? Its rulers cause howling," || A declaration of YHWH, || "And My Name is continually despised all the day. ⁶Therefore My people know My Name, || Therefore, in that day, || Surely I [am] He who is speaking, behold Me." ⁷How lovely on the mountains, || Have been the feet of one proclaiming tidings, || Sounding peace, proclaiming good tidings, || Sounding salvation, || Saying to Zion, "Your God has reigned." ⁸The voice of your watchmen! They have lifted up the voice, together they cry aloud, || Because they see eye to eye, || In YHWH's turning back [to] Zion. ⁹Break forth, sing together, || O ruins of Jerusalem, || For YHWH has comforted His people, || He has redeemed Jerusalem. ¹⁰YHWH has made His holy arm bare || Before the eyes of all the nations, || And all the ends of the earth have seen || The salvation of our God. ¹¹Turn aside, turn aside, go out from there, || Do not touch the unclean, || Go out from her midst, || Be pure, who are carrying the weapons of YHWH. ¹²For you do not go out in haste, || Indeed, you do not go on with flight, || For YHWH [is] going before you, || And the God of Israel [is] gathering you! ¹³"Behold, My Servant acts wisely, || He is high, and has been lifted up, || And has been very high." ¹⁴As many have been astonished at You || (His appearance so marred by man, || And His form by sons of men), ¹⁵So He sprinkles many nations. Kings shut their mouth concerning Him, || For that which was not recounted to them they have seen, || And that which they had not heard they have understood!

CHAPTER 53

¹Who has given credence to that which we heard? And the arm of YHWH, || On whom has it been revealed? ²Indeed, He comes up as a tender plant before Him, || And as a root out of dry land, || He has no form or splendor when we observe Him, || Nor appearance, that we desire Him. ³He is despised, and left of men, || A Man of pains, and acquainted with sickness, || And as one hiding the face from us, || He is despised, and we did not esteem Him. ⁴Surely He has borne our sicknesses, || And our pains—He has carried them, || And we have esteemed Him [as] plagued, struck of God, and afflicted. ⁵And He is pierced for our transgressions, bruised for our iniquities, || The discipline of our peace [is] on Him, || And by His scourging we are healed. ⁶All of us, like sheep, have wandered, || Man has turned to his own way, || And YHWH has laid on Him the punishment of us all. ⁷It has been exacted, and He has answered, || And He does not open His mouth, || He is brought as a lamb to the slaughter, || And as a sheep before its shearers is silent, || So He does not open His mouth. ⁸By restraint and by judgment He has been taken, || And of His generation who meditates, || That He has been cut off from the land of the living? He is plagued by the transgression of My people, ⁹And He appoints His grave with the wicked, || And with the rich at His death, || Because He has done no violence, || Nor [is] deceit in His mouth. ¹⁰And YHWH has delighted to crush Him, || He has made Him sick; If His soul makes an offering for guilt, || He sees [His] seed—He prolongs [His] days, || And the pleasure of YHWH prospers in His hand. ¹¹Of the labor of His soul He sees—He is satisfied, || Through His knowledge My Righteous Servant gives righteousness to many, || And He bears their iniquities. ¹²Therefore I give a portion to Him among the many, || And He apportions spoil with the mighty, || Because that He exposed His soul to death, || And He was numbered with transgressors, || And He has borne the sin of many, || And He intercedes for transgressors.

CHAPTER 54

¹"Sing, O barren, she [who] has not borne! Break forth with singing, and cry aloud, || She [who] has not brought forth! For more [are] the sons of the desolate, || Than the sons of the married one," said YHWH. ²"Enlarge the place of your tent, || And they stretch out the curtains of your dwelling places, || Do not restrain—lengthen your cords, || And make your pins strong. ³For you break forth right and left, || And nations possess your seed, ⁴And they cause desolate cities to be inhabited. Do not fear, for you are not ashamed, || Nor blush, for you are not confounded, || For you forget the shame of your youth, || And the reproach of your widowhood || You do not remember anymore. ⁵For your Maker [is] your husband, || YHWH of Hosts [is] His Name, || And your Redeemer [is] the Holy One of Israel, || He is called God of all the earth. ⁶For as a woman forsaken and grieved in spirit, || YHWH has called you, || Even a youthful wife when she is refused," said your God. ⁷"In a small moment I have forsaken you, || And in great mercies I gather you, ⁸In overflowing wrath I hid My face [for] a moment from you, || And in

ISAIAH

perpetual kindness I have loved you, || Said your Redeemer—YHWH! ⁹For this [is as] the days of Noah to Me, || In that I have sworn that the waters of Noah || Do not pass over the earth again—So I have sworn, || Wrath is not on you, || Nor rebuke against you. ¹⁰For the mountains depart, and the hills remove, || And My kindness does not depart from you, || And the covenant of My peace does not remove," || Says YHWH, your loving one. ¹¹"O afflicted, storm-tossed, not comforted, || Behold, I am laying your stones with cement, || And have founded you with sapphires, ¹²And have made your pinnacles of agate, || And your gates of carbuncle stones, || And all your border of stones of delight, ¹³And all your sons are taught of YHWH, || And the peace of your sons [is] abundant. ¹⁴You establish yourself in righteousness, || Be far from oppression, for you do not fear, || And from ruin, for it does not come near to you. ¹⁵Behold, he diligently assembles without My desire, || Whoever has assembled near you falls by you! ¹⁶Behold, I have created an artisan, || Blowing on a fire of coals, || And bringing out an instrument for his work, || And I have created a destroyer to destroy. ¹⁷No weapon formed against you prospers, || And every tongue rising against you, || You condemn in judgment. This [is] the inheritance of the servants of YHWH, || And their righteousness from Me," a declaration of YHWH!

CHAPTER 55

¹"Behold, every thirsty one, || Come to the waters, || And he who has no money, || Come, buy and eat, || Indeed, come, buy wine and milk || Without money and without price. ²Why do you weigh money for that which is not bread? And your labor for that which is not for satiety? Listen diligently to Me, and eat good, || And your soul delights itself in fatness. ³Incline your ear, and come to Me, || Hear, and your soul lives, || And I make a perpetual covenant for you, || The kind blessings of David that are steadfast. ⁴Behold, I have given him [as] a witness to peoples, || A leader and commander to peoples. ⁵Behold, a nation you do not know, you call, || And a nation who does not know you runs to you, || For the sake of your God YHWH, || And for the Holy One of Israel, || Because He has beautified you." ⁶Seek YHWH while He may be found, || Call Him while He is near, ⁷Let the wicked forsake his way, || And the man of iniquity his thoughts, || And he returns to YHWH, || And He pities him, || And to our God, || For He multiplies to pardon. ⁸"For My thoughts [are] not your thoughts, || Nor your ways My ways," || A declaration of YHWH, ⁹"For [as] high [as] the heavens have been above the earth, || So high have been My ways above your ways, || And My thoughts above your thoughts. ¹⁰For as the shower comes down, || And the snow from the heavens, || And does not return there, || But has watered the earth, || And has caused it to yield, and to spring up, || And has given seed to the sower, and bread to the eater, ¹¹So is My word that goes out of My mouth, || It does not return to Me empty, || But has done that which I desired, || And prosperously effected that [for] which I sent it. ¹²For you go forth with joy, || And you are brought in with peace, || The mountains and the hills || Break forth before you [with] singing, || And all trees of the field clap the hand. ¹³Instead of the thorn comes up fir, || Instead of the brier comes up myrtle, || And it has been to YHWH for a name, || For a perpetual sign—it is not cut off!"

CHAPTER 56

¹Thus said YHWH: "Keep judgment, and do righteousness, || For My salvation [is] near to come, || And My righteousness to be revealed." ²O the blessedness of a man who does this, || And of a son of man who keeps hold on it, || Keeping the Sabbath from defiling it, || And keeping his hand from doing any evil. ³Do not let a son of the stranger speak, || Who is joined to YHWH, saying, "YHWH certainly separates me from His people." Nor let the eunuch say, "Behold, I am a dried up tree," ⁴For thus said YHWH: "To the eunuchs who keep My Sabbaths, || And have fixed on that which I desired, || And are keeping hold on My covenant: ⁵I have given to them in My house, || And within My walls a station and a name, || Better than sons and than daughters, || I give a continuous name to him || That is not cut off. ⁶And sons of the stranger, who are joined to YHWH, || To serve Him, and to love the Name of YHWH, || To be for servants to Him, || All keeping from defiling the Sabbath, || And those keeping hold on My covenant, ⁷I have brought them to My holy mountain, || And caused them to rejoice in My house of prayer, || Their burnt-offerings and their sacrifices || [Are] for a pleasing thing on My altar, || For My house is called a house of prayer for all the peoples." ⁸A declaration of Lord YHWH, || Who is gathering the outcasts of Israel: "Again I gather to him—to his gathered ones." ⁹Every beast of the field, || Come to devour, every beast in the forest. ¹⁰His watchmen [are] blind—all of them, || They have not known, || All of them [are] mute dogs, they are not able to bark, || Dozing, lying down, loving to slumber. ¹¹And the dogs [are] strong of desire, || They have not known sufficiency, || And they [are] shepherds! They have not known understanding, || All of them turned to their own way, || Each to his dishonest gain from his quarter: ¹²"Come, I take wine, || And we drink, gulp strong drink, || And tomorrow has been as this day, || Great—exceedingly abundant!"

CHAPTER 57

¹The righteous has perished, || And there is none laying [it] to heart, || And men of kindness are gathered, || Without any considering that from the face of evil || The righteous one is gathered. ²He enters into peace, they rest on their beds, || [Each] is going straightforward. ³"And you, come near here, || O sons of a sorceress, seed of an adulterer, || Even you commit whoredom. ⁴Against whom do you sport yourselves? Against whom do you enlarge the mouth || [And] prolong the tongue? Are you not children of transgression? A false seed? ⁵Who are inflamed among oaks, under every green tree, || Slaughtering the children in valleys, || Under clefts of the rocks. ⁶Your portion [is] among the smooth things of a brook, || They [are] your lot, || You have also poured out an oblation to them, || You have caused a present to ascend, || Am I comforted in these things? ⁷On a mountain, high and exalted, || You have set your bed, || You have also gone up there to make a sacrifice. ⁸And behind the door, and the post, || You have set up your memorial, || For you have removed from Me, and go up, || You have enlarged your bed, || And cut [a covenant] with them, || You have loved their bed, the station you saw, ⁹And go joyfully to the king in ointment, || And multiply your perfumes, || And send your ambassadors far off, || And humble yourself to Sheol. ¹⁰You have labored in the greatness of your way, || You have not said, It is desperate. You have found the life of your hand, || Therefore you have not been sick. ¹¹And of whom have you been afraid, and fear, || That you lie, and have not remembered Me? You have not laid [it] to your heart, || Am I not silent, even from of old? And you do not fear Me? ¹²I declare your righteousness, and your works, || And they do not profit you. ¹³When you cry, let your gatherings deliver you, || And wind carries all of them away, || Vanity takes away, || And whoever is trusting in Me inherits the land, || And possesses My holy mountain." ¹⁴And He has said, "Raise up, raise up, prepare a way, || Lift a stumbling-block out of the way of My people." ¹⁵For thus said the high and exalted One, || Inhabiting eternity, and His Name [is] holy: "I dwell in the high and holy place, || And with the bruised and humble of spirit, || To revive the spirit of the humble, || And to revive the heart of bruised ones, ¹⁶For I do not strive for all time, nor am I angry forever, || For the spirit is feeble before Me, || And the souls I have made. ¹⁷For the iniquity of his dishonest gain, || I have been angry, and I strike him, || Hiding—and am angry, || And he goes on turning back in the way of his heart. ¹⁸I have seen his ways, and I heal him, indeed, I lead him, || And repay comforts to him and to his mourning ones. ¹⁹Producing the fruit of the lips, || Peace, peace, to the far off, and to the near, || And I have healed him," said YHWH. ²⁰And the wicked [are] as the driven out sea, || For it is not able to rest, || And its waters cast out filth and mire. ²¹"There is no peace," said my God, "for the wicked!"

CHAPTER 58

¹"Call with the throat, do not restrain, lift up your voice as a horn, || And declare to My people their transgression, || And to the house of Jacob their sins; ²They seek Me day by day, || And they desire the knowledge of My ways, || As a nation that has done righteousness, || And has not forsaken the judgment of its God, || They ask of Me judgments of righteousness, || They desire the drawing near of God: ³Why have we fasted, and You have not seen? We have afflicted our soul, and You do not know. Behold, you find pleasure in the day of your

ISAIAH

fast, || And exact all your laborers. ⁴Behold, you fast for strife and debate, || And to strike with the fist of wickedness, || You do not fast as [this] day, || To sound your voice in the high place. ⁵Is this like the fast that I choose? The day of a man's afflicting his soul? To bow his head as a reed, || And spread out sackcloth and ashes? Do you call this a fast, || And a desirable day—to YHWH? ⁶Is this not the fast that I chose—To loose the bands of wickedness, || To shake off the burdens of the yoke, || And to send out the oppressed free, || And draw off every yoke? ⁷Is it not to deal your bread to the hungry, || And bring home the wandering poor, || That you see the naked and cover him, || And do not hide yourself from your own flesh? ⁸Then your light breaks forth as the dawn, || And your health springs up in haste, || Your righteousness has gone before you, || The glory of YHWH gathers you. ⁹Then you call, and YHWH answers, || You cry, and He says, Behold Me. If you turn aside the yoke from your midst, || The sending forth of the finger, || And the speaking of vanity, ¹⁰And bring out your soul to the hungry, || And satisfy the afflicted soul, || Then your light has risen in the darkness, || And your thick darkness [is] as noon. ¹¹And YHWH continually leads you, || And has satisfied your soul in drought, || And He arms your bones, || And you have been as a watered garden, || And as an outlet of waters, whose waters do not lie. ¹²And they have built the ancient ruins from you, || You raise up the foundations of many generations, || And one calls you, Repairer of the breach, || Restorer of paths to rest in. ¹³If you turn your foot from the Sabbath, || [From] doing your own pleasure on My holy day, || And have cried to the Sabbath, A delight, || To the holy of YHWH, Honored, || And have honored it, without doing your own ways, || Without finding your own pleasure, || And speaking a word. ¹⁴Then you delight yourself on YHWH, || And I have caused you to ride on high places of earth, || And have caused you to eat the inheritance of your father Jacob, || For the mouth of YHWH has spoken!"

CHAPTER 59

¹Behold, the hand of YHWH || Has not been shortened from saving, || Nor His ear heavy from hearing. ²But your iniquities have been separating || Between you and your God, || And your sins have hidden || The Presence from you—from hearing. ³For your hands have been defiled with blood, || And your fingers with iniquity, || Your lips have spoken falsehood, || Your tongue mutters perverseness. ⁴There is none calling in righteousness, || And there is none pleading in faithfulness, || Trusting on emptiness, and speaking falsehood, || Conceiving perverseness, and bearing iniquity. ⁵They have hatched eggs of a viper, || And weave webs of a spider, || Whoever is eating their eggs dies, and the crushed hatches a viper. ⁶Their webs do not become a garment, || Nor do they cover themselves with their works, || Their works [are] works of iniquity, || And a deed of violence [is] in their hands. ⁷Their feet run to evil, || And they hurry to shed innocent blood, || Their thoughts [are] thoughts of iniquity, || Spoiling and destruction [are] in their highways. ⁸They have not known a way of peace, || And there is no judgment in their paths, || They have made their paths perverse for themselves, || None treading in it has known peace. ⁹Therefore judgment has been far from us, || And righteousness does not reach us, || We wait for light, and behold, darkness, || For brightness—in thick darkness we go, ¹⁰We feel [for] the wall like the blind, || Indeed, we feel as without eyes, || We have stumbled at noon as at twilight, || In desolate places as the dead. ¹¹We make a noise as bears—all of us, || And we coo severely as doves; We wait for judgment, and there is none, || For salvation—it has been far from us. ¹²For our transgressions have been multiplied before You, || And our sins have testified against us, || For our transgressions [are] with us, || And our iniquities—we have known them. ¹³Transgressing, and lying against YHWH, || And removing from after our God, || Speaking oppression and apostasy, || Conceiving and uttering from the heart || Words of falsehood. ¹⁴And judgment is removed backward, || And righteousness stands far off, || For truth has been feeble in the street, || And straightforwardness is not able to enter, ¹⁵And the truth is lacking, || And whoever is turning aside from evil, || Is making himself a spoil. And YHWH sees, and it is evil in His eyes, || That there is no judgment. ¹⁶And He sees that there is no man, || And is astonished that there is no intercessor, || And His own arm gives salvation to Him, || And His righteousness—it sustained Him. ¹⁷And He puts on righteousness as a breastplate, || And a helmet of salvation on His head, || And He puts on garments of vengeance [for] clothing, || And is covered, as [with] an upper-robe, [with] zeal. ¹⁸According to deeds—so He repays. Fury to His adversaries, [their] deed to His enemies, || To the islands He repays [their] deed. ¹⁹And from the west they fear the Name of YHWH, || And from the rising of the sun—His glory, || When an adversary comes in as a flood, || The Spirit of YHWH has raised an ensign against him. ²⁰"And the Redeemer has come to Zion, || Even to captives of transgression in Jacob," || A declaration of YHWH. ²¹"And I—this [is] My covenant with them," said YHWH, "My Spirit that [is] on you, || And My words that I have put in your mouth, || Do not depart from your mouth, || And from the mouth of your seed, || And from the mouth of your seed's seed," said YHWH, "From now on, even for all time!"

CHAPTER 60

¹Arise, shine, for your light has come, || And the glory of YHWH has risen on you. ²For behold, the darkness covers the earth, || And thick darkness the peoples, || And YHWH rises on you, || And His glory is seen on you. ³And nations have come to your light, || And kings to the brightness of your rising. ⁴"Lift up your eyes around and see, || All of them have been gathered, they have come to you, || Your sons come from afar, || And your daughters are supported on the side. ⁵Then you see, and have become bright, || And your heart has been afraid and enlarged, || For the multitude of the sea turn to you, || The forces of nations come to you. ⁶A multitude of camels covers you, || Dromedaries of Midian and Ephah, || All of them from Sheba come, || They carry gold and frankincense, || And they proclaim the praises of YHWH. ⁷All the flock of Kedar are gathered to you, || The rams of Nebaioth serve you, || They ascend My altar for acceptance, || And I beautify the house of My beauty. ⁸Who [are] these—they fly as a thick cloud, || And as doves to their windows? ⁹Surely islands wait for Me, || And ships of Tarshish first, || To bring your sons from afar, || Their silver and their gold with them, || To the Name of your God YHWH, || And to the Holy One of Israel, || Because He has beautified you. ¹⁰And sons of a stranger have built your walls, || And their kings serve you, || For in My wrath I have struck you, || And in My good pleasure I have pitied you. ¹¹And your gates have continually opened, || They are not shut by day and by night, || To bring the force of nations to you, || Even their kings are led. ¹²For the nation and the kingdom that does not serve you perishes, || Indeed, the nations are utterly desolated. ¹³The glory of Lebanon comes to you, || Fir, pine, and box together, || To beautify the place of My sanctuary, || And I make the place of My feet honorable. ¹⁴And the sons of those afflicting you || Have come to you, bowing down, || And all despising you || Have bowed themselves to the soles of your feet, || And they have cried to you: The City of YHWH, || Zion of the Holy One of Israel! ¹⁵Instead of your being forsaken and hated, || And none passing through, || I have made you for a continuous excellence, || A joy of generation and generation. ¹⁶And you have sucked the milk of nations, || Indeed, you suckle the breast of kings, || And you have known that I, YHWH, Your Savior, and Your Redeemer, || [Am] the Mighty One of Jacob. ¹⁷Instead of the bronze I bring in gold, || And instead of the iron I bring in silver, || And instead of the wood bronze, || And instead of the stone iron, || And I have made your inspection peace, || And your exactors righteousness. ¹⁸Violence is not heard in your land anymore, || Spoiling and destruction in your borders, || And you have called your walls Salvation, || And your gates Praise. ¹⁹The sun is no longer your light by day, || And for brightness the moon does not give light to you, || And YHWH has become to you || A continuous light, and your God your beauty. ²⁰Your sun goes in no more, || And your moon is not removed, || For YHWH becomes a continuous light to you. And the days of your mourning have been completed. ²¹And all your people [are] righteous, || They possess the earth for all time, || A branch of My planting, || A work of My hands, to be beautified. ²²The little one becomes a chief, || And the small one a mighty nation, || I, YHWH, hurry it in its own time!"

ISAIAH

CHAPTER 61

¹"[The] Spirit of Lord Y‍HWH [is] on Me, || Because Y‍HWH anointed Me || To proclaim tidings to the humble, || He sent Me to bind the broken of heart, || To proclaim liberty to the captives, || And an opening of bands to [those] bound. ²To proclaim the year of the favor of Y‍HWH, || And the day of vengeance of our God, || To comfort all mourners. ³To appoint to mourners in Zion, || To give to them beauty instead of ashes, || The oil of joy instead of mourning, || A covering of praise for a faded spirit, || And He is calling to them, Trees of righteousness, || The planting of Y‍HWH—to be beautified." ⁴And they have built the ancient ruins, || They raise up the desolations of the ancients, || And they have renewed ruined cities, || The desolations of generation and generation. ⁵And strangers have stood and fed your flock, || And the sons of a foreigner || [Are] your farmers and your vinedressers. ⁶And you are called priests of Y‍HWH, || It is said of you [that you are] ministers of our God, || You consume the strength of nations, || And you boast yourselves in their glory. ⁷Instead of your shame—double [honor], || And [instead of] confusion, || They rejoice in their portion, || Therefore they take possession in their land a second time, || Continuous joy [is] for them. ⁸"For I [am] Y‍HWH, loving judgment, || Hating plunder for a burnt-offering, || And I have given their wage in truth, || And I make a perpetual covenant for them. ⁹And their seed has been known among the nations, || And their offspring in the midst of the peoples, || All their beholders acknowledge them, || For they [are] a seed Y‍HWH has blessed." ¹⁰I greatly rejoice in Y‍HWH, || My soul rejoices in my God, || For He clothed me with garments of salvation, || [And] covered me with a robe of righteousness, || As a bridegroom prepares ornaments, || And as a bride puts on her jewels. ¹¹For as the earth brings forth her shoots, || And as a garden causes its sown things to shoot up, || So Lord Y‍HWH causes righteousness and praise || To shoot up before all the nations!

CHAPTER 62

¹For Zion's sake I am not silent, || And for Jerusalem's sake I do not rest, || Until her righteousness goes out as brightness, || And her salvation burns as a torch. ²And nations have seen your righteousness, || And all kings your glory, || And He is giving a new name to you, || That the mouth of Y‍HWH defines. ³And you have been a crown of beauty in the hand of Y‍HWH, || And a turban of royalty in the hand of your God, ⁴It is not said of you anymore, "Forsaken!" And of your land it is not said anymore, "Desolate," || For to you is cried, "My delight [is] in her," || And to your land, "Married," || For Y‍HWH has delighted in you, || And your land is married. ⁵For a young man marries a virgin, || Your builders marry you, || With the joy of a bridegroom over a bride, || Your God rejoices over you. ⁶"On your walls, O Jerusalem, I have appointed watchmen, || All the day and all the night, || Continually, they are not silent." O you remembering Y‍HWH, do not keep silence for yourselves, ⁷And do not give silence to Him, || Until He establishes, and until He makes Jerusalem a praise in the earth. ⁸Y‍HWH has sworn by His right hand, || Even by the arm of His strength: "I do not give your grain anymore [as] food for your enemies, || Nor do sons of a stranger drink your new wine, || For which you have labored. ⁹For those gathering it eat it, and have praised Y‍HWH, || And those collecting it drink it in My holy courts." ¹⁰Pass on, pass on through the gates, || Prepare the way of the people, || Raise up, raise up the highway, clear it from stones, || Lift up an ensign over the peoples. ¹¹Behold, Y‍HWH has proclaimed to the end of the earth: "Say to the daughter of Zion, || Behold, your salvation has come, || Behold, His hire [is] with Him, || And His wage before Him." ¹²And they have cried to them, "The People of the Holy One! The Redeemed of Y‍HWH!" Indeed, to you is called, "The sought out one, a city not forsaken!"

CHAPTER 63

¹Who [is] this coming from Edom? With dyed garments from Bozrah? This that is honorable in His clothing, || Traveling in the abundance of His power? "I, speaking in righteousness, mighty to save." ²Why [is] Your clothing red? And Your garments as treading in a winepress? ³"I have trodden a wine vat by Myself, || And of the peoples there is no one with Me, || And I tread them in My anger, || And I trample them in My fury, || Their strength is sprinkled on My garments, || And I have defiled all My clothing. ⁴For the day of vengeance [is] in My heart, || And the year of My redeemed has come. ⁵And I look attentively, and there is none helping, || And I am astonished that there is none supporting, || And My own arm gives salvation to Me. And My wrath—it has supported Me. ⁶And I tread down peoples in My anger, || And I make them drunk in My fury, || And I bring down their strength to earth." ⁷I make mention of the kind acts of Y‍HWH, || The praises of Y‍HWH, || According to all that Y‍HWH has done for us, || And the abundance of the goodness to the house of Israel, || That He has done for them, || According to His mercies, || And according to the abundance of His kind acts. ⁸And He says, "Surely they [are] My people, || Sons—they do not lie," and He is to them for a Savior. ⁹In all their distress [He is] no adversary, || And the Messenger of His Presence saved them, || In His love and in His pity He redeemed them, || And He lifts them up, || And carries them all the days of old. ¹⁰And they have been rebellious and have grieved His Holy Spirit, || And He turns to them for an enemy, || He Himself has fought against them. ¹¹And He remembers the days of old, || Moses—his people. Where [is] He who is bringing them up from the sea, || The shepherd of His flock? Where [is] He who is putting in its midst His Holy Spirit? ¹²Leading by the right hand of Moses, the arm of His glory, || Cleaving waters from before them, || To make to Himself a continuous Name. ¹³Leading them through the depths, || They do not stumble as a horse in a plain. ¹⁴As a beast goes down into a valley, || The Spirit of Y‍HWH causes him to rest, || So You have led Your people, || To make to Yourself a glorious Name. ¹⁵Look attentively from the heavens, || And see from Your holy and beautiful habitation, || Where [is] Your zeal and Your might? The multitude of Your bowels and Your mercies—Are they restrained? ¹⁶For You [are] our Father, || For Abraham has not known us, || And Israel does not acknowledge us, || You, O Y‍HWH, [are] our Father, || Our Redeemer from the Age, [is] Your Name. ¹⁷Why cause us to wander, O Y‍HWH, from Your ways? You harden our heart from Your fear, || Turn back for Your servants' sake, || The tribes of Your inheritance. ¹⁸For a little while Your holy people possessed, || Our adversaries have trodden down Your sanctuary. ¹⁹We have been from of old, || You have not ruled over them, || Your Name is not called on them!

CHAPTER 64

¹Did You not tear the heavens? You came down, || Mountains flowed from Your presence, ²(As fire kindles stubble—Fire causes water to boil), || To make Your Name known to Your adversaries, || Nations tremble from Your presence. ³In Your doing fearful things [that] we do not expect, || You came down, || Mountains flowed from Your presence. ⁴Even from antiquity [men] have not heard, || They have not given ear, || Eye has not seen a God except You, || He works for those waiting for Him. ⁵You have met with the rejoicer || And the doer of righteousness, || In Your ways they remember You, || Behold, You have been angry when we sin, || By them [is] continuance, and we are saved. ⁶And we are as unclean—all of us, || And all our righteous acts [are] as garments of menstruation; And we fade as a leaf—all of us. And our iniquities take us away as wind. ⁷And there is none calling on Your Name, || Stirring himself up to lay hold on You, || For You have hid Your face from us, || And You melt us away by our iniquities. ⁸And now, O Y‍HWH, You [are] our Father, || We [are] the clay, and You [are] our Framer, || And the work of Your hand—all of us. ⁹Do not be angry, O Y‍HWH, very severely, || Nor remember iniquity forever, || Behold, look attentively, we implore You, || We [are] all Your people. ¹⁰Your holy cities have been a wilderness, || Zion has been a wilderness, || Jerusalem a desolation. ¹¹Our holy and our beautiful house, || Where our fathers praised You, || Has become burned with fire, || And all our desirable things have become a ruin. ¹²Do You refrain Yourself for these, Y‍HWH? You are silent, and afflict us very severely!

CHAPTER 65

¹"I have been inquired of by those who did not ask, || I have been found by those who did not seek Me, || I have said, Behold Me, behold Me, || To a nation not calling on My Name. ²I have spread out My hands all the day || To an apostate people, || Who are going in the way [that is] not good, || After their own thoughts. ³The people who are continually provoking

ISAIAH

Me to anger, || To My face, || Sacrificing in gardens, and making incense on the bricks: ⁴Who are dwelling among tombs, || And lodge in reserved places, || Who are eating flesh of the sow, || And a piece of abominations—their vessels. ⁵Who are saying, Keep to yourself, do not come near to me, || For I have declared you unholy. These [are] smoke in My anger, || A fire burning all the day. ⁶Behold, it is written before Me: I am not silent, but have repaid; And I have repaid into their bosom, ⁷Your iniquities, and the iniquities of your fathers together," said YHWH, "Who have made incense on the mountains, || And have reproached Me on the heights, || And I have measured their former work into their bosom." ⁸Thus said YHWH: "As the new wine is found in the cluster, || And one has said, Do not destroy it for a blessing [is] in it, || So I do for My servants' sake, || Not to destroy the whole. ⁹And I have brought out a Seed from Jacob, || And from Judah a Possessor of My mountain, || And My chosen ones possess it, || And My servants dwell there. ¹⁰And Sharon has been for the habitation of a flock, || And the Valley of Achor for the lying down of a herd, || For My people who have sought Me. ¹¹And you [are] those forsaking YHWH, || Who are forgetting My holy mountain, || Who are setting a table in array for Gad, || And who are filling a mixture for Meni. ¹²And I have numbered you for the sword, || And all of you bow down for slaughter, || Because I called, and you have not answered, || I have spoken, and you have not listened, || And you do evil in My eyes, || And on that which I did not desire—fixed." ¹³Therefore, thus said Lord YHWH: "Behold, My servants eat, and you hunger, || Behold, My servants drink, and you thirst, || Behold, My servants rejoice, and you are ashamed, ¹⁴Behold, My servants sing from joy of heart, || And you cry from pain of heart, || And you howl from breaking of spirit. ¹⁵And you have left your name || For an oath for My chosen ones, || And Lord YHWH has put you to death, || And He gives another name to His servants; ¹⁶So that he who is blessing himself in the earth, || Blesses himself in the God of faithfulness, || And he who is swearing in the earth, || Swears by the God of faithfulness, || Because the former distresses have been forgotten, || And because they have been hid from My eyes. ¹⁷For behold, I am creating new heavens and a new earth, || And the former things are not remembered, || Nor do they ascend on the heart. ¹⁸But rejoice, and rejoice forever, that I [am] Creator, || For behold, I am creating Jerusalem [to be] a rejoicing, || And her people a joy. ¹⁹And I have rejoiced in Jerusalem, || And have rejoiced in My people, || And the voice of weeping is not heard in her anymore, and the voice of crying. ²⁰There is not a suckling of [mere] days there anymore, || And an aged man who does not complete his days, || For the youth dies one hundred years old, || And the sinner, one hundred years old, is lightly esteemed. ²¹And they have built houses, and inhabited, || And planted vineyards, and eaten their fruit. ²²They do not build, and another inhabit, || They do not plant, and another eat, || For as the days of a tree [are] the days of My people, || And My chosen wear out the work of their hands. ²³They do not labor for a vain thing, || Nor do they bring forth for trouble, || For they [are] the seed of the blessed of YHWH, || And their offspring with them. ²⁴And it has come to pass, || They do not yet call, and I answer, || They are yet speaking, and I hear. ²⁵Wolf and lamb feed as one, || And a lion eats straw as an ox, || As for the serpent—its food [is] dust, || They do no evil, nor destroy, || In all My holy mountain," said YHWH!

CHAPTER 66

¹Thus said YHWH: "The heavens [are] My throne, || And the earth My footstool, || Where [is] this—the house that you build for Me? And where [is] this—the place—My rest? ²And My hand has made all these, || And all these things are," || A declaration of YHWH! "And to this one I look attentively, || To the humble and bruised in spirit, || And who is trembling at My word. ³Whoever slaughters the ox strikes a man, || Whoever sacrifices the lamb beheads a dog, || Whoever is bringing up a present—The blood of a sow, || Whoever is making mention of frankincense, || Is blessing iniquity. Indeed, they have fixed on their own ways, || And their soul has delighted in their abominations. ⁴I also—I fix on their distress, || And I bring in their fears to them, || Because I have called, and there is none answering, || I spoke, and they have not listened, || And they do evil in My eyes, || And on that which I did not desire—fixed." ⁵Hear a word of YHWH, || You who are trembling at His word: "Your brothers who are hating you, || Who are driving you out for My Name's sake, have said, || YHWH is honored, and we look on your joy, || But they are ashamed." ⁶A voice of noise from the city, || A voice from the temple, || The voice of YHWH, || Giving repayment to His enemies. ⁷"Before she is pained she has brought forth, || Before a pang comes to her, || She has delivered a male. ⁸Who has heard anything like this? Who has seen anything like these? Is earth caused to bring forth in one day? Is a nation born at once? For she has been pained, || Zion has also borne her sons. ⁹Do I bring to the birth, || And not cause to bring forth?" says YHWH, || "Am I not He who is causing to beget? I have also restrained," said your God. ¹⁰"Rejoice with Jerusalem, || And be glad in her, all you loving her, || Rejoice with her for joy, || All you who are mourning for her, ¹¹So that you suckle, and have been satisfied, || From the breast of her consolations, || So that you wring out, and have delighted yourselves || From the abundance of her glory." ¹²For thus said YHWH: "Behold, I am stretching out to her peace as a river, || And the glory of nations as an overflowing stream, || And you have sucked, || You are carried on the side, || And you are dandled on the knees. ¹³As one whom his mother comforts, so do I comfort you, || Indeed, you are comforted in Jerusalem." ¹⁴And you have seen, and your heart has rejoiced, || And your bones flourish as tender grass, || And the hand of YHWH has been known to His servants, || And He has been indignant with His enemies. ¹⁵For behold, YHWH comes in fire, || And His chariots as a windstorm, || To refresh His anger in fury, || And His rebuke in flames of fire. ¹⁶For by fire and by His sword, || YHWH does judgment with all flesh. And many have been YHWH's pierced ones. ¹⁷"Those sanctifying and cleansing themselves [to go] to the gardens, || One after another in the midst, || Eating flesh of the sow, || And of the abomination, and of the muroid, || Are consumed together," || A declaration of YHWH. ¹⁸"And I—their works and their thoughts, || I come to gather all the nations and tongues, || And they have come and seen My glory. ¹⁹And I have set a sign among them, || And have sent out of them those escaping to the nations || (Tarshish, Pul, and Lud, drawing bow, Tubal and Javan, the islands that are far off), || Who have not heard My fame, nor seen My glory, || And they have declared My glory among nations. ²⁰And they have brought all your brothers out of all the nations, || A present to YHWH, || On horses, and on chariot, and on litters, || And on mules, and on dromedaries, || To My holy mountain Jerusalem," said YHWH, "As the sons of Israel bring the present in a clean vessel, || Into the house of YHWH. ²¹And I also take of them for priests, || For Levites," said YHWH. ²²"For as the new heavens and the new earth that I am making, || Are standing before Me," || A declaration of YHWH, || "So your seed and your name remain. ²³And it has been from month to month, || And from Sabbath to Sabbath, || All flesh come to bow themselves before Me," said YHWH. ²⁴"And they have gone forth, || And looked on the carcasses of the men || Who are transgressing against Me, || For their worm does not die, || And their fire is not quenched, || And they have been an abhorrence to all flesh!"

JEREMIAH

CHAPTER 1

¹Words of Jeremiah son of Hilkiah, of the priests who [are] in Anathoth, in the land of Benjamin, ²to whom the word of Yhwh has been in the days of Josiah son of Amon, king of Judah, in the thirteenth year of his reign, ³and it is in the days of Jehoiakim son of Josiah, king of Judah, until the completion of the eleventh year of Zedekiah son of Josiah, king of Judah, until the expulsion of Jerusalem in the fifth month. ⁴And there is a word of Yhwh to me, saying, ⁵"Before I form you in the belly, I have known you; and before you come forth from the womb I have separated you; I have made you a prophet to the nations." ⁶And I say, "Aah! Lord Yhwh! Behold, I have not known—to speak, for I [am] a youth." ⁷And Yhwh says to me, "Do not say, I [am] a youth, for to all to whom I send you—go, and all that I command you—speak. ⁸Do not be afraid of their faces, for I [am] with you to deliver you," a declaration of Yhwh. ⁹And Yhwh puts forth His hand, and strikes against my mouth, and Yhwh says to me, "Behold, I have put My words in your mouth. ¹⁰See, I have charged you this day concerning the nations, and concerning the kingdoms, to pluck up, and to break down, and to destroy, and to throw down, to build, and to plant." ¹¹And there is a word of Yhwh to me, saying, "What are you seeing, Jeremiah?" And I say, "I am seeing a rod of an almond tree." ¹²And Yhwh says to me, "You have seen well: for I am watching over My word to do it." ¹³And there is a word of Yhwh to me a second time, saying, "What are you seeing?" And I say, "I am seeing a blown pot, and its face [is] from the north." ¹⁴And Yhwh says to me, "From the north the evil is loosed against all inhabitants of the land. ¹⁵For behold, I am calling for all families of the kingdoms of the north," a declaration of Yhwh, "And they have come, and each put his throne at the opening of the gates of Jerusalem, and by its walls all around, and by all cities of Judah. ¹⁶And I have spoken My judgments with them concerning all their evil, in that they have forsaken Me, and make incense to other gods, and bow themselves to the works of their own hands. ¹⁷And you, you gird up your loins, and have arisen, and spoken to them all that I command you: do not be frightened because of them, lest I frighten you before them. ¹⁸And I, behold, have given you this day for a fortified city, and for an iron pillar, and for bronze walls over all the land, to the kings of Judah, to its heads, to its priests, and to the people of the land; ¹⁹and they have fought against you, and they do not prevail against you; for I [am] with you," a declaration of Yhwh, "to deliver you."

CHAPTER 2

¹And there is a word of Yhwh to me, saying, ²"Go, and you have called in the ears of Jerusalem, saying, Thus said Yhwh: I have remembered for you || The kindness of your youth, the love of your espousals, || Your going after Me in a wilderness, in a land not sown. ³Israel [is] holy to Yhwh, || The first-fruit of His increase, || All consuming him are guilty, || Calamity comes to them," || A declaration of Yhwh. ⁴Hear a word of Yhwh, O house of Jacob, || And all you families of the house of Israel— ⁵Thus said Yhwh: "What perversity have your fathers found in Me, || That they have gone far off from Me, || And go after vanity, and become vain, ⁶And have not said, Where [is] Yhwh, || Who brings us up out of the land of Egypt, || Who leads us in a wilderness, || In a land of deserts and pits, || In a dry land, and of death-shade, || In a land that none has passed through, || Nor has man dwelt there? ⁷Indeed, I bring you into a land of fruitful fields, || To eat its fruit and its goodness, || And you come in and defile My land, || And have made My inheritance an abomination. ⁸The priests have not said, Where [is] Yhwh? And those handling the Law have not known Me. And the shepherds transgressed against Me, || And the prophets have prophesied by Ba'al, || And have gone after those who do not profit. ⁹Therefore, I yet plead with you," || A declaration of Yhwh, || "And I plead with your sons' sons. ¹⁰For pass to the islands of Chittim and see, || And send to Kedar and consider well, || And see if there has been [anything] like this: ¹¹Has a nation changed gods? (And they [are] no gods!) And My people has changed its glory || For that which does not profit. ¹²Be astonished, you heavens, at this, || Indeed, be frightened, be greatly desolated," || A declaration of Yhwh. ¹³"For My people have done two evils, || They have forsaken Me, a fountain of living waters, || To hew out for themselves wells—broken wells, || That do not contain the waters. ¹⁴[Is] Israel a servant? Is he a child of the house? Why has he been for a prey? ¹⁵Young lions roar against him, || They have given forth their voice, || And make his land become a desolation, || His cities have been burned without inhabitant. ¹⁶Also sons of Noph and Tahapanes || Consume you—the crown of the head! ¹⁷Do you not do this to yourself? [By] your forsaking your God Yhwh, || At the time He is leading you in the way? ¹⁸And now, why do you [go] in the way of Egypt, || To drink the waters of Sihor? And why do you [go] in the way of Asshur, || To drink the waters of the River? ¹⁹Your wickedness instructs you, || And your backslidings reprove you, || Know and see that an evil and a bitter thing [is] your forsaking your God Yhwh, || And My fear not being on you," || A declaration of Lord Yhwh of Hosts. ²⁰"For from of old you have broken your yoke, || Drawn away your bands, and say, I do not serve, || For on every high height, and under every green tree, || You are wandering—a harlot. ²¹And I planted you [as] a choice vine, wholly of true seed, || And how have you been turned || Into the degenerate shoots of a strange vine to Me? ²²But though you wash with natron, || And multiply soap to yourself, || Your iniquity is marked before Me," || A declaration of Lord Yhwh. ²³"How can you say, I have not been defiled, || I have not gone after the Ba'alim? See your way in a valley, know what you have done, || A swift dromedary winding her ways, ²⁴A wild donkey accustomed to a wilderness, || She has swallowed up wind in the desire of her soul, || Her meeting—who turns her back? None seeking her weary themselves, || In her month they find her. ²⁵Withhold your foot from being unshod, || And your throat from thirst, || And you say, It is incurable, || No, for I have loved strangers, and I go after them. ²⁶As the shame of a thief when he is found, || So has the house of Israel been put to shame, || They, their kings, their heads, || And their priests, and their prophets, ²⁷Saying to wood, You [are] my father! And to a stone, You have brought me forth, || For they turned to me the back and not the face, || And in the time of their distress, || They say, Arise, and save us. ²⁸And where [are] your gods, that you have made to yourself? Let them arise, if they may save you, || In the time of your distress, || For—the number of your cities have been your gods, O Judah, ²⁹Why do you strive with Me? All of you have transgressed against Me," || A declaration of Yhwh. ³⁰"I have struck your sons in vain, || They have not accepted instruction, || Your sword has devoured your prophets, || As a destroying lion. ³¹O generation, see the word of Yhwh: Have I been a wilderness to Israel? A land of thick darkness? Why have My people said, || We wandered freely, || We do not come to You again. ³²Does a virgin forget her ornaments? A bride her bands? And My people have forgotten Me [for] days without number. ³³Why do you make your ways pleasing to seek love? Therefore you have even taught the wicked your ways. ³⁴Also the blood of innocent needy souls || Has been found on your skirts, || I have not found them by digging, || But on all these. ³⁵And you say, Because I have been innocent, || Surely His anger has turned back from me? Behold, I have been judged with you, || Because of your saying, I have not sinned. ³⁶What? You are very vile to repeat your way, || You are even ashamed of Egypt, || As you have been ashamed of Asshur, ³⁷Also you go out from this, || And your hands on your head, || For Yhwh has kicked at your confidences, || And you do not give prosperity to them!"

JEREMIAH

CHAPTER 3

¹"Saying, Behold, one sends his wife away, || And she has gone from him, || And she has been to another man, || Does he return to her again? Is that land not greatly defiled? And you have committed whoredom with many lovers, || And turn to Me again," || A declaration of YHWH. ²"Lift your eyes to the high places, and see, || Where have you not been lain with? You have sat for them on the ways, || As an Arab in a wilderness, || And you defile the land, || By your fornications, and by your wickedness. ³And showers are withheld, and there has been no spring rain. You have the forehead of a whorish woman, || You have refused to be ashamed. ⁴Have you not from now on called to Me, || My Father, You [are] the leader of my youth? ⁵Does He keep for all time? Watch forever? Behold, you have spoken these things, || And you do evil, and prevail." ⁶And YHWH says to me, in the days of Josiah the king, "Have you seen that which backsliding Israel has done? She is going on every high mountain, and to the place of every green tree, and commits fornication there. ⁷And I say, after her doing all these, Return to Me, and she has not returned, and her treacherous sister Judah sees it. ⁸And I see that for all the causes whereby backsliding Israel committed adultery, I have sent her away, and I give the bill of her divorce to her; and her treacherous sister Judah has not feared, and goes and commits fornication—she also. ⁹And it has come to pass, from the vileness of her fornication, that the land is defiled, and she commits fornication with stone and with wood. ¹⁰And even in all this her treacherous sister Judah has not turned back to Me with all her heart, but with falsehood," a declaration of YHWH. ¹¹And YHWH says to me: "Backsliding Israel has justified herself, || More than treacherous Judah. ¹²Go, and you have proclaimed these words toward the north, and have said, Return, O backsliding Israel," || A declaration of YHWH! "I do not cause My anger to fall on you, for I [am] kind," || A declaration of YHWH, || "I do not watch for all time. ¹³Only, know your iniquity, || For you have transgressed against your God YHWH, || And you scatter your ways to strangers, || Under every green tree, || And you have not listened to My voice," || A declaration of YHWH. ¹⁴"Return, O backsliding sons," || A declaration of YHWH. "For I have ruled over you, || And taken you—one from a city, and two from a family, || And have brought you to Zion, ¹⁵And I have given shepherds to you || According to My own heart, || And they have fed you with knowledge and understanding. ¹⁶And it has come to pass, when you are multiplied, || And have been fruitful in the land, || In those days," || A declaration of YHWH, || "They no longer say, The Ark of the Covenant of YHWH, || Nor does it go up on the heart, || Nor do they remember concerning it, || Nor do they inspect, nor is it made again. ¹⁷At that time they cry to Jerusalem, O throne of YHWH, || And all the nations have been gathered to her, || For the Name of YHWH, to Jerusalem, || Nor do they go after the stubbornness of their evil heart anymore. ¹⁸In those days the house of Judah || Goes to the house of Israel, || And they come together from the land of the south, || To the land that I caused your fathers to inherit. ¹⁹And I have said, How do I put you among the sons, || And give a desirable land to you, || A beautiful inheritance of the hosts of nations, || And I say, You call Me—My Father, || And you do not turn back from after Me. ²⁰But a woman has deceived her friend, || So you have dealt treacherously with Me, || O house of Israel," || A declaration of YHWH. ²¹A voice is heard on high places—weeping, || Supplications of the sons of Israel, || For they have made their way perverse, || They have forgotten their God YHWH. ²²"Return, O backsliding sons," || I cause your backslidings to cease." "Behold us, we have come to You, || For You [are] our God YHWH. ²³Surely in vain—from the heights, || The multitude of mountains—Surely the salvation of Israel [is] in our God YHWH. ²⁴And the shameful thing has devoured || The labor of our fathers from our youth, || Their flock and their herd, || Their sons and their daughters. ²⁵We have lain down in our shame, and our confusion covers us, || For we have sinned against our God YHWH, || We, and our fathers, from our youth even to this day, || Nor have we listened to the voice of our God YHWH!"

CHAPTER 4

¹"If you return, O Israel," || A declaration of YHWH, || "Return to Me, || And if you turn aside Your abominations from My face, || Then you do not bemoan. ²And you have sworn—YHWH lives, || In truth, in judgment, and in righteousness, || And nations have blessed themselves in Him, || And they boast themselves in Him." ³For thus said YHWH, || To the man of Judah, and to Jerusalem: "Till for yourselves tillage, || And do not sow to the thorns. ⁴Be circumcised to YHWH, || And turn aside the foreskins of your heart, || O man of Judah, and you inhabitants of Jerusalem, || Lest My fury goes out as fire, and has burned, || And there is none quenching, || Because of the evil of your doings." ⁵Declare in Judah, and sound in Jerusalem, and say: "Blow a horn in the land, || Call, Fill up together, || And say, Assemble yourselves and let us go into the fortified cities. ⁶Lift up an ensign toward Zion, || Strengthen yourselves, do not stand still, || For I am bringing evil in from the north, || And a great destruction." ⁷A lion has gone up from his thicket, || And a destroyer of nations has journeyed, || He has come forth from his place || To make your land become a desolation, || Your cities are laid waste, without inhabitant. ⁸For this, gird on sackcloth, lament and howl, || For the fierce anger of YHWH has not turned back from us. ⁹"And it has come to pass in that day," || A declaration of YHWH, || "The heart of the king perishes, || And the heart of the princes, || And the priests have been astonished, || And the prophets wonder." ¹⁰And I say, "Aah! Lord YHWH, || Surely you have entirely forgotten this people and Jerusalem, || Saying, Peace is for you, || And a sword has struck to the soul!" ¹¹At that time it is said of this people, || And of Jerusalem: "A dry wind of high places in the wilderness, || The way of the daughter of My people || (Not for winnowing, nor for cleansing), ¹²A full wind from these comes for Me, || Now also, I speak judgments with them." ¹³"Behold, he comes up as clouds, || And his chariots as a windstorm, || His horses have been lighter than eagles, || Woe to us, for we have been spoiled." ¹⁴Wash evil from your heart, O Jerusalem, || That you may be saved, || Until when do you lodge in your heart || Thoughts of your strength? ¹⁵For a voice is declaring from Dan, || And sounding sorrow from Mount Ephraim: ¹⁶"Make mention to the nations, || Behold, sound to Jerusalem, || Besiegers are coming from the far-off land, || And they give forth their voice against cities of Judah. ¹⁷As the keepers of a field || They have been against her all around, || For she has been rebellious with Me," || A declaration of YHWH. ¹⁸"Your way and your doings have done these to you, || This [is] your distress, for [it is] bitter, || For it has struck to your heart." ¹⁹My bowels, my bowels! I am pained [in] the walls of my heart, || My heart makes a noise for me, I am not silent, || For I have heard the voice of a horn, || O my soul—a shout of battle! ²⁰Destruction on destruction is proclaimed, || For all the land has been spoiled, || My tents have suddenly been spoiled, || In a moment—my curtains. ²¹Until when do I see an ensign? Do I hear the voice of a horn? ²²"For My people [are] foolish, || They have not known Me, || They [are] foolish sons, || Indeed, they [are] not intelligent, || They [are] wise to do evil, || And they have not known to do good." ²³I looked [to] the earth, and behold—formless and void, || And to the heavens, and they [had] no light. ²⁴I have looked [to] the mountains, || And behold, they are trembling. And all the hills moved themselves lightly. ²⁵I have looked, and behold, man is not, || And all birds of the heavens have fled. ²⁶I have looked, and behold, || The fruitful place [is] a wilderness, || And all its cities have been broken down, || Because of YHWH, || Because of the fierceness of His anger. ²⁷For thus said YHWH: "All the land is a desolation, but I do not make a completion. ²⁸For this the earth mourns, || And the heavens above have been black, || Because I have spoken—I have purposed, || And I have not relented, || Nor do I turn back from it. ²⁹From the voice of the horseman, || And of him shooting with the bow, || All the city is fleeing, || They have come into thickets, || And they have gone up on cliffs, || All the city is forsaken, || And there is no one dwelling in them. ³⁰And you, O spoiled one, what do you do? For you put on scarlet, || For you adorn yourself [with] ornaments of gold. For you tear your eyes with pain, || In vain you make yourself beautiful, || Unhealthy ones have kicked against you, || They seek your life. ³¹For I have heard a voice as of a travailing woman, || Distress, as of one bringing forth a firstborn, || The voice of the daughter of Zion, || She laments herself, || She spreads out her hands, || Woe to me now, my soul is weary of slayers!"

JEREMIAH

CHAPTER 5

¹"Go to and fro in streets of Jerusalem, || And see now and know, || And seek in her broad places, || If you find a man, || If there is one doing judgment, || Seeking steadfastness—Then I am propitious to her. ²And if they say, YHWH lives, || Surely they swear to a falsehood." ³YHWH, Your eyes, are they not on steadfastness? You have struck them, and they have not grieved, || You have consumed them, || They have refused to receive instruction, || They made their faces harder than a rock, || They have refused to turn back. ⁴And I said, "Surely these [are] poor, || They have been foolish, || For they have not known the way of YHWH, || The judgment of their God. ⁵I go to the great, and I speak with them, || For they have known the way of YHWH, || The judgment of their God." Surely they have broken the yoke together, || They have drawn away the bands. ⁶Therefore a lion out of the forest has struck them, || A wolf of the deserts spoils them, || A leopard is watching over their cities, || Everyone who is going out of them is torn, || For their transgressions have been many, || Their backslidings have been mighty. ⁷"I am not propitious to you for this, || Your sons have forsaken Me, || And are satisfied by [those who are] not gods, || I satisfy them, and they commit adultery, || And at the house of a harlot || They gather themselves together. ⁸Fed horses—they have been early risers, || They each neigh to the wife of his neighbor. ⁹Do I not lay a charge for these?" A declaration of YHWH, "And on a nation such as this, || Does My soul not avenge itself? ¹⁰Go up on her walls, and destroy, || And I do not make a completion, || Turn her branches aside, || For they [are] not YHWH's, ¹¹For the house of Israel has dealt treacherously against Me, || And the house of Judah," || A declaration of YHWH. ¹²They have lied against YHWH, || And they say, "[It is] not He, || Nor does evil come in against us, || Indeed, we do not see sword and famine. ¹³And the prophets become wind, || And the word is not in them, || Thus it is done to them." ¹⁴Therefore, thus said YHWH, God of Hosts: "Because of your speaking this word, || Behold, I am making My words become fire in your mouth, || And this people wood, || And it has devoured them. ¹⁵Behold, I am bringing against you a nation from afar, || O house of Israel," || A declaration of YHWH, || "It [is] a strong nation, || It [is] an ancient nation, || A nation whose tongue you do not know, || Nor understand what it speaks. ¹⁶Its quiver [is] as an open tomb, || All of them—mighty ones. ¹⁷And it has consumed your harvest and your bread, || They consume your sons, and your daughters, || It consumes your flock, and your herd, || It consumes your vine and your fig tree, || It makes your fortified cities poor, || In which you are trusting—by the sword. ¹⁸And even in those days," || A declaration of YHWH, || "I do not make you a completion. ¹⁹And it has come to pass, when you say, Why has our God YHWH done all these [things] to us? That you have said to them, As you have forsaken Me, || And serve the gods of a foreigner in your land, || So you serve strangers in a land [that is] not yours. ²⁰Declare this in the house of Jacob, || And sound it in Judah, saying, ²¹Now hear this, || O people, foolish and without heart, || They have eyes, and they do not see, || They have ears, and they do not hear. ²²Do you not fear Me?" A declaration of YHWH; "Are you not pained from My presence? Who has made sand the border of the sea, || A perpetual limit, and it does not pass over it, || They shake themselves, and they are not able, || Indeed, its billows have sounded, and they do not pass over. ²³And this people has an apostatizing and rebelling heart, || They have turned aside, and they go on. ²⁴And they have not said in their heart, || Now let us fear our God YHWH, who is giving rain, || The autumn rain and the spring rain, in its season, || He keeps the appointed weeks of harvest for us. ²⁵Your iniquities have turned these away, || And your sins have kept the good from you. ²⁶For the wicked have been found among My people. He watches like one who sets snares, || They have set up a trap—they capture men. ²⁷As a cage full of birds, || So their houses are full of deceit, || Therefore they have been great, and are rich. ²⁸They have been fat, they have shone, || Indeed, they have surpassed the acts of the evil, || They have not judged judgment, || The judgment of the fatherless—and they prosper, || And they have not judged the judgment of the needy. ²⁹Do I not inspect for these," || A declaration of YHWH, || "On a nation such as this, || Does My soul not avenge itself? ³⁰An astonishing and horrible thing has been in the land: ³¹The prophets have prophesied falsely, || And the priests bear rule by their means, || And My people have loved [it] so, || And what do they do at its latter end?"

CHAPTER 6

¹"Strengthen yourselves, sons of Benjamin, || From the midst of Jerusalem, || And blow a horn in Tekoa, || And lift up a flame over Beth-Haccerem, || For evil has been seen from the north, || And great destruction. ²I have cut off the lovely and delicate one, || The daughter of Zion. ³Shepherds and their droves come to her, || They have struck tents by her all around, || They have each fed [in] his own station." ⁴"Sanctify the battle against her, || Rise, and we go up at noon. Woe to us, for the day has turned, || For the shades of evening are stretched out, ⁵Rise, and we go up by night, || And we destroy her palaces." ⁶For thus said YHWH of Hosts: "Cut down her wood, || And pour out a mound against Jerusalem, || She [is] the city to be inspected, || She [is] full of oppression in her midst. ⁷As the digging of a well, is [for] its waters, || So she has dug [for] her wickedness, || Violence and spoil is heard in her, || Sickness and striking [are] continually before My face. ⁸Be instructed, O Jerusalem, || Lest My soul be alienated from you, || Lest I make you a desolation, || A land [that is] not inhabited." ⁹Thus said YHWH of Hosts: "They surely glean, as a vine, the remnant of Israel, || Put your hand back, as a gatherer to the baskets." ¹⁰To whom do I speak, and testify, and they hear? Behold, their ear [is] uncircumcised, || And they are not able to attend. Behold, a word of YHWH has been to them for a reproach, || They do not delight in it. ¹¹And I have been filled with the fury of YHWH || (I have been weary of containing), "To pour [it] on the suckling in the street, || And on the assembly of youths together, || For even husband with wife are captured, || [The] elderly with one full of days, ¹²And their houses have been turned to others, || Fields and wives together, || For I stretch out My hand against the inhabitants of the land," || A declaration of YHWH. ¹³"For from their least to their greatest, || Everyone is gaining dishonest gain, || And from prophet even to priest, || Everyone is dealing falsely, ¹⁴And they heal the breach of the daughter of My people slightly, || Saying, Peace, peace! And there is no peace. ¹⁵They were ashamed when they did abomination! Indeed, they are not at all ashamed, || Indeed, they have not known blushing, || Therefore they fall among those falling, || In the time I have inspected them, || They stumble," said YHWH. ¹⁶Thus said YHWH: "Stand by the ways and see, and ask for paths of old, || Where [is] this—the good way? And go in it, || And find rest for yourselves. And they say, We do not go. ¹⁷And I have raised up watchmen for you, || Attend to the voice of the horn. And they say, We do not attend. ¹⁸Therefore hear, O nations, and know, O congregation, || That which [is] on them. ¹⁹Hear, O earth, behold, I am bringing evil on this people, || The fruit of their plans, || For they gave no attention to My words, || And My law—they kick against it. ²⁰Why [is] this to Me? Frankincense comes from Sheba, || And the sweet cane from a far-off land, || Your burnt-offerings [are] not for acceptance, || And your sacrifices have not been sweet to Me." ²¹Therefore, thus said YHWH: "Behold, I give stumbling blocks to this people, || And fathers and sons have stumbled against them together, || The neighbor and his friend perish." ²²Thus said YHWH: "Behold, a people has come from a north country, || And a great nation is stirred up from the sides of the earth. ²³They take hold of bow and javelin, || It [is] fierce, and they have no mercy, || Their voice sounds as a sea, || And they ride on horses, || Set in array as a man of war, || Against you, O daughter of Zion." ²⁴We have heard its sound, our hands have been feeble, || Distress has seized us, pain as of a travailing woman. ²⁵Do not go forth to the field, || And do not walk in the way, || For the enemy has a sword, || Fear [is] all around. ²⁶O daughter of my people, || Gird on sackcloth, || And roll yourself in ashes, || Make mourning [as for] an only one, || A most bitter lamentation, || For the spoiler suddenly comes against us. ²⁷"I have given you a watchtower, || A fortress among My people, || And you know, and have tried their way. ²⁸All of them are turned aside by apostates, || Walking slanderously—bronze and iron, || All of them are corrupters. ²⁹The bellows have been burned, || The lead has been consumed by fire, || A refiner has refined in vain, || And the wicked have not been drawn away. ³⁰They have called them rejected silver, || For YHWH has kicked against them!"

JEREMIAH

CHAPTER 7

¹The word that has been to Jeremiah from YHWH, saying, ²"Stand in the gate of the house of YHWH, and you have proclaimed this word there, and have said, Hear a word of YHWH, all you of Judah, who are coming in at these gates, to bow before YHWH." ³Thus said YHWH of Hosts, God of Israel: "Amend your ways, and your doings, || And I cause you to dwell in this place. ⁴Do not trust for yourselves || To the words of falsehood, saying, || The temple of YHWH! The temple of YHWH! These [are] the temple of YHWH! ⁵For if you thoroughly amend your ways and your doings, || If you thoroughly do judgment || Between a man and his neighbor, ⁶You do not oppress sojourner, fatherless, and widow, || And innocent blood is not shed in this place, || And [you] do not walk after other gods, for evil to yourselves, ⁷Then I have caused you to dwell in this place, || In the land that I gave to your fathers, || From age even to age. ⁸Behold, you are trusting for yourselves || On the words of falsehood, so as not to profit. ⁹Stealing, murdering, and committing adultery, || And swearing to falsehood, and giving incense to Ba'al, || And going after other gods whom you did not know. ¹⁰And you have come in and stood before Me, || In this house on which My Name is called, || And have said, We have been delivered, || In order to do all these abominations. ¹¹Has this house, || On which My Name is called, || Been a den of burglars in your eyes? Even I, behold, have seen," || A declaration of YHWH. ¹²"But go now to My place that [is] in Shiloh, || Where I caused My Name to dwell at first, || And see that which I have done to it, || For the wickedness of My people Israel. ¹³And now, because of your doing all these works," || A declaration of YHWH, || "And I speak to you, rising early and speaking, || And you have not listened, || And I call you, and you have not answered, ¹⁴I also have done to the house on which My Name is called, || In which you are trusting, || And to the place that I gave to you, and to your fathers, || As I have done to Shiloh. ¹⁵And I have cast you from before My face, || As I have cast out all your brothers, || The whole seed of Ephraim. ¹⁶And you do not pray for this people, || Nor lift up crying and prayer for them, || Nor intercede with Me, for I do not hear you. ¹⁷Are you not seeing what they are doing || In cities of Judah, and in streets of Jerusalem? ¹⁸The sons are gathering wood, || And the fathers are causing the fire to burn, || And the women are kneading dough, || To make cakes to the queen of the heavens, || And to pour out drink-offerings to other gods, || So as to provoke Me to anger. ¹⁹Are they provoking Me to anger?" A declaration of YHWH, "Is it not themselves, || For the shame of their own faces?" ²⁰Therefore, thus said Lord YHWH: "Behold, My anger and My fury is poured out on this place, || On man, and beast, and on tree of the field, || And on fruit of the ground, || And it has burned, and it is not quenched." ²¹Thus said YHWH of Hosts, God of Israel: "Add your burnt-offerings to your sacrifices and eat flesh. ²²For I did not speak with your fathers, || Nor did I command them in the day of My bringing them out of the land of Egypt, || Concerning the matters of burnt-offering and sacrifice, ²³But this thing I commanded them, saying, || Listen to My voice, || And I have been to you for God, || And you are to Me for a people, || And have walked in all the way that I command you, || So that it is well for you. ²⁴And they have not listened, nor inclined their ear, || And they walk in the counsels, || [And] in the stubbornness, of their evil hearts, || And are backward and not forward. ²⁵Even from the day when your fathers || Went out of the land of Egypt until this day, || I send all My servants the prophets to you, || Daily rising early and sending, ²⁶And they have not listened to Me, || Nor inclined their ear—and they harden their neck, || They have done evil above their fathers. ²⁷And you have spoken all these words to them, || And they do not listen to you, || And you have called to them, || And they do not answer you. ²⁸And you have said to them: This [is] the nation that has not listened, || To the voice of its God YHWH, || Nor have they accepted instruction, || Steadfastness has perished, || Indeed, it has been cut off from their mouth. ²⁹Cut off your crown, and cast [it] away, || And lift up lamentation on high places, || For YHWH has rejected, || And He leaves the generation of His wrath. ³⁰For the sons of Judah || Have done evil in My eyes," || A declaration of YHWH, || "They have set their abominations in the house || On which My Name is called—to defile it, ³¹And have built the high places of Tophet, || That [are] in the Valley of the Son of Hinnom, || To burn their sons and their daughters with fire, || Which I did not command, || Nor did it come up on My heart. ³²Therefore, behold, days are coming," || A declaration of YHWH, || "And it is no longer said, The Tophet, || And, Valley of the Son of Hinnom, || But, Valley of the Slaughter, || And they have buried in Tophet—without place. ³³And the carcass of this people has been for food || To a bird of the heavens, and to a beast of the earth, || And there is none troubling. ³⁴And I have caused to cease from cities of Judah, || And from streets of Jerusalem, || The voice of joy, and the voice of gladness, || Voice of bridegroom, and voice of bride, || For the land becomes a desolation!"

CHAPTER 8

¹"At that time," || A declaration of YHWH, || "They bring the bones of the kings of Judah, || And the bones of its princes, || And the bones of the priests, || And the bones of the prophets, || And the bones of inhabitants of Jerusalem, || Out of their graves, ²And have spread them to sun, and to moon, || And to all the host of the heavens, that they have loved, || And that they have served, || And that they have walked after, || And that they have sought, || And to which they have bowed themselves, || They are not gathered, nor buried, || They are for dung on the face of the ground. ³And death is chosen rather than life || By all the remnant who are left of this evil family, || In all the remaining places, to where I have driven them," || A declaration of YHWH of Hosts. ⁴"And you have said to them, Thus said YHWH: Do they fall, and not rise? Does he turn back, and not return? ⁵Why has this people of Jerusalem || Turned back—a continuous backsliding? They have kept hold on deceit, || They have refused to turn back. ⁶I have given attention, indeed, I listen, || They do not speak right, || No man has sighed over his wickedness, || Saying, What have I done? Everyone has turned to his courses, || As a horse is rushing into battle. ⁷Even a stork in the heavens has known her seasons, || And turtle, and swallow, and crane, || Have watched the time of their coming, || And—My people have not known the judgment of YHWH. ⁸How do you say, We [are] wise, || And the Law of YHWH [is] with us? Surely, behold, it has worked falsely, || The false pen of scribes. ⁹The wise have been ashamed, || They have been frightened, and are captured, || Behold, they kicked against a word of YHWH, || And what wisdom do they have? ¹⁰Therefore, I give their wives to others, || Their fields to dispossessors, || For from the least even to the greatest, || Everyone is gaining dishonest gain, || From prophet even to priest, everyone is dealing falsely. ¹¹And they heal the breach of the daughter of My people slightly, || Saying, Peace, peace! And there is no peace. ¹²They were ashamed when they did abomination! Indeed, they are not ashamed at all, || And they have not known blushing, || Therefore, they fall among falling ones, || They stumble in the time of their inspection, said YHWH. ¹³I utterly consume them," || A declaration of YHWH, || "There are no grapes in the vine, || Indeed, there are no figs in the fig tree, || And the leaf has faded, || And the strength they have passes from them. ¹⁴Why are we sitting still? Be gathered, and we go into the fortified cities, || And we are silent there, || For our God YHWH has made us silent, || Indeed, He causes us to drink water of gall, || For we have sinned against YHWH. ¹⁵Looking for peace—and there is no good, || For a time of healing, and behold—terror. ¹⁶The snorting of his horses has been heard from Dan, || From the voice of the neighings of his mighty ones, || All the land has trembled, || And they come in and consume the land and its fullness, || The city and the inhabitants in it. ¹⁷For behold, I am sending serpents among you, || Vipers that have no charmer, || And they have bitten you," || A declaration of YHWH. ¹⁸My sorrow [is] beyond comfort, || My heart [is] sick in me. ¹⁹Behold, the voice of a cry of the daughter of my people from a far-off land, || Is YHWH not in Zion? Is her King not in her? "Why have they provoked Me with their carved images, || With the vanities of a foreigner?" ²⁰Harvest has passed, summer has ended, || And we have not been saved. ²¹For a breach of the daughter of my people I have been broken, || I have been dark, || Astonishment has seized me. ²²Is there no balm in Gilead? Is there no physician there? Why has the health of the daughter of my people not gone up?

CHAPTER 9

¹Who makes my head waters, || And my eye a fountain of tears? And I weep by day and by

JEREMIAH

night, || For the wounded of the daughter of my people. ²Who gives me in a wilderness || A lodging-place for travelers? And I leave my people, and go from them, || For all of them [are] adulterers, || An assembly of treacherous ones. ³"And they bend their tongue, || Their bow [is] a lie, || And they have not been mighty for steadfastness in the land, || For they have gone forth from evil to evil, || And they have not known Me," || A declaration of YHWH! ⁴"You each beware of his friend, || And do not trust any brother, || For every brother utterly supplants, || For every friend slanderously walks, ⁵And they each mock at his friend, || And they do not speak truth, || They taught their tongue to speak falsehood, || They have labored to commit iniquity. ⁶Your dwelling [is] in the midst of deceit, || Through deceit they refused to know Me," || A declaration of YHWH. ⁷Therefore, thus said YHWH of Hosts: "Behold, I am refining them, and have tried them, || For how do I deal with the daughter of My people? ⁸Their tongue [is] a slaughtering arrow, || It has spoken deceit in its mouth, || It speaks peace with its neighbor, || And in its heart it lays its ambush, ⁹Do I not see after them for these things?" A declaration of YHWH, "Does My soul not avenge itself against a nation such as this?" ¹⁰I lift up weeping and wailing for the mountains, || And a lamentation for the habitations of the wilderness, || For they have been burned up without any passing over, || Nor have they heard the voice of livestock, || From the bird of the heavens and to the beast—they have fled, || They have gone. ¹¹"And I make Jerusalem become heaps, || A habitation of dragons, || And I make the cities of Judah a desolation, || Without inhabitant." ¹²Who [is] the wise man? And he understands this, || And he to whom the mouth of YHWH spoke? And he declares it, || For why has the land perished? It has been burned up as a wilderness, || Without any passing through. ¹³And YHWH says: "Because of their forsaking My law that I set before them, || And they have not listened to My voice nor walked in it, ¹⁴And they walk after the stubbornness of their heart, || And after the Ba'alim, || That their fathers taught them," ¹⁵Therefore, thus said YHWH of Hosts, God of Israel: "Behold, I am causing them—this people—to eat wormwood, || And I have caused them to drink water of gall, ¹⁶And I have scattered them among nations || Which they did not know, they and their fathers, || And have sent the sword after them, || Until I have consumed them." ¹⁷Thus said YHWH of Hosts: "Consider, and call for mourning women, || And they come, || And send to the wise women, || And they come, ¹⁸And they hurry, and lift up a wailing for us. And tears run down our eyes, || And waters flow from our eyelids. ¹⁹For a voice of wailing is heard from Zion: How we have been spoiled! We have been greatly ashamed, || Because we have forsaken the land, || Because they have cast down our dwelling places." ²⁰But hear, you women, a word of YHWH, || And your ear receives a word of His mouth, || And teach your daughters wailing, || And each her neighbor lamentation. ²¹For death has come up into our windows, || It has come into our palaces, || To cut off the suckling from outside, || Young men from the broad places. ²²Speak thus, "A declaration of YHWH, || And the carcass of man has fallen, || As dung on the face of the field, || And as a handful after the reaper, || And there is none gathering." ²³Thus said YHWH: "Do not let the wise boast himself in his wisdom, || Nor let the mighty boast himself in his might, || Do not let the rich boast himself in his riches, ²⁴But let the boaster boast himself in this, || In understanding and knowing Me, || For I [am] YHWH, doing kindness, || Judgment, and righteousness, in the earth, || For I have delighted in these," || A declaration of YHWH. ²⁵"Behold, days are coming," || A declaration of YHWH, || "And I have laid a charge on all circumcised in the foreskin, ²⁶On Egypt, and on Judah, and on Edom, || And on the sons of Ammon, and on Moab, || And on all cutting the corner [of the beard], || Who are dwelling in the wilderness, || For all the nations [are] uncircumcised, || And all the house of Israel [are] uncircumcised in heart!"

CHAPTER 10

¹Hear the word, O house of Israel, || That YHWH has spoken for you. ²Thus said YHWH: "Do not accustom yourselves to the way of the nations, || And do not be frightened by the signs of the heavens, || For the nations are frightened by them. ³For the statutes of the peoples are vanity, || For one has cut a tree from a forest, || Work of the hands of a craftsman, with an axe, ⁴They beautify it with silver and with gold, || They fix it with nails and with hammers, || And it does not stumble. ⁵They [are] stiff as a palm, and they do not speak, || They are surely carried, for they do not step, || Do not be afraid of them, for they do no evil, || Indeed, to do good is also not in them." ⁶Because there is none like You, O YHWH, || You [are] great, and Your Name [is] great in might. ⁷Who does not fear You, King of the nations? For it is befitting to You, || For among all the wise of the nations, || And in all their kingdom, there is none like You. ⁸And as one they are brutish and foolish, || An instruction of vanities [is] the tree itself. ⁹Spread-out silver is brought from Tarshish, || And gold from Uphaz, || Work of an artisan, and of the hands of a refiner, || Their clothing [is] blue and purple, || Work of the skillful—all of them. ¹⁰And YHWH [is] a God of truth, || He [is] a living God, and a perpetual King, || The earth shakes from His wrath, || And nations do not endure His indignation. ¹¹Thus you say to them, "The gods who have not made the heavens and earth, || They perish from the earth, || And from under these heavens." ¹²The Maker of the earth by His power, || The Establisher of the world by His wisdom, || Who, by His understanding, stretched forth the heavens— ¹³When He gives forth His voice, || A multitude of waters [is] in the heavens, || And He causes vapors to come up from the end of the earth, || He has made lightnings for rain, || And brings out wind from His treasures. ¹⁴Every man is brutish by knowledge, || Every refiner is put to shame by a carved image, || For his molten image [is] false. And there is no breath in them. ¹⁵They [are] vanity, work of erring ones, || They perish in the time of their inspection. ¹⁶The Portion of Jacob [is] not like these, || For He [is] the Framer of all things, || And Israel [is] the rod of His inheritance, || YHWH of Hosts [is] His Name. ¹⁷Gather your merchandise from the land, || O dweller in the bulwark, ¹⁸For thus said YHWH: "Behold, I am slinging out the inhabitants of the land at this time, || And have been an adversary to them, || So that they are found out." ¹⁹Woe to me for my breaking, || My striking has been grievous, || And I said, "Surely this [is] my sickness, and I bear it." ²⁰My tent has been spoiled, || And all my cords have been broken, || My sons have gone out from me, and they are not, || There is none stretching out my tent anymore, || And raising up my curtains. ²¹For the shepherds have become brutish, || And they have not sought YHWH, || Therefore they have not acted wisely, || And all their flock is scattered. ²²A voice of a report, behold, it has come, || Even a great shaking from the north country, || To make the cities of Judah a desolation, || A habitation of dragons. ²³I have known, O YHWH, that not of man [is] his way, || Not of man [is] the going and establishing of his step. ²⁴Discipline me, O YHWH, only in judgment, || Not in Your anger, lest You make me small. ²⁵Pour out Your fury on the nations that have not known You, || And on the families that have not called on Your Name, || For they have eaten up Jacob, || Indeed, they have eaten him up, indeed, they consume him, || And they have made his habitation desolate!

CHAPTER 11

¹The word that has been to Jeremiah from YHWH, saying, ²"Hear the words of this covenant, and you have spoken to the men of Judah, and to the inhabitants of Jerusalem, ³and you have said to them, Thus said YHWH God of Israel: Cursed [is] the man who does not obey the words of this covenant, ⁴That I commanded your fathers, || In the day of My bringing them out from the land of Egypt, || Out of the iron furnace, saying, Listen to My voice, and you have done them, || According to all that I command you, || And you have been to Me for a people, || And I am to you for God, ⁵In order to establish the oath that I have sworn to your fathers, || To give to them a land flowing with milk and honey, as this day." And I answer and say, "Amen, O YHWH." ⁶And YHWH says to me, "Proclaim all these words in the cities of Judah, and in the streets of Jerusalem, saying, || Hear the words of this covenant, || And you have done them. ⁷For I certainly testified against your fathers, || In the day of My bringing them up out of the land of Egypt—until this day, || Rising early and testifying, saying, Listen to My voice, ⁸And they have not listened nor inclined their ear, || And they each walk in the stubbornness of their evil heart, || And I bring on them all the words of this covenant, || That I commanded to do,

JEREMIAH

and they did not." ⁹And YHWH says to me: "A conspiracy is found in the men of Judah, || And in the inhabitants of Jerusalem. ¹⁰They have turned back to the iniquities of their first fathers, || Who refused to hear My words, || And they have gone after other gods to serve them, || The house of Israel and the house of Judah || Have made void My covenant that I made with their fathers." ¹¹Therefore, thus said YHWH: "Behold, I am bringing calamity on them, || That they are not able to go out from, || And they have cried to Me, || And I do not listen to them. ¹²And the cities of Judah, and inhabitants of Jerusalem have gone, || And they have cried to the gods, || To whom they are making incense, || And they give no deliverance at all to them, || In the time of their distress. ¹³For the number of your cities have been your gods, O Judah, || And [for] the number of the streets of Jerusalem You have placed altars to a shameful thing, || Altars to make incense to Ba'al. ¹⁴And you, you do not pray for this people, || Nor do you lift up cry and prayer for them, || For I do not listen in the time of their calling to Me for their distress. ¹⁵What has My beloved to do in My house, || Her doing wickedness with many, || And does the holy flesh pass over from you? When you do evil, then you exult. ¹⁶An olive, green, beautiful, of good fruit, || Has YHWH called your name, || At the noise of a great tumult He has kindled fire against it, || And its thin branches have been broken. ¹⁷And YHWH of Hosts, who is planting you, || Has spoken calamity concerning you, || For the evil of the house of Israel, and of the house of Judah, || That they have done to themselves, || To provoke Me to anger, to make incense to Ba'al." ¹⁸And, O YHWH, cause me to know, and I know, || Then You have showed me their doings. ¹⁹And I [am] as a trained lamb brought to slaughter, || And I have not known || That they have devised schemes against me: "We destroy the tree with its food, || And cut him off from the land of the living, || And his name is not remembered again." ²⁰And O YHWH of Hosts, judging righteousness, || Trying reins and heart, || I see Your vengeance against them, || For I have revealed my cause to You. ²¹Therefore, thus said YHWH concerning the men of Anathoth, who are seeking your life, saying, "Do not prophesy in the Name of YHWH, and you do not die by our hands." ²²Therefore, thus said YHWH of Hosts: "Behold, I am seeing after them, || The chosen ones die by sword, || Their sons and their daughters die by famine, ²³And they have no remnant, || For I bring calamity to the men of Anathoth, || The year of their inspection!"

CHAPTER 12

¹You [are] righteous, O YHWH, || When I plead toward You, || Only, let me speak judgments with You, || Why did the way of the wicked prosper? All treacherous dealers have been at rest. ²You have planted them, || Indeed, they have taken root, || They go on, indeed, they have made fruit, || You [are] near in their mouth, || And far off from their reins. ³And You, O YHWH, You have known me, || You see me, and have tried my heart with You, || Draw them away as sheep to slaughter, || And separate them for a day of slaughter. ⁴Until when does the earth mourn, || And the herb of the whole field wither? For the wickedness of those dwelling in it, || Beast and bird have been consumed, || Because they said, "He does not see our latter end." ⁵"For you have run with footmen, || And they weary you, || And how you fret yourself with horses! Even in the land of peace, || [In which] you are confident—And how will you do in the rising of Jordan? ⁶For even your brothers and the house of your father, || Even they dealt treacherously against you, || Even they called after you fully, || Do not trust in them when they speak good things to you. ⁷I have forsaken My house, || I have left My inheritance, || I have given the beloved of My soul || Into the hand of her enemies. ⁸My inheritance has been to Me as a lion in a forest, || She gave forth against Me with her voice, || Therefore I have hated her. ⁹[Is] My inheritance a speckled bird to Me? Is the bird around against her? Come, assemble, every beast of the field, || Come for food. ¹⁰Many shepherds destroyed My vineyard, || They have trodden down My portion, || They have made My desirable portion || Become a wilderness—a desolation. ¹¹He has made it become a desolation, || The desolation has mourned to Me, || All the land has been desolated, || But there is no one laying it to heart. ¹²Spoilers have come in on all high places in the plain, || For the sword of YHWH is consuming, || From the end of the land even to the end of the land, || There is no peace to any flesh. ¹³They sowed wheat, and have reaped thorns, || They have become sick—they do not profit, || And they have been ashamed of your increases, || Because of the fierceness of the anger of YHWH." ¹⁴Thus said YHWH: "Concerning all My evil neighbors, who are striking against the inheritance that I caused My people—Israel—to inherit: Behold, I am plucking them from off their ground, || And I pluck the house of Judah out of their midst. ¹⁵And it has been, after My plucking them out, || I turn back, and have pitied them, || And I have brought them back, || Each to his inheritance, and each to his land. ¹⁶And it has come to pass, || If they learn the ways of My people well, || To swear by My Name, YHWH lives, || As they taught My people to swear by Ba'al, || Then they have been built up in the midst of My people. ¹⁷And if they do not listen, || Then I have plucked up that nation, || Plucking up and destroying," || A declaration of YHWH!

CHAPTER 13

¹Thus said YHWH to me: "Go, and you have acquired a girdle of linen for yourself, and have placed it on your loins, and you do not cause it to enter into water." ²And I get the girdle, according to the word of YHWH, and I place [it] on my loins. ³And there is a word of YHWH to me a second time, saying, ⁴"Take the girdle that you have acquired, that [is] on your loins, and rise, go to the Euphrates, and hide it there in a hole of the rock"; ⁵and I go and hide it by the Euphrates, as YHWH commanded me. ⁶And it comes to pass, at the end of many days, that YHWH says to me, "Rise, go to the Euphrates, and take the girdle there, that I commanded you to hide there"; ⁷and I go to the Euphrates, and dig, and take the girdle from the place where I had hid it; and behold, the girdle has been marred, it is not profitable for anything. ⁸And there is a word of YHWH to me, saying, "Thus said YHWH: ⁹Thus I mar the excellence of Judah, || And the great excellence of Jerusalem. ¹⁰This evil people, who refuse to hear My words, || Who walk in the stubbornness of their heart, || And go after other gods to serve them, || And to bow themselves to them, || Indeed it is—as this girdle, that is not profitable for anything. ¹¹For as the girdle cleaves to the loins of a man, || So I caused to cleave to Me || The whole house of Israel, || And the whole house of Judah," || A declaration of YHWH, || "To be to Me for a people, and for a name, || And for praise, and for beauty, || And they have not listened. ¹²And you have said this word to them, || Thus said YHWH, God of Israel: Every bottle is full of wine, || And they have said to you: Do we not certainly know that every bottle is full of wine? ¹³And you have said to them, || Thus said YHWH: Behold, I am filling all the inhabitants of this land, || And the kings who sit for David on his throne, || And the priests, and the prophets, || And all the inhabitants of Jerusalem, || [With] drunkenness, ¹⁴And have dashed them against one another, || And the fathers and the sons together," || A declaration of YHWH, || "I do not pity, nor spare, nor do I have mercy, || So as not to destroy them." ¹⁵Hear, and give ear—do not be haughty, || For YHWH has spoken. ¹⁶Give glory to your God YHWH, || Before He causes darkness, || And before your feet stumble on dark mountains, || And you have waited for light, || And He has made it for death-shade, || And has appointed [it] for thick darkness. ¹⁷And if you do not hear it, || My soul weeps in secret places, because of pride, || Indeed, it weeps and wails, || And the tear comes down my eyes, || For the flock of YHWH has been taken captive. ¹⁸Say to the king and to the mistress: Make yourselves low—sit still, || For your principalities have come down, || The crown of your beauty. ¹⁹The cities of the south have been shut up, || And there is none opening, || Judah has been removed—all of her, || She has been completely removed— ²⁰Lift up your eyes, and see those coming in from the north, || Where [is] the drove given to you, your beautiful flock? ²¹What do you say when He looks after you? And you have taught them [to be] over you—leaders for head? Do pangs not seize you as a travailing woman? ²²And when you say in your heart, "Why have these met me?" For the abundance of your iniquity || Have your skirts been uncovered, || Have your heels suffered violence. ²³"Does a Cushite change his skin? And a leopard his spots? Can you also do good, who are accustomed to do evil? ²⁴And I scatter them as stubble, || Passing away, by a wind of the wilderness. ²⁵This [is] your lot, the portion

of your measures from Me," || A declaration of YHWH, || "Because you have forgotten Me, || And trust in falsehood. ²⁶I have also made your skirts bare before your face, || And your shame has been seen. ²⁷Your adulteries, and your neighings, || The wickedness of your whoredom, on heights in a field, || I have seen your abominations. Woe to you, O Jerusalem, || You are not [yet] made clean—after when [will you be] again?"

CHAPTER 14

¹That which has been the word of YHWH to Jeremiah concerning the matters of the scarcities: ²"Judah has mourned, and her gates have languished, || They have mourned to the earth, || And the cry of Jerusalem has gone up. ³And their majestic ones have sent their little ones to the water, || They have come to ditches, || They have not found water, || They have turned back—their vessels empty! They have been ashamed, || And have blushed and covered their head. ⁴Because the ground has been broken, || For there has been no rain in the land, || Farmers have been ashamed, || They have covered their head. ⁵For even the doe in the field has brought forth—to forsake [it!] || For there has been no grass. ⁶And wild donkeys have stood on high places, || They have swallowed up wind like dragons, || Their eyes have been consumed, for there is no herb." ⁷Surely our iniquities have testified against us, || O YHWH, work for Your Name's sake, || For our backslidings have been many, || We have sinned against You. ⁸O Hope of Israel—its Savior in time of trouble, || Why are You as a sojourner in the land? And as a traveler turned aside to lodge? ⁹Why are You as one mute? As a mighty one not able to save? And You [are] in our midst, O YHWH, || And Your Name is called over us, || Do not leave us. ¹⁰Thus said YHWH concerning this people: "They have loved to wander well, || They have not restrained their feet, || And YHWH has not accepted them, || Now He remembers their iniquity, || And inspects their sin." ¹¹And YHWH says to me: "You do not pray for this people for good. ¹²When they fast, I do not listen to their cry, and when they cause burnt-offering and present to ascend, I do not accept them; for I am consuming them by sword, and by famine, and by pestilence." ¹³And I say, "Aah! Lord YHWH, behold, the prophets are saying to them: You do not see a sword, indeed, famine is not [on] you, for I give true peace to you in this place." ¹⁴And YHWH says to me: "The prophets are prophesying falsehood in My Name. I did not send them, nor command them, nor have I spoken to them. A false vision, and divination, and vanity—indeed, they are prophesying the deceit of their own heart to you. ¹⁵Therefore, thus said YHWH concerning the prophets who are prophesying in My Name and I have not sent them, and they are saying, Sword and famine is not in this land: By sword and by famine are these prophets consumed. ¹⁶And the people to whom they are prophesying are cast into out-places of Jerusalem, because of the famine and the sword, and they have none burying them—them, their wives, and their sons, and their daughters—and I have poured out their evil on them. ¹⁷And you have said this word to them: Tears come down my eyes night and day, || And they do not cease, || For [with] a great breach, || The virgin daughter of my people has been broken, || A very grievous stroke. ¹⁸If I have gone forth to the field, || Then, behold, the pierced of the sword! And if I have entered the city, || Then, behold, the diseased of famine! For both prophet and priest have gone up and down || To a land that they did not know." ¹⁹Have You utterly rejected Judah? Has Your soul loathed Zion? Why have You struck us, || And there is no healing to us? Looking for peace, and there is no good, || And for a time of healing, and behold, terror. ²⁰We have known, O YHWH, our wickedness, || The iniquity of our fathers, || For we have sinned against You. ²¹Do not despise, for Your Name's sake, || Do not dishonor the throne of Your glory, || Remember, do not break Your covenant with us. ²²Are there any among the vanities of the nations causing rain? And do the heavens give showers? Are You not He, O our God YHWH? And we wait for you, for You have done all these!

CHAPTER 15

¹And YHWH says to me: "Though Moses and Samuel should stand before Me, || My soul is not toward this people, || Send from before My face, and they go out. ²And it has come to pass, when they say to you, || To where do we go out? That you have said to them, || Thus said YHWH: Those who [are] for death—to death, || And those who are for the sword—to the sword, || And those who are for famine—to famine, || And those who are for captivity—to captivity. ³And I have appointed four kinds over them," || A declaration of YHWH, || "The sword to slay, and the dogs to drag, || And the bird of the heavens, || And the beast of the earth, to consume and to devour. ⁴And I have given them for a trembling || To all kingdoms of the earth, || Because of Manasseh son of Hezekiah king of Judah, || For that which he did in Jerusalem. ⁵For who has pity on you, O Jerusalem? And who bemoans for you? And who turns aside to ask of your welfare? ⁶You have left Me," || A declaration of YHWH, || "You go backward, || And I stretch out My hand against you, || And I destroy you, || I have been weary of relenting. ⁷And I scatter them with a fan, || In the gates of the land, || I have bereaved [them], || I have destroyed My people, || They did not turn back from their ways. ⁸Its widows have been more to Me than the sand of the seas, || I brought on them—against the mother—A young man—a spoiler—at noon. I caused wrath and trouble to fall on her suddenly. ⁹The bearer of seven has languished, || She has breathed out her spirit, || Her sun has gone in while yet day, || It has been ashamed and confounded, || And I give up their remnant to the sword before their enemies," || A declaration of YHWH. ¹⁰Woe to me, my mother, || For you have borne me, || A man of strife and a man of contention to all the land, || I have not lent on usury, || Nor have they lent on usury to me—All of them are reviling me. ¹¹YHWH said, "Did I not direct you for good? Did I not intercede for you in a time of evil, || In a time of adversity, with the enemy? ¹²Does one break iron, || Northern iron and bronze? ¹³I give your strength and your treasures for a prey—not for price, || Even for all your sins, and in all your borders. ¹⁴And I have caused your enemies || To pass over into the land [that] You have not known, || For a fire has been kindled in My anger, || It burns against you." ¹⁵You, You have known, O YHWH, || Remember me, and inspect me, || And take vengeance for me of my pursuers, || In Your long-suffering do not take me away, || Know [that] I have borne reproach for You. ¹⁶Your words have been found, and I eat them, || And Your word is to me for a joy, || And for the rejoicing of my heart, || For Your Name is called on me, O YHWH, God of Hosts. ¹⁷I have not sat in an assembly of deriders, || Nor do I exult, because of your hand—I have sat alone, || For You have filled me [with] indignation. ¹⁸Why has my pain been continuous? And my wound incurable? It has refused to be healed, || You are surely as a failing stream to me, || Waters [that are] not steadfast. ¹⁹Therefore, thus said YHWH: "If you turn back, then I bring you back, || You stand before Me, || And if you bring out the precious from the vile, || You are as My mouth! They return to you, || And you do not return to them. ²⁰And I have made you to this people || For a wall—bronze—fortified, || And they have fought against you, || And they do not prevail against you, || For I [am] with you to save you, || And to deliver you," || A declaration of YHWH, ²¹"And I have delivered you from the hand of evildoers, || And I have ransomed you || From the hand of the terrible!"

CHAPTER 16

¹And there is a word of YHWH to me, saying, ²"You do not take a wife to yourself, || Nor do you have sons and daughters in this place." ³For thus said YHWH, || Of the sons and of the daughters who are born in this place, || And of their mothers—those bearing them, || And of their fathers—those begetting them in this land: ⁴"They die painful deaths, || They are not lamented, nor are they buried, || For they are dung on the face of the ground, || And are consumed by sword and by famine, || And their carcass has been for food || To the bird of the heavens, || And to the beast of the earth." ⁵For thus said YHWH: "Do not enter the house of a mourning-feast, || Nor go to lament nor bemoan for them, || For I have removed My peace from this people," || A declaration of YHWH, || "The kindness and the mercies. ⁶And great and small have died in this land, || They are not buried, and none lament for them, || Nor does any cut himself, nor become bald for them. ⁷Nor do they deal out to them for mourning, || To comfort him concerning the dead, || Nor cause them to drink a cup of consolations || For his father and for his mother. ⁸You do not enter a house of banqueting, || To sit with them, to eat and to drink," ⁹For thus said YHWH of Hosts, God of

Israel: "Behold, I am causing to cease from this place, || Before your eyes, and in your days, || The voice of joy, and the voice of rejoicing, || The voice of bridegroom and voice of bride. ¹⁰And it has come to pass, || When you declare all these words to this people, || And they have said to you, || Why has YHWH spoken all this great evil against us? Indeed, what [is] our iniquity, and what [is] our sin, || That we have sinned against our God YHWH? ¹¹Then you have said to them: Because that your fathers have forsaken Me, || A declaration of YHWH, || And go after other gods, and serve them, || And they bow themselves to them, || And have forsaken Me, and not kept My law, ¹²You also have done evil above your fathers, || And behold, you are each walking after the stubbornness of his evil heart, || So as not to listen to Me. ¹³And I have cast you from off this land, || On to a land that you have not known, || You and your fathers, || And you have served other gods there by day and by night, || Where I do not give grace to you. ¹⁴Therefore, behold, days are coming," || A declaration of YHWH, || "And it is not said anymore, || YHWH lives, who brought up the sons of Israel out of the land of Egypt, ¹⁵But, YHWH lives, who brought up the sons of Israel out of the land of the north, || And out of all the lands to where He drove them, || And I have brought them back to their land, || That I gave to their fathers. ¹⁶Behold, I am sending for many fishers," || A declaration of YHWH, || "And they have fished them, || And after this I send for many hunters, || And they have hunted them from off every mountain, || And from off every hill, and from holes of the rocks. ¹⁷For My eyes [are] on all their ways, || They have not been hidden from My face, || Nor has their iniquity been concealed from before My eyes. ¹⁸And I have repaid a first—A second time—their iniquity and their sin, || Because of their defiling My land, || With the carcass of their detestable things, || Indeed, their abominations have filled My inheritance." ¹⁹O YHWH, my strength, and my fortress, || And my refuge in a day of adversity, || Nations come to You from the ends of the earth, || And say, "Our fathers only inherited falsehood, || Vanity, and none among them is profitable." ²⁰Does man make gods for himself, || And they—no gods? ²¹"Therefore, behold, I am causing them to know at this time, || I cause them to know My hand and My might, || And they have known that My Name [is] YHWH!"

CHAPTER 17

¹"The sin of Judah is written with a pen of iron, || With the point of a diamond, || Engraved on the tablet of their heart, || And on the horns of your altars, ²As their sons remember their altars and their Asherim, || By the green tree, by the high hills. ³O My mountain in the field—your strength, || All your treasures—I give for a prey, || Your high places for sin in all your borders. ⁴And you have let go—even through yourself, || Of your inheritance that I gave to you, || And I have caused you to serve your enemies, || In a land that you have not known, || For you have kindled a fire in My anger, || It burns for all time." ⁵Thus said YHWH: "Cursed [is] the man who trusts in man, || And has made flesh his arm, || And whose heart turns from YHWH. ⁶And he has been as a naked thing in a desert, || And does not see when good comes, || And has inhabited parched places in a wilderness, || A salt land, and not inhabited. ⁷Blessed [is] the man who trusts in YHWH, || And whose confidence has been YHWH. ⁸And has been as a tree planted by waters, || And he sends forth his roots by a stream, || And he does not see when heat comes, || And his leaf has been green, || And he is not sorrowful in a year of scarcity, || Nor does he cease from making fruit. ⁹The heart [is] deceitful above all things, || And it [is] incurable—who knows it? ¹⁰I, YHWH, search the heart, try the reins, || Even to give to each according to his way, || According to the fruit of his doings. ¹¹A partridge hatching, and not bringing forth, || [Is] one making wealth, and not by right, || In the midst of his days he forsakes it, || And in his latter end—he is a fool." ¹²A throne of glory on high from the beginning, || The place of our sanctuary, ¹³The hope of Israel [is] YHWH, || All forsaking You are ashamed. "And My apostates are written in the earth, || For they have forsaken YHWH, || A fountain of living waters." ¹⁴Heal me, O YHWH, and I am healed, || Save me, and I am saved, || For You [are] my praise. ¹⁵Behold, they are saying to me: "Where [is] the word of YHWH? Pray, let it come." ¹⁶And I did not hurry from feeding after You, || And I have not desired the desperate day, || You have known the produce of my lips, || It has been before Your face, ¹⁷Do not be to me for a terror, || You [are] my hope in a day of calamity. ¹⁸Let my pursuers be ashamed, || And do not let me be ashamed—me! Let them be frightened, || And do not let me be frightened—me! Bring in on them a day of calamity, || And destroy them a second time [with] destruction. ¹⁹Thus said YHWH to me: "Go, and you have stood in the gate of the sons of the people, by which kings of Judah come in, and by which they go out, and in all gates of Jerusalem, ²⁰and you have said to them: Hear a word of YHWH, you kings of Judah, and all Judah, and all inhabitants of Jerusalem, who are coming in by these gates," ²¹Thus said YHWH: "Take heed to yourselves, || And you do not bear a burden on the day of rest, || Nor have you brought [it] in by the gates of Jerusalem. ²²Nor do you take out a burden from your houses on the day of rest, || Indeed, you do not do any work, || And you have sanctified the day of rest, || As I have commanded your fathers. ²³And they have not listened nor inclined their ear, || And they stiffen their neck not to hear, || And not to receive instruction. ²⁴And it has been, if you certainly listen to Me," || A declaration of YHWH, || "So as not to bring in a burden by the gates of this city on the day of rest, || And to sanctify the day of rest, || So as not to do any work in it— ²⁵Then kings and princes have entered by the gates of this city, || Sitting on the throne of David, || Riding in a chariot, and on horses, || They, and their princes, the man of Judah, || And inhabitants of Jerusalem, || And this city has remained for all time. ²⁶And they have come in from cities of Judah, || And from outskirts of Jerusalem, || And from the land of Benjamin, || And from the low country, || And from the hill-country, || And from the south, || Bringing in burnt-offering, and sacrifice, || And present, and frankincense, || And bringing praise [to] the house of YHWH. ²⁷And if you do not listen to Me to sanctify the day of rest, || And so as not to bear a burden, || And to come in at the gates of Jerusalem on the day of rest, || Then I have kindled a fire in its gates, || And it has consumed the high places of Jerusalem, || And it is not quenched!"

CHAPTER 18

¹The word that has been to Jeremiah from YHWH, saying, ²"Rise, and you have gone down [to] the potter's house, and there I cause you to hear My words"; ³and I go down [to] the potter's house, and behold, he is doing a work on the stones, ⁴and the vessel that he is making is marred, as clay in the hand of the potter, and he has turned and he makes it another vessel, as it was right in the eyes of the potter to make. ⁵And there is a word of YHWH to me, saying, ⁶"O house of Israel, am I not able to do to you as this potter?" A declaration of YHWH. "Behold, as clay in the hand of the potter, || So [are] you in My hand, O house of Israel. ⁷The moment I speak concerning a nation, || And concerning a kingdom, || To pluck up and to break down, and to destroy, ⁸And that nation has turned from its evil, || Because I have spoken against it, || Then I have relented of the calamity that I thought to do to it. ⁹And the moment I speak concerning a nation, || And concerning a kingdom, to build, and to plant, ¹⁰And it has done evil in My eyes, || So as not to listen to My voice, || Then I have relented of the good || That I have spoken of doing to it. ¹¹And now, speak now to men of Judah, || And against inhabitants of Jerusalem, saying, || Thus said YHWH: Behold, I am framing calamity against you, || And devising a scheme against you; Please turn back, each from his evil way, || And amend your ways and your doings." ¹²And they have said, "It is incurable, || For we go after our own plans, || And each of us does the stubbornness of his evil heart." ¹³Therefore, thus said YHWH: "Now ask among the nations, || Who has heard such things? The virgin of Israel has done a very horrible thing. ¹⁴Does snow of Lebanon || Cease from the rock of the field? Will the cold strange [waters] that are flowing be forsaken? ¹⁵But My people have forgotten Me, they make incense to a vain thing, || And they cause them to stumble in their ways—paths of old, || To walk in paths—a way not raised up, ¹⁶To make their land become a desolation, || A continuous hissing, || Everyone passing by it is astonished, || And bemoans with his head. ¹⁷I scatter them before an enemy as with an east wind, || I show them the neck and not the face, || In the day of their calamity." ¹⁸And they say, "Come, || And we devise schemes against Jeremiah, || For law does not perish from the priest, || Nor counsel from the wise, || Nor the word from the prophet, || Come, and we strike him with

the tongue, || And we do not attend to any of his words." ¹⁹Give attention, O YHWH, to me, || And listen to the voice of those contending with me. ²⁰Is evil repaid instead of good, || That they have dug a pit for my soul? Remember my standing before You to speak good of them, || To turn back Your wrath from them. ²¹Therefore, give up their sons to famine, || And cause them to run on the sides of the sword, || And their wives are bereaved and widows, || And their men are slain by death, || Their young men [are] struck by sword in battle, ²²A cry is heard from their houses, || For You suddenly bring a troop against them, || For they dug a pit to capture me, || And they have hidden snares for my feet. ²³And You, O YHWH, You have known, || All their counsel against me [is] for death, || You do not cover over their iniquity, || Nor blot out their sin from before You, || And they are made to stumble before You, || Work against them in the time of Your anger!

CHAPTER 19

¹Thus said YHWH: "Go, and you have acquired a potter's earthen vessel, and from [the] elderly of the people, and from [the] elderly of the priests, ²and you have gone forth to the Valley of the Son of Hinnom, that [is] at the opening of the gate of the pottery, and have proclaimed there the words that I speak to you, ³and have said, Hear a word of YHWH, you kings of Judah, and inhabitants of Jerusalem!" Thus said YHWH of Hosts, God of Israel: "Behold, I am bringing in evil on this place, at which the ears of everyone who is hearing it tingles, ⁴because that they have forsaken Me, and make known this place, and make incense in it to other gods, that they did not know, they and their fathers, and the kings of Judah, and they have filled this place [with] innocent blood, ⁵and have built the high places of Ba'al to burn their sons with fire, burnt-offerings to Ba'al, that I did not command, nor spoke of, nor did it come up on My heart. ⁶Therefore, behold, days are coming," a declaration of YHWH, "and this place is no longer called The Tophet and Valley of the Son of Hinnom, but Valley of the Slaughter. ⁷And I have made void the counsel of Judah and Jerusalem in this place, and have caused them to fall by the sword before their enemies, and by the hand of those seeking their life, and I have given their carcass for food to the bird of the heavens, and to the beast of the earth, ⁸and I have made this city for a desolation, and for a hissing, everyone passing by it is astonished, and hisses for all its plagues. ⁹And I have caused them to eat the flesh of their sons, and the flesh of their daughters, and they each eat the flesh of his friend, in the siege and in the constriction with which their enemies constrict them, and those seeking their life." ¹⁰"And you have broken the bottle before the eyes of the men who are going with you, ¹¹and have said to them, Thus said YHWH of Hosts: Thus I break this people and this city, as one breaks the potter's vessel, that is not able to be repaired again, and in Tophet they bury—without place to bury; ¹²so I do to this place—a declaration of YHWH—and to its inhabitants, so as to make this city as Tophet; ¹³and the houses of Jerusalem, and the houses of the kings of Judah, have been as the place of Tophet—defiled, even all the houses on whose roofs they have made incense to all the host of the heavens, so as to pour out oblations to other gods." ¹⁴And Jeremiah comes in from Tophet, to where YHWH had sent him to prophesy, and he stands in the court of the house of YHWH, and he says to all the people: ¹⁵"Thus said YHWH of Hosts, God of Israel: Behold, I am bringing to this city, and on all its cities, all the calamity that I have spoken against it, for they have hardened their neck to not hear My words!"

CHAPTER 20

¹And Pashhur son of Immer the priest—who [is] also overseer, leader in the house of YHWH—hears Jeremiah prophesying these things, ²and Pashhur strikes Jeremiah the prophet, and puts him in the stocks that [are] by the Upper Gate of Benjamin, that [is] by the house of YHWH. ³And it comes to pass on the next day, that Pashhur brings Jeremiah out from the stocks, and Jeremiah says to him, "YHWH has not called your name Pashhur, but Terror on Every Side. ⁴For thus said YHWH: Behold, I am making you for a fear to yourself, || And to all loving you, || And they have fallen by the sword of their enemies, and your eyes are beholding, || And all Judah I give into the hand of the king of Babylon, || And he has removed them to Babylon, || And he has struck them with the sword. ⁵And I have given all the strength of this city, || And all its labor, and all its precious things, || Indeed, I give all the treasures of the kings of Judah into the hand of their enemies, || And they have spoiled them, and taken them, || And have brought them into Babylon. ⁶And you, Pashhur, and all dwelling in your house, || Go into captivity. And you enter Babylon, || And there you die, and there you are buried, || You and all loving you, || To whom you have prophesied falsely." ⁷You have persuaded me, O YHWH, and I am persuaded; You have hardened me, and prevail, || I have been for a laughter all the day, || Everyone is mocking at me, ⁸Because from the time I speak I cry out, I shout, "Violence and destruction!" || For the word of YHWH has been to me || For reproach and for derision all the day. ⁹And I said, "I do not mention Him, || Nor do I speak anymore in His Name," || And it has been in my heart || As a burning fire shut up in my bones, || And I have been weary of containing, || And I am not able. ¹⁰For I have heard the evil report of many, "Fear [is] all around!" "Declare, and we declare it!" All my allies are watching [for] my halting, "Perhaps he is enticed, and we prevail over him, || And we take our vengeance on him." ¹¹And YHWH [is] with me, as a mighty, awesome One, || Therefore my persecutors stumble and do not prevail, || They have been exceedingly ashamed, || For they have not acted wisely, || Continuous confusion is not forgotten. ¹²And, O YHWH of Hosts, trier of the righteous, || Beholder of reins and heart, || I see Your vengeance on them, || For I have revealed my cause to you. ¹³Sing to YHWH, praise YHWH, || For He has delivered the soul of the needy || From the hand of evildoers. ¹⁴Cursed [is] the day in which I was born, || The day that my mother bore me, || Let it not be blessed! ¹⁵Cursed [is] the man who bore tidings [to] my father, || Saying, "A male child has been born to you," || Making him very glad! ¹⁶Then that man has been as the cities, || That YHWH overthrew, and did not relent, || And he has heard a cry in the morning, || And a shout at noontime. ¹⁷Because he has not put me to death from the womb, || And my mother is to me—my grave, || And her womb [is] a perpetual pregnancy. ¹⁸Why [is] this? I have come out from the womb || To see labor and sorrow, || Indeed, my days are consumed in shame!

CHAPTER 21

¹The word that has been to Jeremiah from YHWH, in King Zedekiah's sending to him Pashhur son of Malchiah and Zephaniah son of Maaseiah the priest, saying, ²"Please inquire of YHWH for us, for Nebuchadnezzar king of Babylon has fought against us; perhaps YHWH deals with us according to all His wonders, and causes him to go up from off us." ³And Jeremiah says to them, "Thus you say to Zedekiah, ⁴Thus said YHWH, God of Israel: Behold, I am turning around the weapons of battle || That [are] in your hand, || With which you fight the king of Babylon, || And the Chaldeans, who are laying siege against you, || At the outside of the wall, || And I have gathered them into the midst of this city, ⁵And I have fought against you, || With an outstretched hand, and with a strong arm, || And in anger, and in fury, and in great wrath, ⁶And I have struck the inhabitants of this city, || Both man and beast, || They die by a great pestilence. ⁷And after this," || A declaration of YHWH, || "I give Zedekiah king of Judah, || And his servants, and the people, || And those left in this city, || From the pestilence, from the sword, and from the famine, || Into the hand of Nebuchadnezzar king of Babylon, || And into the hand of their enemies, || And into the hand of those seeking their life, || And he has struck them by the mouth of the sword, || He has no pity on them, || Nor does he spare, nor does he have mercy." ⁸"And you say to this people, Thus said YHWH: Behold, I am setting before you the way of life, || And the way of death! ⁹Whoever is abiding in this city—dies, || By sword, and by famine, and by pestilence, || And whoever is going forth, || And has fallen to the Chaldeans, || Who are laying siege against you—lives, || And his life has been for a spoil to him. ¹⁰For I have set My face against this city for calamity, || And not for good," || A declaration of YHWH. "It is given into the hand of the king of Babylon, || And he has burned it with fire. ¹¹And as for the house of the king of Judah," || Hear a word of YHWH; ¹²O house of David, thus said YHWH: "Decide judgment in the morning, || And deliver the plundered from the hand of the oppressor, || Lest My fury go forth as fire, || And has burned, and none is

quenching, || Because of the evil of your doings. ¹³Behold, I [am] against you," || A declaration of YHWH, || "O inhabitant of the valley, rock of the plain, || Who are saying, Who comes down against us? And who comes into our habitations? ¹⁴And I have laid a charge against you, || According to the fruit of your doings," || A declaration of YHWH, || "And I have kindled a fire in its forest, || And it has consumed all its outskirts!"

CHAPTER 22

¹Thus said YHWH: "Go down [to] the house of the king of Judah, and you have spoken this word there, and have said, ²Hear a word of YHWH, O king of Judah, who are sitting on the throne of David, you, and your servants, and your people, who are coming in at these gates," ³Thus said YHWH: "Do judgment and righteousness, || And deliver the plundered from the hand of the oppressor, || And sojourner, orphan, and widow, you do not oppress nor wrong, || And innocent blood you do not shed in this place. ⁴For if you certainly do this thing, || Then kings sitting for David on his throne || Have come in by the gates of this house, || Riding on chariot, and on horses, || He, and his servants, and his people. ⁵And if you do not hear these words, || I have sworn by Myself," || A declaration of YHWH, || "That this house is for a desolation." ⁶For thus said YHWH concerning the house of the king of Judah: "You [are] Gilead to Me—head of Lebanon, || If not—I make you a wilderness, || Cities [that] are not inhabited. ⁷And I have separated destroyers for you, || Each with his weapons, || And they have cut down the choice of your cedars, || And have cast them on the fire." ⁸And many nations have passed by this city, || And they have each said to his neighbor, "Why has YHWH done thus to this great city?" ⁹And they have said, "Because that they have forsaken || The covenant of their God YHWH, || And bow themselves to other gods, and serve them." ¹⁰You do not weep for the dead, nor bemoan for him, || Weep severely for the traveler, || For he does not return again, || Nor has he seen the land of his birth. ¹¹For thus said YHWH concerning Shallum son of Josiah king of Judah, who is reigning instead of his father Josiah, who has gone forth from this place: "He does not return here again; ¹²For he dies in the place to where they have removed him, || And he does not see this land again. ¹³Woe to him who is building his house by unrighteousness, || And his upper chambers by injustice, || He lays service on his neighbor for nothing, || And he does not give him his wage to him. ¹⁴Who is saying, || I build a large house for myself, || And airy upper chambers, || And he has cut out its windows for himself, || Covered with cedar, and painted with vermillion. ¹⁵Do you reign, because you are fretting yourself in cedar? Your father—did he not eat and drink? Indeed, he did judgment and righteousness, || Then [it is] well with him. ¹⁶He decided the cause of the poor and needy, || Then [it is] well—is it not to know Me?" A declaration of YHWH. ¹⁷"But your eyes and your heart are not, || Except on your dishonest gain, || And on shedding of innocent blood, || And on oppression, and on doing of violence." ¹⁸Therefore, thus said YHWH concerning Jehoiakim son of Josiah king of Judah: "They do not lament for him, || Oh, my brother! And, Oh, my sister! They do not lament for him, || Oh, lord! And, Oh, his splendor! ¹⁹He is buried [with] the burial of a donkey, || Dragged and cast out there to the gates of Jerusalem. ²⁰Go up to Lebanon, and cry, || And give forth your voice in Bashan, || And cry from Abarim, || For all loving you have been destroyed. ²¹I have spoken to you in your ease, || You have said, I do not listen, || This [is] your way from your youth, || For you have not listened to My voice. ²²Wind consumes all your friends, || And your lovers go into captivity, || Surely then you are ashamed, || And have blushed for all your wickedness. ²³O dweller in Lebanon, making a nest among cedars, || How gracious have you been when pangs come to you, || Pain—as of a travailing woman." ²⁴"[As] I live," || A declaration of YHWH, || "Though Coniah son of Jehoiakim king of Judah was a seal on My right hand, surely there I draw you away, ²⁵And I have given you into the hand of those seeking your life, || And into hands of which you are afraid, || Into the hand of Nebuchadnezzar king of Babylon, || And into the hand of the Chaldeans. ²⁶And I have cast you, || And your mother who bore you, to another country, || Where you were not born, and you die there. ²⁷And to the land to where they are lifting up their soul to return, || They do not return there." ²⁸A grief—a despised broken thing—is this man Coniah? A vessel in which there is no pleasure? Why have they been cast up and down, || He and his seed, || Indeed, were they cast on to a land that they did not know? ²⁹Earth, earth, earth, hear a word of YHWH! ³⁰Thus said YHWH: "Write this man down [as] childless, || A man—he does not prosper in his days, || For none of his seed prospers, || Sitting on the throne of David, || And ruling in Judah again!"

CHAPTER 23

¹"Woe to shepherds destroying, || And scattering the flock of My pasture," || A declaration of YHWH. ²Therefore, thus said YHWH, God of Israel, || Against the shepherds who feed My people: "You have scattered My flock, and drive them away, || And have not inspected them, || Behold, I am charging on you the evil of your doings," || A declaration of YHWH. ³"And I gather the remnant of My flock || Out of all the lands to where I drove them, || And have brought them back to their fold, || And they have been fruitful, and multiplied. ⁴And I have raised shepherds for them, || And they have fed them, || And they no longer fear, nor are frightened, || Nor are they lacking," || A declaration of YHWH. ⁵"Behold, days are coming," || A declaration of YHWH, || "And I have raised a righteous shoot to David, || And a king has reigned and acted wisely, || And done judgment and righteousness in the earth. ⁶Judah is saved in His days, and Israel dwells confidently, || And this [is] His Name that YHWH proclaims Him: Our Righteousness. ⁷Therefore, behold, days are coming," || A declaration of YHWH, || "And they no longer say, YHWH lives who brought up || The sons of Israel out of the land of Egypt, ⁸But—YHWH lives, who brought up, || And who brought in, the seed of the house of Israel, || From the land of the north, || And from all the lands to where I drove them, || And they have dwelt on their own ground!" ⁹In reference to the prophets: My heart has been broken in my midst, || All my bones have fluttered, || I have been as a man—a drunkard, || And as a man—wine has passed over him, || Because of YHWH, and of His holy words. ¹⁰For the land has been full of adulterers, || For the land has mourned because of these, || The pleasant places of the wilderness have dried up, || And their course is evil, and their might—not right. ¹¹"For both prophet and priest have been profane, || Indeed, I found their wickedness in My house," || A declaration of YHWH. ¹²"Therefore their way is as slippery places to them, || They are driven into thick darkness, || And they have fallen in it, || For I bring in calamity against them, || The year of their inspection," || A declaration of YHWH. ¹³"And I have seen folly in prophets of Samaria, || They have prophesied by Ba'al, || And cause My people—Israel—to err. ¹⁴And I have seen a horrible thing in prophets of Jerusalem, || Committing adultery, and walking falsely, || Indeed, they strengthened the hands of evildoers, || So that they have not turned back, || Each from his wickedness, || All of them have been as Sodom to me, || And its inhabitants as Gomorrah." ¹⁵Therefore, thus said YHWH of Hosts, concerning the prophets: "Behold, I am causing them to eat wormwood, || And have caused them to drink water of gall, || For from prophets of Jerusalem || Profanity has gone forth to all the land." ¹⁶Thus said YHWH of Hosts: "You do not listen to the words || Of the prophets who are prophesying to you, || They are making you vain things, || They speak a vision of their own heart, || Not from the mouth of YHWH. ¹⁷Diligently saying to those despising, || The word of YHWH: Peace is for you, || And [to] everyone walking in the stubbornness of his heart, they have said: Evil does not come to you." ¹⁸For who has stood in the counsel of YHWH, || And sees and hears His word? Who has regarded My word, and listens? ¹⁹Behold, a whirlwind of YHWH—Fury has gone out, even a piercing whirlwind, || It stays on the head of the wicked. ²⁰The anger of YHWH does not turn back || Until His doing, and until His establishing, || The thoughts of His heart, || In the latter end of the days || You attend to it with understanding. ²¹"I have not sent the prophets, and they have run, || I have not spoken to them, and they have prophesied. ²²But if they stood in My counsel, || Then they cause My people to hear My words, || And they turn them back from their evil way, || And from the evil of their doings. ²³[Am] I a God near," || A declaration of YHWH, || "And not a God far off? ²⁴Is anyone hidden in secret places, || And I do not see him?" A declaration of YHWH, "Do I not fill the heavens

and the earth?" A declaration of YHWH. ²⁵"I have heard that which the prophets said, || Who prophesy falsehood in My Name, saying, || I have dreamed, I have dreamed. ²⁶Until when is it in the heart of the prophets? The prophets of falsehood, || Indeed, prophets of the deceit of their heart, ²⁷Who are devising to cause My people || To forget My Name by their dreams, || That they each recount to his neighbor, || As their fathers forgot My Name for Ba'al. ²⁸The prophet with whom [is] a dream, || Let him recount the dream, || And he with whom [is] My word, || Let him truly speak My word. What does the straw [have to do] with the grain?" A declaration of YHWH. ²⁹"Is it not thus? My word [is] as fire," || A declaration of YHWH. "And as a hammer—it breaks a rock in pieces. ³⁰Therefore, behold, I [am] against the prophets," || A declaration of YHWH, || "Each stealing My words from his neighbor. ³¹Behold, I [am] against the prophets," || A declaration of YHWH, || "Who are making their tongue smooth, || And they affirm—an affirmation. ³²Behold, I [am] against the prophets of false dreams," || A declaration of YHWH, || "And they recount them, and cause My people to err, || By their falsehoods, and by their instability, || And I have not sent them, || Nor have I commanded them, || And they are not profitable to this people at all," || A declaration of YHWH. ³³"And when this people, or the prophet, || Or a priest, asks you, saying, What [is] the burden of YHWH? Then you have said to them: You [are] the burden, and I have left you," || A declaration of YHWH. ³⁴"And the prophet, and the priest, and the people, || That says, The burden of YHWH, || I have seen after that man, and after his house. ³⁵Thus you each say to his neighbor, || And each to his brother: What has YHWH answered? And what has YHWH spoken? ³⁶And you do not mention the burden of YHWH anymore, || For the burden to each is His word, || And you have overturned the words of the living God, YHWH of Hosts, our God. ³⁷Thus you say to the prophet, || What has YHWH answered you? And what has YHWH spoken? ³⁸And if you say, The burden of YHWH, || Therefore, thus said YHWH: Because of your saying this word, || The burden of YHWH, || And I send to you, saying, || You do not say, The burden of YHWH. ³⁹Therefore, behold, I have utterly taken you away, || And I have sent you out, || And the city that I gave to you, || And to your fathers, from before My face, ⁴⁰And I have put continuous reproach on you, || And continuous shame that is not forgotten!"

CHAPTER 24

¹YHWH has showed me, and behold, two baskets of figs, appointed before the temple of YHWH—after the removing by Nebuchadnezzar king of Babylon, of Jeconiah, son of Jehoiakim king of Judah, and the heads of Judah, and the artisan, and the smith, from Jerusalem, when he brings them into Babylon— ²In one basket [are] very good figs, like the first-ripe figs, and in the other basket [are] very bad figs that are not eaten because of badness. ³And YHWH says to me, "What are you seeing, Jeremiah?" And I say, "Figs, the good figs [are] very good, and the bad [are] very bad, that are not eaten because of badness." ⁴And there is a word of YHWH to me, saying, ⁵"Thus said YHWH, God of Israel: Like these good figs so I acknowledge || The expulsion of Judah that I sent from this place, || [To] the land of the Chaldeans—for good. ⁶And I have set My eyes on them for good, || And have brought them back to this land, || And built them up, and I do not throw down, || And have planted them, and do not pluck up. ⁷And have given to them a heart to know Me, || For I [am] YHWH, || And they have been to Me for a people, || And I am to them for God, || For they turned back to Me with all their heart. ⁸And like the bad figs that are not eaten for badness, || Surely thus said YHWH: So I make Zedekiah king of Judah, || And his heads, and the remnant of Jerusalem, || Who are left in this land, || And who are dwelling in the land of Egypt, ⁹And I have given them for a trembling, || For evil—to all kingdoms of the earth, || For a reproach, and for an allegory, || For a byword, and for a reviling, || In all the places to where I drive them. ¹⁰And I have sent the sword against them, || The famine and the pestilence, || Until their consumption from off the ground, || That I gave to them and to their fathers!"

CHAPTER 25

¹The word that has been to Jeremiah concerning all the people of Judah, in the fourth year of Jehoiakim son of Josiah king of Judah—it [is] the first year of Nebuchadnezzar king of Babylon— ²Which Jeremiah the prophet has spoken concerning all the people of Judah, and to all the inhabitants of Jerusalem, saying, ³"From the thirteenth year of Josiah son of Amon king of Judah, and to this day—this twenty-third year—the word of YHWH has been to me, and I speak to you, rising early and speaking, and you have not listened; ⁴and YHWH has sent all His servants to you, the prophets, rising early and sending, and you have not listened, nor inclined your ear to hear, saying, ⁵Please turn back, each from his evil way, and from the evil of your doings, and dwell on the ground that YHWH has given to you and to your fathers from age to age, ⁶and you do not go after other gods to serve them, and to bow yourselves to them, nor do you provoke Me to anger with the work of your hands, and I do no evil to you; ⁷and you have not listened to Me," a declaration of YHWH, "so as to provoke Me to anger with the work of your hands for evil to you. ⁸Therefore, thus said YHWH of Hosts: Because that you have not obeyed My words, ⁹behold, I am sending, and have taken all the families of the north—a declaration of YHWH—even to Nebuchadnezzar king of Babylon, My servant, and have brought them in against this land, and against its inhabitants, and against all these surrounding nations, and have devoted them, and appointed them for an astonishment, and for a hissing, and for continuous ruins. ¹⁰And I have destroyed from them the voice of rejoicing, and the voice of joy, voice of bridegroom and voice of bride, noise of millstones, and the light of lamps. ¹¹And all this land has been for a desolation, for an astonishment, and these nations have served the king of Babylon seventy years. ¹²And it has come to pass, at the fullness of seventy years, I charge against the king of Babylon, and against that nation," a declaration of YHWH, "their iniquity, and against the land of the Chaldeans, and have appointed it for continuous desolations. ¹³And I have brought in on that land all My words that I have spoken against it, all that is written in this scroll, that Jeremiah has prophesied concerning all the nations. ¹⁴For laid service on them—also them—have many nations and great kings, and I have given repayment to them according to their doing, and according to the work of their hands." ¹⁵For thus said YHWH, God of Israel, to me: "Take the wine cup of this fury out of My hand, and you have caused all the nations to drink it to whom I am sending you; ¹⁶and they have drunk, and shaken themselves and shown themselves [to be] foolish, because of the sword that I am sending among them." ¹⁷And I take the cup out of the hand of YHWH, and cause all the nations to drink to whom YHWH sent me: ¹⁸Jerusalem, and the cities of Judah, || And its kings, its heads, || To give them to ruin, to astonishment, || To hissing, and to reviling, as [at] this day; ¹⁹Pharaoh king of Egypt, and his servants, || And his heads, and all his people, ²⁰And all the mixed people, || And all the kings of the land of Uz, || And all the kings of the land of the Philistines, || And Ashkelon, and Gaza, and Ekron, || And the remnant of Ashdod, ²¹Edom, and Moab, and the sons of Ammon, ²²And all the kings of Tyre, || And all the kings of Sidon, || And the kings of the island that [is] beyond the sea, ²³Dedan, and Tema, and Buz, || And all cutting the corners [of the beard], ²⁴And all the kings of Arabia, || And all the kings of the mixed people, || Who are dwelling in the wilderness, ²⁵And all the kings of Zimri, || And all the kings of Elam, || And all the kings of Media, ²⁶And all the kings of the north, || The near and the far off to one another, || And all the kingdoms of the earth, || That [are] on the face of the ground, || And King Sheshach drinks after them. ²⁷"And you have said to them, Thus said YHWH of Hosts, God of Israel: Drink, indeed drink abundantly, || And vomit, and fall, and do not rise, || Because of the sword that I am sending among you. ²⁸And it has come to pass, || When they refuse to receive the cup out of your hand to drink, || That you have said to them, Thus said YHWH of Hosts: You certainly drink. ²⁹For behold, in the city over which My Name is called, || I am beginning to bring ruin, || And are you entirely acquitted? You are not acquitted, for I am proclaiming a sword, || For all inhabitants of the land," || A declaration of YHWH of Hosts. ³⁰"And you, you prophesy all these words to them, and have said to them: YHWH roars from the high place, || And gives forth His voice from His holy habitation, || He surely roars for His habitation, || A shout as those treading [the grapes], || God answers all the inhabitants

of the land, ³¹A rumbling has come to the end of the earth, || For YHWH has a controversy with nations, || He has executed judgment for all flesh, || He has given the wicked to the sword," || A declaration of YHWH. ³²Thus said YHWH of Hosts: "Behold, evil is going out from nation to nation, || And a great whirlwind is stirred up from the sides of the earth. ³³And the pierced of YHWH have been in that day, || From the end of the earth even to the end of the earth, || They are not lamented, nor gathered, nor buried, || For they are dung on the face of the ground. ³⁴Howl, you shepherds, and cry, || And roll yourselves, you majestic of the flock, || For your days have been full || For slaughtering, and [for] your scatterings, || And you have fallen as a desirable vessel. ³⁵And refuge has perished from the shepherds, || And escape from the majestic of the flock. ³⁶A voice of the cry of the shepherds, || And a howling of the majestic of the flock, || For YHWH is spoiling their pasture. ³⁷And the peaceable habitations have been cut down, || Because of the fierceness of the anger of YHWH. ³⁸He has forsaken His covert as a young lion, || Surely their land has become a desolation, || Because of the oppressing fierceness, || And because of the fierceness of His anger!"

CHAPTER 26

¹In the beginning of the reign of Jehoiakim son of Josiah, king of Judah, this word has been from YHWH, saying, ²"Thus said YHWH: Stand in the court of the house of YHWH, and you have spoken to all [those of] the cities of Judah, who are coming to bow themselves in the house of YHWH, all the words that I have commanded you to speak to them—you do not diminish a word. ³Perhaps they listen, and each turns back from his evil way; then I have relented concerning the evil that I am thinking of doing to them, because of the evil of their doings. ⁴And you have said to them, Thus said YHWH: If you do not listen to Me, to walk in My law that I set before you, ⁵to listen to the words of My servants the prophets, whom I am sending to you, indeed, rising early and sending, and you have not listened, ⁶then I have given up this house as Shiloh, and this city I give up for a reviling to all nations of the earth." ⁷And the priests, and the prophets, and all the people, hear Jeremiah speaking these words in the house of YHWH, ⁸and it comes to pass, at the completion of Jeremiah's speaking all that YHWH has commanded him to speak to all the people, that the priests, and the prophets, and all the people catch him, saying, "You surely die! ⁹Why have you prophesied in the Name of YHWH, saying, This house will be as Shiloh, and this city is desolated, without inhabitant?" And all the people are assembled to Jeremiah in the house of YHWH. ¹⁰And the heads of Judah hear these things, and they go up from the house of the king [to] the house of YHWH, and sit in the opening of the New Gate of YHWH. ¹¹And the priests and the prophets speak to the heads, and to all the people, saying, "Judgment of death [is] for this man, for he has prophesied against this city, as you have heard with your ears." ¹²And Jeremiah speaks to all the heads, and to all the people, saying, "YHWH sent me to prophesy concerning this house, and concerning this city, all the words that you have heard. ¹³And now, amend your ways, and your doings, and listen to the voice of your God YHWH, and YHWH relents concerning the evil that He has spoken against you. ¹⁴And I, behold, I [am] in your hand, do to me as is good and as is right in your eyes; ¹⁵only, certainly know that if you are putting me to death, you are surely putting innocent blood on yourselves, and on this city, and on its inhabitants; for YHWH has truly sent me to you to speak all these words in your ears." ¹⁶And the heads and all the people say to the priests and to the prophets, "There is not a judgment of death for this man, for he has spoken to us in the Name of our God YHWH." ¹⁷And men from [the] elderly of the land rise up and speak to all the assembly of the people, saying, ¹⁸"Micah the Morashtite has been prophesying in the days of Hezekiah king of Judah, and he says to all the people of Judah, saying, Thus said YHWH of Hosts: Zion is a plowed field, and Jerusalem is heaps, || And the mountain of the house is for high places of a forest. ¹⁹Did Hezekiah king of Judah and all Judah put him to death? Did he not fear YHWH? Indeed, he appeases the face of YHWH, and YHWH relents concerning the calamity that He spoke against them; and we are doing great evil against our souls." ²⁰And there has also been a man prophesying in the Name of YHWH, Urijah son of Shemaiah, of Kirjath-Jearim, and he prophesies against this city, and against this land according to all the words of Jeremiah, ²¹and King Jehoiakim, and all his mighty ones, and all the heads, hear his words, and the king seeks to put him to death, and Urijah hears, and fears, and flees, and goes to Egypt. ²²And King Jehoiakim sends men to Egypt—Elnathan son of Achbor, and men with him to Egypt— ²³and they bring out Urijah from Egypt, and bring him to King Jehoiakim, and he strikes him with a sword, and casts his corpse to the graves of the sons of the people. ²⁴Only, the hand of Ahikam son of Shaphan has been with Jeremiah so as not to give him up into the hand of the people to put him to death.

CHAPTER 27

¹In the beginning of the reign of Jehoiakim son of Josiah, king of Judah, this word has been to Jeremiah from YHWH, saying, ²"Thus said YHWH to me: Make bands and yokes for yourself, ³and you have put them on your neck, and have sent them to the king of Edom, and to the king of Moab, and to the king of the sons of Ammon, and to the king of Tyre, and to the king of Sidon, by the hand of messengers who are coming to Jerusalem, to Zedekiah king of Judah; ⁴and you have commanded them for their lords, saying, Thus said YHWH of Hosts, God of Israel: ⁵Thus you say to your lords, I have made the earth with man, and the livestock that [are] on the face of the earth, by My great power, and by My outstretched arm, and I have given it to whom it has been right in My eyes. ⁶And now, I have given all these lands into the hand of Nebuchadnezzar king of Babylon, My servant, and I have also given the beast of the field to him to serve him; ⁷and all the nations have served him, and his son, and his son's son, until the coming in of the time of his land, also it; and many nations and great kings have made him serve them. ⁸And it has come to pass, the nation and the kingdom that does not serve him—Nebuchadnezzar king of Babylon—and that which does not put its neck into the yoke of the king of Babylon, with sword, and with famine, and with pestilence, I lay a charge on that nation—a declaration of YHWH—until I consume them by his hand. ⁹And you, you do not listen to your prophets, and to your diviners, and to your dreamers, and to your observers of clouds, and to your sorcerers who are speaking to you, saying, You do not serve the king of Babylon— ¹⁰For they are prophesying falsehood to you, so as to remove you far from your ground, and I have driven you out, and you have perished. ¹¹And the nation that causes its neck to enter into the yoke of the king of Babylon, and has served him—I have left it on its ground—a declaration of YHWH—and it has tilled it, and dwelt in it." ¹²And I have spoken to Zedekiah king of Judah according to all these words, saying, "Cause your necks to enter into the yoke of the king of Babylon, and serve him and his people, and live. ¹³Why do you die, you and your people, by sword, by famine, and by pestilence, as YHWH has spoken concerning the nation that does not serve the king of Babylon? ¹⁴And you do not listen to the words of the prophets who are speaking to you, saying, You do not serve the king of Babylon—for they are prophesying falsehood to you. ¹⁵For I have not sent them—a declaration of YHWH—and they are prophesying falsely in My Name, so as to drive you out, and you have perished, you and the prophets who are prophesying to you." ¹⁶And to the priests, and to all this people, I have spoken, saying, "Thus said YHWH: You do not listen to the words of your prophets, who are prophesying to you, saying, Behold, the vessels of the house of YHWH are now brought back from Babylon in haste, for they are prophesying falsehood to you. ¹⁷You do not listen to them; serve the king of Babylon and live! Why is this city a ruin? ¹⁸And if they are prophets, and if a word of YHWH is with them, let them now intercede with YHWH of Hosts, so that the vessels that are left in the house of YHWH, and [in] the house of the king of Judah, and in Jerusalem, have not gone into Babylon. ¹⁹For thus said YHWH of Hosts concerning the pillars, and concerning the sea, and concerning the bases, and concerning the rest of the vessels that are left in this city, ²⁰that Nebuchadnezzar king of Babylon has not taken, in his removing Jeconiah son of Jehoiakim king of Judah from Jerusalem to Babylon with all the nobles of Judah and Jerusalem, ²¹surely thus said YHWH of Hosts, God of Israel, concerning the vessels that are left of the house of YHWH, and of the house of the king of Judah, and [in] Jerusalem: ²²They are brought to Babylon, and there they

are until the day of My inspecting them—a declaration of Y<small>HWH</small>; then I have brought them up, and have brought them back to this place."

CHAPTER 28

¹And it comes to pass, in that year, in the beginning of the reign of Zedekiah king of Judah, in the fourth year, in the fifth month, Hananiah son of Azur the prophet, who [is] of Gibeon, has spoken to me in the house of Y<small>HWH</small>, before the eyes of the priests, and all the people, saying, ²"Thus spoke Y<small>HWH</small> of Hosts, God of Israel, saying, I have broken the yoke of the king of Babylon; ³within two years of days I am bringing back to this place all the vessels of the house of Y<small>HWH</small> that Nebuchadnezzar king of Babylon has taken from this place, and carries to Babylon, ⁴and Jeconiah son of Jehoiakim, king of Judah, and all the expulsion of Judah, who are entering Babylon, I am bringing back to this place—a declaration of Y<small>HWH</small>; for I break the yoke of the king of Babylon." ⁵And Jeremiah the prophet says to Hananiah the prophet, before the eyes of the priests, and before the eyes of all the people who are standing in the house of Y<small>HWH</small>, ⁶indeed, Jeremiah the prophet says, "Amen! So may Y<small>HWH</small> do; Y<small>HWH</small> establish your words that you have prophesied, to bring back the vessels of the house of Y<small>HWH</small> and all the expulsion from Babylon, to this place. ⁷Only, please hear this word that I am speaking in your ears, and in the ears of all the people. ⁸The prophets who have been before me, and before you, from of old, even they prophesy concerning many lands, and concerning great kingdoms, of battle, and of calamity, and of pestilence. ⁹The prophet who prophesies of peace, by the word of the prophet coming to pass, the prophet is known [as] one whom Y<small>HWH</small> has truly sent." ¹⁰And Hananiah the prophet takes the yoke from off the neck of Jeremiah the prophet, and breaks it, ¹¹and Hananiah speaks before the eyes of all the people, saying, "Thus said Y<small>HWH</small>: Thus I break the yoke of Nebuchadnezzar king of Babylon, within two years of days, from off the neck of all the nations"; and Jeremiah the prophet goes on his way. ¹²And there is a word of Y<small>HWH</small> to Jeremiah after the breaking, by Hananiah the prophet, of the yoke from off the neck of Jeremiah the prophet, saying, ¹³"Go, and you have spoken to Hananiah, saying, Thus said Y<small>HWH</small>: You have broken yokes of wood, and I have made yokes of iron instead of them. ¹⁴For thus said Y<small>HWH</small> of Hosts, God of Israel: I have put a yoke of iron on the neck of all these nations to serve Nebuchadnezzar king of Babylon, and they have served him, and I have also given the beast of the field to him." ¹⁵And Jeremiah the prophet says to Hananiah the prophet, "Now hear, O Hananiah; Y<small>HWH</small> has not sent you, and you have caused this people to trust on falsehood. ¹⁶Therefore, thus said Y<small>HWH</small>: Behold, I am casting you from off the face of the ground; you die this year, for you have spoken apostasy concerning Y<small>HWH</small>." ¹⁷And Hananiah the prophet dies in that year, in the seventh month.

CHAPTER 29

¹And these [are] the words of the letter that Jeremiah the prophet sent from Jerusalem to the remnant of [the] elderly of the expulsion, and to the priests, and to the prophets, and to all the people—whom Nebuchadnezzar removed from Jerusalem to Babylon, ²after the going forth of Jeconiah the king, and the mistress, and the officers, heads of Judah and Jerusalem, and the craftsman, and the smith, from Jerusalem— ³by the hand of Eleasah son of Shaphan, and Gemariah son of Hilkiah, whom Zedekiah king of Judah sent to Babylon, to Nebuchadnezzar king of Babylon, saying, ⁴"Thus said Y<small>HWH</small> of Hosts, God of Israel, to all the expulsion that I removed from Jerusalem to Babylon: ⁵Build houses and abide; and plant gardens and eat their fruit; ⁶take wives and beget sons and daughters; and take wives for your sons, and give your daughters to husbands, and they bear sons and daughters; and multiply there, and you are not few; ⁷and seek the peace of the city to where I have removed you, and pray to Y<small>HWH</small> for it, for in its peace you have peace. ⁸For thus said Y<small>HWH</small> of Hosts, God of Israel: Do not let your prophets who [are] in your midst, and your diviners, lift you up, nor listen to their dreams, that you are causing [them] to dream; ⁹for they are prophesying with falsehood to you in My Name; I have not sent them, a declaration of Y<small>HWH</small>. ¹⁰For thus said Y<small>HWH</small>: Surely at the fullness of Babylon—seventy years—I inspect you, and have established My good word toward you, to bring you back to this place. ¹¹For I have known the thoughts that I am thinking toward you—a declaration of Y<small>HWH</small>; thoughts of peace, and not of evil, to give posterity and hope to you. ¹²And you have called Me, and have gone, and have prayed to Me, and I have listened to you, ¹³and you have sought Me, and have found, for you seek Me with all your heart; ¹⁴and I have been found by you—a declaration of Y<small>HWH</small>; and I have turned back [to] your captivity, and have gathered you out of all the nations, and out of all the places to where I have driven you—a declaration of Y<small>HWH</small>—and I have brought you back to the place from where I removed you. ¹⁵Because you have said, Y<small>HWH</small> has raised up prophets to us in Babylon, ¹⁶surely thus said Y<small>HWH</small> concerning the king who is sitting on the throne of David, and concerning all the people that are dwelling in this city, your brothers who did not go forth with you in the expulsion— ¹⁷thus said Y<small>HWH</small> of Hosts: Behold, I am sending the sword, the famine, and the pestilence among them, and I have given them up as figs that [are] vile, that are not eaten because of badness. ¹⁸And I have pursued after them with sword, with famine, and with pestilence, and have given them for a trembling to all kingdoms of the earth, for a curse and for an astonishment, and for a hissing, and for a reproach among all the nations to where I have driven them, ¹⁹because that they have not listened to My words—a declaration of Y<small>HWH</small>—that I sent to them by My servants the prophets, rising early and sending, and you did not listen—a declaration of Y<small>HWH</small>. ²⁰And you, hear a word of Y<small>HWH</small>, all you of the captivity that I have sent from Jerusalem to Babylon— ²¹thus said Y<small>HWH</small> of Hosts, God of Israel, concerning Ahab son of Kolaiah, and concerning Zedekiah son of Maaseiah, who are prophesying falsehood to you in My Name: Behold, I am giving them into the hand of Nebuchadnezzar king of Babylon, and he has struck them before your eyes, ²²and because of them a reviling has been taken by all the expulsion of Judah that [are] in Babylon, saying, Y<small>HWH</small> sets you as Zedekiah, and as Ahab, whom the king of Babylon roasted with fire; ²³because that they have done folly in Israel, and commit adultery with the wives of their neighbors, and falsely speak a word in My Name that I have not commanded them, and I [am] He who knows and a witness—a declaration of Y<small>HWH</small>. ²⁴And you speak to Shemaiah the Nehelamite, saying, ²⁵Thus said Y<small>HWH</small> of Hosts, God of Israel, saying, Because that you have sent letters in your name to all the people who [are] in Jerusalem, and to Zephaniah son of Maaseiah the priest, and to all the priests, saying, ²⁶Y<small>HWH</small> has made you priest instead of Jehoiada the priest, for there being inspectors of the house of Y<small>HWH</small> over every man [who] is mad and making himself a prophet, and you have put him in the stocks and in the pillory. ²⁷And now, why have you not pushed against Jeremiah of Anathoth, who is making himself a prophet to you? ²⁸Because that he has sent to us [in] Babylon, saying, It [is] long, build houses and abide; and plant gardens and eat their fruit." ²⁹And Zephaniah the priest reads this letter in the ears of Jeremiah the prophet. ³⁰And there is a word of Y<small>HWH</small> to Jeremiah, saying, ³¹"Send to all the expulsion, saying, Thus said Y<small>HWH</small> concerning Shemaiah the Nehelamite: Because that Shemaiah prophesied to you, and I have not sent him, and he causes you to trust on falsehood, ³²therefore, thus said Y<small>HWH</small>: Behold, I am seeing after Shemaiah the Nehelamite, and after his seed, he has none dwelling in the midst of this people, nor does he look on the good that I am doing to My people," a declaration of Y<small>HWH</small>, "for he has spoken apostasy against Y<small>HWH</small>."

CHAPTER 30

¹The word that has been to Jeremiah from Y<small>HWH</small>, saying, ²"Thus spoke Y<small>HWH</small>, God of Israel, saying, Write for yourself all the words that I have spoken to you on a scroll. ³For behold, days are coming—a declaration of Y<small>HWH</small>—and I have turned back [to] the captivity of My people Israel and Judah, said Y<small>HWH</small>, and I have caused them to return to the land that I gave to their fathers, and they possess it." ⁴And these [are] the words that Y<small>HWH</small> has spoken concerning Israel and concerning Judah: ⁵Surely thus said Y<small>HWH</small>: "We have heard a voice of trembling, || Fear—and there is no peace. ⁶Now ask and see, is a male bringing forth? Why have I seen every man || [With] his hands on his loins, as a travailing woman, || And all faces have been turned to paleness? ⁷Woe! For that day [is]

JEREMIAH

great, without any like it, ‖ Indeed, it [is] the time of Jacob's tribulation, ‖ Yet he is saved out of it. ⁸And it has come to pass in that day, ‖ A declaration of YHWH of Hosts, ‖ I break his yoke from off your neck, ‖ And I draw away your bands, ‖ And strangers lay no more service on him. ⁹And they have served their God YHWH, ‖ And David their king whom I raise up to them. ¹⁰And you, do not be afraid, My servant Jacob, ‖ A declaration of YHWH, ‖ Nor be frightened, O Israel, ‖ For behold, I am saving you from afar, ‖ And your seed from the land of their captivity, ‖ And Jacob has turned back and rested, ‖ And is quiet, and there is none troubling. ¹¹For I [am] with you," ‖ A declaration of YHWH, ‖ "To save you, ‖ For I make an end of all the nations ‖ To where I have scattered you, ‖ Only, I do not make an end of you, ‖ And I have disciplined you in judgment, ‖ And do not entirely acquit you." ¹²For thus said YHWH: "Your breach is incurable, your stroke grievous, ¹³There is none judging your cause to bind up, ‖ There are no healing medicines for you. ¹⁴All loving you have forgotten you, ‖ They do not seek you, ‖ For I struck you with the stroke of an enemy, ‖ The discipline of a fierce one, ‖ Because of the abundance of your iniquity, your sins have been mighty! ¹⁵Why do you cry concerning your breach? Your pain [is] incurable, ‖ Because of the abundance of your iniquity, ‖ Your sins have been mighty! I have done these to you. ¹⁶Therefore all consuming you are consumed, ‖ And all your adversaries—all of them—Go into captivity, ‖ And your spoilers have been for a spoil, ‖ And I give up all your plunderers to plunder. ¹⁷For I increase health to you, ‖ And I heal you from your strokes," ‖ A declaration of YHWH, ‖ "For they have called you an outcast, [saying], ‖ It [is] Zion, ‖ There is none seeking for her." ¹⁸Thus said YHWH: "Behold, I turn back [to] the captivity of the tents of Jacob, ‖ And I pity his dwelling places, ‖ And the city has been built on its heap, ‖ And the palace remains according to its ordinance. ¹⁹And thanksgiving has gone forth from them, ‖ And the voice of playful ones, ‖ And I have multiplied them and they are not few, ‖ And made them honorable, and they are not small. ²⁰And his sons have been as before, ‖ And his congregation is established before Me, ‖ And I have seen after all his oppressors. ²¹And his majestic one has been of himself, ‖ And his ruler goes forth from his midst, ‖ And I have caused him to draw near, ‖ And he has drawn near to Me, ‖ For who [is] he who has pledged his heart ‖ To draw near to Me?" A declaration of YHWH. ²²"And you have been to Me for a people, ‖ And I am to you for God." ²³Behold, a whirlwind of YHWH—Fury has gone forth—a cutting whirlwind, ‖ It stays on the head of the wicked. ²⁴The fierceness of the anger of YHWH ‖ Does not turn back until He has done [it], ‖ Indeed, until His establishing the purposes of His heart. In the latter end of the days you consider it!

CHAPTER 31

¹"At that time," a declaration of YHWH, "I am the God of all families of Israel, ‖ And they are My people." ²Thus said YHWH: "A people remaining from the sword ‖ Have found grace in the wilderness ‖ When Israel went to find rest." ³YHWH has appeared to me from afar, "I have loved you with perpetual love, ‖ Therefore I have drawn you [with] kindness. ⁴I build you again, ‖ And you have been built, ‖ O virgin of Israel, ‖ You put on your tambourines again, ‖ And have gone out in the chorus of the playful. ⁵You plant vineyards in mountains of Samaria again, ‖ Planters have planted, and made common. ⁶For there is a day, ‖ Watchmen have cried on Mount Ephraim, ‖ Rise, and we go up to Zion, to our God YHWH"; ⁷For thus said YHWH: "Sing [with] joy for Jacob, ‖ And cry aloud at the head of the nations, ‖ Sound, praise, and say, ‖ Save, O YHWH, Your people, the remnant of Israel. ⁸Behold, I am bringing them in from the north country, ‖ And have gathered them from the sides of the earth, ‖ Blind and lame [are] among them, ‖ Conceiving and travailing one—together, ‖ A great assembly—they return here. ⁹They come in with weeping, ‖ And I bring them with supplications, ‖ I cause them to go to streams of waters, ‖ In a right way—they do not stumble in it, ‖ For I have been a Father to Israel, ‖ And Ephraim—he [is] My firstborn." ¹⁰Hear a word of YHWH, O nations, ‖ And declare among the far off in the islands, and say: He who is scattering Israel gathers him, ‖ And has kept His flock as a shepherd, ¹¹For YHWH has ransomed Jacob, ‖ And redeemed him from a hand stronger than he. ¹²And they have come in, ‖ And have sung in the high place of Zion, ‖ And flowed to the goodness of YHWH, ‖ For wheat, and for new wine, and for oil, ‖ And for the young of the flock and herd, ‖ And their soul has been as a watered garden, ‖ And they do not add to grieve anymore. ¹³"Then a virgin rejoices in a chorus, ‖ Both young men and old men—together, ‖ And I have turned their mourning to joy, ‖ And have comforted them, ‖ And gladdened them above their sorrow, ¹⁴And satisfied the soul of the priests [with] fatness, ‖ And My people are satisfied with My goodness," ‖ A declaration of YHWH. ¹⁵Thus said YHWH: "A voice is heard in Ramah, ‖ Wailing [and] the weeping of bitterness, ‖ Rachel is weeping for her sons, ‖ She has refused to be comforted for her sons, because they are not." ¹⁶Thus said YHWH: "Withhold your voice from weeping, and your eyes from tears, ‖ For there is a reward for your work," ‖ A declaration of YHWH, ‖ "And they have turned back from the land of the enemy. ¹⁷And there is hope for your latter end," ‖ A declaration of YHWH, ‖ "And the sons have turned back [to] their border. ¹⁸I have surely heard Ephraim bemoaning himself, ‖ You have disciplined me, ‖ And I am disciplined, as a heifer [that is] not taught, ‖ Turn me back, and I turn back, ‖ For You [are] my God YHWH. ¹⁹For after my turning back I regretted, ‖ And after my being instructed I struck on the thigh, ‖ I have been ashamed, I have also blushed, ‖ For I have borne the reproach of my youth. ²⁰Is Ephraim a precious son to Me? A child of delights? For since My speaking against him, ‖ I still thoroughly remember him, ‖ Therefore My bowels have been moved for him, ‖ I love him greatly," ‖ A declaration of YHWH. ²¹"Set up signs for yourself, ‖ Make heaps for yourself, ‖ Set your heart to the highway, the way you went, ‖ Turn back, O virgin of Israel, ‖ Turn back to these cities of yours. ²²Until when do you withdraw yourself, O backsliding daughter? For YHWH has prepared a new thing in the land, ‖ Woman surrounds man." ²³Thus said YHWH of Hosts, God of Israel: "Still they say this word in the land of Judah, ‖ And in its cities, ‖ In My turning back [to] their captivity, ‖ YHWH blesses you, habitation of righteousness, ‖ Mountain of holiness. ²⁴And farmers have dwelt in Judah, ‖ And in all its cities together, ‖ And they have journeyed in order. ²⁵For I have satiated the weary soul, ‖ And I have filled every grieved soul." ²⁶On this I have awoken, and I behold, and my sleep has been sweet to me. ²⁷"Behold, days are coming," ‖ A declaration of YHWH, ‖ "And I have sown the house of Israel, ‖ And the house of Judah, ‖ With seed of man and seed of beast. ²⁸And it has been, as I watched over them to pluck up, ‖ And to break down, and to throw down, ‖ And to destroy, and to afflict; So I watch over them to build, and to plant," ‖ A declaration of YHWH. ²⁹"In those days they no longer say: Fathers have eaten unripe fruit, ‖ And the sons' teeth are blunted. ³⁰But—each dies for his own iniquity, ‖ Every man who is eating the unripe fruit, ‖ His teeth are blunted. ³¹Behold, days are coming," ‖ A declaration of YHWH, ‖ "And I have made a new covenant ‖ With the house of Israel ‖ And with the house of Judah, ³²Not like the covenant that I made with their fathers, ‖ In the day of My laying hold on their hand, ‖ To bring them out of the land of Egypt, ‖ In that they made My covenant void, ‖ And I ruled over them," ‖ A declaration of YHWH. ³³"For this [is] the covenant that I make, ‖ With the house of Israel, after those days," ‖ A declaration of YHWH, ‖ "I have given My law in their inward part, ‖ And I write it on their heart, ‖ And I have been their God, ‖ And they are My people. ³⁴And they do not teach anymore ‖ Each his neighbor, and each his brother, ‖ Saying, Know YHWH, ‖ For they all know Me, from their least to their greatest," ‖ A declaration of YHWH; "For I pardon their iniquity, ‖ And I make no more mention of their sin." ³⁵Thus said YHWH, ‖ Who is giving the sun for a light by day, ‖ The statutes of moon and stars for a light by night, ‖ Quieting the sea when its billows roar, ‖ YHWH of Hosts [is] His Name: ³⁶"If these statutes depart from before Me," ‖ A declaration of YHWH, ‖ "Even the seed of Israel ceases ‖ From being a nation before Me [for] all the days." ³⁷Thus said YHWH: "If the heavens above can be measured, ‖ And the foundations of earth searched below, ‖ Even I kick against all the seed of Israel, ‖ For all that they have done," ‖ A declaration of YHWH. ³⁸"Behold, days [are coming]," ‖ A declaration of YHWH, ‖ "And the city has been

built for YHWH, || From the Tower of Hananeel to the Corner Gate. ³⁹And the measuring line has gone out again before it, over the height of Gareb, || And it has gone around to Goah. ⁴⁰And all the valley of the carcasses and of the ashes, || And all the fields to the Brook of Kidron, || To the corner of the Horse Gate eastward, || [Are] holy to YHWH, || It is not plucked up, || Nor is it thrown down anymore for all time!"

CHAPTER 32

¹The word that has been to Jeremiah from YHWH in the tenth year of Zedekiah king of Judah—it [is] the eighteenth year of Nebuchadnezzar— ²And then the forces of the king of Babylon are laying siege against Jerusalem, and Jeremiah the prophet has been shut up in the court of the prison that [is] in the house of the king of Judah, ³where Zedekiah king of Judah has shut him up, saying, "Why are you prophesying, saying, Thus said YHWH: Behold, I am giving this city into the hand of the king of Babylon, and he has captured it; ⁴and Zedekiah king of Judah does not escape out of the hand of the Chaldeans, but is certainly given into the hand of the king of Babylon, and his mouth has spoken with his mouth, and his eyes see his eyes, ⁵and he leads Zedekiah [to] Babylon, and there he is until My inspecting him—a declaration of YHWH—because you fight with the Chaldeans, you do not prosper." ⁶And Jeremiah says, "A word of YHWH has been to me, saying, ⁷Behold, Hanameel son of Shallum, your uncle, is coming to you, saying, Buy my field that [is] in Anathoth for yourself, for the right of redemption [is] yours to buy." ⁸And Hanameel, my uncle's son, comes to me, according to the word of YHWH, to the court of the prison, and says to me, "Please buy my field that [is] in Anathoth, that [is] in the land of Benjamin, for the right of possession [is] yours, and redemption yours—buy [it] for yourself." And I know that it [is] the word of YHWH, ⁹and I buy the field that [is] in Anathoth from Hanameel, my uncle's son, and I weigh the money to him—seventeen shekels of silver. ¹⁰And I write in a scroll, and seal, and cause witnesses to testify, and weigh the silver in balances; ¹¹and I take the purchase scroll, the sealed one, according to law and custom, and the open one; ¹²and I give the purchase scroll to Baruch son of Neriah, son of Maaseiah, before the eyes of Hanameel, my uncle's son, and before the eyes of the witnesses, those writing in the purchase scroll, before the eyes of all the Jews who are sitting in the court of the prison. ¹³And I charge Baruch before their eyes, saying, ¹⁴"Thus said YHWH of Hosts, God of Israel: Take these scrolls, this purchase scroll, both the sealed one and the open one, and you have put them in an earthen vessel, that they may remain many days. ¹⁵For thus said YHWH of Hosts, God of Israel: Houses and fields and vineyards are bought in this land again." ¹⁶And I pray to YHWH after my giving the purchase scroll to Baruch son of Neriah, saying, ¹⁷"Aah! Lord YHWH, behold, You have made the heavens and the earth by Your great power, and by Your outstretched arm; there is nothing too wonderful for You: ¹⁸doing kindness to thousands, and repaying iniquity of fathers into the bosom of their sons after them; God, the great, the mighty, YHWH of Hosts [is] His Name; ¹⁹great in counsel, and mighty in act, in that Your eyes are open on all the ways of the sons of Adam, to give to each according to his ways, and according to the fruit of his doings; ²⁰in that you have done signs and wonders in the land of Egypt to this day, and in Israel, and among men, and You make for Yourself a name as [at] this day. ²¹And You bring forth Your people Israel from the land of Egypt, with signs and with wonders, and by a strong hand, and by an outstretched arm, and by great fear, ²²and you give to them this land that you swore to their fathers to give to them, a land flowing with milk and honey, ²³and they come in, and possess it, and they have not listened to Your voice, and have not walked in Your law, all that which You laid a charge on them to do they have not done, and You proclaim all this calamity [to] them. ²⁴Behold, the [siege] mounds have come to the city to capture it, and the city has been given into the hand of the Chaldeans who are fighting against it, because of the sword, and the famine, and the pestilence; and that which You have spoken has come to pass, and behold, You are seeing. ²⁵Yet You have said to me, O Lord YHWH, Buy the field for yourself with money, and cause witnesses to testify—and the city has been given into the hand of the Chaldeans!" ²⁶And the word of YHWH is to Jeremiah, saying, ²⁷"Behold, I [am] YHWH, God of all flesh: is anything too wonderful for Me?" ²⁸Therefore, thus said YHWH: "Behold, I am giving this city into the hand of the Chaldeans, and into the hand of Nebuchadnezzar king of Babylon, and he has captured it. ²⁹And the Chaldeans who are fighting against this city have come in, and they have set this city on fire, and have burned it—and the houses on whose roofs they made incense to Ba'al, and poured out drink-offerings to other gods, so as to provoke Me to anger. ³⁰For the sons of Israel and the sons of Judah have been doing only evil in My eyes from their youth; for the sons of Israel are surely provoking Me with the work of their hands," a declaration of YHWH. ³¹"For this city has been a cause of My anger and a cause of My fury, even from the day that they built it, and to this day—to turn it aside from before My face, ³²because of all the evil of the sons of Israel, and of the sons of Judah that they have done, so as to provoke Me—they, their kings, their heads, their priests, and their prophets, and the men of Judah, and the inhabitants of Jerusalem. ³³And they turn the neck to Me, and not the face, and teaching them, rising early and teaching, and they are not listening to accept instruction. ³⁴And they set their abominations in the house over which My Name is called, so as to defile it. ³⁵And they build the high places of Ba'al that [are] in the Valley of the Son of Hinnom, to cause their sons and their daughters to pass through to Molech, which I did not command them, nor did it come up on My heart to do this abomination, so as to cause Judah to sin. ³⁶And now, therefore, thus said YHWH, God of Israel, concerning this city, of which you are saying, It has been given into the hand of the king of Babylon by sword, and by famine, and by pestilence: ³⁷Behold, I am gathering them out of all the lands to where I have driven them in My anger, and in My fury, and in great wrath, and I have brought them back to this place, and have caused them to dwell confidently; ³⁸and they have been to Me for a people, and I am to them for God; ³⁹and I have given to them one heart and one way, to fear Me all the days, for the good of them and their sons after them: ⁴⁰and I have made a perpetual covenant for them, in that I do not turn back from after them for My doing them good, and I put My fear in their heart, so as not to turn aside from me; ⁴¹and I have rejoiced over them to do them good, and have planted them in this land in truth, with all my heart, and with all My soul." ⁴²For thus said YHWH: "As I brought to this people all this great calamity, so I am bringing on them all the good that I am speaking concerning them; ⁴³and the field has been bought in this land of which you are saying, It [is] a desolation, without man and beast, it has been given into the hand of the Chaldeans. ⁴⁴They buy fields with money, so as to write in a scroll, and to seal, and to cause witnesses to testify, in the land of Benjamin, and in outskirts of Jerusalem, and in cities of Judah, and in cities of the hill-country, and in cities of the low country, and in cities of the south, for I return their captivity," a declaration of YHWH.

CHAPTER 33

¹And there is a word of YHWH to Jeremiah a second time—and he [is] yet detained in the court of the prison—saying: ²"Thus said YHWH who has made it, YHWH who has formed it, to establish it, YHWH [is] His Name: ³Call to Me, and I answer you, indeed, I declare to you great and inaccessible things—you have not known them. ⁴For thus said YHWH, God of Israel, concerning the houses of this city, and concerning the houses of the kings of Judah that are broken down for the [siege] mounds, and for the tool; ⁵they are coming to fight with the Chaldeans, and to fill them with the carcasses of men, whom I have struck in My anger, and in My fury, and [for] whom I have hidden My face from this city, because of all their evil: ⁶Behold, I am increasing health and cure to it, || And have healed them, and revealed to them || The abundance of peace and truth. ⁷And I have turned back the captivity of Judah, || And the captivity of Israel, || And I have built them as at the first, ⁸And cleansed them from all their iniquity || That they have sinned against Me, || And I have pardoned all their iniquities || That they have sinned against Me, || And that they transgressed against Me. ⁹And it has been for a name of joy to Me, || For praise, and for beauty, to all nations of the earth, || Who hear of all the good that I am doing them, || And they have feared, || And they have trembled for all the good, || And for all the peace, that I am doing to it." ¹⁰Thus said YHWH: "Again is

heard in this place—of which you are saying, It [is] dry, without man and without beast, || In cities of Judah, and in streets of Jerusalem, || That are desolated, without man, || And without inhabitant, and without beast— ¹¹A voice of joy and a voice of gladness, || Voice of bridegroom and voice of bride, || The voice of those saying, || Thank YHWH of Hosts, for YHWH [is] good, || For His kindness [is] for all time, || Who are bringing in thanksgiving to the house of YHWH, || For I return the captivity of the land, || As at the first," said YHWH. ¹²Thus said YHWH of Hosts: "Again there is in this place—that is dry, || Without man and beast, || And in all its cities—a habitation of shepherds, || Causing the flock to lie down. ¹³In the cities of the hill-country, || In the cities of the low country, || And in the cities of the south, || And in the land of Benjamin, || And in the outskirts of Jerusalem, || And in the cities of Judah, || Again the flock passes by under the hands of the numberer," said YHWH. ¹⁴"Behold, days are coming," a declaration of YHWH, "And I have established the good word || That I spoke to the house of Israel, || And concerning the house of Judah. ¹⁵In those days, and at that time, || I cause a Shoot of righteousness to shoot up to David, || And He has done judgment and righteousness in the earth. ¹⁶In those days Judah is saved, || And Jerusalem dwells confidently, || And this [is] what she is called: YHWH [is] Our Righteousness." ¹⁷For thus said YHWH: "A man sitting on the throne of the house of Israel [is] never cut off from David, ¹⁸And to the priests—the Levites, || A man is not cut off from before My face, || Causing a burnt-offering to ascend, || And perfuming a present, and making sacrifice—all the days." ¹⁹And there is a word of YHWH to Jeremiah, saying, ²⁰"Thus said YHWH: If you can break My covenant with the day, || And My covenant with the night, || So that they are not daily and nightly in their season, ²¹My covenant is also broken with My servant David, || So that he does not have a son reigning on his throne, || And with the Levites the priests, My ministers. ²²As the host of the heavens is not numbered, || Nor the sand of the sea measured, || So I multiply the seed of My servant David, || And My ministers the Levites." ²³And there is a word of YHWH to Jeremiah, saying, ²⁴"Have you not considered what this people have spoken, saying, || The two families on which YHWH fixed, || He rejects them? And they despise My people, so that they are no longer a people before them!" ²⁵Thus said YHWH: "If My covenant [is] not with day and night, || [And if] I have not appointed the statutes of the heavens and earth— ²⁶I also reject the seed of Jacob, and My servant David, || From taking rulers from his seed || For the seed of Abraham, Isaac, and Jacob, || For I return their captivity, and have pitied them."

CHAPTER 34

¹The word that has been to Jeremiah from YHWH—and Nebuchadnezzar king of Babylon, and all his force, and all kingdoms of the land of the dominion of his hand, and all the peoples are fighting against Jerusalem, and against all its cities—saying: ²"Thus said YHWH, God of Israel: Go, and you have spoken to Zedekiah king of Judah, and have said to him, Thus said YHWH: Behold, I am giving this city into the hand of the king of Babylon, and he has burned it with fire, ³and you do not escape out of his hand, for you are certainly caught, and you are given into his hand, and your eyes see the eyes of the king of Babylon, and his mouth speaks with your mouth, and you enter Babylon. ⁴Only, hear a word of YHWH, O Zedekiah king of Judah—thus said YHWH to you: You do not die by sword, ⁵you die in peace, and with the burnings of your fathers, the former kings who have been before you, so they make a burning for you; and, Oh, lord, they lament for you, for the word I have spoken—a declaration of YHWH." ⁶And Jeremiah the prophet speaks all these words to Zedekiah king of Judah in Jerusalem, ⁷and the forces of the king of Babylon are fighting against Jerusalem, and against all the cities of Judah that are left—against Lachish, and against Azekah, for these have been left among the cities of Judah, cities of fortresses. ⁸The word that has been to Jeremiah from YHWH, after the making of a covenant by King Zedekiah with all the people who [are] in Jerusalem, to proclaim liberty to them, ⁹to each send out his manservant, and each his maidservant—the Hebrew and the Hebrewess—free, so as not to lay service on them—on any Jew, a brother, a man; ¹⁰and all the heads listen, and all the people who have come into the covenant to each send forth his manservant and each his maidservant free, so as not to lay service on them anymore, indeed, they listen, and send them away; ¹¹and they turn afterward, and cause the menservants and the maidservants to return, whom they had sent forth free, and they subdue them for menservants and for maidservants. ¹²And there is a word of YHWH to Jeremiah from YHWH, saying, ¹³"Thus said YHWH, God of Israel: I made a covenant with your fathers in the day of My bringing them forth from the land of Egypt, from a house of servants, saying, ¹⁴At the end of seven years you each send forth his brother, the Hebrew, who is sold to you, and has served you six years, indeed, you have sent him forth from you free: and your fathers did not listen to Me, nor inclined their ear. ¹⁵And today you turn back and you do that which is right in My eyes, to each proclaim liberty to his neighbor, and you make a covenant before Me in the house over which My Name is called. ¹⁶And you turn back, and defile My Name, and you each cause his manservant and each his maidservant, whom he had sent forth free (at their pleasure), to return, and you subdue them to be for menservants and for maidservants to you." ¹⁷Therefore, thus said YHWH: "You have not listened to Me to proclaim freedom, each to his brother, and each to his neighbor; behold, I am proclaiming to you liberty," a declaration of YHWH, "to the sword, to the pestilence, and to the famine, and I have given you for a trembling to all kingdoms of the earth. ¹⁸And I have given the men who are transgressing My covenant, who have not established the words of the covenant that they have made before Me, by the calf, that they have cut in two, and pass through between its pieces— ¹⁹heads of Judah, and heads of Jerusalem, the officers, and the priests, and all the people of the land who had passed through between the pieces of the calf— ²⁰indeed, I have given them into the hand of their enemies, and into the hand of those seeking their soul, and their carcass has been for food to the bird of the heavens, and to the beast of the earth. ²¹And I give Zedekiah king of Judah and his heads into the hand of their enemies, and into the hand of those seeking their soul, and into the hand of the forces of the king of Babylon that are going up from off you. ²²Behold, I am commanding," a declaration of YHWH, "and have brought them back to this city, and they have fought against it, and captured it, and burned it with fire, and I make the cities of Judah a desolation—without inhabitant."

CHAPTER 35

¹The word that has been to Jeremiah from YHWH, in the days of Jehoiakim son of Josiah king of Judah, saying, ²"Go to the house of the Rechabites, and you have spoken with them, and brought them into the house of YHWH, to one of the chambers, and caused them to drink wine." ³And I take Jaazaniah son of Jeremiah, son of Habazziniah, and his brothers, and all his sons, and all the house of the Rechabites, ⁴and bring them into the house of YHWH, to the chamber of the sons of Hanan son of Igdaliah, a man of God, that [is] near to the chamber of the princes, that [is] above the chamber of Maaseiah son of Shallum, keeper of the threshold; ⁵and I put before the sons of the house of the Rechabites goblets full of wine, and cups, and I say to them, "Drink wine." ⁶And they say, "We do not drink wine: for Jonadab son of Rechab, our father, charged us, saying, You do not drink wine, you and your sons—for all time; ⁷and you do not build a house, and you do not sow seed, and you do not plant a vineyard, nor have of [these]; for you dwell in tents all your days, that you may live many days on the face of the ground to where you are sojourning. ⁸And we listen to the voice of Jonadab son of Rechab, our father, to all that he commanded us, not to drink wine all our days, we, our wives, our sons, and our daughters; ⁹nor to build houses to dwell in; and we have no vineyard, and field, and seed; ¹⁰and we dwell in tents, and we listen, and we do according to all that Jonadab our father commanded us; ¹¹and it comes to pass, in the coming up of Nebuchadnezzar king of Babylon to the land, that we say, Come, and we enter Jerusalem, because of the force of the Chaldeans, and because of the force of Aram—and we dwell in Jerusalem." ¹²And there is a word of YHWH to Jeremiah, saying, "Thus said YHWH of Hosts, God of Israel: ¹³Go, and you have said to the men of Judah and to the inhabitants of Jerusalem: Do you not receive instruction to listen to My words? A declaration of YHWH. ¹⁴The words of Jonadab son of Rechab, when

he commanded his sons not to drink wine, have stood, and they have not drunk to this day, for they have obeyed the command of their father; and I have spoken to you, rising early and speaking, and you have not listened to Me. ¹⁵And I send all My servants the prophets to you, rising early and sending, saying, Please turn back, each from his evil way, and amend your doings, indeed, you do not walk after other gods, to serve them; and dwell on the ground that I have given to you and to your fathers; and you have not inclined your ear, nor listened to Me. ¹⁶Because the sons of Jonadab son of Rechab have stood by the command of their father that he commanded them, and this people have not listened to Me, ¹⁷therefore, thus said YHWH, God of Hosts, God of Israel: Behold, I am bringing to Judah, and to all inhabitants of Jerusalem, all the calamity that I have spoken against them, because I have spoken to them, and they have not listened, indeed, I call to them, and they have not answered." ¹⁸And Jeremiah said to the house of the Rechabites: "Thus said YHWH of Hosts, God of Israel: Because that you have listened to the command of your father Jonadab, and you observe all his commands, and do according to all that he commanded you; ¹⁹therefore, thus said YHWH of Hosts, God of Israel: A man of Jonadab son of Rechab is not cut off [from] standing before Me all the days."

CHAPTER 36

¹And it comes to pass, in the fourth year of Jehoiakim son of Josiah king of Judah, this word has been to Jeremiah from YHWH, saying, ²"Take a roll of a scroll to yourself, and you have written on it all the words that I have spoken to you concerning Israel, and concerning Judah, and concerning all the nations, from the day I spoke to you, from the days of Josiah, even to this day; ³perhaps the house of Israel so hears all the evil that I am thinking of doing to them, so that they each turn back from his evil way, and I have been propitious to their iniquity, and to their sin." ⁴And Jeremiah calls Baruch son of Neriah, and Baruch writes from the mouth of Jeremiah all the words of YHWH, that He has spoken to him, on a roll of a scroll. ⁵And Jeremiah commands Baruch, saying, "I am restrained, I am not able to enter the house of YHWH; ⁶but you have entered—and you have read in the scroll that you have written from my mouth, the words of YHWH, in the ears of the people, in the house of YHWH, in the day of the fast, and you also read them in the ears of all Judah who are coming in from their cities; ⁷perhaps their supplication so falls before YHWH, and they each turn back from his evil way, for the anger and the fury that YHWH has spoken concerning this people [is] great." ⁸And Baruch son of Neriah does according to all that Jeremiah the prophet commanded him, to read in the scroll the words of YHWH in the house of YHWH. ⁹And it comes to pass, in the fifth year of Jehoiakim son of Josiah king of Judah, in the ninth month, they proclaimed a fast before YHWH to all the people in Jerusalem, and to all the people who are coming in from cities of Judah to Jerusalem; ¹⁰and Baruch reads in the scroll the words of Jeremiah in the house of YHWH, in the chamber of Gemariah son of Shaphan, the scribe, in the higher court, at the opening of the New Gate of the house of YHWH, in the ears of all the people. ¹¹And Michaiah son of Gemariah, son of Shaphan, hears all the words of YHWH from off the scroll, ¹²and he goes down [to] the house of the king, to the chamber of the scribe, and behold, there all the heads are sitting: Elishama the scribe, and Delaiah son of Shemaiah, and Elnathan son of Acbor, and Gemariah son of Shaphan, and Zedekiah son of Hananiah, and all the heads. ¹³And Micaiah declares to them all the words that he has heard when Baruch reads in the scroll in the ears of the people; ¹⁴and all the heads send to Baruch, Jehudi son of Nethaniah, son of Shelemiah, son of Cushi, saying, "Take in your hand the scroll, which you have read in the ears of the people, and come." And Baruch son of Neriah takes the scroll in his hand and comes to them, ¹⁵and they say to him, "Please sit down and read it in our ears," and Baruch reads [it] in their ears, ¹⁶and it comes to pass, when they hear all the words, they have been afraid—one to another—and say to Baruch, "We surely declare all these words to the king." ¹⁷And they asked Baruch, saying, "Please declare to us, how did you write all these words from his mouth?" ¹⁸And Baruch says to them, "He pronounces from his mouth all these words to me, and I am writing on the scroll with ink." ¹⁹And the heads say to Baruch, "Go, be hidden, you and Jeremiah, and let no one know where you [are]." ²⁰And they go to the king, to the court, and they have laid up the scroll in the chamber of Elishama the scribe, and they declare all the words in the ears of the king. ²¹And the king sends Jehudi to take the scroll, and he takes it out of the chamber of Elishama the scribe, and Jehudi reads it in the ears of the king, and in the ears of all the heads who are standing by the king; ²²and the king is sitting in the winter-house, in the ninth month, and the stove is burning before him, ²³and it comes to pass, when Jehudi reads three or four leaves, he cuts it out with the scribe's knife, and has cast [it] into the fire that [is] on the stove, until the consumption of all the scroll by the fire that [is] on the stove. ²⁴And the king and all his servants who are hearing all these words have not been afraid, nor torn their garments. ²⁵And also Elnathan, and Delaiah, and Gemariah have interceded with the king not to burn the scroll, and he has not listened to them. ²⁶And the king commands Jerahmeel son of Hammelek, and Seraiah son of Azriel, and Shelemiah son of Abdeel, to take Baruch the scribe and Jeremiah the prophet, and YHWH hides them. ²⁷And there is a word of YHWH to Jeremiah—after the king's burning the scroll, even the words that Baruch has written from the mouth of Jeremiah—saying: ²⁸"Turn, take another scroll to yourself, and write on it all the former words that were on the first scroll that Jehoiakim king of Judah burned, ²⁹and say to Jehoiakim king of Judah, Thus said YHWH: You have burned this scroll, saying, Why have you written on it, saying, The king of Babylon surely comes in, and has destroyed this land, and caused man and beast to cease from it? ³⁰Therefore, thus said YHWH concerning Jehoiakim king of Judah: He has none sitting on the throne of David, and his carcass is cast out to heat by day, and to cold by night; ³¹and I have charged on him, and on his seed, and on his servants, their iniquity; and I have brought in on them, and on the inhabitants of Jerusalem, and to the men of Judah, all the evil that I have spoken to them, and they did not listen." ³²And Jeremiah has taken another scroll, and gives it to Baruch son of Neriah the scribe, and he writes on it from the mouth of Jeremiah all the words of the scroll that Jehoiakim king of Judah has burned in the fire; and again there were added to them many words like these.

CHAPTER 37

¹And King Zedekiah son of Josiah reigns instead of Coniah son of Jehoiakim whom Nebuchadnezzar king of Babylon had caused to reign in the land of Judah, ²and he has not listened—he, and his servants, and the people of the land—to the words of YHWH that He spoke by the hand of Jeremiah the prophet. ³And Zedekiah the king sends Jehucal son of Shelemiah, and Zephaniah son of Maaseiah the priest, to Jeremiah the prophet, saying, "Pray, we implore you, for us to our God YHWH." ⁴And Jeremiah is coming in and going out in the midst of the people (and they have not put him in the prison-house), ⁵and the force of Pharaoh has come out of Egypt, and the Chaldeans who are laying siege against Jerusalem hear their report, and go up from off Jerusalem. ⁶And there is a word of YHWH to Jeremiah the prophet, saying, ⁷"Thus said YHWH, God of Israel: Thus you say to the king of Judah who is sending you to Me, to seek Me: Behold, the force of Pharaoh that is coming out to you for help has turned back to its land, to Egypt, ⁸and the Chaldeans have turned back and fought against this city, and captured it, and burned it with fire. ⁹Thus said YHWH: Do not lift up your souls, saying, The Chaldeans surely go from off us, for they do not go; ¹⁰for though you had struck all the force of the Chaldeans who are fighting with you, and there were left of them wounded men—they rise, each in his tent, and have burned this city with fire." ¹¹And it has come to pass, in the going up of the force of the Chaldeans from off Jerusalem, because of the force of Pharaoh, ¹²that Jeremiah goes out from Jerusalem to go [to] the land of Benjamin, to receive a portion there in the midst of the people. ¹³And it comes to pass, he is at the Gate of Benjamin, and there [is] a master of the ward, and his name is Irijah son of Shelemiah, son of Hananiah; and he catches Jeremiah the prophet, saying, "You are defecting to the Chaldeans!" ¹⁴And Jeremiah says, "Falsehood! I am not defecting to the Chaldeans"; and he has not listened to him, and Irijah lays hold on Jeremiah, and brings him to the heads, ¹⁵and the heads are angry

JEREMIAH

against Jeremiah, and have struck him, and put him in the prison-house—the house of Jonathan the scribe, for they had made it for a prison-house. ¹⁶When Jeremiah has entered into the house of the dungeon, and to the cells, then Jeremiah dwells there many days, ¹⁷and King Zedekiah sends, and takes him, and the king asks him in his house in secret, and says, "Is there a word from YHWH?" And Jeremiah says, "There is," and he says, "You are given into the hand of the king of Babylon." ¹⁸And Jeremiah says to King Zedekiah, "What have I sinned against you, and against your servants, and against this people, that you have put me into a prison-house? ¹⁹And where [are] your prophets who prophesied to you, saying, The king of Babylon does not come in against you, and against this land? ²⁰And now, please listen, O my lord the king; please let my supplication fall before you, and do not cause me to return [to] the house of Jonathan the scribe, that I do not die there." ²¹And King Zedekiah commands, and they commit Jeremiah into the court of the prison, also to give a cake of bread to him daily from the bakers' street, until the consumption of all the bread of the city, and Jeremiah dwells in the court of the prison.

CHAPTER 38

¹And Shephatiah son of Mattan, and Gedaliah son of Pashhur, and Jucal son of Shelemiah, and Pashhur son of Malchiah, hear the words that Jeremiah is speaking to all the people, saying, ²"Thus said YHWH: He who is remaining in this city dies, by sword, by famine, and by pestilence, and he who is going forth to the Chaldeans lives, and his soul has been to him for a prey, and he lives. ³Thus said YHWH: This city is certainly given into the hand of the force of the king of Babylon, and he has captured it." ⁴And the heads say to the king, "Now let this man be put to death, because that he is making feeble the hands of the men of war who are left in this city, and the hands of all the people, by speaking to them according to these words, for this man is not seeking for the peace of this people, but for its calamity." ⁵And King Zedekiah says, "Behold, he [is] in your hand: for the king is not able [to do] anything against you." ⁶And they take Jeremiah, and cast him into the pit of Malchiah son of the king, that [is] in the court of the prison, and they send Jeremiah down with cords; and there is no water in the pit, but mire, and Jeremiah sinks in the mire. ⁷And Ebed-Melech the Cushite, a eunuch who [is] in the king's house, hears that they have put Jeremiah into the pit; and the king is sitting at the Gate of Benjamin, ⁸and Ebed-Melech goes forth from the king's house, and speaks to the king, saying, ⁹"My lord, O king, these men have done evil [in] all that they have done to Jeremiah the prophet, whom they have cast into the pit, and he dies in his place because of the famine, for there is no more bread in the city." ¹⁰And the king commands Ebed-Melech the Cushite, saying, "Take with you thirty men from here, and you have brought up Jeremiah the prophet from the pit, before he dies." ¹¹And Ebed-Melech takes the men with him, and enters the house of the king, to the place of the treasury, and takes there worn-out shreds of cloth, and worn-out rags, and sends them by cords into the pit to Jeremiah. ¹²And Ebed-Melech the Cushite says to Jeremiah, "Now put the worn-out pieces of cloth and rags under your arms, at the place of the cords," and Jeremiah does so, ¹³and they draw Jeremiah out with cords, and bring him up out of the pit, and Jeremiah dwells in the court of the prison. ¹⁴And King Zedekiah sends, and takes Jeremiah the prophet to him, to the third entrance that [is] in the house of YHWH, and the king says to Jeremiah, "I am asking you something, do not hide anything from me." ¹⁵And Jeremiah says to Zedekiah, "When I declare [it] to you, do you not surely put me to death? And when I counsel you, you do not listen to me." ¹⁶And King Zedekiah swears to Jeremiah in secret, saying, "YHWH lives, He who made this soul for us, I do not put you to death, nor give you into the hand of these men who are seeking your soul." ¹⁷And Jeremiah says to Zedekiah, "Thus said YHWH, God of Hosts, God of Israel: If you certainly go forth to the heads of the king of Babylon, then your soul has lived, and this city is not burned with fire, indeed, you have lived, you and your house. ¹⁸And if you do not go forth to the heads of the king of Babylon, then this city has been given into the hand of the Chaldeans, and they have burned it with fire, and you do not escape from their hand." ¹⁹And King Zedekiah says to Jeremiah, "I am fearing the Jews who have fallen to the Chaldeans, lest they give me into their hand, and they have insulted me." ²⁰And Jeremiah says, "They do not give you up; please listen to the voice of YHWH, to that which I am speaking to you, and it is well for you, and your soul lives. ²¹And if you are refusing to go forth, this [is] the thing that YHWH has shown me: ²²That, behold, all the women who have been left in the house of the king of Judah are brought forth to the heads of the king of Babylon, and behold, they are saying: Persuaded you, and prevailed against you, || Have your allies, || Your feet have sunk into mire, || They have been turned backward. ²³And all your wives and your sons are brought forth to the Chaldeans, and you do not escape from their hand, for you are caught by the hand of the king of Babylon, and this city is burned with fire." ²⁴And Zedekiah says to Jeremiah, "Let no man know of these words, and you do not die; ²⁵and when the heads hear that I have spoken with you, and they have come to you, and have said to you, Now declare to us what you spoke to the king, do not hide [it] from us, and we do not put you to death, and what the king spoke to you, ²⁶then you have said to them, I am causing my supplication to fall before the king, not to cause me to return to the house of Jonathan, to die there." ²⁷And all the heads come to Jeremiah, and ask him, and he declares to them according to all these words that the king commanded, and they keep silent from him, for the matter was not heard; ²⁸and Jeremiah dwells in the court of the prison until the day that Jerusalem has been captured, and he was [there] when Jerusalem was captured.

CHAPTER 39

¹In the ninth year of Zedekiah king of Judah, in the tenth month, Nebuchadnezzar king of Babylon and all his force have come to Jerusalem, and they lay siege against it; ²in the eleventh year of Zedekiah, in the fourth month, on the ninth of the month, the city has been broken up; ³and all the heads of the king of Babylon come in, and they sit at the middle gate, Nergal-Sharezer, Samgar-Nebo, Sarsechim, Rab-Saris, Nergal-Sharezer, chief magus, and all the rest of the heads of the king of Babylon. ⁴And it comes to pass, when Zedekiah king of Judah and all the men of war have seen them, that they flee and go forth by night from the city, the way of the king's garden, through the gate between the two walls, and he goes forth the way of the plain. ⁵And the forces of the Chaldeans pursue after them, and overtake Zedekiah in the plains of Jericho, and they take him, and bring him up to Nebuchadnezzar king of Babylon, to Riblah, in the land of Hamath, and he speaks with him—judgments. ⁶And the king of Babylon slaughters the sons of Zedekiah, in Riblah, before his eyes, indeed, the king of Babylon has slaughtered all the nobles of Judah. ⁷And he has blinded the eyes of Zedekiah, and binds him with bronze chains to bring him to Babylon. ⁸And the house of the king, and the house of the people, the Chaldeans have burned with fire, and they have broken down the walls of Jerusalem. ⁹And the remnant of the people who are left in the city, and those defecting who have defected to him, and the remnant of the people who are left, Nebuzar-Adan, chief of the executioners, has removed [to] Babylon. ¹⁰And Nebuzar-Adan, chief of the executioners, has left in the land of Judah the poor people who have nothing, and he gives vineyards and fields to them in that day. ¹¹And Nebuchadnezzar king of Babylon gives a charge concerning Jeremiah, by the hand of Nebuzar-Adan, chief of the executioners, saying, ¹²"Take him, and place your eyes on him, and do no evil thing to him, but as he speaks to you, so do with him." ¹³And Nebuzar-Adan, chief of the executioners, sends, and Nebushazban, chief of the eunuchs, and Nergal-Sharezer, chief magus, and all the chiefs of the king of Babylon, ¹⁴indeed, they send and take Jeremiah out of the court of the prison, and give him to Gedaliah son of Ahikam, son of Shaphan, to carry him home, and he dwells in the midst of the people. ¹⁵And a word of YHWH has been to Jeremiah—in his being detained in the court of the prison—saying: ¹⁶"Go, and you have spoken to Ebed-Melech the Cushite, saying, Thus said YHWH of Hosts, God of Israel: Behold, I am bringing in My words to this city for calamity, and not for good, and they have been before you in that day. ¹⁷And I have delivered you in that day—a declaration of YHWH—and you are not given into the hand of the men of whose face you are afraid, ¹⁸for I certainly deliver you, and you do not fall by sword, and your life has been to you

for a spoil, for you have trusted in Me—a declaration of YHWH."

CHAPTER 40

¹The word that has been to Jeremiah from YHWH, after Nebuzar-Adan, chief of the executioners, has sent him from Ramah, in his taking him—and he a prisoner in chains—in the midst of all the expulsion of Jerusalem and of Judah, who are removed to Babylon. ²And the chief of the executioners takes Jeremiah and says to him, "Your God YHWH has spoken this calamity concerning this place, ³and YHWH brings [it] in, and does as He spoke, because you have sinned against YHWH, and have not listened to His voice, even this thing has been to you. ⁴And now, behold, I have loosed you today from the chains that [are] on your hand; if [it is] good in your eyes to come with me [to] Babylon, come, and I keep my eye on you: and if [it is] evil in your eyes to come with me to Babylon, refrain; see, all the land [is] before you, to where [it is] good, and to where [it is] right in your eyes to go—go." ⁵And while he does not reply—"Or turn back to Gedaliah son of Ahikam, son of Shaphan, whom the king of Babylon has appointed over the cities of Judah, and dwell with him in the midst of the people, or wherever it is right in your eyes to go—go." And the chief of the executioners gives a ration and gift to him, and sends him away, ⁶and Jeremiah comes to Gedaliah son of Ahikam, to Mizpah, and dwells with him in the midst of the people who are left in the land. ⁷And all the heads of the forces that [are] in the field hear, they and their men, that the king of Babylon has appointed Gedaliah son of Ahikam over the land, and that he has charged him [with] men, and women, and infants, and of the poor of the land, of those who have not been removed to Babylon; ⁸and they come to Gedaliah at Mizpah, even Ishmael son of Nethaniah, and Johanan and Jonathan [the] sons of Kareah, and Seraiah son of Tanhumeth, and the sons of Ephai the Netophathite, and Jezaniah son of the Maachathite, they and their men. ⁹And Gedaliah son of Ahikam, son of Shaphan, swears to them and to their men, saying, "Do not be afraid of serving the Chaldeans, abide in the land, and serve the king of Babylon, and it is well for you; ¹⁰and I, behold, I am dwelling in Mizpah to stand before the Chaldeans who have come to us, and you, gather wine, and summer fruit, and oil, and put [them] in your vessels, and dwell in your cities that you have taken." ¹¹And also all the Jews who [are] in Moab, and among the sons of Ammon, and in Edom, and who [are] in all the lands, have heard that the king of Babylon has given a remnant to Judah, and that he has appointed over them Gedaliah son of Ahikam, son of Shaphan, ¹²and all the Jews from all the places to where they have been driven, return and enter the land of Judah, to Gedaliah, to Mizpah, and they gather wine and summer fruit—to multiply abundantly. ¹³And Johanan son of Kareah, and all the heads of the forces that [are] in the field, have come to Gedaliah at Mizpah, and they say to him, "Do you really know that Ba'alis king of the sons of Ammon has sent Ishmael son of Nethaniah to strike your soul?" And Gedaliah son of Ahikam has not given credence to them. ¹⁵And Johanan son of Kareah has spoken to Gedaliah in secret, in Mizpah, saying, "Please let me go, and I strike Ishmael son of Nethaniah, and no one knows; why does he strike your soul? And all Judah who are gathered to you have been scattered, and the remnant of Judah has perished." ¹⁶And Gedaliah son of Ahikam says to Johanan son of Kareah, "You do not do this thing, for you are speaking falsehood concerning Ishmael."

CHAPTER 41

¹And it comes to pass, in the seventh month, Ishmael son of Nethaniah, son of Elishama, of the royal seed, and of the chiefs of the king, and ten men with him, have come to Gedaliah son of Ahikam, to Mizpah, and there they eat bread together in Mizpah. ²And Ishmael son of Nethaniah rises, and the ten men who have been with him, and they strike Gedaliah son of Ahikam, son of Shaphan, with the sword, and he puts him to death whom the king of Babylon has appointed over the land. ³And all the Jews who have been with him, with Gedaliah, in Mizpah, and the Chaldeans who have been found there—the men of war—Ishmael has struck. ⁴And it comes to pass, on the second day of the putting of Gedaliah to death (and no one has known), ⁵that men come in from Shechem, from Shiloh, and from Samaria—eighty men—with shaven beards, and torn garments, and cutting themselves, and [with] an offering and frankincense in their hand, to bring [them] to the house of YHWH. ⁶And Ishmael son of Nethaniah goes forth to meet them, from Mizpah, going on and weeping, and it comes to pass, at meeting them, that he says to them, "Come to Gedaliah son of Ahikam." ⁷And it comes to pass, at their coming into the midst of the city, that Ishmael son of Nethaniah slaughters them, at the midst of the pit, he and the men who [are] with him. ⁸And ten men have been found among them, and they say to Ishmael, "Do not put us to death, for we have things hidden in the field—wheat, and barley, and oil, and honey." And he refrains, and has not put them to death in the midst of their brothers. ⁹And the pit to where Ishmael has cast all the carcasses of the men whom he has struck along with Gedaliah, is that which King Asa made because of Baasha king of Israel—Ishmael son of Nethaniah has filled it with the pierced. ¹⁰And Ishmael takes captive all the remnant of the people who [are] in Mizpah, the daughters of the king, and all the people who are left in Mizpah, whom Nebuzar-Adan, chief of the executioners, has committed [to] Gedaliah son of Ahikam, and Ishmael son of Nethaniah takes them captive, and goes to pass over to the sons of Ammon. ¹¹And Johanan son of Kareah, and all the heads of the forces that [are] with him, hear of all the evil that Ishmael son of Nethaniah has done, ¹²and they take all the men, and go to fight with Ishmael son of Nethaniah, and they find him at the great waters that [are] in Gibeon. ¹³And it comes to pass, when all the people who [are] with Ishmael see Johanan son of Kareah, and all the heads of the forces who [are] with him, that they rejoice. ¹⁴And all the people whom Ishmael has taken captive from Mizpah turn around, indeed, they turn back, and go to Johanan son of Kareah. ¹⁵And Ishmael son of Nethaniah has escaped, with eight men, from the presence of Johanan, and he goes to the sons of Ammon. ¹⁶And Johanan son of Kareah, and all the heads of the forces who [are] with him, take all the remnant of the people whom he has brought back from Ishmael son of Nethaniah, from Mizpah—after he had struck Gedaliah son of Ahikam—mighty ones, men of war, and women, and infants, and eunuchs, whom he had brought back from Gibeon, ¹⁷and they go and abide in the habitations of Chimham, that [are] near Beth-Lehem, to go to enter Egypt, ¹⁸from the presence of the Chaldeans, for they have been afraid of them, for Ishmael son of Nethaniah had struck Gedaliah son of Ahikam, whom the king of Babylon had appointed over the land.

CHAPTER 42

¹And they come near—all the heads of the forces, and Johanan son of Kareah, and Jezaniah son of Hoshaiah, and all the people from the least even to the greatest—²and they say to Jeremiah the prophet, "Please let our supplication fall before you, and pray for us to your God YHWH for all this remnant; for we have been left a few out of many, as your eyes see us; ³and your God YHWH declares to us the way in which we walk, and the thing that we do." ⁴And Jeremiah the prophet says to them, "I have heard: behold, I am praying to your God YHWH according to your words, and it has come to pass, the whole word that YHWH answers you, I declare to you—I do not withhold a word from you." ⁵And they have said to Jeremiah, "YHWH is against us for a true and faithful witness, if—according to all the word with which your God YHWH sends you to us—we do not do so. ⁶Whether [it is] good or evil, to the voice of our God YHWH, to whom we are sending you, we listen; because it is good for us when we listen to the voice of our God YHWH." ⁷And it comes to pass, at the end of ten days, that there is a word of YHWH to Jeremiah, ⁸and he calls to Johanan son of Kareah, and to all the heads of the forces that [are] with him, and to all the people, from the least even to the greatest, ⁹and he says to them, "Thus said YHWH, God of Israel, to whom you sent me, to cause your supplication to fall before Him: ¹⁰If you certainly dwell in this land, then I have built you up, and I do not throw down; and I have planted you, and I do not pluck up; for I have relented concerning the calamity that I have done to you. ¹¹Do not be afraid of the king of Babylon, whom you are afraid of; do not be afraid of him—a declaration of YHWH—for I [am] with you, to save you, and to deliver you from his hand. ¹²And I give mercies to you, and he has pitied you, and caused you to return to your own ground. ¹³And if you are saying, We do not dwell in this land—not to listen to the

voice of your God YHWH, ¹⁴saying, No; but we enter the land of Egypt, that we see no war, and do not hear the sound of a horn, and are not hungry for bread; and we dwell there— ¹⁵And now, therefore, hear a word of YHWH, O remnant of Judah! Thus said YHWH of Hosts, God of Israel: If you really set your faces to enter Egypt, and have gone to sojourn there, ¹⁶then it has come to pass, the sword that you are afraid of, overtakes you there, in the land of Egypt; and the hunger, because of which you are sorrowful, cleaves after you there in Egypt, and there you die. ¹⁷Thus are all the men who have set their faces to enter Egypt to sojourn there; they die—by sword, by hunger, and by pestilence, and there is not a remnant and an escaped one to them, because of the calamity that I am bringing in on them; ¹⁸for thus said YHWH of Hosts, God of Israel: As My anger and My fury have been poured out on the inhabitants of Jerusalem, so My fury is poured out on you in your entering Egypt, and you have been for an execration, and for an astonishment, and for a reviling, and for a reproach, and you do not see this place anymore. ¹⁹YHWH has spoken against you, O remnant of Judah, do not enter Egypt: certainly know that I have testified against you today; ²⁰for you have showed yourselves perverse in your souls, for you sent me to your God YHWH, saying, Pray for us to our God YHWH, and according to all that our God YHWH says, so declare to us, and we have done [it]; ²¹and I declare to you today, and you have not listened to the voice of your God YHWH, and to anything with which He has sent me to you. ²²And now, certainly know that by sword, by famine, and by pestilence you die, in the place that you have desired to go to sojourn there."

CHAPTER 43

¹And it comes to pass, when Jeremiah finishes speaking to all the people all the words of their God YHWH, with which their God YHWH has sent him to them—all these words— ²that Azariah son of Hoshaiah, and Johanan son of Kareah, and all the proud men, speak to Jeremiah, saying, "You are speaking falsehood; our God YHWH has not sent you to say, Do not enter Egypt to sojourn there; ³for Baruch son of Neriah is moving you against us, in order to give us up into the hand of the Chaldeans, to put us to death, and to remove us to Babylon." ⁴And Johanan son of Kareah, and all the heads of the forces, and all the people, have not listened to the voice of YHWH, to dwell in the land of Judah; ⁵and Johanan son of Kareah, and all the heads of the forces, take all the remnant of Judah who have turned from all the nations to where they were driven to sojourn in the land of Judah, ⁶the men, and the women, and the infant, and the daughters of the king, and every person that Nebuzar-Adan, chief of the executioners, had left with Gedaliah son of Ahikam, son of Shaphan, and Jeremiah the prophet, and Baruch son of Neriah, ⁷and they enter the land of Egypt, for they have not listened to the voice of YHWH, and they come as far as Tahpanhes. ⁸And there is a word of YHWH to Jeremiah in Tahpanhes, saying, ⁹"Take great stones in your hand, and you have hidden them in the clay in the brick-kiln, that [is] at the opening of the house of Pharaoh in Tahpanhes, before the eyes of the men of Judah, ¹⁰and you have said to them, Thus said YHWH of Hosts, God of Israel: Behold, I am sending, and I have taken Nebuchadnezzar king of Babylon, My servant, and I have set his throne above these stones that I have hid, and he has stretched out his pavilion over them, ¹¹and he has come, and struck the land of Egypt—those who [are] for death to death, and those who [are] for captivity to captivity, and those who [are] for the sword to the sword. ¹²And I have kindled a fire in the houses of the gods of Egypt, and it has burned them, and he has taken them captive, and covered himself with the land of Egypt, as the shepherd covers himself with his garment, and he has gone forth there in peace; ¹³and he has broken the standing pillars of the house of the sun, that [is] in the land of Egypt, and he burns the houses of the gods of Egypt with fire."

CHAPTER 44

¹The word that has been to Jeremiah concerning all the Jews who are dwelling in the land of Egypt—who are dwelling in Migdol, and in Tahpanhes, and in Noph, and in the land of Pathros—saying, ²"Thus said YHWH of Hosts, God of Israel: You have seen all the calamity that I have brought in on Jerusalem, and on all the cities of Judah, and behold, they [are] a desolation to this day, and there is none dwelling in them, ³because of their wickedness that they have done, by provoking Me to anger, by going to make incense, by serving other gods, that they did not know, they, you, and your fathers. ⁴And I send to you all My servants the prophets, rising early and sending, saying, Please do not do this abomination that I have hated— ⁵and they have not listened nor inclined their ear to turn back from their wickedness, not to make incense to other gods, ⁶and My fury is poured out, and My anger, and it burns in cities of Judah, and in streets of Jerusalem, and they are for a ruin, for a desolation, as [at] this day. ⁷And now, thus said YHWH of Hosts, God of Israel: Why are you doing great evil to your own souls, to cut off man and woman, infant and suckling, from you, from the midst of Judah, so as not to leave a remnant to you: ⁸by provoking Me to anger by the works of your hands, by making incense to other gods in the land of Egypt, to where you are going to sojourn, so as to cut yourselves off, and so as to your being for a reviling and for a reproach among all nations of the earth? ⁹Have you forgotten the wickedness of your fathers, and the wickedness of the kings of Judah, and the wickedness of their wives, and your own wickedness, and the wickedness of your wives, that they have done in the land of Judah, and in streets of Jerusalem? ¹⁰They have not been humbled to this day, nor have they been afraid, nor have they walked in My law, and in My statutes, that I have set before you and before your fathers. ¹¹Therefore, thus said YHWH of Hosts, God of Israel: Behold, I am setting My face against you for calamity, even to cut off all Judah, ¹²and I have taken the remnant of Judah, who have set their faces to enter the land of Egypt to sojourn there, and they have all been consumed in the land of Egypt; they fall by sword [and] are consumed by famine, from the least even to the greatest, they die by sword and by famine, and they have been for an execration, for an astonishment, and for a reviling, and for a reproach. ¹³And I have seen after those dwelling in the land of Egypt, as I saw after Jerusalem, with sword, with famine, and with pestilence, ¹⁴and there is not an escaped and remaining one of the remnant of Judah, who are entering into the land of Egypt to sojourn there, even to turn back to the land of Judah, to where they are lifting up their soul to return to dwell, for they do not turn back, except those escaping." ¹⁵And they answer Jeremiah—all the men who are knowing that their wives are making incense to other gods, and all the women who are remaining, a great assembly, even all the people who are dwelling in the land of Egypt, in Pathros—saying: ¹⁶"The word that you have spoken to us in the Name of YHWH—we are not listening to you; ¹⁷for we certainly do everything that has gone out of our mouth, to make incense to the queen of the heavens, and to pour out drink-offerings to her, as we have done, we, and our fathers, our kings, and our heads, in cities of Judah, and in streets of Jerusalem, and—we are satisfied with bread, and we are well, and we have not seen calamity. ¹⁸And from the time we have ceased to make incense to the queen of the heavens, and to pour out drink-offerings to her, we have lacked all, and we have been consumed by sword and by famine, ¹⁹and when we are making incense to the queen of the heavens, and pouring out drink-offerings to her—have we made cakes for her to idolize her, and to pour out drink-offerings to her, without our husbands?" ²⁰And Jeremiah says to all the people, concerning the men and concerning the women, and concerning all the people who are answering him, saying, ²¹"The incense that you made in the cities of Judah, and in the streets of Jerusalem, you, and your fathers, your kings, and your heads, and the people of the land, has YHWH not remembered it? Indeed, it comes up on His heart. ²²And YHWH is not able to accept [you] anymore, because of the evil of your doings, because of the abominations that you have done, and your land is for a ruin, and for an astonishment, and for a reviling, without inhabitant, as [at] this day. ²³Because that you have made incense, and because you have sinned against YHWH, and have not listened to the voice of YHWH, and have not walked in His law, and in His statutes, and in His testimonies, therefore this calamity has met you as [at] this day." ²⁴And Jeremiah says to all the people, and to all the women, "Hear a word of YHWH, all Judah who [are] in the land of Egypt: ²⁵Thus spoke YHWH of Hosts, God of Israel, saying, You and your wives both speak with your mouth, and with your hands have fulfilled,

JEREMIAH

saying, We certainly execute our vows that we have vowed, to make incense to the queen of the heavens, and to pour out drink-offerings to her. You certainly establish your vows, and certainly execute your vows. ²⁶Therefore, hear a word of YHWH, all Judah who are dwelling in the land of Egypt: Behold, I have sworn by My great Name, said YHWH, My Name is no longer proclaimed by the mouth of any man of Judah, saying, Lord YHWH lives—in all the land of Egypt. ²⁷Behold, I am watching over them for calamity, and not for good, and all the men of Judah who [are] in the land of Egypt have been consumed by sword and by famine, until their consumption. ²⁸And the escaped of the sword turn back out of the land of Egypt to the land of Judah, few in number, and all the remnant of Judah, who are coming into the land of Egypt to sojourn there, have known whose word is established, Mine or theirs. ²⁹And this [is] the sign to you—a declaration of YHWH—that I am seeing after you in this place, so that you know that My words are certainly established against you for calamity— ³⁰thus said YHWH: Behold, I am giving Pharaoh-Hophra king of Egypt into the hand of his enemies, and into the hand of those seeking his life, as I have given Zedekiah king of Judah into the hand of Nebuchadnezzar king of Babylon, his enemy, and who is seeking his life."

CHAPTER 45

¹The word that Jeremiah the prophet has spoken to Baruch son of Neriah, in his writing these words on a scroll from the mouth of Jeremiah, in the fourth year of Jehoiakim son of Josiah king of Judah, saying, ²"Thus said YHWH, God of Israel, concerning you, O Baruch: ³You have said, Woe to me, now, for YHWH has added sorrow to my pain, I have been wearied with my sighing, and I have not found rest. ⁴Thus you say to him, Thus said YHWH: Behold, that which I have built I am throwing down, and that which I have planted I am plucking up, even the whole land itself. ⁵And you seek for great things—do not seek, for behold, I am bringing calamity on all flesh—a declaration of YHWH—and I have given your life to you for a spoil, in all places to where you go."

CHAPTER 46

¹That which has been the word of YHWH to Jeremiah the prophet concerning the nations, ²for Egypt, concerning the force of Pharaoh-Necho king of Egypt, that has been by the Euphrates River, in Carchemish, that Nebuchadnezzar king of Babylon has struck, in the fourth year of Jehoiakim son of Josiah king of Judah: ³"Set shield and buckler in array, || And draw near to battle. ⁴Gird the horses, and go up, you horsemen, || And station yourselves with helmets, || Polish the javelins, put on the coats of mail. ⁵Why have I seen them dismayed [and] turned backward? And their mighty ones are beaten down, || And they have fled [to] a refuge, || And did not turn their face, || Fear [is] all around—a declaration of YHWH. ⁶The swift do not flee, nor do the mighty escape, || Northward, by the side of the Euphrates River, || They have stumbled and fallen. ⁷Who is this? He comes up as a flood, || His waters shake themselves as rivers! ⁸Egypt comes up as a flood, || And the waters shake themselves as rivers. And he says, I go up; I cover the land, I destroy the city and the inhabitants in it. ⁹Go up, you horses; and boast yourselves, you chariots, || And go forth, you mighty, || Cush and Phut handling the shield, || And Lud handling—treading the bow. ¹⁰And that day [is] to Lord YHWH of Hosts || A day of vengeance, || To be avenged of His adversaries, || And the sword has devoured, and been satisfied, || And it has been watered from their blood, || For a sacrifice [is] to Lord YHWH of Hosts, || In the land of the north, by the Euphrates River. ¹¹Go up to Gilead, and take balm, || O virgin daughter of Egypt, || You have multiplied medicines in vain, || There is no healing for you. ¹²Nations have heard of your shame, || And your cry has filled the land, || For the mighty stumbled on the mighty, || Together they have fallen—both of them!" ¹³The word that YHWH has spoken to Jeremiah the prophet concerning the coming in of Nebuchadnezzar king of Babylon, to strike the land of Egypt: ¹⁴"Declare in Egypt, and sound in Migdol, || And sound in Noph, and in Tahpanhes, say, || Stand firm and prepare yourself, || For a sword has devoured around you, ¹⁵Why has your bull been swept away? He has not stood, because YHWH thrust him away. ¹⁶He has multiplied the stumbling, || Indeed, one has fallen on his neighbor, || And they say: Rise, and we return to our people, || And to the land of our birth, || Because of the oppressing sword. ¹⁷They have cried there: Pharaoh king of Egypt [is] a desolation, || The appointed time has passed by. ¹⁸[As] I live—an affirmation of the King, || YHWH of Hosts [is] His Name, || Surely as Tabor [is] among mountains, || And as Carmel by the sea—he comes in, ¹⁹Make goods for yourself for removal, || O inhabitant, daughter of Egypt, || For Noph becomes a desolation, || And has been burned up, without inhabitant. ²⁰Egypt [is] a very beautiful heifer, || Destruction comes into her from the north. ²¹Even her hired ones in her midst [are] as calves of the stall, || For even they have turned, || They have fled together, they have not stood, || For the day of their calamity has come on them, || The time of their inspection. ²²Its voice goes on as a serpent, || For they go with a force, || And they have come in to her with axes, || As hewers of trees. ²³They have cut down her forest, || A declaration of YHWH, || For it is not searched, || For they have been more than the grasshopper, || And they have no numbering. ²⁴The daughter of Egypt has been ashamed, || She has been given into the hand of the people of the north. ²⁵YHWH of Hosts, God of Israel, has said: Behold, I am seeing after Amon of No, || And after Pharaoh, and after Egypt, || And after her gods, and after her kings, || And after Pharaoh, and after those trusting in him, ²⁶And I have given them into the hand of those seeking their life, || And into the hand of Nebuchadnezzar king of Babylon, || And into the hand of his servants, || And afterward it is inhabited, || As [in] days of old—a declaration of YHWH. ²⁷And you, you do not fear, My servant Jacob, || Nor [are] you dismayed, O Israel, || For behold, I am saving you from afar—And your seed from the land of their captivity, || And Jacob has turned back, || And has been at rest, and been at ease, || And there is none disturbing. ²⁸You do not fear, My servant Jacob, || A declaration of YHWH, || For I [am] with you, || For I make an end of all the nations || To where I have driven you, || And I do not make an end of you, || And I have reproved you in judgment, || And do not entirely acquit you!"

CHAPTER 47

¹That which has been the word of YHWH to Jeremiah concerning the Philistines, before Pharaoh strikes Gaza: ²"Thus said YHWH: Behold, waters are going up from the north, || And have been for an overflowing stream, || And they overflow the land and its fullness, || The city, and those dwelling in it, || And men have cried out, || And every inhabitant of the land has howled. ³From the sound of the stamping of the hooves of his mighty ones, || From the rushing of his chariot, || The noise of his wheels, || Fathers have not turned to sons, || From feebleness of hands, ⁴Because of the day that has come to spoil all the Philistines, || To cut off every helping remnant from Tyre and from Sidon. For YHWH is spoiling the Philistines, || The remnant of the island of Caphtor. ⁵Baldness has come to Gaza, || Ashkelon has been cut off, || O remnant of their valley, || Until when do you cut yourself? ⁶Behold, sword of YHWH, until when are you not quiet? Be removed to your sheath, rest and cease. ⁷How will it be quiet, || And YHWH has given a charge to it, || Against Ashkelon and against the seashore? He has appointed it there!"

CHAPTER 48

¹Concerning Moab: "Thus said YHWH of Hosts, God of Israel: Woe to Nebo, for it is spoiled, || Kiriathaim has been captured [and] put to shame, || The high tower has been put to shame, || Indeed, it has been broken down. ²There is no longer praise of Moab, || In Heshbon they devised evil against her: Come, and we cut it off from [being] a nation, || Also, O Madmen, you are cut off, || A sword goes after you. ³A voice of a cry [is] from Horonaim, || Spoiling and great destruction. ⁴Moab has been destroyed, || Her little ones have caused a cry to be heard. ⁵For the ascent of Luhith with weeping, || Weeping goes up, || For in the descent of Horonaim || Adversaries have heard a cry of desolation. ⁶Flee, deliver yourselves, || You are as a naked thing in a wilderness. ⁷For because of your trusting in your works, || And in your treasures, even you are captured, || And Chemosh has gone out in a removal, || His priests and his heads together. ⁸And a spoiler comes to every city, || And no city escapes, || And the valley has perished, || And the plain has been destroyed, as YHWH said. ⁹Give wings to Moab, that she

may go forth and flee away, || And her cities are for a desolation, || Without an inhabitant in them. ¹⁰Cursed [is] he who is doing the work of YHWH slothfully, || And cursed [is] he || Who is withholding his sword from blood. ¹¹Moab is secure from his youth, || And he [is] at rest for his preserved things, || And he has not been emptied out from vessel to vessel, || And he has not gone into captivity, || Therefore his taste has remained in him, || And his fragrance has not been changed. ¹²Therefore, behold, days are coming, || A declaration of YHWH, || And I have sent wanderers to him, || And they have caused him to wander, || And they empty out his vessels, || And they dash his bottles in pieces. ¹³And Moab has been ashamed because of Chemosh, || As the house of Israel has been ashamed || Because of Beth-El, their confidence. ¹⁴How do you say, We [are] mighty, || And men of strength for battle? ¹⁵Moab is spoiled, and has gone up [from] her cities, || And the choice of its young men || Have gone down to slaughter, || An affirmation of the King, || YHWH of Hosts [is] His Name. ¹⁶The destruction of Moab is near to come, || And his calamity has hurried exceedingly. ¹⁷Bemoan for him, all you around him, || And all knowing his name, say, || How it has been broken, the staff of strength, || The rod of beauty! ¹⁸Come down from glory, sit in thirst, || O inhabitant, daughter of Dibon, || For a spoiler of Moab has come up to you, || He has destroyed your fortifications. ¹⁹Stand on the way, and watch, O inhabitant of Aroer, || Ask the fugitive and escaped, || Say, What has happened? ²⁰Moab has been put to shame, || For it has been broken down, || Howl and cry, declare in Arnon, || For Moab is spoiled, ²¹And judgment has come to the land of the plain— to Holon, || And to Jahazah, and on Mephaath, ²²And on Dibon, and on Nebo, || And on Beth-Diblathaim, and on Kirathaim, ²³And on Beth-Gamul, and on Beth-Meon, ²⁴And on Kerioth, and on Bozrah, || And on all cities of the land of Moab, || The far off and the near. ²⁵The horn of Moab has been cut down, || And his arm has been broken, || A declaration of YHWH. ²⁶Declare him drunk, || For he made himself great against YHWH || And Moab has struck in his vomit, || And he has been for a derision— even he. ²⁷And was Israel not the derision to you? Was he found among thieves? For since your words concerning him, || You bemoan yourself. ²⁸Forsake cities, and dwell in a rock, || You inhabitants of Moab, || And be as a dove making a nest in the passages of a pit's mouth. ²⁹We have heard of the arrogance of Moab, || Exceedingly proud! His haughtiness, and his arrogance, || And his pride, and the height of his heart, ³⁰I have known, a declaration of YHWH, || His wrath, and [it is] not right, || His boastings—they have done nothing right. ³¹Therefore I howl for Moab, even for Moab— all of it, || I cry for men of Kir-Heres, it mourns, ³²With the weeping of Jazer, I weep for you, O vine of Sibmah, || Your branches have passed over a sea, || They have come to the Sea of Jazer, || On your summer fruits, and on your harvest, || A spoiler has fallen. ³³And joy and gladness have been removed from the fruitful field, || Even from the land of Moab, || And I have caused wine to cease from winepresses, || Shouting does not proceed, || The shouting [is] not shouting! ³⁴Because of the cry of Heshbon to Elealeh, || They have given their voice to Jahaz, || From Zoar to Horonaim, || A heifer of the third [year], || For even [the] waters of Nimrim become desolations. ³⁵And I have caused to cease in Moab, || A declaration of YHWH, || Him who is offering in a high place, || And him who is making incense to his god. ³⁶Therefore My heart sounds as pipes for Moab, || And My heart sounds as pipes for men of Kir-Heres, || Therefore the abundance he made perished. ³⁷For every head [is] bald, and every beard diminished, || On all hands— cuttings, and on the loins—sackcloth. ³⁸On all roofs of Moab, and in her broad-places, || All of it—lamentation, || For I have broken Moab as a vessel in which there is no pleasure," || A declaration of YHWH. ³⁹"How it has been broken down! They have howled, || How Moab has turned the neck ashamed! And Moab has been for a derision || And for a terror to all around her." ⁴⁰For thus said YHWH: "Behold, he flees as an eagle, || And has spread his wings to Moab. ⁴¹The cities have been captured, || And the strongholds are caught, || And the heart of the mighty of Moab || Has been in that day as the heart of a distressed woman. ⁴²And Moab has been destroyed from [being] a people, || For he exerted himself against YHWH. ⁴³Fear, and a snare, and a trap, [are] for you, || O inhabitant of Moab—a declaration of YHWH, ⁴⁴Whoever is fleeing because of the fear falls into the snare, || And whoever is coming up from the snare is captured by the trap, || For I bring to her—to Moab—The year of their inspection, || A declaration of YHWH. ⁴⁵In the shadow of Heshbon fugitives have stood powerless, || For fire has gone forth from Heshbon, || And a flame from within Sihon, || And it consumes the corner of Moab, || And the crown of the sons of Shaon. ⁴⁶Woe to you, O Moab, || The people of Chemosh have perished, || For your sons were taken with the captives, || And your daughters with the captivity. ⁴⁷And I have turned back [to] the captivity of Moab, || In the latter end of the days," || A declaration of YHWH! "Until now [is] the judgment of Moab."

CHAPTER 49

¹Concerning the sons of Ammon: "Thus said YHWH: Has Israel no sons? Has he no heir? Why has Malcam possessed Gad, || And his people have dwelt in its cities? ²Therefore, behold, days are coming, || A declaration of YHWH, || And I have sounded a shout of battle in Rabbah of the sons of Ammon, || And it has been for a heap—a desolation, || And her daughters are burned with fire, || And Israel has succeeded its heirs, said YHWH. ³Howl, Heshbon, for Ai is spoiled, || Cry, daughters of Rabbah, gird on sackcloth, || Lament, and go to and fro by the hedges, || For Malcam goes into captivity, || His priests and his princes together. ⁴Why do you boast yourself in valleys? Your valley is flowing, || O backsliding daughter, || Who is trusting in her treasures: Who comes to me? ⁵Behold, I am bringing fear in on you, || A declaration of Lord YHWH of Hosts, || From all around you, || And you have each been driven out before it, || And there is no gatherer of the wandering. ⁶And after this I return the captivity of the sons of Ammon, || A declaration of YHWH." ⁷Concerning Edom: "Thus said YHWH of Hosts: Is wisdom no longer in Teman? Has counsel perished from the intelligent? Has their wisdom vanished? ⁸Flee, turn, go deep to dwell, you inhabitants of Dedan, || For I brought the calamity of Esau on him, || The time I inspected him. ⁹If gatherers have come to you, || They do not leave gleanings, || If thieves in the night, || They have destroyed their sufficiency! ¹⁰For I have made Esau bare, || I have uncovered his secret places, || And he is not able to be hidden, || Spoiled [is] his seed, and his brothers, || And his neighbors, and he is not. ¹¹Leave your orphans—I keep alive, || And your widows— trust in Me, ¹²For thus said YHWH: They whose judgment is not to drink of the cup, || Do certainly drink, || And you [are] he that is entirely acquitted! You are not acquitted, for you certainly drink. ¹³For I have sworn by Myself, || A declaration of YHWH, || That for a desolation, for a reproach, || For a dry place, and for a reviling—is Bozrah, || And all her cities are for continuous ruins. ¹⁴I have heard a report from YHWH, || And an ambassador is sent among nations, || Gather yourselves and come in against her, || And rise for battle. ¹⁵For behold, I have made you little among nations, || Despised among men. ¹⁶Your terribleness has lifted you up, || The pride of your heart, || O dweller in clefts of the rock, || Holding the high place of the height, || For you make your nest high as an eagle, || From there I bring you down, || A declaration of YHWH. ¹⁷And Edom has been for a desolation, || Everyone passing by her is astonished, || And hisses because of all her plagues. ¹⁸As the overthrow of Sodom and Gomorrah, || And its neighbors, said YHWH, || No one dwells there, || Nor does a son of man sojourn in her. ¹⁹Behold, he comes up as a lion, || Because of the rising of the Jordan, || To the enduring habitation, || But I cause to rest, || I cause him to run from off her, || And who is chosen? I lay a charge concerning her, || For who is like Me? And who convenes Me? And who [is] this shepherd who stands before Me? ²⁰Therefore, hear the counsel of YHWH, || That He has counseled concerning Edom, || And His plans that He has devised || Concerning the inhabitants of Teman: Do little ones of the flock not drag them out, || Does He not make their habitation desolate? ²¹The earth has shaken from the noise of their fall, || The cry—its voice is heard at the Sea of Suph. ²²Behold, He comes up as an eagle, and flies, || And He spreads His wings over Bozrah, || And the heart of the mighty of Edom has been in that day, || As the heart of a travailing woman." ²³Concerning Damascus: "Hamath and Arpad have been ashamed, || For they have heard an evil report, || They have been melted, sorrow [is] in the sea, || It is not able to be quiet. ²⁴Damascus has been feeble, || She turned to flee, and fear strengthened her, || Distress and

JEREMIAH

pangs have seized her, as a travailing woman. ²⁵How it is not left—the city of praise, ‖ The city of My joy! ²⁶Therefore her young men fall in her broad places, ‖ And all the men of war are cut off in that day, ‖ A declaration of YHWH of Hosts. ²⁷And I have kindled a fire against the wall of Damascus, ‖ And it consumed palaces of Ben-Hadad!" ²⁸Concerning Kedar, and concerning the kingdoms of Hazor that Nebuchadnezzar king of Babylon has struck: "Thus said YHWH: Arise, go up to Kedar, ‖ And spoil the sons of the east. ²⁹They take their tents and their flock, ‖ Their curtains, and all their vessels, ‖ And they carry away their camels for themselves, ‖ And they called concerning them, ‖ Fear [is] all around. ³⁰Flee, bemoan mightily, go deep to dwell, ‖ You inhabitants of Hazor—a declaration of YHWH, ‖ For Nebuchadnezzar king of Babylon has given counsel against you, ‖ Indeed, he devises a scheme against them. ³¹Rise, go up to a nation at rest, ‖ Dwelling confidently, a declaration of YHWH, ‖ It has no double gates nor bar, ‖ They dwell alone. ³²And their camels have been for a prey, ‖ And the multitude of their livestock for a spoil, ‖ And I have scattered them to every wind, ‖ Who cut off the corner [of the beard], ‖ And from all its passages I bring in their calamity, ‖ A declaration of YHWH. ³³And Hazor has been for a habitation of dragons, ‖ A desolation for all time, ‖ No one dwells there, nor does a son of man sojourn in it!" ³⁴That which has been the word of YHWH to Jeremiah the prophet concerning Elam, in the beginning of the reign of Zedekiah king of Judah, saying, ³⁵"Thus said YHWH of Hosts: Behold, I am breaking the bow of Elam, ‖ The beginning of their might. ³⁶And I have brought four winds to Elam, ‖ From the four ends of the heavens, ‖ And have scattered them to all these winds, ‖ And there is no nation to where outcasts of Elam do not come in. ³⁷And I have frightened Elam before their enemies, ‖ And before those seeking their life, ‖ And I have brought calamity on them, ‖ The heat of My anger, ‖ A declaration of YHWH, ‖ And I have sent the sword after them, ‖ Until I have consumed them; ³⁸And I have set My throne in Elam, ‖ And I have destroyed king and princes from there, ‖ A declaration of YHWH. ³⁹And it has come to pass, in the latter end of the days, I return the captivity of Elam, ‖ A declaration of YHWH!"

CHAPTER 50

¹The word that YHWH has spoken concerning Babylon, concerning the land of the Chaldeans, by the hand of Jeremiah the prophet: ²"Declare among nations, and sound, ‖ And lift up an ensign, sound, do not hide, ‖ Say, Babylon has been captured, ‖ Bel has been put to shame, ‖ Merodach has been broken, ‖ Her grievous things have been put to shame, ‖ Her idols have been broken. ³For a nation from the north has come up against her, ‖ It makes her land become a desolation, ‖ And there is not an inhabitant in it. From man even to beast, ‖ They have moved, they have gone. ⁴In those days, and at that time," ‖ A declaration of YHWH, ‖ "Sons of Israel come in, ‖ They and sons of Judah together, ‖ Going on and weeping they go, ‖ And they seek their God YHWH. ⁵They ask the way [to] Zion, ‖ Their faces [are] toward that place: Come in, and we are joined to YHWH, ‖ A perpetual covenant—never forgotten. ⁶My people have been a perishing flock, ‖ Their shepherds have caused them to err, ‖ Causing them to go back [on] the mountains, ‖ They have gone from mountain to hill, ‖ They have forgotten their crouching-place. ⁷All finding them have devoured them, ‖ And their adversaries have said: We are not guilty, ‖ Because that they sinned against YHWH, ‖ The habitation of righteousness, ‖ And the hope of their fathers—YHWH. ⁸Move from the midst of Babylon, ‖ And go out from the land of the Chaldeans; And be as male goats before a flock. ⁹For behold, I am stirring up, ‖ And am causing to come up against Babylon, ‖ An assembly of great nations from [the] land of the north, ‖ And they have set in array against her, ‖ From there she is captured, ‖ Its arrow—as a skillful hero—does not return empty, ¹⁰And Chaldea has been for a spoil, ‖ All her spoilers are satisfied," ‖ A declaration of YHWH. ¹¹"Because you rejoice, because you exult, ‖ O spoilers of My inheritance, ‖ Because you increase as a heifer [at] the tender grass, ‖ And cry aloud as bulls, ¹²Your mother has been greatly ashamed, ‖ She who bore you has been confounded, ‖ Behold, the last of nations [is] a wilderness, ‖ A dry land, and a desert. ¹³Because of the wrath of YHWH it is not inhabited, ‖ And it has been a desolation—all of it. Everyone passing by at Babylon is astonished, ‖ And hisses because of all her plagues. ¹⁴Set yourselves in array against Babylon all around, ‖ All you treading a bow, ‖ Shoot at her, have no pity on the arrow, ‖ For she has sinned against YHWH. ¹⁵Shout against her all around, ‖ She has given forth her hand, ‖ Her foundations have fallen, ‖ Her walls have been thrown down, ‖ For it [is] the vengeance of YHWH, ‖ Be avenged of her, as she did—do to her. ¹⁶Cut off the sower from Babylon, ‖ And him handling the sickle in the time of harvest, ‖ Because of the oppressing sword, ‖ Each to his people—they turn, ‖ And each to his land—they flee. ¹⁷Israel [is as] a scattered sheep, ‖ Lions have driven [him] away, ‖ At first, the king of Asshur devoured him, ‖ And now, at last, Nebuchadnezzar king of Babylon has broken his bone. ¹⁸Therefore, thus said YHWH of Hosts, God of Israel: Behold, I am seeing after the king of Babylon, ‖ And after his land, ‖ As I have seen after the king of Asshur; ¹⁹And I have brought Israel back to his habitation, ‖ And he has fed on Carmel and on Bashan; And his soul is satisfied on Mount Ephraim and on Gilead. ²⁰In those days, and at that time," ‖ A declaration of YHWH, ‖ "The iniquity of Israel is sought, and it is not, ‖ And the sin of Judah, and it is not found, ‖ For I am propitious to those whom I leave! ²¹Against the land of Merathaim, go up against it, ‖ And to the inhabitants of Pekod, ‖ Dry up and devote their posterity," ‖ A declaration of YHWH, ‖ "And do according to all that I have commanded you. ²²A noise of battle [is] in the land, ‖ And of great destruction. ²³How it has been cut and broken, ‖ The hammer of the whole earth! How Babylon has been for a desolation among nations! ²⁴I have laid a snare for you, ‖ And you are also captured, O Babylon, ‖ And you have known, ‖ You have been found, and are also caught, ‖ For you have stirred yourself up against YHWH. ²⁵YHWH has opened His treasury, ‖ And He brings out the weapons of His indignation, ‖ For a work [is] to Lord YHWH of Hosts, ‖ In the land of the Chaldeans. ²⁶Come in to her from the extremity, ‖ Open her storehouses, ‖ Raise her up as heaps, and devote her, ‖ Let her have no remnant. ²⁷Slay all her cows, they go down to slaughter, ‖ Woe [is] on them, for their day has come, ‖ The time of their inspection. ²⁸A voice of fugitives and escaped ones ‖ [Is] from the land of Babylon, ‖ To declare in Zion the vengeance of our God YHWH, ‖ The vengeance of His temple. ²⁹Summon archers to Babylon, all treading the bow, ‖ Encamp against her all around, ‖ Let [her] have no escape; Repay to her according to her work, ‖ According to all that she did—do to her, ‖ For she has been proud against YHWH, ‖ Against the Holy One of Israel. ³⁰Therefore her young men fall in her broad places, ‖ And all her men of war are cut off in that day," ‖ A declaration of YHWH. ³¹"Behold, I [am] against you, O pride," ‖ A declaration of Lord YHWH of Hosts, ‖ "For your day has come, the time of your inspection. ³²And pride has stumbled, ‖ And he has fallen, and has none raising up, ‖ And I have kindled a fire in his cities, ‖ And it has devoured all around him. ³³Thus said YHWH of Hosts: The sons of Israel are oppressed, ‖ And the sons of Judah together, ‖ And all their captors have kept hold on them, ‖ They have refused to send them away. ³⁴Their Redeemer [is] strong, ‖ YHWH of Hosts [is] His Name, ‖ He thoroughly pleads their cause, ‖ So as to cause the land to rest, ‖ And He has given trouble to the inhabitants of Babylon. ³⁵A sword [is] for the Chaldeans," ‖ A declaration of YHWH, ‖ "And it [is] on the inhabitants of Babylon, ‖ And on her heads, and on her wise men; ³⁶A sword [is] on the princes, ‖ And they have become foolish; A sword [is] on her mighty ones, ‖ And they have been broken down; ³⁷A sword [is] on his horses and on his chariot, ‖ And on all the rabble who [are] in her midst, ‖ And they have become women; A sword [is] on her treasuries, ‖ And they have been spoiled; ³⁸A sword [is] on her waters, and they have been dried up, ‖ For it [is] a land of carved images, ‖ And they boast themselves in idols. ³⁹Therefore desert-dwellers dwell with howlers, ‖ Indeed, daughters of the ostrich have dwelt in her, ‖ And it is not inhabited anymore forever, ‖ Nor dwelt in from generation to generation. ⁴⁰As the overthrow by God of Sodom, ‖ And of Gomorrah, and of its neighbors," ‖ A declaration of YHWH, ‖ "None dwell there, ‖ Nor does a son of man sojourn in her. ⁴¹Behold, a people has come from the north, ‖ Even a great nation, ‖ And many kings are stirred up from the sides of the

earth. ⁴²They seize bow and javelin, || They [are] cruel, and they have no mercy, || Their voice sounds as a sea, and they ride on horses, || Set in array as a man for battle, || Against you, O daughter of Babylon. ⁴³The king of Babylon has heard their report, || And his hands have been feeble, || Distress has seized him; pain as a travailing woman. ⁴⁴Behold, he comes up as a lion, || Because of the rising of the Jordan, || To the enduring habitation, || But I cause to rest, I cause them to run from off her. And who is chosen? I lay a charge on her, || For who [is] like Me? And who convenes Me? And who [is] this shepherd who stands before Me? ⁴⁵Therefore, hear the counsel of Yhwh, || That He counseled concerning Babylon, || And His plans that He has devised || Concerning the land of the Chaldeans; Do little ones of the flock not drag them out, || Does He not make the habitation desolate over them? ⁴⁶From the sound of Babylon having been captured, || The earth has been shaken, || And a cry has been heard among nations!"

CHAPTER 51

¹Thus said Yhwh: "Behold, I am stirring up against Babylon, || And the inhabitants of Leb, My withstanders, || A destroying wind, ²And I have sent fanners to Babylon, || And they have fanned her, and they empty her land, || For they have been against her, || All around—in the day of evil. ³Do not let the treader tread his bow, || Nor lift himself up in his coat of mail, || Nor have pity on her young men, || Devote all her host to destruction. ⁴And the wounded have fallen in the land of the Chaldeans, || And the pierced-through in her streets. ⁵For Israel and Judah are not forsaken || By his God—by Yhwh of Hosts, || For their land has been full of guilt, || Against the Holy One of Israel. ⁶Flee from the midst of Babylon, || And let each deliver his soul, || Do not be cut off in her iniquity, || For it [is] a time of vengeance for Yhwh—His, || He is rendering repayment to her. ⁷Babylon [is] a golden cup in the hand of Yhwh, || Making all the earth drunk, || Nations have drunk of her wine, || Therefore nations boast themselves. ⁸Babylon has suddenly fallen, || Indeed, she is broken, howl for her, || Take balm for her pain, perhaps she may be healed. ⁹We healed Babylon, and she was not healed, || Forsake her, and we go, each to his land, || For her judgment has come to the heavens, || And it has been lifted up to the clouds. ¹⁰Yhwh has brought forth our righteousnesses, || Come, and we recount in Zion the work of our God Yhwh. ¹¹Cleanse the arrows, fill the shields, || Yhwh has stirred up the spirit of the kings of Media, || For His purpose [is] against Babylon to destroy her, || For it [is] the vengeance of Yhwh, || The vengeance of His temple. ¹²Lift up an ensign to the walls of Babylon, || Strengthen the watch, || Establish the watchers, prepare the ambush, || For Yhwh has both devised and done that which He spoke, || Concerning the inhabitants of Babylon. ¹³O dweller on many waters, abundant in treasures, || Your end has come—the measure of your dishonest gain. ¹⁴Yhwh of Hosts has sworn by Himself, || That, Surely I have filled you [with] men as the cankerworm, || And they have cried against you—shouting. ¹⁵Making [the] earth by His power, || Establishing [the] world by His wisdom, || Who by His understanding stretched out the heavens, || ¹⁶At the voice He gives forth, || A multitude of waters [are] in the heavens, || And He causes vapors to come up from the end of the earth, || He has made lightnings for rain, || And He brings out wind from His treasures. ¹⁷Every man has been brutish by knowledge, || Everyone has been put to shame—from refining a carved image, || For his molten image [is] falsehood, || And there is no breath in them. ¹⁸They [are] vanity—a work of errors, || They perish in the time of their inspection. ¹⁹The Portion of Jacob [is] not like these, || For He is forming the whole, || And [Israel is] the tribe of His inheritance, || Yhwh of Hosts [is] His Name. ²⁰You [are] My shatterer—weapons of war, || And I have broken in pieces nations by you, || And I have destroyed kingdoms by you, ²¹And I have broken in pieces horse and its rider by you, || And I have broken in pieces chariot and its charioteer by you, ²²And I have broken in pieces man and woman by you, || And I have broken in pieces old and young by you, || And I have broken in pieces young man and virgin by you, ²³And I have broken in pieces shepherd and his drove by you, || And I have broken in pieces farmer and his team by you, || And I have broken in pieces governors and prefects by you. ²⁴And I have repaid to Babylon, || And to all inhabitants of Chaldea, || All the evil that they have done in Zion, || Before your eyes," a declaration of Yhwh. ²⁵"Behold, I [am] against you, O destroying mountain," || A declaration of Yhwh, || "That is destroying all the earth, || And I have stretched out My hand against you, || And I have rolled you from the rocks, || And given you for a burnt mountain. ²⁶And they do not take out of you a stone for a corner, || And a stone for foundations, || For you are continuous desolations," || A declaration of Yhwh. ²⁷"Lift up an ensign in the land, || Blow a horn among nations, || Sanctify nations against it, || Summon against it the kingdoms of Ararat, Minni, and Ashkenaz, || Appoint an infant head against it, || Cause the horse to ascend as the rough cankerworm. ²⁸Sanctify against it the nations with the kings of Media, || Its governors and all its prefects, || And all the land of its dominion. ²⁹And the land shakes, and it is pained, || For the purposes of Yhwh have stood against Babylon, || To make the land of Babylon a desolation without inhabitant. ³⁰The mighty of Babylon have ceased to fight, || They have remained in strongholds, || Their might has failed, they have become [as] women, || They have burned her dwelling places, || Her bars have been broken. ³¹Runner runs to meet runner, || And announcer to meet announcer, || To announce to the king of Babylon, || For his city has been captured—at the extremity. ³²And the passages have been captured, || And they have burned the reeds with fire, || And the men of war have been troubled. ³³For thus said Yhwh of Hosts, God of Israel: The daughter of Babylon [is] as a threshing-floor, || The time of her threshing—yet a little [while], || And the time of her harvest has come. ³⁴Devoured us, crushed us, has Nebuchadnezzar king of Babylon, || He has set us [as] an empty vessel, || He has swallowed us as a dragon, || He has filled his belly with my delicacies, || He has driven us away. ³⁵My wrong, and [that of] my flesh, [is] on Babylon—The inhabitant of Zion says; And my blood [is] on the inhabitants of Chaldea—Jerusalem says. ³⁶Therefore, thus said Yhwh: Behold, I am pleading your cause, || And I have avenged your vengeance, || And dried up her sea, and made her fountains dry. ³⁷And Babylon has been for heaps, || A habitation of dragons, || An astonishment, and a hissing, without inhabitant. ³⁸They roar together as young lions, || They have shaken themselves as lions' whelps. ³⁹In their heat I make their banquets, || And I have caused them to drink, so that they exult, || And have slept a continuous sleep, || And do not awaken," a declaration of Yhwh. ⁴⁰"I cause them to go down as lambs to slaughter, || As rams with male goats. ⁴¹How Sheshach has been captured, || Indeed, the praise of the whole earth is caught, || How Babylon has been for an astonishment among nations. ⁴²The sea has come up over Babylon, || She has been covered with a multitude of its billows. ⁴³Her cities have been for a desolation, || A dry land, and a wilderness, || A land—none dwell in them, || Nor does a son of man pass over into them. ⁴⁴And I have seen after Bel in Babylon, || And I have brought forth that which he swallowed—from his mouth, || And nations no longer flow to him, || Also the wall of Babylon has fallen. ⁴⁵Go forth from her midst, O My people, || And let each deliver his soul, || Because of the fierceness of the anger of Yhwh, ⁴⁶And lest your heart be tender, || And you are afraid of the report that is heard in the land, || And the report has come in [one] year, || And after it [another] report in [another] year, || And violence [is] in the land, ruler against ruler; ⁴⁷Therefore, behold, days are coming, || And I have seen after the carved images of Babylon. And all its land is ashamed, || And all its pierced ones fall in its midst. ⁴⁸And heavens and earth and all that [is] in them || Have cried aloud against Babylon, || For the spoilers come to her from the north," || A declaration of Yhwh. ⁴⁹"As Babylon [has caused the] pierced of Israel to fall, || So they of Babylon have fallen, || You pierced of all the earth. ⁵⁰You escaped of the sword, go on, do not stand, || Remember Yhwh from afar, || And let Jerusalem come up on your heart. ⁵¹We have been ashamed, for we heard reproach, || Shame has covered our faces, || For strangers have come in against the sanctuaries of the house of Yhwh. ⁵²Therefore, behold, days are coming," || A declaration of Yhwh, || "And I have seen after her carved images, || And the wounded groan in all her land. ⁵³Because Babylon goes up to the heavens, || And because she fortifies the high place of her strength, || Spoilers come into her from Me," || A declaration of Yhwh. ⁵⁴"A voice

of a cry [is] from Babylon, || And of great destruction from the land of the Chaldean. ⁵⁵For YHWH is spoiling Babylon, || And has destroyed her great voice, || And her billows have sounded as many waters, || Their voice has given forth a noise. ⁵⁶For a spoiler has come in against her—against Babylon, || And her mighty ones have been captured, || Their bows have been broken, || For the God of recompenses—YHWH—certainly repays. ⁵⁷And I have caused her princes to drink, || And her wise men, her governors, || And her prefects, and her mighty ones, || And they have slept a continuous sleep, || And they do not awaken—an affirmation of the King, || YHWH of Hosts [is] His Name. ⁵⁸Thus said YHWH of Hosts: The wall of Babylon—The broad one—is made utterly bare, || And her high gates are burned with fire, || And peoples labor in vain, || And nations in fire, and have been weary!" ⁵⁹The word that Jeremiah the prophet has commanded Seraiah son of Neriah, son of Maaseiah, in his going with Zedekiah king of Judah to Babylon, in the fourth year of his reign—and Seraiah [is] a quiet prince; ⁶⁰and Jeremiah writes all the calamity that comes to Babylon on one scroll—all these words that are written concerning Babylon. ⁶¹And Jeremiah says to Seraiah, "When you enter Babylon, then you have seen, and have read all these words, ⁶²and have said: YHWH, You have spoken concerning this place, to cut it off, that there is none dwelling in it, from man even to livestock, for it is a continuous desolation. ⁶³And it has come to pass, when you finish reading this scroll, you bind a stone to it, and have cast it into the midst of the Euphrates, ⁶⁴and said, Thus Babylon sinks, and she does not arise, because of the calamity that I am bringing in against it, and they have been weary." Until now [are the] words of Jeremiah.

CHAPTER 52

¹Zedekiah [is] a son of twenty-one years in his reigning, and he has reigned eleven years in Jerusalem, and the name of his mother [is] Hamutal daughter of Jeremiah of Libnah. ²And he does evil in the eyes of YHWH, according to all that Jehoiakim has done, ³for because of the anger of YHWH, it has been in Jerusalem and Judah until He has cast them from before His face, and Zedekiah rebels against the king of Babylon. ⁴And it comes to pass, in the ninth year of his reign, in the tenth month, on the tenth of the month, Nebuchadnezzar king of Babylon has come—he and all his force—against Jerusalem, and they encamp against it, and build against it a fortification all around; ⁵and the city comes into siege until the eleventh year of King Zedekiah. ⁶In the fourth month, on the ninth of the month, when the famine is severe in the city, and there has been no bread for the people of the land, ⁷then the city is broken up, and all the men of war flee, and go forth from the city by night, the way of the gate between the two walls that [is] by the king's garden—and the Chaldeans [are] by the city all around—and they go the way of the plain. ⁸And the forces of the Chaldeans pursue after the king, and overtake Zedekiah in the plains of Jericho, and all his forces have been scattered from him, ⁹and they capture the king, and bring him up to the king of Babylon at Riblah, in the land of Hamath, and he speaks with him—judgments. ¹⁰And the king of Babylon slaughters the sons of Zedekiah before his eyes, and he has also slaughtered all the princes of Judah in Riblah; ¹¹and he has blinded the eyes of Zedekiah, and he binds him in bronze chains, and the king of Babylon brings him to Babylon, and puts him in the house of inspection to the day of his death. ¹²And in the fifth month, on the tenth of the month—it [is] the nineteenth year of King Nebuchadnezzar king of Babylon—Nebuzar-Adan, chief of the executioners, has come; he has stood before the king of Babylon in Jerusalem, ¹³and he burns the house of YHWH, and the house of the king, and all the houses of Jerusalem—even every great house he has burned with fire, ¹⁴and all the forces of the Chaldeans that [are] with the chief of the executioners have broken down all the walls of Jerusalem. ¹⁵And of the poor of the people, and the remnant of the people who are left in the city, and those who are defecting, who have defected to the king of Babylon, and the remnant of the multitude, Nebuzar-Adan, chief of the executioners, has removed; ¹⁶and of the poor of the land, Nebuzar-Adan, chief of the executioners, has left for vinedressers and for farmers. ¹⁷And the pillars of bronze that [are] in the house of YHWH, and the bases, and the bronze sea that [is] in the house of YHWH, the Chaldeans have broken, and they carry away all the bronze of them to Babylon; ¹⁸and the pots, and the shovels, and the snuffers, and the bowls, and the spoons, and all the vessels of bronze with which they minister, they have taken away; ¹⁹and the basins, and the fire-pans, and the bowls, and the pots, and the lampstands, and the spoons, and the cups, the gold of that which [is] gold, and the silver of that which [is] silver, the chief of the executioners has taken. ²⁰The two pillars, the one sea, and the twelve bronze oxen that [are] beneath the bases, that King Solomon made for the house of YHWH, there was no weighing of the bronze of all these vessels. ²¹As for the pillars, eighteen cubits [is] the height of the one pillar, and a cord of twelve cubits goes around it, and its thickness [is] four fingers hollow. ²²And the capital on it [is] of bronze, and the height of the one capital [is] five cubits, and network and pomegranates [are] on the capital all around, the whole [is] of bronze; and like these—the second pillar—and pomegranates. ²³And the pomegranates are ninety-six on a side, all the pomegranates [are] one hundred on the network all around. ²⁴And the chief of the executioners takes Seraiah the head priest, and Zephaniah the second priest, and the three keepers of the threshold, ²⁵and he has taken a certain eunuch out of the city, who has been inspector over the men of war, and seven men of those seeing the king's face, who have been found in the city, and the head scribe of the host, who musters the people of the land, and sixty men of the people of the land, who are found in the midst of the city; ²⁶and Nebuzar-Adan, chief of the executioners, takes them, and brings them to the king of Babylon at Riblah, ²⁷and the king of Babylon strikes them, and puts them to death in Riblah, in the land of Hamath, and he removes Judah from off its own ground. ²⁸This [is] the people whom Nebuchadnezzar has removed: in the seventh year, of Jews, three thousand and twenty-three; ²⁹in the eighteenth year of Nebuchadnezzar—from Jerusalem—eight hundred thirty-two souls; ³⁰in the twenty-third year of Nebuchadnezzar, Nebuzar-Adan, chief of the guard, has removed of Jewish souls, seven hundred forty-five; all the souls [are] four thousand and six hundred. ³¹And it comes to pass, in the thirty-seventh year of the expulsion of Jehoiachin king of Judah, in the twelfth month, on the twenty-fifth of the month, Evil-Merodach king of Babylon has lifted up, in the year of his reign, the head of Jehoiachin king of Judah, and brings him out from the house of restraint, ³²and speaks good things with him, and sets his throne above the throne of the kings who [are] with him in Babylon, ³³and he has changed his prison garments, and he has continually eaten bread before him, all the days of his life. ³⁴And his allowance—a continual allowance—has been given to him by the king of Babylon, the matter of a day in its day, until [the] day of his death—all [the] days of his life.

LAMENTATIONS

CHAPTER 1

¹[ALEPH-BET] How she has sat alone, || The city abounding with people! She has been as a widow, || The mighty among nations! Princes among provinces, || She has become tributary! ²She weeps severely in the night, || And her tear [is] on her cheeks, || There is no comforter for her out of all her lovers, || All her friends dealt treacherously by her, || They have been to her for enemies. ³Removed has Judah because of affliction, || And because of the abundance of her service; She has dwelt among nations, || She has not found rest, || All her pursuers have overtaken her between the straits. ⁴The ways of Zion are mourning, || Without any coming at the appointed time, || All her gates are desolate, her priests sigh, || Her virgins are afflicted—and she has

LAMENTATIONS

bitterness. ⁵Her adversaries have become chief, || Her enemies have been at ease, || For YHWH has afflicted her, || For the abundance of her transgressions, || Her infants have gone captive before the adversary. ⁶And all her honor goes out from the daughter of Zion, || Her princes have been as harts—They have not found pasture, || And they go powerless before a pursuer. ⁷Jerusalem has remembered || [In] the days of her affliction and her mournings, all her desirable things that were from the days of old, || In the falling of her people into the hand of an adversary, || And she has no helper; Adversaries have seen her, || They have laughed at her cessation. ⁸A sin has Jerusalem sinned, || Therefore she has become impure, || All who honored her have esteemed her lightly, || For they have seen her nakedness, || Indeed, she herself has sighed and turns backward. ⁹Her uncleanness [is] in her skirts, || She has not remembered her latter end, || And she comes down wonderfully, || There is no comforter for her. See, O YHWH, my affliction, || For an enemy has exerted himself. ¹⁰His hand has spread out an adversary || On all her desirable things, || For she has seen—Nations have entered her sanctuary, || Concerning which You commanded, || "They do not come into the assembly to you." ¹¹All her people are sighing—seeking bread, || They have given their desirable things || For food to refresh the body; See, O YHWH, and behold attentively, || For I have been lightly esteemed. ¹²[Is it] nothing to you, all you passing by the way? Look attentively, and see, || If there is any pain like my pain, || That He is rolling to me? Whom YHWH has afflicted || In the day of the fierceness of His anger. ¹³From above He has sent fire into my bone, || And it subdues it, He has spread a net for my feet, || He has turned me backward, || He has made me desolate—all the day sick. ¹⁴Bound has been the yoke of my transgressions by His hand, || They are wrapped together, || They have gone up on my neck, || He has caused my power to stumble, || The Lord has given me into hands, I am not able to rise. ¹⁵The Lord has trodden down all my mighty ones in my midst, || He proclaimed an appointed time against me, || To destroy my young men, || The Lord has trodden a winepress, || To the virgin daughter of Judah. ¹⁶For these I am weeping, || My eye, my eye, is running down with waters, || For a comforter has been far from me, || Refreshing my soul, || My sons have been desolate, || For mighty has been an enemy. ¹⁷Zion has spread forth her hands, || There is no comforter for her, || YHWH has charged concerning Jacob, || His neighbors [are] his adversaries, || Jerusalem has become impure among them. ¹⁸YHWH is righteous, || For I have provoked His mouth. Now hear, all you peoples, and see my pain, || My virgins and my young men have gone into captivity. ¹⁹I called for my lovers, they have deceived me, || My priests and my elderly have expired in the city; When they have sought food for themselves, || Then they give back their soul. ²⁰See, O YHWH, for distress [is] to me, || My bowels have been troubled, || My heart has been turned in my midst, || For I have greatly provoked, || From outside the sword has bereaved, || In the house [it is] as death. ²¹They have heard that I have sighed, || There is no comforter for me, || All my enemies have heard of my calamity, || They have rejoiced that You have done [it], || You have brought in the day You have called, || And they are like to me. ²²All their evil comes in before You, || And one is doing to them as You have done to me, || For all my transgressions, || For many [are] my sighs, and my heart [is] sick!

CHAPTER 2

¹[ALEPH-BET] How the Lord clouds in His anger the daughter of Zion, || He has cast from the heavens [to] earth the beauty of Israel, || And has not remembered His footstool in the day of His anger. ²The Lord has swallowed up, || He has not pitied any of the pleasant places of Jacob, || He has broken down in His wrath || The fortresses of the daughter of Judah, || He has caused to come to the earth, || He defiled the kingdom and its princes. ³He has cut off in the heat of anger every horn of Israel, || He has turned backward His right hand || From the face of the enemy, || And He burns against Jacob as a flaming fire, || It has devoured all around. ⁴He has bent His bow as an enemy, || His right hand has stood as an adversary, || And He slays all the desirable ones of the eye, || In the tent of the daughter of Zion, || He has poured out as fire His fury. ⁵The Lord has been as an enemy, || He has swallowed up Israel, || He has swallowed up all her palaces, || He has destroyed His fortresses, || And He multiplies in the daughter of Judah || Mourning and moaning. ⁶And He shakes as a garden His dwelling place, || He has destroyed His appointed place, || YHWH has forgotten in Zion the appointed time and Sabbath, || And despises, in the indignation of His anger, king and priest. ⁷The Lord has cast off His altar, || He has rejected His sanctuary, || He has shut up into the hand of the enemy || The walls of her palaces, || A noise they have made in the house of YHWH || Like a day of appointment. ⁸YHWH has devised to destroy the wall of the daughter of Zion, || He has stretched out a line, || He has not turned His hand from destroying, || And He causes bulwark and wall to mourn, || Together—they have been weak. ⁹Sunk into the earth have her gates, || He has destroyed and broken her bars, || Her king and her princes [are] among the nations, || There is no law, also her prophets || Have not found vision from YHWH. ¹⁰Sit on the earth—[the] elderly of Zion's daughter keep silent, || They have caused dust to go up on their head, || They have girded on sackcloth, || The virgins of Jerusalem have || Put their head down to the earth. ¹¹My eyes have been consumed by tears, || My bowels have been troubled, || My liver has been poured out to the earth, || For the breach of the daughter of my people; In infant and suckling being feeble, || In the broad places of the city, ¹²To their mothers they say, || "Where [are] grain and wine?" In their becoming feeble as a pierced one || In the broad places of the city, || In their soul pouring itself out into the bosom of their mothers. ¹³What do I testify [to] you, what do I liken to you, || O daughter of Jerusalem? What do I equal to you, and I comfort you, || O virgin daughter of Zion? For great as a sea [is] your breach, || Who gives healing to you? ¹⁴Your prophets have seen for you a false and insipid thing, || And have not revealed concerning your iniquity, || To return your captivity, || And they see for you false burdens and causes of expulsion. ¹⁵Everyone passing by the way clapped hands at you, || They have hissed—and they shake the head || At the daughter of Jerusalem: "Is this the city of which they said: The perfection of beauty, a joy to all the land?" ¹⁶Opened against you their mouth have all your enemies, || They have hissed, indeed, they gnash the teeth, || They have said: "We have swallowed [her] up, || Surely this [is] the day that we looked for, || We have found—we have seen." ¹⁷YHWH has done that which He devised, || He has fulfilled His saying || That He commanded from the days of old, || He has broken down and has not pitied, || And causes an enemy to rejoice over you, || He lifted up the horn of your adversaries. ¹⁸Their heart has cried to the Lord; O wall of the daughter of Zion, || Cause to go down tears as a stream daily and nightly, do not give rest to yourself, || Do not let the daughter of your eye stand still. ¹⁹Arise, cry aloud in the night, || At the beginning of the watches. Pour out your heart as water, || Before the face of the Lord, || Lift up to Him your hands, for the soul of your infants, || Who are feeble with hunger at the head of all out-places. ²⁰See, O YHWH, and look attentively, || To whom You have acted thus, || Do women eat their fruit, infants of a handbreadth? Slain in the sanctuary of the Lord are priest and prophet? ²¹Lain on the earth [in] out-places have young and old, || My virgins and my young men have fallen by the sword, || You have slain in a day of Your anger, || You have slaughtered—You have not pitied. ²²You call as [at] a day of appointment, || My fears from all around, || And there has not been in the day of the anger of YHWH, || An escaped and remaining one, || They whom I stretched out and nourished, || My enemy has consumed!

CHAPTER 3

¹[ALEPH-BET] I [am] the man [who] has seen affliction || By the rod of His wrath. ²He has led me, and causes to go [in] darkness, and without light. ³Surely against me He turns back, || He turns His hand all the day. ⁴He has worn out my flesh and my skin. He has broken my bones. ⁵He has built up against me, || And sets around poverty and weariness. ⁶In dark places He has caused me to dwell, || As the dead of old. ⁷He has hedged me in, and I do not go out, || He has made heavy my chain. ⁸Also when I call and cry out, || He has shut out my prayer. ⁹He has hedged my ways with hewn work, || My paths He has made crooked. ¹⁰A bear lying in wait He [is] to me, || A lion in secret hiding places. ¹¹My ways He is turning aside, and He pulls me in pieces, || He has

made me a desolation. ¹²He has bent His bow, || And sets me up as a mark for an arrow. ¹³He has caused to enter into my reins || The sons of His quiver. ¹⁴I have been a derision to all my people, || Their song all the day. ¹⁵He has filled me with bitter things, || He has filled me [with] wormwood. ¹⁶And He breaks with gravel my teeth, || He has covered me with ashes. ¹⁷And You cast off my soul from peace, || I have forgotten prosperity. ¹⁸And I say, My strength and my hope have perished from YHWH. ¹⁹Remember my affliction and my mourning, || Wormwood and gall! ²⁰Remember well, and my soul bows down in me. ²¹This I turn to my heart—therefore I hope. ²²The kindnesses of YHWH! For we have not been consumed, || For His mercies have not ended. ²³New every morning, abundant [is] Your faithfulness. ²⁴My portion [is] YHWH, my soul has said, || Therefore I hope for Him. ²⁵YHWH [is] good to those waiting for Him, || To the soul [that] seeks Him. ²⁶[It is] good when one stays and stands still || For the salvation of YHWH. ²⁷[It is] good for a man that he bears a yoke in his youth. ²⁸He sits alone, and is silent, || For He has laid [it] on him. ²⁹He puts his mouth in the dust, if so be, there is hope. ³⁰He gives to his striker the cheek, || He is filled with reproach. ³¹For the Lord does not cast off for all time. ³²For though He afflicted, yet He has pitied, || According to the abundance of His kindness. ³³For He has not afflicted with His heart, || Nor does He grieve the sons of men. ³⁴To bruise under one's feet any bound ones of earth, ³⁵To turn aside the judgment of a man, || Before the face of the Most High, ³⁶To subvert a man in his cause, the Lord has not approved. ³⁷Who [is] this—he has spoken, and it is, || [And] the Lord has not commanded [it]? ³⁸From the mouth of the Most High does not go forth the evils and the good. ³⁹Why does a living man sigh habitually, || A man for his sin? ⁴⁰We search our ways, and investigate, || And turn back to YHWH. ⁴¹We lift up our heart on the hands to God in the heavens. ⁴²We have transgressed and been rebellious, || You have not forgiven. ⁴³You have covered Yourself with anger, || And pursue us; You have slain—You have not pitied. ⁴⁴You have covered Yourself with a cloud, || So that prayer does not pass through. ⁴⁵Outcast and refuse You make us || In the midst of the peoples. ⁴⁶Opened against us their mouth have all our enemies. ⁴⁷Fear and a snare has been for us, || Desolation and destruction. ⁴⁸Streams of water go down my eye, || For the destruction of the daughter of my people. ⁴⁹My eye is poured out, || And does not cease without intermission, ⁵⁰Until YHWH looks and sees from the heavens, ⁵¹My eye affects my soul, || Because of all the daughters of my city. ⁵²Hunting—my enemies have hunted me without cause like the bird. ⁵³They have cut off my life in a pit, || And they cast a stone against me. ⁵⁴Waters have flowed over my head, I have said, I have been cut off. ⁵⁵I called Your Name, O YHWH, from the lower pit. ⁵⁶You have heard my voice, do not hide Your ear at my breathing—at my cry. ⁵⁷You have drawn near in the day I call You, You have said, Do not fear. ⁵⁸You have pleaded, O Lord, the pleadings of my soul, || You have redeemed my life. ⁵⁹You have seen, O YHWH, my overthrow, || Judge my cause. ⁶⁰You have seen all their vengeance, || All their thoughts of me. ⁶¹You have heard their reproach, O YHWH, || All their thoughts against me, ⁶²The lips of my withstanders, || Even their meditation against me all the day. ⁶³Their sitting down, and their rising up, || Behold attentively, I [am] their song. ⁶⁴You return to them the deed, O YHWH, || According to the work of their hands. ⁶⁵You give to them a covered heart, || Your curse to them. ⁶⁶You pursue in anger, and destroy them, || From under the heavens of YHWH!

CHAPTER 4

¹[ALEPH-BET] How the gold has become dim, || Changed the best—the pure gold! Stones of the sanctuary are poured out || At the head of all out-places. ²The precious sons of Zion, Who are comparable with fine gold, || How they have been reckoned earthen bottles, || Work of the hands of a potter. ³Even dragons have drawn out the breast, || They have suckled their young ones, || The daughter of my people has become cruel, || Like the ostriches in a wilderness. ⁴The tongue of a suckling has cleaved to his palate with thirst, || Infants asked for bread, they have no dealer [of it] out. ⁵Those eating of delicacies have been desolate in out-places, || Those supported on scarlet have embraced dunghills. ⁶And greater is the iniquity of the daughter of my people, || Than the sin of Sodom, || That was overturned as [in] a moment, || And no hands were stayed on her. ⁷Purer were her Nazarites than snow, || Whiter than milk, ruddier of body than rubies, || Of sapphire their form. ⁸Their face has been darker than blackness, || They have not been known in out-places, || Their skin has cleaved to their bone, || It has withered—it has been as wood. ⁹Better have been the pierced of a sword || Than the pierced of famine, || For these flow away, pierced through, || Without the increase of the field. ¹⁰The hands of merciful women have boiled their own children, || They have been for food to them, || In the destruction of the daughter of my people. ¹¹YHWH has completed His fury, || He has poured out the fierceness of His anger, || And He kindles a fire in Zion, || And it devours her foundations. ¹²The kings of earth did not believe, || And any of the inhabitants of the world, || That an adversary and enemy would come || Into the gates of Jerusalem. ¹³Because of the sins of her prophets, || The iniquities of her priests, || Who are shedding in her midst the blood of the righteous, ¹⁴They have wandered naked in out-places, || They have been defiled with blood, || Without [any] being able to touch their clothing, ¹⁵"Turn aside—unclean," they called to them, || "Turn aside, turn aside, do not touch," || For they fled—indeed, they have wandered, || They have said among nations: "They do not add to sojourn." ¹⁶The face of YHWH has divided them, || He does not add to behold them, || They have not lifted up the face of priests, || They have not favored [the] old and elderly. ¹⁷While we exist—consumed are our eyes for our vain help, || In our watchtower we have watched for a nation [that] does not save. ¹⁸They have hunted our steps from going in our broad-places, || Near has been our end, fulfilled our days, || For our end has come. ¹⁹Swifter have been our pursuers, || Than the eagles of the heavens, || On the mountains they have burned [after] us, || In the wilderness they have laid wait for us. ²⁰The breath of our nostrils—the anointed of YHWH, || Has been captured in their pits, of whom we said: "We live among nations in his shadow." ²¹Rejoice and be glad, O daughter of Edom, || Dwelling in the land of Uz, || Even to you a cup passes over, || You are drunk, and make yourself naked. ²²Completed [is] your iniquity, daughter of Zion, || He does not add to remove you, || He has inspected your iniquity, O daughter of Edom, || He has removed [you] because of your sins!

CHAPTER 5

¹Remember, O YHWH, what has befallen us, || Look attentively, and see our reproach. ²Our inheritance has been turned to strangers, || Our houses to foreigners. ³Orphans we have been—without a father, our mothers [are] as widows. ⁴We have drunk our water for money, || Our wood comes for a price. ⁵For our neck we have been pursued, || We have labored—there has been no rest for us. ⁶[To] Egypt we have given a hand, || [To] Asshur, to be satisfied with bread. ⁷Our fathers have sinned—they are not, || We have borne their iniquities. ⁸Servants have ruled over us, || There is no deliverer from their hand. ⁹With our lives we bring in our bread, || Because of the sword of the wilderness. ¹⁰Our skin as an oven has been burning, || Because of the raging of the famine. ¹¹Wives in Zion they have humbled, || Virgins—in cities of Judah. ¹²Princes have been hanged by their hand, || Elderly faces have not been honored. ¹³They have taken young men to grind, || And youths have stumbled with wood. ¹⁴Elderly have ceased from the gate, || Young men from their song. ¹⁵The joy of our heart has ceased, || Our dancing has been turned to mourning. ¹⁶The crown has fallen [from] our head, || Woe [is] now to us, for we have sinned. ¹⁷Our heart has been sick for this, || Our eyes have been dim for these. ¹⁸For the Mount of Zion—that is desolate, || Foxes have gone up on it. ¹⁹You, O YHWH, remain for all time, || Your throne to generation and generation. ²⁰Why do You forget us forever? You forsake us for [the] length of [our] days! ²¹Turn us back, O YHWH, to You, || And we turn back, renew our days as of old. ²²For have You utterly rejected us? You have been angry against us—exceedingly?

EZEKIEL

CHAPTER 1

¹And it comes to pass, in the thirtieth year, in the fourth [month], on the fifth of the month, and I [am] in the midst of the expulsion by the river Chebar, the heavens have been opened, and I see visions of God. ²In the fifth of the month—it is the fifth year of the expulsion of King Jehoiachin— ³the word of YHWH has certainly been to Ezekiel son of Buzi the priest, in the land of the Chaldeans, by the river Chebar, and there is on him there a hand of YHWH. ⁴And I look, and behold, a turbulent wind is coming from the north, a great cloud, and fire catching itself, and brightness to it all around, and out of its midst as the color of electrum, out of the midst of the fire. ⁵And out of its midst [is] a likeness of four living creatures, and this [is] their appearance; a likeness of man [is] to them, ⁶and each had four faces and each of them had four wings, ⁷and their feet [are] straight feet, and the sole of their feet [is] as a sole of a calf's foot, and they are sparkling as the color of bright bronze; ⁸and on their four sides [each had] hands of man under their wings; and [each] of the four had their faces and their wings; ⁹their wings [are] joining to one another, they do not turn around in their going, they each go straight forward. ¹⁰As for the likeness of their faces, [each had] the face of a man, and toward the right the four had the face of a lion, and on the left the four had the face of an ox, and the four had the face of an eagle. ¹¹And their faces and their wings dividing from above, of each [are] two joining together, and two are covering their bodies. ¹²And they each go straight forward, to where the Spirit is to go, they go, they do not turn around in their going. ¹³As for the likeness of the living creatures, their appearances [are] as coals of fire—burning as the appearance of lamps; it is going up and down between the living creatures, and brightness [is] to the fire, and lightning is going forth out of the fire. ¹⁴And the living creatures are running, and turning back, as the appearance of the flash. ¹⁵And I see the living creatures, and behold, one wheel [is] in the earth, near the living creatures, at its four faces. ¹⁶The appearance of the wheels and their works [is] as the color of beryl, and the four of them had one likeness, and their appearances and their works [are] as it were the wheel in the midst of the wheel. ¹⁷On their four sides, in their going they go, they do not turn around in their going. ¹⁸As for their rings, they are both high and fearful, and their rings, of the four of them, [are] full of eyes around them. ¹⁹And in the going of the living creatures, the wheels go beside them, and in the living creatures being lifted up from off the earth, the wheels are lifted up. ²⁰To where the Spirit is to go, they go, there the Spirit [is] to go, and the wheels are lifted up alongside them, for a living spirit [is] in the wheels. ²¹In their going, they go; and in their standing, they stand; and in their being lifted up from off the earth, the wheels are lifted up alongside them; for a living spirit [is] in the wheels. ²²And over the heads of the living creatures—a likeness of an expanse, as the color of the fearful ice, stretched out over their heads from above. ²³And under the expanse their wings [are] straight, one toward [its] sister; two [wings] of each are covering them, and two [wings] of each are covering their bodies. ²⁴And I hear the noise of their wings, as the noise of many waters, as the noise of the Mighty One, in their going—the noise of tumult, as the noise of a camp, in their standing they let their wings fall. ²⁵And there is a voice from above the expanse, that [is] above their head: in their standing they let their wings fall. ²⁶And above the expanse that [is] over their head, as an appearance of a sapphire stone, [is] the likeness of a throne, and on the likeness of the throne a likeness, as the appearance of man on it from above. ²⁷And I see as the color of electrum, as the appearance of fire all around within it, from the appearance of His loins and upward; and from the appearance of His loins and downward, I have seen as the appearance of fire, and brightness [is] all around Him. ²⁸As the appearance of the bow that is in a cloud in a day of rain, so [is] the appearance of the brightness all around.

CHAPTER 2

¹His appearance [was] of the likeness of the glory of YHWH, and I see, and fall on my face, and I hear a voice speaking, and He says to me, "Son of man, stand on your feet, and I speak with you." ²And [the] Spirit comes into me when He has spoken to me, and causes me to stand on my feet, and I hear Him who is speaking to me. ³And He says to me, "Son of man, I am sending you to the sons of Israel, to rebelling nations who have rebelled against Me; they and their fathers have transgressed against Me, to this very day. ⁴And the sons [are] brazen-faced and hard-hearted to whom I am sending you, and you have said to them: Thus said Lord YHWH. ⁵And they—whether they hear, or whether they refrain, for they [are] a house of rebellion—have known that a prophet has been in their midst. ⁶And you, son of man, you are not afraid of them, indeed, you are not afraid of their words, for briers and thorns are with you, and you are dwelling near scorpions, you are not afraid of their words, and you are not frightened of their faces, for they [are] a house of rebellion, ⁷and you have spoken My words to them, whether they hear or whether they refrain, for they [are] a rebellion. ⁸And you, son of man, hear that which I am speaking to you; do not be of rebellion like the house of rebellion, open your mouth and eat that which I am giving to you." ⁹And I look, and behold, a hand [is] sent forth to me, and behold, a roll of a scroll [is] in it, ¹⁰and He spreads it before me, and it is written in front and behind, and written on it [are] lamentations, and mourning, and woe!

CHAPTER 3

¹And He says to me, "Son of man, eat that which you find, eat this scroll, and go, speak to the house of Israel." ²And I open my mouth, and He causes me to eat this scroll. ³And He says to me, "Son of man, feed your belly, and fill your bowels with this scroll that I am giving to you"; and I eat it, and it is as honey for sweetness in my mouth. ⁴And He says to me, "Son of man, go forth, go to the house of Israel, and you have spoken to them with My words. ⁵For you [are] not sent to a people deep of lip and heavy of tongue—to the house of Israel; ⁶not to many peoples, deep of lip and heavy of tongue, whose words you do not understand. If I had not sent you to them—they listen to you, ⁷but the house of Israel are not willing to listen to you, for they are not willing to listen to Me, for all the house of Israel are brazen-faced and strong-hearted. ⁸Behold, I have made your face strong against their face, and your forehead strong against their forehead. ⁹As an adamant, harder than a rock, I have made your forehead; do not fear them, nor are you frightened before them, for they [are] a house of rebellion." ¹⁰And He says to me, "Son of man, all My words that I speak to you, receive with your heart, and hear with your ears; ¹¹and go forth, go to the expulsion, to the sons of your people, and you have spoken to them, and have said to them: Thus said Lord YHWH; whether they hear, or whether they refrain." ¹²And a spirit lifts me up, and I hear a noise behind me, a great rushing—"Blessed [is] the glory of YHWH from His place!" ¹³Even a noise of the wings of the living creatures touching one another, and a noise of the wheels alongside them, even a noise of a great rushing. ¹⁴And [the] Spirit has lifted me up, and takes me away, and I go bitterly, in the heat of my spirit, and the hand of YHWH [is] strong on me. ¹⁵And I come to the expulsion, at Tel-Ahib, who are dwelling at the river Chebar, and where they are dwelling I also dwell [for] seven days, causing astonishment in their midst. ¹⁶And it comes to pass, at the end of seven days, ¹⁷that there is a word of YHWH to me, saying, "Son of man, I have given you [as] a watchman to the house of Israel, and you have heard a word from My mouth, and have warned them from Me. ¹⁸In My saying to the wicked: You surely die; and you have not warned him, nor have spoken to warn the wicked from his wicked way, so that he lives; he—the wicked—dies in his iniquity, and I require his blood from your hand. ¹⁹And you,

because you have warned the wicked, and he has not turned back from his wickedness, and from his wicked way, he dies in his iniquity, and you have delivered your soul. ²⁰And in the turning back of the righteous from his righteousness, and he has done perversity, and I have put a stumbling-block before him, he dies; because you have not warned him, he dies in his sin, and his righteousness that he has done is not remembered, and I require his blood from your hand. ²¹And you, because you have warned him—the righteous—that the righteous does not sin, and he has not sinned, he surely lives, because he has been warned; and you have delivered your soul." ²²And there is a hand of YHWH on me there, and He says to me, "Rise, go forth to the valley, and there I speak with you." ²³And I rise and go forth to the valley, and behold, there the glory of YHWH is standing as the glory that I had seen by the river Chebar, and I fall on my face. ²⁴And [the] Spirit comes into me, and causes me to stand on my feet, and He speaks with me, and says to me, "Go in, be shut up in the midst of your house. ²⁵And you, son of man, behold, they have put thick bands on you, and have bound you with them, and you do not go forth in their midst; ²⁶and I cause your tongue to cleave to your palate, and you have been mute, and are not for a reprover to them, for they [are] a house of rebellion. ²⁷And in My speaking with you, I open your mouth, and you have said to them: Thus said Lord YHWH; the hearer hears, and the refrainer refrains; for they [are] a house of rebellion."

CHAPTER 4

¹"And you, son of man, take a brick for yourself, and you have put it before you, and have carved a city on it—Jerusalem, ²and have placed a siege against it, and built a fortification against it, and poured out a mound against it, and placed camps against it, indeed, set battering-rams against it all around. ³And you, take an iron pan for yourself, and you have made it a wall of iron between you and the city; and you have prepared your face against it, and it has been in a siege, indeed, you have laid siege against it. It [is] a sign to the house of Israel. ⁴And you, lie on your left side, and you have placed the iniquity of the house of Israel on it; the number of the days that you lie on it, you bear their iniquity. ⁵And I have laid the years of their iniquity on you, the number of days, three hundred and ninety days; and you have borne the iniquity of the house of Israel. ⁶And you have completed these, and have lain on your right side, a second time, and have borne the iniquity of the house of Judah forty days—a day for a year—a day for a year I have appointed to you. ⁷And to the siege of Jerusalem you prepare your face, and your arm [is] uncovered, and you have prophesied concerning it. ⁸And behold, I have put thick bands on you, and you do not turn from side to side until your completing the days of your siege. ⁹And you, take for yourself wheat, and barley, and beans, and lentiles, and millet, and spelt, and you have put them in one vessel, and made them for bread for yourself; the number of the days that you are lying on your side—three hundred and ninety days—you eat it. ¹⁰And your food that you eat [is] by weight, twenty shekels daily; from time to time you eat it. ¹¹And you drink water by measure, a sixth part of the hin; from time to time you drink [it]. ¹²And you eat it [as] barley-cake, and it with dung—the filth of man—you bake before their eyes." ¹³And YHWH says, "Thus the sons of Israel eat their defiled bread among the nations to where I drive them." ¹⁴And I say, "Aah! Lord YHWH, behold, my soul is not defiled, and carcass, and torn thing, I have not eaten from my youth, even until now; nor has abominable flesh come into my mouth." ¹⁵And He says to me, "See, I have given to you bullock's dung instead of man's dung, and you have made your bread by it." ¹⁶And He says to me, "Son of man, behold, I am breaking the staff of bread in Jerusalem, and they have eaten bread by weight and with fear; and water by measure and with astonishment, they drink; ¹⁷so that they lack bread and water, and have been astonished with one another, and been consumed in their iniquity."

CHAPTER 5

¹"And you, son of man, take a sharp weapon for yourself, take the barber's razor for yourself, and you have caused [it] to pass over your head, and over your beard, and you have taken weighing scales for yourself, and apportioned them. ²You burn a third part with fire in the midst of the city, at the fullness of the days of the siege; and you have taken the third part, you strike with a weapon around it; and the third part you scatter to the wind, and I draw out a weapon after them. ³And you have taken there a few in number—and have bound them in your skirts; ⁴and you take of them again, and have cast them into the midst of the fire, and have burned them in the fire—out of it comes forth a fire to all the house of Israel." ⁵Thus said Lord YHWH: "This [is] Jerusalem, || I have set her in the midst of the nations, || And the lands [are] around her. ⁶And she changes My judgments into wickedness more than the nations, || And My statutes more than the lands that [are] around her, || For they have kicked against My judgments, || And My statutes—they have not walked in them." ⁷Therefore, thus said Lord YHWH: "Because of your multiplying above the nations that [are] around you, || You have not walked in My statutes, || And you have not done My judgments, || According to the judgments of the nations that [are] around you, you have not done." ⁸Therefore, thus said Lord YHWH: "Behold, I [am] against you, even I, || And I have done judgments in your midst, || Before the eyes of the nations. ⁹And I have done in you that which I have not done, || And the like of which I do not do again, || Because of all your abominations. ¹⁰Therefore fathers eat sons in your midst, || And sons eat their fathers, || And I have done judgments in you, || And have scattered all your remnant to every wind. ¹¹Therefore, [as] I live," a declaration of Lord YHWH, || "Because you have defiled My sanctuary || With all your detestable things, || And with all your abominations, || Therefore I also diminish you, || And My eye does not pity, and I do not spare. ¹²Your third part dies by pestilence, || And are consumed by famine in your midst, || And the third part fall by sword around you, || And the third part I scatter to every wind, || And I draw out a sword after them. ¹³And My anger has been completed, || And I have caused My fury to rest on them, || And I have been comforted, || And they have known that I, YHWH, have spoken in My zeal, || In My completing My fury on them. ¹⁴And I give you for a ruin, || And for a reproach among nations that [are] around you, || Before the eyes of everyone passing by. ¹⁵And it has been a reproach and a reviling, || An instruction and an astonishment, || To nations that [are] around you, || In My doing judgments in you, || In anger and fury, and in furious reproofs, || I, YHWH, have spoken. ¹⁶In My sending the evil arrows of famine among them, || That have been for destruction, || That I send to destroy you, || And I am adding famine on you, || And I have broken your staff of bread. ¹⁷And I have sent famine and evil beasts on you, || And they have bereaved you, || And pestilence and blood pass over on you, || And I bring a sword in against you, || I, YHWH, have spoken!"

CHAPTER 6

¹And there is a word of YHWH to me, saying, ²"Son of man, set your face toward mountains of Israel, and prophesy concerning them: ³And you have said, Mountains of Israel, || Hear a word of Lord YHWH! Thus said Lord YHWH, || To the mountains, and to the hills, || To the streams, and to the valleys: Behold, I am bringing in a sword against you, || And I have destroyed your high places. ⁴And your altars have been desolated, || And your images have been broken, || And I have caused your wounded to fall before your idols, ⁵And I have put the carcasses of the sons of Israel before their idols, || And I have scattered your bones around your altars. ⁶In all your dwellings the cities are laid waste, || And the high places are desolate, || So that your altars are dry and desolate, || Your idols have broken and ceased, || And your images have been cut down, || And your works have been blotted out. ⁷And the wounded has fallen in your midst, || And you have known that I [am] YHWH. ⁸And I have caused [some] to remain, || In their being for you the escaped of the sword among nations, || In your being scattered through lands. ⁹And your escaped have remembered Me among nations, || To where they have been taken captive, || Because I have been broken with their heart that is going whoring, || That has turned aside from off Me, || And with their eyes they are going whoring after their idols, || And they have been loathsome in their own faces, || For the evils that they have done—all their abominations. ¹⁰And they have known that I [am] YHWH, || I have not spoken to do this evil to them for nothing. ¹¹Thus said Lord YHWH: Strike with your palm, and stamp with your

foot, || And say: Aah! For all the evil abominations of the house of Israel, || Which falls by sword, by famine, and by pestilence. ¹²The far-off dies by pestilence, || And the near falls by sword, || And the left and the besieged dies by famine, || And I have completed My fury on them. ¹³And you have known that I [am] YHWH, || In their wounded being in the midst of their idols, || Around their altars, || On every high hill, on all tops of mountains, || And under every green tree, and under every thick oak, || The place where they gave refreshing fragrance to all their idols. ¹⁴And I have stretched out My hand against them, || And have made the land a desolation, || Even a desolation from the wilderness to Diblath, || In all their dwellings, || And they have known that I [am] YHWH!"

CHAPTER 7

¹And there is a word of YHWH to me, saying, "And you, son of man, || Thus said Lord YHWH to the ground of Israel: ²An end, the end has come on the four corners of the land. ³Now [is] the end for you, || And I have sent My anger on you, || And judged you according to your ways, || And set all your abominations against you. ⁴And My eye has no pity on you, nor do I spare, || For I set your ways against you, || And your abominations are in your midst, || And you have known that I [am] YHWH. ⁵Thus said Lord YHWH: Calamity, a single calamity, behold, it has come. ⁶An end has come, the end has come, || It has awoken for you, behold, it has come. ⁷The circlet has come to you, O inhabitant of the land! The time has come, a day of trouble [is] near, || And not the shouting of mountains. ⁸Now shortly I pour out My fury on you, || And have completed My anger against you, || And judged you according to your ways, || And set all your abominations against you. ⁹And My eye does not pity, nor do I spare, || I give to you according to your ways, || And your abominations are in your midst, || And you have known that [it is] I, YHWH, striking. ¹⁰Behold, the day, behold, it has come, || The circlet has gone forth, || The rod has blossomed, the pride has flourished. ¹¹The violence has risen to a rod of wickedness, || There is none of them, nor of their multitude, || Nor of their noise, nor is there wailing for them. ¹²The time has come, the day has arrived, || The buyer does not rejoice, || And the seller does not become a mourner, || For wrath [is] to all its multitude. ¹³For the seller does not turn to the sold thing, || And yet their life [is] among the living, || For the vision [is] to all its multitude, || It does not turn back, || And none strengthens his life by his iniquity. ¹⁴They have blown with a horn to prepare the whole, || And none is going to battle, || For My wrath [is] to all its multitude. ¹⁵The sword [is] outside, || And the pestilence and the famine within, || He who is in a field dies by sword, || And he who is in a city—Famine and pestilence devour him. ¹⁶And their fugitives have escaped away, || And they have been on the mountains || As doves of the valleys, || All of them making a noise—each for his iniquity. ¹⁷All the hands are feeble, and all knees go [as] waters. ¹⁸And they have girded on sackcloth, || And trembling has covered them, || And shame [is] on all faces, || And baldness on all their heads. ¹⁹They cast their silver into outplaces, || And their gold becomes impurity. Their silver and gold are not able to deliver them, || In a day of the wrath of YHWH, || They do not satisfy their soul, || And they do not fill their bowels, || For it has been the stumblingblock of their iniquity. ²⁰As for the beauty of his ornament, || He set it for excellence, || And the images of their abominations, || Their detestable things—they made in it, || Therefore I have given it to them for impurity, ²¹And I have given it into the hand of the strangers for a prey, || And to the wicked of the land for a spoil, || And they have defiled it. ²²And I have turned My face from them, || And they have defiled My hidden place, || Indeed, destroyers have come into it, and defiled it. ²³Make the chain; for the land || Has been full of bloody judgments, || And the city has been full of violence. ²⁴And I have brought in the wicked of the nations, || And they have possessed their houses, || And I have caused the excellence of the strong to cease, || And those sanctifying them have been defiled. ²⁵Destruction has come, || And they have sought peace, and there is none. ²⁶Disaster comes on disaster, and report is on report, || And they have sought a vision from a prophet, || And law perishes from [the] priest, || And counsel from [the] elderly, ²⁷The king becomes a mourner, || And a prince puts on desolation, || And the hands of the people of the land are troubled, || I deal with them from their own way, || And I judge them with their own judgments, || And they have known that I [am] YHWH!"

CHAPTER 8

¹And it comes to pass, in the sixth year, in the sixth [month], on the fifth of the month, I am sitting in my house, and [the] elderly of Judah are sitting before me, and there a hand of Lord YHWH falls on me, ²and I look, and behold, a likeness as the appearance of fire, from the appearance of His loins and downward—fire, and from His loins and upward, as the appearance of brightness, as the color of electrum. ³And He puts forth a form of a hand, and takes me by a lock of my head, and [the] Spirit lifts me up between the earth and the heavens, and brings me to Jerusalem in visions of God, to the opening of the inner gate that is facing the north, where the seat of the figure of jealousy [is] that is making jealous, ⁴and behold, there the glory of the God of Israel [is] as the appearance that I saw in the valley. ⁵And He says to me, "Son of man, now lift up your eyes [toward] the way of the north." And I lift up my eyes [toward] the way of the north, and behold, on the north of the gate of the altar [is] this figure of jealousy, at the entrance. ⁶And He says to me, "Son of man, are you seeing what they are doing? The great abominations that the house of Israel is doing here, to keep far off from My sanctuary; and turn again, [and] see great abominations." ⁷And He brings me to an opening of the court, and I look, and behold, a hole in the wall; ⁸and He says to me, "Son of man, now dig through the wall"; and I dig through the wall, and behold, an opening. ⁹And He says to me, "Go in, and see the evil abominations that they are doing here." ¹⁰And I go in, and look, and behold, every form of creeping thing, and detestable beast—and all the idols of the house of Israel—carved on the wall, all around, ¹¹and seventy men from [the] elderly of the house of Israel—and Jaazaniah son of Shaphan standing in their midst—are standing before them, and each [with] his censer in his hand, and [the] abundance of [the] cloud of the incense is going up. ¹²And He says to me, "Have you seen, son of man, that which elderly of the house of Israel are doing in the darkness, each in [the] inner chambers of his imagery, for they are saying, YHWH is not seeing us, YHWH has forsaken the land?" ¹³And He says to me, "Turn again, [and] see [the] great abominations that they are doing." ¹⁴And He brings me to the opening of the gate of the house of YHWH that [is] at the north, and behold, there the women are sitting, weeping for Tammuz. ¹⁵And He says to me, "Have you seen, son of man? Turn again, [and] see greater abominations than these." ¹⁶And He brings me into the inner court of the house of YHWH, and behold, at the opening of the temple of YHWH, between the porch and the altar, about twenty-five men, their backs toward the temple of YHWH, and their faces eastward, and they are bowing themselves eastward to the sun. ¹⁷And He says to me, "Have you seen, son of man? Has it been a light thing to the house of Judah to do the abomination that they have done here, that they have filled the land with violence, and turn back to provoke Me to anger? And behold, they are putting forth the branch to their nose! ¹⁸And I also deal in fury, My eye does not pity, nor do I spare, and they have cried [with] a loud voice in My ears and I do not hear them."

CHAPTER 9

¹And He cries [with] a loud voice in my ears, saying, "Inspectors of the city have drawn near, and each [with] his destroying weapon in his hand." ²And behold, six men are coming from the way of the upper gate, that is facing the north, and each [with] his slaughter-weapon in his hand, and one man in their midst is clothed with linen, and a scribe's inkhorn at his loins, and they come in, and stand near the bronze altar. ³And the glory of the God of Israel has gone up from off the cherub, on which it has been, to the threshold of the house. ⁴And He calls to the man who is clothed with linen, who has the scribe's inkhorn at his loins, and YHWH says to him, "Pass on into the midst of the city, into the midst of Jerusalem, and you have made a mark on the foreheads of the men who are sighing and who are groaning for all the abominations that are done in its midst." ⁵And to the others he said in my ears, "Pass on into the city after him, and strike; your eye does not pity, nor do you spare; ⁶aged, young man,

EZEKIEL

and virgin, and infant, and women, you slay—to destruction; and against any man on whom [is] the mark you do not go near, and you begin from My sanctuary." ⁷And they begin among the aged men who [are] before the house, and He says to them, "Defile the house, and fill the courts with the wounded, go forth." And they have gone forth and have struck in the city. ⁸And it comes to pass, as they are striking, and I am left—that I fall on my face, and cry, and say, "Aah! Lord YHWH, are You destroying all the remnant of Israel, in Your pouring out Your wrath on Jerusalem?" ⁹And He says to me, "The iniquity of the house of Israel and Judah [is] very, very great, and the land is full of blood, and the city has been full of perverseness, for they have said: YHWH has forsaken the land, and YHWH is not seeing. ¹⁰And I also, My eye does not pity, nor do I spare; I have put their way on their own head." ¹¹And behold, the man clothed with linen, at whose loins [is] the inkhorn, is bringing back word, saying, "I have done as You have commanded me."

CHAPTER 10

¹And I look, and behold, on the expanse that [is] above the head of the cherubim, as a sapphire stone, as the appearance of the likeness of a throne, He has been seen over them. ²And He speaks to the man clothed with linen and says, "Go into the midst of the wheel, to the place of the cherub, and fill your hands with coals of fire from between the cherubim, and scatter over the city." And he goes in before my eyes. ³And the cherubim are standing on the right side of the house, at the going in of the man, and the cloud has filled the inner court, ⁴and the glory of YHWH becomes high above the cherub, over the threshold of the house, and the house is filled with the cloud, and the court has been filled with the brightness of the glory of YHWH. ⁵And a noise of the wings of the cherubim has been heard in the outer court, as the voice of God—the Mighty One—in His speaking. ⁶And it comes to pass, in His commanding the man clothed with linen, saying, "Take fire from between the wheel, from between the cherubim," and he goes in and stands near the wheel, ⁷that the [one] cherub puts forth his hand from between the cherubim to the fire that [is] between the cherubim, and lifts up, and gives [it] into the hands of him who is clothed with linen, and he receives, and comes forth. ⁸And there appears in the cherubim the form of a hand of man under their wings, ⁹and I look, and behold, four wheels near the cherubim, one wheel near one cherub, and another wheel near the other cherub, and the appearance of the wheels [is] as the color of a beryl stone. ¹⁰And [as for] their appearances, [the] four had one likeness, as it were the wheel in the midst of the wheel. ¹¹In their going, they go on their four sides; they do not turn around in their going, for to the place to where the head turns, they go after it, they do not turn around in their going. ¹²And all their flesh, and their backs, and their hands, and their wings, and the wheels, are full of eyes all around—[the] wheels [the] four had. ¹³As for the wheels—they were called "Whirling Wheel" in my ears. ¹⁴And four faces [are] to each; the face of the first [is] the face of the cherub, and the face of the second [is] the face of man, and of the third the face of a lion, and of the fourth the face of an eagle. ¹⁵And the cherubim are lifted up, it [is] the living creature that I saw by the river Chebar. ¹⁶And in the going of the cherubim, the wheels go beside them; and in the cherubim lifting up their wings to be high above the earth, the wheels do not turn around, even they, from being beside them. ¹⁷In their standing they stand, and in their exaltation they are exalted with them: for [the] spirit of the living creature [is] in them. ¹⁸And the glory of YHWH goes forth from off the threshold of the house, and stands over the cherubim, ¹⁹and the cherubim lift up their wings, and are lifted up from the earth before my eyes; in their going forth, the wheels [are] also alongside them, and he stands at the opening of the east gate of the house of YHWH, and the glory of the God of Israel [is] over them from above. ²⁰It [is] the living creature that I saw under the God of Israel by the river Chebar, and I know that they are cherubim. ²¹[The] four—each had four faces, and each had four wings, and the likeness of the hands of man [is] under their wings. ²²And the likeness of their faces, they [are] the faces that I saw by the river Chebar, their appearances and themselves; they each go straight forward.

CHAPTER 11

¹And [the] Spirit lifts me up, and it brings me to the east gate of the house of YHWH, that is facing the east, and behold, at the opening of the gate [are] twenty-five men, and I see in their midst Jaazaniah son of Azzur, and Pelatiah son of Benaiah, heads of the people. ²And He says to me, "Son of man, these [are] the men who are devising iniquity, and who are giving evil counsel in this city; ³who are saying, It [is] not near—to build houses, it [is] the pot, and we [are] the flesh. ⁴Therefore prophesy concerning them, prophesy, son of man." ⁵And [the] Spirit of YHWH falls on me, and He says to me, "Say, Thus said YHWH: You have said correctly, O house of Israel, || And I have known the steps of your spirit. ⁶You multiplied your wounded in this city, || And filled its out-places with the wounded. ⁷Therefore, thus said Lord YHWH: Your wounded whom you placed in its midst, || They [are] the flesh, and it [is] the pot, || And He has brought you out from its midst. ⁸You have feared a sword, || And I bring in a sword against you, || A declaration of Lord YHWH. ⁹And I have brought you out of its midst, || And given you into the hand of strangers, || And I have done judgments among you. ¹⁰You fall by the sword, || I judge you on the border of Israel, || And you have known that I [am] YHWH. ¹¹It is not for a pot for you, || Nor are you for flesh in its midst, || I judge you at the border of Israel. ¹²And you have known that I [am] YHWH, || For you have not walked in My statutes, || And you have not done My judgments, || And according to the judgments of the nations || Who are around you, you have done!" ¹³And it comes to pass, at my prophesying, that Pelatiah son of Benaiah is dying, and I fall on my face, and cry—a loud voice—and say, "Aah! Lord YHWH, You are making an end of the remnant of Israel." ¹⁴And there is a word of YHWH to me, saying, ¹⁵"Son of man, your brothers, your brothers, men of your family, and all the house of Israel—all of it—[are] they to whom inhabitants of Jerusalem have said, Keep far off from YHWH; ¹⁶it [is] ours, the land has been given for an inheritance; therefore say, Thus said Lord YHWH: Because I put them far off among nations, || And because I scattered them through lands, I am also for a little sanctuary to them, || In lands to where they have gone in. ¹⁷Therefore say, Thus said Lord YHWH: And I have assembled you from the peoples, || And I have gathered you from the lands, || Into which you have been scattered, || And I have given the ground of Israel to you. ¹⁸And they have gone in there, || And turned aside all its detestable things, || And all its abominations—out of it. ¹⁹And I have given one heart to them, || And I give a new spirit in your midst, || And I have turned the heart of stone out of their flesh, || And I have given a heart of flesh to them. ²⁰So that they walk in My statutes, || And keep My judgments, and have done them, || And they have been to Me for a people, || And I am to them for God. ²¹As for those whose heart is going to the heart || Of their detestable things and their abominations, || I have put their way on their head, || A declaration of Lord YHWH." ²²And the cherubim lift up their wings, and the wheels [are] alongside them, and the glory of the God of Israel [is] over them from above. ²³And the glory of YHWH goes up from off the midst of the city, and stands on the mountain, that [is] on the east of the city. ²⁴And [the] Spirit has lifted me up, and brings me to Chaldea, to the expulsion, in a vision, by [the] Spirit of God, and the vision that I have seen goes up from off me; ²⁵and I speak to the expulsion all the matters of YHWH that He has showed me.

CHAPTER 12

¹And there is a word of YHWH to me, saying, ²"Son of man, you are dwelling in the midst of the house of rebellion, that have eyes to see, and they have not seen; they have ears to hear, and they have not heard; for they [are] a house of rebellion. ³And you, son of man, make your vessels of removal, and remove by day before their eyes, and you have removed from your place to another place before their eyes, it may be they consider, for they [are] a house of rebellion. ⁴And you have brought forth your vessels as vessels of removal by day before their eyes, and you go forth in the evening before their eyes, as the goings forth of a removal. ⁵You dig through the wall before their eyes, and you have brought forth by it. ⁶Carry on the shoulder before their eyes, bring forth in the darkness, cover your face, and you do not see the earth, for I have given you [as] a sign to the house of Israel." ⁷And I do so, as I

have been commanded; I have brought forth my vessels as vessels of removal by day, and I have dug through the wall with my hand in the evening; I have brought forth in the darkness, I have carried away on the shoulder, before their eyes. ⁸And there is a word of YHWH to me, in the morning, saying, ⁹"Son of man, have they not said to you—the house of Israel—the house of rebellion—What are you doing? ¹⁰Say to them, Thus said Lord YHWH: This burden [concerns] the prince in Jerusalem, and all the house of Israel who are in their midst. ¹¹Say: I [am] your sign; as I have done so it is done to them, into a removal, into a captivity, they go. ¹²As for the prince who [is] in their midst, he carries on the shoulder in the darkness, and he goes forth; they dig through the wall to bring forth by it; he covers his face that he may not look on the very surface of the land. ¹³And I have spread My net for him, and he has been caught in My snare, and I have brought him to Babylon, the land of the Chaldeans, and he does not see it—and he dies there. ¹⁴And all who are around him to help him, and all his bands, I scatter to every wind, and I draw out a sword after them. ¹⁵And they have known that I [am] YHWH, in My scattering them among nations, and I have spread them through lands; ¹⁶and I have left of them, a few in number, from the sword, from the famine, and from the pestilence, so that they recount all their abominations among the nations to where they have come, and they have known that I [am] YHWH." ¹⁷And there is a word of YHWH to me, saying, ¹⁸"Son of man, eat your bread in haste, and drink your water with trembling and with fear; ¹⁹and you have said to the people of the land, Thus said Lord YHWH concerning the inhabitants of Jerusalem, concerning the land of Israel: They eat their bread with fear, and drink their water with astonishment, because its land is desolate, because of its fullness, because of the violence of all who are dwelling in it. ²⁰And the cities that are inhabited are laid waste, and the land is a desolation, and you have known that I [am] YHWH." ²¹And there is a word of YHWH to me, saying, ²²"Son of man, what [is] this allegory to you, concerning the land of Israel, saying, The days are prolonged, and every vision has perished? ²³Therefore say to them, Thus said Lord YHWH: I have caused this allegory to cease, || And they do not use it as an allegory in Israel again, || But speak to them: The days have drawn near, || And every vision has spoken. ²⁴For there is no longer any vain vision, and flattering divination, || In the midst of the house of Israel. ²⁵For I, YHWH, speak, || The word that I speak—it is done, || It is not prolonged anymore, || For in your days, O house of rebellion, I speak a word, and I have done it, || A declaration of Lord YHWH." ²⁶And there is a word of YHWH to me, saying, ²⁷"Son of man, behold, the house of Israel is saying, The vision that he is seeing [is not] for many days, and he is prophesying of far-off times, ²⁸therefore say to them, Thus said Lord YHWH: None of My words are prolonged anymore, || When I speak a word—it is done, || A declaration of Lord YHWH!"

CHAPTER 13

¹And there is a word of YHWH to me, saying, ²"Son of man, prophesy concerning the prophets of Israel who are prophesying, and you have said to those prophesying from their own heart, Hear a word of YHWH! ³Thus said Lord YHWH: Woe to the prophets who are foolish, || Who are going after their own spirit, || And they have seen nothing. ⁴Your prophets have been || As foxes in the wasteland, O Israel. ⁵You have not gone up into breaches, || Nor do you make a wall for the house of Israel, || To stand in battle in a day of YHWH. ⁶They have seen vanity, and lying divination, || Who are saying: A declaration of YHWH, || And YHWH has not sent them, || And they have hoped to establish a word. ⁷Have you not seen a vain vision, || And spoken a lying divination, || When you say, A declaration of YHWH, || And I have not spoken? ⁸Therefore, thus said Lord YHWH: Because you have spoken vanity, and seen a lie, || Therefore, behold, I [am] against you, || A declaration of Lord YHWH. ⁹And My hand has been on the prophets, || Who are seeing vanity, and who are divining a lie, || They are not in the assembly of My people, || And they are not written in the writing of the house of Israel, || And they do not come to the ground of Israel, || And you have known that I [am] Lord YHWH. ¹⁰Because, even because, they caused My people to err, || Saying, Peace! And there is no peace, || And that one is building a wall, || And behold, they are coating it with chalk. ¹¹Say to those coating with chalk—It falls, || There has been an overflowing shower, || And you, O hailstones, fall, || And a turbulent wind breaks out, ¹²And behold, the wall has fallen! Does one not say to you, Where [is] the coating that you coated? ¹³Therefore, thus said Lord YHWH: I have broken with a turbulent wind in My fury, || And an overflowing shower is in My anger, || And hailstones in My fury—to consume. ¹⁴And I have broken down the wall that you coated with chalk, || And have caused it to come to the earth, || And its foundation has been revealed, || And it has fallen, || And you have been consumed in its midst, || And you have known that I [am] YHWH. ¹⁵And I have completed My wrath on the wall, || And on those coating it with chalk, || And I say to you: The wall is not, || And those coating it are not, ¹⁶[These]—the prophets of Israel, who are prophesying concerning Jerusalem, || And who are seeing a vision of peace for her, || And there is no peace, || A declaration of Lord YHWH. ¹⁷And you, son of man, set your face against the daughters of your people, who are prophesying out of their own heart, and prophesy concerning them, ¹⁸And you have said, Thus said Lord YHWH: Woe to those sowing [magic] bands for all joints of the arm, || And to those making the veils || For the head of every stature—to hunt souls, || Do you hunt the souls of My people? And do your souls that live remain alive? ¹⁹Indeed, you pierce Me concerning My people, || For handfuls of barley, || And for pieces of bread, || To put to death souls that should not die, || And to keep alive souls that should not live, || By your lying to My people—listening to lies. ²⁰Therefore, thus said Lord YHWH: Behold, I [am] against your [magic] bands, || With which you are hunting there the souls of the flourishing, || And I have torn them from off your arms, || And have sent away the souls that you are hunting, || The souls of the flourishing. ²¹And I have torn your veils, || And delivered My people out of your hand, || And they are no longer for a prey in your hand, || And you have known that I [am] YHWH. ²²Because of paining the heart of the righteous with falsehood, || And I have not pained it, || And strengthening the hands of the wicked, || So as not to turn [him] back from his evil way, || To keep him alive, ²³Therefore, you do not see vanity, || And you do not divine divination again, || And I have delivered My people out of your hand, || And you have known that I [am] YHWH!"

CHAPTER 14

¹And men from [the] elderly of Israel come to me, and sit before me. ²And there is a word of YHWH to me, saying, ³"Son of man, these men have caused their idols to go up on their heart, and they have put the stumbling-block of their iniquity before their faces; am I inquired of at all by them? ⁴Therefore, speak with them, and you have said to them, Thus said Lord YHWH: Everyone of the house of Israel who causes his idols to go up to his heart, and sets the stumbling-block of his iniquity before his face, and has gone to the prophet—I, YHWH, have given an answer to him for this, for the abundance of his idols, ⁵in order to catch the house of Israel by their heart, in that they have become estranged from off Me by their idols—all of them. ⁶Therefore say to the house of Israel, Thus said Lord YHWH: Turn back, indeed, turn back from your idols, and turn back your faces from all your abominations, ⁷for everyone of the house of Israel, and of the sojourners who sojourn in Israel, who is separated from after Me, and causes his idols to go up to his heart, and sets the stumbling-block of his iniquity before his face, and has come to the prophet to inquire of him concerning Me, I, YHWH, have answered him for Myself; ⁸and I have set My face against that man, and made him for a sign, and for allegories, and I have cut him off from the midst of My people, and you have known that I [am] YHWH. ⁹And the prophet, when he is enticed, and has spoken a word—I, YHWH, have enticed that prophet, and have stretched out My hand against him, and have destroyed him from the midst of My people Israel. ¹⁰And they have borne their iniquity: as the iniquity of the inquirer, so is the iniquity of the prophet; ¹¹so that the house of Israel does not wander from after Me anymore, nor are they defiled with all their transgressions anymore, and they have been to Me for a people, and I am to them for God—a declaration of Lord YHWH." ¹²And there is a word of YHWH to me, saying, ¹³"Son of man, when the land sins against Me to commit a trespass, and I have stretched out My hand against it, and broken the staff of bread for it, and sent famine into it, and cut off man and beast from it— ¹⁴and

[despite] these three men [that] have been in its midst: Noah, Daniel, and Job—they [only] deliver their own soul by their righteousness," a declaration of Lord YHWH. ¹⁵"If I cause an evil beast to pass through the land, and it has bereaved, and it has been a desolation, without any passing through because of the beast— ¹⁶[despite] these three men in its midst—[as] I live," a declaration of Lord YHWH, "they deliver neither sons nor daughters; they alone are delivered, and the land is a desolation. ¹⁷Or [if] I bring a sword in against that land, and I have said: Sword, pass over through the land, and I have cut off man and beast from it— ¹⁸and [despite] these three men in its midst—[as] I live," a declaration of Lord YHWH, "they do not deliver sons and daughters, for they alone are delivered. ¹⁹Or [if] I send pestilence to that land, and I have poured out My fury against it in blood, to cut off man and beast from it— ²⁰and [despite] Noah, Daniel, and Job, in its midst—[as] I live," a declaration of Lord YHWH, "they deliver neither son nor daughter; they, by their righteousness, [only] deliver their own soul." ²¹For thus said Lord YHWH: "Although My four severe judgments—sword, and famine, and wild beast, and pestilence—I have sent to Jerusalem, to cut off man and beast from it, ²²yet, behold, there has been left an escape in it, who are brought forth, sons and daughters, behold, they are coming forth to you, and you have seen their way, and their doings, and have been comforted concerning the calamity that I have brought in against Jerusalem, all that which I have brought in against it. ²³And they have comforted you, for you see their way and their doings, and you have known that I have not done all that which I have done in her for nothing," a declaration of Lord YHWH.

CHAPTER 15

¹And there is a word of YHWH to me, saying, ²"Son of man, || What is the vine-tree more than any tree? The vine-branch that has been, || Among trees of the forest? ³Is wood taken from it to use for work? Do they take a pin of it to hang any vessel on it? ⁴Behold, it has been given to the fire for fuel, || The fire has eaten its two ends, || And its midst has been scorched! Is it profitable for work? ⁵Behold, in its being perfect it is not used for work, || How much less when fire has eaten of it, || And it is scorched, || Has it been used yet for work?" ⁶Therefore, thus said Lord YHWH: "As the vine-tree among trees of the forest, || That I have given to the fire for fuel, || So I have given the inhabitants of Jerusalem. ⁷And I have set My face against them, || They have gone forth from the fire, || And the fire consumes them, || And you have known that I [am] YHWH, || In My setting My face against them. ⁸And I have made the land a desolation, || Because they have committed a trespass," || A declaration of Lord YHWH!

CHAPTER 16

¹And there is a word of YHWH to me, saying, ²"Son of man, cause Jerusalem to know her abominations, and you have said, ³Thus said Lord YHWH to Jerusalem: Your birth and your nativity || [Are] of the land of the Canaanite, || Your father the Amorite, and your mother a Hittite. ⁴As for your nativity, in the day you were born, || Your navel has not been cut, || And you were not washed in water for ease, || And you have not been salted at all, || And you have not been swaddled at all. ⁵No eye has had pity on you, to do any of these to you, || To have compassion on you, || And you are cast on the face of the field, || With loathing of your soul || In the day you were born! ⁶And I pass over by you, || And I see you trodden down in your blood, || And I say to you in your blood, Live! Indeed, I say to you in your blood, Live! ⁷I have made you a myriad as the shoot of the field, || And you are multiplied, and are great, || And come in with an excellent adornment, || Breasts have been formed, and your hair has grown—And you, naked and bare! ⁸And I pass over by you, and I see you, || And behold, your time [is] a time of loves, || And I spread My skirt over you, || And I cover your nakedness, || And I swear to you, and come into a covenant with you, || A declaration of Lord YHWH, || And you become Mine. ⁹And I wash you with water, || And I wash away your blood from off you, || And I anoint you with oil. ¹⁰And I clothe you with embroidery, || And I shoe you with tachash [skin], || And I gird you with fine linen, || And I cover you with figured silk. ¹¹And I adorn you with adornments, || And I give bracelets for your hands, || And a chain for your neck. ¹²And I give a ring for your nose, || And rings for your ears, || And a crown of beauty on your head. ¹³And you put on gold and silver, || And your clothing [is] fine linen, || And figured silk and embroidery, || You have eaten fine flour, and honey, and oil, || And you are very, very beautiful, || And go prosperously to the kingdom. ¹⁴And your name goes forth among nations, || Because of your beauty—for it [is] complete, || In My honor that I have set on you, || A declaration of Lord YHWH. ¹⁵And you trust in your beauty, || And go whoring because of your renown, || And pour out your whoredoms on everyone passing by—to him [that would have] it. ¹⁶And you take from your garments, || And make spotted high-places for yourself, || And go whoring on them, || They are not coming in—nor will it be! ¹⁷And you take your beautiful vessels || Of My gold and My silver that I gave to you, || And make images of a male for yourself, || And go whoring with them, ¹⁸And you take the garments of your embroidery, || And cover them, || And you have set My oil and My incense before them. ¹⁹And My bread, that I gave to you, || Fine flour, and oil, and honey, that I caused you to eat. You have even set it before them, || For a refreshing fragrance—thus it is, || A declaration of Lord YHWH. ²⁰And you take your sons and your daughters whom you have born to Me, || And sacrifice them to them for food. Is it a little thing because of your whoredoms, ²¹that you slaughter My sons, || And give them up in causing them to pass over to them? ²²And with all your abominations and your whoredoms, || You have not remembered the days of your youth, || When you were naked and bare, || You were trodden down in your blood! ²³And it comes to pass, after all your wickedness || (Woe, woe, to you—a declaration of Lord YHWH), ²⁴That you build an arch for yourself, || And make a high place for yourself in every broad place. ²⁵At every head of the way you have built your high place, || And you make your beauty abominable, || And open wide your feet to everyone passing by, || And multiply your whoredoms, ²⁶And go whoring to sons of Egypt, || Your neighbors—great of appetite! And you multiply your whoredoms, || To provoke Me to anger. ²⁷And behold, I have stretched out My hand against you, || And diminish your portion, || And give you to the desire of those hating you, || The daughters of the Philistines, || Who are ashamed of your wicked way. ²⁸And you go whoring to sons of Asshur, || Without your being satisfied, || And you go whoring with them, || And also—you have not been satisfied. ²⁹And you multiply your whoredoms || On the land of Canaan—toward Chaldea, || And even with this you have not been satisfied. ³⁰How weak [is] your heart, || A declaration of Lord YHWH, || In your doing all these, || The work of a domineering, whorish woman. ³¹In your building your arch at the head of every way, || You have made your high place in every broad place, || And have not been as a whore deriding a wage. ³²The wife who commits adultery—Under her husband—receives strangers. ³³They give a gift to all whores, || And you have given your gifts to all your lovers, || And bribe them to come in to you, || From all around—in your whoredoms. ³⁴And you are opposite from [other] women in your whoredoms, || That none go whoring after you; And in your giving a wage, || And a wage has not been given to you; Therefore you are the opposite. ³⁵Therefore, O whore, hear a word of YHWH! ³⁶Thus said Lord YHWH: Because of your bronze being poured forth, || And your nakedness is revealed in your whoredoms near your lovers, || And near all the idols of your abominations, || And according to the blood of your sons, || Whom you have given to them; ³⁷Therefore, behold, I am assembling all your lovers, || To whom you have been sweet, || And all whom you have loved, || Besides all whom you have hated; And I have assembled them by you all around, || And have revealed your nakedness to them, || And they have seen all your nakedness. ³⁸And I have judged you—judgments of adultresses, || And of women shedding blood, || And have given you blood, fury, and jealousy. ³⁹And I have given you into their hand, || And they have thrown down your arch, || And they have broken down your high places, || And they have stripped you of your garments, || And they have taken your beautiful vessels, || And they have left you naked and bare. ⁴⁰And have caused an assembly to come up against you, || And stoned you with stones, || And thrust you through with their swords, ⁴¹And burned your houses with fire, || And done judgments in you before the eyes of many women, || And I have

caused you to cease from going whoring, || And also, you no longer give a wage. ⁴²And I have caused My fury against you to rest, || And My jealousy has turned aside from you, || And I have been quiet, and I am not angry anymore. ⁴³Because you have not remembered the days of your youth, || And give trouble to Me in all these, || Therefore I also—behold—I put your way on [your own] head, || A declaration of Lord YHWH, || And you will not have done—have done this wickedness above all your abominations. ⁴⁴Behold, everyone using the allegory against you, || Uses [this] allegory concerning [you], saying, || As the mother—her daughter! ⁴⁵You [are] your mother's daughter, || Loathing her husband and her sons, || And you [are] your sisters' sister, || Who loathed their husbands and their sons, || Your mother [is] a Hittite, and your father an Amorite. ⁴⁶And your older sister [is] Samaria, she and her daughters, || Who is dwelling at your left hand, || And your younger sister, who is dwelling on your right hand, [is] Sodom and her daughters. ⁴⁷And you have not walked in their ways, || And done according to their abominations, || It has been loathed as a little thing, || Indeed, you do more corruptly than they in all your ways. ⁴⁸[As] I live—a declaration of Lord YHWH, || Your sister Sodom has not done—she and her daughters—As you have done—you and your daughters. ⁴⁹Behold, this has been the iniquity of your sister Sodom, || Arrogancy, fullness of bread, and quiet ease, || Have been to her and to her daughters, || And the hand of the afflicted and needy || She has not strengthened. ⁵⁰And they are haughty and do abomination before Me, || And I turn them aside when I have seen. ⁵¹And Samaria has not sinned even half of your sins, || But you multiply your abominations more than they, || And justify your sisters by all your abominations that you have done. ⁵²You also—bear your shame, || That you have adjudged for your sisters, || Because of your sins that you have done more abominably than they, || They are more righteous than you, || And you, also, be ashamed and bear your shame, || In your justifying your sisters. ⁵³And I have turned back [to] their captivity, || The captivity of Sodom and her daughters, || And the captivity of Samaria and her daughters, || And the captivity of your captives in their midst, ⁵⁴So that you bear your shame, || And have been ashamed of all that you have done, || In your comforting them. ⁵⁵And your sisters, Sodom and her daughters, || Return to their former state, || And Samaria and her daughters return to their former state, || And you and your daughters return to your former state. ⁵⁶And your sister Sodom has not been for a report in your mouth, || In the day of your arrogancy, ⁵⁷Before your wickedness is revealed, || As [at] the time of the reproach of the daughters of Aram, || And of all her neighbors, the daughters of the Philistines, || Who are despising you all around. ⁵⁸Your wicked plans and your abominations, || You have borne them, a declaration of YHWH. ⁵⁹For thus said Lord YHWH: I have dealt with you as you have done, || In that you have despised an oath—to break covenant. ⁶⁰And I have remembered My covenant with you, || In the days of your youth, || And I have established a perpetual covenant for you. ⁶¹And you have remembered your ways, || And you have been ashamed, || In your receiving your sisters—Your older with your younger, || And I have given them to you for daughters, || And not by your covenant. ⁶²And I have established My covenant with you, || And you have known that I [am] YHWH. ⁶³So that you remember, || And you have been ashamed, || And there is not an opening of the mouth to you anymore because of your shame, || In My receiving atonement for you, || For all that you have done, || A declaration of Lord YHWH!"

CHAPTER 17

¹And there is a word of YHWH to me, saying, ²"Son of man, put forth a riddle, and use an allegory to the house of Israel, ³and you have said, Thus said Lord YHWH: The great eagle, great-winged, long-pinioned, || Full of feathers, that has diverse colors, || Has come to Lebanon, || And he takes the foliage of the cedar, ⁴He has cropped the top of its tender twigs, || And he brings it to the land of Canaan. He has placed it in a city of merchants. ⁵And he takes of the seed of the land, || And puts it in a field of seed, || He took [it] by many waters, || He has set it in a conspicuous place. ⁶And it springs up, and becomes a spreading vine, humble of stature, || To turn its thin shoots toward itself, || And its roots are under it, || And it becomes a vine, and makes boughs, || And sends forth beautiful branches. ⁷And there is another great eagle, || Great-winged, and abounding with feathers, || And behold, this vine has bent its roots toward him, || And it has sent out its thin shoots toward him, || To water it from the furrows of its planting, ⁸On a good field, by many waters, it is planted, to make branches, and to bear fruit, to be for a good vine. ⁹Say, Thus said Lord YHWH: It prospers—does he not draw out its roots, || And cut off its fruit, and it is withered? [In] all the leaves of its springing it withers, || And not by great strength, or by numerous people, || To lift it up by its roots. ¹⁰And behold, the planted thing—does it prosper? When the east wind comes against it, does it not utterly wither? On the furrows of its springing it withers." ¹¹And there is a word of YHWH to me, saying, ¹²"Now say to the house of rebellion, || Have you not known what these [are]? Say, Behold, the king of Babylon has come to Jerusalem, || And he takes its king, and its princes, || And brings them to himself to Babylon. ¹³And he takes of the seed of the kingdom, || And makes a covenant with him, || And brings him into an oath, || And he has taken the mighty of the land, ¹⁴That the kingdom may be humble, || That it may not lift itself up, || To keep his covenant—that it may stand. ¹⁵And he rebels against him, || To send his messengers to Egypt, || To give to him horses, and many people, || Does he prosper? Does he who is doing these things escape? And has he broken covenant and escaped? ¹⁶[As] I live—a declaration of Lord YHWH, || Does he not—in the place of the king who is causing him to reign, || Whose oath he has despised, || And whose covenant he has broken—die with him in the midst of Babylon? ¹⁷And not with a great force, and with a numerous assembly, || Does Pharaoh maintain him in battle, || By pouring out a mound, and in building a fortification, || To cut off many souls. ¹⁸And he despised the oath—to break covenant, || And behold, he has given his hand, || And all these he has done—he does not escape. ¹⁹Therefore, thus said Lord YHWH: [As] I live—My oath that he has despised, || And My covenant that he has broken, || Have I not put it on his head? ²⁰And I have spread out My snare for him, || And he has been caught in My net, || And I have brought him to Babylon, || And judged him there [for the] trespass || That he has trespassed against Me. ²¹And all his fugitives, with all his bands, || Fall by sword, and those remaining, || They are spread out to every wind, || And you have known that I, YHWH, have spoken. ²²Thus said Lord YHWH: I have taken of the foliage of the high cedar, || And I have set [it], || I crop a tender one from the top of its tender shoots, || And I have planted [it] on a high and lofty mountain. ²³In a mountain—the high place of Israel, I plant it, || And it has borne boughs, and yielded fruit, || And become a good cedar, || And every bird of every [kind of] wing has dwelt under it, || They dwell in the shade of its thin shoots. ²⁴And all trees of the field have known || That I, YHWH, have made the high tree low, || I have set the low tree on high, || I have dried up the moist tree, || And I have caused the dry tree to flourish, || I, YHWH, have spoken, and have done [it]!"

CHAPTER 18

¹And there is a word of YHWH to me, saying, ²"What [is it] to you [that] you are using this allegory || Concerning the ground of Israel, saying, || Fathers eat unripe fruit, || And the sons' teeth are blunted? ³[As] I live," a declaration of Lord YHWH, "You no longer have the use of this allegory in Israel. ⁴Behold, all the souls are Mine, || As the soul of the father, || So also the soul of the son—they are Mine, || The soul that is sinning—it dies. ⁵And a man, when he is righteous, || And has done judgment and righteousness, ⁶He has not eaten on the mountains, || And has not lifted up his eyes || To idols of the house of Israel, || And did not defile his neighbor's wife, || And did not come near to a separated woman, ⁷He does not oppress a man, || He returns his pledge to the debtor, || He does not take away plunder, || He gives his bread to the hungry, || And covers the naked with a garment, ⁸He does not give in usury, and does not take increase, || He turns back his hand from perversity, || He does true judgment between man and man. ⁹He walks in My statutes, || And he has kept My judgments—to deal truly, || He [is] righteous—he surely lives," || A declaration of Lord YHWH. ¹⁰"And he has begotten a son, || A burglar—a shedder of

blood, || And he has made a brother of one of these, ¹¹And he has not done all those, || For he has even eaten on the mountains, || And he has defiled his neighbor's wife, ¹²He has oppressed the afflicted and needy, || He has taken away plunder violently, || He does not return a pledge, || And he has lifted up his eyes to the idols, || He has done abomination! ¹³He has given in usury, and taken increase, || And he lives? He does not live, || He has done all these abominations, || He surely dies, his blood is on him. ¹⁴And—behold, he has begotten a son, || And he sees all the sins of his father, || That he has done, and he fears, || And does not do like them, ¹⁵He has not eaten on the mountains, || And he has not lifted up his eyes || To idols of the house of Israel, || He has not defiled his neighbor's wife, ¹⁶He has not oppressed a man, || He has not bound a pledge, || And he has not taken away plunder, || He has given his bread to the hungry, || And he covered the naked with a garment, ¹⁷He has turned back his hand from the afflicted, || He has not taken usury and increase, || He has done My judgments, || He has walked in My statutes, || He does not die for the iniquity of his father, || He surely lives. ¹⁸His father—because he used oppression, || Violently plundered a brother, || And did that which [is] not good in the midst of his people, || And behold, he is dying in his iniquity. ¹⁹And you have said, Why has the son not borne of the iniquity of the father? And the son has done judgment and righteousness, || He has kept all My statutes, || And he does them, he surely lives. ²⁰The soul that sins—it dies. A son does not bear of the iniquity of the father, || And a father does not bear of the iniquity of the son, || The righteousness of the righteous is on him, || And the wickedness of the wicked is on him. ²¹And the wicked—when he turns back || From all his sins that he has done, || And he has kept all My statutes, || And has done judgment and righteousness, || He surely lives, he does not die. ²²All his transgressions that he has done || Are not remembered to him, || In his righteousness that he has done he lives. ²³Do I take pleasure [or] delight in the death of the wicked?" A declaration of Lord YHWH, "Is it not in his turning back from his way—And he has lived? ²⁴And in the turning back of the righteous from his righteousness, || And he has done perversity, || According to all the abominations || That the wicked has done, || Does he then live? All his righteous deeds that he has done are not remembered, || For his trespass that he has trespassed, || And for his sin that he has sinned, || For them he dies. ²⁵And you have said, The way of the Lord is not pondered. Now hear, O house of Israel, || My way—is it not pondered? Are not your ways unpondered? ²⁶In the turning back of the righteous from his righteousness, || And he has done perversity, || And he is dying by them, || He dies for his perversity that he has done. ²⁷And in the turning back of the wicked || From his wickedness that he has done, || And he does judgment and righteousness, || He keeps his soul alive. ²⁸And he sees and turns back, || From all his transgressions that he has done, || He surely lives, he does not die, ²⁹And the house of Israel has said, The way of the Lord is not pondered, || My ways—are they not pondered? O house of Israel—are not your ways unpondered? ³⁰Therefore, I judge each according to his ways, || O house of Israel," || A declaration of Lord YHWH, || "Turn back, indeed, turn yourselves back, || From all your transgressions, || And iniquity is not for a stumbling-block to you, ³¹Cast away all your transgressions from over you, || By which you have transgressed, || And make a new heart and a new spirit for yourselves, || And why do you die, || O house of Israel? ³²For I have no pleasure in the death of the dying," || A declaration of Lord YHWH, || "Therefore turn back and live!"

CHAPTER 19

¹"And you, lift up a lamentation to princes of Israel, ²and you have said: What [is] your mother? A lioness, || She has crouched down among lions, || She has multiplied her whelps in the midst of young lions. ³And she brings up one of her whelps, || He has been a young lion, || And he learns to tear prey, || He has devoured man. ⁴And nations hear of him, || He has been caught in their pit, || And they bring him to the land of Egypt in chains. ⁵And as she waited she sees that her hope has perished, || And she takes one of her whelps, || She has made him a young lion. ⁶And he goes up and down in the midst of lions, || He has been a young lion, || And he learns to tear prey, || He has devoured man. ⁷And he knows his forsaken habitations, || And he has laid waste [to] their cities, || And the land and its fullness is desolate, || Because of the voice of his roaring. ⁸And surrounding nations set against him from the provinces. And they spread out their net for him, || He has been caught in their pit. ⁹And they put him in prison—in chains, || And they bring him to the king of Babylon, || They bring him into bulwarks, || So that his voice is not heard || On mountains of Israel anymore. ¹⁰Your mother, like the vine in your blood, || Is being planted by waters, || She was bearing fruit and full of boughs, || Because of many waters. ¹¹And she has strong rods for scepters of rulers, || And she is high in stature above—between thick branches, || And it appears in its height || In the multitude of its thin shoots. ¹²And she is plucked up in fury, || She has been cast to the earth, || And the east wind has dried up her fruit, || [The] rod of her strength has been broken and withered, || Fire has consumed it. ¹³And now she is planted in a wilderness, || In a dry and thirsty land. ¹⁴And fire goes forth from a rod of her boughs, || It has devoured her fruit, || And she has no rod of strength—a scepter to rule, || A lamentation—and she has become for a lamentation!"

CHAPTER 20

¹And it comes to pass, in the seventh year, in the fifth [month], on the tenth of the month, men from [the] elderly of Israel have come in to seek YHWH, and they sit before me; ²and there is a word of YHWH to me, saying, ³"Son of man, speak to the elderly of Israel, and you have said to them, Thus said Lord YHWH: Are you coming in to seek Me? [As] I live—I am not sought by you—a declaration of Lord YHWH. ⁴Do you judge them? Do you judge, son of man? Cause them to know the abominations of their fathers, ⁵and you have said to them, Thus said Lord YHWH: In the day of My fixing on Israel, || I lift up My hand, || To the seed of the house of Jacob, || And am known to them in the land of Egypt, || And I lift up My hand to them, || Saying, I [am] your God YHWH. ⁶In that day I lifted up My hand to them, || To bring them forth from the land of Egypt, || To a land that I spied out for them, || Flowing with milk and honey, || It [is] a beauty to all the lands, ⁷And I say to them, Let each cast away the detestable things of his eyes, || And do not be defiled with the idols of Egypt, || I [am] your God YHWH. ⁸And they rebel against Me, || And have not been willing to listen to Me, || Each has not cast away the detestable things of their eyes, || And have not forsaken the idols of Egypt, || And I speak—to pour out My fury against them, || To complete My anger against them, || In the midst of the land of Egypt. ⁹And I do [it] for My Name's sake, || Not to defile [it] before the eyes of the nations, || In whose midst they [are in], || Before whose eyes I became known to them, || To bring them out from the land of Egypt. ¹⁰And I bring them out of the land of Egypt, || And I bring them into the wilderness, ¹¹And I give My statutes to them, || And I caused them to know My judgments, || Which the man who does—lives by them. ¹²And I have also given My Sabbaths to them, || To be for a sign between Me and them, || To know that I [am] YHWH who is sanctifying them. ¹³And the house of Israel rebels against Me in the wilderness, || They have not walked in My statutes, || And they have despised My judgments, || Which the man who does—lives by them. And they have greatly defiled My Sabbaths, || And I speak—to pour out My fury on them in the wilderness, to consume them. ¹⁴And I do [it] for My Name's sake, || Not to defile [it] before the eyes of the nations, || Before whose eyes I brought them forth. ¹⁵And also, I have lifted up My hand to them in the wilderness, || Not to bring them into the land that I had given, || Flowing with milk and honey, || It [is] a beauty to all the lands, ¹⁶Because they kicked against My judgments, || And they have not walked in My statutes, || And they have defiled My Sabbaths, || For their heart is going after their idols. ¹⁷And My eye has pity on them—against destroying them, || And I have not made an end of them in the wilderness. ¹⁸And I say to their sons in the wilderness: Do not walk in the statutes of your fathers, || And do not observe their judgments, || And do not defile yourselves with their idols. ¹⁹I [am] your God YHWH, walk in My statutes, || And observe My judgments, and do them, ²⁰And sanctify My Sabbaths, || And they have been for a sign between Me and you, || To know that I [am] your God YHWH. ²¹And the sons rebel against Me, || They have not walked in My statutes, || And they have not observed My judgments—to do

them, || Which the man who does—lives by them. They have defiled My Sabbaths, || And I speak—to pour out My fury on them, || To complete My anger against them in the wilderness. ²²And I have turned back My hand, || And I do [it] for My Name's sake, || Not to defile [it] before the eyes of the nations, || Before whose eyes I brought them out. ²³I also, I have lifted up My hand to them in the wilderness, || To scatter them among nations, || And to spread them through lands. ²⁴Because they have not done My judgments, || And they have despised My statutes, || And they have defiled My Sabbaths, || And their eyes have been after [the] idols of their fathers. ²⁵And I also, I have given statutes to them [that are] not good, || And judgments by which they do not live. ²⁶And I defile them by their own gifts, || By causing every opener of a womb to pass away, || So that I make them desolate, || So that they know that I [am] YHWH. ²⁷Therefore, speak to the house of Israel, son of man, and you have said to them, Thus said Lord YHWH: Still in this your fathers have reviled Me, || In their committing a trespass against Me. ²⁸And I bring them into the land, || That I lifted up My hand to give to them, || And they see every high hill, and every thick tree, || And they sacrifice their sacrifices there, || And give the provocation of their offering there, || And make their refreshing fragrance there, || And they pour out their drink-offerings there. ²⁹And I say to them: What [is] the high place to where you are going in?" And its name is called "High Place" to this day. ³⁰"Therefore, say to the house of Israel, Thus said Lord YHWH: Are you defiling yourselves in the way of your fathers? And do you go whoring after their detestable things? ³¹And in the offering of your gifts, || In causing your sons to pass through fire, || You are defiled by all your idols to this day, || And I am sought by you, O house of Israel? [As] I live—a declaration of Lord YHWH, I am not sought by you. ³²And that which is going up on your mind, || It is not at all—in that you are saying: We will be as the nations, as the families of the lands, || To serve wood and stone. ³³[As] I live—a declaration of Lord YHWH, || Do I not, with a strong hand, || And with an outstretched arm, || And with poured out fury—rule over you? ³⁴And I have brought you forth from the peoples, || And assembled you from the lands || In which you have been scattered, || With a strong hand and with an outstretched arm, || And with poured out fury. ³⁵And I have brought you into the wilderness of the peoples, || And have been judged with you there face to face. ³⁶As I was judged with your fathers, || In the wilderness of the land of Egypt, || So I am judged with you, || A declaration of Lord YHWH. ³⁷And I have caused you to pass under the rod, || And brought you into the bond of the covenant, ³⁸And cleared out the rebels from you, || And those transgressing against Me, || I bring them out from the land of their sojournings, || And they do not come to the land of Israel, || And you have known that I [am] YHWH. ³⁹And you, O house of Israel, thus said Lord YHWH: Each go, serve his idols, || And afterward, if you are not listening to Me [anyway], || But you do not defile My holy Name anymore by your gifts, and by your idols. ⁴⁰For on My holy mountain, || On the mountain of the height of Israel, || A declaration of Lord YHWH, || All the house of Israel serves Me there, || All of it, in the land—I accept them there, || And I seek your raised-offerings there, || And with the first-fruit of your gifts, || With all your holy things. ⁴¹With refreshing fragrance I accept you, || In My bringing you out from the peoples, || And I have assembled you from the lands || In which you have been scattered, || And I have been sanctified in you || Before the eyes of the nations. ⁴²And you have known that I [am] YHWH, || In My bringing you to the ground of Israel, || To the land that I lifted up My hand || To give it to your fathers, ⁴³And you have remembered your ways there, || And all your doings, || In which you have been defiled, || And you have been loathsome in your own faces, || For all your evils that you have done. ⁴⁴And you have known that I [am] YHWH, || In My dealing with you for My Name's sake, || Not according to your evil ways, || And according to your corrupt doings, O house of Israel, || A declaration of Lord YHWH." ⁴⁵And there is a word of YHWH to me, saying, ⁴⁶"Son of man, set your face the way of Teman, and prophesy to the south, and prophesy to the forest of the field—the south; ⁴⁷and you have said to the forest of the south, Hear a word of YHWH! Thus said Lord YHWH: Behold, I am kindling a fire in you, || And it has devoured every moist tree in you, and every dry tree, || The glowing flames are not quenched, || And all faces from south to north have been burned by it. ⁴⁸And all flesh has seen, that I, YHWH, have kindled it—it is not quenched." ⁴⁹And I say, "Aah! Lord YHWH, || They are saying of me, || Is he not using allegories?"

CHAPTER 21

¹And there is a word of YHWH to me, saying, ²"Son of man, set your face toward Jerusalem, and prophesy to the holy places, and prophesy to the ground of Israel; ³and you have said to the ground of Israel, Thus said YHWH: Behold, I [am] against you, || And have brought out My sword from its scabbard, || And have cut off righteous and wicked from you. ⁴Because that I have cut off righteous and wicked from you, || Therefore My sword goes out from its scabbard, || To all flesh, from south to north. ⁵And all flesh has known that I, YHWH, || Have brought out My sword from its scabbard, || It does not turn back anymore. ⁶And you, son of man, sigh with breaking of loins, indeed, sigh before their eyes with bitterness, ⁷and it has come to pass, when they say to you, Why are you sighing? That you have said: Because of the report, for it is coming, || And every heart has melted, || And all hands have been feeble, || And every spirit is weak, || And all knees go [as] waters, || Behold, it is coming, indeed, it has been, || A declaration of Lord YHWH." ⁸And there is a word of YHWH to me, saying, ⁹"Son of man, prophesy, and you have said, Thus said YHWH: Say, A sword, a sword is sharpened, and also polished. ¹⁰It is sharpened so as to slaughter a slaughter. It is polished so as to have brightness, || Or do we rejoice? It is despising the scepter of My son [as] every tree. ¹¹And He gives it for polishing, || For laying hold of by the hand. It is sharpened—the sword—and polished, || To give it into the hand of a slayer. ¹²Cry and howl, son of man, || For it has been among My people, || It [is] among all the princes of Israel, || My people have been cast to the sword. Therefore strike on your thigh, ¹³Because [it is] a trier, || And what if it is even despising the scepter? It will not be, a declaration of Lord YHWH. ¹⁴And you, son of man, prophesy, || And strike hand on hand, || And the sword is bent a third time, || The sword of the wounded! It [is] the sword of the wounded—the great one, || That is entering the inner chamber to them. ¹⁵To melt the heart, and to multiply the ruins, || I have set the point of a sword by all their gates. Aah! It is made for brightness, || Wrapped up for slaughter. ¹⁶Take possession of the right, place yourself at the left, || To where your face is appointed. ¹⁷And I also, I strike My hand on My hand, || And have caused My fury to rest; I, YHWH, have spoken." ¹⁸And there is a word of YHWH to me, saying, ¹⁹"And you, son of man, appoint two ways for yourself, for the coming in of the sword of the king of Babylon; they come forth from one land, both of them. And create a station; create [it] at the top of the way of the city. ²⁰Appoint a way for the coming of the sword, || To Rabbath of the sons of Ammon, || And to Judah, in fortified Jerusalem. ²¹For the king of Babylon has stood at the head of the way, || At the top of the two ways, to use divination, || He has moved lightly with the arrows, || He has inquired of the teraphim, || He has looked on the liver. ²²The divination [for] Jerusalem has been at his right, || To place battering-rams, || To open the mouth with slaughter, || To lift up a voice with shouting, || To place battering-rams against the gates, || To pour out a mound, to build a fortification. ²³And it has been to them as a false divination in their eyes, || Who have sworn oaths to them, || But he is causing iniquity to be remembered [so they] are caught. ²⁴Therefore, thus said Lord YHWH: Because of your causing your iniquity to be remembered, || In your transgressions being revealed, || For your sins being seen, in all your doings, || Because of your being remembered, || You are caught by the hand. ²⁵And you, wounded, wicked one, || Prince of Israel, whose day has come, || In the time of the iniquity of the end, ²⁶Thus said Lord YHWH: Turn aside the turban, and carry away the crown, || This—not this—make high the low, || And make low the high. ²⁷An overturn, overturn, overturn, I make it, || Also this has not been until the coming of Him, || Whose [is] the judgment, and I have given it. ²⁸And you, son of man, prophesy, and you have said, Thus said Lord YHWH concerning the sons of Ammon, and concerning their reproach, and you have said: A sword, a sword, open for slaughter, || Polished to the utmost for

brightness! ²⁹In seeing a vain thing for you, || In divining a lie for you, || To put you on the necks of the wounded of the wicked, whose day has come, || In the time of the iniquity of the end. ³⁰Turn [it] back to its scabbard; I judge you || In the place where you were produced, || In the land of your birth. ³¹And I have poured My indignation on you, || I blow against you with [the] fire of My wrath, || And have given you into the hand of brutish men—craftsmen of destruction. ³²You are fuel for the fire, || Your blood is in the midst of the land, || You are not remembered, || For I, YHWH, have spoken!"

CHAPTER 22

¹And there is a word of YHWH to me, saying, ²"And you, son of man, do you judge? Do you judge the city of blood? Then you have caused it to know all its abominations, ³and you have said, Thus said Lord YHWH: The city is shedding blood in its midst, || For the coming in of its time, || And it has made idols on it for defilement. ⁴You have been guilty by your blood that you have shed, || And you have been defiled by your idols that you have made, || And you cause your days to draw near, || And have come to your years, || Therefore I have given you [for] a reproach to nations, || And a derision to all the lands. ⁵The near and the far-off from you scoff at you, || O defiled of name—abounding in trouble. ⁶Behold, princes of Israel—each according to his arm || Have been in you to shed blood. ⁷They have made light of father and mother in you, || They dealt oppressively to a sojourner in your midst, || They oppressed fatherless and widow in you. ⁸You have despised My holy things, || And you have defiled My Sabbaths. ⁹Men of slander have been in you to shed blood, || And they have eaten on the mountains in you, || They have done wickedness in your midst. ¹⁰One has uncovered the nakedness of a father in you, || They humbled the menstruous woman in you. ¹¹And each has done abomination with the wife of his neighbor, || And each has defiled his daughter-in-law through wickedness, || And each has humbled his sister, his father's daughter, in you. ¹²They have taken a bribe to shed blood in you, || You have taken usury and increase, || And cut off your neighbor by oppression, || And you have forgotten Me, || A declaration of Lord YHWH! ¹³And behold, I have struck My hand, || Because of your dishonest gain that you have gained, || And for your blood that has been in your midst. ¹⁴Does your heart stand—are your hands strong, || For the days that I am dealing with you? I, YHWH, have spoken and have done [it]. ¹⁵And I have scattered you among nations, || And have spread you out among lands, || And consumed your uncleanness out of you. ¹⁶And you have been defiled in yourself || Before the eyes of nations, || And you have known that I [am] YHWH." ¹⁷And there is a word of YHWH to me, saying, ¹⁸"Son of man, the house of Israel has been for dross to Me, || All of them [are] bronze, and tin, and iron, and lead, || In the midst of a furnace—silver has been dross, ¹⁹Therefore, thus said Lord YHWH: Because you have all become dross, || Therefore, behold, I am gathering you into the midst of Jerusalem, ²⁰A gathering of silver, and bronze, and iron, and lead, and tin, || Into the midst of a furnace—to blow fire on it, to melt it, || So I gather in My anger and in My fury, || And I have let rest, and have melted you. ²¹And I have heaped you up, || And blown on you in the fire of My wrath, || And you have been melted in its midst. ²²As the melting of silver in the midst of a furnace, || So you are melted in its midst, || And you have known that I, YHWH, have poured out My fury on you." ²³And there is a word of YHWH to me, saying, ²⁴"Son of man, say to it, You [are] a land, || It [is] not cleansed nor rained on in a day of indignation. ²⁵A conspiracy of its prophets [is] in its midst, || As a roaring lion tearing prey; They have devoured the soul, || They have taken wealth and glory, || Its widows have multiplied in its midst. ²⁶Its priests have wronged My law, || And they defile My holy things, || They have not made separation between holy and common, || And they have not made known [the difference] between the unclean and the clean, || And they have hidden their eyes from My Sabbaths, || And I am pierced in their midst. ²⁷Its princes [are] as wolves in its midst, || Tearing prey, to shed blood, to destroy souls, || For the sake of gaining dishonest gain. ²⁸And its prophets have coated with chalk for them, || Seeing a vain thing, and divining a lie for them, || Saying, Thus said Lord YHWH, || And YHWH has not spoken. ²⁹The people of the land have used oppression, || And have taken plunder away violently, || And have oppressed humble and needy, || And oppressed the sojourner without judgment. ³⁰And I seek from them a man making a wall, || And standing in the breach before Me, || In behalf of the land—not to destroy it, || And I have found none. ³¹And I pour out My indignation on them, || I have consumed them by [the] fire of My wrath, || I have put their way on their own head, || A declaration of Lord YHWH!"

CHAPTER 23

¹And there is a word of YHWH to me, saying, "Son of man, ²Two women were daughters of one mother, ³And they go whoring in Egypt, || They have gone whoring in their youth, || There they have bruised their breasts, || And there they have dealt with the loves of their virginity. ⁴And their names [are] Aholah the older, || And Aholibah her sister, || And they are Mine, and bear sons and daughters. As for their names—Samaria [is] Aholah, || And Jerusalem [is] Aholibah. ⁵And Aholah goes whoring under Me, and she lusts on her lovers, on the neighboring Assyrians, ⁶Clothed with blue—governors and prefects, || All of them desirable young men, || Horsemen, riding on horses, ⁷And she gives her whoredoms on them, || The choice of the sons of Asshur, || All of them—even all on whom she lusted, || She has been defiled by all their idols. ⁸And she has not forsaken her whoredoms out of Egypt, || For with her they lay in her youth, || And they dealt with the loves of her virginity, || And they pour out their whoredoms on her. ⁹Therefore I have given her into the hand of her lovers, || Into the hand of sons of Asshur on whom she lusted. ¹⁰They have uncovered her nakedness, || They have taken her sons and her daughters, || And they have slain her by sword, || And she is a name for women, || And they have done judgments with her. ¹¹And her sister Aholibah sees, || And she makes her unhealthy love more corrupt than she, || And her whoredoms than the whoredoms of her sister. ¹²She has lusted on sons of Asshur, || Governors and prefects, || Neighboring ones—clothed in perfection, || Horsemen, riding on horses, || All of them desirable young men. ¹³And I see that she has been defiled, || One way [is] to them both. ¹⁴And she adds to her whoredoms, || And she sees men carved on the wall, || Pictures of Chaldeans, carved with vermillion, ¹⁵Girded with a girdle on their loins, || Dyed attire spread out on their heads, || The appearance of rulers—all of them, || The likeness of sons of Babylon, || Chaldea is the land of their birth. ¹⁶And she lusts on them at the sight of her eyes, || And sends messengers to them, to Chaldea. ¹⁷And sons of Babylon come in to her, || To the bed of loves, || And they defile her with their whoredoms, || And she is defiled with them, || And her soul is alienated from them. ¹⁸And she reveals her whoredoms, || And she reveals her nakedness, || And My soul is alienated from off her, || As My soul was alienated from off her sister. ¹⁹And she multiplies her whoredoms, || To remember the days of her youth, || When she went whoring in the land of Egypt. ²⁰And she lusts on their lovers, || Whose flesh [is] the flesh of donkeys, || And the emission of horses—their emission. ²¹You look after the wickedness of your youth, || In dealing out of Egypt your loves, || For the sake of the breasts of your youth. ²²Therefore, O Aholibah, thus said Lord YHWH: Behold, I am stirring up your lovers against you, || From whom your soul has been alienated, || And have brought them in against you from all around. ²³Sons of Babylon, and of all Chaldea, Pekod, and Shoa, and Koa, || All the sons of Asshur with them, || Desirable young men, governors and prefects, || All of them—rulers and proclaimed ones, || All of them riding on horses. ²⁴And they have come in against you, || With arms, rider, and wheel, || And with an assembly of peoples; Buckler, and shield, and helmet, || They set against you all around, || And I have set judgment before them, || They have judged you in their judgments. ²⁵And I have set My jealousy against you, || And they have dealt with you in fury, || They turn aside your nose and your ears, || And your posterity falls by sword, || They take away your sons and your daughters, || And your posterity is devoured by fire. ²⁶And they have stripped you of your garments, || And have taken your beautiful jewels. ²⁷And I have caused your wickedness to cease from you, || And your whoredoms out of the land of Egypt, || And you do not lift up your eyes to them, || And you do not remember Egypt again. ²⁸For thus said Lord YHWH: Behold, I am giving you into a

EZEKIEL

hand that you have hated, || Into a hand from which you were alienated. ²⁹And they have dealt with you in hatred, || And they have taken all your labor, || And they have left you naked and bare, || And the nakedness of your whoredoms has been revealed, || And the wickedness of your whoredoms. ³⁰To do these things to you, || In your going whoring after nations, || Because you have been defiled with their idols, ³¹You have walked in the way of your sister, || And I have given her cup into your hand. ³²Thus said Lord YHWH: You drink the cup of your sister, || The deep and the wide one || (You are for laughter and for scorn), || Abundant to contain. ³³You are filled with drunkenness and sorrow, || A cup of astonishment and desolation, || The cup of your sister Samaria. ³⁴And you have drunk it, and have drained [it], || And you gnaw its earthen ware, || And you pluck off your own breasts, || For I have spoken, || A declaration of Lord YHWH, ³⁵Therefore, thus said Lord YHWH: Because you have forgotten Me, || And you cast Me behind your back, || Even you also bear your wickedness and your whoredoms." ³⁶And YHWH says to me, "Son of man, || Do you judge Aholah and Aholibah? Then declare their abominations to them. ³⁷For they have committed adultery, || And blood [is] in their hands, || They committed adultery with their idols, || And also their sons whom they bore to Me, || They caused to pass over to them for food. ³⁸Again, they have done this to Me, || They defiled My sanctuary in that day, || And they have defiled My Sabbaths. ³⁹And in their slaughtering their sons to their idols || They also come into My sanctuary in that day to defile it, || And behold, thus they have done in the midst of My house, ⁴⁰And also that they send to men coming from afar, || To whom a messenger is sent, || And behold, they have come in for whom you have washed, || Painted your eyes, and put on adornment. ⁴¹And you have sat on a couch of honor, || And a table arrayed before it, || And placed My incense and My oil on it. ⁴²And the voice of a multitude at ease [is] with her, || And Sabeans from the wilderness are brought in to men of the common people, || And they put bracelets on their hands, || And a beautiful crown on their heads. ⁴³And I say of the worn-out one in adulteries, || Now they commit her whoredoms—she also! ⁴⁴And they come in to her, || As the coming in to a whorish woman, || So they have come in to Aholah, || And to Aholibah—the wicked women. ⁴⁵As for righteous men, they judge them with the judgment of adulteresses, || And the judgment of women shedding blood, || For they [are] adulteresses, || And blood [is] in their hands. ⁴⁶For thus said Lord YHWH: Bring up an assembly against them, || And give them to trembling and to spoiling. ⁴⁷And they have cast the stone of the assembly at them, || And cut them with their swords, || They slay their sons and their daughters, || And they burn their houses with fire. ⁴⁸And I have caused wickedness to cease from the land, || And all the women have been instructed, || And they do not do according to your wickedness. ⁴⁹And they have put your wickedness on you, || And you bear the sins of your idols, || And you have known that I [am] Lord YHWH!"

CHAPTER 24

¹And there is a word of YHWH to me, in the ninth year, in the tenth month, on the tenth of the month, saying, ²"Son of man, write! Write the name of the day for yourself, this very day; the king of Babylon has leaned toward Jerusalem in this very day. ³And use an allegory toward the house of rebellion, and you have said to them, Thus said Lord YHWH: To set on the pot, to set [it] on, and also to pour water into it, ⁴To gather its pieces to it, every good piece, || Thigh and shoulder, to fill in the choice of the bones. ⁵To take the choice of the flock, || And also to pile the bones under it, || Boil it thoroughly, indeed, cook its bones in its midst. ⁶Therefore, thus said Lord YHWH: Woe [to] the city of blood, || A pot whose scum [is] in it, || And its scum has not come out of it, || By piece of it, by piece of it bring it out, a lot has not fallen on it. ⁷For her blood has been in her midst, || She has set it on a clear place of a rock, || She has not poured it on the earth, || To cover it over with dust. ⁸To cause fury to come up to take vengeance, || I have put her blood on a clear place of a rock—not to be covered. ⁹Therefore, thus said Lord YHWH: Woe [to] the city of blood, indeed, I make the pile great. ¹⁰Make the wood abundant, || Kindle the fire, consume the flesh, || And make the compound, || And let the bones be burned. ¹¹And cause it to stand empty on its coals, || So that its bronze is hot and burning, || Its uncleanness has been melted in its midst, || Its scum is consumed. ¹²She has wearied herself [with] sorrows, || And the abundance of her scum does not go out of her, || Her scum [is] in the fire. ¹³Wickedness [is] in your uncleanness, || Because I have cleansed you, || And you have not been cleansed, || You are not cleansed from your uncleanness again, || Until I have caused My fury to rest on you. ¹⁴I, YHWH, have spoken, || It has come, and I have done [it], || I do not free, nor do I spare, nor do I regret, || According to your ways, and according to your acts, || They have judged you, || A declaration of Lord YHWH." ¹⁵And there is a word of YHWH to me, saying, ¹⁶"Son of man, behold, I am taking the desire of your eyes from you by a stroke, and you do not mourn, nor weep, nor let your tear come. ¹⁷Cease to groan [and] make no mourning [for] the dead, bind your headdress on yourself, and put your shoes on your feet, and you do not cover over the upper lip, and you do not eat [the] bread of men." ¹⁸And I speak to the people in the morning, and my wife dies in the evening, and I do in the morning as I have been commanded. ¹⁹And the people say to me, "Do you not declare to us what these [are] to us, that you are doing?" ²⁰And I say to them, "A word of YHWH has been to me, saying, ²¹Say to the house of Israel, Thus said Lord YHWH: Behold, I am defiling My sanctuary, || The excellence of your strength, || The desire of your eyes, and the pitied of your soul, || And your sons and your daughters whom you have left, fall by sword. ²²And you have done as I have done, || You have not covered over the upper lip, || And you do not eat [the] bread of men. ²³And your headdresses [are] on your heads, || And your shoes [are] on your feet, || You do not mourn nor do you weep, || And you have wasted away for your iniquities, || And you have howled to one another. ²⁴And Ezekiel has been for a type to you; according to all that he has done you do. In its coming in—you have known that I [am] Lord YHWH." ²⁵"And you, son of man, is it not in the day of My taking from them their strength, the joy of their beauty, the desire of their eyes, and the song of their soul—their sons and their daughters? ²⁶In that day the escaped one comes to you to cause the ears to hear. ²⁷In that day your mouth is opened with the escaped and you speak, and are not silent anymore, and you have been for a type to them, and they have known that I [am] YHWH."

CHAPTER 25

¹And there is a word of YHWH to me, saying, ²"Son of man, set your face toward the sons of Ammon, and prophesy against them; ³and you have said to the sons of Ammon: Hear a word of Lord YHWH! Thus said Lord YHWH: Because of your saying, Aha, to My sanctuary, || Because it has been defiled, || And to the ground of Israel, || Because it has been desolate, || And to the house of Judah, || Because they have gone into a removal: ⁴Therefore, behold, I am giving you to sons of the east for a possession, || And they set their towers in you, || And have placed their dwelling places in you. They eat your fruit, and they drink your milk, ⁵And I have given Rabbah for a habitation of camels, || And the sons of Ammon for the crouching of a flock, || And you have known that I [am] YHWH. ⁶For thus said Lord YHWH: Because of your clapping the hand, || And of your stamping with the foot, || And you rejoice with all your despite in soul || Against the ground of Israel, ⁷Therefore, behold, I have stretched out My hand against you, || And have given you for a portion to nations, || And I have cut you off from the peoples, || And caused you to perish from the lands; I destroy you, and you have known that I [am] YHWH. ⁸Thus said Lord YHWH: Because of the saying of Moab and Seir: Behold, the house of Judah [is] as all the nations; ⁹Therefore, behold, I am opening the shoulder of Moab—From the cities—from his cities—from his frontier, || The beauty of the land, Beth-Jeshimoth, Ba'al-Meon, and Kiriathaim, ¹⁰To the sons of the east, with the sons of Ammon, || And I have given it for a possession, || So that the sons of Ammon are not remembered among nations. ¹¹And I do judgments in Moab, || And they have known that I [am] YHWH. ¹²Thus said Lord YHWH: Because of the doings of Edom, || In taking vengeance on the house of Judah, || Indeed, they are very guilty, || And they have taken vengeance on them. ¹³Therefore, thus said Lord YHWH: I have stretched out My hand against Edom, || And I have cut off man and beast from it, || And given it up—a ruin, from

Teman even to Dedan, || They fall by sword. ¹⁴And I have given My vengeance on Edom, || By the hand of My people Israel, || And they have done in Edom, || According to My anger, and according to My fury, || And they have known My vengeance, || A declaration of Lord YHWH. ¹⁵Thus said Lord YHWH: Because of the doings of the Philistines in vengeance, || And they take vengeance with despite in soul, || Destruction [with] continuous enmity, ¹⁶Therefore, thus said Lord YHWH: Behold, I am stretching out My hand against the Philistines, || And I have cut off the Cherethim, || And destroyed the remnant of the haven of the sea, ¹⁷And done great vengeance on them with furious reproofs, || And they have known that I [am] YHWH, || In My giving out My vengeance on them!"

CHAPTER 26

¹And it comes to pass, in the eleventh year, on the first of the month, there has been a word of YHWH to me, saying, "Son of man, ²Because that Tyre has said of Jerusalem: Aha, she has been broken, || The doors of the peoples, || She has turned around to me, || I am filled—she has been laid waste, ³Therefore, thus said Lord YHWH: Behold, I [am] against you, O Tyre, || And have caused many nations to come up against you, || As the sea causes its billows to come up. ⁴And they have destroyed the walls of Tyre, || And they have broken down her towers, || And I have scraped her dust from her, || And made her for a clear place of a rock. ⁵She is a spreading place of nets in the midst of the sea, || For I have spoken," || A declaration of Lord YHWH, || "And she has been for a spoil to nations. ⁶And her daughters who [are] in the field, are slain by sword, || And they have known that I [am] YHWH," ⁷For thus said Lord YHWH: "Behold, I am bringing Nebuchadnezzar king of Babylon to Tyre, || From the north—a king of kings, || With horse, and with chariot, and with horsemen, || Even an assembly, and a numerous people. ⁸He slays your daughters in the field by sword, || And he has made a fort against you, || And has poured out a mound against you, || And has raised a buckler against you. ⁹And he places a battering-ram before him against your walls, || And he breaks your towers with his weapons. ¹⁰From the abundance of his horses their dust cover you, || From the noise of horseman, and wheel, and rider, || Your walls shake, in his coming into your gates, || As the coming into a city that has been broken-up. ¹¹He treads all your out-places with [the] hooves of his horses, || He slays your people by sword, || And the pillars of your strength come down to the earth. ¹²And they have spoiled your wealth, || And they have plundered your merchandise, || And they have thrown down your walls, || And they break down your desirable houses, || And your stones, and your wood, and your dust, || They place in the midst of the waters. ¹³And I have caused the noise of your songs to cease, || And the voice of your harps is heard no more. ¹⁴And I have given you up for a clear place of a rock, || You are a spreading-place of nets, || You are not built up anymore, || For I, YHWH, have spoken," || A declaration of Lord YHWH. ¹⁵Thus said Lord YHWH to Tyre: "Do not—from the noise of your fall, || In the groaning of the wounded, || In the slaying of the slaughter in your midst—The islands shake? ¹⁶And all princes of the sea have come down from off their thrones, || And they have turned their robes aside, || And strip off their embroidered garments, || They put on trembling, || They sit on the earth, || And they have trembled every moment, || And they have been astonished at you, ¹⁷And have lifted up a lamentation for you, || And said to you: How you have perished, || That are inhabited from the seas, || The praised city, that was strong in the sea, || She and her inhabitants, || Who put their terror on all her inhabitants! ¹⁸Now the islands tremble [on the] day of your fall; The islands that [are] in the sea have been troubled at your outgoing." ¹⁹For thus said Lord YHWH: "In My making you a city dried up, || Like cities that have not been inhabited, || In bringing up the deep against you, || Then the great waters have covered you. ²⁰And I have caused you to go down, || With those going down to the pit, || To the people of old, || And I have caused you to dwell || In the lower parts of the earth—in ancient ruins, || With those going down to the pit, || So that you are not inhabited, || And I have given beauty in the land of the living. ²¹I make you a terror, and you are not, || And you are sought, and are not found anymore—for all time," || A declaration of Lord YHWH!

CHAPTER 27

¹And there is a word of YHWH to me, saying, ²"And you, son of man, lift up a lamentation concerning Tyre, and you have said to Tyre: ³O dweller on the entrances of the sea, || Merchant of the peoples to many islands, Thus said Lord YHWH: O Tyre, you have said, || I [am] the perfection of beauty. ⁴Your borders [are] in the heart of the seas, || Your builders have perfected your beauty. ⁵They have built of firs from Senir all your double-boarded ships for you, || They have taken of cedars from Lebanon to make a mast for you, ⁶They made your oars of oaks from Bashan, || They have made your bench of ivory, || A branch of Ashurim from islands of Chittim. ⁷Your sail has been of fine linen with embroidery from Egypt, || To be for your ensign, || Your covering has been of blue and purple from islands of Elishah. ⁸Inhabitants of Sidon and Arvad have been rowers for you, || Your wise men, O Tyre, have been in you, || They [are] your pilots. ⁹The elderly of Gebal and its wise men have been in you, || Strengthening your breach; All ships of the sea and their mariners, || Have been in you, to trade your merchandise. ¹⁰Persia and Lud and Phut || Have been in your forces—your men of war. They hung up shield and helmet in you, || They have given out your honor. ¹¹The sons of Arvad, and your force, || [Are] on your walls all around, || And short swordsmen have been in your towers, || They have hung up their shields on your walls all around, || They have perfected your beauty. ¹²Tarshish [is] your merchant, || Because of the abundance of all wealth, || They have given silver, iron, tin, and lead [for] your wares. ¹³Javan, Tubal, and Meshech—they [are] your merchants, || They have given [the] soul of man, and vessels of bronze, [for] your merchandise. ¹⁴Those of the house of Togarmah, || They have given horses, and riding steeds, and mules [for] your wares. ¹⁵Sons of Dedan [are] your merchants, || Many islands [are] the market of your hand, || They sent back horns of ivory and ebony [for] your reward. ¹⁶Aram [is] your merchant, || Because of the abundance of your works, || They have given emerald, purple, and embroidery, || And fine linen, and coral, and agate for your wares. ¹⁷Judah and the land of Israel—they [are] your merchants, || They have given wheat of Minnith, and Pannag, || And honey, and oil, and balm [for] your merchandise. ¹⁸Damascus [is] your merchant, || For the abundance of your works, || Because of the abundance of all wealth, || For wine of Helbon, and white wool. ¹⁹Dan and Javan go about with your wares, || They have given shining iron, cassia, and cane, || It has been in your merchandise. ²⁰Dedan [is] your merchant, || For clothes of freedom for riding. ²¹Arabia, and all princes of Kedar, || They [are] the traders of your hand, || For lambs, and rams, and male goats, || In these your merchants. ²²Merchants of Sheba and Raamah—they [are] your merchants, || They have given the chief of all spices, || And every precious stone, and gold [for] your wares. ²³Haran, and Canneh, and Eden, merchants of Sheba, Asshur—Chilmad—[are] your merchants, ²⁴They [are] your merchants for perfect things, || For wrappings of blue, and embroidery, || And for treasuries of rich apparel, || With cords bound and girded, for your merchandise, ²⁵Ships of Tarshish are journeying [with] your merchandise for you, || And you are filled and honored greatly, || In the heart of the seas. ²⁶Those rowing you have brought you into great waters, || The east wind has broken you in the heart of the seas. ²⁷Your wealth and your wares, || Your merchandise, your mariners, || And your pilots, strengtheners of your breach, || And the traders of your merchandise, || And all your men of war, who [are] in you, || And in all your assembly that [is] in your midst, || Fall into the heart of the seas in the day of your fall, ²⁸At the voice of the cry of your pilots the outskirts shake. ²⁹And all handling an oar come down from their ships, || Mariners [and] all the pilots of the sea stand on the land, ³⁰And have sounded with their voice for you, || And cry bitterly, and cause dust to go up on their heads, || They roll themselves in ashes; ³¹And they have made themselves bald for you, || And they have girded on sackcloth, || And they have wept for you, || In bitterness of soul—a bitter mourning. ³²And their sons have lifted up a lamentation for you, || And they have lamented over you, Who [is] as Tyre? As the cut-off one in the midst of the sea? ³³With the outgoing of your wares from the seas, || You have filled many peoples, || With the abundance of your riches, and your

merchandise, || You have enriched [the] kings of earth. ³⁴At the time of [your] being broken by the seas in the depths of the waters, || Your merchandise and all your assembly have fallen in your midst. ³⁵All inhabitants of the islands have been astonished at you, || And their kings have been severely afraid, || They have been troubled in countenance. ³⁶Merchants among the peoples have shrieked for you, || You have been terrors, and you are not—for all time!"

CHAPTER 28

¹And there is a word of YHWH to me, saying, ²"Son of man, say to the leader of Tyre, Thus said Lord YHWH: Because your heart has been high, || And you say: I [am] a god, || I have inhabited the habitation of God, || In the heart of the seas, || And you [are] man, and not God, || And you give out your heart as the heart of God, ³Behold, you [are] wiser than Daniel, || No hidden thing have they concealed from you. ⁴By your wisdom and by your understanding || You have made wealth for yourself, || And make gold and silver in your treasuries. ⁵By the abundance of your wisdom, || Through your merchandise, || You have multiplied your wealth, || And your heart is high through your wealth. ⁶Therefore, thus said Lord YHWH: Because of your giving out your heart as the heart of God, ⁷Therefore, behold, I am bringing in strangers against you, || The terrible of the nations, || And they have drawn out their swords || Against the beauty of your wisdom, || And they have pierced your brightness. ⁸They bring you down to destruction, || You die by the deaths of the wounded, in the heart of the seas. ⁹Do you really say, I [am] God, || Before him who is slaying you? And you [are] man, and not God, || In the hand of him who is piercing you. ¹⁰You die the deaths of the uncircumcised, || By the hand of strangers, for I have spoken," || A declaration of Lord YHWH. ¹¹And there is a word of YHWH to me, saying, ¹²"Son of man, lift up a lamentation for the king of Tyre, || And you have said to him, Thus said Lord YHWH: You are sealing up a measurement, || Full of wisdom, and perfect in beauty. ¹³You have been in Eden, the garden of God, || Every precious stone [was] your covering, || Ruby, topaz, and diamond, beryl, onyx, and jasper, || Sapphire, emerald, and carbuncle, and gold, || The workmanship of your tambourines and of your pipes, || In you in the day of your being produced, have been created; ¹⁴And I established you as the anointed, covering cherub, || You have been in [the] holy mountain of God, || You have walked up and down in [the] midst of [the] stones of fire. ¹⁵You [were] perfect in your ways, || From [the] day of your being created, || Until perversity was found in you. ¹⁶By [the] abundance of your merchandise || They have filled your midst with violence, || And you sin, || And I thrust you from [the] mountain of God, || And I destroy you, O covering cherub, || From [the] midst of [the] stones of fire. ¹⁷Your heart has been high because of your beauty, || You have corrupted your wisdom because of your brightness, || I have cast you to earth, || I have set you before kings, to look on you, ¹⁸From [the] abundance of your iniquity, || By [the] perversity of your merchandise, || You have defiled your sanctuaries, || And I bring forth fire from your midst, || It has devoured you, || And I make you become ashes on the earth, || In [the] eyes of all beholding you. ¹⁹All knowing you among the peoples || Have been astonished at you, || You have been terrors, and you are not—for all time." ²⁰And there is a word of YHWH to me, saying, ²¹"Son of man, set your face toward Sidon, and prophesy concerning it; ²²and you have said, Thus said Lord YHWH: Behold, I [am] against you, O Sidon, || And I have been honored in your midst, || And they have known that I [am] YHWH, || In My doing judgments in her, || And I have been sanctified in her. ²³And I have sent pestilence into her, || And blood into her out-places, || The wounded has been judged in her midst, || By the sword on her all around, || And they have known that I [am] YHWH. ²⁴And there is no more pricking brier and paining thorn || For the house of Israel, || Of all around them—despising them, || And they have known that I [am] Lord YHWH. ²⁵Thus said Lord YHWH: In My gathering the house of Israel, || Out of the peoples among whom they were scattered, || I have been sanctified in them, || Before the eyes of the nations, || And they have dwelt on their ground, || That I gave to My servant, to Jacob, ²⁶And they have dwelt confidently on it, || And built houses, and planted vineyards, || And dwelt confidently—in My doing judgments, || On all those despising them all around, || And they have known that I [am] their God YHWH!"

CHAPTER 29

¹In the tenth year, in the tenth [month], on the twelfth of the month, a word of YHWH has been to me, saying, ²"Son of man, set your face against Pharaoh king of Egypt, and prophesy concerning him, and concerning Egypt—all of it. ³Speak, and you have said, Thus said Lord YHWH: Behold, I [am] against you, || Pharaoh king of Egypt! The great dragon that is crouching in the midst of his floods, || Who has said, My flood [is] my own, || And I have made it [for] myself. ⁴And I have put hooks in your jaws, || And I have caused the fish of your floods to cleave to your scales, || And I have caused you to come up from the midst of your floods, || And every fish of your floods cleaves to your scales. ⁵And I have left you in the wilderness, || You and every fish of your floods, || You fall on the face of the field, || You are not gathered nor assembled, || I have given you for food to the beast of the earth and to the bird of the heavens. ⁶And all inhabitants of Egypt have known || That I [am] YHWH, || Because of their being a staff of reed to the house of Israel. ⁷In their taking hold of you by your hand, || You crush and have torn every shoulder of theirs, || And in their leaning on you you are broken, || And have caused all their thighs to stand. ⁸Therefore, thus said Lord YHWH: Behold, I am bringing in a sword against you, || And have cut off man and beast from you. ⁹And the land of Egypt has been for a desolation and a ruin, || And they have known that I [am] YHWH, || Because he said: The flood [is] mine, and I made [it]. ¹⁰Therefore, behold, I [am] against you, and against your floods, || And have given the land of Egypt for ruins, || A dry place, a desolation, from Migdol to Syene, || And to the border of Cush. ¹¹A foot of man does not pass over into it, || Indeed, the foot of beast does not pass into it, || Nor is it inhabited forty years. ¹²And I have made the land of Egypt a desolation, || In the midst of desolate lands, || And its cities, in the midst of cities [that are] laid waste, || Are a desolation [for] forty years, || And I have scattered the Egyptians among nations, || And I have dispersed them through lands. ¹³But thus said Lord YHWH: At the end of forty years I gather the Egyptians || Out of the peoples to where they have been scattered, ¹⁴And I have turned back [to] the captivity of Egypt, || And I have brought them back || [To] the land of Pathros, to the land of their birth, || And they have been a low kingdom there. ¹⁵It is lowest of the kingdoms, || And it does not lift itself up above the nations anymore, || And I have made them few, || So as not to rule among nations. ¹⁶And it is no longer for confidence to the house of Israel, || Bringing iniquity to remembrance, || By their turning after them, || And they have known that I [am] Lord YHWH." ¹⁷And it comes to pass, in the twenty-seventh year, in the first [month], on the first of the month, a word of YHWH has been to me, saying, ¹⁸"Son of man, Nebuchadnezzar king of Babylon, || Has caused his force to serve a great service against Tyre, || Every head [is] bald—every shoulder peeled, || And neither he, nor his force, had reward out of Tyre, || For the service that he served against it. ¹⁹Therefore, thus said Lord YHWH: Behold, I am giving the land of Egypt to Nebuchadnezzar king of Babylon, || And he has taken away its store, || And has taken its spoil, and taken its prey, || And it has been a reward to his force. ²⁰I have given to him his wage for which he labored—The land of Egypt, in that they worked for Me, || A declaration of Lord YHWH. ²¹In that day I cause a horn to shoot up for the house of Israel, || And I give an opening to your mouth in their midst, || And they have known that I [am] YHWH!"

CHAPTER 30

¹And there is a word of YHWH to me, saying, ²"Son of man, prophesy, and you have said, Thus said Lord YHWH: Howl, Aah! For the day! ³For a day [is] near, a day [is] near to YHWH! It is a time of cloud [over] the nations. ⁴And a sword has come into Egypt, || And there has been great pain in Cush, || In the falling of the wounded in Egypt, || And they have taken its store, || And its foundations have been broken down. ⁵Cush, and Phut, and Lud, and all the mixture, and Chub, || And the sons of the land of the covenant fall by sword with them, ⁶Thus said YHWH: And those supporting Egypt have fallen, || And the arrogance of her strength has come down, || From Migdol to Syene, they fall by sword in her, || A declaration of Lord YHWH.

⁷And they have been desolated in the midst of desolate lands, || And its cities are in the midst of cities [that are] laid waste. ⁸And they have known that I [am] YHWH, || In My giving fire against Egypt, || And all her helpers have been broken. ⁹In that day messengers go forth from before Me in ships, || To trouble confident Cush, || And there has been great pain among them, || As the day of Egypt, for behold, it has come. ¹⁰Thus said Lord YHWH: I have caused the multitude of Egypt to cease, || By the hand of Nebuchadnezzar king of Babylon, ¹¹He and his people with him—the terrible of nations, || Are brought in to destroy the land, || And they have drawn their swords against Egypt, || And have filled the land [with] the wounded. ¹²And I have made floods a dry place, || And I have sold the land into the hand of evildoers, || And I have made the land desolate, || And its fullness, by the hand of strangers, || I, YHWH, have spoken. ¹³Thus said Lord YHWH: And I have destroyed idols, || And caused vain things to cease from Noph, || And there is no longer a prince of the land of Egypt, || And I give fear in the land of Egypt. ¹⁴And I have made Pathros desolate, || And I have given fire against Zoan, || And I have done judgments in No, ¹⁵And I have poured out My fury on Sin, the stronghold of Egypt, || And I have cut off the multitude of No. ¹⁶And I have given fire against Egypt, || Sin is greatly pained, and No is to be broken, || And Noph has daily distresses. ¹⁷The youths of Aven and Pi-Beseth fall by sword, || And these go into captivity. ¹⁸And the day has been dark in Tehaphnehes, || In My breaking the yokes of Egypt there, || And the excellence of her strength has ceased in her, || Her! A cloud covers her, || And her daughters go into captivity. ¹⁹And I have done judgments in Egypt, || And they have known that I [am] YHWH." ²⁰And it comes to pass, in the eleventh year, in the first [month], on the seventh of the month, a word of YHWH has been to me, saying, "Son of man, ²¹I have broken the arm of Pharaoh, king of Egypt, || And behold, it has not been bound up to give healing, || To put a bandage to bind it, || To strengthen it—to lay hold on the sword. ²²Therefore, thus said Lord YHWH: Behold, I [am] against Pharaoh, king of Egypt, || And I have broken his arms, || The strong one and the broken one, || And have caused the sword to fall out of his hand, ²³And I have scattered the Egyptians among nations, || And have spread them through lands, ²⁴And I have strengthened the arms of the king of Babylon, || And have given My sword into his hand, || And I have broken the arms of Pharaoh, || And he has groaned the groans of a pierced one—before him. ²⁵And I have strengthened the arms of the king of Babylon, || And the arms of Pharaoh fall down, || And they have known that I [am] YHWH, || In My giving My sword into the hand of the king of Babylon, || And he has stretched it out toward the land of Egypt. ²⁶And I have scattered the Egyptians among nations, || And I have spread them through lands, || And they have known that I [am] YHWH!"

CHAPTER 31

¹And it comes to pass, in the eleventh year, in the third [month], on the first of the month, a word of YHWH has been to me, saying, ²"Son of man, say to Pharaoh king of Egypt, and to his multitude: To whom have you been like in your greatness? ³Behold, Asshur, a cedar in Lebanon, || Beautiful in branch, and shading bough, and high in stature, || And its foliage has been between thickets. ⁴Waters have made it great, || The deep has exalted him with its flowings, || Going around its planting, || And it has sent forth its conduits to all trees of the field. ⁵Therefore his stature has been higher than all trees of the field, || And his boughs are multiplied, and his branches are long, || Because of many waters in his shooting forth. ⁶Every bird of the heavens has made a nest in his boughs, || And every beast of the field has brought forth under his branches, || And all great nations dwell in his shade. ⁷And he is beautiful in his greatness, || In the length of his thin shoots, || For his root has been by great waters. ⁸Cedars have not hid him in the garden of God, || Firs have not been like to his boughs, || And plane-trees have not been as his branches, || No tree in the garden of God has been like to him in his beauty, ⁹I have made him beautiful in the multitude of his thin shoots, || And all trees of Eden that [are] in the garden of God envy him. ¹⁰Therefore, thus said Lord YHWH: Because that you have been high in stature, || And he yields his foliage between thickets, || And his heart is high in his haughtiness, ¹¹I give him into the hand of a god of nations, || He deals severely with him, || In his wickedness I have cast him out. ¹²And strangers cut him off, || The terrible of nations, and they leave him, || His thin shoots have fallen on the mountains and in all valleys, || And his boughs are broken at all streams of the land, || And all peoples of the land go down from his shade, and they leave him. ¹³Every bird of the heavens dwells on his ruin, || And all beasts of the field have been on his boughs, ¹⁴In order that none of the trees of the waters || May become haughty because of their stature, || Nor give their foliage between thickets, || Nor any drinking waters stand up to them in their haughtiness, || For all of them are given up to death, || To the lower earth, || In the midst of the sons of men, || To those going down to the pit. ¹⁵Thus said Lord YHWH: I have caused mourning in the day of his going down to Sheol, || I have covered the deep over him, and diminish its flowings, || And many waters are restrained, || And I make Lebanon black for him, || And all trees of the field [have been] a covering for him. ¹⁶I have caused nations to shake at the sound of his fall, || In My causing him to go down to Sheol, || With those going down to the pit, || And all trees of Eden are comforted in the lower earth, || The choice and good of Lebanon—All drinking waters. ¹⁷Those with him have also gone down to Sheol, || To the pierced of the sword, || And—his arm—they dwelt in his shade in the midst of nations. ¹⁸To whom have you been thus like, || In glory and in greatness among the trees of Eden? And you have been brought down with the trees of Eden, || To the lower earth, || You lie in the midst of the uncircumcised, || With the pierced of the sword. This [is] Pharaoh, and all his multitude, || A declaration of Lord YHWH!"

CHAPTER 32

¹And it comes to pass, in the twelfth year, in the twelfth month, on the first of the month, a word of YHWH has been to me, saying, ²"Son of man, lift up a lamentation for Pharaoh king of Egypt, and you have said to him: You have been like a young lion of nations, || And you [are] as a dragon in the seas, || And you come forth with your flowings, || And trouble the waters with your feet, || And you foul their flowings. ³Thus said Lord YHWH: And I have spread out My net for you, || With an assembly of many peoples, || And they have brought you up in My net. ⁴And I have left you in the land, || I cast you out on the face of the field, || And I have caused every bird of the heavens to dwell on you, || And have satisfied every beast of the earth with you. ⁵And I have put your flesh on the mountains, || And filled the valleys [with] your heap, ⁶And watered the land with your flowing, || From your blood—to the mountains, || And streams are filled with you. ⁷And in quenching you I have covered the heavens, || And have made their stars black, || I cover the sun with a cloud, || And the moon does not cause its light to shine. ⁸I make all luminaries of light in the heavens black over you, || And I have given darkness over your land, || A declaration of Lord YHWH, ⁹And I have distressed the heart of many peoples, || In My bringing in your destruction among nations, || To lands that you have not known. ¹⁰And I have made many peoples astonished at you, || And their kings are afraid because of you with trembling, || In My brandishing My sword before their faces, || And they have trembled every moment, || Each for his life—in the day of your fall. ¹¹For thus said Lord YHWH: A sword of the king of Babylon enters you, ¹²I cause your multitude to fall by swords of the mighty, || The terrible of nations—all of them, || And they have spoiled the excellence of Egypt, || And all her multitude has been destroyed. ¹³And I have destroyed all her beasts, || From beside many waters, || And a foot of man does not trouble them anymore, || Indeed, the hooves of beasts do not trouble them. ¹⁴Then I cause their waters to sink, || And I cause their rivers to go as oil, || A declaration of Lord YHWH. ¹⁵In My making the land of Egypt a desolation, || And the land has been desolated of its fullness, || In My striking all the inhabitants in it, || Then they have known that I [am] YHWH. ¹⁶It [is] a lamentation, and they have lamented her, || Daughters of the nations lament her, || For Egypt, and for all her multitude, they lament her, || A declaration of Lord YHWH." ¹⁷And it comes to pass, in the twelfth year, on the fifteenth of the month, a word of YHWH has been to me, saying, ¹⁸"Son of man, || Wail for the multitude of Egypt, || And cause it to go down, || It, and the daughters of majestic nations, || To the lower parts of the earth, || With those going

down to the pit. ¹⁹Whom have you surpassed in beauty? Go down, and be laid with [the] uncircumcised. ²⁰They fall in the midst of the pierced of the sword, || She has been given [to] the sword, || They drew her out, and all her multitude. ²¹The gods of the mighty speak to him out of the midst of Sheol, || With his helpers—they have gone down, || They have lain with the uncircumcised, || The pierced of the sword. ²²There [is] Asshur, and all her assembly, || His graves [are] around him, || All of them [are] wounded, who are falling by sword, ²³Whose graves are appointed in the sides of the pit, || And her assembly is around her grave, || All of them wounded, falling by sword, || Because they gave terror in the land of the living. ²⁴There [is] Elam, and all her multitude, || Around her grave, || All of them wounded, who are falling by sword, || Who have gone down uncircumcised to the lower parts of the earth, || Because they gave their terror in the land of the living, || And they bear their shame with those going down to the pit. ²⁵They have appointed a bed for her in the midst of the wounded, || With all her multitude, || Her graves [are] around them, || All of them uncircumcised, pierced of the sword, || For their terror was given in the land of the living, || And they bear their shame with those going down to the pit, || He has been set in the midst of the pierced. ²⁶There [is] Meshech, Tubal, and all her multitude, || Her graves [are] around them, || All of them uncircumcised, pierced by the sword, || For they gave their terror in the land of the living, ²⁷And they do not lie with the mighty, || Who are falling of the uncircumcised, || Who have gone down to Sheol with their weapons of war, || And they put their swords under their heads, || And their iniquities are on their bones, || For the terror of the mighty [is] in the land of the living. ²⁸And you are broken in the midst of the uncircumcised, || And lie with the pierced of the sword. ²⁹There [is] Edom, her kings, and all her princes, || Who have been given up in their might, || With the pierced of the sword, || They lie with the uncircumcised, || And with those going down to the pit. ³⁰There [are] princes of the north, || All of them, and every Zidonian, || Who have gone down with the pierced in their terror, || They are ashamed of their might, || And they lie uncircumcised with the pierced of the sword, || And they bear their shame with those going down to the pit. ³¹Then Pharaoh sees, || And he has been comforted for all his multitude, || The pierced of the sword—Pharaoh and all his force, || A declaration of Lord YHWH. ³²For I have given his terror in the land of the living, || And he has been laid down in [the] midst of [the] uncircumcised, || With [the] pierced of [the] sword—Pharaoh, and all his multitude, || A declaration of Lord YHWH!"

CHAPTER 33

¹And there is a word of YHWH to me, saying, ²"Son of man, speak to the sons of your people, and you have said to them: When I bring a sword on a land, || And the people of the land have taken one man out of their borders, || And made him their watchman, ³And he has seen the sword coming against the land, || And has blown with a horn, and has warned the people, ⁴And the hearer has heard the voice of the horn, and he has not taken warning, || And the sword comes in, and takes him away, || His blood is on his [own] head. ⁵The voice of the horn he heard, || And he has not taken warning, his blood is on him, || And he who took warning has delivered his soul. ⁶And the watchman, when he sees the sword coming in, || And he has not blown with a horn, || And the people have not been warned, || And a sword comes in, || And takes away a soul from them, || He is taken away in his iniquity, || And I require his blood from the hand of the watchman. ⁷And you, son of man, || I gave you [as] a watchman for the house of Israel, || And you have heard a word from My mouth, || And you have warned them from Me. ⁸In My saying to the wicked, O wicked one—you surely die, || And you have not spoken to warn the wicked from his way, || He—the wicked—dies in his iniquity, || And I require his blood from your hand. ⁹And you, when you have warned the wicked of his way, to turn back from it, || And he has not turned back from his way, || He dies in his iniquity, || And you have delivered your soul. ¹⁰And you, son of man, say to the house of Israel: You have spoken correctly, saying, || Surely our transgressions and our sins [are] on us, || And we are wasting away in them, || How, then, do we live? ¹¹Say to them, [As] I live—a declaration of Lord YHWH, || I do not delight in the death of the wicked, || But in the turning of the wicked from his way, and he has lived. Turn back, turn back, from your evil ways! Indeed, why do you die, O house of Israel? ¹²And you, son of man, say to the sons of your people: The righteousness of the righteous does not deliver him in the day of his transgression, || And the wickedness of the wicked, || He does not stumble for it in the day of his turning from his wickedness, || And the righteous is not able to live in it in the day of his sinning. ¹³In My saying of the righteous: He surely lives, || And—he has trusted on his righteousness, || And he has done perversity, || All his righteous acts are not remembered, || And for his perversity that he has done, || He dies for it. ¹⁴And in My saying to the wicked: You surely die, || And—he has turned back from his sin, || And has done judgment and righteousness, ¹⁵(The wicked restores a pledge, he repays [for] plunder), || He has walked in the statutes of life, || So as not to do perversity, || He surely lives—he does not die. ¹⁶All his sin—his sins that he has sinned—are not remembered against him, || He has done judgment and righteousness, || He surely lives. ¹⁷And the sons of your people have said: The way of the Lord is not pondered, || As for them—their way is not pondered. ¹⁸In the turning back of the righteous from his righteousness, || And he has done perversity—he dies for it. ¹⁹And in the turning back of the wicked from his wickedness, || And he has done judgment and righteousness—he lives by them. ²⁰And you have said, The way of the Lord is not pondered; I judge each of you according to his ways, O house of Israel." ²¹And it comes to pass, in the twelfth year—in the tenth [month], in the fifth of the month—of our removal, one who is escaped from Jerusalem comes to me, saying, "The city has been struck." ²²And the hand of YHWH has been to me in the evening, before the coming in of the escaped one, and He opens my mouth until [his] coming to me in the morning, and my mouth is opened, and I have not been silent again. ²³And there is a word of YHWH to me, saying, ²⁴"Son of man, the inhabitants of these ruins on the ground of Israel are speaking, saying, Abraham has been alone—and he possesses the land, and we [are] many—the land has been given to us for a possession. ²⁵Therefore say to them, Thus said Lord YHWH: You eat with the blood, || And you lift up your eyes to your idols, || And you shed blood, || Should you then inherit the land? ²⁶You have stood on your sword, || You have done abomination, || You have each defiled the wife of his neighbor, || Should you then possess the land? ²⁷Thus you say to them, Thus said Lord YHWH: [As] I live—do they who [are] in the ruins not fall by the sword? And they who [are] on the face of the field, || I have given for food to the beast, || And they who are in strongholds and in caves die by pestilence. ²⁸And I have made the land a desolation and an astonishment, || And the excellence of its strength has ceased, || And mountains of Israel have been desolated, || Without anyone passing through. ²⁹And they have known that I [am] YHWH, || In My making the land a desolation and an astonishment, || For all their abominations that they have done. ³⁰And you, son of man, || The sons of your people who are speaking about you, || By the walls, and in openings of the houses, || Have spoken with one another, each with his brother, || Saying, Please come in, || And hear what the word [is] that comes out from YHWH. ³¹And they come in to you as the coming in of a people, || And they sit before you—My people, || And have heard your words, and they do not do them, || For they are making unhealthy loves with their mouth, || Their heart is going after their dishonest gain. ³²And behold, you [are] as a singer of unhealthy loves to them, || A beautiful voice, and playing well on an instrument, || And they have heard your words, and they are not doing them. ³³And in its coming in—behold, it has come, || And they have known that a prophet has been in their midst!"

CHAPTER 34

¹And there is a word of YHWH to me, saying, ²"Son of man, prophesy concerning shepherds of Israel, prophesy, and you have said to them, Thus said Lord YHWH to the shepherds: Woe [to] the shepherds of Israel, || Who have been feeding themselves! Do the shepherds not feed the flock? ³You eat the fat, and you put on the wool, || You slaughter the fed one, || You do not feed the flock. ⁴You have not strengthened the weak, || And you have not healed the sick one, || And you have not bound

up the broken, || And have not brought back the driven away, || And you have not sought the lost, || And you have ruled them with might and with rigor. ⁵And they are scattered from want of a shepherd, || And are for food to every beast of the field, || Indeed, they are scattered. ⁶My flock goes astray on all the mountains, || And on every high hill, || And My flock has been scattered on [the] whole face of the earth, || And there is none inquiring, and none seeking. ⁷Therefore, shepherds, hear a word of YHWH: ⁸[As] I live—a declaration of Lord YHWH, || If not, because of My flock being for a prey, || Indeed, My flock is for food to every beast of the field, || Because there is no shepherd, || And My shepherds have not sought My flock, || And the shepherds feed themselves, || And they have not fed My flock. ⁹Therefore, O shepherds, hear a word of YHWH! ¹⁰Thus said Lord YHWH: Behold, I [am] against the shepherds, || And have required My flock from their hand, || And caused them to cease from feeding the flock, || And the shepherds feed themselves no more, || And I have delivered My flock from their mouth, || And they are not for food to them. ¹¹For thus said Lord YHWH: Behold, I—even I, have required My flock, || And I have sought it out. ¹²As a shepherd's searching of his drove, || In the day of his being in the midst of his scattered flock, so I seek My flock, || And have delivered them out of all places, || To where they have been scattered, || In a day of cloud and thick darkness. ¹³And I have brought them out from the peoples, || And have gathered them from the lands, || And brought them to their own ground, || And have fed them on mountains of Israel, || By streams, and by all dwellings of the land. ¹⁴I feed them with good pasture, || And their habitation is on mountains of the high place of Israel, || There they lie down in a good habitation, || And they enjoy fat pastures on mountains of Israel. ¹⁵I feed My flock, and cause them to lie down, || A declaration of Lord YHWH. ¹⁶I seek the lost, and bring back the driven away, || And I bind up the broken, and I strengthen the sick, || And I destroy the fat and the strong, || I feed it with judgment. ¹⁷And you, My flock, thus said Lord YHWH: Behold, I am judging between sheep and sheep, || Between rams and male goats. ¹⁸Is it a little thing for you—[that] you enjoy the good pasture, || And tread down the remnant of your pasture with your feet, || And drink a depth of waters, || And trample the remainder with your feet, ¹⁹And My flock consumes the trodden thing of your feet, || And drinks the trampled thing of your feet? ²⁰Therefore, thus said Lord YHWH to them: Behold, I—even I, have judged between fat sheep and lean sheep. ²¹Because you thrust away with side and with shoulder, || And push all the diseased with your horns, || Until you have scattered them to the out-place, ²²Therefore I have given safety to My flock, || And they are not for prey anymore, || And I have judged between sheep and sheep. ²³And have raised up one shepherd over them, || And he has fed them—My servant David, || He feeds them, and he is their shepherd, ²⁴And I, YHWH, am their God, || And My servant David [is] prince in their midst, || I, YHWH, have spoken. ²⁵And I have made a covenant of peace with them, || And caused evil beasts to cease out of the land, || And they have dwelt confidently in a wilderness, || And they have slept in forests. ²⁶And I have given them, and the outskirts of My hill, a blessing, || And caused the shower to come down in its season, || They are showers of blessing. ²⁷And the tree of the field has given its fruit, || And the land gives her increase, || And they have been confident on their land, || And they have known that I [am] YHWH, || In My breaking the bands of their yoke, || And I have delivered them from the hand of those laying service on them. ²⁸And they are no longer a prey to nations, || And the beast of the earth does not devour them, || And they have dwelt confidently, || And there is none troubling. ²⁹And I have raised a plantation of renown for them, || And they are no longer consumed by hunger in the land, || And they no longer bear the shame of the nations. ³⁰And they have known that I, YHWH, their God, [am] with them, || And they—the house of Israel—My people, || A declaration of Lord YHWH. ³¹And you, My flock, the flock of My pasture, || You [are] men [and] I [am] your God, || A declaration of Lord YHWH!"

CHAPTER 35

¹And there is a word of YHWH to me, saying, ²"Son of man, set your face against Mount Seir, and prophesy against it, ³and you have said to it, Thus said Lord YHWH: Behold, I [am] against you, O Mount Seir, || And have stretched out My hand against you, || And made you a desolation and an astonishment. ⁴I make your cities a ruin, and you are a desolation, || And you have known that I [am] YHWH. ⁵Because of your having continuous enmity, || And you saw the sons of Israel, || By the hands of the sword, || In the time of their calamity, || In the time of the iniquity of the end: ⁶Therefore, [as] I live—a declaration of Lord YHWH, || Surely I appoint you for blood, || And blood pursues you, || If you have not hated blood, || Blood also pursues you. ⁷And I have given Mount Seir for a desolation and an astonishment, || And have cut off from it him who is passing over and him who is returning, ⁸And filled his mountains with his wounded, || Your hills, and your valleys, and all your streams, || The pierced of the sword fall into them. ⁹I make you continuous desolations, || And your cities do not return, || And you have known that I [am] YHWH. ¹⁰Because of your saying: The two nations and the two lands are mine, and we have possessed it, || And YHWH has been there; ¹¹Therefore, [as] I live—a declaration of Lord YHWH, || And I have done according to your anger, || And according to your envy, || With which you have worked, || Because of your hatred against them, || And I have been known among them when I judge you. ¹²And you have known that I [am] YHWH, || I have heard all your despisings that you have spoken || Against mountains of Israel, saying, || A desolation—they were given to us for food. ¹³And you magnify yourselves against Me with your mouth, || And have made your words abundant against Me; I have heard. ¹⁴Thus said Lord YHWH: According to the rejoicing of the whole land, || I make a desolation of you. ¹⁵According to your joy at the inheritance of the house of Israel because of desolation, || So I do to you—you are a desolation, || O Mount Seir, and all Edom—all of it, || And they have known that I [am] YHWH!"

CHAPTER 36

¹"And you, son of man, prophesy to mountains of Israel, and you have said, O mountains of Israel, hear a word of YHWH! ²Thus said Lord YHWH: Because the enemy said against you, Aha! The high places of old have also become our possession, ³therefore, prophesy, and you have said, Thus said Lord YHWH: Because, even because, of desolating, || And of swallowing you up from all around, || For your being a possession to the remnant of the nations, || And you are taken up on the tip of the tongue, || And [are] an evil report to the people. ⁴Therefore, O mountains of Israel, || Hear a word of Lord YHWH! Thus said Lord YHWH, to mountains, and to hills, || To streams, and to valleys, || And to ruins that [are] desolate, || And to cities that are forsaken, || That have been for a prey, || And for a scorn, to the remnant of the surrounding nations, ⁵Therefore, thus said Lord YHWH: Have I not, in the fire of My jealousy, || Spoken against the remnant of the nations, || And against Edom—all of it, || Who gave My land to themselves for a possession, || With the joy of the whole heart—with despite of soul, || For the sake of casting it out for a prey? ⁶Therefore, prophesy concerning the ground of Israel, || And you have said to mountains, and to hills, || To streams, and to valleys, || Thus said Lord YHWH: Behold, I, in My jealousy and in My fury, have spoken, || Because you have borne the shame of nations. ⁷Therefore, thus said Lord YHWH: I have lifted up My hand, || Do the nations who [are] surrounding you not bear their own shame? ⁸And you, O mountains of Israel, || You give out your branch, || And you bear your fruits for My people Israel, || For they have drawn near to come. ⁹For behold, I [am] for you, and have turned to you, || And you have been tilled and sown. ¹⁰And I have multiplied men on you, || All the house of Israel—all of it, || And the cities have been inhabited, || And the ruins are built. ¹¹And I have multiplied man and beast on you, || And they have multiplied and been fruitful, || And I have caused you to dwell according to your former states, || And I have done better than at your beginnings, || And you have known that I [am] YHWH. ¹²And I have caused man to walk over you—My people Israel, || And they possess you, and you have been their inheritance, || And you no longer add to bereave them. ¹³Thus said Lord YHWH: Because they are saying to you, You [are] a devourer of men, || And you have been a bereaver of your nations, ¹⁴Therefore, you no longer devour man, || And you do not cause

your nations to stumble anymore, || A declaration of Lord YHWH. ¹⁵And I do not proclaim the shame of the nations to you anymore, || And you no longer bear the reproach of peoples, || And your nations do not stumble anymore, || A declaration of Lord YHWH." ¹⁶And there is a word of YHWH to me, saying, ¹⁷"Son of man, || The house of Israel are dwelling on their land, || And they defile it by their way and by their doings, || Their way has been as the uncleanness of a separated one before Me. ¹⁸And I pour out My fury on them || For the blood that they shed on the land, || And they have defiled it with their idols. ¹⁹And I scatter them among nations, || And they are spread through lands, || According to their way, and according to their doings, || I have judged them. ²⁰And one goes to the nations to where they have gone, || And they defile My holy Name by saying to them, || These [are] the people of YHWH, || And they have gone forth from His land. ²¹And I have pity on My holy Name, || That the house of Israel has defiled || Among the nations to where they have gone in. ²²Therefore, say to the house of Israel, Thus said Lord YHWH: I am not working for your sake, || O house of Israel, but for My holy Name || That you have defiled || Among the nations to where you have gone in. ²³And I have sanctified My great Name, || That is profaned among the nations, || That you have defiled in your midst, || And the nations have known that I [am] YHWH, || A declaration of Lord YHWH, || In My being sanctified in you before your eyes. ²⁴And I have taken you out of the nations, || And have gathered you out of all the lands, || And I have brought you into your land. ²⁵And I have sprinkled clean water over you, || And you have been clean; I cleanse you from all your uncleannesses, || And from all your idols. ²⁶And I have given a new heart to you, || And I give a new spirit in your midst, || And I have turned aside the heart of stone out of your flesh, || And I have given a heart of flesh to you. ²⁷And I give My Spirit in your midst, || And I have done this, so that you walk in My statutes, || And you keep My judgments, and have done them. ²⁸And you have dwelt in the land that I have given to your fathers, || And you have been to Me for a people, || And I am to you for God. ²⁹And I have saved you from all your uncleannesses, || And I have called to the grain, and multiplied it, || And I have put no famine on you. ³⁰And I have multiplied the fruit of the tree, || And the increase of the field, || So that you do not receive a reproach of famine among nations anymore. ³¹And you have remembered your ways that [are] evil, || And your doings that [are] not good, || And have been loathsome in your own faces, || For your iniquities, and for your abominations. ³²I am not working for your sake, || A declaration of Lord YHWH, || Be it known to you, || Be ashamed and confounded, because of your ways, || O house of Israel. ³³Thus said Lord YHWH: In the day of My cleansing you from all your iniquities, || I have caused the cities to be inhabited, || And the ruins have been built, ³⁴And the desolate land is tilled, || Instead of which it was a desolation before the eyes of everyone passing by, ³⁵And they have said: This land, that was desolated, || Has been as the Garden of Eden, || And the cities—the dried up, || And the desolated, and the broken down, || [And the] fortified have remained. ³⁶And the nations who are left around you have known || That I, YHWH, have built the thrown down, || I have planted the desolated: I, YHWH, have spoken, and I have done [it]. ³⁷Thus said Lord YHWH: Yet this I am inquired of by the house of Israel to do for them: I multiply them as a flock of men, ³⁸As a flock of holy ones, as a flock of Jerusalem, || In her appointed times, || So the dried up cities are full of flocks of man, || And they have known that I [am] YHWH!"

CHAPTER 37

¹There has been a hand of YHWH on me, and He takes me forth in [the] Spirit of YHWH, and places me in the midst of the valley, and it is full of bones, ²and He causes me to pass over by them, all around, and behold, very many [are] on the face of the valley, and behold—very dry. ³And He says to me, "Son of man, do these bones live?" And I say, "O Lord YHWH, You have known." ⁴And He says to me, "Prophesy concerning these bones, and you have said to them, O dry bones, hear a word of YHWH! ⁵Thus said Lord YHWH to these bones: Behold, I am bringing a spirit into you, and you have lived, ⁶and I have given sinews on you, and cause flesh to come up on you, and covered you over with skin, and given a spirit in you, and you have lived, and you have known that I [am] YHWH." ⁷And I have prophesied as I have been commanded, and there is a noise as I am prophesying, and behold, a rushing, and the bones draw near, bone to its bone. ⁸And I beheld, and behold, sinews [are] on them, and flesh has come up, and skin covers them over above—and there is no spirit in them. ⁹And He says to me: "Prophesy to the Spirit, prophesy, son of man, and you have said to the Spirit, Thus said Lord YHWH: Come in from the four winds, O Spirit, and breathe on these slain, and they live." ¹⁰And I have prophesied as He commanded me, and the Spirit comes into them, and they live, and stand on their feet—a very, very great force. ¹¹And He says to me, "Son of man, these bones are the whole house of Israel; behold, they are saying, Our bones have dried up, || And our hope has perished, || We have been cut off by ourselves. ¹²Therefore, prophesy, and you have said to them, Thus said Lord YHWH: Behold, I am opening your graves, || And have brought you up out of your graves, O My people, || And brought you into the land of Israel. ¹³And you have known that I [am] YHWH, || In My opening your graves, || And in My bringing you up out of your graves, O My people. ¹⁴And I have given My Spirit in you, and you have lived, || And I have caused you to rest on your land, || And you have known that I, YHWH, have spoken, and I have done [it], || A declaration of YHWH." ¹⁵And there is a word of YHWH to me, saying, ¹⁶"And you, son of man, take one stick for yourself, and write on it, || For Judah, and for the sons of Israel, his companions; and take another stick, and write on it, || For Joseph, the stick of Ephraim, and all the house of Israel, his companions, ¹⁷and bring them near to one another, to you, for one stick, and they have become one in your hand. ¹⁸And when sons of your people speak to you, saying, Do you not declare to us what these [are] to you? ¹⁹Speak to them, Thus said Lord YHWH: Behold, I am taking the stick of Joseph, that [is] in the hand of Ephraim, and the tribes of Israel his companions, and have given them to him, with the stick of Judah, and have made them become one stick, and they have been one in My hand. ²⁰And the sticks on which you write have been in your hand before your eyes, ²¹and speak to them, Thus said Lord YHWH: Behold, I am taking the sons of Israel, || From among the nations to where they have gone, || And have gathered them from all around, || And I have brought them into their land. ²²And I have made them become one nation in the land, on mountains of Israel, || And one king is to them all for king, || And they are no longer as two nations, || Nor are they divided anymore into two kingdoms again. ²³Nor are they defiled anymore with their idols, || And with their abominations, || And with any of their transgressions, || And I have saved them out of all their dwellings, || In which they have sinned, || And I have cleansed them, || And they have been to Me for a people, || And I am to them for God. ²⁴And My servant David [is] king over them, || And they all have one shepherd, || And they go in My judgments, || And they keep My statutes, and have done them. ²⁵And they have dwelt on the land that I gave to My servant, to Jacob, || In which your fathers have dwelt, || And they have dwelt on it, they and their sons, || And their son's sons—for all time, || And My servant David [is] their prince for all time. ²⁶And I have made a covenant of peace with them, || It is a perpetual covenant with them, || And I have placed them, and multiplied them, || And placed My sanctuary in their midst for all time. ²⁷And My dwelling place has been over them, || And I have been to them for God, || And they have been to Me for a people. ²⁸And the nations have known that I, YHWH, am sanctifying Israel, || In My sanctuary being in their midst for all time!"

CHAPTER 38

¹And there is a word of YHWH to me, saying, ²"Son of man, set your face toward Gog, of the land of Magog, chief prince of [[or prince of Rosh,]] Meshech and Tubal, and prophesy concerning him, ³and you have said, Thus says Lord YHWH: Behold, I [am] against you, O Gog, || Chief prince of [[or prince of Rosh,]] Meshech and Tubal, ⁴And I have turned you back, || And I have put hooks in your jaws, || And have brought you out, and all your force, || Horses and horsemen, || All of them clothed in perfection, || A numerous assembly, [with] buckler and shield, || All of them handling swords. ⁵Persia, Cush, and Phut, with them, || All of them [with] shield and helmet. ⁶Gomer and all its bands, || The house of Togarmah

[from] the sides of the north, || And all its bands, many peoples with you, ⁷Be prepared, indeed, prepare yourself, || You and all your assemblies who are assembled to you, || And you have been for a watch for them. ⁸After many days you are appointed, || In the latter end of the years you come into a land brought back from sword—Gathered out of many peoples, || On mountains of Israel, || That have been for a continuous ruin, || And it has been brought out from the peoples, || And all of them have dwelt safely. ⁹And you have gone up—you come in as desolation, || You are as a cloud to cover the land, || You and all your bands, and many peoples with you. ¹⁰Thus said Lord YHWH: And it has come to pass in that day, || Things come up on your heart, || And you have thought an evil thought, ¹¹And you have said: I go up over a land of open places, || I go to those at rest, dwelling confidently, || All of them are dwelling without walls, || And they have no bar and doors— ¹²To take a spoil, and to take a prey, || To turn back your hand on inhabited ruins, || And on a people gathered out of nations, || Making livestock and substance, || Dwelling on a high part of the land. ¹³Sheba, and Dedan, and merchants of Tarshish, || And all its young lions say to you, || Are you coming to take spoil? Have you assembled your assembly to take prey? To carry away silver and gold? To take away livestock and substance? To take a great spoil? ¹⁴Therefore, prophesy, son of man, and you have said to Gog, Thus said Lord YHWH: In that day, in the dwelling of My people Israel safely, || Do you not know? ¹⁵And you have come in out of your place, || From the sides of the north, || You and many peoples with you, || Riding on horses—all of them, || A great assembly, and a numerous force. ¹⁶And you have come up against My people Israel, || As a cloud to cover the land, || It is in the latter end of the days, || And I have brought you in against My land, || In order that the nations may know Me, || In My being sanctified in you before their eyes, O Gog. ¹⁷Thus said Lord YHWH: Are you he of whom I spoke in former days, || By the hand of My servants, prophets of Israel, || Who were prophesying [for] years in those days, || To bring you in against them? ¹⁸And it has come to pass in that day, || In the day of the coming in of Gog against the land of Israel, || A declaration of Lord YHWH, || My fury comes up in My face, ¹⁹And in My zeal, in the fire of My wrath, || I have spoken: Is there not a great rushing on the land of Israel in that day? ²⁰And rushed from My presence have fishes of the sea, || And the bird of the heavens, || And the beast of the field, || And every creeping thing that is creeping on the ground, || And all men who [are] on the face of the ground, || And the mountains have been thrown down, || And the ascents have fallen, || And every wall falls to the earth. ²¹And I have called for a sword against him throughout all My mountains, || A declaration of Lord YHWH, || The sword of each is against his brother. ²²And I have judged him with pestilence and with blood, || And an overflowing rain and hailstones, || I rain fire and brimstone on him, and on his bands, || And on many peoples who [are] with him. ²³And I have magnified Myself, and sanctified Myself, || And I have been known before the eyes of many nations, || And they have known that I [am] YHWH!"

CHAPTER 39

¹"And you, son of man, prophesy concerning Gog, and you have said, Thus said Lord YHWH: Behold, I [am] against you, O Gog, || Chief prince of [[*or* prince of Rosh,]] Meshech and Tubal, ²And have turned you back, and enticed you, || And caused you to come up from the sides of the north, || And brought you in against mountains of Israel, ³And have struck your bow out of your left hand, || Indeed, I cause your arrows to fall out of your right. ⁴You fall on mountains of Israel, || You, and all your bands, and the peoples who [are] with you, || To ravenous bird—a bird of every wing, || And [to] a beast of the field, I have given you for food. ⁵You fall on the face of the field, for I have spoken, || A declaration of Lord YHWH. ⁶And I have sent a fire against Magog, || And against the confident inhabitants of the islands, || And they have known that I [am] YHWH. ⁷And I make My holy Name known in the midst of My people Israel, || And I do not defile My holy Name anymore, || And the nations have known that I, YHWH, the Holy One, [am] in Israel. ⁸Behold, it has come, and it has been done, || A declaration of Lord YHWH, || It [is] the day of which I spoke. ⁹And those dwelling [in the] cities of Israel have gone out, || And they have burned and kindled [a fire], || With armor, and shield, and buckler, || With bow, and with arrows, || And with hand weapon, and with javelin, || And they have caused a fire to burn seven years with them, ¹⁰And they do not take wood out of the field, || Nor do they hew out of the forests, || For they cause the fire to burn with armor, || And they have spoiled their spoilers, || And they have plundered their plunderers, || A declaration of Lord YHWH. ¹¹And it has come to pass in that day, I give a place to Gog there—a grave in Israel, the valley of those passing by, east of the sea, and it is stopping those passing by, and they have buried there Gog, and all his multitude, and have cried, O valley of the multitude of Gog! ¹²And the house of Israel has buried them—in order to cleanse the land—seven months. ¹³Indeed, all the people of the land have buried them, and it has been to them for a name—the day of My being honored—a declaration of Lord YHWH. ¹⁴And they separate men for continual employment, with those passing through, passing on through the land, burying those who are left on the face of the earth, to cleanse it. At the end of seven months they search. ¹⁵And those passing by have passed through the land, and seen a bone of man, and one has constructed a sign near it until those burying have buried it in the valley of the multitude of Gog. ¹⁶And also the name of the city [is] The Multitude; and they have cleansed the land. ¹⁷And you, son of man, thus said Lord YHWH: Say to the bird—every wing, and to every beast of the field: Be assembled and come in, || Be gathered from all around, || For My sacrifice that I am sacrificing for you, || A great sacrifice on mountains of Israel, || And you have eaten flesh, and drunk blood. ¹⁸You eat [the] flesh of [the] mighty, || And you drink [the] blood of [the] princes of the earth, || Of rams, of lambs, and of male goats, || Of calves, fatlings of Bashan—all of them. ¹⁹And you have eaten fat to satiety, || And you have drunk blood—to drunkenness, || Of My sacrifice that I sacrificed for you. ²⁰And you have been satisfied at My table with horse and rider, || Mighty man, and every man of war, || A declaration of Lord YHWH. ²¹And I have given My glory among nations, || And all the nations have seen My judgment that I have done, || And My hand that I have laid on them. ²²And the house of Israel has known that I [am] their God YHWH, || From that day and from now on. ²³And the nations have known || That the house of Israel was removed for their iniquity, || Because they have trespassed against Me, || And I hide My face from them, || And give them into the hand of their adversaries, || And they fall by sword—all of them. ²⁴According to their uncleanness, || And according to their transgressions, I have done with them, || And I hide My face from them. ²⁵Therefore, thus said Lord YHWH: Now I bring back the captivity of Jacob, || And I have pitied all the house of Israel, || And have been zealous for My holy Name. ²⁶And they have forgotten their shame, || And all their trespass that they trespassed against Me, || In their dwelling on their land confidently and none troubling. ²⁷In My bringing them back from the peoples, || I have assembled them from the lands of their enemies, || And I have been sanctified in them before the eyes of the many nations, ²⁸And they have known that I [am] their God YHWH, || In My removing them to the nations, || And I have gathered them to their land, || And I leave none of them there anymore. ²⁹And I do not hide My face from them anymore, || In that I have poured out My Spirit on the house of Israel, || A declaration of Lord YHWH!"

CHAPTER 40

¹In the twenty-fifth year of our removal, in the beginning of the year, on the tenth of the month, in the fourteenth year after which the city was struck, on this very same day a hand of YHWH has been on me, and He brings me in there; ²in visions of God He has brought me into the land of Israel, and causes me to rest on a very high mountain, and on it [is] as the frame of a city from the south. ³And He brings me in there, and behold, a man, his appearance as the appearance of bronze, and a thread of flax in his hand, and a measuring-reed, and he is standing at the gate, ⁴and the man speaks to me: "Son of man, see with your

eyes, || And hear with your ears, || And set your heart to all that I am showing you, || For in order to show [it] you, || You have been brought in here, || Declare all that you are seeing to the house of Israel." ⁵And behold, a wall all around on the outside of the house, and a measuring-reed in the hand of the man, six cubits by a cubit and a handbreadth, and he measures the breadth of the building—one reed, and the height—one reed. ⁶And he comes to the gate whose front [is] eastward, and he goes up by its steps, and he measures the threshold of the gate—one reed broad, even one threshold—one reed broad, ⁷and the little chamber—one reed long and one reed broad, and between the little chambers—five cubits, and the threshold of the gate, from the side of the porch of the gate from within—one reed. ⁸And he measures the porch of the gate from within—one reed, ⁹and he measures the porch of the gate—eight cubits, and its posts—two cubits, and the porch of the gates from within, ¹⁰and the little chambers of the gate eastward, three on this side and three on that side; the three of them—one measure, and the posts—one measure, on this side and on that side. ¹¹And he measures the breadth of the opening of the gate—ten cubits, the length of the gate—thirteen cubits; ¹²and a border before the little chambers—one cubit, and one cubit [is] the border on this side, and the little chamber—six cubits on this side, and six cubits on that side. ¹³And he measures the gate from the roof of the [one] little chamber to the roof of another; the breadth—twenty-five cubits, opening opposite opening. ¹⁴And he makes the posts of sixty cubits, even to the post of the court, the gate all around; ¹⁵and by the front of the gate of the entrance, by the front of the porch of the inner gate—fifty cubits; ¹⁶and narrow windows [are] in the little chambers, and in their posts on the inside of the gate all around—and so to the arches—and windows all around on the inside, and palm-trees [are] on the post. ¹⁷And he brings me into the outer court, and behold, chambers and a pavement made for the court all around—thirty chambers on the pavement— ¹⁸and the pavement to the side of the gates, corresponding to the length of the gates, [is] the lower pavement; ¹⁹and he measures the breadth from before the lower gate, to the front of the inner court, on the outside—one hundred cubits, eastward and northward. ²⁰As for the gate of the outer court whose front [is] northward, he has measured its length and its breadth; ²¹and its little chambers, three on this side and three on that side, and its posts and its arches have been according to the measure of the first gate, its length [is] fifty cubits, and breadth [is] twenty-five by the cubit; ²²and its windows, and its arches, and its palm-trees [are] according to the measure of the gate whose face [is] eastward, and they go up on it by seven steps, and its arches [are] before them. ²³And the gate of the inner court [is] opposite the gate at the north and at the east; and he measures from gate to gate—one hundred cubits. ²⁴And he causes me to go southward, and behold, a gate southward, and he has measured its posts and its arches according to these measurements; ²⁵and windows [are] in it and in its arches all around, like these windows, the length—fifty cubits, and the breadth—twenty-five cubits; ²⁶and seven steps [are] its ascent, and its arches [are] before them, and palm-trees [are] in it, one on this side and one on that side, on its posts; ²⁷and the gate of the inner court [is] southward, and he measures from gate to gate southward, one hundred cubits. ²⁸And he brings me into the inner court by the south gate, and he measures the south gate according to these measurements; ²⁹and its little chambers, and its posts, and its arches [are] according to these measurements, and windows [are] in it and in its arches all around; the length—fifty cubits, and the breadth—twenty-five cubits. ³⁰As for the arches all around, the length—twenty-five cubits, and the breadth—five cubits; ³¹and its arches [are] toward the outer court, and palm-trees [are] on its posts, and eight steps [are] its ascent. ³²And he brings me into the inner court eastward, and he measures the gate according to these measurements; ³³and its little chambers, and its posts, and its arches [are] according to these measurements: and windows [are] in it and in its arches all around, the length—fifty cubits, and the breadth—twenty-five cubits; ³⁴and its arches [are] toward the outer court, and palm-trees [are] toward its posts, on this side and on that side, and eight steps [are] its ascent. ³⁵And he brings me into the north gate, and has measured according to these measurements; ³⁶its little chambers, its posts, and its arches; and windows [are] in it all around: the length—fifty cubits, and the breadth—twenty five cubits; ³⁷and its posts [are] toward the outer court, and palm-trees [are] on its posts, on this side and on that side, and eight steps [are] its ascent. ³⁸And the chamber and its opening [is] by the posts of the gates, there they purge the burnt-offering. ³⁹And in the porch of the gate [are] two tables on this side and two tables on that side, to slaughter on them the burnt-offering, and the sin-offering, and the guilt-offering; ⁴⁰and at the side without, at the going up to the opening of the north gate, [are] two tables; and at the other side that [is] at the porch of the gate, [are] two tables; ⁴¹four tables [are] on this side and four tables on that side, at the side of the gate, eight tables on which they slaughter. ⁴²And the four tables for burnt-offering [are] of hewn stone: the length—one cubit and a half, and the breadth—one cubit and a half, and the height—one cubit; they place on them the instruments with which they slaughter the burnt-offering and the sacrifice. ⁴³And the boundaries [are] one handbreadth, prepared within all around: and the flesh of the offering [is] on the tables. ⁴⁴And on the outside of the inner gate [are] chambers of the singers, in the inner court, that [are] at the side of the north gate, and their fronts [are] southward, one at the side of the east gate [with] front northward. ⁴⁵And he speaks to me: "This chamber, whose front [is] southward, [is] for priests keeping charge of the house; ⁴⁶and the chamber, whose front [is] northward, [is] for priests keeping charge of the altar: they [are] sons of Zadok, who are drawing near of the sons of Levi to YHWH, to serve Him." ⁴⁷And he measures the court: the length—one hundred cubits, and the breadth—one hundred cubits, square, and the altar [is] before the house. ⁴⁸And he brings me to the porch of the house, and he measures the post of the porch—five cubits on this side and five cubits on that side, and the breadth of the gate—three cubits on this side and three cubits on that side; ⁴⁹the length of the porch—twenty cubits, and the breadth—eleven [[or twelve]] cubits; and they go up to it by the [[ten]] steps. And pillars [are] by the posts, one on this side and one on that side.

CHAPTER 41

¹And he brings me into the temple, and he measures the posts, six cubits the breadth on this side and six cubits the breadth on that side—the breadth of the tent. ²And the breadth of the opening [is] ten cubits; and the sides of the opening [are] five cubits on this side and five cubits on that side; and he measures its length—forty cubits, and the breadth—twenty cubits. ³And he has gone inward, and measures the post of the opening—two cubits, and the opening—six cubits, and the breadth of the opening—seven cubits. ⁴And he measures its length—twenty cubits, and the breadth—twenty cubits, to the front of the temple, and he says to me, "This [is] the Holy of Holies." ⁵And he measures the wall of the house—six cubits, and the breadth of the side-chamber—four cubits, all around the house. ⁶And the side-chambers [are] side-chamber by side-chamber, thirty-three times; and they are entering into the wall—which the house has for the side-chambers all around—to be taken hold of, and they are not taken hold of by the wall of the house. ⁷And it has become wider when one has turned even higher toward the side-chambers, for the encompassment of the house [is] even higher all around the house: therefore the breadth of the house [goes] upwards, and so the lower [story] goes up to the higher by the middle. ⁸And I have looked at the height all around the house: the foundations of the side-chambers [are] the fullness of the reed, six cubits by the joining. ⁹The breadth of that wall, of the side-chamber, at the outside, [is] five cubits; and the space remaining of the side-chambers—that of the house, ¹⁰and between the chambers—[is] a breadth of twenty cubits around the house, all around. ¹¹And the opening of the side-chamber [is] to the remaining [space], one opening northward and one opening southward, and the breadth of the remaining space [is] five cubits all around. ¹²As for the building that [is] at the front of the separate place [at] the corner westward, the breadth [is] seventy cubits, and the wall of the building [is] five cubits broad all around, and its length—ninety cubits. ¹³And he has measured the house, the length [is] one

hundred cubits; and the separate place, and the building, and its walls, the length [is] one hundred cubits; ¹⁴and the breadth of the front of the house, and of the separate place eastward—one hundred cubits. ¹⁵And he has measured the length of the building to the front of the separate place that [is] at its back part, and its galleries on this side and on that side—one hundred cubits. And the inner temple and the porches of the court, ¹⁶the thresholds, and the narrow windows, and the galleries around the three of them, opposite the threshold, [were] paneled with wood all around—and the ground to the windows, and the windows were covered, ¹⁷over above the opening, and to the inner-house, and at the outside, and by all the wall all around inside and outside [by] measurements. ¹⁸And it is made [with] cherubim and palm-trees, and a palm-tree [is] between cherub and cherub, and two faces [are] on the cherub; ¹⁹and the face of a man toward the palm-tree on this side and the face of a young lion toward the palm-tree on that side; it is made to all the house all around. ²⁰From the earth to above the opening the cherubim and the palm-trees [were] made, and [on] the wall of the temple. ²¹The doorpost of the temple [is] square, and of the front of the sanctuary, the appearance [is] as that appearance. ²²Of the altar, the wood [is] three cubits in height, and its length—two cubits; and its corners [are] to it, and its length, and its walls [are] of wood, and he speaks to me, "This [is] the table that [is] before YHWH." ²³And the temple and the sanctuary had two doors; ²⁴and the doors had two panels, two turning panels: two on one door, and two panels on the other. ²⁵And made on them, on the doors of the temple, [are] cherubim and palm-trees as are made on the walls, and a thickness of wood [is] at the front of the porch on the outside. ²⁶And narrow windows and palm-trees [are] on this side and on that side, at the sides of the porch, and the side-chambers of the house, and the thick places.

CHAPTER 42

¹And he brings me forth to the outer court, the way northward, and he brings me into the chamber that [is] opposite the separate place, and that [is] opposite the building at the north. ²At the front of the length [is] one hundred cubits [at] the north opening, and the breadth—fifty cubits. ³Opposite the twenty [cubits] that are of the inner court, and opposite the pavement that [is] of the outer court, [is] gallery [with] face toward gallery, in the three [stories]. ⁴And at the front of the chambers [is] a walk of ten cubits in breadth to the inner part, a way of one cubit, and their openings [are] at the north. ⁵And the upper chambers [are] short, for the galleries contain more than these, than the lower, and than the middle one, of the building; ⁶for they [are] threefold, and they have no pillars as the pillars of the court, therefore it has been kept back—more than the lower and than the middle one—from the ground. ⁷As for the wall that [is] at the outside, alongside the chambers, the way of the outer-court at the front of the chambers, its length [is] fifty cubits; ⁸for the length of the chambers that [are] in the outer court [is] fifty cubits, and of those on the front of the temple—one hundred cubits. ⁹And under these chambers [is] the entrance from the east, in one's going into them from the outer court. ¹⁰In the breadth of the wall from the court eastward, to the front of the separate place, and to the front of the building, [are] chambers. ¹¹And the way before them [is] as the appearance of the chambers that [are] northward, according to their length so [is] their breadth, and all their outlets, and according to their fashions, and according to their openings. ¹²And according to the openings of the chambers that [are] southward [is] an opening at the head of the way, the way directly in the front of the wall eastward in entering them. ¹³And he says to me, "The north chambers, the south chambers, that [are] at the front of the separate place, they [are] holy chambers, where the priests (who [are] near to YHWH) eat the most holy things, there they place the most holy things, and the present, and the sin-offering, and the guilt-offering, for the place [is] holy. ¹⁴In the priests' going in, they do not come out from the sanctuary to the outer court, and there they place their garments with which they minister, for they [are] holy, and have put on other garments, and have drawn near to that which [is] for the people." ¹⁵And he has finished the measurements of the inner house, and has brought me forth the way of the gate whose front [is] eastward, and he has measured it all around. ¹⁶He has measured the east side with the measuring-reed, five hundred reeds, with the measuring-reed all around. ¹⁷He has measured the north side, five hundred reeds, with the measuring reed all around. ¹⁸The south side he has measured, five hundred reeds, with the measuring-reed. ¹⁹He has turned around to the west side, he has measured five hundred reeds with the measuring-reed. ²⁰At the four sides he has measured it; it had a wall all around, the length—five hundred, and the breadth—five hundred, to separate between the holy and the profane place.

CHAPTER 43

¹And he causes me to go to the gate, the gate that is looking eastward. ²And behold, the glory of the God of Israel has come from the way of the east, and His voice [is] as the noise of many waters, and the earth has shone from His glory. ³And according to the appearance [is] the appearance that I saw, as the appearance that I saw in my coming in to destroy the city, and the appearances [are] as the appearance that I saw at the river Chebar, and I fall on my face. ⁴And the glory of YHWH has come into the house, the way of the gate whose face [is] eastward. ⁵And [the] Spirit takes me up, and brings me into the inner court, and behold, the glory of YHWH has filled the house. ⁶And I hear one speaking to me from the house, and a man has been standing near me, ⁷and He says to me: "Son of man, the place of My throne, || And the place of the soles of My feet, || Where I dwell in the midst of the sons of Israel for all time, || The house of Israel defiles My holy Name no longer, || They, and their kings, by their whoredom, || And by the carcasses of their kings—their high places. ⁸In their putting their threshold with My threshold, || And their doorpost near My doorpost, || And the wall between Me and them, || And they have defiled My holy Name, || By their abominations that they have done, || And I consume them in My anger. ⁹Now they put their whoredom far off, || And the carcasses of their kings—from Me, || And I have dwelt in their midst for all time. ¹⁰You, son of man, || Show the house of Israel the house, || And they are ashamed of their iniquities, || And they have measured the measurement. ¹¹And since they have been ashamed of all that they have done, || The form of the house, and its measurement, || And its outlets, and its inlets, and all its forms, || And all its statutes, even all its forms, || And all its laws—cause them to know, || And write [it] before their eyes, || And they observe all its forms, || And all its statutes, and have done them. ¹²This [is] a law of the house: on the top of the mountain, all its border all around [is] most holy; behold, this [is] a law of the house. ¹³And these [are] measurements of the altar by cubits: the cubit [is] a cubit and a handbreadth, and the center [is] a cubit, and the breadth a cubit; and its border on its edge around [is] one span, and this [is] the upper part of the altar. ¹⁴And from the center of the ground to the lower border [is] two cubits, and the breadth—one cubit, and from the lesser border to the greater border—four cubits, and the breadth a cubit. ¹⁵And the altar [is] four cubits, and from the altar and upward [are] four horns. ¹⁶And the altar [is] twelve long by twelve broad, square in its four sides. ¹⁷And the border [is] fourteen long by fourteen broad, at its four sides, and the border around it [is] half a cubit, and the center of it [is] a cubit around, and its steps are looking eastward." ¹⁸And He says to me, "Son of man, thus said Lord YHWH: These [are] statutes of the altar in the day of its being made to cause burnt-offering to go up on it, and to sprinkle blood on it. ¹⁹And you have given to the priests, the Levites—who [are] of the seed of Zadok, who are near to Me, a declaration of Lord YHWH, to serve Me—a calf from the herd, for a sin-offering. ²⁰And you have taken of its blood, and have put it on its four horns, and on the four corners of its border, and on the border all around, and have cleansed it, and purified it. ²¹And you have taken the bullock of the sin-offering, and have burned it in the appointed place of the house at the outside of the sanctuary. ²²And on the second day you bring a kid of the goats near, a perfect one, for a sin-offering, and they have cleansed the altar, as they cleansed [it] for the bullock. ²³In your finishing cleansing, you bring a calf near, a son of the herd, a perfect one, and a ram out of the flock, a perfect one. ²⁴And you have brought them near before YHWH, and the priests have cast salt on them, and have caused them to go up, a burnt-offering to YHWH. ²⁵[For] seven

days you prepare a goat daily for a sin-offering; and they also prepare a bullock, a son of the herd, and a ram out of the flock—perfect ones. ²⁶[For] seven days they purify the altar, and have cleansed it, and filled their hand. ²⁷And the days are completed, and it has come to pass on the eighth day, and from now on, the priests prepare your burnt-offerings and your peace-offerings on the altar, and I have accepted you—a declaration of Lord YHWH."

CHAPTER 44

¹And he causes me to turn back the way of the gate of the outer sanctuary that is looking eastward, and it is shut. ²And YHWH says to me, "This gate is shut, it is not opened, and none go in by it, for YHWH, God of Israel, has come in by it, and it has been shut. ³The prince, who [is] prince, he sits by it to eat bread before YHWH, he comes in by the way of the porch of the gate, and by its way he goes out." ⁴And he brings me in the way of the north gate to the front of the house, and I look, and behold, the glory of YHWH has filled the house of YHWH, and I fall on my face. ⁵And YHWH says to me, "Son of man, set your heart, and see with your eyes, and hear with your ears, all that I am speaking with you, all of the statutes of the house of YHWH, and all of its laws; and you have set your heart to the entrance of the house, with all the outlets of the sanctuary, ⁶and have said to [the] rebellion, to the house of Israel, Thus said Lord YHWH: Enough from you—of all your abominations, O house of Israel. ⁷In your bringing in sons of a stranger, uncircumcised of heart, and uncircumcised of flesh, to be in My sanctuary, to defile it, even My house, in your bringing near My bread, fat, and blood, and they break My covenant by all your abominations, ⁸and you have not kept [the] charge of My holy things, and you set [others] for keeping My charge in My sanctuary for you. ⁹Thus said Lord YHWH: No son of a stranger, uncircumcised of heart, and uncircumcised of flesh, comes into My sanctuary, even any son of a stranger, who [is] in the midst of the sons of Israel. ¹⁰And the Levites who have gone far off from Me, in the wandering of Israel when they went astray from Me after their idols, and they have borne their iniquity. ¹¹And they have been servants in My sanctuary, overseers at the gates of the house, and servants at the house; they slay the burnt-offering and the sacrifice for the people, and they stand before them to serve them. ¹²Because that they serve them before their idols, and have been for a stumbling-block of iniquity to the house of Israel, therefore I have lifted up My hand against them—a declaration of Lord YHWH—and they have borne their iniquity. ¹³And they do not draw near to Me to act as My priest, and to draw near to any of My holy things, to the Holy of Holies, and they have borne their shame and their abominations that they have done, ¹⁴and I made them keepers of the charge of the house, for all its service and for all that is done in it. ¹⁵And the priests, the Levites, sons of Zadok, who have kept the charge of My sanctuary in the wandering of the sons of Israel from off Me, they draw near to Me to serve Me, and have stood before Me, to bring fat and blood near to Me—a declaration of Lord YHWH: ¹⁶they come into My sanctuary, and they draw near to My table to serve Me, and they have kept My charge. ¹⁷And it has come to pass, in their going into the gates of the inner court, they put on linen garments; and no wool comes up on them in their ministering in the gates of the inner court and within. ¹⁸Linen headdresses are on their head, and linen trousers are on their loins, they are not restrained with sweat. ¹⁹And in their going forth to the outer court—to the outer court to the people—they strip off their garments, in which they are ministering, and have placed them in the holy chambers, and have put on other garments; and they do not sanctify the people in their own garments. ²⁰And they do not shave their head, and they do not send forth the lock; they certainly trim their heads. ²¹And no priest drinks wine in their coming into the inner court. ²²And they do not take a widow or divorced woman to themselves for wives, but they take virgins of the seed of the house of Israel, and the widow who is widow of a priest. ²³And they direct My people between holy and common, and they cause them to discern between unclean and clean. ²⁴And concerning controversy, they stand up for judgment; they judge it with My judgments; and they keep My law and My statutes in all My appointed places; and they sanctify My Sabbaths. ²⁵And he does not come near to any dead man to be defiled, but if for father, and for mother, and for son, and for daughter, for brother, for sister who has not been to a man, they may defile themselves. ²⁶And after his cleansing, they number seven days to him. ²⁷And in the day of his coming into the sanctuary, into the inner court, to minister in the sanctuary, he brings his sin-offering near—a declaration of Lord YHWH. ²⁸And it has been for an inheritance to them; I [am] their inheritance, and you do not give a possession to them in Israel; I [am] their possession. ²⁹The present, and the sin-offering, and the guilt-offering, they eat, and every devoted thing in Israel is theirs. ³⁰And the first of all the first-fruits of all, and every raised-offering of all, of all your raised-offerings, are the priests'; and you give the first of your dough to the priest, to cause a blessing to rest on your house. ³¹The priests do not eat any carcass or torn thing, from the bird or from the beast."

CHAPTER 45

¹"And in your causing the land to fall into inheritance, you lift up a raised-offering to YHWH, a holy [portion] of the land: the length—twenty-five thousand [is] the length, and the breadth—ten thousand; it [is] holy in all its surrounding border. ²There is of this for the sanctuary five hundred by five hundred, square, around; and fifty cubits of outskirt [is] around it. ³And by this measure you measure: the length—twenty-five thousand, and the breadth—ten thousand: and the sanctuary is in it, the Holy of Holies. ⁴It [is] the holy [portion] of the land; it is for priests, servants of the sanctuary, who are drawing near to serve YHWH; and it has been a place for their houses, and a holy place for the sanctuary. ⁵And of the twenty-five thousand of length, and of the ten thousand of breadth, there is to the Levites, servants of the house, for them—for a possession—twenty chambers. ⁶And of the possession of the city you set [an area] of five thousand breadth, and twenty-five thousand length, alongside the raised-offering of the holy [portion]; it is for all the house of Israel. ⁷And for the prince: on this side and on that side of the raised-offering of the holy place, and of the possession of the city, at the front of the raised-offering of the holy place, and at the front of the possession of the city, from the west corner westward, and from the east corner eastward—and the length [is] corresponding to one of the portions from the west border to the east border— ⁸of the land there is for a possession to him in Israel, and My princes do not oppress My people anymore, and they give the land to the house of Israel according to their tribes." ⁹Thus said Lord YHWH: "Enough from you—princes of Israel; turn violence and spoil aside, and do judgment and righteousness; lift up your exactions from off My people—a declaration of Lord YHWH. ¹⁰You must have just balances, and a just ephah, and a just bath. ¹¹The ephah and the bath is of one measure, for the bath to carry a tenth of the homer, and the ephah a tenth of the homer: its measurement is according to the homer. ¹²And the shekel [is] twenty gerah: twenty shekels, twenty-five shekels, fifteen shekels—is your maneh. ¹³This [is] the raised-offering that you lift up; a sixth part of the ephah of a homer of wheat, also you have given a sixth part of the ephah of a homer of barley, ¹⁴and the portion of oil, the bath of oil, a tenth part of the bath out of the cor, a homer of ten baths—for ten baths [are] a homer; ¹⁵and one lamb out of the flock, out of two hundred, out of the watered country of Israel, for a present, and for a burnt-offering, and for peace-offerings, to make atonement by them—a declaration of Lord YHWH. ¹⁶All the people of the land are at this raised-offering for the prince in Israel. ¹⁷And on the prince are the burnt-offerings, and the present, and the drink-offering, in celebrations, and in new moons, and in Sabbaths, in all appointed times of the house of Israel: he makes the sin-offering, and the present, and the burnt-offering, and the peace-offerings, to make atonement for the house of Israel." ¹⁸Thus said Lord YHWH: "In the first [month], on the first of the month, you take a bullock, a son of the herd, a perfect one, and have cleansed the sanctuary: ¹⁹and the priest has taken from the blood of the sin offering, and has put [it] on the doorpost of the house, and on the four corners of the border of the altar, and on the post of the gate of the inner court. ²⁰And so you do on the seventh of the month, because of each erring one, and because of the simple one—and you have purified the house. ²¹In the first [month], on the fourteenth day of the month, you have the Passover, a celebration of seven days,

unleavened bread is eaten. ²²And the prince has prepared on that day, for himself, and for all the people of the land, a bullock, a sin-offering. ²³And [on] the seven days of the celebration he prepares a burnt-offering to Yhwh, seven bullocks, and seven rams, perfect ones, daily [for] seven days, and a sin-offering, a kid of the goats, daily. ²⁴And he prepares a present of an ephah for a bullock, and an ephah for a ram, and a hin of oil for an ephah. ²⁵In the seventh [month], on the fifteenth day of the month, in the celebration, he does according to these things [for] seven days; as the sin-offering so the burnt-offering, and as the present so also the oil."

CHAPTER 46

¹Thus said Lord Yhwh: "The gate of the inner court that is looking eastward is shut [during] the six days of work, and on the day of rest it is opened, and in the day of the new moon it is opened; ²and the prince has come in the way of the porch of the gate from the outside, and he has stood by the post of the gate, and the priests have made his burnt-offering, and his peace-offerings, and he has bowed himself by the opening of the gate, and has gone forth, and the gate is not shut until the evening. ³And the people of the land have bowed themselves at the opening of that gate, on Sabbaths, and on new moons, before Yhwh. ⁴And the burnt-offering that the prince brings near to Yhwh on the day of rest [is] six lambs, perfect ones, and a ram, a perfect one. ⁵And the present [is] an ephah for a ram, and for the lambs a present, the gift of his hand, and a hin of oil for an ephah. ⁶And on the day of the new moon—a bullock, a son of the herd, a perfect one, and six lambs and a ram; they are perfect. ⁷And with an ephah for a bullock, and an ephah for a ram, he prepares a present, and for the lambs as his hand attains, and a hin of oil for an ephah. ⁸And in the coming in of the prince, he comes in the way of the porch of the gate, and by its way he goes out. ⁹And in the coming in of the people of the land before Yhwh at appointed times, he who has come in the way of the north gate to bow himself, goes out the way of the south gate, and he who has come in the way of the south gate, goes out by the way of the north gate: he does not turn back the way of the gate by which he came in, but he goes out opposite it. ¹⁰And in their coming in the prince in their midst comes in, and in their going out he goes out. ¹¹And in celebrations, and in appointed times, the present is an ephah for a bullock, and an ephah for a ram, and for lambs the gift of his hand, and a hin of oil for an ephah. ¹²And when the prince makes a free-will burnt-offering, or free-will peace-offerings, to Yhwh, then he has opened the gate that is looking eastward for himself, and has made his burnt-offering and his peace-offerings as he does in the day of rest, and he has gone out, and has shut the gate after his going out. ¹³And you make a daily burnt-offering of a lamb, son of a year, a perfect one, to Yhwh; you make it morning by morning. ¹⁴And you make a present with it morning by morning, a sixth part of the ephah, and a third part of the hin of oil, to temper with the fine flour, a present to Yhwh, by a continuous statute—continually; ¹⁵and they prepare the lamb, and the present, and the oil, morning by morning—a continual burnt-offering." ¹⁶Thus said Lord Yhwh: "When the prince gives a gift to any of his sons, it [is] his inheritance, it [is] for his sons; it [is] their possession by inheritance. ¹⁷And when he gives a gift out of his inheritance to one of his servants, then it has been his until the year of freedom, and it has turned back to the prince, only the inheritance of his sons is theirs. ¹⁸And the prince does not take from the people's inheritance to oppress them—from their possession; he causes his sons to inherit out of his own possession, so that My people are not each scattered from his possession." ¹⁹And he brings me in through the entrance that [is] by the side of the gate, to the holy chambers, to the priests, that are looking northward, and behold, there [is] a place in their two sides westward. ²⁰And he says to me, "This [is] the place where the priests boil the guilt-offering and the sin-offering, where they bake the present, so as not to bring [it] out to the outer court, to sanctify the people." ²¹And he brings me out to the outer court, and causes me to pass over to the four corners of the court, and behold, a court in a corner of the court, [moreover] a court in [every] corner of the corner. ²²In the four corners of the court [are] enclosed courts, forty long and thirty broad, [with] one measure for the four corners. ²³And a row [is] all around in them—around the four of them—and made with boilers under the rows all around. ²⁴And he says to me, "These [are] the houses of those boiling where the servants of the house boil the sacrifice of the people."

CHAPTER 47

¹And he causes me to turn back to the opening of the house; and behold, water is coming forth from under the threshold of the house eastward, for the front of the house [is] eastward, and the water is coming down from beneath, from the right side of the house, from south of the altar. ²And he causes me to go out the way of the gate northward, and causes me to turn around the way outside, to the gate that [is] outside, the way that is looking eastward, and behold, water is coming forth from the right side. ³In the going out of the man eastward—and a line in his hand—then he measures one thousand by the cubit, and he causes me to pass over into the waters—waters [to my] ankles. ⁴And he measures one thousand, and causes me to pass over into the waters—waters [to my] knees. And he measures one thousand, and causes me to pass over—waters [to my] loins. ⁵And he measures one thousand—a stream that I am not able to pass over; for the waters have risen—waters to swim in—a stream that is not passed over. ⁶And he says to me, "Have you seen, son of man?" And he leads me, and brings me back to the edge of the stream. ⁷In my turning back, then, behold, at the edge of the stream [are] very many trees, on this side and on that side. ⁸And he says to me, "These waters are going forth to the east circuit, and have gone down to the desert, and have entered the sea; they are brought forth to the sea, and the waters have been healed. ⁹And it has come to pass, every living creature that teems, wherever the streams come, lives: and there has been great abundance of fish, for these waters have come there, and they are healed; and everything to where the stream comes has lived. ¹⁰And it has come to pass, fishers stand by it, from En-Gedi even to En-Eglaim; they are a spreading place for the nets; their fish are of the same kind as the fish of the Great Sea—very many. ¹¹Its miry and its marshy places—they are not healed; they have been given up to salt. ¹²And there comes up by the stream, on its edge, on this side and on that side, every [kind of] fruit-tree whose leaf does not fade, and its fruit is not consumed, it yields first-fruits according to its months, because its waters are coming forth from the sanctuary; and its fruits have been for food, and its leaf for medicine." ¹³Thus said Lord Yhwh: "This [is] the border whereby you inherit the land, according to the twelve tribes of Israel; Joseph [has two] portions. ¹⁴And you have inherited it, one as well as another, in that I have lifted up My hand to give it to your fathers; and this land has fallen to you in inheritance. ¹⁵And this [is] the border of the land at the north quarter; from the Great Sea, the way of Hethlon, at the coming in to Zedad: ¹⁶Hamath, Berothah, Sibraim, that [is] between the border of Damascus and the border of Hamath; Hazar-Hatticon, that [is] at the coast of Havran. ¹⁷And the border from the sea has been Hazar-Enan, the border of Damascus, and Zaphon at the north, and the border of Hamath: and [this is] the north quarter. ¹⁸And the east quarter [is] from between Havran, and Damascus, and Gilead, and the land of Israel, [to] the Jordan; you measure from the border on the Eastern Sea: and [this is] the east quarter. ¹⁹And the south quarter southward [is] from Tamar to the waters of Meriboth-Kadesh, the stream to the Great Sea: and [this is] the south quarter southward. ²⁰And the west quarter [is] the Great Sea, from the border until opposite the coming in to Hamath: this [is] the west quarter. ²¹And you have divided this land to yourselves, according to the tribes of Israel; ²²and it has come to pass, you separate it for an inheritance to yourselves, and to the sojourners who are sojourning in your midst, who have begotten sons in your midst, and they have been to you as native, with the sons of Israel; they are separated with you for an inheritance in the midst of the tribes of Israel. ²³And it has come to pass, in the tribe with which the sojourner sojourns, there you give his inheritance," a declaration of Lord Yhwh.

CHAPTER 48

¹"And these [are] the names of the tribes: from the north end to the side of the way of Hethlon, at the coming in to Hamath, Hazar-Enan, the border of Damascus northward, in the direction of Hamath, and they have been his—

east side to west, Dan, one [portion]; ²and by the border of Dan, from the east side to the west side, Asher, one [portion]; ³and by the border of Asher, from the east side even to the west side, Naphtali, one [portion]; ⁴and by the border of Naphtali, from the east side to the west side, Manasseh, one [portion]; ⁵and by the border of Manasseh, from the east side to the west side, Ephraim, one [portion]; ⁶and by the border of Ephraim, from the east side even to the west side, Reuben, one [portion]; ⁷and by the border of Reuben, from the east side to the west side, Judah, one [portion]; ⁸and by the border of Judah, from the east side to the west side is the raised-offering that you lift up, twenty-five thousand [cubits] broad and long, as one of the parts, from the east side to the west side: and the sanctuary has been in its midst. ⁹The raised-offering that you lift up to YHWH [is] twenty-five thousand long and ten thousand broad. ¹⁰And of these is the holy raised-offering for the priests, northward twenty-five thousand, and westward ten thousand [in] breadth, and eastward ten thousand [in] breadth, and southward twenty-five thousand [in] length: and the sanctuary of YHWH has been in its midst. ¹¹For the priests who are sanctified of the sons of Zadok, who have kept My charge, who did not err in the erring of the sons of Israel, as the Levites erred, ¹²even the raised-offering has been for them, out of the raised-offering of the land, most holy, by the border of the Levites. ¹³And [to] the Levites alongside the border of the priests [are] twenty-five thousand [in] length, and ten thousand [in] breadth, all the length [is] twenty-five thousand, and the breadth ten thousand. ¹⁴And they do not sell of it, nor exchange, nor cause the first-fruit of the land to pass away: for [it is] holy to YHWH. ¹⁵And the five thousand that is left in the breadth, on the front of the twenty-five thousand, is common—for the city, for dwelling, and for outskirt, and the city has been in its midst. ¹⁶And these [are] its measurements: the north side—four thousand and five hundred, and the south side—four thousand and five hundred, and on the east side—four thousand and five hundred, and the west side—four thousand and five hundred. ¹⁷And the outskirt of the city has been northward—two hundred and fifty, and southward—two hundred and fifty, and eastward—two hundred and fifty, and westward—two hundred and fifty. ¹⁸And the remainder in length alongside the raised-offering of the holy [portion is] ten thousand eastward, and ten thousand westward, and it has been alongside the raised-offering of the holy [portion], and its increase has been for food for those serving the city, ¹⁹even [to] him who is serving the city, they serve it out of all the tribes of Israel. ²⁰All the raised-offering [is] twenty-five thousand by twenty-five thousand square—you lift up the raised-offering of the holy [portion] with the possession of the city. ²¹And the remainder [is] for the prince, on this side and on that side of the raised-offering of the holy [portion], and of the possession of the city, on the front of the twenty-five thousand of the raised-offering to the east border, and westward, on the front of the twenty-five thousand on the west border, alongside the portions of the prince; and the raised-offering of the holy [portion], and the sanctuary of the house, has been in its midst. ²²And from the possession of the Levites, from the possession of the city, in the midst of that which is for the prince, between the border of Judah and the border of Benjamin, there is for the prince. ²³As for the rest of the tribes, from the east side to the west side, Benjamin, one [portion]; ²⁴and by the border of Benjamin, from the east side to the west side, Simeon, one [portion]; ²⁵and by the border of Simeon, from the east side to the west side, Issachar, one [portion]; ²⁶and by the border of Issachar, from the east side to the west side, Zebulun, one [portion]; ²⁷and by the border of Zebulun, from the east side to the west side, Gad, one [portion]; ²⁸and by the border of Gad, at the south side southward, the border has been from Tamar [to] the waters of Meriboth-Kadesh, the stream by the Great Sea. ²⁹This [is] the land that you separate by inheritance to the tribes of Israel, and these [are] their divisions," a declaration of Lord YHWH. ³⁰"And these [are] the outgoings of the city: on the north side, four thousand and five hundred measures; ³¹and the gates of the city [are] according to the names of the tribes of Israel; three gates northward—one gate of Reuben, one gate of Judah, one gate of Levi. ³²And on the east side, four thousand and five hundred, and three gates—one gate of Joseph, one gate of Benjamin, one gate of Dan. ³³And the south side, four thousand and five hundred, and three gates—one gate of Simeon, one gate of Issachar, one gate of Zebulun. ³⁴The west side, four thousand and five hundred, [with] their three gates—one gate of Gad, one gate of Asher, one gate of Naphtali. ³⁵[It is] eighteen thousand around, and the renown of the city [is] from the day YHWH [is] there."

DANIEL

CHAPTER 1

¹In the third year of the reign of Jehoiakim king of Judah, Nebuchadnezzar king of Babylon has come to Jerusalem, and lays siege against it; ²and the Lord gives into his hand Jehoiakim king of Judah, and some of the vessels of the house of God, and he brings them in [to] the land of Shinar, [to] the house of his god, and the vessels he has brought in [to] the treasure-house of his god. ³And the king says, to Ashpenaz master of his eunuchs, to bring in out of the sons of Israel (even of the royal seed, and of the chiefs), ⁴boys in whom there is no blemish, and of good appearance, and skillful in all wisdom, and possessing knowledge, and teaching thought, and who have ability to stand in the palace of the king, and to teach them the literature and language of the Chaldeans. ⁵And the king appoints for them a rate, day by day, of the king's portion of food, and of the wine of his drinking, so as to nourish them three years, that at the end thereof they may stand before the king. ⁶And there are among them out of the sons of Judah, Daniel, Hananiah, Mishael, and Azariah, ⁷and the chief of the eunuchs sets names on them, and he sets on Daniel, Belteshazzar; and on Hananiah, Shadrach; and on Mishael, Meshach; and on Azariah, Abed-Nego. ⁸And Daniel purposes in his heart that he will not defile himself with the king's portion of food, and with the wine of his drinking, and he seeks of the chief of the eunuchs that he may not defile himself. ⁹And God gives Daniel for kindness and for mercies before the chief of the eunuchs; ¹⁰and the chief of the eunuchs says to Daniel, "I am fearing my lord the king, who has appointed your food and your drink, for why does he see your faces sadder than [those of] the boys which [are] of your circle? Then you have made my head indebted to the king," ¹¹And Daniel says to the Meltzar, whom the chief of the eunuchs has appointed over Daniel, Hananiah, Mishael, and Azariah, ¹²"Please try your servants [for] ten days; and they give to us from the vegetables and we eat, and water, and we drink; ¹³and our appearance is seen before you, and the appearance of the boys who are eating the king's portion of food, and as you see—deal with your servants." ¹⁴And he listens to them, to this word, and tries them ten days: ¹⁵and at the end of ten days their appearance has appeared better and fatter in flesh then any of the boys who are eating the king's portion of food. ¹⁶And the Meltzar is taking away their portion of food, and the wine of their drink, and is giving to them vegetables. ¹⁷As for these four boys, God has given to them knowledge and understanding in every [kind of] literature, and wisdom; and Daniel has given instruction about every [kind of] vision and dreams. ¹⁸And at the end of the days that the king had said to bring them in, the chief of the eunuchs brings them in before Nebuchadnezzar. ¹⁹And the king speaks with them, and there has not been found among them all like Daniel, Hananiah, Mishael, and Azariah, and they stand before the king; ²⁰and [in] any matter of wisdom [and]

understanding that the king has sought of them, he finds them ten hands above all the enchanters, the conjurers, who [are] in all his kingdom. ²¹And Daniel is to the first year of Cyrus the king.

CHAPTER 2

¹And in the second year of the reign of Nebuchadnezzar, Nebuchadnezzar has dreamed dreams, and his spirit moves itself, and his sleep has been against him; ²and the king says to call for enchanters, and for conjurers, and for sorcerers, and for Chaldeans, to declare to the king his dreams. And they come in and stand before the king; ³and the king says to them, "I have dreamed a dream, and my spirit is moved to know the dream." ⁴And the Chaldeans speak to the king [in] Aramaic, "O king, live for all ages, tell the dream to your servants, and we show the interpretation." ⁵The king has answered and said to the Chaldeans, "The thing is gone from me; if you do not cause me to know the dream and its interpretation, you are made pieces, and your houses are made dunghills; ⁶and if the dream and its interpretation you show, gifts, and fee, and great glory you receive from before me, therefore the dream and its interpretation you show me." ⁷They have answered a second time, and are saying, "Let the king tell the dream to his servants, and we show the interpretation." ⁸The king has answered and said, "Of a truth I know that you are gaining time, because that you have seen that the thing is gone from me, ⁹[so] that, if you do not cause me to know the dream—one is your sentence, seeing a lying and corrupt word you have prepared to speak before me, until the time is changed, therefore tell the dream to me, then I know that you show me its interpretation." ¹⁰The Chaldeans have answered before the king, and are saying, "There is not a man on the earth who is able to show the king's matter; therefore, no king, chief, and ruler, has asked such a thing as this of any scribe, and enchanter, and Chaldean; ¹¹and the thing that the king is asking [is] precious, and there are no others that show it before the king, except the gods, whose dwelling is not with flesh." ¹²Therefore the king has been furious and very angry, and has said to destroy all the wise men of Babylon. ¹³And the sentence has gone forth, and the wise men are being slain, and they have sought Daniel and his companions to be slain. ¹⁴Then Daniel has replied [with] counsel and discretion to Arioch chief of the executioners of the king, who has gone forth to slay the wise men of Babylon. ¹⁵He has answered and said to Arioch the king's captain, "Why [is] the sentence so urgent from before the king?" Then Arioch has made the thing known to Daniel, ¹⁶and Daniel has gone up, and sought of the king that he would give him time to show the interpretation to the king. ¹⁷Then Daniel has gone to his house, and to Hananiah, Mishael, and Azariah, his companions, he has made the thing known, ¹⁸and to seek mercies from before the God of the heavens concerning this secret, that they do not destroy Daniel and his companions with the rest of the wise men of Babylon. ¹⁹Then to Daniel, in a vision of the night, the secret has been revealed. Then Daniel has blessed the God of the heavens. ²⁰Daniel has answered and said, "Let the Name of God be blessed from age even to age, for wisdom and might—for they are His. ²¹And He is changing times and seasons, He is causing kings to pass away, and He is raising up kings; He is giving wisdom to the wise, and knowledge to those possessing understanding. ²²He is revealing deep and hidden things; He has known what [is] in darkness, and light has dwelt with Him. ²³You, O God of my fathers, I am thanking and praising, for wisdom and might You have given to me; and now, You have caused me to know that which we have sought from You, for the king's matter You have caused us to know." ²⁴Therefore Daniel has gone up to Arioch, whom the king has appointed to destroy the wise men of Babylon; he has gone, and thus has said to him, "You do not destroy the wise men of Babylon, bring me up before the king, and I show the interpretation to the king." ²⁵Then Arioch in haste has brought up Daniel before the king, and thus has said to him, "I have found a man of the sons of the expulsion of Judah, who makes known the interpretation to the king." ²⁶The king has answered and said to Daniel, whose name [is] Belteshazzar, "Are you able to cause me to know the dream that I have seen, and its interpretation?" ²⁷Daniel has answered before the king and said, "The secret that the king is asking, the wise men, the enchanters, the scribes, the soothsayers, are not able to show to the king; ²⁸but there is a God in the heavens, a revealer of secrets, and He has made known to King Nebuchadnezzar that which [is] to be in the latter end of the days. Your dream and the visions of your head on your bed are these: ²⁹You, O king, your thoughts on your bed have come up [concerning] that which [is] to be after this, and the Revealer of secrets has caused you to know that which [is] to be. ³⁰As for me—not for [any] wisdom that is in me above any living has this secret been revealed to me; but for the intent that the interpretation to the king they make known, and the thoughts of your heart you know. ³¹You, O king, were looking, and behold, a certain great image. This image [is] mighty, and its brightness excellent; it is standing before you, and its appearance [is] terrible. ³²This image! Its head [is] of fine gold, its breasts and its arms of silver, its belly and its thighs of bronze; ³³its legs of iron, its feet, part of them of iron, and part of them of clay. ³⁴You were looking until a stone has been cut out without hands, and it has struck the image on its feet, that [are] of iron and of clay, and it has broken them small; ³⁵then broken small together have been the iron, the clay, the bronze, the silver, and the gold, and they have been as chaff from the summer threshing-floor, and the wind has carried them away, and no place has been found for them: and the stone that struck the image has become a great mountain, and has filled all the land. ³⁶This [is] the dream, and its interpretation we tell before the king. ³⁷You, O king, are a king of kings, for the God of the heavens a kingdom, strength, and might, and glory, has given to you; ³⁸and wherever sons of men are dwelling, the beast of the field, and the bird of the heavens, He has given into your hand, and has caused you to rule over them all; you [are] this head of gold. ³⁹And after you another kingdom arises lower than those, and another third kingdom of bronze, that rules over all the earth. ⁴⁰And the fourth kingdom is strong as iron, because that iron is breaking small, and making feeble, all [things], even as iron that is breaking all these, it beats small and breaks. ⁴¹As for that which you have seen: the feet and toes, part of them potter's clay, and part of them iron, the kingdom is divided: and some of the standing of the iron [is] to be in it, because that you have seen the iron mixed with miry clay. ⁴²As for the toes of the feet, part of them iron, and part of them clay: some part of the kingdom is strong, and some part of it is brittle. ⁴³Because you have seen iron mixed with miry clay, they are mixing themselves with the seed of men: and they are not adhering with one another, even as iron is not mixed with clay. ⁴⁴And in the days of these kings the God of the heavens raises up a kingdom that is not destroyed for all time, and its kingdom is not left to another people: it beats small and ends all these kingdoms, and it stands for all time. ⁴⁵Because that you have seen that out of the mountain a stone has been cut without hands, and it has beaten the iron small, the bronze, the clay, the silver, and the gold; the great God has made known to the king that which [is] to be after this; and the dream [is] true, and its interpretation steadfast." ⁴⁶Then King Nebuchadnezzar has fallen on his face, and to Daniel he has done homage, and present, and sweet things, he has said to pour out to him. ⁴⁷The king has answered Daniel and said, "Of a truth [it is] that your God is a God of gods, and a Lord of kings, and a revealer of secrets, since you have been able to reveal this secret." ⁴⁸Then the king has made Daniel great, and many great gifts he has given to him, and has caused him to rule over all the province of Babylon, and chief of the prefects over all the wise men of Babylon. ⁴⁹And Daniel has sought from the king, and he has appointed over the work of the province of Babylon, Shadrach, Meshach, and Abed-Nego, and Daniel [is] in the gate of the king.

CHAPTER 3

¹Nebuchadnezzar the king has made an image of gold, its height sixty cubits, its breadth six cubits; he has raised it up in the Valley of Dura, in the province of Babylon; ²and Nebuchadnezzar the king has sent to gather the satraps, the prefects, and the governors, the counselors, the treasurers, the judges, the magistrates, and all the rulers of the province, to come to the dedication of the image that Nebuchadnezzar the king has raised up. ³Then are gathered the satraps, the prefects, and the governors, the counselors, the

treasurers, the judges, the magistrates, and all the rulers of the province, to the dedication of the image that Nebuchadnezzar the king has raised up: and they are standing before the image that Nebuchadnezzar has raised up. ⁴And a crier is calling mightily: "They are saying to you: O peoples, nations, and languages! ⁵At the time that you hear the voice of the horn, the flute, the harp, the lyre, the stringed instrument, the symphony, and all kinds of music, you fall down and pay respect to the golden image that Nebuchadnezzar the king has raised up: ⁶and whoever does not fall down and pay respect, in that hour he is cast into the midst of a burning fiery furnace." ⁷Therefore at that time, when all the peoples are hearing the voice of the horn, the flute, the harp, the lyre, the stringed instrument, and all kinds of music, falling down are all the peoples, nations and languages, worshiping the golden image that Nebuchadnezzar the king has raised up. ⁸Therefore at that time certain Chaldeans have drawn near, and accused the Jews; ⁹they have answered, indeed, they are saying to Nebuchadnezzar the king, "O king, live for all ages! ¹⁰You, O king, have made a decree that every man who hears the voice of the horn, the flute, the harp, the lyre, the stringed instrument, and the symphony, and all kinds of music, falls down and pays respect to the golden image; ¹¹and whoever does not fall down and pay respect, is cast into the midst of a burning fiery furnace. ¹²There are certain Jews whom you have appointed over the work of the province of Babylon—Shadrach, Meshach, and Abed-Nego, these men have not made of you, O king, [any] regard; your gods they are not serving, and to the golden image you have raised up—are not making worship." ¹³Then Nebuchadnezzar, in anger and fury, has said to bring in Shadrach, Meshach, and Abed-Nego. Then these men have been brought in before the king. ¹⁴Nebuchadnezzar has answered and said to them, "Is [it] a laid plan, O Shadrach, Meshach, and Abed-Nego—my gods you are not serving, and to the golden image that I have raised up you are not worshiping? ¹⁵Now behold, you are ready, so that at the time that you hear the voice of the horn, the flute, the harp, the lyre, the stringed instrument, and the symphony, and all kinds of music, you fall down and pay respect to the image that I have made! But if you do not worship—in that hour you are cast into the midst of a burning fiery furnace; who is that God who delivers you out of my hands?" ¹⁶Shadrach, Meshach, and Abed-Nego have answered, indeed, they are saying to King Nebuchadnezzar, "We have no need concerning this matter to answer you. ¹⁷Behold, it is; our God whom we are serving, is able to deliver us from a burning fiery furnace; and from your hand, O king, He delivers. ¹⁸And behold—not! Be it known to you, O king, that we are not serving your gods, and we do not worship the golden image you have raised up." ¹⁹Then Nebuchadnezzar has been full of fury, and the expression of his face has been changed concerning Shadrach, Meshach, and Abed-Nego; he answered and said to heat the furnace seven times above that which it is seen to be heated; ²⁰and to certain mighty men who [are] in his force he has said to bind Shadrach, Meshach, and Abed-Nego, to cast into the burning fiery furnace. ²¹Then these men have been bound in their coats, their tunics, and their turbans, and their clothing, and have been cast into the midst of the burning fiery furnace. ²²Therefore, because that the word of the king is urgent, and the furnace heated exceedingly, those men who have taken up Shadrach, Meshach, and Abed-Nego—the spark of the fire has killed them. ²³And these three men, Shadrach, Meshach, and Abed-Nego, have fallen down in the midst of the burning fiery furnace—bound. ²⁴Then Nebuchadnezzar the king has been astonished, and has risen in haste; he has answered and said to his counselors, "Have we not cast three men into the midst of the fire—bound?" They have answered and are saying to the king, "Certainly, O king." ²⁵He answered and has said, "Behold, I am seeing four men loose, walking in the midst of the fire, and they have no hurt; and the appearance of the fourth [is] like to a son of the gods." ²⁶Then Nebuchadnezzar has drawn near to the gate of the burning fiery furnace; he has answered and said, "Shadrach, Meshach, and Abed-Nego, servants of God Most High come forth, indeed, come"; then Shadrach, Meshach, and Abed-Nego come forth, from the midst of the fire; ²⁷and gathered together, the satraps, the prefects, and the governors, and the counselors of the king, are seeing these men, that the fire has no power over their bodies, and the hair of their head has not been singed, and their coats have not changed, and the smell of fire has not passed on them. ²⁸Nebuchadnezzar has answered and has said, "Blessed [is] the God of Shadrach, Meshach, and Abed-Nego, who has sent His messenger, and has delivered His servants who trusted on Him." And the word of the king changed, and gave up their bodies that they might not serve nor pay respect to any god except to their own God. ²⁹"And by me a decree is made, that any people, nation, and language, that speaks erroneously concerning the God of Shadrach, Meshach, and Abed-Nego, he is made pieces, and its house is made a dunghill, because that there is no other god who is able thus to deliver." ³⁰Then the king has caused Shadrach, Meshach, and Abed-Nego, to prosper in the province of Babylon.

CHAPTER 4

¹"Nebuchadnezzar the king to all peoples, nations, and languages, who are dwelling in all the earth: Your peace be great! ²The signs and wonders that God Most High has done with me, it is good before me to show. ³How great His signs! And how mighty His wonders! His kingdom [is] a continuous kingdom, and His rule [is] with generation and generation. ⁴I, Nebuchadnezzar, have been at rest in my house, and flourishing in my palace; ⁵a dream I have seen, and it makes me afraid, and the conceptions on my bed, and the visions of my head, trouble me. ⁶And by me a decree is made, to cause all the wise men of Babylon to come up before me, that the interpretation of the dream they may cause me to know. ⁷Then coming up are the scribes, the enchanters, the Chaldeans, and the soothsayers, and the dream I have told before them, and its interpretation they are not making known to me. ⁸And at last Daniel has come up before me, whose name [is] Belteshazzar—according to the name of my god—and in whom [is] the spirit of the holy gods, and the dream before him I have told: ⁹O Belteshazzar, master of the scribes, as I have known that the spirit of the holy gods [is] in you, and no secret presses you, the visions of my dream that I have seen, and its interpretation, tell. ¹⁰As for the visions of my head on my bed, I was looking, and behold, a tree in the midst of the earth, and its height [is] great: ¹¹the tree has become great, indeed, strong, and its height reaches to the heavens, and its vision to the end of the whole land; ¹²its leaves [are] beautiful, and its budding great, and food for all [is] in it: under it the beast of the field takes shade, and in its boughs dwell the birds of the heavens, and of it are all flesh fed. ¹³I was looking, in the visions of my head on my bed, and behold, a sifter, even a holy one, from the heavens is coming down. ¹⁴He is calling mightily, and thus has said, Cut down the tree, and cut off its branches, shake off its leaves, and scatter its budding, move away let the beast from under it, and the birds from off its branches; ¹⁵but the stump of its roots leave in the earth, even with a band of iron and bronze, in the tender grass of the field, and with the dew of the heavens is it wet, and with the beasts [is] his portion in the herb of the earth; ¹⁶his heart from man's is changed, and the heart of a beast is given to him, and seven times pass over him; ¹⁷by the decree of the sifters [is] the sentence, and by the saying of the holy ones the requirement, to the intent that the living may know that the Most High is ruler in the kingdom of men, and to whom He wills He gives it, and the lowest of men He raises up over it. ¹⁸This dream I have seen, I King Nebuchadnezzar; and you, O Belteshazzar, tell the interpretation, because that all the wise men of my kingdom are not able to cause me to know the interpretation, and you [are] able, for the spirit of the holy gods [is] in you." ¹⁹Then Daniel, whose name [is] Belteshazzar, has been astonished about one hour, and his thoughts trouble him; the king has answered and said, "O Belteshazzar, do not let the dream and its interpretation trouble you." Belteshazzar has answered and said, "My lord, the dream—to those hating you, and its interpretation—to your enemies! ²⁰The tree that you have seen, that has become great and strong, and its height reaches to the heavens, and its vision to all the land, ²¹and its leaves [are] beautiful, and its budding great, and food for all [is] in it, under it the beast of the field dwells, and on its boughs the birds of the heavens sit. ²²It [is] you, O king, for you have become great and mighty, and your greatness has become great, and has reached to the heavens, and your dominion to the end

of the earth; ²³and that which the king has seen—a sifter, even a holy one, coming down from the heavens, and he has said, Cut down the tree, and destroy it; but the stump of its roots leave in the earth, even with a band of iron and bronze, in the tender grass of the field, and with the dew of the heavens it is wet, and with the beast of the field [is] his portion, until seven times pass over him. ²⁴This [is] the interpretation, O king, and it [is] the decree of the Most High that has come against my lord the king: ²⁵and they are driving you away from men, and your dwelling is with the beast of the field, and they cause you to eat the herb as oxen, and they are wetting you by the dew of the heavens, and pass over you seven times, until you know that the Most High is ruler in the kingdom of men, and to whom He wills He gives it. ²⁶And that which they said—to leave the stump of the roots of the tree; your kingdom abides for you, after that you know that the heavens are ruling. ²⁷Therefore, O king, let my counsel be acceptable to you, and your sins by righteousness break off, and your perversity by pitying the poor, behold, it is a lengthening of your ease." ²⁸All—has come on Nebuchadnezzar the king. ²⁹At the end of twelve months, on the palace of the kingdom of Babylon he has been walking; ³⁰the king has answered and said, "Is this not that great Babylon that I have built, for the house of the kingdom, in the might of my strength, and for the glory of my honor?" ³¹While the word is [in] the king's mouth a voice from the heavens has fallen: "They are saying to you: O Nebuchadnezzar the king, the kingdom has passed from you, ³²and from men they are driving you away, and your dwelling [is] with the beast of the field, they cause you to eat the herb as oxen, and pass over you seven times, until you know that the Most High is ruler in the kingdom of men, and to whom He wills He gives it." ³³In that hour the thing has been fulfilled on Nebuchadnezzar, and from men he is driven, and he eats the herb as oxen, and his body is wet by the dew of the heavens, until his hair has become great as eagles, and his nails as birds. ³⁴"And at the end of the days I, Nebuchadnezzar, have lifted up my eyes to the heavens, and my understanding returns to me, and I have blessed the Most High, and the Perpetual Living One I have praised and honored, whose dominion [is] a continuous dominion, and His kingdom with generation and generation; ³⁵and all who are dwelling on the earth are reckoned as nothing, and according to His will He is doing among the forces of the heavens and those dwelling on the earth, and there is none that claps with his hand and says to Him, What have You done? ³⁶At that time my understanding returns to me, and for the glory of my kingdom, my honor and my brightness return to me, and to me my counselors and my great men seek, and over my kingdom I have been made right, and abundant greatness has been added to me. ³⁷Now I, Nebuchadnezzar, am praising and exalting and honoring the King of the heavens, for all His works [are] truth, and His paths judgment, and those walking in pride He is able to humble."

CHAPTER 5

¹Belshazzar the king has made a great feast to one thousand of his great men, and before the one thousand he is drinking wine; ²Belshazzar has said—while tasting the wine—to bring in the vessels of gold and of silver that his father Nebuchadnezzar had taken from the temple that [is] in Jerusalem, that the king may drink with them, and his great men, his wives, and his concubines. ³Then they have brought in the vessels of gold that had been taken out of the temple of the house of God that [is] in Jerusalem, and the king and his great men, his wives and his concubines, have drunk with them; ⁴they have drunk wine, and have praised the gods of gold, and of silver, of bronze, of iron, of wood, and of stone. ⁵In that hour fingers of a man's hand have come forth, and they are writing in front of the lampstand, on the plaster of the wall of the king's palace: and the king is seeing the extremity of the hand that is writing; ⁶then the king's countenance has changed, and his thoughts trouble him, and the joints of his loins are loosed, and his knees are striking against one another. ⁷The king calls mightily, to bring up the enchanters, the Chaldeans, and the soothsayers. The king has answered and said to the wise men of Babylon, that, "Any man who reads this writing, and shows me its interpretation, he puts on purple, and a bracelet of gold [is] on his neck, and he rules third in the kingdom." ⁸Then all the wise men of the king are coming up, and they are not able to read the writing, and to make known the interpretation to the king; ⁹then King Belshazzar is greatly troubled, and his countenance is changing in him, and his great men are perplexed. ¹⁰The queen, on account of the words of the king and his great men, has come up to the banquet-house. The queen has answered and said, "O king, live for all ages; do not let your thoughts trouble you, nor your countenance be changed: ¹¹there is a man in your kingdom in whom [is] the spirit of the holy gods: and in the days of your father, light, and understanding, and wisdom—as the wisdom of the gods—was found in him; and your father King Nebuchadnezzar, chief of the scribes, enchanters, Chaldeans, soothsayers, established him—your father, O king— ¹²because that an excellent spirit, and knowledge, and understanding, interpreting of dreams, and showing of enigmas, and loosing of knots was found in him, in Daniel, whose name the king made Belteshazzar: now let Daniel be called, and the interpretation he shows." ¹³Then Daniel has been caused to come up before the king; the king has answered and said to Daniel, "You are that Daniel who [is] of the sons of the expulsion of Judah, whom my father the king brought in out of Judah? ¹⁴And I have heard of you, that the spirit of the gods [is] in you, and light, and understanding, and excellent wisdom have been found in you. ¹⁵And now, caused to come up before me have been the wise men, the enchanters, that they may read this writing, and its interpretation to cause me to know: and they are not able to show the interpretation of the thing: ¹⁶and I have heard of you, that you are able to give interpretations, and to loose knots: now, behold—you are able to read the writing, and its interpretation to cause me to know— purple you put on, and a bracelet of gold [is] on your neck, and you rule third in the kingdom." ¹⁷Then Daniel has answered and said before the king, "Your gifts be to yourself, and give your fee to another; nevertheless, the writing I read to the king, and the interpretation I cause him to know; ¹⁸you, O king, God Most High, a kingdom, and greatness, and glory, and honor, gave to your father Nebuchadnezzar: ¹⁹and because of the greatness that He gave to him, all peoples, nations, and languages were trembling and fearing before him: whom he willed he was slaying, and whom he willed he was keeping alive, and whom he willed he was raising up, and whom he willed he was making low; ²⁰and when his heart was high, and his spirit was strong to act proudly, he has been caused to come down from the throne of his kingdom, and his glory they have caused to pass away from him, ²¹and he is driven from the sons of men, and his heart has been like with the beasts, and with the wild donkeys [is] his dwelling; they cause him to eat the herb like oxen, and by the dew of the heavens is his body wet, until he has known that God Most High is ruler in the kingdom of men, and whom He wills He raises up over it. ²²And you, his son, Belshazzar, have not humbled your heart, though all this you have known; ²³and against the Lord of the heavens you have lifted up yourself; and the vessels of His house they have brought in before you, and you, and your great men, your wives, and your concubines, are drinking wine with them, and gods of silver, and of gold, of bronze, of iron, of wood, and of stone, that are not seeing, nor hearing, nor knowing, you have praised: and the God in whose hand [is] your breath, and all your ways, Him you have not honored. ²⁴Then from before Him is the extremity of the hand sent, and the writing is noted down; ²⁵and this [is] the writing that is noted down: Numbered, Numbered, Weighed, and Divided. ²⁶This [is] the interpretation of the thing: Numbered— God has numbered your kingdom, and has finished it. ²⁷Weighed—You are weighed in the balances, and have been found lacking. ²⁸Divided—Your kingdom is divided, and it has been given to the Medes and Persians." ²⁹Then Belshazzar has spoken, and they have clothed Daniel with purple, and a bracelet of gold [is] on his neck, and they have proclaimed concerning him that he is the third ruler in the kingdom. ³⁰In that night Belshazzar king of the Chaldeans is slain, ³¹and Darius the Mede has received the kingdom when a son of sixty-two years.

CHAPTER 6

¹It has been good before Darius, and he has established over the kingdom satraps—one hundred and twenty—that they may be throughout the whole kingdom, ²and three presidents higher than they, of whom Daniel [is] first, that these satraps may give to them an account, and the king have no loss. ³Then this Daniel has been overseer over the presidents and satraps, because that an excellent spirit [is] in him, and the king has thought to establish him over the whole kingdom. ⁴Then the presidents and satraps have been seeking to find a cause of complaint against Daniel concerning the kingdom, and any cause of complaint and corruption they are not able to find, because that he [is] faithful, and any error and corruption have not been found in him. ⁵Then these men are saying, "We do not find against this Daniel any cause of complaint, except we have found [it] against him in the Law of his God." ⁶Then these presidents and satraps have assembled near the king, and thus they are saying to him: "O King Darius, live for all ages! ⁷Taken counsel have all the presidents of the kingdom, the prefects, and the satraps, the counselors, and the governors, to establish a royal statute, and to strengthen an interdict, that any who seeks a petition from any god and man until thirty days, except of you, O king, is cast into a den of lions. ⁸Now, O king, you establish the interdict, and sign the writing, that it is not to be changed, as a law of Media and Persia, that does not pass away." ⁹Therefore King Darius has signed the writing and interdict. ¹⁰And Daniel, when he has known that the writing is signed, has gone up to his house, and the window being opened for him, in his upper chamber, toward Jerusalem, three times in a day he is kneeling on his knees, and praying, and confessing before his God, because that he was doing [it] before this. ¹¹Then these men have assembled, and found Daniel praying and pleading grace before his God; ¹²then they have come near, indeed, they are saying before the king concerning the king's interdict: "Have you not signed an interdict, that any man who seeks from any god and man until thirty days, except of you, O king, is cast into a den of lions?" The king has answered and said, "The thing [is] certain as a law of Media and Persia, that does not pass away." ¹³Then they have answered, indeed, they are saying before the king, that, "Daniel, who [is] of the sons of the expulsion of Judah, has not placed on you, O king, [any] regard, nor on the interdict that you have signed, and three times in a day he is seeking his petition." ¹⁴Then the king, when he has heard the matter, is greatly displeased at himself, and on Daniel he has set the heart to deliver him, and until the going up of the sun he was arranging to deliver him. ¹⁵Then these men have assembled near the king, and are saying to the king, "Know, O king, that the law of Media and Persia [is] that any interdict and statute that the king establishes is not to be changed." ¹⁶Then the king has spoken, and they have brought Daniel, and have cast [him] into a den of lions. The king has answered and said to Daniel, "Your God, whom you are serving continually, delivers you Himself." ¹⁷And a stone has been brought and placed at the mouth of the den, and the king has sealed it with his signet, and with the signet of his great men, that the purpose is not changed concerning Daniel. ¹⁸Then the king has gone to his palace, and he has passed the night fasting, and dahavan have not been brought up before him, and his sleep has fled [from] off him. ¹⁹Then the king rises in the early morning, at the light, and he has gone in haste to the den of lions; ²⁰and at his coming near to the den, to Daniel, with a grieved voice, he cries. The king has answered and said to Daniel, "O Daniel, servant of the living God, your God, whom you are serving continually, is He able to deliver you from the lions?" ²¹Then Daniel has spoken with the king: "O king, live for all ages: ²²my God has sent His messenger, and has shut the lions' mouths, and they have not injured me: because that before Him purity has been found in me; and also before you, O king, injury I have not done." ²³Then was the king very glad for him, and he has commanded Daniel to be taken up out of the den, and Daniel has been taken up out of the den, and no injury has been found in him, because he has believed in his God. ²⁴And the king has spoken, and they have brought those men who had accused Daniel, and to the den of lions they have cast them, they, their sons, and their wives; and they have not come to the lower part of the den until the lions have power over them, and all their bones they have broken small. ²⁵Then Darius the king has written to all the peoples, nations, and languages, who are dwelling in all the land: "Your peace be great! ²⁶From before me a decree is made, that in every dominion of my kingdom they are trembling and fearing before the God of Daniel, for He [is] the living God, and abiding for all ages, and His kingdom that which [is] not destroyed, and His dominion [is] to the end. ²⁷A deliverer, and rescuer, and doer of signs and wonders in the heavens and in earth [is] He who has delivered Daniel from the paw of the lions." ²⁸And this Daniel has prospered in the reign of Darius, and in the reign of Cyrus the Persian.

CHAPTER 7

¹In the first year of Belshazzar king of Babylon, Daniel has seen a dream, and the visions of his head on his bed, then he has written the dream, the chief of the things he has said. ²Daniel has answered and said, "I was seeing in my vision by night, and behold, the four winds of the heavens are coming forth to the Great Sea; ³and four great beasts are coming up from the sea, diverse from one another. ⁴The first [is] like a lion, and it has an eagle's wings. I was seeing until its wings have been plucked, and it has been lifted up from the earth, and on feet as a man it has been caused to stand, and a heart of man is given to it. ⁵And behold, another beast, a second, like to a bear, and to the same authority it has been raised, and three ribs [are] in its mouth, between its teeth, and thus they are saying to it, Rise, consume much flesh. ⁶After this I was seeing, and behold, another like a leopard, and it has four wings of a bird on its back, and the beast has four heads, and dominion is given to it. ⁷After this I was seeing in the visions of the night, and behold, a fourth beast, terrible and fearful, and exceedingly strong; and it has very great iron teeth, it has consumed, indeed, it breaks small, and it has trampled the remnant with its feet; and it [is] diverse from all the beasts that [are] before it; and it has ten horns. ⁸I was considering about the horns, and behold, another horn, a little one, has come up between them, and three of the first horns have been eradicated from before it, and behold, eyes as the eyes of man [are] in this horn, and a mouth speaking great things. ⁹I was seeing until thrones have been thrown down, and the Ancient of Days is seated, His garment [is] white as snow, and the hair of His head [is] as pure wool, His throne flames of fire, its wheels burning fire. ¹⁰A flood of fire is proceeding and coming forth from before Him, one million serve Him and one hundred million rise up before Him, judgment has been set, and the scrolls have been opened. ¹¹I was seeing, then, because of the voice of the great words that the horn is speaking, I was seeing until the beast is slain, and his body has been destroyed, and given to the burning fire; ¹²and the rest of the beasts have caused their dominion to pass away, and a prolongation in life is given to them, until a season and a time. ¹³I was seeing in the visions of the night, and behold, [One] like a Son of Man was coming with the clouds of the heavens, and to the Ancient of Days He has come, and before Him they have brought Him near. ¹⁴And to Him is given dominion, and glory, and a kingdom, and all peoples, nations, and languages serve Him, His dominion [is] a continuous dominion, that does not pass away, and His kingdom that which is not destroyed. ¹⁵My spirit has been pierced—I, Daniel—in the midst of the sheath, and the visions of my head trouble me; ¹⁶I have drawn near to one of those standing, and the certainty I seek from him of all this; and he has spoken to me, indeed, the interpretation of the things he has caused me to know: ¹⁷These great beasts, that [are] four, [are] four kings, they rise up from the earth; ¹⁸and the saints of the Most High receive the kingdom, and they strengthen the kingdom for all time, even for all time and all ages. ¹⁹Then I wished for certainty concerning the fourth beast, that was diverse from them all, exceedingly fearful; its teeth of iron, and its nails of bronze, it has devoured, it breaks small, and it has trampled the remnant with its feet; ²⁰and concerning the ten horns that

DANIEL

[are] in its heads, and of the other that came up, and before which three have fallen, even of that horn that has eyes, and a mouth speaking great things, and whose appearance [is] great above its companions. ²¹I was seeing, and this horn is making war with the saints, and has prevailed over them, ²²until the Ancient of Days has come, and judgment is given to the saints of the Most High, and the time has come, and the saints have strengthened the kingdom. ²³Thus he said: The fourth beast is the fourth kingdom in the earth, that is diverse from all kingdoms, and it consumes all the earth, and treads it down, and breaks it small. ²⁴And the ten horns out of the kingdom [are] ten kings, they rise, and another rises after them, and it is diverse from the former, and it humbles three kings; ²⁵and it speaks words as an adversary of the Most High, and it wears out the saints of the Most High, and it hopes to change seasons and law; and they are given into its hand, until a time, and times, and a division of a time. ²⁶And judgment is set, and they cause his dominion to pass away, to perish, and to be destroyed—to the end; ²⁷and the kingdom, and the dominion, even the greatness of the kingdom under the whole heavens, is given to the people—the saints of the Most High, His kingdom [is] a continuous kingdom, and all dominions serve and obey Him. ²⁸Here [is] the end of the matter. I, Daniel, [am] greatly troubled [by] my thoughts, and my countenance is changed on me, and I have kept the matter in my heart."

CHAPTER 8

¹"In the third year of the reign of Belshazzar the king, a vision has appeared to me—I Daniel—after that which had appeared to me at the beginning. ²And I see in a vision, and it comes to pass, in my seeing, and I [am] in Shushan the palace that [is] in Elam the province, and I see in a vision, and I have been by the stream Ulai. ³And I lift up my eyes, and look, and behold, a certain ram is standing before the stream, and it has two horns, and the two horns [are] high; and one [is] higher than the other, and the high one is coming up last. ⁴I have seen the ram pushing westward, and northward, and southward, and no living creatures stand before it, and there is none delivering out of its hand, and it has done according to its pleasure, and has exerted itself. ⁵And I have been considering, and behold, a young male goat has come from the west, over the face of the whole earth, whom none is touching in the earth; as for the young male goat, a conspicuous horn [is] between its eyes. ⁶And it comes to the ram possessing the two horns, that I had seen standing before the stream, and runs to it in the fury of its power. ⁷And I have seen it coming near the ram, and it becomes embittered at it, and strikes the ram, and breaks its two horns, and there has been no power in the ram to stand before it, and it casts it to the earth, and tramples it down, and there has been no deliverer to the ram out of its power. ⁸And the young male goat has exerted itself very much, and when it is strong, the great horn has been broken; and a vision of four comes up in its place, at the four winds of the heavens. ⁹And from one of them has come forth a little horn, and it exerts itself greatly toward the south, and toward the east, and toward the beautiful [land]; ¹⁰indeed, it exerts to the host of the heavens, and causes to fall to the earth of the host, and of the stars, and tramples them down. ¹¹And to the prince of the host it exerts itself, and the continual [sacrifice] has been taken away by it, and thrown down the base of his sanctuary. ¹²And the host is given up, with the continual [sacrifice], through transgression, and it throws down truth to the earth, and it has worked, and prospered. ¹³And I hear a certain holy one speaking, and a certain holy one says to the wonderful numberer who is speaking: Until when [is] the vision of the continual [sacrifice], and of the transgression, an astonishment, to make a treading down of both sanctuary and host? ¹⁴And he says to me, Until evening—morning two thousand and three hundred, then is the holy place declared right. ¹⁵And it comes to pass in my seeing—I, Daniel—the vision, that I require understanding, and behold, standing before me [is] as the appearance of a mighty one. ¹⁶And I hear a voice of man between [the banks of] Ulai, and he calls and says: Gabriel, cause this [one] to understand the appearance. ¹⁷And he comes in near my station, and at his coming in I have been afraid, and I fall on my face, and he says to me: Understand, son of man, for at the time of the end [is] the vision. ¹⁸And in his speaking with me, I have been in a trance on my face, on the earth; and he comes against me, and causes me to stand on my station, ¹⁹and says: Behold, I am causing you to know that which is in the latter end of the indignation; for at the appointed time [is] the end. ²⁰The ram that you have seen possessing two horns, [are] the kings of Media and Persia. ²¹And the young male goat, the hairy one, [is] the king of Javan; and the great horn that [is] between its eyes is the first king; ²²and that being broken, four stand up in its place, four kingdoms stand up from the nation, and not in its power. ²³And in the latter end of their kingdom, about the perfecting of the transgressors, a king stands up, fierce of face, and understanding hidden things; ²⁴and his power has been mighty, and not by his own power; and he destroys wonderful things, and he has prospered, and worked, and destroyed mighty ones, and the people of the Holy Ones. ²⁵And by his understanding he has also caused deceit to prosper in his hand, and in his heart he exerts himself, and by ease he destroys many; and he stands against the Prince of princes—and he is broken without hand. ²⁶And the appearance of the evening and of the morning, that is told, is true; and you, hide the vision, for [it is] after many days. ²⁷And I, Daniel, have been, indeed, I became sick [for] days, and I rise, and do the king's work, and am astonished at the appearance, and there is none understanding."

CHAPTER 9

¹"In the first year of Darius, son of Ahasuerus, of the seed of the Medes, who has been made king over the kingdom of the Chaldeans, ²in the first year of his reign, I, Daniel, have understood by scrolls the number of the years (in that a word of YHWH has been to Jeremiah the prophet), concerning the fulfilling of the desolations of Jerusalem—seventy years; ³and I set my face toward the Lord God, to seek [by] prayer and supplications, with fasting, and sackcloth, and ashes. ⁴And I pray to my God YHWH, and confess, and say: Ah, now, O Lord God, the great and the fearful, keeping the covenant and the kindness to those loving Him and to those keeping His commands; ⁵we have sinned, and done perversely, and done wickedly, and rebelled, to turn aside from Your commands, and from Your judgments: ⁶and we have not listened to Your servants, the prophets, who have spoken in Your Name to our kings, our heads, and our fathers, and to all the people of the land. ⁷To You, O Lord, [is] the righteousness, and to us the shame of face, as [at] this day, to the men of Judah, and to the inhabitants of Jerusalem, and to all Israel, who are near, and who are far off, in all the lands to where You have driven them, in their trespass that they have trespassed against You. ⁸O Lord, to us [is] the shame of face, to our kings, to our heads, and to our fathers, in that we have sinned against You. ⁹To the Lord our God [are] the mercies and the forgivenesses, for we have rebelled against Him, ¹⁰and have not listened to the voice of our God YHWH, to walk in His laws, that He has set before us by the hand of His servants the prophets; ¹¹and all Israel has transgressed Your law, to turn aside so as not to listen to Your voice; and poured on us is the execration, and the oath, that is written in the Law of Moses, servant of God, because we have sinned against Him. ¹²And He confirms His words that He has spoken against us, and against our judges who have judged us, to bring great calamity on us, in that it has not been done under the whole heavens as it has been done in Jerusalem, ¹³as it is written in the Law of Moses, all this evil has come on us, and we have not appeased the face of our God YHWH to turn back from our iniquities, and to act wisely in Your truth. ¹⁴And YHWH watches for the evil, and brings it on us, for our God YHWH is righteous concerning all His works that He has done, and we have not listened to His voice. ¹⁵And now, O Lord our God, who has brought forth Your people from the land of Egypt by a strong hand, and makes for Yourself a name as at this day, we have sinned, we have done wickedly. ¹⁶O Lord, according to all Your righteous acts, please let Your anger and Your fury turn back from Your city Jerusalem, Your holy mountain, for by our sins, and by the iniquities of our fathers, Jerusalem and Your people [are] for a reproach to all our neighbors; ¹⁷and now, listen, O our God, to the prayer of Your servant, and to his supplication, and cause Your face to shine on Your sanctuary that [is] desolate, for the Lord's sake. ¹⁸Incline, O my God, Your ear, and hear, open Your eyes and

see our desolations, and the city on which Your Name is called; for not for our righteous acts are we causing our supplications to fall before You, but for Your mercies that [are] many. ¹⁹O Lord, hear, O Lord, forgive; O Lord, attend and do; do not delay, for Your own sake, O my God, for Your Name is called on Your city, and on Your people. ²⁰And while I am speaking, and praying, and confessing my sin, and the sin of my people Israel, and causing my supplication to fall before my God YHWH, for the holy mountain of my God, ²¹indeed, while I am speaking in prayer, then that one Gabriel, whom I had seen in vision at the commencement, being caused to fly swiftly, is coming to me at the time of the evening present. ²²And he gives understanding, and speaks with me, and says, O Daniel, now I have come forth to cause you to consider understanding wisely; ²³at the commencement of your supplications the word has come forth, and I have come to declare [it], for you [are] greatly desired, and understand concerning the matter, and consider concerning the appearance. ²⁴Seventy periods of seven are determined for your people and for your holy city, to shut up the transgression, and to seal up sins, and to cover iniquity, and to bring in continuous righteousness, and to seal up vision and prophet, and to anoint the Holy of Holies. ²⁵And you know, and consider wisely, from the going forth of the word to restore and to build Jerusalem until Messiah the Leader [is] seven periods of seven, and sixty-two periods of seven: the broad place has been built again, and the rampart, even in the distress of the times. ²⁶And after the sixty-two periods of seven, Messiah is cut off, but not for Himself, and the people of the leader who is coming destroy the city and the holy place; and its end [is] with a flood, and until the end [is] war, [and] desolations [are] determined. ²⁷And he has strengthened a covenant with many [for] one period of seven, and [in] the midst of the period of seven he causes sacrifice and present to cease, and by the wing of abominations he is making desolate, even until the consummation, and that which is determined is poured on the desolate one."

CHAPTER 10

¹In the third year of Cyrus king of Persia, a thing is revealed to Daniel, whose name is called Belteshazzar, and the thing [is] true, and the warfare [is] great: and he has understood the thing, and has understanding about the appearance. ²"In those days, I, Daniel, have been mourning three weeks of days; ³I have not eaten desirable bread, and no flesh and wine came into my mouth, and I have not anointed myself at all, until the completion of three weeks of days. ⁴And in the twenty-fourth day of the first month, I have been by the side of the great river, that [is] Hiddekel: ⁵and I lift up my eyes, and look, and behold, a certain one clothed in linen, and his loins girt with pure gold of Uphaz, ⁶and his body as a beryl, and his face as the appearance of lightning, and his eyes as lamps of fire, and his arms and his feet as the aspect of bright bronze, and the voice of his words as the voice of a multitude. ⁷And I, Daniel, have seen the vision by myself, and the men who have been with me have not seen the vision, but a great trembling has fallen on them, and they flee to be hidden; ⁸and I have been left by myself, and I see this great vision, and there has been no power left in me, and my splendor has been turned in me to corruption, indeed, I have not retained power. ⁹And I hear the voice of his words, and when I hear the voice of his words, then I have been in a trance on my face, and my face [is] to the earth; ¹⁰and behold, a hand has come against me, and shakes me on my knees and the palms of my hands. ¹¹And he says to me: Daniel, man greatly desired, attend to the words that I am speaking to you, and stand on your station, for now I have been sent to you. And when he speaks with me this word, I have stood trembling. ¹²And he says to me: Do not fear, Daniel, for from the first day that you gave your heart to understand, and to humble yourself before your God, your words have been heard, and I have come because of your words. ¹³And the head of the kingdom of Persia is standing in opposition in front of me [for] twenty-one days, and behold, Michael, first of the chief heads, has come to help me, and I have remained there near the kings of Persia; ¹⁴and I have come to cause you to understand that which happens to your people in the latter end of the days, for yet the vision [is] after days. ¹⁵And when he speaks with me about these things, I have set my face toward the earth, and have been silent; ¹⁶and behold, as the manner of the sons of men, he is striking against my lips, and I open my mouth, and I speak, and say to him who is standing in opposition in front of me: My lord, by the vision my pangs have been turned against me, and I have retained no power. ¹⁷And how is the servant of this my lord able to speak with this my lord? As for me, from now on there remains in me no power, indeed, breath has not been left in me. ¹⁸And he adds, and strikes against me, as the appearance of a man, and strengthens me, ¹⁹and he says: Do not fear, O man greatly desired, peace to you, be strong, indeed, be strong; and when he speaks with me, I have strengthened myself, and I say, Let my lord speak, for you have strengthened me. ²⁰And he says, Have you known why I have come to you? And now I return to fight with the head of Persia; indeed, I am going forth, and behold, the head of Javan has come; ²¹but I declare to you that which is noted down in the Writing of Truth, and there is not one strengthening himself with me, concerning these, except Michael your head."

CHAPTER 11

¹"And I, in the first year of Darius the Mede, my standing [is] for a strengthener, and for a stronghold to him; ²and now, I declare to you truth: Behold, yet three kings are standing for Persia, and the fourth becomes far richer than all, and according to his strength by his riches he stirs up the whole, with the kingdom of Javan. ³And a mighty king has stood, and he has ruled a great dominion, and has done according to his will; ⁴and according to his standing is his kingdom broken, and divided to the four winds of the heavens, and not to his posterity, nor according to his dominion that he ruled, for his kingdom is plucked up—and for others apart from these. ⁵And a king of the south—even of his princes—becomes strong, and prevails against him, and has ruled; a great dominion [is] his dominion. ⁶And at the end of years they join themselves together, and a daughter of the king of the south comes to the king of the north to do upright things; and she does not retain the power of the arm; and he does not stand, nor his arm; and she is given up, she, and those bringing her in, and her child, and he who is strengthening her in [these] times. ⁷And [one] has stood up from a branch of her roots, [in] his station, and he comes to the bulwark, indeed, he comes into a stronghold of the king of the north, and has worked against them, and has done mightily; ⁸and also their gods, with their princes, with their desirable vessels of silver and gold, he brings in captivity [to] Egypt; and he stands more years than the king of the north. ⁹And the king of the south has come into the kingdom, and turned back to his own land; ¹⁰and his sons stir themselves up, and have gathered a multitude of great forces, and he has certainly come in, and overflowed, and passed through, and he turns back, and they stir themselves up to his stronghold. ¹¹And the king of the south becomes embittered, and has gone forth and fought with him, with the king of the north, and has caused a great multitude to stand, and the multitude has been given into his hand, ¹²and he has carried away the multitude, his heart is high, and he has caused myriads to fall, and he does not become strong. ¹³And the king of the north has turned back, and has caused a multitude to stand, greater than the first, and at the end of the times a second time he certainly comes in with a great force, and with much substance; ¹⁴and in those times many stand up against the king of the south, and sons of the destroyers of your people lift themselves up to establish the vision—and they have stumbled. ¹⁵And the king of the north comes in, and pours out a mound, and has captured fortified cities; and the arms of the south do not stand, nor the people of his choice, indeed, there is no power to stand. ¹⁶And he who is coming to him does according to his will, and there is none standing before him; and he stands in the desirable land, and [it is] wholly in his hand. ¹⁷And he sets his face to go in with the strength of his whole kingdom, and upright ones with him; and he has worked, and the daughter of women he gives to him, to corrupt her; and she does not stand, nor is for him. ¹⁸And he turns back his face to the islands, and has captured many; and a prince has caused his reproach of himself to cease; without his reproach he turns [it] back to him. ¹⁹And he turns back his face to the strongholds of his land, and has stumbled and fallen, and is not found. ²⁰And stood up on his station has [one] causing an exactor to pass over the honor of

DANIEL

the kingdom, and in a few days he is destroyed, and not in anger, nor in battle. ²¹And a despicable one has stood up on his station, and they have not given to him the splendor of the kingdom, and he has come in quietly, and has strengthened the kingdom by flatteries. ²²And the arms of the flood are overflowed from before him, and are broken; and also the leader of the covenant. ²³And after they join themselves to him, he works deceit, and has increased, and has been strong by a few of the nation. ²⁴Peaceably even into the fertile places of the province He comes, and he has done that which his fathers did not, nor his fathers' fathers; prey, and spoil, and substance, he scatters to them, and against fortifications he devises his plans, even for a time. ²⁵And he stirs up his power and his heart against the king of the south with a great force, and the king of the south stirs himself up to battle with a very great and mighty force, and does not stand, for they devise plans against him, ²⁶and those eating his portion of food destroy him, and his force overflows, and many wounded have fallen. ²⁷And both of the kings' hearts [are] to do evil, and at one table they speak lies, and it does not prosper, for yet the end [is] at a time appointed. ²⁸And he turns back [to] his land with great substance, and his heart [is] against the holy covenant, and he has worked, and turned back to his land. ²⁹At the appointed time he turns back, and has come against the south, and it is not as the former, and as the latter. ³⁰And ships of Chittim have come in against him, and he has been pained, and has turned back, and has been insolent toward the holy covenant, and has worked, and turned back, and he understands concerning those forsaking the holy covenant. ³¹And strong ones stand up out of him, and have defiled the sanctuary, the stronghold, and have turned aside the continual [sacrifice], and appointed the desolating abomination. ³²And those acting wickedly [against] the covenant, he defiles by flatteries; and the people knowing their God are strong, and have worked. ³³And the teachers of the people give understanding to many; and they have stumbled by sword, and by flame, by captivity, and by spoil—days. ³⁴And in their stumbling, they are helped—a little help, and joined to them have been many with flatteries. ³⁵And some of the teachers stumble for refining by them, and for purifying, and for making white—until the end of the time, for [it is] yet for a time appointed. ³⁶And the king has done according to his will, and exalts himself, and magnifies himself against every god, and he speaks wonderful things against the God of gods, and has prospered until the indignation has been completed, for that which is determined has been done. ³⁷And to the God of his fathers he does not attend, nor to the desire of women, indeed, he does not attend to any god, for he magnifies himself against all. ³⁸And to the god of strongholds, on his station, he gives honor; indeed, to a god whom his fathers did not know he gives honor, with gold, and with silver, and with precious stone, and with desirable things. ³⁹And he has dealt in the fortresses of the strongholds with a strange god whom he has acknowledged; he multiplies honor, and has caused them to rule over many, and the ground he apportions at a price. ⁴⁰And at the time of the end, a king of the south pushes himself forward with him, and a king of the north storms against him, with chariot, and with horsemen, and with many ships; and he has come into the lands, and has overflowed, and passed over, ⁴¹and has come into the desirable land, and many stumble, and these escape from his hand: Edom, and Moab, and the chief of the sons of Ammon. ⁴²And he sends forth his hand on the lands, and the land of Egypt is not for an escape; ⁴³and he has ruled over treasures of gold and of silver, and over all the desirable things of Egypt, and Lubim and Cushim [are] at his steps. ⁴⁴And reports trouble him out of the east and out of the north, and he has gone forth in great fury to destroy, and to devote many to destruction; ⁴⁵and he plants the tents of his palace between the seas and the holy desirable mountain, and has come to his end, and there is no helper to him."

CHAPTER 12

¹"And at that time Michael stands up, the great head, who is standing up for the sons of your people, and there has been a time of distress, such as has not been since there has been a nation until that time, and at that time your people escape, everyone who is found written in the scroll. ²And the multitude of those sleeping in the dust of the ground awake, some to continuous life, and some to reproaches—to continuous abhorrence. ³And those teaching shine as the brightness of the expanse, and those justifying the multitude as stars for all time and forever." ⁴"And you, O Daniel, hide the things, and seal the scroll until the time of the end, many go to and fro, and knowledge is multiplied." ⁵"And I have looked—I, Daniel—and behold, two others are standing, one here at the edge of the flood and one there at the edge of the flood, ⁶and he says to the one clothed in linen, who [is] on the waters of the flood, Until when [is] the end of these wonders? ⁷And I hear the one clothed in linen, who [is] on the waters of the flood, and he lifts up his right hand and his left to the heavens, and swears by Him who is living for all time, that, After a time, times, and a half, and at the completion of the scattering of the power of the holy people, all these are finished. ⁸And I have heard, and I do not understand, and I say, O my lord, what [is] the latter end of these? ⁹And he says, Go, Daniel; for hidden and sealed [are] the things until the time of the end. ¹⁰Purify themselves, indeed, make themselves white, indeed, many are refined: and the wicked have done wickedly, and none of the wicked understand, and those acting wisely understand; ¹¹and from the time of the turning aside of the continuous [sacrifice], and to the giving out of the desolating abomination, [are] one thousand, two hundred, and ninety days. ¹²O the blessedness of him who is waiting earnestly, and comes to the one thousand, three hundred, thirty-five days. ¹³And you, go on to the end, then you rest, and stand in your lot at the end of the days."

HOSEA

CHAPTER 1

¹A word of Y<small>HWH</small> that has been to Hosea, son of Beeri, in the days of Uzziah, Jotham, Ahaz, Hezekiah, kings of Judah, and in the days of Jeroboam son of Joash, king of Israel: ²The commencement of Y<small>HWH</small>'s speaking by Hosea. And Y<small>HWH</small> says to Hosea, "Go, take a woman of whoredoms for yourself, and children of whoredoms, for the land goes utterly whoring from after Y<small>HWH</small>." ³And he goes and takes Gomer daughter of Diblaim, and she conceives and bears a son to him; ⁴and Y<small>HWH</small> says to him, "Call his name Jezreel, for yet a little, and I have charged the blood of Jezreel on the house of Jehu, and have caused the kingdom of the house of Israel to cease; ⁵and it has come to pass in that day that I have broken the bow of Israel in the Valley of Jezreel." ⁶And she conceives again, and bears a daughter, and He says to him, "Call her name Lo-Ruhamah [(Not Loved)], for I no longer pity the house of Israel, for I utterly take them away; ⁷and I pity the house of Judah, and have saved them by their God Y<small>HWH</small>, and do not save them by bow, and by sword, and by battle, by horses, and by horsemen." ⁸And she weans Lo-Ruhamah, and conceives, and bears a son; ⁹and He says, "Call his name Lo-Ammi [(Not My People)], for you [are] not My people, and I am not for you; ¹⁰and the number of the sons of Israel has been as the sand of the sea that is not measured nor numbered, and it has come to pass in the place where it is said to them, You [are] not My people, it is said to them, Sons of the Living God; ¹¹and the sons of Judah and the sons of Israel have been gathered together, and they have appointed one head for themselves, and have gone up from the land, for great [is] the day of Jezreel."

HOSEA

CHAPTER 2

¹"Say to your brothers—Ammi, || And to your sisters—Ruhamah. ²Plead with your mother—plead || (For she [is] not My wife, and I [am] not her husband), || And she turns her whoredoms from before her, || And her adulteries from between her breasts, ³Lest I strip her naked. And have set her up as [in] the day of her birth, || And have made her as a wilderness, || And have set her as a dry land, || And have put her to death with thirst. ⁴And her sons I do not pity, || For they [are] sons of whoredoms, ⁵For their mother has gone whoring, || Their conceiver has acted shamefully, || For she has said, I go after my lovers, || Those giving my bread and my water, || My wool and my flax, my oil and my drink. ⁶Therefore, behold, I am hedging up your way with thorns, || And I have made a wall for her, || And her paths she does not find. ⁷And she has pursued her lovers, || And she does not overtake them, || And has sought them, and does not find [them], || And she has said: I go, and I return to my first husband, || For—better to me then than now. ⁸And she did not know that I had given to her || The grain, and the new wine, and the oil. Indeed, I multiplied silver to her, || And the gold they prepared for Ba'al. ⁹Therefore I return, || And I have taken My grain in its season, || And My new wine in its appointed time, || And I have taken away My wool and My flax, covering her nakedness. ¹⁰And now I reveal her dishonor before the eyes of her lovers, || And none deliver her out of My hand. ¹¹And I have caused all her joy to cease, || Her festival, her new moon, and her Sabbath, || Even all her appointed times, ¹²And made desolate her vine and her fig tree, || Of which she said, They [are] a wage to me, || That my lovers have given to me, || And I have made them for a forest, || And a beast of the field has consumed them. ¹³And I have charged on her the days of the Ba'alim, || To whom she makes incense, || And puts on her ring and her ornament, || And goes after her lovers, || And forgot Me," a declaration of YHWH. ¹⁴"Therefore, behold, I am enticing her, || And have caused her to go to the wilderness, || And I have spoken to her heart, ¹⁵And given to her her vineyards from there, || And the Valley of Achor for an opening of hope, || And she has responded there as in the days of her youth, || And as in the day of her coming up out of the land of Egypt. ¹⁶And it has come to pass in that day," || A declaration of YHWH, || "You call Me: My husband, || And do not call Me anymore: My lord. ¹⁷And I have turned aside the names of the lords from her mouth, || And they are not remembered anymore by their name. ¹⁸And I have made a covenant for them in that day, || With the beast of the field, || And with the bird of the heavens, || And the creeping thing of the ground, || And bow, and sword, and war I break from off the land, || And have caused them to lie down confidently. ¹⁹And I have betrothed you to Me for all time, || And betrothed you to Me in righteousness, || And in judgment, and kindness, and mercies, ²⁰And betrothed you to Me in faithfulness, || And you have known YHWH. ²¹And it has come to pass in that day, I answer," || A declaration of YHWH, || "I answer the heavens, and they answer the earth. ²²And the earth answers the grain, || And the new wine, and the oil, || And they answer Jezreel. ²³And I have sowed her to Me in the land, || And I have pitied Lo-Ruhamah, || And I have said to Lo-Ammi, You [are] My people, || And he says, My God!"

CHAPTER 3

¹And YHWH says to me: "Again, go, love a woman, loved of a friend, and an adulteress, like the loved of YHWH, the sons of Israel, and they are turning to other gods, and are lovers of grape-cakes." ²And I buy her for myself for fifteen pieces of silver, and a homer and a lethech of barley; ³and I say to her, "You remain many days for Me, you do not go whoring, nor become anyone's; and I also [am] for you." ⁴For the sons of Israel remain without a king for many days, and there is no prince, and there is no sacrifice, and there is no standing pillar, and there is no ephod and teraphim. ⁵Afterward the sons of Israel have turned back, and sought their God YHWH, and David their king, and have hurried to YHWH, and to His goodness, in the latter end of the days.

CHAPTER 4

¹"Hear a word of YHWH, sons of Israel, || For a strife [is] to YHWH with inhabitants of the land, || For there is no truth, nor kindness, || Nor knowledge of God in the land; ²Swearing, and lying, and murdering, || And stealing, and committing adultery—have increased, || And blood has touched against blood. ³Therefore the land mourns, || And every dweller is weak in it, || With the beast of the field, || And with the bird of the heavens, || And the fishes of the sea—they are removed. ⁴Only, let no one strive, nor reprove a man, || And your people [are] as those striving with a priest. ⁵And you have stumbled in the day, || And a prophet has also stumbled with you in the night, || And I have cut off your mother. ⁶My people have been cut off for lack of knowledge, || Because you have rejected knowledge, || I reject you from being priest to Me, || And you forget the Law of your God—I forget your sons, I also! ⁷According to their abundance so they sinned against Me, || I change their glory into shame. ⁸The sin of My people they eat, || And to their iniquity lift up their soul. ⁹And it has been, like people, like priest, || And I have charged on it its ways, || And its habitual doings I return to it. ¹⁰And they have eaten, and are not satisfied, || They have gone whoring, and do not increase, || For they have left off taking heed to YHWH. ¹¹Whoredom, and wine, and new wine, take the heart, ¹²My people at its staff asks and its rod declares to it, || For a spirit of whoredoms has caused to err, || And they go whoring from under their God. ¹³On tops of the mountains they sacrifice, || And on the hills they make incense, || Under oak, and poplar, and terebinth, || For good [is] its shade. ¹⁴Therefore your daughters commit whoredom, || And your spouses commit adultery, || I do not see after your daughters when they commit whoredom, || And after your spouses when they commit adultery, || For they with the harlots are separated, || And with the whores they sacrifice, || A people that does not understand kicks. ¹⁵Though you [are] a harlot, O Israel, || Do not let Judah become guilty, || And do not come to Gilgal, nor go up to Beth-Aven, || Nor swear, YHWH lives. ¹⁶For Israel has turned aside as a stubborn heifer, || Now YHWH feeds them as a lamb in a large place. ¹⁷Ephraim is joined to idols, leave him alone. ¹⁸Sour [is] their drink, || They have gone whoring diligently, || Her protectors have thoroughly loved shame. ¹⁹Wind has distressed her with its wings, || And they are ashamed of their sacrifices!"

CHAPTER 5

¹"Hear this, O priests, and attend, O house of Israel, || And, O house of the king, give ear, || For the judgment [is] for you, || For you have been a snare on Mizpah, || And a net spread out on Tabor. ²And to slaughter sinners have gone deep, || And I [am] a chain to them all. ³I have known Ephraim, || And Israel has not been hid from Me, || For now you have gone whoring, Ephraim, || Israel is defiled. ⁴They do not give up their habitual doings, || To turn back to their God, || For a spirit of whoredoms [is] in their midst, || And YHWH they have not known. ⁵And humbled has been the excellence of Israel to his face, || And Israel and Ephraim stumble by their iniquity, || Judah has also stumbled with them. ⁶With their flock and with their herd, || They go to seek YHWH, and do not find, || He has withdrawn from them. ⁷Against YHWH they dealt treacherously, || For they have begotten strange sons, || Now a month consumes them [with] their portions. ⁸Blow a horn in Gibeah, a trumpet in Ramah, || Shout, O Beth-Aven, after you, O Benjamin. ⁹Ephraim is for a desolation in a day of reproof, || I have made known a sure thing among the tribes of Israel. ¹⁰Princes of Judah have been as those removing a border, || I pour out My wrath as water on them. ¹¹Ephraim is oppressed, broken in judgment, || When he pleased he went after the command. ¹²And I [am] as a moth to Ephraim, || And as a rotten thing to the house of Judah. ¹³And Ephraim sees his sickness, and Judah his wound, || And Ephraim goes to Asshur, || And sends to a warlike king, || And he is not able to give healing to you, || Nor does he remove a scar from you. ¹⁴For I [am] as a lion to Ephraim, || And as a young lion to the house of Judah, I tear and go, || I carry away, and there is no deliverer. ¹⁵I go—I return to My place, || Until they are desolate, and have sought My face. In their distress they seek Me speedily!"

CHAPTER 6

¹"Come, and we turn back to YHWH, || For He has torn, and He heals us, || He strikes, and He binds us up. ²He revives us after two days, || In the third day He raises us up, || And we live before Him. ³And we know—we pursue to know YHWH, || His going forth is prepared as the dawn, || And He comes in as a shower to

us, || As spring rain [and] autumn rain to the earth." ⁴"What do I do to you, O Ephraim? What do I do to you, O Judah? Your goodness [is] as a cloud of the morning, || And as dew rising early—going. ⁵Therefore I have hewed by prophets, || I have slain them by sayings of My mouth, || And My judgments go forth to the light. ⁶For kindness I desired, and not sacrifice, || And a knowledge of God above burnt-offerings. ⁷And they, as Adam, transgressed a covenant, || There they dealt treacherously against Me. ⁸Gilead [is] a city of workers of iniquity, || Slippery from blood. ⁹And as bands wait for a man, || A company of priests murder—the way to Shechem, || For they have done wickedness. ¹⁰In the house of Israel I have seen a horrible thing, || There [is] the whoredom of Ephraim—Israel is defiled. ¹¹Also, O Judah, a harvest is appointed to you, || In My turning back [to] the captivity of My people!"

CHAPTER 7

¹"When I give healing to Israel, || Then the iniquity of Ephraim is revealed, || And the wickedness of Samaria, || For they have worked falsehood, || And a thief comes in, || A troop has stripped off in the street, ²And they do not say to their heart, || [That] I have remembered all their evil, || Now their doings have surrounded them, || They have been before My face. ³With their wickedness they make a king glad, || And with their lies—princes. ⁴All of them [are] adulterers, || Like a burning oven of a baker, || He ceases from stirring up after kneading the dough, until its leavening. ⁵A day of our king! Princes have defiled themselves [with] the poison of wine, || He has drawn out his hand with scorners. ⁶For they have drawn near, || Their heart [is] as an oven || In their lying in wait—their baker sleeps all night, || Morning! He is burning as a flaming fire. ⁷All of them are warm as an oven, || And they have devoured their judges, || All their kings have fallen, || There is none calling to Me among them. ⁸Ephraim! He mixes himself among peoples, || Ephraim has been an unturned cake. ⁹Strangers have devoured his power, || And he has not known, || Also old age has sprinkled [itself] on him, || And he has not known. ¹⁰And the excellence of Israel has been humbled to his face, || And they have not turned back to their God YHWH, || Nor have they sought Him for all this. ¹¹And Ephraim is as a simple dove without heart, || Egypt they called on—[to] Asshur they have gone. ¹²When they go I spread over them My net, || As the bird of the heavens I bring them down, || I discipline them as their congregation has heard. ¹³Woe to them, for they wandered from Me, || Destruction to them, for they transgressed against Me, || And I ransom them, and they have spoken lies against Me, ¹⁴And have not cried to Me with their heart, but howl on their beds; They assemble themselves for grain and new wine, || They turn aside against Me. ¹⁵And I instructed—I strengthened their arms, || And concerning Me they think evil! ¹⁶They turn back—not to the Most High, || They have been as a deceitful bow, || Their princes fall by sword, || From the insolence of their tongue, || This [is] their derision in the land of Egypt!"

CHAPTER 8

¹"To your mouth—a horn, || As an eagle against the house of YHWH, || Because they transgressed My covenant, || And against My law they have rebelled. ²To Me they cry, My God, we—Israel—have known You. ³Israel has cast off good, an enemy pursues him. ⁴They have made kings, and not by Me, || They have made princes, and I have not known, || Their silver and their gold they have made to them idols, || So that they are cut off. ⁵Your calf has cast off, O Samaria, || My anger has burned against them; Until when are they not capable of purity? ⁶For even it [is] of Israel; a craftsman made it, || And it [is] not God, || For the calf of Samaria is fragments! ⁷For wind they sow, and a windstorm they reap, || Stalk it has none—a shoot not yielding grain, || If so be it yield—strangers swallow it up. ⁸Israel has been swallowed up, || Now they have been among nations, || As a vessel in which is no delight. ⁹For they have gone up [to] Asshur, A wild donkey alone by himself [is] Ephraim, || They have hired lovers! ¹⁰Also though they hire among nations, || Now I gather them, and they are pained a little, || From the burden of a king of princes. ¹¹Because Ephraim multiplied altars to sin, || They have been to him altars to sin. ¹²I write for him numerous things of My law, || As a strange thing they have been reckoned. ¹³The sacrifices of My offerings! They sacrifice flesh, and they eat, || YHWH has not accepted them, || Now He remembers their iniquity, || And inspects their sin, || They return [to] Egypt. ¹⁴And Israel forgets his Maker, and builds temples, || And Judah has multiplied cities of defense, || And I have sent a fire into his cities, || And it has consumed their palaces!"

CHAPTER 9

¹"Do not rejoice, O Israel, do not be joyful like the peoples, || For you have gone whoring from your God, || You have loved a wage near all floors of grain. ²Floor and winepress do not feed them, || And new wine fails in her, ³They do not abide in the land of YHWH, || And Ephraim has turned back [to] Egypt, || And they eat an unclean thing in Asshur. ⁴They do not pour out wine to YHWH, || Nor are they sweet to Him, || Their sacrifices [are] as bread of mourners to them, || All eating it are unclean: For their bread [is] for themselves, || It does not come into the house of YHWH. ⁵What do you do at the day appointed? And at the day of YHWH's festival? ⁶For behold, they have gone because of destruction, || Egypt gathers them, Moph buries them, || The desirable things of their silver, || Nettles possess them—a thorn [is] in their tents. ⁷The days of inspection have come in, || The days of repayment have come in, Israel knows! The prophet [is] a fool, || Mad [is] the man of the spirit, || Because of the abundance of your iniquity, || And great [is] the hatred. ⁸Ephraim is looking [away] from My God, || The prophet! A snare of a fowler [is] over all his ways, || Hatred [is] in the house of his God. ⁹They have gone deep—have done corruptly, || As [in] the days of Gibeah, || He remembers their iniquity, He inspects their sins. ¹⁰As grapes in a wilderness I found Israel, || As the first-fruit in a fig tree, at its beginning, I have seen your fathers, || They have gone in [to] Ba'al-Peor, || And are separated to a shameful thing, || And have become abominable like their love. ¹¹Ephraim [is] as a bird, their glory flies away, without birth, and without womb, and without conception. ¹²For though they nourish their sons, I have made them childless—without man, || Surely also, woe to them when I turn aside from them. ¹³Ephraim! When I have looked to the rock, || Is planted in comeliness, || And Ephraim [is] to bring out his sons to a slayer. ¹⁴Give to them, YHWH—what do You give? Give to them miscarrying womb, and dry breasts. ¹⁵All their evil [is] in Gilgal, || Surely there I have hated them, || Because of the evil of their doings, || Out of My house I drive them, || I no longer love them, || All their heads [are] apostates. ¹⁶Ephraim has been struck, || Their root has dried up, they do not yield fruit, || Indeed, though they bring forth, || I have put to death the desired of their womb. ¹⁷My God rejects them, || Because they have not listened to Him, || And they are wanderers among nations!"

CHAPTER 10

¹"Israel [is] an empty vine, || He makes fruit like to himself, || According to the abundance of his fruit, || He has multiplied for the altars, || According to the goodness of his land, || They have made good standing-pillars. ²Their heart has been divided, now they are guilty, || He breaks down their altars, || He destroys their standing-pillars. ³For now they say: We have no king, || Because we have not feared YHWH, || And the king—what does he do for us? ⁴They have spoken words, || To swear falsehood in making a covenant, || And flourished as a poisonous herb has judgment, on the furrows of a field. ⁵For the inhabitants of Samaria fear the calves of Beth-Aven, || Surely its people have mourned on account of it, || And its priests leap about on account of it, || Because of its glory, for it has removed from it, ⁶Also, it is carried to Asshur, a present to a warlike king, || Ephraim receives shame, || And Israel is ashamed of its own counsel. ⁷Samaria is cut off! Its king [is] as wrath on the face of the waters. ⁸And high places of Aven have been destroyed, the sin of Israel. Thorn and bramble go up on their altars, || And they have said to hills, Cover us, || And to heights, Fall on us. ⁹From the days of Gibeah you have sinned, O Israel, || There they have stood, || Battle does not overtake them in Gibeah, || Because of sons of perverseness. ¹⁰When I desire, then I bind them, || And peoples have gathered against them, || When they bind themselves to their two iniquities. ¹¹And Ephraim [is] a trained heifer—loving to thresh, || And I have passed over on the goodness of its neck, || I cause [one] to ride Ephraim, || Judah plows, Jacob harrows for

him. ¹²Sow for yourselves in righteousness, || Reap according to loving-kindness, || Till for yourselves tillage of knowledge, || To seek YHWH, || Until He comes and shows righteousness to you. ¹³You have plowed wickedness, || Perversity you have reaped, || You have eaten the fruit of lying, || For you have trusted in your way, || In the abundance of your might. ¹⁴And a tumult rises among your people, || And all your fortresses are spoiled, || As the spoiling of Shalman of Beth-Arbel, || In a day of battle, || Mother against sons dashed in pieces. ¹⁵Thus has Beth-El done to you, || Because of the evil of your wickedness, || In the dawn a king of Israel is utterly cut off!"

CHAPTER 11

¹"Because Israel [is] a youth, and I love him, || Out of Egypt I have called for My Son. ²They have called to them correctly, || They have gone from before them, || They sacrifice to lords, || And make incense to carved images. ³And I have caused Ephraim to go on foot, || Taking them by their arms, || And they have not known that I strengthened them. ⁴I draw them with cords of man, || With thick cords of love, || And I am to them as a raiser up of a yoke on their jaws, || And I incline to him—I feed [him]. ⁵He does not return to the land of Egypt, || And Asshur—he [is] his king, || For they have refused to return. ⁶The sword has been grievous in his cities, || And it has ended his bars, and consumed—from their own counsels. ⁷And My people are hanging in suspense about My returning, || And to the Most High they call, || Together they do not exalt. ⁸How do I give you up, O Ephraim? Do I deliver you up, O Israel? How do I make you as Admah? Do I set you as Zeboim? My heart is turned in Me, || My sympathy has been kindled together. ⁹I do not do the fierceness of My anger, || I do not turn back to destroy Ephraim, || For I [am] God, and not a man—The Holy One in your midst, and I do not enter in enmity. ¹⁰They go after YHWH—He roars as a lion, || When He roars, then the sons from the west tremble. ¹¹They tremble as a sparrow out of Egypt, || And as a dove out of the land of Asshur, || And I have caused them to dwell in their own houses," || A declaration of YHWH. ¹²"Ephraim has surrounded Me with feigning, || And the house of Israel with deceit. And Judah is again ruling with God, || And [is] faithful with the Holy Ones!"

CHAPTER 12

¹"Ephraim is enjoying wind, || And is pursuing an east wind, || All the day he multiplies lying and spoiling, || And they make a covenant with Asshur, || And oil is carried to Egypt. ²And YHWH has a controversy with Judah, || To lay a charge on Jacob according to his ways, || He returns to him according to his doings. ³In the womb he took his brother by the heel, || And by his strength he was a prince with God, ⁴Indeed, he is a prince to the Messenger, || And he overcomes [by] weeping, || And he makes supplication to Him, || At Bethel He finds him, || And there He speaks with us, ⁵Even YHWH, God of the Hosts, YHWH [is] His memorial. ⁶And you, through your God, turn, || Keep kindness and judgment, || And wait on your God continually. ⁷Canaan! In his hand [are] balances of deceit! He has loved to oppress. ⁸And Ephraim says, || Surely I have become rich, I have found wealth for myself, || All my labors—they do not find against me iniquity that [is] sin. ⁹And I—your God YHWH from the land of Egypt, || Again I turn you back into tents, || As in the days of the appointed time. ¹⁰And I have spoken to the prophets, || And I have multiplied vision, || And by the hand of the prophets I use allegories. ¹¹Surely Gilead [is] iniquity, || They have been only vanity, || In Gilead they have sacrificed bullocks, || Also their altars [are] as heaps, on the furrows of a field. ¹²And Jacob flees to the country of Aram, || And Israel serves for a wife, || Indeed, he has kept watch for a wife. ¹³And by a prophet has YHWH brought up Israel out of Egypt, || And by a prophet it has been watched. ¹⁴Ephraim has most bitterly provoked, || And he leaves his blood on himself, || And his Lord turns his reproach back to him!"

CHAPTER 13

¹"When Ephraim speaks tremblingly, || He has been lifted up in Israel, || When he becomes guilty in Ba'al he dies. ²And now they sin, || And make for themselves a molten image of their silver, || By their own understanding—idols, || A work of artisans—all of it, || Of them they say, who [are] sacrificers among men, The calves let them kiss. ³Therefore they are as a cloud of the morning, || And as dew, rising early, going away, || As chaff tossed about out of a floor, || And as smoke out of a window. ⁴And I [am] your God YHWH from the land of Egypt, || And you do not know a God besides Me, || And a Savior—there is none except Me. ⁵I have known you in a wilderness, || In a land of droughts. ⁶They are satiated according to their feedings, || They have been satiated, || And their heart is lifted up, || Therefore they have forgotten Me, ⁷And I am to them as a lion, || I look out as a leopard by the way. ⁸I meet them as a bereaved bear, || And I tear the enclosure of their heart, || And I consume them there as a lioness, || A beast of the field tears them. ⁹You have destroyed yourself, O Israel, || But in Me [is] your help; ¹⁰Where [is] your king now—And he saves you in all your cities? And your judges of whom you said, || Give a king and heads to me? ¹¹I give to you a king in My anger, || And I take away in My wrath. ¹²Bound up [is] the iniquity of Ephraim, || Hidden [is] his sin, ¹³Pangs of a travailing woman come to him, || He [is] not a wise son, || For he does not remain [at] the time for the breaking forth of sons. ¹⁴Will I ransom them from the hand of Sheol? Will I redeem them from death? Where [is] your plague, O death? Where your destruction, O Sheol? Comfort is hid from My eyes. ¹⁵Though he produces fruit among brothers, || An east wind comes in, a wind of YHWH, || From a wilderness it is coming up, || And it dries up his fountain, || And his spring becomes dry, || It—it spoils a treasure—every desirable vessel. ¹⁶Samaria becomes desolate, || Because she has been rebellious against her God, || They fall by sword, || Their sucklings are dashed in pieces, || And its pregnant ones are ripped up!"

CHAPTER 14

¹"Turn back, O Israel, to your God YHWH, || For you have stumbled by your iniquity. ²Take words with you, and turn to YHWH, || Say to Him, Take away all iniquity, and give good, || And we render the fruit of our lips. ³Asshur does not save us, we do not ride on a horse, || Nor do we say anymore, Our god, to the work of our hands, || For in You the fatherless find mercy. ⁴I heal their backsliding, I love them freely, || For My anger has turned back from him. ⁵I am as dew to Israel, he flourishes as a lily, || And he strikes forth his roots as Lebanon. ⁶His shoots go on, || And his splendor is as an olive, || And he has fragrance as Lebanon. ⁷The dwellers return under his shadow, || They revive [as] grain, and flourish as a vine, || His memorial [is] as wine of Lebanon. ⁸O Ephraim, what have I anymore to do with idols? I have answered, and I look after him: I [am] as a green fir-tree, || Your fruit is found from Me. ⁹Who [is] wise, and understands these? Prudent, and knows them? For upright are the ways of YHWH, || And the righteous go on in them, || And the transgressors stumble therein!"

JOEL

CHAPTER 1

¹A word of YHWH that has been to Joel, son of Pethuel: ²Hear this, you aged ones, || And give ear, all you inhabitants of the land, || Has this been in your days? Or in the days of your fathers? ³Concerning it talk to your sons, || And your sons to their sons, || And their sons to another generation. ⁴What is left of the palmer-worm, the locust has eaten, || And what is left of the locust, || The cankerworm has eaten, || And what is left of the cankerworm, || The caterpillar has eaten. ⁵Awake, you drunkards, and weep, || And howl all drinking wine, because of the juice, || For it has been cut off from your mouth. ⁶For a nation has come up on My land, || Strong, and there is no number, || Its teeth [are] the teeth of a lion, || And it has the jaw-teeth of a lioness. ⁷It has made My vine become a desolation, || And My fig tree become a splinter, || It has made it thoroughly bare, and has cast down, || Its branches have been made white. ⁸Wail, as a virgin girds with sackcloth, || For the husband of her youth. ⁹Present and drink-offering have been cut off from the house of YHWH, || The priests have mourned, servants of YHWH. ¹⁰The field is spoiled, || The ground has mourned, || For the grain is spoiled, || New wine has been dried up, oil languishes. ¹¹Be ashamed, you farmers, || Howl, vinedressers, for wheat and for barley, || For the harvest of the field has perished. ¹²The vine has been dried up, || And the fig tree languishes, || Pomegranate, also palm, and apple-tree, || All trees of the field have withered, || For joy has been dried up from the sons of men. ¹³Gird, and lament, you priests, || Howl, you servants of the altar, || Come in, lodge in sackcloth, servants of my God, || For present and drink-offering have been withheld from the house of your God. ¹⁴Sanctify a fast, proclaim a restraint, || Gather [the] elderly [and] all those inhabiting the land, || [Into the] house of your God YHWH, ¹⁵And cry to YHWH, "Aah! For the day! For [the] Day of YHWH [is] near, || And it comes as destruction from [the] Almighty. ¹⁶Is food not cut off before our eyes? Joy and rejoicing from the house of our God? ¹⁷Scattered things have rotted under their clods, || Storehouses have been desolated, || Granaries have been broken down, || For the grain has withered. ¹⁸How livestock have sighed! Perplexed have been droves of oxen, || For there is no pasture for them, || Also droves of sheep have been desolated. ¹⁹To You, O YHWH, I call, || For fire has consumed lovely places of a wilderness, || And a flame has set on fire all trees of the field. ²⁰Also the livestock of the field long for You, || For dried up have been streams of water, || And fire has consumed lovely places of a wilderness!"

CHAPTER 2

¹Blow a horn in Zion, || And shout in My holy hill, || All inhabitants of the earth tremble, || For the Day of YHWH is coming, for [it is] near! ²A day of darkness and thick darkness, || A day of cloud and thick darkness, || As darkness spread on the mountains, || A people numerous and mighty, || Like there has not been from of old, || And after it there is not again—Until the years of generation and generation. ³Before it fire has consumed, || And after it a flame burns, || As the Garden of Eden [is] the land before it, || And after it a wilderness—a desolation! And also there has not been to it an escape, ⁴As the appearance of horses [is] its appearance, || And as horsemen, so they run. ⁵As the noise of chariots, they skip on the tops of the mountains, || As the noise of a flame of fire devouring stubble, || As a mighty people set in array for battle. ⁶Pained are peoples from its face, || All faces have gathered paleness. ⁷They run as mighty ones, || As men of war they go up a wall, || And they each go in his own ways, || And they do not change their paths. ⁸And each does not press his brother, || They each go on in his way, || If they fall by the missile, they are not cut off. ⁹In the city they run to and fro, || On the wall they run, || Into houses they go up by the windows, || They go in as a thief. ¹⁰At their face the earth has trembled, || The heavens have shaken, || Sun and moon have been black, || And stars have gathered up their shining. ¹¹And YHWH has given forth His voice before His force, || For His camp [is] very great, || For mighty [is] the doer of His word, || For great [is] the Day of YHWH—very fearful, || And who bears it? ¹²"And also now," a declaration of YHWH, || "Turn back to Me with all your heart, || And with fasting, and with weeping, || And with lamentation." ¹³And tear your heart, and not your garments, || And turn back to your God YHWH, || For He [is] gracious and merciful, || Slow to anger, and abundant in kindness, || And relenting from evil. ¹⁴Who knows—He turns back, || Indeed—He has relented, || And He has left behind Him a blessing, || A present and drink-offering of your God YHWH? ¹⁵Blow a horn in Zion, || Sanctify a fast—proclaim a restraint. ¹⁶Gather the people, sanctify an assembly, || Assemble the aged, || Gather infants and sucklings of the breasts, || Let a bridegroom go out from his inner chamber, || And a bride out of her closet. ¹⁷Let the priests weep between the porch and the altar, servants of YHWH, || And let them say: "Have pity, O YHWH, on Your people, || And do not give Your inheritance to reproach, || To the ruling over them of nations, || Why do they say among peoples, Where [is] their God?" ¹⁸And let YHWH be zealous for His land, || And have pity on His people. ¹⁹Let YHWH answer and say to His people, || "Behold, I am sending to you the grain, || And the new wine, and the oil, || And you have been satisfied with it, || And I make you no longer a reproach among nations, ²⁰And the northern I put far off from you, || And have driven him to a land dry and desolate, || With his face toward the Eastern Sea, || And his rear to the Western Sea, || And his stink has come up, || And his stench comes up, || For he has exerted himself to work." ²¹Do not fear, O land! Be glad and rejoice, || For YHWH has exerted Himself to work. ²²Do not fear, O livestock of the field! For pastures of a wilderness have sprung up, || For the tree has borne its fruit, || Fig tree and vine have given their strength! ²³And you sons of Zion, || Be glad and rejoice in your God YHWH, || For He has given to you the Teacher for righteousness, || And causes a shower to come down to you, || Early rain and spring rain [as] in the beginning. ²⁴And the floors have been full [with] pure grain, || And the presses have overflown [with] new wine and oil. ²⁵"And I have repaid to you the years that the locust consumed, || The cankerworm, and the caterpillar, and the palmer-worm, || My great force that I sent against you. ²⁶And you have eaten, eating and being satisfied, || And have praised the Name of your God YHWH, || Who has dealt with you wonderfully, || And My people are not ashamed for all time. ²⁷And you have known that I [am] in the midst of Israel, || And I [am] your God YHWH, and there is none else, || And My people are not ashamed for all time. ²⁸And it has come to pass afterward, || I pour out My Spirit on all flesh, || And your sons and your daughters have prophesied, || Your old men dream dreams, || Your young men see visions. ²⁹And also on the menservants and on the maidservants, || In those days I pour out My Spirit. ³⁰And I have given wonders in the heavens and in the earth: Blood, and fire, and columns of smoke. ³¹The sun is turned to darkness, and the moon to blood, || Before the coming of the Day of YHWH, || The great and the fearful. ³²And it has come to pass, || Everyone who calls on the Name of YHWH is delivered, || For in Mount Zion and in Jerusalem there is an escape, || As YHWH has said, || And among the remnants whom YHWH is calling!"

CHAPTER 3

¹"For behold, in those days, and in that time, || When I turn back [to] the captivity of Judah and Jerusalem, ²Then I have gathered all the nations, || And caused them to go down to the Valley of Jehoshaphat, || And I have been in judgment with them there, || Concerning My people and My inheritance—Israel, || Whom they scattered among nations, || And My land they have apportioned. ³And for My people they cast a lot, || And they give the young man for a harlot, || And have sold the young woman for wine, || That they may drink. ⁴And also, what [are] you to Me, O Tyre and Sidon, ||

And all circuits of Philistia? Are you rendering repayment to Me? And if you are giving repayment to Me, || Swiftly, quickly, I return your repayment on your head. ⁵In that My silver and My gold you took, || And My desirable things that are good, || You have brought into your temples. ⁶And sons of Judah, and sons of Jerusalem, || You have sold to the sons of Javan, || To put them far off from their border. ⁷Behold, I am stirring them up out of the place || To where you have sold them, || And I have turned back your repayment on your head, ⁸And have sold your sons and your daughters || Into the hand of the sons of Judah, || And they have sold them to Sabeans, || To a nation far off, for YHWH has spoken." ⁹Proclaim this among nations, || Sanctify a war, stir up the mighty ones, || Come near, come up, let all the men of war. ¹⁰Beat your plowshares to swords, || And your pruning-hooks to javelins, || Let the weak say, "I [am] mighty." ¹¹Hurry, and come in, all you nations around, || And be gathered together, || There cause to come down, O YHWH, || Your mighty ones. ¹²"Let the nations wake and come up to the Valley of Jehoshaphat, || For there I sit to judge all the nations around. ¹³Send forth a sickle, || For harvest has ripened, || Come in, come down, for the press has been filled, || Winepresses have overflowed, || For great [is] their wickedness." ¹⁴Multitudes, multitudes [are] in the Valley of Decision, || For near [is] the Day of YHWH in the Valley of Decision. ¹⁵Sun and moon have been black, || And stars have gathered up their shining. ¹⁶And YHWH roars from Zion, || And gives forth His voice from Jerusalem, || And the heavens and earth have shaken, || And YHWH [is] a refuge to His people, || And a stronghold to sons of Israel. ¹⁷"And you have known that I [am] your God YHWH, || Dwelling in Zion, My holy mountain, || And Jerusalem has been holy, || And strangers do not pass over into it again." ¹⁸And it has come to pass in that day, || The mountains drop down juice, || And the hills flow [with] milk, || And all streams of Judah go [with] water, || And a fountain from the house of YHWH goes forth, || And has watered the Valley of Shittim. ¹⁹"Egypt becomes a desolation, || And Edom becomes a desolation, a wilderness, || For violence [to] sons of Judah, || Whose innocent blood they shed in their land. ²⁰And Judah dwells for all time, || And Jerusalem to generation and generation. ²¹And I have declared their blood innocent, || [That] I did not declare innocent, || And YHWH is dwelling in Zion!"

AMOS

CHAPTER 1

¹Words of Amos—who has been among herdsmen of Tekoa—that he has seen concerning Israel, in the days of Uzziah king of Judah, and in the days of Jeroboam son of Joash king of Israel, two years before the shaking; ²and he says, "YHWH roars from Zion, || And gives forth His voice from Jerusalem, || And pastures of the shepherds have mourned, || And the top of Carmel has withered!" ³And thus said YHWH: "For three transgressions of Damascus, || And for four, I do not reverse it, || Because of their threshing Gilead with sharp-pointed irons, ⁴And I have sent a fire against the house of Hazael, || And it has consumed the palaces of Ben-Hadad. ⁵And I have broken the bar of Damascus, || And cut off the inhabitant from Bikat-Aven, || And a holder of a scepter from Beth-Eden, || And the people of Aram have been removed to Kir," said YHWH. ⁶Thus said YHWH: "For three transgressions of Gaza, || And for four, I do not reverse it, || Because of their removing a complete captivity, || To deliver up to Edom, ⁷And I have sent a fire against the wall of Gaza, || And it has consumed her palaces; ⁸And I have cut off the inhabitant from Ashdod, || And a holder of a scepter from Ashkelon, || And have turned back My hand against Ekron, || And the remnant of the Philistines have perished," said Lord YHWH. ⁹Thus said YHWH: "For three transgressions of Tyre, || And for four, I do not reverse it, || Because of their delivering up a complete captivity to Edom, || And they did not remember the brotherly covenant, ¹⁰And I have sent a fire against the wall of Tyre, || And it has consumed her palaces." ¹¹Thus said YHWH: "For three transgressions of Edom, || And for four, I do not reverse it, || Because of his pursuing his brother with a sword, || And he has destroyed his mercies, || And his anger tears continuously, || And his wrath—he has kept it forever, ¹²And I have sent a fire against Teman, || And it has consumed palaces of Bozrah." ¹³Thus said YHWH: "For three transgressions of the sons of Ammon, || And for four, I do not reverse it, || Because of their ripping up the pregnant ones of Gilead, || To enlarge their border, ¹⁴And I have kindled a fire against the wall of Rabbah, || And it has consumed her palaces, || With a shout in a day of battle, || With a whirlwind in a day of windstorm. ¹⁵And their king has gone in a removal, || He and his heads together," said YHWH!

CHAPTER 2

¹Thus said YHWH: "For three transgressions of Moab, || And for four, I do not reverse it, || Because of his burning the bones of the king of Edom to lime, ²And I have sent a fire against Moab, || And it has consumed the palaces of Kerioth, || And Moab is dying with noise, || With shouting, with voice of a horn. ³And I have cut off judge from her midst, || And I slay all its heads with him," said YHWH. ⁴Thus said YHWH: "For three transgressions of Judah, || And for four, I do not reverse it, || Because of their loathing the Law of YHWH, || And His statutes they have not kept, || And their lies cause them to err, || After which their fathers walked, ⁵And I have sent a fire against Judah, || And it has consumed palaces of Jerusalem." ⁶Thus said YHWH: "For three transgressions of Israel, || And for four, I do not reverse it, || Because of their selling the righteous for silver, || And the needy for a pair of sandals. ⁷Who are panting for the dust of the earth on the head of the poor, || And the way of the humble they turn aside, || And a man and his father go to the girl, || So as to defile My holy Name. ⁸And they stretch themselves on pledged garments near every altar, || And the wine of fined ones they drink [in] the house of their gods. ⁹And I have destroyed the Amorite from before them, || Whose height [is] as the height of cedars, || And he [is] strong as the oaks, || And I destroy his fruit from above, || And his roots from beneath. ¹⁰And I have brought you up from the land of Egypt, || And cause you to go in a wilderness forty years, || To possess the land of the Amorite. ¹¹And I raise of your sons for prophets, || And of your choice ones for Nazarites, || Is this not true, O sons of Israel?" A declaration of YHWH. ¹²"And you cause the Nazarites to drink wine, || And on the prophets you have laid a charge, || Saying, Do not prophesy! ¹³Behold, I am pressing you under, || As the full cart presses a sheaf for itself. ¹⁴And refuge has perished from the swift, || And the strong does not strengthens his power, || And the mighty does not deliver his soul. ¹⁵And the handler of the bow does not stand, || And the swift does not deliver [himself] with his feet, || And the rider of the horse does not deliver his soul. ¹⁶And the courageous of heart among the mighty, || Flees naked in that day," || A declaration of YHWH!

CHAPTER 3

¹Hear this word that YHWH has spoken concerning you, O sons of Israel, concerning all the family that I brought up from the land of Egypt, saying, ²"Only you have I known of all families of the earth, || Therefore I charge on you all your iniquities." ³Do two walk together if they have not met? ⁴Does a lion roar in a forest and he has no prey? Does a young lion give out his voice from his habitation, || If he has not caught? ⁵Does a bird fall into a snare of the earth, || And there is no trap for it? Does a snare go up from the ground, || And it does not capture prey? ⁶Is a horn blown in a city, || And do people not tremble? Is there affliction in a city, || And YHWH has not done [it]? ⁷For Lord YHWH does nothing, || Except He has revealed

AMOS

His counsel to His servants the prophets. ⁸A lion has roared—who does not fear? Lord YHWH has spoken—who does not prophesy? ⁹"Sound to palaces in Ashdod, || And to palaces in the land of Egypt, and say: Be gathered on mountains of Samaria, || And see many troubles within her, || And oppressed ones in her midst. ¹⁰And they have not known to act straightforwardly," || A declaration of YHWH, || "Who are treasuring up violence and spoil in their palaces." ¹¹Therefore, thus said Lord YHWH: "An adversary—and surrounding the land, || And he has brought down your strength from you, || And your palaces have been spoiled." ¹²Thus said YHWH: "As the shepherd delivers from the lion's mouth || Two legs, or a piece of an ear, || So the sons of Israel are delivered, || Who are sitting in Samaria on the corner of a bed, || And in Damascus [on that of] a couch. ¹³Hear and testify to the house of Jacob," || A declaration of Lord YHWH, God of Hosts. ¹⁴"For in the day of My charging the transgressions of Israel on him, I have laid a charge on the altars of Beth-El, || And the horns of the altar have been cut off, || And they have fallen to the earth. ¹⁵And I have struck the winter-house with the summer-house, || And houses of ivory have perished, || And many houses have been consumed," || A declaration of YHWH!

CHAPTER 4

¹Hear this word, you cows of Bashan, || Who [are] on the mountain of Samaria, || Who are oppressing the poor, || Who are bruising the needy, || Who are saying to their lords: "Bring in, and we drink." ²Lord YHWH has sworn by His holiness, || "Behold, days are coming on you, || And He has taken you away with hooks, || And your posterity with fish-hooks. ³And [by] breaches you go forth, || A woman before her, || And you have cast down the high place," || A declaration of YHWH. ⁴"Enter Beth-El, and transgress, || At Gilgal multiply transgression, || And bring in your sacrifices every morning, || Your tithes every third year. ⁵And burn a thank-offering with leaven as incense, || And proclaim willing gifts, sound! For so you have loved, O sons of Israel," || A declaration of Lord YHWH. ⁶"And I also—I have given to you cleanness of teeth in all your cities, || And lack of bread in all your places, || And you have not turned back to Me," || A declaration of YHWH. ⁷"And I also—I have withheld from you the rain, || While yet three months to harvest, || And I have sent rain on one city, || And on another city I do not send rain, || One portion is rained on, || And the portion on which it does not rain withers. ⁸And two or three cities have wandered, || To the same city to drink water, || And they are not satisfied, || And you have not turned back to Me," || A declaration of YHWH. ⁹"I have struck you with blasting and with mildew, || The abundance of your gardens and of your vineyards, || And of your figs, and of your olives, || The palmer-worm eats, || And you have not turned back to Me," || A declaration of YHWH. ¹⁰"I have sent among you pestilence by the way of Egypt, || I have slain your choice ones by sword, || With your captive horses, || And I cause the stink of your camps to come up—Even into your nostrils, || And you have not turned back to Me," || A declaration of YHWH. ¹¹"I have overturned among you, || Like the overturn by God of Sodom and Gomorrah, || And you are as a brand delivered from a burning, || And you have not turned back to Me," || A declaration of YHWH. ¹²"Therefore, thus I do to you, O Israel, at last, || Because this I do to you, || Prepare to meet your God, O Israel." ¹³For behold, the Former of mountains, and Creator of wind, || And the Declarer to man what [is] His thought, || He is making dawn obscurity, || And is treading on high places of earth, || YHWH, God of Hosts, [is] His Name!

CHAPTER 5

¹Hear this word that I am bearing to you, || A lamentation, O house of Israel: ²"Fallen, not to rise again, has the virgin of Israel, || Left on her land—she has none [to] raise [her] up." ³For thus said Lord YHWH: "The city that is going out one thousand, || Leaves one hundred, || And that which is going out one hundred, || Leaves ten to the house of Israel." ⁴For thus said YHWH to the house of Israel: "Seek Me, and live, ⁵And do not seek Beth-El, and do not enter Gilgal, || And do not pass through Beer-Sheba, || For Gilgal utterly removes, || And Beth-El becomes vanity. ⁶Seek YHWH, and live, || Lest He prosper as fire [against] the house of Joseph, || And it has consumed, || And there is no quencher for Beth-El— ⁷You who are turning judgment to wormwood, || And have put down righteousness to the earth!" ⁸The Maker of the Pleiades and Orion, || And He who is turning death-shade to the morning—And He has made day [as] dark [as] night—Who is calling to the waters of the sea, || And pours them on the face of the earth, || YHWH [is] His Name; ⁹Who is brightening up the spoiled against the strong, || And the spoiled comes against a fortress. ¹⁰They have hated a reprover in the gate, || And they detest a plain speaker. ¹¹Therefore, because of your trampling on the poor, || And the tribute of grain you take from him, || Houses of hewn work you have built, || And you do not dwell in them, || Desirable vineyards you have planted, || And you do not drink their wine. ¹²For I have known—many [are] your transgressions, || And mighty your sins, || Adversaries of the righteous, taking ransoms, || And you turned aside the needy in the gate. ¹³Therefore the wise is silent at that time, || For it [is] an evil time. ¹⁴Seek good, and not evil, that you may live, and it is so; YHWH, God of Hosts, [is] with you, as you said. ¹⁵Hate evil, and love good, || And set up judgment in the gate, || It may be YHWH, God of Hosts, pities the remnant of Joseph. ¹⁶Therefore, thus said YHWH, God of Hosts, the Lord: "Lamentation is in all broad places, || And in all out-places they say, Oh! Oh! And called the farmer to mourning, || And the skillful of wailing to lamentation. ¹⁷And in all vineyards [is] lamentation, || For I pass into your midst," said YHWH. ¹⁸Behold, you who are desiring the Day of YHWH, || Why [is] this to you—the Day of YHWH? It is darkness, and not light, ¹⁹As [when] one flees from the face of the lion, || And the bear has met him, || And he has come into the house, || And has leaned his hand on the wall, || And the serpent has bitten him. ²⁰Is not the Day of YHWH darkness and not light, || Even thick darkness that has no brightness? ²¹"I have hated—I have loathed your festivals, || And I am not refreshed by your restraints. ²²For though you cause burnt-offerings and your presents to ascend to Me, || I am not pleased, || And I do not behold the peace-offering of your fatlings. ²³Turn the noise of your songs aside from Me, || Indeed, I do not hear the praise of your stringed instruments. ²⁴And judgment rolls on as waters, || And righteousness as a perennial stream. ²⁵Did you bring sacrifices and offerings near to Me, || In a wilderness forty years, O house of Israel? ²⁶And you bore Succoth your king, and Chiun your images, || The star of your god, that you made for yourselves. ²⁷And I removed you beyond Damascus," said YHWH—God of Hosts [is] His Name.

CHAPTER 6

¹Woe [to] those secure in Zion, || And those confident on the mountain of Samaria, || The marked of the chief of the nations, || And the house of Israel has come to them. ²Pass over [to] Calneh and see, || And go there [to] Hamath the great, || And go down [to] Gath of the Philistines, || Are [they] better than these kingdoms? [Is] their border greater than your border? ³Who are putting away the day of evil, || And you bring the seat of violence near, ⁴Who are lying down on beds of ivory, || And are spread out on their couches, || And are eating lambs from the flock, || And calves from the midst of the stall, ⁵Who are taking part according to the stringed instrument, || Like David they invented for themselves instruments of music; ⁶Who are drinking with bowls of wine, || And anoint themselves [with] chief perfumes, || And have not been pained for the breach of Joseph. ⁷Therefore they now go at the head of the captives, || And the mourning-feast of stretched-out ones is turned aside. ⁸Lord YHWH has sworn by Himself, || A declaration of YHWH, God of Hosts: "I am abominating the excellence of Jacob, || And his high places I have hated, || And I have delivered up the city and its fullness." ⁹And if there are left ten persons in one house, || It has come to pass—that they have died. ¹⁰And his loved one has lifted him up, even his burner, || To bring forth the bones from the house, || And he said to him who [is] in the sides of the house, || "Is there [any] yet with you?" And he said, "None," || Then he said, "Hush! We must not make mention of the Name of YHWH." ¹¹For behold, YHWH is commanding, || And He has struck the great house [with] breaches, || And the little house [with] clefts. ¹²Do horses run on a rock? Does one plow [it] with oxen? For you have turned judgment to gall, || And the fruit of righteousness to wormwood. ¹³O you who are rejoicing at nothing, || Who are saying, "Have we not taken to ourselves horns by our

AMOS

strength?" ¹⁴"Surely, behold, I am raising a nation against you, O house of Israel," || A declaration of YHWH, God of Hosts, || "And they have oppressed you from the coming in to Hamath, || To the stream of the desert."

CHAPTER 7

¹Thus Lord YHWH has showed me, and behold, He is forming locusts at the beginning of the ascending of the latter growth, and behold, the latter growth [is] after the mowings of the king [[*or* King Gog]]; ²and it has come to pass, when it has finished to consume the herb of the land, that I say, "Lord YHWH, please forgive, || How does Jacob arise—for he [is] small?" ³YHWH has relented of this, "It will not be," said YHWH. ⁴Thus has Lord YHWH showed me, and behold, Lord YHWH is calling to contend by the fire, and it consumes the great deep, indeed, it has consumed the portion, and I say, ⁵"Lord YHWH, please cease, || How does Jacob arise—for he [is] small?" ⁶YHWH has relented of this, "It also will not be," said Lord YHWH. ⁷Thus has He showed me, and behold, the Lord is standing by a wall [made according to] a plumb-line, and in His hand a plumb-line; ⁸and YHWH says to me, "What are you seeing, Amos?" And I say, "A plumb-line"; and the Lord says: "Behold, I am setting a plumb-line in the midst of My people Israel, I no longer pass over to it. ⁹And high places of Isaac have been desolated, || And sanctuaries of Israel are dried up, || And I have risen against the house of Jeroboam with a sword." ¹⁰And Amaziah priest of Beth-El sends to Jeroboam king of Israel, saying, "Amos has conspired against you in the midst of the house of Israel; the land is not able to bear all his words, ¹¹for thus said Amos: Jeroboam dies by sword, || And Israel certainly removes from off its land." ¹²And Amaziah says to Amos, "Seer, go, flee to the land of Judah for yourself, and eat bread there, and there you prophesy; ¹³and no longer prophesy [at] Beth-El anymore, for it [is] the king's sanctuary, and it [is] the royal house." ¹⁴And Amos answers and says to Amaziah, "I [am] no prophet, nor [am] I a prophet's son, but I [am] a herdsman, and a cultivator of sycamores, ¹⁵and YHWH takes me from after the flock, and YHWH says to me, Go, prophesy to My people Israel. ¹⁶And now, hear a word of YHWH: You are saying, Do not prophesy against Israel, nor drop [anything] against the house of Isaac, ¹⁷therefore, thus said YHWH: Your wife goes whoring in the city, || And your sons and your daughters fall by sword, || And your land is apportioned by line, || And you die on an unclean land, || And Israel certainly removes from off its land."

CHAPTER 8

¹Thus has Lord YHWH showed me, and behold, a basket of summer-fruit. ²And He says, "What are you seeing, Amos?" And I say, "A basket of summer-fruit." And YHWH says to me: "The end has come to My people Israel, || I no longer pass over to it anymore. ³And female singers have howled of a palace in that day," || A declaration of Lord YHWH, || "Many [are] the carcasses, into any place throw—hush!" ⁴Hear this, you who are swallowing up the needy, || To cause the poor of the land to cease, ⁵Saying, "When does the new moon pass, || And we sell ground grain? And the Sabbath, and we open out pure grain? To make little the ephah, || And to make great the shekel, || And to use balances of deceit perversely. ⁶To purchase the poor with money, || And the needy for a pair of sandals, || Indeed, the refuse of the pure grain we sell." ⁷YHWH has sworn by the excellence of Jacob: "I do not forget any of their works forever. ⁸Does the land not tremble for this, || And every dweller in it has mourned? And all of it has come up as a flood. And it has been cast out, and has sunk, || Like the flood of Egypt. ⁹And it has come to pass in that day," || A declaration of Lord YHWH, || "I have caused the sun to go in at noon, || And caused darkness on the land in a day of light, ¹⁰And have turned your festivals to mourning, || And all your songs to lamentation, || And caused sackcloth to come up on all loins, || And on every head—baldness, || And made it as a mourning of an only one, || And its latter end as a day of bitterness. ¹¹Behold, days are coming," || A declaration of Lord YHWH, || "And I have sent a famine into the land, || Not a famine of bread, nor a thirst of water, || But of hearing the words of YHWH. ¹²And they have wandered from sea to sea, || And from north even to east, || They go to and fro to seek the word of YHWH, || And they do not find [it]. ¹³In that day the beautiful virgins, || And the young men, faint with thirst. ¹⁴Those swearing by the guilt of Samaria, || And who have said, Your god lives, O Dan, || And, The way of Beer-Sheba lives, || Indeed, they have fallen and do not rise again!"

CHAPTER 9

¹I have seen the Lord standing by the altar, and He says, || "Strike the knob, and the thresholds shake, || And cut them off by the head—all of them, || And I slay their posterity with a sword, || None that flee of them flee away, || Nor a fugitive of them escape. ²If they dig through into Sheol, || From there My hand takes them, || And if they go up [to] the heavens, || From there I cause them to come down. ³And if they are hid in the top of Carmel, || From there I search out, and have taken them, || And if they are hid from My eyes in the bottom of the sea, || From there I command the serpent, || And it has bitten them. ⁴And if they go into captivity before their enemies, || From there I command the sword, || And it has slain them, || And I have set My eye on them for evil, || And not for good." ⁵And [it is] the Lord, YHWH of Hosts, || Who is striking against the land, and it melts, || And mourned have all the inhabitants in it, || And all of it has come up as a flood, || And it has sunk—like the flood of Egypt. ⁶Who is building His upper chambers in the heavens; As for His troop, || On earth He has founded it, || Who is calling for the waters of the sea, || And pours them out on the face of the land, || YHWH [is] His Name. ⁷"Are you not as sons of Cushim to Me, O sons of Israel?" A declaration of YHWH. "Did I not bring Israel up out of the land of Egypt? And the Philistines from Caphtor, and Aram from Kir? ⁸Behold, [the] eyes of Lord YHWH [are] on the sinful kingdom, || And I have destroyed it from off the face of the ground, || Only, I do not utterly destroy the house of Jacob," || A declaration of YHWH. ⁹"For behold, I am commanding, || And I have shaken among all the nations the house of Israel, || As [one] shakes with a sieve, || And there does not fall a grain [to] the earth. ¹⁰By sword all sinners of My people die, || Who are saying, || Evil does not overtake, or go before, || For our sakes. ¹¹In that day I raise the dwelling place of David that is fallen, || And I have repaired their breaches, || And I raise up its ruins, || And I have built it up as in days of old, ¹²So that they possess the remnant of Edom, || And all the nations on whom My Name is called," || A declaration of YHWH—the doer of this. ¹³"Behold, days are coming," || A declaration of YHWH, || "And the plowman has come near to the reaper, || And the treader of grapes to the scatterer of seed, || And the mountains have dropped juice, || And all the hills melt. ¹⁴And I have turned back [to] the captivity of My people Israel, || And they have built desolate cities, and inhabited, || And have planted vineyards, and drunk their wine, || And made gardens, and eaten their fruit. ¹⁵And I have planted them on their own ground, || And they are not plucked up anymore from off their own ground, || That I have given to them," said your God YHWH!

OBADIAH

CHAPTER 1

¹Thus said Lord Yʜᴡʜ to Edom || (We have heard a report from Yʜᴡʜ, || And an ambassador among nations was sent, || "Rise, indeed, let us rise against her for battle"): ²"Behold, I have made you little among nations, || You [are] despised exceedingly. ³The pride of your heart has lifted you up, || O dweller in clefts of a rock || (A high place [is] his habitation, || He is saying in his heart: Who brings me down [to] earth?) ⁴If you go up high as an eagle, || And if you set your nest between stars, || From there I bring you down," || A declaration of Yʜᴡʜ. ⁵"If thieves have come in to you, || If spoilers of the night, || How have you been cut off! Do they not steal their sufficiency? If gatherers have come in to you, || Do they not leave gleanings? ⁶How has Esau been searched out! His hidden things have flowed out, ⁷All your allies have sent you to the border, || Forgotten you, prevailed over you, have your friends, || They make your bread a snare under you, || There is no understanding in him! ⁸Is it not in that day," a declaration of Yʜᴡʜ, || "That I have destroyed the wise out of Edom, || And understanding out of the mountain of Esau? ⁹And your mighty ones have been broken down, O Teman, || So that everyone of the mountain of Esau is cut off. ¹⁰For slaughter, for violence [to] your brother Jacob, || Shame covers you, || And you have been cut off for all time. ¹¹In the day of your standing aloof from the opposite [side], || In the day of strangers taking his force captive, || And foreigners have entered his gates, || And have cast a lot for Jerusalem, || Even you [are] as one of them! ¹²And—you do not look on the day of your brother, || On the day of his alienation, || Nor do you rejoice over sons of Judah, || In the day of their destruction, || Nor make your mouth great in a day of distress. ¹³Nor come into a gate of My people in a day of their calamity, || Nor look, even you, on its misfortune in a day of its calamity, || Nor send forth against its force in a day of its calamity, ¹⁴Nor stand by the breach to cut off its escaped, || Nor deliver up its remnant in a day of distress. ¹⁵For near [is] the Day of Yʜᴡʜ, on all the nations, || As you have done, it is done to you, || Your deed turns back on your own head. ¹⁶For—as you have drunk on My holy mountain, || All the nations drink continually, || And they have drunk and have swallowed, || And they have been as [if] they have not been. ¹⁷And in Mount Zion there is an escape, || And it has been holy, || And the house of Jacob has possessed their possessions. ¹⁸And the house of Jacob has been a fire, || And the house of Joseph a flame, || And the house of Esau for stubble, || And they have burned among them, || And they have consumed them, || And there is not a remnant to the house of Esau," || For Yʜᴡʜ has spoken. ¹⁹And they have possessed the south with the mountain of Esau, || And the low country with the Philistines, || And they have possessed the field of Ephraim, || And the field of Samaria, || And Benjamin with Gilead. ²⁰And the expulsion of this force of the sons of Israel, || That [is with] the Canaanites to Zarephat, || And the expulsion of Jerusalem that [is] with the Sepharad, || Possess the cities of the south. ²¹And saviors have gone up on Mount Zion, || To judge the mountain of Esau, || And the kingdom has been to Yʜᴡʜ!

JONAH

CHAPTER 1

¹And there is a word of Yʜᴡʜ to Jonah son of Amittai, saying, ²"Rise, go to Nineveh, the great city, and proclaim against it that their wickedness has come up before Me." ³And Jonah rises to flee to Tarshish from the face of Yʜᴡʜ, and goes down [to] Joppa, and finds a ship going [to] Tarshish, and he gives its fare, and goes down into it, to go with them to Tarshish from the face of Yʜᴡʜ. ⁴And Yʜᴡʜ has cast a great wind on the sea, and there is a great storm in the sea, and the ship has reckoned to be broken; ⁵and the mariners are afraid, and they each cry to his god, and cast the goods that [are] in the ship into the sea, to make [it] light of them; and Jonah has gone down to the sides of the vessel, and he lies down, and is fast asleep. ⁶And the chief of the company draws near to him and says to him, "What are you [doing], O sleeper? Rise, call to your God, it may be God considers Himself of us, and we do not perish." ⁷And they each say to his neighbor, "Come, and we cast lots, and we know on whose account this evil [is] on us." And they cast lots, and the lot falls on Jonah. ⁸And they say to him, "Now declare to us, on whose account [is] this evil on us? What [is] your occupation, and where do you come from? What [is] your country, seeing you are not of this people?" ⁹And he says to them, "I—a Hebrew, and I fear Yʜᴡʜ, God of the heavens, who made the sea and the dry land." ¹⁰And the men fear a great fear, and say to him, "What [is] this you have done!" For the men have known that he is fleeing from the face of Yʜᴡʜ, for he has told them. ¹¹And they say to him, "What do we do to you that the sea may cease from us, for the sea is more and more turbulent?" ¹²And he says to them, "Lift me up, and cast me into the sea, and the sea ceases from you; for I know that on my account this great storm [is] on you." ¹³And the men row to turn back to the dry land, and are not able, for the sea is more and more turbulent against them. ¹⁴And they cry to Yʜᴡʜ, and say, "Ah, now, O Yʜᴡʜ, please do not let us perish for this man's life, and do not lay innocent blood on us! For You, Yʜᴡʜ, as You have pleased, You have done." ¹⁵And they lift up Jonah, and cast him into the sea, and the sea ceases from its raging; ¹⁶and the men fear Yʜᴡʜ [with] a great fear, and sacrifice a sacrifice to Yʜᴡʜ, and vow vows. ¹⁷And Yʜᴡʜ appoints a great fish to swallow up Jonah, and Jonah is in the bowels of the fish three days and three nights.

CHAPTER 2

¹And Jonah prays to his God Yʜᴡʜ from the bowels of the fish. ²And he says: "I called, because of my distress, to Yʜᴡʜ, || And He answers me, || From the belly of Sheol I have cried, || You have heard my voice. ³When You cast me [into] the deep, || Into the heart of the seas, || Then the flood surrounds me, || All Your breakers and Your billows have passed over me. ⁴And I said: I have been cast out from before Your eyes || (Yet I add to look to Your holy temple!) ⁵Waters have surrounded me to the soul, || The deep surrounds me, || The weed is bound to my head. ⁶To the cuttings of mountains I have come down, || The earth, her bars [are] behind me for all time. And You bring my life up from the pit, O Yʜᴡʜ my God. ⁷In the feebleness of my soul within me, || I have remembered Yʜᴡʜ, || And my prayer comes to You, || Into Your holy temple. ⁸Those observing lying vanities forsake their own mercy. ⁹And I—with a voice of thanksgiving—I sacrifice to You, || That which I have vowed I complete, || Salvation [is] of Yʜᴡʜ." ¹⁰And Yʜᴡʜ speaks to the fish, and it vomits Jonah out on the dry land.

CHAPTER 3

¹And there is a word of Yʜᴡʜ to Jonah a second time, saying, ²"Rise, go to Nineveh, the great city, and proclaim to it the proclamation that I am speaking to you"; ³and Jonah rises,

JONAH

and he goes to Nineveh, according to the word of YHWH. And Nineveh has been a great city before God, a journey of three days. ⁴And Jonah begins to go into the city—a journey of one day—and proclaims and says, "Yet forty days and Nineveh is overturned!" ⁵And the men of Nineveh believe in God, and proclaim a fast, and put on sackcloth, from their greatest even to their least, ⁶seeing the word comes to the king of Nineveh, and he rises from his throne, and removes his honorable robe from off him, and spreads out sackcloth, and sits on the ashes, ⁷and he cries and says in Nineveh by a decree of the king and his great ones, saying, "Man and beast, herd and flock—do not let them taste anything, do not let them feed, do not even let them drink water; ⁸and let man and beast cover themselves [with] sackcloth, and let them call to God mightily, and let them each turn back from his evil way, and from the violence that [is] in their hands. ⁹Who knows? He turns back, and God has relented, and has turned back from the heat of His anger, and we do not perish." ¹⁰And God sees their works, that they have turned back from their evil way, and God relents of the evil that He spoke of doing to them, and He has not done [it].

CHAPTER 4

¹And it is grievous to Jonah—a great evil—and he is displeased at it; ²and he prays to YHWH, and he says, "Ah, now, O YHWH, is this not my word while I was in my own land—therefore I was beforehand [going] to flee to Tarshish—that I have known that You [are] a God, gracious and merciful, slow to anger, and abundant in kindness, and relenting of evil? ³And now, O YHWH, please take my soul from me, for better [is] my death than my life." ⁴And YHWH says, "Is doing good displeasing to you?" ⁵And Jonah goes forth from the city, and sits on the east of the city, and makes a shelter for himself there, and sits under it in the shade, until he sees what is in the city. ⁶And YHWH God appoints a gourd, and causes it to come up over Jonah, to be a shade over his head, to give deliverance to him from his affliction, and Jonah rejoices because of the gourd [with] great joy. ⁷And God appoints a worm at the going up of the dawn on the next day, and it strikes the gourd, and it dries up. ⁸And it comes to pass, about the rising of the sun, that God appoints a cutting east wind, and the sun strikes on the head of Jonah, and he wraps himself up, and asks for his soul to die, and says, "Better [is] my death than my life." ⁹And God says to Jonah: "Is doing good displeasing to you, because of the gourd?" And he says, "To do good is displeasing to me—to death." ¹⁰And YHWH says, "You have had pity on the gourd, for which you did not labor, neither did you nourish it, which came up [as] a son of night, and perished [as] a son of night, ¹¹and I—do I not have pity on Nineveh, the great city, in which there are more than one hundred twenty thousand of mankind, who have not known between their right hand and their left—and much livestock?"

MICAH

CHAPTER 1

¹A word of YHWH that has been to Micah the Morashite in the days of Jotham, Ahaz, Hezekiah, kings of Judah, that he has seen concerning Samaria and Jerusalem: ²Hear, O peoples, all of them! Attend, O earth, and its fullness, || And Lord YHWH is against you for a witness, || The Lord from His holy temple. ³For behold, YHWH is going out from His place, || And He has come down, || And has trodden on high places of earth. ⁴The mountains have been melted under Him, || And the valleys split themselves, || As wax from the presence of fire, || As waters cast down by a slope. ⁵For the transgression of Jacob [is] all this, || And for the sins of the house of Israel. What [is] the transgression of Jacob? Is it not Samaria? And what the high places of Judah? Is it not Jerusalem? ⁶"And I have set Samaria for a heap of the field, || For plantations of a vineyard, || And poured out into a valley her stones, || And her foundations I uncover. ⁷And all her carved images are beaten down, || And all her wages are burned with fire, || And all her idols I make a desolation, || For from the wage of a harlot she gathered, and to the wage of a harlot they return." ⁸For this I lament and howl, || I go spoiled and naked, || I make a lamentation like dragons, || And a mourning like daughters of an ostrich. ⁹For mortal [are] her wounds, || For it has come to Judah, || It has come to a gate of My people—to Jerusalem. ¹⁰In Gath do not tell—in Acco do not weep, || In Beth-Aphrah, roll yourself in dust. ¹¹Pass over for you, O inhabitant of Shaphir, || Naked one of shame. The inhabitant of Zaanan has not gone out, || The lamentation of Beth-Ezel takes from you its standing. ¹²For the inhabitant of Maroth has stayed for good, || For calamity has come down from YHWH to the gate of Jerusalem. ¹³Bind the chariot to a swift beast, O inhabitant of Lachish, || The beginning of sin [is] she to the daughter of Zion, || For in you have been found the transgressions of Israel. ¹⁴Therefore you give presents to Moresheth-Gath, || The houses of Achzib become a lying thing to the kings of Israel. ¹⁵Yet I bring the possessor to you, O inhabitant of Mareshah, || The glory of Israel comes to Adullam. ¹⁶Make bald and shave, for your delightful sons, || Enlarge your baldness as an eagle, || For they have removed from you!

CHAPTER 2

¹Woe [to] those devising iniquity, || And working evil on their beds, || In the morning light they do it, || For their hand is—to God. ²And they have desired fields, || And they have taken violently, || And houses, and they have taken away, || And have oppressed a man and his house, || Even a man and his inheritance. ³Therefore, thus said YHWH: "Behold, I am devising against this family calamity, || From which you do not remove your necks, || Nor walk loftily, for it [is] a time of evil. ⁴In that day [one] takes up for you an allegory, || And he has wailed a wailing of woe, || He has said, We have been utterly spoiled, || The portion of my people He changes, || How He moves toward me! To the backslider our fields He apportions." ⁵Therefore, you have no caster of a line by lot || In the assembly of YHWH. ⁶You do not prophesy—they prophesy, || They do not prophesy to these, || It does not remove shame. ⁷[Those] named the house of Jacob: "Has the Spirit of YHWH been shortened? Are these His doings? Do My words not benefit the people that are walking uprightly? ⁸And recently My people raise up as an enemy, || You strip off the honorable ornament from the outer garment, || From the confident passers by, || You who are turning back from war. ⁹The women of My people you cast out from its delightful house, || From its sucklings you take away My honor for all time. ¹⁰Rise and go, for this [is] not the rest, || Because of uncleanness it corrupts, || And corruption is powerful. ¹¹If one is going [with] the wind, || And [with] falsehood has lied: I prophesy to you of wine, and of strong drink, || He has been the prophet of this people! ¹²I surely gather you, O Jacob, all of you, || I surely bring together the remnant of Israel, || Together I set it as the flock of Bozrah, || As a drove in the midst of its pasture, || It makes a noise because of man. ¹³The breaker has gone up before them, || They have broken through, || Indeed, they pass through the gate, || Indeed, they go out through it, || And their king passes on before them, || And YHWH at their head!"

CHAPTER 3

¹And I say, "Now hear, O heads of Jacob, || And you judges of the house of Israel, || Is it not for you to know the judgment? ²You who are hating good, and loving evil, || Taking violently their skin from off them, || And their flesh from off their bones, ³And who have eaten the flesh of My people, || And their skin from off them have stripped, || And their bones they have broken, || And they have spread [them] out as in a pot, || And as flesh in the midst of a

MICAH

cauldron." ⁴Then they cry to YHWH, || And He does not answer them, || And hides His face from them at that time, || As they have made evil their doings. ⁵Thus said YHWH concerning the prophets || Who are causing My people to err, || Who are biting with their teeth, || And have cried "Peace," || And he who does not give to their mouth, || They have sanctified against him war: ⁶"Therefore you have a night without vision, || And you have darkness without divination, || And the sun has gone in on the prophets, || And the day has been black over them. ⁷And the seers have been ashamed, || And the diviners have been confounded, || And all of them have covered their lip, || For there is no answer, O God." ⁸And yet I have been full of power by the Spirit of YHWH, || And of judgment, and of might, || To declare to Jacob his transgression, || And to Israel his sin. ⁹Now hear this, O heads of the house of Jacob, || And you judges of the house of Israel, || Who are making judgment abominable, || And pervert all uprightness. ¹⁰Building up Zion with blood, || And Jerusalem with iniquity. ¹¹Her heads judge for a bribe, || And her priests teach for hire, || And her prophets divine for silver, || And on YHWH they lean, saying, || "Is not YHWH in our midst? Evil does not come in on us." ¹²Therefore, for your sake, Zion is plowed a field, and Jerusalem is heaps, || And the mountain of the house [is] for high places of a forest!

CHAPTER 4

¹And it has come to pass, || In the latter end of the days, || The mountain of the house of YHWH || Is established above the top of the mountains, || And it has been lifted up above the hills, || And flowed to it have peoples. ²And gone have many nations and said, || "Come and we go up to the mountain of YHWH, || And to the house of the God of Jacob, || And He teaches us of His ways, || And we walk in His paths," || For a law goes forth from Zion, || And a word of YHWH from Jerusalem. ³And He has judged between many peoples, || And given a decision to mighty nations far off, || They have beaten their swords to plowshares, || And their spears to pruning-hooks, || Nation does not lift up sword to nation, || Nor do they learn war anymore. ⁴And they have sat each under his vine, || And under his fig tree, || And there is none troubling, || For the mouth of YHWH of Hosts has spoken. ⁵For all the peoples walk, || Each in the name of its god—and we, || We walk in the Name of our God YHWH, || For all time and forever. ⁶"In that day," a declaration of YHWH, || "I gather the halting one, || And the driven away one I bring together, || And she whom I have afflicted. ⁷And I have set the halting for a remnant, || And the far-off for a mighty nation, || And YHWH has reigned over them in Mount Zion, || From now on, and for all time. ⁸And you, O Tower of Eder, || Fort of the daughter of Zion, to you it comes, || Indeed, the former rule has come in, || The kingdom to the daughter of Jerusalem." ⁹Now why do you shout aloud? Is there no king in you? Has your counselor perished, || That pain as of a travailing woman has taken hold of you? ¹⁰Be pained, and bring forth, O daughter of Zion, || As a travailing woman, || For now you go forth from the city, || And you have dwelt in the field, || And you have gone to Babylon, || There you are delivered, || There YHWH redeems you from the hand of your enemies. ¹¹And now, many nations have gathered against you, who are saying: "Let her be defiled, and our eyes look on Zion." ¹²They have not known the thoughts of YHWH, || Nor have they understood His counsel, || For He has gathered them as a sheaf [into] a threshing-floor. ¹³Arise, and thresh, O daughter of Zion, || For I make your horn iron, || And I make your hooves bronze, || And you have beaten small many peoples, || And I have devoted to YHWH their gain, || And their wealth to the Lord of the whole earth!

CHAPTER 5

¹Now gather yourself together, O daughter of troops, || He has laid a siege against us, || They strike [the] judge of Israel on the cheek with a rod. ²"And you, Beth-Lehem Ephratah, || Little to be among the chiefs of Judah! From you He comes forth to Me—to be ruler in Israel, || And His comings forth [are] of old, || From the days of antiquity." ³Therefore He gives them up until the time she who brings forth has brought forth, || And the remnant of His brothers return to the sons of Israel. ⁴And He has stood and delighted in the strength of YHWH, || In the excellence of the Name of His God YHWH, || And they have remained, || For now He is great to the ends of the earth. ⁵And this [One] has been peace. Asshur, when he comes into our land, || And when he treads in our palaces, || We have raised against him seven shepherds, || And eight anointed of man. ⁶And they have afflicted the land of Asshur with the sword, || And the land of Nimrod at its openings, || And He has delivered from Asshur when he comes into our land, || And when he treads in our borders. ⁷And the remnant of Jacob has been in the midst of many peoples, || As dew from YHWH—as showers on the herb, || That does not wait for man, nor stays for the sons of men. ⁸Indeed, the remnant of Jacob has been among nations, || In the midst of many peoples, || As a lion among beasts of a forest, || As a young lion among ranks of a flock, || Which if it has passed through, || Has both trodden down and has torn, || And there is no deliverer. ⁹High is your hand above your adversaries, || And all your enemies are cut off. ¹⁰"And it has come to pass in that day," || A declaration of YHWH, || "I have cut off your horses from your midst, || And I have destroyed your chariots, ¹¹And I have cut off the cities of your land, || And I have thrown down all your fortresses, ¹²And have cut off sorcerers out of your hand, || And observers of clouds—you have none. ¹³And I have cut off your carved images, || And your standing-pillars out of your midst, || And you do not bow yourself anymore || To the work of your hands. ¹⁴And I have plucked up your Asherim out of your midst, || And I have destroyed your enemies. ¹⁵And I have done vengeance in anger and in fury, || With the nations who have not listened!"

CHAPTER 6

¹Now hear that which YHWH is saying: "Rise—strive with the mountains, || And cause the hills to hear your voice. ²Hear, O mountains, the strife of YHWH, || You strong ones—foundations of earth! For a strife [is] to YHWH, with His people, || And with Israel He reasons. ³O My people, what have I done to you? And how have I wearied you? Testify against Me. ⁴For I brought you up from the land of Egypt, || And I have ransomed you from the house of servants, || And I send Moses, Aaron, and Miriam before you. ⁵O My people, please remember || What Balak king of Moab counseled, || What Balaam son of Beor answered him || (From Shittim to Gilgal), || In order to know the righteous acts of YHWH." ⁶With what do I come before YHWH? Do I bow to God Most High? Do I come before Him with burnt-offerings? With calves—sons of a year? ⁷Is YHWH pleased with thousands of rams? With myriads of streams of oil? Do I give my firstborn [for] my transgression? The fruit of my body [for] the sin of my soul? ⁸He has declared to you, O man, what [is] good; Indeed, what is YHWH requiring of you, || Except—to do judgment, and love kindness, || And to walk lowly with your God? ⁹A voice of YHWH calls to the city, || And wisdom fears Your Name, || "Hear the rod, and Him who appointed it. ¹⁰Are there yet [in] the house of the wicked || Treasures of wickedness, || And the abhorred meager ephah? ¹¹Do I reckon [it] pure with balances of wickedness? And with a bag of deceitful stones? ¹²Whose rich ones have been full of violence, || And its inhabitants have spoken falsehood, || And their tongue [is] deceitful in their mouth. ¹³And I also, I have begun to strike you, || To make desolate, because of your sins. ¹⁴You eat, and you are not satisfied, || And your pit [is] in your midst, || And you remove, and do not deliver, || And that which you deliver, I give to a sword. ¹⁵You sow, and you do not reap, || You tread the olive, || And you do not pour out oil, || And new wine—and you do not drink wine. ¹⁶And the statutes of Omri are kept habitually, || And all the work of the house of Ahab, || And you walk in their counsels, || For My giving you for a desolation, || And its inhabitants for a hissing, || And you bear the reproach of My people!"

CHAPTER 7

¹My woe [is] to me, || For I have been as gatherings of summer-fruit, || As gleanings of harvest, || There is no cluster to eat, || The first-ripe fruit has my soul desired. ²The kind have perished out of the land, || And upright among men—there are none, || All of them lie in wait for blood, || They each hunt his brother [with] a net. ³On the evil [are] both hands to do [it] well, || The prince is asking—also the judge—for repayment, || And the great—he is speaking the mischief of his soul, || And they wrap it up. ⁴Their best one [is] as a brier, || The upright one—than a thorn-hedge, || The day

of your watchmen—Your visitation—has come. Now is their perplexity. ⁵Do not believe in a friend, || Do not trust in a leader, || From her who is lying in your bosom keep the openings of your mouth. ⁶For a son is dishonoring a father, || A daughter has stood against her mother, || A daughter-in-law against her mother-in-law, || The enemies of each [are] the men of his house. ⁷And I—in YHWH I watch, || I wait for the God of my salvation, || My God hears me. ⁸You do not rejoice over me, O my enemy, || When I have fallen, I have risen, || When I sit in darkness YHWH is a light to me. ⁹I bear the indignation of YHWH, || For I have sinned against Him, || Until He pleads my cause, || And has executed my judgment, || He brings me forth to the light, || I look on His righteousness. ¹⁰And my enemy sees, || And shame covers her, || Who says to me, "Where [is] your God YHWH?" My eyes look on her, || Now she is for a treading-place, || As mire of the out-places. ¹¹The day to build your walls! That day—removed is the limit. ¹²That day—even to you it comes in, || From Asshur and the cities of the fortress, || And from the fortress even to the river, || And from sea to sea, and mountain to mountain. ¹³And the land has been for a desolation, || Because of its inhabitants, || Because of the fruit of their doings. ¹⁴Rule Your people with Your rod, || The flock of Your inheritance, || Dwelling alone [in] a forest in the midst of Carmel, || They enjoy Bashan and Gilead as in days of old. ¹⁵"According to the days of your coming forth out of the land of Egypt, || I show it wonderful things." ¹⁶Nations see, and they are ashamed of all their might, || They lay a hand on the mouth, their ears are deaf. ¹⁷They lick dust as a serpent, as fearful things of earth, || They tremble from their enclosures, || They are afraid of our God YHWH, || Indeed, they are afraid of You. ¹⁸Who [is] a God like You? Taking away iniquity, || And passing by the transgression of the remnant of His inheritance, || He has not retained His anger forever, || Because He delights [in] kindness. ¹⁹He turns back, He pities us, || He subdues our iniquities, || And You cast all their sins into the depths of the sea. ²⁰You give truth to Jacob, kindness to Abraham, || That You have sworn to our fathers, from the days of antiquity!

NAHUM

CHAPTER 1

¹Burden of Nineveh. The Scroll of the Vision of Nahum the Elkoshite. ²A God zealous and avenging [is] YHWH, || An avenger [is] YHWH, and possessing fury. An avenger [is] YHWH on His adversaries, || And He is watching for His enemies. ³YHWH [is] slow to anger, and great in power, || And YHWH does not entirely acquit, || In a windstorm and in a storm [is] His way, || And a cloud [is] the dust of His feet. ⁴He is pushing against a sea, and dries it up, || Indeed, He has made all the floods dry, || Bashan and Carmel [are] languishing, || Indeed, the flower of Lebanon [is] languishing. ⁵Mountains have shaken because of Him, || And the hills have been melted; And the earth [is] lifted up at His presence, || And the world and all dwelling in it. ⁶Who stands before His indignation? And who rises up in the heat of His anger? His fury has been poured out like fire, || And the rocks have been broken by Him. ⁷Good [is] YHWH for a strong place in a day of distress. And He knows those trusting in Him. ⁸And with a flood passing over, || An end He makes of its place, || And darkness pursues His enemies. ⁹What do we devise against YHWH? He is making an end, distress does not arise twice. ¹⁰For while princes [are] perplexed, || And with their drink are drunken, || They have been consumed as stubble fully dried. ¹¹From you has come forth a deviser of evil || Against YHWH—a worthless counselor. ¹²Thus said YHWH: "Though complete, and thus many, || Yet thus they have been cut off, || And he has passed away. Though I afflicted you, I afflict you no longer. ¹³And now I break his rod from off you, || And your bands I draw away." ¹⁴And YHWH has commanded concerning you, || "No more of your name spreads abroad, || I cut off carved and molten image from the house of your gods, || I appoint your grave, for you have been vile." ¹⁵Behold, on the mountains the feet of one proclaiming tidings, sounding peace! Celebrate, O Judah, your festivals, complete your vows, || For the worthless no longer pass over into you, || He has been completely cut off!

CHAPTER 2

¹A scatterer has come up to your face, || Keep the bulwark, watch the way, || Strengthen the loins, strengthen power mightily. ²For YHWH has turned back to the excellence of Jacob, || As [to] the excellence of Israel, || For emptiers have emptied them out, || And they have marred their branches. ³The shield of his mighty ones has become red, || Men of might [are in] scarlet, || With fiery torches [is] the chariot in a day of his preparation, || And the firs have been caused to tremble. ⁴In out-places the chariots shine, || They go to and fro in broad places, || Their appearances [are] like torches, || As lightnings they run. ⁵He remembers his majestic ones, || They stumble in their goings, || They hurry [to] its wall, || And the covering is prepared. ⁶Gates of the rivers have been opened, || And the palace is dissolved. ⁷And it is established—she has removed, || She has been brought up, || And her handmaids are leading as the voice of doves, || Tabering on their hearts. ⁸And Nineveh [is] as a pool of waters, || From of old it [is]—and they are fleeing! "Stand, stand"; and none is turning! ⁹Seize silver, seize gold, || And there is no end to the prepared things, || [To] the abundance of all desirable vessels. ¹⁰She is empty, indeed, emptiness and waste, || And the heart has melted, || And the knees have struck together, || And great pain [is] in all loins, || And the faces of all of them have gathered paleness. ¹¹Where [is] the habitation of lionesses? And a feeding-place it [is] for young lions || Where a lion has walked, an old lion, || A lion's whelp, and there is none troubling. ¹²The lion is tearing parts [for] his whelps, || And is strangling for his lionesses, || And he fills his holes [with] prey, || And his habitations [with] torn flesh. ¹³"Behold, I [am] against you," || A declaration of YHWH of Hosts, || "And I have burned its chariot in smoke, || And a sword consumes your young lions, || And I have cut off your prey from the land, || And the voice of your messengers is not heard anymore!"

CHAPTER 3

¹Woe [to] the city of blood, || She is all full with lies [and] burglary, || Prey does not depart. ²The sound of a whip, || And the sound of the rattling of a wheel, || And of a prancing horse, and of a bounding chariot, || Of a horseman mounting. ³And the flame of a sword, and the lightning of a spear, || And the abundance of the wounded, || And the weight of carcasses, || Indeed, there is no end to the bodies, || They stumble over their bodies. ⁴Because of the abundance of the fornications of a harlot, || The goodness of the grace of the lady of witchcrafts, || Who is selling nations by her fornications, || And families by her witchcrafts. ⁵"Behold, I [am] against you," || A declaration of YHWH of Hosts, || "And have removed your skirts before your face, || And have showed nations your nakedness, || And kingdoms your shame, ⁶And I have cast on you abominations, || And dishonored you, and made you as a sight. ⁷And it has come to pass, || Each of your beholders flees from you, || And has said: Nineveh is spoiled, || Who bemoans for her? From where do I seek comforters for you?" ⁸Are you better than No-Ammon, || That is dwelling among brooks? Waters she has around her, || Whose bulwark [is] the sea, waters her wall. ⁹Cush her might, and Egypt, and there is no end. Put and Lubim have been for your help. ¹⁰Even she becomes an exile, || She has gone into captivity, || Even her sucklings are dashed to pieces || At the top of all out-places, || And for her honored ones they cast a lot, || And all her great ones have been bound in chains. ¹¹Even you are drunken, you are hidden, || Even you seek a strong place, because of an enemy. ¹²All your

NAHUM

fortresses [are] fig trees with first-fruits, || If they are shaken, || They have fallen into the mouth of the eater. ¹³Behold, your people [are] women in your midst, || To your enemies thoroughly opened || Have been the gates of your land, || Fire has consumed your bars. ¹⁴Waters of a siege draw for yourself, || Strengthen your fortresses, || Enter into mire, and tread on clay, || Make strong a brick-kiln. ¹⁵There a fire consumes you, || A sword cuts you off, || It consumes you as a cankerworm! Make yourself heavy as the cankerworm, || Make yourself heavy as the locust. ¹⁶Multiply your merchants above the stars of the heavens, || The cankerworm has stripped off, and flees away. ¹⁷Your crowned ones [are] as a locust, || And your princes as great grasshoppers, || That encamp in hedges in a day of cold, || The sun has risen, and it flees away, || And its place where they are is not known. ¹⁸Your friends have slumbered, king of Asshur, || Your majestic ones rest, || Your people have been scattered on the mountains, || And there is none gathering. ¹⁹There is no weakening of your destruction, || Your striking [is] grievous, || All hearing your fame have clapped the hand at you, || For over whom did your wickedness not pass continually?

HABAKKUK

CHAPTER 1

¹The burden that Habakkuk the prophet has seen: ²Until when, O YHWH, have I cried, || And You do not hear? I cry to You, "Violence!" And You do not save. ³Why do You show me iniquity, || And cause [me] to behold perversity? And spoiling and violence [are] before me, || And there is strife, and contention lifts [itself] up, ⁴Therefore law ceases, || And judgment does not go forth forever, || For the wicked is surrounding the righteous, || Therefore wrong judgment goes forth. ⁵"Look on nations, and behold and marvel greatly. For a work He is working in your days, || You do not believe though it is declared. ⁶For behold, I am raising up the Chaldeans, || The bitter and hasty nation, || That is going to the broad places of earth, || To occupy dwelling places not his own. ⁷He [is] terrible and fearful, || His judgment and his excellence go forth from him. ⁸His horses have been swifter than leopards, || And sharper than evening wolves, || And his horsemen have increased, || Even his horsemen from afar come in, || They fly as an eagle, hastening to consume. ⁹All for violence—he comes in, || Their faces swallowing up the east wind, || And he gathers a captivity as the sand. ¹⁰And he scoffs at kings, || And princes [are] a laughter to him, || He laughs at every fortification, || And he heaps up dust, and captures it. ¹¹Then the spirit has passed on, || Indeed, he transgresses, || And [ascribes] this—his power—to his god." ¹²Are You not of old, O YHWH, my God, my Holy One? We do not die, O YHWH, || You have appointed him for judgment, || And, O Rock, You have founded him for reproof. ¹³Purer of eyes than to behold evil, || You are not able to look on perverseness, || Why do You behold the treacherous? You keep silent when the wicked || Swallow the more righteous than he, ¹⁴And You make man as fishes of the sea, || As a creeping thing [with] none ruling over him. ¹⁵He has brought up each of them with a hook, || He catches it in his net, and gathers it in his dragnet, || Therefore he delights and rejoices. ¹⁶Therefore he sacrifices to his net, || And makes incense to his dragnet, || For by them [is] his portion fertile, and his food fat. ¹⁷Does he therefore empty his net, || And continually not spare to slay nations?

CHAPTER 2

¹On my charge I stand, and I station myself on a bulwark, and I watch to see what He speaks against me, and what I reply to my reproof. ²And YHWH answers me and says: "Write a vision, and explain on the tablets, || That he may run who is reading it. ³For yet the vision [is] for a season, || And it breathes for the end, and does not lie, || If it lingers, wait for it, || For surely it comes, it is not late. ⁴Behold, a presumptuous one! His soul is not upright within him, || And the righteous lives by his faith. ⁵And also, because the wine [is] treacherous, || A man is haughty, and does not remain at home, || Who has enlarged his soul as Sheol, || And is as death that is not satisfied, || And gathers to itself all the nations, || And assembles to itself all the peoples, ⁶Are these not—all of them—an allegory taken up against him, || And a moral of acute sayings for him, || And say, Woe [to] him who is multiplying [what is] not his? Until when also is he multiplying to himself heavy pledges? ⁷Do your usurers not instantly rise up, || And those shaking you awake, || And you have been a spoil to them? ⁸Because you have spoiled many nations, || All the remnant of the peoples spoil you, || Because of man's blood, and of violence [to] the land, || [To] the city, and [to] all dwelling in it. ⁹Woe [to] him who is gaining evil gain for his house, || To set his nest on high, || To be delivered from the hand of evil, ¹⁰You have counseled a shameful thing to your house, || To cut off many peoples, and your soul [is] sinful. ¹¹For a stone cries out from the wall, || And a beam from the wood answers it. ¹²Woe [to] him who is building a city by blood, || And establishing a city by iniquity. ¹³Behold, is it not from YHWH of Hosts || And peoples are fatigued for fire, || And nations for vanity are weary? ¹⁴For the earth is full of the knowledge of the glory of YHWH, || As the waters cover over a sea. ¹⁵Woe [to] him who is giving drink to his neighbor, || Pouring out your bottle, and also making drunk, || In order to look on their nakedness. ¹⁶You have been filled—shame without honor, || Drink also, and be uncircumcised, || Turn around to you does the cup of the right hand of YHWH, || And shameful spewing [is] on your glory. ¹⁷For violence [done to] Lebanon covers you, || And spoil of beasts frightens them, || Because of man's blood, and of violence [to] the land, || [To] the city, and [to] all dwelling in it. ¹⁸What profit has a carved image given || That its former has hewn it? A molten image and teacher of falsehood, || That the former has trusted on his own formation—to make mute idols? ¹⁹Woe [to] him who is saying to wood, Awake, || To a mute stone, Stir up, || It [is] a teacher! Behold, it is overlaid—gold and silver, || And there is no spirit in its midst. ²⁰And YHWH [is] in His holy temple, || Be silent before Him, all the earth!"

CHAPTER 3

¹A prayer of Habakkuk the prophet, [set] on shigionoth: ²O YHWH, I heard your report, || I have been afraid, O YHWH, || Your work! In midst of years revive it, || In the midst of years You make known, || In anger You remember mercy. ³God comes from Teman, || The Holy One from Mount Paran. Pause! His splendor has covered the heavens, || And His praise has filled the earth. ⁴And the brightness is as the light, || He has rays out of His hand, || And there—the hiding of His strength. ⁵Before Him goes pestilence, || And a burning flame goes forth at His feet. ⁶He has stood, and He measures earth, || He has seen, and He shakes off nations, || And mountains of antiquity scatter themselves, || The hills of old have bowed, || The ways of old [are] His. ⁷Under sorrow I have seen tents of Cushan, || Curtains of the land of Midian tremble. ⁸Has YHWH been angry against rivers? Against rivers [is] Your anger? [Is] Your wrath against the sea? For You ride on Your horses—Your chariots of salvation. ⁹You make Your bow utterly naked, || The tribes have sworn, saying, "Pause!" You cleave the earth [with] rivers. ¹⁰Seen You—pained are mountains, || An inundation of waters has passed over, || The deep has given forth its voice, || It has lifted up its hands high. ¹¹Sun—moon—has stood—a habitation, || Your arrows go on at the light, || At the brightness, the glittering of Your spear. ¹²In indignation You tread earth, || In anger You thresh nations. ¹³You have gone forth for the salvation of Your people, || For salvation with Your Anointed, || You have struck the head of

the house of the wicked, || Laying bare the foundation to the neck. Pause! ¹⁴You have pierced the head of his leaders with his own rods, || They are tempestuous to scatter me, || Their exultation [is] as to consume the poor in secret. ¹⁵You have proceeded through the sea with Your horses—the clay of many waters. ¹⁶I have heard, and my belly trembles, || At the noise have my lips quivered, || Rottenness comes into my bones, || And in my place I tremble, || That I rest for a day of distress, || At the coming up of the people, he overcomes it. ¹⁷Though the fig tree does not flourish, || And there is no produce among vines, || The work of the olive has failed, || And fields have not yielded food, || The flock has been cut off from the fold, || And there is no herd in the stalls, ¹⁸Yet I, in YHWH I exult, || I am joyful in the God of my salvation. ¹⁹YHWH the Lord [is] my strength, || And He makes my feet like does, || And causes me to tread on my high-places. To the overseer with my stringed instruments!

ZEPHANIAH

CHAPTER 1

¹A word of YHWH that has been to Zephaniah son of Cushi, son of Gedaliah, son of Amariah, son of Hezikiah, in the days of Josiah son of Amoz, king of Judah: ²"I utterly consume all from off the face of the ground," || A declaration of YHWH. ³"I consume man and beast, || I consume bird of the heavens, and fishes of the sea, || And the stumbling-blocks—the wicked, || And I have cut off man from the face of the ground," || A declaration of YHWH, ⁴"And I have stretched out My hand against Judah, || And against all inhabiting Jerusalem, || And cut off from this place the remnant of Ba'al, || The name of the idolatrous priests, with the priests, ⁵And those bowing themselves || On the roofs to the host of the heavens, || And those bowing themselves, || Swearing to YHWH, and swearing by Malcham, ⁶And those removing from after YHWH, || And who have not sought YHWH, nor implored Him." ⁷Hush! Because of Lord YHWH, || For near [is the] Day of YHWH, || For YHWH has prepared a sacrifice, || He has sanctified His invited ones. ⁸"And it has come to pass, || In the day of the sacrifice of YHWH, || That I have laid a charge on the heads, || And on sons of the king, || And on all putting on strange clothing. ⁹And I have laid a charge on everyone || Who is leaping over the threshold in that day, || Who are filling the house of their masters || [With] violence and deceit. ¹⁰And there has been in that day," || A declaration of YHWH, || "The noise of a cry from the Fish Gate, || And of a howling from the Second [Quarter], || And of great destruction from the hills. ¹¹Howl, you inhabitants of the hollow place, || For all the merchant people have been cut off, || All carrying silver have been cut off. ¹²And it has come to pass at that time, || I search Jerusalem with lights, || And I have laid a charge on the men || Who are hardened on their preserved things, || Who are saying in their heart: YHWH does no good, nor does He do evil. ¹³And their wealth has been for a spoil, || And their houses for desolation, || And they have built houses, and do not inhabit, || And they have planted vineyards, || And they do not drink their wine." ¹⁴Near [is] the Great Day of YHWH, || Near, and hastening exceedingly, || The noise of the Day of YHWH, || There a mighty one bitterly shrieks. ¹⁵A day of wrath [is] that day, || A day of adversity and distress, || A day of devastation and desolation, || A day of darkness and gloominess, || A day of cloud and thick darkness, ¹⁶A day of horn and shouting against the fortified cities, || And against the high corners. ¹⁷"And I have sent distress to men, || And they have walked as the blind, || For against YHWH they have sinned, || And poured out is their blood as dust, || And their flesh [is] as dung." ¹⁸Even their silver, even their gold, is not able to deliver them in a day of the wrath of YHWH, and in the fire of His jealousy is the whole land consumed, for He makes only a hurried end of all the inhabitants of the land!

CHAPTER 2

¹Bend yourselves, indeed, bend, || O nation not desired, ²Before the bringing forth of a statute, || The day has passed on as chaff, || While the heat of the anger of YHWH has not yet come in on you, || While [the] Day of the anger of YHWH has not yet come in on you, ³Seek YHWH, all you humble of the land, || Who have done His judgment, || Seek righteousness, seek humility, || It may be you are hidden in the Day of the anger of YHWH. ⁴For Gaza is forsaken, || And Ashkelon [is] for a desolation, || Ashdod! At noon they cast her forth, || And Ekron is rooted up. ⁵Behold! O inhabitants of the seacoast, || Nation of the Cherethites, || A word of YHWH [is] against you, || Canaan, land of the Philistines, || "And I have destroyed you without an inhabitant." ⁶And the seacoast has been habitations, || Cottages [for] shepherds, and folds [for] a flock. ⁷And the coast has been for the remnant of the house of Judah, || By them they have pleasure, || In houses of Ashkelon they lie down at evening, || For their God YHWH inspects them, || And He has turned back [to] their captivity. ⁸"I have heard the reproach of Moab, || And the revilings of the sons of Ammon, || With which they reproached My people, || And magnify [themselves] against their border. ⁹Therefore, [as] I live," || A declaration of YHWH of Hosts, God of Israel, || "Surely Moab is as Sodom, || And the sons of Ammon as Gomorrah, || An overrunning of nettles and salt-pits, || And a desolation for all time. A remnant of My people seizes them, || And a remnant of My nation inherits them." ¹⁰This [is] to them for their arrogancy, || Because they have reproached, || And they magnify [themselves] against the people of YHWH of Hosts. ¹¹Fearful [is] YHWH against them, || For He made all gods of the land bare, || And all islanders of the nations bow themselves to Him, || Each from his place. ¹²"Also you, O Cushim, they [are] pierced of My sword." ¹³And He stretches His hand against the north, || And destroys Asshur, || And He sets Nineveh for a desolation, || A dry land like a wilderness. ¹⁴And droves have crouched in her midst, || Every beast of the nation, || Both pelican and hedgehog lodge in her knobs, || A voice sings at the window, || "Destruction [is] at the threshold, || For the cedar-work is exposed." ¹⁵This [is] the exulting city that is dwelling confidently, || That is saying in her heart, || "I [am], and there is none beside me," || How she has been for a desolation, || A crouching-place for beasts, || Everyone passing by her hisses, || He shakes his hand!

CHAPTER 3

¹Woe [to] the rebelling and defiling, || The oppressing city! ²She has not listened to the voice, || She has not accepted instruction, || In YHWH she has not trusted, || She has not drawn near to her God. ³Her heads in her midst [are] roaring lions, || Her judges [are] wolves [as in] evening, || They have not gnawn the bone in the morning. ⁴Her prophets unstable—men of treachery, || Her priests have defiled the sanctuary, || They have violated the Law. ⁵YHWH [is] righteous in her midst, || He does not do perverseness, || Morning by morning His judgment He gives to the light, || It has not been lacking, || And the perverse do not know shame. ⁶"I have cut off nations, || Desolated have been their chief ones, || I have laid waste their out-places without any passing by, || Destroyed have been their cities, || Without man, without inhabitant. ⁷I have said: Only, you fear Me, || You accept instruction, || And her habitation is not cut off, || All that I have appointed for her, || But they have risen early, || They have corrupted all their doings. ⁸Therefore, wait for Me," || A declaration of YHWH, || "For the day of My rising for prey, || For My judgment [is] to gather nations, || To assemble kingdoms, || To pour out on them My indignation, || All the heat of My anger, || For by the fire of My jealousy all the earth is consumed. ⁹For then I turn a pure lip to peoples, || To call all of them by the Name of YHWH, || To serve Him [with]

ZEPHANIAH

one shoulder. ¹⁰From beyond the rivers of Cush, My supplicants, || The daughter of My scattered ones, || Bring My present. ¹¹In that day you are not ashamed because of any of your actions, || With which you have transgressed against Me, || For then I turn aside from your midst || The exulting ones of your excellence, || And you are to be haughty no longer, || In My holy mountain. ¹²And I have left in your midst a people humble and poor, || And they have trusted in the Name of YHWH. ¹³The remnant of Israel does no perversity, nor speaks lies, || Nor is a deceitful tongue found in their mouth, || For they have delight, and have lain down, || And there is none troubling." ¹⁴Cry aloud, O daughter of Zion, shout, O Israel, || Rejoice and exult with the whole heart, O daughter of Jerusalem. ¹⁵YHWH has turned aside your judgments, || He has faced your enemy, || The King of Israel, YHWH, [is] in your midst, || You see evil no more. ¹⁶In that day it is said to Jerusalem, || "Do not fear, O Zion, || Do not let your hands be feeble. ¹⁷Your God YHWH [is] in your midst, || A mighty one [to] save, || He rejoices over you with joy, || He works in His love, || He delights over you with singing." ¹⁸"I have gathered My afflicted from the appointed place, || They have been bearing reproach from you for her sake. ¹⁹Behold, I am dealing with all afflicting you at that time, || And I have saved the halting one, || And I gather the ones driven out, || And have set them for a praise and for a name, || In all the land of their shame. ²⁰At that time I bring you in, || Even at the time of My assembling you, || For I give you for a name, and for a praise, || Among all peoples of the land, || In My turning back [to] your captivity before your eyes," said YHWH!

HAGGAI

CHAPTER 1

¹In the second year of Darius the king, in the sixth month, on the first day of the month, a word of YHWH has been by the hand of Haggai the prophet, to Zerubbabel son of Shealtiel, governor of Judah, and to Joshua son of Josedech, the high priest, saying, ²"Thus spoke YHWH of Hosts, saying, This people—they have said, || The time has not come, || The time the house of YHWH [is] to be built." ³And there is a word of YHWH by the hand of Haggai the prophet, saying, ⁴"Is it time for you to dwell in your covered houses, || And this house to lie waste?" ⁵And now, thus said YHWH of Hosts: "Set your heart to your ways. ⁶You have sown much, and brought in little, || To eat, and not to satiety, || To drink, and not to drunkenness, || To clothe, and none has heat, || And he who is hiring himself out, || Is hiring himself for a bag pierced through." ⁷Thus said YHWH of Hosts: "Set your heart to your ways. ⁸Go up the mountain, and you have brought in wood, || And build the house, and I am pleased with it. And I am honored," said YHWH. ⁹"Looking for much, and behold, little, || And you brought [it] home, and I blew on it—why?" A declaration of YHWH of Hosts, || "Because of My house that is desolate, || And you are running—each to his house, ¹⁰Therefore, over you the heavens have refrained from dew, || And the land has refrained its increase. ¹¹And I proclaim drought on the land, || And on the mountains, and on the grain, || And on the new wine, and on the oil, || And on what the ground brings forth, || And on man, and on beast, || And on all labor of the hands." ¹²And Zerubbabel son of Shealtiel, and Joshua son of Josedech, the high priest, and all the remnant of the people, listen to the voice of their God YHWH, and to the words of Haggai the prophet, as their God YHWH had sent him, and the people are afraid of the face of YHWH. ¹³And Haggai, messenger of YHWH, in messages of YHWH, speaks to the people, saying, "I [am] with you, a declaration of YHWH." ¹⁴And YHWH stirs up the spirit of Zerubbabel son of Shealtiel, governor of Judah, and the spirit of Joshua son of Josedech, the high priest, and the spirit of all the remnant of the people, and they come in, and work in the house of YHWH of Hosts their God, ¹⁵in the twenty-fourth day of the sixth month, in the second year of Darius the king.

CHAPTER 2

¹In the seventh [month], on the twenty-first of the month, a word of YHWH has been by the hand of Haggai the prophet, saying, ²"Now speak to Zerubbabel son of Shealtiel, governor of Judah, and to Joshua son of Josedech, the high priest, and to the remnant of the people, saying, ³Who among you has been left that saw this house in its former glory? And what are you seeing it now? Is it not, compared with it, as nothing in your eyes? ⁴And now, be strong, O Zerubbabel," || A declaration of YHWH, || "And be strong, O Joshua, son of Josedech, the high priest, || And be strong, all you people of the land," || A declaration of YHWH, || "And do, for I [am] with you," || A declaration of YHWH of Hosts. ⁵"The thing that I covenanted with you, || In your coming forth from Egypt, || And My Spirit is remaining in your midst, do not fear." ⁶For thus said YHWH of Hosts: "Yet once more—it [is] a little, || And I am shaking the heavens and the earth, || And the sea, and the dry land, ⁷And I have shaken all the nations, || And they have come [to] the desire of all the nations, || And I have filled this house [with] glory," said YHWH of Hosts. ⁸"The silver [is] Mine, and the gold [is] Mine," || A declaration of YHWH of Hosts. ⁹"Greater is the glory of this latter house, || Than of the former," said YHWH of Hosts, || "And I give peace in this place," || A declaration of YHWH of Hosts. ¹⁰On the twenty-fourth of the ninth [month], in the second year of Darius, a word of YHWH has been by the hand of Haggai the prophet, saying, ¹¹Thus said YHWH of Hosts: "Now ask the priests of the Law, saying, ¹²Behold, [when] one carries holy flesh in the skirt of his garment, and he has come with his skirt against the bread, or against the stew, or against the wine, or against the oil, or against any food—is it holy?" And the priests answer and say, "No." ¹³And Haggai says, "If the unclean of body comes against any of these, is it unclean?" And the priests answer and say, "It is unclean." ¹⁴And Haggai answers and says, "So [is] this people, and so [is] this nation before Me," a declaration of YHWH, "and so [is] every work of their hands, and that which they bring near there—it is unclean. ¹⁵And now, please lay [it] to your heart, || From this day and onward, || Before the laying of stone to stone in the temple of YHWH. ¹⁶From that time [one] has come to a heap of twenty, || And it has been ten, || He has come to the wine vat to draw out fifty measures, || And it has been twenty. ¹⁷I have struck you with blasting, || And with mildew, and with hail—All the work of your hands, || And there is none of you with Me," || A declaration of YHWH. ¹⁸"Now set [it] to your heart, from this day and onward, from the twenty-fourth day of the ninth [month], even from the day that the temple of YHWH has been founded, set [it] to your heart. ¹⁹Is the seed yet in the barn? And until now the vine and the fig, || And the pomegranate, and the olive-tree, || Have not borne—from this day I bless." ²⁰And there is a word of YHWH a second time to Haggai, on the twenty-fourth of the month, saying, ²¹"Speak to Zerubbabel governor of Judah, saying, I am shaking the heavens and the earth, ²²And have overturned the throne of kingdoms, || And I have destroyed the strength of kingdoms of the nations, || And overturned chariot and its charioteers, || And horses and their riders have come down, || Each by the sword of his brother. ²³In that day," a declaration of YHWH of Hosts, || "I take you, Zerubbabel, son of Shealtiel, My servant," || A declaration of YHWH, || "And have set you as a signet, || For I have fixed on you," || A declaration of YHWH of Hosts!

ZECHARIAH

CHAPTER 1

¹In the eighth month, in the second year of Darius, a word of YHWH has been to Zechariah, son of Berechiah, son of Iddo the prophet, saying, ²"YHWH was angry against your fathers—wrath! ³And you have said to them, Thus said YHWH of Hosts: Return to Me, || A declaration of YHWH of Hosts, || And I return to you, said YHWH of Hosts. ⁴You will not be as your fathers, || To whom the former prophets called, || Saying, Thus said YHWH of Hosts: Please turn back from your evil ways and from your evil doings, || And they did not listen, || Nor attend to Me—a declaration of YHWH. ⁵Your fathers—where [are] they? And the prophets—do they live for all time? ⁶Only, My words and My statutes, || That I commanded My servants the prophets, || Have they not overtaken your fathers? And they turn back and say: As YHWH of Hosts designed to do to us, || According to our ways, and according to our doings, || So He has done to us." ⁷On the twenty-fourth day of the eleventh month (it [is] the month of Sebat), in the second year of Darius, a word of YHWH has been to Zechariah, son of Berechiah, son of Iddo the prophet. [He was] saying: ⁸I have seen by night, and behold, one riding on a red horse, and he is standing between the myrtles that [are] in the shade, and behind him [are] horses, red, bay, and white. ⁹And I say, "What [are] these, my lord?" And the messenger who is speaking with me says to me, "I show you what these [are]." ¹⁰And the one who is standing between the myrtles answers and says, "These [are] they whom YHWH has sent to walk up and down in the land." ¹¹And they answer the Messenger of YHWH who is standing between the myrtles, and say, "We have walked up and down in the land, and behold, all the land is sitting still, and at rest." ¹²And the Messenger of YHWH answers and says, "YHWH of Hosts! Until when do You not pity Jerusalem, and the cities of Judah, that You have abhorred these seventy years?" ¹³And YHWH answers the messenger, who is speaking with me, good words, comfortable words. ¹⁴And the messenger who is speaking with me, says to me, "Call, saying, Thus said YHWH of Hosts: I have been zealous for Jerusalem, || And for Zion [with] great zeal. ¹⁵And [with] great wrath I am angry against the nations who are at ease, || For I was a little angry, and they assisted—for evil. ¹⁶Therefore, thus said YHWH: I have turned to Jerusalem with mercies, || My house is built in it, || A declaration of YHWH of Hosts, || And a line is stretched over Jerusalem. ¹⁷Again call, saying, || Thus said YHWH of Hosts: Again My cities overflow from good, || And YHWH has again comforted Zion, || And He has fixed again on Jerusalem." ¹⁸And I lift up my eyes, and look, and behold, four horns. ¹⁹And I say to the messenger who is speaking with me, "What [are] these?" And he says to me, "These [are] the horns that have scattered Judah, Israel, and Jerusalem." ²⁰And YHWH shows me four artisans. ²¹And I say, "What [are] these coming to do?" And He speaks, saying, "These [are] the horns that have scattered Judah, so that no one has lifted up his head, and these come to trouble them, to cast down the horns of the nations who are lifting up a horn against the land of Judah—to scatter it."

CHAPTER 2

¹And I lift up my eyes, and look, and behold, a man, and in his hand a measuring line. ²And I say, "To where are you going?" And he says to me, "To measure Jerusalem, to see how much [is] its breadth and how much its length." ³And behold, the messenger who is speaking with me is going out, and another messenger is going out to meet him, ⁴and he says to him, "Run, speak to this young man, saying, || Jerusalem is inhabited [as] open places, || From the abundance of man and beast in her midst. ⁵And I am to her—a declaration of YHWH—A wall of fire all around, || And I am for glory in her midst. ⁶Behold, and flee from the land of the north, || A declaration of YHWH, || For as the four winds of the heavens, || I have spread you abroad, || A declaration of YHWH. ⁷Behold, Zion, be delivered who are dwelling [with] the daughter of Babylon. ⁸For thus said YHWH of Hosts: He has sent Me after glory to the nations who are spoiling you, || For he who is coming against you, || Is coming against the pupil of His eye. ⁹For behold, I am waving My hand against them, || And they have been a spoil to their servants. And you have known that YHWH of Hosts has sent Me. ¹⁰Sing, and rejoice, O daughter of Zion, || For behold, I am coming, and have dwelt in your midst, || A declaration of YHWH. ¹¹And many nations have been joined to YHWH in that day, || And they have been to Me for a people, || And I have dwelt in your midst, || And you have known that YHWH of Hosts has sent Me to you. ¹²And YHWH has inherited Judah, || His portion on the holy ground, || And He has fixed again on Jerusalem. ¹³Hush, all flesh, because of YHWH, || For He has been roused up from His holy habitation!"

CHAPTER 3

¹And he shows me Joshua the high priest standing before the Messenger of YHWH, and Satan standing at his right hand, to be an adversary to him. ²And YHWH says to Satan: "YHWH pushes against you, O Satan, || Indeed, YHWH pushes against you, || Who is fixing on Jerusalem, || Is not this a brand delivered from fire?" ³And Joshua was clothed with filthy garments, and is standing before the Messenger. ⁴And He answers and speaks to those standing before Him, saying, "Turn aside the filthy garments from off him." And He says to him, "See, I have caused your iniquity to pass away from off you, so as to clothe you with costly apparel." ⁵He also said, "Let them set a pure turban on his head." And they set the pure turban on his head, and clothe him with garments. And the Messenger of YHWH is standing, ⁶and the Messenger of YHWH protests to Joshua, saying, ⁷"Thus said YHWH of Hosts: If you walk in My ways, || And if you keep My charge, || Then also you judge My house, || And also you keep My courts, || And I have given to you conductors among these standing by. ⁸Now hear, O Joshua the high priest, || You and your companions sitting before you || (For men of type [are] they), || For behold, I am bringing in My servant—a Shoot. ⁹For behold, the stone that I put before Joshua, || On one stone [are] seven eyes, || Behold, I am engraving its engraving, || A declaration of YHWH of Hosts, || And I have removed the iniquity of that land in one day. ¹⁰In that day—a declaration of YHWH of Hosts, || You call, each to his neighbor, || To the place of the vine, || And to the place of the fig tree!"

CHAPTER 4

¹And the messenger who is speaking with me turns back, and stirs me up as one who is stirred up out of his sleep, ²and he says to me, "What are you seeing?" And I say, "I have looked, and behold, a lampstand of gold—all of it, and its bowl [is] on its top, and its seven lamps [are] on it, and twice seven pipes [are] to the lights that [are] on its top, ³and two olive-trees [are] by it, one on the right of the bowl and one on its left." ⁴And I answer and speak to the messenger who is speaking with me, saying, "What [are] these, my lord?" ⁵And the messenger who is speaking with me answers and says to me, "Have you not known what these [are]?" And I say, "No, my lord." ⁶And he answers and speaks to me, saying, "This [is] a word of YHWH to Zerubbabel, saying, || Not by a force, nor by power, || But—by My Spirit, said YHWH of Hosts. ⁷Who [are] you, O great mountain || Before Zerubbabel—for a plain! And he has brought forth the topstone, || Cries of Grace, grace—[are] to it." ⁸And there is a word of YHWH to me, saying, ⁹"Hands of Zerubbabel founded this house, || And his hands finish it, || And you have known that YHWH of Hosts || Has sent Me to you. ¹⁰For who trampled on the day of small things, || They have rejoiced, || And seen the tin weight in the hand of Zerubbabel, || These seven [are] the eyes of YHWH, || They are going to and fro in all the land." ¹¹And I answer and say to him, "What [are] these two olive-trees, on the right of the lampstand, and on its left?" ¹²And I answer a second time, and say to him, "What [are] the two branches of the olive trees that, by means of the two golden pipes, are

ZECHARIAH

emptying out of themselves the oil?" ¹³And he speaks to me, saying, "Have you not known what these [are]?" And I say, "No, my lord." ¹⁴And he says, "These [are] the two sons of the oil, who are standing by the Lord of the whole earth."

CHAPTER 5

¹And I turn back, and lift up my eyes, and look, and behold, a flying scroll. ²And he says to me, "What are you seeing?" And I say, "I am seeing a flying scroll, its length [is] twenty by the cubit, and its breadth [is] ten by the cubit." ³And he says to me, "This [is] the execration that is going forth over the face of all the land, for everyone who is stealing, on the one side, according to it, has been declared innocent, and everyone who has sworn, on the other side, according to it, has been declared innocent." ⁴"I have brought it out," a declaration of YHWH of Hosts, "and it has come into the house of the thief, and into the house of him who has sworn in My Name with a falsehood, and it has remained in the midst of his house, and has consumed it, both its wood and its stones." ⁵And the messenger who is speaking with me goes forth and says to me, "Now lift up your eyes, and [do you] see what this [is] that is coming forth?" ⁶And I say, "What [is] it?" And he says, "This—the ephah that is coming forth." And he says, "This [is] their aspect in all the land. ⁷And behold, a disc of lead lifted up; and this [is] a woman sitting in the midst of the ephah." ⁸And he says, "This [is] the wicked woman." And he casts her into the midst of the ephah, and casts the weight of lead on its mouth. ⁹And I lift up my eyes, and see, and behold, two women are coming forth, and wind [is] in their wings; and they have wings like wings of the stork, and they lift up the ephah between the earth and the heavens. ¹⁰And I say to the messenger who is speaking with me, "To where [are] they causing the ephah to go?" ¹¹And he says to me, "To build a house for it in the land of Shinar." And it has been prepared and has been placed there on its base.

CHAPTER 6

¹And I turn back, and lift up my eyes, and look, and behold, four chariots are coming forth from between two of the mountains, and the mountains [are] mountains of bronze. ²In the first chariot [are] red horses, and in the second chariot brown horses, ³and in the third chariot white horses, and in the fourth chariot strong spotted horses. ⁴And I answer and say to the messenger who is speaking with me, "What [are] these, my lord?" ⁵And the messenger answers and says to me, "These [are] four spirits of the heavens coming forth from presenting themselves before the Lord of the whole earth. ⁶The brown horses that [are] therein, are coming forth to the land of the north; and the white have come forth to their back part; and the spotted have come forth to the land of the south; ⁷and the strong ones have come forth, and they seek to go to walk up and down in the earth"; and he says, "Go, walk up and down in the earth"; and they walk up and down in the earth. ⁸And he calls me, and speaks to me, saying, "See, those coming forth to the land of the north have caused My Spirit to rest in the land of the north." ⁹And there is a word of YHWH to me, saying, ¹⁰"Take of the captivity (who came from Babylon) from Heldai, from Tobijah, and from Jedaiah, and you have come in—you, in that day, indeed, you have come into the house of Josiah son of Zephaniah, ¹¹and you have taken silver and gold, and have made a crown, and have placed [it] on the head of Joshua son of Josedech, the high priest, ¹²and have spoken to him, saying, || Thus spoke YHWH of Hosts, saying, || Behold, the Man! A Shoot—[is] His Name, || And from His place He shoots up, || And He has built the temple of YHWH. ¹³Indeed, He builds the temple of YHWH, || And He carries away splendor, || And He has sat and ruled on His throne, || And has been a priest on His throne, || And a counsel of peace is between both. ¹⁴And the crown is to Helem, and to Tobijah, and to Jedaiah, and to Hen son of Zephaniah, for a memorial in the temple of YHWH. ¹⁵And the far-off come in, and they have built in the temple of YHWH, and you have known that YHWH of Hosts has sent me to you, indeed, it has come to pass, if you certainly listen to the voice of your God YHWH."

CHAPTER 7

¹And it comes to pass, in the fourth year of Darius the king, a word of YHWH has been to Zechariah, in the fourth of the ninth month, in Chisleu. ²And Beth-El sends Sherezer and Regem-Melech, and its men, to appease the face of YHWH, ³speaking to the priests who [are] at the house of YHWH of Hosts, and to the prophets, saying, "Do I weep in the fifth month—being separated—as I have done these so many years?" ⁴And there is a word of YHWH of Hosts to me, saying, ⁵"Speak to all the people of the land, and to the priests, saying, ⁶When you fasted with mourning in the fifth and in the seventh [months]—even these seventy years—did you keep the fast [to] Me? And when you eat, and when you drink, is it not you who are eating, and you who are drinking? ⁷Are [these] not the words that YHWH proclaimed by the hand of the former prophets, in Jerusalem's being inhabited, and [in] safety, and its cities around it, and the south and the plain—abiding?" ⁸And there is a word of YHWH to Zechariah, saying, ⁹"Thus spoke YHWH of Hosts, saying, || Judge [with] true judgment, || And do kindness and mercy with one another. ¹⁰And do not oppress widow, and fatherless, || Sojourner, and poor, || And you do not devise the calamity of one another in your heart. ¹¹And they refuse to attend, || And they give a stubborn shoulder, || And their ears are made heavy against hearing. ¹²And their heart they have made adamant, || Against hearing the Law, and the words, || That YHWH of Hosts sent by His Spirit, || By the hand of the former prophets, || And there is great wrath from YHWH of Hosts. ¹³And it comes to pass, as He called, || And they have not listened, || So they call, and I do not listen," said YHWH of Hosts. ¹⁴"And I toss them on all the nations, || That they have not known, || The land has been desolate behind them, || Of any passing by and turning back, || And they set a desirable land for a desolation!"

CHAPTER 8

¹And there is a word of YHWH of Hosts, saying, ²"Thus said YHWH of Hosts: I have been zealous for Zion with great zeal, || With great heat I have been zealous for her. ³Thus said YHWH: I have turned back to Zion, || And I have dwelt in the midst of Jerusalem, || And Jerusalem has been called The City of Truth, || And The Mountain of YHWH of Hosts, || The Holy Mountain. ⁴Thus said YHWH of Hosts: Again old men and old women dwell || In broad places of Jerusalem, || And each his staff in his hand, || Because of abundance of days. ⁵And broad places of the city are full of boys and girls, || Playing in its broad places. ⁶Thus said YHWH of Hosts: Surely it is wonderful in the eyes of the remnant of this people in those days, || Also in My eyes it is wonderful, || A declaration of YHWH of Hosts. ⁷Thus said YHWH of Hosts: Behold, I am saving My people from the land of the rising, || And from the land of the going in, of the sun, ⁸And I have brought them in, || They have dwelt in the midst of Jerusalem, || And they have been to Me for a people, || And I am to them for God, || In truth and in righteousness. ⁹Thus said YHWH of Hosts: Let your hands be strong, || You who are hearing in these days these words from the mouth of the prophets, || That in the day the house of YHWH of Hosts has been founded, || The temple [is] to be built. ¹⁰For before those days there has been no hiring of man, || Indeed, a hiring of beasts there is none; And to him who is going out, || And to him who is coming in, || There is no peace because of the adversary, || And I send all men—each against his neighbor. ¹¹And now, not as [in] the former days [am] I to the remnant of this people, || A declaration of YHWH of Hosts. ¹²Because of the sowing of peace, || The vine gives her fruit, || And the earth gives her increase, || And the heavens give their dew, || And I have caused the remnant of this people || To inherit all these. ¹³And it has come to pass, || As you have been a reviling among nations, || O house of Judah, and house of Israel, || So I save you, and you have been a blessing, || Do not fear, let your hands be strong. ¹⁴For thus said YHWH of Hosts: As I purposed to do evil to you, || When your fathers made Me angry—said YHWH of Hosts—And I did not relent, ¹⁵So I have turned back, I have purposed, in these days, || To do good with Jerusalem, || And with the house of Judah—do not fear! ¹⁶These [are] the things that you do: Each speak truth with his neighbor, || Judge [with] truth and peaceful judgment in your gates, ¹⁷And do not devise the evil of his neighbor in your heart, || And do not love a false oath, || For all these [are] things that I have hated, || A declaration of YHWH." ¹⁸And there is a word of YHWH of Hosts to me, saying, ¹⁹"Thus said YHWH of Hosts: The fast of the fourth, and the fast of the fifth, and the fast of the seventh, and the fast of the tenth [months], are to the house of Judah for joy and

ZECHARIAH

for rejoicing, and for pleasant appointed times, and the truth and the peace they have loved. ²⁰Thus said YHWH of Hosts: Yet peoples come, and inhabitants of many cities, ²¹Indeed, inhabitants of one || Have gone to another, saying, || We go diligently, || To appease the face of YHWH, || To seek YHWH of Hosts—I go, even I. ²²Indeed, many peoples have come in, and mighty nations, || To seek YHWH of Hosts in Jerusalem, || And to appease the face of YHWH. ²³Thus said YHWH of Hosts: In those days ten men of all languages of the nations take hold, || Indeed, they have taken hold on the skirt of a man, a Jew, saying, || We go with you, for we heard God [is] with you!"

CHAPTER 9

¹The burden of a word of YHWH against the land of Hadrach, and Demmeseh—his place of rest: (When to YHWH [is] the eye of man, || And of all the tribes of Israel). ²And also Hamath borders thereon, || Tyre and Sidon, for—very wise! ³And Tyre builds a bulwark for herself, || And heaps silver as dust, || And gold as mire of out-places. ⁴Behold, the Lord dispossesses her, || And He has struck her force in the sea, || And she is consumed with fire. ⁵Ashkelon sees and fears, || Also Gaza, and she is exceedingly pained, || Also Ekron—for her expectation dried up, || And a king has perished from Gaza, || And Ashkelon does not remain, ⁶"And a foreigner has dwelt in Ashdod, || And I have cut off the excellence of the Philistines. ⁷And turned aside his blood from his mouth, || His abominations from between his teeth, || And he has remained, even he, to our God, || And he has been as a leader in Judah, || And Ekron as a Jebusite. ⁸And I have pitched a camp for My house, || Because of the passer through, and of the returner, || And an exactor does not pass through against them again, || For now, I have seen with My eyes. ⁹Rejoice exceedingly, O daughter of Zion, || Shout, O daughter of Jerusalem, || Behold, your King comes to you, || Righteous and having salvation, || Afflicted—and riding on a donkey, || And on a colt—a son of female donkeys. ¹⁰And I have cut off the chariot from Ephraim, || And the horse from Jerusalem, || Indeed, the bow of battle has been cut off, || And He has spoken peace to nations, || And His rule [is] from sea to sea, || And from the river to the ends of the earth. ¹¹Also You—by the blood of Your covenant, || I have sent Your prisoners out of the pit, || There is no water in it. ¹²Return to a stronghold, || You prisoners of the hope, || Even today a second announcer I restore to you. ¹³For I have trodden for Myself with Judah, || I have filled a bow [with] Ephraim, || And I have stirred up your sons, O Zion, || Against your sons, O Javan, || And I have set you as the sword of a hero." ¹⁴And YHWH appears for them, || And His arrow has gone forth as lightning, || And Lord YHWH blows with a horn, || And He has gone with whirlwinds of the south. ¹⁵YHWH of Hosts covers them over, || And they consumed, and subdued sling-stones, || Indeed, they have drunk, || They have made a noise as wine, || And they have been full as a bowl, || As corners of an altar. ¹⁶And their God YHWH has saved them in that day, || As a flock of His people, || For stones of a crown are displaying themselves over His ground. ¹⁷For what His goodness! And what His beauty! Grain the young men, || And new wine the virgins—make fruitful!

CHAPTER 10

¹They asked of YHWH rain || In a time of spring rain, || YHWH is making lightnings, || And He gives to them rain [in] showers. To each—the herb in the field. ²Because the teraphim spoke iniquity, || And the diviners have seen a falsehood, || And dreams of the vanity they speak, || [With] vanity they give comfort, || Therefore they have journeyed as a flock, || They are afflicted, for there is no shepherd. ³"My anger burned against the shepherds, || And I lay a charge against the male goats, || For YHWH of Hosts has inspected His flock, the house of Judah, || And set them as His splendid horse in battle. ⁴From him [is] a cornerstone, || From him a nail, from him a battle-bow, || From him goes forth every exactor together. ⁵And they have been as heroes, || Treading in mire of out-places in battle, || And they have fought, for YHWH [is] with them, || And have put to shame riders of horses. ⁶And I have made the house of Judah mighty, || And I save the house of Joseph, || And I have caused them to dwell, for I have loved them, || And they have been as [if] I had not cast them off, || For I [am] their God YHWH, || And I answer them. ⁷And Ephraim has been as a hero, || And their heart has rejoiced as wine, || And their sons see, and they have rejoiced, || Their heart rejoices in YHWH. ⁸I hiss for them, and I gather them, || For I have redeemed them, || And they have multiplied as they multiplied. ⁹And I sow them among peoples, || And in far-off places they remember Me, || And they have lived with their sons, || And they have turned back. ¹⁰And I have brought them back from the land of Egypt, || And I gather them from Asshur, || And I bring them into the land of Gilead and Lebanon, || And [space] is not found for them there. ¹¹And He has passed over through the sea, || And has pressed and struck billows in the sea, || And all depths of a flood have been dried up, || And the excellence of Asshur has been brought down, || And the rod of Egypt turns aside. ¹²And I have made them mighty in YHWH, || And in His Name they walk up and down," || A declaration of YHWH!

CHAPTER 11

¹Open, O Lebanon, your doors, || And fire devours among your cedars. ²Howl, O fir, for the cedar has fallen, || For their majestic ones were destroyed, || Howl, you oaks of Bashan, || For the enclosed forest has come down, ³A voice of the howling of the shepherds! For their robe of honor was destroyed, || A voice of the roaring of young lions! For the excellence of Jordan was destroyed. ⁴Thus said my God YHWH: "Feed the flock of the slaughter, ⁵Whose buyers slay them, and are not guilty, || And their sellers say, Blessed [is] YHWH, || And I am rich, || And their shepherds have no pity on them. ⁶For I no longer have pity on inhabitants of the land, || A declaration of YHWH, || And behold, I am causing man to come forth, || Each into the hand of his neighbor, || And into the hand of his king, || And they have beaten down the land, || And I do not deliver out of their hand." ⁷And I feed the flock of slaughter, even you, you afflicted of the flock; and I take two staffs to myself; I have called one Pleasantness, and I have called the other Bands, and I feed the flock. ⁸And I cut off the three shepherds in one month, and my soul is grieved with them, and also their soul has abhorred me. ⁹And I say, "I do not feed you, the dying, let die; and the cut off, let be cut off; and the remaining ones, let each eat the flesh of its neighbor." ¹⁰And I take my staff Pleasantness, and cut it apart, to make void my covenant that I had made with all the peoples: ¹¹and it is broken in that day, and the afflicted of the flock who are observing me know well, that it [is] a word of YHWH. ¹²And I say to them: "If good in your eyes, give my hire, and if not, refrain"; and they weigh out my hire—thirty pieces of silver. ¹³And YHWH says to me, "Cast it to the potter"; the good price that I have been prized at by them, and I take the thirty pieces of silver, and cast them [into] the house of YHWH, to the potter. ¹⁴And I cut apart my second staff, Bands, || To break the unity between Judah and Israel. ¹⁵And YHWH says to me, "Again take to yourself the instrument of a foolish shepherd. ¹⁶For behold, I am raising up a shepherd in the land, || The cut off he does not inspect, || The shaken off he does not seek, || And the broken he does not heal, || The standing he does not sustain, || And the flesh of the fat he eats, || And their hooves he breaks off. ¹⁷Woe [to] the worthless shepherd, forsaking the flock, || A sword [is] on his arm, and on his right eye, || His arm is utterly dried up, || And his right eye is very dim!"

CHAPTER 12

¹The burden of a word of YHWH on Israel. A declaration of YHWH, || Stretching out the heavens, and founding earth, || And forming the spirit of man in his midst: ²"Behold, I am making Jerusalem a cup of reeling || To all the surrounding peoples, || And it is also against Judah, || In the siege against Jerusalem. ³And it has come to pass in that day, || I make Jerusalem a burdensome stone to all the peoples, || All loading it are completely pressed down, || And gathered against it have been all nations of the earth. ⁴In that day," a declaration of YHWH, || "I strike every horse with astonishment, || And its rider with madness, || And on the house of Judah I open My eyes, || And every horse of the peoples I strike with blindness. ⁵And leaders of Judah have said in their heart, || The inhabitants of Jerusalem [are] strength to me, || In YHWH of Hosts their God. ⁶In that day I make the leaders of Judah || As a hearth of fire among trees, || And as a torch of fire in a sheaf, || And they have consumed—on the right and on the left—all the surrounding peoples, || And

ZECHARIAH

Jerusalem has again inhabited her place in Jerusalem. ⁷And YHWH has saved the tents of Judah first, || So that the beauty of the house of David does not become great against Judah, || And the beauty of the inhabitant of Jerusalem. ⁸In that day YHWH covers over the inhabitant of Jerusalem, || And the stumbling among them has been in that day as David, || And the house of David as God—As the Messenger of YHWH—before them. ⁹And it has come to pass in that day, || I seek to destroy all the nations || Who are coming in against Jerusalem, ¹⁰And I have poured on the house of David, || And on the inhabitant of Jerusalem, || The Spirit of grace and supplications, || And they have looked to Me whom they pierced, || And they have mourned over Him, || Like a mourning over the only one, || And they have been in bitterness for Him, || Like a bitterness over the firstborn. ¹¹In that day, great is the mourning of Jerusalem, || As the mourning of Hadadrimmon in the Valley of Megiddon, ¹²And the land has mourned—every family apart, || The family of the house of David apart, || And their women apart; The family of the house of Nathan apart, || And their women apart; ¹³The family of the house of Levi apart, || And their women apart; The family of Shimei apart, || And their women apart, ¹⁴All the families that are left, || Every family apart, and their women apart!"

CHAPTER 13

¹"In that day there is a fountain opened || To the house of David || And to the inhabitants of Jerusalem, || For sin and for impurity. ²And it has come to pass in that day," || A declaration of YHWH of Hosts, || "I cut off the names of the idols from the land, || And they are not remembered anymore, || And also the prophets and the spirit of uncleanness || I cause to pass away from the land. ³And it has been, when one prophesies again, || That his parents, his father and his mother, || Have said to him, You do not live, || For you have spoken falsehood in the Name of YHWH, || And his father and his mother, his parents, || Have pierced him through in his prophesying. ⁴And it has come to pass in that day, || The prophets are ashamed, each of his vision, in his prophesying, || And they do not put on a hairy robe to deceive. ⁵And [one] has said, I am not a prophet, || A man—I am a tiller of ground, || For ground [is] my possession from my youth. ⁶And [one] has said to him, || What [are] these wounds in your hands? And he has said, Because I was struck [at] home by my lovers. ⁷Sword, awake against My Shepherd, || And against a hero—My Fellow," || A declaration of YHWH of Hosts. "Strike the Shepherd, and the flock is scattered, || And I have put back My hand on the little ones. ⁸And it has come to pass, || In all the land," a declaration of YHWH, || "Two parts in it are cut off—they expire, || And the third is left in it. ⁹And I have brought the third into fire, || And refined them like a refining of silver, || And have tried them like a trying of gold, || It calls in My Name, and I answer it, || I have said, It [is] My people, || And it says, YHWH [is] my God!"

CHAPTER 14

¹Behold, a day has come to YHWH, || And your spoil has been divided in your midst. ²And I have gathered all the nations to Jerusalem to battle, || And the city has been captured, || And the houses have been spoiled, || And the women are lain with, || Half the city has gone forth in a removal, || And the remnant of the people are not cut off from the city. ³And YHWH has gone forth, || And He has fought against those nations, || As in the day of His fighting in a day of conflict. ⁴And His feet have stood, in that day, || On the Mount of Olives, || That [is] eastward before Jerusalem, || And the Mount of Olives has been cleft at its midst, || To the east, and to the west, a very great valley, || And half of the mountain is removed toward the north, || And half toward the south. ⁵And you have fled [to] the valley of My mountains, || For the valley of the mountains joins to Azal, || And you have fled as you fled before the shaking, || In the days of Uzziah king of Judah, || And my God YHWH has come in, || All holy ones [are] with You. ⁶And it has come to pass in that day, || The precious light is not, it is dense darkness, ⁷And there has been one day, || It is known to YHWH, not day nor night, || And it has been at evening-time—there is light. ⁸And it has come to pass in that day, || Living waters go forth from Jerusalem, || Half of them to the Eastern Sea, || And half of them to the Western Sea, || It is in summer and in winter. ⁹And YHWH has become King over all the earth, || In that day YHWH is one, and His Name one. ¹⁰All the land is changed as a plain, || From Gebo to Rimmon, south of Jerusalem, || And she has been high, and has dwelt in her place, || Even from the Gate of Benjamin || To the place of the first gate, to the front gate, || And from the Tower of Hananeel, || To the wine-vats of the king. ¹¹And they have dwelt in her, || And destruction is no more, || And Jerusalem has dwelt confidently. ¹²And this is the plague with which YHWH plagues all the peoples who have warred against Jerusalem: He has consumed away its flesh, || And it is standing on its feet, || And its eyes are consumed in their holes, || And its tongue is consumed in their mouth. ¹³And it has come to pass in that day, || A great destruction [from] YHWH is among them, || And they have each seized the hand of his neighbor, || And his hand has gone up against the hand of his neighbor. ¹⁴And also Judah is fought with in Jerusalem, || And the force of all the surrounding nations has been gathered, || Gold, and silver, and apparel, in great abundance. ¹⁵And so is the plague of the horse, of the mule, || Of the camel, and of the donkey, || And of all the livestock that are in these camps, || As this plague. ¹⁶And it has come to pass, || Everyone who has been left of all the nations, || Who are coming in against Jerusalem, || They have also gone up from year to year, || To bow themselves to the King, YHWH of Hosts, || And to celebrate the Celebration of the Shelters. ¹⁷And it has come to pass, || That he who does not go up of the families of the land to Jerusalem, || To bow himself to the King, YHWH of Hosts, || Even on them there is no shower. ¹⁸And if the family of Egypt does not go up, nor come in, || Then on them is the plague || With which YHWH plagues the nations || That do not go up to celebrate the Celebration of Shelters. ¹⁹This is the punishment of the sin of Egypt, || And the punishment of the sin of all the nations, || That do not go up to celebrate the Celebration of Shelters. ²⁰In that day "Holy to YHWH" is [engraved] on bells of the horse, || And the pots in the house of YHWH || Have been as bowls before the altar. ²¹And every pot in Jerusalem and in Judah, || Have been holy to YHWH of Hosts, || And all those sacrificing have come in, || And have taken of them, and boiled in them, || And in that day there is no merchant anymore in the house of YHWH of Hosts!

MALACHI

CHAPTER 1

¹The burden of a word of YHWH to Israel by the hand of Malachi: ²"I have loved you, said YHWH, || And you have said, || In what have You loved us? ³Is not Esau Jacob's brother?" A declaration of YHWH, || "And I love Jacob, and Esau I have hated, || And I make his mountains a desolation, || And his inheritance for dragons of a wilderness. ⁴Because Edom says, We have been made poor, || And we return and we build the ruins, || Thus said YHWH of Hosts: They build, and I destroy, || And [men] have called to them, || O region of wickedness, || O people whom YHWH defied for all time. ⁵And your eyes see, and you say, || YHWH is magnified beyond the border of Israel, ⁶A son honors a father, and a servant his master. And if I [am] a father, where [is] My glory? And if I [am] a master, where [is] My fear? Said YHWH of Hosts to you, || O priests, despising My Name! And you have said, In what have we despised Your Name? ⁷You are bringing defiled bread near on My altar, || And you have said, In what have we defiled You? In your saying, The table of YHWH—it [is]

MALACHI

despicable, ⁸And when you bring the blind near for sacrifice, [saying], || There is no evil, || And when you bring the lame and sick near, [saying], || There is no evil; Now bring it near to your governor—Does he accept you? Or does he lift up your face?" said YHWH of Hosts. ⁹"And now, please appease the face of God, || And He favors us; This has been from your own hand, || Does He accept your faces?" said YHWH of Hosts. ¹⁰"Who [is] even among you, || And he shuts the double doors? Indeed, you do not kindle My altar for nothing, || I have no pleasure in you," said YHWH of Hosts, || "And I do not accept a present of your hand. ¹¹For from the rising of the sun to its going in, || Great [is] My Name among nations, || And in every place incense is brought near for My Name, and a pure present, || For great [is] My Name among nations," said YHWH of Hosts. ¹²"And you are defiling it in your saying, || The table of YHWH—it is defiled, || As for its fruit—its food is despicable. ¹³And you have said, Behold, what a weariness, || And you have puffed at it," said YHWH of Hosts, || "And you have brought in plunder, || And the lame and the sick, || And you have brought in the present! Do I accept it from your hand?" said YHWH. ¹⁴"And a deceiver [is] cursed, who has in his drove a male, || And is vowing, and is sacrificing a marred thing to the Lord, || For I [am] a great King," said YHWH of Hosts, || "And My Name [is] revered among nations!"

CHAPTER 2

¹"And now, to you [is] this charge, O priests, ²If you do not listen, and if you do not lay [it] to heart, || To give glory to My Name," said YHWH of Hosts, || "I have sent the curse against you, || And I have cursed your blessings, || Indeed, I have also cursed it, || Because you are not laying [it] to heart. ³Behold, I am pushing away the seed before you, || And have scattered dung before your faces, || Dung of your festivals, || And it has taken you away with it. ⁴And you have known that I have sent this charge to you, || For My covenant being with Levi," said YHWH of Hosts. ⁵"My covenant has been of life and of peace with him, || And I make them a fear to him, and he fears Me, || And because of My Name he has been frightened. ⁶The law of truth has been in his mouth, || And perverseness has not been found in his lips, || In peace and in uprightness he walked with Me, || And he brought back many from iniquity. ⁷For the lips of a priest preserve knowledge, || And they seek law from his mouth, || For he [is] a messenger of YHWH of Hosts. ⁸And you, you have turned from the way, || You have caused many to stumble in the Law, || You have corrupted the covenant of Levi," said YHWH of Hosts. ⁹"And I also, I have made you despised and low before all the people, || Because you are not keeping My ways, || And are accepting by superficial things in the Law." ¹⁰Have we not all one Father? Has not our God created us? Why do we deal treacherously, || Each against his brother, || To defile the covenant of our fathers? ¹¹Judah has dealt treacherously, || And abomination has been done in Israel and in Jerusalem, || For Judah has defiled the holy thing of YHWH that He has loved, || And has married the daughter of a strange god. ¹²YHWH cuts off the man who does it, || Tempter and tempted—from the tents of Jacob, || Even he who is bringing a present near to YHWH of Hosts. ¹³And you do this a second time, || Covering the altar of YHWH with tears, || With weeping and groaning, || Because there is no more turning to the present, || Or receiving of a pleasing thing from your hand. ¹⁴And you have said, "Why?" Because YHWH has testified between you || And the wife of your youth, || That you have dealt treacherously against her, || And she [is] your companion, and your covenant-wife. ¹⁵And He did not make one [only], || And a remnant of the Spirit [is] for him. And what [is] the one [alone]! He is seeking a godly seed. And you have been watchful over your spirit, || And with the wife of your youth, || None deal treacherously. ¹⁶"For He hates sending away," said YHWH, God of Israel, || "And he [who] has covered violence with his clothing," said YHWH of Hosts, || "And you have been watchful over your spirit, || And you do not deal treacherously." ¹⁷You have wearied YHWH with your words, || And you have said, "In what have we wearied Him?" In your saying, "Every evildoer [is] good in the eyes of YHWH, || And He is delighting in them," || Or, "Where [is] the God of judgment?"

CHAPTER 3

¹"Behold, I am sending My messenger, || And he has prepared a way before Me, || And suddenly the Lord whom you are seeking comes into His temple, || Even the Messenger of the Covenant, || Whom you are desiring, || Behold, He is coming," said YHWH of Hosts. ²"And who is bearing the day of His coming? And who is standing in His appearing? For He [is] as fire of a refiner, || And as soap of a fuller. ³And He has sat, a refiner and purifier of silver, || And He has purified the sons of Levi, || And has refined them as gold and as silver, || And they have been bringing a present near to YHWH in righteousness. ⁴And the present of Judah and Jerusalem has been sweet to YHWH, || As in days of old, and as in former years. ⁵And I have drawn near to you for judgment, || And I have been a witness, || Making haste against sorcerers, and against adulterers, || And against swearers to a falsehood, || And against oppressors of the hire of a hired worker, || Of a widow, and of a fatherless one, || And those turning aside a sojourner, || And who do not fear Me," said YHWH of Hosts. ⁶"For I, YHWH, have not changed, || And you, the sons of Jacob, || You have not been consumed. ⁷Even from the days of your fathers You have turned aside from My statutes, || And you have not taken heed. Return to Me, and I return to you," said YHWH of Hosts. "And you have said, || In what do we turn back? ⁸Does man deceive God? But you are deceiving Me, || And you have said, || In what have we deceived You? The tithe and the raised-offering! ⁹You are cursed with a curse! And you are deceiving Me—this nation—all of it. ¹⁰Bring in all the tithe to the treasure-house, || And there is food in My house; When you have tried Me, now, with this," said YHWH of Hosts, || "Do I not open the windows of the heavens to you? Indeed, I have emptied on you a blessing until there is no space. ¹¹And I have pushed against the consumer for you, || And He does not destroy the fruit of your ground, || Nor does the vine in the field miscarry to you," said YHWH of Hosts. ¹²"And all the nations have declared you blessed, || For you are a delightful land," said YHWH of Hosts. ¹³"Your words have been hard against Me," said YHWH, || "And you have said, What have we spoken against You? ¹⁴You have said, A vain thing to serve God! And what gain when we kept His charge? And when we have gone in black, || Because of YHWH of Hosts? ¹⁵And now, we are declaring the proud blessed, || Indeed, those doing wickedness have been built up, || Indeed, they have tempted God, and escape. ¹⁶Then have those fearing YHWH spoken to one another, || And YHWH attends and hears, || And a scroll of memorial is written before Him || Of those fearing YHWH, || And of those esteeming His Name. ¹⁷And they have been to Me," said YHWH of Hosts, || "In the day that I am appointing—a peculiar treasure, || And I have had pity on them, || As one has pity on his son who is serving him. ¹⁸And you have turned back and considered, || Between the righteous and the wicked, || Between the servant of God and him who is not His servant."

CHAPTER 4

¹"For behold, the day has come, burning as a furnace, || When all the proud and all those doing wickedness have been stubble, || And the day that came has burned them," said YHWH of Hosts, || "That there is not left to them root or branch, ²But for you fearing My Name, || The Sun of Righteousness has risen with healing in His wings, || And you have gone forth, || And have bounded as calves of a stall. ³And you have trodden down the wicked, || For they are ashes under the soles of your feet, || In the day that I am appointing," said YHWH of Hosts. ⁴"Remember the Law of My servant Moses, || That I commanded him in Horeb, || For all Israel—statutes and judgments. ⁵Behold, I am sending Elijah the prophet to you, || Before the coming of the great and fearful Day of YHWH. ⁶And he has turned back the heart of fathers to sons, || And the heart of sons to their fathers, || Before I come and have utterly struck the land!"

360

THE NEW TESTAMENT
Of our Lord, Savior, and God Jesus Christ, faithfully translated from the Greek

MATTHEW

CHAPTER 1

¹[The] scroll of the birth of Jesus Christ, Son of David, Son of Abraham. ²Abraham begot Isaac, and Isaac begot Jacob, and Jacob begot Judah and his brothers, ³and Judah begot Perez and Zerah of Tamar, and Perez begot Hezron, and Hezron begot Ram, ⁴and Ram begot Amminadab, and Amminadab begot Nahshon, and Nahshon begot Salmon, ⁵and Salmon begot Boaz of Rahab, and Boaz begot Obed of Ruth, and Obed begot Jesse, ⁶and Jesse begot David the king. And David the king begot Solomon, of her [who had been] Uriah's, ⁷and Solomon begot Rehoboam, and Rehoboam begot Abijah, and Abijah begot Asa, ⁸and Asa begot Jehoshaphat, and Jehoshaphat begot Joram, and Joram begot Uzziah, ⁹and Uzziah begot Jotham, and Jotham begot Ahaz, and Ahaz begot Hezekiah, ¹⁰and Hezekiah begot Manasseh, and Manasseh begot Amon, and Amon begot Josiah, ¹¹and Josiah begot Jeconiah and his brothers, at the Babylonian removal. ¹²And after the Babylonian removal, Jeconiah begot Shealtiel, and Shealtiel begot Zerubbabel, ¹³and Zerubbabel begot Abiud, and Abiud begot Eliakim, and Eliakim begot Azor, ¹⁴and Azor begot Sadok, and Sadok begot Achim, and Achim begot Eliud, ¹⁵and Eliud begot Eleazar, and Eleazar begot Matthan, and Matthan begot Jacob, ¹⁶and Jacob begot Joseph, the husband of Mary, of whom was begotten Jesus, who is named Christ. ¹⁷All the generations, therefore, from Abraham to David [are] fourteen generations, and from David to the Babylonian removal fourteen generations, and from the Babylonian removal to the Christ, fourteen generations. ¹⁸And of Jesus Christ, the birth was thus: for His mother Mary having been betrothed to Joseph, before their coming together she was found to have conceived from the Holy Spirit, ¹⁹and her husband Joseph being righteous, and not willing to make her an example, resolved to send her away privately. ²⁰And on his thinking of these things, behold, a messenger of the LORD appeared to him in a dream, saying, "Joseph, son of David, you may not fear to receive your wife Mary, for that which was begotten in her is of [the] Holy Spirit, ²¹and she will bring forth a Son, and you will call His Name Jesus, for He will save His people from their sins." ²²And all this has come to pass, that it may be fulfilled that was spoken by the LORD through the prophet, saying, ²³"Behold, the virgin will conceive, and she will bring forth a Son, and they will call His Name Emmanuel," which is, being interpreted, "God with us." ²⁴And Joseph, having risen from sleep, did as the messenger of the LORD directed him, and received his wife, ²⁵and did not know her until she brought forth her Son—the firstborn, and he called His Name Jesus.

CHAPTER 2

¹And Jesus having been born in Beth-Lehem of Judea, in the days of Herod the king, behold, magi from the east came to Jerusalem, ²saying, "Where is He who was born King of the Jews? For we saw His star in the east, and we came to worship Him." ³And Herod the king having heard, was stirred, and all Jerusalem with him, ⁴and having gathered all the chief priests and scribes of the people, he was inquiring from them where the Christ is born. ⁵And they said to him, "In Beth-Lehem of Judea, for thus it has been written through the prophet: ⁶And you, Beth-Lehem, the land of Judah, you are by no means the least among the leaders of Judah, for out of you will come One leading, who will feed My people Israel." ⁷Then Herod, having called the magi privately, inquired exactly from them the time of the appearing star, ⁸and having sent them to Beth-Lehem, he said, "Having gone—inquire exactly for the Child, and whenever you may have found, bring me back word, that I also having come may worship Him." ⁹And they, having heard the king, departed, and behold, the star, that they saw in the east, went before them, until, having come, it stood over where the Child was. ¹⁰And having seen the star, they rejoiced with exceedingly great joy, ¹¹and having come into the house, they found the Child with His mother Mary, and having fallen down they worshiped Him, and having opened their treasures, they presented to Him gifts, gold, and frankincense, and myrrh, ¹²and having been divinely warned in a dream not to return to Herod, through another way they withdrew to their own region. ¹³And on their having withdrawn, behold, a messenger of the LORD appears in a dream to Joseph, saying, "Having risen, take the Child and His mother, and flee to Egypt, and be there until I may speak to you, for Herod is about to seek the Child to destroy Him." ¹⁴And he, having risen, took the Child and His mother by night, and withdrew to Egypt, ¹⁵and he was there until the death of Herod, that it might be fulfilled that was spoken by the LORD through the prophet, saying, "Out of Egypt I called My Son." ¹⁶Then Herod, having seen that he was deceived by the magi, was very angry, and having sent forth, he slew all the male children in Beth-Lehem, and in all its borders, from two years and under, according to the time that he inquired exactly from the magi. ¹⁷Then was fulfilled that which was spoken by Jeremiah the prophet, saying, ¹⁸"A voice in Ramah was heard—weeping and much mourning—Rachel weeping [for] her children, and she would not be comforted because they are not." ¹⁹And Herod having died, behold, a messenger of the LORD appears in a dream to Joseph in Egypt, ²⁰saying, "Having risen, take the Child and His mother, and be going to the land of Israel, for they have died—those seeking the life of the Child." ²¹And he, having risen, took the Child and His mother, and came to the land of Israel, ²²and having heard that Archelaus reigns over Judea instead of his father Herod, he was afraid to go there, and having been divinely warned in a dream, he withdrew to the parts of Galilee, ²³and coming, he dwelt in a city named Nazareth, that it might be fulfilled that was spoken through the Prophets, that "He will be called a Nazarene."

CHAPTER 3

¹And in those days John the Immerser comes, proclaiming in the wilderness of Judea, ²and saying, "Convert, for the kingdom of the heavens has come near," ³for this is he having been spoken of by Isaiah the prophet, saying, "A voice of one crying in the wilderness: Prepare the way of the LORD, || Make His paths straight." ⁴And this John had his clothing of camel's hair, and a girdle of skin around his loins, and his nourishment was locusts and honey of the field. ⁵Then were going forth to him Jerusalem, and all Judea, and all the region around the Jordan, ⁶and they were immersed in the Jordan by him, confessing their sins. ⁷And having seen many of the Pharisees and Sadducees coming about his immersion, he said to them, "Brood of vipers! Who showed you to flee from the coming wrath? ⁸Bear, therefore, fruits worthy of conversion, ⁹and do not think to say in yourselves, We have a father—Abraham, for I say to you that God is able to raise children to Abraham out of these stones, ¹⁰and now also, the axe is laid to the root of the trees, therefore, every tree not bearing good fruit is cut down, and is cast into fire. ¹¹I indeed immerse you in water for conversion, but He who is coming after me is mightier than I, of whom I am not worthy to carry the sandals, He will immerse you in the Holy Spirit and fire, ¹²whose fan [is] in His hand, and He will thoroughly cleanse His floor, and will gather His wheat into the storehouse, but He will burn the chaff with unquenchable fire." ¹³Then Jesus comes from Galilee to John at the Jordan, to be immersed by him, ¹⁴but John was forbidding Him, saying, "I have need to be immersed by You—and You come to me?" ¹⁵But Jesus answering said to him, "Permit [it] now, for thus it is fitting to us to fulfill all righteousness," then he permits Him. ¹⁶And having been immersed, Jesus

immediately went up from the water, and behold, the heavens were opened to Him, and He saw the Spirit of God descending as a dove, and coming on Him, ¹⁷and behold, a voice out of the heavens, saying, "This is My Son, the Beloved, in whom I delighted."

CHAPTER 4

¹Then Jesus was led up to the wilderness by the Spirit, to be tempted by the Devil, ²and having fasted forty days and forty nights, afterward He hungered. ³And the tempting [one], having come to Him, said, "If You are the Son of God—speak that these stones may become loaves." ⁴But He answering said, "It has been written: Man does not live on bread alone, but on every word coming forth from the mouth of God." ⁵Then the Devil takes Him to the [holy] city, and sets Him on the pinnacle of the temple, ⁶and says to Him, "If You are the Son of God—cast Yourself down, for it has been written that, His messengers He will charge concerning you, and on hands they will bear you up, that you may not dash your foot on a stone." ⁷Jesus said to him again, "It has been written: You will not tempt the LORD your God." ⁸Again the Devil takes Him to a very high mountain, and shows to Him all the kingdoms of the world and their glory, ⁹and says to Him, "All these I will give to You, if falling down You may worship me." ¹⁰Then Jesus says to him, "Go—Satan, for it has been written: You will worship the LORD your God, and Him only will you serve." ¹¹Then the Devil leaves Him, and behold, messengers came and were ministering to Him. ¹²And Jesus, having heard that John was delivered up, withdrew to Galilee, ¹³and having left Nazareth, having come, He dwelt at Capernaum that is by the sea, in the borders of Zebulun and Naphtali, ¹⁴that it might be fulfilled that was spoken through Isaiah the prophet, saying, ¹⁵"Land of Zebulun and land of Naphtali, way of the sea, beyond the Jordan, Galilee of the nations! ¹⁶The people that is sitting in darkness saw a great light, and to those sitting in a region and shadow of death—light arose to them." ¹⁷From that time Jesus began to proclaim and to say, "Convert, for the kingdom of the heavens has come near." ¹⁸And Jesus, walking by the Sea of Galilee, saw two brothers, Simon named Peter and his brother Andrew, casting a drag into the sea—for they were fishers— ¹⁹and He says to them, "Come after Me, and I will make you fishers of men," ²⁰and they, immediately, having left the nets, followed Him. ²¹And having advanced from there, He saw two other brothers, James of Zebedee, and his brother John, in the boat with their father Zebedee, refitting their nets, and He called them, ²²and they, immediately, having left the boat and their father, followed Him. ²³And Jesus was going in all of Galilee teaching in their synagogues, and proclaiming the good news of the kingdom, and healing every disease and every sickness among the people, ²⁴and His fame went forth to all Syria, and they brought to Him all the ill having manifold oppressing diseases and torments—and demoniacs, and lunatics, and paralytics—and He healed them. ²⁵And there followed Him many multitudes from Galilee, and Decapolis, and Jerusalem, and Judea, and beyond the Jordan.

CHAPTER 5

¹And having seen the multitudes, He went up to the mountain, and He having sat down, His disciples came to Him, ²and having opened His mouth, He was teaching them, saying, ³"Blessed the poor in spirit—because theirs is the kingdom of the heavens. ⁴Blessed the mourning—because they will be comforted. ⁵Blessed the meek—because they will inherit the land. ⁶Blessed those hungering and thirsting for righteousness—because they will be filled. ⁷Blessed the kind—because they will find kindness. ⁸Blessed the clean in heart—because they will see God. ⁹Blessed the peacemakers—because they will be called sons of God. ¹⁰Blessed those persecuted for righteousness' sake—because theirs is the kingdom of the heavens. ¹¹Blessed are you whenever they may reproach you, and may persecute, and may say any evil thing against you falsely for My sake— ¹²rejoice and be glad, because your reward [is] great in the heavens, for thus they persecuted the prophets who were before you. ¹³You are the salt of the earth, but if the salt may lose savor, in what will it be salted? It is good for nothing from now on, except to be cast outside, and to be trodden down by men. ¹⁴You are the light of the world, a city set on a mountain is not able to be hid; ¹⁵nor do they light a lamp and put it under the measure, but on the lampstand, and it shines to all those in the house; ¹⁶so let your light shine before men, that they may see your good works, and may glorify your Father who [is] in the heavens. ¹⁷Do not suppose that I came to throw down the Law or the Prophets—I did not come to throw down, but to fulfill; ¹⁸for truly I say to you, until the heaven and the earth may pass away, one iota or one tittle may not pass away from the Law, until all may come to pass. ¹⁹Therefore whoever may loose one of these commands—the least—and may teach men so, he will be called least in the kingdom of the heavens, but whoever may do and may teach [them], he will be called great in the kingdom of the heavens. ²⁰For I say to you that if your righteousness may not abound above that of the scribes and Pharisees, you may not enter into the kingdom of the heavens. ²¹You heard that it was said to the ancients: You will not murder, and whoever may murder will be in danger of the judgment; ²²but I say to you that everyone who is angry at his brother without cause will be in danger of the judgment, and whoever may say to his brother, Stupid, will be in danger of the Sanhedrin, and whoever may say, Moron, will be in danger of the Gehenna of fire. ²³If, therefore, you may bring your gift to the altar, and there may remember that your brother has anything against you, ²⁴leave there your gift before the altar, and go—first be reconciled to your brother, and then having come, bring your gift. ²⁵Be agreeing with your opponent quickly, while you are in the way with him, that the opponent may not deliver you to the judge, and the judge may deliver you to the officer, and you may be cast into prison; ²⁶truly I say to you, you may not come forth from there until you may pay the last penny. ²⁷You heard that it was said to the ancients: You will not commit adultery; ²⁸but I say to you that everyone who is looking on a woman to desire her, already committed adultery with her in his heart. ²⁹But if your right eye causes you to stumble, pluck it out and cast from you, for it is good to you that one of your members may perish, and not your whole body be cast into Gehenna. ³⁰And if your right hand causes you to stumble, cut it off, and cast from you, for it is good to you that one of your members may perish, and not your whole body be cast into Gehenna. ³¹And it was said that, Whoever may put away his wife, let him give to her a writing of divorce; ³²but I say to you that whoever may put away his wife, except for the matter of whoredom, makes her to commit adultery; and whoever may marry her who has been put away commits adultery. ³³Again, you heard that it was said to the ancients: You will not swear falsely, but you will pay to the LORD your oaths; ³⁴but I say to you not to swear at all; neither by Heaven, because it is the throne of God, ³⁵nor by the earth, because it is His footstool, nor by Jerusalem, because it is [the] city of [the] great King, ³⁶nor may you swear by your head, because you are not able to make one hair white or black; ³⁷but let your word be, Yes, Yes, No, No, and that which is more than these is of the evil [one]. ³⁸You heard that it was said: Eye for eye, and tooth for tooth; ³⁹but I say to you not to resist the evil, but whoever will slap you on your right cheek, turn to him also the other; ⁴⁰and whoever is willing to take you to law, and to take your coat—also permit to him the cloak. ⁴¹And whoever will impress you one mile, go with him two; ⁴²to him who is asking of you be giving, and him who is willing to borrow from you, you may not turn away. ⁴³You heard that it was said: You will love your neighbor, and will hate your enemy; ⁴⁴but I say to you, love your enemies, bless those cursing you, do good to those hating you, and pray for those accusing you falsely, and persecuting you, ⁴⁵that you may be sons of your Father in the heavens, because He causes His sun to rise on evil and good, and He sends rain on righteous and unrighteous. ⁴⁶For if you may love those loving you, what reward do you have? Do the tax collectors not also do the same? ⁴⁷And if you may greet your brothers only, what do you do abundant? Do the nations not also do so? ⁴⁸You will therefore be perfect, as your Father who [is] in the heavens is perfect."

CHAPTER 6

¹ "Take heed not to do your kindness before men, to be seen by them, and if not—you have no reward from your Father who [is] in the heavens; ² whenever, therefore, you may do kindness, you may not sound a trumpet before you as the hypocrites do, in the synagogues, and in the streets, that they may have glory from men; truly I say to you, they have their reward! ³ But you, doing kindness, do not let your left hand know what your right hand does, ⁴ that your kindness may be in secret, and your Father who is seeing in secret will reward you Himself. ⁵ And when you may pray, you will not be as the hypocrites, because they cherish to pray standing in the synagogues and in the corners of the broad places, that they may be seen of men; truly I say to you that they have their reward. ⁶ But you, when you may pray, go into your chamber, and having shut your door, pray to your Father who [is] in secret, and your Father who is seeing in secret will reward you. ⁷ And—praying—you may not use vain repetitions like the nations, for they think that in their speaking much they will be heard, ⁸ therefore do not be like them, for your Father knows those things that you have need of before your asking Him; ⁹ therefore pray thus: Our Father who [is] in the heavens, hallowed be Your Name. ¹⁰ Your kingdom come, Your will come to pass, as in Heaven also on the earth. ¹¹ Give us today our appointed bread. ¹² And forgive us our debts, as we also forgive our debtors. ¹³ And may You not lead us into temptation, but deliver us from the evil [one], because Yours is the kingdom, and the power, and the glory—for all ages. Amen. ¹⁴ For if you may forgive men their trespasses He also will forgive you—your Father who [is] in the heavens; ¹⁵ but if you may not forgive men their trespasses, neither will your Father forgive your trespasses. ¹⁶ And when you may fast, do not be as the hypocrites, of sour countenances, for they disfigure their faces, that they may appear to men fasting; truly I say to you that they have their reward. ¹⁷ But you, fasting, anoint your head, and wash your face, ¹⁸ that you may not appear to men fasting, but to your Father who [is] in secret, and your Father, who is seeing in secret, will reward you. ¹⁹ Do not treasure up to yourselves treasures on the earth, where moth and rust disfigure, and where thieves break through and steal, ²⁰ but treasure up to yourselves treasures in Heaven, where neither moth nor rust disfigure, and where thieves do not break through nor steal, ²¹ for where your treasure is, there will your heart be also. ²² The lamp of the body is the eye, if, therefore, your eye may be perfect, all your body will be enlightened, ²³ but if your eye may be evil, all your body will be dark; if, therefore, the light that [is] in you is darkness—the darkness, how great! ²⁴ None is able to serve two lords, for either he will hate the one and love the other, or he will hold to the one, and despise the other; you are not able to serve God and wealth. ²⁵ Because of this I say to you, do not be anxious for your life, what you may eat, and what you may drink, nor for your body, what you may put on. Is not life more than nourishment, and the body than clothing? ²⁶ Look to the birds of the sky, for they do not sow, nor reap, nor gather into storehouses, and your heavenly Father nourishes them; are you not much better than they? ²⁷ And who of you, being anxious, is able to add to his age one cubit? ²⁸ And why are you anxious about clothing? Consider well the lilies of the field; how do they grow? They do not labor, nor do they spin; ²⁹ and I say to you that not even Solomon in all his glory was clothed as one of these. ³⁰ And if the herb of the field, that today is, and tomorrow is cast into the furnace, God so clothes—not much more you, O you of little faith? ³¹ Therefore you may not be anxious, saying, What may we eat? Or, What may we drink? Or, [With] what may we be clothed? ³² For the nations seek for all these, for your heavenly Father knows that you have need of all these; ³³ but seek first the Kingdom of God and His righteousness, and all these will be added to you. ³⁴ Therefore do not be anxious for tomorrow, for tomorrow will be anxious for its own things; sufficient for the day [is] the evil of it."

CHAPTER 7

¹ "Do not judge, that you may not be judged, ² for in what judgment you judge, you will be judged, and in what measure you measure, it will be measured to you. ³ And why do you behold the speck that [is] in your brother's eye, and do not consider the beam that [is] in your own eye? ⁴ Or, how will you say to your brother, Permit [that] I may cast out the speck from your eye, and behold, the beam [is] in your own eye? ⁵ Hypocrite, first cast out the beam out of your own eye, and then you will see clearly to cast out the speck out of your brother's eye. ⁶ You may not give that which is [holy] to the dogs, nor cast your pearls before the pigs, that they may not trample them among their feet, and having turned—may tear you apart. ⁷ Ask, and it will be given to you; seek, and you will find; knock, and it will be opened to you; ⁸ for everyone who is asking receives, and he who is seeking finds, and to him who is knocking it will be opened. ⁹ Or what man is of you, of whom, if his son may ask [for] a loaf—a stone will he present to him? ¹⁰ And if he may ask [for] a fish—a serpent will he present to him? ¹¹ If, therefore, you being evil, have known to give good gifts to your children, how much more will your Father who [is] in the heavens give good things to those asking Him? ¹² All things, therefore, whatever you may will that men may be doing to you, so also do to them, for this is the Law and the Prophets. ¹³ Go in through the narrow gate, because wide [is] the gate and broad the way that is leading to the destruction, and many are those going in through it; ¹⁴ how narrow [is] the gate and compressed the way that is leading to life, and few are those finding it! ¹⁵ But take heed of the false prophets who come to you in sheep's clothing, and inwardly are ravenous wolves. ¹⁶ From their fruits you will know them; do [men] gather grapes from thorns? Or figs from thistles? ¹⁷ So every good tree yields good fruits, but the bad tree yields evil fruits. ¹⁸ A good tree is not able to yield evil fruits, nor a bad tree to yield good fruits. ¹⁹ Every tree not yielding good fruit is cut down and is cast into fire: ²⁰ therefore from their fruits you will know them. ²¹ Not everyone who is saying to Me, Lord, Lord, will come into the kingdom of the heavens, but he who is doing the will of My Father who is in the heavens. ²² Many will say to Me in that day, Lord, Lord, have we not prophesied in Your Name? And in Your Name cast out demons? And in Your Name done many mighty things? ²³ And then I will acknowledge to them, that—I never knew you, depart from Me you who are working lawlessness. ²⁴ Therefore, everyone who hears these words of Mine, and does them, I will liken him to a wise man who built his house on the rock; ²⁵ and the rain descended, and the streams came, and the winds blew, and they beat on that house, and it did not fall, for it had been founded on the rock. ²⁶ And everyone who is hearing these words of Mine, and is not doing them, will be likened to a foolish man who built his house on the sand; ²⁷ and the rain descended, and the streams came, and the winds blew, and they beat on that house, and it fell, and its fall was great." ²⁸ And it came to pass, when Jesus finished these words, the multitudes were astonished at His teaching, ²⁹ for He was teaching them as having authority, and not as the scribes.

CHAPTER 8

¹ And when He came down from the mountain, great multitudes followed Him, ² and behold, a leper having come, was prostrating to Him, saying, "Lord, if You are willing, You are able to cleanse me"; ³ and having stretched forth the hand, Jesus touched him, saying, "I will, be cleansed," and immediately his leprosy was cleansed. ⁴ And Jesus says to him, "See, you may tell no one, but go, show yourself to the priest, and bring the gift that Moses commanded for a testimony to them." ⁵ And Jesus having entered into Capernaum, there came to Him a centurion calling on Him, ⁶ and saying, "Lord, my young man has been laid in the house a paralytic, fearfully afflicted," ⁷ and Jesus says to him, "I, having come, will heal him." ⁸ And the centurion answering said, "Lord, I am not worthy that You may enter under my roof, but only say a word, and my servant will be healed; ⁹ for I also am a man under authority, having under myself soldiers, and I say to this one, Go, and he goes, and to another, Be coming, and he comes, and to my servant, Do this, and he does [it]." ¹⁰ And Jesus having heard, wondered, and said to those following,

"Truly I say to you, not even in Israel have I found such great faith; ¹¹and I say to you that many from east and west will come and recline with Abraham, and Isaac, and Jacob, in the kingdom of the heavens, ¹²but the sons of the kingdom will be cast forth into the outer darkness—there will be the weeping and the gnashing of the teeth." ¹³And Jesus said to the centurion, "Go, and as you believed let it be to you"; and his young man was healed in that hour. ¹⁴And Jesus having come into the house of Peter, saw his mother-in-law laid, and fevered, ¹⁵and He touched her hand, and the fever left her, and she arose, and was ministering to them. ¹⁶And evening having come, they brought to Him many demoniacs, and He cast out the spirits with a word, and healed all who were ill, ¹⁷that it might be fulfilled that was spoken through Isaiah the prophet, saying, "He took our sicknesses Himself, and bore the diseases." ¹⁸And Jesus having seen great multitudes around Him, commanded to depart to the other side; ¹⁹and a certain scribe having come, said to Him, "Teacher, I will follow You wherever You may go"; ²⁰and Jesus says to him, "The foxes have holes, and the birds of the sky places of rest, but the Son of Man has nowhere He may lay the head." ²¹And another of His disciples said to Him, "Lord, permit me first to depart and to bury my father"; ²²and Jesus said to him, "Follow Me, and permit the dead to bury their own dead." ²³And when He entered into the boat His disciples followed Him, ²⁴and behold, a great storm arose in the sea, so that the boat was being covered by the waves, but He was sleeping, ²⁵and His disciples having come to Him, awoke Him, saying, "Lord, save us! We are perishing!" ²⁶And He says to them, "Why are you fearful, O you of little faith?" Then having risen, He rebuked the winds and the sea, and there was a great calm; ²⁷and the men wondered, saying, "What kind—is this, that even the wind and the sea obey Him?" ²⁸And He having come to the other side, to the region of the Gergesenes, there met Him two demoniacs, coming forth out of the tombs, very fierce, so that no one was able to pass over by that way, ²⁹and behold, they cried out, saying, "What [regards] us and You, [[Jesus,]] Son of God? Did You come here to afflict us before the time?" ³⁰And there was a herd of many pigs feeding far off from them, ³¹and the demons were calling on Him, saying, "If You cast us forth, permit us to go away into the herd of the pigs"; ³²and He says to them, "Go." And having come forth, they went into the herd of the pigs, and behold, the whole herd of the pigs rushed down the steep, into the sea, and died in the waters, ³³and those feeding fled, and having gone into the city, they declared all, and the matter of the demoniacs. ³⁴And behold, all the city came forth to meet Jesus, and having seen Him, they called on [Him] that He might depart from their borders.

CHAPTER 9

¹And having gone into the boat, He passed over, and came to His own city, ²and behold, they were bringing to Him a paralytic, laid on a bed, and Jesus having seen their faith, said to the paralytic, "Take courage, child, your sins have been forgiven." ³And behold, certain of the scribes said within themselves, "This One speaks evil." ⁴And Jesus, having known their thoughts, said, "Why think evil in your hearts? ⁵For which is easier? To say, Your sins are forgiven; or to say, Rise and walk? ⁶But that you may know that the Son of Man has power on the earth to forgive sins—(then He says to the paralytic)—Having risen, take up your bed, and go to your house." ⁷And he, having risen, went to his house, ⁸and the multitudes having seen, wondered, and glorified God, who gave such power to men. ⁹And Jesus passing on from there saw a man sitting at the tax office named Matthew, and says to him, "Follow Me," and he, having risen, followed Him. ¹⁰And it came to pass, He reclining in the house, that behold, many tax collectors and sinners having come, were dining with Jesus and His disciples, ¹¹and the Pharisees having seen, said to His disciples, "Why does your teacher eat with the tax collectors and sinners?" ¹²And Jesus having heard, said to them, "They who are whole have no need of a physician, but they who are ill; ¹³but having gone, learn what [this] is: Kindness I will, and not sacrifice; for I did not come to call righteous men, but sinners." ¹⁴Then the disciples of John come to Him, saying, "Why do we and the Pharisees fast much, and Your disciples do not fast?" ¹⁵And Jesus said to them, "Can the sons of the bride-chamber mourn, so long as the bridegroom is with them? But days will come when the bridegroom may be taken from them, and then they will fast. ¹⁶And no one puts a patch of undressed cloth on an old garment, for its filling up takes from the garment, and a worse split is made. ¹⁷Nor do they put new wine into old skins, and if not—the skins burst, and the wine runs out, and the skins are destroyed, but they put new wine into new skins, and both are preserved together." ¹⁸While He is speaking these things to them, behold, a ruler having come, was prostrating to Him, saying that "My daughter just now died, but having come, lay Your hand on her, and she will live." ¹⁹And Jesus having risen, followed him, also His disciples, ²⁰and behold, a woman having a flow of blood [for] twelve years, having come to Him behind, touched the fringe of His garments, ²¹for she said within herself, "If only I may touch His garment, I will be saved." ²²And Jesus having turned, and having seen her, said, "Take courage, daughter, your faith has saved you," and the woman was saved from that hour. ²³And Jesus having come into the house of the ruler, and having seen the pipers and the multitude making tumult, ²⁴He says to them, "Withdraw, for the girl did not die, but sleeps," and they were deriding Him; ²⁵but when the multitude was put forth, having gone in, He took hold of her hand, and the girl arose, ²⁶and the fame of this went forth to all the land. ²⁷And Jesus passing on from there, two blind men followed Him, calling and saying, "Deal kindly with us, Son of David!" ²⁸And He having come into the house, the blind men came to Him, and Jesus says to them, "Do you believe that I am able to do this?" They say to Him, "Yes, Lord." ²⁹Then He touched their eyes, saying, "According to your faith let it be to you," ³⁰and their eyes were opened, and Jesus strictly charged them, saying, "See, let no one know"; ³¹but they, having gone forth, spread His fame in all that land. ³²And as they are coming forth, behold, they brought to Him a man mute, a demoniac, ³³and the demon having been cast out, the mute spoke, and the multitude wondered, saying that "It was never so seen in Israel," ³⁴but the Pharisees said, "By the ruler of the demons He casts out the demons." ³⁵And Jesus was going up and down all the cities and the villages, teaching in their synagogues, and proclaiming the good news of the kingdom, and healing every disease and every sickness among the people. ³⁶And having seen the multitudes, He was moved with compassion for them, that they were faint and cast aside, as sheep not having a shepherd; ³⁷then He says to His disciples, "The harvest indeed [is] abundant, but the workmen few; ³⁸therefore implore the Lord of the harvest that He may put forth workmen to His harvest."

CHAPTER 10

¹And having called His twelve disciples to Himself, He gave to them power over unclean spirits, so as to be casting them out, and to be healing every disease and every sickness. ²And of the twelve apostles the names are these: first, Simon, who is called Peter, and his brother Andrew; James of Zebedee, and his brother John; ³Philip, and Bartholomew; Thomas, and Matthew the tax collector; James of Alpheus, and Lebbeus who was surnamed Thaddeus; ⁴Simon the Zealot, and Judas Iscariot, who also delivered Him up. ⁵These twelve Jesus sent forth, having given command to them, saying, "Do not go away to the way of the nations, and do not go into a city of the Samaritans, ⁶and be going rather to the lost sheep of the house of Israel. ⁷And going on, proclaim, saying that the kingdom of the heavens has come near; ⁸be healing [those] ailing, raising the dead, cleansing lepers, casting out demons—freely you received, freely give. ⁹Do not provide gold, nor silver, nor brass in your girdles, ¹⁰nor leather pouch for the way, nor two coats, nor sandals, nor staff—for the workman is worthy of his nourishment. ¹¹And into whatever city or village you may enter, inquire who in it is worthy, and abide there, until you may go forth. ¹²And coming into the house greet it, ¹³and if indeed the house is worthy, let your peace come on it; and if it is not worthy, let your peace return to you. ¹⁴And whoever may not receive you nor hear your words, coming forth from that house or city, shake off the dust of your feet, ¹⁵truly I say to you, it will be more tolerable for the land of Sodom and Gomorrah in the day of judgment than for that city. ¹⁶Behold, I send you forth as sheep in the midst of wolves, therefore be wise as the serpents, and pure as the doves. ¹⁷And take heed of men, for they will give you up to

Sanhedrins, and in their synagogues they will scourge you, ⁱ⁸and before governors and kings you will be brought for My sake, for a testimony to them and to the nations. ¹⁹And whenever they may deliver you up, do not be anxious how or what you may speak, for it will be given you in that hour what you will speak; ²⁰for you are not the speakers, but the Spirit of your Father that is speaking in you. ²¹And brother will deliver up brother to death, and father child, and children will rise up against parents, and will put them to death, ²²and you will be hated by all because of My Name, but he who has endured to the end, he will be saved. ²³And whenever they may persecute you in this city, flee to the other, for truly I say to you, you may not have finished [going through] the cities of Israel until the Son of Man may come. ²⁴A disciple is not above the teacher, nor a servant above his lord; ²⁵sufficient to the disciple that he may be as his teacher, and the servant as his lord; if the master of the house they called Beelzebul, how much more those of his household? ²⁶You may not, therefore, fear them, for there is nothing covered that will not be revealed, and hid that will not be known; ²⁷that which I tell you in the darkness, speak in the light, and that which you hear at the ear, proclaim on the housetops. ²⁸And do not be afraid of those killing the body, and are not able to kill the soul, but rather fear Him who is able to destroy both soul and body in Gehenna. ²⁹Are not two sparrows sold for an assarion? And one of them will not fall on the ground without your Father; ³⁰and of you—even the hairs of the head are all numbered; ³¹therefore, do not be afraid, you are better than many sparrows. ³²Everyone, therefore, who will confess in Me before men, I also will confess in him before My Father who is in the heavens; ³³and whoever will deny Me before men, I also will deny him before My Father who is in the heavens. ³⁴You may not suppose that I came to put peace on the earth; I did not come to put peace, but a sword; ³⁵for I came to set a man at variance against his father, and a daughter against her mother, and a daughter-in-law against her mother-in-law, ³⁶and the enemies of a man are those of his household. ³⁷He who is cherishing father or mother above Me, is not worthy of Me, and he who is cherishing son or daughter above Me, is not worthy of Me, ³⁸and whoever does not receive his cross and follow after Me, is not worthy of Me. ³⁹He who found his life will lose it, and he who lost his life for My sake will find it. ⁴⁰He who is receiving you receives Me, and he who is receiving Me receives Him who sent Me; ⁴¹he who is receiving a prophet in the name of a prophet, will receive a prophet's reward, and he who is receiving a righteous man in the name of a righteous man, will receive a righteous man's reward, ⁴²and whoever may give to drink to one of these little ones a cup of cold water only in the name of a disciple, truly I say to you, he may not lose his reward."

MATTHEW

CHAPTER 11

¹And it came to pass, when Jesus finished directing His twelve disciples, He departed from there to teach and to preach in their cities. ²And John having heard in the prison the works of the Christ, having sent two of his disciples, ³said to Him, "Are You He who is coming, or do we look for another?" ⁴And Jesus answering said to them, "Having gone, declare to John the things that you hear and see, ⁵blind receive sight, and lame walk, lepers are cleansed, and deaf hear, dead are raised, and poor have good news proclaimed, ⁶and blessed is he who may not be stumbled in Me." ⁷And as they are going, Jesus began to say to the multitudes concerning John, "What did you go out to the wilderness to view? A reed shaken by the wind? ⁸But what did you go out to see? A man clothed in soft garments? Behold, those wearing the soft things are in the kings' houses. ⁹But what did you go out to see? A prophet? Yes, I say to you, and more than a prophet, ¹⁰for this is he of whom it has been written: Behold, I send My messenger before Your face, who will prepare Your way before You. ¹¹Truly I say to you, there has not risen, among those born of women, [one] greater than John the Immerser, but he who is least in the kingdom of the heavens is greater than he. ¹²And from the days of John the Immerser until now, the kingdom of the heavens suffers violence, and violent men seize it by force, ¹³for all the Prophets and the Law prophesied until John, ¹⁴and if you are willing to receive [it], he is Elijah who was about to come; ¹⁵he who is having ears to hear—let him hear. ¹⁶And to what will I liken this generation? It is like little children in marketplaces, sitting and calling to others, ¹⁷and saying, We piped to you, and you did not dance, we lamented to you, and you did not strike the breast. ¹⁸For John came neither eating nor drinking, and they say, He has a demon; ¹⁹the Son of Man came eating and drinking, and they say, Behold, a man, a glutton, and a wine-drinker, a friend of tax collectors and sinners; and wisdom was justified of her children." ²⁰Then He began to reproach the cities in which were done most of His mighty works, because they did not convert. ²¹"Woe to you, Chorazin! Woe to you, Bethsaida! Because, if in Tyre and Sidon had been done the mighty works that were done in you, long ago in sackcloth and ashes they had converted; ²²but I say to you, to Tyre and Sidon it will be more tolerable in [the] day of judgment than for you. ²³And you, Capernaum, which were exalted to Heaven, will be brought down to Hades, because if the mighty works that were done in you had been done in Sodom, it had remained to this day; ²⁴but I say to you, to the land of Sodom it will be more tolerable in [the] day of judgment than to you." ²⁵At that time Jesus answering said, "I confess to You, Father, Lord of the heavens and of the earth, that You hid these things from wise and understanding ones, and revealed them to babies. ²⁶Yes, Father, because so it was good pleasure before You. ²⁷All things were delivered to Me by My Father, and none know the Son, except the Father, nor does any know the Father, except the Son, and he to whom the Son may resolve to reveal [Him]. ²⁸Come to Me, all you laboring and burdened ones, and I will give you rest; ²⁹take up My yoke on you, and learn from Me, because I am meek and humble in heart, and you will find rest to your souls, ³⁰for My yoke [is] easy, and My burden is light."

CHAPTER 12

¹At that time Jesus went on the Sabbaths through the grainfields, and His disciples were hungry, and they began to pluck ears, and to eat, ²and the Pharisees having seen, said to Him, "Behold, Your disciples do that which it is not lawful to do on a Sabbath." ³And He said to them, "Did you not read what David did when he was hungry, himself and those with him— ⁴how he went into the house of God, and ate the Bread of the Presentation, which it is not lawful to him to eat, nor to those with him, except to the priests alone? ⁵Or did you not read in the Law that on the Sabbaths the priests in the temple profane the Sabbath and are blameless? ⁶And I say to you that [One] greater than the temple is here; ⁷and if you had known what [this] is: Kindness I will, and not sacrifice—you had not condemned the blameless, ⁸for the Son of Man is Lord even of the Sabbath." ⁹And having departed from there, He went to their synagogue, ¹⁰and behold, there was a man having the hand withered, and they questioned Him, saying, "Is it lawful to heal on the Sabbaths?" That they might accuse Him. ¹¹And He said to them, "What man will be of you who will have one sheep, and if this may fall on the Sabbaths into a ditch, will not lay hold on it and raise [it]? ¹²How much better, therefore, is a man than a sheep? So that it is lawful on the Sabbaths to do good." ¹³Then He says to the man, "Stretch forth your hand," and he stretched [it] forth, and it was restored whole as the other. ¹⁴And the Pharisees having gone forth, held a consultation against Him, how they might destroy Him, ¹⁵and Jesus having known, withdrew from there, and there followed Him great multitudes, and He healed them all, ¹⁶and charged them that they might not make Him apparent, ¹⁷that it might be fulfilled that was spoken through Isaiah the prophet, saying, ¹⁸"Behold, My Servant, whom I chose, || My Beloved, in whom My soul delighted, || I will put My Spirit on Him, || And He will declare judgment to the nations; ¹⁹He will not strive nor cry, || Nor will any hear His voice in the broad places; ²⁰A bruised reed He will not break, || And smoking flax He will not quench, || Until He may put forth judgment to victory, ²¹And in His Name will nations hope." ²²Then was brought to Him a demoniac, blind and mute, and He healed him, so that the blind and mute both spoke and saw. ²³And all the multitudes were amazed and said, "Is this the Son of David?" ²⁴But the Pharisees having heard, said, "This One does not cast out demons, except by Beelzebul, ruler of the demons." ²⁵And Jesus, knowing their thoughts, said to them, "Every kingdom having been

MATTHEW

divided against itself is desolated, and no city or house having been divided against itself stands, ²⁶and if Satan casts out Satan, against himself he was divided, how then does his kingdom stand? ²⁷And if I, by Beelzebul, cast out the demons, your sons—by whom do they cast out? Because of this they will be your judges. ²⁸But if I, by the Spirit of God, cast out the demons, then the Kingdom of God has already come to you. ²⁹Or how is one able to go into the house of the strong man, and to snatch his goods, if first he may not bind the strong man? And then his house he will plunder. ³⁰He who is not with Me is against Me, and he who is not gathering with Me, scatters. ³¹Because of this I say to you, all sin and slander will be forgiven to men, but the slander of the Spirit will not be forgiven to men. ³²And whoever may speak a word against the Son of Man it will be forgiven to him, but whoever may speak against the Holy Spirit, it will not be forgiven him, neither in this age, nor in that which is coming. ³³Either make the tree good, and its fruit good, or make the tree bad, and its fruit bad, for from the fruit is the tree known. ³⁴Brood of vipers! How are you able to speak good things—being evil? For out of the abundance of the heart the mouth speaks. ³⁵The good man out of the good treasure of the heart puts forth the good things, and the evil man out of the evil treasure puts forth evil things. ³⁶And I say to you that every idle word that men may speak, they will give for it a reckoning in [the] day of judgment; ³⁷for from your words you will be declared righteous, and from your words you will be declared unrighteous." ³⁸Then certain of the scribes and Pharisees answered, saying, "Teacher, we will to see a sign from You." ³⁹And He answering said to them, "A generation, evil and adulterous, seeks a sign, and a sign will not be given to it, except the sign of Jonah the prophet; ⁴⁰for as Jonah was in the belly of the fish three days and three nights, so will the Son of Man be in the heart of the earth three days and three nights. ⁴¹Men of Nineveh will stand up in the judgment with this generation, and will condemn it, for they converted at the proclamation of Jonah, and behold, [One] greater than Jonah [is] here! ⁴²A queen of the south will rise up in the judgment with this generation, and will condemn it, for she came from the ends of the earth to hear the wisdom of Solomon, and behold, [One] greater than Solomon [is] here! ⁴³And when the unclean spirit may go forth from the man, it walks through dry places seeking rest and does not find; ⁴⁴then it says, I will return to my house from where I came forth; and having come, it finds [it] unoccupied, swept, and adorned: ⁴⁵then it goes, and takes with itself seven other spirits more evil than itself, and having gone in they dwell there, and the last of that man becomes worse than the first; so will it also be to this evil generation." ⁴⁶And while He was yet speaking to the multitudes, behold, His mother and brothers had stood outside, seeking to speak to Him, ⁴⁷and one said to Him, "Behold, Your mother and Your brothers stand outside, seeking to speak to You." ⁴⁸And He answering said to him who spoke to Him, "Who is My mother? And who are My brothers?" ⁴⁹And having stretched forth His hand toward His disciples, He said, "Behold, My mother and My brothers! ⁵⁰For whoever may do the will of My Father who is in the heavens, He is My brother, and sister, and mother."

CHAPTER 13

¹And in that day Jesus, having gone forth from the house, was sitting by the sea, ²and gathered together to Him were many multitudes, so that He having gone into the boat sat down, and all the multitude on the beach stood, ³and He spoke to them many things in allegories, saying, "Behold, the sower went forth to sow, ⁴and in his sowing, some indeed fell by the way, and the birds having come, devoured them, ⁵and others fell on the rocky places where they did not have much earth, and immediately they sprang forth, through having no depth of earth, ⁶and the sun having risen they were scorched, and through having no root, they withered, ⁷and others fell on the thorns, and the thorns came up and choked them, ⁸and others fell on the good ground, and were giving fruit, some indeed a hundredfold, and some sixty, and some thirty. ⁹He who is having ears to hear—let him hear." ¹⁰And the disciples having come near, said to Him, "Why do You speak to them in allegories?" ¹¹And He answering said to them that, "To you it has been given to know the secrets of the kingdom of the heavens, and to these it has not been given, ¹²for whoever has, it will be given to him, and he will have overabundance, and whoever has not, even that which he has will be taken from him. ¹³Because of this, in allegories I speak to them, because seeing they do not see, and hearing they do not hear, nor understand, ¹⁴and fulfilled on them is the prophecy of Isaiah that says, With hearing you will hear, and you will not understand, and seeing you will see, and you will not perceive, ¹⁵for the heart of this people was made obtuse, and with the ears they barely heard, and they closed their eyes, lest they might see with the eyes, and might hear with the ears, and understand with the heart, and turn back, and I might heal them. ¹⁶And blessed are your eyes because they see, and your ears because they hear, ¹⁷for truly I say to you that many prophets and righteous men desired to see that which you look on, and they did not see, and to hear that which you hear, and they did not hear. ¹⁸You, therefore, hear the allegory of the sower: ¹⁹Everyone hearing the word of the kingdom, and not understanding—the evil one comes, and snatches that which has been sown in his heart; this is that sown by the way. ²⁰And that sown on the rocky places, this is he who is hearing the word, and immediately with joy is receiving it, ²¹and he has no root in himself, but is temporary, and persecution or tribulation having happened because of the word, immediately he is stumbled. ²²And that sown toward the thorns, this is he who is hearing the word, and the anxiety of this age, and the deceitfulness of the riches, chokes the word, and it becomes unfruitful. ²³And that sown on the good ground: this is he who is hearing the word, and is understanding, who indeed bears fruit, and makes, some indeed a hundredfold, and some sixty, and some thirty." ²⁴Another allegory He set before them, saying, "The kingdom of the heavens was likened to a man sowing good seed in his field, ²⁵and while men are sleeping, his enemy came and sowed darnel in the midst of the wheat, and went away, ²⁶and when the herb sprang up, and yielded fruit, then appeared also the darnel. ²⁷And the servants of the householder, having come near, said to him, Lord, did you not sow good seed in your field? From where then does it have the darnel? ²⁸And he says to them, A man, an enemy, did this; and the servants said to him, Will you, then, [that] having gone away we may gather it up? ²⁹And he said, No, lest—gathering up the darnel—you root up with it the wheat; ³⁰permit both to grow together until the harvest, and in the time of the harvest I will say to the reapers, Gather up first the darnel, and bind it in bundles, to burn it, and the wheat gather up into my storehouse." ³¹Another allegory He set before them, saying, "The kingdom of the heavens is like to a grain of mustard, which a man having taken, sowed in his field, ³²which less, indeed, is than all the seeds, but when it may be grown, is greatest of the herbs, and becomes a tree, so that the birds of the sky come and rest in its branches." ³³Another allegory He spoke to them: "The kingdom of the heavens is like to leaven, which a woman having taken, hid in three measures of meal, until the whole was leavened." ³⁴All these things Jesus spoke in allegories to the multitudes, and without an allegory He was not speaking to them, ³⁵that it might be fulfilled that was spoken through the prophet, saying, "I will open in allegories My mouth, || I will utter things having been hidden from the foundation of the world." ³⁶Then having let away the multitudes, Jesus came into the house, and His disciples came near to Him, saying, "Explain to us the allegory of the darnel of the field." ³⁷And He answering said to them, "He who is sowing the good seed is the Son of Man, ³⁸and the field is the world, and the good seed, these are the sons of the kingdom, and the darnel are the sons of the evil one, ³⁹and the enemy who sowed them is the Devil, and the harvest is [the] full end of the age, and the reapers are messengers. ⁴⁰As, then, the darnel is gathered up, and is burned with fire, so will it be in the full end of this age; ⁴¹the Son of Man will send forth His messengers, and they will gather up out of His kingdom all the stumbling-blocks, and those doing the lawlessness, ⁴²and will cast them into the furnace of the fire; there will be the weeping and the gnashing of the teeth. ⁴³Then will the righteous shine forth as the sun in the kingdom of their Father. He who is having ears to hear—let him hear. ⁴⁴Again, the kingdom of the heavens is like to treasure hid in the field, which a man having found, hid, and from his joy goes, and all, as much as he

has, he sells, and buys that field. ⁴⁵Again, the kingdom of the heavens is like to a man, a merchant, seeking good pearls, ⁴⁶who having found one pearl of great price, having gone away, has sold all, as much as he had, and bought it. ⁴⁷Again, the kingdom of the heavens is like to a net that was cast into the sea, and gathered together of every kind, ⁴⁸which, when it was filled, having drawn up again on the beach, and having sat down, they gathered the good into vessels, and the bad they cast out, ⁴⁹so will it be in the full end of the age, the messengers will come forth and separate the evil out of the midst of the righteous, ⁵⁰and will cast them into the furnace of the fire; there will be the weeping and the gnashing of the teeth." ⁵¹Jesus says to them, "Did you understand all these?" They say to Him, "Yes, Lord." ⁵²And He said to them, "Because of this, every scribe having been discipled in regard to the kingdom of the heavens is like to a man, a householder, who brings forth out of his treasure things new and old." ⁵³And it came to pass, when Jesus finished these allegories, He removed from there, ⁵⁴and having come to His own country, He was teaching them in their synagogue, so that they were astonished, and were saying, "From where to this One this wisdom and the mighty works? ⁵⁵Is this not the carpenter's Son? Is His mother not called Mary, and His brothers James, and Joses, and Simon, and Judas? ⁵⁶And His sisters—are they not all with us? From where, then, to this One all these?" ⁵⁷And they were stumbled at Him. And Jesus said to them, "A prophet is not without honor except in his own country, and in his own house": ⁵⁸and He did not do many mighty works there, because of their unbelief.

CHAPTER 14

¹At that time Herod the tetrarch heard the fame of Jesus, ²and said to his servants, "This is John the Immerser, he rose from the dead, and because of this the mighty energies are working in him." ³For Herod having laid hold on John, bound him, and put him in prison, because of Herodias, his brother Philip's wife, ⁴for John was saying to him, "It is not lawful to you to have her," ⁵and willing to kill him, he feared the multitude, because as a prophet they were holding him. ⁶But the birthday of Herod being kept, the daughter of Herodias danced in the midst, and pleased Herod, ⁷after which with an oath he professed to give her whatever she might ask. ⁸And she, having been instigated by her mother, says, "Give me here on a plate the head of John the Immerser"; ⁹and the king was grieved, but because of the oaths and of those dining with him, he commanded [it] to be given; ¹⁰and having sent, he beheaded John in the prison, ¹¹and his head was brought on a plate, and was given to the girl, and she brought [it] near to her mother. ¹²And his disciples having come, took up the body, and buried it, and having come, they told Jesus, ¹³and Jesus having heard, withdrew from there in a boat to a desolate place by Himself, and the multitudes having heard followed Him on land from the cities. ¹⁴And Jesus having come forth, saw a great multitude, and was moved with compassion on them, and healed their sick; ¹⁵and evening having come, His disciples came to Him, saying, "The place is desolate, and the hour has now past, let away the multitudes that, having gone into the villages, they may buy food for themselves." ¹⁶And Jesus said to them, "They have no need to go away—you give them to eat." ¹⁷And they say to Him, "We have nothing here except five loaves and two fishes." ¹⁸And He said, "Bring them to Me here." ¹⁹And having commanded the multitudes to recline on the grass, and having taken the five loaves and the two fishes, having looked up to the sky, He blessed, and having broken, He gave the loaves to the disciples, and the disciples [gave] to the multitudes, ²⁰and they all ate, and were filled, and they took up what was over of the broken pieces twelve handbaskets full; ²¹and those eating were about five thousand men, apart from women and children. ²²And immediately Jesus constrained His disciples to go into the boat, and to go before Him to the other side, until He might let away the multitudes; ²³and having let away the multitudes, He went up to the mountain by Himself to pray, and evening having come, He was there alone, ²⁴and the boat was now in the midst of the sea, distressed by the waves, for the wind was contrary. ²⁵And in the fourth watch of the night Jesus went away to them, walking on the sea, ²⁶and the disciples having seen Him walking on the sea, were troubled, saying, "It is an apparition," and from the fear they cried out; ²⁷and immediately Jesus spoke to them, saying, "Take courage! I AM; do not be afraid." ²⁸And Peter answering Him said, "Lord, if it is You, command me to come to You on the waters"; ²⁹and He said, "Come"; and having gone down from the boat, Peter walked on the waters to come to Jesus, ³⁰but seeing the vehement wind, he was afraid, and having begun to sink, he cried out, saying, "Lord, save me!" ³¹And immediately Jesus, having stretched forth the hand, laid hold of him and says to him, "Little faith! For why did you waver?" ³²And they having gone into the boat, the wind stilled, ³³and those in the boat having come, worshiped Him, saying, "You are truly God's Son." ³⁴And having passed over, they came into the land of Gennesaret, ³⁵and having recognized Him, the men of that place sent forth to all that surrounding region, and they brought to Him all who were ill, ³⁶and were calling on Him that they might only touch the fringe of His garment, and as many as touched were saved.

CHAPTER 15

¹Then they come to Jesus from Jerusalem—scribes and Pharisees—saying, ²"Why do Your disciples transgress the tradition of the elders? For they do not wash their hands when they may eat bread." ³And He answering said to them, "Why also do you transgress the command of God because of your tradition? ⁴For God commanded, saying, Honor your father and mother; and, He who is speaking evil of father or mother—let him die the death; ⁵but you say, Whoever may say to father or mother, An offering [is] whatever you may be profited by me— ⁶and he may not honor his father or his mother, and you set aside the command of God because of your tradition. ⁷Hypocrites, Isaiah prophesied well of you, saying, ⁸This people draws near to Me with their mouth, and with the lips it honors Me, but their heart is far off from Me; ⁹and in vain they worship Me, teaching teachings—commands of men." ¹⁰And having called near the multitude, He said to them, "Hear and understand: ¹¹[it is] not that which is coming into the mouth [that] defiles the man, but that which is coming forth from the mouth, this defiles the man." ¹²Then His disciples having come near, said to Him, "Have You known that the Pharisees, having heard the word, were stumbled?" ¹³And He answering said, "Every plant that My heavenly Father did not plant will be rooted up; ¹⁴leave them alone, they are guides—blind of blind; and if blind may guide blind, both will fall into a ditch." ¹⁵And Peter answering said to Him, "Explain to us this allegory." ¹⁶And Jesus said, "Are you also yet without understanding? ¹⁷Do you not understand that all that is going into the mouth passes into the belly, and is cast forth into the drain? ¹⁸But the things coming forth from the mouth come forth from the heart, and these defile the man; ¹⁹for out of the heart come forth evil thoughts, murders, adulteries, whoredoms, thefts, false witnessings, slanders; ²⁰these are the things defiling the man; but to eat with unwashed hands does not defile the man." ²¹And Jesus having come forth from there, withdrew to the parts of Tyre and Sidon, ²²and behold, a woman, a Canaanite, having come forth from those borders, called to Him, saying, "Deal kindly with me, Lord, Son of David; my daughter is miserably demonized." ²³And He did not answer her a word; and His disciples having come to Him, were asking Him, saying, "Let her away, because she cries after us"; ²⁴and He answering said, "I was not sent except to the lost sheep of the house of Israel." ²⁵And having come, she was worshiping Him, saying, "Lord, help me"; ²⁶and He answering said, "It is not good to take the children's bread, and to cast to the little dogs." ²⁷And she said, "Yes, Lord, for even the little dogs eat of the crumbs that are falling from their lords' table"; ²⁸then answering, Jesus said to her, "O woman, great [is] your faith, let it be to you as you will"; and her daughter was healed from that hour. ²⁹And having departed from there, Jesus came near to the Sea of Galilee, and having gone up to the mountain, He was sitting there, ³⁰and there came to Him great multitudes, having with them lame, blind, mute, maimed, and many others, and they cast them at the feet of Jesus, and He healed them, ³¹so that the

multitudes wondered, seeing mute ones speaking, maimed whole, lame walking, and blind seeing; and they glorified the God of Israel. ³²And Jesus having called near His disciples, said, "I have compassion on the multitude, because now three days they continue with Me, and they do not have what they may eat; and to let them away fasting I will not, lest they faint in the way." ³³And His disciples say to Him, "From where to us in a wilderness [will we get] so many loaves, as to fill so great a multitude?" ³⁴And Jesus says to them, "How many loaves do you have?" And they said, "Seven, and a few little fishes." ³⁵And He commanded the multitudes to sit down on the ground, ³⁶and having taken the seven loaves and the fishes, having given thanks, He broke, and gave to His disciples, and the disciples [gave] to the multitude. ³⁷And they all ate, and were filled, and they took up what was over of the broken pieces seven baskets full, ³⁸and those eating were four thousand men, apart from women and children. ³⁹And having let away the multitudes, He went into the boat, and came to the borders of Magdala.

CHAPTER 16

¹And the Pharisees and Sadducees having come, tempting, questioned Him, to show to them a sign from Heaven, ²and He answering said to them, "Evening having come, you say, Fair weather, for the sky is red, ³and at morning, Foul weather today, for the sky is red—gloomy; hypocrites, you indeed know to discern the face of the sky, but the signs of the times you are not able! ⁴An evil and adulterous generation seeks a sign, and a sign will not be given to it, except the sign of Jonah the prophet"; and having left them He went away. ⁵And His disciples having come to the other side, forgot to take loaves, ⁶and Jesus said to them, "Beware, and take heed of the leaven of the Pharisees and Sadducees"; ⁷and they were reasoning in themselves, saying, "Because we took no loaves." ⁸And Jesus having known, said to them, "Why reason you in yourselves, you of little faith, because you took no loaves? ⁹Do you not yet understand, nor remember the five loaves of the five thousand, and how many hand-baskets you took up? ¹⁰Nor the seven loaves of the four thousand, and how many baskets you took up? ¹¹How do you not understand that I did not speak to you of bread—to take heed of the leaven of the Pharisees and Sadducees?" ¹²Then they understood that He did not say to take heed of the leaven of the bread, but of the teaching of the Pharisees and Sadducees. ¹³And Jesus, having come to the parts of Caesarea Philippi, was asking His disciples, saying, "Who do men say I am—the Son of Man?" ¹⁴And they said, "Some, John the Immerser, and others, Elijah, and others, Jeremiah, or one of the prophets." ¹⁵He says to them, "And you—who do you say I am?" ¹⁶And Simon Peter answering said, "You are the Christ, the Son of the living God." ¹⁷And Jesus answering said to him, "Blessed are you, Simon Bar-Jona, because flesh and blood did not reveal [it] to you, but My Father who is in the heavens. ¹⁸And I also say to you that you are Peter, and on this rock I will build My Assembly, and [the] gates of Hades will not prevail against it; ¹⁹and I will give to you the keys of the kingdom of the heavens, and whatever you may bind on the earth will be having been bound in the heavens, and whatever you may loose on the earth will be having been loosed in the heavens." ²⁰Then He charged His disciples that they may say to no one that He is Jesus the Christ. ²¹From that time Jesus began to show to His disciples that it is necessary for Him to go away to Jerusalem, and to suffer many things from the elders, and chief priests, and scribes, and to be put to death, and the third day to rise. ²²And having taken Him aside, Peter began to rebuke Him, saying, "Be kind to Yourself, Lord; this will not be to You"; ²³and He having turned, said to Peter, "Get behind Me, Satan! You are a stumbling-block to Me, for you do not mind the things of God, but the things of men." ²⁴Then Jesus said to His disciples, "If anyone wills to come after Me, let him disown himself, and take up his cross, and follow Me, ²⁵for whoever may will to save his life will lose it, and whoever may lose his life for My sake will find it; ²⁶for what is a man profited if he may gain the whole world, but of his life suffer loss? Or what will a man give as an exchange for his life? ²⁷For the Son of Man is about to come in the glory of His Father, with His messengers, and then He will reward each according to his work. ²⁸Truly I say to you, there are certain of those standing here who will not taste of death until they may see the Son of Man coming in His kingdom."

CHAPTER 17

¹And after six days Jesus takes Peter, and James, and his brother John, and brings them up to a high mountain by themselves, ²and He was transfigured before them, and His face shone as the sun, and His garments became white as the light, ³and behold, Moses and Elijah appeared to them, talking together with Him. ⁴And Peter answering said to Jesus, "Lord, it is good to us to be here; if You will, we may make three shelters here: one for You, and one for Moses, and one for Elijah." ⁵While he is yet speaking, behold, a bright cloud overshadowed them, and behold, a voice out of the cloud, saying, "This is My Son, the Beloved, in whom I delighted; hear Him." ⁶And the disciples having heard, fell on their face, and were exceedingly afraid, ⁷and Jesus having come near, touched them, and said, "Rise, do not be afraid," ⁸and having lifted up their eyes, they saw no one, except Jesus only. ⁹And as they are coming down from the mountain, Jesus charged them, saying, "Say to no one the vision, until the Son of Man may rise out of the dead." ¹⁰And His disciples questioned Him, saying, "Why then do the scribes say that Elijah must come first?" ¹¹And Jesus answering said to them, "Elijah does indeed come first, and will restore all things, ¹²and I say to you, Elijah already came, and they did not know him, but did with him whatever they would, so also the Son of Man is about to suffer by them." ¹³Then the disciples understood that He spoke to them concerning John the Immerser. ¹⁴And when they came to the multitude, there came to Him a man, kneeling down to Him, ¹⁵and saying, "Lord, deal kindly with my son, for he is [a] lunatic, and suffers miserably, for he often falls into the fire, and often into the water, ¹⁶and I brought him near to Your disciples, and they were not able to heal him." ¹⁷And Jesus answering said, "O generation, unsteadfast and perverse, until when will I be with you? Until when will I bear you? Bring him to Me here"; ¹⁸and Jesus rebuked him, and the demon went out of him, and the boy was healed from that hour. ¹⁹Then the disciples having come to Jesus by Himself, said, "Why were we not able to cast him out?" ²⁰And Jesus said to them, "Through your want of faith; for truly I say to you, if you may have faith as a grain of mustard, you will say to this mountain, Move from here to there, and it will move, and nothing will be impossible to you, ²¹[[and this kind does not go forth except in prayer and fasting."]] ²²And while they are living in Galilee, Jesus said to them, "The Son of Man is about to be delivered up into the hands of men, ²³and they will kill Him, and the third day He will rise," and they were exceedingly sorry. ²⁴And they having come to Capernaum, those receiving the didrachmas came near to Peter and said, "Your teacher—does He not pay the didrachmas?" He says, "Yes." ²⁵And when he came into the house, Jesus anticipated him, saying, "What do you think, Simon? The kings of the earth—from whom do they receive custom or poll-tax? From their sons or from the strangers?" ²⁶Peter says to Him, "From the strangers." Jesus said to him, "Then the sons are free; ²⁷but that we may not cause them to stumble, having gone to the sea, cast a hook, and the fish that has come up first take up, and having opened its mouth, you will find a stater, that having taken, give to them for Me and you."

CHAPTER 18

¹At that hour the disciples came near to Jesus, saying, "Who, now, is greater in the kingdom of the heavens?" ²And Jesus having called near a child, set him in the midst of them, ³and said, "Truly I say to you, if you may not be turned and become as the children, you may not enter into the kingdom of the heavens; ⁴whoever then may humble himself as this child, he is the greater in the kingdom of the heavens. ⁵And he who may receive one such child in My Name, receives Me, ⁶and whoever may cause to stumble one of those little ones who are believing in Me, it is better for him that a weighty millstone may be hanged on his neck, and he may be sunk in the depth of the sea. ⁷Woe to the world from the stumbling-blocks! For there is necessity for the stumbling-blocks to come, but woe to that man through whom the stumbling-block comes! ⁸And if your hand or your foot causes you to stumble, cut them off and cast [them] from you; it is good for you to enter into life lame or maimed, rather than having two hands or two feet, to be cast into the

MATTHEW

continuous fire. ⁹And if your eye causes you to stumble, pluck it out and cast from you; it is good for you to enter into life one-eyed, rather than having two eyes to be cast into the Gehenna of fire. ¹⁰Beware! You may not despise one of these little ones, for I say to you that their messengers in the heavens always behold the face of My Father who is in the heavens, ¹¹[[for the Son of Man came to save the lost.]] ¹²What do you think? If a man may have one hundred sheep, and there may go astray one of them, does he not—having left the ninety-nine, having gone on the mountains—seek that which is gone astray? ¹³And if it may come to pass that he finds it, truly I say to you that he rejoices over it more than over the ninety-nine that have not gone astray; ¹⁴so it is not [the] will in [the] presence of your Father who is in the heavens that one of these little ones may perish. ¹⁵And if your brother may sin against you, go and show him his fault between you and him alone, if he may hear you, you gained your brother; ¹⁶and if he may not hear, take with you yet one or two, that by the mouth of two witnesses or three every word may stand. ¹⁷And if he may not hear them, say [it] to the assembly, and if also the assembly he may not hear, let him be to you as the heathen man and the tax collector. ¹⁸Truly I say to you, whatever things you may bind on the earth will be having been bound in the heavens, and whatever things you may loose on the earth will be having been loosed in the heavens. ¹⁹Again, I say to you that if two of you may agree on the earth concerning anything, whatever they may ask—it will be done to them from My Father who is in the heavens, ²⁰for where there are two or three gathered together—to My Name, there am I in the midst of them." ²¹Then Peter having come near to Him, said, "Lord, how often will my brother sin against me, and I forgive him—until seven times?" ²²Jesus says to him, "I do not say to you until seven times, but until seventy times seven. ²³Because of this was the kingdom of the heavens likened to a man, a king, who willed to take reckoning with his servants, ²⁴and he having begun to take account, there was brought near to him one debtor of a myriad of talents, ²⁵and he having nothing to pay, his lord commanded him to be sold, and his wife, and the children, and all, whatever he had, and payment to be made. ²⁶The servant then, having fallen down, was prostrating to him, saying, Lord, have patience with me, and I will pay you all; ²⁷and the lord of that servant having been moved with compassion released him, and the debt he forgave him. ²⁸And that servant having come forth, found one of his fellow-servants who was owing him one hundred denarii, and having laid hold, he took him by the throat, saying, Pay me that which you owe. ²⁹His fellow-servant then, having fallen down at his feet, was calling on him, saying, Have patience with me, and I will pay you all; ³⁰and he would not, but having gone away, he cast him into prison, until he might pay that which was owing. ³¹And his fellow-servants having seen the things that were done, were grieved exceedingly, and having come, showed fully to their lord all the things that were done; ³²then having called him, his lord says to him, Evil servant! All that debt I forgave you, seeing you called on me; ³³did it not seem necessary to you to have dealt kindly with your fellow servant, as I also dealt kindly with you? ³⁴And having been angry, his lord delivered him to the inquisitors, until he might pay all that was owing to him; ³⁵so also My heavenly Father will do to you, if you may not forgive each one his brother from your hearts their trespasses."

CHAPTER 19

¹And it came to pass, when Jesus finished these words, He removed from Galilee, and came to the borders of Judea, beyond the Jordan, ²and great multitudes followed Him, and He healed them there. ³And the Pharisees came near to Him, tempting Him, and saying to Him, "Is it lawful for a man to put away his wife for every cause?" ⁴And He answering said to them, "Did you not read that He who made [them] from the beginning, made them a male and a female, ⁵and said, For this cause will a man leave father and mother, and cleave to his wife, and they will be—the two—for one flesh? ⁶So that they are no longer two, but one flesh; what therefore God joined together, let no man separate." ⁷They say to Him, "Why then did Moses command to give a roll of divorce, and to put her away?" ⁸He says to them, "Moses for your stiffness of heart permitted you to put away your wives, but from the beginning it has not been so. ⁹And I say to you that whoever may put away his wife, if not for whoredom, and may marry another, commits adultery; and he who married her that has been put away, commits adultery." ¹⁰His disciples say to Him, "If the case of the man with the woman is so, it is not good to marry." ¹¹And He said to them, "All do not receive this word, but those to whom it has been given; ¹²for there are eunuchs who from the mother's womb were so born; and there are eunuchs who were made eunuchs by men; and there are eunuchs who kept themselves eunuchs because of the kingdom of the heavens: he who is able to receive [it]—let him receive." ¹³Then were brought near to Him children that He might put hands on them and pray, and the disciples rebuked them. ¹⁴But Jesus said, "Permit the children, and do not forbid them to come to Me, for of such is the kingdom of the heavens"; ¹⁵and having laid [His] hands on them, He departed from there. ¹⁶And behold, one having come near, said to Him, "Good Teacher, what good thing will I do that I may have continuous life?" ¹⁷And He said to him, "Why do you call Me good? No one [is] good except one—God; but if you will to enter into life, keep the commands." ¹⁸He says to Him, "What kind?" And Jesus said, "You will not murder, You will not commit adultery, You will not steal, You will not bear false witness, ¹⁹Honor your father and mother, and, You will love your neighbor as yourself." ²⁰The young man says to Him, "All these I kept from my youth; what yet do I lack?" ²¹Jesus said to him, "If you will to be perfect, go away, sell what you have, and give to the poor, and you will have treasure in Heaven, and come, follow Me." ²²And the young man, having heard the word, went away sorrowful, for he had many possessions; ²³and Jesus said to His disciples, "Truly I say to you that hardly will a rich man enter into the kingdom of the heavens; ²⁴and again I say to you, it is easier for a camel to go through the eye of a needle, than for a rich man to enter into the Kingdom of God." ²⁵And His disciples having heard, were exceedingly amazed, saying, "Who, then, is able to be saved?" ²⁶And Jesus having earnestly beheld, said to them, "With men this is impossible, but with God all things are possible." ²⁷Then Peter answering said to Him, "Behold, we left all, and followed You, what then will we have?" ²⁸And Jesus said to them, "Truly I say to you that you who followed Me, in the regeneration, when the Son of Man may sit on a throne of His glory, will sit—you also—on twelve thrones, judging the twelve tribes of Israel; ²⁹and everyone who left houses, or brothers, or sisters, or father, or mother, or wife, or children, or fields, for My Name's sake, will receive a hundredfold, and will inherit continuous life; ³⁰and many first will be last, and last first."

CHAPTER 20

¹"For the kingdom of the heavens is like to a man, a householder, who went forth with the morning to hire workmen for his vineyard, ²and having agreed with the workmen for a denarius a day, he sent them into his vineyard. ³And having gone forth about the third hour, he saw others standing in the marketplace idle, ⁴and to these he said, Go—also you—to the vineyard, and whatever may be righteous I will give you; ⁵and they went away. Again, having gone forth about the sixth and the ninth hour, he did in like manner. ⁶And about the eleventh hour, having gone forth, he found others standing idle and says to them, Why have you stood here idle all day? ⁷They say to him, Because no one hired us; he says to them, Go—you also—to the vineyard, and whatever may be righteous you will receive. ⁸And evening having come, the lord of the vineyard says to his steward, Call the workmen, and pay them the reward, having begun from the last—to the first. ⁹And they of about the eleventh hour having come, each received a denarius. ¹⁰And the first having come, supposed that they will receive more, and they received, they also, each a denarius, ¹¹and having received [it], they were murmuring against the householder, saying, ¹²that, These, the last, worked one hour, and you made them equal to us, who were bearing the burden of the day—and the heat. ¹³And he answering said to one of them, Friend, I do no unrighteousness to you; did you not agree with me for a denarius? ¹⁴Take that which is yours, and go; and I will to give to this, the last, also as to you; ¹⁵is it not lawful to me to do what I will in my own? Is your eye evil because I am good? ¹⁶So the last will be first, and the first last, for many are called, and few chosen."

¹⁷And Jesus going up to Jerusalem, took the twelve disciples by themselves in the way and said to them, ¹⁸"Behold, we go up to Jerusalem, and the Son of Man will be delivered to the chief priests and scribes, ¹⁹and they will condemn Him to death, and will deliver Him to the nations to mock, and to scourge, and to crucify, and the third day He will rise again." ²⁰Then came near to Him the mother of the sons of Zebedee, with her sons, prostrating and asking something from Him, ²¹and He said to her, "What do you will?" She says to Him, "Say that they may sit—these two sons of mine—one on Your right hand and one on the left, in Your kingdom." ²²And Jesus answering said, "You have not known what you ask for yourselves; are you able to drink of the cup that I am about to drink? And with the immersion that I am immersed with, to be immersed?" They say to Him, "We are able." ²³And He says to them, "Of My cup indeed you will drink, and with the immersion that I am immersed with you will be immersed; but to sit on My right hand and on My left is not Mine to give, but—to those for whom it has been prepared by My Father." ²⁴And the ten having heard, were much displeased with the two brothers, ²⁵and Jesus having called them near, said, "You have known that the rulers of the nations exercise lordship over them, and those [who are] great exercise authority over them, ²⁶but not so will it be among you, but whoever may will among you to become great, let him be your servant; ²⁷and whoever may will among you to be first, let him be your servant; ²⁸even as the Son of Man did not come to be ministered to, but to minister, and to give His life [as] a ransom for many." ²⁹And they going forth from Jericho, there followed Him a great multitude, ³⁰and behold, two blind men sitting by the way, having heard that Jesus passes by, cried, saying, "Deal kindly with us, Lord—Son of David." ³¹And the multitude charged them that they might be silent, and they cried out the more, saying, "Deal kindly with us Lord—Son of David." ³²And having stood, Jesus called them and said, "What do you will [that] I may do to you?" ³³They say to Him, "Lord, that our eyes may be opened"; ³⁴and having been moved with compassion, Jesus touched their eyes, and immediately their eyes received sight, and they followed Him.

CHAPTER 21

¹And when they came near to Jerusalem, and came to Bethphage, to the Mount of Olives, then Jesus sent two disciples, ²saying to them, "Go on into the village in front of you, and immediately you will find a donkey bound, and a colt with her—having loosed, you bring to Me; ³and if anyone may say anything to you, you will say that the LORD has need of them, and immediately He will send them." ⁴And all this came to pass, that it might be fulfilled that was spoken through the prophet, saying, ⁵"Tell the daughter of Zion, Behold, your King comes to you, meek, and mounted on a donkey, and a colt, a foal of a beast of burden." ⁶And the disciples having gone and having done as Jesus commanded them, ⁷brought the donkey and the colt, and put on them their garments, and set [Him] on them; ⁸and the very great multitude spread their own garments in the way, and others were cutting branches from the trees, and were strewing in the way, ⁹and the multitudes who were going before, and who were following, were crying, saying, "Hosanna to the Son of David, blessed is He who is coming in the Name of the LORD; Hosanna in the highest!" ¹⁰And He having entered into Jerusalem, all the city was moved, saying, "Who is this?" ¹¹And the multitudes said, "This is Jesus the prophet, who [is] from Nazareth of Galilee." ¹²And Jesus entered into the temple of God, and cast forth all those selling and buying in the temple, and the tables of the money-changers He overturned, and the seats of those selling the doves, ¹³and He says to them, "It has been written: My house will be called a house of prayer; but you made it a den of robbers." ¹⁴And there came to Him blind and lame men in the temple, and He healed them, ¹⁵and the chief priests and the scribes having seen the wonderful things that He did, and the children crying in the temple, and saying, "Hosanna to the Son of David," were much displeased; ¹⁶and they said to Him, "Do You hear what these say?" And Jesus says to them, "Yes, did you never read, that, Out of the mouth of babies and sucklings You prepared praise?" ¹⁷And having left them, He went forth out of the city to Bethany, and lodged there, ¹⁸and in the morning turning back to the city, He hungered, ¹⁹and having seen a certain fig tree on the way, He came to it, and found nothing in it except leaves only, and He says to it, "No more fruit may be from you—throughout the age"; and instantly the fig tree withered. ²⁰And the disciples having seen, wondered, saying, "How did the fig tree instantly wither?" ²¹And Jesus answering said to them, "Truly I say to you, if you may have faith, and may not doubt, not only this of the fig tree will you do, but even if to this mountain you may say, Be lifted up and be cast into the sea, it will come to pass; ²²and all—as much as you may ask in the prayer, believing, you will receive." ²³And He having come into the temple, there came to Him when teaching the chief priests and the elders of the people, saying, "By what authority do You do these things? And who gave You this authority?" ²⁴And Jesus answering said to them, "I will ask you—I also—one word, which if you may tell Me, I also will tell you by what authority I do these things; ²⁵the immersion of John, from where was it? From Heaven, or from men?" And they were reasoning with themselves, saying, "If we should say, From Heaven, He will say to us, Why, then, did you not believe him? ²⁶And if we should say, From men, we fear the multitude, for all hold John as a prophet." ²⁷And answering Jesus they said, "We have not known." He said to them—He also, "Neither do I tell you by what authority I do these things. ²⁸And what do you think? A man had two children, and having come to the first, he said, Child, go, today be working in my vineyard. ²⁹And he answering said, I will not, but at last, having regretted, he went. ³⁰And having come to the second, he said in the same manner, and he answering said, I [go], lord, and did not go; ³¹which of the two did the will of the father?" They say to Him, "The first." Jesus says to them, "Truly I say to you that the tax collectors and the prostitutes go before you into the Kingdom of God, ³²for John came to you in the way of righteousness, and you did not believe him, and the tax collectors and the prostitutes believed him, and you, having seen, did not regret at last—to believe him. ³³Hear another allegory: There was a certain man, a householder, who planted a vineyard, and put a hedge around it, and dug in it a winepress, and built a tower, and gave it out to farmers, and went abroad. ³⁴And when the season of the fruits came near, he sent his servants to the farmers, to receive the fruits of it, ³⁵and the farmers having taken his servants, one they scourged, and one they killed, and one they stoned. ³⁶Again he sent other servants more than the first, and they did to them in the same manner. ³⁷And at last he sent to them his son, saying, They will respect my son; ³⁸and the farmers having seen the son, said among themselves, This is the heir, come, we may kill him, and may possess his inheritance; ³⁹and having taken him, they cast [him] out of the vineyard, and killed him; ⁴⁰whenever therefore the lord of the vineyard may come, what will he do to these farmers?" ⁴¹They say to Him, "Evil men—he will grievously destroy them, and will give out the vineyard to other farmers who will give back to him the fruits in their seasons." ⁴²Jesus says to them, "Did you never read in the Writings: A stone that the builders disallowed, it became head of a corner; from the LORD has this come to pass, and it is wonderful in our eyes? ⁴³Because of this I say to you that the Kingdom of God will be taken from you, and given to a nation bringing forth its fruit; ⁴⁴and he who is falling on this stone will be broken, and on whomsoever it may fall it will crush him to pieces." ⁴⁵And the chief priests and the Pharisees having heard His allegories, knew that He speaks of them, ⁴⁶and seeking to lay hold on Him, they feared the multitudes, seeing they were holding Him as a prophet.

CHAPTER 22

¹And Jesus answering, again spoke to them in allegories, saying, ²"The kingdom of the heavens was likened to a man, a king, who made wedding feasts for his son, ³and he sent forth his servants to call those having been called to the wedding feasts, and they were not willing to come. ⁴Again he sent forth other servants, saying, Say to those who have been called: Behold, I prepared my early meal, my oxen and the fatlings have been killed, and all things [are] ready, come to the wedding feasts; ⁵and they, having disregarded [it], went away, one to his own field, and the other to his merchandise; ⁶and the rest, having laid hold on his servants, mistreated and slew [them]. ⁷And the king having heard, was angry, and having sent forth his soldiers, he destroyed

MATTHEW

those murderers, and their city he set on fire; ⁸then he says to his servants, The wedding feast indeed is ready, and those called were not worthy, ⁹be going, then, on to the cross-ways, and as many as you may find, call to the wedding feasts. ¹⁰And those servants, having gone forth to the ways, gathered all, as many as they found, both bad and good, and the wedding was filled with those reclining. ¹¹And the king having come in to view those reclining, saw there a man not clothed with wedding clothes, ¹²and he says to him, Friend, how did you come in here, not having wedding clothes? And he was speechless. ¹³Then the king said to the servants, Having bound his feet and hands, take him up and cast forth into the outer darkness, there will be the weeping and the gnashing of the teeth; ¹⁴for many are called, and few chosen." ¹⁵Then the Pharisees having gone, took counsel how they might ensnare Him in words, ¹⁶and they send to Him their disciples with the Herodians, saying, "Teacher, we have known that You are true, and the way of God in truth You teach, and You are not caring for anyone, for You do not look to the face of men; ¹⁷tell us, therefore, what do You think? Is it lawful to give tribute to Caesar or not?" ¹⁸And Jesus having known their wickedness, said, "Why do you tempt Me, hypocrites? ¹⁹Show Me the tribute-coin." And they brought to Him a denarius; ²⁰and He says to them, "Whose [is] this image and the inscription?" ²¹They say to Him, "Caesar's"; then He says to them, "Render therefore the things of Caesar to Caesar, and the things of God to God"; ²²and having heard they wondered, and having left Him they went away. ²³In that day there came near to Him Sadducees who are saying there is not a resurrection, and they questioned Him, saying, ²⁴"Teacher, Moses said if anyone may die having no children, his brother will marry his wife, and will raise up seed to his brother. ²⁵And there were with us seven brothers, and the first having married died, and having no seed, he left his wife to his brother; ²⁶in like manner also the second, and the third, to the seventh, ²⁷and last of all the woman also died; ²⁸therefore in the resurrection, of which of the seven will she be wife—for all had her?" ²⁹And Jesus answering said to them, "You go astray, not knowing the Writings, nor the power of God; ³⁰for in the resurrection they do not marry, nor are they given in marriage, but are as messengers of God in Heaven. ³¹And concerning the resurrection of the dead, did you not read that which was spoken to you by God, saying, ³²I am the God of Abraham, and the God of Isaac, and the God of Jacob? God is not a God of dead men, but of living." ³³And having heard, the multitudes were astonished at His teaching; ³⁴and the Pharisees, having heard that He silenced the Sadducees, were gathered together to Him; ³⁵and one of them, a lawyer, questioned, tempting Him, and saying, ³⁶"Teacher, which [is] the great command in the Law?" ³⁷And Jesus said to him, "You will love the LORD your God with all your heart, and with all your soul, and with all your understanding— ³⁸this is a first and great command; ³⁹and the second [is] like to it: You will love your neighbor as yourself; ⁴⁰on these—the two commands—all the Law and the Prophets hang." ⁴¹And the Pharisees having been gathered together, Jesus questioned them, ⁴²saying, "What do you think concerning the Christ? Of whom is He Son?" They say to Him, "Of David." ⁴³He says to them, "How then does David in the Spirit call Him Lord, saying, ⁴⁴The LORD said to my Lord, || Sit at My right hand, || Until I may make Your enemies Your footstool? ⁴⁵If then David calls Him Lord, how is He his son?" ⁴⁶And no one was able to answer Him a word, nor did any dare question Him from that day [on].

CHAPTER 23

¹Then Jesus spoke to the multitudes, and to His disciples, ²saying, "On the seat of Moses sat down the scribes and the Pharisees; ³all, then, as much as they may say to you to observe, observe and do, but according to their works do not do, for they say, and do not do; ⁴for they bind together burdens [too] heavy and grievous to bear, and lay [them] on the shoulders of men, but with their finger they will not move them. ⁵And all their works they do to be seen by men, and they make broad their phylacteries, and enlarge the fringes of their garments, ⁶they also cherish the first couches at the banquets, and the first seats in the synagogues, ⁷and the salutations in the marketplaces, and to be called by men, Rabbi, Rabbi. ⁸And you may not be called Rabbi, for one is your teacher—the Christ, and you are all brothers; ⁹and you may not call [any] your father on the earth, for one is your Father, who is in the heavens, ¹⁰nor may you be called teachers, for one is your teacher—the Christ. ¹¹And the greater of you will be your servant, ¹²and whoever will exalt himself will be humbled, and whoever will humble himself will be exalted. ¹³Woe to you, scribes and Pharisees, hypocrites! Because you shut up the kingdom of the heavens before men, for you do not go in, nor do you permit those going in to enter. ¹⁴[[Woe to you, scribes and Pharisees, hypocrites! Because you eat up the houses of the widows, and for a pretense make long prayers, because of this you will receive more abundant judgment.]] ¹⁵Woe to you, scribes and Pharisees, hypocrites! Because you go around the sea and the dry land to make one proselyte, and whenever it may happen—you make him a son of Gehenna twofold more than yourselves. ¹⁶Woe to you, blind guides, who are saying, Whoever may swear by the temple, it is nothing, but whoever may swear by the gold of the temple—is debtor! ¹⁷Fools and blind! For which [is] greater, the gold, or the temple that is sanctifying the gold? ¹⁸And, Whoever may swear by the altar, it is nothing, but whoever may swear by the gift that is on it—is debtor! ¹⁹Fools and blind! For which [is] greater, the gift, or the altar that is sanctifying the gift? ²⁰He therefore who swore by the altar, swears by it, and by all things on it; ²¹and he who swore by the temple, swears by it, and by Him who is dwelling in it; ²²and he who swore by Heaven, swears by the throne of God, and by Him who is sitting on it. ²³Woe to you, scribes and Pharisees, hypocrites! Because you give tithe of the mint, and the dill, and the cumin, and neglected the weightier things of the Law—judgment, and kindness, and faith; these it was necessary to do, and those not to neglect. ²⁴Blind guides! Who are straining out the gnat, and are swallowing the camel. ²⁵Woe to you, scribes and Pharisees, hypocrites! Because you make clean the outside of the cup and the plate, and within they are full of robbery and self-indulgence. ²⁶Blind Pharisee! First cleanse the inside of the cup and the plate, that the outside of them may also become clean. ²⁷Woe to you, scribes and Pharisees, hypocrites! Because you are like to whitewashed graves, which outwardly indeed appear beautiful, and within are full of bones of dead men, and of all uncleanness; ²⁸so also you outwardly indeed appear to men righteous, and within you are full of hypocrisy and lawlessness. ²⁹Woe to you, scribes and Pharisees, hypocrites! Because you build the graves of the prophets, and adorn the tombs of the righteous, ³⁰and say, If we had been in the days of our fathers, we would not have been partakers with them in the blood of the prophets. ³¹So that you testify to yourselves that you are sons of them who murdered the prophets; ³²and you fill up the measure of your fathers. ³³Serpents! Brood of vipers! How may you escape from the judgment of Gehenna? ³⁴Because of this, behold, I send to you prophets, and wise men, and scribes, and of them you will kill and crucify, and of them you will scourge in your synagogues, and will pursue from city to city, ³⁵that on you may come all the righteous blood being poured out on the earth from the blood of Abel the righteous, to the blood of Zacharias son of Barachias, whom you murdered between the temple and the altar: ³⁶truly I say to you, all these things will come on this generation. ³⁷Jerusalem, Jerusalem, that are killing the prophets, and stoning those sent to you, how often I willed to gather your children together, as a hen gathers her own chickens under the wings, and you did not will. ³⁸Behold, your house is left to you desolate; ³⁹for I say to you, you may not see Me from now on, until you may say, Blessed [is] He who is coming in the Name of the LORD."

CHAPTER 24

¹And having gone forth, Jesus departed from the temple, and His disciples came near to show Him the buildings of the temple, ²and Jesus said to them, "Do you not see all these? Truly I say to you, there may not be left here a stone on a stone that will not be thrown down." ³And when He is sitting on the Mount of Olives, the disciples came near to Him by Himself, saying, "Tell us, when will these be? And what [is] the sign of Your coming, and of the full end of the age?" ⁴And Jesus answering said to them, "Take heed that no one may lead you astray, ⁵for many will come in My Name, saying, I am the Christ, and they will lead

many astray, ⁶and you will begin to hear of wars, and reports of wars; see, do not be troubled, for it is necessary for all [these] to come to pass, but the end is not yet. ⁷For nation will rise against nation, and kingdom against kingdom, and there will be famines, and pestilences, and earthquakes, in various places; ⁸and all these [are the] beginning of travails; ⁹then they will deliver you up to tribulation, and will kill you, and you will be hated by all the nations because of My Name; ¹⁰and then will many be stumbled, and they will deliver up one another, and will hate one another. ¹¹And many false prophets will arise, and will lead many astray; ¹²and because of the abounding of the lawlessness, the love of the many will become cold; ¹³but he who endured to the end, he will be saved; ¹⁴and this good news of the kingdom will be proclaimed in all the world, for a testimony to all the nations, and then will the end arrive. ¹⁵Whenever, therefore, you may see the abomination of the desolation, that was spoken of through Daniel the prophet, standing in the holy place (whoever is reading let him observe) ¹⁶then those in Judea—let them flee to the mountains; ¹⁷he on the housetop—do not let him come down to take up anything out of his house; ¹⁸and he in the field—do not let him turn back to take his garments. ¹⁹And woe to those with child, and to those giving suck in those days; ²⁰and pray that your flight may not be in winter, nor on a Sabbath; ²¹for there will then be great tribulation, such as was not from the beginning of the world until now, no, nor may be. ²²And if those days were not shortened, no flesh would have been saved; but because of the chosen will those days be shortened. ²³Then if anyone may say to you, Behold, here [is] the Christ! Or, Here! You may not believe; ²⁴for there will arise false Christs, and false prophets, and they will give great signs and wonders, so as to lead astray, if possible, also the chosen. ²⁵Behold, I told you beforehand. ²⁶If therefore they may say to you, Behold, He is in the wilderness, you may not go forth; Behold, in the inner chambers, you may not believe; ²⁷for as the lightning comes forth from the east, and appears to the west, so will also be the coming of the Son of Man; ²⁸for wherever the carcass may be, there the eagles will be gathered together. ²⁹And immediately after the tribulation of those days, the sun will be darkened, and the moon will not give her light, and the stars will fall from the sky, and the powers of the heavens will be shaken; ³⁰and then will appear the sign of the Son of Man in the sky; and then will all the tribes of the earth strike the breast, and they will see the Son of Man coming on the clouds of Heaven, with power and much glory; ³¹and He will send His messengers with a great sound of a trumpet, and they will gather together His chosen from the four winds, from the ends of the heavens to the ends thereof. ³²And from the fig tree learn the allegory: when its branch may have already become tender, and it may put forth the leaves, you know that summer [is] near, ³³so also you, when you may see all these, you know that it is near—at the doors. ³⁴Truly I say to you, this generation may not pass away until all these may come to pass. ³⁵The heaven and the earth will pass away, but My words will not pass away. ³⁶And concerning that day and the hour no one has known—not even the messengers of the heavens—except My Father only; ³⁷and as the days of Noah—so will also be the coming of the Son of Man; ³⁸for as they were, in the days before the flood, eating, and drinking, marrying, and giving in marriage, until the day Noah entered into the Ark, ³⁹and they did not know until the flood came and took all away, so will also be the coming of the Son of Man. ⁴⁰Then two [men] will be in the field: one is received, and one is left; ⁴¹two [women] will be grinding in the mill: one is received, and one is left. ⁴²Watch therefore, because you have not known in what hour your Lord comes; ⁴³and know this, that if the master of the house had known in what watch the thief comes, he had watched, and did not permit his house to be broken through; ⁴⁴because of this also you, become ready, because in what hour you do not think, the Son of Man comes. ⁴⁵Who, then, is the servant, faithful and wise, whom his lord set over his household, to give them the nourishment in season? ⁴⁶Blessed that servant, whom his lord, having come, will find doing so; ⁴⁷truly I say to you that he will set him over all his substance. ⁴⁸And if that evil servant may say in his heart, My lord delays to come, ⁴⁹and may begin to beat the fellow-servants, and to eat and to drink with the drunken, ⁵⁰the lord of that servant will arrive in a day when he does not expect, and in an hour of which he does not know, ⁵¹and will cut him off, and will appoint his portion with the hypocrites; there will be the weeping and the gnashing of the teeth."

CHAPTER 25

¹"Then will the kingdom of the heavens be likened to ten virgins, who, having taken their lamps, went forth to meet the bridegroom; ²and five of them were prudent, and five foolish; ³they who were foolish having taken their lamps, did not take with themselves oil; ⁴and the prudent took oil in their vessels, with their lamps. ⁵And the bridegroom lingering, they all nodded and were sleeping, ⁶and in the middle of the night a cry was made, Behold, the bridegroom comes; go forth to meet him! ⁷Then all those virgins rose, and trimmed their lamps, ⁸and the foolish said to the prudent, Give us of your oil, because our lamps are going out; ⁹and the prudent answered, saying, Lest there may not be sufficient for us and you, go rather to those selling, and buy for yourselves. ¹⁰And while they are going away to buy, the bridegroom came, and those ready went in with him to the wedding feasts, and the door was shut; ¹¹and afterward come also the rest of the virgins, saying, Lord, lord, open to us; ¹²and he answering said, Truly I say to you, I have not known you. ¹³Watch therefore, for you have not known the day nor the hour in which the Son of Man comes. ¹⁴For—as a man going abroad called his own servants, and delivered to them his substance, ¹⁵and to one he gave five talents, and to another two, and to another one, to each according to his several ability, went abroad immediately. ¹⁶And he who received the five talents, having gone, worked with them, and made five other talents; ¹⁷in like manner also he who [received] the two, he gained, also he, other two; ¹⁸and he who received the one, having gone away, dug in the earth, and hid his lord's money. ¹⁹And after a long time comes the lord of those servants, and takes reckoning with them; ²⁰and he who received the five talents, having come, brought five other talents, saying, Lord, you delivered five talents to me; behold, I gained five other talents besides them. ²¹And his lord said to him, Well done, good and faithful servant, you were faithful over a few things, I will set you over many things; enter into the joy of your lord. ²²And he also, who received the two talents, having come, said, Lord, you delivered to me two talents; behold, I gained two other talents besides them. ²³His lord said to him, Well done, good and faithful servant, you were faithful over a few things, I will set you over many things; enter into the joy of your lord. ²⁴And he also who has received the one talent, having come, said, Lord, I knew you, that you are a hard man, reaping where you did not sow, and gathering from where you did not scatter; ²⁵and having been afraid, having gone away, I hid your talent in the earth; behold, you have your own! ²⁶And his lord answering said to him, Evil servant, and slothful, you had known that I reap where I did not sow, and I gather from where I did not scatter! ²⁷It was necessary [for] you then to put my money to the money-lenders, and having come I had received my own with increase. ²⁸Take therefore from him the talent, and give to him having the ten talents, ²⁹for to everyone having will be given, and he will have overabundance, and from him who is not having, even that which he has will be taken from him; ³⁰and cast forth the unprofitable servant into the outer darkness; there will be the weeping and the gnashing of the teeth. ³¹And whenever the Son of Man may come in His glory, and all the holy messengers with Him, then He will sit on a throne of His glory; ³²and all the nations will be gathered together before Him, and He will separate them from one another, as the shepherd separates the sheep from the goats, ³³and He will set the sheep indeed on His right hand, and the goats on the left. ³⁴Then the King will say to those on His right hand, Come, the blessed of My Father, inherit the kingdom that has been prepared for you from the foundation of the world; ³⁵for I hungered, and you gave Me to eat; I thirsted, and you gave Me

to drink; I was a stranger, and you received Me; ³⁶naked, and you clothed Me; I was sick, and you looked after Me; I was in prison, and you came to Me. ³⁷Then will the righteous answer Him, saying, Lord, when did we see You hungering, and we nourished? Or thirsting, and we gave to drink? ³⁸And when did we see You a stranger, and we received? Or naked, and we clothed? ³⁹And when did we see You ailing or in prison, and we came to You? ⁴⁰And the King answering, will say to them, Truly I say to you, inasmuch as you did [it] to one of these My brothers—the least— you did [it] to Me. ⁴¹Then will He say also to those on the left hand, Go from Me, the cursed, into the continuous fire that has been prepared for the Devil and his messengers; ⁴²for I hungered, and you gave Me nothing to eat; I thirsted, and you gave Me nothing to drink; ⁴³I was a stranger, and you did not receive Me; naked, and you did not clothe Me; sick and in prison, and you did not look after Me. ⁴⁴Then they will answer, they also, saying, Lord, when did we see You hungering, or thirsting, or a stranger, or naked, or sick, or in prison, and we did not minister to You? ⁴⁵Then will He answer them, saying, Truly I say to you, inasmuch as you did [it] not to one of these, the least, you did [it] not to Me. ⁴⁶And these will go away into continuous punishment, but the righteous into continuous life."

CHAPTER 26

¹And it came to pass, when Jesus finished all these words, He said to His disciples, ²"You have known that after two days the Passover comes, and the Son of Man is delivered up to be crucified." ³Then were gathered together the chief priests, and the scribes, and the elders of the people, into the court of the chief priest who was called Caiaphas; ⁴and they consulted together that they might take Jesus by guile, and kill [Him], ⁵and they said, "Not in the celebration, that there may not be a tumult among the people." ⁶And Jesus having been in Bethany, in the house of Simon the leper, ⁷there came to Him a woman having an alabaster box of ointment, very precious, and she poured on His head as He is reclining. ⁸And having seen [it], His disciples were much displeased, saying, "To what purpose [is] this waste? ⁹For this ointment could have been sold for much, and given to the poor." ¹⁰And Jesus having known, said to them, "Why do you give trouble to the woman? For a good work she worked for Me; ¹¹for you always have the poor with you, and you do not always have Me; ¹²for she having put this ointment on My body—for My burial she did [it]. ¹³Truly I say to you, wherever this good news may be proclaimed in the whole world, what this [one] did will also be spoken of—for a memorial of her." ¹⁴Then one of the Twelve, who is called Judas Iscariot, having gone to the chief priests, said, ¹⁵"What are you willing to give me, and I will deliver Him up to you?" And they weighed out to him thirty pieces of silver, ¹⁶and from that time he was seeking a convenient season to deliver Him up. ¹⁷And on the first [day] of the Unleavened [Bread] the disciples came near to Jesus, saying to Him, "Where will You [that] we may prepare for You to eat the Passover?" ¹⁸And He said, "Go away into the city, to such a one, and say to him, The Teacher says, My time is near; near you I keep the Passover with My disciples"; ¹⁹and the disciples did as Jesus appointed them, and prepared the Passover. ²⁰And evening having come, He was reclining with the Twelve, ²¹and while they are eating, He said, "Truly I say to you that one of you will deliver Me up." ²²And being grieved exceedingly, they began to say to Him, each of them, "Is it I, Lord?" ²³And He answering said, "He who dipped with Me the hand in the dish, he will deliver Me up; ²⁴the Son of Man indeed goes, as it has been written concerning Him, but woe to that man through whom the Son of Man is delivered up! It were good for him if that man had not been born." ²⁵And Judas—he who delivered Him up—answering said, "Is it I, Rabbi?" He says to him, "You have said." ²⁶And while they were eating, Jesus having taken the bread, and having blessed, broke, and was giving [it] to the disciples, and said, "Take, eat, this is My body"; ²⁷and having taken the cup, and having given thanks, He gave to them, saying, "Drink of it—all; ²⁸for this is My blood of the New Covenant, that is being poured out for many, for forgiveness of sins; ²⁹and I say to you that I may not drink from now on this produce of the vine, until that day when I may drink it with you new in the kingdom of My Father." ³⁰And having sung a hymn, they went forth to the Mount of Olives; ³¹then Jesus says to them, "All you will be stumbled at Me this night; for it has been written: I will strike the Shepherd, and the sheep of the flock will be scattered abroad; ³²but after My having risen, I will go before you to Galilee." ³³And Peter answering said to Him, "Even if all will be stumbled at You, I will never be stumbled." ³⁴Jesus said to him, "Truly I say to you that this night, before rooster-crowing, three times you will deny Me." ³⁵Peter says to Him, "Even if it may be necessary for me to die with You, I will not deny You"; in like manner also said all the disciples. ³⁶Then Jesus comes with them to a place called Gethsemane, and He says to the disciples, "Sit here, until having gone away, I will pray over there." ³⁷And having taken Peter and the two sons of Zebedee, He began to be sorrowful, and to be very heavy; ³⁸then He says to them, "Exceedingly sorrowful is My soul—to death; abide here, and watch with Me." ³⁹And having gone forward a little, He fell on His face, praying, and saying, "My Father, if it be possible, let this cup pass from Me; nevertheless, not as I will, but as You." ⁴⁰And He comes to the disciples, and finds them sleeping, and He says to Peter, "So! You were not able to watch with Me one hour! ⁴¹Watch, and pray, that you may not enter into temptation: the spirit indeed is forward, but the flesh weak." ⁴²Again, a second time, having gone away, He prayed, saying, "My Father, if this cup cannot pass away from Me except I drink it, Your will be done"; ⁴³and having come, He finds them again sleeping, for their eyes were heavy. ⁴⁴And having left them, having gone away again, He prayed a third time, saying the same word; ⁴⁵then He comes to His disciples and says to them, "Sleep on from now on, and rest! Behold, the hour has come near, and the Son of Man is delivered up into the hands of sinners. ⁴⁶Rise, let us go; behold, he who is delivering Me up has come near." ⁴⁷And while He is yet speaking, behold, Judas, one of the Twelve came, and with him a great multitude, with swords and sticks, from the chief priests and elders of the people. ⁴⁸And he who delivered Him up gave them a sign, saying, "Whomsoever I will kiss, it is He, lay hold on Him"; ⁴⁹and immediately, having come to Jesus, he said, "Greetings, Rabbi," and kissed Him; ⁵⁰and Jesus said to him, "Friend, for what are you present?" Then having come near, they laid hands on Jesus, and took hold on Him. ⁵¹And behold, one of those with Jesus, having stretched forth the hand, drew his sword, and having struck the servant of the chief priest, he took off his ear. ⁵²Then Jesus says to him, "Turn back your sword to its place; for all who took the sword will perish by the sword; ⁵³do you think that I am not able now to call on My Father, and He will place beside Me more than twelve legions of messengers? ⁵⁴How then may the Writings be fulfilled, that thus it must happen?" ⁵⁵In that hour Jesus said to the multitudes, "Did you come forth as against a robber, with swords and sticks, to take Me? Daily I was with you sitting, teaching in the temple, and you did not lay hold on Me; ⁵⁶but all this has come to pass, that the Writings of the prophets may be fulfilled"; then all the disciples, having left Him, fled. ⁵⁷And those laying hold on Jesus led [Him] away to Caiaphas the chief priest, where the scribes and the elders were gathered together, ⁵⁸and Peter was following Him far off, to the court of the chief priest, and having gone in within, he was sitting with the officers, to see the end. ⁵⁹And the chief priests, and the elders, and all the council, were seeking false witness against Jesus, that they might put Him to death, ⁶⁰and they did not find; and many false witnesses having come near, they did not find; and at last two false witnesses having come near, ⁶¹said, "This One said, I am able to throw down the temple of God, and after three days to build it." ⁶²And the chief priest having stood up, said to Him, "Nothing You answer? What do these witness against You?" ⁶³And Jesus was silent. And the chief priest answering said to Him, "I adjure You, by the living God, that You may say to us if You are the Christ—the Son of God." ⁶⁴Jesus says to him, "You have said; nevertheless I say to you, hereafter you will see the Son of Man sitting on the right hand of the Power and coming on the clouds of Heaven." ⁶⁵Then the chief priest tore his garments, saying, "He has slandered; what need have we yet of witnesses? Behold, now you heard His slander; ⁶⁶what do you think?" And they answering said, "He is worthy of death." ⁶⁷Then they spit in His face and punched Him, and others slapped, ⁶⁸saying, "Declare to us, O Christ, who he is that

struck You?" ⁶⁹And Peter was sitting in the court outside, and there came near to him a certain maid, saying, "And you were with Jesus of Galilee!" ⁷⁰And he denied before all, saying, "I have not known what you say." ⁷¹And he having gone forth to the porch, another female saw him, and says to those there, "And this one was with Jesus of Nazareth"; ⁷²and again he denied with an oath, "I have not known the Man." ⁷³And after a while those standing near having come, said to Peter, "Truly you also are of them, for even your speech makes you evident." ⁷⁴Then he began to curse, and to swear, "I have not known the Man"; and immediately a rooster crowed, ⁷⁵and Peter remembered the saying of Jesus, He having said to him, "Before rooster-crowing, you will deny Me three times"; and having gone outside, he wept bitterly.

CHAPTER 27

¹And morning having come, all the chief priests and the elders of the people took counsel against Jesus, so as to put Him to death; ²and having bound Him, they led [Him] away, and delivered Him up to Pontius Pilate, the governor. ³Then Judas—he who delivered Him up—having seen that He was condemned, having regretted, brought back the thirty pieces of silver to the chief priests and to the elders, saying, ⁴"I sinned, having delivered up innocent blood"; and they said, "What [is that] to us? You will see!" ⁵And having cast down the pieces of silver in the temple, he departed, and having gone away, he strangled himself. ⁶And the chief priests having taken the pieces of silver, said, "It is not lawful to put them into the treasury, seeing it is the price of blood"; ⁷and having taken counsel, they bought the potter's field with them, for the burial of strangers; ⁸therefore that field was called, "Field of Blood," to this day. ⁹Then was fulfilled that spoken through Jeremiah the prophet, saying, "And I took the thirty pieces of silver, the price of Him who has been priced, whom they of the sons of Israel priced, ¹⁰and gave them for the potter's field, as the LORD appointed to me." ¹¹And Jesus stood before the governor, and the governor questioned Him, saying, "Are You the King of the Jews?" And Jesus said to him, "You say [it]." ¹²And in His being accused by the chief priests and the elders, He did not answer anything; ¹³then Pilate says to Him, "Do You not hear how many things they witness against You?" ¹⁴And He did not answer him, not even to one word, so that the governor wondered greatly. ¹⁵And at the celebration the governor had been accustomed to release one to the multitude, a prisoner, whom they willed, ¹⁶and they had a noted prisoner then, called Barabbas, ¹⁷therefore they having been gathered together, Pilate said to them, "Whom do you will [that] I may release to you? Barabbas or Jesus who is called Christ?" ¹⁸For he had known that they had delivered Him up because of envy. ¹⁹And as he is sitting on the judgment seat, his wife sent to him, saying, "Nothing—to you and to that Righteous One, for I suffered many things today in a dream because of Him." ²⁰And the chief priests and the elders persuaded the multitudes that they might ask for themselves Barabbas, and might destroy Jesus; ²¹and the governor answering said to them, "Which of the two will you [that] I may release to you?" And they said, "Barabbas." ²²Pilate says to them, "What then will I do with Jesus who is called Christ?" They all say to him, "Let [Him] be crucified!" ²³And the governor said, "Why, what evil did He do?" And they were crying out the more, saying, "Let [Him] be crucified!" ²⁴And Pilate having seen that it profits nothing, but rather a tumult is made, having taken water, he washed the hands before the multitude, saying, "I am innocent from the blood of this Righteous One; you will see [to it] yourselves"; ²⁵and all the people answering said, "His blood [is] on us, and on our children!" ²⁶Then he released Barabbas to them, and having scourged Jesus, he delivered [Him] up that He may be crucified; ²⁷then the soldiers of the governor having taken Jesus to the Praetorium, gathered to Him all the band; ²⁸and having unclothed Him, they put a crimson cloak around Him, ²⁹and having plaited Him a garland out of thorns they put [it] on His head, and [put] a reed in His right hand, and having kneeled before Him, they were mocking Him, saying, "Hail, the King of the Jews!" ³⁰And having spit on Him, they took the reed, and were striking on His head; ³¹and when they had mocked Him, they took off the cloak from Him, and put His own garments on Him, and led Him away to crucify [Him]. ³²And coming forth, they found a man, a Cyrenian, by name Simon: they impressed him that he might carry His cross; ³³and having come to a place called Golgotha, which is called "Place of [the] Skull," ³⁴they gave Him vinegar mixed with gall to drink, and having tasted, He would not drink. ³⁵And having crucified Him, they divided His garments, casting a lot, [[that it might be fulfilled which was spoken by the prophet: "They divided My garments to themselves, and they cast a lot over My clothing";]] ³⁶and sitting down, they were watching Him there, ³⁷and they put up over His head, His accusation written: "THIS IS JESUS, THE KING OF THE JEWS." ³⁸Then two robbers are crucified with Him, one on the right hand and one on the left, ³⁹and those passing by kept slandering Him, wagging their heads, ⁴⁰and saying, "You that are throwing down the temple, and in three days building [it], save Yourself; if You are the Son of God, come down from the cross." ⁴¹And in like manner also the chief priests mocking, with the scribes and elders, said, ⁴²"He saved others; He is not able to save Himself! If He is King of Israel, let Him come down now from the cross, and we will believe Him; ⁴³He has trusted on God, let Him now deliver Him if He wants Him, because He said, I am [the] Son of God"; ⁴⁴with the same also the robbers, who were crucified with Him, were reproaching Him. ⁴⁵And from the sixth hour darkness came over all the land to the ninth hour, ⁴⁶and about the ninth hour Jesus cried out with a great voice, saying, "Eli, Eli, lama sabachthani?" That is, "My God, My God, why did You forsake Me?" ⁴⁷And certain of those standing there having heard, said, "He calls Elijah"; ⁴⁸and immediately, one of them having run, and having taken a sponge, having filled [it] with vinegar, and having put [it] on a reed, was giving Him to drink, ⁴⁹but the rest said, "Let alone, let us see if Elijah comes—about to save Him." ⁵⁰And Jesus having again cried with a great voice, yielded the spirit; ⁵¹and behold, the veil of the temple was torn in two from top to bottom, and the earth quaked, and the rocks were split, ⁵²and the tombs were opened, and many bodies of the holy ones who have fallen asleep, arose, ⁵³and having come forth out of the tombs after His rising, they went into the holy city, and appeared to many. ⁵⁴And the centurion, and those with him watching Jesus, having seen the earthquake, and the things that were done, were exceedingly afraid, saying, "Truly this was God's Son." ⁵⁵And there were there many women beholding from afar, who followed Jesus from Galilee, ministering to Him, ⁵⁶among whom was Mary the Magdalene, and Mary the mother of James and of Joses, and the mother of the sons of Zebedee. ⁵⁷And evening having come, there came a rich man from Arimathea named Joseph, who also himself was discipled to Jesus, ⁵⁸he having gone near to Pilate, asked for himself the body of Jesus; then Pilate commanded the body to be given back. ⁵⁹And having taken the body, Joseph wrapped it in clean linen, ⁶⁰and laid it in his new tomb that he hewed in the rock, and having rolled a great stone to the door of the tomb, he went away; ⁶¹now Mary the Magdalene was there, and the other Mary, sitting opposite the grave. ⁶²And on the next day that is after the Preparation, the chief priests and the Pharisees were gathered together to Pilate, ⁶³saying, "Lord, we have remembered that this deceiver said while yet living, After three days I rise; ⁶⁴command, then, the grave to be made secure until the third day, lest His disciples, having come by night, may steal Him away, and may say to the people, He rose from the dead, and the last deceit will be worse than the first." ⁶⁵And Pilate said to them, "You have a guard, go away, make [it] secure—as you have known"; ⁶⁶and they, having gone, made the grave secure, having sealed the stone, together with the guard.

CHAPTER 28

¹Now after [the] Sabbaths, it being dawn, toward the first [day] of the weeks, Mary the Magdalene came, and the other Mary, to see the grave, ²and behold, there came a great earthquake, for a messenger of the LORD, having come down out of Heaven, having

MATTHEW

come, rolled away the stone from the door, and was sitting on it, ³and his countenance was as lightning, and his clothing white as snow, ⁴and from the fear of him the keepers shook, and they became as dead men. ⁵And the messenger answering said to the women, "Do not fear, for I have known that you seek Jesus who has been crucified; ⁶He is not here, for He rose, as He said; come, see the place where the LORD was lying; ⁷and having gone quickly, say to His disciples that He rose from the dead; and behold, He goes before you to Galilee, there you will see Him; behold, I have told you." ⁸And having gone forth quickly from the tomb, with fear and great joy, they ran to tell His disciples; ⁹and as they were going to tell His disciples, then behold, Jesus met them, saying, "Greetings!" And having come near, they laid hold of His feet, and worshiped Him. ¹⁰Then Jesus says to them, "Do not fear, go away, tell My brothers that they may go away to Galilee, and there they will see Me." ¹¹And while they are going on, behold, certain of the guard having come into the city, reported to the chief priests all the things that happened, ¹²and having been gathered together with the elders, having also taken counsel, they gave much money to the soldiers, ¹³saying, "Say that His disciples having come by night, stole Him—we being asleep; ¹⁴and if this is heard by the governor, we will persuade him, and you keep free from anxiety." ¹⁵And they, having received the money, did as they were taught, and this account was spread abroad among Jews until this day. ¹⁶And the eleven disciples went to Galilee, to the mountain where Jesus appointed them, ¹⁷and having seen Him, they worshiped Him, but some wavered. ¹⁸And having come near, Jesus spoke to them, saying, "All authority in Heaven and on earth was given to Me; ¹⁹having gone, then, disciple all the nations, immersing them into the Name of the Father, and of the Son, and of the Holy Spirit, ²⁰teaching them to observe all, whatever I commanded you, and behold, I am with you all the days—until the full end of the age."

MARK

CHAPTER 1

¹A beginning of the good news of Jesus Christ, Son of God. ²As it has been written in the Prophets: "Behold, I send My messenger before Your face, || Who will prepare Your way before You. ³A voice of one calling in the wilderness: Prepare the way of the LORD, || Make His paths straight." ⁴John came immersing in the wilderness, and proclaiming an immersion of conversion for forgiveness of sins, ⁵and there were going forth to him all the region of Judea, and they of Jerusalem, and they were all immersed by him in the river Jordan, confessing their sins. ⁶And John was clothed with camel's hair, and a girdle of skin around his loins, and eating locusts and honey of the field, ⁷and he proclaimed, saying, "He comes—who is mightier than I—after me, of whom I am not worthy—having stooped down—to loose the strap of His sandals; ⁸I indeed immersed you in water, but He will immerse you in the Holy Spirit." ⁹And it came to pass in those days, Jesus came from Nazareth of Galilee, and was immersed by John in the Jordan; ¹⁰and immediately coming up from the water, He saw the heavens dividing, and the Spirit coming down on Him as a dove; ¹¹and a voice came out of the heavens, "You are My Son, the Beloved, in whom I delighted." ¹²And immediately the Spirit puts Him forth into the wilderness, ¹³and He was there in the wilderness forty days, being tempted by Satan, and He was with the beasts, and the messengers were ministering to Him. ¹⁴And after the delivering up of John, Jesus came to Galilee, proclaiming the good news of the Kingdom of God, ¹⁵and saying, "The time has been fulfilled, and the Kingdom of God has come near, convert and believe in the good news." ¹⁶And walking by the Sea of Galilee, He saw Simon, and his brother Andrew, casting a drag into the sea, for they were fishers, ¹⁷and Jesus said to them, "Come after Me, and I will make you to become fishers of men"; ¹⁸and immediately, having left their nets, they followed Him. ¹⁹And having gone on there a little, He saw James of Zebedee, and his brother John, and they were in the boat refitting the nets, ²⁰and immediately He called them, and having left their father Zebedee in the boat with the hired servants, they went away after Him. ²¹And they go on to Capernaum, and immediately, on the Sabbaths, having gone into the synagogue, He was teaching, ²²and they were astonished at His teaching, for He was teaching them as having authority, and not as the scribes. ²³And there was in their synagogue a man with an unclean spirit, and he cried out, ²⁴saying, "What [regards] us and You, Jesus the Nazarene? You came to destroy us; I have known You, who You are—the Holy One of God." ²⁵And Jesus rebuked him, saying, "Be silenced, and come forth out of him," ²⁶and the unclean spirit having convulsed him, and having cried with a great voice, came forth out of him, ²⁷and they were all amazed, so as to reason among themselves, saying, "What is this? What new teaching [is] this? That with authority He also commands the unclean spirits, and they obey Him!" ²⁸And the fame of Him went forth immediately to all the region of Galilee. ²⁹And immediately, having come forth out of the synagogue, they went into the house of Simon and Andrew, with James and John, ³⁰and the mother-in-law of Simon was lying fevered, and immediately they tell Him about her, ³¹and having come near, He raised her up, having laid hold of her hand, and the fever left her immediately, and she was ministering to them. ³²And evening having come, when the sun set, they brought to Him all who were ill and who were demoniacs, ³³and the whole city was gathered together near the door, ³⁴and He healed many who were ill of manifold diseases, and He cast forth many demons, and was not permitting the demons to speak, because they knew Him. ³⁵And very early, it being yet night, having risen, He went forth, and went away to a desolate place, and was praying there; ³⁶and Simon and those with him went in quest of Him, ³⁷and having found Him, they say to Him, "All seek You"; ³⁸and He says to them, "We may go into the next towns, that there also I may preach, for—for this I came forth." ³⁹And He was preaching in their synagogues, in all Galilee, and is casting out the demons, ⁴⁰and there comes to Him a leper, calling on Him, and kneeling to Him, and saying to Him, "If You may will, You are able to cleanse me." ⁴¹And Jesus having been moved with compassion, having stretched forth the hand, touched him and says to him, "I will, be cleansed"; ⁴²and He having spoken, immediately the leprosy went away from him, and he was cleansed. ⁴³And having sternly charged him, immediately He put him forth, ⁴⁴and says to him, "See [that] you may say nothing to anyone, but go away, show yourself to the priest, and bring near for your cleansing the things Moses directed, for a testimony to them." ⁴⁵And he, having gone forth, began to proclaim much, and to spread the thing abroad, so that He was no longer able to openly enter into the city, but He was outside in desolate places, and they were coming to Him from every quarter.

CHAPTER 2

¹And again He entered into Capernaum, after [some] days, and it was heard that He is in the house, ²and immediately many were gathered together, so that there was no more room, not even at the door, and He was speaking to them the word. ³And they come to Him, bringing a paralytic, carried by four, ⁴and not being able to come near to Him because of the multitude, they uncovered the roof where He was, and having broken [it] up, they let down the pallet on which the paralytic was lying, ⁵and Jesus having seen their faith, says to the paralytic, "Child, your sins have been forgiven you." ⁶And there were certain of the scribes sitting there, and reasoning in their hearts, ⁷"Why does this One thus speak evil words? Who is

MARK

able to forgive sins except one—God?" ⁸And immediately Jesus, having known in His spirit that they thus reason in themselves, said to them, "Why do you reason these things in your hearts? ⁹Which is easier? To say to the paralytic, Your sins are forgiven; or to say, Rise, and take up your pallet, and walk? ¹⁰And that you may know that the Son of Man has authority on the earth to forgive sins—(He says to the paralytic)— ¹¹I say to you, rise, and take up your pallet, and go away to your house"; ¹²and he rose immediately, and having taken up the pallet, he went forth before all, so that all were astonished, and glorify God, saying, "Never thus did we see." ¹³And He went forth again by the sea, and all the multitude was coming to Him, and He was teaching them, ¹⁴and passing by, He saw Levi of Alpheus sitting at the tax office, and says to him, "Follow Me," and he, having risen, followed Him. ¹⁵And it came to pass, in His reclining in his house, that many tax collectors and sinners were dining with Jesus and His disciples, for there were many, and they followed Him. ¹⁶And the scribes and the Pharisees, having seen Him eating with the tax collectors and sinners, said to His disciples, "Why—that with the tax collectors and sinners He eats and drinks?" ¹⁷And Jesus, having heard, says to them, "They who are strong have no need of a physician, but they who are ill; I did not come to call righteous men, but sinners." ¹⁸And the disciples of John and those of the Pharisees were fasting, and they come and say to Him, "Why do the disciples of John and those of the Pharisees fast, and Your disciples do not fast?" ¹⁹And Jesus said to them, "Are the sons of the bride-chamber able, while the bridegroom is with them, to fast? As long a time [as] they have the bridegroom with them they are not able to fast; ²⁰but days will come when the bridegroom may be taken from them, and then they will fast—in those days. ²¹And no one sews a patch of undressed cloth on an old garment, and if not—the new, filling it up, takes from the old and the split becomes worse; ²²and no one puts new wine into old skins, and if not—the new wine bursts the skins, and the wine is poured out, and the skins will be destroyed; but new wine is to be put into new skins." ²³And it came to pass—He is going along on the Sabbaths through the grainfields—and His disciples began to make a way, plucking the ears, ²⁴and the Pharisees said to Him, "Behold, why do they do on the Sabbaths that which is not lawful?" ²⁵And He said to them, "Did you never read what David did when he had need and was hungry, he and those with him? ²⁶How he went into the house of God, in [the days of] Abiathar the chief priest, and ate the Bread of the Presentation, which it is not lawful to eat, except to the priests, and he also gave to those who were with him?" ²⁷And He said to them, "The Sabbath was made for man, not man for the Sabbath, ²⁸so that the Son of Man is also Lord of the Sabbath."

CHAPTER 3

¹And He entered again into the synagogue, and there was there a man having the hand withered, ²and they were watching Him, whether on the Sabbaths He will heal him, that they might accuse Him. ³And He says to the man having the hand withered, "Rise up in the midst." ⁴And He says to them, "Is it lawful on the Sabbaths to do good, or to do evil? To save life, or to kill?" But they were silent. ⁵And having looked around on them with anger, being grieved for the hardness of their heart, He says to the man, "Stretch forth your hand"; and he stretched forth, and his hand was restored whole as the other; ⁶and the Pharisees having gone forth, immediately, with the Herodians, were taking counsel against Him how they might destroy Him. ⁷And Jesus withdrew with His disciples to the sea, and a great multitude from Galilee followed Him, and from Judea, ⁸and from Jerusalem, and from Idumea and beyond the Jordan; and they around Tyre and Sidon—a great multitude—having heard how He was doing great things, came to Him. ⁹And He said to His disciples that a little boat may wait on Him, because of the multitude, that they may not press on Him, ¹⁰for He healed many, so that they threw themselves on Him, in order to touch Him—as many as had plagues; ¹¹and the unclean spirits, when they were seeing Him, were falling down before Him, and were crying, saying, "You are the Son of God"; ¹²and many times He was charging them that they might not make Him apparent. ¹³And He goes up to the mountain, and calls near whom He willed, and they went away to Him; ¹⁴and He appointed twelve, that they may be with Him, and that He may send them forth to preach, ¹⁵and to have power to heal the sicknesses, and to cast out the demons. ¹⁶And He put on Simon the name Peter; ¹⁷and James of Zebedee, and John the brother of James, and He put on them names—Boanerges, that is, "Sons of thunder"; ¹⁸and Andrew, and Philip, and Bartholomew, and Matthew, and Thomas, and James of Alpheus, and Thaddeus, and Simon the Zealot, ¹⁹and Judas Iscariot, who also delivered Him up; and they come into a house. ²⁰And a multitude comes together again, so that they are not even able to eat bread; ²¹and those alongside Him having heard, went forth to lay hold on Him, for they said that He was beside Himself, ²²and the scribes who [are] from Jerusalem having come down, said, "He has Beelzebul," and, "By the ruler of the demons He casts out the demons." ²³And having called them near, He said to them in allegories, "How is Satan able to cast out Satan? ²⁴And if a kingdom is divided against itself, that kingdom cannot be made to stand; ²⁵and if a house is divided against itself, that house cannot be made to stand; ²⁶and if Satan rose against himself, and has been divided, he cannot be made to stand, but has an end. ²⁷No one is able to spoil the vessels of the strong man, having entered into his house, if first he may not bind the strong man, and then he will spoil his house. ²⁸Truly I say to you that all sins will be forgiven to the sons of men, and slanders with which they might have slandered, ²⁹but whoever may slander in regard to the Holy Spirit has no forgiveness—throughout the age, but is in danger of continuous judgment; ³⁰because they said, He has an unclean spirit." ³¹Then His brothers and mother come, and standing outside, they sent to Him, calling Him, ³²and a multitude was sitting around Him, and they said to Him, "Behold, Your mother and Your brothers seek You outside." ³³And He answered them, saying, "Who is My mother, or My brothers?" ³⁴And having looked around in a circle to those sitting around Him, He says, "Behold, My mother and My brothers! ³⁵For whoever may do the will of God, he is My brother, and My sister, and mother."

CHAPTER 4

¹And again He began to teach by the sea, and there was gathered to Him a great multitude, so that He, having gone into the boat, sat in the sea, and all the multitude was near the sea, on the land, ²and He taught them many things in allegories, and He said to them in His teaching: ³"Listen, behold, the sower went forth to sow; ⁴and it came to pass, in the sowing, some fell by the way, and the birds of the sky came and devoured it; ⁵and other fell on the rocky ground, where it did not have much earth, and immediately it sprang forth, because of having no depth of earth, ⁶and the sun having risen, it was scorched, and because of having no root it withered; ⁷and other fell toward the thorns, and the thorns came up and choked it, and it gave no fruit; ⁸and other fell to the good ground, and was giving fruit, coming up and increasing, and it was bearing, one thirty-fold, and one sixty, and one a hundred." ⁹And He said to them, "He who is having ears to hear—let him hear." ¹⁰And when He was alone, those around Him, with the Twelve, asked Him of the allegory, ¹¹and He said to them, "To you it has been given to know the secret of the Kingdom of God, but to those who are outside, in allegories are all the things done, ¹²that seeing they may see and not perceive, and hearing they may hear and not understand, lest they may turn, and the sins may be forgiven them." ¹³And He says to them, "Have you not known this allegory? And how will you know all the allegories? ¹⁴He who is sowing sows the word; ¹⁵and these are they by the way where the word is sown: and whenever they may hear, Satan immediately comes, and he takes away the word that has been sown in their hearts. ¹⁶And these are they, in like manner, who are sown on the rocky ground: who, whenever they may hear the word, immediately receive it with joy, ¹⁷and have no root in themselves, but are temporary; afterward tribulation or persecution having come because of the word, immediately they are stumbled. ¹⁸And these are they who are sown toward the thorns: these are they who are hearing the word, ¹⁹and the anxieties of this age, and the deceitfulness of the riches, and the desires concerning the other things, entering in, choke the word, and it becomes unfruitful.

MARK

[20]And these are they who on the good ground have been sown: who hear the word, and receive, and bear fruit, one thirty-fold, and one sixty, and one a hundred." [21]And He said to them, "Does the lamp come that it may be put under the measure, or under the bed—not that it may be put on the lampstand? [22]For there is not anything hid that may not be revealed, nor was anything kept hid but that it may come to light. [23]If any has ears to hear—let him hear." [24]And He said to them, "Take heed what you hear; in what measure you measure, it will be measured to you; and to you who hear it will be added; [25]for whoever may have, there will be given to him, and whoever has not, also that which he has will be taken from him." [26]And He said, "Thus is the Kingdom of God: as if a man may cast the seed on the earth, [27]and may sleep, and may rise night and day, and the seed springs up and grows, he has not known how; [28]for of itself the earth bears fruit, first a blade, afterward an ear, afterward full grain in the ear; [29]and whenever the fruit may yield itself, immediately he sends forth the sickle, because the harvest has come." [30]And He said, "To what may we liken the Kingdom of God, or in what allegory may we compare it? [31]As a grain of mustard, which, whenever it may be sown on the earth, is less than any of the seeds that are on the earth; [32]and whenever it may be sown, it comes up, and becomes greater than any of the herbs, and makes great branches, so that under its shade the birds of the sky are able to rest." [33]And with many such allegories He was speaking to them the word, as they were able to hear, [34]and without an allegory He was not speaking to them, and by themselves, to His disciples He was expounding all. [35]And He says to them on that day, evening having come, "We may pass over to the other side"; [36]and having let away the multitude, they take Him up as He was in the boat, and other little boats were also with Him. [37]And there comes a great storm of wind, and the waves were beating on the boat, so that it is now being filled, [38]and He Himself was on the stern, sleeping on the pillow, and they wake Him up, and say to Him, "Teacher, are You not caring that we perish?" [39]And having awoken, He rebuked the wind and said to the sea, "Peace, be stilled"; and the wind stilled, and there was a great calm; [40]and He said to them, "Why are you so fearful? How have you no faith?" [41]And they feared a great fear and said to one another, "Who, then, is this, that even the wind and the sea obey Him?"

CHAPTER 5

[1]And they came to the other side of the sea, to the region of the Gadarenes, [2]and He having come forth out of the boat, immediately there met Him out of the tombs a man with an unclean spirit, [3]who had his dwelling in the tombs, and not even with chains was anyone able to bind him, [4]because that many times he had been bound with shackles and chains, and the chains had been pulled in pieces by him, and the shackles broken in pieces, and none was able to tame him, [5]and always, night and day, he was in the mountains, and in the tombs, crying and cutting himself with stones. [6]And having seen Jesus from afar, he ran and prostrated to Him, [7]and having called with a loud voice, he said, "What [regards] me and You, Jesus, Son of God the Most High? I adjure You by God, may You not afflict me!" [8]For He said to him, "Come forth, unclean spirit, out of the man!" [9]And He was questioning him, "What [is] your name?" And he answered, saying, "Legion [is] my name, because we are many"; [10]and he was calling on Him much, that He may not send them out of the region. [11]And there was there, near the mountains, a great herd of pigs feeding, [12]and all the demons called on Him, saying, "Send us to the pigs, that into them we may enter"; [13]and immediately Jesus gave them leave, and having come forth, the unclean spirits entered into the pigs, and the herd rushed down the steep place to the sea—and they were about two thousand—and they were choked in the sea. [14]And those feeding the pigs fled, and told in the city, and in the fields, and they came forth to see what it is that has been done; [15]and they come to Jesus, and see the demoniac, sitting, and clothed, and right-minded—him having had the legion—and they were afraid; [16]and those having seen [it], declared to them how it had come to pass to the demoniac, and about the pigs; [17]and they began to call on Him to go away from their borders. [18]And He having gone into the boat, the demoniac was calling on Him that he may be with Him, [19]and Jesus did not permit him, but says to him, "Go away to your house, to your own [friends], and tell them how the LORD did great things to you, and dealt kindly with you"; [20]and he went away, and began to proclaim in the Decapolis how Jesus did great things to him, and all were wondering. [21]And Jesus having passed over in the boat again to the other side, there was gathered a great multitude to Him, and He was near the sea, [22]and behold, there comes one of the chiefs of the synagogue, by name Jairus, and having seen Him, he falls at His feet, [23]and he was calling on Him much, saying, "My little daughter is at the last extremity—that having come, You may lay on her [Your] hands, so that she may be saved, and she will live"; [24]and He went away with him. And there was following Him a great multitude, and they were thronging Him, [25]and a certain woman, being with a flow of blood [for] twelve years, [26]and having suffered many things under many physicians, and having spent all that she had, and having profited nothing, but rather having come to the worse, [27]having heard about Jesus, having come in the multitude behind, she touched His garment, [28]for she said, "If I may even touch His garments, I will be saved"; [29]and immediately the fountain of her blood was dried up, and she knew in the body that she has been healed of the plague. [30]And immediately Jesus having known in Himself that power had gone forth out of Him, having turned in the multitude, said, "Who touched My garments?" [31]And His disciples said to Him, "You see the multitude thronging You, and You say, Who touched Me!" [32]And He was looking around to see her who did this, [33]and the woman, having been afraid, and trembling, knowing what was done on her, came, and fell down before Him, and told Him all the truth, [34]and He said to her, "Daughter, your faith has saved you; go away in peace, and be whole from your plague." [35]As He is yet speaking, there come from the chief of the synagogue's [house, certain], saying, "Your daughter died, why do you still harass the Teacher?" [36]And Jesus immediately, having heard the word that is spoken, says to the chief of the synagogue, "Do not be afraid, only believe." [37]And He did not permit anyone to follow with Him, except Peter, and James, and John the brother of James; [38]and He comes into the house of the chief of the synagogue, and sees a tumult, much weeping and wailing; [39]and having gone in He says to them, "Why do you make a tumult, and weep? The child did not die, but sleeps"; [40]and they were laughing at Him. And He, having put all forth, takes the father of the child, and the mother, and those with Him, and goes in where the child is lying, [41]and having taken the hand of the child, He says to her, "Talitha cumi"; which is, being interpreted, "Girl (I say to you), arise." [42]And immediately the girl arose, and was walking, for she was twelve years [old]; and they were amazed with a great amazement, [43]and He charged them much, that no one may know this thing, and He said that there be given to her to eat.

CHAPTER 6

[1]And He went forth from there, and came to His own country, and His disciples follow Him, [2]and Sabbath having come, He began to teach in the synagogue, and many hearing were astonished, saying, "From where [did] this One [hear] these things? And what [is] the wisdom that was given to Him, that also such mighty works are done through His hands? [3]Is this not the carpenter, the Son of Mary, and brother of James, and Joses, and Judas, and Simon? And are His sisters not here with us?" And they were being stumbled at Him. [4]And Jesus said to them, "A prophet is not without honor, except in his own country, and among his relatives, and in his own house"; [5]and He was not able to do any mighty work there, except having put hands on a few sick, He healed [them]; [6]and He wondered because of their unbelief. And He was going around the

villages, in a circle, teaching, ⁷and He calls near the Twelve, and He began to send them forth two by two, and He was giving them power over the unclean spirits, ⁸and He commanded them that they may take nothing for the way, except a staff only—no leather pouch, no bread, no brass in the girdle, ⁹but having been shod with sandals, and you may not put on two coats. ¹⁰And He said to them, "Whenever you may enter into a house, remain there until you may depart from there, ¹¹and as many as may not receive you nor hear you, going out from there, shake off the dust that is under your feet for a testimony to them; [[truly I say to you, it will be more tolerable for Sodom or Gomorrah in [the] day of judgment than for that city."]] ¹²And having gone forth they were preaching that [men] might convert, ¹³and they were casting out many demons, and they were anointing many sick with oil, and they were healing [them]. ¹⁴And King Herod heard (for His Name became public), and he said, "John the Immerser was raised out of the dead, and because of this the mighty powers are working in him." ¹⁵Others said, "It is Elijah," and others said, "It is a prophet, or as one of the prophets." ¹⁶And Herod having heard, said, "He whom I beheaded—John—this is he; he was raised out of the dead." ¹⁷For Herod himself, having sent forth, laid hold on John, and bound him in the prison, because of Herodias, the wife of his brother Philip, because he married her, ¹⁸for John said to Herod, "It is not lawful for you to have the wife of your brother"; ¹⁹and Herodias was having a quarrel with him, and was willing to kill him, and was not able, ²⁰for Herod was fearing John, knowing him [to be] a righteous and holy man, and was keeping watch over him, and having heard him, was doing many things, and hearing him gladly. ²¹And a seasonable day having come when Herod on his birthday was making a banquet to his great men, and to the chiefs of thousands, and to the first men of Galilee, ²²and the daughter of that Herodias having come in, and having danced, and having pleased Herod and those dining with him, the king said to the girl, "Ask of me whatever you will, and I will give to you," ²³and he swore to her, "Whatever you may ask me, I will give to you—to the half of my kingdom." ²⁴And she, having gone forth, said to her mother, "What will I ask for myself?" And she said, "The head of John the Immerser"; ²⁵and having come in immediately with haste to the king, she asked, saying, "I will that you may immediately give me the head of John the Immerser on a plate." ²⁶And the king, made very sorrowful because of the oaths and of those reclining with him, would not put her away, ²⁷and immediately the king having sent a guardsman, commanded his head to be brought, ²⁸and he having gone, beheaded him in the prison, and brought his head on a plate, and gave it to the girl, and the girl gave it to her mother; ²⁹and having heard, his disciples came and took up his corpse, and laid it in the tomb. ³⁰And the apostles are gathered together to Jesus, and they told Him all, and how many things they did, and how many things they taught, ³¹and He said to them, "Come yourselves apart to a desolate place, and rest a little," for those coming and those going were many, and not even to eat had they opportunity, ³²and they went away to a desolate place, in the boat, by themselves. ³³And the multitudes saw them going away, and many recognized Him, and they ran there by land from all the cities, and went before them, and came together to Him, ³⁴and having come forth, Jesus saw a great multitude, and was moved with compassion on them, that they were as sheep not having a shepherd, and He began to teach many things. ³⁵And now the hour being advanced, His disciples having come near to Him, say, "The place is desolate, and the hour is now advanced, ³⁶let them away, that having gone away into the surrounding fields and villages, they may buy loaves for themselves, for they do not have what they may eat." ³⁷And He answering said to them, "You give them to eat," and they say to Him, "Having gone away, may we buy two hundred denarii worth of loaves, and give to them to eat?" ³⁸And He says to them, "How many loaves do you have? Go and see"; and having known, they say, "Five, and two fishes." ³⁹And He commanded them to make all recline in companies on the green grass, ⁴⁰and they sat down in squares, by hundreds, and by fifties. ⁴¹And having taken the five loaves and the two fishes, having looked up to the sky, He blessed, and broke the loaves, and was giving [them] to His disciples, that they may set [them] before them, and the two fishes He divided to all, ⁴²and they all ate, and were filled, ⁴³and they took up of broken pieces twelve hand-baskets full, and of the fishes, ⁴⁴and those eating of the loaves were about five thousand men. ⁴⁵And immediately He constrained His disciples to go into the boat, and to go before [Him] to the other side, to Bethsaida, until He may let the multitude away, ⁴⁶and having taken leave of them, He went away to the mountain to pray. ⁴⁷And evening having come, the boat was in the midst of the sea, and He alone on the land; ⁴⁸and He saw them harassed in the rowing, for the wind was against them, and about the fourth watch of the night He comes to them walking on the sea, and wished to pass by them. ⁴⁹And they having seen Him walking on the sea, thought [it] to be an apparition, and cried out, ⁵⁰for they all saw Him, and were troubled, and immediately He spoke with them, and says to them, "Take courage! I AM; do not be afraid." ⁵¹And He went up to them into the boat, and the wind stilled, and greatly out of measure they were amazed in themselves, and were wondering, ⁵²for they did not understand concerning the loaves, for their heart has been hard. ⁵³And having passed over, they came on the land of Gennesaret, and drew to the shore, ⁵⁴and they having come forth out of the boat, immediately having recognized Him, ⁵⁵they ran around through all that surrounding region, and they began to carry around on the pallets those being ill, where they were hearing that He is, ⁵⁶and wherever He was going, to villages, or cities, or fields, in the marketplaces they were laying the ailing, and were calling on Him, that they may touch if it were but the fringe of His garment, and as many as were touching Him were saved.

CHAPTER 7

¹And gathered together to Him are the Pharisees, and certain of the scribes, having come from Jerusalem, ²and having seen certain of His disciples with defiled hands—that is, unwashed—eating bread, they found fault; ³for the Pharisees, and all the Jews, if they do not wash the hands to the wrist, do not eat, holding the tradition of the elders, ⁴and [coming] from the marketplace, if they do not immerse themselves, they do not eat; and many other things there are that they received to hold, immersions of cups, and pots, and bronze vessels, and couches. ⁵Then the Pharisees and the scribes question Him, "Why do Your disciples not walk according to the tradition of the elders, but eat the bread with unwashed hands?" ⁶And He answering said to them, "Well did Isaiah prophesy concerning you, hypocrites, as it has been written: This people honors Me with the lips, and their heart is far from Me; ⁷and in vain they worship Me, teaching teachings, commands of men; ⁸for having put away the command of God, you hold the tradition of men, immersions of pots and cups; and many other such like things you do." ⁹And He said to them, "Well do you put away the command of God that you may keep your tradition; ¹⁰for Moses said, Honor your father and your mother; and, He who is speaking evil of father or mother—let him die the death; ¹¹and you say, If a man may say to father or to mother, Korban (that is, a gift), [is] whatever you may be profited out of mine, ¹²and you no longer permit him to do anything for his father or for his mother, ¹³setting aside the word of God for your tradition that you delivered; and many such like things you do." ¹⁴And having called near all the multitude, He said to them, "Listen to Me, you all, and understand; ¹⁵there is nothing from outside the man entering into him that is able to defile him, but the things coming out from him, those are the things defiling the man. ¹⁶[[If any has ears to hear—let him hear."]] ¹⁷And when He entered into a house from the multitude, His disciples were questioning Him about the allegory, ¹⁸and He says to them, "So also you are without understanding! Do you not perceive that nothing from outside entering into the man is able to defile him? ¹⁹Because it does not enter into his heart, but into the belly, and into the drain it goes out, purifying all the meats." ²⁰And He said, "That which is coming out from the man, that defiles the man; ²¹for from within, out of the heart of men, the evil

reasonings come forth, adulteries, whoredoms, murders, ²²thefts, covetous desires, wickedness, deceit, arrogance, an evil eye, slander, pride, foolishness; ²³all these evils come forth from within, and they defile the man." ²⁴And from there having risen, He went away to the borders of Tyre and Sidon, and having entered into the house, He wished none to know, and He was not able to be hid, ²⁵for a woman having heard about Him, whose little daughter had an unclean spirit, having come, fell at His feet— ²⁶and the woman was a Greek, a Syro-Phoenician by nation—and was asking Him that He may cast forth the demon out of her daughter. ²⁷And Jesus said to her, "First permit the children to be filled, for it is not good to take the children's bread, and to cast [it] to the little dogs." ²⁸And she answered and says to Him, "Yes, Lord; for the little dogs under the table also eat of the children's crumbs." ²⁹And He said to her, "Because of this word, go; the demon has gone forth out of your daughter"; ³⁰and having come away to her house, she found the demon gone forth, and the daughter laid on the bed. ³¹And again, having gone forth from the coasts of Tyre and Sidon, He came to the Sea of Galilee, through the midst of the coasts of Decapolis, ³²and they bring to Him a deaf, stuttering man, and they call on Him that He may put the hand on him. ³³And having taken him away from the multitude by Himself, He put His fingers to his ears, and having spit, He touched his tongue, ³⁴and having looked to the sky, He sighed, and says to him, "Ephphatha," that is, "Be opened"; ³⁵and immediately his ears were opened, and the string of his tongue was loosed, and he was speaking plain. ³⁶He charged them that they may tell no one, but the more He was charging them, the more abundantly they were proclaiming [it], ³⁷and they were being astonished beyond measure, saying, "He has done all things well; He makes both the deaf to hear, and the mute to speak."

CHAPTER 8

¹In those days the multitude being very great, and not having what they may eat, Jesus having called near His disciples, says to them, ²"I have compassion on the multitude, because now three days they continue with Me, and they have not what they may eat; ³and if I will let them away fasting to their home, they will faint in the way, for certain of them are come from far." ⁴And His disciples answered Him, "From where will anyone be able to feed these here in a wilderness with bread?" ⁵And He was questioning them, "How many loaves do you have?" And they said, "Seven." ⁶And He commanded the multitude to sit down on the ground, and having taken the seven loaves, having given thanks, He broke, and was giving to His disciples that they may set before [them]; and they set before the multitude. ⁷And they had a few small fishes, and having blessed, He said to set them also before [them]; ⁸and they ate and were filled, and they took up that which was over of broken pieces—seven baskets; ⁹and those eating were about four thousand. And He let them away, ¹⁰and immediately having entered into the boat with His disciples, He came to the parts of Dalmanutha, ¹¹and the Pharisees came forth, and began to dispute with Him, seeking from Him a sign from Heaven, tempting Him; ¹²and having sighed deeply in His spirit, He says, "Why does this generation seek after a sign? Truly I say to you, no sign will be given to this generation." ¹³And having left them, having entered again into the boat, He went away to the other side; ¹⁴and they forgot to take loaves, and except one loaf they had nothing with them in the boat, ¹⁵and He was charging them, saying, "Take heed, beware of the leaven of the Pharisees, and of the leaven of Herod," ¹⁶and they were reasoning with one another, saying, "Because we have no loaves." ¹⁷And Jesus having known, says to them, "Why do you reason, because you have no loaves? Do you not yet perceive, nor understand, yet have you hardened your heart? ¹⁸Having eyes, do you not see? And having ears, do you not hear? And do you not remember? ¹⁹When I broke the five loaves to the five thousand, how many hand-baskets full of broken pieces did you take up?" They say to Him, "Twelve." ²⁰"And when the seven to the four thousand, how many hand-baskets full of broken pieces did you take up?" And they said, "Seven." ²¹And He said to them, "How do you not understand?" ²²And He comes to Bethsaida, and they bring to Him one blind, and call on Him that He may touch him, ²³and having taken the hand of the blind man, He led him forth outside the village, and having spit on his eyes, having put [His] hands on him, He was questioning him if he beholds anything: ²⁴and he, having looked up, said, "I behold men, as I see trees, walking." ²⁵Afterward again He put [His] hands on his eyes, and made him look up, and he was restored, and discerned all things clearly, ²⁶and He sent him away to his house, saying, "Neither may you go into the village, nor tell [it] to any in the village." ²⁷And Jesus went forth, and His disciples, into the villages of Caesarea Philippi, and in the way He was questioning His disciples, saying to them, "Who do men say I am?" ²⁸And they answered, "John the Immerser, and others Elijah, but others one of the prophets." ²⁹And He says to them, "And you—who do you say I am?" And Peter answering says to him, "You are the Christ." ³⁰And He strictly charged them that they may tell no one about it, ³¹and began to teach them that it is necessary for the Son of Man to suffer many things, and to be rejected by the elders, and chief priests, and scribes, and to be killed, and to rise again after three days; ³²and openly He was speaking the word. And Peter having taken Him aside, began to rebuke Him, ³³and He, having turned, and having looked on His disciples, rebuked Peter, saying, "Get behind Me, Satan, because you do not mind the things of God, but the things of men." ³⁴And having called near the multitude, with His disciples, He said to them, "Whoever wills to come after Me—let him disown himself, and take up his cross, and follow Me; ³⁵for whoever may will to save his life will lose it; and whoever may lose his life for My sake and for the good news' sake, he will save it; ³⁶for what will it profit a man, if he may gain the whole world, and forfeit his life? ³⁷Or what will a man give as an exchange for his life? ³⁸For whoever may be ashamed of Me, and of My words, in this adulterous and sinful generation, the Son of Man will also be ashamed of him when He may come in the glory of His Father with the holy messengers."

CHAPTER 9

¹And He said to them, "Truly I say to you that there are certain of those standing here, who may not taste of death until they see the Kingdom of God having come in power." ²And after six days Jesus takes Peter, and James, and John, and brings them up to a high mountain by themselves, alone, and He was transfigured before them, ³and His garments became glittering, exceedingly white, as snow, so as a launderer on the earth is not able to whiten [them]. ⁴And there appeared to them Elijah with Moses, and they were talking with Jesus. ⁵And Peter answering says to Jesus, "Rabbi, it is good to us to be here; and we may make three shelters, for You one, and for Moses one, and for Elijah one": ⁶for he was not knowing what he might say, for they were greatly afraid. ⁷And there came a cloud overshadowing them, and there came a voice out of the cloud, saying, "This is My Son, the Beloved, hear Him"; ⁸and suddenly, having looked around, they saw no one anymore, but Jesus only with themselves. ⁹And as they are coming down from the mountain, He charged them that they may declare to no one the things that they saw, except when the Son of Man may rise out of the dead; ¹⁰and the thing they kept to themselves, questioning together what the rising out of the dead is. ¹¹And they were questioning Him, saying that the scribes say that Elijah must come first. ¹²And He answering said to them, "Elijah indeed, having come first, restores all things; and how has it been written concerning the Son of Man, that He may suffer many things, and be set at nothing? ¹³But I say to you that also Elijah has come, and they did to him what they willed, as it has been written of him." ¹⁴And having come to the disciples, He saw a great multitude around them, and scribes questioning with them, ¹⁵and immediately, all the multitude having seen Him, were amazed, and running near, were greeting Him. ¹⁶And He questioned the scribes, "What do you dispute with them?" ¹⁷And one out of the multitude answering said, "Teacher, I brought my son to You, having a mute spirit, ¹⁸and wherever it seizes him, it tears him, and he foams, and gnashes his teeth, and pines away; and I spoke to Your disciples that they may cast it out, and they were not able." ¹⁹And He answering him, said, "O generation unbelieving, until when will I be with you? Until when will I suffer you? Bring him to Me"; ²⁰and they brought him to Him, and he having seen Him, immediately the spirit convulsed him, and he, having fallen on the earth, was wallowing—foaming. ²¹And He questioned his father, "How much time is it

MARK

since this came to him?" And he said, "From childhood, ²²and many times it also cast him into fire, and into water, that it might destroy him; but If You are able to do anything, help us, having compassion on us." ²³And Jesus said to him, "If you are able to believe! All things are possible to the one that is believing"; ²⁴and immediately the father of the child, having cried out with tears, said, "I believe, Lord; be helping my unbelief." ²⁵Jesus having seen that a multitude runs together, rebuked the unclean spirit, saying to it, "Spirit—mute and deaf—I charge you, come forth out of him, and you may no longer enter into him"; ²⁶and having cried, and convulsed him much, it came forth, and he became as dead, so that many said that he was dead, ²⁷but Jesus, having taken him by the hand, lifted him up, and he arose. ²⁸And He having come into the house, His disciples were questioning Him by Himself, "Why were we not able to cast it forth?" ²⁹And He said to them, "This kind is able to come forth with nothing except with prayer and fasting." ³⁰And having gone forth there, they were passing through Galilee, and He did not wish that any may know, ³¹for He was teaching His disciples, and He said to them, "The Son of Man is being delivered into the hands of men, and they will kill Him, and having been killed, the third day He will rise," ³²but they were not understanding the saying, and they were afraid to question Him. ³³And He came to Capernaum, and being in the house, He was questioning them, "What were you reasoning in the way among yourselves?" ³⁴And they were silent, for they reasoned with one another in the way who is greater; ³⁵and having sat down He called the Twelve, and He says to them, "If any wills to be first, he will be last of all, and minister of all." ³⁶And having taken a child, He set him in the midst of them, and having taken him in His arms, said to them, ³⁷"Whoever may receive one of such children in My Name, receives Me, and whoever may receive Me, does not receive Me, but Him who sent Me." ³⁸And John answered Him, saying, "Teacher, we saw a certain one casting out demons in Your Name, who does not follow us, and we forbade him, because he does not follow us." ³⁹And Jesus said, "Do not forbid him, for there is no one who will do a mighty work in My Name, and will be readily able to speak evil of Me: ⁴⁰for he who is not against us is for us; ⁴¹for whoever may give you to drink a cup of water in My Name, because you are Christ's, truly I say to you, he may not lose his reward; ⁴²and whoever may cause to stumble one of the little ones believing in Me, better is it for him if a millstone is hanged around his neck, and he has been cast into the sea. ⁴³And if your hand may cause you to stumble, cut it off; it is better for you to enter into life maimed, than having the two hands, to go away into Gehenna, into the fire—the unquenchable— ⁴⁴[[where their worm is not dying, and the fire is not being quenched.]] ⁴⁵And if your foot may cause you to stumble, cut it off; it is better for you to enter into life lame, than having the two feet to be cast into Gehenna, into the fire—the unquenchable— ⁴⁶[[where their worm is not dying, and the fire is not being quenched.]] ⁴⁷And if your eye may cause you to stumble, cast it out; it is better for you to enter into the Kingdom of God one-eyed, than having two eyes, to be cast into the Gehenna of fire— ⁴⁸where their worm is not dying, and the fire is not being quenched; ⁴⁹for everyone will be salted with fire, and every sacrifice will be salted with salt. ⁵⁰The salt [is] good, but if the salt may become saltless, in what will you season [it]? Have in yourselves salt, and have peace in one another."

CHAPTER 10

¹And having risen from there, He comes to the coasts of Judea, through the other side of the Jordan, and again multitudes come together to Him, and as He had been accustomed, again He was teaching them. ²And the Pharisees, having come near, questioned Him if it is lawful for a husband to put away a wife, tempting Him, ³and He answering said to them, "What did Moses command you?" ⁴And they said, "Moses permitted to write a bill of divorce, and to put away." ⁵And Jesus answering said to them, "For the stiffness of your heart he wrote you this command, ⁶but from the beginning of the creation God made them a male and a female; ⁷on this account will a man leave his father and mother, and will cleave to his wife, ⁸and they will be—the two—for one flesh, so that they are no longer two, but one flesh; ⁹what God therefore joined together, do not let man separate." ¹⁰And in the house His disciples again questioned Him of the same thing, ¹¹and He says to them, "Whoever may put away his wife, and may marry another, commits adultery against her; ¹²and if a woman may put away her husband, and is married to another, she commits adultery." ¹³And they were bringing to Him children that He might touch them, and the disciples were rebuking those bringing them, ¹⁴and Jesus having seen, was much displeased, and He said to them, "Permit the children to come to Me, and do not forbid them, for of such is the Kingdom of God; ¹⁵truly I say to you, whoever may not receive the Kingdom of God as a child—he may not enter into it"; ¹⁶and having taken them in His arms, having put [His] hands on them, He was blessing them. ¹⁷And as He is going forth into the way, one having run and having kneeled to Him, was questioning Him, "Good Teacher, what may I do that I may inherit continuous life?" ¹⁸And Jesus said to him, "Why do you call Me good? No one [is] good except one—God; ¹⁹you have known the commands: You may not commit adultery, You may not murder, You may not steal, You may not bear false witness, You may not defraud, Honor your father and mother." ²⁰And he answering said to Him, "Teacher, all these I have kept from my youth." ²¹And Jesus having looked on him, loved him, and said to him, "One thing you lack: go away, whatever you have—sell, and give to the poor, and you will have treasure in Heaven, and come, follow Me, having taken up the cross." ²²And he—gloomy at the word—went away sorrowing, for he was having many possessions. ²³And Jesus having looked around, says to His disciples, "How hardly will they who have riches enter into the Kingdom of God!" ²⁴And the disciples were astonished at His words, and Jesus again answering says to them, "Children, how hard it is to those trusting on riches to enter into the Kingdom of God! ²⁵It is easier for a camel to enter through the eye of the needle, than for a rich man to enter into the Kingdom of God." ²⁶And they were astonished beyond measure, saying to themselves, "And who is able to be saved?" ²⁷And Jesus, having looked on them, says, "With men it is impossible, but not with God; for all things are possible with God." ²⁸And Peter began to say to Him, "Behold, we left all, and we followed You." ²⁹And Jesus answering said, "Truly I say to you, there is no one who left house, or brothers, or sisters, or father, or mother, or wife, or children, or fields, for My sake, and for the good news', ³⁰who may not receive a hundredfold now in this time, houses, and brothers, and sisters, and mothers, and children, and fields, with persecutions, and in the age that is coming, continuous life; ³¹and many first will be last, and the last first." ³²And they were in the way going up to Jerusalem, and Jesus was going before them, and they were amazed, and following they were afraid. And having again taken the Twelve, He began to tell them the things about to happen to Him: ³³"Behold, we go up to Jerusalem, and the Son of Man will be delivered to the chief priests, and to the scribes, and they will condemn Him to death, and will deliver Him to the nations, ³⁴and they will mock Him, and scourge Him, and spit on Him, and kill Him, and the third day He will rise again." ³⁵And there come near to Him James and John, the sons of Zebedee, saying, "Teacher, we wish that whatever we may ask for ourselves, You may do for us"; ³⁶and He said to them, "What do you wish Me to do for you?" ³⁷And they said to Him, "Grant to us that, one on Your right hand and one on Your left, we may sit in Your glory"; ³⁸and Jesus said to them, "You have not known what you ask; are you able to drink of the cup that I drink of, and with the immersion that I am immersed with—to be immersed?" ³⁹And they said to Him, "We are able"; and Jesus said to them, "Of the cup indeed that I drink of, you will drink, and with the immersion that I am immersed with, you will be immersed; ⁴⁰but to sit on My right and on My left is not Mine to give, but—to those for whom it has been prepared." ⁴¹And the ten having heard, began to be much displeased at James and John, ⁴²but Jesus having called them near, says to them, "You have known that they who are considered to rule the nations exercise lordship over them, and their great ones exercise authority on them; ⁴³but not so will it be among you; but whoever may will to become great among you, he will be your minister, ⁴⁴and whoever of you may will to become first, he will be servant of all; ⁴⁵for even the Son of Man did not come to be ministered to, but to minister, and to give His life [as] a ransom for many." ⁴⁶And

MARK

they come to Jericho, and as He is going forth from Jericho with His disciples and a great multitude, a son of Timaeus—Bartimaeus the blind—was sitting beside the way begging, ⁴⁷and having heard that it is Jesus the Nazarene, he began to cry out, and to say, "The Son of David—Jesus! Deal kindly with me"; ⁴⁸and many were rebuking him that he might keep silent, but the more abundantly he cried out, "Son of David, deal kindly with me." ⁴⁹And Jesus having stood, He commanded him to be called, and they call the blind man, saying to him, "Take courage, rise, He calls you"; ⁵⁰and he, having cast away his garment, having risen, came to Jesus. ⁵¹And answering, Jesus says to him, "What do you will I may do to you?" And the blind man said to Him, "Rabboni, that I may see again"; ⁵²and Jesus said to him, "Go, your faith has saved you": and immediately he saw again, and was following Jesus in the way.

CHAPTER 11

¹And when they come near to Jerusalem, to Bethphage, and Bethany, to the Mount of Olives, He sends forth two of His disciples, ²and says to them, "Go away into the village that is in front of you, and immediately, entering into it, you will find a colt tied, on which no one of men has sat, having loosed it, bring [it]: ³and if anyone may say to you, Why do you do this? Say that the LORD has need of it, and immediately He will send it here." ⁴And they went away, and found the colt tied at the door outside, by the two ways, and they loose it, ⁵and certain of those standing there said to them, "What do you—loosing the colt?" ⁶And they said to them as Jesus commanded, and they permitted them. ⁷And they brought the colt to Jesus, and cast their garments on it, and He sat on it, ⁸and many spread their garments in the way, and others were cutting down branches from the trees, and were strewing in the way. ⁹And those going before and those following were crying out, saying, "Hosanna! Blessed [is] He who is coming in the Name of the LORD; ¹⁰blessed is the coming kingdom, in the Name of the LORD, of our father David; Hosanna in the highest!" ¹¹And Jesus entered into Jerusalem, and into the temple, and having looked around on all things, it being now evening, He went forth to Bethany with the Twelve. ¹²And on the next day, they having come forth from Bethany, He hungered, ¹³and having seen a fig tree far off having leaves, He came, if perhaps He will find anything in it, and having come to it, He found nothing except leaves, for it was not a time of figs, ¹⁴and Jesus answering said to it, "No longer from you—throughout the age—may any eat fruit"; and His disciples were hearing. ¹⁵And they come to Jerusalem, and Jesus having gone into the temple, began to cast forth those selling and buying in the temple, and He overthrew the tables of the money-changers and the seats of those selling the doves, ¹⁶and He did not permit that any might carry a vessel through the temple, ¹⁷and He was teaching, saying to them, "Has it not been written: My house will be called a house of prayer for all the nations? And you made it a den of robbers!" ¹⁸And the scribes and the chief priests heard, and they were seeking how they will destroy Him, for they were afraid of Him, because all the multitude was astonished at His teaching; ¹⁹and when evening came, He was going forth outside the city. ²⁰And in the morning, passing by, they saw the fig tree having been dried up from the roots, ²¹and Peter having remembered says to Him, "Rabbi, behold, the fig tree that You cursed is dried up." ²²And Jesus answering says to them, "Have faith from God; ²³for truly I say to you that whoever may say to this mountain, Be taken up, and be cast into the sea, and may not doubt in his heart, but may believe that the things that he says come to pass, it will be to him whatever he may say. ²⁴Because of this I say to you, all whatever—praying—you ask, believe that you receive, and it will be to you. ²⁵And whenever you may stand praying, forgive, if you have anything against anyone, that your Father who is in the heavens may also forgive you your trespasses; ²⁶[[and, if you do not forgive, neither will your Father who is in the heavens forgive your trespasses."]] ²⁷And they come again to Jerusalem, and in the temple, as He is walking, there come to Him the chief priests, and the scribes, and the elders, ²⁸and they say to Him, "By what authority do You do these things? And who gave You this authority that You may do these things?" ²⁹And Jesus answering said to them, "I will question you—I also—one word; and answer Me, and I will tell you by what authority I do these things; ³⁰the immersion of John—was it from Heaven or from men? Answer Me." ³¹And they were reasoning with themselves, saying, "If we may say, From Heaven, He will say, Why then did you not believe him? ³²But if we may say, From men…" They were fearing the people, for all were holding that John was indeed a prophet; ³³and answering they say to Jesus, "We have not known"; and Jesus answering says to them, "Neither do I tell you by what authority I do these things."

CHAPTER 12

¹And He began to speak to them in allegories: "A man planted a vineyard, and put a hedge around, and dug a wine vat, and built a tower, and gave it out to farmers, and went abroad; ²and he sent to the farmers at the due time a servant, that from the farmers he may receive from the fruit of the vineyard, ³and they, having taken him, severely beat [him], and sent him away empty. ⁴And again he sent to them another servant, and having cast stones at that one, they wounded [him] in the head, and sent [him] away—dishonored. ⁵And again he sent another, and that one they killed; and many others, some beating, and some killing. ⁶Having yet therefore one son—his beloved—he also sent him to them last, saying, They will respect my son; ⁷and those farmers said among themselves, This is the heir, come, we may kill him, and the inheritance will be ours; ⁸and having taken him, they killed, and cast [him] forth outside the vineyard. ⁹What therefore will the lord of the vineyard do? He will come and destroy the farmers, and will give the vineyard to others. ¹⁰And this Writing you did not read: A stone that the builders rejected, it became the head of a corner; ¹¹this was from the LORD, and it is wonderful in our eyes." ¹²And they were seeking to lay hold on Him, and they feared the multitude, for they knew that He spoke the allegory against them, and having left Him, they went away; ¹³and they send to Him certain of the Pharisees and of the Herodians, that they may ensnare Him in discourse, ¹⁴and they having come, say to Him, "Teacher, we have known that You are true, and You are not caring for anyone, for You do not look to the face of men, but in truth teach the way of God; is it lawful to give tribute to Caesar or not? May we give, or may we not give?" ¹⁵And He, knowing their hypocrisy, said to them, "Why do you tempt Me? Bring Me a denarius, that I may see"; ¹⁶and they brought, and He says to them, "Whose [is] this image, and the inscription?" And they said to Him, "Caesar's"; ¹⁷and Jesus answering said to them, "Give back the things of Caesar to Caesar, and the things of God to God"; and they wondered at Him. ¹⁸And the Sadducees come to Him, who say there is not a resurrection, and they questioned Him, saying, ¹⁹"Teacher, Moses wrote to us that if anyone's brother may die, and may leave a wife, and may leave no children, that his brother may take his wife, and raise up seed to his brother. ²⁰There were then seven brothers, and the first took a wife, and dying, he left no seed; ²¹and the second took her, and died, not having left seed, and the third in like manner, ²²and the seven took her, and left no seed, last of all the woman also died; ²³in the resurrection, then, whenever they may rise, of which of them will she be wife—for the seven had her as wife?" ²⁴And Jesus answering said to them, "Do you not go astray because of this, not knowing the Writings, nor the power of God? ²⁵For when they may rise out of the dead, they neither marry nor are they given in marriage, but are as messengers who are in the heavens. ²⁶And concerning the dead, that they rise: have you not read in the Scroll of Moses (at the bush), how God spoke to him, saying, I [am] the God of Abraham, and the God of Isaac, and the God of Jacob; ²⁷He is not the God of dead men, but a God of living men; you then go greatly astray." ²⁸And one of the scribes having come near, having heard them disputing, knowing that He answered them well, questioned Him, "Which is the first command of all?" ²⁹And Jesus answered him, "The first of all the commands—Hear, O Israel: The LORD is our God, the LORD is one; ³⁰and you will love the LORD your God out of all your heart, and out of all your soul, and out of all your understanding, and out of all your strength—this [is] the first command; ³¹and the second [is] like [it], this, You will love your neighbor as yourself—there is no other command greater than these." ³²And the scribe said to Him, "Well, Teacher, in truth You have spoken that there is one God, and there is none other but He; ³³and to love Him out of all the heart, and

out of all the understanding, and out of all the soul, and out of all the strength, and to love one's neighbor as one's self, is more than all the whole burnt-offerings and the sacrifices." ³⁴And Jesus, having seen him that he answered with understanding, said to him, "You are not far from the Kingdom of God"; and no one dared question Him anymore. ³⁵And Jesus answering said, teaching in the temple, "How do the scribes say that the Christ is son of David? ³⁶For David himself said in the Holy Spirit, The LORD said to my Lord, || Sit on My right hand, || Until I place Your enemies—Your footstool; ³⁷therefore David himself calls Him Lord, and from where is He his son?" And the great multitude were hearing Him gladly, ³⁸and He was saying to them in His teaching, "Beware of the scribes who will to walk in long robes, and love salutations in the marketplaces, ³⁹and first seats in the synagogues, and first couches at the banquets, ⁴⁰who are devouring the widows' houses, and for a pretense are making long prayers; these will receive more abundant judgment." ⁴¹And Jesus having sat down opposite the treasury, was beholding how the multitude puts brass into the treasury, and many rich were putting in much, ⁴²and having come, a poor widow put in two mites, which are a penny. ⁴³And having called near His disciples, He says to them, "Truly I say to you that this poor widow has put in more than all those putting into the treasury; ⁴⁴for all, out of their abundance, put in, but she, out of her want, put in all that she had—all her living."

CHAPTER 13

¹And as He is going forth out of the temple, one of His disciples says to Him, "Teacher, see! What stones! And what buildings!" ²And Jesus answering said to him, "See these great buildings? There may not be left a stone on a stone that may not be thrown down." ³And as He is sitting at the Mount of Olives, opposite the temple, Peter, and James, and John, and Andrew, were questioning Him by Himself, ⁴"Tell us when these things will be? And what [is] the sign when all these may be about to be fulfilled?" ⁵And Jesus answering them, began to say, "Take heed lest anyone may lead you astray, ⁶for many will come in My Name, saying, I am [He], and many they will lead astray; ⁷and when you may hear of wars and reports of wars, do not be troubled, for these ought to be, but the end [is] not yet; ⁸for nation will rise against nation, and kingdom against kingdom, and there will be earthquakes in various places, and there will be famines and troubles; these [are the] beginning of travails. ⁹And take heed to yourselves, for they will deliver you up to Sanhedrins, and to synagogues, you will be beaten, and before governors and kings you will be set for My sake, for a testimony to them; ¹⁰and to all the nations it is first necessary that the good news be proclaimed. ¹¹And when they may lead you, delivering up, do not be anxious beforehand what you may speak, nor premeditate, but whatever may be given to you in that hour, that speak, for it is not you who are speaking, but the Holy Spirit. ¹²And brother will deliver up brother to death, and father child, and children will rise up against parents, and will put them to death, ¹³and you will be hated by all because of My Name, but he who has endured to the end—he will be saved. ¹⁴And when you may see the abomination of the desolation, that was spoken of by Daniel the prophet, standing where it should not (whoever is reading let him understand), then those in Judea, let them flee to the mountains; ¹⁵and he on the housetop, do not let him come down into the house, nor come in to take anything out of his house; ¹⁶and he who is in the field, do not let him turn to the things behind, to take up his garment. ¹⁷And woe to those with child, and to those giving suck, in those days; ¹⁸and pray that your flight may not be in winter, ¹⁹for those days will be tribulation, such as has not been from the beginning of the creation that God created, until now, and may not be [again]; ²⁰and if the LORD did not shorten the days, no flesh had been saved; but because of the chosen, whom He chose to Himself, He shortened the days. ²¹And then, if any may say to you, Behold, here [is] the Christ, or, Behold, there, you may not believe; ²²for there will rise false Christs and false prophets, and they will give signs and wonders, to seduce, if possible, also the chosen; ²³and you, take heed; behold, I have foretold you all things. ²⁴But in those days, after that tribulation, the sun will be darkened, and the moon will not give her light, ²⁵and the stars of the sky will be falling, and the powers that are in the heavens will be shaken. ²⁶And then they will see the Son of Man coming in clouds with much power and glory, ²⁷and then He will send His messengers, and gather together His chosen from the four winds, from the end of the earth to the end of heaven. ²⁸And from the fig tree learn the allegory: when the branch may already become tender, and may put forth the leaves, you know that the summer is near; ²⁹so you, also, when you may see these coming to pass, you know that it is near, at the doors. ³⁰Truly I say to you that this generation may not pass away until all these things may come to pass; ³¹the heaven and the earth will pass away, but My words will not pass away. ³²And concerning that day and the hour no one has known—not even the messengers who are in Heaven, not even the Son—except the Father. ³³Take heed, watch and pray, for you have not known when the time is; ³⁴as a man who is gone abroad, having left his house, and given to his servants the authority, and to each one his work, also commanded the doorkeeper that he may watch; ³⁵watch, therefore, for you have not known when the lord of the house comes, at evening, or at midnight, or at rooster-crowing, or at the morning; ³⁶lest, having come suddenly, he may find you sleeping; ³⁷and what I say to you, I say to all, Watch!"

CHAPTER 14

¹And the Passover and the Unleavened [Bread] were after two days, and the chief priests and the scribes were seeking how, by guile, having taken hold of Him, they might kill Him; ²and they said, "Not in the celebration, lest there will be a tumult of the people." ³And He, being in Bethany, in the house of Simon the leper, at His reclining, there came a woman having an alabaster box of ointment, of spikenard, very precious, and having broken the alabaster box, poured [it] on His head; ⁴and there were certain much displeased within themselves, and saying, "For what has this waste of the ointment been made? ⁵For this could have been sold for more than three hundred denarii, and given to the poor"; and they were murmuring at her. ⁶And Jesus said, "Leave her alone; why are you giving her trouble? She worked a good work on Me; ⁷for you always have the poor with you, and whenever you may will you are able to do them good, but you do not always have Me; ⁸she did what she could, she anticipated to anoint My body for the embalming. ⁹Truly I say to you, wherever this good news may be proclaimed in the whole world, what this woman did will also be spoken of—for a memorial of her." ¹⁰And Judas the Iscariot, one of the Twelve, went away to the chief priests that he might deliver Him up to them, ¹¹and having heard, they were glad, and promised to give him money, and he was seeking how, conveniently, he might deliver Him up. ¹²And the first day of the Unleavened [Bread], when they were killing the Passover, His disciples say to Him, "Where will You, [that] having gone, we may prepare, that You may eat the Passover?" ¹³And He sends forth two of His disciples and says to them, "Go away into the city, and there a man carrying a pitcher of water will meet you, follow him; ¹⁴and wherever he may go in, say to the master of the house: The Teacher says, Where is the guest-chamber, where the Passover, with My disciples, I may eat? ¹⁵And he will show you a large upper room, furnished, prepared—make ready for us there." ¹⁶And His disciples went forth, and came into the city, and found as He said to them, and they made ready the Passover. ¹⁷And evening having come, He comes with the Twelve, ¹⁸and as they are reclining, and eating, Jesus said, "Truly I say to you that one of you who is eating with Me will deliver Me up." ¹⁹And they began to be sorrowful, and to say to Him one by one, "Is it I?" And another, "Is it I?" ²⁰And He answering said to them, "One of the Twelve who is dipping with Me in the dish; ²¹the Son of Man indeed goes, as it has been written concerning Him, but woe to that man through whom the Son of Man is delivered up; it were good to him if that man had not been born." ²²And as they are eating, Jesus having taken bread, having blessed, broke, and gave to them, and said, "Take, eat; this is My body." ²³And having taken the cup, having given thanks, He gave to them, and they drank of it—all; ²⁴and He said to them, "This is My blood of the New Covenant, which is being poured out for many; ²⁵truly I say to you that I may drink no more of the produce of the vine until that day when I may drink it new in the Kingdom of God." ²⁶And having sung a hymn, they went

forth to the Mount of Olives, ²⁷and Jesus says to them, "All of you will be stumbled at Me this night, because it has been written: I will strike the Shepherd, and the sheep will be scattered abroad; ²⁸but after My having risen I will go before you to Galilee." ²⁹And Peter said to Him, "And if all will be stumbled, yet not I." ³⁰And Jesus said to him, "Truly I say to you that today, this night, before a rooster will crow twice, three times you will deny Me." ³¹And he spoke the more vehemently, "If it may be necessary for me to die with You—I will in no way deny You"; and in like manner also said they all. ³²And they come to a spot, the name of which [is] Gethsemane, and He says to His disciples, "Sit here until I may pray"; ³³and He takes Peter, and James, and John with Him, and began to be amazed, and to be very heavy, ³⁴and He says to them, "My soul is exceedingly sorrowful—to death; remain here, and watch." ³⁵And having gone forward a little, He fell on the earth, and was praying that, if it be possible, the hour may pass from Him, ³⁶and He said, "Abba, Father; all things are possible to You; make this cup pass from Me; but not what I will, but what You [will]." ³⁷And He comes, and finds them sleeping, and says to Peter, "Simon, you sleep! You were not able to watch one hour! ³⁸Watch and pray, that you may not enter into temptation; the spirit indeed is forward, but the flesh weak." ³⁹And again having gone away, He prayed, saying the same word; ⁴⁰and having returned, He found them sleeping again, for their eyes were heavy, and they had not known what they might answer Him. ⁴¹And He comes the third time and says to them, "Sleep on from now on, and rest—it is over; the hour came; behold, the Son of Man is delivered up into the hands of the sinful; ⁴²rise, we may go, behold, he who is delivering Me up has come near." ⁴³And immediately—while He is yet speaking—Judas comes near, one of the Twelve, and with him a great multitude with swords and sticks, from the chief priests, and the scribes, and the elders; ⁴⁴and he who is delivering Him up had given a token to them, saying, "Whomsoever I will kiss, it is He, lay hold on Him, and lead Him away safely," ⁴⁵and having come, immediately, having gone near Him, he says, "Rabbi, Rabbi," and kissed Him. ⁴⁶And they laid on Him their hands, and kept hold on Him; ⁴⁷and a certain one of those standing by, having drawn the sword, struck the servant of the chief priest, and took off his ear. ⁴⁸And Jesus answering said to them, "As against a robber you came out, with swords and sticks, to take Me! ⁴⁹Daily I was with you teaching in the temple, and you did not lay hold on Me—but that the Writings may be fulfilled." ⁵⁰And having left Him they all fled; ⁵¹and a certain young man was following Him, having cast a linen cloth on [his] naked [body], and the young men lay hold on him, ⁵²and he, having left the linen cloth, fled from them naked. ⁵³And they led Jesus away to the chief priest, and all the chief priests, and the elders, and the scribes come together; ⁵⁴and Peter followed Him far off, to the inside of the hall of the chief priest, and he was sitting with the officers, and warming himself near the fire. ⁵⁵And the chief priests and all the Sanhedrin were seeking testimony against Jesus—to put Him to death, and they were not finding, ⁵⁶for many were bearing false testimony against Him, and their testimonies were not alike. ⁵⁷And certain having risen up, were bearing false testimony against Him, saying, ⁵⁸"We heard Him saying, I will throw down this temple made with hands, and by three days, I will build another made without hands"; ⁵⁹and neither so was their testimony alike. ⁶⁰And the chief priest, having risen up in the midst, questioned Jesus, saying, "You do not answer anything! Why do these testify against You?" ⁶¹And He was keeping silent and did not answer anything. Again the chief priest was questioning Him and says to Him, "Are You the Christ—the Son of the Blessed?" ⁶²And Jesus said, "I AM; and you will see the Son of Man sitting on the right hand of the Power and coming with the clouds of Heaven." ⁶³And the chief priest, having torn his garments, says, "What need have we yet of witnesses? ⁶⁴You heard the slander, what appears to you?" And they all condemned Him to be worthy of death, ⁶⁵and certain began to spit on Him, and to cover His face, and to punch Him, and to say to Him, "Prophesy"; and the officers were striking Him with their palms. ⁶⁶And Peter being in the hall beneath, there comes one of the maids of the chief priest, ⁶⁷and having seen Peter warming himself, having looked on him, she said, "And you were with Jesus of Nazareth!" ⁶⁸And he denied, saying, "I have not known [Him], neither do I understand what you say"; and he went forth outside to the porch, and a rooster crowed. ⁶⁹And the maid having seen him again, began to say to those standing near, "This is of them"; ⁷⁰and he was again denying. And after a while again, those standing near said to Peter, "Truly you are of them, for you also are a Galilean, and your speech is alike"; ⁷¹and he began to curse, and to swear, "I have not known this Man of whom you speak"; ⁷²and a second time a rooster crowed, and Peter remembered the saying that Jesus said to him, "Before a rooster crows twice, you may deny Me three times"; and having thought thereon—he was weeping.

CHAPTER 15

¹And immediately, in the morning, the chief priests having made a consultation with the elders, and scribes, and the whole Sanhedrin, having bound Jesus, led [Him] away, and delivered [Him] to Pilate; ²and Pilate questioned Him, "Are You the King of the Jews?" And He answering said to him, "You say [it]." ³And the chief priests were accusing Him of many things, [but He answered nothing.] ⁴And Pilate again questioned Him, saying, "You do not answer anything? Behold, how many things they testify against You!" ⁵And Jesus no longer answered anything, so that Pilate wondered. ⁶And at every celebration he was releasing to them one prisoner, whomsoever they were asking for; ⁷and there was [one] named Barabbas, bound with those making insurrection with him, who had committed murder in the insurrection. ⁸And the multitude having cried out, began to ask for themselves as he was always doing to them, ⁹and Pilate answered them, saying, "Will you [that] I will release to you the King of the Jews?" ¹⁰For he knew that the chief priests had delivered Him up because of envy; ¹¹and the chief priests moved the multitude that he might rather release Barabbas to them. ¹²And Pilate answering, again said to them, "What, then, will you [that] I will do to Him whom you call King of the Jews?" ¹³And they again cried out, "Crucify Him!" ¹⁴And Pilate said to them, "Why—what evil did He do?" And they cried out the more vehemently, "Crucify Him!" ¹⁵And Pilate, resolving to do that which [was] satisfactory to the multitude, released Barabbas to them, and delivered up Jesus—having scourged [Him]—that He might be crucified. ¹⁶And the soldiers led Him away into the hall, which is [the] Praetorium, and call together the whole band, ¹⁷and clothe Him with purple, and having plaited a garland of thorns, they put [it] on Him, ¹⁸and began to greet Him, "Hail, King of the Jews!" ¹⁹And they were striking Him on the head with a reed, and were spitting on Him, and having bent the knee, were prostrating to Him, ²⁰and when they [had] mocked Him, they took the purple from off Him, and clothed Him in His own garments, and they led Him forth, that they may crucify Him. ²¹And they impress a certain one passing by—Simon, a Cyrenian, coming from the field, the father of Alexander and Rufus—that he may carry His cross, ²²and they bring Him to the place [called] Golgotha, which is, being interpreted, "Place of [the] Skull"; ²³and they were giving Him wine mingled with myrrh to drink, and He did not receive [it]. ²⁴And having crucified Him, they were dividing His garments, casting a lot on them, what each may take; ²⁵and it was the third hour, and they crucified Him; ²⁶and the inscription of His accusation was written above: "THE KING OF THE JEWS." ²⁷And they crucify two robbers with Him, one on the right hand and one on His left, ²⁸[[and the Writing was fulfilled that is saying, "And He was numbered with lawless ones."]] ²⁹And those passing by were slandering Him, shaking their heads, and saying, "Ha! The [One] throwing down the temple, and building [it] in three days! ³⁰Save Yourself, and come down from the cross!" ³¹And in like manner also the chief priests, mocking with one another, with the scribes, said, "He saved others; He is not able to save Himself. ³²The Christ! The King of Israel—let Him come down now from the cross, that we may see and believe"; and those crucified with Him were reproaching Him. ³³And the sixth hour having come, darkness came over the whole land until the ninth hour, ³⁴and at the ninth hour Jesus cried with a great voice, saying, "Eloi, Eloi, lamma sabachthani?" Which is, being interpreted, "My God, My God, why did You forsake Me?" ³⁵And certain of those standing by, having heard, said, "Behold, He calls Elijah"; ³⁶and one having run, and having filled a sponge with vinegar, having also put

MARK

[it] on a reed, was giving Him to drink, saying, "Let alone, let us see if Elijah comes to take Him down." ³⁷And Jesus having uttered a loud cry, yielded the spirit, ³⁸and the veil of the temple was torn in two from top to bottom, ³⁹and the centurion who was standing opposite Him, having seen that, having so cried out, He yielded the spirit, said, "Truly this Man was [the] Son of God." ⁴⁰And there were also women beholding far off, among whom was also Mary the Magdalene, and Mary of James the less, and of Joses, and Salome, ⁴¹who also, when He was in Galilee, were following Him and were ministering to Him, and many other women who came up with Him to Jerusalem. ⁴²And now evening having come, seeing it was the Preparation, that is, before Sabbath, ⁴³Joseph of Arimathea, an honorable counselor, who also himself was waiting for the Kingdom of God, came, boldly entered in to Pilate, and asked for the body of Jesus. ⁴⁴And Pilate wondered if He were already dead, and having called near the centurion, questioned him if He were long dead, ⁴⁵and having known [it] from the centurion, he granted the body to Joseph. ⁴⁶And he, having brought fine linen, and having taken Him down, wrapped Him in the linen, and laid Him in a tomb that had been hewn out of a rock, and he rolled a stone to the door of the tomb, ⁴⁷and Mary the Magdalene, and Mary of Joses, were beholding where He is laid.

CHAPTER 16

¹And the Sabbath having past, Mary the Magdalene, and Mary of James, and Salome, bought spices, that having come, they may anoint Him, ²and early in the morning of the first [day] of the weeks, they come to the tomb, at the rising of the sun, ³and they said among themselves, "Who will roll away the stone out of the door of the tomb for us?" ⁴And having looked, they see that the stone has been rolled away—for it was very great, ⁵and having entered into the tomb, they saw a young man sitting on the right hand, clothed in a long white robe, and they were amazed. ⁶And he says to them, "Do not be amazed, you seek Jesus the Nazarene, the crucified [One]: He rose—He is not here; behold the place where they laid Him! ⁷And go, say to His disciples and Peter that He goes before you to Galilee; there you will see Him, as He said to you." ⁸And having come forth quickly, they fled from the tomb, and trembling and amazement had seized them, and they said to no one anything, for they were afraid. [[⁹And He, having risen in the morning of the first of the week, appeared first to Mary the Magdalene, out of whom He had cast seven demons; ¹⁰she having gone, told those who had been with Him, mourning and weeping; ¹¹and they, having heard that He is alive, and was seen by her, did not believe. ¹²And after these things, to two of them, as they are going into a field, walking, He appeared in another form, ¹³and they having gone, told [it] to the rest; not even them did they believe. ¹⁴Afterward, as they are reclining, He appeared to the Eleven, and reproached their unbelief and stiffness of heart, because they did not believe those having seen Him being raised; ¹⁵and He said to them, "Having gone into all the world, proclaim the good news to all the creation; ¹⁶he who has believed and has been immersed will be saved; and he who has not believed will be condemned. ¹⁷And signs will accompany those believing these things: they will cast out demons in My Name; they will speak with new tongues; ¹⁸they will take up serpents; and if they may drink any deadly thing, it will not hurt them; they will lay hands on the ailing, and they will be well." ¹⁹The LORD, then, indeed, after speaking to them, was received up to Heaven, and sat on the right hand of God; ²⁰and they, having gone forth, preached everywhere, the LORD working with [them], and confirming the word, through the signs following. Amen.]]

LUKE

CHAPTER 1

¹Seeing that many took in hand to set in order a narration of the matters that have been fully assured among us, ²as they delivered to us, who from the beginning became eyewitnesses, and officers of the word, ³it seemed good also to me, having followed from the first after all things exactly, to write to you in order, most noble Theophilus, ⁴that you may know the certainty of the things wherein you were instructed. ⁵There was in the days of Herod, the king of Judea, a certain priest, by name Zacharias, of the division of Abijah, and his wife of the daughters of Aaron, and her name Elizabeth; ⁶and they were both righteous before God, going on in all the commands and righteousnesses of the LORD blameless, ⁷and they had no child, because that Elizabeth was barren, and both were advanced in their days. ⁸And it came to pass, in his acting as priest, in the order of his division before God, ⁹according to the custom of the priesthood, his lot was to make incense, having gone into the temple of the LORD, ¹⁰and all the multitude of the people were praying outside, at the hour of the incense. ¹¹And there appeared to him a messenger of the LORD standing on the right side of the altar of the incense, ¹²and Zacharias, having seen, was troubled, and fear fell on him; ¹³and the messenger said to him, "Do not fear, Zacharias, for your supplication was heard, and your wife Elizabeth will bear a son to you, and you will call his name John, ¹⁴and there will be joy to you, and gladness, and many will rejoice at his birth, ¹⁵for he will be great before the LORD, and wine and strong drink he may not drink, and he will be full of the Holy Spirit, even from his mother's womb; ¹⁶and he will turn many of the sons of Israel to the LORD their God, ¹⁷and he will go before Him, in the spirit and power of Elijah, to turn hearts of fathers to children, and disobedient ones to the wisdom of righteous ones, to make ready for the LORD, a people prepared." ¹⁸And Zacharias said to the messenger, "Whereby will I know this? For I am aged, and my wife is advanced in her days?" ¹⁹And the messenger answering said to him, "I am Gabriel, who has been standing near before God, and I was sent to speak to you, and to proclaim this good news to you, ²⁰and behold, you will be silent, and not able to speak, until the day that these things will come to pass, because you did not believe my words that will be fulfilled in their season." ²¹And the people were waiting for Zacharias, and wondering at his lingering in the temple, ²²and having come out, he was not able to speak to them, and they perceived that he had seen a vision in the temple, and he was beckoning to them, and remained mute. ²³And it came to pass, when the days of his service were fulfilled, he went away to his house, ²⁴and after those days, his wife Elizabeth conceived, and hid herself five months, saying, ²⁵"Thus the LORD has done to me, in days in which He looked on [me], to take away my reproach among men." ²⁶And in the sixth month the messenger Gabriel was sent by God, to a city of Galilee, the name of which [is] Nazareth, ²⁷to a virgin, betrothed to a man, whose name [is] Joseph, of the house of David, and the name of the virgin [is] Mary. ²⁸And the messenger having come in to her, said, "Greetings, favored one, the LORD [is] with you; blessed [are] you among women"; ²⁹and she, having seen, was troubled at his word, and was reasoning of what kind this salutation may be. ³⁰And the messenger said to her, "Do not fear, Mary, for you have found favor with God; ³¹and behold, you will conceive in the womb, and will bring forth a Son, and call His Name Jesus; ³²He will be great, and He will be called Son of the Highest, and the LORD God will give Him the throne of His father David, ³³and He will reign over the house of Jacob for all ages; and of His kingdom there will be no end." ³⁴And Mary said to the messenger, "How will this be, seeing I do not know a husband?" ³⁵And the messenger answering said to her, "The Holy Spirit will come on you, and the power of the Highest will overshadow you, therefore also the holy-begotten thing will be

LUKE

called Son of God; ³⁶and behold, Elizabeth, your relative, she also has conceived a son in her old age, and this is the sixth month to her who was called barren; ³⁷because nothing will be impossible with God." ³⁸And Mary said, "Behold, the maidservant of the LORD; let it be to me according to your saying," and the messenger went away from her. ³⁹And Mary having arisen in those days, went into the hill-country, with haste, to a city of Judea, ⁴⁰and entered into the house of Zacharias, and greeted Elizabeth. ⁴¹And it came to pass, when Elizabeth heard the salutation of Mary, the baby leapt in her womb; and Elizabeth was filled with the Holy Spirit, ⁴²and spoke out with a loud voice and said, "Blessed [are] you among women, and blessed [is] the Fruit of your womb; ⁴³and from where [is] this to me, that the mother of my Lord might come to me? ⁴⁴For behold, when the voice of your salutation came to my ears, the baby in my womb leapt in gladness; ⁴⁵and blessed [is] she who believed, for there will be a completion to the things spoken to her from the LORD." ⁴⁶And Mary said, "My soul magnifies the LORD, ⁴⁷And my spirit was glad on God my Savior, ⁴⁸Because He looked on the lowliness of His maidservant, || For behold, from now on all the generations will call me blessed, ⁴⁹For He who is mighty did great things to me, || And holy [is] His Name, ⁵⁰And His kindness [is] to generations of generations, || To those fearing Him; ⁵¹He did powerfully with His arm, || He scattered abroad the proud in the thought of their heart, ⁵²He brought down the mighty from thrones, || And He exalted the lowly, ⁵³He filled the hungry with good, || And the rich He sent away empty; ⁵⁴He has taken hold of His servant Israel, || To remember kindness, ⁵⁵As He spoke to our fathers, || To Abraham and to his seed throughout the age." ⁵⁶And Mary remained with her about three months, and turned back to her house. ⁵⁷And to Elizabeth was the time fulfilled for her bringing forth, and she bore a son, ⁵⁸and the neighbors and her relatives heard that the LORD was making His kindness great with her, and they were rejoicing with her. ⁵⁹And it came to pass, on the eighth day, they came to circumcise the child, and they were calling him by the name of his father, Zacharias, ⁶⁰and his mother answering said, "No, but he will be called John." ⁶¹And they said to her, "There is none among your relatives who is called by this name," ⁶²and they were making signs to his father, what he would wish him to be called, ⁶³and having asked for a tablet, he wrote, saying, "John is his name"; and they all wondered; ⁶⁴and his mouth was opened immediately, and his tongue, and he was speaking, praising God. ⁶⁵And fear came on all those dwelling around them, and in all the hill-country of Judea were all these sayings spoken of, ⁶⁶and all who heard laid them up in their hearts, saying, "What then will this child be?" And the hand of the LORD was with him. ⁶⁷And his father Zacharias was filled with the Holy Spirit, and prophesied, saying, ⁶⁸"Blessed [is] the LORD, the God of Israel, || Because He looked on, || And worked redemption for His people, ⁶⁹And raised a horn of salvation to us, || In the house of His servant David, ⁷⁰As He spoke by the mouth of His holy prophets, || Which have been from the age; ⁷¹Salvation from our enemies, || And out of the hand of all hating us, ⁷²To do kindness with our fathers, || And to be mindful of His holy covenant, ⁷³An oath that He swore to Abraham our father, ⁷⁴To give to us, without fear, || Having been delivered out of the hand of our enemies, ⁷⁵To serve Him, in holiness and righteousness || Before Him, all the days of our life. ⁷⁶And you, child, || Prophet of the Highest will you be called; For you will go before the face of the LORD, || To prepare His ways. ⁷⁷To give knowledge of salvation to His people || In forgiveness of their sins, ⁷⁸Through the yearnings of our God, || In which the rising from on high looked on us, ⁷⁹To give light to those sitting in darkness and death-shade, || To guide our feet to a way of peace." ⁸⁰And the child grew, and was strengthened in spirit, and he was in the deserts until the day of his showing to Israel.

CHAPTER 2

¹And it came to pass in those days, there went forth a decree from Caesar Augustus that all the world be registered— ²this census first came to pass when Quirinius was governor of Syria— ³and all were going to be registered, each to his proper city, ⁴and Joseph also went up from Galilee, out of the city of Nazareth, to Judea, to the city of David, that is called Beth-Lehem, because of his being of the house and family of David, ⁵to register himself with Mary his betrothed wife, being with Child. ⁶And it came to pass, in their being there, the days were fulfilled for her bringing forth, ⁷and she brought forth her Son—the firstborn, and wrapped Him up, and laid Him down in the manger, because there was not a place for them in the guest-chamber. ⁸And there were shepherds in the same region, lodging in the field and keeping the night-watches over their flock, ⁹and behold, a messenger of the LORD stood over them, and the glory of the LORD shone around them, and they feared [with] a great fear. ¹⁰And the messenger said to them, "Do not fear, for behold, I bring you good news of great joy that will be to all the people, ¹¹because today in the city of David a Savior was born to you, who is Christ the LORD! ¹²And this [is] the sign to you: you will find a Baby wrapped up, lying in the manger." ¹³And suddenly there came with the messenger a multitude of the heavenly host, praising God, and saying, ¹⁴"Glory in the highest to God, and on earth peace, among men—good will!" ¹⁵And it came to pass, when the messengers were gone away from them to the heavens, that the men, the shepherds, said to one another, "We may indeed go over to Beth-Lehem and see this thing that has come to pass, that the LORD made known to us!" ¹⁶And they came, having hurried, and found both Mary, and Joseph, and the Baby lying in the manger, ¹⁷and having seen, they made known abroad concerning the saying spoken to them concerning the Child. ¹⁸And all who heard [it] wondered concerning the things spoken to them by the shepherds; ¹⁹and Mary was preserving all these things, pondering [them] in her heart; ²⁰and the shepherds turned back, glorifying and praising God for all those things they heard and saw, as it was spoken to them. ²¹And when eight days were fulfilled to circumcise the Child, then was His Name called Jesus, having been so called by the messenger before His being conceived in the womb. ²²And when the days of their purification were fulfilled, according to the Law of Moses, they brought Him up to Jerusalem, to present to the LORD, ²³as it has been written in the Law of the LORD: "Every male opening a womb will be called holy to the LORD," ²⁴and to give a sacrifice, according to that said in the Law of the LORD: "A pair of turtle-doves, or two young pigeons." ²⁵And behold, there was a man in Jerusalem whose name [is] Simeon, and this man is righteous and devout, looking for the comforting of Israel, and the Holy Spirit was on him, ²⁶and it has been divinely told him by the Holy Spirit—not to see death before he may see the Christ of the LORD. ²⁷And he came in the Spirit into the temple, and in the parents bringing in the child Jesus, for their doing according to the custom of the Law regarding Him, ²⁸then he took Him in his arms, and blessed God, and he said, ²⁹"Now You send Your servant away, O LORD, according to Your word, in peace, ³⁰because my eyes saw Your salvation, ³¹which You prepared before the face of all the peoples, ³²a light to the uncovering of nations, and the glory of Your people Israel." ³³And Joseph and His mother were wondering at the things spoken concerning Him, ³⁴and Simeon blessed them and said to His mother Mary, "Behold, this [One] is set for the falling and rising again of many in Israel, and for a sign spoken against— ³⁵(and also a sword will pass through your own soul)—that the reasonings of many hearts may be revealed." ³⁶And there was Anna, a prophetess, daughter of Phanuel, of the tribe of Asher, she was much advanced in days, having lived with a husband seven years from her virginity, ³⁷and she [is] a widow of about eighty-four years, who did not depart from the temple, serving with fasts and supplications, night and day, ³⁸and she, at that hour, having come in, was confessing, likewise, to the LORD, and was speaking concerning Him to all those looking for redemption in Jerusalem. ³⁹And when they completed all things according to the Law of the LORD, they turned back to Galilee, to their city of Nazareth; ⁴⁰and the Child grew and was strengthened in spirit, being filled with wisdom, and the grace of God was on Him. ⁴¹And His parents were going yearly to Jerusalem, at the Celebration of the Passover, ⁴²and when He became twelve years old, they

having gone up to Jerusalem according to the custom of the celebration, ⁴³and having finished the days, in their returning the child Jesus remained behind in Jerusalem, and Joseph and His mother did not know, ⁴⁴and having supposed Him to be in the company, they went a day's journey, and were seeking Him among the relatives and among the acquaintances, ⁴⁵and having not found Him, they turned back to Jerusalem seeking Him. ⁴⁶And it came to pass, after three days they found Him in the temple, sitting in the midst of the teachers, both hearing them and questioning them, ⁴⁷and all those hearing Him were astonished at His understanding and answers. ⁴⁸And having seen Him, they were amazed, and His mother said to Him, "Child, why did You do this to us? Behold, Your father and I, sorrowing, were seeking You." ⁴⁹And He said to them, "Why [is it] that you were seeking Me? Did you not know that it is necessary for Me to be in the things of My Father?" ⁵⁰And they did not understand the saying that He spoke to them, ⁵¹and He went down with them, and came to Nazareth, and He was subject to them, and His mother was keeping all these sayings in her heart, ⁵²and Jesus was advancing in wisdom, and in stature, and in favor with God and men.

CHAPTER 3

¹And in the fifteenth year of the government of Tiberius Caesar—Pontius Pilate being governor of Judea, and Herod tetrarch of Galilee, and his brother Philip, tetrarch of Ituraea and of the region of Trachonitis, and Lysanias tetrarch of Abilene, ²[and] Annas and Caiaphas being chief priests—there came a word of God to John the son of Zacharias, in the wilderness, ³and he came to all the region around the Jordan, proclaiming an immersion of conversion for forgiveness of sins, ⁴as it has been written in the scroll of the words of Isaiah the prophet: "A voice of one crying in the wilderness: Prepare the way of the LORD, || Make His paths straight; ⁵Every valley will be filled, || And every mountain and hill will be made low, || And the crooked will become straightness, || And the rough become smooth ways; ⁶And all flesh will see the salvation of God." ⁷Then he said to the multitudes coming forth to be immersed by him, "Brood of vipers! Who prompted you to flee from the coming wrath? ⁸Make, therefore, fruits worthy of conversion, and do not begin to say within yourselves, We have a father—Abraham; for I say to you that God is able to raise children to Abraham out of these stones; ⁹and also the axe is already laid to the root of the trees, every tree, therefore, not making good fruit is cut down, and it is cast into fire." ¹⁰And the multitudes were questioning him, saying, "What, then, will we do?" ¹¹And he answering says to them, "He having two coats, let him impart to him having none; and he having food, let him do in like manner." ¹²And there also came tax collectors to be immersed, and they said to him, "Teacher, what will we do?" ¹³And he said to them, "Exact no more than that directed you." ¹⁴And also questioning him were those warring, saying, "And we, what will we do?" And he said to them, "Do violence to no one, nor accuse falsely, and be content with your wages." ¹⁵And the people are looking forward, and all are reasoning in their hearts concerning John, whether or not he may be the Christ; ¹⁶John answered, saying to all, "I indeed immerse you in water, but He comes who is mightier than I, of whom I am not worthy to loose the strap of His sandals—He will immerse you in the Holy Spirit and fire; ¹⁷whose winnowing shovel [is] in His hand, and He will thoroughly cleanse His floor, and will gather the wheat into His storehouse, and He will burn the chaff with unquenchable fire." ¹⁸And therefore, indeed, with many other things, exhorting, he was proclaiming good news to the people, ¹⁹and Herod the tetrarch, being reproved by him concerning Herodias, the wife of his brother Philip, and concerning all the evils that Herod did, ²⁰added also this to all, that he shut up John in the prison. ²¹And it came to pass, in all the people being immersed, Jesus also being immersed, and praying, Heaven was opened, ²²and the Holy Spirit came down in a bodily appearance, as if a dove, on Him, and a voice came out of Heaven, saying, "You are My Son, the Beloved, in You I delighted." ²³And Jesus Himself was beginning to be about thirty years of age, being, as was supposed, Son of Joseph, ²⁴the [son] of Eli, the [son] of Matthat, the [son] of Levi, the [son] of Melchi, the [son] of Janna, the [son] of Joseph, ²⁵the [son] of Mattathias, the [son] of Amos, the [son] of Nahum, the [son] of Esli, ²⁶the [son] of Naggai, the [son] of Maath, the [son] of Mattathias, the [son] of Semei, the [son] of Joseph, the [son] of Judah, ²⁷the [son] of Joanna, the [son] of Rhesa, the [son] of Zerubbabel, the [son] of Shealtiel, ²⁸the [son] of Neri, the [son] of Melchi, the [son] of Addi, the [son] of Cosam, the [son] of Elmodam, the [son] of Er, ²⁹the [son] of Jose, the [son] of Eliezer, the [son] of Jorim, the [son] of Matthat, ³⁰the [son] of Levi, the [son] of Simeon, the [son] of Judah, the [son] of Joseph, the [son] of Jonan, the [son] of Eliakim, ³¹the [son] of Melea, the [son] of Mainan, the [son] of Mattatha, the [son] of Nathan, ³²the [son] of David, the [son] of Jesse, the [son] of Obed, the [son] of Boaz, the [son] of Salmon, the [son] of Nahshon, ³³the [son] of Amminadab, the [son] of Aram, the [son] of Esrom, the [son] of Perez, ³⁴the [son] of Judah, the [son] of Jacob, the [son] of Isaac, the [son] of Abraham, the [son] of Terah, the [son] of Nahor, ³⁵the [son] of Serug, the [son] of Reu, the [son] of Peleg, the [son] of Eber, ³⁶the [son] of Salah, the [son] of Cainan, the [son] of Arphaxad, the [son] of Shem, the [son] of Noah, the [son] of Lamech, ³⁷the [son] of Methuselah, the [son] of Enoch, the [son] of Jared, the [son] of Mahalaleel, ³⁸the [son] of Cainan, the [son] of Enos, the [son] of Seth, the [son] of Adam, the [son] of God.

CHAPTER 4

¹And Jesus, full of the Holy Spirit, turned back from the Jordan, and was brought in the Spirit into the wilderness, ²being tempted by the Devil forty days, and He did not eat anything in those days, and they having been ended, He afterward hungered, ³and the Devil said to Him, "If You are [the] Son of God, speak to this stone that it may become bread." ⁴And Jesus answered him, saying, "It has been written, that, Not on bread only will man live, but on every saying of God." ⁵And the Devil having brought Him up to a high mountain, showed to Him all the kingdoms of the world in a moment of time, ⁶and the Devil said to Him, "To You I will give all this authority, and their glory, because to me it has been delivered, and to whomsoever I will, I give it; ⁷You, then, if You may worship me—all will be Yours." ⁸And Jesus answering him said, "[[Get behind Me, Satan, for]] it has been written: You will worship the LORD your God, and Him only you will serve." ⁹And he brought Him to Jerusalem, and set Him on the pinnacle of the temple, and said to Him, "If You are the Son of God, cast Yourself down from here, ¹⁰for it has been written: To His messengers He will give charge concerning you, to guard over you; ¹¹and: On hands they will bear you up, lest at any time you may dash your foot against a stone." ¹²And Jesus answering said to him, "It has been said, You will not tempt the LORD your God." ¹³And having ended all temptation, the Devil departed from Him until a convenient season. ¹⁴And Jesus turned back in the power of the Spirit to Galilee, and a fame went forth through all the surrounding region concerning Him, ¹⁵and He was teaching in their synagogues, being glorified by all. ¹⁶And He came to Nazareth, where He has been brought up, and He went in, according to His custom, on the day of the Sabbaths, into the synagogue, and stood up to read; ¹⁷and there was given over to Him a scroll of Isaiah the prophet, and having unfolded the scroll, He found the place where it has been written: ¹⁸"The Spirit of the LORD [is] on Me, || Because He anointed Me || To proclaim good news to the poor, || Sent Me to heal the broken of heart, || To proclaim to captives deliverance, || And to blind receiving of sight, || To send the bruised away with deliverance, ¹⁹To proclaim the acceptable year of the LORD." ²⁰And having folded the scroll, having given [it] back to the officer, He sat down, and the eyes of all in the synagogue were gazing on Him. ²¹And He began to say to them, "Today this writing has been fulfilled in your ears"; ²²and all were bearing testimony to Him, and were wondering at the gracious words that are coming forth out of His mouth, and they said, "Is this not the Son of Joseph?" ²³And He said to them, "Certainly you will say to Me this allegory, Physician, heal yourself; as great things as we heard done in Capernaum, do also here in Your country"; ²⁴and He said, "Truly I say to you, no prophet is accepted in

his own country; ²⁵and of a truth I say to you, many widows were in the days of Elijah, in Israel, when the sky was shut for three years and six months, when great famine came on all the land, ²⁶and to none of them was Elijah sent, but—to Sarepta of Sidon, to a woman, a widow; ²⁷and many lepers were in the time of Elisha the prophet, in Israel, and none of them was cleansed, but—Naaman the Syrian." ²⁸And all in the synagogue were filled with wrath, hearing these things, ²⁹and having risen, they put Him forth outside the city, and brought Him to the brow of the hill on which their city had been built—to cast Him down headlong, ³⁰and He, having gone through the midst of them, went away. ³¹And He came down to Capernaum, a city of Galilee, and was teaching them on the Sabbaths, ³²and they were astonished at His teaching, because His word was with authority. ³³And in the synagogue was a man having a spirit of an unclean demon, and he cried out with a great voice, ³⁴"Aah! What [regards] us and You, Jesus, O Nazarene? You came to destroy us; I have known who You are—the Holy One of God!" ³⁵And Jesus rebuked him, saying, "Be silenced, and come forth out of him"; and the demon having cast him into the midst, came forth from him, having hurt him nothing; ³⁶and amazement came on all, and they were speaking together with one another, saying, "What [is] this word, that with authority and power He commands the unclean spirits, and they come forth?" ³⁷And there was going forth a fame concerning Him to every place of the surrounding region. ³⁸And having risen out of the synagogue, He entered into the house of Simon, and the mother-in-law of Simon was pressed with a great fever, and they asked Him about her, ³⁹and having stood over her, He rebuked the fever, and it left her, and immediately, having risen, she was ministering to them. ⁴⁰And at the setting of the sun, all, as many as had any ailing with manifold diseases, brought them to Him, and He, having put hands on each one of them, healed them. ⁴¹And demons were also coming forth from many, crying out and saying, "You are the Christ, the Son of God"; and rebuking, He did not permit them to speak, because they knew Him to be the Christ. ⁴²And day having come, having gone forth, He went on to a desolate place, and the multitudes were seeking Him, and they came to Him, and were restraining Him—not to go on from them, ⁴³and He said to them, "Also to the other cities it is necessary for Me to proclaim good news of the Kingdom of God, because for this I have been sent"; ⁴⁴and He was preaching in the synagogues of Galilee.

CHAPTER 5

¹And it came to pass, in the multitude pressing on Him to hear the word of God, that He was standing beside the Lake of Gennesaret, ²and He saw two boats standing beside the lake, and the fishers, having gone away from them, were washing the nets, ³and having entered into one of the boats, that was Simon's, He asked him to put back a little from the land, and having sat down, was teaching the multitudes out of the boat. ⁴And when He left off speaking, He said to Simon, "Put back into the deep, and let down your nets for a catch"; ⁵and Simon answering said to Him, "Master, through the whole night, having labored, we have taken nothing, but at Your saying I will let down the net." ⁶And having done this, they enclosed a great multitude of fishes, and their net was breaking, ⁷and they beckoned to the partners who [are] in the other boat, having come, to help them; and they came, and filled both the boats, so that they were sinking. ⁸And Simon Peter having seen, fell down at the knees of Jesus, saying, "Depart from me, because I am a sinful man, O Lord"; ⁹for astonishment seized him, and all those with him, at the catch of the fishes that they took, ¹⁰and in like manner also James and John, sons of Zebedee, who were partners with Simon; and Jesus said to Simon, "Do not fear, from now on you will be catching men"; ¹¹and they, having brought the boats on the land, having left all, followed Him. ¹²And it came to pass, in His being in one of the cities, that behold, a man full of leprosy, and having seen Jesus, having fallen on [his] face, he implored Him, saying, "Lord, if You may will, You are able to cleanse me"; ¹³and having stretched forth [His] hand, He touched him, having said, "I will, be cleansed"; and immediately the leprosy went away from him. ¹⁴And He charged him to tell no one, "But having gone away, show yourself to the priest, and bring near for your cleansing according as Moses directed, for a testimony to them"; ¹⁵but the more was the report going abroad concerning Him, and great multitudes were coming together to hear, and to be healed by Him of their sicknesses, ¹⁶and He was withdrawing Himself in the desolate places and was praying. ¹⁷And it came to pass, on one of the days, that He was teaching, and there were sitting by Pharisees and teachers of the Law, who were come out of every village of Galilee, and Judea, and Jerusalem, and the power of the LORD was—to heal them. ¹⁸And behold, men carrying a man on a bed, who has been struck with palsy, and they were seeking to bring him in, and to place before Him, ¹⁹and having not found by what way they may bring him in because of the multitude, having gone up on the housetop, through the tiles they let him down with the little bed, into the midst before Jesus, ²⁰and He having seen their faith, said to him, "Man, your sins have been forgiven you." ²¹And the scribes and the Pharisees began to reason, saying, "Who is this that speaks evil words? Who is able to forgive sins, except God only?" ²²And Jesus having known their reasonings, answering, said to them, "What reason you in your hearts? ²³Which is easier—to say, Your sins have been forgiven you? Or to say, Arise, and walk? ²⁴And that you may know that the Son of Man has authority on the earth to forgive sins—(He said to the one struck with palsy)—I say to you, arise, and having taken up your little bed, be going on to your house." ²⁵And immediately having risen before them, having taken up [that] on which he was lying, he went away to his house, glorifying God, ²⁶and astonishment took all, and they were glorifying God, and were filled with fear, saying, "We saw strange things today." ²⁷And after these things He went forth, and beheld a tax collector, by name Levi, sitting at the tax office, and said to him, "Follow Me"; ²⁸and he, having left all, having arisen, followed Him. ²⁹And Levi made a great entertainment to Him in his house, and there was a great multitude of tax collectors and others who were with them reclining, ³⁰and the scribes and the Pharisees among them were murmuring at His disciples, saying, "Why do You eat and drink with tax collectors and sinners?" ³¹And Jesus answering said to them, "They who are well have no need of a physician, but they that are ill: ³²I did not come to call righteous men, but sinners, to conversion." ³³And they said to Him, "Why do the disciples of John fast often, and make supplications—in like manner also those of the Pharisees—but Yours eat and drink?" ³⁴And He said to them, "Are you able to make the sons of the bride-chamber—in the Bridegroom being with them—to fast? ³⁵But days will come, and when the Bridegroom may be taken away from them, then they will fast in those days." ³⁶And He spoke also an allegory to them: "No one puts a patch of new clothing on old clothing, and if otherwise, the new also makes a split, and with the old the patch does not agree, that [is] from the new. ³⁷And no one puts new wine into old skins, and if otherwise, the new wine will burst the skins, and itself will be poured out, and the skins will be destroyed; ³⁸but new wine is to be put into new skins, and both are preserved together; ³⁹and no one having drunk old, immediately wishes new, for he says, The old is better."

CHAPTER 6

¹And it came to pass, on a Sabbath, as He is going through the grainfields, that His disciples were plucking the ears, and were eating, rubbing with the hands, ²and certain of the Pharisees said to them, "Why do you do that which is not lawful to do on the Sabbaths?" ³And Jesus answering said to them, "Did you not read even this that David did when he hungered, himself and those who are with him, ⁴how he went into the house of God, and took the Bread of the Presentation, and ate, and gave also to those with him, which it is not lawful to eat, except only to the priests?" ⁵And He said to them, "The Son of Man is Lord also of the Sabbath." ⁶And it came to pass also, on another Sabbath, that He goes into the synagogue, and teaches, and there was there a man, and his right hand was withered, ⁷and the scribes and the Pharisees were watching Him, if on the Sabbath He will heal, that they might find an accusation against Him. ⁸And He Himself had known their reasonings and said to the man having the withered hand, "Rise, and stand in the midst"; and he having risen, stood. ⁹Then Jesus said to them, "I will question you something: is it lawful on the Sabbaths to do good, or to do evil? To save life or to kill?" ¹⁰And having looked around on them all, He said to the man,

"Stretch forth your hand"; and he did so, and his hand was restored whole as the other; ¹¹and they were filled with madness, and were speaking with one another what they might do to Jesus. ¹²And it came to pass in those days, He went forth to the mountain to pray, and was passing the night in the prayer of God, ¹³and when it became day, He called near His disciples, also having chosen twelve from them, whom He also named apostles: ¹⁴Simon, whom He also named Peter, and his brother Andrew, James and John, Philip and Bartholomew, ¹⁵Matthew and Thomas, James of Alphaeus, and Simon called Zealot, ¹⁶Judas of James, and Judas Iscariot, who also became betrayer. ¹⁷And having come down with them, He stood on a level spot; and a crowd of His disciples, and a great multitude of the people from all Judea, and Jerusalem, and the seacoast of Tyre and Sidon, ¹⁸who came to hear Him and to be healed of their diseases, [gathered]. And those harassed by unclean spirits [also gathered] and were healed. ¹⁹And all the multitude were seeking to touch Him, because power was going forth from Him, and He was healing all. ²⁰And He, having lifted up His eyes to His disciples, said: "Blessed the poor—because yours is the Kingdom of God. ²¹Blessed those hungering now—because you will be filled. Blessed those weeping now—because you will laugh. ²²Blessed are you when men will hate you, and when they will separate you, and will reproach, and will cast forth your name as evil, for the Son of Man's sake— ²³rejoice in that day, and leap, for behold, your reward [is] great in Heaven, for according to these things were their fathers doing to the prophets. ²⁴But woe to you—the rich, because you have gotten your comfort. ²⁵Woe to you who have been filled—because you will hunger. Woe to you who are laughing now—because you will mourn and weep. ²⁶Woe to you when all men will speak well of you—for according to these things were their fathers doing to false prophets. ²⁷But I say to you who are hearing, love your enemies, do good to those hating you, ²⁸bless those cursing you, pray for those maligning you; ²⁹and to him striking you on the cheek, give also the other, and from him taking away from you the mantle, also the coat you may not keep back. ³⁰And to everyone who is asking of you, be giving; and from him who is taking away your goods, do not be asking again; ³¹and as you wish that men may do to you, do also to them in like manner; ³²and—if you love those loving you, what grace is it to you? For also the sinful love those loving them; ³³and if you do good to those doing good to you, what grace is it to you? For also the sinful do the same; ³⁴and if you lend [to those] of whom you hope to receive back, what grace is it to you? For also the sinful lend to sinners—that they may receive again as much. ³⁵But love your enemies, and do good, and lend, hoping for nothing again, and your reward will be great, and you will be sons of the Highest, because He is kind to the ungracious and evil; ³⁶be therefore merciful, as also your Father is merciful. ³⁷And do not judge, and you may not be judged; do not condemn, and you may not be condemned; release, and you will be released. ³⁸Give, and it will be given to you; good measure, pressed, and shaken, and running over, they will give into your bosom; for with that measure with which you measure, it will be measured to you again." ³⁹And He spoke an allegory to them, "Is blind able to lead blind? Will they not both fall into a pit? ⁴⁰A disciple is not above his teacher, but everyone perfected will be as his teacher. ⁴¹And why do you behold the speck that is in your brother's eye, and do not consider the beam that [is] in your own eye? ⁴²Or how are you able to say to your brother, Brother, permit, I may take out the speck that [is] in your eye—yourself not beholding the beam in your own eye? Hypocrite, first take the beam out of your own eye, and then you will see clearly to take out the speck that [is] in your brother's eye. ⁴³For there is not a good tree making bad fruit, nor a bad tree making good fruit; ⁴⁴for each tree is known from its own fruit, for they do not gather figs from thorns, nor do they crop a grape from a bramble. ⁴⁵The good man out of the good treasure of his heart brings forth that which [is] good; and the evil man out of the evil treasure of his heart brings forth that which [is] evil; for out of the abounding of the heart his mouth speaks. ⁴⁶And why do you call Me, Lord, Lord, and do not do what I say? ⁴⁷Everyone who is coming to Me, and is hearing My words, and is doing them, I will show you to whom he is like: ⁴⁸he is like to a man building a house, who dug and deepened, and laid a foundation on the rock, and a flood having come, the stream broke forth on that house, and was not able to shake it, for it had been founded on the rock. ⁴⁹And he who heard and did not, is like to a man having built a house on the earth, without a foundation, against which the stream broke forth, and immediately it fell, and the ruin of that house became great."

CHAPTER 7

¹And when He completed all His sayings in the ears of the people, He went into Capernaum; ²and a certain centurion's servant being ill, was about to die, who was much valued by him, ³and having heard about Jesus, he sent to Him elders of the Jews, imploring Him, that having come He might thoroughly save his servant. ⁴And they, having come near to Jesus, were calling on Him earnestly, saying, "He is worthy to whom You will do this, ⁵for he loves our nation, and he built to us the synagogue." ⁶And Jesus was going on with them, and now when He is not far distant from the house the centurion sent to Him friends, saying to Him, "Lord, do not be troubled, for I am not worthy that You may enter under my roof; ⁷for this reason I did not consider myself worthy to come to You, but say in a word, and my boy will be healed; ⁸for I also am a man placed under authority, having under myself soldiers, and I say to this [one], Go, and he goes; and to another, Be coming, and he comes; and to my servant, Do this, and he does [it]." ⁹And having heard these things Jesus wondered at him, and having turned to the multitude following Him, He said, "I say to you, not even in Israel did I find so much faith"; ¹⁰and those sent, having turned back to the house, found the ailing servant in health. ¹¹And it came to pass, on the next day, He was going on to a city called Nain, and there were going with Him many of His disciples, and a great multitude, ¹²and as He came near to the gate of the city, then, behold, one dead was being carried forth, an only son of his mother, and she a widow, and a great multitude of the city was with her. ¹³And the LORD having seen her, was moved with compassion toward her and said to her, "Do not be weeping"; ¹⁴and having come near, He touched the bier, and those carrying [it] stood still, and He said, "Young man, to you I say, Arise"; ¹⁵and the dead sat up, and began to speak, and He gave him to his mother; ¹⁶and fear took hold of all, and they were glorifying God, saying, "A great prophet has risen among us," and, "God looked on His people." ¹⁷And the account of this went forth in all Judea about Him, and in all the region around. ¹⁸And the disciples of John told him about all these things, ¹⁹and John having called near a certain two of his disciples, sent to Jesus, saying, "Are You He who is coming, or do we look for another?" ²⁰And having come near to Him, the men said, "John the Immerser sent us to You, saying, Are You He who is coming, or do we look for another?" ²¹And in that hour He cured many from diseases, and plagues, and evil spirits, and He granted sight to many blind. ²²And Jesus answering said to them, "Having gone on, report to John what you saw and heard, that blind men see again, lame walk, lepers are cleansed, deaf hear, dead are raised, poor have good news proclaimed; ²³and blessed is he whoever may not be stumbled in Me." ²⁴And the messengers of John having gone away, He began to say to the multitudes concerning John: "What have you gone forth into the wilderness to look on? A reed shaken by the wind? ²⁵But what have you gone forth to see? A man clothed in soft garments? Behold, they in splendid clothing, and living in luxury, are in the houses of kings! ²⁶But what have you gone forth to see? A prophet? Yes, I say to you, and much more than a prophet: ²⁷this is he concerning whom it has been written: Behold, I send My messenger before Your face, who will prepare Your way before You; ²⁸for I say to you, there is not a greater prophet, among those born of women, than John the Immerser; but the least in the Kingdom of God is greater than he." ²⁹And all the people having heard, and the tax collectors, declared God righteous, having been immersed with the immersion of John, ³⁰but the Pharisees and the lawyers put away the counsel of God for themselves, having not

been immersed by him. ³¹And the LORD said, "To what, then, will I liken the men of this generation? And to what are they like? ³²They are like to children, to those sitting in a marketplace, and calling to one another, and saying, We piped to you, and you did not dance, we mourned to you, and you did not weep! ³³For John the Immerser came neither eating bread nor drinking wine, and you say, He has a demon; ³⁴the Son of Man came eating and drinking, and you say, Behold, a man, a glutton, and a wine drinker, a friend of tax collectors and sinners; ³⁵and the wisdom was justified from all her children." ³⁶And a certain one of the Pharisees was asking Him that He might eat with him, and having gone into the house of the Pharisee He reclined, ³⁷and behold, a woman in the city, who was a sinner, having known that He reclines in the house of the Pharisee, having provided an alabaster box of ointment, ³⁸and having stood behind, beside His feet, weeping, she began to wet His feet with the tears, and with the hairs of her head she was wiping, and was kissing His feet, and was anointing with the ointment. ³⁹And the Pharisee who called Him, having seen, spoke within himself, saying, "This One, if He were a prophet, would have known who and of what kind [is] the woman who touches Him, that she is a sinner." ⁴⁰And Jesus answering said to him, "Simon, I have something to say to you"; and he says, "Teacher, say on." ⁴¹"Two debtors were to a certain creditor; one was owing five hundred denarii, and the other fifty; ⁴²and they not having [with which] to give back, he forgave both; which of them then, do you say, will love him more?" ⁴³And Simon answering said, "I suppose that to whom he forgave the more"; and He said to him, "You judged correctly." ⁴⁴And having turned to the woman, He said to Simon, "See this woman? I entered into your house; you did not give water for My feet, but this woman wet My feet with tears, and wiped with the hairs of her head; ⁴⁵you did not give a kiss to Me, but this woman, from what [time] I came in, did not cease kissing My feet; ⁴⁶you did not anoint My head with oil, but this woman anointed My feet with oil; ⁴⁷therefore I say to you, her many sins have been forgiven, because she loved much; but to whom is forgiven little, loves little." ⁴⁸And He said to her, "Your sins have been forgiven"; ⁴⁹and those dining with Him began to say within themselves, "Who is this, who also forgives sins?" ⁵⁰And He said to the woman, "Your faith has saved you, be going on to peace."

CHAPTER 8

¹And it came to pass thereafter, that He was going through every city and village, preaching and proclaiming good news of the Kingdom of God, and the Twelve [are] with Him, ²and certain women who were healed of evil spirits and sicknesses, Mary who is called Magdalene, from whom seven demons had gone forth, ³and Joanna wife of Chuza, steward of Herod, and Susanna, and many others, who were ministering to Him from their substance. ⁴And a great multitude having gathered, and those who from city and city were coming to Him, He spoke by an allegory: ⁵"The sower went forth to sow his seed, and in his sowing some indeed fell beside the way, and it was trodden down, and the birds of the sky devoured it. ⁶And other fell on the rock, and having sprung up, it withered, through having no moisture. ⁷And other fell amidst the thorns, and the thorns having sprung up with it, choked it. ⁸And other fell on the good ground, and having sprung up, it made fruit a hundredfold." Saying these things, He was calling, "He having ears to hear—let him hear." ⁹And His disciples were questioning Him, saying, "What may this allegory be?" ¹⁰And He said, "To you it has been given to know the secrets of the Kingdom of God, but to the rest in allegories, that seeing they may not see, and hearing they may not understand. ¹¹And this is the allegory: the seed is the word of God, ¹²and those beside the way are those hearing, then comes the Devil, and takes up the word from their heart, lest having believed, they may be saved. ¹³And those on the rock: they who, when they may hear, receive the word with joy, and these have no root, who for a time believe, and in time of temptation fall away. ¹⁴And that which fell to the thorns: these are they who have heard, and going forth, through anxieties, and riches, and pleasures of life, are choked, and do not bear to completion. ¹⁵And that in the good ground: these are they who in an upright and good heart, having heard the word, retain [it], and bear fruit in continuance. ¹⁶And no one having lighted a lamp covers it with a vessel, or puts [it] under a bed; but he puts [it] on a lampstand, that those coming in may see the light, ¹⁷for nothing is secret, that will not become visible, nor hid, that will not be known and become visible. ¹⁸See, therefore, how you hear, for whoever may have, there will be given to him, and whoever may not have, also what he seems to have will be taken from him." ¹⁹And there came to Him His mother and brothers, and they were not able to get to Him because of the multitude, ²⁰and it was told Him, saying, "Your mother and Your brothers stand outside, wishing to see You"; ²¹and He answering said to them, "My mother and My brothers! They are those who are hearing the word of God, and doing." ²²And it came to pass, on one of the days, that He Himself went into a boat with His disciples, and He said to them, "We may go over to the other side of the lake"; and they set forth, ²³and as they are sailing He fell deeply asleep, and there came down a storm of wind to the lake, and they were filling, and were in peril. ²⁴And having come near, they awoke Him, saying, "Master, Master, we perish!" And He, having arisen, rebuked the wind and the raging of the water, and they ceased, and there came a calm, ²⁵and He said to them, "Where is your faith?" And they being afraid wondered, saying to one another, "Who, then, is this, that He even commands the winds and the water, and they obey Him?" ²⁶And they sailed down to the region of the Gadarenes that is opposite Galilee, ²⁷and He having gone forth on the land, there met Him a certain man, out of the city, who had demons for a long time, and was not clothed with a garment, and was not abiding in a house, but in the tombs, ²⁸and having seen Jesus, and having cried out, he fell before Him, and with a loud voice, said, "What [regards] me and You, Jesus, Son of God Most High? I implore You, may You not afflict me!" ²⁹For He commanded the unclean spirit to come forth from the man, for many times it had caught him, and he was being bound with chains and shackles—guarded, and breaking apart the bonds he was driven by the demons into the deserts. ³⁰And Jesus questioned him, saying, "What is your name?" And he said, "Legion," because many demons were entered into him, ³¹and he was calling on Him that He may not command them to go away into the abyss, ³²and there was there a herd of many pigs feeding on the mountain, and they were calling on Him that He might permit them to enter into these, and He permitted them, ³³and the demons having gone forth from the man, entered into the pigs, and the herd rushed down the steep into the lake, and were drowned. ³⁴And those feeding [them], having seen what was come to pass, fled, and having gone, told [it] to the city, and to the fields; ³⁵and they came forth to see what was come to pass, and they came to Jesus, and found the man sitting, out of whom the demons had gone forth, clothed, and right-minded, at the feet of Jesus, and they were afraid; ³⁶and those also having seen [it], told them how the demoniac was saved. ³⁷And the whole multitude of the region of the Gadarenes asked Him to go away from them, because they were pressed with great fear, and He having entered into the boat, turned back. ³⁸And the man from whom the demons had gone forth was imploring of Him to be with Him, and Jesus sent him away, saying, ³⁹"Return to your house, and tell how God did great things to you"; and he went away through all the city proclaiming how Jesus did great things to him. ⁴⁰And it came to pass, in the turning back of Jesus, the multitude received Him, for they were all looking for Him, ⁴¹and behold, there came a man whose name [is] Jairus, and he was a chief of the synagogue, and having fallen at the feet of Jesus, was calling on Him to come to his house, ⁴²because he had an only daughter about twelve years [old], and she was dying. And in His going away, the multitudes were thronging Him, ⁴³and a woman, being with a flow of blood for twelve years, who, having spent all her living on physicians, was not able to be healed by any, ⁴⁴having come near behind, touched the fringe of His garment, and immediately the flow of her blood stood still. ⁴⁵And Jesus said, "Who [is] it that touched Me?" And all denying, Peter and those with him said, "Master, the multitudes press You, and throng [You], and You say, Who [is] it that touched Me?" ⁴⁶And Jesus said, "Someone touched Me, for I knew power having gone forth from Me." ⁴⁷And the woman, having seen that she was not hid, trembling, came, and having fallen before Him, for what cause she touched Him declared to Him before all the

people, and how she was healed instantly; ⁴⁸and He said to her, "Take courage, daughter, your faith has saved you, be going on to peace." ⁴⁹While He is yet speaking, there comes a certain one from the chief of the synagogue's [house], saying to him, "Your daughter has died, do not harass the Teacher"; ⁵⁰and Jesus having heard, answered him, saying, "Do not be afraid, only believe, and she will be saved." ⁵¹And having come into the house, He permitted no one to go in, except Peter, and James, and John, and the father of the child, and the mother; ⁵²and they were all weeping, and beating themselves for her, and He said, "Do not weep, she did not die, but sleeps"; ⁵³and they were deriding Him, knowing that she died; ⁵⁴and He having put all forth outside, and having taken hold of her hand, called, saying, "Child, arise"; ⁵⁵and her spirit came back, and she arose immediately, and He directed that there be given to her to eat; ⁵⁶and her parents were amazed, but He charged them to say to no one what had come to pass.

CHAPTER 9

¹And having called together His twelve disciples, He gave them power and authority over all the demons, and to cure diseases, ²and He sent them to proclaim the Kingdom of God, and to heal the ailing. ³And He said to them, "Take nothing for the way, neither staff, nor leather pouch, nor bread, nor money; neither have two coats each; ⁴and into whatever house you may enter, remain there, and depart from there; ⁵and as many as may not receive you, going forth from that city, even the dust from your feet shake off, for a testimony against them." ⁶And going forth they were going through the several villages, proclaiming good news, and healing everywhere. ⁷And Herod the tetrarch heard of all the things being done by Him, and was perplexed, because it was said by some that John has been raised out of the dead, ⁸and by some that Elijah appeared, and by others, that a prophet, one of the ancients, was risen; ⁹and Herod said, "I beheaded John, but who is this concerning whom I hear such things?" And he was seeking to see Him. ¹⁰And the apostles having turned back, declared to Him how they did great things, and having taken them, He withdrew by Himself into a city called Bethsaida, ¹¹and the multitudes having known followed Him, and having received them, He was speaking to them concerning the Kingdom of God, and He cured those having need of service. ¹²And the day began to decline, and the Twelve having come near, said to Him, "Let away the multitude, that having gone into the surrounding villages and the fields, they may lodge and may find provision, because here we are in a desolate place." ¹³And He said to them, "You give them to eat"; and they said, "We have no more than five loaves and two fishes: except, having gone, we may buy food for all this people"; ¹⁴for they were about five thousand men. And He said to His disciples, "Cause them to recline in companies, in each fifty"; ¹⁵and they did so, and made all to recline; ¹⁶and having taken the five loaves and the two fishes, having looked up to the sky, He blessed them, and broke, and was giving to the disciples to set before the multitude; ¹⁷and they ate, and were all filled, and there was taken up what was over to them of broken pieces, twelve baskets. ¹⁸And it came to pass, as He is praying alone, the disciples were with Him, and He questioned them, saying, "Who do the multitudes say I am?" ¹⁹And they answering said, "John the Immerser; and others, Elijah; and others, that a prophet, one of the ancients, was risen"; ²⁰and He said to them, "And you—who do you say I am?" And Peter answering said, "The Christ of God." ²¹And having charged them, He commanded [them] to say this to no one, ²²saying, "It is necessary for the Son of Man to suffer many things, and to be rejected by the elders, and chief priests, and scribes, and to be killed, and to be raised the third day." ²³And He said to all, "If anyone wills to come after Me, let him disown himself, and take up his cross daily, and follow Me; ²⁴for whoever may will to save his life will lose it, and whoever may lose his life for My sake, he will save it; ²⁵for what is a man profited, having gained the whole world, and having lost or having forfeited himself? ²⁶For whoever may be ashamed of Me and of My words, of this one will the Son of Man be ashamed when He may come in His glory, and the Father's, and the holy messengers'; ²⁷and I say to you, truly, there are certain of those standing here who will not taste of death until they may see the Kingdom of God." ²⁸And it came to pass, after these words, as it were eight days, that having taken Peter, and John, and James, He went up to the mountain to pray, ²⁹and it came to pass, in His praying, the appearance of His face became altered, and His clothing became flashing white. ³⁰And behold, two men were speaking together with Him, who were Moses and Elijah, ³¹who having appeared in glory, spoke of His outgoing that He was about to fulfill in Jerusalem, ³²but Peter and those with him were heavy with sleep, and having awoken, they saw His glory, and the two men standing with Him. ³³And it came to pass, in their parting from Him, Peter said to Jesus, "Master, it is good to us to be here; and we may make three shelters: one for You, and one for Moses, and one for Elijah," not knowing what he says: ³⁴and as he was speaking these things, there came a cloud, and overshadowed them, and they feared in their entering into the cloud, ³⁵and a voice came out of the cloud, saying, "This is My Son, the Beloved; hear Him"; ³⁶and when the voice was past, Jesus was found alone; and they were silent, and declared to no one in those days anything of what they have seen. ³⁷And it came to pass on the next day, they having come down from the mountain, a great multitude met Him there, ³⁸and behold, a man from the multitude cried out, saying, "Teacher, I implore You, look on my son, because he is my only begotten; ³⁹and behold, a spirit takes him, and suddenly he cries out, and it convulses him, with foaming, and it hardly departs from him, bruising him, ⁴⁰and I implored Your disciples that they might cast it out, and they were not able." ⁴¹And Jesus answering said, "O generation, unsteadfast and perverse, until when will I be with you, and endure you? Bring your son near here"; ⁴²and as he is yet coming near, the demon threw him down, and convulsed [him], and Jesus rebuked the unclean spirit, and healed the youth, and gave him back to his father. ⁴³And they were all amazed at the greatness of God, and while all are wondering at all things that Jesus did, He said to His disciples, ⁴⁴"Lay to your ears these words, for the Son of Man is about to be delivered up into the hands of men." ⁴⁵And they were not knowing this saying, and it was veiled from them, that they might not perceive it, and they were afraid to ask Him about this saying. ⁴⁶And there entered a reasoning among them, this—who may be greater of them. ⁴⁷And Jesus having seen the reasoning of their heart, having taken hold of a child, set him beside Him, ⁴⁸and said to them, "Whoever may receive this child in My Name, receives Me, and whoever may receive Me, receives Him who sent Me, for he who is least among you all—he will be great." ⁴⁹And John answering said, "Master, we saw a certain one casting forth the demons in Your Name, and we forbade him, because he does not follow with us"; ⁵⁰and Jesus said to him, "Do not forbid, for he who is not against us, is for us." ⁵¹And it came to pass, in the completing of the days of His being taken up, that He fixed His face to go on to Jerusalem, ⁵²and He sent messengers before His face, and having gone on, they went into a village of Samaritans, to make ready for Him, ⁵³and they did not receive Him, because His face was going on to Jerusalem. ⁵⁴And His disciples James and John having seen, said, "Lord, will You [that] we may command fire to come down from Heaven, and to consume them, as Elijah also did?" ⁵⁵And having turned, He rebuked them and said, "You have not known of what spirit you are, ⁵⁶for the Son of Man did not come to destroy men's lives, but to save"; and they went on to another village. ⁵⁷And it came to pass, as they are going on in the way, a certain one said to Him, "I will follow You wherever You may go, Lord"; ⁵⁸and Jesus said to him, "The foxes have holes, and the birds of the sky places of rest, but the Son of Man has nowhere He may recline the head." ⁵⁹And He said to another, "Follow Me"; and he said, "Lord, permit me, having gone away, to first bury my father"; ⁶⁰and Jesus said to him, "Permit the dead to bury their own dead, and you, having gone away, publish the Kingdom of God." ⁶¹And another also said, "I will follow You, Lord, but first permit me to take leave of those in my house"; ⁶²and Jesus said to him, "No one having put his hand on a plow, and looking back, is fit for the Kingdom of God."

CHAPTER 10

¹And after these things, the LORD also appointed seventy others, and sent them by twos before His face, to every city and place to where He Himself was about to come, ²then He said to them, "The harvest [is] indeed

abundant, but the workmen few; implore then the Lord of the harvest, that He may put forth workmen to His harvest. ³Go away; behold, I send you forth as lambs in the midst of wolves; ⁴carry no bag, no leather pouch, nor sandals; and greet no one on the way; ⁵and into whatever house you enter, first say, Peace to this house; ⁶and if indeed there may be there the son of peace, your peace will rest on it; and if not so, it will turn back on you. ⁷And remain in that house, eating and drinking the things they have, for worthy [is] the workman of his hire; do not go from house to house, ⁸and into whatever city you enter, and they may receive you, eat the things set before you, ⁹and heal the ailing in it, and say to them, The Kingdom of God has come near to you. ¹⁰And into whatever city you enter, and they may not receive you, having gone forth to its broad places, say, ¹¹And the dust that has cleaved to us from your city, we wipe off against you, but know this, that the Kingdom of God has come near to you; ¹²and I say to you that it will be more tolerable for Sodom in that day than for that city. ¹³Woe to you, Chorazin; woe to you, Bethsaida; for if the mighty works that were done in you had been done in Tyre and Sidon, they had converted long ago, sitting in sackcloth and ashes; ¹⁴but it will be more tolerable for Tyre and Sidon in the judgment than for you. ¹⁵And you, Capernaum, which were exalted to Heaven, you will be brought down to Hades. ¹⁶He who is hearing you, hears Me; and he who is putting you away, puts Me away; and he who is putting Me away, puts away Him who sent Me." ¹⁷And the seventy turned back with joy, saying, "Lord, and the demons are being subjected to us in Your Name"; ¹⁸and He said to them, "I was beholding Satan having fallen as lightning from Heaven; ¹⁹behold, I give to you the authority to tread on serpents and scorpions, and on all the power of the enemy, and nothing by any means will hurt you; ²⁰but do not rejoice in this, that the spirits are subjected to you, but rejoice rather that your names were written in the heavens." ²¹In that hour Jesus was glad in the Spirit and said, "I confess to You, Father, Lord of Heaven and of earth, that You hid these things from wise men and understanding, and revealed them to babies; yes, Father, because so it became good pleasure before You. ²²All things were delivered up to Me by My Father, and no one knows who the Son is, except the Father, and who the Father is, except the Son, and he to whom the Son may resolve to reveal [Him]." ²³And having turned to the disciples, He said, by themselves, "Blessed the eyes that are perceiving what you perceive; ²⁴for I say to you that many prophets and kings wished to see what you perceive, and did not see, and to hear what you hear, and did not hear." ²⁵And behold, a certain lawyer stood up, trying Him, and saying, "Teacher, what having done, will I inherit continuous life?" ²⁶And He said to him, "In the Law what has been written? How do you read [it]?" ²⁷And he answering said, "You will love the LORD your God out of all your heart, and out of all your soul, and out of all your strength, and out of all your understanding, and your neighbor as yourself." ²⁸And He said to him, "You answered correctly; do this, and you will live." ²⁹And he, willing to declare himself righteous, said to Jesus, "And who is my neighbor?" ³⁰And Jesus having taken up [the word], said, "A certain man was going down from Jerusalem to Jericho, and fell among robbers, and having stripped him and inflicted blows, they went away, leaving [him] half dead. ³¹And by a coincidence a certain priest was going down in that way, and having seen him, he passed over on the opposite side; ³²and in like manner also, a Levite, having been around the place, having come and seen, passed over on the opposite side. ³³But a certain Samaritan, journeying, came along him, and having seen him, he was moved with compassion, ³⁴and having come near, he bound up his wounds, pouring on oil and wine, and having lifted him up on his own beast, he brought him to an inn, and was careful of him; ³⁵and on the next day, going forth, taking out two denarii, he gave to the innkeeper and said to him, Be careful of him, and whatever you may spend more, I, in my coming again, will give back to you. ³⁶Who, then, of these three, seems to you to have become neighbor of him who fell among the robbers?" ³⁷And he said, "He who did the kindness with him," then Jesus said to him, "Be going on, and you be doing in like manner." ³⁸And it came to pass, in their going on, that He entered into a certain village, and a certain woman, by name Martha, received Him into her house, ³⁹and she also had a sister, called Mary, who also, having seated herself beside the feet of Jesus, was hearing the word, ⁴⁰and Martha was distracted about much serving, and having stood by Him, she said, "Lord, do You not care that my sister left me alone to serve? Say then to her that she may partake along with me." ⁴¹And Jesus answering said to her, "Martha, Martha, you are anxious and disquieted about many things, ⁴²but of one thing there is need, and Mary chose the good part; that will not be taken away from her."

CHAPTER 11

¹And it came to pass, in His being in a certain place praying, as He ceased, a certain one of His disciples said to Him, "Lord, teach us to pray, as also John taught his disciples." ²And He said to them, "When you may pray, say: Our Father who is in the heavens, hallowed be Your Name; Your kingdom come, Your will come to pass, as in Heaven also on earth; ³be giving us daily our appointed bread; ⁴and forgive us our sins, for we also ourselves forgive everyone indebted to us; and may You not bring us into temptation, but deliver us from the evil [one]." ⁵And He said to them, "Who of you will have a friend, and will go on to him at midnight, and may say to him, Friend, lend me three loaves, ⁶seeing a friend of mine came out of the way to me, and I have not what I will set before him, ⁷and he from within answering may say, Do not give me trouble, the door has already been shut, and my children are with me in the bed, I am not able, having risen, to give to you. ⁸I say to you, even if he will not give to him, having risen, because of his being his friend, yet because of his persistence, having risen, he will give him as many as he needs; ⁹and I say to you, ask, and it will be given to you; seek, and you will find; knock, and it will be opened to you; ¹⁰for everyone who is asking receives; and he who is seeking finds; and to him who is knocking it will be opened. ¹¹And of which of you—the father—[if] the son will ask [for] a loaf, will present to him a stone? And [if] a fish, instead of a fish, will present to him a serpent? ¹²And [if] he may ask [for] an egg, will present to him a scorpion? ¹³If, then, you, being evil, have known to be giving good gifts to your children, how much more will the Father who is from Heaven give the Holy Spirit to those asking Him!" ¹⁴And He was casting forth a demon, and it was mute, and it came to pass, the demon having gone forth, the mute man spoke, and the multitudes wondered, ¹⁵and certain of them said, "By Beelzebul, ruler of the demons, He casts forth the demons"; ¹⁶and others, tempting, were asking [for] a sign out of Heaven from Him. ¹⁷And He, knowing their thoughts, said to them, "Every kingdom having been divided against itself is desolated; and house against house falls; ¹⁸and if Satan was also divided against himself, how will his kingdom be made to stand? For you say by Beelzebul is My casting forth the demons, ¹⁹but if I, by Beelzebul, cast forth the demons—your sons, by whom do they cast forth? Because of this they will be your judges; ²⁰but if by the finger of God I cast forth the demons, then the Kingdom of God came unaware on you. ²¹When the strong man may keep his hall armed, his goods are in peace; ²²but when the stronger than he, having come on [him], may overcome him, he takes away his whole armor in which he had trusted, and he distributes his spoils; ²³he who is not with Me is against Me, and he who is not gathering with Me scatters. ²⁴When the unclean spirit may go forth from the man, it walks through waterless places seeking rest, and not finding, it says, I will return to my house from where I came forth; ²⁵and having come, it finds [it] swept and adorned; ²⁶then it goes, and takes to it seven other spirits more evil than itself, and having entered, they dwell there, and the last of that man becomes worse than the first." ²⁷And it came to pass, in His saying these things, a certain woman having lifted up the voice out of the multitude, said to Him, "Blessed the womb that carried You, and the breasts that You sucked!" ²⁸And He said, "Indeed, rather, blessed those hearing the word of God, and keeping [it]!" ²⁹And the multitudes crowding together on Him, He began to say, "This generation is evil, it seeks after a sign, and a sign will not be given to it, except the sign of Jonah the prophet, ³⁰for as Jonah became a sign to the Ninevites, so also will the Son of Man be to this generation. ³¹A queen of the south will rise up in the judgment with the men of this generation, and will condemn them, because she came from the ends of the earth to hear the wisdom of

Solomon; and behold, [One] greater than Solomon [is] here! ³²Men of Nineveh will stand up in the judgment with this generation, and will condemn it, because they converted at the proclamation of Jonah; and behold, [One] greater than Jonah [is] here! ³³And no one having lighted a lamp, puts [it] in a secret place, nor under the measure, but on the lampstand, that those coming in may behold the light. ³⁴The lamp of the body is the eye, when then your eye may be simple, your whole body is also lightened; and when it may be evil, your body is also darkened; ³⁵take heed, then, lest the light that [is] in you is darkness; ³⁶if then your whole body is lightened, not having any part darkened, the whole will be lightened, as when the lamp by the brightness may give you light." ³⁷And in [His] speaking, a certain Pharisee was asking Him that He might dine with him, and having gone in, He reclined, ³⁸and the Pharisee having seen, wondered that He did not first immerse Himself before the early meal. ³⁹And the LORD said to him, "Now you, the Pharisees, make the outside of the cup and of the plate clean, but your inward part is full of robbery and wickedness. ⁴⁰Unthinking [ones]! Did He who made the outside not also make the inside? ⁴¹But what you have given [as] alms, and behold, all things are clean to you. ⁴²But woe to you, the Pharisees, because you tithe the mint, and the rue, and every herb, and you pass by the judgment and the love of God; these things [you] should do, and those not to be neglecting. ⁴³Woe to you, the Pharisees, because you love the first seats in the synagogues and the salutations in the marketplaces. ⁴⁴Woe to you, scribes and Pharisees, hypocrites, because you are as the unseen tombs, and the men walking above have not known." ⁴⁵And one of the lawyers answering, says to Him, "Teacher, saying these things, You also insult us"; ⁴⁶and He said, "And to you, the lawyers, woe! Because you burden men with burdens [too] grievous to bear, and you yourselves do not touch the burdens with one of your fingers. ⁴⁷Woe to you, because you build the tombs of the prophets, and your fathers killed them. ⁴⁸Then you testify, and are well pleased with the works of your fathers, because they indeed killed them, and you build their tombs; ⁴⁹because of this also the wisdom of God said: I will send to them prophets, and apostles, and some of them they will kill and persecute, ⁵⁰that the blood of all the prophets, that is being poured forth from the foundation of the world, may be required from this generation— ⁵¹from the blood of Abel to the blood of Zacharias, who perished between the altar and the house; yes, I say to you, it will be required from this generation. ⁵²Woe to you, the lawyers, because you took away the key of the knowledge; you yourselves did not enter; and you hindered those coming in." ⁵³And in His speaking these things to them, the scribes and the Pharisees began fearfully to urge and to press Him to speak about many things, ⁵⁴laying wait for Him, and seeking to catch something out of His mouth, that they might accuse Him.

CHAPTER 12

¹At which time the myriads of the multitude having been gathered together, so as to tread on one another, He began to say to His disciples, first, "Take heed to yourselves of the leaven of the Pharisees, which is hypocrisy; ²and there is nothing covered that will not be revealed, and hid that will not be known; ³because whatever you said in the darkness will be heard in the light, and what you spoke to the ear in the inner-chambers will be proclaimed on the housetops. ⁴And I say to you, my friends, do not be afraid of those killing the body, and after these things are not having anything more to do; ⁵but I will show to you whom you may fear: fear Him who, after the killing, is having authority to cast into Gehenna; yes, I say to you, fear Him. ⁶Are not five sparrows sold for two assaria? And one of them is not forgotten before God, ⁷but even the hairs of your head have all been numbered; therefore do not fear, you are of more value than many sparrows. ⁸And I say to you, everyone who may confess in Me before men, the Son of Man will also confess in him before the messengers of God, ⁹and he who has denied Me before men, will be denied before the messengers of God, ¹⁰and everyone who will say a word to the Son of Man, it will be forgiven to him, but the [one] having slandered to the Holy Spirit will not be forgiven. ¹¹And when they bring you before the synagogues, and the rulers, and the authorities, do not be anxious how or what you may reply, or what you may say, ¹²for the Holy Spirit will teach you in that hour what [you] should say." ¹³And a certain one out of the multitude said to Him, "Teacher, say to my brother to divide with me the inheritance." ¹⁴And He said to him, "Man, who set Me a judge or a divider over you?" ¹⁵And He said to them, "Observe, and beware of the covetousness, because his life is not in the abundance of one's goods." ¹⁶And He spoke an allegory to them, saying, "Of a certain rich man the field brought forth well; ¹⁷and he was reasoning within himself, saying, What will I do, because I have nowhere I will gather together my fruits? ¹⁸And he said, This I will do, I will take down my storehouses, and I will build greater ones, and I will gather together there all my products and my good things, ¹⁹and I will say to my soul, Soul, you have many good things laid up for many years, be resting, eat, drink, be merry. ²⁰And God said to him, Unthinking [one]! This night your life is required of you, and what things you prepared—to whom will they be [given]? ²¹So [is] he who is treasuring up to himself, and is not rich toward God." ²²And He said to His disciples, "Because of this, to you I say, do not be anxious for your life, what you may eat; nor for the body, what you may put on; ²³life is more than nourishment, and the body than clothing. ²⁴Consider the ravens, that they do not sow, nor reap, to which there is no barn nor storehouse, and God nourishes them; how much better are you than the birds? ²⁵And who of you, being anxious, is able to add to his age one cubit? ²⁶If, then, you are not able for the least—why are you anxious for the rest? ²⁷Consider the lilies, how do they grow? They do not labor, nor do they spin, and I say to you, not even Solomon in all his glory was clothed as one of these; ²⁸and if the herbage in the field, that today is, and tomorrow is cast into an oven, God so clothes, how much more you of little faith? ²⁹And you—do not seek what you may eat, or what you may drink, and do not be in suspense, ³⁰for the nations of the world seek after all these things, and your Father has known that you have need of these things; ³¹but seek the Kingdom of God, and all these things will be added to you. ³²Do not fear, little flock, because your Father delighted to give you the kingdom; ³³sell your goods, and give alms, make to yourselves bags that do not become old, a treasure unfailing in the heavens, where thief does not come near, nor moth destroy; ³⁴for where your treasure is, there your heart will be also. ³⁵Let your loins be girded, and the lamps burning, ³⁶and you [be] like to men waiting for their lord when he will return out of the wedding feasts, that he having come and knocked, immediately they may open to him. ³⁷Blessed those servants, whom the lord, having come, will find watching; truly I say to you that he will gird himself, and will cause them to recline, and having come near, will minister to them; ³⁸and if he may come in the second watch, and in the third watch he may come, and may find [it] so, blessed are those servants. ³⁹And know this, that if the master of the house had known what hour the thief comes, he would have watched, and would not have permitted his house to be broken through; ⁴⁰and you, then, become ready, because at the hour you do not think, the Son of Man comes." ⁴¹And Peter said to Him, "Lord, do You speak this allegory to us, or also to all?" ⁴²And the LORD said, "Who, then, is the faithful and prudent steward whom the lord will set over his household, to give in season the wheat measure? ⁴³Blessed that servant, whom his lord, having come, will find doing so; ⁴⁴truly I say to you that he will set him over all his goods. ⁴⁵And if that servant may say in his heart, My lord delays to come, and may begin to beat the menservants and the maidservants, to eat also, and to drink, and to be drunken, ⁴⁶the lord of that servant will come in a day in which he does not look for [him], and in an hour that he does not know, and will cut him off, and he will appoint his portion with the unfaithful. ⁴⁷And that servant, who having known his lord's will, and having not prepared, nor having gone according to his will, will be beaten with many stripes, ⁴⁸and he who, not having known, and having done things worthy of stripes, will be beaten with few; and to everyone to whom much was given, much will be required from him; and to whom they committed much, more abundantly they will ask of him. ⁴⁹I came to cast fire to the earth, and what I wish [is] if it were already kindled! ⁵⁰But I have an immersion to be immersed with, and how I

am pressed until it may be accomplished! ⁵¹Do you think that I came to give peace in the earth? No, I say to you, but rather division; ⁵²for there will be from now on five in one house divided—three against two, and two against three; ⁵³a father will be divided against a son, and a son against a father, a mother against a daughter, and a daughter against a mother, a mother-in-law against her daughter-in-law, and a daughter-in-law against her mother-in-law." ⁵⁴And He also said to the multitudes, "When you may see the cloud rising from the west, immediately you say, A shower comes, and it is so; ⁵⁵and when a south wind is blowing, you say that there will be heat, and it is; ⁵⁶hypocrites! You have known to discern the face of the earth and of the sky, but how do you not discern this time? ⁵⁷And why, also, of yourselves, do you not judge what is righteous? ⁵⁸For as you are going away with your opponent to the ruler, in the way give diligence to be released from him, lest he may drag you to the judge, and the judge may deliver you to the officer, and the officer may cast you into prison; ⁵⁹I say to you, you may not come forth from there until even the last mite you may give back."

CHAPTER 13

¹And there were some present at that time, telling Him about the Galileans, whose blood Pilate mingled with their sacrifices; ²and Jesus answering said to them, "Do you think that these Galileans became sinners beyond all the Galileans, because they have suffered such things? ³No—I say to you, but if you may not convert, even so will all you perish. ⁴Or those eighteen on whom the tower in Siloam fell, and killed them, do you think that these became debtors beyond all men who are dwelling in Jerusalem? ⁵No—I say to you, but if you may not convert, all you will perish in like manner. ⁶And He spoke this allegory: "A certain one had a fig tree planted in his vineyard, and he came seeking fruit in it, and he did not find; ⁷and he said to the vinedresser, Behold, three years I come seeking fruit in this fig tree, and do not find [it], cut it off, why does it also render the ground useless? ⁸And he answering says to him, Lord, permit it also this year, until I may dig around it, and cast in dung; ⁹and if indeed it may bear fruit—and if not so, thereafter you will cut it off." ¹⁰And He was teaching in one of the synagogues on the Sabbath, ¹¹and behold, there was a woman having a spirit of disability [for] eighteen years, and she was bent together, and not able to bend back at all, ¹²and Jesus having seen her, called [her] near and said to her, "Woman, you have been loosed from your disability"; ¹³and He laid on her [His] hands, and immediately she was set upright, and was glorifying God. ¹⁴And the chief of the synagogue answering—much displeased that on the Sabbath Jesus healed—said to the multitude, "Six days there are in which it is necessary to be working; in these, then, coming, be healed, and not on the day of the Sabbath." ¹⁵Then the LORD answered him and said, "Hypocrite, do not each of you loose his ox or donkey from the stall on the Sabbath, and having led [it] away, water [it]? ¹⁶And this one, being a daughter of Abraham, whom Satan bound eighteen years, behold, did [she] not ought to be loosed from this bond on the day of the Sabbath?" ¹⁷And He saying these things, all who were opposed to Him were being ashamed, and all the multitude were rejoicing over all the glorious things that are being done by Him. ¹⁸And He said, "To what is the Kingdom of God like? And to what will I liken it? ¹⁹It is like to a grain of mustard, which a man having taken, cast into his garden, and it increased, and came to a great tree, and the birds of the heavens rested in its branches." ²⁰And again He said, "To what will I liken the Kingdom of God? ²¹It is like leaven, which a woman, having taken, hid in three measures of meal, until all was leavened." ²²And He was going through cities and villages, teaching, and making progress toward Jerusalem; ²³and a certain one said to Him, "Lord, are those saved few?" And He said to them, ²⁴"Be striving to go in through the straight gate, because many, I say to you, will seek to go in, and will not be able; ²⁵from the time the Master of the house may have risen up, and may have shut the door, and you may begin to stand outside, and to knock at the door, saying, Lord, Lord, open to us, and He answering will say to you, I have not known you from where you are, ²⁶then you may begin to say, We ate before You, and drank, and You taught in our broad places; ²⁷and He will say, I say to you, I have not known you from where you are; depart from Me, all you workers of the unrighteousness. ²⁸There will be there the weeping and the gnashing of the teeth when you may see Abraham, and Isaac, and Jacob, and all the prophets, in the Kingdom of God, and yourselves being cast outside; ²⁹and they will come from east and west, and from north and south, and will recline in the Kingdom of God, ³⁰and behold, there are last who will be first, and there are first who will be last." ³¹On that day there came near certain Pharisees, saying to Him, "Go forth, and be going on from here, for Herod wishes to kill You"; ³²and He said to them, "Having gone, say to that fox, Behold, I cast forth demons, and perfect cures today and tomorrow, and the third [day] I am being perfected; ³³but it is necessary for Me today, and tomorrow, and the [day] following, to go on, because it is not possible for a prophet to perish out of Jerusalem. ³⁴Jerusalem, Jerusalem, that is killing the prophets, and stoning those sent to her, how often I willed to gather together your children, as a hen [gathers] her brood under the wings, and you did not will. ³⁵Behold, your house is being left to you desolate, and truly I say to you, you may not see Me, until it may come when you may say, Blessed [is] He who is coming in the Name of the LORD."

CHAPTER 14

¹And it came to pass, on His going into the house of a certain one of the chiefs of the Pharisees, on a Sabbath, to eat bread, that they were watching Him, ²and behold, there was a certain dropsical man before Him; ³and Jesus answering spoke to the lawyers and Pharisees, saying, "Is it lawful to heal on the Sabbath?" ⁴And they were silent, and having taken hold of [him], He healed him, and let [him] go; ⁵and answering them He said, "Of which of you will a donkey or ox fall into a pit, and he will not immediately draw it up on the Sabbath day?" ⁶And they were not able to answer Him again to these things. ⁷And He spoke an allegory to those called, marking how they were choosing out the first couches, saying to them, ⁸"When you may be called by anyone to wedding feasts, you may not recline on the first couch, lest [one] more honorable than you may have been called by him, ⁹and he who called you and him having come will say to you, Give to this one [your] place, and then you may begin to occupy the last place with shame. ¹⁰But when you may be called, having gone on, recline in the last place, that when he who called you may come, he may say to you, Friend, come up higher; then you will have glory before those dining with you; ¹¹because everyone who is exalting himself will be humbled, and he who is humbling himself will be exalted." ¹²And He also said to him who called Him, "When you may make an early meal or a dinner, do not be calling your friends, nor your brothers, nor your relatives, nor rich neighbors, lest they may also call you again, and a repayment may come to you; ¹³but when you may make a feast, be calling poor, maimed, lame, blind, ¹⁴and you will be blessed, because they have nothing to repay you, for it will be repaid to you in the resurrection of the righteous." ¹⁵And one of those dining with Him, having heard these things, said to Him, "Blessed [is] he who will eat bread in the Kingdom of God"; ¹⁶and He said to him, "A certain man made a great dinner, and called many, ¹⁷and he sent his servant at the hour of the dinner to say to those having been called, Be coming, because now all things are ready. ¹⁸And all began with one [voice] to excuse themselves. The first said to him, I bought a field, and I have need to go forth and see it; I beg of you, have me excused. ¹⁹And another said, I bought five yoke of oxen, and I go on to prove them; I beg of you, have me excused. ²⁰And another said, I married a wife, and because of this I am not able to come. ²¹And that servant having come, told these things to his lord, then the master of the house, having been angry, said to his servant, Go forth quickly into the broad places and lanes of the city, and the poor, and maimed, and lame, and blind, bring in here. ²²And the servant said, Lord, it has been done as you commanded, and still there is room. ²³And the lord said to the servant, Go forth into the ways and hedges, and constrain to come in, that my house may be filled; ²⁴for I say to you that none of those men who have been called will taste of my dinner." ²⁵And there were going on with Him great multitudes, and having turned, He said to them, ²⁶"If anyone comes to Me, and does not hate his own father, and mother, and wife, and children, and brothers, and sisters, and yet even his own life, he is not able to be My disciple; ²⁷and

whoever does not carry his cross, and come after Me, is not able to be My disciple. ²⁸For who of you, willing to build a tower, does not first, having sat down, count the expense, whether he has the things for completing? ²⁹Lest that he having laid a foundation, and not being able to finish, all who are beholding may begin to mock him, ³⁰saying, This man began to build, and was not able to finish. ³¹Or what king going on to engage with another king in war, does not, having sat down, first consult if he with ten thousand is able to meet him who is coming against him with twenty thousand? ³²And if not so—he being yet a long way off—having sent a delegation, he asks the things for peace. ³³So, then, everyone of you who does not take leave of all that he himself has, is not able to be My disciple. ³⁴The salt [is] good, but if the salt becomes tasteless, with what will it be seasoned? ³⁵It is neither fit for land nor for manure—they cast it outside. He who is having ears to hear—let him hear."

CHAPTER 15

¹And all the tax collectors and sinners were coming near to Him, to hear Him, ²and the Pharisees and the scribes were murmuring, saying, "This One receives sinners, and eats with them." ³And He spoke to them this allegory, saying, ⁴"What man of you having one hundred sheep, and having lost one out of them, does not leave behind the ninety-nine in the wilderness, and go on after the lost one, until he may find it? ⁵And having found, he lays [it] on his shoulders rejoicing, ⁶and having come into the house, he calls together the friends and the neighbors, saying to them, Rejoice with me, because I found my sheep—the lost one. ⁷I say to you that [more] joy will be in Heaven over one sinner converting, rather than over ninety-nine righteous men who have no need of conversion. ⁸Or what woman having ten drachmas, if she may lose one drachma, does not light a lamp, and sweep the house, and seek carefully until she may find? ⁹And having found, she calls together the female friends and the neighbors, saying, Rejoice with me, for I found the drachma that I lost. ¹⁰So I say to you, joy comes before the messengers of God over one sinner converting." ¹¹And He said, "A certain man had two sons, ¹²and the younger of them said to the father, Father, give me the portion of the substance falling to [me], and he divided to them the living. ¹³And not many days after, having gathered all together, the younger son went abroad to a far country, and there he scattered his substance, living riotously; ¹⁴and he having spent all, there came a mighty famine on that country, and himself began to be in want; ¹⁵and having gone on, he joined himself to one of the citizens of that country, and he sent him into the fields to feed pigs, ¹⁶and he was desirous to fill his belly from the husks that the pigs were eating, and no one was giving to him. ¹⁷And having come to himself, he said, How many hired workers of my father have a superabundance of bread, and I am perishing here with hunger! ¹⁸Having risen, I will go on to my father, and will say to him, Father, I sinned—to Heaven, and before you, ¹⁹and I am no longer worthy to be called your son; make me as one of your hired workers. ²⁰And having risen, he went to his own father, and he being yet far distant, his father saw him, and was moved with compassion, and having ran he fell on his neck and kissed him; ²¹and the son said to him, Father, I sinned—to Heaven, and before you, and I am no longer worthy to be called your son. ²²And the father said to his servants, Bring forth the foremost robe, and clothe him, and give a ring for his hand, and sandals for the feet; ²³and having brought the fatted calf, kill [it], and having eaten, we may be merry, ²⁴because this son of mine was dead, and lived again, and he was lost, and was found; and they began to be merry. ²⁵And his elder son was in a field, and as, coming, he drew near to the house, he heard music and dancing, ²⁶and having called near one of the young men, he was inquiring what these things might be, ²⁷and he said to him, Your brother has arrived, and your father killed the fatted calf, because he received him back in health. ²⁸And he was angry, and would not go in, therefore his father, having come forth, was pleading him; ²⁹and he answering said to the father, Behold, so many years I serve you, and never did I transgress your command, and you never gave to me a kid that I might make merry with my friends; ³⁰but when your son—this one who devoured your living with prostitutes—came, you killed to him the fatted calf. ³¹And he said to him, Child, you are always with me, and all my things are yours; ³²but to be merry, and to be glad, it was necessary, because this your brother was dead, and lived again, he was lost, and was found."

CHAPTER 16

¹And He also said to His disciples, "A certain man was rich, who had a steward, and he was accused to him as scattering his goods; ²and having called him, he said to him, What [is] this I hear about you? Render the account of your stewardship, for you may not be steward any longer. ³And the steward said in himself, What will I do, because my lord takes away the stewardship from me? I am not able to dig, I am ashamed to beg— ⁴I have known what I will do, that, when I may be removed from the stewardship, they may receive me to their houses. ⁵And having called near each one of his lord's debtors, he said to the first, How much do you owe to my lord? ⁶And he said, One hundred baths of oil; and he said to him, Take your bill, and having sat down write fifty. ⁷Afterward to another he said, And you, how much do you owe? And he said, One hundred cors of wheat; and he says to him, Take your bill, and write eighty. ⁸And the lord commended the unrighteous steward that he did prudently, because the sons of this age are more prudent than the sons of the light in respect to their generation. ⁹And I say to you, make to yourselves friends out of the wealth of unrighteousness, that when you may fail, they may receive you into the continuous dwelling places. ¹⁰He who is faithful in the least, [is] also faithful in much; and he who in the least [is] unrighteous, is also unrighteous in much; ¹¹if, then, in the unrighteous wealth you did not become faithful—who will entrust to you the true? ¹²And if in the other's you did not become faithful—who will give to you your own? ¹³No servant is able to serve two lords, for either he will hate the one, and he will love the other; or one he will hold to, and of the other he will be heedless; you are not able to serve God and wealth." ¹⁴And also the Pharisees, being lovers of money, were hearing all these things, and were deriding Him, ¹⁵and He said to them, "You are those declaring yourselves righteous before men, but God knows your hearts; because that which is high among men [is] abomination before God; ¹⁶the Law and the Prophets [are] until John; since then the good news of the Kingdom of God is proclaimed, and everyone presses into it; ¹⁷and it is easier for the heaven and the earth to pass away, than one tittle to fall of the Law. ¹⁸Everyone who is sending his wife away, and marrying another, commits adultery; and everyone who is marrying her sent away from a husband commits adultery. ¹⁹And—a certain man was rich, and was clothed in purple and fine linen, making merry sumptuously every day, ²⁰and there was a certain poor man, by name Lazarus, who was laid at his porch, full of sores, ²¹and desiring to be filled from the crumbs that are falling from the table of the rich man; indeed, also the dogs, coming, were licking his sores. ²²And it came to pass, that the poor man died, and that he was carried away by the messengers into the bosom of Abraham—and the rich man also died, and was buried; ²³and having lifted up his eyes in Hades, being in torments, he sees Abraham far off, and Lazarus in his bosom, ²⁴and having cried, he said, Father Abraham, deal kindly with me, and send Lazarus, that he may dip the tip of his finger in water, and may cool my tongue, because I am distressed in this flame. ²⁵And Abraham said, Child, remember that you received your good things in your life, and Lazarus in like manner the evil things, and now he is comforted, and you are distressed; ²⁶and besides all these things, between us and you a great chasm is fixed, so that they who are willing to go over from here to you are not able, nor do they pass through from there to us. ²⁷And he said, I ask, then, father, that you may send him to the house of my father, ²⁸for I have five brothers, so that he may thoroughly testify to them, that they also may not come to this place of torment. ²⁹Abraham says to him, They have Moses and the prophets, let them hear them; ³⁰and he said, No, father Abraham, but if anyone from the dead may go to them, they will convert. ³¹And he said to him, If they do not hear Moses

and the prophets, neither will they be persuaded if one may rise out of the dead."

CHAPTER 17

¹And He said to the disciples, "It is impossible for the stumbling blocks not to come, but woe [to him] through whom they come; ²it is more profitable to him if a weighty millstone is put around his neck, and he has been cast into the sea, than that he may cause one of these little ones to stumble. ³Take heed to yourselves, and if your brother may sin in regard to you, rebuke him, and if he may change his mind, forgive him, ⁴and if seven times in the day he may sin against you, and seven times in the day may return to you, saying, I change my mind, you will forgive him." ⁵And the apostles said to the LORD, "Add to us faith"; ⁶and the LORD said, "If you had faith as a grain of mustard, you would have said to this sycamine, Be uprooted, and be planted in the sea, and it would have obeyed you. ⁷But who is he of you—having a servant plowing or feeding—who, to him having come in out of the field, will say, Having come, recline at once? ⁸But will not [rather] say to him, Prepare what I may dine, and having girded yourself around, minister to me, until I eat and drink, and after these things you will eat and drink? ⁹Does he have favor to that servant because he did the things directed? I think not. ¹⁰So also you, when you may have done all the things directed you, say, We are unprofitable servants, because that which we owed to do we have done." ¹¹And it came to pass, in His going on to Jerusalem, that He passed through the midst of Samaria and Galilee, ¹²and He entering into a certain village, there ten leprous men met Him, who stood far off, ¹³and they lifted up the voice, saying, "Jesus, Master, deal kindly with us"; ¹⁴and having seen [them], He said to them, "Having gone on, show yourselves to the priests"; and it came to pass, in their going, they were cleansed, ¹⁵and one of them having seen that he was healed turned back, glorifying God with a loud voice, ¹⁶and he fell on [his] face at His feet, giving thanks to Him, and he was a Samaritan. ¹⁷And Jesus answering said, "Were not the ten cleansed, and the nine—where? ¹⁸There were none found who turned back to give glory to God, except this foreigner"; ¹⁹and He said to him, "Having risen, be going on, your faith has saved you." ²⁰And having been questioned by the Pharisees when the Kingdom of God comes, He answered them and said, "The Kingdom of God does not come with observation; ²¹nor will they say, Behold, here; or, Behold, there; for behold, the Kingdom of God is within you." ²²And He said to His disciples, "Days will come when you will desire to see one of the days of the Son of Man and you will not behold [it]; ²³and they will say to you, Behold, here; or, Behold, there; you may not go away, nor follow; ²⁴for as the lightning is flashing out of one [part] under the sky [and] shines to the other [part] under the sky, so will the Son of Man also be in His day; ²⁵and first it is necessary for Him to suffer many things, and to be rejected by this generation. ²⁶And as it came to pass in the days of Noah, so will it also be in the days of the Son of Man; ²⁷they were eating, they were drinking, they were marrying, they were given in marriage, until the day that Noah entered into the Ark, and the flood came, and destroyed all; ²⁸in like manner also, as it came to pass in the days of Lot; they were eating, they were drinking, they were buying, they were selling, they were planting, they were building; ²⁹and on the day Lot went forth from Sodom, He rained fire and brimstone from the sky, and destroyed all. ³⁰According to these things it will be, in the day the Son of Man is revealed; ³¹in that day, he who will be on the housetop, and his vessels in the house, do not let him come down to take them away; and he in the field, in like manner, do not let him turn backward; ³²remember the wife of Lot. ³³Whoever may seek to save his life, will lose it; and whoever may lose it, will preserve it. ³⁴I say to you, in that night there will be two [men] on one bed: one will be taken, and the other will be left; ³⁵two [women] will be grinding at the same place together: one will be taken, and the other will be left; ³⁶[[two [men] will be in the field: one will be taken, and the other left."]] ³⁷And they answering say to Him, "Where, Lord?" And He said to them, "Where the body [is], there the eagles will be gathered together."

CHAPTER 18

¹And He also spoke an allegory to them, that it is always necessary to pray and not to faint, ²saying, "A certain judge was in a certain city—he is not fearing God, and he is not regarding man— ³and a widow was in that city, and she was coming to him, saying, Do me justice on my opponent, ⁴and he would not for a time, but after these things he said in himself, Even if I do not fear God, and do not regard man, ⁵yet because this widow gives me trouble, I will do her justice, lest, continuously coming, she may bruise me." ⁶And the LORD said, "Hear what the unrighteous judge says: ⁷and will God not execute justice to His chosen ones, who are crying to Him day and night—bearing long in regard to them? ⁸I say to you that He will execute justice to them quickly; but the Son of Man having come, will He find faith on the earth?" ⁹And He also spoke to some who have been trusting in themselves that they were righteous, and have been despising the rest, this allegory: ¹⁰"Two men went up to the temple to pray, one a Pharisee, and the other a tax collector; ¹¹the Pharisee having stood by himself, thus prayed: God, I thank You that I am not as the rest of men, rapacious, unrighteous, adulterers, or even as this tax collector; ¹²I fast twice in the week, I give tithes of all things—as many as I possess. ¹³And the tax collector, having stood far off, would not even lift up the eyes to the sky, but was striking on his breast, saying, God be propitious to me—the sinner! ¹⁴I say to you, this one went down declared righteous, to his house, rather than that one: for everyone who is exalting himself will be humbled, and he who is humbling himself will be exalted." ¹⁵And they were also bringing the babies near, that He may touch them, and the disciples having seen, rebuked them, ¹⁶and Jesus having called them near, said, "Permit the little children to come to Me, and do not forbid them, for of such is the Kingdom of God; ¹⁷truly I say to you, whoever may not receive the Kingdom of God as a little child, may not enter into it." ¹⁸And a certain ruler questioned Him, saying, "Good Teacher, what having done—will I inherit continuous life?" ¹⁹And Jesus said to him, "Why do you call Me good? No one [is] good, except one—God; ²⁰you have known the commands: You may not commit adultery, You may not murder, You may not steal, You may not bear false witness, Honor your father and your mother." ²¹And he said, "All these I kept from my youth"; ²²and having heard these things, Jesus said to him, "Yet one thing to you is lacking: all things—as many as you have—sell, and distribute to the poor, and you will have treasure in Heaven, and come, follow Me"; ²³and he, having heard these things, became very sorrowful, for he was exceedingly rich. ²⁴And Jesus having seen him become very sorrowful, said, "How hardly will those having riches enter into the Kingdom of God! ²⁵For it is easier for a camel to enter through the eye of a needle, than for a rich man to enter into the Kingdom of God." ²⁶And those who heard, said, "And who is able to be saved?" ²⁷And He said, "The things impossible with men are possible with God." ²⁸And Peter said, "Behold, we left all, and followed You"; ²⁹and He said to them, "Truly I say to you that there is not one who left house, or parents, or brothers, or wife, or children, for the sake of the Kingdom of God, ³⁰who may not receive back manifold more in this time, and in the coming age, continuous life." ³¹And having taken the Twelve aside, He said to them, "Behold, we go up to Jerusalem, and all things will be accomplished that have been written through the prophets to the Son of Man, ³²for He will be delivered up to the nations, and will be mocked, and insulted, and spit on, ³³and having scourged they will put Him to death, and on the third day He will rise again." ³⁴And they understood none of these things, and this saying was hid from them, and they were not knowing the things said. ³⁵And it came to pass, in His coming near to Jericho, a certain blind man was sitting beside the way begging, ³⁶and having heard a multitude going by, he was inquiring what this may be, ³⁷and they brought him word that Jesus the Nazarene passes by, ³⁸and he cried out, saying, "Jesus, Son of David, deal kindly with me"; ³⁹and those going before were rebuking him, that he might be silent, but he was crying out much more, "Son of David, deal kindly with me!" ⁴⁰And Jesus having stood, commanded him to be brought

to Him, and he having come near, He questioned him, ⁴¹saying, "What do you will I will do to you?" And he said, "Lord, that I may receive sight." ⁴²And Jesus said to him, "Receive your sight; your faith has saved you"; ⁴³and instantly he received sight, and was following Him, glorifying God; and all the people, having seen, gave praise to God.

CHAPTER 19

¹And having entered, He was passing through Jericho, ²and behold, a man, by name called Zaccheus, and he was a chief tax collector, and he was rich, ³and he was seeking to see Jesus, who He is, and was not able for the multitude, because he was small in stature, ⁴and having run forward before, he went up on a sycamore, that he may see Him, because through that [way] He was about to pass by. ⁵And as Jesus came up to the place, having looked up, He saw him and said to him, "Zaccheus, having hurried, come down, for it is necessary for Me to remain in your house today"; ⁶and he having hurried came down, and received Him rejoicing; ⁷and having seen [it], they were all murmuring, saying, "He went in to lodge with a sinful man!" ⁸And Zaccheus having stood, said to the LORD, "Behold, half of my goods, Lord, I give to the poor, and if I took by false accusation anything of anyone, I give back fourfold." ⁹And Jesus said to him, "Today salvation came to this house, inasmuch as he also is a son of Abraham; ¹⁰for the Son of Man came to seek and to save the lost." ¹¹And while they are hearing these things, having added He spoke an allegory, because of His being near to Jerusalem, and of their thinking that the Kingdom of God is immediately about to appear. ¹²He therefore said, "A certain man of birth went on to a far country, to take to himself a kingdom, and to return, ¹³and having called ten servants of his own, he gave ten minas to them and said to them, Do business—until I come; ¹⁴and his citizens were hating him, and sent a delegation after him, saying, We do not wish this one to reign over us. ¹⁵And it came to pass, on his coming back, having taken the kingdom, that he commanded these servants to be called to him, to whom he gave the money, that he might know what anyone had done in business. ¹⁶And the first came near, saying, Lord, your mina gained ten minas; ¹⁷and he said to him, Well done, good servant, because you became faithful in a very little, be having authority over ten cities. ¹⁸And the second came, saying, Lord, your mina made five minas; ¹⁹and he also said to this one, And you, become [ruler] over five cities. ²⁰And another came, saying, Lord, behold, your mina, that I had lying away in a napkin; ²¹for I was afraid of you, because you are an austere man; you take up what you did not lay down, and reap what you did not sow. ²²And he says to him, Out of your mouth I will judge you, evil servant: you knew that I am an austere man, taking up what I did not lay down, and reaping what I did not sow! ²³And why did you not give my money to the bank, and I, having come, might have received it with interest? ²⁴And to those standing by he said, Take the mina from him, and give to him having the ten minas— ²⁵(and they said to him, Lord, he has ten minas)— ²⁶for I say to you that to everyone having will be given, and from him not having, also what he has will be taken from him, ²⁷but those my enemies, who did not wish me to reign over them, bring here and slay before me." ²⁸And having said these things, He went on before, going up to Jerusalem. ²⁹And it came to pass, as He came near to Bethphage and Bethany, to that called the Mount of Olives, He sent two of His disciples, ³⁰having said, "Go away into the village in front of [you], in which, entering in, you will find a colt bound, on which no one of men ever sat, having loosed it, bring [it]; ³¹and if anyone questions you, Why do you loose [it]? Thus you will say to him: The LORD has need of it." ³²And those sent, having gone away, found according as He said to them, ³³and while they are loosing the colt, its owners said to them, "Why do you loose the colt?" ³⁴And they said, "The LORD has need of it"; ³⁵and they brought it to Jesus, and having cast their garments on the colt, they sat Jesus on it. ³⁶And as He is going, they were spreading their garments in the way, ³⁷and as He is coming near now, at the descent of the Mount of Olives, the whole multitude of the disciples began rejoicing to praise God with a great voice for all the mighty works they had seen, ³⁸saying, "Blessed [is] the King coming in the Name of the LORD; peace in Heaven, and glory in the highest!" ³⁹And certain of the Pharisees from the multitude said to Him, "Teacher, rebuke Your disciples"; ⁴⁰and He answering said to them, "I say to you that if these will be silent, the stones will cry out!" ⁴¹And when He came near, having seen the city, He wept over it, ⁴²saying, "If you knew, even you, at least in this your day, the things for your peace; but now they were hid from your eyes. ⁴³Because days will come on you, and your enemies will cast a rampart around you, and surround you around, and press you on every side, ⁴⁴and lay you low, and your children within you, and they will not leave in you a stone on a stone, because you did not know the time of your inspection." ⁴⁵And having entered into the temple, He began to cast forth those selling in it, and those buying, ⁴⁶saying to them, "It has been written, My house is a house of prayer—but you made it a den of robbers." ⁴⁷And He was teaching daily in the temple, but the chief priests and the scribes were seeking to destroy Him—also the chiefs of the people— ⁴⁸and they were not finding what they will do, for all the people were hanging on Him, hearing Him.

CHAPTER 20

¹And it came to pass, on one of those days, as He is teaching the people in the temple, and proclaiming good news, the chief priests and the scribes, with the elders, came on [Him], ²and spoke to Him, saying, "Tell us by what authority You do these things? Or who is he that gave to You this authority?" ³And He answering said to them, "I will question you—I also—one thing, and tell Me: ⁴the immersion of John, was it from Heaven, or from men?" ⁵And they reasoned with themselves, saying, "If we may say, From Heaven, He will say, Why, then, did you not believe him? ⁶And if we may say, From men, all the people will stone us, for they are having been persuaded John to be a prophet." ⁷And they answered that they did not know from where [it was], ⁸and Jesus said to them, "Neither do I say to you by what authority I do these things." ⁹And He began to speak to the people this allegory: "A certain man planted a vineyard, and gave it out to farmers, and went abroad for a long time, ¹⁰and at the season he sent a servant to the farmers, that they may give to him from the fruit of the vineyard, but the farmers having beat him, sent [him] away empty. ¹¹And he added to send another servant, and they also having beaten and dishonored that one, sent [him] away empty; ¹²and he added to send a third, and this one also, having wounded, they cast out. ¹³And the owner of the vineyard said, What will I do? I will send my son, the beloved, perhaps having seen this one, they will respect [him]; ¹⁴and having seen him, the farmers reasoned among themselves, saying, This is the heir; come, we may kill him, that the inheritance may become ours; ¹⁵and having cast him outside of the vineyard, they killed [him]; what, then, will the owner of the vineyard do to them? ¹⁶He will come, and destroy these farmers, and will give the vineyard to others." And having heard, they said, "Let it not be!" ¹⁷And He, having looked on them, said, "What, then, is this that has been written: A stone that the builders rejected—this became head of a corner? ¹⁸Everyone who has fallen on that stone will be broken, and on whom it may fall, it will crush him to pieces." ¹⁹And the chief priests and the scribes sought to lay hands on Him in that hour, and they feared the people, for they knew that He spoke this allegory against them. ²⁰And having watched [Him], they sent forth ones lying in wait, feigning themselves to be righteous, that they might take hold of His word, to deliver Him up to the rule and to the authority of the governor, ²¹and they questioned Him, saying, "Teacher, we have known that You say and teach correctly, and do not receive a person, but in truth teach the way of God. ²²Is it lawful to us to give tribute to Caesar or not?" ²³And He, having perceived their craftiness, said to them, "Why do you tempt Me? ²⁴Show Me a denarius; of whom does it have an image and inscription?" And they answering said, "Of Caesar": ²⁵and He said to them, "Give back, therefore, the things of Caesar to Caesar, and the things of God to God"; ²⁶and they were not able to take hold on His saying before the people, and having wondered at His answer, they were silent. ²⁷And certain of the Sadducees, who are denying that there is a resurrection, having come near, questioned Him, ²⁸saying, "Teacher, Moses wrote to us if anyone's brother may die, having a wife, and he may die childless—that his brother may take the wife, and may raise up seed to his brother. ²⁹There were, then, seven brothers,

LUKE

and the first having taken a wife, died childless, ³⁰and the second took the wife, and he died childless, ³¹and the third took her, and in like manner also the seven—they left no children, and they died; ³²and last of all the woman also died: ³³in the resurrection, then, of which of them does she become wife? For the seven had her as wife." ³⁴And Jesus answering said to them, "The sons of this age marry and are given in marriage, ³⁵but those accounted worthy to obtain that age, and the resurrection that is out of the dead, neither marry, nor are they given in marriage; ³⁶for neither are they able to die anymore—for they are like messengers—and they are sons of God, being sons of the resurrection. ³⁷And that the dead are raised, even Moses showed at the Bush, since he calls the LORD the God of Abraham, and the God of Isaac, and the God of Jacob; ³⁸and He is not a God of dead men, but of living, for all live to Him." ³⁹And certain of the scribes answering said, "Teacher, You said well"; ⁴⁰and they no longer dared question Him anything. ⁴¹And He said to them, "How do they say the Christ is [the] son of David, ⁴²and David himself says in [the] Scroll of Psalms, The LORD said to my Lord, || Sit on My right hand, ⁴³Until I will make Your enemies Your footstool; ⁴⁴David, then, calls Him Lord, and how is He his son?" ⁴⁵And all the people hearing, He said to His disciples, ⁴⁶"Take heed of the scribes, who are wishing to walk in long robes, and are cherishing salutations in the markets, and first seats in the synagogues, and first couches at the banquets, ⁴⁷who devour the houses of the widows, and make long prayers for a pretense, these will receive more abundant judgment."

CHAPTER 21

¹And having looked up, He saw those who cast their gifts into the treasury—rich men, ²and He also saw a certain poor widow casting two mites there, ³and He said, "Truly I say to you that this poor widow cast in more than all; ⁴for all these out of their superabundance cast into the gifts to God, but this one out of her want, all the living that she had, cast in." ⁵And [as] some were speaking about the temple, that it has been adorned with good stones and devoted things, He said, ⁶"These things that you behold—days will come in which there will not be left a stone on a stone that will not be thrown down." ⁷And they questioned Him, saying, "Teacher, when, then, will these things be? And what [is] the sign when these things may be about to happen?" ⁸And He said, "See—you may not be led astray, for many will come in My Name, saying, I am [He], and the time has come near; do not then go on after them; ⁹and when you may hear of wars and uprisings, do not be terrified, for it is necessary for these things to happen first, but the end [is] not immediately." ¹⁰Then He said to them, "Nation will rise against nation, and kingdom against kingdom, ¹¹also great shakings, and there will be famines and pestilences in every place; also there will be fearful things and great signs from the sky; ¹²and before all these, they will lay on you their hands, and persecute, delivering up to synagogues and prisons, being brought before kings and governors for My Name's sake; ¹³and it will become to you for a testimony. ¹⁴Settle, then, to your hearts, not to meditate beforehand to reply, ¹⁵for I will give to you a mouth and wisdom that all your opposers will not be able to refute or resist. ¹⁶And you will be delivered up also by parents, and brothers, and relatives, and friends, and they will put [some] of you to death; ¹⁷and you will be hated by all because of My Name— ¹⁸and a hair out of your head will not perish; ¹⁹in your patience possess your souls. ²⁰And when you may see Jerusalem surrounded by encampments, then know that her desolation has come near; ²¹then those in Judea, let them flee to the mountains; and those in her midst, let them depart out; and those in the countries, do not let them come in to her; ²²because these are days of vengeance, to fulfill all things that have been written. ²³And woe to those with child, and to those giving suck, in those days; for there will be great distress on the land, and wrath on this people; ²⁴and they will fall by the mouth of the sword, and will be led captive to all the nations, and Jerusalem will be trodden down by nations, until the times of nations be fulfilled. ²⁵And there will be signs in sun, and moon, and stars, and on the earth distress of nations with perplexity, sea and wave roaring; ²⁶men fainting at heart from fear, and expectation of the things coming on the world, for the powers of the heavens will be shaken. ²⁷And then they will see the Son of Man coming in a cloud, with power and much glory; ²⁸and these things beginning to happen, bend yourselves back, and lift up your heads, because your redemption draws near." ²⁹And He spoke an allegory to them: "See the fig tree, and all the trees, ³⁰when they may now cast forth, having seen, of yourselves you know that now the summer is near; ³¹so also you, when you may see these things happening, you know that the Kingdom of God is near; ³²truly I say to you, this generation may not pass away until all may have come to pass; ³³the sky and the earth will pass away, but My words may not pass away. ³⁴And take heed to yourselves lest your hearts may be weighed down with carousing, and drunkenness, and anxieties of life, and suddenly that day may come on you, ³⁵for it will come as a snare on all those dwelling on the face of all the earth, ³⁶watch, then, in every season, praying that you may be accounted worthy to escape all these things that are about to come to pass, and to stand before the Son of Man." ³⁷And He was teaching in the temple during the days, and during the nights, going forth, He was lodging at [that] called the Mount of Olives; ³⁸and all the people were coming early to Him in the temple to hear Him.

CHAPTER 22

¹And the Celebration of the Unleavened [Bread] was coming near, that is called Passover, ²and the chief priests and the scribes were seeking how they may take Him up, for they were afraid of the people. ³And Satan entered into Judas, who is surnamed Iscariot, being of the number of the Twelve, ⁴and he, having gone away, spoke with the chief priests and the magistrates, how he might deliver Him up to them, ⁵and they rejoiced, and covenanted to give him money, ⁶and he agreed, and was seeking a favorable season to deliver Him up to them without tumult. ⁷And the day of the Unleavened [Bread] came, in which it was necessary [for] the Passover to be sacrificed, ⁸and He sent Peter and John, saying, "Having gone on, prepare to us the Passover, that we may eat"; ⁹and they said to Him, "Where do You will that we might prepare?" ¹⁰And He said to them, "Behold, in your entering into the city, a man will meet you there, carrying a pitcher of water, follow him into the house where he goes in, ¹¹and you will say to the master of the house, The Teacher says to you, Where is the guest-chamber where I may eat the Passover with My disciples? ¹²And he will show you a large upper room furnished, make ready there"; ¹³and they, having gone away, found as He has said to them, and they made the Passover ready. ¹⁴And when the hour was come, He reclined, and the twelve apostles with Him, ¹⁵and He said to them, "With desire I desired to eat this Passover with you before My suffering, ¹⁶for I say to you that I may eat of it no longer until it may be fulfilled in the Kingdom of God." ¹⁷And having taken a cup, having given thanks, He said, "Take this and divide to yourselves, ¹⁸for I say to you that I may not drink of the produce of the vine until the Kingdom of God may come." ¹⁹And having taken bread, having given thanks, He broke and gave to them, saying, "This is My body, that is being given for you, do this in remembrance of Me." ²⁰In like manner, also, the cup after the dining, saying, "This cup [is] the New Covenant in My blood, that is being poured forth for you. ²¹But behold, the hand of him delivering Me up [is] with Me on the table, ²²and, indeed, the Son of Man goes according to what has been determined; but woe to that man through whom He is being delivered up." ²³And they began to reason among themselves who then of them it may be who is about to do this thing. ²⁴And there happened also a strife among them—who of them is accounted to be greater. ²⁵And He said to them, "The kings of the nations exercise lordship over them, and those exercising authority on them are called benefactors; ²⁶but you [are] not so, but he who is greater among you—let him be as the younger; and he who is leading, as he who is ministering; ²⁷for who is greater? He who is reclining, or he who is ministering? Is it not he who is reclining? And I am in your midst as He who is ministering. ²⁸And you are those who have remained with Me in My temptations, ²⁹and I appoint to you a kingdom, as My Father appointed to Me, ³⁰that you may eat and may drink at My table, in My kingdom, and may sit on thrones, judging the twelve tribes of Israel." ³¹And the LORD said, "Simon, Simon, behold, Satan asked for himself to sift you as the wheat, ³²and I implored for you that your faith may not fail; and you, when you turned,

strengthen your brothers." ³³And he said to Him, "Lord, I am ready to go with You both to prison and to death"; ³⁴and He said, "I say to you, Peter, a rooster will not crow today, before you may disown knowing Me three times." ³⁵And He said to them, "When I sent you without bag, and leather pouch, and sandals, did you lack anything?" And they said, "Nothing." ³⁶Then He said to them, "But now, he who is having a bag, let him take [it] up, and in like manner also a leather pouch; and he who is not having, let him sell his garment, and buy a sword, ³⁷for I say to you that this which has been written is necessary to be accomplished in Me: And He was reckoned with lawless ones; for also the things concerning Me have an end." ³⁸And they said, "Lord, behold, here [are] two swords"; and He said to them, "It is sufficient." ³⁹And having gone forth, He went on, according to custom, to the Mount of Olives, and His disciples also followed Him, ⁴⁰and having come to the place, He said to them, "Pray to not enter into temptation." ⁴¹And He was withdrawn from them, as it were a stone's cast, and having fallen on the knees He was praying, ⁴²saying, "Father, if You are willing, remove this cup from Me, but not My will, but Yours be done." ⁴³And there appeared to Him a messenger from Heaven strengthening Him; ⁴⁴and having been in agony, He was more earnestly praying, and His sweat became, as it were, great drops of blood falling on the ground. ⁴⁵And having risen up from the prayer, having come to the disciples, He found them sleeping from the sorrow, ⁴⁶and He said to them, "Why do you sleep? Having risen, pray that you may not enter into temptation." ⁴⁷And while He is speaking, behold, a multitude, and he who is called Judas, one of the Twelve, was coming before them, and he came near to Jesus to kiss Him, ⁴⁸and Jesus said to him, "Judas, do you deliver up the Son of Man with a kiss?" ⁴⁹And those around Him, having seen what was about to be, said to Him, "Lord, will we strike with a sword?" ⁵⁰And a certain one of them struck the servant of the chief priest, and took off his right ear, ⁵¹and Jesus answering said, "Permit thus far," and having touched his ear, He healed him. ⁵²And Jesus said to those having come on Him—chief priests, and magistrates of the temple, and elders, "Have you come forth with swords and sticks as on a robber? ⁵³While daily I was with you in the temple, you stretched forth no hands against Me; but this is your hour and the power of the darkness." ⁵⁴And having taken Him, they led and brought Him into the house of the chief priest. And Peter was following far off, ⁵⁵and they having kindled a fire in the midst of the court, and having sat down together, Peter was sitting in the midst of them, ⁵⁶and a certain maid having seen him sitting at the light, and having earnestly looked at him, she said, "And this one was with Him!" ⁵⁷And he disowned Him, saying, "Woman, I have not known Him." ⁵⁸And after a while, another having seen him, said, "And you are of them!" And Peter said, "Man, I am not." ⁵⁹And one hour, as it were, having intervened, a certain other was confidently affirming, saying, "Of a truth this one also was with Him, for he is also a Galilean"; ⁶⁰and Peter said, "Man, I have not known what you say"; and immediately, while he is speaking, a rooster crowed. ⁶¹And the LORD, having turned, looked on Peter, and Peter remembered the word of the LORD, how He said to him, "Before a rooster will crow, you may disown Me three times"; ⁶²and Peter having gone outside, wept bitterly. ⁶³And the men who were holding Jesus were mocking Him, beating [Him]; ⁶⁴and having blindfolded Him, they were striking Him on the face, and were questioning Him, saying, "Prophesy who he is who struck You?" ⁶⁵And many other things, slandering, they spoke in regard to Him. ⁶⁶And when it became day there was gathered together the eldership of the people, chief priests also, and scribes, and they led Him up to their own Sanhedrin, ⁶⁷saying, "If You are the Christ, tell us." And He said to them, "If I may tell you, you will not believe; ⁶⁸and if I also question [you], you will not answer Me or send Me away; ⁶⁹from now on, there will be the Son of Man sitting on the right hand of the power of God." ⁷⁰And they all said, "You, then, are the Son of God?" And He said to them, "You say [it], because I AM"; ⁷¹and they said, "What need do we have yet of testimony? For we ourselves heard [it] from His mouth."

CHAPTER 23

¹And having risen, the whole multitude of them led Him to Pilate, ²and began to accuse Him, saying, "We found this One perverting the nation, and forbidding to give tribute to Caesar, saying Himself to be Christ, a king." ³And Pilate questioned Him, saying, "You are the King of the Jews?" And He answering him, said, "You say [it]." ⁴And Pilate said to the chief priests and the multitude, "I find no fault in this Man"; ⁵and they were the more urgent, saying, "He stirs up the people, teaching throughout the whole of Judea—having begun from Galilee—to this place." ⁶And Pilate having heard of Galilee, questioned if the Man is a Galilean, ⁷and having known that He is from the jurisdiction of Herod, he sent Him back to Herod, he also being in Jerusalem in those days. ⁸And Herod rejoiced exceedingly having seen Jesus, for he was wishing to see Him for a long [time], because of hearing many things about Him, and he was hoping to see some sign done by Him, ⁹and was questioning Him in many words, and He answered him nothing. ¹⁰And the chief priests and the scribes stood vehemently accusing Him, ¹¹and Herod with his soldiers having set Him at nothing, and having mocked, having cast radiant apparel around Him, sent Him back to Pilate, ¹²and both Pilate and Herod became friends with one another on that day, for they were previously at enmity between themselves. ¹³And Pilate having called together the chief priests, and the rulers, and the people, ¹⁴said to them, "You brought this Man to me as perverting the people, and behold, I having examined [Him] before you, found no fault in this Man in those things you bring forward against Him; ¹⁵no, neither Herod, for he sent Him back to us, and behold, nothing worthy of death is having been done by Him; ¹⁶having corrected, therefore, I will release Him," ¹⁷[[for it was necessary for him to release to them one at every celebration,]] ¹⁸and they cried out—the whole multitude—saying, "Away with this One, and release Barabbas to us," ¹⁹who had been cast into prison, because of a certain sedition made in the city, and murder. ²⁰Pilate again then—wishing to release Jesus—called to them, ²¹but they were calling out, saying, "Crucify! Crucify Him!" ²²And he said to them a third time, "Why, what evil did He do? I found no cause of death in Him; having corrected Him, then, I will release [Him]." ²³And they were pressing with loud voices asking Him to be crucified, and their voices, and those of the chief priests, were prevailing, ²⁴and Pilate gave judgment for their request being done, ²⁵and he released him who because of sedition and murder has been cast into the prison, whom they were asking for, and he gave up Jesus to their will. ²⁶And as they led Him away, having taken hold on Simon, a certain Cyrenian, coming from the field, they put the cross on him to carry [it] behind Jesus. ²⁷And a great multitude of the people were following Him, and of women, who also were beating themselves and lamenting Him, ²⁸and Jesus having turned to them, said, "Daughters of Jerusalem, do not weep for Me, but weep for yourselves and for your children; ²⁹for behold, days come in which they will say, Blessed the barren, and wombs that did not bear, and breasts that did not give suck; ³⁰then they will begin to say to the mountains, Fall on us, and to the hills, Cover us; ³¹for if they do these things in the green tree, what may happen in the dry?" ³²And there were also others—two evildoers—with Him, to be put to death; ³³and when they came to the place that is called "[Place] of [the] Skull," there they crucified Him and the evildoers, one on the right hand and one on the left. ³⁴And Jesus said, "Father, forgive them, for they have not known what they do"; and parting His garments they cast a lot. ³⁵And the people were standing, looking on, and the rulers were also sneering with them, saying, "He saved others, let Him save Himself, if this be the Christ, the Chosen One of God." ³⁶And the soldiers were also mocking Him, coming near and offering vinegar to Him, ³⁷and saying, "If You are the King of the Jews, save Yourself." ³⁸And there was also an inscription written over Him [[in letters of Greek, and Latin, and Hebrew]]: "THIS IS THE KING OF THE JEWS." ³⁹And one of the evildoers who were hanged was slandering Him, saying, "If You are the Christ, save Yourself and us." ⁴⁰And the other answering, was rebuking him, saying, "Do you not even fear God, that you are in the same judgment? ⁴¹And we indeed justly, for we are receiving back [things] worthy of what we did, but this One did nothing out of place"; ⁴²and he said to Jesus, "Remember me, Lord, when You may come in Your kingdom"; ⁴³and Jesus said to him, "Truly I say to you, today you will be with Me in Paradise." ⁴⁴And it was, as it were, the sixth

LUKE

hour, and darkness came over all the land until the ninth hour, ⁴⁵and the sun was darkened, and the veil of the temple was torn in the middle, ⁴⁶and having cried with a loud voice, Jesus said, "Father, into Your hands I commit My spirit"; now having said this, He breathed His last. ⁴⁷And the centurion having seen what was done, glorified God, saying, "Truly this Man was righteous"; ⁴⁸and all the multitudes having come together to this sight, beholding the things that came to pass, turned back striking their breasts; ⁴⁹and all His acquaintances stood far off, and women who followed Him from Galilee, beholding these things. ⁵⁰And behold, a man, by name Joseph, being a counselor, a man good and righteous, ⁵¹from Arimathea, a city of the Jews, who also himself was expecting the Kingdom of God, he was not consenting to their counsel and deed, ⁵²he having gone near to Pilate, asked for the body of Jesus, ⁵³and having taken it down, he wrapped it in fine linen, and placed it in a hewn out tomb, where no one was yet laid. ⁵⁴And it was [the] Day of Preparation, and Sabbath was approaching, ⁵⁵and the women who also have come with Him out of Galilee having followed after, beheld the tomb, and how His body was placed, ⁵⁶and having turned back, they made ready spices and ointments, and on the Sabbath, indeed, they rested, according to the command.

CHAPTER 24

¹And on the first [day] of the weeks, at early dawn, they came to the tomb, carrying the spices they made ready, and certain [others] with them, ²and they found the stone having been rolled away from the tomb, ³and having gone in, they did not find the body of the Lord Jesus. ⁴And it came to pass, while they are perplexed about this, that behold, two men stood by them in clothing—flashing [with light]; ⁵and on their having become afraid, and having inclined the face to the earth, they said to them, "Why do you seek the living with the dead? ⁶He is not here, but was raised; remember how He spoke to you, being yet in Galilee, ⁷saying, It is necessary for the Son of Man to be delivered up into the hands of sinful men, and to be crucified, and to rise again [on] the third day." ⁸And they remembered His sayings, ⁹and having turned back from the tomb, told all these things to the Eleven, and to all the rest. ¹⁰And it was Mary the Magdalene, and Joanna, and Mary of James, and the other women with them, who told these things to the apostles, ¹¹and their sayings appeared before them as idle talk, and they were not believing them. ¹²And Peter having risen, ran to the tomb, and having stooped down he sees the linen clothes lying alone, and he went away to his own home, wondering at that having come to pass. ¹³And behold, two of them were going on during that day to a village, being sixty stadia distant from Jerusalem, the name of which [is] Emmaus, ¹⁴and they were conversing with one another about all these things that have happened. ¹⁵And it came to pass in their conversing and reasoning together, that Jesus Himself, having come near, was going on with them, ¹⁶and their eyes were restrained so as not to know Him, ¹⁷and He said to them, "What [are] these words that you exchange with one another, walking, and you are sad?" ¹⁸And one, whose name was Cleopas, answering, said to Him, "Are You alone visiting Jerusalem and have not known the things having come to pass in it in these days?" ¹⁹And He said to them, "What things?" And they said to Him, "The things about Jesus of Nazareth, who became a man—a prophet—powerful in deed and word, before God and all the people, ²⁰how also the chief priests and our rulers delivered Him up to a judgment of death, and crucified Him; ²¹and we were hoping that it is He who is about to redeem Israel, and also with all these things, this third day is passing today since these things happened. ²²And certain of our women also astonished us, coming early to the tomb, ²³and having not found His body, they came, saying to have also seen an apparition of messengers who say He is alive, ²⁴and certain of those with us went away to the tomb, and found [it] so, even as the women said, and they did not see Him." ²⁵And He said to them, "O inconsiderate and slow in heart to believe on all that the prophets spoke! ²⁶Was it not necessary [for] the Christ to suffer these things, and to enter into His glory?" ²⁷And having begun from Moses, and from all the Prophets, He was expounding to them in all the Writings the things about Himself. ²⁸And they came near to the village to where they were going, and He made an appearance of going on further, ²⁹and they constrained Him, saying, "Remain with us, for it is toward evening," and the day declined, and He went in to remain with them. ³⁰And it came to pass, in His reclining with them, having taken the bread, He blessed, and having broken, He was giving to them, ³¹and their eyes were opened, and they recognized Him, and He became unseen by them. ³²And they said to one another, "Was our heart not burning within us as He was speaking to us in the way, and as He was opening the Writings up to us?" ³³And they, having risen up the same hour, turned back to Jerusalem, and found the Eleven gathered together, and those with them, ³⁴saying, "The Lord was indeed raised, and was seen by Simon"; ³⁵and they were expounding the things in the way, and how He was made known to them in the breaking of the bread, ³⁶and as they are speaking these things, Jesus Himself stood in the midst of them, and says to them, "Peace to you"; ³⁷and being amazed, and becoming frightened, they were thinking themselves to see a spirit. ³⁸And He said to them, "Why are you troubled? And why do reasonings come up in your hearts? ³⁹See My hands and My feet, that I am He; handle Me and see, because a spirit does not have flesh and bones as you see Me having." ⁴⁰And having said this, He showed the hands and the feet to them, ⁴¹and while they are not believing from the joy, and wondering, He said to them, "Do you have anything here to eat?" ⁴²And they gave to Him part of a broiled fish, and of a honeycomb, ⁴³and having taken, He ate before them, ⁴⁴and He said to them, "These [are] the words that I spoke to you, being yet with you, that it is necessary to be fulfilled all the things that are written in the Law of Moses, and the Prophets, and the Psalms, about Me." ⁴⁵Then He opened up their understanding to understand the Writings, ⁴⁶and He said to them, "Thus it has been written, and thus it was necessary [for] the Christ to suffer, and to rise out of the dead [on] the third day, ⁴⁷and conversion and forgiveness of sins is to be proclaimed in His Name to all the nations, beginning from Jerusalem: ⁴⁸and you are witnesses of these things. ⁴⁹And behold, I send the promise of My Father on you, but you—abide in the city of Jerusalem until you are clothed with power from on high." ⁵⁰And He led them forth outside—to Bethany, and having lifted up His hands He blessed them, ⁵¹and it came to pass, in His blessing them, He was parted from them, and was carried up into Heaven; ⁵²and they, having worshiped Him, turned back to Jerusalem with great joy, ⁵³and were continually in the temple, praising and blessing God. Amen.

JOHN

CHAPTER 1

¹In the beginning was the Word, and the Word was with God, and the Word was God; ²this One was in the beginning with God; ³all things happened through Him, and without Him not even one thing happened that has happened. ⁴In Him was life, and the life was the light of men, ⁵and the light shined in the darkness, and the darkness did not perceive it. ⁶There came a man—having been sent from God—whose name [is] John, ⁷this one came for testimony, that he might testify about the Light, that all might believe through him; ⁸that one was not the Light, but—that he might testify about the Light. ⁹He was the true Light, which enlightens every man, coming into the world; ¹⁰He was in the world, and the world was made through Him, and the world did not know Him: ¹¹He came to [His] own, and [His] own did not receive Him; ¹²but as many as received Him, to them He gave authority to become sons of God—to those believing in His Name, ¹³who were begotten, not of blood, nor of will of flesh, nor of will of man, but of God. ¹⁴And the Word

became flesh, and dwelt among us, and we beheld His glory, glory as of [the] only begotten of [the] Father, full of grace and truth. ¹⁵John testifies concerning Him, and has cried, saying, "This was He of whom I said, He who is coming after me has come before me, for He was before me." ¹⁶And we all received out of His fullness, and grace for grace; ¹⁷for the Law was given through Moses, the grace and the truth came through Jesus Christ. ¹⁸No one has ever seen God; the only begotten God who is on the bosom of the Father—He has expounded [Him]. ¹⁹And this is the testimony of John when the Jews sent priests and Levites out of Jerusalem, that they might question him, "Who are you?" ²⁰And he confessed and did not deny, and confessed, "I am not the Christ." ²¹And they questioned him, "What then? Are you Elijah?" And he says, "I am not." "Are you the prophet?" And he answered, "No." ²²Then they said to him, "Who are you, that we may give an answer to those sending us? What do you say concerning yourself?" ²³He said, "I [am] a voice of one crying in the wilderness: Make straight the way of the LORD, as Isaiah the prophet said." ²⁴And those sent were of the Pharisees, ²⁵and they questioned him and said to him, "Why, then, do you immerse, if you are not the Christ, nor Elijah, nor the prophet?" ²⁶John answered them, saying, "I immerse in water, but in the midst of you has stood He whom you have not known, it is this One who is coming after me, who has been before me, ²⁷of whom I am not worthy that I may loose the strap of His sandal." ²⁸These things came to pass in Bethabara, beyond the Jordan, where John was immersing. ²⁹On the next day John sees Jesus coming to him and says, "Behold, the Lamb of God, who is taking away the sin of the world; ³⁰this is He concerning whom I said, After me comes a Man who has come before me, because He was before me: ³¹and I did not know Him, but that He might be revealed to Israel, because of this I came immersing in water." ³²And John testified, saying, "I have seen the Spirit coming down out of Heaven as a dove, and [that] One remained on Him; ³³and I did not know Him, but He who sent me to immerse in water, He said to me, On whomsoever you may see the Spirit coming down, and remaining on Him, this is He who is immersing in the Holy Spirit; ³⁴and I have seen, and have testified, that this is the Son of God." ³⁵On the next day, again, John was standing, and two of his disciples, ³⁶and having looked on Jesus walking, he says, "Behold, the Lamb of God"; ³⁷and the two disciples heard him speaking, and they followed Jesus. ³⁸And Jesus having turned, and having beheld them following, says to them, "What do you seek?" And they said to Him, "Rabbi" (which is, being interpreted, Teacher), "where do You remain?" ³⁹He says to them, "Come and see"; they came and saw where He remains, and they remained with Him that day and the hour was about the tenth. ⁴⁰Andrew, the brother of Simon Peter, was one of the two who heard from John, and followed Him; ⁴¹this one first finds his own brother Simon and says to him, "We have found the Messiah," (which is, being interpreted, Anointed One), ⁴²and he brought him to Jesus: and having looked on him, Jesus says, "You are Simon, the son of Jonas, you will be called Cephas," (which is interpreted, A rock). ⁴³On the next day He willed to go forth to Galilee, and He finds Philip and says to him, "Follow Me." ⁴⁴And Philip was from Bethsaida, of the city of Andrew and Peter; ⁴⁵Philip finds Nathanael and says to him, "Him of whom Moses wrote in the Law, and the Prophets, we have found, Jesus the Son of Joseph, who [is] from Nazareth!" ⁴⁶And Nathanael said to him, "Is any good thing able to be out of Nazareth?" Philip said to him, "Come and see." ⁴⁷Jesus saw Nathanael coming to Him, and He says concerning him, "Behold, truly an Israelite, in whom is no guile"; ⁴⁸Nathanael says to Him, "From where do You know me?" Jesus answered and said to him, "Before Philip's calling you, being under the fig tree, I saw you." ⁴⁹Nathanael answered and says to Him, "Rabbi, You are the Son of God, You are the King of Israel." ⁵⁰Jesus answered and said to him, "Because I said to you, I saw you under the fig tree, you believe; you will see greater things than these"; ⁵¹and He says to him, "Truly, truly, I say to you, from now on you will see Heaven opened, and the messengers of God going up and coming down on the Son of Man."

CHAPTER 2

¹And [on] the third day a wedding happened in Cana of Galilee, and the mother of Jesus was there, ²and also Jesus was called, and His disciples, to the wedding; ³and wine having failed, the mother of Jesus says to Him, "They have no wine"; ⁴Jesus says to her, "What [is that] to Me and to you, woman? My hour is not yet come." ⁵His mother says to the servants, "Whatever He may say to you—do." ⁶And there were six water-jugs of stone there, placed according to the purifying of the Jews, holding each two or three measures. ⁷Jesus says to them, "Fill the water-jugs with water"; and they filled them—to the brim; ⁸and He says to them, "Draw out, now, and carry to the headwaiter"; and they bore. ⁹And as the headwaiter tasted the water become wine, and did not know where it is from (but the servants knew, who have drawn the water), the headwaiter calls the bridegroom, ¹⁰and says to him, "Every man, at first, sets forth the good wine; and when they may have drunk freely, then the inferior; you kept the good wine until now." ¹¹This [is the] beginning of the signs Jesus did in Cana of Galilee, and revealed His glory, and His disciples believed in Him; ¹²after this He went down to Capernaum, He, and His mother, and His brothers, and His disciples; and they did not remain there many days. ¹³And the Passover of the Jews was near, and Jesus went up to Jerusalem, ¹⁴and He found in the temple those selling oxen, and sheep, and doves, and the money-changers sitting, ¹⁵and having made a whip of small cords, He put all forth out of the temple, also the sheep, and the oxen; and He poured out the coins of the money-changers, and He overthrew the tables, ¹⁶and He said to those selling the doves, "Take these things from here; do not make the house of My Father a house of merchandise." ¹⁷And His disciples remembered that it is written: "The zeal of Your house ate Me up"; ¹⁸the Jews then answered and said to Him, "What sign do You show to us—that You do these things?" ¹⁹Jesus answered and said to them, "Destroy this temple, and in three days I will raise it up." ²⁰The Jews, therefore, said, "This temple was built [in] forty-six years, and will You raise it up in three days?" ²¹But He spoke concerning the temple of His body; ²²when, then, He was raised out of the dead, His disciples remembered that He said this to them, and they believed the Writing, and the word that Jesus said. ²³And as He was in Jerusalem, in the Passover, in the celebration, many believed in His Name, beholding His signs that He was doing; ²⁴and Jesus Himself was not trusting Himself to them, because of His knowing all [men], ²⁵and because He had no need that any should testify concerning man, for He Himself was knowing what was in man.

CHAPTER 3

¹And there was a man of the Pharisees, his name Nicodemus, a ruler of the Jews; ²this one came to Him by night and said to Him, "Rabbi, we have known that You have come from God—a teacher, for no one is able to do these signs that You do, if God may not be with him." ³Jesus answered and said to him, "Truly, truly, I say to you, if anyone may not be born from above, he is not able to see the Kingdom of God"; ⁴Nicodemus says to Him, "How is a man able to be born, being old? Is he able to enter into the womb of his mother a second time, and to be born?" ⁵Jesus answered, "Truly, truly, I say to you, if anyone may not be born of water and the Spirit, he is not able to enter into the Kingdom of God; ⁶that which has been born of the flesh is flesh, and that which has been born of the Spirit is spirit. ⁷You may not wonder that I said to you, It is required for you to be born from above; ⁸the Spirit blows where [that] One wills, and you hear [that] One's voice, but you have not known from where [that] One comes, and to where [that] One goes; thus is everyone who has been born of the Spirit." ⁹Nicodemus answered and said to Him, "How are these things able to happen?" ¹⁰Jesus answered and said to him,

"You are the teacher of Israel and you do not know these things? ¹¹Truly, truly, I say to you, what We have known We speak, and what We have seen We testify, and you do not receive Our testimony; ¹²if I spoke to you of the earthly things, and you do not believe, how, if I will speak to you of the heavenly things, will you believe? ¹³And no one has gone up to Heaven, except He who came down out of Heaven—the Son of Man who is in Heaven. ¹⁴And as Moses lifted up the serpent in the wilderness, so it is necessary for the Son of Man to be lifted up, ¹⁵that everyone who is believing in Him may not perish, but may have continuous life, ¹⁶for God so loved the world that He gave the only begotten Son, that everyone who is believing in Him may not perish, but may have continuous life. ¹⁷For God did not send His Son into the world that He may judge the world, but that the world may be saved through Him; ¹⁸he who is believing in Him is not judged, but he who is not believing has been judged already, because he has not believed in the Name of the only begotten Son of God. ¹⁹And this is the judgment, that the light has come into the world, and men loved the darkness rather than the light, for their works were evil; ²⁰for everyone who is doing wicked things hates the light, and does not come into the light, that his works may not be detected; ²¹but he who is doing the truth comes into the light, that his works may be revealed, that in God they are having been worked." ²²After these things Jesus and His disciples came into the land of Judea, and there He tarried with them, and was immersing; ²³and John was also immersing in Aenon, near to Salem, because there were many waters there, and they were coming and were being immersed— ²⁴for John was not yet cast into the prison—²⁵there arose then a question from the disciples of John with [some] Jews about purifying, ²⁶and they came to John and said to him, "Rabbi, He who was with you beyond the Jordan, to whom you testified, behold, this One is immersing, and all are coming to Him." ²⁷John answered and said, "A man is not able to receive anything if it may not have been given him from Heaven; ²⁸you yourselves testify to me that I said, I am not the Christ, but that I am having been sent before Him; ²⁹He who is having the bride is bridegroom, and the friend of the bridegroom, who is standing and hearing Him, rejoices with joy because of the voice of the bridegroom; this, then, my joy has been fulfilled. ³⁰It is necessary [for] Him to increase, and me to become less; ³¹He who is coming from above is above all; he who is from the earth, from the earth he is, and from the earth he speaks; He who is coming from Heaven is above all. ³²And what He has seen and heard—this He testifies, and none receives His testimony; ³³he who is receiving His testimony sealed that God is true; ³⁴for He whom God sent, He speaks the sayings of God; for God does not give the Spirit by measure; ³⁵the Father loves the Son, and has given all things into His hand; ³⁶he who is believing in the Son has continuous life; and he who is not believing the Son will not see life, but the wrath of God remains on him."

CHAPTER 4

¹When therefore the Lord knew that the Pharisees heard that Jesus makes and immerses more disciples than John, ²(though indeed Jesus Himself was not immersing, but His disciples), ³He left Judea and went away again to Galilee, ⁴and it was necessary [for] Him to go through Samaria. ⁵He comes, therefore, to a city of Samaria, called Sychar, near to the place that Jacob gave to his son Joseph; ⁶and there was there a well of Jacob. Jesus therefore having been weary from the journeying, was thus sitting on the well; it was as it were the sixth hour; ⁷there comes a woman out of Samaria to draw water. Jesus says to her, "Give Me to drink"; ⁸for His disciples were gone away into the city that they may buy food; ⁹the Samaritan woman therefore says to Him, "How do You, being a Jew, ask drink from me, being a Samaritan woman?" For Jews have no dealing with Samaritans. ¹⁰Jesus answered and said to her, "If you had known the gift of God, and who it is who is saying to you, Give Me to drink, you would have asked Him, and He would have given you living water." ¹¹The woman says to Him, "Lord, You do not even have a vessel to draw with, and the well is deep; from where, then, have You the living water? ¹²Are You greater than our father Jacob, who gave us the well, and himself drank out of it, and his sons, and his livestock?" ¹³Jesus answered and said to her, "Everyone who is drinking of this water will thirst again; ¹⁴but whoever may drink of the water that I will give him, may not thirst—throughout the age; and the water that I will give him will become in him a well of water, springing up to continuous life." ¹⁵The woman says to Him, "Lord, give me this water, that I may not thirst, nor come here to draw." ¹⁶Jesus says to her, "Go, call your husband, and come here"; ¹⁷the woman answered and said, "I do not have a husband." Jesus says to her, "Well did you say—I do not have a husband; ¹⁸for you have had five husbands, and now, he whom you have is not your husband; you have said this correctly." ¹⁹The woman says to Him, "Lord, I perceive that You are a prophet; ²⁰our fathers worshiped in this mountain, and You say that in Jerusalem is the place where it is required to worship." ²¹Jesus says to her, "Woman, believe Me, that there comes an hour when neither in this mountain, nor in Jerusalem, will you worship the Father; ²²you worship what you have not known; we worship what we have known, because salvation is of the Jews; ²³but there comes an hour, and it now is, when the true worshipers will worship the Father in spirit and truth, for the Father also seeks such to worship Him; ²⁴God [is] Spirit, and those worshiping Him should worship in spirit and truth." ²⁵The woman says to Him, "I have known that Messiah comes, who is called Christ, when that One may come, He will tell us all things"; ²⁶Jesus says to her, "I who am speaking to you am [He]." ²⁷And on this came His disciples, and were wondering that He was speaking with a woman, no one, however, said, "What do You seek?" Or "Why do You speak with her?" ²⁸The woman then left her water-jug and went away into the city, and says to the men, ²⁹"Come, see a Man who told me all things—as many as I did; is this the Christ?" ³⁰They went forth therefore out of the city, and were coming to Him. ³¹And in the meanwhile His disciples were asking Him, saying, "Rabbi, eat"; ³²and He said to them, "I have food to eat that you have not known." ³³The disciples then said to one another, "Did anyone bring Him anything to eat?" ³⁴Jesus says to them, "My food is that I may do the will of Him who sent Me, and may finish His work; ³⁵do not say that it is yet four months, and the harvest comes; behold, I say to you, lift up your eyes, and see the fields, that they are white to harvest already. ³⁶And he who is reaping receives a reward, and gathers fruit to continuous life, that both he who is sowing and he who is reaping may rejoice together; ³⁷for in this the saying is the true one, that one is the sower and another the reaper. ³⁸I sent you to reap on that which you have not labored; others labored, and you have entered into their labor." ³⁹And many from that city believed in Him, of the Samaritans, because of the word of the woman testifying, "He told me all things—as many as I did." ⁴⁰When, then, the Samaritans came to Him, they were asking Him to remain with them, and He remained there two days; ⁴¹and many more believed because of His word, ⁴²and said to the woman, "We no longer believe because of your speaking; for we ourselves have heard and known that this is truly the Savior of the world—the Christ." ⁴³And after the two days He went forth from there, and went away to Galilee, ⁴⁴for Jesus Himself testified that a prophet will not have honor in his own country; ⁴⁵when then, He came to Galilee, the Galileans received Him, having seen all things that He did in Jerusalem in the celebration—for they also went to the celebration. ⁴⁶Jesus came, therefore, again to Cana of Galilee, where He made the water wine, and there was a certain attendant, whose son was ailing in Capernaum, ⁴⁷he, having heard that Jesus comes out of Judea to Galilee, went away to Him, and was asking Him that He may come down and may heal his son, for he was about to die. ⁴⁸Jesus then said to him, "If you may not see signs and wonders, you will not believe." ⁴⁹The attendant says to Him, "Lord, come down before my child dies"; ⁵⁰Jesus says to him, "Be going on; your son lives." And the man believed the word that Jesus said to him, and was going on, ⁵¹and he now going down, his servants met him, and told, saying, "Your child lives"; ⁵²he inquired then of them the

hour in which he became better, and they said to him, "Yesterday at the seventh hour the fever left him"; ⁵³then the father knew that [it was] in that hour in which Jesus said to him, "Your son lives," and he himself believed, and his whole house; ⁵⁴this again [was] a second sign Jesus did, having come out of Judea to Galilee.

CHAPTER 5

¹After these things there was a celebration of the Jews, and Jesus went up to Jerusalem, ²and there is in Jerusalem by the sheep-[gate] a pool that is called in Hebrew Bethesda, having five porches, ³in these were lying a great multitude of the ailing, blind, lame, withered, [[waiting for the moving of the water, ⁴for a messenger at a set time was going down in the pool, and was troubling the water, the first then having gone in after the troubling of the water, became whole of whatever sickness he was held.]] ⁵And there was a certain man there being in ailment thirty-eight years, ⁶him Jesus having seen lying, and having known that he is already a long time, He says to him, "Do you wish to become whole?" ⁷The ailing man answered Him, "Lord, I have no man, that, when the water may be troubled, he may put me into the pool, and while I am coming, another goes down before me." ⁸Jesus says to him, "Rise, take up your pallet, and be walking"; ⁹and immediately the man became whole, and he took up his pallet, and was walking, and it was a Sabbath on that day, ¹⁰the Jews then said to him that has been healed, "It is a Sabbath; it is not lawful to you to take up the pallet." ¹¹He answered them, "He who made me whole—that One said to me, Take up your pallet, and be walking"; ¹²they questioned him, then, "Who is the Man who is saying to you, Take up your bed and be walking?" ¹³But he that was healed had not known who He is, for Jesus moved away, a multitude being in the place. ¹⁴After these things, Jesus finds him in the temple and said to him, "Behold, you have become whole; sin no more, lest something worse may happen to you." ¹⁵The man went away, and told the Jews that it is Jesus who made him whole, ¹⁶and because of this were the Jews persecuting Jesus, and seeking to kill Him, because these things He was doing on a Sabbath. ¹⁷And Jesus answered them, "My Father works until now, and I work"; ¹⁸because of this, then, were the Jews seeking the more to kill Him, because not only was He breaking the Sabbath, but He also called God His own Father, making Himself equal to God. ¹⁹Jesus therefore responded and said to them, "Truly, truly, I say to you, the Son is not able to do anything of Himself, if He may not see the Father doing anything; for whatever things He may do, these also the Son does in like manner; ²⁰for the Father cherishes the Son, and shows to Him all things that He Himself does; and greater works than these He will show Him, that you may wonder. ²¹For as the Father raises the dead, and makes alive, so also the Son makes alive whom He wills; ²²for neither does the Father judge anyone, but all the judgment He has given to the Son, ²³that all may honor the Son according as they honor the Father; he who is not honoring the Son, does not honor the Father who sent Him. ²⁴Truly, truly, I say to you, he who is hearing My word, and is believing Him who sent Me, has continuous life, and he does not come into judgment, but has passed out of death into life. ²⁵Truly, truly, I say to you, [that] there comes an hour, and it now is, when the dead will hear the voice of the Son of God, and those having heard will live; ²⁶for as the Father has life in Himself, so He gave also to the Son to have life in Himself, ²⁷and authority He gave Him also to do judgment, because He is Son of Man. ²⁸Do not wonder at this, because there comes an hour in which all those in the tombs will hear His voice, ²⁹and they will come forth; those who did good things to a resurrection of life, and those who practiced evil things to a resurrection of judgment. ³⁰I am not able of Myself to do anything; according as I hear I judge, and My judgment is righteous, because I do not seek My own will, but the will of the Father who sent Me. ³¹If I testify concerning Myself, My testimony is not true; ³²there is another who is testifying concerning Me, and I have known that the testimony that He testifies concerning Me is true; ³³you have sent to John, and he has testified to the truth. ³⁴But I do not receive testimony from man, but these things I say that you may be saved; ³⁵he was the burning and shining lamp, and you willed to be glad, for an hour, in his light. ³⁶But I have the testimony greater than John's, for the works that the Father gave Me, that I might finish them, the works themselves that I do, they testify concerning Me, that the Father has sent Me. ³⁷And the Father who sent Me has testified Himself concerning Me; you have neither heard His voice at any time, nor have you seen His appearance; ³⁸and you do not have His word remaining in you, because you do not believe Him whom He sent. ³⁹You search the Writings, because you think in them to have continuous life, and these are they that are testifying concerning Me; ⁴⁰and you do not will to come to Me, that you may have life; ⁴¹I do not receive glory from man, ⁴²but I have known you, that you do not have the love of God in yourselves. ⁴³I have come in the Name of My Father, and you do not receive Me; if another may come in his own name, him you will receive; ⁴⁴how are you able—you—to believe, receiving glory from one another, and the glory that [is] from God alone you do not seek? ⁴⁵Do not think that I will accuse you to the Father; there is [one] who is accusing you, Moses—in whom you have hoped; ⁴⁶for if you were believing Moses, you would have been believing Me, for he wrote concerning Me; ⁴⁷but if you do not believe his writings, how will you believe My sayings?"

CHAPTER 6

¹After these things Jesus went away beyond the Sea of Galilee (of Tiberias), ²and there was following Him a great multitude, because they were seeing His signs that He was doing on the ailing; ³and Jesus went up to the mountain, and He was sitting with His disciples there, ⁴and the Passover was near, the celebration of the Jews. ⁵Jesus then having lifted up [His] eyes and having seen that a great multitude comes to Him, says to Philip, "From where will we buy loaves, that these may eat?" ⁶And this He said, trying him, for He Himself had known what He was about to do. ⁷Philip answered Him, "Two hundred denarii worth of loaves are not sufficient to them, that each of them may receive some little"; ⁸one of His disciples—Andrew, the brother of Simon Peter—says to Him, ⁹"There is one little boy here who has five barley loaves and two fishes, but these—what are they to so many?" ¹⁰And Jesus said, "Make the men to sit down"; and there was much grass in the place, the men then sat down, in number, as it were, five thousand, ¹¹and Jesus took the loaves, and having given thanks He distributed [them] to the disciples, and the disciples to those reclining, in like manner, also of the little fishes as much as they wished. ¹²And when they were filled, He says to His disciples, "Gather together the broken pieces that are left over, that nothing may be lost"; ¹³they gathered together, therefore, and filled twelve hand-baskets with broken pieces, from the five barley loaves that were over to those having eaten. ¹⁴The men, then, having seen the sign that Jesus did, said, "This is truly the Prophet who is coming into the world"; ¹⁵Jesus, therefore, having known that they are about to come, and to seize Him by force that they may make Him king, retired again to the mountain Himself alone. ¹⁶And when evening came, His disciples went down to the sea, ¹⁷and having entered into the boat, they were going over the sea to Capernaum, and darkness had already come, and Jesus had not come to them, ¹⁸the sea also—a great wind blowing—was being raised, ¹⁹having pushed onward, therefore, about twenty-five or thirty stadia, they behold Jesus walking on the sea, and coming near to the boat, and they were afraid; ²⁰and He says to them, "I AM; do not be afraid"; ²¹they were willing then to receive Him into the boat, and immediately the boat came to the land to which they were going. ²²On the next day, the multitude that was standing on the other side of the sea, having seen that there was no other little boat there except one—that into which His disciples entered—and that Jesus did not go in with His disciples into the little boat, but His disciples went away alone ²³(and other little boats came from Tiberias, near the place where they ate the bread, the LORD having given thanks), ²⁴when therefore the multitude saw that Jesus is not there, nor His disciples, they also entered into the boats themselves, and came

to Capernaum seeking Jesus; ²⁵and having found Him on the other side of the sea, they said to Him, "Rabbi, when have You come here?" ²⁶Jesus answered them and said, "Truly, truly, I say to you, you seek Me, not because you saw signs, but because you ate of the loaves, and were satisfied; ²⁷do not work for the food that is perishing, but for the food that is remaining to continuous life, which the Son of Man will give to you, for the Father sealed Him—[even] God." ²⁸Therefore they said to Him, "What may we do that we may work the works of God?" ²⁹Jesus answered and said to them, "This is the work of God, that you may believe in Him whom He sent." ³⁰Therefore they said to Him, "What sign, then, do You do, that we may see and may believe You? What do You work? ³¹Our fathers ate the manna in the wilderness, according as it is having been written: He gave them bread out of Heaven to eat." ³²Jesus, therefore, said to them, "Truly, truly, I say to you, Moses did not give you the bread out of Heaven, but My Father gives you the true bread out of Heaven; ³³for the bread of God is Him coming down out of Heaven, and giving life to the world." ³⁴Therefore they said to Him, "Lord, always give us this bread." ³⁵And Jesus said to them, "I AM the bread of life; he who is coming to Me may not hunger, and he who is believing in Me may not thirst—at any time; ³⁶but I said to you that you also have seen Me, and you do not believe; ³⁷all that the Father gives to Me will come to Me; and him who is coming to Me, I will never cast outside, ³⁸because I have come down out of Heaven, not that I may do My will, but the will of Him who sent Me. ³⁹And this is the will of the Father who sent Me, that all that He has given to Me, I may lose none of it, but may raise it up in the last day; ⁴⁰and this is the will of Him who sent Me, that everyone who is beholding the Son, and is believing in Him, may have continuous life, and I will raise him up in the last day." ⁴¹The Jews, therefore, were murmuring at Him, because He said, "I AM the bread that came down out of Heaven"; ⁴²and they said, "Is this not Jesus, the Son of Joseph, whose father and mother we have known? How then does this One say, I have come down out of Heaven?" ⁴³Jesus answered, therefore, and said to them, "Do not murmur with one another; ⁴⁴no one is able to come to Me if the Father who sent Me may not draw him, and I will raise him up in the last day; ⁴⁵it is having been written in the Prophets: And they will all be taught of God; everyone, therefore, who heard from the Father, and learned, comes to Me; ⁴⁶not that anyone has seen the Father, except He who is from God, He has seen the Father. ⁴⁷Truly, truly, I say to you, he who is believing in Me has continuous life; ⁴⁸I AM the bread of life; ⁴⁹your fathers ate the manna in the wilderness and they died; ⁵⁰this is the bread that is coming down out of Heaven, that anyone may eat of it, and not die. ⁵¹I AM the living bread that came down out of Heaven; if anyone may eat of this bread he will live—throughout the age; and the bread also that I will give is My flesh, that I will give for the life of the world." ⁵²The Jews, therefore, were striving with one another, saying, "How is this One able to give us [His] flesh to eat?" ⁵³Jesus, therefore, said to them, "Truly, truly, I say to you, if you may not eat the flesh of the Son of Man, and may not drink His blood, you have no life in yourselves; ⁵⁴he who is eating My flesh, and is drinking My blood, has continuous life, and I will raise him up in the last day; ⁵⁵for My flesh is truly food, and My blood is truly drink; ⁵⁶he who is eating My flesh, and is drinking My blood, remains in Me, and I in him. ⁵⁷According as the living Father sent Me, and I live because of the Father, he also who is eating Me, even that one will live because of Me; ⁵⁸this is the bread that came down out of Heaven; not as your fathers ate the manna, and died; he who is eating this bread will live—throughout the age." ⁵⁹He said these things in a synagogue, teaching in Capernaum; ⁶⁰many, therefore, of His disciples having heard, said, "This word is hard; who is able to hear it?" ⁶¹And Jesus having known in Himself that His disciples are murmuring about this, said to them, "Does this stumble you? ⁶²If then you may behold the Son of Man going up where He was before? ⁶³It is the Spirit that is giving life; the flesh does not profit anything; the sayings that I speak to you are spirit, and they are life; ⁶⁴but there are certain of you who do not believe"; for Jesus had known from the beginning who they are who are not believing, and who is he who will deliver Him up, ⁶⁵and He said, "Because of this I have said to you, No one is able to come to Me if it may not have been given him from My Father." ⁶⁶From this [time] many of His disciples went away backward, and were no longer walking with Him, ⁶⁷Jesus, therefore, said to the Twelve, "Do you also wish to go away?" ⁶⁸Simon Peter, therefore, answered Him, "Lord, to whom will we go? You have sayings of continuous life; ⁶⁹and we have believed, and we have known, that You are the Christ, the Son of the living God." ⁷⁰Jesus answered them, "Did I not choose you—the Twelve? And of you—one is a devil." ⁷¹And He spoke of Judas, [son] of Simon Iscariot, for he was about to deliver Him up, being one of the Twelve.

CHAPTER 7

¹And Jesus was walking after these things in Galilee, for He did not wish to walk in Judea, because the Jews were seeking to kill Him, ²and the celebration of the Jews was near—that of Shelters— ³His brothers, therefore, said to Him, "Depart from here, and go away to Judea, that Your disciples may also behold Your works that You do; ⁴for no one does anything in secret, and himself seeks to be in public; if you do these things—reveal Yourself to the world"; ⁵for not even His brothers were believing in Him. ⁶Jesus, therefore, says to them, "My time is not yet present, but your time is always ready; ⁷the world is not able to hate you, but it hates Me, because I testify concerning it that its works are evil. ⁸You—go up to this celebration; I do not yet go up to this celebration, because My time has not yet been fulfilled"; ⁹and saying these things to them, He remained in Galilee. ¹⁰And when His brothers went up, then also He Himself went up to the celebration, not openly, but as in secret; ¹¹the Jews, therefore, were seeking Him in the celebration, and said, "Where is that One?" ¹²And there was much murmuring about Him among the multitudes, some indeed said, "He is good"; and others said, "No, but He leads the multitude astray"; ¹³no one, however, was speaking freely about Him, through fear of the Jews. ¹⁴And it being now the middle of the celebration, Jesus went up to the temple, and He was teaching, ¹⁵and the Jews were wondering, saying, "How has this One known letters—having not learned?" ¹⁶Jesus answered them and said, "My teaching is not Mine, but His who sent Me; ¹⁷if anyone may will to do His will, he will know concerning the teaching, whether it is of God, or—[if] I speak from Myself. ¹⁸He who is speaking from himself seeks his own glory, but he who is seeking the glory of him who sent him, this one is true, and unrighteousness is not in him; ¹⁹has not Moses given you the Law? And none of you does the Law; why do you seek to kill Me?" ²⁰The multitude answered and said, "You have a demon, who seeks to kill You?" ²¹Jesus answered and said to them, "I did one work, and you all wonder, ²²because of this, Moses has given you the circumcision—not that it is of Moses, but of the fathers—and on a Sabbath you circumcise a man; ²³if a man receives circumcision on a Sabbath that the Law of Moses may not be broken, are you angry with Me that I made a man all whole on a Sabbath? ²⁴Do not judge according to appearance, but the righteous judgment judge." ²⁵Certain, therefore, of the Jerusalemites said, "Is this not He whom they are seeking to kill? ²⁶And behold, He speaks freely, and they say nothing to Him; did the rulers truly know that this is the Christ? ²⁷But this One—we have known where He is from; and the Christ, when He comes, no one knows where He is from." ²⁸Jesus cried, therefore, in the temple, teaching and saying, "You have both known Me, and you have known from where I am; and I have not come of Myself, but He who sent Me is true, whom you have not known; ²⁹and I have known Him, because I am from Him, and He sent Me." ³⁰They were seeking, therefore, to seize Him, and no one laid the hand on Him, because His hour had not yet come, ³¹and many out of the multitude believed in Him and said, "The Christ—when He may come—will He do more signs than these that this One did?" ³²The Pharisees heard the multitude murmuring these things concerning Him, and the Pharisees and the chief priests sent officers that they may take Him; ³³Jesus, therefore, said to them, "Yet a short time I am with you, and I go away to Him who sent Me; ³⁴you will seek Me, and you will not find; and where I am, you are not able to come." ³⁵The Jews, therefore, said among themselves, "To where is this One about to go that we will not find Him? Is He about to go to the dispersion of the Greeks, and to teach the Greeks? ³⁶What is this word that He said, You will seek Me, and you will not find? And, Where I am, you are

JOHN

not able to come?" ³⁷And in the last, the great day of the celebration, Jesus stood and cried, saying, "If anyone thirsts, let him come to Me and drink; ³⁸he who is believing in Me, according as the Writing said, Rivers of living water will flow out of his belly"; ³⁹and this He said of the Spirit, which those believing in Him were about to receive; for not yet was the Holy Spirit, because Jesus was not yet glorified. ⁴⁰Many, therefore, out of the multitude, having heard the word, said, "This is truly the Prophet"; ⁴¹others said, "This is the Christ"; and others said, "Why, does the Christ come out of Galilee? ⁴²Did the Writing not say that out of the seed of David, and from Beth-Lehem—the village where David was—the Christ comes?" ⁴³A division, therefore, arose among the multitude because of Him. ⁴⁴And certain of them were willing to seize Him, but no one laid hands on Him; ⁴⁵the officers came, therefore, to the chief priests and Pharisees, and they said to them, "Why did you not bring Him?" ⁴⁶The officers answered, "Never so spoke man—as this Man." ⁴⁷The Pharisees, therefore, answered them, "Have you also been led astray? ⁴⁸Did anyone out of the rulers believe in Him? Or out of the Pharisees? ⁴⁹But this multitude, that is not knowing the Law, is accursed." ⁵⁰Nicodemus says to them—he who came by night to Him—being one of them, ⁵¹"Does our law judge the Man, if it may not hear from Him first, and know what He does?" ⁵²They answered and said to him, "Are you also out of Galilee? Search and see that a prophet has not risen out of Galilee"; [[⁵³and each one went on to his house, but Jesus went on to the Mount of Olives.

CHAPTER 8

¹And at dawn He came again to the temple [courts], ²and all the people were coming to Him, and having sat down, He was teaching them; ³and the scribes and the Pharisees bring to Him a woman having been taken in adultery, and having set her in the midst, ⁴they say to Him, "Teacher, this woman was taken in the very crime [of] committing adultery, ⁵and in the Law, Moses commanded us that such be stoned; You, therefore, what do You say?" ⁶And this they said, trying Him, that they might have to accuse Him. And Jesus, having stooped down, with the finger He was writing on the ground, ⁷and when they continued asking Him, having bent Himself back, He said to them, "The sinless of you—let him cast the first stone at her"; ⁸and again having stooped down, He was writing on the ground, ⁹and they having heard, and being convicted by the conscience, were going forth one by one, having begun from the elders—to the last; and Jesus was left alone, and the woman standing in the midst. ¹⁰And Jesus having bent Himself back, and having seen no one but the woman, said to her, "Woman, where are those—your accusers? Did no one pass sentence on you?" ¹¹And she said, "No one, Lord"; and Jesus said to her, "Neither do I pass sentence on you; be going on, and sin no more."]] ¹²Again, therefore, Jesus spoke to them, saying, "I AM the light of the world; he who is following Me will not walk in the darkness, but he will have the light of life." ¹³The Pharisees, therefore, said to Him, "You testify of Yourself, Your testimony is not true"; ¹⁴Jesus answered and said to them, "And if I testify of Myself—My testimony is true, because I have known from where I came, and to where I go, and you have not known from where I come, or to where I go. ¹⁵You judge according to the flesh; I do not judge anyone, ¹⁶and even if I do judge My judgment is true, because I am not alone, but I and the Father who sent Me; ¹⁷and also in your law it has been written that the testimony of two men is true; ¹⁸I am [One] who is testifying of Myself, and the Father who sent Me testifies of Me." ¹⁹They said, therefore, to Him, "Where is Your father?" Jesus answered, "You have neither known Me nor My Father: if you had known Me, you had also known My Father." ²⁰Jesus spoke these sayings in the treasury, teaching in the temple, and no one seized Him, because His hour had not yet come; ²¹therefore Jesus said again to them, "I go away, and you will seek Me, and you will die in your sin; to where I go away, you are not able to come." ²²The Jews, therefore, said, "Will He kill Himself, because He says, To where I go away, you are not able to come?" ²³And He said to them, "You are from beneath, I am from above; you are of this world, I am not of this world; ²⁴I said, therefore, to you, that you will die in your sins, for if you may not believe that I AM, you will die in your sins." ²⁵They said, therefore, to Him, "You—who are You?" And Jesus said to them, "Even what I spoke of to you at the beginning; ²⁶many things I have to speak concerning you and to judge, but He who sent Me is true, and I—what things I heard from Him—these I say to the world." ²⁷They did not know that He spoke to them of the Father; ²⁸Jesus, therefore, said to them, "When you may lift up the Son of Man then you will know that I AM; and I do nothing of Myself, but according as My Father taught Me, these things I speak; ²⁹and He who sent Me is with Me; the Father did not leave Me alone, because I always do the things pleasing to Him." ³⁰As He is speaking these things, many believed in Him; ³¹Jesus, therefore, said to the Jews who believed in Him, "If you may remain in My word, you are truly My disciples, ³²and you will know the truth, and the truth will make you free." ³³They answered Him, "We are seed of Abraham; and we have been servants to no one at any time; how do You say—You will become free?" ³⁴Jesus answered them, "Truly, truly, I say to you, everyone who is committing sin, is a servant of sin, ³⁵and the servant does not remain in the house—throughout the age, the Son remains—throughout the age; ³⁶if then the Son may make you free, in reality you will be free. ³⁷I have known that you are seed of Abraham, but you seek to kill Me, because My word has no place in you; ³⁸I speak that which I have seen with My Father, and you, therefore, do that which you have seen with your father." ³⁹They answered and said to Him, "Our father is Abraham"; Jesus says to them, "If you were children of Abraham, the works of Abraham you were doing; ⁴⁰and now, you seek to kill Me—a Man who has spoken to you the truth I heard from God; Abraham did not do this; ⁴¹you do the works of your father." They said, therefore, to Him, "We have not been born of whoredom; we have one Father—God"; ⁴²Jesus then said to them, "If God were your father, you were loving Me, for I came forth from God, and am come; for neither have I come of Myself, but He sent Me; ⁴³why do you not know My speech? Because you are not able to hear My word. ⁴⁴You are of a father—the Devil, and the desires of your father you will do; he was a manslayer from the beginning, and he has not stood in the truth, because there is no truth in him; when one may speak the falsehood, he speaks of his own, because he is a liar—also his father. ⁴⁵And because I say the truth, you do not believe Me. ⁴⁶Who of you convicts Me of sin? And if I speak truth, why do you not believe Me? ⁴⁷He who is of God, he hears the sayings of God; because of this you do not hear, because you are not of God." ⁴⁸The Jews, therefore, answered and said to Him, "Do we not say well, that You are a Samaritan, and have a demon?" ⁴⁹Jesus answered, "I do not have a demon, but I honor My Father, and you dishonor Me; ⁵⁰and I do not seek My own glory; there is [One] who is seeking and is judging; ⁵¹truly, truly, I say to you, if anyone may keep My word, he may not see death—throughout the age." ⁵²The Jews, therefore, said to Him, "Now we have known that You have a demon; Abraham died, and the prophets, and You say, If anyone may keep My word, he will not taste of death—throughout the age! ⁵³Are You greater than our father Abraham, who died? And the prophets died; whom do You make Yourself?" ⁵⁴Jesus answered, "If I glorify Myself, My glory is nothing; it is My Father who is glorifying Me, of whom you say that He is your God; ⁵⁵and you have not known Him, and I have known Him, and if I say that I have not known Him, I will be like you—speaking falsely; but I have known Him, and I keep His word; ⁵⁶your father Abraham was glad that he might see My day; and he saw, and rejoiced." ⁵⁷The Jews, therefore, said to Him, "You are not yet fifty years old, and You have seen Abraham?" ⁵⁸Jesus said to them, "Truly, truly, I say to you, before Abraham's coming—I AM"; ⁵⁹they took up, therefore, stones that they may cast at Him, but Jesus hid Himself, and went forth out of the temple, going through the midst of them, and so passed by.

CHAPTER 9

¹And passing by, He saw a man blind from birth, ²and His disciples asked Him, saying, "Rabbi, who sinned, this one or his parents,

that he should be born blind?" ³Jesus answered, "Neither this one sinned nor his parents, but that the works of God may be revealed in him; ⁴it is necessary for Me to be working the works of Him who sent Me while it is day; night comes when no one is able to work: ⁵when I am in the world, I AM [the] light of the world." ⁶Saying these things, He spat on the ground, and made clay of the spittle, and rubbed the clay on the eyes of the blind man, and said to him, ⁷"Go away, wash at the pool of Siloam," which is, interpreted, Sent. He went away, therefore, and washed, and came seeing; ⁸the neighbors, therefore, and those seeing him before, that he was blind, said, "Is this not he who is sitting and begging?" ⁹Others said, "This is he"; and others, "He is like to him"; he himself said, "I am [he]." ¹⁰They said, therefore, to him, "How were your eyes opened?" ¹¹He answered and said, "A man called Jesus made clay, and rubbed my eyes, and said to me, Go away to the pool of Siloam, and wash; and having gone away and having washed, I received sight"; ¹²they said, therefore, to him, "Where is that One?" He says, "I have not known." ¹³They bring him who once [was] blind to the Pharisees, ¹⁴and it was a Sabbath when Jesus made the clay, and opened his eyes. ¹⁵Again, therefore, the Pharisees also were asking him how he received sight, and he said to them, "He put clay on my eyes, and I washed—and I see." ¹⁶Certain of the Pharisees therefore said, "This Man is not from God, because He does not keep the Sabbath"; others said, "How is a man—a sinful one—able to do such signs?" And there was a division among them. ¹⁷They said to the blind man again, "You—what do you say of Him—that He opened your eyes?" ¹⁸And he said, "He is a prophet." The Jews, therefore, did not believe concerning him that he was blind and received sight, until they called the parents of him who received sight, ¹⁹and they asked them, saying, "Is [this] your son, of whom you say that he was born blind? How then does he now see?" ²⁰His parents answered them and said, "We have known that this is our son, and that he was born blind; ²¹and how he now sees, we have not known; or who opened his eyes, we have not known; he is of age, ask him; he himself will speak concerning himself." ²²His parents said these things, because they were afraid of the Jews, for the Jews had already agreed together, that if anyone may confess Him—Christ, he may be put out of the synagogue; ²³because of this his parents said, "He is of age, ask him." ²⁴They called, therefore, the man who was blind a second time, and they said to him, "Give glory to God, we have known that this Man is a sinner"; ²⁵he answered, therefore, and said, "If He is a sinner—I have not known, one thing I have known, that, being blind, now I see." ²⁶And they said to him again, "What did He do to you? How did He open your eyes?" ²⁷He answered them, "I told you already, and you did not hear; why do you wish to hear [it] again? Do you also wish to become His disciples?" ²⁸They reviled him, therefore, and said, "You are His disciple, and we are Moses' disciples; ²⁹we have known that God has spoken to Moses, but this One—we have not known where He is from." ³⁰The man answered and said to them, "Why, in this is a wonderful thing, that you have not known where He is from, and He opened my eyes! ³¹And we have known that God does not hear sinners, but if anyone may be a worshiper of God, and may do His will, He hears him; ³²from the age it was not heard that anyone opened eyes of one who has been born blind; ³³if this One were not from God, He were not able to do anything." ³⁴They answered and said to him, "In sins you were born altogether, and you teach us?" And they cast him forth outside. ³⁵Jesus heard that they cast him forth outside, and having found him, He said to him, "Do you believe in the Son of God?" ³⁶He answered and said, "Who is He, Lord, that I may believe in Him?" ³⁷And Jesus said to him, "You have both seen Him, and He who is speaking with you is He"; ³⁸and he said, "I believe, Lord," and worshiped Him. ³⁹And Jesus said, "I came to this world for judgment, that those not seeing may see, and those seeing may become blind." ⁴⁰And those of the Pharisees who were with Him heard these things, and they said to Him, "Are we also blind?" ⁴¹Jesus said to them, "If you were blind, you were not having had sin, but now you say—We see, therefore your sin remains."

CHAPTER 10

¹"Truly, truly, I say to you, he who is not entering through the door to the fold of the sheep, but is going up from another side, that one is a thief and a robber; ²and he who is entering through the door is shepherd of the sheep; ³the doorkeeper opens to this one, and the sheep hear his voice, and his own sheep he calls by name, and leads them forth; ⁴and when he may put forth his own sheep, he goes on before them, and the sheep follow him, because they have known his voice; ⁵and they will not follow a stranger, but will flee from him, because they have not known the voice of strangers." ⁶Jesus spoke this allegory to them, and they did not know what the things were that He was speaking to them; ⁷Jesus therefore said again to them, "Truly, truly, I say to you, I AM the door of the sheep; ⁸all, as many as came before Me, are thieves and robbers, but the sheep did not hear them; ⁹I AM the door, if anyone may come in through Me, he will be saved, and he will come in, and go out, and find pasture. ¹⁰The thief does not come, except that he may steal, and kill, and destroy; I came that they may have life, and may have [it] abundantly. ¹¹I AM the good shepherd; the good shepherd lays His life down for the sheep; ¹²and the hired worker, and not being a shepherd, whose own the sheep are not, beholds the wolf coming, and leaves the sheep, and flees; and the wolf snatches them, and scatters the sheep; ¹³and the hired worker flees because he is a hired worker, and is not caring for the sheep. ¹⁴I AM the good shepherd, and I know My [sheep], and am known by Mine, ¹⁵according as the Father knows Me, and I know the Father, and My life I lay down for the sheep, ¹⁶and other sheep I have that are not of this fold, these also it is necessary for Me to bring, and My voice they will hear, and there will become one flock—one shepherd. ¹⁷Because of this the Father loves Me, because I lay down My life, that again I may take it; ¹⁸no one takes it from Me, but I lay it down of Myself; authority I have to lay it down, and authority I have again to take it; this command I received from My Father." ¹⁹Therefore, again, there came a division among the Jews, because of these words, ²⁰and many of them said, "He has a demon, and is mad, why do you hear Him?" ²¹Others said, "These sayings are not those of a demoniac; is a demon able to open blind men's eyes?" ²²And the Dedication in Jerusalem came, and it was winter, ²³and Jesus was walking in the temple, in the porch of Solomon, ²⁴the Jews, therefore, came around Him and said to Him, "Until when do You hold our soul in suspense? If You are the Christ, tell us freely." ²⁵Jesus answered them, "I told you, and you do not believe; the works that I do in the Name of My Father, these testify concerning Me; ²⁶but you do not believe, for you are not of My sheep, ²⁷according as I said to you: My sheep hear My voice, and I know them, and they follow Me, ²⁸and I give continuous life to them, and they will not perish—throughout the age, and no one will snatch them out of My hand; ²⁹My Father, who has given to Me, is greater than all, and no one is able to snatch out of the hand of My Father; ³⁰I and the Father are one." ³¹Therefore, again, the Jews took up stones that they may stone Him; ³²Jesus answered them, "I showed you many good works from My Father; because of which work of them do you stone Me?" ³³The Jews answered Him, saying, "We do not stone You for a good work, but for slander, and because You, being a man, make Yourself God." ³⁴Jesus answered them, "Is it not having been written in your law: I said, you are gods? ³⁵If He called them gods to whom the word of God came (and the Writing is not able to be broken), ³⁶of Him whom the Father sanctified and sent into the world, do you say—You slander, because I said, I am [the] Son of God? ³⁷If I do not do the works of My Father, do not believe Me; ³⁸and if I do, even if you may not believe Me, believe the works, that you may know and may believe that the Father [is] in Me, and I in Him." ³⁹Therefore they were seeking again to seize Him, and He went forth out of their hand, ⁴⁰and went away again to the other side of the Jordan, to the place where John was at first immersing, and remained there, ⁴¹and many came to Him and said, "John, indeed, did no sign, and all things, as many as John said about this One were true"; ⁴²and many believed in Him there.

CHAPTER 11

¹And there was a certain one ailing, Lazarus, from Bethany, of the village of Mary and Martha her sister— ²and it was Mary who anointed the LORD with ointment, and wiped His feet with her hair, whose brother Lazarus was ailing— ³therefore the sisters sent to Him,

saying, "Lord, behold, he whom You cherish is ailing"; ⁴and Jesus having heard, said, "This ailment is not to death, but for the glory of God, that the Son of God may be glorified through it." ⁵And Jesus was loving Martha, and her sister, and Lazarus, ⁶when, therefore, He heard that he is ailing, then indeed He remained in the place in which He was two days, ⁷then after this, He says to the disciples, "We may go to Judea again"; ⁸the disciples say to Him, "Rabbi, the Jews were just seeking to stone You, and again You go there?" ⁹Jesus answered, "Are there not twelve hours in the day? If anyone may walk in the day, he does not stumble, because he sees the light of this world; ¹⁰and if anyone may walk in the night, he stumbles, because the light is not in him." ¹¹He said these things, and after this He says to them, "Our friend Lazarus has fallen asleep, but I go on that I may awake him"; ¹²therefore His disciples said, "Lord, if he has fallen asleep, he will be saved"; ¹³but Jesus had spoken about his death, but they thought that He speaks about the repose of sleep. ¹⁴Then, therefore, Jesus said to them freely, "Lazarus has died; ¹⁵and I rejoice, for your sake (that you may believe), that I was not there; but we may go to him"; ¹⁶therefore Thomas, who is called Didymus, said to the fellow-disciples, "We may go—we also, that we may die with Him," ¹⁷Jesus, therefore, having come, found him having already been four days in the tomb. ¹⁸And Bethany was near to Jerusalem, about fifteen stadia off, ¹⁹and many of the Jews had come to Martha and Mary, that they might comfort them concerning their brother; ²⁰Martha, therefore, when she heard that Jesus comes, met Him, and Mary kept sitting in the house. ²¹Martha, therefore, said to Jesus, "Lord, if You had been here, my brother had not died; ²²but even now, I have known that whatever You may ask of God, God will give to You"; ²³Jesus says to her, "Your brother will rise again." ²⁴Martha says to Him, "I have known that he will rise again in the resurrection in the last day"; ²⁵Jesus said to her, "I AM the resurrection, and the life; he who is believing in Me, even if he may die, will live; ²⁶and everyone who is living and believing in Me will not die—throughout the age; ²⁷do you believe this?" She says to Him, "Yes, Lord, I have believed that You are the Christ, the Son of God, who is coming into the world." ²⁸And having said these things, she went away, and called Mary her sister privately, saying, "The Teacher is present, and calls you"; ²⁹she, when she heard, rises up quickly, and comes to Him; ³⁰and Jesus had not yet come into the village, but was in the place where Martha met Him; ³¹the Jews, therefore, who were with her in the house, and were comforting her, having seen Mary that she rose up quickly and went forth, followed her, saying, "She goes away to the tomb, that she may weep there." ³²Mary, therefore, when she came where Jesus was, having seen Him, fell at His feet, saying to Him, "Lord, if You had been here, my brother had not died"; ³³Jesus, therefore, when He saw her weeping, and the Jews who came with her weeping, groaned in the spirit, and troubled Himself, and He said, ³⁴"Where have you laid him?" They say to Him, "Lord, come and see"; ³⁵Jesus wept. ³⁶The Jews, therefore, said, "Behold, how He was cherishing him!" ³⁷And certain of them said, "Was not this One, who opened the eyes of the blind man, also able to cause that this one might not have died?" ³⁸Jesus, therefore, again groaning in Himself, comes to the tomb, and it was a cave, and a stone was lying on it, ³⁹Jesus says, "Take away the stone"; the sister of him who has died—Martha—says to Him, "Lord, he already stinks, for he is four days dead"; ⁴⁰Jesus says to her, "Did I not say to you that if you may believe, you will see the glory of God?" ⁴¹Therefore they took away the stone where the dead was laid, and Jesus lifted His eyes upwards, and said, "Father, I thank You that You heard Me; ⁴²and I knew that You always hear Me, but because of the multitude that is standing by, I said [it], that they may believe that You sent Me." ⁴³And saying these things, He cried out with a loud voice, "Lazarus, come forth!" ⁴⁴And he who died came forth, feet and hands being bound with grave-clothes, and his face was bound around with a napkin; Jesus says to them, "Loose him, and permit to go." ⁴⁵Many, therefore, of the Jews who came to Mary, and beheld what Jesus did, believed in Him; ⁴⁶but certain of them went away to the Pharisees, and told them what Jesus did; ⁴⁷the chief priests, therefore, and the Pharisees, gathered together [the] Sanhedrin and said, "What may we do? Because this Man does many signs? ⁴⁸If we may leave Him alone thus, all will believe in Him; and the Romans will come, and will take away both our place and nation." ⁴⁹And a certain one of them, Caiaphas, being chief priest of that year, said to them, "You have not known anything, ⁵⁰nor reason that it is good for us that one man may die for the people, and not the whole nation perish." ⁵¹And he did not say this of himself, but being chief priest of that year, he prophesied that Jesus was about to die for the nation, ⁵²and not for the nation only, but that also the children of God, who have been scattered abroad, He may gather together into one. ⁵³From that day, therefore, they took counsel together that they may kill Him; ⁵⁴Jesus, therefore, was no longer freely walking among the Jews, but went away from there into the region near the wilderness, to a city called Ephraim, and there He tarried with His disciples. ⁵⁵And the Passover of the Jews was near, and many went up to Jerusalem out of the country before the Passover, that they might purify themselves; ⁵⁶therefore they were seeking Jesus and said with one another, standing in the temple, "What appears to you—that He may not come to the celebration?" ⁵⁷And both the chief priests and the Pharisees had given a command, that if anyone may know where He is, he may show [it], so that they may seize Him.

CHAPTER 12

¹Jesus, therefore, six days before the Passover, came to Bethany, where Lazarus was, who had died, whom He raised out of the dead; ²they made, therefore, a dinner to Him there, and Martha was ministering, and Lazarus was one of those reclining together with Him; ³Mary, therefore, having taken a pound of ointment of spikenard, of great price, anointed the feet of Jesus and wiped His feet with her hair, and the house was filled from the fragrance of the ointment. ⁴Therefore one of His disciples—Judas Iscariot, of Simon, who is about to deliver Him up—says, ⁵"Why was this ointment not sold for three hundred denarii, and given to the poor?" ⁶And he said this, not because he was caring for the poor, but because he was a thief, and had the bag, and what things were put in he was carrying. ⁷Jesus, therefore, said, "Permit her; she has kept it for the day of My embalming, ⁸for you always have the poor with yourselves, and you do not always have Me." ⁹Therefore, a great multitude of the Jews knew that He is there, and they came, not only because of Jesus, but that they may also see Lazarus, whom He raised out of the dead; ¹⁰and the chief priests took counsel, that they may also kill Lazarus, ¹¹because on account of him many of the Jews were going away, and were believing in Jesus. ¹²On the next day, a great multitude that came to the celebration, having heard that Jesus comes to Jerusalem, ¹³took the branches of the palms, and went forth to meet Him, and were crying, "Hosanna! Blessed [is] He who is coming in the Name of the LORD—the King of Israel"; ¹⁴and Jesus having found a young donkey sat on it, according as it is written, ¹⁵"Do not fear, daughter of Zion, behold, your King comes, sitting on a colt of a donkey." ¹⁶And His disciples did not know these things at first, but when Jesus was glorified, then they remembered that these things were having been written about Him, and these things they did to Him. ¹⁷The multitude, therefore, who are with Him, were testifying that He called Lazarus out of the tomb, and raised him out of the dead; ¹⁸because of this the multitude also met Him, because they heard of His having done this sign, ¹⁹therefore the Pharisees said among themselves, "You see that you do not gain anything, behold, the world went after Him." ²⁰And there were certain Greeks out of those coming up that they may worship in the celebration, ²¹these then came near to Philip, who [is] from Bethsaida of Galilee, and were asking him, saying, "Lord, we wish to see Jesus"; ²²Philip comes and tells Andrew, and again Andrew and Philip tell Jesus. ²³And Jesus responded to them, saying, "The hour has

come that the Son of Man may be glorified; ²⁴truly, truly, I say to you, if the grain of the wheat, having fallen to the earth, may not die, itself remains alone; and if it may die, it bears much fruit; ²⁵he who is cherishing his life will lose it, and he who is hating his life in this world will keep it to continuous life; ²⁶if anyone may minister to Me, let him follow Me, and where I am, there My servant will be also; and if anyone may minister to Me—the Father will honor him. ²⁷Now My soul has been troubled; and what will I say—Father, save Me from this hour? But because of this I came to this hour; ²⁸Father, glorify Your Name." Therefore there came a voice out of Heaven, "I both glorified, and again I will glorify [it]"; ²⁹the multitude, therefore, having stood and heard, were saying that there has been thunder; others said, "A messenger has spoken to Him." ³⁰Jesus answered and said, "This voice has not come because of Me, but because of you; ³¹now is a judgment of this world, now will the ruler of this world be cast forth; ³²and I, if I may be lifted up from the earth, will draw all men to Myself." ³³And this He said signifying by what death He was about to die; ³⁴the multitude answered Him, "We heard that the Christ remains out of the Law—throughout the age; and how do You say that it is required that the Son of Man be lifted up? Who is this—the Son of Man?" ³⁵Therefore Jesus said to them, "Yet a short time is the light with you; walk while you have the light, that darkness may not overtake you; and he who is walking in the darkness has not known where he goes; ³⁶while you have the light, believe in the light, that you may become sons of light." Jesus spoke these things, and having gone away, He was hid from them, ³⁷yet He, having done so many signs before them, they were not believing in Him, ³⁸that the word of Isaiah the prophet might be fulfilled, which he said, "LORD, who gave credence to our report? And the arm of the LORD—to whom was it revealed?" ³⁹Because of this they were not able to believe, that again Isaiah said, ⁴⁰"He has blinded their eyes, and hardened their heart, that they might not see with the eyes, and understand with the heart, and turn, and I might heal them"; ⁴¹Isaiah said these things when he saw His glory, and spoke of Him. ⁴²Still, however, out of the rulers many also believed in Him, but because of the Pharisees they were not confessing, that they might not be put out of the synagogue, ⁴³for they loved the glory of men more than the glory of God. ⁴⁴And Jesus cried and said, "He who is believing in Me, does not believe in Me, but in Him who sent Me; ⁴⁵and He who is beholding Me, beholds Him who sent Me; ⁴⁶I—light to the world—have come, that everyone who is believing in Me may not remain in the darkness; ⁴⁷and if anyone may hear My sayings, and not believe, I do not judge him, for I did not come that I might judge the world, but that I might save the world. ⁴⁸He who is rejecting Me, and not receiving My sayings, has one who is judging him, the word that I spoke, that will judge him in the last day, ⁴⁹because I did not speak from Myself, but the Father who sent Me, He gave Me a command, what I may say, and what I may speak, ⁵⁰and I have known that His command is continuous life; what, therefore, I speak, according as the Father has said to Me, so I speak."

CHAPTER 13

¹And before the Celebration of the Passover, Jesus knowing that His hour has come, that He may depart out of this world to the Father, having loved His own who [are] in the world—to the end He loved them. ²And dinner having come, the Devil already having put [it] into the heart of Judas of Simon, Iscariot, that he may deliver Him up, ³Jesus knowing that all things the Father has given to Him—into [His] hands, and that He came forth from God, and He goes to God, ⁴rises from the dinner, and lays down His garments, and having taken a towel, He girded Himself; ⁵afterward He puts water into the basin, and began to wash the feet of His disciples, and to wipe with the towel with which He was being girded. ⁶He comes, therefore, to Simon Peter, and that one says to Him, "Lord, You—do You wash my feet?" ⁷Jesus answered and said to him, "That which I do you have not known now, but you will know after these things"; ⁸Peter says to Him, "You may not wash my feet—throughout the age." Jesus answered him, "If I may not wash you, you have no part with Me"; ⁹Simon Peter says to Him, "Lord, not my feet only, but also the hands and the head." ¹⁰Jesus says to him, "He who has been bathed has no need except to wash his feet, but he is clean altogether; and you are clean, but not all"; ¹¹for He knew him who is delivering Him up; because of this He said, "You are not all clean." ¹²When, therefore, He washed their feet, and took His garments, having reclined again, He said to them, "Do you know what I have done to you? ¹³You call Me the Teacher and the LORD, and you say well, for I am; ¹⁴if then I washed your feet—the LORD and the Teacher—you also ought to wash one another's feet. ¹⁵For I gave to you an example, that, according as I did to you, you also may do; ¹⁶truly, truly, I say to you, a servant is not greater than his lord, nor an apostle greater than he who sent him; ¹⁷if you have known these things, you are blessed if you may do them; ¹⁸I do not speak concerning you all; I have known whom I chose for Myself; but that the Writing may be fulfilled: He who is eating the bread with Me, lifted up his heel against Me. ¹⁹From this time I tell you, before its coming to pass, that, when it may come to pass, you may believe that I AM; ²⁰truly, truly, I say to you, he who is receiving whomsoever I may send, receives Me; and he who is receiving Me, receives Him who sent Me." ²¹Having said these things, Jesus was troubled in the spirit, and testified and said, "Truly, truly, I say to you that one of you will deliver Me up"; ²²the disciples were looking, therefore, at one another, doubting concerning of whom He speaks. ²³And there was one of His disciples reclining in the bosom of Jesus, whom Jesus was loving; ²⁴Simon Peter, then, beckons to this one, to inquire who he may be concerning whom He speaks, ²⁵and that one having leaned back on the breast of Jesus, responds to Him, "Lord, who is it?" ²⁶Jesus answers, "It is that one to whom I, having dipped the morsel, will give it"; and having dipped the morsel, He gives [it] to Judas of Simon, Iscariot. ²⁷And after the morsel, then Satan entered into that one. Jesus, therefore, says to him, "What you do—do quickly"; ²⁸and none of those reclining to eat knew for what intent He said this to him, ²⁹for certain [of them] were thinking, since Judas had the bag, that Jesus says to him, "Buy what we have need of for the celebration"; or that he may give something to the poor; ³⁰having received, therefore, the morsel, that one immediately went forth, and it was night. ³¹When, therefore, he went forth, Jesus says, "Now was the Son of Man glorified, and God was glorified in Him; ³²if God was glorified in Him, God will also glorify Him in Himself; indeed, He will immediately glorify Him. ³³Little children, yet a little [while] am I with you; you will seek Me, and according as I said to the Jews, I also say to you now: To where I go away, you are not able to come. ³⁴A new command I give to you, that you love one another; according as I loved you, that you also love one another; ³⁵in this will all know that you are My disciples, if you may have love one to another." ³⁶Simon Peter says to Him, "Lord, to where do You go away?" Jesus answered him, "To where I go away, you are not able now to follow Me, but afterward you will follow Me." ³⁷Peter says to Him, "Lord, why am I not able to follow You now? I will lay down my life for You"; ³⁸Jesus answered him, "You will lay down your life for Me? Truly, truly, I say to you, a rooster will not crow until you may deny Me three times."

CHAPTER 14

¹"Do not let your heart be troubled, believe in God, believe also in Me; ²in the house of My Father are many rooms; and if not, I would have told you; I go on to prepare a place for you; ³and if I go on and prepare a place for you, I come again, and will receive you to Myself, that where I am you also may be; ⁴and to where I go away you have known, and the way you have known." ⁵Thomas says to Him, "Lord, we have not known to where You go away, and how are we able to know the way?" ⁶Jesus says to him, "I AM the way, and the truth, and the life, no one comes to the Father, if not through Me; ⁷if you had known Me, you would also have known My Father, and from this time you have known Him, and have seen Him." ⁸Philip says to Him, "Lord, show to us the Father, and it is enough for us"; ⁹Jesus says to him, "Such [a] long time am I with you, and you have not known Me, Philip? He who has seen Me has seen the Father; and how do you say, Show to us the Father? ¹⁰Do you not believe that I [am] in the Father, and the Father is in Me? The sayings that I speak to you, I do not speak from Myself, and the Father who is abiding in Me does the works Himself; ¹¹believe Me, that I [am] in the Father, and the Father in Me; and if not, because of the works themselves, believe Me. ¹²Truly, truly, I

say to you, he who is believing in Me, the works that I do—that one will also do, and greater than these he will do, because I go on to My Father; ¹³and whatever you may ask in My Name, I will do, that the Father may be glorified in the Son; ¹⁴if you ask anything in My Name I will do [it]. ¹⁵If you love Me, keep My commands, ¹⁶and I will ask the Father, and He will give to you another Comforter, that He may remain with you throughout the age: ¹⁷the Spirit of truth, whom the world is not able to receive, because it does not see nor know [this] One, and you know [this] One, because [this] One remains with you, and will be in you. ¹⁸I will not leave you bereaved, I come to you; ¹⁹yet a little [while] and the world beholds Me no more, and you behold Me, because I live, and you will live; ²⁰in that day you will know that I [am] in My Father, and you in Me, and I in you; ²¹he who is having My commands, and is keeping them, that one it is who is loving Me, and he who is loving Me will be loved by My Father, and I will love him, and will manifest Myself to him." ²²Judas says to Him (not the Iscariot), "Lord, what has come to pass, that You are about to manifest Yourself to us, and not to the world?" ²³Jesus answered and said to him, "If anyone may love Me, he will keep My word, and My Father will love him, and We will come to him, and We will make [an] abode with him; ²⁴he who is not loving Me does not keep My words; and the word that you hear is not Mine, but the Father's who sent Me. ²⁵These things I have spoken to you, remaining with you, ²⁶and the Comforter, the Holy Spirit, whom the Father will send in My Name, He will teach you all things, and remind you of all things that I said to you. ²⁷Peace I leave to you; My peace I give to you. Not according as the world gives do I give to you. Do not let your heart be troubled, nor let it be afraid. ²⁸You heard that I said to you, I go away, and I come to you. If you loved Me, you would have rejoiced that I said, I go on to the Father, because My Father is greater than I. ²⁹And now I have said [it] to you before it comes to pass, that when it may come to pass, you may believe. ³⁰I will no longer talk much with you, for the ruler of this world comes, and he has nothing in Me; ³¹but that the world may know that I love the Father, and according as the Father gave Me command, so I do; arise, we may go from here."

CHAPTER 15

¹"I AM the true vine, and My Father is the vinedresser; ²every branch not bearing fruit in Me, He takes it away, and everyone bearing fruit, He cleanses by pruning it, that it may bear more fruit; ³you are already clean, because of the word that I have spoken to you; ⁴remain in Me, and I in you, as the branch is not able to bear fruit of itself, if it may not remain in the vine, so neither you, if you may not remain in Me. ⁵I AM the vine, you the branches; he who is remaining in Me, and I in him, this one bears much fruit, because apart from Me you are not able to do anything; ⁶if anyone may not remain in Me, he was cast forth outside as the branch, and was withered, and they gather them, and cast into fire, and they are burned; ⁷if you may remain in Me, and My sayings may remain in you, whatever you may wish you will ask, and it will be done to you. ⁸In this was My Father glorified, that you may bear much fruit, and you will become My disciples. ⁹According as the Father loved Me, I also loved you, remain in My love; ¹⁰if you may keep My commands, you will remain in My love, according as I have kept the commands of My Father, and remain in His love; ¹¹these things I have spoken to you, that My joy in you may remain, and your joy may be full. ¹²This is My command, that you love one another, according as I loved you; ¹³greater love has no one than this, that anyone may lay down his life for his friends; ¹⁴you are My friends if you may do whatever I command you; ¹⁵I no longer call you servants, because the servant has not known what his lord does, and I have called you friends, because all things that I heard from My Father, I made known to you. ¹⁶You did not choose Me, but I chose you, and appointed you, that you might go away, and might bear fruit, and your fruit might remain, that whatever you may ask of the Father in My Name, He may give you. ¹⁷These things I command you, that you love one another; ¹⁸if the world hates you, you know that it has hated Me before you; ¹⁹if you were of the world, the world would have been cherishing its own, but because you are not of the world, but I chose [you] out of the world—because of this the world hates you. ²⁰Remember the word that I said to you: A servant is not greater than his lord; if they persecuted Me, they will also persecute you; if they kept My word, they will also keep yours; ²¹but all these things will they do to you, because of My Name, because they have not known Him who sent Me; ²²if I had not come and spoken to them, they were not having sin; but now they have no pretext for their sin. ²³He who is hating Me, hates My Father also; ²⁴if I did not do among them the works that no other has done, they were not having sin, and now they have both seen and hated both Me and My Father; ²⁵but—that the word may be fulfilled that was written in their law—They hated Me without a cause. ²⁶And when the Comforter may come, whom I will send to you from the Father—the Spirit of truth, who comes forth from the Father, He will testify of Me; ²⁷and you also testify, because you are with Me from the beginning."

CHAPTER 16

¹"These things I have spoken to you, that you may not be stumbled. ²They will put you out of the synagogues, but an hour comes that everyone who has killed you may think to offer service to God; ³and these things they will do to you, because they did not know the Father, nor Me. ⁴But these things I have spoken to you, that when the hour may come, you may remember them, that I said [them] to you, and I did not say these things to you from the beginning, because I was with you; ⁵and now I go away to Him who sent Me, and none of you asks Me, To where do you go? ⁶But because I have said to you these things, the sorrow has filled your heart. ⁷But I tell you the truth; it is better for you that I go away, for if I may not go away, the Comforter will not come to you, and if I go on, I will send Him to you; ⁸and having come, He will convict the world concerning sin, and concerning righteousness, and concerning judgment; ⁹concerning sin indeed, because they do not believe in Me; ¹⁰and concerning righteousness, because I go away to My Father, and you behold Me no more; ¹¹and concerning judgment, because the ruler of this world has been judged. ¹²I have yet many things to say to you, but you are not able to bear [them] now; ¹³and when He may come—the Spirit of truth—He will guide you to all the truth, for He will not speak from Himself, but as many things as He will hear He will speak, and the coming things He will tell you; ¹⁴He will glorify Me, because He will take of Mine, and will tell to you. ¹⁵All things, as many as the Father has, are Mine; because of this I said that He will take of Mine, and will tell to you; ¹⁶a little while, and you do not behold Me, and again a little while, and you will see Me, because I go away to the Father." ¹⁷Therefore [some] of His disciples said to one another, "What is this that He says to us, A little while, and you do not behold Me, and again a little while, and you will see Me, and, Because I go away to the Father?" ¹⁸They said then, "What is this He says—the little while? We have not known what He says." ¹⁹Jesus, therefore, knew that they were wishing to ask Him, and He said to them, "Concerning this do you seek with one another, because I said, A little while, and you do not behold Me, and again a little while, and you will see Me? ²⁰Truly, truly, I say to you that you will weep and lament, and the world will rejoice; and you will be sorrowful, but your sorrow will become joy. ²¹The woman, when she may bear, has sorrow, because her hour came, and when she may bear the child, she no longer remembers the anguish, because of the joy that a man was born into the world. ²²And you, therefore, now indeed have sorrow; and again I will see you, and your heart will rejoice, and no one takes your joy from you, ²³and in that day you will question nothing of Me; truly, truly, I say to you, as many things as you may ask of the Father in My Name, He will give you; ²⁴until now you asked nothing in My Name; ask, and you will receive, that your joy may be full. ²⁵I have spoken these things in allegories to you, but there comes an hour when I will no longer speak to you in allegories, but will tell you freely of the Father. ²⁶In that day you will make request in My Name, and I do not say to you that I will ask the Father for you, ²⁷for the Father Himself cherishes you, because you have cherished Me, and you have believed that I came forth from God; ²⁸I came forth from the Father, and have come into the world; again I leave the world, and go on to the Father." ²⁹His disciples say to Him, "Behold, now You speak freely, and You do not speak allegory; ³⁰now we have known that You have known all things, and have no need that

JOHN

anyone questions You; in this we believe that You came forth from God." ³¹Jesus answered them, "Now do you believe? Behold, there comes an hour, ³²and now it has come, that you may be scattered, each to his own things, and you may leave Me alone, and I am not alone, because the Father is with Me; ³³these things I have spoken to you, that in Me you may have peace, in the world you will have tribulation, but take courage—I have overcome the world."

CHAPTER 17

¹These things Jesus spoke, and lifted up His eyes to the sky, and said, "Father, the hour has come, glorify Your Son, that Your Son may also glorify You, ²according as You gave to Him authority over all flesh, that—all that You have given to Him—He may give to them continuous life; ³and this is the continuous life, that they may know You, the only true God, and Him whom You sent—Jesus Christ; ⁴I glorified You on the earth, having completed the work that You have given Me, that I should do. ⁵And now, glorify Me, You Father, with Yourself, with the glory that I had with You before the world was; ⁶I revealed Your Name to the men whom You have given to Me out of the world; they were Yours, and You have given them to Me, and they have kept Your word; ⁷now they have known that all things, as many as You have given to Me, are from You, ⁸because the sayings that You have given to Me, I have given to them, and they themselves received, and have known truly, that I came forth from You, and they believed that You sent Me. ⁹I ask in regard to them; I do not ask in regard to the world, but in regard to those whom You have given to Me, because they are Yours, ¹⁰and all Mine are Yours, and Yours [are] Mine, and I have been glorified in them; ¹¹and I am no longer in the world, and these are in the world, and I come to You. Holy Father, keep them in Your Name, whom You have given to Me, that they may be one as We [are one]; ¹²when I was with them in the world, I was keeping them in Your Name; I guarded those whom You have given to Me, and none of them were destroyed, except the son of the destruction, that the Writing may be fulfilled. ¹³And now I come to You, and these things I speak in the world, that they may have My joy fulfilled in themselves; ¹⁴I have given Your word to them, and the world hated them, because they are not of the world, as I am not of the world; ¹⁵I do not ask that You may take them out of the world, but that You may keep them out of the evil. ¹⁶They are not of the world, as I am not of the world; ¹⁷sanctify them in Your truth, Your word is truth; ¹⁸as You sent Me into the world, I also sent them into the world; ¹⁹and I sanctify Myself for them, that they also may be sanctified in truth themselves. ²⁰And I do not ask in regard to these alone, but also in regard to those who will be believing in Me through their word, ²¹that they all may be one, as You Father [are] in Me, and I in You, that they also may be one in Us, that the world may believe that You sent Me. ²²And I have given to them the glory that You have given to Me, that they may be one as We are one— ²³I in them, and You in Me, that they may be perfected into one, and that the world may know that You sent Me, and loved them as You loved Me. ²⁴Father, those whom You have given to Me, I will that where I am they also may be with Me, that they may behold My glory that You gave to Me, because You loved Me before the foundation of the world. ²⁵Righteous Father, also the world did not know You, and I knew You, and these have known that You sent Me, ²⁶and I made known to them Your Name, and will make known, that the love with which You loved Me may be in them, and I in them."

CHAPTER 18

¹Having said these things, Jesus went forth with His disciples beyond the Brook of Kidron, where [there] was a garden, into which He entered, Himself and His disciples, ²and Judas also, who delivered Him up, had known the place, because Jesus assembled there with His disciples many times. ³Judas, therefore, having taken the band and officers out of the chief priests and Pharisees, comes there with torches and lamps, and weapons; ⁴Jesus, therefore, knowing all things that are coming on Him, having gone forth, said to them, "Whom do you seek?" ⁵They answered Him, "Jesus the Nazarene"; Jesus says to them, "I AM"; and Judas who delivered Him up was standing with them. ⁶When, therefore, He said to them, "I AM," they went away backward, and fell to the ground. ⁷Again, therefore, He questioned them, "Whom do you seek?" And they said, "Jesus the Nazarene"; ⁸Jesus answered, "I said to you that I AM; if, then, you seek Me, permit these to go away"; ⁹that the word might be fulfilled that He said, "Those whom You have given to Me, I did not lose even one of them." ¹⁰Simon Peter, therefore, having a sword, drew it, and struck the chief priest's servant, and cut off his right ear—and the name of the servant was Malchus— ¹¹Jesus, therefore, said to Peter, "Put the sword into the sheath; the cup that the Father has given to Me, may I not drink it?" ¹²The band, therefore, and the captain, and the officers of the Jews, took hold on Jesus, and bound Him, ¹³and they led Him away to Annas first, for he was father-in-law of Caiaphas, who was chief priest of that year, ¹⁴and Caiaphas was he who gave counsel to the Jews that it is good for one man to perish for the people. ¹⁵And following Jesus was Simon Peter, and the other disciple, and that disciple was known to the chief priest, and he entered with Jesus into the hall of the chief priest, ¹⁶and Peter was standing at the door outside, therefore the other disciple who was known to the chief priest went forth, and he spoke to the doorkeeper, and he brought in Peter. ¹⁷Then the maid, the doorkeeper, says to Peter, "Are you also of the disciples of this Man?" He says, "I am not"; ¹⁸and the servants and the officers were standing, having made a fire of coals, because it was cold, and they were warming themselves, and Peter was standing with them, and warming himself. ¹⁹The chief priests, therefore, questioned Jesus concerning His disciples, and concerning His teaching; ²⁰Jesus answered him, "I spoke freely to the world, I always taught in a synagogue, and in the temple, where the Jews always come together; and I spoke nothing in secret; ²¹why do you question Me? Question those having heard what I spoke to them; behold, these have known what I said." ²²And He having said these things, one of the officers standing by gave Jesus a slap, saying, "Thus do You answer the chief priest?" ²³Jesus answered him, "If I spoke ill, testify concerning the ill; and if well, why do you strike Me?" ²⁴Annas then sent Him bound to Caiaphas the chief priest. ²⁵And Simon Peter was standing and warming himself, then they said to him, "Are you also of His disciples?" He denied and said, "I am not." ²⁶One of the servants of the chief priest, being a relative of him whose ear Peter cut off, says, "Did I not see you in the garden with Him?" ²⁷Again, therefore, Peter denied, and immediately a rooster crowed. ²⁸They led, therefore, Jesus from Caiaphas into the Praetorium, and it was early, and they themselves did not enter into the Praetorium, that they might not be defiled, but that they might eat the Passover; ²⁹Pilate, therefore, went forth to them and said, "What accusation do you bring against this Man?" ³⁰They answered and said to him, "If He were not doing evil, we had not delivered Him to you." ³¹Pilate, therefore, said to them, "Take Him—you—and judge Him according to your law"; the Jews, therefore, said to him, "It is not lawful to us to put anyone to death"; ³²that the word of Jesus might be fulfilled which He said, signifying by what death He was about to die. ³³Pilate, therefore, entered into the Praetorium again, and called Jesus, and said to Him, "You are the King of the Jews?" ³⁴Jesus answered him, "Do you say this from yourself? Or did others say it to you about Me?" ³⁵Pilate answered, "Am I a Jew? Your nation and the chief priests delivered You up to me; what did You do?" ³⁶Jesus answered, "My kingdom is not of this world; if My kingdom were of this world, My officers had struggled that I might not be delivered up to Jews; but now My kingdom is not from here." ³⁷Pilate, therefore, said to Him, "Are You then a king?" Jesus answered, "You say [it], because I am a king; I have been born for this, and I have come into the world for this, that I may testify to the truth; everyone who is of the truth, hears My voice." ³⁸Pilate says to Him, "What is truth?" And having said this, again he went forth to the Jews and says to them, "I find no fault in Him; ³⁹and you have a custom that I will release to you one in the Passover; do you determine, therefore, [that] I will release to you the King of the Jews?" ⁴⁰Therefore they all cried out again, saying, "Not this One—but Barabbas"; and Barabbas was a robber.

CHAPTER 19

¹Then, therefore, Pilate took Jesus and scourged [Him], ²and the soldiers having plaited a garland of thorns, placed [it] on His head, and they cast a purple garment around Him, ³and said, "Hail! The King of the Jews"; and they were giving Him slaps. ⁴Pilate, therefore, again went forth outside and says to them, "Behold, I bring Him to you outside, that you may know that I find no fault in Him"; ⁵Jesus, therefore, came forth outside, bearing the thorny garland and the purple garment; and he says to them, "Behold, the Man!" ⁶When, therefore, the chief priests and the officers saw Him, they cried out, saying, "Crucify! Crucify!" Pilate says to them, "Take Him yourselves and crucify, for I find no fault in Him"; ⁷the Jews answered him, "We have a law, and according to our law He ought to die, for He made Himself Son of God." ⁸When, therefore, Pilate heard this word, he was more afraid, ⁹and entered again into the Praetorium and says to Jesus, "Where are You from?" And Jesus gave him no answer. ¹⁰Pilate, therefore, says to Him, "Do You not speak to me? Have You not known that I have authority to crucify You, and I have authority to release You?" ¹¹Jesus answered, "You would have no authority against Me if it were not having been given you from above; because of this, he who is delivering Me up to you has greater sin." ¹²From this [time] Pilate was seeking to release Him, and the Jews were crying out, saying, "If you may release this One, you are not a friend of Caesar; everyone making himself a king speaks against Caesar." ¹³Pilate, therefore, having heard this word, brought Jesus outside—and he sat down on the judgment seat—to a place called, "Pavement," and in Hebrew, Gabbatha; ¹⁴and it was the Preparation of the Passover, and as it were the sixth hour, and he says to the Jews, "Behold, your King!" ¹⁵And they cried out, "Take away! Take away! Crucify Him!" Pilate says to them, "Will I crucify your King?" The chief priests answered, "We have no king except Caesar." ¹⁶Then, therefore, he delivered Him up to them, that He may be crucified, and they took Jesus and led [Him] away, ¹⁷and carrying His cross, He went forth to the [place] called "Place of [the] Skull," which is called in Hebrew, Golgotha— ¹⁸where they crucified Him, and with Him two others, on this side and on that side, but Jesus in the middle. ¹⁹And Pilate also wrote a title, and put [it] on the cross, and it was written: "JESUS THE NAZARENE, THE KING OF THE JEWS"; ²⁰therefore many of the Jews read this title, because the place was near to the city where Jesus was crucified, and it was having been written in Hebrew, in Greek, in Latin. ²¹The chief priests of the Jews therefore said to Pilate, "Do not write, The King of the Jews, but that this One said, I am King of the Jews"; ²²Pilate answered, "What I have written, I have written." ²³The soldiers, therefore, when they crucified Jesus, took His garments, and made four parts, to each soldier a part, also the coat, and the coat was seamless, from the top woven throughout; ²⁴they said, therefore, to one another, "We may not tear it, but cast a lot for it, whose it will be"; that the Writing might be fulfilled, that is saying, "They divided My garments to themselves, and they cast a lot for My clothing"; the soldiers, therefore, indeed, did these things. ²⁵And there stood by the cross of Jesus His mother, and His mother's sister, Mary of Cleopas, and Mary the Magdalene; ²⁶Jesus, therefore, having seen [His] mother, and the disciple standing by, whom He was loving, He says to His mother, "Woman, behold, your son"; ²⁷afterward He says to the disciple, "Behold, your mother"; and from that hour the disciple took her to his own [home]. ²⁸After this, Jesus knowing that all things have now been accomplished, that the Writing may be fulfilled, says, "I thirst"; ²⁹a vessel, therefore, was placed full of vinegar, and having filled a sponge with vinegar, and having put [it] around a hyssop stalk, they put [it] to His mouth; ³⁰when, therefore, Jesus received the vinegar, He said, "It has been accomplished." And having bowed the head, gave up the spirit. ³¹The Jews, therefore, that the bodies might not remain on the cross on the Sabbath, since it was the Preparation (for that Sabbath day was a great one), asked of Pilate that their legs may be broken, and they [are] taken away. ³²The soldiers, therefore, came, and they indeed broke the legs of the first and of the other who was crucified with Him, ³³and having come to Jesus, when they saw Him already having been dead, they did not break His legs; ³⁴but one of the soldiers pierced His side with a spear, and immediately there came forth blood and water; ³⁵and he who has seen has testified, and his testimony is true, and that one has known that he speaks true things, that you also may believe. ³⁶For these things came to pass, that the Writing may be fulfilled, "A bone of Him will not be broken"; ³⁷and again another Writing says, "They will look to Him whom they pierced." ³⁸And after these things, Joseph of Arimathea—being a disciple of Jesus, but concealed, through the fear of the Jews—asked of Pilate, that he may take away the body of Jesus, and Pilate gave leave; he came, therefore, and took away the body of Jesus, ³⁹and Nicodemus also came—who came to Jesus by night at the first—carrying a mixture of myrrh and aloes, as it were, one hundred pounds. ⁴⁰Therefore they took the body of Jesus, and bound it with linen clothes with the spices, according as it was the custom of the Jews to prepare for burial; ⁴¹and there was a garden in the place where He was crucified, and a new tomb in the garden, in which no one was yet laid; ⁴²therefore, because the tomb was near, there they laid Jesus because of the Preparation of the Jews.

CHAPTER 20

¹And on the first [day] of the weeks, Mary the Magdalene comes early (there being yet darkness) to the tomb, and she sees the stone having been taken away out of the tomb; ²she runs, therefore, and comes to Simon Peter, and to the other disciple whom Jesus was cherishing, and says to them, "They took away the Lord out of the tomb, and we have not known where they laid Him." ³Peter, therefore, went forth, and the other disciple, and they were coming to the tomb, ⁴and the two were running together, and the other disciple ran forward more quickly than Peter, and came first to the tomb, ⁵and having stooped down, sees the linen clothes lying, yet, indeed, he did not enter. ⁶Simon Peter, therefore, comes, following him, and he entered into the tomb, and beholds the linen clothes lying [there], ⁷and the napkin that was on His head not lying with the linen clothes, but apart, having been folded up, in one place; ⁸then, therefore, the other disciple who came first to the tomb entered also, and he saw and believed; ⁹for they did not yet know the Writing, that it was necessary for Him to rise again out of the dead. ¹⁰The disciples therefore went away again to their own friends, ¹¹and Mary was standing near the tomb, weeping outside; as she was weeping, then, she stooped down into the tomb, and beholds two messengers in white, sitting, ¹²one at the head and one at the feet, where the body of Jesus had been laid. ¹³And they say to her, "Woman, why do you weep?" She says to them, "Because they took away my Lord, and I have not known where they laid Him"; ¹⁴and having said these things, she turned backward, and sees Jesus standing, and she had not known that it is Jesus. ¹⁵Jesus says to her, "Woman, why do you weep? Whom do you seek?" She, supposing that He is the gardener, says to Him, "Lord, if You carried Him away, tell me where You laid Him, and I will take Him away"; ¹⁶Jesus says to her, "Mary!" Having turned, she says to Him, "Rabboni!" That is to say, "Teacher." ¹⁷Jesus says to her, "Do not be touching Me, for I have not yet ascended to My Father; and be going on to My brothers, and say to them, I ascend to My Father and your Father, and [to] My God and your God." ¹⁸Mary the Magdalene comes, reporting to the disciples that she has seen the LORD, and [that] He said these things to her. ¹⁹It being, therefore, evening, on that day, the first [day] of the weeks, and the doors having been shut where the disciples were assembled through fear of the Jews, Jesus came and stood in the midst, and says to them, "Peace to you"; ²⁰and having said this, He showed them His hands and side; the disciples, therefore, rejoiced,

having seen the LORD. ²¹Jesus, therefore, said to them again, "Peace to you; according as the Father has sent Me, I also send you"; ²²having said this, He breathed on [them], and says to them, "Receive the Holy Spirit; ²³if you may forgive the sins of any, they are forgiven them; if you may retain of any, they have been retained." ²⁴And Thomas, one of the Twelve, who is called Didymus, was not with them when Jesus came; ²⁵the other disciples, therefore, said to him, "We have seen the Lord!" And he said to them, "If I may not see the mark of the nails in His hands, and may [not] put my finger into the mark of the nails, and may [not] put my hand into His side, I will not believe." ²⁶And after eight days, again His disciples were within, and Thomas [was] with them; Jesus comes, the doors having been shut, and He stood in the midst and said, "Peace to you!" ²⁷Then He says to Thomas, "Bring your finger here, and see My hands, and bring your hand, and put [it] into My side, and do not become unbelieving, but believing." ²⁸And Thomas answered and said to Him, "My Lord and my God!" ²⁹Jesus says to him, "Because you have seen Me, Thomas, you have believed; blessed [are] those having not seen, and having believed." ³⁰Many indeed, therefore, other signs Jesus also did before His disciples that are not written in this scroll; ³¹and these have been written that you may believe that Jesus is the Christ, the Son of God, and that believing, you may have life in His Name.

CHAPTER 21

¹After these things Jesus Himself again appeared to the disciples on the Sea of Tiberias, and He revealed Himself thus: ²Simon Peter, and Thomas who is called Didymus, and Nathanael from Cana of Galilee, and the [sons] of Zebedee, and two of His other disciples were together. ³Simon Peter says to them, "I go away to fish"; they say to him, "We go—we also—with you"; they went forth and immediately entered into the boat, and on that night they caught nothing. ⁴And morning having now come, Jesus stood at the shore, yet indeed the disciples did not know that it is Jesus; ⁵Jesus, therefore, says to them, "Boys, do you have any meat?" ⁶They answered Him, "No"; and He said to them, "Cast the net at the right side of the boat, and you will find [some]"; they cast, therefore, and no longer were they able to draw it, from the multitude of the fishes. ⁷That disciple, therefore, whom Jesus was loving says to Peter, "It is the Lord!" Simon Peter, therefore, having heard that it is the LORD, girded on the outer coat (for he was naked), and cast himself into the sea; ⁸and the other disciples came by the little boat, for they were not far from the land, but about two hundred cubits away, dragging the net of the fishes; ⁹when, therefore, they came to the land, they behold a fire of coals lying [there], and a fish lying on it, and bread. ¹⁰Jesus says to them, "Bring from the fishes that you caught now"; ¹¹Simon Peter went up, and drew the net up on the land, full of great fishes—one hundred fifty-three; and though they were so many, the net was not split. ¹²Jesus says to them, "Come, dine"; and none of the disciples were venturing to inquire of Him, "Who are You?" Knowing that it is the LORD; ¹³Jesus, therefore, comes and takes the bread and gives [it] to them, and the fish in like manner; ¹⁴this [is] now a third time Jesus was revealed to His disciples, having been raised from the dead. ¹⁵When, therefore, they dined, Jesus says to Simon Peter, "Simon, [son] of Jonas, do you love Me more than these?" He says to Him, "Yes, Lord; You have known that I cherish You"; He says to him, "Feed My lambs." ¹⁶He says to him again, a second time, "Simon, [son] of Jonas, do you love Me?" He says to Him, "Yes, Lord; You have known that I cherish You"; He says to him, "Tend My sheep." ¹⁷He says to him the third time, "Simon, [son] of Jonas, do you cherish Me?" Peter was grieved that He said to him the third time, "Do you cherish Me?" And he said to Him, "Lord, You have known all things; You know that I cherish You." Jesus says to him, "Feed My sheep; ¹⁸truly, truly, I say to you, when you were younger, you were girding yourself and were walking to where you willed, but when you may be old, you will stretch forth your hands, and another will gird you, and will carry [you] to where you do not will"; ¹⁹and this He said, signifying by what death he will glorify God; and having said this, He says to him, "Follow Me." ²⁰And having turned, Peter sees the disciple whom Jesus was loving following (who also reclined in the dinner on His breast and said, "Lord, who is he who is delivering You up?") ²¹Having seen this one, Peter says to Jesus, "Lord, and what of this one?" ²²Jesus says to him, "If I will him to remain until I come, what [is that] to you? Follow Me." ²³This word, therefore, went forth to the brothers that this disciple does not die, yet Jesus did not say to him that he does not die, but, "If I will him to remain until I come, what [is that] to you?" ²⁴This is the disciple who is testifying concerning these things, and he wrote these things, and we have known that his testimony is true. ²⁵And there are also many other things—as many as Jesus did—which, if they may be written one by one, I think the world itself does not even have place for the scrolls written. Amen.

ACTS

CHAPTER 1

¹The former account, indeed, I made concerning all things, O Theophilus, that Jesus began both to do and to teach, ²until the day in which, having given command through the Holy Spirit to the apostles whom He chose out, He was taken up, ³to whom He also presented Himself alive after His suffering, in many certain proofs, being seen by them through forty days, and speaking the things concerning the Kingdom of God. ⁴And being assembled together with them, He commanded them not to depart from Jerusalem, but to wait for the promise of the Father, "Which you heard from Me; ⁵because John, indeed, immersed in water, but you will be immersed in the Holy Spirit not many days after these." ⁶They, therefore, indeed, having come together, were questioning Him, saying, "Lord, do You at this time restore the kingdom to Israel?" ⁷And He said to them, "It is not yours to know times or seasons that the Father appointed in His own authority; ⁸but you will receive power at the coming of the Holy Spirit on you, and you will be witnesses for Me both in Jerusalem, and in all Judea and Samaria, and to the end of the earth." ⁹And having said these things—they beholding—He was taken up, and a cloud received Him up from their sight; ¹⁰and as they were looking steadfastly to the sky in His going on, then, behold, two men stood by them in white clothing, ¹¹who also said, "Men, Galileans, why do you stand gazing into the sky? This Jesus who was received up from you into Heaven, will so come in what manner you saw Him going on to Heaven." ¹²Then they returned to Jerusalem from [that] called the Mount of Olives, that is near Jerusalem, a Sabbath's journey; ¹³and when they came in, they went up into the upper room, where were abiding both Peter, and James, and John, and Andrew, Philip, and Thomas, Bartholomew, and Matthew, James, of Alphaeus, and Simon the Zealot, and Judas, of James; ¹⁴these were all continuing with one accord in prayer and supplication, with women, and Mary the mother of Jesus, and with His brothers. ¹⁵And in these days, Peter having risen up in the midst of the disciples, said (also the multitude of the names at the same place was, as it were, one hundred and twenty), ¹⁶"Men, brothers, it was necessary [for] this Writing to be fulfilled that the Holy Spirit spoke beforehand through the mouth of David, concerning Judas, who

became guide to those who took Jesus, ¹⁷because he was numbered among us, and received the share in this ministry. ¹⁸(This one, indeed, then, purchased a field out of the reward of unrighteousness, and falling headlong, burst apart in the midst, and all his bowels gushed forth, ¹⁹and it became known to all those dwelling in Jerusalem, insomuch that this place is called, in their proper dialect, Aceldama, that is, Field of Blood.) ²⁰For it has been written in [the] Scroll of Psalms: Let his lodging-place become desolate, and let no one be dwelling in it, and let another take his oversight. ²¹It is necessary, therefore, of the men who went with us during all the time in which the Lord Jesus went in and went out among us, ²²beginning from the immersion of John, to the day in which He was received up from us, one of these to become with us a witness of His resurrection." ²³And they set two, Joseph called Barsabas, who was surnamed Justus, and Matthias, ²⁴and having prayed, they said, "You, LORD, who are knowing the heart of all, show which one You chose of these two, ²⁵to receive the share of this ministry and apostleship, from which Judas, by transgression, fell, to go on to his proper place"; ²⁶and they gave their lots, and the lot fell on Matthias, and he was numbered with the eleven apostles.

CHAPTER 2

¹And in the day of the Pentecost being fulfilled, they were all with one accord at the same place, ²and there came suddenly out of the sky a sound as of a violent rushing wind, and it filled all the house where they were sitting, ³and there appeared to them divided tongues, as it were of fire; it also sat on each one of them, ⁴and they were all filled with the Holy Spirit, and began to speak with other tongues, according as the Spirit was giving them to declare. ⁵And there were Jews dwelling in Jerusalem, devout men from every nation of those under the heaven, ⁶and the rumor of this having come, the multitude came together, and was confounded, because they were, each one, hearing them speaking in his proper dialect, ⁷and they were all amazed, and wondered, saying to one another, "Behold, are not all these who are speaking Galileans? ⁸And how do we hear, each in our proper dialect, in which we were born? ⁹Parthians, and Medes, and Elamites, and those dwelling in Mesopotamia, in Judea also, and Cappadocia, Pontus, and Asia, ¹⁰Phrygia also, and Pamphylia, Egypt, and the parts of Libya that [are] along Cyrene, and the strangers of Rome, both Jews and proselytes, ¹¹Cretes and Arabians, we heard them speaking the great things of God in our tongues." ¹²And they were all amazed, and were in doubt, saying to one another, "What would this wish to be?" ¹³And others mocking said, "They are full of sweet wine"; ¹⁴and Peter having stood up with the Eleven, lifted up his voice and declared to them: "Men—Jews, and all those dwelling in Jerusalem! Let this be known to you, and listen to my sayings, ¹⁵for these are not drunken, as you take it up, for it is the third hour of the day. ¹⁶But this is that which has been spoken through the prophet Joel: ¹⁷And it will be in the last days, says God, || I will pour out of My Spirit on all flesh, || And your sons and your daughters will prophesy, || And your young men will see visions, || And your old men will dream dreams; ¹⁸And also on My menservants, and on My maidservants, || In those days, I will pour out of My Spirit, || And they will prophesy; ¹⁹And I will give wonders in the sky above, || And signs on the earth beneath—Blood, and fire, and vapor of smoke; ²⁰The sun will be turned to darkness, || And the moon to blood, || Before the coming of the Day of the LORD—the great and conspicuous; ²¹And it will be, everyone who, if he may have called on the Name of the LORD, will be saved. ²²Men, Israelites! Hear these words: Jesus the Nazarene, a man approved of God among you by mighty works, and wonders, and signs, that God did through Him in the midst of you, according as also you yourselves have known, ²³this One, by the determinate counsel and foreknowledge of God, being given out, having been taken by lawless hands, having been crucified—you slew, ²⁴whom God raised up, having loosed the travails of death, because it was not possible for Him to be held by it; ²⁵for David says in regard to Him: I foresaw the LORD always before me—Because He is on my right hand—That I may not be moved; ²⁶Because of this was my heart cheered, || And my tongue was glad, || And yet—my flesh will also rest on hope, ²⁷Because You will not leave my soul to Hades, || Nor will You give Your Holy One to see corruption; ²⁸You made known to me ways of life, || You will fill me with joy with Your countenance. ²⁹Men, brothers! It is permitted to speak with freedom to you concerning the patriarch David, that he both died and was buried, and his tomb is among us to this day; ³⁰therefore, being a prophet, and knowing that God swore to him with an oath, out of the fruit of his loins, according to the flesh, to raise up the Christ, to sit on his throne, ³¹having foreseen, he spoke concerning the resurrection of the Christ, that His soul was not left to Hades, nor did His flesh see corruption. ³²God raised up this Jesus, of which we are all witnesses; ³³then having been exalted at the right hand of God—also having received the promise of the Holy Spirit from the Father—He poured forth this which you now see and hear; ³⁴for David did not go up into the heavens, and he says himself: The LORD says to my Lord, || Sit at My right hand, ³⁵Until I make Your enemies Your footstool; ³⁶assuredly, therefore, let all the house of Israel know that God made Him both Lord and Christ—this Jesus whom you crucified." ³⁷And having heard, they were pricked to the heart; they also say to Peter and to the rest of the apostles, "What will we do, men, brothers?" ³⁸And Peter said to them, "Convert, and each of you be immersed on the Name of Jesus Christ, for forgiveness of sins, and you will receive the gift of the Holy Spirit, ³⁹for the promise is to you and to your children, and to all those far off, as many as the LORD our God will call." ⁴⁰Also with many more other words he was testifying and exhorting, saying, "Be saved from this perverse generation"; ⁴¹then those, indeed, who gladly received his word were immersed, and there were added on that day, as it were, three thousand souls, ⁴²and they were continuing steadfastly in the teaching of the apostles, and the fellowship, and the breaking of the bread, and the prayers. ⁴³And fear came on every soul, also many wonders and signs were being done through the apostles, ⁴⁴and all those believing were at the same place, and had all things common, ⁴⁵and they were selling the possessions and the goods, and were parting them to all, according as anyone had need. ⁴⁶Also continuing daily with one accord in the temple, also breaking bread at every house, they were partaking of food in gladness and simplicity of heart, ⁴⁷praising God, and having favor with all the people, and the LORD was adding those being saved every day to the Assembly.

CHAPTER 3

¹And Peter and John were going up at the same time into the temple, at the hour of the prayer, the ninth [hour], ²and a certain man, being lame from the womb of his mother, was being carried, whom they were laying every day at the gate of the temple, called Beautiful, to ask a kindness from those entering into the temple, ³who, having seen Peter and John about to go into the temple, was begging to receive a kindness. ⁴And Peter, having looked steadfastly toward him with John, said, "Look toward us"; ⁵and he was giving heed to them, looking to receive something from them; ⁶and Peter said, "I have no silver and gold, but what I have, that I give to you; in the Name of Jesus Christ of Nazareth, rise up and be walking." ⁷And having seized him by the right hand, he raised [him] up, and instantly his feet and ankles were strengthened, ⁸and springing up, he stood, and was walking, and entered with them into the temple, walking and springing, and praising God; ⁹and all the people saw him walking and praising God, ¹⁰and they knew him, that this it was who for a kindness was sitting at the Beautiful Gate of the temple, and they were filled with wonder and amazement at what has happened to him. ¹¹And at the lame man who was healed holding Peter and John, all the people ran together to them in the porch called Solomon's—greatly amazed, ¹²and Peter having seen, answered to the people, "Men, Israelites! Why do you wonder at this? Or why do you look on us so earnestly, as if by our own power or piety we have made him to walk? ¹³The God of Abraham, and of Isaac, and of Jacob, the God of our fathers, glorified His child Jesus, whom you delivered up, and denied Him in the presence of Pilate,

he having given judgment to release [Him], ¹⁴and you denied the Holy and Righteous One, and desired a man—a murderer—to be granted to you, ¹⁵and the Prince of life you killed, whom God raised out of the dead, of which we are witnesses; ¹⁶and on the faith of His Name, this one whom you see and have known, His Name made strong, even the faith that [is] through Him gave to him this perfect soundness before you all. ¹⁷And now, brothers, I have known that through ignorance you did [it], as also your rulers; ¹⁸and God, what things He had declared before through the mouth of all His prophets, that the Christ should suffer, He thus fulfilled; ¹⁹convert, therefore, and turn back, for your sins being blotted out, that times of refreshing may come from the presence of the LORD, ²⁰and He may send Jesus Christ who before has been preached to you, ²¹whom Heaven required, indeed, to receive until times of a restitution of all things, of which God spoke through the mouth of all His holy prophets from the age. ²²For Moses, indeed, said to the fathers—The LORD your God will raise up a Prophet to you out of your brothers, like to me; you will hear Him in all things, as many as He may speak to you; ²³and it will be, every soul that may not hear that Prophet will be utterly destroyed out of the people; ²⁴and also all the prophets from Samuel and those following in order, as many as spoke, also foretold of these days. ²⁵You are sons of the prophets, and of the covenant that God made to our fathers, saying to Abraham: And in your Seed will all the families of the earth be blessed; ²⁶to you first, God, having raised up His child Jesus, sent Him, blessing you, in the turning away of each one from your evil ways."

CHAPTER 4

¹And as they are speaking to the people, there came to them the priests, and the magistrate of the temple, and the Sadducees— ²being grieved because of their teaching the people, and preaching in Jesus the resurrection out of the dead— ³and they laid hands on them, and put them in custody until the next day, for it was evening already; ⁴and many of those hearing the word believed, and the number of the men became, as it were, five thousand. ⁵And it came to pass the next day, there were gathered together of them the rulers, and elders, and scribes, to Jerusalem, ⁶and Annas the chief priest, and Caiaphas, and John, and Alexander, and as many as were of the family of the chief priest, ⁷and having set them in the midst, they were inquiring, "In what power, or in what name did you do this?" ⁸Then Peter, having been filled with the Holy Spirit, said to them: "Rulers of the people, and elders of Israel, ⁹if we are examined today concerning the good deed to the ailing man, by whom he has been saved, ¹⁰be it known to all of you, and to all the people of Israel, that in the Name of Jesus Christ of Nazareth, whom you crucified, whom God raised out of the dead, in Him has this one stood by before you whole. ¹¹This is the stone that was set at nothing by you—the builders, that became head of a corner; ¹²and there is not salvation in any other, for there is no other name under Heaven that has been given among men, in which it is required of us to be saved." ¹³And beholding the openness of Peter and John, and having perceived that they are illiterate men and commoners, they were wondering—they were also taking knowledge of them that they had been with Jesus— ¹⁴and seeing the man standing with them who has been healed, they had nothing to say against [it], ¹⁵and having commanded them to go away out of the Sanhedrin, they took counsel with one another, ¹⁶saying, "What will we do to these men? Because that, indeed, a notable sign has been done through them [is] apparent to all those dwelling in Jerusalem, and we are not able to deny [it]; ¹⁷but that it may spread no further toward the people, let us strictly threaten them to no longer speak in this Name to any man." ¹⁸And having called them, they charged them not to speak at all, nor to teach, in the Name of Jesus, ¹⁹and Peter and John answering to them said, "Whether it is righteous before God to listen to you rather than to God, judge; ²⁰for we cannot but speak what we saw and heard." ²¹And they having further threatened [them], let them go, finding no way how they may punish them, because of the people, because all were glorifying God for that which has been done, ²²for above forty years of age was the man on whom had been done this sign of the healing. ²³And being let go, they went to their own friends, and declared whatever the chief priests and the elders said to them, ²⁴and they having heard, lifted up the voice to God with one accord and said, "LORD, You [are] God, who made the heaven, and the earth, and the sea, and all that [are] in them, ²⁵who, through the mouth of Your servant David, said, Why did nations rage, and peoples meditate vain things? ²⁶The kings of the earth stood up, and the rulers were gathered together against the LORD and against His Christ; ²⁷for gathered together of a truth against Your holy child Jesus, whom You anointed, were both Herod and Pontius Pilate, with nations and peoples of Israel, ²⁸to do whatever Your hand and Your counsel determined before to come to pass. ²⁹And now, LORD, look on their threatenings, and grant to Your servants to speak Your word with all freedom, ³⁰in the stretching forth of Your hand, for healing, and signs, and wonders, to come to pass through the Name of Your holy child Jesus." ³¹And they having prayed, the place was shaken in which they were gathered together, and they were all filled with the Holy Spirit, and were speaking the word of God with freedom, ³²and of the multitude of those who believed, the heart and the soul were one, and not one was saying that anything of the things he had was his own, but all things were in common to them. ³³And with great power the apostles were giving the testimony to the resurrection of the Lord Jesus, great grace was also on them all, ³⁴for there was not anyone among them who lacked, for as many as were possessors of fields, or houses, selling [them], were bringing the prices of the thing sold, ³⁵and were laying them at the feet of the apostles, and distribution was being made to each according as anyone had need. ³⁶And Joses, who was surnamed by the apostles Barnabas—which is, having been interpreted, Son of Comfort—a Levite, of Cyprus by birth, ³⁷a field being his, having sold [it], brought the money and laid [it] at the feet of the apostles.

CHAPTER 5

¹And a certain man, Ananias by name, with his wife Sapphira, sold a possession, ²and kept back of the price—his wife also knowing—and having brought a certain part, he laid [it] at the feet of the apostles. ³And Peter said, "Ananias, why did Satan fill your heart, for you to lie to the Holy Spirit, and to keep back of the price of the place? ⁴While it remained, did it not remain yours? And having been sold, was it not in your authority? Why [is] it that you put this thing in your heart? You did not lie to men, but to God"; ⁵and Ananias hearing these words, having fallen down, expired, and great fear came on all who heard these things, ⁶and having risen, the younger men wound him up, and having carried forth, they buried [him]. ⁷And it came to pass, about three hours after, that his wife, not knowing what has happened, came in, ⁸and Peter answered her, "Tell me if for so much you sold the place"; and she said, "Yes, for so much." ⁹And Peter said to her, "How was it agreed by you to tempt the Spirit of the LORD? Behold, the feet of those who buried your husband [are] at the door, and they will carry you forth"; ¹⁰and immediately she fell down at his feet, and expired, and the young men having come in, found her dead, and having carried forth, they buried [her] by her husband; ¹¹and great fear came on all the Assembly, and on all who heard these things. ¹²And through the hands of the apostles came many signs and wonders among the people, and they were all with one accord in the porch of Solomon; ¹³and of the rest no one was daring to join himself to them, but the people were magnifying them, ¹⁴(and the more were believers added to the LORD, multitudes of both men and women), ¹⁵so as to bring forth the ailing into the broad places, and to lay [them] on beds and pallets, that at the coming of Peter, even [his] shadow might overshadow someone of them; ¹⁶and there were also coming together the people of the surrounding cities to Jerusalem, carrying ailing persons, and those harassed by unclean spirits—who were all healed. ¹⁷And having risen, the chief priest, and all those with him—being the sect of the Sadducees—were filled with zeal, ¹⁸and laid their hands on the apostles, and put them in a public prison; ¹⁹but through the night a messenger of the LORD opened the doors of the prison, having also brought them forth, he said, ²⁰"Go on, and standing, speak in the temple to the people all the sayings of this life"; ²¹and having heard, they entered into the temple at the dawn, and were teaching. And the chief priest having come, and those with him, they called together the Sanhedrin and all the Senate of the sons of Israel, and they sent to the prison

to have them brought, ²²and the officers having come, did not find them in the prison, and having turned back, they told, ²³saying, "We indeed found the prison shut in all safety, and the keepers standing outside before the doors, and having opened—we found no one within." ²⁴And as the priest, and the magistrate of the temple, and the chief priests, heard these words, they were doubting concerning them to what this would come; ²⁵and coming near, a certain one told them, saying, "Behold, the men whom you put in the prison are in the temple standing and teaching the people"; ²⁶then the magistrate having gone away with officers, brought them without violence, for they were fearing the people, lest they should be stoned; ²⁷and having brought them, they set [them] in the Sanhedrin, and the chief priest questioned them, ²⁸saying, "Did we not strictly command you not to teach in this Name? And behold, you have filled Jerusalem with your teaching, and you intend to bring on us the blood of this Man." ²⁹And Peter and the apostles answering, said, "It is required to obey God, rather than men; ³⁰and the God of our fathers raised up Jesus, whom you slew, having hanged on a tree; ³¹this One, God, a Prince and a Savior, has exalted with His right hand, to give conversion to Israel, and forgiveness of sins; ³²and we are His witnesses of these sayings, and the Holy Spirit also, whom God gave to those obeying Him." ³³And they having heard, were cut [to the heart], and were intending to slay them, ³⁴but a certain one, having risen up in the Sanhedrin—a Pharisee, by name Gamaliel, a teacher of law honored by all the people—commanded to put the apostles forth a little, ³⁵and said to them, "Men, Israelites, take heed to yourselves about these men, what you are about to do, ³⁶for before these days Theudas rose up, saying that he was someone, to whom a number of men joined themselves, as it were four hundred, who was slain, and all, as many as were obeying him, were scattered, and came to nothing. ³⁷After this one, Judas the Galilean rose up, in the days of the census, and drew away people after him, and that one perished, and all, as many as were obeying him, were scattered; ³⁸and now I say to you, refrain from these men, and leave them alone, because if this counsel or this work may be of men, it will be overthrown, ³⁹and if it be of God, you are not able to overthrow it, lest perhaps you are also found fighting against God." ⁴⁰And to him they agreed, and having called near the apostles, having beaten [them], they commanded [them] not to speak in the Name of Jesus, and let them go; ⁴¹they, indeed, then, departed from the presence of the Sanhedrin, rejoicing that for His Name they were counted worthy to suffer dishonor, ⁴²also every day in the temple, and in every house, they were not ceasing teaching and proclaiming good news—Jesus the Christ.

CHAPTER 6

¹And in these days, the disciples multiplying, there came a murmuring of the Hellenists at the Hebrews, because their widows were being overlooked in the daily ministry, ²and the Twelve, having called near the multitude of the disciples, said, "It is not pleasing that we, having left the word of God, minister at tables; ³look out, therefore, brothers, seven men of you who are testified well of, full of the Holy Spirit and wisdom, whom we may set over this necessity, ⁴and we to prayer, and to the ministry of the word, will give ourselves continually." ⁵And the thing was pleasing before all the multitude, and they chose Stephen, a man full of faith and the Holy Spirit, and Philip, and Prochorus, and Nicanor, and Timon, and Parmenas, and Nicolaus, a proselyte of Antioch, ⁶whom they set before the apostles, and they, having prayed, laid [their] hands on them. ⁷And the word of God increased, and the number of the disciples multiplied in Jerusalem exceedingly; a great multitude of the priests were also obedient to the faith. ⁸And Stephen, full of faith and power, was doing great wonders and signs among the people, ⁹and there arose certain of those of the synagogue, the [one] called Libertines (and Cyrenians, and Alexandrians, and of those from Cilicia, and Asia), disputing with Stephen, ¹⁰and they were not able to resist the wisdom and the Spirit with which he was speaking; ¹¹then they suborned men, saying, "We have heard him speaking slanderous sayings in regard to Moses and God." ¹²They also stirred up the people, and the elders, and the scribes, and having come on [him], they caught him, and brought [him] to the Sanhedrin; ¹³they also set up false witnesses, saying, "This one does not cease to speak evil sayings against this holy place and the Law, ¹⁴for we have heard him saying that this Jesus the Nazarean will overthrow this place, and will change the customs that Moses delivered to us"; ¹⁵and gazing at him, all those sitting in the Sanhedrin saw his face as it were the face of a messenger.

CHAPTER 7

¹And the chief priest said, "Are then these things so?" ²And he said, "Men, brothers, and fathers, listen! The God of glory appeared to our father Abraham, being in Mesopotamia, before his dwelling in Haran, ³and He said to him, Go forth out of your land, and out of your relatives, and come to a land that I will show you. ⁴Then having come forth out of the land of the Chaldeans, he dwelt in Haran, and from there, after the death of his father, He removed him to this land wherein you now dwell, ⁵and He gave him no inheritance in it, not even a footstep, and promised to give it to him for a possession, and to his seed after him—he having no child. ⁶And God spoke thus, that his seed will be sojourning in a strange land, and they will cause it to serve, and will do it evil [for] four hundred years. ⁷And the nation whom they will serve I will judge, said God; And after these things they will come forth and will do Me service in this place. ⁸And He gave to him a covenant of circumcision, and so he begot Isaac, and circumcised him on the eighth day, and Isaac [begot] Jacob, and Jacob—the twelve patriarchs; ⁹and the patriarchs, having been moved with jealousy, sold Joseph to Egypt, and God was with him, ¹⁰and delivered him out of all his tribulations, and gave him favor and wisdom before Pharaoh king of Egypt, and he set him—governor over Egypt and all his house. ¹¹And there came a scarcity on all the land of Egypt and Canaan, and great tribulation, and our fathers were not finding sustenance, ¹²and Jacob having heard that there was grain in Egypt, sent forth our fathers a first time; ¹³and at the second time was Joseph made known to his brothers, and Joseph's family became disclosed to Pharaoh, ¹⁴and Joseph having sent, called for his father Jacob, and all his relatives—with seventy-five souls— ¹⁵and Jacob went down to Egypt, and died, himself and our fathers, ¹⁶and they were carried over into Shechem, and were laid in the tomb that Abraham bought for a price in money from the sons of Emmor, of Shechem. ¹⁷And according as the time of the promise was drawing near, which God swore to Abraham, the people increased and multiplied in Egypt, ¹⁸until another king rose, who had not known Joseph; ¹⁹this one, having dealt subtly with our family, did evil to our fathers, causing to expose their babies, that they might not live; ²⁰in which time Moses was born, and he was fair to God, and he was brought up [for] three months in the house of his father; ²¹and having been set outside, the daughter of Pharaoh took him up, and reared him to herself for a son; ²²and Moses was taught in all wisdom of the Egyptians, and he was powerful in words and in works. ²³And when forty years were fulfilled to him, it came on his heart to look after his brothers, the sons of Israel; ²⁴and having seen a certain one suffering injustice, he defended, and did justice to the oppressed, having struck the Egyptian; ²⁵and he was supposing his brothers to understand that God gives salvation through his hand; and they did not understand. ²⁶On the succeeding day, also, he showed himself to them as they are striving, and urged them to peace, saying, Men, you are brothers, why do you do injustice to one another? ²⁷And he who is doing injustice to the neighbor, thrusted him away, saying, Who set you a ruler and a judge over us? ²⁸Do you wish to kill me, as you killed the Egyptian yesterday? ²⁹And Moses fled at this word, and became a sojourner in the land of Midian, where he begot two sons, ³⁰and forty years having been fulfilled, there appeared to him in the wilderness of Mount Sinai [the] Messenger of the LORD, in a flame of fire of a bush, ³¹and Moses having seen, wondered at the sight; and he drawing near to behold, there came a voice of the LORD to him, ³²I [am] the God of your fathers; the God of Abraham, and the God of Isaac, and the God of Jacob. And Moses having become terrified, did not dare behold, ³³and the LORD said to him, Loose the sandal of your feet, for the place in which you have stood is holy ground; ³⁴seeing I have seen the affliction of My people that [is] in Egypt, and I heard their groaning, and came down to deliver them; and now come, I will send you to

Egypt. ³⁵This Moses, whom they refused, saying, Who set you a ruler and a judge? This one God sent [as] a ruler and a redeemer, by the hand of [the] Messenger who appeared to him in the bush; ³⁶this one brought them forth, having done wonders and signs in the land of Egypt, and in the Red Sea, and in the wilderness forty years; ³⁷this is the Moses who said to the sons of Israel: The LORD your God will raise up to you a Prophet out of your brothers, like to me, Him will you hear. ³⁸This is he who was in the assembly in the wilderness, with the Messenger who is speaking to him in Mount Sinai, and with our fathers who received the living oracles to give to us; ³⁹to whom our fathers did not wish to become obedient, but thrusted away, and turned back in their hearts to Egypt, ⁴⁰saying to Aaron, Make to us gods who will go on before us, for this Moses, who brought us forth out of the land of Egypt, we have not known what has happened to him. ⁴¹And they made a calf in those days, and brought a sacrifice to the idol, and were rejoicing in the works of their hands, ⁴²and God turned, and gave them up to do service to the host of Heaven, according as it has been written in the scroll of the Prophets: Did you offer slain beasts and sacrifices to Me forty years in the wilderness, O house of Israel? ⁴³And you took up the dwelling place of Moloch, and the star of your god Remphan—the figures that you made to worship them, and I will remove your dwelling beyond Babylon. ⁴⁴The Dwelling Place of the Testimony was among our fathers in the wilderness, according as He directed, who is speaking to Moses, to make it according to the figure that he had seen; ⁴⁵which also our fathers having in succession received, brought in with Joshua, into the possession of the nations whom God drove out from the presence of our fathers, until the days of David, ⁴⁶who found favor before God, and requested to find a dwelling place for the God of Jacob; ⁴⁷and Solomon built Him a house. ⁴⁸But the Most High does not dwell in sanctuaries made with hands, according as the prophet says: ⁴⁹Heaven [is] My throne, || And the earth My footstool, || What house will you build to Me? Says the LORD; Or what [is] the place of My rest? ⁵⁰Has My hand not made all these things? ⁵¹You stiff-necked and uncircumcised in heart and in ears! You always resist the Holy Spirit; as your fathers—also you; ⁵²which of the prophets did your fathers not persecute? And they killed those who declared before about the coming of the Righteous One, of whom you have now become betrayers and murderers, ⁵³who received the Law by arrangement of messengers, and did not keep [it]." ⁵⁴And hearing these things, they were cut to the hearts, and gnashed the teeth at him; ⁵⁵and being full of the Holy Spirit, having looked steadfastly to the sky, he saw the glory of God, and Jesus standing on the right hand of God, ⁵⁶and he said, "Behold, I see the heavens having been opened, and the Son of Man standing on the right hand of God." ⁵⁷And they, having cried out with a loud voice, stopped their ears, and rushed with one accord on him, ⁵⁸and having cast him forth outside of the city, they were stoning [him]—and the witnesses put down their garments at the feet of a young man called Saul— ⁵⁹and they were stoning Stephen, [as he was] calling and saying, "Lord Jesus, receive my spirit"; ⁶⁰and having bowed the knees, he cried with a loud voice, "LORD, may You not lay to them this sin"; and having said this, he fell asleep.

CHAPTER 8

¹And Saul was assenting to his death, and there came in that day a great persecution on the Assembly in Jerusalem, all were also scattered abroad in the regions of Judea and Samaria, except the apostles; ²and devout men carried Stephen away, and made great lamentation over him; ³and Saul was making havoc of the Assembly, entering into every house, and dragging away men and women, giving them up to prison; ⁴they then indeed, having been scattered, went abroad proclaiming good news—the word. ⁵And Philip having gone down to a city of Samaria, was preaching the Christ to them; ⁶the multitudes were also giving heed to the things spoken by Philip, with one accord, in their hearing and seeing the signs that he was doing, ⁷for unclean spirits came forth from many who were possessed, crying with a loud voice, and many who have been paralytic and lame were healed, ⁸and there was great joy in that city. ⁹And a certain man, by name Simon, was previously in the city using magic, and amazing the nation of Samaria, saying himself to be a certain great one, ¹⁰to whom they were all giving heed, from small to great, saying, "This one is the great power of God"; ¹¹and they were giving heed to him, because of his having amazed them for a long time with deeds of magic. ¹²And when they believed Philip, proclaiming good news, the things concerning the Kingdom of God and the Name of Jesus Christ, they were immersed—both men and women; ¹³and Simon himself also believed, and having been immersed, he was continuing with Philip, beholding also signs and mighty acts being done, he was amazed. ¹⁴And the apostles in Jerusalem having heard that Samaria has received the word of God, sent Peter and John to them, ¹⁵who having come down prayed concerning them, that they may receive the Holy Spirit— ¹⁶for as yet He was fallen on none of them, and only they have been immersed—into the Name of the Lord Jesus; ¹⁷then they were laying hands on them, and they received the Holy Spirit. ¹⁸And Simon, having beheld that through the laying on of the hands of the apostles the Holy Spirit is given, brought money before them, ¹⁹saying, "Give also to me this authority, that on whomsoever I may lay the hands, he may receive the Holy Spirit." ²⁰And Peter said to him, "Your silver with you—may it be to destruction! Because you thought to possess the gift of God through money; ²¹you have neither part nor lot in this thing, for your heart is not right before God; ²²convert, therefore, from this your wickedness, and implore God, if then the purpose of your heart may be forgiven you, ²³for in the gall of bitterness, and bond of unrighteousness, I perceive you being." ²⁴And Simon answering, said, "Implore for me to the LORD, that nothing may come on me of the things you have spoken." ²⁵They indeed, therefore, having testified fully, and spoken the word of the LORD, turned back to Jerusalem; they also proclaimed good news in many villages of the Samaritans. ²⁶And a messenger of the LORD spoke to Philip, saying, "Arise, and go on toward the south, on the way that is going down from Jerusalem to Gaza." (This is desolate.) ²⁷And having arisen, he went on, and behold, a man of Ethiopia, a eunuch, a man of rank, of Candace the queen of the Ethiopians, who was over all her treasure, who had come to Jerusalem to worship; ²⁸he was also returning, and is sitting on his chariot, and he was reading the prophet Isaiah. ²⁹And the Spirit said to Philip, "Go near, and be joined to this chariot"; ³⁰and Philip having run near, heard him reading the prophet Isaiah and said, "Do you then know what you read?" ³¹And he said, "Why, how am I able, if someone may not guide me?" He called Philip also, having come up, to sit with him. ³²And the passage of the Writing that he was reading was this: "He was led as a sheep to slaughter, || And as a lamb before his shearer is silent, || So He does not open His mouth; ³³In His humiliation His judgment was taken away, || And His generation who will declare? Because His life is taken from the earth." ³⁴And the eunuch answering Philip said, "I beg you, about whom does the prophet say this? About himself, or about some other one?" ³⁵And Philip having opened his mouth, and having begun from this Writing, proclaimed good news to him—Jesus. ³⁶And as they were going on the way, they came on some water, and the eunuch said, "Behold, water; what hinders me to be immersed?" ³⁷[[And Philip said, "If you believe out of all the heart, it is lawful"; and he answering said, "I believe Jesus Christ to be the Son of God";]] ³⁸and he commanded the chariot to stand still, and they both went down to the water, both Philip and the eunuch, and he immersed him; ³⁹and when they came up out of the water, Spirit of the LORD snatched up Philip, and the eunuch saw him no more, for he was going on his way rejoicing; ⁴⁰and Philip was found at Azotus, and passing through, he was proclaiming good news to all the cities, until his coming to Caesarea.

CHAPTER 9

¹And Saul, yet breathing of threatening and slaughter to the disciples of the LORD, having gone to the chief priest, ²asked from him letters to Damascus, to the synagogues, that if he may find any being of The Way, both men and women, he may bring them bound to Jerusalem. ³And in the going, he came near to Damascus, and suddenly there shone around him a light from Heaven, ⁴and having fallen on the earth, he heard a voice saying to him, "Saul, Saul, why do you persecute Me?" ⁵And he said, "Who are You, Lord?" And the LORD said, "I am Jesus whom you persecute; [[hard for you to kick at the goads"; ⁶trembling also, and astonished, he said, "Lord, what do You wish me to do?" And the LORD [said] to him,]] "Arise, and enter into the city, and it will be told [to] you what you must do." ⁷And the men who are journeying with him stood speechless, indeed hearing the voice but seeing no one, ⁸and Saul arose from the earth, and his eyes having been opened, he beheld no one, and leading him by the hand they brought him to Damascus, ⁹and he was three days without seeing, and he neither ate nor drank. ¹⁰And there was a certain disciple in Damascus, by name Ananias, and the LORD said to him in a vision, "Ananias"; and he said, "Behold me, Lord"; ¹¹and the LORD [says] to him, "Having risen, go on to the street that is called Straight, and seek in the house of Judas, [one] by name Saul of Tarsus, for behold, he prays, ¹²and he saw in a vision a man, by name Ananias, coming in, and putting a hand on him, that he may see again." ¹³And Ananias answered, "LORD, I have heard from many about this man, how many evils he did to Your holy ones in Jerusalem, ¹⁴and here he has authority from the chief priests, to bind all those calling on Your Name." ¹⁵And the LORD said to him, "Go, because this one is a chosen vessel to Me, to carry My Name before nations and kings—also the sons of Israel; ¹⁶for I will show him how many things he must suffer for My Name." ¹⁷And Ananias went away, and entered into the house, and having put on him [his] hands, said, "Saul, brother, the LORD has sent me—Jesus who appeared to you in the way in which you were coming—that you may see again, and may be filled with the Holy Spirit." ¹⁸And immediately there fell from his eyes as it were scales, he also saw again instantly, and having risen, was immersed, ¹⁹and having received nourishment, was strengthened, and Saul was with the disciples in Damascus certain days, ²⁰and immediately he was preaching the Christ in the synagogues, that He is the Son of God. ²¹And all those hearing were amazed and said, "Is this not he who laid waste in Jerusalem those calling on this Name, and here to this intent had come, that he might bring them bound to the chief priests?" ²²And Saul was still more strengthened, and he was confounding the Jews dwelling in Damascus, proving that this is the Christ. ²³And when many days were fulfilled, the Jews took counsel together to kill him, ²⁴and their counsel against [him] was known to Saul; they were also watching the gates both day and night, that they may kill him, ²⁵and the disciples having taken him, by night let him down by the wall, letting down in a basket. ²⁶And Saul, having come to Jerusalem, tried to join himself to the disciples, and they were all afraid of him, not believing that he is a disciple, ²⁷and Barnabas having taken him, brought [him] to the apostles, and declared to them how he saw the LORD in the way, and that He spoke to him, and how in Damascus he was speaking boldly in the Name of Jesus. ²⁸And he was with them, coming in and going out in Jerusalem, ²⁹and speaking boldly in the Name of the Lord Jesus; he was both speaking and disputing with the Hellenists, and they were taking in hand to kill him, ³⁰and the brothers having known, brought him down to Caesarea, and sent him forth to Tarsus. ³¹Then, indeed, the assemblies throughout all Judea, and Galilee, and Samaria, had peace, being built up, and going on in the fear of the LORD, and in the comfort of the Holy Spirit, they were multiplied. ³²And it came to pass that Peter, passing throughout all [quarters], also came down to the holy ones who were dwelling at Lydda, ³³and he found there a certain man, Aeneas by name—for eight years laid on a pallet—who was paralytic, ³⁴and Peter said to him, "Aeneas, Jesus the Christ heals you; arise and spread for yourself"; and immediately he rose, ³⁵and all those dwelling at Lydda and Saron saw him, and turned to the LORD. ³⁶And in Joppa there was a certain female disciple, by name Tabitha (which interpreted, is called Dorcas); this woman was full of good works and kind acts that she was doing; ³⁷and it came to pass in those days she, having ailed, died, and having bathed her, they laid her in an upper chamber, ³⁸and Lydda being near to Joppa, the disciples having heard that Peter is in that [place], sent two men to him, calling on him not to delay to come through to them. ³⁹And Peter having risen, went with them, whom having come, they brought into the upper chamber, and all the widows stood by him weeping, and showing coats and garments, as many as Dorcas was making while she was with them. ⁴⁰And Peter having put them all forth outside, having bowed the knees, prayed, and having turned to the body, said, "Tabitha, arise"; and she opened her eyes, and having seen Peter, she sat up, ⁴¹and having given her [his] hand, he lifted her up, and having called the holy ones and the widows, he presented her alive, ⁴²and it became known throughout all Joppa, and many believed on the LORD; ⁴³and it came to pass, that he remained many days in Joppa, with a certain one, Simon a tanner.

CHAPTER 10

¹And there was a certain man in Caesarea, by name Cornelius, a centurion from a cohort that is called Italian, ²pious, and fearing God with all his house, also doing many kind acts to the people, and always imploring God; ³he saw in a vision openly, as it were the ninth hour of the day, a messenger of God coming in to him, and saying to him, "Cornelius"; ⁴and he having looked earnestly on him, and becoming afraid, said, "What is it, Lord?" And he said to him, "Your prayers and your kind acts came up for a memorial before God, ⁵and now send men to Joppa, and send for a certain one Simon, who is surnamed Peter; ⁶this one lodges with a certain Simon a tanner, whose house is by the sea; this one will speak to you what you must do." ⁷And when the messenger who is speaking to Cornelius went away, having called two of his servants, and a pious soldier of those waiting on him continually, ⁸and having expounded all things to them, he sent them to Joppa. ⁹And on the next day, as these are proceeding on the way, and are drawing near to the city, Peter went up on the housetop to pray, about the sixth hour, ¹⁰and he became very hungry, and wished to eat; and they making ready, there fell on him a trance, ¹¹and he beholds Heaven opened, and a certain vessel descending to him, as a great sheet, bound at the four corners, and let down on the earth, ¹²in which were all the four-footed beasts of the earth, and the wild beasts, and the creeping things, and the birds of the sky, ¹³and there came a voice to him: "Having risen, Peter, slay and eat." ¹⁴And Peter said, "Not so, Lord; because at no time did I eat anything common or unclean"; ¹⁵and [there is] a voice again a second time to him: "What God cleansed, you do not declare common"; ¹⁶and this was done three times, and again was the vessel received up to Heaven. ¹⁷And as Peter was perplexed in himself what the vision that he saw might be, then, behold, the men who have been sent from Cornelius, having made inquiry for the house of Simon, stood at the gate, ¹⁸and having called, they were asking if Simon, who is surnamed Peter, lodges here. ¹⁹And Peter thinking about the vision, the Spirit said to him, "Behold, three men seek you; ²⁰but having risen, go down and go on with them, doubting nothing, because I have sent them"; ²¹and Peter having come down to the men who have been sent from Cornelius to him, said, "Behold, I am he whom you seek, what [is] the cause for which you are present?" ²²And they said, "Cornelius, a centurion, a man righteous and fearing God, well testified to, also, by all the nation of the Jews, was divinely warned by a holy messenger to send for you, to his house, and to hear sayings from you." ²³Having called them in, therefore, he lodged them, and on the next day Peter went forth with them, and certain of the brothers from Joppa went with him, ²⁴and on the next day they entered into Caesarea; and Cornelius was waiting for them, having called together his relatives and near friends, ²⁵and as it came that Peter entered in, Cornelius having met him, having fallen at

[his] feet, worshiped [him]; ²⁶and Peter raised him, saying, "Stand up; I am also a man myself"; ²⁷and talking with him he went in, and finds many having come together. ²⁸And he said to them, "You know how it is unlawful for a man, a Jew, to keep company with, or to come to, one of another race, but God showed to me to call no man common or unclean; ²⁹therefore also without contradicting I came, having been sent for; I ask, therefore, for what matter you sent for me?" ³⁰And Cornelius said, "Four days ago until this hour, I was fasting, and [at] the ninth hour praying in my house, and behold, a man stood before me in radiant clothing, ³¹and he said, Cornelius, your prayer was heard, and your kind acts were remembered before God; ³²send, therefore, to Joppa, and call for Simon, who is surnamed Peter; this one lodges in the house of Simon a tanner, by the sea, who having come, will speak to you; ³³at once, therefore, I sent to you; you also did well, having come; now, therefore, we are all present before God to hear all things that have been commanded you by God." ³⁴And Peter having opened his mouth, said, "Of a truth, I perceive that God is not favoring by appearance, ³⁵but in every nation he who is fearing Him, and is working righteousness, is acceptable to Him; ³⁶the word that He sent to the sons of Israel, proclaiming good news—peace through Jesus Christ (this One is Lord of all), ³⁷you have known the word that came throughout all Judea, having begun from Galilee, after the immersion that John preached; ³⁸Jesus who [is] from Nazareth—how God anointed Him with the Holy Spirit and power; who went through, doing good, and healing all those oppressed by the Devil, because God was with Him; ³⁹and we are witnesses of all things that He did, both in the country of the Jews, and in Jerusalem—whom they slew, having hanged [Him] on a tree. ⁴⁰This One God raised up [on] the third day, and gave Him to become visible, ⁴¹not to all the people, but to witnesses, to those having been chosen before by God—to us who ate with [Him], and drank with Him, after His rising out of the dead; ⁴²and He commanded us to preach to the people, and to fully testify that it is He who has been ordained judge of living and dead by God— ⁴³to this One do all the Prophets testify, that through His Name everyone that is believing in Him receives forgiveness of sins." ⁴⁴While Peter is yet speaking these sayings, the Holy Spirit fell on all those hearing the word, ⁴⁵and those of circumcision [who were] believing were astonished—as many as came with Peter—because the gift of the Holy Spirit has also been poured out on the nations, ⁴⁶for they were hearing them speaking with tongues and magnifying God. ⁴⁷Then Peter answered, "Is anyone able to forbid the water, that these may not be immersed, who received the Holy Spirit—even as us also?" ⁴⁸He commanded them to also be immersed in the Name of the LORD; then they implored him to remain certain days.

CHAPTER 11

¹And the apostles and the brothers who are in Judea heard that the nations also received the word of God, ²and when Peter came up to Jerusalem, those of circumcision were contending with him, ³saying, "You went in to uncircumcised men, and ate with them!" ⁴And Peter having begun, set [it] forth to them in order, saying, ⁵"I was in the city of Joppa praying, and I saw in a trance a vision, a certain vessel coming down, as a great sheet by four corners being let down out of Heaven, and it came to me; ⁶at which having looked steadfastly, I was considering, and I saw the four-footed beasts of the earth, and the wild beasts, and the creeping things, and the birds of the sky; ⁷and I heard a voice saying to me, Having risen, Peter, slay and eat; ⁸and I said, Not so, Lord, because anything common or unclean has at no time entered into my mouth; ⁹and a voice answered me a second time out of Heaven, What God cleansed, you do not declare common. ¹⁰And this happened three times, and again was all drawn up to Heaven, ¹¹and behold, immediately, three men stood at the house in which I was, having been sent from Caesarea to me, ¹²and the Spirit said to me to go with them, doubting nothing, and these six brothers also went with me, and we entered into the house of the man, ¹³he also declared to us how he saw the messenger standing in his house, and saying to him, Send men to Joppa, and call for Simon, who is surnamed Peter, ¹⁴who will speak sayings by which you will be saved, you and all your house. ¹⁵And in my beginning to speak, the Holy Spirit fell on them, even as also on us in the beginning, ¹⁶and I remembered the saying of the LORD, how He said, John indeed immersed in water, but you will be immersed in the Holy Spirit; ¹⁷if then God gave to them the equal gift as also to us, having believed on the Lord Jesus Christ, I—how was I able to withstand God?" ¹⁸And they, having heard these things, were silent, and were glorifying God, saying, "Then, indeed, God also gave conversion to life to the nations." ¹⁹Those, indeed, therefore, having been scattered abroad, from the tribulation that came after Stephen, went through to Phoenicia, and Cyprus, and Antioch, speaking the word to none except to Jews only; ²⁰and there were certain of them, men of Cyprus and Cyrene, who having entered into Antioch, were speaking to the Hellenists, proclaiming good news—the Lord Jesus, ²¹and the hand of the LORD was with them, a great number also, having believed, turned to the LORD. ²²And the account was heard in the ears of the assembly that [is] in Jerusalem concerning them, and they sent forth Barnabas to go through to Antioch, ²³who, having come, and having seen the grace of God, was glad, and was exhorting all with purpose of heart to cleave to the LORD, ²⁴because he was a good man, and full of the Holy Spirit, and of faith, and a great multitude was added to the LORD. ²⁵And Barnabas went forth to Tarsus, to seek for Saul, ²⁶and having found him, he brought him to Antioch, and it came to pass that they assembled together a whole year in the assembly, and taught a great multitude, and the disciples were first called Christians in Antioch. ²⁷And in those days there came from Jerusalem prophets to Antioch, ²⁸and one of them, by name Agabus, having stood up, signified through the Spirit a great scarcity is about to be throughout all the world—which also came to pass in the time of Claudius Caesar— ²⁹and the disciples, according as anyone was prospering, determined each of them to send for ministry to the brothers dwelling in Judea, ³⁰which also they did, having sent to the elders by the hand of Barnabas and Saul.

CHAPTER 12

¹And about that time, Herod the king put forth his hands to do evil to certain of those of the Assembly, ²and he killed James, the brother of John, with the sword, ³and having seen that it is pleasing to the Jews, he added to lay hold of Peter also—and they were the days of the Unleavened [Bread]— ⁴whom also having seized, he put in prison, having delivered [him] to four squads of four soldiers to guard him, intending to bring him forth to the people after the Passover. ⁵Peter, therefore, indeed, was kept in the prison, and fervent prayer was being made by the Assembly to God for him, ⁶and when Herod was about to bring him forth, the same night was Peter sleeping between two soldiers, having been bound with two chains, guards were also keeping the prison before the door, ⁷and behold, a messenger of the LORD stood by, and a light shone in the buildings, and having struck Peter on the side, he raised him up, saying, "Rise in haste," and his chains fell from off [his] hands. ⁸The messenger also said to him, "Gird yourself, and bind on your sandals"; and he did so; and he says to him, "Cast your garment around and follow me"; ⁹and having gone forth, he was following him, and he did not know that it is true that which is done through the messenger, and was thinking he saw a vision, ¹⁰and having passed through a first ward, and a second, they came to the iron gate that is leading into the city, which opened to them of its own accord, and having gone forth, they went on through one street, and immediately the messenger departed from him. ¹¹And Peter having come to himself, said, "Now I have known of a truth that the LORD sent forth His messenger, and delivered me out of the hand of Herod, and all the expectation of the people of the Jews"; ¹²also, having considered, he came to the house of Mary, the mother of John, who is surnamed Mark, where there were many thronged together and praying. ¹³And Peter having knocked at the door of the porch, there came a girl to listen, by name Rhoda, ¹⁴and having known the voice of Peter, from the joy she did not open the porch, but having run in, told of the standing of Peter before the porch, ¹⁵and they said to her, "You are mad"; and she was confidently affirming [it] to be so, and they said, "It is his messenger"; ¹⁶and Peter was continuing knocking, and having opened, they saw him, and were astonished, ¹⁷and having

beckoned to them with the hand to be silent, he declared to them how the LORD brought him out of the prison, and he said, "Declare these things to James and to the brothers"; and having gone forth, he went on to another place. ¹⁸And day having come, there was not a little stir among the soldiers what then was become of Peter, ¹⁹and Herod having sought for him, and having not found, having examined the guards, commanded [them] to be led away to punishment, and having gone down from Judea to Caesarea, he was abiding [there]. ²⁰And Herod was highly displeased with the Tyrians and Sidonians, and with one accord they came to him, and having made a friend of Blastus, who [is] over the bedchambers of the king, they were asking peace, because of their country being nourished from the king's; ²¹and on a set day, Herod having clothed himself in kingly clothing, and having sat down on the judgment seat, was making an oration to them, ²²and the populace were shouting, "The voice of a god, and not of a man!" ²³And immediately a messenger of the LORD struck him in return for that he did not give the glory to God, and having been eaten of worms, he expired. ²⁴And the word of God grew and multiplied, ²⁵and Barnabas and Saul turned back out of Jerusalem, having fulfilled the ministry, having also taken John with [them], who was surnamed Mark.

CHAPTER 13

¹And there were certain in Antioch, in the assembly there, prophets and teachers: both Barnabas, and Simeon who is called Niger, and Lucius the Cyrenian, Manaen also—Herod the tetrarch's foster-brother—and Saul; ²and in their ministering to the LORD and fasting, the Holy Spirit said, "Separate to Me both Barnabas and Saul to the work to which I have called them," ³then having fasted, and having prayed, and having laid the hands on them, they sent [them] away. ⁴These, indeed, then, having been sent forth by the Holy Spirit, went down to Seleucia, and from there they sailed to Cyprus, ⁵and having come to Salamis, they declared the word of God in the synagogues of the Jews, and they also had John [as] a servant; ⁶and having gone through the island to Paphos, they found a certain magus, a false prophet, a Jew, whose name [is] Bar-Jesus; ⁷who was with the proconsul Sergius Paulus, an intelligent man; this one having called for Barnabas and Saul, desired to hear the word of God, ⁸and there withstood them Elymas the magus—for so is his name interpreted—seeking to pervert the proconsul from the faith. ⁹And Saul—who also [is] Paul—having been filled with the Holy Spirit, and having looked steadfastly on him, ¹⁰said, "O full of all guile, and all recklessness, son of a devil, enemy of all righteousness, will you not cease perverting the right ways of the LORD? ¹¹And now, behold, a hand of the LORD [is] on you, and you will be blind, not seeing the sun for a season"; and instantly there fell on him a mist and darkness, and he, going around, was seeking some to lead [him] by the hand; ¹²then the proconsul having seen what has come to pass, believed, being astonished at the teaching of the LORD. ¹³And those around Paul having set sail from Paphos, came to Perga of Pamphylia, and John having departed from them, turned back to Jerusalem, ¹⁴and they having gone through from Perga, came to Antioch of Pisidia, and having gone into the synagogue on the day of the Sabbaths, they sat down, ¹⁵and after the reading of the Law and of the Prophets, the chief men of the synagogue sent to them, saying, "Men, brothers, if there be a word in you of exhortation to the people—say on." ¹⁶And Paul having risen, and having beckoned with the hand, said, "Men, Israelites, and those fearing God, listen: ¹⁷the God of this people Israel chose our fathers, and He exalted the people in their sojourning in the land of Egypt, and He brought them out of it with a high arm; ¹⁸and about a period of forty years He endured their conduct in the wilderness, ¹⁹and having destroyed seven nations in the land of Canaan, He divided their land to them by lot. ²⁰And after these things, about four hundred and fifty years, He gave judges—until Samuel the prophet; ²¹and thereafter they asked for a king, and God gave to them Saul, son of Kish, a man of the tribe of Benjamin, for forty years; ²²and having removed him, He raised up to them David for king, to whom also having testified, He said, I found David, the [son] of Jesse, a man according to My heart, who will do all My will. ²³Of this one's seed, God, according to promise, raised to Israel a Savior—Jesus, ²⁴John having first preached, before His coming, an immersion of conversion to all the people of Israel; ²⁵and as John was fulfilling the course, he said, Whom do you suppose I am? I am not [He], but behold, He comes after me, of whom I am not worthy to loose the sandal of [His] feet. ²⁶Men, brothers, sons of the race of Abraham, and those among you fearing God, to you was the word of this salvation sent, ²⁷for those dwelling in Jerusalem, and their chiefs, having not known this One, also the voices of the Prophets, which are being read every Sabbath—having judged [Him]—fulfilled, ²⁸and having found no cause of death, they asked of Pilate that He should be slain, ²⁹and when they fulfilled all the things written about Him, having taken [Him] down from the tree, they laid Him in a tomb; ³⁰and God raised Him out of the dead, ³¹and He was seen for many days of those who came up with Him from Galilee to Jerusalem, who are His witnesses to the people. ³²And we proclaim good news to you—that the promise made to the fathers, ³³God has completed this in full to us their children, having raised up Jesus, as also in the second Psalm it has been written: You are My Son—I have begotten You today. ³⁴And that He raised Him up out of the dead, to no longer return to corruption, He has said this: I will give to You the holy [blessings] of David [that are] faithful; ³⁵for what reason He also says in another [place]: You will not give Your Holy One to see corruption; ³⁶for David, indeed, having served his own generation by the will of God, fell asleep, and was added to his fathers, and saw corruption, ³⁷but He whom God raised up, did not see corruption. ³⁸Let it therefore be known to you, men, brothers, that the forgiveness of sins is declared to you through this One, ³⁹and from all things in the Law of Moses from which you were not able to be declared righteous, everyone who is believing in this One is declared righteous; ⁴⁰see, therefore, it may not come on you that has been spoken in the Prophets: ⁴¹See, you despisers, and wonder, and perish, because I work a work in your days, a work in which you may not believe, though anyone may declare [it] to you." ⁴²And having gone forth out of the synagogue of the Jews, the nations were calling on [them] that on the next Sabbath these sayings may be spoken to them, ⁴³and the synagogue having been dismissed, many of the Jews and of the devout proselytes followed Paul and Barnabas, who, speaking to them, were persuading them to remain in the grace of God. ⁴⁴And on the coming Sabbath, almost all the city was gathered together to hear the word of God, ⁴⁵and the Jews having seen the multitudes, were filled with zeal, and contradicted the things spoken by Paul—contradicting and slandering. ⁴⁶And speaking boldly, Paul and Barnabas said, "It was necessary that the word of God be first spoken to you, and seeing you thrust it away, and do not judge yourselves worthy of the continuous life, behold, we turn to the nations; ⁴⁷for¹ so the LORD has commanded us: I have set you for a light of nations—for your being for salvation to the end of the earth." ⁴⁸And the nations hearing were glad, and were glorifying the word of the LORD, and believed—as many as were appointed to continuous life; ⁴⁹and the word of the LORD was spread abroad through all the region. ⁵⁰And the Jews stirred up the devout and honorable women, and the first men of the city, and raised persecution against Paul and Barnabas, and put them out from their borders; ⁵¹and having shaken off the dust of their feet against them, they came to Iconium, ⁵²and the disciples were filled with joy and the Holy Spirit.

CHAPTER 14

¹And it came to pass in Iconium, that they entered together into the synagogue of the Jews, and spoke, so that there believed a great multitude of both Jews and Greeks; ²and the unbelieving Jews stirred up and made the souls of the nations evil against the brothers; ³[for a] long time, indeed, therefore, they abided speaking boldly in the LORD, who is testifying to the word of His grace, and granting signs and wonders to come to pass through their hands. ⁴And the multitude of the city was divided, and some were with the

Jews, and some with the apostles, ⁵and when there was a purpose both of the nations and of the Jews with their rulers to mistreat [them], and to stone them, ⁶they having become aware, fled to the cities of Lycaonia, Lystra, and Derbe, and the surrounding region, ⁷and there they were proclaiming good news. ⁸And a certain man in Lystra, impotent in the feet, was sitting, being lame from the womb of his mother—who never had walked; ⁹this one was hearing Paul speaking, who, having steadfastly beheld him, and having seen that he has faith to be saved, ¹⁰said with a loud voice, "Stand up on your feet upright"; and he was springing and walking, ¹¹and the multitudes having seen what Paul did, lifted up their voice in the speech of Lycaonia, saying, "The gods, having become like men, came down to us"; ¹²they were also calling Barnabas Zeus, and Paul Hermes, since he was the leader in speaking. ¹³And the priest of the Zeus that is before their city, having brought oxen and garlands to the porches, wished to sacrifice with the multitudes, ¹⁴and having heard, the apostles Barnabas and Paul, having torn their garments, sprung into the multitude, crying ¹⁵and saying, "Men, why do you do these things? And we are similar-feeling men with you, proclaiming good news to you, to turn to the living God from these vanities, who made the heaven, and the earth, and the sea, and all the things in them; ¹⁶who in the past generations permitted all the nations to go on in their ways, ¹⁷though, indeed, He did not leave Himself without witness, doing good—giving rains to us from Heaven, and fruitful seasons, filling our hearts with food and gladness"; ¹⁸and saying these things, they scarcely restrained the multitudes from sacrificing to them. ¹⁹And there came there, from Antioch and Iconium, Jews, and they having persuaded the multitudes, and having stoned Paul, drew him outside of the city, having supposed him to be dead; ²⁰and the disciples having surrounded him, having risen he entered into the city, and on the next day he went forth with Barnabas to Derbe. ²¹Having also proclaimed good news to that city, and having discipled many, they turned back to Lystra, and Iconium, and Antioch, ²²confirming the souls of the disciples, exhorting to remain in the faith, and that it is required of us to enter into the Kingdom of God through many tribulations, ²³and having appointed to them elders in every assembly by vote, having prayed with fastings, they commended them to the LORD in whom they had believed. ²⁴And having passed through Pisidia, they came to Pamphylia, ²⁵and having spoken the word in Perga, they went down to Attalia, ²⁶and [from] there sailed to Antioch, from where they had been given by the grace of God for the work that they fulfilled; ²⁷and having come and gathered the assembly together, they declared as many things as God did with them, and that He opened a door of faith to the nations; ²⁸and they abided there with the disciples [for] not a short time.

CHAPTER 15

¹And certain having come down from Judea, were teaching the brothers, "If you are not circumcised after the custom of Moses, you are not able to be saved"; ²there having been, therefore, not a little dissension and debate to Paul and Barnabas with them, they arranged for Paul and Barnabas, and certain others of them, to go up to the apostles and elders to Jerusalem about this question; ³they indeed, then, having been sent forward by the assembly, were passing through Phoenicia and Samaria, declaring the conversion of the nations, and they were causing great joy to all the brothers. ⁴And having come to Jerusalem, they were received by the assembly, and the apostles, and the elders; they also declared as many things as God did with them; ⁵and there rose up certain of those of the sect of the Pharisees who believed, saying, "It is required to circumcise them, to command them also to keep the Law of Moses." ⁶And there were gathered together the apostles and the elders, to see about this matter, ⁷and there having been much disputing, Peter having risen up said to them, "Men, brothers, you know that from former days God made choice among us, through my mouth, for the nations to hear the word of the good news, and to believe; ⁸and the heart-knowing God bore them testimony, having given to them the Holy Spirit, even as also to us, ⁹and also put no difference between us and them, having purified their hearts by faith; ¹⁰now, therefore, why do you tempt God, to put a yoke on the neck of the disciples, which neither our fathers nor we were able to bear? ¹¹But through the grace of the Lord Jesus Christ, we believe to be saved, even as also they." ¹²And all the multitude kept silence and were listening to Barnabas and Paul expounding as many signs and wonders as God did among the nations through them; ¹³and after they were silent, James answered, saying, "Men, brothers, listen to me: ¹⁴Simeon expounded how at first God looked on [us] to take a people out of [the] nations for His Name, ¹⁵and to this the words of the Prophets agree, as it has been written: ¹⁶After these things I will return, || And I will rebuild the dwelling place of David that has fallen down, || And I will rebuild its ruins, || And will set it upright— ¹⁷That the remnant of men may seek after the LORD, || And all the nations on whom My Name has been called, || Says the LORD, who is doing all these things. ¹⁸Known from the ages to God are all His works. ¹⁹For this reason I judge: not to trouble those who turn back to God from the nations, ²⁰but to write to them to abstain from the defilements of the idols, and the whoredom, and the strangled thing, and the blood; ²¹for Moses has those preaching him from former generations in every city—being read every Sabbath in the synagogues." ²²Then it seemed good to the apostles and the elders, with the whole assembly, to send to Antioch with Paul and Barnabas chosen men out of themselves—Judas surnamed Barsabas, and Silas, leading men among the brothers— ²³having written through their hand thus: "The apostles, and the elders, and the brothers, to those in Antioch, and Syria, and Cilicia, brothers, who [are] of the nations, greeting; ²⁴seeing we have heard that some having gone forth from us troubled you with words, subverting your souls, saying to be circumcised and to keep the Law, to whom we gave no charge, ²⁵it seemed good to us, having come together with one accord, to send to you chosen men, with our beloved Barnabas and Paul— ²⁶men who have given up their lives for the Name of our Lord Jesus Christ— ²⁷we have sent, therefore, Judas and Silas, and they are telling the same things by word. ²⁸For it seemed good to the Holy Spirit, and to us, to lay no more burden on you, except these necessary things: ²⁹to abstain from things offered to idols, and blood, and a strangled thing, and whoredom; keeping yourselves from which, you will do well; be strong!" ³⁰They then, indeed, having been let go, went to Antioch, and having brought the multitude together, delivered the letter, ³¹and having read [it] they rejoiced for the consolation; ³²Judas also and Silas, also being prophets themselves, through much discourse exhorted the brothers, and confirmed, ³³and having passed some time, they were let go with peace from the brothers to the apostles; ³⁴[[and it seemed good to Silas to remain there still.]] ³⁵And Paul and Barnabas continued in Antioch, teaching and proclaiming good news—with many others also—the word of the LORD; ³⁶and after certain days, Paul said to Barnabas, "Having turned back again, we may look after our brothers, in every city in which we have preached the word of the LORD—how they are." ³⁷And Barnabas resolved to take with [them] John called Mark, ³⁸and Paul was not thinking it good to take him with them who withdrew from them from Pamphylia, and did not go with them to the work; ³⁹there came, therefore, a sharp contention, so that they were parted from one another, and Barnabas having taken Mark, sailed to Cyprus, ⁴⁰and Paul having chosen Silas, went forth, having been given up to the grace of God by the brothers; ⁴¹and he went through Syria and Cilicia, confirming the assemblies.

CHAPTER 16

¹And he came to Derbe and Lystra, and behold, a certain disciple was there, by name Timotheus, son of a certain woman, a believing Jewess, but of a father, a Greek, ²who was well testified to by the brothers in Lystra and Iconium; ³Paul wished this one to go forth with him, and having taken [him], he circumcised him, because of the Jews who are in those places, for they all knew his father—that he was a Greek. ⁴And as they were going on through the cities, they were delivering to them the decrees to keep, that have been judged by the apostles and the elders who [are] in Jerusalem, ⁵then, indeed, were the assemblies established in the faith, and were abounding in number every day; ⁶and having gone through Phrygia and the region of Galatia, having been forbidden by the Holy Spirit to speak the word in Asia, ⁷having gone

toward Mysia, they were trying to go on toward Bithynia, and the Spirit did not permit them, ⁸and having passed by Mysia, they came down to Troas. ⁹And a vision through the night appeared to Paul—a certain man of Macedonia was standing, calling on him, and saying, "Having passed through to Macedonia, help us." ¹⁰And when he saw the vision, immediately we endeavored to go forth to Macedonia, assuredly gathering that the LORD has called us to preach good news to them, ¹¹having set sail, therefore, from Troas, we came with a straight course to Samothracia, on the next day also to Neapolis, ¹²there also to Philippi, which is a principal city of the part of Macedonia—a colony. And we were abiding in this city some days; ¹³on the day of the Sabbaths we also went forth outside of the city, by a river, where there used to be prayer, and having sat down, we were speaking to the women who came together, ¹⁴and a certain woman, by name Lydia, a seller of purple, of the city of Thyatira, worshiping God, was hearing, whose heart the LORD opened to attend to the things spoken by Paul; ¹⁵and when she was immersed, and her household, she called on us, saying, "If you have judged me to be faithful to the LORD, having entered into my house, remain"; and she constrained us. ¹⁶And it came to pass in our going on to prayer, a certain maid, having a spirit of Python, met us, who brought much employment to her masters by soothsaying; ¹⁷she having followed Paul and us, was crying, saying, "These men are servants of the Most High God, who declare to us [the] way of salvation!" ¹⁸And this she was doing for many days, but Paul having been grieved, and having turned, said to the spirit, "I command you, in the Name of Jesus Christ, to come forth from her"; and it came forth the same hour. ¹⁹And her masters having seen that the hope of their employment was gone, having caught Paul and Silas, drew [them] into the marketplace, to the rulers, ²⁰and having brought them to the magistrates, they said, "These men being Jews exceedingly trouble our city; ²¹and they proclaim customs that are not lawful for us to receive nor to do, being Romans." ²²And the multitude rose up together against them, and the magistrates having torn their garments from them, were commanding to beat [them] with rods, ²³having also laid on them many blows, they cast them into prison, having given charge to the jailor to keep them safely, ²⁴who having received such a charge, put them into the inner prison, and fastened their feet in the stocks. ²⁵And at midnight Paul and Silas praying, were singing hymns to God, and the prisoners were hearing them, ²⁶and suddenly a great earthquake came, so that the foundations of the prison were shaken, also all the doors were immediately opened, and of all—the bands were loosed; ²⁷and the jailor having come out of sleep, and having seen the doors of the prison open, having drawn a sword, was about to kill himself, supposing the prisoners to have fled, ²⁸and Paul cried out with a loud voice, saying, "You may not do yourself any harm, for we are all here!" ²⁹And having asked for a light, he sprang in, and he fell down before Paul and Silas trembling, ³⁰and having brought them forth, said, "Lords, what must I do that I may be saved?" ³¹And they said, "Believe on the Lord Jesus Christ, and you will be saved—you and your household." ³²And they spoke to him the word of the LORD, and to all those in his household; ³³and having taken them, in that hour of the night, he bathed [them] from the blows, and immediately he and all of his were immersed, ³⁴having also brought them into his house, he set food before [them], and was glad with all the household, he having believed in God. ³⁵And day having come, the magistrates sent the rod-bearers, saying, "Let those men go"; ³⁶and the jailor told these words to Paul, "The magistrates have sent, that you may be let go; now, therefore, having gone forth go on in peace"; ³⁷and Paul said to them, "Having beaten us publicly uncondemned—men, being Romans—they cast [us] to prison, and now privately they cast us forth! Why no! But having come themselves, let them bring us forth." ³⁸And the rod-bearers told these sayings to the magistrates, and they were afraid, having heard that they are Romans, ³⁹and having come, they implored them, and having brought [them] forth, they were asking [them] to go forth from the city; ⁴⁰and they, having gone forth out of the prison, entered into [the house of] Lydia, and having seen the brothers, they comforted them, and went forth.

CHAPTER 17

¹And having passed through Amphipolis, and Apollonia, they came to Thessalonica, where the synagogue of the Jews was, ²and according to the custom of Paul, he went in to them, and for three Sabbaths he was reasoning with them from the Writings, ³opening and alleging that it was necessary [for] the Christ to suffer, and to rise again out of the dead, and that "this is the Christ—Jesus whom I proclaim to you." ⁴And certain of them believed, and attached themselves to Paul and to Silas, also a great multitude of the worshiping Greeks, also not a few of the principal women. ⁵And the Jews, having been moved with envy, and having taken to themselves certain evil men of the agitators, and having made a crowd, were setting the city in an uproar; having also assailed the house of Jason, they were seeking them to bring [them] to the populace, ⁶and having not found them, they drew Jason and certain brothers to the city rulers, calling aloud, "These, having put the world in commotion, are also present here, ⁷whom Jason has received; and all these do contrary to the decrees of Caesar, saying another to be king—Jesus." ⁸And they troubled the multitude and the city rulers, hearing these things, ⁹and having taken security from Jason and the rest, they let them go. ¹⁰And the brothers immediately, through the night, sent forth both Paul and Silas to Berea, who having come, went into the synagogue of the Jews; ¹¹and these were more noble than those in Thessalonica; they received the word with all readiness of mind, examining the Writings every day [to see] whether those things were so; ¹²therefore, many of them, indeed, believed, and not a few of the honorable Greek women and men. ¹³And when the Jews from Thessalonica knew that also in Berea was the word of God declared by Paul, they came there also, agitating the multitudes; ¹⁴and then immediately the brothers sent forth Paul, to go on as it were to the sea, but both Silas and Timotheus were remaining there. ¹⁵And those conducting Paul, brought him to Athens, and having received a command to Silas and Timotheus that with all speed they may come to him, they departed; ¹⁶and Paul waiting for them in Athens, his spirit was stirred in him, beholding the city wholly given to idolatry, ¹⁷therefore, indeed, he was reasoning in the synagogue with the Jews, and with the worshiping persons, and in the marketplace every day with those who met with him. ¹⁸And certain of the Epicurean and of the Stoic philosophers, were meeting together to see him, and some were saying, "What would this seed picker wish to say?" And others, "He seems to be an announcer of strange demons"; because he proclaimed to them Jesus and the resurrection as good news, ¹⁹having also taken him, they brought [him] to the Areopagus, saying, "Are we able to know what this new teaching [is] that is spoken by you, ²⁰for you bring certain strange things to our ears? We resolve, then, to know what these things would wish to be"; ²¹and all Athenians, and the strangers sojourning, for nothing else were at leisure but to say something, and to hear some newer thing. ²²And Paul, having stood in the midst of the Areopagus, said, "Men, Athenians, in all things I perceive you as over-religious; ²³for passing through and contemplating your objects of worship, I also found an altar on which had been inscribed: To God—unknown; whom, therefore—not knowing—you worship, this One I announce to you. ²⁴God, who made the world, and all things in it, this One, being Lord of Heaven and of earth, does not dwell in temples made with hands, ²⁵neither is He served by the hands of men—needing anything, He giving life to all, and breath, and all things; ²⁶He also made every nation of man of one blood, to dwell on all the face of the earth—having ordained times before appointed, and the bounds of their dwellings—²⁷to seek the LORD, if perhaps they felt after Him and found, though, indeed, He is not far from each one of us, ²⁸for in Him we live, and move, and are; as certain of your poets have also said: For we are also His offspring. ²⁹Being, therefore, offspring of God, we ought not to think the Godhead to be like to gold, or silver, or stone, [an] engraving of art and imagination of man; ³⁰therefore indeed God, having overlooked the times of ignorance, now commands all men everywhere to convert, ³¹because He set a day in which He is about to judge the world in righteousness, by a Man whom He ordained, having given assurance to all, having raised Him out of the

dead." ³²And having heard of a resurrection of the dead, some, indeed, were mocking, but others said, "We will hear you again concerning this"; ³³and so Paul went forth from the midst of them, ³⁴and certain men having cleaved to him, believed, among whom [is] also Dionysius the Areopagite, and a woman, by name Damaris, and others with them.

CHAPTER 18

¹And after these things, Paul having departed out of Athens, came to Corinth, ²and having found a certain Jew, by name Aquilas, of Pontus by birth, lately come from Italy, and his wife Priscilla—because of Claudius having directed all the Jews to depart out of Rome—he came to them, ³and because of being of the same craft, he remained with them, and was working, for they were tentmakers as to craft; ⁴and he was reasoning in the synagogue every Sabbath, persuading both Jews and Greeks. ⁵And when both Silas and Timotheus came down from Macedonia, Paul was pressed in the Spirit, testifying fully to the Jews Jesus the Christ; ⁶and on their resisting and slandering, having shaken [his] garments, he said to them, "Your blood [is] on your head—I am clean; from now on I will go on to the nations." ⁷And having departed from there, he went to the house of a certain one, by name Justus, a worshiper of God, whose house was adjoining the synagogue, ⁸and Crispus, the ruler of the synagogue believed in the LORD with all his house, and many of the Corinthians hearing were believing, and they were being immersed. ⁹And the LORD said through a vision in the night to Paul, "Do not be afraid, but be speaking and you may not be silent; ¹⁰because I am with you, and no one will set on you to do evil [to] you, because I have many people in this city"; ¹¹and he continued a year and six months, teaching the word of God among them. ¹²And Gallio being proconsul of Achaia, the Jews made a rush with one accord on Paul, and brought him to the judgment seat, ¹³saying, "This one persuades men to worship God against the Law"; ¹⁴and Paul being about to open [his] mouth, Gallio said to the Jews, "If, indeed, then, it was anything unrighteous, or an act of wicked recklessness, O Jews, according to reason I had borne with you, ¹⁵but if it is a question concerning words and names, and of your law, look [to it] yourselves, for I do not intend to be a judge of these things," ¹⁶and he drives them from the judgment seat; ¹⁷and all the Greeks having taken Sosthenes, the chief man of the synagogue, were beating [him] before the judgment seat, and Gallio was not even caring for these things. ¹⁸And Paul having remained yet a good many days, having taken leave of the brothers, was sailing to Syria—and with him [are] Priscilla and Aquilas—having shorn [his] head in Cenchera, for he had a vow; ¹⁹and he came down to Ephesus, and left them there, and he himself having entered into the synagogue reasoned with the Jews: ²⁰and they having requested [him] to remain a longer time with them, he did not consent, ²¹but took leave of them, saying, "It is necessary for me by all means to keep the coming celebration at Jerusalem, and again I will return to you—God willing." And he sailed from Ephesus, ²²and having come down to Caesarea, having gone up, and having greeted the assembly, he went down to Antioch. ²³And having stayed some time, he went forth, going successively through the region of Galatia and Phrygia, strengthening all the disciples. ²⁴And a certain Jew, Apollos by name, an Alexandrian by birth, a man of eloquence, being mighty in the Writings, came to Ephesus; ²⁵this one was instructed in the way of the LORD, and being fervent in the Spirit, was speaking and teaching exactly the things about the LORD, knowing only the immersion of John; ²⁶this one also began to speak boldly in the synagogue, and Aquilas and Priscilla having heard of him, took him to [them], and more exactly set forth to him The Way of God, ²⁷and he resolving to go through into Achaia, the brothers wrote to the disciples, having exhorted them to receive him, who having come, helped them much who have believed through grace, ²⁸for he was powerfully refuting the Jews publicly, showing through the Writings Jesus to be the Christ.

CHAPTER 19

¹And it came to pass, in Apollos being in Corinth, Paul having gone through the upper parts, came to Ephesus, and having found certain disciples, ²he said to them, "Having believed, did you receive the Holy Spirit?" And they said to him, "But we did not even hear whether there is any Holy Spirit"; ³and he said to them, "Into what, then, were you immersed?" And they said, "Into John's immersion." ⁴And Paul said, "John, indeed, immersed with an immersion of conversion, saying to the people that they should believe in Him who is coming after him—that is, in the Christ—Jesus"; ⁵and they, having heard, were immersed into the Name of the Lord Jesus, ⁶and Paul having laid [his] hands on them, the Holy Spirit came on them, they were also speaking with tongues, and prophesying, ⁷and all the men were, as it were, twelve. ⁸And having gone into the synagogue, he was speaking boldly for three months, reasoning and persuading the things concerning the Kingdom of God, ⁹and when certain were hardened and were disbelieving, speaking evil of The Way before the multitude, having departed from them, he separated the disciples, reasoning every day in the school of a certain Tyrannus. ¹⁰And this happened for two years so that all those dwelling in Asia heard the word of the Lord Jesus, both Jews and Greeks, ¹¹also mighty works—not common—God was working through the hands of Paul, ¹²so that even to the ailing were brought from his body handkerchiefs or aprons, and the diseases departed from them; the evil spirits also went forth from them. ¹³And certain of the wandering exorcist Jews, took on [them] to name over those having the evil spirits the Name of the Lord Jesus, saying, "We adjure you by Jesus, whom Paul preaches"; ¹⁴and there were certain—seven sons of Sceva, a Jew, a chief priest—who are doing this thing; ¹⁵and the evil spirit, answering, said, "I know Jesus, and I am acquainted with Paul; and you—who are you?" ¹⁶And the man, in whom was the evil spirit, leaping on them, and having overcome them, prevailed against them, so that they fled naked and wounded out of that house, ¹⁷and this became known to all, both Jews and Greeks, who are dwelling at Ephesus, and fear fell on them all, and the Name of the Lord Jesus was being magnified; ¹⁸many also of those who believed were coming, confessing and declaring their acts, ¹⁹and many of those who had practiced the superfluous arts, having brought the scrolls together, were burning [them] before all; and they reckoned together the prices of them, and found [it] fifty thousand pieces of silver, ²⁰so powerfully was the word of God increasing and prevailing. ²¹And when these things were fulfilled, Paul purposed in the Spirit, having gone through Macedonia and Achaia, to go on to Jerusalem, saying, "After my being there, it is also necessary for me to see Rome"; ²²and having sent to Macedonia two of those ministering to him—Timotheus and Erastus—he himself stayed a time in Asia. ²³And there came, at that time, not a little stir about The Way, ²⁴for a certain one, Demetrius by name, a worker in silver, making silver sanctuaries of Artemis, was bringing to the craftsmen not a little gain, ²⁵whom, having brought in a crowd together, and those who worked around such things, he said, "Men, you know that by this work we have our wealth; ²⁶and you see and hear, that not only at Ephesus, but almost in all Asia, this Paul, having persuaded, turned away a great multitude, saying that they who are made by hands are not gods; ²⁷and not only is this department in danger for us of coming into disregard, but also, that of the great goddess Artemis, the temple is to be reckoned for nothing, and also her greatness is about to be brought down, whom all Asia and the world worships." ²⁸And having heard, and having become full of wrath, they were crying out, saying, "Great [is] the Artemis of the Ephesians!" ²⁹And the whole city was filled with confusion; they rushed also with one accord into the theater, having caught Gaius and Aristarchus, Macedonians, Paul's fellow-travelers. ³⁰And on Paul's resolving to enter in to the populace, the disciples were not permitting him, ³¹and also some of the chief men of Asia, being his friends, having sent to him, were pleading [with] him not to venture into the theater himself. ³²Some indeed, therefore, were calling out one thing, and some another, for the assembly was confused, and the greater part did not know for what they had come together; ³³and out of the multitude they put forward Alexander—the Jews thrusting him forward—and Alexander having beckoned with the hand, wished to make defense to the populace, ³⁴and having known that he is a Jew, one voice came out of all, for about two hours, crying, "Great [is] the Artemis of the Ephesians!" ³⁵And the public

clerk having quieted the multitude, says, "Men, Ephesians, why, who is the man that does not know that the city of the Ephesians is temple-keeper of the great goddess Artemis, and of that which fell down from Zeus? ³⁶These things, then, being undeniable, it is necessary for you to be quiet, and to do nothing rashly. ³⁷For you brought these men, who are neither temple-robbers nor slandering of your goddess; ³⁸if indeed, therefore, Demetrius and the craftsmen with him have a matter with anyone, court [days] are held, and there are proconsuls; let them accuse one another. ³⁹And if you seek after anything concerning other matters, it will be determined in the legal assembly; ⁴⁰for we are also in peril of being accused of insurrection in regard to this day, there being no occasion by which we will be able to give an account of this concourse"; ⁴¹and having said these things, he dismissed the assembly.

CHAPTER 20

¹And after the ceasing of the tumult, Paul having called near the disciples, and having embraced [them], went forth to go on to Macedonia; ²and having gone through those parts, and having exhorted them with many words, he came to Greece; ³and having continued three months—a counsel of the Jews having been against him—being about to set forth to Syria, there came [to him] a resolution of returning through Macedonia. ⁴And there were accompanying him to Asia, Sopater of Pyrrhus from Berea, and of Thessalonians Aristarchus and Secundus, and Gaius of Derbe, and Timotheus, and of Asians Tychicus and Trophimus; ⁵these, having gone before, remained for us in Troas, ⁶and we sailed, after the days of the Unleavened [Bread], from Philippi, and came to them to Troas in five days, where we abided seven days. ⁷And on the first [day] of the weeks, the disciples having been gathered together to break bread, Paul was discoursing to them, about to depart on the next day, he was also continuing the discourse until midnight, ⁸and there were many lamps in the upper chamber where they were gathered together, ⁹and there a certain youth was sitting, by name Eutychus, on the window—being borne down by a deep sleep, Paul discoursing long—he having sunk down from the sleep, fell down from the third story, and was lifted up dead. ¹⁰And Paul, having gone down, fell on him, and having embraced [him], said, "Make no tumult, for his life is in him"; ¹¹and having come up, and having broken bread, and having tasted, for a long time also having talked—until daylight, so he went forth, ¹²and they brought up the boy alive, and were comforted in no ordinary measure. ¹³And we having gone before to the ship, sailed to Assos, there intending to take in Paul, for so he had arranged, intending himself to go on foot; ¹⁴and when he met with us at Assos, having taken him up, we came to Mitylene, ¹⁵and there having sailed, on the next day we came opposite Chios, and the next day we arrived at Samos, and having remained in Trogyllium, on the following day we came to Miletus, ¹⁶for Paul decided to sail past Ephesus, that there may not be to him a loss of time in Asia, for he was hurrying, if it were possible for him, to be at Jerusalem on the day of the Pentecost. ¹⁷And from Miletus, having sent to Ephesus, he called for the elders of the assembly, ¹⁸and when they were come to him, he said to them, "You know from the first day in which I came to Asia, how I was with you at all times; ¹⁹serving the LORD with all humility, and many tears, and temptations, that befell me in the counsels of the Jews against [me]; ²⁰how I kept back nothing of what things are profitable, not to declare to you, and to teach you publicly, and in every house, ²¹testifying fully both to Jews and Greeks, conversion toward God, and faith toward our Lord Jesus Christ. ²²And now, behold, I—bound in the Spirit—go on to Jerusalem, not knowing the things that will befall me in it, ²³except that the Holy Spirit fully testifies in every city, saying that bonds and tribulations remain for me; ²⁴but I make account of none of these, neither do I count my life precious to myself, so that I finish my course with joy, and the ministry that I received from the Lord Jesus, to fully testify [to] the good news of the grace of God. ²⁵And now, behold, I have known that you will no longer see my face, among all you [to] whom I went preaching the Kingdom of God; ²⁶for this reason I take you to witness this day, that I [am] clear from the blood of all, ²⁷for I did not keep back from declaring to you all the counsel of God. ²⁸Take heed, therefore, to yourselves, and to all the flock, among which the Holy Spirit made you overseers, to feed the Assembly of God that He acquired through His own blood, ²⁹for I have known this, that there will enter in, after my departing, grievous wolves to you, not sparing the flock, ³⁰and there will arise men of your own selves, speaking perverse things, to draw away the disciples after them. ³¹Therefore, watch, remembering that three years, night and day, I did not cease with tears warning each one; ³²and now, I commend you, brothers, to God, and to the word of His grace, that is able to build up, and to give you an inheritance among all those sanctified. ³³I coveted the silver or gold or clothing of no one; ³⁴and you yourselves know that to my necessities, and to those who were with me, these hands ministered; ³⁵I showed you all things, that, thus laboring, it is necessary to partake with the ailing, to also be mindful of the words of the Lord Jesus, that He Himself said: It is more blessed to give than to receive." ³⁶And having said these things, having bowed his knees, with them all, he prayed, ³⁷and there came a great weeping to all, and having fallen on the neck of Paul, they were kissing him, ³⁸sorrowing most of all for the word that he had said—that they are about to see his face no longer; and they were accompanying him to the ship.

CHAPTER 21

¹And it came to pass, at our sailing, having been parted from them, having run direct, we came to Coos, and the succeeding [day] to Rhodes, and there to Patara, ²and having found a ship passing over to Phoenicia, having gone on board, we sailed, ³and having discovered Cyprus, and having left it on the left, we were sailing to Syria, and landed at Tyre, for there was the ship discharging the cargo. ⁴And having found out the disciples, we tarried there seven days, and they said to Paul, through the Spirit, not to go up to Jerusalem; ⁵but when it came that we completed the days, having gone forth, we went on, all bringing us on the way, with women and children, to the outside of the city, and having bowed the knees on the shore, we prayed, ⁶and having embraced one another, we embarked in the ship, and they returned to their own friends. ⁷And we, having finished the course, from Tyre came down to Ptolemais, and having greeted the brothers, we remained one day with them; ⁸and on the next day Paul and his company having gone forth, we came to Caesarea, and having entered into the house of Philip the evangelist—who is of the seven—we remained with him, ⁹and this one had four daughters, virgins, prophesying. ¹⁰And we remaining many more days, there came down a certain one from Judea, a prophet, by name Agabus, ¹¹and he having come to us, and having taken up the girdle of Paul, having also bound his own hands and feet, said, "Thus says the Holy Spirit: The man whose is this girdle—so will the Jews in Jerusalem bind, and they will deliver [him] up into the hands of nations." ¹²And when we heard these things, we called on [him]—both we, and those of that place—not to go up to Jerusalem, ¹³and Paul answered, "Why are you weeping, and crushing my heart? For I am ready, not only to be bound, but also to die at Jerusalem for the Name of the Lord Jesus"; ¹⁴and he not being persuaded, we were silent, saying, "The will of the LORD be done." ¹⁵And after these days, having taken [our] vessels, we were going up to Jerusalem, ¹⁶and there went also of the disciples from Caesarea with us, bringing with them him with whom we may lodge, a certain Mnason of Cyprus, an aged disciple. ¹⁷And we having come to Jerusalem, the brothers gladly received us, ¹⁸and on the next day Paul was going in with us to James, all the elders also came, ¹⁹and having greeted them, he was expounding, one by one, each of the things God did among the nations through his ministry, ²⁰and they having heard, were glorifying the LORD. They also said to him, "You see, brother, how many myriads there are of Jews who have believed, and all are zealous of the Law, ²¹and they are instructed concerning you, that you teach departure from Moses to all Jews among the nations, saying not to circumcise the children, nor to walk after the customs; ²²what then is it? Certainly the multitude must come together, for they will hear that you have come. ²³This, therefore, that we say to you, do. We have four men having a vow on themselves, ²⁴having taken these, be purified with them, and be at expense with them, that they may shave the head, and all

may know that the things of which they have been instructed concerning you are nothing, but you walk—yourself also—keeping the Law. ²⁵And concerning those of the nations who have believed, we have written, having given judgment, that they observe no such thing, except to keep themselves both from idol-sacrifices, and blood, and a strangled thing, and whoredom." ²⁶Then Paul, having taken the men, on the following day, having purified himself with them, was entering into the temple, announcing the fulfillment of the days of the purification, until the offering was offered for each one of them. ²⁷And as the seven days were about to be fully ended, the Jews from Asia having beheld him in the temple, were stirring up all the multitude, and they laid hands on him, ²⁸crying out, "Men, Israelites, help! This is the man who, against the people, and the Law, and this place, is teaching all everywhere; and further, also, he brought Greeks into the temple, and has defiled this holy place"; ²⁹for they had seen before Trophimus, the Ephesian, in the city with him, whom they were supposing that Paul brought into the temple. ³⁰All the city was also moved and there was a running together of the people, and having laid hold on Paul, they were drawing him out of the temple, and immediately were the doors shut, ³¹and they seeking to kill him, a rumor came to the chief captain of the band that all Jerusalem has been thrown into confusion, ³²who, at once, having taken soldiers and centurions, ran down on them, and they having seen the chief captain and the soldiers, left off beating Paul. ³³Then the chief captain, having come near, took him, and commanded [him] to be bound with two chains, and was inquiring who he may be, and what it is he has been doing, ³⁴and some were crying out one thing, and some another, among the multitude, and not being able to know the certainty because of the tumult, he commanded him to be carried into the stronghold, ³⁵and when he came on the steps, it happened he was carried by the soldiers, because of the violence of the multitude, ³⁶for the crowd of the people was following after, crying, "Away with him." ³⁷And Paul being about to be led into the stronghold, says to the chief captain, "Is it permitted to me to say anything to you?" And he said, "Do you know Greek? ³⁸Are you not, then, the Egyptian who made an uprising before these days, and led the four thousand men of the assassins into the desert?" ³⁹And Paul said, "I, indeed, am a man, a Jew, of Tarsus of Cilicia, a citizen of no insignificant city; and I implore you, permit me to speak to the people." ⁴⁰And he having given him leave, Paul having stood on the stairs, beckoned with the hand to the people, and there having been a great silence, he spoke to them in the Hebrew dialect, saying:

CHAPTER 22

¹"Men, brothers, and fathers, hear my defense now to you." ²and they having heard that he was speaking to them in the Hebrew dialect, they became even more silent, and he says, ³"I, indeed, am a man, a Jew, having been born in Tarsus of Cilicia, and brought up in this city at the feet of Gamaliel, having been taught according to the exactness of a law of the fathers, being zealous of God, as all you are today. ⁴And this Way I persecuted to death, binding and delivering up to prisons both men and women, ⁵as also the chief priest testifies to me, and all the eldership; from whom also having received letters to the brothers, to Damascus, I was going on, to bring also those there bound to Jerusalem that they might be punished, ⁶and it came to pass, in my going on and coming near to Damascus, about noon, suddenly out of Heaven there shone a great light around me; ⁷I also fell to the ground, and I heard a voice saying to me, Saul, Saul, why do you persecute Me? ⁸And I answered, Who are You, Lord? And He said to me, I am Jesus the Nazarene whom you persecute— ⁹and they who are with me saw the light, and became afraid, and they did not hear the voice of Him who is speaking to me— ¹⁰and I said, What will I do, Lord? And the LORD said to me, Having risen, go on to Damascus, and there it will be told you concerning all things that have been appointed for you to do. ¹¹And when I did not see from the glory of that light, being led by the hand by those who are with me, I came to Damascus, ¹²and a certain one, Ananias, a pious man according to the Law, being testified to by all the Jews dwelling [there], ¹³having come to me and stood by [me], said to me, Saul, brother, look up; and the same hour I looked up to him; ¹⁴and he said, The God of our fathers chose you beforehand to know His will, and to see the Righteous One, and to hear a voice out of His mouth, ¹⁵because you will be His witness to all men of what you have seen and heard; ¹⁶and now, why do you linger? Having risen, immerse yourself, and wash away your sins, calling on the Name of the LORD. ¹⁷And it came to pass, when I returned to Jerusalem, and while I was praying in the temple, I came into a trance, ¹⁸and I saw Him saying to me, Hurry and go forth in haste out of Jerusalem, because they will not receive your testimony concerning Me; ¹⁹and I said, LORD, they know that I was imprisoning and was scourging those believing on You in every synagogue; ²⁰and when the blood of your witness Stephen was being poured forth, I was also standing by and assenting to his death, and keeping the garments of those putting him to death; ²¹and He said to me, Go, because I will send you to far-off nations." ²²And they were hearing him to this word, and they lifted up their voice, saying, "Away from the earth with such a one; for it is not fit for him to live." ²³And they crying out and casting up their garments, and throwing dust into the air, ²⁴the chief captain commanded him to be brought into the stronghold, saying, "Let him be examined by scourges," that he might know for what cause they were crying so against him. ²⁵And as he was stretching him with the straps, Paul said to the centurion who was standing by, "Is it lawful to you to scourge a man, a Roman, uncondemned?" ²⁶And the centurion having heard, having gone near to the chief captain, told, saying, "Take heed what you are about to do, for this man is a Roman"; ²⁷and the chief captain having come near, said to him, "Tell me, are you a Roman?" And he said, "Yes"; ²⁸and the chief captain answered, "I, with a great sum, obtained this citizenship"; but Paul said, "But I have even been born [so]." ²⁹Immediately, therefore, they departed from him, those being about to examine him, and the chief captain was also afraid, having learned that he is a Roman, and because he had bound him, ³⁰and the next day, intending to know the certainty for what reason he is accused by the Jews, he loosed him from the bonds, and commanded the chief priests and all their Sanhedrin to come, and having brought down Paul, he set [him] before them.

CHAPTER 23

¹And Paul having earnestly beheld the Sanhedrin, said, "Men, brothers, I have lived to God in all good conscience to this day"; ²and the chief priest Ananias commanded those standing by him to strike him on the mouth, ³then Paul said to him, "God is about to strike you, you whitewashed wall, and you sit judging me according to the Law, and violating law, order me to be struck!" ⁴And those who stood by said, "Do you revile the chief priest of God?" ⁵And Paul said, "I did not know, brothers, that he is chief priest, for it has been written: You will not speak evil of the ruler of your people"; ⁶and Paul having known that one part are Sadducees, and the other Pharisees, cried out in the Sanhedrin, "Men, brothers, I am a Pharisee—son of a Pharisee—concerning [the] hope and resurrection of [the] dead I am judged." ⁷And he having spoken this, there came a dissension of the Pharisees and of the Sadducees, and the crowd was divided, ⁸for Sadducees, indeed, say there is no resurrection, nor messenger, nor spirit, but Pharisees confess both. ⁹And there came a great cry, and the scribes of the Pharisees' part having arisen, were striving, saying, "We find no evil in this man; and if a spirit spoke to him, or a messenger, we may not fight against God"; ¹⁰and a great dissension having come, the chief captain having been afraid lest Paul may be pulled to pieces by them, commanded the army, having gone down, to seize him out of their midst, and to bring [him] into the stronghold. ¹¹And on the following night, the LORD having stood by him, said, "Take courage, Paul, for as you fully testified [to] the things concerning Me at Jerusalem, so you must also testify at Rome." ¹²And day having come, certain of the Jews having made a concourse, cursed themselves, saying neither to eat nor to drink until they may kill Paul; ¹³and they were more than forty who made this conspiracy by oath, ¹⁴who having come near to the chief priests and to the elders said, "With a curse we accursed ourselves—to taste nothing until we have killed Paul; ¹⁵now, therefore, you, signify to the chief captain, with the Sanhedrin, that tomorrow he may bring him down to you, as being about to know more exactly the things concerning him; and

we, before his coming near, are ready to put him to death." ¹⁶And the son of Paul's sister having heard of the lying in wait, having gone and entered into the stronghold, told Paul, ¹⁷and Paul having called near one of the centurions, said, "Lead this young man to the chief captain, for he has something to tell him." ¹⁸He indeed, then, having taken him, brought him to the chief captain and says, "The prisoner Paul, having called me near, asked [me] to bring to you this young man, having something to say to you." ¹⁹And the chief captain having taken him by the hand, and having withdrawn by themselves, inquired, "What is that which you have to tell me?" ²⁰And he said, "The Jews agreed to request you, that tomorrow you may bring down Paul to the Sanhedrin, as being about to inquire something more exactly concerning him; ²¹you, therefore, may you not yield to them, for there more than forty men of them lie in wait for him, who cursed themselves—not to eat nor to drink until they kill him, and now they are ready, waiting for the promise from you." ²²The chief captain, then, indeed, let the young man go, having charged [him], "Tell no one that you have shown these things to me"; ²³and having called a certain two of the centurions near, he said, "Make ready two hundred soldiers, that they may go on to Caesarea, and seventy horsemen, and two hundred spearmen, from the third hour of the night; ²⁴also provide beasts, that, having set Paul on, they may bring him safe to Felix the governor"; ²⁵he having written a letter after this description: ²⁶"Claudius Lysias, to the most noble governor Felix, greetings: ²⁷This man having been taken by the Jews, and being about to be killed by them—having come with the army, I rescued him, having learned that he is a Roman; ²⁸and intending to know the cause for which they were accusing him, I brought him down to their Sanhedrin, ²⁹whom I found accused concerning questions of their law, and having no accusation worthy of death or bonds; ³⁰and a plot having been intimated to me against this man—about to be of the Jews—I sent to you at once, having also given command to the accusers to say the things against him before you; be strong." ³¹Then, indeed, the soldiers according to that directed them, having taken up Paul, brought him through the night to Antipatris, ³²and on the next day, having permitted the horsemen to go on with him, they returned to the stronghold; ³³those having entered into Caesarea, and delivered the letter to the governor, also presented Paul to him. ³⁴And the governor having read [it], and inquired of what province he is, and understood that [he is] from Cilicia; ³⁵"I will hear you," he said, "when your accusers may also have come"; he also commanded him to be kept in the Praetorium of Herod.

CHAPTER 24

¹And after five days the chief priest Ananias came down, with the elders, and a certain orator—Tertullus, and they disclosed to the governor [the things] against Paul; ²and he having been called, Tertullus began to accuse [him], saying, "Enjoying much peace through you, and worthy deeds being done to this nation through your forethought, ³always, also, and everywhere we receive it, most noble Felix, with all thankfulness; ⁴and that I may not be further tedious to you, I exhort you to hear us concisely in your gentleness; ⁵for having found this man a pestilence, and moving a dissension to all the Jews through the world—also a ringleader of the sect of the Nazarenes— ⁶who also tried to profane the temple, whom we also took, [[and wished to judge according to our law, ⁷and Lysias the chief captain having come near, took away out of our hands with much violence, ⁸having commanded his accusers to come to you,]] from whom you may be able, yourself having examined, to know concerning all these things of which we accuse him"; ⁹and the Jews also agreed, professing these things to be so. ¹⁰And Paul—the governor having beckoned to him to speak—answered, "Knowing [that] for many years you have been a judge to this nation, I answer more cheerfully the things concerning myself; ¹¹you being able to know that it is not more than twelve days to me since I went up to worship in Jerusalem, ¹²and neither did they find me reasoning with anyone in the temple, or making a dissension of the multitude, nor in the synagogues, nor in the city; ¹³nor are they able to prove against me the things concerning which they now accuse me. ¹⁴And I confess this to you, that, according to The Way that they call a sect, so I serve the God of the fathers, believing all things that have been written in the Law and the Prophets, ¹⁵having hope toward God, which they themselves also wait for, [that] there is about to be a resurrection of the dead, both of righteous and unrighteous; ¹⁶and in this I exercise myself, to always have a conscience void of offense toward God and men. ¹⁷And after many years I came, about to do kind acts to my nation, and offerings, ¹⁸in which certain Jews from Asia found me purified in the temple, not with multitude, nor with tumult, ¹⁹whom it is necessary to be present before you, and to accuse, if they had anything against me, ²⁰or let these same say if they found any unrighteousness in me in my standing before the Sanhedrin, ²¹except concerning this one voice, in which I cried, standing among them—Concerning a resurrection of the dead I am judged by you today." ²²And having heard these things, Felix delayed them—having known more exactly of the things concerning The Way—saying, "When Lysias the chief captain may come down, I will know fully the things concerning you"; ²³having also given a direction to the centurion to keep Paul, to let [him] also have liberty, and to forbid none of his own friends to minister or to come near to him. ²⁴And after certain days, Felix having come with his wife Drusilla, being a Jewess, he sent for Paul, and heard him concerning faith toward Christ, ²⁵and he reasoning concerning righteousness, and self-control, and the judgment that is about to be, Felix, having become afraid, answered, "For the present be going, and having time, I will call for you"; ²⁶and at the same time also hoping that money will be given to him by Paul, that he may release him, therefore, also sending for him often, he was conversing with him; ²⁷and two years having been fulfilled, Felix received a successor, Porcius Festus; Felix also willing to lay a favor on the Jews, left Paul bound.

CHAPTER 25

¹Festus, therefore, having come into the province, after three days went up to Jerusalem from Caesarea, ²and the chief priest and the principal men of the Jews disclosed to him [the things] against Paul, and were calling on him, ³asking favor against him, that he may send for him to Jerusalem, making an ambush to put him to death in the way. ⁴Then, indeed, Festus answered that Paul is kept in Caesarea, and is himself about to go forth speedily, ⁵"Therefore those able among you," he says, "having come down together, if there be anything in this man—let them accuse him"; ⁶and having tarried among them more than ten days, having gone down to Caesarea, on the next day having sat on the judgment seat, he commanded Paul to be brought; ⁷and he having come, there stood around the Jews who have come down from Jerusalem—many and weighty charges they are bringing against Paul, which they were not able to prove, ⁸he making defense, [said,] "Neither in regard to the Law of the Jews, nor in regard to the temple, nor in regard to Caesar—did I commit any sin." ⁹And Festus willing to lay on the Jews a favor, answering Paul, said, "Are you willing, having gone up to Jerusalem, to be judged before me there concerning these things?" ¹⁰And Paul said, "At the judgment seat of Caesar I am standing, where it is necessary for me to be judged; I did no unrighteousness to Jews, as you also very well know; ¹¹for if I am indeed unrighteous, and have done anything worthy of death, I do not deprecate to die; and if there is none of the things of which these accuse me, no one is able to make a favor of me to them; I appeal to Caesar!" ¹²Then Festus, having communed with the council, answered, "To Caesar you have appealed; to Caesar you will go." ¹³And certain days having passed, Agrippa the king, and Bernice, came down to Caesarea greeting Festus, ¹⁴and as they were continuing there more days, Festus submitted to the king the things concerning Paul, saying, "There is a certain man, left by Felix, a prisoner, ¹⁵about whom, in my being at Jerusalem, the chief priests and the elders of the Jews laid information, asking a decision against him, ¹⁶to whom I answered, that it is not a custom of Romans to make a favor of any man to die, before that he who is accused may have the accusers face to face, and may receive place of defense in regard to the charge laid against [him]. ¹⁷They, therefore, having come together—I, making no delay, on the succeeding [day] having sat on the judgment seat, commanded the man to be brought, ¹⁸concerning whom the accusers, having stood up, were bringing against [him] no

accusation of the things I was thinking of, ¹⁹but certain questions concerning their own religion they had against him, and concerning a certain Jesus who was dead, whom Paul affirmed to be alive; ²⁰and I, doubting in regard to the question concerning this, asked if he was willing to go on to Jerusalem, and to be judged there concerning these things— ²¹but Paul having appealed to be kept to the hearing of Sebastus, I commanded him to be kept until I might send him to Caesar." ²²And Agrippa said to Festus, "I was also intending to hear the man myself"; and he said, "Tomorrow you will hear him"; ²³on the next day, therefore—on the coming of Agrippa and Bernice with much display, and they having entered into the audience chamber, with the chief captains also, and the principal men of the city, and Festus having ordered—Paul was brought forth. ²⁴And Festus said, "King Agrippa, and all men who are present with us, you see this one, about whom all the multitude of the Jews dealt with me, both in Jerusalem and here, crying out, He ought not to live any longer; ²⁵and I, having found him to have done nothing worthy of death, and he also himself having appealed to Sebastus, I decided to send him, ²⁶concerning whom I have no certain thing to write to [my] lord, for what reason I brought him forth before you, and especially before you, King Agrippa, that the examination having been made, I may have something to write; ²⁷for it seems to me irrational, sending a prisoner, not to also signify the charges against him."

CHAPTER 26

¹And Agrippa said to Paul, "It is permitted to you to speak for yourself"; then Paul having stretched forth the hand, was making a defense: ²"Concerning all things of which I am accused by Jews, King Agrippa, I have thought myself blessed, being about to make a defense before you today, ³especially knowing you to be acquainted with all things—both customs and questions—among Jews; for this reason, I implore you to hear me patiently. ⁴The manner of my life then, indeed, from youth—which from the beginning was among my nation, in Jerusalem—all the Jews know, ⁵knowing me before from the first (if they may be willing to testify), that after the most exact sect of our worship, I lived a Pharisee; ⁶and now for the hope of the promise made to the fathers by God, I have stood judged, ⁷to which our twelve tribes, intently serving night and day, hope to come, concerning which hope I am accused, King Agrippa, by the Jews; ⁸why is it judged incredible with you if God raises the dead? ⁹I indeed, therefore, thought with myself that it was necessary [for me] to do many things against the Name of Jesus of Nazareth, ¹⁰which I also did in Jerusalem, and I shut up many of the holy ones in prison, having received the authority from the chief priests; they also being put to death, I gave my vote against them, ¹¹and in every synagogue, often punishing them, I was constraining [them] to speak evil, being also exceedingly mad against them, I was also persecuting [them] even to strange cities. ¹²In which things, also, going on to Damascus—with authority and commission from the chief priests— ¹³at midday, I saw in the way, O king, out of Heaven, above the brightness of the sun, shining around me a light—and those going on with me; ¹⁴and we all having fallen to the earth, I heard a voice speaking to me, and saying in the Hebrew dialect, Saul, Saul, why do you persecute Me? [It is] hard for you to kick against goads! ¹⁵And I said, Who are You, Lord? And He said, I am Jesus whom you persecute; ¹⁶but rise, and stand on your feet, for this I appeared to you, to appoint you an officer and a witness both of the things you saw, and of the things [in which] I will appear to you, ¹⁷delivering you from the people, and the nations, to whom I now send you, ¹⁸to open their eyes, to turn [them] from darkness to light, and [from] the authority of Satan to God, for their receiving forgiveness of sins, and a lot among those having been sanctified by faith that [is] toward Me. ¹⁹After which, King Agrippa, I was not disobedient to the heavenly vision, ²⁰but to those in Damascus first, and to those in Jerusalem, also to all the region of Judea, and to the nations, I was preaching to convert, and to turn back to God, doing works worthy of conversion; ²¹because of these things the Jews—having caught me in the temple—were endeavoring to kill [me]. ²²Having obtained, therefore, help from God, until this day, I have stood witnessing both to small and to great, saying nothing besides the things that both the prophets and Moses spoke of as about to come, ²³that the Christ is to suffer, whether first by a resurrection from the dead, He is about to proclaim light to the people and to the nations." ²⁴And he thus making a defense, Festus said with a loud voice, "You are mad, Paul; much learning turns you mad!" ²⁵And he says, "I am not mad, most noble Festus, but of truth and soberness I speak forth the sayings; ²⁶for the king knows concerning these things, before whom I also speak boldly, for none of these things, I am persuaded, are hidden from him; for this thing has not been done in a corner; ²⁷do you believe, King Agrippa, the prophets? I have known that you believe!" ²⁸And Agrippa said to Paul, "In [so] little you persuade me to become a Christian?" ²⁹And Paul said, "I would have wished to God, both in a little, and in much, not only you, but also all those hearing me today, to become such as I also am—except these bonds." ³⁰And he having spoken these things, the king rose up, and the governor, Bernice also, and those sitting with them, ³¹and having withdrawn, they were speaking to one another, saying, "This man does nothing worthy of death or of bonds"; ³²and Agrippa said to Festus, "This man might have been released if he had not appealed to Caesar."

CHAPTER 27

¹And when our sailing to Italy was determined, they were delivering up both Paul and certain others, prisoners, to a centurion, by name Julius, of the band of Sebastus, ²and having embarked in a ship of Adramyttium, we, being about to sail by the coasts of Asia, set sail, there being with us Aristarchus, a Macedonian of Thessalonica, ³on the next [day] also we touched at Sidon, and Julius, courteously treating Paul, permitted [him], having gone on to friends, to receive [their] care. ⁴And there, having set sail, we sailed under Cyprus, because of the winds being contrary, ⁵and having sailed over the sea down by Cilicia and Pamphylia, we came to Myria of Lycia, ⁶and there the centurion having found a ship of Alexandria, sailing to Italy, put us into it, ⁷and having sailed slowly many days, and with difficulty coming down by Cnidus, the wind not permitting us, we sailed under Crete, down by Salmone, ⁸and hardly passing it, we came to a certain place called Fair Havens, near to which was the city of Lasaea. ⁹And much time being spent, and the sailing now being dangerous—because of the fast also being already past—Paul was admonishing, ¹⁰saying to them, "Men, I perceive that with hurt, and much damage, not only of the load and of the ship, but also of our lives—the voyage is about to be"; ¹¹but the centurion gave more credence to the pilot and to the shipowner than to the things spoken by Paul; ¹²and the haven being not well placed to winter in, the greater part gave counsel to sail from there, if somehow they might be able, having attained to Phoenix, to winter [there], [which is] a haven of Crete, looking to the southwest and northwest, ¹³and a south wind blowing softly, having thought they had obtained [their] purpose, having lifted anchor, they sailed close by Crete, ¹⁴and not long after, there came down from it a turbulent wind [that] is called the Euroclydon, ¹⁵and the ship being caught, and not being able to bear up against the wind, having given [her] up, we were carried on, ¹⁶and having run under a certain little island called Clauda, we were hardly able to become masters of the boat, ¹⁷which having taken up, they were using helps, undergirding the ship, and fearing lest they may fall into the [sandbars of] Syrtis, having let down the mast—so were carried on. ¹⁸And we, being exceedingly storm-tossed, the succeeding [day] they were making a clearing, ¹⁹and on the third [day] we cast out the tackling of the ship with our own hands, ²⁰and neither sun nor stars appearing for more days, and not a little storm lying on us, from then on all hope was taken away of our being saved. ²¹And there having been long fasting, then Paul having stood in the midst of them, said, "It was necessary, indeed, O men—having listened to me—not to set sail from Crete, and to save this hurt and damage; ²²and now I exhort you to be of good cheer, for there will be no loss of life among you—but of the ship; ²³for this night there stood by me a messenger of God—whose I am, and whom I serve— ²⁴saying, Do not be afraid Paul; it is necessary for you to stand before Caesar; and behold, God has granted to you all those sailing with you; ²⁵for this reason be of good cheer, men! For I believe God, that so it will be, even as it has been spoken to me, ²⁶and on a

certain island it is necessary for us to be cast." ²⁷And when the fourteenth night came—we being carried up and down in the Adria—toward the middle of the night the sailors were supposing that some country drew near to them; ²⁸and having sounded they found twenty fathoms, and having gone a little farther, and again having sounded, they found fifteen fathoms, ²⁹and fearing lest we may fall on rough places, having cast four anchors out of the stern, they were wishing day to come. ³⁰And the sailors seeking to flee out of the ship, and having let down the boat to the sea, in pretense as [if] out of the prow they are about to cast anchors, ³¹Paul said to the centurion and to the soldiers, "If these do not remain in the ship—you are not able to be saved"; ³²then the soldiers cut off the ropes of the boat, and permitted it to fall off. ³³And until the day was about to be, Paul was calling on all to partake of nourishment, saying, "Fourteen days today, waiting, you continue fasting, having taken nothing, ³⁴for this reason I call on you to take nourishment, for this is for your safety, for of not one of you will a hair fall from the head"; ³⁵and having said these things, and having taken bread, he gave thanks to God before all, and having broken [it], he began to eat; ³⁶and all having become of good cheer, also took food themselves, ³⁷(and we were—all the souls in the ship—two hundred, seventy-six), ³⁸and having eaten sufficient nourishment, they were lightening the ship, casting forth the wheat into the sea. ³⁹And when the day came, they were not discerning the land, but were perceiving a certain bay having a beach, into which they took counsel, if possible, to thrust forward the ship, ⁴⁰and having taken up the anchors, they were committing [it] to the sea, at the same time—having loosed the bands of the rudders, and having hoisted up the foresail to the wind—they were making for the shore, ⁴¹and having fallen into a place of two seas, they ran the ship aground, and the prow, indeed, having stuck fast, remained immoveable, but the stern was broken by the violence of the waves. ⁴²And the soldiers' counsel was that they should kill the prisoners, lest anyone having swam out should escape, ⁴³but the centurion, resolving to save Paul, hindered them from the counsel, and commanded those able to swim, having cast themselves out first—to get to the land, ⁴⁴and the rest, some indeed on boards, and some on certain things of the ship; and thus it came to pass that all came safe to the land.

CHAPTER 28

¹And having been saved, then they knew that the island is called Malta, ²and the foreigners were showing us no ordinary kindness, for having kindled a fire, they received us all, because of the pressing rain, and because of the cold; ³but Paul having gathered together a quantity of sticks, and having laid [them] on the fire, a viper—having come out of the heat—fastened on his hand. ⁴And when the foreigners saw the beast hanging from his hand, they said to one another, "Certainly this man is a murderer, whom, having been saved out of the sea, the justice did not permit to live"; ⁵he then, indeed, having shaken off the beast into the fire, suffered no evil, ⁶and they were expecting him to be about to be inflamed, or to suddenly fall down dead, and they, expecting [it] a long time, and seeing nothing uncommon happening to him, changing [their] minds, said he was a god. ⁷And in the neighborhood of that place were lands of the principal man of the island, by name Publius, who, having received us, courteously lodged [us for] three days; ⁸and it came to pass, the father of Publius was lying, oppressed with fevers and dysentery, to whom Paul, having entered and having prayed, having laid [his] hands on him, healed him; ⁹this, therefore, being done, also the others in the island having sicknesses were coming and were healed; ¹⁰who also honored us with many honors, and we setting sail—they were loading [us] with the things that were necessary. ¹¹And after three months, we set sail in a ship (that had wintered in the island) of Alexandria, with the sign Dioscuri, ¹²and having landed at Syracuse, we remained three days, ¹³there having gone around, we came to Rhegium, and after one day, a south wind having sprung up, the second [day] we came to Puteoli, ¹⁴where, having found brothers, we were called on to remain with them seven days, and thus we came to Rome; ¹⁵and there, the brothers having heard the things concerning us, came forth to meet us, as far as [the] Forum of Appius, and Three Taverns—whom Paul having seen, having given thanks to God, took courage. ¹⁶And when we came to Rome, the centurion delivered up the prisoners to the captain of the barracks, but Paul was permitted to remain by himself, with the soldier guarding him. ¹⁷And it came to pass after three days, Paul called together those who are the principal men of the Jews, and they having come together, he said to them: "Men, brothers, I—having done nothing contrary to the people, or to the customs of the fathers—a prisoner from Jerusalem, was delivered up into the hands of the Romans; ¹⁸who having examined me, were willing to release [me], because of there being no cause of death in me, ¹⁹and the Jews having spoken against [it], I was constrained to appeal to Caesar—not as having anything to accuse my nation of; ²⁰for this cause, therefore, I called for you to see and to speak with [you], for because of the hope of Israel I am bound with this chain." ²¹And they said to him, "We neither received letters concerning you from Judea, nor did anyone who came of the brothers declare or speak any evil concerning you, ²²and we think it good from you to hear what you think, for indeed, concerning this sect it is known to us that it is spoken against everywhere"; ²³and having appointed him a day, more of them came to him, to the lodging, to whom he was setting [it] forth, testifying fully the Kingdom of God, persuading them also of the things concerning Jesus, both from the Law of Moses, and the Prophets, from morning until evening, ²⁴and some, indeed, were believing the things spoken, and some were not believing. ²⁵And not being agreed with one another, they were going away, Paul having spoken one word, "The Holy Spirit spoke well through Isaiah the prophet to our fathers, ²⁶saying, Go on to this people and say, With hearing you will hear, and you will not understand, and seeing you will see, and you will not perceive, ²⁷for the heart of this people was made obtuse, and with the ears they barely heard, and they closed their eyes, lest they may see with the eyes, and may understand with the heart, and should turn, and I may heal them. ²⁸Be it known, therefore, to you, that the salvation of God was sent to the nations, these also will hear it"; ²⁹[[and he having said these things, the Jews went away, having much debate among themselves;]] ³⁰and Paul remained an entire two years in his own hired [house], and was receiving all those coming in to him, ³¹preaching the Kingdom of God, and teaching the things concerning the Lord Jesus Christ with all boldness—unforbidden.

ROMANS

CHAPTER 1

¹Paul, a servant of Jesus Christ, a called apostle, having been separated to the good news of God, ²which He announced before through His prophets in holy writings, ³concerning His Son—who has come of the seed of David according to the flesh, ⁴who is marked out [as the] Son of God in power, according to the Spirit of sanctification, by the resurrection from the dead—Jesus Christ our Lord; ⁵through whom we received grace and apostleship, for obedience of faith among all the nations, in behalf of His Name; ⁶among whom are also you, the called of Jesus Christ; ⁷to all who are in Rome, beloved of God, called holy ones: Grace to you and peace from God our Father and the Lord Jesus Christ! ⁸First, indeed, I thank my God through Jesus Christ for you all, that your faith is proclaimed in the whole world; ⁹for God is my witness, whom I serve in my spirit in the good news of His Son, how unceasingly I make mention of you, ¹⁰always in my prayers imploring, if by any means now at length I will have a prosperous journey, by the will of God, to come to you, ¹¹for I long to see you, that I may impart to you some spiritual gift, that you may be

established; ¹²and that is, that I may be comforted together among you, through faith in one another, both yours and mine. ¹³And I do not wish you to be ignorant, brothers, that many times I purposed to come to you—and was hindered until the present time—that some fruit I might have also among you, even as also among the other nations. ¹⁴Both to Greeks and to foreigners, both to wise and to thoughtless, I am a debtor, ¹⁵so, as much as in me is, I am ready also to you who [are] in Rome to proclaim good news, ¹⁶for I am not ashamed of the good news of the Christ, for it is the power of God to salvation to everyone who is believing, both to Jew first, and to Greek. ¹⁷For the righteousness of God in it is revealed from faith to faith, according as it has been written: "And the righteous one will live by faith," ¹⁸for the wrath of God is revealed from Heaven on all impiety and unrighteousness of men, holding down the truth in unrighteousness. ¹⁹Because that which is known of God is revealed among them, for God revealed [it] to them, ²⁰for the invisible things of Him from the creation of the world, by the things made being understood, are plainly seen, both His eternal power and Godhead—to their being inexcusable; ²¹because, having known God they did not glorify [Him] as God, nor gave thanks, but were made vain in their reasonings, and their unintelligent heart was darkened, ²²professing to be wise, they were made fools, ²³and changed the glory of the incorruptible God into the likeness of an image of corruptible man, and of birds, and of quadrupeds, and of reptiles. ²⁴For this reason also God gave them up, in the desires of their hearts, to uncleanness, to dishonor their bodies among themselves; ²⁵who changed the truth of God into the lie, and honored and served the creature rather than the Creator, who is blessed for all ages. Amen. ²⁶Because of this God gave them up to dishonorable affections, for even their females changed the natural use into that against nature; ²⁷and in like manner also the males having left the natural use of the female, burned in their longing toward one another; males with males working shame, and the repayment of their error that was fit, in themselves receiving. ²⁸And according as they did not approve of having God in knowledge, God gave them up to a disapproved mind, to do the things not seemly; ²⁹having been filled with all unrighteousness, whoredom, wickedness, covetousness, malice; full of envy, murder, strife, deceit, evil dispositions; whisperers, ³⁰evil-speakers, God-haters, insulting, proud, boasters, inventors of evil things, disobedient to parents, ³¹unintelligent, faithless, without natural affection, implacable, unmerciful; ³²who the righteous judgment of God having known—that those practicing such things are worthy of death—not only do them, but also have delight with those practicing them.

CHAPTER 2

¹Therefore, you are inexcusable, O man—everyone who is judging—for in that in which you judge the other, yourself you condemn, for the same things you practice who are judging, ²and we have known that the judgment of God is according to truth, on those practicing such things. ³And do you think this, O man, who are judging those who such things are practicing, and are doing them, that you will escape the judgment of God? ⁴Or the riches of His goodness, and forbearance, and long-suffering, do you despise, not knowing that the goodness of God leads you to conversion? ⁵But according to your hardness and impenitent heart, you treasure up wrath to yourself in [the] day of wrath and of the revelation of the righteous judgment of God, ⁶who will render to each according to his works; ⁷to those, indeed, who in continuance of a good work, seek glory, and honor, and incorruptibility—continuous life; ⁸and to those contentious, and disobedient, indeed, to the truth, and obeying the unrighteousness—indignation and wrath, ⁹tribulation and distress, on every soul of man that is working the evil, both of Jew first, and of Greek; ¹⁰and glory, and honor, and peace, to everyone who is working the good, both to Jew first, and to Greek. ¹¹For there is no favor by appearance with God, ¹²for as many as sinned without law, will also perish without law, and as many as sinned in law, through law will be judged, ¹³for not the hearers of the Law [are] righteous before God, but the doers of the Law will be declared righteous. ¹⁴For when nations that have no law, by nature may do the things of the Law, these not having a law—to themselves are a law, ¹⁵who show the work of the Law written in their hearts, their conscience also witnessing with them, and between one another the thoughts accusing or else defending, ¹⁶in the day when God will judge the secrets of men, according to my good news, through Jesus Christ. ¹⁷Behold, you are named a Jew, and rest on the Law, and boast in God, ¹⁸and know the will, and approve the distinctions, being instructed out of the Law, ¹⁹and have confidence that you yourself are a leader of blind ones, a light of those in darkness, ²⁰a corrector of foolish ones, a teacher of babies, having the form of the knowledge and of the truth in the Law. ²¹You, then, who are teaching another, do you not teach yourself? ²²You who are preaching not to steal, do you steal? You who are saying not to commit adultery, do you commit adultery? You who are abhorring the idols, do you rob temples? ²³You who boast in the Law, through the transgression of the Law do you dishonor God? ²⁴For evil is spoken of the Name of God among the nations because of you, according as it has been written. ²⁵For circumcision, indeed, profits, if you may practice law, but if you may be a transgressor of law, your circumcision has become uncircumcision. ²⁶If, therefore, the uncircumcision may keep the righteousness of the Law, will not his uncircumcision be reckoned for circumcision? ²⁷And the uncircumcision, by nature, fulfilling the Law, will judge you who, through letter and circumcision, [are] a transgressor of law. ²⁸For he is not a Jew who is [so] outwardly, neither [is] circumcision that which is outward in flesh; ²⁹but a Jew [is] he who is [so] inwardly, and circumcision [is] of the heart, in spirit, not in letter, of which the praise is not of men, but of God.

CHAPTER 3

¹What, then, [is] the superiority of the Jew? Or what the profit of the circumcision? ²Much in every way; for first, indeed, that they were entrusted with the oracles of God; ³for what, if certain were faithless? Will their faithlessness make the faithfulness of God useless? ⁴Let it not be! And let God become true, and every man false, according as it has been written: "That You may be declared righteous in Your words, and may overcome in Your being judged." ⁵And if our unrighteousness establishes God's righteousness, what will we say? Is God unrighteous who is inflicting the wrath? (I speak after the manner of a man.) ⁶Let it not be! Since how will God judge the world? ⁷For if the truth of God in my falsehood abounded more to His glory, why am I also yet judged as a sinner? ⁸And not, as we are spoken evil of, and as certain affirm us to say, "We may do the evil things, that the good ones may come?" Whose judgment is righteous. ⁹What, then? Are we better? Not at all! For we charged before both Jews and Greeks with being all under sin, ¹⁰according as it has been written: "There is none righteous, not even one; ¹¹there is none who is understanding, there is none who is seeking after God. ¹²All went out of the way, together they became unprofitable, there is none doing good, there is not even one. ¹³Their throat [is] an opened grave; with their tongues they used deceit; poison of cobras [is] under their lips—¹⁴whose mouth is full of cursing and bitterness. ¹⁵Their feet [are] swift to shed blood. ¹⁶Ruin and misery [are] in their ways. ¹⁷And a way of peace they did not know. ¹⁸There is no fear of God before their eyes." ¹⁹And we have known that as many things as the Law says, to those in the Law it speaks, that every mouth may be stopped, and all the world may come under judgment to God; ²⁰for this reason by works of law will no flesh be declared righteous before Him, for through law is a knowledge of sin. ²¹And now apart from law the righteousness of God has been revealed, testified to by the Law and the Prophets, ²²and the righteousness of God [is] through the faith of Jesus Christ to all, and on all those believing—for there is no difference, ²³for all have sinned and fall short of the glory of God— ²⁴being declared righteous freely by His grace through the redemption that [is] in Christ Jesus, ²⁵whom God set forth [as] a propitiatory covering, through faith in His blood, for the showing forth of His righteousness, because of the passing over of the former sins in the forbearance of God—²⁶for the showing forth of His righteousness in the present time, for His being righteous, and declaring him righteous who [is] of the faith of Jesus. ²⁷Where then [is] the boasting? It was excluded; by what law? Of works? No, but by a law of faith: ²⁸therefore we reckon a man to

be declared righteous by faith, apart from works of law. ²⁹[Is He] only the God of Jews, and not also of nations? ³⁰Yes, also of nations; since [there is] one God who will declare righteous circumcision by faith, and uncircumcision through faith. ³¹Do we then make law useless through faith? Let it not be! Indeed, we establish law.

CHAPTER 4

¹What, then, will we say Abraham our father to have found, according to flesh? ²For if Abraham was declared righteous by works, he has to boast—but not before God; ³for what does the writing say? "And Abraham believed God, and it was reckoned to him for righteousness"; ⁴and to him who is working, the reward is not reckoned of grace, but of debt; ⁵and to him who is not working, and is believing on Him who is declaring righteous the impious, his faith is reckoned for righteousness— ⁶even as David also speaks of the blessedness of the man to whom God reckons righteousness apart from works: ⁷"Blessed [are] they whose lawless acts were forgiven, || And whose sins were covered; ⁸Blessed [is] the man || To whom the LORD may not reckon sin." ⁹[Is] this blessedness, then, on the circumcision, or also on the uncircumcision—for we say that faith was reckoned to Abraham for righteousness? ¹⁰How then was it reckoned? He being in circumcision, or in uncircumcision? Not in circumcision, but in uncircumcision; ¹¹and he received a sign of circumcision, a seal of the righteousness of faith in the uncircumcision, for his being father of all those believing through uncircumcision, for the righteousness also being reckoned to them, ¹²and father of circumcision to those not of circumcision only, but who also walk in the steps of faith, that [is] in the uncircumcision of our father Abraham. ¹³For not through law [is] the promise to Abraham, or to his seed, of his being heir of the world, but through the righteousness of faith; ¹⁴for if they who are of law [are] heirs, faith has been made void, and the promise has been made useless; ¹⁵for the Law works wrath; for where law is not, neither [is] transgression. ¹⁶Because of this [it is] of faith, that [it may be] according to grace, for the promise being sure to all the seed, not to that which [is] of the Law only, but also to that which [is] of the faith of Abraham, ¹⁷who is father of us all (according as it has been written: "A father of many nations I have set you,") before Him whom he believed—God, who is quickening the dead, and is calling the things that are not as being. ¹⁸Who, against hope, believed in hope, for his becoming father of many nations according to that spoken: "So will your seed be"; ¹⁹and having not been weak in faith, he did not consider his own body, already become dead (being about one hundred years old), and the deadness of Sarah's womb, ²⁰and at the promise of God did not stagger in unbelief, but was strengthened in faith, having given glory to God, ²¹and having been fully persuaded that what He has promised He is also able to do: ²²for this reason also it was reckoned to him for righteousness. ²³And it was not written on his account alone that it was reckoned to him, ²⁴but also on ours, to whom it is about to be reckoned—to us believing on Him who raised up Jesus our Lord out of the dead, ²⁵who was delivered up because of our offenses, and was raised up because of our being declared righteous.

CHAPTER 5

¹Having been declared righteous, then, by faith, we have peace toward God through our Lord Jesus Christ, ²through whom also we have the access by faith into this grace in which we have stood, and we boast on the hope of the glory of God. ³And not only [so], but we also boast in the tribulations, knowing that the tribulation works endurance; ⁴and the endurance, experience; and the experience, hope; ⁵and the hope does not make ashamed, because the love of God has been poured forth in our hearts through the Holy Spirit that has been given to us. ⁶For in our being still ailing, Christ in due time died for the impious; ⁷for scarcely for a righteous man will anyone die, for the good man perhaps someone also dares to die; ⁸and God commends His own love to us, that, in our being still sinners, Christ died for us; ⁹much more, then, having been declared righteous now in His blood, we will be saved through Him from the wrath; ¹⁰for if, being enemies, we have been reconciled to God through the death of His Son, much more, having been reconciled, we will be saved in His life. ¹¹And not only [so], but we are also boasting in God, through our Lord Jesus Christ, through whom we now received the reconciliation; ¹²because of this, even as through one man sin entered into the world, and through sin—death; and thus to all men death passed through, for that all sinned; ¹³for until law sin was in the world: and sin is not reckoned when there is not law; ¹⁴but death reigned from Adam until Moses, even on those having not sinned in the likeness of Adam's transgression, who is a type of Him who is coming. ¹⁵But not as the offense so also [is] the free gift; for if by the offense of the one the many died, much more the grace of God, and the free gift in grace of the one man Jesus Christ, abound to the many; ¹⁶and not as through one who sinned [is] the free gift, for the judgment indeed [is] of one to condemnation, but the gift [is] of many offenses to a declaration of "Righteous," ¹⁷for if by the offense of the one death reigned through the one, much more those who are receiving the abundance of grace and of the free gift of righteousness, in life will reign through the one—Jesus Christ. ¹⁸So, then, as through one offense to all men [it is] to condemnation, so also through one declaration of "Righteous" [it is] to all men to justification of life; ¹⁹for as through the disobedience of the one man, the many were constituted sinners: so also through the obedience of the One, will the many be constituted righteous. ²⁰And law came in, that the offense might abound, and where sin abounded, grace hyper-abounded, ²¹that even as sin reigned in death, so also grace may reign, through righteousness, to continuous life, through Jesus Christ our Lord.

CHAPTER 6

¹What, then, will we say? Will we continue in sin that grace may abound? ²Let it not be! We who died to sin—how will we still live in it? ³Are you ignorant that we, as many as were immersed into Christ Jesus, were immersed into His death? ⁴We were buried together, then, with Him through the immersion into death, that even as Christ was raised up out of the dead through the glory of the Father, so we also might walk in newness of life. ⁵For if we have become planted together to the likeness of His death, [so] we also will be of the resurrection; ⁶knowing this, that our old man was crucified with [Him], that the body of sin may be made useless, for our no longer serving sin, ⁷for he who has died has been set free from sin. ⁸And if we died with Christ, we believe that we also will live with Him, ⁹knowing that Christ, having been raised up out of the dead, dies no more; death has no more lordship over Him; ¹⁰for in that He died, He died to sin once, and in that He lives, He lives to God; ¹¹so also you, reckon yourselves to be dead indeed to sin, and living to God in Jesus Christ our Lord. ¹²Do not let then sin reign in your mortal body, to obey it in its desires; ¹³neither present your members instruments of unrighteousness to sin, but present yourselves to God as living out of the dead, and your members instruments of righteousness to God; ¹⁴for sin will not have lordship over you, for you are not under law, but under grace. ¹⁵What then? Will we sin because we are not under law but under grace? Let it not be! ¹⁶Have you not known that to whom you present yourselves servants for obedience, servants you are to him to whom you obey, whether of sin to death, or of obedience to righteousness? ¹⁷And thanks to God, that you were servants of sin, and—were obedient from the heart to the form of teaching to which you were delivered up; ¹⁸and having been freed from sin, you became servants to righteousness. ¹⁹I speak in a human [way], because of the weakness of your flesh, for even as you presented your members servants to the uncleanness and to the lawlessness—to the lawlessness, so now present your members servants to

righteousness—to sanctification, ²⁰for when you were servants of sin, you were free from righteousness. ²¹What fruit, therefore, were you having then, in the things of which you are now ashamed? For the end of those [is] death. ²²And now, having been freed from sin, and having become servants to God, you have your fruit—to sanctification, and the end continuous life; ²³for the wages of sin [is] death, and the gift of God [is] continuous life in Christ Jesus our Lord.

CHAPTER 7

¹Are you ignorant, brothers—for to those knowing law I speak—that the law has lordship over the man as long as he lives? ²For the married woman to the living husband has been bound by law, and if the husband may die, she has been free from the law of the husband; ³so then, the husband being alive, she will be called an adulteress if she may become another man's; and if the husband may die, she is free from the law, so as not to be an adulteress, having become another man's. ⁴So that, my brothers, you also were made dead to the law through the body of the Christ, for your becoming another's, who was raised up out of the dead, that we might bear fruit to God; ⁵for when we were in the flesh, the passions of sins, that [are] through the Law, were working in our members, to bear fruit to death; ⁶and now we have ceased from the Law, that being dead in which we were held, so that we may serve in newness of spirit, and not in oldness of letter. ⁷What, then, will we say? The Law [is] sin? Let it not be! But I did not know sin except through law, for also the covetousness I had not known if the Law had not said: ⁸"You will not covet"; and sin having received an opportunity, through the command, worked in me all covetousness—for apart from law sin is dead. ⁹And I was alive apart from law once, and the command having come, sin revived, and I died; ¹⁰and the command that [is] for life, this was found by me for death; ¹¹for sin, having received an opportunity, through the command, deceived me, and through it, slew [me], ¹²so that the Law, indeed, [is] holy, and the command holy, and righteous, and good. ¹³That which is good then, has it become death to me? Let it not be! But sin, that it might appear sin, through the good, working death to me, that sin might become exceedingly sinful through the command. ¹⁴For we have known that the Law is spiritual, and I am fleshly, sold by sin; ¹⁵for that which I work, I do not acknowledge; for not what I will, this I practice, but what I hate, this I do. ¹⁶And if what I do not will, this I do, I consent to the Law that [it is] good, ¹⁷and now it is no longer I that work it, but sin dwelling in me, ¹⁸for I have known that there does not dwell in me, that is, in my flesh, good: for to will is present with me, and I do not find to work that which is right, ¹⁹for the good that I will, I do not do; but the evil that I do not will, this I practice. ²⁰And if what I do not will, this I do, it is no longer I that work it, but sin that is dwelling in me. ²¹I find, then, the law, that when I desire to do what is right, the evil is present with me, ²²for I delight in the Law of God according to the inward man, ²³and I behold another law in my members, warring against the law of my mind, and bringing me into captivity to the law of sin that [is] in my members. ²⁴A wretched man I [am]! Who will deliver me out of the body of this death? ²⁵I thank God—through Jesus Christ our Lord; so then, I myself indeed serve the Law of God with the mind, and with the flesh, the law of sin.

CHAPTER 8

¹There is, then, now no condemnation to those in Christ Jesus, who walk not according to the flesh, but according to the Spirit, ²for the law of the Spirit of life in Christ Jesus set me free from the law of sin and of death; ³for what the Law was not able to do, in that it was weak through the flesh, God, His own Son having sent in the likeness of sinful flesh, and for sin, condemned sin in the flesh, ⁴that the righteousness of the Law may be fulfilled in us, who do not walk according to the flesh, but according to the Spirit. ⁵For those who are according to the flesh, mind the things of the flesh; and those according to the Spirit, the things of the Spirit; ⁶for the mind of the flesh [is] death, and the mind of the Spirit—life and peace; ⁷because the mind of the flesh [is] enmity to God, for to the Law of God it does not subject itself, ⁸for neither is it able; and those who are in the flesh are not able to please God. ⁹And you are not in the flesh, but in the Spirit, if indeed the Spirit of God dwells in you; and if anyone does not have the Spirit of Christ—this one is not His; ¹⁰and if Christ [is] in you, the body, indeed, [is] dead because of sin, and the Spirit [is] life because of righteousness, ¹¹and if the Spirit of Him who raised up Jesus out of the dead dwells in you, He who raised up the Christ out of the dead will also quicken your dying bodies, through His Spirit dwelling in you. ¹²So, then, brothers, we are debtors, not to the flesh, to live according to the flesh; ¹³for if according to the flesh you live, you are about to die; and if, by the Spirit, the deeds of the body you put to death, you will live; ¹⁴for as many as are led by the Spirit of God, these are the sons of God; ¹⁵for you did not receive a spirit of bondage again for fear, but you received [the] Spirit of adoption in which we cry, "Abba! Father!" ¹⁶[This] One—the Spirit—testifies with our spirit, that we are children of God; ¹⁷and if children, also heirs, heirs, indeed, of God, and heirs together of Christ—if, indeed, we suffer together, that we may also be glorified together. ¹⁸For I reckon that the sufferings of the present time [are] not worthy [to be compared] with the glory about to be revealed in us; ¹⁹for the earnest looking out of the creation expects the revelation of the sons of God; ²⁰for to vanity was the creation made subject—not of its will, but because of Him who subjected [it]—in hope, ²¹that also the creation itself will be set free from the servitude of the corruption to the liberty of the glory of the children of God; ²²for we have known that all the creation groans together, and travails in pain together until now. ²³And not only [so], but also we ourselves, having the first-fruit of the Spirit, we also ourselves groan in ourselves, expecting adoption—the redemption of our body; ²⁴for in hope we were saved, and hope beheld is not hope; for what anyone beholds, why does he also hope for [it]? ²⁵And if what we do not behold we hope for, through continuance we expect [it]. ²⁶And in like manner also, the Spirit helps our weaknesses; for what we may pray for, as it is necessary, we have not known, but [this] One—the Spirit—makes intercession for us with unutterable groanings, ²⁷and He who is searching the hearts has known what [is] the mind of the Spirit, because according to God He intercedes for holy ones. ²⁸And we have known that to those loving God all things work together for good, to those who are called according to purpose; ²⁹because whom He foreknew, He also foreordained, conformed to the image of His Son, that He might be firstborn among many brothers; ³⁰and whom He foreordained, these also He called; and whom He called, these also He declared righteous; and whom He declared righteous, these also He glorified. ³¹What, then, will we say to these things? If God [is] for us, who [is] against us? ³²He who indeed did not spare His own Son, but delivered Him up for us all, how will He not also with Him grant to us all things? ³³Who will lay a charge against the chosen ones of God? God [is] He that is declaring righteous; ³⁴who [is] he that is condemning? Christ [is] He that died, indeed, rather also, was raised up; who is also on the right hand of God—who also interceded for us. ³⁵Who will separate us from the love of the Christ? Tribulation, or distress, or persecution, or famine, or nakedness, or peril, or sword? ³⁶According as it has been written: "For Your sake we are put to death all the day long; we were reckoned as sheep of slaughter." ³⁷But in all these we more than conquer, through Him who loved us; ³⁸for I am persuaded that neither death, nor life, nor messengers, nor principalities, nor powers, nor things present, ³⁹nor things about to be, nor height, nor depth, nor any other created thing, will be able to separate us from the love of God that [is] in Christ Jesus our Lord.

CHAPTER 9

¹Truth I say in Christ, I do not lie, my conscience bearing testimony with me in the Holy Spirit, ²that I have great grief and unceasing pain in my heart— ³for I was wishing, I myself, to be accursed from the Christ—for my brothers, my relatives, according to the flesh, ⁴who are Israelites, whose [is] the adoption, and the glory, and the covenants, and the lawgiving, and the service, and the promises, ⁵whose [are] the fathers,

and of whom [is] the Christ, according to the flesh, who is God over all, blessed for all ages. Amen. ⁶And it is not possible that the word of God has failed; for not all who [are] of Israel are these of Israel; ⁷nor because they are seed of Abraham [are] all children, but, "in Isaac will a seed be called to you"; ⁸that is, the children of the flesh—these [are] not children of God; but the children of the promise are reckoned for seed; ⁹for the word of promise [is] this: "According to this time I will come, and there will be to Sarah a son." ¹⁰And not only [so], but also Rebecca, having conceived by one—our father Isaac ¹¹(for they being not yet born, neither having done anything good or evil, that the purpose of God, according to [divine] selection, might remain; not of works, but of Him who is calling), ¹²it was said to her, "The greater will serve the less"; ¹³according as it has been written: "Jacob I loved, and Esau I hated." ¹⁴What, then, will we say? Unrighteousness [is] with God? Let it not be! ¹⁵For to Moses He says, "I will do kindness to whom I do kindness, and I will have compassion on whom I have compassion"; ¹⁶so then—not of him who is willing, nor of him who is running, but of God who is doing kindness; ¹⁷for the Writing says to Pharaoh, "For this very thing I raised you up, that I might show in you My power, and that My Name might be declared in all the land"; ¹⁸so then, to whom He wills, He does kindness, and to whom He wills, He hardens. ¹⁹You will say, then, to me, "Why does He yet find fault? For who has resisted His counsel?" ²⁰No, but, O man, who are you that are answering again to God? Will the thing formed say to Him who formed [it], Why did you make me thus? ²¹Does the potter not have authority over the clay, out of the same lump to make one vessel to honor and one to dishonor? ²²And if God, willing to show the wrath and to make known His power, endured, in much long suffering, vessels of wrath fitted for destruction, ²³and that He might make known the riches of His glory on vessels of kindness, that He before prepared for glory, whom also He called—us— ²⁴not only out of Jews, but also out of nations, ²⁵as also in Hosea He says, "I will call what [is] not My people—My people; and her not beloved—Beloved, ²⁶and it will be—in the place where it was said to them, You [are] not My people; there they will be called sons of the living God." ²⁷And Isaiah cries concerning Israel, "If the number of the sons of Israel may be as the sand of the sea, the remnant will be saved; ²⁸for a matter He is finishing, and is cutting short in righteousness, because a matter cut short will the LORD do on the land." ²⁹And according as Isaiah says before, "Except the LORD of Hosts left to us a seed, we had become as Sodom, and we had been made like Gomorrah." ³⁰What, then, will we say? That nations who are not pursuing righteousness attained to righteousness, and righteousness that [is] of faith, ³¹and Israel, pursuing a law of righteousness, did not arrive at a law of righteousness; ³²why? Because—not by faith, but as by works of law; for they stumbled at the stone of stumbling, ³³according as it has been written: "Behold, I place in Zion a stone of stumbling and a rock of offense; and everyone who is believing thereon will not be ashamed."

CHAPTER 10

¹Brothers, the pleasure indeed of my heart, and my supplication that [is] to God for Israel, is—for salvation; ²for I bear them testimony that they have a zeal of God, but not according to knowledge, ³for not knowing the righteousness of God, and seeking to establish their own righteousness, they did not submit to the righteousness of God. ⁴For Christ is an end of law for righteousness to everyone who is believing, ⁵for Moses describes the righteousness that [is] of the Law, that, "The man who did them will live in them," ⁶and the righteousness of faith thus speaks: "You may not say in your heart, Who will go up to Heaven?" (that is, to bring Christ down) ⁷or, "Who will go down to the abyss?" (that is, to bring up Christ out of the dead). ⁸But what does it say? "The saying is near you—in your mouth, and in your heart": that is, the saying of the faith that we preach; ⁹that if you may confess with your mouth that Jesus [is] LORD, and may believe in your heart that God raised Him out of the dead, you will be saved, ¹⁰for with the heart [one] believes to righteousness, and with the mouth is confession made to salvation; ¹¹for the Writing says, "Everyone who is believing on Him will not be ashamed," ¹²for there is no difference between Jew and Greek, for the same Lord of all [is] rich to all those calling on Him, ¹³for "Everyone who, if he may have called on the Name of the LORD, will be saved." ¹⁴How then will they call on [Him] in whom they did not believe? And how will they believe [on Him] of whom they did not hear? And how will they hear apart from one preaching? ¹⁵And how will they preach, if they may not be sent? According as it has been written: "How beautiful the feet of those proclaiming good tidings of peace, of those proclaiming good tidings of the good things!" ¹⁶But they were not all obedient to the good tidings, for Isaiah says, "LORD, who gave credence to our report?" ¹⁷So then faith [is] by a report, and the report through a saying of God, ¹⁸but I say, did they not hear? Yes, indeed, "their voice went forth to all the earth, and their sayings to the ends of the habitable world." ¹⁹But I say, did Israel not know? First Moses says, "I will provoke you to jealousy by [that which is] not a nation, || By an unintelligent nation I will anger you," ²⁰and Isaiah is very bold and says, "I was found by those not seeking Me; I became visible to those not inquiring after Me"; ²¹and to Israel He says, "All the day I stretched out My hands to a people unbelieving and contradicting."

CHAPTER 11

¹I say then, did God cast away His people? Let it not be! For I am also an Israelite, of the seed of Abraham, of the tribe of Benjamin: ²God did not cast away His people whom He knew before; have you not known—in Elijah—what the Writing says? How he pleads with God concerning Israel, saying, ³"LORD, they killed Your prophets, and they dug down Your altars, and I was left alone, and they seek my life"; ⁴but what does the divine answer say to him? "I left to Myself seven thousand men who did not bow a knee to Ba'al." ⁵So then also in the present time there has been a remnant according to the [divine] selection of grace; ⁶and if by grace, no longer of works, otherwise grace becomes no longer grace; and if of works, it is no longer grace, otherwise work is no longer work. ⁷What then? What Israel seeks after, this it did not obtain, and the chosen obtained, and the rest were hardened, ⁸according as it has been written: "God gave to them a spirit of deep sleep, eyes not to see, and ears not to hear, to this very day," ⁹and David says, "Let their table become for a snare, and for a trap, and for a stumbling-block, and for a repayment to them; ¹⁰let their eyes be darkened—not to behold, and You always bow down their back." ¹¹I say then, did they stumble that they might fall? Let it not be! But by their fall the salvation [is] to the nations, to arouse them to jealousy; ¹²and if their fall [is] the riches of [the] world, and their diminishment the riches of nations, how much more their fullness? ¹³For to you I speak—to the nations—inasmuch as I am indeed an apostle of nations, I glorify my ministry; ¹⁴if I will arouse my own flesh to jealousy by any means, and will save some of them, ¹⁵for if the casting away of them [is] a reconciliation of the world, what the reception—if not life out of the dead? ¹⁶And if the first-fruit [is] holy, the lump also; and if the root [is] holy, the branches also. ¹⁷And if certain of the branches were broken off, and you, being a wild olive tree, were grafted in among them, and became a fellow-partaker of the root and of the fatness of the olive tree—¹⁸do not boast against the branches; and if you boast, you do not bear the root, but the root you! ¹⁹You will say, then, "The branches were broken off, that I might be grafted in"; right! ²⁰By unbelief they were broken off, and you have stood by faith; do not be high-minded, but be fearing; ²¹for if God did not spare the natural branches—lest perhaps He also will not spare you. ²²Behold, then, goodness and severity of God—on those indeed who fell, severity; and on you, goodness, if you may remain in the goodness, otherwise, you also will be cut off. ²³And those also, if they may not remain in unbelief, will be grafted in, for God is able to graft them in again; ²⁴for if you, out of the olive tree, wild by nature, were cut out, and contrary to nature, were grafted into a good olive tree, how much rather will they, who [are] according to nature, be grafted into their own olive tree? ²⁵For I do not wish you to be ignorant, brothers, of this secret—that you may not be wise in your own conceits—that hardness in part to Israel has happened until the fullness of the nations may come in; ²⁶and so all Israel will be saved, according as it has been written: "There will come forth out of Zion He who is delivering, and He will turn away impiety from Jacob, ²⁷and this to them [is] the covenant from Me when I may take

away their sins." ²⁸As regards, indeed, the good tidings, [they are] enemies on your account; and as regards the [divine] selection—beloved on account of the fathers; ²⁹for the gifts and the calling of God are irrevocable; ³⁰for as you also once did not believe in God, and now found kindness by the unbelief of these, ³¹so also these now did not believe, that in your kindness they also may find kindness; ³²for God shut up together the whole to unbelief, that to the whole He might do kindness. ³³O depth of riches, and wisdom and knowledge of God! How unsearchable His judgments, and untraceable His ways! ³⁴For who knew the mind of the LORD? Or who became His counselor? ³⁵Or who first gave to Him, and it will be given back to him again? ³⁶Because of Him, and through Him, and to Him [are] all things; to Him [is] the glory—for all ages. Amen.

CHAPTER 12

¹I call on you, therefore, brothers, through the compassions of God, to present your bodies [as] a sacrifice—living, sanctified, acceptable to God—your intelligent service; ²and do not be conformed to this age, but be transformed by the renewing of your mind, for your proving what [is] the will of God—the good, and acceptable, and perfect. ³For I say, through the grace that was given to me, to everyone who is among you, not to think above what it ought to think; but to think so as to think wisely, as to each God dealt a measure of faith, ⁴for as in one body we have many members, and all the members do not have the same office, ⁵so we, the many, are one body in Christ, and members of one another—each one. ⁶And having gifts, different according to the grace that was given to us: whether prophecy, according to the proportion of faith; ⁷or ministry, in the ministry; or he who is teaching, in the teaching; ⁸or he who is exhorting, in the exhortation; he who is sharing, in simplicity; he who is leading, in diligence; he who is doing kindness, in cheerfulness. ⁹The love unhypocritical: abhorring the evil; cleaving to the good; ¹⁰in the love of brothers, to one another kindly affectioned: in the honor going before one another; ¹¹in the diligence not slothful; in the spirit fervent; serving the LORD; ¹²in the hope rejoicing; in the tribulation enduring; in the prayer persevering; ¹³to the necessities of the holy ones communicating; the hospitality pursuing. ¹⁴Bless those persecuting you; bless, and do not curse; ¹⁵to rejoice with the rejoicing, and to weep with the weeping, ¹⁶of the same mind toward one another, not minding the high things, but with the lowly going along; do not become wise in your own conceit; ¹⁷giving back to no one evil for evil; providing right things before all men. ¹⁸If possible—so far as in you—with all men being in peace; ¹⁹not avenging yourselves, beloved, but give place to the wrath, for it has been written: "Vengeance [is] Mine, ²⁰I will repay again, says the LORD"; if, then, your enemy hungers, feed him; if he thirsts, give him drink; for doing this, you will heap coals of fire on his head. ²¹Do not be overcome by the evil, but overcome, in the good, the evil.

CHAPTER 13

¹Let every soul be subject to the higher authorities, for there is no authority except from God, and the authorities existing are appointed by God, ²so that he who is setting himself against the authority, has resisted against God's ordinance; and those resisting will receive judgment to themselves. ³For those ruling are not a terror to the good works, but to the evil; and do you wish to not be afraid of the authority? Be doing that which is good, and you will have praise from it, ⁴for it is a servant of God to you for good; and if you may do that which is evil, be fearing, for it does not bear the sword in vain; for it is a servant of God, an avenger for wrath to him who is doing that which is evil. ⁵For this reason it is necessary to be subject, not only because of the wrath, but also because of the conscience, ⁶for because of this you also pay tribute; for they are servants of God, on this very thing attending continually; ⁷render, therefore, to all [their] dues; to whom tribute, the tribute; to whom custom, the custom; to whom fear, the fear; to whom honor, the honor. ⁸To no one owe anything, except to love one another; for he who is loving the other—he has fulfilled law, ⁹for, "You will not commit adultery, You will not murder, You will not steal, You will not bear false testimony, You will not covet"; and if there is any other command, in this word it is summed up, in this: "You will love your neighbor as yourself"; ¹⁰the love to the neighbor works no ill; the love, therefore, [is] the fullness of law. ¹¹And this, knowing the time, that for us, the hour already [is] to be aroused out of sleep, for now our salvation [is] nearer than when we believed; ¹²the night advanced, and the day came near; let us lay aside, therefore, the works of the darkness, and let us put on the armor of the light; ¹³as in daytime, let us walk properly; not in reveling and drunkenness, not in promiscuity and licentiousness, not in strife and jealousy; ¹⁴but put on the Lord Jesus Christ, and take no forethought for the flesh—for desires.

CHAPTER 14

¹And receive him who is weak in the faith—not to determinations of reasonings; ²one believes that he may eat all things—and he who is weak eats herbs; ³do not let him who is eating despise him who is not eating: and do not let him who is not eating judge him who is eating, for God received him. ⁴You—who are you that are judging another's domestic [affairs]? To his own master he stands or falls; and he will be made to stand, for God is able to make him stand. ⁵One judges one day above another, and another judges every day [alike]; let each be fully assured in his own mind. ⁶He who is regarding the day, he regards [it] to the LORD, and he who is not regarding the day, he does not regard [it] to the LORD. He who is eating, he eats to the LORD, for he gives thanks to God; and he who is not eating, he does not eat to the LORD, and gives thanks to God. ⁷For none of us lives to himself, and none dies to himself; ⁸for both, if we may live, we live to the LORD; if also we may die, we die to the LORD; both then if we may live, also if we may die, we are the LORD's; ⁹for because of this Christ both died and rose again, and lived again, that He may be Lord both of dead and of living. ¹⁰And you, why do you judge your brother? Or again, you, why do you set at nothing your brother? For we will all stand at the judgment seat of the Christ; ¹¹for it has been written: "I live! Says the LORD—Every knee will bow to Me, and every tongue will confess to God"; ¹²so, then, each of us will give reckoning to God concerning himself; ¹³therefore, may we judge one another no longer, but rather judge this, not to put a stumbling-stone before the brother, or an offense. ¹⁴I have known, and am persuaded, in the Lord Jesus, that nothing [is] unclean of itself, except to him who is reckoning anything to be unclean—to that one [it is] unclean; ¹⁵and if your brother is grieved through food, you no longer walk according to love; do not destroy with your food that one for whom Christ died. ¹⁶Do not let, then, evil be spoken of your good, ¹⁷for the Kingdom of God is not eating and drinking, but righteousness, and peace, and joy in the Holy Spirit; ¹⁸for he who in these things is serving the Christ, [is] acceptable to God and approved of men. ¹⁹So, then, may we pursue the things of peace, and the things of building up one another. ²⁰Do not cast down the work of God for the sake of food; all things, indeed, [are] pure, but evil [is] to the man who is eating through stumbling. ²¹[It is] not right to eat flesh, nor to drink wine, nor to [do anything] in which your brother stumbles, or is made to fall, or is weak. ²²You have faith! Have [it] to yourself before God; blessed is he who is not judging himself in what he approves, ²³and he who is making a difference, if he may eat, has been condemned, because [it is] not of faith; and all that [is] not of faith is sin.

CHAPTER 15

¹And we ought—we who are strong—to bear the weaknesses of the powerless, and not to please ourselves; ²for let each one of us please the neighbor for good, for edification, ³for even the Christ did not please Himself, but according as it has been written: "The reproaches of those reproaching You fell on Me"; ⁴for as many things as were written before, for our instruction were written before, that through the endurance, and the exhortation of the Writings, we might have the hope. ⁵And may the God of the endurance, and of the exhortation, give to you to have the same mind toward one another, according to Christ Jesus, ⁶that with one accord—with one mouth—you may glorify the God and Father of our Lord Jesus Christ; ⁷for this reason receive one another, according as also the Christ received us, to the glory of God. ⁸And I say Jesus Christ to have become a servant of circumcision for the truth of God, to confirm the promises to the fathers, ⁹and the nations for kindness to glorify God, according as it has

been written: "Because of this I will confess to You among nations, and to Your Name I will sing praise"; ¹⁰and again it says, "Rejoice you nations, with His people"; ¹¹and again, "Praise the Lord, all you nations; and laud Him, all you peoples"; ¹²and again, Isaiah says, "There will be the root of Jesse, and He who is rising to rule nations—on Him will nations hope"; ¹³and the God of the hope will fill you with all joy and peace in the believing, for your abounding in the hope in power of the Holy Spirit. ¹⁴And I am persuaded, my brothers—I myself also—concerning you, that you yourselves also are full of goodness, having been filled with all knowledge, also able to admonish one another; ¹⁵and the more boldly I wrote to you, brothers, in part, as putting you in mind, because of the grace that is given to me by God, ¹⁶for my being a servant of Jesus Christ to the nations, acting as priest in the good news of God, that the offering up of the nations may become acceptable, sanctified by the Holy Spirit. ¹⁷I have, then, a boasting in Christ Jesus, in the things pertaining to God, ¹⁸for I will not dare to speak anything of the things that Christ did not work through me, to obedience of nations, by word and deed, ¹⁹in power of signs and wonders, in power of the Spirit of God; so that I, from Jerusalem, and in a circle as far as Illyricum, have fully preached the good news of the Christ; ²⁰and so counting it honor to proclaim good news, not where Christ was named—that on another's foundation I might not build— ²¹but according as it has been written: "To whom it was not told concerning Him, they will see; and they who have not heard, will understand." ²²For this reason, also, I was hindered many times from coming to you, ²³and now, no longer having place in these parts, and having a longing to come to you for many years, ²⁴when I may go on to Spain I will come to you, for I hope in going through, to see you, and by you to be set forward there, if of you first, in part, I will be filled. ²⁵And now, I go on to Jerusalem, ministering to the holy ones; ²⁶for it pleased Macedonia and Achaia well to make a certain contribution for the poor of the holy ones who [are] in Jerusalem; ²⁷for it pleased well, and their debtors they are, for if the nations participated in their spiritual things, they ought also, in the fleshly things, to minister to them. ²⁸This, then, having finished, and having sealed to them this fruit, I will return through you, to Spain; ²⁹and I have known that coming to you—in the fullness of the blessing of the good news of Christ I will come. ³⁰And I call on you, brothers, through our Lord Jesus Christ, and through the love of the Spirit, to strive together with me in the prayers for me to God, ³¹that I may be delivered from those not believing in Judea, and that my ministry, that [is] for Jerusalem, may become acceptable to the holy ones; ³²that in joy I may come to you, through the will of God, and may be refreshed with you, ³³and the God of peace [be] with you all. Amen.

CHAPTER 16

¹And I commend you to Phoebe our sister—being a servant of the assembly that [is] in Cenchrea— ²that you may receive her in the Lord, worthily of the holy ones, and may assist her in whatever matter she may have need of you, for she also became a leader of many, and of myself. ³Greet Priscilla and Aquilas, my fellow-workmen in Christ Jesus— ⁴who laid down their own neck for my life, to whom not only I give thanks, but also all the assemblies of the nations— ⁵and the assembly at their house; greet Epaenetus, my beloved, who is first-fruit of Achaia to Christ. ⁶Greet Mary, who labored much for us; ⁷greet Andronicus and Junias, my relatives, and my fellow-captives, who are of note among the apostles, who also have been in Christ before me. ⁸Greet Amplias, my beloved in the Lord; ⁹greet Arbanus, our fellow-workman in Christ, and Stachys, my beloved; ¹⁰greet Apelles, the approved in Christ; greet those of the [household] of Aristobulus; ¹¹greet Herodion, my relative; greet those of the [household] of Narcissus, who are in the Lord; ¹²greet Tryphaena, and Tryphosa, who are laboring in the Lord; greet Persis, the beloved, who labored much in the Lord. ¹³Greet Rufus, the chosen one in the Lord, and his mother and mine, ¹⁴greet Asyncritus, Phlegon, Hermas, Patrobas, Hermes, and the brothers with them; ¹⁵greet Philologus, and Julias, Nereus, and his sister, and Olympas, and all the holy ones with them; ¹⁶greet one another in a holy kiss; the assemblies of Christ greet you. ¹⁷And I call on you, brothers, to mark those who are causing the divisions and the stumbling-blocks, contrary to the teaching that you learned, and turn away from them; ¹⁸for such do not serve our Lord Jesus Christ, but their own belly; and through the good word and fair speech they deceive the hearts of the harmless. ¹⁹For your obedience reached to all; I rejoice, therefore, as regards you, and I wish you to be wise, indeed, as to the good, and pure as to the evil; ²⁰and the God of peace will bruise Satan under your feet quickly; the grace of our Lord Jesus Christ [be] with you. Amen! ²¹Timotheus greets you, my fellow-workman, and Lucius, and Jason, and Sosipater, my relatives; ²²I, Tertius, greet you (who wrote the letter) in the Lord; ²³Gaius greets you, my host, and of the whole Assembly; Erastus greets you, the steward of the city, and Quartus the brother. ²⁴[[The grace of our Lord Jesus Christ [be] with you all! Amen.]] ²⁵And to Him who is able to establish you, according to my good news, and the preaching of Jesus Christ, according to the revelation of the secret, having been kept secret in the times of the ages, ²⁶and now having been revealed, also, through prophetic writings, according to a command of the perpetual God, having been made known to all the nations for obedience of faith— ²⁷to the only wise God, through Jesus Christ, to Him [be] glory for all ages. Amen.

1 CORINTHIANS

CHAPTER 1

¹Paul, a called apostle of Jesus Christ, through the will of God, and Sosthenes the brother, ²to the Assembly of God that is in Corinth, to those sanctified in Christ Jesus, called holy ones, with all those calling on the Name of our Lord Jesus Christ in every place—both theirs and ours: ³Grace to you and peace from God our Father and the Lord Jesus Christ! ⁴I give thanks to my God always concerning you for the grace of God that was given to you in Christ Jesus, ⁵that in everything you were enriched in Him, in all discourse and all knowledge, ⁶according as the testimony of the Christ was confirmed in you, ⁷so that you are not behind in any gift, waiting for the revelation of our Lord Jesus Christ; ⁸who also will confirm you to the end—unblamable in the day of our Lord Jesus Christ; ⁹faithful [is] God, through whom you were called into the fellowship of His Son Jesus Christ our Lord. ¹⁰And I call on you, brothers, through the Name of our Lord Jesus Christ, that the same thing you may all say, and there may not be divisions among you, and you may be perfected in the same mind, and in the same judgment, ¹¹for it was signified to me concerning you, my brothers, by those of Chloe, that contentions are among you; ¹²and I say this, that each one of you says, "I, indeed, am of Paul," and "I of Apollos," and "I of Cephas," and "I of Christ." ¹³Has the Christ been divided? Was Paul crucified for you? Or were you immersed into the name of Paul? ¹⁴I give thanks to God that I immersed no one of you, except Crispus and Gaius— ¹⁵that no one may say that to my own name I immersed; ¹⁶and I also immersed Stephanas' household—further, I have not known if I immersed any other. ¹⁷For Christ did not send me to immerse, but to proclaim good news, not in wisdom of discourse, that the Cross of the Christ may not be made of no effect; ¹⁸for the word of the Cross to those indeed perishing is foolishness, and to us—those being saved—it is the power of God, ¹⁹for it has been written: "I will destroy the wisdom of the wise, and the intelligence of the intelligent I will bring to nothing"; ²⁰where [is] the wise? Where the scribe? Where a disputer of this age? Did God not make foolish the wisdom of this world? ²¹For seeing in the wisdom of God the world through the wisdom did not know God, it pleased God through the foolishness of the preaching to save those believing. ²²Since also Jews ask a sign, and Greeks seek wisdom, ²³also we preach Christ crucified, to Jews,

1 CORINTHIANS

indeed, a stumbling-block, and to Greeks foolishness, ²⁴and to those called—both Jews and Greeks—Christ the power of God, and the wisdom of God, ²⁵because the foolishness of God is wiser than men, and the weakness of God is stronger than men; ²⁶for see your calling, brothers, that not many [are] wise according to the flesh, not many mighty, not many noble; ²⁷but God chose the foolish things of the world that He may put the wise to shame; and God chose the weak things of the world that He may put the strong to shame; ²⁸and God chose the base things of the world, and the things despised, and the things that are not, that He may make useless the things that are— ²⁹that no flesh may glory before Him; ³⁰but out of Him you are in Christ Jesus, who became to us from God wisdom, righteousness also, and sanctification, and redemption, ³¹that, according as it has been written: "He who is glorying—let him glory in the LORD."

CHAPTER 2

¹And I, having come to you, brothers, came—not in superiority of discourse or wisdom—declaring to you the testimony of God, ²for I decided not to know anything among you, except Jesus Christ, and Him crucified; ³and I, in weakness, and in fear, and in much trembling, was with you; ⁴and my word and my preaching was not in persuasive words of wisdom, but in demonstration of the Spirit and of power— ⁵that your faith may not be in the wisdom of men, but in the power of God. ⁶And wisdom we speak among the perfect, and wisdom not of this age, nor of the rulers of this age—of those becoming useless, ⁷but we speak the hidden wisdom of God in a secret, that God foreordained before the ages to our glory, ⁸which no one of the rulers of this age knew, for if they had known, they would not have crucified the Lord of Glory; ⁹but according as it has been written: "What eye did not see, and ear did not hear, and on the heart of man did not come up, what God prepared for those loving Him"; ¹⁰but God revealed [them] to us through His Spirit, for the Spirit searches all things, even the depths of God, ¹¹for who of men has known the things of the man, except the spirit of the man that [is] in him? So also the things of God no one has known, except the Spirit of God. ¹²And we did not receive the spirit of the world, but the Spirit that [is] of God, that we may know the things conferred by God on us, ¹³which things we also speak, not in words taught by human wisdom, but in those taught by the Holy Spirit, comparing spiritual things with spiritual things, ¹⁴and the natural man does not receive the things of the Spirit of God, for they are foolishness to him, and he is not able to know [them], because they are discerned spiritually; ¹⁵and he who is spiritual, indeed discerns all things, and he himself is discerned by no one; ¹⁶for who knew the mind of the LORD that he will instruct Him? And we have the mind of Christ.

CHAPTER 3

¹And I, brothers, was not able to speak to you as to spiritual, but as to fleshly—as to babies in Christ; ²with milk I fed you, and not with meat, for you were not yet able, but not even yet are you now able, ³for yet you are fleshly, for where [there is] among you envying, and strife, and divisions, are you not fleshly, and walk in the manner of men? ⁴For when one may say, "I, indeed, am of Paul," and another, "I—of Apollos," are you not fleshly? ⁵Who, then, is Paul, and who Apollos, but servants through whom you believed, and to each as the LORD gave? ⁶I planted, Apollos watered, but God was giving growth; ⁷so that neither is he who is planting anything, nor he who is watering, but He who is giving growth—God; ⁸and he who is planting and he who is watering are one, and each will receive his own reward according to his own labor, ⁹for we are fellow-workmen of God; you are God's tillage, God's building. ¹⁰According to the grace of God that was given to me, as a wise master-builder, I have laid a foundation, and another builds on [it], ¹¹for no one is able to lay another foundation except that which is laid, which is Jesus the Christ; ¹²and if anyone builds on this foundation gold, silver, precious stones, wood, hay, straw— ¹³the work will become visible of each, for the day will declare [it], because it is revealed in fire, and the work of each, what kind it is, the fire will prove; ¹⁴if the work of anyone remains that he built on [it], he will receive a wage; ¹⁵if the work of any is burned up, he will suffer loss, but himself will be saved, but so as through fire. ¹⁶Have you not known that you are a temple of God, and the Spirit of God dwells in you? ¹⁷If anyone ruins the temple of God, God will ruin him; for the temple of God is holy, which you are. ¹⁸Let no one deceive himself; if anyone seems to be wise among you in this age—let him become a fool, that he may become wise, ¹⁹for the wisdom of this world is foolishness with God, for it has been written: "Who is taking the wise in their craftiness"; ²⁰and again, "The LORD knows the reasonings of the wise, that they are vain." ²¹So then, let no one glory in men, for all things are yours, ²²whether Paul, or Apollos, or Cephas, or the world, or life, or death, or things present, or things about to be—all are yours, ²³and you [are] Christ's, and Christ [is] God's.

CHAPTER 4

¹Let a man so reckon us as officers of Christ, and stewards of the secrets of God, ²and as to the rest, it is required in the stewards that one may be found faithful, ³and to me it is for a very little thing that by you I may be judged, or by man's Day, but I do not even judge myself, ⁴for I have been conscious of nothing for myself, but I have not been declared right in this—and He who is discerning me is the LORD; ⁵so, then, judge nothing before the time, until the LORD may come, who will both bring to light the hidden things of the darkness, and will reveal the counsels of the hearts, and then the praise will come to each from God. ⁶And these things, brothers, I transferred to myself and to Apollos because of you, that in us you may learn not to think above that which has been written, that you may not be puffed up one for one against the other, ⁷for who makes you to differ? And what do you have, that you did not receive? And if you also received, why do you glory as not having received? ⁸Already you are having been filled, already you were rich, apart from us you reigned, and I also wish you reigned, that we also may reign together with you, ⁹for I think that God set forth us the apostles last—as appointed to death, because we became a spectacle to the world, and messengers, and men; ¹⁰we [are] fools because of Christ, and you wise in Christ; we [are] ailing, and you strong; you glorious, and we dishonored; ¹¹to the present hour we both hunger, and thirst, and are naked, and are battered, and wander, ¹²and labor, working with [our] own hands; being reviled, we bless; being persecuted, we endure; ¹³being spoken evil of, we plead; we became as filth of the world—of all things an outcast—until now. ¹⁴Not [as] putting you to shame do I write these things, but I admonish as my beloved children, ¹⁵for if a myriad of child-conductors you may have in Christ, yet not many fathers; for in Christ Jesus, through the good news, I begot you; ¹⁶I call on you, therefore, become followers of me; ¹⁷because of this I sent to you Timotheus, who is my child, beloved and faithful in the LORD, who will remind you of my ways in Christ, according as everywhere in every assembly I teach. ¹⁸And some were puffed up as if I were not coming to you; ¹⁹but I will come quickly to you, if the LORD may will, and I will not know the word of those puffed up, but the power; ²⁰for not in word is the Kingdom of God, but in power. ²¹What do you wish? Will I come to you with a rod, or in love, also with a spirit of meekness?

CHAPTER 5

¹Whoredom is actually heard of among you, and such whoredom as is not even named among the nations—as that one has the wife of the father! ²And you are having been puffed up, and did not rather mourn, that he may be removed out of the midst of you who did this work, ³for I indeed, as being absent as to the body, and present as to the spirit, have already judged, as being present, him who so worked this thing: ⁴in the Name of our Lord Jesus Christ—you being gathered together, also my spirit—with the power of our Lord Jesus Christ, ⁵to deliver up such a one to Satan for the destruction of the flesh, that the spirit may be saved in the Day of the Lord Jesus. ⁶Your glorying [is] not good; have you not known that a little leaven leavens the whole lump? ⁷Cleanse out, therefore, the old leaven, that you may be a new lump, according as you are

unleavened, for our Passover was sacrificed for us also—Christ, ⁸so that we may keep the celebration, not with old leaven, nor with the leaven of evil and wickedness, but with unleavened [bread] of sincerity and truth. ⁹I wrote to you in the letter, not to keep company with whoremongers— ¹⁰and certainly not with the whoremongers of this world, or with the covetous, or extortioners, or idolaters, seeing you ought then to go forth out of the world— ¹¹and now, I wrote to you not to keep company with [him], if anyone, being named a brother, may be a whoremonger, or covetous, or an idolater, or a railer, or a drunkard, or an extortioner—do not even eat together with such a one; ¹²for what have I also to judge those outside? Do you not judge those within? ¹³And judge those without God; and put away the evil from among yourselves.

CHAPTER 6

¹Dare anyone of you, having a matter with the other, go to be judged before the unrighteous, and not before the holy ones? ²Have you not known that the holy ones will judge the world? And if the world is judged by you, are you unworthy of the smaller judgments? ³Have you not known that we will judge messengers? Why not then the things of life? ⁴Of the things of life, indeed, then, if you may have judgment, those despised in the Assembly—these you cause to sit; ⁵I speak to your shame: so there is not among you one wise man, not even one, who will be able to discern in the midst of his brothers! ⁶But brother with brother goes to be judged, and this before unbelievers! ⁷Already, indeed, then, there is altogether a fault among you, that you have judgments with one another; why do you not rather suffer injustice? Why not be defrauded? ⁸But you do injustice, and you defraud, and these—brothers! ⁹Have you not known that the unrighteous will not inherit the Kingdom of God? Do not be led astray; neither whoremongers, nor idolaters, nor adulterers, nor effeminate, nor sodomites, ¹⁰nor thieves, nor covetous, nor drunkards, nor revilers, nor extortioners, will inherit the Kingdom of God. ¹¹And certain of you were these! But you were washed, but you were sanctified, but you were declared righteous, in the Name of the Lord Jesus, and in the Spirit of our God. ¹²All things are lawful to me, but all things are not profitable; all things are lawful to me, but I will not be under authority by any; ¹³the meats [are] for the belly, and the belly for the meats. And God will make useless both this and these; and the body [is] not for whoredom, but for the LORD, and the LORD for the body; ¹⁴and God raised both the LORD, and will raise us up through His power. ¹⁵Have you not known that your bodies are members of Christ? Having taken, then, the members of the Christ, will I make [them] members of a prostitute? Let it not be! ¹⁶Have you not known that he who is joined to the prostitute is one body? For it says, "The two will be into one flesh." ¹⁷And he who is joined to the LORD is one spirit; ¹⁸flee the whoredom; every sin—whatever a man may commit—is outside the body, and he who is committing whoredom sins against his own body. ¹⁹Have you not known that your body is a temple of the Holy Spirit in you, which you have from God? And you are not your own, ²⁰for you were bought with a price; glorify, then, God in your body and in your spirit, which are God's.

CHAPTER 7

¹And concerning the things of which you wrote to me: [it is] good for a man not to touch a woman, ²and because of the whoredom let each man have his own wife, and let each woman have her proper husband; ³to the wife let the husband render the due benevolence, and in like manner also the wife to the husband; ⁴the wife does not have authority over her own body, but the husband; and in like manner also, the husband does not have authority over his own body, but the wife. ⁵Do not defraud one another, except by consent for a time, that you may be free for fasting and prayer, and again may come together, that Satan may not tempt you because of your self-indulgence; ⁶and this I say by way of concurrence—not of command, ⁷for I wish all men to be even as I myself [am]; but each has his own gift of God, one indeed thus and one thus. ⁸And I say to the unmarried and to the widows: it is good for them if they may remain even as I [am]; ⁹and if they do not have continence—let them marry, for it is better to marry than to burn; ¹⁰and to the married I announce—not I, but the LORD—do not let a wife separate from a husband: ¹¹but, and if she may separate, let her remain unmarried, or let her be reconciled to the husband, and do not let a husband send a wife away. ¹²And to the rest I speak—not the LORD—if any brother has an unbelieving wife, and she is pleased to dwell with him, do not let him send her away; ¹³and a woman who has an unbelieving husband, and he is pleased to dwell with her, do not let her send him away; ¹⁴for the unbelieving husband has been sanctified in the wife, and the unbelieving wife has been sanctified in the husband; otherwise your children are unclean, but now they are holy. ¹⁵And if the unbelieving separates himself—let him separate himself: the brother or the sister is not under servitude in such [cases], and in peace has God called us; ¹⁶for what, have you known, O wife, whether you will save the husband? Or what, have you known, O husband, whether you will save the wife? ¹⁷If not, as God distributed to each, as the LORD has called each—so let him walk; and thus I direct in all the assemblies: ¹⁸being circumcised—was anyone called? Do not let him become uncircumcised; in uncircumcision was anyone called? Do not let him be circumcised; ¹⁹the circumcision is nothing, and the uncircumcision is nothing—but a keeping of the commands of God. ²⁰Each in the calling in which he was called—in this let him remain; ²¹a servant—were you called? Do not be anxious; but if also you are able to become free—use [it] rather; ²²for he who [is] in the LORD—having been called a servant—is the LORD's freedman: in like manner also he the freeman, having been called, is servant of Christ: ²³you were bought with a price, do not become servants of men; ²⁴each, in that in which he was called, brothers, in this let him remain with God. ²⁵And concerning the virgins, I do not have a command of the LORD; and I give judgment as having obtained kindness from the LORD to be faithful. ²⁶I suppose, therefore, this to be good because of the present necessity, that [it is] good for a man that the matter be thus: ²⁷Have you been bound to a wife? Do not seek to be loosed; have you been loosed from a wife? Do not seek a wife. ²⁸But, and if you may marry, you did not sin; and if the virgin may marry, she did not sin; and such will have tribulation in the flesh: and I spare you. ²⁹And this I say, brothers, the time from now on is having been shortened—that both those having wives may be as not having; ³⁰and those weeping, as not weeping; and those rejoicing, as not rejoicing; and those buying, as not possessing; ³¹and those using this world, as not using [it] up; for the [present] form of this world is passing away. ³²And I wish you to be without anxiety; the unmarried is anxious for the things of the LORD, how he will please the LORD; ³³and the married is anxious for the things of the world, how he will please the wife. ³⁴The wife and the virgin have been distinguished: the unmarried is anxious for the things of the LORD, that she may be holy both in body and in spirit, and the married is anxious for the things of the world, how she will please the husband. ³⁵And this I say for your own profit: not that I may cast a noose on you, but for the seemliness and devotedness to the LORD, undistractedly, ³⁶and if anyone thinks [it] to be unseemly to his virgin, if she may be beyond the bloom of age, and it ought to be so, what he wills let him do; he does not sin—let him marry. ³⁷And he does well who has stood steadfast in the heart—not having necessity—and has authority over his own will, and he has determined this in his heart—to keep his own virgin; ³⁸so that both he who is giving in marriage does well, and he who is not giving in marriage does better. ³⁹A wife has been bound by law [for] as long [a] time as her husband may live, and if her husband may sleep, she is free to be married to whom she will—only in the LORD; ⁴⁰and she is happier if she may so remain—according to my judgment; and I think I also have the Spirit of God.

CHAPTER 8

¹And concerning the things sacrificed to idols, we have known that we all have knowledge: knowledge puffs up, but love builds up; ²and if anyone thinks to know anything, he has not yet known anything according as it is required to know; ³and if anyone loves God, this one has been known by Him. ⁴Concerning the eating then of the things sacrificed to idols, we have known that an idol [is] nothing in the world, and that there is no other God except one; ⁵for even if there are those called gods, whether in Heaven, whether on earth—as there are

many gods and many lords— ⁶yet to us [is] one God, the Father, of whom [are] all things, and we to Him; and one Lord, Jesus Christ, through whom [are] all things, and we through Him; ⁷but not in all men [is] the knowledge, and certain with conscience of the idol, until now, eat [it] as a thing sacrificed to an idol, and their conscience, being weak, is defiled. ⁸But food does not commend us to God, for neither if we may eat are we in advance; nor if we may not eat, are we behind; ⁹but see, lest this privilege of yours may become a stumbling-block to the weak, ¹⁰for if anyone may see you that have knowledge in an idol's temple reclining to eat, will not his conscience—he being weak—be emboldened to eat the things sacrificed to idols? ¹¹For the [one] being weak—the brother for whom Christ died—will perish by your knowledge. ¹²And thus sinning in regard to the brothers, and striking their weak conscience—you sin in regard to Christ; ¹³for this reason, if food causes my brother to stumble, I may not eat flesh—throughout the age—that I may not cause my brother to stumble.

CHAPTER 9

¹Am I not an apostle? Am I not free? Have I not seen Jesus Christ our Lord? Are you not my work in the LORD? ²If I am not an apostle to others—yet doubtless I am to you; for you are the seal of my apostleship in the LORD. ³My defense to those who examine me in this: ⁴do we not have authority to eat and to drink? ⁵Do we not have authority to lead about a sister— a wife—as also the other apostles, and the brothers of the LORD, and Cephas? ⁶Or do only Barnabas and I have no authority not to work? ⁷Who serves as a soldier at his own expense at any time? Who plants a vineyard and does not eat of its fruit? Or who feeds a flock and does not eat of the milk of the flock? ⁸Do I speak these things according to man? Or does the Law not also say these things? ⁹For in the Law of Moses it has been written: "you will not muzzle an ox treading out grain"; does God care for the oxen? ¹⁰Or by all means does He say [it] because of us? Yes, because of us it was written, because in hope ought the plower to plow, and he who is treading [ought] of his hope to partake in hope. ¹¹If we sowed to you the spiritual things—[is it] great if we reap your fleshly things? ¹²If others partake of the authority over you—[do] we not more? But we did not use this authority, but we bear all things, that we may give no hindrance to the good news of the Christ. ¹³Have you not known that those working about the things of the temple eat of the temple, and those waiting at the altar are partakers with the altar? ¹⁴So also the LORD directed to those proclaiming the good news to live of the good news. ¹⁵And I have used none of these things; neither did I write these things that it may be so done in my case, for [it is] good for me rather to die, than that anyone may make my glorying void; ¹⁶for if I may proclaim good news, it is no glorying for me, for necessity is laid on me, and woe is to me if I may not proclaim good news; ¹⁷for if I do this willingly, I have a reward; and if unwillingly—I have been entrusted with a stewardship! ¹⁸What, then, is my reward? That proclaiming good news, without charge I will make the good news of the Christ, not to abuse my authority in the good news; ¹⁹for being free from all men, I made myself servant to all men, that the more I might gain; ²⁰and to the Jews I became like a Jew, that I might gain Jews; to those under law as under law, that I might gain those under law; ²¹to those without law, as without law—(not being without law to God, but within law to Christ)—that I might gain those without law; ²²to the weak I became weak, that I might gain the weak; to all men I have become all things, that by all means I may save some. ²³And I do this because of the good news, that I may become a fellow-partaker of it; ²⁴have you not known that those running in a race—all indeed run, but one receives the prize? So run that you may obtain; ²⁵and everyone who is striving is temperate in all things; these, indeed, then, that they may receive a corruptible garland, but we an incorruptible; ²⁶I, therefore, thus run, not as uncertainly, thus I fight, as not beating air; ²⁷but I bruise my body, and bring [it] into servitude, lest by any means, having preached to others—I myself may become disapproved.

CHAPTER 10

¹And I do not wish you to be ignorant, brothers, that all our fathers were under the cloud, and all passed through the sea, ²and all were immersed into Moses in the cloud, and in the sea; ³and all ate the same spiritual food, ⁴and all drank the same spiritual drink, for they were drinking of a spiritual rock following them, and the rock was the Christ; ⁵but in the most of them God was not well pleased, for they were strewn in the wilderness, ⁶and those things became types of us, for our not passionately desiring evil things, as also these desired. ⁷Neither become idolaters, as certain of them, as it has been written: "The people sat down to eat and to drink, and stood up to play"; ⁸neither may we commit whoredom, as certain of them committed whoredom, and there fell in one day twenty-three thousand; ⁹neither may we tempt the Christ, as also certain of them tempted, and perished by the serpents; ¹⁰neither murmur, as also some of them murmured, and perished by the destroyer. ¹¹And all these things happened to those persons as types, and they were written for our admonition, to whom the end of the ages came, ¹²so that he who is thinking to stand— let him observe, lest he fall. ¹³No temptation has taken you—except that of man; and God is faithful, who will not permit you to be tempted above what you are able, but He will make, with the temptation, also the outlet, for your being able to bear [it]. ¹⁴For this reason, my beloved, flee from the idolatry; ¹⁵as to wise men I speak—judge what I say. ¹⁶The cup of the blessing that we bless—is it not the fellowship of the blood of the Christ? The bread that we break—is it not the fellowship of the body of the Christ? ¹⁷Because one bread, one body, are we the many—for we all partake of the one bread. ¹⁸See Israel according to the flesh! Are those not eating the sacrifices in the fellowship of the altar? ¹⁹What do I say then? That an idol is anything? Or that a sacrifice offered to an idol is anything? ²⁰[No,] but that the things that the nations sacrifice— they sacrifice to demons and not to God; and I do not wish you to come into the fellowship of the demons. ²¹You are not able to drink the cup of the LORD and the cup of demons; you are not able to partake of the table of the LORD and of the table of demons; ²²do we arouse the LORD to jealousy? Are we stronger than He? ²³All things are lawful to me, but not all things are profitable; all things are lawful to me, but not all things build up; ²⁴let no one seek his own— but each another's. ²⁵Eat whatever is sold in the meat-market, not inquiring, because of the conscience, ²⁶for the earth and its fullness [are] the LORD's; ²⁷and if anyone of the unbelieving calls you, and you wish to go, eat all that is set before you, inquiring nothing, because of the conscience; ²⁸and if anyone may say to you, "This is a thing sacrificed to an idol," do not eat, because of that one who showed [it], and of the conscience, for the LORD's [is] the earth and its fullness: ²⁹and conscience, I say, not of yourself, but of the other, for why [is it] that my liberty is judged by another's conscience? ³⁰And if I partake thankfully, why am I spoken of [as] evil, for that for which I give thanks? ³¹Whether, then, you eat, or drink, or do anything, do all to the glory of God; ³²become offenseless, both to Jews and Greeks, and to the Assembly of God; ³³as I also please all in all things, not seeking my own profit, but that of many—that they may be saved.

CHAPTER 11

¹Become followers of me, as I also [am] of Christ. ²And I praise you, brothers, that in all things you remember me, and according as I delivered to you, you keep the deliverances, ³and I wish you to know that the Christ is the head of every man, and the head of a woman is the husband, and the head of Christ is God. ⁴Every man praying or prophesying, having the head covered, dishonors his head, ⁵and every woman praying or prophesying with the head uncovered, dishonors her own head, for it is one and the same thing with her being shaven, ⁶for if a woman is not covered—then let her be shorn, and if [it is] a shame for a woman to be shorn or shaven—let her be covered; ⁷for a man, indeed, ought not to cover the head, being the image and glory of God, and a woman is the glory of a man, ⁸for a man is not of a woman, but a woman [is] of a man, ⁹for also was a man not created because of the woman, but a woman because of the man; ¹⁰because of this the woman ought to have [a token of] authority on the head, because of the messengers; ¹¹but neither [is] a man apart from a woman, nor a woman apart from a man, in the LORD, ¹²for as the woman [is] of the man, so also the man [is] through the woman, and all the things [are] of God. ¹³Judge in your

own selves: is it seemly for a woman to pray to God uncovered? ¹⁴Does not even nature itself teach you, that if a man indeed has long hair, it is a dishonor to him? ¹⁵And a woman, if she has long hair, it is a glory to her, because the hair has been given to her instead of a covering; ¹⁶and if anyone thinks to be contentious, we have no such custom, neither the assemblies of God. ¹⁷And declaring this, I give no praise, because you do not come together for the better, but for the worse; ¹⁸for first, indeed, coming together in an assembly, I hear of divisions being among you, and I partly believe [it], ¹⁹for it is also necessary for sects to be among you, that those approved may become visible among you; ²⁰you, then, coming together at the same place—it is not to eat the LORD's Dinner; ²¹for each takes his own dinner before in the eating, and one is hungry, and another is drunk; ²²why, do you not have houses to eat and to drink in? Or do you despise the Assembly of God, and shame those not having? What may I say to you? Will I praise you in this? I do not praise! ²³For I received from the LORD that which I also delivered to you, that the Lord Jesus in the night in which He was delivered up, took bread, ²⁴and having given thanks, He broke, and said, "Take, eat, this is My body that is being broken for you; do this—to the remembrance of Me." ²⁵In like manner also the cup after the supping, saying, "This cup is the New Covenant in My blood; do this, as often as you may drink [it]—to the remembrance of Me"; ²⁶for as often as you may eat this bread, and may drink this cup, you show forth the death of the LORD—until He may come; ²⁷so that whoever may eat this bread or may drink the cup of the LORD unworthily, he will be guilty of the body and blood of the LORD: ²⁸and let a man be proving himself, and so let him eat of the bread, and let him drink of the cup; ²⁹for he who is eating and drinking unworthily, he eats and drinks judgment to himself—not discerning the body of the LORD. ³⁰Because of this many [are] weak and sickly among you, and many sleep; ³¹for if we were discerning ourselves, we would not be being judged, ³²and being judged by the LORD, we are disciplined, that we may not be condemned with the world; ³³so then, my brothers, coming together to eat, wait for one another; ³⁴and if anyone is hungry, let him eat at home, that you may not come together to judgment; and the rest, whenever I may come, I will arrange.

CHAPTER 12

¹And concerning the spiritual things, brothers, I do not wish you to be ignorant; ²you have known that you were nations, being carried away as you were led to the mute idols; ³for this reason, I give you to understand that no one, speaking in the Spirit of God, says Jesus [is] accursed, and no one is able to say Jesus [is] LORD, except in the Holy Spirit. ⁴And there are diversities of gifts, and the same Spirit; ⁵and there are diversities of ministries, and the same Lord; ⁶and there are diversities of workings, and it is the same God—who is working all in all. ⁷And to each has been given the manifestation of the Spirit for profit; ⁸for to one through the Spirit has been given a word of wisdom, and to another a word of knowledge, according to the same Spirit; ⁹and to another faith in the same Spirit, and to another gifts of healings in the same Spirit; ¹⁰and to another in-workings of mighty deeds; and to another prophecy; and to another discernings of spirits; and to another [various] kinds of tongues; and to another interpretation of tongues: ¹¹and the one and the same Spirit works all these, dividing to each individually as He intends. ¹²For even as the body is one, and has many members, and all the members of the one body, being many, are one body, so also [is] the Christ, ¹³for also in one Spirit we were all immersed into one body, whether Jews or Greeks, whether servants or freemen, and all were made to drink one Spirit, ¹⁴for also the body is not one member, but many. ¹⁵If the foot may say, "Because I am not a hand, I am not of the body," is it not, because of this, not of the body? ¹⁶And if the ear may say, "Because I am not an eye, I am not of the body," is it not, because of this, not of the body? ¹⁷If the whole body [were] an eye, where the hearing? If the whole hearing, where the smelling? ¹⁸And now, God set the members, each one of them in the body, according as He willed, ¹⁹and if all were one member, where [is] the body? ²⁰And now, indeed, [are] many members, but one body; ²¹and an eye is not able to say to the hand, "I have no need of you"; nor again the head to the feet, "I have no need of you." ²²But much more the members of the body seeming to be weaker are necessary, ²³and those that we think to be less honorable of the body, around these we put more abundant honor, and our unseemly things have more abundant seemliness, ²⁴and our seemly things have no need; but God tempered the body together, having given more abundant honor to the lacking part, ²⁵that there may be no division in the body, but that the members may have the same anxiety for one another, ²⁶and whether one member suffers, all the members suffer with [it], or one member is glorified, all the members rejoice with [it]; ²⁷and you are the body of Christ, and members in particular. ²⁸And some, indeed, God set in the Assembly: first apostles, secondly prophets, thirdly teachers, afterward powers, afterward gifts of healings, helpings, governings, various kinds of tongues. ²⁹[Are] all apostles? [Are] all prophets? [Are] all teachers? [Are] all powers? ³⁰[Do] all have gifts of healings? Do all speak with tongues? Do all interpret? ³¹And earnestly desire the better gifts; and yet I show to you a far [more] excelling way:

CHAPTER 13

¹If I speak with the tongues of men and of messengers, and do not have love, I have become sounding brass, or a clanging cymbal; ²and if I have prophecy, and know all the secrets, and all the knowledge, and if I have all faith, so as to remove mountains, and do not have love, I am nothing; ³and if I give away all my goods to feed others, and if I give up my body that I may be burned, and do not have love, I am profited nothing. ⁴Love is long-suffering, it is kind, love does not envy, love does not vaunt itself, is not puffed up, ⁵does not act unseemly, does not seek its own things, is not provoked, does not impute evil, ⁶[does] not rejoice over unrighteousness, and rejoices with the truth; ⁷it bears all things, it believes all, it hopes all, it endures all. ⁸Love never fails; and whether [there be] prophecies, they will become useless; whether tongues, they will cease; whether knowledge, it will become useless; ⁹for we know in part, and we prophesy in part; ¹⁰and when that which is perfect may come, then that which [is] in part will become useless. ¹¹When I was a child, I was speaking as a child, I was thinking as a child, I was reasoning as a child, and when I have become a man, I have made useless the things of the child; ¹²for we now see obscurely through a mirror, and then face to face; now I know in part, and then I will fully know, as I was also known; ¹³and now there remains faith, hope, love—these three; and the greatest of these [is] love.

CHAPTER 14

¹Pursue love, and earnestly seek the spiritual things, and rather that you may prophesy, ²for he who is speaking in an [unknown] tongue—he does not speak to men, but to God, for no one listens, and he speaks secrets in spirit; ³and he who is prophesying to men speaks edification, and exhortation, and comfort; ⁴he who is speaking in an [unknown] tongue, edifies himself, and he who is prophesying, edifies the Assembly; ⁵and I wish you all to speak with tongues, and more that you may prophesy, for greater is he who is prophesying than he who is speaking with tongues, except one may interpret, that the Assembly may receive edification. ⁶And now, brothers, if I may come to you speaking tongues, what will I profit you, except I will speak to you either in revelation, or in knowledge, or in prophesying, or in teaching? ⁷Yet the things without life giving sound—whether pipe or harp—if they may not give a difference in the sounds, how will be known that which is piped or that which is harped? ⁸For also, if a trumpet may give an uncertain sound, who will prepare himself for battle? ⁹So also you, if you may not give speech easily understood through the tongue—how will that which is spoken be known? For you will be speaking to air. ¹⁰There are, it may be, so many kinds of voices in the world, and none of them is unmeaning. ¹¹If, then, I do not know the power of the voice, I will be a foreigner to him who is speaking, and he who is speaking is a foreigner to me; ¹²so you also, since you are earnestly desirous of spiritual gifts, seek for the building up of the Assembly that you may abound; ¹³for this reason he who is speaking in an [unknown] tongue—let him pray that he may interpret; ¹⁴for if I pray in an [unknown] tongue, my spirit prays, and my understanding is unfruitful. ¹⁵What then is it? I will pray [in] the spirit, and I will also pray [with] understanding; I will sing psalms [in]

the spirit, and I will also sing psalms [with] understanding; ¹⁶since, if you may bless in spirit, he who is filling the place of the commoner, how will he say the Amen at your giving of thanks, since he has not known what you say? ¹⁷For you, indeed, give thanks well, but the other is not built up! ¹⁸I give thanks to my God—more than you all with tongues speaking— ¹⁹but I wish to speak five words in an assembly through my understanding, that I also may instruct others, rather than myriads of words in an [unknown] tongue. ²⁰Brothers, do not become children in the understanding, but in the evil be children, and in the understanding become perfect; ²¹in the Law it has been written, that, "With other tongues and with other lips I will speak to this people, and even so they will not hear Me, says the LORD"; ²²so that the tongues are for a sign, not to the believing, but to the unbelieving; and the prophecy [is] not for the unbelieving, but for the believing. ²³If, therefore, the whole assembly may come together to the same place, and all may speak with tongues, and there may come in commoners or unbelievers, will they not say that you are mad? ²⁴And if all may prophesy, and anyone may come in, an unbeliever or commoner, he is convicted by all, he is discerned by all, ²⁵and so the secrets of his heart become visible, and so having fallen on [his] face, he will worship God, declaring that God really is among you. ²⁶What then is it, brothers? Whenever you may come together, each of you has a psalm, has a teaching, has a tongue, has a revelation, has an interpretation. Let all things be for building up; ²⁷if anyone speaks an [unknown] tongue, by two, or at the most, by three, and in turn, and let one interpret; ²⁸and if there may be no interpreter, let him be silent in an assembly, and let him speak to himself, and to God. ²⁹And prophets—let two or three speak, and let the others discern, ³⁰and if [anything] may be revealed to another [who is] sitting, let the first be silent; ³¹for you are able, one by one, all to prophesy, that all may learn, and all may be exhorted, ³²and the spiritual gift of prophets are subject to prophets, ³³for God is not [a God] of tumult, but of peace, as in all the assemblies of the holy ones. ³⁴Your women, let them be silent in the assemblies, for it has not been permitted to them to speak, but to be subject, as the Law also says; ³⁵and if they wish to learn anything, let them question their own husbands at home, for it is a shame to women to speak in an assembly. ³⁶Did the word of God come forth from you? Or did it come to you alone? ³⁷If anyone thinks to be a prophet, or spiritual, let him acknowledge the things that I write to you—that they are commands of the LORD; ³⁸and if anyone is ignorant—let him be ignorant; ³⁹so that, brothers, earnestly desire to prophesy, and do not forbid to speak with tongues; ⁴⁰let all things be done decently and in order.

CHAPTER 15

¹And I make known to you, brothers, the good news that I proclaimed to you, which you also received, in which you also have stood, ²through which you are also being saved, if you hold fast [to] the word—what I proclaimed as good news to you—unless you believed in vain. ³For I delivered to you as most important what I also received: that Christ died for our sins according to the Writings, ⁴and that He was buried, and that He has risen on the third day according to the Writings, ⁵and that He appeared to Cephas, then to the Twelve, ⁶afterward He appeared to above five hundred brothers at once, of whom the greater part remain until now, and some also fell asleep; ⁷afterward He appeared to James, then to all the apostles. ⁸And last of all—as to the untimely birth—He also appeared to me, ⁹for I am the least of the apostles, who am not worthy to be called an apostle, because I persecuted the Assembly of God, ¹⁰and by the grace of God I am what I am, and His grace that [is] toward me did not come in vain, but I labored more abundantly than they all, yet not I, but the grace of God that [is] with me; ¹¹whether, then, I or they, so we preach, and so you believed. ¹²And if Christ is preached, that He has risen out of the dead, how [do] certain among you say that there is no resurrection of [the] dead? ¹³And if there is no resurrection of [the] dead, neither has Christ risen; ¹⁴and if Christ has not risen, then our preaching [is] void, and your faith [is] also void, ¹⁵and we are also found [to be] false witnesses of God, because we testified of God that He raised up the Christ, whom He did not raise if then dead persons do not rise; ¹⁶for if dead persons do not rise, neither has Christ risen, ¹⁷and if Christ has not risen, your faith is vain, you are yet in your sins; ¹⁸then, also, those having fallen asleep in Christ perished; ¹⁹if we only have hope in Christ in this life, we are to be most pitied of all men. ²⁰And now, Christ has risen out of the dead—He became the first-fruits of those sleeping, ²¹for since through man [is] death, also through Man [is] a resurrection of the dead, ²²for even as in Adam all die, so also in the Christ all will be made alive, ²³and each in his proper order: Christ, a first-fruit, afterward those who are the Christ's in His coming, ²⁴then—the end, when He may deliver up the kingdom to God, even the Father, when He may have made all rule useless, and all authority and power. ²⁵For it is necessary for Him to reign until He may have put all the enemies under His feet. ²⁶The last enemy is done away with—death. ²⁷For He put all things under His feet, and when one may say that all things have been subjected, [it is] evident that He is excepted who subjected all things to Him, ²⁸and when all things may be subjected to Him, then also the Son Himself will be subject to Him, who subjected to Him all things, that God may be the all in all. ²⁹Seeing what will they do who are immersed for the dead, if the dead do not rise at all? Why are they also immersed for the dead? ³⁰Why do we also stand in peril every hour? ³¹I die every day, by the glorying of you that I have in Christ Jesus our Lord. ³²If I fought with wild beasts in Ephesus after the manner of a man, what [is] the advantage to me if the dead do not rise? Let us eat and drink, for tomorrow we die! ³³Do not be led astray; evil communications corrupt good manners; ³⁴wake up, as is right, and do not sin; for some have an ignorance of God; I say [it] to you for shame. ³⁵But someone will say, "How do the dead rise?" ³⁶Unwise! You—what you sow is not quickened except it may die; ³⁷and that which you sow, you do not sow the body that will be, but a bare grain, it may be of wheat, or of someone of the others, ³⁸and God gives a body to it according as He willed, and its proper body to each of the seeds. ³⁹All flesh [is] not the same flesh, but there is one flesh of men, and another flesh of beasts, and another of fishes, and another of birds; ⁴⁰and [there are] heavenly bodies and earthly bodies; but one [is] the glory of the heavenly, and another that of the earthly; ⁴¹one glory of sun, and another glory of moon, and another glory of stars, for star differs from star in glory. ⁴²So also [is] the resurrection of the dead: it is sown in corruption, it is raised in incorruption; ⁴³it is sown in dishonor, it is raised in glory; it is sown in weakness, it is raised in power; ⁴⁴it is sown a natural body, it is raised a spiritual body; there is a natural body, and there is a spiritual body; ⁴⁵so also it has been written: "The first man Adam became a living creature," the last Adam [is] for a life-giving spirit, ⁴⁶but that which is spiritual [is] not first, but that which [was] natural, afterward that which [is] spiritual. ⁴⁷The first man [is] out of the earth—earthly; the second Man [is] the LORD out of Heaven; ⁴⁸as [is] the earthly, such [are] also the earthly; and as [is] the heavenly, such [are] also the heavenly; ⁴⁹and according as we bore the image of the earthly, we will also bear the image of the heavenly. ⁵⁰And this I say, brothers, that flesh and blood are not able to inherit the Kingdom of God, nor does the corruption inherit the incorruption. ⁵¹Behold, I tell you a secret: we indeed will not all sleep, but we will all be changed; ⁵²in a moment, in the twinkling of an eye, in the last trumpet, for it will sound, and the dead will be raised incorruptible, and we will be changed; ⁵³for it is necessary for this corruptible to put on incorruption, and this mortal to put on immortality; ⁵⁴and when this corruptible may have put on incorruption, and this mortal may have put on immortality, then will be brought to pass the word that has been written: "Death was swallowed up—to victory; ⁵⁵Where, O Death, your sting? Where, O Death [[or Hades]], your victory?" ⁵⁶And the sting of death [is] sin, and the power of sin the Law; ⁵⁷and to God—thanks, to Him who is giving us

1 CORINTHIANS

the victory through our Lord Jesus Christ; ³⁸so that, my beloved brothers, become steadfast, unmovable, abounding in the work of the LORD at all times, knowing that your labor in the LORD is not vain.

CHAPTER 16

¹And concerning the collection that [is] for the holy ones, as I directed to the assemblies of Galatia, so also you—do; ²on every first [day] of the week, let each one of you lay by him, treasuring up whatever he may have prospered, that when I may come then collections may not be made; ³and whenever I may come, whomsoever you may approve, through letters, these I will send to carry your favor to Jerusalem; ⁴and if it be worthy for me also to go, with me they will go. ⁵And I will come to you when I pass through Macedonia—for I pass through Macedonia—⁶and with you, it may be, I will abide, or even winter, that you may send me forward wherever I go, ⁷for I do not wish to see you now in the passing, but I hope to remain a certain time with you, if the LORD may permit; ⁸and I will remain in Ephesus until the Pentecost, ⁹for a door has been opened to me—great and effectual—and withstanders [are] many. ¹⁰And if Timotheus may come, see that he may become without fear with you, for he works the work of the LORD, even as I, ¹¹no one, then, may despise him; and send him forward in peace, that he may come to me, for I expect him with the brothers; ¹²and concerning Apollos our brother, I begged him much that he may come to you with the brothers, and it was not at all [his] will that he may come now, and he will come when he may find convenient. ¹³Watch, stand in the faith; be men, be strong; ¹⁴let all your things be done in love. ¹⁵And I beg you, brothers, you have known the household of Stephanas, that it is the first-fruit of Achaia, and they set themselves to the ministry to the holy ones—¹⁶that you also be subject to such, and to everyone who is working with [us] and laboring; ¹⁷and I rejoice over the coming of Stephanas, and Fortunatus, and Achaicus, because these filled up the lack of you; ¹⁸for they refreshed my spirit and yours; acknowledge, therefore, those who [are] such. ¹⁹The assemblies of Asia greet you; Aquilas and Priscilla greet you much in the LORD, with the assembly in their house; ²⁰all the brothers greet you; greet one another in a holy kiss. ²¹The salutation of [me], Paul, with my hand; ²²if anyone does not cherish the Lord Jesus Christ—let him be accursed! The LORD has come! ²³The grace of the Lord Jesus Christ [is] with you; ²⁴my love [is] with you all in Christ Jesus! Amen.

2 CORINTHIANS

CHAPTER 1

¹Paul, an apostle of Jesus Christ, through the will of God, and Timotheus the brother, to the Assembly of God that is in Corinth, with all the holy ones who are in all Achaia: ²Grace to you and peace from God our Father and the Lord Jesus Christ! ³Blessed [is] God, even the Father of our Lord Jesus Christ, the Father of mercies, and God of all comfort, ⁴who is comforting us in all our tribulation, for our being able to comfort those in any tribulation through the comfort with which we are comforted ourselves by God; ⁵because, as the sufferings of the Christ abound to us, so through the Christ our comfort also abounds; ⁶and whether we be in tribulation, [it is] for your comfort and salvation, that is worked in the enduring of the same sufferings that we also suffer; whether we are comforted, [it is] for your comfort and salvation; ⁷and our hope [is] steadfast for you, knowing that even as you are partakers of the sufferings—so also of the comfort. ⁸For we do not wish you to be ignorant, brothers, of our tribulation that happened to us in Asia, that we were exceedingly burdened above [our] power, so that we even despaired of life; ⁹but we ourselves have had the sentence of death in ourselves, that we may not be trusting on ourselves, but on God, who is raising the dead, ¹⁰who delivered us out of so great a death, and delivers, in whom we have hoped that even yet He will deliver; ¹¹you also working together for us by your supplication, that the gift through many persons to us, through many, may be thankfully acknowledged for us. ¹²For our glorying is this: the testimony of our conscience, that in simplicity and sincerity of God, not in fleshly wisdom, but in the grace of God, we conducted ourselves in the world, and more abundantly toward you; ¹³for no other things do we write to you, but what you either read or also acknowledge, and I hope that you will also acknowledge to the end, ¹⁴according as you also acknowledged us in part, that we are your glory, even as also you [are] ours, in the Day of the Lord Jesus; ¹⁵and in this confidence I was intending to come to you before, that you might have a second favor, ¹⁶and to pass to Macedonia through you, and to come to you again from Macedonia, and to be sent forward by you to Judea. ¹⁷This, therefore, intending, did I then use the lightness; or the things that I counsel, [did] I counsel according to the flesh, that it may be with me Yes, yes, and No, no? ¹⁸And God [is] faithful, that our word to you did not become Yes and No, ¹⁹for the Son of God, Jesus Christ, having been preached through us among you—through me and Silvanus and Timotheus—did not become Yes and No, but in Him it has become Yes; ²⁰for as many as [are] promises of God, in Him [are] the Yes, and in Him the Amen, for glory to God through us; ²¹and He who is confirming you with us into Christ, and anointed us, [is] God, ²²who also sealed us, and gave the deposit of the Spirit in our hearts. ²³And I call on God for a witness on my soul, that sparing you, I did not come to Corinth yet; ²⁴not that we are lords over your faith, but we are workers together with your joy, for by faith you stand.

CHAPTER 2

¹And I decided this to myself, not to come again to you in sorrow, ²for if I make you sorry, then who is he who is making me glad, except he who is made sorry by me? ³And I wrote to you this same thing, that having come, I may not have sorrow from them of whom it was necessary [for] me to have joy, having confidence in you all, that my joy is of you all, ⁴for out of much tribulation and pressure of heart I wrote to you through many tears, not that you might be made sorry, but that you might know the love that I have more abundantly toward you. ⁵And if anyone has caused sorrow, he has not caused sorrow to me, but in part, that I may not burden you all; ⁶sufficient to such a one is this punishment, that [is] by the greater part, ⁷so that, on the contrary, [it is] rather for you to forgive and to comfort, lest by over abundant sorrow such a one may be swallowed up; ⁸for this reason, I call on you to confirm love to him, ⁹for this also I wrote, that I might know your proof, whether you are obedient in regard to all things. ¹⁰And to whom you forgive anything—I also; for I also, if I have forgiven anything, to whom I have forgiven [it], because of you—in the person of Christ—[I forgive it,] ¹¹that we may not be over-reached by Satan, for we are not ignorant of his schemes. ¹²And having come to Troas for the good news of the Christ, and a door having been opened to me in the LORD, ¹³I have not had rest to my spirit, on my not finding my brother Titus, but having taken leave of them, I went forth to Macedonia; ¹⁴and to God [is] thanks, who at all times is leading us in triumph in the Christ, and the fragrance of His knowledge He is revealing through us in every place; ¹⁵we are a refreshing fragrance to God because of Christ, in those being saved, and in those being lost; ¹⁶to one, indeed, a fragrance of death to death, and to the other, a fragrance of life to life; and who is sufficient for these things? ¹⁷For we are not as the many, adulterating the word of God, but as of sincerity—but as of God; in the presence of God, in Christ we speak.

2 CORINTHIANS

CHAPTER 3

¹Do we begin again to recommend ourselves, except we need, as some, letters of recommendation to you, or from you? ²You are our letter, having been written in our hearts, known and read by all men, ³revealed that you are a letter of Christ ministered by us, not written with ink, but with the Spirit of the living God, not in the tablets of stone, but in fleshy tablets of the heart, ⁴and such trust we have through the Christ toward God, ⁵not that we are sufficient of ourselves to think anything, as of ourselves, but our sufficiency [is] of God, ⁶who also made us sufficient [to be] servants of the New Covenant, not of letter, but of the Spirit; for the letter kills, and the Spirit makes alive. ⁷And if the ministry of death, in letters, engraved in stones, came in glory, so that the sons of Israel were not able to look steadfastly into the face of Moses, because of the glory of his face—which was being made useless, ⁸how will the ministry of the Spirit not be more in glory? ⁹For if the ministry of the condemnation [is] glory, much more does the ministry of righteousness abound in glory; ¹⁰for also even that which has been glorious, has not been glorious—in this respect, because of the superior glory; ¹¹for if that which is being made useless [is] through glory, much more that which is remaining [is] in glory. ¹²Having, then, such hope, we use much freedom of speech, ¹³and [are] not as Moses, who was putting a veil on his own face, for the sons of Israel not to look steadfastly into the end of that which is being made useless, ¹⁴but their minds were hardened, for to this day the same veil at the reading of the Old Covenant remains unwithdrawn—which in Christ is being made useless— ¹⁵but until today, when Moses is read, a veil lies on their heart, ¹⁶and whenever they may turn to the LORD, the veil is taken away. ¹⁷And the LORD is the Spirit; and where the Spirit of the LORD [is], there [is] liberty; ¹⁸and we all, with unveiled face, beholding the glory of the LORD in a mirror, are being transformed into the same image, from glory to glory, even as by the Spirit of the LORD.

CHAPTER 4

¹Because of this, having this ministry, according as we received kindness, we do not faint, ²but renounced for ourselves the hidden things of shame, not walking in craftiness, nor deceitfully using the word of God, but by the manifestation of the truth recommending ourselves to every conscience of men, before God; ³and if our good news is also veiled, it is veiled in those perishing, ⁴in whom the god of this age blinded the minds of the unbelieving, that there does not shine forth to them the enlightening of the good news of the glory of the Christ, who is the image of God; ⁵for we do not preach ourselves, but Christ Jesus—LORD, and [we are] ourselves your servants because of Jesus; ⁶because [it is] God who said, "Light will shine out of darkness," who shined in our hearts, for the enlightening of the knowledge of the glory of God in the face of Jesus Christ. ⁷And we have this treasure in earthen vessels, that the excellence of the power may be of God, and not of us, ⁸being in tribulation in every [way], but not crushed; perplexed, but not despairing; ⁹persecuted, but not forsaken; cast down, but not destroyed; ¹⁰at all times carrying around in the body the dying of the Lord Jesus, that the life of Jesus may also be revealed in our body, ¹¹for we who are living are always delivered up to death because of Jesus, that the life of Jesus may also be revealed in our dying flesh, ¹²so that, death indeed works in us, and life in you. ¹³And having the same spirit of faith, according to that which has been written: "I believed, therefore I spoke"; we also believe, therefore we also speak; ¹⁴knowing that He who raised up the Lord Jesus, will also raise us up through Jesus, and will present [us] with you, ¹⁵for all things [are] because of you, that the grace having been multiplied, because of the thanksgiving of the more, may abound to the glory of God; ¹⁶for this reason, we do not faint, but if our outward man also decays, yet the inward is renewed day by day; ¹⁷for the momentary light matter of our tribulation works out for us more and more an exceedingly continuous weight of glory— ¹⁸we [are] not looking to the things seen, but to the things not seen; for the things seen [are] temporary, but the things not seen [are] continuous.

CHAPTER 5

¹For we have known that if the tent of our earthly house may be thrown down, we have a building from God, a house not made with hands—perpetual—in the heavens, ²for also in this we groan, earnestly desiring to clothe ourselves with our dwelling that is from Heaven, ³if so be that, having clothed ourselves, we will not be found naked, ⁴for we also who are in the tent groan, being burdened, seeing we do not wish to unclothe ourselves, but to clothe ourselves, that the mortal may be swallowed up of life. ⁵And He who worked us to this very thing [is] God, who also gave to us the deposit of the Spirit; ⁶having courage, then, at all times, and knowing that being at home in the body, we are away from home from the LORD— ⁷for we walk through faith, not through sight— ⁸we have courage, and are well pleased, rather, to be away from the home of the body, and to be at home with the LORD. ⁹We are also ambitious for this reason, whether at home or away from home, to be well pleasing to Him, ¹⁰for it is necessary for all of us to have appeared before the judgment seat of the Christ, that each one may receive the things [done] through the body, in reference to the things that he did, whether good or evil; ¹¹having known, therefore, the fear of the LORD, we persuade men, and we are revealed to God, and I also hope to have been revealed in your consciences; ¹²for we do not again recommend ourselves to you, but we are giving occasion to you of glorifying in our behalf, that you may have [something] in reference to those glorifying in face and not in heart; ¹³for whether we were beside ourselves, [it was] to God; whether we be of sound mind, [it is] to you, ¹⁴for the love of the Christ constrains us, having judged thus: that if one died for all, then the whole died, ¹⁵and He died for all, that those living may no longer live to themselves, but to Him who died for them, and was raised again. ¹⁶So that we, from now on, have known no one according to the flesh, and even if we have known Christ according to the flesh, yet now we know Him [thus] no longer; ¹⁷so that if anyone [is] in Christ—[he is] a new creature; the old things passed away, behold, all things have become new. ¹⁸And all things [are] of God, who reconciled us to Himself through Jesus Christ, and gave to us the ministry of the reconciliation, ¹⁹how that God was in Christ—reconciling the world to Himself, not reckoning to them their trespasses; and having put in us the word of the reconciliation, ²⁰in behalf of Christ, then, we are ambassadors, as if God were calling through us, we implore, in behalf of Christ, "Be reconciled to God"; ²¹He made Him having not known sin [to be] sin in our behalf, that we may become the righteousness of God in Him.

CHAPTER 6

¹And also working together we call on [you] that you do not receive the grace of God in vain— ²for He says, "In an acceptable time I heard you, and in a day of salvation I helped you, behold, now [is] a well-accepted time; behold, now, a day of salvation." ³In nothing giving any cause of offense, that the ministry may not be blamed, ⁴but in everything recommending ourselves as God's servants; in much patience, in tribulations, in necessities, in distresses, ⁵in stripes, in imprisonments, in insurrections, in labors, in watchings, in fastings, ⁶in pureness, in knowledge, in long-suffering, in kindness, in the Holy Spirit, in unhypocritical love, ⁷in the word of truth, in the power of God, through the armor of righteousness, on the right and on the left, ⁸through glory and dishonor, through evil report and good report, as leading astray, and true; ⁹as unknown, and recognized; as dying, and behold, we live; as disciplined, and not put to death; ¹⁰as sorrowful, and always rejoicing; as poor, and making many rich; as having nothing, and possessing all things. ¹¹Our mouth has been open to you, O Corinthians, our heart has been enlarged! ¹²You are not restricted in us, and

2 CORINTHIANS

you are restricted in your [own] yearnings, ¹³and [as] a repayment of the same kind (as to children I say [it]), be enlarged—also you! ¹⁴Do not become yoked with others—unbelievers, for what partaking [is there] to righteousness and lawlessness? ¹⁵And what fellowship to light with darkness? And what concord to Christ with Belial? Or what part to a believer with an unbeliever? ¹⁶And what agreement to the temple of God with idols? For you are a temple of the living God, according as God said, "I will dwell in them, and will walk among [them], and I will be their God, and they will be My people, ¹⁷for this reason, come forth out of the midst of them, and be separated, says the LORD, and do not touch an unclean thing, and I will receive you, ¹⁸and I will be for a Father to you, and you will be sons and daughters to Me, says the LORD Almighty."

CHAPTER 7

¹Having, then, these promises, beloved, may we cleanse ourselves from every defilement of flesh and spirit, perfecting sanctification in the fear of God; ²receive us; no one did we wrong; no one did we ruin; no one did we defraud; ³I do not say [it] to condemn you, for I have said before that you are in our hearts to die together and to live together; ⁴great [is] my freedom of speech to you, great my glory on your behalf; I have been filled with the comfort, I hyper-abound with the joy on all our tribulation, ⁵for we also, having come to Macedonia, our flesh has had no relaxation, but on every side we are in tribulation: fightings outside, fears within; ⁶but He who is comforting the cast-down—God—He comforted us in the coming of Titus; ⁷and not only in his coming, but also in the comfort with which he was comforted over you, declaring to us your longing desire, your lamentation, your zeal for me, so that I rejoiced the more, ⁸because even if I made you sorry in the letter, I do not regret—if even I regretted—for I perceive that the letter, even if for an hour, made you sorry. ⁹I now rejoice, not that you were made sorry, but that you were made sorry to conversion, for you were made sorry toward God, that you might receive damage from us in nothing; ¹⁰for sorrow toward God works conversion to salvation without regret, and the sorrow of the world works death, ¹¹for behold, this same thing—your being made sorry toward God—how much diligence it works in you! But defense, but displeasure, but fear, but longing desire, but zeal, but revenge; in everything you approved yourselves to be pure in the matter. ¹²If, then, I also wrote to you—not for his cause who did wrong, nor for his cause who suffered wrong, but for our diligence in your behalf being revealed to you before God— ¹³because of this we have been comforted in your comfort, and more abundantly the more we rejoiced in the joy of Titus, that his spirit has been refreshed from you all; ¹⁴because if I have boasted anything to him in your behalf, I was not put to shame; but as we spoke to you all things in truth, so also our boasting before Titus became truth, ¹⁵and his yearnings are more abundantly toward you, remembering the obedience of you all, how you received him with fear and trembling; ¹⁶I rejoice, therefore, that in everything I have courage in you.

CHAPTER 8

¹And we make known to you, brothers, the grace of God, that has been given in the assemblies of Macedonia, ²because in much trial of tribulation the abundance of their joy, and their deep poverty, abounded to the riches of their liberality; ³because, according to [their] power, I testify, and above [their] power, they were willing of themselves, ⁴with much plea calling on us to receive the favor and the fellowship of the ministry to the holy ones, ⁵and not according as we expected, but they gave themselves first to the LORD, and to us, through the will of God, ⁶so that we exhorted Titus, that, according as he began before, so also he may also finish this favor to you, ⁷but even as in everything you abound, in faith, and word, and knowledge, and all diligence, and in your love to us, that also in this grace you may abound; ⁸I do not speak according to command, but because of the diligence of others, and proving the genuineness of your love, ⁹for you know the grace of our Lord Jesus Christ, that because of you He became poor—being rich, that you may become rich by that poverty. ¹⁰And I give an opinion in this: for this [is] expedient to you, who not only to do, but also to will, began before—a year ago, ¹¹and now also finish doing [it], that even as [there is] the readiness of the will, so also the finishing, out of that which you have, ¹²for if the willing mind is present, it is well-accepted according to that which anyone may have, not according to that which he does not have; ¹³for I do not speak that for others [to be] released, and you pressured, ¹⁴but by equality, at the present time your abundance—for their want, that also their abundance may be for your want, that there may be equality, ¹⁵according as it has been written: "He who [gathered] much, had nothing over; and he who [gathered] little, had no lack." ¹⁶And thanks to God, who is putting the same diligence for you in the heart of Titus, ¹⁷because he indeed accepted the exhortation, and being more diligent, he went forth to you of his own accord, ¹⁸and we sent with him the brother, whose praise in the good news [is] through all the assemblies, ¹⁹and not only so, but who was also appointed by vote by the assemblies, our fellow-traveler, with this favor that is ministered by us, to the glory of the same Lord, and your willing mind; ²⁰avoiding this, lest anyone may blame us in this abundance that is ministered by us, ²¹providing right things, not only before the LORD, but also before men; ²²and we sent our brother with them, whom we proved being diligent many times in many things, and now much more diligent, by the great confidence that is toward you, ²³whether—about Titus—my partner and fellow-worker toward you, whether—our brothers, apostles of assemblies—glory of Christ; ²⁴the showing therefore of your love, and of our boasting on your behalf, show to them, even in the face of the assemblies.

CHAPTER 9

¹For indeed, concerning the ministry that [is] for the holy ones, it is superfluous for me to write to you, ²for I have known your readiness of mind, which in your behalf I boast of to Macedonians, that Achaia has been prepared a year ago, and your zeal stirred up the greater part, ³and I sent the brothers, that our boasting on your behalf may not be made vain in this respect; that, according as I said, you may be ready, ⁴lest if Macedonians may come with me, and find you unprepared, we may be put to shame (that we do not say—you) in this same confidence of boasting. ⁵Therefore I thought [it] necessary to exhort the brothers, that they may go before to you, and may make up before your formerly announced blessing, that this be ready, as a blessing, and not as covetousness. ⁶And [remember] this: he who is sowing sparingly, will also reap sparingly; and he who is sowing in blessings, will also reap in blessings; ⁷each one, according as he purposes in heart, not out of sorrow or out of necessity, for God loves a cheerful giver, ⁸and God [is] able to cause all grace to abound to you, that in everything always having all sufficiency, you may abound to every good work, ⁹according as it has been written: "He dispersed abroad, He gave to the poor, His righteousness remains throughout the age," ¹⁰and may He who is supplying seed to the sower, and bread for food, supply and multiply your seed sown, and increase the fruits of your righteousness, ¹¹being enriched to all liberality in everything, which works thanksgiving through us to God, ¹²because the ministry of this service not only is supplying the wants of the holy ones, but is also abounding through many thanksgivings to God, ¹³through the proof of this ministry glorifying God for the subjection of your confession to the good news of the Christ, and [for] the liberality of the fellowship to them and to all, ¹⁴and by their supplication in your behalf, longing after you because of the exceeding grace of God on you; ¹⁵thanks also to God for His unspeakable gift!

CHAPTER 10

¹And I, Paul, myself, call on you—through the meekness and gentleness of the Christ—who in presence [am] indeed humble among you, and being absent, have courage toward you, ²and I implore [you], that, being present, I may not have courage, with the confidence with which I reckon to be bold against certain reckoning us as walking according to the flesh; ³for walking in the flesh, we do not war according to the flesh, ⁴for the weapons of our warfare [are] not fleshly, but powerful to God for bringing down of strongholds, ⁵bringing down reasonings, and every high thing lifted up against the knowledge of God, and bringing into captivity every thought to the obedience of the Christ, ⁶and being in readiness to avenge every disobedience whenever your obedience may be fulfilled. ⁷You see the

outward appearance. If anyone has trusted in himself to be Christ's, let him reckon this again from himself, that according as he is Christ's, so also we [are] Christ's; ⁸for even if I will also boast anything more abundantly concerning our authority, that the LORD gave us for building up, and not for casting you down, I will not be ashamed, ⁹that I may not seem as if I would terrify you through the letters, ¹⁰"because the letters indeed," says one, "[are] weighty and strong, and the bodily presence weak, and the speech despicable." ¹¹This one—let him reckon thus: that such as we are in word, through letters, being absent, such also, being present, [we are] in deed. ¹²For we do not make bold to rank or to compare ourselves with certain of those commending themselves, but they, measuring themselves among themselves, and comparing themselves with themselves, are not wise, ¹³and we will not boast ourselves in regard to the unmeasured things, but after the measure of the line that the God of measure appointed to us—to reach even to you; ¹⁴for we do not stretch ourselves too much, as not reaching to you, for even to you we came in the good news of the Christ, ¹⁵not boasting of the things not measured, in other men's labors, and having hope—your faith increasing—in you to be enlarged, according to our line—into abundance, ¹⁶to proclaim good news in the [places] beyond you, not in another's line in regard to the things made ready, to boast; ¹⁷and he who is boasting—let him boast in the LORD; ¹⁸for he who is commending himself is not approved, but he whom the LORD commends.

CHAPTER 11

¹O that you were bearing with me a little of the folly, but you also bear with me: ²for I am zealous for you with zeal of God, for I betrothed you to one Husband, a pure virgin, to present to Christ, ³and I fear, lest, as the serpent deceived Eve in his subtlety, so your minds may be corrupted from the simplicity that [is] in the Christ; ⁴for if, indeed, he who is coming preaches another Jesus whom we did not preach, or you receive another spirit which you did not receive, or other good news which you did not accept—well were you bearing [it], ⁵for I reckon that I have been nothing behind the very chiefest apostles, ⁶and even if a commoner in speech—yet not in knowledge, but in everything we were made evident in all things to you. ⁷Did I do sin—humbling myself that you might be exalted, because I freely proclaimed the good news of God to you? ⁸I robbed other assemblies, having taken wages, for your ministry; ⁹and being present with you, and having been in want, I was chargeable to no one, for the brothers supplied my lack—having come from Macedonia—and I kept myself burdenless to you in everything, and will keep. ¹⁰The truth of Christ is in me, because this boasting will not be stopped in regard to me in the regions of Achaia; ¹¹for what reason? Because I do not love you? God has known! ¹²And what I do, I also will do, that I may cut off the occasion of those wishing an occasion, that in that which they boast they may be found according as we also; ¹³for those such [are] false apostles, deceitful workers, transforming themselves into apostles of Christ, ¹⁴and no wonder—for even Satan transforms himself into a messenger of light; ¹⁵[it is] no great thing, then, if his servants also transform themselves as servants of righteousness—whose end will be according to their works. ¹⁶Again I say, may no one think me to be a fool; and if otherwise, receive me even as a fool, that I also may boast a little. ¹⁷That which I speak, I do not speak according to the LORD, but as in foolishness, in this the confidence of boasting; ¹⁸since many boast according to the flesh, I also will boast: ¹⁹for you gladly bear with the fools—being wise, ²⁰for you bear, if anyone is bringing you under bondage, if anyone devours, if anyone takes away, if anyone exalts himself, if anyone strikes you on the face; ²¹I speak in reference to dishonor, how that we were weak, and in whatever anyone is bold—in foolishness I say [it]—I also am bold. ²²Are they Hebrews? I also! Are they Israelites? I also! Are they seed of Abraham? I also! ²³Are they servants of Christ? As [if] beside myself I speak—I [am] more; in labors more abundantly, in stripes above measure, in prisons more frequently, in deaths many times. ²⁴Five times I received from Jews forty [stripes] except one; ²⁵three times I was beaten with rods, once I was stoned, three times I was shipwrecked, I have passed a night and a day in the deep; ²⁶journeys many times, perils of rivers, perils of robbers, perils from [my own] race, perils from nations, perils in city, perils in wilderness, perils in sea, perils among false brothers; ²⁷in laboriousness and painfulness, many times in watchings, in hunger and thirst, many times in fastings, in cold and nakedness; ²⁸apart from the things without—the crowding on me that is daily—the care of all the assemblies. ²⁹Who is weak, and I am not weak? Who is stumbled, and I am not burned? ³⁰If it is necessary to boast, I will boast of the things of my weakness; ³¹the God and Father of our Lord Jesus Christ—who is blessed for all ages—has known that I do not lie! ³²In Damascus the governor [under] Aretas the king was watching the city of the Damascenes, wishing to seize me, ³³and I was let down through a window in a rope basket, through the wall, and fled out of his hands.

CHAPTER 12

¹To boast, really, is not profitable for me, for I will come to visions and revelations of the LORD. ²I have known a man in Christ, fourteen years ago—whether in the body I have not known, whether out of the body I have not known, God has known—such a one being snatched up to the third heaven; ³and I have known such a man—whether in the body, whether out of the body, I have not known, God has known— ⁴that he was snatched up to the paradise, and heard unutterable sayings, that it is not possible for man to speak. ⁵Of such a one I will boast, and of myself I will not boast, except in my weaknesses, ⁶for if I may wish to boast, I will not be a fool, for I will say truth; but I refrain, lest in regard to me anyone may think anything above what he sees me, or hears anything of me; ⁷and that by the exceeding greatness of the revelations I might not be exalted too much, there was given to me a thorn in the flesh, a messenger of Satan, that he might batter me, that I might not be exalted too much. ⁸I called on the LORD three times concerning this thing, that it might depart from me, ⁹and He said to me, "My grace is sufficient for you, for My power is perfected in weakness"; most gladly, therefore, will I rather boast in my weaknesses, that the power of the Christ may rest on me: ¹⁰for this reason I am well pleased in weaknesses, in damages, in necessities, in persecutions, in distresses—for Christ; for whenever I may be weak, then I am powerful; ¹¹I have become a fool—boasting; you compelled me; for I ought to have been commended by you, for I was behind the very chiefest apostles in nothing—even if I am nothing. ¹²The signs, indeed, of the apostle were worked among you in all patience, in signs, and wonders, and mighty deeds, ¹³for what is there in which you were inferior to the rest of the assemblies, except that I myself was not a burden to you? Forgive me this injustice! ¹⁴Behold, a third time I am ready to come to you, and I will not be a burden to you, for I do not seek yours, but you, for the children ought not to lay up for the parents, but the parents for the children, ¹⁵and I will most gladly spend and be entirely spent for your souls, even if, loving you more abundantly, I am loved less. ¹⁶And be it [so], I did not burden you, but being crafty, I took you with guile; ¹⁷anyone of those whom I have sent to you—did I take advantage of you by him? ¹⁸I begged Titus, and sent with [him] the brother; did Titus take advantage of you? Did we not walk in the same Spirit? Did we not [walk] in the same steps? ¹⁹Again, [do] you think that we are making defense to you? We speak before God in Christ; and all things, beloved, [are] for your up-building, ²⁰for I fear lest, having come, I may not find you such as I wish, and I may be found by you such as you do not wish, lest there be strifes, envyings, wraths, revelries, slanders, whisperings, puffings up, insurrections, ²¹lest again having come, my God may humble me in regard to you, and I may mourn many of those having sinned before, and having not changed their mind concerning the uncleanness, and whoredom, and licentiousness, that they practiced.

CHAPTER 13

¹I come to you this third time; on the mouth of two or three witnesses will every saying be

established; ²I have said before, and I say [it] before, as being present, the second time, and being absent, now, I write to those having sinned before, and to all the rest, that if I come again, I will not spare, ³since you seek a proof of the Christ speaking in me, who is not weak to you, but is powerful in you, ⁴for even if He was crucified from weakness, yet He lives from the power of God; for we also are weak in Him, but we will live with Him from the power of God toward you. ⁵Try yourselves, if you are in the faith; prove yourselves; do you not know yourselves, that Jesus Christ is in you, if you are not disapproved of in some respect? ⁶And I hope that you will know that we are not disapproved of; ⁷and I pray before God that you do no evil, not that we may appear approved, but that you may do that which is right, and we may be as disapproved; ⁸for we are not able to do anything against the truth, but for the truth; ⁹for we rejoice when we may be weak, but you may be powerful; and we also pray for this—your perfection! ¹⁰Because of this, these things—being absent—I write, that being present, I may not treat [any] sharply, according to the authority that the LORD gave me for building up, and not for casting down. ¹¹From now on, brothers, rejoice; be made perfect, be comforted, be of the same mind, be at peace, and the God of love and peace will be with you. ¹²Greet one another in a holy kiss. ¹³All the holy ones greet you. ¹⁴The grace of the Lord Jesus Christ, and the love of God, and the fellowship of the Holy Spirit, [is] with you all! Amen.

GALATIANS

CHAPTER 1

¹Paul, an apostle—not from men, nor through man, but through Jesus Christ, and God the Father, who raised Him out of the dead— ²and all the brothers with me, to the assemblies of Galatia: ³Grace to you and peace from God the Father and our Lord Jesus Christ, ⁴who gave Himself for our sins, that He might deliver us out of the present evil age, according to the will of our God and Father, ⁵to whom [is] the glory through the ages of the ages. Amen. ⁶I wonder that you are so quickly removed from Him who called you in the grace of Christ to another good news— ⁷not that there is another, except there are certain who are troubling you, and wishing to pervert the good news of the Christ; ⁸but even if we or a messenger out of Heaven may proclaim good news to you different from what we proclaimed to you—let him be accursed! ⁹As we have said before, and now say again: if anyone may proclaim to you good news different from what you received—let him be accursed! ¹⁰For do I now persuade men, or God? Or do I seek to please men? For if I yet pleased men—I should not be Christ's servant. ¹¹And I make known to you, brothers, the good news that was proclaimed by me, that it is not according to man, ¹²for neither did I receive it from man, nor was I taught [it], but through a revelation of Jesus Christ, ¹³for you heard of my behavior once in Judaism, that I was exceedingly persecuting the Assembly of God, and destroying it, ¹⁴and I was advancing in Judaism above many equals in age in my own race, being more abundantly zealous of my fathers' deliverances, ¹⁵and when God was well pleased—having separated me from the womb of my mother, and having called [me] through His grace— ¹⁶to reveal His Son in me, that I might proclaim Him as good news among the nations, I did not immediately confer with flesh and blood, ¹⁷nor did I go up to Jerusalem to those who were apostles before me, but I went away to Arabia, and again returned to Damascus; ¹⁸then, after three years I went up to Jerusalem to inquire about Peter, and remained with him fifteen days, ¹⁹and I did not see [any] other of the apostles, except James, the brother of the LORD. ²⁰And the things that I write to you, behold, before God—I do not lie; ²¹then I came into the regions of Syria and of Cilicia, ²²and was unknown by face to the assemblies of Judea, that [are] in Christ, ²³and they were only hearing that "he who is persecuting us then, now proclaims good news—the faith that he was then destroying"; ²⁴and they were glorifying God in me.

CHAPTER 2

¹Then after fourteen years again I went up to Jerusalem with Barnabas, having also taken Titus with me; ²and I went up by revelation, and submitted the good news to them that I preach among the nations, and privately to those esteemed, lest I ran or might run in vain; ³but not even Titus, who [is] with me, being a Greek, was compelled to be circumcised— ⁴and [that] because of the false brothers brought in unaware, who came in secretly to spy out our liberty that we have in Christ Jesus, that they might bring us under bondage, ⁵to whom not even for an hour we gave place by subjection, that the truth of the good news might remain to you. ⁶And from those who were esteemed to be something—whatever they were then, it makes no difference to me. God does not accept the face of man, for to me those esteemed added nothing, ⁷but on the contrary, having seen that I have been entrusted with the good news of the uncircumcision, as Peter with [that] of the circumcision, ⁸for He who worked with Peter to the apostleship of the circumcision, worked also in me in regard to the nations, ⁹and having known the grace that was given to me, James, and Cephas, and John, who were esteemed to be pillars, they gave to me a right hand of fellowship, and to Barnabas, that we may go to the nations, and they to the circumcision, ¹⁰only, that we should be mindful of the poor, which I also was diligent—this very thing—to do. ¹¹And when Peter came to Antioch, I stood up against him to the face, because he was blameworthy, ¹²for before the coming of some from James, he was eating with the nations, and when they came, he was withdrawing and separating himself, fearing those of circumcision, ¹³and the other Jews acted hypocritically with him, so that Barnabas was also carried away by their hypocrisy. ¹⁴But when I saw that they are not walking uprightly to the truth of the good news, I said to Peter before all, "If you, being a Jew, live in the manner of the nations, and not in the manner of the Jews, how do you compel the nations to live like Jews? ¹⁵We by nature Jews, and not sinners of the nations, ¹⁶having also known that a man is not declared righteous by works of law, but through faith from Jesus Christ, we also believed in Christ Jesus, that we might be declared righteous by faith from Christ, and not by works of law, because no flesh will be declared righteous by works of law." ¹⁷And if, seeking to be declared righteous in Christ, we were also ourselves found sinners, [is] Christ then a servant of sin? Let it not be! ¹⁸For if the things I threw down, these again I build up, I set myself forth [as] a transgressor; ¹⁹for I died through law that I may live to God; ²⁰I have been crucified with Christ, and I no longer live, but Christ lives in me; and that which I now live in the flesh—I live in the faith of the Son of God, who loved me and gave Himself for me; ²¹I do not make the grace of God void, for if righteousness [is] through law—then Christ died in vain.

CHAPTER 3

¹O thoughtless Galatians, who bewitched you, not to obey the truth—before whose eyes [it] was previously written [about] Jesus Christ having been crucified? ²I only wish to learn this from you: did you receive the Spirit by works of the Law, or by the hearing of faith? ³Are you so thoughtless? Having begun in the Spirit, do you now end in the flesh? ⁴So many things you suffered in vain! If, indeed, even in

GALATIANS

vain. ⁵He, therefore, who is supplying the Spirit to you and working mighty acts among you—[is it] by works of law or by the hearing of faith? ⁶According as Abraham believed God, and it was reckoned to him for righteousness; ⁷know, then, that those of faith—these are sons of Abraham, ⁸and the Writing, having foreseen that God declares righteous the nations by faith, foretold the good news to Abraham: ⁹"All the nations will be blessed in you"; so that those of faith are blessed with the believing Abraham, ¹⁰for as many as are of works of law are under a curse, for it has been written: "Cursed [is] everyone who is not remaining in all things that have been written in the Scroll of the Law—to do them," ¹¹and [it] is evident that in law no one is declared righteous with God, because "The righteous will live by faith"; ¹²and the Law is not by faith, rather, "The man who did them will live in them." ¹³Christ redeemed us from the curse of the Law, having become a curse for us, for it has been written: "Cursed is everyone who is hanging on a tree," ¹⁴that the blessing of Abraham may come to the nations in Christ Jesus, that we may receive the promise of the Spirit through faith. ¹⁵Brothers, I say [it] as a man, no one even makes void or adds to a confirmed covenant of man, ¹⁶and to Abraham were the promises spoken, and to his Seed; He does not say, "And to seeds," as of many, but as of one, "And to your Seed," which is Christ; ¹⁷and this I say, a covenant confirmed before by God to Christ, the Law, that came four hundred and thirty years after, does not set aside, to make void the promise, ¹⁸for if the inheritance [is] by law, [it is] no longer by promise, but God granted [it] to Abraham through promise. ¹⁹Why, then, the Law? It was added on account of the transgressions, until the Seed might come to which the promise has been made, having been set in order through messengers in the hand of a mediator— ²⁰and the mediator is not of one, but God is one. ²¹[Is] the Law, then, against the promises of God? Let it not be! For if a law was given that was able to make alive, truly there would have been righteousness by law, ²²but the Writing shut up the whole under sin, that the promise by faith of Jesus Christ may be given to those believing. ²³And before the coming of faith, we were being kept under law, shut up to the faith about to be revealed, ²⁴so that the Law became our tutor—to Christ, that we may be declared righteous by faith, ²⁵and faith having come, we are no longer under a tutor, ²⁶for you are all sons of God through faith in Christ Jesus, ²⁷for as many as were immersed into Christ put on Christ; ²⁸there is neither Jew nor Greek, there is neither servant nor freeman, there is neither male and female, for you are all one in Christ Jesus; ²⁹and if you [are] of Christ then you are seed of Abraham, and heirs according to promise.

CHAPTER 4

¹And I say, now as much time as the heir is a child, he differs nothing from a servant, [though] being lord of all, ²but is under tutors and stewards until the time appointed of the father, ³so we also, when we were children, were in servitude under the elements of the world, ⁴and when the fullness of time came, God sent forth His Son, come of a woman, come under law, ⁵that He may redeem those under law, that we may receive the adoption as sons; ⁶and because you are sons, God sent forth the Spirit of His Son into your hearts, crying, "Abba! Father!" ⁷So that you are no longer a servant, but a son, and if a son, also an heir of God through Christ. ⁸But then, indeed, having not known God, you were in servitude to those [that are] not by nature gods, ⁹and now, having known God—and rather being known by God—how [do] you turn again to the weak and poor elements to which you desire anew to be in servitude? ¹⁰You observe days, and months, and times, and years! ¹¹I am afraid for you, lest I labored in vain for you. ¹²I implore you, brothers, become as I [am]—because I also [am] as you; you did not hurt me; ¹³and you have known that through weakness of the flesh I proclaimed good news to you at the first, ¹⁴and you did not despise nor reject my trial that [is] in my flesh, but you received me as a messenger of God—as Christ Jesus; ¹⁵what then was your blessedness? For I testify to you, that if possible, having plucked out your eyes, you would have given [them] to me; ¹⁶so have I become your enemy, being true to you? ¹⁷They are zealous for you—[yet] not well, but they wish to shut us out, that you may be zealous for them; ¹⁸and [it is] good to be zealously regarded, in what is good, at all times, and not only in my being present with you; ¹⁹my little children, of whom I travail in birth again until Christ may be formed in you, ²⁰indeed I was wishing to be present with you now, and to change my voice, because I am in doubt about you. ²¹Tell me, you who are willing to be under law, do you not hear the Law? ²²For it has been written that Abraham had two sons, one by the maidservant and one by the free [woman], ²³but he who [is] of the maidservant has been according to flesh, but he who [is] of the free [woman], through the promise, ²⁴which things are allegorized, for these are the two covenants: one, indeed, from Mount Sinai, bringing forth to servitude, which is Hagar; ²⁵for this Hagar is Mount Sinai in Arabia, and corresponds to the Jerusalem that now [is], and is in servitude with her children, ²⁶and the Jerusalem above is the free [woman], which is mother of us all, ²⁷for it has been written: "Rejoice, O barren, who is not bearing; break forth and cry, you who are not travailing, because many [are] the children of the desolate—more than of her having the husband." ²⁸And we, brothers, as Isaac, are children of promise, ²⁹but as he then who was born according to the flesh persecuted him [born] according to the Spirit, so also now; ³⁰but what does the Writing say? "Cast forth the maidservant and her son, for the son of the maidservant may not be heir with the son of the free [woman]"; ³¹then, brothers, we are not a maidservant's children, but the free [woman's].

CHAPTER 5

¹In the freedom, then, with which Christ made you free—stand, and do not be held fast again by a yoke of servitude. ²Behold! I, Paul, say to you, that if you are [to be] circumcised, Christ will profit you nothing; ³and I testify again to every man circumcised, that he is a debtor to do the whole law; ⁴you were voided from the Christ, you who are declared righteous in law; you fell away from grace; ⁵for we by the Spirit, by faith, wait for a hope of righteousness, ⁶for in Christ Jesus neither circumcision avails anything, nor uncircumcision, but faith working through love. ⁷You were running well; who hindered you [so as] not to obey the truth? ⁸The persuasion [is] not of Him who is calling you! ⁹A little leaven leavens the whole lump; ¹⁰I have confidence in regard to you in the LORD that you will not be otherwise minded; and he who is troubling you will bear the judgment, whoever he may be. ¹¹And I, brothers, if I still preach circumcision, why am I still persecuted? Then the stumbling-block of the Cross has been done away [with]; ¹²O that even they would cut themselves off who are unsettling you! ¹³For you were called to freedom, brothers, only the freedom [is] not for an occasion to the flesh, but serve one another through the love, ¹⁴for all the Law is fulfilled in one word—in this: "You will love your neighbor as yourself"; ¹⁵and if you bite and devour one another, see that you may not be consumed by one another. ¹⁶And I say, walk in the Spirit, and you may not fulfill the desire of the flesh; ¹⁷for the flesh desires contrary to the Spirit, and the Spirit contrary to the flesh, and these are opposed to one another, that the things that you may will—these you may not do; ¹⁸and if you are led by the Spirit, you are not under law. ¹⁹And the works of the flesh are also evident, which are: adultery, whoredom, uncleanness, licentiousness, ²⁰idolatry, witchcraft, enmities, strife, jealousy, wraths, rivalries, dissensions, sects, ²¹envyings, murders, drunkenness, reveling, and such like, of which I tell you before, as I also said before, that those doing such things will not inherit the Kingdom of God. ²²And the fruit of the Spirit is: love, joy, peace, long-suffering, kindness, goodness, faith, ²³meekness, [and] self-control. Against such there is no law; ²⁴and those who are of Christ Jesus have crucified the flesh with the affections and the desires; ²⁵if we may live in the Spirit, we may also walk in the Spirit; ²⁶let us not become vainglorious—provoking one another, envying one another!

CHAPTER 6

¹Brothers, even if a man may be overtaken in any trespass, you who [are] spiritual restore such a one in a spirit of meekness, considering

yourself—lest you also may be tempted. ²Bear the burdens of one another, and so fill up the law of the Christ, ³for if anyone thinks [himself] to be something—being nothing—he deceives himself; ⁴and let each one prove his own work, and then he will have the glorying in regard to himself alone, and not in regard to the other, ⁵for each one will bear his own burden. ⁶And let him who is instructed in the word share with him who is instructing in all good things. ⁷Do not be led astray: God is not mocked; for what a man may sow—that he will also reap, ⁸because he who is sowing to his own flesh, of the flesh will reap corruption; and he who is sowing to the Spirit, of the Spirit will reap continuous life; ⁹and in doing good we should not be weary, for at the proper time we will reap—not desponding; ¹⁰therefore, then, as we have opportunity, may we work the good to all, and especially to those of the household of faith. ¹¹You see in how large letters I have written to you with my own hand; ¹²as many as are willing to make a good appearance in the flesh, these constrain you to be circumcised—only that they may not be persecuted for the Cross of the Christ, ¹³for neither do those circumcised keep the Law themselves, but they wish you to be circumcised, that they may glory in your flesh. ¹⁴And for me, let it not be—to glory, except in the Cross of our Lord Jesus Christ, through which the world has been crucified to me, and I to the world; ¹⁵for in Christ Jesus neither circumcision avails anything, nor uncircumcision, but a new creation; ¹⁶and as many as walk by this rule—peace on them, and kindness, and on the Israel of God! ¹⁷From now on, let no one give me trouble, for I carry the scars of the Lord Jesus in my body. ¹⁸The grace of our Lord Jesus Christ [is] with your spirit, brothers! Amen.

EPHESIANS

CHAPTER 1

¹Paul, an apostle of Jesus Christ through the will of God, to the holy ones who are in Ephesus, and to the faithful in Christ Jesus: ²Grace to you and peace from God our Father and the Lord Jesus Christ! ³Blessed [is] the God and Father of our Lord Jesus Christ, who blessed us in every spiritual blessing in the heavenly [places] in Christ, ⁴according as He chose us in Him before the foundation of the world, for our being holy and unblemished before Him, in love, ⁵having foreordained us to the adoption of sons through Jesus Christ to Himself, according to the good pleasure of His will, ⁶to the praise of the glory of His grace, in which He made us accepted in the beloved, ⁷in whom we have the redemption through His blood, the forgiveness of the trespasses, according to the riches of His grace, ⁸in which He abounded toward us in all wisdom and prudence, ⁹having made known to us the secret of His will, according to His good pleasure, that He purposed in Himself, ¹⁰in regard to the dispensation of the fullness of the times, to bring into one the whole in the Christ, both the things in the heavens, and the things on the earth—in Him; ¹¹in whom also we obtained an inheritance, being foreordained according to the purpose of Him who is working all things according to the counsel of His will, ¹²for our being to the praise of His glory, [even] those who first hoped in the Christ, ¹³in whom you also, having heard the word of the truth—the good news of your salvation—in whom also having believed, you were sealed with the Holy Spirit of the promise, ¹⁴which is a deposit of our inheritance, to the redemption of the acquired possession, to the praise of His glory. ¹⁵Because of this I also, having heard of your faith in the Lord Jesus, and the love to all the holy ones, ¹⁶do not cease giving thanks for you, making mention of you in my prayers, ¹⁷that the God of our Lord Jesus Christ, the Father of the glory, may give to you a spirit of wisdom and revelation in the recognition of Him, ¹⁸the eyes of your understanding being enlightened, for your knowing what is the hope of His calling, and what the riches of the glory of His inheritance in the holy ones, ¹⁹and what the exceeding greatness of His power to us who are believing, according to the working of the power of His might, ²⁰which He worked in the Christ, having raised Him out of the dead, and sat [Him] at His right hand in the heavenly [places], ²¹far above all principality, and authority, and might, and lordship, and every name named, not only in this age, but also in the coming one; ²²and He put all things under His feet, and gave Him—head over all things to the Assembly, ²³which is His body, the fullness of Him who is filling all in all.

CHAPTER 2

¹Also you—being dead in trespasses and sins, ²in which you once walked according to the age of this world, according to the ruler of the authority of the air, of the spirit that is now working in the sons of disobedience, ³among whom we also all walked once in the desires of our flesh, doing the wishes of the flesh and of the thoughts, and were by nature children of wrath—as also the others, ⁴but God, being rich in kindness, because of His great love with which He loved us, ⁵even being dead in the trespasses, made us alive together with the Christ (by grace you are saved), ⁶and raised [us] up together, and sat [us] together in the heavenly [places] in Christ Jesus, ⁷that He might show, in the ages that are coming, the exceeding riches of His grace in kindness toward us in Christ Jesus, ⁸for by grace you are saved, through faith, and this [is] not of yourselves—[it is] the gift of God, ⁹not of works, that no one may boast; ¹⁰for we are His workmanship, created in Christ Jesus on good works, which God prepared before, that we may walk in them. ¹¹For this reason, remember, that you [were] once the nations in the flesh, who are called Uncircumcision by that called Circumcision in the flesh made by hands, ¹²that you were at that time apart from Christ, having been alienated from the commonwealth of Israel, and strangers to the covenants of the promise, having no hope, and without God in the world; ¹³but now, in Christ Jesus, you being once far off became near in the blood of the Christ, ¹⁴for He is our peace, who made both one, and broke down the middle wall of the partition of hostility, ¹⁵the enmity in His flesh, having done away [with] the Law of the commands in ordinances, that He might create the two into one new man in Himself, making peace, ¹⁶and might reconcile both in one body to God through the Cross, having slain the enmity by it, ¹⁷and having come, He proclaimed good news—peace to you—the far-off and the near, ¹⁸because through Him we have the access—we both—in one Spirit to the Father. ¹⁹Then, therefore, you are no longer strangers and foreigners, but fellow-citizens of the holy ones, and of the household of God, ²⁰being built on the foundation of the apostles and prophets, Jesus Christ Himself being chief corner-[stone], ²¹in whom all the building fitly framed together increases to a holy temple in the LORD, ²²in whom you also are built together, for a habitation of God in the Spirit.

CHAPTER 3

¹For this cause, I Paul, the prisoner of Christ Jesus for you the nations, ²if, indeed, you heard of the dispensation of the grace of God that was given to me in regard to you, ³that by revelation He made known to me the secret, according as I wrote before in few [words]— ⁴in regard to which you are able, reading [it], to understand my knowledge in the secret of the Christ, ⁵which in other generations was not made known to the sons of men, as it was now revealed to His holy apostles and prophets in the Spirit— ⁶that the nations are fellow-heirs, and of the same body, and partakers of His promise in the Christ, through the good news, ⁷of which I became a servant, according to the gift of the grace of God that was given to me, according to the working of His power; ⁸to me—the less than the least of all the holy ones—was given this grace, among the nations to proclaim good news—the untraceable riches of the Christ,

EPHESIANS

⁹and to cause all to see what [is] the fellowship of the secret that has been hid from the ages in God, who created all things by Jesus Christ, ¹⁰that there might be made known now to the principalities and the authorities in the heavenly [places], through the Assembly, the manifold wisdom of God, ¹¹according to a purpose of the ages, which He made in Christ Jesus our Lord, ¹²in whom we have the freedom and the access in confidence through the faith of Him, ¹³for this reason, I ask [you] not to faint in my tribulations for you, which is your glory. ¹⁴For this cause I bow my knees to the Father of our Lord Jesus Christ, ¹⁵of whom the whole family in the heavens and on earth is named, ¹⁶that He may give to you, according to the riches of His glory, to be strengthened through His Spirit with might, in regard to the inner man, ¹⁷that the Christ may dwell through the faith in your hearts, having been rooted and founded in love, ¹⁸that you may be in strength to comprehend, with all the holy ones, what [is] the breadth, and length, and depth, and height, ¹⁹to know also the love of the Christ that is exceeding the knowledge, that you may be filled—to all the fullness of God; ²⁰and to Him who is able to do exceedingly [and] abundantly above all things that we ask or think, according to the power that is working in us, ²¹to Him [is] the glory in the Assembly in Christ Jesus, to all the generations of the age of the ages. Amen.

CHAPTER 4

¹I, the prisoner of the LORD, then call on you to walk worthily of the calling with which you were called, ²with all lowliness and meekness, with long-suffering, bearing with one another in love, ³being diligent to keep the unity of the Spirit in the bond of peace; ⁴one body and one Spirit, according as you were also called in one hope of your calling; ⁵one Lord, one faith, one immersion, ⁶one God and Father of all, who [is] over all, and through all, and in you all, ⁷and to each one of you was given grace, according to the measure of the gift of Christ, ⁸for this reason, it says, "Having gone up on high He led captive captivity, and gave gifts to men." ⁹And that, He went up, what is it except that He also went down first into the lower parts of the earth? ¹⁰He who went down is the same who also went up far above all the heavens, that He may fill all things— ¹¹and He gave some [as] apostles, and some [as] prophets, and some [as] proclaimers of good news, and some [as] shepherds and teachers, ¹²to the perfecting of the holy ones, for a work of ministry, for a building up of the body of the Christ, ¹³until we may all come to the unity of faith and of the recognition of the Son of God, to a perfect man, to a measure of stature of the fullness of the Christ, ¹⁴that we may no longer be children, being tossed by waves and being carried around by every wind of the teaching, in the cunning of men, in craftiness, to the scheming of leading astray, ¹⁵and [speaking] truth in love, we may increase to Him [in] all things, who is the head—the Christ; ¹⁶from whom the whole body, being fitly joined together and united, through the supply of every joint, according to the working in the measure of each single part, the increase of the body makes for the building up of itself in love. ¹⁷This, then, I say, and I testify in the LORD: you are no longer to walk, as also the other nations walk, in the vanity of their mind, ¹⁸being darkened in the understanding, being alienated from the life of God, because of the ignorance that is in them, because of the hardness of their heart, ¹⁹who, having ceased to feel, gave themselves up to the licentiousness, for the working of all uncleanness in greediness; ²⁰and you did not so learn the Christ, ²¹if [it] so be [that] you heard Him, and were taught in Him, as truth is in Jesus; ²²concerning the former behavior you are to put off the old man, that is corrupt according to the desires of the deceit, ²³and to be renewed in the spirit of your mind, ²⁴and to put on the new man, which, according to God, was created in righteousness and kindness of the truth. ²⁵For this reason, putting away the lying, each speak truth with his neighbor, because we are members of one another; ²⁶be angry and do not sin; do not let the sun go down on your wrath, ²⁷neither give place to the Devil; ²⁸whoever is stealing let him no longer steal, but rather let him labor, working the thing that is good with the hands, that he may have to impart to him having need. ²⁹Let no corrupt word go forth out of your mouth, but what is good to the necessary building up, that it may give grace to the hearers; ³⁰and do not make the Holy Spirit of God sorrowful, in which you were sealed to [the] day of redemption. ³¹Let all bitterness, and wrath, and anger, and clamor, and slander, be put away from you, with all malice, ³²and become kind to one another, tender-hearted, forgiving one another, according as God also forgave you in Christ.

CHAPTER 5

¹Become, then, followers of God, as beloved children, ²and walk in love, as the Christ also loved us, and gave Himself for us, an offering and a sacrifice to God for an odor of a refreshing fragrance, ³and whoredom, and all uncleanness, or covetousness, do not let it even be named among you, as is proper to holy ones; ⁴also filthiness, and foolish talking, or jesting—the things not fit—but rather thanksgiving; ⁵for you know this, that every whoremonger, or unclean, or covetous person, who is an idolater, has no inheritance in the kingdom of the Christ and God. ⁶Let no one deceive you with vain words, for because of these things comes the anger of God on the sons of the disobedience; ⁷do not become, then, partakers with them, ⁸for you were once darkness, and now light in the LORD; walk as children of light, ⁹for the fruit of the light [is] in all goodness, and righteousness, and truth, ¹⁰proving what is well-pleasing to the LORD; ¹¹and have no fellowship with the unfruitful works of the darkness and rather even convict, ¹²for it is a shame even to speak of the things done by them in secret, ¹³and all the things reproved by the light are revealed, for everything that is revealed is light; ¹⁴for this reason it says, "Arouse yourself, you who are sleeping, and arise out of the dead, and the Christ will shine on you." ¹⁵See, then, how exactly you walk, not as unwise, but as wise, ¹⁶redeeming the time, because the days are evil; ¹⁷do not become fools because of this, but—understanding what [is] the will of the LORD, ¹⁸and do not be drunk with wine, in which is wastefulness, but be filled in the Spirit, ¹⁹speaking to yourselves in psalms and hymns and spiritual songs, singing and making melody in your heart to the LORD, ²⁰always giving thanks for all things, in the Name of our Lord Jesus Christ, to the God and Father, ²¹subjecting yourselves to one another in the fear of Christ. ²²The wives: [subject yourselves] to your own husbands, as to the LORD, ²³because the husband is head of the wife, as also the Christ [is] head of the Assembly, and He is Savior of the body, ²⁴but even as the Assembly is subject to Christ, so also [are] the wives [subject] to their own husbands in everything. ²⁵The husbands: love your own wives, as the Christ also loved the Assembly, and gave Himself for it, ²⁶that He might sanctify it, having cleansed [it] with the bathing of the water in the saying, ²⁷that He might present the Assembly to Himself in glory, having no spot or wrinkle, or any of such things, but that it may be holy and unblemished; ²⁸so ought the husbands to love their own wives as their own bodies: he who is loving his own wife—he loves himself; ²⁹for no one ever hated his own flesh, but nourishes and nurtures it, as also the LORD—the Assembly, ³⁰because we are members of His body, [[of His flesh, and of His bones.]] ³¹"For this cause will a man leave his father and mother, and will be joined to his wife, and the two will be into one flesh"; ³²this secret is great, and I speak in regard to Christ and to the Assembly; ³³but you also, everyone in particular—let each so love his own wife as himself, and the wife—that she may revere the husband.

CHAPTER 6

¹The children: obey your parents in the LORD, for this is right; ²honor your father and mother, ³which is the first command with a promise, "That it may be well with you, and you may live a long time on the land." ⁴And the fathers: do not provoke your children, but nourish them in the instruction and admonition of the LORD. ⁵The servants: obey the masters according to the flesh with fear and trembling, in the simplicity of your heart, as to the Christ; ⁶not with eye-service as men-pleasers, but as servants of the Christ, doing the will of God out of [your] soul, ⁷serving with goodwill, as to the LORD, and not to men, ⁸having known that whatever good thing each one may do, this he will receive from the LORD, whether servant or freeman. ⁹And the masters! Do the same things to them, letting threatening alone, having also known that your Master is in the heavens, and favor by appearance is not with Him. ¹⁰As to the rest, my brothers, be strong in the LORD, and in the power of His might; ¹¹put on the whole armor

of God, so you are able to stand against the schemes of the Devil, ¹²because our wrestling is not with flesh and blood, but with the principalities, with the authorities, with the world-rulers of the darkness of this age, with the spiritual [forces] of evil in the heavenly [places]; ¹³because of this take up the whole armor of God, that you may be able to resist in the day of the evil, and having done all things—to stand. ¹⁴Stand, therefore, having your loins girded around in truth, and having put on the breastplate of righteousness, ¹⁵and having the feet shod in the preparation of the good news of peace; ¹⁶in all, having taken up the shield of faith, in which you will be able to quench all the fiery darts of the evil one, ¹⁷and receive the helmet of the salvation, and the sword of the Spirit, which is the word of God, ¹⁸through all prayer and supplication praying at all times in the Spirit, and in this, watching in all perseverance and supplication for all the holy ones— ¹⁹and in behalf of me, that to me may be given a word in the opening of my mouth, in freedom, to make known the secret of the good news, ²⁰for which I am an ambassador in a chain, that in it I may speak freely—as it is necessary for me to speak. ²¹And that you may know—you also—the things concerning me—what I do, Tychicus will make all things known to you, the beloved brother and faithful servant in the LORD, ²²whom I sent to you for this very thing, that you might know the things concerning us, and that he might comfort your hearts. ²³Peace to the brothers, and love, with faith, from God the Father, and the Lord Jesus Christ! ²⁴The grace with all those loving our Lord Jesus Christ—undecayingly! Amen.

PHILIPPIANS

CHAPTER 1

¹Paul and Timotheus, servants of Jesus Christ, to all the holy ones in Christ Jesus who are in Philippi, with overseers and servants: ²Grace to you and peace from God our Father and the Lord Jesus Christ! ³I give thanks to my God on all the remembrance of you, ⁴always, in every supplication of mine for you all, with joy making the supplication, ⁵for your contribution to the good news from the first day until now, ⁶having been confident of this very thing, that He who began a good work in you, will complete [it] until [the] day of Jesus Christ, ⁷according as it is righteous for me to think this in behalf of you all, because of my having you in the heart, both in my bonds, and [in] the defense and confirmation of the good news, all of you being fellow-partakers with me of grace. ⁸For God is my witness, how I long for you all with [the] yearnings of Jesus Christ, ⁹and this I pray, that your love may abound yet more and more in full knowledge, and all discernment, ¹⁰for your proving the things that differ, that you may be pure and offenseless—to [the] Day of Christ, ¹¹being filled with the fruit of righteousness, that [is] through Jesus Christ, to the glory and praise of God. ¹²And I intend you to know, brothers, that the things concerning me, rather have come to an advancement of the good news, ¹³so that my bonds have become evident in Christ in the whole Praetorium, and to all the other places, ¹⁴and the greater part of the brothers in the LORD, having confidence by my bonds, are more abundantly bold to fearlessly speak the word. ¹⁵Certain, indeed, even through envy and contention, and certain also through goodwill, preach the Christ; ¹⁶one, indeed, of rivalry proclaims the Christ, not purely, supposing to add affliction to my bonds, ¹⁷and the other out of love, having known that I am set for defense of the good news: ¹⁸what then? In every way, whether in pretense or in truth, Christ is proclaimed—and I rejoice in this, indeed, and will rejoice. ¹⁹For I have known that this will turn out to me for salvation, through your supplication, and the supply of the Spirit of Christ Jesus, ²⁰according to my earnest expectation and hope, that I will be ashamed in nothing, and in all freedom, as always, also Christ will now be magnified in my body, whether through life or through death, ²¹for to me to live [is] Christ, and to die [is] gain. ²²And if to live in the flesh [is] to me a fruit of work, then what will I choose? I do not know; ²³for I am pressed by the two, having the desire to depart, and to be with Christ, for it is far better, ²⁴and to remain in the flesh is more necessary on your account, ²⁵and being persuaded of this, I have known that I will remain and continue with you all, to your advancement and joy of the faith, ²⁶that your boasting may abound in Christ Jesus in me through my coming again to you. ²⁷Only conduct yourselves worthily of the good news of the Christ, that, whether having come and seen you, whether being absent I may hear of the things concerning you, that you stand fast in one spirit, with one soul, striving together for the faith of the good news, ²⁸and not be terrified in anything by those opposing, which is indeed a token of destruction to them, and to you of salvation, and that from God; ²⁹because to you it was granted, on behalf of Christ, not only to believe in Him, but also to suffer on behalf of Him; ³⁰having the same conflict, such as you saw in me, and now hear of in me.

CHAPTER 2

¹If, then, any exhortation [is] in Christ, if any comfort of love, if any fellowship of [the] Spirit, if any yearnings and mercies, ²fulfill my joy, that you may mind the same thing—having the same love—of one soul—minding the one thing, ³nothing in rivalry or vainglory, but in humility of mind counting one another more excellent than yourselves— ⁴do not each look to your own, but each also to the things of others. ⁵For let this mind be in you that [is] also in Christ Jesus, ⁶who, being in the form of God, thought [it] not something to be seized to be equal to God, ⁷but emptied Himself, having taken the form of a servant, having been made in the likeness of men, ⁸and having been found in appearance as a man, He humbled Himself, having become obedient to death—even death of a cross, ⁹for this reason, also, God highly exalted Him, and gave to Him a Name that [is] above every name, ¹⁰that in the Name of Jesus every knee may bow—of heavenlies, and earthlies, and what are under the earth— ¹¹and every tongue may confess that Jesus Christ [is] LORD, to the glory of God the Father. ¹²So that, my beloved, as you always obey, not as in my presence only, but now much more in my absence, work out your own salvation with fear and trembling, ¹³for it is God who is working in you both to will and to work for His good pleasure. ¹⁴Do all things without murmurings and deliberations, ¹⁵that you may become blameless and pure children of God, unblemished in the midst of a crooked and perverse generation, among whom you appear as luminaries in the world, ¹⁶holding forth the word of life, for rejoicing to me in regard to [the] Day of Christ, that I did not run in vain, nor did I labor in vain; ¹⁷but if I also am poured forth on the sacrifice and service of your faith, I rejoice and am glad with you all, ¹⁸because of this you also rejoice and are glad with me. ¹⁹And I hope, in the Lord Jesus, to send Timotheus to you quickly, that I also may be of good spirit, having known the things concerning you, ²⁰for I have no one like-minded, who will sincerely care for the things concerning you, ²¹for the whole seek their own things, not the things of Christ Jesus, ²²and you know his proof, that as a child [serves] a father, he served with me in regard to the good news; ²³I indeed hope to send him, when I may see through the things concerning me—immediately; ²⁴and I trust in the LORD that I will also come quickly myself. ²⁵And I thought [it] necessary to send to you Epaphroditus—my brother and fellow-workman and fellow-soldier, and your apostle and servant to my need, ²⁶seeing he was longing after you all, and in heaviness, because you heard that he ailed, ²⁷for he also ailed near to death, but God dealt kindly with him, and not with him only, but also with me, that I might not have sorrow on sorrow. ²⁸The more eagerly, therefore, I sent him, that having seen him again you may

PHILIPPIANS

rejoice, and I may be less sorrowful; ²⁹receive him, therefore, in the LORD, with all joy, and hold such in honor, ³⁰because on account of the work of the Christ he drew near to death, having hazarded life that he might fill up your deficiency of service to me.

CHAPTER 3

¹As to the rest, my brothers, rejoice in the LORD; indeed, [it] is not tiresome to me to write to you the same things, and for you [is] sure. ²Look out for the dogs! Look out for the evil-workers! Look out for the mutilation! ³For we are the circumcision, who are serving God by the Spirit, and glorying in Christ Jesus, and having no trust in flesh, ⁴though I also have [cause of] trust in flesh. If any other one thinks to have trust in flesh, I more: ⁵circumcision on the eighth day! Of the race of Israel! Of the tribe of Benjamin! A Hebrew of Hebrews! According to law—a Pharisee! ⁶According to zeal—persecuting the Assembly! According to righteousness that is in law—becoming blameless! ⁷But what things were gains to me, these I have counted loss, because of the Christ; ⁸yes, indeed, and I count all things to be loss, because of the excellence of the knowledge of Christ Jesus my Lord, because of whom I suffered loss of all things, and count them to be refuse, that I may gain Christ, and be found in Him, ⁹not having my righteousness, which [is] of law, but that which [is] through faith from Christ—the righteousness that is of God by faith, ¹⁰to know Him, and the power of His resurrection, and the fellowship of His sufferings, being conformed to His death, ¹¹if anyhow I may attain to the resurrection of the dead. ¹²Not that I already obtained, or have already been perfected, but I pursue, if I also may lay hold of that for which I was also laid hold of by Christ Jesus; ¹³brothers, I do not reckon myself to have laid hold [of it], but one thing [I do]—indeed forgetting the things behind, and stretching forth to the things before— ¹⁴I pursue to the mark for the prize of the high calling of God in Christ Jesus. ¹⁵As many, therefore, as [are] perfect—let us think this, and if [in] anything you think otherwise, this also will God reveal to you, ¹⁶but to what we have attained—walk by the same rule, think the same thing; ¹⁷together become my followers, brothers, and observe those thus walking, according as you have us—a pattern; ¹⁸for many walk of whom I told you [about] many times—and now also weeping tell—[they are] the enemies of the Cross of the Christ, ¹⁹whose end [is] destruction, whose god [is] the belly, and whose glory [is] in their shame, who are minding the things on earth. ²⁰For our citizenship is in the heavens, from where we also await a Savior—the Lord Jesus Christ— ²¹who will transform the body of our humiliation to its becoming conformed to the body of His glory, according to the working of His power, even to subject all things to Himself.

CHAPTER 4

¹So then, my brothers, beloved and longed for, my joy and garland, so stand in the LORD, beloved. ²I exhort Euodia, and I exhort Syntyche, to be of the same mind in the LORD; ³and I also ask you, genuine yoke-fellow, be assisting those women who strove along with me in the good news, with Clement also, and the others, my fellow-workers, whose names [are] in [the] Scroll of Life. ⁴Rejoice in the LORD always; again I will say, rejoice! ⁵Let your reasonableness be known to all men; the LORD [is] near; ⁶be anxious for nothing, but in everything by prayer, and by supplication, with thanksgiving, let your requests be made known to God; ⁷and the peace of God, that is surpassing all understanding, will guard your hearts and your thoughts in Christ Jesus. ⁸As to the rest, brothers, as many things as are true, as many as [are] revered, as many as [are] righteous, as many as [are] pure, as many as [are] lovely, as many as [are] of good report, if any worthiness, and if any praise, think on these things; ⁹the things that you also learned, and receive, and hear, and saw in me, do those, and the God of peace will be with you. ¹⁰And I rejoiced in the LORD greatly, that now at length you flourished again in caring for me, for which also you were caring, and lacked opportunity; ¹¹I do not say that in respect of want, for I learned in the things in which I am—to be content; ¹²I have known both to be abased, and I have known to abound; in everything and in all things I have been initiated, both to be full and to be hungry, both to abound and to be in want. ¹³I have strength for all things, in Christ's strengthening me; ¹⁴but you did well, having shared in my tribulation; ¹⁵and you have known, even you Philippians, that in the beginning of the good news when I went forth from Macedonia, no assembly communicated with me in regard to giving and receiving except you only; ¹⁶because in Thessalonica also, both once and again you sent to my need; ¹⁷not that I seek after the gift, but I seek after the fruit that is overflowing to your account; ¹⁸and I have all things, and abound; I am filled, having received from Epaphroditus the things from you—an odor of a refreshing fragrance—a sacrifice acceptable, well-pleasing to God: ¹⁹and my God will supply all your need, according to His riches in glory in Christ Jesus; ²⁰and to God, even our Father, [is] the glory through the ages of the ages. Amen. ²¹Every holy one in Christ Jesus greets you; the brothers with me greet you; ²²all the holy ones greet you, and especially those of Caesar's house. ²³The grace of our Lord Jesus Christ [is] with you all! Amen.

COLOSSIANS

CHAPTER 1

¹Paul, an apostle of Jesus Christ through the will of God, and Timotheus the brother, ²to the holy ones in Colossae, and to the faithful brothers in Christ: Grace to you and peace from God our Father and the Lord Jesus Christ! ³We give thanks to the God and Father of our Lord Jesus Christ, always praying for you, ⁴having heard of your faith in Christ Jesus, and of the love that [is] to all the holy ones, ⁵because of the hope that is laid up for you in the heavens, which you heard of beforehand by the word of the truth of the good news, ⁶which has come to you, as also in all the world, and is bearing fruit, as also in you, from the day in which you heard, and knew the grace of God in truth, ⁷as you also learned from Epaphras, our beloved fellow-servant, who is a faithful servant of the Christ for you, ⁸who also declared to us your love in the Spirit. ⁹Because of this, we also, from the day in which we heard, do not cease praying for you, and asking that you may be filled with the full knowledge of His will in all wisdom and spiritual understanding, ¹⁰to walk worthily of the LORD, pleasing in all, being fruitful in every good work, and increasing in the knowledge of God, ¹¹in all might being made mighty according to the power of His glory, to all endurance and long-suffering with joy. ¹²Giving thanks to the Father who has qualified us for the participation of the inheritance of the holy ones in the light, ¹³who rescued us out of the authority of the darkness, and translated [us] into the kingdom of the Son of His love, ¹⁴in whom we have the redemption [[through His blood]], the forgiveness of sins, ¹⁵who is the image of the invisible God, firstborn of all creation, ¹⁶because all things were created in Him, those in the heavens, and those on the earth, those visible, and those invisible, whether thrones, whether lordships, whether principalities, whether authorities; all things have been created through Him and for Him, ¹⁷and He is before all, and all things have consisted in Him. ¹⁸And He is the head of the body—the Assembly—who is a beginning, a firstborn out of the dead, that He might become first in all [things] Himself, ¹⁹because all the fullness was pleased to dwell in Him, ²⁰and through Him to reconcile all things to Himself—having made peace through the blood of His Cross—through Him, whether the things on the earth, whether the things in the heavens. ²¹And you—once being alienated, and enemies in the mind, in the evil works, yet now He reconciled, ²²in the body of His flesh through death, to present you holy, and unblemished, and unblameable before Himself, ²³if you also remain in the faith, being founded and settled, and not moved away from the hope of the good news, which you heard, which was

preached in all the creation that [is] under Heaven, of which I, Paul, became a servant. ²⁴I now rejoice in my sufferings for you, and fill up the things lacking of the tribulations of the Christ in my flesh for His body, which is the Assembly, ²⁵of which I became a servant according to the dispensation of God, that was given to me for you, to fulfill the word of God, ²⁶the secret that has been hid from the ages and from the generations, but now was revealed to His holy ones, ²⁷to whom God willed to make known what [is] the riches of the glory of this secret among the nations—which is Christ in you, the hope of the glory, ²⁸whom we proclaim, warning every man, and teaching every man, in all wisdom, that we may present every man perfect in Christ Jesus, ²⁹for which I also labor, striving according to His working that is working in me in power.

CHAPTER 2

¹For I wish you to know how great a conflict I have for you and those in Laodicea, and as many as have not seen my face in the flesh, ²that their hearts may be comforted, being united in love, and to all riches of the full assurance of the understanding, to the full knowledge of the secret of the God and Father, and of the Christ, ³in whom are all the treasures of the wisdom and the knowledge hid, ⁴and this I say, that no one may deceive you with enticing words, ⁵for if even in the flesh I am absent—yet in the spirit I am with you, rejoicing and beholding your order, and the steadfastness of your faith in regard to Christ; ⁶as, then, you received Christ Jesus the LORD, walk in Him, ⁷being rooted and built up in Him, and confirmed in the faith, as you were taught—abounding in it in thanksgiving. ⁸See that no one will be carrying you away as spoil through philosophy and vain deceit, according to the tradition of men, according to the rudiments of the world, and not according to Christ, ⁹because in Him dwells all the fullness of the Godhead bodily, ¹⁰and you are made full in Him, who is the head of all principality and authority, ¹¹in whom you also were circumcised with a circumcision not made with hands, in the putting off of the body of sins of the flesh by the circumcision of the Christ, ¹²being buried with Him in the immersion, in which you also rose with [Him] through the faith of the working of God, who raised Him out of the dead. ¹³And you—being dead in the trespasses and the uncircumcision of your flesh—He made alive together with Him, having forgiven you all the trespasses, ¹⁴having blotted out the handwriting in the ordinances that is against us, that was contrary to us, and He has taken it out of the way, having nailed it to the Cross; ¹⁵having stripped the principalities and the authorities, He made a show of them openly—having triumphed over them by it. ¹⁶Let no one, then, judge you in eating or in drinking, or in respect of a celebration, or of a new moon, or of Sabbaths, ¹⁷which are a shadow of the coming things, but the body [is] of the Christ; ¹⁸let no one deceive you of your prize, delighting in humble-mindedness and [in] worship of the messengers, intruding into the things he has not seen, being vainly puffed up by the mind of his flesh, ¹⁹and not holding the Head, from which all the body—gathering supply through the joints and bands, and being knit together—may increase with the increase of God. ²⁰If, then, you died with the Christ from the rudiments of the world, why, as living in the world, are you subject to ordinances—²¹you may not touch, nor taste, nor handle—²²which are all for destruction with the using, after the commands and teachings of men, ²³which are, indeed, having a matter of wisdom in self-willed religion, and humble-mindedness, and neglecting of body—not of any value to satisfying the flesh.

CHAPTER 3

¹If, then, you were raised with the Christ, seek the things above, where the Christ is, seated on the right hand of God; ²mind the things above, not the things on the earth, ³for you died, and your life has been hid with the Christ in God; ⁴when the Christ—our life—may have appeared, then we will also appear with Him in glory. ⁵Put to death, then, your members that [are] on the earth—whoredom, uncleanness, passion, evil desire, and the covetousness, which is idolatry— ⁶because of which things comes the anger of God on the sons of the disobedience, ⁷in which you also—you once walked, when you lived in them; ⁸but now put off, even you, the whole—anger, wrath, malice, slander, filthy talking—out of your mouth. ⁹Do not lie to one another, having put off the old man with his practices, ¹⁰and having put on the new, which is renewed in regard to knowledge, after the image of Him who created him, ¹¹where there is not Greek and Jew, circumcision and uncircumcision, foreigner, Scythian, servant, freeman, but Christ [is] all and in all. ¹²Put on, therefore, as chosen ones of God, holy and beloved, yearnings of mercies, kindness, humble-mindedness, meekness, long-suffering, ¹³bearing with one another, and forgiving each other, if anyone may have a quarrel with anyone, as the Christ also forgave you—so also you; ¹⁴and above all these things, [have] love, which is a bond of the perfection, ¹⁵and let the peace of God rule in your hearts, to which you were also called in one body, and become thankful. ¹⁶Let the word of Christ dwell in you richly, in all wisdom, teaching and admonishing each other, in psalms, and hymns, and spiritual songs, in grace singing in your hearts to the LORD; ¹⁷and all, whatever you may do in word or in work, [do] all things in the Name of the Lord Jesus—giving thanks to the God and Father, through Him. ¹⁸The wives: be subject to your own husbands, as is fit in the LORD; ¹⁹the husbands: love your wives, and do not be bitter with them; ²⁰the children: obey the parents in all things, for this is well-pleasing to the LORD; ²¹the fathers: do not distress your children, lest they be discouraged; ²²the servants: obey those who are masters in all things according to the flesh, not in eye-service as men-pleasers, but in simplicity of heart, fearing God; ²³and all, whatever you may do—out of soul work—as to the LORD, and not to men, ²⁴having known that you will receive the repayment of the inheritance from the LORD—for you serve the LORD Christ; ²⁵and he who is doing unrighteously will receive what he did unrighteously, and there is no favor by appearance.

CHAPTER 4

¹The masters: give that which is righteous and equal to the servants, having known that you also have a Master in the heavens. ²Continue in the prayer, watching in it in thanksgiving, ³also praying for us at the same time, that God may open to us a door for the word, to speak the secret of the Christ, because of which I have also been bound, ⁴that I may reveal it, as it is necessary for me to speak. ⁵Walk in wisdom toward those outside, redeeming the time, ⁶your word always being seasoned with salt in grace—to know how it is necessary for you to answer each one. ⁷Tychicus will make known to you all the things concerning me—the beloved brother, and faithful servant, and fellow-servant in the LORD— ⁸whom I sent to you for this very thing, that he might know the things concerning you, and might comfort your hearts, ⁹with Onesimus the faithful and beloved brother, who is of you; they will make known to you all things that [are] here. ¹⁰Aristarchus greets you, my fellow-captive, and Marcus, the nephew of Barnabas (concerning whom you received commands—if he may come to you, receive him), ¹¹and Jesus who is called Justus, who are of circumcision: these [are the] only fellow-workers for the Kingdom of God who become a comfort to me. ¹²Epaphras greets you, who [is] of you, a servant of Christ, always striving for you in the prayers, that you may stand perfect and made full in all the will of God, ¹³for I testify to him that he has much zeal for you, and those in Laodicea, and those in Hierapolis. ¹⁴Lucas greets you, the beloved physician, and Demas; ¹⁵those in Laodicea greet you—brothers, and Nymphas, and the assembly in his house; ¹⁶and when the letter may be read with you, cause that it may also be read in the assembly of the Laodiceans, and the [letter] from Laodicea that you also may read; ¹⁷and say to Archippus, "See to the ministry that you received in the LORD, that you may fulfill it." ¹⁸The salutation [is] by my hand, Paul. Remember my bonds. The grace [is] with you! Amen.

1 THESSALONIANS

CHAPTER 1

¹Paul, and Silvanus, and Timotheus, to the assembly of Thessalonians in God the Father and the Lord Jesus Christ: Grace to you and peace from God our Father and the Lord Jesus Christ! ²We always give thanks to God for you all, making mention of you in our prayers, ³unceasingly remembering your work of faith, and the labor of the love, and the endurance of the hope, of our Lord Jesus Christ, in the presence of our God and Father, ⁴having known, beloved brothers, by God, your [divine] selection, ⁵because our good news did not come to you in word only, but also in power, and in the Holy Spirit, and in much assurance, even as you have known of what sort we became among you for your sake, ⁶and you became imitators of us and of the LORD, having received the word in much tribulation with joy of the Holy Spirit, ⁷so that you became patterns to all those believing in Macedonia and Achaia, ⁸for from you has sounded forth the word of the LORD, not only in Macedonia and Achaia, but also in every place your faith toward God went forth, so that we have no need to say anything, ⁹for they themselves declare concerning us what entrance we had to you, and how you turned to God from the idols, to serve a living and true God, ¹⁰and to wait for His Son from the heavens, whom He raised out of the dead—Jesus, who is rescuing us from the anger that is coming.

CHAPTER 2

¹For you have known, brothers, that our entrance to you has not been in vain, ²but having both suffered before, and having been mistreated (as you have known) in Philippi, we were bold in our God to speak to you the good news of God in much conflict, ³for our exhortation [is] not out of deceit, nor out of uncleanness, nor in guile, ⁴but as we have been approved by God to be entrusted with the good news, so we speak, not as pleasing men, but God, who is proving our hearts, ⁵for at no time did we come with speech of flattery (as you have known), nor in a pretext for covetousness (God [is] witness), ⁶nor seeking glory from men, neither from you nor from others, being able to be burdensome, as Christ's apostles. ⁷But we became gentle in your midst, as a nurse may nurture her own children, ⁸so being desirous of you, we are well-pleased to impart to you not only the good news of God, but also our own souls, because you have become beloved to us, ⁹for you remember, brothers, our labor and travail, for working night and day not to be a burden on any of you, we preached the good news of God to you; ¹⁰you [are] witnesses—God also—how piously and righteously and blamelessly we became to you who believe, ¹¹even as you have known how we are exhorting each one of you, as a father his own children, and comforting, and testifying, ¹²for your walking worthily of God, who is calling you to His own kingdom and glory. ¹³And because of this we also continually give thanks to God, that, having received the word of God [by] your hearing from us, you accepted, not the word of men, but as it truly is, the word of God, who also works in you who believe; ¹⁴for you became imitators, brothers, of the assemblies of God that are in Judea in Christ Jesus, because you suffered such things, even you, from your own countrymen, as they also from the Jews, ¹⁵who put to death both the Lord Jesus and their own prophets, and persecuted us, and they are not pleasing God, and [are] contrary to all men, ¹⁶forbidding us to speak to the nations that they might be saved, so as to always fill up their sins, but [God's] anger came on them—to the end! ¹⁷And we, brothers, having been taken from you for the space of an hour—in presence, not in heart—hurried more abundantly to see your face in much desire; ¹⁸for this reason we wished to come to you (I, indeed, Paul), both once and again, and Satan hindered us; ¹⁹for what [is] our hope, or joy, or garland of rejoicing? Are not even you before our Lord Jesus Christ at His coming? ²⁰For you are our glory and joy.

CHAPTER 3

¹For this reason, enduring no longer, we thought good to be left in Athens alone, ²and sent Timotheus—our brother, and a servant of God, and our fellow-workman in the good news of the Christ—to establish you, and to comfort you concerning your faith, ³that no one be moved in these tribulations, for you have known that we are set for this, ⁴for even when we were with you, we said to you beforehand that we are about to suffer tribulation, as it also came to pass, and you have known [it]; ⁵because of this also, I, no longer enduring, sent to know your faith, lest he who is tempting tempted you, and our labor might be in vain. ⁶And Timotheus now having come to us from you, and having declared good news to us of your faith and love, and that you always have a good remembrance of us, desiring much to see us, as we also [to see] you, ⁷because of this we were comforted, brothers, over you, in all our tribulation and necessity, through your faith, ⁸because now we live, if you may stand fast in the LORD. ⁹For what thanks are we able to repay to God for you, for all the joy with which we delight because of you in the presence of our God, ¹⁰exceedingly imploring night and day, that we might see your face, and perfect the things lacking in your faith? ¹¹And our God and Father Himself, and our Lord Jesus Christ, direct our way to you, ¹²and the LORD cause you to increase and to abound in the love to one another, and to all, even as we also to you, ¹³in order to have established your hearts, blameless in sanctification before our God and Father, at the coming of our Lord Jesus Christ with all His holy ones.

CHAPTER 4

¹As to the rest, then, brothers, we request, and call on you in the Lord Jesus, as you received from us how it is necessary for you to walk and to please God, that you may abound the more, ²for you have known what commands we gave you through the Lord Jesus; ³for this is the will of God—your sanctification: that you abstain from the whoredom, ⁴that each of you know to possess his own vessel in sanctification and honor, ⁵not in the affection of desire, as also the nations that were not knowing God, ⁶that no one goes beyond and defrauds his brother in the matter, because the LORD [is] an avenger of all these, as we also spoke to you before and testified, ⁷for God did not call us to uncleanness, but in sanctification. ⁸He, therefore, who is despising, does not despise man, but God, who also gave His Holy Spirit to us. ⁹And concerning the brotherly love, you have no need of [my] writing to you, for you yourselves are God-taught to love one another, ¹⁰for you do it also to all the brothers who [are] in all Macedonia; and we call on you, brothers, to abound still more, ¹¹and to study to be quiet, and to do your own business, and to work with your own hands, as we commanded you, ¹²that you may walk properly to those outside, and may have lack of nothing. ¹³And I do not wish you to be ignorant, brothers, concerning those who have fallen asleep, that you may not sorrow, as also the rest who have no hope, ¹⁴for if we believe that Jesus died and rose again, so also God will bring with Him those asleep through Jesus, ¹⁵for we say this to you in the word of the LORD, that we who are living—who remain over to the coming of the LORD—may not precede those asleep, ¹⁶because the LORD Himself, with a shout, with the voice of a chief-messenger, and with the trumpet of God, will come down from Heaven, and the dead in Christ will rise first; ¹⁷then we who are living, who are remaining over, will be snatched up together with them in [the] clouds to meet the LORD in [the] air, and so we will always be with the LORD; ¹⁸so, then, comfort one another with these words.

CHAPTER 5

¹And concerning the times and the seasons, brothers, you have no need of my writing to you, ²for you have thoroughly known that the Day of the LORD so comes as a thief in the night, ³for when they may say, "Peace and security,"

then sudden destruction comes [on] them, as the travail [on] her who is with child, and they will not escape; ⁴but you, brothers, are not in darkness, that the Day may catch you as a thief; ⁵you are all sons of light, and sons of day; we are not of night, nor of darkness, ⁶so, then, we may not sleep as also the others, but watch and be sober, ⁷for those sleeping, sleep by night, and those making themselves drunk, are drunken by night, ⁸and we, being of the day—let us be sober, putting on a breastplate of faith and love, and a helmet—a hope of salvation, ⁹because God did not appoint us to anger, but to the acquiring of salvation through our Lord Jesus Christ, ¹⁰who died for us, that whether we wake—whether we sleep—we may live together with Him; ¹¹for this reason, comfort one another, and build up one another, as also you do. ¹²And we ask you, brothers, to know those laboring among you and leading you in the LORD and admonishing you, ¹³and to esteem them very abundantly in love, because of their work; be at peace among yourselves, ¹⁴and we exhort you, brothers, admonish the disorderly, comfort the feeble-minded, support the weak, be patient to all; ¹⁵see [that] no one may render evil for evil to anyone, but always pursue that which is good, both to one another and to all; ¹⁶always rejoice; ¹⁷continually pray; ¹⁸give thanks in everything, for this [is] the will of God in Christ Jesus in regard to you. ¹⁹Do not quench the Spirit; ²⁰do not despise prophesyings; ²¹prove all things; hold fast [to] that which is good; ²²abstain from all appearance of evil; ²³and may the God of peace Himself sanctify you wholly, and may your whole spirit and soul and body be preserved, unblameably at the coming of our Lord Jesus Christ; ²⁴He who is calling you is steadfast, who also will do [it]. ²⁵Brothers, pray for us. ²⁶Greet all the brothers with a holy kiss. ²⁷I charge you [by] the LORD, that the letter be read to all the holy brothers. ²⁸The grace of our Lord Jesus Christ [is] with you! Amen.

2 THESSALONIANS

CHAPTER 1

¹Paul, and Silvanus, and Timotheus, to the assembly of Thessalonians in God our Father, and the Lord Jesus Christ: ²Grace to you and peace from God our Father and the Lord Jesus Christ! ³We always ought to give thanks to God for you, brothers, as it is fitting, because your faith increases greatly, and the love of each one of you all abounds to one another, ⁴so that we ourselves glory in you in the assemblies of God, for your endurance and faith in all your persecutions and tribulations that you bear— ⁵a token of the righteous judgment of God, for your being counted worthy of the Kingdom of God, for which you also suffer, ⁶since [it is] a righteous thing with God to give back to those troubling you—tribulation, ⁷and to you who are troubled—rest with us in the revelation of the Lord Jesus from Heaven, with messengers of His power, ⁸in flaming fire, giving vengeance to those not knowing God, and to those not obeying the good news of our Lord Jesus Christ, ⁹who will suffer justice—continuous destruction—from the face of the LORD, and from the glory of His strength, ¹⁰when He may come to be glorified in His holy ones, and to be wondered at by all those believing—because our testimony was believed among you—in that day; ¹¹for which we also always pray for you, that our God may count you worthy of the calling, and may fulfill all the good pleasure of goodness, and the work of faith in power, ¹²that the Name of our Lord Jesus Christ may be glorified in you, and you in Him, according to the grace of our God and Lord Jesus Christ.

CHAPTER 2

¹And we ask you, brothers, in regard to the coming of our Lord Jesus Christ, and of our gathering together to Him, ²that you are not quickly shaken in mind, nor be troubled, neither through spirit, neither through word, neither through letters as through us, as that the Day of the LORD has arrived; ³do not let anyone deceive you in any way, because if the departure may not come first, the man of lawlessness may [not] be revealed—the son of destruction, ⁴who is opposing and is raising himself up above all called god or worshiped, so as for him to have sat down in the temple of God, proclaiming that he is God. ⁵Do you not remember that, yet being with you, I said these things to you? ⁶And now, you have known what is restraining, for his being revealed in his own time, ⁷for the secret of lawlessness already works, only the [One] now restraining [will do so] until He may come out of [the] midst, ⁸and then the lawless one will be revealed, whom the LORD will consume with the Spirit of His mouth, and will nullify at the appearance of His coming, ⁹whose coming is according to the working of Satan, in all power, and signs, and lying wonders, ¹⁰and in all deceitfulness of the unrighteousness in those perishing, because they did not receive the love of the truth for their being saved, ¹¹and because of this God will send to them a working of delusion, for their believing the lie, ¹²that they may be judged—all who did not believe the truth, but were well pleased in the unrighteousness. ¹³And we ought to give thanks to God always for you, brothers, beloved by the LORD, that God chose you from the beginning to salvation, in sanctification of the Spirit, and belief of the truth, ¹⁴to which He called you through our good news, to the acquiring of the glory of our Lord Jesus Christ; ¹⁵so, then, brothers, stand fast, and hold the traditions that you were taught, whether through word, whether through our letter; ¹⁶and may our Lord Jesus Christ Himself, and our God and Father, who loved us, and gave continuous comfort, and good hope in grace, ¹⁷comfort your hearts, and establish you in every good word and work.

CHAPTER 3

¹As to the rest, pray, brothers, concerning us, that the word of the LORD may run and may be glorified, as also with you, ²and that we may be delivered from the unreasonable and evil men, for not all [are] of the faith; ³but faithful is the LORD who will establish you, and will guard [you] from the evil [one]; ⁴and we now have confidence in the LORD, that which we command you both do and will do; ⁵and the LORD direct your hearts to the love of God, and to the endurance of the Christ. ⁶And we command you, brothers, in the Name of our Lord Jesus Christ, to withdraw yourselves from every brother walking disorderly, and not after the tradition that you received from us, ⁷for you have known how it is necessary to imitate us, because we did not act disorderly among you; ⁸nor did we eat bread of anyone for nothing, but in labor and in travail, working night and day, not to be chargeable to any of you; ⁹not because we have no authority, but that we might give ourselves to you [as] a pattern, to imitate us; ¹⁰for even when we were with you, this we commanded you, that if anyone is not willing to work, neither let him eat, ¹¹for we hear of some walking disorderly among you, working nothing, but being busybodies, ¹²and such we command and exhort through our Lord Jesus Christ, that working with quietness, they may eat their own bread; ¹³and you, brothers, may you not be weary doing well, ¹⁴and if anyone does not obey our word through the letter, note this one, and have no company with him, that he may be ashamed, ¹⁵and do not count as an enemy, but admonish as a brother; ¹⁶and may the LORD of peace Himself always give to you peace in every way; the LORD [is] with you all! ¹⁷The salutation by the hand of me, Paul, which is a sign in every letter; thus I write. ¹⁸The grace of our Lord Jesus Christ [is] with you all! Amen.

1 TIMOTHY

CHAPTER 1

¹Paul, an apostle of Jesus Christ, according to a command of God our Savior, and of the Lord Jesus Christ our hope, ²to Timotheus—genuine child in faith: Grace, kindness, peace, from God our Father and Christ Jesus our Lord! ³According as I exhorted you to remain in Ephesus—I going on to Macedonia—that you might charge certain [ones] not to teach any other thing, ⁴nor to give heed to fables and endless genealogies, that cause questions rather than [the] stewardship of God which [is] in faith. ⁵And the end of the charge is love out of a pure heart, and of a good conscience, and of unhypocritical faith, ⁶from which certain [men], having swerved, turned aside to vain discourse, ⁷willing to be teachers of law, not understanding either the things they say, nor concerning what they confidently assert, ⁸and we have known that the Law [is] good, if anyone may use it lawfully; ⁹having known this, that law is not set for a righteous man, but for lawless and insubordinate persons, ungodly and sinners, impious and profane, murderers of fathers and murderers of mothers, manslayers, ¹⁰whoremongers, homosexuals, enslavers, liars, perjured persons, and if there be any other thing that is adverse to sound doctrine, ¹¹according to the good news of the glory of the blessed God, with which I was entrusted. ¹²And I give thanks to Him who enabled me—Christ Jesus our Lord—that He reckoned me steadfast, having put [me] to the ministry, ¹³who before was speaking slander, and persecuting, and insulting, but I found kindness, because, being ignorant, I did [it] in unbelief, ¹⁴and the grace of our Lord exceedingly abounded, with faith and love that [is] in Christ Jesus. ¹⁵The word [is] steadfast, and worthy of all acceptance, that Christ Jesus came into the world to save sinners—of whom I am first; ¹⁶but because of this I found kindness, that Jesus Christ might first show forth all long-suffering in me, for a pattern of those about to believe on Him to continuous life. ¹⁷And to the King of the ages, the incorruptible, invisible, only wise God, [is] honor and glory through the ages of the ages! Amen. ¹⁸I commit to you this charge, child Timotheus, according to the prophecies that went before on you, that you may war in them the good warfare, ¹⁹having faith and a good conscience, which some having thrust away, made shipwreck concerning the faith, ²⁰of whom are Hymenaeus and Alexander, whom I delivered to Satan, that they might be instructed not to speak evil.

CHAPTER 2

¹I exhort, then, first of all, there be made supplications, prayers, intercessions, thanksgivings, for all men— ²for kings, and all who are in authority, that we may lead a quiet and peaceable life in all piety and gravity, ³for this [is] right and acceptable before God our Savior, ⁴who wills all men to be saved, and to come to the full knowledge of the truth; ⁵for [there is] one God, also one mediator of God and of men—the man Christ Jesus, ⁶who gave Himself [as] a ransom for all—the testimony in its own times— ⁷in regard to which I was set a preacher and apostle—truth I say in Christ, I do not lie—a teacher of nations, in faith and truth. ⁸I intend, therefore, that men pray in every place, lifting up holy hands, apart from anger and deliberation; ⁹also the women in like manner, in orderly apparel, to adorn themselves with modesty and sobriety, not in braided hair, or gold, or pearls, or clothing of great price, ¹⁰but—which becomes women professing godly piety—through good works. ¹¹Let a woman learn in quietness in all subjection, ¹²and I do not allow a woman to teach, nor to rule a husband, but to be in quietness, ¹³for Adam was formed first, then Eve, ¹⁴and Adam was not deceived, but the woman, having been deceived, came into transgression, ¹⁵and she will be saved through the childbearing, if they remain in faith, and love, and sanctification, with sobriety.

CHAPTER 3

¹The word [is] steadfast: If anyone longs for overseership, he desires a right work; ²it is required, therefore, the overseer to be blameless, a husband of one wife, vigilant, sober, respectable, a friend of strangers, apt to teach, ³not given to wine, not a striker, but gentle, not contentious, not a lover of money, ⁴leading his own house well, having children in subjection with all dignity, ⁵(and if anyone has not known [how] to lead his own house, how will he take care of an assembly of God?) ⁶not a new convert, lest having been puffed up he may fall to a judgment of the Devil; ⁷and it is required of him also to have a good testimony from those outside, that he may not fall into reproach and a snare of the Devil. ⁸Servants, in like manner, dignified, not double-tongued, not given to much wine, not given to shameful gain, ⁹having the secret of the faith in a pure conscience, ¹⁰and let these also first be proved, then let them minister, being unblameable. ¹¹Women, in like manner, dignified, not false accusers, vigilant, faithful in all things. ¹²Servants—let them be husbands of one wife, leading the children well, and their own houses, ¹³for those who ministered well acquire a good step to themselves, and much boldness in faith that [is] in Christ Jesus. ¹⁴I write to you these things, hoping to come to you soon, ¹⁵and if I delay, that you may know how it is required to conduct yourself in the house of God, which is an assembly of the living God—a pillar and foundation of the truth, ¹⁶and confessedly, great is the secret of piety: who was revealed in flesh, declared righteous in [the] Spirit, seen by messengers, preached among nations, believed on in the world, taken up in glory!

CHAPTER 4

¹And the Spirit expressly says that in latter times some will depart from the faith, giving heed to seducing spirits and teachings of demons, ²speaking lies in hypocrisy, being seared in their own conscience, ³forbidding to marry—to abstain from meats that God created to be received with thanksgiving by those believing and acknowledging the truth, ⁴because every creature of God [is] good, and nothing [is] to be rejected, with thanksgiving being received, ⁵for it is sanctified through the word of God and intercession. ⁶Placing these things before the brothers, you will be a good servant of Jesus Christ, being nourished by the words of the faith, and of the good teaching, which you followed after, ⁷but reject the profane and old women's fables, and exercise yourself to piety, ⁸for bodily exercise is to little profit, but piety is profitable to all things, having promise of the life that now is, and of that which is coming; ⁹the word [is] steadfast, and worthy of all acceptance; ¹⁰for this we both labor and are reproached, because we hope on the living God, who is Savior of all men—especially of those believing. ¹¹Charge these things, and teach; ¹²let no one despise your youth, but become a pattern of those believing in word, in behavior, in love, in spirit, in faith, in purity; ¹³until I come, give heed to the reading, to the exhortation, to the teaching; ¹⁴do not be careless of the gift in you, that was given you through prophecy, with laying on of the hands of the eldership; ¹⁵be careful of these things; be in these things, that your advancement may be evident in all things; ¹⁶take heed to yourself and to the teaching; remain in them, for doing this thing, you will save both yourself and those hearing you.

CHAPTER 5

¹You may not rebuke an elder, but exhort [him] as a father, younger persons as brothers, ²aged women as mothers, younger ones as sisters—in all purity; ³honor widows who are really widows; ⁴and if any widow has children or grandchildren, let them first learn to show piety to their own house, and to give back a repayment to the parents, for this is right and acceptable before God. ⁵And she who is really a widow and desolate, has hoped on God, and remains in the supplications and in the prayers night and day, ⁶but she given to luxury [while] living has died; ⁷and charge these things, that they may be blameless; ⁸and if anyone does not provide for his own, and especially for those of the household, he has denied the faith, and he is worse than an unbeliever. ⁹A widow—do not let her be enrolled under sixty years of age, having been a wife of one husband, ¹⁰being testified to in good works: if she brought up children, if she entertained strangers, if she washed holy ones' feet, if she relieved those in tribulation, if she followed after every good work; ¹¹and be

refusing younger widows, for when they may revel against the Christ, they wish to marry, ¹²having judgment, because they cast away the first faith, ¹³and also at the same time, they learn [to be] idle, going around the houses; and not only so, but also tattlers and busybodies, speaking things they should not; ¹⁴I intend, therefore, younger ones to marry, to bear children, to be mistress of the house, to give no occasion to the opposer of reviling; ¹⁵for some already turned aside after Satan. ¹⁶If any believing man or believing woman has widows, let them relieve them, and do not let the assembly be burdened, that it may relieve those [who are] really widows. ¹⁷Let them, the well-leading elders, be counted worthy of double honor, especially those laboring in word and teaching, ¹⁸for the Writing says, "You will not muzzle an ox treading out," and, "Worthy [is] the workman of his reward." ¹⁹Do not receive an accusation against an elder, except on two or three witnesses. ²⁰Reprove those sinning before all, that the others may also have fear; ²¹I fully testify, before God and the Lord Jesus Christ, and the chosen messengers, that you may keep these things, without prejudging, doing nothing by partiality. ²²Be quickly laying hands on no one, nor be having fellowship with [the] sins of others; be keeping yourself pure; ²³no longer be drinking water, but be using a little wine, because of your stomach and of your frequent sicknesses; ²⁴the sins of certain men are evident beforehand, leading before to judgment, but some also they follow after; ²⁵in like manner the right works are also evident beforehand, and those that are otherwise are not able to be hid.

CHAPTER 6

¹As many as are servants under a yoke, let them reckon their own masters worthy of all honor, that evil may not be spoken of the Name of God and the teaching; ²and those having believing masters, do not let them slight [them], because they are brothers, but rather let them serve, because they are steadfast and beloved, who are partaking of the benefit. Be teaching and exhorting these things; ³if anyone be teaching otherwise, and does not consent to sound words—those of our Lord Jesus Christ—and to the teaching according to piety, ⁴he is proud, knowing nothing, but unhealthy about questions and word-striving, out of which come envy, strife, slanders, evil-surmisings, ⁵wranglings of men wholly corrupted in mind, and destitute of the truth, supposing the piety to be gain; depart from such; ⁶but it is great gain—the piety with contentment; ⁷for we brought nothing into the world—because neither are we able to carry out anything; ⁸but having food and raiment—with these we will suffice ourselves; ⁹and those intending to be rich fall into temptation and a snare, and many desires, foolish and hurtful, that sink men into ruin and destruction, ¹⁰for the love of money is a root of all the evils, which certain [ones] longing for went astray from the faith, and pierced themselves through with many sorrows; ¹¹and you, O man of God, flee these things, and pursue righteousness, piety, faith, love, endurance, meekness. ¹²Be striving the good strife of the faith; be laying hold on the continuous life to which you also were called, and did profess the right profession before many witnesses. ¹³I charge you, before God, who is making all things alive, and of Christ Jesus, who testified the right profession before Pontius Pilate, ¹⁴that you keep the command unspotted, unblameable, until the appearing of our Lord Jesus Christ, ¹⁵which He will show in His own times—the blessed and only sovereign, the King of the kings and Lord of the lords, ¹⁶having immortality alone, dwelling in unapproachable light, whom no one of men saw, nor is able to see, to whom [is] honor and perpetual might! Amen. ¹⁷Charge those rich in the present age not to be high-minded, nor to hope in the uncertainty of riches, but in the living God, who is giving to us all things richly for enjoyment— ¹⁸to do good, to be rich in good works, to be ready to impart, willing to communicate, ¹⁹treasuring up to themselves a right foundation for the time to come, that they may lay hold on [that which is] truly life. ²⁰O Timotheus, guard the thing entrusted, avoiding the profane vain-words and opposition of the falsely-named knowledge, ²¹which certain [ones] professing—swerved concerning the faith. The grace [is] with you! Amen.

2 TIMOTHY

CHAPTER 1

¹Paul, an apostle of Jesus Christ, through the will of God, according to a promise of life that [is] in Christ Jesus, ²to Timotheus, beloved child: Grace, kindness, peace, from God the Father and Christ Jesus our Lord! ³I am thankful to God, whom I serve from progenitors in a pure conscience, that I unceasingly have remembrance concerning you in my supplications night and day, ⁴desiring to see you greatly, being mindful of your tears, that I may be filled with joy, ⁵taking remembrance of the unhypocritical faith that is in you, that first dwelt in your grandmother Lois, and your mother Eunice, and I am persuaded that also in you. ⁶For which cause I remind you to stir up the gift of God that is in you through the putting on of my hands, ⁷for God did not give us a spirit of fear, but of power, and of love, and of a sound mind; ⁸therefore you may not be ashamed of the testimony of our Lord, nor of me His prisoner, but you suffer evil along with the good news according to the power of God, ⁹who saved us, and called with a holy calling, not according to our works, but according to His own purpose and grace, that was given to us in Christ Jesus, before the times of the ages, ¹⁰and was made visible now through the appearing of our Savior Jesus Christ, who indeed abolished death, and enlightened life and immortality through the good news, ¹¹to which I was placed a preacher and an apostle, and a teacher of nations, ¹²for which cause these things I also suffer, but I am not ashamed, for I have known in whom I have believed, and have been persuaded that He is able to guard that which I have committed to Him—to that day. ¹³Hold the pattern of sound words, which you heard from me, in faith and love that [is] in Christ Jesus; ¹⁴guard the good thing committed through the Holy Spirit that is dwelling in us; ¹⁵you have known this, that they turned from me—all those in Asia, of whom are Phygellus and Hermogenes; ¹⁶may the LORD give kindness to the house of Onesiphorus, because he refreshed me many times, and was not ashamed of my chain, ¹⁷but being in Rome, he sought me very diligently and found [me]; ¹⁸may the LORD give to him to find kindness from the LORD in that day; and you very well know how much he ministered in Ephesus.

CHAPTER 2

¹You, therefore, my child, be strong in the grace that [is] in Christ Jesus, ²and the things that you heard from me through many witnesses, be committing these things to steadfast men, who will also be sufficient to teach others; ³you, therefore, suffer evil as a good soldier of Jesus Christ; ⁴no one serving as a soldier entangles himself with the affairs of life, that he may please him who enlisted him; ⁵and if anyone also may strive, he is not crowned, except he may strive lawfully; ⁶it is first necessary [for] the laboring farmer to partake of the fruits; ⁷be considering what things I say, for the LORD gives to you understanding in all things. ⁸Remember Jesus Christ, raised out of the dead, of the seed of David, according to my good news, ⁹in which I suffer evil—to bonds, as an evildoer, but the word of God has not been bound; ¹⁰because of this I endure all things, because of the chosen ones, that they also may obtain salvation that [is] in Christ Jesus, with perpetual glory. ¹¹The word [is] steadfast: For if we died together—we will also live together; ¹²if we endure together—we will also reign together; if we deny [Him], He will also deny us; ¹³if we are not steadfast, He remains steadfast; He is not able to deny Himself. ¹⁴Remind [them] of these things, testifying fully before the LORD—not to strive about words to nothing profitable, but to the subversion of those hearing; ¹⁵be diligent to present yourself approved to

2 TIMOTHY

God—a workman not ashamed, straightly cutting the word of truth; ¹⁶and stand aloof from the profane vain talkings, for they will advance to more impiety, ¹⁷and their word will have pasture as a gangrene, of whom is Hymenaeus and Philetus, ¹⁸who swerved concerning the truth, saying the resurrection to have already been, and overthrows the faith of some; ¹⁹sure, nevertheless, the foundation of God has stood, having this seal: "The LORD has known those who are His," and, "Let him depart from unrighteousness—everyone who is naming the Name of Christ." ²⁰And in a great house there are not only vessels of gold and of silver, but also of wood and of earth, and some to honor, and some to dishonor: ²¹if, then, anyone may cleanse himself from these, he will be a vessel to honor, sanctified and profitable to the master—having been prepared to every good work; ²²and flee the youthful lusts, and pursue righteousness, faith, love, peace, with those calling on the LORD out of a pure heart; ²³and be avoiding the foolish and uninstructed questions, having known that they beget strife, ²⁴and a servant of the LORD must not quarrel, but to be gentle to all, apt to teach, patient under evil, ²⁵instructing those opposing in meekness—if perhaps God may give to them conversion to an acknowledging of the truth, ²⁶and they may awake out of the Devil's snare, having been caught by him at his will.

CHAPTER 3
¹And know this, that in the last days there will come perilous times, ²for men will be lovers of themselves, lovers of money, boasters, proud, slanderous, disobedient to parents, unthankful, unkind, ³without natural affection, implacable, false accusers, without control, barbaric, not lovers of those who are good, ⁴traitors, reckless, lofty, lovers of pleasure more than lovers of God, ⁵having a form of piety, but having denied its power; and be turning away from these, ⁶for of these there are those coming into the houses and leading captive the weak women, loaded with sins, led away with manifold desires, ⁷always learning, and never able to come to a knowledge of truth, ⁸and even as Jannes and Jambres stood against Moses, so these also stand against the truth, men corrupted in mind, disapproved concerning the faith; ⁹but they will not advance any further, for their folly will be evident to all, as theirs also became. ¹⁰And you have followed after my teaching, manner of life, purpose, faith, long-suffering, love, endurance, ¹¹the persecutions, the afflictions, that befell me in Antioch, in Iconium, in Lystra; what persecutions I endured! And the LORD delivered me out of all. ¹²And all who will to live piously in Christ Jesus will also be persecuted, ¹³and evil men and impostors will advance to the worse, leading astray and being led astray. ¹⁴And you—remain in the things which you learned and were entrusted with, having known from whom you learned, ¹⁵and because you have known the Holy Writings from infancy, which are able to make you wise—to salvation, through faith that [is] in Christ Jesus. ¹⁶Every Writing [is] God-breathed, and profitable for teaching, for conviction, for correction, for instruction that [is] in righteousness, ¹⁷that the man of God may be fitted—having been completed for every good work.

CHAPTER 4
¹I fully testify, then, before God, and the Lord Jesus Christ, who is about to judge [the] living and dead at His appearing and His Kingdom— ²preach the word; be earnest in season, out of season; convict, rebuke, exhort, in all long-suffering and teaching, ³for there will be a season when they will not endure the sound teaching, but they will heap up teachers according to their own desires—having an itching ear, ⁴and, indeed, they will turn away from hearing the truth, and they will be turned aside to the fables. ⁵But you—watch in all things; suffer evil; do the work of one proclaiming good news; make full assurance of your ministry, ⁶for I am already being poured out, and the time of my release has arrived; ⁷I have striven the good strife, I have finished the course, I have kept the faith; ⁸from now on there is laid up for me the garland of righteousness that the LORD—the Righteous Judge—will give to me in that day, and not only to me, but also to all those loving His appearing. ⁹Be diligent to come to me quickly, ¹⁰for Demas forsook me, having loved the present age, and went on to Thessalonica, Crescens to Galatia, Titus to Dalmatia; ¹¹only Lucas is with me; having taken Mark, bring [him] with you, for he is profitable to me for ministry; ¹²and I sent Tychicus to Ephesus; ¹³coming, bring the cloak that I left in Troas with Carpus and the scrolls—especially the parchments. ¹⁴Alexander the coppersmith did me much evil; may the LORD repay to him according to his works, ¹⁵of whom you also beware, for he has greatly stood against our words; ¹⁶no one stood with me in my first defense, but all forsook me (may it not be reckoned to them), ¹⁷but the LORD stood by me, and strengthened me, that the preaching might be fully assured through me, and all the nations might hear, and I was freed out of the mouth of a lion, ¹⁸and the LORD will free me from every evil work, and will save [me]—to His heavenly kingdom; to whom [is] the glory through the ages of the ages! Amen. ¹⁹Greet Prisca and Aquilas, and Onesiphorus' household; ²⁰Erastus remained in Corinth, and I left Trophimus ailing in Miletus; ²¹be diligent to come before winter. Eubulus greets you, and Pudens, and Linus, and Claudia, and all the brothers. ²²The Lord Jesus Christ [is] with your spirit. The grace [is] with you! Amen.

TITUS

CHAPTER 1
¹Paul, a servant of God, and an apostle of Jesus Christ, according to the faith of the chosen ones of God, and an acknowledging of truth that [is] according to piety, ²on hope of continuous life, which God, who does not lie, promised before times of ages ³(and He revealed His word in [His] own times), in preaching, which I was entrusted with, according to a charge of God our Savior, ⁴to Titus—true child according to a common faith: Grace, [[kindness,]] peace, from God the Father and the Lord Jesus Christ our Savior! ⁵For this cause I left you in Crete, that you may arrange the things lacking, and may set elders down in every city, as I appointed to you, ⁶if anyone is blameless, a husband of one wife, having believing children, not under accusation of riotous living or insubordinate— ⁷for it is required of the overseer to be blameless, as God's steward, not self-pleased, nor prone to anger, not given to wine, not an abuser, not given to shameful gain, ⁸but a lover of strangers, a lover of [the] good, sober-minded, righteous, holy, self-controlled, ⁹holding—according to the teaching—to the steadfast word, that he may also be able to exhort in the sound teaching, and to convict the deniers; ¹⁰for there are many both insubordinate, vain-talkers, and mind-deceivers—especially those of the circumcision— ¹¹whose mouths must be covered, who overturn whole households, teaching what things it should not, for [the] sake of shameful gain. ¹²A certain one of them, a prophet of their own, said, "Cretans! Always liars, evil beasts, lazy bellies!" ¹³This testimony is true; for which cause convict them sharply, that they may be sound in the faith, ¹⁴not giving heed to Jewish fables and commands of men, turning themselves away from the truth. ¹⁵All things, indeed, [are] pure to the pure, and nothing [is] pure to the defiled and unsteadfast, but even the mind and the conscience of them [is] defiled. ¹⁶They profess

TITUS

to know God, but they deny [Him] by their works, being abominable, and disobedient, and disapproved to every good work.

CHAPTER 2

¹But you—speak what is suitable [according] to the sound teaching. ²Elders [are] to be temperate, dignified, sober, sound in faith, in the love, in the endurance. ³Aged women, in like manner, in behavior as becomes sacred persons, not false accusers, not enslaved to much wine, teachers of good things, ⁴that they may make the young women sober-minded, to be lovers of [their] husbands, lovers of [their] children, ⁵sober, pure, keepers of [their own] houses, good, subject to their own husbands, that evil may not be spoken of the word of God. ⁶The younger men, in like manner, exhort [them] to be sober-minded. ⁷Concerning all things, present yourself [as] a pattern of good works—in the teaching [with] uncorruptedness, dignity, ⁸sound discourse [that is] blameless, so that he who is of the contrary may be ashamed, having nothing evil to say concerning you. ⁹Servants [are] to be subject to their own masters, to be well-pleasing in all things, not contradicting, ¹⁰not stealing, but showing all good steadfastness, that the teaching of God our Savior they may adorn in all things. ¹¹For the saving grace of God has appeared to all men, ¹²teaching us, that denying the impiety and the worldly desires, we may live soberly, and righteously, and piously in the present age, ¹³waiting for the blessed hope and appearing of the glory of our great God and Savior Jesus Christ, ¹⁴who gave Himself for us, that He might ransom us from all lawlessness, and might purify to Himself a special people, zealous of good works. ¹⁵Speak these things, and exhort and convict with all authority; let no one despise you!

CHAPTER 3

¹Remind them to be subject to principalities and authorities, to obey rule, to be ready to every good work, ²to speak evil of no one, not to be quarrelsome—gentle, showing all meekness to all men, ³for we, also, were once thoughtless, disobedient, led astray, serving manifold desires and pleasures, living in malice and envy, odious—hating one another; ⁴and when the kindness and the love to men of God our Savior appeared ⁵(not by works that [are] in righteousness that we did but according to His kindness), He saved us, through a bathing of regeneration, and a renewing of the Holy Spirit, ⁶which He poured on us richly, through Jesus Christ our Savior, ⁷that having been declared righteous by His grace, we may become heirs according to the hope of continuous life. ⁸The word [is] steadfast; and concerning these things I intend you to affirm fully, that they may be thoughtful, to be leading in good works—who have believed God; these are the good and profitable things to men, ⁹but stand away from foolish questions, and genealogies, and contentions, and strivings about law—for they are unprofitable and vain. ¹⁰Reject a heretical man, after a first and second admonition, ¹¹having known that he has been subverted who [is] such, and sins, being self-condemned. ¹²When I will send Artemas to you, or Tychicus, be diligent to come to me to Nicopolis, for I have determined to winter there. ¹³Diligently send forth Zenas the lawyer and Apollos on their way, that nothing to them may be lacking, ¹⁴and let them learn—ours also—to be leading in good works to the necessary uses, that they may not be unfruitful. ¹⁵All those with me greet you. Greet those cherishing us in faith. The grace [is] with you all!

PHILEMON

CHAPTER 1

¹Paul, a prisoner of Christ Jesus, and Timotheus the brother, to Philemon our beloved and fellow-worker, ²and Apphia the beloved, and Archippus our fellow-soldier, and the assembly in your house: ³Grace to you and peace from God our Father and the Lord Jesus Christ! ⁴I give thanks to my God, always making mention of you in my prayers, ⁵hearing of your love and faith that you have to the Lord Jesus and toward all the holy ones, ⁶that the fellowship of your faith may become working in the full knowledge of every good thing that [is] in you toward Christ Jesus; ⁷for we have much joy and comfort in your love, because the yearnings of the holy ones have been refreshed through you, brother. ⁸For this reason, having in Christ much boldness to command you that which is fit— ⁹because of the love I rather plead, being such a one as Paul the aged, and now also a prisoner of Jesus Christ; ¹⁰I beg you concerning my child—whom I begot in my bonds—Onesimus, ¹¹who once was to you unprofitable, and now is profitable to me and to you, ¹²whom I sent again to you—he who is my own heart, ¹³whom I intended to retain to myself, that in your behalf he might minister to me in the bonds of the good news, ¹⁴but apart from your mind I willed to do nothing, so that your good deed may not be as of necessity, but of willingness, ¹⁵for perhaps because of this he departed for an hour, that you may have him continuously, ¹⁶no longer as a servant, but above a servant—a beloved brother, especially to me, and how much more to you, both in the flesh and in the LORD! ¹⁷If, then, you have fellowship with me, receive him as me, ¹⁸and if he did hurt to you, or owes anything, charge this to me; ¹⁹I, Paul, wrote with my hand, I will repay; besides, that I may not say that you also owe to me yourself. ²⁰Yes, brother, may I have profit of you in the LORD; refresh my yearnings in the LORD; ²¹I wrote to you having been confident in your obedience, having known that you will also do above what I may say; ²²and at the same time also prepare for me a lodging, for I hope that through your prayers I will be granted to you. ²³Epaphras greets you (my fellow-captive in Christ Jesus), ²⁴Marcus, Aristarchus, Demas, Lucas, my fellow-workmen! ²⁵The grace of our Lord Jesus Christ [is] with your spirit! Amen.

HEBREWS

CHAPTER 1

¹In many parts and many ways, God, having spoken long ago to the fathers by the prophets, ²in these last days speaks to us in [His] Son, whom He appointed heir of all things, through whom He also made the ages; ³who being the brightness of the glory, and the impress of His subsistence, bearing up also all things by the saying of His might—having made a cleansing of our sins through Himself, sat down at the right hand of the Greatness in the highest, ⁴having become so much better than the messengers, as He inherited a more excellent name than them. ⁵For to which of the messengers did He ever say, "You are My Son—today I have begotten You?" And again, "I will be to Him for a Father, and He will be to Me for a Son?" ⁶And when again He may bring the firstborn into the world, He says, "And let them worship Him—all messengers of God"; ⁷and to the messengers, indeed, He says, "The [One] who is making His messengers spirits, and His ministers a flame of fire"; ⁸but to the Son: "Your throne, O God, [is] throughout the age of the age; The scepter of righteousness [is the] scepter of Your kingdom; ⁹You loved righteousness, and hated lawlessness; Because of this He anointed You—God, Your God—With oil of gladness above Your partners"; ¹⁰and, "You, LORD, founded the earth at the beginning, || And the heavens are a work of Your hands. ¹¹These will perish, but You remain, || And all will become old as a

HEBREWS

garment, ¹²And You will roll them together as a mantle, and they will be changed, || But You are the same, and Your years will not fail." ¹³And to which of the messengers did He ever say, "Sit at My right hand, || Until I may make Your enemies Your footstool?" ¹⁴Are they not all spirits of service—being sent forth for ministry because of those about to inherit salvation?

CHAPTER 2

¹Because of this it is more abundantly necessary to take heed to the things heard, lest we may drift away, ²for if the word being spoken through messengers became steadfast, and every transgression and disobedience received a just repayment, ³how will we escape, having neglected such great salvation? Which having received [that] spoken through the LORD [from] the beginning, was confirmed to us by those having heard, ⁴God also bearing joint-witness both with signs and wonders, and manifold powers, and distributions of the Holy Spirit, according to His will. ⁵For He did not subject the coming world to messengers, concerning which we speak, ⁶and one in a certain place testified fully, saying, "What is man, that You are mindful of him, || Or a son of man, that You look after him? ⁷You made him [a] little less than messengers, || You crowned him with glory and honor, || And set him over the works of Your hands, ⁸You put all things in subjection under his feet," for in the subjecting to Him all things, He left nothing to Him unsubjected, but now we do not yet see all things subjected to Him, ⁹and we see Him who was made [a] little less than messengers—Jesus—because of the suffering of death, having been crowned with glory and honor, that by the grace of God He might taste of death for everyone. ¹⁰For it was fitting to Him, because of whom [are] all things, and through whom [are] all things, bringing many sons to glory, to make the author of their salvation perfect through sufferings, ¹¹for both He who is sanctifying and those sanctified [are] all of one, for which cause He is not ashamed to call them brothers, ¹²saying, "I will declare Your Name to My brothers, || In the midst of an assembly I will sing praise to You"; and again, "I will be trusting on Him"; ¹³and again, "Behold, I and the children that God gave to Me." ¹⁴Seeing, then, the children have partaken of flesh and blood, He Himself also took part of the same in like manner, that through death He might destroy him having the power of death—that is, the Devil— ¹⁵and might deliver those, whoever, with fear of death, throughout all their life, were subjects of bondage, ¹⁶for doubtless, He does not lay hold of messengers, but He lays hold of [the] seed of Abraham, ¹⁷for this reason it seemed necessary to Him to be made like the brothers in all things, that He might become a kind and faithful Chief Priest in the things related to God, to make propitiation for the sins of the people, ¹⁸for in that He suffered, Himself being tempted, He is able to help those who are tempted.

CHAPTER 3

¹For this reason, holy brothers, partakers of a heavenly calling, consider the Apostle and Chief Priest of our profession, Christ Jesus, ²being faithful to Him who appointed Him, as also Moses [was] in all His house. ³For this One has been counted worthy of more glory than Moses, inasmuch as He who builds it has more honor than the house. ⁴For every house is built by someone, and He who built all things [is] God, ⁵and Moses [was] indeed steadfast in all His house, as an attendant, for a testimony of those things that were to be spoken— ⁶but Christ, as a Son over His house, whose house we are, if we hold fast the boldness and the rejoicing of the hope to the end. ⁷For this reason, as the Holy Spirit says, "Today, if you may hear His voice— ⁸you may not harden your hearts, as in the provocation, in the day of the temptation in the wilderness, ⁹in which your fathers tempted Me; they proved Me, and saw My works [for] forty years; ¹⁰for this reason I was grieved with that generation and said, They always go astray in [their] heart, and these have not known My ways; ¹¹so I swore in My anger, They will [not] enter into My rest." ¹²Watch out, brothers, lest there will be in any of you an evil heart of unbelief in the falling away from the living God, ¹³but exhort one another every day, while [it] is called "Today," that none of you may be hardened by the deceitfulness of sin, ¹⁴for we have become partakers of the Christ, if we may hold fast the confidence [we had] at the beginning to the end, ¹⁵as it is said, "Today, if you may hear His voice, you may not harden your hearts, as in the provocation." ¹⁶For who [were those], having heard, [that] provoked, but not all those having come out of Egypt through Moses? ¹⁷But with whom was He grieved forty years? Was it not with those who sinned, whose carcasses fell in the wilderness? ¹⁸And to whom did He swear that they will not enter into His rest, except to those who did not believe? ¹⁹And we see that they were not able to enter in because of unbelief.

CHAPTER 4

¹We may fear, then, lest a promise being left of entering into His rest, anyone of you may seem to have come short, ²for we also are having good news proclaimed, even as they, but the word heard did not profit them, not being mixed with faith in those who heard, ³for we enter into the rest—we who believed, as He said, "So I swore in My anger, They will [not] enter into My rest"; and yet the works were done from the foundation of the world, ⁴for He spoke in a certain place concerning the seventh [day] thus: "And God rested in the seventh day from all His works"; ⁵and in this [place] again, "They will [not] enter into My rest"; ⁶since then, it remains for some to enter into it, and those who first heard good news did not enter in because of unbelief— ⁷again He limits a certain day, "Today," in David saying, after so long a time, as it has been said, "Today, if you may hear His voice, you may not harden your hearts," ⁸for if Joshua had given them rest, He would not have spoken after these things concerning another day; ⁹there remains, then, a Sabbath rest to the people of God, ¹⁰for he who entered into His rest, he also rested from his works, as God from His own. ¹¹May we be diligent, then, to enter into that rest, that no one may fall in the same example of the unbelief, ¹²for the Word of God is living, and working, and sharper—beyond every two-edged sword—and piercing as far as [the] division of soul and spirit, of joints and also marrows, and a discerner of thoughts and intents of the heart; ¹³and there is not a created thing hidden before Him, but all things [are] naked and open to His eyes—with whom is our reckoning. ¹⁴Having, then, a great Chief Priest having passed through the heavens—Jesus the Son of God—may we hold fast the profession, ¹⁵for we do not have a Chief Priest unable to sympathize with our weaknesses, but [One] tempted in all things in like manner, [yet] without sin; ¹⁶we may come near, then, with freedom, to the throne of grace, that we may receive kindness, and find grace—for seasonable help.

CHAPTER 5

¹For every chief priest taken out of men is set in things [pertaining] to God in behalf of men, that he may offer both gifts and sacrifices for sins, ²being able to be gentle to those being ignorant and going astray, since he is also surrounded with weakness; ³and because of this [weakness] he ought, just as for the people, so also for himself, to bring forward [sacrifices] for sins; ⁴and no one takes the honor to himself, but he who is called by God, as also Aaron. ⁵So also the Christ did not glorify Himself to become Chief Priest, but He who spoke to Him: "You are My Son, today I have begotten You"; ⁶just as He also says in another [place], "You [are] a priest throughout the age, according to the order of Melchizedek"; ⁷who in the days of His flesh having offered up both prayers and supplications with strong crying and tears to Him who was able to save Him from death, and having been heard in respect to that which He feared, ⁸though being a Son, [He] learned obedience by the things which He suffered, ⁹and having been made perfect, He became the cause of continuous salvation to all those obeying Him, ¹⁰having been called by God a Chief Priest according to the order of Melchizedek, ¹¹concerning the Word, of whom we have much [to speak], and of hard explanation to say, since you have become dull of hearing, ¹²for even owing to be teachers, because of the time, again you have need that one teach you what [are] the elements of the beginning of the oracles of God, and you have become having need of milk, and not of strong food, ¹³for everyone who is partaking of milk [is] unskilled in the word of righteousness—for he is an infant, ¹⁴and the strong food is of perfect men, who because of the use are having the senses exercised, to both the discernment of good and of evil.

CHAPTER 6

¹For this reason, having left the word of the beginning of the Christ, we may advance to

perfection, not laying again a foundation of conversion from dead works, and of faith on God, ²of the teaching of immersions, also of laying on of hands, also of [the] resurrection of the dead, and of continuous judgment, ³and this we will do, if God may permit, ⁴for [it is] impossible for those once enlightened, having also tasted of the heavenly gift, and having become partakers of the Holy Spirit, ⁵and tasted the good saying of God, also the powers of the coming age, ⁶and having fallen away, to renew [them] again to conversion, having crucified to themselves the Son of God again, and exposed to public shame. ⁷For the earth, having drunk in the rain coming on it many times, and is bringing forth herbs fit for those because of whom it is also dressed, partakes of blessing from God, ⁸but that which is bearing thorns and briers [is] disapproved of, and near to cursing, whose end [is] for burning; ⁹but we are persuaded, concerning you, beloved, the things that are better, and accompanying salvation, though even thus we speak, ¹⁰for God is not unrighteous to forget your work, and the labor of love that you showed to His Name, having ministered to the holy ones and ministering; ¹¹and we desire each one of you to show the same diligence, to the full assurance of the hope to the end, ¹²that you may not become slothful, but followers of those who through faith and patient endurance are inheriting the promises. ¹³For God, having made promise to Abraham, seeing He was not able to swear by [any] greater, swore by Himself, ¹⁴saying, "Blessing I will indeed bless you, and multiplying I will multiply you"; ¹⁵and so, having patiently endured, he obtained the promise; ¹⁶for men swear by the greater, and the oath [is] for confirmation of the end of all their controversy, ¹⁷in which God, more abundantly willing to show to the heirs of the promise the immutability of His counsel, interposed by an oath, ¹⁸that through two immutable things, in which [it is] impossible for God to lie, we may have a strong comfort, having fled for refuge, to lay hold on the hope being set before [us], ¹⁹which we have, as an anchor of the soul, both sure and steadfast, and entering into that within the veil, ²⁰to where a forerunner entered for us—Jesus, having become Chief Priest throughout the age after the order of Melchizedek.

CHAPTER 7

¹For this Melchizedek, king of Salem, priest of God Most High, who met Abraham turning back from the striking of the kings, and blessed him, ²to whom also Abraham divided a tenth of all (first, indeed, being interpreted, "King of righteousness," and then also, "King of Salem," which is, King of Peace), ³without father, without mother, without genealogy, having neither beginning of days nor end of life, and having been like the Son of God, remains a priest continually. ⁴And see how great this one [is], to whom Abraham the patriarch also gave a tenth out of the best of the spoils, ⁵and those, indeed, out of the sons of Levi receiving the priesthood, have a command to take tithes from the people according to the Law, that is, their brothers, even though they came forth out of the loins of Abraham; ⁶and he who was not reckoned by genealogy of them, received tithes from Abraham, and he has blessed him having the promises, ⁷and apart from all controversy, the less is blessed by the better— ⁸and here, indeed, men who die receive tithes, and there [he] who is testified to that he was living, ⁹and so to speak, through Abraham even Levi who is receiving tithes, has paid tithes, ¹⁰for he was yet in the loins of the father when Melchizedek met him. ¹¹If indeed, then, perfection were through the Levitical priesthood—for the people under it had received law—what further need, according to the order of Melchizedek, for another priest to arise, and not to be called according to the order of Aaron? ¹²For the priesthood being changed, of necessity also, a change comes of the Law, ¹³for He of whom these things are said in another tribe has had part, of whom no one gave attendance at the altar, ¹⁴for [it is] evident that out of Judah has arisen our Lord, in regard to which tribe Moses spoke nothing concerning priesthood. ¹⁵And it is yet more abundantly most evident, if according to the likeness of Melchizedek there arises another priest, ¹⁶who did not come according to the law of a fleshly command, but according to the power of an endless life, ¹⁷for He testifies, "You [are] a priest—throughout the age, according to the order of Melchizedek"; ¹⁸for an annulling indeed comes of the command going before because of its weakness, and unprofitableness ¹⁹(for nothing did the Law perfect), and the bringing in of a better hope, through which we draw near to God. ²⁰And inasmuch as [it is] not apart from oath ²¹(for those indeed apart from oath have become priests, and He [became priest] with an oath through Him who is saying to Him, "The LORD swore, and will not regret, You [are] a priest throughout the age, according to the order of Melchizedek"), ²²by so much also has Jesus become guarantee of a better covenant, ²³and those indeed are many who have become priests, because by death they are hindered from remaining; ²⁴and He, because of His remaining throughout the age, has the inviolable priesthood, ²⁵from where also He is able to save to the very end, those coming through Him to God—ever living to make intercession for them. ²⁶For also such a Chief Priest was fitting for us—holy, innocent, undefiled, separate from the sinners, and having become higher than the heavens, ²⁷who has no daily necessity, as the chief priests, to first offer up sacrifice for His own sins, then for those of the people; for this He did once, having offered up Himself; ²⁸for the Law appoints men [as] chief priests, having weakness, but the word of the oath that [is] after the Law [appoints] the Son having been perfected throughout the age.

CHAPTER 8

¹And the sum concerning the things spoken of [is]: we have such a Chief Priest, who sat down at the right hand of the throne of the Greatness in the heavens, ²a servant of the holy places, and of the true dwelling place, which the LORD set up, and not man, ³for every chief priest is appointed to offer both gifts and sacrifices, from where [it is] necessary for this One to also have something that He may offer; ⁴for if, indeed, He were on earth, He would not be a priest (there being the priests who are offering the gifts according to the Law, ⁵who to an example and shadow serve of the heavenly things, as Moses has been divinely warned, being about to construct the Dwelling Place, for, "See," He says, "[that] you will make all things according to the pattern that was shown to you on the mountain"), ⁶but now He has obtained a more excellent service, how much He is also mediator of a better covenant, which has been sanctioned on better promises, ⁷for if that first were faultless, a place would not have been sought for a second. ⁸For finding fault, He says to them, "Behold, days come, says the LORD, and I will complete with the house of Israel, and with the house of Judah, a new covenant, ⁹not according to the covenant that I made with their fathers, in the day of My taking [them] by their hand, to bring them out of the land of Egypt—because they did not remain in My covenant, and I did not regard them, says the LORD— ¹⁰because this [is] the covenant that I will make with the house of Israel, after those days, says the LORD, giving My laws into their mind, and I will write them on their hearts, and I will be to them for a God, and they will be to Me for a people; ¹¹and they will not each teach his neighbor, and each his brother, saying, Know the LORD, because they will all know Me—from the small one of them to the great one of them, ¹²because I will be merciful to their unrighteousness, and I will remember their sins and their lawlessnesses no more." ¹³In the saying "new," He has made the first obsolete, and what is becoming obsolete and growing old [is] near disappearing.

CHAPTER 9

¹It had, indeed, then (even the first dwelling place) ordinances of service, also a worldly sanctuary, ²for a dwelling place was prepared, the first, in which was both the lampstand, and the table, and the Bread of the Presentation—which is called "Holy"; ³and after the second veil a dwelling place that is called "Holy of Holies," ⁴having a golden censer, and the Ark of the Covenant overlaid all over with gold, in which [is] the golden pot having the manna, and the rod of Aaron that budded, and the tablets of the covenant, ⁵and over it cherubim of the glory, overshadowing the propitiatory covering, concerning which we are not to particularly speak now. ⁶And these things having been thus prepared, into

the first dwelling place, indeed, the priests go in at all times, performing the services, ⁷and into the second, once in the year, only the chief priest, not apart from blood, which he offers for himself and the errors of the people. ⁸By this the Holy Spirit was making evident that the way of the holy [places] has not yet been revealed, the first dwelling place yet having a standing, ⁹which [is] an allegory in regard to the present time, in which both gifts and sacrifices are offered, which are not able, in regard to conscience, to make perfect him who is serving, ¹⁰only on the basis of food, and drinks, and different immersions, and fleshly ordinances—until the time of reformation imposed on [them]. ¹¹But Christ having come, Chief Priest of the coming good things, through the greater and more perfect dwelling place not made with hands—that is, not of this creation— ¹²neither through blood of goats and calves, but through His own blood, entered in once into the holy places, having obtained continuous redemption; ¹³for if the blood of bulls, and goats, and ashes of a heifer, sprinkling those defiled, sanctifies to the purifying of the flesh, ¹⁴how much more will the blood of the Christ (who through the perpetual Spirit offered Himself unblemished to God) purify your conscience from dead works to serve the living God? ¹⁵And because of this, He is mediator of a new covenant, that [His] death having come for redemption of the transgressions under the first covenant, those called may receive the promise of the continuous inheritance, ¹⁶for where a covenant [is], [it is] necessary to establish the death of the [one] having made [it], ¹⁷for a covenant is affirmed at death, since it is not in force at all when the [one] having made [it] lives, ¹⁸for which reason, not even the first has been initiated apart from blood, ¹⁹for every command having been spoken, according to law, by Moses, to all the people, having taken the blood of the calves and goats, with water, and scarlet wool, and hyssop, he sprinkled both the scroll itself and all the people, ²⁰saying, "This [is] the blood of the covenant that God enjoined to you," ²¹and he sprinkled both the Dwelling Place and all the vessels of the service with blood in like manner, ²²and with blood almost all things are purified according to the Law, and forgiveness does not come apart from blood-shedding. ²³[It is] necessary, therefore, the pattern indeed of the things in the heavens to be purified with these, and the heavenly things themselves with better sacrifices than these; ²⁴for the Christ did not enter into holy places made with hands—figures of the true—but into Heaven itself, now to be manifested in the presence of God for us; ²⁵nor that He may offer Himself many times, even as the chief priest enters into the holy places every year with blood of others, ²⁶otherwise it was necessary for Him to suffer many times from the foundation of the world, but now He has been revealed once, at the full end of the ages, for [the] annulling of sin through His sacrifice; ²⁷and as it is reserved for men to die once, and after this—judgment, ²⁸so also the Christ, having been offered once to bear the sins of many, will appear a second time, apart from a sin-offering, for salvation to those waiting for Him!

CHAPTER 10

¹For the Law having a shadow of the good things coming—not the very image of the matters, every year, by the same sacrifices that they offer continually, is never able to make perfect those coming near, ²since, would they not have ceased to be offered, because of those serving having no more conscience of sins, having been purified once? ³But in those [sacrifices] is a remembrance of sins every year, ⁴for it is impossible for blood of bulls and goats to take away sins. ⁵For this reason, coming into the world, He says, "Sacrifice and offering You did not will, and a body You prepared for Me; ⁶in burnt-offerings, and concerning sin-offerings, You did not delight. ⁷Then I said, Behold, I come (in a volume of the scroll it has been written concerning Me), to do, O God, Your will"; ⁸saying above, "Sacrifice, and offering, and burnt-offerings, and concerning sin-offering You did not will, nor delight in" (which are offered according to the Law), ⁹then He said, "Behold, I come to do, O God, Your will"; He takes away the first that He may establish the second; ¹⁰in which will, we have been sanctified through the offering of the body of Jesus Christ once for all, ¹¹and every priest, indeed, has daily stood serving, and offering the same sacrifices many times, that are never able to take away sins. ¹²But He, having offered one sacrifice for sin—to the end, sat down at the right hand of God— ¹³as to the rest, expecting until He may place His enemies [as] His footstool, ¹⁴for by one offering He has perfected to the end those being sanctified; ¹⁵and the Holy Spirit also testifies to us, for after that He has said before, ¹⁶"This [is] the covenant that I will make with them after those days, says the LORD, giving My laws on their hearts, and I will write them on their minds," ¹⁷and, "I will remember their sins and their lawlessness no more"; ¹⁸and where [there is] forgiveness of these, there is no longer offering for sin. ¹⁹Having, therefore, brothers, boldness for the entrance into the holy places, by the blood of Jesus, ²⁰which [is] the way He initiated for us—new and living, through the veil, that is, His flesh— ²¹and a Great Priest over the house of God, ²²may we draw near with a true heart, in full assurance of faith, having the hearts sprinkled from an evil conscience, and having the body bathed with pure water; ²³may we hold fast the unwavering profession of the hope (for He who promised [is] faithful), ²⁴and may we consider to provoke one another to love and to good works, ²⁵not forsaking the assembling of ourselves together, as [is] a custom of some, but exhorting, and so much the more as you see the Day coming near. ²⁶For [if] we are sinning willingly after receiving the full knowledge of the truth—there remains no more sacrifice for sins, ²⁷but a certain fearful looking for of judgment, and fiery zeal, about to devour the opposers; ²⁸anyone having set aside a law of Moses dies without mercies on the basis of two or three witnesses. ²⁹Of how much worse punishment will he be counted worthy who trampled on the Son of God, and counted the blood of the covenant a common thing, by which he was sanctified, and having insulted the Spirit of grace? ³⁰For we have known Him who is saying, "Vengeance [is] Mine, I will repay, says the LORD"; and again, "The LORD will judge His people." ³¹[It is] fearful to fall into [the] hands of [the] living God. ³²But call to your remembrance the former days, in which, having been enlightened, you endured much conflict of sufferings; ³³this indeed, being made spectacles with both insults and afflictions, now this, having become partners of those so living, ³⁴for you also sympathized with my bonds, and the robbery of your goods you received with joy, knowing that you have in yourselves a better substance in the heavens, and an enduring one. ³⁵You may not cast away, then, your boldness, which has great repayment of reward, ³⁶for you have need of patience, that having done the will of God, you may receive the promise. ³⁷"For yet [in] a very, very little [while], He who is coming will come, and will not linger," ³⁸but, "The righteous will live by faith; and if he may draw back, My soul has no pleasure in him." ³⁹But we are not of those drawing back to destruction, but of those believing to a preserving of soul.

CHAPTER 11

¹Now faith is [the] substance of things hoped for, [the] proof of matters not being seen, ²for by this, the elders were well-attested. ³By faith we understand the ages to have been prepared by a saying of God, in regard to the things seen having not come out of things appearing. ⁴By faith Abel offered a better sacrifice to God than Cain, through which he was testified to be righteous, God testifying of his gifts, and through it, he being dead, yet speaks. ⁵By faith Enoch was translated—not to see death, and was not found, because God translated him; for before his translation he had been testified to—that he had pleased God well, ⁶and apart from faith it is impossible to please [Him], for it is required of him who is coming to God to believe that He exists and [that] He becomes a rewarder to those seeking Him. ⁷By faith Noah, having been divinely warned concerning the things not yet

seen, having feared, prepared an ark to the salvation of his house, through which he condemned the world, and he became heir of the righteousness according to faith. ⁸By faith Abraham, being called, obeyed, to go forth into the place that he was about to receive for an inheritance, and he went forth, not knowing to where he goes. ⁹By faith he sojourned in the land of the promise as a strange country, having dwelt in dwelling places with Isaac and Jacob, fellow-heirs of the same promise, ¹⁰for he was looking for the city having the foundations, whose craftsman and constructor [is] God. ¹¹And by faith Sarah, herself barren, received power to conceive seed even after the time of life, seeing she judged Him who promised faithful; ¹²for this reason, also, from one—and that of one who had become dead—were begotten as the stars of the sky in multitude, and innumerable as the sand that [is] by the seashore. ¹³All these died in faith, having not received the promises, but having seen them from afar, and having been persuaded, and having greeted [them], and having confessed that they are strangers and sojourners on the earth, ¹⁴for those saying such things make apparent that they seek a country; ¹⁵and if, indeed, they had been mindful of that from which they came forth, they might have had an opportunity to return, ¹⁶but now they long for better, that is, heavenly, for this reason God is not ashamed of them, to be called their God, for He prepared a city for them. ¹⁷By faith Abraham has offered up Isaac, being tried, even the [one] having received the promises offered up his only begotten, ¹⁸of whom it was said, "In Isaac will your Seed be called," ¹⁹reckoning that God is even able to raise up out of the dead, from where also in a figurative sense he received [him]. ²⁰By faith, concerning coming things, Isaac blessed Jacob and Esau. ²¹By faith Jacob, dying, blessed each of the sons of Joseph and worshiped on the top of his staff. ²²By faith Joseph, dying, made mention concerning the outgoing of the sons of Israel, and gave command concerning his bones. ²³By faith Moses, having been born, was hid three months by his parents, because they saw the child beautiful, and were not afraid of the decree of the king. ²⁴By faith Moses, having become great, refused to be called a son of the daughter of Pharaoh, ²⁵having chosen rather to be afflicted with the people of God, than to have sin's pleasure for a season, ²⁶having reckoned the reproach of the Christ greater wealth than the treasures in Egypt, for he looked to the repayment of reward. ²⁷By faith he left Egypt behind, having not been afraid of the wrath of the king, for as seeing the Invisible One—he endured. ²⁸By faith he kept the Passover, and the sprinkling of the blood, so that He who is destroying the firstborn might not touch them. ²⁹By faith they passed through the Red Sea as through dry land, which having made an attempt [to cross], the Egyptians were swallowed up. ³⁰By faith the walls of Jericho fell, having been surrounded for seven days. ³¹By faith Rahab the prostitute did not perish with those who disbelieved, having received the spies with peace. ³²And what yet will I say? For the time will fail me recounting about Gideon, also Barak, and Samson, and Jephthah, also David, and Samuel, and the prophets, ³³who through faith subdued kingdoms, worked righteousness, obtained promises, stopped mouths of lions, ³⁴quenched the power of fire, escaped the mouth of the sword, were made powerful out of weakness, became strong in battle, caused armies of the foreigners to give way; ³⁵women received their dead by a resurrection, and others were tortured, not accepting the redemption, that they might receive a better resurrection, ³⁶and others received trial of mockings and scourgings, and yet of bonds and imprisonment; ³⁷they were stoned, they were sawn apart, they were tried; they died in the killing of the sword; they went around in sheepskins, in goatskins—being destitute, afflicted, injuriously treated, ³⁸of whom the world was not worthy; wandering in deserts, and mountains, and caves, and the holes of the earth; ³⁹and all these, having been testified to through faith, did not receive the promise, ⁴⁰God, having provided something better for us, that apart from us they might not be made perfect.

CHAPTER 12
¹Therefore, we also having so great a cloud of witnesses set around us, having put off every weight, and the closely besetting sin, may we run the contest that is set before us through endurance, ²looking to the Author and Perfecter of the faith—Jesus, who, for the joy set before Him, endured a cross, having despised shame, and sat down at the right hand of the throne of God; ³for again consider Him who endured such contradiction from the sinners to Himself, that you may not be wearied in your souls—being faint. ⁴You did not yet resist to blood—striving with sin; ⁵and you have forgotten the exhortation that speaks fully to you as to sons, "My son, do not despise [the] discipline of [the] LORD, nor be faint, being reproved by Him, ⁶for whom the LORD loves He disciplines, and He scourges every son whom He receives"; ⁷if you endure discipline, God bears Himself to you as to sons, for who is a son whom a father does not discipline? ⁸And if you are apart from discipline, of which all have become partakers, then you are bastards, and not sons. ⁹Then, indeed, we have had fathers of our flesh, correctors, and we respected [them]; will we not much rather be subject to the Father of the spirits, and live? ¹⁰For they, indeed, for a few days, according to what seemed good to them, were disciplining, but He for profit, to be partakers of His separation; ¹¹and all discipline for the present, indeed, does not seem to be of joy, but of sorrow, yet afterward it yields the peaceable fruit of righteousness to those exercised through it. ¹²For this reason, lift up the hanging-down hands and the loosened knees; ¹³and make straight paths for your feet, so that which is lame may not be turned aside, but rather be healed; ¹⁴pursue peace with all, and the separation, apart from which no one will see the LORD, ¹⁵observing lest anyone be failing of the grace of God, lest any root of bitterness springing up may give trouble, and through this many may be defiled; ¹⁶lest anyone be a fornicator, or a profane person, as Esau, who in exchange for one morsel of food sold his birthright, ¹⁷for you know that also afterward, wishing to inherit the blessing, he was disapproved of, for he did not find a place of conversion, though having sought it with tears. ¹⁸For you did not come near to the mountain touched and scorched with fire, and to blackness, and darkness, and storm, ¹⁹and a sound of a trumpet, and a voice of sayings, which those having heard begged that a word might not be added to them, ²⁰for they were not bearing that which is commanded, "And if a beast may touch the mountain, it will be stoned, or shot through with an arrow," ²¹and (so terrible was the sight), Moses said, "I am exceedingly fearful, and trembling." ²²But you came to Mount Zion, and to [the] city of the living God, to the heavenly Jerusalem, and to myriads of messengers, ²³to the assembly-place and Assembly of the Firstborn registered in Heaven, and to God the judge of all, and to spirits of righteous men made perfect, ²⁴and to a mediator of a new covenant—Jesus, and to blood of sprinkling, speaking better things than that of Abel! ²⁵Watch out lest you refuse Him who is speaking, for if those did not escape who refused him who was divinely speaking on earth—much less we who turn away from Him who [speaks] from Heaven, ²⁶whose voice shook the earth then, and now He has promised, saying, "Yet once [more]—I shake not only the earth, but also Heaven"; ²⁷and this, "Yet once [more]," makes evident the removal of the things shaken, as of things having been made, that the things not shaken may remain; ²⁸for this reason, receiving a kingdom that cannot be shaken, may we have grace, through which we may serve God well-pleasingly, with reverence and fear, ²⁹for our God [is] also a consuming fire.

CHAPTER 13
¹Let brotherly love remain. ²Do not be forgetful of hospitality, for through this some entertained messengers unaware. ³Be mindful of those in bonds, as having been bound with them, of those maltreated, as yourselves also being in the body. ⁴The marriage [is to be] honored by all, and the bed undefiled, for God will judge whoremongers and adulterers. ⁵[Be] without covetous behavior, being content with the things present, for He has said, "No, I will not leave, no, nor forsake you," ⁶so that we boldly say, "The LORD [is] to me a helper, and I will not fear what man will do to me." ⁷Be mindful of those leading you, who spoke to you the word of God, who, considering the outcome of [their] behavior, imitate [their] faith: ⁸Jesus Christ—the same yesterday and today and for all ages. ⁹Do not be carried away with strange and manifold teachings, for [it is] good that by grace the heart is confirmed, not with meats,

HEBREWS

in which they who were occupied were not profited; ¹⁰we have an altar from which they who are serving the Dwelling Place have no authority to eat, ¹¹for those beasts whose blood is brought for sin into the holy places through the chief priest—of these the bodies are burned outside the camp. ¹²For this reason, also Jesus—that He might sanctify the people through [His] own blood—suffered outside the gate; ¹³now then, may we go forth to Him outside the camp, bearing His reproach; ¹⁴for we have no abiding city here, but we seek the coming one. ¹⁵Through Him, then, we may always offer up a sacrifice of praise to God, that is, the fruit of lips, giving thanks to His Name. ¹⁶And do not be forgetful of doing good and of fellowship, for God is well-pleased with such sacrifices. ¹⁷Be obedient to those leading you, and be subject, for these watch for your souls, as about to give account, that they may do this with joy, and not sighing, for this [is] unprofitable to you. ¹⁸Pray for us, for we trust that we have a good conscience, willing to behave well in all things, ¹⁹and I call on [you] to do this more abundantly, that I may be restored to you more quickly. ²⁰And the God of peace, who brought up the Great Shepherd of the sheep out of the dead—by the blood of a perpetual covenant—our Lord Jesus, ²¹make you perfect in every good work to do His will, doing in you that which is well-pleasing before Him, through Jesus Christ, to whom [is] the glory through the ages of the ages! Amen. ²²And I beg you, brothers, endure the word of the exhortation, for I have also written to you through few words. ²³Know that the brother Timotheus is released, with whom I will see you, if he may come more shortly. ²⁴Greet all those leading you, and all the holy ones. Those from Italy greet you. ²⁵The grace [is] with you all! Amen.

JAMES

CHAPTER 1

¹James, a servant of God and of the Lord Jesus Christ, to the twelve tribes who are in the dispersion: Greetings! ²Count [it] all joy, my brothers, when you may fall into manifold temptations, ³knowing that the proof of your faith works endurance, ⁴and let the endurance have a perfect work, that you may be perfect and complete, lacking in nothing. ⁵And if any of you lacks wisdom, let him ask from God, who is giving to all generously, and not reproaching, and it will be given to him; ⁶but let him ask in faith, doubting nothing, for he who is doubting has been like a wave of the sea, driven by wind and tossed; ⁷for do not let that man suppose that he will receive anything from the LORD— ⁸a soul-split man [is] unstable in all his ways. ⁹And let the brother who is low rejoice in his exaltation, ¹⁰but the rich in his becoming low, because he will pass away as a flower of grass; ¹¹for the sun rose with the burning heat, and withered the grass, and the flower of it fell, and the beauty of its appearance perished, so also the rich in his way will fade away! ¹²Blessed [is] the man who endures temptation, because, becoming approved, he will receive the garland of life, which the LORD promised to those loving Him. ¹³Let no one who is being tempted say, "I am tempted from God," for God is not tempted by evils, and Himself tempts no one, ¹⁴but each one is tempted, being led away and enticed by his own desires; ¹⁵afterward the desire having conceived, gives birth to sin, and sin having been perfected, brings forth death. ¹⁶Do not be led astray, my beloved brothers. ¹⁷Every good giving, and every perfect gift, is from above, coming down from the Father of lights, with whom is no variation, or shadow of turning; ¹⁸having willed [it], He begot us with a word of truth, for our being a certain first-fruit of His creatures. ¹⁹So then, my beloved brothers, let every man be swift to hear, slow to speak, slow to anger, ²⁰for the wrath of a man does not work the righteousness of God; ²¹for this reason, having put aside all filthiness and superabundance of evil, receive the implanted word in meekness, that is able to save your souls; ²²and become doers of the word, and not hearers only, deceiving yourselves, ²³because, if anyone is a hearer of the word and not a doer, this one has been like to a man viewing his natural face in a mirror, ²⁴for he viewed himself, and has gone away, and immediately he forgot what kind of [man] he was; ²⁵but he who looked into [the] perfect law—that of liberty, and continued there, not becoming a forgetful hearer, but a doer of work—this one will be blessed in his doing. ²⁶If anyone thinks to be religious among you, not bridling his tongue, but deceiving his heart, the religion of this one [is] vain; ²⁷religion pure and undefiled with the God and Father is this: to look after orphans and widows in their tribulation—to keep himself unspotted from the world.

CHAPTER 2

¹My brothers, do not hold the faith of the glory of our Lord Jesus Christ in favor by appearance, ²for if there may come into your synagogue a man with gold ring, in radiant clothing, and there may also come in a poor man in vile clothing, ³and you may look on him bearing the radiant clothing, and may say to him, "You—sit here well," and may say to the poor man, "You—stand there," or, "Sit here under my footstool," ⁴you did not judge fully in yourselves, and became ill-reasoning judges. ⁵Listen, my beloved brothers, did God not choose the poor of this world, rich in faith, and heirs of the kingdom that He promised to those loving Him? ⁶But you dishonored the poor one. Do the rich not oppress you and themselves draw you to judgment-seats? ⁷Do they not themselves speak evil of the good Name having been called on you? ⁸If, indeed, you fulfill royal law, according to the Writing: "You will love your neighbor as yourself," you do well; ⁹but if you favor by appearance, you work sin, being convicted by the Law as transgressors; ¹⁰for whoever will keep the whole Law, but will stumble in one [point], he has become guilty of all; ¹¹for He who is saying, "You may not commit adultery," also said, "You may not murder"; but if you will not commit adultery, but will commit murder, you have become a transgressor of law; ¹²thus, speak and so act as [one] about to be judged by a law of liberty, ¹³for the judgment without mercy [is] to him having not done mercy, and mercy exults over judgment. ¹⁴What [is] the profit, my brothers, if anyone may speak of having faith, but he may not have works? Is that faith able to save him? ¹⁵And if a brother or sister may be naked, and may be destitute of daily food, ¹⁶and anyone of you may say to them, "Depart in peace, be warmed, and be filled," but may not give to them the things necessary for the body, what [is] the profit? ¹⁷So also faith, if it may not have works, is dead by itself. ¹⁸But someone may say, "You have faith, and I have works." Show me your faith without works, and I will show you my faith out of works. ¹⁹You believe that God is one; you do well! The demons also believe—and shudder! ²⁰And do you wish to know, O vain man, that faith apart from works is dead? ²¹Was not our father Abraham considered righteous out of works, having brought up his son Isaac on the altar? ²²Do you see that faith was working with his works, and faith was perfected out of the works? ²³And the Writing was fulfilled that is saying, "And Abraham believed God, and it was reckoned to him for righteousness"; and, "Friend of God" he was called. ²⁴You see, then, that man is considered righteous out of works, and not out of faith only; ²⁵and in like manner also Rahab the prostitute—was she not considered righteous out of works, having received the messengers, and having sent [them] forth by another way? ²⁶For as the body apart from [the] spirit is dead, so also the faith apart from works is dead.

CHAPTER 3

¹Do not let many be teachers, my brothers, having known that we will receive greater judgment, ²for we all make many stumbles; if anyone does not stumble in word, this one [is]

JAMES

a perfect man, able to also bridle the whole body; ³behold, the bits we put into the mouths of the horses for their obeying us, and we direct their whole body; ⁴behold, also the ships, being so great, and being driven by fierce winds, are directed by a very small rudder, wherever the impulse of the [one] steering wills, ⁵so also the tongue is a little member, and boasts greatly; behold, how much forest a little fire kindles! ⁶And the tongue [is] a fire, the world of the unrighteousness, so the tongue is set in our members, which is spotting our whole body, and is setting on fire the course of nature, and is set on fire by Gehenna. ⁷For every nature, both of beasts and of birds, both of creeping things and things of the sea, is subdued, and has been subdued, by the human nature, ⁸but no one of men is able to subdue the tongue—[it is] an unruly evil, full of deadly poison; ⁹with it we bless the God and Father, and with it we curse the men made according to [the] likeness of God; ¹⁰out of the same mouth comes forth blessing and cursing; it does not need, my brothers, these things to so happen; ¹¹does the fountain out of the same opening pour forth the sweet and the bitter? ¹²Is a fig tree able, my brothers, to make olives? Or a vine figs? Neither is salty [water able] to have made sweet water. ¹³Who [is] wise and intelligent among you? Let him show his works out of good behavior in meekness of wisdom, ¹⁴yet, if you have bitter zeal, and rivalry in your heart, do not glory, nor lie against the truth; ¹⁵this wisdom is not descending from above, but earthly, physical, demon-like, ¹⁶for where zeal and rivalry [are], there is insurrection and every evil matter; ¹⁷but the wisdom from above, first, indeed, is pure, then peaceable, gentle, well-convinced, full of kindness and good fruits, uncontentious, and unhypocritical— ¹⁸and the fruit of righteousness in peace is sown to those making peace.

CHAPTER 4

¹From where [are] wars and fightings among you? [Is it] not from here, out of your passions warring in your members? ²You desire, and do not have, [so] you murder; and you are zealous, and are not able to attain, [so] you fight and war; and you do not have, because of your not asking; ³you ask, and you do not receive, because you ask badly, that you may spend [it] in your pleasures. ⁴Adulterers and adulteresses! Have you not known that friendship of the world is enmity with God? Whoever, then, may intend to be a friend of the world, he is designated [as] an enemy of God. ⁵Or, do you think that the Writing says emptily, "The Spirit that has dwelt in us yearns with envy," ⁶but [God] gives greater grace, for this reason it says, "God sets Himself up against proud ones, and He gives grace to lowly ones." ⁷Be subject, then, to God; stand up against the Devil, and he will flee from you; ⁸draw near to God, and He will draw near to you; cleanse hands, you sinners! And purify hearts, you split-souled! ⁹Be exceedingly afflicted, and mourn, and weep, let your laughter be turned to mourning, and the joy to heaviness; ¹⁰be made low before the LORD, and He will exalt you. ¹¹Do not speak against one another, brothers; he who is speaking against a brother, and is judging his brother, speaks against law, and judges law, and if you judge law, you are not a doer of law but a judge. ¹²One is the lawgiver, who is able to save and to destroy; you—who are you that judges the other? ¹³Go, now, you who are saying, "Today and tomorrow we will go on to such a city, and will pass there one year, and traffic, and make gain," ¹⁴who does not know the thing of tomorrow; for what is your life? For it is a vapor that is appearing for a little [while], and then is vanishing; ¹⁵instead, you [ought] to say, "If the LORD may will, we will live, and do this or that"; ¹⁶but now you glory in your pride; all such glorying is evil; ¹⁷to him, then, knowing to do good, and not doing [it], it is sin to him.

CHAPTER 5

¹Go, now, you rich! Weep, howling over your miseries that are coming on [you]; ²your riches have rotted, and your garments have become moth-eaten; ³your gold and silver have rotted, and the rust of them will be to you for a testimony, and will eat your flesh as fire. You have stored up treasure in the last days! ⁴Behold, the reward of the workmen cries out, of those who in-gathered your fields, which has been fraudulently kept back by you, and the exclamations of those who reaped have entered into the ears of the LORD of Hosts; ⁵you lived in luxury on the earth, and were wanton; you nourished your hearts, as in a day of slaughter; ⁶you condemned—you murdered the righteous; he does not resist you. ⁷Be patient, then, brothers, until the coming of the LORD; behold, the farmer expects the precious fruit of the earth, being patient for it, until he may receive rain—early and latter; ⁸you also be patient; establish your hearts, because the coming of the LORD has drawn near; ⁹do not murmur against one another, brothers, that you may not be condemned; behold, the Judge has stood before the door. ¹⁰Brothers, [as] an example of the suffering of evil and of patience, take the prophets who spoke in the Name of the LORD; ¹¹behold, we call those who are enduring blessed; you heard of the endurance of Job, and you have seen the end from the LORD, that the LORD is very compassionate, and pitying. ¹²And before all things, my brothers, do not swear, neither by Heaven, neither by the earth, neither by any other oath, but let your "Yes" be yes, and the "No," no, that you may not fall under judgment. ¹³Does anyone suffer evil among you? Let him pray; is anyone of good cheer? Let him sing psalms; ¹⁴is anyone sick among you? Let him call for the elders of the assembly, and let them pray over him, having anointed him with oil, in the Name of the LORD, ¹⁵and the prayer of faith will save the distressed one, and the LORD will raise him up, and if he may have committed sins, they will be forgiven to him. ¹⁶Be confessing to one another the trespasses, and be praying for one another, that you may be healed; very strong is a working supplication of a righteous man; ¹⁷Elijah was a similar-feeling man as us, and with prayer he prayed—not to rain, and it did not rain on the land three years and six months; ¹⁸and again he prayed, and the sky gave rain, and the land brought forth her fruit. ¹⁹Brothers, if anyone among you may go astray from the truth, and anyone may turn him back, ²⁰let him know that he who turned back a sinner from the straying of his way will save a soul from death, and will cover a multitude of sins.

1 PETER

CHAPTER 1

¹Peter, an apostle of Jesus Christ, to the chosen sojourners of the dispersion of Pontus, Galatia, Cappadocia, Asia, and Bithynia, ²according to [the] foreknowledge of God the Father, by [the] sanctification of the Spirit, to [the] obedience and sprinkling of the blood of Jesus Christ: Grace and peace be multiplied to you! ³Blessed [is] the God and Father of our Lord Jesus Christ, who, according to the abundance of His kindness begot us again to a living hope, through the resurrection of Jesus Christ out of the dead, ⁴to an incorruptible inheritance, and undefiled, and unfading, reserved for you in the heavens, ⁵who, in the power of God are being guarded, through faith, to salvation, ready to be revealed in the last time, ⁶in which you are glad, a little now, if it be necessary, being made to sorrow in various trials, ⁷so that the proof of your faith—much more precious than gold that is perishing, and being approved through fire—may be found to [result in] praise, and honor, and glory, at the revelation of Jesus Christ, ⁸whom, having not seen, you love, in whom, now believing [although] not seeing, you are glad with unspeakable joy and have been filled with glory, ⁹receiving the outcome of the faith—salvation of your souls; ¹⁰concerning which salvation [the] prophets sought out and

1 PETER

searched out, who prophesied concerning the grace toward you, ¹¹searching in regard to what or what manner of time the Spirit of Christ that was in them was signifying, testifying beforehand of the sufferings of Christ and the glory after these, ¹²to whom it was revealed, that not to themselves, but to us they were ministering these, which now were told to you (through those who proclaimed good news to you), by the Holy Spirit sent from Heaven, to which things messengers desire to look into intently. ¹³For this reason, having girded up the loins of your mind, being sober, hope perfectly on the grace that is being brought to you in the revelation of Jesus Christ, ¹⁴as obedient children, not fashioning yourselves to the former desires in your ignorance, ¹⁵but according as He who called you [is] holy, you also, become holy in all behavior, ¹⁶because it has been written: "Become holy, because I am holy"; ¹⁷and if you call on the Father, who is judging without favoritism according to the work of each, pass the time of your sojourn in fear, ¹⁸having known that, not with corruptible things—silver or gold—were you redeemed from your foolish behavior inherited from our forefathers, ¹⁹but with precious blood, as of a lamb unblemished and unspotted—Christ's— ²⁰foreknown, indeed, before the foundation of the world, and revealed in the last times because of you, ²¹who through Him believe in God who raised [Him] out of the dead, and gave glory to Him, so that your faith and hope may be in God. ²²Having purified your souls in the obedience of the truth through the Spirit to unhypocritical brotherly love, love one another earnestly out of a pure heart, ²³being begotten again, not out of corruptible seed, but incorruptible, through a word of God—living and remaining—throughout the age; ²⁴because all flesh [is] as grass, and all glory of man as flower of grass; the grass withered, and the flower of it fell away, ²⁵but the saying of the LORD remains—throughout the age; and this is the saying of good news that was proclaimed to you.

CHAPTER 2

¹Having put aside, then, all evil, and all guile, and hypocrisies, and envyings, and all evil speakings, ²as newborn babies, desire the reasonable, unspoiled milk, so that you may grow up to salvation, ³if [it] so be [that] you tasted that the LORD [is] good, ⁴to whom coming—a living stone—having indeed been disapproved of by men, but with God—choice [and] precious, ⁵and you yourselves are built up as living stones [into] a spiritual house, a holy priesthood, to offer up spiritual sacrifices acceptable to God through Jesus Christ. ⁶For this reason, also, it is contained in the Writing: "Behold, I lay in Zion a chief cornerstone, choice, precious, and he who is believing on Him may not be put to shame"; ⁷to you, then, who are believing—the preciousness; but to the unbelieving, [the] stone that the builders disapproved of—this One has become the head of [the] corner, ⁸and a stone of stumbling and a rock of offense—who are stumbling at the word, being unbelieving—to which they were also set. ⁹But you [are] a chosen race, a royal priesthood, a holy nation, a people acquired, that you may show forth the excellencies of Him who called you out of darkness into His wonderful light, ¹⁰who [were] once not a people, but [are] now the people of God; who had not found mercy, but now have found mercy. ¹¹Beloved, I call on [you], as strangers and sojourners, to keep from the fleshly desires that war against the soul, ¹²having your behavior right among the nations, so that whenever they speak against you as evildoers, seeing [your] good works, they may glorify God in [the] day of inspection. ¹³Be subject, then, to every human creation, because of the LORD, whether to a king, as the highest, ¹⁴whether to governors, as to those sent through him, for punishment, indeed, of evildoers, and a praise of those doing good; ¹⁵because, so is the will of God, doing good, to put to silence the ignorance of the foolish men— ¹⁶as free, and not having freedom as the cloak of evil, but as servants of God; ¹⁷give honor to all; love the brotherhood; fear God; honor the king. ¹⁸Servants, be subject in all fear to the masters, not only to the good and gentle, but also to the crooked; ¹⁹for this [is] grace: if anyone endures sorrows because of conscience toward God, suffering unrighteously; ²⁰for what renown [is it], if sinning and being battered, you endure [it]? But if, doing good and suffering [for it], you endure, this [is] grace with God, ²¹for to this you were called, because Christ also suffered for you, leaving to you an example, that you may follow His steps, ²²who did not commit sin, nor was guile found in His mouth, ²³who being reviled—was not reviling again, suffering—was not threatening, and was committing Himself to Him who is judging righteously, ²⁴who Himself bore our sins in His body on the tree, that having died to sins, we may live to righteousness, by whose stripes you were healed; ²⁵for you were as sheep going astray, but now you turned back to the Shepherd and Overseer of your souls.

CHAPTER 3

¹Wives, be subject to your own husbands in like manner, that even if some are disobedient to the word, they may be won through the behavior of the wives without the word, ²having beheld your pure behavior in fear, ³whose adorning—let it not be that which is outward, of braiding of hair, and of putting around of things of gold, or of putting on of garments, ⁴but—the hidden man of the heart, by the incorruptible [thing] of the meek and quiet spirit, which is of great value before God, ⁵for thus once also the holy women who hoped on God were adorning themselves, being subject to their own husbands, ⁶as Sarah was obedient to Abraham, calling him "lord," of whom you became daughters, doing good, and not fearing any terror. ⁷Husbands, in like manner, dwelling with [them], according to knowledge, as to a weaker vessel—to the wife—imparting honor, as also being heirs together of the grace of life, that your prayers are not hindered. ⁸And finally, be all of one mind, having fellow-feeling, loving as brothers, compassionate, courteous, ⁹not giving back evil for evil, or reviling for reviling, but on the contrary, blessing, having known that you were called to this, that you may inherit a blessing; ¹⁰for "he who is willing to love life, and to see good days, let him guard his tongue from evil, and his lips—not to speak guile; ¹¹let him turn aside from evil, and do good, let him seek peace and pursue it; ¹²because the eyes of the LORD [are] on the righteous, and His ears—to their supplication, but the face of the LORD [is] against those doing evil"; ¹³and who [is] he who will be doing you evil, if you may become imitators of Him who is good? ¹⁴But if you also should suffer because of righteousness, [you are] blessed! And do not be afraid of their fear, nor be troubled, ¹⁵but sanctify the LORD God in your hearts. And always [be] ready for defense to everyone who is asking of you an account concerning the hope that [is] in you, with meekness and fear, ¹⁶having a good conscience, so that whenever they speak against you as evildoers, they may be ashamed—[those] who are maligning your good behavior in Christ; ¹⁷for if the will of God wills it, [it is] better to suffer doing good, than doing evil; ¹⁸also because Christ suffered once for sin—righteous for unrighteous—that He might lead us to God, indeed having been put to death in the flesh, but having been made alive in the Spirit, ¹⁹by which, having gone, He also preached to the spirits in prison, ²⁰who sometime [ago] disobeyed when once the long-suffering of God waited, in [the] days of Noah—an ark being prepared—in which few, that is, eight souls, were saved through water, ²¹also an antitype to immersion which now saves you—not a putting away of the filth of flesh, but the question of a good conscience in regard to God, through the resurrection of Jesus Christ, ²²who is at the right hand of God, having gone on to Heaven—messengers, and authorities, and powers, having been subjected to Him.

CHAPTER 4

¹Christ, then, having suffered for us in the flesh, you also arm yourselves with the same mind, because he who suffered in the flesh has finished [with] sin, ²no longer in the desires of men, but in the will of God, to live the rest of the time in the flesh; ³for the time has sufficiently passed to have carried out the will of the nations, having walked in licentiousness, lusts, excesses of wines, revelings, drinking-bouts, and unlawful idolatries, ⁴in which they think it strange—your not running with them to the same excess of wastefulness, slandering [you]— ⁵who will give an account to Him who is ready to judge [the] living and [the] dead, ⁶for this also was good news proclaimed to dead men, that they may be judged, indeed, according to men in the flesh, but may live according to God in the Spirit. ⁷Now the end of all things has come near; be sober-minded, then, and be sober in [your] prayers. ⁸Before all things,

1 PETER

having earnest love among yourselves, because love covers a multitude of sins; ⁹[be] hospitable to one another, without murmuring; ¹⁰each [one], according as he received a gift, ministering it to one another, as good stewards of the manifold grace of God; ¹¹if anyone speaks, [speak] as oracles of God; if anyone ministers, [minister] as of the strength which God supplies, so that in all things God may be glorified through Jesus Christ, to whom is the glory and the power through the ages of the ages. Amen. ¹²Beloved, do not think it strange at the fiery suffering among you that is coming to try you, as if a strange thing were happening to you, ¹³but according as you have fellowship with the sufferings of the Christ, rejoice, that you may also rejoice in the revelation of His glory—exulting; ¹⁴if you are reproached in the Name of Christ—[you are] blessed, because the Spirit of glory and of God rests on you; in regard, indeed, to them, is evil spoken of Him, and in regard to you, He is glorified; ¹⁵for let none of you suffer as a murderer, or thief, or evildoer, or as a meddler into other men's matters; ¹⁶and if as a Christian, do not let him be ashamed, but let him glorify God in this respect; ¹⁷because it is the time of the judgment to have begun from the house of God, and if first from us, what [is] the end of those disobedient to the good news of God? ¹⁸And if the righteous man is scarcely saved, where will the ungodly and sinner appear? ¹⁹So that those also suffering according to the will of God, as to a steadfast Creator, let them commit their own souls in doing good.

CHAPTER 5

¹Elders who [are] among you, I exhort [you], [as] a fellow-elder, and a witness of the sufferings of the Christ, and a partaker of the glory about to be revealed, ²feed the flock of God that [is] among you, overseeing not by compulsion, but willingly, neither for shameful gain, but eagerly, ³neither as exercising lordship over the heritages, but becoming patterns for the flock, ⁴and the Chief Shepherd having appeared, you will receive the unfading garland of glory. ⁵In like manner, you young [ones], be subject to elders, and all subjecting yourselves to one another; clothe yourselves with humble-mindedness, because God resists the proud, but He gives grace to the humble; ⁶be humbled, then, under the powerful hand of God, that He may exalt you in good time, ⁷having cast all your care on Him, because He cares for you. ⁸Be sober, vigilant, because your opponent the Devil walks around as a roaring lion, seeking whom he may swallow up, ⁹whom you must resist, steadfast in the faith, having known the same sufferings of your brotherhood to be accomplished in the world. ¹⁰And the God of all grace, who called you to His perpetual glory in Christ Jesus, having suffered a little, Himself make you perfect, establish, strengthen, settle [you]; ¹¹to Him [is] the glory and the power through the ages and the ages! Amen. ¹²Through Silvanus, the faithful brother as I reckon, I wrote through few [words] to you, exhorting and testifying this to be the true grace of God in which you have stood. ¹³She in Babylon chosen with you greets you, and my son Marcus. ¹⁴Greet one another in a kiss of love. Peace to you all who [are] in Christ Jesus! Amen.

2 PETER

CHAPTER 1

¹Simeon Peter, a servant and an apostle of Jesus Christ, to those who obtained an equally precious faith with us in the righteousness of our God and Savior Jesus Christ: ²Grace and peace be multiplied to you in the acknowledgment of God and of Jesus our Lord! ³As His divine power has given to us all things pertaining to life and piety, through the acknowledgment of Him who called us through glory and virtue, ⁴through which the most great and precious promises have been given to us, that through these you may become partakers of a divine nature, having escaped from the corruption [and] lust in the world. ⁵And [for] this same [reason] also, having brought in all diligence, supplement your faith with virtue, and with virtue—knowledge, ⁶and with knowledge—self-control, and with self-control—endurance, and with endurance—piety, ⁷and with piety—brotherly kindness, and with brotherly kindness—love; ⁸for these things being in you and abounding, make [you] neither inert nor unfruitful in regard to the knowledge of our Lord Jesus Christ, ⁹for he with whom these things are not present is blind, dim-sighted, having become forgetful of the cleansing of his old sins; ¹⁰therefore, rather, brothers, be diligent to make steadfast your calling and [divine] selection, for doing these things you may never stumble; ¹¹in this way the entrance into the continuous kingdom of our Lord and Savior Jesus Christ will be richly supplemented to you. ¹²Therefore, I will always be ready to remind you about these things, although you have known [them] and have been established in the present truth, ¹³and I think right, so long as I am in this tent, to stir you up in reminding [you], ¹⁴having known that the laying aside of my tent is soon, even as our Lord Jesus Christ also showed to me. ¹⁵And I will also be diligent [to ensure] that you always have a remembrance to make of these things after my departure. ¹⁶For having not followed out skillfully devised fables, we made known to you the power and coming of our Lord Jesus Christ, but having become eyewitnesses of His majesty— ¹⁷for having received honor and glory from God the Father, such a voice being borne to Him by the Excellent Glory: "This is My Son, the Beloved, in whom I delighted"; ¹⁸and we heard this voice borne out of Heaven, being with Him at the holy mountain. ¹⁹And we have a more firm prophetic word, to which we do well giving heed, as to a lamp shining in a dark place, until day may dawn, and [the] morning star may arise in your hearts; ²⁰knowing this first, that no prophecy of the Writing comes of private exposition, ²¹for prophecy never came by [the] will of man, but men spoke from God, being brought by the Holy Spirit.

CHAPTER 2

¹But there also came false prophets among the people, as there will also be false teachers among you, who will stealthily bring in destructive sects, even denying the Master who bought them, bringing quick destruction to themselves, ²and many will follow out their destructive ways, because of whom the way of the truth will be spoken of [as] evil, ³and in covetousness, with forged words, they will make merchandise of you, whose judgment of old is not idle, and their destruction does not slumber. ⁴For if God did not spare messengers having sinned, but having cast [them] down to Tartarus with chains of deepest gloom, delivered [them], having been reserved to judgment, ⁵and did not spare the old world, but kept the eighth person, Noah, a preacher of righteousness, having brought a flood on the world of the impious, ⁶and having turned the cities of Sodom and Gomorrah to ashes, condemned with an overthrow, having set [them as] an example to those about to be impious, ⁷and He rescued righteous Lot, worn down by the conduct of the lawless in licentiousness, ⁸for the righteous [man] dwelling among them was tormented in [his] righteous soul, day by day, in seeing and hearing unlawful works— ⁹the LORD has known to rescue [the] pious out of temptation, and to keep [the] unrighteous being punished to [the] day of judgment, ¹⁰and chiefly those following after the flesh in lust [and] defilement, and despising lordship. Bold, self-pleased, they are not afraid to speak evil of glorious ones, ¹¹whereas messengers, being greater in strength and power, do not bear a slanderous judgment against them before the LORD; ¹²and these, as irrational natural beasts, made to be caught and destroyed—in what things they are ignorant of, slandering—in their destruction will be destroyed; ¹³doing unjustly, [they will receive] a reward of unrighteousness, esteeming pleasure in the day, [and] luxury—[they are] spots and blemishes, reveling in their deceits, feasting with you, ¹⁴having eyes full of adultery, and unable to cease from sin, enticing unstable souls, having a heart exercised in covetousnesses, children of a curse, ¹⁵having

forsaken a right way, they went astray, having followed in the way of Balaam the [son] of Bosor, who loved a reward of unrighteousness, ¹⁶and had a rebuke of his own iniquity—a mute donkey, having spoken in man's voice, forbid the madness of the prophet. ¹⁷These are wells without water, and clouds driven by a storm, to whom the deepest gloom of darkness has been kept throughout the age; ¹⁸for speaking swollen words of vanity, they entice in desires of the flesh—licentiousness, those who had truly escaped from those conducting themselves in error, ¹⁹promising liberty to them, themselves being servants of corruption, for by whom anyone has been overcome, he has been brought to servitude to this one also; ²⁰for if having escaped from the defilements of the world, in the acknowledging of the LORD and Savior Jesus Christ, and again being entangled by these things, they have been overcome, the last things have become worse to them than the first, ²¹for it were better to them not to have acknowledged the way of righteousness, than having acknowledged [it], to turn back from the holy command delivered to them, ²²and that of the true proverb has happened to them: "A dog turned back on his own vomit," and, "A sow having bathed herself—to rolling in mire."

CHAPTER 3

¹This [is] now, beloved, a second letter I write to you, in both which I stir up your pure mind in reminding [you] ²to be mindful of the sayings said before by the holy prophets, and of the command of us the apostles of the LORD and Savior, ³knowing this first, that there will come scoffers in the last days, going on according to their own desires, ⁴and saying, "Where is the promise of His coming? For since the fathers fell asleep, all things so remain from the beginning of the creation"; ⁵for this they willingly conceal, that the heavens existed long ago, and the earth having been established by the word of God out of water and through water, ⁶through which the world then, having been flooded by water, was destroyed; ⁷and by the same word, the present heavens and earth, having been stored up for fire, are being preserved until [the] day of judgment and destruction of impious men. ⁸And do not let this one thing be concealed from you, beloved, that one day with the LORD [is] as one thousand years and one thousand years as one day; ⁹the LORD is not slow in regard to the promise, as some count slowness, but is long-suffering to us, not intending any to be lost, but all to come to conversion, ¹⁰and it will come—the Day of the LORD—as a thief in the night, in which the heavens will pass away with a rushing noise, and the elements will be dissolved with burning heat, and [the] earth and the works in it will not be found. ¹¹All these, then, being dissolved, what kind of persons ought you to be in holy behaviors and pious acts, ¹²waiting for and hurrying the coming of the Day of God, by which the heavens, being on fire, will be dissolved, and the elements will melt with burning heat? ¹³And we wait for new heavens and a new earth according to His promise, in which righteousness dwells; ¹⁴for this reason, beloved, waiting for these things, be diligent, spotless and unblameable, to be found by Him in peace, ¹⁵and count the long-suffering of our Lord [as] salvation, according as also our beloved brother Paul—according to the wisdom given to him—wrote to you, ¹⁶as also in all the letters, speaking in them concerning these things, among which are some things [that are] hard to be understood, which the untaught and unstable twist, as also the other Writings, to their own destruction. ¹⁷You, then, beloved, knowing before, take heed, lest, together with the error of the impious being led away, you may fall from your own steadfastness, ¹⁸and increase in grace, and in the knowledge of our Lord and Savior Jesus Christ; to Him [is] the glory both now, and to the day of the age! Amen.

1 JOHN

CHAPTER 1

¹That which was from the beginning, that which we have heard, that which we have seen with our eyes, that which we beheld, and our hands handled, concerning the Word of Life— ²and the Life appeared, and we have seen, and testify, and declare to you the continuous Life, which was with the Father, and was revealed to us— ³we declare to you that which we have seen and heard, that you also may have fellowship with us, and our fellowship [is] with the Father, and with His Son Jesus Christ; ⁴and these things we write to you, that your joy may be full. ⁵And this is the message that we have heard from Him, and announce to you, that God is light, and darkness is not in Him at all; ⁶if we may say, "We have fellowship with Him," and may walk in the darkness—we lie, and do not [speak] the truth; ⁷and if we may walk in the light, as He is in the light—we have fellowship with one another, and the blood of His Son Jesus Christ cleanses us from every sin; ⁸if we may say, "We have no sin," we lead ourselves astray, and the truth is not in us; ⁹if we may confess our sins, He is steadfast and righteous that He may forgive us the sins, and may cleanse us from every unrighteousness; ¹⁰if we may say, "We have not sinned," we make Him a liar, and His word is not in us.

CHAPTER 2

¹My little children, these things I write to you that you may not sin: and if anyone may sin, we have an Advocate with the Father, Jesus Christ, [the] Righteous One, ²and He is [the] propitiation for our sins, and not only for ours, but also for the whole world, ³and in this we know that we have known Him, if we may keep His commands; ⁴he who is saying, "I have known Him," and is not keeping His commands, is a liar, and the truth is not in him; ⁵and whoever may keep His word, truly the love of God has been perfected in him; in this we know that we are in Him. ⁶He who is saying he remains in Him, himself ought to also walk according as He walked. ⁷Beloved, I do not write a new command to you, but an old command, that you had from the beginning—the old command is the word that you heard from the beginning; ⁸again, a new command I write to you, which is true in Him and in you, because the darkness is passing away, and the true light now shines; ⁹he who is saying he is in the light, and is hating his brother, he is in the darkness until now; ¹⁰he who is loving his brother, he remains in the light, and there is not a stumbling-block in him; ¹¹but he who is hating his brother, he is in the darkness, and he walks in the darkness, and he has not known where he goes, because the darkness blinded his eyes. ¹²I write to you, little children, because sins have been forgiven you through His Name; ¹³I write to you, fathers, because you have known Him who [is] from the beginning; I write to you, young men, because you have overcome the evil [one]; I write to you, little youths, because you have known the Father; ¹⁴I wrote to you, fathers, because you have known Him who [is] from the beginning; I wrote to you, young men, because you are strong, and the word of God remains in you, and you have overcome the evil [one]. ¹⁵Do not love the world, nor the things in the world; if anyone loves the world, the love of the Father is not in him, ¹⁶because all that [is] in the world—the desire of the flesh, and the desire of the eyes, and the ostentation of [one's] life—is not of the Father, but of the world, ¹⁷and the world is passing away, and the desire of it, but he who is doing the will of God, he remains—throughout the age. ¹⁸Little youths, it is the last hour; and even as you heard that the antichrist comes, even now antichrists have become many—whereby we know that it is [the] last hour; ¹⁹they went forth out of us, but they were not of us, for if they had been of us, they would have remained with us; but [they went out] so that they might be revealed that they are not all of us. ²⁰And you have an anointing from the Holy One, and have known all things; ²¹I did not write to you because you have not known the truth, but because you have known it, and because no lie is of the truth. ²²Who is the liar, except he who is denying that Jesus is the Christ? This one is the antichrist who is denying the Father and the Son; ²³everyone who is denying the Son, neither has the Father; he who is confessing the Son has the Father also. ²⁴You, then, that which you heard from the beginning, let it remain in you; if that which you heard from

the beginning may remain in you, you also will remain in the Son and in the Father, ²⁵and this is the promise that He promised us—the continuous life. ²⁶These things I wrote to you concerning those leading you astray; ²⁷and you, the anointing that you received from Him, it remains in you, and you have no need that anyone may teach you, but as the same anointing teaches you concerning all, and is true, and is not a lie, and even as was taught you, you will remain in Him. ²⁸And now, little children, remain in Him, so that when He may have appeared, we may have boldness, and may not be ashamed before Him, at His coming; ²⁹if you know that He is righteous, know that everyone doing righteousness, has been begotten of Him.

CHAPTER 3

¹See what love the Father has given to us, that we may be called children of God; because of this the world does not know us, because it did not know Him. ²Beloved, now, we are children of God, and it was not yet revealed what we will be. We have known that if He may have appeared, we will be like Him, because we will see Him as He is; ³and everyone who is having this hope on Him, purifies himself, even as He is pure. ⁴Everyone who is doing sin, he also does lawlessness, and sin is lawlessness, ⁵and you have known that He appeared that He may take away our sins, and sin is not in Him; ⁶everyone who is remaining in Him does not sin; everyone who is sinning, has not seen Him, nor known Him. ⁷Little children, let no one lead you astray; he who is doing righteousness is righteous, even as He is righteous, ⁸he who is doing sin, he is of the Devil, because the Devil sins from the beginning; for this [reason] the Son of God appeared, that He may undo the works of the Devil; ⁹everyone who has been begotten of God, he does not sin, because His seed remains in him, and he is not able to sin, because he has been begotten of God. ¹⁰In this are revealed the children of God, and the children of the Devil; everyone who is not doing righteousness, is not of God, and he who is not loving his brother, ¹¹because this is the message that you heard from the beginning, that we may love one another, ¹²not as Cain—he was of the evil one, and he slew his brother. And for [what] reason did he slay him? Because his works were evil, and those of his brother [were] righteous. ¹³Do not wonder, my brothers, if the world hates you; ¹⁴we have known that we have passed out of death into life, because we love the brothers; he who is not loving [his] brother remains in death. ¹⁵Everyone who is hating his brother is a manslayer, and you have known that no manslayer has continuous life remaining in him; ¹⁶in this we have known love, because He laid down His life for us, and we ought to lay down [our] lives for the brothers; ¹⁷and whoever may have the goods of the world, and may view his brother having need, and may shut up his yearnings from him—how does the love of God remain in him? ¹⁸My little children, may we not love in word nor in tongue, but in work and in truth! ¹⁹And in this we know that we are of the truth, and before Him we will assure our hearts, ²⁰because if our heart may condemn—because greater is God than our heart, and He knows all things. ²¹Beloved, if our heart may not condemn us, we have boldness toward God, ²²and whatever we may ask, we receive from Him, because we keep His commands, and we do the things pleasing before Him, ²³and this is His command, that we may believe in the Name of His Son Jesus Christ, and may love one another, even as He gave command to us, ²⁴and he who is keeping His commands, remains in Him, and He in him; and in this we know that He remains in us, from the Spirit that He gave us.

CHAPTER 4

¹Beloved, do not believe every spirit, but prove the spirits, if they are of God, because many false prophets have gone forth into the world. ²In this you know the Spirit of God: every spirit that confesses Jesus Christ having come in the flesh, it is of God, ³and every spirit that does not confess Jesus Christ having come in the flesh, it is not of God; and this is that of the antichrist, which you heard that it comes, and now it is already in the world. ⁴You are of God, little children, and you have overcome them; because greater is He who [is] in you, than he who is in the world. ⁵They are of the world, because they speak of this from the world, and the world hears them; ⁶we are of God; he who is knowing God hears us; he who is not of God, does not hear us; from this we know the Spirit of truth and the spirit of error. ⁷Beloved, may we love one another, because love is of God, and everyone loving has been begotten of God, and knows God; ⁸he who is not loving did not know God, because God is love. ⁹In this was revealed the love of God in us, because God has sent His only begotten Son into the world, that we may live through Him; ¹⁰in this is love, not that we loved God, but that He loved us, and sent His Son [as] the propitiation for our sins. ¹¹Beloved, if God so loved us, we also ought to love one another; ¹²no one has ever seen God; if we may love one another, God remains in us, and His love is having been perfected in us; ¹³in this we know that we remain in Him, and He in us, because of His Spirit He has given us. ¹⁴And we have seen and testify that the Father has sent the Son [as] Savior of the world; ¹⁵whoever may confess that Jesus is the Son of God, God remains in him, and he in God; ¹⁶and we have known and believed the love that God has in us; God is love, and he who is remaining in love, remains in God, and God in him. ¹⁷In this, love has been perfected with us, that we may have boldness in the day of judgment, because even as He is, we also are in this world. ¹⁸There is no fear in love, but perfect love casts out fear, because fear involves punishment, and he who is fearing has not been made perfect in love; ¹⁹we love Him, because He first loved us; ²⁰if anyone may say, "I love God," and may hate his brother, he is a liar; for he who is not loving his brother whom he has seen, how is he able to love God whom he has not seen? ²¹And this [is] the command we have from Him, that he who is loving God, may also love his brother.

CHAPTER 5

¹Everyone who is believing that Jesus is the Christ has been begotten of God, and everyone who is loving Him who begot, also loves him who is begotten of Him. ²In this we know that we love the children of God, when we may love God and may keep His commands; ³for this is the love of God, that we may keep His commands, and His commands are not burdensome; ⁴because everyone who is begotten of God overcomes the world, and this is the victory that overcame the world—our faith. ⁵Who is he who is overcoming the world, if not he who is believing that Jesus is the Son of God? ⁶This One is He who came through water and blood—Jesus the Christ, not in water only, but in the water and the blood; and the Spirit is the [One] testifying, because the Spirit is the truth, ⁷because [there] are three who are testifying [[in Heaven: the Father, the Word, and the Holy Spirit, and these three are one; ⁸and [there] are three who are testifying in the earth]]: the Spirit, and the water, and the blood, and the three are into the one. ⁹If we receive the testimony of men, the testimony of God is greater, because this is the testimony of God that He has testified concerning His Son. ¹⁰He who is believing in the Son of God has the testimony in himself; he who is not believing God has made Him a liar, because he has not believed in the testimony that God has testified concerning His Son; ¹¹and this is the testimony, that God gave continuous life to us, and this life is in His Son; ¹²he who is having the Son has life; he who is not having the Son of God does not have life. ¹³I wrote these things to you who are believing in the Name of the Son of God, that you may know that you have continuous life, and that you may believe in the Name of the Son of God. ¹⁴And this is the boldness that we have toward Him, that if we may ask anything according to His will, He hears us, ¹⁵and if we have known that He hears us, whatever we may ask, we have known that we have the requests that we have requested from Him. ¹⁶If anyone may see his brother sinning a sin [that is] not to death, he will ask, and He will give life to him—to those not

1 JOHN

sinning to death; there is sin to death—I do not say that he may ask concerning it; ¹⁷all unrighteousness is sin, and there is sin [that is] not to death. ¹⁸We have known that everyone who has been begotten of God does not sin, but He who was begotten of God keeps him, and the evil one does not touch him; ¹⁹we have known that we are of God, and the whole world lies [under the power] of the evil [one]; ²⁰but we have known that the Son of God has come, and has given us a mind that we may know Him who is true, and we are in Him who is true, in His Son Jesus Christ; this One is the true God and the continuous Life! ²¹Little children, guard yourselves from idols! Amen.

2 JOHN

CHAPTER 1

¹The elder to the chosen lady, and to her children, whom I love in truth, and not only I, but also all those having known the truth, ²because of the truth that is remaining in us, and will be with us throughout the age, ³there will be with you grace, mercy, [and] peace from God the Father, and from the Lord Jesus Christ, the Son of the Father, in truth and love. ⁴I rejoiced exceedingly that I have found of your children walking in truth, even as we received a command from the Father; ⁵and now I implore you, lady, not as writing to you a new command, but which we had from the beginning, that we may love one another, ⁶and this is love, that we may walk according to His commands; this is the command, even as you heard from the beginning, that you may walk in it, ⁷because many deceivers entered into the world, who are not confessing Jesus Christ coming in flesh; this one is he who is leading astray, and the antichrist. ⁸See to yourselves that you may not lose the things that we worked for, but may receive a full reward; ⁹everyone who is transgressing, and is not remaining in the teaching of the Christ, does not have God; he who is remaining in the teaching of the Christ, this one has both the Father and the Son; ¹⁰if anyone comes to you, and does not bear this teaching, do not receive him into the house, and do not say to him, "Greetings!" ¹¹For he who is saying to him, "Greetings," has fellowship with his evil works. ¹²Having many things to write to you, I did not intend [it] with paper and ink, but I hope to come to you, and speak mouth to mouth, that our joy may be full. ¹³The children of your chosen sister greet you. Amen.

3 JOHN

CHAPTER 1

¹The elder to Gaius the beloved, whom I love in truth! ²Beloved, I desire you to prosper concerning all things, and to be in health, even as your soul prospers, ³for I rejoiced exceedingly, brothers coming and testifying of the truth in you, even as you walk in truth; ⁴I have no joy greater than these things, that I may hear of my children walking in truth. ⁵Beloved, you act faithfully in whatever you may do toward the brothers and the one [among] strangers, ⁶who testified of your love before an assembly, whom you will do well, having sent forward worthily of God, ⁷because they went forth for [His] Name, receiving nothing from the nations; ⁸we, then, ought to receive such, that we may become fellow-workers to the truth. ⁹I wrote to the assembly, but he who is loving to be first among them—Diotrephes—does not receive us; ¹⁰because of this, if I may come, I will cause him to remember his works that he does, talking nonsense against us with evil words; and not content with these, neither does he himself receive the brothers, and he forbids those intending [to receive them], and he casts [them] out of the assembly. ¹¹Beloved, do not be following that which is evil, but that which is good; he who is doing good, he is of God, [but] he who is doing evil has not seen God; ¹²testimony has been given to Demetrius by all, and by the truth itself, and we also—we testify, and you have known that our testimony is true. ¹³Many things I had to write, but I do not wish to write to you through ink and pen, ¹⁴and I hope to see you soon, and we will speak mouth to mouth. Peace to you! The friends greet you. Be greeting the friends by name.

JUDE

CHAPTER 1

¹Judas, a servant of Jesus Christ, and brother of James, to those called, having been loved in God [the] Father, and having been kept in Jesus Christ, ²mercy and peace and love be multiplied to you! ³Beloved, using all diligence to write to you concerning our common salvation, I had necessity to write to you, exhorting [you] to fight for the faith once delivered to the holy ones, ⁴for there came in certain men stealthily, having been written beforehand to this judgment long ago, impious, perverting the grace of our God to licentiousness, and denying our only Master and Lord—Jesus Christ. ⁵Now I intend to remind you, you once having known all this, that Jesus, having saved a people out of the land of Egypt, He secondly destroyed those not having believed; ⁶messengers also, those who did not keep their own principality, but left their proper dwelling, He has kept in eternal bonds under darkness until [the] judgment of [the] great day, ⁷as Sodom and Gomorrah, and the cities around them, in like manner to these [messengers], having given themselves to whoredom, and having gone after other flesh, have been set before [as] an example, undergoing the justice of continuous fire. ⁸In like manner, nevertheless, those dreaming indeed defile the flesh, and they disregard lordship, and they speak evil of glorious [ones], ⁹yet Michael, the chief messenger, when disputing with the Devil, reasoning about the body of Moses, did not dare to bring against [him] a judgment of slander, but said, "The LORD rebuke you!" ¹⁰But these, indeed, whatever [things] they have not known, they speak evil of; and whatever [they know], like the irrational beasts, they understand naturally—in these they are corrupted; ¹¹woe to them! Because they went on in the way of Cain, and they rushed to the deceit of Balaam for reward, and in the controversy of Korah they perished. ¹²These are stains at your love-feasts, feasting together with you without fear, shepherding themselves; waterless clouds, being carried away by winds; autumnal trees without fruit, having died twice, having been uprooted; ¹³wild waves of a sea, foaming up their own shameful [deeds]; stars going astray, for whom the gloom of the darkness throughout the age has been kept. ¹⁴And Enoch, the seventh from Adam, also prophesied to these, saying, "Behold, the LORD has come with myriads of His holy ones, ¹⁵to do judgment against all, and to convict all their impious ones, concerning all their works of impiety that they did impiously, and concerning all the harsh [words] that impious sinners spoke against Him." ¹⁶These are discontented grumblers, walking according to their own lusts; and their mouth speaks swollen words,

JUDE

giving admiration to persons for the sake of profit; ¹⁷but you, beloved, remember the sayings spoken before by the apostles of our Lord Jesus Christ, ¹⁸that they said to you, that in the last time there will be scoffers, following after their own lusts of impieties, ¹⁹these are those causing divisions, natural men, not having the Spirit. ²⁰But you, beloved, building yourselves up on your most holy faith, praying in the Holy Spirit, ²¹keep yourselves in the love of God, waiting for the mercy of our Lord Jesus Christ [resulting] in continuous life; ²²and, indeed, show mercy to those who are doubting, ²³and rescue others by snatching [them] out of fire; but show mercy to others in fear, hating even the coat having been stained from the flesh. ²⁴And to Him who is able to guard you without stumbling, and to set [you] in the presence of His glory unblemished, in gladness, ²⁵to the only wise God our Savior, [is] glory and greatness, power and authority, both now and forever! Amen.

REVELATION

CHAPTER 1

¹A revelation of Jesus Christ that God gave to Him to show to His servants what things must quickly come to pass; and He signified [it], having sent through His messenger to His servant John, ²who testified [to] the word of God, and the testimony of Jesus Christ, as many things as he also saw. ³Blessed is he who is reading, and those hearing the words of the prophecy, and keeping the things written in it, for the time is near! ⁴John, to the seven assemblies that [are] in Asia: Grace to you, and peace, from Him who is, and who was, and who is coming, and from the Seven Spirits that are before His throne, ⁵and from Jesus Christ, the faithful witness, the firstborn out of the dead, and the ruler of the kings of the earth; to Him loving us and having released us from our sins in His blood, ⁶[He] has also made us kings and priests to His God and Father, to Him—the glory and the power through the ages of the ages! Amen. ⁷Behold, He comes with the clouds, and every eye will see Him, even those who pierced Him, and all the tribes of the land will wail because of Him. Yes! Amen! ⁸"I am the Alpha and the Omega, beginning and end, says the LORD, who is, and who was, and who is coming—the Almighty." ⁹I, John, who [am] also your brother, and fellow-partner in the tribulation, and in the kingdom and endurance of Jesus Christ, was in the island that is called Patmos, because of the word of God, and because of the testimony of Jesus Christ; ¹⁰I was in the Spirit on the LORD's Day, and I heard a great voice behind me, as of a trumpet, saying, ¹¹"I am the Alpha and the Omega, the First and the Last," and, "Write what you see in a scroll, and send [it] to the seven assemblies that [are] in Asia: to Ephesus, and to Smyrna, and to Pergamos, and to Thyatira, and to Sardis, and to Philadelphia, and to Laodicea." ¹²And I turned to see the voice that spoke with me, and having turned, I saw seven golden lampstands, ¹³and in the midst of the seven lampstands, [One] like a Son of Man, clothed to the foot, and having been girded around at the breasts with a golden girdle, ¹⁴and His head and hairs [were] white, as if white wool—as snow, and His eyes as a flame of fire; ¹⁵and His feet like to frankincense-colored brass, as having been fired in a furnace, and His voice as a sound of many waters; ¹⁶and having seven stars in His right hand, and out of His mouth a sharp two-edged sword is proceeding, and His countenance—as the sun shining in its might. ¹⁷And when I saw Him, I fell at His feet as dead, and He placed His right hand on me, saying to me, "Do not be afraid; I am the First and the Last, ¹⁸and He who is living, and I became dead, and behold, I am living through the ages of the ages. Amen! And I have the keys of Hades and of death. ¹⁹Write the things that you have seen, and the things that are, and the things that are about to come after these things; ²⁰the secret of the seven stars that you have seen on My right hand, and the seven golden lampstands: the seven stars are messengers of the seven assemblies, and the seven lampstands that you have seen are seven assemblies."

CHAPTER 2

¹"To the messenger of the Ephesian assembly write: These things says He who is holding the seven stars in His right hand, who is walking in the midst of the seven golden lampstands: ²I have known your works, and your labor, and your endurance, and that you are not able to bear evil ones, and that you have tried those saying themselves to be apostles and are not, and have found them liars, ³and you bore, and have endurance, and have toiled because of My Name, and have not been weary. ⁴But I have against you that you left your first love! ⁵Remember, then, from where you have fallen, and convert, and do the first works; and if not, I come to you quickly, and will remove your lampstand from its place—if you may not convert; ⁶but this you have, that you hate the works of the Nicolaitans, that I also hate. ⁷He who is having an ear—let him hear what the Spirit says to the assemblies: To him who is overcoming—I will give to him to eat of the Tree of Life that is in the midst of the paradise of God. ⁸And to the messenger of the assembly of the Smyrneans write: These things says the First and the Last, who became dead and lived: ⁹I have known your works, and tribulation, and poverty—yet you are rich—and the slander of those saying themselves to be Jews, and are not, but [are] a synagogue of Satan. ¹⁰Do not be afraid of the things that you are about to suffer; behold, the Devil is about to cast [some] of you into prison, that you may be tried, and you will have tribulation ten days; become faithful to death, and I will give to you the garland of life. ¹¹He who is having an ear—let him hear what the Spirit says to the assemblies: He who is overcoming may not be injured of the second death. ¹²And to the messenger of the assembly in Pergamos write: These things says He who is having the sharp two-edged sword: ¹³I have known your works, and where you dwell—where the throne of Satan [is]—and you hold fast My Name, and you did not deny My faith, even in the days in which Antipas [was] My faithful witness, who was put to death beside you, where Satan dwells. ¹⁴But I have a few things against you: that you have there those holding the teaching of Balaam, who taught Balak to cast a stumbling-block before the sons of Israel, to eat idol-sacrifices, and to commit whoredom; ¹⁵so have you, even you, those holding the teaching of the Nicolaitans—which thing I hate. ¹⁶Convert! And if not, I come to you quickly, and will fight against them with the sword of My mouth. ¹⁷He who is having an ear—let him hear what the Spirit says to the assemblies: To him who is overcoming, I will give to him to eat from the hidden manna, and will give to him a white stone, and on the stone a new name written, that no one knew except him who is receiving [it]. ¹⁸And to the messenger of the assembly of Thyatira write: These things says the Son of God, who is having His eyes as a flame of fire, and His feet like to frankincense-colored brass: ¹⁹I have known your works, and love, and ministry, and faith, and your endurance, and your works—and the last [are] more than the first. ²⁰But I have a few things against you: that you allow the woman Jezebel, who is calling herself a prophetess, to teach, and to lead astray, My servants to commit whoredom, and to eat idol-sacrifices; ²¹and I gave to her a time that she might convert from her whoredom, and she did not convert; ²²behold, I will cast her into a bed, and those committing adultery with her into great tribulation—if they may not convert from her works, ²³and I

will kill her children in death, and all the assemblies will know that I am He who is searching affections and hearts; and I will give to you—to each—according to your works. ²⁴And to you I say, and to the rest who are in Thyatira, as many as do not have this teaching, and who did not know the depths of Satan, as they say—I will not put on you another burden, ²⁵but hold that which you have, until I may come; ²⁶and he who is overcoming, and who is keeping My works to the end, I will give to him authority over the nations, ²⁷and he will rule them with a rod of iron—they will be broken as the vessels of the potter—as I have also received from My Father; ²⁸and I will give to him the morning star. ²⁹He who is having an ear—let him hear what the Spirit says to the assemblies."

CHAPTER 3

¹"And to the messenger of the assembly in Sardis write: These things says He who is having the Seven Spirits of God, and the seven stars: I have known your works, and that you have the name that you live, and you are dead; ²be watching, and strengthen the rest of the things that are about to die, for I have not found your works fulfilled before God. ³Remember, then, what you have received and heard, and keep [it] and convert: if, then, you may not watch, I will come on you as a thief, and you may not know what hour I will come on you. ⁴You have a few names even in Sardis who did not defile their garments, and they will walk with Me in white, because they are worthy. ⁵The [one] thus overcoming will be clothed in white garments, and I will not blot out his name from the Scroll of Life, and I will confess his name before My Father, and before His messengers. ⁶He who is having an ear—let him hear what the Spirit says to the assemblies. ⁷And to the messenger of the assembly in Philadelphia write: These things says the Holy [One], the True [One], having the key of David, the [One] opening and no one will shut, and shutting and no one opens: ⁸I have known your works; behold, I have set before you a door having been opened, which no one is able to shut it, because you have little power, and yet have kept My word, and have not denied My Name; ⁹behold, I give from the synagogue of Satan—those saying themselves to be Jews, and are not, but lie—behold, I will make them that they may come and prostrate before your feet, and may know that I loved you. ¹⁰Because you kept the word of My endurance, I also will keep you from the hour of the trial that is about to come on all the world, to try those dwelling on the earth. ¹¹Behold, I come quickly, be holding fast that which you have, that no one may receive your garland. ¹²He who is overcoming—I will make him a pillar in the temple of My God, and he may not go outside anymore, and I will write on him the Name of My God, and the name of the city of My God, the New Jerusalem, that comes down out of Heaven from My God—also My new Name. ¹³He who is having an ear—let him hear what the Spirit says to the assemblies. ¹⁴And to the messenger of the assembly of the Laodiceans write: These things says the Amen, the Witness—the Faithful and True—the Chief of the creation of God: ¹⁵I have known your works, that you are neither cold nor hot; I wish you were cold or hot. ¹⁶So—because you are lukewarm, and neither cold nor hot, I am about to vomit you out of My mouth; ¹⁷because you say—I am rich, and have grown rich, and have need of nothing, and have not known that you are the wretched, and miserable, and poor, and blind, and naked; ¹⁸I counsel you to buy from Me gold fired by fire, that you may be rich, and white garments that you may be clothed, and the shame of your nakedness may not be revealed, and with eye-salve anoint your eyes, that you may see. ¹⁹As many as I cherish, I convict and discipline; be zealous, then, and convert; ²⁰behold, I have stood at the door, and I knock; if anyone may hear My voice, and may open the door, I will come in to him, and will dine with him, and he with Me. ²¹He who is overcoming—I will give to him to sit with Me in My throne, as I also overcame and sat down with My Father in His throne. ²²He who is having an ear—let him hear what the Spirit says to the assemblies."

CHAPTER 4

¹After these things I saw, and behold, a door opened in the sky, and the first voice that I heard—as of a trumpet speaking with me, saying, "Come up here, and I will show you what must come to pass after these things"; ²and immediately I was in [the] Spirit, and behold, a throne was set in Heaven, and on the throne is [One] sitting, ³and He who is sitting was in appearance like a stone, jasper and sardine: and a rainbow was around the throne in appearance like an emerald. ⁴And around the throne [are] twenty-four thrones, and sitting on the thrones I saw twenty-four elders, having been clothed in white garments, and on their heads golden garlands; ⁵and out of the throne proceed lightnings, and thunders, and voices; and seven lamps of fire are burning before the throne, which are the Seven Spirits of God, ⁶and before the throne—a sea of glass like to crystal, and in the midst of the throne, and around the throne—four living creatures, full of eyes before and behind; ⁷and the first living creature—like a lion; and the second living creature—like a calf; and the third living creature has the face as a man; and the fourth living creature—like an eagle flying. ⁸And the four living creatures, one by one of them had six wings respectively, around and within [are] full of eyes, and they have no rest day and night, saying, "HOLY, HOLY, HOLY, the LORD God, the Almighty, who was, and who is, and who is coming"; ⁹and when the living creatures give glory, and honor, and thanksgiving, to the [One] sitting on the throne, the [One] living through the ages of the ages, ¹⁰the twenty-four elders will fall down before the [One] sitting on the throne, and worship the [One] living through the ages of the ages, and they will cast their garlands before the throne, saying, ¹¹"Worthy are You, our Lord and God, to receive the glory, and the honor, and the power, because You created all things, and because of Your will they existed and were created."

CHAPTER 5

¹And I saw a scroll on the right hand of Him who is sitting on the throne, written within and on the back, sealed with seven seals; ²and I saw a strong messenger crying with a great voice, "Who is worthy to open the scroll and to loose its seals?" ³And no one was able in Heaven, nor on the earth, nor under the earth, to open the scroll, nor to behold it. ⁴And I was weeping much, because no one was found worthy to open and to read the scroll, nor to behold it, ⁵and one of the elders says to me, "Do not weep; behold, the Lion of the tribe of Judah, the root of David, has overcome to open the scroll, and to loose its seven seals"; ⁶and I saw, and behold, in the midst of the throne, and of the four living creatures, and in the midst of the elders, a Lamb standing as having been slain, having seven horns and seven eyes, which are the Seven Spirits of God, which are sent to all the earth, ⁷and He came and took the scroll out of the right hand of Him who is sitting on the throne. ⁸And when He took the scroll, the four living creatures and the twenty-four elders fell before the Lamb, each one having harps and golden bowls full of incenses, which are the prayers of the holy ones, ⁹and they sing a new song, saying, "Worthy are You to take the scroll, and to open its seals, because You were slain, and You purchased us to God in Your blood, out of every tribe, and tongue, and people, and nation, ¹⁰and made them [to be] to our God kings and priests, and they will reign on the earth." ¹¹And I saw, and I heard the voice of many messengers around the throne, and the living creatures, and the elders—and the number of them was myriads of myriads, and thousands of thousands— ¹²saying with a great voice, "Worthy is the Lamb that was slain to receive the power, and riches, and wisdom, and strength, and honor, and glory, and blessing!" ¹³And every creature that is in Heaven, and on the earth, and under the earth, and the things that are on the sea, and all things in them, I heard saying, "To Him who is sitting on the throne and to the Lamb—the blessing, and the honor, and the glory, and the might—through the ages of the ages!" ¹⁴And the four living creatures said, "Amen!" And the twenty-four elders fell down and they worship Him who is living through the ages of the ages.

CHAPTER 6

¹And I saw when the Lamb opened one of the seals, and I heard one of the four living creatures saying, as it were a voice of thunder,

"Come and behold!" ²And I saw, and behold, a white horse, and he who is sitting on it is having a bow, and there was given to him a garland, and he went forth overcoming, and that he may overcome. ³And when He opened the second seal, I heard the second living creature saying, "Come and behold!" ⁴And there went forth another horse—fire-colored, and to him who is sitting on it, there was given to him to take peace from the earth, and that they may slay one another, and there was given to him a great sword. ⁵And when He opened the third seal, I heard the third living creature saying, "Come and behold!" And I saw, and behold, a black horse, and he who is sitting on it is having a balance in his hand, ⁶and I heard a voice in the midst of the four living creatures saying, "A measure of wheat for a denarius, and three measures of barley for a denarius, and you may not injure the oil and the wine." ⁷And when He opened the fourth seal, I heard the voice of the fourth living creature saying, "Come and behold!" ⁸And I saw, and behold, a pale horse, and he who is sitting on him—his name is Death, and Hades follows with him, and there was given to them authority to kill over the fourth part of the earth with sword, and with hunger, and with death, and by the beasts of the earth. ⁹And when He opened the fifth seal, I saw under the altar the souls of those slain because of the word of God, and because of the testimony that they held, ¹⁰and they were crying with a great voice, saying, "Until when, O Master, the Holy and the True, do You not judge and take vengeance of our blood from those dwelling on the earth?" ¹¹And there was given to each one a white robe, and it was said to them that they may rest themselves yet a short time, until may also be fulfilled their fellow-servants and their brothers, who are about to be killed—even as they. ¹²And I saw when He opened the sixth seal, and behold, a great earthquake came, and the sun became black as sackcloth of hair, and the moon became as blood, ¹³and the stars of Heaven fell to the earth—as a fig tree casts her unripe figs, being shaken by a great wind— ¹⁴and the sky departed as a scroll rolled up, and every mountain and island were moved out of their places; ¹⁵and the kings of the earth, and the great men, and the rich, and the chiefs of thousands, and the mighty, and every servant, and every freeman, hid themselves in the dens, and in the rocks of the mountains, ¹⁶and they say to the mountains and to the rocks, "Fall on us, and hide us from the face of Him who is sitting on the throne, and from the anger of the Lamb," ¹⁷because the great day of His anger has come, and who is able to stand?

CHAPTER 7

¹And after these things I saw four messengers, standing on the four corners of the earth, holding the four winds of the earth, that the wind may not blow on the earth, nor on the sea, nor on any tree; ²and I saw another messenger going up from the rising of the sun, having a seal of the living God, and he cried with a great voice to the four messengers, to whom it was given to injure the land and the sea, saying, ³"Do not injure the land, nor the sea, nor the trees, until we may seal the servants of our God on their foreheads." ⁴And I heard the number of those sealed—one hundred forty-four thousand, having been sealed out of every tribe of the sons of Israel: ⁵of the tribe of Judah twelve thousand were sealed; of the tribe of Reuben twelve thousand were sealed; of the tribe of Gad twelve thousand were sealed; ⁶of the tribe of Asher twelve thousand were sealed; of the tribe of Naphtali twelve thousand were sealed; of the tribe of Manasseh twelve thousand were sealed; ⁷of the tribe of Simeon twelve thousand were sealed; of the tribe of Levi twelve thousand were sealed; of the tribe of Issachar twelve thousand were sealed; ⁸of the tribe of Zebulun twelve thousand were sealed; of the tribe of Joseph twelve thousand were sealed; of the tribe of Benjamin twelve thousand were sealed. ⁹After these things I saw, and behold, a great multitude, which no one was able to number, out of all nations, and tribes, and peoples, and tongues, standing before the throne, and before the Lamb, having been clothed [in] white robes, and palms in their hands, ¹⁰and crying with a great voice, saying, "Salvation to our God, the [One] sitting on the throne, and to the Lamb!" ¹¹And all the messengers stood around the throne, and the elders and the four living creatures, and they fell on their faces and worshiped God, ¹²saying, "Amen! The blessing, and the glory, and the wisdom, and the thanksgiving, and the honor, and the power, and the strength, [are] to our God through the ages of the ages! Amen!" ¹³And one of the elders answered, saying to me, "These having been clothed with the white robes, who are they, and from where have they come?" ¹⁴And I have said to him, "Lord, you have known"; and he said to me, "These are those who are coming out of the Great Tribulation, and they washed their robes, and they made their robes white in the blood of the Lamb; ¹⁵because of this they are before the throne of God, and they do service to Him day and night in His temple, and He who is sitting on the throne will dwell over them; ¹⁶they will not hunger anymore, nor may the sun fall on them, nor any heat, ¹⁷because the Lamb that [is] in the midst of the throne will feed them, and will lead them to living fountains of waters, and God will wipe away every tear from their eyes."

CHAPTER 8

¹And when He opens the seventh seal, there came silence in Heaven about half an hour, ²and I saw the seven messengers who have stood before God, and there were given to them seven trumpets, ³and another messenger came, and he stood at the altar, having a golden censer, and there was given to him much incense, that he may give [it] to the prayers of all the holy ones on the golden altar that [is] before the throne, ⁴and the smoke of the incenses, with the prayers of the holy ones, went up before God out of the hand of the messenger; ⁵and the messenger took the censer, and filled it out of the fire of the altar, and cast [it] to the earth, and there came voices, and thunders, and lightnings, and an earthquake. ⁶And the seven messengers who are having the seven trumpets prepared themselves that they may sound the trumpets; ⁷and the first messenger sounded the trumpet, and there came hail and fire, mingled with blood, and it was cast to the earth, and the third of the trees were burned up, and all the green grass was burned up. ⁸And the second messenger sounded the trumpet, and [something] like a great mountain burning with fire was cast into the sea, and the third of the sea became blood, ⁹and the third of the creatures that [are] in the sea died, those having life, and the third of the ships were destroyed. ¹⁰And the third messenger sounded the trumpet, and there fell out of the sky a great star, burning as a lamp, and it fell on the third of the rivers, and on the fountains of waters, ¹¹and the name of the star is called Wormwood, and the third of the waters become wormwood, and many of the men died [because] of the waters, because they were made bitter. ¹²And the fourth messenger sounded the trumpet, and the third of the sun was struck, and the third of the moon, and the third of the stars, that the third of them may be darkened, and that the day may not shine—the third of it, and the night in like manner. ¹³And I saw, and I heard one messenger, flying in midair, saying with a great voice, "Woe, woe, woe, to those dwelling on the earth because of the rest of the voices of the trumpet of the three messengers being about to sound trumpets."

CHAPTER 9

¹And the fifth messenger sounded the trumpet, and I saw a star having fallen to the earth out of Heaven, and there was given to him the key of the pit of the abyss, ²and [he] opened the pit of the abyss, and there came up a smoke out of the pit as smoke of a great furnace, and the sun and the air were darkened from the smoke of the pit. ³And out of the smoke came forth locusts to the earth, and there was given to them authority, as scorpions of the earth have authority, ⁴and it was said to them that they may not injure the grass of the earth, nor any green thing, nor any tree, but only the men who do not have the seal of God on their foreheads, ⁵and it was given to them that they may not kill them, but that they may be tormented five months, and their torment—as the torment of a scorpion—when it may strike a man; ⁶and in those days men will seek death and they will not find it, and they will desire to die, and death will flee from them. ⁷And the likenesses

of the locusts—like to horses made ready to battle, and on their heads [something] as garlands like gold, and their faces as faces of men, ⁸and they had hair as hair of women, and their teeth were as [those] of lions, ⁹and they had breastplates as breastplates of iron, and the noise of their wings—as the noise of chariots of many horses running to battle; ¹⁰and they have tails like to scorpions, and stings were in their tails; and their authority [is] to injure men five months; ¹¹and they have over them a king—the messenger of the abyss—a name [is] to him in Hebrew, Abaddon, and in the Greek he has a name, Apollyon. ¹²The first woe went forth, behold, there yet come two woes after these things. ¹³And the sixth messenger sounded the trumpet, and I heard a voice out of the four horns of the altar of gold that is before God, ¹⁴saying to the sixth messenger who had the trumpet, "Loose the four messengers who are bound at the great river Euphrates"; ¹⁵and the four messengers were loosed, who have been made ready for the hour, and day, and month, and year, that they may kill the third of mankind; ¹⁶and the number of the forces of the horsemen—twice ten thousand ten thousands, and I heard the number of them. ¹⁷And thus I saw the horses in the vision, and those sitting on them, having breastplates of fire, and jacinth, and brimstone; and the heads of the horses [are] as heads of lions, and out of their mouths proceed fire, and smoke, and brimstone; ¹⁸by these three plagues the third of mankind was killed, from the fire, and from the smoke, and from the brimstone, that is proceeding out of their mouths, ¹⁹for the power of the horses are in their mouth, and in their tails, for their tails [are] like serpents, having heads, and they injure with them. ²⁰And the rest of mankind, who were not killed in these plagues, neither converted from the works of their hands, that they may not worship the demons, and idols, those of gold, and those of silver, and those of brass, and those of stone, and those of wood, that are neither able to see, nor to hear, nor to walk, ²¹and they did not convert from their murders, nor from their sorceries, nor from their whoredoms, nor from their thefts.

CHAPTER 10

¹And I saw another strong messenger coming down out of Heaven, clothed with a cloud, and a rainbow on the head, and his face as the sun, and his feet as pillars of fire, ²and he had in his hand a little scroll opened, and he placed his right foot on the sea, and the left on the land, ³and he cried with a great voice, as a lion roars, and when he cried, the seven thunders spoke out their voices; ⁴and when the seven thunders spoke their voices, I was about to write, and I heard a voice out of Heaven saying to me, "Seal the things that the seven thunders spoke," and, "You may not write these things." ⁵And the messenger whom I saw standing on the sea, and on the land, lifted up his hand to the sky, ⁶and swore by Him who lives through the ages of the ages, who created the sky and the things in it, and the land and the things in it, and the sea and the things in it—that time will not be yet, ⁷but in the days of the voice of the seventh messenger, when he may be about to sound the trumpet, and the secret of God may be accomplished, as He declared to His own servants, to the prophets. ⁸And the voice that I heard out of Heaven is again speaking with me, and saying, "Go, take the little scroll that is open in the hand of the messenger who has been standing on the sea, and on the land": ⁹and I went away to the messenger, saying to him, "Give me the little scroll"; and he says to me, "Take, and eat it up, and it will make your belly bitter, but in your mouth it will be sweet as honey." ¹⁰And I took the little scroll out of the hand of the messenger, and ate it up, and it was in my mouth sweet as honey, and when I ate it my belly was made bitter; ¹¹and he says to me, "You must again prophesy about many peoples, and nations, and tongues, and kings."

CHAPTER 11

¹And there was given to me a reed like to a rod, [[and the messenger stood,]] saying, "Rise, and measure the temple of God, and the altar, and those worshiping in it; ²and leave out the court that is outside the temple, and you may not measure it, because it was given to the nations, and they will tread down the holy city forty-two months; ³and I will give to My two witnesses, and they will prophesy one thousand, two hundred, sixty days, clothed with sackcloth"; ⁴these are the two olive [trees], and the two lampstands that stand before the God of the earth; ⁵and if anyone may will to injure them, fire proceeds out of their mouth, and devours their enemies, and if anyone may will to injure them, thus it is required of him to be killed. ⁶These have authority to shut the sky, that rain may not rain in the days of their prophecy, and they have authority over the waters to turn them to blood, and to strike the land with every plague, as often as they may will. ⁷And when they may finish their testimony, the beast that is coming up out of the abyss will make war with them, and overcome them, and kill them, ⁸and their body [is] on the street of the great city that is called spiritually Sodom and Egypt, where also their Lord was crucified, ⁹and they gaze—[those] of the peoples, and tribes, and tongues, and nations—on their dead bodies three and a half days, and they will not allow their dead bodies to be put into tombs, ¹⁰and those dwelling on the earth will rejoice over them, and will make merry, and they will send gifts to one another, because these—the two prophets—tormented those dwelling on the earth. ¹¹And after the three and a half days, [the] Spirit of life from God entered into them, and they stood on their feet, and great fear fell on those beholding them, ¹²and they heard a great voice out of Heaven saying to them, "Come up here"; and they went up to Heaven in the cloud, and their enemies beheld them; ¹³and in that hour a great earthquake came, and the tenth of the city fell, and seven thousand names of men were killed in the earthquake, and the rest became frightened, and they gave glory to the God of Heaven. ¹⁴The second woe went forth, behold, the third woe comes quickly. ¹⁵And the seventh messenger sounded the trumpet, and there came great voices in Heaven, saying, "The kingdoms of the world became [those] of our Lord and of His Christ, and He will reign through the ages of the ages!" ¹⁶And the twenty-four elders, who are sitting on their thrones before God, fell on their faces and worshiped God, ¹⁷saying, "We give thanks to You, O LORD God, the Almighty, who is, and who was, and who is coming, because You have taken Your great power and reigned; ¹⁸and the nations were angry, and Your anger came, and the time of the dead to be judged, and to give the reward to Your servants, to the prophets, and to the holy ones, and to those fearing Your Name, to the small and to the great, and to destroy those who are destroying the earth." ¹⁹And the temple of God was opened in Heaven, and the Ark of His Covenant was seen in His temple, and there came lightnings, and voices, and thunders, and an earthquake, and great hail.

CHAPTER 12

¹And a great sign was seen in the sky: a woman clothed with the sun, and the moon under her feet, and on her head a garland of twelve stars, ²and having [a child] in [her] womb she cries out, travailing and being in pain to bring forth. ³And there was seen another sign in the sky, and behold, a great fire-colored dragon, having seven heads and ten horns, and seven crowns on his heads, ⁴and his tail draws the third of the stars of the sky, and he cast them to the earth; and the dragon stood before the woman who is about to bring forth, that when she may bring forth, he may devour her child; ⁵and she brought forth a male son, who is about to rule all the nations with a rod of iron, and her child was snatched up to God and to His throne, ⁶and the woman fled into the wilderness, where she has a place made ready from God, that there they may nourish her—one thousand, two hundred, sixty days. ⁷And there came war in Heaven: Michael and his messengers warred against the dragon, and the dragon and his messengers warred, ⁸and they did not prevail, nor was their place found anymore in Heaven; ⁹and the great dragon was cast forth—the old serpent, who is called "Devil," and "Satan," who is leading the whole world astray—he was cast forth to the earth, and his messengers were cast forth with him. ¹⁰And I heard a great voice saying in Heaven, "Now came the salvation, and the power, and the kingdom, of our God, and the authority of His Christ, because the accuser of our brothers was cast down, who is accusing them before

REVELATION

our God day and night; ¹¹and they overcame him because of the blood of the Lamb, and because of the word of their testimony, and they did not love their life—to death; ¹²because of this be glad, you heavens, and those who dwell in them; woe to those inhabiting the earth and the sea, because the Devil went down to you, having great wrath, having known that he has [a] short time." ¹³And when the dragon saw that he was cast forth to the earth, he pursued the woman who brought forth the male, ¹⁴and there were given to the woman two wings of the great eagle, that she may fly into the wilderness, to her place, where she is nourished a time, and times, and half a time, from the face of the serpent; ¹⁵and the serpent cast forth out of his mouth water as a river after the woman, that he may cause her to be carried away by the river, ¹⁶and the earth helped the woman, and the earth opened its mouth and swallowed up the river that the dragon cast forth out of his mouth; ¹⁷and the dragon was angry against the woman, and went away to make war with the rest of her seed, those keeping the commands of God, and having the testimony of Jesus.

CHAPTER 13

¹And I stood on the sand of the sea, and I saw a beast coming up out of the sea, having seven heads and ten horns, and ten crowns on its horns, and on its heads names of slander, ²and the beast that I saw was like to a leopard, and its feet as of a bear, and its mouth as the mouth of a lion, and the dragon gave to it his power, and his throne, and great authority. ³And I saw one of its heads as slain to death, and its deadly wound was healed, and all the earth wondered after the beast, ⁴and they worshiped the dragon who gave authority to the beast, and they worshiped the beast, saying, "Who [is] like to the beast? Who is able to war with it?" ⁵And there was given to it a mouth speaking great things, and slanders, and there was given to it authority to make war forty-two months, ⁶and it opened its mouth for slander toward God, to slander His Name, and of His dwelling place, and of those who dwell in Heaven, ⁷and there was given to it to make war with the holy ones, and to overcome them, and there was given to it authority over every tribe, and tongue, and nation. ⁸And all who are dwelling on the earth will worship him, whose names have not been written in the Scroll of Life of the Lamb slain from the foundation of the world; ⁹if anyone has an ear—let him hear: ¹⁰if anyone [goes] into captivity, into captivity he goes; if anyone is to be killed with sword, it is necessary of him by sword to be killed; here is the endurance and the faith of the holy ones. ¹¹And I saw another beast coming up out of the earth, and it had two horns like a lamb, and it was speaking as a dragon, ¹²and all the authority of the first beast does it do before it, and it makes the earth and those dwelling in it that they will worship the first beast, whose deadly wound was healed, ¹³and it does great signs, that fire also it may make to come down from the sky to the earth before men, ¹⁴and it leads astray those dwelling on the earth, because of the signs that were given it to do before the beast, saying to those dwelling on the earth to make an image to the beast that has the wound of the sword and lived, ¹⁵and there was given to it to give a spirit to the image of the beast, that also the image of the beast may speak, and it may cause as many as will not worship the image of the beast, that they may be killed. ¹⁶And it makes all, the small, and the great, and the rich, and the poor, and the freemen, and the servants, that it may give to them a mark on their right hand or on their foreheads, ¹⁷and that no one may be able to buy, or to sell, except he who is having the mark, or the name of the beast, or the number of his name. ¹⁸Here is the wisdom! He who is having the understanding, let him count the number of the beast, for it is the number of a man, and its number: six hundred sixty-six.

CHAPTER 14

¹And I saw, and behold, a Lamb was standing on Mount Zion, and with Him one hundred forty-four thousand, having the Name of His Father written on their foreheads; ²and I heard a voice out of Heaven, as a voice of many waters, and as a voice of great thunder, and I heard a voice of harpists harping with their harps, ³and they sing, as it were, a new song before the throne, and before the four living creatures, and the elders, and no one was able to learn the song except the one hundred forty-four thousand who have been bought from the earth; ⁴these are they who were not defiled with women, for they are virgin; these are they who are following the Lamb wherever He may go; these were bought from among men—a first-fruit to God and to the Lamb— ⁵and in their mouth there was not found guile, for they are unblemished before the throne of God. ⁶And I saw another messenger flying in midair, having continuous good news to proclaim to those dwelling on the earth, and to every nation, and tribe, and tongue, and people, ⁷saying in a great voice, "Fear God, and give to Him glory, because the hour of His judgment came, and worship Him who made the sky, and the land, and sea, and fountains of waters." ⁸And another messenger followed, saying, "Fallen, fallen is Babylon the great, because of the wine of the wrath of her whoredom she has given to all nations to drink." ⁹And a third messenger followed them, saying in a great voice, "If anyone worships the beast and his image, and receives a mark on his forehead or on his hand, ¹⁰he also will drink of the wine of the wrath of God that has been mingled unmixed in the cup of His anger, and he will be tormented in fire and brimstone before the holy messengers, and before the Lamb, ¹¹and the smoke of their torment goes up through ages of ages; and they have no rest day and night, who are worshiping the beast and his image, also if any receive the mark of his name. ¹²Here is endurance of the holy ones; here [are] those keeping the commands of God, and the faith of Jesus." ¹³And I heard a voice out of Heaven saying to me, "Write: Blessed are the dead who are dying in the LORD from this time!" "Yes," says the Spirit, "That they may rest from their labors—and their works follow them!" ¹⁴And I saw, and behold, a white cloud, and on the cloud [One] sitting like [a] Son of Man, having on His head a golden garland, and in His hand a sharp sickle; ¹⁵and another messenger came forth out of the temple crying in a great voice to Him who is sitting on the cloud, "Send forth Your sickle and reap, because the hour of reaping has come to You, because the harvest of the earth has been ripe"; ¹⁶and He who is sitting on the cloud put forth His sickle on the earth, and the earth was reaped. ¹⁷And another messenger came forth out of the temple that [is] in Heaven, having—he also—a sharp sickle, ¹⁸and another messenger came forth out from the altar, having authority over the fire, and he called with a great cry to him having the sharp sickle, saying, "Send forth your sharp sickle, and gather the clusters of the vine of the earth, because her grapes have come to perfection"; ¹⁹and the messenger put forth his sickle to the earth, and gathered the vine of the earth, and cast [it] into the great winepress of the wrath of God; ²⁰and the winepress was trodden outside of the city, and blood came forth out of the winepress—to the bridles of the horses, one thousand six hundred stadia.

CHAPTER 15

¹And I saw another sign in the sky, great and wonderful: seven messengers having the seven last plagues, because in these the wrath of God was completed, ²and I saw as a sea of glass mingled with fire, and those who gain the victory over the beast, and his image, and his mark, [and] the number of his name, standing by the sea of the glass, having harps of God, ³and they sing the song of Moses, servant of God, and the song of the Lamb, saying, "Great and wonderful [are] Your works, O LORD God, the Almighty, righteous and true [are] Your ways, O King of holy ones! ⁴Who may not fear You, O LORD, and glorify Your Name? Because You alone [are] holy, because all the nations will come and worship before You, because Your righteous acts were revealed." ⁵And after these things I saw, and behold, the temple of the Dwelling Place of the Testimony was opened in Heaven; ⁶and the seven messengers having the seven plagues came forth out of the temple, clothed in linen, pure and radiant, and girded around the breasts with golden girdles: ⁷and one of the four living creatures gave to the seven messengers seven golden bowls, full of the wrath of God, who is living through the ages of the ages; ⁸and the temple was filled with smoke from the glory of God, and from His power, and no one was able to enter into the temple until the seven plagues of the seven messengers may be completed.

CHAPTER 16

¹And I heard a great voice out of the temple saying to the seven messengers, "Go away, and pour out the bowls of the wrath of God

into the earth"; ²and the first went away, and poured out his bowl into the earth, and there came a sore—bad and grievous—to men, those having the mark of the beast, and those worshiping his image. ³And the second messenger poured out his bowl into the sea, and it became blood as of [one] dead, and every living soul in the sea died. ⁴And the third messenger poured out his bowl into the rivers, and into the fountains of the waters, and there came blood, ⁵and I heard the messenger of the waters, saying, "Righteous, O LORD, are You, who is, and who was, [[and who will be,]] the Holy [One], because You judged these things, ⁶because they poured out [the] blood of holy ones and prophets, and You gave to them blood to drink, for they are worthy"; ⁷and I heard another out of the altar, saying, "Yes, LORD God, the Almighty, true and righteous [are] Your judgments." ⁸And the fourth messenger poured out his bowl on the sun, and there was given to him to scorch men with fire, ⁹and men were scorched with great heat, and they slandered the Name of God, who has authority over these plagues, and they did not convert—to give to Him glory. ¹⁰And the fifth messenger poured out his bowl on the throne of the beast, and his kingdom became darkened, and they were gnawing their tongues from the pain, ¹¹and they slandered the God of Heaven, from their pains, and from their sores, and they did not convert from their works. ¹²And the sixth messenger poured out his bowl on the great river, the Euphrates, and its water was dried up, that the way of the kings who are from the rising of the sun may be made ready; ¹³and I saw [come] out of the mouth of the dragon, and out of the mouth of the beast, and out of the mouth of the false prophet, three unclean spirits like frogs— ¹⁴for they are spirits of demons, doing signs—which go forth to the kings of the earth, and of the whole world, to bring them together to the battle of that great day of God the Almighty. ¹⁵("Behold, I come as a thief; blessed [is] he who is watching, and keeping his garments, that he may not walk naked, and they may see his unseemliness.") ¹⁶And they brought them together to the place that is called in Hebrew Armageddon. ¹⁷And the seventh messenger poured out his bowl on the air, and there came forth a great voice from the temple of Heaven, from the throne, saying, "It is done!" ¹⁸And there came voices, and thunders, and lightnings; and a great earthquake came, such as has not come since men came on the earth, so mighty an earthquake—so great! ¹⁹And it came—the great city—into three parts, and the cities of the nations fell, and Babylon the great was remembered before God, to give to her the cup of the wine of the wrath of His anger, ²⁰and every island fled away, and mountains were not found, ²¹and great hail (as of talent weight) comes down out of the sky on men, and men slandered God because of the plague of the hail, because its plague is very great.

REVELATION

CHAPTER 17

¹And there came one of the seven messengers, who were having the seven bowls, and he spoke with me, saying to me, "Come, I will show to you the judgment of the great whore, who is sitting on the many waters, ²with whom the kings of the earth committed whoredom; and those inhabiting the earth were made drunk from the wine of her whoredom"; ³and he carried me away to a wilderness in the Spirit, and I saw a woman sitting on a scarlet-colored beast, full of names of slander, having seven heads and ten horns, ⁴and the woman was clothed with purple and scarlet-color, and gilded with gold, and precious stone, and pearls, having a golden cup in her hand full of abominations and uncleanness of her whoredom, ⁵and on her forehead was a name written: "SECRET, BABYLON THE GREAT, THE MOTHER OF THE WHORES, AND THE ABOMINATIONS OF THE EARTH." ⁶And I saw the woman drunken from the blood of the holy ones, and from the blood of the witnesses of Jesus, and I wondered—having seen her—with great wonder; ⁷and the messenger said to me, "For this reason did you wonder? I will tell you the secret of the woman and of the beast that [is] carrying her, which has the seven heads and the ten horns. ⁸The beast that you saw: it was, and it is not, and it is about to come up out of the abyss, and to go away to destruction, and those dwelling on the earth will wonder, whose names have not been written on the Scroll of Life from the foundation of the world, beholding the beast that was, and is not, although it is. ⁹Here [is] the mind that is having wisdom: the seven heads are seven mountains on which the woman sits, ¹⁰and there are seven kings, the five fell, and the one is, the other did not yet come, and when he may come, it is necessary for him to remain a short time; ¹¹and the beast that was, and is not, he also is eighth, and he is out of the seven, and he goes away to destruction. ¹²And the ten horns that you saw are ten kings who did not yet receive a kingdom, but receive authority as kings one hour with the beast; ¹³these have one mind, and they will give over their own power and authority to the beast; ¹⁴these will make war with the Lamb, and the Lamb will overcome them, because He is Lord of lords, and King of kings, and those with Him are called, and chosen, and steadfast." ¹⁵And he says to me, "The waters that you saw, where the whore sits, are peoples, and multitudes, and nations, and tongues; ¹⁶and the ten horns that you saw, and the beast, these will hate the whore, and will make her desolate and naked, and will eat her flesh, and will burn her in fire, ¹⁷for God gave into their hearts to do His purpose, and to make one purpose, and to give their kingdom to the beast until the sayings of God may be fulfilled, ¹⁸and the woman that you saw is the great city that is having reign over the kings of the earth."

CHAPTER 18

¹And after these things I saw another messenger coming down out of Heaven, having great authority, and the earth was lightened from his glory, ²and he cried in might [with] a great voice, saying, "Fallen, fallen is Babylon the great! And she became a habitation of demons, and a hold of every unclean spirit, and a hold of every unclean and hateful bird, ³because all the nations have drunk of the wine of the wrath of her whoredom, and the kings of the earth committed whoredom with her, and merchants of the earth were made rich from the power of her indulgence." ⁴And I heard another voice out of Heaven, saying, "Come forth out of her, My people, that you may not partake with her sins, and that you may not receive of her plagues, ⁵because her sins have reached up to Heaven, and God remembered her unrighteousness. ⁶Render to her as she also rendered to you, and double to her twofold according to her works; in the cup that she mingled mingle to her double. ⁷As much as she glorified herself and indulged, so much torment and sorrow give to her, because in her heart she says, I sit [as] queen, and I am not a widow, and I will not see sorrow; ⁸because of this, in one day, will come her plagues: death, and sorrow, and famine; and she will be utterly burned in fire, because strong [is] the LORD God who is judging her; ⁹and the kings of the earth will weep over her and strike themselves for her, who committed whoredom and indulged with her, when they may see the smoke of her burning, ¹⁰having stood from afar because of the fear of her torment, saying, Woe, woe, the great city! Babylon, the strong city! Because in one hour your judgment came. ¹¹And the merchants of the earth will weep and mourn over her, because no one buys their cargo anymore; ¹²cargo of gold, and silver, and precious stone, and pearls, and fine linen, and purple, and silk, and scarlet, and all fragrant wood, and every vessel of ivory, and every vessel of most precious wood, and brass, and iron, and marble, ¹³and cinnamon, and amomum, and incense, and ointment, and frankincense, and wine, and oil, and fine flour, and wheat, and cattle, and sheep, and of horses, and of chariots, and of bodies and souls of men. ¹⁴And the fruits of the desire of your soul went away from you, and all things—the sumptuous and the radiant—went away from you, and no more at all may you find them. ¹⁵The merchants of these things, who were made rich by her, will stand far off because of the fear of her torment, weeping, and mourning, ¹⁶and saying, Woe, woe, the great city, that was clothed with fine linen, and purple, and scarlet, and gilded in gold, and precious stone, and pearls— ¹⁷because in one hour so much riches were made desolate! And every shipmaster, and all the company on the ships, and sailors, and as many as work the sea, stood far off, ¹⁸and were crying, seeing the smoke of her burning, saying, What [city is] like to the great city? ¹⁹And they cast dust on their heads, and were crying out, weeping and mourning, saying, Woe, woe, the great city! In which were made rich all having ships in the sea, out of her costliness—for in one hour was

she made desolate. ²⁰Be glad over her, O Heaven, and you holy apostles and prophets, because God judged your judgment of her!" ²¹And one strong messenger took up a stone as a great millstone, and cast [it] into the sea, saying, "Thus with violence will Babylon be cast, the great city, and may not be found anymore at all; ²²and voice of harpists, and musicians, and pipers, and trumpeters, may not be heard at all in you anymore; and any craftsman of any craft may not be found at all in you anymore; and noise of a millstone may not be heard at all in you anymore; ²³and light of a lamp may not shine at all in you anymore; and voice of bridegroom and of bride may not be heard at all in you anymore; because your merchants were the great ones of the earth, because all the nations were led astray in your sorcery, ²⁴and in her blood of prophets and of holy ones was found, and of all those who have been slain on the earth."

CHAPTER 19

¹And after these things I heard a great voice of a great multitude in Heaven, saying, "Hallelujah! The salvation, and the glory, and the power [belong] to the LORD our God; ²because true and righteous [are] His judgments, because He judged the great whore who corrupted the earth in her whoredom, and He avenged the blood of His servants at her hand"; ³and a second time they said, "Hallelujah"; and her smoke comes up through the ages of the ages! ⁴And the twenty-four elders and the four living creatures fell down and they worshiped God who is sitting on the throne, saying, "Amen! Hallelujah!" ⁵And a voice out of the throne came forth, saying, "Praise our God, all you His servants, and those fearing Him, both the small and the great"; ⁶and I heard as the voice of a great multitude, and as the voice of many waters, and as the voice of mighty thunderings, saying, "Hallelujah! Because our Lord, the God, the Almighty, has reigned! ⁷May we rejoice and exult, and give the glory to Him, because the marriage of the Lamb has come, and His wife has made herself ready; ⁸and there was given to her that she may be clothed with fine linen, pure and radiant, for the fine linen is the righteous acts of the holy ones." ⁹And he says to me, "Write: Blessed [are] they who have been called to the banquet of the marriage of the Lamb"; and he says to me, "These [are] the true words of God"; ¹⁰and I fell before his feet to worship him, and he says to me, "Behold—No! I am your fellow servant, and of your brothers, those having the testimony of Jesus; worship God, for the testimony of Jesus is the spirit of the prophecy." ¹¹And I saw Heaven having been opened, and behold, a white horse, and He who is sitting on it is called Faithful and True, and in righteousness He judges and makes war, ¹²and His eyes [are] as a flame of fire, and on His head [are] many crowns—having a Name written that no one has known, except Himself, ¹³and He is clothed with a garment covered with blood, and His Name is called, The Word of God. ¹⁴And the armies in Heaven were following Him on white horses, clothed in fine linen—white and pure; ¹⁵and out of His mouth proceeds a sharp sword, that with it He may strike the nations, and He will rule them with a rod of iron, and He treads the press of the wine of the wrath and the anger of God the Almighty, ¹⁶and He has on the garment and on His thigh the name written: "KING OF KINGS, AND LORD OF LORDS." ¹⁷And I saw one messenger standing in the sun, and he cried [with] a great voice, saying to all the birds that are flying in midair, "Come and be gathered together to the banquet of the great God [[or the great banquet of God]], ¹⁸that you may eat flesh of kings, and flesh of chiefs of thousands, and flesh of strong men, and flesh of horses, and of those sitting on them, and the flesh of all—freemen and servants—both small and great." ¹⁹And I saw the beast, and the kings of the earth, and their armies, having been gathered together to make war with Him who is sitting on the horse, and with His army; ²⁰and the beast was taken, and with him the false prophet who did the signs before him, in which he led astray those who received the mark of the beast, and those who worshiped his image; the two were cast living into the lake of the fire that is burning with brimstone; ²¹and the rest were killed with the sword of Him who is sitting on the horse, which is proceeding out of His mouth, and all the birds were filled with their flesh.

CHAPTER 20

¹And I saw a messenger coming down out of Heaven, having the key of the abyss, and a great chain over his hand, ²and he laid hold on the dragon, the ancient serpent, who is [the] Devil and Satan, and bound him one thousand years, ³and he cast him into the abyss, and shut him up, and put a seal on him, that he may no longer lead the nations astray, until the one thousand years may be completed; and after these it is necessary for him to be loosed a short time. ⁴And I saw thrones, and they [that] sat on them, and judgment was given to them, and the souls of those who have been beheaded because of the testimony of Jesus, and because of the word of God, and who did not worship the beast, nor his image, and did not receive the mark on their forehead and on their hand, and they lived and reigned with the Christ one thousand years; ⁵and the rest of the dead did not live again until the one thousand years may be completed; this [is] the first resurrection. ⁶Blessed and holy—he who is having part in the first resurrection; the second death has no authority over these, but they will be priests of God and of the Christ, and will reign with Him one thousand years. ⁷And when the one thousand years may be completed, Satan will be loosed out of his prison, ⁸and he will go forth to lead the nations astray, that are in the four corners of the earth—Gog and Magog—to gather them together to war, of whom the number—as the sand of the sea; ⁹and they went up over the breadth of the land, and surrounded the camp of the holy ones, and the beloved city, and there came down fire from God out of Heaven, and devoured them; ¹⁰and the Devil, who is leading them astray, was cast into the lake of fire and brimstone where the beast and the false prophet [are], and they will be tormented day and night through the ages of the ages. ¹¹And I saw a great white throne, and Him who is sitting on it, from whose face the earth and the sky fled away, and no place was found for them; ¹²and I saw the dead, small and great, standing before God, and scrolls were opened, and another scroll was opened, which is that of the life, and the dead were judged out of the things written in the scrolls—according to their works; ¹³and the sea gave up those dead in it, and death and Hades gave up the dead in them, and they were judged, each one according to their works; ¹⁴and death and Hades were cast into the lake of the fire—this [is] the second death; ¹⁵and if anyone was not found written in the Scroll of Life, he was cast into the lake of the fire.

CHAPTER 21

¹And I saw a new heaven and a new earth, for the first heaven and the first earth passed away, and the sea is no more; ²and I saw the holy city, New Jerusalem, coming down from God out of Heaven, made ready as a bride adorned for her husband; ³and I heard a great voice out of Heaven, saying, "Behold, the dwelling place of God [is] with men, and He will dwell with them, and they will be His peoples, and God Himself will be with them [as] their God, ⁴and God will wipe away every tear from their eyes, and there will be no more death, nor sorrow, nor crying, nor will there be anymore pain, because the first things passed away." ⁵And He who is sitting on the throne said, "Behold, I make all things new"; and He says to me, "Write, because these words are true and steadfast"; ⁶and He said to me, "It is done! I am the Alpha and the Omega, the Beginning and the End. To him who is thirsting, I will give of the fountain of the water of life freely. ⁷The [one] who is overcoming will inherit all things, and I will be his God, and he will be My son. ⁸But to fearful, and unsteadfast, and abominable, and murderers, and whoremongers, and sorcerers, and idolaters, and all the liars, their part [is] in the lake that is burning with fire and brimstone, which is the second death." ⁹And one of the seven messengers, having the seven bowls

that are full of the seven last plagues, came and spoke with me, saying, "Come, I will show you the bride, the wife of the Lamb," [10]and he carried me away in the Spirit to a mountain great and high, and showed me the great city, the holy Jerusalem, coming down out of Heaven from God, [11]having the glory of God, and her light—like a most precious stone, as a jasper stone clear as crystal, [12]also having a great and high wall, having twelve gates, and at the gates twelve messengers, and names written thereon, which are [those] of the twelve tribes of the sons of Israel— [13]at the east three gates, at the north three gates, at the south three gates, at the west three gates; [14]and the wall of the city had twelve foundations, and on them names of the twelve apostles of the Lamb. [15]And he who is speaking with me had a golden reed, that he may measure the city, and its gates, and its wall; [16]and the city lies square, and the length of it is as great as the breadth; and he measured the city with the reed—twelve thousand stadia; the length, and the breadth, and the height of it are equal. [17]And he measured its wall—one hundred forty-four cubits, the measure of a man, that is, of the messenger; [18]and the building of its wall was jasper, and the city [is] pure gold—like to pure glass. [19]And the foundations of the wall of the city have been adorned with every precious stone: the first foundation jasper, the second sapphire, the third chalcedony, the fourth emerald, [20]the fifth sardonyx, the sixth sardius, the seventh chrysolite, the eighth beryl, the ninth topaz, the tenth chrysoprase, the eleventh jacinth, the twelfth amethyst. [21]And the twelve gates [are] twelve pearls, each one of the gates respectively was of one pearl; and the street of the city [is] pure gold—as transparent glass. [22]And I did not see a temple in it, for the LORD God, the Almighty, and the Lamb, are its temple. [23]And the city has no need of the sun, nor of the moon, that they may shine in it; for the glory of God lightens it, and the lamp of it—the Lamb; [24]and the nations will walk by its light, and the kings of the earth bring their glory and honor into it, [25]and its gates will never be shut by day, for night will not be there; [26]and they will bring the glory and the honor of the nations into it; [27]and there may never enter into it anything defiling and doing abomination, and a lie, if not those written in the Lamb's Scroll of Life.

CHAPTER 22

[1]And he showed me [the] river of [the] water of life, radiant as crystal, going forth out of the throne of God and of the Lamb [2]in the midst of its street, and of the river on this side and on that—[the] Tree of Life, producing twelve fruits, yielding its fruit according to each month, and the leaves of the tree [are] for the healing of the nations; [3]and there will no longer be any curse, and the throne of God and of the Lamb will be in it, and His servants will serve Him, [4]and they will see His face, and His Name [is] on their foreheads, [5]and there will be no night there, and they have no need of [the] light of a lamp and of [the] light of [the] sun, because the LORD God gives them light, and they will reign through the ages of the ages. [6]And he said to me, "These words [are] steadfast and true, and the LORD God of the holy prophets sent His messenger to show to His servants the things that must come quickly. [7]Behold, I come quickly; blessed [is] he who is keeping the words of the prophecy of this scroll." [8]And I, John, am he who is seeing these things and hearing, and when I heard and beheld, I fell down to worship before the feet of the messenger who is showing me these things; [9]and he says to me, "Behold—No! For I am your fellow servant, and of your brothers the prophets, and of those keeping the words of this scroll; worship God." [10]And He says to me, "You may not seal the words of the prophecy of this scroll, because the time is near. [11]The [one] being unrighteous—let him be unrighteous still; and the filthy—let him be filthy still; and the righteous—let him do righteousness still; and the holy—let him be holy still. [12]Behold, I come quickly, and My reward [is] with Me, to render to each as his work will be; [13]I am the Alpha and the Omega—the Beginning and End—the First and the Last. [14]Blessed are those washing their robes that the authority will be theirs to the Tree of Life, and they may enter into the city by the gates; [15]and outside [are] the dogs, and the sorcerers, and the whoremongers, and the murderers, and the idolaters, and everyone cherishing and doing falsehood. [16]I, Jesus, sent My messenger to testify to you these things concerning the assemblies; I am the root and the offspring of David, the radiant morning star! [17]And the Spirit and the bride say, Come! And he who is hearing—let him say, Come! And he who is thirsting—let him come; and he who is willing—let him take the water of life freely. [18]For I testify to everyone hearing the words of the prophecy of this scroll, if anyone may add to these, God will add to him the plagues that have been written in this scroll, [19]and if anyone may take away from the words of the scroll of this prophecy, God will take away his part from the Scroll of Life, and out of the holy city, and the things that have been written in this scroll." [20]The [One] testifying [to] these things says, "Yes, I come quickly!" Amen. Come, Lord Jesus! [21]The grace of our Lord Jesus Christ [is] with all [[the holy ones. Amen.]]

476

THE APOCRYPHA
Containing the disputed, non-canonical, and pseudepigraphical writings

APOCRYPHAL ESTHER

The Septuagint (LXX) version of Esther contains a number of sections not found in the Hebrew version of the text (chs. 11–16). These Greek chapters are canonical in a variety of traditions.

CHAPTER 11

¹In the fourth year of the reign of Ptolemy and Cleopatra, Dositheus, who said he was a priest, and of the Levitical race, and Ptolemy his son brought this letter of Purim, which they said Lysimachus the son of Ptolemy had interpreted in Jerusalem. ²In the second year of the reign of Artaxerxes the great, in the first day of the month of Nisan, Mordecai the son of Jair, the son of Semei, the son of Cis, of the tribe of Benjamin: ³a Jew who dwelt in the city of Shushan, a great man and among the first of the king's court, had a dream. ⁴Now he was of the number of the captives, whom Nebuchadnezzar king of Babylon had carried away from Jerusalem with Jehoiachin king of Judah: ⁵And this was his dream: Behold, there were voices, and tumults, and thunders, and earthquakes, and a disturbance on the earth. ⁶And behold, two great dragons came forth ready to fight against one another. ⁷And at their cry all nations were stirred up to fight against the nation of the just. ⁸And that was a day of darkness and danger, of tribulation and distress, and great fear on the earth. ⁹And the nation of the just was troubled fearing their own evils and was prepared for death. ¹⁰And they cried to God: and as they were crying, a little fountain grew into a very great river, and abounded into many waters. ¹¹The light and the sun rose up, and the humble were exalted, and they devoured the glorious. ¹²And when Mordecai had seen this, and arose out of his bed, he was thinking what God would do: and he kept it fixed in his mind, desirous to know what the dream should signify.

CHAPTER 12

¹And he abode at that time in the king's court with Bagatha and Thara, the king's eunuchs, who were porters of the palace. ²And when he understood their designs, and had diligently searched into their projects, he learned that they went about to lay violent hands on King Artaxerxes, and he told the king thereof. ³Then the king had them both examined, and after they had confessed, commanded them to be put to death. ⁴But the king made a record of what was done: and Mordecai also committed the memory of the thing to writing. ⁵And the king commanded him to abide in the court of the palace, and gave him presents for the information. ⁶But Haman, the son of Amadathi the Bugite, was in great honor with the king, and sought to hurt Mordecai and his people, because of the two eunuchs of the king who were put to death.

CHAPTER 13

¹And this was the copy of the letter: Artaxerxes, the great king who reigns from India to Ethiopia, to the princes and governors of the one hundred and twenty-seven provinces that are subject to his empire, greetings. ²Whereas I reigned over many nations, and had brought all the world under my dominion, I was not willing to abuse the greatness of my power, but to govern my subjects with clemency and leniency, that they might live quietly without any terror, and might enjoy peace, which is desired by all men. ³But when I asked my counselors how this might be accomplished, one that excelled the rest in wisdom and fidelity, and was second after the king, Haman by name, ⁴he told me that there was a people scattered through the whole world, which used new laws, and acted against the customs of all nations, despised the commands of kings, and violated by their opposition the concord of all nations. ⁵For what reason having learned this, and seeing one nation in opposition to all mankind using perverse laws, and going against our commands, and disturbing the peace and concord of the provinces subject to us, ⁶we have commanded that all whom Haman will mark out, who is chief over all the provinces, and second after the king, and whom we honor as a father, will be utterly destroyed by their enemies, with their wives and children, and that none will have pity on them, on the fourteenth day of the twelfth month Adar of this present year: ⁷that these wicked men going down to Hades in one day, may restore to our empire the peace which they had disturbed. ⁸But Mordecai implored the LORD, remembering all His works, ⁹and said, "O LORD, LORD, almighty King, for all things are in Your power, and there is none that can resist Your will, if You determine to save Israel. ¹⁰You have made the heavens and earth, and all things that are under the cover of Heaven. ¹¹You are Lord of all, and there is none that can resist Your majesty. ¹²You know all things, and You know that it was not out of pride and contempt, or any desire of glory, that I refused to worship the proud Haman, ¹³(for I would willingly and readily for the salvation of Israel have kissed even the steps of his feet,) ¹⁴but I feared lest I should transfer the honor of my God to a man, and lest I should adore anyone except my God. ¹⁵And now, O LORD, O King, O God of Abraham, have mercy on Your people, because our enemies resolve to destroy us, and extinguish Your inheritance. ¹⁶Do not despise Your portion, which You have redeemed for Yourself out of Egypt. ¹⁷Hear my supplication, and be merciful to Your lot and inheritance, and turn our mourning into joy, that we may live and praise Your Name, O LORD, and do not shut the mouths of them that sing to You." ¹⁸And all Israel with like mind and supplication cried to the LORD, because they saw certain death hanging over their heads.

CHAPTER 14

¹Queen Esther also, fearing the danger that was at hand, had recourse to the LORD. ²And when she had laid away her royal apparel, she put on garments suitable for weeping and mourning: instead of various precious ointments, she covered her head with ashes and dung, and she humbled her body with fasts: and all the places in which before she was accustomed to rejoice, she filled with her torn hair. ³And she prayed to the LORD, the God of Israel, saying, "O my LORD, who alone are our King, help me, a desolate woman, and who has no other helper but You. ⁴My danger is in my hands. ⁵I have heard from my father that You, O LORD, took Israel from among all nations, and our fathers from all their predecessors, to possess them as a perpetual inheritance, and You have done to them as You have promised. ⁶We have sinned in Your sight, and therefore You have delivered us into the hands of our enemies: ⁷For we have worshiped their gods. You are just, O LORD. ⁸And now they are not content to oppress us with most hard bondage, but attributing the strength of their hands to the power of their idols, ⁹they design to change Your promises, and destroy Your inheritance, and shut the mouths of them that praise You, and extinguish the glory of Your temple and altar, ¹⁰that they may open the mouths of nations, and praise the strength of idols, and magnify a carnal king forever. ¹¹Do not give, O LORD, Your scepter to them that are nothing, lest they laugh at our ruin, but turn their counsel on themselves, and destroy him that has begun to rage against us. ¹²Remember, O LORD, and show Yourself to us in the time of our tribulation, and give me boldness, O LORD, King of gods, and of all power: ¹³give me a well-ordered speech in my mouth in the presence of the lion, and turn his heart to the hatred of our enemy, that both he himself may perish, and the rest that consent to him. ¹⁴But deliver us by Your hand, and help me, who has no other helper, but You, O LORD, who has the knowledge of all things. ¹⁵And You know that I hate the glory of the wicked, and abhor the bed of the uncircumcised, and of every stranger. ¹⁶You know my necessity, that I abominate the sign of my pride and glory, which is on my head in the days of my public appearance, and detest it as a menstruous rag, and do not wear it in the days of my silence, ¹⁷and that I have not eaten at Haman's table, nor has the king's banquet pleased me, and that I have not drunk the wine of the drink offerings: ¹⁸And that Your handmaid has never

APOCRYPHAL ESTHER

rejoiced, since I was brought here to this day, but in You, O LORD, the God of Abraham. ¹⁹O God, who is mighty above all, hear the voice of them that have no other hope, and deliver us from the hand of the wicked, and deliver me from my fear."

CHAPTER 15

¹And he [(Mordecai)] commanded her to go to the king, and petition for her people, and for her country. ²"Remember," [he said,] "the days of your low estate, how you were brought up by my hand, because Haman—the second after the king—has spoken against us to [put us to] death. ³And you [must] call on the LORD, and speak to the king for us, and deliver us from death." ⁴And on the third day she laid away the garments she wore, and put on her glorious apparel. ⁵And glittering in royal robes, after she had called on God the Ruler and Savior of all, she took two maids with her, ⁶and she leaned on one of them, as if for delicateness and excessive tenderness she were not able to bear up her own body. ⁷And the other maid followed her lady, bearing up her train flowing on the ground. ⁸But she with a rosy color in her face, and with gracious and bright eyes, hid a mind full of anguish, and exceeding great fear. ⁹So going in she passed through all the doors in order, and stood before the king, where he sat on his royal throne, clothed with his royal robes, and glittering with gold, and precious stones, and he was terrible to behold. ¹⁰And when he had lifted up his countenance, and with burning eyes had shown the wrath of his heart, the queen sunk down, and her color turned pale, and she rested her weary head on her handmaid. ¹¹And God changed the king's spirit into mildness, and all in haste and in fear he leaped from his throne, and holding her up in his arms, until she came to herself, caressed her with these words: ¹²"What is the matter, Esther? I am your brother, do not fear. ¹³You will not die, for this law is not made for you, but for all others. ¹⁴Come near then, and touch the scepter." ¹⁵And as she held her peace, he took the golden scepter, and laid it on her neck, and kissed her, and said, "Why do you not speak to me?" ¹⁶She answered, "I saw you, my lord, as a messenger of God, and my heart was troubled for fear of your majesty. ¹⁷For you, my lord, are very admirable, and your face is full of graces." ¹⁸And while she was speaking, she fell down again, and was almost in a swoon. ¹⁹But the king was troubled, and all his servants comforted her.

CHAPTER 16

¹The great King Artaxerxes, from India to Ethiopia, to the governors and princes of one hundred and twenty-seven provinces, which obey our command, sends greetings. ²Many have abused to pride the goodness of princes, and the honor that has been bestowed on them: ³and not only endeavor to oppress the king's subjects, but not bearing the glory that is given them, take in hand to practice also against them that gave it. ⁴Neither are they content not to return thanks for benefits received, and to violate in themselves the laws of humanity, but they think they can also escape the justice of God who sees all things. ⁵And they break out into such great madness, as to endeavor to undermine by lies such as observe diligently the offices committed to them, and do all things in such manner as to be worthy of all men's praise, ⁶while, with crafty fraud, they deceive the ears of princes that are well meaning, and judge of others by their own nature. ⁷Now this is proved both from ancient histories, and by the things which are done daily, how the good designs of kings are depraved by the evil suggestions of certain men. ⁸For what reason we must provide for the peace of all provinces. ⁹Neither must you think, if we command different things, that it comes from the levity of our mind, but that we give sentence according to the quality and necessity of times, as the profit of the commonwealth requires. ¹⁰Now that you may more plainly understand what we say, I, Haman, the son of Amadathi, a Macedonian both in mind and country, and having nothing of the Persian blood, but with his cruelty staining our goodness, was received, being a stranger by us: ¹¹and found our humanity so great toward him, that he was called our father, and was worshiped by all as the next man after the king, ¹²but he was so far puffed up with arrogancy, as to go about to deprive us of our kingdom and life. ¹³For with certain new and unheard-of devices he has sought the destruction of Mordecai, by whose fidelity and good services our life was saved, and of Esther the partner of our kingdom, with all their nation, ¹⁴thinking that after they were slain, he might work treason against us left alone without friends, and might transfer the kingdom of the Persians to the Macedonians. ¹⁵But we have found that the Jews, who were by that most wicked man appointed to be slain, are in no fault at all, but to the contrary, use just laws, ¹⁶and are the children of the highest and the greatest, and the ever-living God, by whose benefit the kingdom was given both to our fathers and to us, and is kept to this day. ¹⁷For what reason, know that those letters which he sent in our name are void and of no effect. ¹⁸For which crime both he himself that devised it, and all his relatives hang on gallows, before the gates of this city Shushan—not us, but God repaying him as he deserved. ¹⁹But this edict, which we now send, will be published in all cities, that the Jews may freely follow their own laws. ²⁰And you will aid them that they may kill those who had prepared themselves to kill them, on the thirteenth day of the twelfth month, which is called Adar. ²¹For the Almighty God has turned this day of sadness and mourning into joy to them. ²²For what reason you will also count this day among other festival days, and celebrate it with all joy, that it may be known also in times to come, ²³that all they who faithfully obey the Persians, receive a worthy reward for their fidelity, but they that are traitors to their kingdom, are destroyed for their wickedness. ²⁴And let every province and city, that will not be partaker of this solemnity, perish by the sword and by fire, and be destroyed in such manner as to be made unpassable, both to men and beasts, for an example of contempt, and disobedience.

APOCRYPHAL PSALMS

Psalm 151 is a short psalm found in most copies of the Septuagint but not in the Hebrew Bible. The Greek title given to this psalm indicates that it is supernumerary. It is also included in some manuscripts of the Peshitta. The psalm concerns the story of David and Goliath. The Eastern Orthodox Church, as well as the Coptic Orthodox Church, Armenian Apostolic Church, and the Armenian Catholic Church accept Psalm 151 as deuterocanonical. Psalms 152–155 are found extant in two Syriac manuscripts and appear to have been composed in the pre-Christian era. Psalms 154 and 155 have also been found in Hebrew in the Dead Sea Scrolls. Psalms 156–160 come from the Great Psalms Scroll (11Q5) and 4Q88. Probable interpolations are made in a number of instances to make the text more readable.

I. THIS PSALM IS ASCRIBED TO DAVID AND IS OUTSIDE THE NUMBER. WHEN HE SLEW GOLIATH IN A DUEL.

PSALM 151

¹I was the youngest among my brothers, || And a youth in my father's house. ²I used to feed my father's flock, || And I found a lion and a wolf, || And slew them and tore them. ³My hands made an organ, || And my fingers fashioned a harp. ⁴Who will show me my Lord? He, my Lord, has become my God. ⁵He sent His messenger and took me away from my father's flock, || And anointed me with the oil of anointing. ⁶My brothers, the fair and the tall, || In them the LORD had no pleasure. ⁷And I went forth to meet the Philistine, || And he cursed me by his idols. ⁸But I drew his sword and cut off his head, || And took away the reproach from the sons of Israel.

APOCRYPHAL PSALMS

II. THE PRAYER OF HEZEKIAH WHEN ENEMIES SURROUNDED HIM.

PSALM 152

¹With a loud voice glorify God; In the assembly of many proclaim His glory. ²Amid the multitude of the upright glorify His praise; And speak of His glory with the righteous. ³Join your soul to the good and to the perfect, || To glorify the Most High. ⁴Gather yourselves together to make known His strength; And do not be slow in showing forth His deliverance and His glory to all babies. ⁵That the honor of the LORD may be known, wisdom has been given; And to tell of His works it has been made known to men: ⁶To make known to babies His strength, || And to make them that lack understanding [[or heart]] to comprehend His glory; ⁷Who are far from His entrances and distant from His gates: ⁸Because the Lord of Jacob is exalted, || And His glory is on all His works. ⁹And a man who glorifies the Most High, in him will He take pleasure; As in one who offers fine meal, || And as in one who offers male goats and calves; ¹⁰And as in one who makes fat the altar with a multitude of burnt-offerings; And as the smell of incense from the hands of the just. ¹¹From your upright gates will be heard His voice, || And from the voice of the upright admonition. ¹²And in their eating will be satisfying in truth, || And in their drinking, when they share together. ¹³Their dwelling is in the law of the Most High, || And their speech is to make known His strength. ¹⁴How far from the wicked is speech of Him, || And from all transgressors to know Him! ¹⁵Behold, the eye of the LORD takes pity on the good, || And to them that glorify Him will He multiply mercy, || And from the time of evil will He deliver their soul. ¹⁶Blessed is the LORD, who has delivered the wretched from the hand of the wicked; Who raises up a horn out of Jacob and a judge of the nations out of Israel; ¹⁷That He may prolong His dwelling in Zion, || And may adorn our age in Jerusalem.

III. WHEN THE PEOPLE OBTAINED PERMISSION FROM CYRUS TO RETURN HOME.

PSALM 153

¹O LORD, I have cried to You; Listen to me. ²I have lifted up my hands to Your holy dwelling-place; Incline Your ear to me. ³And grant me my request; Do not withhold my prayer from me. ⁴Build up my soul, and do not destroy it; And do not lay it bare before the wicked. ⁵Them that repay evil things—turn [them] away from me, O judge of truth. ⁶O LORD, do not judge me according to my sins, || Because no flesh is innocent before You. ⁷Make plain to me, O LORD, Your law, || And teach me Your judgments; ⁸And many will hear of Your works, || And the nations will praise Your honor. ⁹Remember me and do not forget me; And do not lead me into things that are too hard for me. ¹⁰Make the sins of my youth pass from me, || And my discipline—do not let them remember [it] against me. ¹¹Cleanse me, O LORD, from the evil leprosy, || And let it no longer come to me. ¹²Dry up its roots from me, || And do not let its leaves sprout within me. ¹³Great are You, O LORD; Therefore, my request will be fulfilled from before You. ¹⁴To whom will I complain that he may give to me? And what can the strength of men add [to me]? ¹⁵From before You, O LORD, is my confidence; I cried to the LORD and He heard me, and healed the breaking of my heart. ¹⁶I slumbered and slept; I dreamed and was helped, and the LORD sustained me. ¹⁷They severely pained my heart; I will return thanks because the LORD delivered me. ¹⁸Now I will rejoice in their shame; I have hoped in You, and I will not be ashamed. ¹⁹Give You honor for all time—even forever and ever! ²⁰Deliver Israel, Your chosen one, || And them of the house of Jacob Your proved one.

IV. SPOKEN BY DAVID WHEN HE WAS CONTENDING WITH THE LION AND THE WOLF WHICH TOOK A SHEEP FROM HIS FLOCK.

PSALM 154

¹O God, O God, come to my aid; Help me and save me; Deliver my soul from the slayer. ²Will I go down to Sheol by the mouth of the lion? Or will the wolf confound me? ³Was it not enough for them that they lay in wait for my father's flock, || And tore in pieces a sheep of my father's drove, || But they were also wishing to destroy my soul? ⁴Have pity, O LORD, and save Your holy one from destruction; That he may rehearse Your glories in all his times, || And may praise Your great Name: ⁵When You have delivered him from the hands of the destroying lion and of the ravening wolf, || And when You have rescued my captivity from the hands of the wild beasts. ⁶Quickly, O my Lord, send a deliverer from before You, || And draw me out of the gaping pit, || Which imprisons me in its depths.

V. SPOKEN BY DAVID WHEN RETURNING THANKS TO GOD, WHO HAD DELIVERED HIM FROM THE LION AND THE WOLF AND HE HAD SLAIN BOTH OF THEM.

PSALM 155

¹Praise the LORD, all you nations; Glorify Him, and bless His Name— ²Who rescued the soul of His chosen one from the hands of death, || And delivered His holy one from destruction, ³And saved me from the nets of Sheol, || And my soul from the pit that cannot be fathomed. ⁴Because, before my deliverance could go forth from before Him, || I was well nearly torn in two pieces by two wild beasts. ⁵But He sent His messenger, || And shut up from me the gaping mouths, || And rescued my life from destruction. ⁶My soul will glorify Him and exalt Him, || Because of all His kindnesses which He has done and will do to me.

VI. A PLEA FOR DELIVERANCE.

PSALM 156

¹A worm does not thank You, || Nor can a maggot recount Your loving-kindness. ²Only the living thank You, || All they whose feet stumble thank You, || When You make Your loving-kindness known to them, || And cause them to understand Your righteousness; ³For the soul of all the living is in Your hand, || And You have given breath to all flesh. ⁴O LORD, do to us according to Your goodness, || According to the greatness of Your mercies, || And according to the greatness of Your righteous works. ⁵The LORD listens to the voice of all who love His Name, || And He does not permit His loving-kindness to depart from them. ⁶Blessed be the LORD, || Who does righteous works, || Who crowns His holy ones with loving-kindness and mercies. ⁷My soul shouts to praise Your Name, || To praise Your mercies with gladness, || To announce Your faithfulness; For there is no limit to Your praises. ⁸I belonged to death because of my sins, || And my iniquities had sold me to Sheol; ⁹But You saved me, O LORD, || According to the greatness of Your mercies, || And according to the greatness of Your righteous works. ¹⁰I have, indeed, loved Your Name, || And have taken refuge in Your shadow. ¹¹My heart is strengthened when I remember Your power, || And I rely on Your mercies. ¹²Forgive my sins, O LORD, || And purify me of my iniquity. ¹³Grant me a spirit of faithfulness and knowledge; Do not let me be dishonored in ruin. ¹⁴Do not allow the evil one || Or an unclean spirit to overtake me, || And do not allow pain || Or the evil inclination to possess my bones; ¹⁵For You, O LORD, are my praise, || And I hope in You every day. ¹⁶My brothers rejoice with me, || And the house of my father is astounded by Your graciousness. ¹⁷I will always rejoice in You.

VII. A LOVE SONG FOR ZION.

PSALM 157

¹I will remember you, O Zion, for a blessing. I love you with all My strength, || For your memory is to be blessed forever. ²Your hope is great, O Zion—Peace and your expected salvation will come. ³Generation after generation will dwell in you, || And generations of the righteous will be your decoration. ⁴They who desire the day of your salvation || Will rejoice in the greatness of your glory. ⁵They will be suckled on the fullness of your glory, || And in your beautiful streets they will make ringing sounds. ⁶You will remember the righteous works of your prophets, || And will glorify yourself in the works of your righteous ones. ⁷Cleanse violence from your midst; May lying and iniquity be cut off from [within] you. ⁸Your sons will rejoice within you, || And your cherished ones will be joined to you. How much have they hoped in your salvation? ⁹How much have your perfect ones mourned for you? ¹⁰Your hope, O Zion, will not perish, || And your expectation will not be forgotten. ¹¹Is there a righteous man who has perished? Is there a man who has escaped his iniquity? ¹²Man is tried according to his way—Each is repaid according to his works. ¹³Your oppressors will be cut off from around you, O Zion, || And all who hate you will be scattered.

APOCRYPHAL PSALMS

¹⁴Your praise is pleasing, O Zion; It rises up in all the world. ¹⁵I will remember you many times for a blessing, || And I will bless you with all My heart. ¹⁶You will attain to continuous righteousness, || And will receive blessings from the noble. ¹⁷Take the vision which speaks of you, || And the dreams of the prophets requested for you. ¹⁸Be exalted and increase, O Zion, || And praise the Most High, your Redeemer! May my soul rejoice in your glory!

VIII. A PSALM FOR THE NAME OF THE LORD.

PSALM 158

¹In the midst of the congregation || They will praise the Name of the LORD, ²For He has come to judge every action, || To remove the wicked from the earth, || So that the children of iniquity will no longer be found. ³The heavens will give their dew, || And there will be no drought within their boundaries. ⁴The earth will give its fruit in its season, || And its produce will never fail. ⁵The fruit trees will give of the fruit of its vineyards, || And the ground will not cheat of its produce. ⁶The poor will eat, || And those who fear God will be filled.

IX. A PSALM FOR JUDAH.

PSALM 159

¹The heavens and earth will give praise together. Let all the stars of the evening give praise! ²Rejoice, Judah, rejoice! Rejoice, rejoice and be glad with gladness! ³Celebrate your feasts and pay your vows, || For there is no wickedness in your midst. ⁴Raise your hand and fortify your right hand! ⁵Behold, the enemy will perish, || And all the workers of iniquity will be scattered; ⁶But You, O LORD, are forever, || And Your glory will be forever and ever. Praise the LORD!

X. A PSALM FOR THE CREATOR.

PSALM 160

¹The LORD is great and holy—The most holy for generation after generation. ²Majesty goes before Him, || And abundance of many waters comes after Him. ³Loving-kindness and truth surround His face; Truth, judgment, and righteousness are the foundation of His throne. ⁴He divides light from the unknown, || And He establishes the dawn || By the knowledge of His heart. ⁵All His messengers sang when they saw it, || For He showed them that which they had not known. ⁶He crowns the mountains with fruit, || With good food for all the living. ⁷May the Lord of the earth be blessed, || Along with His power, || For He establishes the world by His wisdom. ⁸He stretches out the heavens by His understanding, || And brings forth wind from His treasures. ⁹He made lightnings for the rain || And raised mist from the ends of the earth.

APOCRYPHAL DANIEL

The Septuagint (LXX) version of Daniel contains three sections not found in the Hebrew version of the text. These are known as "The Prayer of Azariah and Song of the Three Holy Children" (often placed as vv. 3:24–90), "Susanna and the Elders" (Ch. 13), and "Bel and the Dragon" (Ch. 14). All three are included in the LSV, with "The Prayer of Azariah" versified as 3B:1–68, which can be read between verses 3:23 and 3:24 of the standard text of Daniel. This particular book is an account of the prayer of Azariah (Abednego) while in the midst of the fire and the song that he and his two other companions sung in praise to God while in the furnace. "Susanna and the Elders" portrays the lovely and virtuous wife Susanna as sexually accosted by two conniving elders. They falsely accuse her of adultery, but the prophet Daniel cross-examines them, exposing them as liars, and then they are put to death. "Bel and the Dragon" recounts Daniel's confrontation with the followers of the false god Bel during the reign of King Cyrus of Persia, which results in their execution. Later in the narrative Daniel slays a much-revered dragon and is thrust into a lion's den as a result. God intervenes to deliver him.

SECTION 1:

THE PRAYER OF AZARIAH AND SONG OF THE THREE HOLY CHILDREN

CHAPTER 3B

¹They walked in the midst of the fire, praising God, and blessing the LORD. ²Then Azariah stood and prayed like this—opening his mouth in the midst of the fire, he said: ³"Blessed are You, O LORD, You God of our fathers! Your Name is worthy to be praised and glorified forevermore; ⁴For You are righteous in all the things that You have done. Yes, all Your works are true. Your ways are right, and all Your judgments are truth. ⁵In all the things that You have brought on us, and on the holy city of our fathers, Jerusalem, || You have executed true judgments. For according to truth and justice You have brought all these things on us because of our sins. ⁶For we have sinned and committed iniquity in departing from You. ⁷In all things we have trespassed, and not obeyed Your commands or kept them. We have not done as You have commanded us, that it might go well with us. ⁸Therefore all that You have brought on us, and everything that You have done to us, || You have done in true judgment. ⁹You delivered us into the hands of lawless enemies, most hateful rebels, || And to an unjust king who is the most wicked in all the world. ¹⁰And now we cannot open our mouth. Shame and reproach have come on Your servants and those who worship You. ¹¹Do not utterly deliver us up, for Your Name's sake. Do not annul Your covenant. ¹²Do not cause Your mercy to depart from us, || For the sake of Abraham who is loved by You, || And for the sake of Isaac Your servant, and Israel Your holy one, ¹³To whom You promised that You would multiply their offspring as the stars of the sky, || And as the sand that is on the seashore. ¹⁴For we, O LORD, have become less than any nation, || And are kept under this day in all the world because of our sins. ¹⁵There is not at this time prince, or prophet, or leader, or burnt-offering, || Or sacrifice, or oblation, or incense, or place to offer before You, and to find mercy. ¹⁶Nevertheless, in a contrite heart and a humble spirit let us be accepted, ¹⁷Like the burnt-offerings of rams and bullocks, and like tens of thousands of fat lambs—So let our sacrifice be in Your sight this day, that we may wholly go after You, || For they will not be ashamed who put their trust in You. ¹⁸And now we follow You with all our heart. We fear You and seek Your face. ¹⁹Do not put us to shame; but deal with us after Your kindness, || And according to the multitude of Your mercy. ²⁰Deliver us also according to Your marvelous works, and give glory to Your Name, O LORD. Let all those who harm Your servants be confounded. ²¹Let them be ashamed of all their power and might, and let their strength be broken. ²²Let them know that You are the LORD, the only God, || And [are] glorious over the whole world." ²³The king's servants who put them in did not stop making the furnace hot with naphtha, pitch, tinder, and small wood, ²⁴so that the flame streamed out forty-nine cubits above the furnace. ²⁵It spread and burned those Chaldeans whom it found around the furnace. ²⁶But the Messenger of the LORD came down into the furnace together with Azariah and his fellows, and He struck the flame of the fire out of the furnace, ²⁷and made the midst of the furnace as it had been a moist whistling wind, so that the fire did not touch them at all. It neither hurt nor troubled them. ²⁸Then the three, as out of one mouth, praised, glorified, and blessed God in the furnace, saying, ²⁹"Blessed are You, O LORD, You God of our fathers, || To be praised and exalted above all forever! ³⁰Blessed is Your glorious and holy Name, || To be praised and exalted above all forever! ³¹Blessed are You in the temple of Your holy glory, || To be praised and glorified above all forever! ³²Blessed are

You who see the depths and sit on the cherubim, || To be praised and exalted above all forever! ³³Blessed are You on the throne of Your kingdom, || To be praised and extolled above all forever! ³⁴Blessed are You in the expanse of Heaven, || To be praised and glorified forever! ³⁵O all you works of the LORD, bless the LORD! Praise and exalt Him above all forever! ³⁶O you heavens, bless the LORD! Praise and exalt Him above all forever! ³⁷O you messengers of the LORD, bless the LORD! Praise and exalt Him above all forever! ³⁸O all you waters that are above the sky, bless the LORD! Praise and exalt Him above all forever! ³⁹O all you powers of the LORD, bless the LORD! Praise and exalt Him above all forever! ⁴⁰O you sun and moon, bless the LORD! Praise and exalt Him above all forever! ⁴¹O you stars of the heavens, bless the LORD! Praise and exalt Him above all forever! ⁴²O every shower and dew, bless the LORD! Praise and exalt Him above all forever! ⁴³O all you winds, bless the LORD! Praise and exalt Him above all forever! ⁴⁴O you fire and heat, bless the LORD! Praise and exalt Him above all forever! ⁴⁵O you winter and summer, bless the LORD! Praise and exalt Him above all forever! ⁴⁶O you dews and storms of snow, bless the LORD! Praise and exalt Him above all forever! ⁴⁷O you nights and days, bless the LORD! Praise and exalt Him above all forever! ⁴⁸O you light and darkness, bless the LORD! Praise and exalt Him above all forever! ⁴⁹O you cold and heat, bless the LORD! Praise and exalt Him above all forever! ⁵⁰O you frost and snow, bless the LORD! Praise and exalt Him above all forever! ⁵¹O you lightnings and clouds, bless the LORD! Praise and exalt Him above all forever! ⁵²O let the earth bless the LORD! Let it praise and exalt Him above all forever! ⁵³O you mountains and hills, bless the LORD! Praise and exalt Him above all forever! ⁵⁴O all you things that grow on the earth, bless the LORD! Praise and exalt Him above all forever! ⁵⁵O sea and rivers, bless the LORD! Praise and exalt Him above all forever! ⁵⁶O you springs, bless the LORD! Praise and exalt Him above all forever! ⁵⁷O you whales and all that move in the waters, bless the LORD! Praise and exalt Him above all forever! ⁵⁸O all you birds of the air, bless the LORD! Praise and exalt Him above all forever! ⁵⁹O all you beasts and cattle, bless the LORD! Praise and exalt Him above all forever! ⁶⁰O you children of men, bless the LORD! Praise and exalt Him above all forever! ⁶¹O let Israel bless the LORD! Praise and exalt Him above all forever. ⁶²O you priests of the LORD, bless the LORD! Praise and exalt Him above all forever! ⁶³O you servants of the LORD, bless the LORD! Praise and exalt Him above all forever! ⁶⁴O you spirits and souls of the righteous, bless the LORD! Praise and exalt Him above all forever! ⁶⁵O you who are holy and humble of heart, bless the LORD! Praise and exalt Him above all forever! ⁶⁶O Hananiah, Mishael, and Azariah, bless the LORD! Praise and exalt Him above all forever; For He has rescued us from Hades and saved us from the hand of death! He has delivered us out of the midst of the furnace and burning flame. He has delivered us out of the midst of the fire. ⁶⁷O give thanks to the LORD, for He is good; For His mercy is forever. ⁶⁸O all you who worship the LORD, bless the God of gods, praise Him, and give Him thanks; for His mercy is forever!"

SECTION 2:

SUSANNA AND THE ELDERS

CHAPTER 13

¹A man lived in Babylon, and his name was Jehoiakim. ²He took a wife, whose name was Susanna, the daughter of Hilkiah, a very fair woman, and one who feared the LORD. ³Her parents were also righteous and taught their daughter according to the Law of Moses. ⁴Now Jehoiakim was a great rich man, and had a fair garden joining to his house. The Jews used to come to him, because he was more honorable than all others. ⁵The same year two of the elders of the people were appointed to be judges, such as the LORD spoke of, that wickedness came from Babylon from elders who were judges, who were supposed to govern the people. ⁶These were often at Jehoiakim's house. All that had any suits in law came to them. ⁷When the people departed away at noon, Susanna went into her husband's garden to walk. ⁸The two elders saw her going in every day, and walking; and they were inflamed with lust for her. ⁹They perverted their own mind and turned away their eyes, that they might not look to Heaven, nor remember just judgments. ¹⁰And although they both were wounded with lust for her yet dared not show the other his grief. ¹¹For they were ashamed to declare their lust, that they desired to have to do with her. ¹²Yet they watched jealously from day to day to see her. ¹³The one said to the other, "Let us go home, now; for it is dinner time." ¹⁴So when they had gone out, they parted company, and turning back again, they came to the same place. After they had asked one another the cause, they acknowledged their lust. Then they appointed a time both together, when they might find her alone. ¹⁵It happened, as they watched on an opportune day, she went in as before with only two maids, and she desired to wash herself in the garden; for it was hot. ¹⁶There was nobody there except the two elders who had hid themselves and watched her. ¹⁷Then she said to her maids, "Bring me oil and washing balls, and shut the garden doors, that I may wash myself." ¹⁸They did as she asked them, and shut the garden doors, and went out themselves at the side doors to fetch the things that she had commanded them. They did not see the elders, because they were hidden. ¹⁹Now when the maids had gone out, the two elders rose up, and ran to her, saying, ²⁰"Behold, the garden doors are shut, that no man can see us, and we are in love with you. Therefore, consent to us, and lie with us. ²¹If you will not, we will testify against you, that a young man was with you; therefore, you sent your maids away from you." ²²Then Susanna sighed, and said, "I am trapped; for if I do this thing, it is death to me. If I do not do it, I cannot escape your hands. ²³It is better for me to fall into your hands, and not do it, than to sin in the sight of the LORD." ²⁴With that Susanna cried with a loud voice; and the two elders cried out against her. ²⁵Then one of them ran and opened the garden doors. ²⁶So when the servants of the house heard the cry in the garden, they rushed in at the side door, to see what had happened to her. ²⁷But when the elders had told their tale, the servants were greatly ashamed; for there was never such a report made of Susanna. ²⁸It came to pass on the next day, when the people assembled to her husband Jehoiakim, the two elders came full of their wicked intent against Susanna to put her to death, ²⁹and said before the people, "Send for Susanna, the daughter of Hilkiah, Jehoiakim's wife." So they sent; ³⁰and she came with her father and mother, her children, and all her relatives. ³¹Now Susanna was a very delicate woman, and beautiful to behold. ³²These wicked men commanded her to be unveiled, for she was veiled, that they might be filled with her beauty. ³³Therefore her friends and all who saw her wept. ³⁴Then the two elders stood up in the midst of the people and laid their hands on her head. ³⁵She, weeping, looked up toward Heaven; for her heart trusted in the LORD. ³⁶The elders said, "As we walked in the garden alone, this woman came in with two maids, shut the garden doors, and sent the maids away. ³⁷Then a young man, who was hidden there, came to her and lay with her. ³⁸And we, being in a corner of the garden, saw this wickedness and ran to them. ³⁹And when we saw them together, we could not hold the man; for he was stronger than we, and opened the doors, and leapt out. ⁴⁰But having taken this woman, we asked who the young man was, but she would not tell us. We testify these things." ⁴¹Then the assembly believed them, as those who were elders of the people and judges; so they condemned her to death. ⁴²Then Susanna cried out with a loud voice, and said, "O perpetual God, You know the secrets, and know all things before they happen, ⁴³You know that they have testified falsely against me. Behold, I must die, even though I never did such things as these men have maliciously invented against me." ⁴⁴The LORD heard her voice. ⁴⁵Therefore when she was led away to be put to death, God raised up the holy spirit of a young youth, whose name was Daniel. ⁴⁶He cried with a loud voice, "I am clear from the blood of this woman!" ⁴⁷Then all the people turned them toward him, and said, "What do these words that you have spoken mean?" ⁴⁸So he, standing in the midst of them, said, "Are you all such fools, you sons of Israel, that without examination or knowledge of the truth you have condemned a daughter of Israel? ⁴⁹Return again to the place of judgment; for these have testified falsely against her." ⁵⁰Therefore all the people turned again in haste, and the elders said to him, "Come, sit down among us, and show it to us, seeing God has given you the honor of an elder." ⁵¹Then Daniel said to them, "Put them far apart from each another, and I will examine them." ⁵²So when they were put apart

from one another, he called one of them, and said to him, "O you who have become old in wickedness, now your sins have returned which you have committed before, ⁵³in pronouncing unjust judgment, condemning the innocent, and letting the guilty go free; although the LORD says, You will not kill the innocent and righteous. ⁵⁴Now then, if you saw her, tell me, under which tree did you see them companying together?" He answered, "Under a mastick tree." ⁵⁵And Daniel said, "You have certainly lied against your own head; for even now the messenger of God has received the sentence of God and will cut you in two." ⁵⁶So he put him aside, and commanded to bring the other, and said to him, "O you seed of Canaan, and not of Judah, beauty has deceived you, and lust has perverted your heart. ⁵⁷Thus you have dealt with the daughters of Israel, and they for fear were intimate with you; but the daughter of Judah would not tolerate your wickedness. ⁵⁸Now therefore, tell me, under which tree did you take them being intimate together?" He answered, "Under an evergreen oak tree." ⁵⁹Then Daniel said to him, "You have also certainly lied against your own head; for the messenger of God waits with the sword to cut you in two, that he may destroy you." ⁶⁰With that, all the assembly cried out with a loud voice, and blessed God, who saves those who hope in him. ⁶¹Then they arose against the two elders, for Daniel had convicted them of false testimony out of their own mouth. ⁶²According to the Law of Moses they did to them in such sort as they maliciously intended to do to their neighbor. They put them to death, and the innocent blood was saved the same day. ⁶³Therefore Hilkiah and his wife praised God for their daughter Susanna, with Jehoiakim her husband, and all the relatives, because there was no dishonesty found in her. ⁶⁴And from that day out, Daniel was held in high regard in the sight of the people.

SECTION 3:
BEL AND THE DRAGON

CHAPTER 14

¹King Astyages was gathered to his fathers, and Cyrus the Persian received his kingdom. ²Daniel lived with the king and was honored above all his friends. ³Now the Babylonians had an idol, called Bel, and every day twelve great measures of fine flour, forty sheep, and six firkins of wine were spent on him. ⁴And the king honored it and went daily to worship it; but Daniel worshiped his own God. The king said to him, "Why do you not worship Bel?" ⁵He said, "Because I may not honor idols made with hands, but only the living God, who has created the sky and the earth, and has sovereignty over all flesh." ⁶Then the king said to him, "Do you not think that Bel is a living god? Do you not see how much he eats and drinks every day?" ⁷Then Daniel laughed, and said, "O king, do not be deceived; for this is just clay inside, and brass outside, and never ate or drank anything." ⁸So the king was angry, and called for his priests, and said to them, "If you do not tell me who this is who devours these expenses, you will die. ⁹But if you can show me that Bel devours them, then Daniel will die; for he has spoken blasphemy against Bel." Daniel said to the king, "Let it be according to your word." ¹⁰Now there were seventy priests of Bel, besides their wives and children. The king went with Daniel into Bel's temple. ¹¹So Bel's priests said, "Behold, we will leave; but you, O king, set out the meat, and mix the wine and set it out, shut the door securely, and seal it with your own signet. ¹²When you come in the morning, if you do not find that Bel has eaten everything, we will suffer death, or else Daniel, who speaks falsely against us." ¹³They were not concerned, for under the table they had made a secret entrance, whereby they entered in continually, and consumed those things. ¹⁴It happened, when they had gone out, the king set the meat before Bel. Now Daniel had commanded his servants to bring ashes, and they scattered them all over the temple in the presence of the king alone. Then they went out, shut the door, sealed it with the king's signet, and so departed. ¹⁵Now in the night, the priests came with their wives and children, as they usually did, and ate and drank it all. ¹⁶In the morning, the king arose, and Daniel with him. ¹⁷The king said, "Daniel, are the seals whole?" He said, "Yes, O king, they are whole." ¹⁸And as soon as he had opened the door, the king looked at the table, and cried with a loud voice, "You are great, O Bel, and with you is no deceit at all!" ¹⁹Then Daniel laughed, and held the king that he should not go in, and said, "Behold now the pavement, and mark well whose footsteps these are." ²⁰The king said, "I see the footsteps of men, women, and children." Then the king was angry, ²¹and took the priests with their wives and children, who showed him the secret doors, where they came in, and consumed the things that were on the table. ²²Therefore the king killed them, and delivered Bel into Daniel's power, who overthrew him and his temple. ²³In that same place there was a great dragon, which the people of Babylon worshiped. ²⁴The king said to Daniel, "Will you also say that this is of brass? Behold, he lives, eats, and drinks. You cannot say that he is no living god. Therefore, worship him." ²⁵Then Daniel said, "I will worship the LORD my God; for He is a living God. ²⁶But allow me, O king, and I will kill this dragon without sword or staff." The king said, "I allow you." ²⁷Then Daniel took pitch, fat, and hair, and melted them together, and made lumps of them. He put these in the dragon's mouth, so the dragon ate and burst apart. Daniel said, "Behold, these are the gods you all worship." ²⁸When the people of Babylon heard that, they took great indignation, and conspired against the king, saying, "The king has become a Jew. He has pulled down Bel, slain the dragon, and put the priests to the sword." ²⁹So they came to the king, and said, "Deliver Daniel to us, or else we will destroy you and your house." ³⁰Now when the king saw that they trapped him, being constrained, the king delivered Daniel to them. ³¹They cast him into the lion's den, where he was six days. ³²There were seven lions in the den, and they had been giving them two carcasses and two sheep every day, which then were not given to them, intending that they would devour Daniel. ³³Now there was in Jewry the prophet Habakkuk, who had made stew, and had broken bread into a bowl. He was going into the field to bring it to the reapers. ³⁴But the messenger of the LORD said to Habakkuk, "Go, carry the dinner that you have into Babylon—to Daniel in the lions' den." ³⁵Habakkuk said, "Lord, I never saw Babylon. I do not know where the den is." ³⁶Then the messenger of the LORD took him by the crown and lifted him up by the hair of his head, and with the blast of his breath set him in Babylon over the den. ³⁷Habakkuk cried, saying, "O Daniel, Daniel, take the dinner which God has sent you." ³⁸Daniel said, "You have remembered me, O God! You have not forsaken those who love you!" ³⁹So Daniel arose and ate; and the messenger of God immediately set Habakkuk in his own place again. ⁴⁰On the seventh day, the king came to mourn for Daniel. When he came to the den, he looked in, and behold, Daniel was sitting. ⁴¹Then the king cried with a loud voice, saying, "Great are You, O LORD, You God of Daniel, and there is no other besides You!" ⁴²So he drew him out, and cast those that were the cause of his destruction into the den; and they were devoured in a moment before his face.

ACTS 29

Acts 29, also known as the Lost Chapter of the Acts of the Apostles and the Sonnini Manuscript, is a short text purporting to be the translation of a manuscript containing the 29th chapter of the Acts of the Apostles, detailing Paul the Apostle's journey to Britannia, where he preached to a tribe of Israelites on Mount Lud (Ludgate Hill), later the site of St. Paul's Cathedral, and met with druids, who proved to him that they were descended from Jews. Thereafter, Paul preached in Gaul and Belgium, and then to Switzerland (Helvetia), where a miraculous earthquake occurred at the site of Pontius Pilate's supposed suicide. The canonical book of Acts ends rather abruptly with Paul kept under house arrest in chapter 28, which has led to various theories about the history of the text. The text made its first appearance in London in 1871. According to the editor, it was translated in the late 18th century by the French naturalist Sonnini de Manoncourt from a Greek manuscript discovered in the archives at Constantinople and presented to him by the Sultan Abdoul Achmet. However, no trace of any such manuscript has been found, and from internal evidence, mainstream philology considers it to most likely be a fraud, thus it is classed among the pseudepigrapha.

CHAPTER 29

¹And Paul, full of the blessings of Christ, and abounding in the Spirit, departed out of Rome, determining to go into Spain, for he had proposed to journey toward there for a long time, and was also intending to go from there to Britain. ²For he had heard in Phoenicia that certain of the children of Israel, about the time of the Assyrian captivity, had escaped by sea to "The Isles far off" as spoken by the Prophet Esdras, and called by the Romans—Britain. ³And the LORD commanded the good news to be preached far hence to the nations, and to the lost sheep of the House of Israel. ⁴And no man hindered Paul; for he testified boldly of Jesus before the tribunes and among the people; and he took with him cetain of the brothers which dwelt with him at Rome, and they embarked at Ostrium; and having fair winds, they were brought safely into a haven of Spain. ⁵And many people were gathered together from the towns, and villages, and the hill country, for they had heard of the conversion to the Apostles, and the many miracles which he had worked. ⁶And Paul preached mightily in Spain, and great multitudes believed and were converted, for they perceived he was an apostle sent from God. ⁷And they departed out of Spain, and Paul and his company finding a ship in Armorica sailing to Britain, they were therein, and passing along the southern coast, they reached a port called Raphinus. ⁸Now when it was voiced abroad that the apostle had landed on their coast, great multitudes of the inhabitants met him, and they treated Paul courteously, and he entered in at the east gate of their city and lodged in the house of a Hebrew—and one of his own nation. ⁹And in the morning he came and stood on Mount Lud, and the people crowded at the gate, and assembled in the broadway, and he preached Christ to them, and they believed the word and the testimony of Jesus. ¹⁰And in the evening the Holy Spirit fell on Paul, and he prophesied, saying, "Behold, in the last days the God of Peace will dwell in the cities, and the inhabitants thereof will be numbered: and in the seventh numbering of the people, their eyes will be opened, and the glory of their inheritance will shine forth before them. The nations will come up to worship on the mount that testifies of the patience and long suffering of a servant of the LORD. ¹¹And in the latter days, new tidings of the good news will issue forth out of Jerusalem, and the hearts of the people will rejoice, and behold, fountains will be opened, and there will be no more plague. ¹²In those days there will be wars and rumors of war; and a king will arise, and his sword will be for the healing of the nations, and his peacemaking will remain, and the glory of his kingdom [will be] a wonder among princes." ¹³And it came to pass that certain of the druids came to Paul privately and showed by their rites and ceremonies [that] they were descended from the Jews which escaped from bondage in the land of Egypt, and the apostle believed these things, and he gave them the kiss of peace. ¹⁴And Paul remained in his lodgings [for] three months, confirming in the faith and preaching Christ continually. ¹⁵And after these things, Paul and his brothers departed from Raphinus and sailed to Atium in Gaul. ¹⁶And Paul preached in the Roman garrison and among the people, exhorting all men to convert and confess their sins. ¹⁷And there came to him certain of the Belgae to inquire of him of the new doctrine, and of the man Jesus; and Paul opened his heart to them and told them all things that had befallen him, how it was that Christ Jesus came into the world to save sinners; and they departed, pondering among themselves on the things which they had heard. ¹⁸And after much preaching and toil, Paul and his fellow laborers passed into Helvetia, and came to Mount Pontius Pilate, where he who condemned the Lord Jesus dashed himself down headlong, and so miserably perished. ¹⁹Immediately a torrent gushed out of the mountain and washed his body, broken in pieces, into a lake. ²⁰And Paul stretched forth his hands on the water, and prayed to the Lord, saying, "O LORD God, give a sign to all nations that here Pontius Pilate, who condemned Your only begotten Son, plunged down headlong into the pit." ²¹And while Paul was yet speaking, behold, there came a great earthquake, and the face of the waters was changed, and the form of the lake like to the Son of Man hanging in agony on the Cross. ²²And a voice came out of Heaven, saying, "Even Pilate has escaped the wrath to come, for he washed his hands before the multitude at the blood-shedding of the Lord Jesus." ²³When, therefore, Paul and those that were with him saw the earthquake, and heard the voice of the angel, they glorified God, [and] they were mightily strengthened in the Spirit. ²⁴And they journeyed and came to Mount Julius where two pillars stood—one on the right hand and one on the left hand, erected by Caesar Augustus. ²⁵And Paul, filled with the Holy Spirit, stood up between the two pillars, saying, "Men and brothers! These stones which you see this day will testify of my journey here; and truly I say [to you]: they will remain until the outpouring of the Spirit on all nations, neither will the way be hindered throughout all generations." ²⁶And they went forth and came unto Illtricum, intending to go by Macedonia into Asia, and grace was found in all the assemblies, and they prospered and had peace. Amen.

TOBIT

The Book of Tobit, named after its principal character, combines Jewish piety and morality with folklore in a fascinating story that has enjoyed wide popularity in both Jewish and Christian circles. Prayers, psalms, and words of wisdom, as well as the skillfully constructed story itself, provide valuable insights into the faith and the religious milieu of its unknown author. The book was probably written early in the 2nd century BC; it is not known where.

CHAPTER 1

¹The scroll of the words of Tobit, the son of Tobiel, the son of Ananiel, the son of Aduel, the son of Gabael, of the seed of Asiel, of the tribe of Naphtali; ²who in the days of Enemessar king of the Assyrians was carried away captive out of Thisbe, which is on the right side of Kedesh Naphtali in Galilee above Asher. ³I, Tobit, walked in the ways of truth and righteousness all the days of my life, and I did many kind acts to my countrymen and my nation, who went with me into the land of the Assyrians, to Nineveh. ⁴When I was in my own country, in the land of Israel, while I was yet young, all the tribe of my father Naphtali fell away from the house of Jerusalem, which was chosen out of all the tribes of Israel, that all the tribes should sacrifice there, and the temple of the habitation of the Most High was hallowed and built therein for all ages. ⁵All the tribes which fell away together sacrificed to the heifer Ba'al, and so did the house of my father Naphtali. ⁶I alone went often to Jerusalem at the feasts, as it has been ordained to all Israel by a perpetual decree, having the first-fruits and the tenths of my increase, and that which was first shorn; and I gave them to the priests at the altar, the sons of Aaron. ⁷I gave a tenth part of all my increase to the sons of Levi, who ministered at Jerusalem. A second tenth part I sold away, and went, and spent it each year at Jerusalem. ⁸A third tenth I gave to them to whom it was appropriate, as Deborah my father's mother had commanded me, because I was left an orphan by my father. ⁹When I became a man, I took as wife Anna of the seed of our own family. With her, I became the father of Tobias. ¹⁰When I was carried away captive to Nineveh, all my countrymen and my family ate of the bread of the nations; ¹¹but I kept myself from eating, ¹²because I remembered God with all my soul. ¹³So the Most High gave me grace and favor in the sight of Enemessar, and I was his purchasing agent. ¹⁴And I went into Media and left ten talents of silver in trust with Gabael, the brother of Gabrias, at Rages of Media. ¹⁵And when Enemessar was dead, Sennacherib his son reigned in his place. In his time, the highways were troubled, and I could no longer go into Media. ¹⁶In the days of Enemessar, I did many kind acts to my countrymen: I gave my bread to the hungry, ¹⁷and my garments to the naked. If I saw any of my race dead, and thrown out on the wall of Nineveh, I buried him. ¹⁸If Sennacherib the king killed any, when he came fleeing from Judea, I buried them privately; for in his wrath he killed many; and the bodies were sought for by the king and were not found. ¹⁹But one of the Ninevites went and showed to the king concerning me, how I buried them, and hid myself; and when I knew that I was sought for to be put to death, I withdrew myself for fear. ²⁰And all my goods were forcibly taken away, and there was nothing left to me, save my wife Anna and my son Tobias. ²¹No more than fifty-five days passed before two of his sons killed him, and they fled into the mountains of Ararat. And Esarhaddon his son reigned in his place; and he appointed Ahikar, my brother Anael's son, over all the accounts of his kingdom, and over all his affairs. ²²Ahikar requested me, and I came to Nineveh. Now Ahikar was cupbearer, keeper of the signet, steward, and overseer of the accounts. Esarhaddon appointed him next to himself, but he was my brother's son.

CHAPTER 2

¹Now when I had come home again, and my wife Anna was restored to me, and my son Tobias, in the Celebration of Pentecost, which is the holy celebration of the seven weeks, there was a good dinner prepared [for] me, and I sat down to eat. ²I saw abundance of meat, and I said to my son, "Go and bring whatever poor man you find of our countrymen, who is mindful of the LORD. Behold, I wait for you." ³Then he came, and said, "Father, one of our race is strangled, and has been cast out in the marketplace." ⁴Before I had tasted anything, I sprang up, and took him up into a chamber until the sun had set. ⁵Then I returned, washed myself, ate my bread in heaviness, ⁶and remembered the prophecy of Amos, as he said, "Your feasts will be turned into mourning, and all your mirth into lamentation." ⁷So I wept: and when the sun had set, I went and dug a grave, and buried him. ⁸My neighbors mocked me, and said, "He is no longer afraid to be put to death for this matter; and yet he fled away. Behold, he buries the dead again." ⁹The same night I returned from burying him, and slept by the wall of my courtyard, being polluted; and my face was uncovered. ¹⁰I did not know that there were sparrows in the wall. My eyes were open, and the sparrows dropped warm dung into my eyes, and white films came over my eyes. I went to the physicians, and they did not help me; but Ahikar nourished me, until I went into Elymais. ¹¹My wife Anna wove cloth in the women's chambers, ¹²and sent the work back to the owners. They on their part paid her wages, and also gave her a kid. ¹³But when it came to my house, it began to cry, and I said to her, "Where did this kid come from? Is it stolen? Give it back to the owners; for it is not lawful to eat anything that is stolen." ¹⁴But she said, "It has been given to me for a gift more than the wages." I did not believe her, and I asked her to return it to the owners; and I was ashamed of her. But she answered and said to me, "Where are your alms and your righteous deeds? Behold, you and all your works are known."

CHAPTER 3

¹I was grieved and wept, and prayed in sorrow, saying, ²"O LORD, You are righteous, || And all Your works and all Your ways are mercy and truth, || And You judge true and righteous judgment forever. ³Remember me and look at me. Do not take vengeance on me for my sins and my ignorance, || And the sins of my fathers who sinned before You. ⁴For they disobeyed Your commands. You gave us as plunder, for captivity, for death, || And for a proverb of reproach to all the nations among whom we are dispersed. ⁵Now Your judgments are many and true; That You should deal with me according to my sins and the sins of my fathers; Because we did not keep Your commands, || For we did not walk in truth before You. ⁶Now deal with me according to that which is pleasing in Your sight. Command my spirit to be taken from me, || That I may be released, and become earth. For it is more profitable for me to die rather than to live, || Because I have heard false reproaches, || And there is much sorrow in me. Command that I be released from my distress, now, || And go to the agelong place. Do not turn Your face away from me." ⁷The same day it happened to Sarah, the daughter of Raguel, in Ecbatana of Media, that she also was reproached by her father's maidservants; ⁸because that she had been given to seven husbands, and Asmodeus the evil spirit killed them, before they had lain with her. And they said to her, "Do you not know that you strangle your husbands? You have already had seven husbands, and you have not borne the name of any of them. ⁹Why do you scourge us? If they are dead, go your ways with them. Let us never see either son or daughter from you." ¹⁰When she heard these things, she was grieved exceedingly, so that she thought about hanging herself. Then she said, "I am the only daughter of my father. If I do this, it will be a reproach to him, and I will bring down his old age with sorrow to the grave." ¹¹Then she prayed by the window, and said, "Blessed are You, O LORD my God, || And blessed is Your holy and honorable Name forever! Let all Your works praise You forever! ¹²And now, LORD, I have set my eyes and my face toward You. ¹³Command that I be released from the

earth, || And that I no longer hear reproach. ¹⁴You know, LORD, that I am pure from all sin with man, ¹⁵And that I never polluted my name or the name of my father, || In the land of my captivity. I am the only daughter of my father, || And he has no child that will be his heir, nor brother near him, || Nor son belonging to him, that I should keep myself for a wife to him. Seven husbands of mine are dead already. Why should I live? If it does not please You to kill me, || Command some regard to be had of me, and pity taken of me, || And that I hear no more reproach." ¹⁶The prayer of both was heard before the glory of the great God. ¹⁷Raphael, also, was sent to heal them both, to scale away the white films from Tobit's eyes, and to give Sarah the daughter of Raguel for a wife to Tobias the son of Tobit, and to bind Asmodeus the evil spirit; because it belonged to Tobias that he should inherit her. At that very time, Tobit returned and entered into his house, and Sarah the daughter of Raguel came down from her upper chamber.

CHAPTER 4

¹In that day Tobit remembered the money which he had left in trust with Gabael in Rages of Media, ²and he said to himself, I have asked for death; why do I not call my son Tobias, that I may explain to him about the money before I die? ³And he called him, and said, "My child, if I die, bury me. Do not despise your mother. Honor her all the days of your life, and do that which is pleasing to her, and do not grieve her. ⁴Remember, my child, that she has seen many dangers for you, when you were in her womb. When she is dead, bury her by me in one grave. ⁵My child, be mindful of the LORD our God all your days, and do not let your will be set to sin and to transgress His commands: do righteousness all the days of your life, and do not follow the ways of unrighteousness. ⁶For if you do what is true, your deeds will prosperously succeed for you, and for all those who do righteousness. ⁷Give alms from your possessions. When you give alms, do not let your eye be envious. Do not turn your face away from any poor man, and the face of God will not be turned away from you. ⁸As your possessions are, give alms of it according to your abundance. If you have little, do not be afraid to give alms according to that little; ⁹for you lay up a good treasure for yourself against the day of necessity; ¹⁰because kindness delivers from death, and does not allow you to come into darkness. ¹¹Alms is a good gift in the sight of the Most High for all that give it. ¹²Beware, my child, of all whoredom, and take first a wife of the seed of your fathers. Do not take a strange wife, who is not of your father's tribe; for we are the descendants of the prophets. Remember, my child, that Noah, Abraham, Isaac, and Jacob, our fathers from antiquity, all took wives of their countrymen, and were blessed in their children, and their seed will inherit the land. ¹³And now, my child, love your relatives, and do not scorn your countrymen and the sons and the daughters of your people in your heart, to take a wife of them; for in scornfulness is destruction and much trouble, and in naughtiness is decay and great lack; for naughtiness is the mother of famine. ¹⁴Do not let the wages of any man who works for you wait with you but give it to him out of hand. If you serve God, you will be rewarded. Take heed to yourself, my child, in all your works, and be discreet in all your behavior. ¹⁵And what you yourself hate, do to no man. Do not drink wine to drunkenness, and do not let drunkenness go with you on your way. ¹⁶Give of your bread to the hungry, and of your garments to those who are naked. Give alms from all your abundance. Do not let your eye be envious when you give alms. ¹⁷Pour out your bread on the burial of the just and give nothing to sinners. ¹⁸Ask counsel of every man who is wise, and do not despise any counsel that is profitable. ¹⁹Bless the LORD your God at all times and ask of Him that your ways may be made straight, and that all your paths and counsels may prosper; for every nation has no counsel; but the LORD Himself gives all good things, and He humbles whom He will, as He will. And now, my child, remember my commands, and do not let them be blotted out of your mind. ²⁰And now I explain to you about the ten talents of silver, which I left in trust with Gabael the son of Gabrias at Rages of Media. ²¹And do not fear, my child, because we are made poor. You have much wealth, if you fear God, and depart from all sin, and do that which is pleasing in His sight."

CHAPTER 5

¹Then Tobias answered and said to him, "Father, I will do all things, whatever you have commanded me. ²But how could I receive the money, since I do not know him?" ³He gave him the handwriting, and said to him, "Seek a man who will go with you, and I will give him wages, while I yet live; and go and receive the money." ⁴He went to seek a man and found Raphael who was a messenger; ⁵and he did not know it. He said to him, "Can I go with you to Rages of Media? Do you know those places well?" ⁶The messenger said to him, "I will go with you. I know the way well. I have lodged with our brother Gabael." ⁷Tobias said to him, "Wait for me, and I will tell my father." ⁸He said to him, "Go, and do not wait." And he went in and said to his father, "Behold, I have found someone who will go with me." But he said, "Call him to me, that I may know of what tribe he is, and whether he is a trustworthy man to go with you." ⁹So he called him, and he came in, and they saluted one another. ¹⁰And Tobit said to him, "Brother, of what tribe and of what family are you? Tell me." ¹¹He said to him, "Do you seek a tribe and a family, or a hired man which will go with your son?" And Tobit said to him, "I want to know, brother, your relatives and your name." ¹²And he said, "I am Azariah, the son of Ananias the great, of your relatives." ¹³And he said to him, "Welcome, brother. Do not be angry with me, because I sought to know your tribe and family. You are my brother, of an honest and good lineage; for I knew Ananias and Jathan, the sons of Shemaiah the great, when we went together to Jerusalem to worship, and offered the firstborn, and the tenths of our increase; and they did not go astray in the error of our countrymen. My brother, you are of a great stock. ¹⁴But tell me, what wages will I give you? A drachma a day, and those things that are necessary for you, as to my son? ¹⁵And moreover, if you both return safe and sound, I will add something to your wages." ¹⁶And so they agreed. And he said to Tobias, "Prepare yourself for the journey. May God prosper you." So, his son prepared what was needful for the journey, and his father said to him, "Go with this man; but God, who dwells in Heaven, will prosper your journey. May His messenger go with you." Then they both departed, and the young man's dog went with them. ¹⁷But Anna his mother wept, and said to Tobit, "Why have you sent our child away? Is he not the staff of our hand, in going in and out before us? ¹⁸Do not be greedy to add money to money; but let it be as refuse compared to our child. ¹⁹For what the LORD has given us to live is enough for us." ²⁰Tobit said to her, "Do not worry, my sister. He will return safe and sound, and your eyes will see him. ²¹For a good messenger will go with him. His journey will be prospered, and he will return safe and sound." ²²So she stopped weeping.

CHAPTER 6

¹Now as they went on their journey, they came at evening to the River Tigris, and they lodged there. ²But the young man went down to wash himself, and a fish leaped out of the river, and would have swallowed up the young man. ³But the messenger said to him, "Grab the fish!" So the young man grabbed the fish, and hauled it up onto the land. ⁴And the messenger said to him, "Cut the fish open, and take the heart, the liver, and the bile, and keep them with you." ⁵And the young man did as the messenger commanded him; but they roasted the fish and ate it. And they both went on their way, until they drew near to Ecbatana. ⁶The young man said to the messenger, "Brother Azariah, of what use is the heart, the liver, and the bile of the fish?" ⁷He said to him, "About the heart and the liver: If a demon or an evil spirit troubles anyone, we must burn those and make smoke of them before the man or the woman, and the affliction will flee. ⁸But as for the bile, it is good to anoint a man that has white films in his eyes, and he will be healed." ⁹But when they drew near to Rages, ¹⁰the messenger said to the young man, "Brother, today we will lodge with Raguel. He is your relative. He has an only daughter named Sarah. I will speak about her, that she should be given to you for a wife. ¹¹For her inheritance belongs to you, and you only are of her relatives. ¹²The maid is fair and wise. And now hear me, and I will speak to her father. When we return from Rages we will celebrate the marriage; for I know that Raguel may in no way marry her to another according to the Law of Moses, or else he would be liable to death, because it belongs to you to take the inheritance, rather than any

other." ¹³Then the young man said to the messenger, "Brother Azariah, I have heard that this maid has been given to seven men, and that they all perished in the bride-chamber. ¹⁴Now I am the only son of my father, and I am afraid, lest I go in and die, even as those before me. For a demon loves her, which harms no man, but those which come to her. Now I fear lest I die and bring my father's and my mother's life to the grave with sorrow because of me. They have no other son to bury them." ¹⁵But the messenger said to him, "Do not you remember the words which your father commanded you, that you should take a wife of your own relatives? Now hear me, brother; for she will be your wife. Do not worry about the demon; for this night she will be given you as wife. ¹⁶And when you come into the bride-chamber, you will take the ashes of incense, and will lay on them some of the heart and liver of the fish and will make smoke with them. ¹⁷The demon will smell it, and flee away, and never come again anymore. But when you go near to her, both of you rise up, and cry to God who is merciful. He will save you and have mercy on you. Do not be afraid, for she was prepared for you from the beginning; and you will save her, and she will go with you. And I suppose that you will have children with her." When Tobias heard these things, he loved her, and his soul was strongly joined to her.

CHAPTER 7

¹They came to Ecbatana and arrived at the house of Raguel. But Sarah met them; and she greeted them, and they her. Then she brought them into the house. ²Raguel said to Edna his wife, "This young man really resembles Tobit my cousin!" ³And Raguel asked them, "Where are you two from, countrymen?" They said to him, "We are of the sons of Naphtali, who are captives in Nineveh." ⁴He said to them, "Do you know Tobit our brother?" They said, "We know him." Then he said to them, "Is he in good health?" ⁵They said, "He is both alive, and in good health." Tobias said, "He is my father." ⁶And Raguel sprang up, and kissed him, wept, ⁷blessed him, and said to him, "You are the son of an honest and good man." When he had heard that Tobit had lost his sight, he was grieved, and wept; ⁸and Edna his wife and Sarah his daughter wept. They received them gladly; and they killed a ram of the flock and served them meat. But Tobias said to Raphael, "Brother Azariah, speak of those things of which you talked about in the way, and let the matter be finished." ⁹So he communicated the thing to Raguel. Raguel said to Tobias, "Eat, drink, and make merry: ¹⁰for it belongs to you to take my child. However, I will tell you the truth. ¹¹I have given my child to seven men of our countrymen, and whenever they came in to her, they died in the night. But for the present be merry." And Tobias said, "I will taste nothing here, until you all make a covenant and enter into that covenant with me." ¹²Raguel said, "Take her to yourself from now on according to custom. You are her relative, and she is yours. The merciful God will give all good success to you." ¹³And he called his daughter Sarah, and took her by the hand, and gave her to be wife of Tobias, and said, "Behold, take her to yourself after the Law of Moses, and lead her away to your father." And he blessed them. ¹⁴He called Edna his wife, then took a scroll, wrote a contract, and sealed it. ¹⁵Then they began to eat. ¹⁶And Raguel called his wife Edna, and said to her, "Sister, prepare the other chamber, and bring her in there." ¹⁷She did as he asked her, and brought her in there. She wept, and she received the tears of her daughter, and said to her, ¹⁸"Be comforted, my child. May the Lord of the heavens and earth give you favor for this your sorrow. Be comforted, my daughter."

CHAPTER 8

¹When they had finished their supper, they brought Tobias in to her. ²But as he went, he remembered the words of Raphael, and took the ashes of the incense, and put the heart and the liver of the fish on them and made smoke with them. ³When the demon smelled that smell, it fled into the uppermost parts of Egypt, and the messenger bound him. ⁴But after they were both shut in together, Tobias rose up from the bed, and said, "Sister, arise, and let us pray that the LORD may have mercy on us." ⁵And Tobias began to say, "Blessed are You, O God of our fathers, || And blessed is Your holy and glorious Name forever. Let the heavens bless You, and all Your creatures. ⁶You made Adam and gave him Eve his wife for a helper and support. From them came the seed of men. You said, It is not good that the man should be alone. Let Us make him a helper like him. ⁷And now, O LORD, I do not take this my sister for lust, but in truth. Command that I may find mercy and grow old with her." ⁸She said with him, "Amen." And they both slept that night. ⁹Raguel arose, and went and dug a grave, ¹⁰saying, "Lest he also should die." ¹¹And Raguel came into his house, ¹²and said to Edna his wife, "Send one of the maidservants, and let them see if he is alive. If not, we will bury him, and no man will know it." ¹³So the maidservant opened the door, and went in, and found them both sleeping, ¹⁴and came out, and told them that he was alive. ¹⁵Then Raguel blessed God, saying, "Blessed are You, O God, with all pure and holy blessing! Let Your saints bless You, and all Your creatures! Let all Your messengers and Your chosen ones bless You forever! ¹⁶Blessed are You, because You have made me glad; and it has not happened to me as I suspected; but You have dealt with us according to Your great mercy. ¹⁷Blessed are You, because You have had mercy on two that were the only begotten children of their parents. Show them mercy, O LORD. Fulfill their life in health with gladness and mercy." ¹⁸He commanded his servants to fill the grave. ¹⁹He kept the wedding feast for them fourteen days. ²⁰Before the days of the wedding feast were finished, Raguel swore to him that he should not depart until the fourteen days of the wedding feast were fulfilled; ²¹and that then he should take half of his goods and go in safety to his father; "and the rest," he said, "when my wife and I die."

CHAPTER 9

¹And Tobias called Raphael, and said to him, ²"Brother Azariah, take a servant and two camels with you, and go to Rages of Media to Gabael, and receive the money for me, and bring him to the wedding feast, ³because Raguel has sworn that I must not depart. ⁴My father counts the days; and if I wait long, he will be very grieved." ⁵So Raphael went on his way, and lodged with Gabael, and gave him the handwriting; so he brought out the bags with their seals, and gave them to him. ⁶Then they rose up early in the morning together and came to the wedding feast. Tobias blessed his wife.

CHAPTER 10

¹Tobit his father counted every day. When the days of the journey were expired, and they did not come, ²he said, "Is he perhaps detained? Or is Gabael perhaps dead, and there is no one to give him the money?" ³He was very grieved. ⁴But his wife said to him, "The child has perished, seeing he waits long." She began to mourn him, and said, ⁵"I care about nothing, my child, since I have let you go, the light of my eyes." ⁶Tobit said to her, "Hold your peace. Do not worry. He is in good health." ⁷And she said to him, "Hold your peace. Do not deceive me. My child has perished." And she went out every day into the way by which they went, and ate no bread in the daytime, and did not stop mourning her son Tobias for whole nights, until the fourteen days of the wedding feast were expired, which Raguel had sworn that he should spend there. Then Tobias said to Raguel, "Send me away, for my father and my mother no longer look to see me." ⁸But his father-in-law said to him, "Stay with me, and I will send to your father, and they will declare to him how things go with you." ⁹Tobias said, "No. Send me away to my father." ¹⁰Raguel arose, and gave him Sarah his wife, and half his goods, servants and cattle and money; ¹¹and he blessed them, and sent them away, saying, "The God of Heaven will prosper you, my children, before I die." ¹²And he said to his daughter, "Honor your father-in-law and your mother-in-law. They are now your parents. Let me hear a good report of you." Then he kissed her. Edna said to Tobias, "May the Lord of Heaven restore you, dear brother, and grant to me that I may see your children of my daughter Sarah, that I may rejoice before the LORD. Behold, I commit my daughter to you in special trust. Do not cause her grief."

CHAPTER 11

¹After these things Tobias also went his way, blessing God because He had prospered his journey; and he blessed Raguel and Edna his wife. Then he went on his way until they drew near to Nineveh. ²Raphael said to Tobias, "Do you not know, brother, how you left your father? ³Let us run forward before your wife and prepare the house. ⁴But take in your hand the bile of the fish." So they went their way,

and the dog went after them. ⁵Anna sat looking around toward the path for her son. ⁶She saw him coming, and said to his father, "Behold, your son is coming with the man that went with him!" ⁷Raphael said, "I know, Tobias, that your father will open his eyes. ⁸Therefore anoint his eyes with the bile, and being pricked with it, he will rub, and will make the white films fall away. Then he will see you." ⁹Anna ran to him, and fell on the neck of her son, and said to him, "I have seen you, my child! I am ready to die." They both wept. ¹⁰Tobit went toward the door and stumbled; but his son ran to him, ¹¹and took hold of his father. He rubbed the bile on his father's eyes, saying, "Cheer up, my father." ¹²When his eyes began to hurt, he rubbed them. ¹³Then the white films peeled away from the corners of his eyes; and he saw his son and fell on his neck. ¹⁴He wept, and said, "Blessed are You, O God, || And blessed is Your Name forever! Blessed are all Your holy messengers! ¹⁵For You scourged and had mercy on me. Behold, I see my son Tobias." And his son went in rejoicing and told his father the great things that had happened to him in Media. ¹⁶Tobit went out to meet his daughter-in-law at the gate of Nineveh, rejoicing, and blessing God. Those who saw him go marveled, because he had received his sight. ¹⁷Tobit gave thanks before them, because God had shown mercy on him. When Tobit came near to Sarah his daughter-in-law, he blessed her, saying, "Welcome, daughter! Blessed is God who has brought you to us and blessed are your father and your mother." And there was joy among all his relatives who were at Nineveh. ¹⁸Ahikar and Nasbas his brother's son came. ¹⁹Tobias' wedding feast was kept seven days with great gladness.

CHAPTER 12

¹And Tobit called his son Tobias, and said to him, "See, my child, that the man which went with you have his wages, and you must give him more." ²And he said to him, "Father, it is no harm to me to give him the half of those things which I have brought; ³for he has led me for you in safety, and he cured my wife, and brought my money, and likewise cured you." ⁴The old man said, "It is due to him." ⁵And he called the messenger, and said to him, "Take half of all that you all have brought." ⁶Then he called them both privately, and said to them, "Bless God, and give Him thanks, and magnify Him, and give Him thanks in the sight of all that live, for the things which He has done with you. It is good to bless God and exalt His Name, showing out with honor the works of God. Do not be slack to give Him thanks. ⁷It is good to keep close the secret of a king, but to reveal gloriously the works of God. Do good, and evil will not find you. ⁸Good is prayer with fasting, kindness, and righteousness. A little with righteousness is better than much with unrighteousness. It is better to give alms than to lay up gold. ⁹Kindness delivers from death, and it purges away all sin. Those who give alms and do righteousness will be filled with life; ¹⁰but those who sin are enemies to their own life. ¹¹Surely I will keep nothing closed from you. I have said, It is good to keep close the secret of a king, but to reveal gloriously the works of God. ¹²And now, when you prayed, and Sarah your daughter-in-law, I brought the memorial of your prayer before the Holy One. When you buried the dead, I was with you likewise. ¹³And when you did not delay to rise up, and leave your dinner, that you might go and cover the dead, your good deed was not hidden from me. I was with you. ¹⁴And now God sent me to heal you and your daughter-in-law Sarah. ¹⁵I am Raphael, one of the seven holy messengers, which present the prayers of the saints, and go in before the glory of the Holy One." ¹⁶And they were both troubled and fell on their faces; for they were afraid. ¹⁷And he said to them, "Do not be afraid. You will all have peace; but bless God forever. ¹⁸For I did not come of any favor of my own, but by the will of your God. Therefore, bless Him forever. ¹⁹All these days I appeared to you, I did not eat or drink, but you all saw a vision. ²⁰Now give God thanks, because I ascend to Him that sent me. Write in a scroll all the things which have been done." ²¹Then they rose up and saw him no longer. ²²They confessed the great and wonderful works of God, and how the messenger of the LORD had appeared to them.

CHAPTER 13

¹And Tobit wrote a prayer for rejoicing, and said, "Blessed is God who lives forever! Blessed is His kingdom! ²For He scourges and shows mercy. He leads down to the grave and brings up again. There is no one that will escape His hand. ³Give thanks to Him before the nations, all you sons of Israel! For He has scattered us among them. ⁴Declare His greatness there. Extol Him before all the living; because He is our Lord, and God is our Father forever. ⁵He will scourge us for our iniquities, || And will again show mercy, || And will gather us out of all the nations among whom you are all scattered. ⁶If you turn to Him with your whole heart and with your whole soul, || To do truth before Him, || Then He will turn to you, || And will not hide His face from you. See what He will do with you. Give Him thanks with your whole mouth. Bless the Lord of righteousness. Exalt the perpetual King. I give Him thanks in the land of my captivity, || And show His strength and majesty to a nation of sinners. Turn, you sinners, and do righteousness before Him. Who can tell if He will accept you and have mercy on you? ⁷I exalt my God. My soul exalts the King of Heaven and rejoices in His greatness. ⁸Let all men speak and let them give Him thanks in Jerusalem. ⁹O Jerusalem, the holy city, He will scourge you for the works of your sons, || And will again have mercy on the sons of the righteous. ¹⁰Give thanks to the LORD with goodness, || And bless the perpetual King, || That His dwelling place may be built in you again with joy, || And that He may make glad in you those who are captives, || And love in you forever those who are miserable. ¹¹Many nations will come from afar to the Name of the LORD God with gifts in their hands, || Even gifts to the King of Heaven. Generations of generations will praise you and sing songs of rejoicing. ¹²All those who hate you are cursed. All those who love you forever will be blessed. ¹³Rejoice and be exceedingly glad for the sons of the righteous; For they will be gathered together and will bless the Lord of the righteous. ¹⁴Oh blessed are those who love you. They will rejoice for your peace. Blessed are all those who sorrowed for all your scourges; Because they will rejoice for you when they have seen all your glory. They will be made glad forever. ¹⁵Let my soul bless God the great King. ¹⁶For Jerusalem will be built with sapphires, emeralds, and precious stones; Your walls and towers and battlements with pure gold. ¹⁷The streets of Jerusalem will be paved with beryl, carbuncle, and stones of Ophir. ¹⁸All her streets will say, Hallelujah! And give praise, saying, Blessed is God, who has exalted you forever!"

CHAPTER 14

¹Then Tobit finished giving thanks. ²He was fifty-eight years old when he lost his sight. After eight years, he received it again. He gave alms and he feared the LORD God more and more and gave thanks to Him. ³Now he grew very old; and he called his son with the six sons of his son, and said to him, "My child, take your sons. Behold, I have grown old, and am ready to depart out of this life. ⁴Go into Media, my child, for I surely believe all the things which Jonah the prophet spoke of Nineveh, that it will be overthrown, but in Media there will rather be peace for a season. Our countrymen will be scattered in the earth from the good land. Jerusalem will be desolate, and the house of God in it will be burned up and will be desolate for a time. ⁵God will again have mercy on them, and bring them back into the land, and they will build the house, but not like to the former house, until the times of that age are fulfilled. Afterward they will return from the places of their captivity and build up Jerusalem with honor. The house of God will be built in it forever with a glorious building, even as the prophets spoke concerning it. ⁶And all the nations will turn to fear the LORD God in truth and will bury their idols. ⁷All the nations will bless the LORD, and His people will give thanks to God, and the LORD will exalt His people; and all those who love the LORD God in truth and righteousness will rejoice, showing mercy to our countrymen. ⁸And now, my child, depart from Nineveh, because those things which the prophet Jonah spoke will surely come to pass. ⁹But you must keep the law and the ordinances, and show yourself merciful and righteous, that it may be well with you. ¹⁰Bury me decently, and your mother with me. Do not stay at Nineveh. See, my child, what Nadab did to Ahikar that nourished him, how out of light he brought him into darkness, and all the repayment that he made him. Ahikar was saved, but the other had his repayment, and he went down into darkness. Manasseh gave alms and escaped the snare of death which he set for him; but Nadab fell into the snare and

TOBIT

perished. ¹¹And now, my children, consider what kindness does, and how righteousness delivers." While he was saying these things, he gave up the spirit in the bed; but he was one hundred fifty-eight years old. Tobias buried him magnificently. ¹²When Anna died, he buried her with his father. But Tobias departed with his wife and his sons to Ecbatana to Raguel his father-in-law, ¹³and he grew old in honor, and he buried his father-in-law and mother-in-law magnificently, and he inherited their possessions, and his father Tobit's. ¹⁴He died at Ecbatana of Media, being one hundred twenty-seven years old. ¹⁵Before he died, he heard of the destruction of Nineveh, which Nebuchadnezzar and Ahasuerus took captive. Before his death, he rejoiced over Nineveh.

JUDITH

The Book of Judith relates the story of God's deliverance of the Jewish people. This was accomplished "by the hand of a female"—a constant motif (cf. 8:33; 9:9, 10; 12:4; 13:4, 14, 15; 15:10; 16:5) meant to recall the "hand" of God in the Exodus narrative (cf. Ex. 15:6). The work may have been written around 100 BC. There are four Greek recensions of Judith (Septuagint codices Vaticanus, Sinaiticus, Alexandrinus, and Basiliano-Vaticanus), four ancient translations (Old Latin, Syriac, Sahidic, and Ethiopic), and some late Hebrew versions, apparently translated from the Vulgate. Despite Jerome's claim to have translated an Aramaic text, no ancient Aramaic or Hebrew manuscripts have been found. The oldest extant text of Judith is the preservation of 15:1–7 inscribed on a 3rd-century AD potsherd. Whatever the reasons, the rabbis did not count Judith among their scriptures, and the Reformers adopted that position.

CHAPTER 1

¹In the twelfth year of the reign of Nebuchadnezzar, who reigned over the Assyrians in Nineveh, the great city, in the days of Arphaxad, who reigned over the Medes in Ecbatana, ²and built around Ecbatana walls of hewn stones three cubits broad and six cubits long, and made the height of the wall seventy cubits, and its breadth fifty cubits; ³and set its towers at its gates, one hundred cubits high, and its breadth in the foundation was sixty cubits; ⁴and made its gates, even gates that were raised to the height of seventy cubits, and their breadth forty cubits, for his mighty army to go out of, and the setting in array of his footmen—⁵even in those days King Nebuchadnezzar made war with King Arphaxad in the great plain. This plain is on the borders of Ragau. ⁶There came to meet him all that lived in the hill country, and all that lived by Euphrates, Tigris, and Hydaspes, and in the plain of Arioch the king of the Elymaeans. Many nations of the sons of Chelod assembled themselves to the battle. ⁷And Nebuchadnezzar king of the Assyrians sent to all who lived in Persia, and to all who lived westward, to those who lived in Cilicia, Damascus, Libanus, and Antilibanus, and to all who lived along the seacoast, ⁸and to those among the nations that were of Carmel and Gilead, and to the higher Galilee and the great plain of Esdraelon, ⁹and to all who were in Samaria and its cities, and beyond Jordan to Jerusalem, Betane, Chellus, Kadesh, the river of Egypt, Tahpanhes, Rameses, and all the land of Goshen, ¹⁰until you come above Tanis and Memphis, and to all that lived in Egypt, until you come to the borders of Ethiopia. ¹¹All those who lived in all the land made light of the command of Nebuchadnezzar king of the Assyrians and did not go with him to the war; for they were not afraid of him, but he was before them as one man. They turned away his messengers from their presence without effect, and with disgrace. ¹²And Nebuchadnezzar was exceedingly angry with all this land, and he swore by his throne and kingdom, that he would surely be avenged on all the coasts of Cilicia, Damascus, and Syria, that he would kill with his sword all the inhabitants of the land of Moab, and the children of Ammon, all Judea, and all that were in Egypt, until you come to the borders of the two seas. ¹³And he set the battle in array with his army against King Arphaxad in the seventeenth year; and he prevailed in his battle, and turned to flight all the army of Arphaxad, with all his horses and all his chariots. ¹⁴He became master of his cities, and he came even to Ecbatana, and took the towers, plundered its streets, and turned its beauty into shame. ¹⁵He took Arphaxad in the mountains of Ragau, struck him through with his darts, and utterly destroyed him, to this day. ¹⁶He returned with them to Nineveh, he and all his company of various nations, an exceedingly great multitude of men of war, and there he took his ease and banqueted, he and his army, for one hundred twenty days.

CHAPTER 2

¹In the eighteenth year, the twenty-second day of the first month, there was talk in the house of Nebuchadnezzar king of the Assyrians, that he should be avenged on all the land, even as he spoke. ²He called together all his servants and all his great men, and communicated with them his secret counsel, and concluded the afflicting of all the land out of his own mouth. ³They decreed to destroy all flesh which did not follow the word of his mouth. ⁴It came to pass, when he had ended his counsel, Nebuchadnezzar king of the Assyrians called Holofernes the chief captain of his army, which was next after himself, and said to him, ⁵"The great king, the lord of all the earth, says: Behold, you will go out from my presence, and take with you men who trust in their strength, to one hundred twenty thousand footmen and twelve thousand horses with their riders. ⁶And you will go out against all the west country, because they disobeyed the command of my mouth. ⁷You will declare to them that they should prepare earth and water, because I will go out in my wrath against them and will cover the whole face of the earth with the feet of my army, and I will give them as plunder to them. ⁸Their slain will fill their valleys and brooks, and the river will be filled with their dead until it overflows. ⁹I will lead them captives to the utmost parts of all the earth. ¹⁰But you will go out and take all their coasts for me first. If they will yield themselves to you, then you must reserve them for me until the day of their reproof. ¹¹As for those who are disobedient, your eye will not spare; but you will give them up to be slain and to be plundered in all your land. ¹²For as I live, and by the power of my kingdom, I have spoken, and I will do this with my hand. ¹³Moreover, you will not transgress anything of the commands of your lord, but you will surely accomplish them, as I have commanded you. You will not defer to do them." ¹⁴So Holofernes went out from the presence of his lord, and called all the governors, the captains, and officers of the army of Asshur. ¹⁵He counted chosen men for the battle, as his lord had commanded him, to one hundred twenty thousand, with twelve thousand archers on horseback. ¹⁶He arranged them as a great multitude is ordered for the war. ¹⁷He took camels and donkeys and mules for their baggage, an exceedingly great multitude, and sheep and oxen and goats without number for their provision, ¹⁸and great store of rations for every man, and exceedingly much gold and silver out of the king's house. ¹⁹He went out, he and all his army, on their journey, to go before King Nebuchadnezzar, and to cover all the face of the earth westward with their chariots, horsemen, and chosen footmen. ²⁰A great company of various nations went out with them like locusts, and like the sand of the earth. For they could not be counted by reason of their multitude. ²¹And they departed out of Nineveh three days' journey toward the plain of Bectileth and encamped from Bectileth near the mountain which is at the left hand of the upper Cilicia. ²²And he took all his army, his footmen, horsemen, and chariots, and went away from there into the hill country, ²³and

destroyed Put and Lud, and plundered all the children of Rasses and the children of Ishmael, which were along the wilderness to the south of the land of the Chellians. ²⁴And he went over Euphrates, and went through Mesopotamia, and broke down all the high cities that were on the River Arbonai, until you come to the sea. ²⁵And he took possession of the borders of Cilicia, and killed all that resisted him, and came to the borders of Japheth, which were toward the south, opposite Arabia. ²⁶He surrounded all the children of Midian, and set their tents on fire, and plundered their sheepfolds. ²⁷He went down into the plain of Damascus in the days of wheat harvest, and set all their fields on fire, and utterly destroyed their flocks and herds, and plundered their cities, laid their plains waste, and struck all their young men with the edge of the sword. ²⁸And the fear and the dread of him fell on those who lived on the seacoast, on those who were in Sidon and Tyre, those who lived in Sur and Ocina, and all who lived in Jemnaan. Those who lived in Azotus and Ashkelon feared him exceedingly.

CHAPTER 3

¹And they sent to him messengers with words of peace, saying, ²"Behold, we the servants of Nebuchadnezzar the great king lie before you. Use us as it is pleasing in your sight. ³Behold, our dwellings, and all our country, and all our fields of wheat, and our flocks and herds, and all the sheepfolds of our tents, lie before your face. Use them as it may please you. ⁴Behold, even our cities and those who dwell in them are your servants. Come and deal with them as it is good in your eyes." ⁵So the men came to Holofernes and declared to him according to these words. ⁶He came down toward the seacoast, he and his army, and set garrisons in the high cities, and took out of them chosen men for allies. ⁷They received him, they and all the country around them, with garlands and dances and timbrels. ⁸He cast down all their borders and cut down their sacred groves. It had been given to him to destroy all the gods of the land, that all the nations would worship Nebuchadnezzar only, and that all their tongues and their tribes would call on him as god. ⁹Then he came toward Esdraelon near to Dotaea, which is opposite the great ridge of Judea. ¹⁰He encamped between Geba and Scythopolis. He was there a whole month, that he might gather together all the baggage of his army.

CHAPTER 4

¹The sons of Israel that lived in Judea heard all that Holofernes the chief captain of Nebuchadnezzar king of the Assyrians had done to the nations, and how he had plundered all their temples and destroyed them utterly. ²They were exceedingly afraid before him, and were troubled for Jerusalem, and for the temple of the LORD their God; ³because they had newly come up from the captivity, and all the people of Judea were recently gathered together; and the vessels, the altar, and the house were sanctified after being profaned. ⁴And they sent into every coast of Samaria, to Konae, to Beth-Horon, Belmaim, Jericho, to Choba, Aesora, and to the Valley of Salem; ⁵and they occupied beforehand all the tops of the high mountains, fortified the villages that were in them, stored supplies for the provision of war; for their fields were newly reaped. ⁶Jehoiakim the chief priest, who was in those days at Jerusalem, wrote to those who lived in Bethulia, and Betomesthaim, which is opposite Esdraelon toward the plain that is near to Doesaim, ⁷charging them to seize on the ascents of the hill country; because by them was the entrance into Judea, and it was easy to stop them from approaching, since the approach was narrow, with space for two men at the most. ⁸And the sons of Israel did as Jehoiakim the chief priest had commanded them, as did the senate of all the people of Israel, which lived at Jerusalem. ⁹And every man of Israel cried to God with great earnestness, and with great earnestness they humbled their souls. ¹⁰They, their wives, their children, their cattle, and every sojourner, hireling, and servant bought with their money put sackcloth on their loins. ¹¹Every man and woman of Israel, and the little children, and the inhabitants of Jerusalem, fell before the temple, and cast ashes on their heads, and spread out their sackcloth before the LORD. They put sackcloth around the altar. ¹²They cried to the God of Israel earnestly with one consent, that He would not give their children as prey, their wives as plunder, the cities of their inheritance to destruction, and the sanctuary to being profaned and being made a reproach, for the nations to rejoice at. ¹³The LORD heard their voice and looked at their affliction. The people continued fasting many days in all Judea and Jerusalem before the sanctuary of the LORD Almighty. ¹⁴And Jehoiakim the chief priest, and all the priests that stood before the LORD, and those who ministered to the LORD, had their loins dressed in sackcloth, and offered the continual burnt-offering, the vows, and the free gifts of the people. ¹⁵They had ashes on their hats. They cried to the LORD with all their power, that He would look on all the house of Israel for good.

CHAPTER 5

¹Holofernes, the chief captain of the army of Asshur, was told that the sons of Israel had prepared for war, had shut up the passages of the hill country, had fortified all the tops of the high hills, and had laid impediments in the plains. ²Then he was exceedingly angry, and he called all the princes of Moab, and the captains of Ammon, and all the governors of the seacoast, ³and he said to them, "Tell me now, you sons of Canaan, who are these people who dwell in the hill country? What are the cities that they inhabit? How large is their army? Where is their power and their strength? What king is set over them, to be the leader of their army? ⁴Why have they turned their backs, that they should not come and meet me, more than all that dwell in the west?" ⁵Then Achior, the leader of all the children of Ammon, said to him, "Let my lord now hear a word from the mouth of your servant, and I will tell you the truth concerning these people who dwell in this hill country, near to the place where you dwell. No lie will come out of the mouth of your servant. ⁶These people are descended from the Chaldeans. ⁷They sojourned before this in Mesopotamia, because they did not want to follow the gods of their fathers, which were in the land of the Chaldeans. ⁸They departed from the way of their parents, and worshiped the God of Heaven, the God whom they knew. Their parents cast them out from the face of their gods, and they fled into Mesopotamia, and sojourned there many days. ⁹Then their God commanded them to depart from the place where they sojourned, and to go into the land of Canaan. They lived there, and prospered with gold and silver, and with exceedingly much cattle. ¹⁰Then they went down into Egypt, for a famine covered all the land of Canaan. They sojourned there until they had grown up. They became a great multitude there, so that one could not count the population of their nation. ¹¹Then the king of Egypt rose up against them, and dealt subtly with them, and brought them low, making them labor in brick, and made them slaves. ¹²They cried to their God, and He struck all the land of Egypt with incurable plagues; so the Egyptians cast them out of their sight. ¹³God dried up the Red Sea before them, ¹⁴and brought them into the way of Sinai Kadesh-Barnea, and they cast out all that lived in the wilderness. ¹⁵They lived in the land of the Amorites, and they destroyed by their strength everyone in Heshbon. Passing over Jordan, they possessed all the hill country. ¹⁶They cast out before them the Canaanite, the Perizzite, the Jebusite, the Shechemite, and all the Girgashites, and they lived in that country many days. ¹⁷And while they did not sin before their God, they prospered, because God who hates iniquity was with them. ¹⁸But when they departed from the way which He appointed them, they were destroyed in many severe battles, and were led captives into a land that was not theirs. The temple of their God was cast to the ground, and their cities were taken by their adversaries. ¹⁹And now they have returned to their God and have come up from the dispersion where they were dispersed, and have possessed Jerusalem, where their sanctuary is, and are seated in the hill country; for it was desolate. ²⁰And now, my lord and master, if there is any error in this people, and they sin against their God, we will consider what this thing is in which they stumble, and we will go up and overcome them. ²¹But if there is no lawlessness in their nation, let my lord now pass by, lest their Lord defend them, and their God be for them, and we will be a reproach before all the earth." ²²It came to pass, when Achior had finished speaking these words, all the people standing around the tent murmured. The great men of Holofernes, and all that lived by the seaside and in Moab, said that he should kill him. ²³For, they said, "We will not be afraid of the sons of

Israel, because, behold, they are a people that has no power nor might to make the battle strong. ²⁴Therefore now we will go up, and they will be a prey to be devoured by all your army, Lord Holofernes."

CHAPTER 6

¹And when the disturbance of the men that were around the council had ceased, Holofernes the chief captain of the army of Asshur said to Achior and to all the children of Moab before all the people of the foreigners, ²"And who are you, Achior, and the hirelings of Ephraim, that you have prophesied among us as today, and have said that we should not make war with the race of Israel, because their God will defend them? And who is God but Nebuchadnezzar? ³He will send out his might and will destroy them from the face of the earth, and their God will not deliver them; but we his servants will strike them as one man. They will not sustain the might of our horses. ⁴For with them we will burn them up. Their mountains will be drunken with their blood. Their plains will be filled with their dead bodies. Their footsteps will not stand before us, but they will surely perish, says King Nebuchadnezzar, lord of all the earth; for he said, The words that I have spoken will not be in vain. ⁵But you, Achior, hireling of Ammon, who have spoken these words in the day of your iniquity, will see my face no longer from this day, until I am avenged of the race of those that came out of Egypt. ⁶And then the sword of my army, and the multitude of those who serve me, will pass through your sides, and you will fall among their slain when I return. ⁷Then my servants will bring you back into the hill country and will set you in one of the cities of the ascents. ⁸You will not perish until you are destroyed with them. ⁹And if you hope in your heart that they will not be taken, do not let your countenance fall. I have spoken it, and none of my words will fall to the ground." ¹⁰Then Holofernes commanded his servants who waited in his tent to take Achior, and bring him back to Bethulia, and deliver him into the hands of the sons of Israel. ¹¹So his servants took him and brought him out of the camp into the plain, and they moved from the midst of the plains into the hill country and came to the springs that were under Bethulia. ¹²When the men of the city saw them on the top of the hill, they took up their weapons, and went out of the city against them to the top of the hill. Every man that used a sling kept them from coming up and cast stones against them. ¹³They took cover under the hill, bound Achior, cast him down, left him at the foot of the hill, and went away to their lord. ¹⁴But the sons of Israel descended from their city, and came to him, untied him, led him away into Bethulia, and presented him to the rulers of their city; ¹⁵which were in those days Ozias the son of Micah, of the tribe of Simeon, and Chabris the son of Gothoniel, and Charmis the son of Melchiel. ¹⁶Then they called together all the elders of the city; and all their young men ran together, with their women, to the assembly. They set Achior in the midst of all their people. Then Ozias asked him what had happened. ¹⁷He answered and declared to them the words of the council of Holofernes, and all the words that he had spoken in the midst of the princes of the children of Asshur, and all the great words that Holofernes had spoken against the house of Israel. ¹⁸Then the people fell down and worshiped God, and cried, saying, ¹⁹"O Lord God of Heaven, behold their arrogance, and pity the low estate of our race. Look on the face of those who are sanctified to You this day." ²⁰They comforted Achior and praised him exceedingly. ²¹Then Ozias took him out of the assembly into his house and made a feast for the elders. They called on the God of Israel for help all that night.

CHAPTER 7

¹The next day Holofernes commanded all his army and all the people who had come to be his allies, that they should move their camp toward Bethulia, take beforehand the ascents of the hill country, and make war against the sons of Israel. ²Every mighty man of them moved that day. The army of their men of war was one hundred seventy thousand footmen, plus twelve thousand horsemen, besides the baggage, and the men that were on foot among them: an exceedingly great multitude. ³They encamped in the valley near Bethulia, by the fountain. They spread themselves in breadth over Doesaim even to Belmaim, and in length from Bethulia to Cyamon, which is near Esdraelon. ⁴But the sons of Israel, when they saw the multitude of them, were troubled exceedingly, and everyone said to his neighbor, "Now these men will lick up the face of all the earth. Neither the high mountains, nor the valleys, nor the hills will be able to bear their weight." ⁵Every man took up his weapons of war, and when they had kindled fires on their towers, they remained and watched all that night. ⁶But on the second day Holofernes led out all his cavalry in the sight of the sons of Israel which were in Bethulia, ⁷viewed the ascents to their city, and searched out the springs of the waters, seized on them, and set garrisons of men of war over them. Then he departed back to his people. ⁸All the rulers of the children of Esau, all the leaders of the people of Moab, and the captains of the seacoast came to him and said, ⁹"Let our lord now hear a word, that there not be losses in your army. ¹⁰For this people of the sons of Israel do not trust in their spears, but in the height of the mountains wherein they dwell, for it is not easy to come up to the tops of their mountains. ¹¹And now, my lord, do not fight against them as men fight who join battle, and there will not so much as one man of your people perish. ¹²Remain in your camp and keep every man of your army safe. Let your servants get possession of the water spring, which flows from the foot of the mountain, ¹³because all the inhabitants of Bethulia get their water from there. Then thirst will kill them, and they will give up their city. Then we and our people will go up to the tops of the mountains that are near, and will encamp on them, to watch that not one man gets out of the city. ¹⁴They will be consumed with famine, they and their wives and their children. Before the sword comes against them, they will be laid low in the streets where they dwell. ¹⁵And you will pay them back with evil, because they rebelled, and did not meet your face in peace." ¹⁶Their words were pleasing in the sight of Holofernes and in the sight of all his servants; and he ordered them to do as they had spoken. ¹⁷And the army of the children of Ammon moved, and with them five thousand of the children of Asshur, and they encamped in the valley. They seized the waters and the springs of the waters of the sons of Israel. ¹⁸The children of Esau went up with the children of Ammon and encamped in the hill country near Doesaim. They sent some of them toward the south, and toward the east, near Ekrebel, which is near Chusi, that is on the brook Mochmur. The rest of the army of the Assyrians encamped in the plain and covered all the face of the land. Their tents and baggage were pitched on it in a great crowd. They were an exceedingly great multitude. ¹⁹The sons of Israel cried to the Lord their God, for their spirit fainted; for all their enemies had surrounded them. There was no way to escape out from among them. ²⁰All the army of Asshur remained around them, their footmen and their chariots and their horsemen, thirty-four days. All their vessels of water ran dry for all the inhabitants of Bethulia. ²¹The cisterns were emptied, and they had no water to drink their fill for one day; for they rationed drink by measure. ²²Their young children were discouraged. The women and the young men fainted for thirst. They fell down in the streets of the city, and in the passages of the gates. There was no longer any strength in them. ²³All the people, including the young men, the women, and the children, were gathered together against Ozias, and against the rulers of the city. They cried with a loud voice, and said before all the elders, ²⁴"God be judge between all of you and us, because you have done us great wrong, in that you have not spoken words of peace with the children of Asshur. ²⁵Now we have no helper; but God has sold us into their hands, that we should be laid low before them with thirst and great destruction. ²⁶And now summon them and deliver up the whole city as prey to the people of Holofernes, and to all his army. ²⁷For it is better for us to be made a plunder to them. For we will be servants, and our souls will live, and we will not see the death of our babies before our eyes, and our wives and our children fainting in death. ²⁸We take to witness against you the heavens and the earth, and our God and the Lord of our fathers, who punishes us according to our sins and the sins of our fathers. Do what we have said today!" ²⁹And there was great weeping of all with one consent in the midst of the assembly; and they cried to the Lord God with a loud voice. ³⁰And Ozias said to them, "Brothers, be of good courage! Let us endure five more days, during which the Lord our God will turn His mercy toward us; for He will not forsake us utterly.

JUDITH

31 But if these days pass, and no help comes to us, I will do what you say." **32** Then he dispersed the people, every man to his own camp; and they went away to the walls and towers of their city. He sent the women and children into their houses. They were brought very low in the city.

CHAPTER 8

1 In those days Judith heard about this. She was the daughter of Merari, the son of Ox, the son of Joseph, the son of Oziel, the son of Elkiah, the son of Ananias, the son of Gideon, the son of Raphaim, the son of Ahitub, the son of Elihu, the son of Eliab, the son of Nathanael, the son of Salamiel, the son of Salasadai, the son of Israel. **2** Her husband was Manasseh, of her tribe and of her family. He died in the days of barley harvest. **3** For he stood over those who bound sheaves in the field, and the heat came on his head, and he fell on his bed, and died in his city Bethulia. So they buried him with his fathers in the field which is between Doesaim and Balamon. **4** Judith was a widow in her house three years and four months. **5** She made herself a tent on the roof of her house and put on sackcloth on her loins. The garments of her widowhood were on her. **6** And she fasted all the days of her widowhood, except the eves of the Sabbaths, the Sabbaths, the eves of the new moons, the new moons, and the feasts and joyful days of the house of Israel. **7** She was of an attractive countenance, and exceedingly beautiful to behold. Her husband Manasseh had left her gold, silver, menservants, maidservants, cattle, and lands. She remained on those lands. **8** No one said anything evil about her; for she feared God exceedingly. **9** She heard the evil words of the people against the governor, because they fainted for lack of water; and Judith heard all the words that Ozias spoke to them, how he swore to them that he would deliver the city to the Assyrians after five days. **10** So she sent her maid, who was over all things that she had, to summon Ozias, Chabris, and Charmis, the elders of her city. **11** They came to her, and she said to them, "Hear me now, O you rulers of the inhabitants of Bethulia, for your word that you have spoken before the people this day is not right. You have set the oath which you have pronounced between God and you and have promised to deliver the city to our enemies, unless within these days the LORD turns to help you. **12** Now who are you that you have tempted God this day, and stand in the place of God among the children of men? **13** Now try the LORD Almighty, and you will never know anything. **14** For you will not find the depth of the heart of man, and you will not perceive the things that he thinks. How will you search out God, who has made all these things, and know His mind, and comprehend His purpose? No, my countrymen, do not provoke the LORD our God to anger! **15** For if He has not decided to help us within these five days, He has power to defend us in such time as He will, or to destroy us before the face of our enemies. **16** But do not pledge the counsels of the LORD our God! For God is not as man, that He should be threatened; neither as the son of man, that He should be turned by entreaty. **17** Therefore let us wait for the salvation that comes from Him and call on Him to help us. He will hear our voice, if it pleases Him. **18** For there arose none in our age, neither is there any of us today, tribe, or countrymen, or family, or city, which worship gods made with hands, as it was in the former days; **19** for this reason our fathers were given to the sword, and for plunder, and fell with a great fall before our enemies. **20** But we know no other god besides Him. Therefore, we hope that He will not despise us, nor any of our race. **21** For if we are taken so, all Judea will sit on the ground, and our sanctuary will be plundered; and He will require our blood for profaning it. **22** And the slaughter of our countrymen, and the captivity of the land, and the desolation of our inheritance, He will turn on our heads among the nations, wherever we will be in bondage. We will be an offense and a reproach before those who take us for a possession. **23** For our bondage will not be ordered to favor; but the LORD our God will turn it to dishonor. **24** And now, countrymen, let us show an example to our countrymen, because their soul hangs on us, and the sanctuary, the house, and the altar rest on us. **25** Besides all this, let us give thanks to the LORD our God, who tries us, even as He did our fathers also. **26** Remember all the things which He did to Abraham, and all the things in which He tried Isaac, and all the things which happened to Jacob in Mesopotamia of Syria, when he kept the sheep of Laban his mother's brother. **27** For He has not tried us in the fire, as He did them, to search out their hearts, neither has He taken vengeance on us; but the LORD does scourge them that come near to Him, to admonish them." **28** And Ozias said to her, "All that you have spoken, you have spoken with a good heart. There is no one who will deny your words. **29** For this is not the first day wherein your wisdom is manifested; but from the beginning of your days all the people have known your understanding, because the disposition of your heart is good. **30** But the people were exceedingly thirsty and compelled us to do as we spoke to them, and to bring an oath on ourselves, which we will not break. **31** And now pray for us, because you are a godly woman, and the LORD will send us rain to fill our cisterns, and we will faint no more." **32** Then Judith said to them, "Hear me, and I will do a thing, which will go down to all generations among the children of our race. **33** You will all stand at the gate tonight. I will go out with my maid. Within the days after which you said that you would deliver the city to our enemies, the LORD will visit Israel by my hand. **34** But you will not inquire of my act; for I will not declare it to you, until the things are finished that I will do." **35** Then Ozias and the rulers said to her, "Go in peace. May the LORD God be before you, to take vengeance on our enemies." **36** So they returned from the tent and went to their stations.

CHAPTER 9

1 But Judith fell on her face, and put ashes on her head, and uncovered the sackcloth with which she was clothed. The incense of that evening was now being offered at Jerusalem in the house of God, and Judith cried to the LORD with a loud voice, and said, **2** "O LORD God of my father Simeon, into whose hand You gave a sword to take vengeance on the strangers who loosened the belt of a virgin to defile her, uncovered the thigh to her shame, and profaned the womb to her reproach; for You said, It will not be so; and they did so. **3** Therefore You gave their rulers to be slain, and their bed, which was ashamed for her who was deceived, to be dyed in blood, and struck the servants with their masters, and the masters on their thrones; **4** and gave their wives for a prey, and their daughters to be captives, and all their spoils to be divided among Your dear children; which were moved with zeal for You, and abhorred the pollution of their blood, and called on You for aid. O God, O my God, hear me who am also a widow. **5** For You did the things that were before those things, and those things, and such as come after; and You planned the things which are now, and the things which are to come. The things which You planned came to pass. **6** Yes, the things which You determined stood before You, and said, Behold, we are here; for all Your ways are prepared, and Your judgment is with foreknowledge. **7** For behold, the Assyrians are multiplied in their power. They are exalted with horse and rider. They were proud of the strength of their footmen. They have trusted in shield, spear, bow, and sling. They do not know that You are the LORD who breaks the battles. The LORD is Your Name. **8** Break their strength in Your power and bring down their force in Your wrath; for they intend to profane Your sanctuary, and to defile the dwelling place where Your glorious Name rests, and to destroy the horn of Your altar with the sword. **9** Look at their pride and send Your wrath on their heads. Give into my hand, which am a widow, the might that I have conceived. **10** Strike by the deceit of my lips the servant with the prince, and the prince with his servant. Break down their arrogance by the hand of a woman. **11** For Your power stands not in multitude, nor Your might in strong men, but You are a God of the afflicted. You are a helper of the minorities, a helper of the weak, a protector of the forsaken, a Savior of those who are without hope. **12** Yes, yes, God of my father, and God of the inheritance of Israel, Lord of the heavens and of the earth. Creator of the waters, King of every creature, hear my prayer. **13** Make my speech and deceit to be their wound and stripe, who intend hard things against Your covenant, Your holy house, the top of Zion, and the house of the possession of Your children. **14** Make every nation and tribe of Yours to know that You are God, the God of all power and might, and that there is none other that protects the race of Israel but You."

JUDITH

CHAPTER 10

¹ It came to pass, when she had ceased to cry to the God of Israel, and had finished saying all these words, ² that she rose up where she had fallen down, called her maid, and went down into the house that she used to live in on the Sabbath days and on her feast days. ³ She pulled off the sackcloth which she had put on, took off the garments of her widowhood, washed her body all over with water, anointed herself with rich ointment, braided the hair of her head, and put a tiara on it. She put on her garments of gladness, which she used to wear in the days of the life of Manasseh her husband. ⁴ She took sandals for her feet, and put her chains around her, and her bracelets, her rings, her earrings, and all her jewelry, and decked herself bravely, to deceive the eyes of all men who would see her. ⁵ She gave her maid a leather container of wine and a flask of oil, and filled a bag with parched corn, lumps of figs, and fine bread. She packed all her vessels together and laid them on her. ⁶ They went out to the gate of the city of Bethulia, and found Ozias and the elders of the city, Chabris and Charmis standing by it. ⁷ But when they saw her, that her countenance was altered, and her apparel was changed, they wondered at her beauty very exceedingly, and said to her, ⁸ "May the God of our fathers give you favor and accomplish your purposes to the glory of the sons of Israel, and to the exaltation of Jerusalem." Then she worshiped God, ⁹ and said to them, "Command that they open the gate of the city for me, and I will go out to accomplish the things you spoke with me about." And they commanded the young men to open to her, as she had spoken; ¹⁰ and they did so. Then Judith went out, she, and her handmaid with her. The men of the city watched her until she had gone down the mountain, until she had passed the valley, and they could see her no longer. ¹¹ They went straight onward in the valley. The watch of the Assyrians met her; ¹² and they took her, and asked her, "Of what people are you? Where are you coming from? Where are you going?" She said, "I am a daughter of the Hebrews. I am fleeing away from their presence, because they are about to be given to you to be consumed. ¹³ I am coming into the presence of Holofernes the chief captain of your army, to declare words of truth. I will show him a way that he can go and win all the hill country, and there will not be lacking of his men one person, nor one life." ¹⁴ Now when the men heard her words, and considered her countenance, the beauty thereof was exceedingly marvelous in their eyes. They said to her, ¹⁵ "You have saved your life, in that you have hurried to come down to the presence of our master. Now come to his tent. Some of us will guide you until they deliver you into his hands. ¹⁶ But when you stand before him, do not be afraid in your heart, but declare to him according to your words; and he will treat you well." ¹⁷ They chose out of them one hundred men, and appointed them to accompany her and her maid; and they brought them to the tent of Holofernes. ¹⁸ And there was great excitement throughout all the camp, for her coming was reported among the tents. They came and surrounded her as she stood outside Holofernes' tent, until they told him about her. ¹⁹ They marveled at her beauty and marveled at the sons of Israel because of her. Each one said to his neighbor, "Who would despise this people, that have among them such women? For it is not good that one man of them be left, seeing that, if they are let go, they will be able to deceive the whole earth." ²⁰ Those who lay near Holofernes, and all his servants, went out and brought her into the tent. ²¹ And Holofernes was resting on his bed under the canopy, which was woven with purple, gold, emeralds, and precious stones. ²² And they told him about her; and he came out into the space before his tent, with silver lamps going before him. ²³ But when Judith had come before him and his servants, they all marveled at the beauty of her countenance. She fell down on her face, and bowed down to him, but his servants raised her up.

CHAPTER 11

¹ Holofernes said to her, "Woman, take courage. Do not be afraid in your heart; for I never hurt anyone who has chosen to serve Nebuchadnezzar, the king of all the earth. ² And now, if your people who dwell in the hill country had not slighted me, I would not have lifted up my spear against them; but they have done these things to themselves. ³ And now tell me why you fled from them and came to us; for you have come to save yourself. Take courage! You will live tonight, and hereafter; ⁴ for there is no one that will wrong you, but all will treat you well, as is done to the servants of King Nebuchadnezzar my lord." ⁵ And Judith said to him, "Receive the words of your servant, and let your handmaid speak in your presence, and I will declare no lie to my lord this night. ⁶ If you will follow the words of your handmaid, God will bring the thing to pass perfectly with you; and my lord will not fail to accomplish his purposes. ⁷ As Nebuchadnezzar king of all the earth lives, and as his power lives, who has sent you for the preservation of every living thing, not only do men serve him by you, but also the beasts of the field, the cattle, and the birds of the sky will live through your strength, in the time of Nebuchadnezzar and of all his house. ⁸ For we have heard of your wisdom and the subtle plans of your soul. It has been reported in all the earth that you only are brave in all the kingdom, mighty in knowledge, and wonderful in feats of war. ⁹ And now as concerning the matter which Achior spoke in your council, we have heard his words; for the men of Bethulia saved him, and he declared to them all that he had spoken before you. ¹⁰ Therefore, O lord and master, do not neglect his word; but lay it up in your heart, for it is true; for our race will not be punished, neither will the sword prevail against them, unless they sin against their God. ¹¹ And now, that my lord not be defeated and frustrated of his purpose, and that death may fall on them, their sin has overtaken them, with which they will provoke their God to anger, whenever they do wickedness. ¹² Since their food failed them, and all their water was scant, they took counsel to lay hands on their cattle, and determined to consume all those things which God charged them by his laws that they should not eat. ¹³ They are resolved to spend the first-fruits of the corn, and the tenths of the wine and the oil, which they had sanctified and reserved for the priests who stand before the face of our God in Jerusalem; which things it is not fitting for any of the people so much as to touch with their hands. ¹⁴ They have sent some to Jerusalem, because they also that dwell there have done this thing, to bring them permission from the council of elders. ¹⁵ It will be, when word comes to them and they do it, they will be given to you to be destroyed the same day. ¹⁶ Therefore I, your servant, knowing all this, fled away from their presence. God sent me to work things with you, at which all the earth will be astonished, even as many as hear it. ¹⁷ For your servant is religious and serves the God of Heaven day and night. Now, my lord, I will stay with you, and your servant will go out by night into the valley. I will pray to God, and He will tell me when they have committed their sins. ¹⁸ Then I will come and show it also to you. Then you will go out with all your army, and there will be none of them that will resist you. ¹⁹ And I will lead you through the midst of Judea, until you come to Jerusalem. I will set your seat in the midst of it. You will drive them as sheep that have no shepherd, and a dog will not so much as open his mouth before you; for these things were told me according to my foreknowledge, and were declared to me, and I was sent to tell you." ²⁰ Her words were pleasing in the sight of Holofernes and of all his servants. They marveled at her wisdom, and said, ²¹ "There is not such a woman from one end of the earth to the other, for beauty of face and wisdom of words." ²² Holofernes said to her, "God did well to send you before the people, that might would be in our hands, and destruction among those who slighted my lord. ²³ And now you are beautiful in your countenance, and wise in your words. If you will do as you have spoken, your God will be my God, and you will dwell in the house of King Nebuchadnezzar and will be renowned through the whole earth."

CHAPTER 12

¹ He commanded that she should be brought in where his silver vessels were set and asked that his servants should prepare some of his own meats for her, and that she should drink from his own wine. ² And Judith said, "I will not eat of it, lest there be an occasion of stumbling, but provision will be made for me of the things that have come with me." ³ And Holofernes said to her, "But if the things that are with you should fail, from where will we be able to give you more like it? For there is none of your race with us." ⁴ And Judith said to him, "As your soul lives, my lord, your servant will not spend those things that are with me, until the LORD

works by my hand the things that He has determined." ⁵Then Holofernes' servants brought her into the tent, and she slept until midnight. Then she rose up toward the morning watch, ⁶and sent to Holofernes, saying, "Let my lord now command that they allow your servant to go out to pray." ⁷Holofernes commanded his guards that they should not stop her. She stayed in the camp three days and went out every night into the Valley of Bethulia and washed herself at the fountain of water in the camp. ⁸And when she came up, she implored the LORD God of Israel to direct her way to the raising up of the children of His people. ⁹She came in clean, and remained in the tent, until she ate her food toward evening. ¹⁰It came to pass on the fourth day, that Holofernes made a feast for his own servants only and called none of the officers to the banquet. ¹¹And he said to Bagoas the eunuch, who had charge over all that he had, "Go now, and persuade this Hebrew woman who is with you that she come to us and eat and drink with us. ¹²For behold, it is a shame for our person, if we will let such a woman go, not having had her company; for if we do not draw her to ourselves, she will laugh us to scorn." ¹³Bagoas went from the presence of Holofernes, and came in to her, and said, "Let this fair lady not fear to come to my lord, and to be honored in his presence, and to drink wine and be merry with us, and to be made this day as one of the daughters of the children of Asshur, which wait in the house of Nebuchadnezzar." ¹⁴Judith said to him, "Who am I, that I should contradict my lord? For whatever would be pleasing in his eyes, I will do speedily, and this will be my joy to the day of my death." ¹⁵She arose and decked herself with her apparel and all her woman's attire; and her servant went and laid fleeces on the ground for her next to Holofernes, which she had received from Bagoas for her daily use, that she might sit and eat on them. ¹⁶Judith came in and sat down, and Holofernes' heart was ravished with her. His soul was moved, and he exceedingly desired her company. He was watching for a time to deceive her, from the day that he had seen her. ¹⁷Holofernes said to her, "Drink now, and be merry with us." ¹⁸Judith said, "I will drink now, my lord, because my life is magnified in me this day more than all the days since I was born." ¹⁹Then she took and ate and drank before him what her servant had prepared. ²⁰Holofernes took great delight in her, and drank exceedingly much wine, more than he had drunk at any time in one day since he was born.

CHAPTER 13

¹But when the evening had come, his servants hurried to depart. Bagoas shut the tent outside and dismissed those who waited from the presence of his lord. They went away to their beds; for they were all weary, because the feast had been long. ²But Judith was left alone in the tent, with Holofernes lying alone on his bed; for he was drunk with wine. ³Judith had said to her servant that she should stand outside her bedchamber, and wait for her to come out, as she did daily; for she said she would go out to her prayer. She spoke to Bagoas according to the same words. ⁴All went away from her presence, and none was left in the bedchamber, small or great. Judith, standing by his bed, said in her heart, O LORD God of all power, look in this hour on the works of my hands for the exaltation of Jerusalem. ⁵For now is the time to help Your inheritance, and to do the thing that I have purposed to the destruction of the enemies which have risen up against us. ⁶She came to the rail of the bed, which was at Holofernes' head, and took down his scimitar from there. ⁷She drew near to the bed, took hold of the hair of his head, and said, "Strengthen me, O LORD God of Israel, this day." ⁸She struck twice on his neck with all her might, and took away his head from him, ⁹tumbled his body down from the bed, and took down the canopy from the pillars. After a little while she went out and gave Holofernes' head to her maid; ¹⁰and she put it in her bag of food. They both went out together to prayer, according to their custom. They passed through the camp, circled around that valley, and went up to the mountain of Bethulia, and came to its gates. ¹¹Judith said far off to the watchmen at the gates, "Open, open the gate, now. God is with us, even our God, to show His power yet in Israel, and His might against the enemy, as He has done even this day." ¹²It came to pass, when the men of her city heard her voice, they hurried to go down to the gate of their city, and they called together the elders of the city. ¹³They all ran together, both small and great, for it was strange to them that she had come. They opened the gate and received them, making a fire to give light, and surrounded them. ¹⁴She said to them with a loud voice, "Praise God! Praise Him! Praise God, who has not taken away His mercy from the house of Israel but has destroyed our enemies by my hand tonight!" ¹⁵Then she took the head out of the bag and showed it, and said to them, "Behold, the head of Holofernes, the chief captain of the army of Asshur, and behold, the canopy, in which he laid in his drunkenness. The LORD struck him by the hand of a woman. ¹⁶And as the LORD lives, who preserved me in my way that I went, my countenance deceived him to his destruction, and he did not commit sin with me, to defile and shame me." ¹⁷All the people were exceedingly amazed, and bowed themselves, and worshiped God, and said with one accord, "Blessed are You, O our God, which have this day brought to nothing the enemies of Your people." ¹⁸Ozias said to her, "Blessed are you, daughter, in the sight of the Most High God, above all the women on the earth; and blessed is the LORD God, who created the heavens and the earth, who directed you to cut off the head of the prince of our enemies. ¹⁹For your hope will not depart from the heart of men that remember the strength of God forever. ²⁰May God turn these things to you for a perpetual praise, to visit you with good things, because you did not spare your life by reason of the affliction of our race, but avenged our fall, walking a straight way before our God." And all the people said, "Amen! Amen!"

CHAPTER 14

¹Judith said to them, "Hear me now, my countrymen, and take this head, and hang it on the battlement of your wall. ²It will be, so soon as the morning appears, and the sun comes up on the earth, you will each take up his weapons of war, and every valiant man of you go out of the city. You will set a captain over them, as though you would go down to the plain toward the watch of the children of Asshur; but you men will not go down. ³These will take up their full armor and will go into their camp and rouse up the captains of the army of Asshur. They will run together to Holofernes' tent. They will not find him. Fear will fall on them, and they will flee before your face. ⁴You men, and all that inhabit every coast of Israel, will pursue them and overthrow them as they go. ⁵But before you do these things, summon Achior the Ammonite to me, that he may see and know him that despised the house of Israel, and that sent him to us, as it were to death." ⁶And they called Achior out of the house of Ozias; but when he came and saw the head of Holofernes in a man's hand in the assembly of the people, he fell on his face, and his spirit failed. ⁷But when they had recovered him, he fell at Judith's feet, and bowed down to her, and said, "Blessed are you in every tent of Judah, and in every nation, which hearing your name will be troubled. ⁸Now tell me all the things that you have done in these days." And Judith declared to him in the midst of the people all the things that she had done, from the day that she went out until the time that she spoke to them. ⁹But when she finished speaking, the people shouted with a loud voice, and made a joyful noise in their city. ¹⁰But when Achior saw all the things that the God of Israel had done, he believed in God exceedingly, and circumcised the flesh of his foreskin, and was joined to the house of Israel, to this day. ¹¹But as soon as the morning arose, they hanged the head of Holofernes on the wall, and every man took up his weapons, and they went out by bands to the ascents of the mountain. ¹²But when the children of Asshur saw them, they sent word to their leaders; but they went to their captains and tribunes, and to each of their rulers. ¹³They came to Holofernes' tent, and said to him that was over all that he had, "Wake our lord up, now; for the slaves have been bold to come down against us to battle, that they may be utterly destroyed." ¹⁴Bagoas went in and knocked at the outer door of the tent; for he supposed that he was sleeping with Judith. ¹⁵But when no one listened to him, he opened it, and went into the bedchamber, and found him cast on the threshold dead, and his head had been taken from him. ¹⁶He cried with a loud voice, with weeping and groaning and a mighty cry, and tore his garments. ¹⁷He entered into the tent where Judith lodged, and he did not find her. He leaped out to the people, and cried aloud, ¹⁸"The slaves have

dealt treacherously! One woman of the Hebrews has brought shame on the house of King Nebuchadnezzar; for behold, Holofernes lies on the ground, and his head is not on him!" ¹⁹But when the rulers of the army of Asshur heard the words, they tore their coats, and their soul was troubled exceedingly. There was a cry and an exceedingly great noise in the midst of the camp.

CHAPTER 15

¹When those who were in the tents heard, they were amazed at what happened. ²Trembling and fear fell on them, and no man dared stay anymore in the sight of his neighbor, but rushing out with one accord, they fled into every way of the plain and of the hill country. ³Those who had encamped in the hill country around Bethulia fled away. And then the sons of Israel, everyone who was a warrior among them, rushed out on them. ⁴Ozias sent to Betomasthaim, Bebai, Chobai, and Chola, and to every coast of Israel, to tell about the things that had been accomplished, and that all should rush on their enemies to destroy them. ⁵But when the sons of Israel heard, they all fell on them with one accord, and struck them to Chobai. Yes, and in like manner also they of Jerusalem and of all the hill country came (for men had told them about what happened in their enemies' camp), and those who were in Gilead and in Galilee fell on their flank with a great slaughter, until they were past Damascus and its borders. ⁶The rest of the people who lived at Bethulia fell on the camp of Asshur, and plundered them, and were enriched exceedingly. ⁷The sons of Israel returned from the slaughter and got possession of that which remained. The villages and the cities that were in the hill country and in the plain country, took many spoils; for there was an exceedingly great supply. ⁸Jehoiakim the chief priest, and the elders of the sons of Israel who lived in Jerusalem, came to see the good things which the LORD had showed to Israel, and to see Judith, and to salute her. ⁹When they came to her, they all blessed her with one accord, and said to her, "You are the exaltation of Jerusalem! You are the great glory of Israel! You are the great rejoicing of our race! ¹⁰You have done all these things by your hand. You have done with Israel the things that are good, and God is pleased with it. Blessed are you with the Almighty LORD forever." And all the people said, "Amen!" ¹¹And the people plundered the camp for the space of thirty days: and they gave Holofernes' tent to Judith, along with all his silver cups, his beds, his bowls, and all his furniture. She took them, and placed them on her mule, and prepared her wagons, and heaped them on it. ¹²And all the women of Israel ran together to see her; and they blessed her and made a dance among them for her. She took branches in her hand and distributed them to the women who were with her. ¹³Then they made themselves garlands of olive, she and those who were with her, and she went before all the people in the dance, leading all the women. All the men of Israel followed in their armor with garlands, and with songs in their mouths.

CHAPTER 16

¹And Judith began to sing this song of thanksgiving in all Israel, and all the people sang with loud voices this song of praise. ²Judith said, "Begin a song to my God with timbrels. Sing to my Lord with cymbals. Make melody to Him with psalm and praise. Exalt Him and call on His Name. ³For the LORD is the God that crushes battles. For in His armies in the midst of the people, || He delivered me out of the hand of those who persecuted me. ⁴Asshur came out of the mountains from the north. He came with tens of thousands of his army. Its multitude stopped the torrents. Their horsemen covered the hills. ⁵He said that he would burn up my borders, || Kill my young men with the sword, || Throw my nursing children to the ground, || Give my infants up as prey, || And make my virgins a plunder. ⁶The Almighty LORD brought them to nothing by the hand of a woman. ⁷For their mighty one did not fall by young men, || Neither did sons of the Titans strike him. Tall giants did not attack him, || But Judith the daughter of Merari made him weak with the beauty of her countenance. ⁸For she put off the apparel of her widowhood || For the exaltation of those who were distressed in Israel. She anointed her face with ointment, || Bound her hair in a tiara, || And took a linen garment to deceive him. ⁹Her sandal ravished his eye. Her beauty took his soul prisoner. The scimitar passed through his neck. ¹⁰The Persians quaked at her daring. The Medes were daunted at her boldness. ¹¹Then my lowly ones shouted aloud. My weak ones were terrified and trembled for fear. They lifted up their voice, and they fled. ¹²The sons of ladies pierced them through and wounded them as fugitives' children. They perished by the battle of my Lord. ¹³I will sing to my God a new song: O LORD, You are great and glorious, || Marvelous in strength, invincible. ¹⁴Let all Your creation serve You; For You spoke, and they were made. You sent out Your Spirit, || And it built them. There is no one who can resist Your voice. ¹⁵For the mountains will be moved from their foundations with the waters, || And the rocks will melt as wax at your presence, || But You are yet merciful to those who fear You. ¹⁶For all sacrifice is little for a sweet savor, || And all the fat is very little for a whole burnt-offering to You; But he who fears the LORD is great continually. ¹⁷Woe to the nations who rise up against my race! The LORD Almighty will take vengeance on them in the Day of Judgment, || To put fire and worms in their flesh; And they will weep and feel their pain forever." ¹⁸Now when they came to Jerusalem, they worshiped God. When the people were purified, they offered their whole burnt-offerings, their free will offerings, and their gifts. ¹⁹Judith dedicated all Holofernes' stuff, which the people had given her, and gave the canopy, which she had taken for herself out of his bedchamber, for a gift to the LORD. ²⁰And the people continued feasting in Jerusalem before the sanctuary for three months, and Judith remained with them. ²¹But after these days, everyone departed to his own inheritance. Judith went away to Bethulia, and remained in her own possession, and was honorable in her time in all the land. ²²Many desired her, and no man knew her all the days of her life, from the day that Manasseh her husband died and was gathered to his people. ²³She increased in greatness exceedingly; and she grew old in her husband's house, to one hundred five years, and let her maid go free. Then she died in Bethulia. They buried her in the cave of her husband Manasseh. ²⁴The house of Israel mourned for her seven days. She distributed her goods before she died to all those who were nearest relatives to Manasseh her husband, and to those who were nearest of her own relatives. ²⁵There was no one that made the sons of Israel afraid anymore in the days of Judith, nor a long time after her death.

WISDOM

Otherwise known as the Wisdom of Solomon, the Book of Wisdom was written as late as fifty years before the coming of Christ. Its author, whose name is not known to us, was probably a member of the Jewish community at Alexandria, in Egypt. He wrote in Greek, in a style patterned on that of Hebrew verse. At times he speaks in the person of Solomon, placing his teachings on the lips of the wise king of Hebrew tradition in order to emphasize their value.

CHAPTER 1

¹Love righteousness, all you who are judges of the earth. Think of the LORD with a good mind. Seek Him in singleness of heart. ²Because He is found by those who do not tempt Him and is manifested to those who trust Him. ³For crooked thoughts separate from God. His Power convicts when it is tested and exposes the foolish. ⁴Because wisdom will not enter into a soul that devises evil, || Nor dwell in a body that is enslaved by sin. ⁵For a holy spirit of discipline will flee deceit, || And will depart from thoughts that are without understanding, || And will be ashamed when unrighteousness has come in. ⁶For wisdom is

a spirit who loves man, || And she will not hold a blasphemer guiltless for his lips; Because God is [the] witness of his innermost self, || And is [the] true overseer of his heart, and a hearer of his tongue: ⁷Because the Spirit of the LORD has filled the world, || And that which holds all things together knows what is said. ⁸Therefore no one who utters unrighteous things will be unseen; Neither will justice, when it convicts, pass him by. ⁹For in his counsels the ungodly will be searched out, || And the sound of his words will come to the LORD to bring his lawless deeds to conviction; ¹⁰Because a jealous ear listens to all things, || And the noise of murmurings is not hidden. ¹¹Beware then of unprofitable murmuring and keep your tongue from slander, || Because no secret utterance will go on its way void, || And a lying mouth destroys a soul. ¹²Do not court death in the error of your life; And do not draw destruction on yourselves by the works of your hands, ¹³Because God did not make death; Neither does He delight when the living perish. ¹⁴For He created all things that they might have being. The generative powers of the world are wholesome, || And there is no poison of destruction in them, || Nor does Hades have royal dominion on earth; ¹⁵For righteousness is immortal, ¹⁶But ungodly men, by their hands and their words, summon death; Deeming him a friend, they wear themselves out [for him]. They made a covenant with him, || Because they are worthy to belong with him.

CHAPTER 2

¹For they said within themselves, with unsound reasoning, "Our life is short and sorrowful. There is no healing when a man comes to his end, || And no one was ever known who was released from Hades, ²Because we were born by mere chance, || And hereafter we will be as though we had never been; Because the breath in our nostrils is smoke, || And reason is a spark kindled by the beating of our heart, ³Which being extinguished, the body will be turned into ashes, || And the spirit will be dispersed as thin air. ⁴Our name will be forgotten in time. No one will remember our works. Our life will pass away as the traces of a cloud, || And will be scattered as is a mist, when it is chased by the rays of the sun and overcome by its heat. ⁵For our allotted time is the passing of a shadow, and our end does not retreat, || Because it is securely sealed, and no one turns it back. ⁶Come therefore and let us enjoy the good things that exist. Let us use the creation earnestly as in our youth. ⁷Let us fill ourselves with costly wine and perfumes || And let no Spring flower pass us by. ⁸Let us crown ourselves with rosebuds before they wither. ⁹Let none of us go without his share in our proud revelry. Let us leave signs of mirth everywhere, || Because this is our portion, and this is our lot. ¹⁰Let us oppress the righteous poor. Let us not spare the widow, || Nor give reverence to the gray hair of the old man. ¹¹But let our strength be a law of righteousness; For that which is weak is proven useless. ¹²But let us lie in wait for the righteous man, || Because he annoys us, is contrary to our works, reproaches us with sins against the law, and charges us with sins against our training. ¹³He professes to have knowledge of God and calls himself a child of the LORD. ¹⁴He became to us a reproof of our thoughts. ¹⁵He is grievous to us even to look at, || Because his life is unlike other men's, and his paths are strange. ¹⁶We were regarded by him as worthless metal, || And he abstains from our ways as from uncleanness. He calls the latter end of the righteous happy. He boasts that God is his father. ¹⁷Let us see if his words are true. Let us test what will happen at the end of his life. ¹⁸For if the righteous man is God's son, He will uphold him, || And He will deliver him out of the hand of his adversaries. ¹⁹Let us test him with outrage and torture, || That we may find out how gentle he is and test his patience. ²⁰Let us condemn him to a shameful death, || For he will be overseen according to his words." ²¹So they reasoned, and they were led astray; For their wickedness blinded them, ²²And they did not know the mysteries of God, || Neither did they hope for wages of holiness, || Nor did they discern that there is a prize for blameless souls. ²³Because God created man for incorruption || And made Him an image of His own perpetuity; ²⁴But death entered into the world by the envy of the Devil, || And those who belong to him experience it.

CHAPTER 3

¹But the souls of the righteous are in the hand of God, || And no torment will touch them. ²In the eyes of the foolish they seemed to have died. Their departure was considered affliction, ³And their travel away from us ruin; But they are in peace. ⁴For even if they are punished in the sight of men, || Their hope is full of immortality. ⁵Having borne a little disciplining, they will receive great good, || Because God tested them and found them worthy of Himself. ⁶He tested them like gold in the furnace, || And He accepted them as a whole burnt-offering. ⁷In the time of their visitation they will shine. They will run back and out like sparks among stubble. ⁸They will judge nations and have dominion over peoples. The LORD will reign over them forever. ⁹Those who trust Him will understand truth. The faithful will live with Him in love, || Because grace and mercy are with His chosen ones. ¹⁰But the ungodly will be punished even as they reasoned, || Those who neglected righteousness and revolted from the LORD; ¹¹For he who despises wisdom and discipline is miserable. Their hope is void and their toils unprofitable. Their works are useless. ¹²Their wives are foolish and their children are wicked. ¹³Their descendants are cursed, || Because the barren woman who is undefiled is happy—she who has not conceived in transgression. She will have fruit in the visitation of souls. ¹⁴So is the eunuch which has done no lawless deed with his hands, || Nor imagined wicked things against the LORD; For a precious gift will be given to him for his faithfulness—a special favor, and a delightful inheritance in the LORD's sanctuary. ¹⁵For good labors have fruit of great renown. The root of understanding cannot fail. ¹⁶But children of adulterers will not come to maturity. The seed of an unlawful bed will vanish away. ¹⁷For if they live long, they will not be esteemed, || And in the end, their old age will be without honor. ¹⁸If they die quickly, they will have no hope, || Nor consolation in the day of decision. ¹⁹For the end of an unrighteous generation is always grievous.

CHAPTER 4

¹It is better to be childless with virtue, || For immortality is in the memory of virtue, || Because it is recognized both before God and before men. ²When it is present, people imitate it. They long after it when it has departed. Throughout all time it marches crowned in triumph—Victorious in the competition for the prizes that are undefiled. ³But the multiplying brood of the ungodly will be of no profit, || And their illegitimate offshoots will not take deep root, || Nor will they establish a sure hold. ⁴For even if they grow branches and flourish for a season, || Standing unsure, they will be shaken by the wind. They will be uprooted by the violence of winds. ⁵Their branches will be broken off before they come to maturity. Their fruit will be useless—Never ripe to eat and fit for nothing. ⁶For unlawfully conceived children are witnesses of wickedness against parents when they are investigated. ⁷But a righteous man, even if he dies before his time, will be at rest. ⁸For honorable old age is not that which stands in length of time, || Nor is its measure given by number of years, ⁹But understanding is gray hair to men, || And an unspotted life is ripe old age. ¹⁰Being found well-pleasing to God, he was loved; While living among sinners he was transported. ¹¹He was caught away, lest evil should change his understanding, || Or guile deceive his soul. ¹²For the witchcraft of worthlessness obscures the things which are good, || And the whirl of desire perverts an innocent mind. ¹³Being made perfect quickly, he filled a long time; ¹⁴For his soul was pleasing to the LORD. Therefore, he hurried out of the midst of wickedness. ¹⁵But as for the peoples seeing and not understanding, || They are not considering this: that grace and mercy are with His chosen, || And that He visits His holy ones. ¹⁶But a righteous man who is dead will condemn the ungodly who are living, || And youth that is quickly perfected will condemn the many years of an unrighteous man's old age. ¹⁷For the ungodly will see a wise man's end, || And will not understand what the LORD planned for him, and why He safely kept him. ¹⁸They will see, and they will despise; But the LORD will laugh them to scorn. After this, they will become a dishonored carcass and a reproach among the dead forever, ¹⁹Because He will dash them speechless to the ground || And will shake them from the foundations. They will lie utterly waste. They will be in anguish and their memory will perish. ²⁰They will come with cowardly fear when their sins

WISDOM

are counted. Their lawless deeds will convict them to their face.

CHAPTER 5

¹Then the righteous man will stand in great boldness ‖ Before the face of those who afflicted him, ‖ And those who make his labors of no account. ²When they see him, they will be troubled with terrible fear, ‖ And will be amazed at the marvel of salvation. ³They will speak among themselves converting, ‖ And for distress of spirit they will groan, ‖ "This was he whom we used to hold in derision, as an allegory of reproach. ⁴We fools considered his life madness, and his end without honor. ⁵How was he counted among sons of God? How is his lot among saints? ⁶Truly we went astray from the way of truth. The light of righteousness did not shine for us. The sun did not rise for us. ⁷We took our fill of the paths of lawlessness and destruction. We traveled through trackless deserts, ‖ But we did not know the Lord's way. ⁸What did our arrogance profit us? What good have riches and boasting brought us? ⁹Those things all passed away as a shadow, ‖ Like a message that runs by, ¹⁰Like a ship passing through the billowy water, ‖ Which, when it has gone by, there is no trace to be found, ‖ No pathway of its keel in the billows. ¹¹Or it is like when a bird flies through the air [and] no evidence of its passage is found, ‖ But the light wind, lashed with the stroke of its pinions, ‖ And torn apart with the violent rush of the moving wings, is passed through. Afterward no sign of its coming remains. ¹²Or it is like when an arrow is shot at a mark [and] the parted air closes up again immediately, ‖ So that men do not know where it passed through. ¹³So we also, as soon as we were born, ceased to be; And we had no sign of virtue to show, but we were utterly consumed in our wickedness." ¹⁴Because the hope of the ungodly man is like chaff carried by the wind, ‖ And as foam vanishing before a tempest; And [it] is scattered like smoke by the wind, ‖ And passes by as the remembrance of a guest that waits but a day. ¹⁵But the righteous live forever. Their reward is in the Lord, ‖ And the care for them with the Most High. ¹⁶Therefore they will receive the crown of royal dignity ‖ And the diadem of beauty from the Lord's hand; Because He will cover them with His right hand, ‖ And He will shield them with His arm. ¹⁷He will take His jealousy as complete armor ‖ And will make the whole creation His weapons to punish His enemies: ¹⁸He will put on righteousness as a breastplate ‖ And will wear impartial judgment as a helmet. ¹⁹He will take holiness as an invincible shield. ²⁰He will sharpen stern wrath for a sword. The world will go with Him to fight against His frenzied enemies. ²¹Shafts of lightning will fly with true aim. They will leap to the mark from the clouds, as from a well-drawn bow. ²²Hailstones full of wrath will be hurled from an engine of war. The water of the sea will be angered against them. Rivers will sternly overwhelm them. ²³A mighty blast will encounter them. It will winnow them away like a tempest. So lawlessness will make all the land desolate. Their evildoing will overturn the thrones of princes.

CHAPTER 6

¹Hear therefore, you kings, and understand. Learn, you judges of the ends of the earth. ²Give ear, you rulers who have dominion over many people, ‖ And [who] make your boast in multitudes of nations, ³Because your dominion was given to you from the Lord, ‖ And your sovereignty from the Most High. He will search out your works and will inquire about your plans; ⁴Because, being officers of His kingdom, you did not judge rightly, ‖ Nor did you keep law, nor did you walk according to God's counsel. ⁵He will come on you awfully and swiftly, ‖ Because a stern judgment comes on those who are in high places. ⁶For the man of low estate may be pardoned in mercy, ‖ But mighty men will be mightily tested. ⁷For the Sovereign Lord of all will not be impressed with anyone, ‖ Neither will He show deference to greatness; Because it is He who made both small and great, and cares about them all; ⁸But the scrutiny that comes on the powerful is strict. ⁹Therefore, my words are to you, O princes, ‖ That you may learn wisdom and not fall away. ¹⁰For those who have kept the things that are holy in holiness will be made holy. Those who have been taught them will find what to say in defense. ¹¹Therefore set your desire on my words. Long for them, and you princes will be instructed. ¹²Wisdom is radiant and does not fade away, ‖ And is easily seen by those who love her ‖ And found by those who seek her. ¹³She anticipates those who desire her, making herself known. ¹⁴He who rises up early to seek her will not have difficulty, ‖ For he will find her sitting at his gates. ¹⁵For to think on her is perfection of understanding, ‖ And he who watches for her will quickly be free from care; ¹⁶Because she herself goes around, seeking those who are worthy of her, ‖ And in their paths she appears to them graciously, ‖ And in every purpose she meets them. ¹⁷For her true beginning is desire for instruction; And desire for instruction is love. ¹⁸And love is observance of her laws. To give heed to her laws confirms immortality. ¹⁹Immortality brings closeness to God. ²⁰So then, desire for wisdom promotes to a kingdom. ²¹If, therefore, you delight in thrones and scepters—you princes of peoples—Honor wisdom, that you may reign forever. ²²But what wisdom is, and how she came into being, I will declare. I will not hide mysteries from you; But I will explore from her first beginning; [I will] bring the knowledge of her into clear light, ‖ And I will not pass by the truth. ²³Indeed, I will not go with consuming envy, ‖ Because envy will have no fellowship with wisdom. ²⁴But a multitude of wise men is salvation to the world, ‖ And an understanding king is stability for his people. ²⁵Therefore be instructed by my words, and you will profit.

CHAPTER 7

¹I myself am also mortal, like everyone else, ‖ And am a descendant of one formed first and born of the earth. ²I [was] molded into flesh in the time of ten months in my mother's womb, ‖ Being compacted in blood from the seed of man and pleasure that came with sleep. ³I also, when I was born, drew in the common air, and fell on the related earth, ‖ Uttering, like all, for my first voice, the same cry. ⁴I was nursed with care in swaddling clothes. ⁵For no king had any other first beginning; ⁶But all men have one entrance into life, and a common departure. ⁷For this reason I prayed, and understanding was given to me. I asked, and a spirit of wisdom came to me. ⁸I preferred her before scepters and thrones. I considered riches nothing in comparison to her. ⁹Neither did I liken to her any priceless gem, ‖ Because all gold in her presence is a little sand, ‖ And silver will be considered as clay before her. ¹⁰I loved her more than health and beauty, ‖ And I chose to have her rather than light, ‖ Because her bright shining is never laid to sleep. ¹¹All good things came to me with her, ‖ And innumerable riches are in her hands. ¹²And I rejoiced over them all because wisdom leads them, ‖ Although I did not know that she was their mother. ¹³As I learned without guile, I impart without grudging. I do not hide her riches. ¹⁴For she is a treasure for men that does not fail, ‖ And those who use it obtain friendship with God, ‖ Commended by the gifts which they present through discipline. ¹⁵But may God grant that I may speak His judgment, ‖ And to conceive thoughts worthy of what has been given me; Because He is one who guides even wisdom and who corrects the wise. ¹⁶For both we and our words are in His hand, ‖ With all understanding and skill in various crafts. ¹⁷For He Himself gave me an unerring knowledge of the things that are, ‖ To know the structure of the universe and the operation of the elements; ¹⁸The beginning, end, and middle of times; The alternations of the solstices and the changes of seasons; ¹⁹The circuits of years and the positions of stars; ²⁰The natures of living creatures and the raging of wild beasts; The violence of winds and the thoughts of men; The diversities of plants and the virtues of roots. ²¹All things that are either secret or manifest I learned, ²²For wisdom, that is the architect of all things, taught me. For there is a spirit in her that is quick to understand, ‖ Holy, unique, manifold, subtle, freely moving, clear in utterance, ‖ Unpolluted, distinct, unharmed, loving what is good, keen, unhindered, ²³Beneficent, loving toward man, steadfast, sure, free from care, all-powerful, all-surveying, ‖ And penetrating through all spirits that are quick to understand, pure, most subtle: ²⁴For wisdom is more mobile than any motion. Yes, she pervades and penetrates all things by reason of her purity. ²⁵For she is a breath of the power of God, ‖ And a clear effluence of the glory of the Almighty. Therefore, nothing defiled can find entrance into her. ²⁶For she is a reflection of continuous light, ‖ An unspotted mirror of the working of God, ‖ And an image of His

goodness. ²⁷She, being one, has power to do all things. Remaining in herself, she renews all things. From generation to generation passing into holy souls, || She makes friends of God and prophets. ²⁸For God loves nothing as much as one who dwells with wisdom. ²⁹For she is fairer than the sun, and above all the constellations of the stars. She is better than light. ³⁰For daylight yields to night, but evil does not prevail against wisdom.

CHAPTER 8

¹But she reaches from one end to the other with full strength and orders all things well. ²I loved her and sought her from my youth. I sought to take her for my bride. I became enamored by her beauty. ³She glorifies her noble birth by living with God. The Sovereign Lord of all loves her. ⁴For she is initiated into the knowledge of God, || And she chooses His works. ⁵But if riches are a desired possession in life, || What is richer than wisdom, which makes all things? ⁶And if understanding works, || Who more than wisdom is an architect of the things that exist? ⁷If a man loves righteousness, the fruits of wisdom's labor are virtues, || For she teaches soberness, understanding, righteousness, and courage. There is nothing in life more profitable for people than these. ⁸And if anyone longs for wide experience, || She knows the things of old, and infers the things to come. She understands subtleties of speeches and interpretations of dark sayings. She foresees signs and wonders, and the issues of seasons and times. ⁹Therefore I determined to take her to live with me, || Knowing that she is one who would give me good counsel, || And encourage me in cares and grief. ¹⁰Because of her, I will have glory among multitudes, || And honor in the sight of elders, though I am young. ¹¹I will be found keen when I give judgment. I will be admired in the presence of rulers. ¹²When I am silent, they will wait for me. When I open my lips, they will heed what I say. If I continue speaking, they will put their hands on their mouths. ¹³Because of her, I will have immortality, || And leave behind a continuous memory to those who come after me. ¹⁴I will govern peoples. Nations will be subjected to me. ¹⁵Dreaded monarchs will fear me when they hear of me. Among the people, I will show myself to be good and courageous in war. ¹⁶When I come into my house, I will find rest with her. For conversation with her has no bitterness, || And living with her has no pain, but gladness and joy. ¹⁷When I considered these things in myself || And thought in my heart how immortality is in kinship to wisdom, ¹⁸And in her friendship is good delight, || And in the labors of her hands is wealth that does not fail, || And understanding is in her companionship, || And great renown in having fellowship with her words, || I went around seeking how to take her to myself. ¹⁹Now I was a clever child and received a good soul. ²⁰Or rather, being good, I came into an undefiled body. ²¹But perceiving that I could not otherwise possess wisdom unless God gave her to me—Yes, and to know and understand by whom the grace is given—I pleaded with the Lord and implored Him, and with my whole heart I said:

CHAPTER 9

¹"O God of the fathers, and Lord of mercy, who made all things by Your word; ²And by Your wisdom You formed man, that he should have dominion over the creatures that were made by You, ³And rule the world in holiness and righteousness, and execute judgment in uprightness of soul; ⁴Give me wisdom—her who sits by You on Your thrones. Do not reject me from among Your servants, ⁵Because I am Your servant and the son of Your handmaid, || A weak and short-lived man, with little power to understand judgment and laws. ⁶For even if a man is perfect among the sons of men, || If the wisdom that comes from You is not with him, he will count for nothing. ⁷You chose me to be king of Your people, || And a judge for Your sons and daughters. ⁸You gave a command to build a sanctuary on Your holy mountain, || And an altar in the city where You pitch Your tent—A copy of the holy tent which You prepared from the beginning. ⁹Wisdom is with You and knows Your works, || And was present when You were making the world, || And understands what is pleasing in Your eyes, || And what is right according to Your commands. ¹⁰Send her from the holy heavens and ask her to come from the throne of Your glory, || That being present with me she may work, || And I may learn what pleases You well. ¹¹For she knows all things and understands, || And she will guide me soberly in my actions. She will guard me in her glory. ¹²So my works will be acceptable. I will judge Your people righteously, || And I will be worthy of my father's throne. ¹³For what man will know the counsel of God? Or who will conceive what the Lord wills? ¹⁴For the thoughts of mortals are unstable, and our plans are prone to fail. ¹⁵For a corruptible body weighs down the soul. The earthy frame lies heavy on a mind that is full of cares. ¹⁶We can hardly guess the things that are on earth, || And we find the things that are close at hand with labor; But who has traced out the things that are in the heavens? ¹⁷Who gained knowledge of Your counsel, || Unless You gave wisdom, and sent Your Holy Spirit from the highest? ¹⁸It was so that the ways of those who are on earth were corrected, || And men were taught the things that are pleasing to You. They were saved through wisdom."

CHAPTER 10

¹Wisdom guarded to the end the first formed father of the world, || Who was created alone, and delivered him out of his own transgression, ²And gave him strength to get dominion over all things. ³But when an unrighteous man fell away from her in his anger, || He perished himself in the rage with which he killed his brother. ⁴When for his cause the earth was drowning with a flood, || Wisdom again saved it, guiding the righteous man's course by a poor piece of wood. ⁵Moreover, when nations consenting together in wickedness had been confounded, || Wisdom knew the righteous man, and preserved him blameless to God, || And kept him strong when his heart yearned toward his child. ⁶While the ungodly were perishing, wisdom delivered a righteous man, || When he fled from the fire that descended out of Heaven on [the] five cities— ⁷To whose wickedness a smoking waste still witnesses, || And plants bearing fair fruit that does not ripen, || A disbelieving soul has a memorial: a standing pillar of salt. ⁸For having passed wisdom by, || Not only were they disabled from recognizing the things which are good, || But they also left behind them for their life a monument of their folly, || To the end that where they stumbled, they might fail even to be unseen; ⁹But wisdom delivered those who waited on her out of troubles. ¹⁰When a righteous man was a fugitive from a brother's wrath, || Wisdom guided him in straight paths. She showed him God's Kingdom and gave him knowledge of holy things. She prospered him in his toils and multiplied the fruits of his labor. ¹¹When in their covetousness men dealt harshly with him, || She stood by him and made him rich. ¹²She guarded him from enemies, || And she kept him safe from those who lay in wait. Over his severe conflict, she watched as judge, || That he might know that godliness is more powerful than everyone. ¹³When a righteous man was sold, || Wisdom did not forsake him, but she delivered him from sin. She went down with him into a dungeon, ¹⁴And in bonds she did not depart from him, || Until she brought him the scepter of a kingdom, and authority over those that dealt unjustly with him. She also showed those who had mockingly accused him to be false and gave him continuous glory. ¹⁵Wisdom delivered a holy people and a blameless seed from a nation of oppressors. ¹⁶She entered into the soul of a servant of the Lord || And withstood terrible kings in wonders and signs. ¹⁷She rendered to holy men a reward of their toils. She guided them along a marvelous way || And became to them a covering in the daytime, || And a flame of stars through the night. ¹⁸She brought them over the Red Sea and led them through much water; ¹⁹But she drowned their enemies, and she cast them up from the bottom of the deep. ²⁰Therefore the righteous plundered the ungodly, || And they sang praise to Your holy Name, O Lord, || And extolled with one accord Your hand that fought for them, ²¹Because wisdom opened the mouth of the mute, || And made the tongues of babies to speak clearly.

CHAPTER 11

¹She prospered their works in the hand of a holy prophet. ²They traveled through a desert without inhabitant, || And they pitched their tents in trackless regions. ³They withstood enemies and repelled enemies. ⁴They thirsted, and they called on You, || And water was given to them out of the flinty rock, || And healing of their thirst out of the hard stone. ⁵For by what

things their enemies were punished, || By these they in their need were benefited. ⁶When enemies were troubled with clotted blood instead of a river's ever-flowing fountain, ⁷To rebuke the decree for the slaying of babies, You gave them abundant water beyond all hope, ⁸Having shown by the thirst which they had suffered how You punished the adversaries. ⁹For when they were tried, although disciplined in mercy, || They learned how the ungodly were tormented, being judged with wrath. ¹⁰For You tested these as a father admonishing them; But You searched out those as a stern king condemning them. ¹¹Yes, and whether they were far off or near, they were equally distressed; ¹²For a double grief seized them, || And a groaning at the memory of things past. ¹³For when they heard that through their own punishments the others benefited, || They recognized the LORD. ¹⁴For him who long before was thrown out and exposed they stopped mocking. In the end of what happened, they marveled, || Having thirsted in another manner than the righteous. ¹⁵But in return for the senseless imaginings of their unrighteousness, || Wherein they were led astray to worship irrational reptiles and wretched vermin, || You sent on them a multitude of irrational creatures for vengeance, ¹⁶That they might learn that by what things a man sins, by these he is punished. ¹⁷For Your all-powerful hand that created the world out of formless matter || Did not lack means to send on them a multitude of bears, fierce lions, ¹⁸Or newly-created and unknown wild beasts, full of rage, || Either breathing out a blast of fiery breath, or belching out smoke, || Or flashing dreadful sparks from their eyes, ¹⁹Which had power not only to consume them by their violence, || But to destroy them even by the terror of their sight. ²⁰Yes, and without these they might have fallen by a single breath, || Being pursued by justice, and scattered abroad by the breath of Your power; But You arranged all things by measure, number, and weight. ²¹For to be greatly strong is Yours at all times. Who could withstand the might of Your arm? ²²Because the whole world before You is as a grain in a balance, || And as a drop of dew that comes down on the earth in the morning. ²³But You have mercy on all men, || Because You have power to do all things, || And You overlook the sins of men to the end that they may convert. ²⁴For You love all things that are || And abhor none of the things which You made; For You never would have formed anything if You hated it. ²⁵How would anything have endured unless You had willed it? Or that which was not called by You, how would it have been preserved? ²⁶But You spare all things, because they are Yours, || O Sovereign LORD—You lover of lives.

CHAPTER 12

¹For Your incorruptible Spirit is in all things— ²Why [indeed] You convict little by little those who fall from the right way, || And, putting them in remembrance by the things wherein they sin, You admonish them, || That escaping from their wickedness they may believe in You, O LORD. ³For truly the old inhabitants of Your holy land, ⁴Hating them because they practiced detestable works of enchantments and unholy rites— ⁵Merciless slaughters of children and sacrificial banquets of men's flesh and of blood— ⁶Allies in an impious fellowship, and murderers of their own helpless babies, || It was Your counsel to destroy [them] by the hands of our fathers, ⁷That the land which in Your sight is most precious of all might receive a worthy colony of God's servants. ⁸Nevertheless, You even spared these as men, || And You sent hornets as forerunners of Your army, || To cause them to perish little by little; ⁹Not that You were unable to subdue the ungodly under the hand of the righteous in battle, || Or by terrible beasts, or by a stern word to make away with them at once; ¹⁰But judging them little by little, You gave them a chance to convert, || Not being ignorant that their nature by birth was evil, their wickedness inborn, || And that their manner of thought would never be changed. ¹¹For they were a cursed seed from the beginning. It was not through fear of any that You left them unpunished for their sins. ¹²For who will say, "What have You done?" Or "Who will withstand Your judgment?" Who will accuse You for the perishing of nations which You caused? Or who will come and stand before You as an avenger for unrighteous men? ¹³For there is not any God besides You that cares for all, || That You might show that You did not judge unrighteously. ¹⁴No king or prince will be able to look You in the face || For those whom You have punished. ¹⁵But being righteous, You rule all things righteously, || Deeming it a thing alien from Your power to condemn one that does not deserve to be punished. ¹⁶For Your strength is the beginning of righteousness, || And Your sovereignty over all makes You to forbear all. ¹⁷For when men do not believe that You are perfect in power, || You show Your strength, || And in dealing with those who think this, || You confuse their boldness. ¹⁸But You, being sovereign over strength, || Judge in gentleness and govern us with great forbearance; For the power is Yours whenever You desire it. ¹⁹But You taught Your people by such works as these, || How the righteous must be a lover of men. You made Your sons to have good hope, || Because You give conversion when men have sinned. ²⁰For if on those who were enemies of Your servants, || And due to death, You took vengeance with so great deliberation and indulgence, || Giving them times and opportunities when they might escape from their wickedness— ²¹With how much greater carefulness You judged Your sons, || To whose fathers You gave oaths and covenants of good promises! ²²Therefore, while You discipline us, || You scourge our enemies ten thousand times more, || To the intent that we may ponder Your goodness when we judge, || And when we are judged may look for mercy. ²³Why also the unrighteous that lived in folly of life, || You tormented through their own abominations. ²⁴For truly they went very far astray in the ways of error, || Taking as gods those animals which even among their enemies were held in dishonor, || Deceived like foolish babies. ²⁵Therefore, as to unreasoning children, || You sent Your judgment to mock them. ²⁶But those who would not be admonished by a mocking correction as of children, || Will experience a judgment worthy of God. ²⁷For through the sufferings they were indignant of, || Being punished in these creatures which they supposed to be gods, || They saw and recognized as the true God Him whom they refused to know. Therefore, the result of condemnation also came on them.

CHAPTER 13

¹For truly all men who had no perception of God were vain by nature || And did not gain power to know Him who exists from the good things that are seen. They did not recognize the Architect from His works. ²But they thought that either fire, or wind, or swift air, || Or circling stars, or raging water, or luminaries of the heavens were gods that rule the world. ³If it was through delight in their beauty that they took them to be gods, || Let them know how much better their Sovereign LORD is than these, || For the first Author of beauty created them. ⁴But if it was through astonishment at their power and influence, || Then let them understand from them how much more powerful He who formed them is. ⁵For from the greatness of the beauty of created things, || Mankind forms the corresponding image of their Maker. ⁶But yet for these men there is but small blame, || For they too perhaps go astray while they are seeking God and desiring to find Him. ⁷For they diligently search while living among His works, || And they trust their sight that the things that they look at are beautiful. ⁸But again even they are not to be excused. ⁹For if they had power to know so much, || That they should be able to explore the world, || How is it that they did not find the Sovereign LORD sooner? ¹⁰But they [were] miserable—And their hopes [were] in dead things—Who called them gods which are works of men's hands: Gold and silver, skillfully made, and likenesses of animals, || Or a useless stone, the work of an ancient hand; ¹¹Yes, and if some woodcutter, having sawn down a tree that is easily moved, || Skillfully strips away all its bark, and fashioning it in attractive form, || Makes a useful vessel to serve his life's needs. ¹²Burning the scraps from his handiwork to cook his food, he eats his fill. ¹³Taking a discarded scrap which served no purpose, || A crooked piece of wood and full of knots, || He carves it with the diligence of his idleness, || And shapes it by the skill of his idleness. He shapes it in the image of a man, ¹⁴Or makes it like some paltry animal, || Smearing it with something red, || Painting it red, and smearing over every stain in it. ¹⁵Having made a worthy chamber for it, || He sets it in a wall, securing it with iron. ¹⁶He plans for it that it may not fall down, || Knowing that it is unable to help itself; For it is truly an image, and needs [his]

help. ¹⁷When he makes his prayer concerning goods and his marriage and children, || He is not ashamed to speak to that which has no life. ¹⁸Yes, for health, he calls on that which is weak. For life, he implores that which is dead. For aid, he supplicates that which has no experience. For a good journey, he asks that which cannot so much as move a step. ¹⁹And for profit in business and good success of his hands, || He asks ability from that which has hands with no ability.

CHAPTER 14

¹Again, one preparing to sail, and about to journey over raging waves, || Calls on a piece of wood more rotten than the vessel that carries him. ²For the hunger for profit planned it, || And wisdom was the craftsman who built it. ³Your providence, O Father, guides it along, || Because even in the sea You gave a way, || And in the waves a sure path, ⁴Showing that You can save out of every danger, || That even a man without skill may put to sea. ⁵It is Your will that the works of Your wisdom should not be idle. Therefore, men also entrust their lives to a little piece of wood, || And passing through the surge on a raft come safely to land. ⁶For in the old time also, when proud giants were perishing, || The hope of the world, taking refuge on a raft, || Your hand guided the seed of generations of the race of men. ⁷For blessed is [the] wood through which comes righteousness; ⁸But the idol made with hands is accursed—Itself and he that made it; Because his was the working, || And the corruptible thing was called a god; ⁹For both the ungodly and his ungodliness are alike hateful to God; ¹⁰For the deed will truly be punished together with him who committed it. ¹¹Therefore there will also be a visitation among the idols of the nation, || Because, though formed of things which God created, || They were made an abomination, stumbling blocks to the souls of men, || And a snare to the feet of the foolish. ¹²For the devising of idols was the beginning of fornication, || And the invention of them the corruption of life. ¹³For they did not exist from the beginning, || And they will not exist forever. ¹⁴For by the vain pride of men they entered into the world, || And therefore a speedy end was planned for them. ¹⁵For a father worn with untimely grief, making an image of the child quickly taken away, || Now honored him as a god which was then a dead man, || And delivered to those that were under him mysteries and solemn rites. ¹⁶Afterward the ungodly custom, in process of time grown strong, was kept as a law, || And the engraved images received worship by the commands of princes. ¹⁷And when men could not honor them in presence because they lived far off, imagining the likeness from afar, || They made a visible image of the king whom they honored, || That by their zeal they might flatter the absent as if present. ¹⁸But worship was raised to a yet higher pitch, || Even by those who did not know him, urged forward by the ambition of the architect; ¹⁹For he, wishing perhaps to please one in authority, || Used his art to force the likeness toward a greater beauty. ²⁰So the multitude, allured by reason of the grace of his handiwork, || Now consider an object of devotion him that a little while before was honored as a man. ²¹And this became an ambush, because men, in bondage either to calamity or to tyranny, || Invested stones and stocks with the incommunicable Name. ²²Afterward it was not enough for them to go astray concerning the knowledge of God, || But also, while they live in a great war of ignorance, they call a multitude of evils peace. ²³For either slaughtering children in solemn rites, || Or celebrating secret mysteries, || Or holding frantic revels of strange ordinances, ²⁴No longer do they guard either life or purity of marriage, || But one brings on another: Either death by treachery, or anguish by adultery. ²⁵And all things confusedly are filled with blood and murder, || Theft and deceit, corruption, faithlessness, tumult, perjury, ²⁶Confusion about what is good, forgetfulness of favors, ingratitude for benefits, || Defiling of souls, confusion of sex, disorder in marriage, adultery and wantonness. ²⁷For the worship of idols that may not be named || Is a beginning, and cause, and end of every evil. ²⁸For their worshipers either make merry to madness, || Or prophesy lies, or live unrighteously, or lightly commit perjury. ²⁹For putting their trust in lifeless idols, when they have sworn a wicked oath, || They do not expect to suffer harm. ³⁰But for both, the just doom will pursue them, || Because they had evil thoughts of God by giving heed to idols || And swore unrighteously in deceit through contempt for holiness. ³¹For it is not the power of them by whom men swear, || But it is the just penalty for those who sin that always visits the transgression of the unrighteous.

CHAPTER 15

¹But You, our God, are gracious and true, || Patient, and ordering all things in mercy. ²For even if we sin, we are Yours, knowing Your dominion; But we will not sin, knowing that we have been accounted Yours. ³For to be acquainted with You is perfect righteousness, || And to know Your dominion is the root of immortality. ⁴For we were not led astray by any evil plan of men's, || Nor yet by painters' fruitless labor, a form stained with varied colors, ⁵The sight of which leads fools into lust. Their desire is for the breathless form of a dead image. ⁶Lovers of evil things, and worthy of such hopes, || Are those who make, desire, and worship them. ⁷For a potter, kneading soft earth, laboriously molds each article for our service. He fashions out of the same clay both the vessels that minister to clean uses, || And those of a contrary sort, all in like manner. What will be the use of each article of either sort—the potter is the judge. ⁸Also, laboring to an evil end, he molds a vain god out of the same clay, || He who, having but a little while before been made of earth, || After a short span goes his way to the earth out of which he was taken, || When he is required to render back the soul which was lent him. ⁹However, he has anxious care, not because his powers must fail, || Nor because his span of life is short; But he compares himself with goldsmiths and silversmiths, || And he imitates molders in brass, || And esteems it glory that he molds counterfeits. ¹⁰His heart is ashes. His hope is of less value than earth. His life is of less honor than clay; ¹¹Because he was ignorant of Him who molded him, || And of Him that inspired into him an active soul || And breathed into him a vital spirit. ¹²But he accounted our life to be a game, || And our lifetime a festival for profit; For, he says, one must get gain however one can, even if it is by evil. ¹³For this man knows that he sins beyond all others, || Making brittle vessels and graven images out of earthly matter. ¹⁴But most foolish and more miserable than a baby, || Are the enemies of Your people, who oppressed them; ¹⁵Because they even considered all the idols of the nations to be gods, || Which have neither the use of eyes for seeing, nor nostrils for drawing breath, || Nor ears to hear, nor fingers for handling, and their feet are helpless for walking. ¹⁶For a man made them, and one whose own spirit is borrowed molded them; For no one has power as a man to mold a god like to himself. ¹⁷But, being mortal, he makes a dead thing by the work of lawless hands; For he is better than the objects of his worship, || Since he indeed had life, but they never did. ¹⁸Yes, and they worship the creatures that are most hateful, || For, being compared as to lack of sense, these are worse than all others; ¹⁹Neither, as seen beside other creatures, are they beautiful, so that one should desire them, || But they have escaped both the praise of God and His blessing.

CHAPTER 16

¹For this reason, they were deservedly punished through creatures like those which they worship || And tormented through a multitude of vermin. ²Instead of this punishment, You, giving benefits to Your people, || Prepared quails for food, a delicacy to satisfy the desire of their appetite, ³To the end that Your enemies, desiring food, || Might for the hideousness of the creatures sent among them, || Loathe even the necessary appetite; But these, Your people, having suffered lack for a short time, || Might even partake of delicacies. ⁴For it was necessary that inescapable lack should come on those oppressors, || But that to these it should only be showed how their enemies were tormented. ⁵For even when terrible raging of wild beasts came on Your people, || And they were perishing by the bites of crooked serpents, || Your wrath did not continue to the uttermost; ⁶But for admonition they were troubled for a short time, || Having a token of salvation to put them in remembrance of the command of Your law; ⁷For he who turned toward it was not saved because of that which was seen, || But because of You, the Savior of all. ⁸Yes, and in this You persuaded our enemies || That You are He who delivers out of every evil. ⁹For the bites of locusts and flies truly killed them. No healing for their life was found, || Because they were worthy to be punished by such things. ¹⁰But Your children

WISDOM

were not overcome by the very teeth of venomous dragons, || For Your mercy passed by where they were and healed them. ¹¹For they were bitten to put them in remembrance of Your oracles, || And were quickly saved, lest, falling into deep forgetfulness, || They should become unable to respond to Your kindness. ¹²For truly it was neither herb nor mollifying plaster that cured them, || But Your word, O LORD, which heals all things. ¹³For You have authority over life and death, || And You lead down to the gates of Hades and lead up again. ¹⁴But though a man kills by his wickedness, || He cannot retrieve the spirit that has departed or release the imprisoned soul. ¹⁵But it is not possible to escape Your hand; ¹⁶For ungodly men, refusing to know You, || Were scourged in the strength of Your arm, || Pursued with strange rains, and hails, and relentless storms, || And utterly consumed with fire. ¹⁷For, what was most marvelous, || In the water which quenches all things, the fire burned hotter; For the world fights for the righteous. ¹⁸For at one time the flame lost its fierceness, || That it might not burn up the creatures sent against the ungodly, || But that these themselves as they looked might see || That they were chased through the judgment of God. ¹⁹At another time even in the midst of water it burns above the power of fire, || That it may destroy the produce of an unrighteous land. ²⁰Instead of these things, You gave Your people messengers' food to eat, || And You provided ready-to-eat bread for them from Heaven without toil, || Having the virtue of every pleasant flavor, || And agreeable to every taste. ²¹For Your nature showed Your sweetness toward Your children, || While that bread, serving the desire of the eater, changed itself according to every man's choice. ²²But snow and ice endured fire, and did not melt, || That people might know that fire was destroying the fruits of the enemies, || Burning in the hail and flashing in the rains; ²³And that this fire again, in order that righteous people may be nourished, || Has even forgotten its own power. ²⁴For the creation, ministering to You its Maker, || Strains its force against the unrighteous for punishment || And slackens it on behalf of those who trust in You, for kindness. ²⁵Therefore at that time also, converting itself into all forms, || It ministered to Your all-nourishing bounty, according to the desire of those who had need, ²⁶That Your sons, whom You loved, O LORD, || Might learn that it is not the growth of crops that nourishes a man, || But that Your word preserves those who trust You. ²⁷For that which was not marred by fire, || When it was simply warmed by a faint sunbeam melted away, ²⁸That it might be known that we must rise before the sun to give You thanks || And must plead with You at the dawning of the light; ²⁹For the hope of the unthankful will melt as the winter's hoarfrost || And will flow away as water that has no use.

CHAPTER 17

¹For Your judgments are great, and hard to interpret; Therefore, undisciplined souls went astray. ²For when lawless men had supposed that they held a holy nation in their power, || They, prisoners of darkness, and bound in the chains of a long night, || Kept close beneath their roofs, [and] lay exiled from the perpetual providence. ³For while they thought that they were unseen in [their] secret sins, || They were divided from one another by a dark curtain of forgetfulness, || Stricken with terrible awe, and very troubled by apparitions. ⁴For neither did the dark recesses that held them guard them from fears, || But terrifying sounds rang around them, || And dismal phantoms appeared with unsmiling faces. ⁵And no force of fire prevailed to give light, || Neither were the brightest flames of the stars strong enough to illuminate that gloomy night; ⁶But only the glimmering of a self-kindled fire appeared to them, full of fear. In terror, they considered the things which they saw || To be worse than that sight, on which they could not gaze. ⁷The mockeries of their magic arts were powerless now, || And a shameful rebuke of their boasted understanding: ⁸For those who promised to drive away terrors and disorders from a sick soul, || These were sick with a ludicrous fearfulness. ⁹For even if no troubling thing frightened them, || Yet, scared with the creeping of vermin and hissing of serpents, ¹⁰They perished trembling in fear, || Refusing even to look at the air, which could not be escaped on any side. ¹¹For wickedness, condemned by a witness within, is a cowardly thing, || And, being pressed hard by conscience, has always added forecasts of the worst. ¹²For fear is nothing else but a surrender of the help which reason offers; ¹³And from within, the expectation of being less || Makes of greater account the ignorance of the cause that brings the torment. ¹⁴But they, all through the night which was powerless indeed, || And which came on them out of the recesses of powerless Hades, || Sleeping the same sleep, ¹⁵Now were haunted by monstrous apparitions, || And now were paralyzed by their soul's surrendering; For sudden and unexpected fear came on them. ¹⁶So then, whoever it might be, sinking down in his place, || Was kept captive, shut up in that prison which was not barred with iron; ¹⁷For whether he was a farmer, or a shepherd, or a laborer whose toils were in the wilderness, || He was overtaken, and endured that inevitable necessity; For they were all bound with one chain of darkness. ¹⁸Whether there was a whistling wind, || Or a melodious sound of birds among the spreading branches, || Or a measured fall of water running violently, ¹⁹Or a harsh crashing of rocks hurled down, || Or the swift course of animals bounding along unseen, || Or the voice of wild beasts harshly roaring, || Or an echo rebounding from the hollows of the mountains, || All these things paralyzed them with terror. ²⁰For the whole world was illuminated with clear light, || And was occupied with unhindered works, ²¹While over them alone was spread a heavy night, || An image of the darkness that should afterward receive them; But to themselves, they were heavier than darkness.

CHAPTER 18

¹But there was great light for Your holy ones. Their enemies, hearing their voice but not seeing their form, || Counted it a happy thing that they too had suffered, ²Yet for that they do not hurt them, || Though wronged by them before, they are thankful; And because they had been at variance with them, they begged for pardon. ³Whereas You provided a burning pillar of fire to be a guide for Your people's unknown journey, || And a harmless sun for their glorious exile. ⁴For the Egyptians well deserved to be deprived of light and imprisoned by darkness, || They who had imprisoned Your children, through whom the incorruptible light of the Law was to be given to the race of men. ⁵After they had taken counsel to kill the babies of the holy ones, || And when a single child had been abandoned and saved to convict them of their sin, || You took their multitude of children away from them, || And destroyed all their army together in a mighty flood. ⁶Our fathers were made aware of that night beforehand, || That, having sure knowledge, they might be cheered by the oaths which they had trusted. ⁷Salvation of the righteous and destruction of the enemies was expected by Your people. ⁸For as You took vengeance on the adversaries, || By the same means, calling us to Yourself, You glorified us. ⁹For holy children of good men offered sacrifice in secret, || And with one consent they took on themselves the covenant of the Divine Law, || That they would partake alike in the same good things and the same perils, || The fathers already leading the sacred songs of praise. ¹⁰But the discordant cry of the enemies echoed back, || And a pitiful voice of lamentation for children was spread abroad. ¹¹Both servant and master were punished with the same just doom, || And the commoner suffering the same as king; ¹²Yes, they all together, under one form of death, had corpses without number. For the living were not even sufficient to bury them, || Since at a single stroke, their most cherished offspring was consumed. ¹³For while they were disbelieving all things by reason of the enchantments, || On the destruction of the firstborn they confessed the people to be God's son. ¹⁴For while peaceful silence wrapped all things, || And night in her own swiftness was in mid-course, ¹⁵Your all-powerful word leapt from Heaven out of the royal thrones—A stern warrior, into the midst of the doomed land, ¹⁶Bearing Your authentic command as a sharp sword; And standing, it filled all things with death, || And while it touched the heavens it stood on the earth. ¹⁷Then immediately apparitions in dreams troubled them terribly, || And unexpected fears came on them. ¹⁸And each—one thrown here half dead, another there—Made known why he was dying; ¹⁹For the dreams, disturbing them, forewarned them of this, || That they might not perish without knowing why they were afflicted. ²⁰But

WISDOM

experience of death also touched the righteous, || And a multitude were destroyed in the wilderness; However, the wrath did not last long. ²¹For a blameless man hurried to be their champion, || Bringing the weapon of his own ministry: Prayer and the atoning sacrifice of incense. He withstood the indignation, and set an end to the calamity, || Showing that he was your servant. ²²And he overcame the anger, || Not by strength of body, not by force of weapons, || But he subdued him who was punishing by word, || By bringing to remembrance oaths and covenants made with the fathers. ²³For when the dead had already fallen in heaps on one another, || Standing between, he stopped the wrath, || And cut off the way to the living. ²⁴For the whole world was on his long robe, || And the glories of the fathers were on the engraving of the four rows of precious stones, || And Your majesty was on the diadem of his head. ²⁵The destroyer yielded to these, and they feared; For it was enough only to test the wrath.

CHAPTER 19

¹But indignation without mercy came on the ungodly to the end; For God also foreknew their future, ²How, having changed their minds to let Your people go, || And having sped them eagerly on their way, || They would change their minds and pursue them. ³For while they were yet in the midst of their mourning, || And lamenting at the graves of the dead, || They drew on themselves another counsel of folly, || And pursued as fugitives those whom they had begged to leave and driven out. ⁴For the doom which they deserved was drawing them to this end, || And it made them forget the things that had happened to them, || That they might fill up the punishment which was yet lacking to their torments, ⁵And that Your people might journey on by a marvelous road, || But they themselves might find a strange death. ⁶For the whole creation, each part in its diverse kind, || Was made new again, complying with Your commands, || That Your servants might be kept unharmed. ⁷Then the cloud that overshadowed the camp was seen, || And dry land rising up out of what had been water, || Out of the Red Sea an unhindered highway, || And a grassy plain out of the violent surge, ⁸By which they passed over with all their army, || These who were covered with Your hand, having seen strange marvels. ⁹For like horses they roamed at large, || And they skipped about like lambs, || Praising You, O LORD, who was their deliverer. ¹⁰For they still remembered the things that happened in the time of their sojourning, || How instead of bearing cattle, the land brought out lice, || And instead of fish, the river spewed out a multitude of frogs. ¹¹But afterward, they also saw a new kind of birds, || When, led on by desire, they asked for luxurious delicacies; ¹²For, to comfort them, quails came up for them from the sea. ¹³Punishments came on the sinners, || Not without the signs that were given beforehand by the force of the thunders; For they justly suffered through their own wickedness, || For the hatred which they practiced toward guests was grievous indeed. ¹⁴For whereas the others did not receive the strangers when they came to them, || The Egyptians made slaves of guests who were their benefactors. ¹⁵And not only so, but God will visit the men of Sodom another way, || Since they received as enemies those who were aliens; ¹⁶Whereas these first welcomed with feastings, || And then afflicted with dreadful toils—Those who had already shared with them in the same rights. ¹⁷And moreover, they were stricken with loss of sight, || Even as were those others at the righteous man's doors, || When, being surrounded with yawning darkness, || They each looked for the passage through his own door. ¹⁸For as the notes of a lute vary the character of the rhythm, || Even so the elements—Changing their order with one another, continuing always in its sound, || As may clearly be conjectured from the sight of the things that have happened. ¹⁹For creatures of the dry land were turned into creatures of the waters, || And creatures that swim moved on the land. ²⁰Fire kept the mastery of its own power in water, || And water forgot its quenching nature. ²¹On the contrary, flames did not consume flesh of perishable creatures that walked among them, || Neither did they melt the ice-like grains of ambrosial food that were apt to melt. ²²For in all things, O LORD, You magnified Your people, || And You glorified them and did not lightly regard them, || Standing by their side in every time and place.

SIRACH

Otherwise known as Ecclesiasticus, the Wisdom of Ben Sira derives its title from the author, "Yeshua [Jesus], son of Eleazar, son of Sira" (50:27). This seems to be the earliest title of the book. The designation Liber Ecclesiasticus, meaning "Church Book," appended to some Greek and Latin manuscripts, is perhaps due to the extensive use the church made of this book in presenting moral teaching to catechumens and to the faithful. The author, a sage who lived in Jerusalem, was thoroughly imbued with love for the wisdom tradition, and also for the law, priesthood, Temple, and divine worship. Written in Hebrew in the early years of the 2nd century BC, the book was finished by approximately 175.

CHAPTER 1

¹All wisdom comes from the LORD and is with Him forever. ²Who can count the sand of the seas, || The drops of rain, and the days of [the] age? ³Who will search out the height of the sky, || The breadth of the earth, the deep, and wisdom? ⁴Wisdom has been created before all things, || And the understanding of prudence from perpetuity. ⁵… ⁶To whom has the root of wisdom been revealed? Who has known her shrewd counsels? ⁷… ⁸There is one wise, greatly to be feared, sitting on His throne: The LORD. ⁹He created her. He saw and measured her. He poured her out on all His works. ¹⁰She is with all flesh according to His gift. He gave her freely to those who love Him. ¹¹The fear of the LORD is glory, || Exultation, and gladness, and a crown of rejoicing. ¹²The fear of the LORD will delight the heart, || And will give gladness, joy, and length of days. ¹³Whoever fears the LORD, || It will go well with him at the end. He will be blessed in the day of his death. ¹⁴To fear the LORD is the beginning of wisdom. It was created together with the faithful in the womb. ¹⁵She laid a perpetual foundation with men. She will be trusted among their offspring. ¹⁶To fear the LORD is the fullness of wisdom. She inebriates men with her fruits. ¹⁷She will fill all her house with desirable things, || And her storehouses with her produce. ¹⁸The fear of the LORD is the crown of wisdom, || Making peace and perfect health to flourish. ¹⁹He both saw and measured her. He rained down skill and knowledge of understanding || And exalted the honor of those who hold her fast. ²⁰To fear the LORD is the root of wisdom. Her branches are length of days. ²¹… ²²Unjust wrath can never be justified, || For the sway of his wrath is his downfall. ²³A man that is patient will resist for a season, || And afterward gladness will spring up to him. ²⁴He will hide his words for a season, || And the lips of many will tell of his understanding. ²⁵An allegory of knowledge is in the treasures of wisdom; But godliness is an abomination to a sinner. ²⁶If you desire wisdom, keep the commands || And the LORD will give her to you freely; ²⁷For the fear of the LORD is wisdom and instruction. Faith and humility are His good pleasure. ²⁸Do not disobey the fear of the LORD. Do not come to Him with a double heart. ²⁹Do not be a hypocrite in the mouths of men. Keep watch over your lips. ³⁰Do not exalt yourself, || Lest you fall and bring dishonor on your soul. The LORD will reveal your secrets || And will cast you down in the midst of the

congregation, || Because you did not come to the fear of the LORD || And your heart was full of deceit.

CHAPTER 2

¹My son, if you come to serve the LORD, || Prepare your soul for temptation. ²Set your heart correctly, || Constantly endure, || And do not hurry in time of calamity. ³Cling to Him, and do not depart, || That you may be increased at your latter end. ⁴Accept whatever is brought on you || And be patient when you suffer humiliation. ⁵For gold is tried in the fire, || And acceptable men in the furnace of humiliation. ⁶Put your trust in Him, || And He will help you. Make your ways straight || And set your hope on Him. ⁷All you who fear the LORD, || Wait for His mercy. Do not turn aside, lest you fall. ⁸All you who fear the LORD, || Put your trust in Him, || And your reward will not fail. ⁹All you who fear the LORD, || Hope for good things, || And for continuous gladness and mercy. ¹⁰Look at the generations of old, and see: Who ever put his trust in the LORD, and was ashamed? Or who remained in His fear, and was forsaken? Or who called on Him, and He despised him? ¹¹For the LORD is full of compassion and mercy. He forgives sins and saves in time of affliction. ¹²Woe to fearful hearts, to faint hands, || And to the sinner that goes two ways! ¹³Woe to the faint heart! For it does not believe. Therefore, it will not be defended. ¹⁴Woe to you who have lost your patience! And what will you all do when the LORD visits you? ¹⁵Those who fear the LORD will not disobey His words. Those who love Him will keep His ways. ¹⁶Those who fear the LORD will seek His good pleasure. Those who love Him will be filled with the Law. ¹⁷Those who fear the LORD will prepare their hearts || And will humble their souls in His sight. ¹⁸We will fall into the hands of the LORD, || And not into the hands of men; For as His majesty is, so also is His mercy.

CHAPTER 3

¹Hear me, your father, O my children, || And do what you hear, that you all may be saved. ²For the LORD has given the father glory concerning the children || And has confirmed the judgment of the mother concerning the sons. ³He who honors his father will make atonement for sins. ⁴He that gives glory to his mother is as one who lays up treasure. ⁵Whoever honors his father will have joy in his own children. He will be heard in the day of his prayer. ⁶He who gives glory to his father will have length of days. He who listens to the LORD will bring rest to his mother, ⁷And will serve under his parents, as to masters. ⁸Honor your father in deed and word, || That a blessing may come on you from him. ⁹For the blessing of the father establishes the houses of children, || But the curse of the mother roots out the foundations. ¹⁰Do not glorify yourself in the dishonor of your father, || For your father's dishonor is no glory to you. ¹¹For the glory of a man is from the honor of his father, || And a mother in dishonor is a reproach to her children. ¹²My son, help your father in his old age, || And do not grieve him as long as he lives. ¹³If he fails in understanding, have patience with him. Do not dishonor him in your full strength. ¹⁴For the relieving of your father will not be forgotten. Instead of sins it will be added to build you up. ¹⁵In the day of your affliction it will remember you; As fair weather on ice, so will your sins also melt away. ¹⁶He who forsakes his father is as a blasphemer. He who provokes his mother is cursed by the LORD. ¹⁷My son, go on with your business in humility; So you will be loved by an acceptable man. ¹⁸The greater you are, humble yourself [all] the more, || And you will find favor before the LORD. ¹⁹... ²⁰For the power of the LORD is great, || And He is glorified by those who are lowly. ²¹Do not seek things that are too hard for you, || And do not search out things that are above your strength. ²²Think about the things that have been commanded you, || For you have no need of the things that are secret. ²³Do not be overly busy in your superfluous works, || For more things are showed to you than men can understand. ²⁴For the conceit of many has led them astray. Evil opinion has caused their judgment to slip. ²⁵There is no light without eyes. There is no wisdom without knowledge. ²⁶A stubborn heart will do badly at the end. He who loves danger will perish in it. ²⁷A stubborn heart will be burdened with troubles. The sinner will heap sin on sins. ²⁸The calamity of the proud is no healing, || For a weed of wickedness has taken root in him. ²⁹The heart of the prudent will understand an allegory. A wise man desires the ear of a listener. ³⁰Water will quench a flaming fire; Kindness will make atonement for sins. ³¹He who repays with kind acts is mindful of that which comes afterward. In the time of his falling, he will find a support.

CHAPTER 4

¹My son, do not deprive the poor of his living. Do not make the needy eyes wait long. ²Do not make a hungry soul sorrowful || Or provoke a man in his distress. ³Do not add more trouble to a heart that is provoked. Do not put off giving to him who is in need. ⁴Do not reject a suppliant in his affliction. Do not turn your face away from a poor man. ⁵Do not turn your eye away from one who asks. Give no occasion to a man to curse you. ⁶For if he curses you in the bitterness of his soul, || He who made him will hear his supplication. ⁷Endear yourself to the assembly. Bow your head to a great man. ⁸Incline your ear to a poor man. Answer him with peaceful words in humility. ⁹Deliver him who is wronged from the hand of him that wrongs him; Do not be faint-hearted in giving judgment. ¹⁰Be as a father to the fatherless, || And like a husband to their mother. So you will be as a son of the Most High, || And He will love you more than your mother does. ¹¹Wisdom exalts her sons || And takes hold of those who seek her. ¹²He who loves her loves life. Those who seek her early will be filled with gladness. ¹³He who holds her fast will inherit glory. Where he enters, the LORD will bless. ¹⁴Those who serve her minister to the Holy One. The LORD loves those who love her. ¹⁵He who gives ear to her will judge the nations. He who heeds her will dwell securely. ¹⁶If he trusts her, he will inherit her, || And his generations will possess her. ¹⁷For at the first she will walk with him in crooked ways, || And will bring fear and dread on him, || And torment him with her discipline, || Until she may trust his soul, and try him by her judgments. ¹⁸Then she will return him again to the straight way, || And will gladden him, and reveal to him her secrets. ¹⁹If he goes astray, she will forsake him, || And hand him over to his fall. ²⁰Observe the opportunity and beware of evil. Do not be ashamed of your soul. ²¹For there is a shame that brings sin, || And there is a shame that is glory and grace. ²²Do not show partiality against your soul. Do not revere any man to your falling. ²³Do not refrain from speaking when it is for safety. Do not hide your wisdom for the sake of seeming fair. ²⁴For wisdom will be known by speech, || And instruction by the word of the tongue. ²⁵Do not speak against the truth and be shamed for your ignorance. ²⁶Do not be ashamed to confess your sins. Do not fight the river's current. ²⁷Do not lay yourself down for a fool to tread on. Do not be partial to one that is mighty. ²⁸Strive for the truth to death, || And the LORD God will fight for you. ²⁹Do not be hasty with your tongue, || Or slack and negligent in your deeds. ³⁰Do not be like a lion in your house, || Or suspicious of your servants. ³¹Do not let your hand be stretched out to receive || And closed when you should repay.

CHAPTER 5

¹Do not set your heart on your goods. Do not say, "They are sufficient for me." ²Do not follow your own mind and your strength || To walk in the desires of your heart. ³Do not say, "Who will have dominion over me?" For the LORD will surely take vengeance on you. ⁴Do not say, "I sinned, and what happened to me?" For the LORD is patient. ⁵Do not be so confident of atonement that you add sin on sins. ⁶Do not say, "His compassion is great. He will be pacified for the multitude of my sins," || For mercy and wrath are with Him, || And His indignation will rest on sinners. ⁷Do not wait to turn to the LORD. Do not put off from day to day; For the wrath of the LORD will suddenly come on you, || And you will perish in the time of vengeance. ⁸Do not set your heart on unrighteous gains, || For you will profit nothing in the day of calamity. ⁹Do not winnow with every wind. Do not walk in every path. This is what the sinner who has a double tongue does. ¹⁰Be steadfast in your understanding. Let your speech be consistent. ¹¹Be swift to hear and answer with patience. ¹²If you have understanding, answer your neighbor; But if not, put your hand over your mouth. ¹³Glory and dishonor is in talk. A man's tongue may be his downfall. ¹⁴Do not be called a whisperer. Do not lie in wait with your tongue; For shame is on the thief, || And an evil condemnation is on him who has a double tongue. ¹⁵Do not be ignorant in a great or small matter.

SIRACH

CHAPTER 6

¹Do not become an enemy instead of a friend; For an evil name will inherit shame and reproach. So it is with the sinner who has a double tongue. ²Do not exalt yourself in the counsel of your soul, || That your soul is not torn in pieces as a bull. ³You will eat up your leaves, destroy your fruit, || And leave yourself as a dry tree. ⁴A wicked soul will destroy him who has it || And will make him a laughing-stock to his enemies. ⁵Sweet words will multiply a man's friends. A gracious tongue will multiply courtesies. ⁶Let those that are at peace with you be many, || But your advisers one of one thousand. ⁷If you want to gain a friend, get him in a time of testing, || And do not be in a hurry to trust him. ⁸For there is a friend just for an occasion. He will not continue in the day of your affliction. ⁹And there is a friend who turns into an enemy. He will discover strife to your reproach. ¹⁰And there is a friend who is a companion at the table, || But he will not continue in the day of your affliction. ¹¹In your prosperity he will be as yourself || And will be bold over your servants. ¹²If you are brought low, he will be against you, || And will hide himself from your face. ¹³Separate yourself from your enemies and beware of your friends. ¹⁴A faithful friend is a strong defense. He who has found him has found a treasure. ¹⁵There is nothing that can be taken in exchange for a faithful friend. His excellency is beyond price. ¹⁶A faithful friend is a life-saving medicine. Those who fear the LORD will find Him. ¹⁷He who fears the LORD directs his friendship properly; For as he is, so is his neighbor also. ¹⁸My son, gather instruction from your youth up. Even when you have gray hair you will find wisdom. ¹⁹Come to her as one who plows and sows || And wait for her good fruit; For your toil will be little in her tillage, || And you will soon eat of her fruit. ²⁰How exceedingly harsh she is to the unlearned! He who is without understanding will not remain in her. ²¹She will rest on him as a mighty stone of trial. He will not hesitate to cast her from him. ²²For wisdom is according to her name. She is not manifest to many. ²³Give ear, my son, and accept my judgment. Do not refuse my counsel. ²⁴Bring your feet into her chains, || And your neck into her chain. ²⁵Put your shoulder under her and bear her. Do not be grieved with her bonds. ²⁶Come to her with all your soul. Keep her ways with your whole power. ²⁷Search and seek, and she will be made known to you. When you get hold of her, do not let her go. ²⁸For at the end you will find her rest; And she will be turned into gladness for you. ²⁹Her chains will be to you for a covering of strength, || And her chains for a robe of glory. ³⁰For there is a golden ornament on her, || And her bonds [are] a purple ribbon. ³¹You will put her on as a robe of glory || And will put her on as a crown of rejoicing. ³²My son, if you are willing, you will be instructed. If you will yield your soul, you will be prudent. ³³If you love to hear, you will receive. If you incline your ear, you will be wise. ³⁴Stand in the multitude of the elders. Attach yourself to whoever is wise. ³⁵Be willing to listen to every godly discourse. Do not let the proverbs of understanding escape you. ³⁶If you see a man of understanding, get to him early. Let your foot wear out the steps of his doors. ³⁷Let your mind dwell on the ordinances of the LORD || And meditate continually on His commands. He will establish your heart || And your desire for wisdom will be given to you.

CHAPTER 7

¹Do no evil, so no evil will overtake you. ²Depart from wrong, and it will turn away from you. ³My son, do not sow on the furrows of unrighteousness, || And you will not reap them sevenfold. ⁴Do not seek preeminence from the LORD, || Nor the seat of honor from the king. ⁵Do not justify yourself in the presence of the LORD, || And do not display your wisdom before the king. ⁶Do not seek to be a judge, || Lest you not be able to take away iniquities, || Lest perhaps you fear the person of a mighty man || And lay a stumbling block in the way of your uprightness. ⁷Do not sin against the multitude of the city. Do not cast yourself down in the crowd. ⁸Do not commit a sin twice, || For even in one you will not be unpunished. ⁹Do not say, "He will look on the multitude of my gifts. When I make an offering to the Most High God, He will accept it." ¹⁰Do not be faint-hearted in your prayer. Do not neglect to give alms. ¹¹Do not laugh a man to scorn when he is in the bitterness of his soul, || For there is one who humbles and exalts. ¹²Do not devise a lie against your brother or do the same to a friend. ¹³Do not love to make any manner of lie, for that is not a good habit. ¹⁴Do not babble in the multitude of elders. Do not repeat your words in your prayer. ¹⁵Do not hate hard labor or farm work, which the Most High has created. ¹⁶Do not number yourself among the multitude of sinners. Remember that wrath will not wait. ¹⁷Humble your soul greatly, || For the punishment of the ungodly man is fire and the worm. ¹⁸Do not exchange a friend for something, || Neither a true brother for the gold of Ophir. ¹⁹Do not deprive yourself of a wise and good wife, || For her grace is worth more than gold. ²⁰Do not abuse a servant who works faithfully, || Or a hireling who gives you his life. ²¹Let your soul love a wise servant. Do not defraud him of liberty. ²²Do you have cattle? Look after them. If they are profitable to you, let them stay by you. ²³Do you have children? Correct them and bow their necks from their youth. ²⁴Do you have daughters? Take care of their bodies, || And do not be overly indulgent toward them. ²⁵Give your daughter in marriage, || And you will have accomplished a great matter. Give her to a man of understanding. ²⁶Do you have a wife after your mind? Do not cast her out. But do not entrust yourself to one who is hateful. ²⁷Give glory to your father with your whole heart, || And do not forget the birth pangs of your mother. ²⁸Remember that you were born of them. What will you repay them for the things that they have done for you? ²⁹Fear the LORD with all your soul; Also revere His priests. ³⁰With all your strength love Him who made you. Do not forsake His ministers. ³¹Fear the LORD and honor the priest. Give him his portion, even as it is commanded you: The first-fruits, the trespass offering, the gift of the shoulders, || The sacrifice of sanctification, and the first-fruits of holy things. ³²Also stretch out your hand to the poor man, || That your blessing may be perfected. ³³A gift has grace in the sight of every living man. Do not withhold grace for a dead man. ³⁴Do not be lacking to those who weep, || And mourn with those who mourn. ³⁵Do not be slow to visit a sick man, || For by such things you will gain love. ³⁶In all your words, remember eternity, || And you will never sin.

CHAPTER 8

¹Do not contend with a mighty man, lest perhaps you fall into his hands. ²Do not strive with a rich man, lest perhaps he overpowers you; For gold has destroyed many and turned away the hearts of kings. ³Do not contend with a talkative man. Do not heap wood on his fire. ⁴Do not jest with a rude man, lest your ancestors be dishonored. ⁵Do not reproach a man when he turns from sin. Remember that we are all worthy of punishment. ⁶Do not dishonor a man in his old age; For some of us are also growing old. ⁷Do not rejoice over one who is dead. Remember that we all die. ⁸Do not neglect the discourse of the wise. Be conversant with their proverbs; For from them you will learn instruction || And how to minister to great men. ⁹Do not miss the discourse of the aged, || For they also learned from their fathers, || Because from them you will learn understanding, || And [how] to give an answer in time of need. ¹⁰Do not kindle the coals of a sinner, || Lest you be burned with the flame of his fire. ¹¹Do not rise up from the presence of an insolent man, || Lest he lie in wait as an ambush for your mouth. ¹²Do not lend to a man who is mightier than yourself; And if you lend, be as one who has lost. ¹³Do not be a guarantee above your power. If you are a guarantee, think as one who will have to pay. ¹⁴Do not go to law with a judge; For according to his honor they will give judgment for him. ¹⁵Do not go in the way with a rash man, || Lest he be burdensome to you; For he will do according to his own will, || And you will perish with his folly. ¹⁶Do not fight with a wrathful man. Do not travel with him through the desert, || For blood is as nothing in his sight. Where there is no help, he will overthrow you. ¹⁷Do not take counsel with a fool, || For he will not be able to conceal the matter. ¹⁸Do no secret thing before a stranger, || For you do not know what it will cause. ¹⁹Do not open your heart to every man. Do not let him return you a favor.

CHAPTER 9

¹Do not be jealous over the wife of your bosom, || And do not teach her an evil lesson against yourself. ²Do not give your soul to a woman, || That she should set her foot on your strength. ³Do not go to meet a woman who plays the prostitute, || Lest perhaps you fall into her snares. ⁴Do not use the company of a

woman who is a singer, || Lest perhaps you be caught by her attempts. ⁵Do not gaze at a maid, || Lest perhaps you be trapped in her penalties. ⁶Do not give your soul to prostitutes, || That you may not lose your inheritance. ⁷Do not look around you in the streets of the city, || Neither wander in its solitary places. ⁸Turn your eye away from a beautiful woman, || And do not gaze at another's beauty. Many have been led astray by the beauty of a woman; And with this, affection is kindled as a fire. ⁹Do not sit at all with a woman who has a husband, || Or revel with her at the wine, || Lest perhaps your soul turns away to her, || And with your spirit you slide into destruction. ¹⁰Do not forsake an old friend; For the new is not comparable to him. A new friend is like new wine: If it becomes old, you will drink it with gladness. ¹¹Do not envy the glory of a sinner; For you do not know what his overthrow will be. ¹²Do not delight in the delights of the ungodly. Remember, they will not go to the grave unpunished. ¹³Keep yourself far from the man who has power to kill, || And you will have no suspicion of the fear of death. If you come to him, commit no fault, || Lest he takes your life away. Surely know that you go about in the midst of snares || And walk on the battlements of a city. ¹⁴As well as you can, aim to know your neighbors, || And take counsel with the wise. ¹⁵Let your conversation be with men of understanding. Let all your discourse be in the Law of the Most High. ¹⁶Let just men be companions at your table. Let your glorying be in the fear of the LORD. ¹⁷A work is commended because of the hand of the artisan; So he who rules the people will be considered wise for his speech. ¹⁸A talkative man is dangerous in his city. He who is headlong in his speech will be hated.

CHAPTER 10

¹A wise judge will instruct his people. The government of a man of understanding will be well ordered. ²As is the judge of his people, || So are his ministers. As the city's ruler is, || So are all those who dwell in it. ³An uninstructed king will destroy his people. A city will be established through the understanding of the powerful. ⁴The authority of the earth is in the LORD's hand. In due time, He will raise up over it one who is profitable. ⁵A man's prosperity is in the LORD's hand. He will lay his honor on the person of the scribe. ⁶Do not be angry with your neighbor for every wrong. Do nothing by works of violence. ⁷Pride is hateful before the LORD and men. Unrighteousness is abhorrent in the judgment of both. ⁸Sovereignty is transferred from nation to nation || Because of iniquities, deeds of violence, and greed for money. ⁹Why are dirt and ashes proud? Because in life, my body decays. ¹⁰A long disease mocks the physician. He is a king today, and tomorrow he will die. ¹¹For when a man is dead, || He will inherit creeping things, and beasts, and worms. ¹²It is the beginning of pride when a man departs from the LORD. His heart has departed from Him who made him. ¹³For the beginning of pride is sin. He who keeps it will pour out abomination. For this reason, the LORD brought strange calamities on them || And utterly overthrew them. ¹⁴The LORD cast down the thrones of rulers || And set the meek in their place. ¹⁵The LORD plucked up the roots of nations || And planted the lowly in their place. ¹⁶The LORD overthrew the lands of nations || And destroyed them to the foundations of the earth. ¹⁷He took some of them away || And destroyed them and made their memorial to cease from the earth. ¹⁸Pride has not been created for men, || Nor wrathful anger for the offspring of women. ¹⁹What manner of seed has honor? The seed of man, those who fear the LORD. What manner of seed has no honor? The seed of man, those who transgress the commands. ²⁰In the midst of countrymen he who rules them has honor. Those who fear the LORD have honor in his eyes. ²¹… ²²The rich man, the honorable, and the poor || All glory in the fear of the LORD. ²³It is not right to dishonor a poor man who has understanding. It is not fitting to glorify a man who is a sinner. ²⁴The great man, the judge, and the mighty man will be glorified. There is not one of them greater than he who fears the LORD. ²⁵Free men will minister to a wise servant. A man who has knowledge will not complain. ²⁶Do not flaunt your wisdom in doing your work. Do not glorify yourself in the time of your distress. ²⁷Better is he who labors and abounds in all things, || Than he who glorifies himself and lacks bread. ²⁸My son, glorify your soul in humility, || And esteem yourself honor according to your true worth. ²⁹Who will justify him who sins against his own soul? Who will glorify him who dishonors his own life? ³⁰A poor man is glorified for his knowledge. A rich man is glorified for his riches. ³¹But he who is glorified in poverty, how much more in riches? He who is dishonored in riches, how much more in poverty?

CHAPTER 11

¹The wisdom of the lowly will lift up his head || And make him sit in the midst of great men. ²Do not commend a man for his beauty. Do not abhor a man for his outward appearance. ³The bee is little among flying creatures, || But what it produces is the best of confections. ⁴Do not boast about the clothes you wear, || And do not exalt yourself in the day of honor; For the LORD's works are wonderful, || And His works are hidden among men. ⁵Many kings have sat down on the ground, || But one who was never thought of has worn a crown. ⁶Many mighty men have been greatly disgraced. Men of renown have been delivered into other men's hands. ⁷Do not blame before you investigate. Understand first, and then rebuke. ⁸Do not answer before you have heard. Do not interrupt while someone else is speaking. ⁹Do not argue about a matter that does not concern you. Do not sit with sinners when they judge. ¹⁰My son, do not be busy about many matters; For if you meddle much, || You will not be unpunished. If you pursue, you will not overtake, || And you will not escape by fleeing. ¹¹There is one who toils, labors, and makes haste, || And is even more behind. ¹²There is one who is sluggish, and needs help, lacking in strength, and who abounds in poverty, || But the LORD's eyes looked on him for good, || And He raised him up from his low condition, ¹³And lifted up his head so that many marveled at him. ¹⁴Good things and evil, life and death, || Poverty and riches, are from the LORD. ¹⁵… ¹⁶… ¹⁷The LORD's gift remains with the godly. His good pleasure will prosper forever. ¹⁸One grows rich by his diligence and self-denial, || And this is the portion of his reward: ¹⁹When he says, "I have found rest, and now I will eat of my goods!" He does not know how much time will pass || Until he leaves them to others and dies. ²⁰Be steadfast in your covenant || And be doing it and grow old in your work. ²¹Do not marvel at the works of a sinner, || But trust the LORD and stay in your labor; For it is an easy thing in the sight of the LORD || To swiftly and suddenly make a poor man rich. ²²The LORD's blessing is in the reward of the godly. He makes his blessing flourish in an hour that comes swiftly. ²³Do not say, "What use is there of me? What further good things can be mine?" ²⁴Do not say, "I have enough. What harm could happen to me now?" ²⁵In the day of good things, || Evil things are forgotten. In the day of evil things, || A man will not remember things that are good. ²⁶For it is an easy thing in the sight of the LORD || To reward a man in the day of death according to his ways. ²⁷The affliction of an hour causes delights to be forgotten. In the end, a man's deeds are revealed. ²⁸Call no man happy before his death. A man will be known in his children. ²⁹Do not bring every man into your house, || For many are the plots of a deceitful man. ³⁰Like a decoy partridge in a cage, || So is the heart of a proud man. Like a spy, he looks for your weakness. Like a spy, he lies in wait to turn things that are good into evil || And assigns blame in things that are praiseworthy. ³²From a spark of fire, a heap of many coals is kindled, || And a sinful man lies in wait for blood. ³³Take heed of an evildoer, for he plans wicked things, || Lest perhaps he ruins your reputation forever. ³⁴Receive a stranger into your house, || And he will distract you with arguments and estrange you from your own.

CHAPTER 12

¹If you do good, know to whom you do it, || And your good deeds will have thanks. ²Do good to a godly man, and you will find a reward—If not from him, then from the Most High. ³No good will come to him who continues to do evil, || Nor to him who gives no alms. ⁴Give to the godly man, || And do not help the sinner. ⁵Do good to one who is lowly. Do not give to an ungodly man. Keep back his bread, and do not give it to him, || Lest he subdue you with it; For you would receive twice as much evil || For all the good you would have done to him. ⁶For the Most High also hates sinners || And will repay vengeance to the ungodly. ⁷Give to the good man, and do not help the sinner. ⁸A man's friend will not be fully tried in prosperity. His enemy will not be hidden in adversity. ⁹In a man's prosperity, his

enemies are grieved. In his adversity, even his friend leaves. ¹⁰Never trust your enemy, || For his wickedness is like corrosion in copper. ¹¹Though he humbles himself and walks bowed down, || Still be careful and beware of him. You will be to him as one who has wiped a mirror, || To be sure it does not completely tarnish. ¹²Do not set him next to you, || Lest he overthrow you and stand in your place. Do not let him sit on your right hand, || Lest he seek to take your seat, || And at the last you acknowledge my words, || And be pricked with my sayings. ¹³Who will pity a charmer that is bitten by a snake, || Or any who come near wild beasts? ¹⁴Even so, who will pity him who goes to a sinner, || And is associated with him in his sins? ¹⁵For a while he will stay with you, || And if you falter, he will not stay. ¹⁶The enemy will speak sweetly with his lips, || And in his heart plan to throw you into a pit. The enemy may weep with his eyes, || But if he finds opportunity, he will want more blood. ¹⁷If adversity meets you, || You will find him there before you. Pretending to help you, he will trip you. ¹⁸He will shake his head, clap his hands, || Whisper much, and change his countenance.

CHAPTER 13

¹He who touches pitch will be defiled. He who has fellowship with a proud man will become like him. ²Do not take up a burden above your strength. Have no fellowship with one who is mightier and richer than yourself. What fellowship would the earthen pot have with the kettle? The kettle will strike, || And the pot will be dashed in pieces. ³The rich man does a wrong and threatens. The poor is wronged and apologizes. ⁴If you are profitable, || He will make merchandise of you. If you are in lack, || He will forsake you. ⁵If you own something, || He will live with you. He will drain you bare and will not be sorry. ⁶Does he need you? Then he will deceive you, || Smile at you, and give you hope. He will speak kindly to you and say, "What do you need?" ⁷He will shame you by his meats || Until he has made you bare twice or three times, || And in the end he will laugh you to scorn. Afterward he will see you, || Will forsake you, and shake his head at you. ⁸Beware that you are not deceived || And brought low in your mirth. ⁹If a mighty man invites you, be reserved, || And he will invite you more. ¹⁰Do not press him, lest you be thrust back. Do not stand far off, lest you be forgotten. ¹¹Do not try to speak with him as an equal, || And do not believe his many words; For he will test you with much talk || And will examine you in a smiling manner. ¹²He who does not keep secrets to himself is unmerciful. He will not hesitate to harm and to bind. ¹³Keep them to yourself and be careful, || For you walk in danger of falling. ¹⁴... ¹⁵Every living creature loves its own kind, || And every man loves his neighbor. ¹⁶All flesh associates with their own kind. A man will stick to people like himself. ¹⁷What fellowship would the wolf have with the lamb? So is the sinner to the godly. ¹⁸What peace is there between a hyena and a dog? What peace is there between a rich man and the poor? ¹⁹Wild donkeys are the prey of lions in the wilderness; Likewise, poor men are feeding grounds for the rich. ²⁰Lowliness is an abomination to a proud man; Likewise, a poor man is an abomination to the rich. ²¹When a rich man is shaken, || He is supported by his friends, || But when one of low degree is down, || He is pushed away even by his friends. ²²When a rich man falls, there are many helpers. He speaks things not to be spoken, || And men justify him. A man of low degree falls, and men rebuke him. He utters wisdom and is not listened to. ²³A rich man speaks, and all keep silence. They extol what he says to the clouds. A poor man speaks, and they say, "Who is this?" If he stumbles, they will help to overthrow him. ²⁴Riches are good if they have no sin. Poverty is evil in the mouth of the ungodly. ²⁵The heart of a man changes his countenance, || Whether it is for good or for evil. ²⁶A cheerful countenance is a sign of a prosperous heart. Devising proverbs takes strenuous thinking.

CHAPTER 14

¹Blessed is the man who has not slipped with his mouth || And does not suffer from sorrow for sins. ²Blessed is he whose soul does not condemn him, || And who has not given up hope. ³Riches are not appropriate for a stingy person. What would an envious man do with money? ⁴He who gathers by denying himself gathers for others. Others will revel in his goods. ⁵If one is mean to himself, || To whom will he be good? He will not enjoy his possessions. ⁶There is none more evil than he who is stingy with himself. This is a punishment for his wickedness. ⁷Even if he does good, he does it in forgetfulness. In the end, he reveals his wickedness. ⁸A miser is evil. He turns away and disregards souls. ⁹A covetous man's eye is not satisfied with his portion. Wicked injustice dries up his soul. ¹⁰A miser begrudges bread, || And it is lacking at his table. ¹¹My son, according to what you have, treat yourself well, || And bring worthy offerings to the LORD. ¹²Remember that death will not wait, || And that the covenant of Hades has not been shown to you. ¹³Do good to your friend before you die. According to your ability, reach out and give to him. ¹⁴Do not defraud yourself of a good day. Do not let the portion of a good desire pass you by. ¹⁵Will you not leave your labors to another, || And your toils be divided by lot? ¹⁶Give, take, and treat yourself well, || Because there is no seeking of luxury in Hades. ¹⁷All flesh grows old like a garment, || For the covenant from the beginning is, "You must die." ¹⁸Like the leaves flourishing on a thick tree—Some it sheds, and some grow—So also are the generations of flesh and blood: One comes to an end and another is born. ¹⁹Every work rots and falls away, || And its builder will depart with it. ²⁰Blessed is the man who meditates on wisdom, || And who reasons by his understanding. ²¹He who considers her ways in his heart || Will also have knowledge of her secrets. ²²Go after her like one who tracks || And lie in wait in her ways. ²³He who pries in at her windows || Will also listen at her doors. ²⁴He who lodges close to her house || Will also fasten a nail in her walls. ²⁵He will pitch his tent near at hand to her || And will lodge in a lodging where good things are. ²⁶He will set his children under her shelter || And will rest under her branches. ²⁷By her he will be covered from heat || And will lodge in her glory.

CHAPTER 15

¹He who fears the LORD will do this. He who has possession of the Law will obtain her. ²As a mother, she will meet him || And receive him as a wife married in her virginity. ³She will feed him with bread of understanding || And give him water of wisdom to drink. ⁴He will be stayed on her and will not be moved. He will rely on her and will not be confounded. ⁵She will exalt him above his neighbors. She will open his mouth in the midst of the congregation. ⁶He will inherit joy, a crown of gladness, and a perpetual name. ⁷Foolish men will not obtain her. Sinners will not see her. ⁸She is far from pride. Liars will not remember her. ⁹Praise is not attractive in the mouth of a sinner; For it was not sent to him from the LORD. ¹⁰For praise will be spoken in wisdom; The LORD will prosper it. ¹¹Do not say, "It is through the LORD that I fell away"; For you will not do the things that He hates. ¹²Do not say, "It is He that caused me to err"; For He has no need of a sinful man. ¹³The LORD hates every abomination; And those who fear Him do not love them. ¹⁴He Himself made man from the beginning || And left him in the hand of his own counsel. ¹⁵If you will, you will keep the commands. To be faithful is good pleasure. ¹⁶He has set fire and water before you. You will stretch out your hand to whichever you desire. ¹⁷Before man is life and death. Whichever he likes, it will be given to him. ¹⁸For great is the wisdom of the LORD. He is mighty in power and sees all things. ¹⁹His eyes are on those who fear Him. He knows every work of man. ²⁰He has not commanded any man to be ungodly. He has not given any man license to sin.

CHAPTER 16

¹Do not desire a multitude of unprofitable children, || Neither delight in ungodly sons. ²If they multiply, do not delight in them || Unless the fear of the LORD is in them. ³Do not trust in their life. Do not rely on their condition. For one is better than one thousand, || And to die childless than to have ungodly children. ⁴For from one who has understanding, a city will be populated, || But a race of wicked men will be made desolate. ⁵I have seen many such things with my eyes. My ear has heard mightier things than these. ⁶In the congregation of sinners, a fire will be kindled. In a disobedient nation, wrath is kindled. ⁷He was not pacified toward the giants of ancient time, || Who revolted in their strength. ⁸He did not spare Lot's neighbors, || Whom He abhorred for their pride. ⁹He did not pity the people of perdition || Who were taken away in their sins, ¹⁰Or in like manner, the six hundred

thousand footmen || Who were gathered together in the hardness of their hearts. ¹¹Even if there is one stiff-necked person, || It is a marvel if he will be unpunished, || For mercy and wrath are both with Him who is mighty to forgive, || And He pours out wrath. ¹²As His mercy is great, || So is His correction also. He judges a man according to his works. ¹³The sinner will not escape with plunder. The perseverance of the godly will not be frustrated. ¹⁴He will make room for every work of mercy. Each man will receive according to his works. ¹⁵The LORD made the king of Egypt so stubborn || That he would not acknowledge the LORD, || In order that the world might know the LORD's works. ¹⁶He shows His mercy to all creation; He has divided His light from darkness with a plumb line. ¹⁷Do not say, "I will be hidden from the LORD," || And "Who will remember me from on high?" I will not be known among so many people, || For what is my soul in a boundless creation? ¹⁸Behold, the Heaven—the Heaven of heavens—The deep, and the earth, will be moved when He visits. ¹⁹The mountains and the foundations of the earth together || Are shaken with trembling when He looks at them. ²⁰No heart will think about these things. Who could comprehend His ways? ²¹Like a tempest which no man can see, || Yes, the majority of His works are hidden. ²²Who will declare His works of righteousness? Who will endure them? For His covenant is far off. ²³He who is lacking in understanding thinks about these things. An unwise and erring man thinks follies. ²⁴My son, listen to me, learn knowledge, || And heed my words with your heart. ²⁵I will impart instruction with precision || And declare knowledge exactly. ²⁶In the judgment of the LORD are His works from the beginning. From the making of them He determined their parts. ²⁷He arranged His works for all time, || And their beginnings to their generations. They are not hungry or weary, || And they do not cease from their works. ²⁸No one thrusts aside his neighbor. They will never disobey His word. ²⁹After this the LORD also looked at the earth || And filled it with His blessings. ³⁰All manner of living things covered its face, || And into it is their return.

CHAPTER 17

¹The LORD created mankind out of the earth || And turned them back to it again. ²He gave them days by number, and a set time, || And gave them authority over the things that are on it. ³He endowed them with strength appropriate for them || And made them according to His own image. ⁴He put the fear of man on all flesh || And gave him dominion over beasts and birds. ⁵The LORD gave them the five senses, || But He also gave them a sixth—intelligence, || And a seventh—reason, || Which enables them to interpret what comes to them through the senses. ⁶He gave them counsel, tongue, eyes, ears, || And heart to have understanding. ⁷He filled them with the knowledge of wisdom || And showed them good and evil. ⁸He set His eye on their hearts, || To show them the majesty of His works. ⁹And He allowed them to take pride forever in His marvelous deeds. ¹⁰And they will praise the Name of His holiness, || That they may declare the majesty of His works. ¹¹He added to them knowledge || And gave them a law of life for a heritage. ¹²He made a perpetual covenant with them || And showed them His judgments. ¹³Their eyes saw the majesty of His glory. Their ears heard the glory of His voice. ¹⁴He said to them, "Beware of all unrighteousness." So He gave them command—Each man concerning his neighbor. ¹⁵Their ways are ever before Him. They will not be hidden from His eyes. ¹⁶From childhood on they tend to be evil; Their heart is like stone, || And they do not seem to be able to make it more human. ¹⁷He divided the nations of the whole earth. For every nation He appointed a ruler, || But Israel is the LORD's portion. ¹⁸Israel is His firstborn, || Whom He disciplines as He brings him up. He gives him the light of His love and never neglects him. ¹⁹All their works are as clear as the sun before Him. His eyes are continually on their ways. ²⁰Their iniquities are not hidden from Him. All their sins are before the LORD. ²¹But the LORD is gracious and knows His creatures; So He has spared them rather than abandon them. ²²With Him the kindness of a man is as a signet. He will keep the bounty of a man as the apple of the eye. ²³Afterward He will rise up, and repay them, || And render their repayment on their head. ²⁴However, to those who convert He grants a return. He comforts those who are losing patience. ²⁵Return to the LORD and forsake sins. Make your prayer before His face offend less. ²⁶Turn to the Most High again || And turn away from iniquity. Greatly hate the abominable thing. ²⁷Who will give praise to the Most High in Hades, || In place of those who live and return thanks? ²⁸Thanksgiving perishes from the dead, || As from one who does not exist. He who is in life and health will praise the LORD. ²⁹How great is the mercy of the LORD, || And His forgiveness to those who turn to Him! ³⁰For all things cannot be in men, || Because the son of man is not immortal. ³¹What is brighter than the sun? Yet even this fails. An evil man thinks about flesh and blood. ³²He looks on the power of the height of Heaven, || While all men are earth and ashes.

CHAPTER 18

¹He who lives forever created all things in common. ²The LORD alone will be justified || And there is no other besides Him. ³He guides the world with His hand, || And everything obeys Him. He is the King of all things, || And His power separates what is holy from what is not. ⁴He has given power to declare His works to no one. Who could trace out His mighty deeds? ⁵Who could measure the strength of His majesty? Who could also proclaim His mercies? ⁶As for the wondrous works of the LORD, || It is not possible to take from them nor add to them, || Neither is it possible to explore them. ⁷When a man has finished, || Then he is just at the beginning. When he ceases, || Then he will be in perplexity. ⁸What is mankind, and what purpose do they serve? What is their good, and what is their evil? ⁹The number of man's days at the most are one hundred years. ¹⁰As a drop of water from the sea, and a pebble from the sand, || So are a few years in the day [[or time]] of [the] age. ¹¹For this reason the LORD was patient over them || And poured out His mercy on them. ¹²He saw and perceived their end, || That it is evil. Therefore, He multiplied His forgiveness. ¹³The mercy of a man is on his neighbor; But the mercy of the LORD is on all flesh: Reproving, disciplining, teaching, and bringing back, || As a shepherd does his flock. ¹⁴He has mercy on those who accept disciplining, || And that diligently seek after His judgments. ¹⁵My son, add no blemish to your good deeds, || And no grief of words in any of your giving. ¹⁶Does the dew not relieve the scorching heat? So a word is better than a gift. ¹⁷Behold, is a word not better than a gift? Both are with a gracious man. ¹⁸A fool is ungracious and abusive. The gift of an envious man consumes the eyes. ¹⁹Learn before you speak. Take care of your health before you are sick. ²⁰Before judgment examine yourself, || And in the hour of visitation you will find forgiveness. ²¹Humble yourself before you become sick. In the time of sins, show conversion. ²²Let nothing hinder you to pay your vow in due time. Do not wait until death to be justified. ²³Before you make a vow, prepare yourself. Do not be like a man who tempts the LORD. ²⁴Think about the wrath coming in the days of the end, || And the time of vengeance, when He turns away His face. ²⁵In the days of fullness remember the time of hunger. Remember poverty and lack in the days of wealth. ²⁶From morning until evening, the time changes. All things are speedy before the LORD. ²⁷A wise man is cautious in everything. In days of sinning, he will beware of offense. ²⁸Every man of understanding knows wisdom. He will give thanks to him who found her. ²⁹They who were of understanding in sayings || Also became wise themselves and poured out apt proverbs. ³⁰Do not go after your lusts. Refrain yourself from your appetites. ³¹If you give fully to your soul the delight of her desire, || She will make you the laughing-stock of your enemies. ³²Do not make merry in much luxury, || Neither be tied to the expense thereof. ³³Do not be made a beggar by banqueting on borrowing || When you have nothing in your purse.

CHAPTER 19

¹A workman who is a drunkard will not become rich. He who despises small things will fall little by little. ²Wine and women will make men of understanding fall away. And he who joins with prostitutes will be more reckless. ³Moths and worms will have him as their heritage. A reckless soul will be taken away. ⁴He who is hasty to trust is shallow-minded. He who sins will offend against his own soul. ⁵He who makes merry in his heart will be condemned: ⁶He who hates talk has less wickedness. ⁷Never repeat what is told you, || And you will not be lacking. ⁸Whether it is of friend or enemy, do not tell it. Unless it is

a sin to you, do not reveal it. ⁹For he has heard you and observed you, || And when the time comes, he will hate you. ¹⁰Have you heard a word? Let it die with you. Be of good courage: it will not burst you. ¹¹A fool will travail in pain with a word, || As a woman in labor with a child. ¹²As an arrow that sticks in the flesh of the thigh, || So is a word in a fool's belly. ¹³Reprove a friend: It may be [that] he did not do it. If he did something, || It may be [that] he may not do it again. ¹⁴Reprove your neighbor: It may be [that] he did not say it. If he has said it, || It may be [that] he may not say it again. ¹⁵Reprove a friend: For many times there is slander. Do not trust every word. ¹⁶There is one who slips, and not from the heart. Who is he who has not sinned with his tongue? ¹⁷Reprove your neighbor before you threaten him; And give place to the Law of the Most High; And do not be angry. ¹⁸Fearing the LORD is the first step toward His accepting you; He will love you if you are wise. ¹⁹Learn the LORD's commands. It is a discipline that gives life. Those who do what pleases Him || Enjoy the fruit of the tree of immortality. ²⁰All wisdom is the fear of the LORD. In all wisdom is the doing of the Law || And what the knowledge of His omnipotence means. ²¹If a servant refuses to obey his master, but later does obey, || The master is still angry. ²²The knowledge of wickedness is not wisdom. The prudence of sinners is not counsel. ²³There is a wickedness, and it is abomination. There is a fool lacking in wisdom. ²⁴Better is one who has small understanding, and fears, || Than one who has much prudence, and transgresses the Law. ²⁵There is an exquisite subtlety, and it is unjust. And there is one who perverts favor to gain a judgment. ²⁶There is one who does wickedly, || Who hangs down his head with mourning, || But inwardly he is full of deceit, ²⁷Bowing his face down, || And making [it seem] as if he were deaf of one ear. Where he is not known, || He will be beforehand with you. ²⁸And if for lack of power he is hindered from sinning, || If he finds opportunity, he will do mischief. ²⁹A man will be known by his look; One who has understanding will be known by his face when you meet him. ³⁰A man's attire, grinning laughter, || And gait show what he is.

CHAPTER 20

¹There is a reproof that is not timely; And there is a man who keeps silent and is wise. ²How good it is to reprove, rather than to be angry. He who confesses will be kept back from hurt. ³Admit when you are wrong, || And you will avoid embarrassment. ⁴As is the lust of a eunuch to deflower a virgin, || So is he who executes judgments with violence. ⁵There is one who keeps silent and is found wise; And there is one who is hated for his much talk. ⁶There is one who keeps silent, || For he has no answer to make; And there is one who keeps silent, as knowing his time. ⁷A wise man will be silent until his time has come, || But the braggart and fool will miss his time. ⁸He who uses many words will be abhorred. He who takes authority for himself will be hated in it. ⁹There is a prosperity that a man finds in misfortunes; And there is a gain that turns to loss. ¹⁰There is a gift that will not profit you; And there is a gift [that] pays back double. ¹¹There is an abasement because of glory; And there is one who has lifted up his head from a low estate. ¹²There is one who buys much for a little and pays for it again sevenfold. ¹³He who is wise in words will make himself beloved; But the pleasantries of fools will be wasted. ¹⁴The gift of a fool will not profit you; For his eyes are many instead of one. ¹⁵He will give little and insult much. He will open his mouth like a crier. Today he will lend, || And tomorrow he will ask for it back. Such a one is a hateful man. ¹⁶The fool will say, "I have no friend, || And I have no thanks for my good deeds. They who eat my bread are of evil tongue." ¹⁷How often, and of how many, will he be laughed to scorn! ¹⁸A slip on a pavement is better than a slip with the tongue. So the fall of the wicked will come speedily. ¹⁹A man without grace is a tale out of season. It will be continually in the mouth of the ignorant. ²⁰An allegory from a fool's mouth will be rejected; For he will not speak it in its season. ²¹There is one who is hindered from sinning through lack. When he rests, he will not be troubled. ²²There is one who destroys his soul through bashfulness. By a foolish countenance, he will destroy it. ²³There is one who for bashfulness makes promises to his friend; And he makes him his enemy for nothing. ²⁴A lie is a foul blot in a man. It will be continually in the mouth of the ignorant. ²⁵A thief is better than a man who is continually lying, || But they will both inherit destruction. ²⁶The disposition of a liar is dishonor. His shame is with him continually. ²⁷He who is wise in words will advance himself. And one who is prudent will please great men. ²⁸He who tills his land will raise his heap high. He who pleases great men will get pardon for iniquity. ²⁹Presents and gifts blind the eyes of the wise, || And as a muzzle on the mouth, turn away reproofs. ³⁰Wisdom that is hidden, and treasure that is out of sight— What profit is in them both? ³¹Better is a man who hides his folly || Than a man who hides his wisdom.

CHAPTER 21

¹My son, have you sinned? Add no more to it; And ask forgiveness for your past sins. ²Flee from sin as from the face of a serpent; For if you draw near, it will bite you. Its teeth are lion's teeth, slaying men's souls. ³All iniquity is as a two-edged sword. Its stroke has no healing. ⁴Terror and violence will lay waste riches. So the house of an arrogant man will be laid waste. ⁵Supplication from a poor man's mouth reaches to the ears of God, || And his judgment comes speedily. ⁶One who hates reproof is in the path of the sinner. He who fears the LORD will turn again in his heart. ⁷He who is mighty in tongue is known far away, || But the man of understanding knows when he slips. ⁸He who builds his house with other men's money || Is like one who gathers stones for his own tomb. ⁹The congregation of wicked men is as a bundle of tow || With a flame of fire at the end of them. ¹⁰The way of sinners is paved with stones, || And at the end of it is the pit of Hades. ¹¹He who keeps the Law becomes master of its intent. The end of the fear of the LORD is wisdom. ¹²He who is not clever will not be instructed. There is a cleverness which makes bitterness abound. ¹³The knowledge of a wise man will be made to abound as a flood, || And his counsel as a fountain of life. ¹⁴The inward parts of a fool are like a broken vessel. He will hold no knowledge. ¹⁵If a man of knowledge hears a wise word, || He will commend it and add to it. The wanton man hears it, and it displeases him, || So he puts it away behind his back. ¹⁶The discourse of a fool is like a burden in the way, || But grace will be found on the lips of the wise. ¹⁷The mouth of the prudent man will be sought for in the congregation. They will ponder his words in their heart. ¹⁸As a house that is destroyed, || So is wisdom to a fool. The knowledge of an unwise man is talk without sense. ¹⁹Instruction is as chains on the feet of an unwise man, || And as shackles on the right hand. ²⁰A fool lifts up his voice with laughter, || But a clever man smiles quietly. ²¹Instruction is to a prudent man as an ornament of gold, || And as a bracelet on his right arm. ²²The foot of a fool rushes into a house, || But a man of experience will be ashamed of entering. ²³A foolish man peers into the door of a house, || But a man who is instructed will stand outside. ²⁴It is a lack of instruction in a man to listen at a door, || But a prudent man will be grieved with the disgrace. ²⁵The lips of strangers will be grieved at these things, || But the words of prudent men will be weighed in the balance. ²⁶The heart of fools is in their mouth, || But the mouth of wise men is their heart. ²⁷When the ungodly curses Satan, || He curses his own soul. ²⁸A whisperer defiles his own soul || And will be hated wherever he travels.

CHAPTER 22

¹A slothful man is compared to a stone that is defiled. Everyone will hiss at him in his disgrace. ²A slothful man is compared to the filth of a dunghill. Every man who takes it up will shake out his hand. ³An uninstructed child is a disgrace to his father, || And a foolish daughter is born to his loss. ⁴A prudent daughter will inherit a husband of her own. She who brings shame is the grief of her father. ⁵She who is bold brings shame on father and husband. She will be despised by both of them. ⁶Unseasonable discourse is as music in mourning, || But stripes and correction are wisdom in every season. ⁷He who teaches a fool is as one who glues a potsherd together, || Even as one who wakes a sleeper out of a deep sleep. ⁸He who teaches a fool is as one who teaches a man who slumbers. In the end he will say, "What is it?" ⁹Children who are brought up well || Do not show the humble origin of their parents. ¹⁰Children who are not brought up well, || Who are arrogant and conceited, || Are a stain on the noblest family. ¹¹Weep for the dead, for he lacks light. Weep for a fool, for he lacks understanding. Weep more sweetly for the

dead, because he has found rest, || But the life of the fool is worse than death. ¹²Mourning for the dead lasts seven days, || But for a fool and an ungodly man, all the days of his life. ¹³Do not talk much with a foolish man, || And do not go to one that has no understanding: Beware of him, lest you have trouble and be defiled in his onslaught. Turn away from him, and you will find rest, || And you will not be wearied in his madness. ¹⁴What would be heavier than lead? What is its name, but a fool? ¹⁵Sand, salt, and a mass of iron are easier to bear || Than a man without understanding. ¹⁶Timber girded and bound into a building || Will not be released with shaking. So a heart established in due season on well advised counsel || Will not be afraid. ¹⁷A heart settled on a thoughtful understanding || Is as an ornament of plaster on a polished wall. ¹⁸Fences set on a high place || Will not stand against the wind; So a fearful heart in the imagination of a fool || Will not stand against any fear. ¹⁹He who pricks the eye will make tears fall. He who pricks the heart makes it show feeling. ²⁰Whoever casts a stone at birds scares them away. He who insults a friend will dissolve friendship. ²¹If you have drawn a sword against a friend, do not despair, || For there may be a way back. ²²If you have opened your mouth against a friend, do not be afraid, || For there may be reconciliation, || Unless it is for insulting, arrogance, disclosing of a secret, or a treacherous blow—For any friend will flee these things. ²³Gain trust with your neighbor in his poverty, || That in his prosperity you may have gladness. Stay steadfast to him in the time of his affliction, || That you may be heir with him in his inheritance. ²⁴Before fire is the vapor and smoke of a furnace, || So insults precede bloodshed. ²⁵I will not be ashamed to shelter a friend. I will not hide myself from his face; ²⁶If any evil happens to me because of him, || Everyone that hears it will beware of him. ²⁷Who will set a watch over my mouth, || And a seal of shrewdness on my lips, || That I do not fall from it, || And that my tongue does not destroy me?

CHAPTER 23

¹O LORD, Father and Master of my life, || Do not abandon me to their counsel. Do not let me fall by them. ²Who will set scourges over my thought, || And a discipline of wisdom over my heart, || That they do not spare me for my errors, || And not overlook their [[*or* my]] sins? ³Otherwise my errors might be multiplied, || And my sins abound, || [And] I fall before my adversaries, || And my enemy rejoice over me. ⁴O LORD, Father and God of my life, || Do not give me haughty eyes, ⁵And turn evil desire away from me. ⁶Let neither gluttony nor lust overtake me. Do not give me over to a shameless mind. ⁷Listen, my children, to the discipline of the mouth. He who keeps it will not be taken. ⁸The sinner will be overpowered through his lips. By them, the insulter and the arrogant will stumble. ⁹Do not accustom your mouth to an oath, || And do not be accustomed to naming the Holy One, ¹⁰For as a servant who is continually scourged will not lack a bruise, || So he also who swears and continually utters the Name || Will not be cleansed from sin. ¹¹A man of many oaths will be filled with iniquity. The scourge will not depart from his house. If he offends, his sin will be on him. If he disregards it, he has sinned doubly. If he has sworn in vain, he will not be justified, || For his house will be filled with calamities. ¹²There is a manner of speech that is clothed with death. Do not let it be found in the heritage of Jacob, || For all these things will be far from the godly, || And they will not wallow in sins. ¹³Do not accustom your mouth to gross rudeness, || For it involves sinful speech. ¹⁴Remember your father and your mother, || For you sit in the midst of great men, || That you are not forgetful before them, || And become a fool by your custom; So you may wish that you had not been born, || And curse the day of your nativity. ¹⁵A man who is accustomed to words of reproach || Will not be corrected all the days of his life. ¹⁶Two sorts of people multiply sins, || And the third will bring wrath: A hot mind, as a burning fire, || Will not be quenched until it is consumed; A fornicator, in the body of his flesh, || Will never cease until he has burned out the fire. ¹⁷All bread is sweet to a fornicator. He will not cease until he dies. ¹⁸A man who goes astray from his own bed, || Says in his heart, "Who sees me? Darkness is around me, and the walls hide me. No one sees me. Of whom am I afraid? The Most High will not remember my sins." ¹⁹The eyes of men are his terror. He does not know that the eyes of the LORD || Are ten thousand times brighter than the sun, || Seeing all the ways of men, || And looking into secret places. ²⁰All things were known to Him before they were created, || And also after they were completed. ²¹This man will be punished in the streets of the city. He will be seized where he least expects it. ²²So also is a wife who leaves her husband || And brings in an heir by a stranger. ²³For first, she was disobedient in the Law of the Most High. Second, she trespassed against her own husband. Third, she played the adulteress in whoredom, || And brought in children by a stranger. ²⁴She will be brought out into the congregation. Her punishment will extend to her children. ²⁵Her children will not take root. Her branches will bear no fruit. ²⁶She will leave her memory for a curse. Her reproach will not be blotted out. ²⁷And those who are left behind || Will know that there is nothing better than the fear of the LORD, || And nothing sweeter than to heed the commands of the LORD.

CHAPTER 24

¹Wisdom will praise her own soul || And will proclaim her glory in the midst of her people. ²She will open her mouth in the congregation of the Most High || And proclaim her glory in the presence of His power. ³"I came out of the mouth of the Most High || And covered the earth as a mist. ⁴I lived in high places, || And my throne is in the pillar of the cloud. ⁵Alone I surrounded the circuit of Heaven || And walked in the depth of the abyss. ⁶In the waves of the sea, and in all the earth, || And in every people and nation, I got a possession. ⁷With all these I sought rest. In whose inheritance will I lodge? ⁸Then the Creator of all things gave me a command. He who created me made my dwelling place to rest, || And said, Let your dwelling place be in Jacob, || And your inheritance in Israel. ⁹He created me from the beginning before the world. For all ages, I will not cease to exist. ¹⁰In the holy Dwelling Place, I ministered before Him. So I was established in Zion. ¹¹In the beloved city, likewise He gave me rest. In Jerusalem was my domain. ¹²I took root in a people that was glorified, || Even in the portion of the LORD's own inheritance. ¹³I was exalted like a cedar in Lebanon, || And like a cypress tree on the mountains of Hermon. ¹⁴I was exalted like a palm tree on the seashore, || And as rose plants in Jericho, || And as a fair olive tree in the plain. I was exalted as a plane tree. ¹⁵As cinnamon and as palathus, || I have given a scent to perfumes. As choice myrrh, I spread abroad a pleasant fragrance, || As galbanum, onyx, stacte, || And as the smell of frankincense in the Dwelling Place. ¹⁶As the terebinth, I stretched out my branches. My branches are branches of glory and grace. ¹⁷As the vine, I put out grace. My flowers are the fruit of glory and riches. ¹⁸I am the mother of beautiful love, || Of fear, knowledge, and holy hope. Since I am perpetual, || I am given to all my children, who are named by Him. ¹⁹Come to me, all you who desire me, || And be filled with my fruits. ²⁰For my memorial is sweeter than honey, || And my inheritance [is sweeter] than the honeycomb. ²¹Those who eat me will be hungry for more. Those who drink me will be thirsty for more. ²²He who obeys me will not be ashamed. Those who work in me will not sin." ²³All these things are the Scroll of the Covenant of the Most High God, || The Law which Moses commanded us for an inheritance for the assemblies of Jacob. ²⁴Always be strong in the LORD; Stay with Him, so that He may make you strong. There is no God but the LORD Almighty, || And no savior except Him. ²⁵It is He who makes wisdom abundant, || As Pishon, and as Tigris in the days of first-fruits. ²⁶He makes understanding as full as [the] Euphrates, || And as [the] Jordan in the days of harvest, ²⁷Who makes instruction shine out as the light, || As [the] Gihon in the days of vintage. ²⁸The first man did not know her perfectly. In like manner, the last has not explored her. ²⁹For her thoughts are filled from the sea, || And her counsels from the great deep. ³⁰"I came out as a canal stream from a river, || And as an irrigation ditch into a garden. ³¹I said, I will water my garden, || And will drench my garden bed. Behold, my stream became a river, || And my river became a sea. ³²I will yet bring instruction to light as the morning || And will make these things clear from far away. ³³I will continue to pour out doctrine like prophecy || And leave it to generations of ages. ³⁴Behold that I have not labored for myself only, || But for all those who diligently seek her."

SIRACH

CHAPTER 25

¹ In three things I was beautified || And stood up beautiful before the LORD and men: The concord of relatives, || And friendship of neighbors, || And a woman and her husband that walk together in agreement. ² But three sorts [of men] my soul hates, || And I am greatly offended at their life: A poor man that is arrogant, || And a rich man that is a liar, || [And] an old man that is an adulterer lacking understanding. ³ In [your] youth you have not gathered, || And how should you find in your old age? ⁴ How beautiful a thing is judgment for gray hairs, || And for elders to know counsel! ⁵ How beautiful is the wisdom of old men, || And thought and counsel to men that are in honor! ⁶ Much experience is the crown of old men; And their glorying is the fear of the LORD. ⁷ There are nine things that I have thought of, || And in my heart counted happy; And the tenth I will utter with my tongue: A man that rejoices in his children; A man that lives and looks on the fall of his enemies; ⁸ Happy is he that dwells with a wife of understanding; And he that has not slipped with his tongue; And he that has not served a man that is unworthy of him; ⁹ Happy is he that has found prudence; And he that speaks in the ears of those who listen. ¹⁰ How great is he that has found wisdom! Yet there is none above him that fears the LORD. ¹¹ The fear of the LORD passes all things: He that holds it—To whom will he be likened? ¹² Fearing the LORD is the first step toward loving Him, || And faith is the first step toward loyalty to Him. ¹³ [Give me] any plague but the plague of the heart; And any wickedness but the wickedness of a woman; ¹⁴ Any calamity, but a calamity from those who hate me; And any vengeance, but the vengeance of enemies. ¹⁵ There is no head above the head of a serpent; And there is no wrath above the wrath of an enemy. ¹⁶ I would rather dwell with a lion and a dragon, || Than keep house with a wicked woman. ¹⁷ The wickedness of a woman changes her look || And darkens her countenance as a bear does. ¹⁸ Her husband will sit at meat among his neighbors, || And when he hears it he sighs bitterly. ¹⁹ All malice is but little to the malice of a woman: Let the portion of a sinner fall on her. ²⁰ [As] the going up a sandy way [is] to the feet of the aged, || So is a wife full of words to a quiet man. ²¹ Do not throw yourself on the beauty of a woman; And do not desire a woman for her beauty. ²² There is anger, and impudence, and great reproach, || If a woman supports her husband. ²³ A wicked woman is a dejection of heart, || And sadness of countenance, and a wounded heart: A woman that will not make her husband happy || Is [as] hands that hang down, and palsied knees. ²⁴ From a woman [was] the beginning of sin; And because of her we all die. ²⁵ Do not give water an outlet; Neither [give] freedom of speech to a wicked woman. ²⁶ If she does not go as you would have her, || Cut her off from your flesh.

CHAPTER 26

¹ Happy is the husband of a good wife; And the number of his days will be doubled. ² A brave woman rejoices her husband; And he will fulfill his years in peace. ³ A good wife is a good portion: She will be given in the portion of such as fear the LORD. ⁴ Whether a man is rich or poor, || A good heart [makes] a cheerful countenance at all times. ⁵ Of three things my heart was afraid; And concerning the fourth kind I made supplication: The slander of a city, || And the assembly of a multitude, || And a false accusation: All these are more grievous than death. ⁶ A grief of heart and sorrow is a woman that is jealous of [another] woman, || And the scourge of a tongue communicating to all. ⁷ A wicked woman is [as] a yoke of oxen shaken to and fro: He that takes hold of her is as one that grasps a scorpion. ⁸ A drunken woman [causes] great wrath; And she will not cover her own shame. ⁹ The whoredom of a woman is in the lifting up of her eyes; And it will be known by her eyelids. ¹⁰ Keep strict watch on a headstrong daughter, || Lest she finds liberty for herself, and uses it. ¹¹ Look well after an impudent eye; And do not marvel if it trespasses against you. ¹² She will open her mouth as a thirsty traveler, || And drink of every water that is near: She will sit down at every post || And open her quiver against [any] arrow. ¹³ The grace of a wife will delight her husband; And her knowledge will fatten his bones. ¹⁴ A silent woman is a gift of the LORD; And there is nothing worth so much as a well-instructed soul. ¹⁵ A modest woman is grace on grace; And there is no price worthy of a continent soul. ¹⁶ As the sun when it arises in the highest places of the LORD, || So is the beauty of a good wife in the ordering of a man's house. ¹⁷ As the lamp that shines on the holy candlestick, || So is the beauty of the face in ripe age. ¹⁸ As the golden pillars are on a base of silver, || So are beautiful feet with the breasts of one that is steadfast. ¹⁹ My child, stay healthy while you are young, || And do not give your strength to strangers. ²⁰ Search the whole land for a fertile field, || And plant it with your own seed, || Trusting your own good stock. ²¹ Then your children will survive || And grow up confident of their good family. ²² A prostitute is like spit; A married woman who has affairs brings death to her lovers. ²³ A lawless man will get a godless wife, as he deserves, || But a man who honors the LORD will have a devout wife. ²⁴ A shameless wife enjoys making a disgrace of herself, || But a modest wife will act modestly even alone with her husband. ²⁵ A self-willed woman is a dog, || But a woman with a sense of decency honors the LORD. ²⁶ A wife who honors her husband will seem wise to everyone; But if she dishonors him by her overbearing attitude, || Everyone will know that she is ungodly. The husband of a good wife is fortunate, || Because he will live twice as long. ²⁷ A loud-mouthed, talkative woman is like a trumpet sounding the signal for attack, || And any man who has such a wife will spend his life at war. ²⁸ For two things my heart is grieved; And for the third anger comes on me: A man of war that suffers for poverty; And men of understanding that are counted as refuse; One that turns back from righteousness to sin—The LORD will prepare him for the sword. ²⁹ A merchant will hardly keep himself from wrongdoing; And a huckster will not be acquitted of sin.

CHAPTER 27

¹ Many have sinned for a thing indifferent; And he that seeks to multiply [gain] will turn his eye away. ² A nail will stick fast between the joining of stones; And sin will thrust itself in between buying and selling. ³ Unless [a man] holds on diligently in the fear of the LORD, || His house will soon be overthrown. ⁴ In the shaking of a sieve, the refuse remains; So is the filth of man in his reasoning. ⁵ The furnace will prove the potter's vessels; And the trial of a man is in his reasoning. ⁶ The fruit of a tree declares the farming thereof; So is the utterance of the thought of the heart of a man. ⁷ Praise no man before [you hear him] reason; For this is the trial of men. ⁸ If you follow righteousness, you will obtain her, || And put her on, as a long robe of glory. ⁹ Birds will return to their like; And truth will return to those who practice her. ¹⁰ The lion lies in wait for prey; So does sin for those who work iniquity. ¹¹ The discourse of a godly man is always wisdom, || But the foolish man changes as the moon. ¹² Among men void of understanding observe the opportunity; But continually stay among the thoughtful. ¹³ The discourse of fools is an offense; And their laughter is in the wantonness of sin. ¹⁴ The talk of a man of many oaths will make the hair stand upright; And their strife makes one stop his ears. ¹⁵ The strife of the proud is a shedding of blood; And their reviling of each other is a grievous thing to hear. ¹⁶ He that reveals secrets destroys credit || And will not find a friend to his mind. ¹⁷ Love a friend and keep faith with him, || But if you reveal his secrets, || You will not pursue after him; ¹⁸ For as a man has destroyed his enemy, || So have you destroyed the friendship of your neighbor. ¹⁹ And as a bird which you have released out of your hand, || So have you let your neighbor go, || And you will not catch him again: ²⁰ Do not pursue him, for he has gone far away, || And has escaped as a gazelle out of the snare. ²¹ For a wound may be bound up, || And after reviling there may be a reconcilement; But he that reveals secrets has lost hope. ²² One that winks with the eye contrives evil things; And no man will remove him from it. ²³ When you are present, he will speak sweetly, || And will admire your words; But afterward he will writhe his mouth || And set a trap [for you] in your words. ²⁴ I have hated many things, || But nothing like him; And the LORD will hate him. ²⁵ One that casts a stone on high casts it on his own head; And a deceitful stroke will open wounds. ²⁶ He that digs a pit will fall into it; And he that sets a snare will be taken therein. ²⁷ He that does evil things, they will roll on him, || And he will not know from where they have come to him. ²⁸ Mockery and reproach are from the arrogant; And vengeance, as a lion, will lie in wait for him. ²⁹ They that rejoice at the

fall of the godly || Will be taken in a snare; And anguish will consume them before they die. ³⁰Wrath and anger, these are also abominations; And a sinful man will possess them.

CHAPTER 28

¹He that takes vengeance will find vengeance from the LORD; And he will surely make firm his sins. ²Forgive your neighbor the hurt that he has done [you]; And then your sins will be pardoned when you pray. ³Man cherishes anger against man; And does he [then] seek healing from the LORD? ⁴On a man like himself he has no mercy; And does he [then] make supplication for his own sins? ⁵He being himself flesh nourishes wrath: Who will make atonement for his sins? ⁶Remember your last end, || And cease from enmity: [Remember] corruption and death, || And remain in the commands. ⁷Remember the commands || And do not be angry with your neighbor; And [remember] the covenant of the Highest, || And wink at ignorance. ⁸Abstain from strife, and you will diminish your sins, || For a passionate man will kindle strife; ⁹And a man that is a sinner will trouble friends || And will make debate among those who are at peace. ¹⁰As is the fuel of the fire, so will it burn; And as the stoutness of the strife is, [so] will it burn; As is the strength of the man, [so] will be his wrath; And as is his wealth, [so] he will exalt his anger. ¹¹A contention begun in haste kindles a fire; And a hasty fighting sheds blood. ¹²If you blow a spark, it will burn; And if you spit on it, it will be quenched: And both these will come out of your mouth. ¹³Curse the whisperer and double-tongued, || For he has destroyed many that were at peace. ¹⁴A third person's tongue has shaken many || And dispersed them from nation to nation; And it has pulled down strong cities || And overthrown the houses of great men. ¹⁵A third person's tongue has cast out brave women || And deprived them of their labors. ¹⁶He that listens to it will not find rest, || Nor will he dwell quietly. ¹⁷The stroke of a whip makes a mark in the flesh; But the stroke of a tongue will break bones. ¹⁸Many have fallen by the edge of the sword: Yet not so many as those who have fallen because of the tongue. ¹⁹Happy is he that is sheltered from it, || Who has not passed through the wrath thereof; Who has not drawn its yoke, || And has not been bound with its bands. ²⁰For the yoke thereof is a yoke of iron, || And the bands thereof are bands of brass. ²¹The death thereof is an evil death; And Hades would be better than it. ²²It will not have rule over godly men; And they will not be burned in its flame. ²³They that forsake the LORD will fall into it; And it will burn among them and will not be quenched: It will be sent out on them as a lion; And as a leopard it will destroy them. ²⁴See to it that you hedge around your possession with thorns; Bind up your silver and your gold; ²⁵And make a balance and a weight for your words; And make a door and a bar for your mouth. ²⁶Take heed lest you slip therein; Lest you fall before one that lies in wait.

CHAPTER 29

¹He that shows mercy will lend to his neighbor; And he that strengthens him with his hand keeps the commands. ²Lend to your neighbor in time of his need; And pay your neighbor again in due season. ³Confirm your word and keep faith with him; And at all seasons you will find what you need. ⁴Many have reckoned a loan as a windfall || And have given trouble to those that helped them. ⁵Until he has received, he will kiss a man's hands; And for his neighbor's money he will speak submissively: And when payment is due, he will prolong the time, || And return words of heaviness, and complain of the times. ⁶If he prevails, he will hardly receive the half; And he will count it as a windfall: If not, he has deprived him of his money, || And he has gotten him for an enemy without cause: He will pay him with cursing and railing; And he will pay him disgrace for honor. ⁷Many on account of [men's] ill-dealing have turned away; They have feared to be defrauded for nothing. ⁸However, be patient with a man in poor estate; And do not let him wait for [your] kindness. ⁹Help a poor man for the command's sake; And according to his need, do not send him away empty. ¹⁰Lose [your] money for a brother and a friend; And do not let it rust under the stone to be lost. ¹¹Bestow your treasure according to the commands of the Most High, || And it will profit you more than gold. ¹²Shut up alms in your storechambers, || And it will deliver you out of all affliction: ¹³It will fight for you against your enemy || Better than a mighty shield and a ponderous spear. ¹⁴A good man will be a guarantee for his neighbor; And he that has lost shame will fail him. ¹⁵Do not forget the good offices of your guarantor; For he has given his life for you. ¹⁶A sinner will overthrow the good estate of his guarantor; ¹⁷And he that is of an unthankful mind will fail him that delivered him. ¹⁸Suretyship has undone many that were prospering || And shaken them as a wave of the sea: It has driven mighty men from their homes; And they wandered among strange nations. ¹⁹A sinner that falls into suretyship, || And undertakes contracts for work, || Will fall into lawsuits. ²⁰Help your neighbor according to your power || And take heed to yourself that you do not fall [the same way]. ²¹The chief thing for life is water, and bread, || And a garment, and a house to cover shame. ²²Better is the life of a poor man under a shelter of logs, || Than sumptuous fare in another man's house. ²³With little or with much, be well satisfied. ²⁴It is a miserable life to go from house to house: And where you are a sojourner, || You will not [dare to] open your mouth. ²⁵You will entertain, and give to drink, and have no thanks: And in addition to this, you will hear bitter words. ²⁶"Come here, you sojourner, furnish a table, || And if you have anything in your hand, feed me with it. ²⁷Go out, you sojourner, from the face of honor; My brother has come to be my guest; I have need of my house." ²⁸These things are grievous to a man of understanding: The scolding of [the] household, || And the reproaching of the money-lender.

CHAPTER 30

¹He that loves his son will continue to lay stripes on him, || That he may rejoice in him in the end. ²He that disciplines his son will profit from him || And will boast of him among his acquaintance. ³He that teaches his son will provoke his enemy to jealousy; And he will rejoice in him before friends. ⁴His father dies and is as though he had not died; For he has left one behind him like himself. ⁵In his life, he saw and rejoiced [in him]; And when he died, he did not sorrow: ⁶He left behind him an avenger against his enemies, || And one to repay kindness to his friends. ⁷He that makes too much of his son will bind up his wounds; And his heart will be troubled at every cry. ⁸An unbroken horse becomes stubborn; And a son left at large becomes headstrong. ⁹Pamper your child, and he will make you afraid: Play with him, and he will grieve you. ¹⁰Do not laugh with him, lest you have sorrow with him; And you will gnash your teeth in the end. ¹¹Give him no liberty in his youth, || And do not wink at his follies. ¹²Bow his neck down in his youth || And beat him on the sides while he is a child, || Lest he wax stubborn, and be disobedient to you; And there will be sorrow to your soul. ¹³Discipline your son, and take pains with him, || Lest his shameless behavior be an offense to you. ¹⁴Better is a poor man, being sound and strong of constitution, || Than a rich man that is plagued in his body. ¹⁵Health and a good constitution are better than all gold; And a strong body than wealth without measure. ¹⁶There is no riches better than health of body; And there is no gladness above the joy of the heart. ¹⁷Death is better than a bitter life, || And perpetual rest than a continual sickness. ¹⁸Good things poured out on a mouth that is closed || Are [as] messes of meat laid on a grave. ¹⁹What does an offering profit an idol? For neither will it eat nor smell; So is he that is afflicted of the LORD, ²⁰Seeing with his eyes and groaning, || As a eunuch embracing a virgin and groaning. ²¹Do not give your soul over to sorrow; And do not afflict yourself in your own counsel. ²²Gladness of heart is the life of a man; And the joyfulness of a man is length of days. ²³Love your own soul and comfort your heart: And remove sorrow far from you; For sorrow has destroyed many, || And there is no profit therein. ²⁴Envy and wrath shorten [a man's] days; And care brings old age before the time. ²⁵A cheerful and good heart || Will have a care of his meat and diet.

CHAPTER 31

¹Wakefulness that comes of riches consumes the flesh, || And the anxiety thereof puts away sleep. ²Wakeful anxiety will crave slumber; And in a severe disease sleep will be broken. ³A rich man toils in gathering money together; And when he rests, he is filled with his good things. ⁴A poor man toils in lack of substance; And when he rests, he becomes needy. ⁵He that loves gold will not be justified; And he that follows destruction will himself have his fill [of

it]. ⁶Many have been given over to ruin for the sake of gold; And their perdition meets them face to face. ⁷It is a stumbling block to those who sacrifice to it; And every fool will be taken with that. ⁸Blessed is the rich who is found without blemish, || And who does not go after gold. ⁹Who is he? And we will call him blessed; For he has done wonderful things among his people. ¹⁰Who has been tried by it, and found perfect? Then let him glory. Who has had the power to transgress, and has not transgressed? And to do evil, and has not done it? ¹¹His goods will be made sure, || And the congregation will declare his alms. ¹²Do you sit at a great table? Do not be greedy on it, || And do not say, "There are many things on it." ¹³Remember that an evil eye is a wicked thing: What has been created more evil than an eye? Therefore, it sheds tears from every face. ¹⁴Do not stretch your hand wherever it looks || And do not thrust yourself with it into the dish. ¹⁵Consider your neighbor's [liking] by your own; And be discreet in every point. ¹⁶Eat, as [becomes] a man, || Those things which are set before you; And do not eat greedily, lest you be hated. ¹⁷Be first to leave off for manners' sake; And do not be insatiable, lest you offend. ¹⁸And if you sit among many, || Do not reach out your hand before them. ¹⁹How sufficient to a well-mannered man is a very little, || And he does not breathe hard on his bed. ²⁰Healthy sleep comes of moderate eating; He rises early, and his wits are with him: The pain of wakefulness, and colic, and griping, || Are with an insatiable man. ²¹And if you have been forced to eat, || Rise up in the midst thereof, and you will have rest. ²²Hear me, my son, and do not despise me, || And at the end you will find my words [true]: In all your works be quick, || And no disease will come to you. ²³Him that is liberal of his meat the lips will bless; And the testimony of his excellence will be believed. ²⁴The city will murmur at him who is stingy with his meat; And the testimony of his stinginess will be sure. ²⁵Do not show yourself valiant in wine, || For wine has destroyed many. ²⁶The furnace proves the temper [of steel] by dipping; So does wine [prove] hearts in the quarreling of the proud. ²⁷Wine is as good as life to men, || If you drink it in its measure: What life is there to a man that is without wine? And it has been created to make men glad. ²⁸Wine drunk in season, to satisfy, || Is joy of heart and gladness of soul: ²⁹Wine drunk abundantly is bitterness of soul, || With provocation and conflict. ³⁰Drunkenness increases the rage of a fool to his hurt; It diminishes strength and adds wounds. ³¹Do not rebuke your neighbor at a banquet of wine, || Neither set him at nothing in his mirth; Do not speak a word of reproach to him, || And do not press on him by asking back [a debt].

CHAPTER 32

¹Have they made you ruler [of a feast]? Do not be lifted up; Be among them as one of them; Take thought for them, and so sit down. ²And when you have done all your office, take your place, || That you may be gladdened on their account, || And receive a crown for your well ordering. ³Speak, you that are the elder, || For it is suitable for you, [but] with sound knowledge; And do not hinder music. ⁴Do not pour out talk where there is a performance of music, || And do not display your wisdom out of season. ⁵[As] a signet of carbuncle in a setting of gold, || [So] is a concert of music in a banquet of wine. ⁶[As] a signet of emerald in a work of gold, || [So] is a strain of music with pleasant wine. ⁷Speak, young man, if there is need of you; [Yet] scarcely if you be twice asked. ⁸Sum up your speech, many things in few words; Be as one that knows and yet holds his tongue. ⁹[If you be] among great men, || Do not behave as their equal; And when another is speaking, || Do not make much babbling. ¹⁰Lightning speeds before thunder; And before a modest man favor will go out. ¹¹Rise up on time and do not be the last; Get home quickly and do not loiter: ¹²Take your pastime there and do what is in your heart; And do not sin by proud speech: ¹³And for these things bless Him that made you || And gives you to drink freely of His good things. ¹⁴He that fears the LORD will receive [His] discipline; And those who seek [Him] early will find favor. ¹⁵He that seeks the Law will be filled with that, || But the hypocrite will stumble at that. ¹⁶They that fear the LORD will find judgment || And will kindle righteous acts as a light. ¹⁷A sinful man shuns reproof || And will find a judgment according to his will. ¹⁸A man of counsel will not neglect a thought; A strange and proud man will not crouch in fear, || Even after he has done a thing by himself without counsel. ¹⁹Do nothing without counsel; And when you have once done [it], || Do not convert [from it]. ²⁰Do not go in a way of conflict; And do not stumble in stony places. ²¹Do not be confident in a smooth way. ²²And beware of your own children. ²³In every work trust your own soul; For this is the keeping of the commands. ²⁴He that believes the Law gives heed to the command; And he that trusts in the LORD will suffer no loss.

CHAPTER 33

¹No evil will happen to him that fears the LORD, || But in temptation He will once again deliver him. ²A wise man will not hate the Law; But he that is a hypocrite therein is as a ship in a storm. ³A man of understanding will put his trust in the Law; And the Law is faithful to him, || As when one asks at the oracle. ⁴Prepare [your] speech, and so will you be heard; Bind up instruction and make your answer. ⁵The heart of a fool is [as] a cartwheel; And his thoughts like a rolling axle-tree. ⁶A stallion horse is as a mocking friend; He neighs under everyone that sits on him. ⁷Why does one day excel [over] another, || When all the light of every day in the year is of the sun? ⁸By the knowledge of the LORD they were distinguished; And He varied seasons and feasts: ⁹Some of them He exalted and hallowed, || And some of them He has made ordinary days. ¹⁰And all men are from the ground, || And Adam was created of earth. ¹¹In the abundance of His knowledge the LORD distinguished them || And made their ways various: ¹²Some of them He blessed and exalted, || And some of them He hallowed and brought near to Himself; Some of them He cursed and brought low, || And overthrew them from their place. ¹³As the clay of the potter in his hand, || All his ways are according to his good pleasure; So men are in the hand of Him that made them, || To render to them according to His judgment. ¹⁴Good is the opposite of evil, || And life is the opposite of death; So the sinner is the opposite of the godly. ¹⁵And so look on all the works of the Most High: Two and two, one against another. ¹⁶And I awoke last, as one that gleans after the grape gatherers: By the blessing of the LORD I got before them, || And filled my winepress as one that gathers grapes. ¹⁷Consider that I did not labor for myself alone, || But for all those who seek instruction. ¹⁸Hear me, you great men of the people, || And listen with your ears, you rulers of the congregation. ¹⁹To son and wife, to brother and friend, || Do not give power over yourself while you live; And do not give your goods to another, || Lest you convert and make supplication for them [again]. ²⁰While you yet live, and breath is in you, || Do not give yourself over to anybody. ²¹For it is better that your children should supplicate you, || Than that you should look to the hand of your sons. ²²In all your works keep the upper hand; Do not bring a stain on your honor. ²³In the day that you end the days of your life, || And in the time of death, distribute your inheritance. ²⁴Fodder, a stick, and burdens, for a donkey; Bread, and discipline, and work, for a servant. ²⁵Set your servant to work, and you will find rest: Leave his hands idle, and he will seek liberty. ²⁶Yoke and thong will bow the neck: And for an evil servant there are racks and tortures. ²⁷Send him to labor, that he may not be idle; For idleness teaches much mischief. ²⁸Set him to work, as is fit for him; And if he does not obey, make his chains heavy. ²⁹And do not be excessive toward any; And do nothing without judgment. ³⁰If you have a servant, let him be as yourself, || Because you have bought him with blood. ³¹If you have a servant, treat him as yourself, || For you will have need of him as your own soul: If you treat him ill, and he departs and runs away, || Which way will you go to seek him?

CHAPTER 34

¹Vain and false hopes are for a man void of understanding; And dreams give wings to fools. ²As one that catches at a shadow, || And follows after the wind, || So is he that sets his mind on dreams. ³The vision of dreams is [as] this thing against that, || The likeness of a face near a face. ⁴Of an unclean thing what will be cleansed? And of that which is false what will be true? ⁵Divinations, and soothsayings, and dreams, are vain: And the heart has fantasies, as a woman's in travail. ⁶If they are not sent from the Most High in [your] visitation, || Do not give your heart to them. ⁷For dreams have led many astray: And they have failed by putting their hope in them. ⁸Without lying the

SIRACH

Law will be accomplished; And wisdom is perfection to a faithful mouth. ⁹A well-instructed man knows many things; And he that has much experience will declare understanding. ¹⁰He that has no experience knows few things, || But he that has wandered will increase [his] skill. ¹¹In my wandering I have seen many things; And my understanding is more than my words. ¹²I was often in danger even to death; And I was preserved because of these things. ¹³The spirit of those that fear the LORD will live; For their hope is on Him that saves them. ¹⁴Whoever fears the LORD will not be afraid || And will not play the coward; For He is his hope. ¹⁵Blessed is the soul of him that fears the LORD: To whom does he give heed? And who is his stay? ¹⁶The eyes of the LORD are on those who love Him, || A mighty protection and strong stay, || A cover from the hot blast, and a cover from the noonday, || A guard from stumbling, and a help from falling. ¹⁷He raises up the soul, and enlightens the eyes: He gives healing, life, and blessing. ¹⁸He that sacrifices of a thing wrongfully gotten—His offering is made in mockery; And the mockeries of wicked men are not well-pleasing. ¹⁹The Most High has no pleasure in the offerings of the ungodly; Neither is He pacified for sins by the multitude of sacrifices. ²⁰[As] one that kills the son before his father's eyes || Is he that brings a sacrifice from the goods of the poor. ²¹The bread of the needy is the life of the poor: He that deprives him thereof is a man of blood. ²²[As] one that slays his neighbor || Is he that takes away his living; And [as] a shedder of blood || Is he that deprives a hireling of his hire. ²³One building, and another pulling down—What profit have they had but toil? ²⁴One praying, and another cursing—Whose voice will the LORD listen to? ²⁵He that washes himself after [touching] a dead body, and touches it again—What profit does he have in his washing? ²⁶Even so a man fasting for his sins, and going again, and doing the same—Who will listen to his prayer? And what profit does he have in his humiliation?

CHAPTER 35

¹He that keeps the Law multiplies offerings; He that takes heed to the commands sacrifices a peace offering. ²He that returns a favor offers fine flour; And he that gives alms sacrifices a thank offering. ³To depart from wickedness is a thing pleasing to the LORD; And to depart from unrighteousness is an atoning sacrifice. ⁴See that you do not appear in the presence of the LORD empty. ⁵For all these things [are to be done] because of the command. ⁶The offering of the righteous makes the altar fat; And the sweet savor thereof [is] before the Most High. ⁷The sacrifice of a righteous man is acceptable; And the memorial thereof will not be forgotten. ⁸Glorify the LORD with a good eye, || And do not limit the first-fruits of your hands. ⁹In every gift show a cheerful countenance || And dedicate your tithe with gladness. ¹⁰Give to the Most High according as He has given; And as your hand has found, [give] with a good eye. ¹¹For the LORD rewards, || And He will reward you sevenfold. ¹²Do not think to corrupt with gifts, || For He will not receive them: And do not set your mind on an unrighteous sacrifice, || For the LORD is judge, || And with Him is no respect of persons. ¹³He will not accept any person against a poor man; And He will listen to the prayer of him that is wronged. ¹⁴He will in no way despise the supplication of the fatherless; Nor the widow, when she pours out her tale. ¹⁵Do the tears of the widow not run down her cheek? And is her cry not against him that has caused them to fall? ¹⁶He that serves [God] according to His good pleasure will be accepted, || And his supplication will reach to the clouds. ¹⁷The prayer of the humble pierces the clouds; And until it comes near, he will not be comforted; And he will not depart, until the Most High will visit; And He will judge righteously and execute judgment. ¹⁸And the LORD will not be slack, || Neither will He be patient toward them, || Until He has crushed the loins of the unmerciful; And He will repay vengeance to the heathen, || Until He has taken away the multitude of the arrogant, || And broken in pieces the scepters of the unrighteous; ¹⁹Until He has rendered to [every] man according to his doings, || And [to] the works of men according to their plans; Until He has judged the cause of His people; And He will make them to rejoice in His mercy. ²⁰Mercy is seasonable in the time of His afflicting [them], || As clouds of rain in the time of drought.

CHAPTER 36

¹Have mercy on us, O LORD the God of all, and behold; ²And send Your fear on all the nations: ³Lift up Your hand against the strange nations; And let them see Your mighty power. ⁴As You were sanctified in us before them, || So be magnified in them before us. ⁵And let them know You, as we also have known You, || That there is no God but only You, O God. ⁶Show new signs and work various wonders; Glorify Your hand and Your right arm. ⁷Raise up indignation, and pour out wrath; Take away the adversary, and destroy the enemy. ⁸Hasten the time and remember the oath; And let them declare Your mighty works. ⁹Let him that escapes be devoured by the rage of fire; And may those who harm Your people find destruction. ¹⁰Crush the heads of the rulers of the enemies, || That say, "There is none but us." ¹¹Gather all the tribes of Jacob together, || And take them for Your inheritance, as from the beginning. ¹²O LORD, have mercy on the people that is called by Your Name, || And on Israel, whom You did liken to a firstborn. ¹³Have compassion on the city of Your sanctuary: Jerusalem, the place of Your rest. ¹⁴Fill Zion; exalt Your oracles || And [fill] Your people with Your glory. ¹⁵Give testimony to those that were Your creatures in the beginning || And raise up the prophecies that have been in Your Name. ¹⁶Give reward to those who wait for You: And men will put their trust in Your prophets. ¹⁷Listen, O LORD, to the prayer of Your suppliants, || According to the blessing of Aaron concerning Your people; And all those who are on the earth will know || That You are the LORD, the perpetual God. ¹⁸The belly will eat any meat; Yet one meat is better than another. ¹⁹The mouth tastes meats taken in hunting; So does an understanding heart false speeches. ²⁰A contrary heart will cause heaviness: And a man of experience will reward him. ²¹A woman will receive any man; But one daughter is better than another. ²²The beauty of a woman cheers the countenance; And a man desires nothing so much. ²³If there is mercy and meekness on her tongue, || Her husband is not like the sons of men. ²⁴He that gets a wife enters on a possession: A help appropriate for him, and a pillar of rest. ²⁵Where no hedge is, the possession will be laid waste; And he that has no wife will mourn as he wanders up and down. ²⁶For who will trust a nimble robber || Who skips from city to city? Even so, [who will trust] a man that has no nest, || And [who] lodges wherever he finds himself at nightfall?

CHAPTER 37

¹Every friend will say, "I am also his friend," || But there is a friend who is only a friend in name. ²Is there not a grief in it even to death, || When a companion and friend is turned to enmity? ³O wicked imagination, from where did you come, || Rolling in to cover the dry land with deceitfulness? ⁴There is a companion who rejoices in the gladness of a friend, || But in time of affliction will be against him. ⁵There is a companion who for the belly's sake labors with his friend, || [But] in the face of battle will take up the buckler. ⁶Do not forget a friend in your soul; And do not be unmindful of him in your riches. ⁷Every counselor extols counsel; But there is [one] who counsels for himself. ⁸Let your soul beware of a counselor || And know beforehand what his interest is, || For he will take counsel for himself; Lest he casts the lot on you, ⁹And says to you, "Your way is good": And he will stand near you, || To see what will happen to you. ¹⁰Take no counsel with one that looks suspiciously at you; And hide your counsel from such as are jealous of you. ¹¹[Take no counsel] with a woman about her rival; Neither with a coward about war; Nor with a merchant about exchange; Nor with a buyer about selling; Nor with an envious man about thankfulness; Nor with an unmerciful man about kindness; Nor with a sluggard about any kind of work; Nor with a hireling in your house about finishing [his work]; Nor with an idle servant about much business: Give no heed to these in any matter of counsel, ¹²But rather be continually with a godly man, || Whom you will have known to be a keeper of the commands, || Who in his soul is as your own soul, || And who will grieve with you, if you will miscarry. ¹³And make the counsel of your heart to stand; For there is none more faithful to you than it. ¹⁴For a man's soul is sometimes accustomed to bring him tidings—More than seven watchmen that sit up high on a watchtower. ¹⁵And above all this, entreat the Most High, || That He may direct your way in truth. ¹⁶Let reason be the beginning of every work, || And let counsel go

before every action. ⁱ⁷As a token of the changing of the heart, ¹⁸Four manner of things rise up: Good and evil, life and death; And that which rules over them continually is the tongue. ¹⁹There is one that is shrewd [and] the instructor of many, ǁ And yet is unprofitable to his own soul. ²⁰There is [one] that is subtle in words and is hated; He will be destitute of all food: ²¹For grace was not given to him from the LORD, ǁ Because he is deprived of all wisdom. ²²There is one that is wise to his own soul, ǁ And the fruits of his understanding are trustworthy in the mouth. ²³A wise man will instruct his own people, ǁ And the fruits of his understanding are trustworthy. ²⁴A wise man will be filled with blessing, ǁ And all those who see him will call him happy. ²⁵The life of man is counted by days, ǁ And the days of Israel are innumerable. ²⁶The wise man will inherit confidence among his people, ǁ And his name will live forever. ²⁷My son, prove your soul in your life, ǁ And see what is evil for it, and do not give that to it. ²⁸For all things are not profitable for all men, ǁ Neither does every soul have pleasure in everything. ²⁹Do not be insatiable in any luxury, ǁ And do not be greedy in the things that you eat. ³⁰For in multitude of meats there will be disease, ǁ And gorging will come near to colic. ³¹Because of gorging many have perished; But he that takes heed will prolong his life.

CHAPTER 38

¹Honor a physician according to your need [of him] ǁ With the honors due to him; For the LORD has truly created him. ²For from the Most High comes healing; And from the king he will receive a gift. ³The skill of the physician will lift up his head; And in the sight of great men he will be admired. ⁴The LORD created medicines out of the earth; And a prudent man will have no disgust at them. ⁵Was water not made sweet with wood, ǁ That the virtue thereof might be known? ⁶And He gave men skill, ǁ That they might be glorified in His marvelous works. ⁷With them He heals [a man and] takes away his pain. ⁸With these the apothecary will make a confection; And his works will not be brought to an end; And from him is peace on the face of the earth. ⁹My son, in your sickness do not be negligent; But pray to the LORD, and He will heal you. ¹⁰Put away wrongdoing, ǁ And order your hands correctly, ǁ And cleanse your heart from all manner of sin. ¹¹Give a sweet savor, and a memorial of fine flour; And make fat your offering, as one that is not. ¹²Then give place to the physician, ǁ For the LORD has truly created him; And do not let him go from you, for you have need of him. ¹³There is a time when in their very hands is the issue for good. ¹⁴For they will also implore the LORD, ǁ That He may prosper them in [giving] relief and in healing for the maintenance of life. ¹⁵He that sins before his Maker, ǁ Let him fall into the hands of the physician. ¹⁶My son, let your tears fall over the dead, ǁ And as one that suffers grievously begin lamentation; And wind up his body according to his due, ǁ And do not neglect his burial. ¹⁷Make bitter weeping, and make passionate wailing, ǁ And let your mourning be according to his merit—For one day or two, ǁ Lest you be spoken evil of: And so be comforted for your sorrow. ¹⁸For of sorrow comes death, ǁ And sorrow of heart will bow down the strength. ¹⁹In calamity sorrow also remains: And the poor man's life is grievous to the heart. ²⁰Do not give your heart to sorrow. Put it away, remembering the latter end. ²¹Do not forget it, ǁ For there is no returning again: You will not profit him, ǁ And you will hurt yourself. ²²Remember the sentence on him; For so yours will also be; Yesterday for me, and today for you. ²³When the dead is at rest, ǁ Let his remembrance rest; And be comforted for him, ǁ When his spirit departs from him. ²⁴The wisdom of the scribe comes by opportunity of leisure; And he that has little business will become wise. ²⁵How will he become wise that holds the plow, ǁ That glories in the shaft of the goad, ǁ That drives oxen, and is occupied in their labors, ǁ And whose discourse is of the stock of bulls? ²⁶He will set his heart on turning his furrows; And his wakefulness is to give his heifers their fodder. ²⁷So is every craftsman and master workman, ǁ That passes his time by night as by day; They that cut gravings of signets, ǁ And his diligence is to make great variety; He will set his heart to preserve likeness in his portraiture ǁ And will be wakeful to finish his work. ²⁸So is the smith sitting by the anvil and considering the unworked iron: The vapor of the fire will waste his flesh; And in the heat of the furnace he will wrestle [with his work]: The noise of the hammer will be ever in his ear, ǁ And his eyes are on the pattern of the vessel; He will set his heart on perfecting his works, ǁ And he will be wakeful to adorn them perfectly. ²⁹So is the potter sitting at his work, ǁ And turning the wheel around with his feet; ǁ Who is always anxiously set at his work, ǁ And all his handiwork is by number; ³⁰He will fashion the clay with his arm ǁ And will bend its strength in front of his feet; He will apply his heart to finish the glazing; And he will be wakeful to make clean the furnace. ³¹All these put their trust in their hands; And each becomes wise in his own work. ³²Without these a city will not be inhabited, ǁ And men will not sojourn nor walk up and down [therein]. ³³They will not be sought for in the council of the people, ǁ And in the assembly, they will not mount on high; They will not sit on the seat of the judge, ǁ And they will not understand the covenant of judgment: Neither will they declare instruction and judgment; And where allegories are, they will not be found. ³⁴But they will maintain the fabric of the world; And in the handiwork of their craft is their prayer.

CHAPTER 39

¹Not so he that has applied his soul ǁ And meditates in the Law of the Most High; He will seek out the wisdom of all the ancients ǁ And will be occupied in prophecies. ²He will keep the discourse of the men of renown ǁ And will enter in amidst the subtleties of allegories. ³He will seek out the hidden meaning of proverbs ǁ And be conversant in the dark sayings of allegories. ⁴He will serve among great men ǁ And appear before him that rules. He will travel through the land of strange nations; For he has tried good things and evil among men. ⁵He will apply his heart to return early to the LORD that made him, ǁ And will make supplication before the Most High, ǁ And will open his mouth in prayer, ǁ And will make supplication for his sins. ⁶If the great LORD wills, ǁ He will be filled with the spirit of understanding: He will pour out the words of his wisdom, ǁ And in prayer give thanks to the LORD. ⁷He will direct his counsel and knowledge, ǁ And in His secrets he will meditate. ⁸He will show out the instruction which he has been taught ǁ And will glory in the Law of the covenant of the LORD. ⁹Many will commend his understanding; And so long as the world endures, ǁ It will not be blotted out: His memorial will not depart, ǁ And his name will live from generation to generation. ¹⁰Nations will declare his wisdom, ǁ And the congregation will tell out his praise. ¹¹If he continues, he will leave a greater name than one thousand, ǁ And if he dies, he adds to that. ¹²Yet more I will utter, which I have thought on; And I am filled as the moon at the full. ¹³Listen to me, you holy children, ǁ And bud out as a rose growing by a brook of water: ¹⁴And give a sweet savor as frankincense, ǁ And put out flowers as a lily; Spread abroad a sweet smell, ǁ And sing a song of praise; Bless the LORD for all His works. ¹⁵Magnify His Name, and give utterance to His praise ǁ With the songs of your lips, and with harps; And so will you say when you utter [His praise]: ¹⁶"All the works of the LORD are exceedingly good, ǁ And every command will be [accomplished] in his season." ¹⁷None can say, "What is this? What is that?" For in his season they will all be sought out. At His word the waters stood as a heap, ǁ And the receptacles of waters at the word of His mouth. ¹⁸At His command all His good pleasure is [done]; And there is none that will hinder His salvation. ¹⁹The works of all flesh are before Him; And it is not possible to be hid from His eyes. ²⁰He sees from age to age; And there is nothing wonderful before Him. ²¹None can say, "What is this? What is that?" For all things are created for their uses. ²²His blessing covered the dry land as a river ǁ And saturated it as a flood. ²³As He has made the waters salty, ǁ So the heathen will inherit His wrath. ²⁴His ways are plain to the holy, ǁ So are they stumbling blocks to the wicked. ²⁵Good things are created from the beginning for the good, ǁ So are evil things for sinners. ²⁶The chief of all things necessary for the life of man ǁ Are water, and fire, and iron, and salt, ǁ And flour of wheat, and honey, and milk, ǁ The blood of the grape, and oil, and clothing. ²⁷All these things are for good to the godly; So to the sinners they will be turned into evil. ²⁸There are winds that are created for vengeance, ǁ And in their fury their scourges lay on heavily; In the time of consummation they pour out their strength ǁ And will appease the wrath of Him that made them. ²⁹Fire, and hail, and famine, and death—All these are created for

vengeance— ³⁰Teeth of wild beasts, and scorpions and adders, || And a sword punishing the ungodly to destruction. ³¹They will rejoice in His command, || And will be made ready on earth when there is need; And in their seasons they will not transgress [His] word. ³²Therefore, I was resolved from the beginning, || And I considered [this, and] left it in writing; ³³All the works of the LORD are good: And He will supply every need in its season. ³⁴And none can say, "This is worse than that," || For they will all be well approved in their season. ³⁵And now with all your heart and mouth || Sing praises and bless the Name of the LORD.

CHAPTER 40

¹Great travail is created for every man, || And a heavy yoke is on the sons of Adam, || From the day of their coming out from their mother's womb, || Until the day for their burial in the mother of all things. ²The expectation of things to come, and the day of death, || [Trouble] their thoughts, and [cause] fear of heart— ³From him that sits on a lofty throne, || Even to him that is humbled in earth and ashes; ⁴From him that wears purple and a crown, || Even to him that is clothed with a hempen gown. ⁵[There is] wrath, and jealousy, and trouble, and disquiet, || And fear of death, and anger, and strife; And in the time of rest on his bed || His night sleep changes his knowledge. ⁶Little or nothing is his resting, || And afterward in his sleep, as in a day of keeping watch, || He is troubled in the vision of his heart, || As one that has escaped from the front of battle. ⁷In the very time of his deliverance he awakens, || And marvels that the fear is nothing. ⁸[It is so] with all flesh, from man to beast, || And on sinners sevenfold more. ⁹Death, and bloodshed, and strife, and sword, || Calamities, famine, suffering, and the scourge— ¹⁰All these things were created for the wicked, || And because of them the Flood came. ¹¹All things that are of the earth return to the earth again, || And [all things that are] of the waters return into the sea. ¹²All bribery and injustice will be blotted out; And good faith will stand forever. ¹³The goods of the unjust will be dried up like a river, || And like a great thunder in rain will go off in noise. ¹⁴In opening his hands, [a man] will be made glad; So will transgressors utterly fail. ¹⁵The children of the ungodly will not put out many branches; And [they are as] unclean roots on a sheer rock. ¹⁶The sedge [that grows] on every water and bank of a river || Will be plucked up before all grass. ¹⁷Bounty is as a garden of blessings, || And kindness endures forever. ¹⁸The life of one that labors, and is content, will be made sweet; And he that finds a treasure is above both. ¹⁹Children and the building of a city establish a name; And a blameless wife is counted above both. ²⁰Wine and music make the heart rejoice; And the love of wisdom is above both. ²¹The pipe and the lute make pleasant melody; And a pleasant tongue is above both. ²²Your eye will desire grace and beauty; And above both— the green blade of corn. ²³A friend and a companion never meet wrongly; And a wife with her husband is above both. ²⁴Brothers and help are for a time of affliction; And kindness is a deliverer above both. ²⁵Gold and silver will make the foot stand sure; And counsel is esteemed above them both. ²⁶Riches and strength will lift up the heart; And the fear of the LORD is above both: There is nothing lacking in the fear of the LORD, || And there is no need to seek help therein. ²⁷The fear of the LORD is as a garden of blessing || And [it] covers a man above all glory. ²⁸My son, do not lead a beggar's life; It is better to die than to beg. ²⁹A man that looks to the table of another, || His life is not to be counted for a life; He will pollute his soul with another man's meats, || But a man wise and well-instructed will beware thereof. ³⁰In the mouth of the shameless, begging will be sweet; And in his belly a fire will be kindled.

CHAPTER 41

¹O death, how bitter is the remembrance of you || To a man that is at peace in his possessions, || To the man that has nothing to distract him, || And [who] has prosperity in all things, || And who still has strength to receive meat! ²O death, your sentence is acceptable to a man that is needy, || And that fails in strength, that is in extreme old age, || And is distracted about all things, and is perverse, and has lost patience! ³Do not be afraid of the sentence of death; Remember those who have been before you, || And that come after: This is the sentence from the LORD over all flesh. ⁴And why do you refuse, || When it is the good pleasure of the Most High? Whether it be ten, or one hundred, or one thousand years, || There is no inquisition of life in the grave. ⁵The children of sinners are abominable children, || And they frequent the dwellings of the ungodly. ⁶The inheritance of sinners' children will perish, || And a perpetual reproach will be with their posterity. ⁷Children will complain of an ungodly father, || Because they will be reproached for his sake. ⁸Woe to you, ungodly men, || Which have forsaken the Law of the Most High God! ⁹If you are born, you will be born to a curse; If you die, a curse will be your portion. ¹⁰All things that are of the earth will go back to the earth; So the ungodly will go from a curse to perdition. ¹¹The mourning of men is about their bodies, || But the name of sinners being evil will be blotted out. ¹²Have regard for your name, || For it continues with you longer than one thousand great treasures of gold. ¹³A good life has its number of days; And a good name continues forever. ¹⁴My children, keep instruction in peace, || But wisdom that is hid, and a treasure that is not seen, || What profit is in them both? ¹⁵Better is a man that hides his foolishness || Than a man that hides his wisdom. ¹⁶Why show reverence to my word, || For it is not good to retain every kind of shame; And not all things are approved by all in good faith. ¹⁷Be ashamed of whoredom before father and mother, || And of a lie before a prince and a mighty man; ¹⁸Of an offense before a judge and ruler; Of iniquity before the congregation and the people; Of unjust dealing before a partner and friend; ¹⁹And of theft in regard of the place where you sojourn, || And in regard of the truth of God and His covenant; And of leaning with your elbow at meat; And of vulgarity in the matter of giving and taking; ²⁰And of silence before those who salute you; And of looking on a woman that is a prostitute; ²¹And of turning your face away from a relative; Of taking away a portion or a gift; And of gazing on a woman that has a husband; ²²Of being over-busy with his maid—And do not come near her bed; Of scolding speeches before friends; And after you have given, do not scold; ²³Of repeating and speaking what you have heard; And of revealing of secrets. ²⁴So you will be truly modest and find favor in the sight of every man.

CHAPTER 42

¹Do not be ashamed of these things, || And accept no man's person to sin [by it]: ²Of the Law of the Most High, and His covenant; And of judgment to do justice to the ungodly; ³Of reckoning with a partner and with travelers; And of a gift from the heritage of friends; ⁴Of exactness of balance and weights; And of getting much or little; ⁵Of indifferent selling of merchants; And of much correction of children; And of making the side of an evil servant to bleed. ⁶Keeping a seal is good where an evil wife is; And where many hands are, shut [things] closed. ⁷Whatever you hand over, || Let it be by number and weight; And in giving and receiving, || Let all be in writing. ⁸[Do not be ashamed] to instruct the unwise and foolish, || And one of extreme old age that contends with those that are young; And so you will be well instructed indeed, || And approved in the sight of every living man. ⁹A daughter is a secret cause of wakefulness to a father; And the care for her puts away sleep in her youth, || Lest she pass the flower of her age; And when she is married, || Lest she should be hated; ¹⁰In her virginity, || Lest she should be defiled || And be with child in her father's house; And when she has a husband, || Lest she should transgress; And when she is married, || Lest she should be barren. ¹¹Keep a strict watch over a headstrong daughter, || Lest she makes you a laughing-stock to your enemies, || A byword in the city and notorious among the people, || And shame you before the multitude. ¹²Do not look on everybody in regard of beauty || And do not sit in the midst of women; ¹³For from garments comes a moth, || And from a woman a woman's wickedness. ¹⁴Better is the wickedness of a man || Than a pleasant-dealing woman, || And a woman which puts you to shameful reproach. ¹⁵I will now make mention of the works of the LORD || And will declare the things that I have seen: In the words of the LORD are His works. ¹⁶The sun that gives light looks on all things; And the work of the LORD is full of His glory. ¹⁷The LORD has not given power to the saints || To declare all His marvelous works, || Which the Almighty LORD firmly settled, || That whatever exists might be established in His glory. ¹⁸He searches out the

SIRACH

deep, and the heart, || And He has understanding of their cunning plans; For the Most High knows all knowledge, || And He looks into the signs of the world, ¹⁹Declaring the things that are past, || And the things that will be, || And revealing the traces of hidden things. ²⁰No thought escapes Him; There is no word hidden from Him. ²¹He has ordered the mighty works of His wisdom—[He] who is from age to age: Nothing has been added to them, || Nor diminished from them; And He had no need of any counselor. ²²How desirable are all His works! One may behold [this] even to a spark. ²³All these things live and remain forever in all manner of uses, || And they are all obedient. ²⁴All things are double—one against another: And He has made nothing imperfect. ²⁵One thing establishes the good things of another; And who will be filled with beholding His glory?

CHAPTER 43

¹The pride of the height is the expanse in its clearness, || The appearance of Heaven, in the spectacle of its glory. ²The sun when he appears, || Bringing tidings as he goes out, || Is a marvelous instrument, the work of the Most High: ³At his noon he dries up the country, || And who will stand against his burning heat? ⁴A man blowing a furnace is in works of heat, || [But] the sun [is] three times more: Burning up the mountains, || Breathing out fiery vapors, || And sending out bright beams—he dims the eyes. ⁵Great is the LORD that made him; And at His word he hastens his course. ⁶The moon is also in all things for her season, || For a declaration of times, and a sign of the world. ⁷From the moon is the sign of the feast day—A light that wanes when she has come to the full. ⁸The month is called after her name, || Increasing wonderfully in her changing; An instrument of the army on high, || Shining out in the expanse of Heaven; ⁹The beauty of Heaven, the glory of the stars, || An ornament giving light in the highest places of the LORD. ¹⁰At the word of the Holy One they will stand in due order, || And they will not faint in their watches. ¹¹Look on the rainbow and praise Him that made it—Exceedingly beautiful in the brightness thereof. ¹²It encircles the Heaven around with a circle of glory; The hands of the Most High have stretched it. ¹³By His command He makes the snow to fall speedily || And swiftly sends the lightnings of His judgment. ¹⁴By reason thereof the treasure-houses are opened; And clouds fly out as birds. ¹⁵By His mighty power He makes the clouds strong, || And the hailstones are broken small: ¹⁶And at His appearing the mountains will be shaken, || And at His will the south wind will blow. ¹⁷The voice of His thunder makes the earth to travail; So does the northern storm and the whirlwind. As birds flying down, He sprinkles the snow; And as the lighting of the locust is the falling down thereof: ¹⁸The eye will marvel at the beauty of its whiteness, || And the heart will be astonished at the raining of it. ¹⁹He also pours the hoarfrost on the earth as salt; And when it is congealed, it is [as] points of thorns. ²⁰The cold north wind will blow, || And the ice will be congealed on the water: It will lodge on every gathering of water, || And the water will put it on as [if] it were a breastplate. ²¹It will devour the mountains, and burn up the wilderness, || And consume the green herb as fire. ²²A mist coming speedily is the healing of all things; A dew coming after heat will bring cheerfulness. ²³By His counsel He has stilled the deep, || And planted islands therein. ²⁴They that sail on the sea tell of the danger thereof; And when we hear it with our ears, we marvel. ²⁵Therein are also those strange and wondrous works, || A variety of all that has life—the race of sea-monsters. ²⁶By reason of Him his end has success, || And by His word all things consist. ²⁷We may say many things, || Yet we will not attain [to them]; And the sum of our words is, "He is all." ²⁸How will we have strength to glorify Him? For He Himself is the great one above all His works. ²⁹The LORD is terrible and exceedingly great; And His power is marvelous. ³⁰When you glorify the LORD, || Exalt Him as much as you can; For even yet He will exceed: And when you exalt Him, put out your full strength: Do not be weary, for you will never attain. ³¹Who has seen Him, that he may declare Him? And who will magnify Him as He is? ³²Many things are hidden greater than these; For we have seen but a few of His works. ³³For the LORD made all things; And He gave wisdom to the godly.

CHAPTER 44

¹Let us now praise famous men, || And our fathers that became the father of us. ²The LORD manifested [in them] great glory, || [Even] His mighty power from the beginning: ³Such as bore rule in their kingdoms, || And were men renowned for their power, || Giving counsel by their understanding; Such as have brought tidings in prophecies; ⁴Leaders of the people by their counsels, || And by their understanding [men of] learning for the people—Wise [were] their words in their instruction; ⁵Such as sought out musical tunes, || And set out verses in writing; ⁶Rich men furnished with ability, || Living peaceably in their habitations: ⁷All these were honored in their generations, || And were a glory in their days. ⁸There is of them, that have left a name behind them, || To declare their praises. ⁹And there are some which have no memorial, || Who have perished as though they had not been || And have become as though they had not been born—And their children after them. ¹⁰But these were men of mercy, || Whose righteous deeds have not been forgotten. ¹¹A good inheritance will remain with their seed continually; Their children [are] within the covenants. ¹²Their seed stands fast, || And their children for their sakes. ¹³Their seed will remain forever, || And their glory will not be blotted out. ¹⁴Their bodies were buried in peace, || And their name lives to all generations. ¹⁵Peoples will declare their wisdom, || And the congregation tells out their praise. ¹⁶Enoch pleased the LORD, and was translated, || [Being] an example of conversion to all generations. ¹⁷Noah was found perfect [and] righteous; In the season of wrath, he was taken in exchange [for the world]; Therefore a remnant was left to the earth when the Flood came. ¹⁸Perpetual covenants were made with him, || That all flesh should no longer be blotted out by a flood. ¹⁹Abraham was a great father of a multitude of nations; And there was none found like him in glory, ²⁰Who kept the Law of the Most High || And was taken into covenant with Him: In his flesh he established the covenant; And when he was tested, he was found faithful. ²¹Therefore He assured him by an oath, || That the nations should be blessed in his seed; That He would multiply him as the dust of the earth, || And exalt his seed as the stars, || And cause them to inherit from sea to sea, || And from the River to the utmost part of the earth. ²²In Isaac He also established likewise, for his father Abraham's sake, || The blessing of all men, and the covenant: ²³And He made it rest on the head of Jacob; He acknowledged him in His blessings, || And gave to him by inheritance, and divided his portions; He parted them among [the] twelve tribes.

CHAPTER 45

¹And He brought out of him a man of mercy, || Which found favor in the sight of all flesh; A man beloved of God and men—Even Moses, whose memorial is blessed. ²He made him like to the glory of the saints || And magnified him in the fears of his enemies. ³By his words He caused the wonders to cease; He glorified him in the sight of kings; He gave him command for his people || And showed him part of His glory. ⁴He sanctified him in his faithfulness and meekness; He chose him out of all flesh. ⁵He made him to hear His voice, || And led him into the thick darkness, || And gave him commands face to face—Even the law of life and knowledge, || That he might teach Jacob the covenant, || And Israel His judgments. ⁶He exalted Aaron, a holy man like to him, || Even his brother, of the tribe of Levi. ⁷He established a perpetual covenant for him || And gave him the priesthood of the people; He beautified him with attractive ornaments || And girded him around with a robe of glory. ⁸He clothed him with the perfection of exultation, || And strengthened him with apparel of honor: The linen trousers, the long robe, and the ephod. ⁹And He compassed him with pomegranates of gold, || And with many bells around—To send out a sound as he went, || To make a sound that might be heard in the temple, || For a memorial to the children of his people— ¹⁰With a holy garment, || With gold, and blue, and purple, the work of the embroiderer, || With an oracle of judgment, || With the Lights and Perfections; ¹¹With twisted scarlet, the work of the craftsman, || With precious stones graven like a signet, || In a setting of gold, the work of the jeweler, || For a memorial engraved in writing, || After the number of the tribes of Israel; ¹²With a crown of gold on the miter, || Having graven on it, as on a signet, HOLINESS, || An ornament of honor, a work of might, || The desires of the eyes, attractive and

SIRACH

beautiful. ¹³There have never been any such before him; No stranger put them on, || But his sons only, and his offspring perpetually. ¹⁴His sacrifices will be wholly consumed every day—twice continually. ¹⁵Moses consecrated him and anointed him with holy oil: It was to him for a perpetual covenant, || And to his seed, all the days of Heaven, || To minister to Him, and also to execute the priest's office, || And to bless His people in His Name. ¹⁶He chose him out of all living to offer sacrifice to the LORD, || Incense, and a sweet savor, for a memorial, || To make reconciliation for Your people. ¹⁷He gave His commands to him—Authority in the covenants of judgments, || To teach Jacob the testimonies, || And to enlighten Israel in His law. ¹⁸Strangers gathered themselves together against him, || And envied him in the wilderness, || [Even] Dathan and Abiram with their company, || And the congregation of Korah, with wrath and anger. ¹⁹The LORD saw it, and it displeased Him; And in the wrath of His anger they were destroyed: He did wonders on them, || To consume them with flaming fire. ²⁰And He added glory to Aaron and gave him a heritage: He divided to him the first-fruits of the increase; [And] first he prepared bread in abundance: ²¹For they will eat the sacrifices of the LORD, || Which He gave to him and to his seed. ²²However, in the land of the people he will have no inheritance, || And he has no portion among the people; For He Himself is your portion [and] inheritance. ²³And Phinehas the son of Eleazar is the third in glory, || In that he was zealous in the fear of the LORD, || And stood fast in the good forwardness of his soul when the people turned away, || And he made reconciliation for Israel. ²⁴Therefore there was a covenant of peace established for him, || [That he should be] leader of the saints and of His people; That he and his seed should have the dignity of the priesthood forever. ²⁵Also [He made] a covenant with David the son of Jesse, of the tribe of Judah; The inheritance of the king is his alone from son to son; So the inheritance of Aaron is also to his seed. ²⁶[God] give you wisdom in your heart to judge His people in righteousness, || That their good things may not be abolished, || And [that] their glory [may endure] for all their generations.

CHAPTER 46

¹Joshua the son of Nun was valiant in war || And was the successor of Moses in prophecies: Who according to his name was made great for the saving of God's chosen ones, || To take vengeance of the enemies that rose up against them, || That he might give Israel their inheritance. ²How he was glorified in lifting up his hands, || And in stretching out his sword against the cities! ³Who before him so stood fast? For the LORD Himself brought his enemies to him. ⁴Did the sun not go back by his hand? And did one day not become as two? ⁵He called on the Most High [and] Mighty One, || When his enemies pressed him around; And the great LORD heard him. ⁶With hailstones of mighty power || He caused war to break violently on the nation, || And in the going down he destroyed those who resisted, || That the nations might know his armor, || How that he fought in the sight of the LORD; For he followed after the Mighty One. ⁷Also in the time of Moses he did a work of mercy—He and Caleb the son of Jephunneh, || In that they withstood the adversary, || Hindered the people from sin, || And stilled the murmuring of wickedness. ⁸And of six hundred thousand people on foot, || They two alone were preserved to bring them into the heritage, || Even into a land flowing with milk and honey. ⁹Also the LORD gave strength to Caleb, || And it remained with him to his old age, || So that he entered on the height of the land, || And his seed obtained it for a heritage: ¹⁰That all the sons of Israel might see || That it is good to walk after the LORD. ¹¹Also the judges, everyone by His Name—All whose hearts did not go whoring, || And who did not turn away from the LORD—May their memorial be blessed, ¹²May their bones again flourish out of their place, || And may the name of those who have been honored be renewed on their children. ¹³Samuel, the prophet of the LORD, beloved of his Lord, || Established a kingdom, and anointed princes over His people. ¹⁴By the Law of the LORD he judged the congregation, || And the LORD visited Jacob. ¹⁵By his faithfulness he was proved to be a prophet, || And by his words he was known to be faithful in vision. ¹⁶Also when his enemies pressed around him, || He called on the LORD, the Mighty One, || With the offering of the sucking lamb. ¹⁷And the LORD thundered from Heaven, || And made His voice to be heard with a mighty sound. ¹⁸And He utterly destroyed the rulers of the Tyrians, || And all the princes of the Philistines. ¹⁹Also before the time of his long sleep || He made protestations in the sight of the LORD and [His] anointed: "I have not taken any man's goods, so much as a sandal": And no man did accuse him. ²⁰And after he fell asleep, he prophesied, || And showed the king his end, || And lifted up his voice from the earth in prophecy, || To blot out the wickedness of the people.

CHAPTER 47

¹And after him, Nathan rose up to prophesy in the days of David. ²As is the fat when it is separated from the peace offering, || So was David [separated] from the sons of Israel. ³He played with lions as with kids, || And with bears as with lambs of the flock. ⁴In his youth did he not kill a giant, || And take away reproach from the people, || When he lifted up his hand with a sling stone, || And beat down the boasting of Goliath? ⁵For he called on the Most High LORD; And He gave him strength in his right hand, || To kill a man mighty in war, || To exalt the horn of His people. ⁶So they glorified him for [his] tens of thousands, || And praised him for the blessings of the LORD, || In that there was given to him a diadem of glory. ⁷For he destroyed the enemies on every side, || And brought to nothing the Philistines his adversaries, || [And] broke their horn in pieces to this day. ⁸In every work of his || He gave thanks to the Holy One Most High with words of glory; With his whole heart he sang praise || And loved Him that made him. ⁹He also set singers before the altar, || So as to make sweet melody by their music. ¹⁰He gave beauty to the feasts, || And set in order the seasons to perfection, || While they praised His holy Name, || And the sanctuary sounded from early morning. ¹¹The LORD took away his sins, || And exalted his horn forever, || And gave him a covenant of kings, || And a throne of glory in Israel. ¹²After him, [his] son rose up—a man of understanding; And for his sake he lived at large. ¹³Solomon reigned in days of peace; And God gave to him rest around, || That he might set up a house for His Name || And prepare a sanctuary forever. ¹⁴How wise you were made in your youth || And filled as a river with understanding! ¹⁵Your soul covered the earth, || And you filled it with dark allegories. ¹⁶Your name reached to the isles far off; And you were beloved for your peace. ¹⁷For your songs, and proverbs, and allegories, || And for your interpretations, the countries marveled at you. ¹⁸By the Name of the LORD God, which is called the God of Israel, || You gathered gold as tin and multiplied silver as lead. ¹⁹You bowed your loins to women, || And in your body you were brought into subjection. ²⁰You blemished your honor and profaned your seed, || To bring wrath on your children; And I was grieved for your folly, ²¹So that the sovereignty was divided, || And out of Ephraim a disobedient kingdom ruled. ²²But the LORD will never forsake His mercy; And He will not destroy any of His works, || Nor blot out the posterity of His chosen ones; And the seed of him that loved Him He will not take away; And He gave a remnant to Jacob, || And to David a root out of him. ²³And [so] rested Solomon with his fathers; And of his seed he left behind him Rehoboam—[Even] the foolishness of the people, || And one that lacked understanding, || Who made the people to revolt by his counsel. Also Jeroboam the son of Nebat, || Who made Israel to sin, and gave to Ephraim a way of sin. ²⁴And their sins were multiplied exceedingly, || To remove them from their land. ²⁵For they sought out all manner of wickedness, || Until vengeance should come on them.

CHAPTER 48

¹Also there arose Elijah the prophet as fire, || And his word burned like a torch: ²Who brought a famine on them, || And by his zeal made them few in number. ³By the word of the LORD he shut up the Heaven: Three times he so brought down fire. ⁴How you were glorified, O Elijah, in your wondrous deeds! And who will [have] glory like to you? ⁵Who raised up a dead man from death, || And from the place of the dead, by the word of the Most High; ⁶Who brought down kings to destruction, || And honorable men from their bed; ⁷Who heard rebuke in Sinai, || And judgments of vengeance in Horeb; ⁸Who anointed kings for retribution, || And prophets to succeed after him; ⁹Who was taken up in a tempest of fire, || In a chariot of

fiery horses; ¹⁰Who was recorded for reproofs in their seasons, || To pacify anger, before it broke out into wrath; To turn the heart of the father to the son, || And to restore the tribes of Jacob. ¹¹Blessed are those who saw you, || And those who have been beautified with love; For we also will surely live. ¹²[It was] Elijah who was wrapped in a tempest, || And Elisha was filled with his spirit; And in [all] his days he was not moved by [the fear of] any ruler, || And no one brought him into subjection. ¹³Nothing was too high for him; And when he was laid on sleep his body prophesied. ¹⁴As in his life he did wonders, || So in death his works were marvelous. ¹⁵For all this the people did not convert, || And they did not depart from their sins, || Until they were carried away as a plunder from their land || And were scattered through all the earth; And the people were left very few in number, || And a ruler [was left] in the house of David. ¹⁶Some of them did that which was pleasing [to God], || [And] some multiplied sins. ¹⁷Hezekiah fortified his city || And brought in water into the midst of them: He dug the sheer rock with iron || And built up wells for waters. ¹⁸In his days Sennacherib came up, || And sent Rabshakeh, and departed; And he lifted up his hand against Zion || And boasted great things in his arrogance. ¹⁹Then their hearts and their hands were shaken, || And they were in pain, as women in travail; ²⁰And they called on the LORD, who is merciful, || Spreading out their hands to Him: And the Holy One heard them speedily out of Heaven, || And delivered them by the hand of Isaiah. ²¹He struck the camp of the Assyrians, || And His messenger utterly destroyed them. ²²For Hezekiah did that which was pleasing to the LORD || And was strong in the ways of his father David, || Which Isaiah the prophet commanded, || Who was great and faithful in his vision. ²³In his days the sun went backward; And he added life to the king. ²⁴He saw by an excellent spirit what should come to pass at the end; And he comforted those who mourned in Zion. ²⁵He showed the things that should be to the end of time, || And the hidden things before they came.

CHAPTER 49

¹The memorial of Josiah is like the composition of incense || Prepared by the work of the apothecary: It will be sweet as honey in every mouth, || And as music at a banquet of wine. ²He behaved himself uprightly in the conversion of the people || And took away the abominations of iniquity. ³He set his heart right toward the LORD; In the days of wicked men, || He made godliness to prevail. ⁴Except David, and Hezekiah, and Josiah, all committed trespass; For they forsook the Law of the Most High; The kings of Judah failed. ⁵For they gave their power to others, || And their glory to a strange nation. ⁶They set the chosen city of the sanctuary on fire, || And made her streets desolate, [as it was written] by the hand of Jeremiah. ⁷For they mistreated him; And yet he was sanctified in the womb to be a prophet, || To root out, and to afflict, and to destroy; [And] in like manner to build and to plant. ⁸[It was] Ezekiel who saw the vision of glory, || Which [God] showed him on the chariot of the cherubim. ⁹For truly he remembered the enemies in storm, || And to do good to those who directed their ways correctly. ¹⁰Also of the twelve prophets || May the bones flourish again out of their place. And he comforted Jacob and delivered them by confidence of hope. ¹¹How will we magnify Zerubbabel? And he was as a signet on the right hand: ¹²So was Jesus the son of Josedek: Who in their days built the house, || And exalted a people holy to the LORD, prepared for continuous glory. ¹³Also of Nehemiah the memorial is great: Who raised up for us the walls that were fallen, || And set up the gates and bars, and raised up our homes again. ¹⁴No man was created on the earth such as was Enoch; For he was taken up from the earth. ¹⁵Neither was there a man born like to Joseph, || A governor of his countrymen, a support of the people: Yes, his bones were visited. ¹⁶Shem and Seth were glorified among men; And above every living thing in the creation is Adam.

CHAPTER 50

¹[It was] Simon, the son of Onias, the great priest, || Who in his life repaired the house, || And in his days strengthened the temple: ²And by him was built from the foundation the height of the double [wall], || The lofty underworks of the enclosure of the temple: ³In his days the cistern of waters was diminished, || The brazen vessel in compass as the sea. ⁴[It was] he that took thought for his people that they should not fall || And fortified the city against besieging; ⁵How glorious was he when the people gathered around him || At his coming out of the sanctuary— ⁶As the morning star in the midst of a cloud, || As the moon at the full; ⁷As the sun shining out on the temple of the Most High, || And as the rainbow giving light in clouds of glory; ⁸As the flower of roses in the days of new [fruits], || As lilies at the water spring, || As the shoot of the frankincense tree in the time of summer; ⁹As fire and incense in the censer, || As a vessel all of beaten gold, || Adorned with all manner of precious stones; ¹⁰As an olive tree budding out fruits, || And as a cypress growing high among the clouds. ¹¹When he took up the robe of glory, || And put on the perfection of exultation, || In the ascent of the holy altar, || He made the precinct of the sanctuary glorious. ¹²And when he received the portions out of the priests' hands, || Himself also standing by the hearth of the altar, || His countrymen as a garland around him, || He was as a young cedar in Libanus; And as stems of palm trees compassed around him, ¹³And all the sons of Aaron in their glory, || And the LORD's offering in their hands, || Before all the congregation of Israel. ¹⁴And finishing the service at the altars, || That he might adorn the offering of the Most High, the Almighty, ¹⁵He stretched out his hand to the cup, || And poured out the cup of the grape; He poured out at the foot of the altar || A sweet smelling savor to the Most High, the King of all. ¹⁶Then the sons of Aaron shouted, || They sounded the trumpets of beaten work, || They made a great noise to be heard, || For a remembrance before the Most High. ¹⁷Then all the people hurried together || And fell down on the earth on their faces to worship their Lord—The Almighty, God Most High. ¹⁸The singers also praised Him with their voices; In the whole house sweet melody was made. ¹⁹And the people implored the LORD Most High, || In prayer before Him that is merciful, || Until the worship of the LORD should be ended; And so, they accomplished His service. ²⁰Then he went down and lifted up his hands || Over the whole congregation of the sons of Israel, || To give blessing to the LORD with his lips, || And to glory in His Name. ²¹And he bowed himself down in worship the second time, || To declare the blessing from the Most High. ²²And now bless the God of all, who everywhere does great things, || Who exalts our days from the womb, || And deals with us according to His mercy. ²³May He grant us joyfulness of heart, || And that peace may be in our days in Israel for the days of [the] age: ²⁴To entrust His mercy with us; And let Him deliver us in His time! ²⁵With two nations is my soul vexed, || And the third is no nation: ²⁶They that sit on the mountain of Samaria, and the Philistines, || And that foolish people that dwells in Shechem. ²⁷I have written in this scroll the instruction of understanding and knowledge, || I, Jesus, the son of Sirach Eleazar, of Jerusalem, || Who out of his heart poured out wisdom. ²⁸Blessed is he that will be exercised in these things; And he that lays them up in his heart will become wise. ²⁹For if he does them, he will be strong for all things; For the light of the LORD is his guide.

CHAPTER 51

A PRAYER OF JESUS THE SON OF SIRACH. ¹I will give thanks to You, O LORD, O King, || And will praise You, O God my Savior: I give thanks to Your Name, ²For You were my protector and helper, || And You delivered my body out of destruction, || And out of the snare of a slanderous tongue, || From lips that forge lies, || And were my helper before those who stood by; ³And You delivered me, || According to the abundance of Your mercy, and [greatness] of Your Name, || From the gnashing [of teeth] ready to devour, || Out of the hand of such as sought my life, || Out of the manifold afflictions which I had; ⁴From the choking of a fire on every side, || And out of the midst of fire which I did not kindle; ⁵Out of the depth of the belly of the grave, || And from an unclean tongue, and from lying words— ⁶The slander of an unrighteous tongue to the king. My soul drew near even to death, || And my life was near to the grave beneath. ⁷They compassed me on every side, || And there was none to help [me]. I was looking for the help of men, and it was not. ⁸And I remembered Your mercy, O LORD, || And Your working which has been from perpetuity, || How You deliver those who wait for You, || And save them out of the hand of the enemies. ⁹And I lifted up my supplication from the earth || And prayed for deliverance from death. ¹⁰I called on the LORD, the Father of my Lord, || That He would not forsake me in the days of affliction, || In the time when there was no help against the proud. ¹¹I will praise Your Name continually || And will sing praise with thanksgiving; And my supplication was heard: ¹²For You saved me from destruction, || And delivered me from the evil time. Therefore, I will give thanks and praise to You, || And bless the Name of the LORD. ¹³When I was yet young, before I went abroad, || I sought wisdom openly in my prayer. ¹⁴Before the temple I asked for her, || And I will seek her out even to the end. ¹⁵From [her] flower, as from the ripening grape, || My heart delighted in her; My foot trod in uprightness, || From my youth I tracked her out. ¹⁶I bowed my ear down a little, and received her, || And found for myself much instruction. ¹⁷I profited in her: To Him that gives me wisdom I will give glory. ¹⁸For I purposed to practice her, || And I was zealous for that which is good; And I will never be put to shame. ¹⁹My soul has wrestled in her, || And in my doing I was exact: I spread out my hands to the Heaven above || And mourned my ignorance of her. ²⁰I set my soul properly to her, || And in pureness I found her. I got myself a heart [joined] with her from the beginning: Therefore, I will not be forsaken. ²¹My inward part was also troubled to seek her: Therefore, I have gotten a good possession. ²²The LORD gave me a tongue for my reward; And I will praise Him with that. ²³Draw near to me, you unlearned, || And lodge in the house of instruction. ²⁴Say, "Why are you lacking in these things, || And your souls are very thirsty?" ²⁵I opened my mouth, and spoke, || "Get her for yourselves without money. ²⁶Put your neck under the yoke, || And let your soul receive instruction: She is hard at hand to find. ²⁷Behold with your eyes, how that I labored but a little, || And found for myself much rest. ²⁸Get instruction with a great sum of silver || And gain much gold by her. ²⁹May your soul rejoice in His mercy, || And may you not be put to shame in praising Him. ³⁰Work your work before the time comes, || And in His time, He will give you your reward."

1 BARUCH

Called Baruch by most, but 1 Baruch in the LSV for distinction, the opening verses ascribe the book to the well-known assistant to Jeremiah (Jer. 32:12; 36:4, 32; 45:1). It is a collection of four very different compositions, ending with a work entitled "The Letter of Jeremiah," which circulated separately in major manuscripts of the Greek tradition. The original language was likely Hebrew, but only the Greek and other versions have been preserved. The setting is Babylon, where Baruch reads his scroll to King Jechoniah (Jehoiachin) and the exiles; they react by sending gifts and the scroll to Jerusalem (1:1–14), presumably by the hand of Baruch (1:7). No certain date can be given for the book, but it may have been edited in final form during the last two centuries BC.

CHAPTER 1

¹These are the words of the scroll, which Baruch the son of Neriah, the son of Mahseiah, the son of Zedekiah, the son of Hasadiah, the son of Hilkiah, wrote in Babylon, ²in the fifth year, [and] in the seventh day of the month, at the time the Chaldeans took Jerusalem, and burned it with fire. ³And Baruch read the words of this scroll in the hearing of Jehoiachin the son of Jehoiakim king of Judah, and in the hearing of all the people that came to [hear] the scroll, ⁴and in the hearing of the mighty men, and of the kings' sons, and in the hearing of the elders, and in the hearing of all the people, from the least to the greatest, even of all those who lived at Babylon by the River Sud. ⁵And they wept, and fasted, and prayed before the LORD; ⁶they also made a collection of money according to every man's power: ⁷and they sent [it] to Jerusalem to Jehoiakim the [high] priest, the son of Hilkiah, the son of Salom, and to the priests, and to all the people which were found with him at Jerusalem, ⁸at the same time when he took the vessels of the house of the LORD, that had been carried out of the temple, to return [them] into the land of Judah, the tenth day of the [month] Sivan, [namely,] silver vessels, which Zedekiah the son of Josiah king of Judah had made, ⁹after Nebuchadnezzar king of Babylon had carried away Jehoiachin, and the princes, and the captives, and the mighty men, and the people of the land, from Jerusalem, and brought them to Babylon. ¹⁰And they said: "Behold, we have sent you money; therefore buy with the money burnt-offerings, and sin offerings, and incense, and prepare an oblation, and offer on the altar of the LORD our God; ¹¹and pray for the life of Nebuchadnezzar king of Babylon, and for the life of his son Belshazzar, that their days may be as the days of Heaven above the earth: ¹²and the LORD will give us strength, and lighten our eyes, and we will live under the shadow of Nebuchadnezzar king of Babylon, and under the shadow of his son Belshazzar, and we will serve them many days, and find favor in their sight. ¹³Pray for us also to the LORD our God, for we have sinned against the LORD our God; and to this day the wrath of the LORD and His indignation is not turned from us. ¹⁴And you will read this scroll which we have sent to you, to make confession in the house of the LORD, on the day of the feast and on the days of the solemn assembly." ¹⁵And you will say: To the LORD our God [belongs] righteousness, but to us confusion of face, as at this day, to the men of Judah, and to the inhabitants of Jerusalem, ¹⁶and to our kings, and to our princes, and to our priests, and to our prophets, and to our fathers: ¹⁷for that we have sinned before the LORD, ¹⁸and disobeyed Him, and have not listened to the voice of the LORD our God, to walk in the commands of the LORD that He has set before us: ¹⁹since the day that the LORD brought our fathers out of the land of Egypt, to this present day, we have been disobedient to the LORD our God, and we have dealt unadvisedly in not listening to His voice. ²⁰Why the plagues cleaved to us, and the curse, which the LORD commanded Moses His servant [to pronounce] in the day that He brought our fathers out of the land of Egypt, to give us a land that flows with milk and honey, as at this day. ²¹Nevertheless, we did not listen to the voice of the LORD our God, according to all the words of the prophets, whom He sent to us, ²²but we walked—every man—in the imagination of his own wicked heart, to serve strange gods, and to do that which is evil in the sight of the LORD our God.

CHAPTER 2

¹Therefore the LORD has made good His word, which He pronounced against us, and against our judges that judged Israel, and against our kings, and against our princes, and against the men of Israel and Judah, ²to bring on us great plagues, such as never happened under the whole Heaven, as it came to pass in Jerusalem, according to the things that are written in the Law of Moses; ³That we should eat—every man—the flesh of his own son, and every man the flesh of his own daughter. ⁴Moreover, He has given them to be in subjection to all the kingdoms that are around us, to be a reproach and a desolation among all the surrounding people, where the LORD has scattered them. ⁵So were they cast down, and not exalted, because we sinned against the LORD our God, in not listening to His voice. ⁶To the LORD our God [belongs] righteousness, but to us and to our fathers confusion of face, as at this day. ⁷[For] all these plagues have come on us, which the LORD has pronounced against us. ⁸Yet we have not entreated the favor of the LORD, in turning everyone from the thoughts of his wicked heart. ⁹Therefore the LORD has kept watch over the plagues, and the LORD has brought [them] on us; for the LORD is righteous in all His works which He has commanded us. ¹⁰Yet we have not listened to His voice, to walk in the commands of the LORD that He has set before us. ¹¹And now, O LORD, You God of Israel, that have brought Your people out of the land of Egypt with a mighty hand, and with signs, and with wonders, and with great power, and with a high arm, and have gotten Yourself a Name, as at this day: ¹²O LORD our God, we have sinned, we have been ungodly, we have dealt unrighteously in all Your ordinances. ¹³Let Your wrath turn from us, for we are but a few

left among the heathen, where You have scattered us. ¹⁴Hear our prayer, O LORD, and our petition, and deliver us for Your own sake, and give us favor in the sight of them which have led us away captive, ¹⁵that all the earth may know that You are the LORD our God, because Israel and his posterity is called by Your Name. ¹⁶O LORD, look down from Your holy house, and consider us: incline Your ear, O LORD, and hear: ¹⁷open Your eyes, and behold, for the dead that are in the grave, whose breath is taken from their bodies, will give to the LORD neither glory nor righteousness: ¹⁸but the soul that is greatly vexed, which goes stooping and feeble, and the eyes that fail, and the hungry soul, will give You glory and righteousness, O LORD. ¹⁹For we do not present our supplication before You, O LORD our God, for the righteousness of our fathers, and of our kings. ²⁰For You have sent Your wrath and Your indignation on us, as You have spoken by Your servants the prophets, [saying,] ²¹"The LORD says, Bow your shoulders to serve the king of Babylon, and remain in the land that I gave to your fathers. ²²But if you will not hear the voice of the LORD, to serve the king of Babylon, ²³I will cause to cease out of the cities of Judah, and from the region near Jerusalem, the voice of mirth, and the voice of gladness, the voice of the bridegroom, and the voice of the bride: and the whole land will be desolate without inhabitant." ²⁴But we would not listen to Your voice, to serve the king of Babylon: therefore You have made good Your words that You spoke by Your servants the prophets, [namely,] that the bones of our kings, and the bones of our fathers, should be taken out of their places. ²⁵And behold, they are cast out to the heat by day, and to the frost by night, and they died in great miseries by famine, by sword, and by pestilence. ²⁶And the house which is called by Your Name have You laid [waste], as at this day, for the wickedness of the house of Israel and the house of Judah. ²⁷Yet, O LORD our God, You have dealt with us after all Your kindness, and according to all Your great mercy, ²⁸as You spoke by Your servant Moses in the day when You commanded him to write Your law before the sons of Israel, saying, ²⁹"If you will not hear My voice, surely this very great multitude will be turned into a small [number] among the nations, where I will scatter them. ³⁰For I know that they will not hear Me, because it is a stiff-necked people, but in the land of their captivity they will take it to heart, ³¹and will know that I am the LORD their God: and I will give them a heart, and ears to hear: ³²and they will praise Me in the land of their captivity, and think on My Name, ³³and will return from their stiff neck, and from their wicked deeds, for they will remember the way of their fathers, which sinned before the LORD. ³⁴And I will bring them again into the land which I swore to their fathers, to Abraham, to Isaac, and to Jacob, and they will be lords of it: and I will increase them, and they will not be diminished. ³⁵And I will make a perpetual covenant with them to be their God, and they will be My people: and I will no longer remove My people Israel out of the land that I have given them."

CHAPTER 3

¹O LORD Almighty, You God of Israel, the soul in anguish, the troubled spirit, cries to You. ²Hear, O LORD, and have mercy; for You are a merciful God: yes, have mercy on us, because we have sinned before You. ³For You sit [as king] forever, and we perish forevermore. ⁴O LORD Almighty, You God of Israel, hear now the prayer of the dead Israelites, and of the children of them which were sinners before You, that did not listen to the voice of You their God, for this reason these plagues cleaved to us. ⁵Do not remember the iniquities of our fathers, but remember Your power and Your Name [now] at this time. ⁶For You are the LORD our God, and You, O LORD, will we praise. ⁷For this reason You have put Your fear in our hearts, to the intent that we should call on Your Name, and we will praise You in our captivity, for we have called to mind all the iniquity of our fathers, that sinned before You. ⁸Behold, we are yet this day in our captivity, where You have scattered us, for a reproach and a curse, and to be subject to penalty, according to all the iniquities of our fathers, which departed from the LORD our God. ⁹Hear, O Israel, the commands of life: give ear to understand wisdom. ¹⁰How is it, O Israel, that you are in your enemies' land, that you have become old in a strange country, that you are defiled with the dead, ¹¹that you are counted with those who [go down] into the grave? ¹²You have forsaken the fountain of wisdom. ¹³[For] if you had walked in the way of God, you should have dwelled in peace forever. ¹⁴Learn where is wisdom, where is strength, where is understanding; that you may also know where is length of days, and life, where is the light of the eyes, and peace. ¹⁵Who has found out her place? And who has come into her treasuries? ¹⁶Where are the princes of the heathen, and such as ruled the beasts that are on the earth; ¹⁷those who had their pastime with the birds of the air, and those who hoarded up silver and gold, wherein men trust; and of whose getting there is no end? ¹⁸For those who made in silver, and were so careful, and whose works are past finding out, ¹⁹they are vanished and gone down to the grave, and others have come up in their steads. ²⁰Younger men have seen the light and lived on the earth, but the way of knowledge they have not known, ²¹neither did they understand the paths thereof, neither have their children embraced it: they are far off from their way. ²²It has not been heard of in Canaan, neither has it been seen in Teman. ²³The sons also of Agar that seek understanding, which are in the land, the merchants of Merran and Teman, and the authors of fables, and the searchers out of understanding; none of these have known the way of wisdom or remembered her paths. ²⁴O Israel, how great is the house of God! And how large is the place of His possession! ²⁵[It is] great, and has no end; high, and unmeasurable. ²⁶There were the giants born that were famous of old, great of stature, [and] expert in war. ²⁷God did not choose these, nor did He give the way of knowledge to them; ²⁸so they perished, because they had no wisdom, they perished through their own foolishness. ²⁹Who has gone up into Heaven, and taken her, and brought her down from the clouds? ³⁰Who has gone over the sea, and found her, and will bring her for choice gold? ³¹There is none that knows her way, nor any that comprehends her path. ³²But He that knows all things knows her, He found her out with His understanding: He that prepared the earth forevermore has filled it with four-footed beasts: ³³He that sends out the light, and it goes; He called it, and it obeyed Him with fear: ³⁴and the stars shone in their watches, and were glad when He called them, they said, "Here we are." They shone with gladness to Him that made them. ³⁵This is our God, [and] there will none other be accounted of in comparison of Him. ³⁶He has found out all the way of knowledge, and has given it to His servant Jacob, and to Israel that is beloved of Him. ³⁷Afterward she appeared on earth and was conversant with men.

CHAPTER 4

¹This is the scroll of the commands of God, and the law that endures forever: All those who hold it fast [are appointed] to life; but such as leave it will die. ²Turn, O Jacob, and take hold of it: walk toward her shining in the presence of the light thereof. ³Do not give your glory to another, nor the things that are profitable to you to a strange nation. ⁴O Israel, happy are we, for the things that are pleasing to God are made known to us. ⁵Be of good cheer, my people, the memorial of Israel. ⁶You were sold to the nations, |but| not for destruction: because you moved God to wrath, you were delivered to your adversaries. ⁷For you provoked Him that made you by sacrificing to demons, and not to God. ⁸You forgot the perpetual God that brought you up; you also grieved Jerusalem that nursed you. ⁹For she saw the wrath that has come on you from God, and said, "Listen, you [women] that dwell about Zion, for God has brought on me great mourning; ¹⁰for I have seen the captivity of my sons and daughters, which the Perpetual has brought on them. ¹¹For with joy I nourished them, but sent them away with weeping and mourning. ¹²Let no man rejoice over me, a widow, and forsaken of many, for the sins of my children I am left desolate, because they turned away from the law of God, ¹³and had no regard to His statutes, neither did they walk in the ways of God's commands, nor trod in the paths of discipline in His righteousness. ¹⁴Let those who dwell about Zion come, and remember the captivity of my sons and daughters, which the Perpetual has brought on them. ¹⁵For He has brought a nation on them from far, a shameless nation, and of a strange language, who neither gave reverence to old man, nor pitied child. ¹⁶And they have carried away the dear beloved sons of the widow and left her that was alone desolate of

her daughters. ¹⁷But I—how can I help you? ¹⁸For He that brought these plagues on you will deliver you from the hand of your enemies. ¹⁹Go your way, O my children, go your way, for I am left desolate. ²⁰I have put off the garment of peace and put on myself the sackcloth of my petition: I will cry to the Perpetual as long as I live. ²¹Be of good cheer, O my children, cry to God, and He will deliver you from the power and hand of the enemies. ²²For I have trusted in the Perpetual, that He will save you; and joy has come to me from the Holy One, because of the mercy which will soon come to you from your continuous Savior. ²³For I sent you out with mourning and weeping, but God will give you to me again with joy and gladness forever. ²⁴For like as now those who dwell about Zion have seen your captivity, so they will shortly see your salvation from our God, which will come on you with great glory, and brightness of the Perpetual. ²⁵My children, suffer patiently the wrath that has come on you from God, for your enemy has persecuted you; but shortly you will see his destruction, and will tread on their necks. ²⁶My delicate ones have gone rough ways; they were taken away as a flock carried off by the enemies. ²⁷Be of good cheer, O my children, and cry to God, for you will be remembered of Him that has brought [these things] on you. ²⁸For as it was your mind to go astray from God, return and seek Him ten times more. ²⁹For He that brought these plagues on you will bring you continuous joy again with your salvation." ³⁰Be of good cheer, O Jerusalem, for He that called you by name will comfort you. ³¹Miserable are those who afflicted you and rejoiced at your fall. ³²Miserable are the cities which your children served; miserable is she that received your sons. ³³For as she rejoiced at your fall, and was glad of your ruin, so she will be grieved for her own desolation. ³⁴And I will take away her exultation in her great multitude, and her boasting will be turned into mourning. ³⁵For fire will come on her from the Perpetual, long to endure; and she will be inhabited of devils for a great time. ³⁶O Jerusalem look around you toward the east and behold the joy that comes to you from God. ³⁷Behold, your sons come, whom you sent away, they come gathered together from the east to the west at the word of the Holy One, rejoicing in the glory of God.

CHAPTER 5

¹Put off, O Jerusalem, the garment of your mourning and affliction, and put on the beauty of the glory that [comes] from God forever. ²Cast about you the robe of the righteousness which [comes] from God; set a diadem on your head of the glory of the Perpetual. ³For God will show your brightness to every [region] under Heaven. ⁴For your name will be called of God forever, THE PEACE OF RIGHTEOUSNESS, and, THE GLORY OF GODLINESS. ⁵Arise, O Jerusalem, and stand on the height, and look around you toward the east, and behold your children gathered from the going down of the sun to the rising thereof at the word of the Holy One, rejoicing that God has remembered them. ⁶For they went from you on foot, being led away of their enemies, but God brings them in to you, borne on high with glory, as [on] a royal throne. ⁷For God has appointed that every high mountain, and the perpetual hills, should be made low, and the valleys filled up, to make plain the ground, that Israel may go safely in the glory of God. ⁸Moreover the woods and every sweet-smelling tree have overshadowed Israel by the command of God. ⁹For God will lead Israel with joy in the light of His glory with the mercy and righteousness that comes from Him.

EPISTLE OF JEREMIAH

CHAPTER 6

¹A COPY OF A LETTER, WHICH JEREMIAH SENT TO THEM WHICH WERE TO BE LED CAPTIVES INTO BABYLON BY THE KING OF THE BABYLONIANS, TO CERTIFY THEM, AS IT WAS COMMANDED HIM OF GOD. ²Because of the sins which you have committed before God, you will be led away captives to Babylon by Nebuchadnezzar king of the Babylonians. ³So when you come to Babylon, you will remain there many years, and for a long season, even for seven generations: and after that I will bring you out peaceably from there. ⁴But now you will see in Babylon gods of silver, and of gold, and of wood, borne on shoulders, which cause the nations to fear. ⁵Beware, therefore, that you in no way become like to the strangers, neither let fear take hold on you because of them, when you see the multitude before them and behind them, worshiping them. ⁶But say in your hearts, "O LORD, we must worship You." ⁷For My messenger is with you, and I Myself care for your souls. ⁸For their tongue is polished by the workman, and they themselves are overlaid with gold and with silver; yet they are but false and cannot speak. ⁹And taking gold, as it were for a virgin that loves to be happy, they make crowns for the heads of their gods: ¹⁰and sometimes also the priests carry from their gods gold and silver and bestow it on themselves; ¹¹and will even give thereof to the common prostitutes: and they deck them as men with garments, [even] the gods of silver, and gods of gold, and of wood. ¹²Yet these gods cannot save themselves from rust and moths, though they are covered with purple raiment. ¹³They wipe their faces because of the dust of the temple, which is thick on them. ¹⁴And he that cannot put to death one that offends against him holds a scepter, as though he were judge of a country. ¹⁵He also has a dagger in his right hand, and an axe, but cannot deliver himself from war and robbers. ¹⁶Whereby they are not known to be gods: therefore, do not fear them. ¹⁷For like as a vessel that a man uses is worth nothing when it is broken, even so it is with their gods: when they are set up in the temples their eyes are full of dust through the feet of those who come in. ¹⁸And as the courts are made sure on every side on him that offends the king, as being committed to suffer death, [even so] the priests make fast their temples with doors, with locks, and bars, lest they are carried off by robbers. ¹⁹They light the candles, yes, more than for themselves, of which they cannot see one. ²⁰They are as one of the beams of the temple; and men say their hearts are eaten out, when things creeping out of the earth devour both them and their raiment: ²¹they do not feel it when their faces are blackened through the smoke that comes out of the temple: ²²bats, swallows, and birds land on their bodies and heads; and in like manner the cats also. ²³Whereby you may know that they are no gods: therefore, do not fear them. ²⁴Notwithstanding the gold with which they are beset to make them beautiful, except one wipe off the rust, they will not shine, for not even when they were molten did they feel it. ²⁵Things wherein there is no breath are bought at any cost. ²⁶Having no feet, they are borne on shoulders, whereby they declare to men that they are worth nothing. ²⁷They also that serve them are ashamed, for if they fall to the ground at any time, they cannot rise up again of themselves; neither, if they are bowed down, can they make themselves straight, but the offerings are set before them, as if they were dead men. ²⁸And the things that are sacrificed to them, their priests sell and spend; and in like manner their wives also lay up part thereof in salt; but to the poor and to the impotent they will give nothing thereof. ²⁹The menstruous woman and the woman in childbirth touch their sacrifices, knowing, therefore, by these things, that they are not gods, [and so] do not fear them. ³⁰For how can they be called gods? Because women set meat before the gods of silver, gold, and wood. ³¹And in their temples the priests sit on seats, having their clothes torn, and their heads and beards shaven, and nothing on their heads. ³²They roar and cry before their gods, as men do at the feast when one is dead. ³³The priests also take off garments from them and clothe their wives and children in addition. ³⁴Whether it be evil that one does to them, or good, they are not able to repay it: they can neither set up a king, nor put him down. ³⁵In like manner, they can neither give riches nor money; though a man makes a vow to them, and does not keep it, they will never exact it. ³⁶They can save no man from death, neither deliver the weak from the mighty. ³⁷They cannot restore a blind man to his sight, nor deliver any that is in distress. ³⁸They can show no mercy to the widow, nor do good to the fatherless. ³⁹They are like the stones that are [hewn] out of the mountain, [these gods] of wood, and that are overlaid with gold and with silver. Those who minister to them will be confounded. ⁴⁰How should a man then think or say that they are gods, when even the Chaldeans themselves dishonor them? ⁴¹Who if they will see one mute that cannot speak, they bring him, and entreat him to call on Bel, as though he were able to understand. ⁴²Yet they cannot perceive this themselves and forsake them, for they have no understanding. ⁴³The women also with cords around them sit in the ways, burning bran for incense, but if any of them,

1 BARUCH

drawn by some that passes by, lies with him, she reproaches her fellow, that she was not thought as worthy as herself, nor her cord broken. ⁴⁴Whatever is done among them is false. How should a man then think or say that they are gods? ⁴⁵They are fashioned by carpenters and goldsmiths—they can be nothing else than the workmen will have them to be. ⁴⁶And they themselves that fashioned them can never continue long; how then should the things that are fashioned by them? ⁴⁷For they have left lies and reproaches to those who come after. ⁴⁸For when there comes any war or plague on them, the priests consult with themselves, where they may be hidden with them. ⁴⁹How then can men not understand that they are not gods, which can neither save themselves from war, nor from plague? ⁵⁰For seeing they are but of wood, and overlaid with gold and with silver, it will be known hereafter that they are false; ⁵¹and it will be manifest to all nations and kings that they are no gods, but the works of men's hands, and that there is no work of God in them. ⁵²Who then may not know that they are no gods? ⁵³For neither can they set up a king in a land, nor give rain to men. ⁵⁴Neither can they judge their own cause, nor redress a wrong, being unable, for they are as crows between the heavens and earth. ⁵⁵For even when fire falls on the house of gods of wood, or overlaid with gold or with silver, their priests will flee away, and escape, but they themselves will be burned apart like beams. ⁵⁶Moreover they cannot withstand any king or enemies. How should a man then allow or think that they are gods? ⁵⁷Neither are those gods of wood, and overlaid with silver or with gold, able to escape either from thieves or robbers. ⁵⁸Whose gold, and silver, and garments with which they are clothed, they that are strong will take from them, and go away with [them]; neither will they be able to help themselves. ⁵⁹Therefore it is better to be a king that shows his manhood, or else a vessel in a house profitable for that of which the owner will have need, than such false gods; or even a door in a house, to keep the things safe that are therein, than such false gods; or a pillar of wood in a palace, than such false gods. ⁶⁰For sun, and moon, and stars, being bright and sent to do their offices, are obedient. ⁶¹Likewise also, the lightning when it glitters is fair to see; and after the same manner the wind also blows in every country. ⁶²And when God commands the clouds to go over the whole world, they do as they are told. ⁶³And the fire sent from above to consume mountains and woods does as it is commanded, but these are to be likened to them neither in show nor power. ⁶⁴Why a man should neither think nor say that they are gods, seeing they are neither able to judge causes, nor to do good to men. ⁶⁵Knowing, therefore, that they are not gods, do not fear them. ⁶⁶For they can neither curse nor bless kings; ⁶⁷neither can they show signs in the heavens among the nations, nor shine as the sun, nor give light as the moon. ⁶⁸The beasts are better than they, for they can get under a covert and help themselves. ⁶⁹In no way then is it manifest to us that they are gods. Therefore, do not fear them. ⁷⁰For as a scarecrow in a garden of cucumbers that keeps nothing, so are their gods of wood, and overlaid with gold and with silver. ⁷¹Likewise also, their gods of wood, and overlaid with gold and with silver, are like to a white thorn in an orchard, that every bird sits on; as also to a dead body that is cast out into the dark. ⁷²And you will know them to be no gods by the bright purple that rots on them: And they themselves afterward will be consumed and will be a reproach in the country. ⁷³Better therefore is the just man that has no idols, for he will be far from reproach.

1 MACCABEES

The name Maccabee, probably meaning "hammer," is actually applied in the Books of Maccabees to only one man, Judas, third son of the priest Mattathias and first leader of the revolt against the Seleucid kings who persecuted the Jews (1 Mc. 2:4, 66; 2 Mc. 8:5, 16; 10:1, 16). Traditionally the name has come to be extended to the brothers of Judas, his supporters, and even to other Jewish heroes of the period, such as the seven brothers (2 Mc. 7). First Maccabees was written about 100 BC in Hebrew, but the original has not come down to us. Instead, we have an early, pre-Christian, Greek translation full of Hebrew idioms. The author, probably a Jew, is unknown. He was familiar with the traditions and sacred books of his people and had access to much reliable information on their recent history (from 175 to 134 BC). He may well have played some part in it himself in his youth. His purpose in writing is to record the deliverance of Israel that God worked through the family of Mattathias (5:62)—especially through his three sons, Judas, Jonathan, and Simon, and his grandson, John Hyrcanus.

CHAPTER 1

¹It came to pass, after that Alexander the Macedonian, the son of Philip, who came out of the land of Chittim, and struck Darius king of the Persians and Medes, [it came to pass,] after he had struck him, that he reigned in his stead, in former time, over Greece. ²And he fought many battles, and won many strongholds, and killed the kings of the earth, ³and went through to the ends of the earth and took spoils of a multitude of nations. And the earth was quiet before him, and he was exalted, and his heart was lifted up, ⁴and he gathered together an exceedingly strong army, and ruled over countries and nations and principalities, and they became tributary to him. ⁵And after these things he fell sick, and perceived that he should die. ⁶And he called his servants, which were honorable, which had been brought up with him from his youth, and he divided to them his kingdom, while he was yet alive. ⁷And Alexander reigned twelve years, and he died. ⁸And his servants bare rule, each one in his place. ⁹And they did all put diadems on themselves after that he was dead, and so did their sons after them many years: and they multiplied evils in the earth. ¹⁰And there came out of them a sinful root, Antiochus Epiphanes, son of Antiochus the king, who had been a hostage at Rome, and he reigned in the one hundred and thirty-seventh year of the kingdom of the Greeks. ¹¹In those days came there out of Israel transgressors of the law, and persuaded many, saying, let us go and make a covenant with the nations that are around us; for since we were parted from them many evils have befallen us. ¹²And the saying was good in their eyes. ¹³And certain of the people were forward [here in] land went to the king, and he gave them license to do after the ordinances of the nations. ¹⁴And they built a place of exercise in Jerusalem according to the laws of the nations; ¹⁵and they made themselves uncircumcised, and forsook the holy covenant, and joined themselves to the nations, and sold themselves to do evil. ¹⁶And the kingdom was well ordered in the sight of Antiochus, and he thought to reign over Egypt, that he might reign over the two kingdoms. ¹⁷And he entered into Egypt with a great multitude, with chariots, and with elephants, and with horsemen, and with a great navy; ¹⁸and he made war against Ptolemy king of Egypt; and Ptolemy was put to shame before him and fled; and many fell wounded to death. ¹⁹And they got possession of the strong cities in the land of Egypt; and he took the spoils of Egypt. ²⁰And Antiochus, after he had struck Egypt, returned in the one hundred and forty-third year, and went up against Israel and Jerusalem with a great multitude, ²¹and entered presumptuously into the sanctuary, and took the golden altar, and the candlestick of the light, and all that pertained to that, ²²and the table of the Bread of the Presentation, and the cups to pour with, and the bowls, and the golden censers, and the veil, and the crowns, and the adorning of gold which was on the face of the temple, and he peeled it all off. ²³And

he took the silver and the gold and the precious vessels; and he took the hidden treasures which he found. ²⁴And when he had taken all, he went away into his own land, and he made a great slaughter, and spoke very presumptuously. ²⁵And there came great mourning on Israel, in every place where they were; ²⁶and the rulers and elders groaned, the virgins and young men were made feeble, and the beauty of the women was changed. ²⁷Every bridegroom took up lamentation, she that sat in the marriage chamber was in heaviness. ²⁸And the land was moved for the inhabitants thereof, and all the house of Jacob was clothed with shame. ²⁹And after two full years the king sent a chief collector of tribute to the cities of Judah, and he came to Jerusalem with a great multitude. ³⁰And he spoke words of peace to them in subtlety, and they gave him credence: and he fell on the city suddenly, and struck it very severely, and destroyed much people out of Israel. ³¹And he took the spoils of the city, and set it on fire, and pulled down the houses thereof and the walls thereof on every side. ³²And they led captive the women and the children, and the cattle they took in possession. ³³And they built the city of David with a great and strong wall, with strong towers, and it became to them a citadel. ³⁴And they put there a sinful nation, transgressors of the law, and they strengthened themselves therein. ³⁵And they stored up arms and food, and gathering together the spoils of Jerusalem, they laid them up there, and they became a severe snare; ³⁶and it became a place to lie in wait in against the sanctuary, and an evil adversary to Israel continually. ³⁷And they shed innocent blood on every side of the sanctuary and defiled the sanctuary. ³⁸And the inhabitants of Jerusalem fled because of them; and she became a habitation of strangers, and she became strange to those who were born in her, and her children forsook her. ³⁹Her sanctuary was laid waste like a wilderness, her feasts were turned into mourning, her Sabbaths into reproach, her honor into contempt. ⁴⁰According to her glory, so was her dishonor multiplied, and her high estate was turned into mourning. ⁴¹And King Antiochus wrote to his whole kingdom, that all should be one people, ⁴²and that each should forsake his own laws. And all the nations agreed according to the word of the king; ⁴³and many of Israel consented to his worship, and sacrificed to the idols, and profaned the Sabbath. ⁴⁴And the king sent letters by the hand of messengers to Jerusalem and the cities of Judah, that they should follow laws strange to the land, ⁴⁵and should forbid whole burnt-offerings and sacrifice and drink offerings in the sanctuary; and should profane the Sabbaths and feasts, ⁴⁶and pollute the sanctuary and those who were holy; ⁴⁷that they should build altars, and temples, and shrines for idols, and should sacrifice swine's flesh and unclean beasts: ⁴⁸and that they should leave their sons uncircumcised, that they should make their souls abominable with all manner of uncleanness and profanation; ⁴⁹so that they might forget the law, and change all the ordinances. ⁵⁰And whoever will not do according to the word of the king, he will die. ⁵¹According to all these words wrote he to his whole kingdom; and he appointed overseers over all the people, and he commanded the cities of Judah to sacrifice, city by city. ⁵²And from the people were gathered together to them many, everyone that had forsaken the law; and they did evil things in the land; ⁵³and they made Israel to hide themselves in every place of refuge which they had. ⁵⁴And on the fifteenth day of Kislev, in the one hundred and forty-fifth year, they built an abomination of desolation on the altar, and in the cities of Judah on every side they built [idol] altars. ⁵⁵And at the doors of the houses and in the streets they burned incense. ⁵⁶And they tore in pieces the scrolls of the law which they found and set them on fire. ⁵⁷And wherever was found with any a scroll of the Covenant, and if any consented to the law, the king's sentence delivered him to death. ⁵⁸So did they in their might to Israel, to those that were found month by month in the cities. ⁵⁹And on the twenty-fifth day of the month they sacrificed on the [idol] altar [of God]. ⁶⁰And the women that had circumcised their children they put to death according to the command. ⁶¹And they hanged their babies about their necks, and [destroyed] their houses, and those who had circumcised them. ⁶²And many in Israel were fully resolved and confirmed in themselves not to eat unclean things. ⁶³And they chose to die, that they might not be defiled with the meats, and that they might not profane the holy covenant: and they died. ⁶⁴And there came exceedingly great wrath on Israel.

CHAPTER 2

¹In those days Mattathias rose up, the son of John, the son of Simeon, a priest of the sons of Joarib, from Jerusalem; and he lived at Modin. ²And he had five sons, John, who was surnamed Gaddis; ³Simon, who was called Thassi; ⁴Judas, who was called Maccabaeus; ⁵Eleazar, who was called Avaran; Jonathan, who was called Apphus. ⁶And he saw the blasphemies that were committed in Judah and in Jerusalem, ⁷and he said, "Woe is me! Why was I born to see the destruction of my people, and the destruction of the holy city, and to dwell there, when it was given into the hand of the enemy, the sanctuary into the hand of aliens? ⁸Her temple is become as a man that was glorious; ⁹her vessels of glory are carried away into captivity, her infants are slain in her streets, her young men with the sword of the enemy. ¹⁰What nation has not inherited her palaces, and gotten possession of her spoils? ¹¹Her adorning is all taken away; instead of a free woman she is become a bond woman: ¹²and behold, our holy things and our beauty and our glory are laid waste, and the nations have profaned them. ¹³Why should we live any longer?" ¹⁴And Mattathias and his sons tore their clothes, and put on sackcloth, and mourned exceedingly. ¹⁵And the king's officers, that were enforcing the apostasy, came into the city Modin to sacrifice. ¹⁶And many of Israel came to them, and Mattathias and his sons were gathered together. ¹⁷And the king's officers answered and spoke to Mattathias, saying, "You are a ruler and an honorable and great man in this city, and strengthened with sons and relatives: ¹⁸now therefore, come first and do the command of the king, as all the nations have done, and the men of Judah, and those who remain in Jerusalem: and you and your house will be in the number of the king's friends, and you and your sons will be honored with silver and gold and many gifts." ¹⁹And Mattathias answered and said with a loud voice, "If all the nations that are in the house of the king's dominion listen to him, to each one fall away from the worship of his fathers, and have made choice to follow his commands, ²⁰yet I and my sons and my relatives will walk in the covenant of our fathers. ²¹Heaven forbid that we should forsake the law and the ordinances. ²²We will not listen to the king's words, to go aside from our worship, on the right hand, or on the left." ²³And when he had left speaking these words, there came a Jew in the sight of all to sacrifice on the altar which was at Modin, according to the king's command. ²⁴And Mattathias saw it, and his zeal was kindled, and his reins trembled, and he showed out his wrath according to judgment, and ran, and killed him on the altar. ²⁵And the king's officer, who compelled men to sacrifice, he killed at that time, and pulled down the altar. ²⁶And he was zealous for the law, even as Phinehas did to Zimri the son of Salu. ²⁷And Mattathias cried out in the city with a loud voice, saying, "Whoever is zealous for the law, and maintains the covenant, let him come out after me." ²⁸And he and his sons fled into the mountains and forsook all that they had in the city. ²⁹Then many that sought after justice and judgment went down into the wilderness, to dwell there, ³⁰they, and their sons, and their wives, and their cattle; because evils were multiplied on them. ³¹And it was told the king's officers, and the forces that were in Jerusalem, the city of David, that certain men, who had broken the king's command, were gone down into the secret places in the wilderness; ³²and many pursued after them, and having overtaken them, they encamped against them, and set the battle in array against them on the Sabbath day. ³³And they said to them, so far, "Come out, and do according to the word of the king, and you will live." ³⁴And they said, "We will not come out, neither will we do the word of the king, to profane the Sabbath day." ³⁵And they hurried to give them battle. ³⁶And they did not answer them, neither did they cast a stone at them, nor stopped up the secret places, ³⁷saying, "Let us die all in our innocence: the heavens and earth witness over us, that you put us to death without trial." ³⁸And they rose up against them in battle on the Sabbath, and they died, they and their wives and their children, and their cattle, to the number of one thousand souls. ³⁹And Mattathias and his friends knew it, and they mourned over them exceedingly. ⁴⁰And one

said to another, "If we all do as our countrymen have done, and fight not against the nations for our lives and our ordinances, they will now quickly destroy us from off the earth." ⁴¹And they took counsel on that day, saying, "Whoever will come against us to battle on the Sabbath day, let us fight against him, and we will in no way all die, as our countrymen died in the secret places." ⁴²Then were gathered together to them a company of Hasidaeans, mighty men of Israel, everyone that offered himself willingly for the law. ⁴³And all those who fled from the evils were added to them and became a stay to them. ⁴⁴And they mustered an army, and struck sinners in their anger, and lawless men in their wrath: and the rest fled to the nations for safety. ⁴⁵And Mattathias and his friends went around and pulled down the altars; ⁴⁶and they circumcised by force the children that were uncircumcised, as many as they found in the coasts of Israel. ⁴⁷And they pursued after the sons of pride, and the work prospered in their hand. ⁴⁸And they rescued the law out of the hand of the nations, and out of the hand of the kings, neither suffered they the sinner to triumph. ⁴⁹And the days of Mattathias drew near that he should die, and he said to his sons, "Now have pride and rebuke gotten strength, and a season of overthrow, and wrath of indignation. ⁵⁰And now, my children, be zealous for the law, and give your lives for the covenant of your fathers. ⁵¹And call to remembrance the deeds of our fathers which they did in their generations; and receive great glory and a perpetual name. ⁵²Was not Abraham found faithful in temptation, and it was reckoned to him for righteousness? ⁵³Joseph in the time of his distress kept the command and became lord of Egypt. ⁵⁴Phinehas our father, for that he was zealous exceedingly, obtained the covenant of a perpetual priesthood. ⁵⁵Joshua for fulfilling the word became a judge in Israel. ⁵⁶Caleb for bearing witness in the congregation obtained a heritage in the land. ⁵⁷David for being merciful inherited the throne of a kingdom forever and ever. ⁵⁸Elijah, for that he was exceedingly zealous for the law, was taken up into Heaven. ⁵⁹Hananiah, Azariah, Mishael, believed, and were saved out of the flame. ⁶⁰Daniel for his innocence was delivered from the mouth of lions. ⁶¹And so consider you from generation to generation, that none that put their trust in him will lack for strength. ⁶²And do not be afraid of the words of a sinful man; for his glory will be dung and worms. ⁶³Today he will be lifted up, and tomorrow he will in no way be found, because he is returned to his dust, and his thought is perished. ⁶⁴And you, my children, be strong, and show yourselves men in behalf of the law; for therein will you obtain glory. ⁶⁵And behold, Simon your brother, I know that he is a man of counsel; give ear to him always: he will be a father to you. ⁶⁶And Judas Maccabaeus, he has been strong and mighty from his youth: he will be your captain and will fight the battle of the people. ⁶⁷And take to yourself all the doers of the law and avenge the wrong of your people. ⁶⁸Render a repayment to the nations and take heed to the commands of the law." ⁶⁹And he blessed them and was gathered to his fathers. ⁷⁰And he died in the one hundred and forty-sixth year, and his sons buried him in the tombs of his fathers at Modin, and all Israel made great lamentation for him.

CHAPTER 3

¹And his son Judas, who was called Maccabaeus, rose up in his stead. ²And all his countrymen helped him, and so did all those who cleaved to his father, and they fought with gladness the battle of Israel. ³And he got his people great glory, and put on a breastplate as a giant, and girded his warlike harness about him, and set battles in array, protecting the army with his sword. ⁴And he was like a lion in his deeds, and as a lion's whelp roaring for prey. ⁵And he pursued the lawless, seeking them out, and he burned up those that troubled his people. ⁶And the lawless shrunk for fear of him, and all the workers of lawlessness were severely troubled, and salvation prospered in his hand. ⁷And he angered many kings, and made Jacob glad with his acts, and his memorial is blessed forever. ⁸And he went around among the cities of Judah, and destroyed the ungodly out of the land, and turned away wrath from Israel: ⁹and he was renowned to the utmost part of the earth, and he gathered together such as were ready to perish. ¹⁰And Apollonius gathered the nations together, and a great army from Samaria, to fight against Israel. ¹¹And Judas perceived it, and he went out to meet him, and struck him, and killed him: and many fell wounded to death, and the rest fled. ¹²And they took their spoils, and Judas took the sword of Apollonius, and with that he fought all his days. ¹³And Seron, the commander of the army of Syria, heard it said that Judas had gathered a gathering and a congregation of faithful men with him, and of such as went out to war; ¹⁴And he said, I will make myself a name and get me glory in the kingdom; and I will fight against Judas and those who are with him, that set at nothing the word of the king. ¹⁵And there went up with him also a mighty army of the ungodly to help him, to take vengeance on the sons of Israel. ¹⁶And he came near to the going up of Bethhoron, and Judas went out to meet him with a small company. ¹⁷But when they saw the army coming to meet them, they said to Judas, "What? Will we be able, being a small company, to fight against so great and strong a multitude? And we for our part are faint, having tasted no food this day." ¹⁸And Judas said, "It is an easy thing for many to be shut up in the hands of a few; and with Heaven it is all one, to save by many or by few: ¹⁹for victory in battle stands not in the multitude of an army; but strength is from Heaven. ²⁰They come to us in fullness of insolence and lawlessness, to destroy us and our wives and our children, for to plunder us: ²¹but we fight for our lives and our laws. ²²And he himself will defeat them before our face, but as for you, do not be afraid of them." ²³Now when he had left off speaking, he leapt suddenly on them, and Seron and his army were defeated before him. ²⁴And they pursued them in the going down of Bethhoron to the plain, and there fell of them about eight hundred men; but the residue fled into the land of the Philistines. ²⁵And the fear of Judas and his countrymen, and the dread of them, began to fall on the nations around them: ²⁶and his name came near even to the king, and every nation told of the battles of Judas. ²⁷But when King Antiochus heard these words, he was full of indignation: and he sent and gathered together all the forces of his realm, an exceedingly strong army. ²⁸And he opened his treasury, and gave his forces pay for a year, and commanded them to be ready for every need. ²⁹And he saw that the money failed from his treasures, and that the tributes of the country were small, because of the dissension and plague which he had brought on the land, to the end that he might take away the laws which had been from the first days; ³⁰and he feared that he should not have enough as at other times for the charges and the gifts which he gave previously with a liberal hand, and he abounded above the kings that were before him. ³¹And he was exceedingly perplexed in his mind, and he determined to go into Persia, and to take the tributes of the countries, and to gather much money. ³²And he left Lysias, an honorable man, and one of the seed royal, to be over the affairs of the king from the River Euphrates to the borders of Egypt, ³³and to bring up his son Antiochus, until he came again. ³⁴And he delivered to him the half of his forces, and the elephants, and gave him charge of all the things that he would have done, and concerning those who lived in Judea and in Jerusalem, ³⁵that he should send an army against them, to root out and destroy the strength of Israel, and the remnant of Jerusalem, and to take away their memorial from the place; ³⁶And that he should make strangers to dwell on all their coasts, and should divide their land to them by lot. ³⁷And the king took the half that remained of the forces, and removed from Antioch, from his royal city, the one hundred and forty-seventh year; and he passed over the River Euphrates and went through the upper countries. ³⁸And Lysias chose Ptolemy the son of Dorymenes, and Nicanor, and Gorgias, mighty men of the king's friends; ³⁹and with them he sent forty thousand footmen, and seven thousand horse, to go into the land of Judah, and to destroy it, according to the word of the king. ⁴⁰And they removed with all their army and came and pitched near to Emmaus in the plain country. ⁴¹And the merchants of the country heard the fame of them, and took silver and gold exceedingly much, with chains, and came into the camp to take the sons of Israel for servants: and there were added to them the forces of Syria and of the land of the Philistines. ⁴²And Judas and his countrymen saw that evils were multiplied, and that the forces were encamping in their borders; and they took knowledge of the king's words which he had commanded, to destroy the

people and make an end of them; ⁴³and they said each man to his neighbor, "Let us raise up the ruin of our people, and let us fight for our people and the holy place." ⁴⁴And the congregation was gathered together, that they might be ready for battle, and that they might pray, and ask for mercy and compassion. ⁴⁵And Jerusalem was without inhabitant as a wilderness, there was none of her offspring that went in or went out; and the sanctuary was trodden down, and the sons of strangers were in the citadel, the nations lodged therein; and joy was taken away from Jacob, and the pipe and the harp ceased. ⁴⁶And they gathered themselves together, and came to Mizpeh, near Jerusalem; for in Mizpeh was there a place of prayer previously for Israel. ⁴⁷And they fasted that day, and put on sackcloth, and [put] ashes on their heads, and tore their clothes, ⁴⁸and laid open the Scroll of the Law, concerning which the nations were accustomed to inquire, seeking the likenesses of their idols. ⁴⁹And they brought the priests' garments, and the first-fruits, and the tithes: and they stirred up the Nazarites, who had accomplished their days. ⁵⁰And they cried aloud toward Heaven, saying, "What will we do with these men, and where will we carry them away? ⁵¹And your holy place is trodden down and profaned, and your priests are in heaviness and brought low. ⁵²And behold, the nations are assembled together against us to destroy us: you know what things they imagine against us. ⁵³How will we be able to stand before them, except you be our help?" ⁵⁴And they sounded with the trumpets and cried with a loud voice. ⁵⁵And after this Judas appointed leaders of the people, captains of thousands, and captains of hundreds, and captains of fifties, and captains of tens. ⁵⁶And he said to those who were building houses, and were betrothing wives, and were planting vineyards, and were fearful, that they should return, each man to his own house, according to the law. ⁵⁷And the army removed and encamped on the south side of Emmaus. ⁵⁸And Judas said, "Gird yourselves, and be valiant men, and be in readiness against the morning, that you may fight with these nations, that are assembled together against us to destroy us, and our holy place: ⁵⁹for it is better for us to die in battle, than to look on the evils of our nation and the holy place. ⁶⁰Nevertheless, as may be the will in Heaven, so will he do."

CHAPTER 4

¹And Gorgias took five thousand footmen, and one thousand chosen horse, and the army removed by night, ²that it might fall on the army of the Jews and strike them suddenly: and the men of the citadel were his guides. ³And Judas heard thereof, and removed, he and the valiant men, that he might strike the king's army which was at Emmaus, ⁴while as yet the forces were dispersed from the camp. ⁵And Gorgias came into the camp of Judas by night and found no man; and he sought them in the mountains; for he said, "These men flee from us." ⁶And as soon as it was day, Judas appeared in the plain with three thousand men: however, they did not have the armor and swords they desired. ⁷And they saw the camp of the nations strong [and] fortified, and horsemen compassing it around; and these were expert in war. ⁸And Judas said to the men that were with him, "Do not fear their multitude, neither be afraid of their onset. ⁹Remember how our fathers were saved in the Red Sea, when Pharaoh pursued them with an army. ¹⁰And now let us cry to Heaven, if He will have us, and will remember the covenant of our fathers, and destroy this army before our face today: ¹¹and all the nations will know that there is one who redeems and saves Israel." ¹²And the strangers lifted up their eyes and saw them coming near them: ¹³and they went out of the camp to battle. And those who were with Judas sounded their trumpets, ¹⁴and joined battle, and the nations were defeated, and fled into the plain. ¹⁵But all the furthest back fell by the sword: and they pursued them to Gazara, and to the plains of Idumaea and Azotus and Jamnia, and there fell of them about three thousand men. ¹⁶And Judas and his army returned from pursuing after them, ¹⁷and he said to the people, "Do not be greedy of the spoils, inasmuch as there is a battle before us; ¹⁸and Gorgias and his army are near to us in the mountain. But stand you now against our enemies, and fight against them, and afterward take the spoils with boldness." ¹⁹While Judas was yet making an end of these words, there appeared a part of them looking out from the mountain: ²⁰and they saw that their army had been put to flight, and that the Jews were burning the camp; for the smoke that was seen declared what was done. ²¹But when they perceived these things, they were severely afraid; and perceiving also the army of Judas in the plain ready for battle, ²²they fled—all of them—into the land of the Philistines. ²³And Judas returned to plunder the camp, and they got much gold, and silver, and blue, and sea purple, and great riches. ²⁴And they returned home, and sang a song of thanksgiving, and gave praise to Heaven; because [His mercy] is good, because His mercy endures forever. ²⁵And Israel had a great deliverance that day. ²⁶But the strangers, as many as had escaped, came and told Lysias all the things that had happened: ²⁷but when he heard thereof, he was confounded and discouraged, because neither had such things as he desired been done to Israel, nor had such things as the king commanded him come to pass. ²⁸And in the next year he gathered together sixty thousand chosen footmen, and five thousand horse, that he might subdue them. ²⁹And they came into Idumaea and encamped at Bethsura; and Judas met them with ten thousand men. ³⁰And he saw that the army was strong, and he prayed and said, "Blessed are You, O Savior of Israel, who quelled the onset of the mighty man by the hand of Your servant David, and delivered the army of the Philistines into the hands of Jonathan the son of Saul, and of his armor bearer: ³¹shut up this army in the hand of Your people Israel, and let them be ashamed for their army and their horsemen: ³²give them faintness of heart, and cause the boldness of their strength to melt away, and let them quake at their destruction: ³³cast them down with the sword of those who love You, and let all that know Your Name praise You with thanksgiving." ³⁴And they joined battle; and there fell of the army of Lysias about five thousand men, and they fell down near them. ³⁵But when Lysias saw that his array was put to flight, and the boldness that had come on those who were with Judas, and how they were ready either to live or to die nobly, he removed to Antioch, and gathered together hired soldiers, that he might come again into Judea with even a greater company. ³⁶But Judas and his countrymen said, "Behold, our enemies are defeated: let us go up to cleanse the holy place, and to dedicate it afresh." ³⁷And all the army was gathered together, and they went up to Mount Zion. ³⁸And they saw the sanctuary laid desolate, and the altar profaned, and the gates burned up, and shrubs growing in the courts as in a forest or as on one of the mountains, and the priests' chambers pulled down; ³⁹and they tore their clothes, and made great lamentation, and put ashes on their heads, ⁴⁰and fell on their faces to the ground, and blew with the solemn trumpets, and cried toward Heaven. ⁴¹Then Judas appointed certain men to fight against those that were in the citadel, until he should have cleansed the holy place. ⁴²And he chose blameless priests, such as had pleasure in the law: ⁴³and they cleansed the holy place and bare out the stones of defilement into an unclean place. ⁴⁴And they took counsel concerning the altar of burnt-offerings, which had been profaned, what they should do with it: ⁴⁵and there came into their mind a good counsel, that they should pull it down, lest it should be a reproach to them, because the nations had defiled it: and they pulled down the altar, ⁴⁶and laid up the stones in the mountain of the house in a convenient place, until there should come a prophet to give an answer concerning them. ⁴⁷And they took whole stones according to the law and built a new altar after the fashion of the former; ⁴⁸and they built the holy place, and the inner parts of the house; and they hallowed the courts. ⁴⁹And they made the holy vessels new, and they brought the candlestick, and the altar of burnt-offerings and of incense, and the table, into the temple. ⁵⁰And they burned incense on the altar, and they lighted the lamps that were on the candlestick, and they gave light in the temple. ⁵¹And they set loaves on the table, and spread out the veils, and finished all the works which they made. ⁵²And they rose up early in the morning, on the twenty-fifth day of the ninth month, which is the month Kislev, in the one hundred and forty-eighth year, ⁵³and offered sacrifice according to the law on the new altar of burnt-offerings which they had made. ⁵⁴At what time and on what day the nations had profaned it, even on that [day] was it dedicated afresh, with songs and harps and lutes, and with cymbals. ⁵⁵And all the people fell on their faces, and worshiped, and gave praise to Heaven,

which had given them good success. ⁵⁶And they kept the dedication of the altar eight days, and offered burnt-offerings with gladness, and sacrificed a sacrifice of deliverance and praise. ⁵⁷And they decked the forefront of the temple with crowns of gold and small shields, and dedicated afresh the gates and the priests' chambers, and made doors for them. ⁵⁸And there was exceedingly great gladness among the people, and the reproach of the nations was turned away. ⁵⁹And Judas and his countrymen and the whole congregation of Israel ordained, that the days of the dedication of the altar should be kept in their seasons from year to year by the space of eight days, from the twenty-fifth day of the month Kislev, with gladness and joy. ⁶⁰And at that season they built up Mount Zion with high walls and strong towers around, lest perhaps the nations should come and tread them down, as they had done previously. ⁶¹And he set there a force to keep it, and they fortified Bethsura to keep it; that the people might have a stronghold near Idumaea.

CHAPTER 5

¹And it came to pass, when the surrounding nations heard that the altar was built, and the sanctuary dedicated as previously, they were exceedingly angry. ²And they took counsel to destroy the race of Jacob that was in the midst of them, and they began to kill and destroy among the people. ³And Judas fought against the children of Esau in Idumaea at Akrabattine, because they besieged Israel: and he struck them with a great slaughter, and brought down their pride, and took their spoils. ⁴And he remembered the wickedness of the children of Baean, who were to the people a snare and a stumbling block, lying in wait for them in the ways. ⁵And they were shut up by him in the towers; and he encamped against them, and destroyed them utterly, and burned with fire the towers of the place, with all that were therein. ⁶And he passed over to the children of Ammon, and found a mighty band, and much people, with Timotheus for their leader. ⁷And he fought many battles with them, and they were defeated before his face; and he struck them, ⁸and got possession of Jazer, and the villages thereof, and returned again into Judea. ⁹And the nations that were in Gilead gathered themselves together against the Israelites that were on their borders, to destroy them. And they fled to the stronghold of Dathema, ¹⁰and sent letters to Judas and his countrymen, saying, "The nations that are around us are gathered together against us to destroy us: ¹¹and they are preparing to come and get possession of the stronghold whereto we have fled for refuge, and Timotheus is the leader of their army. ¹²Now therefore come and deliver us from their hand, for many of us are fallen. ¹³And all our countrymen that were in the land of Tubias have been put to death; and they have carried into captivity their wives and their children and their stuff; and they destroyed there about one thousand men." ¹⁴While the letters were yet being read, behold, there came other messengers from Galilee with their clothes torn, bringing a report in this way, ¹⁵saying that there were gathered together against them those of Ptolemais, and of Tyre, and of Sidon, and all Galilee of the nations to consume them. ¹⁶Now when Judas and the people heard these words, there assembled together a great congregation, to consult what they should do for their countrymen, that were in suffering, and were assaulted of them. ¹⁷And Judas said to Simon his brother, "Choose out men, and go and deliver your countrymen that are in Galilee, but my brother Jonathan and I will go into the land of Gilead." ¹⁸And he left Joseph the son of Zechariah, and Azariah, as leaders of the people, with the remnant of the army, in Judea, for to keep it. ¹⁹And he gave command to them, saying, "Take you the charge of this people, and fight no battle with the nations until that we come again." ²⁰And to Simon were divided three thousand men to go into Galilee, but to Judas eight thousand men [to go] into the land of Gilead. ²¹And Simon went into Galilee, and fought many battles with the nations, and the nations were defeated before him. ²²And he pursued them to the gate of Ptolemais; and there fell of the nations about three thousand men, and he took their spoils. ²³And they took to them those that were in Galilee, and in Arbatta, with their wives and their children, and all that they had, and brought them into Judea with great gladness. ²⁴And Judas Maccabaeus and his brother Jonathan passed over Jordan, and went three days' journey in the wilderness; ²⁵and they met with the Nabathaeans, and these met them in a peaceful manner, and told them all things that had befallen their countrymen in the land of Gilead: ²⁶and how that many of them were shut up in Bosora, and Bosor, and Alema, Casphor, Maked, and Carnaim; all these cities are strong and great: ²⁷and how that they were shut up in the rest of the cities of the land of Gilead, and that tomorrow they have appointed to encamp against the strongholds, and to take them, and to destroy all these men in one day. ²⁸And Judas and his army turned suddenly by the way of the wilderness to Bosora; and he took the city and killed all the males with the edge of the sword, and took all their spoils, and burned the city with fire. ²⁹And he left from there by night and went until he came to the stronghold. ³⁰And the morning came, and they lifted up their eyes, and behold, much people which could not be counted, bearing ladders and engines of war, to take the stronghold; and they were fighting against them. ³¹And Judas saw that the battle was begun, and that the cry of the city went up to Heaven, with trumpets and a great sound, ³²and he said to the men of his army, "Fight this day for your countrymen." ³³And he went out behind them in three companies, and they sounded with their trumpets, and cried out in prayer. ³⁴And the army of Timotheus perceived that it was Maccabaeus, and they fled from before him: and he struck them with a great slaughter; and there fell of them on that day about eight thousand men. ³⁵And he turned away to Mizpeh and fought against it, and took it, and killed all the males thereof, and took the spoils thereof, and burned it with fire. ³⁶From there he left, and took Casphor, Maked, Bosor, and the other cities of the land of Gilead. ³⁷Now after these things Timotheus gathered another army and encamped near Raphon beyond the brook. ³⁸And Judas sent men to spy on the army; and they brought him word, saying, "All the nations that are around us are gathered together to them, an exceedingly great army. ³⁹And they have hired Arabians to help them, and are encamping beyond the brook, ready to come against you to battle." And Judas went to meet them. ⁴⁰And Timotheus said to the captains of his army, when Judas and his army drew near to the brook of water, "If he passes over first to us, we will not be able to withstand him; for he will mightily prevail against us: ⁴¹but if he be afraid, and encamp beyond the river, we will cross over to him, and prevail against him." ⁴²Now when Judas came near to the brook of water, he caused the scribes of the people to remain by the brook, and gave command to them, saying, "Permit no man to encamp, but let all come to the battle." ⁴³And he crossed over the first against them, and all the people after him: and all the nations were defeated before his face, and cast away their arms, and fled to the temple at Carnaim. ⁴⁴And they took the city, and burned the temple with fire, together with all that were therein. And Carnaim was subdued, neither could they stand any longer before the face of Judas. ⁴⁵And Judas gathered together all Israel, those who were in the land of Gilead, from the least to the greatest, and their wives, and their children, and their stuff, an exceedingly great army, that they might come into the land of Judah. ⁴⁶And they came as far as Ephron, and this same city was great, [and it was] in the way as they should go, exceedingly strong: they could not turn away from it on the right hand or on the left but must necessarily pass through the midst of it. ⁴⁷And they of the city shut them out and stopped up the gates with stones. ⁴⁸And Judas sent to them with words of peace, saying, "We will pass through your land to go into our own land, and none will do you any harm, we will only pass by on our feet." And they would not open to him. ⁴⁹And Judas commanded proclamation to be made in the army, that each man should encamp in the place where he was. ⁵⁰And the men of the army encamped and fought against the city all that day and all that night, and the city was delivered into his hands; ⁵¹and he destroyed all the males with the edge of the sword, and razed the city, and took the spoils thereof, and passed through the city over those who were slain. ⁵²And they

went over Jordan into the great plain near Bethshan. ⁵³And Judas gathered together those that lagged behind, and encouraged the people all the way through, until he came into the land of Judah. ⁵⁴And they went up to Mount Zion with gladness and joy, and offered whole burnt-offerings, because not so much as one of them was slain until they returned in peace. ⁵⁵And in the days when Judas and Jonathan were in the land of Gilead, and Simon his brother in Galilee before Ptolemais, ⁵⁶Joseph the son of Zechariah, and Azariah, rulers of the army, heard of their exploits and of the war, what things they had done; ⁵⁷and they said, "Let us also get us a name, and let us go fight against the nations that are around us." ⁵⁸And they gave charge to the men of the army that was with them and went toward Jamnia. ⁵⁹And Gorgias and his men came out of the city to meet them in battle. ⁶⁰And Joseph and Azariah were put to flight and were pursued to the borders of Judea; and there fell on that day of the people of Israel about two thousand men. ⁶¹And there was a great overthrow among the people, because they did not listen to Judas and his countrymen, thinking to do some exploit. ⁶²But they were not of the seed of those men, by whose hand deliverance was given to Israel. ⁶³And the man Judas and his countrymen were glorified exceedingly in the sight of all Israel, and of all the nations, wherever their name was heard of; ⁶⁴and men gathered together to them, acclaiming them. ⁶⁵And Judas and his countrymen went out and fought against the children of Esau in the land toward the south; and he struck Hebron and the villages thereof, and pulled down the strongholds thereof, and burned the towers thereof. ⁶⁶And he left to go into the land of the Philistines, and he went through Samaria. ⁶⁷In that day certain priests, desiring to do exploits there, were slain in battle, when he went out to battle unadvisedly. ⁶⁸And Judas turned toward Azotus, to the land of the Philistines, and pulled down their altars, and burned the carved images of their gods with fire, and took the plunder of their cities, and returned into the land of Judah.

CHAPTER 6

¹And King Antiochus was journeying through the upper countries; and he heard it said that in Elymais in Persia there was a city renowned for riches, for silver and gold; ²and that the temple which was in it was exceedingly rich, and that therein were golden shields, and breastplates, and arms, which Alexander, son of Philip, the Macedonian king, who reigned first among the Greeks, left behind there. ³And he came and sought to take the city, and to pillage it; and he was not able, because the thing was known to them of the city, ⁴and they rose up against him to battle: and he fled, and left from there with great heaviness, to return to Babylon. ⁵And there came one bringing him tidings into Persia, that the armies, which went against the land of Judah, had been put to flight; ⁶and that Lysias went first with a strong army, and was put to shame before them; and that they had waxed strong by reason of arms and power, and with store of spoils, which they took from the armies that they had cut off; ⁷and that they had pulled down the abomination which he had built on the altar that was in Jerusalem; and that they had compassed about the sanctuary with high walls, as before, and Bethsura, his city. ⁸And it came to pass, when the king heard these words, he was astonished and moved exceedingly: and he laid down on his bed, and fell sick for grief, because it had not befallen him as he looked for. ⁹And he was there many days, because great grief was renewed on him, and he made account that he should die. ¹⁰And he called for all his friends, and said to them, "Sleep departs from my eyes, and my heart fails for care. ¹¹And I said in my heart, To what suffering am I come, and how great a flood is it, wherein I now am! For I was gracious and beloved in my power. ¹²But now I remember the evils which I did at Jerusalem, and that I took all the vessels of silver and gold that were therein and sent out to destroy the inhabitants of Judah without a cause. ¹³I perceive that on this account these evils have come on me, and behold, I perish through great grief in a strange land." ¹⁴And he called for Philip, one of his Friends, and set him over all his kingdom, ¹⁵and gave him his diadem, and his robe, and his signet ring, to the end he should bring Antiochus his son, and nourish him up that he might be king. ¹⁶And King Antiochus died there in the one hundred and forty-ninth year. ¹⁷And Lysias knew that the king was dead, and he set up Antiochus his son to reign, whom he had nourished up being young, and he called his name Eupator. ¹⁸And those who were in the citadel shut up Israel around the sanctuary, and sought always their hurt, and the strengthening of the nations. ¹⁹And Judas thought to destroy them and called all the people together to besiege them. ²⁰And they were gathered together, and besieged them in the one hundred and fiftieth year, and he made mounds to shoot from, and engines of war. ²¹And there came out some of those who were shut up, and there were joined to them certain ungodly men of Israel. ²²And they went to the king, and said, "How long will you not execute judgment, and avenge our countrymen? ²³We were willing to serve your father, and to walk after his words, and to follow his commands; ²⁴and for this reason the children of our people besieged the citadel and were alienated from us; but as many of us as they could descend on they killed and plundered our inheritances. ²⁵And not against us only did they stretch out their hand, but also against all their borders. ²⁶And behold, they are encamped this day against the citadel at Jerusalem, to take it: and they have fortified the sanctuary and Bethsura. ²⁷And if you are not beforehand with them quickly, they will do greater things than these, and you will not be able to control them." ²⁸And when the king heard this, he was angry, and gathered together all his friends, [even the] rulers of his army, and those who were over the horse. ²⁹And there came to him from other kingdoms, and from isles of the sea, bands of hired soldiers. ³⁰And the number of his forces was one hundred thousand footmen, and twenty thousand horsemen, and thirty-two elephants trained for war. ³¹And they went through Idumaea, and encamped against Bethsura, and fought against it many days, and made engines of war; and they [of Bethsura] came out, and burned them with fire, and fought valiantly. ³²And Judas left from the citadel, and encamped at Bethzacharias, near the king's camp. ³³And the king rose early in the morning and sent his army at full speed along the road to Bethzacharias, and his forces made them ready to battle, and sounded with the trumpets. ³⁴And they showed the elephants the blood of grapes and mulberries, that they might prepare them for the battle. ³⁵And they divided the beasts among the phalanxes, and they set by each elephant one thousand men armed with coats of mail, and helmets of brass on their heads; and for each beast were appointed five hundred chosen horsemen. ³⁶These were ready beforehand, wherever the beast was; and wherever the beast went, they went with him; they did not depart from him. ³⁷And towers of wood were on them, strong [and] covered, one on each beast, girded fast on him with cunning contrivances; and on each [beast] were thirty-two valiant men that fought on them, beside his Indian ³⁸(and the residue of the horsemen he set on this side and that side at the two parts of the army), striking terror [into the enemy], and protected by the phalanxes. ³⁹Now when the sun shone on the shields of gold and brass, the mountains shone with them, and blazed like torches of fire. ⁴⁰And a part of the king's army was spread on the high mountains, and some on the low ground, and they went on firmly and in order. ⁴¹And all that heard the noise of their multitude, and the marching of the multitude, and the rattling of the arms, did quake, for the army was exceedingly great and strong. ⁴²And Judas and his army drew near for battle, and there fell of the king's army six hundred men. ⁴³And Eleazar, who was [called] Avaran, saw one of the beasts armed with royal breastplates, and he was higher than all the beasts, and the king seemed to be on him; ⁴⁴and he gave himself to deliver his people, and to get himself a perpetual name; ⁴⁵and he ran on him courageously into the midst of the phalanx, and killed on the right hand and on the left, and they separated apart from him on this side and on that. ⁴⁶And he crept under the elephant, and thrust him from beneath, and killed him; and the [elephant] fell to the earth on him, and he died there. ⁴⁷And they saw the strength of the kingdom, and the fierce onset of the army, and turned away from them. ⁴⁸But they of the king's army went up to Jerusalem to meet them, and the king encamped toward Judea, and toward Mount Zion. ⁴⁹And he made peace with them of Bethsura; and he came out of the city, because they had no food there to endure the siege, because it was a Sabbath to the land. ⁵⁰And the king took Bethsura and appointed a garrison there to keep it. ⁵¹And he

encamped against the sanctuary many days; and set there mounds to shoot from, and engines of war, and instruments for casting fire and stones, and pieces to cast darts, and slings. ⁵²And they also made engines against their engines and fought for many days. ⁵³But there was no food in the sanctuary, because it was the seventh year, and those who fled for safety into Judea from among the nations had eaten up the residue of the store; ⁵⁴and there were but a few left in the sanctuary, because the famine prevailed against them, and they were scattered, each man to his own place. ⁵⁵And Lysias heard it said that Philip, whom Antiochus the king, while he was yet alive, appointed to nourish up his son Antiochus, that he might be king, ⁵⁶had returned from Persia and Media, and with him the forces that went with the king, and that he was seeking to take the government to himself. ⁵⁷And he hurried, and gave consent to depart; and he said to the king and the leaders of the army and to the men, "We decay daily, and our food is scant, and the place where we encamp is strong, and the affairs of the kingdom lie on us: ⁵⁸now therefore let us give the right hand to these men, and make peace with them and with all their nation, ⁵⁹and covenant with them, that they will walk after their own laws, as previously, for because of their laws which we abolished they were angered, and did all these things." ⁶⁰And the saying pleased the king and the princes, and he sent to them to make peace; and they accepted thereof. ⁶¹And the king and the princes swore to them: immediately they came out from the stronghold. ⁶²And the king entered into Mount Zion; and he saw the strength of the place and set at nothing the oath which he had sworn and gave command to pull down the wall around. ⁶³And he left in haste, and returned to Antioch, and found Philip master of the city; and he fought against him and took the city by force.

CHAPTER 7

¹In the one hundred and fiftieth year, Demetrius the son of Seleucus came out from Rome and went up with a few men to a city by the sea and reigned there. ²And it came to pass, when he would go into the house of the kingdom of his fathers, that the army laid hands on Antiochus and Lysias, to bring them to him. ³And the thing was known to him, and he said, "Do not show me their faces." ⁴And the army killed them. And Demetrius sat on the throne of his kingdom. ⁵And there came to him all the lawless and ungodly men of Israel; and Alcimus was their leader, desiring to be chief priest; ⁶and they accused the people to the king, saying, "Judas and his countrymen have destroyed all your friends, and have scattered us from our own land. ⁷Now therefore send a man whom you trust and let him go and see all the havock which he has made of us, and of the king's country, and [how] he has punished them and all that helped them." ⁸And the king chose Bacchides, one of the king's friends, who was ruler in the country beyond the river, and was a great man in the kingdom, and faithful to the king. ⁹And he sent him, and that ungodly Alcimus, and made sure to him the chief priesthood, and he commanded him to take vengeance on the sons of Israel. ¹⁰And they went and came with a great army into the land of Judah, and he sent messengers to Judas and his countrymen with words of peace deceitfully. ¹¹And they gave no heed to their words; for they saw that they were come with a great army. ¹²And there were gathered together to Alcimus and Bacchides a company of scribes, to seek for justice. ¹³And the Hasidaeans were the first among the sons of Israel that sought peace of them; ¹⁴for they said, "One that is a priest of the seed of Aaron has come with the forces, and he will do us no wrong." ¹⁵And he spoke with them words of peace, and swore to them, saying, "We will seek the hurt neither of you nor your friends." ¹⁶And they gave him credence: and he laid hands on sixty men of them, and killed them in one day, according to the word which [the psalmist] wrote, ¹⁷"The flesh of your saints [they cast out, and] their blood they shed around Jerusalem; And there was no man to bury them." ¹⁸And the fear and the dread of them fell on all the people, for they said, "There is neither truth nor judgment in them; for they have broken the covenant and the oath which they swore." ¹⁹And Bacchides left from Jerusalem and encamped in Bezeth; and he sent and took away many of the deserters that were with him, and certain of the people, and he killed them, and [cast them] into the great pit. ²⁰And he made sure the country to Alcimus and left with him a force to aid him; and Bacchides went away to the king. ²¹And Alcimus strove for his chief priesthood. ²²And there were gathered to him all those who troubled their people, and they got the mastery of the land of Judah and did great hurt in Israel. ²³And Judas saw all the mischief that Alcimus and his company had done among the sons of Israel, [even] above the nations, ²⁴and he went out into all the surrounding coasts of Judea and took vengeance on the men that had deserted from him, and they were restrained from going out into the country. ²⁵But when Alcimus saw that Judas and his company waxed strong and knew that he was not able to withstand them, he returned to the king, and brought evil accusations against them. ²⁶And the king sent Nicanor, one of his honorable princes, a man that hated Israel and was their enemy, and commanded him to destroy the people. ²⁷And Nicanor came to Jerusalem with a great army; and he sent to Judas and his countrymen deceitfully with words of peace, saying, ²⁸"Let there be no battle between me and you; I will come with a few men, that I may see your faces in peace." ²⁹And he came to Judas, and they saluted one another peaceably. And the enemies were ready to take away Judas by violence. ³⁰And the thing was known to Judas, that he came to him with deceit, and he was severely afraid of him, and would see his face no longer. ³¹And Nicanor knew that his counsel was discovered; and he went out to meet Judas in battle beside Capharsalama; ³²and there fell of Nicanor's side about five hundred men, and they fled into the city of David. ³³And after these things Nicanor went up to Mount Zion: and there came some of the priests out of the sanctuary, and some of the elders of the people, to salute him peaceably, and to show him the whole burned sacrifice that was being offered for the king. ³⁴And he mocked them, and laughed at them, and entreated them shamefully, and spoke haughtily, ³⁵and swore in a rage, saying, "Unless Judas and his army are now delivered into my hands, it will be that, if I come again in peace, I will burn up this house"; and he went out in a great rage. ³⁶And the priests entered in and stood before the altar and the temple; and they wept, and said, ³⁷"You chose this house to be called by Your Name, to be a house of prayer and supplication for Your people: ³⁸take vengeance on this man and his army, and let them fall by the sword: remember their blasphemies, and do not allow them to live any longer." ³⁹And Nicanor went out from Jerusalem, and encamped in Bethhoron, and there met him the army of Syria. ⁴⁰And Judas encamped in Adasa with three thousand men: and Judas prayed and said, ⁴¹"When those who came from the king blasphemed, your messenger went out, and struck among them one hundred and eighty-five thousand. ⁴²Even so defeat this army before us today and let all the rest know that he has spoken wickedly against Your sanctuary and judge him according to his wickedness." ⁴³And on the thirteenth day of the month Adar the armies joined battle: and Nicanor's army was defeated, and he himself was the first to fall in the battle. ⁴⁴Now when his army saw that Nicanor was fallen, they cast away their arms, and fled. ⁴⁵And they pursued after them a day's journey from Adasa until you come to Gazara, and they sounded an alarm after them with the solemn trumpets. ⁴⁶And they came out of all the surrounding villages of Judea and closed them in; and these turned them back on those, and they all fell by the sword, and there was not one of them left. ⁴⁷And they took the spoils, and the plunder, and they struck off Nicanor's head, and his right hand, which he stretched out so haughtily, and brought them, and hanged them up beside Jerusalem. ⁴⁸And the people were exceedingly glad, and they kept that day as a day of great gladness. ⁴⁹And they ordained to keep this day year by year, the thirteenth day of Adar. ⁵⁰And the land of Judah had rest a little while.

CHAPTER 8

¹And Judas heard of the fame of the Romans, that they are valiant men, and have pleasure in all that join themselves to them and make friends with all such as come to them, ²and that they are valiant men. And they told him of their wars and exploits which they do among the Gauls, and how that they conquered them, and brought them under tribute; ³and what things they did in the land of Spain, that they might become masters of the mines of silver and gold which were there; ⁴and how that by

their policy and persistence they conquered all the place (and the place was exceedingly far from them), and the kings that came against them from the uttermost part of the earth, until they had defeated them, and struck them very severely; and how the rest give them tribute year by year: ⁵and Philip, and Perseus, king of Chittim, and those who lifted up themselves against them, did they defeat in battle, and conquered them: ⁶Antiochus also, the great king of Asia, who came against them to battle, having one hundred and twenty elephants, with horse, and chariots, and an exceedingly great army, and he was defeated by them, ⁷and they took him alive, and appointed that both he and such as reigned after him should give them a great tribute, and should give hostages, and a parcel [of land], ⁸the country of India, and Media, and Lydia, and of the attractive of their countries; and they took them from him, and gave them to King Eumenes: ⁹and how they of Greece took counsel to come and destroy them; ¹⁰and the thing was known to them, and they sent against them a captain, and fought against them, and many of them fell down wounded to death, and they made captive their wives and their children, and plundered them, and conquered their land, and pulled down their strongholds, and plundered them, and brought them into bondage to this day: ¹¹and the residue of the kingdoms and of the isles, as many as rose up against them at any time, they destroyed and made them to be their servants; ¹²but with their friends and such as relied on them they stayed friends; and they conquered the kingdoms that were near and those that were far off, and all that heard of their fame were afraid of them: ¹³moreover, whoever they will to help and to make kings, these do they make kings; and whoever they will, do they depose; and they are exalted exceedingly: ¹⁴and for all this none of them ever put on a diadem, neither did they clothe themselves with purple, to be magnified by it: ¹⁵and how they had made for themselves a senate house, and day by day three hundred and twenty men sat in council, always consulting for the people, to the end they might be well ordered: ¹⁶and how they commit their government to one man year by year, that he should rule over them, and be lord over all their country, and all are obedient to that one, and there is neither envy nor emulation among them. ¹⁷And Judas chose Eupolemus the son of John, the son of Accos, and Jason the son of Eleazar, and sent them to Rome, to establish friendship and alliance with them, ¹⁸and that they should take the yoke from them; for they saw that the kingdom of the Greeks kept Israel in bondage. ¹⁹And they went to Rome (and the way was exceedingly long), and they entered into the senate house, and answered and said, ²⁰Judas, who is also [called] Maccabaeus, and his countrymen, and the people of the Jews, have sent us to you, to make a confederacy and peace with you, and that we might be registered your allies and friends. ²¹And the thing was well-pleasing in their sight. ²²And this is the copy of the writing which they wrote back again on tablets of brass, and sent to Jerusalem, that it might be with them there for a memorial of peace and confederacy: ²³"Good success be to the Romans, and to the nation of the Jews, by sea and by land forever: the sword also and the enemy be far from them. ²⁴But if war arise for Rome first, or any of their allies in all their dominion, ²⁵the nation of the Jews will help them as allies, as the occasion will prescribe to them, with all their heart: ²⁶and to those who make war on them they will not give, neither supply, food, arms, money, or ships, as it has seemed good to Rome, and they will keep their ordinances without taking anything therefore. ²⁷In the same manner, moreover, if war comes first on the nation of the Jews, the Romans will help them as allies with all their soul, as the occasion will prescribe to them: ²⁸and to those who are allies [with their enemies] there will not be given food, arms, money, or ships, as it has seemed good to Rome; and they will keep these ordinances, and that without deceit. ²⁹According to these words have the Romans made a covenant with the people of the Jews. ³⁰But if hereafter the one party and the other will take counsel to add or diminish anything, they will do it at their pleasure, and whatever they will add or take away will be established. ³¹And as touching the evils which King Demetrius does to them, we have written to him, saying, Why have you made your yoke heavy on our friends and allies the Jews? ³²If, therefore, they plead anymore against you, we will do them justice, and fight with you by sea and by land."

CHAPTER 9

¹And Demetrius heard that Nicanor was fallen with his forces in battle, and he sent Bacchides and Alcimus again into the land of Judah a second time, and the right wing [of his army] with them: ²and they went by the way that leads to Gilgal, and encamped against Mesaloth, which is in Arbela, and got possession of it, and destroyed many people. ³And the first month of the one hundred and fifty-second year they encamped against Jerusalem: ⁴and they left, and went to Berea, with twenty thousand footmen and two thousand horses. ⁵And Judas was encamped at Elasa, and three thousand chosen men with him: ⁶and they saw the multitude of the forces, that they were many, and they feared exceedingly: and many slipped away out of the army; there were not left of them more than eight hundred men. ⁷And Judas saw that his army slipped away, and that the battle pressed on him, and he was severely troubled in heart, for that he had no time to gather them together, and he waxed faint. ⁸And he said to those who were left, "Let us arise and go up against our adversaries, if perhaps we may be able to fight with them." ⁹And they would have dissuaded him, saying, "We will in no way be able, but let us rather save our lives now: let us return again, [we] and our countrymen, and fight against them, but we are few." ¹⁰And Judas said, "Do not let it be so that I should do this thing, to flee from them: and if our time has come, let us die in a manly way for our countrymen's sake, and not leave a cause of reproach against our glory." ¹¹And the army went from the camp, and stood to encounter them, and the horse was parted into two companies, and the slingers and the archers went before the army, and all the mighty men that fought in the front of the battle. ¹²But Bacchides was in the right wing; and the phalanx drew near on the two parts, and they blew with their trumpets. ¹³And the men of Judas' side, even they sounded with their trumpets, and the earth shook with the shout of the armies, and the battle was joined, and continued from morning until evening. ¹⁴And Judas saw that Bacchides and the strength of his army were on the right side, and there went with him all that were brave in heart, ¹⁵and the right wing was defeated by them, and he pursued after them to Mount Azotus. ¹⁶And those who were on the left wing saw that the right wing was defeated, and they turned and followed on the footsteps of Judas and of those that were with him: ¹⁷and the battle waxed severe, and many on both parts fell wounded to death. ¹⁸And Judas fell, and the rest fled. ¹⁹And Jonathan and Simon took Judas their brother and buried him in the tomb of his fathers at Modin. ²⁰And they mourned him, and all Israel made great lamentation for him, and mourned many days, and said, ²¹"How is the mighty fallen, the savior of Israel!" ²²And the rest of the acts of Judas, and his wars, and the valiant deeds which he did, and his greatness, they are not written; for they were exceedingly many. ²³And it came to pass after the death of Judas, that the lawless put out their heads in all the coasts of Israel, and all those who did iniquity rose up ²⁴(in those days there was an exceedingly great famine), and the country went over with them. ²⁵And Bacchides chose out the ungodly men and made them lords of the country. ²⁶And they sought out and searched for the friends of Judas, and brought them to Bacchides, and he took vengeance on them, and used them despitefully. ²⁷And there was great suffering in Israel, such as was not since the time that no prophet appeared to them. ²⁸And all the friends of Judas were gathered together, and they said to Jonathan, ²⁹Since your brother Judas has died, we have no man like him to go out against our enemies, and Bacchides, and among them of our nation that hate us. ³⁰Now therefore, we have chosen you this day to be our prince and leader in his stead, that you may fight our battles. ³¹And Jonathan took the governance on him at that time and rose up in the stead of his brother Judas. ³²And Bacchides knew it, and he sought to kill him. ³³And Jonathan, and Simon his brother, and all that were with him, knew it; and they fled into the wilderness of Tekoah, and encamped by the water of the pool Asphar. ³⁴And Bacchides knew it on the Sabbath day, and came, he and all his army, over Jordan. ³⁵And [Jonathan] sent his brother, a leader of the multitude, and implored his friends the Nabathaeans, that they might leave with them their baggage,

which was much. ³⁶And the children of Jambri came out of Medaba, and took John, and all that he had, and went their way with it. ³⁷But after these things they brought word to Jonathan and Simon his brother, that the children of Jambri were making a great marriage and were bringing the bride from Nadabath with a great train, a daughter of one of the great nobles of Canaan. ³⁸And they remembered John their brother, and went up, and hid themselves under the covert of the mountain: ³⁹and they lifted up their eyes, and saw, and behold, a great ado and much baggage: and the bridegroom came out, and his friends and his countrymen, to meet them with timbrels, and minstrels, and many weapons. ⁴⁰And they rose up against them from their ambush, and killed them, and many fell wounded to death, and the remnant fled into the mountain, and they took all their spoils. ⁴¹And the marriage was turned into mourning, and the voice of their minstrels into lamentation. ⁴²And they avenged fully the blood of their brother, and turned back to the marsh of Jordan. ⁴³And Bacchides heard it, and he came on the Sabbath day to the banks of Jordan with a great army. ⁴⁴And Jonathan said to his company, "Let us stand up now and fight for our lives, for it is not [with us] today, as yesterday and the day before. ⁴⁵For behold, the battle is before us and behind us; moreover, the water of the Jordan is on this side and on that side, and marsh and wood; and there is no place to escape. ⁴⁶Now therefore, cry to Heaven, that you may be delivered out of the hand of your enemies." ⁴⁷And the battle was joined, and Jonathan stretched out his hand to strike Bacchides, and he turned away back from him. ⁴⁸And Jonathan and those who were with him leapt into the Jordan and swam over to the other side: and they did not pass over Jordan against them. ⁴⁹And there fell of Bacchides' company that day about one thousand men; ⁵⁰and he returned to Jerusalem. And they built strong cities in Judea, the stronghold that was in Jericho, and Emmaus, and Bethhoron, and Bethel, and Timnath, Pharathon, and Tephon, with high walls and gates and bars. ⁵¹And in them he set a garrison, to vex Israel. ⁵²And he fortified the city Bethsura, and Gazara, and the citadel, and put forces in them, and store of food. ⁵³And he took the sons of the chief men of the country for hostages and put them in ward in the citadel at Jerusalem. ⁵⁴And in the one hundred and fifty-third year, in the second month, Alcimus commanded to pull down the wall of the inner court of the sanctuary; he pulled down also the works of the prophets; ⁵⁵and he began to pull down. At that time was Alcimus stricken, and his works were hindered; and his mouth was stopped, and he was taken with a palsy, and he could no longer speak anything and give order concerning his house. ⁵⁶And Alcimus died at that time with great torment. ⁵⁷And Bacchides saw that Alcimus was dead, and he returned to the king: and the land of Judah had rest two years. ⁵⁸And all the lawless men took counsel, saying, "Behold, Jonathan and they of his part are dwelling at ease, and in security: now therefore we will bring Bacchides, and he will lay hands on them all in one night." ⁵⁹And they went and consulted with him. ⁶⁰And he went, and came with a great army, and sent letters privily to all his allies that were in Judea, that they should lay hands on Jonathan and those that were with him: and they could not, because their counsel was known to them. ⁶¹And [those who were of Jonathan's part] laid hands on about fifty of the men of the country, that were authors of the wickedness, and he killed them. ⁶²And Jonathan, and Simon, and those who were with him, got them away to Bethbasi, which is in the wilderness, and he built up that which had been pulled down thereof, and they made it strong. ⁶³And Bacchides knew it, and he gathered together all his multitude, and sent word to those who were of Judea. ⁶⁴And he went and encamped against Bethbasi, and fought against it many days, and made engines of war. ⁶⁵And Jonathan left his brother Simon in the city, and went out into the country, and he went with a few men. ⁶⁶And he struck Odomera and his relatives, and the children of Phasiron in their tent. ⁶⁷And they began to strike them, and to go up with their forces. And Simon and those who were with him went out of the city, and set on fire the engines of war, ⁶⁸and fought against Bacchides, and he was defeated by them, and they afflicted him severely; for his counsel was in vain, and his inroad. ⁶⁹And they were very angry with the lawless men that gave him counsel to come into the country, and they killed many of them. And he took counsel to depart into his own land. ⁷⁰And Jonathan had knowledge thereof, and sent ambassadors to him, to the end that they should make peace with him, and that he should restore to them the captives. ⁷¹And he accepted the thing, and did according to his words, and swore to him that he would not seek his hurt all the days of his life. ⁷²And he restored to him the captives which he had taken previously out of the land of Judah, and he returned and departed into his own land, and came not anymore into their borders. ⁷³And the sword ceased from Israel. And Jonathan lived at Michmash; and Jonathan began to judge the people; and he destroyed the ungodly out of Israel.

CHAPTER 10

¹And in the one hundred and sixtieth year, Alexander Epiphanes, the son of Antiochus, went up and took possession of Ptolemais: and they received him, and he reigned there. ²And King Demetrius heard thereof, and he gathered together exceedingly great forces, and went out to meet him in battle. ³And Demetrius sent letters to Jonathan with words of peace, so as to magnify him. ⁴For he said, "Let us go beforehand to make peace with them, before he makes peace with Alexander against us: ⁵for he will remember all the evils that we have done against him, and to his countrymen and to his nation." ⁶And he gave him authority to gather together forces, and to provide arms, and that he should be his ally: and he commanded that they should deliver up to him the hostages that were in the citadel. ⁷And Jonathan came to Jerusalem and read the letters in the audience of all the people, and of those who were in the citadel: ⁸and they were severely afraid, when they heard that the king had given him authority to gather together an army. ⁹And they of the citadel delivered up the hostages to Jonathan, and he restored them to their parents. ¹⁰And Jonathan lived in Jerusalem and began to build and renew the city. ¹¹And he commanded those who did the work to build the walls and Mount Zion around with square stones for defense; and they did so. ¹²And the strangers, that were in the strongholds which Bacchides had built, fled away; ¹³and each man left his place, and departed into his own land. ¹⁴Only at Bethsura were there left certain of those that had forsaken the law and the commands; for it was a place of refuge to them. ¹⁵And King Alexander heard all the promises which Demetrius had sent to Jonathan: and they told him of the battles and the valiant deeds which he and his countrymen had done, and of the toils which they had endured; ¹⁶And he said, "Will we find such another man? And now we will make him our friend and ally." ¹⁷And he wrote letters, and sent them to him, according to these words, saying, ¹⁸"King Alexander to his brother Jonathan, greetings: ¹⁹We have heard of you, that you are a mighty man of valor, and meet to be our friend. ²⁰And now we have appointed you this day to be chief priest of your nation, and to be called the king's friend (and he sent to him a purple robe and a crown of gold), and to take our part, and to keep friendship with us." ²¹And Jonathan put on the holy garments in the seventh month of the one hundred and sixtieth year, at the Celebration of Shelters, and he gathered together forces, and provided arms in abundance. ²²And Demetrius heard these things, and he was grieved, and said, ²³"What is this that we have done, that Alexander has been beforehand with us in establishing friendship with the Jews, to strengthen himself? ²⁴I also will write to them words of encouragement and of honor and of gifts, that they may be with me to aid me." ²⁵And he sent to them according to these words: "King Demetrius to the nation of the Jews, greetings: ²⁶Forasmuch as you have kept your covenants with us, and continued in our friendship, and have not joined yourselves to our enemies, we have heard of this, and are glad. ²⁷And now continue still to keep faith with us, and we will repay to you good things in return for your dealings with us, ²⁸and will grant you many immunities, and give you gifts. ²⁹And now I free you, and release all the Jews, from the tributes, and from the customs of salt, and from the crowns. ³⁰And instead of the third part of the seed, and instead of the half of the fruit of the trees, which falls to me to receive, I release it from this day and from now on, so that I will not take it from the land of Judah, and from the three governments which are added to that from the country of Samaria and Galilee, from this day out and for all time. ³¹And

let Jerusalem be holy and free, and her borders; the tenths and the tolls [also]. ³²I yield up also my authority over the citadel which is at Jerusalem, and give it to the chief priest, that he may appoint in it such men as he will choose to keep it. ³³And every soul of the Jews, that has been carried captive from the land of Judah into any part of my kingdom, I set at liberty without price; and let all remit the tributes of their cattle also. ³⁴And all the feasts, and the Sabbaths, and new moons, and appointed days, and three days before a feast, and three days after a feast, let them all be days of immunity and release for all the Jews that are in my kingdom. ³⁵And no man will have authority to exact from any of them, or to trouble them concerning any matter. ³⁶And let there be enrolled among the king's forces about thirty thousand men of the Jews, and pay will be given to them, as belongs to all the king's forces. ³⁷And of them some will be placed in the king's great strongholds, and some of them will be placed over the affairs of the kingdom, which are of trust: and let those that are over them, and their rulers, be of themselves, and let them walk after their own laws, even as the king has commanded in the land of Judah. ³⁸And the three governments that have been added to Judea from the country of Samaria, let them be added to Judea, that they may be reckoned to be under one, that they may not obey other authority than the chief priest's. ³⁹As for Ptolemais, and the land pertaining to that, I have given it as a gift to the sanctuary that is at Jerusalem, for the expenses that befit the sanctuary. ⁴⁰And I give every year fifteen thousand shekels of silver from the king's revenues from the places that are convenient. ⁴¹And all the overplus, which those who manage the king's affairs paid not in as in the first years, they will give from now on toward the works of the house. ⁴²And besides this, the five thousand shekels of silver, which they received from the uses of the sanctuary from the revenue year by year, this is also released, because it pertains to the priests that minister. ⁴³And whoever will flee to the temple that is at Jerusalem, and [be found] within all the borders thereof, whether one owes money to the king, or any other matter, let them go free, and all that they have in my kingdom. ⁴⁴And for the building and renewing of the works of the sanctuary the expense will be given also out of the king's revenue. ⁴⁵And for the building of the walls of Jerusalem, and the fortifying thereof around, will the expense be given also out of the king's revenue, and for the building of the walls in Judea." ⁴⁶Now when Jonathan and the people heard these words, they gave no credence to them, nor received them, because they remembered the great evil which he had done in Israel, and that he had afflicted them very severely. ⁴⁷And they were well pleased with Alexander, because he was the first that spoke words of peace to them, and they were allies with him always. ⁴⁸And King Alexander gathered together great forces and encamped near Demetrius. ⁴⁹And the two kings joined battle, and the army of Alexander fled; and Demetrius followed after him and prevailed against them. ⁵⁰And he strengthened the battle exceedingly until the sun went down: and Demetrius fell that day. ⁵¹And Alexander sent ambassadors to Ptolemy king of Egypt according to these words, saying, ⁵²"Forasmuch as I am returned to my kingdom, and am set on the throne of my fathers, and have gotten the dominion, and have overthrown Demetrius, and have gotten possession of our country; ⁵³yes, I joined the battle with him, and he and his army were defeated by us, and we sat on the throne of his kingdom: ⁵⁴now also let us make friends with one another, and give me now your daughter to wife: and I will be joined with you, and will give both you and her gifts worthy of you." ⁵⁵And Ptolemy the king answered, saying, "Happy is the day wherein you returned into the land of your fathers, and sat on the throne of their kingdom. ⁵⁶And now I will do to you as you have written, but meet me at Ptolemais, that we may see one another; and I will join with you, even as you have said." ⁵⁷And Ptolemy went out of Egypt, himself and Cleopatra his daughter, and came to Ptolemais in the one hundred and sixty-second year: ⁵⁸and King Alexander met him, and he bestowed on him his daughter Cleopatra, and celebrated her wedding at Ptolemais with great pomp, as the manner of kings is. ⁵⁹And King Alexander wrote to Jonathan, that he should come to meet him. ⁶⁰And he went with pomp to Ptolemais, and met the two kings, and gave them and their friends silver and gold, and many gifts, and found favor in their sight. ⁶¹And there were gathered together against him certain pernicious fellows out of Israel, men that were transgressors of the law, to complain against him: and the king gave no heed to them. ⁶²And the king commanded, and they took off Jonathan's garments, and clothed him in purple: and so they did. ⁶³And the king made him sit with him, and said to his princes, "Go out with him into the midst of the city, and make proclamation, that no man complains against him of any matter, and let no man trouble him for any manner of cause." ⁶⁴And it came to pass, when those who complained against him saw his glory according as [the herald] made proclamation, and [saw] him clothed in purple, they all fled away. ⁶⁵And the king gave him honor, and wrote him among his chief friends, and made him a captain, and governor of a province. ⁶⁶And Jonathan returned to Jerusalem with peace and gladness. ⁶⁷And in the one hundred and sixty-fifth year came Demetrius, son of Demetrius, out of Crete into the land of his fathers: ⁶⁸and King Alexander heard thereof, and he grieved exceedingly, and returned to Antioch. ⁶⁹And Demetrius appointed Apollonius, who was over Coele-Syria, and he gathered together a great army, and encamped in Jamnia, and sent to Jonathan the chief priest, saying, ⁷⁰"You alone lift up yourself against us, but I am had in derision and in reproach because of you. And why do you vaunt your power against us in the mountains? ⁷¹Now therefore, if you trust in your forces, come down to us into the plain, and there let us try the matter together; for with me is the power of the cities. ⁷²Ask and learn who I am, and the rest that help us; and they say your foot cannot stand before our face; for your fathers have been twice put to flight in their own land. ⁷³And now you will not be able to withstand the horse and such an army as this in the plain, where is neither stone nor flint, nor place to flee to." ⁷⁴Now when Jonathan heard the words of Apollonius, he was moved in his mind, and he chose out ten thousand men, and went out from Jerusalem, and Simon his brother met him for to help him. ⁷⁵And he encamped against Joppa: and they of the city shut him out, because Apollonius had a garrison in Joppa. ⁷⁶and they fought against it. And they of the city were afraid and opened to him: and Jonathan became master of Joppa. ⁷⁷And Apollonius heard, and he gathered an army of three thousand horses, and a great army, and went to Azotus as though he were on a journey, and immediately drew onward into the plain, because he had a multitude of horse, and trusted therein. ⁷⁸And he pursued after him to Azotus, and the armies joined battle. ⁷⁹And Apollonius had left one thousand horses behind them privily. ⁸⁰And Jonathan knew that there was an ambush behind him. And they compassed round his army, and cast their darts at the people, from morning until evening: ⁸¹but the people stood still, as Jonathan commanded them: and their horses were wearied. ⁸²And Simon drew out his army and joined battle with the phalanx (for the horsemen were spent), and they were defeated by him, and fled. ⁸³And the horsemen were scattered in the plain, and they fled to Azotus, and entered into Beth-Dagon, their idol's temple, to save themselves. ⁸⁴And Jonathan burned Azotus, and the surrounding cities, and took their spoils; and the temple of Dagon, and those who fled into it, he burned with fire. ⁸⁵And those who had fallen by the sword, with those who were burned, were about eight thousand men. ⁸⁶And from there Jonathan left, and encamped against Ashkelon, and they of the city came out to meet him with great pomp. ⁸⁷And Jonathan, with those who were on his side, returned to Jerusalem, having many spoils. ⁸⁸And it came to pass, when King Alexander heard these things, he honored Jonathan yet more; ⁸⁹and he sent to him a buckle of gold, as the use is to give to such as are of the relatives of the kings: and he gave him Ekron and all the coasts thereof for a possession.

CHAPTER 11

¹And the king of Egypt gathered together great forces, as the sand which is by the seashore, and many ships, and sought to make himself master of Alexander's kingdom by deceit, and to add it to his own kingdom. ²And he went out into Syria with words of peace, and they of the cities opened to him, and met him; For King Alexander's command was that they should meet him, because he was his father-in-law. ³Now as he entered into the

cities of Ptolemais, he set his forces for a garrison in each city. ⁴But when he came near to Azotus, they showed him the temple of Dagon burned with fire, and Azotus and the pasture lands thereof pulled down, and the bodies cast abroad, and those who had been burned, whom he burned in the war, for they had made heaps of them in his way. ⁵And they told the king what things Jonathan had done, that they might cast blame on him: and the king held his peace. ⁶And Jonathan met the king with pomp at Joppa, and they saluted one another, and they slept there. ⁷And Jonathan went with the king as far as the river that is called Eleutherus and returned to Jerusalem. ⁸But King Ptolemy became master of the cities on the seacoast, to Selucia which is by the sea, and he devised evil plans concerning Alexander. ⁹And he sent ambassadors to King Demetrius, saying, "Come! Let us make a covenant with one another, and I will give you my daughter whom Alexander has, and you will reign over your father's kingdom; ¹⁰for I have changed my mind that I gave my daughter to him, for he sought to kill me." ¹¹And he cast blame on him, because he coveted his kingdom. ¹²And taking his daughter from him, he gave her to Demetrius, and was estranged from Alexander, and their enmity was openly seen. ¹³And Ptolemy entered into Antioch and put on himself the diadem of Asia; and he put two diadems on his head, the diadem of Egypt and that of Asia. ¹⁴But King Alexander was in Cilicia at that season, because they of those parts were in revolt. ¹⁵And Alexander heard of it, and he came against him in war: and Ptolemy led out [his army, and] met him with a strong force, and put him to flight. ¹⁶And Alexander fled into Arabia, that he might be sheltered there; but King Ptolemy was exalted. ¹⁷And Zabdiel the Arabian took off Alexander's head and sent it to Ptolemy. ¹⁸And King Ptolemy died the third day after, and those who were in his strongholds were slain by those who were in the strongholds. ¹⁹And Demetrius reigned in the one hundred and sixty-seventh year. ²⁰In those days Jonathan gathered together them of Judea, to take the citadel that was at Jerusalem: and he made many engines of war against it. ²¹And certain that hated their own nation, men that transgressed the law, went to the king, and reported to him that Jonathan was besieging the citadel. ²²And he heard, and was angered; but when he heard it, he set out immediately, and came to Ptolemais, and wrote to Jonathan, that he should not besiege it, and that he should meet him and speak with him at Ptolemais with all speed. ²³But when Jonathan heard this, he commanded to besiege it [still]: and he chose certain of the elders of Israel and of the priests, and put himself in peril, ²⁴and taking silver and gold and raiment and various presents besides, went to Ptolemais to the king. And he found favor in his sight. ²⁵And certain lawless men of those who were of the nation made complaints against him, ²⁶and the king did to him even as his predecessors had done to him and exalted him in the sight of all his friends, ²⁷and confirmed to him the chief priesthood, and all the other honors that he had before, and gave him preeminence among his chief friends. ²⁸And Jonathan requested of the king, that he would make Judea free from tribute, and the three provinces, and the country of Samaria; and promised him three hundred talents. ²⁹And the king consented and wrote letters to Jonathan concerning all these things after this manner: ³⁰"King Demetrius to his brother Jonathan, and to the nation of the Jews, greetings: ³¹The copy of the letter which we wrote to Lasthenes our countryman concerning you, we have written also to you, that you may see it. ³²King Demetrius to Lasthenes his father, greetings: ³³We have determined to do good to the nation of the Jews, who are our friends, and observe what is just toward us, because of their good will toward us. ³⁴We have confirmed therefore to them the borders of Judea, and also the three governments of Aphaerema and Lydda and Ramathaim ([these] were added to Judea from the country of Samaria), and all things pertaining to them, for all such as do sacrifice in Jerusalem, instead of the king's dues which the king received of them yearly previously from the produce of the earth and the fruits of trees. ³⁵And as for the other things that pertain to us from now on, of the tenths and the tolls that pertain to us, and the salt pits, and the crowns that pertain to us, all these we will bestow on them. ³⁶And not one of these things will be annulled from this time out and forever. ³⁷Now therefore, be careful to make a copy of these things, and let it be given to Jonathan, and let it be set up on the holy mount in an appropriate and conspicuous place." ³⁸And King Demetrius saw that the land was quiet before him, and that no resistance was made to him, and he sent away all his forces, each man to his own place, except the foreign forces, which he had raised from the isles of the nations: and all the forces of his fathers hated him. ³⁹Now Tryphon was of those who previously had been of Alexander's part, and he saw that all the forces murmured against Demetrius, and he went to Imalcue the Arabian, who was nourishing up Antiochus the young child of Alexander, ⁴⁰and pressed severely on him that he should deliver him to him, that he might reign in his father's stead: and he told him all that Demetrius had done, and the hatred with which his forces hated him; and he dwelt there many days. ⁴¹And Jonathan sent to King Demetrius, that he should cast out of Jerusalem them of the citadel, and those who were in the strongholds; for they fought against Israel continually. ⁴²And Demetrius sent to Jonathan, saying, "I will not only do this for you and your nation, but I will greatly honor you and your nation, if I find fair occasion. ⁴³Now therefore you will do well, if you send me men who will fight for me; for all my forces are revolted." ⁴⁴And Jonathan sent him three thousand valiant men to Antioch: and they came to the king, and the king was glad at their coming. ⁴⁵And they of the city gathered themselves together into the midst of the city, to the number of one hundred and twenty thousand men, and they were inclined to kill the king. ⁴⁶And the king fled into the court of the palace, and they of the city seized the passages of the city and began to fight. ⁴⁷And the king called the Jews to help him, and they were gathered together to him all at once, and they dispersed themselves in the city, and killed that day to the number of one hundred thousand. ⁴⁸And they set the city on fire, and got many spoils that day, and saved the king. ⁴⁹And they of the city saw that the Jews had made themselves masters of the city as they would, and they waxed faint in their hearts, and they cried out to the king with supplication, saying, ⁵⁰"Give us your right hand, and let the Jews cease from fighting against us and the city." ⁵¹And they cast away their arms and made peace; and the Jews were glorified in the sight of the king, and before all that were in his kingdom; and they returned to Jerusalem, having many spoils. ⁵²And King Demetrius sat on the throne of his kingdom, and the land was quiet before him. ⁵³And he lied in all that he spoke, and estranged himself from Jonathan, and did not repay him according to the benefits with which he had repaid him and afflicted him exceedingly. ⁵⁴Now after this, Tryphon returned, and with him the young child Antiochus; and he reigned and put on a diadem. ⁵⁵And there were gathered to him all the forces which Demetrius had sent away with disgrace, and they fought against him, and he fled and was put to the rout. ⁵⁶And Tryphon took the elephants and became master of Antioch. ⁵⁷And the young Antiochus wrote to Jonathan, saying, "I confirm to you the chief priesthood, and appoint you over the four governments, and to be one of the king's friends." ⁵⁸And he sent to him golden vessels and furniture for the table, and gave him leave to drink in golden vessels, and to be clothed in purple, and to have a golden buckle. ⁵⁹And his brother Simon he made captain from the Ladder of Tyre to the borders of Egypt. ⁶⁰And Jonathan went out and took his journey beyond the river and through the cities; and all the forces of Syria gathered themselves to him for to be his allies. And he came to Ashkelon, and they of the city met him honorably. ⁶¹And he departed from there to Gaza, and they of Gaza shut him out; and he laid siege to it, and burned the pasture lands thereof with fire, and plundered them. ⁶²And they of Gaza made request to Jonathan, and he gave them his right hand, and took the sons of their princes for hostages, and sent them away to Jerusalem; and he passed through the country as far as Damascus. ⁶³And Jonathan heard that Demetrius' princes were come to Kedesh, which is in Galilee, with a great army, purposing to remove him from his office; ⁶⁴and he went to meet them, but Simon his brother he left in the country. ⁶⁵And Simon encamped against Bethsura, and fought against it many days, and shut it up: ⁶⁶and they made request to him that he would give them his right hand, and he gave it to them; and he put them out from there, and took possession of the city, and set a garrison over it. ⁶⁷And

Jonathan and his army encamped at the water of Gennesareth, and early in the morning they got them to the plain of Hazor. ⁶⁸And behold, an army of strangers met him in the plain, and they laid an ambush for him in the mountains, but themselves met him face to face. ⁶⁹But those who lay in ambush rose out of their places and joined battle; and all those who were of Jonathan's side fled: ⁷⁰not one of them was left, except Mattathias, the son of Absalom, and Judas the son of Chalphi, captains of the forces. ⁷¹And Jonathan tore his clothes, and put earth on his head, and prayed. ⁷²And he turned again to them in battle, and put them to the rout, and they fled. ⁷³And they of his side that fled saw it, and returned to him, and pursued with him to Kedesh to their camp, and they encamped there. ⁷⁴And there fell of the strangers on that day about three thousand men: and Jonathan returned to Jerusalem.

CHAPTER 12

¹And Jonathan saw that the time served him, and he chose men, and sent them to Rome, to confirm and renew the friendship that they had with them. ²And to the Spartans, and to other places, he sent letters after the same manner. ³And they went to Rome, and entered into the senate house, and said, "Jonathan the chief priest, and the nation of the Jews, have sent us, to renew for them the friendship and the confederacy, as in former time." ⁴And they gave them letters to the men in every place, that they should bring them on their way to the land of Judah in peace. ⁵And this is the copy of the letters which Jonathan wrote to the Spartans: ⁶"Jonathan the chief priest, and the senate of the nation, and the priests, and the rest of the people of the Jews, to their countrymen the Spartans, greetings: ⁷Even before this time were letters sent to Onias the chief priest from Arius, who was reigning among you, to signify that you are our countrymen, as the copy written below shows. ⁸And Onias entreated honorably the man that was sent, and received the letters, wherein declaration was made of confederacy and friendship. ⁹Therefore we also, albeit we need none of these things, having for our encouragement the holy scrolls which are in our hands, ¹⁰have determined to send that we might renew our brotherhood and friendship with you, to the end that we should not become estranged from you altogether, for a long time has passed since you sent to us. ¹¹We therefore, at all times without ceasing, both in our feasts, and on the other convenient days, remember you in the sacrifices which we offer, and in our prayers, as it is right and appropriate to be mindful of countrymen: ¹²and moreover are glad for your glory. ¹³But as for ourselves, many afflictions and many wars have encompassed us, and the kings that are around us have fought against us. ¹⁴We were not inclined therefore to be troublesome to you, and to the rest of our allies and friends, in these wars; ¹⁵for we have the help which is from Heaven to help us, and we have been delivered from our enemies, and our enemies have been brought low. ¹⁶We chose, therefore, Numenius the son of Antiochus, and Antipater the son of Jason, and have sent them to the Romans, to renew the friendship that we had with them, and the former confederacy. ¹⁷We commanded them, therefore, to go also to you, and to salute you, and to deliver you our letters concerning the renewing [of friendship] and our brotherhood. ¹⁸And now you will do well if you give us an answer to that. ¹⁹And this is the copy of the letters which they sent to Onias: ²⁰Arius, king of the Spartans, to Onias the chief priest, greetings: ²¹It has been found in writing, concerning the Spartans and the Jews, that they are countrymen, and that they are of the stock of Abraham: ²²and now, since this has come to our knowledge, you will do well to write to us of your prosperity. ²³And we moreover write on our part to you, that your cattle and goods are ours, and ours are yours. We command, therefore, that they make report to you concerning this." ²⁴And Jonathan heard that Demetrius' princes were returned to fight against him with a greater army than before, ²⁵and he went from Jerusalem, and met them in the country of Hamath; for he gave them no respite to set foot in his country. ²⁶And he sent spies into his camp, and they came again, and reported to him that they were appointed in such and such a way to fall on them in the night season. ²⁷But as soon as the sun was down, Jonathan commanded his men to watch, and to be in arms, that all the night long they might be ready for battle: and he put out sentinels around the camp. ²⁸And the adversaries heard that Jonathan and his men were ready for battle, and they feared, and trembled in their hearts, and they kindled fires in their camp, ²⁹but Jonathan and his men did not know it until the morning; for they saw the lights burning. ³⁰And Jonathan pursued after them and overtook them not; for they were gone over the River Eleutherus. ³¹And Jonathan turned toward the Arabians, who are called Zabadaeans, and struck them, and took their spoils. ³²And he came out from there, and came to Damascus, and took his journey through all the country. ³³And Simon went out, and took his journey as far as Ashkelon, and the strongholds that were near to it. And he turned toward Joppa and took possession of it; ³⁴for he had heard that they were determined to deliver the stronghold to the men of Demetrius; and he set a garrison there to keep it. ³⁵And Jonathan returned, and called the elders of the people together; and he took counsel with them to build strongholds in Judea, ³⁶and to make the walls of Jerusalem higher, and to raise a great mound between the citadel and the city, for to separate it from the city, that so it might be all alone, that men might neither buy nor sell. ³⁷And they were gathered together to build the city, and there fell down part of the wall of the brook that is on the east side, and he repaired that which is called Chaphenatha. ³⁸And Simon also built Adida in the plain country, and made it strong, and set up gates and bars. ³⁹And Tryphon sought to reign over Asia and to put on himself the diadem, and to stretch out his hand against Antiochus the king. ⁴⁰And he was afraid lest perhaps Jonathan should not permit him, and lest he should fight against him; and he sought a way how to take him, that he might destroy him. And he went and came to Bethshan. ⁴¹And Jonathan came out to meet him with forty thousand men chosen for battle and came to Bethshan. ⁴²And Tryphon saw that he came with a great army, and he was afraid to stretch out his hand against him: ⁴³and he received him honorably, and commended him to all his friends, and gave him gifts, and commanded his forces to be obedient to him, as to himself. ⁴⁴And he said to Jonathan, "Why have you put all this people to trouble, seeing there is no war between us? ⁴⁵And now send them away to their homes but choose for yourself a few men who will be with you, and come you with me to Ptolemais, and I will give it up to you, and the rest of the strongholds and the rest of the forces, and all the king's officers: and I will return and depart; for this is the cause of my coming." ⁴⁶And he put his trust in him, and did even as he said, and sent away his forces, and they departed into the land of Judah. ⁴⁷But he reserved to himself three thousand men, of whom he left two thousand in Galilee, but one thousand went with him. ⁴⁸Now as soon as Jonathan entered into Ptolemais, they of Ptolemais shut the gates, and laid hands on him; and all those who came in with him they killed with the sword. ⁴⁹And Tryphon sent forces and horsemen into Galilee, and into the great plain, to destroy all Jonathan's men. ⁵⁰And they perceived that he was taken and had perished, and those who were with him; and they encouraged one another, and went on their way close together, prepared to fight. ⁵¹And those who followed on them saw that they were ready to fight for their lives and turned back again. ⁵²And they all came in peace into the land of Judah, and they mourned for Jonathan, and those who were with him, and they were severely afraid; and all Israel mourned with a great mourning. ⁵³And all the nations that were around them sought to destroy them utterly, for they said, "They have no ruler, nor any to help them: now therefore, let us fight against them and take away their memorial from among men."

CHAPTER 13

¹And Simon heard that Tryphon had gathered together a mighty army to come into the land of Judah and destroy it utterly. ²And he saw that the people trembled and were in great fear; and he went up to Jerusalem, and gathered the people together; ³and he encouraged them, and said to them, "You yourselves know all the things that I, and my countrymen, and my father's house, have done for the laws and the sanctuary, and the battles and the distresses which we have seen: ⁴by reason of this all my countrymen have perished for Israel's sake, and I am left alone. ⁵And now be it far from me, that I should spare my own life in any time of affliction; for I am not better than my

countrymen. ⁶However, I will take vengeance for my nation, and for the sanctuary, and for our wives and children, because all the nations are gathered to destroy us of very [great] hatred." ⁷And the spirit of the people revived, as soon as they heard these words. ⁸And they answered with a loud voice, saying, "You are our leader instead of Judas and Jonathan your brother. ⁹Fight our battles, and all that you will say to us, that will we do." ¹⁰And he gathered together all the men of war, and hurried to finish the walls of Jerusalem, and he fortified it around. ¹¹And he sent Jonathan the son of Absalom, and with him a great army, to Joppa; and he cast out those who were therein and dwelt there in it. ¹²And Tryphon left from Ptolemais with a mighty army to enter into the land of Judah, and Jonathan was with him in ward. ¹³But Simon encamped at Adida, near the plain. ¹⁴And Tryphon knew that Simon was risen up instead of his brother Jonathan, and meant to join battle with him, and he sent ambassadors to him, saying, ¹⁵"It is for money which Jonathan your brother owed to the king's treasure, by reason of the offices which he had, that we hold him fast. ¹⁶And now send one hundred talents of silver, and two of his sons for hostages, that when he is set at liberty he may not revolt from us, and we will set him at liberty." ¹⁷And Simon knew that they spoke to him deceitfully; and he sent the money and the children, lest perhaps he should procure to himself great hatred of the people, ¹⁸and they should say, "Because I did not send him the money and the children, he perished." ¹⁹And he sent the children and the hundred talents. And he dealt falsely and did not set Jonathan at liberty. ²⁰And after this Tryphon came to invade the land, and destroy it, and he went around by the way that leads to Adora: and Simon and his army marched near him to every place, wherever he went. ²¹Now they of the citadel sent to Tryphon ambassadors, hastening him to come to them through the wilderness, and to send them food. ²²And Tryphon made ready all his horse to come: and on that night there fell a very great snow, and he came not by reason of the snow. And he left and came into the country of Gilead. ²³But when he came near to Bascama, he killed Jonathan, and he was buried there. ²⁴And Tryphon returned and went away into his own land. ²⁵And Simon sent, and took the bones of Jonathan his brother, and buried him at Modin, the city of his fathers. ²⁶And all Israel made great lamentation over him and mourned for him many days. ²⁷And Simon built [a monument] on the tomb of his father and his relatives, and raised it aloft to the sight, with polished stone behind and before. ²⁸And he set up seven pyramids, one near another, for his father, and his mother, and his four relatives. ²⁹And for these he made cunning devices, setting around them great pillars, and on the pillars he fashioned all manner of arms for a perpetual memory, and beside the arms ships carved, that they should be seen of all that sail on the sea. ³⁰This is the tomb which he made at Modin, and [it is there] to this day. ³¹Now Tryphon dealt deceitfully with the young King Antiochus, and killed him, ³²and reigned in his stead, and put the diadem of Asia on himself, and brought a great calamity on the land. ³³And Simon built the strongholds of Judea, and fenced them about with high towers, and great walls, and gates, and bars; and he laid up food in the strongholds. ³⁴And Simon chose men, and sent to King Demetrius, to the end he should give the country an immunity, because all that Tryphon did was to plunder. ³⁵And King Demetrius sent to him according to these words, and answered him, and wrote a letter to him, after this manner: ³⁶"King Demetrius to Simon the chief priest and friend of kings, and to the elders and nation of the Jews, greetings: ³⁷The golden crown, and the palm branch, which you sent, we have received: and we are ready to make a steadfast peace with you, yes, and to write to our officers, to grant immunities to you. ³⁸And whatever things we confirmed to you, they are confirmed; and the strongholds, which you have built, let them be your own. ³⁹As for any oversights and faults committed to this day, we forgive them, and the crown which you owed us: and if there were any other toll exacted in Jerusalem, let it be exacted no longer. ⁴⁰And if there are any among you appropriate to be enrolled in our court, let them be enrolled, and let there be peace between us." ⁴¹In the one hundred and seventieth year was the yoke of the heathen taken away from Israel. ⁴²And the people began to write in their instruments and contracts, "In the first year of Simon, the great chief priest and captain and leader of the Jews." ⁴³In those days he encamped against Gazara and compassed it around with armies; and he made an engine of siege, and brought it up to the city, and struck a tower, and took it. ⁴⁴And those who were in the engine leaped out into the city; and there was a great uproar in the city: ⁴⁵and they of the city tore their clothes and went up on the walls with their wives and children, and cried with a loud voice, making request to Simon to give them his right hand. ⁴⁶And they said, "Do not deal with us according to our wickedness, but according to your mercy." ⁴⁷And Simon was reconciled to them and did not fight against them: and he put them out of the city, and cleansed the houses wherein the idols were, and so entered into it with singing and giving praise. ⁴⁸And he put all uncleanness out of it and placed in it such men as would keep the law, and made it stronger than it was before, and built therein a dwelling place for himself. ⁴⁹But they of the citadel in Jerusalem were hindered from going out, and from going into the country, and from buying and selling; and they hungered exceedingly, and a great number of them perished through famine. ⁵⁰And they cried out to Simon, that he should give them his right hand; and he gave it to them: and he put them out from there, and he cleansed the citadel from its pollutions. ⁵¹And he entered into it on the twenty-third day of the second month, in the one hundred and seventy-first year, with praise and palm branches, and with harps, and with cymbals, and with lutes, and with hymns, and with songs: because a great enemy was destroyed out of Israel. ⁵²And he ordained that they should keep that day every year with gladness. And the hill of the temple that was by the citadel he made stronger than before, and there he lived, himself and his men. ⁵³And Simon saw that John his son was a [valiant] man, and he made him leader of all his forces: and he lived in Gazara.

CHAPTER 14

¹And in the one hundred and seventy-second year, King Demetrius gathered his forces together, and went into Media, to get himself help, that he might fight against Tryphon. ²And Arsaces, the king of Persia and Media, heard that Demetrius had come into his borders, and he sent one of his princes to take him alive: ³and he went and struck the army of Demetrius, and took him, and brought him to Arsaces; and he put him in ward. ⁴And the land had rest all the days of Simon: and he sought the good of his nation; and his authority and his glory was well-pleasing to them all his days. ⁵And amid all his glory he took Joppa for a haven and made it an entrance for the isles of the sea; ⁶and he enlarged the borders of his nation and got possession of the country; ⁷and he gathered together a great number of captives, and got the dominion of Gazara, and Bethsura, and the citadel, and he took away from it its uncleanness; and there was none that resisted him. ⁸And they tilled their land in peace, and the land gave her increase, and the trees of the plains their fruit. ⁹The ancient men sat in the streets, they communed—all of them—together of good things, and the young men put on glorious and warlike apparel. ¹⁰He provided food for the cities, and furnished them with all manner of munition, until the name of his glory was named to the end of the earth. ¹¹He made peace in the land, and Israel rejoiced with great joy; ¹²and each man sat under his vine and his fig tree, and there was none to make them afraid; ¹³and there ceased in the land any that fought against them: and the kings were defeated in those days. ¹⁴And he strengthened all those of his people that were brought low: the law he searched out, and every lawless and wicked person he took away. ¹⁵He glorified the sanctuary, and the vessels of the temple he multiplied. ¹⁶And it was heard at Rome that Jonathan was dead, and even to Sparta, and they were exceedingly sorry. ¹⁷But as soon as they heard that his brother Simon was made chief priest in his stead, and ruled the country, and the cities therein, ¹⁸they wrote to him on tablets of brass, to renew with him the friendship and the confederacy which they had confirmed with Judas and Jonathan his relatives; ¹⁹and they were read before the congregation at Jerusalem. ²⁰And this is the copy of the letters which the Spartans sent: "The rulers of the Spartans, and the city, to Simon the chief priest, and to the elders, and the priests, and the residue of the people of the Jews, our countrymen, greetings: ²¹The ambassadors

that were sent to our people made report to us of your glory and honor: and we were glad for their coming, ²²and we registered the things that were spoken by them in the public records after this manner: Numenius son of Antiochus, and Antipater son of Jason, the Jews' ambassadors, came to us to renew the friendship they had with us." ²³And it pleased the people to entertain the men honorably, and to put the copy of their words in the public records, to the end that the people of the Spartans might have a memorial thereof: moreover, they wrote a copy of these things to Simon the chief priest. ²⁴After this Simon sent Numenius to Rome with a great shield of gold of one-thousand-pound weight, in order to confirm the confederacy with them. ²⁵But when the people heard these things, they said, "What thanks will we give to Simon and his sons? ²⁶For he and his countrymen and the house of his father have made themselves strong and have chased away in fight the enemies of Israel from them, and confirmed liberty to Israel." ²⁷And they wrote on tablets of brass, and set them on pillars in Mount Zion: and this is the copy of the writing: "On the eighteenth day of Elul, in the one hundred and seventy-second year, and this is the third year of Simon the chief priest, ²⁸in Asaramel, in a great congregation of priests and people and princes of the nation, and of the elders of the country, was it notified to us: ²⁹Forasmuch as oftentimes there have been wars in the country, but Simon the son of Mattathias, the son of the sons of Joarib, and his countrymen, put themselves in danger, and withstood the enemies of their nation, that their sanctuary and the law might be established, and glorified their nation with great glory: ³⁰and Jonathan assembled their nation together, and became their chief priest, and was gathered to his people: ³¹and their enemies purposed to invade their country, that they might destroy their country utterly, and stretch out their hands against their sanctuary: ³²then rose up Simon, and fought for his nation, and spent much of his own substance, and armed the valiant men of his nation, and gave them wages: ³³and he fortified the cities of Judea, and Bethsura that lies on the borders of Judea, where the arms of the enemies were previously, and set there a garrison of Jews: ³⁴and he fortified Joppa which is on the sea, and Gazara which is on the borders of Azotus, wherein the enemies lived previously, and placed Jews there, and set therein all things convenient for their restoration: ³⁵and the people saw the faith of Simon, and the glory which he thought to bring to his nation, and they made him their leader and chief priest, because he had done all these things, and for the justice and the faith which he kept to his nation, and for that he sought by all means to exalt his people: ³⁶and in his days things prospered in his hands, so that the nations were taken away out of their country, and they also that were in the city of David, those who were in Jerusalem, who had made themselves a citadel, out of which they issued, and polluted all things around the sanctuary, and did great hurt to its purity; ³⁷and he placed Jews therein, and fortified it for the safety of the country and the city, and made high the walls of Jerusalem: ³⁸and King Demetrius confirmed to him the chief priesthood according to these things, ³⁹and made him one of his friends, and honored him with great honor; ⁴⁰for he had heard it said that the Jews had been called by the Romans friends and allies and countrymen, and that they had met the ambassadors of Simon honorably; ⁴¹and that the Jews and the priests were well pleased that Simon should be their leader and chief priest forever, until there should arise a faithful prophet; ⁴²and that he should be captain over them, and should take charge of the sanctuary, to set them over their works, and over the country, and over the arms, and over the strongholds; and that he should take charge of the sanctuary, ⁴³and that he should be obeyed by all, and that all instruments in the country should be written in his name, and that he should be clothed in purple, and wear gold; ⁴⁴and that it should not be lawful for any of the people or of the priests to set at nothing any of these things, or to deny the words that he should speak, or to gather an assembly in the country without him, or to be clothed in purple, or wear a buckle of gold; ⁴⁵but whoever should do otherwise, or set at nothing any of these things, he should be liable to punishment." ⁴⁶All the people consented to ordain for Simon that he should do according to these words; ⁴⁷and Simon accepted this, and consented to be chief priest, and to be captain and governor of the Jews and of the priests, and to be protector of all. ⁴⁸And they commanded to put this writing on tablets of brass, and to set them up within the precinct of the sanctuary in a conspicuous place; ⁴⁹and moreover to put the copies thereof in the treasury, to the end that Simon and his sons might have them.

CHAPTER 15

¹And Antiochus son of Demetrius the king sent letters from the isles of the sea to Simon the priest and governor of the Jews, and to all the nation; ²and the contents thereof were after this manner: "King Antiochus to Simon the chief priest and governor, and to the nation of the Jews, greetings: ³Forasmuch as certain pernicious fellows have made themselves masters of the kingdom of our fathers, but my purpose is to claim the kingdom, that I may restore it as it was before; and moreover I have raised a multitude of foreign soldiers, and have prepared ships of war; ⁴moreover I am inclined to land in the country, that I may punish those who have destroyed our country, and those who have made many cities in the kingdom desolate: ⁵Now therefore, I confirm to you all the exactions which the kings that were before me remitted to you, and whatever gifts besides they remitted to you: ⁶and I give you leave to coin money for your country with your own stamp, ⁷but that Jerusalem and the sanctuary should be free: and all the arms that you have prepared, and the strongholds that you have built, which you have in your possession, let them remain to you: ⁸and everything owing to the king, and the things that will be owing to the king from now on and forevermore, let them be remitted to you: ⁹moreover, when we will have established our kingdom, we will glorify you and your nation and the temple with great glory, so that your glory will be made manifest in all the earth." ¹⁰In the one hundred and seventy-fourth year Antiochus went out into the land of his fathers; and all the forces came together to him, so that there were few men with Tryphon. ¹¹And King Antiochus pursued him, and he came, as he fled, to Dor, which is by the sea: ¹²for he knew that troubles were come on him all at once, and that his forces had forsaken him. ¹³And Antiochus encamped against Dor, and with him one hundred and twenty thousand men of war, and eight thousand horses. ¹⁴And he compassed the city around, and the ships joined in the attack from the sea; and he vexed the city by land and sea, and suffered no man to go out or in. ¹⁵And Numenius and his company came from Rome, having letters to the kings and to the countries, wherein were written these things: ¹⁶"Lucius, consul of the Romans, to King Ptolemy, greetings: ¹⁷The Jews' ambassadors came to us as our friends and allies, to renew the old friendship and confederacy, being sent from Simon the chief priest, and from the people of the Jews: ¹⁸moreover they brought a shield of gold of one thousand pounds. ¹⁹It pleased us therefore to write to the kings and to the countries, that they should not seek their hurt, nor fight against them, and their cities, and their country, nor be allies with such as fight against them. ²⁰Moreover it seemed good to us to receive the shield from them. ²¹If, therefore, any pernicious fellows have fled from their country to you, deliver them to Simon the chief priest, that he may take vengeance on them according to their law." ²²And he wrote the same things to Demetrius the king, and to Attalus, and to Arathes, and to Arsaces, ²³and to all the countries, and to Sampsames, and to the Spartans, and to Delos, and to Myndos, and to Sicyon, and to Caria, and to Samos, and to Pamphylia, and to Lycia, and to Halicarnassus, and to Rhodes, and to Phaselis, and to Cos, and to Side, and to Aradus, and Gortyna, and Cnidus, and Cyprus, and Cyrene. ²⁴But they wrote this copy to Simon the chief priest. ²⁵But Antiochus the king encamped against Dor the second day, bringing his forces up to it continually, and making engines of war, and he shut up Tryphon from going in or out. ²⁶And Simon sent him two thousand chosen men to fight on his side; and silver, and gold, and instruments of war in abundance. ²⁷And he would not receive them but set at nothing all the covenants which he had made with him previously and was estranged from him. ²⁸And he sent to him Athenobius, one of his friends, to commune with him, saying, "You hold possession of Joppa and Gazara, and the citadel that is in Jerusalem, cities of my kingdom. ²⁹The borders thereof you have

wasted, and done great hurt in the land, and gotten the dominion of many places in my kingdom. ³⁰Now therefore, deliver up the cities which you have taken, and the tributes of the places of which you have gotten dominion without the borders of Judea: ³¹or else give me for them five hundred talents of silver; and for the harm that you have done, and the tributes of the cities, other five hundred talents: or else we will come and subdue you." ³²And Athenobius the king's friend came to Jerusalem; and he saw the glory of Simon, and the cupboard of gold and silver vessels, and his great attendance, and he was amazed; and he reported to him the king's words. ³³And Simon answered, and said to him, "We have neither taken other men's land, nor have we possession of that which pertains to others, but of the inheritance of our fathers; however, it was had in possession of our enemies wrongfully for a certain time. ³⁴But we, having opportunity, hold fast the inheritance of our fathers. ³⁵But as touching Joppa and Gazara, which you demand, they did great harm among the people throughout our country, we will give one hundred talents for them." And he did not answer him a word, ³⁶but returned in a rage to the king, and reported to him these words, and the glory of Simon, and all that he had seen: and the king was exceedingly angry. ³⁷But Tryphon embarked on board a ship and fled to Orthosia. ³⁸And the king appointed Cendebaeus chief captain of the seacoast and gave him forces of foot and horse: ³⁹and he commanded him to encamp before Judea, and he commanded him to build up Kidron, and to fortify the gates, and that he should fight against the people, but the king pursued Tryphon. ⁴⁰And Cendebaeus came to Jamnia, and began to provoke the people, and to invade Judea, and to take the people captive, and to kill them. ⁴¹And he built Kidron, and set horsemen there, and forces of foot, to the end that issuing out they might make excursions on the ways of Judea, according as the king commanded him.

CHAPTER 16

¹And John went up from Gazara and told his father Simon what Cendebaeus was doing. ²And Simon called his two oldest sons, Judas and John, and said to them, I and my countrymen and my father's house have fought the battles of Israel from our youth, even to this day; and things have prospered in our hands, that we should deliver Israel oftentimes. ³But now I am old, and you moreover, by [His] mercy, are of a sufficient age: be instead of me and my brother and go out and fight for our nation; but let the help which is from Heaven be with you. ⁴And he chose out of the country twenty thousand men of war and horsemen, and they went against Cendebaeus, and slept at Modin. ⁵And rising up in the morning, they went into the plain, and behold, a great army came to meet them, of footmen and horsemen: and there was a brook between them. ⁶And he encamped near them, he and his people: and he saw that the people were afraid to pass over the brook, and he passed over first, and the men saw him, and passed over after him. ⁷And he divided the people and [set] the horsemen in the midst of the footmen, but the enemies' horsemen were exceedingly many. ⁸And they sounded with the trumpets; and Cendebaeus and his army were put to the rout, and there fell of them many wounded to death, but those who were left fled to the stronghold: ⁹at that time was Judas, John's brother, wounded, but John pursued after them, until he came to Kidron, which [Cendebaeus] had built; ¹⁰and they fled to the towers that are in the fields of Azotus; and he burned it with fire; and there fell of them about two thousand men. And he returned into Judea in peace. ¹¹And Ptolemy the son of Abubus had been appointed captain for the plain of Jericho, and he had much silver and gold; ¹²for he was the chief priest's son-in-law. ¹³And his heart was lifted up, and he was inclined to make himself master of the country, and he took counsel deceitfully against Simon and his sons, to make away with them. ¹⁴Now Simon was visiting the cities that were in the country, and taking care for the good ordering of them; and he went down to Jericho, himself and Mattathias and Judas his sons, in the one hundred and seventy-seventh year, in the eleventh month, which is the month Sebat: ¹⁵and the son of Abubus received them deceitfully into the little stronghold that is called Dok, which he had built, and made them a great banquet, and hid men there. ¹⁶And when Simon and his sons had drunk freely, Ptolemy and his men rose up, and took their arms, and came in on Simon into the banqueting place, and killed him, and his two sons, and certain of his servants. ¹⁷And he committed a great iniquity, and repaid evil for good. ¹⁸And Ptolemy wrote these things, and sent to the king, that he should send him forces to aid him, and should deliver him, their country, and the cities. ¹⁹And he sent others to Gazara to make away with John: and to the captains of thousands, he sent letters to come to him, that he might give them silver and gold and gifts. ²⁰And others he sent to take possession of Jerusalem, and the mount of the temple. ²¹And one ran before to Gazara and told John that his father and countrymen were perished, and he has sent to kill you also. ²²And when he heard, he was severely amazed; and he laid hands on the men that came to destroy him and killed them; for he perceived that they were seeking to destroy him. ²³And the rest of the acts of John, and of his wars, and of his valiant deeds which he did, and of the building of the walls which he built, and of his doings, ²⁴behold, they are written in the chronicles of his chief priesthood, from the time that he was made chief priest after his father.

2 MACCABEES

2 Maccabees is a deuterocanonical book which focuses on the Maccabean Revolt against Antiochus IV Epiphanes and concludes with the defeat of the Seleucid empire general Nicanor in 161 BC by Judas Maccabeus, the hero of the work. Unlike 1 Maccabees, 2 Maccabees was written in Koine Greek, probably in Alexandria, Egypt, circa 124 BC. It presents a revised version of the historical events recounted in the first seven chapters of 1 Maccabees, adding material from the Pharisaic tradition, including prayer for the dead and a resurrection on Judgment Day. Jews and Protestants reject most of the doctrinal issues present in the work, while Catholics and Eastern Orthodox consider the work to be deuterocanonical.

CHAPTER 1

¹The countrymen, the Jews that are in Jerusalem and those who are in the country of Judea, send greetings to the countrymen, the Jews that are throughout Egypt, and [wish them] good peace: ²and may God do good to you, and remember His covenant with Abraham, and Isaac, and Jacob, His faithful servants; ³and give you all a heart to worship Him and do His pleasure with a great heart and a willing soul; ⁴and open your heart in His law and in His statutes, and make peace, ⁵and listen to your requests, and be reconciled with you, and not forsake you in an evil time. ⁶And now we here are praying for you. ⁷In the reign of Demetrius, in the one hundred [and] sixty-ninth year, we the Jews have [already] written to you in the suffering and in the extremity that has come on us in these years, from the time that Jason and his company revolted from the holy land and the kingdom, ⁸and set the gate on fire, and shed innocent blood: and we implored the LORD, and were heard; and we offered sacrifice and meal [offering, and] we lighted the lamps, and we set out the Bread of the Presentation. ⁹And now [see] that you keep the days of the Celebration of Shelters of the month Kislev. ¹⁰[Written] in the one hundred eighty-eighth year. They that are in Jerusalem and those who are in Judea and the senate and Judas, to Aristobulus, King Ptolemy's teacher, who is also of the stock of the anointed priests, and to the Jews that are in Egypt, send greetings and health. ¹¹Having been saved by God out of great perils, as men arrayed against a king, we thank Him greatly. ¹²For He cast out into Persia those who arrayed themselves [against us] in the holy

city. ¹³For when the prince had come, [and] the army with him that seemed irresistible, they were cut to pieces in the temple of Nanaea by the treachery of Nanaea's priests. ¹⁴For Antiochus, on the pretense that he would marry her, came into the place, he and his friends that were with him, that they might take a great part of the treasures in name of a dowry. ¹⁵And when the priests of Nanaea's temple had set the treasures out, and he had come there with a small company within the wall of the precincts, they shut to the temple when Antiochus had come in: ¹⁶and opening the secret door of the paneled ceiling, they threw stones and struck down the prince, and they hewed [him and his company] in pieces, and struck off their heads, and cast them to those that were without. ¹⁷Blessed [be] our God in all things, who gave [for a prey] those who had committed impiety. ¹⁸Whereas we are now about to keep the purification of the temple in the [month] Kislev, on the twenty-fifth day, we thought it necessary to certify you thereof, that you also may keep [the] Celebration of Shelters, and [a memorial] of the fire [which was given] when Nehemiah offered sacrifices, after he had built both the temple and the altar. ¹⁹For indeed when our fathers were about to be led into the land of Persia, the godly priests of that time took of the fire of the altar and hid it privily in the hollow of a well that was without water, wherein they made [it] sure, so that the place was unknown to all men. ²⁰Now after many years, when it pleased God, Nehemiah, having received a charge from the king of Persia, sent in quest of the fire the descendants of the priests that hid it. When they declared to us that they had found no fire, but thick water, ²¹he commanded them to draw out thereof and bring [to him]: and when the sacrifices had been offered, Nehemiah commanded the priests to sprinkle with the water both the wood and the things laid immediately. ²²And when it was done, and some time had passed, and the sun shone out, which before was hid with clouds, there was kindled a great blaze, so that all men marveled. ²³And the priests made a prayer while the sacrifice was consuming, both the priests and all [others], Jonathan leading and the rest answering, as Nehemiah did. ²⁴And the prayer was after this manner: "O LORD, LORD God, the Creator of all things, who are terrible and strong and righteous and merciful, who alone are King and gracious, ²⁵who alone supplies [every need], who alone are righteous, and almighty, and continuous, You that save Israel out of all evil, who made the fathers [your] chosen, and sanctified them: ²⁶accept the sacrifice for all Your people Israel, and guard Your own portion, and consecrate it. ²⁷Gather together our dispersion, set at liberty those who are in bondage among the heathen, look on those who are despised and abhorred, and let the heathen know that You are our God. ²⁸Torment those who oppress us and in arrogance shamefully entreat us. ²⁹Plant Your people in Your holy place, even as Moses said." ³⁰And immediately the priests sang the hymns. ³¹And as soon as the sacrifice was consumed, then Nehemiah commanded to pour [on] great stones the water that was left. ³²And when this was done, a flame was kindled; but when the light from the altar shone near it, [all] was consumed. ³³And when the matter became known, and it was told the king of the Persians, that, in the place where the priests that were led away had hid the fire, there appeared the water, with which also Nehemiah and those who were with him purified the sacrifice, ³⁴then the king, enclosing [the place], made it sacred, after he had proved the matter. ³⁵And when the king would show favor to any, he would take [from them] many presents and give them some of [this water]. ³⁶And Nehemiah and those who were with him called this thing Nephthar, which is by interpretation, "Cleansing"; but most men call it Nephthai.

CHAPTER 2

¹It is also found in the records, that Jeremiah the prophet commanded those who were carried away to take of the fire, as has been signified [above]: ²and how that the prophet charged those who were carried away, having given them the law, that they should not forget the statutes of the LORD, neither be led astray in their minds, when they saw images of gold and silver, and the adornment thereof. ³And with other such words exhorted he them, that the law should not depart from their heart. ⁴And it was [contained] in the writing, that the prophet, being warned of God, commanded that the Dwelling Place and the Ark should follow with him, when he went out into the mountain where Moses went up and saw the heritage of God. ⁵And Jeremiah came and found a chamber in the rock, and there he brought in the Dwelling Place, and the Ark, and the altar of incense; and he made fast the door. ⁶And some of those that followed with him came there that they might mark the way and could not find it. ⁷But when Jeremiah perceived it, he blamed them, saying, "Yes, and the place will be unknown until God gathers the people again together, and mercy comes: ⁸and then will the LORD disclose these things, and the glory of the LORD will be seen, and the cloud." As also it was shown with Moses; as also Solomon implored that the place might be consecrated greatly, ⁹and it was also declared that he, having wisdom, offered a sacrifice of dedication, and of the finishing of the temple; [so we would have it now.] ¹⁰As Moses prayed to the LORD, and fire came down out of Heaven and consumed the sacrifice, even so prayed Solomon also, and the fire came down and consumed the burnt-offerings ¹¹(and Moses said, "Because the sin offering had not been eaten, it was consumed in like manner [with the rest]"); ¹²and Solomon kept the eight days. ¹³And the same things were related both in the public archives and in the records that concern Nehemiah; and how he, founding a library, gathered together the scrolls about the kings and prophets, and the [scrolls] of David, and letters of kings about sacred gifts. ¹⁴And in like manner Judas also gathered together for us all those [writings] that had been scattered by reason of the war that befell, and they are [still] with us. ¹⁵If, therefore, you have need thereof, send some to fetch them to you. ¹⁶Seeing then that we are about to keep the purification, we write to you; you will therefore do well if you keep the days. ¹⁷Now God, who saved all His people, and restored the heritage to all, and the kingdom, and the priesthood, and the hallowing, ¹⁸even as He promised through the law—in God we have hope, that He will quickly have mercy on us, and gather [us] together out of all the earth to the holy place, for He delivered us out of great evils, and purified the place. ¹⁹Now the things concerning Judas Maccabaeus and his countrymen, and the purification of the great temple, and the dedication of the altar, ²⁰and further the wars against Antiochus Epiphanes, and Eupator his son, ²¹and the manifestations that came from Heaven to those that vied with one another in courageous deeds for the religion of the Jews; so that, being but a few, they rescued the whole country, and chased the barbarous multitudes, ²²and recovered again the temple renowned all the world over, and freed the city, and restored the laws which were like to be overthrown, seeing the LORD became gracious to them with all forbearance: ²³[these things, I say,] which have been declared by Jason of Cyrene in five scrolls, we will determine to abridge in one work. ²⁴For having in view the confused mass of the numbers, and the difficulty which awaits those who would enter into the narratives of the history, by reason of the abundance of the matter, ²⁵we were careful that they who choose to read may be attracted, and that they who wish well [to our cause] may find it easy to recall [what we have written, and] that all readers may have profit. ²⁶And although to us, who have taken on us the painful labor of the abridgement, the task is not easy, but [matter] of sweat and watching ²⁷(even as it is no light thing to him that prepares a banquet, and seeks the benefit of others); yet for the sake of the gratitude of the many we will gladly endure the painful labor, ²⁸leaving to the historian the exact handling of every particular, and again having no strength to fill in the outlines of our abridgement. ²⁹For as the master builder of a new house must care for the whole structure, and again he that undertakes to decorate and paint it must seek out the things fit for the adorning thereof; even so I think it is also with us. ³⁰To occupy the ground, and to indulge in long discussions, and to be curious in particulars, becomes the first author of the history: ³¹but to strive after brevity of expression, and to avoid a labored fullness in the treatment, is to be granted to him that would bring a writing into a new form. ³²Here then let us begin the narration, only adding so much to that which has been already said; for it is a foolish thing to make a long prologue to the history, and to abridge the history [itself].

CHAPTER 3

¹When the holy city was inhabited with all peace, and the laws were kept very well, because of the godliness of Onias the chief priest, and his hatred of wickedness, ²it came to pass that even the kings themselves did honor the place and glorify the temple with the noblest presents; ³insomuch that even Seleucus the king of Asia of his own revenues bare all the costs belonging to the services of the sacrifices. ⁴But one Simon of the tribe of Benjamin, having been made guardian of the temple, fell out with the chief priest about the ruling of the market in the city. ⁵And when he could not overcome Onias, he got him to Apollonius [the son] of Thrasaeus, who at that time was governor of Coele-Syria and Phoenicia: ⁶and he brought him word how that the treasury in Jerusalem was full of untold sums of money, so that the multitude of the funds was innumerable, and that they did not pertain to the account of the sacrifices, but that it was possible that these should fall under the king's power. ⁷And when Apollonius met the king, he informed him of the money of which he had been told; and the king appointed Heliodorus, who was his chancellor, and sent him with a command to accomplish the removal of the previously mentioned money. ⁸So out with Heliodorus took his journey, under a color of visiting the cities of Coele-Syria and Phoenicia, but in fact to execute the king's purpose. ⁹And when he had come to Jerusalem and had been courteously received by the chief priest of the city, he laid before [the man] account of the information which had been given [him and] declared why he had come; and he inquired if in truth these things were so. ¹⁰And the chief priest explained to him that there were [in the treasury] deposits of widows and orphans, ¹¹and moreover some [money] belonging to Hyrcanus the [son] of Tobias, a man in very high place, and [that the case] was not as that impious Simon falsely alleged; and that in all there were four hundred talents of silver and two hundred of gold; ¹²and that it was altogether impossible that wrong should be done to them that had put trust in the holiness of the place, and in the majesty and inviolable sanctity of the temple, honored over all the world. ¹³But Heliodorus, because of the king's commands given him, said that in any case this [money] must be confiscated for the king's treasury. ¹⁴So having appointed a day, he entered in to direct the inquiry concerning these matters; and there was no small distress throughout the whole city. ¹⁵And the priests, prostrating themselves before the altar in their priestly garments, and [looking] toward Heaven, called on him that gave the law concerning deposits, that he should preserve these [treasures] safe for those that had deposited them. ¹⁶And whoever saw the mien of the chief priest was wounded in mind; for his countenance and the change of his color betrayed the distress of his soul. ¹⁷For a terror and a shuddering of the body had come over the man, whereby the pain that was in his heart was plainly shown to those who looked on him. ¹⁸And those who were in the houses rushed flocking out to make a universal supplication, because the place was like to come into contempt. ¹⁹And the women, girded with sackcloth under their breasts, thronged the streets, and the virgins that were kept in ward ran together, some to the gates, others to the walls, and some looked out through the windows. ²⁰And all, stretching out their hands toward Heaven, made their solemn supplication. ²¹Then it would have pitied a man to see the multitude prostrating themselves all mixed together, and the expectation of the chief priest in his severe distress. ²²While therefore they called on the Almighty LORD to keep the things entrusted [to them] safe and sure for those that had entrusted them, ²³Heliodorus went on to execute that which had been decreed. ²⁴But when he was already present there with his guards near the treasury, the Sovereign of spirits and of all authority caused a great apparition, so that all that had presumed to come [in] with him, stricken with dismay at the power of God, fainted and were severely afraid. ²⁵For there was seen by them a horse with a terrible rider on him, and adorned with beautiful trappings, and he rushed fiercely and struck at Heliodorus with his forefeet, and it seemed that he that sat on the horse had complete armor of gold. ²⁶Two others also appeared to him, young men notable in their strength, and beautiful in their glory, and splendid in their apparel, who stood by him on either side, and scourged him unceasingly, inflicting on him many severe stripes. ²⁷And when he had fallen suddenly to the ground, and great darkness had come over him, [his guards] caught him up and put him into a litter, ²⁸and carried him, him that had just now entered with a great train and all his guard into the previously mentioned treasury, himself now brought to utter helplessness, manifestly made to recognize the sovereignty of God. ²⁹And so, while he, through the working of God, speechless and deprived of all hope and deliverance, lay prostrate, ³⁰they blessed the LORD, that made marvelous his own place; and the temple, which a little before was full of terror and alarm, was filled with joy and gladness after the Almighty LORD appeared. ³¹But quickly certain of Heliodorus' familiar friends implored Onias to call on the Most High, and grant life to him who lay quite at the last gasp. ³²And the chief priest, secretly fearing lest the king might come to think that some treachery toward Heliodorus had been perpetrated by the Jews, brought a sacrifice for the deliverance of the man. ³³But as the chief priest was making the atoning sacrifice, the same young men appeared again to Heliodorus, arrayed in the same garments; and they stood and said, "Give Onias the chief priest great thanks, for his sake the LORD has granted you life; ³⁴and do you, since you have been scourged from Heaven, publish to all men the sovereign majesty of God." And when they had spoken these words, they vanished out of sight. ³⁵So Heliodorus, having offered a sacrifice to the LORD and vowed great vows to him that had saved his life, and having graciously received Onias, returned with his army to the king. ³⁶And he testified to all men the works of the great God which he had seen with his eyes. ³⁷And when the king asked Heliodorus, what manner of man was fit to be sent yet once again to Jerusalem, he said, ³⁸"If you have any enemy or conspirator against the state, send him there, and you will receive him back well scourged, if he even escapes with his life; because of a truth there is about the place a power of God. ³⁹For He that has His dwelling in Heaven Himself has His eyes on that place and helps it; and those who come to hurt it He strikes and destroys." ⁴⁰And such was the history of Heliodorus and the keeping of the treasury.

CHAPTER 4

¹But the previously mentioned Simon, he who had given information of the money, and [had betrayed] his country, slandered Onias, [saying] that it was he who had incited Heliodorus, and made himself the author of these evils. ²And him that was the benefactor of the city, and the guardian of his fellow countrymen, and a zealot for the laws, he dared to call a conspirator against the state. ³But when the growing enmity [between them] waxed so great, that even murders were perpetrated through one of Simon's trusted followers, ⁴Onias, seeing the danger of the contention, and that Apollonius [the son] of Menestheus, the governor of Coele-Syria and Phoenicia, was increasing Simon's malice, ⁵went himself to the king, not to be an accuser of his fellow-citizens, but looking to the good of all the people, both public and private; ⁶for he saw that without the king's providence it was impossible for the state to obtain peace anymore, and that Simon would not cease from his madness. ⁷But when Seleucus was deceased, and Antiochus, who was called Epiphanes, succeeded to the kingdom, Jason the brother of Onias supplanted [his brother] in the chief priesthood, ⁸having promised to the king at an audience three hundred and sixty talents of silver, and [out] of another fund eighty talents; ⁹and besides this, he undertook to assign one hundred and fifty more, if it might be allowed him through the king's authority to set him up a [Greek] place of exercise and [form] a body of youths [to be trained therein, and] to register the inhabitants of Jerusalem as [citizens] of Antioch. ¹⁰And when the king had given assent, and he had gotten possession of the office, he out with brought over them of his own race to the Greek fashion. ¹¹And setting aside the royal ordinances of special favor to the Jews, granted by the means of John the father of Eupolemus, who went on the delegation to the Romans for friendship and alliance, and seeking to overthrow the lawful modes of life, he brought in new customs forbidden by the law: ¹²for he eagerly established a [Greek] place of exercise under the citadel itself; and caused the noblest of the young men to wear the [Greek] cap. ¹³And so there was an extreme of hellenization, and an

advance of an alien religion, by reason of the exceeding profaneness of Jason, that ungodly man and no chief priest; [14]so that the priests had no longer any zeal for the services of the altar, but despising the sanctuary, and neglecting the sacrifices, they hastened to enjoy that which was unlawfully provided in the palaestra, after the summons of the discus; [15]making of no account the honors of their fathers, and thinking the glories of the Greeks best of all. [16]By reason of which severe calamity beset them; and the men whose ways of living they earnestly followed, and to whom they desired to be made like in all things, these became their enemies and punished them. [17]For it is not a light thing to do impiously against the laws of God, but these things the time following will declare. [18]Now when certain games that came every fifth year were kept at Tyre, and the king was present, [19]the vile Jason sent sacred envoys, as being Antiochians of Jerusalem, bearing three hundred drachmas of silver to the sacrifice of Hercules, which even the bearers thereof thought not right to use for [any] sacrifice, because it was not fit, but to expend on another charge. [20]And though in the purpose of the sender this [money was for] the sacrifice of Hercules, yet on account of present circumstances it went to the equipment of the galleys. [21]Now when Apollonius the [son] of Menestheus was sent into Egypt for the enthronement of [Ptolemy] Philometor as king, Antiochus, learning that [Ptolemy] had shown himself ill affected toward the state, took thought for the security of his realm; for that reason, going [by sea] to Joppa, he traveled on to Jerusalem. [22]And being magnificently received by Jason and the city, he was brought in with torches and shouting. This done, he afterward led his army down into Phoenicia. [23]Now after a space of three years Jason sent Menelaus, the previously mentioned Simon's brother, to bear the money to the king, and to make reports concerning some necessary matters. [24]But he, being commended to the king, and having glorified himself by the display of his authority, got the chief priesthood for himself, outbidding Jason by three hundred talents of silver. [25]And having received the royal mandates he came [to Jerusalem], bringing nothing worthy the chief priesthood, but having the passion of a cruel tyrant, and the rage of a savage beast. [26]And whereas Jason, who had supplanted his own brother, was supplanted by another and driven as a fugitive into the country of the Ammonites, [27]Menelaus had possession of the office, but of the money that had been promised to the king nothing was duly paid, and that though Sostratus the governor of the citadel demanded it [28](for to him pertained the gathering of the revenues); for this reason they were both called by the king to his presence. [29]And Menelaus left his own brother Lysimachus for his deputy in the chief priesthood; and Sostratus [left] Crates, who was over the Cyprians. [30]Now while such was the state of things, it came to pass that they of Tarsus and Mallus made insurrection, because they were to be given as a present to Antiochis, the king's concubine. [31]The king therefore came [to Cilicia] in all haste to settle matters, leaving for his deputy Andronicus, a man of high rank. [32]And Menelaus, supposing that he had gotten a favorable opportunity, presented to Andronicus certain vessels of gold belonging to the temple, which he had stolen: other [vessels] also he had already sold into Tyre and the surrounding cities. [33]And when Onias had sure knowledge [of this], he sharply reproved him, having withdrawn himself into a sanctuary at Daphne, that lies by Antioch. [34]For that reason, Menelaus, taking Andronicus apart, begged him to kill Onias. And coming to Onias, and being persuaded to use treachery, and being received as a friend, Andronicus gave him his right hand with oaths [of fidelity, and], though he was suspected, persuaded him to come out of the sanctuary; and out with he dispatched him without regard of justice. [35]For this reason, not only Jews, but many also of the other nations, had indignation and displeasure at the unjust murder of the man. [36]And when the king had come back again from the places in Cilicia, the Jews that were in the city pleaded before him [against Andronicus] (the Greeks also joining with them in hatred of the wickedness), urging that Onias had been wrongfully slain. [37]Antiochus therefore was heartily sorry, and was moved to pity, and wept, because of the sober and well-ordered life of him that was dead; [38]and being inflamed with passion, out with he stripped off Andronicus' purple robe, and tore off his under garments, and when he had led him round through the whole city to that very place where he had committed impiety against Onias, there he put the murderer out of the way, the LORD rendering to him the punishment he had deserved. [39]Now when many sacrileges had been committed in the city by Lysimachus with the consent of Menelaus, and when the report of them was spread abroad outside, the people gathered themselves together against Lysimachus, after many vessels of gold had been already dispersed. [40]And when the multitudes were rising against [him, and] were filled with anger, Lysimachus armed about three thousand men, and with unrighteous violence began [the conflict], one Hauran, a man far gone in years and no less also in madness, leading [the attack]. [41]But when they perceived the assault of Lysimachus, some caught up stones, others logs of wood, and some took handfuls of the ashes that lay near, and they flung them all pell-mell on Lysimachus and those who were with him; [42]by reason of which they wounded many of them, and some they struck to the ground, and all [of them] they forced to flee, but the author of the sacrilege himself they killed beside the treasury. [43]But touching these matters there was an accusation laid against Menelaus. [44]And when the king had come to Tyre, the three men that were sent by the senate pleaded the cause before him. [45]But Menelaus, seeing himself now defeated, promised much money to Ptolemy the [son] of Dorymenes, that he might win over the king. [46]After which Ptolemy taking the king aside into a cloister, as it were to take the air, brought him to be of another mind; [47]and him that was the cause of all the evil, Menelaus, he discharged from the accusations; but these hapless men, who, if they had pleaded even before Scythians, would have been discharged uncondemned, them he sentenced to death. [48]Soon then did those who were spokesmen for the city and the families [of Israel] and the holy vessels suffer that unrighteous penalty. [49]For this reason even certain Tyrians, moved with hatred of the wickedness, provided magnificently for their burial. [50]But Menelaus through the covetous dealings of those who were in power remained still in his office, growing in wickedness, as a great conspirator against his fellow-citizens.

CHAPTER 5

[1]Now about this time Antiochus made his second inroad into Egypt. [2]And it [so] befell that throughout all the city, for the space of almost forty days, there appeared in the midst of the sky horsemen in swift motion, wearing robes inworked with gold and [carrying] spears, equipped in troops for battle; [3]and drawing of swords; and [on the other side] squadrons of horse in array; and encounters and pursuits of both [armies]; and shaking of shields, and multitudes of lances, and casting of darts, and flashing of golden trappings, and girding on of all sorts of armor. [4]For that reason, all men implored that the vision might have been given for good. [5]But when a false rumor had arisen that Antiochus was deceased, Jason took not less than one thousand men, and suddenly made an assault on the city; and those who were on the wall being routed, and the city being now at length well near taken, Menelaus took refuge in the citadel. [6]But Jason slaughtered his own citizens without mercy, not considering that good success against countrymen is the greatest ill success, but supposing himself to be setting up trophies over enemies, and not over fellow countrymen. [7]The office [however] he did not get, but, receiving shame as the end of his conspiracy, he passed again a fugitive into the country of the Ammonites. [8]At the last therefore he met with a miserable end: having been shut up at the court of Aretas the prince of the Arabians, fleeing from city to city, pursued of all men, hated as an apostate from the laws, and held in abomination as the butcher of his country and his fellow-citizens, he was cast out into Egypt; [9]and he that had driven many from their own country into strange lands perished [himself] in a strange land, having crossed the sea to the Lacedaemonians, as thinking to find shelter [there] because they were related; [10]and he that had cast out a multitude unburied had none to mourn for him, nor had he any funeral at all, or place in the tomb of his fathers. [11]Now when tidings came to the king concerning that which was done, he thought that Judea was in

revolt; after which setting out from Egypt in a furious mind, he took the city by force of arms, ¹²and commanded his soldiers to cut down without mercy such as came in their way, and to kill such as went up on the houses; ¹³and there was killing of young and old, making away of boys, women, and children, slaying of virgins and infants. ¹⁴And in all the three days [of the slaughter] there were destroyed eighty thousand, [where of] forty thousand [were slain] in close combat, and no fewer were sold than slain. ¹⁵But not content with this, he presumed to enter into the most holy temple of all the earth, having Menelaus for his guide (him that had proved himself a traitor both to the laws and to his country), ¹⁶even taking the sacred vessels with his polluted hands, and dragging down with his profane hands the offerings that had been dedicated by other kings to the augmentation and glory and honor of the place. ¹⁷And Antiochus was lifted up in mind, not seeing that because of the sins of those who lived in the city the Sovereign LORD had been provoked to anger a little, and therefore His eye was [then] turned away from the place. ¹⁸But had it not so been that they were already bound by many sins, this man, even as Heliodorus who was sent by Seleucus the king to view the treasury, would, so soon as he pressed forward, have been scourged and turned back from his daring deed. ¹⁹However, the LORD did not choose the nation for the place's sake, but the place for the nation's sake. ²⁰For that reason, also the place itself, having shared in the calamities that befell the nation, did afterward share in [its] benefits; and the [place] which was forsaken in the wrath of the Almighty was, at the reconciliation of the great Sovereign, restored again with all glory. ²¹As for Antiochus, when he had carried away out of the temple one thousand and eight hundred talents, he departed in all haste to Antioch, thinking in his arrogance to make the land navigable and the sea passable by foot, because his heart was lifted up. ²²And moreover he left governors to afflict the race: at Jerusalem, Philip, by race a Phrygian, and in character more barbarous than him that set him there; ²³and at Gerizim, Andronicus; and besides these, Menelaus, who worse than all the rest exalted himself against his fellow-citizens. And having a malicious mind toward the Jews—his citizens, ²⁴he sent that lord of pollutions Apollonius with an army of twenty-two thousand, commanding him to kill all those that were of full age, and to sell the women and the younger men. ²⁵And he, coming to Jerusalem, and playing the man of peace, waited until the holy day of the Sabbath, and finding the Jews at rest from work, he commanded his men to parade in arms. ²⁶And he put to the sword all those who came out to the spectacle; and running into the city with the armed men he killed great multitudes. ²⁷But Judas, who is also Maccabaeus, with nine others or thereabout, withdrew himself, and with his company kept himself alive in the mountains after the manner of wild beasts; and they continued feeding on such poor herbs as grew there, that they might not be partakers of the pollution.

CHAPTER 6

¹And not long after this the king sent out an old man of Athens to compel the Jews to depart from the laws of their fathers, and not to live after the laws of God; ²and also to pollute the sanctuary in Jerusalem, and to call it by the name of Jupiter Olympius, and [to call] the [sanctuary] in Gerizim by the name of Jupiter the Protector of strangers, even as they were that lived in the place. ³But severe and utterly grievous was the visitation of this evil. ⁴For the temple was filled with riot and reveling by the heathen, who dallied with prostitutes, and had to do with women within the sacred precincts, and moreover brought inside things that were not befitting; ⁵and the place of sacrifice was filled with those abominable things which had been prohibited by the laws. ⁶And a man could neither keep the Sabbath, nor observe the feasts of the fathers, nor so much as confess himself to be a Jew. ⁷And on the day of the king's birth every month they were led along with bitter constraint to eat of the sacrifices; and when the Festival of Bacchus came, they were compelled to go in procession in honor of Bacchus, wearing wreaths of ivy. ⁸A decree went out to the neighboring Greek cities, by the suggestion of Ptolemy, that they should observe the same conduct against the Jews and should make them eat of the sacrifices; ⁹and that they should kill such as did not choose to go over to the Greek rites. So the present misery was for all to see: ¹⁰for two women were brought up for having circumcised their children; and these, when they had led them publicly around the city, with the babies hung from their breasts, they cast down headlong from the wall. ¹¹And others, that had run together into the caves nearby to keep the seventh day secretly, being betrayed to Philip, were all burned together, because they hesitated to defend themselves, from regard to the honor of that most solemn day. ¹²I implore, therefore, those that read this scroll, that they not be discouraged because of the calamities, but account that these punishments were not for the destruction, but for the disciplining of our race. ¹³For indeed that those who act impiously are not left alone any long time, but immediately meet with retribution, is a sign of great beneficence. ¹⁴For in the case of the other nations the Sovereign LORD does with patience forbear, until that He punishes them when they have attained to the full measure of [their] sins; but not so judged He as touching us, ¹⁵that He may not take vengeance on us afterward, when we come to the height of our sins. ¹⁶For that reason, He never withdraws His mercy from us; but though He chastens with calamity, yet He does not forsake His own people. ¹⁷However, let this that we have spoken suffice to put [you] in remembrance; but after [these] few words we must come to the narrative. ¹⁸Eleazar, one of the principal scribes, a man already well stricken in years, and of a noble countenance, was compelled to open his mouth to eat swine's flesh. ¹⁹But he, welcoming death with renown rather than life with pollution, advanced of his own accord to the instrument of torture, but first spat out [the flesh], ²⁰[coming forward] as men should come that are resolute to repel such things as not [even] for the natural love of life is it lawful to taste. ²¹But those who had the charge of that forbidden sacrificial feast took the man aside, for the acquaintance which of old times they had with him, and privately implored him to bring flesh of his own providing, such as was befitting for him to use, and to make as if he did eat of the flesh from the sacrifice, as had been commanded by the king; ²²that by so doing he might be delivered from death, and for his ancient friendship with them might be treated kindly. ²³But he, having formed a high resolve, and one that became his years, and the dignity of old age, and the gray hairs which he had reached with honor, and his excellent education from a child, or rather [that became] the holy laws of God's ordaining, declared his mind accordingly, bidding them quickly send him to Hades. ²⁴"For it does not become our years to deceive," [he said,] "that [through this] many of the young should suppose that Eleazar, the man of eighty years and ten, had gone over to an alien religion; ²⁵and [so] they, by reason of my deception, and for the sake of this brief and momentary life, should be led astray because of me, and [so] I get to myself a pollution and a stain of my old age. ²⁶For even if for the present time I will remove from myself the punishment of men, yet I will not escape the hands of the Almighty, either living or dead. ²⁷For that reason, by courageously parting with my life now, I will show myself worthy of my old age, ²⁸and leave behind a noble example to the young to die willingly and nobly a glorious death for the reverend and holy laws." And when he had said these words, he went immediately to the instrument of torture. ²⁹And when they changed the good will they bore toward him a little before into ill will, because these words of his were, as they thought, sheer madness, ³⁰and when he was at the point to die with the stripes, he groaned aloud and said, "To the LORD, who has the holy knowledge, it is manifest that, whereas I might have been delivered from death, I endure severe pains in my body by being scourged; but in soul I gladly suffer these things for my fear of Him." ³¹So this man also died after this manner, leaving his death for an example of nobleness and a memorial of virtue, not only to the young but also to the great body of his nation.

CHAPTER 7

¹And it came to pass that seven brothers also with their mother were at the king's command taken and shamefully handled with scourges and cords, to compel them to taste of the abominable swine's flesh. ²But one of them made himself the spokesman and said, "What would you ask and learn of us? For we are ready to die rather than transgress the laws of our fathers." ³And the king fell into a rage and commanded to heat pans and

cauldrons: ⁴and when these were heated, he commanded to cut out the tongue of him that had been their spokesman, and to scalp him, and to cut off his extremities, the rest of his brothers and his mother looking on. ⁵And when he was utterly maimed, [the king] commanded to bring him to the fire, being yet alive, and to fry him in the pan. And as the vapor of the pan spread far, they and their mother also exhorted one another to die nobly, saying, ⁶"The LORD God sees, and in truth is entreated for us, as Moses declared in his song, which witnesses against [the people] to their faces, saying, And He will be treated for His servants." ⁷And when the first had died after this manner, they brought the second to the mocking; and they pulled off the skin of his head with the hair and asked him, "Will you eat, before your body is punished in every limb?" ⁸But he answered in the language of his fathers and said to them, "No." Therefore he also underwent the next torture in succession, as the first had done. ⁹And when he was at the last gasp, he said, "You—miscreant—release us out of this present life, but the King of the world will raise us up, who have died for His laws, to a continuous renewal of life." ¹⁰And after him the third was made a laughingstock. And when he was required, he quickly put out his tongue, and stretched out his hands courageously, ¹¹and nobly said, "From Heaven I possess these; and for His laws' sake I treat these with contempt; and from Him I hope to receive these back again": ¹²insomuch that the king himself and those who were with him were astonished at the young man's soul, for he regarded the pain as nothing. ¹³And when he too was dead, they shamefully handled and tortured the fourth in like manner. ¹⁴And having come near to death he said, "It is good to die at the hands of men and look for the hopes which are [given] by God, that we will be raised up again by Him; for as for you, you will have no resurrection to life." ¹⁵And next after him they brought the fifth, and shamefully handled him. ¹⁶But he looked toward the king and said, "Because you have authority among men, though you are [yourself] corruptible, you do what you will; yet do not think that our race has been forsaken of God; ¹⁷but hold on your way, and behold His sovereign majesty, how it will torture you and your seed." ¹⁸And after him they brought the sixth. And when he was at the point to die he said, "Do not be vainly deceived, for we suffer these things for our own doings, as sinning against our own God: marvelous things have come to pass; ¹⁹but do not think that you will be unpunished, having determined to fight against God." ²⁰But above all was the mother marvelous and worthy of honorable memory; for when she looked on seven sons perishing within the space of one day, she bare [the sight] with good courage for the hopes [that she had set] on the LORD. ²¹And she exhorted each one of them in the language of their fathers, filled with a noble temper and stirring up her womanish thought with manly passion, saying to them, ²²"I do not know how you came into my womb, neither was it I that bestowed on you your spirit and your life, and it was not I that brought into order the first elements of each one of you. ²³Therefore the Creator of the world, who fashioned the generation of man and devised the generation of all things, in mercy gives back to you again both your spirit and your life, as you now treat yourselves with contempt for His laws' sake." ²⁴But Antiochus, thinking himself to be despised, and suspecting the reproachful voice, while the youngest was yet alive did not only make his appeal [to him] by words, but also at the same time promised with oaths that he would enrich him and raise him to high estate, if he would turn from the [customs] of his fathers, and that he would take him for his friend and entrust him with affairs. ²⁵But when the young man would in no way give heed, the king called to him his mother, and exhorted her that she would counsel the youth to save himself. ²⁶And when he had exhorted her with many words, she undertook to persuade her son. ²⁷But bending toward him, laughing the cruel tyrant to scorn, she spoke this in the language of her fathers: "My son, have pity on me that carried you nine months in my womb, and gave you suck three years, and nourished and brought you up to this age, and sustained you. ²⁸I implore you, my child, to lift your eyes to the Heaven and the earth, and to see all things that are in it, and so to recognize that God made them not of things that were, and [that] the race of men in this way comes into being. ²⁹Do not be afraid of this butcher, but, proving yourself worthy of your brothers, accept your death, that in the mercy [of God] I may receive you again with your brothers." ³⁰But before she had yet ended speaking, the young man said, "Whom do you wait for? I do not obey the command of the king, but I listen to the command of the law that was given to our fathers through Moses. ³¹But you, that have devised all manner of evil against the Hebrews, will in no way escape the hands of God. ³²For we are suffering because of our own sins; ³³and if for rebuke and disciplining our living Lord has been angered a little while, yet He will again be reconciled with His own servants. ³⁴But you, O unholy man and of all most vile, do not be vainly lifted up in your wild pride with uncertain hopes, raising your hand against the heavenly children; ³⁵for not yet have you escaped the judgment of the Almighty God that sees [all things]. ³⁶For these our brothers, having endured a short pain that brings continuous life, have now died under God's covenant; but you, through the judgment of God, will receive in just measure the penalties of your arrogance. ³⁷But I, as my brothers, give up both body and soul for the laws of our fathers, calling on God that He may speedily become gracious to the nation; and that you amidst trials and plagues may confess that He alone is God; ³⁸and that in me and my brothers you may stay the wrath of the Almighty, which has been justly brought on our whole race." ³⁹But the king, falling into a rage, handled him worse than all the rest, being exasperated at his mocking. ⁴⁰So he also died pure [from pollution], putting his whole trust in the LORD. ⁴¹And last of all, after her sons, the mother died. ⁴²Let it then suffice to have said so much concerning the sacrificial feasts and the [king's] exceeding barbarities.

CHAPTER 8

¹But Judas, who is also [called] Maccabaeus, and those who were with him, making their way privily into the villages, called to them their countrymen; and taking to them such as had continued in the Jews' religion, gathered together as many as six thousand. ²And they called on the LORD, [imploring Him] to look on the people that was oppressed by all; and to also have compassion on the sanctuary that had been profaned by the ungodly men; ³and to have pity on the city also that was suffering ruin and ready to be made level with the ground; and to listen to the blood that cried to Him; ⁴and to remember also the lawless slaughter of the innocent infants, and the blasphemies that had been committed against His Name; and to show His hatred of wickedness. ⁵And when Maccabaeus had trained his men for service, the heathen at once found him irresistible, for that the wrath of the LORD was turned into pity. ⁶And coming unawares he set fire to cities and villages. And in winning back the most important positions, putting to flight no small number of the enemies, ⁷he especially took advantage of the nights for such assaults. And his courage was loudly talked of everywhere. ⁸But when Philip saw the man gaining ground little by little, and increasing more and more in his prosperity, he wrote to Ptolemy, the governor of Coele-Syria and Phoenicia, that he should support the king's cause. ⁹And [Ptolemy] quickly appointed Nicanor the [son] of Patroclus, one of the king's chief friends, and sent him, in command of no fewer than twenty thousand of all nations, to destroy the whole race of Judea; and with him he joined Gorgias also, a captain and one that had experience in matters of war. ¹⁰And Nicanor undertook by [the sale of the] captive Jews to make up for the king the tribute of two thousand talents which he was to pay to the Romans. ¹¹And immediately he sent to the cities on the seacoast, inviting them to buy Jewish slaves, promising to allow ninety slaves for a talent, not expecting the judgment that was to follow on him from the Almighty. ¹²But tidings came to Judas concerning the inroad of Nicanor; and when he communicated to those who were with him the presence of the army, ¹³those who were cowardly and distrustful of the judgment of God ran away and left the country. ¹⁴And others sold all that was left over to them, and in addition implored the LORD to deliver those who had been sold [as slaves] by the impious Nicanor before he ever met them; ¹⁵and, if not for their own sakes, yet for the covenants made with their fathers, and because he had called them by his reverend and glorious name. ¹⁶And Maccabaeus gathered his men together, six thousand in number, and exhorted them not to be stricken with dismay at the enemy, nor to fear the

great multitude of the heathen who came wrongfully against them; but to contend nobly, ¹⁷setting before their eyes the outrage that had been lawlessly perpetrated on the holy place, and the shameful handling of the city that had been turned to mockery, and further the overthrow of the mode of life received from their ancestors. ¹⁸"For they," he said, "trust to arms, and in addition to deeds of daring; but we trust on the Almighty God, since He is able at a beckoning to cast down those who are coming against us, and even the whole world." ¹⁹And moreover He recounted to them the help given from time to time in the days of their ancestors, both the [help given] in the days of Sennacherib, how that one hundred and eighty-five thousand perished, ²⁰and the [help given] in the land of Babylon, even the battle that was fought against the Gauls, how that they came to the engagement eight thousand in all, with four thousand Macedonians, and [how that,] the Macedonians being hard-pressed, the six thousand destroyed the one hundred and twenty thousand, because of the help which they had from Heaven, and took great plunder. ²¹And when he had with these words made them of good courage, and ready to die for the laws and their country, he divided his army into four parts; ²²appointing his relatives to be leaders with himself of the several bands—Simon, and Joseph, and Jonathan—giving each the command of fifteen hundred men, ²³and moreover Eleazer also: [then,] having read aloud the sacred scroll, and having given as a watchword, THE HELP OF GOD, leading the first band himself, he joined battle with Nicanor. ²⁴And, since the Almighty fought on their side, they killed of the enemy above nine thousand, and wounded and disabled the greater part of Nicanor's army and compelled all to flee: ²⁵and they took the money of those that had come there to buy them. And after they had pursued them for some distance, they returned, being constrained by the time of the day; ²⁶for it was the day before the Sabbath, and for this reason they made no effort to chase them far. ²⁷And when they had gathered the arms of the enemy together, and had stripped off their spoils, they occupied themselves about the Sabbath, blessing and thanking the LORD exceedingly, who had saved them to this day, for that He had caused a beginning of mercy to distill on them. ²⁸And after the Sabbath, when they had given of the spoils to the maimed, and to the widows and orphans, the residue they distributed among themselves and their children. ²⁹And when they had accomplished these things, and had made a common supplication, they implored the merciful LORD to be wholly reconciled with His servants. ³⁰And having had an encounter with the forces of Timotheus and Bacchides, they killed above twenty thousand of them, and made themselves masters of strongholds exceedingly high, and divided very much plunder, giving the maimed and orphans and widows, and moreover the aged also, an equal share with themselves. ³¹And when they had gathered the arms of the enemy together, they stored them all up carefully in the most important positions, and the residue of the spoils they carried to Jerusalem. ³²And they killed the phylarch of Timotheus' forces, a most unholy man, and one who had done the Jews much hurt. ³³And as they celebrated [the] victory in the city of their fathers, they burned those that had set the sacred gates on fire, and [among them] Callisthenes, who had fled into an outhouse; and [so] they received the suitable reward of their impiety. ³⁴And the three times-accursed Nicanor, who had brought the thousand merchants to buy the Jews [for slaves], ³⁵being through the help of the LORD humbled by them who in his eyes were held to be of least account, put off his glorious apparel, and [passing] through the midland, shunning all company like a fugitive slave, arrived at Antioch, having, [as he thought,] had the greatest possible good fortune, though his army was destroyed. ³⁶And he that had taken on himself to make tribute sure for the Romans by the captivity of the men of Jerusalem published abroad that the Jews had One who fought for them, and that because this was so the Jews were invulnerable, because they followed the laws ordained by Him.

CHAPTER 9

¹Now about that time it befell that Antiochus had returned in disorder from the region of Persia. ²For he had entered into the city called Persepolis, and he determined to rob a temple and to hold down the city. After which there was an onset of the multitudes, and [Antiochus and his men] turned to make defense with arms; and it came to pass that Antiochus was put to flight by the people of the country and broke up his camp with disgrace. ³And while he was at Ecbatana, news was brought him what had happened to Nicanor and the forces of Timotheus. ⁴And being lifted up by his passion he thought to make the Jews suffer even for the evildoing of those that had put him to rout. For that reason, the judgment from Heaven even now accompanying him, he gave order to his charioteer to drive without ceasing and dispatch the journey; for so he arrogantly spoke: I will make Jerusalem a common graveyard of Jews, when I come there. ⁵But the All-seeing Lord, the God of Israel, struck him with a fatal and invisible stroke; and as soon as he had ceased speaking this word, an incurable pain of the bowels seized him, and bitter torments of the inner parts; ⁶and that most justly, for he had tormented other men's bowels with many and strange sufferings. ⁷But he in no way ceased from his rude insolence; no, still more was he filled with arrogance, breathing fire in his passion against the Jews, and commanding to hasten the journey. But it came to pass moreover that he fell from his chariot as it rushed along, and having a grievous fall was racked in all the members of his body. ⁸And he that but now supposed himself to have the waves of the sea at his bidding, so vainglorious was he beyond the condition of a man, and that thought to weigh the heights of the mountains in a balance, was now brought to the ground and carried in a litter, showing to all that the power was manifestly God's; ⁹so that out of the body of the impious man worms swarmed, and while he was still living in anguish and pains, his flesh fell off, and by reason of the stench all the army turned with loathing from his corruption. ¹⁰And the man that a little before supposed himself to touch the stars of the heavens, no one could endure to carry for his intolerable stench. ¹¹Therefore he began in great part to cease from his arrogance, being broken [in spirit, and] to come to knowledge under the scourge of God, his pains increasing every moment. ¹²And when he himself could not stand his own smell, he said these words: "It is right to be subject to God, and that one who is mortal should not be inclined arrogantly." ¹³And the vile man vowed to the Sovereign LORD, who now no longer would have pity on him, saying concerning this ¹⁴that the holy city, to which he was going in haste, to lay it even with the ground and to make it a common graveyard, he would declare free; ¹⁵and as touching the Jews, whom he had decided not even to count worthy of burial, but to cast them out to the beasts with their infants, for the birds to devour, he would make them all equal to citizens of Athens; ¹⁶and the holy sanctuary, which before he had plundered, he would adorn with excellent offerings, and would restore all the sacred vessels many times multiplied, and out of his own revenues would defray the charges that were required for the sacrifices; ¹⁷and, besides all this, that he would become a Jew, and would visit every inhabited place, publishing abroad the might of God. ¹⁸But when his sufferings did in no way cease, for the judgment of God had come on him in righteousness, having given up all hope of himself, he wrote to the Jews the letter written below, having the nature of a supplication, to this effect: ¹⁹"To the worthy Jews, his fellow-citizens, Antiochus, king and general, wishes much joy and health and prosperity. ²⁰May you and your children fare well; and your affairs will be to your mind. Having my hope in Heaven, ²¹I remembered with affection your honor and good will [toward me]. Returning out of the region of Persia, and being taken with a ghastly sickness, I deemed it necessary to take thought for the common safety of all, ²²not despairing of myself, but having great hope to escape from the sickness. ²³But considering that my father also, at what time he led an army into the upper country, appointed his successor, ²⁴to the end that, if anything fell out contrary to expectation, or if any unwelcome tidings were brought, they [that remained] in the country, knowing to whom the state had been left, might not be troubled; ²⁵and, besides all this, observing how that the princes that are borderers and neighbors to my kingdom watch opportunities, and look for the future event, I have appointed my son Antiochus [to be] king, whom I often committed and commended to

most of you, when I was hastening to the upper provinces; and I have written to him what is written below. ²⁶I exhort you therefore and implore you, having in your remembrance the benefits done to you in common and separately, to preserve each of you your present good will toward me and my son. ²⁷For I am persuaded that he, in gentleness and kindness, will follow my purpose and treat you with indulgence." ²⁸So the murderer and blasphemer, having endured the most intense sufferings, even as he had dealt with other men, ended his life among the mountains by a most piteous fate in a strange land. ²⁹And Philip his foster brother carried the body [home]; and then, fearing the son of Antiochus, he went himself to Ptolemy Philometor in Egypt.

CHAPTER 10

¹And Maccabaeus and those who were with him, the LORD leading them on, recovered the temple and the city; ²and they pulled down the altars that had been built in the marketplace by the aliens, and also sacred enclosures. ³And having cleansed the sanctuary they made another altar of sacrifice; and striking stones and taking fire out of them, they offered sacrifices, after two years, and [burned] incense, and [lighted] lamps, and set out the Bread of the Presentation. ⁴And when they had done these things, they fell prostrate and implored the LORD that they might no longer fall into such evils; but that, if ever they should sin, they might be disciplined by Him with forbearance, and not be delivered to blaspheming and barbarous heathen. ⁵Now on the same day that the sanctuary was profaned by aliens, on that very day it came to pass that the cleansing of the sanctuary was made, even on the twenty-fifth day of the same month, which is Kislev. ⁶And they kept eight days with gladness in the manner [of the Celebration] of Shelters, remembering how that not long before, during the Celebration of Shelters, they were wandering in the mountains and in the caves after the manner of wild beasts. ⁷For that reason, bearing wands wreathed with leaves, and fair boughs, and palms also, they offered up hymns of thanksgiving to him that had prosperously brought to pass the cleansing of his own place. ⁸They ordained also with a common statute and decree, for all the nation of the Jews, that they should keep these days every year. ⁹And such was the end of Antiochus, who was called Epiphanes. ¹⁰But now we will declare what came to pass under Antiochus [named] Eupator, who proved himself a [true] son of that ungodly man and will gather up briefly the successive evils of the wars. ¹¹For this man, when he succeeded to the kingdom, appointed one Lysias—chancellor, and supreme governor of Coele-Syria and Phoenicia. ¹²For Ptolemy that was called Macron, setting an example of observing justice toward the Jews because of the wrong that had been done to them, endeavored to conduct his dealings with them on peaceful terms. ¹³After which being accused by the king before Eupator, and hearing himself called traitor at every turn, because he had abandoned Cyprus which Philometor had entrusted to him, and had withdrawn himself to Antiochus [called] Epiphanes, and failing to uphold the honor of his office, he took poison and made away with himself. ¹⁴But Gorgias, when he was made governor of the district, maintained a force of mercenaries, and at every turn kept up war with the Jews. ¹⁵And together with him the Idumaeans also, being masters of important strongholds, harassed the Jews; and receiving to them those that had taken refuge [there] from Jerusalem, they determined to keep up war. ¹⁶But Maccabaeus and his men, having made solemn supplication and having implored God to fight on their side, rushed on the strongholds of the Idumaeans; ¹⁷and assaulting them vigorously they made themselves masters of the positions, and kept off all that fought on the wall, and killed those that fell in their way, and killed no fewer than twenty thousand. ¹⁸And because no less than nine thousand were fled into two towers exceedingly strong and having all things [needed] for a siege, ¹⁹Maccabaeus, having left Simon and Joseph, and Zacchaeus besides and those who were with him, a force sufficient to besiege them, departed himself to places where he was most needed. ²⁰But Simon and those who were with him, yielding to covetousness, were bribed by certain of those that were in the towers, and receiving seventy thousand drachmas let some of them slip away. ²¹But when word was brought to Maccabaeus of what was done, he gathered the leaders of the people together, and accused [those men] of having sold their countrymen for money, by setting their enemies free [to fight] against them. ²²So he killed these men for having turned traitors, and out with took possession of the two towers. ²³And prospering with his arms in all things he took in hand, he destroyed in the two strongholds more than twenty thousand. ²⁴Now Timotheus, who had been before defeated by the Jews, having gathered together foreign forces in great multitudes, and having collected the horsemen which belonged to Asia, not a few, came as though he would take Judea by force of arms. ²⁵But as he drew near, Maccabaeus and his men sprinkled earth on their heads and girded their loins with sackcloth, in supplication to God, ²⁶and falling down on the step in front of the altar, implored Him to become gracious to them, and be an enemy to their enemies and an adversary to their adversaries, as the law declares. ²⁷And rising from their prayer they took up their arms and advanced some distance from the city; and when they had come near to their enemies they halted. ²⁸And when the dawn was now spreading, the two [armies] joined battle; the one part having this, besides [their] virtue, for a pledge of success and victory, that they had fled to the LORD for refuge, the others making their passion their leader in the strife. ²⁹But when the battle waxed strong, there appeared out of Heaven to their adversaries five men on horses with bridles of gold, [in] splendid [array]; and two of them, leading on the Jews, ³⁰and taking Maccabaeus in the midst of them, and covering him with their own armor, guarded him from wounds, while on the adversaries they shot out arrows and thunderbolts; by reason of which they were blinded and thrown into confusion, and were cut to pieces, filled with bewilderment. ³¹And there were slain twenty thousand and five hundred, beside six hundred horsemen. ³²But Timotheus himself fled into a stronghold called Gazara, a fortress of exceeding strength, Chaereas being in command there. ³³But Maccabaeus and his men were glad and laid siege to the fortress twenty-four days. ³⁴And those who were within, trusting to the strength of the place, blasphemed exceedingly, and hurled out impious words. ³⁵But at dawn of the twenty-fifth day certain young men of the company of Maccabaeus, inflamed with passion because of the blasphemies, assaulted the wall with masculine force and with furious passion, and cut down whoever came in their way. ³⁶And others climbing up in like manner, while [the besieged] were distracted with them [that had made their way] within, set fire to the towers, and kindling fires burned the blasphemers alive; while others broke open the gates, and, having given entrance to the rest of the band, occupied the city. ³⁷And they killed Timotheus, who was hidden in a cistern, and his brother Chaereas, and Apollophanes. ³⁸And when they had accomplished these things, they blessed the LORD with hymns and thanksgiving, Him who does great benefits to Israel, and gives them the victory.

CHAPTER 11

¹Now after a very short time, Lysias, the king's guardian and countryman and chancellor, being severely displeased for the things that had come to pass, ²collected about eighty thousand [footmen] and all his horsemen and came against the Jews, thinking to make the city a place for Greeks to dwell in, ³and to levy tribute on the temple, as of the other sacred places of the nations, and to put up the chief priesthood to sale every year; ⁴holding in no account the might of God, but puffed up with his tens of thousands of footmen, and his thousands of horsemen, and his eighty elephants. ⁵And coming into Judea and drawing near to Bethsuron, which was a strong place and distant from Jerusalem about five leagues, he pressed it hard. ⁶But when Maccabaeus and his men learned that he was besieging the strongholds, they and all the people with lamentations and tears made supplication to the LORD to send a good messenger to save Israel. ⁷And Maccabaeus himself took up arms first and exhorted the others to put themselves in danger together with him and help their countrymen; and they went out with him very willingly. ⁸And as they were there, close to Jerusalem, there appeared at their head one on horseback in white apparel, brandishing weapons of gold. ⁹And they all together praised the merciful

God and were yet more strengthened in heart: being ready to assail not men only but the wildest beasts, and walls of iron, ¹⁰they advanced in array, having Him that is in Heaven to fight on their side, for the LORD had mercy on them. ¹¹And hurling [themselves] like lions on the enemy, they killed of them eleven thousand [footmen] and sixteen hundred horsemen and forced all [the rest] to flee. ¹²But the greater part of them escaped wounded [and] naked; and Lysias also himself escaped by shameful flight. ¹³But as he was a man not void of understanding, weighing with himself the defeat which had befallen him, and considering that the Hebrews could not be overcome, because the Almighty God fought on their side, he sent again [to them], ¹⁴and persuaded them to come to terms on condition that all their rights were acknowledged, and [promised] that he would also persuade the king to become their friend. ¹⁵And Maccabaeus gave consent on all the conditions which Lysias proposed to him, being careful of the [common] good; for whatever [requests] Maccabaeus delivered in writing to Lysias concerning the Jews the king allowed. ¹⁶For the letters written to the Jews from Lysias were to this effect: "Lysias to the people of the Jews, greetings. ¹⁷John and Absalom, who were sent from you, having delivered the petition written below, made request concerning the things signified therein. ¹⁸Whatever things therefore had need to be brought before the king I declared [to him, and] what things were possible he allowed. ¹⁹If then you will preserve your good will toward the state, henceforward I will also endeavor to contribute to [your] good. ²⁰And on this behalf, I have given order in detail, both to these men and to those [that are sent] from me, to confer with you. ²¹Farewell. [Written] in the one hundred [and] forty-eighth year, on the twenty-fourth day of the [month] Dioscorinthius." ²²And the king's letter was in these words: "King Antiochus to his brother Lysias, greetings. ²³Seeing that our father passed to the gods having the wish that the subjects of his kingdom should be undisturbed and give themselves to the care of their own affairs, ²⁴we, having heard that the Jews do not consent to our father's purpose to turn them to the [customs] of the Greeks, but choose rather their own manner of living, and make request that the [customs] of their law be allowed to them— ²⁵choosing therefore that this nation also should be free from disturbance, we determine that their temple be restored to them, and that they live according to the customs that were in the days of their ancestors. ²⁶You will therefore do well to send [messengers] to them and give them the right hand [of friendship], that they, knowing our mind, may be of good heart, and gladly occupy themselves with the conduct of their own affairs." ²⁷And to the nation the king's letter was after this manner: "King Antiochus to the senate of the Jews and to the other Jews, greetings. ²⁸If you fare well, we have our desire: we ourselves are also in good health. ²⁹Menelaus informed us that your desire was to return home and follow your own business. ³⁰They therefore that depart home up to the thirtieth day of Xanthicus will have [our] friendship, with full permission ³¹that the Jews use their own [proper] meats and [observe their own] laws, even as formerly; and none of them will be in any way molested for the things that have been ignorantly done. ³²Moreover I have sent Menelaus also, that he may encourage you. ³³Farewell. [Written] in the one hundred [and] forty-eighth year, on the fifteenth day of Xanthicus." ³⁴And the Romans also sent to them a letter in these words: "Quintus Memmius [and] Titus Manius, ambassadors of the Romans, to the people of the Jews, greetings. ³⁵In regard to the things which Lysias the king's countryman granted you, we also give consent. ³⁶But as for the things which he judged should be referred to the king, send one out with, after you have advised thereof, that we may publish such [decrees] as befit your case; for we are on our way to Antioch. ³⁷For that reason, send some with speed, that we also may learn what is your mind. ³⁸Farewell. [Written] in the one hundred [and] forty-eighth year, on the fifteenth day of Xanthicus."

CHAPTER 12

¹So when these covenants had been made, Lysias departed to the king, and the Jews went about their farming. ²But [certain] of the governors of districts, Timotheus, and Apollonius the [son] of Gennaeus, and Hieronymus also, and Demophon, and besides them, Nicanor the governor of Cyprus would not permit them to enjoy tranquility and live in peace. ³And men of Joppa perpetrated this great impiety: they invited the Jews that lived among them to go with their wives and children into the boats which they had provided, as though they had no ill will toward them; ⁴and when the Jews, relying on the common decree of the city, accepted [the invitation], as men desiring to live in peace and suspecting nothing, they took them out to sea and drowned them—not less than two hundred. ⁵But when Judas heard of the cruelty done to his fellow-countrymen, giving command to the men that were with him ⁶and calling on God the righteous Judge, he came against the murderers of his countrymen, and set the haven on fire by night, and burned the boats, and put to the sword those that had fled there. ⁷But when the town was closed [against him], he withdrew, intending to come again to root out the whole community of the men of Joppa. ⁸But learning that the men of Jamnia were inclined to do in like manner to the Jews that sojourned among them, ⁹he fell on the Jamnites also by night, and set fire to the haven together with the fleet, so that the glare of the light was seen at Jerusalem, two hundred and forty furlongs distant. ¹⁰Now when they had drawn off nine furlongs from there, as they marched against Timotheus, [an] army] of Arabians attacked him, no fewer than five thousand [footmen] and five hundred horsemen. ¹¹And when a severe battle had been fought, and Judas and his company by the help of God had good success, the nomads being overcome implored Judas to grant them friendship, promising to give [him] cattle, and to help his people in all other ways. ¹²So Judas, thinking that they would indeed be profitable in many things, agreed to live in peace with them; and receiving pledges of friendship they departed to their tents. ¹³And he also fell on a certain city, Gephyrun, strong and fenced about with walls, and inhabited by a mixed multitude of various nations; and it was named Caspin. ¹⁴But those who were within, trusting to the strength of the walls and to their store of provisions, behaved themselves rudely toward Judas and those who were with him, railing, and furthermore blaspheming and speaking impious words. ¹⁵But Judas and his company, calling on the great Sovereign of the world, who without rams and cunning engines of war hurled down Jericho in the times of Joshua, rushed wildly against the wall; ¹⁶and having taken the city by the will of God, they made unspeakable slaughter, insomuch that the adjoining lake, which was two furlongs broad, appeared to be filled with the flood of blood. ¹⁷And when they had drawn off seven hundred and fifty furlongs from there, they made their way to Charax, to the Jews that are called Tubieni. ¹⁸And they did not find Timotheus in occupation of that district, for he had then departed from the district without accomplishing anything, but had left behind a garrison, and that a very strong one, in a certain post. ¹⁹But Dositheus and Sosipater, who were of Maccabaeus' captains, went out and destroyed those that had been left by Timotheus in the stronghold, above ten thousand men. ²⁰And Maccabaeus, ranging his own army by bands, set these two over the bands, and marched in haste against Timotheus, who had with him one hundred and twenty thousand footmen and two thousand and five hundred horsemen. ²¹But when Timotheus heard of the inroad of Judas, he at once sent away the women and the children and also the baggage into the [fortress] called Carnion; for the place was hard to besiege and difficult of access by reason of the narrowness of the approaches on all sides. ²²But when the band of Judas, who led the van, appeared in sight, and when terror came on the enemy and fear, because the manifestation of him who sees all things came on them, they fled a main, carried this way and that, so that they were often hurt of their own men, and pierced with the points of their swords. ²³And Judas continued in hot pursuit, putting the wicked wretches to the sword, and he destroyed as many as thirty thousand men. ²⁴But Timotheus himself, falling in with the company of Dositheus and Sosipater, implored them with much crafty guile to let him go with his life, because he had in [his power] the parents of many [of them] and the relatives of some: otherwise, [he said,] little regard will be shown to these. ²⁵So when he had with many words confirmed the agreement to restore them without harm,

they let him go that they might save their relatives. ²⁶And [Judas], marching against Carnion and the temple of Atergatis, killed twenty-five thousand persons. ²⁷And after he had put these to flight and destroyed them, he also marched against Ephron, a strong city, wherein were multitudes of people of all nations; and stalwart young men placed on the walls made a vigorous defense; and there were great stores of engines and darts there. ²⁸But calling on the Sovereign who with might breaks in pieces the strength of the enemy, they got the city into their hands, and killed as many as twenty-five thousand of those who were within. ²⁹And setting out from there they marched in haste against Scythopolis, which is distant from Jerusalem six hundred furlongs. ³⁰But when the Jews that were settled there testified of the good will that the Scythopolitans had shown toward them, and of their kindly bearing [toward them] in the times of their misfortune, ³¹they gave thanks, and further exhorted them to remain well-affected toward the race for the future; and they went up to Jerusalem, the Celebration of Weeks being close to hand. ³²But after the [festival] called Pentecost they marched in haste against Gorgias the governor of Idumaea: ³³and he came out with three thousand footmen and four hundred horsemen. ³⁴And when they had set themselves in array, it came to pass that a few of the Jews fell. ³⁵And a certain Dositheus, one of Bacenor's company, who was on horseback and a strong man, pressed hard on Gorgias, and taking hold of his cloak drew him along by main force; and while he was inclined to take the accursed man alive, one of the Thracian horsemen bore down on him and disabled his shoulder, and so Gorgias escaped to Marisa. ³⁶And when those who were with Esdris had been fighting long and were wearied out, Judas called on the LORD to show Himself, fighting on their side and leading the van of the battle; ³⁷and [then] in the language of his fathers he raised the battle-cry joined with hymns, and rushing unawares on the troops of Gorgias put them to flight. ³⁸And Judas gathering his army came to the city of Adullam; and as the seventh day was coming on, they purified themselves according to the custom, and kept the Sabbath there. ³⁹And on the day following, at which time it had become necessary, Judas and his company came to take up the bodies of those who had fallen, and in company with their countrymen to bring them back to the tombs of their fathers. ⁴⁰But under the garments of each one of the dead they found consecrated signs of the idols of Jamnia, which the law forbids the Jews to have anything to do with; and it became clear to all that it was for this reason that they had fallen. ⁴¹All therefore, blessing the [works] of the LORD, the righteous Judge, who makes manifest the things that are hid, ⁴²went themselves to supplication, imploring that the sin committed might be wholly blotted out. And the noble Judas exhorted the multitude to keep themselves from sin, for so much as they had seen before their eyes what things had come to pass because of the sin of those who had fallen. ⁴³And when he had made a collection—man by man—to the sum of two thousand drachmas of silver, he sent to Jerusalem to offer a sacrifice for sin, doing therein right well and honorably, in that he took thought for a resurrection. ⁴⁴For if he were not expecting that those who had fallen would rise again, it was superfluous and idle to pray for the dead. ⁴⁵(And if [he did it] looking to an honorable memorial of gratitude laid up for those who die in godliness, holy and godly was the thought.) For that reason, he made the atoning sacrifice for those who had died, that they might be released from their sin.

CHAPTER 13

¹In the one hundred and forty-ninth year, tidings were brought to Judas and his company that Antiochus Eupator was coming with [great] multitudes against Judea, ²and with him Lysias his guardian and chancellor, each having a Greek force, one hundred and ten thousand footmen, and five thousand and three hundred horsemen, and twenty-two elephants, and three hundred chariots armed with scythes. ³And Menelaus also joined himself with them, and with great deception encouraged Antiochus, not for the saving of his country, but because he thought that he would be set over the government. ⁴But the King of kings stirred up the passion of Antiochus against the wicked wretch; and when Lysias informed him that this man was the cause of all the evils, [the king] commanded to bring him to Beroea, and to put him to death after the manner of that place. ⁵Now there is in that place a tower of fifty cubits high, full of ashes, and it had all around it a gallery descending sheer on every side into the ashes. ⁶Here him that is guilty of sacrilege or has attained a preeminence in any other evil deeds, they all push forward into destruction. ⁷By such a fate it befell the breaker of the law, Menelaus, to die, without obtaining so much as [a grave in] the earth, and that right justly; ⁸for since he had perpetrated many sins against the altar, whose fire and whose ashes were holy, in ashes he received his death. ⁹Now the king, infuriated in spirit, was coming with intent to inflict on the Jews the very worst of the sufferings that had befallen [them] in his father's time. ¹⁰But when Judas heard of these things, he gave charge to the multitude to call on the LORD day and night, [imploring Him,] if ever at any other time, so now to help those who were at the point to be deprived of the law and their country and the holy temple, ¹¹and not to permit the people that had been but now a little while revived to fall into the hands of those profane heathen. ¹²So when they had all done the same thing together, imploring the merciful Lord with weeping, and fasting, and prostration for three days without ceasing, Judas exhorted them and commanded they should join him. ¹³And having gone apart with the elders, he resolved that, before the king's army should enter into Judea and make themselves masters of the city, they should go out and try the matter [in fight] by the help of God. ¹⁴And committing the decision to the Lord of the world and exhorting those who were with him to contend nobly even to death for laws, temple, city, country, commonwealth, he pitched his camp by Modin. ¹⁵And given out to his men the watchword, VICTORY IS GOD'S, with a chosen body of the bravest young men he fell on [the camp] by night [and penetrated] to the king's tent and killed [of] the army as many as two thousand men and brought down the mightiest elephant with him that was in the tower on him. ¹⁶And at last they filled the army with terror and alarm and departed with good success. ¹⁷And this had been accomplished when the day was but now dawning, because of the LORD's protection that gave Judas help. ¹⁸But the king, having had a taste of the exceeding boldness of the Jews, made attempts by stratagem on their positions; ¹⁹and [on] a strong fortress of the Jews at Bethsura, he advanced, was turned back, failed, was defeated, ²⁰and Judas carried such things as were necessary to those who were within. ²¹But Rhodocus, from the Jewish ranks, made known to the enemy the secrets [of his countrymen]. He was sought out, and taken, and shut up in prison. ²²The king treated with them in Bethsura the second time, gave his hand, took theirs, departed, attacked the forces of Judas, was given a worse [outcome], ²³heard that Philip, who had been left as chancellor in Antioch, had become reckless, was confounded, made to the Jews an overture [of peace], submitted himself, and swore to acknowledge all their rights, came to terms with them and offered sacrifice, honored the sanctuary and the place, ²⁴showed kindness and graciously received Maccabaeus, left Hegemonides governor from Ptolemais even to the Gerrenians, ²⁵[and] came to Ptolemais. The men of Ptolemais were displeased at the treaty, for they had exceedingly great indignation [against the Jews]: they desired to annul the articles of the agreement. ²⁶Lysias came forward to speak, made the best defense that was possible, persuaded, pacified, made them well-affected, [and] departed to Antioch. This was the issue of the inroad and departure of the king.

CHAPTER 14

¹Now after a space of three years tidings were brought to Judas and his company that Demetrius the [son] of Seleucus, having sailed into the haven of Tripolis with a mighty army and a fleet, ²had gotten possession of the country, having made away with Antiochus and his guardian Lysias. ³But one Alcimus, who had formerly been chief priest, and had willfully polluted himself in the times when there was no mingling [with the nations], considering that there was no deliverance for him in any way, nor any more access to the holy altar, ⁴came to King Demetrius in about the one hundred [and] fifty-first year, presenting to him a crown of gold and a palm, and beside these some of the festal olive boughs of the temple. And for that day he held

his peace; ⁵but having gotten opportunity to further his own madness, being called by Demetrius into a meeting of his council and asked how the Jews stood affected and what they purposed, he answered to that. ⁶Those of the Jews that he called Hasidaeans, whose leader is Judas Maccabaeus, keep up war, and are seditious, not suffering the kingdom to find tranquility. ⁷For that reason, having laid aside my ancestral glory, I mean the chief priesthood, I have now come here; ⁸first, for the genuine care I have for the things that concern the king, and secondly, because I also have regard to my own fellow-citizens; for, through the unadvised dealing of those of whom I spoke before, our whole race is in no small misfortune. ⁹But do you, O king, having informed yourself of these things separately, take thought both for our country and for our race, which is surrounded [by enemies], according to the gracious kindness with which you receive all? ¹⁰For as long as Judas remains alive, it is impossible that the state should find peace. ¹¹And when he had spoken such words as these, at once the rest of the [king's] friends, having ill will against Judas, inflamed Demetrius yet more. ¹²And then appointing Nicanor, who had been master of the elephants, and making him governor of Judea, he sent him out, ¹³giving him written instructions to make away with Judas himself and to scatter those who were with him, and to set up Alcimus as chief priest of the great temple. ¹⁴And those in Judea that had [before] driven Judas into exile thronged to Nicanor in flocks, supposing that the misfortunes and calamities of the Jews would be successes to themselves. ¹⁵But when [the Jews] heard of Nicanor's inroad and the assault of the heathen, they sprinkled earth [on their heads] and made solemn supplication to him who had established His own people forevermore, and who always, making manifest His presence, upholds [those who are] His own portion. ¹⁶And when the leader had given [his] commands, he immediately set out from there, and joined battle with them at a village [called] Lessau. ¹⁷But Simon, the brother of Judas, had encountered Nicanor, yet not until late, having received a check by reason of the sudden consternation caused by his adversaries. ¹⁸Nevertheless Nicanor, hearing of the manliness of those who were with Judas, and their courage in fighting for their country, shrank from bringing the matter to the decision of the sword. ¹⁹For that reason, he sent Posidonius, and Theodotus, and Mattathias to give and receive pledges of friendship. ²⁰So when these proposals had been long considered, and the leader had made the troops acquainted with them, and it appeared that they were all of like mind, they consented to the covenants. ²¹And they appointed a day on which to meet together by themselves. And a litter was borne forward from each [army]; they set chairs of state; ²²Judas stationed armed men ready in convenient places, lest perhaps there should suddenly be treachery on the part of the enemy; they held such conference as was suitable. ²³Nicanor waited in Jerusalem, and did nothing to cause disturbance, but dismissed the flocks of people that had gathered together. ²⁴And he kept Judas always in his presence; he had gained a hearty affection for the man; ²⁵he urged him to marry and beget children; he married, settled quietly, took part in common life. ²⁶But Alcimus, perceiving the good will that was between them, and having gotten possession of the covenants that had been made, came to Demetrius and told him that Nicanor was ill-affected toward the state, for he had appointed that conspirator against his kingdom, Judas, to be his successor. ²⁷And the king, falling into a rage, and being exasperated by the false accusations of that most wicked man, wrote to Nicanor, signifying that he was displeased at the covenants, and commanding him to send Maccabaeus prisoner to Antioch in all haste. ²⁸And when this message came to Nicanor, he was confounded, and was severely troubled at the thought of annulling the articles that had been agreed on, the man having done no wrong; ²⁹but because there was no dealing against the king, he watched his time to execute this purpose by stratagem. ³⁰But Maccabaeus, when he perceived that Nicanor was behaving more harshly in his dealings with him, and that he had become ruler in his customary bearing, understanding that this harshness came not of good, gathered together not a few of his men, and concealed himself from Nicanor. ³¹But the other, when he became aware that he had been bravely defeated by the stratagem of Judas, came to the great and holy temple, while the priests were offering the usual sacrifices, and commanded them to deliver the man up. ³²And when they declared with oaths that they had no knowledge where the man was whom he sought, ³³he stretched out his right hand toward the sanctuary and swore this oath: "If you will not deliver up to me Judas as a prisoner, I will lay this temple of God even with the ground, and will break down the altar, and I will erect here a temple to Bacchus for all to see." ³⁴And having said this, he departed. But the priests, stretching out their hands toward Heaven, called on Him that ever fights for our nation, in these words: ³⁵"You, O Lord of the universe, who in Yourself have need of nothing, was well pleased that a sanctuary of Your habitation should be set among us; ³⁶so now, O holy Lord of all hallowing, keep undefiled forever this house that has been lately cleansed." ³⁷Now information was given to Nicanor against one Razis, an elder of Jerusalem, as being a lover of his countrymen and a man of very good report, and one called "Father of the Jews" for his good will [toward them]. ³⁸For in the former times when there was no mingling [with the nations] he had been accused of [cleaving to the] Jews' religion, and had endangered body and life with all earnestness for the religion of the Jews. ³⁹And Nicanor, wishing to make evident the ill will that he bore to the Jews, sent above five hundred soldiers to take him; ⁴⁰for he thought by taking him to inflict a calamity on them. ⁴¹But when the troops were on the point of taking the tower, and were forcing the door of the court, and commanded to bring fire and burn the doors, he being surrounded on every side, fell on his sword, ⁴²choosing rather to die nobly than to fall into the hands of the wicked wretches, and suffer outrage unworthy of his own nobleness: ⁴³but since he missed his stroke through the excitement of the struggle, and the crowds were now rushing within the door, he ran bravely up to the wall and cast himself down courageously among the crowds. ⁴⁴But as they quickly gave back, a space was made, and he fell on the middle of his side. ⁴⁵And having yet breath within him, and being inflamed with passion, he rose up, and though his blood gushed out in streams and his wounds were grievous, he ran through the crowds, and standing on a steep rock, ⁴⁶when as his blood was now well near spent, he drew out his bowels [through the wound, and] taking them in both his hands he shook them at the crowds; and calling on Him who is Lord of the life and the spirit to restore these again, he thus died.

CHAPTER 15

¹But Nicanor, hearing that Judas and his company were in the region of Samaria, resolved to set on them with all security on the day of rest. ²And when the Jews that were compelled to follow him said, "Do not destroy so savagely and barbarously, but give due glory to the day which He that sees all things has honored and hallowed above [other days]"; ³then the three times-accursed wretch asked if there were a Sovereign in Heaven that had commanded to keep the Sabbath day. ⁴And when they declared, "There is the LORD, living Himself [as the] Sovereign in Heaven, who commanded [us] to observe the seventh day"; ⁵then the other says, "I also am a sovereign on the earth, who [now] command to take up arms and execute the king's business." Nevertheless, he did not prevail to execute his cruel purpose. ⁶And Nicanor, bearing himself haughtily in all vain pride, had determined to set up a monument of complete victory over Judas and all those who were with him: ⁷but Maccabaeus still trusted unceasingly, with all hope that he should obtain help from the LORD. ⁸And he exhorted his company not to be fearful at the inroad of the heathen, but, keeping in mind the help which of old they had oftentimes received from Heaven, so now also to look for the victory which would come to them from the Almighty; ⁹and comforting them out of the Law and the Prophets, and in addition, putting them in mind of the conflicts that they had maintained, he made them more eager [for the battle]. ¹⁰And when he had roused their spirit, he gave them [his] commands, at the same time pointing out the disloyalty of the heathen and their breach of their oaths. ¹¹And arming each one of them, not so much with the sure defense of shields and spears as with the encouragement [that lies] in good words, and moreover relating to them a dream

worthy to be believed, he made them all exceedingly glad. ¹²And the vision of that [dream] was this: [He saw] Onias, him that was chief priest, a noble and good man, reverend in bearing, yet gentle in manner and well-spoken, and exercised from a child in all points of virtue, with outstretched hands invoking [blessings] on the whole body of the Jews: ¹³there on [he saw] a man appear, of venerable age and exceeding glory, and wonderful and most majestic was the dignity around him: ¹⁴and Onias answered and said, "This is the lover of the countrymen, he who prays much for the people and the holy city, Jeremiah the prophet of God": ¹⁵and Jeremiah stretching out his right hand delivered to Judas a sword of gold, and in giving it addressed [him], saying, ¹⁶"Take the holy sword, a gift from God, with which you will strike down the adversaries." ¹⁷And being encouraged by the words of Judas, which were of a lofty strain, and able to incite to virtue and to stir the souls of the young to manly courage, they determined not to carry on a campaign, but nobly to bear down on [the enemy, and] fighting hand to hand with all courage bring the matter to an issue, because the city and the sanctuary and the temple were in danger. ¹⁸For their fear for wives and children, and furthermore for relatives and countrymen, was in less account with them; but greatest and first was their fear for the consecrated sanctuary. ¹⁹And they also that were shut up in the city were in no light distress, being troubled because of the encounter in the open ground. ²⁰And when all were now waiting for the decision of the issue, and the enemy had already joined battle, and the army had been set in array, and the elephants brought back to a convenient post, and the horsemen drawn on the flank, ²¹Maccabaeus, perceiving the presence of the troops, and the various arms with which they were equipped, and the savageness of the elephants, holding up his hands to Heaven called on the LORD that works wonders, recognizing that [success] comes not by arms, but that, according as [the LORD] will judge, He gains the victory for those who are worthy. ²²And calling on [God], he said after this manner: "You, O Sovereign LORD, sent Your messenger in the time of Hezekiah king of Judea, and he killed of the army of Sennacherib as many as one hundred and eighty-five thousand; ²³so now also, O Sovereign of the heavens, send a good messenger before us to bring terror and trembling: ²⁴through the greatness of Your arm let them be stricken with dismay that have come here against Your holy people with blasphemy." And as he ended with these words, ²⁵Nicanor and his company advanced with trumpets and victory songs; ²⁶but Judas and his company joined battle with the enemy with invocation and prayers. ²⁷And contending with their hands, and praying to God with their hearts, they killed no less than thirty-five thousand men, being made exceedingly glad by the manifestation of God. ²⁸And when the engagement was over, and they were returning again with joy, they recognized Nicanor lying dead in full armor; ²⁹and there arose a shout and tumult, and then they blessed the Sovereign [LORD] in the language of their fathers. ³⁰And he that in all things was in body and soul the foremost champion of his fellow-citizens, he that kept through life the good will of his youth toward his countrymen, commanded to cut off Nicanor's head, and his hand with the shoulder, and bring them to Jerusalem. ³¹And when he had arrived there, and had called his countrymen together and set the priests before the altar, he sent for those who were in the citadel; ³²and showing the head of the vile Nicanor, and the hand of that profane man, which with proud brags he had stretched out against the holy house of the Almighty, ³³and cutting out the tongue of the impious Nicanor, he said that he would give it by pieces to the birds, and hang up the rewards of his madness near the sanctuary. ³⁴And they all, [looking up] to Heaven, blessed the LORD who had manifested Himself, saying, "Blessed is He that has preserved His own place undefiled." ³⁵And he hanged Nicanor's head and shoulder from the citadel, a sign, evident to all and manifest, of the help of the LORD. ³⁶And they all ordained with a common decree in no way to let this day pass undistinguished, but to mark with honor the thirteenth day of the twelfth month (it is called Adar in the Syrian tongue), the day before the day of Mordecai. ³⁷This then having been the issue of the attempt of Nicanor, and the city having from those times been held by the Hebrews, I will also here make an end of my scroll. ³⁸And if [I have written] well and to the point in my story, this is what I myself desired; but if meanly and indifferently, this is all I could attain to. ³⁹For as it is distasteful to drink wine alone and in like manner again [to drink] water [alone], while the mingling of wine with water at once gives full pleasantness to the flavor; so also, the fashioning of the language delights the ears of those who read the story. And here will be the end.

1 ESDRAS

1 Esdras, also called Greek Esdras, Greek Ezra, or 3 Esdras, is an ancient Greek version of the biblical Book of Ezra in use among the early church, and many modern Christians with varying degrees of canonicity. First Esdras is substantially the same as Masoretic Ezra. As part of the Septuagint translation of the Old Testament, it is regarded as deuterocanonical in the churches of the East, but apocryphal in the West. First Esdras is found in Origen's Hexapla. Greek and related versions of the Bible include both Esdras A (English title: 1 Esdras) and Esdras B (Ezra–Nehemiah) in parallel.

CHAPTER 1

¹Josiah held the Passover in Jerusalem to his Lord and offered the Passover [on] the fourteenth day of the first month; ²having set the priests according to their daily courses, being arrayed in their vestments, in the temple of the LORD. ³And he spoke to the Levites, the temple-servants of Israel, that they should make themselves holy to the LORD, to set the holy Ark of the LORD in the house that King Solomon the son of David had built, ⁴[and he said,] "You will no longer have need to bear it on your shoulders: now therefore, serve the LORD your God, and minister to His people Israel, and prepare after your fathers' houses and relatives, ⁵according to the writing of David, king of Israel, and according to the magnificence of his son Solomon: and standing in the holy place according to the several divisions of the families of you the Levites, who [minister] in the presence of your countrymen the sons of Israel, ⁶offer the Passover in order, and make the sacrifices ready for your countrymen, and keep the Passover according to the command of the LORD, which was given to Moses." ⁷And to the people which were present Josiah gave thirty thousand lambs and kids, and three thousand calves: these things were given of the king's substance, according as he promised, to the people, and to the priests and Levites. ⁸And Hilkiah, and Zechariah, and Esyelus, the rulers of the temple, gave to the priests for the Passover two thousand [and] six hundred sheep, and three hundred calves. ⁹And Jeconias, and Samaias, and his brother Nathanael, and Sabias, and Ochielus, and Joram, captains over thousands, gave to the Levites for the Passover five thousand sheep, and seven hundred calves. ¹⁰And when these things were done, the priests and Levites, having the unleavened bread, stood in agreeable order according to the countrymen, ¹¹and according to the several divisions by fathers' houses, before the people, to offer to the LORD, as it is written in the Scroll of Moses: and so [they] did [in] the morning. ¹²And they roasted the Passover with fire, as pertains: and they boiled the sacrifices in the brazen vessels and cauldrons with a good savor, ¹³and set them before all the people; and afterward they prepared for themselves, and for their relatives the priests, the sons of Aaron. ¹⁴For the priests offered the fat until night: and the Levites prepared for themselves, and for their relatives the priests, the sons of Aaron. ¹⁵The holy singers also, the sons of Asaph, were in their order, according to the appointment of David, Asaph, Zechariah, and Eddinus, who was of the king's retinue. ¹⁶Moreover, the

gatekeepers were at every gate; none had need to depart from his daily course, for their relatives the Levites prepared for them. ¹⁷So were the things that belonged to the sacrifices of the LORD accomplished in that day, in holding the Passover, ¹⁸and offering sacrifices on the altar of the LORD, according to the command of King Josiah. ¹⁹So the sons of Israel, which were present at that time, held the Passover and the Celebration of Unleavened Bread [for] seven days. ²⁰And such a Passover was not held in Israel since the time of the prophet Samuel. ²¹Yes, all the kings of Israel had not held such a Passover as Josiah, and the priests, and the Levites, and the Jews, with all Israel that were present in their dwelling place at Jerusalem. ²²In the eighteenth year of the reign of Josiah this Passover was held. ²³And the works of Josiah were upright before his Lord with a heart full of godliness. ²⁴Moreover, the things that came to pass in his days have been written in times past, concerning those that sinned, and did wickedly against the LORD above every people and kingdom, and how they grieved Him exceedingly, so that the words of the LORD were confirmed against Israel. ²⁵Now after all these acts of Josiah, it came to pass that Pharaoh the king of Egypt came to raise war at Carchemish on [the] Euphrates: and Josiah went out against him. ²⁶But the king of Egypt sent to him, saying, "What have I to do with you, O king of Judea? ²⁷I am not sent out from the LORD God against you; for my war is on [the] Euphrates: and now the LORD is with me, yes, the LORD is with me hastening me forward. Depart from me and do not be against the LORD." ²⁸However, Josiah did not turn back to his chariot, but undertook to fight with him, not regarding the words of the prophet Jeremiah [spoken] by the mouth of the LORD, ²⁹but he joined battle with him in the plain of Megiddo, and the princes came down against King Josiah. ³⁰Then the king said to his servants, "Carry me away out of the battle; for I am very weak. And immediately his servants carried him away out of the army." ³¹Then he got up on his second chariot; and being brought back to Jerusalem he died and was buried in the tomb of his fathers. ³²And in all Jewry they mourned for Josiah; and the prophet Jeremiah lamented for Josiah, and the chief men with the women made lamentation for him, to this day: and this was given out for an ordinance to be done continually in all the nation of Israel. ³³These things are written in the Scroll of the Histories of the Kings of Judea, and each of the acts that Josiah did, and his glory, and his understanding in the Law of the LORD, and the things that he had done before, and the things now [recited], are reported in the Scroll of the Kings of Israel and Judah. ³⁴And the people took Joachaz, the son of Josiah, and made him king instead of his father Josiah, when he was twenty-three years old. ³⁵And he reigned in Judah and in Jerusalem three months: and then the king of Egypt deposed him from reigning in Jerusalem. ³⁶And he set a tax on the people of one hundred talents of silver and one talent of gold. ³⁷The king of Egypt also made King Jehoiakim, his brother, king of Judea and Jerusalem. ³⁸And Jehoiakim bound the nobles, but he apprehended his brother Zarakes and brought him up out of Egypt. ³⁹Jehoiakim was twenty-five years old when he began to reign in Judea and Jerusalem; and he did that which was evil in the sight of the LORD. ⁴⁰And Nebuchadnezzar the king of Babylon came up against him, and bound him with a chain of brass, and carried him to Babylon. ⁴¹Nebuchadnezzar also took of the holy vessels of the LORD, and carried them away, and set them up in his own temple at Babylon. ⁴²But those things that are reported of him, and of his uncleanness and impiety, are written in the Chronicles of the Kings. ⁴³And his son Jehoiakim reigned in his stead; for when he was made king he was eighteen years old; ⁴⁴and he reigned three months and ten days in Jerusalem; and did that which was evil before the LORD. ⁴⁵So after a year Nebuchadnezzar sent and caused him to be brought to Babylon with the holy vessels of the LORD, ⁴⁶and he made Zedekiah king of Judea and Jerusalem when he was twenty-one years old; and he reigned eleven years: ⁴⁷and he also did that which was evil in the sight of the LORD and did not care for the words that were spoken by the prophet Jeremiah from the mouth of the LORD. ⁴⁸And after King Nebuchadnezzar had made him to swear by the Name of the LORD, he renounced it, and rebelled; and hardening his neck and his heart, he transgressed the laws of the LORD, the God of Israel. ⁴⁹Moreover, the governors of the people and of the priests did many things wickedly, and surpassed all the pollutions of all nations, and defiled the temple of the LORD, which was sanctified in Jerusalem. ⁵⁰And the God of their fathers sent by His messenger to call them back, because He had compassion on them and on His dwelling place. ⁵¹But they mocked His messengers; and in the day when the LORD spoke [to them], they scoffed at His prophets, ⁵²so much so that He, being angry with His people for their great ungodliness, commanded to bring up the kings of the Chaldeans against them, ⁵³who killed their young men with the sword, around their holy temple, and spared neither young man nor maid, old man nor child; but He delivered all into their hands. ⁵⁴And they took all the holy vessels of the LORD, both great and small, with the vessels of the Ark of the LORD, and the king's treasures, and carried them away to Babylon. ⁵⁵And they burned the house of the LORD, and broke down the walls of Jerusalem, and burned the towers thereof with fire. ⁵⁶And as for her glorious things, they never ceased until they had brought them all to nothing; and the people that were not slain with the sword he carried to Babylon, ⁵⁷and they were servants to him and to his children, until the Persians reigned, to fulfill the word of the LORD by the mouth of Jeremiah: ⁵⁸"Until the land has enjoyed her Sabbaths, the whole time of her desolation she will keep Sabbath, to fulfill seventy years."

CHAPTER 2

¹In the first year of Cyrus king of the Persians, that the word of the LORD by the mouth of Jeremiah might be accomplished, ²the LORD stirred up the spirit of Cyrus king of the Persians, and he made proclamation through all his kingdom, and also by writing, ³saying, "Cyrus king of the Persians says: The Lord of Israel, the Most High LORD, has made me king of the whole world, ⁴and commanded me to build Him a house at Jerusalem that is in Judea. ⁵If, therefore, there are any of you that are of His people, let the LORD, even his Lord, be with him, and let him go up to Jerusalem that is in Judea, and build the house of the LORD of Israel: He is the LORD that dwells in Jerusalem. ⁶Of such therefore as dwell in various places, let those who are in his own place help each one with gold, and with silver, ⁷with gifts, also with horses and cattle, besides the other things which have been added by vow for the temple of the LORD which is in Jerusalem." ⁸Then the chief of the families of Judah and of the tribe of Benjamin stood up; the priests also, and the Levites, and all they whose spirit the LORD had stirred to go up, to build the house for the LORD which is in Jerusalem. ⁹And those who lived around them helped them in all things with silver and gold, with horses and cattle, and with very many gifts that were vowed of a great number whose minds were stirred up. ¹⁰King Cyrus also brought out the holy vessels of the LORD, which Nebuchadnezzar had carried away from Jerusalem, and had set up in his temple of idols. ¹¹Now when Cyrus king of the Persians had brought them out, he delivered them to his treasurer Mithradates, ¹²and they were delivered by him to Sanabassar the governor of Judea. ¹³And this was the number of them: one thousand golden cups, one thousand cups of silver, twenty-nine censers of silver, thirty vials of gold, and of silver—two thousand four hundred and ten, and other vessels—one thousand. ¹⁴So all the vessels of gold and of silver were brought up, even five thousand four hundred and sixty-nine, ¹⁵and were carried back by Sanabassar, together with them of the captivity, from Babylon to Jerusalem. ¹⁶But in the time of Artaxerxes king of the Persians, Belemus, and Mithradates, and Tabellius, and Rathumus, and Beeltethmus, and Samellius the scribe, with the others that were in commission with them, dwelling in Samaria and other places, wrote to him against those who lived in Judea and Jerusalem the following letter: ¹⁷"To King Artaxerxes our Lord, Your servants, Rathumus the recorder, and Samellius the scribe, and the rest of their council, and the judges that are in Coele-Syria and Phoenicia. ¹⁸Be it now known to our lord the king, that the Jews that have come up from you to us, having come to Jerusalem, are building that rebellious and wicked city, and are repairing its marketplaces and walls, and are laying the foundation of a temple. ¹⁹Now if this city is built and the walls [thereof] are finished, they will not only refuse to give tribute, but will even stand up against kings. ²⁰And forasmuch

as the things pertaining to the temple are now in hand, we think it suitable not to neglect such a matter, ²¹but to speak to our lord the king, to the intent that, if it be your pleasure, search may be made in the scrolls of your fathers: ²²and you will find in the chronicles what is written concerning these things, and will understand that that city was rebellious, troubling both kings and cities, ²³and that the Jews were rebellious, and always raised wars therein of former time; for this reason even this city was laid waste. ²⁴For that reason, now we declare to you, O lord the king, that if this city is built again, and the walls thereof set up anew, you will from now on have no passage into Coele-Syria and Phoenicia." ²⁵Then the king wrote back again to Rathumus the recorder, and Beeltethmus, and Samellius the scribe, and to the rest that were in commission, and lived in Samaria, and Syria, and Phoenicia, after this manner: ²⁶"I have read the letter which you have sent to me; therefore, I commanded to make search, and it has been found that that city of former time has made insurrection against kings; ²⁷and the men were given to rebellion and war therein; and that fierce and mighty kings were in Jerusalem, who reigned and exacted tribute in Coele-Syria and Phoenicia. ²⁸Now therefore, I have commanded to hinder those men from building the city, and heed to be taken that there is nothing done contrary to this [order]; ²⁹and that those wicked doings proceed no further to the annoyance of kings. ³⁰Then King Artaxerxes, his letters being read, Rathumus, and Samellius the scribe, and the rest that were in commission with them, removing in haste to Jerusalem with horsemen and a multitude of people in battle array, began to hinder the builders; and the building of the temple in Jerusalem ceased until the second year of the reign of Darius king of the Persians.

CHAPTER 3

¹Now King Darius made a great feast to all his subjects, and to all that were born in his house, and to all the princes of Media and of Persia, ²and to all the local governors, and captains, and governors that were under him, from India to Ethiopia, in the one hundred [and] twenty-seven provinces. ³And when they had eaten and drunken, and being satisfied were gone home, then Darius the king went into his bedchamber, and slept, and awoke out of his sleep. ⁴Then the three young men of the bodyguard, that kept the king's person, spoke to one another: ⁵"Let each of us say one thing which will be strongest; and he whose sentence will seem wiser than the others, to him Darius the king will give great gifts, and great honors in token of victory: ⁶as, to be clothed in purple, to drink in gold, and to sleep on gold, and a chariot with bridles of gold, and a turban of fine linen, and a chain around his neck; ⁷and he will sit next to Darius because of his wisdom, and will be called cousin of Darius." ⁸And then they each wrote his sentence, and set to their seals, and laid [the writing] under [the] pillow of King Darius, ⁹and said, "When the king is risen, some will give him the writing; and of whose side the king and the three princes of Persia will judge that his sentence is the wisest, to him will the victory be given, as it is written." ¹⁰The first wrote, "Wine is the strongest." ¹¹The second wrote, "The king is strongest." ¹²The third wrote, "Women are strongest, but above all things Truth bears away the victory." ¹³Now when the king was risen up, they took the writing, and gave it to him, and so he read it: ¹⁴and sending out he called all the princes of Persia and of Media, and the local governors, and the captains, and the governors, and the chief officers, ¹⁵and he sat down in the royal seat of judgment, and the writing was read before them. ¹⁶And he said, "Call the young men, and they will explain their own sentences." So they were called, and came in. ¹⁷And they said to them, "Declare to us your mind concerning the things you have written." Then began the first, who had spoken of the strength of wine, ¹⁸and said, "O lords, how exceedingly strong is wine! It causes all men to err that drink it: ¹⁹it makes the mind of the king and of the fatherless child to be all one; of the bondman and of the freeman, of the poor man and of the rich; ²⁰it also turns every thought into cheer and mirth, so that a man remembers neither sorrow nor debt; ²¹and it makes every heart rich, so that a man remembers neither king nor local governor; and it makes all things to speak by talents; ²²and when they are in their cups, they forget their love both to friends and relatives, and a little after draw their swords, ²³but when they awake from their wine, they do not remember what they have done. ²⁴O lords, is not wine the strongest, seeing that it enforces to do so?" And when he had so spoken, he held his peace.

CHAPTER 4

¹Then the second, that had spoken of the strength of the king, began to say, ²"O lords, do men not excel in strength, that bear rule over the sea and land, and all things in them? ³But yet is the king stronger: and he is their lord and has dominion over them; and in whatever he commands them they obey him. ⁴If he commands them to make war—the one against the other—they do it; and if he sends them out against the enemies, they go, and overcome mountains, walls, and towers. ⁵They kill and are slain, and [still] do not transgress the king's command: if they get the victory, they bring everything to the king, as well as the plunder, as everything else. ⁶Likewise for those that are not soldiers, and have nothing to do with wars, but are farming, when they have again reaped that which they had sown, they bring it to the king, and compel one another to pay tribute to the king. ⁷And he is but one man: if he commands to kill, they kill; if he commands to spare, they spare; ⁸if he commands to strike, they strike; if he commands to make desolate, they make desolate; if he commands to build, they build; ⁹if he commands to cut down, they cut down; if he commands to plant, they plant. ¹⁰So all his people and his armies obey him: furthermore, he lies down, he eats and drinks, and takes his rest, ¹¹and these keep watch around him, neither may anyone depart and do his own business, neither do they disobey him in [anything]. ¹²O lords, how should the king not be strongest, seeing that in such sort he is obeyed? And he held his peace. ¹³Then the third, who had spoken of women and of truth (this was Zerubbabel), began to speak. ¹⁴"O lords, is not the king great, and men are many, and wine is strong? Who is it then that rules them, or has the lordship over them? Are they not women? ¹⁵Women have borne the king and all the people that bear rule by sea and land. ¹⁶Even from them they came: and they nourished them up that planted the vineyards, from where the wine comes. ¹⁷These also make garments for men; these bring glory to men; and without women men cannot be. ¹⁸Yes, and if men have gathered together gold, and silver, and any other attractive thing, and see a woman which is attractive in favor and beauty, ¹⁹they let all those things go, and stare after her, and even with open mouth fix their eyes fast on her; and they have all [the] more desire for her than for gold or silver, or any other attractive thing. ²⁰A man leaves his own father that brought him up, and his own country, and joins with his wife. ²¹And with his wife he ends his days, and remembers neither father, nor mother, nor country. ²²By this also you must know that women have dominion over you: do you not labor and toil, and give and bring all to women? ²³Yes, a man takes his sword, and goes out to make excursions, and to rob and to steal, and to sail on the sea and on rivers; ²⁴and looks on a lion and walks in the darkness; and when he has stolen, plundered, and robbed, he brings it to his love. ²⁵For that reason, a man loves his wife better than father or mother. ²⁶Yes, there are many that have run out of their wits for women and become bondmen for their sakes. ²⁷Many have also perished, have stumbled, and sinned, for women. ²⁸And now do you not believe me? Is the king not great in his power? Do all regions not fear to touch him? ²⁹Yet I saw him and the king's concubine Apame, the daughter of the illustrious Barticus, sitting at the right hand of the king, ³⁰and taking the crown from the king's head, and setting it on her own head; yes, she struck the king with her left hand: ³¹and immediately the king stared and gazed on her with open mouth. If she laughed on him, he also laughed, but if she took any displeasure at him, he was glad to flatter, that she might be reconciled to him again. ³²O lords, how can it be but women should be strong, seeing they do so?" ³³Then the king and the nobles looked on one another, so he began to speak concerning truth. ³⁴"O lords, are women not strong? Great is the earth, high is the Heaven, swift is the sun in his course, for he encircles the heavens around, and fetches his course again to his own place in one day. ³⁵Is He not great that makes these things? Therefore, great is truth, and stronger than all things. ³⁶All the earth calls on truth, and the Heaven blesses her; all works shake and tremble, but with her is no

unrighteous thing. ³⁷Wine is unrighteous, the king is unrighteous, women are unrighteous, all the children of men are unrighteous, and all such works of theirs are unrighteous; and there is no truth in them; in their unrighteousness also, they will perish. ³⁸But truth remains and is strong forever; she lives and conquers forevermore. ³⁹With her there is no accepting of persons or rewards; but she does the things that are just, and [refrains] from all unrighteous and wicked things; and all men do well like of her works. ⁴⁰Neither is any unrighteousness in her judgment; and she is the strength, and the kingdom, and the power, and the majesty, of all ages. Blessed is the God of truth." ⁴¹And with that he held his tongue. And all the people then shouted, and said, "Great is truth, and strong above all things." ⁴²Then the king said to him, "Ask what you will more than is appointed in writing, and we will give it to you, inasmuch as you are found wisest; and you will sit next to me, and will be called my cousin." ⁴³Then he said to the king, "Remember your vow, which you vowed to build Jerusalem, in the day when you came to your kingdom, ⁴⁴and to send away all the vessels that were taken out of Jerusalem, which Cyrus set apart, when he vowed to destroy Babylon, and vowed to send them there again. ⁴⁵You also vowed to build up the temple, which the Edomites burned when Judea was made desolate by the Chaldeans. ⁴⁶And now, O lord the king, this is that which I require, and which I desire of you, and this is the princely generosity that will proceed from you: I pray therefore that you make good the vow, the performance of which you have vowed to the King of Heaven with your own mouth." ⁴⁷Then Darius the king stood up, and kissed him, and wrote letters for him to all the treasurers, and governors, and captains, and local governors, that they should safely bring on their way both him, and all those that should go up with him to build Jerusalem. ⁴⁸He also wrote letters to all the governors that were in Coele-Syria and Phoenicia, and to them in Libanus, that they should bring cedar wood from Libanus to Jerusalem, and that they should build the city with him. ⁴⁹Moreover, he wrote for all the Jews that should go out of his realm up into Jewry, concerning their freedom, that no officer, no governor, no local governor, nor treasurer, should forcibly enter into their doors; ⁵⁰and that all the country which they occupied should be free to them without tribute; and that the Edomites should give over the villages of the Jews which they then held; ⁵¹and that there should be yearly given twenty talents to the building of the temple, until the time that it were built; ⁵²and ten more talents yearly, for burnt-offerings to be presented on the altar every day, as they had a command to offer seventeen: ⁵³and that all those who should come from Babylonia to build the city should have their freedom—they as well as their posterity, and all the priests that came. ⁵⁴He also wrote [to give them] their charges, and the priests' vestments wherein they minister; ⁵⁵and for the Levites he wrote that their charges should be given them until the day that the house were finished, and Jerusalem built up. ⁵⁶And he commanded to give to all that kept the city lands and wages. ⁵⁷He also sent away all the vessels from Babylon that Cyrus had set apart; and all that Cyrus had given in command, he also charged to be done, and sent to Jerusalem. ⁵⁸Now when this young man had gone out, he lifted up his face to Heaven toward Jerusalem, and praised the King of Heaven, ⁵⁹and said, "From You comes victory, from You comes wisdom, and Yours is the glory, and I am Your servant. ⁶⁰Blessed are You, who have given me wisdom: and to You I give thanks, O LORD of our fathers." ⁶¹And so he took the letters, and went out, and came to Babylon, and told it [to] all his countrymen. ⁶²And they praised the God of their fathers, because He had given them freedom and liberty ⁶³to go up, and to build Jerusalem, and the temple which is called by His Name: and they feasted with instruments of music and gladness [for] seven days.

CHAPTER 5

¹After this the chiefs of fathers' houses were chosen to go up according to their tribes, with their wives, and sons, and daughters, with their menservants and maidservants, and their cattle. ²And Darius sent one thousand horsemen with them, until they had brought them back to Jerusalem safely, and with musical instruments, tabrets, and flutes. ³And all their countrymen played, and he made them go up together with them. ⁴And these are the names of the men which went up, according to their families among their tribes, after their several divisions. ⁵The priests, the sons of Phinehas, the sons of Aaron: Jesus the son of Josedek, the son of Saraias, and Jehoiakim the son of Zerubbabel, the son of Salathiel, of the house of David, of the lineage of Phares, of the tribe of Judah; ⁶who spoke wise sentences before Darius the king of Persia in the second year of his reign, in the month Nisan, which is the first month. ⁷And these are they of Jewry that came up from the captivity, where they lived as strangers, whom Nebuchadnezzar the king of Babylon had carried away to Babylon. ⁸And they returned to Jerusalem, and to the other parts of Jewry, every man to his own city, who came with Zerubbabel, with Jesus, Nehemiah, and Zerahiah, Resaias, Eneneus, Mardocheus, Beelsarus, Aspharsus, Reelias, Roimus, and Baana, their leaders. ⁹The number of them of the nation, and their leaders: the sons of Phoros, two thousand one hundred and seventy-two; the sons of Saphat, four hundred and seventy-two; ¹⁰the sons of Ares, seven hundred and fifty-six; ¹¹the sons of Phaath-Moab, of the sons of Jesus and Joab, two thousand eight hundred and twelve; ¹²the sons of Elam, one thousand two hundred and fifty-four; the sons of Zathui, nine hundred and forty-five; the sons of Chorbe, seven hundred and five; the sons of Bani, six hundred and forty-eight; ¹³the sons of Bebai, six hundred and twenty-three; the sons of Astad, one thousand three hundred and twenty-two; ¹⁴the sons of Adonikam, six hundred and sixty-seven; the sons of Bagoi, two thousand and sixty-six; the sons of Adinu, four hundred and fifty-four; ¹⁵the sons of Ater, of Ezekias, ninety-two; the sons of Kilan and Azetas, sixty-seven; the sons of Azaru, four hundred and thirty-two; ¹⁶the sons of Annis, one hundred and one; the sons of Arom, of the sons of Bassai, three hundred and twenty-three; the sons of Arsiphurith, one hundred and twelve; ¹⁷the sons of Baiterus, three thousand and five; the sons of Bethlomon, one hundred and twenty-three; ¹⁸they of Netophas, fifty-five; they of Anathoth, one hundred and fifty-eight; they of Bethasmoth, forty-two; ¹⁹they of Kariathiarius, twenty-five; they of Caphira and Beroth, seven hundred and forty-three; ²⁰the Chadiasai and Ammidioi, four hundred and twenty-two; they of Kirama and Gabbe, six hundred and twenty-one; ²¹they of Macalon, one hundred and twenty-two; they of Betolion, fifty-two; the sons of Niphis, one hundred and fifty-six; ²²the sons of Calamolalus and Onus, seven hundred and twenty-five; the sons of Jerechu, three hundred and forty-five; ²³the sons of Sanaas, three thousand three hundred and thirty. ²⁴The priests: the sons of Jeddu, the son of Jesus, among the sons of Sanasib, nine hundred and seventy-two; the sons of Emmeruth, one thousand and fifty-two; ²⁵the sons of Phassurus, one thousand two hundred and forty-seven; the sons of Charme, one thousand and seventeen. ²⁶The Levites: the sons of Jesus, and Kadmiel, and Bannas, and Sudias, seventy-four. ²⁷The holy singers: the sons of Asaph, one hundred and twenty-eight. ²⁸The gatekeepers: the sons of Salum, the sons of Atar, the sons of Tolman, the sons of Dacubi, the sons of Ateta, the sons of Sabi, in all one hundred and thirty-nine. ²⁹The temple servants: the sons of Esau, the sons of Asipha, the sons of Tabaoth, the sons of Keras, the sons of Sua, the sons of Phaleas, the sons of Labana, the sons of Aggaba. ³⁰The sons of Acud, the sons of Uta, the sons of Ketab, the sons of Accaba, the sons of Subai, the sons of Anan, the sons of Cathua, the sons of Geddur, ³¹the sons of Jairus, the sons of Daisan, the sons of Noeba, the sons of Chaseba, the sons of Gazera, the sons of Ozias, the sons of Phinoe, the sons of Asara, the sons of Basthai, the sons of Asana, the sons of Maani, the sons of Naphisi, the sons of Acub, the sons of Achipha, the sons of Asur, the sons of Pharakim, the sons of Basaloth, ³²the sons of Meedda, the sons of Cutha, the sons of Charea, the sons of Barchus, the sons of Serar, the sons of Thomei, the sons of Nasi, the sons of Atipha. ³³The sons of the servants of Solomon: the sons of Assaphioth, the sons of Pharida, the sons of Jeeli, the sons of Lozon, the sons of Isdael, the sons of Saphuthi, ³⁴the sons of Agia, the sons of Phacareth, the sons of Sabie, the sons of Sarothie, the sons of Masias, the sons of Gas, the sons of Addus, the sons of Subas, the sons of Apherra, the sons of Barodis, the sons of Saphat, the sons of Allon. ³⁵All the temple-servants, and the sons of the servants of Solomon, were three hundred and seventy-

two. ³⁶These came up from Thermeleth, and Thelersas, Charaathalan leading them, and Allar; ³⁷and they could not show their families, nor their stock, how they were of Israel: the sons of Dalan the son of Ban, the sons of Nekodan, six hundred and fifty-two. ³⁸And of the priests, those who usurped the office of the priesthood and were not found: the sons of Obdia, the sons of Akkos, the sons of Jaddus, who married Augia one of the daughters of Zorzelleus, and was called after his name. ³⁹And when the description of the relatives of these men was sought in the register, and was not found, they were removed from executing the office of the priesthood: ⁴⁰for Nehemiah and Attharias said to them that they should not be partakers of the holy things, until there arose up a chief priest wearing Lights and Perfections. ⁴¹So all those of Israel, from twelve years old [and upward], besides menservants and maidservants, were in [number forty] and two thousand three hundred and sixty. ⁴²Their menservants and handmaids were seven thousand three hundred and thirty-seven; the minstrels and singers, two hundred and forty-five; ⁴³four hundred and thirty-five camels, seven thousand and thirty-six horses, two hundred and forty-five mules, five thousand five hundred and twenty-five beasts of burden. ⁴⁴And certain of the chief men of their families, when they came to the temple of God that is in Jerusalem, vowed to set up the house again in its own place according to their ability, ⁴⁵and to give into the holy treasury of the works one thousand pounds of gold, five thousand of silver, and one hundred priestly vestments. ⁴⁶And the priests, and the Levites, and those who were of the people lived in Jerusalem and the country; the holy singers also, and the gatekeepers, and all Israel in their villages. ⁴⁷But when the seventh month was at hand, and when the sons of Israel were each in his own place, they all came together with one consent into the broad place before the first porch which is toward the east. ⁴⁸Then Jesus the son of Josedek arose, and his relatives the priests, and Zerubbabel the son of Salathiel, and his relatives, and they made the altar of the God of Israel ready, ⁴⁹to offer burned sacrifices on it, according as it is expressly commanded in the Scroll of Moses the man of God. ⁵⁰And certain [ones] were gathered to them out of the other nations of the land, and they erected the altar on its own place, because all the nations of the land were at enmity with them and oppressed them; and they offered sacrifices according to the time and burnt-offerings to the LORD, both morning and evening. ⁵¹They also held the Celebration of Shelters, as it is commanded in the Law, and [offered] sacrifices daily, as was suitable; ⁵²and after that, the continual oblations, and the sacrifices of the Sabbaths, and of the new moons, and of all the consecrated feasts. ⁵³And all those who had made any vow to God began to offer sacrifices to God from the new moon of the seventh month, although the temple of God was not yet built. ⁵⁴And they gave money to the masons and carpenters, and meat and drink, ⁵⁵and carts to them of Sidon and Tyre, that they should bring cedar trees from Libanus, and transport them in floats to the haven of Joppa, according to the command which was written for them by Cyrus king of the Persians. ⁵⁶And in the second year after his coming to the temple of God at Jerusalem, in the second month, Zerubbabel the son of Salathiel, and Jesus the son of Josedek, and their relatives, and the Levitical priests, and all those who had come to Jerusalem out of the captivity commenced: ⁵⁷and they laid the foundation of the temple of God on the new moon of the second month, in the second year after they had come to Jewry and Jerusalem. ⁵⁸And they appointed the Levites from twenty years old over the works of the LORD. Then Jesus arose, and his sons and relatives, and his brother Kadmiel, and the sons of Jesus, Emadabun, and the sons of Joda the son of Iliadun, and their sons and relatives, all the Levites, started the undertaking with one accord, laboring to advance the works in the house of God. So the builders built the temple of the LORD. ⁵⁹And the priests stood arrayed in their vestments with musical instruments and trumpets, and the Levites, the sons of Asaph, with their cymbals, ⁶⁰singing songs of thanksgiving, and praising the LORD, after the order of David king of Israel. ⁶¹And they sang aloud, praising the LORD in songs of thanksgiving, because His goodness and His glory are forever in all Israel. ⁶²And all the people sounded trumpets, and shouted with a loud voice, singing songs of thanksgiving to the LORD for the rearing up of the house of the LORD. ⁶³Also of the Levitical priests, and of the heads of their families, the ancients who had seen the former house, came to the building of this with lamentation and great weeping. ⁶⁴But many with trumpets and joy [shouted] with a loud voice, ⁶⁵insomuch that the people did not hear the trumpets for the weeping of the people; for the multitude sounded marvelously, so that it was heard far off. ⁶⁶For that reason, when the enemies of the tribe of Judah and Benjamin heard it, they came to know what that noise of trumpets should mean. ⁶⁷And they perceived that those who were of the captivity built the temple to the LORD, the God of Israel. ⁶⁸So they went to Zerubbabel and Jesus, and to the chief men of the families, and said to them, "We will build together with you. ⁶⁹For we likewise, as you, obey your Lord, and sacrifice to Him from the days of Asbasareth the king of the Assyrians, who brought us here." ⁷⁰Then Zerubbabel, and Jesus, and the chief men of the families of Israel said to them, "It is not for you to build the house to the LORD our God. ⁷¹We ourselves alone will build to the LORD of Israel, according as Cyrus the king of the Persians has commanded us." ⁷²But the heathen of the land lying heavy on the inhabitants of Judea, and holding them constricted, hindered their building; ⁷³and by their secret plots, and popular persuasions, and commotions, hindered the finishing of the building all the time that King Cyrus lived; so they were hindered from building for the space of two years, until the reign of Darius.

CHAPTER 6

¹Now in the second year of the reign of Darius, Haggai and Zechariah, the [grand]son of Iddo, the prophets, prophesied to the Jews in Jewry and Jerusalem; in the Name of the LORD, the God of Israel, [they prophesied] to them. ²Then Zerubbabel the son of Salathiel and Jesus the son of Josedek stood up and began to build the house of the LORD at Jerusalem, the prophets of the LORD being with them, and helping them. ³At the same time, Sisinnes the governor of Syria and Phoenicia came to them, with Sathrabuzanes and his companions, and said to them, ⁴"By whose appointment do you build this house and this roof, and perform all the other things? And who are the builders that perform these things?" ⁵Nevertheless, the elders of the Jews obtained favor, because the LORD had visited the captivity; ⁶and they were not hindered from building, until such time as communication was made to Darius concerning them, and his answer signified. ⁷The copy of the letter which Sisinnes, governor of Syria and Phoenicia, and Sathrabuzanes, with their companions, the rulers in Syria and Phoenicia, wrote and sent to Darius: ⁸"To King Darius, greetings: Let all things be known to our lord the king, that having come into the country of Judea, and having entered into the city of Jerusalem, we found in the city of Jerusalem the elders of the Jews that were of the captivity ⁹building a house to the LORD, great [and] new, of hewn and costly stones, with timber laid in the walls. ¹⁰And those works are done with great speed, and the work goes on prosperously in their hands, and it is accomplished with all glory and diligence. ¹¹Then we asked these elders, saying, By whose command do you build this house, and lay the foundations of these works? ¹²Therefore, to the intent that we might give knowledge to you by writing who were the chief doers, we questioned them, and we required of them the names in writing of their principal men. ¹³So they gave us this answer: We are the servants of the LORD which made the heavens and earth. ¹⁴And as for this house, it was built many years ago by a great and mighty king of Israel and was completed. ¹⁵But when our fathers sinned against the LORD of Israel, who is in Heaven, and provoked Him to wrath, He gave them over into the hands of Nebuchadnezzar king of Babylon, king of the Chaldeans; ¹⁶and they pulled down the house, and burned it, and carried the people away [as] captives to Babylon. ¹⁷But in the first year that Cyrus reigned over the country of Babylon, King Cyrus wrote [an edict] to build up this house. ¹⁸And the holy vessels of gold and of silver, that Nebuchadnezzar had carried away out of the house at Jerusalem, and had set up in his own temple, those Cyrus the king brought out again out of the temple in Babylonia, and they were delivered to Zerubbabel and to Sanabassarus the governor, ¹⁹with command that he should carry away all these vessels and put them in the temple at Jerusalem; and that the temple of the LORD should be built in its

place. ²⁰Then Sanabassarus, having come here, laid the foundations of the house of the LORD which is in Jerusalem; and from that time to this being still a building, it is not yet fully ended. ²¹Now therefore, if it seems good, O king, let search be made among the royal archives of our lord the king that are in Babylon; ²²and if it is found that the building of the house of the LORD which is in Jerusalem has been done with the consent of King Cyrus, and it seems good to our lord the king, let him signify to us thereof." ²³Then King Darius commanded to seek among the archives that were laid up at Babylon: and so at Ekbatana the palace, which is in the country of Media, there was found a scroll where these things were recorded: ²⁴"In the first year of the reign of Cyrus, King Cyrus commanded to build up the house of the LORD which is in Jerusalem, where they sacrifice with continual fire: ²⁵whose height will be sixty cubits, and the breadth sixty cubits, with three rows of hewn stones, and one row of new wood of that country; and the expenses thereof to be given out of the house of King Cyrus; ²⁶and that the holy vessels of the house of the LORD, both gold and silver, that Nebuchadnezzar took out of the house at Jerusalem, and carried away to Babylon, should be restored to the house at Jerusalem, and be set in the place where they were before." ²⁷And also, he commanded that Sisinnes the governor of Syria and Phoenicia, and Sathrabuzanes, and their companions, and those which were appointed rulers in Syria and Phoenicia, should be careful not to meddle with the place, but permit Zerubbabel, the servant of the LORD, and governor of Judea, and the elders of the Jews, to build that house of the LORD in its place. ²⁸"And I also command to have it built up whole again; and that they look diligently to help those that be of the captivity of Judea, until the house of the LORD is finished; ²⁹and that out of the tribute of Coele-Syria and Phoenicia a portion be carefully given these men for the sacrifices of the LORD, [that is,] to Zerubbabel the governor, for bullocks, and rams, and lambs; ³⁰and also corn, salt, wine, and oil—and that continually every year without further question, according as the priests that are in Jerusalem will signify to be daily spent, ³¹that drink offerings may be made to the Most High God for the king and for his children, and that they may pray for their lives. ³²And that command [will] be given that whoever will transgress, yes, or neglect anything written here, out of his own [house] will a tree be taken, and he [will] be hanged on it, and all his goods seized for the king. ³³May the LORD therefore, whose Name is there called on, utterly destroy every king and nation that will stretch out his hand to hinder or damage that house of the LORD in Jerusalem. ³⁴I, Darius the king, have ordained that according to these things it [will] be done with diligence."

CHAPTER 7

¹Then Sisinnes the governor of Coele-Syria and Phoenicia, and Sathrabuzanes, with their companions, following the commands of King Darius, ²very carefully oversaw the holy works, assisting the elders of the Jews and rulers of the temple. ³And so the holy works prospered, while Haggai and Zechariah the prophets prophesied. ⁴And they finished these things by the command of the LORD, the God of Israel, and with the consent of Cyrus, Darius, and Artaxerxes, kings of the Persians. ⁵[And so] the house was finished by the twenty-third [[or third]] day of the month Adar, in the sixth year of King Darius. ⁶And the sons of Israel, the priests, and the Levites, and the others that were of the captivity, that were added [to them], did according to the things [written] in the Scroll of Moses. ⁷And for the dedication of the temple of the LORD they offered one hundred bullocks, two hundred rams, [and] four hundred lambs; ⁸[and also] twelve male goats for the sin of all Israel, according to the number of the twelve princes of the tribes of Israel. ⁹The priests and the Levites also stood arrayed in their vestments, according to their relatives, for the services of the LORD, the God of Israel, according to the Scroll of Moses: and the gatekeepers at every gate. ¹⁰And the sons of Israel that came out of the captivity held the Passover [on] the fourteenth day of the first month, when the priests and the Levites were sanctified together, ¹¹and all those who were of the captivity; for they were sanctified. For the Levites were all sanctified together, ¹²and they offered the Passover for all those of the captivity, and for their relatives the priests, and for themselves. ¹³And the sons of Israel that came out of the captivity ate, even all those who had separated themselves from the abominations of the heathen of the land and sought the LORD. ¹⁴And they kept the Celebration of Unleavened Bread seven days, making merry before the LORD, ¹⁵for that He had turned the counsel of the king of Assyria toward them, to strengthen their hands in the works of the LORD, the God of Israel.

CHAPTER 8

¹And after these things, when Artaxerxes the king of the Persians reigned, Ezra came, the son of Seraiah, the son of Azariah, the son of Hilkiah, the son of Salem, ²the son of Zadok, the son of Ahitob, the son of Amariah, the son of Ozias, the son of Memeroth, the son of Zerahiah, the son of Savias, the son of Boccas, the son of Abisne, the son of Phinehas, the son of Eleazar, the son of Aaron, the chief priest. ³This Ezra went up from Babylon, as being a ready scribe in the Law of Moses that was given by the God of Israel. ⁴And the king honored him, for he found grace in his sight in all his requests. ⁵There also went up with him certain of the sons of Israel, and of the priests, and Levites, and holy singers, and gatekeepers, and temple servants, to Jerusalem, ⁶in the seventh year of the reign of Artaxerxes, in the fifth month, this was the king's seventh year; for they went from Babylon on the new moon of the first month, and came to Jerusalem, according to the prosperous journey which the LORD gave them for His sake. ⁷For Ezra had very great skill, so that he omitted nothing of the law and commands of the LORD but taught all Israel the ordinances and judgments. ⁸Now the commission, which was written from Artaxerxes the king, came to Ezra the priest and reader of the Law of the LORD, of which this that follows is a copy: ⁹"King Artaxerxes to Ezra the priest and reader of the Law of the LORD, greetings: ¹⁰Having determined to deal graciously, I have given order that such of the nation of the Jews, and of the priests and Levites, and of those within our realm, as are willing and desirous, should go with you to Jerusalem. ¹¹Therefore, as many as have a mind [to this purpose], let them depart with you, as it has seemed good both to me and my seven friends the counselors, ¹²that they may look to the affairs of Judea and Jerusalem, agreeably to that which is in the Law of the LORD, ¹³and carry the gifts to the LORD of Israel to Jerusalem, which my friends and I have vowed; and that all the gold and silver that can be found in the country of Babylonia for the LORD in Jerusalem, ¹⁴with that also which is given of the people for the temple of the LORD their God that is at Jerusalem, be collected: even the gold and silver for bullocks, rams, and lambs, and things pertaining to that, ¹⁵to the end that they may offer sacrifices to the LORD on the altar of the LORD their God, which is in Jerusalem— ¹⁶and whatever you and your relatives are inclined to do with gold and silver, that perform, according to the will of your God. ¹⁷And the holy vessels of the LORD, which are given to you for the use of the temple of your God, which is in Jerusalem, ¹⁸and anything else you will remember for the use of the temple of your God, you will give it out of the king's treasury. ¹⁹And I, King Artaxerxes, have also commanded the keepers of the treasures in Syria and Phoenicia, that whatever Ezra the priest and reader of the Law of the Most High God will send for, they should give it to him with all diligence, ²⁰to the sum of one hundred talents of silver, likewise also of wheat even to one hundred measures, and one hundred firkins of wine, and salt in abundance. ²¹Let all things be diligently performed after the Law of God—to the Most High God—that wrath does not come on the kingdom of the king and his sons. ²²I also command you that no tax, nor any other imposition, be laid on any of the priests, or Levites, or holy singers, or gatekeepers, or temple servants, or any that have employment in this temple, and that no man have authority to impose anything on them. ²³And you, Ezra, according to the wisdom of God, ordain judges and justices, that they may judge in all Syria and Phoenicia all those that know the law of your God; and you will teach those that do not know it. ²⁴And whoever will transgress the law of your God, and of the king, will be punished diligently, whether it be by death, or other punishment, by penalty of money, or by imprisonment." ²⁵Then Ezra the scribe said, "Blessed is the only Lord, the God of my fathers, who has put these things into the heart of the king, to glorify His house that is in Jerusalem, ²⁶and has honored

me in the sight of the king, and his counselors, and all his friends and nobles. ²⁷Therefore, I was encouraged by the help of the LORD my God and gathered together out of Israel men to go up with me. ²⁸And these are the chiefs, according to their families and the several divisions thereof, that went up with me from Babylon in the reign of King Artaxerxes: ²⁹of the sons of Phinehas, Gerson; of the sons of Ithamar, Gamael; of the sons of David, Attus the son of Sechenias; ³⁰of the sons of Phoros, Zechariah, and with him were counted one hundred and fifty men; ³¹of the sons of Phaath-Moab, Eliehoenai the son of Zerahiah, and with him two hundred men; ³²of the sons of Zathoes, Sechenias the son of Jezelus, and with him three hundred men; of the sons of Adin, Obeth the son of Jonathan, and with him two hundred and fifty men; ³³of the sons of Elam, Jesias son of Gotholia, and with him seventy men; ³⁴of the sons of Saphatias, Zerahiah son of Michael, and with him seventy men; ³⁵of the sons of Joab, Obadiah son of Jehiel, and with him two hundred and twelve men; ³⁶of the sons of Banias, Salimoth son of Josaphias, and with him one hundred and sixty men; ³⁷of the sons of Babi, Zechariah son of Bebai, and with him twenty-eight men; ³⁸of the sons of Azgad, Joannes son of Hakkatan, and with him one hundred and ten men; ³⁹of the sons of Adonikam, the last, and these are the names of them—Eliphalat, Jeuel, and Shemaiah, and with them seventy men; ⁴⁰of the sons of Bigvai, Uthi the son of Istalcurus, and with him seventy men. ⁴¹And I gathered them together to the river called Theras; and there we pitched our tents three days, and I surveyed them. ⁴²But when I had found there none of the priests and Levites, ⁴³then I sent to Eleazar, and Iduel, and Maasmas, ⁴⁴and Elnathan, and Samaias, and [Jarib], Nathan, Ennatan, Zechariah, and Mosollamus, principal men and men of understanding. ⁴⁵And I commanded those who should go to [Iddo], Loddeus the captain, who was in the place of [Casiphia], the treasury; ⁴⁶and I commanded them that they should speak to Loddeus, and to his relatives, and to the treasurers in that place, to send us such men as might execute the priests' office in the house of our Lord. ⁴⁷And by the mighty hand of our Lord they brought to us men of understanding of the sons of Mooli the son of Levi, the son of Israel, Asebebias, and his sons, and his relatives, who were eighteen, ⁴⁸and Asebias, and Annuus, and Osaias his brother, of the sons of Chanuneus, and their sons were twenty men; ⁴⁹and of the temple-servants whom David and the principal men had appointed for the servants of the Levites, two hundred and twenty temple-servants, the catalogue of all their names was shown. ⁵⁰And there I vowed a fast for the young men before our Lord, to desire of Him a prosperous journey both for us and for our children, and [for the] cattle that were with us: ⁵¹for I was ashamed to ask of the king footmen, and horsemen, and conduct for protection against our adversaries. ⁵²For we had said to the king that the power of our Lord would be with those who seek Him, to support them in all ways. ⁵³And again we implored our Lord as touching these things and found Him favorable [to us]. ⁵⁴Then I separated twelve men of the chiefs of the priests: Eserebias, and Assamias, and ten men of their relatives with them; ⁵⁵and I weighed them the silver, and the gold, and the holy vessels of the house of our Lord, which the king, and his counselors, and the nobles, and all Israel, had given. ⁵⁶And when I had weighed it, I delivered to them six hundred and fifty talents of silver, and silver vessels of one hundred talents, and one hundred talents of gold, ⁵⁷and twenty golden vessels, and twelve vessels of brass, even of fine brass, glittering like gold. ⁵⁸And I said to them, "You are holy to the LORD and the vessels are holy—both—and the gold and the silver are a vow to the LORD, the Lord of our fathers. ⁵⁹Watch and keep them until you deliver them to the chiefs of the priests and Levites, and to the principal men of the families of Israel, in Jerusalem, in the chambers of the house of our Lord." ⁶⁰So the priests and the Levites, who received the silver, and the gold, and the vessels which were in Jerusalem, brought them into the temple of the LORD. ⁶¹And from the River Theras we departed [on] the twelfth day of the first month, until we came to Jerusalem, by the mighty hand of our Lord which was on us: and the LORD delivered us from [assault by] the way, from every enemy, and so we came to Jerusalem. ⁶²And when we had been there three days, the silver and gold was weighed and delivered in the house of our Lord on the fourth day to Marmoth the priest, the son of Urias. ⁶³And with him was Eleazar the son of Phinehas, and with them were Josabdus the son of Jesus and Moeth the son of Sabannus, the Levites: all [was delivered to them] by number and weight. ⁶⁴And all the weight of them was written up the same hour. ⁶⁵Moreover, those who had come out of the captivity offered sacrifices to the LORD, the God of Israel, even twelve bullocks for all Israel, [and] ninety-six rams, ⁶⁶seventy-two lambs, goats for a peace offering—twelve; all of them a sacrifice to the LORD. ⁶⁷And they delivered the king's commands to the king's stewards, and to the governors of Coele-Syria and Phoenicia; and they honored the people and the temple of the LORD. ⁶⁸Now when these things were done, the principal men came to me, and said, ⁶⁹"The nation of Israel, and the princes, and the priests, and the Levites, have not put away the strange people of the land, nor the uncleanness of the nations—of the Canaanites, Hittites, Perizzites, Jebusites, and the Moabites, Egyptians, and Edomites. ⁷⁰For both they and their sons have married with their daughters, and the holy seed is mixed with the strange people of the land; and from the beginning of this matter the rulers and the nobles have been partakers of this iniquity." ⁷¹And as soon as I had heard these things, I tore my clothes and my holy garment, and plucked the hair from off my head and beard, and sat myself down sad and full of heaviness. ⁷²So all those who were moved at the word of the LORD, the God of Israel, assembled to me, while I mourned for the iniquity, but I sat still full of heaviness until the evening sacrifice. ⁷³Then rising up from the fast with my clothes and my holy garment torn, and bowing my knees, and stretching out my hands to the LORD, ⁷⁴I said, "O LORD, I am ashamed and confounded before Your face, ⁷⁵for our sins are multiplied above our heads, and our errors have reached up to Heaven, ⁷⁶ever since the time of our fathers; and we are in great sin, even to this day. ⁷⁷And for our sins and our fathers' we with our relatives, and our kings, and our priests were given up to the kings of the earth, to the sword, and to captivity, and for a prey with shame, to this day. ⁷⁸And now in some measure mercy has been shown to us from You, O LORD, that a root and a name should be left for us in the place of Your sanctuary, ⁷⁹and to discover a light for us in the house of the LORD our God, and to give us food in the time of our servitude. ⁸⁰Yes, when we were in bondage, we were not forsaken of our Lord, but He made us gracious before the kings of Persia, so that they gave us food, ⁸¹and glorified the temple of our Lord, and raised up the desolate Zion, to give us a sure dwelling in Jewry and Jerusalem. ⁸²And now, O LORD, what will we say, having these things? For we have transgressed Your commands, which You gave by the hand of Your servants the prophets, saying, ⁸³The land, which you enter into to possess as a heritage, is a land polluted with the pollutions of the strangers of the land, and they have filled it with their uncleanness. ⁸⁴Therefore now, you will not join your daughters to their sons, neither will you take their daughters to your sons, ⁸⁵neither will you seek to have peace with them forever, that you may be strong, and eat the good things of the land, and that you may leave it for an inheritance to your children forevermore. ⁸⁶And all that has befallen [us] is done to us for our wicked works and great sins, for You, O LORD, made our sins light, ⁸⁷and gave to us such a root, [but] we have turned back again to transgress Your law, in mingling ourselves with the uncleanness of the heathen of the land. ⁸⁸You were not angry with us to destroy us, until You had left us neither root, seed, nor name. ⁸⁹O LORD of Israel, You are true, for we are left a root to this day. ⁹⁰Behold, now we are before You in our iniquities, for we cannot stand any longer before You by reason of these things." ⁹¹And as Ezra made his confession in his prayer, weeping and lying flat on the ground before the temple, there gathered to him from Jerusalem a very great crowd of men, and women, and children, for there was great weeping among the multitude. ⁹²Then Jehoiachin the son of Jeelus, one of the sons of Israel, called out, and said, "O Ezra, we have sinned against the LORD God, we have married strange women of the heathen of the land, and now is all Israel aloft. ⁹³Let us make an oath to the LORD herein, that we will put away all our wives, which [we have taken] of the strangers, with their children, ⁹⁴like as seems good to you, and to as many as obey the Law of the LORD. ⁹⁵Arise and execute this, for this matter pertains to you, and we will be with you to do valiantly." ⁹⁶So Ezra arose, and took an oath of the chief of the priests and Levites of all Israel to do after these things; and [so] they swore.

CHAPTER 9

¹Then Ezra, rising from the court of the temple, went to the chamber of Jonas the son of Eliasib, ²and lodged there, and ate no bread nor drank water, mourning for the great iniquities of the multitude. ³And there was made proclamation in all Jewry and Jerusalem to all those who were of the captivity, that they should be gathered together at Jerusalem, ⁴and that whoever did not meet there within two or three days, according as the elders that bore rule appointed, their cattle should be seized to the use of the temple, and himself cast out from the multitude of those who were of the captivity. ⁵And in three days all those of the tribe of Judah and Benjamin were gathered together at Jerusalem: this was the ninth month, on the twentieth day of the month. ⁶And all the multitude sat together trembling in the broad place before the temple because of the present foul weather. ⁷So Ezra arose and said to them, "You have transgressed the Law and married strange wives to increase the sins of Israel. ⁸And now make confession and give glory to the LORD, the God of our fathers, ⁹and do His will, and separate yourselves from the heathen of the land, and from the strange women." ¹⁰Then the whole multitude cried, and said with a loud voice, "Just as you have spoken, so we will do. ¹¹But forasmuch as the multitude is great, and it is foul weather, so that we cannot stand outside, this indeed is not a work of one day or two, seeing our sin in these things is spread far: ¹²therefore, let the rulers of the multitude stay, and let all those of our habitations that have strange wives come at the time appointed, ¹³and with them the rulers and judges of every place, until we turn the wrath of the LORD away from us for this matter." ¹⁴[Then] Jonathan the son of Azael and Ezekias the son of Thocanus took the matter on them accordingly; and Mosollamus, and Levis, and Sabbateus were assessors to them. ¹⁵And those who were of the captivity did according to all these things. ¹⁶And Ezra the priest chose principal men for himself of their families, all by name: and on the new moon of the tenth month, they were shut in together to examine the matter. ¹⁷So their cause that held strange wives was brought to an end by the new moon of the first month. ¹⁸And there were found of the priests that had come together and had strange wives, ¹⁹of the sons of Jesus the son of Josedek, and his relatives: Mathelas, and Eleazar, and Joribus, and Joadanus. ²⁰And they gave their hands to put away their wives, and to [offer] rams to make reconciliation for their error. ²¹And of the sons of Emmer: Ananias, and Zabdeus, and Manes, and Sameus, and Hiereel, and Azariah. ²²And of the sons of Phaisur: Elionas, Massias, Ishmael, and Nathanael, and Ocidelus, and Saloas. ²³And of the Levites: Jozabdus, and Semeis, and Colius, who was called Calitas, and Patheus, and Judas, and Jonas. ²⁴Of the holy singers: Eliasibus [and] Bacchurus. ²⁵Of the gatekeepers: Sallumus and tolbanes. ²⁶Of Israel, of the sons of Phoros: Hiermas, and Ieddias, and Melchias, and Maelus, and Eleazar, and Asibas, and Banneas. ²⁷Of the sons of Ela: Matthanias, Zechariah, and Jezrielus, and Oabdius, and Hieremoth, and Aedias. ²⁸And of the sons of Zamoth: Eliadas, Eliasimus, Othonias, Jarimoth, and Sabathus, and Zardeus. ²⁹Of the sons of Bebai: Joannes, and Ananias, and Jozabdus, and Ematheis. ³⁰Of the sons of Mani: Olamus, Mamuchus, Jedeus, Jasubas, and Jasaelus, and Hieremoth. ³¹And of the sons of Addi: Naathus, and Moossias, Laccunus, and Naidus, and Matthanias, and Sesthel, Balnuus, and Manasseas. ³²And of the sons of Annas: Elionas, and Aseas, and Melchias, and Sabbeus, and Simon Chosameus. ³³And of the sons of Asom: Maltanneus, and Mattathias, and Sabanneus, Eliphalat, and Manasseh, and Semei. ³⁴And of the sons of Baani: Jeremias, Momdis, Ismacrus, Juel, Mamdai, and Pedias, and Anos, Carabasion, and Enasibus, and Mamnitamenus, Eliasis, Bannus, Eliali, someis, Selemias, Nathanias. And of the sons of Ezora: Sesis, Ezril, Azaelus, Samatus, Zambri, Josephus. ³⁵And of the sons of Nooma: Mazitias, Zabadeas, Edos, Juel, Banaias. ³⁶All these had taken strange wives, and they put them away with their children. ³⁷And the priests and Levites, and those who were of Israel, lived in Jerusalem, and in the country, on the new moon of the seventh month, and the sons of Israel in their habitations. ³⁸And the whole multitude were gathered together with one accord into the broad place before the porch of the temple toward the east; ³⁹and they said to Ezra the priest and reader, "Bring the Law of Moses, that was given of the LORD, the God of Israel." ⁴⁰So Ezra the chief priest brought the Law to the whole multitude of both men and women, and to all the priests, to hear the Law on the new moon of the seventh month. ⁴¹And he read in the broad place before the porch of the temple from morning to midday, before both men and women; and all the multitude gave heed to the Law. ⁴²And Ezra the priest and reader of the Law stood up on the pulpit of wood, which was made [for that purpose]. ⁴³And there stood up by him Mattathias, Sammus, Ananias, Azariah, Urias, Ezekias, Ba'alsamus, on the right hand; ⁴⁴and on his left hand: Phaldeus, Misael, Melchias, Lothasubus, Nabarias, [and] Zechariah. ⁴⁵Then Ezra took the Scroll of the Law before the multitude and sat honorably in the first place before all. ⁴⁶And when he opened the Law, they all stood straight up. So Ezra blessed the LORD God Most High, the God of armies, Almighty. ⁴⁷And all the people answered, "Amen"; and lifting up their hands they fell to the ground and worshiped the LORD. ⁴⁸Also Jesus, Annus, Sarabias, Iadinus, Jacubus, Sabateus, Auteas, Maiannas, and Calitas, Azariah, and Jozabdus, and Ananias, Phalias, the Levites, taught the Law of the LORD, and read the Law of the LORD to the multitude, in addition, making them to understand it. ⁴⁹Then Attharates said to Ezra the chief priest and reader, and to the Levites that taught the multitude, even to all, ⁵⁰"This day is holy to the LORD"—now they all wept when they heard the Law—⁵¹"go then, and eat the fat, and drink the sweet, and send portions to those who have nothing, ⁵²for the day is holy to the LORD; and do not be sorrowful, for the LORD will bring you to honor." ⁵³So the Levites published all things to the people, saying, "This day is holy; do not be sorrowful." ⁵⁴Then they went their way, everyone to eat, and drink, and make merry, and to give portions to those who had nothing, and to make great cheer, ⁵⁵because they understood the words wherein they were instructed, and for which they had been assembled.

2 ESDRAS

2 Esdras (also called 4 Esdras, Latin Esdras, or Latin Ezra) is the name of an apocalyptic book in many English versions of the Bible. Its authorship is ascribed to Ezra, a scribe and priest of the 5th century BC, although modern scholarship places its composition between AD 70 and 218. It is reckoned among the apocrypha by Roman Catholics, Protestants, and most Eastern Orthodox Christians. Although 2 Esdras was preserved in Latin as an appendix to the Vulgate and passed down as a unified book, it is generally considered to be a tripartite work.

CHAPTER 1

¹The second scroll of the prophet Ezra, the son of Saraias, the son of Azariah, the son of Hilkiah, the son of Salemas, the son of Zadok, the son of Ahitob, ²the son of Achias, the son of Phinehas, the son of Eli, the son of Amariah, the son of Aziei, the son of Marimoth, the son of Arna, the son of Ozias, the son of Borith, the son of Abissei, the son of Phinehas, the son of Eleazar, ³the son of Aaron, of the tribe of Levi, which was captive in the land of the Medes, in the reign of Artaxerxes king of the Persians. ⁴And the word of the LORD came to me, saying, ⁵"Go your way, and show My people their sinful deeds, and their children their wickedness which they have done against Me, that they may tell their children's children, ⁶because the sins of their fathers are increased in them, for they have forgotten Me, and have

done sacrifice to strange gods. ⁷Did I not bring them out of the land of Egypt, out of the house of bondage? But they have provoked Me to wrath and have despised My counsels. ⁸Shake then the hair of your head, and cast all evils on them, for they have not been obedient to My law, but it is a rebellious people. ⁹How long will I forbear them, to whom I have done so much good? ¹⁰I have overthrown many kings for their sakes; I have struck down Pharaoh with his servants and all his army. ¹¹I have destroyed all the nations before them, and in the east, I have scattered the people of two provinces, even of Tyre and Sidon, and have slain all their adversaries. ¹²Therefore, speak to them, saying, ¹³The LORD says, Of a truth I brought you through the sea, and where there was no path I made highways for you; I gave you Moses for a leader, and Aaron for a priest. ¹⁴I gave you light in a pillar of fire, and I have done great wonders among you; yet you have forgotten Me, says the LORD." ¹⁵The LORD Almighty says, "The quails were for a token to you; I gave you a camp for your protection, nevertheless you murmured there: ¹⁶and you did not triumph in My Name for the destruction of your enemies, but ever to this day you yet murmur. ¹⁷Where are the benefits that I have done for you? When you were hungry and thirsty in the wilderness, did you not cry to Me, ¹⁸saying, Why have You brought us into this wilderness to kill us? It had been better for us to have served the Egyptians, than to die in this wilderness. ¹⁹I had pity on your mourning and gave you manna for food; you ate messengers' bread. ²⁰When you were thirsty, did I not cleave the rock, and waters flowed out to your fill? For the heat I covered you with the leaves of the trees. ²¹I divided fruitful lands among you; I cast out the Canaanites, the Perizzites, and the Philistines, before you: what will I yet do more for you?" Says the LORD. ²²The LORD Almighty says, "When you were in the wilderness, at the bitter river, being thirsty, and blaspheming My Name, ²³I did not give you fire for your blasphemies, but cast a tree in the water, and made the river sweet. ²⁴What will I do to you, O Jacob? You, Judah, would not obey Me: I will turn Myself to other nations, and I will give My Name to them, that they may keep my statutes. ²⁵Seeing you have forsaken Me, I will also forsake you; when you ask me to be merciful to you, I will have no mercy on you. ²⁶Whenever you will call on Me, I will not hear you, for you have defiled your hands with blood, and your feet are swift to commit manslaughter. ²⁷You have not as it were forsaken Me, but your own selves," says the LORD. ²⁸The LORD Almighty says, "Have I not pleaded with you as a father his sons, as a mother her daughters, and a nurse her young babies, ²⁹that you would be My people, and I should be your God; that you would be My children, and I should be your Father? ³⁰I gathered you together, as a hen [gathers] her chickens under her wings, but now, what will I do to you? I will cast you out from My presence. ³¹When you offer oblations to Me, I will turn My face from you, for your solemn feast days, your new moons, and your circumcisions of the flesh, I have rejected. ³²I sent My servants the prophets to you, whom you have taken and slain, and torn their bodies in pieces, whose blood I will require [of your hands]," says the LORD. ³³The LORD Almighty says, "Your house is desolate, I will cast you out as the wind does stubble. ³⁴And your children will not be fruitful; for they have neglected My command to you and done that which is evil before Me. ³⁵I will give your houses to a people that will come, which having not heard of Me, yet believe Me; they to whom I have showed no signs will do that which I have commanded. ³⁶They have seen no prophets, yet they will call their former estate to remembrance. ³⁷I take to witness the grace of the people that will come, whose little ones rejoice with gladness: and though they do not see Me with bodily eyes, yet in spirit they will believe the thing that I say. ³⁸And now, O father, behold with glory; and see the people that come from the east, ³⁹to whom I will give for leaders: Abraham, Isaac, and Jacob, Hosea, Amos, and Micah, Joel, Obadiah, and Jonah, ⁴⁰Nahum, and Habakkuk, Zephaniah, Haggai, Zechariah, and Malachi, which is also called the Messenger of the LORD."

CHAPTER 2

¹The LORD says, "I brought this people out of bondage, and I gave them My commands by My servants the prophets; whom they would not hear but set My counsels at nothing. ²The mother that bears them says to them, Go your way, O my children; for I am a widow and forsaken. ³I brought you up with gladness, and with sorrow and heaviness I have lost you; for you have sinned before the LORD God and done that which is evil before me. ⁴But what will I now do to you? For I am a widow and forsaken: go your way, O my children, and ask mercy of the LORD. ⁵As for Me, O father, I call on you for a witness over the mother of [these] children, because they would not keep My covenant, ⁶that you bring them to confusion, and their mother to a plunder, that there may be no offspring of them. ⁷Let them be scattered abroad among the heathen, let their names be blotted out of the earth; for they have despised My covenant. ⁸Woe to you, Asshur, you that hide the unrighteous with you! O you wicked nation, remember what I did to Sodom and Gomorrah, ⁹whose land lies in clods of pitch and heaps of ashes: even so I will also do to those who have not listened to Me," says the LORD Almighty. ¹⁰The LORD says to Ezra, "Tell My people that I will give them the kingdom of Jerusalem, which I would have given to Israel. ¹¹I will also take their glory, and give these the continuous dwelling places, which I had prepared for them. ¹²They will have the Tree of Life for an ointment of sweet savor; they will neither labor, nor be weary. ¹³Ask, and you will receive: pray for few days for you, that they may be shortened: the kingdom is already prepared for you: watch. ¹⁴Take the heavens and earth to witness, take them to witness; for I have given up the evil, and created the good; for I live," says the LORD. ¹⁵"Mother, embrace your children; I will bring them out with gladness like a dove; establish their feet; for I have chosen you," says the LORD. ¹⁶"And I will raise those who are dead up again from their places and bring them out from their tombs; for I have known My Name in them. ¹⁷Do not be afraid, you mother of the children, for I have chosen you," says the LORD. ¹⁸"For your help I will send My servants Isaiah and Jeremiah, after whose counsel I have sanctified and prepared for you twelve trees laden with various fruits, ¹⁹and as many springs flowing with milk and honey, and seven mighty mountains, after which there grow roses and lilies, whereby I will fill your children with joy. ²⁰Do right to the widow, judge the fatherless, give to the poor, defend the orphan, clothe the naked, ²¹heal the broken and the weak, do not laugh a lame man to scorn, defend the maimed, and let the blind man come to the sight of My glory. ²²Keep the old and young within your walls. ²³Wherever you find the dead, set a sign on them and commit them to the grave, and I will give you the first place in My resurrection. ²⁴Stay still, O My people, and take your rest, for your quietness will come. ²⁵Nourish your children, O you good nurse, and establish their feet. ²⁶As for the servants whom I have given you, not one of them will perish, for I will require them from among your number. ²⁷Do not be careful excessively, for when the day of suffering and anguish comes, others will weep and be sorrowful, but you will be merry and have abundance. ²⁸The nations will envy you, but they will be able to do nothing against you," says the LORD. ²⁹"My hands will cover you, so that your children do not see Gehenna. ³⁰Be joyful, O you mother, with your children; for I will deliver you," says the LORD. ³¹"Remember your children that sleep, for I will bring them out of the secret places of the earth and show mercy to them, for I am merciful," says the LORD Almighty. ³²"Embrace your children until I come and proclaim mercy to them, for My wells run over, and My grace will not fail." ³³I, Ezra, received a charge from the LORD on Mount Horeb, that I should go to Israel; but when I came to them, they would have none of me, and rejected the command of the LORD. ³⁴And therefore I say to you, O you nations that hear and understand: look for your Shepherd; He will give you continuous rest; for He is near at hand who will come in the end of the world. ³⁵Be ready to the rewards of the kingdom, for the continuous light will shine on you forevermore. ³⁶Flee the shadow of this world, receive the joyfulness of your glory: I call to witness my Savior openly. ³⁷O receive that which is given to you of the LORD, and be joyful, giving thanks to Him that has called you to heavenly kingdoms. ³⁸Arise, and stand, and behold the number of those that are sealed in the celebration of the LORD; ³⁹those who withdrew themselves from the shadow of the world have received glorious garments of the LORD. ⁴⁰Look on your number, O Zion, and make up the reckoning of those of you that are

clothed in white, which have fulfilled the Law of the LORD. ⁴¹The number of your children, whom you long for, is fulfilled: implore the power of the LORD, that your people, which have been called from the beginning, may be hallowed. ⁴²I, Ezra, saw on Mount Zion a great multitude, whom I could not number, and they all praised the LORD with songs. ⁴³And in the midst of them there was a young Man of a high stature, taller than all the rest, and on each of their heads He set crowns and was more exalted. I marveled greatly at this. ⁴⁴So I asked the Messenger, and said, "What are these, my Lord?" ⁴⁵He answered and said to me, "These are those who have put off the mortal clothing, and put on the immortal, and have confessed the Name of God: now they are crowned, and receive palms." ⁴⁶Then I said to the Messenger, "What young Man is He that sets crowns on them, and gives them palms in their hands?" ⁴⁷So He answered and said to me, "It is the Son of God, whom they have confessed in the world." Then I began to greatly commend those who stood so stiffly for the Name of the LORD. ⁴⁸Then the Messenger said to me, "Go your way, and tell My people what manner of things, and how great wonders of the LORD God you have seen."

CHAPTER 3

¹In the thirty years after the ruin of the city, I, Salathiel (also called Ezra), was in Babylon, and lay troubled on my bed, and my thoughts came up over my heart: ²for I saw the desolation of Zion, and the wealth of those who lived at Babylon. ³And my spirit was severely moved, so that I began to speak words full of fear to the Most High, and said, ⁴"O LORD that bears rule, did You not speak at the beginning, when You fashioned the earth, and that Yourself alone, and commanded the dust? ⁵And it gave You Adam, a body without a soul? Yet it was the workmanship of Your hands, and You breathed into him the breath of life, and he was made living before You. ⁶And You led him into paradise, which Your right hand planted, before the earth ever came forward. ⁷And You gave to him Your one command, which he transgressed, and immediately You appointed death for him and in his generations; and there were born of him nations and tribes, peoples and relatives, out of number. ⁸And every nation walked after their own will, and did ungodly things before You, and despised [Your commands, and] You did not forbid them. ⁹Nevertheless, again in [the] process of time You brought the Flood on those that lived in the world and destroyed them. ¹⁰And it came to pass, that the same fortune befell them; like as death was to Adam, so was the Flood to these. ¹¹Nevertheless, one of them You left—Noah with his household, [even] all the righteous men [that came] of him. ¹²And it came to pass, that when those who lived on the earth began to multiply, they also multiplied children, and peoples, and many nations, and again began to be more ungodly than the first. ¹³And it came to pass, when they did wickedly before You, You chose one from among them, whose name was Abraham; ¹⁴and You loved him, and only to him did You show the end of the times secretly by night, ¹⁵and made a perpetual covenant with him, promising him that You would never forsake his seed. ¹⁶And to him You gave Isaac, and to Isaac You gave Jacob and Esau. And You set Jacob apart for Yourself, but put [him] by Esau: and Jacob became a great multitude. ¹⁷And it came to pass, that when You led his seed out of Egypt, You brought them up to Mount Sinai. ¹⁸You also bowed the heavens, and shook the earth, and moved the whole world, and made the depths to tremble, and troubled the [course of that] age. ¹⁹And Your glory went through four gates: of fire, and of earthquake, and of wind, and of cold, that You might give the Law to the seed of Jacob, and the command to the generation of Israel. ²⁰And yet You did not take away from them [their] wicked heart, that Your law might bring out fruit in them. ²¹For the first Adam bearing a wicked heart transgressed, and was overcome; [and not only him,] but also all of them that are born of him. ²²Therefore disease was made permanent; and the Law was in the heart of the people along with the wickedness of the root; so the good departed away, and that which was wicked dwelt still. ²³So the times passed away, and the years were brought to an end: then You raised up a servant, called David, ²⁴whom You commanded to build a city to Your Name, and to offer oblations to You therein of Your own. ²⁵When this was done [for] many years, then those who inhabited the city did evil, ²⁶in all things doing even as Adam and all his generations had done; for they also bore a wicked heart: ²⁷and so You gave Your city over into the hands of Your enemies. ²⁸And then I said in my heart, Are their deeds any better that inhabit Babylon? And does she therefore have dominion over Zion? ²⁹For it came to pass when I came here, that I also saw impieties without number, and my soul saw many evildoers in this thirtieth year, so that my heart failed me. ³⁰For I have seen how You permit them sinning, and have spared the ungodly doers, and have destroyed Your people, and have preserved Your enemies; and You have not signified to any how Your way may be comprehended. ³¹Are the deeds of Babylon better than those of Zion? ³²Or is there any other nation that knows You besides Israel? Or what tribes have so believed Your covenants as these [tribes of] Jacob? ³³And yet their reward does not appear, and their labor has no fruit, for I have gone here and there through the nations, and I see that they abound [in wealth, and] do not think on Your commands. ³⁴Therefore, weigh our iniquities in the balance now, and also theirs that dwell in the world, and so it will be found which way the scale inclines. ³⁵Or when was it that they which dwell on the earth have not sinned in Your sight? Or what nation has so kept Your commands? ³⁶You will find that men [who may be reckoned] by name have kept Your precepts; but nations You will not find."

CHAPTER 4

¹And the messenger that was sent to me, whose name was Uriel, gave me an answer, ²and said to me, "Your heart has utterly failed you in [regard to] this world, and do you think to comprehend the way of the Most High?" ³Then I said, "Yes my Lord." And he answered me, and said, "I have been sent to show you three ways, and to set out three similitudes before you: ⁴of which if you can declare me one, I also will show you the way that you desire to see, and I will teach you why the heart is wicked." ⁵And I said, "Speak, my Lord." Then he said to me, "Go forth, weigh me a weight of fire, or measure me a measure of wind, or call me again the day that is past." ⁶Then I answered and said, "Who of the sons [of men] is able to do this, that you should ask me of such things?" ⁷And he said to me, "If I had asked you, saying, How many dwellings are there in the heart of the sea? Or how many springs are there at the fountain head of the deep? Or how many ways are above the expanse? Or which are the exits of Hades? Or which are the paths of paradise? ⁸Perhaps you would say to me, I never went down into the deep, nor as yet into Hades, neither did I ever climb up into Heaven. ⁹Nevertheless, now I have asked you but only of the fire and wind, and of the day, things you have experienced, and without which you cannot be, and yet you have given me no answer about them." ¹⁰Moreover, he said to me, "Your own things, that are grown up with you, you cannot know; ¹¹how then can you comprehend the way of the Most High? And how can he that is already worn out with the corrupted world understand incorruption?" ¹²And when I heard these things I fell on my face, and said to him, "It would be better that we were not here at all, than that we should come here and live in the midst of ungodliness, and suffer, and not know why." ¹³He answered me, and said, "The woods of the trees of the field went out, and took counsel together, ¹⁴and said, Come! Let us go and make war against the sea, that it may depart away before us, and that we may make ourselves more woods. ¹⁵The waves of the sea also in like manner took counsel together, and said, Come! Let us go up and subdue the wood of the plain, that we may make ourselves another country there also. ¹⁶The counsel of the wood was in vain, for the fire came and consumed it; ¹⁷likewise also, the counsel of the waves of the sea, for the sand stood up and stopped them. ¹⁸If you were judge now between these two, whom would you justify, or whom condemn?" ¹⁹I answered and said, "It is a foolish counsel that they both have taken, for the ground is given to the wood, and the place of the sea [is given] to bear his waves." ²⁰Then he answered me, and said, "You have given a right judgment, and why do you not judge in your own case? ²¹For just as the ground is given to the wood, and the sea to his waves, even so those who dwell on the earth may understand nothing but that which is on the earth: and he [only that dwells] above the heavens [may understand the] things that are above the height of the heavens." ²²Then I

answered and said, "I implore you, O Lord, why is the power of understanding given to me? ²³For it was not in my mind to be curious of the ways above, but of such things as pass by us daily, because Israel is given up as a reproach to the heathen, and the people whom you have loved is given over to ungodly nations, and the Law of our forefathers is made of no effect, and the written covenants are nowhere [regarded], ²⁴and we pass away out of the world as grasshoppers, and our life is as a vapor, neither are we worthy to obtain mercy. ²⁵What will He then do for His Name whereby we are called? Of these things have I asked." ²⁶Then he answered me, and said, "If you are [alive] you will see, and if you live long, you will marvel, for the world hastens quickly to pass away. ²⁷For it is not able to bear the things that are promised to the righteous in the times [to come], for this world is full of sadness and infirmities. ²⁸For the evil of which you asked me is sown, but the gathering thereof has not yet come. ²⁹If, therefore, that which is sown has not reaped, and if the place where the evil is sown has not passed away, there cannot come the field where the good is sown. ³⁰For a grain of evil seed was sown in the heart of Adam from the beginning, and how much wickedness has it brought out to this time! And how much will it yet bring out until the time of threshing comes! ³¹Now ponder [this] by yourself: how great a fruit of wickedness a grain of evil seed has brought out. ³²When the ears which are without number will be sown, how great a floor they will fill!" ³³Then I answered and said, "How long? And when will these things come to pass? Why are our years few and evil?" ³⁴And he answered me, and said, "You do not hasten more than the Most High, for your haste is for your own self, but He that is above hastens on behalf of many. ³⁵Did the souls of the righteous not ask questions of these things in their chambers, saying, How long are we here? When does the fruit of the threshing time of our reward come?" ³⁶And to them Jeremiel the chief-messenger gave answer, and said, "When the number is fulfilled of those who are like to you. For He has weighed the world in the balance; ³⁷and by measure He has measured the times, and by number He has counted the seasons; and He will not move nor stir them until the said measure is fulfilled." ³⁸Then I answered and said, "O Lord that bears rule, yet even we are all full of impiety: ³⁹and for our sakes perhaps it is that the threshing time of the righteous is kept back, because of the sins of those who dwell on the earth." ⁴⁰So he answered me, and said, "Go your way to a woman with child, and ask of her when she has fulfilled her nine months, if her womb may keep the birth any longer within her." ⁴¹Then I said, "No, Lord, that it cannot." And he said to me, "In the grave the chambers of souls are like the womb: ⁴²for like as a woman that travails hurries to escape the anguish of the travail, even so do these places hasten to deliver those things that are committed to them from the beginning. ⁴³Then it will be shown to you concerning those things which you desire to see." ⁴⁴Then I answered and said, "If I have found favor in your sight, and if it is possible, and if I am therefore suitable, ⁴⁵show me this also, whether there are more to come than are past, or whether the greater part has [already] gone over us. ⁴⁶For what is gone I know, but what is still to come I do not know." ⁴⁷And he said to me, "Stand up on the right side, and I will expound the similitude to you." ⁴⁸So I stood, and saw, and behold, a hot burning oven passed by before me: and it happened, that when the flame was gone by, I looked, and behold, the smoke remained still. ⁴⁹After this there passed by before me a watery cloud and it sent down much rain with a storm; and when the stormy rain was past, the drops remained therein still. ⁵⁰Then he said to me, "Consider with yourself; as the rain is more than the drops, and the fire is greater than the smoke, so the quantity which is past did exceed more; but the drops and the smoke remained still." ⁵¹Then I prayed, and said, "Will I live until that time? Or who will be alive in those days?" ⁵²He answered me, and said, "As for the signs of which you asked me, I may tell you of them in part, but as touching your life, I am not sent to show you; for I do not know it."

CHAPTER 5

¹"Nevertheless, as concerning the signs, behold, the days will come, that they which dwell on earth will be taken with great amazement, and the way of truth will be hidden, and the land will be barren of faith. ²But iniquity will be increased above that which you now see, or that you have heard of long ago. ³And the land, that you now see to have rule, will be waste and untrodden, and men will see it desolate. ⁴But if the Most High grants you to live, you will see that which is after the third [kingdom] to be troubled; and the sun will suddenly shine out in the night, and the moon in the day; ⁵and blood will drop out of wood, and the stone will give his voice, and the peoples will be troubled; and their goings will be changed; ⁶and he will rule, whom those who dwell on the earth do not look for, and the birds will take their flight away together; ⁷and the Sodomite sea will cast out fish, and make a noise in the night, which many have not known, but all will hear the voice thereof. ⁸There will also be chaos in many places, and the fire will often be sent out, and the wild beasts will change their places, and women will bring out monsters; ⁹and salt waters will be found in the sweet, and all friends will destroy one another; then sense will hide itself, and understanding withdraw itself into its chamber; ¹⁰and it will be sought of [by] many, and will not be found; and unrighteousness and incontinency will be multiplied on earth. ¹¹One land will also ask another, and say, Has righteousness—has a man that does righteousness—gone through you? And it will say, No. ¹²And it will come to pass at that time that men will hope, but will not obtain: they will labor, but their ways will not prosper. ¹³To show you such signs I have [taken] leave; and if you will pray again, and weep as now, and fast [for] seven days, you will hear yet greater things than these." ¹⁴Then I awoke, and an extreme trembling went through my body, and my mind was troubled, so that it fainted. ¹⁵So the messenger that had come to talk with me held me, comforted me, and set me up on my feet. ¹⁶And in the second night it came to pass, that Phaltiel the captain of the people came to me, saying, "Where have you been? And why is your countenance sad? ¹⁷Or do you not know that Israel is committed to you in the land of their captivity? ¹⁸Get up then, and eat some bread, and do not forsake us, as the shepherd [that leaves the flock] in the hands of cruel wolves." ¹⁹Then I said to him, "Go your ways from me, and do not come near me for seven days, and then you will come to me." And he heard what I said and went from me. ²⁰And so I fasted seven days, mourning and weeping, just as Uriel the messenger commanded me. ²¹And after seven days, so it was, that the thoughts of my heart were very grievous to me again, ²²and my soul recovered the spirit of understanding, and I began to speak words before the Most High again, ²³and said, "O LORD that bears rule, of all the woods of the earth, and of all the trees thereof, You have chosen one vine for Yourself; ²⁴and of all the lands of the world You have chosen one country for Yourself; and of all the flowers of the world You have chosen one lily for Yourself; ²⁵and of all the depths of the sea You have filled one river for Yourself; and of all built cities You have hallowed Zion for Yourself; ²⁶and of all the birds that are created You have named one dove for Yourself; and of all the cattle that are made You have provided one sheep for Yourself; ²⁷and among all the multitudes of peoples You have gotten one people for Yourself; and to this people, whom You loved, You gave a law that is approved of all. ²⁸And now, O LORD, why have You given this one people over to many, and have dishonored the one root above others, and have scattered Your only one among many? ²⁹And they which denied Your promises have trodden them down that believed Your covenants. ³⁰If You hate Your people so much, they should be punished with Your own hands." ³¹Now when I had spoken these words, the Messenger that came to me a previous night was sent to me, ³²and said to me, "Hear Me, and I will instruct you; listen to Me, and I will tell you more." ³³And I said, "Speak, my Lord." Then He said to me, "You are severely troubled in mind for Israel's sake: do you [love] that people better than He that made them?" ³⁴And I said, "No, Lord, but I have spoken in great grief, for my reins torment me every hour, while I labor to comprehend the way of the Most High, and to seek out part of His judgment." ³⁵And he said to me, "You cannot." And I said, "Why, Lord, or for what purpose was I born? Or why was my mother's womb not then my grave, that I might not have seen the travail of Jacob, and the wearisome toil of the stock of Israel?" ³⁶And He said to me, "Number to Me those who have not yet come, gather together to Me the drops that are scattered abroad, make for Me the

flowers green again that are withered, ³⁷open to Me the chambers that are closed, and bring out to Me the winds that in them are shut up, or show Me the image of a voice: and then I will declare to you the travail that you asked to see." ³⁸And I said, "O LORD that bears rule, who may know these things, but He that does not have his dwelling with men? ³⁹As for me, I am unwise: how may I then speak of these things of which You asked me?" ⁴⁰Then He said to me, "Just as you can do none of these things that I have spoken of, even so you cannot find out My judgment, or the end of the love that I have promised to My people." ⁴¹And I said, "But, behold, O LORD, You have made the promise to those who are in the end: and what will they do that have been before us, or we [that are now], or those who will come after us?" ⁴²And He said to me, "I will liken My judgment to a ring: just as there is no slackness of those who are last, even so there is no swiftness of those who are first." ⁴³So I answered and said, "Could You not make them [to be] at once that have been made, and that are now, and that are still to come; that You might show Your judgment sooner?" ⁴⁴Then He answered me, and said, "The creature may not hasten above the Creator; neither may the world hold them at once that will be created therein." ⁴⁵And I said, "How have You said to Your servant that You will surely make alive at once the creature that You have created? If, therefore, they will be alive at once, and the creature will sustain them, even so it might now also support them to be present at once." ⁴⁶And He said to me, "Ask the womb of a woman, and say to her, If you bring out ten children, why [do you do it] several times? Pray instead to bring out ten children at once." ⁴⁷And I said, "She cannot, but must do it by distance of time." ⁴⁸Then He said to me, "Even so have I given the womb of the earth to those that are sown therein in their several times. ⁴⁹For just as a young child may not bring out, neither may she that has grown old [bring out] any more, even so—I have disposed the world which I created." ⁵⁰And I asked, and said, "Seeing You have now showed me the way, I will speak before You: Is our mother, of whom You have told me, still young? Or does she now draw near to age?" ⁵¹He answered me, and said, "Ask a woman that bears children, and she will tell you. ⁵²Say to her, Why are they whom you have now not brought out like those that were before, but of less stature? ⁵³And she will also answer you, They that are born in the strength of youth are of one fashion, and those who are born in the time of age, when the womb fails, are otherwise. ⁵⁴Therefore, also consider yourself, how that you are of less stature than those that were before you. ⁵⁵And so are those who come after you less than you, as [born] of the creature which now begins to be old and is past the strength of youth." ⁵⁶Then I said, "Lord, I implore You, if I have found favor in Your sight, show Your servant by whom You visit Your creature."

2 ESDRAS

CHAPTER 6

¹And He said to me, "In the beginning, when the earth was made, before the portals of the world were fixed, or the gatherings of the winds ever blew, ²before the voices of the thunder sounded, and before the flashes of the lightning shone, or the foundations of paradise were ever laid, ³before the fair flowers were seen, or the powers of the earthquake were ever established, before the innumerable army of messengers were gathered together, ⁴or the heights of the air were ever lifted up, before the measures of the expanse were named, or the footstool of Zion was ever established, ⁵and before the present years were sought out, and or the imaginations of those who now sin were ever estranged, before they were sealed that have gathered faith for a treasure— ⁶then I considered these things, and they were all made through Me alone, and through none other: as by Me they will also be ended, and by none other." ⁷Then I answered and said, "What will be the separating apart of the times? Or when will be the end of the first, and the beginning of it that follows?" ⁸And He said to me, "From Abraham to Abraham, inasmuch as Jacob and Esau were born of him, for Jacob's hand held the heel of Esau from the beginning. ⁹For Esau is the end of this world, and Jacob is the beginning of it that follows. ¹⁰The beginning of a man is his hand, and the end of a man is his heel; between the heel and the hand do not seek anything else, Ezra. ¹¹I answered then and said, "O LORD that bears rule, If I have found favor in Your sight, ¹²I implore You, show Your servant the end of Your signs, of which You showed me part the last night." ¹³So He answered and said to me, "Stand up on your feet, and you will hear a mighty sounding voice; ¹⁴and if the place you stand on is greatly moved, ¹⁵when it speaks, do not be afraid, for the word is of the end, and the foundations of the earth will understand, ¹⁶that the speech is of them: they will tremble and be moved, for they know that their end must be changed." ¹⁷And it happened, that when I had heard it I stood up on my feet, and listened, and behold, there was a voice that spoke, and the sound of it was like the sound of many waters. ¹⁸And it said, "Behold, the days come, and it will be that when I draw near to visit those who dwell on the earth, ¹⁹and when I will make inquisition of those who have done hurt unjustly with their unrighteousness, and when the affliction of Zion will be fulfilled, ²⁰and when the seal will be set on the world that is to pass away, then I will show these signs: the scrolls will be opened before the expanse, and all will see together; ²¹and the children of a year old will speak with their voices, [and] the women with child will bring out untimely children at three or four months, and they will live, and dance; ²²and suddenly the sown places will appear unsown, [and] the full storehouses will suddenly be found empty; ²³and the trumpet will give a sound, which when every man hears, they will be suddenly afraid. ²⁴At that time friends will make war against one another like enemies, and the earth will stand in fear with those that dwell therein; the springs of the springs will stand still, so that for three hours they will not run. ²⁵And it will be that whoever remains after all these things that I have told you of, he will be saved, and will see My salvation and the end of My world. ²⁶And they will see the men that have been taken up, who have not tasted death from their birth: and the heart of the inhabitants will be changed and turned into another meaning. ²⁷For evil will be blotted out, and deceit will be quenched; ²⁸and faith will flourish, and corruption will be overcome, and the truth, which has been so long without fruit, will be declared." ²⁹And when He talked with me, behold, little by little the place I stood on rocked to and fro. ³⁰And He said to me, "These things I came to show you this night. ³¹If, therefore, you will pray yet again, and fast [for] seven more days, I will yet tell you greater things than these. ³²For your voice has surely been heard before the Most High, for the Mighty has seen your righteous dealing; He has also previously seen your chastity, which you have had ever since your youth. ³³And therefore He has sent Me to show you all these things, and to say to you, Be of good comfort, and do not fear. ³⁴And do not be hasty in [regard of the] former times, to think vain things, that you may not hasten in the latter times." ³⁵And it came to pass after this, that I wept again, and fasted [for] seven days in like manner, that I might fulfill the three weeks which He told me. ³⁶And in the eighth night my heart was vexed within me again, and I began to speak before the Most High. ³⁷For my spirit was greatly set on fire, and my soul was in distress. ³⁸And I said, "O LORD, of a truth You spoke at the beginning of the creation, on the first day, and said this: Let the heavens and earth be made; and Your word perfected the work. ³⁹And then the Spirit was fluttering, and darkness and silence were on every side; the sound of man's voice was not yet [heard]. ⁴⁰Then You commanded a ray of light to be brought out of Your treasures, that Your works might then appear. ⁴¹On the second day again You made the spirit of the expanse and commanded it to separate apart, and to make a division between the waters, that the one part might go up, and the other remain beneath. ⁴²On the third day You commanded that the waters should be gathered together in the seventh part of the earth: six parts You dried up, and You keep them, to the intent that of these some being both planted and tilled might serve before You. ⁴³For as soon as Your word went out the work was done. ⁴⁴For immediately there came out great and innumerable fruit, and manifold pleasures for the taste, and flowers of inimitable color, and aromas of most exquisite smell: and this was done the third day. ⁴⁵On the fourth day You commanded that the sun should shine, and the moon give her light, and the stars should be in their order: ⁴⁶and You gave them a charge to do service to man that was to be made. ⁴⁷On the fifth day You said to the seventh part, where the water was gathered together, that it should bring out living

creatures—birds and fishes: and so it came to pass, ⁴⁸that the mute water—and without life—brought out living things as it was told, that the peoples might therefore praise Your wondrous works. ⁴⁹Then You preserved two living creatures, the one You called Behemoth, and the other you called Leviathan; ⁵⁰and You separated the one from the other; for the seventh part, namely, where the water was gathered together, might not hold them both. ⁵¹To Behemoth You gave one part, which was dried up on the third day, that he should dwell in it, wherein are one thousand hills, ⁵²but to Leviathan You gave the seventh part, namely, the moist; and You have kept them to be devoured of whom You will, and when. ⁵³But on the sixth day You gave command to the earth, that it should bring out cattle, beasts, and creeping things before You: ⁵⁴and over these [is] Adam, whom You ordain lord over all the works that You have made; of him we all come—the people whom You have chosen. ⁵⁵I have spoken all this before You, O LORD, because You have said that You have made this world for our sakes. ⁵⁶As for the other nations, which also come of Adam, You have said that they are nothing, and are like to spittle: and You have likened the abundance of them to a drop that falls from a vessel. ⁵⁷And now, O LORD, behold [how] these nations, which are regarded as nothing, are lords over us, and devour us. ⁵⁸But we Your people, whom You have called Your firstborn, Your only begotten, and Your fervent lover, are given into their hands. ⁵⁹If the world is now made for our sakes, why do we not possess our world for an inheritance? How long will this endure?"

CHAPTER 7

¹And when I had made an end of speaking these words, there was sent to me the Messenger which had been sent to me the nights before, ²and He said to me, "Get up, Ezra, and hear the words that I have come to tell you." ³And I said, "Speak, my Lord." Then He said to me, "There is a sea set in a wide place, that it might be broad and vast. ⁴But the entrance thereof will be set in a narrow place so as to be like a river; ⁵whoever then should desire to go into the sea to look on it, or to rule it, if he did not go through the narrow, how could he come into the broad? ⁶Another thing also: there is a city built and set in a plain country, and full of all good things; ⁷but the entrance thereof is narrow and is set in a dangerous place to fall, having a fire on the right hand, and on the left a deep water; ⁸and there is only one path between them both, even between the fire and the water, [so small] that there could [be] but one man [who could] go there at once. ⁹If this city is now given to a man for an inheritance, if the heir does not pass the danger before him, how will he receive his inheritance?" ¹⁰And I said, "It is so, Lord." Then He said to me, "Even so is Israel's portion also. ¹¹Because for their sakes I made the world; and when Adam transgressed My statutes, then was decreed that [which] now is done. ¹²Then the entrances of this world were made narrow, and sorrowful, and toilsome: they are but few and evil, full of perils, and charged with great toils. ¹³For the entrances of the greater world are wide, and sure, and bring out fruit of immortality. ¹⁴If then those who live do not enter these narrow and vain things, they can never receive those that are laid up for them. ¹⁵Now therefore, why do you disquiet yourself, seeing you are but a corruptible man? And why are you moved, whereas you are but mortal? ¹⁶And why have you not considered in your mind that which is to come, rather than that which is present?" ¹⁷Then I answered and said, "O LORD that bears rule, behold, You have ordained in Your law that the righteous should inherit these things, but that the ungodly should perish. ¹⁸The righteous will therefore suffer narrow things, and hope for wide, but those who have done wickedly have suffered the narrow things, and yet will not see the wide." ¹⁹And He said to me, "You are not a judge above God, neither have you understanding above the Most High. ²⁰Yes, rather let many that now are perish, than that the Law of God which is set before them be despised. ²¹For God strictly commanded such as came, even as they came, what they should do to live, and what they should observe to avoid punishment. ²²Nevertheless, they were not obedient to Him, but spoke against Him and imagined for themselves vain things, ²³and framed cunning plans of wickedness, and said, moreover, of the Most High, that He is not, and did not know His ways, ²⁴but they despised His law and denied His covenants; they have not been faithful to His statutes and have not performed His works. ²⁵Therefore, Ezra, for the empty are empty things, and for the full are the full things. ²⁶For behold, the time will come, and it will be, when these signs of which I told you before will come to pass: that the bride will appear, even the city coming out, and she will be seen that now is withdrawn from the earth. ²⁷And whoever is delivered from the previously mentioned evils will see My wonders. ²⁸For My Son the Christ will be revealed with those that are with Him and will rejoice with those who remain four hundred years. ²⁹After these years My Son the Christ will die, and all those that have the breath of life. ³⁰And the world will be turned into the primordial silence [for] seven days, just as in the first beginning, so that no man will remain. ³¹And after seven days, the world that has not yet awaken will be raised up, and that which is corruptible will die. ³²And the earth will restore those that are asleep in her, and so will the dust those that dwell therein in silence, and the secret places will deliver those souls that were committed to them. ³³And the Most High will be revealed on the seat of judgment, and compassion will pass away, and patience will be withdrawn, ³⁴but only judgment will remain, truth will stand, and faith will wax strong; ³⁵and the work will follow, and the reward will be shown, and good deeds will awake, and wicked deeds will not sleep. ³⁶And the pit of torment will appear, and near it will be the place of rest; and the furnace will be shown, and near it the paradise of delight. ³⁷And then the Most High will say to the nations that are raised from the dead: See and understand whom you have denied, or whom you have not served, or whose commands you have despised. ³⁸Look on this side and on that: here is delight and rest, and there fire and torments. He will speak this to them in the Day of Judgment: ³⁹this is a day that has neither sun, nor moon, nor stars, ⁴⁰neither cloud, nor thunder, nor lightning, neither wind, nor water, nor air, neither darkness, nor evening, nor morning, ⁴¹neither summer, nor spring, nor heat, nor winter, neither frost, nor cold, nor hail, nor rain, nor dew, ⁴²neither noon, nor night, nor dawn, neither shining, nor brightness, nor light, save only the splendor of the glory of the Most High, whereby all will see the things that are set before them, ⁴³for it will endure as it were a week of years. ⁴⁴This is My judgment and the ordinance thereof; but only to you have I showed these things." ⁴⁵And I answered, I said even then, "O LORD, and I say now: blessed are those who are now alive and keep the [statutes] ordained of You. ⁴⁶But as touching them for whom my prayer was made, [what will I say]? For who is there of those who are alive that has not sinned, and who of the sons [of men] that has not transgressed Your covenant? ⁴⁷And now I see that the world to come will bring delight to few, but torments to many. ⁴⁸For an evil heart has grown up in us, which has led us astray from these [statutes, and] has brought us into corruption and into the ways of death, has showed us the paths of perdition, and removed us far from life—and that, not a few only, but well near all that have been created." ⁴⁹And He answered me, and said, "Listen to Me, and I will instruct you; and I will admonish you yet again: ⁵⁰for this reason the Most High has not made one world, but two. ⁵¹For whereas you have said that the just are not many, but few, and the ungodly abound, hear [the answer] to that. ⁵²If you have exceedingly few choice stones, will you set for yourself near them, according to their number, [things of] lead and clay?" ⁵³And I said, "Lord, how will this be?" ⁵⁴And He said to me, "Not only this, but ask the earth, and she will tell you; entreat her, and she will declare to you. ⁵⁵For you will say to her, You bring out gold, and silver, and brass, and iron also, and lead, and clay; ⁵⁶but silver is more abundant than gold, and brass than silver, and iron than brass, lead than iron, and clay than lead. ⁵⁷Therefore judge which things are precious and to be desired, what is abundant or what is rare." ⁵⁸And I said, "O LORD that bears rule, that which is plentiful is of less worth, for that which is more rare is more precious." ⁵⁹And He answered me, and said, "Weigh within yourself the things that you have thought, for he that has what is hard to get rejoices over him that has what is plentiful. ⁶⁰So also is the judgment which I have promised, for I will rejoice over the few that will be saved, inasmuch as these are those who have made My glory now to prevail, and of whom My Name is now named. ⁶¹And I will

not grieve over the multitude of those who perish; for these are those who are now like to vapor and have become as flame and smoke; they are set on fire and burn hotly and are quenched." ⁶²And I answered and said, "O you earth, why have you brought out, if the mind is made out of dust, like as all other created things? ⁶³For it were better that the dust itself had been unborn, so that the mind might not have been made from it. ⁶⁴But now the mind grows with us, and by reason of this we are tormented, because we perish and know it. ⁶⁵Let the race of men lament and the beasts of the field be glad; let all that are born lament, but let the four-footed beasts and the cattle rejoice. ⁶⁶For it is far better with them than with us; for they do not look for judgment, neither do they know of torments or of salvation promised to them after death. ⁶⁷For what does it profit us, that we will be preserved alive, but yet be afflicted with torment? ⁶⁸For all that are born are defiled with iniquities, and are full of sins, and laden with offenses; ⁶⁹and if after death we were not to come into judgment, perhaps it had been better for us." ⁷⁰And He answered me, and said, "When the Most High made the world, and Adam and all those who came of him, He first prepared the judgment and the things that pertain to the judgment. ⁷¹And now understand from your own words, for you have said that the mind grows with us. ⁷²Therefore, they that dwell on the earth will be tormented for this reason, that having understanding, they have done iniquity, and receiving commands, have not kept them, and having obtained a law, they dealt unfaithfully with that which they received. ⁷³What then will they have to say in the judgment, or how will they answer in the last times? ⁷⁴For how great a time has the Most High been patient with those who inhabit the world, and not for their sakes, but because of the times which He has foreordained!" ⁷⁵And I answered and said, "If I have found grace in Your sight, O LORD, show this to Your servant also, whether after death, even now when each of us gives up his soul, we will be kept in rest until those times come, in which You will renew the creation, or whether we will be tormented immediately." ⁷⁶And He answered me, and said, "I will show you this also, but do not join yourself with those who are scorners, nor count yourself with those who are tormented. ⁷⁷For you have a treasure of [good] works laid up with the Most High, but it will not be shown to you until the last times. ⁷⁸For concerning death the teaching is: When the determinate sentence has gone out from the Most High that a man should die, as the spirit leaves the body to return again to Him who gave it, it adores the glory of the Most High first of all. ⁷⁹And if it is one of those that have been scorners and have not kept the way of the Most High, and that have despised His law, and that hate those who fear God, ⁸⁰these spirits will not enter into habitations, but will wander and be in torments immediately, ever grieving and sad, in seven ways. ⁸¹The first way, because they have despised the Law of the Most High. ⁸²The second way, because they cannot now make a good returning that they may live. ⁸³The third way, they will see the reward laid up for those who have believed the covenants of the Most High. ⁸⁴The fourth way, they will consider the torment laid up for themselves in the last days. ⁸⁵The fifth way, they will see the dwelling places of the others guarded by messengers, with great quietness. ⁸⁶The sixth way, they will see how some of them will immediately pass into torment. ⁸⁷The seventh way, which is more grievous than all the previously mentioned ways, because they will pine away in confusion, and be consumed with shame, and will be withered up by fears, seeing the glory of the Most High before whom they have sinned while living, and before whom they will be judged in the last times. ⁸⁸Now this is the order of those who have kept the ways of the Most High, when they will be separated from the corruptible vessel. ⁸⁹In the time that they lived therein they painfully served the Most High, and were in danger every hour, that they might keep the Law of the Lawgiver perfectly. ⁹⁰Here then is the teaching concerning them: ⁹¹First of all, they will see with great joy the glory of Him who takes them up, for they will have rest in seven orders. ⁹²The first order, because they have labored with great effort to overcome the evil thought which was fashioned together with them, that it might not lead them astray from life into death. ⁹³The second order, because they see the perplexity in which the souls of the ungodly wander, and the punishment that awaits them. ⁹⁴The third order, they see the witness which He that fashioned them bears concerning them, that while they lived they kept the Law which was given them in trust. ⁹⁵The fourth order, they understand the rest which, being gathered in their chambers, they now enjoy with great quietness, guarded by messengers, and the glory that awaits them in the last days. ⁹⁶The fifth order, they rejoice, [seeing] how they have now escaped from that which is corruptible, and how they will inherit that which is to come, while they see moreover the narrowness and the painfulness from which they have been delivered, and the large room which they will receive with joy and immortality. ⁹⁷The sixth order, when it is showed to them how their face will shine as the sun, and how they will be made like to the light of the stars, being from now on incorruptible. ⁹⁸The seventh order, which is greater than all the previous orders, because they will rejoice with confidence, and because they will be bold without confusion, and will be glad without fear, for they hasten to behold the face of Him whom in their lifetime they served, and from whom they will receive [their] reward in glory. ⁹⁹This is the order of the souls of the just, as from now on is announced to them, and announced are the ways of torture which those who would not give heed will suffer from now on." ¹⁰⁰And I answered and said, "Will time therefore be given to the souls after they are separated from the bodies, that they may see what You have spoken to me?" ¹⁰¹And He said, "Their freedom will be for seven days, that for seven days they may see the things that you have been told, and afterward they will be gathered together in their habitations." ¹⁰²And I answered and said, "If I have found favor in Your sight, show further to me Your servant whether in the Day of Judgment the just will be able to intercede for the ungodly or to entreat the Most High for them, ¹⁰³whether fathers for children, or children for parents, or relatives for relatives, or countrymen for countrymen, or friends for those who are most dear." ¹⁰⁴And He answered me, and said, "Since you have found favor in My sight, I will show you this also: the Day of Judgment is a day of decision, and displays to all the seal of truth; even as now a father does not send his son, or a son his father, or a master his slave, or a friend him that is most dear, that in his stead he may be sick, or sleep, or eat, or be healed, ¹⁰⁵so never will anyone pray for another in that day, neither will one lay a burden on another, for then everyone will bear his own righteousness or unrighteousness." ¹⁰⁶And I answered and said, "How do we now find that first Abraham prayed for the people of Sodom, and Moses for the fathers that sinned in the wilderness, ¹⁰⁷and Joshua after him for Israel in the days of Achar, ¹⁰⁸and Samuel in the days of Saul, and David for the plague, and Solomon for those who [should worship] in the sanctuary, ¹⁰⁹and Elijah for those that received rain, and for the dead, that he might live, ¹¹⁰and Hezekiah for the people in the days of Sennacherib, and many for many? ¹¹¹If, therefore now, when corruption is grown up, and unrighteousness increased, the righteous have prayed for the ungodly, why will it not be so then also?" ¹¹²He answered me, and said, "This present world is not the end; the full glory does not remain therein. Therefore, they who were able have prayed for the weak, ¹¹³but the Day of Judgment will be the end of this time, and the beginning of the immortality to come, wherein corruption has passed away, ¹¹⁴intemperance is at an end, infidelity is cut off, but righteousness has grown, and truth has sprung up. ¹¹⁵Then no man will be able to have mercy on him that is cast in judgment, nor to thrust down him that has gotten the victory." ¹¹⁶I answered then and said, "This is my first and last saying, that it had been better that the earth had not given Adam: or else, when it had given [him], to have restrained him from sinning. ¹¹⁷For what profit is it for all that are in this present time to live in heaviness, and after death to look for punishment? ¹¹⁸O you Adam! What have you done? For though it was you that sinned, the evil is not fallen on you alone, but on all of us that come of you. ¹¹⁹For what profit is it to us, if there is promised us an immortal time, whereas we have done the works that bring death? ¹²⁰And that there has been promised us a continuous hope, whereas we have become most miserably vain? ¹²¹And that there are reserved habitations of health and safety, whereas we have lived wickedly? ¹²²And that the glory of the Most High will defend them which have led a pure life, whereas we have walked in the most wicked ways of all? ¹²³And that there will be showed a paradise, whose fruit endures without decay, wherein is abundance and healing, but we will not enter into it, ¹²⁴for we have walked in unpleasant places? ¹²⁵And that the faces of them which have used abstinence will shine above the stars, whereas our faces will be blacker than darkness? ¹²⁶For while we lived and committed iniquity, we did not consider what we should have to suffer after death." ¹²⁷Then He answered and said, "This is the condition of the battle, which man that is born on the earth will fight; ¹²⁸that, if he is overcome, he will suffer as you have said, but if he gets the victory, he will receive the thing that I say. ¹²⁹For this is the way of which Moses spoke to the people while he lived, saying, Choose life, that you may live. ¹³⁰Nevertheless, they did not believe him, nor yet the prophets after him, no, nor Me which have spoken to them, ¹³¹so that there will not be such heaviness in their destruction, as there will be joy over those who are persuaded to salvation." ¹³²I answered then and said, "I know, Lord, that the Most High is now called merciful, in that He has mercy on them which have not yet come into the world; ¹³³and compassionate, in that He has compassion on those that turn to His law; ¹³⁴and patient, for that He long endures those that have sinned, as His creatures; ¹³⁵and bountiful, for that He is ready to give rather than to exact; ¹³⁶and of great mercy, for that He multiplies more and more mercies to those who are present, and that are past, and also to them which are to come ¹³⁷(for if He did not multiply [His mercies], the world would not continue with those who dwell therein); ¹³⁸and one that forgives, for if He did not forgive of His goodness, that they which have committed iniquities might be eased of them, the ten-thousandth part of men would not remain living; ¹³⁹and a judge, [for] if He did not pardon those who were created by His word, and blot out the multitude of offenses, ¹⁴⁰there would perhaps be very few left in an innumerable multitude."

CHAPTER 8

¹And He answered me, and said, "The Most High has made this world for many, but the world to come for few. ²I will now tell you a similitude, Ezra: [just] as when you ask the earth, it will say to you that it gives very much mold of which earthen vessels are made, and little dust that gold comes of, even so is the course of the present world. ³There are many created, but few will be saved." ⁴And I answered and said, "Swallow down understanding then, O my soul, and let [my heart] devour wisdom. ⁵For you have come here without your will and depart when you would not, for there is given to you no more space than only to live a short time. ⁶O LORD, You that are over us, permit Your servant, that we may pray before You, and give us seed to our heart, and culture to our understanding, that there may come fruit of it, whereby each one will live that is corrupt, who bears the likeness of a man. ⁷For You are alone, and we are all one workmanship of Your hands, just as You have said. ⁸Forasmuch as You give life to the body that is fashioned now in the womb, and give it members, Your creature is preserved in fire and water, and [for] nine months Your workmanship endures Your creature which is created in her. ⁹But that which keeps and that which is kept will both be kept by Your keeping: and when the womb gives up again that which has grown in it, ¹⁰You have commanded that out of the parts of the body, that is to say, out of the breasts, be given milk, which is the fruit of the breasts, ¹¹that the thing which is fashioned may be nourished for a time, and afterward You will order it in Your mercy. ¹²Yes, You have brought it up in Your righteousness, and nurtured it in Your law, and corrected it with Your judgment. ¹³And You will mortify it as Your creature and give it life as Your work. ¹⁴If, therefore, You will lightly and suddenly destroy him which with so great labor was fashioned by Your command, to what purpose was he made? ¹⁵Now therefore, I will speak; touching man in general, You know best; but touching Your people [I will speak], for whose sake I am sorry; ¹⁶and for Your inheritance, for whose cause I mourn; and for Israel, for whom I am heavy; and for the seed of Jacob, for whose sake I am troubled; ¹⁷therefore I will begin to pray before You for myself and for them, for I see the falls of us that dwell in the land, ¹⁸but I have heard the swiftness of the judgment which is to come. ¹⁹Therefore hear my voice, and understand my saying, and I will speak before You." The beginning of the words of Ezra, before he was taken up. And he said, ²⁰"O LORD, You who remain forever, whose eyes are exalted, and whose chambers are in the air; ²¹whose throne is inestimable; whose glory may not be comprehended; before whom the army of messengers stand with trembling, ²²at whose bidding they are changed to wind and fire; whose word is sure, and sayings constant; whose ordinance is strong, and command fearful; ²³whose look dries up the depths, and whose indignation makes the mountains to melt away, and whose truth bears witness: ²⁴hear, O LORD, the prayer of Your servant, and give ear to the petition of Your handiwork; ²⁵attend to my words, for so long as I live I will speak, and so long as I have understanding I will answer. ²⁶Do not look on the sins of Your people, but on those who have served You in truth. ²⁷Do not regard the doings of those who deal wickedly, but of those who have kept Your covenants in affliction. ²⁸Do not think on those that have walked ungenuine before You, but remember them which have willingly known Your fear. ²⁹Do not let it be Your will to destroy them which have lived like cattle, but look on those who have clearly taught Your law. ³⁰Take no indignation at them which are deemed worse than beasts, but love those who have always put their trust in Your glory. ³¹For we and our fathers have passed our lives in ways that bring death, but You, because of us sinners, are called merciful. ³²For if You have a desire to have mercy on us, then You will be called merciful, to us, namely, that have no works of righteousness. ³³For the just, which have many [good] works laid up with You, will for their own deeds receive reward. ³⁴For what is man that You should take displeasure at him? Or what is a corruptible race that You should be so bitter toward it? ³⁵For in truth there is no man among those who are born, but he [who] has dealt wickedly; and among them that have lived there is none which have not done wrong. ³⁶For in this, O LORD, Your righteousness and Your goodness will be declared, if You are merciful to them which have no store of good works." ³⁷Then He answered me, and said, "You have spoken some things correctly, and according to your words so it will come to pass. ³⁸For indeed, I will not think on the fashioning of them which have sinned, or their death, their judgment, or their destruction, ³⁹but I will rejoice over the framing of the righteous, their pilgrimage also, and the salvation and the reward that they will have. ⁴⁰Therefore, just as I have spoken, so it will be. ⁴¹For as the farmer sows much seed on the ground, and plants many trees, and yet not all that is sown will come up in due season, neither will all that is planted take root: even so those who are sown in the world will not all be saved." ⁴²I answered then and said, "If I have found favor, let me speak before You. ⁴³Forasmuch as the farmer's seed, if it does not come up, seeing that it has not received Your rain in due season, or if it is corrupted through too much rain, so perishes, ⁴⁴likewise man, which is formed with Your hands, and is called Your own image, because he is made like [You], for whose sake You have formed all things, even him you have made like to the farmer's seed. ⁴⁵Do not be angry with us, but spare Your people, and have mercy on Your inheritance; for You have mercy on Your own creation." ⁴⁶Then He answered me, and said, "Things present are for those who now are, and things to come for such as will be hereafter. ⁴⁷For you come far short that you should be able to love My creature more than Me. But you have brought yourself full near to the unrighteous—never! ⁴⁸Yet in this you will be admirable to the Most High: ⁴⁹in that you have humbled yourself, as it is appropriate for you, and have not judged yourself [worthy to be] among the righteous, so as to be much glorified. ⁵⁰For many grievous miseries will fall on those who in the last times dwell in the world, because they have walked in great pride. ⁵¹But understand for yourself, and of such as are like you—seek out the glory. ⁵²For to you paradise is opened, the Tree of Life planted, the time to come is prepared, bounty is made ready, a city is built, and rest is allowed, goodness is perfected, wisdom being perfect beforehand. ⁵³The root [of evil] is sealed up from you, weakness is done away from you, and [death] is hidden; Hades and corruption have fled into forgetfulness; ⁵⁴sorrows have passed away, and in the end, the treasure of immortality is shown. ⁵⁵Therefore, do not ask any more questions

concerning the multitude of them that perish. ⁵⁶For when they had received liberty, they despised the Most High, thought scorn of His law, and forsook His ways. ⁵⁷Moreover, they have trodden down His righteous, ⁵⁸and said in their heart that there is no God; yes, and that knowing they must die. ⁵⁹For as the things previously stated you will receive, so thirst and pain which are prepared [they will receive], for the Most High did not will that men should come to nothing, ⁶⁰but they which are created have themselves defiled the Name of Him that made them and were unthankful to Him which prepared life for them. ⁶¹And therefore My judgment is now at hand, ⁶²which I have not showed to all men, but to you, and a few like you." Then I answered and said, ⁶³"Behold, O LORD, now You have showed me the multitude of the wonders, which You will do in the last times, but at what time, You have not showed me."

CHAPTER 9

¹And He answered me, and said, "Measure diligently within yourself: and when you see that a certain part of the signs are past, which have been told to you beforehand, ²then you will understand that it is the very time wherein the Most High will visit the world which was made by Him. ³And when there will be seen in the world earthquakes, disquietude of peoples, plans of nations, wavering of leaders, disquietude of princes, ⁴then you will understand that the Most High spoke of these things from the days that were previously from the beginning. ⁵For just as of all that is made in the world, the beginning is evident and the end manifest, ⁶so also are the times of the Most High: the beginnings are manifest in wonders and mighty works, and the end in effects and signs. ⁷And everyone that will be saved, and will be able to escape by his works, or by faith, whereby he has believed, ⁸will be preserved from the stated perils, and will see My salvation in My land, and within My borders, which I have sanctified for Myself from the beginning. ⁹Then those which have now abused My ways will be amazed, and those who have despitefully cast them away will dwell in torments. ¹⁰For as many as in their life have received benefits, and yet have not known Me, ¹¹and as many as have scorned My law while they still had liberty, and, when conversion was open to them, did not understand, but despised [it], ¹²must know [it] after death by torment. ¹³And therefore, no longer be curious how the ungodly will be punished, but inquire how the righteous will be saved, they whose the world [is, and] for whom the world [was created]." ¹⁴And I answered and said, ¹⁵"I have said before, and now speak, and will speak it also hereafter, that there are more of them which perish, than of those which will be saved: ¹⁶just as a wave is greater than a drop." ¹⁷And He answered me, saying, "Just as the field is, so also the seed; and as the flowers are, such are the colors also; and such as the work is, such is the judgment [on it] also; and as is the farmer, so is his threshing floor also. For there was a time in the world, ¹⁸even then when I was preparing for those who now live, before the world was made for them to dwell in; and then no man spoke against Me— ¹⁹there was not any; but now they which are created in this world that is prepared, both with a table that does not fail, and a law which is unsearchable, are corrupted in their manners. ²⁰So I considered My world, and behold, it was destroyed, and My earth, and behold, it was in peril, because of the plans that had come into it. ²¹And I saw, and spared them, but not greatly, and saved Myself a grape out of a cluster, and a plant out of a great forest. ²²Let the multitude which was born in vain perish then; and let My grape be saved, and My plant; for I have made them perfect with great labor. ²³Nevertheless, if you will cease yet seven more days, (however you will not fast in them, ²⁴but will go into a field of flowers, where no house is built, and eat only of the flowers of the field; and you will taste no flesh, and will drink no wine, but [will eat] flowers only;) ²⁵and pray to the Most High continually, then I will come and talk with you." ²⁶So I went my way, just as He commanded me, into the field which is called Ardat; and there I sat among the flowers, and ate of the herbs of the field, and its meat satisfied me. ²⁷And it came to pass after seven days that I lay on the grass, and my heart was vexed again just as before; ²⁸and my mouth was opened, and I began to speak before the LORD Most High, and said, ²⁹"O LORD, You showed Yourself among us, to our fathers in the wilderness, when they went out of Egypt, and when they came into the wilderness, where no man treads and which bears no fruit; ³⁰and You said, Hear Me, Israel; and mark My words, O seed of Jacob. ³¹For behold, I sow My law in you, and it will bring out fruit in you, and you will be glorified in it forever. ³²But our fathers, which received the Law, did not keep it, and did not observe the statutes: and the fruit of the Law did not perish, neither could it, for it was Yours; ³³yet those who received it perished, because they did not keep the thing that was sown in them. ³⁴And behold, it is a custom that when the ground has received seed, or the sea a ship, or any vessel meat or drink, and when it comes to pass that that which is sown, or that which is launched, ³⁵or the things which have been received, should come to an end, these come to an end, but the receptacles remain: yet with us it has not happened so. ³⁶For we that have received the Law will perish by sin, and also our heart which received it. ³⁷Notwithstanding, the Law does not perish, but remains in its honor." ³⁸And when I spoke these things in my heart, I looked around me with my eyes, and on the right side I saw a woman, and behold, she mourned and wept with a loud voice, and was greatly grieved in mind, and her clothes were torn, and she had ashes on her head. ³⁹Then I let my thoughts go wherein I was occupied, and I turned to her, ⁴⁰and said to her, "Why do you weep? And why are you grieved in your mind?" ⁴¹And she said to me, "Leave me alone, my lord, that I may mourn myself, and add to my sorrow, for I am severely vexed in my mind, and brought very low." ⁴²And I said to her, "What ails you? Tell me." ⁴³She said to me, "I, your servant, was barren, and had no child, though I had a husband [for] thirty years. ⁴⁴And every hour and every day these thirty years I made my prayer to the Most High day and night. ⁴⁵And it came to pass after thirty years, that God heard me, your handmaid, and looked on my low estate, and considered my trouble, and gave me a son: and I rejoiced in him greatly—me, and my husband, and all my neighbors—and we gave great honor to the Mighty. ⁴⁶And I nourished him with great travail. ⁴⁷So when he grew up, and I came to take a wife for him, I made him a feast day."

CHAPTER 10

¹"And so it came to pass, that when my son had entered into his wedding chamber, he fell down and died. ²Then we all overthrew the lights, and all my neighbors rose up to comfort me: and I remained quiet to the second day at night. ³And it came to pass when they had all ceased to comfort me, to the end I might be quiet, then I arose by night, and fled, and came here into this field, as you see. ⁴And now I do not purpose to return into the city, but to stay here, and neither to eat nor drink, but to continually mourn and fast until I die." ⁵Then I left the meditations wherein I was, and answered her in anger, and said, ⁶"You foolish woman above all others! Do you not see our mourning, and what has happened to us? ⁷How Zion, the mother of us all, is full of sorrow, and greatly humbled. ⁸It is right to mourn very severely now, seeing we all mourn, and to be sorrowful, seeing we are all in sorrow, but you mourn for one son. ⁹For ask the earth, and she will tell you that it is she which should mourn for so many that grow on her. ¹⁰For out of her all had their beginnings, and others will come; and behold, almost all of them walk into destruction, and the multitude of them is utterly rooted out. ¹¹Who then should make more mourning: she that has lost so great a multitude, or you which are grieved but for one? ¹²But if you say to me, My lamentation is not like the earth's, for I have lost the fruit of my womb, which I brought out with pains, and bore with sorrows, ¹³but [it is with the] earth after the manner of the earth—the multitude present in it is gone, as it came: ¹⁴then I say to you, just as you have brought out with sorrow, even so the earth has also given her fruit, namely, man, ever since the beginning to Him that made her. ¹⁵Now therefore, keep your sorrow to yourself, and bear with a good courage the adversities which have befallen you. ¹⁶For if you will acknowledge the decree of God to be just, you will both receive your son in time, and will be praised among women. ¹⁷Go your way then into the city to your husband." ¹⁸And she said to me, "I will not do that. I will not go into the city, but I will die here." ¹⁹So I proceeded to speak further to her, and said, ²⁰"Do not do that, but permit yourself to be prevailed on by reason of the adversities of Zion; and be comforted by reason of the

sorrow of Jerusalem. ²¹For you see that our sanctuary is laid waste, our altar broken down, our temple destroyed; ²²our lute is brought low, our song is put to silence, our rejoicing is at an end; the light of our candlestick is put out, the Ark of our covenant is plundered, our holy things are defiled, and the name that is called on us is profaned; our freemen are despitefully treated, our priests are burned, our Levites have gone into captivity, our virgins are defiled, and our wives ravished; our righteous men carried away, our little ones betrayed, our young men are brought into bondage, and our strong men have become weak; ²³and, what is more than all, the seal of Zion—for she has now lost the seal of her honor, and is delivered into the hands of those who hate us. ²⁴Therefore, shake off your great heaviness, and put away from yourself the multitude of sorrows, that the Mighty may be merciful to you again, and the Most High may give you rest, even ease from your travails." ²⁵And it came to pass, while I was talking with her, behold, her face suddenly shined exceedingly, and her countenance radiated like lightning, so that I was terrified of her, and wondered what this might be; ²⁶and behold, she suddenly made a great [and] very fearful cry, so that the earth shook at the noise. ²⁷And I looked, and behold, the woman appeared to me no longer, but there [where she was] a city was built, and a place showed itself from large foundations. Then I was afraid, and cried with a loud voice, and said, ²⁸"Where is Uriel the messenger, who came to me at the first? For he has caused me to fall into this great trance, and my end is turned into corruption, and my prayer to rebuke." ²⁹And as I was speaking these words, behold, the messenger who had come to me at the first came to me, and he looked on me; ³⁰and behold, I lay as one that had been dead, and my understanding was taken from me; and he took me by the right hand, and comforted me, and set me on my feet, and said to me, ³¹"What ails you? And why are you so disquieted? And why is your understanding troubled, and the thoughts of your heart?" ³²And I said, "Because you have forsaken me: yet I did according to your words, and went into the field, and behold, I have seen, and yet see, that which I am not able to express." ³³And he said to me, "Stand up like a man, and I will advise you." ³⁴Then I said, "Speak, my Lord; only do not forsake me, lest I die without hope. ³⁵For I have seen and heard that [which] I do not understand. ³⁶Or is my sense deceived, or my soul in a dream? ³⁷Now therefore, I implore you to show your servant concerning this vision." ³⁸And he answered me, and said, "Hear me, and I will inform you, and tell you concerning the things of which you are afraid. For the Most High has revealed many secret things to you. ³⁹He has seen that your way is right, for that you continually mourn for your people and make great lamentation for Zion. ⁴⁰Therefore, this is the meaning of the vision: ⁴¹the woman which appeared to you a little while ago—whom you saw mourning, and began to comfort her, ⁴²but now you no longer see the likeness of the woman, but there appeared to you a city in building, ⁴³and whereas she told you of the death of her son—this is the solution: ⁴⁴this woman, whom you saw, is Zion, whom you now see as a city built. ⁴⁵And whereas she said to you that she has been barren [for] thirty years, [it is] because there were three thousand years in the world wherein there was no offering as yet offered in her. ⁴⁶And it came to pass after three thousand years, that Solomon built the city and offered offerings: then it was that the barren [woman] bore a son. ⁴⁷And whereas she told you that she nourished him with travail: that was the dwelling in Jerusalem. ⁴⁸And whereas she said to you, My son coming into his marriage chamber died, and that misfortune befell her: this was the destruction that came to Jerusalem. ⁴⁹And behold, you saw her likeness, how she mourned for her son, and you began to comfort her for what has befallen her: these were the things to be opened to you. ⁵⁰For now the Most High, seeing that you are grieved, and suffer from your whole heart for her, has showed you the brightness of her glory, and the attractiveness of her beauty: ⁵¹and therefore I commanded you to remain in the field where no house was built, ⁵²for I knew that the Most High would show this to you. ⁵³Therefore I commanded you to come into the field where no foundation of any building was. ⁵⁴For in the place wherein the city of the Most High was to be shown, the work of no man's building could stand. ⁵⁵Therefore, do not fear, nor let your heart be frightened, but go your way in, and see the beauty and greatness of the building, as much as your eyes are able to see, ⁵⁶and then you will hear as much as your ears may comprehend. ⁵⁷For you are blessed above many, and are called by name with the Most High, like as but few. ⁵⁸But tomorrow at night you will remain here; ⁵⁹and so the Most High will show you those visions in dreams, of what the Most High will do to those who dwell on the earth in the last days." So I slept that night and another, just as he commanded me.

CHAPTER 11

¹And it came to pass the second night that I saw a dream, and behold, there came up from the sea an eagle which had twelve feathered wings and three heads. ²And I saw, and behold, she spread her wings over all the earth, and all the winds of the sky blew on her, and the clouds were gathered together against her. ³And I saw, and out of her wings there grew [other] wings near them; and they became little wings and small. ⁴But her heads were at rest: the head in the midst was greater than the other heads yet rested with them. ⁵Moreover, I saw, and behold, the eagle flew with her wings, to reign over the earth, and over those who dwell therein. ⁶And I saw how all things under Heaven were subject to her, and no man spoke against her, no, not one creature on earth. ⁷And I saw, and behold, the eagle rose on her talons, and uttered her voice to her wings, saying, ⁸"Do not watch all at once: everyone sleep in his own place, and watch by course; ⁹but let the heads be preserved for the last." ¹⁰And I saw, and behold, the voice did not go out of her heads, but from the midst of her body. ¹¹And I counted her wings that were near the other, and behold, there were eight of them. ¹²And I saw, and behold, on the right side there arose one wing, and it reigned over all the earth; ¹³and so it was, that when it reigned, the end of it came and it did not appear, so that the place thereof appeared no longer; and following [it], the next rose up and reigned, and it ruled a great time; ¹⁴and it happened, that when it reigned, the end of it also came, so that it appeared no longer, just as the first. ¹⁵And behold, there came a voice to it, and said, ¹⁶"Hear—you that have borne rule over the earth all this time; this I proclaim to you, before you will appear no longer: ¹⁷none after you will attain to your time, neither to the half thereof." ¹⁸Then the third arose, and had the rule as the others before, and it also appeared no longer. ¹⁹So it went with all the wings, one after another, as that each one bore rule, and then appeared no longer. ²⁰And I saw, and behold, in process of time the wings that followed were set up on the right side, that they might also rule; and some of them ruled, but within a while they appeared no longer; ²¹some of them also rose up, but did not rule. ²²After this I saw, and behold, the twelve wings appeared no longer, nor two of the little wings, ²³and there was no longer left on the eagle's body, but the three heads that rested, and six little wings. ²⁴And I saw, and behold, two little wings divided themselves from the six, and remained under the head that was on the right side, but four remained in their place. ²⁵And I saw, and behold, these wings under thought to set themselves up, and to have the rule. ²⁶And I saw, and behold, there was one set up, but within a while it appeared no longer. ²⁷A second also, and it was gone sooner than the first. ²⁸And I saw, and behold, the two that remained also thought in themselves to reign; ²⁹and while they so thought, behold, there awakened one of the heads that were at rest, [namely, it] that was in the midst; for that was greater than the two [other] heads. ³⁰And I saw how it joined the two [other] heads with it. ³¹And behold, the head was turned with those who were with it, and it ate up the two wings under that thought to have reigned. ³²But this head held the whole earth in possession, and bore rule over those that dwell therein with much oppression; and it had the governance of the world more than all the wings that had been. ³³And after this I saw, and behold, the head that was in the midst also suddenly appeared no longer, just as the wings. ³⁴But there remained the two heads, which also in like manner reigned over the earth, and over those that dwell therein. ³⁵And I saw, and behold, the head on the right side devoured it that was on the left side. ³⁶Then I heard a voice, which said to me, "Look before you, and consider the thing that you see." ³⁷And I saw, and behold, as it were a lion roused out of the wood roaring; and I heard how that he sent out a man's voice to the eagle,

and spoke, saying, ³⁸"Hear! I will talk with you, and the Most High will say to you, ³⁹Are you not it that remains of the four beasts, whom I made to reign in My world, that the end of My times might come through them? ⁴⁰And the fourth came, and overcame all the beasts that were past, and held the world in governance with great trembling, and the whole circle of the earth with grievous oppression; and for such a long time he lived on the earth with deceit. ⁴¹And you have judged the earth, but not with truth. ⁴²For you have afflicted the meek, you have hurt the peaceful, you have hated those who speak truth, you have loved liars, and destroyed the dwellings of those who brought out fruit, and cast down the walls of such as did you no harm. ⁴³Therefore your insolent dealing has come up to the Most High, and your pride to the Mighty. ⁴⁴The Most High has also looked on His times, and behold, they are ended, and His ages are fulfilled. ⁴⁵And therefore, appear no longer you eagle, nor your horrible wings, nor your evil little wings, nor your cruel heads, nor your hurtful talons, nor all your vain body, ⁴⁶that all the earth may be refreshed, and be eased, being delivered from your violence, and that she may hope for the judgment and mercy of Him that made her."

CHAPTER 12

¹And it came to pass while the lion spoke these words to the eagle, I saw, ²and behold, the head that remained appeared no longer, and the two wings which went over to it arose and set themselves up to reign, and their kingdom was small, and full of uproar. ³And I saw, and behold, they appeared no longer, and the whole body of the eagle was burned, so that the earth was in great fear: then I awoke by reason of great ecstasy of mind, and from great fear, and said to my spirit, ⁴"Behold, you have done this to me, in that you search out the ways of the Most High. ⁵Behold, I am yet weary in my mind, and very weak in my spirit; nor is there the least strength in me, because of the great fear with which I was frightened this night. ⁶Therefore, I will now implore the Most High, that He will strengthen me to the end." ⁷And I said, "O LORD that bears rule, if I have found favor in Your sight, and if I am justified with You above many others, and if my prayer has indeed come up before Your face, ⁸strengthen me then and show me, Your servant, the interpretation and plain meaning of this fearful vision, that You may perfectly comfort my soul. ⁹For You have judged me worthy to show me the end of time and the last times." ¹⁰And He said to me, "This is the interpretation of this vision which you saw: ¹¹the eagle, whom you saw come up from the sea, is the fourth kingdom which appeared in vision to your brother Daniel. ¹²But it was not expounded to him, as I now expound it to you or have expounded it. ¹³Behold, the days come that there will rise up a kingdom on earth, and it will be feared above all the kingdoms that were before it. ¹⁴Twelve kings will reign in it, one after another, ¹⁵of which the second will begin to reign and will have a longer time than [any of the] twelve. ¹⁶This is the interpretation of the twelve wings, which you saw. ¹⁷And whereas you heard a voice which spoke, not going out from the heads, but from the midst of the body thereof, this is the interpretation: ¹⁸that after the time of that kingdom there will arise no small contentions, and it will stand in peril of falling; nevertheless, it will not then fall, but will be restored again to its first estate. ¹⁹And whereas you saw the eight wings under sticking to her wings, this is the interpretation: ²⁰that there will arise eight kings in it, whose times will be but small, and their years swift. ²¹And two of them will perish when the middle time approaches; four will be kept for awhile until the time of the ending thereof will approach; but two will be kept to the end. ²²And whereas you saw three heads resting, this is the interpretation: ²³in the last days thereof, the Most High will raise up three kingdoms, and renew many things therein, and they will bear rule over the earth, ²⁴and over those that dwell therein, with much oppression, above all those that were before them. Therefore they are called the heads of the eagle. ²⁵For these are those who will accomplish her wickedness, and that will finish her last end. ²⁶And whereas you saw that the great head appeared no longer, [it signifies] that one of them will die on his bed, and yet with pain. ²⁷But for the two that remained, the sword will devour them. ²⁸For the sword of the one will devour him that was with him, but he will also fall by the sword in the last days. ²⁹And whereas you saw two wings under passing over to the head that is on the right side, ³⁰this is the interpretation: these are they whom the Most High has kept to His end; this is the small kingdom and full of trouble, as you saw. ³¹And the lion, whom you saw rising up out of the wood, and roaring, and speaking to the eagle, and rebuking her for her unrighteousness, and all her words which you have heard: ³²this is the Anointed One, whom the Most High has kept to the end of days, who will spring up out of the seed of David, and He will come and speak to them, and reprove them for their wickedness and unrighteousness, and will heap up before them their contemptuous dealings. ³³For at the first He will set them alive in His judgment, and when He has reproved them, He will destroy them. ³⁴For He will deliver the rest of My people with mercy, those that have been preserved throughout My borders, and He will make them joyful until the coming of the end, even the Day of Judgment, of which I have spoken to you from the beginning. ³⁵This is the dream that you saw, and this is the interpretation thereof: ³⁶and you alone have been chosen to know the secret of the Most High. ³⁷Therefore, write all these things that you have seen in a scroll and put them in a secret place, ³⁸and you will teach them to the wise of your people, whose hearts you know are able to comprehend and keep these secrets. ³⁹But wait here yourself yet seven more days, that there may be showed to you whatever it pleases the Most High to show you." And He departed from me. ⁴⁰And it came to pass, when all the people saw that the seven days were past, and I had not come into the city again, they gathered themselves all together, from the least to the greatest, and came to me, and spoke to me, saying, ⁴¹"How have we offended you? And what evil have we done against you that you have utterly forsaken us, and sit in this place? ⁴²For of all the prophets you alone are left to us, as a cluster of the vintage, and as a lamp in a dark place, and as a haven for a ship saved from the tempest. ⁴³Are the evils which have come to us not sufficient? ⁴⁴If you will forsake us, how much better had it been for us if we had also been consumed in the burning of Zion! ⁴⁵For we are not better than those who died there." And they wept with a loud voice. And I answered them, and said, ⁴⁶"Be of good comfort, O Israel; and do not be sorrowful, you house of Jacob: ⁴⁷for the Most High has you in remembrance, and the Mighty has not forgotten you forever. ⁴⁸As for me, I have not forsaken you, neither have I departed from you, but have come into this place to pray for the desolation of Zion, and that I might seek mercy for the low estate of your sanctuary. ⁴⁹And now go your way, every man to his own house, and after these days I will come to you." ⁵⁰So the people went their way into the city, just as I said to them, ⁵¹but I sat in the field seven days, as [the messenger] commanded me; and in those days I ate only of the flowers of the field and had my meat of the herbs.

CHAPTER 13

¹And it came to pass after seven days, I dreamed a dream by night: ²and behold, there arose a wind from the sea, that it moved all the waves thereof. ³And I saw, and behold, this wind caused to come up from the midst of the sea as it were the likeness of a Man, and I saw, and behold, that Man flew with the clouds of Heaven; and when He turned His countenance to look, all things trembled that were seen under Him. ⁴And whenever the voice went out of His mouth, all those that heard His voice burned, just as the wax melts when it feels the fire. ⁵And after this I saw, and behold, there was gathered together a multitude of men, out of number, from the four winds of the sky, to make war against the Man that came out of the sea. ⁶And I saw, and behold, He carved Himself a great mountain, and flew on it. ⁷But I sought to see the region or place where the mountain was graven, and I could not. ⁸And after this I saw, and behold, all they which were gathered together to fight against Him were severely afraid, and yet dared fight. ⁹And behold, as He saw the assault of the multitude that came, He neither lifted up His hand, nor held spear, nor any instrument of war, ¹⁰but only I saw how that He sent out of His mouth as it had been a flood of fire, and out of His lips a flaming breath, and out of His tongue He cast out sparks of the storm. ¹¹And these were all mixed together: the flood of fire, the flaming breath, and the great storm; and they fell on the assault of the multitude which was prepared to fight, and burned all of them up, so that suddenly

nothing of [the] innumerable multitude was to be seen, but only dust of ashes and smell of smoke. When I saw this, I was amazed. ¹²Afterward I saw the same Man come down from the mountain, and call to Himself another multitude which was peaceful. ¹³And many people came to Him, of which some were glad, some were sorry, some of them were bound, and some brought of those who were offered. Then through great fear I awakened, and prayed to the Most High, and said, ¹⁴"You have showed Your servant these wonders from the beginning, and have counted me worthy that You should receive my prayer: ¹⁵and now show me, moreover, the interpretation of this dream. ¹⁶For as I conceive in my understanding, woe to those who will be left in those days! And much more, woe to those who are not left! ¹⁷For those who were not left will be in heaviness, ¹⁸understanding the things that are laid up in the latter days, but not attaining to them. ¹⁹But also woe to them that are left, for this reason; for they will see great perils and many necessities, just as these dreams declare. ²⁰Yet it is better for one to be in peril and to come into these things, than to pass away as a cloud out of the world, and not to see the things that will happen in the last days." And He answered to me, and said, ²¹"I will tell you the interpretation of the vision, and I will also open to you the things of which you have made mention. ²²Whereas you have spoken of those who are left behind, this is the interpretation: ²³He that will endure the peril in that time will keep those who have fallen into danger, even such as have works and faith toward the Almighty. ²⁴Therefore, know that they which are left behind are more blessed than those who are dead. ²⁵These are the interpretations of the vision: whereas you saw a Man coming up from the midst of the sea, ²⁶this is He whom the Most High has kept a great season, which by His own self will deliver His creature; and He will order those who are left behind. ²⁷And whereas you saw that out of His mouth there came wind, and fire, and storm, ²⁸and whereas He held neither spear, nor any instrument of war, but destroyed the assault of that multitude which came to fight against Him, this is the interpretation: ²⁹behold, the days come when the Most High will begin to deliver those who are on the earth. ³⁰And there will come astonishment of mind on those who dwell on the earth. ³¹And one will think to war against another—city against city, place against place, people against people, and kingdom against kingdom. ³²And it will be, when these things will come to pass, and the signs will happen which I showed you before, then My Son will be revealed, whom you saw [as] a Man ascending. ³³And it will be, when all the nations hear His voice, every man will leave his own land and the battle they have against one another. ³⁴And an innumerable multitude will be gathered together, as you saw, desiring to come and to fight against Him. ³⁵But He will stand on the top of Mount Zion. ³⁶And Zion will come, and will be shown to all men, being prepared and built, just as you saw the mountain graven without hands. ³⁷And He, My Son, will rebuke the nations which have come for their wickedness, [with plagues] that are like to a tempest; ³⁸and He will taunt them to their face with their evil thoughts, and the torments with which they will be tormented, which are likened to a flame; and He will destroy them without labor by the Law, which is likened to fire. ³⁹And whereas you saw that He gathered to Himself another multitude that was peaceful: ⁴⁰these are the ten tribes, which were led away out of their own land in the time of Hoshea the king, whom Salmananser the king of the Assyrians led away captive, and he carried them beyond the River, and they were carried into another land. ⁴¹But they took this counsel among themselves, that they would leave the multitude of the heathen, and go out into a further country, where mankind never lived, ⁴²that they might keep their statutes there, which they had not kept in their own land. ⁴³And they entered by the narrow passages of the River Euphrates. ⁴⁴For the Most High then performed signs for them, and held back the springs of the River until they had passed over. ⁴⁵For through that country there was a great way to go, namely, of a year and a half: and the same region is called Arzareth. ⁴⁶Then they lived there until the latter time; and now when they begin to come again, ⁴⁷the Most High holds back the springs of the River again, that they may go through: therefore you saw the multitude gathered together with peace. ⁴⁸But those that are left behind of your people are those who are found within My holy border. ⁴⁹It will be, therefore, when He will destroy the multitude of the nations that are gathered together, He will defend the people that remain. ⁵⁰And then He will show them very many wonders." ⁵¹Then I said, "O LORD that bears rule, show me this: why I have seen the Man coming up from the midst of the sea." ⁵²And He said to me, "Just as one can neither seek out nor know what is in the deep of the sea, even so can no man on earth see My Son, or those that are with Him, but in the time of His day. ⁵³This is the interpretation of the dream which you saw, and for this you only are enlightened herein. ⁵⁴For you have forsaken your own [ways, and] applied your diligence to Mine, and have sought out My law. ⁵⁵You have ordered your life in wisdom and have called understanding your mother. ⁵⁶And therefore I have showed you this; for there is a reward laid up with the Most High; and it will be, after another three days I will speak other things to you and declare to you mighty and wondrous things." ⁵⁷Then I went out and passed into the field, greatly giving praise and thanks to the Most High because of His wonders, which He did from time to time, ⁵⁸and because He governs the time, and such things as fall in their seasons. And there I sat three days.

CHAPTER 14

¹And it came to pass on the third day, I sat under an oak, and behold, there came a voice out of a bush near me, and said, "Ezra, Ezra." ²And I said, "Here I am, Lord." And I stood up on my feet. ³Then He said to me, "In the bush I manifestly revealed Myself, and talked with Moses when My people were in bondage in Egypt: ⁴and I sent him, and he led My people out of Egypt; and I brought him up to [the] mountain of Sinai, where I kept him near Me for many days, ⁵and told him many wondrous things, and showed him the secrets of the times, and the end of the seasons, and commanded him, saying, ⁶You will publish these words openly, and these you will hide. ⁷And now I say to you, ⁸lay up in your heart the signs that I have showed, and the dreams that you have seen, and the interpretations which you have heard: ⁹for you will be taken away from men, and from now on you will remain with My Son, and with such as are like you, until the times are ended. ¹⁰For the world has lost its youth, and the times begin to wax old. ¹¹For the world is divided into twelve parts, and ten parts of it are already gone, even the half of the tenth part: ¹²and there remains of it two parts after the middle of the tenth part. ¹³Now therefore, set your house in order, and reprove your people, comfort the lowly among them, and instruct such of them as are wise, and now renounce the life that is corruptible, ¹⁴and let go from the mortal thoughts, cast yourself away from the burdens of man, put off now your weak nature, ¹⁵and lay aside the thoughts that are most grievous to you, and hasten to depart from these times. ¹⁶For yet worse evils than those which you have seen happen will be done hereafter. ¹⁷For see how much the world will be weaker through age—so much the more will evils increase on those who dwell therein. ¹⁸For the truth will withdraw itself further off, and falsehood will be hard at hand; for now the eagle which you saw in [the] vision hastens to come." ¹⁹Then I answered and said, "I will speak before You, O LORD. ²⁰Behold, I will go, as You have commanded me, and reprove the people that now are, but those who will be born afterward, who will admonish them? For the world is set in darkness, and those who dwell therein are without light. ²¹For Your law is burned, therefore no man knows the things that You have done, or the works that will be done. ²²But if I have found favor before You, send the Holy Spirit to me, and I will write all that has been done in the world since the beginning, even the things that were written in Your law, that men may be able to find the path, and that they which would live in the latter days may live." ²³And He answered me and said, "Go your way, gather the people together, and say to them that they may not seek you for forty days. ²⁴But prepare many tablets, and take with you Sarea, Dabria, Selemia, Ethanus, and Asiel, these five, which are ready to write swiftly; ²⁵and come here, and I will light a lamp of understanding in your heart, which will not be put out until the things which you will write are ended. ²⁶And when you have done this, some things you will publish openly, and some things you will deliver in secret to the

wise. Tomorrow at this hour you will begin to write." ²⁷Then I went out, as He commanded me, and gathered all the people together, and said, ²⁸"Hear these words, O Israel. ²⁹At the beginning our fathers were strangers in Egypt, and they were delivered from there, ³⁰and received the law of life, which they did not keep, which you also have transgressed after them. ³¹Then the land, even the land of Zion, was given to you for a possession, but you yourselves, and your fathers, have done unrighteousness, and have not kept the ways which the Most High commanded you. ³²And forasmuch as He is a righteous judge, He took from you for awhile the thing that He had given to you. ³³And now you are here, and your relatives are among you. ³⁴Therefore, if [it] so be that you will rule over your own understanding, and instruct your hearts, you will be kept alive, and after death you will obtain mercy. ³⁵For after death the judgment will come when we will live again; and then the names of the righteous will be manifest, and the works of the ungodly will be declared. ³⁶Therefore, let no man come to me now, nor seek after me these forty days." ³⁷So I took the five men as He commanded me, and we went out into the field and remained there. ³⁸And it came to pass on the next day that, behold, a voice called me, saying, "Ezra, open your mouth, and drink what I give you to drink." ³⁹Then I opened my mouth, and behold, there was given to me a full cup, which was full as it were with water, but the color of it was like fire. ⁴⁰And I took it and drank. And when I had drunk of it, my heart uttered understanding, and wisdom grew in my breast, for my spirit retained its memory; ⁴¹and my mouth was opened and no longer shut. ⁴²The Most High gave understanding to the five men, and they wrote by course the things that were told them, in characters which they did not know, and they sat [for] forty days. Now they wrote in the daytime, and at night they ate bread. ⁴³As for me, I spoke in the day, and I did not hold my tongue by night. ⁴⁴So in forty days ninety-four scrolls were written. ⁴⁵And it came to pass, when the forty days were fulfilled, that the Most High spoke to me, saying, "The first that you have written publish openly, and let the worthy and unworthy read it, ⁴⁶but keep the seventy last, that you may deliver them to such as are wise among your people, ⁴⁷for in them is the spring of understanding, the fountain of wisdom, and the stream of knowledge." ⁴⁸And I did so.

CHAPTER 15

¹"Behold, speak in the ears of My people the words of prophecy, which I will put in your mouth," says the LORD; ²"and cause them to be written in paper, for they are faithful and true. ³Do not be afraid of their imaginations against you, do not let the unbelief of them that speak against you trouble you. ⁴For all the unbelievers will die in their unbelief. ⁵Behold," says the LORD, "I bring calamities on the whole earth: sword, and famine, and death, and destruction. ⁶For wickedness has prevailed over every land, and their hurtful works have come to the full. ⁷Therefore," says the LORD, ⁸"I will no longer hold My peace as touching their wickedness, which they profanely commit, neither will I permit them in these things, which they wickedly practice. Behold, the innocent and righteous blood cries to Me, and the souls of the righteous cry out continually. ⁹I will surely avenge them," says the LORD, "and will receive to Myself all the innocent blood from among them. ¹⁰Behold, My people are led as a flock to the slaughter: I will not permit them to now dwell in the land of Egypt, ¹¹but I will bring them out with a mighty hand and with a high arm, and will strike Egypt with plagues, as previously, and will destroy all the land thereof. ¹²Let Egypt mourn, and the foundations thereof, for the plague of the discipline and the punishment that God will bring on it. ¹³Let the farmers that till the ground mourn, for their seeds will fail and their trees will be laid waste through the blasting, and hail, and a terrible storm. ¹⁴Woe to the world and those who dwell therein! ¹⁵For the sword and their destruction draws near, and nation will rise up against nation to battle with weapons in their hands. ¹⁶For there will be sedition among men; and waxing strong against one another, they will not regard their king nor the chief of their great ones, in their might. ¹⁷For a man will desire to go into a city and will not be able. ¹⁸For because of their pride the cities will be troubled, the houses will be destroyed, and men will be afraid. ¹⁹A man will have no pity on his neighbor but will make an assault on their houses with the sword, and plunder their goods, because of the lack of bread, and for great suffering. ²⁰Behold," says God, "I call together all the kings of the earth, to stir up those who are from the rising of the sun, from the south, from the east, and Libanus, to turn themselves against one another, and repay the things that they have done to them. ²¹Just as they yet do this day to My chosen, so I will do also, and repay in their bosom." The LORD God says: ²²"My right hand will not spare the sinners, and My sword will not cease over those who shed innocent blood on the earth. ²³And a fire has gone out from His wrath, and has consumed the foundations of the earth, and the sinners, like the straw that is kindled. ²⁴Woe to those who sin and do not keep My commands!" says the LORD. ²⁵"I will not spare them. Go your way, you rebellious children, do not defile My sanctuary. ²⁶For the LORD knows all those who trespass against Him, therefore He has delivered them to death and destruction. ²⁷For now the calamities have come on the whole earth, and you will remain in them, for God will not deliver you, because you have sinned against Him. ²⁸Behold, a horrible vision, and the appearance thereof from the east! ²⁹And the nations of the dragons of Arabia will come out with many chariots, and from the day that they set out the hissing of them is carried over the earth, so that all they which will hear them may also fear and tremble. ³⁰Also the Carmonians raging in wrath will go out as the wild boars of the wood, and they will come with great power and join battle with them, and will waste a portion of the land of the Assyrians with their teeth. ³¹And then the dragons will have the upper hand, remembering their nature; and if they will turn themselves, conspiring together in great power to persecute them, ³²then these will be troubled, and keep silence through their power, and will turn and flee. ³³And from the land of the Assyrians the ambusher in wait will besiege them, and consume one of them, and on their army will be fear and trembling, and sedition against their kings. ³⁴Behold, clouds from the east and from the north to the south, and they are very horrible to look on—full of wrath and storm. ³⁵They will dash one against another, and they will pour out a plentiful storm on the earth, even their own storm; and there will be blood from the sword to the horse's belly, ³⁶and to the thigh of man, and to the camel's hock. ³⁷And there will be fearfulness and great trembling on earth: and they that see that wrath will be afraid, and trembling will take hold on them. ³⁸And after this there will be stirred up great storms from the south, and from the north, and another part from the west. ³⁹And strong winds will arise from the east, and will shut it up, even the cloud which He raised up in wrath; and the storm that was to cause destruction by the east wind will be violently driven toward the south and west. ⁴⁰And great clouds, indeed mighty and full of wrath, will be lifted up—and the storm—that they may destroy all the earth, and those who dwell therein; and they will pour out over every high and eminent one a terrible storm, ⁴¹[with] fire, and hail, and flying swords, and many waters, that all plains may be full, and all rivers, with the abundance of those waters. ⁴²And they will break down the cities and walls, mountains and hills, trees of the wood, and grass of the meadows, and their corn. ⁴³And they will go on steadfastly to Babylon and destroy her. ⁴⁴They will come to her and surround her; they will pour out the storm and all wrath on her; then the dust and smoke will rise up to the sky, and all those who are around her will mourn her. ⁴⁵And those who remain will do service to those who have put her in fear. ⁴⁶And you, Asia, that are partaker in the beauty of Babylon, and in the glory of her person: ⁴⁷woe to you, you wretch, because you have made yourself like to her; you have decked your daughters in whoredom, that they might please and glory in your lovers, which have always desired you to commit whoredom with! ⁴⁸You have followed her that is hateful in all her works and inventions: therefore," says God, ⁴⁹"I will send evils on you: widowhood, poverty, famine, sword, and pestilence, to waste your houses to destruction and death. ⁵⁰And the glory of your power will be dried up as a flower, when the heat will arise that is sent over you. ⁵¹You will be weakened as a poor woman with stripes, and as one disciplined with wounds, so that you will not be able to receive your mighty ones and [your] lovers. ⁵²Would I with jealousy have so proceeded against you," says the LORD, ⁵³"if you had not always slain My chosen, exalting the stroke of

your hands, and saying over their dead, when you were drunken, ⁵⁴Set out the beauty of your countenance? ⁵⁵The reward of a prostitute will be in your bosom, therefore you will receive repayment. ⁵⁶Just as you will do to My chosen," says the LORD, "even so God will do to you, and will deliver you into mischief. ⁵⁷And your children will die of hunger, and you will fall by the sword, and your cities will be broken down, and all yours will perish by the sword in the field. ⁵⁸And those who are in the mountains will die of hunger, and eat their own flesh, and drink [their own] blood, for great hunger of bread, and thirst of water. ⁵⁹You, unhappy above all, will come and will receive calamities again. ⁶⁰And in the passage, they will rush on the idle city, and will destroy some portion of your land, and mar part of your glory, and will again return to Babylon that was destroyed. ⁶¹And you will be cast down by them as stubble, and they will be to you as fire, ⁶²and will devour you, and your cities, your land, and your mountains; they will burn up all your woods and your fruitful trees with fire. ⁶³They will carry your children away captive, and will plunder your wealth, and mar the glory of your face."

CHAPTER 16

¹"Woe to you, Babylon and Asia! Woe to you, Egypt and Syria! ²Gird yourselves with sackcloth and garments of hair, and mourn your children, and lament; for your destruction is at hand. ³A sword is sent on you, and who is he that may turn it back? ⁴A fire is sent on you, and who is he that may quench it? ⁵Calamities are sent on you, and who is he that may drive them away? ⁶May one drive away a hungry lion in the wood? Or may one quench the fire in stubble, when it has once begun to burn? ⁷May one turn again the arrow that is shot of a strong archer? ⁸The LORD God sends the evils, and who will drive them away? ⁹A fire will go out from His wrath, and who is he that may quench it? ¹⁰He will cast lightning, and who will not fear? He will thunder, and who will not tremble? ¹¹The LORD will threaten, and who will not be utterly broken in pieces at His presence? ¹²The earth quakes, and the foundations thereof; the sea arises with waves from the deep, and the waves of it will be troubled, and also the fishes thereof, at the presence of the LORD, and before the glory of His power: ¹³for strong is His right hand that bends the bow; His arrows that He shoots are sharp, and will not miss, when they begin to be shot into the ends of the world. ¹⁴Behold, the calamities are sent out, and will not return again, until they come on the earth. ¹⁵The fire is kindled, and will not be put out, until it consumes the foundations of the earth. ¹⁶Just as an arrow which is shot by a mighty archer does not return backward, even so the calamities that are sent out on earth will not return again. ¹⁷Woe is me! Woe is me! Who will deliver me in those days? ¹⁸The beginning of sorrows, and the great mourning; the beginning of famine, and many will perish; the beginning of wars, and the powers will stand in fear; the beginning of calamities, and all will tremble! What will they do in [all] this when the calamities will come? ¹⁹Behold, famine and plague, suffering and anguish! They are sent as scourges for amendment. ²⁰But for all these things they will not turn them from their wickedness, nor be always mindful of the scourges. ²¹Behold, food will be so cheap on earth that they will think themselves to be in a good case, and even then, calamities will grow on earth: sword, famine, and great confusion. ²²For many of those who dwell on earth will perish of famine; and the other, that escape the famine, will the sword destroy. ²³And the dead will be cast out as dung, and there will be no man to comfort them, for the earth will be left desolate, and the cities thereof will be cast down. ²⁴There will be no farmer left to till the earth, and to sow it. ²⁵The trees will give fruit, and who will gather them? ²⁶The grapes will ripen, and who will tread them? For in [all] places there will be a great forsaking: ²⁷for one man will desire to see another, or to hear his voice. ²⁸For of a city there will be ten left, and two of the field, which have hidden themselves in the thick groves, and in the clefts of the rocks. ²⁹As in an orchard of olives on every tree there are left three or four olives, ³⁰or as when a vineyard is gathered there are some clusters left by those who diligently seek through the vineyard; ³¹even so in those days there will be three or four left by those who search their houses with the sword. ³²And the earth will be left desolate, and the fields thereof will be for briers, and her ways and all her paths will bring out thorns, because no sheep will pass through there. ³³The virgins will mourn, having no bridegrooms; the women will mourn, having no husbands; their daughters will mourn, having no helpers. ³⁴In the wars their bridegrooms will be destroyed, and their husbands will perish of famine. ³⁵Now hear these things, and understand them, you servants of the LORD. ³⁶Behold, the word of the LORD, receive it: do not disbelieve the things of which the LORD speaks. ³⁷Behold, the calamities draw near, and are not slack. ³⁸Just as a woman with child in the ninth month, when the hour of her delivery draws near, within two or three hours sorrowful pains surround her womb, and when the child comes out from the womb, there will be no waiting for [even] a moment: ³⁹even so the calamities will not be slack to come on the earth, and the world will groan, and sorrows will take hold of it on every side. ⁴⁰O My people, hear My word: make ready for the battle, and in those calamities be even as pilgrims on the earth. ⁴¹He that sells, let him be as he that flees away; and he that buys, as one that will lose; ⁴²he that occupies merchandise, as he that has no profit by it; and he that builds, as he that will not dwell therein; ⁴³he that sows, as if he should not reap; so also he that prunes [the vines], as he that will not gather the grapes; ⁴⁴those who marry, as those who will get no children; and those who do not marry, as the widowed. ⁴⁵Because of this, those who labor labor in vain; ⁴⁶for strangers will reap their fruits, and plunder their goods, overthrow their houses, and take their children captive, for in captivity and famine they will beget their children; ⁴⁷and those who traffic traffic to become a plunder—the more they deck their cities, their houses, their possessions, and their own persons, ⁴⁸the more I will hate them for their sins," says the LORD. ⁴⁹"Just as a rightly honest and virtuous woman hates a prostitute, ⁵⁰so righteousness will hate iniquity when she decks herself, and will accuse her to her face when He comes that will defend him that diligently searches out every sin on earth. ⁵¹Therefore, do not be like them, nor do the works thereof. ⁵²For yet a little while, and iniquity will be taken away out of the earth, and righteousness will reign over us. ⁵³Do not let the sinner say that he has not sinned, for he will burn coals of fire on his head, which says, I have not sinned before God and His glory. ⁵⁴Behold, the LORD knows all the works of men, their imaginations, their thoughts, and their hearts— ⁵⁵[He] who said, Let the earth be made, and it was made; [and,] Let the heaven be made, and it was made; ⁵⁶and at His word the stars were established, and He knows the number of the stars; ⁵⁷who searches the deep, and the treasures thereof; He has measured the sea, and what it contains; ⁵⁸who has shut the sea in the midst of the waters, and with His word He has hanged the earth on the waters; ⁵⁹who spreads out the sky like a vault; He has established it on the waters; ⁶⁰who has made springs of water in the desert, and pools on the tops of the mountains, to send out rivers from the height to water the earth; ⁶¹who framed man and put a heart in the midst of the body, and gave him breath, life, and understanding— ⁶²yes, the Spirit of God Almighty. He who made all things, and searches out hidden things in hidden places, ⁶³surely He knows your imagination, and what you think in your hearts. Woe to those who sin and would gladly hide their sin! ⁶⁴Because of this, the LORD will exactly search out all your works, and He will put you all to shame. ⁶⁵And when your sins are brought out before men, you will be ashamed, and your own iniquities will stand as your accusers in that day. ⁶⁶What will you do? Or how will you hide your sins before God and His messengers? ⁶⁷Behold, God is the judge—fear Him: depart from your sins, and forget your iniquities, to no longer meddle with them forever, so God will lead you out, and deliver you from all suffering. ⁶⁸For behold, the burning wrath of a great multitude is kindled over you, and they will take away certain of you, and feed you with that which is slain to idols. ⁶⁹And those who consent to them will be held in derision and in reproach and will be trodden under their foot. ⁷⁰For there will be in various places, and in the next cities, a great insurrection on those that fear the LORD. ⁷¹They will be like mad men, sparing none, but spoiling and destroying those who still fear the LORD. ⁷²For they will waste and take away their goods and cast them out of their houses. ⁷³Then the trial of My chosen ones will be manifested, even as the gold that is tried in the fire. ⁷⁴Hear, O you My chosen ones," says the LORD: "behold, the days of

suffering are at hand, and I will deliver you from them. ⁷⁵Do not be afraid, neither doubt; for God is your guide. ⁷⁶And you who keep My commands and precepts," says the LORD God, "do not let your sins weigh you down, and do not let your iniquities lift themselves up. ⁷⁷Woe to those who are fast bound with their sins, and covered with their iniquities, like as a field is fast bound with bushes, and the path thereof covered with thorns, that no man may travel through! ⁷⁸It is even shut off and given up to be consumed by fire."

3 MACCABEES

The book of 3 Maccabees is found in most Orthodox Bibles as a part of the deuterocanon. Catholics consider it to be an example of pseudepigrapha and do not regard it as canonical. Protestants, with the exception of the Moravian Brothers who include it in the Apocrypha of the Czech Kralice Bible and Polish Gdańsk Bible, likewise regard it as non-canonical. Despite the title, the book has nothing to do with the Maccabees or their revolt against the Seleucid Empire, as described in 1 Maccabees and 2 Maccabees. Instead, it tells the story of persecution of the Jews under Ptolemy IV Philopator (222-205 BC), some decades before the Maccabean uprising. The name of the book apparently comes from the similarities between this book and the stories of the martyrdom of Eleazar and the Maccabean youths in 2 Maccabees; the chief priest Shimon is also mentioned.

CHAPTER 1

¹When Philopator learned from those who came back that Antiochus had made himself master of the places which belonged to himself, he sent orders to all his footmen and horsemen, took his sister Arsinoe with him, and marched out as far as the parts of Raphia, where Antiochus and his forces encamped. ²And one Theodotus, intending to carry out his design, took with him the bravest of the armed men who had been previously committed to his trust by Ptolemy, and got through at night to the tent of Ptolemy, to kill him on his own responsibility, and so to end the war. ³But Dositheus, called the son of Drimulus, by birth a Jew, afterward a renegade from the laws and observances of his country, carried Ptolemy away, and made an obscure person lie down in his place in the tent. It befell this man to receive the fate which was meant for the other. ⁴A fierce battle then took place, and the men of Antiochus prevailing, Arsinoe continually went up and down the ranks, and with disheveled hair, with tears and pleadings, begged the soldiers to fight courageously for themselves, their children, and wives; and promised that if they proved conquerors, she would give them each two minas of gold. ⁵It then happened that their enemies were defeated in hand-to-hand encounter, and that many of them were taken prisoners. ⁶Having vanquished this attempt, the king then decided to proceed to the neighboring cities and encourage them. ⁷By doing this, and by making donations to their temples, he inspired his subjects with confidence. ⁸The Jews sent some of their council and of their elders to him. The greetings, gifts of welcome, and commendations of the past, bestowed by them, filled him with the greater eagerness to visit their city. ⁹Having arrived at Jerusalem, sacrificed, and offered thank-offerings to the greatest God, and done whatever else was suitable to the sanctity of the place, and entered the inner court, ¹⁰he was so struck with the magnificence of the place, and so wondered at the orderly arrangements of the temple, that he considered entering the sanctuary itself. ¹¹And when they told him that this was not permissible, none of the nation, no, nor even the priests in general, but only the supreme chief priest of all, and he only once in a year, being allowed to go in, he would by no means give way. ¹²Then they read the Law to him; but he persisted in obtruding himself, exclaiming that he should be allowed, and saying, "Be it that they were deprived of this honor, I should not be." ¹³And he put the question, "Why, when he entered all the temples, did none of the priests who were present forbid him?" ¹⁴He was thoroughly answered by someone, that he did wrong to boast of this. ¹⁵"Well; since I have done this," he said, "be the cause what it may, will I not enter with or without your consent?" ¹⁶And when the priests fell down in their sacred vestments imploring the greatest God to come and help in time of need, and to avert the violence of the fierce aggressor, and when they filled the temple with lamentations and tears, ¹⁷then those who had been left behind in the city were scared, and rushed out, uncertain of the event. ¹⁸Virgins, who had been shut up within their chambers, came out with their mothers, scattering dust and ashes on their heads, and filling the streets with outcries. ¹⁹Women, but recently separated off, left their bridal chambers, left the reserve that suited them, and ran around the city in a disorderly manner. ²⁰Newborn babies were deserted by the mothers or nurses who waited on them; some here, some there—in houses, or in fields; these now, with a zeal which could not be checked, swarmed into the most high temple. ²¹Manifold prayers were offered up by those who assembled in this place, on account of the unholy attempt of the king. ²²Along with these there were some of the citizens who took courage, and would not submit to his obstinacy, and his intention of carrying out his purpose. ²³Calling out to arms, and to die bravely in defense of the law of their fathers, they created a great uproar in the place, and were with difficulty brought back by the aged and the elders to the station of prayer which they had occupied before. ²⁴During this time, the multitude kept on praying. ²⁵The elders who surrounded the king tried in many ways to divert his arrogant mind from the design which he had formed. ²⁶He, in his hardened mood, insensible to all persuasion, was going onward with the view of carrying out this design. ²⁷Yet even his own officers, when they saw this, joined the Jews in an appeal to Him who has all power, to aid in the present crisis, and not to wink at such overconfident lawlessness. ²⁸Such was the frequency and the vehemence of the cry of the assembled crowd, that an indescribable noise ensued. ²⁹Not the men only, but the very walls and floor seemed to sound out—all things preferring dissolution rather than to see the place defiled.

CHAPTER 2

¹Then the chief priest Simon bowed his knees near the holy place, and spread out his hands in reverent form, and uttered the following supplication: ²"O LORD, LORD, King of the heavens, and Ruler of the whole creation, Holy among the holy, sole Governor, Almighty, give ear to us who are oppressed by a wicked and profane one, who celebrates in his confidence and strength. ³It is You, the Creator of all, the Lord of the universe, who are a righteous Governor, and judge all who act with pride and insolence. ⁴It was You who destroyed the former workers of unrighteousness, among whom were the giants, who trusted in their strength and daring, by covering them with a measureless flood. ⁵It was You who made the Sodomites, those workers of exceeding iniquity, men notorious for their vices, an example to following generations, when You covered them with fire and brimstone. ⁶You made Your power known when You caused the bold Pharaoh, the enslaver of Your people, to pass through the ordeal of many and diverse afflictions. ⁷And You rolled the depths of the sea over him, when he made pursuit with chariots, and with a multitude of followers, and gave a safe passage to those who put their trust in You, the Lord of the whole creation. ⁸These saw and felt the works of Your hands, and praised You, the Almighty. ⁹You, O King, when You created the limitless and measureless earth, chose out this city: You made this place sacred to Your Name, albeit You need nothing. You glorified it with Your illustrious presence, after constructing it to the glory of Your great and honorable Name. ¹⁰And You promised, out of love, to the people of Israel, that should we fall away from You, and become afflicted, and then come to this house and pray, You would hear our prayer. ¹¹Truly You are faithful and true. ¹²And when You often aided our fathers when hard-

pressed, and in low estate, and delivered them out of great dangers, ¹³see now, holy King, how through our many and great sins we are borne down, and made subject to our enemies, and have become weak and powerless. ¹⁴We being in this low condition, this bold and profane man seeks to dishonor this, Your holy place, consecrated out of the earth to the Name of Your Majesty. ¹⁵Your dwelling place, the Heaven of heavens, is indeed unapproachable to men. ¹⁶But since it seemed good to You to exhibit Your glory among Your people Israel, You sanctified this place. ¹⁷Do not punish us by means of the uncleanness of their men, nor discipline us by means of their profanity, lest the lawless ones should boast in their rage, and exult in exuberant pride of speech, and say, ¹⁸We have trampled on the holy house, as idolatrous houses are trampled on. ¹⁹Blot out our iniquities, and do away with our errors, and show forth Your compassion in this hour. ²⁰Let Your mercies quickly go before us. Grant us peace, that the cast down and brokenhearted may praise You with their mouth." ²¹At that time God, who sees all things, who is beyond all Holy among the holy, heard that prayer, so suitable, and scourged the man greatly uplifted with scorn and insolence. ²²Shaking him to and fro as a reed is shaken with the wind, He cast him on the pavement, powerless, with limbs paralyzed, by a righteous judgment deprived [him] of the faculty of speech. ²³His friends and bodyguards, beholding the swift repayment which had suddenly overtaken him, struck with exceeding terror, and fearing that he would die, speedily removed him. ²⁴When in [the] course of time he had come to himself, this severe check caused no conversion within him, but he departed with bitter threats. ²⁵He proceeded to Egypt, grew worse in wickedness through his aforementioned companions in wine, who were lost to all goodness; ²⁶and not satisfied with countless acts of impiety, his audacity so increased that he raised evil reports there, and many of his friends, watching his purpose attentively, joined in furthering his will. ²⁷His purpose was to indict a public stigma on our race; for that reason, he erected a pillar at the tower-porch, and caused the following inscription to be engraved on it: ²⁸"THE ENTRANCE TO THEIR TEMPLE IS TO BE REFUSED TO ALL THOSE WHO WILL NOT SACRIFICE; ALL THE JEWS ARE TO BE REGISTERED AMONG THE COMMON PEOPLE; THOSE WHO RESIST ARE TO BE FORCIBLY SEIZED AND PUT TO DEATH; ²⁹THOSE WHO ARE SO REGISTERED, ARE TO BE MARKED ON THEIR PERSONS BY THE IVY-LEAF SYMBOL OF DIONYSUS, AND TO BE SET APART WITH THESE LIMITED RIGHTS." ³⁰To do away with the appearance of hating them all, he had it written underneath: "IF ANY OF THEM SHOULD CHOOSE TO ENTER THE COMMUNITY OF THOSE INITIATED IN THE RITES, THESE SHOULD HAVE EQUAL RIGHTS WITH THE ALEXANDRIANS." ³¹Some of those who were over the city, therefore, abhorring any approach to the city of piety, unhesitatingly gave in to the king, and expected to derive some great honor from a future connection with him. ³²A nobler spirit, however, prompted the majority to cling to their religious observances, and by paying money that they might live unmolested, these sought to escape the registration. ³³Cheerfully looking forward to future aid, they abhorred their own apostates, considering them to be national enemies, and were debarring them from the common usages of social intercourse.

CHAPTER 3

¹On discovering this, so incensed was the wicked king that he no longer confined his rage to the Jews in Alexandria. Laying his hand more heavily on those who lived in the country, he gave orders that they should be quickly collected into one place, and most cruelly deprived of their lives. ²While this was going on, an invidious rumor was uttered abroad by men who had banded together to injure the Jewish race. The purport of their charge was that the Jews kept them away from the ordinances of the law. ³Now, while the Jews always maintained a feeling of unwavering loyalty toward the kings, ⁴yet, as they worshiped God, and observed His law, they made certain distinctions, and avoided certain things. Hence some persons held them in revulsion; ⁵although, as they adorned their conversation with works of righteousness, they had established themselves in the good opinion of the world. ⁶What all the rest of mankind said, was, however, made of no account by the foreigners, ⁷who said much of the exclusiveness of the Jews with regard to their worship and meats; they alleged that they were unsociable men, hostile to the king's interests, refusing to associate with him or his troops. By this way of speaking, they brought much odium on them. ⁸Nor was this unexpected uproar and sudden conflux of people unobserved by the Greeks who lived in the city, concerning men who had never harmed them: yet to aid them was not in their power, since there was oppression all around, but they encouraged them in their troubles, and expected a favorable turn of affairs. ⁹He who knows all things, will not, [they said,] disregard so great a people. ¹⁰Some of the neighbors, friends, and fellow dealers of the Jews, even called them secretly to an interview, pledged them their assistance, and promised to do their very utmost for them. ¹¹Now the king, elated with his prosperous fortune, and not regarding the superior power of God, but thinking to persevere in his present purpose, wrote the following letter to the prejudice of the Jews: ¹²"King Ptolemy Philopator, to the commanders and soldiers in Egypt, and in all places, health and happiness! ¹³I am right [and] well; and so, too, are my affairs. ¹⁴Since our Asiatic campaign, the particulars of which you know, and which by the aid of the gods, not lightly given, and by our own vigor, has been brought to a successful issue according to our expectation, ¹⁵we resolved, not with strength of spear, but with gentleness and much humanity, as it were to nurse the inhabitants of Coele-Syria and Phoenicia, and to be their willing benefactors. ¹⁶So, having bestowed considerable sums of money on the temples of the several cities, we proceeded even as far as Jerusalem, and went up to honor the temple of these wretched beings who never cease from their folly. ¹⁷To outward appearance they received us willingly, but belied that appearance by their deeds. When we were eager to enter their temple, and to honor it with the most beautiful and exquisite gifts, ¹⁸they were so carried away by their old arrogance, as to forbid us the entrance; while we, out of our forbearance toward all men, refrained from exercising our power on them. ¹⁹And so, exhibiting their enmity against us, they alone among the nations lift up their heads against kings and benefactors, as men unwilling to submit to anything reasonable. ²⁰We then, having endeavored to make allowance for the madness of these persons, and on our victorious return treating all people in Egypt courteously, acted in a manner which was befitting. ²¹Accordingly, bearing no ill-will against their countrymen [at Jerusalem], but rather remembering our connection with them, and the numerous matters with sincere heart from a remote period entrusted to them, we wished to venture a total alteration of their state, by giving them the rights of citizens of Alexandria, and to admit them to the continuous rites of our solemnities. ²²All this, however, they have taken in a very different spirit. With their innate malignity, they have spurned the fair offer; and constantly inclining to evil, ²³have rejected the inestimable rights. Not only so, but by using speech, and by refraining from speech, they abhor the few among them who are heartily disposed toward us, ever deeming that their ignoble course of procedure will force us to do away with our reform. ²⁴Having then received certain proofs that these [Jews] bear us every sort of ill-will, we must look forward to the possibility of some sudden tumult among ourselves, when these impious men may turn traitors and barbarous enemies. ²⁵As soon, therefore, as the contents of this letter become known to you, in that same hour we order those [Jews] who dwell among you, with wives and children, to be sent to us, vilified and abused, in chains of iron, to undergo a death, cruel and ignominious, suitable to disaffected men. ²⁶For by the punishment of them in one body we perceive that we have found the only means of establishing our affairs for the future on a firm and satisfactory basis. ²⁷Whoever will shield a Jew, whether it be old man, child, or nursing baby, will with his whole house be tortured to death. ²⁸Whoever will inform against the [Jews], besides receiving the property of the person charged, will be presented with two thousand drachmas from the royal treasury, will be made free, and will be crowned. ²⁹Whatever place will shelter a Jew, will, when he is hunted out, be put under the ban of fire, and be forever rendered useless to every living being

for all time to come." ³⁰Such was the purport of the king's letter.

CHAPTER 4

¹Wherever this decree was received, the people kept up a revelry of joy and shouting, as if their long-pent-up, hardened hatred, was now to show itself openly. ²The Jews suffered great throes of sorrow and wept much, while their hearts, all things around being lamentable, were set on fire as they mourned the sudden destruction which was decreed against them. ³What home, or city, or place at all inhabited, or what streets were there, which their condition did not fill with wailing and lamentation? ⁴They were sent out unanimously by the generals in the several cities, with such stern and pitiless feeling, that the exceptional nature of the infliction moved even some of their enemies. These influenced by sentiments of common humanity, and reflecting on the uncertain issue of life, shed tears at this miserable expulsion of theirs. ⁵A multitude of aged, gray-haired old men, were driven along with halting [and] bending feet, urged onward by the impulse of a violent, shameless force to quick speed. ⁶Girls who had entered the bridal chamber quite lately, to enjoy the partnership of marriage, exchanged pleasure for misery, and with dust scattered on their myrrh-anointed heads, were hurried along unveiled, and, in the midst of outlandish insults, set up a lamentable cry with one accord instead of the marriage hymn. ⁷Bound, and exposed to public gaze, they were violently hurried on board ship. ⁸The husbands of these, in the prime of their youthful vigor, wore halters around their necks instead of crowns; instead of feasting and youthful celebration, they spent the rest of their nuptial days in wailing, and saw only the grave at hand. ⁹They were dragged along by unyielding chains, like wild beasts; of these, some had their necks thrust into the benches of the rowers, while the feet of others were enclosed in hard chains. ¹⁰The planks of the deck above them blocked out the light, and shut out the day on every side, so that they might be treated like traitors during the whole voyage. ¹¹They were accordingly transported in this vessel, and at the end of it arrived at Schedia. The king had ordered them to be cast into the vast hippodrome, which was built in front of the city. This place was well adapted by its situation to expose them to the gaze of all those coming into the city, and of those who went from the city into the country. So they could hold no communication with his forces, no, [and] were deemed unworthy of any civilized accommodation. ¹²When this was done, the king, hearing that their relatives in the city often went out and lamented the melancholy distress of these victims, ¹³was full of rage, and commanded that they should be carefully subjected to the same (and not one bit milder) treatment. ¹⁴The whole nation was now to be registered. Every individual was to be specified by name, not for that hard servitude of labor which we have shortly before mentioned, but that he might expose them to the previously mentioned tortures; and finally, in the short space of a day, might eradicate them by his cruelties. ¹⁵The registering of these men was carried on cruelly, zealously, assiduously, from the rising of the sun to its going down, and was not brought to an end in forty days. ¹⁶The king was filled with great and constant joy, and celebrated banquets before the temple idols. His erring heart, far from the truth, and his profane mouth, gave glory to idols, deaf and incapable of speaking or aiding, and uttered unworthy speech against the greatest God. ¹⁷At the end of the above-mentioned interval of time, the registrars brought word to the king that the multitude of the Jews was too great for registration, ¹⁸inasmuch as there were many still left in the land, of whom some were in inhabited houses, and others were scattered around in various places, so that all the commanders in Egypt were insufficient for the work. ¹⁹The king threatened them, and charged them with taking bribes, in order to contrive the escape of the Jews, but was clearly convinced of the truth of what had been said. ²⁰They said, and proved, that paper and pens had failed them for the carrying out of their purpose. ²¹Now this was an active interference of the unconquerable providence which assisted the Jews from Heaven.

CHAPTER 5

¹Then he called Hermon, who had charge of the elephants. Full of rage, altogether fixed in his furious design, ²he commanded him, with a quantity of unmixed wine and handfuls of incense [infused] to drug the elephants early on the following day. These five hundred elephants were, when infuriated by the copious draughts of frankincense, to be led up to the execution of death on the Jews. ³The king, after issuing these orders, went to his feasting and gathered together all those of his friends and of the army who hated the Jews the most. ⁴The master of the elephants, Hermon, fulfilled his commission punctually. ⁵The underlings appointed for the purpose went out about evening and bound the hands of the miserable victims, and took other precautions for their security at night, thinking that the whole race would perish together. ⁶The heathen believed the Jews to be destitute of all protection, for chains bound them around. ⁷They invoked the Almighty LORD, and ceaselessly implored with tears their merciful God and Father, Ruler of all, Lord of every power, ⁸to overthrow the evil purpose which had gone out against them, and to deliver them by extraordinary manifestation from that death which was in store for them. ⁹Their litany so earnest went up to Heaven. ¹⁰Then Hermon, who had filled his merciless elephants with copious draughts of mixed wine and frankincense, came early to the palace to certify the kind thereof. ¹¹He, however, who has sent His good creature sleep from all time, by night or by day, so gratifying whom He wills, now diffused a portion thereof on the king. ¹²By this sweet and profound influence of the LORD he was held fast, and so his unjust purpose was quite frustrated, and his unflinching resolve greatly falsified. ¹³But the Jews, having escaped the hour which had been fixed, praised their holy God, and again begged Him who is easily reconciled to display the power of His powerful hand to the overconfident nations. ¹⁴The middle of the tenth hour had well near arrived, when the person who sent invitations, seeing the guests who were invited present, came and shook the king. ¹⁵He gained his attention with difficulty, and hinting that the mealtime was getting past, talked the matter over with him. ¹⁶The king listened to this, and then turning aside to his drinking, commanded the guests to sit down before him. ¹⁷This done, he asked them to enjoy themselves, and to indulge in mirth at this somewhat late hour of the banquet. ¹⁸Conversation grew on, and the king sent for Hermon, and inquired of him, with fierce denunciations, why the Jews had been allowed to outlive that day. ¹⁹Hermon explained that he had done his bidding over night; and in this he was confirmed by his friends. ²⁰The king, then, with a barbarity exceeding that of Phalaris, said that they might thank his sleep of that day: "Lose no time, and get the elephants ready against tomorrow, as you did before, for the destruction of these accursed Jews." ²¹When the king said this, the company present were glad, and approved; and then each man went to his own home. ²²Nor did they employ the night in sleep, so much as in contriving cruel mockeries for those deemed miserable. ²³The morning cock had just crowed, and Hermon, having harnessed the brutes, was stimulating them in the great colonnade. ²⁴The city crowds were collected together to see the hideous spectacle and waited impatiently for the dawn. ²⁵The Jews, breathless with momentary suspense, stretched out their hands, and prayed to the greatest God, in mournful strains, to quickly help them again. ²⁶The sun's rays were not yet shed abroad, and the king was waiting for his friends, when Hermon came to him, calling him out, and saying that his desires could now be realized. ²⁷The king, receiving him, was astonished at his unusual exit, and overwhelmed with a spirit of oblivion about everything, inquired [regarding] the object of this earnest preparation. ²⁸But this was the working of that Almighty God who had made him forget all his purpose. ²⁹Hermon and all his friends pointed out the preparation of the animals. "They are ready, O king, according to your own strict injunction." ³⁰The king was filled with fierce anger at these words, for, by the providence of God regarding these things, his mind had become entirely confused. He looked hard at Hermon, and threatened him as follows: ³¹"Your parents or your children, were they here, should have been furnished [as] a large meal for these wild beasts—not these innocent Jews, who my forefathers and I have loyally served. ³²Had it not been for familiar friendship, and the claims of your office, your life should have gone for theirs.

³³Hermon, being threatened in this unexpected and alarming manner, was troubled in visage, and depressed in countenance. ³⁴The friends, too, slipped out one by one, and dismissed the assembled multitudes to their respective occupations. ³⁵The Jews, having heard of these events, praised the glorious God and King of kings, because they too had obtained this help from Him. ³⁶Now the king arranged another banquet after the same manner and proclaimed an invitation to mirth. ³⁷And he summoned Hermon to his presence, and said, with threats, "How often, O wretch, must I repeat my orders to you about these same persons? ³⁸Once more, arm the elephants for the extermination of the Jews tomorrow." ³⁹His countrymen, who were reclining with him, wondered at his instability, and so expressed themselves: ⁴⁰"O king, how long do you make trial of us, as of men deprived of reason? This is the third time that you have ordered their destruction. When the thing is to be done, you change your mind, and recall your instructions. ⁴¹For this reason the feeling of expectation causes tumult in the city: it swarms with factions and is continually at the point of being plundered." ⁴²The king, just like another Phalaris, a prey to thoughtlessness, made no account of the changes which his own mind had undergone, issuing in the deliverance of the Jews. He swore a fruitless oath, and firmly determined to send them to Hades, crushed by the knees and feet of the elephants. ⁴³He would also invade Judea, and level its towns with fire and the sword, and destroy that temple which the heathen might not enter, and prevent sacrifices from ever being offered up there. ⁴⁴Joyfully his friends broke up, together with his countrymen, and, trusting in his determination, arranged their forces in guard at the most convenient places of the city. ⁴⁵And the master of the elephants urged the beasts into an almost maniacal state, drenched them with incense and wine, and decked them with frightful instruments. ⁴⁶About early morning, when the city was now filled with an immense number of people at the hippodrome, he entered the palace and called the king to the business at hand. ⁴⁷The king's heart teemed with impious rage, and he rushed out with the mass, along with the elephants. With feelings unsoftened, and eyes pitiless, he longed to gaze at the hard and wretched doom of the above-mentioned [Jews]. ⁴⁸But the [Jews], when the elephants went out at the gate, followed by the armed force; and when they saw the dust raised by the throng, and heard the loud cries of the crowd, ⁴⁹thought that they had come to the last moment of their lives, to the end of what they had tremblingly expected. They gave way, therefore, to lamentations and moans; they kissed each other; those related to each other hung around one another's necks: fathers around their sons, mothers [around] their daughters; other women held their infants to their breasts, which drew what seemed their last milk. ⁵⁰Nevertheless, when they reflected on the help previously granted them from Heaven, they prostrated themselves with one accord, even removed the sucking children from the breasts, ⁵¹and sent up an exceedingly great cry asking the Lord of all power to reveal Himself and have mercy on those who now lay at the gates of Hades.

CHAPTER 6

¹And Eleazar, an illustrious priest of the country, who had attained to length of days, and whose life had been adorned with virtue, caused the elders who were around him to cease to cry out to the holy God, and prayed this: ²"O King, mighty in power, Most High, Almighty God, who regulates the whole creation with Your tender mercy, ³look on the seed of Abraham, on the children of the sanctified Jacob, Your sanctified inheritance, O Father, now being wrongfully destroyed as strangers in a strange land. ⁴You destroyed Pharaoh, with his army of chariots, when that lord of this same Egypt was uplifted with lawless daring and a loud-sounding tongue. Shedding the beams of Your mercy on the race of Israel, You overwhelmed him with his proud army. ⁵When Sennacherib, the grievous king of the Assyrians, exulting in his countless army, had subdued the whole land with his spear, and was lifting himself against Your holy city, with boastings [too] grievous to be endured, You, O LORD, demolished him and showed Your might to many nations. ⁶When the three friends in the land of Babylon of their own will exposed their lives to the fire rather than serve vain things, You sent a moist coolness through the fiery furnace and brought the fire on all their adversaries. ⁷It was You who, when Daniel was hurled—through slander and envy—as a prey to lions down below, brought him back up to [the] light unharmed. ⁸When Jonah was pining away in the belly of the sea-bred monster, You looked on him, O Father, and restored him to the sight of his own. ⁹And now, You who hate insolence; You who abound in mercy; You who are the protector of all things: appear quickly to those of the race of Israel, who are insulted by abhorred, lawless nations. ¹⁰If our life has been stained with iniquity during our exile, deliver us from the hand of the enemy, and destroy us, O LORD, by the death which You prefer. ¹¹Do not let the vain-minded congratulate vain idols at the destruction of Your beloved, saying, "Neither did their God deliver them." ¹²You, who are All-powerful and Almighty, O Perpetual One, behold! Have mercy on us who are being withdrawn from life, like traitors, by the unreasoning insolence of lawless men. ¹³Let the heathen cower before Your invincible might today, O glorious One, who has all power to save the race of Jacob. ¹⁴The whole band of infants and their parents implore You with tears. ¹⁵Let it be shown to all the nations that You are with us, O LORD, and have not turned Your face away from us; but as You said that You would not forget them even in the land of their enemies, so fulfill this saying, O LORD. ¹⁶Now, at the time that Eleazar had ended his prayer, the king came along to the hippodrome, with the wild beasts, and with his tumultuous power. ¹⁷When the Jews saw this, they uttered a loud cry to Heaven, so that the adjacent valleys resounded, and caused an irrepressible lamentation throughout the army. ¹⁸Then the all-glorious, all-powerful, and true God, displayed His holy countenance, and opened the gates of Heaven, from which two messengers, dreadful of form, came down and were visible to all but the Jews. ¹⁹And they stood opposite and filled the enemies' army with confusion and cowardice, and bound them with immoveable chains. ²⁰And a cold shudder came over the person of the king, and oblivion paralyzed the vehemence of his spirit. ²¹They turned the animals back on the armed forces which followed them, and the animals trod them down and destroyed them. ²²The king's wrath was converted into compassion, and he wept at his own machinations. ²³For when he heard the cry, and saw them all on the verge of destruction, he angrily threatened his friends with tears, saying, ²⁴"You have governed badly, and have exceeded tyrants in cruelty; and me, your benefactor, you have labored to deprive of my dominion and my life at once, by secretly devising measures injurious to the kingdom. ²⁵Who has gathered here, unreasonably removing each from his home, those who, in fidelity to us, had held the fortresses of the country? ²⁶Who has so consigned to unmerited punishments those who in good will toward us from the beginning have in all things surpassed all nations, and who often have engaged in the most dangerous undertakings? ²⁷Loose, loose the unjust bonds; send them to their homes in peace, and deprecate what has been done. ²⁸Release the sons of the almighty living God of Heaven, who from our ancestors' times until now has granted a glorious and uninterrupted prosperity to our affairs. ²⁹He said these things, and they, released the same moment, having now escaped death, praised God their holy Savior. ³⁰The king then departed to the city, and called his financier to him, and asked him to provide a seven days' quantity of wine and other materials for feasting for the Jews. He decided that they should keep a joyful festival of deliverance in the very place in which they expected to meet with their destruction. ³¹Then they who were previously despised and near to Hades, yes, rather advanced into it, partook of the cup of salvation, instead of a grievous and lamentable death. Full of exultation, they parted out the place intended for their fall and burial into banqueting shelters. ³²Ceasing their miserable strain of woe, they took up the subject of their fatherland, singing praise to God, their wonder-working Savior. All groans, all wailing, were laid aside: they formed dances as a sign of serene joy. ³³So also the king—he collected a number of guests for the occasion and returned unceasing thanks with much magnificence for the unexpected deliverance afforded him. ³⁴Those who had marked them out as for death and for carrion, and had registered them with joy, howled aloud, and

were clothed with shame, and had the fire of their rage ingloriously put out. ³⁵But the Jews, as we just said, instituted a dance, and then gave themselves up to feasting, glad thanksgiving, and psalms. ³⁶They made a public ordinance to commemorate these things for generations to come, as long as they should be sojourners. Therefore, they established these days as days of mirth, not for the purpose of drinking or luxury, but because God had saved them. ³⁷They requested the king to send them back to their homes. ³⁸They were being enrolled from the twenty-fifth of Pachon to the fourth of Epiphi—a period of forty days. The measures taken for their destruction lasted from the fifth of Epiphi until the seventh—that is, three days. ³⁹The Ruler over all gloriously manifested His mercy during this time and delivered them all together unharmed. ⁴⁰They feasted on the king's provision up to the fourteenth day, and then asked to be sent away. ⁴¹The king commended them and wrote the following letter, of magnanimous importance for them, to the commanders of every city:

CHAPTER 7

¹"King Ptolemy Philopator to the commanders throughout Egypt, and to all who are set over affairs—joy and strength. ²We ourselves and our children are well, and God has directed our affairs as we wish. ³Certain of our friends vehemently urged us from malice to punish the Jews of our realm in a body, with the infliction of a monstrous punishment. ⁴They pretended that our affairs would never be in a good state until this took place. Such, they said, was the hatred borne by the Jews to all other people. ⁵They brought them bound in grievous chains as slaves, no, as traitors. Without inquiry or examination, they endeavored to annihilate them. They buckled themselves with a savage cruelty, worse than Scythian custom. ⁶For this reason we severely threatened them; yet, with the clemency which we are accustomed to extend to all men, we at length permitted them to live. Finding that the God of Heaven cast a shield of protection over the Jews so as to preserve them, and that He fought for them as a father always fights for his sons, ⁷and taking into consideration their constancy and fidelity toward us and toward our ancestors, we have, as we should, acquitted them of every sort of charge. ⁸And we have dismissed them to their various homes, bidding all men everywhere to do them no wrong, or unrighteously revile them about the past. ⁹Know that should we conceive any evil design, or in any way aggrieve them, we will ever have as our opposite, not man, but the highest God, the ruler of all might. From Him there will be no escape, as the avenger of such deeds. Farewell." ¹⁰When they had received this letter, they were not hurried to depart immediately. They petitioned the king to be allowed to inflict fitting punishment on those of their race who had willingly transgressed the holy God, and the Law of God. ¹¹They alleged that men who had for their bellies' sake transgressed the ordinances of God, would never be faithful to the interests of the king. ¹²The king admitted the truth of this reasoning and commended them. Full power was given them, without warrant or special commission, to destroy those who had transgressed the Law of God boldly in every part of the king's dominions. ¹³Their priests, then, as it was suitable, saluted him with good wishes, and all the people echoed with the "Hallelujah." They then joyfully departed. ¹⁴Then they punished and destroyed with ignominy every polluted Jew that fell in their way; ¹⁵slaying therefore, in that day, more than three hundred men, and esteeming this destruction of the wicked a season of joy. ¹⁶They themselves having held fast their God to death, and having enjoyed a full deliverance, departed from the city garlanded with sweet-flowered wreaths of every kind. Uttering exclamations of joy, with songs of praise and melodious hymns, they thanked the God of their fathers, the perpetual Savior of Israel. ¹⁷Having arrived at Ptolemais, called from the specialty of that district Rose-bearing, where the fleet, in accordance with the general wish, waited seven days for them, ¹⁸they partook of a banquet of deliverance, for the king generously granted them separately the means of securing a return home. ¹⁹They were accordingly brought back in peace, while they gave utterance to appropriate thanks; and they determined to keep these days during their sojourn as days of joyfulness. ²⁰These they registered as sacred on a pillar, when they had dedicated the place of their festivity to be one of prayer. They departed unharmed, free, abundant in joy, preserved by the king's command, by land, by sea, and by river, each to his own home. ²¹They had more weight than before among their enemies, and were honored and feared, and no one in any way robbed them of their goods. ²²Every man received back his own, according to inventory, [from] those who had obtained their goods, giving them up with the greatest terror. For the greatest God made perfect wonders for their salvation. ²³Blessed is the Redeemer of Israel to [the] age. Amen.

4 MACCABEES

The book of 4 Maccabees is a homily or philosophic discourse praising the supremacy of pious reason over passion. It is not in the Bible for most churches, but is an appendix to the Greek Bible, and in the canon of the Georgian Orthodox Bible. It was included in the 1688 Romanian Orthodox and the 18th-century Romanian Catholic Bibles where it was called "Iosip" (Joseph). It is no longer printed in Romanian Bibles today. The book was ascribed to Josephus by Eusebius and Jerome, and this opinion was accepted for many years, leading to its inclusion in many editions of Josephus' works. Scholars have, however, pointed to perceived differences of language and style. The book is generally dated between AD 20 and 130, likely in the later half of that range.

CHAPTER 1

¹As I am going to demonstrate a most philosophical proposition, namely, that religious reasoning is absolute master of the passions, I would willingly advise you to give the utmost heed to philosophy. ²For reason is necessary to everyone as a step to science: and it more especially embraces the praise of prudence, the highest virtue. ³If then reasoning appears to hold the mastery over the passions which stand in the way of temperance, such as gluttony and lust, ⁴it also surely and manifestly has the rule over the affections which are contrary to justice, such as malice; and of those which are hindrances to manliness, as wrath, and pain, and fear. ⁵How then is it, perhaps some may say, that reasoning, if it rules the affections, is not also master of forgetfulness and ignorance? They attempt a ridiculous argument. ⁶For reasoning does not rule over its own affections, but over such as are contrary to justice, and manliness, and temperance, and prudence; and yet over these, so as to withstand, without destroying them. ⁷I might prove to you, from many other considerations, that religious reasoning is sole master of the passions; ⁸but I will prove it with the greatest force from the fortitude of Eleazar, and seven brothers, and their mother, who suffered death in defense of virtue. ⁹For all these, treating pains with contempt even to death, by this contempt, demonstrated that reasoning has command over the passions. ¹⁰For their virtues, then, it is right that I should commend those men who died with their mother at this time in behalf of rectitude; and for their honors, I may count them happy. ¹¹For they, winning admiration not only from men in general, but even from the persecutors, for their manliness and endurance, became the means of the destruction of the tyranny against their nation, having conquered the tyrant by their endurance, so that by them their country was purified. ¹²But we may now at once enter on the question, having commenced, as is our custom, with laying down the doctrine, and so proceed to the account of these persons, giving glory to the all-wise God. ¹³Therefore the question is whether reasoning is absolute master of the passions. ¹⁴Let us determine, then, what reasoning is, and what passion [is],

and how many forms of the passions, and whether reasoning bears sway over all of these. ¹⁵Reasoning is, then, intellect accompanied by a life of rectitude, putting foremost the consideration of wisdom. ¹⁶And wisdom is a knowledge of divine and human things, and of their causes. ¹⁷And this is contained in the education of the Law, by means of which we learn divine things reverently, and human things profitably. ¹⁸And the forms of wisdom are prudence, and justice, and manliness, and temperance. ¹⁹The leading one of these is prudence, by whose means, indeed, it is that reasoning bears rule over the passions. ²⁰Of the passions, pleasure and pain are the two most comprehensive, and they also by nature refer to the soul. ²¹And there are many attendant affections surrounding pleasure and pain. ²²Before pleasure is lust, and after pleasure, joy. ²³And before pain is fear, and after pain is sorrow. ²⁴Wrath is an affection, common to pleasure and to pain, if anyone will pay attention when it comes on him. ²⁵And there exists in pleasure a malicious disposition, which is the most multiform of all the affections. ²⁶In the soul it is arrogance, and love of money, and vain pride, and contention, and faithlessness, and the evil eye. ²⁷In the body it is greediness, and gorging, and solitary gluttony. ²⁸As pleasure and pain are, therefore, two growths of the body and the soul, so there are many offshoots of these passions. ²⁹And reasoning, the universal farmer, purging, and pruning these separately, and binding around, and watering, and transplanting, in every way improves the materials of the morals and affections. ³⁰For reasoning is the leader of the virtues, but it is the sole ruler of the passions. Observe then first, through the very things which stand in the way of temperance, that reasoning is absolute ruler of the passions. ³¹Now temperance consists of a command over the lusts. ³²But of the lusts, some belong to the soul, others to the body: and over each of these classes the reasoning appears to bear sway. ³³For where is it, otherwise, that when urged on to forbidden meats, we reject the gratification which would ensue from them? Is it not because reasoning is able to command the appetites? I believe so. ³⁴Hence it is, then, that when lusting after aquatic animals and birds, and four-footed beasts, and all kinds of food which are forbidden us by the Law, we withhold ourselves through the mastery of reasoning. ³⁵For the affections of our appetites are resisted by the temperate understanding, and bent back again, and all the impulses of the body are reined in by reasoning.

CHAPTER 2

¹And what wonder [is it] if the lusts of the soul, after participation with what is beautiful, are frustrated? ²On this ground, therefore, the temperate Joseph is praised in that by reasoning he subdued, on reflection, the indulgence of sense. ³For, although young, and ripe for sexual intercourse, he abrogated by reasoning the stimulus of his passions. ⁴And it is not merely the stimulus of sensual indulgence, but that of every desire, that reasoning is able to master. ⁵For instance, the Law says, "You will not covet your neighbor's wife, nor anything that belongs to your neighbor." ⁶Now, then, since it is the Law which has forbidden us to desire, I will much more easily persuade you that reasoning is able to govern our lusts, just as it does the affections which are impediments to justice. ⁷Since in what way is a solitary eater, and a glutton, and a drunkard reclaimed, unless it is clear that reasoning is lord of the passions? ⁸Therefore, a man who regulates his course by the Law, even if he is a lover of money, immediately puts force on his own disposition; lending to the needy without interest and cancelling the debt of the incoming Sabbath. ⁹And should a man be parsimonious, he is ruled by the Law acting through reasoning, so that he does not glean his harvest crops, nor vintage: and in reference to other points we may perceive that it is reasoning that conquers his passions. ¹⁰For the Law conquers even affection toward parents, not surrendering virtue on their account. ¹¹And it prevails over marriage love, condemning it when transgressing Law. ¹²And it lords it over the love of parents toward their children, for they punish them for vice; and it domineers over the intimacy of friends, reproving them when wicked. ¹³And do not think it a strange assertion that reasoning can in behalf of the Law conquer even enmity. ¹⁴It does not allow [one] to cut down the cultivated herbage of an enemy, but preserves it from the destroyers, and collects their fallen ruins. ¹⁵And reason appears to be master of the more violent passions, such as love of power, and empty boasting, and slander. ¹⁶For the temperate understanding repels all these malignant passions, as it does wrath, for it masters even this. ¹⁷So Moses, when angered against Dathan and Abiram, did nothing to them in wrath, but regulated his anger by reasoning. ¹⁸For the temperate mind is able, as I said, to be superior to the passions, and to transfer some, and destroy others. ¹⁹For why else does our most wise father Jacob blame Simeon and Levi for having irrationally slain the whole race of the Shechemites, saying, "Cursed be their anger"? ²⁰For if reasoning did not possess the power of subduing angry affections, he would not have spoken like this. ²¹For at the time when God created man, He implanted within him his passions and moral nature. ²²And at that time He enthroned above all the holy leader mind, through the medium of the senses. ²³And He gave a law to this mind, by living according to which it will maintain a temperate, and just, and good, and manly reign. ²⁴How [is it] then [that] a man might say that if reasoning is master of the passions, it has no control over forgetfulness and ignorance?

CHAPTER 3

¹The argument is exceedingly ridiculous, for reasoning does not appear to bear sway over its own affections, but over those of the body, ²in such a way as that anyone of you may not be able to root out desire, but reasoning will enable you to avoid being enslaved to it. ³One may not be able to root out anger from the soul, but it is possible to withstand anger. ⁴Anyone of you may not be able to eradicate malice, but reasoning has force to work with you to prevent you yielding to malice. ⁵For reasoning is not an eradicator, but an antagonist of the passions. ⁶And this may be more clearly comprehended from the thirst of King David. ⁷For after David had been attacking the Philistines the whole day, he with the soldiers of his nation killed many of them; ⁸then when evening came, sweating and very weary, he came to the royal tent, around which the entire army of our ancestors was encamped. ⁹Now all the rest of them were at supper, ¹⁰but the king, being very much thirsty, although he had numerous springs, could not by their means quench his thirst, ¹¹but a certain irrational longing for the water in the enemy's camp grew stronger and fiercer on him, and consumed him with languish. ¹²For that reason, his bodyguards being troubled at this longing of the king, two valiant young soldiers, reverencing the desire of the king, put on their armor, and taking a pitcher, got over the ramparts of the enemies: ¹³and unperceived by the guardians of the gate, they went throughout the whole camp of the enemy in quest. ¹⁴And having boldly discovered the fountain, they filled out of it the draught for the king. ¹⁵But he, though parched with thirst, reasoned that a draught regarded of equal value to blood, would be terribly dangerous to his soul. ¹⁶For that reason, setting up reasoning in opposition to his desire, he poured out the draught to God. ¹⁷For the temperate mind has power to conquer the pressure of the passions, and to quench the fires of excitement, ¹⁸and to wrestle down the pains of the body, however excessive; and, through the excellency of reasoning, to abominate all the assaults of the passions. ¹⁹But the occasion now invites us to give an illustration of temperate reasoning from history. ²⁰For at a time when our fathers were in possession of undisturbed peace through obedience to the Law, and were prosperous, so that Seleucus Nicanor, the king of Asia, both assigned them money for divine service, and accepted their form of government, ²¹then certain persons, bringing in new things contrary to the general unanimity, fell into calamities in various ways.

CHAPTER 4

¹For a certain man named Simon, who was in opposition to Onias, who once held the chief priesthood for life, and was an honorable and good man, after slandering him in every way, he could not injure him with the people, went away as an exile, with the intention of betraying his country. ²When coming to Apollonius, the military governor of Syria, and Phoenicia, and Cilicia, he said, ³"Having good will to the king's affairs, I have come to inform you that infinite private wealth is laid up in the treasuries of Jerusalem which do not belong to the temple but pertain to King Seleucus."

⁴Apollonius, acquainting himself with the particulars of this, praised Simon for his care of the king's interests, and going up to Seleucus informed him of the treasure; ⁵and getting authority over it, and quickly advancing into our country with the accursed Simon and a very heavy force, ⁶he said that he came with the commands of the king that he should take the private money of the treasure. ⁷And the nation, indignant at this proclamation, and replying to the effect that it was extremely unfair that those who had committed deposits to the sacred treasury should be deprived of them, resisted as well as they could. ⁸But Apollonius went away with threats into the temple. ⁹And the priests, with the women and children, having supplicated God to throw His shield over the holy, despised place, ¹⁰and Apollonius going up with his armed force to the seizure of the treasure, there appeared from Heaven messengers riding on horseback, all radiant in armor, filling them with much fear and trembling. ¹¹And Apollonius fell half dead on the court which is open to all nations, and extended his hands to Heaven, and implored the Hebrews, with tears, to pray for him, and propitiate the heavenly army. ¹²For he said that he had sinned, so as to be consequently worthy of death; and that if he were saved, he would celebrate to all men the blessedness of the holy place. ¹³Onias the chief priest, induced by these words, although for other reasons anxious that King Seleucus should not suppose that Apollonius was slain by human device and not by Divine punishment, prayed for him; ¹⁴and he being unexpectedly saved, departed to manifest to the king what had happened to him. ¹⁵But on the death of Seleucus the king, his son Antiochus Epiphanes succeeds to the kingdom: a man of arrogant pride and terrible, ¹⁶who having deposed Onias from the chief priesthood, appointed his brother Jason to be chief priest, ¹⁷who had made a covenant to pay three thousand six hundred and sixty talents yearly if he would give him this authority. ¹⁸And he committed the chief priesthood and rulership over the nation to him. ¹⁹And he both changed the manner of living of the people and perverted their civil customs into all lawlessness, ²⁰so that he not only erected a gymnasium on the very citadel of our country, but [neglected] the guardianship of the temple. ²¹At which Divine vengeance being grieved, instigated Antiochus himself against them. ²²For being at war with Ptolemy in Egypt, he heard that on a report of his death being spread abroad, the inhabitants of Jerusalem had exceedingly rejoiced, and he quickly marched against them. ²³And having subdued them, he established a decree that if any of them lived according to the laws of his country he should die. ²⁴And when he could by no means destroy by his decrees the obedience to the law of the nation, but saw all his threats and punishments without effect, ²⁵for even women, because they continued to circumcise their children, were flung down a precipice along with them, knowing beforehand of the punishment. ²⁶When, therefore, his decrees were disregarded by the people, he himself compelled by means of tortures everyone of this race, by tasting forbidden meats, to renounce the Jewish religion.

CHAPTER 5

¹The tyrant Antiochus, therefore, sitting in public state with his assessors on a certain lofty place, with his armed troops standing in a circle around him, ²commanded his spear-bearers to seize everyone of the Hebrews, and to compel them to taste swine's flesh, and things offered to idols. ³And should any of them be unwilling to eat the accursed food, they were to be tortured on the wheel, and so killed. ⁴And when many had been seized, a foremost man of the assembly, a Hebrew, by name Eleazar, a priest by family, by profession a lawyer, and advanced in years, and for this reason known to many of the king's followers, was brought near to him. ⁵And Antiochus seeing him, said, ⁶"I would counsel you, old man, before your tortures begin, to taste the swine's flesh, and save your life; for I feel respect for your age and gray head, which since you have had so long, you appear to me to be no philosopher in retaining the superstition of the Jews. ⁷For that reason, since nature has conferred on you the most excellent flesh of this animal, do you loathe it? ⁸It seems senseless not to enjoy what is pleasant, yet not disgraceful; and from notions of sinfulness, to reject the boons of nature. ⁹And you will be acting, I think, still more senselessly, if you follow vain conceits about the truth. ¹⁰And you will, moreover, be despising me to your own punishment. ¹¹Will you not awake from your trifling philosophy, and give up the folly of your notions, and regaining understanding worthy of your age, search into the truth of an expedient course, ¹²and reverencing my kindly admonition, have pity on your own years? ¹³For bear in mind that if there is any power which watches over this religion of yours, it will pardon you for all transgressions of the Law which you commit through compulsion." ¹⁴While the tyrant incited him in this manner to the unlawful eating of flesh, Eleazar begged permission to speak. ¹⁵And having received power to speak, he began to deliver himself like this: ¹⁶"We, O Antiochus, who are persuaded that we live under a divine law, consider no compulsion to be so forcible as obedience to that law; ¹⁷for this reason we consider that we should not in any point transgress the Law. ¹⁸And indeed, were our law (as you suppose) not truly divine, and if we wrongly think it divine, we should have no right even in that case to destroy our sense of religion. ¹⁹Do not think eating the unclean, then, a trifling offense. ²⁰For transgression of the Law, whether in small or great matters, is of equal moment, ²¹for in either case the Law is equally slighted. ²²But you deride our philosophy, as though we lived irrationally in it. ²³Yet it instructs us in temperance, so that we are superior to all pleasures and lusts; and it exercises us in manliness, so that we cheerfully undergo every grievance. ²⁴And it instructs us in justice, so that in all our dealings we render what is due; and it teaches us piety, so that we worship the one [and] only God as is appropriate. ²⁵For it is that reason we do not eat the unclean; for believing that the Law was established by God, we are convinced that the Creator of the world, in giving His laws, sympathizes with our nature. ²⁶Those things which are convenient to our souls, He has directed us to eat, but those which are repugnant to them, He has interdicted. ²⁷But, tyrant-like, you not only force us to break the Law, but also to eat, that you may ridicule us as we so profanely eat; ²⁸but you will not have this cause of laughter against me, ²⁹nor will I transgress the sacred oaths of my forefathers to keep the Law. ³⁰No, not if you pluck out my eyes, and consume my entrails. ³¹I am not so old, and void of manliness, but that my rational powers are youthful in defense of my religion. ³²Now then, prepare your wheels and kindle a fiercer flame. ³³I will not so pity my old age, as on my account to break the law of my country. ³⁴I will not betray you, O law, my instructor! Or forsake you, O beloved self-control! ³⁵I will not put you to shame, O philosopher reason! Or deny you, O honored priesthood, and science of the law. ³⁶Mouth! You will not pollute my old age, nor the full stature of a perfect life. ³⁷My fathers will receive me pure, not having cowered before your compulsion, though to death. ³⁸For you will tyrannize over the ungodly, but you will not lord it over my thoughts about religion, either by your arguments, or through deeds.

CHAPTER 6

¹When Eleazar had answered the exhortations of the tyrant in this manner, the spear-bearers came up and violently dragged Eleazar to the instruments of torture. ²And first they stripped the old man, adorned as he was with the beauty of piety. ³Then tying back his arms and hands, they disdainfully abused him with stripes, ⁴[while] a herald opposite was crying out, "Obey the commands of the king!" ⁵But Eleazar, the high-minded and truly noble, as one tortured in a dream, did not regard it at all. ⁶But raising his eyes on high to Heaven, the old man's flesh was stripped off by the scourges, and his blood streamed down, and his sides were pierced through. ⁷And falling on the ground, from his body having no power to support the pains, he yet kept his reasoning upright and unbending. ⁸Then one of the harsh spear-bearers leaped on his belly as he was falling, to force him upright. ⁹But he endured the pains, and despised the cruelty, and persevered through the indignities; ¹⁰and like a noble athlete, the old man, when struck, vanquished his torturers. ¹¹His countenance sweating, and panting for breath, he was admired by the very torturers for his courage. ¹²For that reason, partly in pity for his old age, ¹³partly from the sympathy of acquaintance, and partly in admiration of his endurance, some of the attendants of the king said, ¹⁴"Why do you

unreasonably destroy yourself, O Eleazar, with these miseries? ¹⁵We will bring you some meat cooked by yourself, and you can save yourself by pretending that you have eaten swine's flesh." ¹⁶And Eleazar, as though the advice more painfully tortured him, cried out, ¹⁷"Do not let us who are children of Abraham be so wickedly advised as by giving way to make use of an inappropriate pretense; ¹⁸for it were irrational, if having lived up to old age in all truth, and having scrupulously guarded our character for it, we should now turn back, ¹⁹and ourselves should become a pattern of impiety to the young, as being an example of eating pollution. ²⁰It would be disgraceful if we should live for some short time—and that scorned by all men for cowardice— ²¹and be condemned by the tyrant for unmanliness, by not contending to the death for our Divine Law. ²²For this reason, you, O children of Abraham, die nobly for your religion. ²³You spear-bearers of the tyrant, why do you linger?" ²⁴Beholding him so high-minded against misery, and not changing at their pity, they led him to the fire: ²⁵then with their wickedly contrived instruments they burned him on the fire and poured stinking fluids down into his nostrils. ²⁶And he being at length burned down to the bones, and about to expire, raised his eyes toward God, and said, ²⁷"You know, O God, that when I might have been saved, I am slain for the sake of the Law by tortures of fire. ²⁸Be merciful to Your people and be satisfied with my punishment on their account. ²⁹Let my blood be a purification for them and take my life in repayment for theirs." ³⁰Therefore speaking, the holy man departed, noble in his torments, and even to the agonies of death resisted in his reasoning for the sake of the Law. ³¹Confessedly, therefore, religious reasoning is master of the passions. ³²For had the passions been superior to reasoning, I would have given them the witness of this mastery. ³³But now, since reasoning conquered the passions, we befittingly awarded it the authority of first place. ³⁴And it is but fair that we should allow that the power belongs to reasoning, since it masters external miseries. ³⁵It would be ridiculous were it not so; and I prove that reasoning has not only mastered pains, but that it is also superior to the pleasures, and withstands them.

CHAPTER 7

¹The reasoning of our father Eleazar, like a first-rate pilot, steering the vessel of piety in the sea of passions, ²and flouted by the threats of the tyrant, and overwhelmed with the breakers of torture, ³in no way shifted the rudder of piety until it sailed into the harbor of victory over death. ⁴A city has never, when besieged, held out against many and various machines as that holy man did when his pious soul was tried with the fiery trial of tortures and racking, [and when] he moved his besiegers through the religious reasoning that shielded him. ⁵For father Eleazar, projecting his disposition, broke the raging waves of the passions as with a jutting promontory. ⁶O priest worthy of the priesthood! You did not pollute your sacred teeth, nor make your appetite, which had always embraced the clean and lawful, a partaker of profanity. ⁷O harmonizer with the Law, and sage devoted to a divine life! ⁸Of such a character should those be who perform the duties of the Law at the risk of their own blood and defend it with generous sweat by sufferings even to death. ⁹You, father, have gloriously established our right government by your endurance, and making our past service of much account, prevented its destruction, and, by your deeds, have made the words of philosophy credible. ¹⁰O aged man of more power than tortures, elder more vigorous than fire, greatest king over the passions, Eleazar! ¹¹For as father Aaron, armed with a censer, hastening through the consuming fire, vanquished the flame-bearing messenger, ¹²so Eleazar, the descendant of Aaron, wasted away by the fire, did not give up his reasoning. ¹³And what is most wonderful, though an old man, though the labors of his body were now spent, and his muscles were relaxed, and his sinews worn out, he recovered youth. ¹⁴By the spirit of reasoning, and the reasoning of Isaac, he rendered the many-headed instrument powerless. ¹⁵O blessed old age, and venerable gray head, and life obedient to the Law, which the faithful seal of death perfected. ¹⁶If then an old man, through religion, despised tortures even to death, confessedly religious reasoning is ruler of the passions. ¹⁷But perhaps some might say, "It is not all who conquer passions, as all do not possess wise reasoning." ¹⁸But they who have meditated on religion with their whole heart, these alone can master the passions of the flesh— ¹⁹they who believe that they do not die to God; for as our forefathers Abraham, Isaac, [and] Jacob, they live to God. ²⁰This circumstance, then, is by no means an objection, that some who have weak reasoning are governed by their passions: ²¹since what person, walking religiously by the whole rule of philosophy, and believing in God, ²²and knowing that it is a blessed thing to endure all kinds of hardships for virtue, would not, for the sake of religion, master his passion? ²³For only the wise and brave man is lord over his passions. ²⁴From where it is that even boys, trained with the philosophy of religious reasoning, have conquered still more bitter tortures:

CHAPTER 8

¹For when the tyrant was manifestly vanquished in his first attempt, in being unable to force the old man to eat the unclean thing, then indeed, vehemently swayed with passion, he commanded others of the adult Hebrews to be brought, and if they would eat of the unclean thing, to let them go when they had eaten, but if they objected, to torment them more grievously. ²The tyrant having given this charge, seven brothers were brought into his presence, along with their aged mother, handsome, and modest, and well-born, and altogether beautiful. ³When the tyrant saw them encircling their mother as in a dance, he was pleased at them; and being struck with their appropriate and innocent manner, smiled on them, and calling them near, said, ⁴"O youths, with favorable feelings I admire the beauty of each of you; and greatly honoring such a numerous a band of brothers, I not only counsel you not to share the madness of the old man who has been tortured before, ⁵but I beg you to yield and to enjoy my friendship; for I possess the power, not only of punishing those who disobey my commands, but of doing good to those who obey them. ⁶Put confidence in me, then, and you will receive places of authority in my government if you forsake your national ordinance, ⁷and, conforming to the Greek mode of life, alter your rule, and revel in youth's delights. ⁸For if you provoke me by your disobedience, you will compel me to destroy you—everyone—with terrible punishments by tortures. ⁹Have mercy, then, on your own selves, whom I, although an enemy, pity for your age and attractive appearance. ¹⁰Will you not reason on this— that if you disobey, there will be nothing left for you but to die in tortures?" ¹¹So speaking, he ordered the instruments of torture to be brought forward, that great fear might prevail on them to eat unclean meat. ¹²And when the spearman brought forward the wheels, and the racks, and the hooks, and catapults, and cauldrons, pans, and finger-racks, and iron hands and wedges, and bellows, the tyrant continued: ¹³"Fear, young men, and the righteousness which you worship will be merciful to you if you err from compulsion." ¹⁴Now, they having listened to these words of persuasion and seeing the fearful instruments, not only were not afraid, but even answered the arguments of the tyrant, and through their good reasoning destroyed his power. ¹⁵Now let us consider the matter: had any of them been weak-spirited and cowardly among them, what reasoning would they have employed but these? ¹⁶"O wretched that we are, and exceedingly senseless! When the king exhorts us, and calls us to his bounty, should we not obey him? ¹⁷Why do we cheer ourselves with vain counsels, and venture on a disobedience bringing death? ¹⁸Will we not fear, O brothers, the instruments of torture, and weigh the threats of torment, and shun this vainglory and destructive pride? ¹⁹Let us have compassion on our age and relent over the years of our mother. ²⁰And let us bear in mind that we will be dying as rebels. ²¹And Divine Justice will pardon us if we fear the king through necessity. ²²Why withdraw ourselves from a most sweet life, and deprive ourselves of this pleasant world? ²³Let us not oppose necessity, nor seek vainglory by our own excruciation. ²⁴The Law itself is not forward to put us to death if we dread torture. ²⁵From where has such angry zeal taken root in us, and such fatal obstinacy approved itself to us, when we might live unmolested by the king?" ²⁶But nothing of this kind did the young men say or think when about to be tortured. ²⁷For they were well aware of the sufferings and

were masters of the pains. ²⁸... ²⁹So that as soon as the tyrant had ceased counseling them to eat the unclean, they all with one voice, as from the same heart, said:

CHAPTER 9

¹"Why do you delay, O tyrant? For we are more ready to die than to transgress the injunctions of our fathers. ²And we should be disgracing our fathers if we did not obey the Law and take knowledge for our guide. ³O tyrant, counselor of law-breaking, do not, hating us as you do, pity us more than we pity ourselves. ⁴For we account escape to be worse than death. ⁵And you think to scare us, by threatening us with death by tortures, as though you had learned nothing by the death of Eleazar. ⁶But if aged men of the Hebrews have died in the cause of religion after enduring torture, more rightly should we younger men die, scorning your cruel tortures, which our aged instructor overcame. ⁷Make the attempt, then, O tyrant; and if you put us to death for our religion, do not think that you harm us by torturing us. ⁸For we through this mistreatment and endurance will bear off the rewards of virtue. ⁹But you, for the wicked and despotic slaughter of us, will, from the Divine vengeance, endure continuous torture by fire." ¹⁰When they had so spoken, the tyrant was not only exasperated against them as being refractory, but enraged with them as being ungrateful. ¹¹So that, at his bidding, the torturers brought out the oldest of them, and tearing through his tunic, bound his hands and arms on each side with thongs. ¹²And when they had labored hard without effect in scourging him, they hurled him on the wheel. ¹³And the noble youth, extended on this, became dislocated. ¹⁴And with every member disjointed, he exclaimed in protest: ¹⁵"O most accursed tyrant, and enemy of heavenly justice, and cruel-hearted, I am no murderer, nor sacrilegious man, whom you so mistreated, but a defender of the Divine law." ¹⁶And when the spearmen said, "Consent to eat, that you may be released from your tortures," ¹⁷he answered, "Not so powerful, O accursed ministers, is your wheel, as to stifle my reasoning; cut my limbs, and burn my flesh, and twist my joints. ¹⁸For through all my torments I will convince you that the children of the Hebrews are alone unconquered in behalf of virtue." ¹⁹While he was saying this, they heaped up fuel, and setting fire to it, strained him on the wheel still more. ²⁰And the wheel was defiled all over with blood, and the hot ashes were quenched by the droppings of gore, and pieces of flesh were scattered around the axles of the machine. ²¹And although the framework of his bones was now destroyed, the high-minded and Abrahamic youth did not groan. ²²But, as though transformed by fire into immortality, he nobly endured the racking, saying, ²³"Imitate me, O brothers, [and] never desert your station, nor renounce our courageous brotherhood: fight the holy and honorable fight of religion, ²⁴by which means our just and paternal Providence, becoming merciful to the nation, will punish the pernicious tyrant." ²⁵And saying this, the revered youth abruptly closed his life. ²⁶And when all admired his courageous soul, the spearmen brought forward him who was second in point of age, and having put on iron hands, bound him with pointed hooks to the torture device. ²⁷And when, on inquiring whether he would eat before he was tortured, they heard his noble sentiment, ²⁸after they with the iron hands had violently dragged all the flesh from the neck to the chin—the panther-like beasts tore off the very skin of his head, but he, bearing this misery with firmness, said, ²⁹"How sweet is every form of death for the religion of our fathers!" And he said to the tyrant, ³⁰"Do you think, most cruel of all tyrants, that you are now tortured more than I, finding your overconfident conception of tyranny conquered by our perseverance in behalf of our religion? ³¹For I lighten my suffering by the pleasures which are connected with virtue. ³²But you are tortured with threats for impiety; and you will not escape, most corrupt tyrant, the vengeance of Divine wrath."

CHAPTER 10

¹Now this one, having endured this praiseworthy death, the third was brought along, and exhorted by many to taste and save his life. ²But he cried out and said, "Do you not know that the father of those who are dead, became the father of me also, and that the same mother bore me, and that I was brought up in the same tenets? ³I do not renounce the noble relationship of my brothers. ⁴Now then, whatever instrument of vengeance you have, apply it to my body, for you are not able to touch, even if you wish it, my soul. ⁵But they, highly incensed at his boldness of speech, dislocated his hands and feet with racking engines, and wrenching them from their sockets, dismembered him." ⁶And they dragged around his fingers, and his arms, and his legs, and his ankles. ⁷And not being able by any means to strangle him, they tore off his skin, together with the extreme tips of his fingers and then dragged him to the wheel, ⁸around which his vertebral joints were loosened, and he saw his own flesh torn to shreds, and streams of blood flowing from his entrails. ⁹And when about to die, he said, ¹⁰"We, O accursed tyrant, suffer this for the sake of Divine education and virtue. ¹¹But you, for your impiety and blood shedding, will endure indissoluble torments." ¹²And having died worthily of his brothers, they dragged forward the fourth, saying, ¹³"Do not share the madness of your brothers, but give regard to the king, and save yourself." ¹⁴But he said to them, "You do not have a fire so scorching as to make me play the coward. ¹⁵By the blessed death of my brothers, and the continuous punishment of the tyrant, and the glorious life of the pious, I will not repudiate the noble brotherhood. ¹⁶Invent, O tyrant, tortures, that you may learn, even through them, that I am the brother of those tormented before." ¹⁷When he had said this, the blood-thirsty, and murderous, and unhallowed Antiochus ordered his tongue to be cut out. ¹⁸But he said, "Even if you take away the organ of speech, yet God hears the silent. ¹⁹Behold, my tongue is extended, cut it off; for by that you will not halt my reasoning. ²⁰We gladly lose our limbs in behalf of God. ²¹But God will swiftly find you, since you cut off the tongue—the instrument of divine melody."

CHAPTER 11

¹And when he had died, disfigured in his torments, the fifth leaped forward, and said, ²"I do not intend, O tyrant, to get excused from the torment which is in behalf of virtue. ³But I have come of my own accord, that by my death you may owe heavenly vengeance a punishment for more crimes. ⁴O you hater of virtue and of men! What have we done that you so revel in our blood? ⁵Does it seem evil to you that we worship the Founder of all things, and live according to His surpassing law? ⁶But this is worthy of honors, not torments, ⁷had you been capable of the higher feelings of men and possessed the hope of salvation from God. ⁸Behold now, being alien from God, you make war against those who are religious toward God." ⁹As he said this, the spear-bearers bound him and drew him to the torture device, ¹⁰to which binding him at his knees, and fastening them with iron chains, they bent down his loins on the wedge of the wheel; and his body was then dismembered, scorpion-fashion. ¹¹With his breath so confined, and his body strangled, he said, ¹²"A great favor you bestow on us, O tyrant, by enabling us to manifest our adherence to the Law by means of nobler sufferings." ¹³He also being dead, the sixth, quite a youth, was brought out; and on the tyrant asking him whether he would eat and be delivered, he said, ¹⁴"I am indeed younger than my brothers, but I am as old in understanding; ¹⁵for having been born and reared to the same end, we are also bound to die in behalf of the same cause. ¹⁶So that if you think proper to torment us for not eating the unclean, then torment!" ¹⁷As he said this, they brought him to the wheel, ¹⁸extended on which, with limbs racked and dislocated, he was gradually roasted from beneath. ¹⁹And having heated sharp spits, they approached them to his back; and having transfixed his sides, they burned away his entrails. ²⁰And he, while tormented, said, "O period good and holy, in which, for the sake of religion, we brothers have been called to the contest of pain, and have not been conquered! ²¹For religious understanding, O tyrant, is unconquered. ²²Armed with upright virtue, I will also depart with my brothers. ²³I, too, [am] bearing with myself a great Avenger, O inventor of tortures and enemy of the truly pious! ²⁴We six youths have destroyed your tyranny. ²⁵For is not your inability to overrule our reasoning, and to compel us to eat the unclean, your destruction? ²⁶Your fire is cold to us, your devices are painless, and your violence harmless. ²⁷For the guards not of a tyrant but of a divine law are our defenders:

through this we keep our reasoning unconquered."

CHAPTER 12

¹When he, too, had undergone blessed martyrdom, and died in the cauldron into which he had been thrown, the seventh, the youngest of all, came forward, ²whom the tyrant pitying, though he had been dreadfully reproached by his brothers, ³seeing him already encompassed with chains, had him brought nearer, and endeavored to counsel him, saying, ⁴"You see the end of the madness of your brothers, for they have died in torture through disobedience; and you, if disobedient, having been miserably tormented, will yourself perish prematurely. ⁵But if you obey, you will be my friend, and have a charge over the affairs of the kingdom." ⁶And having so exhorted him, he sent for the mother of the boy, that, by condoling with her for the loss of so many sons, he might incline her, through the hope of safety, to render the survivor obedient. ⁷And he, after his mother had urged him on in the Hebrew tongue (as we will soon relate), says, ⁸"Release me that I may speak to the king and all his friends." ⁹And they, rejoicing exceedingly at the promise of the youth, quickly let him go. ¹⁰And he, running up to the pans, said, ¹¹"Impious tyrant, and most blasphemous man, were you not ashamed, having received prosperity and a kingdom from God, to kill His servants, and to rack the doers of godliness? ¹²For this reason the Divine vengeance is reserving you for continuous fire and torments, which will cling to you for all time. ¹³Were you not ashamed, man as you are, yet most savage, to cut out the tongues of men of like feeling and origin, and having so abused to torture them? ¹⁴But they, bravely dying, fulfilled their religion toward God. ¹⁵But you will groan according to your deserts for having slain the champions of virtue without cause." ¹⁶"For this reason," he continued, "I myself, being about to die, ¹⁷will not forsake my brothers. ¹⁸And I call on the God of my fathers to be merciful to my race. ¹⁹But you, both living and dead, He will punish." ²⁰So having prayed, he hurled himself into the pans, and so expired.

CHAPTER 13

¹If then the seven brothers despised troubles even to death, it is confessed on all sides that righteous reasoning is absolute master over the passions. ²For just as if, had they as slaves to the passions eaten of the unholy, we should have said that they had been conquered; ³now it is not so, but by means of the reasoning which is praised by God, they mastered their passions. ⁴And it is impossible to overlook the leadership of reflection, for it gained the victory over both passions and troubles. ⁵How then can we avoid, according to these men, mastery of passion through right reasoning, since they did not draw back from the pains of fire? ⁶For just as by means of towers projecting in front of harbors men break the threatening waves, and therefore assure a still course to vessels entering port, ⁷so that seven-towered right-reasoning of the young men, securing the harbor of religion, conquered the intemperance of passions. ⁸For having arranged a holy choir of piety, they encouraged one another, saying, ⁹"Brothers, may we die brotherly for the Law. Let us imitate the three young men in Assyria who despised the equally afflicting furnace. ¹⁰Let us not be cowards in the manifestation of piety." ¹¹And one said, "Courage, brother"; and another, "Nobly endure." ¹²And another, "Remember of what stock you are—and by the hand of our father Isaac who endured to be slain for the sake of piety." ¹³And one and all, looking on each other serene and confident, said, "Let us sacrifice with all our heart our souls to God who gave them, and employ our bodies for the keeping of the Law. ¹⁴Let us not fear him who thinks he kills, ¹⁵for great is the trial of soul and danger of continuous torment laid up for those who transgress the command of God. ¹⁶Let us therefore arm ourselves in the self-control, which is divine reasoning. ¹⁷If we suffer like this, Abraham, and Isaac, and Jacob will receive us, and all the fathers will commend us." ¹⁸And as each one of the brothers was hauled away, the rest exclaimed, "Do not disgrace us, O brother, nor falsify those who died before you. ¹⁹Now you are not ignorant of the charm of brotherhood, which the Divine and all-wise Providence has imparted through fathers to children and has engendered through the mother's womb." ²⁰In which these brothers having remained an equal time, and having been formed for the same period, and been increased by the same blood, and having been perfected through the same principle of life, ²¹and having been brought out at equal intervals, and having sucked milk from the same springs, their brotherly souls are reared up lovingly together, ²²and increase [all] the more powerfully by reason of this simultaneous rearing, and by daily companionship, and by other education, and exercise in the law of God. ²³Brotherly love being so sympathetically constituted, the seven brothers had a more sympathetic mutual harmony. ²⁴For being educated in the same law, and practicing the same virtues, and reared up in a just course of life, they increased this harmony with each other. ²⁵For a like zeal for what is right and honorable increased their fellow-feeling toward each other. ²⁶For it acting along with religion, made their brotherly feeling more desirable to them. ²⁷And yet, although nature, and companionship, and virtuous morals increased their brotherly love, those who were left endured to behold their brothers, who were mistreated for their religion [and] tortured even to death.

CHAPTER 14

¹And more than this, they even urged them on to this mistreatment, so that they not only despised pains themselves, but they even got the better of their affections of brotherly love. ²O reasoning, more royal than a king and freer than freemen! ³O sacred and harmonious concord of the seven brothers as concerning piety! ⁴None of the seven youths turned cowardly or shrank back from death. ⁵But all of them, as though running the road to immortality, hastened on to death through tortures. ⁶For just as hands and feet are moved sympathetically with the directions of the soul, so those holy youths agreed to death for religion's sake, as through the immortal soul of religion. ⁷O holy seven—harmonious brothers! For as the seven days of creation, about religion, ⁸so the youths, circling around the number seven, annulled the fear of torments. ⁹We now shudder at the recital of the affliction of those young men, but they not only saw, and not only heard the immediate execution of the threat, but undergoing it, persevered—and that through the pains of fire. ¹⁰And what could be more painful? For the power of fire, being sharp and quick, speedily dissolved their bodies. ¹¹And do not think it wonderful that reasoning bore rule over those men in their torments, when even a woman's mind despised more manifold pains. ¹²For the mother of those seven youths endured the rackings of each of her children. ¹³And consider how comprehensive the love for offspring is, which draws everyone to sympathy of affection, ¹⁴where irrational animals possess a similar sympathy and love for their offspring with men. ¹⁵The tame birds frequenting the roofs of our houses, defend their fledglings. ¹⁶Others build their nests and hatch their young in the tops of mountains, and in the precipices of valleys, and the holes and tops of trees, and keep off the intruder. ¹⁷And if not able to do this, they fly circling around them in agony of affection, calling out in their own note, and save their offspring in whatever manner they are able. ¹⁸But why should we point attention to the sympathy toward children shown by irrational animals? ¹⁹The very bees, at the season of honey-making, attack all who approach, and pierce with their sting, as with a sword, those who draw near their hive, and repel them even to death. ²⁰But sympathy for her children did not turn away the mother of the young men—[she] who had a spirit related with that of Abraham.

CHAPTER 15

¹O reasoning of the sons, lord over the passions, and religion more desirable to a mother than progeny! ²The mother, when two things were set before her—religion and the safety of her seven sons for a time on the conditional promise of a tyrant— ³rather chose the religion which according to God preserves to continuous life. ⁴O in what way can I describe ethically the affections of parents toward their children, the resemblance of soul and of form engrafted into the small type of a child in a wonderful manner, especially through the greater sympathy of mothers with the feelings of those born of them! ⁵For by how much mothers are by nature weak in disposition and prolific in offspring, by so much the fonder they are of children. ⁶And of all mothers the mother of the seven was the

fondest of children, who in seven childbirths had deeply engendered love toward them, ⁷and through her many pains undergone in connection with each one, was compelled to feel sympathy with them, ⁸yet, through fear of God, she neglected the temporary salvation of her children. ⁹Not [only] that, but on account of the excellent disposition to the Law, her maternal affection toward them was increased. ¹⁰For they were both just and temperate, and manly, and high-minded, and fond of their brothers, and so fond of their mother that even to death they obeyed her by observing the Law. ¹¹And yet, though there were so many circumstances connected with love of children to draw on a mother to sympathy, in the case of none of them were the various tortures able to pervert her principle. ¹²But she inclined each one separately and all together to death for religion. ¹³O holy nature and parental feeling, and reward of bringing up children, and unconquerable maternal affection! ¹⁴At the racking and roasting of each one of them, the observant mother was prevented by religion from changing. ¹⁵She saw her children's flesh dissolving around the fire, and their extremities quivering on the ground, and the flesh of their heads dropped forward down to their beards, like masks. ¹⁶O you mother who was tried at this time with bitterer pangs than those of childbirth! ¹⁷O you only woman who has brought out perfect holiness! ¹⁸Your firstborn, expiring, did not sway you; nor the second, looking miserable in his torments; nor the third, breathing out his soul. ¹⁹Nor did you weep when you beheld the eyes of each of them looking sternly on their tortures, and their nostrils foreboding death! ²⁰When you saw children's flesh heaped on children's flesh that had been torn off, heads decapitated on heads, dead falling on the dead, and a choir of children turned through torture into a burying ground, you did not lament. ²¹Not so do siren melodies or songs of swans attract the hearers to listening [as did the] voices of [you] children calling on your mother in the midst of torments! ²²O with what and what manner of torments was the mother herself tortured as her sons were undergoing the wheel and the fires! ²³But religious reasoning, having strengthened her courage in the midst of sufferings, enabled her to forego, for the time, parental love. ²⁴Although beholding the destruction of seven children, the noble mother, after one embrace, stripped off [her feelings] through faith in God. ²⁵For just as in a council-room, beholding in her own soul vehement counselors—nature, and parentage, and love of her children, and the racking of her children— ²⁶she holding two votes, one for the death, the other for the preservation of her children, ²⁷did not lean to that which would have saved her children for the safety of a brief space. ²⁸But this daughter of Abraham remembered his holy fortitude. ²⁹O holy mother of a nation, avenger of the Law, and defender of religion, and prime bearer in the battle of the affections! ³⁰O you nobler in endurance than males, and more manly than men in perseverance! ³¹For as the Ark of Noah, bearing the world in the world-filling flood, bore up against the waves, ³²so you, the guardian of the Law, when surrounded on every side by the flood of passions, and constricted by violent storms which were the torments of those children, nobly bore up against the storms against religion.

CHAPTER 16

¹If then, even a woman, and that an aged one and the mother of seven children, endured to see her children's torments even to death, confessedly religious reasoning is master even of the passions. ²I have proved, then, that not only men have obtained the mastery of their passions, but also that a woman despised the greatest torments. ³And not so fierce were the lions around Daniel, nor the furnace of Mishael burning with most vehement fires as that natural love of children burned within her, when she saw her seven sons tortured. ⁴But with the reasoning of religion, the mother quenched passions so great and powerful. ⁵For we must consider this also: that, had the woman been faint-hearted, as being their other, she would have lamented over them, and perhaps might have spoken like this: ⁶"Ah! Wretched me, and many times miserable, who having born seven sons, have become the mother of none. ⁷O seven useless childbirths, and seven profitless periods of labor, and fruitless giving of suck, and miserable nursing at the breast. ⁸Vainly, for your sakes, O sons, have I endured many pangs, and the more difficult anxieties of rearing. ⁹Aah! Of my children, some of you unmarried, and some who have married to no profit, I will not see your children, nor be congratulated as a grandmother. ¹⁰Ah! That I who had many and fair children, should be a lone widow full of sorrows! ¹¹Nor, should I die, will I have a son to bury me." But with such a lament as this the holy and God-fearing mother mourned none of them. ¹²Nor did she divert any of them from death, nor grieve for them as for the dead. ¹³But as one possessed with an adamantine mind, and as one bringing out again her full number of sons to immortality, she rather with supplication exhorted them to death in behalf of religion. ¹⁴O woman, soldier of God for religion, you, aged and a female, have even conquered a tyrant through endurance; and though but weak, have been found more powerful in deeds and words. ¹⁵For when you were seized along with your children, you stood looking on Eleazar in torments, and said to your sons in the Hebrew tongue, ¹⁶"O sons, the contest is noble to which you are being called as a witness for the nation, [to which] you strive zealously for the laws of your country. ¹⁷For it were disgraceful that this old man should endure pains for the sake of righteousness, and that you who are younger should be afraid of the tortures. ¹⁸Remember that through God you obtained existence and have enjoyed it. ¹⁹And on this second account you should bear every affliction because of God, ²⁰for whom our father Abraham was also forward to sacrifice our progenitor Isaac, and did not shudder at the sight of his own paternal hand descending down with the sword on him. ²¹And the righteous Daniel was cast to the lions; and Hananiah, and Azariah, and Mishael were slung out into a furnace of fire, yet they endured through God. ²²You, then, having the same faith toward God, do not be troubled. ²³For it is unreasonable that they who know religion should not stand up against troubles. ²⁴With these arguments, the mother of seven, exhorting each of her sons, over-persuaded them from transgressing the command of God. ²⁵And they also saw this, that they who die for God live to God, as Abraham, and Isaac, and Jacob, and all the patriarchs.

CHAPTER 17

¹And some of the spear-bearers said that when she herself was about to be seized for the purpose of being put to death, she threw herself on the pile, rather than that they should touch her person. ²O you mother, who together with seven children destroyed the violence of the tyrant, and rendered his wicked intentions void, and exhibited the nobleness of faith! ³For you, as a house bravely built on the pillar of your children, bore the shock of tortures without swaying. ⁴Be of good cheer, therefore, O holy-minded mother, holding the firm [substance of the] hope of your steadfastness with God. ⁵The moon does not appear with the stars in the sky as gracious as you are: established honorable before God, and fixed in the expanse with your sons who you illuminated with religion to the stars. ⁶For your bearing of children was after the fashion of a child of Abraham. ⁷And, were it lawful for us to paint as on a tablet the religion of your story, the spectators would not shudder at beholding the mother of seven children enduring, for the sake of religion, various tortures even to death. ⁸And it had been a worthy thing to have inscribed on the tomb itself these words as a memorial to those of the nation: ⁹"HERE AN AGED PRIEST, AND AN AGED WOMAN, AND SEVEN SONS, ARE BURIED THROUGH THE VIOLENCE OF A TYRANT, WHO WISHED TO DESTROY THE SOCIETY OF THE HEBREWS. ¹⁰THESE ALSO AVENGED THEIR NATION, LOOKING TO GOD AND ENDURING TORMENTS TO DEATH." ¹¹For it was truly a divine contest which was carried through by them. ¹²For at that time virtue presided over the contest, approving the victory through endurance, namely, immortality [and] continuous life. ¹³Eleazar was the first to contend, and [then] the mother of the seven children entered the contest, and [then] the brothers contended. ¹⁴The tyrant was the opposite; and the world and living men were the spectators. ¹⁵And reverence for God conquered and crowned her own athletes. ¹⁶Who did not admire those champions of true legislation? Who were not astonished? ¹⁷The tyrant himself, and all their council, admired their endurance; ¹⁸through which, also, they now stand beside the divine throne, and live a blessed life. ¹⁹For Moses says, "And all the

saints are under Your hands." ²⁰These, therefore, having been sanctified through God, have been honored not only with this honor, but that also by their means the enemy did not overcome our nation, ²¹and that the tyrant was punished, and their country purified. ²²For they became the ransom to the sin of the nation, and the Divine Providence saved Israel, previously afflicted, by the blood of those pious ones, and the propitiatory death. ²³For the tyrant Antiochus, looking to their manly virtue, and to their endurance in torture, proclaimed that endurance as an example to his soldiers. ²⁴And they proved to him to be noble and brave for land battles and for sieges; and he conquered and stormed the towns of all his enemies.

CHAPTER 18

¹O Israeli children, descendants of the seed of Abraham, obey this law, and in every way be religious, ²knowing that religious reasoning is lord of the passions, and those not only inward but outward. ³When those persons were giving up their bodies to pains for the sake of religion, they were not only admired by men, but were deemed worthy of a divine portion. ⁴And the nation obtained peace through them, and having renewed the observance of the Law in their country, they drove the enemy out of the land. ⁵And the tyrant Antiochus was both punished on earth and is punished now [that] he is dead; for when he was quite unable to compel the Israelites to adopt foreign customs and to desert the manner of life of their fathers, ⁶then, departing from Jerusalem, he made war against the Persians. ⁷And the righteous mother of the seven children also spoke as follows to her offspring: "I was a pure virgin and did not go beyond my father's house, but I took care of the built-up rib. ⁸No destroyer of the desert [or] ravisher of the plain injured me; nor did the destructive, deceitful snake make plunder of my pure virginity; and I remained with my husband during the period of my prime. ⁹And these children of mine, having arrived at maturity, their father died: he was blessed! For having sought out a life of fertility in children, he was not grieved with a period of loss of children. ¹⁰And he used to teach you, when yet with you, the Law and the Prophets. ¹¹He used to read to you the slaying of Abel by Cain, and the offering up of Isaac, and the imprisonment of Joseph. ¹²And he used to tell you of the zealous Phinehas; and informed you of Hananiah, and Azariah, and Mishael in the fire. ¹³And he used to glorify Daniel, who was in the den of lions, and pronounce him blessed. ¹⁴And he used to put you in mind of the Writing of Isaiah, which says, Even if you pass through the fire, it will not burn you. ¹⁵He chanted to you David, the hymn-writer, who says, Many are the afflictions of the just. ¹⁶He declared the proverbs of Solomon, who says, He is a Tree of Life to all those who do His will. ¹⁷He used to verify Ezekiel, who said, Will these dry bones live? ¹⁸For he did not forget the song which Moses taught, proclaiming, I will kill, and I will make to live. ¹⁹This is our life, and the length of our days." ²⁰O that bitter—and yet not bitter—day when the bitter tyrant of the Greeks, quenching fire with fire in his cruel cauldrons, brought with boiling rage the seven sons of the daughter of Abraham to the torture device, and to all his torments! ²¹He pierced the balls of their eyes, and cut out their tongues, and put them to death with varied tortures. ²²For this reason divine retribution pursued and will [still] pursue the pernicious wretch. ²³But the children of Abraham, with their victorious mother, are assembled together to the choir of their father, having received pure and immortal souls from God, ²⁴to whom be glory forever and ever. Amen.

PRAYER OF MANASSEH

The Prayer of Manasseh (or Manasses) is a short work of 15 verses recording a penitential prayer attributed to King Manasseh of Judah. Most scholars believe that the Prayer of Manasseh was written in Greek in the 1st or 2nd century BC. Another work by the same title, written in Hebrew and containing distinctly different content, was found among the Dead Sea Scrolls.

CHAPTER 1

¹O LORD Almighty, that are in Heaven, You God of our fathers, of Abraham, and Isaac, and Jacob, and of their righteous seed; ²who have made the heavens and earth, with all the ornament thereof; ³who have bound the sea by the word of Your command; who have shut up the deep, and sealed it by Your terrible and glorious Name; ⁴whom all things fear, yes, tremble before Your power; ⁵for the majesty of Your glory cannot be borne, and the anger of Your threatening toward sinners is importable: ⁶Your merciful promise is unmeasurable and unsearchable; ⁷for You are the LORD Most High, of great compassion, patient and abundant in mercy, and relenting of bringing evils on men. ⁸You, O LORD, according to Your great goodness have promised conversion and forgiveness to those who have sinned against You: and of Your infinite mercies have appointed conversion to sinners, that they may be saved. You, therefore, O LORD, that are the God of the just, have not appointed conversion to the just, to Abraham, and Isaac, and Jacob, which have not sinned against You; but You have appointed conversion to me that am a sinner: ⁹for I have sinned above the number of the sands of the sea. My transgressions are multiplied, O LORD: my transgressions are multiplied, and I am not worthy to behold and see the height of Heaven for the multitude of my iniquities. ¹⁰I am bowed down with many iron bands, that I cannot lift up my head by reason of my sins, neither do I have any respite, for I have provoked Your wrath and done that which is evil before You: I did not do Your will, neither did I keep Your commands: I have set up abominations and have multiplied detestable things. ¹¹Now therefore, I bow the knee of my heart, imploring You of grace. ¹²I have sinned, O LORD, I have sinned, and I acknowledge my iniquities: ¹³but, I humbly implore You, forgive me, O LORD, forgive me, and do not destroy me with my iniquities. Do not be angry with me forever, by reserving evil for me; neither condemn me into the lower parts of the earth. For You, O LORD, are the God of those who convert; ¹⁴and in me You will show all Your goodness, for You will save me, that am unworthy, according to Your great mercy. ¹⁵And I will praise You forever all the days of my life, for all the army of Heaven sings Your praise, and Yours is the glory forever and ever. Amen.

TESTAMENTS OF THE TWELVE PATRIARCHS

The Testaments of the Twelve Patriarchs are apocryphal works purporting to contain the last words of the twelve sons of Jacob. These are part of the Oskan Armenian Orthodox Bible. Fragments of similar writings were found at Qumran, and scholarship maintains that the Testaments were written in Hebrew or Greek, possibly in the 2nd century BC, and reached their final form in the 2nd century AD.

THE TESTAMENT OF REUBEN

THE FIRSTBORN SON OF JACOB AND LEAH

CHAPTER 1

¹The copy of the Testament of Reuben, even the commands which he gave his sons before he died in the one hundred and twenty-fifth year of his life. ²Two years after the death of his brother Joseph, when Reuben fell sick, his sons and his sons' sons were gathered together to visit him. ³And he said to them, "My children, behold, I am dying, and I go the way of my fathers." ⁴And seeing his brothers Judah, and Gad, and Asher there, he said to them, "Raise me up, that I may tell to my brothers and to my children what things I have hidden in my heart, for behold, now at length I am passing away." ⁵And he arose and kissed them, and said to them, "Hear, my brothers, and my children, give ear to your father Reuben in the commands which I give to you. ⁶And behold, I call the God of Heaven to witness against you this day, that you may not walk in the sins of youth and fornication, wherein I was poured out, and defiled the bed of my father Jacob. ⁷And I tell you that He struck me with a sore plague in my loins for seven months, and had my father Jacob not prayed for me to the LORD, the LORD would have destroyed me. ⁸For I was thirty years old when I worked the evil thing before the LORD, and I was sick to death for seven months. ⁹And after this I converted with set purpose of my soul for seven years before the LORD. ¹⁰And I did not drink wine and strong drink, and flesh did not enter into my mouth, and I did not eat pleasant food; but I mourned over my sin, for it was great—such as had not been in Israel."

CHAPTER 2

¹"And now hear me, my children, what things I saw concerning the seven spirits of deceit, when I converted. ²Therefore seven spirits are appointed against man, and they are the leaders in the works of youth. [[³And seven other spirits are given to him at his creation, that through them should be done every work of man. ⁴The first is the spirit of life, with which the constitution [of man] is created. ⁵The second is the sense of sight, with which arises desire. The third is the sense of hearing, with which comes teaching. ⁶The fourth is the sense of smell, with which tastes are given to draw air and breath. The fifth is the power of speech, with which comes knowledge. ⁷The sixth is the sense of taste, with which comes the eating of meats and drinks; and by it strength is produced, for in food is the foundation of strength. ⁸The seventh is the power of procreation and sexual intercourse, with which through love of pleasure sins enter in. ⁹For what reason it is the last in order of creation, and the first in that of youth, because it is filled with ignorance, and leads the youth as a blind man to a pit, and as a beast to a precipice."

CHAPTER 3

¹"Besides all these there is an eighth spirit of sleep, with which is brought about the trance of nature and the image of death. With these spirits are mingled the spirits of error.]] ²First, the spirit of fornication is seated in the nature and in the senses; the second, the spirit of insatiableness, in the belly; ³the third, the spirit of fighting, in the liver and gall; ⁴the fourth is the spirit of groveling and trickery, that through overbearing attention one may [falsely] seem fair; ⁵the fifth is the spirit of pride, that one may be boastful and arrogant; ⁶the sixth is the spirit of lying, to practice deceits in perdition and jealousy, and concealments from kindred and friends; ⁷the seventh is the spirit of injustice, with which are thefts and acts of rapacity, that a man may fulfill the desire of his heart; for injustice works together with the other spirits by the taking of gifts. ⁸And with all these the spirit of sleep is joined which is [that] of error and fantasy. And so perishes every young man, darkening his mind from the truth, and not understanding the Law of God, nor obeying the admonitions of his fathers as also befell me in my youth. ⁹And now, my children, love the truth, and it will preserve you: hear the words of your father Reuben. ¹⁰Pay no heed to the face of a woman, nor associate with another man's wife, nor meddle with affairs of womankind. ¹¹For had I not seen Bilhah bathing in a covered place, I would not have fallen into this great iniquity. ¹²For my mind, taking in the thought of the woman's nakedness, did not permit me to sleep until I had worked the abominable thing. ¹³For while our father Jacob had gone to his father Isaac, when we were in Eder, near to Ephrath in Beth-Lehem, Bilhah became drunk and was asleep uncovered in her chamber. ¹⁴Therefore, having gone in and beheld [her] nakedness, I worked the impiety without her perceiving it, and leaving her sleeping, I departed. ¹⁵And immediately a messenger of God revealed to my father concerning my impiety, and he came and mourned over me, and touched her no longer."

CHAPTER 4

¹"Pay no heed, therefore, my children, to the beauty of women, nor set your mind on their affairs; but walk in singleness of heart in the fear of the LORD, and expend labor on good works, and on study, and on your flocks, until the LORD gives you a wife, whom He will, that you do not permit as I did. ²For until my father's death, I did not have boldness to look in his face, or to speak to any of my brothers, because of the reproach. ³Even until now, my conscience causes me anguish on account of my impiety. ⁴And yet my father comforted me much and prayed for me to the LORD, that the anger of the LORD might pass from me, even as the LORD showed. ⁵And from then until now, I have been on my guard and have not sinned. Therefore, my children, I say to you: observe all things, whatever I command you, and you will not sin. ⁶For the sin of fornication is a pit to the soul, separating it from God, and bringing it near to idols, because it deceives the mind and understanding, and leads young men into Hades before their time. ⁷For fornication has destroyed many, because, though a man may be old or noble, or rich or poor, he brings reproach on himself with the sons of men and derision with Belial. ⁸For you heard regarding Joseph how he guarded himself from a woman, and purged his thoughts from all fornication, and found favor in the sight of God and men. ⁹For the Egyptian woman did many things to him, and summoned magicians, and offered him love potions, but the purpose of his soul admitted no evil desire. ¹⁰Therefore the God of your fathers delivered him from every evil [and] hidden death. For if fornication does not overcome your mind, neither can Belial overcome you."

CHAPTER 5

¹"For women are evil, my children; and since they have no power or strength over man, they use schemes by outward attractions, that they may draw him to themselves. ²And whom they cannot bewitch by outward attractions, they overcome him by craft. ³For moreover, concerning them, the messenger of the LORD told me, and taught me, that women are overcome by the spirit of fornication more than men, and they plot against men in their heart; and by means of their adornment they first deceive their minds, and by the glance of the eye instill the poison, and then through the accomplished act, they take them captive. ⁴For a woman cannot force a man openly, but by a harlot's bearing she deceives him. ⁵Flee, therefore, fornication, my children, and command your wives and your daughters, that they do not adorn their heads and faces to deceive the mind, because every woman who

uses these schemes has been reserved for continuous punishment; ⁶for thus they allured the Watchers who were before the Flood; for as these continually beheld them, they lusted after them, and they conceived the act in their mind; for they changed themselves into the shape of men, and appeared to them when they were with their husbands. ⁷And the women, lusting in their minds after their forms, gave birth to giants, for the Watchers appeared to them as reaching even to Heaven."

CHAPTER 6

¹"Beware, therefore, of fornication; and if you wish to be pure in mind, guard your senses from every woman. ²And likewise command the women not to associate with men, that they may also be pure in mind. ³For constant meetings, even though the ungodly deed is not worked, are an irremediable disease to them, and to us a destruction of Belial and a continuous reproach. ⁴For in fornication there is neither understanding nor godliness, and all jealousy dwells in the lust thereof. ⁵Therefore, I say to you then: you will be jealous against the sons of Levi and will seek to be exalted over them, but you will not be able. ⁶For God will avenge them, and you will die by an evil death. ⁷For God gave the sovereignty to Levi, [[and to Judah with him, and to me also, and to Dan and Joseph, that we should be for rulers;]] ⁸therefore I command you to listen to Levi, because he will know the Law of the LORD, and will give ordinances for judgment, and will sacrifice for all Israel until the consummation of the times, as the anointed chief priest, of whom the LORD spoke, ⁹I adjure you by the God of Heaven to do truth—each one to his neighbor, and to entertain love—each one for his brother. ¹⁰And draw near to Levi in humbleness of heart, that you may receive a blessing from his mouth. ¹¹For he will bless Israel and Judah, because the LORD has chosen him to be king over all the nation. ¹²And bow down before his seed, for on our behalf it will die in wars, visible and invisible, and will be among you [as] a perpetual king."

CHAPTER 7

¹And Reuben died, having given these commands to his sons. ²And they placed him in a coffin until they carried him up from Egypt and buried him in Hebron in the cave where his father was.

THE TESTAMENT OF SIMEON

THE SECOND SON OF JACOB AND LEAH

CHAPTER 1

¹The copy of the words of Simeon, the things which he spoke to his sons before he died, in the one hundred and twentieth year of his life, at which time his brother Joseph died. ²For when Simeon was sick, his sons came to visit him, and he strengthened himself and sat up and kissed them, and said:

CHAPTER 2

¹"Listen, my children, to your father Simeon, and I will declare to you what things I have in my heart. ²I was born of Jacob as my father's second son; and my mother Leah called me Simeon, because the LORD had heard her prayer. ³Moreover, I became exceedingly strong; I shrank from no achievement, nor was I afraid of anything. ⁴For my heart was hard, and my liver was immovable, and my bowels [were] without compassion, ⁵because valor has also been given from the Most High to men in soul and body. ⁶For in the time of my youth I was jealous in many things of Joseph, because my father loved him beyond all. ⁷And I set my mind against him to destroy him, because the prince of deceit sent forth the spirit of jealousy and blinded my mind, so that I did not regard him as a brother, nor did I even spare my father Jacob. ⁸But his God and the God of his fathers sent forth His messenger and delivered him out of my hands. ⁹For when I went to Shechem to bring ointment for the flocks, and Reuben to Dothan, where our necessities and all our stores were, my brother Judah sold him to the Ishmaelites. ¹⁰And when Reuben heard these things, he was grieved, for he wished to restore him to his father. ¹¹But on hearing this I was exceedingly angry against Judah in that he let him go away alive, and for five months I continued being wrathful against him. ¹²But the LORD restrained me and withheld from me the power of my hands, for my right hand was half withered for seven days. ¹³And I knew, my children, that this had befallen me because of Joseph, and I converted and wept; and I implored the LORD God that my hand might be restored, and that I might hold aloof from all pollution, and envy, and from all folly. ¹⁴For I knew that I had devised an evil thing before the LORD and my father Jacob, on account of my brother Joseph, in that I envied him."

CHAPTER 3

¹"And now, my children, listen to me and beware of the spirit of deceit and envy. ²For envy rules over the whole mind of a man and permits him neither to eat, nor to drink, nor to do any good thing. ³But it always suggests [to him] to destroy him that he envies; and so long as he that is envied flourishes, he that envies fades away. ⁴Therefore, I afflicted my soul with fasting in the fear of the LORD [for] two years, and I learned that deliverance from envy comes by the fear of God. ⁵For if a man flees to the LORD, the evil spirit runs away from him, and his mind is lightened. ⁶And henceforward he sympathizes with him whom he envied and forgives those who are hostile to him, and so ceases from his envy."

CHAPTER 4

¹"And my father asked concerning me, because he saw that I was sad; and I said to him, I am pained in my liver. ²For I mourned more than all of them, because I was guilty of the selling of Joseph. ³And when we went down into Egypt, and he bound me as a spy, I knew that I was suffering justly, and I did not grieve. ⁴Now Joseph was a good man and had the Spirit of God within him: being compassionate and pitiful, he bore no malice against me, but loved me even as the rest of his brothers. ⁵Beware, therefore, my children, of all jealousy and envy, and walk in singleness of soul and with good heart, keeping in mind Joseph, your father's brother, that God may also give you grace and glory, and blessing on your heads, even as you saw in Joseph's case. ⁶All his days he did not reproach us concerning this thing, but loved us as his own soul, and glorified us beyond his own sons, and gave us riches, and cattle, and fruits. ⁷You also, my children, must love his brother—each one—with a good heart, and the spirit of envy will withdraw from you. ⁸For this [[(envy)]] makes the soul savage and destroys the body; it causes anger and war in the mind, and stirs up to deeds of blood, and leads the mind into frenzy, and does not permit prudence to act in men; moreover, it takes away sleep, [[and causes tumult to the soul and trembling to the body]]. ⁹For even in sleep, some malicious jealousy, deluding him, gnaws and with wicked spirits disturbs his soul, and causes the body to be troubled, and wakes the mind from sleep in confusion; and as a wicked and poisonous spirit, so it appears to men."

CHAPTER 5

¹"Therefore Joseph was handsome in appearance and attractive to look on, because no wickedness dwelt in him; for the face manifests some of the trouble of the spirit. ²And now, my children, make your hearts good before the LORD and your ways straight before men, and you will find grace before the LORD and men. ³Beware, therefore, of fornication, for fornication is a mother of all evils, separating from God and bringing near to Belial. ⁴For I have seen it inscribed in the writing of Enoch that your sons will be corrupted in fornication, ⁵and will do harm to the sons of Levi with the sword. But they will not be able to withstand Levi; ⁶for he will wage the war of the LORD and will conquer all your hosts. And they will be few in number, divided in Levi and Judah, and there will be none of you for sovereignty, even as our father also prophesied in his blessings."

CHAPTER 6

¹"Behold, I have told you all things that I may be acquitted of your sin. ²Now, if you remove your envy and all stiff-neckedness from yourselves, || My bones will flourish in Israel as a rose, || And my flesh in Jacob as a lily, || And my fragrance will be as the fragrance of Libanus; And holy ones will be multiplied from me as cedars forever, || And their branches will stretch far off. ³Then the seed of Canaan will perish, || And a remnant will not be to Amalek, || And all the Cappadocians will perish, || And all the Hittites will be utterly destroyed. ⁴Then the land of Ham will fail, || And all the people will perish. Then all the earth will rest from trouble, || And all the world under Heaven from war. ⁵Then the

Mighty One of Israel will glorify Shem, || For the LORD God will appear on earth, || And [He] Himself will save men. ⁶Then all the spirits of deceit will be given to be trodden under foot, || And men will rule over wicked spirits. ⁷Then I will arise in joy, || And will bless the Most High because of His marvelous works, [[|| Because God has taken a body and eaten with men and saved men.]]"

CHAPTER 7

¹"And now, my children, obey Levi and Judah, and do not be lifted up against these two tribes, for from them the salvation of God will arise to you. ²For the LORD will raise up from Levi as it were a Chief Priest, and from Judah as it were a King—[[God and man;]] He will save all [[the nations and]] the race of Israel. ³Therefore I give you these commands that you may also command your children that they may observe them throughout their generations."

CHAPTER 8

¹And when Simeon had made an end of commanding his sons, he slept with his fathers, ²being one hundred and twenty years old. ²And they laid him in a wooden coffin, to take up his bones to Hebron. ³And they took them up secretly during a war of the Egyptians. ⁴For the Egyptians guarded the bones of Joseph in the tombs of the kings. ⁵For the sorcerers told them that on the departure of the bones of Joseph there should be darkness and gloom throughout all the land, and an exceedingly great plague to the Egyptians, so that even with a lamp a man should not recognize his brother.

CHAPTER 9

¹And the sons of Simeon lamented their father. ²And they were in Egypt until the day of their departure by the hand of Moses.

THE TESTAMENT OF LEVI

THE THIRD SON OF JACOB AND LEAH

CHAPTER 1

¹The copy of the words of Levi, the things which he ordained to his sons, according to all that they should do, and what things should befall them until the Day of Judgment. ²He was sound in health when he called them to himself; for it had been revealed to him that he should die. And when they were gathered together, he said to them:

CHAPTER 2

¹"I, Levi, was born in Haran, and I came with my father to Shechem. ²And I was young, about twenty years of age, when, with Simeon, I worked vengeance on Hamor for our sister Dinah. ³And when I was feeding the flocks in Abel-Maul, the spirit of understanding of the LORD came on me, and I saw all men corrupting their way, and that unrighteousness had built walls for itself, and lawlessness sat on towers. ⁴And I was grieving for the race of the sons of men, and I prayed to the LORD that I might be saved. ⁵Then there fell on me a sleep, and I beheld a high mountain, and I was on it. ⁶And behold, the heavens were opened and a messenger of God said to me, Levi, enter. ⁷And I entered from the first heaven, and I saw a great sea hanging there. ⁸And further, I saw a second heaven far brighter and more brilliant, for there was a boundless light also therein. ⁹And I said to the messenger, Why is this so? And the messenger said to me, Do not marvel at this, for you will see another heaven more brilliant and incomparable. ¹⁰And when you have ascended there, you will stand near the LORD, and will be His minister, and will declare His mysteries to men, and will proclaim concerning Him who will redeem Israel. ¹¹And by you and Judah the LORD will appear among men, saving every race of men. ¹²And from the LORD's portion will be your life, and He will be your field, and vineyard, and fruits, gold, and silver."

CHAPTER 3

1 "Hear, therefore, regarding the heavens which have been shown to you. The lowest is for this reason gloomy to you, in that it beholds all the unrighteous deeds of men. ²And it has fire, snow, and ice made ready for the Day of Judgment, in the righteous judgment of God; for in it are all the spirits of the retributions for vengeance on men. ³And in the second are the hosts of the armies which are ordained for the Day of Judgment, to work vengeance on the spirits of deceit and of Belial. And above them are the holy ones. ⁴And in the highest of all dwells the Great Glory, far above all holiness. ⁵In [[the heaven next to]] it are the chief-messengers, who minister and make propitiation to the LORD for all the sins of ignorance of the righteous, offering a sweet-smelling savor to the LORD, a reasonable and a bloodless offering. ⁷And [[in the heaven below this]] are the messengers who bear answers to the messengers of the presence of the LORD. ⁸And in the heaven next to this are thrones and dominions, in which they always offer praise to God. ⁹When, therefore, the LORD looks on us, all of us are shaken; yes, the heavens, and the earth, and the abysses are shaken at the presence of His majesty. ¹⁰But the sons of men, having no perception of these things, sin and provoke the Most High."

CHAPTER 4

¹"Now, therefore, know that the LORD will execute judgment on the sons of men. Because when the rocks are being split, and the sun quenched, and the waters dried up, and the fire cowering, and all creation troubled, and the invisible spirits melting away, and Hades takes spoils through the visitations of the Most High, men will be unbelieving and persist in their iniquity. On this account they will be judged with punishment. ²Therefore the Most High has heard your prayer, to separate you from iniquity, and that you should become a son to Him, and a servant, and a minister of His presence. ³You will light the light of knowledge in Jacob, and you will be as the sun to all the seed of Israel. ⁴And a blessing will be given to you and to all your seed until the LORD will visit all the nations in His tender mercies forever. ⁵And therefore counsel and understanding have been given to you that you might instruct your sons concerning this, ⁶because they that bless Him will be blessed, and they that curse Him will perish."

CHAPTER 5

¹"And thereon the Messenger opened the gates of Heaven to me, and I saw the holy temple, and the Most High on a throne of glory. ²And He said to me, Levi, I have given you the blessings of the priesthood until I come and sojourn in the midst of Israel. ³Then the Messenger brought me down to the earth, and gave me a shield and a sword, and said to me, ⁴Execute vengeance on Shechem because of your sister Dinah, and I will be with you because the LORD has sent Me. ⁵And I destroyed the sons of Hamor at that time, as it is written in the heavenly tablets. ⁶And I said to Him, Please, O Lord, tell me Your Name, that I may call on You in a day of tribulation. ⁷And He said, I am the Messenger who intercedes for the nation of Israel that they may not be utterly smitten, for every evil spirit attacks it. ⁸And after these things I awoke, and blessed the Most High and the Messenger who intercedes for the nation of Israel and for all the righteous."

CHAPTER 6

¹"And when I was going to my father, I found a brazen shield—also for what reason the name of the mountain is Aspis, which is near Gebal, to the south of Abila. And I kept these words in my heart. ²And after this I counseled my father and my brother Reuben to command the sons of Hamor not to be circumcised, ³for I was zealous because of the abomination which they had worked on my sister. ⁴And I slew Shechem first, and Simeon slew Hamor. ⁵And after this my brothers came and struck that city with the edge of the sword. ⁶And my father heard these things and was angry, and he was grieved in that they had received the circumcision, and after that had been put to death, and in his blessings he looked wrongly on us. ⁷For we sinned because we had done this thing against his will, and he was sick on that day. ⁸But I saw that the sentence of God was for evil on Shechem, for they sought to do to Sarah and Rebekah as they had done to our sister Dinah, but the LORD prevented them. ⁹And they persecuted our father Abraham when he was a stranger, and they vexed his flocks when they were big with young; and Eblaen, who was born in his house, they most shamefully handled. ¹⁰And thus they did to all strangers, taking away their wives by force, and they banished them. ¹¹But the wrath of the LORD came on them to the uttermost."

CHAPTER 7

¹"And I said to my father Jacob, By you the LORD will plunder the Canaanites, and will give their land to you and to your seed after you. ²For from this day forward Shechem will be called a city of imbeciles; for as a man mocks a fool, so we mocked them. ³Because they had also worked folly in Israel by defiling my sister. ⁴And we departed and came to Bethel."

CHAPTER 8

¹"And there again I saw a vision as the former, after we had spent seventy days there. ²And I saw seven men in white raiment saying to me, Arise, put on the robe of the priesthood, and the crown of righteousness, and the breastplate of understanding, and the garment of truth, and the plate of faith, and the turban of the head, and the ephod of prophecy. ³And they carried [these things] separately, and put [them] on me, and said to me, From now on become a priest of the LORD—you and your seed forever. ⁴And the first anointed me with holy oil and gave the staff of judgment to me. ⁵The second washed me with pure water, and fed me with bread and wine (the most holy things), and clad me with a holy and glorious robe. ⁶The third clothed me with a linen vestment like an ephod. ⁷The fourth put a girdle around me like to purple. ⁸The fifth gave me a branch of rich olive. ⁹The sixth placed a crown on my head. ¹⁰The seventh placed a diadem of priesthood on my head and filled my hands with incense that I might serve as priest to the LORD God. ¹¹And they said to me, Levi, your seed will be divided into three offices for a sign of the glory of the LORD who is to come: ¹²and the first portion will be great; yes, there will be none greater than it; ¹³the second will be in the priesthood; ¹⁴and the third will be called by a new name, because a King will arise in Judah, and will establish a new priesthood, after the fashion of the nations [[or to all the nations]]. ¹⁵And His presence is beloved, as a prophet of the Most High, of the seed of our father Abraham. ¹⁶Therefore, every desirable thing in Israel will be for you and for your seed, and you will eat everything fair to look on, and your seed will apportion the table of the LORD. ¹⁷And some of them will be high priests, and judges, and scribes, for the holy place will be guarded by their mouth. ¹⁸And when I awoke, I understood that this [dream] was like the first dream. ¹⁹And I also hid this in my heart and did not tell it to any man on the earth."

CHAPTER 9

¹"And after two days Judah and I went up with our father Jacob to Isaac, our father's father. ²And my father's father blessed me according to all the words of the visions which I had seen. ³And he would not come with us to Bethel. And when we came to Bethel, my father saw a vision concerning me, that I should be their priest to God. ⁴And he rose up early in the morning, and paid tithes of all to the LORD through me. ⁵And so we came to Hebron to dwell there. ⁶And Isaac called me continually to put me in remembrance of the Law of the LORD, even as the Messenger of the LORD showed to me. ⁷And he taught me the law of the priesthood, of sacrifices, whole burnt-offerings, first-fruits, freewill-offerings, peace-offerings. ⁸And each day he was instructing me, and was busy on my behalf before the LORD, and said to me, ⁹Beware of the spirit of fornication, for this will continue and will pollute the holy place by your seed. ¹⁰Therefore, take a wife for yourself without blemish or pollution, while you are yet young, and not of the race of strange nations. ¹¹And before entering into the holy place, bathe; and when you offer the sacrifices, wash; ¹²and again, when you finish the sacrifice, wash; of twelve trees having leaves, offer to the LORD as Abraham also taught me. ¹³And of every clean beast and bird, offer a sacrifice to the LORD. ¹⁴And of all your first-fruits and of wine, offer the first as a sacrifice to the LORD God; and you will salt every sacrifice with salt."

CHAPTER 10

¹"Now, therefore, observe whatever I command you, children, for whatever things I have heard from my fathers I have declared to you. ²And behold, I am clear from your ungodliness and transgression, which you will commit in the end of the ages [[against the Savior of the world, Christ, acting godlessly]], deceiving Israel, and stirring up against it great calamities from the LORD. ³And you will deal lawlessly together with Israel, so He will not bear with Jerusalem because of your wickedness; but the veil of the temple will be torn, so as not to cover your shame. ⁴And you will be scattered as captives among the nations and will be for a reproach and for a curse there. ⁵For the house which the LORD will choose will be called Jerusalem, as is contained in the scroll of Enoch the righteous."

CHAPTER 11

¹"Therefore, when I took a wife, I was twenty-eight years old, and her name was Melcha. ²And she conceived and bore a son, and I called his name Gershom, for we were sojourners in our land. ³And I saw concerning him that he would not be in the first rank. ⁴And Kohath was born in the thirty-fifth year of my life, toward sunrise. ⁵And I saw in a vision that he was standing on high in the midst of all the congregation, ⁶therefore I called his name Kohath [[(which is, beginning of majesty and instruction)]]. ⁷And she bore me a third son, in the fortieth year of my life; and since his mother bore him with difficulty, I called him Merari (which is, my bitterness), because he was also like to death. ⁸And Jochebed was born in Egypt, in my sixty-fourth year, for I was renowned then in the midst of my brothers."

CHAPTER 12

¹"And Gershom took a wife, and she bore Lomni and Semei to him. ²And the sons of Kohath: Ambram, Issachar, Hebron, and Ozeel. ³And the sons of Merari: Mooli and Mouses. ⁴And in the ninety-fourth year, Ambram took my daughter Jochebed to himself to be [his] wife, for they were born in one day, he and my daughter. ⁵I was eight years old when I went into the land of Canaan, and [was] eighteen years when I slew Shechem, and at nineteen years I became priest, and at twenty-eight years I took a wife, and at forty-eight I went into Egypt. ⁶And behold, my children, you are a third generation. ⁷In my one hundred and eighteenth year Joseph died."

CHAPTER 13

¹"And now, my children, I command you: fear the LORD your God with your whole heart and walk in simplicity according to all His law. ²And also teach your children letters that they may have understanding all their life, reading the Law of God unceasingly. ³For everyone that knows the Law of the LORD will be honored, || And will not be a stranger wherever he goes. ⁴Yes, he will gain many more friends than his parents, || And many men will desire to serve him, || And to hear the Law from his mouth. ⁵Work righteousness, therefore, my children, on the earth, || That you may have [it] as a treasure in Heaven. ⁶And sow good things in your souls, || That you may find them in your life. But if you sow evil things, || You will reap every trouble and affliction. ⁷Get wisdom in the fear of God with diligence; For though there is a leading into captivity, || And cities and lands are destroyed, || And gold, and silver, and every possession perish, || Nothing can take away the wisdom of the wise, || Save the blindness of ungodliness, and the callousness of sin. ⁸For if one keeps oneself from these evil things, || Then even among his enemies wisdom will be a glory to him, || And in a strange country a fatherland, || And in the midst of foes will prove a friend. ⁹Whosoever teaches noble things and does them, || Will be enthroned with kings, || As was also my brother Joseph."

CHAPTER 14

¹"Therefore, my children, I have learned that at the end of the ages you will transgress against the LORD, stretching out hands to wickedness [[against Him]]; and you will become a scorn to all the nations. ²For our father Israel is pure from the transgressions of the chief priests [[who will lay their hands on the Savior of the world]]. ³For as the Heaven is purer in the LORD's sight than the earth, so also are you, the lights of Israel, [purer] than all the nations. ⁴But if you are darkened through transgressions, what, therefore, will all the nations do living in blindness? Yes, you will bring a curse on our race, because the light of the Law which was given to lighten every man—this you desire to destroy by teaching commandments contrary to the ordinances of God. ⁵You will rob the offerings of the LORD, and you will steal choice portions from His portion, eating [them] contemptuously with harlots. ⁶And out of covetousness you will teach the commandments of the LORD; you will pollute wedded women, and you will defile the virgins of Jerusalem, and you will be joined with harlots and adulteresses, and you

will take the daughters of the nations to be [your] wives, purifying them with an unlawful purification; and your union will be like to Sodom and Gomorrah. ⁷And you will be puffed up because of your priesthood, lifting yourselves up against men, and not only so, but also against the commands of God. ⁸For you will despise the holy things with jests and laughter."

CHAPTER 15
¹"Therefore the temple, which the LORD will choose, will be laid waste through your uncleanness, and you will be captives throughout all nations. ²And you will be an abomination to them, and you will receive reproach and everlasting shame from the righteous judgment of God. ³And all who hate you will rejoice at your destruction. ⁴And if you were not to receive mercy through Abraham, Isaac, and Jacob, our fathers, not one of our seed should be left on the earth.

CHAPTER 16
¹And now I have learned that for seventy weeks you will go astray, and profane the priesthood, and pollute the sacrifices. ²And you will make the Law void, and set at nothing the words of the prophets by evil perverseness. ³And you will persecute righteous men and hate the godly; you will abhor the words of the faithful. [[⁴And a man who renews the Law in the power of the Most High, you will call a deceiver; and at last you will rush [on him] to slay him, not knowing his dignity, taking innocent blood through [the] wickedness on your heads.]] ⁵And your holy places will be laid waste even to the ground because of him. ⁶And you will have no place that is clean, but you will be a curse and a dispersion among the nations until He will again visit you and in pity will receive you [[through faith and water]]."

CHAPTER 17
¹"And whereas you have heard concerning the seventy weeks, hear also concerning the priesthood. ²For in each jubilee there will be a priesthood. And in the first jubilee, the first who is anointed to the priesthood will be great and will speak to God as to a father. And his priesthood will be perfect with the LORD, [[and in the day of his gladness he will arise for the salvation of the world]]. ³In the second jubilee, he that is anointed will be conceived in the sorrow of beloved ones; and his priesthood will be honored and will be glorified by all. ⁴And the third priest will be taken hold of by sorrow. ⁵And the fourth will be in pain, because unrighteousness will gather itself against him exceedingly, and all Israel will hate his neighbor—each one. ⁶The fifth will be taken hold of by darkness. Likewise also the sixth and the seventh. ⁷And in the seventh will be such pollution as I cannot express before men, for they will know it who do these things. ⁸Therefore they will be taken captive and become a prey, and their land and their substance will be destroyed. ⁹And in the fifth week they will return to their desolate country and will renew the house of the LORD. ¹⁰And in the seventh week they will become priests, [who are] idolaters, adulterers, lovers of money, proud, lawless, lascivious, abusers of children and beasts."

CHAPTER 18
¹"And after their punishment will have come from the LORD, the priesthood will fail. ²Then the LORD will raise up a new priest. And to him all the words of the LORD will be revealed; And He will execute a righteous judgment on the earth for a multitude of days. ³And His star will arise in Heaven as of a King—Lighting up the light of knowledge as the sun [lights] the day, || And He will be magnified in the world. ⁴He will shine forth as the sun on the earth, || And will remove all darkness from under Heaven, || And there will be peace in all the earth. ⁵The heavens will exult in His days, || And the earth will be glad, || And the clouds will rejoice, || And the knowledge of the LORD will be poured forth on the earth, || As the water of the seas; And the messengers of the glory of the presence of the LORD will be glad in Him. ⁶The heavens will be opened, || And sanctification will come on Him from the temple of glory, || With the Father's voice as from Abraham to Isaac. ⁷And the glory of the Most High will be uttered over Him, || And the Spirit of understanding and sanctification will rest on Him [in the water]. ⁸For He will give the majesty of the LORD to His sons in truth forevermore; And none will succeed Him for all generations forever. ⁹And in His priesthood the nations will be multiplied in knowledge on the earth, || And enlightened through the grace of the LORD: In His priesthood sin will come to an end, || And the lawless will cease to do evil, [[And the just will rest in Him.]] ¹⁰And He will open the gates of paradise, || And will remove the threatening sword against Adam. ¹¹And He will give to the saints to eat from the Tree of Life, || And the Spirit of holiness will be on them. ¹²And Belial will be bound by Him, || And He will give power to His children to tread on the evil spirits. ¹³And the LORD will rejoice in His children, || And be well pleased in His beloved ones forever. ¹⁴Then Abraham, and Isaac, and Jacob will exult, || And I will be glad, || And all the saints will clothe themselves with joy."

CHAPTER 19
¹"And now, my children, you have heard all; therefore, choose for yourselves either the light or the darkness, either the Law of the LORD or the works of Belial." ²And his sons answered him, saying, ³"We will walk before the LORD according to His law." And their father said to them, "The LORD is a witness, and His messengers are witnesses, and you are witnesses, and I am a witness, concerning the word of your mouth." ⁴And his sons said to him, "We are witnesses." ⁵And thus Levi ceased commanding his sons; and he stretched out his feet on the bed, and was gathered to his fathers, after he had lived one hundred and thirty-seven years. ⁶And they laid him in a coffin, and afterward they buried him in Hebron, with Abraham, Isaac, and Jacob.

THE TESTAMENT OF JUDAH
THE FOURTH SON OF JACOB AND LEAH

CHAPTER 1
¹The copy of the words of Judah, what things he spoke to his sons before he died. ²They gathered themselves together, therefore, and came to him, and he said to them, ³"Listen, my children, to your father Judah. I was the fourth son born to my father Jacob; and my mother Leah named me Judah, saying, ⁴'I give thanks to the LORD, because He has given me a fourth son also.' ⁵I was swift in my youth, and obedient to my father in everything. And I honored my mother and my mother's sister. ⁶And it came to pass, when I became a man, that my father blessed me, saying, You will be a king, prospering in all things."

CHAPTER 2
¹"And the LORD showed me favor in all my works, both in the field and in the house. ²I know that I raced a doe, and caught it, and prepared the meat for my father, and he ate. ³And I used to master the roes in the chase and overtake all that were in the plains. ⁴I overtook a wild mare, and caught it, and tamed it. I slew a lion and plucked a kid out of its mouth. ⁵I took a bear by its paw and hurled it down the cliff, and it was crushed. I outran the wild boar, and seizing it as I ran, I tore it apart. ⁶A leopard in Hebron leaped on my dog, and I caught it by the tail, and hurled it on the rocks, and it was broken in half. ⁷I found a wild ox feeding in the fields, and seizing it by the horns, and whirling it around and stunning it, I cast it from myself and slew it."

CHAPTER 3
¹"And when the two kings of the Canaanites came sheathed in armor against our flocks, and many people with them, I rushed on the king of Hazor single-handedly, ²and struck him on the greaves, and dragged him down, and so I slew him. And the other, the king of Tappuah, as he sat on his horse, ³[[I slew, and so I scattered all his people. Achor the king,]] a man of giant stature, I found hurling javelins before and behind as he sat on horseback, and I took up a stone of sixty pounds weight, and hurled it, and struck his horse, and killed it. ⁴And I fought with [this] other for two hours; and I cleaved his shield in half, and I chopped off his feet, and killed him. ⁵And as I was stripping off his breastplate, behold, nine men, his companions, began to fight with me. ⁶And I wound my garment on my hand; and I slung stones at them, and killed four of them, and the rest fled. ⁷And my father Jacob slew Beelesath, king of all the kings, a giant in strength—twelve cubits high. ⁸And fear fell on them, and they ceased warring against us. ⁹Therefore my father was free from anxiety in the wars when I was with my brothers. ¹⁰For he saw in a vision concerning me that a

messenger of might followed me everywhere, that I should not be overcome."

CHAPTER 4

[1] "And in the south, there came on us a greater war than that in Shechem; and I joined in battle array with my brothers, and pursued one thousand men, and slew of them two hundred men and four kings. [2] And I went up on the wall, and I slew four mighty men. [3] And so we captured Hazor and took all the spoil."

CHAPTER 5

[1] "On the next day we departed to Aretan, a city strong, and walled, and inaccessible, threatening us with death. [2] But Gad and I approached on the east side of the city, and Reuben and Levi on the west. [3] And they that were on the wall, thinking that we were alone, were drawn down against us. [4] And so my brothers secretly climbed up the wall on both sides by stakes and entered the city while the men did not know it. [5] And we took it with the edge of the sword. And as for those who had taken refuge in the tower, we set fire to the tower and took both it and them. [6] And as we were departing, the men of Tappuah set on our spoil, and delivering it up to our sons, we fought with them as far as Tappuah. [7] And we slew them, and burned their city, and took all that was in it as spoil."

CHAPTER 6

[1] "And when I was at the waters of Kozeba, the men of Jobel came against us to battle. [2] And we fought with them and routed them, and we slew their allies from Shiloh, and we did not leave them power to come in against us. [3] And the men of Makir came on us the fifth day to seize our spoil; and we attacked them and overcame them in fierce battle, for there was a host of mighty men among them, [4] and we slew them before they had gone up the ascent. [5] And when we came to their city, their women rolled stones on us from the brow of the hill on which the city stood, [6] and Simeon and I hid ourselves behind the town, and seized on the heights, and destroyed this city also."

CHAPTER 7

[1] "And the next day it was told to us that the king of the city of Gaash was coming against us with a mighty host. [2] Therefore Dan and I pretended we were Amorites and went into their city as [if] allies. [3] And in the depth of night our brothers came and we opened the gates to them; and we destroyed all the men and their substance, and we took all that was theirs for a prey, and we cast down their three walls. [4] And we drew near to Thamna, where all the substance of the hostile kings was. [5] Then being insulted by them, I was therefore angry, and rushed against them to the summit; and they kept slinging stones and darts against me. [6] And had my brother Dan not aided me, they would have slain me. [7] We came on them, therefore, with wrath, and they all fled; and passing by another way, they implored my father, and he made peace with them. [8] And we did no harm to them, and they became tributary to us, and we restored their spoil to them. [9] And I built Thamna, and my father built Pabael. [10] I was twenty years old when this war occurred. And the Canaanites feared me and my brothers."

CHAPTER 8

[1] "And I had many cattle, and I had Iram the Adullamite for [my] chief herdsman. [2] And when I went to him, I saw Parsaba, king of Adullam, and he spoke to us, and he made us a feast; [3] and when I was heated, he gave me his daughter Bathshua to be [my] wife. [4] She bore me Er, and Onan, and Shelah; and the LORD struck two of them, for Shelah lived, and you are his children."

CHAPTER 9

[1] "And [for] eighteen years my father abode in peace with his brother Esau, and his sons with us, after we had come from Mesopotamia, from Laban. [2] And when eighteen years were fulfilled, in the fortieth year of my life, Esau, the brother of my father, came on us with a mighty and strong people. [3] And Jacob struck Esau with an arrow, and he was taken up wounded on Mount Seir, and as he went, he died at Anoniram, and we pursued after the sons of Esau. [4] Now they had a city with walls of iron and gates of brass; and we could not enter into it, and we encamped around, and besieged it. [5] And when they did not open to us in twenty days, I set up a ladder in the sight of all, and I went up with my shield on my head, sustaining the assault of stones—upwards of three talents weight; [6] and I slew four of their mighty men. And Reuben and Gad slew six others. [7] Then they asked [for] terms of peace from us; and having taken counsel with our father, we received them as tributaries. [8] And they gave us five hundred cors of wheat, five hundred baths of oil, five hundred measures of wine, until the famine, when we went down into Egypt."

CHAPTER 10

[1] "And after these things my son Er took Tamar, from Mesopotamia, a daughter of Aram, to be [his] wife. [2] Now Er was wicked, and he was in need concerning Tamar, because she was not of the land of Canaan. [3] And on the third night a messenger of the LORD struck him. And he had not known her according to the evil craftiness of his mother, for he did not wish to have children by her. [4] In the days of the wedding-feast I gave Onan to her in marriage; and he also in wickedness did not know her, though he spent a year with her. [5] And when I threatened him, he went in to her, but he spilled the seed on the ground, according to the command of his mother, and he also died through wickedness. [6] And I wished to give Shelah to her also, but his mother did not permit it; for she worked evil against Tamar, because she was not of the daughters of Canaan, as she also herself was."

CHAPTER 11

[1] "And I knew that the race of the Canaanites was wicked, but the impulse of youth blinded my mind. [2] And when I saw her pouring out wine, owing to the intoxication of wine, I was deceived and took her although my father had not counseled [it]. [3] And while I was away, she went and took a wife for Shelah from Canaan. [4] And when I knew what she had done, I cursed her in the anguish of my soul. [5] And she also died through her wickedness together with her sons."

CHAPTER 12

[1] "And after these things, while Tamar was a widow, she heard after two years that I was going up to shear my sheep, and adorned herself in bridal array, and sat in the city Enaim by the gate. [2] For it was a law of the Amorites that she who was about to marry should sit in fornication seven days by the gate. [3] Therefore being drunk with wine, I did not recognize her; and her beauty deceived me, through the fashion of her adorning. [4] And I turned aside to her, and said, Let me go in to you. And she said, What will you give me? And I gave her my staff, and my girdle, and the diadem of my kingdom in pledge. [5] And I went in to her, and she conceived. And not knowing what I had done, I wished to slay her; but she privily sent my pledges and put me to shame. [6] And when I called her, I also heard the secret words which I spoke when lying with her in my drunkenness; [7] and I could not slay her, because it was from the LORD. [8] For I said, Lest perhaps she did it in subtlety, having received the pledge from another woman. [9] But I did not come near her again while I lived, because I had done this abomination in all Israel. [10] Moreover, they who were in the city said there was no harlot in the gate, because she came from another place, and sat for a while in the gate. [11] And I thought that no one knew that I had gone in to her. [12] And after this, we came into Egypt to Joseph, because of the famine. And I was forty-six years old, and I lived in Egypt seventy-three years."

CHAPTER 13

[1] "And now I command you, my children, listen to your father Judah, and keep my sayings to perform all the ordinances of the LORD, and to obey the commands of God. [2] And do not walk after your lusts, nor in the imaginations of your thoughts in haughtiness of heart; and do not glory in the deeds and strength of your youth, for this is also evil in the eyes of the LORD. [3] Since I also gloried that in wars no beautiful woman's face ever enticed me, and reproved my brother Reuben concerning Bilhah, the wife of my father, the spirits of jealousy and of fornication arrayed themselves against me until I lay with Bathshua the Canaanite, and Tamar, who was espoused to my sons. [4] For I said to my father-in-law, I will take counsel with my father, and so I will take your daughter. And he was unwilling, but he showed me a boundless store of gold in his daughter's behalf, for he was a king. [5] And he adorned her with gold and pearls and caused her to pour out wine for us at the feast with the beauty of women. [6] And the wine turned my eyes aside, and pleasure

blinded my heart. ⁷And I became enamored, and I laid with her, and transgressed the commandment of the LORD and the commandment of my fathers, and I took her to be [my] wife. ⁸And the LORD rewarded me according to the imagination of my heart, inasmuch as I had no joy in her children."

CHAPTER 14

¹"And now, my children, I say to you: do not be drunk with wine, for wine turns the mind away from the truth, and inspires the passion of lust, and leads the eyes into error. ²For the spirit of fornication has wine as a minister to give pleasure to the mind; for these two also take away the mind of man. ³For if a man drinks wine to drunkenness, it disturbs the mind with filthy thoughts leading to fornication and heats the body to carnal union; and if the occasion of the lust is present, he works the sin, and is not ashamed. ⁴Such is the inebriated man, my children; for he who is drunken reveres no man. ⁵For behold, it also made me to err, so that I was not ashamed of the multitude in the city, in that I turned aside to Tamar before the eyes of all, and I worked a great sin, and I uncovered the covering of my sons' shame. ⁶After I had drunk wine, I did not revere the commandment of God, and I took a woman of Canaan to be [my] wife. ⁷For the man who drinks wine needs much discretion, my children; and herein is discretion in drinking wine: a man may drink so long as he preserves modesty. ⁸But if he goes beyond this limit, the spirit of deceit attacks his mind, and it makes the drunkard to talk filthily, and to transgress and not to be ashamed, but even to glory in his shame, and to account himself honorable."

CHAPTER 15

¹"He that commits fornication is not aware when he suffers loss and is not ashamed when put to dishonor. ²For even though a man is a king and commits fornication, he is stripped of his kingship by becoming the slave of fornication, as I myself also suffered. ³For I gave my staff, that is, the stay of my tribe; and my girdle, that is, my power; and my diadem, that is, the glory of my kingdom. ⁴And I indeed converted of these things; I did not eat wine and flesh until my old age, nor did I behold any joy. ⁵And the messenger of God showed me that women bear rule over king and beggar alike forever. ⁶And from the king they take away his glory, and from the valiant man his might, and from the beggar even that little which is the stay of his poverty."

CHAPTER 16

¹"Therefore observe, my children, the right limit in wine; for there are four evil spirits in it: of lust, of hot desire, of profligacy, [and] of shameful gain. ²If you drink wine in gladness, be modest in the fear of God. For if in [your] gladness the fear of God departs, then drunkenness arises and shamelessness steals in. ³But if you would live soberly, do not touch wine at all, lest you sin in words of outrage, and in fightings and slanders, and transgressions of the commandments of God, and you perish before your time. ⁴Moreover, wine reveals the mysteries of God and men, even as I also revealed the commandments of God and the mysteries of my father Jacob to the Canaanite woman Bathshua, which God commanded me not to reveal. ⁵And wine is a cause both of war and confusion."

CHAPTER 17

¹"And now, I command you, my children, not to love money, nor to gaze on the beauty of women, because for the sake of money and beauty I was led astray to Bathshua the Canaanite. [[²For I know that because of these two things my race will fall into wickedness. ³For they will even mar wise men among my sons and will cause the kingdom of Judah to be diminished, which the LORD gave me because of my obedience to my father. ⁴For I never caused grief to my father Jacob, for all things, whatever he commanded, I did. ⁵And Isaac, the father of my father, blessed me to be king in Israel, and Jacob further blessed me in like manner. ⁶And I know that the kingdom will be established from me."

CHAPTER 18

¹"And I know what evils you will do in the last days.]] ²Beware, therefore, my children, of fornication, and the love of money, and listen to your father Judah. ³For these things withdraw you from the Law of God, || And blind the inclination of the soul, || And teach arrogance, || And do not permit a man to have compassion on his neighbor. ⁴They rob his soul of all goodness, || And oppress him with toils and troubles, || And drive away sleep from him, || And devour his flesh. ⁵And he hinders the sacrifices of God; And he does not remember the blessing of God, || He does not listen to a prophet when he speaks, || And resents the words of godliness. ⁶For he is a slave to two contrary passions, || And cannot obey God, || Because they have blinded his soul, || And he walks in the day as in the night."

CHAPTER 19

¹"My children, the love of money leads to idolatry, because, when led astray through money, men name as gods those who are not gods, and it causes him who has it to fall into madness. ²For the sake of money I lost my children and did not have my conversion and my humiliation; and had the prayers of my father [not] been accepted, I should have died childless. ³But the God of my fathers had mercy on me, because I did it in ignorance. ⁴And the prince of deceit blinded me, and I sinned as a man and as flesh, being corrupted through sins; and I learned my own weakness while thinking myself invincible."

CHAPTER 20

¹"Know, therefore, my children, that two spirits wait on man: the Spirit of truth and the spirit of deceit. ²And in the midst is the spirit of understanding of the mind, to which it belongs to turn wherever it will. ³And the works of truth and the works of deceit are written on the hearts of men, and the LORD knows each one of them. ⁴And there is no time at which the works of men can be hid, for on the heart itself they have been written down before the LORD. ⁵And the Spirit of truth testifies all things and accuses all; and the sinner is burned up by his own heart and cannot raise his face to the Judge."

CHAPTER 21

¹"And now, my children, I command you: love Levi, that you may abide, and do not exalt yourselves against him, lest you be utterly destroyed. ²For the LORD gave the kingdom to me, and the priesthood to him, and He set the kingdom beneath the priesthood. ³He gave the things on the earth to me [and] the things in the heavens to him. ⁴As the Heaven is higher than the earth, so is the priesthood of God higher than the earthly kingdom, unless it falls away through sin from the LORD and is dominated by the earthly kingdom. ⁵For the messenger of the LORD said to me, The LORD chose him rather than you to draw near to Him, and to eat of His table, and to offer Him the first-fruits of the choice things of the sons of Israel, but you will be king of Jacob. ⁶And you will be among them as the sea. For as, on the sea, [both] just and unjust are tossed around—some taken into captivity while some are enriched—so also will every race of men be in you; some will be impoverished, being taken captive, and others will grow rich by plundering the possessions of others. ⁷For the kings will be as sea-monsters; They will swallow men like fishes, || They will enslave the sons and daughters of free men, || They will plunder houses, lands, flocks, money, ⁸And with the flesh of many they will wrongfully feed the ravens and the cranes; And they will advance in evil, uplifted in covetousness, ⁹And there will be false prophets like tempests, || And they will persecute all righteous men."

CHAPTER 22

¹"And the LORD will bring on them divisions against one another. And there will be continual wars in Israel; ²And from among men of another race my kingdom will be brought to an end, || Until the salvation of Israel will come, || Until the appearing of the God of righteousness, || That Jacob [[and all the nations]] may rest in peace. ³And He will guard the might of my kingdom forever; For the LORD swore to me with an oath || That He would not destroy the kingdom from my seed forever."

CHAPTER 23

¹"Now I have much grief, my children, because of your lewdness, and witchcrafts, and idolatries which you will practice against the kingdom, following them that have familiar spirits, diviners, and demons of error. ²You will make your daughters singing girls and harlots, and you will mingle in the abominations of the nations. ³For which things' sake the LORD will bring on you famine and pestilence, death and the sword,

besieging by enemies, and revilings of friends, the slaughter of children, the rape of wives, the plundering of possessions, the burning of the temple of God, the laying waste of the land, the enslavement of yourselves among the nations. And they will make some of you eunuchs for their wives, ⁵until the LORD visits you, when with perfect heart you convert and walk in all His commandments, and He brings you up from captivity among the nations."

CHAPTER 24

¹"And after these things a star will arise to you from Jacob in peace, || And a Man will arise [[from my seed]], || Like the Sun of Righteousness, || Walking with the sons of men in meekness and righteousness; And no sin will be found in Him. ²And the heavens will be open to Him, || To pour out the Spirit, || [Even] the blessing of the Holy Father; ³And He will pour out the Spirit of grace on you; And you will be to Him sons in truth, || And you will walk in His commandments first and last— [[⁴This Branch of God Most High, || And this Fountain giving life to all.]] ⁵Then the scepter of my kingdom will shine forth; And a stem will arise from your root; ⁶And a rod of righteousness will grow from it to the nations, || To judge and to save all that call on the LORD."

CHAPTER 25

¹"And after these things Abraham, and Isaac, and Jacob will arise to life, and my brothers and I will be chiefs of the tribes of Israel: Levi first, I the second, Joseph third, Benjamin fourth, Simeon fifth, Issachar sixth, and so all in order. ²And the LORD blessed Levi; and the Messenger of the Presence, me; the powers of glory, Simeon; the Heaven, Reuben; the earth, Issachar; the sea, Zebulun; the mountains, Joseph; the Dwelling Place, Benjamin; the luminaries, Dan; Eden, Naphtali; the sun, Gad; the moon, Asher. ³And you will be the people of the LORD and have one tongue, and there will be no spirit of deceit of Belial there, for he will be cast into the fire forever. ⁴And they who have died in grief will arise in joy, || And they who were poor for the LORD's sake will be made rich, || And they who are put to death for the LORD's sake will awake to life. ⁵And the deer of Jacob will run in joyfulness, || And the eagles of Israel will fly in gladness; And all the people will glorify the LORD forever."

CHAPTER 26

¹"Therefore observe, my children, all the Law of the LORD, for there is hope for all them who hold fast to His ways." ²And he said to them, "Behold, I die before your eyes this day—one hundred and nineteen years old. ³Let no one bury me in costly apparel, nor tear open my bowels, for this is what they who are kings do; and carry me up to Hebron with you." ⁴And Judah, when he had said these things, fell asleep; and his sons did according to everything he commanded them, and they buried him in Hebron, with his fathers.

THE TESTAMENT OF ISSACHAR
THE FIFTH SON OF JACOB AND LEAH

CHAPTER 1

¹The copy of the words of Issachar. For he called his sons and said to them, ²"Listen, my children, to your father Issachar; give ear to the words of him who is beloved of the LORD. ³I was born the fifth son to Jacob, by way of hire for the mandrakes. ⁴For my brother Reuben brought in mandrakes from the field, and Rachel met him and took them. And Reuben wept, and at his voice my mother Leah came forth. ⁵Now these [mandrakes] were sweet-smelling apples which were produced in the land of Haran below a ravine of water. ⁶And Rachel said, I will not give them to you, but they will be to me instead of children. ⁷For the LORD has despised me, and I have not borne children to Jacob. Now there were two apples, and Leah said to Rachel, ⁸Is it enough for you that you have taken my husband? Will you take these also? ⁹And Rachel said to her, You will have Jacob this night for the mandrakes of your son. And Leah said to her, ¹⁰Jacob is mine, for I am the wife of his youth. But Rachel said, Do not boast, and do not vaunt yourself; for he espoused me before you, and he served our father fourteen years for my sake. ¹¹And had craft not increased on the earth and had the wickedness of men [not] prospered, you would not now see the face of Jacob."

CHAPTER 2

¹"Then a messenger of the LORD appeared to Jacob, saying, Rachel will bear two children, inasmuch as she has refused company with her husband, and has chosen continency. ²And had my mother Leah not paid for the two apples for the sake of his company, she would have borne eight sons; for this reason, she bore six, and Rachel bore the two. For on account of the mandrakes the LORD visited her. ³For He knew that for the sake of children she wished to company with Jacob, and not for lust of pleasure. ⁴For also on the next day she again gave up Jacob. Because of the mandrakes, ⁵therefore, the LORD listened to Rachel. For though she desired them, she did not eat them, but offered them in the house of the LORD, presenting them to who was the priest of the Most High at that time."

CHAPTER 3

¹"When, therefore, I grew up, my children, I walked in uprightness of heart, and I became a farmer for my father and my brothers, and I brought in fruits from the field according to their season. ²And my father blessed me, for he saw that I walked in rectitude before him. ³And I was not a busybody in my doings, nor envious and malicious against my neighbor. ⁴I never slandered anyone, nor did I censure the life of any man, walking as I did in singleness of eye. ⁵Therefore, when I was thirty-five years old, I took a wife for myself, for my labor wore away my strength, and I never thought on pleasure with women, but owing to my toil, sleep overcame me. ⁶And my father always rejoiced in my rectitude, because I offered all first-fruits through the priest to the LORD—then to my father also. ⁷And the LORD increased ten thousandfold His benefits in my hands; and also Jacob, my father, knew that God aided my singleness. ⁸For on all the poor and oppressed I bestowed the good things of the earth in the singleness of my heart."

CHAPTER 4

¹"And now, listen to me, my children, || And walk in singleness of your heart, || For I have seen in it all that is well-pleasing to the LORD. ²The single-[minded] man does not covet gold, || He does not overreach his neighbor, || He does not long after manifold delicacies, || He does not delight in varied apparel. ³He does not desire to live a long life, || But only waits for the will of God. ⁴And the spirits of deceit have no power against him, || For he does not look on the beauty of women, || Lest he should pollute his mind with corruption. ⁵There is no envy in his thoughts; [[No malicious person makes his soul to pine away, ||]] Nor worry with insatiable desire in his mind. ⁶For he walks in singleness of soul, || And beholds all things in uprightness of heart, || Shunning eyes [made] evil through the error of the world, || Lest he should see the perversion of any of the commandments of the LORD."

CHAPTER 5

¹"Therefore, my children, keep the Law of God, || And get singleness. And walk in guilelessness, || Not playing the busybody with the business of your neighbor, ²But love the LORD and your neighbor, || Have compassion on the poor and weak. ³Bow down your back to farming, || And toil in labors in all manner of farming, || Offering gifts to the LORD with thanksgiving. ⁴For the LORD will bless you with the first-fruits of the earth, even as He blessed all the saints from Abel even until now. ⁵For no other portion is given to you than of the fatness of the earth, whose fruits are raised by toil. ⁶For our father Jacob blessed me with blessings of the earth and of first-fruits. ⁷And Levi and Judah were glorified by the LORD even among the sons of Jacob, for the LORD gave them an inheritance: indeed, He gave the priesthood to Levi and the kingdom to Judah. ⁸And you must therefore obey them and walk in the singleness of your father, [[for it has been given to Gad to destroy the troops that are coming on Israel]]."

CHAPTER 6

¹"Therefore, my children, know that in the last times Your sons will forsake singleness, || And will cleave to insatiable desire; And leaving guilelessness will draw near to malice; And forsaking the commandments of the LORD, || They will cleave to Belial. ²And leaving farming, || They will follow after their own wicked devices, || And they will be dispersed among the nations, || And will serve their enemies. ³And, therefore, give these

commands to your children, that, if they sin, they may [even] more quickly return to the LORD; ⁴for He is merciful, and will deliver them, even to bring them back into their land."

CHAPTER 7

¹"Behold, therefore, as you see, I am one hundred and twenty-six years old and am not conscious of committing any sin. ²I have not known any woman except my wife; I never committed fornication by the uplifting of my eyes. ³I did not drink wine to be led astray thereby; I did not covet any desirable thing that was my neighbor's. ⁴Guile did not arise in my heart; A lie did not pass through my lips. ⁵If any man was in distress, || I joined my sighs with his, || And I shared my bread with the poor. I worked godliness, || [And] all my days I kept truth. ⁶I loved the LORD; Likewise also every man with all my heart. ⁷So you must also do these things, my children, || And every spirit of Belial will flee from you, || And no deed of wicked men will rule over you; And you will subdue every wild beast || Since you have the God of the heavens and earth with you; [And] walk with men in singleness of heart." ⁸And having said these things, he commanded his sons that they should carry him up to Hebron, and bury him there in the cave with his fathers. And he stretched out his feet and died at a good old age; with every limb sound, and with strength unabated, he slept the continuous sleep.

THE TESTAMENT OF ZEBULUN

THE SIXTH SON OF JACOB AND LEAH

CHAPTER 1

¹The copy of the words of Zebulun, which he enjoined on his sons before he died in the one hundred and fourteenth year of his life, two years after the death of Joseph. ²And he said to them, "Listen to me, you sons of Zebulun, attend to the words of your father. ³I, Zebulun, was born [as] a good gift to my parents. For when I was born my father was increased very exceedingly, both in flocks and herds, when with the straked rods he had his portion. ⁴I am not conscious that I have sinned all my days, save in thought. ⁵Nor yet do I remember that I have done any iniquity, except the sin of ignorance which I committed against Joseph; for I covenanted with my brothers not to tell my father what had been done. ⁶But I wept [for] many days in secret on account of Joseph, for I feared my brothers, because they had all agreed that if anyone should declare the secret, he should be slain. ⁷But when they wished to kill him, I adjured them much with tears not to be guilty of this sin."

CHAPTER 2

¹"For Simeon and Gad came against Joseph to kill him, and he said to them with tears: ²Pity me, my brothers, have mercy on the bowels of our father Jacob. Do not lay your hands on me to shed innocent blood, for I have not sinned against you. ³And if I have indeed sinned, discipline me with disciplining, my brothers, but do not lay your hand on me for the sake of our father Jacob. ⁴And as he spoke these words, wailing as he did so, I was unable to bear his lamentations, and began to weep, and my liver was poured out, and all the substance of my bowels was loosened. ⁵And I wept with Joseph, and my heart sounded, and the joints of my body trembled, and I was not able to stand. ⁶And when Joseph saw me weeping with him, and them coming against him to slay him, he fled behind me, imploring them. ⁷But meanwhile Reuben arose and said, Come, my brothers, let us not slay him, but let us cast him into one of these dry pits, which our fathers dug and found no water. ⁸For this reason the LORD forbade that water should rise up in them, in order that Joseph should be preserved. And they did so, until they sold him to the Ishmaelites."

CHAPTER 3

¹"For I had no share in his price, my children. ²But Simeon, and Gad, and six other of our brothers took the price of Joseph, and bought sandals for themselves, and their wives, and their children, saying, ³We will not eat of it, for it is the price of our brother's blood, but we will assuredly tread it under foot, because he said that he would be king over us, and so let us see what will become of his dreams. ⁴Therefore it is written in the writing of the Law of Moses that whosoever will not raise up seed to his brother, his sandal should be unloosed, and they should spit in his face. ⁵And the brothers of Joseph did not wish that their brother should live, and the LORD loosed from them the sandal which they wore against Joseph their brother. ⁶For when they came into Egypt they were unloosed by the servants of Joseph outside the gate, and so they paid respect to Joseph after the fashion of King Pharaoh. ⁷And not only did they pay respect to him, but were also spit on, falling down before him immediately, and so they were put to shame before the Egyptians. ⁸For after this the Egyptians heard all the evils that they had done to Joseph."

CHAPTER 4

¹"And after he was sold, my brothers sat down to eat and drink. ²But I, through pity for Joseph, did not eat, but watched the pit, since Judah feared lest Simeon, Dan, and Gad should rush off and slay him. ³But when they saw that I did not eat, they set me to watch him, until he was sold to the Ishmaelites. ⁴And when Reuben came and heard that [Joseph] had been sold while he was away, he tore his garments, [and] mourning, said, ⁵How will I look on the face of my father Jacob? ⁶And he took the money and ran after the merchants, but as he failed to find them, he returned grieving. But the merchants had left the broad road and marched through the Troglodytes by a short cut. ⁷But Reuben was grieved and ate no food that day. ⁸Therefore Dan came to him and said, Do not weep, neither grieve; for we have found what we can say to our father Jacob. ⁹Let us slay a kid of the goats and dip the coat of Joseph in it; ¹⁰and let us send it to Jacob, saying, Know, is this the coat of your son? ¹¹And they did so. For they stripped off from Joseph his coat when they were selling him and put the garment of a slave on him. ¹²Now Simeon took the coat, and would not give it up, for he wished to tear it with his sword, as he was angry that Joseph lived and that he had not slain him. ¹³Then we all rose up and said to him, If you do not give up the coat, we will say to our father that you alone did this evil thing in Israel. And so he gave it to them, and they did even as Dan had said."

CHAPTER 5

¹"And now, my children, I bid you to keep the commands of the LORD, and to show mercy to your neighbors, and to have compassion toward all, not toward men only, but also toward beasts. ²For all this thing's sake the LORD blessed me, and when all my brothers were sick, I escaped without sickness, for the LORD knows the purposes of each. ³Therefore, have compassion in your hearts, my children, because even as a man does to his neighbor, even so will the LORD do to him also. ⁴For the sons of my brothers were getting sick and dying on account of Joseph, because they did not show mercy in their hearts; but my sons were preserved without sickness, as you know. ⁵And when I was in the land of Canaan, by the seacoast, I made a catch of fish for my father Jacob; and when many were drowned in the sea, I continued unharmed."

CHAPTER 6

¹"I was the first to make a boat to sail on the sea, for the LORD gave me understanding and wisdom therein. ²And I let down a rudder behind it, and I stretched a sail on another upright piece of wood in the midst. ³And I sailed therein along the shores, catching fish for the house of my father until we came to Egypt. ⁴[[And through compassion I shared my catch with every stranger. And if a man was a stranger, or sick, or aged, I boiled the fish, and dressed them well, and offered them to all men, as every man had need, grieving with and having compassion on them. ⁵For this reason the LORD also satisfied me with abundance of fish when catching fish; for he that shares with his neighbor receives manifold more from the LORD.]] ⁶For five years I caught fish [[and gave thereof to every man whom I saw, ⁸and enough for all the house of my father]]. ⁷And in the summer I caught fish, and in the winter I kept sheep with my brothers."

CHAPTER 7

[[¹"Now I will declare to you what I did: I saw a man in distress through nakedness in wintertime, and had compassion on him, and secretly stole a garment from my father's house, and gave it to him who was in distress. ²Therefore, my children, from that which God bestows on you, show compassion and mercy without hesitation to all men, and give to every man with a good heart. ³And if you do not have the means to give to him that needs, have compassion for him in yearnings of mercy. ⁴I know that my hand did not find the means to give to him that needed, and I walked with him weeping for seven furlongs, and my bowels yearned toward him in compassion."

CHAPTER 8

¹"Have, therefore, yourselves also, my children, compassion toward every man with mercy, that the LORD may also have compassion and mercy on you. ²Because also in the last days God will send His compassion on the earth, and wheresoever He finds yearnings of mercy He dwells in him. ³For in the degree in which a man has compassion on his neighbors, in the same degree the LORD also has [compassion] on him.]] ⁴And when we went down into Egypt, Joseph bore no malice against us. ⁵To whom taking heed, you also, my children, must approve yourselves without malice, and love one another; and do not set down in account—each one of you—evil against his brother. ⁶For this breaks unity and divides all kindred, and troubles the soul, and wears away the countenance."

CHAPTER 9

¹"Therefore, observe the waters and know when they flow together—they sweep along stones, trees, ²earth, and other things. But if they are divided into many streams, the earth swallows them up, and they vanish away. ³So you will also be if you are divided. ⁴Do not be, therefore, divided into two heads, for everything which the LORD made has but one head, and two shoulders, two hands, two feet, and all the remaining members. ⁵For I have learned in the writing of my fathers that you will be divided in Israel, and will follow two kings, and will work every abomination. ⁶And your enemies will lead you captive, and you will be treated evil among the nations with many infirmities and tribulations. ⁷And after these things you will remember the LORD, and convert, [[And He will cause you to return]]; for He is merciful and compassionate. And He does not set down in account evil to the sons of men, because they are flesh, and the spirits of deceit deceive them in all their deeds. ⁸And after these things the LORD Himself will arise to you—the Light of righteousness—[[and healing and compassion will be in His wings. He will redeem all the captivity of the sons of men from Belial, and every spirit of deceit will be trodden down]]. And He will bring back all the nations into zeal for Him. And you will return to your land. And you will see Him in Jerusalem, for His Name's sake. ⁹And again through the wickedness of your works you will provoke Him to anger, and you will be cast away by Him to the time of consummation."

CHAPTER 10

¹"And now, my children, do not grieve that I am dying, nor be cast down in that I am coming to my end. ²For I will rise again in the midst of you, as a ruler in the midst of his sons; and I will rejoice in the midst of my tribe, as many as will keep the Law of the LORD and the commandments of their father Zebulun. ³But the LORD will bring continuous fire on the ungodly and destroy them throughout all generations. ⁴But I am now hastening away to my rest, as my fathers also did. ⁵But fear the LORD our God with all your strength all the days of your life." ⁶And when he had said these things, he fell asleep at a good old age. ⁷And his sons laid him in a wooden coffin. And afterward they carried him up and buried him in Hebron with his fathers.

THE TESTAMENT OF DAN

THE SEVENTH SON OF JACOB AND BILHAH

CHAPTER 1

¹The copy of the words of Dan, which he spoke to his sons in his last days, in the one hundred and twenty-fifth year of his life. ²For he called together his family, and said, "Listen to my words, you sons of Dan; and give heed to the words of your father. ³I have proved in my heart, and in my whole life, that truth with just dealing is good and well pleasing to God, and that lying and anger are evil, because they teach man all wickedness. ⁴I confess, therefore, this day to you, my children, that in my heart I resolved on the death of my brother Joseph, the true and good man. [[⁵And I rejoiced that he was sold, because his father loved him more than us.]] ⁶For the spirit of jealousy and vainglory said to me, You yourself are also his son. ⁷And one of the spirits of Belial stirred me up, saying, Take this sword, and slay Joseph with it, so your father will love you when he is dead. ⁸Now this is the spirit of anger that persuaded me to crush Joseph as a leopard crushes a kid. ⁹But the God of my fathers did not permit him to fall into my hands, so that I should find him alone and slay him and cause a second tribe to be destroyed in Israel."

CHAPTER 2

¹"And now, my children, behold, I am dying, and I tell you of a truth, that unless you keep yourselves from the spirit of lying and of anger, and love truth and longsuffering, you will perish. ²For anger is blindness and does not permit one to see the face of any man with truth. ³For though it may be a father or a mother, he behaves toward them as enemies; though it may be a brother, he does not know him; though it may be a prophet of the LORD, he disobeys him; though a righteous man, he does not regard him; though a friend, he does not acknowledge him. ⁴For the spirit of anger encompasses him with the net of deceit, and blinds his eyes, and through lying, darkens his mind, and gives him its own peculiar vision. ⁵And with which encompasses it—his eyes? With hatred of heart, so as to be envious of his brother."

CHAPTER 3

¹"For anger is an evil thing, my children, for it troubles even the soul itself. ²And it makes the body of the angry man its own, and it gets the mastery over his soul, and it bestows power on the body that it may work all iniquity. ³And when the body does all these things, the soul justifies what is done, since it does not see right. ⁴Therefore he that is wrathful, if he is a mighty man, has a threefold power in his anger: one by the help of his servants; and a second by his wealth, whereby he persuades and overcomes wrongfully; and, thirdly, having his own natural power, he thereby works the evil. ⁵And though the wrathful man may be weak, yet he has a power twofold of that which is by nature, for wrath always aids such in lawlessness. ⁶This spirit always goes with lying at the right hand of Satan, that with cruelty and lying his works may be worked."

CHAPTER 4

¹"Therefore, understand the power of wrath, that it is vain. ²For it first of all gives provocation by word; then by deeds it strengthens him who is angry, and with sharp losses disturbs his mind, and so stirs up his soul with great wrath. ³Therefore, when anyone speaks against you, do not be moved to anger, [[and if any man praises you as holy men, do not be uplifted: do not be moved either to delight or to disgust]]. ⁴For first it pleases the hearing, and so makes the mind keen to perceive the grounds for provocation; and then being enraged, he thinks that he is justly angry. ⁵If you fall into any loss or ruin, my children, do not be afflicted, for this very spirit makes [a man] desire that which is perishable in order that he may be enraged through the affliction. ⁶And if you suffer loss voluntarily, or involuntarily, do not be vexed, for from vexation arises wrath with lying. ⁷Moreover, a twofold mischief is wrath with lying; and they assist one another in order to disturb the heart; and when the soul is continually disturbed, the LORD departs from it, and Belial rules over it."

CHAPTER 5

¹"Therefore observe, my children, the commandments of the LORD, and keep His law. Depart from wrath and hate lying, that the LORD may dwell among you and Belial may flee from you. ²Speak truth, each one, with his neighbor; so you will not fall into wrath and confusion, but you will be in peace, having the God of peace, so no war will prevail over you. ³Love the LORD throughout all your life, and [love] one another with a true heart. ⁴I know that in the last days you will depart from the LORD, and provoke Levi to anger, and fight against Judah, but you will not prevail against them, for a messenger of the LORD will guide them both; for by them Israel will stand. ⁵And whenever you depart from the LORD, you will walk in all evil and work the abominations of the nations, going whoring after women of the lawless ones while the spirits of wickedness work in you with all wickedness. [[⁶For I have read in the scroll of Enoch, the righteous, that

your prince is Satan, and that all the spirits of wickedness and pride will conspire to attend constantly on the sons of Levi, to cause them to sin before the Lord. ⁷And my sons will draw near to Levi, and sin with them in all things. And the sons of Judah will be covetous, plundering other men's goods like lions.]] ⁸Therefore you will be led away [with them] into captivity, || And you will receive all the plagues of Egypt there, || And all the evils of the nations. ⁹And so when you return to the Lord you will obtain mercy, || And He will bring you into His sanctuary, || And He will give you peace. ¹⁰And there will arise to you from the tribe of [[Judah and of]] Levi the Salvation of the Lord; And He will make war against Belial || And execute an everlasting vengeance on our enemies; ¹¹And He will take the captivity from Belial—[[the souls of the saints]], || And turn disobedient hearts to the Lord, || And give continuous peace to them that call on Him. ¹²And the saints will rest in Eden, || And the righteous will rejoice in the New Jerusalem, || And it will be to the glory of God forever. ¹³And Jerusalem will no longer endure desolation, || Nor will Israel be led captive, || For the Lord will be in the midst of it [[living among men]], || And the Holy One of Israel will reign over it [[in humility and in poverty; And he who believes on Him will reign among men in truth]]."

CHAPTER 6

¹"And now, fear the Lord, my children, and beware of Satan and his spirits. ²Draw near to God and to the Messenger that intercedes for you, for He is a mediator between God and man, and for the peace of Israel He will stand up against the kingdom of the enemy. ³Therefore the enemy is eager to destroy all that call on the Lord. ⁴For he knows that on the day on which Israel will convert, the kingdom of the enemy will be brought to an end. ⁵For this very Messenger of peace will strengthen Israel, that it does not fall into the extremity of evil. ⁶And it will be in the time of the lawlessness of Israel that the Lord will not depart from them, but will transform them into a nation that does His will, for none of the messengers will be equal to Him. ⁷And His Name will be in every place in Israel and among the nations. ⁸Therefore keep yourselves, my children, from every evil work, and cast away wrath and all lying, and love truth and long-suffering. ⁹And also impart to your children the things which you have heard from your father [[that the Savior of the nations may receive you, for He is true and long-suffering, meek and lowly, and teaches the Law of God by His works]]. ¹⁰Therefore, depart from all unrighteousness, and cleave to the righteousness of God, and your race will be saved forever. And bury me near my fathers."

CHAPTER 7

¹And when he had said these things, he kissed them and fell asleep at a good old age. ²And his sons buried him, and after that they carried up his bones, and placed them near Abraham, and Isaac, and Jacob. [[³Nevertheless, Dan prophesied to them that they should forget their God and should be alienated from the land of their inheritance, and from the race of Israel, and from the family of their seed.]]

THE TESTAMENT OF NAPHTALI

THE EIGHTH SON OF JACOB AND BILHAH

CHAPTER 1

¹The copy of the testament of Naphtali, which he ordained at the time of his death in the one hundred and thirtieth year of his life. ²When his sons were gathered together in the seventh month, on the first day of the month, while still in good health, he made them a feast of food and wine. ³And after he was awake in the morning, he said to them, "I am dying"; and they did not believe him. ⁴And as he glorified the Lord, he grew strong and said that after yesterday's feast he should die. ⁵And he then began to say, "Hear, my children—you sons of Naphtali—hear the words of your father. ⁶I was born from Bilhah, and because Rachel dealt craftily, and gave Bilhah in place of herself to Jacob, and she conceived and bore me on Rachel's knees, therefore she called my name Naphtali. ⁷For Rachel loved me very much because I was born on her lap; and when I was still young, she was accustomed to kiss me, and say, ⁸May I have a brother of yours from my own womb, like to you. ⁹From where also Joseph was like to me in all things, according to the prayers of Rachel. Now my mother was Bilhah, daughter of Rotheus, the brother of Deborah, Rebekah's nurse, who was born on one and the same day with Rachel. ¹⁰And Rotheus was of the family of Abraham, a Chaldean, God-fearing, free-born, and noble. ¹¹And he was taken captive and was bought by Laban; and he gave him his handmaid Euna to be [his] wife, and she bore a daughter and called her name Zilpah after the name of the village in which he had been taken captive. ¹²And next she bore Bilhah, saying, My daughter hastens after what is new, for as soon as she was born she seized the breast and hastened to suck it."

CHAPTER 2

¹"And I was swift on my feet like the deer, and my father Jacob appointed me for all messages, and he gave me his blessing as a deer. ²For as the potter knows how much the vessel is to contain, and brings clay accordingly, so also the Lord makes the body after the likeness of the spirit, and He implants the spirit according to the capacity of the body. ³And the one does not fall short of the other by a third part of a hair; for by weight, and measure, and rule was all the creation made. ⁴And as the potter knows the use of each vessel, what it is appropriate for, so also the Lord knows the body, how far it will persist in goodness, and when it begins in evil. ⁵For there is no inclination or thought which the Lord does not know, for He created every man after His own image. ⁶As a man's strength, so also is his work; and as his mind, so also is his skill; and as his purpose, so also is his achievement; and as his heart, so also is his mouth; as his eye, so also is his sleep; as his soul, so also is his word, either in the Law of the Lord or in the works of Belial. ⁷And as there is a division between light and darkness, between seeing and hearing, so also is there a division between man and man, and between woman and woman; and it is not to be said that the one is like the other, either in face or in mind. ⁸For God made all things good in their order: the five senses in the head (and He joined the neck to the head, also adding the hair to it for comeliness and glory), then the heart for understanding, the belly for excrement, and the stomach for [grinding], the windpipe for taking in [the breath], the liver for wrath, the gall for bitterness, the spleen for laughter, the reins for prudence, the muscles of the loins for power, the lungs for drawing in, the loins for strength, and so forth. ⁹So then, my children, let all your works be done in order with good intent in the fear of God, and do nothing disorderly in scorn or out of its due season. ¹⁰For if you command the eye to hear, it cannot; so neither can you do the works of light while you are in darkness."

CHAPTER 3

¹"Therefore, do not be eager to corrupt your doings through covetousness or to deceive your souls with vain words, because if you keep silence in purity of heart, you will understand how to hold fast the will of God and to cast away the will of Belial. ²Sun, and moon, and stars do not change their order; so you also must not change the Law of God in the disorderliness of your doings. ³The nations went astray, and forsook the Lord, and changed their order, and obeyed stocks and stones, spirits of deceit. ⁴But you will not be so, my children, recognizing in the expanse, in the earth, and in the sea, and in all created things, the Lord who made all things, that you do not become as Sodom, which changed the order of nature. ⁵In like manner the Watchers also changed the order of their nature, whom the Lord cursed at the Flood, on whose account He made the earth without inhabitants and fruitless."

CHAPTER 4

¹"These things I say to you, my children, for I have read in the writing of Enoch that you yourselves will also depart from the Lord, walking according to all the lawlessness of the nations, and you will do according to all the wickedness of Sodom. ²And the Lord will bring captivity on you, and there you will serve your enemies, and you will be bowed down with every affliction and tribulation, until the Lord has consumed you all. ³And after you have become diminished and made few, you will return and acknowledge the Lord your God, and He will bring you back into your land, according to His abundant mercy. ⁴And it will be that after they come into the land of their fathers, they will again forget the Lord and become ungodly. ⁵And the Lord

will scatter them on the face of all the earth, until the Compassion of the LORD will come—a Man working righteousness and working mercy to all of them that are far off, and to them that are near."

CHAPTER 5
¹"For in the fortieth year of my life, I saw a vision on the Mount of Olives, on the east of Jerusalem, that the sun and the moon were standing still. ²And behold, Isaac, the father of my father, said to us, Run and lay hold of them, each one according to his strength; and the sun and moon will belong to him that seizes them. ³And all of us ran together, and Levi laid hold of the sun, and Judah outstripped the others and seized the moon, and both of them were lifted up with them. ⁴And when Levi became as [the] sun, behold, a certain young man gave twelve palm branches to him; ⁵and Judah was bright as the moon, and under their feet were twelve rays. [[⁶And the two, Levi and Judah, ran, and laid hold of them,]] ⁷and a bull on the earth, with two great horns, and an eagle's wings on its back; and we wished to seize him, but could not. ⁸But Joseph came, and seized him, and ascended up with him on high. And I saw, for I was there, and behold, a holy writing appeared to us, saying, Assyrians, Medes, Persians, [[Chaldeans,]] [and] Syrians will possess in captivity the twelve tribes of Israel."

CHAPTER 6
¹"And again after seven days I saw our father Jacob standing by the Sea of Jamnia, and we were with him. ²And behold, there came a ship sailing by, without sailors or pilot; and there was written on the ship: THE SHIP OF JACOB. ³And our father said to us, Come, let us embark on our ship. ⁴And when he had gone on board, there arose a vehement storm, and a mighty tempest of wind; and our father, who was holding the helm, departed from us. ⁵And we, being tossed with the tempest, were borne along over the sea; and the ship was filled with water, [and was] pounded by mighty waves, until it was broken up. ⁶And Joseph fled away on a little boat, and we were all divided on nine planks, and Levi and Judah were together. ⁷And we were all scattered to the ends of the earth. ⁸Then Levi, girt around with sackcloth, prayed for us all to the LORD. ⁹And when the storm ceased, the ship reached the land as it were in peace. ¹⁰And our father came, and we all rejoiced with one accord."

CHAPTER 7
¹"I told these two dreams to my father; and he said to me, These things must be fulfilled in their season, after Israel has endured many things. ²Then my father says to me, I believe God that Joseph lives, for I see that the LORD always numbers him with you. ³And he said, weeping, Ah me! My son Joseph, you live, though I do not see you, and you do not see Jacob who begot you. ⁴He caused me also, therefore, to weep by these words, and I burned in my heart to declare that Joseph had been sold, but I feared my brothers."

CHAPTER 8
¹"And behold, my children, I have shown the last times to you, how everything will come to pass in Israel. ²Therefore, also charge your children that they should be united to Levi and to Judah: For salvation will arise to Israel through them, || And Jacob will be blessed in them. ³For through their tribes God will appear [dwelling among men] on earth, || To save the race of Israel, || And to gather together the righteous from among the nations. ⁴If you work that which is good, my children, || Both men and messengers will bless you; And God will be glorified among the nations through you, || And the Devil will flee from you, || And the wild beasts will fear you, || And the LORD will love you, || [[And the messengers will cleave to you]]. ⁵As a man who has trained a child well is kept in kindly remembrance, || So also for a good work there is a good remembrance before God. ⁶But him that does not [do] that which is good, || Both messengers and men will curse, || And God will be dishonored among the nations through him, || And the Devil will make him as his own peculiar instrument, || And every wild beast will master him, || And the LORD will hate him. ⁷For the commandments of the Law are twofold, || And through prudence they must be fulfilled. ⁸For there is a season for a man to embrace his wife, || And a season to abstain from that for his prayer. ⁹So then, there are two commandments, and unless they are done in due order, they bring very great sin on men. ¹⁰So it is also with the other commandments. Therefore, be wise in God, my children, and prudent, understanding the order of His commandments and the laws of every word that the LORD may love you."

CHAPTER 9
¹And when he had charged them with many such words, he exhorted them that they should remove his bones to Hebron, and that they should bury him with his fathers. ²And when he had eaten and drunken with a merry heart, he covered his face and died. ³And his sons did according to all that their father Naphtali had commanded them.

THE TESTAMENT OF GAD

THE NINTH SON OF JACOB AND ZILPAH

CHAPTER 1
¹The copy of the testament of Gad, what things he spoke to his sons in the one hundred and twenty-fifth year of his life, saying to them, ²"Listen, my children. I was the ninth son born to Jacob, and I was valiant in keeping the flocks. ³Accordingly, I guarded the flock at night; and whenever the lion came, or the wolf, or any wild beast against the fold, I pursued it, and overtaking [it], I seized its foot with my hand and hurled it about a stone's throw, and so killed it. ⁴Now my brother Joseph was feeding the flock with us for upwards of thirty days, and being young, he fell sick by reason of the heat. ⁵And he returned to Hebron to our father, who made him lie down near him, because he loved him greatly. ⁶And Joseph told our father that the sons of Zilpah and Bilhah were slaying the best of the flock and eating them against the judgment of Reuben and Judah. ⁷For he saw that I had delivered a lamb out of the mouth of a bear and put the bear to death, but had slain the lamb, being grieved concerning it that it could not live, and that we had eaten it. ⁸And regarding this matter, I was angry with Joseph until the day that he was sold, ⁹and the spirit of hatred was in me, and I did not wish either to hear of Joseph with the ears or see him with the eyes, because he rebuked us to our faces, saying that we were eating of the flock without Judah. For whatever things he told our father, he believed him."

CHAPTER 2
¹"I now confess my sin, my children, that oftentimes I wished to kill him, because I hated him from my heart. ²Moreover, I hated him even more for his dreams; and I wished to lick him out of the land of the living, even as an ox licks up the grass of the field. ³Therefore Simeon and I sold him to the Ishmaelites [[for thirty pieces of gold, and ten of them we hid, and showed the twenty to our brothers]] ⁴And thus we were bent on slaying him through covetousness. ⁵And the God of my fathers delivered him from my hands, that I should not work lawlessness in Israel."

CHAPTER 3
¹"And now, my children, listen to the words of truth to work righteousness, and all the Law of the Most High, and do not go astray through the spirit of hatred, for it is evil in all the doings of men. ²Whatever a man does, the hater abominates himself: and though a man works the Law of the LORD, he does not praise Him; though a man fears the LORD, and takes pleasure in that which is righteous, he does not love Him. ³He disparages the truth, he envies him that prospers, he welcomes evil-speaking, he loves arrogance, for hatred blinds his soul—as I also then looked on Joseph."

CHAPTER 4
¹"Therefore, beware of hatred, my children, for it even works lawlessness against the LORD Himself. ²For it will not hear the words of His commandments concerning the loving of one's neighbor, and it sins against God. ³For if a brother stumbles, it immediately delights to proclaim it to all men, and is urgent that he should be judged for it, and be punished, and be put to death. ⁴And if it is a servant, it stirs him up against his master, and with every affliction it devises against him [that], if it were possible, he can be put to death. ⁵For hatred also works with envy against them that prosper; so long as it hears of or sees their success, it always languishes. ⁶For as love would even give life to the dead and would call back them that are condemned to die, so hatred would slay the living, and it would not permit those that had sinned to live. ⁷For the

spirit of hatred works together with Satan, through hastiness of spirit, in all things to men's death; but the spirit of love works together with the Law of God in long-suffering to the salvation of men."

CHAPTER 5

¹"Therefore hatred is evil, for it constantly mates with lying, speaking against the truth; and it makes small things to be great, and causes the light to be darkness, and calls the sweet bitter, and teaches slander, and kindles wrath, and stirs up war, and violence, and all covetousness; ²it fills the heart with evils and devilish poison. Therefore, I say these things to you from experience, my children, that you may drive hatred away, which is of the Devil, and cleave to the love of God. Righteousness casts out hatred, humility destroys envy. ³For he that is just and humble is ashamed to do what is unjust, not being reproved by another, but by his own heart, because the LORD looks on his inclination. ⁴He does not speak against a holy man, because the fear of God overcomes hatred. ⁵For fearing lest he should offend the LORD, he will not do wrong to any man, even in thought. ⁶I learned these things at last, after I had converted concerning Joseph. ⁷For true conversion after a godly sort [[destroys ignorance, and]] drives away the darkness, and enlightens the eyes, and gives knowledge to the soul, and leads the mind to salvation. ⁸And those things which it has not learned from man, it knows through conversion. ⁹For God brought a disease of the liver on me; and had the prayers of my father Jacob not aided me, my spirit would have surely departed. ¹⁰For by what things a man transgresses, by the same he is also punished. ¹¹Since, therefore, my liver was mercilessly set against Joseph, I too suffered in my liver mercilessly, and was judged for eleven months, for so long a time as I had been angry against Joseph."

CHAPTER 6

¹"And now, my children, I exhort each one of you to love his brother and put away hatred from your hearts. Love one another in deed, and in word, and in the inclination of the soul. ²For I spoke peaceably to Joseph in the presence of my father, and when I had gone out, the spirit of hatred darkened my mind, and stirred up my soul to slay him. ³Therefore love one another from the heart; and if a man sins against you, cast out the poison of hate and speak peaceably to him, and do not hold guile in your soul; and if he confesses and converts, forgive him. ⁴But if he denies it, do not get into a passion with him, lest catching the poison from you, he takes to swearing and so you sin doubly. [[⁵Do not let another man hear your secrets when engaged in legal strife, lest he comes to hate you, and becomes your enemy, and commits a great sin against you; for oftentimes he addresses you cunningly or busies himself concerning you with wicked intent.]] ⁶And though he denies it and yet has a sense of shame when reproved, give over reproving him. ⁷For he who denies may convert so as not to wrong you again; yes, he may also honor you, and be at peace with you. ⁸And if he is shameless and persists in his wrongdoing, even so forgive him from the heart, and leave the avenging to God."

CHAPTER 7

¹"If a man prospers more than you, do not be vexed, but also pray for him, that he may have perfect prosperity. ²For so it is expedient for you. And if he is further exalted, do not be envious of him, remembering that all flesh will die; and offer praise to God, who gives good and profitable things to all men. ³Seek out the judgments of the LORD and your mind will rest and be at peace. ⁴And though a man becomes rich by evil means, even as Esau, the brother of my father, do not be jealous, ⁵but wait for the end from the LORD. For if he takes away [from a man] wealth (gotten by evil means), He forgives him if he converts, but the unconverted is reserved for continuous punishment. ⁶For the poor man, if free from envy, pleases the LORD in all things—he is blessed beyond all men, because he does not have the travail of vain men. ⁷Therefore put away jealousy from your souls and love one another with uprightness of heart."

CHAPTER 8

¹"Therefore, tell these things to your children, that they may honor Judah and Levi, for the LORD will raise up salvation to Israel from them. [[²For I know that at the end your children will depart from Him, and will walk in all wickedness, and affliction, and corruption before the LORD.]]" ³And when he had rested for a little while, he said again, "My children, obey my father, and bury me near to my fathers." ⁴And he drew up his feet and fell asleep in peace. ⁵And after five years they carried him up to Hebron and laid him with his fathers.

THE TESTAMENT OF ASHER

THE TENTH SON OF JACOB AND ZILPAH

CHAPTER 1

¹The copy of the Testament of Asher, what things he spoke to his sons in the one hundred and twenty-fifth year of his life. ²For while he was still in health, he said to them, "Listen, you children of Asher, to your father, and I will declare to you all that is upright in the sight of the LORD. ³God has given two ways to the sons of men, and two inclinations, and two kinds of action, and two modes [of action], and two issues. ⁴Therefore all things are by twos—one over against the other. ⁵For there are two ways of good and evil, and with these are the two inclinations in our breasts discriminating them. ⁶Therefore if the soul takes pleasure in the good [inclination], all its actions are in righteousness; and if it sins it immediately converts. ⁷For, having its thoughts set on righteousness, and casting away wickedness, it immediately overthrows the evil, and uproots the sin. ⁸But if it inclines to the evil inclination, all its actions are in wickedness, and it drives away the good, and cleaves to the evil, and is ruled by Belial; even though it works what is good, he perverts it to evil. ⁹For whenever it begins to do good, he forces the issue of the action into evil for him, seeing that the treasure of the inclination is filled with an evil spirit."

CHAPTER 2

¹"A person may then with words help the good for the sake of the evil, yet the issue of the action leads to mischief. ²There is a man who shows no compassion on him who serves his turn in evil; and this thing has two aspects, but the whole is evil. ³And there is a man that loves him that works evil, because he would prefer even to die in evil for his sake; and concerning this it is clear that it has two aspects, but the whole is an evil work. ⁴Though indeed he has love, yet he is wicked who conceals what is evil for the sake of the good name, but the end of the action tends to evil. ⁵Another steals, does unjustly, plunders, defrauds, and moreover pities the poor: this too has a twofold aspect, but the whole is evil. ⁶He who defrauds his neighbor provokes God, and swears falsely against the Most High, and yet pities the poor: he sets the LORD who commands the Law at nothing and provokes [Him], and yet he refreshes the poor. ⁷He defiles the soul, and makes the body happy; he kills many, and pities a few: this, too, has a twofold aspect, but the whole is evil. ⁸Another commits adultery and fornication, and abstains from meats, and when he fasts, he does evil, and by the power of his wealth overwhelms many; and notwithstanding his excessive wickedness, he does the commandments: this, too, has a twofold aspect, but the whole is evil. ⁹Such men are hares—clean, like those that divide the hoof, but in very deed are unclean. ¹⁰For God has thus declared in the tablets of the commandments."

CHAPTER 3

¹"But do not, my children, wear two faces like to them—of goodness and of wickedness; but cleave to goodness only, for God has His habitation therein, and men desire it. ²But flee away from wickedness, destroying the [evil] inclination by your good works; ³for they that are double-faced do not serve God, but their own lusts, so that they may please Belial and men like to themselves."

CHAPTER 4

¹"For good men, even they that are of single face, though they are thought by them that are double-faced to sin, are just before God. ²For many in killing the wicked do two works, of good and evil; but the whole is good, because he has uprooted and destroyed that which is evil. ³One man hates the merciful and unjust man, and the man who commits adultery and fasts: this, too, has a twofold aspect, but the whole work is good, because he follows the LORD's example, in that he does not accept the seemingly good as the genuine good. ⁴Another

does not desire to see a good day with them that riot, lest he defile his body and pollute his soul: this, too, is double-faced, but the whole is good. ⁵For such men are like to stags and to hinds, because in the manner of wild animals they seem to be unclean, but they are altogether clean, because they walk in zeal for the LORD and abstain from what God also hates and forbids by His commandments, warding off the evil from the good."

CHAPTER 5

¹"You see, my children, how that there are two in all things—one against the other, and the one is hidden by the other: in wealth [is hidden] covetousness, in conviviality drunkenness, in laughter grief, in wedlock profligacy. ²Death succeeds to life, dishonor to glory, night to day, and darkness to light; [[and all things are under the day, just things under life, unjust things under death;]] ³for what reason also, continuous life awaits death. Nor may it be said that truth is a lie, nor right wrong, for all truth is under the light, even as all things are under God. ⁴All these things, therefore, I proved in my life, and I did not wander from the truth of the LORD, and I searched out the commandments of the Most High, walking according to all my strength with singleness of face to that which is good."

CHAPTER 6

¹"Therefore, you also take heed, my children, to the commandments of the LORD, following the truth with singleness of face. ²For they that are double-faced are guilty of a twofold sin, for they both do the evil thing and they have pleasure in them that do it, following the example of the spirits of deceit, and striving against mankind. ³Therefore, my children, keep the Law of the LORD and do not give heed to evil as to good, but look to the thing that is really good and keep it in all commandments of the LORD, having your conversation therein, and resting therein. ⁴For the latter ends of men show their righteousness [[or unrighteousness]], when they meet the messengers of the LORD and of Satan. ⁵For when the soul departs troubled, it is tormented by the evil spirit which it also served in lusts and evil works. ⁶But if he is peaceful with joy, he meets the messenger of peace, and he leads him into continuous life."

CHAPTER 7

¹"Do not become, my children, as Sodom, which sinned against the messengers of the LORD, and perished forever. ²For I know that you will sin, and be delivered into the hands of your enemies, and your land will be made desolate, and your holy places destroyed, and you will be scattered to the four corners of the earth. ³And you will be set at nothing in the dispersion, vanishing away as water ⁴until the Most High will visit the earth, coming Himself [[as a Man, eating and drinking with men, and breaking the head of the dragon in the water. ⁵He will save Israel and all the nations—God speaking in the person of [this] Man. ⁶Therefore you also, my children, tell these things to your children that they do not disobey Him. For I have known that you will assuredly be disobedient, and assuredly act ungodly, not giving heed to the Law of God, but to the commandments of men, being corrupted through wickedness. ⁷And therefore you will be scattered as my brothers Gad and Dan, and you will not know your lands, tribe, and tongue. ⁸But the LORD will gather you together in faith through His tender mercy, and for the sake of Abraham, Isaac, and Jacob.]]"

CHAPTER 8

¹And when he had said these things to them, he commanded them, saying, "Bury me in Hebron." ²And he fell asleep and died at a good old age. And his sons did as he had commanded them, and they carried him up to Hebron and buried him with his fathers.

THE TESTAMENT OF JOSEPH

THE ELEVENTH SON OF JACOB AND RACHEL

CHAPTER 1

¹The copy of the Testament of Joseph. When he was about to die, he called his sons and his brothers together and said to them, ²"My brothers and my children, || Listen to Joseph, the beloved of Israel; Give ear, my sons, to your father. ³I have seen in my life envy and death, || Yet I did not go astray, but persevered in the truth of the LORD. ⁴These brothers of mine hated me, but the LORD loved me; They wished to slay me, but the God of my fathers guarded me; They let me down into a pit, and the Most High brought me up again; ⁵I was sold into slavery, and the Lord of all made me free; I was taken into captivity, and His strong hand aided me; I was beset with hunger, and the LORD Himself nourished me; ⁶I was alone, and God comforted me; I was sick, and the LORD visited me; I was in prison, and my God showed favor to me; In bonds, and He released me; ⁷Slandered, and He pleaded my cause; Bitterly spoken against by the Egyptians, and He delivered me; Envied by my fellow-slaves, and He exalted me."

CHAPTER 2

¹"And this chief captain of Pharaoh entrusted his house to me. ²And I struggled against a shameless woman, urging me to transgress with her, but the God of my father Israel delivered me from the burning flame. ³I was cast into prison, I was beaten, I was mocked, but the LORD granted me to find mercy in the sight of the keeper of the prison. ⁴For the LORD does not forsake them that fear Him, || Neither in darkness, nor in bonds, nor in tribulations, nor in necessities. ⁵For God is not put to shame as a man, || Nor as the son of man is He afraid, || Nor as one that is earth-born is He [weak or] frightened. ⁶But in all those things He gives protection, || And He comforts in various ways, || [Though] for a short time He departs to try the inclination of the soul. ⁷In ten temptations He showed me approved, || And in all of them I endured; For endurance is a mighty charm, || And patience gives many good things."

CHAPTER 3

¹"How often did the Egyptian woman threaten me with death! How often did she give me over to punishment, and then call me back and threaten me, and when I was unwilling to company with her, she said to me, ²You will be lord of me, and all that is in my house, if you will give yourself to me, and you will be as our master. ³But I remembered the words of my father, and going into my chamber, I wept and prayed to the LORD. ⁴And I fasted in those seven years, and I appeared to the Egyptians as one living delicately, for they that fast for God's sake receive beauty of face. ⁵And if my lord was away from home, I drank no wine; nor for three days did I take my food, but I gave it to the poor and sick. ⁶And I sought the LORD early, and I wept for the Egyptian woman of Memphis, for she troubled me very unceasingly, for she also came to me at night under pretense of visiting me. ⁷And because she had no male child, she pretended to regard me as a son, and so I prayed to the LORD, and she bore a male child. ⁸And for a time she embraced me as a son, and I did not know it, but later, she sought to draw me into fornication. ⁹And when I perceived it, I sorrowed to death; and when she had gone out, I came to myself, and lamented for her many days, because I recognized her guile and her deceit. ¹⁰And I declared the words of the Most High to her, if perhaps she would turn from her evil lust."

CHAPTER 4

¹"Therefore, she often flattered me with words as a holy man, and guilefully in her talk praised my chastity before her husband, while desiring to ensnare me when we were alone. ²For she lauded me openly as chaste, and in secret she said to me, Do not fear my husband, for he is persuaded concerning your chastity. For even should one tell him concerning us, he would not believe [it]. ³Owing to all these things, I lay on the ground, and implored God that the LORD would deliver me from her deceit. ⁴And when she had not prevailed thereby, she came to me again under the plea of instruction, that she might learn the word of God. ⁵And she said to me, If you will that I should leave my idols, lie with me, and I will persuade my husband to depart from his idols, and we will walk in the Law of your Lord. ⁶And I said to her, The LORD does not will that those who revere Him should be in uncleanness, nor does He take pleasure in them that commit adultery, ⁷but in those that approach Him with a pure heart and undefiled lips. ⁷But she held her peace, longing to accomplish her evil desire. ⁸And I gave myself even more to fasting and prayer, that the LORD might deliver me from her."

CHAPTER 5

¹"And again, at another time she said to me, If you will not commit adultery, I will kill my

husband by poison and take you to be my husband. ²I therefore, when I heard this, tore my garments, and said to her, Woman, revere God, and do not do this evil deed, lest you be destroyed; ³for indeed know that I will declare this scheme of yours to all men. ⁴She therefore, being afraid, implored that I would not declare this scheme. And she departed, soothing me with gifts, and sending to me every delight of the sons of men."

CHAPTER 6

¹"And afterward she sent me food mingled with enchantments. ²And when the eunuch who brought it came, I looked up and beheld a terrible man giving me a sword with the dish, and I perceived that [her] scheme was to deceive me. ³And when he had gone out, I wept, nor did I taste that or any other of her food. ⁴So then after one day she came to me and observed the food, ⁵and said to me, Why is it that you have not eaten of the food? And I said to her, It is because you have filled it with deadly enchantments; and how you said, I do not come near to idols, but to the LORD alone. ⁶Now therefore know that the God of my father has revealed your wickedness to me by His messenger, and I have kept it to convict you, if perhaps you may see and convert. ⁷But that you may learn that the wickedness of the ungodly has no power over them that worship God with chastity, behold, I will take of it and eat before you. And having said so, I prayed thus: The God of my fathers and the Messenger of Abraham, be with me; and [then] I ate. ⁸And when she saw this she fell on her face at my feet, weeping; and I raised her up and admonished her. And she promised to do this iniquity no longer."

CHAPTER 7

¹"But her heart was still set on evil, and she looked around [regarding] how to ensnare me, and sighing deeply, she became downcast, though she was not sick. ²And when her husband saw her, he said to her, Why is your countenance fallen? And she said to him, I have a pain at my heart, and the groanings of my spirit oppress me; and so he comforted her who was not sick. ³Then, accordingly seizing an opportunity, she rushed to me while her husband was still outside, and said to me, I will hang myself or cast myself over a cliff if you will not lie with me. ⁴And when I saw the spirit of Belial was troubling her, I prayed to the LORD and said to her, ⁵Why, wretched woman, are you troubled and disturbed, blinded through sins? Remember that if you kill yourself, Asteho, the concubine of your husband, your rival, will beat your children, and you will destroy your memorial from off the earth. ⁶And she said to me, Behold, then you love me; let this be enough for me: only strive for my life and my children, ⁷and I expect that I will also enjoy my desire. But she did not know that I spoke this because of my lord, and not because of her. ⁸For if a man has fallen before the passion of a wicked desire and become enslaved by it even as she, whatever good thing he may hear with regard to that passion, he receives it with a view to his wicked desire."

CHAPTER 8

¹"Therefore, I declare to you, my children, that it was about the sixth hour when she departed from me; and I knelt before the LORD all day, and all the night; and about dawn I arose, weeping and praying for a release from her. ²At last, then, she laid hold of my garments, forcibly dragging me to have relations with her. ³Therefore, when I saw that in her madness she was holding fast to my garment, I left it behind, and fled away naked. ⁴And holding fast to the garment, she falsely accused me, and when her husband came, he cast me into [the] prison in his house; and on the next day he scourged me and sent me into Pharaoh's prison. ⁵And when I was in bonds, the Egyptian woman was oppressed with grief, and she came and heard how I gave thanks to the LORD and sang praises in the abode of darkness, and with glad voice rejoiced, glorifying my God that I was delivered from the lustful desire of the Egyptian woman."

CHAPTER 9

¹"And often she sent to me, saying, Consent to fulfill my desire, and I will release you from your bonds, and I will free you from the darkness. And not even in thought did I incline to her. ²For God loves him who in a den of wickedness combines fasting with chastity, rather than the man who in kings' chambers combines luxury with license. And if a man lives in chastity, and also desires glory, and the Most High knows that it is expedient for him, He also bestows this on me. ³How often, though she were sick, did she come down to me at [the] unwatched times, and listened to my voice as I prayed! ⁴And when I heard her groanings I held my peace. ⁵For when I was in her house, she was accustomed to bare her arms, and breasts, and legs, that I might lie with her, for she was very beautiful, splendidly adorned in order to deceive me. And the LORD guarded me from her devices."

CHAPTER 10

¹"You see, therefore, my children, how great things patience works, and prayer with fasting. ²So you too, if you follow after chastity and purity with patience and prayer, with fasting in humility of heart, the LORD will dwell among you, because He loves chastity. ³And wheresoever the Most High dwells, even though envy, or slavery, or slander befalls [a man], the LORD who dwells in him, for the sake of his chastity, not only delivers him from evil, but also exalts him even as me. ⁴For in every way the man is lifted up, whether in deed, or in word, or in thought. ⁵My brothers knew how my father loved me, and yet I did not exalt myself in my mind; although I was a child, I had the fear of God in my heart, for I knew that all things would pass away. ⁶And I did not raise myself [against them] with evil intent, but I honored my brothers; and out of respect for them, even when I was being sold, I refrained from telling the Ishmaelites that I was a son of Jacob, a great and mighty man."

CHAPTER 11

¹"My children, have the fear of God in all your works before your eyes, and honor your brothers. ²For everyone who does the Law of the LORD will be loved by Him. And when I came to the Indocolpitae with the Ishmaelites, they asked me, saying, Are you a slave? ³And I said that I was a homeborn slave, that I might not put my brothers to shame. And the eldest of them said to me, You are not a slave, for even your appearance makes it manifest. ⁴But I said that I was their slave. Now when we came into Egypt, they strove concerning me, which of them should buy me and take me. ⁵Therefore it seemed good to all that I should remain in Egypt with the merchant of their trade, until they should return bringing merchandise. ⁶And the LORD gave me favor in the eyes of the merchant, and he entrusted his house to me. ⁷And God blessed him by my means and increased him in gold, and silver, and in household servants. ⁸And I was with him three months and five days."

CHAPTER 12

¹"And about that time the Memphian woman, the wife of Potiphar, came down in a chariot with great pomp, because she had heard from her eunuchs concerning me. ²And she told her husband that the merchant had become rich by means of a young Hebrew, and they say that he had assuredly been stolen out of the land of Canaan. ³Now therefore, render justice to him, and take the youth away to your house, so the God of the Hebrews will bless you, for grace from Heaven is on him."

CHAPTER 13

¹"And Potiphar was persuaded by her words, and commanded the merchant to be brought, and said to him, What is this that I hear concerning you, that you steal persons out of the land of Canaan and sell them for slaves? ²But the merchant fell at his feet and implored him, saying, ³I implore you, my lord, I do not know what you say. And Potiphar said to him, From where, then, is the Hebrew slave? And he said, The Ishmaelites entrusted him to me until they should return. ⁴But he did not believe him, but commanded him to be stripped and beaten. ⁵And when he persisted in this statement, Potiphar said, Let the youth be brought. ⁶And when I was brought in, I paid respect to Potiphar (for he was third in rank of the officers of Pharaoh). ⁷And he took me apart from him, and said to me, Are you a slave or free? And I said, A slave. And he said, Whose? ⁸And I said, The Ishmaelites. And he said, How did you become their slave? ⁹And I said, They bought me out of the land of Canaan. And he said to me, You truly lie; and immediately he commanded me to be stripped and beaten."

CHAPTER 14

¹"Now the Memphian woman was looking through a window at me while I was being

beaten, for her house was near, and she sent to him, saying, Your judgment is unjust, for you punish a free man who has been stolen, as though he were a transgressor. ²And when I made no change in my statement, though I was beaten, he ordered me to be imprisoned, until, he said, the owners of the boy should come. ³And the woman said to her husband, For what reason do you detain the captive and well-born youth in bonds, who ought rather to be set at liberty, and be waited on? ⁴For she wished to see me out of a desire of sin, but I was ignorant concerning all these things. ⁵And he said to her, It is not the custom of the Egyptians to take that which belongs to others before proof is given. ⁶This, therefore, he said concerning the merchant; [and he said,] But as for the youth, he must be imprisoned."

CHAPTER 15

¹"Now after twenty-four days the Ishmaelites came, for they had heard that my father Jacob was mourning much concerning me. ²And they came and said to me, How is it that you said that you were a slave? And behold, we have learned that you are the son of a mighty man in the land of Canaan, and your father still mourns for you in sackcloth and ashes. ³When I heard this, my bowels were dissolved, and my heart melted, and I greatly desired to weep, but I restrained myself, that I should not put my brothers to shame. And I said to them, I do not know, I am a slave. ⁴Then, therefore, they took counsel to sell me, that I should not be found in their hands. ⁵For they feared my father, lest he [should come and] execute on them a grievous vengeance. ⁶For they had heard that he was mighty with God and with men. ⁷Then the merchant said to them, Release me from the judgment of Potiphar. ⁸And they came and requested me, saying, Say that you were bought by us with money, and he will set us free."

CHAPTER 16

¹"Now the Memphian woman said to her husband, Buy the youth; for I hear, she said, that they are selling him. ²And she immediately sent a eunuch to the Ishmaelites and asked them to sell me. ³But since the eunuch would not agree to buy me [at their price], he returned, having made trial of them, and he made known to his mistress that they requested a large price for their slave. ⁴And she sent another eunuch, saying, Even though they demand two minas, give [it to] them, do not spare the gold; only buy the boy, and bring him to me. ⁵The eunuch therefore went and gave them eighty pieces of gold, and he received me; but he said to the Egyptian woman, I have given one hundred. ⁶And though I knew [this], I held my peace, lest the eunuch should be put to shame."

CHAPTER 17

¹"You see, therefore, my children, what great things I endured that I should not put my brothers to shame. ²You also, therefore, love one another, and with long-suffering hide one another's faults. ³For God delights in the unity of brothers, and in the purpose of a heart that takes pleasure in love. ⁴And when my brothers came into Egypt, they learned that I had returned their money to them and had not scolded them, and I comforted them. ⁵And I loved them more abundantly after the death of my father Jacob; and all things, whatever he commanded, I did very abundantly for them, ⁶and I did not allow them to be afflicted in the smallest matter; and I gave all that was in my hand to them. ⁷And their children were my children, and my children as their servants; and their life was my life, and all their suffering was my suffering, and all their sickness was my infirmity. ⁸My land was their land, and their counsel my counsel. And I did not exalt myself among them in arrogance because of my worldly glory, but I was among them as one of the least."

CHAPTER 18

¹"Therefore, if you also walk in the commandments of the LORD, my children, He will exalt you there, and will bless you with good things forever and ever. ²And if anyone seeks to do evil to you, do well to him, and pray for him, and you will be redeemed of the LORD from all evil. ³Behold, you see that out of my humility and long-suffering I took the daughter of the priest of Heliopolis to be [my] wife. ⁴And one hundred talents of gold were given to me with her, and the LORD made them to serve me. ⁵And He also gave me beauty as a flower beyond the beautiful ones of Israel; and He preserved me to old age in strength and in beauty, because I was like in all things to Jacob."

CHAPTER 19

¹"Therefore, hear my vision which I saw: ²I saw twelve deer feeding. And nine of them were dispersed. Now the three were preserved, but on the following day they were also dispersed. ³And I saw that the three deer became three lambs, and they cried to the LORD, and He brought them forth into a flourishing and well-watered place, yes, He brought them out of darkness into light. ⁴And there they cried to the LORD until there gathered together to them the nine deer, and they became as twelve sheep, and after a short time they increased and became many flocks. ⁵And after these things I saw and behold, twelve bulls were sucking one cow, which produced a sea of milk, and there drank thereof the twelve flocks and innumerable herds. ⁶And the horns of the fourth bull went up to Heaven and became as a wall for the flocks, and in the midst of the two horns there grew another horn. ⁷And I saw a bull calf which surrounded them twelve times, and it became a help to all the bulls. ⁸And I saw in the midst of the horns a virgin [[wearing a many-colored garment, and from her]] went forth a lamb; and on his right [[was as it were a lion; and]] all the beasts and all the reptiles rushed [against him], and the lamb overcame them and destroyed them. ⁹And the bulls rejoiced because of him, and the cow [and the deer] exulted together with them. ¹⁰And these things must come to pass in their season. Therefore, my children, observe the commandments of the LORD, and honor Levi and Judah; ¹¹for from them will arise to you [[the Lamb of God, who takes away the sin of the world]]—One who saves [[all the nations and]] Israel. ¹²For His kingdom is an everlasting kingdom, which will not pass away; but my kingdom among you will come to an end as a watcher's hammock, which disappears after the summer."

CHAPTER 20

¹"For I know that after my death the Egyptians will afflict you, but God will avenge you, and will bring you into that which He promised to your fathers. ²But you will carry up my bones with you; for when my bones are being taken up there, the LORD will be with you in light, and Belial will be in darkness with the Egyptians. ³And carry your mother Asenath to the Hippodrome and bury her near your mother Rachel." ⁴And when he had said these things, he stretched out his feet and died at a good old age. ⁵And all Israel mourned for him, and all Egypt, with a great mourning. ⁶And when the sons of Israel went out of Egypt, they took the bones of Joseph with them, and they buried him in Hebron with his fathers, and the years of his life were one hundred and ten years.

THE TESTAMENT OF BENJAMIN

THE TWELFTH SON OF JACOB AND RACHEL

CHAPTER 1

¹The copy of the words of Benjamin, which he commanded his sons to observe after he had lived one hundred and twenty-five years. ²And he kissed them, and said, "As Isaac was born to Abraham in his old age, so was I also to Jacob. ³And since my mother Rachel died in giving me birth, I had no milk; therefore I was suckled by her handmaid Bilhah. ⁴For Rachel remained barren for twelve years after she had borne Joseph; and she prayed [to] the LORD with fasting [for] twelve days, and she conceived and bore me. ⁵For my father loved Rachel dearly, and prayed that he might see two sons born from her. ⁶Therefore I was called Benjamin, that is, a son of days."

CHAPTER 2

¹"And when I went into Egypt, to Joseph, and my brother recognized me, he said to me, ²What did they tell my father when they sold me? And I said to him, They dabbled your coat with blood and sent it, and said, Do you know whether this is your son's coat? ³And Joseph said to me, Even so, brother, the Canaanite merchants stole me by force, ⁴and it came to pass that as they went on their way they concealed my garment as though a wild beast had met me and slain me. ⁵And so his associates sold me to the Ishmaelites. ⁶And they did not lie in saying this. For he wished to conceal the deeds of my brothers from me. And he called his brothers to himself and said, ⁷Do not tell my father what you have done to

me, but tell him as I have told Benjamin. ⁸And let the thoughts among you be such, and do not let these things come to the heart of my father."

CHAPTER 3

¹"Therefore, my children, you must also love the LORD God of the heavens and earth, and keep His commandments, following the example of the good and holy man Joseph. ²And let your mind be to good, even as you know me; for he that has his mind right sees all things rightly. ³Fear the LORD and love your neighbor; and even though the spirits of Belial claim you to afflict you with every evil, yet they will not have dominion over you, even as they did not have [dominion] over my brother Joseph. ⁴How many men wished to slay him, and God shielded him! For he that fears God and loves his neighbor cannot be smitten by the spirit of Belial, being shielded by the fear of God. ⁵Nor can he be ruled over by the device of men or beasts, for he is helped by the LORD through the love which he has toward his neighbor. ⁶For Joseph also implored our father that he would pray for his brothers, that the LORD would not impute to them as sin whatever evil they had done to him. ⁷And thus Jacob cried out: My good child, you have prevailed over the yearnings of your father Jacob. And he embraced him, and kissed him for two hours, saying, ⁸In you the prophecy of Heaven will be fulfilled [[concerning the Lamb of God, and Savior of the world]], and that a blameless One will be delivered up for lawless men, and a sinless One will die for ungodly men [[in the blood of the covenant, for the salvation of the nations and of Israel, and will destroy Belial and his servants]]."

CHAPTER 4

¹"Therefore, my children, do you see the end of the good man? Be followers of his compassion, therefore, with a good mind, that you may also wear crowns of glory. ²For the good man does not have a dark eye, for he shows mercy to all men, even though they are sinners. ³And though they devise with evil intent concerning him, by doing good he overcomes evil, being shielded by God: and he loves the righteous as his own soul. ⁴If anyone is glorified, he does not envy him; if anyone is enriched, he is not jealous; if anyone is valiant, he praises him; he praises the virtuous man; he has mercy on the poor man; he has compassion on the weak; he sings praises to God. ⁵As for him who has the fear of God, he protects him as with a shield; he helps him that loves God; he admonishes and turns back him that rejects the Most High; and he loves him that has the grace of a good spirit as his own soul."

CHAPTER 5

¹"Therefore, if you also have a good mind, then will both wicked men be at peace with you, and the profligate will revere you and turn to good; ²and the covetous will not only cease from their inordinate desire, but even give the objects of their covetousness to them that are afflicted. ³If you do well, even the unclean spirits will flee from you, and the beasts will dread you. For where there is reverence for good works and light in the mind, even darkness flees away from him. ⁴For if anyone does violence to a holy man, he converts; for the holy man is merciful to his reviler and holds his peace. ⁵And if anyone betrays a righteous man, the righteous man prays: though for a little while he is humbled, yet not long after he appears far more glorious, as was my brother Joseph."

CHAPTER 6

¹"The inclination of the good man is not in the power of the deceit of the spirit of Belial, for the messenger of peace guides his soul. ²And he does not gaze passionately on corruptible things, nor gathers together riches through a desire of pleasure. ³He does not delight in pleasure, [[he does not grieve for what is his neighbor's]], he does not satisfy himself with luxuries, he does not err in the uplifting of the eyes; the LORD is his portion. ⁴The good inclination does not receive glory nor dishonor from men, and it does not know any guile, or lie, or fighting, or reviling; for the LORD dwells in him and lights up his soul, and he always rejoices toward all men. ⁵The good mind does not have two tongues, of blessing and of cursing, of insolence and of honor, of sorrow and of joy, of quietness and of confusion, of hypocrisy and of truth, [[of poverty and of wealth]], but it has one disposition, uncorrupt and pure, concerning all men. ⁶It has no double sight, nor double hearing, for in everything which he does, or speaks, or sees, he knows that the LORD looks on his soul. ⁷And he cleanses his mind that he may not be condemned by men as well as by God. And in like manner, the works of Belial are twofold, and there is no singleness in them."

CHAPTER 7

¹"Therefore, my children, I tell you: flee the malice of Belial, for he gives a sword to them that obey him. ²And the sword is the mother of seven evils: first the mind conceives through Belial, and first there is bloodshed; secondly, ruin; thirdly, tribulation; fourthly, exile; fifthly, scarcity; sixthly, panic; seventhly, destruction. ³Therefore Cain was also delivered over to seven vengeances by God, for in every hundred years the LORD brought one plague on him. ⁴And when he was two hundred years old, he began to suffer, and in the nine-hundredth year he was destroyed. For on account of his brother Abel, he was judged with all the evils—but Lamech with seventy times seven. ⁵Because those who are like Cain in envy and hatred of brothers, will be punished with the same judgment forever."

CHAPTER 8

¹"And you, my children, must flee evildoing, envy, and hatred of brothers, and cleave to goodness and love. ²He that has a pure mind in love does not look after a woman with a view to fornication, for he has no defilement in his heart, because the Spirit of God rests on him. ³For as the sun is not defiled by shining on dung and mire, but rather dries up both and drives away the evil smell, so also the pure mind, though encompassed by the defilements of earth, rather cleanses [them] and is not itself defiled."

CHAPTER 9

¹"And I believe that there will also be evildoings among you, according to the words of Enoch the righteous—that you will commit fornication with the fornication of Sodom, and will perish, all except a few, and will renew wanton deeds with women; and the Kingdom of the LORD will not be among you, for He will immediately take it away. ²Nevertheless, the temple of God will be in your portion, and the last [temple] will be more glorious than the first. And the twelve tribes will be gathered together there, and all the nations, until the Most High will send forth His salvation in the visitation of an only begotten Prophet. [[³And He will enter into the temple, and there the LORD will be treated with outrage, and He will be lifted up on a tree. ⁴And the veil of the temple will be torn, and the Spirit of God will pass on to the nations as fire poured forth. ⁵And He will ascend from Hades and will pass from earth into Heaven. And I know how lowly He will be on earth, and how glorious in Heaven.]]"

CHAPTER 10

¹"Now when Joseph was in Egypt, I longed to see his figure and the form of his countenance, and through the prayers of my father Jacob I saw him while awake in the daytime, even his entire figure exactly as he was. ²And when he had said these things, he said to them, Therefore, my children, know that I am dying. ³Therefore, do truth and righteousness, each one to his neighbor, and judgment to confirmation, and keep the Law of the LORD and His commandments. ⁴For I leave you these things instead of an inheritance. Therefore, you must also give them to your children for an everlasting possession, for so did both Abraham, and Isaac, and Jacob. ⁵For they gave us all these things for an inheritance, saying, Keep the commandments of God until the LORD will reveal His salvation to all nations. ⁶And then you will see Enoch, Noah, and Shem, and Abraham, and Isaac, and Jacob, rising on the right hand in gladness. ⁷Then we will also rise, each one over our tribe, worshiping the King of Heaven [[who appeared on earth in the form of a Man in humility. And as many as believe on Him will rejoice with Him on the earth]]. ⁸Then all men will also rise, some to glory and some to shame. And the LORD will judge Israel first, for their unrighteousness, [[for when He appeared as God in the flesh to deliver them they did not believe Him]]. ⁹And then He will judge all the nations, [[as many as did not believe Him when He appeared on earth]]. ¹⁰And He will convict Israel through the chosen ones of the nations, even as He

reproved Esau through the Midianites, who deceived their brothers, [[so that they fell into fornication, and idolatry; and they were alienated from God]], therefore becoming children in the portion of them that fear the LORD. ¹¹If you therefore, my children, walk in holiness according to the commandments of the LORD, you will again dwell securely with me, and all Israel will be gathered to the LORD."

CHAPTER 11

¹"And I will no longer be called a ravening wolf on account of your ravages, but [[a worker of the LORD, distributing food to them that work what is good. ²And there will rise up from my seed in the latter times One]] beloved of the LORD, [[hearing His voice on the earth,]] and a doer of the good pleasure of His will, [[enlightening all the nations with new knowledge, even the light of knowledge, bursting in on Israel for salvation, and tearing away from them like a wolf, and giving to the synagogue of the nations. ³Until the consummation of the age He will be in the synagogues of the nations, and among their rulers, as a strain of music in the mouth of all. ⁴And He will be inscribed in the holy scrolls, both His work and His word, and He will be [the] Chosen One of God forever. ⁵And through them He will go to and fro as my father Jacob, saying, He will fill up that which lacks of your tribe]]."

CHAPTER 12

¹And when he finished his words, he said, "I command you, my children, carry up my bones out of Egypt, and bury me at Hebron, near my fathers." ²So Benjamin died one hundred and twenty-five years old, at a good old age, and they placed him in a coffin. ³And in the ninety-first year from the entrance of the sons of Israel into Egypt, they and their brothers secretly brought up the bones of their fathers during the Canaanite war, and they buried them in Hebron by the feet of their fathers. ⁴And they returned from the land of Canaan and dwelt in Egypt until the day of their departure from the land of Egypt.

JUBILEES

The Book of Jubilees, sometimes called Lesser Genesis (Leptogenesis), is an ancient Jewish religious work of 50 chapters, considered canonical by the Ethiopian Orthodox Church as well as Beta Israel (Ethiopian Jews), where it is known as the Book of Division. Jubilees is considered one of the pseudepigrapha by Protestant, Roman Catholic, and Eastern Orthodox Churches. It is also not considered canonical within Judaism outside of Beta Israel. It is generally dated to the 2nd century BC and its primary purpose seems to be in promoting the use of a 364-day calendar in Israel (a year equally divided into 52 weeks of seven days each). With no intercalary method given, the year would not synchronize with the seasons in the long-term. The book also reimagines some of the history of Genesis and introduces a concept foreign to Judeo-Christianity in which certain sins are unatonable.

THIS IS THE HISTORY OF THE DIVISION OF THE DAYS OF THE LAW AND OF THE TESTIMONY, OF THE EVENTS OF THE YEARS, OF THEIR PERIODS OF SEVEN, OF THEIR JUBILEES THROUGHOUT ALL THE YEARS OF THE WORLD, AS THE LORD SPOKE TO MOSES ON MOUNT SINAI WHEN HE WENT UP TO RECEIVE THE TABLETS OF THE LAW AND OF THE COMMAND, ACCORDING TO THE VOICE OF GOD AS HE SAID TO HIM, "GO UP TO THE TOP OF THE MOUNTAIN."

CHAPTER 1

¹And it came to pass in the first year of the exodus of the sons of Israel out of Egypt, in the third month, on the sixteenth day of the month, that God spoke to Moses, saying, "Come up to Me on the mountain, and I will give you two tablets of stone, of the Law and of the command, which I have written, that you may teach them." ²And Moses went up into the mountain of God, and the glory of the LORD abode on Mount Sinai, and a cloud overshadowed it [for] six days. ³And He called to Moses on the seventh day out of the midst of the cloud, and the appearance of the glory of the LORD was like a flaming fire on the top of the mountain. ⁴And Moses was on the mountain [for] forty days and forty nights, and God taught him the earlier and the later history of the division of all the days of the Law and of the Testimony. ⁵And He said, "Incline your heart to every word which I will speak to you on this mountain and write them in a scroll in order that their generations may see how I have not forsaken them for all the evil which they have worked in transgressing the covenant which I establish between Me and you for their generations this day on Mount Sinai. ⁶And thus it will come to pass when all these things come on them, that they will recognize that I am more righteous than they in all their judgments and in all their actions, and they will recognize that I have truly been with them. ⁷And write for yourself all these words which I declare to you this day, for I know their rebellion and their stiff neck, before I bring them into the land of which I swore to their fathers, to Abraham, and to Isaac, and to Jacob, saying, To your seed I will give a land flowing with milk and honey. ⁸And they will eat and be satisfied, and they will turn to strange gods, to [gods] which cannot deliver them from any of their tribulation: and this witness will be heard for a witness against them. ⁹For they will forget all My commands, [even] all that I command them, and they will walk after the nations, and after their uncleanness, and after their shame, and will serve their gods, and these will prove to them an offense, and a tribulation, and an affliction, and a snare. ¹⁰And many will perish, and they will be taken captive, and will fall into the hands of the enemy, because they have forsaken My ordinances and My commands, and the festivals of My covenant, and My Sabbaths, and My holy place which I have hallowed for Myself in their midst, and My Dwelling Place, and My sanctuary, which I have hallowed for Myself in the midst of the land, that I should set My Name on it, and that it should dwell [there]. ¹¹And they will make to themselves high places, and groves, and graven images, and they will worship, each his own [graven image], so as to go astray, and they will sacrifice their children to demons, and to all the works of the error of their hearts. ¹²And I will send witnesses to them that I may witness against them, but they will not hear, and will slay the witnesses also, and they will persecute those who seek the Law, and they will abrogate and change everything so as to work evil before My eyes. ¹³And I will hide My face from them, and I will deliver them into the hand of the nations for captivity, and for a prey, and for devouring, and I will remove them from the midst of the land, and I will scatter them among the nations. ¹⁴And they will forget all My law, and all My commands, and all My judgments, and will go astray as to new moons, and Sabbaths, and festivals, and jubilees, and ordinances. ¹⁵And after this they will turn to Me from among the nations with all their heart, and with all their soul, and with all their strength, and I will gather them from among all the nations, and they will seek Me, so that I will be found by them when they seek Me with all their heart and with all their soul. ¹⁶And I will disclose to them abounding peace with righteousness, and I will remove them—the plant of uprightness—with all My heart and with all My soul, and they will be for a blessing and not for a curse, and they will be the head and not the tail. ¹⁷And I will build My sanctuary in their midst, and I will dwell with them, and I will be their God and they will be My people in truth and righteousness. ¹⁸And I will not forsake them nor fail them; for I am the LORD their God." ¹⁹And Moses fell on his face and prayed and said, "O LORD my God, do not forsake Your people and Your inheritance, so that they should wander in the error of their hearts, and do not deliver them into the

hands of their enemies, the nations, lest they should rule over them and cause them to sin against You. ²⁰Let Your mercy, O LORD, be lifted up on Your people, and create an upright spirit in them, and do not let the spirit of Belial rule over them to accuse them before You, and to ensnare them from all the paths of righteousness, so that they may perish from before Your face. ²¹But they are Your people and Your inheritance, which You have delivered with Your great power from the hands of the Egyptians: create in them a clean heart and a holy spirit, and do not let them be ensnared in their sins from now on [and] forever." ²²And the LORD said to Moses, "I know their contrariness, and their thoughts, and their stubbornness, and they will not be obedient until they confess their own sin and the sin of their fathers. ²³And after this they will turn to Me in all uprightness and with all [their] heart and with all [their] soul, and I will circumcise the foreskin of their heart and the foreskin of the heart of their seed, and I will create in them a holy spirit, and I will cleanse them so that they will not turn away from Me from that day [and] continuously. ²⁴And their souls will cleave to Me and to all My commands, and they will fulfill My commands, and I will be their Father and they will be My children. ²⁵And they will all be called children of the living God, and every messenger and every spirit will know, yes, they will know that these are My children, and that I am their Father in uprightness and righteousness, and that I love them. ²⁶And write down for yourself all these words which I declare to you on this mountain, the first and the last, which will come to pass in all the divisions of the days in the Law, and in the Testimony, and in the periods of seven, and the jubilees continuously, until I descend and dwell with them forever." ²⁷And He said to the Messenger of the Presence, "Write for Moses from the beginning of creation until My sanctuary has been built among them for all ages. ²⁸And the LORD will appear to the eyes of all, and all will know that I am the God of Israel and the Father of all the children of Jacob, and King on Mount Zion for all ages. And Zion and Jerusalem will be holy." ²⁹And the Messenger of the Presence who went before the camp of Israel took the tablets of the divisions of the years—from the time of the creation—of the Law, and of the Testimony of the periods of seven, of the jubilees, according to the individual years, according to all the number of the jubilees [according to the individual years], from the day of the [new] creation when the heavens and the earth will be renewed and all their creation according to the powers of the heavens, and according to all the creation of the earth, until the sanctuary of the LORD will be made in Jerusalem on Mount Zion, and all the luminaries are renewed for healing, and for peace, and for blessing for all the chosen of Israel, and that thus it may be from that day and to all the days of the earth.

CHAPTER 2

¹And the Messenger of the Presence spoke to Moses according to the word of the LORD, saying, Write the complete history of the creation, how in six days the LORD God finished all His works and all that He created, and kept Sabbath on the seventh day and hallowed it for all ages, and appointed it as a sign for all His works. ²For on the first day He created the heavens which are above, and the earth, and the waters, and all the spirits which serve before Him—the messengers of the presence, and the messengers of sanctification, and the messengers [[of the spirit of fire, and the messengers]] of the spirit of the winds, and the messengers of the spirit of the clouds, and of darkness, and of snow, and of hail, and of hoarfrost, and the messengers of the voices, and of the thunder, and of the lightning, and the messengers of the spirits of cold, and of heat, and of winter, and of spring, and of autumn, and of summer, and of all the spirits of His creatures which are in the heavens and on the earth, [He created] the abysses and the darkness, evening [and night], and the light, dawn and day, which He has prepared in the knowledge of His heart. ³And we immediately saw His works, and praised Him, and lauded before Him on account of all His works; for He created seven great works on the first day. ⁴And on the second day He created the expanse in the midst of the waters, and the waters were divided on that day—half of them went up above and half of them went down below the expanse [that was] in the midst over the face of the whole earth. And this was the only work [God] created on the second day. ⁵And on the third day He commanded the waters to pass from off the face of the whole earth into one place, and the dry land to appear. ⁶And the waters did so as He commanded them, and they retired from off the face of the earth into one place outside of this expanse, and the dry land appeared. ⁷And on that day, He created for them all the seas according to their separate gathering-places, and all the rivers, and the gatherings of the waters in the mountains and on all the earth, and all the lakes, and all the dew of the earth, and the seed which is sown, and all sprouting things, and fruit-bearing trees, and trees of the wood, and the Garden of Eden, in Eden, and all [plants after their kind]. These four great works God created on the third day. ⁸And on the fourth day He created the sun, and the moon, and the stars, and set them in the expanse of the heavens, to give light on all the earth, and to rule over the day and the night, and divide the light from the darkness. ⁹And God appointed the sun to be a great sign on the earth for days, and for Sabbaths, and for months, and for feasts, and for years, and for Sabbaths of years, and for jubilees, and for all seasons of the years. ¹⁰And it divides the light from the darkness [and] for prosperity, that all things may prosper which shoot and grow on the earth. These three kinds He made on the fourth day. ¹¹And on the fifth day He created great sea monsters in the depths of the waters, for these were the first things of flesh that were created by His hands, the fish and everything that moves in the waters, and everything that flies—the birds and all their kind. ¹²And the sun rose above them to prosper [them], and above everything that was on the earth, everything that shoots out of the earth, and all fruit-bearing trees, and all flesh. These three kinds He created on the fifth day. ¹³And on the sixth day He created all the animals of the earth, and all cattle, and everything that moves on the earth. ¹⁴And after all this He created man, a man and a woman He created them, and gave him dominion over all that is on the earth, and in the seas, and over everything that flies, and over beasts and over cattle, and over everything that moves on the earth, and over the whole earth, and over all this He gave him dominion. And these four kinds He created on the sixth day. ¹⁵And there were altogether twenty-two kinds. ¹⁶And He finished all His work on the sixth day—all that is in the heavens and on the earth, and in the seas and in the abysses, and in the light and in the darkness, and in everything. ¹⁷And He gave us a great sign, the Sabbath day, that we should work six days, but keep Sabbath on the seventh day from all work. ¹⁸And all the messengers of the presence, and all the messengers of sanctification, these two great classes—He has bidden us to keep the Sabbath with Him in the heavens and on earth. ¹⁹And He said to us, "Behold, I will separate a people to Myself from among all the peoples, and these will keep the Sabbath day, and I will sanctify them to Myself as My people and will bless them; as I have sanctified the Sabbath day and sanctify [it] to Myself, even so will I bless them, and they will be My people and I will be their God. ²⁰And I have chosen the seed of Jacob from among all that I have seen, and have written him down as My firstborn son, and have sanctified him to Myself forever and ever; and I will teach them the Sabbath day, that they may keep Sabbath thereon from all work." ²¹And thus He created therein a sign in accordance with which they should keep Sabbath with us on the seventh day, to eat and to drink, and to bless Him who has created all things as He has blessed and sanctified to Himself a peculiar people above all peoples, and that they should keep Sabbath together with us. ²²And He caused His commands to ascend as a sweet savor acceptable before Him all the days. ²³There [were] twenty-two heads of mankind from Adam to Jacob, and twenty-two kinds of work were made until the seventh day; this is blessed and holy; and the former is also blessed and holy; and this one serves with that one for sanctification and blessing. ²⁴And to these [(Jacob and his seed)] it was granted that they should always be the blessed and holy ones of the first testimony and law, even as He had sanctified and blessed the Sabbath day on the seventh day. ²⁵He created the heavens, and earth, and everything that He created in six days, and God made the seventh day holy for all His works; therefore, He

commanded on its behalf that whoever does any work thereon will die, and that he who defiles it will surely die. ²⁶For that reason, command the sons of Israel to observe this day that they may keep it holy and not do any work thereon, and not to defile it, as it is holier than all other days. ²⁷And whoever profanes it will surely die, and whoever does any work thereon will surely die forever, that the sons of Israel may observe this day throughout their generations, and not be rooted out of the land; for it is a holy day and a blessed day. ²⁸And everyone who observes it and keeps Sabbath thereon from all his work will be holy and blessed throughout all days like to us. ²⁹Declare and say to the sons of Israel the law of this day, both that they should keep Sabbath thereon, and that they should not forsake it in the error of their hearts; [and] that it is not lawful to do any work thereon which is unseemly, to do their own pleasure thereon, and that they should not prepare anything thereon to be eaten or drunk, and [that it is not lawful] to draw water or bring in or take out thereon through their gates any burden, which they had not prepared for themselves on the sixth day in their dwellings. ³⁰And they will not bring in nor take out from house to house on that day; for that day is more holy and blessed than any jubilee day of the jubilees: on this we kept Sabbath in the heavens before it was made known to any flesh to keep Sabbath thereon on the earth. ³¹And the Creator of all things blessed it, but He did not sanctify all peoples and nations to keep Sabbath thereon, but Israel alone: them alone He permitted to eat and drink and to keep Sabbath thereon on the earth. ³²And the Creator of all things blessed this day which He had created for a blessing, and a sanctification, and a glory above all days. ³³This law and testimony was given to the sons of Israel as a law forever to their generations.

CHAPTER 3

¹And on the six days of the second week we brought, according to the word of God, to Adam all the beasts, and all the cattle, and all the birds, and everything that moves on the earth, and everything that moves in the water, according to their kinds, and according to their types: the beasts on the first day; the cattle on the second day; the birds on the third day; and all that which moves on the earth on the fourth day; and that which moves in the water on the fifth day. ²And Adam named them all by their respective names, and as he called them, so was their name. ³And on these five days Adam saw all these, male and female, according to every kind that was on the earth, but he was alone and found no helpmate for him. ⁴And the LORD said to us, "It is not good that the man should be alone: let us make a helpmate for him." ⁵And the LORD our God caused a deep sleep to fall on him, and he slept, and He took for the woman one rib from among his ribs, and this rib was the origin of the woman from among his ribs, and He built up the flesh in its stead, and built the woman. ⁶And He awoke Adam out of his sleep and on awaking he rose on the sixth day, and He brought her to him, and he knew her, and said to her, "This is now bone of my bones and flesh of my flesh; she will be called Woman, because she was taken from Man." ⁷Therefore man and wife will be one, and therefore a man will leave his father and his mother, and cleave to his wife, and they will be one flesh. ⁸In the first week Adam was created, and the rib—his wife; in the second week He showed her to him: and for this reason, the command was given to keep in their defilement, for a male seven days, and for a female twice seven days. ⁹And after Adam had completed forty days in the land where he had been created, we brought him into the Garden of Eden to till and keep it, but they brought his wife in on the eightieth day, and after this she entered into the Garden of Eden. ¹⁰And for this reason the command is written on the heavenly tablets in regard to her that gives birth: "If she bears a male, she will remain in her uncleanness seven days according to the first week of days, and thirty-three days she will remain in the blood of her purifying, and she will not touch any hallowed thing, nor enter into the sanctuary, until she accomplishes these days which [are prescribed] in the case of a male child. ¹¹But in the case of a female child she will remain in her uncleanness two weeks of days, according to the first two weeks, and sixty-six days in the blood of her purification, and they will be in all eighty days." ¹²And when she had completed these eighty days, we brought her into the Garden of Eden, for it is holier than all the earth besides, and every tree that is planted in it is holy. ¹³Therefore, there was ordained regarding her who bears a male or a female child the statute of those days that she should touch no hallowed thing, nor enter into the sanctuary until these days for the male or female child are accomplished. ¹⁴This is the law and testimony which was written down for Israel, in order that they should observe [it] all the days. ¹⁵And in the first week of the first jubilee, Adam and his wife were in the Garden of Eden for seven years tilling and keeping it, and we gave him work and we instructed him to do everything that is suitable for tillage. ¹⁶And he tilled [the garden], and was naked and did not know it, and was not ashamed, and he protected the garden from the birds, and beasts, and cattle, and gathered its fruit, and ate, and put aside the residue for himself and for his wife. ¹⁷And after the completion of the seven years, which he had completed there, seven years exactly, and in the second month, on the seventeenth day [of the month], the serpent came and approached the woman, and the serpent said to the woman, "Has God commanded you, saying, you will not eat of every tree of the garden?" ¹⁸And she said to it, "Of all the fruit of the trees of the garden God has said to us, Eat; but of the fruit of the tree which is in the midst of the garden God has said to us, You will not eat thereof, neither will you touch it, lest you die." ¹⁹And the serpent said to the woman, "You will not surely die, for God knows that on the day you will eat thereof, your eyes will be opened, and you will be as gods, and you will know good and evil." ²⁰And the woman saw the tree that it was agreeable and pleasant to the eye, and that its fruit was good for food, and she took thereof and ate. ²¹And when she had first covered her shame with fig-leaves, she gave thereof to Adam and he ate, and his eyes were opened, and he saw that he was naked. ²²And he took fig-leaves and sewed [them] together, and made an apron for himself, and covered his shame. ²³And God cursed the serpent and was angry with it forever. ²⁴And He was angry with the woman because she listened to the voice of the serpent and ate; and He said to her, "I will greatly multiply your sorrow and your pains; in sorrow you will bring out children, and your return will be to your husband [[or Man]], and he [[or He]] will rule over you." ²⁵And He also said to Adam, "Because you have listened to the voice of your wife, and have eaten of the tree of which I commanded you that you should not eat thereof, the ground is cursed for your sake: it will bring out thorns and thistles to you, and you will eat your bread in the sweat of your face, until you return to the earth from where you were taken; for earth you are, and to earth you will return." ²⁶And He made coats of skin for them, and clothed them, and sent them out from the Garden of Eden. ²⁷And on that day on which Adam went out from the garden, he offered as a sweet savor an offering: frankincense, galbanum, and stacte, and spices in the morning with the rising of the sun from the day when he covered his shame. ²⁸And on that day the mouth of all beasts, and of cattle, and of birds, and of whatever walks, and of whatever moves was closed, so that they could no longer speak, for they had all spoken with one another with one lip and with one tongue. ²⁹And He sent out of the Garden of Eden all flesh that was in the Garden of Eden, and all flesh was scattered according to its kinds, and according to its types to the places which had been created for them. ³⁰And to man alone did He give [the means] to cover his shame, of all the beasts and cattle. ³¹On this account, it is prescribed on the heavenly tablets as touching all those who know the judgment of the Law, that they should cover their shame, and should not uncover themselves as the nations uncover themselves. ³²And on the new moon of the fourth month, Adam and his wife went out from the Garden of Eden, and they dwelt in the land of 'Eldâ, in the land of their creation. ³³And Adam called the name of his wife Eve. ³⁴And they had no son until the first jubilee, and after this he knew her. ³⁵Now he tilled the land as he had been instructed in the Garden of Eden.

CHAPTER 4

¹And in the third week in the second jubilee she gave birth to Cain, and in the fourth she gave birth to Abel, and in the fifth she gave birth to her daughter 'Âwân. ²And in the first [year] of the third jubilee, Cain slew Abel because [God] accepted the sacrifice of Abel

and did not accept the offering of Cain. ³And he slew him in the field: and his blood cried from the ground to Heaven, complaining because he had slain him. ⁴And the LORD reproved Cain because of Abel, because he had slain him, and he made him a fugitive on the earth because of the blood of his brother, and he cursed him on the earth. ⁵And on this account, it is written on the heavenly tablets: "Cursed is he who strikes his neighbor treacherously, and let all who have seen and heard it say so; and the man who has seen and not declared [it], let him be accursed as the other." And for this reason, we announce when we come before the LORD our God all the sin which is committed in the heavens and on earth, and in light and in darkness, and everywhere. ⁷And Adam and his wife mourned for Abel four weeks of years, and in the fourth year of the fifth week they became joyful, and Adam knew his wife again, and she bore him a son, and he called his name Seth, for he said, "God has raised up a second seed to us on the earth instead of Abel, for Cain slew him." ⁸And in the sixth week he begot his daughter 'Azûrâ. ⁹And Cain took his sister 'Âwân to be his wife and she bore him Enoch at the close of the fourth jubilee. And in the first year of the first week of the fifth jubilee, houses were built on the earth, and Cain built a city, and called its name after the name of his son Enoch. ¹⁰And Adam knew his wife Eve and she bore nine more sons. ¹¹And in the fifth week of the fifth jubilee Seth took his sister 'Azûrâ to be his wife, and in the fourth [year of the sixth week] she bore him Enos. ¹²He began to call on the Name of the LORD on the earth. ¹³And in the seventh jubilee in the third week Enos took his sister Nôâm to be his wife, and she bore him a son in the third year of the fifth week, and he called his name Kenan. ¹⁴And at the close of the eighth jubilee Kenan took his sister Mûalêlêth to be his wife, and she bore him a son in the ninth jubilee, in the first week in the third year of this week, and he called his name Mahalalel. ¹⁵And in the second week of the tenth jubilee Mahalalel took to himself Dînâh to be [his] wife, the daughter of Barâkî'êl, the daughter of his father's brother, and she bore him a son in the third week in the sixth year, and he called his name Jared, for in his days the messengers of the LORD descended on the earth, those who are named the Watchers, that they should instruct the children of men, and that they should do judgment and uprightness on the earth. ¹⁶And in the eleventh jubilee Jared took to himself a wife, and her name was Bâraka, the daughter of Râsûjâl, a daughter of his father's brother, in the fourth week of this jubilee, and she bore him a son in the fifth week, in the fourth year of the jubilee, and he called his name Enoch. ¹⁷And he was the first among men that are born on earth who learned writing, and knowledge, and wisdom, and who wrote down the signs of the heavens according to the order of their months in a scroll, that men might know the seasons of the years according to the order of their separate months. ¹⁸And he was the first to write a testimony, and he testified to the sons of men among the generations of the earth, and recounted the weeks of the jubilees, and made known to them the days of the years, and set in order the months, and recounted the Sabbaths of the years as we made [them] known to him. ¹⁹And what was and what will be he saw in a vision of his sleep, as it will happen to the children of men throughout their generations until the Day of Judgment; he saw and understood everything, and wrote his testimony, and placed the testimony on earth for all the children of men and for their generations. ²⁰And in the twelfth jubilee, in the seventh week thereof, he took to himself a wife, and her name was Ednî, the daughter of Dânêl, the daughter of his father's brother, and in the sixth year in this week she bore him a son and he called his name Methuselah. ²¹And he was moreover with the messengers of God these six jubilees of years, and they showed him everything which is on earth and in the heavens, the rule of the sun, and he wrote down everything. ²²And he testified to the Watchers who had sinned with the daughters of men, for these had begun to unite themselves [with them], so as to be defiled with the daughters of men, and Enoch testified against [them] all. ²³And he was taken from among the children of men, and we conducted him into the Garden of Eden in majesty and honor, and behold, there he wrote down the condemnation and judgment of the world, and all the wickedness of the children of men. ²⁴And on account of it [God] brought the waters of the Flood on all the land of Eden; for there he was set as a sign and that he should testify against all the children of men, that he should recount all the deeds of the generations until the day of condemnation. ²⁵And he burned the incense of the sanctuary, [even] sweet spices, acceptable before the LORD on the mountain. ²⁶For the LORD has four places on the earth: the Garden of Eden, and the mountain of the East, and this mountain on which you are this day, Mount Sinai, and Mount Zion [which] will be sanctified in the new creation for a sanctification of the earth; through it the earth will be sanctified from all [its] guilt and its uncleanness throughout the generations of the world. ²⁷And in the fourteenth jubilee Methuselah took to himself a wife, Ednâ the daughter of 'Âzrîâl, the daughter of his father's brother, in the third week, in the first year of this week, and he begot a son and called his name Lamech. ²⁸And in the fifteenth jubilee in the third week Lamech took to himself a wife, and her name was Bêtênôs, the daughter of Bârâkî'îl, the daughter of his father's brother, and in this week she bore him a son and he called his name Noah, saying, "This one will comfort me for my trouble, and all my work, and for the ground which the LORD has cursed." ²⁹And at the close of the nineteenth jubilee, in the seventh week in the sixth year thereof, Adam died, and all his sons buried him in the land of his creation, and he was the first to be buried in the earth. ³⁰And he lacked seventy years of one thousand years; for one thousand years are as one day in the testimony of the heavens and therefore it was written concerning the Tree of Knowledge: "On the day that you eat thereof you will die." For this reason, he did not complete the years of this day, for he died during it. ³¹At the close of this jubilee Cain was killed after him in the same year, for his house fell on him and he died in the midst of his house, and he was killed by its stones, for with a stone he had killed Abel, and by a stone he was killed in righteous judgment. ³²For this reason it was ordained on the heavenly tablets: "With the instrument with which a man kills his neighbor with the same he will be killed; after the manner that he wounded him, in like manner they will deal with him." ³³And in the twenty-fifth jubilee Noah took to himself a wife, and her name was 'Ĕmzârâ, the daughter of Râkê'êl, the daughter of his father's brother, in the first year in the fifth week: and in the third year thereof she bore him Shem, in the fifth year thereof she bore him Ham, and in the first year in the sixth week she bore him Japheth.

CHAPTER 5

¹And it came to pass when the children of men began to multiply on the face of the earth and daughters were born to them, that the messengers of God saw them on a certain year of this jubilee, that they were beautiful to look on; and they took wives [for] themselves of all whom they chose, and they bore sons to them and they were giants. ²And lawlessness increased on the earth and all flesh corrupted its way—men, and cattle, and beasts, and birds, and everything that walks on the earth alike—all of them corrupted their ways and their orders, and they began to devour each other, and lawlessness increased on the earth, and every imagination of the thoughts of all men was evil continually. ³And God looked on the earth, and behold it was corrupt, and all flesh had corrupted its orders, and all that were on the earth had worked all manner of evil before His eyes. ⁴And He said that He would destroy man and all flesh on the face of the earth which He had created. ⁵But Noah found grace before the eyes of the LORD. ⁶And against the messengers whom He had sent on the earth, He was exceedingly angry, and He gave command to root them out of all their dominion, and He commanded us to bind them in the depths of the earth, and behold, they are bound in the midst of them and are [kept] separate. ⁷And a command went out against their sons from before His face that they should be smitten with the sword and be removed from under the heavens. ⁸And He said, "My Spirit will not always abide on man, for they are also flesh and their days will be one hundred and twenty years." ⁹And He sent His sword into their midst that each should slay his neighbor, and they began to slay each other until they all fell by the sword and were destroyed from the earth. ¹⁰And their fathers were witnesses [of their destruction], and after this they were bound in the depths of the earth forever, until the day of the great condemnation, when judgment is executed

on all those who have corrupted their ways and their works before the Lord. ¹¹And He destroyed all from their places, and there was not left [even] one of them whom He did not judge according to all their wickedness. ¹²And He made for all His works a new and righteous nature, so that they should not sin in their whole nature forever but should be all righteous—each in his kind always. ¹³And the judgment of all is ordained and written on the heavenly tablets in righteousness—even [the judgment of] all who depart from the path which is ordained for them to walk in; and if they do not walk therein, judgment is written down for every creature and for every kind. ¹⁴And there is nothing in the heavens or on earth, or in light or in darkness, or in Sheol or in the depth, or in the place of darkness [which is not judged]; and all their judgments are ordained, and written, and engraved. ¹⁵In regard to all He will judge, the great according to his greatness, and the small according to his smallness, and each according to his way. ¹⁶And He is not one who will regard the person [of any], nor is He one who will receive gifts, if He says that He will execute judgment on each: if one gave everything that is on the earth, He will not regard the gifts or the person [of any], nor accept anything at his hands, for He is a righteous judge. ¹⁷And of the sons of Israel it has been written and ordained [that] if they turn to Him in righteousness, He will forgive all their transgressions and pardon all their sins. ¹⁸It is written and ordained that He will show mercy to all who turn from all their guilt once each year. ¹⁹And as for all those who corrupted their ways and their thoughts before the Flood, no man's person was accepted save that of Noah alone; for his person was accepted in behalf of his sons, whom [God] saved from the waters of the Flood on his account; for his heart was righteous in all his ways, according as it was commanded regarding him, and he had not departed from anything that was ordained for him. ²⁰And the Lord said that He would destroy everything which was on the earth, both men, and cattle, and beasts, and birds of the air, and that which moves on the earth. ²¹And He commanded Noah to make himself an ark, that he might save himself from the waters of the Flood. ²²And Noah made the Ark in all respects as He commanded him, in the twenty-seventh jubilee of years, in the fifth week in the fifth year [[on the new moon of the first month]]. [1307 A.M.] ²³And he entered in the sixth [year] thereof [1308 A.M.], in the second month, on the new moon of the second month, until the sixteenth; and he entered, and all that we brought to him, into the Ark, and the Lord closed it from outside on the seventeenth evening. ²⁴And the Lord opened seven floodgates of [the] heavens, and the mouths of the fountains of the great deep—seven mouths in number. ²⁵And the floodgates began to pour down water from the heavens forty days and forty nights, and the fountains of the deep also sent up waters, until the whole world was full of water. ²⁶And the waters increased on the earth: the waters rose fifteen cubits above all the high mountains, and the Ark was lifted up above the earth, and it moved on the face of the waters. ²⁷And the water prevailed on the face of the earth five months—one hundred and fifty days. ²⁸And the Ark went and rested on the top of Lûbâr, one of the mountains of Ararat. ²⁹And [on the new moon] in the fourth month the fountains of the great deep were closed and the floodgates of the heavens were restrained; and on the new moon of the seventh month all the mouths of the abysses of the earth were opened, and the water began to descend into the deep below. ³⁰And on the new moon of the tenth month the tops of the mountains were seen, and on the new moon of the first month the earth became visible. ³¹And the waters disappeared from above the earth in the fifth week in the seventh year [1309 A.M.] thereof, and on the seventeenth day in the second month the earth was dry. ³²And on the twenty-seventh thereof he opened the Ark, and sent out from it beasts, and cattle, and birds, and every moving thing.

CHAPTER 6

¹And on the new moon of the third month he went out from the Ark and built an altar on that mountain. ²And he made atonement for the earth and took a kid and made atonement by its blood for all the guilt of the earth; for everything that had been on it had been destroyed, save those that were in the Ark with Noah. ³And he placed the fat thereof on the altar, and he took an ox, and a goat, and a sheep and kids, and salt, and a turtle-dove, and the young of a dove, and placed a burnt sacrifice on the altar, and poured an offering mingled with oil thereon, and sprinkled wine and scattered frankincense over everything, and caused an attractive savor to arise, acceptable before the Lord. ⁴And the Lord smelled the attractive savor, and He made a covenant with him that there should not be a flood to destroy the earth anymore; that all the days of the earth, seed-time and harvest, should never cease; cold and heat, and summer and winter, and day and night should not change their order, nor cease forever. ⁵"And you: increase and multiply on the earth, and become many on it, and be a blessing on it. The fear of you and the dread of you I will inspire in everything that is on earth and in the sea. ⁶And behold, I have given to you all beasts, and all winged things, and everything that moves on the earth, and the fish in the waters, and all things for food; as the green herbs, I have given you all things to eat. ⁷But flesh, with the life thereof, with the blood, you will not eat; for the life of all flesh is in the blood, lest your blood of your lives be required. At the hand of every man, at the hand of every [beast], I will require the blood of man. ⁸Whoever sheds man's blood by man his blood will be shed, for in the image of God He made man. ⁹And you: increase and multiply on the earth." ¹⁰And Noah and his sons swore that they would not eat any blood that was in any flesh, and he made a covenant before the Lord God forever throughout all the generations of the earth in this month. ¹¹On this account He spoke to you that you should make a covenant with the sons of Israel in this month on the mountain with an oath, and that you should sprinkle blood on them because of all the words of the covenant, which the Lord made with them forever. ¹²And this testimony is written concerning you that you should observe it continually, so that you should not eat on any day any blood of beasts, or birds, or cattle during all the days of the earth, and the man who eats the blood of beast, or of cattle, or of birds during all the days of the earth, he and his seed will be rooted out of the land. ¹³And command the sons of Israel to eat no blood, so that their names and their seed may continually be before the Lord our God. ¹⁴And for this law there is no limit of days, for it is forever. They will observe it throughout their generations, so that they may continue supplicating on your behalf with blood before the altar; every day and at the time of morning and evening they will seek forgiveness on your behalf perpetually before the Lord that they may keep it and not be rooted out. ¹⁵And He gave a sign to Noah and his sons that there should not be a flood on the [whole] earth again. ¹⁶He set His bow in the cloud for a sign of the perpetual covenant that there should not again be a flood on the earth to destroy it all the days of the earth. ¹⁷For this reason it is ordained and written on the heavenly tablets that they should celebrate the Celebration of Weeks in this month once a year, to renew the covenant every year. ¹⁸And this whole festival was celebrated in Heaven from the day of creation until the days of Noah—twenty-six jubilees and five weeks of years: and Noah and his sons observed it for seven jubilees and one week of years, until the day of Noah's death, and from the day of Noah's death his sons did away with [it] until the days of Abraham, and they ate blood. ¹⁹But Abraham observed it, and Isaac, and Jacob, and his children observed it up to your days, and in your days the sons of Israel forgot it until you celebrated it anew on this mountain. ²⁰And command the sons of Israel to observe this festival in all their generations for a command to them: one day in the year in this month they will celebrate the festival. ²¹For it is the Celebration of Weeks and the Celebration of First-Fruits: this feast is twofold and of a double nature. According to what is written and engraved concerning it, celebrate it. ²²For I have written in the scroll of the first law, in that which I have written for you, that you should celebrate it in its season, one day in the year, and I explained to you its sacrifices that the sons of Israel should remember and should celebrate it throughout their generations in this month, one day in every year. ²³And on the new moon of the first month, and on the new moon of the fourth month, and on the new moon of the seventh month, and on the new moon of the tenth month are the days of remembrance, and the days of the seasons in the four divisions of the year. These are written and ordained as a testimony forever. ²⁴And Noah ordained them

for himself as feasts for the generations forever, so that they have thereby become a memorial to him. ²⁵And on the new moon of the first month he was commanded to make for himself an ark, and on that [day] the earth became dry, and he opened [the Ark], and saw the earth. ²⁶And on the new moon of the fourth month the mouths of the depths of the abysses beneath were closed. And on the new moon of the seventh month all the mouths of the abysses of the earth were opened, and the waters began to descend into them. ²⁷And on the new moon of the tenth month the tops of the mountains were seen, and Noah was glad. ²⁸And on this account, he ordained them for himself as feasts for a memorial forever, and thus they are ordained. ²⁹And they placed them on the heavenly tablets; each had thirteen weeks; from one to another—their memorial, from the first to the second, and from the second to the third, and from the third to the fourth. ³⁰And all the days of the command will be fifty-two weeks of days, and [these will make] the entire year complete. ³¹Thus it is engraved and ordained on the heavenly tablets. And there is no neglecting [this command] for a single year or from year to year. ³²And command the sons of Israel that they observe the years according to this reckoning—three hundred and sixty-four days, and [these] will constitute a complete year, and they will not disturb its time from its days and from its feasts; for everything will fall out in them according to their testimony, and they will not leave out any day nor disturb any feasts. ³³But if they neglect and do not observe them according to His command, then they will disturb all their seasons, and the years will be dislodged from this [order], and they will neglect their ordinances. ³⁴And all the sons of Israel will forget, and will not find the path of the years, and will forget the new moons, and seasons, and Sabbaths, and they will go wrong as to all the order of the years. ³⁵For I know and from now on will declare it to you, and it is not of My own devising, for the scroll [lies] written before Me, and on the heavenly tablets the division of days is ordained, lest they forget the feasts of the covenant and walk according to the feasts of the nations after their error and after their ignorance. ³⁶For there will be those who will assuredly make observations of the moon—how [it] disturbs the seasons and comes in from year to year ten days too soon. ³⁷For this reason the years will come on them when they will disturb [the order] and make an abominable [day] the day of testimony, and an unclean day a feast day, and they will confound all the days, the holy with the unclean, and the unclean day with the holy; for they will go wrong as to the months, and Sabbaths, and feasts, and jubilees. ³⁸For this reason I command and testify to you that you may testify to them; for after your death your children will disturb [them], so that they will not make the year three hundred and sixty-four days only, and for this reason they will go wrong as to the new moons, and seasons, and Sabbaths, and festivals, and they will eat all kinds of blood with all kinds of flesh.

CHAPTER 7

¹And in the seventh week in the first year thereof, in this jubilee, Noah planted vines on the mountain on which the Ark had rested, named Lûbâr, one of the Ararat Mountains, and they produced fruit in the fourth year, and he guarded their fruit, and gathered it in this year in the seventh month. ²And he made wine from that and put it into a vessel, and kept it until the fifth year, until the first day, on the new moon of the first month. ³And he celebrated with joy the day of this feast, and he made a burnt sacrifice to the LORD—one young ox, and one ram, and seven sheep, each a year old, and a kid of the goats, that he might make atonement thereby for himself and his sons. ⁴And he prepared the kid first and placed some of its blood on the flesh that was on the altar which he had made, and all the fat he laid on the altar where he made the burnt sacrifice, and the ox, and the ram, and the sheep, and he laid all their flesh on the altar. ⁵And he placed all their offerings mingled with oil on it, and afterward he sprinkled wine on the fire which he had previously made on the altar, and he placed incense on the altar and caused a sweet savor to ascend acceptable before the LORD his God. ⁶And he rejoiced and drank of this wine—he and his children with joy. ⁷And it was evening, and he went into his tent, and being drunken, he lay down and slept, and was uncovered in his tent as he slept. ⁸And Ham saw his father Noah naked and went out and told his two brothers outside. ⁹And Shem took his garment and arose, he and Japheth, and they placed the garment on their shoulders and went backward and covered the shame of their father, and their faces were backward. ¹⁰And Noah awoke from his sleep and knew all that his younger son had done to him, and he cursed his son and said, "Cursed be Canaan; he will be an enslaved servant to his brothers." ¹¹And he blessed Shem and said, "Blessed is the LORD God of Shem, and Canaan will be his servant. ¹²God will enlarge Japheth, and God will dwell in the dwelling of Shem, and Canaan will be his servant." ¹³And Ham knew that his father had cursed his younger son, and he was displeased that he had cursed his son, and he parted from his father, he and his sons with him—Cush, and Mizraim, and Put, and Canaan. ¹⁴And he built a city for himself and called its name after the name of his wife Nê'êlâtamâ'ûk. ¹⁵And Japheth saw it, and became envious of his brother, and he too built a city for himself, and he called its name after the name of his wife 'Adâtanêsês. ¹⁶And Shem dwelt with his father Noah, and he built a city close to his father on the mountain, and he too called its name after the name of his wife Sêdêqêtêlĕbâb. ¹⁷And behold, these three cities are near Mount Lûbâr: Sêdêqêtêlĕbâb, fronting the mountain on its east, and Na'êlâtamâ'ûk on the south, [and] 'Adatanêsês toward the west. ¹⁸And these are the sons of Shem: Elam, and Asshur, and Arphaxad (this [son] was born two years after the Flood), and Lud, and Aram. ¹⁹The sons of Japheth: Gomer, and Magog, and Madai, and Javan, Tubal, and Meshech, and Tiras. These are the sons of Noah. ²⁰And in the twenty-eighth jubilee Noah began to prescribe on his sons' sons the ordinances and commands, and all the judgments that he knew, and he exhorted his sons to observe righteousness, and to cover the shame of their flesh, and to bless their Creator, and honor father and mother, and love their neighbor, and guard their souls from fornication, and uncleanness, and all iniquity. ²¹For owing to these three things the Flood came on the earth, namely, owing to the fornication wherein the Watchers against the law of their ordinances went whoring after the daughters of men, and took wives [for] themselves of all which they chose: and they made the beginning of uncleanness. ²²And they begot sons, the Nâphîdîm, and they were all different, and they devoured one another: and the Giants slew the Nâphîl, and the Nâphîl slew the Eljô, and the Eljô mankind, and one man another. ²³And everyone sold himself to work iniquity and to shed much blood, and the earth was filled with iniquity. ²⁴And after this they sinned against the beasts, and birds, and all that moves and walks on the earth: and much blood was shed on the earth, and every imagination and desire of men they imagined [was] vanity and evil continually. ²⁵And the LORD destroyed everything from off the face of the earth; because of the wickedness of their deeds, and because of the blood which they had shed in the midst of the earth He destroyed everything. ²⁶"And we were left, you and I, my sons, and everything that entered with us into the Ark, and behold, I see your works before me that you do not walk in righteousness; for you have begun to walk in the path of destruction, and you are parting from one another, and are envious of one another, and [so it is] that you are not in harmony, my sons, each with his brother. ²⁷For I see and behold [that] the demons have begun [their] seductions against you and against your children, and now I fear on your behalf that after my death you will shed the blood of men on the earth, and that you, too, will be destroyed from the face of the earth. ²⁸For whoever sheds man's blood, and whoever eats the blood of any flesh, will all be destroyed from the earth. ²⁹And there will not be left any man that eats blood or that sheds the blood of man on the earth, nor will there be left to him any seed or descendants living under the heavens; for they will go into Sheol, and they will descend into the place of condemnation. And into the darkness of the deep they will all be removed by a violent death. ³⁰No blood will be seen on you of all the blood there will be all the days in which you have killed any beasts, or cattle, or whatever flies on the earth; and work a good work for your souls by covering that which has been shed on the face of the earth. ³¹And you will not be like him who eats with blood, but guard yourselves that none may eat blood before you: cover the blood, for thus I have been commanded to testify to you and your children, together with all flesh. ³²And do not permit the soul to be eaten with the flesh, that

your blood, which is your life, may not be required at the hand of any flesh that sheds [it] on the earth. ³³For the earth will not be clean from the blood which has been shed on it; for [only] through the blood of him that shed it will the earth be purified throughout all its generations. ³⁴And now, my children, listen: work judgment and righteousness that you may be planted in righteousness over the face of the whole earth, and your glory [will be] lifted up before my God, who saved me from the waters of the Flood. ³⁵And behold, you will go and build cities for yourselves, and plant in them all the plants that are on the earth, and moreover all fruit-bearing trees. ³⁶For three years the fruit of everything that is eaten will not be gathered: and in the fourth year its fruit will be accounted holy, acceptable before the Most High God, who created the heavens, and earth, and all things. Let them offer in abundance the first of the wine and oil [as] first-fruits on the altar of the LORD, who receives it, and let the servants of the house of the LORD eat what is left before the altar which receives [it]. ³⁷And in the fifth year make the release so that you release it in righteousness and uprightness, and you will be righteous, and all that you plant will prosper. ³⁸For thus did Enoch, the father of your father command Methuselah, his son, and Methuselah his son Lamech, and Lamech commanded me all the things which his fathers commanded him. ³⁹And I also will give you command, my sons, as Enoch commanded his son in the first jubilees: while still living, the seventh in his generation, he commanded and testified to his son and to his sons' sons until the day of his death."

CHAPTER 8

¹In the twenty-ninth jubilee, in the first week, in the beginning thereof, Arphaxad took to himself a wife and her name was Râsû'ĕjâ, [the daughter of Sûsân,] the daughter of Elam, and she bore him a son in the third year in this week, and he called his name Kâinâm. ²And the son grew, and his father taught him writing, and he went to seek for himself a place where he might seize for himself a city. ³And he found a writing which former [generations] had carved on the rock, and he read what was thereon, and he transcribed it and sinned owing to it; for it contained the teaching of the Watchers in accordance with which they used to observe the omens of the sun, and moon, and stars in all the signs of the heavens. ⁴And he wrote it down and said nothing regarding it; for he was afraid to speak to Noah about it lest he should be angry with him on account of it. ⁵And in the thirtieth jubilee, in the second week, in the first year thereof, he took to himself a wife, and her name was Mêlkâ, the daughter of Madai, the son of Japheth, and in the fourth year he begot a son, and called his name Shelah, for he said, "Truly I have been sent." ⁶[And in the fourth year he was born], and Shelah grew up and took to himself a wife, and her name was Mû'ak, the daughter of Kêsêd, his father's brother, in the thirty-first jubilee, in the fifth week, in the first year thereof. ⁷And she bore him a son in the fifth year thereof, and he called his name Eber: and he took to himself a wife, and her name was 'Azûrâd, the daughter of Nêbrôd, in the thirty-second jubilee, in the seventh week, in the third year thereof. ⁸And in the sixth year thereof, she bore him a son, and he called his name Peleg, for in the days when he was born the children of Noah began to divide the earth among themselves; for this reason he called his name Peleg. ⁹And they divided [it] secretly among themselves and told it to Noah. ¹⁰And it came to pass in the beginning of the thirty-third jubilee that they divided the earth into three parts, for Shem, and Ham, and Japheth, according to the inheritance of each, in the first year in the first week, when one of us, who had been sent, was with them. ¹¹And he called his sons, and they drew near to him, they and their children, and he divided the earth into the lots, which his three sons were to take in possession, and they reached out their hands, and took the writing out of the bosom of their father Noah. ¹²And there came out on the writing as Shem's lot the middle of the earth which he should take as an inheritance for himself and for his sons, for the perpetual generations, from the middle of the mountain range of Râfâ, from the mouth of the water from the River Tînâ, and his portion goes toward the west through the midst of this river, and it extends until it reaches the water of the abysses, out of which this river goes out and pours its waters into the sea Mê'at, and this river flows into the Great Sea. And all that is toward the north is Japheth's, and all that is toward the south belongs to Shem. ¹³And it extends until it reaches Kârâsô: this is in the bosom of the tongue which looks toward the south. ¹⁴And his portion extends along the Great Sea, and it extends in a straight line until it reaches the west of the tongue which looks toward the south; for this sea is called the tongue of the Egyptian Sea. ¹⁵And it turns from here toward the south toward the mouth of the Great Sea on the shore of [its] waters, and it extends to the west to 'Afrâ and it extends until it reaches the waters of the River Gihon, and to the south of the waters of Gihon, to the banks of this river. ¹⁶And it extends toward the east until it reaches the Garden of Eden, to the south thereof, [to the south] and from the east of the whole land of Eden and of the whole east [thereof], it turns to the east, and proceeds until it reaches the east of the mountain named Râfâ, and it descends to the bank of the mouth of the River Tînâ. ¹⁷This portion came out by lot for Shem and his sons, that they should possess it forever to his generations forevermore. ¹⁸And Noah rejoiced that this portion came out for Shem and for his sons, and he remembered all that he had spoken with his mouth in prophecy; for he had said, "Blessed is the LORD God of Shem, and may the LORD dwell in the dwelling of Shem." ¹⁹And he knew that the Garden of Eden is the Holy of Holies and the dwelling of the LORD, and Mount Sinai—the center of the desert, and Mount Zion—the center of the navel of the earth: these three were created as holy places facing each other. ²⁰And he blessed the God of gods who had put the word of the LORD into his mouth, and [blessed] the LORD forevermore. ²¹And he knew that a blessed portion and a blessing had come to Shem and his sons to the generations forever—the whole land of Eden and the whole land of the Red Sea, and the whole land of the east, and India, and on the Red Sea and the mountains thereof, and all the land of Bashan, and all the land of Lebanon and the islands of Kaftûr, and all the mountains of Sanîr and 'Amânâ, and the mountains of Asshur in the north, and all the land of Elam, Asshur, and Bâbêl, and Sûsân, and Mâ'ĕdâi, and all the mountains of Ararat, and all the region beyond the sea, which is beyond the mountains of Asshur toward the north, a blessed and spacious land, and all that is in it is very good. ²²And for Ham came out the second portion, beyond the Gihon toward the south to the right of the Garden, and it extends toward the south and it extends to all the mountains of fire, and it extends toward the west to the Sea of 'Atêl and it extends toward the west until it reaches the Sea of Mâ'ûk—that [sea] into which everything which is not destroyed descends. ²³And it goes out toward the north to the limits of Gâdîr, and it goes out to the coast of the waters of the sea to the waters of the Great Sea until it draws near to the River Gihon and goes along the River Gihon until it reaches the right of the Garden of Eden. ²⁴And this is the land which came out for Ham as the portion which he was to occupy forever for himself and his sons to their generations forever. ²⁵And for Japheth came out the third portion beyond the River Tînâ to the north of the outflow of its waters, and it extends northeastward to the whole region of Gog and to all the country east thereof. ²⁶And it extends northward to the north, and it extends to the mountains of Qêlt toward the north, and toward the Sea of Mâ'ûk, and it goes out to the east of Gâdîr as far as the region of the waters of the sea. ²⁷And it extends until it approaches the west of Fârâ, and it returns toward 'Afêrâg, and it extends eastward to the waters of the Sea of Mê'at. ²⁸And it extends to the region of the River Tînâ in a northeasterly direction until it approaches the boundary of its waters toward the mountain Râfâ, and it turns toward the north. ²⁹This is the land which came out for Japheth and his sons as the portion of his inheritance which he should possess for himself and his sons, for their generations forever: five great islands, and a great land in the north. ³⁰But it is cold, and the land of Ham is hot, and the land of Shem is neither hot nor cold, but it is of blended cold and heat.

CHAPTER 9

¹And Ham divided among his sons, and the first portion came out for Cush toward the east, and to the west of him for Mizraim, and to the west of him for Put, and to the west of him [and to the west thereof] on the sea for Canaan. ²And Shem also divided among his

sons, and the first portion came out for Elam and his sons, to the east of the River Tigris until it approaches the east, the whole land of India, and on the Red Sea on its coast, and the waters of Dêdân, and all the mountains of Mebrî and 'Êlâ, and all the land of Sûsân and all that is on the side of Pharnâk to the Red Sea and the River Tînâ. ³And for Asshur came out the second portion, all the land of Asshur, and Nineveh, and Shinar, and to the border of India, and it ascends and skirts the river. ⁴And for Arphaxad came out the third portion, all the land of the region of the Chaldees to the east of the Euphrates, bordering on the Red Sea, and all the waters of the desert close to the tongue of the sea which looks toward Egypt, all the land of Lebanon, and Sanîr, and 'Amânâ to the border of the Euphrates. ⁵And for Aram there came out the fourth portion, all the land of Mesopotamia between the Tigris and the Euphrates to the north of the Chaldees to the border of the mountains of Asshur and the land of 'Arârâ. ⁶And there came out for Lud the fifth portion, the mountains of Asshur and all pertaining to them until it reaches the Great Sea, and until it reaches the east of his brother Asshur. ⁷And Japheth also divided the land of his inheritance among his sons. ⁸And the first portion came out for Gomer to the east from the north side to the River Tînâ; and in the north there came out for Magog all the inner portions of the north until it reaches to the Sea of Mê'at. ⁹And for Madai came out as his portion that he should possess from the west of his two brothers to the islands, and to the coasts of the islands. ¹⁰And for Javan came out the fourth portion, every island and the islands which are toward the border of Lud. ¹¹And for Tubal there came out the fifth portion in the midst of the tongue which approaches toward the border of the portion of Lud to the second tongue, to the region beyond the second tongue to the third tongue. ¹²And for Meshech came out the sixth portion, all the region beyond the third tongue until it approaches the east of Gâdîr. ¹³And for Tiras there came out the seventh portion: four great islands in the midst of the sea, which reach to the portion of Ham [[and the islands of Kamâtûrî came out by lot for the sons of Arphaxad as his inheritance]]. ¹⁴And thus the sons of Noah divided to their sons in the presence of their father Noah, and he bound them all by an oath, invoking a curse on everyone that sought to seize the portion which had not fallen [to him] by his lot. ¹⁵And they all said, "So be it; so be it," for themselves and their sons forever throughout their generations until the Day of Judgment, on which the LORD God will judge them with a sword and with fire, for all the unclean wickedness of their errors, with which they have filled the earth with transgression, and uncleanness, and fornication, and sin.

CHAPTER 10

¹And in the third week of this jubilee the unclean demons began to lead the children of the sons of Noah astray, and to make [them] to err, and destroy them. ²And the sons of Noah came to their father Noah, and they told him concerning the demons which were leading astray, and blinding, and slaying his sons' sons. ³And he prayed before the LORD his God, and said, "God of the spirits of all flesh, || Who has shown mercy to me, || And has saved me and my sons from the waters of the Flood, || And has not caused me to perish as you did the sons of perdition, || For Your grace has been great toward me, || And great has been Your mercy to my soul: Let Your grace be lifted up on my sons, || And do not let wicked spirits rule over them || Lest they should destroy them from the earth. ⁴But bless me and my sons, || That we may increase, and multiply, and replenish the earth. ⁵And You know how Your Watchers, || The fathers of these spirits, acted in my day: And as for these spirits which are living, || Imprison them and hold them fast in the place of condemnation, || And do not let them bring destruction on the sons of Your servant, my God; For these are malevolent, and created in order to destroy. ⁶And do not let them rule over the spirits of the living, || For You alone can exercise dominion over them. And do not let them have power over the sons of the righteous || From now on and forevermore." ⁷And the LORD our God commanded us to bind all. ⁸And the chief of the spirits, Mastêmâ, came and said, "LORD, Creator, let some of them remain before me, and let them listen to my voice, and do all that I will say to them; for if some of them are not left to me, I will not be able to execute the power of my will on the sons of men; for these are for corruption and leading astray before my judgment, for great is the wickedness of the sons of men." ⁹And He said, "Let the tenth part of them remain before him, and let nine parts descend into the place of condemnation." ¹⁰And He commanded that one of us should teach Noah all their medicines; for He knew that they would not walk in uprightness, nor strive in righteousness. ¹¹And we did according to all His words: we bound all the malevolent evil ones in the place of condemnation, and a tenth part of them we left that they might be subject before Satan on the earth. ¹²And we explained to Noah all the medicines of their diseases, together with their seductions, how he might heal them with herbs of the earth. ¹³And Noah wrote down all things in a scroll as we instructed him concerning every kind of medicine. Thus, the evil spirits were precluded from [hurting] the sons of Noah. ¹⁴And he gave all that he had written to Shem, his eldest son, for he loved him exceedingly above all his sons. ¹⁵And Noah slept with his fathers and was buried on Mount Lûbâr in the land of Ararat. ¹⁶Nine hundred and fifty years he completed in his life—nineteen jubilees, and two weeks, and five years. ¹⁷And in his life on earth he excelled the children of men, save Enoch because of the righteousness wherein he was perfect. For Enoch's office was ordained for a testimony to the generations of the world, so that he should recount all the deeds of generation to generation, until the Day of Judgment. ¹⁸And in the thirty-third jubilee, in the first year in the second week, Peleg took to himself a wife, whose name was Lômnâ, the daughter of Sînâ'ar, and she bore him a son in the fourth year of this week, and he called his name Reu, for he said, "Behold, the children of men have become evil through the wicked purpose of building for themselves a city and a tower in the land of Shinar." ¹⁹For they departed from the land of Ararat eastward to Shinar, for in his days they built the city and the tower, saying, "Go forth; let us ascend thereby into the heavens." ²⁰And they began to build, and in the fourth week they made brick with fire, and the bricks served them for stone, and the clay with which they cemented them together was asphalt, which comes out of the sea and out of the fountains of water in the land of Shinar. ²¹And they built it; forty-three years they were building it; its breadth was two hundred and three bricks, and the height [of a brick] was the third of one; its height amounted to five thousand and four hundred and thirty-three cubits and two palms, and [the extent of one wall was] thirteen stadia [[and of the other thirty stadia]]. ²²And the LORD our God said to us, "Behold, they are one people, and they begin to do [this], and now nothing will be withheld from them. Go forth; let us go down and confound their language that they may not understand one another's speech, and they may be dispersed into cities and nations, and one purpose will no longer abide with them until the Day of Judgment." ²³And the LORD descended, and we descended with Him to see the city and the tower which the children of men had built. ²⁴And He confounded their language, and they no longer understood one another's speech, and then they ceased to build the city and the tower. ²⁵For this reason the whole land of Shinar is called Babel, because the LORD confounded all the language of the children of men there, and from there they were dispersed into their cities, each according to his language and his nation. ²⁶And the LORD sent a mighty wind against the tower and overthrew it on the earth, and behold, it was between Asshur and Babylon in the land of Shinar, and they called its name "Overthrow." ²⁷In the fourth week, in the first year, in the beginning thereof, in the thirty-fourth jubilee, they were dispersed from the land of Shinar. ²⁸And Ham and his sons went into the land which he was to occupy, which he acquired as his portion in the land of the south. ²⁹And Canaan saw the land of Lebanon to the river of Egypt that it was very good, and he did not go into the land of his inheritance to the west [that is to] the sea, and he dwelt in the land of Lebanon, eastward and westward from the border of Jordan and from the border of the sea. ³⁰And his father Ham, and his brothers Cush and Mizraim, said to him, "You have settled in a land which is not yours, and which did not fall to us by lot: do not do so; for if you do so, you and your sons will fall in the land and [be] accursed through sedition; for by sedition you have settled, and by sedition your children will fall, and you will be rooted out

forever. ³¹Do not dwell in the dwelling of Shem, for to Shem and to his sons did it come by their lot. ³²Cursed are you and cursed will you be beyond all the sons of Noah, by the curse by which we bound ourselves by an oath in the presence of the Holy Judge, and in the presence of our father Noah." ³³But he did not listen to them and dwelt in the land of Lebanon from Hamath to the entering of Egypt—he and his sons until this day. ³⁴And for this reason that land is named Canaan. ³⁵And Japheth and his sons went toward the sea and dwelt in the land of their portion, and Madai saw the land of the sea and it did not please him, and he begged [for] a [portion] from Elam, and Asshur, and Arphaxad, his wife's brother, and he dwelt in the land of Media, near to his wife's brother, until this day. ³⁶And he called his dwelling-place and the dwelling-place of his sons Media, after the name of their father Madai.

CHAPTER 11

¹And in the thirty-fifth jubilee, in the third week, in the first year thereof, Reu took to himself a wife, and her name was 'Ôrâ, the daughter of 'Ûr, the son of Kêsêd, and she bore him a son, and he called his name Sêrôḫ, in the seventh year of this week in this jubilee. ²And the sons of Noah began to war on each other, to take captive and to slay each other, and to shed the blood of men on the earth, and to eat blood, and to build strong cities, and walls, and towers, and individuals [began] to exalt themselves above the nation, and to found the beginnings of kingdoms, and to go to war—people against people, and nation against nation, and city against city, and all [began] to do evil, and to acquire arms, and to teach their sons war, and they began to capture cities, and to sell menservants and maidservants. ³And 'Ûr, the son of Kêsêd, built the city of 'Arâ of the Chaldees, and called its name after his own name and the name of his father. ⁴And they made molten images for themselves, and they each worshiped the idol, the molten image which they had made for themselves, and they began to make graven images and unclean statues, and malevolent spirits assisted and seduced [them] into committing transgression and uncleanness. ⁵And the prince Mastêmâ exerted himself to do all this, and he sent out other spirits, those which were put under his hand, to do all manner of wrong and sin, and all manner of transgression, to corrupt and destroy, and to shed blood on the earth. ⁶For this reason he called the name of Sêrôḫ, Serug, for everyone turned to do all manner of sin and transgression. ⁷And he grew up and dwelt in Ur of the Chaldees, near to the father of his wife's mother, and he worshiped idols, and he took to himself a wife in the thirty-sixth jubilee, in the fifth week, in the first year thereof, and her name was Mêlkâ, the daughter of Kâbêr, the daughter of his father's brother. ⁸And she bore him Nahor in the first year of this week, and he grew and dwelt in Ur of the Chaldees, and his father taught him the research of the Chaldees to divine and portend, according to the signs of the heavens. ⁹And in the thirty-seventh jubilee, in the sixth week, in the first year thereof, he took to himself a wife, and her name was 'Îjâskâ, the daughter of Nêstâg of the Chaldees. ¹⁰And she bore him Terah in the seventh year of this week. ¹¹And the prince Mastêmâ sent ravens and birds to devour the seed which was sown in the land, in order to destroy the land, and rob the children of men of their labors. Before they could plow in the seed, the ravens picked [it] from the surface of the ground. ¹²And for this reason he called his name Terah, because the ravens and the birds reduced them to destitution and devoured their seed. ¹³And the years began to be barren, owing to the birds, and they devoured all the fruit of the trees from the trees: it was only with great effort that they could save a little of all the fruit of the earth in their days. ¹⁴And in this thirty-ninth jubilee, in the second week in the first year, Terah took to himself a wife, and her name was 'Êdnâ, the daughter of 'Abrâm, the daughter of his father's sister. ¹⁵And in the seventh year of this week she bore him a son, and he called his name Abram, by the name of the father of his mother, for he had died before his daughter had conceived a son. ¹⁶And the child began to understand the errors of the earth, that all went astray after graven images and after uncleanness, and his father taught him writing, and he was two weeks of years old, and he separated himself from his father that he might not worship idols with him. ¹⁷And he began to pray to the Creator of all things that He might save him from the errors of the children of men, and that his portion should not fall into error after uncleanness and vileness. ¹⁸And the seed-time came for the sowing of seed on the land, and they all went out together to protect their seed against the ravens, and Abram went out with those that went, and the child was a youth of fourteen years. ¹⁹And a cloud of ravens came to devour the seed, and Abram ran to meet them before they settled on the ground and cried to them before they settled on the ground to devour the seed, and said, "Do not descend! Return to the place where you came!" And they proceeded to turn back. ²⁰And he caused the clouds of ravens to turn back that day seventy times, and of all the ravens throughout all the land where Abram was there settled there not so much as one. ²¹And all who were with him throughout all the land saw him cry out, and all the ravens turn back, and his name became great in all the land of the Chaldees. ²²And there came to him this year all those that wished to sow, and he went with them until the time of sowing ceased: and they sowed their land, and that year they brought enough grain home and ate and were satisfied. ²³And in the first year of the fifth week Abram taught those who made implements for oxen, the craftsmen in wood, and they made a vessel above the ground, facing the frame of the plow, in order to put the seed thereon, and the seed fell down from that on the share of the plow, and was hidden in the earth, and they no longer feared the ravens. ²⁴And after this manner they made [vessels] above the ground on all the frames of the plows, and they sowed and tilled all the land, according as Abram commanded them, and they no longer feared the birds.

CHAPTER 12

¹And it came to pass in the sixth week, in the seventh year thereof, that Abram spoke to his father Terah, saying, "Father!" And he said, "Behold, here I am, my son." ²And he said, "What help and profit do we have from those idols which you worship, and before which you bow yourself? ³For there is no spirit in them, for they are mute forms, and a misleading of the heart. Do not worship them: ⁴worship the God of Heaven, who causes the rain and the dew to descend on the earth, and does everything on the earth, and has created everything by His word, and all life is from before His face. ⁵Why do you worship things that have no spirit in them? For they are the work of [men's] hands, and you bear them on your shoulders, and you have no help from them, but they are a great cause of shame to those who make them, and a misleading of the heart to those who worship them: do not worship them." ⁶And his father said to him, "I also know it, my son, but what will I do with a people who have made me to serve before them? ⁷And if I tell them the truth, they will slay me, for their soul cleaved to them to worship them and honor them. Keep silent, my son, lest they slay you." ⁸And he spoke these words to his two brothers, and they were angry with him and he kept silent. ⁹And in the fortieth jubilee, in the second week, in the seventh year thereof, Abram took to himself a wife, and her name was Sarai, the daughter of his father, and she became his wife. ¹⁰And his brother Haran took to himself a wife in the third year of the third week, and she bore him a son in the seventh year of this week, and he called his name Lot. ¹¹And his brother Nahor took to himself a wife. ¹²And in the sixtieth year of the life of Abram, that is, in the fourth week, in the fourth year thereof, Abram arose by night, and burned the house of the idols, and he burned all that was in the house, and no man knew it. ¹³And they arose in the night and sought to save their gods from the midst of the fire. ¹⁴And Haran tried to save them, but the fire flamed over him, and he was burned in the fire, and he died in Ur of the Chaldees before his father Terah, and they buried him in Ur of the Chaldees. ¹⁵And Terah went out from Ur of the Chaldees, he and his sons, to go into the land of Lebanon and into the land of Canaan, and he dwelt in the land of Haran, and Abram dwelt with his father Terah in Haran [for] two weeks of years. ¹⁶And in the sixth week, in the fifth year thereof, Abram sat up throughout the night on the new moon of the seventh month to observe the stars from the evening to the morning, in order to see what the nature of the year would be with regard to the rains, and he was alone as he sat and observed. ¹⁷And a word came into his heart and he said, "All the signs of the stars, and the signs of the moon and of the sun are

all in the hand of the LORD. Why do I search [them] out? ¹⁸If He desires, He causes it to rain, morning and evening; and if He desires, He withholds it, and all things are in His hand." ¹⁹And he prayed that night and said, "My God, God Most High, You alone are my God, and I have chosen You and Your dominion. And You have created all things, and all things that exist are the work of Your hands. ²⁰Deliver me from the hands of evil spirits who have sway over the thoughts of men's hearts, and do not let them lead me astray from You, my God. And establish me and my seed forever so that we do not go astray from now and forevermore." ²¹And he said, "Will I return to Ur of the Chaldees who seek my face that I may return to them, or am I to remain here in this place? The right path before You—prosper it in the hands of Your servant that he may fulfill [it] and that I may not walk in the deceitfulness of my heart, O my God." ²²And he made an end of speaking and praying, and behold, the word of the LORD was sent to him through me, saying, "Go forth from your country, and from your relatives, and from the house of your father to a land which I will show you, and I will make you a great and numerous nation. ²³And I will bless you, and I will make your name great, and you will be blessed in the earth, and all [the] families of the earth will be blessed in you, and I will bless them that bless you, and curse them that curse you. ²⁴And I will be God to you and your son, and to your son's son, and to all your seed: do not fear, from now and to all generations of the earth I am your God." ²⁵And the LORD God said, "Open his mouth and his ears that he may hear and speak with his mouth, with the language which has been revealed," for it had ceased from the mouths of all the children of men from the day of the overthrow [of Babel]. ²⁶And I opened his mouth, and his ears, and his lips, and I began to speak with him in Hebrew in the tongue of the creation. ²⁷And he took the scrolls of his fathers, and these were written in Hebrew, and he transcribed them, and he began from then on to study them, and I made known to him that which he could not [understand], and he studied them during the six rainy months. ²⁸And it came to pass in the seventh year of the sixth week that he spoke to his father and informed him that he would leave Haran to go into the land of Canaan to see it and [then] return to him. ²⁹And his father Terah said to him, "Go in peace; may the perpetual God make your path straight, and the LORD [[be with you, and]] protect you from all evil, and grant grace, mercy, and favor to you before those who see you, and may none of the children of men have power over you to harm you; go in peace. ³⁰And if you see a land pleasant to your eyes to dwell in, then arise and take me to you, and take Lot, the son of your brother Haran, with you as your own son: the LORD be with you. ³¹And leave your brother Nahor with me until you return in peace, and we all go with you together."

CHAPTER 13

¹And Abram journeyed from Haran, and he took his wife Sarai, and Lot, his brother Haran's son, to the land of Canaan, and he came into Asshur, and proceeded to Shechem, and dwelt near a lofty oak. ²And he saw, and behold, the land was very pleasant from the entering of Hamath to the lofty oak. ³And the LORD said to him, "To you and to your seed I will give this land." ⁴And he built an altar there, and he offered a burnt sacrifice thereon to the LORD, who had appeared to him. ⁵And he left from there to the mountain [with] Bethel on the west and Ai on the east and pitched his tent there. ⁶And he saw, and behold, the land was very wide and good, and everything grew thereon—vines, and figs, and pomegranates, oaks, and hollies, and terebinths, and oil trees, and cedars, and cypresses, and date trees, and all trees of the field, and there was water on the mountains. ⁷And he blessed the LORD who had led him out of Ur of the Chaldees and had brought him to this land. ⁸And it came to pass in the first year, in the seventh week, on the new moon of the first month, that he built an altar on this mountain, and called on the Name of the LORD: "You, the perpetual God, are my God." ⁹And he offered a burnt sacrifice to the LORD on the altar that He should be with him and not forsake him all the days of his life. ¹⁰And he left from there and went toward the south, and he came to Hebron, and Hebron was built at that time, and he dwelt there two years, and he went into the land of the south, to Bealoth, and there was a famine in the land. ¹¹And Abram went into Egypt in the third year of the week, and he dwelt in Egypt five years before his wife was torn away from him. ¹²Now Tanis [(Zoan)] in Egypt was at that time built—seven years after Hebron. ¹³And it came to pass when Pharaoh seized Sarai, the wife of Abram, that the LORD plagued Pharaoh and his house with great plagues because of Sarai, Abram's wife. ¹⁴And Abram was very glorious by reason of possessions in sheep, and cattle, and donkeys, and horses, and camels, and menservants, and maidservants, and in exceeding silver and gold. And Lot also, his brother's son, was wealthy. ¹⁵And Pharaoh gave back Sarai, the wife of Abram, and he sent him out of the land of Egypt, and he journeyed to the place where he had pitched his tent at the beginning, to the place of the altar, with Ai on the east and Bethel on the west, and he blessed the LORD his God who had brought him back in peace. ¹⁶And it came to pass in the forty-first jubilee, in the third year of the first week, that he returned to this place and offered a burnt sacrifice there, and called on the Name of the LORD, and said, "You, the Most High God, are my God forever and ever." ¹⁷And in the fourth year of this week Lot parted from him, and Lot dwelt in Sodom, and the men of Sodom were sinners exceedingly. ¹⁸And it grieved him in his heart that his brother's son had parted from him, for he had no children. ¹⁹In that year, when Lot was taken captive, the LORD said to Abram after Lot had parted from him, in the fourth year of this week: "Lift up your eyes from the place where you are dwelling—northward, and southward, and westward, and eastward. ²⁰For all the land which you see I will give to you and to your seed forever, and I will make your seed as the sand of the sea: though a man may number the dust of the earth, yet your seed will not be numbered. ²¹Arise, walk in the length of it and the breadth of it, and see it all; for to your seed I will give it." And Abram went to Hebron and dwelt there. ²²And in this year Chedorlaomer, king of Elam, and Amraphel, king of Shinar, and Arioch, king of Sêllâsar and Têrgâl, king of nations, came and slew the king of Gomorrah, and the king of Sodom fled, and many fell through wounds in the Valley of Siddim, by the Salt Sea. ²³And they took Sodom, and Adam, and Zeboim captive, and they took Lot captive also, the son of Abram's brother, and all his possessions, and they went to Dan. ²⁴And one who had escaped came and told Abram that his brother's son had been taken captive and [Abram] armed his household servants. ²⁵For Abram, and for his seed, a tenth of the first-fruits to the LORD, and the LORD ordained it as an ordinance forever that they should give it to the priests who served before Him, that they should possess it forever. ²⁶And to this law there is no limit of days; for He has ordained it for the generations forever that they should give to the LORD the tenth of everything, of the seed, and of the wine, and of the oil, and of the cattle, and of the sheep. ²⁷And He gave [it] to His priests to eat and to drink with joy before Him. ²⁸And the king of Sodom came to him and bowed himself before him, and said, "Our Lord Abram, give to us the souls which you have rescued, but let the plunder be yours." ²⁹And Abram said to him, "I lift up my hands to the Most High God, that from a thread to a shoe-strap I will not take anything that is yours, lest you should say, I have made Abram rich—save only what the young men have eaten, and the portion of the men who went with me—Aner, Eschol, and Mamre. These will take their portion."

CHAPTER 14

¹After these things, in the fourth year of this week, on the new moon of the third month, the word of the LORD came to Abram in a dream, saying, "Do not fear, Abram; I am your defender, and your reward will be exceedingly great." ²And he said, "Lord YHWH, what will You give me, seeing I go childless, and the son of Mâsêq, the son of my handmaid, is the Demmesek Eliezer: he will be my heir, and to me You have not given seed." ³And He said to him, "This [man] will not be your heir, but one that will come out of your own bowels, he will be your heir." ⁴And He brought him out abroad, and said to him, "Look toward the heavens and number the stars, if you are able to number them." ⁵And he looked toward the heavens and beheld the stars. And He said to him, "So will your seed be." ⁶And he believed in the LORD, and it was counted to him for righteousness. ⁷And He said to him, "I am the LORD that brought you out of Ur of the Chaldees, to give you the land

of the Canaanites to possess it forever; and I will be God to you and to your seed after you." ⁸And he said, "Lord YHWH, whereby will I know that I will inherit [it]?" ⁹And He said to him, "Take Me a heifer of three years, and a goat of three years, and a sheep of three years, and a turtle-dove, and a pigeon." ¹⁰And he took all these in the middle of the month; and he dwelt at the oak of Mamre, which is near Hebron. ¹¹And he built an altar there and sacrificed all these; and he poured their blood on the altar, and divided them in the midst, and laid them over against each other, but he did not divide the birds. ¹²And birds came down on the pieces, and Abram drove them away, and did not permit the birds to touch them. ¹³And it came to pass, when the sun had set, that an ecstasy fell on Abram, and behold, a horror of great darkness fell on him, and it was said to Abram: "Know for sure that your seed will be a stranger in a land [that is] not theirs, and they will bring them into bondage, and afflict them four hundred years. ¹⁴And the nation to whom they will be in bondage I will also judge, and after that they will come out from there with much substance. ¹⁵And you will go to your fathers in peace and be buried in a good old age. ¹⁶But in the fourth generation they will return here, for the iniquity of the Amorites is not yet full." ¹⁷And he awoke from his sleep, and he arose, and the sun had set; and there was a flame, and behold, a furnace was smoking, and a flame of fire passed between the pieces. ¹⁸And on that day the LORD made a covenant with Abram, saying, "To your seed I will give this land, from the river of Egypt to the great river, the River Euphrates—the Kenites, the Kenizzites, the Kadmonites, the Perizzites, and the Rephaim, the Phakorites, and the Hivites, and the Amorites, and the Canaanites, and the Girgashites, and the Jebusites." ¹⁹And the day passed, and Abram offered the pieces, and the birds, and their fruit-offerings, and their drink-offerings, and the fire devoured them. ²⁰And on that day we made a covenant with Abram, according as we had covenanted with Noah in this month; and Abram renewed the festival and ordinance for himself forever. ²¹And Abram rejoiced and made all these things known to his wife Sarai; and he believed that he would have seed, but she did not bear. ²²And Sarai advised her husband Abram and said to him, "Go in to Hagar, my Egyptian maid: it may be that I will build up seed to you by her." ²³And Abram listened to the voice of his wife Sarai and said to her, "Do [so]." And Sarai took Hagar, her maid, the Egyptian, and gave her to her husband Abram to be his wife. ²⁴And he went in to her, and she conceived and bore him a son, and he called his name Ishmael, in the fifth year of this week; and this was the eighty-sixth year in the life of Abram.

CHAPTER 15

¹And in the fifth year of the fourth week of this jubilee, in the third month, in the middle of the month, Abram celebrated the Celebration of the First-Fruits of the grain harvest. ²And he offered new offerings on the altar, the first-fruits of the produce, to the LORD: a heifer, and a goat, and a sheep on the altar as a burnt sacrifice to the LORD; their fruit-offerings and their drink-offerings he offered on the altar with frankincense. ³And the LORD appeared to Abram and said to him, "I am God Almighty; approve yourself before Me and be perfect. ⁴And I will make My covenant between Me and you, and I will multiply you exceedingly." ⁵And Abram fell on his face, and God talked with him, and said, ⁶"Behold, My ordinance is with you, and you will be the father of many nations. ⁷Neither will your name be called Abram anymore, but your name from now on, even forever, will be Abraham. For I have made you the father of many nations. ⁸And I will make you very great, and I will make you into nations, and kings will come out from you. ⁹And I will establish My covenant between Me and you, and your seed after you, throughout their generations, for a perpetual covenant, so that I may be a God to you, and to your seed after you. ¹⁰[[And I will give to you and to your seed after you]] the land where you have been a sojourner, the land of Canaan, that you may possess it forever, and I will be their God." ¹¹And the LORD said to Abraham, "And as for you: keep My covenant, you and your seed after you, and circumcise every male among you, and circumcise your foreskins, and it will be a token of a perpetual covenant between Me and you. ¹²And you will circumcise the child on the eighth day, every male throughout your generations—him that is born in the house, or whom you have bought with money from any stranger, whom you have acquired who is not of your seed. ¹³He that is born in your house will surely be circumcised, and those whom you have bought with money will be circumcised, and My covenant will be in your flesh for a perpetual ordinance. ¹⁴And the uncircumcised male who is not circumcised in the flesh of his foreskin on the eighth day, that soul will be cut off from his people, for he has broken My covenant." ¹⁵And God said to Abraham, "As for Sarai your wife, her name will no longer be called Sarai, but Sarah will be her name. ¹⁶And I will bless her, and give you a son by her, and I will bless him, and he will become a nation, and kings of nations will proceed from him." ¹⁷And Abraham fell on his face, and rejoiced, and said in his heart, "Will a son be born to him that is one hundred years old, and will Sarah, who is ninety years old, bring out?" ¹⁸And Abraham said to God, "O that Ishmael might live before you!" ¹⁹And God said, "Yes, and Sarah will also bear you a son, and you will call his name Isaac, and I will establish My covenant with him, a perpetual covenant, and for his seed after him. ²⁰And as for Ishmael, I have also heard you, and behold, I will bless him, and make him great, and multiply him exceedingly, and he will beget twelve princes, and I will make him a great nation. ²¹But I will establish My covenant with Isaac, whom Sarah will bear to you, in these days, in the next year." ²²And He left off speaking with him, and God went up from Abraham. ²³And Abraham did according as God had said to him, and he took his son Ishmael, and all that were born in his house, and whom he had bought with his money, every male in his house, and circumcised the flesh of their foreskin. ²⁴And on the same day Abraham was circumcised, indeed, all the men of his house and all those whom he had bought with money from the children of the stranger were circumcised with him. ²⁵This law is for all the generations forever, and there is no circumcision of the days, and no omission of one day out of the eight days, for it is a perpetual ordinance, ordained and written on the heavenly tablets. ²⁶And everyone that is born, the flesh of whose foreskin is not circumcised on the eighth day, does not belong to the children of the covenant which the LORD made with Abraham, but to the children of destruction; nor is there, moreover, any sign on him that he is the LORD's, but [he is destined] to be destroyed and slain from the earth, and to be rooted out of the earth, for he has broken the covenant of the LORD our God. ²⁷For all the messengers of the presence and all the messengers of sanctification have been so created from the day of their creation, and before the messengers of the presence and the messengers of sanctification, He has sanctified Israel, that they should be with Him and with His holy messengers. ²⁸And command the sons of Israel and let them observe the sign of this covenant for their generations as a perpetual ordinance, and they will not be rooted out of the land. ²⁹For the command is ordained for a covenant, that they should observe it forever among all the sons of Israel. ³⁰For Ishmael, and his sons, and his brothers, and Esau, the LORD did not cause to approach Him, and He did not choose them because they are the children of Abraham, because He knew them, but He chose Israel to be His people. ³¹And He sanctified it and gathered it from among all the children of men; for there are many nations and many peoples, and all are His, and over all He has placed spirits in authority to lead them astray from Him. ³²But over Israel He did not appoint any messenger or spirit, for He alone is their ruler, and He will preserve them and require them at the hand of His messengers and His spirits, and at the hand of all His powers in order that He may preserve them and bless them, and that they may be His and He may be theirs from now on and forever. ³³And now I announce to you that the sons of Israel will not keep true to this ordinance, and they will not circumcise their sons according to all this law, for in the flesh of their circumcision they will omit this circumcision of their sons, and all of them, sons of Belial, will leave their sons uncircumcised as they were born. ³⁴And there will be great wrath from the LORD against the sons of Israel, because they have forsaken His covenant and turned aside from His word, and provoked and blasphemed, inasmuch as they do not observe the ordinance of this law, for they have treated their members like the nations, so that they may be removed and

JUBILEES

rooted out of the land. And there will no longer be pardon or forgiveness to them for all the sin of this continuous error.

CHAPTER 16

¹And on the new moon of the fourth month we appeared to Abraham, at the oak of Mamre, and we talked with him, and we announced to him that a son would be given to him by his wife Sarah. ²And Sarah laughed, for she heard that we had spoken these words with Abraham, and we admonished her, and she became afraid, and denied that she had laughed on account of the words. ³And we told her the name of her son, as his name [(Isaac)] is ordained and written in the heavenly tablets, ⁴and [that] when we returned to her at a set time, she would have conceived a son. ⁵And in this month the LORD executed His judgments on Sodom, and Gomorrah, and Zeboim, and all the region of the Jordan, and He burned them with fire and brimstone, and destroyed them until this day, even as I have declared to you all their works, that they are sinners and exceedingly wicked, and that they defile themselves and commit fornication in their flesh, and work uncleanness on the earth. ⁶And, in like manner, God will execute judgment on the places where they have done according to the uncleanness of the Sodomites, like to the judgment of Sodom. ⁷But we saved Lot, for God remembered Abraham and sent him out from the midst of the overthrow. ⁸And he and his daughters committed sin on the earth, such as had not been on the earth since the days of Adam until his time, for the man lay with his daughters. ⁹And behold, it was commanded and engraved concerning all his seed, on the heavenly tablets, to remove them and root them out, and to execute judgment on them like the judgment of Sodom, and to leave no seed of the man on earth on the day of condemnation. ¹⁰And in this month Abraham moved from Hebron and departed and dwelt between Kadesh and Shur in the mountains of Gerar. ¹¹And in the middle of the fifth month he moved from there and dwelt at the Well of the Oath. ¹²And in the middle of the sixth month the LORD visited Sarah and did to her as He had spoken, and she conceived. ¹³And she bore a son in the third month, and in the middle of the month, at the time of which the LORD had spoken to Abraham, on the festival of the first-fruits of the harvest, Isaac was born. ¹⁴And Abraham circumcised his son on the eighth day: he was the first that was circumcised according to the covenant which is ordained forever. ¹⁵And in the sixth year of the fourth week we came to Abraham, to the Well of the Oath, and we appeared to him [[as we had told Sarah that we should return to her, and she would have conceived a son. ¹⁶And we returned in the seventh month, and found Sarah with child before us,]] and we blessed him, and we announced to him all the things which had been decreed concerning him: that he should not die until he should beget six more sons, and should see [them] before he died, but [that] in Isaac should his name and seed be called, ¹⁷and [that] all the seed of his sons should be nations, and be reckoned with the nations, but from the sons of Isaac one should become a holy seed and should not be reckoned among the nations. ¹⁸For he should become the portion of the Most High, and all his seed had fallen into the possession of God, that it should be to the LORD a people for [His] possession above all nations and that it should become a kingdom, and priests, and a holy nation. ¹⁹And we went our way, and we announced to Sarah all that we had told him, and they both rejoiced with exceedingly great joy. ²⁰And he built an altar there to the LORD who had delivered him, and who was making him rejoice in the land of his sojourning, and he celebrated a festival of joy in this month [for] seven days, near the altar which he had built at the Well of the Oath. ²¹And he built shelters for himself and for his servants on this festival, and he was the first to celebrate the Celebration of Shelters on the earth. ²²And during these seven days he brought each day to the altar a burnt-offering to the LORD: two oxen, two rams, seven sheep, one male goat, for a sin-offering, that he might atone for himself and for his seed thereby. ²³And as a thank-offering: seven rams, seven kids, seven sheep, and seven male goats, and their fruit-offerings and their drink-offerings; and he burned all the fat thereof on the altar, a chosen offering to the LORD for a sweet-smelling savor. ²⁴And morning and evening he burned fragrant substances: frankincense, and galbanum, and stacte, and nard, and myrrh, and spice, and costum; all these seven he offered crushed, mixed together in equal parts, [and] pure. ²⁵And he celebrated this feast during seven days, rejoicing with all his heart and with all his soul, he and all those who were in his house; and there was no stranger with him, nor any that was uncircumcised. ²⁶And he blessed his Creator who had created him in his generation, for He had created him according to His good pleasure, for He knew and perceived that from him would arise the Plant of Righteousness for the continuous generations, and from him a holy Seed, so that it should become like Him who had made all things. ²⁷And he blessed and rejoiced, and he called the name of this festival the Festival of the LORD, a joy acceptable to the Most High God. ²⁸And we blessed him forever, and all his seed after him throughout all the generations of the earth, because he celebrated this festival in its season, according to the testimony of the heavenly tablets. ²⁹For this reason it is ordained on the heavenly tablets concerning Israel that they will celebrate the Celebration of Shelters [for] seven days with joy, in the seventh month, acceptable before the LORD—a statute forever throughout their generations every year. ³⁰And to this there is no limit of days, for it is ordained forever regarding Israel that they should celebrate it and dwell in shelters, and set wreaths on their heads, and take leafy boughs, and willows from the brook. ³¹And Abraham took branches of palm trees, and the fruit of attractive trees, and every day going around the altar with the branches seven times [a day] in the morning, he praised and gave thanks to his God for all things in joy.

CHAPTER 17

¹And in the first year of the fifth week Isaac was weaned in this jubilee, and Abraham made a great banquet in the third month, on the day his son Isaac was weaned. ²And Ishmael, the son of Hagar the Egyptian, was before the face of his father Abraham, in his place, and Abraham rejoiced and blessed God because he had seen his sons and had not died childless. ³And he remembered the words which He had spoken to him on the day on which Lot had parted from him, and he rejoiced because the LORD had given him seed on the earth to inherit the earth, and he blessed the Creator of all things with all his mouth. ⁴And Sarah saw Ishmael playing and dancing and Abraham rejoicing with great joy, and she became jealous of Ishmael and said to Abraham, "Cast out this bondwoman and her son, for the son of this bondwoman will not be heir with my son Isaac." ⁵And the thing was grievous in Abraham's sight, because of his maidservant and because of his son, that he should drive them from him. ⁶And God said to Abraham, "Do not let it be grievous in your sight, because of the child and because of the bondwoman; in all that Sarah has said to you, listen to her words and do [them], for in Isaac will your name and seed be called. ⁷But as for the son of this bondwoman, I will make him a great nation, because he is of your seed." ⁸And Abraham rose up early in the morning and took bread and a bottle of water and placed them on the shoulders of Hagar and the child and sent her away. ⁹And she departed and wandered in the wilderness of Beersheba, and the water in the bottle was spent, and the child thirsted, and was not able to go on, and fell down. ¹⁰And his mother took him and cast him under an olive tree, and went and sat her down over against him, at the distance of a bow-shot; for she said, "Let me not see the death of my child," and as she sat, she wept. ¹¹And a messenger of God, one of the holy ones, said to her, "Why do you weep, Hagar? Arise, take the child, and hold him in your hand, for God has heard your voice, and has seen the child." ¹²And she opened her eyes, and she saw a well of water, and she went and filled her bottle with water, and she gave her child to drink, and she arose and went toward the wilderness of Paran. ¹³And the child grew and became an archer, and God was with him; and his mother took a wife [for] him from among the daughters of Egypt. ¹⁴And she bore him a son, and he called his name Nebaioth, for she said, "The LORD was near to me when I called on Him." ¹⁵And it came to pass in the seventh week, in the first year thereof, in the first month in this jubilee, on the twelfth of this month, there were voices in Heaven regarding Abraham, that he was faithful in all that He told him, and that he loved the LORD, and that in every affliction he was faithful. ¹⁶And the prince Mastêmâ came and said

before God, "Behold, Abraham loves his son Isaac, and he delights in him above all other things; command him to offer him as a burnt-offering on the altar, and You will see if he will do this command, and You will know if he is faithful in everything wherein You try him." ¹⁷And the LORD knew that Abraham was faithful in all his afflictions, for He had tried him through his country and with famine, and had tried him with the wealth of kings, and had tried him again through his wife, when she was torn [from him], and with circumcision, and had tried him through Ishmael and Hagar, his maidservant, when he sent them away. ¹⁸And in everything wherein He had tried him, he was found faithful, and his soul was not impatient, and he was not slow to act, for he was faithful and a lover of the LORD.

CHAPTER 18

¹And God said to him, "Abraham, Abraham"; and he said, "Behold, [here] I am." ²And He said, "Take your beloved son whom you love, [even] Isaac, and go to the high country, and offer him on one of the mountains which I will point out to you." ³And he rose early in the morning and saddled his donkey, and took his two young men with him, and his son Isaac, and cleaved the wood of the burnt-offering, and he went to the place on the third day, and he saw the place far off. ⁴And he came to a well of water, and he said to his young men, "Abide here with the donkey, and the youth and I will go [over there], and when we have worshiped we will come again to you." ⁵And he took the wood of the burnt-offering and laid it on his son Isaac, and he took in his hand the fire and the knife, and both of them went together to that place. ⁶And Isaac said to his father, "Father"; and he said, "Here I am, my son." And he said to him, "Behold the fire, and the knife, and the wood, but where is the sheep for the burnt-offering, father?" ⁷And he said, "God will provide for Himself a sheep for a burnt-offering, my son." And he drew near to the place of the mount of God. ⁸And he built an altar, and he placed the wood on the altar, and bound his son Isaac, and placed him on the wood which was on the altar, and stretched out his hand to take the knife to slay his son Isaac. ⁹And I stood before him, and before the prince of the Mastêmâ, and the LORD said, "Command him not to lay his hand on the youth, nor to do anything to him, for I have shown that he fears the LORD." ¹⁰And I called to him from Heaven, and said to him, "Abraham! Abraham!" And he was terrified and said, "Behold, [here] I am." ¹¹And I said to him, "Do not lay your hand on the youth, neither do anything to him, for now I have shown that you fear the LORD, and have not withheld your son, your firstborn [[or only]] son, from Me." ¹²And the prince of the Mastêmâ was put to shame, and Abraham lifted up his eyes and looked, and behold, a single ram was caught by his horns, and Abraham went and took the ram and offered it for a burnt-offering in the place of his son. ¹³And Abraham called that place "The LORD has seen," so that it is said, "[in the mount] the LORD has seen": that is Mount Zion. ¹⁴And the LORD called Abraham by his name a second time from Heaven, as He caused us to appear to speak to him in the Name of the LORD. ¹⁵And He said, "By Myself I have sworn, says the LORD, because you have done this thing, and have not withheld your son, your beloved son, from Me, that in blessing I will bless you, and in multiplying I will multiply your seed as the stars of the heavens, and as the sand which is on the seashore. And your Seed will inherit the cities of its enemies, ¹⁶and in your Seed all nations of the earth will be blessed; because you have obeyed My voice, and I have shown to all that you are faithful to Me in all that I have said to you: go in peace." ¹⁷And Abraham went to his young men, and they arose and went together to Beersheba, and Abraham dwelt by the Well of the Oath. ¹⁸And he celebrated this festival every year [for] seven days with joy, and he called it the Festival of the LORD according to the seven days during which he went and returned in peace. ¹⁹And accordingly it has been ordained and written on the heavenly tablets regarding Israel and its seed that they should observe this festival [for] seven days with the joy of festival.

CHAPTER 19

¹And in the first year of the first week, in the forty-second jubilee, Abraham returned and dwelt opposite Hebron, that is Kirjath-Arba, two weeks of years. ²And in the first year of the third week of this jubilee the days of the life of Sarah were accomplished, and she died in Hebron. ³And Abraham went to mourn over her and bury her, and we tried him [to see] if his spirit was patient and he was not indignant in the words of his mouth, and he was found patient in this and was not disturbed. ⁴For in patience of spirit he conversed with the children of Heth, to the intent that they should give him a place in which to bury his dead. ⁵And the LORD gave him grace before all who saw him, and he implored in gentleness the sons of Heth, and they gave him the land of the double cave over against Mamre, that is Hebron, for four hundred pieces of silver. ⁶And they implored him, saying, "We will give it to you for nothing," but he would not take it from their hands for nothing, for he gave the price of the place, the money in full, and he bowed down before them twice; and after this he buried his dead in the double cave. ⁷And all the days of the life of Sarah were one hundred and twenty-seven years, that is, two jubilees and four weeks and one year: these are the days of the years of the life of Sarah. ⁸This is the tenth trial with which Abraham was tried, and he was found faithful, patient in spirit. ⁹And he said not a single word regarding the rumor in the land, how that God had said that He would give it to him and to his seed after him, and he begged [for] a place there to bury his dead, for he was found faithful and was recorded on the heavenly tablets as the friend of God. ¹⁰And in the fourth year thereof he took a wife for his son Isaac and her name was Rebekah [[the daughter of Bethuel, the son of Nahor, the brother of Abraham,]] the sister of Laban and daughter of Bethuel; and Bethuel was the son of Mêlcâ, who was the wife of Nahor, the brother of Abraham. ¹¹And Abraham took to himself a third wife—and her name was Keturah—from among the daughters of his household servants, for Hagar had died before Sarah. ¹²And she bore him six sons: Zimram, and Jokshan, and Medan, and Midian, and Ishbak, and Shuah, in the two weeks of years. ¹³And in the sixth week, in the second year thereof, Rebekah bore to Isaac two sons, Jacob and Esau, and Jacob was a smooth and upright man, and Esau was fierce, a man of the field, and hairy, and Jacob dwelt in tents. ¹⁴And the youths grew, and Jacob learned to write, but Esau did not learn, for he was a man of the field and a hunter, and he learned war, and all his deeds were fierce. ¹⁵And Abraham loved Jacob, but Isaac loved Esau. ¹⁶And Abraham saw the deeds of Esau, and he knew that in Jacob should his name and seed be called; and he called Rebekah and gave command regarding Jacob, for he knew that she [too] loved Jacob much more than Esau. ¹⁷And he said to her, "My daughter, watch over my son Jacob, for he will be in my stead on the earth, and for a blessing in the midst of the children of men, and for the glory of the whole seed of Shem. ¹⁸For I know that the LORD will choose him to be a people for possession to Himself, above all peoples that are on the face of the earth. ¹⁹And behold, my son Isaac loves Esau more than Jacob, but I see that you truly love Jacob. ²⁰Add still further to your kindness to him, and let your eyes be on him in love, for he will be a blessing to us on the earth from now on and to all generations of the earth. ²¹Let your hands be strong and let your heart rejoice in your son Jacob, for I have loved him far beyond all my sons. He will be blessed forever, and his seed will fill the whole earth. ²²If a man can number the sand of the earth, his seed will also be numbered. ²³And all the blessings with which the LORD has blessed me and my seed will belong to Jacob and his seed always. ²⁴And in his seed my name will be blessed, and the name of my fathers: Shem, and Noah, and Enoch, and Mahalalel, and Enos, and Seth, and Adam. ²⁵And these will serve to lay the foundations of the heavens, and to strengthen the earth, and to renew all the luminaries which are in the expanse." ²⁶And he called Jacob before the eyes of his mother Rebekah, and kissed him, and blessed him, and said, ²⁷"Jacob, my beloved son, whom my soul loves, may God bless you from above the expanse, and may He give you all the blessings with which He blessed Adam, and Enoch, and Noah, and Shem; and all the things of which He told me, and all the things which He promised to give me, may He cause to cleave to you and to your seed forever, according to the days of Heaven above the earth. ²⁸And the spirits of Mastêmâ will not rule over you or over your seed to turn you from the LORD, who is your God from now on and forever. ²⁹And may the LORD God be a father to you—and you [being] the firstborn

son—and to the people always. Go in peace, my son." ³⁰And they both went out together from Abraham. ³¹And Rebekah loved Jacob with all her heart and with all her soul, very much more than Esau, but Isaac loved Esau much more than Jacob.

CHAPTER 20

¹And in the forty-second jubilee, in the first year of the seventh week, Abraham called Ishmael, and his twelve sons, and Isaac and his two sons, and the six sons of Keturah, and their sons. ²And he commanded them that they should observe the way of the LORD, that they should work righteousness, and each love his neighbor, and act on this manner among all men, that they should each so walk with regard to them as to do judgment and righteousness on the earth, ³[and] that they should circumcise their sons according to the covenant which He had made with them, and not deviate to the right hand or the left of all the paths which the LORD had commanded us, and that we should keep ourselves from all fornication and uncleanness. ⁴"And if any woman or maid may commit fornication among you, burn her with fire, and do not let them commit fornication with her after their eyes and their heart; and do not let them take to themselves wives from the daughters of Canaan, for the seed of Canaan will be rooted out of the land." ⁵And he told them of the judgment of the giants, and the judgment of the Sodomites, how they had been judged on account of their wickedness, and had died on account of their fornication, and uncleanness, and mutual corruption through fornication. ⁶"And guard yourselves from all fornication and uncleanness, and from all pollution of sin, lest you make our name a curse, and your whole life a hissing, and all your sons be destroyed by the sword, and you become accursed like Sodom, and all your remnant as the sons of Gomorrah. ⁷I implore you, my sons: love the God of Heaven, and cleave to all His commands. And do not walk after their idols, and after their uncleanness, ⁸and do not make for yourselves molten or graven gods, for they are vanity, and there is no spirit in them, for they are [the] work of [men's] hands, and all who trust in them, trust in nothing. Do not serve them, nor worship them, ⁹but serve the Most High God, and worship Him continually. And hope for His countenance always, and work uprightness and righteousness before Him, that He may have pleasure in you and grant you His mercy, and send rain on you morning and evening, and bless all your works which you have worked on the earth, and bless your bread and your water, and bless the fruit of your womb and the fruit of your land, and the herds of your cattle, and the flocks of your sheep. ¹⁰And you will be for a blessing on the earth, and all nations of the earth will desire you, and bless your sons in my name, that they may be blessed as I am." ¹¹And he gave to Ishmael, and to his sons, and to the sons of Keturah, gifts, and sent them away from his son Isaac, and he gave everything to his son Isaac. ¹²And Ishmael and his sons, and the sons of Keturah and their sons, went together and dwelt from Paran to the entering in of Babylon in all the land which is toward the east facing the desert. ¹³And these mingled with each other, and their name was called Arabs, and Ishmaelites.

CHAPTER 21

¹And in the sixth year of the seventh week of this jubilee, Abraham called his son Isaac and commanded him, saying, "I have become old, and I do not know the day of my death, and am full of my days. ²And behold, I am one hundred and seventy-five years old, and throughout all the days of my life I have remembered the LORD and sought with all my heart to do His will, and to walk uprightly in all His ways. ³My soul has hated idols, [[and I have despised those that served them, and I have given my heart and spirit]] that I might observe to do the will of Him who created me. ⁴For He is the living God, and He is holy and faithful, and He is righteous beyond all, and there is with Him no accepting of [men's] persons and no accepting of gifts, for God is righteous and executes judgment on all those who transgress His commands and despise His covenant. ⁵And you, my son, observe His commands, and His ordinances, and His judgments, and do not walk after the abominations, and after the graven images, and after the molten images. ⁶And eat no blood at all of animals, or cattle, or of any bird which flies in the heavens. ⁷And if you slay a victim as an acceptable peace-offering, slay it, and pour out its blood on the altar, and all the fat of the offering offer on the altar with fine flour [and the meat-offering] mingled with oil, with its drink-offering—offer them all together on the altar of burnt-offering; it is a sweet savor before the LORD. ⁸And you will offer the fat of the sacrifice of thank-offerings on the fire which is on the altar, and the fat which is on the belly, and all the fat on the innards and the two kidneys, and all the fat that is on them, and on the loins and liver you will remove together with the kidneys. ⁹And offer all these for a sweet savor acceptable before the LORD, with its meat-offering and with its drink-offering, for a sweet savor, the bread of the offering to the LORD, ¹⁰and eat its meat on that day and on the second day, and do not let the sun go down on it on the second day until it is eaten, and let nothing be left over for the third day, for it is not acceptable; and let it no longer be eaten, and all who eat thereof will bring sin on themselves, for thus I have found it written in the scrolls of my forefathers, and in the words of Enoch, and in the words of Noah. ¹¹And on all your oblations you will scatter salt, and do not let the salt of the covenant be lacking in all your oblations before the LORD. ¹²And as regards the wood of the sacrifices, beware lest you bring [other] wood for the altar in addition to these: cypress, dêfrân, sagâd, pine, fir, cedar, savin, palm, olive, myrrh, laurel, and citron, juniper, and balsam. ¹³And of these kinds of wood lay on the altar under the sacrifice, such as have been tested as to their appearance, and do not lay any split or dark wood [on it], [but] hard and clean, without fault—a sound and new growth; and do not lay old wood [on it], for there is no longer fragrance in it as before. ¹⁴Besides these kinds of wood, there is no other that you will place [on the altar], for the fragrance is dispersed, and the smell of its fragrance does not go up to Heaven. ¹⁵Observe this command and do it, my son, that you may be upright in all your deeds. ¹⁶And at all times be clean in your body, and wash yourself with water before you approach to offer on the altar, and wash your hands and your feet before you draw near to the altar; and when you are done sacrificing, wash your hands and your feet again. ¹⁷And let no blood appear on you nor on your clothes; be on your guard, my son, against blood, be on your guard exceedingly; cover it with dust. ¹⁸And do not eat any blood, for it is the soul; eat no blood whatsoever. ¹⁹And take no gifts for the blood of man, lest it be shed with impunity, without judgment, for it is the blood that is shed that causes the earth to sin, and the earth cannot be cleansed from the blood of man save by the blood of him who shed it. ²⁰And take no present or gift for the blood of man, blood for blood, that you may be accepted before the LORD, the Most High God—for He is the defense of the good—and that you may be preserved from all evil, and that He may save you from every kind of death. ²¹I see, my son, that all the works of the children of men are sin and wickedness, and all their deeds are uncleanness, and an abomination, and a pollution, and there is no righteousness with them. ²²Beware, lest you should walk in their ways, and tread in their paths, and sin a sin to death before the Most High God. Otherwise He will [[hide His face from you, and]] give you back into the hands of your transgression, and root you out of the land, and your seed likewise from under Heaven, and your name and your seed will perish from the whole earth. ²³Turn away from all their deeds and all their uncleanness, and observe the ordinance of the Most High God, and do His will, and be upright in all things. ²⁴And He will bless you in all your deeds and will raise up from you the plant of righteousness through all the earth, throughout all generations of the earth, and my name and your name will not be forgotten under Heaven forever. ²⁵Go, my son, in peace. May the Most High God, my God and your God, strengthen you to do His will, and may He bless all your seed and the residue of your seed for the generations forever, with all righteous blessings, that you may be a blessing on all the earth." ²⁶And he went out from him rejoicing.

CHAPTER 22

¹And it came to pass in the first week, in the forty-fourth jubilee, in the second year, that is, the year in which Abraham died, that Isaac and Ishmael came from the Well of the Oath to celebrate the Celebration of Weeks—that is, the celebration of the first-fruits of the harvest—to their father Abraham, and Abraham rejoiced because his two sons had

come. ²For Isaac had many possessions in Beersheba, and Isaac was accustomed to go and see his possessions and to return to his father. ³And in those days Ishmael came to see his father, and they both came together, and Isaac offered a sacrifice for a burnt-offering, and presented it on the altar of his father which he had made in Hebron. ⁴And he offered a thank-offering and made a feast of joy before his brother Ishmael: and Rebekah made new cakes from the new grain and gave them to her son Jacob to take them to his father Abraham, from the first-fruits of the land, that he might eat and bless the Creator of all things before he died. ⁵And Isaac, too, sent by the hand of Jacob to Abraham a best thank-offering, that he might eat and drink. ⁶And he ate, and drank, and blessed the Most High God who has created the heavens and earth, who has made all the fat things of the earth and given them to the children of men that they might eat, and drink, and bless their Creator. ⁷"And now I give thanks to you, my God, because You have caused me to see this day: behold, I am one hundred and seventy-five years [old], an old man and full of days, and all my days have been peace to me. ⁸The sword of the adversary has not overcome me in all that You have given me and my children all the days of my life until this day. ⁹My God, may Your mercy and Your peace be on Your servant and on the seed of his sons, that they may be to You a chosen nation and an inheritance from among all the nations of the earth from now on and to all the days of the generations of the earth—to all the ages." ¹⁰And he called Jacob and said, "My son Jacob, may the God of all bless you and strengthen you to do righteousness and His will before Him, and may He choose you and your seed that you may become a people for His inheritance according to His will always. And my son Jacob: draw near and kiss me." ¹¹And he drew near and kissed him, and he said, "Blessed is my son Jacob, and all the sons of God Most High, to all the ages. May God give to you [the] Seed of righteousness; and may He sanctify some of your sons in the midst of the whole earth. May nations serve you, and all the nations bow themselves before your Seed. ¹²Be strong in the presence of men, and exercise authority over all the seed of Seth. Then your ways and the ways of your sons will be justified, so that they will become a holy nation. ¹³May the Most High God give you all the blessings with which He has blessed me and with which He blessed Noah and Adam. May they rest on the sacred head of your Seed from generation to generation forever. ¹⁴And may He cleanse you from all unrighteousness and impurity, that you may be forgiven of all [your] transgressions [and] your sins of ignorance. And may He strengthen you and bless you. And may you inherit the whole earth; ¹⁵and may He renew His covenant with you, that you may be to Him a nation for His inheritance for all the ages, and that He may be to you and to your seed a God in truth and righteousness throughout all the days of the earth. ¹⁶And my son Jacob: remember my words and observe the commands of your father Abraham: separate yourself from the nations, and do not eat with them, and do not do according to their works, and do not become their associate, for their works are unclean, and all their ways are a pollution, and an abomination, and uncleanness. ¹⁷They offer their sacrifices to the dead, and they worship evil spirits, and they eat over the graves, and all their works are vanity and nothingness. ¹⁸They have no heart to understand, and their eyes do not see what their works are, and how they err in saying to a piece of wood, You are my God; and to a stone, You are my lord and you are my deliverer. [[And they have no heart.]] ¹⁹And as for you, my son Jacob: may the Most High God help you, and the God of Heaven bless you and remove you from their uncleanness and from all their error. ²⁰Beware, my son Jacob, of taking a wife from any seed of the daughters of Canaan, for all his seed is to be rooted out of the earth. ²¹For, owing to the transgression of Ham, Canaan erred, and all his seed will be destroyed from off the earth and all the residue thereof, and none springing from him will be saved on the Day of Judgment. ²²And as for all the worshipers of idols and the profane: there will be no hope for them in the land of the living and there will be no remembrance of them on the earth, for they will descend into Sheol, and they will go into the place of condemnation; as the children of Sodom were taken away from the earth, so will all those who worship idols be taken away. ²³Do not fear, my son Jacob, and do not be dismayed, O son of Abraham: may the Most High God preserve you from destruction, and may He deliver you from all the paths of error. ²⁴I have built this house for myself that I might put my name on it in the earth: [[it is given to you and to your seed forever]], and it will be named the House of Abraham; it is given to you and to your seed forever, for you will build my house and establish my name before God forever: your seed and your name will stand throughout all generations of the earth." ²⁵And he ceased commanding him and blessing him. ²⁶And the two lay together on one bed, and Jacob slept in the bosom of Abraham, his father's father, and he kissed him seven times, and his affection and his heart rejoiced over him. ²⁷And he blessed him with all his heart and said, "The Most High God, the God of all and Creator of all, who brought me out from Ur of the Chaldees that He might give me this land to inherit it forever, and that I might establish a holy Seed—blessed is the Most High forever." ²⁸And he blessed Jacob and said [to God], "My son, over whom with all my heart and my affection I rejoice, may Your grace and Your mercy be lifted up on him and on his seed always. ²⁹And do not forsake him, nor set him at nothing from now on and to the days of [all] ages, and may Your eyes be opened on him and on his seed, that You may preserve him, and bless him, and may sanctify him as a nation for Your inheritance; ³⁰and bless him with all Your blessings from now on and to all the days of [the] ages, and renew Your covenant and Your grace with him and with his seed according to all Your good pleasure to all the generations of the earth."

CHAPTER 23

¹And he placed two of Jacob's fingers on his eyes, and he blessed the God of gods, and he covered his face, and stretched out his feet, and slept the continuous sleep, and was gathered to his fathers. ²And notwithstanding all this, Jacob was lying in his bosom, and did not know that Abraham, his father's father, was dead. ³And Jacob awoke from his sleep, and behold, Abraham was cold as ice, and he said, "Father! Father!" But there was none that spoke, and he knew that he was dead. ⁴And he arose from his bosom and ran and told his mother Rebekah; and Rebekah went to Isaac in the night and told him; and they went together, and Jacob with them, and a lamp was in his hand, and when they had gone in they found Abraham lying dead. ⁵And Isaac fell on the face of his father, and wept, and kissed him. ⁶And the voices were heard in the house of Abraham, and his son Ishmael arose, and went to his father Abraham, and wept over his father Abraham—he and all the house of Abraham—and they wept with a great weeping. ⁷And his sons Isaac and Ishmael buried him in the double cave near his wife Sarah, and they wept for him forty days, all the men of his house, and Isaac and Ishmael, and all their sons, and all the sons of Keturah in their places, and the days of weeping for Abraham were ended. ⁸And he lived three jubilees and four weeks of years—one hundred and seventy-five years—and completed the days of his life, being old and full of days. ⁹For the days of the forefathers, of their life, were nineteen jubilees; and after the Flood they began to grow less than nineteen jubilees, and to decrease in jubilees, and to grow old quickly, and to be full of their days by reason of manifold tribulation and the wickedness of their ways, with the exception of Abraham. ¹⁰For Abraham was perfect in all his deeds with the LORD, and well-pleasing in righteousness all the days of his life; and behold, he did not complete four jubilees in his life when he had grown old by reason of the wickedness [in the world] and was full of his days. ¹¹And all the generations which will arise from this time until the Day of the Great Judgment will grow old quickly before they complete two jubilees, and their knowledge will forsake them by reason of their old age. ¹²And in those days, if a man lives [for] a jubilee and a half of years, they will say regarding him: "He has lived long, and the greater part of his days are pain, and sorrow, and tribulation, and there is no peace, ¹³for calamity follows on calamity, and wound on wound, and tribulation on tribulation, and evil tidings on evil tidings, and sickness on sickness, and all evil judgments such as these, with one another—sickness, and overthrow, and snow, and frost, and ice, and fever, and chills, and torpor, and famine, and death, and sword, and captivity, and all kinds of calamities and pains." ¹⁴And all these will come on an evil

generation, which transgresses on the earth: their works are uncleanness, and fornication, and pollution, and abominations. ¹⁵Then they will say, "The days of the forefathers were many, [even] to one thousand years, and were good, but behold, the days of our life, if a man has lived many, are sixty years and ten, and, if he is strong, eighty years, and those [are] evil and there is no peace in the days of this evil generation." ¹⁶And in that generation the sons will convict their fathers and their elders of sin and unrighteousness, and of the words of their mouth and the great wickedness which they perpetrate, and concerning their forsaking the covenant which the LORD made between them and Him, that they should observe and do all His commands, and His ordinances, and all His laws, without departing either to the right hand or to the left. ¹⁷For all have done evil, and every mouth speaks iniquity, and all their works are an uncleanness and an abomination, and all their ways are pollution, uncleanness, and destruction. ¹⁸Behold, the earth will be destroyed on account of all their works, and there will be no seed of the vine and no oil, for their works are altogether faithless, and they will all perish together: beasts, and cattle, and birds, and all the fish of the sea, on account of the children of men. ¹⁹And they will strive with one another, the young with the old, and the old with the young, the poor with the rich, and the lowly with the great, and the beggar with the prince, on account of the Law and the Covenant, for they have forgotten command, and covenant, and feasts, and months, and Sabbaths, and jubilees, and all judgments. ²⁰And they will stand [[with bows and]] swords, and war to turn them back into the way, but they will not return until much blood has been shed on the earth by one another. ²¹And those who have escaped will not return from their wickedness to the way of righteousness, but they will all exalt themselves to deceit and wealth, that they may each take all that is his neighbor's, and they will name the Great Name, but not in truth and not in righteousness, and they will defile the Holy of Holies with their uncleanness and the corruption of their pollution. ²²And a great punishment will befall the deeds of this generation from the LORD, and He will give them over to the sword, and to judgment, and to captivity, and to be plundered and devoured. ²³And He will wake up against them the sinners of the nations who have neither mercy nor compassion, and who will respect the person of none, neither old nor young, nor anyone, for they are more wicked and strong to do evil than all the children of men. And they will use violence against Israel and transgression against Jacob, and much blood will be shed on the earth, and there will be none to gather and none to bury. ²⁴In those days they will cry aloud, and call and pray that they may be saved from the hand of the sinners, the nations, but none will be saved. ²⁵And the heads of the children will be white with grey hair, and a child of three weeks will appear old like a man of one hundred years, and their stature will be destroyed by tribulation and oppression. ²⁶And in those days the children will begin to study the laws, and to seek the commands, and to return to the path of righteousness. ²⁷And the days will begin to grow many and increase among those children of men [until] their days draw near to one thousand years, and to a greater number of years than were the number of the days [before]. ²⁸And there will be no old man nor one who is not satisfied with his days, for all will be [as] children and youths. ²⁹And they will complete all their days and live in peace and in joy, and there will be no adversary, nor any evil destroyer, for all their days will be days of blessing and healing, ³⁰and at that time the LORD will heal His servants, and they will rise up and see great peace, and drive out their adversaries. And the righteous will see and be thankful, and rejoice with joy forever and ever, and will see all their judgments and all their curses on their enemies. ³¹And their bones will rest in the earth, and their spirits will have much joy, and they will know that it is the LORD who executes judgment and shows mercy to hundreds, and thousands, and to all that love Him. ³²And you, Moses, write down these words, for thus are they written, and they record [them] on the heavenly tablets for a testimony for the generations forever.

CHAPTER 24

¹And it came to pass after the death of Abraham, that the LORD blessed his son Isaac, and he arose from Hebron and went and dwelt at the Well of the Vision in the first year of the third week of this jubilee [for] seven years. ²And in the first year of the fourth week a famine began in the land, besides the first famine which had been in the days of Abraham. ³And Jacob prepared lentil stew, and Esau came from the field hungry. And he said to his brother Jacob, "Give me of this red stew." And Jacob said to him, "Sell your birthright to me and I will give you bread and also some of this lentil stew." ⁴And Esau said in his heart: "I will die; of what profit to me is this birthright?" And he said to Jacob, "I give it to you." ⁵And Jacob said, "Swear to me, this day," and he swore to him. ⁶And Jacob gave his brother Esau bread and stew, and he ate until he was satisfied, and Esau despised his birthright; for this reason Esau's name was called Edom on account of the red stew which Jacob gave him for his birthright. ⁷And Jacob became the elder, and Esau was brought down from his dignity. ⁸And the famine was over the land, and Isaac departed to go down into Egypt in the second year of this week, and he went to the king of the Philistines, to Gerar, to Abimelech. ⁹And the LORD appeared to him and said to him, "Do not go down into Egypt; dwell in the land that I will tell you of, and sojourn in this land, and I will be with you and bless you. ¹⁰For to you and to your seed I will give all this land, and I will establish My oath which I swore to your father Abraham, and I will multiply your seed as the stars of the heavens, and I will give to your seed all this land. ¹¹And in your Seed will all the nations of the earth be blessed, because your father obeyed My voice, and kept My charge, and My commands, and My laws, and My ordinances, and My covenant; and now obey My voice and dwell in this land." ¹²And he dwelt in Gerar three weeks of years. ¹³And Abimelech charged concerning him, and concerning all that was his, saying, "Any man that will touch him or anything that is his will surely die." ¹⁴And Isaac waxed strong among the Philistines, and he got many possessions: oxen, and sheep, and camels, and donkeys, and a great household. ¹⁵And he sowed in the land of the Philistines and brought in a hundredfold, and Isaac became exceedingly great, and the Philistines envied him. ¹⁶Now all the wells which the servants of Abraham had dug during the life of Abraham, the Philistines had stopped them after the death of Abraham and filled them with earth. ¹⁷And Abimelech said to Isaac, "Go from us, for you are much mightier than us"; and Isaac departed from there in the first year of the seventh week and sojourned in the valleys of Gerar. ¹⁸And they dug the wells of water again which the servants of his father Abraham had dug, and which the Philistines had closed after the death of his father Abraham, and he called their names as his father Abraham had named them. ¹⁹And the servants of Isaac dug a well in the valley, and found living water, and the shepherds of Gerar strove with the shepherds of Isaac, saying, "The water is ours"; and Isaac called the name of the well "Perversity," because they had been perverse with us. ²⁰And they dug a second well, and they strove for that also, and he called its name "Enmity." And he arose from there and they dug another well, and for that they did not strive, and he called the name of it "Room," and Isaac said, "Now the LORD has made room for us, and we have increased in the land." ²¹And he went up from there to the Well of the Oath in the first year of the first week, in the forty-fourth jubilee. ²²And the LORD appeared to him that night, on the new moon of the first month, and said to him, "I am the God of your father Abraham; do not fear, for I am with you, and will bless you and will surely multiply your seed as the sand of the earth, for the sake of my servant Abraham." ²³And he built an altar there, which his father Abraham had first built, and he called on the Name of the LORD, and he offered sacrifice to the God of his father Abraham. ²⁴And they dug a well and they found living water. ²⁵And the servants of Isaac dug another well and did not find water, and they went and told Isaac that they had not found water, and Isaac said, "I have sworn this day to the Philistines and this thing has been announced to us." ²⁶And he called the name of that place the "Well of the Oath," for there he had sworn to Abimelech, and his friend Ahuzzath, and Phicol, the prefect of his host. ²⁷And Isaac knew that day that under constraint he had sworn to them to make peace with them. ²⁸And on that day Isaac cursed the Philistines and said, "Cursed are the Philistines to the day of wrath and

indignation from the midst of all nations; may God make them a derision, and a curse, and an object of wrath and indignation in the hands of the sinners—the nations—and in the hands of the Kittim. ²⁹And whoever escapes the sword of the enemy and the Kittim, may the righteous nation root out in judgment from under Heaven, for they will be the enemies, and enemies of my children, throughout their generations on the earth. ³⁰And no remnant will be left to them, nor one that will be saved on the day of the wrath of judgment, for destruction, and rooting out, and expulsion from the earth is the whole seed of the Philistines [reserved], and there will no longer be left for these Caphtorim a name or a seed on the earth. ³¹For though he ascends into Heaven, from there he will be brought down, and though he makes himself strong on earth, from there he will be dragged out, and though he hides himself among the nations, even from there he will be rooted out, and though he descends into Sheol, there also will his condemnation be great, and there also he will have no peace. ³²And if he goes into captivity, by the hands of those that seek his life they will slay him on the way, and neither name nor seed will be left to him on all the earth, for he will depart into a continuous curse." ³³And thus is it written and engraved concerning him on the heavenly tablets, to do to him on the Day of Judgment, so that he may be rooted out of the earth.

CHAPTER 25

¹And in the second year of this week, in this jubilee, Rebekah called her son Jacob and spoke to him, saying, "My son, do not take a wife for yourself of the daughters of Canaan, as your brother Esau, who took two wives of the daughters of Canaan for himself, and they have embittered my soul with all their unclean deeds, for all their deeds are fornication and lust, and there is no righteousness with them, for [their deeds] are evil. ²And I, my son, love you exceedingly, and my heart and my affection bless you every hour of the day and watch of the night. ³And now, my son, listen to my voice, and do the will of your mother, and do not take a wife for yourself of the daughters of this land, but only of the house of my father, and of my father's relatives; you will take a wife of the house of my father, and the Most High God will bless you, and your children will be a righteous generation and a holy seed." ⁴And then Jacob spoke to his mother Rebekah, and said to her, "Behold, mother, I am nine weeks of years old, and I neither know nor have I touched any woman, nor have I betrothed myself to any, nor even think of taking a wife for myself of the daughters of Canaan. ⁵For I remember, mother, the words of our father Abraham, for he commanded me not to take a wife of the daughters of Canaan, but to take a wife for myself from the seed of my father's house and from my relatives. ⁶I have heard before that daughters have been born to your brother Laban, and I have set my heart on them to take a wife from among them. ⁷And for this reason I have guarded myself in my spirit against sinning or being corrupted in all my ways throughout all the days of my life, for with regard to lust and fornication, my father Abraham gave me many commands. ⁸And despite all that he has commanded me, these twenty-two years my brother has striven with me, and spoken frequently to me, and said, My brother, take a sister of my two wives to be [your] wife; but I refuse to do as he has done. ⁹I swear before you, mother, that all the days of my life I will not take a wife for myself from the daughters of the seed of Canaan, and I will not act wickedly as my brother has done. ¹⁰Do not fear, mother; be assured that I will do your will, and walk in uprightness, and not corrupt my ways forever." ¹¹And immediately she lifted up her face to Heaven, and extended the fingers of her hands, and opened her mouth, and blessed the Most High God who had created the heavens and the earth, and she gave Him thanks and praise. ¹²And she said, "Blessed is the LORD God, and may His holy Name be blessed forever and ever, who has given me Jacob as a pure son and a holy seed; for He is Yours, and his seed will be Yours continually and throughout all the generations forevermore. ¹³Bless him, O LORD, and place in my mouth the blessing of righteousness, that I may bless him." ¹⁴And at that hour, when the Spirit of righteousness descended into her mouth, she placed both her hands on the head of Jacob, and said, ¹⁵"Blessed are You, LORD of righteousness and God of the ages. And may He bless you beyond all the generations of men. May He give you, my son, the path of righteousness, and reveal righteousness to your seed. ¹⁶And may He make your sons many during your life, and may they arise according to the number of the months of the year. And may their sons become many and great beyond the stars of the heavens, and their numbers be more than the sand of the sea. ¹⁷And may He give them this excellent land—as He said He would give it to Abraham and to his seed after him always—and may they hold it as a possession forever. ¹⁸And may I see [born] to you, my son, blessed children during my life, and a blessed and holy seed may all your seed be. ¹⁹And as you have refreshed your mother's spirit during my life, the womb of her that bore you blesses you, and my breasts bless you, and my mouth and my tongue praise you greatly. ²⁰Increase and spread over the earth, and may your seed be perfect in the joy of the heavens and earth forever; and may your seed rejoice, and on the great day of peace may it have peace. ²¹And may your name and your seed endure to all the ages, and may the Most High God be their God, and may the God of righteousness dwell with them, and by them may His sanctuary be built to all the ages. ²²Blessed is he that blesses you, and all flesh that curses you falsely—may it be cursed." ²³And she kissed him and said to him, "May the Lord of the world love you just as the heart of your mother and her affection rejoices in you and blesses you." And she ceased from blessing.

CHAPTER 26

¹And in the seventh year of this week Isaac called Esau, his elder son, and said to him, "I am old, my son, and behold, my eyes are dim in seeing, and I do not know the day of my death. ²And now take your hunting weapons, your quiver and your bow, and go out to the field, and hunt and catch me [game], my son, and make me savory meat, such as my soul loves, and bring it to me that I may eat, and that my soul may bless you before I die." ³But Rebekah heard Isaac speaking to Esau. ⁴And Esau went out early to the field to hunt, and catch, and bring home to his father. ⁵And Rebekah called her son Jacob and said to him, "Behold, I heard your father Isaac speak to your brother Esau, saying, Hunt for me, and make me savory meat, and bring [it] to me that I may eat and bless you before the LORD before I die. ⁶And now, my son, obey my voice in that which I command you: go to your flock and fetch me two good kids of the goats, and I will make him savory meat for your father, such as he loves, and you will bring [it] to your father that he may eat and bless you before the LORD before he die, and that you may be blessed." ⁷And Jacob said to his mother Rebekah, "Mother, I will not withhold anything which my father would eat, and which would please him: only I fear, my mother, that he will recognize my voice and wish to touch me. ⁸And you know that I am smooth, and my brother Esau is hairy, and I will appear before his eyes as an evildoer, and will do a deed which he had not commanded me, and he will be angry with me, and I will bring a curse on myself, and not a blessing." ⁹And his mother Rebekah said to him, "Your curse be on me, my son, only obey my voice." ¹⁰And Jacob obeyed the voice of his mother Rebekah, and went and fetched two good and fat kids of the goats, and brought them to his mother, and his mother made them [savory meat] such as he loved. ¹¹And Rebekah took the attractive raiment of her elder son Esau, which was with her in the house, and she clothed her younger son Jacob [with them], and she put the skins of the kids on his hands and on the exposed parts of his neck. ¹²And she gave the meat and the bread which she had prepared into the hand of her son Jacob. ¹³And Jacob went in to his father and said, "I am your son: I have done according as you commanded me. Arise, and sit, and eat of that which I have caught, father, that your soul may bless me." ¹⁴And Isaac said to his son, "How have you found [game] so quickly, my son?" ¹⁵And Jacob said, "Because [the LORD] your God caused me to find [it]." ¹⁶And Isaac said to him, "Come near, that I may feel you, my son, if you are my son Esau or not." ¹⁷And Jacob went near to his father Isaac, and he felt him, and said, ¹⁸"The voice is Jacob's voice, but the hands are the hands of Esau," and he did not discern him, because it was a dispensation from Heaven to remove his power of perception, and Isaac did not discern, for his hands were as hairy as [his brother] Esau's, so that he blessed him. ¹⁹And he said, "Are you my son Esau?" and he said, "I am your son,"

and he said, "Bring [it] near to me that I may eat of that which you have caught, my son, that my soul may bless you." ²⁰And he brought [it] near to him, and he ate, and he brought him wine and he drank. ²¹And his father Isaac said to him, "Come near and kiss me, my son." And he came near and kissed him. ²²And he smelled the smell of his raiment, and he blessed him, and said, "Behold, the smell of my son is as the smell of a [full] field which the LORD has blessed. ²³And may the LORD give you of the dew of the heavens and of the dew of the earth, and plenty of corn and oil: Let nations serve you || And peoples bow down to you. ²⁴Be lord over your brothers || And let your mother's sons bow down to you; And may all the blessings with which the LORD has blessed me and blessed my father Abraham || Be imparted to you and to your seed forever. Cursed is he that curses you, || And blessed is he that blesses you." ²⁵And it came to pass as soon as Isaac had made an end of blessing his son Jacob and Jacob had gone out from his father Isaac, he hid himself, and his brother Esau came in from his hunting. ²⁶And he also made savory meat, and brought [it] to his father, and said to his father, "Let my father arise and eat of my venison that your soul may bless me." ²⁷And his father Isaac said to him, "Who are you?" And he said to him, "I am your firstborn, your son Esau: I have done as you have commanded me." ²⁸And Isaac was very greatly astonished, and said, "Who is he that has hunted, and caught, and brought [it] to me? And I have eaten of all before you came and have blessed him: [and] he will be blessed, and all his seed forever." ²⁹And it came to pass when Esau heard the words of his father Isaac that he cried with an exceedingly great and bitter cry, and said to his father, "Bless me, me also, father!" ³⁰And he said to him, "Your brother came with guile, and has taken away your blessing." And he said, "Now I know why his name is named Jacob: behold, he has supplanted me these two times; he took away my birthright, and now he has taken away my blessing." ³¹And he said, "Have you not reserved a blessing for me, father?" And Isaac answered and said to Esau, "Behold, I have made him your lord, and I have given all his brothers to him for servants, and I have strengthened him with plenty of corn, and wine, and oil: and what now will I do for you, my son?" ³²And Esau said to his father Isaac, "Have you but one blessing, O father? Bless me, [even] me also, father!" And Esau lifted up his voice and wept. ³³And Isaac answered and said to him, "Behold, your dwelling will be far from the dew of the earth, and far from the dew of the heavens from above. ³⁴And you will live by your sword, and you will serve your brother. And it will come to pass when you become great, and shake his yoke from off your neck, you will sin a complete sin to death, and your seed will be rooted out from under Heaven." ³⁵And Esau kept threatening Jacob because of the blessing with which his father blessed him, and he said in his heart, "May the days of mourning for my father now come, so that I may slay my brother Jacob."

CHAPTER 27

¹And the words of her elder son Esau were told to Rebekah in a dream, and Rebekah sent and called her younger son Jacob, and said to him, ²"Behold, your brother Esau will take vengeance on you so as to kill you. ³Now, therefore, my son, obey my voice, and arise and flee to my brother Laban, to Haran, and tarry with him a few days until your brother's anger turns away, and he removes his anger from you, and forgets all that you have done; then I will send and fetch you from there." ⁴And Jacob said, "I am not afraid; if he wishes to kill me, I will kill him." ⁵But she said to him, "Let me not be deprived of both my sons on one day." ⁶And Jacob said to his mother Rebekah, "Behold, you know that my father has become old and does not see because his eyes are dull, and if I leave him it will be evil in his eyes, because I leave him and go away from you, and my father will be angry, and will curse me. I will not go; when he sends me, then only will I go." ⁷And Rebekah said to Jacob, "I will go in and speak to him, and he will send you away." ⁸And Rebekah went in and said to Isaac, "I loathe my life because of the two daughters of Heth, whom Esau has taken to himself as wives; and if Jacob takes a wife from among the daughters of the land such as these, for what further purpose do I live? For the daughters of Canaan are evil." ⁹And Isaac called Jacob and blessed him, and admonished him, and said to him, ¹⁰"Do not take a wife for yourself of any of the daughters of Canaan; arise and go to Mesopotamia, to the house of Bethuel, your mother's father, and take a wife for yourself from there of the daughters of Laban, your mother's brother. ¹¹And may God Almighty bless you, and increase and multiply you, that you may become a company of nations, and give you the blessings of my father Abraham—to you and to your seed after you—that you may inherit the land of your sojournings and all the land which God gave to Abraham. Go, my son, in peace." ¹²And Isaac sent Jacob away, and he went to Mesopotamia, to Laban the son of Bethuel the Syrian, the brother of Rebekah, Jacob's mother. ¹³And it came to pass after Jacob had arisen to go to Mesopotamia that the spirit of Rebekah was grieved after her son, and she wept. ¹⁴And Isaac said to Rebekah, "My sister, do not weep on account of my son Jacob, for he goes in peace, and in peace he will return. ¹⁵The Most High God will preserve him from all evil and will be with him, for He will not forsake him all his days, ¹⁶for I know that his ways will be prospered in all things wherever he goes, until he returns to us in peace and we see him in peace. ¹⁷Do not fear on his account, my sister, for he is on the upright path and he is a perfect man: and he is faithful and will not perish. Do not weep." ¹⁸And Isaac comforted Rebekah on account of her son Jacob and blessed him. ¹⁹And Jacob went from the Well of the Oath to go to Haran on the first year of the second week, in the forty-fourth Jubilee, and he came to Luz on the mountains, that is, Bethel, on the new moon of the first month of this week, and he came to the place at evening and turned from the way to the west of the road that night: and he slept there, for the sun had set. ²⁰And he took one of the stones of that place and laid it [at his head] under the tree, and he was journeying alone, and he slept. ²¹And he dreamt that night, and behold, a ladder [was] set up on the earth, and the top of it reached to Heaven, and behold, the messengers of the LORD ascended and descended on it: and behold, the LORD stood on it. ²²And He spoke to Jacob and said, "I am the LORD God of your father Abraham and the God of Isaac; the land on which you are sleeping, to you I will give it, and to your seed after you. ²³And your seed will be as the dust of the earth, and you will increase to the west and to the east, to the north and the south, and in you and in your Seed all the families of the nations will be blessed. ²⁴And behold, I will be with you, and will keep you wherever you go, and I will bring you into this land again in peace, for I will not leave you until I do everything that I told you of." ²⁵And Jacob awoke from his sleep, and said, "Truly this place is the house of the LORD, and I did not know it." And he was afraid and said, "This place is dreadful, which is none other than the house of God, and this is the gate of Heaven." ²⁶And Jacob arose early in the morning and took the stone which he had put under his head and set it up as a pillar for a sign, and he poured oil on the top of it. And he called the name of that place Bethel, but the name of the place was Luz at the first. ²⁷And Jacob vowed a vow to the LORD, saying, "If the LORD will be with me, and will keep me in this way that I go, and give me bread to eat and raiment to put on, so that I come to my father's house again in peace, then the LORD will be my God, and this stone which I have set up as a pillar for a sign in this place will be the LORD's house, and of all that You give me, I will give the tenth to You, my God."

CHAPTER 28

¹And he went on his journey, and came to the land of the east, to Laban, the brother of Rebekah, and he was with him, and served him for his daughter Rachel [for] one week. ²And in the first year of the third week he said to him, "Give me my wife, for whom I have served you seven years"; and Laban said to Jacob, "I will give you your wife." ³And Laban made a feast, and took his elder daughter Leah, and gave [her] to Jacob as a wife, and gave her his handmaid Zilpah for a handmaid, and Jacob did not know, for he thought that she was Rachel. ⁴And he went in to her, and behold, she was Leah; and Jacob was angry with Laban, and said to him, "Why have you dealt thus with me? Did I not serve you for Rachel and not for Leah? Why have you wronged me? Take your daughter, and I will go, for you have done evil to me." ⁵For Jacob loved Rachel more than Leah, for Leah's eyes were weak, but her form was very attractive, but Rachel had beautiful eyes and a beautiful and very attractive form. ⁶And Laban said to Jacob, "It is not so done in our country, to give the younger before the elder." And it is not

right to do this, for thus it is ordained and written in the heavenly tablets that no one should give his younger daughter before the elder—but he gives the elder one first and after her the younger—and the man who does so, they set down guilt against him in Heaven, and none is righteous that does this thing, for this deed is evil before the LORD. ⁷And command the sons of Israel that they do not do this thing; let them neither take nor give the younger before they have given the elder, for it is very wicked. ⁸And Laban said to Jacob, "Let the seven days of the celebration of this one pass by, and I will give you Rachel, that you may serve me another seven years, that you may pasture my sheep as you did in the former week." ⁹And on the day when the seven days of the celebration of Leah had passed, Laban gave Rachel to Jacob, that he might serve him another seven years, and he gave to Rachel Bilhah, the sister of Zilpah, as a handmaid. ¹⁰And he served yet another seven years for Rachel, for Leah had been given to him for nothing. ¹¹And the LORD opened the womb of Leah, and she conceived and bore Jacob a son, and he called his name Reuben, on the fourteenth day of the ninth month, in the first year of the third week. ¹²But the womb of Rachel was closed, for the LORD saw that Leah was hated and Rachel loved. ¹³And again Jacob went in to Leah, and she conceived, and bore Jacob a second son, and he called his name Simeon, on the twenty-first of the tenth month, and in the third year of this week. ¹⁴And again Jacob went in to Leah, and she conceived, and bore him a third son, and he called his name Levi, in the new moon of the first month, in the sixth year of this week. ¹⁵And again Jacob went in to her, and she conceived, and bore him a fourth son, and he called his name Judah, on the fifteenth of the third month, in the first year of the fourth week. ¹⁶And on account of all this, Rachel envied Leah, for she did not bear, and she said to Jacob, "Give me children"; and Jacob said, "Have I withheld from you the fruits of your womb? Have I forsaken you?" ¹⁷And when Rachel saw that Leah had borne four sons to Jacob—Reuben, and Simeon, and Levi, and Judah—she said to him, "Go in to my handmaid Bilhah, and she will conceive, and bear a son to me." ¹⁸And he went in to her, and she conceived, and bore him a son, and he called his name Dan, on the ninth of the sixth month, in the sixth year of the third week. ¹⁹And Jacob went in again to Bilhah a second time, and she conceived, and bore Jacob another son, and Rachel called his name Naphtali, on the fifth of the seventh month, in the second year of the fourth week. ²⁰And when Leah saw that she had become sterile and did not bear, she envied [Rachel] and she also gave her handmaid Zilpah to Jacob to be [his] wife, and she conceived, and bore a son, and Leah called his name Gad, on the twelfth of the eighth month, in the third year of the fourth week. ²¹And he went in again to her, and she conceived, and bore him a second son, and Leah called his name Asher, on the second of the eleventh month, in the fifth year of the fourth week. ²²And Jacob went in to Leah, and she conceived, and bore a son, and she called his name Issachar, on the fourth of the fifth month, in the fourth year of the fourth week, and she gave him to a nurse. ²³And Jacob went in again to her, and she conceived, and bore two [children], a son and a daughter, and she called the name of the son Zebulun, and the name of the daughter Dinah, in the seventh of the seventh month, in the sixth year of the fourth week. ²⁴And the LORD was gracious to Rachel, and opened her womb, and she conceived, and bore a son, and she called his name Joseph, on the new moon of the fourth month, in the sixth year in this fourth week. ²⁵And in the days when Joseph was born, Jacob said to Laban, "Give me my wives and sons, and let me go to my father Isaac, and let me make myself a house, for I have completed the years in which I have served you for your two daughters, and I will go to the house of my father." ²⁶And Laban said to Jacob, "Tarry with me for your wages, and pasture my flock for me again, and take your wages." ²⁷And they agreed with one another that he should give him as his wages those of the lambs and kids which were born black, and spotted, and white; [these] were to be his wages. ²⁸And all the sheep brought out spotted, and speckled, and black, variously marked, and they brought out again lambs like themselves, and all that were spotted were Jacob's and those which were not were Laban's. ²⁹And Jacob's possessions multiplied exceedingly, and he possessed oxen, and sheep, and donkeys, and camels, and menservants, and maidservants. ³⁰And Laban and his sons envied Jacob, and Laban took back his sheep from him, and he observed him with evil intent.

CHAPTER 29

¹And it came to pass when Rachel had borne Joseph, that Laban went to shear his sheep, for they were distant from him a three days' journey. ²And Jacob saw that Laban was going to shear his sheep, and Jacob called Leah and Rachel, and spoke kindly to them that they should come with him to the land of Canaan. ³For he told them how he had seen everything in a dream, even all that He had spoken to him that he should return to his father's house, and they said, "To every place where you go we will go with you." ⁴And Jacob blessed the God of his father Isaac, and the God of Abraham, his father's father, and he arose and mounted his wives and his children, and took all his possessions and crossed the river, and came to the land of Gilead, and Jacob hid his intention from Laban and did not tell him. ⁵And in the seventh year of the fourth week Jacob turned [his face] toward Gilead in the first month, on the twenty-first thereof. And Laban pursued after him and overtook Jacob in the mountain of Gilead in the third month, on the thirteenth thereof. ⁶And the LORD did not permit him to injure Jacob, for He appeared to him in a dream by night. And Laban spoke to Jacob, ⁷and on the fifteenth of those days Jacob made a feast for Laban and for all who came with him, and Jacob swore to Laban that day, and Laban also to Jacob, that neither should cross the mountain of Gilead to the other with evil purpose. ⁸And he made a heap there for a witness; for that reason the name of that place is called "The Heap of Witness," after this heap. ⁹But before [that] they used to call the land of Gilead the land of the Rephaim, for it was the land of the Rephaim, and the Rephaim were born [there]—giants whose height was ten, nine, eight, [and] down to seven cubits. ¹⁰And their habitation was from the land of the children of Ammon to Mount Hermon, and the seats of their kingdom were Karnaim, and Ashtaroth, and Edrei, and Mîsûr, and Beon. ¹¹And the LORD destroyed them because of the evil of their deeds, for they were very malevolent, and the Amorites dwelt in their stead, wicked and sinful, and there is no people today which has worked to the measure of all their sins, and they have no more length of life on the earth. ¹²And Jacob sent Laban away, and he departed into Mesopotamia, the land of the east, and Jacob returned to the land of Gilead. ¹³And he passed over the Jabbok in the ninth month, on the eleventh thereof. And on that day his brother Esau came to him, and he was reconciled to him, and departed from him to the land of Seir, but Jacob dwelt in tents. ¹⁴And in the first year of the fifth week in this jubilee he crossed the Jordan, and dwelt beyond the Jordan, and he pastured his sheep from the sea of the heap to Bethshan, and to Dothan, and to the forest of Akrabbim. ¹⁵And he sent to his father Isaac of all his substance: clothing, and food, and meat, and drink, and milk, and butter, and cheese, and some dates of the valley; ¹⁶and also to his mother Rebekah four times a year, between the times of the months, between plowing and reaping, and between autumn and the rain [season], and between winter and spring, to the tower of Abraham. ¹⁷For Isaac had returned from the Well of the Oath and gone up to the tower of his father Abraham, and he dwelt there apart from his son Esau. ¹⁸For in the days when Jacob went to Mesopotamia, Esau took to himself Mahalath, the daughter of Ishmael, to be [his] wife, and he gathered together all the flocks of his father and his wives, and went up and dwelt on Mount Seir, and left his father Isaac at the Well of the Oath alone. ¹⁹And Isaac went up from the Well of the Oath and dwelt in the tower of his father Abraham on the mountains of Hebron, ²⁰and there Jacob sent all that he sent to his father and his mother from time to time—all they needed—and they blessed Jacob with all their heart and with all their soul.

CHAPTER 30

¹And in the first year of the sixth week he went up to Salem, to the east of Shechem, in peace, in the fourth month. ²And there they carried off Dinah, the daughter of Jacob, into the house of Shechem, the son of Hamor, the Hivite, the prince of the land, and he lay with her and defiled her, and she was a little girl, a child of twelve years. ³And he implored his father and her brothers that she might be given to him to

be [his] wife. And Jacob and his sons were angry because of the men of Shechem, for they had defiled their sister Dinah, and they spoke to them with evil intent, and dealt deceitfully with them, and deceived them. ⁴And Simeon and Levi came stealthily to Shechem, and executed judgment on all the men of Shechem, and slew all the men whom they found in it, and left not a single one remaining in it: they slew all in torments because they had dishonored their sister Dinah. ⁵And thus do not let it be done again from now on that a daughter of Israel is defiled, for judgment is ordained in Heaven against them that they should destroy with the sword all the men of the Shechemites because they had worked shame in Israel. ⁶And the LORD delivered them into the hands of the sons of Jacob that they might exterminate them with the sword, and execute judgment on them, and that it might not thus be done again in Israel that a virgin of Israel should be defiled. ⁷And if there is any man in Israel who wishes to give his daughter or his sister to any man who is of the seed of the nations, he will surely die, and they will stone him with stones, for he has worked shame in Israel; and they will burn the woman with fire, because she has dishonored the name of the house of her father, and she will be rooted out of Israel. ⁸And do not let an adulteress be found, and no uncleanness, in Israel, throughout all the days of the generations of the earth, for Israel is holy to the LORD, and every man who has defiled [it] will surely die: they will stone him with stones. ⁹For thus it has been ordained and written in the heavenly tablets regarding all the seed of Israel: he who defiles [it] will surely die, and he will be stoned with stones. ¹⁰And to this law there is no limit of days, and no forgiveness, nor any atonement, but the man who has defiled his daughter will be rooted out in the midst of all Israel, because he has given of his seed to Moloch, and worked impiously so as to defile it. ¹¹And you, Moses, command the sons of Israel and exhort them not to give their daughters to the nations, and not to take any of the daughters of the nations for their sons, for this is abominable before the LORD. ¹²For this reason I have written for you in the words of the Law all the deeds of the Shechemites, which they worked against Dinah, and how the sons of Jacob spoke, saying, "We will not give our daughter to a man who is uncircumcised, for that would be a reproach to us." ¹³And it is a reproach to Israel to those who give and to those who take the daughters of the nations, for this is unclean and abominable to Israel. ¹⁴And Israel will not be free from this uncleanness if it has a wife of the daughters of the nations or has given any of its daughters to a man who is of any of the nations. ¹⁵For there will be plague on plague, and curse on curse, and every judgment, and plague, and curse will come [on him] if he does this thing, or hides his eyes from those who commit uncleanness, or those who defile the sanctuary of the LORD, or those who profane His holy Name, [for] the whole nation will be judged together for all the uncleanness and desecration of this [man]. ¹⁶And there will be no respect of persons, and no receiving at his hands of fruits, and offerings, and burnt-offerings, and fat, nor the fragrance of sweet savor, so as to accept it: and likewise for every man or woman in Israel who defiles the sanctuary. ¹⁷For this reason I have commanded you, saying, "Testify this testimony to Israel: see how the Shechemites and their sons fared, how they were delivered into the hands of two sons of Jacob, and they slew them under tortures, and it was [reckoned] to them for righteousness, and it is written down to them for righteousness. ¹⁸And the seed of Levi was chosen for the priesthood, and to be Levites, that they might minister before the LORD, as we, continually, and that Levi and his sons may be blessed forever, for he was zealous to execute righteousness, and judgment, and vengeance on all those who arose against Israel. ¹⁹And so they inscribe as a testimony in his favor on the heavenly tablets blessing and righteousness before the God of all; ²⁰and we remember the righteousness which the man fulfilled during his life, at all periods of the year; until one thousand generations they will [still] record it, and it will come to him and to his descendants after him, and he has been recorded on the heavenly tablets as a friend and a righteous man. ²¹All this account I have written for you and have commanded you to say to the sons of Israel, that they should not commit sin, nor transgress the ordinances, nor break the covenant which has been ordained for them, [but] that they should fulfill it and be recorded as friends. ²²But if they transgress and work uncleanness in every way, they will be recorded on the heavenly tablets as adversaries, and they will be destroyed out of the Scroll of Life, and they will be recorded in the scroll of those who will be destroyed and with those who will be rooted out of the earth. ²³And on the day when the sons of Jacob slew Shechem, a writing was recorded in their favor in Heaven that they had executed righteousness, and uprightness, and vengeance on the sinners, and it was written for a blessing. ²⁴And they brought their sister Dinah out of the house of Shechem, and they took everything captive that was in Shechem: their sheep, and their oxen, and their donkeys, and all their wealth, and all their flocks; and they brought them all to their father Jacob. ²⁵And he reproached them because they had put the city to the sword, for he feared those who dwelt in the land, the Canaanites and the Perizzites. ²⁶And the dread of the LORD was on all the cities which are around Shechem, and they did not rise to pursue after the sons of Jacob, for terror had fallen on them."

CHAPTER 31

¹And on the new moon of the month Jacob spoke to all the people of his house, saying, "Purify yourselves and change your garments, and let us arise and go up to Bethel, where I vowed a vow to Him on the day when I fled from the face of my brother Esau, because He has been with me and has brought me into this land in peace, and put away the strange gods that are among you." ²And they gave up the strange gods, and that which was in their ears and which was on their necks, and the idols which Rachel stole from her father Laban she wholly gave to Jacob. And he burned and broke them to pieces, and destroyed them, and hid them under an oak which is in the land of Shechem. ³And he went up on the new moon of the seventh month to Bethel. And he built an altar at the place where he had slept, and he set up a pillar there, and he sent word to his father Isaac to come to him to his sacrifice, and to his mother Rebekah. ⁴And Isaac said, "Let my son Jacob come, and let me see him before I die." ⁵And Jacob went to his father Isaac and to his mother Rebekah, to the house of his father Abraham, and he took two of his sons with him, Levi and Judah, and he came to his father Isaac and to his mother Rebekah. ⁶And Rebekah came out from the tower to the front of it to kiss Jacob and embrace him, for her spirit had revived when she heard: "Behold, your son Jacob has come!" And she kissed him. ⁷And she saw his two sons, and she recognized them, and said to him, "Are these your sons, my son?" and she embraced them, and kissed them, and blessed them, saying, "In you the seed of Abraham will become illustrious, and you will prove a blessing on the earth." ⁸And Jacob went in to his father Isaac, to the chamber where he lay, and his two sons were with him, and he took the hand of his father, and stooping down, he kissed him, and Isaac clung to the neck of his son Jacob and wept on his neck. ⁹And the darkness left the eyes of Isaac, and he saw the two sons of Jacob, Levi and Judah, and he said, "Are these your sons, my son? For they are like you." ¹⁰And he said to him that they were truly his sons: "And you have truly seen that they are truly my sons." ¹¹And they came near to him, and he turned and kissed them, and embraced them both together. ¹²And the spirit of prophecy came down into his mouth, and he took Levi by his right hand and Judah by his left. ¹³And he turned to Levi first, and began to bless him first, and said to him, "May the God of all, the very Lord of all the ages, || Bless you and your children throughout all the ages. ¹⁴And may the LORD give greatness and great glory to you and to your seed, || And cause you and your seed, from among all flesh, to approach Him || To serve in His sanctuary as the messengers of the presence and as the holy ones. [Even] as they, may the seed of your sons be for glory, and greatness, and holiness, || And may He make them great to all the ages. ¹⁵And they will be princes and judges, || And chiefs of all the seed of the sons of Jacob; They will speak the word of the LORD in righteousness, || And they will judge all His judgments in righteousness. And they will declare My ways to Jacob, || And My paths to Israel. The blessing of the LORD will be given in their mouths || To bless all the seed of the beloved. ¹⁶Your mother has called your name Levi, || And justly has she called your name; You will be joined to the LORD, || And be the companion of all the sons of Jacob; Let His

table be yours || And you and your sons will eat thereof; And may your table be full to all generations, || And your food will not fail to all the ages. ¹⁷And let all who hate you fall down before you, || And let all your adversaries be rooted out and perish; And blessed is he that blesses you || And cursed is every nation that curses you." ¹⁸And to Judah he said, "May the LORD give you strength and power || To tread down all that hate you; You will be a prince—you and one of your sons, || Over the sons of Jacob; May your name and the name of your sons || Go out and traverse every land and region. Then the nations will fear before your face, || And all the nations [[*or* peoples]] will quake. ¹⁹In you will be the help of Jacob, || And in you will be found the salvation of Israel. ²⁰And when you sit on the throne of the honor of your righteousness, || There will be great peace for all the seed of the sons of the beloved, || And he that blesses you will be blessed; And all that hate you, and afflict you, and curse you || Will be rooted out and destroyed from the earth and accursed." ²¹And turning, he kissed him again and embraced him, and greatly rejoiced, for he had seen the sons of his son Jacob in exceeding truth. ²²And he went out from between his feet and fell down and worshiped him. And he blessed them. And [Jacob] rested there with his father Isaac that night, and they ate and drank with joy. ²³And he made the two sons of Jacob sleep—the one on his right hand and the other on his left, and it was counted to him for righteousness. ²⁴And Jacob told his father everything during the night, how the LORD had shown him great mercy, and how He had prospered [him in] all his ways and protected him from all evil. ²⁵And Isaac blessed the God of his father Abraham who had not withdrawn His mercy and His righteousness from the sons of His servant Isaac. ²⁶And in the morning, Jacob told his father Isaac the vow which he had vowed to the LORD, and the vision which he had seen, and that he had built an altar, and that everything was ready for the sacrifice to be made before the LORD as he had vowed, and that he had come to set him on a donkey. ²⁷And Isaac said to his son Jacob, "I am not able to go with you, for I am old and not able to bear the way: go, my son, in peace, for I am one hundred and sixty-five years [old] this day; I am no longer able to journey. Set your mother [on a donkey] and let her go with you. ²⁸And I know, my son, that you have come on my account, and may this day be blessed on which you have seen me alive, and I also have seen you, my son. ²⁹May you prosper and fulfill the vow which you have vowed, and do not put off your vow, for you will be called to account as touching the vow. Now, therefore, make sure to perform it, and may He be pleased who has made all things, to whom you have vowed the vow." ³⁰And he said to Rebekah, "Go with your son Jacob"; and Rebekah went with her son Jacob, and Deborah with her, and they came to Bethel. ³¹And Jacob remembered the prayer with which his father had blessed him and his two sons, Levi and Judah, and he rejoiced and blessed the God of his fathers Abraham and Isaac. ³²And he said, "Now I know that I have a continuous hope, and my sons also, before the God of all"; and thus it is ordained concerning the two; and they record it as a perpetual testimony to them on the heavenly tablets how Isaac blessed them.

CHAPTER 32

¹And he stayed that night at Bethel, and Levi dreamed that they had ordained and made him the priest of the Most High God, him and his sons forever; and he awoke from his sleep and blessed the LORD. ²And Jacob rose early in the morning, on the fourteenth of this month, and he gave a tithe of all that came with him, both of men and cattle, both of gold and every vessel and garment, yes, he gave tithes of all. ³And in those days Rachel became pregnant with her son Benjamin. And Jacob counted his sons from him upwards and Levi fell to the portion of the LORD, and his father clothed him in the garments of the priesthood and filled his hands. ⁴And on the fifteenth of this month, he brought to the altar fourteen oxen from among the cattle, and twenty-eight rams, and forty-nine sheep, and seven lambs, and twenty-one kids of the goats as a burnt-offering on the altar of sacrifice, well pleasing for a sweet savor before God. ⁵This was his offering, in consequence of the vow which he had vowed that he would give a tenth, with their fruit-offerings and their drink-offerings. ⁶And when the fire had consumed it, he burned incense on the fire over the fire, and for a thank-offering two oxen, and four rams, and four sheep, four male goats, and two sheep of a year old, and two kids of the goats; and thus he did daily for seven days. ⁷And he, and all his sons, and his men were eating [this] with joy there for seven days and were blessing and thanking the LORD who had delivered him out of all his tribulation and had given him his vow. ⁸And he tithed all the clean animals, and made a burnt sacrifice, but he did [not] give the unclean animals to his son Levi, and he gave him all the souls of the men. ⁹And Levi discharged the priestly office at Bethel before his father Jacob in preference to his ten brothers, and he was a priest there, and Jacob gave his vow: thus he tithed the tithe to the LORD again and sanctified it, and it became holy to Him. ¹⁰And for this reason it is ordained on the heavenly tablets as a law for the tithing the tithe again to eat before the LORD from year to year in the place where it is chosen that His Name should dwell, and to this law there is no limit of days forever. ¹¹This ordinance is written that it may be fulfilled from year to year in eating the second tithe before the LORD in the place where it has been chosen, and nothing will remain over from it from this year to the year following. ¹²For in its year the seed will be eaten until the days of the gathering of the seed of the year, and the wine until the days of the wine, and the oil until the days of its season. ¹³And all that is left thereof and becomes old, let it be regarded as polluted: let it be burned with fire, for it is unclean. ¹⁴And thus let them eat it together in the sanctuary and do not let them permit it to become old. ¹⁵And all the tithes of the oxen and sheep will be holy to the LORD, and will belong to His priests, which they will eat before Him from year to year, for thus it is ordained and engraved regarding the tithe on the heavenly tablets. ¹⁶And on the following night, on the twenty-second day of this month, Jacob resolved to build that place, and to surround the court with a wall, and to sanctify it and make it holy forever, for himself and his children after him. ¹⁷And the LORD appeared to him by night, and blessed him, and said to him, "Your name will not be called Jacob, but Israel they will name your name." ¹⁸And He said to him again, "I am the LORD who created the heavens and the earth, and I will increase you and multiply you exceedingly, and kings will come out from you, and they will judge everywhere, wherever the foot of the sons of men has trodden. ¹⁹And I will give to your seed all the earth which is under the heavens, and they will judge all the nations according to their desires, and after that, they will get possession of the whole earth and inherit it forever." ²⁰And He finished speaking with him, and He went up from him, and Jacob looked until He had ascended into Heaven. ²¹And he saw in a vision of the night, and behold, a messenger descended from Heaven with seven tablets in his hands, and he gave them to Jacob, and he read them and knew all that was written therein which would befall him and his sons throughout all the ages. ²²And he showed him all that was written on the tablets and said to him, "Do not build this place, and do not make it a perpetual sanctuary, and do not dwell here, for this is not the place. Go to the house of your father Abraham and dwell with your father Isaac until the day of the death of your father. ²³For in Egypt you will die in peace, and you will be buried in this land with honor in the tomb of your fathers, with Abraham and Isaac. ²⁴Do not fear, for as you have seen and read it, thus it will all be; and write down everything as you have seen and read." ²⁵And Jacob said, "Lord, how can I remember all that I have read and seen?" And he said to him, "I will bring all things to your remembrance." ²⁶And he went up from him, and he awoke from his sleep, and he remembered everything which he had read and seen, and he wrote down all the words which he had read and seen. ²⁷And he celebrated there yet another day, and he sacrificed thereon according to all that he sacrificed on the former days, and called its name "Addition," for this day was added, and the former days he called "The Feast." ²⁸And thus it was manifested that it should be, and it is written on the heavenly tablets, for that reason it was revealed to him that he should celebrate it and add it to the seven days of the feast. ²⁹And its name was called "Addition," because that it was recorded among the days of the feast days, according to the number of the days of the year. ³⁰And in the night, on the twenty-third of this month, Rebekah's nurse Deborah died, and they buried her beneath the city under the oak of the river, and he

called the name of this place, "The river of Deborah," and the oak, "The oak of the mourning of Deborah." ³¹And Rebekah went and returned to her house, to his father Isaac, and Jacob sent by her hand rams, and sheep, and male goats that she should prepare a meal for his father such as he desired. ³²And he went after his mother until he came to the land of Kabrâtân, and he dwelt there. ³³And Rachel bore a son in the night and called his name "Son of my sorrow," for she suffered in giving him birth, but his father called his name Benjamin, on the eleventh of the eighth month, in the first of the sixth week of this jubilee. ³⁴And Rachel died there, and she was buried in the land of Ephrath, the same is Beth-Lehem, and Jacob built a pillar on the grave of Rachel, on the road above her grave.

CHAPTER 33

¹And Jacob went and dwelt to the south of Magdalâdrâ'êf. And he went to his father Isaac, he and his wife Leah, on the new moon of the tenth month. ²And Reuben saw Bilhah, Rachel's maid, the concubine of his father, bathing in water in a secret place, and he loved her. ³And he hid himself at night, and he entered the house of Bilhah [at night], and he found her sleeping alone on a bed in her house. ⁴And he lay with her, and she awoke and saw, and behold, Reuben was lying with her in the bed, and she uncovered the border of her covering and seized him, and cried out, and discovered that it was Reuben. ⁵And she was ashamed because of him, and released her hand from him, and he fled. ⁶And she lamented exceedingly because of this thing and did not tell it to anyone. ⁷And when Jacob returned and sought her, she said to him, "I am not clean for you, for I have been defiled as regards you, for Reuben has defiled me, and has lain with me in the night, and I was asleep, and did not discover [it] until he uncovered my skirt and slept with me." ⁸And Jacob was exceedingly angry with Reuben because he had lain with Bilhah, because he had uncovered his father's skirt. ⁹And Jacob did not approach her again because Reuben had defiled her. And as for any man who uncovers his father's skirt: his deed is exceedingly wicked, for he is abominable before the LORD. ¹⁰For this reason it is written and ordained on the heavenly tablets that a man should not lie with his father's wife, and should not uncover his father's skirt, for this is unclean: they will surely die together, the man who lies with his father's wife and the woman also, for they have worked uncleanness on the earth. ¹¹And there will be nothing unclean before our God in the nation which He has chosen for Himself as a possession. ¹²And again, it is written a second time: "Cursed is he who lies with the wife of his father, for he has uncovered his father's shame"; and all the holy ones of the LORD said, "So be it; so be it." ¹³And you, Moses, command the sons of Israel that they observe this word, for it [entails] a punishment of death; and it is unclean, and there is no atonement forever to atone for the man who has committed this, but he is to be put to death and slain, and stoned with stones, and rooted out from the midst of the people of our God. ¹⁴For to no man who does so in Israel is it permitted to remain alive a single day on the earth, for he is abominable and unclean. ¹⁵And do not let them say, "Life and forgiveness were granted to Reuben after he had lain with his father's concubine, and to her also though she had a husband, and her husband Jacob, his father, was still alive." ¹⁶For until that time there had not been revealed the ordinance, and judgment, and law in its completeness for all, but in your days [it has been revealed] as a law of seasons and of days, and a continuous law for the perpetual generations. ¹⁷And for this law there is no consummation of days, and no atonement for it, but they must both be rooted out in the midst of the nation: on the day on which they committed it they will slay them. ¹⁸And you, Moses, write [it] down for Israel that they may observe it, and do according to these words, and not commit a sin to death, for the LORD our God is judge, who does not respect persons and does not accept gifts. ¹⁹And tell them these words of the covenant, that they may hear and observe, and be on their guard with respect to them, and not be destroyed and rooted out of the land; for an uncleanness, and an abomination, and a contamination, and a pollution are all they who commit it on the earth before our God. ²⁰And there is no greater sin than the fornication which they commit on earth, for Israel is a holy nation to the LORD its God, and a nation of inheritance, and a priestly and royal nation, and for [His own] possession; and no such uncleanness will appear in the midst of the holy nation. ²¹And in the third year of this sixth week Jacob and all his sons went and dwelt in the house of Abraham, near his father Isaac and his mother Rebekah. ²²And these were the names of the sons of Jacob: the firstborn Reuben, Simeon, Levi, Judah, Issachar, Zebulun—the sons of Leah; and the sons of Rachel: Joseph and Benjamin; and the sons of Bilhah: Dan and Naphtali; and the sons of Zilpah: Gad and Asher; and Dinah, the daughter of Leah, the only daughter of Jacob. ²³And they came and bowed themselves to Isaac and Rebekah, and when they saw them, they blessed Jacob and all his sons, and Isaac rejoiced exceedingly, for he saw the sons of Jacob, his younger son, and he blessed them.

CHAPTER 34

¹And in the sixth year of this week, of this forty-fourth jubilee, Jacob sent his sons to pasture their sheep, and his servants with them, to the pastures of Shechem. ²And the seven kings of the Amorites assembled themselves together against them, to slay them, hiding themselves under the trees, and to take their cattle as a prey. ³And Jacob, and Levi, and Judah, and Joseph were in the house with their father Isaac, for his spirit was sorrowful, and they could not leave him; and Benjamin was the youngest, and for this reason remained with his father. ⁴And there came the king[s] of Tâphû, and the king[s] of 'Arêsa, and the king[s] of Sêragân, and the king[s] of Sêlô, and the king[s] of Gâ'as, and the king of Bêthôrôn, and the king of Ma'anîsâkîr, and all those who dwell in these mountains [and] who dwell in the woods in the land of Canaan. ⁵And they announced this to Jacob, saying, "Behold, the kings of the Amorites have surrounded your sons, and plundered their herds." ⁶And he arose from his house—he, and his three sons, and all the servants of his father, and his own servants—and he went against them with six thousand men who carried swords. ⁷And he slew them in the pastures of Shechem, and pursued those who fled, and he slew them with the edge of the sword, and he slew 'Arêsa, and Tâphû, and Sêragân, and Sêlô, and Ma'anîsâkîr, and Gâ'as, and he recovered his herds. ⁸And he prevailed over them, and imposed tribute on them that they should pay him tribute, five fruit products of their land, and he built Rôbêl and Tamnâtârês, ⁹and he returned in peace, and made peace with them, and they became his servants until the day that he and his sons went down into Egypt. ¹⁰And in the seventh year of this week he sent Joseph from his house to the land of Shechem to learn about the welfare of his brothers, and he found them in the land of Dothan. ¹¹And they dealt treacherously with him, and formed a plot against him to slay him, but changing their minds, they sold him to Ishmaelite merchants, and they brought him down into Egypt, and they sold him to Potiphar, the eunuch of Pharaoh, the chief of the cooks, priest of the city of 'Êlêw. ¹²And the sons of Jacob slaughtered a kid, and dipped the coat of Joseph in the blood, and sent [it] to their father Jacob on the tenth of the seventh month. ¹³And he mourned all that night, for they had brought it to him in the evening, and he became feverish with mourning for his death, and he said, "An evil beast has devoured Joseph"; and all the members of his house were grieving and mourning with him that whole day. ¹⁴And his sons and his daughter rose up to comfort him, but he refused to be comforted for his son. ¹⁵And on that day, Bilhah heard that Joseph had perished, and she died mourning [for] him, and she was living in Qafrâtêf and Dinah also, his daughter, died after Joseph had perished. And these three mournings came on Israel in one month. ¹⁶And they buried Bilhah over against the tomb of Rachel, and Dinah also, his daughter, they buried there. ¹⁷And he mourned for Joseph one year, and did not cease, for he said, "Let me go down to the grave mourning for my son." ¹⁸For this reason it is ordained for the sons of Israel that they should afflict themselves on the tenth of the seventh month—on the day that the news which made him weep for Joseph came to Jacob his father—that they should make atonement for themselves thereon with a young goat on the tenth of the seventh month, once a year, for their sins, for they had grieved the affection of their father regarding his son Joseph. ¹⁹And this day has been ordained that they should grieve thereon for their sins, and for all their transgressions, and for all their errors, so that

they might cleanse themselves on that day once a year. ²⁰And after Joseph perished, the sons of Jacob took wives for themselves. The name of Reuben's wife is 'Adâ; and the name of Simeon's wife is 'Adîbâ'a, a Canaanite; and the name of Levi's wife is Mêlkâ, of the daughters of Aram, of the seed of the sons of Terah; and the name of Judah's wife, Bêtasû'êl, a Canaanite; and the name of Issachar's wife, Hêzaqâ; and the name of Zebulun's wife, Nî'îmân; and the name of Dan's wife, 'Êglâ; and the name of Naphtali's wife, Rasû'û, of Mesopotamia; and the name of Gad's wife, Mâka; and the name of Asher's wife, 'Îjônâ; and the name of Joseph's wife, Asenath, the Egyptian; and the name of Benjamin's wife, 'Îjasaka. ²¹And Simeon converted, and took a second wife from Mesopotamia as his brothers.

CHAPTER 35

¹And in the first year of the first week of the forty-fifth jubilee, Rebekah called her son Jacob and commanded him regarding his father and regarding his brother, that he should honor them all the days of his life. ²And Jacob said, "I will do everything as you have commanded me, for this thing will be honor and greatness to me, and righteousness before the LORD, that I should honor them. ³And you, mother, also know from the time I was born until this day, all my deeds and all that is in my heart, that I always think good concerning all. ⁴And how should I not do this thing which you have commanded me, that I should honor my father and my brother! ⁵Tell me, mother, what perversity have you seen in me and I will turn away from it, and mercy will be on me." ⁶And she said to him, "My son, I have not seen in you all my days anything perverse, but [only] upright deeds. And yet I will tell you the truth, my son: I will die this year, and I will not survive this year in my life, for I have seen in a dream the day of my death, that I should not live beyond one hundred and fifty-five years; and behold, I have completed all the days of my life which I am to live." ⁷And Jacob laughed at the words of his mother, because his mother had said to him that she should die; and she was sitting opposite to him in possession of her strength, and she was not weak in her strength, for she went in and out and saw, and her teeth were strong, and no ailment had touched her all the days of her life. ⁸And Jacob said to her, "Blessed am I, mother, if my days approach the days of your life, and my strength remains with me thus as your strength: and you will not die, for you are idly jesting with me regarding your death." ⁹And she went in to Isaac and said to him, "One petition I make to you: make Esau swear that he will not injure Jacob, nor pursue him with enmity, for you know that Esau's thoughts are perverse from his youth, and there is no goodness in him, for he desires to kill him after your death. ¹⁰And you know all that he has done since the day his brother Jacob went to Haran until this day, how he has forsaken us with his whole heart and has done evil to us; he has taken your flocks to himself and carried off all your possessions from before your face. ¹¹And when we implored and entreated him for what was our own, he did as a man who was taking pity on us. ¹²And he is bitter against you because you blessed Jacob, your perfect and upright son; for there is no evil but only goodness in him, and since he came from Haran to this day, he has not robbed us of anything, for he always brings us everything in its season, and rejoices with all his heart when we take at his hands, and he blesses us, and has not parted from us since he came from Haran until this day, and he continually remains at home with us, honoring us." ¹³And Isaac said to her, "I, too, know and see the deeds of Jacob who is with us, how that he honors us with all his heart, but I formerly loved Esau more than Jacob, because he was the firstborn, but now I love Jacob more than Esau, for he has done manifold evil deeds, and there is no righteousness in him, for all his ways are unrighteousness and violence. ¹⁴And now my heart is troubled because of all his deeds, and neither he nor his seed is to be saved, for they are those who will be destroyed from the earth, and who will be rooted out from under the heavens, for he has forsaken the God of Abraham and gone after his wives, and after their uncleanness, and after their error—he and his children. ¹⁵And you command me to make him swear that he will not slay his brother Jacob; even if he swears, he will not abide by his oath, and he will not do good but only evil. ¹⁶But if he desires to slay his brother Jacob, he will be given into Jacob's hands, and he will not escape from his hands. ¹⁷And do not fear on account of Jacob, for the guardian of Jacob is great, and powerful, and honored, and praised more than the guardian of Esau." ¹⁸And Rebekah sent and called Esau, and he came to her, and she said to him, "I have a petition, my son, to make to you, and do you promise to do it, my son?" ¹⁹And he said, "I will do everything that you say to me, and I will not refuse your petition." ²⁰And she said to him, "I ask you that the day I die, you will take me in and bury me near Sarah, your father's mother, and that you and Jacob will love each other, and that neither will desire evil against the other, but mutual love only, and [so] you will prosper, my sons, and be honored in the midst of the land, and no enemy will rejoice over you, and you will be a blessing and a mercy in the eyes of all those that love you." ²¹And he said, "I will do all that you have told me, and I will bury you on the day you die near Sarah, my father's mother, as you have desired, that her bones may be near your bones. ²²And I will also love my brother Jacob above all flesh, for I have no brother in all the earth but him only; and this is no great merit for me if I love him, for he is my brother, and we were sown together in your body, and together we came out from your womb, and if I do not love my brother, whom will I love? ²³And I, myself, beg you to exhort Jacob concerning me and concerning my sons, for I know that he will assuredly be king over me and my sons, for on the day my father blessed him he made him the higher and me the lower. ²⁴And I swear to you that I will love him, and not desire evil against him all the days of my life, but good only." And he swore to her regarding all this matter. ²⁵And she called Jacob before the eyes of Esau and gave him command according to the words which she had spoken to Esau. ²⁶And he said, "I will do your pleasure; believe me that no evil will proceed from me or from my sons against Esau, and I will be first in nothing save in love only." ²⁷And she and her sons ate and drank that night, and she died—three jubilees and one week and one year old—on that night, and her two sons, Esau and Jacob, buried her in the double cave near Sarah, their father's mother.

CHAPTER 36

¹And in the sixth year of this week Isaac called his two sons, Esau and Jacob, and they came to him, and he said to them, "My sons, I am going the way of my fathers, to the continuous house where my fathers are. ²For that reason, bury me near my father Abraham, in the double cave in the field of Ephron the Hittite, where Abraham purchased a tomb to bury in; in the tomb which I dug for myself, bury me there. ³And this I command you, my sons, that you practice righteousness and uprightness on the earth, so that the LORD may bring on you all that the LORD said that He would do to Abraham and to his seed. ⁴And, my sons, love one another—your brother—as a man who loves his own soul, and let each seek in what [way] he may benefit his brother, and act together on the earth; and let them love each other as their own souls. ⁵And concerning the question of idols, I command and admonish you to reject them, and hate them, and not to love them, for they are full of deception for those that worship them and for those that bow down to them. ⁶Remember, my sons, the LORD God of your father Abraham, and how I also worshiped Him and served Him in righteousness and in joy, that He might multiply you and increase your seed as the stars of the heavens in multitude and establish you on the earth as the plant of righteousness which will not be rooted out to all the generations forever. ⁷And now I will make you swear a great oath—for there is no oath which is greater than it, by the glorious, and honored, and great, and splendid, and wonderful, and mighty Name, which created the heavens, and the earth, and all things together—that you will fear Him and worship Him, ⁸and that each will love his brother with affection and righteousness, and that neither will desire evil against his brother from now on and forever, all the days of your life, so that you may prosper in all your deeds and not be destroyed. ⁹And if either of you devises evil against his brother, know that from now on everyone that devises evil against his brother will fall into his hand, and will be rooted out of the land of the living, and his seed will be destroyed from under the heavens. ¹⁰But on the day of turbulence, and execration, and indignation, and anger, with flaming devouring fire as He burned Sodom, so

likewise He will burn his land, and his city, and all that is his, and he will be blotted out of the scroll of the discipline of the children of men, and not be recorded in the Scroll of Life, but in that which is appointed to destruction, and he will depart into continuous execration, so that their condemnation may always be renewed in hate, and in execration, and in wrath, and in torment, and in indignation, and in plagues, and in disease forever. ¹¹I say and testify to you, my sons, according to the judgment which will come on the man who wishes to injure his brother." ¹²And he divided all his possessions between the two on that day, and he gave the larger portion to him that was the firstborn, and the tower and all that was around it, and all that Abraham possessed at the Well of the Oath. ¹³And he said, "I will give this larger portion to the firstborn." ¹⁴And Esau said, "I have sold to Jacob and given my birthright to Jacob; let it be given to him, and I have not a single word to say regarding it, for it is his." ¹⁵And Isaac said, "May a blessing rest on you, my sons, and on your seed this day, for you have given me rest, and my heart is not pained concerning the birthright, lest you should work wickedness on account of it. ¹⁶May the Most High God bless the man that works righteousness—him and his seed forever." ¹⁷And he ended commanding them and blessing them, and they ate and drank together before him, and he rejoiced because there was one mind between them, and they went out from him, and rested that day, and slept. ¹⁸And Isaac slept on his bed that day rejoicing; and he slept the continuous sleep and died one hundred and eighty years old. He completed twenty-five weeks and five years; and his two sons Esau and Jacob buried him. ¹⁹And Esau went to the land of Edom, to the mountains of Seir, and dwelt there. ²⁰And Jacob dwelt in the mountains of Hebron, in the tower of the land of the sojournings of his father Abraham, and he worshiped the LORD with all his heart and according to the visible commands according as He had divided the days of his generations. ²¹And his wife Leah died in the fourth year of the second week of the forty-fifth jubilee, and he buried her in the double cave near his mother Rebekah, to the left of the grave of Sarah, his father's mother. ²²And all her sons and his sons came to mourn over his wife Leah with him, and to comfort him regarding her, for he was lamenting her. ²³For he loved her exceedingly after her sister Rachel died, for she was perfect and upright in all her ways and honored Jacob, and all the days that she lived with him he did not hear from her mouth a harsh word, for she was gentle, and peaceable, and upright, and honorable. ²⁴And he remembered all her deeds which she had done during her life, and he lamented her exceedingly, for he loved her with all his heart and with all his soul.

CHAPTER 37

¹And on the day that Isaac the father of Jacob and Esau died, the sons of Esau heard that Isaac had given the portion of the elder to his younger son Jacob and they were very angry. ²And they strove with their father, saying, "Why has your father given Jacob the portion of the elder and passed over you, although you are the elder and Jacob the younger?" ³And he said to them, "Because I sold my birthright to Jacob for a small mess of lentils; and on the day my father sent me to hunt, and catch, and bring him something that he should eat and bless me, he came with guile and brought my father food and drink, and my father blessed him and put me under his hand. ⁴And now our father has caused us to swear—me and him—that we will not mutually devise evil, either against his brother, and that we will each continue in love and in peace with his brother and not make our ways corrupt." ⁵And they said to him, "We will not listen to you to make peace with him, for our strength is greater than his strength, and we are more powerful than he; we will go against him and slay him, and destroy him and his sons. And if you will not go with us, we will do harm to you also. ⁶And now listen to us: let us send to Aram, and Philistia, and Moab, and Ammon, and let us choose for ourselves chosen men who are ardent for battle, and let us go against him and do battle with him, and let us exterminate him from the earth before he grows strong." ⁷And their father said to them, "Do not go and do not make war with him lest you fall before him." ⁸And they said to him, "This, too, is exactly your mode of action from your youth until this day, and you are putting your neck under his yoke. We will not listen to these words." ⁹And they sent to Aram and to 'Adurâm, to the friend of their father, and they hired along with them one thousand fighting men, chosen men of war. ¹⁰And there came to them from Moab and from the children of Ammon those who were hired, one thousand chosen men; and from Philistia, one thousand chosen men of war; and from Edom and from the Horites, one thousand chosen fighting men; and from the Kittim, mighty men of war. ¹¹And they said to their father, "Go out with them and lead them, else we will slay you." ¹²And he was filled with wrath and indignation on seeing that his sons were forcing him to go before [them] to lead them against his brother Jacob. ¹³But afterward he remembered all the evil which lay hidden in his heart against his brother Jacob, and he did not remember the oath which he had sworn to his father and to his mother that he would devise no evil all his days against his brother Jacob. ¹⁴And notwithstanding all this, Jacob did not know that they were coming against him to battle, and he was mourning for his wife Leah until they approached very near to the tower with four thousand warriors and chosen men of war. ¹⁵And the men of Hebron sent to him, saying, "Behold, your brother has come against you, to fight you, with four thousand girt with the sword, and they carry shields and weapons"; for they loved Jacob more than Esau. So they told him, for Jacob was a more liberal and merciful man than Esau. ¹⁶But Jacob would not believe [it] until they came very near to the tower. ¹⁷And he closed the gates of the tower; and he stood on the battlements, and spoke to his brother Esau, and said, "Noble is the comfort with which you have come to comfort me for my wife who has died. Is this the oath that you swore to your father and again to your mother before they died? You have broken the oath, and on the moment that you swore to your father you were condemned." ¹⁸And then Esau answered and said to him, "Neither the children of men nor the beasts of the earth have any oath of righteousness which in swearing they have sworn forever, but every day they devise evil against one another, and how each may slay his adversary and enemy. ¹⁹And you hate me and my children forever. And there is no observing the tie of brotherhood with you. ²⁰Hear these words which I declare to you, If the boar can change its skin and make its bristles as soft as wool, or if it can cause horns to sprout out on its head like the horns of a stag or of a sheep, then I will observe the tie of brotherhood with you. [[And if the breasts separated themselves from their mother; for you have not been a brother to me.]] ²¹And if the wolves make peace with the lambs so as not to devour or do them violence, and if their hearts are toward them for good, then there will be peace in my heart toward you. ²²And if the lion becomes the friend of the ox and makes peace with him, and if he is bound under one yoke with him and plows with him, then I will make peace with you. ²³And when the raven becomes white as the râzâ, then know that I have loved you and will make peace with you. You will be rooted out, and your sons will be rooted out, and there will be no peace for you." ²⁴And when Jacob saw that he was [so] evilly disposed toward him with [all] his heart and with all his soul as to slay him, and that he had come springing like the wild boar which comes on the spear that pierces and kills it, and does not recoil from it, ²⁵then he spoke to his own and to his servants that they should attack him and all his companions.

CHAPTER 38

¹And after that, Judah spoke to his father Jacob, and said to him, "Bend your bow, father, and send out your arrows, and cast down the adversary, and slay the enemy; and may you have the power, for we will not slay your brother, for he is such as you, and he is like you: let us give him [this] honor." ²Then Jacob bent his bow, and sent out the arrow, and struck his brother Esau [[on his right breast]], and slew him. ³And again he sent out an arrow and struck 'Adôrân the Aramaean, on the left breast, and drove him backward and slew him. ⁴And then the sons of Jacob went out—they and their servants—dividing themselves into companies on the four sides of the tower. ⁵And Judah went out in front, and Naphtali and Gad with him, and fifty servants with him on the south side of the tower, and they slew all they found before them, and not one individual of them escaped. ⁶And Levi, and Dan, and Asher went out on the east side of the tower, and fifty [men] with them, and they slew the fighting men of Moab and Ammon.

⁷And Reuben, and Issachar, and Zebulun went out on the north side of the tower, and fifty men with them, and they slew the fighting men of the Philistines. ⁸And Simeon, and Benjamin, and Enoch, Reuben's son, went out on the west side of the tower, and fifty [men] with them, and they slew of Edom and of the Horites four hundred men, stout warriors; and six hundred fled, and four of the sons of Esau fled with them, and left their father lying slain, as he had fallen on the hill which is in 'Adûrâm. ⁹And the sons of Jacob pursued after them to the mountains of Seir. And Jacob buried his brother on the hill which is in 'Adûrâm, and he returned to his house. ¹⁰And the sons of Jacob pressed hard on the sons of Esau in the mountains of Seir and bowed their necks so that they became servants of the sons of Jacob. ¹¹And they sent to their father [to inquire] whether they should make peace with them or slay them. ¹²And Jacob sent word to his sons that they should make peace, and they made peace with them, and placed the yoke of servitude on them, so that they always paid tribute to Jacob and to his sons. ¹³And they continued to pay tribute to Jacob until the day that he went down into Egypt. ¹⁴And the sons of Edom have not gotten rid of the yoke of servitude which the twelve sons of Jacob had imposed on them until this day. ¹⁵And these are the kings that reigned in Edom, in the land of Edom, before any king reigned over the sons of Israel: ¹⁶and Bâlâq, the son of Beor, reigned in Edom, and the name of his city was Danâbâ; ¹⁷and Bâlâq died, and Jobab, the son of Zârâ of Bôsêr, reigned in his stead; ¹⁸and Jobab died, and 'Asâm, of the land of Têmân, reigned in his stead; ¹⁹and 'Asâm died, and 'Adâth, the son of Barad, who slew Midian in the field of Moab, reigned in his stead, and the name of his city was Avith; ²⁰and 'Adâth died, and Salman, from 'Amâsêqâ, reigned in his stead; ²¹and Salman died, and Saul of Râ'abôth [by the] river, reigned in his stead; ²²and Saul died, and Ba'êlûnân, the son of Achbor, reigned in his stead; ²³and Ba'êlûnân, the son of Achbor, died, and 'Adâth reigned in his stead, and the name of his wife was Maiṭabîth, the daughter of Mâṭarat, the daughter of Mêtabêdzâ'ab. ²⁴These are the kings who reigned in the land of Edom.

CHAPTER 39

¹And Jacob dwelt in the land of his father's sojournings in the land of Canaan. ²These are the generations of Jacob. And Joseph was seventeen years old when they took him down into the land of Egypt, and Potiphar, [[a eunuch of Pharaoh,]] the chief cook [[or chief executioner]] bought him. ³And he set Joseph over all his house, and the blessing of the LORD came on the house of the Egyptian on account of Joseph, and the LORD prospered him in all that he did. ⁴And the Egyptian committed everything into the hands of Joseph, for he saw that the LORD was with him, and that the LORD prospered him in all that he did. ⁵And Joseph's appearance was handsome, and his appearance was very beautiful, and his master's wife lifted up her eyes and saw Joseph, and she loved him, and implored him to lie with her. ⁶But he did not surrender his soul, and he remembered the LORD and the words which his father Jacob used to read from among the words of Abraham, that no man should commit fornication with a woman who has a husband, that the punishment of death has been ordained in the heavens for him before the Most High God, and the sin will be continually recorded against him in the perpetual scrolls before the LORD. ⁷And Joseph remembered these words and refused to lie with her. ⁸And she implored him for a year, but he refused and would not listen. ⁹But she embraced him and held him fast in the house in order to force him to lie with her, and she closed the doors of the house and held him fast, but he left his garment in her hands, and broke through the door, and fled outside from her presence. ¹⁰And the woman saw that he would not lie with her, and she accused him in the presence of his lord, saying, "Your Hebrew servant, whom you love, sought to force me so that he might lie with me; and it came to pass when I lifted up my voice, that he fled and left his garment in my hands when I held him, and he broke through the door." ¹¹And the Egyptian saw the garment of Joseph and the broken door, and heard the words of his wife, and cast Joseph into prison into the place where the prisoners were kept whom the king imprisoned. ¹²And he was there in the prison, and the LORD gave Joseph favor in the sight of the chief of the prison guards and compassion before him, for he saw that the LORD was with him, and that the LORD made all that he did to prosper. ¹³And he committed all things into his hands, and the chief of the prison guards knew of nothing that was with him, for Joseph did everything, and the LORD perfected it. ¹⁴And he remained there two years. And in those days Pharaoh, king of Egypt, was angry against his two eunuchs, against the chief butler and against the chief baker, and he put them in ward in the house of the chief cook, in the prison where Joseph was kept. ¹⁵And the chief of the prison guards appointed Joseph to serve them; and he served before them. ¹⁶And they both dreamed a dream, the chief butler and the chief baker, and they told it to Joseph. ¹⁷And as he interpreted [the dreams] to them, so it befell them, and Pharaoh restored the chief butler to his office, and he slew the [chief] baker, as Joseph had interpreted to them. ¹⁸But the chief butler forgot Joseph in the prison, although he had informed him what would befall him, and did not remember to inform Pharaoh how Joseph had told him, for he forgot.

CHAPTER 40

¹And in those days Pharaoh dreamed two dreams in one night concerning a famine which was to be in all the land, and he awoke from his sleep and called all the interpreters of dreams that were in Egypt, and magicians, and told them his two dreams, and they were not able to declare [the interpretation]. ²And then the chief butler remembered Joseph and spoke of him to the king, and he brought him out from the prison, and he told his two dreams before him. ³And he said before Pharaoh that his two dreams were one, and he said to him, "Seven years of plenty will come over all the land of Egypt, and after that, seven years of famine—such a famine as has not been in all the land. ⁴And now let Pharaoh appoint overseers in all the land of Egypt, and let them store up food in every city throughout the days of the years of plenty, and there will be food for the seven years of famine, and the land will not perish through the famine, for it will be very severe." ⁵And the LORD gave Joseph favor and mercy in the eyes of Pharaoh, and Pharaoh said to his servants, "We will not find such a wise and discreet man as this man, for the Spirit of the LORD is with him." ⁶And he appointed him the second in all his kingdom and gave him authority over all Egypt, and caused him to ride in the second chariot of Pharaoh. ⁷And he clothed him with flax garments, and he put a gold chain on his neck, and [a herald] proclaimed before him "'Êl 'Êl wa' Abîrĕr," and he placed a ring on his hand, and made him ruler over all his house, and magnified him, and said to him, "Only on the throne will I be greater than you." ⁸And Joseph ruled over all the land of Egypt, and all the princes of Pharaoh, and all his servants, and all who did the king's business loved him, for he walked in uprightness, for he was without pride and arrogance, and he had no respect of persons, and did not accept gifts, but he judged all the people of the land in uprightness. ⁹And the land of Egypt was at peace before Pharaoh because of Joseph, for the LORD was with him, and gave him favor and mercy for all his generations before all those who knew him and those who heard concerning him, and Pharaoh's kingdom was well ordered, and there was no adversary and no evil person [therein]. ¹⁰And the king called Joseph's name Sĕphânṭîphâns and gave Joseph the daughter of Potiphar to be [his] wife, the daughter of the priest of Heliopolis, the chief cook [[or chief executioner]]. ¹¹And on the day that Joseph stood before Pharaoh, he was thirty years old. ¹²And in that year Isaac died. And it came to pass as Joseph had said in the interpretation of his two dreams, according as he had said it, there were seven years of plenty over all the land of Egypt, and the land of Egypt produced abundantly, one measure [producing] eighteen hundred measures. ¹³And Joseph gathered food into every city until they were full of corn until they could no longer count and measure it for its multitude.

CHAPTER 41

¹And in the forty-fifth jubilee, in the second week, [and] in the second year, Judah took a wife for his firstborn Er named Tamar, from the daughters of Aram. ²But he hated [her] and did not lie with her, because his mother was of the daughters of Canaan, and he wished to take a wife [for] himself of the countrymen of his mother, but his father Judah would not permit him. ³And this Er, the

firstborn of Judah, was wicked, and the LORD slew him. ⁴And Judah said to his brother Onan, "Go in to your brother's wife and perform the duty of a husband's brother to her, and raise up seed to your brother." ⁵And Onan knew that the seed would not be his, [but] his brother's only, and he went into the house of his brother's wife, and spilled the seed on the ground, and he was wicked in the eyes of the LORD, and He slew him. ⁶And Judah said to his daughter-in-law Tamar, "Remain in your father's house as a widow until my son Shelah is grown up, and I will give you to him to be [his] wife." ⁷And he grew up, but Bêdsû'êl, the wife of Judah, did not permit her son Shelah to marry. And Bêdsû'êl, the wife of Judah, died in the fifth year of this week. ⁸And in the sixth year Judah went up to shear his sheep at Timnah. And they told Tamar, "Behold, your father-in-law goes up to Timnah to shear his sheep." ⁹And she put off her widow's clothes, and put on a veil, and adorned herself, and sat in the gate adjoining the way to Timnah. ¹⁰And as Judah was going along, he found her, and thought her to be a harlot, and he said to her, "Let me come in to you"; and she said to him, "Come in," and he went in. ¹¹And she said to him, "Give me my hire"; and he said to her, "I have nothing in my hand except my ring that is on my finger, and my necklace, and my staff which is in my hand." ¹²And she said to him, "Give them to me until you send me my hire"; and he said to her, "I will send a kid of the goats to you"; and he gave them to her, [and he went in to her,] and she conceived by him. ¹³And Judah went to his sheep, and she went to her father's house. ¹⁴And Judah sent a kid of the goats by the hand of his shepherd, an Adullamite, and he did not find her; and he asked the people of the place, saying, "Where is the harlot who was here?" And they said to him, "There is no harlot here with us." ¹⁵And he returned, and informed him, and said to him that he had not found her; "I asked the people of the place, and they said to me, There is no harlot here." And he said, "Let her keep [them] lest we become a cause of derision." ¹⁶And when she had completed three months, it was manifest that she was with child, and they told Judah, saying, "Behold, your daughter-in-law Tamar is with child by whoredom." ¹⁷And Judah went to the house of her father, and said to her father and her brothers, "Bring her out, and let them burn her, for she has worked uncleanness in Israel." ¹⁸And it came to pass when they brought her out to burn her that she sent to her father-in-law the ring, and the necklace, and the staff, saying, "Discern whose these are, for I am with child by him." ¹⁹And Judah acknowledged [them] and said, "Tamar is more righteous than I am. And therefore, let them not burn her." ²⁰And for that reason she was not given to Shelah, and he did not approach her again. ²¹And after that she bore two sons, Perez and Zerah, in the seventh year of this second week. ²²And immediately the seven years of fruitfulness of which Joseph spoke to Pharaoh were accomplished. ²³And Judah acknowledged that the deed which he had done was evil, for he had lain with his daughter-in-law, and he esteemed it hateful in his eyes, and he acknowledged that he had transgressed and gone astray, for he had uncovered the skirt of his son, and he began to lament and to supplicate before the LORD because of his transgression. ²⁴And we told him in a dream that it was forgiven him because he supplicated earnestly, and lamented, and did not commit it again. ²⁵And he received forgiveness because he turned from his sin and from his ignorance, for he greatly transgressed before our God; and everyone that acts this way, everyone who lies with his mother-in-law, let them burn him with fire that he may burn therein, for there is uncleanness and pollution on them; let them burn them with fire. ²⁶And you command the sons of Israel that there is no uncleanness among them, for everyone who lies with his daughter-in-law or with his mother-in-law has worked uncleanness; let them burn the man who has lain with her with fire, and likewise the woman, and he will turn away wrath and punishment from Israel. ²⁷And to Judah we said that his two sons had not lain with her, and for this reason his seed was established for a second generation and would not be rooted out. ²⁸For in singleness of eye he had gone and sought for punishment, namely, according to the judgment of Abraham, which he had commanded his sons, Judah had sought to burn her with fire.

CHAPTER 42

¹And in the first year of the third week of the forty-fifth jubilee the famine began to come into the land, and the rain refused to be given to the earth, for none fell whatsoever. ²And the earth grew barren, but in the land of Egypt there was food, for Joseph had gathered the seed of the land in the seven years of plenty and had preserved it. ³And the Egyptians came to Joseph that he might give them food, and he opened the storehouses where the grain of the first year was, and he sold it to the people of the land for gold. ⁴[[Now the famine was very severe in the land of Canaan]], and Jacob heard that there was food in Egypt, and he sent his ten sons that they should procure food for him in Egypt, but he did not send Benjamin; and they arrived [in Egypt] among those that went [there.] ⁵And Joseph recognized them, but they did not recognize him, and he spoke to them and questioned them, and he said to them, "Are you not spies, and have you not come to explore the approaches of the land?" And he put them in ward. ⁶And after that, he set them free again, and detained Simeon alone, and sent off his nine brothers. ⁷And he filled their sacks with corn, and he put their gold in their sacks, and they did not know. ⁸And he commanded them to bring their younger brother, for they had told him their father was living and [also] their younger brother. ⁹And they went up from the land of Egypt and they came to the land of Canaan; and they told their father all that had befallen them, and how the lord of the country had spoken roughly to them and had seized Simeon until they should bring Benjamin. ¹⁰And Jacob said, "You have bereaved me of my children! Joseph is not, and Simeon is also not, and you will take Benjamin away. Your wickedness has come on me." ¹¹And he said, "My son will not go down with you lest perhaps he falls sick, for their mother gave birth to two sons, and one has perished, and you will also take this one from me. If perhaps he took a fever on the road, you would bring down my old age with sorrow to death." ¹²For he saw that their money had been returned to each man in his sack, and for this reason he feared to send him. ¹³And the famine increased and became severe in the land of Canaan, and in all lands except in the land of Egypt, for many of the children of the Egyptians had stored up their seed for food from the time when they saw Joseph gathering seed together, and putting it in storehouses, and preserving it for the years of famine. ¹⁴And the people of Egypt fed themselves thereon during the first year of their famine. ¹⁵But when Israel saw that the famine was very severe in the land and there was no deliverance, he said to his sons, "Go again, and procure food for us that we do not die." ¹⁶And they said, "We will not go; unless our youngest brother goes with us, we will not go." ¹⁷And Israel saw that if he did not send him with them, they should all perish by reason of the famine. ¹⁸And Reuben said, "Give him into my hand, and if I do not bring him back to you, slay my two sons instead of his soul." And he said to him, "He will not go with you." ¹⁹And Judah came near and said, "Send him with me, and if I do not bring him back to you, let me bear the blame before you all the days of my life." ²⁰And he sent him with them in the second year of this week, on the first day of the month, and they came to the land of Egypt with all those who went, and [they had] presents in their hands: stacte, and almonds, and terebinth nuts, and pure honey. ²¹And they went and stood before Joseph, and he saw his brother Benjamin, and he knew him, and said to them, "Is this your youngest brother?" And they said to him, "It is he." And he said, "The LORD be gracious to you, my son!" ²²And he sent him into his house, and brought Simeon out to them, and he made a feast for them, and they presented the gift to him which they had brought in their hands. ²³And they ate before him and he gave them all a portion, but the portion of Benjamin was seven times larger than that of any of theirs. ²⁴And they ate, and drank, and arose, and remained with their donkeys. ²⁵And Joseph devised a plan whereby he might learn their thoughts as to whether thoughts of peace prevailed among them, and he said to the steward who was over his house: "Fill all their sacks with food, and return their money to them into their vessels, and my cup, the silver cup out of which I drink, put it in the sack of the youngest, and send them away."

CHAPTER 43

¹And he did as Joseph had told him and filled all their sacks for them with food, and put their money in their sacks, and put the cup in

Benjamin's sack. ²And early in the morning they departed, and it came to pass that, when they had gone from there, Joseph said to the steward of his house, "Pursue them, run and seize them, saying, For good you have repaid me with evil; you have stolen from me the silver cup out of which my lord drinks. And bring back their youngest brother to me, and fetch [him] quickly before I go out to my seat of judgment." ³And he ran after them and said to them according to these words. ⁴And they said to him, "God forbid that your servants should do this thing, and steal from the house of your lord any utensil, and also the money which we found in our sacks the first time, we, your servants, brought back from the land of Canaan. ⁵How then should we steal any utensil? Behold, here we are and our sacks; search, and wherever you find the cup in the sack of any man among us, let him be slain, and we and our donkeys will serve your lord." ⁶And he said to them, "Not so; the man with whom I find [it], him only will I take as a servant, and you will return to your house in peace." ⁷And as he was searching in their vessels, beginning with the eldest and ending with the youngest, it was found in Benjamin's sack. ⁸And they tore their garments, and loaded their donkeys, and returned to the city, and came to the house of Joseph, and they all bowed themselves on their faces to the ground before him. ⁹And Joseph said to them, "You have done evil." And they said, "What will we say and how will we defend ourselves? Our lord has discovered the transgression of his servants; behold, we are the servants of our lord, and our donkeys also." ¹⁰And Joseph said to them, "I also fear the LORD; as for you, go to your homes and let your brother be my servant, for you have done evil. Do you not know that a man delights in his cup as I with this cup? And yet you have stolen it from me." ¹¹And Judah said, "O my lord, please let your servant speak a word in my lord's ear; your servant's mother bore two brothers to our father; one went away and was lost, and has not been found, and he alone is left of his mother, and your servant, our father, loves him, and his life is also bound up with the life of this [youth]. ¹²And it will come to pass, when we go to your servant, our father, and the youth is not with us, that he will die, and we will bring down our father with sorrow to death. ¹³Now rather let me, your servant, abide instead of the boy as a bondsman to my lord, and let the youth go with his brothers, for I became a guarantee for him at the hand of your servant, our father, and if I do not bring him back, your servant will bear the blame to our father forever." ¹⁴And Joseph saw that they were all in accord in goodness with one another, and he could not refrain himself, and he told them that he was Joseph. ¹⁵And he conversed with them in the Hebrew tongue and fell on their neck and wept. But they did not recognize him, and they began to weep. ¹⁶And he said to them, "Do not weep over me, but hurry and bring my father to me; and you see that it is my mouth that speaks, and the eyes of my brother Benjamin see. ¹⁷For behold, this is the second year of the famine, and there are still five years without harvest, or fruit, of trees, or plowing. ¹⁸Come down quickly, you and your households, so that you do not perish through the famine, and do not be grieved for your possessions, for the LORD sent me before you to set things in order that many people might live. ¹⁹And tell my father that I am still alive, and you, behold, you see that the LORD has made me as a father to Pharaoh, and ruler over his house and over all the land of Egypt. ²⁰And tell my father of all my glory, and all the riches and glory that the LORD has given Me." ²¹And by the command of the mouth of Pharaoh he gave them chariots and provisions for the way, and he gave them all many-colored raiment[s] and silver. ²²And to their father he sent raiment, and silver, and ten donkeys which carried corn, and he sent them away. ²³And they went up and told their father that Joseph was alive and was measuring out corn to all the nations of the earth, and that he was ruler over all the land of Egypt. ²⁴And their father did not believe it, for he was beside himself in his mind, but when he saw the wagons which Joseph had sent, the life of his spirit revived, and he said, "It is enough for me if Joseph lives; I will go down and see him before I die."

CHAPTER 44

¹And Israel took his journey from Haran from his house on the new moon of the third month, and he went on the way of the Well of the Oath, and he offered a sacrifice to the God of his father Isaac on the seventh of this month. ²And Jacob remembered the dream that he had seen at Bethel, and he feared to go down into Egypt. ³And while he was thinking of sending word to Joseph to come to him, and that he would not go down, he remained there seven days, if perhaps he should see a vision as to whether he should remain or go down. ⁴And he celebrated the harvest festival of the first-fruits with old grain, for in all the land of Canaan there was not [even] a handful of seed, for the famine was over all the beasts, and cattle, and birds, and also over man. ⁵And on the sixteenth [day] the LORD appeared to him, and said to him, "Jacob, Jacob"; and he said, "Here I am." And He said to him, "I am the God of your fathers, the God of Abraham and Isaac; do not fear to go down into Egypt, for I will make of you a great nation there. ⁶I will go down with you, and I will bring you up [again], and you will be buried in this land, and Joseph will put his hands on your eyes. Do not fear; go down into Egypt." ⁷And his sons rose up, and his sons' sons, and they placed their father and their possessions on wagons. ⁸And Israel rose up from the Well of the Oath on the sixteenth [day] of this third month, and he went to the land of Egypt. ⁹And Israel sent Judah before him to his son Joseph to examine the land of Goshen, for Joseph had told his brothers that they should come and dwell there that they might be near him. ¹⁰And this was the excellent [land] in the land of Egypt, and near to him, for all [of them] and also for the cattle. ¹¹And these are the names of the sons of Jacob who went into Egypt with their father Jacob: ¹²Reuben, the firstborn of Israel; and these are the names of his sons: Enoch, and Pallu, and Hezron, and Carmi—five. ¹³Simeon and his sons; and these are the names of his sons: Jemuel, and Jamin, and Ohad, and Jachin, and Zohar, and Shaul, the son of the Zephathite woman—seven. ¹⁴Levi and his sons; and these are the names of his sons: Gershon, and Kohath, and Merari—four. ¹⁵Judah and his sons; and these are the names of his sons: Shela, and Perez, and Zerah—four. ¹⁶Issachar and his sons; and these are the names of his sons: Tola, and Phûa, and Jâsûb, and Shimron—five. ¹⁷Zebulun and his sons; and these are the names of his sons: Sered, and Elon, and Jahleel—four. ¹⁸And these are the sons of Jacob, and their sons, whom Leah bore to Jacob in Mesopotamia—six, and their one sister, Dinah. And all the souls of the sons of Leah, and their sons, who went with their father Jacob into Egypt, were twenty-nine, and their father Jacob being with them, they were thirty. ¹⁹And the sons of Zilpah, Leah's handmaid, the wife of Jacob, whom she bore to Jacob: Gad and Asher. ²⁰And these are the names of their sons who went with him into Egypt: the sons of Gad: Ziphion, and Haggi, and Shuni, and Ezbon, [and Eri,] and Areli, and Arodi—eight. ²¹And the sons of Asher: Imnah, and Ishvah, [and Ishvi], and Beriah, and Serah, their one sister—six. ²²All the souls were fourteen, and all those of Leah were forty-four. ²³And the sons of Rachel, the wife of Jacob: Joseph and Benjamin. ²⁴And there were born to Joseph in Egypt, before his father came into Egypt, those whom Asenath, daughter of Potiphar priest of Heliopolis, bore to him: Manasseh and Ephraim—three. ²⁵And the sons of Benjamin: Bela, and Becher, and Ashbel, Gera, and Naaman, and Ehi, and Rosh, and Muppim, and Huppim, and Ard—eleven. ²⁶And all the souls of Rachel were fourteen. ²⁷And the sons of Bilhah, the handmaid of Rachel, the wife of Jacob, whom she bore to Jacob, were Dan and Naphtali. ²⁸And these are the names of their sons who went with them into Egypt: and the sons of Dan were Hushim, and Sâmôn, and Asûdî, and 'Îjâka, and Salômôn—six. ²⁹And they died the year in which they entered into Egypt, and there was left to Dan Hushim alone. ³⁰And these are the names of the sons of Naphtali: Jahziel, and Guni, and Jezer, and Shallum, and 'Îv. ³¹And 'Îv, who was born after the years of famine, died in Egypt. ³²And all the souls of Rachel were twenty-six. ³³And all the souls of Jacob which went into Egypt were seventy souls. These are his children and his children's children, seventy in all; but five died in Egypt before Joseph and had no children. ³⁴And in the land of Canaan two sons of Judah died, Er and Onan, and they had no children, and the sons of Israel buried those who perished, and they were reckoned among the seventy nations.

CHAPTER 45

¹And Israel went into the country of Egypt, into the land of Goshen, on the new moon of the fourth month, in the second year of the

third week of the forty-fifth jubilee. ²And Joseph went to meet his father Jacob, to the land of Goshen, and he fell on his father's neck and wept. ³And Israel said to Joseph, "Now let me die since I have seen you, and now may the LORD God of Israel be blessed, the God of Abraham and the God of Isaac who has not withheld His mercy and His grace from His servant Jacob. ⁴It is enough for me that I have seen your face while I am yet alive; yes, the vision which I saw at Bethel is true. Blessed is the LORD my God forever and ever and blessed is His Name." ⁵And Joseph and his brothers ate bread before their father and drank wine, and Jacob rejoiced with exceedingly great joy because he saw Joseph eating with his brothers and drinking before him, and he blessed the Creator of all things who had preserved him and had preserved his twelve sons for him. ⁶And Joseph had given to his father and to his brothers as a gift the right of dwelling in the land of Goshen, and in Rameses, and all the surrounding region, which he ruled over before Pharaoh. And Israel and his sons dwelt in the land of Goshen, the best part of the land of Egypt; and Israel was one hundred and thirty years old when he came into Egypt, ⁷and Joseph nourished his father, and his brothers, and also their possessions with as much bread as they needed for the seven years of the famine. ⁸And the land of Egypt suffered by reason of the famine, and Joseph acquired all the land of Egypt for Pharaoh in return for food, and he got possession of the people, and their cattle, and everything for Pharaoh. ⁹And the years of the famine were accomplished, and Joseph gave seed and food to the people in the land that they might sow in the eighth year, for the river had overflowed all the land of Egypt. ¹⁰For in the seven years of the famine it had not overflowed and had irrigated only a few places on the banks of the river, but now it overflowed, and the Egyptians sowed the land, and it bore much corn that year. ¹¹And this was the first year of the fourth week of the forty-fifth jubilee. ¹²And Joseph took the fifth part of the corn of the harvest for the king and left four parts for them for food and for seed, and Joseph made it an ordinance for the land of Egypt until this day. ¹³And Israel lived in the land of Egypt [for] seventeen years, and all the days which he lived were three jubilees, one hundred and forty-seven years, and he died in the fourth year of the fifth week of the forty-fifth jubilee. ¹⁴And Israel blessed his sons before he died and told them everything that would befall them in the land of Egypt; and he made known to them what would come on them in the last days, and blessed them, and gave two portions to Joseph in the land. ¹⁵And he slept with his fathers, and he was buried in the double cave in the land of Canaan, near his father Abraham in the grave which he dug for himself in the double cave in the land of Hebron. ¹⁶And he gave all his scrolls and the scrolls of his fathers to his son Levi that he might preserve them and renew them for his children until this day.

CHAPTER 46

¹And it came to pass that after Jacob died, the sons of Israel multiplied in the land of Egypt, and they became a great nation, and they were of one accord in heart, so that brother loved brother and every man helped his brother, and they increased abundantly and multiplied exceedingly [for] ten weeks of years, all the days of the life of Joseph. ²And there was no adversary nor any evil all the days of the life of Joseph which he lived after his father Jacob, for all the Egyptians honored the sons of Israel all the days of the life of Joseph. ³And Joseph died being one hundred and ten years old; he lived seventeen years in the land of Canaan, and he was a servant [for] ten years, and [he was] in prison [for] three years, and he was under the king [for] eighty years, ruling all the land of Egypt. ⁴And he died, and all his brothers, and all that generation. ⁵And he commanded the sons of Israel before he died that they should carry his bones with them when they went out from the land of Egypt. ⁶And he made them swear regarding his bones, for he knew that the Egyptians would not again bring out and bury him in the land of Canaan, for Mâkamârôn, king of Canaan, while dwelling in the land of Assyria, fought in the valley with the king of Egypt and slew him there, and pursued after the Egyptians to the gates of 'Ěrmôn. ⁷But he was not able to enter, for another, a new king, had become king of Egypt, and he was stronger than he, and he returned to the land of Canaan, and the gates of Egypt were closed, and none went out and none came into Egypt. ⁸And Joseph died in the forty-sixth jubilee, in the sixth week, in the second year, and they buried him in the land of Egypt, and his brothers died after him. ⁹And the king of Egypt went out to war with the king of Canaan in the forty-seventh jubilee, in the second week in the second year, and the sons of Israel brought out all the bones of the children of Jacob save the bones of Joseph, and they buried them in the field in the double cave in the mountain. ¹⁰And most [of them] returned to Egypt, but a few of them remained in the mountains of Hebron, and your father Amram remained with them. ¹¹And the king of Canaan was victorious over the king of Egypt, and he closed the gates of Egypt. ¹²And he devised an evil scheme against the sons of Israel of afflicting them; and he said to the people of Egypt, ¹³"Behold, the people of the sons of Israel have increased and multiplied more than we. Come and let us deal wisely with them before they become too many, and let us afflict them with slavery before war comes on us and before they, too, fight against us, otherwise they will join themselves to our enemies; and get them out of our land, for their hearts and faces are toward the land of Canaan." ¹⁴And he set taskmasters over them to afflict them with slavery; and they built strong cities for Pharaoh, Pithom and Raamses, and they built all the walls and all the fortifications which had fallen in the cities of Egypt. ¹⁵And they made them serve with rigor, and the more they dealt evilly with them, the more they increased and multiplied. ¹⁶And the people of Egypt despised the sons of Israel.

CHAPTER 47

¹And in the seventh week, in the seventh year, in the forty-seventh jubilee, your father went out from the land of Canaan, and you were born in the fourth week, in the sixth year thereof, in the forty-eighth jubilee; this was the time of tribulation on the sons of Israel. ²And Pharaoh, king of Egypt, issued a command regarding them that they should cast all their male children which were born into the river. ³And they cast them in for seven months until the day that you were born. And your mother hid you for three months, and they told [the Egyptians] regarding her. ⁴And she made an ark for you, and covered it with pitch and asphalt, and placed it in the flags on the bank of the river, and she placed you in it [for] seven days, and your mother came by night and suckled you, and by day your sister Miriam guarded you from the birds. ⁵And in those days Tharmuth, the daughter of Pharaoh, came to bathe in the river, and she heard your voice crying, and she told her maidens to bring you out, and they brought you to her. ⁶And she took you out of the ark, and she had compassion on you. ⁷And your sister said to her, "Will I go and call to you one of the Hebrew women to nurse and suckle this baby for you?" And she said, "Go." ⁸And she went and called your mother Jochebed, and she gave her wages, and she nursed you. ⁹And afterward, when you were grown up, they brought you to the daughter of Pharaoh, and you became her son, and your father Amram taught you writing, and after you had completed three weeks, they brought you into the royal court. ¹⁰And you were three weeks of years at court until the time when you went out from the royal court and saw an Egyptian striking your friend who was of the sons of Israel, and you slew him and hid him in the sand. ¹¹And on the second day you found two of the sons of Israel striving together, and you said to him who was doing the wrong: "Why do you strike your brother?" ¹²And he was angry and indignant, and said, "Who made you a prince and a judge over us? Do you think to kill me as you killed the Egyptian yesterday?" And you were afraid and fled on account of these words.

CHAPTER 48

¹And in the sixth year of the third week of the forty-ninth jubilee you departed and dwelt in the land of Midian [for] five weeks and one year. And you returned into Egypt in the second week, in the second year, in the fiftieth jubilee. ²And you yourself know what He spoke to you on Mount Sinai, and what prince Mastêmâ desired to do with you when you were returning into Egypt on the way when you met him at the lodging-place. ³Did he not, with all his power, seek to slay you and deliver the Egyptians out of your hand when he saw that you were sent to execute judgment and vengeance on the Egyptians? ⁴And I delivered

you out of his hand, and you performed the signs and wonders which you were sent to perform in Egypt against Pharaoh, and against all his house, and against his servants and his people. ⁵And the LORD executed a great vengeance on them for Israel's sake, and struck them through blood and frogs, lice and biting flies, and malignant boils breaking out in blisters, and their cattle by death, and by hailstones, thereby He destroyed everything that grew for them, and by locusts which devoured the residue which had been left by the hail, and by darkness, and [by the death] of the firstborn of men and animals, and on all their idols the LORD took vengeance and burned them with fire. ⁶And everything was sent through your hand, that you should declare [these things] before they were done, and you spoke with the king of Egypt before all his servants and before his people. ⁷And everything took place according to your words; ten great and terrible judgments came on the land of Egypt that you might execute vengeance on it for Israel. ⁸And the LORD did everything for Israel's sake, and according to His covenant, which He had ordained with Abraham that He would take vengeance on them as they had brought them into bondage by force. ⁹And the prince of the Mastêmâ stood up against you and sought to cast you into the hands of Pharaoh, and he helped the Egyptian sorcerers, and they stood up and worked before you. ¹⁰We indeed permitted them to work the evils, but we did not allow the remedies to be worked by their hands. ¹¹And the LORD struck them with malignant ulcers, and they were not able to stand, for we destroyed them so that they could not perform a single sign. ¹²And notwithstanding all [these] signs and wonders, the prince of the Mastêmâ was not put to shame because he took courage and cried to the Egyptians to pursue after you with all the powers of the Egyptians, with their chariots, and with their horses, and with all the hosts of the peoples of Egypt. ¹³And I stood between the Egyptians and Israel, and we delivered Israel out of his hand, and out of the hand of his people, and the LORD brought them through the midst of the sea as if it were dry land. ¹⁴And all the peoples whom he brought to pursue after Israel, the LORD our God cast them into the midst of the sea, into the depths of the abyss beneath the sons of Israel, even as the people of Egypt had cast their children into the river. He took vengeance on one million of them, and one thousand strong and energetic men were destroyed on account of one suckling of the children of your people which they had thrown into the river. ¹⁵And on the fourteenth day, and on the fifteenth, and on the sixteenth, and on the seventeenth, and on the eighteenth, the prince of the Mastêmâ was bound and imprisoned behind the sons of Israel that he might not accuse them. ¹⁶And on the nineteenth [day] we let them loose that they might help the Egyptians and pursue the sons of Israel. ¹⁷And He hardened their hearts and made them stubborn, and the device was devised by the LORD our God that He might strike the Egyptians and cast them into the sea. ¹⁸And on the fourteenth [day] we bound him that he might not accuse the sons of Israel on the day when they asked the Egyptians for vessels and garments, vessels of silver, and vessels of gold, and vessels of bronze, in order to despoil the Egyptians in return for the bondage in which they had forced them to serve. ¹⁹And we did not lead out the sons of Israel from Egypt empty-handed.

CHAPTER 49

¹Remember the command which the LORD commanded you concerning the Passover, that you should celebrate it in its season on the fourteenth of the first month, that you should kill it before it is evening, and that they should eat it by night on the evening of the fifteenth from the time of the setting of the sun. ²For on this night—the beginning of the festival and the beginning of the joy—you were eating the Passover in Egypt, when all the powers of Mastêmâ had been let loose to slay all the firstborn in the land of Egypt, from the firstborn of Pharaoh to the firstborn of the captive maidservant in the mill, and to the cattle. ³And this is the sign which the LORD gave them: into every house on the lintels of which they saw the blood of a lamb of the first year, into [that] house they should not enter to slay, but should pass by [it], that all those should be saved that were in the house because the sign of the blood was on its lintels. ⁴And the powers of the LORD did everything according as the LORD commanded them, and they passed by all the sons of Israel, and the plague did not come on them to destroy any soul from among them, either of cattle, or man, or dog. ⁵And the plague was very grievous in Egypt, and there was no house in Egypt where there was not someone dead, and weeping, and lamentation. ⁶And all Israel was eating the flesh of the Passover lamb, and drinking the wine, and was lauding and blessing, and giving thanks to the LORD God of their fathers, and was ready to go out from under the yoke of Egypt and from the evil bondage. ⁷And remember this day all the days of your life and observe it from year to year all the days of your life, once a year, on its day, according to all the law thereof, and do not adjourn [it] from day to day, or from month to month. ⁸For it is a perpetual ordinance and engraved on the heavenly tablets regarding all the sons of Israel that they should observe it every year, on its day, once a year, throughout all their generations; and there is no limit of days, for this is ordained forever. ⁹And the man who is free from uncleanness and does not come to observe it on occasion of its day so as to bring an acceptable offering before the LORD, and to eat and to drink before the LORD on the day of its festival, that man who is clean and close at hand will be cut off, because he did not offer the oblation of the LORD in its appointed season; he will take the guilt on himself. ¹⁰Let the sons of Israel come and observe the Passover on the day of its fixed time, on the fourteenth day of the first month, between the evenings, from the third part of the day to the third part of the night, for two portions of the day are given to the light, and a third part to the evening. ¹¹That is that which the LORD commanded you that you should observe it between the evenings. ¹²And it is not permissible to slay it during any period of the light, but during the period bordering on the evening, and let them eat it at the time of the evening until the third part of the night, and whatever is leftover of all its flesh from the third part of the night and onwards, let them burn it with fire. ¹³And they will not cook it with water, nor will they eat it raw, but roast on the fire: they will eat it with diligence, its head with the inwards thereof and its feet they will roast with fire, and not break any bone thereof, for no bone of the sons of Israel will be crushed. ¹⁴For this reason the LORD commanded the sons of Israel to observe the Passover on the day of its fixed time, and they will not break a bone thereof, for it is a festival day, and a day commanded, and there may be no passing over from day to day, and month to month, but on the day of its festival let it be observed. ¹⁵And command the sons of Israel to observe the Passover throughout their days, every year, once a year on the day of its fixed time, and it will come for a memorial well pleasing before the LORD, and no plague will come on them to slay or to strike in that year in which they celebrate the Passover in its season in every respect according to His command. ¹⁶And they will not eat it outside the sanctuary of the LORD, but before the sanctuary of the LORD, and all the people of the congregation of Israel will celebrate it in its appointed season. ¹⁷And every man who has come on its day will eat it in the sanctuary of your God before the LORD from twenty years old and upward, for thus it is written and ordained that they should eat it in the sanctuary of the LORD. ¹⁸And when the sons of Israel come into the land which they are to possess, into the land of Canaan, and set up the Dwelling Place of the LORD in the midst of the land in one of their tribes until the sanctuary of the LORD has been built in the land, let them come and celebrate the Passover in the midst of the Dwelling Place of the LORD, and let them slay it before the LORD from year to year. ¹⁹And in the days when the house has been built in the Name of the LORD in the land of their inheritance, they will go there and slay the Passover in the evening, at sunset, at the third part of the day. ²⁰And they will offer its blood on the threshold of the altar and will place its fat on the fire which is on the altar, and they will eat its flesh roasted with fire in the court of the house which has been sanctified in the Name of the LORD. ²¹And they may not celebrate the Passover in their cities, nor in any place except before the Dwelling Place of the LORD, or before His house where His Name has dwelt; and they will not go astray from the LORD. ²²And you, Moses: command the sons of Israel to observe the ordinances of the Passover, as it was commanded to you; declare to them every year and the day of its days, and the festival of unleavened bread, that they should eat unleavened bread [for]

seven days, [and] that they should observe its festival, and that they bring an oblation every day during those seven days of joy before the LORD on the altar of your God. ²³For you celebrated this festival when you went out from Egypt until you entered into the wilderness of Shur, for you completed it on the shore of the sea.

CHAPTER 50

¹And after this law I made known to you the days of the Sabbaths in the wilderness of Zin, which is between Elim and Sinai. ²And I told you of the Sabbaths of the land on Mount Sinai, and I told you of the jubilee years in the Sabbaths of years, but the year thereof I have not told you until you enter the land which you are to possess. ³And the land will also keep its Sabbaths while they dwell on it, and they will know the jubilee year. ⁴For that reason I have ordained for you the year-weeks, and the years, and the jubilees: there are forty-nine jubilees from the days of Adam until this day, and one week and two years, and there are yet forty years more for learning the commands of the LORD, until they pass over into the land of Canaan, crossing the Jordan to the west. ⁵And the jubilees will pass by, until Israel is cleansed from all guilt of fornication, and uncleanness, and pollution, and sin, and error, and dwells with confidence in all the land, and there will no longer be an adversary or any evil one, and the land will be clean from that time forevermore. ⁶And behold, the command regarding the Sabbaths—I have written [them] down for you and all the judgments of its laws. ⁷Six days you will labor, but on the seventh day is the Sabbath of the LORD your God. In it you will do no manner of work—you, and your sons, and your menservants, and your maidservants, and all your cattle, and the sojourner who is also with you. ⁸And the man that does any work on it will die: whoever desecrates that day, whoever lies with [his] wife, or whoever says he will do something on it, that he will set out on a journey thereon in regard to any buying or selling, and whoever draws water thereon which he had not prepared for himself on the sixth day, and whoever takes up any burden to carry it out of his tent or out of his house will die. ⁹You will do no work whatsoever on the Sabbath day except [to utilize] what you have prepared for yourselves on the sixth day, so as to eat, and drink, and rest, and keep Sabbath from all work on that day, and to bless the LORD your God who has given you a day of festival, and a holy day; and a day of the holy kingdom for all Israel is this day among their days forever. ¹⁰For great is the honor which the LORD has given to Israel that they should eat, and drink, and be satisfied on this festival day, and rest thereon from all labor which belongs to the labor of the children of men, except burning frankincense and bringing oblations and sacrifices before the LORD for days and for Sabbaths. ¹¹Only this work will be done on the Sabbaths in the sanctuary of the LORD your God, that they may atone for Israel with sacrifice continually from day to day for a memorial well-pleasing before the LORD, and that He may always receive them from day to day according as you have been commanded. ¹²And every man who does any work thereon, or goes on a journey, or tills [his] farm, whether in his house or any other place, and whoever lights a fire, or rides on any beast, or travels by ship on the sea, and whoever strikes or kills anything, or slaughters a beast or a bird, or whoever catches an animal, or a bird, or a fish, or whoever fasts or makes war on the Sabbaths: ¹³the man who does any of these things on the Sabbath will die, so that the sons of Israel will observe the Sabbaths according to the commands regarding the Sabbaths of the land, as it is written in the tablets, which He gave into My hands that I should write out for you—the laws of the seasons and the seasons according to the division of their days. The account of the division of the days is completed.

1 ENOCH

The Book of Enoch (also called 1 Enoch) is an ancient Jewish religious work, ascribed by tradition to Enoch, the great-grandfather of Noah. Enoch contains unique material on the origins of supernatural demons and giants, why some messengers fell from Heaven, an explanation of why the Great Flood was morally necessary, and prophetic exposition of the thousand-year reign of the Messiah. It is wholly extant only in the Ge'ez language, with Aramaic fragments from the Dead Sea Scrolls and a few Greek and Latin fragments. Jude 1:14–15 is a direct quote of Enoch 1:9 (see also 1 Enoch 60:8). Enoch is composed of five sections.

SECTION 1:
THE BOOK OF THE WATCHERS

CHAPTER 1

¹THE WORDS OF THE BLESSING OF ENOCH, WITH WHICH HE BLESSED THE CHOSEN ONES AND RIGHTEOUS, WHO WILL BE LIVING IN THE DAY OF TRIBULATION, WHEN ALL THE WICKED AND GODLESS ARE TO BE REMOVED. ²And he took up his allegory and spoke—Enoch a righteous man, whose eyes were opened by God, saw the vision of the Holy One in the heavens, which the messengers showed me, and from them I heard everything, and from them I understood as I saw, but not for this generation, but for a remote one which is to come. ³Concerning the chosen ones, I spoke and took up my allegory concerning them: The Holy Great One will come out from His dwelling, ⁴And the perpetual God will tread on the earth, [even] on Mount Sinai, || And appear in the strength of His might from the Heaven of heavens. ⁵And all will be smitten with fear, || And the Watchers will quake, || And great fear and trembling will seize them to the ends of the earth. ⁶And the high mountains will be shaken, || And the high hills will be made low || And will melt like wax before the flame, ⁷And the earth will be wholly split apart, || And all that is on the earth will perish, || And there will be a judgment on all [men]. ⁸But with the righteous He will make peace, || And will protect the chosen ones, || And mercy will be on them. And they will all belong to God, || And they will be prospered, || And they will all be blessed. And He will help them all, || And light will appear to them, || And He will make peace with them. ⁹And behold, He comes with myriads of His holy ones to execute judgment on all, || And to destroy all the ungodly, || And to convict all flesh of all the works of their ungodliness which they have ungodly committed, || And of all the hard things which ungodly sinners have spoken against Him.

CHAPTER 2

¹Observe everything that takes place in the heavens, how they do not change their orbits, and the luminaries which are in the heavens, how they all rise and set in order, each in its season, and do not transgress against their appointed order. ²Behold the earth and give heed to the things which take place on it from first to last, how steadfast they are, how none of the things on earth change, but all the works of God appear to you. ³Behold the summer and the winter, how the whole earth is filled with water, and clouds, and dew, and rain lie on it.

CHAPTER 3

¹Observe and see how [in the winter] all the trees seem as though they had withered and shed all their leaves, ²except fourteen trees, which do not lose their foliage but retain the

1 ENOCH

old foliage from two to three years until the new comes.

CHAPTER 4
¹And again, observe the days of summer, how the sun is above the earth—over against it. ²And you seek shade and shelter by reason of the heat of the sun, and the earth also burns with growing heat, and so you cannot tread on the earth, or on a rock by reason of its heat.

CHAPTER 5
¹Observe how the trees cover themselves with green leaves and bear fruit; for what reason, take heed and know with regard to all His works and recognize how He that lives forever has made them so. ²And all His works go on like this from year to year forever, and all the tasks which they accomplish for Him, and their tasks do not change, but according as God has ordained so it is done. ³And behold how the sea and the rivers accomplish [their tasks] in like manner and do not change their tasks from His commands. ⁴But you have not been steadfast, || Nor done the commands of the LORD, || But you have turned away and spoken proud and hard words || With your impure mouths against His greatness. O you hard-hearted! You will find no peace. ⁵Therefore you will execrate your days, || And the years of your life will perish, || And the years of your destruction will be multiplied in continuous execration, || And you will find no mercy. ⁶In those days you will make your names a continuous execration to all the righteous, || And by you will all who curse, curse, || And all the sinners and godless will imprecate by you, || And for you, the godless, there will be a curse. And all the [righteous] will rejoice, || And there will be forgiveness of sins, || And every mercy, and peace, and forbearance: There will be salvation to them, an excellent light. And for all of you sinners there will be no salvation, || But a curse will abide on all of you. ⁷But for the chosen ones there will be light, and joy, and peace, || And they will inherit the earth. ⁸And then wisdom will be bestowed on the chosen ones, || And they will all live and never again sin, || Either through ungodliness or through pride, || But they who are wise will be humble. ⁹And they will not transgress again, || Nor will they sin all the days of their life, || Nor will they die of [the divine] anger or wrath, || But they will complete the number of the days of their life. And their lives will be increased in peace, || And the years of their joy will be multiplied, || In continuous gladness and peace, all the days of their life.

CHAPTER 6
¹And it came to pass when the children of men had multiplied that in those days were born to them beautiful and attractive daughters. ²And the messengers, the children of the heavens, saw and lusted after them, and said to one another, "Come, let us choose wives [for] ourselves from among the children of men and beget children [for] ourselves." ³And Semjaza, who was their leader, said to them, "Indeed, I fear you will not agree to do this deed, and I alone will have to pay the penalty of a great sin." ⁴And they all answered him and said, "Let us all swear an oath, and all bind ourselves by mutual imprecations not to abandon this plan but to do this thing." ⁵Then they all swore together and bound themselves by mutual imprecations on it. ⁶And they were two hundred in all who descended in the days of Jared on the summit of Mount Hermon, and they called it Mount Hermon, because they had sworn and bound themselves by mutual imprecations on it. ⁷And these are the names of their leaders: their leader Semjaza, [and] Araklba, Rameel, Kokablel, Tamlel, Ramlel, Danel, Ezeqeel, Baraqijal, Asael, Armaros, Batarel, Ananel, Zaqiel, Samsapeel, Satarel, Turel, Jomjael, [and] Sariel. ⁸These are their chiefs of tens.

CHAPTER 7
¹And all the others took wives to themselves together with them, and each chose one for himself, and they began to go in to them and to defile themselves with them, and they taught them charms and enchantments, and the cutting of roots, and made them acquainted with plants. ²And they became pregnant, and they bore great giants, whose height was [[three thousand ells]], ³who consumed all the acquisitions of men. And when men could no longer sustain them, ⁴the giants turned against them and devoured mankind. ⁵And they began to sin against birds, and beasts, and reptiles, and fish, and to devour one another's flesh, and drink the blood. ⁶Then the earth laid accusation against the lawless ones.

CHAPTER 8
¹And Azazel taught men to make swords, and knives, and shields, and breastplates, and made known to them the metals of the earth and the craft of working them, and bracelets, and ornaments, and the use of antimony, and the beautifying of the eyelids, and all kinds of costly stones, and all coloring tinctures. ²And there arose much godlessness, and they committed fornication, and they were led astray, and became corrupt in all their ways. ³Semjaza taught enchantments and root-cuttings, 'Armaros the resolving of enchantments, Baraqijal [taught] astrology, Kokabel the constellations, Ezeqeel the knowledge of the clouds, Araqiel the signs of the earth, Shamsiel the signs of the sun, and Sariel the course of the moon. And as men perished, they cried, and their cry went up to Heaven.

CHAPTER 9
¹And then Michael, Uriel, Raphael, and Gabriel looked down from Heaven and saw much blood being shed on the earth, and all lawlessness being worked on the earth. ²And they said to one another, "The earth made without inhabitant cries the voice of their crying up to the gates of Heaven." ³And now to you, the holy ones of Heaven, the souls of men make their suit, saying, "Bring our cause before the Most High." ⁴And they said to the Lord of the ages, "Lord of lords, God of gods, King of kings, and God of the ages, the throne of Your glory stands to all the generations of the ages, and Your Name [is] holy, and glorious, and blessed to all the ages! ⁵You have made all things and have power over all things: and all things are naked and open in Your sight, and You see all things, and nothing can hide itself from You. ⁶You see what Azazel has done, who has taught all unrighteousness on earth and revealed the perpetual secrets which were [preserved] in Heaven, which men were striving to learn— ⁷and Semjaza, to whom You have given authority to bear rule over his associates. ⁸And they have gone to the daughters of men on the earth, and have slept with the women, and have defiled themselves, and revealed to them all kinds of sins. ⁹And the women have borne giants, and the whole earth has thereby been filled with blood and unrighteousness. ¹⁰And now, behold, the souls of those who have died are crying and making their suit to the gates of Heaven, and their lamentations have ascended, and they cannot cease because of the lawless deeds which are worked on the earth. ¹¹And You know all things before they come to pass, and You see these things and You permit them, and You do not say to us what we are to do to them in regard to these."

CHAPTER 10
¹Then the Most High uttered, the Holy and Great One spoke, and sent Uriel to the son of Lamech, and said to him: ²"Go to Noah and tell him in My Name: Hide yourself! And reveal to him the end that is approaching, that the whole earth will be destroyed, and a flood is about to come on the whole earth and will destroy all that is on it. ³And now instruct him that he may escape and his seed may be preserved for all the generations of the world." ⁴And again, the LORD said to Raphael, "Bind Azazel hand and foot and cast him into the darkness, and make an opening in the desert, which is in Dudael, and cast him therein. ⁵And place rough and jagged rocks over him, and cover him with darkness, and let him abide there forever, and cover his face that he may not see light. ⁶And on the Day of the Great Judgment he will be cast into the fire. ⁷And heal the earth which the messengers have corrupted, and proclaim the healing of the earth, that they may heal the plague, and that all the children of men may not perish through all the secret things that the Watchers have disclosed and have taught their sons. ⁸And the whole earth has been corrupted through the works that were taught by

Azazel: to him ascribe all sin." ⁹And to Gabriel the Lord said, "Proceed against the bastards and the reprobates, and against the children of fornication, and destroy the children of the Watchers from among men. Send them against one another that they may destroy each other in battle, for they will not have length of days. ¹⁰And no request that they make of you will be granted to their fathers on their behalf, for they hope to live a continuous life, and that each one of them will live five hundred years." ¹¹And the Lord said to Michael, "Go, bind Semjaza and his associates who have united themselves with women so as to have defiled themselves with them in all their uncleanness. ¹²And when their sons have slain one another, and they have seen the destruction of their beloved ones, bind them fast for seventy generations in the valleys of the earth, until the day of their judgment and of their consummation, until the judgment that is forever and ever is consummated. ¹³In those days they will be led off to the abyss of fire, and to the torment and the prison in which they will be confined forever. ¹⁴And whoever will be condemned and destroyed will from then on be bound together with them to the end of all generations. ¹⁵And destroy all the spirits of the reprobate and the children of the Watchers, because they have wronged mankind. ¹⁶Destroy all wrong from the face of the earth and let every evil work come to an end; and let the plant of righteousness and truth appear: and it will prove a blessing; the works of righteousness and truth will be planted in truth and joy forevermore. ¹⁷And then all the righteous will escape and will live until they beget thousands of children, and they will complete all the days of their youth and their old age in peace. ¹⁸And then the whole earth will be tilled in righteousness and will all be planted with trees and be full of blessing. ¹⁹And all desirable trees will be planted on it, and they will plant vines on it, and the vine which they plant thereon will yield wine in abundance. And as for all the seed which is sown thereon, each measure [of it] will bear one thousand, and each measure of olives will yield ten presses of oil. ²⁰And you will cleanse the earth from all oppression, and from all unrighteousness, and from all sin, and from all godlessness: and destroy all the uncleanness that is worked on the earth from off the earth. ²¹And all the children of men will become righteous, and all nations will offer adoration and will praise Me, and all will worship Me. ²²And the earth will be cleansed from all defilement, and from all sin, and from all punishment, and from all torment, and I will never again send [them] on it from generation to generation and forever."

CHAPTER 11

¹"And in those days I will open the store chambers of blessing which are in the heavens, so as to send them down on the earth over the work and labor of the children of men. ²And truth and peace will be associated together throughout all the days of the world and throughout all the generations of men."

CHAPTER 12

¹Before these things Enoch was hidden, and no one of the children of men knew where he was hidden, and where he dwelt, and what had become of him. ²And his activities had to do with the Watchers, and his days were with the holy ones. ³And I, Enoch, was blessing the Lord of majesty and the King of the ages, and the Watchers called me—Enoch the scribe—and said to me, ⁴"Enoch, you scribe of righteousness, go, declare to the Watchers of the heavens who have left the high Heaven, the holy perpetual place, and have defiled themselves with women, and have done as the children of earth do, and have taken wives to themselves: ⁵You have worked great destruction on the earth, and you will have no peace nor forgiveness of sin; ⁶and inasmuch as they delight themselves in their children, they will see the murder of their beloved ones, and they will lament over the destruction of their children, and will make supplication continuously; but you will not attain mercy and peace."

CHAPTER 13

¹And Enoch went and said, "Azazel, you will have no peace: a severe sentence has gone out against you to put you in bonds, ²and you will not have toleration nor request granted to you, because of the unrighteousness which you have taught, and because of all the works of godlessness, and unrighteousness, and sin which you have shown to men." ³Then I went and spoke to them all together, and they were all afraid, and fear and trembling seized them. ⁴And they implored me to draw up a petition for them that they might find forgiveness, and to read their petition in the presence of the Lord of Heaven. ⁵For from that point forward they could not speak [with Him] nor lift up their eyes to Heaven for shame of their sins for which they had been condemned. ⁶Then I wrote out their petition, and the prayer in regard to their spirits and their deeds individually, and in regard to their requests that they should have forgiveness and length. ⁷And I went off and sat down at the waters of Dan, in the land of Dan, to the south of the west of Hermon, [and there] I read their petition until I fell asleep. ⁸And behold, a dream came to me, and visions fell down on me, and I saw visions of discipline, and a voice came bidding me to tell it to the sons of Heaven and reprimand them. ⁹And when I awoke, I came to them, and they were all sitting gathered together, weeping in 'Abelsjail, which is between Lebanon and Seneser, with their faces covered. ¹⁰And I recounted before them all the visions which I had seen in sleep, and I began to speak the words of righteousness, and to reprimand the heavenly Watchers.

CHAPTER 14

¹The Scroll of the Words of Righteousness, and of the Reprimand of the Perpetual Watchers in accordance with the command of the Holy Great One in that vision. ²I saw in my sleep what I will now say with a tongue of flesh and with the breath of my mouth, which the Great One has given to men to converse with and understand with the heart. ³As He has created and given to man the power of understanding, the word of wisdom, so He has also created me and given me the power of reprimanding the Watchers, the children of Heaven. ⁴I wrote out your petition, and in my vision it appeared like this, that your petition will not be granted to you throughout all the days of the age, and that judgment has been finally passed on you: yes, [your petition] will not be granted to you. ⁵And from now on you will not ascend into Heaven for all ages, and in bonds of the earth the decree has gone out to bind you for all the days of the world. ⁶And you will have seen the destruction of your beloved sons beforehand and you will have no pleasure in them, but they will fall before you by the sword. ⁷And your petition on their behalf will not be granted, nor yet on your own, even though you weep, and pray, and speak all the words contained in the writing which I have written. ⁸And the vision was shown to me like this: behold, in the vision clouds invited me and a mist summoned me, and the course of the stars and the lightnings sped toward me, and the winds in the vision caused me to fly and lifted me upward and bore me into Heaven. ⁹And I went in until I drew near to a wall which is built of crystals and surrounded by tongues of fire: and it began to frighten me. ¹⁰And I went into the tongues of fire and drew near to a large house which was built of crystals: and the walls of the house were like a tessellated floor [made] of crystals, and its groundwork was of crystal. ¹¹Its ceiling was like the path of the stars and the lightnings, and between them were fiery cherubim, and their heaven was [as clear as] water. ¹²A flaming fire surrounded the walls, and its portals blazed with fire. ¹³And I entered into that house, and it was hot as fire and cold as ice: ¹⁴there were no delights of life therein; fear covered me, and trembling took hold of me. ¹⁵And as I quaked and trembled, I fell on my face. And I beheld a vision, and behold, there was a second house, greater than the former, and the entire portal stood open before me, and it was built of flames of fire. ¹⁶And in every respect it so excelled in splendor, and magnificence, and extent that I cannot describe to you its splendor and its extent. ¹⁷And its floor was of fire, and above it were lightnings and the path of the stars, and its ceiling was also flaming fire. ¹⁸And I looked and saw a lofty throne therein: its appearance was as crystal, and the wheels thereof as the shining sun, and there was the vision of cherubim. ¹⁹And from underneath the throne came streams of flaming fire so that I could not look thereon. ²⁰And the Great Glory sat thereon, and His raiment shone more brightly than the sun and was whiter than any snow. ²¹None of the messengers could enter and behold His face by reason of the magnificence and glory, and no flesh could behold Him. ²²The flaming fire was around Him, and a great

fire stood before Him, and none around could draw near Him: myriads of myriads [stood] before Him, yet He needed no counselor. ²³And the most holy ones who were near to Him did not leave by night nor depart from Him. ²⁴And until then I had been prostrate on my face, trembling: and the LORD called me with His own mouth, and said to me, "Come here, Enoch, and hear My word." ²⁵And one of the holy ones came to me and waked me, and He made me rise up and approach the door, and I bowed my face downwards.

CHAPTER 15

¹And He answered and said to me, and I heard His voice: "Do not fear, Enoch, you righteous man and scribe of righteousness: approach here and hear My voice. ²And go, say to the Watchers of the heavens, who have sent you to intercede for them: You should intercede for men, and not men for you! ³Why have you left the high, holy, and perpetual Heaven, and lain with women, and defiled yourselves with the daughters of men, and taken wives to yourselves, and done like the children of earth, and begotten giants [as your] sons? ⁴And though you were holy [and] spiritual, living the continuous life, you have defiled yourselves with the blood of women, and have begotten [children] with the blood of flesh, and, as the children of men, have lusted after flesh and blood as those who die and perish also do. ⁵Therefore I have also given them wives that they might impregnate them, and beget children by them, that nothing might be wanting to them on earth. ⁶But you were formerly spiritual, living the continuous life, and immortal for all generations of the world. ⁷And, therefore, I have not appointed wives for you; for as for the spiritual ones of the heavens, their dwelling is in the heavens. ⁸And now the giants, who are produced from the spirits and flesh, will be called evil spirits on the earth, and their dwelling will be on the earth. ⁹Evil spirits have proceeded from their bodies, because they are born from men and their beginning and primal origin is from the holy Watchers; they will be evil spirits on earth, and they will be called evil spirits. ¹⁰[[As for the spirits of Heaven, their dwelling will be in Heaven, but as for the spirits of the earth which were born on the earth, their dwelling will be on the earth.]] ¹¹And the spirits of the giants afflict, oppress, destroy, attack, do battle, and work destruction on the earth, and cause trouble: they take no food, but nevertheless hunger and thirst, and cause offenses. ¹²And these spirits will rise up against the children of men and against the women, because they have proceeded from them."

CHAPTER 16

¹From the days of the slaughter, and destruction, and death of the giants—from the souls of whose flesh the spirits, having gone out, will destroy without incurring judgment—they will therefore destroy until the Day of the Consummation, the Great Judgment in which the age will be consummated over the Watchers and the godless; yes, [it] will be wholly consummated. ²And now as to the Watchers who have sent you to intercede for them, who had previously been in Heaven, [say to them]: ³"You have been in Heaven, but all the mysteries had not yet been revealed to you, and you knew worthless ones, and you have made these known to the women in the hardness of your hearts, and through these mysteries women and men work much evil on earth." ⁴Therefore, say to them: "You have no peace."

CHAPTER 17

¹And they took and brought me to a place in which those who were there were like flaming fire, and they appeared as men when they wished. ²And they brought me to the place of darkness, and to a mountain the point of whose summit reached to Heaven. ³And I saw the places of the luminaries, and the treasuries of the stars and of the thunder, and in the uttermost depths where there were a fiery bow, and arrows, and their quiver, and a fiery sword and all the lightnings. ⁴And they took me to the living waters, and to the fire of the west, which receives every setting of the sun. ⁵And I came to a river of fire in which the fire flows like water and discharges itself into the Great Sea toward the west. ⁶I saw the great rivers and came to the great river and to the great darkness and went to the place where no flesh walks. ⁷I saw the mountains of the darkness of winter and the place from where all the waters of the deep flow. ⁸I saw the mouths of all the rivers of the earth and the mouth of the deep.

CHAPTER 18

¹I saw the treasuries of all the winds: I saw how He had furnished the whole creation and the firm foundations of the earth with them. ²And I saw the cornerstone of the earth: I saw the four winds which bear [the earth and] the expanse of the heavens. ³And I saw how the winds stretch out the vaults of the heavens and have their station between the heavens and earth: these are the pillars of the heavens. ⁴I saw the winds of the heavens which turn and bring the circumference of the sun and all the stars to their setting. ⁵I saw the winds on the earth carrying the clouds. I saw the paths of the messengers. ⁶I saw at the end of the earth the expanse of the heavens above. And I proceeded and saw a place which burns day and night, where there are seven mountains of magnificent stones: three toward the east and three toward the south. ⁷And as for those toward the east: [one] was of colored stone, and one of pearl, and one of jacinth; and those toward the south [were] of red stone. ⁸But the middle one reached to the heavens like the throne of God, of alabaster, and the summit of the throne was of sapphire. ⁹And I saw a flaming fire. ¹⁰And beyond these mountains is a region at the end of the great earth: there the heavens were completed. ¹¹And I saw a deep abyss with columns of heavenly fire, and among them I saw columns of fire fall, which were beyond measure alike toward the height and toward the depth. ¹²And beyond that abyss I saw a place which had no expanse of the heavens above, and no firmly founded earth beneath it: there was no water on it, and no birds, but it was a waste and horrible place. ¹³I saw seven stars there like great burning mountains, and to me, when I inquired regarding them, ¹⁴the messenger said, "This place is the end of the heavens and earth: this has become a prison for the stars and the host of Heaven. ¹⁵And the stars which roll over the fire are they which have transgressed the command of the LORD in the beginning of their rising, because they did not come out at their appointed times. ¹⁶And He was angry with them and bound them until the time when their guilt should be consummated for ten thousand years."

CHAPTER 19

¹And Uriel said to me, "The messengers who have connected themselves with women will stand here, and their spirits assuming many different forms are defiling mankind and will lead them astray into sacrificing to demons as gods; [[they will stand here]] until the Day of the Great Judgment in which they will be judged until they are made an end of. ²And also, the women of the messengers who went astray will become sirens." ³And only I, Enoch, saw the vision, the ends of all things: and no man will see as I have seen.

CHAPTER 20

¹And these are the names of the holy messengers who watch: ²Uriel, one of the holy messengers, who is over the world and over Tartarus; ³Raphael, one of the holy messengers, who is over the spirits of men; ⁴Raguel, one of the holy messengers who takes vengeance on the world of the luminaries; ⁵Michael, one of the holy messengers, namely, he that is set over the best part of mankind and over chaos; ⁶Saraqael, one of the holy messengers, who is set over the spirits who sin in the spirit; ⁷Gabriel, one of the holy messengers, who is over Paradise, and the serpents, and the cherubim; ⁸Remiel, one of the holy messengers, whom God set over those who rise.

CHAPTER 21

¹And I proceeded to where things were chaotic, ²and I saw something horrible there: I saw neither a heaven above nor a firmly founded earth, but a chaotic and horrible place. ³And there I saw seven stars of the heavens bound together in it, like great mountains and burning with fire. ⁴Then I said, "For what sin are they bound, and on what account have they been cast in here?" ⁵Then Uriel, one of the holy messengers who was with me, and was chief over them, spoke and said, "Enoch, why do you ask, and why are you eager for the truth? ⁶These are of the number of the stars of the heavens which have transgressed the command of the LORD and are bound here until ten thousand years, the time entailed by their sins, are consummated." ⁷And from there I went to another place,

which was still more horrible than the former, and I saw a horrible thing: a great fire there which burned and blazed, and the place was cleft as far as the abyss, being full of great descending columns of fire: I could see neither its extent or magnitude, nor could I conjecture. ⁸Then I said, "How fearful is the place and how terrible to look on!" ⁹Then Uriel answered me, one of the holy messengers who was with me, and said to me, "Enoch, why do you have such fear and fright?" And I answered, "Because of this fearful place, and because of the spectacle of the pain." ¹⁰And he said to me, "This place is the prison of the messengers, and they will be imprisoned here forever."

CHAPTER 22

¹And then I went to another place—the mountain of hard rock. ²And there were four hollow places in it, deep, and wide, and very smooth. O how smooth the hollow places are, and deep and dark to look at! ³Then Raphael answered, one of the holy messengers who was with me, and said to me, "These hollow places have been created for this very purpose, that the spirits of the souls of the dead should assemble therein, yes, that all the souls of the children of men should assemble here. ⁴And these places have been made to receive them until the day of their judgment and until their appointed period, until the Great Judgment [comes] on them." ⁵I saw [the spirit of] a dead man making suit, and his voice went out to Heaven and made suit. ⁶And I asked Raphael, the messenger who was with me, and I said to him, "This spirit which makes suit, whose is it, whose voice goes out and makes suit to Heaven?" ⁷And he answered me, saying, "This is the spirit which went out from Abel, whom his brother Cain slew, and he makes his suit against him until his seed is destroyed from the face of the earth, and his seed is annihilated from among the seed of men." ⁸Then I asked regarding it, and regarding all the hollow places: "Why is one separated from the other?" ⁹And he answered me and said to me, "These three have been made that the spirits of the dead might be separated. And such a division has been made [for] the spirits of the righteous, in which there is the bright spring of water. ¹⁰And such has been made for sinners when they die and are buried in the earth and judgment has not been executed on them in their lifetime. ¹¹Here their spirits will be set apart in this great pain until the Great Day of Judgment; and [there will be] punishment and torment of those who are cursed forever, and retribution for their spirits. ¹²There He will bind them forever. And such a division has been made for the spirits of those who make their suit, who make disclosures concerning their destruction, when they were slain in the days of the sinners. ¹³Such has been made for the spirits of men who were not righteous but sinners, who were complete in transgression, and they will be companions of the transgressors, but their spirits will not be slain in the Day of Judgment nor will they be raised from there." ¹⁴Then I blessed the Lord of Glory and said, "Blessed is my Lord, the Lord of righteousness, who rules forever."

CHAPTER 23

¹From there I went to another place to the west of the ends of the earth. ²And I saw a burning fire which ran without resting and did not cease from its course day or night, but [ran] regularly. ³And I asked, saying, "What is this which does not rest?" ⁴Then Raguel, one of the holy messengers who was with me, answered me and said to me, "This course of fire which you have seen is the fire in the west which persecutes all the luminaries of the heavens."

CHAPTER 24

¹And from there I went to another place of the earth, and he showed me a mountain range of fire which burned day and night. ²And I went beyond it and saw seven magnificent mountains, all differing from each other, and the stones [thereof] were magnificent and beautiful, magnificent as a whole, of glorious appearance and fair exterior: three toward the east, one founded on the other, and three toward the south, one on the other, and deep rough ravines, not one of which joined with any other. ³And the seventh mountain was in the midst of these, and it excelled them in height, resembling the seat of a throne: and fragrant trees encircled the throne. ⁴And among them was a tree such as I had never yet smelled, neither was any among them nor were others like it: it had a fragrance beyond all fragrance, and its leaves, and blooms, and wood do not wither forever, and its fruit is beautiful, and its fruit resembles the dates of a palm. ⁵Then I said, "O how beautiful and fragrant this tree is! And its leaves are fair, and its blooms [are] very delightful in appearance!" ⁶Then Michael, one of the holy and honored messengers who was with me and was their leader, answered.

CHAPTER 25

¹And he said to me, "Enoch, why do you ask me regarding the fragrance of the tree, and why do you wish to learn the truth?" ²Then I answered him, saying, "I wish to know about everything, but especially about this tree." ³And he answered, saying, "This high mountain which you have seen, whose summit is like the throne of God, is His throne, where the Holy Great One, the Lord of Glory, the perpetual King will sit when He will come down to visit the earth with goodness. ⁴And as for this fragrant tree, no mortal is permitted to touch it until the Great Judgment when He will take vengeance on all and bring [everything] to its consummation forever. ⁵It will then be given to the righteous and holy. Its fruit will be for food to the chosen ones: it will be transplanted to the holy place, to the temple of the LORD, the perpetual King. ⁶Then they will rejoice with joy and be glad, || And they will enter into the holy place; And its fragrance will be in their bones, || And they will live a long life on earth, || Such as your fathers lived: And in their days no sorrow, or plague, || Or torment, or calamity will touch them." ⁷Then I blessed the God of Glory, the perpetual King, who has prepared such things for the righteous, and has created them and promised to give to them.

CHAPTER 26

¹And I went from there to the middle of the earth, and I saw a blessed place in which there were trees with branches abiding and blooming. ²And there I saw a holy mountain, and underneath the mountain to the east there was a stream and it flowed toward the south. ³And I saw another mountain higher than this toward the east, and between them a deep and narrow ravine: in it also ran a stream underneath the mountain. ⁴And to the west thereof there was another mountain, lower than the former and of small elevation, and a deep and dry ravine between them: and another deep and dry ravine was at the extremities of the three mountains. ⁵And all the ravines were deep and narrow, [being formed] of hard rock, and trees were not planted on them. ⁶And I marveled at the rocks, and I marveled at the ravine, yes, I marveled very much.

CHAPTER 27

¹Then I said, "For what purpose is this blessed land, which is entirely filled with trees, and this accursed valley between?" ²Then Uriel, one of the holy messengers who was with me, answered and said, "This accursed valley is for those who are accursed forever. Here all the accursed will be gathered together who utter unseemly words with their lips against the LORD and speak hard things of His glory. Here they will be gathered together, and here will be their place of judgment. ³In the last days there will be the spectacle of righteous judgment on them in the presence of the righteous forever: here the merciful will bless the Lord of Glory, the perpetual King. ⁴In the days of judgment over the former, they will bless Him for the mercy in accordance with which He has assigned them [their lot]." ⁵Then I blessed the Lord of Glory and set out His glory and lauded Him gloriously.

CHAPTER 28

¹And then I went toward the east, into the midst of the mountain range of the desert, and I saw a wilderness and it was solitary, full of trees and plants. ²And water gushed out from above. ³Rushing like a copious watercourse [which flowed] toward the northwest, it caused clouds and dew to ascend on every side.

CHAPTER 29

¹And then I went to another place in the desert and approached to the east of this mountain range. ²And there I saw aromatic trees exhaling the fragrance of frankincense and myrrh, and the trees were also similar to the almond tree.

1 ENOCH

CHAPTER 30

¹And beyond these, I went far to the east, and I saw another place, a valley [full] of water. ²And therein there was a tree, the color of fragrant trees such as the mastic. ³And on the sides of those valleys I saw fragrant cinnamon. And beyond these I proceeded to the east.

CHAPTER 31

¹And I saw other mountains, and among them were groves of trees, and nectar flowed out from them, which is called sarara and galbanum. ²And beyond these mountains I saw another mountain to the east of the ends of the earth, on which were aloe-trees, and all the trees were full of stacte, being like almond-trees. ³And when one burned it, it smelled sweeter than any refreshing fragrance.

CHAPTER 32

¹And after these fragrant odors, as I looked toward the north over the mountains, I saw seven mountains full of choice nard, and fragrant trees, and cinnamon, and pepper. ²And then I went over the summits of all these mountains, far toward the east of the earth, and passed above the Erythraean Sea, and went far from it and passed over the messenger Zotiel. ³And I came to the Garden of Righteousness and saw beyond those trees many large trees growing there and of attractive fragrance, large, very beautiful and glorious, and the Tree of Wisdom of which they eat and know great wisdom. ⁴That tree is in height like the fir, and its leaves are like [those of] the Carob tree, and its fruit is like the clusters of the vine, very beautiful, and the fragrance of the tree penetrates far. ⁵Then I said, "How beautiful is the tree, and how attractive is its look!" ⁶Then Raphael, the holy messenger, who was with me, answered me and said, "This is the Tree of Wisdom, of which your ancient father and your ancient mother, who were before you, have eaten, and they learned wisdom, and their eyes were opened, and they knew that they were naked, and they were driven out of the garden."

CHAPTER 33

¹And from there I went to the ends of the earth and saw great beasts there, and each differed from the other, and also birds differing in appearance, and beauty, and voice—the one differing from the other. ²And to the east of those beasts I saw the ends of the earth on which the heavens rest, and the portals of the heavens open. ³And I saw how the stars of the heavens come out, and I counted the portals out of which they proceed, and wrote down all their outlets, of each individual star by itself, according to their number and their names, their courses and their positions, and their times and their months, as Uriel, the holy messenger who was with me, showed me. ⁴He showed all things to me and wrote them down for me. He also wrote their names, and their laws, and their companies for me.

CHAPTER 34

¹And from there I went toward the north to the ends of the earth, and there I saw a great and glorious device at the ends of the whole earth. ²And here I saw three portals of heaven open in the heavens: north winds proceed through each of them. When they blow there is cold, hail, frost, snow, dew, and rain. ³And out of one portal they blow for good, but when they blow through the other two portals, it is with violence and affliction on the earth, and they blow with violence.

CHAPTER 35

¹And from there I went toward the west, to the ends of the earth, and saw three portals of heaven open there such as I had seen in the east, the same number of portals, and the same number of outlets.

CHAPTER 36

¹And from there I went to the south, to the ends of the earth, and saw three portals of heaven open there: and then there came dew, rain, and wind. ²And from there I went to the east, to the ends of the heavens, and saw the three eastern portals of heaven open here, and small portals [were] above them. ³Through each of these small portals the stars of the heavens pass and run their course to the west on the path which is shown to them. ⁴And as often as I saw, I always blessed the Lord of Glory, and I continued to bless the Lord of Glory who has worked great and glorious wonders, to show the greatness of His work to the messengers, and to spirits, and to men, that they might praise His work and all His creation, that they might see the work of His might, and praise the great work of His hands, and bless Him forever.

SECTION 2:

THE BOOK OF ALLEGORIES OF ENOCH

CHAPTER 37

¹THE SECOND VISION WHICH HE SAW, THE VISION OF WISDOM, WHICH ENOCH THE SON OF JARED, THE SON OF MAHALALEL, THE SON OF CAINAN, THE SON OF ENOS, THE SON OF SETH, THE SON OF ADAM, SAW. ²And this is the beginning of the words of wisdom which I lifted up my voice to speak and say to those which dwell on earth: "Hear, you men of ancient time, and see, you that come after, the words of the Holy One which I will speak before the Lord of Spirits." ³It were better to declare [them only] to the men of ancient time, but even from those that come after we will not withhold the beginning of wisdom. ⁴Until the present day such wisdom has never been given by the Lord of Spirits as I have received according to my insight, according to the good pleasure of the Lord of Spirits by whom the lot of continuous life has been given to me. ⁵Now three allegories were imparted to me, and I lifted up my voice and recounted them to those that dwell on the earth.

CHAPTER 38

¹THE FIRST ALLEGORY. When the congregation of the righteous will appear, and sinners will be judged for their sins, and will be driven from the face of the earth, ²and when the Righteous One will appear before the eyes of the righteous, whose chosen works hang on the Lord of Spirits, and light will appear to the righteous and the chosen ones who dwell on the earth, where then will be the dwelling of the sinners, and where the resting-place of those who have denied the Lord of Spirits? It had been good for them if they had not been born. ³When the secrets of the righteous will be revealed and the sinners judged, and the godless driven from the presence of the righteous and chosen ones, ⁴from that time those that possess the earth will no longer be powerful and exalted, and they will not be able to behold the face of the holy, for the Lord of Spirits has caused His light to appear on the face of the holy, righteous, and chosen ones. ⁵Then the kings and the mighty will perish and be given into the hands of the righteous and holy. ⁶And from then on none will seek for themselves mercy from the Lord of Spirits, for their life is at an end.

CHAPTER 39

¹[[And it will come to pass in those days that chosen ones and holy children will descend from the high Heaven, and their seed will become one with the children of men. ²And in those days Enoch received scrolls of zeal and wrath, and scrolls of disquiet and expulsion.]] "And mercy will not be accorded to them," says the Lord of Spirits. ³And in those days a whirlwind carried me off from the earth and set me down at the end of the heavens. ⁴And there I saw another vision, the dwelling-places of the holy, and the resting-places of the righteous. ⁵Here my eyes saw their dwellings with His righteous messengers, and their resting-places with the holy. And they petitioned, and interceded, and prayed for the children of men, and righteousness flowed before them as water, and mercy like dew on the earth; so it is among them forever and ever. ⁶And in that place my eyes saw the Chosen One of righteousness and of faith, and I saw His dwelling-place under the wings of the Lord of Spirits. And righteousness will prevail in His days, and the righteous and chosen ones will be without number before Him forever and ever. ⁷And all the righteous and chosen ones before Him will be strong as fiery lights, and their mouth will be full of blessing, and their lips extol the Name of the Lord of Spirits, and righteousness will never fail before Him. ⁸I wished to dwell there, and my spirit longed for that dwelling-place; and my portion has been there until now, for so it has been established concerning me before the Lord of Spirits. ⁹In those days I praised and extolled the Name of the Lord of Spirits with blessings and praises, because He has destined me for blessing and glory according to the good pleasure of the Lord of Spirits. ¹⁰For a long time my eyes regarded that place, and I blessed Him and praised Him, saying,

"Blessed is He, and may He be blessed from the beginning and forevermore. ¹¹And before Him there is no ceasing. He knows before the world was created what is forever and what will be from generation to generation. ¹²Those who do not sleep bless You: they stand before Your glory and bless, praise, and extol, saying, HOLY, HOLY, HOLY, is the Lord of Spirits: He fills the earth with spirits." And here my eyes saw all those who do not sleep: they stand before Him, and bless, and say, "Blessed are You and blessed is the Name of the LORD forever and ever." And my face was changed, for I could no longer behold.

CHAPTER 40

¹And after that I saw thousands of thousands and ten thousand times ten thousand, I saw a multitude beyond number and reckoning, who stood before the Lord of Spirits. ²And on the four sides of the Lord of Spirits I saw four presences, different from those that do not sleep, and I learned their names, for the messenger that went with me made their names known to me and showed me all the hidden things. ³And I heard the voices of those four presences as they uttered praises before the Lord of Glory. ⁴The first voice blesses the Lord of Spirits forever and ever. ⁵And the second voice I heard blessing the Chosen One and the chosen ones who hang on the Lord of Spirits. ⁶And the third voice I heard pray and intercede for those who dwell on the earth and supplicate in the Name of the Lord of Spirits. ⁷And I heard the fourth voice fending off the devils and forbidding them to come before the Lord of Spirits to accuse them who dwell on the earth. ⁸After that I asked the messenger of peace who went with me, who showed me everything that is hidden: "Who are these four presences which I have seen and whose words I have heard and written down?" ⁹And he said to me, "This first is Michael, the merciful and long-suffering; and the second, who is set over all the diseases and all the wounds of the children of men, is Raphael; and the third, who is set over all the powers, is Gabriel; and the fourth, who is set over the conversion to hope of those who inherit continuous life, is named Phanuel." ¹⁰And these are the four messengers of the Lord of Spirits and the four voices I heard in those days.

CHAPTER 41

¹And after that I saw all the secrets of the heavens, and how the kingdom is divided, and how the actions of men are weighed in the balance. ²And there I saw the mansions of the chosen ones and the mansions of the holy, and there my eyes saw all the sinners which deny the Name of the Lord of Spirits being driven from there and being dragged off: and they could not abide because of the punishment which proceeds from the Lord of Spirits. ³And there my eyes saw the secrets of the lightning and of the thunder, and the secrets of the winds, how they are divided to blow over the earth, and the secrets of the clouds and dew, and there I saw from where they proceed in that place and from where they saturate the dusty earth. ⁴And there I saw closed chambers out of which the winds are divided: the chamber of the hail and winds, the chamber of the mist, and of the clouds, and the cloud thereof hovers over the earth from the beginning of the world. ⁵And I saw the chambers of the sun and moon, from where they proceed and where they come again, and their glorious return, and how one is superior to the other, and their stately orbit, and how they do not leave their orbit, and they add nothing to their orbit and they take nothing from it, and they keep faith with each other in accordance with the oath by which they are bound together. ⁶And first the sun goes out and traverses his path according to the command of the Lord of Spirits, and mighty is His Name forever and ever. ⁷And after that I saw the hidden and the visible path of the moon, and she accomplishes the course of her path in that place by day and by night—the one holding a position opposite to the other before the Lord of Spirits. And they give thanks and praise and do not rest, for their thanksgiving is rest to them. ⁸For the sun often changes for a blessing or a curse, and the course of the path of the moon is light to the righteous and darkness to the sinners in the Name of the LORD, who made a separation between the light and the darkness, and divided the spirits of men, and strengthened the spirits of the righteous, in the name of His righteousness. ⁹For no messenger hinders and no power is able to hinder, for He appoints a judge for them all and He judges them all before Him.

CHAPTER 42

¹Wisdom found no place where she might dwell; then a dwelling-place was assigned to her in the heavens. ²Wisdom went out to make her dwelling among the children of men and found no dwelling-place: Wisdom returned to her place and took her seat among the messengers. ³And unrighteousness went out from her chambers; whom she did not seek she found and dwelt with them, as rain in a desert and dew on a thirsty land.

CHAPTER 43

¹And I saw other lightnings and the stars of the heavens, and I saw how He called them all by their names and they listened to Him. ²And I saw how they are weighed in a righteous balance according to their proportions of light. [I saw] the width of their spaces, and the day of their appearing, and how their revolution produces lightning; and [I saw] their revolution according to the number of the messengers, and [how] they keep faith with each other. ³And I asked the messenger who went with me, who showed me what was hidden: "What are these?" ⁴And he said to me, "The Lord of Spirits has showed you their allegorical meaning: these are the names of the holy who dwell on the earth and believe in the Name of the Lord of Spirits forever and ever."

CHAPTER 44

¹I also saw another phenomenon in regard to the lightnings: how some of the stars arise and become lightnings and cannot part with their new form.

CHAPTER 45

¹AND THIS IS THE SECOND ALLEGORY CONCERNING THOSE WHO DENY THE NAME OF THE DWELLING OF THE HOLY ONES AND THE LORD OF SPIRITS. ²And they will not ascend into the heavens, and they will not come on the earth: such will be the lot of the sinners who have denied the Name of the Lord of Spirits, who are therefore preserved for the day of suffering and tribulation. ³On that day My Chosen One will sit on the throne of glory and will try their works, and their places of rest will be innumerable. And their souls will grow strong within them when they see My chosen ones, and those who have called on My glorious Name. ⁴Then I will cause My Chosen One to dwell among them. And I will transform Heaven and make it a continuous blessing and light, and I will transform the earth and make it a blessing, ⁵and I will cause My chosen ones to dwell on it, but the sinners and evildoers will not set foot thereon. ⁶For I have provided and satisfied My righteous ones with peace and have caused them to dwell before Me, but for the sinners there is judgment impending with Me, so that I will destroy them from the face of the earth.

CHAPTER 46

¹And there I saw One who had a head of days, and His head was white like wool, and another being was with Him whose countenance had the appearance of a Man, and His face was full of graciousness, like one of the holy messengers. ²And I asked the messenger who went with me and showed me all the hidden things, concerning that Son of Man, who He was, and from where He was, [and] why He went with the Head of Days? ³And he answered and said to me, "This is the Son of Man who has righteousness, with whom dwells righteousness, and who reveals all the treasures of that which is hidden, because the Lord of Spirits has chosen Him, and whose lot has the preeminence before the Lord of Spirits in uprightness forever. ⁴And this Son of Man whom you have seen || Will raise up the kings and the mighty from their seats, [[|| And the strong from their thrones,]] || And will loosen the reins of the strong || And break the teeth of the sinners. ⁵[[And He will put down the kings from their thrones and kingdoms,]] || Because they do not extol and praise Him, nor humbly acknowledge from where the kingdom was bestowed on them. ⁶And He will put down the countenance of the strong || And will fill them with shame. And darkness will be their dwelling, || And worms will be their bed, || And they will have no hope of rising from their beds, || Because they do not extol the Name of the Lord of Spirits. ⁷[[And they raise their hands against the Most High,]] || And tread on the earth and dwell on it. And all their deeds manifest

unrighteousness, || And their power rests on their riches, || And their faith is in the gods which they have made with their hands, || And they deny the Name of the Lord of Spirits, ⁸And they persecute the houses of His congregations, || And the faithful who hang on the Name of the Lord of Spirits."

CHAPTER 47

¹And in those days the prayer of the righteous and the blood of the righteous will have ascended from the earth before the Lord of Spirits. ²In those days the holy ones who dwell above in the heavens will unite with one voice, and supplicate, and pray, [[and praise,]] and give thanks, and bless the Name of the Lord of Spirits on behalf of the blood of the righteous which has been shed, and that the prayer of the righteous may not be in vain before the Lord of Spirits, that judgment may be done to them, and that they may not have to suffer forever. ³In those days I saw the Head of Days when He seated himself on the throne of His glory, and the scrolls of the living were opened before Him, and all His host which is in Heaven above and His counselors stood before Him, ⁴And the hearts of the holy were filled with joy, because the number of the righteous had been offered, and the prayer of the righteous had been heard, and the blood of the righteous had been required before the Lord of Spirits.

CHAPTER 48

¹And in that place I saw the fountain of righteousness which was inexhaustible, and many fountains of wisdom were around it. And all the thirsty drank of them, and were filled with wisdom, and their dwellings were with the righteous, and holy, and chosen ones. ²And at that hour that Son of Man was named in the presence of the Lord of Spirits, and His Name before the Head of Days. ³Yes, before the sun and the signs were created, before the stars of the heavens were made, His Name was named before the Lord of Spirits. ⁴He will be a staff to the righteous on which to stay themselves and not fall, and He will be the light of the nations, and the hope of those who are troubled of heart. ⁵All who dwell on earth will fall down and worship before Him and will praise, and bless, and celebrate the Lord of Spirits with song. ⁶And for this reason He has been chosen and hidden before Him, before the creation of the world and forevermore. ⁷And the wisdom of the Lord of Spirits has revealed Him to the holy and righteous, for He has preserved the lot of the righteous, because they have hated and despised this world of unrighteousness and have hated all its works and ways in the Name of the Lord of Spirits; for they are saved in His Name, and it has been in regard to their life according to His good pleasure. ⁸In these days the kings of the earth and the strong who possess the land will have become downcast in countenance because of the works of their hands, for on the day of their anguish and affliction they will not [be able to] save themselves. ⁹And I will give them over into the hands of My chosen ones as straw in the fire, so they will burn before the face of the holy. They will sink as lead in the water before the face of the righteous, and no trace of them will be found anymore. ¹⁰And on the day of their affliction there will be rest on the earth, and they will fall before them and not rise again, and there will be no one to take them with his hands and raise them, for they have denied the Lord of Spirits and His Anointed. The Name of the Lord of Spirits be blessed.

CHAPTER 49

¹For wisdom is poured out like water, and glory does not fail before Him forevermore. ²For He is mighty in all the secrets of righteousness, and unrighteousness will disappear as a shadow and have no continuance, because the Chosen One stands before the Lord of Spirits, and His glory is forever and ever, and His might to all generations. ³And in Him dwells the Spirit of wisdom, and the Spirit which gives insight, and the Spirit of understanding and of might, and the Spirit of those who have fallen asleep in righteousness. ⁴And He will judge the secret things, and none will be able to utter a lying word before Him, for He is the Chosen One before the Lord of Spirits according to His good pleasure.

CHAPTER 50

¹And in those days a change will take place for the holy and chosen ones, and the light of days will abide on them, and glory and honor will turn to the holy, on the day of affliction on which evil will have been treasured up against the sinners. ²And the righteous will be victorious in the Name of the Lord of Spirits, and He will cause the others to witness [this] that they may convert and forgo the works of their hands. ³They will have no honor through the Name of the Lord of Spirits, yet they will be saved through His Name, and the Lord of Spirits will have compassion on them, for His compassion is great. ⁴And He is also righteous in His judgment, and also in the presence of His glory unrighteousness will not maintain itself: at His judgment the unconverted will perish before Him. ⁵"And from now on I will have no mercy on them," says the Lord of Spirits.

CHAPTER 51

¹And in those days the earth will also give back that which has been entrusted to it, and Sheol will also give back that which it has received, and destruction will give back that which it owes. For in those days the Chosen One will arise, ²and He will choose the righteous and holy from among them, for the day has drawn near that they should be saved. ³And the Chosen One will sit on My throne in those days, and His mouth will pour out all the secrets of wisdom and counsel, for the Lord of Spirits has given [them] to Him and has glorified Him. ⁴And in those days the mountains will leap like rams, and the hills will also skip like lambs satisfied with milk, and the faces of [all] the messengers in Heaven will be lit up with joy. ⁵And the earth will rejoice, and the righteous will dwell on it, and the chosen ones will walk thereon.

CHAPTER 52

¹And after those days in that place where I had seen all the visions of that which is hidden, I had been carried off in a whirlwind and they had borne me toward the west. ²There my eyes saw all the secret things of Heaven that will be, a mountain of iron, and a mountain of copper, and a mountain of silver, and a mountain of gold, and a mountain of soft metal, and a mountain of lead. ³And I asked the messenger who went with me, saying, "What things are these which I have seen in secret?" ⁴And he said to me, "All these things which you have seen will serve the dominion of His Anointed that He may be potent and mighty on the earth." ⁵And that messenger of peace answered, saying to me, "Wait a little, and all the secret things which surround the Lord of Spirits will be revealed to you. ⁶And these mountains which your eyes have seen—the mountain of iron, and the mountain of copper, and the mountain of silver, and the mountain of gold, and the mountain of soft metal, and the mountain of lead—all these will be in the presence of the Chosen One as wax before the fire, and like the water which streams down from above, and they will become powerless before His feet. ⁷And it will come to pass in those days that none will be saved, either by gold or by silver, and none will be able to escape. ⁸And there will be no iron for war, nor will one clothe oneself with a breastplate. Bronze will be of no service, and tin will not be esteemed, and lead will not be desired. ⁹And all these things will be destroyed from the surface of the earth when the Chosen One will appear before the face of the Lord of Spirits."

CHAPTER 53

¹My eyes saw a deep valley with open mouths there, and all who dwell on the earth, and sea, and islands will bring gifts, and presents, and signs of homage to Him, but that deep valley will not become full. ²And their hands commit lawless deeds, and the sinners devour all whom they lawlessly oppress, yet the sinners will be destroyed before the face of the Lord of Spirits, and they will be banished from off the face of His earth, and they will perish forever and ever. ³For I saw all the messengers of punishment abiding [there] and preparing all the instruments of Satan. ⁴And I asked the messenger of peace who went with me: "For whom are they preparing these instruments?" ⁵And he said to me, "They prepare these for the kings and the mighty of this earth, that they may thereby be destroyed. ⁶And after this the Righteous and Chosen One will cause the house of His congregation to appear: from now on they will no longer be hindered in the Name of the Lord of Spirits. ⁷And these mountains will not stand as the earth before His righteousness, but the hills will be as a fountain of water, and the righteous will have rest from the oppression of sinners."

1 ENOCH

CHAPTER 54

¹And I looked and turned to another part of the earth and saw a deep valley with burning fire there. ²And they brought the kings and the mighty and began to cast them into this deep valley. ³And there my eyes saw how they made these instruments of theirs iron chains of immeasurable weight. ⁴And I asked the messenger of peace who went with me, saying, "For whom are these chains being prepared?" And he said to me, "These are being prepared for the hosts of Azazel, so that they may take them and cast them into the abyss of complete condemnation, and they will cover their jaws with rough stones as the Lord of Spirits commanded. ⁶And Michael, and Gabriel, and Raphael, and Phanuel will take hold of them on that great day, and cast them on that day into the burning furnace, that the Lord of Spirits may take vengeance on them for their unrighteousness in becoming subject to Satan and leading those who dwell on the earth astray." ⁷And in those days punishment will come from the Lord of Spirits, and He will open all the chambers of waters which are above the heavens, and of the fountains which are beneath the earth. ⁸And all the waters will be joined with the waters: that which is above the heavens is the masculine, and the water which is beneath the earth is the feminine. ⁹And they will destroy all who dwell on the earth and those who dwell under the ends of the heavens. ¹⁰And when they have recognized their unrighteousness which they have worked on the earth, then by these they will perish.

CHAPTER 55

¹And after that the Head of Days regretted and said, "I have destroyed all who dwell on the earth in vain." ²And He swore by His great Name: "From now on I will not do so to all who dwell on the earth, and I will set a sign in the heavens: and this will be a pledge of good faith between Me and them forever, so long as the heavens are above the earth. And this is in accordance with My command. ³When I have desired to take hold of them by the hand of the messengers on the day of tribulation and pain because of this, I will cause My discipline and My wrath to abide on them," says God, the Lord of Spirits. ⁴"You mighty kings who dwell on the earth, you will have to behold My Chosen One, how He sits on the throne of glory and judges Azazel, and all his associates, and all his hosts in the Name of the Lord of Spirits."

CHAPTER 56

¹And I saw there the hosts of the messengers of punishment going, and they held scourges and chains of iron and bronze. ²And I asked the messenger of peace who went with me, saying, "To whom are these who hold the scourges going?" ³And he said to me, "To their chosen and beloved ones, that they may be cast into the chasm of the abyss of the valley. ⁴And then that valley will be filled with their chosen and beloved ones, and the days of their lives will be at an end, and the days of their leading astray will no longer be reckoned. ⁵And in those days the messengers will return and hurl themselves to the east on the Parthians and Medes: they will stir up the kings, so that a spirit of unrest will come on them, and they will rouse them from their thrones, that they may break out as lions from their lairs, and as hungry wolves among their flocks. ⁶And they will go up and tread underfoot the land of His chosen ones, [[and the land of His chosen ones will be a threshing-floor and a highway before them,]] ⁷but the city of my righteous will be a hindrance to their horses. And they will begin to fight among themselves, and their right hand will be strong against themselves, and a man will not know his brother, nor a son his father or his mother, until there is no number of the corpses through their slaughter, and their punishment is not in vain. ⁸In those days Sheol will open its jaws, and they will be swallowed up therein, and their destruction will be at an end; Sheol will devour the sinners in the presence of the chosen ones."

CHAPTER 57

¹And it came to pass after this that I saw another host of wagons, and men riding thereon, and coming on the winds from the east, and from the west to the south. ²And the noise of their wagons was heard, and when this turmoil took place the holy ones from Heaven noted it, and the pillars of the earth were moved from their place, and the sound thereof was heard from one end of the heavens to the other, in one day. ³And they will all fall down and worship the Lord of Spirits. And this is the end of the second allegory.

CHAPTER 58

¹AND I BEGAN TO SPEAK THE THIRD ALLEGORY CONCERNING THE RIGHTEOUS AND CHOSEN ONES. ²Blessed are you, you righteous and chosen ones, || For your lot will be glorious. ³And the righteous will be in the light of the sun, || And the chosen ones in the light of continuous life: The days of their life will be unending, || And the days of the holy without number. ⁴And they will seek the light and find righteousness || With the Lord of Spirits: There will be peace to the righteous in the Name of the Perpetual Lord. ⁵And after this it will be said to the holy in Heaven || That they should seek out the secrets of righteousness, || The heritage of faith; For it has become bright as the sun on earth, || And the darkness is past. ⁶And there will be a light that never ends, || And they will not come to a limit of days, || For the darkness will have first been destroyed, || And the light [[of uprightness]] established forever before the Lord of Spirits.

CHAPTER 59

¹[[In those days my eyes saw the secrets of the lightnings, and of the lights, and the judgments they execute: and they lighten for a blessing or a curse as the Lord of Spirits wills. ²And there I saw the secrets of the thunder, and how when it resounds above in the heavens, the sound thereof is heard, and he caused me to see the judgments executed on the earth, whether they are for well-being and blessing, or for a curse according to the word of the Lord of Spirits. ³And after that all the secrets of the lights and lightnings were shown to me, and they lighten for blessing and for satisfying.]]

CHAPTER 60

¹In the five hundredth year, in the seventh month, on the fourteenth day of the month in the life of Enoch, in that allegory I saw how a mighty quaking made the Heaven of heavens to quake, and the host of the Most High, and the messengers—one million and [even] one hundred million—were disquieted with a great disquiet. ²And the Head of Days sat on the throne of His glory, and the messengers and the righteous stood around Him. ³And a great trembling seized me, and fear took hold of me, and my loins gave way, and my reins were dissolved, and I fell on my face. ⁴And Michael sent another messenger from among the holy ones and he raised me up, and when he had raised me up my spirit returned, for I had not been able to endure the look of this host, and the commotion and the quaking of Heaven. ⁵And Michael said to me, "Why are you disquieted with such a vision? The day of His mercy lasted until this day; and He has been merciful and long-suffering toward those who dwell on the earth. ⁶And when the day, and the power, and the punishment, and the judgment come, which the Lord of Spirits has prepared for those who do not bow to the righteous law, and for those who deny the righteous judgment, and for those who take His Name in vain—that day is prepared: a covenant for the chosen ones, but an inquisition for sinners. When the punishment of the Lord of Spirits will rest on them, it will rest in order that the punishment of the Lord of Spirits may not come in vain, and it will slay the children with their mothers and the children with their fathers. Afterward the judgment will take place according to His mercy and His patience." ⁷And on that day two monsters were parted: a female monster named Leviathan, to dwell in the abysses of the ocean over the fountains of the waters, ⁸but the male is named Behemoth, who occupied with his breast a waste wilderness named Duidain, on the east of the garden where the chosen ones and righteous dwell, where my grandfather was taken up—the seventh from Adam, the first man whom the Lord of Spirits created. ⁹And I sought the other messenger that he should show me the might of those monsters, how they were parted on one day and cast, the one into the abysses of the sea, and the other onto the dry land of the wilderness. ¹⁰And he said to me, "You son of man, herein you seek to know what is hidden." ¹¹And the other messenger who went with me and showed me what was hidden told me what is first and last in the height of Heaven, and beneath the earth in the depth, and at the ends of the heavens, and on the foundation of the heavens; ¹²and the chambers of the winds, and how the winds

are divided, and how they are weighed, and [how] the portals of the winds are reckoned, each according to the power of the wind, and the power of the lights of the moon, and according to the power that is fitting, and the divisions of the stars according to their names, and how all the divisions are divided; ¹³and the thunders according to the places where they fall, and all the divisions that are made among the lightnings that it may lighten, and their host that they may immediately obey. ¹⁴For the thunder has places of rest [which] are assigned [to it] while it is waiting for its peal; and the thunder and lightning are inseparable, and although not one and undivided, they both go together through the spirit and do not separate. ¹⁵For when the lightning lightens, the thunder utters its voice, and the spirit enforces a pause during the peal, and divides equally between them; for the treasury of their peals is like the sand, and each one of them as it peals is held in with a bridle, and turned back by the power of the spirit, and pushed forward according to the many quarters of the earth. ¹⁶And the spirit of the sea is masculine and strong, and according to the might of his strength he draws it back with a rein, and in like manner it is driven forward and disperses amid all the mountains of the earth. ¹⁷And the spirit of the hoarfrost is his own messenger, and the spirit of the hail is a good messenger. ¹⁸And the spirit of the snow has forsaken his chambers on account of his strength. There is a special spirit therein, and that which ascends from it is like smoke, and its name is frost. ¹⁹And the spirit of the mist is not united with them in their chambers, but it has a special chamber, for its course is glorious both in light and in darkness, and in winter and in summer, and a messenger is in its chamber. ²⁰And the spirit of the dew has its dwelling at the ends of the heavens, and is connected with the chambers of the rain, and its course is in winter and summer: and its clouds and the clouds of the mist are connected, and the one gives to the other. ²¹And when the spirit of the rain goes out from its chamber, the messengers come and open the chamber and lead it out, and when it is diffused over the whole earth it unites with the water on the earth. ²²For the waters are for those who dwell on the earth, for they are nourishment for the earth from the Most High who is in Heaven. Therefore, there is a measure for the rain, and the messengers take it in charge. ²³And these things I saw toward the Garden of the Righteous. ²⁴And the messenger of peace who was with me said to me, "These two monsters, prepared conformably to the greatness of God, will feed."

CHAPTER 61

¹And I saw in those days how long cords were given to those messengers, and they took wings for themselves and flew, and they went toward the north. ²And I asked the messenger, saying to him, "Why have those [messengers] taken these cords and gone off?" And he said to me, "They have gone to measure." ³And the messenger who went with me said to me, "These will bring the measures of the righteous and the ropes of the righteous to the righteous, that they may stay themselves on the Name of the Lord of Spirits forever and ever. ⁴The chosen ones will begin to dwell with the chosen ones, and those are the measures which will be given to faith and which will strengthen righteousness. ⁵And these measures will reveal all the secrets of the depths of the earth, and those who have been destroyed by the desert, and those who have been devoured by the beasts, and those who have been devoured by the fish of the sea, that they may return and stay themselves on the day of the Chosen One, for none will be destroyed before the Lord of Spirits, and none can be destroyed. ⁶And all who dwell above in Heaven received a command, and power, and one voice, and one light like to fire. ⁷And they blessed that One [with] their first words, and extolled and lauded with wisdom, and they were wise in utterance and in the spirit of life. ⁸And the Lord of Spirits placed the Chosen One on the throne of glory, and He will judge all the works of the holy above in Heaven, and their deeds will be weighed in the balance, ⁹and when He will lift up His countenance to judge their secret ways according to the word of the Name of the Lord of Spirits, and their path according to the way of the righteous judgment of the Lord of Spirits, then with one voice they will all speak, and bless, and glorify, and extol, and sanctify the Name of the Lord of Spirits. ¹⁰And He will summon all the host of the heavens, and all the holy ones above, and the host of God, the cherubim, seraphim, and ophanim, and all the messengers of power, and all the messengers of principalities, and the Chosen One, and the other powers on the earth [and] over the water. ¹¹They will raise one voice on that day and bless, and glorify, and exalt in the Spirit of faith, and in the Spirit of wisdom, and in the Spirit of patience, and in the Spirit of mercy, and in the Spirit of judgment and of peace, and in the Spirit of goodness, and will all say with one voice: Blessed is He and may the Name of the Lord of Spirits be blessed forever and ever! ¹²All who do not sleep above in Heaven will bless Him: All the holy ones who are in Heaven will bless Him, || And all the chosen ones who dwell in the garden of life, || And every spirit of light || Who is able to bless, and glorify, and extol, and hallow Your blessed Name, || And all flesh will glorify and bless Your Name beyond measure forever and ever. ¹³For great is the mercy of the Lord of Spirits, and He is long-suffering, and all His works and all that He has created He has revealed to the righteous and chosen ones in the Name of the Lord of Spirits."

CHAPTER 62

¹And so the LORD commanded the kings, and the mighty, and the exalted, and those who dwell on the earth, and said, "Open your eyes and lift up your horns if you are able to recognize the Chosen One." ²And the Lord of Spirits seated Him on the throne of His glory, and the Spirit of righteousness was poured out on Him, and the word of His mouth slays all the sinners, and all the unrighteous are destroyed from before His face. ³And all the kings, and the mighty, and the exalted, and those who hold the earth will stand up in that day, and they will see and recognize how He sits on the throne of His glory, and righteousness is judged before Him, and no lying word is spoken before Him. ⁴Then pain will come on them as on a woman in travail when her child enters the mouth of the womb and she has pain in bringing out. ⁵And one portion of them will look on the other, and they will be terrified, and they will be downcast of countenance, and pain will seize them when they see that Son of Man Sitting on the throne of His glory. ⁶And the kings, and the mighty, and all who possess the earth will bless, and glorify, and extol Him who rules over all, who was hidden. ⁷For from the beginning the Son of Man was hidden, and the Most High preserved Him in the presence of His might and revealed Him to the chosen ones. ⁸And the congregation of the chosen and holy ones will be sown, and all the chosen ones will stand before Him on that day. ⁹And all the kings, and the mighty, and the exalted, and those who rule the earth will fall down before Him on their faces, and worship and set their hope on that Son of Man, and petition Him, and supplicate for mercy at His hands. ¹⁰Nevertheless, that Lord of Spirits will so press them that they will have to go out from His presence, and their faces will be filled with shame, and the darkness will grow deeper on their faces. ¹¹And He will deliver them to the messengers for punishment, to execute vengeance on them because they have oppressed His children and His chosen ones, ¹²and they will be a spectacle for the righteous and for His chosen ones: they will rejoice over them, because the wrath of the Lord of Spirits rests on them, and His sword is drunk with their blood. ¹³And the righteous and chosen ones will be saved on that day, and they will never again see the face of the sinners and unrighteous. ¹⁴And the Lord of Spirits will abide over them, and they will eat, and lie down, and rise up with that Son of Man forever and ever. ¹⁵And the righteous and chosen ones will have risen from the earth and ceased to be of downcast countenance. And they will have been clothed with garments of glory, ¹⁶and these will be the garments of life from the Lord of Spirits: and your garments will not grow old, nor your glory pass away before the Lord of Spirits.

CHAPTER 63

¹In those days the mighty and the kings who possess the earth will implore [Him] to grant them a little respite from His messengers of punishment to whom they were delivered, that they might fall down and worship before the Lord of Spirits and confess their sins before Him. ²And they will bless and glorify the Lord of Spirits and say, "Blessed is the Lord of Spirits and the Lord of kings, || And the Lord of the mighty and the Lord of the rich, || And the Lord of Glory and the Lord of wisdom,

³And splendid in every secret thing is Your power from generation to generation, || And Your glory forever and ever. All Your secrets are deep and innumerable, || And Your righteousness is beyond reckoning. ⁴We have now learned that we should glorify and bless the Lord of kings and Him who is King over all kings." ⁵And they will say, "If only we had rest to glorify, and give thanks, and confess our faith before His glory! ⁶And now we long for a little rest but do not find it; We follow hard on and do not obtain [it]; And light has vanished from before us, || And darkness is our dwelling-place forever and ever, ⁷For we have not believed before Him || Nor glorified the Name of the Lord of Spirits, || But our hope was in the scepter of our kingdom, || And in our glory. ⁸And in the day of our suffering and tribulation || He does not save us, || And we find no respite for confession that our Lord is true in all His works, || And in His judgments and His justice, || And His judgments have no respect of persons. And we pass away from before His face on account of our works, || And all our sins are reckoned up in righteousness." ¹⁰Now they will say to themselves, "Our souls are full of unrighteous gain, but it does not prevent us from descending from the midst thereof into the burden of Sheol." ¹¹And after that their faces will be filled with darkness and shame before that Son of Man, and they will be driven from His presence, and the sword will abide before His face in their midst. ¹²So spoke the Lord of Spirits: "This is the ordinance and judgment with respect to the mighty, and the kings, and the exalted, and those who possess the earth before the Lord of Spirits."

CHAPTER 64

¹And I saw other forms hidden in that place. ²I heard the voice of the messenger, saying, "These are the messengers who descended to the earth, and revealed what was hidden to the children of men, and seduced the children of men into committing sin."

CHAPTER 65

¹And in those days Noah saw that the earth had sunk down and its destruction was near. ²And he arose from there and went to the ends of the earth, and he cried aloud to his grandfather Enoch, ³and with an embittered voice Noah said three times, "Hear me! Hear me! Hear me!" And I said to him, "Tell me what it is that is falling out on the earth that the earth is in such an evil plight and shaken, lest perhaps I will perish with it?" ⁴And there was a great commotion on the earth, and a voice was heard from Heaven, and I fell on my face. ⁵And my grandfather Enoch came and stood by me, and said to me, "Why have you cried to me with a bitter cry and weeping? ⁶Indeed, a command has gone out from the presence of the LORD concerning those who dwell on the earth that their ruin is accomplished because they have learned all the secrets of the messengers, and all the violence of the devils, and all their powers—the most secret ones—and all the power of those who practice sorcery, and the power of witchcraft, and the power of those who make molten images for the whole earth, ⁷and how silver is produced from the dust of the earth, and how soft metal originates in the earth. ⁸For lead and tin are not produced from the earth like the first: it is a fountain that produces them, and a messenger stands therein, and that messenger is preeminent." ⁹And after that, my grandfather Enoch took hold of me by my hand and raised me up, and said to me, "Go, for I have asked the Lord of Spirits concerning this commotion on the earth." ¹⁰And He said to me, "Because of their unrighteousness their judgment has been determined and will not be withheld by Me forever. Because of the sorceries which they have searched out and learned, the earth and those who dwell on it will be destroyed. ¹¹And these—they have no place of conversion forever, because they have shown them what was hidden, and they are the damned; but as for you, my son, the Lord of Spirits knows that you are pure and guiltless of this reproach concerning the secrets. ¹²And He has destined your name to be among the holy, and will preserve you among those who dwell on the earth, and has destined your righteous Seed both for kingship and for great honors, and from your Seed will proceed a fountain of the righteous and holy without number forever."

CHAPTER 66

¹And after that he showed me the messengers of punishment who are prepared to come and let loose all the powers of the waters which are beneath in the earth in order to bring judgment and destruction on all who [abide and] dwell on the earth. ²And the Lord of Spirits gave command to the messengers who were going out, that they should not cause the waters to rise but should hold them in check, for those messengers were over the powers of the waters. ³And I went away from the presence of Enoch.

CHAPTER 67

¹And in those days the word of God came to me, and He said to me, "Noah, your lot has come up before Me, a lot without blame, a lot of love and uprightness. ²And now the messengers are making a wooden [vessel], and when they have completed that task, I will place My hand on it and preserve it, and the seed of life will come out from it, and a change will set in so that the earth will not remain without inhabitant. ³And I will make your seed firm before Me forever and ever, and I will spread abroad those who dwell with you: it will not be unfruitful on the face of the earth, but it will be blessed and multiply on the earth in the Name of the LORD." ⁴And He will imprison those messengers who have shown unrighteousness in that burning valley which my grandfather Enoch had formerly shown to me, in the west among the mountains of gold, and silver, and iron, and soft metal, and tin. ⁵And I saw that valley in which there was a great convulsion and a convulsion of the waters. ⁶And when all this took place, a smell of sulfur was produced from that fiery molten metal and from the convulsion thereof in that place, and it was connected with those waters, and that valley of the messengers who had led [mankind] astray burned beneath that land. ⁷And streams of fire proceed through its valleys where these messengers who had led those who dwell on the earth astray are punished. ⁸But in those days those waters will serve for the kings, and the mighty, and the exalted, and those who dwell on the earth, [not] for the healing of the body, but for the punishment of the spirit; now their spirit is full of lust, that they may be punished in their body, for they have denied the Lord of Spirits and see their punishment daily, and yet do not believe in His Name. ⁹And in proportion as the burning of their bodies becomes severe, a corresponding change will take place in their spirit forever and ever, for none will utter an idle word before the Lord of Spirits; ¹⁰for the judgment will come on them, because they believe in the lust of their body and deny the Spirit of the LORD. ¹¹And those same waters will undergo a change in those days, for when those messengers are punished in these waters, these water-springs will change their temperature, and when the messengers ascend, this water of the springs will change and become cold. ¹²And I heard Michael answering, and saying, "This judgment with which the messengers are judged is a testimony for the kings and the mighty who possess the earth." ¹³Because these waters of judgment minister to the healing of the body of the kings and the lust of their body, therefore, they will not see and will not believe that those waters will change and become a fire which burns forever.

CHAPTER 68

¹And after that my grandfather Enoch gave me the teaching of all the secrets in the scroll, in the allegories which had been given to him, and he put them together for me in the words of the Scroll of the Allegories. ²And on that day Michael answered Raphael and said, "The power of the Spirit transports and makes me to tremble because of the severity of the judgment of the secrets, the judgment of the messengers: who can endure the severe judgment which has been executed, and before which they melt away?" ³And Michael answered again, and said to Raphael, "Who is he whose heart is not softened concerning it, and whose reins are not troubled by this word of judgment [that] has gone out on them because of those who have so led them out?" ⁴And it came to pass when he stood before the Lord of Spirits, Michael said this to Raphael: "I will not take their part under the eye of the LORD, for the Lord of Spirits has been angry with them because they do as if they were the LORD. ⁵Therefore all that is hidden will come on them forever and ever; for neither messenger nor man will have his portion [in it], but they alone have received their judgment forever and ever."

1 ENOCH

CHAPTER 69

¹And after this judgment they will terrify and make them to tremble because they have shown this to those who dwell on the earth. ²And behold the names of those messengers, [[and these are their names: the first of them is Semjaza, the second Artaqifa, and the third Armen, the fourth Kokabel, the fifth Turael, the sixth Rumjal, the seventh Danjal, the eighth Neqael, the ninth Baraqel, the tenth Azazel, the eleventh Armaros, the twelfth Batarjal, the thirteenth Busasejal, the fourteenth Hananel, the fifteenth Turel, and the sixteenth Simapesiel, the seventeenth Jetrel, the eighteenth Tumael, the nineteenth Turel, the twentieth Rumael, the twenty-first Azazel. ³And these are the chiefs of their messengers, and their names, and their chief ones over hundreds, and over fifties, and over tens.]] ⁴The name of the first Jeqon: that is, the one who led astray [all] the sons of God, and brought them down to the earth, and led them astray through the daughters of men. ⁵And the second was named Asbeel: he imparted to the holy sons of God evil counsel and led them astray so that they defiled their bodies with the daughters of men. ⁶And the third was named Gadreel: it is he who showed the children of men all the blows of death, and he led Eve astray, and showed the shield, and the coat of mail, and the sword for battle, and all the weapons of death to the children of men; ⁷and they have proceeded from his hand against those who dwell on the earth from that day and forevermore. ⁸And the fourth was named Penemue: he taught the children of men the bitter and the sweet, and he taught them all the secrets of their wisdom, ⁹and he instructed mankind in writing with ink and paper, and thereby many sinned from age to age and until this day, ¹⁰for men were not created for such a purpose, to give confirmation to their good faith with pen and ink. ¹¹For men were created exactly like the messengers, to the intent that they should continue pure and righteous, and death, which destroys everything, could not have taken hold of them, but through this knowledge of theirs they are perishing, and through this power it is consuming me. ¹²And the fifth was named Kasdeja: this is he who showed the children of men all the wicked striking of spirits and demons, and the striking of the embryo in the womb that it may pass away, and the striking of the soul [by] the bites of the serpent, and the striking which befalls through the noontide heat, the son of the serpent named Taba'et. ¹³And this is the task of Kasbeel, the chief of the oath which he showed to the holy ones when he dwelt high above in glory, and its name is Biqa. ¹⁴This [messenger] requested Michael to show him the hidden name, that he might enunciate it in the oath, so that those might quake before that name and oath who revealed all that was in secret to the children of men. ¹⁵And this is the power of this oath, for it is powerful and strong, and he placed this oath of Akae in the hand of Michael. ¹⁶And these are the secrets of this oath, and they are strong through his oath: and Heaven was suspended before the world was created—and forever, ¹⁷and through it the earth was founded on the water, and from the secret recesses of the mountains come beautiful waters, from the creation of the world and continuously. ¹⁸And through that oath the sea was created, and at its foundation He set for it the sand against the time of [its] anger, and it does not dare pass beyond it from the creation of the world [and] continuously. ¹⁹And through that oath the depths are made fast, and abide, and do not stir from their place from age to age. ²⁰And through that oath the sun and moon complete their course and do not deviate from their ordinance from age to age. ²¹And through that oath the stars complete their course, and He calls them by their names, and they answer Him from age to age. ²²[[And in like manner the spirits of the water, and of the winds, and of all zephyrs, and [their] paths from all the quarters of the winds. ²³And the voices of the thunder and the light of the lightnings are preserved; and the chambers of the hail, and the chambers of the hoarfrost, and the chambers of the mist, and the chambers of the rain and the dew are preserved. ²⁴And all these believe and give thanks before the Lord of Spirits, and glorify [Him] with all their power, and their food is in every act of thanksgiving: they thank, and glorify, and extol the Name of the Lord of Spirits forever and ever.]] ²⁵And this oath is mighty over them, and their paths are preserved through it, and their course is not destroyed. ²⁶And there was great joy among them, and they blessed, and glorified, and extolled, because the Name of that Son of Man had been revealed to them. ²⁷And He sat on the throne of His glory, and the sum of judgment was given to the Son of Man, and He caused the sinners to pass away and be destroyed from off the face of the earth, and those who have led the world astray. ²⁸They will be bound with chains, and in their gathering place of destruction they will be imprisoned, and all their works will vanish from the face of the earth. ²⁹And from now on there will be nothing corruptible, for that Son of Man has appeared and has seated Himself on the throne of His glory, and all evil will pass away before His face, and the word of that Son of Man will go out and be strong before the Lord of Spirits.

CHAPTER 70

¹And it came to pass after this that his name during his lifetime was raised aloft to that Son of Man and to the Lord of Spirits from among those who dwell on the earth. ²And he was raised aloft on the chariots of the Spirit and his name vanished among them. ³And from that day I was no longer numbered among them: and He set me between the two winds, between the north and the west, where the messengers took the cords to measure for me the place for the chosen ones and righteous. ⁴And there I saw the first fathers and the righteous who dwell in that place from the beginning.

CHAPTER 71

¹And it came to pass after this that my spirit was translated, and it ascended into the heavens, and I saw the holy sons of God: they were stepping on flames of fire, their garments were white, and their faces shone like snow. ²And I saw two streams of fire, and the light of that fire shone like hyacinth, and I fell on my face before the Lord of Spirits. ³And the messenger Michael, [[one of the chief-messengers,]] seized me by my right hand, and lifted me up, and led me out into all the secrets, and he showed me all the secrets of righteousness. ⁴And he showed me all the secrets of the ends of the heavens, and all the chambers of all the stars, and all the luminaries, from where they proceed before the face of the holy ones. ⁵And he translated my spirit into the Heaven of heavens, and I saw there as it were a structure built of crystals, and between those crystals, tongues of living fire. ⁶And my spirit saw the girdle which girt that house of fire, and on its four sides were streams full of living fire, and they girt that house. ⁷And around were seraphim, cherubim, and ophanim: and these are they who do not sleep, and they guard the throne of His glory. ⁸And I saw messengers who could not be counted—one million and [even] one hundred million—encircling that house. And Michael, and Raphael, and Gabriel, and Phanuel, and the holy messengers who are above the heavens, go in and out of that house. ⁹And they came out from that house, and [also] Michael and Gabriel, Raphael and Phanuel, and many holy messengers without number, ¹⁰and with them the Head of Days, His head white and pure as wool, and His raiment indescribable. ¹¹And I fell on my face, and my whole body became relaxed, and my spirit was transfigured; and I cried with a loud voice, with the spirit of power, and blessed, and glorified, and extolled. ¹²And these blessings which went out of my mouth were well pleasing before that Head of Days. ¹³And that Head of Days came with Michael and Gabriel, Raphael and Phanuel, [and] thousands and myriads of messengers without number. ¹⁴And He came to me and greeted me with His voice, and said to me, "This is the Son of Man who is born to righteousness, and righteousness abides over Him, and the righteousness of the Head of Days does not forsake Him." ¹⁵And He said to me, "He proclaims peace to you in the name of the world to come, for peace has proceeded from there since the creation of the world, and so it will be to you forever and ever. ¹⁶And all will walk in His ways since righteousness never forsakes Him: their dwelling-places will be with Him, and their heritage with Him, and they will not be separated from Him forever and ever. And so there will be length of days with that Son of Man, and the righteous will have peace and an upright way in the Name of the Lord of Spirits forever and ever."

SECTION 3:

THE ASTRONOMICAL BOOK

CHAPTER 72

¹THE SCROLL OF THE COURSES OF THE LUMINARIES OF THE HEAVENS, the relations of each, according to their classes, their dominion and their seasons, according to their names and places of origin, and according to their months, which Uriel, the holy messenger who was with me, who is their guide, showed me; and he showed me all their laws exactly as they are, and how it is with regard to all the years of the world and continuously, until the new creation is accomplished which endures forever. ²And this is the first law of the luminaries: the luminary [named] the Sun has its rising in the eastern portals of heaven, and its setting in the western portals of heaven. ³And I saw six portals in which the sun rises, and six portals in which the sun sets, and the moon rises and sets in these portals, and the leaders of the stars and those whom they lead: six in the east and six in the west, and all following each other in accurately corresponding order: also, many windows to the right and left of these portals. ⁴And first there goes out the great luminary named the Sun, and his circumference is like the circumference of heaven, and he is quite filled with illuminating and heating fire. ⁵The chariot on which he ascends, the wind drives, and the sun goes down from heaven and returns through the north in order to reach the east and is so guided that he comes to the appropriate portal and shines in the face of heaven. ⁶In this way he rises in the first month in the great portal, which is the fourth. ⁷And in that fourth portal from which the sun rises in the first month are twelve window-openings, from which proceed a flame when they are opened in their season. ⁸When the sun rises in heaven, he comes out through that fourth portal [for] thirty mornings in succession, and sets accurately in the fourth portal in the west of heaven. ⁹And during this period the day becomes daily longer and the night nightly shorter to the thirtieth morning. ¹⁰On that day the day is longer than the night by a ninth part, and the day amounts exactly to ten parts and the night to eight parts. ¹¹And the sun rises from that fourth portal, and sets in the fourth, and returns to the fifth portal of the east [for] thirty mornings, and rises from it, and sets in the fifth portal. ¹²And then the day becomes longer by two parts and amounts to eleven parts, and the night becomes shorter and amounts to seven parts. ¹³And it returns to the east and enters into the sixth portal, and rises, and sets in the sixth portal [for] thirty-one mornings on account of its sign. ¹⁴On that day the day becomes longer than the night, and the day becomes double the night, and the day becomes twelve parts, and the night is shortened and becomes six parts. ¹⁵And the sun mounts up to make the day shorter and the night longer, and the sun returns to the east and enters into the sixth portal, and rises from it, and sets [for] thirty mornings. ¹⁶And when thirty mornings are accomplished, the day decreases by exactly one part, and becomes eleven parts, and the night seven. ¹⁷And the sun goes out from that sixth portal in the west, and goes to the east, and rises in the fifth portal for thirty mornings, and sets in the west again in the fifth western portal. ¹⁸On that day the day decreases by two parts and amounts to ten parts and the night to eight parts. ¹⁹And the sun goes out from that fifth portal, and sets in the fifth portal of the west, and rises in the fourth portal for thirty-one mornings on account of its sign, and sets in the west. ²⁰On that day the day is equalized with the night, and the night amounts to nine parts and the day to nine parts. ²¹And the sun rises from that portal, and sets in the west, and returns to the east, and rises [for] thirty mornings in the third portal, and sets in the west in the third portal. ²²And on that day the night becomes longer than the day, and night becomes longer than [the previous] night, and day shorter than [the previous] day until the thirtieth morning, and the night amounts exactly to ten parts and the day to eight parts. ²³And the sun rises from that third portal, and sets in the third portal in the west, and returns to the east, and for thirty mornings rises in the second portal in the east, and in like manner sets in the second portal in the west of heaven. ²⁴And on that day the night amounts to eleven parts and the day to seven parts. ²⁵And the sun rises on that day from that second portal, and sets in the west in the second portal, and returns to the east into the first portal for thirty-one mornings, and sets in the first portal in the west of heaven. ²⁶And on that day the night becomes longer and amounts to the double of the day: and the night amounts exactly to twelve parts and the day to six. ²⁷And the sun has traversed the divisions of his orbit, and turns again on those divisions of his orbit, and enters that portal [for] thirty mornings, and also sets in the west opposite to it. ²⁸And on that night the night has decreased in length by a ninth part, and the night has become eleven parts and the day seven parts. ²⁹And the sun has returned and entered into the second portal in the east, and returns on those divisions of his orbit for thirty mornings, rising and setting. ³⁰And on that day the night decreases in length, and the night amounts to ten parts and the day to eight. ³¹And on that day the sun rises from that portal, and sets in the west, and returns to the east, and rises in the third portal for thirty-one mornings, and sets in the west of heaven. ³²On that day the night decreases and amounts to nine parts, and the day to nine parts, and the night is equal to the day, and the year is exactly as to its days three hundred and sixty-four. ³³And the length of the day and of the night, and the shortness of the day and of the night arise through the course of the sun [where] these distinctions are made. ³⁴So it comes that its course becomes daily longer, and its course nightly shorter. ³⁵And this is the law and the course of the sun, and his return as often as he returns sixty times and rises—the great luminary, which is named the Sun, forever and ever. ³⁶And that which rises is the great luminary, and is so named according to its appearance, according as the LORD commanded. ³⁷As he rises, so he sets, and does not decrease and does not rest, but runs day and night, and his light is sevenfold brighter than that of the moon, but as regards size, they are both equal.

CHAPTER 73

¹And after this law I saw another law dealing with the smaller luminary, which is named the Moon. ²And her circumference is like the circumference of heaven, and her chariot in which she rides is driven by the wind, and light is given to her in [definite] measure. ³And her rising and setting change every month: and her days are like the days of the sun, and when her light is uniform it amounts to the seventh part of the light of the sun. ⁴And so she rises. And her first phase in the east comes out on the thirtieth morning: and on that day she becomes visible and constitutes for you the first phase of the moon on the thirtieth day, together with the sun in the portal where the sun rises. ⁵And the one half of her goes out by a seventh part, and her whole circumference is empty, without light, with the exception of one-seventh part of it, [and] the fourteenth part of her light. ⁶And when she receives one-seventh part of the half of her light, her light amounts to one-seventh part and the half thereof. ⁷And she sets with the sun, and when the sun rises, the moon rises with him and receives the half of one part of light, and in that night, in the beginning of her morning, the moon sets with the sun and is invisible that night with the fourteen parts and the half of one of them. ⁸And she rises on that day with exactly a seventh part, and comes out, and recedes from the rising of the sun, and in her remaining days she becomes bright in the [remaining] thirteen parts.

CHAPTER 74

¹And I saw another course, a law for her, [and] how according to that law she performs her monthly revolution. ²And Uriel, the holy messenger who is the leader of them all, showed all these to me, and their positions, and I wrote down their positions as he showed them to me, and I wrote down their months as they were, and the appearance of their lights until fifteen days were accomplished. ³In each seventh part she accomplishes all her light in the east, and in each seventh part accomplishes all her darkness in the west. ⁴And in certain months she alters her settings, and in certain months she pursues her own peculiar course. ⁵In two months the moon sets with the sun: in those two middle portals, the third and the fourth. ⁶She goes out for seven days, and turns around, and returns again through the portal where the sun rises and accomplishes all her light: and she recedes from the sun, and in eight days enters the sixth portal from which the sun goes out. ⁷And when the sun goes out from the fourth portal, she goes out seven

days, until she goes out from the fifth, and turns back again in seven days into the fourth portal and accomplishes all her light: and she recedes and enters into the first portal in eight days. ⁸And she returns again in seven days into the fourth portal from which the sun goes out. ⁹So I saw their position—how the moon rose and the sun set in those days. ¹⁰And if five years are added together the sun has a surplus of thirty days, and all the days which accrue to it for one of those five years, when they are full, amount to three hundred and sixty-four days. ¹¹And the surplus of the sun and of the stars amounts to six days: in five years six days every year comes to thirty days, and the moon falls behind the sun and stars to the number of thirty days. ¹²And the sun and the stars bring in all the years exactly, so that they do not advance or delay their position by a single day [and] continuously, but complete the years with perfect justice in three hundred and sixty-four days. ¹³In three years there are one thousand and ninety-two days, and in five years one thousand and eight hundred and twenty days, so that in eight years there are two thousand and nine hundred and twelve days. ¹⁴For the moon alone the days amount in three years to one thousand and sixty-two days, and in five years she falls fifty days behind: there is [the sum of these five] to be added to [the] one thousand and sixty-two days. ¹⁵And in five years there are one thousand and seven hundred and seventy days, so that for the moon the days in eight years amount to two thousand and eight hundred and thirty-two days. ¹⁶[For in eight years she falls behind to the amount of eighty days]; all the days she falls behind in eight years are eighty. ¹⁷And the year is accurately completed in conformity with their world-stations and the stations of the sun, which rises from the portals through which it rises and sets [for] thirty days.

CHAPTER 75

¹And the leaders of the heads of the thousands, who are placed over the whole creation and over all the stars, also have to do with the four intercalary days, being inseparable from their office, according to the reckoning of the year, and these render service on the four days which are not reckoned in the reckoning of the year. ²And owing to them men go wrong therein, for those luminaries truly render service on the world-stations, one in the first portal, one in the third portal of heaven, one in the fourth portal, and one in the sixth portal, and the exactness of the year is accomplished through its separate three hundred and sixty-four stations. ³For the signs, and the times, and the years, and the days the messenger Uriel showed to me, whom the Lord of Glory has set forever over all the luminaries of the heavens, in the heavens and in the world, that they should rule on the face of the heavens and be seen on the earth, and be leaders for the day and the night—the sun, moon, and stars, and all the ministering creatures which make their revolution in all the chariots of the heavens.

⁴In like manner, Uriel showed me twelve doors open in the circumference of the sun's chariot in the heavens, through which the rays of the sun break out: and from them warmth is diffused over the earth when they are opened at their appointed seasons— ⁵[[and for the winds and the spirit of the dew when they are opened, standing open in the heavens, at the ends.]] ⁶As for the twelve portals in the heavens at the ends of the earth, out of which go out the sun, moon, and stars, and all the works of heaven in the east and in the west, ⁷there are many windows open to the left and right of them, and one window at its [appointed] season produces warmth, corresponding [as these do] to those doors from which the stars come out according as He has commanded them, and wherein they set corresponding to their number. ⁸And I saw chariots in the heavens, running in the world, above those portals in which revolve the stars that never set. ⁹And one is larger than all the rest, and it is that which makes its course through the entire world.

CHAPTER 76

¹And at the ends of the earth I saw twelve portals open to all the quarters [of the heavens], from which the winds go out and blow over the earth. ²Three of them are open on the face [(the east)] of the heavens, and three in the west, and three on the right [(the south)] of the heavens, and three on the left [(the north)]. ³And the three first are those of the east, and three are of the north, and three of the south, and three of the west. ⁴Through four of these come winds of blessing and prosperity, and from those eight come hurtful winds: when they are sent, they bring destruction on all the earth, and on the water on it, and on all who dwell thereon, and on everything which is in the water and on the land. ⁵And the first wind from those portals, called the East Wind, comes out through the first portal which is in the east, inclining toward the south: desolation, drought, heat, and destruction come out from it. ⁶And through the second portal in the middle comes what is fitting: and rain, and fruitfulness, and prosperity, and dew come from it. And through the third portal which lies toward the north come cold and drought. ⁷And after these, the south winds come out through three portals: through the first portal of them inclining to the east a hot wind comes out. ⁸And through the middle portal next to it, fragrant smells, and dew, and rain, and prosperity, and health come out. ⁹And through the third portal lying to the west, dew and rain, locusts and desolation come out. ¹⁰And after these, the north winds: from the seventh portal in the east come dew and rain, locusts and desolation. ¹¹And from the middle portal, health, and rain, and dew, and prosperity come in a direct direction. And through the third portal in the west come cloud, and hoarfrost, and snow, and rain, and dew, and locusts. ¹²And after these [four] are the west winds: through the first portal adjoining the north, dew, and hoarfrost, and cold, and snow, and frost come out. ¹³And from the middle portal, dew, and rain, and prosperity, and blessing come out. And through the last portal which adjoins the south, drought, and desolation, and burning, and destruction come out. ¹⁴And the twelve portals of the four quarters of the heavens are completed with that, and I have shown all their laws, and all their plagues, and all their benefactions to you, my son Methuselah.

CHAPTER 77

¹And the first quarter is called the East, because it is the first. And the second, the South, because the Most High will descend there—yes, there in quite a special sense will He who is blessed forever descend. ²And the west quarter is named the Diminished, because all the luminaries of the heavens wane and go down there. ³And the fourth quarter, named the North, is divided into three parts: the first of them is for the dwelling of men; and the second contains seas of water, and the abysses, and forests, and rivers, and darkness, and clouds; and the third part contains the Garden of Righteousness. ⁴I saw seven high mountains, higher than all the mountains which are on the earth: and there comes out hoarfrost, and days, seasons, and years pass away. ⁵I saw seven rivers on the earth larger than all the rivers: one of them coming from the west pours its waters into the Great Sea. ⁶And these two come from the north to the sea and pour their waters into the Erythraean Sea in the east. ⁷And the remaining four come out on the side of the north to their own sea—two of them to the Erythraean Sea and two into the Great Sea—and discharge themselves there [[or into the desert]]. ⁸I saw seven great islands in the sea and in the mainland: two in the mainland and five in the Great Sea.

CHAPTER 78

¹And the names of the sun are the following: the first Orjares, and the second Tomas. ²And the moon has four names: the first name is Asonja, the second Ebla, the third Benase, and the fourth Erae. ³These are the two great luminaries; their circumference is like the circumference of heaven, and the size of the circumference of both is alike. ⁴In the circumference of the sun there are seven portions of light which are added to it more than to the moon, and it is transferred in definite measures until the seventh portion of the sun is exhausted. ⁵And they set and enter the portals of the west, and make their revolution by the north, and come out through the eastern portals on the face of the heavens. ⁶And when the moon rises, one-fourteenth part appears in the heavens; on the fourteenth day she accomplishes her light. ⁷And fifteen parts of light are transferred to her until the fifteenth day [when] her light is accomplished, according to the sign of the year, and she becomes fifteen parts, and the moon grows by fourteen parts. ⁸And in her waning [the moon] decreases on the first day to fourteen parts of her light, on the second to

thirteen parts of light, on the third to twelve, on the fourth to eleven, on the fifth to ten, on the sixth to nine, on the seventh to eight, on the eighth to seven, on the ninth to six, on the tenth to five, on the eleventh to four, on the twelfth to three, on the thirteenth to two, on the fourteenth to the half of a seventh, and all her remaining light disappears wholly on the fifteenth. ⁹And in certain months the month has twenty-nine days and once twenty-eight. ¹⁰And Uriel showed me another law [regarding] when light is transferred to the moon, and on which side it is transferred to her by the sun. ¹¹During all the period during which the moon is growing in her light, she is transferring it to herself when opposite to the sun during fourteen days; and when she is illuminated throughout, her light is fully accomplished in the heavens. ¹²And on the first day she is called the new moon, for on that day the light rises on her. ¹³She becomes a full moon exactly on the day when the sun sets in the west, and from the east she rises at night, and the moon shines the whole night through until the sun rises over against her and the moon is seen over against the sun. ¹⁴On the side from where the light of the moon comes out, there again she wanes until all the light vanishes and all the days of the month are at an end, and her circumference is empty, void of light. ¹⁵And three months she makes of thirty days, and at her time she makes three months of twenty-nine days each, in which she accomplishes her waning in the first period of time, and in the first portal for one hundred and seventy-seven days. ¹⁶And in the time of her going out she appears for three months [of] thirty days each, and for three months she appears [of] twenty-nine each. ¹⁷At night she appears like a man for twenty days each time, and by day she appears like the heavens, and there is nothing else in her except her light [(the light of day)].

CHAPTER 79

¹"And now, my son, I have shown you everything, and the law of all the stars of the heavens is completed." ²And he showed me all the laws of these for every day, and for every season of bearing rule, and for every year, and for its going out, and for the order prescribed to it every month and every week; ³and the waning of the moon which takes place in the sixth portal; for in this sixth portal her light is accomplished, and after that there is the beginning of the waning; ⁴[and the waning] which takes place in the first portal in its season, until one hundred and seventy-seven days are accomplished, reckoned according to weeks—twenty-five [weeks] and two days. ⁵She falls behind the sun and the order of the stars exactly five days in the course of one period, and when this place which you see has been traversed. ⁶Such is the picture and sketch of every luminary which the chief-messenger Uriel, who is their leader, showed to me.

CHAPTER 80

¹And in those days the messenger Uriel answered and said to me, "Behold, I have shown you everything, Enoch, and I have revealed everything to you that you should see this sun and this moon, and the leaders of the stars of the heavens and all those who turn them, their tasks, and times, and departures. ²And in the days of the sinners the years will be shortened, and their seed will be late on their lands and fields, and all things on the earth will alter, and will not appear in their time: And the rain will be kept back, || And the heavens will withhold [it]. ³And in those times the fruits of the earth will be backward, || And will not grow in their time, || And the fruits of the trees will be withheld in their time. ⁴And the moon will alter her order, || And not appear at her time. ⁵[[And in those days the sun will be seen, || And he will journey in the evening || On the extremity of the great chariot in the west,]] || And will shine more brightly than accords with the order of light. ⁶And many chiefs of the stars || Will transgress the order [prescribed]. And these will alter their orbits and tasks, || And not appear at the seasons prescribed to them. ⁷And the whole order of the stars will be concealed from the sinners, || And the thoughts of those on the earth will err concerning them, [[|| And they will be altered from all their ways,]] || Yes, they will err and take them to be gods. ⁸And evil will be multiplied on them, || And punishment will come on them so as to destroy all."

CHAPTER 81

¹And he said to me, "Enoch, observe these heavenly tablets, and read what is written thereon, and mark every individual fact." ²And I observed the heavenly tablets, and read everything which was written [thereon], and understood everything, and read the scroll of all the deeds of mankind, and of all the children of flesh that will be on the earth to the most remote generations. ³And thereon I blessed the great LORD, the King of glory, forever, in that He has made all the works of the world, and I extolled the LORD because of His patience, and blessed Him because of the children of men. ⁴And after that I said, "Blessed is the man who dies in righteousness and goodness, concerning whom there is no scroll of unrighteousness written, and against whom no Day of Judgment will be found." ⁵And those seven holy ones brought me and placed me on the earth before the door of my house, and said to me, "Declare everything to your son Methuselah, and show to all your children that no flesh is righteous in the sight of the LORD, for He is their Creator. ⁶One year we will leave you with your son, until you give your [last] commands, that you may teach your children, and record [it] for them, and testify to all your children; and in the second year they will take you from their midst. ⁷Let your heart be strong, || For the good will announce righteousness to the good; The righteous will rejoice with the righteous || And will offer congratulations to one another. ⁸But the sinners will die with the sinners, || And the apostate goes down with the apostate. ⁹And those who practice righteousness || Will die on account of the deeds of men || And be taken away on account of the doings of the godless." ¹⁰And in those days they ceased to speak to me, and I came to my people, blessing the Lord of the world.

CHAPTER 82

¹And now, my son Methuselah, all these things I am recounting to you and writing down for you! And I have revealed everything to you, and given you scrolls concerning all these; so preserve, my son Methuselah, the scrolls from your father's hand, and [see] that you deliver them to the generations of the world. ²I have given wisdom to you and to your children, [[|| And your children that will be to you,]] || That they may give it to their children for generations—This wisdom that surpasses their thought. ³And those who understand it will not sleep, || But will listen with the ear that they may learn this wisdom, || And it will please those that eat thereof better than good food. ⁴Blessed are all the righteous, blessed are all those who walk in the way of righteousness and do not sin as the sinners in the reckoning of all their days in which the sun traverses the heavens, entering into and departing from the portals for thirty days with the heads of thousands of the order of the stars, together with the four which are intercalated, which divide the four portions of the year, which lead them and enter with them four days. ⁵Owing to them, men will be at fault and not reckon them in the whole reckoning of the year: yes, men will be at fault, and not recognize them accurately. ⁶For they belong to the reckoning of the year and are truly recorded [thereon] forever, one in the first portal, and one in the third, and one in the fourth, and one in the sixth, and the year is completed in three hundred and sixty-four days. ⁷And the account thereof is accurate and the recorded reckoning thereof exact, for the luminaries, and months, and festivals, and years, and days, Uriel has shown and revealed to me, to whom the Lord of the whole creation of the world has subjected the host of Heaven. ⁸And he has power over night and day in the heavens to cause the light to give light to men—sun, moon, and stars, and all the powers of the heavens which revolve in their circular chariots. ⁹And these are the orders of the stars, which are set in their places, and in their seasons, and festivals, and months. ¹⁰And these are the names of those who lead them, who watch that they enter at their times, in their orders, in their seasons, in their months, in their periods of dominion, and in their positions. ¹¹Their four leaders who divide the four parts of the year enter first; and after them the twelve leaders of the orders who divide the months; and for the three hundred and sixty [days] there are heads over thousands who divide the days; and for the four intercalary days there are the leaders which split the four parts of the year. ¹²And these heads over thousands are intercalated between leader and leader, each behind a station, but their leaders make the division. ¹³And these are the names of the leaders who

divide the four parts of the year which are ordained: Milki'el, Hel'emmelek, and Mel'ejal, and Narel. ¹⁴And the names of those who lead them: Adnar'el, and Ijasusa'el, and 'Elome'el—these three follow the leaders of the orders, and there is one that follows the three leaders of the orders which follow those leaders of stations that divide the four parts of the year. ¹⁵In the beginning of the year Melkejal rises first and rules, who is named Tam'aini and Sun, and all the days of his dominion while he bears rule are ninety-one days. ¹⁶And these are the signs of the days which are to be seen on earth in the days of his dominion: sweat, and heat, and stillness; and all the trees bear fruit, and leaves are produced on all the trees, and the harvest of wheat, and the rose-flowers, and all the flowers which come out in the field, but the trees of the winter season become withered. ¹⁷And these are the names of the leaders which are under them: Berka'el, Zelebs'el, and another who is added, a head of one thousand called Hilujaseph: and the days of the dominion of this [leader] are at an end. ¹⁸The next leader after him is Hel'emmelek, whom one names the Shining Sun, and all the days of his light are ninety-one days. ¹⁹And these are the signs of [his] days on the earth: glowing heat and dryness, and the trees ripen their fruits and produce all their fruits ripe and ready, and the sheep pair and become pregnant, and all the fruits of the earth are gathered in, as well as everything that is in the fields and the winepress: these things take place in the days of his dominion. ²⁰These are the names, and the orders, and the leaders of those heads of thousands: Gida'ljal, Ke'el, and He'el, and the name of the head of one thousand which is added to them, Asfa'el: and the days of his dominion are at an end.

SECTION 4:
THE BOOK OF DREAM VISIONS

CHAPTER 83

¹And now, my son Methuselah, I will show you all my visions which I have seen, recounting them before you. ²I saw two visions before I took a wife, and the one was quite unlike the other: the first when I was learning to write; the second before I took your mother, [when] I saw a terrible vision. ³And I prayed to the LORD regarding them. I had laid myself down in the house of my grandfather Mahalalel [when] I saw in a vision how heaven collapsed and was borne off and fell to the earth. ⁴And when it fell to the earth, I saw how the earth was swallowed up in a great abyss, and mountains were suspended on mountains, and hills sank down on hills, and high trees were torn from their stems, and hurled down, and sunk in the abyss. ⁵And a word suddenly fell into my mouth, and I lifted up [my voice] to cry aloud, and said, "The earth is destroyed!" ⁶And my grandfather Mahalalel waked me as I lay near him, and said to me, "Why do you cry so, my son, and why do you make such lamentation?" ⁷And I recounted to him the whole vision which I had seen, and he said to me, "You have seen a terrible thing, my son, and of grave moment is your dream-vision as to the secrets of all the sin of the earth: it must sink into the abyss and be destroyed with a great destruction. ⁸And now, my son, arise and make petition to the Lord of Glory, since you are a believer, that a remnant may remain on the earth, and that He may not destroy the whole earth. ⁹My son, all this will come on the earth from Heaven, and there will be great destruction on the earth." ¹⁰After that I arose, and prayed, and implored, and sought, and wrote down my prayer for the generations of the world, and I will show everything to you, my son Methuselah. ¹¹And when I had gone out below and seen the heavens, and the sun rising in the east, and the moon setting in the west, and a few stars, and the whole earth, and everything as He had known it in the beginning, then I blessed the Lord of judgment and extolled Him because He had made the sun to go out from the windows of the east, and he ascended and rose on the face of the heavens, and set out and kept traversing the path shown to him.

CHAPTER 84

¹And I lifted up my hands in righteousness and blessed the Holy and Great One, and spoke with the breath of my mouth, and with the tongue of flesh, which God has made for the children of the flesh of men, that they should speak with [it], and He gave them breath, and a tongue, and a mouth that they should speak with [them]: ²"Blessed are You, O LORD, || King, great and mighty in Your greatness, || Lord of the whole creation of the heavens, || King of kings and God of the whole world. And Your power, and kingship, and greatness || Abide forever and ever, || And throughout all generations Your dominion; And all the heavens are Your throne forever, || And the whole earth Your footstool forever and ever. ³For You have made and You rule all things, || And nothing is too hard for You; Wisdom does not depart from the place of Your throne, || Nor turns away from Your presence. And You know, and see, and hear everything, || And there is nothing hidden from You. ⁴And now the messengers of Your heavens are guilty of trespass, || And Your wrath abides on the flesh of men until the great Day of Judgment. ⁵And now, O God, and Lord, and Great King, I exceedingly implore You to fulfill my prayer, to leave me a posterity on earth, and not destroy all the flesh of man, and make the earth without inhabitant, so that there should be a continuous destruction. ⁶And now, my Lord, destroy from the earth the flesh which has aroused Your wrath, but establish the flesh of righteousness and uprightness as a plant of the continuous seed, and do not hide Your face from the prayer of Your servant, O LORD."

CHAPTER 85

¹And after this I saw another dream, and I will show the whole dream to you, my son. ²And Enoch lifted up [his voice] and spoke to his son Methuselah: "To you, my son, I will speak: hear my words and incline your ear to the dream-vision of your father. ³Before I took your mother Edna, I saw in a vision on my bed, and behold, a bull came out from the earth, and that bull was white; and after it a heifer came out, and along with this [heifer] two bulls came out: one of them black and the other red. ⁴And that black bull gored the red one and pursued him over the earth, and immediately I could no longer see that red bull. ⁵But that black bull grew, and that heifer went with him, and I saw that many oxen proceeded from him which resembled and followed him. ⁶And that cow, that first one, went from the presence of that first bull in order to seek that red one, but did not find him, and lamented with a great lamentation over him and sought him. ⁷And I looked until that first bull came to her and quieted her, and from that time onward she no longer cried. ⁸And after that, she bore another white bull, and after him she bore many bulls and black cows. ⁹And I saw in my sleep that white bull likewise grows and becomes a great white bull, and from him proceeded many white bulls, and they resembled him. ¹⁰And they began to beget many white bulls, which resembled them, one following the other, [even] many."

CHAPTER 86

¹"And again, I saw with my eyes as I slept, and I saw the heavens above, and behold, a star fell from Heaven, and it arose, and ate, and pastured among those oxen. ²And after that I saw the large and the black oxen, and behold, they all changed their stalls, and pastures, and their cattle, and began to live with each other. ³And again, I saw in the vision, and looked toward the heavens, and behold, I saw many stars descend and cast themselves down from Heaven to that first star, and they became bulls among those cattle and pastured among them. ⁴And I looked at them and saw, and behold, they all let out their genitals like horses, and began to cover the cows of the oxen, and they all became pregnant and bore elephants, camels, and donkeys. ⁵And all the oxen feared them, and were frightened at them, and began to bite with their teeth, and to devour, and to gore with their horns. ⁶And they began, moreover, to devour those oxen; and behold, all the children of the earth began to tremble and quake before them and to flee from them."

CHAPTER 87

¹"And again, I saw how they began to gore each other and to devour each other, and the earth began to cry aloud. ²And I raised my eyes again to Heaven, and I saw in the vision, and behold, there came out from Heaven beings who were like white men: and four went out from that place and three with them. ³And those three that had last come out grasped me by my hand and took me up, away from the generations of the earth, and raised me up to a lofty place, and showed me a tower raised high above the earth, and all the hills were lower. ⁴And one said to me, Remain here

until you see everything that befalls those elephants, camels, and donkeys, and the stars, and the oxen, and all of them."

CHAPTER 88

¹ "And I saw one of those four who had come out first, and he seized that first star which had fallen from Heaven, and bound it hand and foot, and cast it into an abyss: now that abyss was narrow, and deep, and horrible, and dark. ² And one of them drew a sword and gave it to those elephants, and camels, and donkeys: then they began to strike each other, and the whole earth quaked because of them. ³ And as I was beholding in the vision, one of those four who had come out from Heaven stoned [them], and gathered [them], and took all the great stars whose genitals were like those of horses, and bound them all hand and foot, and cast them in an abyss of the earth."

CHAPTER 89

¹ "And one of those four went to that white bull and instructed him in a secret, without his being terrified: he was born a bull, and became a man, and built a great vessel for himself, and dwelt thereon; and three bulls dwelt with him in that vessel, and they were enclosed inside. ² And again, I raised my eyes toward the heavens and saw a lofty roof with seven water torrents thereon, and those torrents flowed with much water into an enclosure. ³ And I saw again, and behold, fountains were opened on the surface of that great enclosure, and that water began to swell and rise on the surface, and I saw that enclosure until all its surface was covered with water. ⁴ And the water, the darkness, and mist increased on it; and as I looked at the height of that water, that water had risen above the height of that enclosure, and was streaming over that enclosure, and it stood on the earth. ⁵ And all the cattle of that enclosure were gathered together until I saw how they sank, and were swallowed up, and perished in that water. ⁶ But that vessel floated on the water, while all the oxen, and elephants, and camels, and donkeys sank to the bottom with all the animals, so that I could no longer see them, and they were not able to escape, [but] perished and sank into the depths. ⁷ And again, I saw in the vision until those water torrents were removed from that high roof, and the chasms of the earth were leveled up, and other abysses were opened. ⁸ Then the water began to run down into these until the earth became visible, but that vessel settled on the earth, and the darkness retired, and light appeared. ⁹ But that white bull which had become a man came out of that vessel, and the three bulls with him, and one of those three was white like that bull, and one of them was red as blood, and one black: and that white bull departed from them. ¹⁰ And they began to bring out beasts of the field and birds, so that there arose different genera: lions, tigers, wolves, dogs, hyenas, wild boars, foxes, squirrels, swine, falcons, vultures, kites, eagles, and ravens; and a white bull was born among them. ¹¹ And they began to bite one another, but that white bull which was born among them begot a wild donkey and a white bull with it, and the wild donkeys multiplied. ¹² But that bull which was born from him begot a black wild boar and a white sheep; and the former begot many boars, but that sheep begot twelve sheep. ¹³ And when those twelve sheep had grown, they gave up one of them to the donkeys, and those donkeys again gave up that sheep to the wolves, and that sheep grew up among the wolves. ¹⁴ And the LORD brought the eleven sheep to live with it and to pasture with it among the wolves: and they multiplied and became many flocks of sheep. ¹⁵ And the wolves began to fear them, and they oppressed them until they destroyed their little ones, and they cast their young into a river of much water, but those sheep began to cry aloud on account of their little ones, and to complain to their Lord. ¹⁶ And a sheep which had been saved from the wolves fled and escaped to the wild donkeys; and I saw how the sheep lamented, and cried, and implored their Lord with all their might until that Lord of the sheep descended at the voice of the sheep from a lofty abode, and came to them, and pastured them. ¹⁷ And He called that sheep which had escaped the wolves and spoke with it concerning the wolves that it should admonish them not to touch the sheep. ¹⁸ And the sheep went to the wolves according to the word of the LORD, and another sheep met it and went with it, and the two went and entered together into the assembly of those wolves, and spoke with them, and admonished them not to touch the sheep from now on. ¹⁹ And immediately I saw the wolves, and how they oppressed the sheep exceedingly with all their power; and the sheep cried aloud. ²⁰ And the LORD came to the sheep and they began to strike those wolves: and the wolves began to make lamentation, but the sheep became quiet and then ceased to cry out. ²¹ And I saw the sheep until they departed from among the wolves, but the eyes of the wolves were blinded, and those wolves departed in pursuit of the sheep with all their power. ²² And the Lord of the sheep went with them, as their leader, and all His sheep followed Him: and his face was dazzling, and glorious, and terrible to behold. ²³ But the wolves began to pursue those sheep until they reached a sea of water. ²⁴ And that sea was divided, and the water stood on this side and on that before their face, and their Lord led them and placed Himself between them and the wolves. ²⁵ And as those wolves did not yet see the sheep, they proceeded into the midst of that sea, and the wolves followed the sheep, and [those wolves] ran after them into that sea. ²⁶ And when they saw the Lord of the sheep, they turned to flee before His face, but that sea gathered itself together, and became as it had been created, and the water swelled and rose until it covered those wolves. ²⁷ And I saw until all the wolves who pursued those sheep perished and were drowned. ²⁸ But the sheep escaped from that water and went out into a wilderness, where there was no water and no grass; and they began to open their eyes and to see; and I saw the Lord of the sheep pasturing them and giving them water and grass, and that sheep going and leading them. ²⁹ And that sheep ascended to the summit of that lofty rock, and the Lord of the sheep sent it to them. ³⁰ And after that I saw the Lord of the sheep who stood before them, and His appearance was great, and terrible, and majestic, and all those sheep saw Him and were afraid before His face. ³¹ And they all feared and trembled because of Him, and they cried to that sheep with them [which was among them]: We are not able to stand before our Lord or to behold Him! ³² And that sheep which led them again ascended to the summit of that rock, but the sheep began to be blinded and to wander from the way which he had showed them, but that sheep was not aware. ³³ And the Lord of the sheep was exceedingly wrathful against them, and that sheep discovered it, and went down from the summit of the rock, and came to the sheep, and found the greatest part of them blinded and fallen away. ³⁴ And when they saw it, they feared and trembled at its presence and desired to return to their folds. ³⁵ And that sheep took other sheep with it, and came to those sheep which had fallen away, and began to slay them; and the sheep feared its presence, and so that sheep brought back those sheep that had fallen away, and they returned to their folds. ³⁶ And I saw in this vision until that sheep became a man, and built a house for the Lord of the sheep, and placed all the sheep in that house. ³⁷ And I saw until this sheep which had met that sheep which led them fell asleep: and I saw until all the great sheep perished and little ones arose in their place, and they came to a pasture, and approached a stream of water. ³⁸ Then that sheep, their leader which had become a man, withdrew from them and fell asleep, and all the sheep sought it and cried over it with a great crying. ³⁹ And I saw until they ceased from crying for that sheep and crossed that stream of water, and there arose the two sheep as leaders in the place of those which had led them and fallen asleep. ⁴⁰ And I saw until the sheep came to an attractive place, and a pleasant and glorious land, and I saw until those sheep were satisfied; and that house stood among them in the pleasant land. ⁴¹ And sometimes their eyes were opened, and sometimes blinded, until another sheep arose and led them and brought them all back, and their eyes were opened. ⁴² And the dogs, and the foxes, and the wild boars began to devour those sheep until the Lord of the sheep raised up a ram from their midst, which led them. ⁴³ And that ram began to butt those dogs, foxes, and wild boars on either side until he had destroyed them all. ⁴⁴ And that sheep whose eyes were opened saw that ram, which was among the sheep, until it forsook its glory and began to butt those sheep, and trampled on them, and behaved unseemly itself. ⁴⁵ And the Lord of the sheep sent the lamb to another lamb and raised it to be a ram and leader of the sheep instead of that ram which had forsaken its glory. ⁴⁶ And it went to it and spoke

to it alone, and raised it to be a ram, and made it the prince and leader of the sheep, but during all these things those dogs oppressed the sheep. ⁴⁷And the first ram pursued that second ram, and that second ram arose and fled before it, and I saw until those dogs pulled down the first ram. ⁴⁸And that second ram arose and led the [little] sheep. And those sheep grew and multiplied, but all the dogs, and foxes, and wild boars feared and fled before it, and that ram butted and killed the wild beasts, and those wild beasts no longer had any power among the sheep and no longer robbed them of anything. ⁴⁹And that ram begot many sheep and fell asleep; and a little sheep became ram in its stead and became prince and leader of those sheep. ⁵⁰And that house became great and broad, and it was built for those sheep: [and] a great and lofty tower was built on the house for the Lord of the sheep, and that house was low, but the tower was elevated and lofty, and the Lord of the sheep stood on that tower and they offered a full table before Him. ⁵¹And again I saw that those sheep again erred and went many ways, and forsook that house of theirs, and the Lord of the sheep called some from among the sheep and sent them to the sheep, but the sheep began to slay them. ⁵²And one of them was saved and was not slain, and it sped away and cried aloud over the sheep; and they sought to slay it, but the Lord of the sheep saved it from the sheep, and brought it up to me, and caused it to dwell there. ⁵³And He sent many other sheep to those sheep to testify to them and lament over them. ⁵⁴And after that, I saw that when they forsook the house of the LORD and His tower they fell away entirely, and their eyes were blinded; and I saw how the Lord of the sheep worked much slaughter among them in their herds until those sheep invited that slaughter and betrayed His place. ⁵⁵And He gave them over into the hands of the lions, and tigers, and wolves, and hyenas, and into the hand of the foxes, and to all the wild beasts, and those wild beasts began to tear those sheep in pieces. ⁵⁶And I saw that He forsook their house and their tower and gave them all into the hand of the lions and into the hand of all the wild beasts to tear and devour them. ⁵⁷And I began to cry aloud with all my power, and to appeal to the Lord of the sheep, and to represent to Him in regard to the sheep that they were devoured by all the wild beasts. ⁵⁸But He remained unmoved, though He saw it, and rejoiced that they were devoured, and swallowed, and robbed, and He left them to be devoured in the hand of all the beasts. ⁵⁹And He called seventy shepherds and cast those sheep to them that they might pasture them, and He spoke to the shepherds and their companions: Let each individual among you pasture the sheep from now on and do everything that I will command you to do. And I will deliver them over to you rightly numbered and tell you which of them are to be destroyed: and destroy them. ⁶⁰And He gave those sheep over to them. ⁶¹And He called another and spoke to him: Observe and record everything that the shepherds will do to those sheep, for they will destroy more of them than I have commanded them. ⁶²And every excess and the destruction which will be worked through the shepherds, record—how many they destroy according to My command, and how many according to their own caprice: record against every individual shepherd all the destruction he effects. ⁶³And read out before Me by number how many they destroy and how many they deliver over for destruction, that I may have this as a testimony against them, and know every deed of the shepherds, that I may comprehend and see what they do, whether or not they abide by My command which I have commanded them. ⁶⁴But they will not know it, and you will not declare it to them, nor admonish them, but only record against each individual all the destruction which each of the shepherds effect in his time, and lay it all before Me. ⁶⁵And I saw until those shepherds pastured in their season, and they began to slay and to destroy more than they were commanded, and they delivered those sheep into the hand of the lions. ⁶⁶And the lions and tigers ate and devoured the greater part of those sheep, and the wild boars ate along with them; and they burned that tower and demolished that house. ⁶⁷And I became exceedingly sorrowful over that tower because that house of the sheep was demolished, and afterward I was unable to see if those sheep entered that house. ⁶⁸And the shepherds and their associates delivered those sheep over to all the wild beasts to devour them, and each one of them received a definite number in his time: it was written by the other in a scroll how many of them each one of them destroyed. ⁶⁹And each one slew and destroyed many more than was prescribed, and I began to weep and lament on account of those sheep. ⁷⁰And so in the vision I saw how that one who wrote wrote down everyone that was destroyed by those shepherds day by day, and he carried [it] up, and laid [it] down, and actually showed the whole scroll to the Lord of the sheep—[even] everything that they had done, and all that each one of them had made away with, and all that they had given over to destruction. ⁷¹And the scroll was read before the Lord of the sheep, and He took the scroll from his hand, and read it, and sealed it, and laid it down. ⁷²And then I saw how the shepherds pastured for twelve hours, and behold, three of those sheep turned back, and came, and entered, and began to build up all that had fallen down of that house, but the wild boars tried to hinder them, but they were not able. ⁷³And they began to build again as before, and they reared up that tower, and it was named the high tower; and they began to place a table again before the tower, but all the bread on it was polluted and not pure. ⁷⁴And as concerning all this, the eyes of those sheep were blinded so that they did not see, and [the eyes of] their shepherds likewise; and they delivered them in large numbers to their shepherds for destruction, and they trampled the sheep with their feet and devoured them. ⁷⁵And the Lord of the sheep remained unmoved until all the sheep were dispersed over the field and mingled with them, and they did not save them out of the hand of the beasts. ⁷⁶And this one who wrote the scroll carried it up, and showed it, and read it before the Lord of the sheep, and implored Him on their account as he showed Him all the doings of the shepherds and gave testimony before Him against all the shepherds. ⁷⁷And he took the actual scroll, and laid it down beside Him, and departed."

CHAPTER 90

¹"And I saw until thirty-five shepherds undertook the pasturing [of the sheep] in this manner, and they separately completed their periods as did the first; and others received them into their hands, to pasture them for their period, each shepherd in his own period. ²And after that, I saw in my vision all the birds of the heavens coming: the eagles, the vultures, the kites, the ravens; but the eagles led all the birds, and they began to devour those sheep, and to pick out their eyes, and to devour their flesh. ³And the sheep cried out because their flesh was being devoured by the birds, and as for me, I looked and lamented in my sleep over that shepherd who pastured the sheep. ⁴And I saw until those sheep were devoured by the dogs, and eagles, and kites, and they left neither flesh, nor skin, nor sinew remaining on them until only their bones stood there: and their bones also fell to the earth and the sheep became few. ⁵And I saw until twenty-three had undertaken the pasturing and completed fifty-eight times in their several periods. ⁶But behold, lambs were borne by those white sheep, and they began to open their eyes and to see, and to cry to the sheep. ⁷Yes, they cried to them, but they did not listen to what they said to them, but were exceedingly deaf, and their eyes were very exceedingly blinded. ⁸And I saw in the vision how the ravens flew on those lambs, and took one of those lambs, and dashed the sheep in pieces, and devoured them. ⁹And I saw until horns grew on those lambs, and the ravens cast down their horns; and I saw until there sprouted a great horn of one of those sheep, and their eyes were opened. ¹⁰And it looked at them [and their eyes opened], and it cried to the sheep, and the rams saw it, and all ran to it. ¹¹And notwithstanding all this, those eagles, and vultures, and ravens, and kites still kept tearing the sheep, and swooping down on them, and devouring them: still the sheep remained silent, but the rams lamented and cried out. ¹²And those ravens fought and battled with it and sought to lay its horn low, but they had no power over it. ¹³And I saw until the shepherds, and eagles, and those vultures and kites came, and they cried to the ravens that they should break the horn of that ram, and they battled and fought with it, and it battled with them and cried that its help might come. ¹⁴And I saw until that man, who wrote down the names of the shepherds [and] carried [it] up into the presence of the Lord of the sheep, [[came and helped it and showed it everything: he had come down for the help of

that ram.**]]** ¹⁵And I saw until the Lord of the sheep came to them in wrath, and all who saw Him fled, and they all fell into His shadow from before His face. ¹⁶All the eagles, and vultures, and ravens, and kites were gathered together, and there came with them all the sheep of the field, yes, they all came together, and helped each other to break that horn of the ram. ¹⁷And I saw until that man, who wrote the scroll according to the command of the Lord, opened that scroll concerning the destruction which those twelve last shepherds had worked, and showed before the Lord of the sheep that they had destroyed much more than their predecessors. ¹⁸And I saw until the Lord of the sheep came to them and took in His hand the staff of His wrath, and struck the earth, and the earth split apart, and all the beasts and all the birds of the heavens fell from among those sheep, and were swallowed up in the earth, and it covered them. ¹⁹And I saw until a great sword was given to the sheep, and the sheep proceeded against all the beasts of the field to slay them, and all the beasts and the birds of the heavens fled before their face. ²⁰And I saw until a throne was erected in the pleasant land, and the Lord of the sheep sat Himself thereon, and the other took the sealed scrolls and opened those scrolls before the Lord of the sheep. ²¹And the Lord called those men, [those] seven first white ones, and commanded that they should bring before Him, beginning with the first star which led the way, all the stars whose genitals were like those of horses, and they brought them all before Him. ²²And He spoke to that man who wrote before Him, being one of those seven white ones, and said to him, Take those seventy shepherds to whom I delivered the sheep, and who taking them on their own authority slew more than I commanded them. ²³And behold, I saw [that] they were all bound, and they all stood before Him. ²⁴And the judgment was first held over the stars, and they were judged and found guilty, and went to the place of condemnation, and they were cast into an abyss, full of fire and flaming, and full of pillars of fire. ²⁵And those seventy shepherds were judged and found guilty, and they were cast into that fiery abyss. ²⁶And I saw at that time how a similar abyss was opened in the midst of the earth, full of fire, and they brought those blinded sheep, and they were all judged, and found guilty, and cast into this fiery abyss, and they burned; now this abyss was to the right of that house. ²⁷And I saw those sheep burning and their bones burning. ²⁸And I stood up to see until they folded up that old house, and carried off all the pillars, and all the beams and ornaments of the house were at the same time folded up with it, and they carried it off and laid it in a place in the south of the land. ²⁹And I saw until the Lord of the sheep brought a new house greater and loftier than that first and set it up in the place of the first which had been folded up: all its pillars were new, and its ornaments were new and larger than those of the first, the old one which He had taken away, and all the sheep were within it. ³⁰And I saw all the sheep which had been left, and all the beasts on the earth, and all the birds of the heavens falling down and doing homage to those sheep, and making petition to and obeying them in everything. ³¹And thereafter those three who were clothed in white and had seized me by my hand, [who had taken me up before], and the hand of that ram also seizing hold of me, they took me up and set me down in the midst of those sheep before the judgment took place. ³²And those sheep were all white, and their wool was abundant and clean. ³³And all that had been destroyed and dispersed, and all the beasts of the field, and all the birds of the heavens assembled in that house, and the Lord of the sheep rejoiced with great joy because they were all good and had returned to His house. ³⁴And I saw until they laid down that sword which had been given to the sheep, and they brought it back into the house, and it was sealed before the presence of the Lord, and all the sheep were invited into that house, but it did not hold them. ³⁵And their eyes were all opened, and they saw the good, and there was not one among them that did not see. ³⁶And I saw that that house was large, and broad, and very full. ³⁷And I saw that a white bull was born, with large horns and all the beasts of the field and all the birds of the air feared him and made petition to him all the time. ³⁸And I saw until all their generations were transformed, and they all became white bulls; and the first among them became a lamb, and that lamb became a great animal and had great black horns on its head; and the Lord of the sheep rejoiced over it and over all the oxen. ³⁹And I slept in their midst: and I awoke and saw everything. ⁴⁰This is the vision which I saw while I slept, and I awoke and blessed the Lord of righteousness and gave Him glory. ⁴¹Then I wept with a great weeping and my tears were unrestrained until I could no longer endure it: when I saw, they flowed on account of what I had seen, for everything will come and be fulfilled, and all the deeds of men in their order were shown to me. ⁴²On that night I remembered the first dream, and I wept because of it, and was troubled because I had seen that vision."

SECTION 5:

THE EPISTLE OF ENOCH

CHAPTER 91

¹"And now, my son Methuselah, call all your brothers to me and gather together all the sons of your mother to me; for the word calls me, and the Spirit is poured out on me, that I may show you everything that will befall you forever." ²And there on Methuselah went and summoned to himself all his brothers and assembled his relatives. ³And he spoke to all the children of righteousness and said, "Hear, you sons of Enoch, all the words of your father, and listen to the voice of my mouth; for I exhort you and say to you, beloved: ⁴Love uprightness and walk therein. And do not draw near to uprightness with a double heart, || And do not associate with those of a double heart, || But walk in righteousness, my sons. And it will guide you on good paths, || And righteousness will be your companion. ⁵For I know that violence must increase on the earth, || And a great discipline will be executed on the earth, || Yes, it will be cut off from its roots, || And its whole structure will be destroyed. ⁶And unrighteousness will again be consummated on the earth, || And all the deeds of unrighteousness, and of violence, and transgression || Will prevail in a twofold degree. ⁷And when sin, and unrighteousness, and blasphemy, and violence || Increase in all kinds of deeds, || And apostasy, and transgression, and uncleanness increase, || A great discipline will come from Heaven on all these, || And the holy Lord will come out with wrath and discipline || To execute judgment on earth. ⁸In those days violence will be cut off from its roots, || And the roots of unrighteousness together with deceit, || And they will be destroyed from under the heavens. ⁹And all the idols of the heathen will be abandoned, || And the temples burned with fire, || And they will remove them from the whole earth, || And they will be cast into the judgment of fire || And will perish in wrath and in grievous judgment forever. ¹⁰And the righteous will arise from their sleep, || And wisdom will arise and be given to them. **[[**And after that the roots of unrighteousness will be cut off, || And the sinners will be destroyed by the sword || [And] will be cut off from the blasphemers in every place, || And those who plan violence and those who commit blasphemy || Will perish by the sword.**]]** ¹²And after that there will be another, the eighth week—That of righteousness—And a sword will be given to it || That a righteous judgment may be executed on the oppressors, || And sinners will be delivered into the hands of the righteous. ¹³And at its close they will acquire houses through their righteousness, || And a house will be built for the Great King in glory forevermore, || And all mankind will look to the path of uprightness. ¹⁴And after that, in the ninth week, || The righteous judgment will be revealed to the whole world, || And all the works of the godless will vanish from all the earth, || And the world will be written down for destruction. ¹⁵And after this, in the tenth week, in the seventh part, || There will be the great continuous judgment, || In which He will execute vengeance among the messengers. ¹⁶And the first heaven will depart and pass away, || And a new heaven will appear, || And all the powers of the heavens will give sevenfold light. ¹⁷And after that there will be many weeks without number forever, || And all will be in goodness and righteousness, || And sin will no longer be mentioned forever. ¹⁸And now I tell you, my sons, || And show you the paths of righteousness and the paths of violence. Yes, I will show them to you again || That you may know what will come to pass. ¹⁹And now, listen to me, my sons, || And walk in the paths of righteousness, || And do not walk in the paths of violence, || For all who walk in the paths of unrighteousness will perish forever."

CHAPTER 92

¹The scroll written by Enoch—[[Enoch indeed wrote this complete doctrine of wisdom, [which is] praised of all men and a judge of all the earth]]—for all my children who will dwell on the earth, and for the future generations who will observe uprightness and peace. ²Do not let your spirit be troubled on account of the times; For the Holy and Great One has appointed days for all things. ³And the righteous one will arise from sleep || And walk in the paths of righteousness, || And all his path and conversation || Will be in continuous goodness and grace. ⁴He will be gracious to the righteous || And give him continuous uprightness, || And He will give him power || So that he will be [endowed] with goodness and righteousness. And he will walk in perpetual light. ⁵And sin will perish in darkness forever || And will no longer be seen from that day forevermore.

CHAPTER 93

¹And after that, Enoch both gave and began to recount from the scrolls. ²And Enoch said, "Concerning the children of righteousness, and concerning the chosen ones of the world, and concerning the plant of uprightness, I will speak these things; yes, I, Enoch, will declare [them] to you, my sons, according to that which appeared to me in the heavenly vision, and which I have known through the word of the holy messengers, and have learned from the heavenly tablets." ³And Enoch began to recount from the scrolls and said, "I was born the seventh in the first week, while judgment and righteousness still endured. ⁴And great wickedness will arise after me in the second week, and deceit will have sprung up, and the first end will be in it. And a man will be saved in it; and after it is ended, unrighteousness will grow up, and a law will be made for the sinners. ⁵And after that, in the third week, at its close, a man will be chosen as the plant of righteous judgment, and his posterity will become the plant of righteousness forevermore. ⁶And after that, in the fourth week, at its close, visions of the holy and righteous will be seen, and a law for all generations and an enclosure will be made for them. ⁷And after that, in the fifth week, at its close, the house of glory and dominion will be built forever. ⁸And after that, in the sixth week, all who live in it will be blinded, and the hearts of all of them will godlessly forsake wisdom. And a man will ascend in it; and at its close the house of dominion will be burned with fire, and the whole race of the chosen root will be dispersed. ⁹And after that, in the seventh week, an apostate generation will arise, and its [wicked] deeds will be many, and all its deeds will be apostate. ¹⁰And at its close the chosen righteous of the continuous plant of righteousness will be selected to receive sevenfold instruction concerning all His creation. ¹¹[[For who is there of all the children of men that is able to hear the voice of the Holy One without being troubled? And who can think His thoughts? And who is there that can behold all the works of Heaven? ¹²And how should there be one who could behold Heaven, and who is there that could understand the things of Heaven, and see a soul or a spirit, and could tell thereof, or ascend and see all their ends and think them or do like them? ¹³And who is there of all men that could know what the breadth and the length of the earth is? And to whom has been shown the measure of all of them? ¹⁴Or is there anyone who could discern the length of the heavens and how great its height is, and on what it is founded, and how great the number of the stars is, and where all the luminaries rest?]]"

CHAPTER 94

¹And now I say to you, my sons, love righteousness and walk therein, for the paths of righteousness are worthy of acceptance, but the paths of unrighteousness will suddenly be destroyed and vanish. ²And the paths of violence and death will be revealed to certain men of a generation, and they will hold themselves far from them, and will not follow them. ³And now I say to you, the righteous: do not walk in the paths of wickedness, nor in the paths of death, and do not draw near to them, lest you be destroyed. ⁴But seek and choose for yourselves righteousness and a chosen life, and walk in the paths of peace, and you will live and prosper. ⁵And hold fast my words in the thoughts of your hearts and do not allow them to be effaced from your hearts, for I know that sinners will tempt men to mistreat wisdom, so that no place may be found for her, and no manner of temptation may diminish. ⁶Woe to those who build unrighteousness and oppression and lay deceit as a foundation, for they will be suddenly overthrown, and they will have no peace. ⁷Woe to those who build their houses with sin, for they will be overthrown from all their foundations, and they will fall by the sword. [[And those who acquire gold and silver will suddenly perish in judgment.]] ⁸Woe to you, you rich, for you have trusted in your riches, and you will depart from your riches, because you have not remembered the Most High in the days of your riches. ⁹You have committed blasphemy and unrighteousness, and have become ready for the day of slaughter, and the day of darkness, and the Day of the Great Judgment. ¹⁰So I speak and declare to you: He who has created you will overthrow you, and there will be no compassion for your fall, and your Creator will rejoice at your destruction. ¹¹And your righteous ones will be a reproach to the sinners and the godless in those days.

CHAPTER 95

¹Oh that my eyes were [a cloud of] waters that I might weep over you || And pour down my tears as a cloud of waters—So that I might rest from my troubled heart! ²Who has permitted you to practice reproaches and wickedness? And so judgment will overtake you sinners. ³Do not fear the sinners, you righteous, || For the LORD will deliver them into your hands again, || That you may execute judgment on them according to your desires. ⁴Woe to you who fulminate anathemas which cannot be reversed: Healing will therefore be far from you because of your sins. ⁵Woe to you who repay your neighbor with evil, || For you will be repaid according to your works. ⁶Woe to you, lying witnesses, and to those who weigh out injustice, || For you will suddenly perish. ⁷Woe to you, sinners, for you persecute the righteous, || For you will be delivered up and persecuted because of injustice, || And its yoke will be heavy on you.

CHAPTER 96

¹Be hopeful, you righteous, || For the sinners will suddenly perish before you, || And you will have lordship over them according to your desires. ²[[And in the day of the tribulation of the sinners, || Your children will mount and rise as eagles, || And your nest will be higher than the vultures, || And you will ascend and enter the crevices of the earth, || And the clefts of the rock forever as coneys before the unrighteous, || And the sirens will sigh and weep because of you.]] ³So do not fear, you that have suffered, || For healing will be your portion, || And a bright light will enlighten you, || And you will hear the voice of rest from Heaven. ⁴Woe to you, you sinners, || For your riches make you appear like the righteous, || But your hearts convict you of being sinners, || And this fact will be a testimony against you for a memorial of [your] evil deeds. ⁵Woe to you who devour the finest of the wheat, || And drink wine in large bowls, || And tread the lowly underfoot with your might. ⁶Woe to you who drink water from every fountain, || For you will suddenly be consumed and wither away, || Because you have forsaken the fountain of life. ⁷Woe to you who work unrighteousness, and deceit, and blasphemy: It will be a memorial against you for evil. ⁸Woe to you, you mighty, who oppress the righteous with might, || For the day of your destruction is coming. In those days many and good days will come to the righteous—In the day of your judgment.

CHAPTER 97

¹Believe, you righteous, that the sinners will become a shame and perish in the day of unrighteousness. ²Be it known to you, [you sinners,] that the Most High is mindful of your destruction, and the messengers of Heaven rejoice over your destruction. ³What will you do, you sinners, and where will you flee on that Day of Judgment, when you hear the voice of the prayer of the righteous? ⁴Yes, you will fare like to them, against whom this word will be a testimony: "You have been companions of sinners." ⁵And in those days the prayer of the righteous will reach to the LORD, and for you the days of your judgment will come. ⁶And all the words of your unrighteousness will be read out before the Great Holy One, and your faces will be covered with shame, and He will reject every work which is grounded on unrighteousness. ⁷Woe to you, you sinners, who live in the midst of [the] ocean and on the dry land, whose remembrance is evil against you. ⁸Woe to you

1 ENOCH

who acquire silver and gold in unrighteousness, and say, "We have become rich with riches, and have possessions, and have acquired everything we have desired. ⁹And now, let us do what we purposed, for we have gathered silver, and there are many farmers in our houses. And our granaries are brimful as with water, ¹⁰yes, and like water your lies will flow away; for your riches will not abide but speedily ascend from you, for you have acquired it all in unrighteousness, and you will be given over to a great curse.

CHAPTER 98

¹And now I swear to you—to the wise and to the foolish—for you will have manifold experiences on the earth. ²For you men will put on more adornments than a woman, and more colored garments than a virgin. They will be poured out as water in royalty, and in grandeur, and in power, and in silver, and in gold, and in purple, and in splendor, and in food. ³Therefore they will be wanting in doctrine and wisdom, and they will thereby perish together with their possessions, and with all their glory, and their splendor; and in shame, and in slaughter, and in great destitution, their spirits will be cast into the furnace of fire. ⁴I have sworn to you, you sinners, as a mountain has not become a slave, and a hill does not become the handmaid of a woman, even so sin has not been sent on the earth, but man has created it of himself, and they who commit it will fall under a great curse. ⁵And barrenness has not been given to the woman, but she dies without children on account of the deeds of her own hands. ⁶I have sworn to you, you sinners, by the Holy Great One, that all your evil deeds are revealed in the heavens, and that none of your deeds of oppression are covered and hidden. ⁷And do not think in your spirit nor say in your heart that you do not know and that you do not see that every sin is recorded every day in Heaven in the presence of the Most High. ⁸From now on you know that all your oppression with which you oppress is written down every day until the day of your judgment. ⁹Woe to you, you fools, for you will perish through your folly; and you transgress against the wise, and so good fortune will not be your portion. ¹⁰And now, know that you are prepared for the day of destruction. For that reason, do not hope to live, you sinners, but you will depart and die; for you know no ransom; for you are prepared for the Day of the Great Judgment, for the day of tribulation and great shame for your spirits. ¹¹Woe to you, you obstinate of heart, who work wickedness and eat blood: from where do you have good things to eat, and to drink, and to be filled? From all the good things which the LORD, the Most High, has placed in abundance on the earth. Therefore, you will have no peace. ¹²Woe to you who love the deeds of unrighteousness: why do you hope for good for yourselves? Know that you will be delivered into the hands of the righteous, and they will cut off your necks, and slay you, and have no mercy on you. ¹³Woe to you who rejoice in the tribulation of the righteous, for no grave will be dug for you. ¹⁴Woe to you who set as nothing the words of the righteous, for you will have no hope of life. ¹⁵Woe to you who write down lying and godless words, for they write down their lies that men may hear them and act godlessly toward [their] neighbor. ¹⁶Therefore, they will have no peace, but will die a sudden death.

CHAPTER 99

¹Woe to you who work godlessness, and glory in lying and extol them: you will perish, and no happy life will be yours. ²Woe to them who pervert the words of uprightness, and transgress the perpetual law, and transform themselves into what they were not: they will be trodden underfoot on the earth. ³In those days make ready, you righteous, to raise your prayers as a memorial, and place them as a testimony before the messengers, that they may place the sin of the sinners for a memorial before the Most High. ⁴In those days the nations will be stirred up, and the families of the nations will arise on the day of destruction. ⁵And in those days the destitute will go out and carry off their children, and they will abandon them, so that their children will perish through them: yes, they will abandon their children—sucklings, and not return to them, and will have no pity on their beloved ones. ⁶And again I swear to you, you sinners, that sin is prepared for a day of unceasing bloodshed. ⁷And they who worship stones, and grave images of gold, and silver, and wood, and clay, and those who worship impure spirits and demons, and all kinds of idols not according to knowledge, will get no manner of help from them. ⁸And they will become godless by reason of the folly of their hearts, and their eyes will be blinded through the fear of their hearts and through visions in their dreams. ⁹They will become godless and fearful through these, for they will have worked all their work in a lie and will have worshiped a stone. Therefore, they will perish in an instant. ¹⁰But in those days, blessed are all they who accept the words of wisdom, and understand them, and observe the paths of the Most High, and walk in the path of His righteousness, and do not become godless with the godless, for they will be saved. ¹¹Woe to you who spread evil to your neighbors, for you will be slain in Sheol. ¹²Woe to you who make deceitful and false measures, and who cause bitterness on the earth, for they will thereby be utterly consumed. ¹³Woe to you who build your houses through the grievous toil of others, and all their building materials are the bricks and stones of sin; I tell you that you will have no peace. ¹⁴Woe to them who reject the measure and agelong heritage of their fathers and whose souls follow after idols, for they will have no rest. ¹⁵Woe to them who work unrighteousness, and help oppression, and slay their neighbors until the Day of the Great Judgment. ¹⁶For He will cast down your glory, and bring affliction on your hearts, and will arouse His fierce indignation, and destroy all of you with the sword; and all the holy and righteous will remember your sins.

CHAPTER 100

¹And in those days in one place the fathers will be smitten together with their sons and brothers will fall in death with one another until the streams flow with their blood. ²For a man will not withhold his hand from slaying his sons and his sons' sons, and the sinner will not withhold his hand from his honored brother: they will slay one another from dawn until sunset. ³And the horse will walk up to the breast in the blood of sinners, and the chariot will be submerged to its height. ⁴In those days the messengers will descend into the secret places and gather together into one place all those who brought down sin, and the Most High will arise on that Day of Judgment to execute great judgment among sinners. ⁵And He will appoint guardians over all the righteous and holy from among the holy messengers to guard them as the apple of [His] eye, until He makes an end of all wickedness and all sin, and though the righteous sleep a long sleep, they have nothing to fear. ⁶And [then] the children of the earth will see the wise in security, and will understand all the words of this scroll, and recognize that their riches will not be able to save them in the overthrow of their sins. ⁷Woe to you, sinners, on the day of strong anguish—you who afflict the righteous and burn them with fire: you will be repaid according to your works. ⁸Woe to you, you obstinate of heart, who watch in order to devise wickedness: therefore, fear will come on you and there will be none to help you. ⁹Woe to you, you sinners, on account of the words of your mouth, and on account of the deeds of your hands which your godlessness has worked: you will burn in blazing flames worse than fire. ¹⁰And now, know that He will inquire from the messengers in Heaven regarding your deeds, [and] from the sun, and from the moon, and from the stars in reference to your sins, because on the earth you execute judgment on the righteous. ¹¹And He will summon every cloud, and mist, and dew, and rain to testify against you, for they will all be withheld from descending on you because of you, and they will be mindful of your sins. ¹²And now give presents to the rain that it is not withheld from descending on you, nor yet the dew, when it has received gold and silver from you, that it may descend. ¹³When the hoarfrost and snow with their frigidness, and all the snowstorms with all their plagues fall on you, in those days you will not be able to stand before them.

CHAPTER 101

¹Observe the heavens, you children of Heaven, and every work of the Most High, and fear Him and work no evil in His presence. ²If He closes the windows of the heavens, and withholds the rain and the dew from descending on the earth on your account, what will you do then? ³And if He sends His anger on you because of your deeds, you cannot petition Him, for you spoke proud and

insolent words against His righteousness: therefore, you will have no peace. ⁴And do you not see the sailors of the ships, how their ships are tossed to and fro by the waves, and are shaken by the winds, and are in severe trouble? ⁵And therefore, they fear because all their excellent possessions go on the sea with them, and they have evil forebodings of heart that the sea will swallow them, and they will perish therein. ⁶Are the entire sea, and all its waters, and all its movements, not the work of the Most High, and has He not set limits to its doings, and confined it throughout by the sand? ⁷And at His reproof it is afraid and dries up, and all its fish die and all that is in it, but you sinners that are on the earth do not fear Him. ⁸Has He not made the heavens, and the earth, and all that is therein? Who has given understanding and wisdom to everything that moves on the earth and in the sea? ⁹Do the sailors of the ships not fear the sea? Yet sinners do not fear the Most High.

CHAPTER 102

¹In those days when He has brought a grievous fire on you, where will you flee, and where will you find deliverance? And when He launches out His Word against you will you not be frightened and fear? ²And all the luminaries will be frightened with great fear, and all the earth will be frightened, and tremble, and be alarmed. ³And all the messengers will execute their commands and will seek to hide themselves from the presence of the Great Glory, and the children of earth will tremble and quake; and you sinners will be cursed forever, and you will have no peace. ⁴Do not fear, you souls of the righteous, and be hopeful, you that have died in righteousness. ⁵And do not grieve if your soul has descended into Sheol in grief, and that in your life your body did not fare according to your goodness, but wait for the day of the judgment of sinners and for the day of cursing and discipline. ⁶And yet when you die, the sinners speak over you: "As we die, so the righteous die, and what benefit do they reap for their deeds? ⁷Behold, so they die even as we, in grief and darkness, and what have they more than we? From now on we are equal. ⁸And what will they receive and what will they see forever? Behold, they have also died, and from now on and forever they will see no light." ⁹I tell you, you sinners, you are content to eat and drink, and rob and sin, and strip men naked, and acquire wealth and see good days. ¹⁰Have you seen the righteous, how their end falls out, that no manner of violence is found in them until their death? ¹¹"Nevertheless, they perished and became as though they had not been, and their spirits descended into Sheol in tribulation."

CHAPTER 103

¹Now, therefore, I swear to you, the righteous, by the glory of the Great and Honored and Mighty One in dominion, and by His greatness I swear to you. ²I know a mystery and have read the heavenly tablets, and have seen the holy scrolls, and have found written therein and inscribed regarding them ³that all goodness, and joy, and glory are prepared for them and written down for the spirits of those who have died in righteousness, and that manifold good will be given to you in reward for your labors, and that your lot is abundantly beyond the lot of the living. ⁴And the spirits of you who have died in righteousness will live and rejoice, and their spirits will not perish, nor their memorial from before the face of the Great One to all the generations of the world. For that reason, no longer fear their insolence. ⁵Woe to you, you sinners, when you have died, if you die in the wealth of your sins! And those who are like you say regarding you, "Blessed are the sinners: they have seen all their days. ⁶And how they have died in prosperity and in wealth and have not seen tribulation or murder in their life. And they have died in honor, and judgment has not been executed on them during their life." ⁷Know that their souls will be made to descend into Sheol, and they will be wretched in their great tribulation. ⁸And your spirits will enter into darkness, and chains, and a burning flame where there is grievous judgment; and the Great Judgment will be for all the generations of the world. Woe to you, for you will have no peace. ⁹Do not say in regard to the righteous and good who are in life, "In our troubled days we have toiled laboriously, and experienced every trouble, and met with much evil, and been consumed, and have become few and our spirit small. ¹⁰And we have been destroyed and have not found any to help us even with a word. We have been tortured and have not hoped to see life from day to day. ¹¹We hoped to be the head and have become the tail. We have toiled laboriously and had no satisfaction in our toil. And we have become the food of the sinners and the unrighteous, and they have laid their yoke heavily on us. ¹²They who hated us have had dominion over us and struck us; and we have bowed our necks to those that hated us, but they did not pity us. ¹³We desired to get away from them that we might escape and be at rest, but we found no place where we should flee and be safe from them. ¹⁴And we complained to the rulers in our tribulation and cried out against those who devoured us, but they did not attend to our cries and would not listen to our voice. ¹⁵And they helped those who robbed us and devoured us and those who made us few; and they concealed their oppression, and they did not remove from us the yoke of those that devoured us, and dispersed us, and murdered us, and they concealed their murder, and did not remember that they had lifted up their hands against us."

CHAPTER 104

¹I swear to you that the messengers in Heaven remember you for good before the glory of the Great One, and your names are written before the glory of the Great One. ²Be hopeful, for you were previously put to shame through ill and affliction, but now you will shine as the lights of the heavens; you will shine, and you will be seen, and the portals of the heavens will be opened to you. ³And in your cry, cry for judgment, and it will appear to you, for all your tribulation will be visited on the rulers, and on all who helped those who plundered you. ⁴Be hopeful and do not cast away your hopes, for you will have great joy as the messengers of Heaven. ⁵What will you be obliged to do? You will not have to hide on the Day of the Great Judgment, and you will not be found as sinners, and the continuous judgment will be far from you for all the generations of the world. ⁶And now, do not fear, you righteous, when you see the sinners growing strong and prospering in their ways: do not be companions with them, but keep far from their violence, for you will become companions of the hosts of Heaven. ⁷And, although you sinners say, "All our sins will not be searched out and written down," nevertheless, they will write down all your sins every day. ⁸And now I show to you that light and darkness, day and night, see all your sins. ⁹Do not be godless in your hearts, and do not lie, and do not alter the words of uprightness, nor charge the words of the Holy Great One with lying, nor take account of your idols, for all your lying and all your godlessness do not issue in righteousness but in great sin. ¹⁰And now I know this mystery, that sinners will alter and pervert the words of righteousness in many ways, and will speak wicked words, and lie, and practice great deceits, and write scrolls concerning their words. ¹¹But when they write down all my words truthfully in their languages, and do not change or diminish from my words, but write them all down truthfully, all that I first testified concerning them, ¹²then—I know another mystery—scrolls will be given to the righteous and the wise to become a cause of joy, and uprightness, and much wisdom. ¹³And the scrolls will be given to them, and they will believe in them and rejoice over them, and then all the righteous who have learned from all the paths of uprightness will be repaid.

CHAPTER 105

¹In those days the LORD commanded [them] to summon and testify to the children of earth concerning their wisdom: "Show [it] to them, for you are their guides and a repayment over the whole earth. ²For My Son and I will be united with them forever in the paths of uprightness in their lives, and you will have peace. Rejoice, you children of uprightness! Amen."

CHAPTER 106

¹And after some days my son Methuselah took a wife for his son Lamech, and she became pregnant by him and bore a son. ²And his body was white as snow and red as the blooming of a rose, and the hair of his head and his long locks were white as wool, and his eyes beautiful. And when he opened his eyes, he lighted up the whole house like the sun, and the whole house was very bright. ³And he immediately arose in the hands of the midwife, opened his mouth, and conversed with the Lord of Righteousness. ⁴And his

1 ENOCH

father Lamech was afraid of him, and fled, and came to his father Methuselah. ⁵And he said to him, "I have begotten a strange son, diverse from and unlike man, and resembling the sons of the God of Heaven, and his nature is different, and he is not like us, and his eyes are as the rays of the sun, and his countenance is glorious. ⁶And it seems to me that he is not sprung from me but from the messengers, and I fear that a wonder may be worked on the earth in his days. ⁷And now, my father, I am here to petition and implore you that you may go to our father Enoch and learn the truth from him, for his dwelling-place is among the messengers." ⁸And when Methuselah heard the words of his son, he came to me at the ends of the earth, for he had heard that I was there, and he cried aloud, and I heard his voice, and I came to him. And I said to him, "Behold, here I am, my son, why have you come to me?" ⁹And he answered and said, "I have come to you because of a great cause of anxiety, and I have approached because of a disturbing vision. ¹⁰And now, my father, hear me: a son has been born to my son Lamech, the like of whom there is none, and his nature is not like man's nature, and the color of his body is whiter than snow and redder than the bloom of a rose, and the hair of his head is whiter than white wool, and his eyes are like the rays of the sun, and he opened his eyes and immediately lighted up the whole house. ¹¹And he arose in the hands of the midwife, and opened his mouth, and blessed the Lord of Heaven. ¹²And his father Lamech became afraid, and fled to me, and did not believe that he was sprung from him, but that he was in the likeness of the messengers of Heaven; and behold, I have come to you that you may make the truth known to me." ¹³And I, Enoch, answered and said to him, "The LORD will do a new thing on the earth, and I have already seen this in a vision, and I make known to you that in the generation of my father Jared some of the messengers of Heaven transgressed the word of the LORD. ¹⁴And behold, they commit sin, and transgress the law, and have united themselves with women, and commit sin with them, and have married some of them, and have begot children by them. And they will produce giants on the earth, not according to the spirit, but according to the flesh, and there will be a great punishment on the earth, and the earth will be cleansed from all impurity. ¹⁵Yes, there will come a great destruction over the whole earth, and there will be a flood and a great destruction for one year. ¹⁶And this son who has been born to you will be left on the earth, ¹⁷and his three children will be saved with him when all mankind that are on the earth will die. ¹⁸And now, make [it] known to your son Lamech that he who has been born is truly his son and call his name Noah, for he will be left to you, and he and his sons will be saved from the destruction which will come on the earth on account of all the sin and all the unrighteousness which will be consummated on the earth in his days. ¹⁹And after that there will still be more unrighteousness than that which was first consummated on the earth, for I know the mysteries of the holy ones; for He, the LORD, has showed me and informed me, and I have read [them] in the heavenly tablets."

CHAPTER 107

¹"And I saw written on them that generation on generation will transgress, until a generation of righteousness arises, and transgression is destroyed, and sin passes away from the earth, and all manner of good comes on it. ²And now, my son, go and make [it] known to your son Lamech that this son which has been born is truly his son, and that [this] is no lie." ³And when Methuselah had heard the words of his father Enoch—for he had shown everything to him in secret—he returned and showed [them] to him and called the name of that son Noah, for he will comfort the earth after all the destruction.

CHAPTER 108

¹Another scroll which Enoch wrote for his son Methuselah and for those who will come after him and keep the Law in the last days. ²You who have done good will wait for those days until an end is made of those who work evil and an end of the might of the transgressors. ³And indeed, wait until sin has passed away, for their names will be blotted out of the Scroll of Life and out of the holy scrolls, and their seed will be destroyed forever, and their spirits will be slain, and they will cry and make lamentation in a place that is a chaotic wilderness, and they will burn in the fire, for there is no earth there. ⁴And I saw something like an invisible cloud there, for by reason of its depth I could not look over, and I saw a flame of fire blazing brightly, and things like shining mountains circling and sweeping to and fro. ⁵And I asked one of the holy messengers who was with me, and said to him, "What is this shining thing? For it is not a heaven but only the flame of a blazing fire, and the voice of weeping, and crying, and lamentation, and strong pain." ⁶And he said to me, "[Into] this place which you see here are cast the spirits of sinners, and blasphemers, and of those who work wickedness, and of those who pervert everything that the LORD has spoken through the mouth of the prophets—[even] the things that will be. ⁷For some of them are written and inscribed above in Heaven in order that the messengers may read them and know that which will befall the sinners, and the spirits of the humble, and of those who have afflicted their bodies and been repaid by God, and of those who have been put to shame by wicked men, ⁸[those] who love God and loved neither gold, nor silver, nor any of the good things which are in the world, but gave their bodies over to torture. ⁹Who, since they came into being, did not long after earthly food, but regarded everything as a passing breath, and lived accordingly, and the LORD tried them much, and their spirits were found pure so that they should bless His Name. ¹⁰And I have recounted all the blessings destined for them in the scrolls. And He has assigned them their reward, because they have been found to be such as loved Heaven more than their life in the world, and though they were trodden under [the] foot of wicked men, and experienced abuse and reviling from them, and were put to shame, yet they blessed Me. ¹¹And now I will summon the spirits of the good who belong to the generation of light, and I will transform those who were born in darkness, who in the flesh were not repaid with such honor as their faithfulness deserved. ¹²And I will bring out those who have loved My holy Name in shining light, and I will seat each on the throne of his honor. ¹³And they will be resplendent for infinite ages, for righteousness is the judgment of God; for He will give faithfulness to the faithful in the habitation of upright paths. ¹⁴And they will see those who were born in darkness led into darkness, while the righteous will be resplendent. ¹⁵And the sinners will cry aloud and see them resplendent, and they will indeed go where days and seasons are prescribed for them."

2 ENOCH

2 Enoch, also called Slavonic Enoch or the Secrets of Enoch, is thought to have been written between the 1st century BC and the 1st century AD. It deals with Enoch's rapture and ascent through the ten heavenly dimensions.

CHAPTER 1

¹There was a wise man, a great craftsman, and the LORD conceived love for him and received him, that he should behold the uppermost dwellings and be an eyewitness of the wise, and great, and inconceivable, and immutable realm of God Almighty, of the very wonderful, and glorious, and bright, and many-eyed station of the LORD's servants, and of the inaccessible throne of the LORD, and of the degrees and manifestations of the incorporeal hosts, and of the ineffable service of the multitude of the elements, and of the various apparition[s] and inexpressible singing of the host of cherubim, and of the boundless light. ²At that time he said: When my one hundred and sixty-fifth year was completed, I begot my son Methuselah. ³After this I also lived two

2 ENOCH

hundred years and completed, of all the years of my life, three hundred and sixty-five years. ⁴On the first day of the month I was in my house alone, and was resting on my bed, and slept. ⁵And when I was asleep, great distress came up into my heart, and I was weeping with my eyes in sleep, and I could not understand what this distress was, or what would happen to me. ⁶And two men appeared to me, exceedingly big, so that I never saw such on earth; their faces were shining like the sun, their eyes were also like a burning light, and fire was coming forth from their lips; with clothing… in appearance purple, their wings were brighter than gold, their hands whiter than snow. ⁷They were standing at the head of my bed and began to call me by my name. ⁸And I arose from my sleep and clearly saw those two men standing in front of me. ⁹And I saluted them, and was seized with fear, and the appearance of my face was changed from terror, and those men said to me, ¹⁰"Have courage, Enoch, do not fear; the perpetual God sent us to you, and behold, you will ascend with us into Heaven today, and you will tell your sons and all your household all that they will do without you on earth in your house, and let no one seek you until the LORD returns you to them." ¹¹And I hurried to obey them, and went out from my house, and made for the doors as it was commanded me, and summoned my sons Methuselah, and Regim, and Gaidad, and made all the marvels those men had told me known to them.

CHAPTER 2

¹Listen to me, my children: I do not know where I go, or what will befall me; now therefore, my children, I tell you: do not turn from God before the face of the vain, who did not make the heavens and earth, for these will perish and those who worship them, and may the LORD make your hearts confident in the fear of Him. And now, my children, let no one think to seek me until the LORD returns me to you.

CHAPTER 3

¹It came to pass, when Enoch had told [this to] his sons, that the messengers took him on to their wings and bore him up on to the first heaven and placed him on the clouds. And there I looked, and again I looked higher, and saw the ether, and they placed me on the first heaven and showed me a very great sea, greater than the earthly sea.

CHAPTER 4

¹They brought the elders and rulers of the stellar orders before my face, and showed me two hundred messengers who rule the stars and their services to the heavens, and fly with their wings, and come around all those who sail.

CHAPTER 5

¹And here I looked down and saw the treasure-houses of the snow, and the messengers who keep their terrible storehouses, and the clouds from where they come out and into which they go.

CHAPTER 6

¹They showed me the treasure-house of the dew, like oil of the olive, and the appearance of its form, as of all the flowers of the earth; furthermore, many messengers guarding the treasure-houses of these things, and how they are made to shut and open.

CHAPTER 7

¹And those men took me and led me up on to the second heaven, and showed me darkness, greater than earthly darkness, and there I saw prisoners hanging, watched, awaiting the great and boundless judgment, and these messengers were dark-looking, more than earthly darkness, and unceasingly making weeping through all hours. ²And I said to the men who were with me, "For what reason are these unceasingly tortured?" They answered me: "These are God's apostates who did not obey God's commands, but took counsel with their own will, and turned away with their prince who is also fastened on the fifth heaven." ³And I felt great pity for them, and they saluted me, and said to me, "Man of God, pray for us to the LORD"; and I answered to them: "Who am I, a mortal man, that I should pray for messengers? Who knows where I go, or what will befall me? Or who will pray for me?"

CHAPTER 8

¹And those men took me there, and led me up on to the third heaven, and placed me there; and I looked downwards and saw the produce of these places, such as has never been known for goodness. ²And I saw all the sweet-flowering trees and beheld their fruits, which were sweet-smelling, and all the foods borne by them bubbling with fragrant exhalation. ³And in the midst of the trees, that of Life, in that place whereon the LORD rests, when He goes up into paradise; and this tree is of ineffable goodness and fragrance and adorned more than every existing thing; and on all sides it is gold-looking, and vermillion, and fire-like in form and covers all, and it has produce from all fruits. ⁴Its root is in the garden at the earth's end. ⁵And paradise is between corruptibility and incorruptibility. ⁶And two springs come out which send forth honey and milk, and their springs send forth oil and wine, and they separate into four parts, and go around with quiet course, and go down into the Paradise of Eden, between corruptibility and incorruptibility. ⁷And there they go forth along the earth and have a revolution to their circle even as other elements. ⁸And here there is no unfruitful tree, and every place is blessed. ⁹And there are three hundred very bright messengers who keep the garden, and with unceasing sweet singing and never-silent voices serve the LORD throughout all days and hours. ¹⁰And I said, "How very sweet this place is!" And those men said to me:

CHAPTER 9

¹"This place, O Enoch, is prepared for the righteous, who endure all manner of offense from those that exasperate their souls, who avert their eyes from iniquity, and make righteous judgment, and give bread to the hungering, and cover the naked with clothing, and raise up the fallen, and help injured orphans, and who walk without fault before the face of the LORD, and serve Him alone, and for them this place is prepared for continuous inheritance."

CHAPTER 10

¹And those two men led me up on to the northern side, and showed me a very terrible place there, and there were all manner of tortures in that place: cruel darkness and unilluminated gloom, and there is no light there, but murky fire constantly flaming aloft, and there is a fiery river coming forth, and that whole place is fire everywhere, and everywhere there is frost and ice, thirst and shivering, while the bonds are very cruel, and the messengers fearful and merciless, bearing angry weapons [for] merciless torture, and I said, ²"Woe, woe! How very terrible this place is! ³And those men said to me, "This place, O Enoch, is prepared for those who dishonor God, who practice sin against nature on earth, which is child-corruption after the sodomitic fashion, magic-making, enchantments, and devilish witchcrafts, and who boast of their wicked deeds—stealing, lies, slanders, envy, malice, fornication, murder—and who, cursed, steal the souls of men; who, seeing the poor, take away their goods and themselves wax rich, injuring them for other men's goods; who being able to satisfy the empty, made the hungering to die; being able to clothe, stripped the naked; and who did not know their Creator, and bowed to the soulless and lifeless gods—who cannot see nor hear, vain gods— who also built hewn images and bow down to unclean handiwork; this place is prepared for all these for a continuous inheritance."

CHAPTER 11

¹Those men took me, and led me up on to the fourth heaven, and showed me all the successive goings, and all the rays of the light of sun and moon. ²And I measure their goings, and compared their light, and saw that the sun's light is greater than the moon's. ³Its circle and the wheels on which it goes always, like the wind going past with very marvelous speed, and day and night it has no rest. ⁴Its passage and return are accompanied by four great stars, and each star has one thousand stars under it, to the right of the sun's wheel, and by four to the left, each having one thousand stars under it—eight thousand altogether, issuing with the sun continually. ⁵And by day, fifteen myriads of messengers attend it, and by night one thousand. ⁶And six-winged ones issue with the messengers before the sun's wheel into the fiery flames, and one hundred messengers kindle the sun and set it gleaming.

CHAPTER 12

¹And I looked and saw other flying elements of the sun, whose names are phoenixes and

chalkydri, marvelous and wonderful, with feet and tails in the form of a lion, and a crocodile's head, their appearance is empurpled, like the rainbow; their size is nine hundred measures; their wings are like those of messengers, each has twelve, and they attend and accompany the sun, bearing heat and dew as it is commanded to them from God. ²Thus the sun revolves and goes, and rises under the heavens, and its course goes under the earth with the light of its rays unceasingly.

CHAPTER 13

¹Those men bore me away to the east, and placed me at the sun's gates, where the sun goes forth according to the regulation of the seasons, and the circuit of the months of the whole year, and the number of the hours, day and night. ²And I saw six gates open, each gate having sixty-one stadia and a quarter of one stadium, and I measured them accurately, and understood their size to be so great, through which the sun goes forth, and goes to the west, and is made even, and rises throughout all the months, and turns back again from the six gates according to the succession of the seasons; thus, the period of the whole year is finished after the returns of the four seasons.

CHAPTER 14

¹And again those men led me away to the western parts and showed me six great gates open corresponding to the eastern gates, opposite to where the sun sets, according to the number of the days—three hundred and sixty-five and a quarter. ²Thus again it goes down to the western gates, and draws away its light, the greatness of its brightness, under the earth; for since the crown of its shining is in Heaven with the LORD, and guarded by four hundred messengers, while the sun goes around [the] wheel under the earth, and stands seven great hours in night, and spends half its course under the earth, when it comes to the eastern approach in the eighth hour of the night, it brings its lights, and the crown of shining, and the sun flames forth more than fire.

CHAPTER 15

¹Then the elements of the sun, called phoenixes and chalkydri, break into song; therefore, every bird flutters with its wings, rejoicing at the giver of light, and they broke into song at the command of the LORD. ²The giver of light comes to give brightness to the whole world, and the morning guard takes shape, which is the rays of the sun, and the sun of the earth goes out, and receives its brightness to light up the whole face of the earth, and they showed me this calculation of the sun's going. ³And the gates which it enters, these are the great gates of the calculation of the hours of the year; for this reason, the sun is a great creation, whose circuit lasts twenty-eight years, and begins again from the beginning.

CHAPTER 16

¹Those men showed me the other course, that of the moon, twelve great gates, crowned from west to east, by which the moon goes in and out of the customary times. ²It goes in at the first gate to the western places of the sun, by the first gates with thirty-one days exactly, by the second gates with thirty-one days exactly, by the third with thirty days exactly, by the fourth with thirty days exactly, by the fifth with thirty-one days exactly, by the sixth with thirty-one days exactly, by the seventh with thirty days exactly, by the eighth with thirty-one days perfectly, by the ninth with thirty-one days exactly, by the tenth with thirty days perfectly, by the eleventh with thirty-one days exactly, by the twelfth with twenty-eight days exactly. ³And it goes through the western gates in the order and number of the eastern and accomplishes the three hundred and sixty-five and a quarter days of the solar year, while the lunar year has three hundred fifty-four, and there are twelve days of the solar circle lacking to it, which are the lunar epacts of the whole year. ⁴Thus, too, the great circle contains five hundred and thirty-two years. ⁵The quarter of a day is omitted for three years, the fourth fulfills it exactly. ⁶Therefore they are taken outside of the heavens for three years and are not added to the number of days, because they change the time of the years to two new months toward completion, to two others toward diminution. ⁷And when the western gates are finished, it returns and goes to the eastern, to the lights, and thus goes around the heavenly circles day and night, lower than all circles, swifter than the heavenly winds, and spirits, and elements, and messengers flying; each messenger has six wings. ⁸It has a sevenfold course in nineteen years.

CHAPTER 17

¹I saw armed soldiers in the midst of the heavens serving the LORD with drums and pipes, with unceasing voice, with sweet voice, with sweet and unceasing voice and various singing, which it is impossible to describe, and which astonishes every mind, so wonderful and marvelous is the singing of those messengers, and I was delighted listening to it.

CHAPTER 18

¹The men took me on to the fifth heaven and placed me [there], and there I saw many countless soldiers called Grigori, of human appearance, and their size was greater than that of great giants, and their faces [were] withered, and the silence of their mouths [was] perpetual, and there was no service on the fifth heaven, and I said to the men who were with me, ²"For what reason are these very withered, and their faces melancholy, and their mouths silent, and for what reason is there no service on this heaven?" ³And they said to me, "These are the Grigori, who with their prince Satanael rejected the Lord of light, and after them are those who are held in great darkness on the second heaven, and three of them went down on to earth from the LORD's throne, to the place Hermon, and broke through their vows on the shoulder of Mount Hermon, and saw how pleasing the daughters of men are, and took wives to themselves, and polluted the earth with their deeds, who in all times of their age made lawlessness and mixing, and giants are born, and marvelous large men, and great enmity. ⁴And therefore God judged them with great judgment, and they weep for their brothers, and they will be punished on [the] Great Day of the LORD." ⁵And I said to the Grigori, "I saw your brothers, and their works, and their great torments, and I prayed for them, but the LORD has condemned them to be under the earth until the existing heavens and earth will end forever." ⁶And I said, "For what reason do you wait, brothers, and do not serve before the LORD's face, and have not put your services before the LORD's face, lest you utterly anger your Lord?" ⁷And they listened to my admonition, and spoke to the four ranks in Heaven, and behold, as I stood with those two men, four trumpets trumpeted together with great voice, and the Grigori broke into song with one voice, and their voice went up before the LORD pitifully and movingly.

CHAPTER 19

¹And there those men took me and bore me up on to the sixth heaven, and I saw seven bands of messengers there, very bright and very glorious, and their faces shining more than the sun's shining—glistening, and there is no difference in their faces, or behaviour, or manner of dress; and these make the orders, and learn the goings of the stars, and the alteration of the moon, or revolution of the sun, and the good government of the world. ²And when they see evildoing, they make commandments and instruction, and sweet and loud singing, and all songs of praise. ³These are the chief-messengers who are above messengers, [who] measure all life in Heaven and on earth, and the messengers who are appointed over seasons and years, the messengers who are over rivers and sea, and who are over the fruits of the earth, and the messengers who are over every grass, giving food to all, to every living thing, and the messengers who write all the souls of men, and all their deeds, and their lives before the LORD's face; six phoenixes, and six cherubim, and six six-winged ones are in their midst, continually singing with one voice, and it is not possible to describe their singing, and they rejoice before the LORD at His footstool.

CHAPTER 20

¹And those two men lifted me up there on to the seventh heaven, and I saw a very great light there, and fiery troops of great chief-messengers, incorporeal forces, and dominions, orders and governments, cherubim and seraphim, thrones and many-eyed ones, nine regiments, the YAH-favored stations of light, and I became afraid, and began to tremble with great terror, and those men took me, and led me after them, and said to me, ²"Have courage, Enoch, do not fear," and

showed me the LORD from afar, sitting on His very high throne. For what is there on the tenth heaven, since the LORD dwells there? ³On the tenth heaven is God, in the Hebrew tongue He is called Aravat. ⁴And all the heavenly troops would come and stand on the ten steps according to their rank, and would bow down to the LORD, and would go to their places again in joy and bliss, singing songs in the boundless light with small and tender voices, gloriously serving Him.

CHAPTER 21

¹And the cherubim and seraphim [are] standing around the throne; the six-winged and many-eyed ones do not depart, standing before the LORD's face, doing His will, and they cover His whole throne, singing with a gentle voice before the LORD's face: "HOLY, HOLY, HOLY, LORD, Ruler of Hosts, the heavens and earth are full of Your glory." ²When I saw all these things, those men said to me, "Enoch, thus far it is commanded us to journey with you," and those men went away from me and thereon I did not see them. ³And I remained alone at the end of the seventh heaven, and became afraid, and fell on my face, and said to myself, "Woe is me! What has befallen me?" ⁴And the LORD sent one of His glorious ones, the chief-messenger Gabriel, and he said to me, "Have courage, Enoch, do not fear; arise before the LORD's face into eternity; arise, come with me." ⁵And I answered him, and said in myself: "My Lord, my soul has departed from me from terror and trembling, and I called to the men who led me up to this place, I relied on them, and it is with them I go before the LORD's face." ⁶And Gabriel caught me up, as a leaf caught up by the wind, and placed me before the LORD's face. ⁷And I saw the eighth heaven, which is called in the Hebrew tongue Muzaloth, changer of the seasons, of drought, and of wet, and of the twelve constellations of the circle of the expanse, which are above the seventh heaven. ⁸And I saw the ninth heaven, which is called in Hebrew Kuchavim, where the heavenly homes of the twelve constellations of the circle of the expanse are.

CHAPTER 22

¹On the tenth heaven, which is called Aravoth, I saw the appearance of the LORD's face, like iron made to glow in fire, and brought out, emitting sparks, and it burns. ²Thus in a moment of eternity I saw the LORD's face, but the LORD's face is ineffable, marvelous and very awful, and very, very terrible. ³And who am I to tell of the LORD's unspeakable being, and of His very wonderful face? And I cannot tell the quantity of His many instructions, and various voices—the LORD's throne is very great and not made with hands—nor the quantity of those standing around Him, troops of cherubim and seraphim, nor their unceasing singing, nor His immutable beauty. And who will tell of the ineffable greatness of His glory? ⁴And I fell prone and bowed down to the LORD, and the LORD said to me with His lips: ⁵"Have courage, Enoch, do not fear; arise and stand before My face into eternity." ⁶And the chief-general Michael lifted me up and led me to before the LORD's face. ⁷And the LORD said to His servants, trying them: "Let Enoch stand before My face into eternity," and the glorious ones bowed down to the LORD, and said, "Let Enoch go according to Your word." ⁸And the LORD said to Michael, "Go and take Enoch from out of his earthly garments, and anoint him with My sweet ointment, and put him into the garments of My glory." ⁹And Michael did thus, as the LORD told him. He anointed me, and dressed me, and the appearance of that ointment is more than the great light, and His ointment is like sweet dew, and its smell mild, shining like the sun's ray, and I looked at myself, and I was like one of His glorious ones. ¹⁰And the LORD summoned one of His chief-messengers, Pravuel by name, whose knowledge was quicker in wisdom than the other chief-messengers, who wrote all the deeds of the LORD; and the LORD said to Pravuel, "Bring out the scrolls from My storehouses, and a reed of quick-writing, and give it to Enoch, and deliver to him the choice and comforting scrolls out of your hand."

CHAPTER 23

¹And he was telling me all the works of Heaven, earth and sea, and all the elements, their passages and goings, and the thunderings of the thunders, the sun and moon, the goings and changes of the stars, the seasons, years, days, and hours, the risings of the wind, the numbers of the messengers, and the formation of their songs, and all human things, the tongue of every human song and life, the commandments, instructions, and sweet-voiced singings, and all things that it is fitting to learn. ²And Pravuel told me: "All the things that I have told you, we have written. Sit and write all the souls of mankind, however many of them are born, and the places prepared for them to eternity; for all souls are prepared to eternity, before the formation of the world." ³And [I wrote] all [this for] two periods of thirty days and thirty nights; and I wrote out all things exactly, and wrote three hundred and sixty-six scrolls.

CHAPTER 24

¹And the LORD summoned me, and said to me, "Enoch, sit down on My left with Gabriel." ²And I bowed down to the LORD, and the LORD spoke to me: "Enoch, beloved, all that you see, all things that are standing finished, I tell to you even before the very beginning, all that I created from non-being, and visible things from invisible. ³Hear, Enoch, and take in these words of Mine, for I have not told My secret to My messengers, and I have not told them their rise, nor My endless realm, nor have they understood My creating, which I tell you today. ⁴For before all things were visible, I alone used to go around in the invisible things, like the sun from east to west, and from west to east. ⁵But even the sun has peace in itself, while I found no peace, because I was creating all things, and I conceived the thought of placing foundations, and of creating visible creation."

CHAPTER 25

¹"I commanded in the very lowest parts that visible things should come down from invisible, and Adoil came down very great, and I beheld him, and behold, he had a belly of great light. ²And I said to him, Become undone, Adoil, and let the visible come out of you. ³And he came undone, and a great light came out. And I was in the midst of the great light, and as there is born light from light, there came forth a great age, and [it] showed all creation, which I had thought to create. ⁴And I saw that it was good. ⁵And I placed a throne for Myself, and took My seat on it, and said to the light, Go up higher and fix yourself high above the throne, and be a foundation to the highest things. ⁶And there is nothing else above the light, and then I bent up and looked up from My throne."

CHAPTER 26

¹"And I summoned the very lowest a second time, and said, Let Archas come forth hard, and he came forth hard from the invisible. ²And Archas came forth, hard, heavy, and very red. ³And I said, Be opened, Archas, and let there be born from you; and [when] he came undone, a very great and very dark age came forth, bearing the creation of all lower things, and I saw that it was good, and said to him, ⁴Go down below, and make yourself firm, and be a foundation for the lower things; and it happened, and he went down and fixed himself, and became the foundation for the lower things, and there is nothing else below the darkness."

CHAPTER 27

¹"And I commanded that there should be taken from light and darkness, and I said, Be thick, and it became thus, and I spread it out with the light, and it became water, and I spread it out over the darkness, below the light, ²and then I made the waters firm, that is to say, the bottomless, and I made a foundation of light around the water, and created seven circles from inside, and imaged the water like crystal, wet and dry, that is to say, like glass, and the circumcession of the waters and the other elements, ³and I showed each one of them its road, and the seven stars, each one of them in its heaven, that they go thus, and I saw that it was good. ⁴And I separated between light and between darkness, that is to say, in the midst of the water here and there, and I said to the light that it should be the day, and to the darkness, that it should be the night, and there was evening and there was morning the first day."

CHAPTER 28

¹"And then I made the heavenly circle firm, and made the lower water which is under the heavens collect itself together into one whole, and [made] the chaos become dry, and it became so. ²Out of the waves I created rock, hard and big, and from the rock I piled up the dry, and the dry I called Earth, and the midst of the earth I called Abyss, that is to say, the bottomless; I collected the sea in one place and bound it together with a yoke. ³And I said

to the sea, Behold, I give you your perpetual limits, and you will not break loose from your component parts. ⁴Thus I made the expanse steady. This day I called the first-created [(Sunday)]."

CHAPTER 29

¹"And for all the heavenly troops I imaged the image and essence of fire, and My eye looked at the very hard, firm rock, and from the gleam of My eye the lightning received its wonderful nature, which is both fire in water and water in fire, and one does not put out the other, nor does the one dry up the other; therefore, the lightning is brighter than the sun, softer than water, and firmer than hard rock. ²And from the rock I cut off a great fire, and from the fire I created the orders of the incorporeal ten troops of messengers, and their weapons are fiery and their raiment a burning flame, and I commanded that each one should stand in his order. ³And one from out of the order of messengers, having turned away with the order that was under him, conceived an impossible thought: to place his throne higher than the clouds above the earth, that he might become equal in rank to My power. ⁴And I threw him out from the height with his messengers, and he was continuously flying in the air above the bottomless [pit]."

CHAPTER 30

¹"On the third day I commanded the earth to make great and fruitful trees grow, and hills, and seed to sow, and I planted Paradise, and enclosed it, and placed flaming messengers as armed guardians, and thus I created renewal. ²Then there came evening, and there came morning—the fourth day [(Wednesday)]. ³On the fourth day I commanded that there should be great lights on the heavenly circles. ⁴On the first uppermost circle I placed the stars [and] Kronos [(Saturn)], and on the second Aphrodite [(Venus)], on the third Ares [(Mars)], on the fifth Zeus [(Jupiter)], on the sixth Hermes [(Mercury)], on the lesser seventh the moon, and adorned it with the lesser stars. ⁵And on the lower I placed the sun for the illumination of day, and the moon and stars for the illumination of night— ⁶the sun that it should go according to each constellation, twelve, and I appointed the succession of the months and their names and lives, their thunderings, and their hour-markings, how they should succeed. ⁷Then there came evening, and there came morning—the fifth day [(Thursday)]. ⁸On the fifth day I commanded the sea, that it should bring forth fishes, and feathered birds of many varieties, and all animals creeping over the earth, going forth over the earth on four legs, and soaring in the air, male and female, and every soul breathing the breath of life. ⁹And there came evening, and there came morning—the sixth day [(Friday)]. ¹⁰On the sixth day I commanded My wisdom to create man from seven consistencies: one, his flesh from the earth; two, his blood from the dew; three, his eyes from the sun; four, his bones from stone; five, his intelligence from the swiftness of the messengers and from cloud; six, his veins and his hair from the grass of the earth; seven, his soul from My breath and from the wind. ¹¹And I gave him seven natures: to the flesh hearing, the eyes for sight, to the soul smell, the veins for touch, the blood for taste, the bones for endurance, to the intelligence sweetness [(enjoyment)]. ¹²I conceived a cunning saying to say, I created man from invisible and from visible nature, of both are his death, and life, and image; he knows speech like some created thing, small in greatness and again great in smallness, and I placed him on earth, a second messenger, honorable, great and glorious, and I appointed him as ruler to rule on earth and to have My wisdom, and there was none like him of earth of all My existing creatures. ¹³And I appointed him a name from the four component parts: from east, from west, from south, from north; and I appointed four special stars for him, and I called his name Adam, and showed him the two ways, the light and the darkness, and I told him: ¹⁴This is good, and that bad, that I should learn whether he has love or hatred toward Me, that it might be clear which in his race love Me. ¹⁵For I have seen his nature, but he has not seen his own nature; therefore, through not seeing he will sin worse, and I said, After sin what is there but death? ¹⁶And I put sleep into him, and he fell asleep. And I took a rib from him and created him a wife, that death should come to him by his wife, and I took his last word and called her name mother, that is to say, Eva [(Eve)]."

CHAPTER 31

¹"Adam has life on earth, and I created a garden in Eden in the east, that he should observe the testament and keep the command. ²I made the heavens open to him, that he should see the messengers singing the song of victory, and the gloomless light. ³And he was continuously in paradise, and the Devil understood that I wanted to create another world, because Adam was lord on earth, to rule and control it. ⁴The Devil is the evil spirit of the lower places; as a fugitive from the heavens, he became Satan, as his name was Satanael; thus he became different from the messengers, but his nature did not change his intelligence as far as his understanding of righteous and sinful things. ⁵And he understood his condemnation and the sin which he had sinned before, therefore he conceived a thought against Adam, in such form he entered and seduced Eve, but did not touch Adam. ⁶But I cursed ignorance, but what I had blessed previously, those I did not curse: I did not curse man, nor the earth, nor other creatures, but man's evil fruit, and his works."

CHAPTER 32

¹"I said to him: Earth you are, and into the earth from where I took you, you will go, and I will not ruin you, but send you from where I took you. ²Then I can receive you again at My second coming. ³And I blessed all My creatures visible and invisible. And Adam was in paradise [for] five and a half hours. ⁴And I blessed the seventh day, which is the Sabbath [(Saturday)], on which He rested from all His works."

CHAPTER 33

¹"And I appointed the eighth day also, that the eighth day should be the first-created after my work, and that the first seven revolve in the form of the seven thousand [years], and that at the beginning of the eighth thousand there should be a time of not-counting—endless, with neither years, nor months, nor weeks, nor days, nor hours. ²And now, Enoch, all that I have told you, all that you have understood, all that you have seen of heavenly things, all that you have seen on earth, and all that I have written in scrolls by My great wisdom, all these things I have devised and created from the uppermost foundation to the lower and to the end, and there is no counselor nor inheritor to My creations. ³I am self-continuous, not made with hands, and without change. ⁴My thought is My counselor, My wisdom and My word are prepared, and My eyes observe how all things stand here and tremble with terror. ⁵If I turn away My face, then all things will be destroyed. ⁶And apply your mind, Enoch, and know Him who is speaking to you, and take there the scrolls which you yourself have written. ⁷And I give you Samuel and Raguel, who led you up, and the scrolls, and go down to earth, and tell your sons all that I have told you, and all that you have seen, from the lower heaven up to My throne, and all the troops. ⁸For I created all forces, and there is none that resists Me or that does not subject himself to Me. For all subject themselves to My monarchy, and labor for My sole rule. ⁹Give them the scrolls of the handwriting, and they will read them, and will know Me as the Creator of all things, and will understand how there is no other God but Me. ¹⁰And let them distribute the scrolls of your handwriting—children to children, generation to generation, nations to nations. ¹¹And I will give you, Enoch, My intercessor, the chief-general Michael, for the handwritings of your fathers Adam, Seth, Enos, Cainan, Mahalaleel, and your father Jared."

CHAPTER 34

¹"They have rejected My commandments and My yoke; worthless seed has come up, not fearing God, and they would not bow down to Me, but have begun to bow down to vain gods, and denied My unity, and have laden the whole earth with untruths, offenses, abominable lecheries, namely one with another, and all manner of other unclean wickedness, which are disgusting to relate. ²And therefore I will bring down a flood on the earth and will destroy all men, and the whole earth will crumble together into great darkness."

CHAPTER 35

¹"Behold, another generation will arise from their seed, much afterward, but of them many will be very insatiate. ²He who raises that

generation will reveal to them the scrolls of your handwriting, of your fathers, to them to whom he must point out the guardianship of the world, to the faithful men and workers of My pleasure, who do not acknowledge My Name in vain. ³And they will tell another generation, and those others, having read, will be glorified thereafter, more than the first."

CHAPTER 36

¹"Now, Enoch, I give you the term of thirty days to spend in your house, and tell your sons and all your household, that all may hear from My face what is told them by you, that they may read and understand how there is no other God but Me, ²and that they may always keep My commandments, and begin to read and take in the scrolls of your handwriting. ³And after thirty days I will send My messenger for you, and he will take you from earth and from your sons to Me."

CHAPTER 37

¹And the LORD called on one of the older messengers, terrible and menacing, and placed him by me, in appearance white as snow, and his hands like ice, having the appearance of great frost, and he froze my face, because I could not endure the terror of the LORD, just as it is not possible to endure a stove's fire, and the sun's heat, and the frost of the air. ²And the LORD said to me, "Enoch, if your face is not frozen here, no man will be able to behold your face."

CHAPTER 38

¹And the LORD said to those men who first led me up: "Let Enoch go down on to earth with you, and await him until the determined day." ²And they placed me on my bed by night. ³And Methuselah, expecting my coming, keeping watch by day and by night at my bed, was filled with awe when he heard my coming, and I told him, "Let all my household come together, that I tell them everything."

CHAPTER 39

¹Oh my children, my beloved ones, hear the admonition of your father, as much as is according to the LORD's will. ²I have been allowed to come to you today, and announce to you, not from my lips, but from the LORD's lips, all that is, and was, and all that is now, and all that will be until Judgment Day. ³For the LORD has let me come to you; you therefore hear the words of my lips, of a man made big for you, but I am one who has seen the LORD's face: like iron made to glow from fire, it sends forth sparks and burns. ⁴You now look on my eyes, the eyes of a man big with meaning for you, but I have seen the LORD's eyes, shining like the sun's rays and filling the eyes of man with awe. ⁵You see now, my children, the right hand of a man that helps you, but I have seen the LORD's right hand filling Heaven as He helped me. ⁶You see the compass of my work like your own, but I have seen the LORD's limitless and perfect compass, which has no end. ⁷You hear the words of my lips, as I heard the words of the LORD, like great thunder unceasingly with hurling of clouds. ⁸And now, my children, hear the discourses of the father of the earth, how fearful and awful it is to come before the face of the ruler of the earth, how much more terrible and awful it is to come before the face of the ruler of Heaven, the controller of quick and dead, and of the heavenly troops. Who can endure that endless pain?

CHAPTER 40

¹And now, my children, I know all things, for this is from the LORD's lips, and my eyes have seen this from beginning to end. ²I know all things and have written all things into scrolls: the heavens, and their end, and their plenitude, and all the armies and their marchings. ³I have measured and described the stars, the great countless multitude of them. ⁴What man has seen their revolutions and their entrances? For not even the messengers see their number, while I have written all their names. ⁵And I measured the sun's circle, and measured its rays, [and] counted the hours; I also wrote down all things that go over the earth; I have written the things that are nourished, and all seed sown and unsown, which the earth produces, and all plants, and every grass and every flower, and their sweet smells, and their names, and the dwelling-places of the clouds, and their composition, and their wings, and how they bear rain and raindrops. ⁶And I investigated all things and wrote the road of the thunder and of the lightning, and they showed me the keys and their guardians, their rise, the way they go; it is let out gently in measure by a chain, lest by a heavy chain and violence it hurls the angry clouds down and destroys all things on earth. ⁷I wrote the treasure-houses of the snow, and the storehouses of the cold and the frosty airs, and I observed their season's key-holder; he fills the clouds with them and does not exhaust the treasure-houses. ⁸And I wrote the resting-places of the winds and observed and saw how their key-holders bear weighing-scales and measures; first, they put them in one weighing-scale, then in the other, the weights, and they let them out according to measure cunningly over the whole earth, lest by heavy breathing they make the earth to rock. ⁹And I measured out the whole earth, its mountains, and all hills, fields, trees, stones, rivers; I wrote down all existing things: the height from earth to the seventh heaven, and downwards to the very lowest [part of] Hades, and the judgment-place, and the very great, open, and weeping depth. ¹⁰And I saw how the prisoners are in pain, expecting the limitless judgment. ¹¹And I wrote down all those being judged by the judge, and all their judgment, and sentences, and all their works.

CHAPTER 41

¹And I saw all forefathers from all time with Adam and Eve, and I sighed, and broke into tears, and said of the ruin of their dishonor: ²"Woe to me for my infirmity and for that of my forefathers!" And I thought in my heart and said, ³"Blessed is the man who has not been born or who has been born and will not sin before the LORD's face, that he does not come into this place, nor bears the yoke of this place."

CHAPTER 42

¹I saw the key-holders and guards of the gates of Hades standing like great serpents, and their faces like extinguishing lamps, and their eyes of fire, their sharp teeth, and I saw all the LORD's works, how they are right, while some [of] the works of man are good, and others bad, and in their works are known those who lie evilly.

CHAPTER 43

¹I, my children, measured and wrote out every work, and every measure, and every righteous judgment. ²As one year is more honorable than another, so is one man more honorable than another: some for great possessions, some for wisdom of heart, some for particular intellect, some for cunning, one for silence of lip, another for cleanliness, one for strength, another for comeliness, one for youth, another for sharp wit, one for shape of body, another for sensibility. Let it be heard everywhere that there is none better than he who fears God; he will be more glorious in [the] time to come.

CHAPTER 44

¹The LORD, having created man with His hands, in the likeness of His own face, the LORD made him small and great. ²Whoever reviles the ruler's face, and abhors the LORD's face, has despised the LORD's face, and he who vents anger on any man without injury, the LORD's great anger will cut him down; he who spits on the face of man reproachfully will be cut down at the LORD's Great Judgment. ³Blessed is the man who does not direct his heart with malice against any man, and helps the injured and condemned, and raises the broken down, and will do charity to the needy, ⁴because on the Day of the Great Judgment every weight, every measure, and every makeweight will be as in the market, that is to say, they are hung on scales and stand in the market, and everyone will learn his own measure, and according to his measure will take his reward.

CHAPTER 45

¹Whoever hastens to make offerings before the LORD's face, the LORD, for His part, will hasten that offering by granting of his work. ²But whoever increases his lamp before the LORD's face and does not make true judgment, the LORD will not increase his treasure in the realm of the highest. ³When the LORD demands bread, or candles, or the flesh of beasts, or any other sacrifice, then that is nothing; but God demands pure hearts, and with all that, only tests the heart of man.

CHAPTER 46

¹Hear, my people, and take in the words of my lips. ²If anyone brings any gifts to an earthly ruler, and has disloyal thoughts in his heart,

and the ruler know this, will he not be angry with him, and will he not refuse his gifts, and will he not give him over to judgment? ³Or if one man makes himself appear good to another by deceit of tongue, but has evil in his heart, then will the other not understand the treachery of his heart, and himself be condemned, since his untruth was plain to all? ⁴And when the LORD will send a great light, then there will be judgment for the just and the unjust, and no one will escape notice there.

CHAPTER 47

¹And now, my children, lay thought on your hearts; mark well the words of your father, which have all come to you from the LORD's lips. ²Take these scrolls of your father's handwriting and read them. ³For the scrolls are many, and in them you will learn all the LORD's works, all that has been from the beginning of creation, and will be until the end of time. ⁴And if you will observe my handwriting, you will not sin against the LORD, because there is no other except the LORD, neither in Heaven, nor in earth, nor in the very lowest places, nor in one foundation. ⁵The LORD has placed the foundations in the unknown and has spread forth heavens visible and invisible; He fixed the earth on the waters and created countless creatures. ⁶And who has counted the water and the foundation of the unfixed, or the dust of the earth, or the sand of the sea, or the drops of the rain, or the morning dew, or the wind's breathings? Who has filled earth, and sea, and the indissoluble winter? ⁷"I cut the stars out of fire, and decorated Heaven, and put it in their midst."

CHAPTER 48

¹So the sun goes along the seven heavenly circles, which are the appointment of one hundred and eighty-two thrones that it goes down on a short day, and again one hundred and eighty-two that it goes down on a big day; and he has two thrones on which he rests, revolving here and there above the thrones of the months, from the seventeenth day of the month Sivan it goes down to the month Thevan, [and] from the seventeenth of Thevan it goes up. ²And thus it goes close to the earth; then the earth is glad and makes its fruits grow, and when it goes away, then the earth is sad, and trees and all fruits have no florescence. ³All this He measured with a good measurement of hours, and fixed a measure by His wisdom, of the visible and the invisible. ⁴From the invisible He made all things visible, Himself being invisible. ⁵Thus I make known to you, my children, and distribute the scrolls to your children, into all your generations, and among the nations who will have the sense to fear God: let them receive them, and may they come to love them more than any food or earthly sweets, and read them, and apply themselves to them. ⁶And those who do not understand the LORD, who do not fear God, who do not accept, but reject, who do not receive the scrolls—a terrible judgment awaits these. ⁷Blessed is the man who will bear their yoke and will drag them along, for he will be released on the Day of the Great Judgment.

CHAPTER 49

¹I swear to you, my children, but I swear not by any oath, neither by Heaven nor by earth, nor by any other creature which God created. ²The LORD said, "There is no curse [[or oath]] in Me, nor injustice, but truth." ³If there is no truth in men, let them swear by the words, Yes, yes, or else, No, no. ⁴And I swear to you, yes, yes, that there has been no man in his mother's womb, except which [was] already [prepared] beforehand, even to each one there is a place prepared for the repose of that soul, and a measure fixed how much it is intended that a man be tried in this world. ⁵Yes, children, do not deceive yourselves, for a place has been previously prepared for every soul of man.

CHAPTER 50

¹I have put every man's work in writing, and none born on earth can remain hidden nor his works remain concealed. I see all things. ²Now therefore, my children, spend the number of your days in patience and meekness, so that you inherit endless life. ³Endure every wound, every injury, every evil word and attack for the sake of the LORD. ⁵If retaliations befall you, do not return them either to neighbor or enemy, because the LORD will return them for you and be your avenger on the Day of Great Judgment, that there is no avenging here among men. ⁶Whoever of you spends gold or silver for his brother's sake, he will receive ample treasure in the world to come. ⁷Harm neither widows, nor orphans, nor strangers, lest God's wrath come on you.

CHAPTER 51

¹Stretch out your hands to the poor according to your strength. ²Do not hide your silver in the earth. ³Help the faithful man in affliction, and affliction will not find you in the time of your trouble. ⁴And every grievous and cruel yoke that comes on you—bear all for the sake of the LORD, and thus you will find your reward in the Day of Judgment. ⁵It is good to go morning, midday, and evening into the LORD's dwelling, for the glory of your Creator, ⁶because every breathing thing glorifies Him, and every creature, visible and invisible, returns Him praise.

CHAPTER 52

¹Blessed is the man who opens his lips in praise of [the] God of Hosts and praises the LORD with his heart. ²Cursed [is] every man who opens his lips for the bringing into contempt and slander of his neighbor, because he brings God into contempt. ³Blessed is he who opens his lips blessing and praising God. ⁴Cursed is he before the LORD, all the days of his life, who opens his lips to curse and abuse. ⁵Blessed is he who blesses all the LORD's works. ⁶Cursed is he who brings the LORD's creation into contempt. ⁷Blessed is he who looks down and raises the fallen. ⁸Cursed is he who looks to and is eager for the destruction of what is not his. ⁹Blessed is he who keeps the foundations of his fathers made firm from the beginning. ¹⁰Cursed is he who perverts the decrees of his forefathers. ¹¹Blessed is he who imparts peace and love. ¹²Cursed is he who disturbs those that love their neighbors. ¹³Blessed is he who speaks with a humble tongue and heart to all. ¹⁴Cursed is he who speaks peace with his tongue, while in his heart there is no peace but a sword. ¹⁵For all these things will be laid bare in the weighing-scales and in the scrolls on the Day of the Great Judgment.

CHAPTER 53

¹And now, my children, do not say, "Our father is standing before God and is praying for our sins," for there is no helper there of any man who has sinned. ²You see how I wrote all works of every man, before his creation, all that is done among all men for all time, and none can tell or relate my handwriting, because the LORD sees all imaginings of man, how they are vain, where they lie in the treasure-houses of the heart. ³And now, my children, mark well all the words of your father that I tell you, lest you regret, saying, "Why did our father not tell us?"

CHAPTER 54

¹At that time, not understanding this, let these scrolls which I have given you be for an inheritance of your peace. ²Hand them to all who want them, and instruct them, that they may see the LORD's very great and marvelous works.

CHAPTER 55

¹My children, behold, the day of my term and time have approached. ²For the messengers who will go with me are standing before me and urge me to my departure from you; they are standing here on earth, awaiting what has been told them. ³For tomorrow I will go up on to Heaven, to the uppermost Jerusalem—to my continuous inheritance. ⁴Therefore I command you: before the LORD's face do all His good pleasure.

CHAPTER 56

¹Methuselah, having answered his father Enoch, said, "What is agreeable to your eyes, father, that I may make before your face, that you may bless our dwellings, and your sons, and that your people may be made glorious through you, and then that you may thus depart as the LORD said?" ²Enoch answered to his son Methuselah and said, "Hear, child: from the time when the LORD anointed me with the ointment of His glory, there has been no food in me, and my soul does not remember earthly enjoyment, neither do I want anything earthly."

CHAPTER 57

¹"My child Methuselah, summon all your brothers, and all your household, and the elders of the people, that I may talk to them and depart, as is planned for me." ²And

Methuselah hurried, and summoned his brothers Regim, Riman, Uchan, Chermion, Gaidad, and all the elders of the people before the face of his father Enoch; and he blessed them, and said to them:

CHAPTER 58

¹Listen to me, my children, today. ²In those days when the LORD came down on to earth for Adam's sake, and visited all His creatures which He created Himself, after all these He created Adam, and the LORD called all the beasts of the earth, all the reptiles, and all the birds that soar in the air, and brought them all before the face of our father Adam. ³And Adam gave the names to all things living on earth. ⁴And the LORD appointed him ruler over all, and subjected to him all things under his hands, and made them dumb and made them dull that they can be commanded of man, and be in subjection and obedience to him. ⁵Thus the LORD also created every man lord over all His possessions. ⁶The LORD will not judge a single soul of beast for man's sake, but adjudicates the souls of men to their beasts in this world, for men have a special place. ⁷And as every soul of man is according to number, similarly beasts will not perish, nor all souls of beasts which the LORD created, until the Great Judgment, and they will accuse man if he fed them ill.

CHAPTER 59

¹Whoever defiles the soul of beasts, defiles his own soul. ²For man brings clean animals to make sacrifice for sin, that he may have cure of his soul. ³And if they bring for sacrifice clean animals, and birds, man has a cure—he cures his soul. ⁴All is given to you for food; bind it by the four feet, that is to make good the cure—he cures his soul. ⁵But whoever kills beast without wounds, kills his own souls and defiles his own flesh. ⁶And he who does any beast any injury whatever, in secret, it is evil practice, and he defiles his own soul.

CHAPTER 60

¹He who works the killing of a man's soul, kills his own soul, and kills his own body, and there is no cure for him for all time. ²He who puts a man in any snare, will stick in it himself, and there is no cure for him for all time. ³He who puts a man in any vessel, his retribution will not be wanting at the Great Judgment for all time. ⁴He who works crookedly or speaks evil against any soul will not make justice for himself for all time.

CHAPTER 61

¹And now, my children, keep your hearts from every injustice, which the LORD hates. Just as a man asks something for his own soul from God, so let him do to every living soul, because I know all things, how in the great time to come there is much inheritance prepared for men, good for the good, and bad for the bad, without number—many. ²Blessed are those who enter the good houses, for in the bad houses there is no peace nor return from them. ³Hear, my children, small and great: when man puts a good thought in his heart [and] brings gifts from his labors before the LORD's face, but his hands did not make them, then the LORD will turn His face away from the labor of his hand, and that man cannot find the labor of his hands. ⁴And if his hands made it, but his heart murmurs, and his heart does not cease making murmur unceasingly, he does not have any advantage.

CHAPTER 62

¹Blessed is the man who in his patience brings his gifts with faith before the LORD's face, because he will find forgiveness of sins. ²But if he takes back his words before the time, there is no conversion for him; and if the time passes and he does not do what is promised of his own will, there is no conversion after death. ³Because every work which man does before the time is all deceit before men and sin before God.

CHAPTER 63

¹When man clothes the naked and fills the hungry, he will find reward from God. ²But if his heart murmurs, he commits a double evil: ruin of himself and of that which he gives; and for him there will be no finding of reward on account of that. ³And if his own heart is filled with his food and his own flesh clothed with his own clothing, he commits contempt, and will forfeit all his endurance of poverty, and will not find reward of his good deeds. ⁴Every proud and grandiose man, and every false speech clothed in untruth, is hateful to the LORD; it will be cut with the blade of the sword of death, and thrown into the fire, and will burn for all time.

CHAPTER 64

¹When Enoch had spoken these words to his sons, all people far and near heard how the LORD was calling Enoch. They took counsel together: ²"Let us go and kiss Enoch," and two thousand men came together and came to the place [called] Achuzan where Enoch and his sons were. ³And the elders of the people, the whole assembly, came and bowed down and began to kiss Enoch and said to him: ⁴"Our father Enoch, may you be blessed of the LORD, the perpetual ruler, and now bless your sons and all the people, that we may be glorified today before your face. ⁵For you will be glorified before the LORD's face for all time, since the LORD chose you, rather than all men on earth, and designated you writer of all His creation, visible and invisible, and redeemed of the sins of man, and helper of your household."

CHAPTER 65

¹And Enoch answered all his people, saying, "Hear, my children: before all creatures were created, the LORD created the visible and invisible things. ²And as much time as there was and went past, understand that after all that, He created man in the likeness of His own form, and put into him eyes to see, and ears to hear, and heart to reflect, and intellect with which to deliberate. ³And the LORD saw all man's works, and created all His creatures, and divided time: from time He fixed the years, and from the years He appointed the months, and from the months He appointed the days, and of days He appointed seven, ⁴and in those He appointed the hours, [and] measured them out exactly, that man might reflect on time and count years, months, and hours, their alternation, beginning, and end, and that he might count his own life, from the beginning until death, and reflect on his sin, and write his work, [whether] bad and good, because no work is hidden before the LORD, that every man might know his works, and never transgress all His commandments, and keep my handwriting from generation to generation. ⁵When all creation visible and invisible, as the LORD created it, will end, then every man goes to the Great Judgment, and then all time will perish, and the years, and from then on there will be neither months, nor days, nor hours; they will adhere together and will not be counted. ⁶There will be one age, and all the righteous who will escape the LORD's Great Judgment will be collected in the Great Age; the Great Age will begin for the righteous, and they will live continuously, and then there will also be among them neither labor, nor sickness, nor humiliation, nor anxiety, nor need, nor brutality, nor night, nor darkness, but great light. ⁷And they will have a great indestructible wall, and a bright and incorruptible paradise, for all corruptible things will pass away, and there will be continuous life."

CHAPTER 66

¹And now, my children, keep your souls from all injustice, such as the LORD hates. ²Walk before His face with terror and trembling and serve Him alone. ³Bow down to the true God, not to dumb idols, but bow down to His similitude, and bring all just offerings before the LORD's face. The LORD hates what is unjust. ⁴For the LORD sees all things; when man takes thought in his heart, then He counsels the intellects, and every thought is always before the LORD who made the earth firm and put all creatures on it. ⁵If you look to Heaven, the LORD is there; if you take thought of the sea's deep and all under the earth, the LORD is there. ⁶For the LORD created all things. Do not bow down to things made by man, leaving the LORD of all creation, because no work can remain hidden before the LORD's face. ⁷Walk, my children, in long-suffering, in meekness, honesty, in provocation, in grief, in faith, and in truth, in reliance on promises, in sickness, in abuse, in wounds, in temptation, in nakedness, in privation, loving one another, until you go out from this age of ills, that you become inheritors of endless time. ⁸Blessed are the just who will escape the Great Judgment, for they will shine forth more than the sun sevenfold, for in this world the seventh part is taken off from all: light, darkness, food, enjoyment, sorrow, paradise, torture, fire, frost, and other things; he put all down in writing, that you might read and understand.

CHAPTER 18

¹R. Ishmael said: Metatron, the messenger, the Prince of the Presence, the glory of all Heaven, said to me: "'The messengers of the first heaven, whenever they see their prince, they dismount from their horses and fall on their faces. And the prince of the first heaven, when he sees the prince of the second heaven, removes, dismounts, he sees the prince of the second heaven. And the prince of the second heaven, when he sees the prince of the third heaven, he removes the crown of glory from his head and falls on his face. And the prince of the third heaven, when he sees the prince of the fourth heaven, he removes the crown of glory from his head and falls on his face. And the prince of the fourth heaven, when he sees the prince of the fifth heaven, he removes the crown of glory from his head and falls on his face. And the prince of the fifth heaven, when he sees the prince of the sixth heaven, he removes the crown of glory from his head and falls on his face. And the prince of the sixth heaven, when he sees the prince of the seventh heaven, he removes the crown of glory from his head and falls on his face. ²And he sees the seventy-two princes of kingdoms, he sees the seventy-two princes of kingdoms in the Araboth Raqia in the highest, they remove the royal crown from their heads and fall on their faces. And the doorkeepers of the First Hall, when they see the doorkeepers of the Second Hall, they remove the crown of glory from their head and fall on their faces. And the doorkeepers of the Second Hall, when they see the doorkeepers of the Third Hall, they remove the crown of glory from their head and fall on their faces. And the doorkeepers of the Third Hall, when they see the doorkeepers of the Fourth Hall, they remove the crown of glory from their head and fall on their faces. And the doorkeepers of the Fourth Hall, when they see the doorkeepers of the Fifth Hall, when they see the doorkeepers of the Fifth Hall, they remove the crown of glory from their head and fall on their faces. And the doorkeepers of the Fifth Hall, when they see the doorkeepers of the Sixth Hall, they remove the crown of glory from their head and fall on their faces. And the doorkeepers of the Sixth Hall, when they see the doorkeepers of the Seventh Hall, they remove the crown of glory from their head and fall on their faces. ⁴And the doorkeepers of the Seventh Hall, when they see the four great princes, the honored ones, who are appointed over the four camps of Shekinah, they remove the crowns of glory from their head and fall on their faces. ⁵And the four great princes, when they see Tag'as, the prince, great and honored of Heaven, they remove the crown of glory from their head and fall on their faces. ⁶And Tag'as, the great and honored prince, when he sees Baratiel, the great prince of three fingers in the height of Araboth, the highest Heaven, he removes the crown of glory from his head and falls on his face. ⁷And Baratiel, the great prince, when he sees Hamon, the great prince, the fearful and honored, pleasant and terrible one who makes all the children of Heaven to tremble, when the time draws near for the saying of the Thrice Holy—as it is written: At the noise of the tumult the peoples are fled; at the lifting up of Yourself the nations are scattered—he removes the crown of glory from his head and falls on his face. ⁸And Hamon, the great prince, when he sees Tutresiel, the great prince, he removes the crown of glory from his head and falls on his face. ⁹And Tutresiel-YHWH, the great prince, when he sees Atrugiel, the great prince, he removes the crown of glory from his head and falls on his face. ¹⁰And Atrugiel, the great prince, when he sees Na'aririel-YHWH, the great prince, he removes the crown of glory from his head and falls on his face. ¹¹And Na'aririel-YHWH, the great prince, when he sees Sasnigiel, the great prince, he removes the crown of glory from his head and falls on his face. ¹²And Sasnigiel-YHWH, when he sees the great prince, he removes

660

the crown of glory from his head and falls on his face. ¹³And Zazriel-YHWH, the prince, when he sees Geburatiel-YHWH, the prince, he removes the crown of glory from his head and falls on his face. ¹⁴And Geburatiel-YHWH, the prince, when he sees 'Araphiel-YHWH, the prince, he removes the crown of glory from his head and falls on his face. ¹⁵And 'Araphiel-YHWH, the prince, when he sees Ashruylu, the prince, who presides in all the sessions of children of Heaven, he removes the crown of glory from his head and falls on his face. ¹⁶And Ashruylu-YHWH, the prince, when he sees Gallisur-YHWH, the prince, who reveals all the secrets of the Law, he removes the crown of glory from his head and falls on his face. ¹⁷And Gallisur-YHWH, the prince, when he sees Zakzakiel-YHWH, the prince who is appointed to write down the merits of Israel on the Throne of Glory, he removes the crown of glory from his head and falls on his face. ¹⁸And Zakzakiel-YHWH, the great prince, when he sees 'Anaphiel-YHWH, the prince who keeps the keys of the heavenly halls, he removes the crown of glory from his head and falls on his face. Why is he called by the name of 'Anaphiel? Because the bough of his honor and majesty and his own, and his splendor and his brilliance cover all the chambers of Araboth Raqia on high even as the Maker of the world overshadows them, just as it is written with regard to the Maker of the world: His glory covered the heavens, and the earth was full of His praise—even so do the honor and majesty of 'Anaphiel cover all the glories of Araboth the highest. ¹⁹And when he sees Sother 'Ashiel-YHWH, the prince, the great, fearful, and honored one, he removes the crown of glory from his face. Why is he called Sother 'Ashiel? Because he is appointed over the four heads of the fiery river over against the Throne of Glory; and every single prince who goes out or enters before the Shekinah, only goes out or enters by his permission. For the seals of the fiery river are entrusted to him. And furthermore, his height is seven thousand myriads of parasangs. And he stirs up the fire of the river; and he goes out and enters before the Shekinah to expound what is written concerning the inhabitants of the world, according as it is written: The judgment was set, and the scrolls were opened. ²⁰And Sother 'Ashiel, the prince, when he sees Shoqed Chozi, the great prince, the mighty, terrible and honored one, he removes the crown of glory from his head and falls on his face. And why is he called Shoqed Chozi? Because he weighs all the merits of man in a balance in the presence of the Holy One, blessed is He. ²¹And when he sees Zehanpuryu-YHWH, the great prince, the mighty and terrible one, honored, glorified, and feared in all the heavenly household, he removes the crown of glory from his head and falls on his face. Why is he called Zehanpuryu? Because he rebukes the fiery river and pushes it back to its place. ²²And when he sees Azbuga-YHWH, the great prince, glorified, revered, honored, adorned, wonderful, exalted, beloved, and feared among all the

CHAPTER 11

¹R. Ishmael said: Metatron, the messenger, the Prince of the Presence, said to me: "Henceforth, the Holy One, blessed is He, revealed to me all the mysteries of instruction, and all the secrets of wisdom, and all the depths of the Perfect Law; and all living beings' thoughts of heart, and all the secrets of the universe, and all the secrets of creation were revealed to me even as they are revealed to the Maker of creation. ²And I watched intently to behold the secrets of the depth and the wonderful mystery. Before a man thought, I knew what was in his thought. ³And there is no thing above on high nor below in the deep hidden from me."

CHAPTER 12

¹R. Ishmael said: Metatron, the Prince of the Presence, said to me: "By reason of the love with which the Holy One, blessed is He, loved me more than all the children of Heaven, He made me a garment of glory on which were fixed all kinds of lights, and He clad me in it. ²And He made me a robe of honor on which were fixed all kinds of beauty, splendor, brilliance, and majesty. ³And He made me a royal crown in which were fixed forty-nine costly stones like to the light of the globe of the sun. ⁴For its splendor went forth in the four quarters of the Arabboth Raqia', and in through the seven heavens, and in the four quarters of the world. And he put it on my head. ⁵And He called me THE LESSER YHWH in the presence of all His heavenly household; as it is written: For My Name is in him."

CHAPTER 13

¹R. Ishmael said: Metatron, the messenger, the Prince of the Presence, the glory of all heavens, said to me: "Because of the great love and mercy with which the Holy One, blessed is He, loved and cherished me more than all the children of Heaven, He wrote with His finger with a flaming style on the crown on my head the letters by which the heavens and earth, the seas and rivers, the mountains and hills, the planets and constellations, the lightnings, winds, earthquakes and voices, the snow and hail, the storm-wind and the tempest were created—the letters by which all the needs of the world and all the orders of creation were created. ²And every single letter sent forth time after time as it were lightnings, time after time as it were torches, time after time as it were flames, time after time as if

were flames of fire, time after time rays like as the rising of the sun, and the moon and the planets."

CHAPTER 14

¹R. Ishmael said: Metatron, the messenger, the Prince of the Presence, said to me: "When the Holy One, blessed is He, put this crown on my head, [then] all the princes of kingdoms who are in the height of 'Arabboth Raqia' and all the hosts of every heaven trembled before me; and even the princes of the elim, the princes of the er'elim, and the princes of the taphsarim, who are greater than all the ministering messengers who minister before the Throne of Glory, feared, and trembled before me when they beheld me. ²Even Sammael, the prince of the accusers, who is greater than all the princes of kingdoms on high, feared and trembled before me. ³And even the messenger of fire, and the messenger of hail, and the messenger of the wind, and the messenger of the lightning, and the messenger of anger, and the messenger of the thunder, and the messenger of the snow, and the messenger of the rain, and the messenger of the day, and the messenger of the night, and the messenger of the sun, and the messenger of the moon, and the messenger of the planets, and the messenger of the constellations who rule the world under their hands, feared, and trembled, and were frightened before me when they beheld me. ⁴These are the names of the rulers of the world: Gabriel, the messenger of the fire, Baradiel, the messenger of the hail, Ruchiel who is appointed over the wind, Baragiel who is appointed over the lightnings, Za'amiel who is appointed over the vehemence, Ziqiel who is appointed over the sparks, Zi'iel who is appointed over the commotion, Za'aphiel who is appointed over the storm-wind, Ra'amiel who is appointed over the thunders, Ra'ashiel who is appointed over the earthquake, Shalgiel who is appointed over the snow, Matariel who is appointed over the rain, Shimshiel who is appointed over the day, Lailiel who is appointed over the night, Galgalliel who is appointed over the globe of the sun, 'Ophanniel who is appointed over the globe of the moon, Kokbiel who is appointed over the planets, [and] Rahatiel who is appointed over the constellations. ⁵And they all fell prostrate when they saw me. And they were not able to behold me because of the majestic glory and beauty of the appearance of the shining light of the crown of glory on my head."

CHAPTER 15

¹R. Ishmael said: Metatron, the messenger, the Prince of the Presence, the glory of all heavens, said to me: "As soon as the Holy One, blessed is He, took me in His service to attend the Throne of Glory, and the wheels of the Merkaba, and the needs of Shekinah, my flesh was immediately changed into flames, my sinews into flaming fire, my bones into coals of burning juniper, the light of my eyelids into [the] splendor of lightnings, my eyeballs into firebrands, the hair of my head into hot flames,

all my limbs into wings of burning fire, and the whole of my body into glowing fire. ²And on my right were divisions of fiery flames, on my left firebrands were burning around me, storm-wind and tempest were blowing, and in front of me and behind me was roaring of thunder with earthquake."

CHAPTER 16

¹R. Ishmael said: Metatron, the messenger, the Prince of the Presence, the glory of all Heaven, said to me: "At first I was sitting on a great throne at the door of the Seventh Hall, and I was judging all the children of Heaven, the household on high by authority of the Holy One, blessed is He. And I divided Greatness, Kingship, Dignity, Rulership, Honor and Praise, and Diadem and Crown of Glory to all the princes of kingdoms, while I was presiding in the Celestial Court, and the princes of kingdoms were standing before me, on my right and on my left by authority of the Holy One, blessed is He. ²But when Acher came to behold the vision of the Merkaba and fixed his eyes on me, he feared and trembled before me and his soul was frightened even to departing from him, because of [the] fear, horror, and dread of me when he beheld me sitting on a throne like a king with all the ministering messengers standing by me as my servants and all the princes of kingdoms adorned with crowns surrounding me. ³In that moment he opened his mouth and said: Indeed, there are two Divine Powers in Heaven! ⁴Immediately Bath Qol, the Divine Voice, went forth from Heaven from before the Shekinah and said: Return, you backsliding children, except Acher! ⁵Then Aniyel, the prince—the honored, glorified, beloved, wonderful, revered, and fearful one—came in commission from the Holy One, blessed is He, and gave me sixty strokes with lashes of fire and made me stand on my feet."

CHAPTER 17

¹R. Ishmael said: Metatron, the messenger, the Prince of the Presence, the glory of all heavens, said to me: "There are seven princes—the great, beautiful, revered, wonderful, and honored ones—who are appointed over the seven heavens. And they are these: Michael, and Gabriel, and Shatqiel, and Baradiel, and Shachaqiel, and Baraqiel, and Sidriel. ²And each of them is the prince of the host of one heaven. And each one of them is accompanied by four hundred ninety-six thousand myriads of ministering messengers. ³Michael, the great prince, is appointed over the seventh heaven, the highest one, which is in the 'Arabboth. Gabriel, the prince of the host, is appointed over the sixth heaven which is in Makon. Shataqiel, prince of the host, is appointed over the fifth heaven which is in Ma'on. Shahaqi'el, prince of the host, is appointed over the fourth heaven which is in Zebul. Badari'el, prince of the host, is appointed over the third heaven which is in Shehaqim. Baraki'el, prince of the host, is appointed over the second heaven which is in the height of Merom. Pazriel, prince of the host, is appointed over the first

they saw me, they said before Him: Lord of the Universe, what is this one that he should ascend to the height of heights? Is he not one from among the sons of the sons of those who perished in the days of the Flood? What is he doing in the Raqia'? ⁸Again, the Holy One, blessed is He, answered and said to them: What are you, that you enter and speak in my presence? I delight in this one more than in all of you, and hence he will be a prince and a ruler over you in the high heavens. ⁹Immediately all stood up and went out to meet me, prostrated themselves before me, and said, Happy are you and happy is your father, for your Creator favors you. ¹⁰And because I am small and a youth among them in days, months, and years, therefore they call me Youth."

CHAPTER 5

¹R. Ishmael said: Metatron, the Prince of the Presence, said to me: "From the day when the Holy One, blessed is He, expelled the first Adam from the Garden of Eden and onwards, Shekinah was dwelling on a cherub under the Tree of Life. ²And the ministering messengers were gathering together and going down from Heaven in parties, from the Raqia in companies, and from the heavens in camps to do His will in the whole world. ³And the first man and his generation were sitting outside the gate of the Garden to behold the radiant appearance of the Shekinah. ⁴For the splendor of the Shekinah traversed the world from one end to the other with a splendor three hundred sixty-five thousand times that of the globe of the sun. And everyone who made use of the splendor of the Shekinah, on him no flies and no gnats rested, neither was he sick nor did he suffer any pain. No demons got power over him, neither were they able to injure him. ⁵When the Holy One, blessed is He, went out and went in from the Garden to Eden, from Eden to the Garden, from the Garden to Raqia, and from Raqia to the Garden of Eden, then all and everyone beheld the splendor of His Shekinah and they were not injured, ⁶until the time of the generation of Enosh who was the head of all idol worshipers of the world. ⁷And what did the generation of Enosh do? They went from one end of the world to the other, and each one brought silver, gold, precious stones, and pearls in heaps like to mountains and hills, making idols out of them throughout all the world. And they erected the idols in every quarter of the world: the size of each idol was one thousand parasangs. ⁸And they brought down the sun, the moon, planets, and constellations, and placed them before the idols on their right hand and on their left, to attend them even as they attend the Holy One, blessed is He, as it is written: And all the host of Heaven were standing by Him on His right hand and on His left. ⁹What power was in them that they were able to bring them down? They would not have been able to bring them down but for 'Uzza, 'Azza, and 'Azzielis who taught them sorceries whereby they brought them down and made use of them. ¹⁰In that time the ministering messengers brought charges against them before the Holy One, blessed is He, saying before Him: Master of the World! ¹¹What have You to do with the children of men? As it is written: What is man that You are mindful of him? MAH ADAM is not written here, but MAH ENOSH, for he is the head of the idol worshipers. Why have You left the highest of the high heavens, which are filled with the majesty of Your glory and are high, uplifted, and exalted, and the high and exalted Throne in the Raqia' Araboth on high, and have gone and dwell with the children of men who worship idols and equate You to the idols? ¹²Now You are on earth and the idols likewise. What have You to do with the inhabitants of the earth who worship idols? ¹³Immediately the Holy One, blessed is He, lifted up His Shekinah from the earth, from their midst. ¹⁴In that moment the ministering messengers came, the troops of hosts and the armies of 'Araboth, in one thousand camps and ten thousand hosts: they fetched trumpets, and took the horns in their hands, and surrounded the Shekinah with all kinds of songs. And He ascended to the high heavens, as it is written: God has gone up with a shout, the LORD with the sound of a trumpet."

CHAPTER 6

¹R. Ishmael said: Metatron, the messenger, the Prince of the Presence, said to me: "When the Holy One, blessed is He, desired to lift me up on high, He first sent 'Anaphiel H, the prince, and he took me from their midst in their sight and carried me in great glory on a fiery chariot with fiery horses, servants of glory. And he lifted me up to the high heavens together with the Shekinah. ²As soon as I reached the high heavens, the holy chayyoth, the ophanim, the seraphim, the cherubim, the wheels of the Merkaba, the galgallim, and the ministers of the consuming fire, perceiving my smell from a distance of three hundred sixty-five thousand myriads of parasangs, said, What smell of one born of woman and what taste of a white drop is this that ascends on high, and behold, he is merely a gnat among those who divide flames of fire? ³The Holy One, blessed is He, answered and spoke to them: My servants, My hosts, My cherubim, My ophanim, My seraphim! Do not be displeased on account of this! Since all the children of men have denied Me and My great Kingdom and have gone worshiping idols, I have removed My Shekinah from among them and have lifted it up on high. But this one whom I have taken from among them is a chosen one among the inhabitants of the world, and he is equal to all of them in faith, righteousness, and perfection of deed, and I have taken him as a tribute from My world under all the heavens."

CHAPTER 7

¹R. Ishmael said: Metatron, the messenger, the Prince of the Presence, said to me: "When the Holy One, blessed is He, took me away from the generation of the Flood, He lifted me on the wings of the wind of Shekinah to the highest Heaven and brought me into the great palaces of the 'Araboth Raqia' on high, ²where the glorious Throne of Shekinah, the Merkaba, the troops of anger, the armies of vehemence, the fiery shin'anim, the flaming cherubim, and the burning ophanim, the flaming servants, the flashing chashmallim, and the lightening seraphim are. And He placed me there to attend the Throne of Glory day after day."

CHAPTER 8

¹R. Ishmael said: Metatron, the Prince of the Presence, said to me: "Before He appointed me to attend the Throne of Glory, the Holy One, blessed is He, opened to me three hundred thousand gates of understanding, three hundred thousand gates of subtlety, three hundred thousand gates of life, three hundred thousand gates of grace and loving-kindness, three hundred thousand gates of love, three hundred thousand gates of instruction, three hundred thousand gates of meekness, three hundred thousand gates of maintenance, three hundred thousand gates of mercy, [and] three hundred thousand gates of fear of Heaven. ²In that hour the Holy One, blessed is He, added in me wisdom to wisdom, understanding to understanding, subtlety to subtlety, knowledge to knowledge, mercy to mercy, instruction to instruction, love to love, loving-kindness to loving-kindness, goodness to goodness, meekness to meekness, power to power, strength to strength, might to might, brilliance to brilliance, beauty to beauty, splendor to splendor, and I was honored and adorned with all these good and praiseworthy things more than all the children of Heaven."

CHAPTER 9

¹R. Ishmael said: Metatron, the Prince of the Presence, said to me: "After all these things the Holy One, blessed is He, put His hand on me and blessed me with five hundred thirty-six blessings. ²And I was raised and enlarged to the size of the length and width of the world. ³And He caused seventy-two wings to grow on me, thirty-six on each side. And each wing was as the whole world. ⁴And He fixed three hundred sixty-five eyes on me: each eye was as the great luminary. ⁵And He left no kind of splendor, brilliance, radiance, [or] beauty in of all the lights of the universe that He did not fix on me."

CHAPTER 10

¹R. Ishmael said: Metatron, the Prince of the Presence, said to me: "All these things the Holy One, blessed is He, made for me: He made me a throne, similar to the Throne of Glory. And He spread a curtain of splendor and brilliant appearance over me—of beauty, grace, and mercy, similar to the curtain of the Throne of Glory; and all kinds of lights in the universe were fixed on it. ²And He placed it at the door of the Seventh Hall and seated me on it. ³And the herald went forth into every Heaven, saying, This is My servant Metatron. I have made him into a prince and a ruler over all the princes of My kingdoms and over all the children of Heaven, except the eight great princes, the honored and revered ones who are called LORD, by the Name of their King.

2 ENOCH

CHAPTER 67

¹When Enoch had talked to the people, the LORD sent out darkness on to the earth, and there was darkness, and it covered those men standing with Enoch, and they took Enoch up on to the highest Heaven where the LORD is; and He received him and placed him before His face, and the darkness went off from the earth, and light came again. ²And the people did not see and understand how Enoch had been taken, and they glorified God, and they found a roll in which was traced "The Invisible God"; and all went to their dwelling places.

CHAPTER 68

¹Enoch was born on the sixth day of the month Sivan and lived three hundred and sixty-five years. ²He was taken up to Heaven on the first day of the month Sivan and remained in Heaven sixty days. ³He wrote all these signs of all creation, which the LORD created, and wrote three hundred and sixty-six scrolls, and handed them over to his sons, and remained on earth thirty days, and was taken up to Heaven again on the sixth day of the month Sivan, on the very day and hour when he was born. ⁴As every man's nature in this life is dark, so also are his conception, birth, and departure from this life. ⁵At what hour he was conceived, at that hour he was born, and at that hour too he died. ⁶Methuselah and his brothers, all the sons of Enoch, hurried and erected an altar at that place called Achuzan, from which and where Enoch had been taken up to Heaven. ⁷And they took sacrificial oxen, and summoned all people, and sacrificed the sacrifice before the LORD's face. ⁸All people, the elders of the people and the whole assembly, came to the feast and brought gifts to the sons of Enoch. ⁹And they made a great feast, rejoicing and making merry [for] three days, praising God who had given them such a sign through Enoch, who had found favor with Him, ¹⁰and that they should hand it on to their sons from generation to generation, from age to age. Amen.

3 ENOCH

3 Enoch, also called Hebrew Enoch, The Revelation of Metatron, or The Book of the Palaces, was likely written in the 1st or 2nd century AD by either Ishmael ben Elisha ha-Kohen or Rabbi Yishmael ben Elisha. Its Jewish author has an otherworldly experience where he ascends into the heavens and beholds the glorified Enoch (Metatron). Metatron has become the heavenly scribe and among the highest-ranking angels.

CHAPTER 1

¹Rabbi Ishmael said: When I ascended on high to behold the vision of the Merkaba and had entered the six halls, one within the other, ²as soon as I reached the door of the Seventh Hall I stood still in prayer before the Holy One, blessed is He, and, lifting up my eyes on high toward the Divine Majesty, I said, ³"Lord of the Universe, please, that the merit of Aaron, the son of Amram, the lover of peace and pursuer of peace, who received the crown of priesthood from Your Glory on Mount Sinai, be valid for me in this hour, so that Cassiel, the prince, and the messengers with him may not get power over me nor throw me down from the heavens." ⁴Immediately the Holy One, blessed is He, sent Metatron to me, his servant the messenger, the Prince of the Presence, and he, spreading his wings, came to meet me with great joy so as to save me from their hand. ⁵And he took me by his hand in their sight, saying to me: "Enter in peace before the high and exalted King and behold the picture of the Merkaba." ⁶Then I entered the Seventh Hall, and he led me to the camps of Shekinah and placed me before the Holy One, blessed is He, to behold the Merkaba. ⁷As soon as the princes of the Merkaba and the flaming seraphim perceived me, they fixed their eyes on me. Trembling and shuddering instantly seized me, and I fell down and was benumbed by the radiant image of their eyes and the splendid appearance of their faces, until the Holy One, blessed is He, rebuked them, saying, ⁸"My servants, my seraphim, my cherubim, and my ophanim! Cover your eyes before Ishmael, my son, my friend, my beloved one, and my glory, so he does not tremble or shudder!" ⁹Immediately Metatron, the Prince of the Presence, came and restored my spirit and put me on my feet. ¹⁰After that moment there was not strength enough in me to say a song before the Throne of Glory of the glorious King, the mightiest of all kings, the most excellent of all princes, until after the hour had passed. ¹¹After one hour had passed, the Holy One, blessed is He, opened to me the gates of Shekinah, the gates of Peace, the gates of Wisdom, the gates of Strength, the gates of Power, the gates of Speech, the gates of Song, the gates of Holiness, the gates of Chant. ¹²And he enlightened my eyes and my heart by words of psalm, song, praise, exaltation, thanksgiving, extolment, glorification, hymn, and eulogy. And as I opened my mouth, uttering a song before the Holy One, blessed is He, the holy chayyoth beneath and above the Throne of Glory answered and said, "HOLY" and, "Blessed is the glory of the LORD from His place!"

CHAPTER 2

¹R. Ishmael said: In that hour the eagles of the Merkaba, the flaming ophanim and the seraphim of consuming fire, asked Metatron, saying to him: ²"Youth! Why permit one born of woman to enter and behold the Merkaba? From which nation, from which tribe is this one? What is his character?" ³Metatron answered and said to them: "From the nation of Israel whom the Holy One, blessed is He, chose for His people from among seventy tongues, from the tribe of Levi, whom He set aside as a contribution to His Name and from the seed of Aaron whom the Holy One, blessed is He, chose for his servant and put on him the crown of priesthood on Sinai." ⁴Immediately they spoke and said, "Indeed, this one is worthy to behold the Merkaba." And they said, "Happy is the people that is in such a case!"

CHAPTER 3

¹R. Ishmael said: In that hour I asked Metatron, the messenger, the Prince of the Presence: "What is your name?" ²He answered me: "I have seventy names, corresponding to the seventy tongues of the world, and all of them are based on the name Metatron, Messenger of the Presence; but my King calls me Youth."

CHAPTER 4

¹R. Ishmael said: I asked Metatron and said to him: "Why are you called by the Name of your Creator, by seventy names? You are greater than all the princes, higher than all the messengers, more beloved than all the servants, honored above all the mighty ones in kingship, greatness, and glory: why do they call you Youth in the high heavens?" ²He answered and said to me: "Because I am Enoch, the son of Jared. ³For when the generation of the Flood sinned and were confounded in their deeds, saying to God, Depart from us, for we do not desire the knowledge of Your ways, then the Holy One, blessed is He, removed me from their midst to be a witness against them in the high heavens to all the inhabitants of the world, that they may not say: The Merciful One is cruel. What sins had they committed, all those multitudes? Or, let it be they sinned—what had their sons and their daughters, their mules and their cattle sinned? And likewise, all the animals, domestic and wild, and the birds in the world that God destroyed from the world? ⁵Hence the Holy One, blessed is He, lifted me up in their lifetime before their eyes to be a witness against them to the future world. And the Holy One, blessed is He, assigned me for a prince and a ruler among the ministering messengers. ⁶In that hour three of the ministering messengers, 'Uzza, 'Azza, and 'Azzael came forth and brought charges against me in the high heavens, saying before the Holy One, blessed is He: Did the Ancient Ones not rightly say before You, Do not create man? The Holy One, blessed is He, answered and said to them: I have made, and I will bear, yes, I will carry and will deliver. ⁷As soon as

great princes who know the mystery of the Throne of Glory, he removes the crown of glory from his head and falls on his face. Why is he called 'Azbuga? Because in the future he will gird the righteous and pious of the world with the garments of life and wrap them in the cloak of life, that they may live a continuous life in them. ²³And when he sees the two great princes, the strong and glorified ones who are standing above him, he removes the crown of glory from his head and falls on his face. And these are the names of the two princes: Sopheriel-YHWH Who Kills, the great prince, the honored, glorified, blameless, venerable, ancient, and mighty one; and Sopheriel-YHWH Who Makes Alive, the great prince, the honored, glorified, blameless, ancient, and mighty one. ²⁴Why is he called Sopheriel-YHWH Who Kills? Because he is appointed over the scrolls of the dead, so that everyone, when the day of his death draws near, he writes him in the scrolls of the dead. ²⁵Why is he called Sopheriel-YHWH Who Makes Alive? Because he is appointed over the scrolls of the living, so that everyone whom the Holy One, blessed is He, will bring into life, he writes him in the Scroll of the Living, by authority of MAQOM. ²⁶You might perhaps say: Since the Holy One, blessed is He, is sitting on a throne, they are also sitting when writing. Answer: the Writing teaches us: And all the host of Heaven are standing by Him. ²⁷It is said, The host of Heaven, in order to show us that even the great princes—like whom there is none in the high heavens—do not fulfill the requests of the Shekinah otherwise than standing. ²⁸But how is it they are able to write when they are standing? It is like this: one is standing on the wheels of the tempest and the other is standing on the wheels of the storm-wind. ²⁹The one is clad in kingly garments, the other is clad in kingly garments. The one is wrapped in a mantle of majesty and the other is wrapped in a mantle of majesty. The one is crowned with a royal crown and the other is crowned with a royal crown. The one's body is full of eyes and the other's body is full of eyes. ³⁰The appearance of one is like to the appearance of lightnings and the appearance of the other is like to the appearance of lightnings. The eyes of the one are like the sun in its might and the eyes of the other are like the sun in its might. The one's height is like the height of the seven heavens and the other's height is like the height of the seven heavens. ³¹The wings of the one are as many as the days of the year and the wings of the other are as many as the days of the year. The wings of the one extend over the breadth of Raqia' and the wings of the other extend over the breadth of Raqia'. ³²The lips of the one are as the gates of the east and the lips of the other are as the gates of the east. The tongue of the one is as high as the waves of the sea and the tongue of the other is as high as the waves of the sea. ³³From the mouth of the one a flame goes forth and from the mouth of the other a flame goes forth. From the mouth of the one there go forth lightnings and from the mouth of the other there go forth lightnings. ³⁴From the sweat of the one fire is kindled and from the perspiration of the other fire is kindled. From the one's tongue a torch is burning and from the tongue of the other a torch is burning. ³⁵On the head of the one there is a sapphire stone and on the head of the other there is a sapphire stone. On the shoulders of the one there is a wheel of a swift cherub and on the shoulders of the other there is a wheel of a swift cherub. ³⁶One has a burning scroll in his hand, the other has a burning scroll in his hand. The one has a flaming style in his hand, the other has a flaming style in his hand. ³⁷The length of the scroll is three thousand myriads of parasangs; the size of the style is three thousand myriads of parasangs; the size of every single letter that they write is three hundred sixty-five parasangs."

CHAPTER 19

¹R. Ishmael said: Metatron, the messenger, the Prince of the Presence, said to me: "Above these three messengers, these great princes, there is one prince, distinguished, honored, noble, glorified, adorned, fearful, valiant, strong, great, magnified, glorious, crowned, wonderful, exalted, blameless, beloved, lordly, high and lofty, ancient and mighty, like to whom there is none among the princes. His name is Rikbiel-YHWH, the great and revered prince who is standing by the Merkaba. ²And why is he called Rikbiel? Because he is appointed over the wheels of the Merkaba, and they are given in his charge. ³And how many are the wheels? Eight; two in each direction. And there are four winds compassing them around. And these are their names: the Storm-Wind, the Tempest, the Strong Wind, and the Wind of Earthquake. ⁴And there are four fiery rivers continually running under them, one fiery river on each side. And around them, between the rivers, four clouds are planted, and they are these: clouds of fire, clouds of lamps, clouds of coal, [and] clouds of brimstone, and they are standing beside their wheels. ⁵And the feet of the chayyoth are resting on the wheels. And between one wheel and the other, earthquake is roaring, and thunder is thundering. ⁶And when the time draws near for the recital of the Song, then the multitudes of wheels are moved, the multitude of clouds tremble, all the chieftains are made afraid, all the horsemen rage, all the mighty ones are excited, all the hosts are frightened, all the troops are in fear, all the appointed ones hurry away, all the princes and armies are dismayed, all the servants faint, and all the messengers and divisions travail with pain. ⁷And one wheel makes a sound to be heard to the other, and one cherub to another, one chayya to another, one seraph to another, saying, Extol Him that rides in 'Araboth, by His Name YHWH, and rejoice before Him!"

CHAPTER 20

¹R. Ishmael said: Metatron, the messenger, the Prince of the Presence, said to me: "Above these there is one great and mighty prince. His name is Chayyliel-YHWH, a noble and revered prince, a glorious and mighty prince, a great and revered prince, a prince before whom all the children of Heaven tremble, a prince who is able to swallow up the whole earth in one moment. ²And why is he called Chayyliel-YHWH? Because he is appointed over the holy chayyoth and strikes the chayyoth with lashes of fire, and glorifies them when they give praise, and glory, and rejoicing, and he causes them to hurry to say HOLY and BLESSED IS THE GLORY OF YHWH FROM HIS PLACE!"

CHAPTER 21

¹R. Ishmael said: Metatron, the messenger, the Prince of the Presence, said to me: "Four [are] the chayyoth corresponding to the four winds. Each chayya is as the space of the whole world. And each one has four faces; and each face is as the face of the east. ²Each one has four wings, and each wing is like the cover of the universe. ³And each one has faces in the middle of faces and wings in the middle of wings. The size of the faces is as the size of two hundred forty-eight faces, and the size of the wings is as the size of three hundred sixty-five wings. ⁴And each one is crowned with two thousand crowns on his head. And each crown is like to the bow in the cloud. And its splendor is like to the splendor of the globe of the sun. And the sparks that go forth from each one are like the splendor of the morning star in the east."

CHAPTER 22 (A)

¹R. Ishmael said: Metatron, the messenger, the Prince of the Presence, said to me: "Above these there is one prince: noble, wonderful, strong, and praised with all kinds of praise. His name is Kerubiel-YHWH, a mighty prince, full of power and strength, a prince of highness, and with him there is a righteous prince of righteousness, and with him a holy prince of holiness, and with him there is a prince glorified by one thousand hosts, exalted by ten thousand armies. ²At his wrath the earth trembles, at his anger the camps are moved, from fear of him the foundations are shaken, at his rebuke the 'Araboth trembles. ³His stature is full of burning coals. The height of his stature is as the height of the seven heavens, the breadth of his stature is as the wideness of the seven heavens, and the thickness of his stature is as the seven heavens. ⁴The opening of his mouth is like a lamp of fire. His tongue is a consuming fire. His eyebrows are like to the splendor of the lightning. His eyes are like sparks of brilliance. His countenance is like a burning fire. ⁵And there is a crown of holiness on his head on which the Explicit Name is graven—and lightnings go forth from it. And the bow of Shekinah is between his shoulders. And his sword is like to lightning, and on his loins there are arrows like to a flame, and on his armor and shield there is a consuming fire, and on his neck there are coals of burning juniper, and also around him there are coals of burning juniper. ⁷And the splendor of Shekinah is on his face, and the horns of majesty on his wheels, and a royal diadem on

his skull. ⁸And his body is full of eyes. And wings are covering the whole of his high stature. ⁹On his right hand a flame is burning, and on his left a fire is glowing; and coals are burning from it. And firebrands go forth from his body. And lightnings are cast forth from his face. With him there is always thunder on thunder, by his side there is always earthquake on earthquake. ¹⁰And the two princes of the Merkaba are together with him. ¹¹Why is he called Kerubiel-YHWH, the prince? Because he is appointed over the chariot of the cherubim. And the mighty cherubim are given in his charge. And he adorns the crowns on their heads and polishes the diadem on their skull. ¹²He magnifies the glory of their appearance. And he glorifies the beauty of their majesty. And he increases the greatness of their honor. He causes the song of their praise to be sung. He intensifies their beautiful strength. He causes the brilliance of their glory to shine forth. He beautifies their excellent mercy and loving-kindness. He frames the fairness of their radiance. He makes their merciful beauty even more beautiful. He glorifies their upright majesty. He extols the order of their praise, to establish the dwelling place of Him who dwells on the cherubim. ¹³And the cherubim are standing by the holy chayyoth, and their wings are raised up to their heads, and Shekinah is resting on them, and the brilliance of the Glory is on their faces, and song and praise [are] in their mouth, and their hands are under their wings, and their feet are covered by their wings, and horns of glory are on their heads, and the splendor of Shekinah on their face, and Shekinah is resting on them, and sapphire stones are around them, and columns of fire [are] on their four sides, and columns of firebrands beside them. ¹⁴There is one sapphire on one side and another sapphire on another side, and under the sapphires there are coals of burning juniper. ¹⁵And one cherub is standing in each direction, but the wings of the cherubim encircle each other above their skulls in glory; and they spread them to sing a song with them to Him that inhabits the clouds and to praise the fearful majesty of the King of kings with them. ¹⁶And Kerubiel-YHWH, the prince who is appointed over them, he arrays them in attractive, beautiful, and pleasant orders, and he exalts them in all manner of exaltation, dignity, and glory. And he hastens them in glory and might to do the will of their Creator every moment. For above their lofty heads continually abides the glory of the High King who dwells on the cherubim."

CHAPTER 22 (B)

¹R. Ishmael said: Metatron, the Prince of the Presence said to me: "What is the distance between one bridge and another? Twelve myriads of parasangs. Their ascent is myriads of parasangs, and their descent myriads of parasangs. ²The distance between the rivers of dread and the rivers of fear is twenty-two myriads of parasangs; between the rivers of hail and the rivers of darkness, thirty-six myriads of parasangs; between the chambers of lightnings and the clouds of compassion, forty-two myriads of parasangs; between the clouds of compassion and the Merkaba, eighty-four myriads of parasangs; between the Merkaba and the cherubim, one hundred forty-eight myriads of parasangs; between the cherubim and the ophanim, twenty-four myriads of parasangs; between the ophanim and the chambers of chambers, twenty-four myriads of parasangs; between the chambers of chambers and the holy chayyoth, forty thousand myriads of parasangs; between one wing of the chayyoth and another, twelve myriads of parasangs; and the breadth of each one wing is of that same measure; and the distance between the holy chayyoth and the Throne of Glory is thirty thousand myriads of parasangs. ³And from the foot of the Throne to the seat there are forty thousand myriads of parasangs. And the Name of Him that sits on it: let the Name be sanctified! ⁴And the arches of the Bozv are set above the 'Araboth, and they are one million and one hundred million parasangs high. Their measure is after the measure of the 'Irin and Qaddishin, that is, the Watchers and the Holy Ones. As it is written: I have set My bow in the cloud. It is not written here: I will set, but: I have set—already— clouds that surround the Throne of Glory. As His clouds pass by, the messengers of hail turn into burning coal. ⁵And a fire of the voice goes down from by the holy chayyoth. And because of the breath of that voice, they run to another place, fearing lest it command them to go; and they return lest it injure them from the other side. Therefore, [as it is written:] They run and return. ⁶And these arches of the bow are more beautiful and radiant than the radiance of the sun during the summer solstice, and they are whiter than a flaming fire, and they are great and beautiful. ⁷Above the arches of the bow are the wheels of the ophanim. Their height is one million and one hundred million units of measure after the measure of the seraphim and the troops."

CHAPTER 23

¹R. Ishmael said: Metatron, the messenger, the Prince of the Presence, said to me: "There are numerous winds blowing under the wings of the cherubim. The Fluttering Wind blows there, as it is written: And the Spirit of God was fluttering on the face of the waters. ²The Strong Wind blows there, as it is said: And the LORD caused the sea to go back by a strong east wind all that night. ³The East Wind blows there, as it is written: The east wind brought the locusts. ⁴The Wind of Quails blows there, as it is written: And there went forth a wind from the LORD and brought quails. ⁵The Wind of Jealousy blows there, as it is written: And the wind of jealousy came on him. ⁶The Wind of Earthquake blows there, as it is written: And after that, the wind of the earthquake, but the LORD was not in the earthquake. ⁷The Wind of YHWH blows there, as it is written: And He carried me out by the Spirit of the LORD and set me down. ⁸The Evil Wind blows there, as it is written: And the evil wind departed from him. ⁹The Wind of Wisdom, and the Wind of Understanding, and the Wind of Knowledge, and the Wind of the Fear of YHWH blow there, as it is written: And the Spirit of the LORD will rest on Him, || The Spirit of wisdom and understanding, || The Spirit of counsel and might, || The Spirit of knowledge and of the fear. ¹⁰The Wind of Rain blows there, as it is written: The north wind brings forth rain. ¹¹The Wind of Lightnings blows there, as it is written: He makes lightnings for the rain and brings forth the wind out of His treasuries. ¹²The Wind, Breaking the Rocks, blows there, as it is written: The LORD passed by and a great and strong wind split the mountains and broke in pieces the rocks before the LORD. ¹³The Wind of Assuagement of the Sea blows there, as it is written: And God made a wind to pass over the earth, and the waters assuaged. ¹⁴The Wind of Wrath blows there, as it is written: And behold, there came a great wind from the wilderness and [it] struck the four corners of the house and it fell. ¹⁵The Storm-Wind blows there, as it is written: Storm-wind, fulfilling His word. ¹⁶And Satan is standing among these winds, for Storm-Wind is nothing else but Satan, and all these winds do not blow but under the wings of the cherubim, as it is written: And He rode on a cherub and flew, yes, and He flew swiftly on the wings of the wind. ¹⁷And where do all these winds go? The Writing teaches us that they go out from under the wings of the cherubim and descend on the globe of the sun, as it is written: The wind goes toward the south and turns around to the north; it turns around continually in its course and the wind returns again to its circuits. And from the globe of the sun they return and descend on the rivers and the seas, on the mountains and on the hills, as it is written: For behold, He that forms the mountains and creates the wind. ¹⁸And from the mountains and the hills they return and descend to the seas and the rivers; and from the seas and the rivers they return and descend on the cities and provinces; and from the cities and provinces they return and descend into the Garden, and from the Garden they return and descend to Eden, as it is written: Walking in the Garden in the wind of day. ¹⁹And in the midst of the Garden they join together and blow from one side to the other and are perfumed with the spices of the Garden even from its remotest parts, until they separate from each other, and, filled with the scent of the pure spices, they bring the fragrance from the remotest parts of Eden and the spices of the Garden to the righteous and godly who in the time to come will inherit the Garden of Eden and the Tree of Life, ²⁰as it is written: Awake, O north wind; and come you south; blow on my garden, that the spices thereof may flow out. Let my beloved come into his garden and eat his precious fruits."

CHAPTER 24

¹R. Ishmael said: Metatron, the messenger, the Prince of the Presence, the glory of all Heaven, said to me: "The Holy One, blessed is He, has numerous chariots: He has the Chariots of the Cherubim, as it is written: And he rode on a

cherub and flew. ²He has the Chariots of Wind, as it is written: And he flew swiftly on the wings of the wind. ³He has the Chariots of the Swift Cloud, as it is written: Behold, the LORD rides on a swift cloud. ⁴He has the Chariots of Clouds, as it is written: Behold, I come to you in a cloud. ⁵He has the Chariots of the Altar, as it is written: I saw the LORD standing on the altar. ⁶He has the Chariots of Myriads, as it is written: The chariots of God are myriads, thousands of messengers. ⁷He has the Chariots of the Tent, as it is written: And the LORD appeared in the tent in a pillar of cloud. ⁸He has the Chariots of the Dwelling Place, as it is written: And the LORD spoke to him out of the Dwelling Place. ⁹He has the Chariots of the Propitiatory Covering, as it is written: Then he heard the voice speaking to him from on the propitiatory covering. ¹⁰He has the Chariots of Sapphire Stone, as it is written: And there was under His feet as it were a paved work of sapphire stone. ¹¹He has the Chariots of Eagles, as it is written: I bare you on eagles' wings. (Eagles are not literally meant here but they that fly swiftly as eagles.) ¹²He has the chariots of Shout, as it is written: God has gone up with a shout. ¹³He has the Chariots of 'Araboth, as it is written: Extol Him that rides on the 'Araboth. ¹⁴He has the Chariots of Thick Clouds, as it is written: Who makes the thick clouds His chariot. ¹⁵He has the Chariots of the Chayyoth, as it is written: And the chayyoth ran and returned. They run by permission and return by permission, for Shekinah is above their heads. ¹⁶He has the Chariots of Wheels, as it is written: And He said, Go in between the whirling wheels. ¹⁷He has the Chariots of a Swift Cherub, as it is written: Riding on a swift cherub. And at the time when He rides on a swift cherub, as He sets one of His feet on him, before He sets the other foot on his back, He looks through eighteen thousand worlds at one glance. And He discerns and sees into them all and knows what is in all of them and then he sets down the other foot on him, according as it is written: Around eighteen thousand. From where do we know that He looks through every one of them every day? It is written: He looked down from Heaven on the children of men to see if there were any that understood, that seek after God. ¹⁸He has the Chariots of the Ophanim, as it is written: And the ophanim were full of eyes around. ¹⁹He has the Chariots of His Holy Throne, as it is written: God sits on His holy throne. ²⁰He has the chariots of the Throne of YAH, as it is written: Because a hand is lifted up on the throne of YAH. ²¹He has the Chariots of the Throne of Judgment, as it is written: But the LORD of Hosts will be exalted in judgment. ²²He has the Chariots of the Throne of Glory, as it is written: The throne of glory, set on high from the beginning, is the place of our sanctuary. ²³He has the Chariots of the High and Exalted Throne, as it is written: I saw the LORD sitting on the high and exalted throne."

CHAPTER 25

¹R. Ishmael said: Metatron, the messenger, the Prince of the Presence, said to me: "Above these there is one great prince, revered, high, lordly, fearful, ancient, and strong. 'Ophphanniel-YHWH is his name. ²He has sixteen faces, four faces on each side, one hundred wings on each side. And he has eight thousand four hundred sixty-six eyes, corresponding to the days of the year. Two thousand one hundred and ninety and some say two thousand one hundred sixteen on each side. ³And those two eyes of his face—in each one of them lightnings are flashing, and from each one of them firebrands are burning, and no creature is able to behold them. For anyone who looks at them is burned instantly. ⁴His height is as the distance of two thousand five hundred years' journey. No eye can behold and no mouth can tell the mighty power of his strength except the King of kings, the Holy One, blessed is He, alone. ⁵Why is he called 'Ophphanniel? Because he is appointed over the ophanim and the ophanim are given in his charge. He stands every day, and attends, and beautifies them. And he exalts and orders their apartment, and polishes their standing-place, and makes their dwellings bright, [and] makes their corners even, and cleanses their seats. And he waits on them early and late, by day and by night, to increase their beauty, to make their dignity great, and to make them diligent in praise of their Creator. ⁶And all the ophanim are full of eyes, and they are all full of brightness; seventy-two sapphire stones are fixed on their garments on their right side and seventy-two sapphire stones are fixed on their garments on their left side. ⁷And four carbuncle stones are fixed on the crown of every single one, the splendor of which proceeds in the four directions of 'Araboth even as the splendor of the globe of the sun proceeds in all the directions of the universe. And why is it called Carbuncle? Because its splendor is like the appearance of lightning. And tents of splendor, tents of brilliance, [and] tents of brightness as of sapphire and carbuncle enclose them because of the shining appearance of their eyes."

CHAPTER 26

¹R. Ishmael said: Metatron, the messenger, the Prince of the Presence, said to me: "Above these there is one prince, wonderful, noble, great, honorable, mighty, terrible, a chief, and leader, and a swift scribe, glorified, honored, and beloved. ²He is altogether filled with splendor, full of praise and shining; and he is wholly full of brilliance, of light and of beauty; and the whole of him is filled with goodliness and greatness. ³His countenance is altogether like that of messengers, but his body is like an eagle's body. ⁴His splendor is like to lightnings, his appearance like firebrands, his beauty like to sparks, his honor like fiery coals, his majesty like electrum, his radiance like the light of the planet Venus. The image of him is like to the Greater Light. His height is as the seven heavens. The light from his eyebrows is like the sevenfold light. ⁵The sapphire stone on his head is as great as the whole universe and like to the splendor of the very heavens in radiance. ⁶His body is full of eyes like the stars of the sky, innumerable and unsearchable. Every eye is like the planet Venus. Yet, there are some of them like the Lesser Light and some of them like to the Greater Light. From his ankles to his knees, they are like to stars of lightning; from his knees to his thighs like to the planet Venus; from his thighs to his loins like to the moon; from his loins to his neck like the sun; from his neck to his skull like to the Imperishable Light. ⁷The crown on his head is like to the splendor of the Throne of Glory. The measure of the crown is the distance of five hundred and two years' journey. There is no kind of splendor, no kind of brilliance, no kind of radiance, no kind of light in the universe but is fixed on that crown. ⁸The name of that prince is Seraphiel-YHWH. And the crown on his head, its name is the Prince of Peace. And why is he called by the name of Seraphiel-YHWH? Because he is appointed over the seraphim. And the flaming seraphim are given in his charge. And he presides over them by day and by night and teaches them song, praise, proclamation of beauty, might, and majesty, that they may proclaim the beauty of their King in all manner of praise and sanctification. ⁹How many are the seraphim? Four, corresponding to the four winds of the world. And how many wings does each one of them have? Six, corresponding to the six days of Creation. And how many faces do they have? Each one of them [has] four faces. ¹⁰The measure of the seraphim and the height of each one of them correspond to the height of the seven heavens. The size of each wing is like the measure of all Raqia'. The size of each face is like that of the face of the east. ¹¹And each one of them gives forth light like to the splendor of the Throne of Glory, so that not even the holy chayyoth, the honored ophanim, nor the majestic cherubim are able to behold it. For everyone who beholds it, his eyes are darkened because of its great splendor. ¹²Why are they called seraphim? Because they burn the writing tablets of Satan: every day Satan is sitting, together with Sammael, the Prince of Rome, and with Dubbiel, the Prince of Persia, and they write the iniquities of Israel on writing tablets which they hand over to the seraphim in order that they may present them before the Holy One, blessed is He, so that He may destroy Israel from the world. But the seraphim know from the secrets of the Holy One, blessed is He, that He does not desire that this people Israel should perish. What do the seraphim do? Every day they receive them from the hand of Satan and burn them in the burning fire beside the high and exalted Throne in order that they may not come before the Holy One, blessed is He, at the time when He is sitting on the Throne of Judgment, judging the whole world in truth."

CHAPTER 27

¹R. Ishmael said: Metatron, the messenger of YHWH, the Prince of the Presence, said to me:

"Above the seraphim there is one prince, exalted above all the princes, wondrous more than all the servants. His name is Radweriel-YHWH, who is appointed over the treasuries of the scrolls. ²He fetches forth the Case of Writings with the Scroll of Records in it, and brings it before the Holy One, blessed is He. And he breaks the seals of the case, opens it, takes out the scrolls, and delivers them before the Holy One, blessed is He. And the Holy One, blessed is He, receives them from his hand and gives them in his sight to the Scribes that they may read them in the Great House of Judgment in the height of 'Araboth Raqia', before the heavenly household. ³And why is he called Radweriel? Because out of every word that goes forth from his mouth a messenger is created: and he stands in the singing company of the ministering messengers and utters a song before the Holy One, blessed is He, when the time draws near for the recitation of the Thrice Holy."

CHAPTER 28

¹R. Ishmael said: Metatron, the messenger, the Prince of the Presence, said to me: "Above all these there are four great princes, Watchers and Holy Ones by name: high, honored, revered, beloved, wonderful, and glorious ones, greater than all the children of Heaven. There is none like to them among all the celestial princes and none their equal among all the servants. For each one of them is equal to all the rest together. ²And their dwelling is beside the Throne of Glory, and their standing place beside the Holy One, blessed is He, so that the brilliance of their dwelling is a reflection of the brilliance of the Throne of Glory. And the splendor of their countenance is a reflection of the splendor of Shekinah. ³And they are glorified by the glory of the Divine Majesty and praised by the praise of Shekinah. ⁴And not only that, but the Holy One, blessed is He, does nothing in His world without first consulting them, but after that He does it. As it is written: The sentence is by the decree of the watchers and the demand by the word of the holy ones. ⁵The watchers are two and the holy ones are two. And how are they standing before the Holy One, blessed is He? It is to be understood that one watcher is standing on one side and the other watcher on the other side, and one holy one is standing on one side and the other on the other side. ⁶And they always exalt the humble, and they abase to the ground those that are proud, and they exalt to the height those that are humble. ⁷And every day, as the Holy One, blessed is He, is sitting on the Throne of Judgment and judges the whole world, and the scrolls of the living and the scrolls of the dead are opened before Him, then all the children of Heaven are standing before Him in fear, dread, awe, and trembling. At that time, when the Holy One, blessed is He, is sitting on the Throne of Judgment to execute judgment, His garment is white as snow, the hair on His head as pure wool, and the whole of His cloak is like the shining light. And He is covered with righteousness all over as with a coat of mail. ⁸And those watchers and holy ones are standing before Him like court officers before the judge. And they raise and argue every case and close the case that comes before the Holy One, blessed is He, in judgment, according as it is written: The sentence is by the decree of the watchers and the demand by the word of the holy ones. ⁹Some of them argue and others pass the sentence in the Great House of Judgment in 'Araboth. Some of them make the requests from before the Divine Majesty and some close the cases before the Most High. Others finish by going down and executing the sentences on earth below. According as it is written: Behold, a watcher and a holy one came down from Heaven, and cried aloud, and said thus: Hew down the tree, and cut off his branches, shake off his leaves, and scatter his fruit: let the beasts get away from under it, and the birds from his branches. ¹⁰Why are they called watchers and holy ones? By reason that they sanctify the body and the spirit with lashes of fire on the third day of the judgment, as it is written: After two days He will revive us, || On the third [[day]] He will raise us up, || And we will live before Him."

CHAPTER 29

¹R. Ishmael said: Metatron, the messenger, the Prince of the Presence, said to me: "Each one of them has seventy names corresponding to the seventy tongues of the world. And all of them are based on the Name of the Holy One, blessed is He. And every name is written with a flaming style on the Fearful Crown which is on the head of the high and exalted King. ²And sparks and lightnings go forth from each one of them. And each one of them is beset with horns of splendor around. From each one lights are shining forth, and each one is surrounded by tents of brilliance so that not even the seraphim and the chayyoth who are greater than all the [other] children of Heaven are able to behold them."

CHAPTER 30

¹R. Ishmael said: Metatron, the messenger, the Prince of the Presence, said to me: "Whenever the Great House of Judgment is seated in the 'Araboth Raqia' on high there is no opening of the mouth for anyone in the world except those great princes who are called YHWH by the Name of the Holy One, blessed is He. ²How many are those princes? Seventy-two princes of the kingdoms of the world besides the Prince of the World who speaks in favor of the world before the Holy One, blessed is He, every day, at the hour when the scroll is opened in which all the doings of the world are recorded, according as it is written: The judgment was set and the scrolls were opened."

CHAPTER 31

¹R. Ishmael said: Metatron, the messenger, the Prince of the Presence, said to me: "At the time when the Holy One, blessed is He, is sitting on the Throne of Judgment, then Justice is standing on His right, and Mercy on His left, and Truth before His face. ²And when man enters before Him to judgment, then a staff, as it were, comes forth from the splendor of the Mercy toward him and stands in front of him. Immediately man falls on his face, and all the messengers of destruction fear and tremble before Him, according as it is written: And with mercy will the throne be established, and He will sit on it in truth."

CHAPTER 32

¹R. Ishmael said: Metatron, the messenger, the Prince of the Presence, said to me: "When the Holy One, blessed is He, opens the Scroll—half of which is fire and half flame—then they go out from before Him in every moment to execute the judgment on the wicked by His sword that is drawn forth out of its sheath and the splendor of which shines like lightning and pervades the world from one end to the other, as it is written: For the LORD will plead by fire and with all flesh by His sword. ²And all the inhabitants of the world fear and tremble before Him when they behold His sharpened sword like to lightning from one end of the world to the other, and sparks and flashes of the size of the stars of Raqia' going out from it, according as it is written: If I sharpen the lightning of My sword."

CHAPTER 33

¹R. Ishmael said: Metatron, the messenger, the Prince of the Presence, said to me: "At the time that the Holy One, blessed is He, is sitting on the Throne of Judgment, then the messengers of Mercy are standing on His right, the messengers of Peace are standing on His left, and the messengers of Destruction are standing in front of Him. ²And one scribe is standing beneath Him, and another scribe above Him. ³And the glorious seraphim surround the Throne on its four sides with walls of lightnings, and the ophanim surround them with firebrands around the Throne of Glory. And clouds of fire and clouds of flames surround them to the right and to the left; and the holy chayyoth carry the Throne of Glory from below: each one with three fingers. The measure of the fingers of each one is eight hundred thousand and seven hundred times one hundred, and sixty-six thousand parasangs. ⁴And underneath the feet of the chayyoth seven fiery rivers are running and flowing. And the breadth of each river is three hundred sixty-five thousand parasangs and its depth is two hundred forty-eight thousand myriads of parasangs. Its length is unsearchable and immeasurable. ⁵And each river turns around in a bow in the four directions of 'Araboth Raqia', and from there it falls down to Ma'on and is stayed, and from Ma'on to Zebul, from Zebul to Shechaqim, from Shechaqim to Raqia', from Raqia' to Shamayim, and from Shamayim on the heads of the wicked who are in Gehenna, ⁶as it is written: Behold, a whirlwind of the LORD, even His fury, is gone, yes, a whirling tempest; it will burst on the head of the wicked."

3 ENOCH

CHAPTER 34

¹R. Ishmael said: Metatron, the messenger, the Prince of the Presence, said to me: "The hooves of the chayyoth are surrounded by seven clouds of burning coals. The clouds of burning coals are surrounded on the outside by seven walls of flames. The seven walls of flames are surrounded on the outside by seven walls of hailstones. The hailstones are surrounded on the outside by stones of hail. The stones of hail are surrounded on the outside by stones of the wings of the tempest. The stones of the wings of the tempest are surrounded on the outside by flames of fire. The flames of fire are surrounded by the chambers of the whirlwind. The chambers of the whirlwind are surrounded on the outside by the fire and the water. ²Around the fire and the water are those who utter the HOLY. Around those who utter the HOLY are those who utter the BLESSED. Around those who utter the BLESSED are the bright clouds. The bright clouds are surrounded on the outside by coals of burning juniper; and on the outside surrounding the coals of burning juniper there are one thousand camps of fire and ten thousand hosts of flames. And between every camp and every host there is a cloud, so that they may not be burned by the fire."

CHAPTER 35

¹R. Ishmael said: Metatron, the messenger, the Prince of the Presence, said to me: "The Holy One, blessed is He, has five hundred and six thousand myriads of camps in the height of 'Araboth Raqia'. And each camp is composed of four hundred ninety-six thousand messengers. ²And every single messenger, the height of his stature is as the Great Sea; and the appearance of their countenance is as the appearance of the lightning, and their eyes as lamps of fire, and their arms and their feet like in color to polished brass, and the roaring voice of their words like the voice of a multitude. ³And they are all standing before the Throne of Glory in four rows. And the princes of the army are standing at the head of each row. ⁴And some of them utter the HOLY and others utter the BLESSED, some of them run as messengers, others are standing in attendance, according as it is written: One million ministered to Him and one hundred million stood before him, the judgment was set, and the scrolls were opened. ⁵And in the hour when the time draws near for [them] to say the HOLY, then first there goes forth a whirlwind from before the Holy One, blessed is He, and bursts on the camp of Shekinah and there arises a great commotion among them, as it is written: Behold, the whirlwind of the LORD goes forth with fury—a continuing commotion. ⁶At that moment one million of them are changed into sparks, one million of them into firebrands, one million into flashes, one million into flames, one million into males, one million into females, one million into winds, one million into burning fires, one million into flames, one million into sparks, one million into chashmals of light, until they take on themselves the yoke of the Kingdom of the heavens, the high and lifted up, of the Creator of them all, with fear, dread, awe, and trembling, with commotion, anguish, terror, and trepidation. Then they are changed again into their former shape to always have the fear of their King before them, as they have set their hearts on saying the Song continually, as it is written: And one cried to another and said, HOLY, HOLY, HOLY."

CHAPTER 36

¹R. Ishmael said: Metatron, the messenger, the Prince of the Presence, said to me: "At the time when the ministering messengers desire to say the Song, then the fiery stream rises with many thousand[s] of thousands and myriads of myriads of messengers of power and strength of fire and it runs and passes under the Throne of Glory, between the camps of the ministering messengers and the troops of 'Araboth. ²And all the ministering messengers first go down into Nehar di-Nur, and they dip themselves in the fire and dip their tongue and their mouth seven times; and after that they go up and put on the garment of 'Machaqe Samal, and cover themselves with cloaks of chashmal, and stand in four rows beside the Throne of Glory, in all the heavens."

CHAPTER 37

¹R. Ishmael said: Metatron, the messenger, the Prince of the Presence, said to me: "There are four chariots of Shekinah standing in the seven Halls, and the four camps of Shekinah are standing before each one. Between each camp a river of fire is continually flowing. ²Between each river there are bright clouds surrounding them, and pillars of brimstone are put up between each cloud. Flaming wheels are standing between one pillar and another, surrounding them. And between one wheel and another there are flames of fire around. Between one flame and another there are treasuries of lightnings; behind the treasuries of lightnings are the wings of the storm wind. Behind the wings of the storm-wind are the chambers of the tempest; behind the chambers of the tempest there are winds, voices, thunders, sparks on sparks, and earthquakes on earthquakes."

CHAPTER 38

¹R. Ishmael said: Metatron, the messenger, the Prince of the Presence, said to me: "At the time when the ministering messengers utter the Thrice Holy, then all the pillars of the heavens and their sockets tremble, and the gates of the Halls of 'Araboth Raqia' are shaken, and the foundations of Shechaqim and the universe are moved, and the orders of Ma'on and the chambers of Makon quiver, and all the orders of Raqia', and the constellations, and the planets are dismayed, and the globes of the sun and the moon hurry away, and flee out of their courses, and run twelve thousand parasangs, and seek to throw themselves down from the heavens ²by reason of the roaring voice of their chant, and the noise of their praise, and the sparks and lightnings that go forth from their faces; as it is written: The voice of Your thunder was in the heavens and the lightnings lightened the world, the earth trembled and shook. ³Until the Prince of the World calls them, saying, Be quiet in your place! Do not fear because of the ministering messengers who sing the Song before the Holy One, blessed is He. As it is written: When the morning stars sang together, || And all the sons of Heaven [[or God]] shouted for joy."

CHAPTER 39

¹R. Ishmael said: Metatron, the messenger, the Prince of the Presence, said to me: "When the ministering messengers utter the HOLY, then all the explicit names that are graven with a flaming style on the Throne of Glory fly off like eagles, with sixteen wings. And they surround and encircle the Holy One, blessed is He, on the four sides of the place of His Shekinah. ²And the messengers of the host, and the flaming servants, and the mighty ophanim, and the cherubim of the Shekinah, and the holy chayyoth, and the seraphim, and the er'elim, and the taphsarim and the troops of consuming fire, and the fiery armies, and the flaming hosts, and the holy princes, adorned with crowns, clad in kingly majesty, wrapped in glory, girt with loftiness, fall on their faces three times, saying, Blessed is the name of His glorious Kingdom forever and ever."

CHAPTER 40

¹R. Ishmael said: Metatron, the messenger, the Prince of the Presence, said to me: "When the ministering messengers say HOLY before the Holy One, blessed is He, in the proper way, then the servants of His Throne, the attendants of His Glory, go forth with great mirth from under the Throne of Glory. ²And they all carry in their hands—each one of them—one million and one hundred million crowns of stars, similar in appearance to the planet Venus, and put them on the ministering messengers and the great princes who utter the HOLY. They put three crowns on each one of them: one crown because they say HOLY, another crown because they say HOLY, HOLY, and a third crown because they say HOLY, HOLY, HOLY, is the LORD of Hosts. ³And in the moment that they do not utter the HOLY in the right order, a consuming fire goes forth from the little finger of the Holy One, blessed is He, and falls down in the midst of their ranks and is divided into four hundred ninety-six thousand parts corresponding to the four camps of the ministering messengers, and consumes them in one moment, as it is written: A fire goes before Him and burns up His adversaries around. ⁴After that, the Holy One, blessed is He, opens His mouth, and speaks one word, and creates others in their stead—new ones like them. And each one stands before His Throne of Glory, uttering the HOLY, as it is written: They are new every morning; great is Your faithfulness."

CHAPTER 41

¹R. Ishmael said: Metatron, the messenger, the Prince of the Presence, said to me: "Come and behold the letters by which the heavens and

the earth were created, the letters by which the mountains and hills were created, the letters by which the seas and rivers were created, the letters by which the trees and herbs were created, the letters by which the planets and the constellations were created, the letters by which the globe of the moon and the globe of the sun, Orion, the Pleiades, and all the different luminaries of Raqia' were created, ²the letters by which the Throne of Glory and the wheels of the Merkaba were created, the letters by which the necessities of the worlds were created, ³the letters by which wisdom, understanding, knowledge, prudence, meekness, and righteousness were created, by which the whole world is sustained." ⁴And I walked by his side, and he took me by his hand, and raised me on his wings, and showed me those letters, all of them, that are graven with a flaming style on the Throne of Glory: and sparks go forth from them and cover all the chambers of 'Araboth.

CHAPTER 42

¹R. Ishmael said: Metatron, the messenger, the Prince of the Presence, said to me: "Come, and I will show you where the waters are suspended in the highest, where fire is burning in the midst of hail, where lightnings lighten out of the midst of snowy mountains, where thunders are roaring in the celestial heights, where a flame is burning in the midst of the burning fire, and where voices make themselves heard in the midst of thunder and earthquake." ²Then I went by his side, and he took me by his hand, and lifted me up on his wings, and showed me all those things. I beheld the waters suspended on high in 'Araboth Raqia', by the Name YAH 'EHYE 'ASHER 'EHYE, that is, YAH, I AM THAT I AM; and [I beheld] their fruits going down from Heaven and watering the face of the world, as it is written: "He waters the mountains from His chambers: the earth is satisfied with the fruit of Your work." ³And I saw fire, and snow, and hailstone that were mingled together within each other and yet were not damaged, by the name 'Esh 'Okela, as it is written: "For the Lord your God is a consuming fire." ⁴And I saw lightnings that were lightening out of mountains of snow and yet were not damaged, by the name YAH Sur 'Olamim, as it is written: "For in YAH, the LORD, the everlasting rock." ⁵And I saw thunders and voices that were roaring in the midst of fiery flames and were not damaged, by the name 'EL-SHADDAI RABBA, as it is written: "I am God Almighty." ⁶And I beheld a flame and a glow that were flaming and glowing in the midst of burning fire, and yet were not damaged, by the name YAD 'AL KES YAH, as it is written: "And he said, For the hand is on the Throne of the LORD." ⁷And I beheld rivers of fire in the midst of rivers of water and they were not damaged, by the name 'OSE SHALOM, as it is written: "He makes peace in His high places." For He makes peace between the fire and the water, between the hail and the fire, between the wind and the cloud, between the earthquake and the sparks.

CHAPTER 43

¹R. Ishmael said: Metatron said to me: "Come, and I will show you where the spirits of the righteous are that have been created and have returned, and the spirits of the righteous that have not yet been created." ²And he lifted me up to his side, took me by his hand, and lifted me up near the Throne of Glory by the place of the Shekinah; and he revealed the Throne of Glory to me, and he showed me the spirits that have been created and had returned: and they were flying above the Throne of Glory before the Holy One, blessed is He. ³After that I went to interpret the following verse of Writing and I found in what is written: "For the spirit clothed itself before me, and the souls I have made"—that means the spirits that have been created in the chamber of creation of the righteous and that have returned before the Holy One, blessed is He; and the words "and the souls I have made" refer to the spirits of the righteous that have not yet been created in the chamber, or Guph.

CHAPTER 44

¹R. Ishmael said: Metatron, the messenger, the Prince of the Presence, said to me: "Come, and I will show you where the spirits of the wicked and the spirits of the intermediate are standing, and the spirits of the intermediate, where they go down, and the spirits of the wicked, where they go down." ²And he said to me: "The spirits of the wicked go down to Sheol by the hands of two messengers of destruction: their names are Za'aphiel and Simkiel. ³Simkiel is appointed over the intermediate to support them and purify them because of the great mercy of the Prince of the Place. Za'aphiel is appointed over the spirits of the wicked in order to cast them down from the presence of the Holy One, blessed is He, and from the splendor of the Shekinah to Sheol, to be punished in the fire of Gehenna with staves of burning coal." ⁴And I went by his side, and he took me by his hand and showed me all of them with his fingers. ⁵And I beheld the appearance of their faces, and, behold, it was as the appearance of children of men, and their bodies like eagles. And not only that, but furthermore the color of the countenance of the intermediate was like pale grey on account of their deeds, for there are stains on them until they have become cleaned from their iniquity in the fire. ⁶And the color of the wicked was like the bottom of a pot on account of the wickedness of their doings. ⁷And I saw the spirits of the Patriarchs—Abraham, Isaac, and Jacob—and the rest of the righteous whom they have brought up out of their graves and who have ascended to Heaven. And they were praying before the Holy One, blessed is He, saying in their prayer: "Lord of the Universe! How long will You sit on Your Throne like a mourner in the days of his mourning with Your right hand behind You and not deliver Your children and reveal Your Kingdom in the world? And for how long will You have no pity on Your children who are made slaves among the nations of the world? Nor on Your right hand that is behind You with which You stretched out the heavens, and the earth, and the heavens of heavens? When will You have compassion?" ⁸Then the Holy One, blessed is He, answered each of them, saying, "Since these wicked sin so and so, and transgress with such and such transgressions against Me, how could I deliver My Great Right Hand in the downfall by their hands?" ⁹In that moment Metatron called me and spoke to me: "My servant! Take the scrolls and read their evil doings!" Immediately I took the scrolls and read their doings and there were to be found thirty-six transgressions written down with regard to each wicked one and besides that they have transgressed all the letters in the Torah, as it is written: "Yes, all Israel has transgressed Your law." It is not written "'al torateka" but, "'et torateka," for they have transgressed from Aleph to Taw; they have transgressed forty statutes for each letter. ¹⁰Immediately Abraham, Isaac, and Jacob wept. Then the Holy One, blessed is He, said to them: "Abraham, My beloved, Isaac, My chosen one, Jacob, My firstborn! How can I now deliver them from among the nations of the world?" And immediately Michael, the prince of Israel, cried and wept with a loud voice and said, "Why do You stand far off, O LORD?"

CHAPTER 45

¹R. Ishmael said: Metatron said to me: "Come, and I will show you the curtain of the Divine Majesty which is spread before the Holy One, blessed is He, and whereon are graven all the generations of the world and all their doings, both what they have done and what they will do until the end of all generations." ²And I went, and he showed it to me, pointing it out with his fingers like a father who teaches his children the letters of Torah. And I saw each generation, the rulers of each generation, and the heads of each generation, the shepherds of each generation, the oppressors of each generation, the keepers of each generation, the scourgers of each generation, the overseers of each generation, the judges of each generation, the court officers of each generation, the teachers of each generation, the supporters of each generation, the chiefs of each generation, the presidents of academies of each generation, the magistrates of each generation, the princes of each generation, the counselors of each generation, the nobles of each generation, and the men of might of each generation, the elders of each generation, and the guides of each generation. ³And I saw Adam, his generation, their doings and their thoughts; Noah and his generation, their doings and their thoughts; and the generation of the Flood, their doings and their thoughts; Shem and his generation, their doings and their thoughts; Nimrod and the generation of the confusion of tongues, and his generation, their doings and their thoughts; Abraham and his generation, their doings and their thoughts; Isaac and his generation, their doings and their thoughts; Ishmael and his generation, their doings and

their thoughts; Jacob and his generation, their doings and their thoughts; Joseph and his generation, their doings and their thoughts; the tribes and their generation, their doings and their thoughts; Amram and his generation, their doings and their thoughts; Moses and his generation, their doings and their thoughts; ⁴Aaron and Miriam, their works and their doings; the princes and the elders, their works and doings; Joshua and his generation, their works and doings; the judges and their generation, their works and doings; Eli and his generation, their works and doings; Phinehas, their works and doings; Elkanah and his generation, their works and their doings; Samuel and his generation, their works and doings; the kings of Judah with their generations, their works and their doings; the kings of Israel and their generations, their works and their doings; the princes of Israel, their works and their doings; the princes of the nations of the world, their works and their doings; the heads of the councils of Israel, their works and their doings; the heads of the councils in the nations of the world, their generations, their works and their doings; the rulers of Israel and their generation, their works and their doings; the nobles of Israel and their generation, their works and their doings; the nobles of the nations of the world and their generations, their works and their doings; the men of reputation in Israel, their generation, their works and their doings; the judges of Israel, their generation, their works and their doings; the judges of the nations of the world and their generation, their works and their doings; the teachers of children in Israel, their generations, their works and their doings; the teachers of children in the nations of the world, their generations, their works and their doings; the counselors of Israel, their generation, their works and their doings; the counselors of the nations of the world, their generation, their works and their doings; all the prophets of Israel, their generation, their works and their doings; all the prophets of the nations of the world, their generation, their works and their doings; ⁵and all the fights and wars that the nations of the world worked against the people of Israel in the time of their kingdom. And I saw Messiah, son of Joseph, and His generation, and their works and their doings that they will do against the nations of the world. And I saw Messiah, son of David, and His generation, and all the fights and wars, and their works and their doings that they will do with Israel both for good and evil. And I saw all the fights and wars that Gog and Magog will fight in the days of Messiah, and all that the Holy One, blessed is He, will do with them in the time to come. ⁶And all the rest of all the leaders of the generations and all the works of the generations both in Israel and in the nations of the world, both what is done and what will be done hereafter to all generations until the end of time, all were graven on the curtain of MAQOM. And I saw all these things with my eyes; and after I had seen it, I opened my mouth in praise of MAQOM, the Divine Majesty saying thus: "For the King's word has power and who may say to Him: What are You doing? Whosoever keeps the commandments will know no evil thing." And I said, "O LORD, how manifold are Your works!"

CHAPTER 46

¹R. Ishmael said: Metatron said to me: "Come, and I will show you the space of the stars that are standing in Raqia' night by night in fear of the Almighty and I will show you where they go and where they stand." ²I walked by his side, and he took me by his hand and pointed out all to me with his fingers. And they were standing on sparks of flames around the Merkaba of the Almighty. What did Metatron do? At that moment he clapped his hands and chased them off from their place. Immediately they flew off on flaming wings, rose, and fled from the four sides of the Throne of the Merkaba, and as they flew he told me the names of every single one. As it is written: "He tells the number of the stars, || He gives them all their names," teaching that the Holy One, blessed is He, has given a name to each one of them. ³And they all enter in counted order under the guidance of Rahatiel to Raqia' ha-Shamayim to serve the world. And they go out in counted order to praise the Holy One, blessed is He, with songs and hymns, according as it is written: "The heavens declare the glory of God." ⁴But in the time to come the Holy One, blessed is He, will create them anew, as it is written: "They are new every morning." And they open their mouth and utter a song. Which is the song that they utter? "When I consider Your heavens."

CHAPTER 47

¹R. Ishmael said: Metatron said to me: "Come, and I will show you the souls of the messengers and the spirits of the ministering servants whose bodies have been burned in the fire of the Almighty that goes forth from His little finger. And they have been made into fiery coals in the midst of the fiery river. But their spirits and their souls are standing behind the Shekinah. ²Whenever the ministering messengers utter a song at a wrong time or as not appointed to be sung, they are burned and consumed by the fire of their Creator and by a flame from their Maker, in the places of the whirlwind, for it blows on them and drives them into the Nehar di-Nur; and there they are made into numerous mountains of burning coal. But their spirit and their soul return to their Creator, and all are standing behind their Master." ³And I went by his side, and he took me by his hand and showed me all the souls of the messengers and the spirits of the ministering servants who were standing behind the Shekinah on wings of the whirlwind and walls of fire surrounding them. ⁴At that moment Metatron opened the gates of the walls to me within which they were standing behind the Shekinah, and I lifted up my eyes and saw them, and behold, the likeness of each one was as that of messengers and their wings like birds' wings, made out of flames, the work of burning fire. In that moment I opened my mouth in praise of MAQOM and said, "How great are Your works, O LORD."

CHAPTER 48 (A)

¹R. Ishmael said: Metatron said to me: "Come, and I will show you the Right Hand of MAQOM, laid behind Him because of the destruction of the holy temple, from which all kinds of splendor and light shine forth and by which the nine hundred fifty-five heavens were created, and whom not even the seraphim and the ophanim are permitted to behold until the day of salvation will arrive." ²And I went by his side, and he took me by his hand and showed me the Right Hand of MAQOM, with all manner of praise, rejoicing, and song: and no mouth can tell its praise, and no eye can behold it, because of its greatness, dignity, majesty, glory, and beauty. ³And not only that, but all the souls of the righteous who are counted worthy to behold the joy of Jerusalem, they are standing by it, praising and praying before it three times every day, saying, "Awake, awake, put on strength, O arm of the LORD," according as it is written: "He caused His glorious arm to go at the right hand of Moses." ⁴In that moment the Right Hand of MAQOM was weeping. And there went forth from its five fingers five rivers of tears, and they fell down into the Great Sea, and shook the whole world, according as it is written: "The earth is utterly broken down, || The earth is clean dissolved, || The earth is utterly moved, || The earth will stagger like a drunken man, || And will be moved to and fro like a lodge," five times corresponding to the fingers of His Great Right Hand. ⁵But when the Holy One, blessed is He, sees that there is no righteous man in the generation, and no pious man on earth, and no justice in the hands of men, and that there is no man like to Moses, and no intercessor as Samuel who could pray before MAQOM for the salvation and for the deliverance, and for His Kingdom, that it might be revealed in the whole world, and for His Great Right Hand that He put it before Himself again to work great salvation for Israel by it, ⁶then immediately the Holy One, blessed is He, will remember His own justice, favor, mercy, and grace, and He will deliver His Great Arm by Himself, and His righteousness will support Him, according as it is written: "And He saw that there was no man" (that is, like to Moses who prayed countless times for Israel in the desert and averted the Divine decrees from them) "and He wondered that there was no intercessor"—like to Samuel who entreated the Holy One, blessed is He, and called to Him and He answered him and fulfilled his desire, even if it was not fit in accordance with the Divine plan, according as it is written: "Is it not wheat-harvest today? I will call to the LORD." ⁷And not only that, but He joined fellowship with Moses in every place, as it is written: "Moses and Aaron among His priests." And again it is written: "Though Moses and Samuel stood before Me, || My own arm brought salvation to Me." ⁸The Holy One, blessed is He,

said in that hour: "How long will I wait for the children of men to work salvation according to their righteousness for My arm? For My own sake and for the sake of My merit and righteousness I will deliver [with] My arm and redeem My children by it from among the nations of the world, as it is written: For My own sake I will do it. For why should My Name be profaned?" ⁹In that moment the Holy One, blessed is He, will reveal His Great Arm and show it to the nations of the world, for its length is as the length of the world and its breadth is as the width of the world. And the appearance of its splendor is like to the splendor of the sunshine in its might, in the summer solstice. ¹⁰Immediately Israel will be saved from among the nations of the world. And Messiah will appear to them and He will bring them up to Jerusalem with great joy. And not only that, but they will eat and drink, for they will glorify the Kingdom of Messiah, the house of David, in the four quarters of the world. And the nations of the world will not prevail against them, as it is written: "The LORD has made His holy arm bare || In the eyes of all the nations, || And all the ends of the earth will see || The salvation of our God." And again: "The LORD alone led him, || And there was no strange god with him." [And again:] "And the LORD will be King over all the earth."

CHAPTER 48 (B)

¹Metatron has seventy names which the Holy One, blessed is He, took from His own Name and put on him. And they are these: (1) YEHOEL YAH, (2) YEHOEL, (3) YOPHIEL, and (4) YOPHPHIEL, and (5) 'APHPHIEL, and (6) MARGEZIEL, (7) GIPPUYEL, (8) PA'AZIEL, (9) 'A'AH, (10) PERIEL, (11) TATRIEL, (12) TABKIEL, (13) 'W, (14) YHWH, (15) DH, (16) WHYH, (17) 'EBED, (18) DIBBURIEL, (19) 'APH'APIEL, (20) SPPIEL, (21) PASPASIEL, (22) SENEGRON, (23) METATRON, (24) SOGDIN, (25) 'ADRIGON, (26) 'ASUM, (27) SAQPAM, (28) SAQTAM, (29) MIGON, (30) MITTON, (31) MOTTRON, (32) ROSPHIM, (33) QINOTH, (34) CHATATYAH, (35) DEGAZYAH, (36) PSPYAH, (37) BSKNYH, (38) MGRG, (39) BARAD, (40) MKRKK, (41) MSPRD, (42) CHSHG, (43) CHSHG, (43) CHSHB, (44) MNRTTT, (45) BSYRM, (46) MITMON, (47) TITMON, (48) PISQON, (49) SAPHSAPHYAH', (50) ZRCH, (51) ZRCHYAH, (52) B, (53) BEYAH, (54) HBHBEYAH, (55) PELET, (56) PLTYAH, (57) RABRABYAH, (58) CHAS, (59) CHASYAH, (60) TAPHTAPHYAH, (61) TAMTAMYAH, (62) SEHASYAH, (63) IRURYAH, (64) 'AL'ALYAH, (65) BAZRIDYAH, (66) SATSATKYAH, (67) SASDYAH, (68) RAZRAZYAH, (69) BAZRAZYAH, (70) 'ARIMYAH, (71) SBHYAH, (72) SBIBKHYH, (73) SIMKAM, (74) YAHSEYAH, (75) SSBIBYAH, (76) SABKASBEYAH, (77) QELILQALYAH, (78) KIHHH, (79) HHYH, (80) WH, (81) WHYH, (82) ZAKKLKYAH, (83) TUTRISYAH, (84) SURYAH, (85) ZEH, (86) PENIRHYAH, (87) Z'ZI'H, (88) GAL RAZAYYA, (89) MAMLIKYAH, (90) TTYAH, (91) 'EMEQ, (92) QAMYAH, (93) MEKAPPERYAH, (94) PERISHYAH, (95) SEPHAM, (96) GBIR, (97) GIBBORYAH, (98) GOR, (99) GORYAH, (100) ZIW, (101) 'OKBAR, (102) THE LESSER YHWH, after the Name of his Master, "for My Name is in him," (103) RABIBIEL, (104) TUMIEL, (105) SEGANSAKKIEL, THE PRINCE OF WISDOM. ²And why is he called by the name SAGNESAKIEL? Because all the treasuries of wisdom are committed in his hand. ³And all of them were opened to Moses on Sinai, so that he learned them during the forty days, while he was standing: the Torah in the seventy aspects of the seventy tongues, the Prophets in the seventy aspects of the seventy tongues, the Writings in the seventy aspects of the seventy tongues, the Halakhas in the seventy aspects of the seventy tongues, the Traditions in the seventy aspects of the seventy tongues, the Haggadahs in the seventy aspects of the seventy tongues, and the Toseftas in the seventy aspects of the seventy tongues. ⁴But as soon as the forty days were ended, he forgot all of them in one moment. Then the Holy One, blessed is He, called Yephiphyah, the Prince of the Law, and [through him] they were given to Moses as a gift. As it is written: "And the LORD gave them to me." And after that it remained with him. And from where do we know that it remained in his memory? Because it is written: "Remember the Law of My servant Moses which I commanded to him in Horeb for all Israel, even My statutes and judgments." The Law of Moses: that is, the Teaching; the Prophets and the Writings—[the] statutes: that is, the Halakhas and Traditions; Judgments: that is, the Haggadahs and the Toseftas. And all of them were given to Moses on high on Sinai. ⁵These seventy names are a reflection of the Explicit Names on the Merkaba which are graven on the Throne of Glory. For the Holy One, blessed is He, took from His Explicit Names and put seventy names of His on the name of Metatron by which the ministering messengers call the King of the kings of kings, blessed is He, in the high heavens, and twenty-two letters that are on the ring on His finger with which the destinies of the princes of kingdoms on high are sealed in greatness and power and with which the lots of the Messenger of Death are sealed, and the destinies of every nation and tongue. ⁶Metatron, the messenger, the Prince of the Presence; the messenger, the Prince of the Wisdom; the messenger, the Prince of the Understanding; the messenger, the Prince of the Kings; the messenger, the Prince of the Rulers; the messenger, the Prince of the Glory; the messenger, the Prince of the High Ones; and of the princes—the exalted, great, and honored ones, in Heaven and on earth—said: ⁷"YHWH, the God of Israel, is my witness in this thing, that when I revealed this secret to Moses, then all the hosts in every heaven on high raged against me and said to me: ⁸Why do you reveal this secret to a son of man, born of woman, tainted and unclean, a man of a decaying drop—the secret by which the heavens and earth, the sea and the dry land, the mountains and hills, the rivers and springs, Gehenna of fire and hail, the Garden of Eden and the Tree of Life were created; and by which Adam and Eve, and the cattle, and the wild beasts, and the bird of the air, and the fish of the sea, and Behemoth and Leviathan, and the creeping things, the worms, the dragons of the sea, and the creeping things of the deserts, and the Torah, and Wisdom, and Knowledge, and Thought, and the Knowledge of things above, and the fear of Heaven were formed? Why do you reveal this to flesh and blood? Have you obtained authority from MAQOM? And again: Have you received permission? The Explicit Names went forth from before me with lightnings of fire and flaming chashmallim. ⁹But they were not appeased until the Holy One, blessed is He, rebuked them and drove them away with rebuke from before Him, saying to them: I delight in, and have set My love on, and have entrusted and committed to Metatron, My servant, alone, for he is one unique among all the children of Heaven." ¹⁰And Metatron brought them out from his house of treasuries and committed them to Moses, and Moses to Joshua, and Joshua to the elders, and the elders to the prophets, and the prophets to the men of the Great Synagogue, and the men of the Great Synagogue to Ezra, and Ezra the Scribe to Hillel the elder, and Hillel the elder to R. Abbahu, and R. Abbahu to R. Zera, and R. Zera to the men of faith, and the men of faith committed them to give warning and to heal by them all diseases that rage in the world, as it is written: "If you will diligently listen to the voice of the LORD your God and will do that which is right in His eyes, and will give ear to His commandments, and keep all His statutes, I will put none of the diseases on you which I have put on the Egyptians, for I am the LORD that heals you." Ended and finished. Praise be to the Creator of the World.

BOOK OF GIANTS

Once thought to be nothing more than a 3rd-century Manichaean corruption of biblical and Jewish legends, a primordial Aramaic form was found among the Dead Sea Scrolls. This much older Book of Giants was composed hundreds of years before Christ's first advent—*at the latest*—and shares Enochian similarities. In this LSV reconstruction of the DSS Book of Giants, instead of presenting each fragmentary section, the narrative is pieced together in a plausible chronological order by chapter, so some fragments are grouped together. The fragment identifiers are listed before each set of verses belonging to that fragment.

CHAPTER 1
[The rebellious Watchers (messengers) descend to earth, bringing secret knowledge and wickedness. Their hybrid offspring are giants.]

[(1Q23)] ¹… they knew the secrets of… ²… sin was great in the earth … ³… and they killed many… ⁴… [they begot] giants…

CHAPTER 2
[The messengers observe all the creatures on earth, including human beings.]

[(4Q531)] ¹… [everything that the] earth produced … ²… the great fish … ³… the sky with all that grew… ⁴… [fruit of] the earth and all kinds of grain and all the trees… ⁵… beasts and reptiles… all creeping things of the earth, ⁶and they observed all… ⁷… every harsh deed and … utterance … ⁸… male and female, and among humans…

CHAPTER 3
[The messengers choose two hundred specimens from each of a variety of creatures on which to perform ungodly acts.]

[(1Q23)] ¹… [two hundred] donkeys, two hundred mules, two hundred … ²… rams of the flock, two hundred goats, two hundred … ³… [beasts of the] field from every animal, ⁴from every [bird]… ⁵… for interbreeding…

CHAPTER 4
[Giants, monsters, and corruption fill the earth as a result of angelic interbreeding.]

[(4Q531)] ¹… they defiled … ²… [they begot] giants and monsters … ³… they begot, and behold, all [the earth was corrupted] … ⁴… with its blood and by the hand of… ⁵… which did not suffice for them and … ⁶… and they were seeking to devour many … ⁷… the monsters attacked it.

CHAPTER 5
[(4Q532)] ¹… flesh … ²… all … monsters … will be … ³… they would arise … lacking in true knowledge … because … ⁴… the earth [grew corrupt] … mighty … ⁵… they were considering… ⁶… from the messengers on … ⁷… in the end it will perish and die… ⁸… they caused great corruption in the [earth] … ⁹… [this did not] suffice to … ¹⁰"They will be…"

CHAPTER 6
[The giants are troubled by dreams and visions which hint at a coming judgment on them. In one dream, a stone tablet is drenched in water and emerges with only three names still inscribed (presumably the names of Noah's sons).]

[(2Q26)] ¹… they drenched the tablet in the water … ²… the waters went up over the [tablet]… ³… they lifted the tablet out from the water of…

CHAPTER 7
[(4Q530)] ¹… [the vision] is for cursing and sorrow. I am the one who confessed… ²… the whole group of the castaways that I will go to … ³… the spirits of the slain, complaining about their killers and crying out… ⁴… that we will die together and be made an end of… ⁵… much and I will be sleeping, and bread … ⁶… for my dwelling; ⁷the vision and also … entered into the gathering of the giants … [6Q8] ⁸… Ohya, and he said to Mahway… ⁹"… without trembling. Who showed you all this vision, brother?" ¹⁰… "Barakel, my father, was with me." ¹¹… Before Mahway had finished telling what [he had seen] … ¹²… [said] to him, "Now I have heard wonders! If a barren woman gives birth …" [4Q530] ¹³Thereon Ohya said to Ha[hya], ¹⁴"… [will be destroyed] from on the earth and … ¹⁵… [the] earth." ¹⁶When… ¹⁷… they wept before [the giants] … ¹⁸"… your strength …" ¹⁹… Thereon Ohya [said] to Hahya, ²⁰… Then he answered, "It is not for us, but for Azaiel, ²¹for he did … [the offspring of the] messengers are the giants, ²²[and they would not let all their loved ones] be neglected … ²³… [we have] not been cast down; you have strength …

CHAPTER 8
[A giant boasts about his strength, but realizes he is not stronger than the faithful messengers of Heaven. One of the speakers is apparently the giant hybrid Gilgamesh from Sumerian myth.]

[(4Q531)] ¹"… I am a giant, and by the mighty strength of my arm and my own great strength … ²… anyone mortal, and I have made war against them; ³but I am not … able to stand against them, for my opponents… ⁴… reside in Heaven, and they dwell in the holy places. ⁵And not … [they] are stronger than me. ⁶… of the wild beast has come, and they call [me] the wild man." ⁷… Then Ohya said to him, "I have been forced to have a dream … the sleep of my eyes [vanished], to let me see a vision. Now I know that on…" ⁸… Gilgamesh …

CHAPTER 9
[Ohya has a dream in which a tree is uprooted, but three roots remain. This is presumably the same message as the dream of the stone tablet.]

[(6Q8)] ¹… three of its roots … ²… [while] I was [watching], there came … ³… [the roots were moved into] this garden, all of them, and not…

CHAPTER 10
[Bothered by the dreams and visions, Ohya suggests the message is actually judgment on another group.]

[(4Q530)] ¹… concerns the death of our souls … ²… and all his comrades, [and] Ohya told them what Gilgamesh said to him… ³… and it was said … "… concerning … the leader has cursed the potentates." ⁴And the giants were glad at his words. Then he turned and left…

CHAPTER 11
[Dreamers recount yet more dreams, first to the assembly of monsters, and second to the assembly of giants.]

[(4Q530)] ¹Thereon two of them had dreams and the sleep of their eye fled from them, ²and they arose and came to… ³… [and recounted] their dreams, and said in the assembly of [the giants and] the monsters, ⁴"[In] my dream I was watching this very night, ⁵[and within a garden there were] gardeners and they were watering… ⁶… [two hundred trees and] large shoots came out of their root … ⁷… all the water, and the fire burned all [the trees]…" ⁸… They found the giants to tell them [of the dream]…

CHAPTER 12
[Mahway is petitioned to seek Enoch for an interpretation of the dream, and then flies to him with the request.]

[(4Q530)] ¹"[Go to Enoch,] the noted scribe, and he will interpret the dream for us." ²Thereon his companion Ohya declared [this], and said to the giants, "I too had a dream this night, O giants, and behold, the Ruler of Heaven came down to earth … ³… and such is the end of the dream." ⁴[Then] all the giants [and monsters] grew afraid and called Mahway. ⁵He came to them and the giants pleaded with him and sent him to Enoch … ⁶They said to him, "Go … to you that … you have heard his voice." ⁷And he said to him, "He will … interpret the dreams … ⁸… how long the giants have to live."

BOOK OF GIANTS

CHAPTER 13
[(4Q530)] ¹…[he moved through the air] like strong winds, ²and flew with his hands like eagles … [he left] the inhabited world and passed over Desolation, the great desert…. ³… and Enoch saw him and hailed him, ⁴and Mahway said to him … ⁵… here and there a second time to Mahway … ⁶"The giants await your words, and all the monsters of the earth. ⁷If … has been carried … from the days of … their … and they will be added … ⁸… we would know from you their meaning … ⁹… [two hundred] trees that [came down] from Heaven…"

CHAPTER 14
[Enoch grants the request and sends Mahway with a stone tablet containing the interpretation.]
[(4Q530)] ¹The scribe [Enoch] … ²… a copy of the second tablet that [Enoch] sent … ³… in the very handwriting of Enoch the noted scribe… ⁴"[In the Name of God the great] and Holy One, to Shemihaza and all [his companions] … ⁵… let it be known to you that not… ⁶and the things you have done, and that your wives … ⁷… they and their sons and the wives of [their sons] … ⁸… by your licentiousness on the earth, and there has been on you… ⁹… [and the earth is crying out] and complaining about you and the deeds of your children, ¹⁰[and] the harm that you have done to it. ¹¹… until Raphael arrives, behold, destruction [is coming, a great flood, and it will destroy all living things] ¹²and whatever is in the deserts and the seas. ¹³And the meaning of the matter … ¹⁴… on you for evil. ¹⁵But now, loosen the bonds binding [you to evil]… and pray."

CHAPTER 15
[(4Q531)] ¹… [great fear] seized me, and I fell on my face; I heard his voice … ²… he dwelt among human beings but he did not learn from them…

LIFE OF ADAM AND EVE

The Life of Adam and Eve, also known in its Greek version as the Apocalypse of Moses, is a Jewish apocryphal group of writings. It recounts the lives of Adam and Eve from after their expulsion from the Garden of Eden to their deaths. It provides more detail about the Fall of Man, including Eve's version of the story. Satan explains that he rebelled when God commanded him to bow down to Adam. After Adam dies, he and all his descendants are promised a resurrection. The extant version comes from the 1st to 5th centuries AD, but there is widespread consensus that the original work was composed in the 1st century or earlier.

CHAPTER 1
¹This is the story of Adam and Eve after they had gone out of Paradise. ²And Adam knew his wife Eve and went upwards to the sun-rising and abode there eighteen years and two months. ³And Eve conceived and bore two sons: Adiaphotos, who is called Cain, and Amilabes, who is called Abel.

CHAPTER 2
¹And after this, Adam and Eve were with one another and while they were sleeping, Eve said to Adam her lord, "My lord, Adam, behold, ²I have seen in a dream this night the blood of my son Amilabes, who is styled Abel, being poured into the mouth of his brother Cain, and he went on drinking it without pity. But he begged him to leave him a little of it. ³Yet he did not listen to him, but gulped down the whole; nor did it stay in his stomach, but came out of his mouth." ⁴And Adam said, "Let us arise and go and see what has happened to them. [I fear] lest the adversary may be assailing them somewhere."

CHAPTER 3
¹And they both went and found Abel murdered by the hand of his brother Cain. ²And God says to the chief-messenger Michael, "Say to Adam: Do not reveal the secret that you know to Cain your son, for he is a son of wrath. But do not grieve, for I will give you another son in his stead; he will show [to you] all that you will do. Do not tell him anything." Thus spoke the chief-messenger to Adam. ³But he kept the word in his heart, and with him also Eve, though they grieved concerning their son Abel.

CHAPTER 4
¹And after this, Adam knew his wife Eve, and she conceived and bore Seth. ²And Adam said to Eve, "See! We have begotten a son in place of Abel, whom Cain slew, let us give glory and sacrifice to God."

CHAPTER 5
¹And Adam begot thirty sons and thirty daughters, and Adam lived nine hundred and thirty years; ²and he fell sick and cried with a loud voice and said, "Let all my sons come to me that I may see them before I die." ³And all assembled, for the earth was divided into three parts. And his son Seth said to him, ⁴"Father Adam, what is your complaint?" ⁵And he says, "My children, I am crushed by the burden of trouble." And they say to him, "What is trouble?"

CHAPTER 6
¹And Seth answered and said to him, "Have you called to mind, father, the fruit of paradise of which you used to eat, and have been grieved in yearning for it? ²If this be so, tell me—I will go and bring you fruit from paradise. For I will set dung on my head and will weep and pray that the LORD will listen to me and send His messenger (and bring me a plant from paradise), and I will bring it to you that your trouble may cease from you." ³Adam says to him, "No, my son Seth, but I have [much] sickness and trouble!" Seth says to him, "And how has this come on you?"

CHAPTER 7
¹And Adam said to him, "When God made us, me and your mother, through whom also I die, He gave us power to eat of every tree which is in paradise, but, concerning that one only, He charged us not to eat of it, and through this one we are to die. ²And the hour drew near for the messengers who were guarding your mother to go up and worship the LORD, and I was far from her, and the enemy knew that she was alone and gave to her, and she ate of the tree of which she had been told not to eat. ³Then she also gave to me to eat."

CHAPTER 8
¹"And God was angry with us, and the LORD came into paradise and called me in a terrible voice and said, Adam, where are you and why do you hide from My face? Will the house be able to hide itself from its builder? And He says to me, Since you have abandoned My covenant, I have brought on your body seventy-two strokes; the trouble of the first stroke is a pain of the eyes, the second stroke an affection of the hearing, and likewise in turn all the strokes will befall you."

CHAPTER 9
¹As he said this to his sons, Adam groaned sore and said, "What will I do? I am in great distress." ²And Eve wept and said, "My lord Adam, rise up and give me half of your trouble and I will endure it; for it is on my account that this has happened to you, on my account you are beset with toils and troubles." ³But Adam said to Eve, "Arise and go with my son Seth near to paradise, and put earth on your heads and weep and pray [to] God to have mercy on me and [to] send His messenger to paradise, and give me of the tree out of which the oil flows, and bring it me, and I will anoint myself and will have rest from my complaint."

CHAPTER 10
¹Then Seth and Eve went toward paradise, and Eve saw her son, and a wild beast assailing him, and Eve wept and said, ²"Woe is me! If I come to the day of the resurrection, all those who have sinned will curse me, saying, Eve has not kept the commandment of God." ³And she spoke to the beast: "You wicked beast, do you not fear to fight with the image of God? How was your mouth opened? How were your teeth made strong? How did you

LIFE OF ADAM AND EVE

not call to mind your subjection? For long ago you were made subject to the image of God." ⁴Then the beast cried out and said:

CHAPTER 11
¹"It is not our concern, Eve, your greed and your wailing, but your own; for [it is] from you that the rule of the beasts has arisen. ²How was your mouth opened to eat of the tree concerning which God enjoined you not to eat of it? On this account, our nature has also been transformed. ³Now therefore, you cannot endure it if I begin to reprove you."

CHAPTER 12
¹Then Seth speaks to the beast, "Close your mouth and be silent and stand off from the image of God until the Day of Judgment." ²Then the beast says to Seth: "Behold, I stand off from the image of God." And he went to his lair.

CHAPTER 13
¹And Seth went with Eve near paradise, and they wept there, and prayed [to] God to send His messenger and give them the oil of mercy. ²And God sent the chief-messenger Michael and he spoke to Seth: "Seth, man of God, do not weary yourself with prayers and entreaties concerning the tree which flows with oil to anoint your father Adam. For it will not be yours now, but in the end of the times. ³Then will all flesh be raised up from Adam until that great day—all that will be of the holy people. ⁴Then the delights of paradise will be given to them and God will be in their midst. ⁵And they will no longer sin before His face, for the evil heart will be taken from them and there will be given them a heart understanding the good and to serve God only. ⁶But you go back to your father. For the term of his life has been fulfilled and he will live three days from today and will die. ⁷But when his soul is departing, you will behold the awful [scene of] his passing."

CHAPTER 14
¹Thus spoke the messenger and departed from them. And Seth and Eve came to the hut where Adam was laid. ²And Adam says to Eve, "Eve, what have you worked in us? You have brought on us great wrath, which is death, [[lording it over all our race]]." ³And he says to her, "Call all our children and our children's children and tell them the manner of our transgression."

CHAPTER 15
¹Then Eve says to them, "Hear, all my children and children's children, and I will relate to you how the enemy deceived us. ²It befell that we were guarding paradise—each of us the portion allotted to us from God. ³Now I guarded in my lot, the west and the south. But the Devil went to Adam's lot, where the male creatures were. [[For God divided the creatures; all the males he gave to your father and all the females he gave to me.]]"

CHAPTER 16
¹"And the Devil spoke to the serpent, saying, ²Rise up, come to me, and I will tell you a word whereby you may have profit. And he arose and came to him. And the Devil says to him, ³I hear that you are wiser than all the beasts, and I have come to counsel you. Why do you eat of Adam's tares and not of paradise? ⁴Rise up and we will cause him to be cast out of paradise, even as we were cast out through him. The serpent says to him, I fear lest the LORD be angry with me. ⁵The Devil says to him, Do not fear, only be my vessel and I will speak through your mouth words to deceive him."

CHAPTER 17
¹"And instantly he hung himself from the wall of paradise, and when the messengers ascended to worship God, then Satan appeared in the form of a messenger and sang hymns like the messengers. ²And I bent over the wall and saw him, like a messenger. But he says to me, Are you Eve? ³And I said to him, I am. [He said,] What are you doing in paradise? And I said to him, God set us to guard and to eat of it. ⁴The Devil answered through the mouth of the serpent: You do well, but you do not eat of every plant. ⁵And I said, Yes, we eat of all, save one only, which is in the midst of paradise, concerning which, God charged us not to eat of it; for, He said to us, On the day on which you eat of it, you will die the death."

CHAPTER 18
¹"Then the serpent says to me, May God live! But I am grieved on your account, for I would not have you ignorant. ²But arise, [come] here, listen to me and eat and mind the value of that tree. ³But I said to him, I fear lest God be angry with me as He told us. And he says to me, Do not fear, for as soon as you eat of it, you too will be as God, in that you will know good and evil. ⁴But God perceived this that you would be like Him, so he envied you and said, You will not eat of it. ⁵No, give heed to the plant and you will see its great glory. ⁶Yet I feared to take of the fruit. And he says to me, Come here, and I will give it you. Follow me."

CHAPTER 19
¹"And I opened to him and he walked a little way, then turned and said to me, ²I have changed my mind and I will not give you to eat until you swear to me to give also to your husband. [And] I said, What sort of oath will I swear to you? Yet what I know, I say to you: ³By the throne of the Master, and by the cherubim and the Tree of Life! I will also give to my husband to eat. ⁴And when he had received the oath from me, he went and poured on the fruit the poison of his wickedness, which is lust, the root and beginning of every sin, and he bent the branch on the earth, and I took of the fruit and I ate."

CHAPTER 20
¹"And in that very hour my eyes were opened, ²and immediately I knew that I was bare of the righteousness with which I had been clothed [on], and I wept and said to him, ³Why have you done this to me in that you have deprived me of the glory with which I was clothed? But I also wept about the oath, which I had sworn. But he descended from the tree and vanished. ⁴And I began to seek, in my nakedness, in my part for leaves to hide my shame, but I found none, for, as soon as I had eaten, the leaves showered down from all the trees in my part, except the fig tree only. ⁵But I took leaves from it and made for myself a girdle and it was from the very same plant of which I had eaten."

CHAPTER 21
¹"And I cried out in that very hour, Adam, Adam! Where are you? ²Rise up, come to me and I will show you a great secret. ³But when your father came, I spoke to him words of transgression [[which have brought us down from our great glory]]. For, when he came, I opened my mouth and the Devil was speaking, and I began to exhort him and said, ⁴Come here, my lord Adam, listen to me and eat of the fruit of the tree of which God told us not to eat of it, and you will be as a God. And your father answered and said, I fear lest God be angry with me. ⁵And I said to him, Do not fear, for as soon as you have eaten you will know good and evil. And speedily I persuaded him, and he ate and immediately his eyes were opened, and he too knew his nakedness. ⁶And to me he says, O wicked woman! What have I done to you that you have deprived me of the glory of God?"

CHAPTER 22
¹"And in that same hour, we heard the chief-messenger Michael blowing with his trumpet and calling to the messengers, and saying, ²Thus says the LORD: Come with me to Paradise and hear the judgment with which I will judge Adam. ³And when God appeared in paradise, mounted on the chariot of His cherubim with the messengers proceeding before Him and singing hymns of praises, all the plants of paradise, both of your father's lot and mine, broke out into flowers. ⁴And the throne of God was fixed where the Tree of Life was."

CHAPTER 23
¹"And God called Adam, saying, Adam, where are you? Can the house be hidden from the presence of its builder? ²Then your father answered, It is not because we do not think to be found by you, LORD, that we hide, but I was afraid, because I am naked, and I was ashamed before Your might, [my] Master. ³God says to him, Who showed you that you are naked, unless you have forsaken My commandment, which I delivered you to keep? ⁴Then Adam called to mind the word which I spoke to him, [saying,] I will make you secure before God. And he turned and said to me, Why have you done this? And I said, The serpent deceived me."

CHAPTER 24
¹"God says to Adam, Since you have disregarded My commandment and have listened to your wife, cursed is the earth in

your labors. ²You will work it and it will not give its strength: thorns and thistles will spring up for you, and in the sweat of your face you will eat your bread. [[You will be in manifold toils; you will be crushed by bitterness, but you will not taste of sweetness.]] ³You will be weary and will not rest; you will be tired by heat; you will be straightened by cold: you will busy yourself abundantly, but you will not be rich; and you will grow fat, but come to no end. ⁴The beasts, over whom you ruled, will rise up in rebellion against you, for you have not kept My commandment."

CHAPTER 25

¹"And the LORD turned to me and said, Since you have listened to the serpent, and turned a deaf ear to My commandment, ²you will be in throes of travail and intolerable agonies; you will bear children in much trembling and in one hour you will come to the birth, and lose your life, ³from your sore trouble and anguish. But you will confess and say: ⁴LORD, LORD, save me, and I will no longer turn to the sin of the flesh. And on this account, from your own words I will judge you, by reason of the enmity which the enemy has planted in you."

CHAPTER 26

¹"But He turned to the serpent and said, Since you have done this, and become a thankless vessel until you have deceived the innocent hearts, cursed are you among all beasts. ²You will be deprived of the victual of which you ate and will feed on dust all the days of your life: ³on your breast and your belly you will walk and be robbed of hands and feet. ⁴There will not be left [to] you ear nor wing, nor one limb of all that with which you ensnared them in your malice and caused them to be cast out of paradise; ⁵and I will put enmity between you and his Seed: He will bruise your head and you will bruise His heel until the Day of Judgment."

CHAPTER 27

¹"Thus He spoke and commanded the messengers have us cast out of paradise: and as we were being driven out amid our loud lamentations, your father Adam implored the messengers and said, ²Leave me a little [space] that I may entreat the LORD that He have compassion on me and pity me, for I only have sinned. ³And they left off driving him and Adam cried aloud and wept, saying, Pardon me, O LORD, my deed. ⁴Then the LORD says to the messengers, Why have you ceased from driving Adam from paradise? Why do you not cast him out? Is it I who have done wrong? ⁵Or is My judgment badly judged? ⁶Then the messengers fell down on the ground and worshiped the LORD, saying, You are just, O LORD, and You judge righteous judgment."

CHAPTER 28

¹"But the LORD turned to Adam and said, I will not permit you henceforward to be in paradise. ²And Adam answered and said, Grant me, O LORD, of the Tree of Life that I may eat of it, before I be cast out. ³Then the LORD spoke to Adam, You will not take of it now, for I have commanded the cherubim with the flaming sword that turns [every way] to guard it from you that you do not taste of it; ⁴but you have the war which the adversary has put into you, yet when you are gone out of paradise, if you should keep yourself from all evil, as one about to die, when again the resurrection has come to pass, I will raise you up and then there will be given to you the Tree of Life."

CHAPTER 29

¹"Thus spoke the LORD and ordered us to be cast out of paradise. ²But your father Adam wept before the messengers opposite paradise and the messengers say to him, What would you have us to do, Adam? ³And your father says to them, Behold, you cast me out. Please, allow me to take away fragrant herbs from paradise, so that I may offer an offering to God after I have gone out of paradise that he [may] hear me." ⁴And the messengers approached God and said, YAH'EL, Perpetual King, command, my Lord, that there be given to Adam incense of sweet fragrance from paradise and seeds for his food. ⁵And God commanded Adam go in and take sweet spices and fragrant herbs from paradise and seeds for his food. ⁶And the messengers let him go and he took four kinds: crocus, and nard, and calamus, and cinnamon, and the other seeds for his food; ⁷and, after taking these, he went out of paradise. And we were on the earth."

CHAPTER 30

¹"Now then, my children, I have shown you the way in which we were deceived; and you [must] guard yourselves from transgressing against the good."

CHAPTER 31

¹And when Eve had said this in the midst of her sons, while Adam was lying sick and bound to die after a single day from the sickness which had fastened on him, she says to him, ²"How is it that you die and I live or how long have I to live after you are dead? Tell me." ³And Adam says to her, "Do not pay heed to this, for you do not tarry after me, but even both of us are to die together. And she will lie in my place. ⁴But when I die, anoint me and let no man touch me until the messenger of the LORD will speak somewhat concerning me. ⁵For God will not forget me, but will seek His own creature; and now arise rather, and pray to God until I give up my spirit into His hands who gave it me. ⁶For we do not know how we are to meet our Maker, whether He is angry with us, or is merciful and intends to pity and receive us."

CHAPTER 32

¹And Eve rose up and went outside and fell on the ground and began to say: "I have sinned, O God, I have sinned, O God of All, I have sinned against You. ²I have sinned against the chosen messengers. I have sinned against the cherubim. I have sinned against Your fearful and unshakable Throne. I have sinned before You and all sin has begun through my doing in the creation." ³Even thus prayed Eve on her knees; [and] behold, the messenger of humanity came to her, and raised her up and said, ⁴"Rise up, Eve, for behold, your husband Adam has gone out of his body. Rise up and behold his spirit borne aloft to his Maker."

CHAPTER 33

¹And Eve rose up and wiped off her tears with her hand, and the messenger says to her, ²"Lift yourself up from the earth." And she gazed steadfastly into Heaven, and beheld a chariot of light, borne by four bright eagles, [and] it was impossible for any man born of woman to tell the glory of them or behold their face— ³and messengers going before the chariot— and when they came to the place where your father Adam was, the chariot halted and the seraphim. ⁴And I beheld golden censers, between your father and the chariot, and all the messengers with censers and frankincense came in haste to the incense-offering and blew on it and the smoke of the incense veiled the expanses. ⁵And the messengers fell down and worshiped God, crying aloud, and saying, "YAH'EL, Holy One, have pardon, for he is Your image, and the work of Your holy hands."

CHAPTER 34

¹And I, Eve, beheld two great and fearful wonders standing in the presence of God and I wept for fear, ²and I cried aloud to my son Seth and said, "Rise up, Seth, from the body of your father Adam and come to me, and you will see a spectacle which no man's eye has yet beheld."

CHAPTER 35

¹Then Seth arose and came to his mother and to her he says, "What is your trouble? Why do you weep?" [And] she says to him, ²"Look up and see with your eyes the seven heavens opened, and see how the soul of your father lies on its face and all the holy messengers are praying on his behalf, and saying, Pardon him, Father of All, for he is Your image. ³Pray, my child Seth, what will this mean? And will he one day be delivered into the hands of the Invisible Father, even our God? ⁴But who are the two dark ones who stand by at the prayers for your father Adam?"

CHAPTER 36

¹And Seth tells his mother that, "They are the sun and moon, and they fall down and pray on behalf of my father Adam." ²Eve says to him, "And where is their light and why have they taken on such a black appearance?" ³And Seth answers her, "The light has not left them, but they cannot shine before the Light of the Universe, the Father of Light; and on this account their light has been hidden from them."

CHAPTER 37

¹Now while Seth was saying this to his mother, behold, a messenger blew the trumpet, and there stood up all the messengers, [and they

were] lying on their faces, and they cried aloud in an awful voice and said, ²"Blessed [is] the glory of the LORD from the works of His making, for He has pitied Adam, the creature of His hands." ³But when the messengers had said these words, behold, there came one of the seraphim with six wings and snatched up Adam and carried him off to the Acherusian lake, and washed him three times, in the presence of God.

CHAPTER 38

¹And God says to him, "Adam, what have you done? If you had kept My commandment, there would now be no rejoicing among those who are bringing you down to this place. ²Yet, I tell you that I will turn their joy to grief, and I will turn your grief to joy, and I will transform you to your former glory and set you on the throne of your deceiver. ³But he will be cast into this place to see you sitting above him, then he will be condemned and they that heard him, and he will be sorely grieved when he sees you sitting on his honorable throne."

CHAPTER 39

¹And he stayed there three hours, lying down, and thereafter the Father of all, sitting on His holy throne, stretched out His hand, and took Adam and handed him over to the chief-messenger Michael, saying, ²"Lift him up into Paradise to the third heaven, and leave him there until that fearful day of My reckoning, which I will make in the world." ³Then Michael took Adam and left him where God told him.

CHAPTER 40

¹But after all this, the chief-messenger asked concerning the laying out of the remains. ²And God commanded that all the messengers should assemble in His presence, each in his order, and all the messengers assembled, some having censers in their hands, and others trumpets. ³And behold, the LORD of Hosts came on and four winds drew Him, and cherubim mounted on the winds and the messengers from Heaven [were] escorting Him, and they came on the earth where the body of Adam was. ⁴And they came to paradise and all the leaves of paradise were stirred so that all men begotten of Adam slept from the fragrance save Seth alone, because he was born according to the appointment of God. ⁵Then Adam's body lay there in paradise on the earth and Seth grieved exceedingly over him.

CHAPTER 41

¹Then God spoke to the chief-messenger[[s]] Michael, [[Gabriel, Uriel, and Raphael]]: ²"Go away to Paradise in the third heaven, and spread linen clothes and cover the body of Adam, and bring oil of the oil of fragrance and pour it over him." ³And they acted thus—the three great messengers—and they prepared him for burial. And God said, "Let the body of Abel also be brought." ⁴And they brought other linen clothes and prepared his [body] also. For he was unburied since the day when his brother Cain slew him; for wicked Cain took great pains to conceal [him] but could not, for the earth would not receive him for the body sprang up from the earth and a voice went out of the earth, saying, ⁵"I will not receive a companion body, until the earth which was taken and fashioned in me comes to me." At that time, the messengers took it and placed it on a rock, until his father Adam was buried. ⁶And both were buried, according to the commandment of God, in the spot where God found the dust, and He caused the place to be dug for two. ⁷And God sent seven messengers to paradise and they brought many fragrant spices and placed them in the earth, and they took the two bodies and placed them in the spot which they had dug and built.

CHAPTER 42

¹And God called and said, "Adam, Adam." And the body answered from the earth and said, "Here I am, Lord." ²And God says to him, "I told you [that] you are earth and to earth you will return. ³Again I promise to you the resurrection; I will raise you up in the resurrection with every man who is of your seed."

CHAPTER 43

¹After these words, God made a seal and sealed the tomb, that no one might do anything to him for six days until his rib should return to him. Then the LORD and His messengers went to their place. ²And Eve also, when the six days were fulfilled, fell asleep. ³But while she was living, she wept bitterly about Adam's falling on sleep, for she did not know where he was laid. For when the LORD came to paradise to bury Adam, she was asleep, and her sons too, except Seth, until He commanded Adam be prepared for burial; and no man knew on earth, except her son Seth. ⁴And Eve prayed in the hour of her death that she might be buried in the place where her husband Adam was. And after she had finished her prayer, she says, ⁵"LORD, Master, God of all rule, do not estrange me, Your handmaid, from the body of Adam, for from his members You made me. ⁶But deem me worthy, even me, unworthy that I am, and a sinner, to enter into his dwelling place, even as I was with him in paradise, both without separation from each other; just as in our transgression, we were led astray, and transgressed Your command, but were not separated. ⁷Even so, Lord, do not separate us now." But after she had prayed, she gazed heavenwards and groaned aloud and struck her breast and said, ⁸"God of all, receive my spirit," and immediately she delivered up her spirit to God.

CHAPTER 44

¹And Michael came and taught Seth how to prepare Eve for burial. And there came three messengers and they buried her [body] where Adam's body was and Abel's. ²And thereafter Michael spoke to Seth and says, "Lay out in this way every man that dies until the day of the resurrection." ³And after giving him this rule he says to him, "Do not mourn beyond six days, but on the seventh day, rest and rejoice on it, because on that very day, God rejoices, and we messengers, with the righteous soul, who has passed away from the earth." ⁴Even thus spoke the messenger, and ascended into Heaven, glorifying [God], and saying, "Hallelujah! ⁵[[HOLY, HOLY, HOLY is the LORD, in the glory of God the Father, for to Him it is appropriate to give glory, honor and worship, with the continuous life-giving Spirit now, and always, and forever. Amen. HOLY, HOLY, HOLY is the LORD of Hosts. To whom be glory and power forever and forever. Amen." ⁶Then the chief-messenger Joel glorified God, saying, "HOLY, HOLY, HOLY Lord, the heavens and earth are full of Your glory."]]

BOOK OF CREATION

The Sefer Yetzirah ("Book of Formation" or "Book of Creation") is the title of the earliest extant book on Jewish mysticism, although some early commentators treated it as a treatise on mathematical and linguistic theory as opposed to Kabbalah. The book is traditionally ascribed to the patriarch Abraham, although others attribute its writing to Rabbi Akiva. Modern scholars have not reached a consensus on the question of its origins and tend to date it between the 2nd century BC and 2nd century AD.

CHAPTER 1

¹In thirty-two mysterious paths of wisdom YAH—the LORD of Hosts, the God of Israel, the living God, the King of ages, the merciful and gracious God, the Exalted One, the Dweller in eternity, Most High and holy—engraved His Name by the three Sepharim: numbers, letters, and sounds. ²Ten are the ineffable Sephiroth. Twenty-two are the letters, the foundation of all things; there are three mothers, seven double, and twelve simple letters. ³The ineffable Sephiroth are ten, as are the numbers; and as there are in man five fingers over against five, so over them is established a covenant of strength, by word of mouth, and by the circumcision of the flesh. ⁴Ten is the number of the ineffable Sephiroth—ten and not nine, ten and not eleven. Understand this wisdom and be wise by the perception. Search out concerning it, restore the word to its creator, and pass from Him who formed it on His throne. ⁵The ten ineffable Sephiroth have ten vast regions bound to them—boundless in origin and having no ending; an abyss of good and of ill; measureless height and depth; boundless to the east and the west; boundless to the north and south; and the LORD, the only God, the faithful King, rules all these from His holy seat, forever and ever. ⁶The ten ineffable Sephiroth have the appearance of the lightning flash, their origin is unseen, and no end is perceived. The Word is in them as they rush forth and as they return, they speak as from the whirlwind, and returning fall prostrate in adoration before the Throne. ⁷The ten ineffable Sephiroth, whose ending is even as their origin, are like as a flame arising from a burning coal. For God is superlative in his unity; there is none equal to Him: what number can you place before one? ⁸Ten are the ineffable Sephiroth; seal up your lips lest you speak of them, and guard your heart as you consider them; and if your mind escapes from you, bring it back to your control; even as it was said, "running and returning"—[(the living creatures ran and returned)]—and hence was the Covenant made. ⁹The ineffable Sephiroth give forth the ten numbers. First, the Spirit of the God of the living; blessed and more than blessed is the living God of ages. The Voice, the Spirit, and the Utterance—these are the Holy Spirit. ¹⁰Second, from the Spirit He produced air, and formed in it twenty-two sounds—the letters; three are mothers, seven are double, and twelve are simple; but the Spirit is first and above these. Third, from the air He formed the waters, and from the formless and void He made mire and clay, and designed surfaces on them, and hewed recesses in them, and formed the strong material foundation. Fourth, from the water He formed fire and made for Himself a throne of glory with auphanim, seraphim, and cherubim, as His ministering messengers; and with these three He completed His dwelling, as it is written: "Who makes His messengers spirits and His ministers a flaming fire." ¹¹He selected three letters from among the simple ones and sealed them and formed them into a great Name: Y-H-W; and with this He sealed the universe in six directions. ¹²Fifth, He looked above, and sealed the height with Y-H-W. ¹³Sixth, He looked below, and sealed the depth with Y-W-H. ¹⁴Seventh, He looked forward, and sealed the east with H-Y-W. ¹⁵Eighth, He looked backward, and sealed the west with H-W-Y. ¹⁶Ninth, He looked to the right, and sealed the south with W-Y-H. ¹⁷Tenth, He looked to the left, and sealed the north with W-H-Y. ¹⁸Behold! From the ten ineffable Sephiroth proceed the one Spirit of the living God, air, water, fire, and also height, depth, east, west, south, and north.

CHAPTER 2

¹The twenty-two sounds and letters are the foundation of all things. Three mothers, seven doubles, and twelve simples. The three mothers are Aleph, Mem, and Shin; they are air, water, and fire. Water is silent, fire is sibilant, and air derived from the Spirit is as the tongue of a balance standing between these contraries which are in equilibrium, reconciling and mediating between them. ²He has formed, weighed, and composed with these twenty-two letters every created thing, and the form of everything which will hereafter be. ³These twenty-two sounds or letters are formed by the voice, impressed on the air, and audibly modified in five places: in the throat, in the mouth, by the tongue, through the teeth, and by the lips. ⁴These twenty-two letters, which are the foundation of all things, He arranged as on a sphere with two hundred and thirty-one gates, and the sphere may be rotated forward or backward, whether for good or for evil; from the good comes true pleasure, from evil nothing but torment. ⁵For He showed the combination of these letters, each with the other: Aleph with all, and all with Aleph; Beth with all, and all with Beth. Thus, in combining all together in pairs, the two hundred and thirty-one gates of knowledge are produced. ⁶And from the non-existent He made something, and all forms of speech and everything that has been produced; from the empty void He made the material world, and from the inert earth He brought forth everything that has life. ⁷He hewed, as it were, vast columns out of the intangible air, and by the power of His Name made every creature and everything that is; and the production of all things from the twenty-two letters is the proof that they are all but parts of one living body.

CHAPTER 3

¹The foundation of all the other sounds and letters is provided by the three mothers: Aleph, Mem, and Shin; they resemble a balance, on the one hand the guilty, on the other hand the purified, and Aleph—the air—is like the tongue of a balance standing between them. ²The three mothers, Aleph, Mem, and Shin, are a great Mystery, very admirable and most recondite, and sealed as with six rings; and from them proceed air, fire, and water, which divide into active and passive forces. The three mothers, Aleph, Mem, and Shin, are the foundation, from them spring three fathers, and from these have proceeded all things that are in the world. ³The three mothers in the world are Aleph, Mem, and Shin: the heavens were produced from fire; the earth from the eater; and the air from the Spirit is as a reconciler between the fire and the water. ⁴The three mothers, Aleph, Mem, and Shin—fire, water, and air—are shown in the year: from the fire came heat, from the waters came cold, and from the air was produced the temperate state, again a mediator between them. The three mothers, Aleph, Mem, and Shin—fire, water, and air—are found in man: from the fire was formed the head, from the water the belly, and from the air was formed the chest, again placed as a mediator between the others. ⁵He produced and designed these three mothers and combined them; and He sealed them as the three mothers in the universe, in the year and in man—both male and female. ⁶He caused the letter Aleph to reign in air and crowned it, and combining it with the others He sealed it, as air in the world, as the temperate [climate] of the year, and as the breath in the chest in man: the male with Aleph, Mem, Shin, the female with Shin, Mem, Aleph. ⁷He caused the letter Mem to reign in water, crowned it, and combining it with the others, formed the earth in the world, cold in the year, and the belly in man, male and female, the former with Mem, Aleph, Shin, the latter with Mem, Shin, Aleph. ⁸He caused Shin to reign in fire, and crowned it, and combining it with the others, sealed with it the heavens in the universe, heat in the year, and the head in man, male and female.

CHAPTER 4

¹The seven double letters, Beth, Gimel, Daleth, Kaph, Pe, Resh, and Taw, each have two sounds associated with them. They are referred to [as] life, peace, wisdom, riches, grace, fertility, and power. The two sounds of each letter are the hard and the soft—the aspirated and the softened. They are called double, because each letter presents a contrast or permutation; thus, life and death, peace and war, wisdom and folly, riches and poverty, grace and indignation, fertility and solitude, power and servitude. ²These seven double letters point out seven localities: above, below, east, west, north, south, and the palace of holiness in the midst of them sustaining all things. ³He designed, produced, and combined these seven double letters, and formed with them the planets of this world, the days of the week, and the gates of the soul [[the orifices of perception]] in man. From these seven He has produced the seven heavens, the seven earths, the seven Sabbaths; for this reason, He has loved and blessed the number seven more than all things under Heaven. ⁴Two letters produce two houses; three form six; four form twenty-four; five form one hundred and twenty; six form seven hundred and twenty; seven form five thousand and forty; and beyond this their numbers increase so that the mouth can hardly utter them, nor the ear hear the number of them. ⁵So now, behold the stars of our world, the planets which are seven: the Sun, Venus, Mercury, Moon, Saturn, Jupiter, and Mars. The seven are also the seven days of creation and the seven gateways of the soul of man—the two eyes, the two ears, the mouth, and the two nostrils. So with the seven are formed the seven heavens, the seven earths, and the seven periods of time; and so has He preferred the number seven above all things under His Heaven. [[⁶He produced Beth, and connected it to wisdom; He crowned it, combined and formed with it the Moon in the universe, the first day of the week, and the right eye of man. ⁷He produced Gimel, and connected it to health; He crowned it, combined and joined with it Mars in the universe, the second day of the week, and the right ear of man. ⁸He produced Daleth, and connected it to fertility; He crowned it, combined and formed with it the Sun in the universe, the third day of the week, and the right nostril of man. ⁹He produced Kaph, and connected it to life; He crowned it, combined and formed with it Venus in the universe, the fourth day of the week, and the left eye of man. ¹⁰He produced Pe, and connected it to power; He crowned it, combined and formed with it Mercury in the universe, the fifth day of the week, and the left ear of man. ¹¹He produced Resh, and connected it to peace; He crowned it, combined and formed with it Saturn in the universe, the sixth day of the week, and the left nostril of man. ¹²He produced Taw, and connected it to beauty; He crowned it, combined and formed with it Jupiter in the universe, the seventh day of the week, and the mouth of man. ¹³By these seven letters were also made seven worlds, seven heavens, seven earths, seven seas, seven rivers, seven deserts, seven days, seven weeks from Passover to Pentecost, and every seventh year a Jubilee.]]

CHAPTER 5

¹The twelve simple letters are He, Waw, Zayin, Heth, Teth, Yod, Lamed, Nun, Samekh, Ayin, Tsade, and Qof; they are the foundations of these twelve properties: sight, hearing, smell, speech, taste, sexual love, work, movement, anger, mirth, imagination, and sleep. ²These twelve are also allotted to the directions in space: northeast, southeast, the east above, the east below, the north above, the north below, the southwest, the northwest, the west above, the west below, the south above, and the south below; these diverge to infinity, and are as the arms of the universe. ³He designed and combined these twelve simple letters, and formed with them the twelve celestial constellations—the twelve signs. ⁴The twelve are also the months of the year: Nisan, Iyar, Sivan, Tammuz, Av, Elul, Tishri, Cheshvan, Kislev, Tevet, Shevat, and Adar. ⁵The twelve are also the twelve organs of living creatures: the two hands, the two feet, the two kidneys, the spleen, the liver, the gall, private parts, stomach, and intestines. ⁶He made these, as it were provinces, and arranged them as in order of battle for warfare. And God also made one from the region of the other. ⁷Three mothers and three fathers; and from there issue fire, air, and water. Three mothers, seven doubles, and twelve simple letters and sounds. ⁸Behold, now these are the twenty-two letters from which YAH—the LORD of Hosts, the living God, the God of Israel, exalted and sublime, the Dweller in eternity—formed and established all things; high and holy is His Name. [[⁹God produced He predominant in speech, crowned it, combined and formed with it Aries in the universe, Nisan in the year, and the right foot of man. ¹⁰He produced Waw, predominant in mind, crowned it, combined and formed with it Taurus in the universe, Iyar in the year, and the right kidney of man. ¹¹He produced Zayin, predominant in movement, crowned it, combined and formed with it Gemini in the universe, Sivan in the year, and the left foot of man. ¹²He produced Heth, predominant in sight, crowned it, combined and formed with it Cancer in the universe, Tammuz in the year, and the right hand of man. ¹³He produced Teth, predominant in hearing, crowned it, combined and formed with it Leo in the universe, Av in the year, and the left kidney in man. ¹⁴He produced Yod, predominant in work, crowned it, combined and formed with it Virgo in the universe, Elul in the year, and the left hand of man. ¹⁵He produced Lamed, predominant in sexual desire, crowned it, combined and formed with it Libra in the universe, Tishri in the year, and the private parts of man. ¹⁶He produced Nun, predominant in smell, crowned it, combined and formed with it Scorpio in the universe, Cheshvan in the year, and the intestines of man. ¹⁷He produced Samekh, predominant in sleep, crowned it, combined and formed with it Sagittarius in the universe, Kislev in the year, and the stomach of man. ¹⁸He produced Ayin, predominant in anger, crowned it, combined and formed with it Capricornus in the universe, Tevet in the year, and the liver of man. ¹⁹He produced Tsade, predominant in taste, crowned it, combined and formed with it Aquarius in the year, and the gullet in man. ²⁰He produced Qof, predominant in mirth, crowned it, combined and formed with it Pisces in the universe, Adar in the year, and the spleen of man.]]

CHAPTER 6

¹Three fathers and their generations, seven conquerors and their armies, and twelve bounds of the universe. See now, of these words, the faithful witnesses are the universe, the year, and man. The dodecad, the heptad, and the triad with their provinces; above is the Celestial Dragon, T-L-Y, and below is the world, and lastly the heart of man. The three are water, air, and fire—fire above, water below, and air conciliating between them; and the sign of these things is that the fire sustains the waters; Mem is mute, Shin is sibilant, and Aleph is the mediator and as it were a friend placed between them. ²The Celestial Dragon, T-L-Y, is placed over the universe like a king on the throne; the revolution of the year is as a king over his dominion; the heart of man is as a king in warfare. Moreover, He made all things, one from the other; and God set good over against evil, and made good things from good, and evil things from evil: with the good He tested the evil, and with the evil He tried the good. Happiness is reserved for the good, and misery is kept for the wicked. ³The three are one, and that one stands above. The seven are divided: three are over against three, and one stands between the triads. The twelve stand as in warfare: three are friends, three are enemies, three are life givers, [and] three are destroyers. The three friends are the heart, the ears, and the mouth; the three enemies are the liver, the gall, and the tongue; while God the faithful King rules over all. One above three, three above seven, and seven above twelve: and all are connected—the one with the other. ⁴And after that our father Abraham had perceived and understood, and had taken down and engraved all these things, the LORD Most High revealed Himself, and called him His beloved, and made a covenant with him and his seed; and Abraham believed on Him and it was imputed to him for righteousness. And He made this Covenant as between the ten toes of the feet—this is that of circumcision; and as between the ten fingers of the hands and this is that of the tongue. And He formed the twenty-two letters into speech and showed him all the mysteries of them. He drew them through the waters; He burned them in the fire; He vibrated them in the air; seven planets in the heavens, and twelve celestial constellations of the stars of the twelve signs.

TESTAMENT OF ABRAHAM

The Testament of Abraham was probably composed sometime in the 1st or 2nd century AD and is extant in Greek in two recensions (one long, the other short). The long recension is included here. The Testament of Abraham is often humorous in tone, indicating the text might actually be an entertaining fiction extrapolating on the life of the patriarch— even in the first verse we see Abraham's enormously exaggerated age. Though not necessarily composed by the same author, the *Testaments* (of Abraham, Isaac, and Jacob, *respectively*) are closely related works and are often grouped together.

CHAPTER 1

¹Abraham lived the measure of his life, nine hundred and ninety-five years, and having lived all the years of his life in quietness, gentleness, and righteousness, the righteous one was exceedingly hospitable; ²for, pitching his tent in the crossways at the oak of Mamre, he received everyone, both rich and poor, kings and rulers, the maimed and the helpless, friends and strangers, neighbors and travelers, all alike did the devout, all-holy, righteous, and hospitable Abraham entertain. ³Even on him, however, there came the common, inexorable, bitter lot of death, and the uncertain end of life. ⁴Therefore the LORD God, summoning His chief-messenger Michael, said to him, "Go down, chief-captain Michael, to Abraham and speak to him concerning his death, that he may set his affairs in order, ⁵for I have blessed him as the stars of the heavens, and as the sand by the seashore, and he is in abundance of long life and many possessions, and is becoming exceedingly rich. ⁶Beyond all men, moreover, he is righteous in every goodness, hospitable and loving to the end of his life; ⁷but you, chief-messenger Michael, go to Abraham, my beloved friend, and announce to him his death and assure him thus: You will at this time depart from this vain world, and will quit the body, and go to your own Lord among the good."

CHAPTER 2

¹And the chief-captain departed from before the face of God, and went down to Abraham to the oak of Mamre, and found the righteous Abraham in the field close by, sitting beside yokes of oxen for plowing, together with the sons of Masek and other servants, to the number of twelve. ²And behold, the chief-captain came to him, and Abraham, seeing the chief-captain Michael coming from afar, like to a very handsome warrior, arose and met him as was his custom, meeting and entertaining all strangers. ³And the chief-captain saluted him and said, "Greetings, most honored father, righteous soul chosen of God, true son of the heavenly one." ⁴Abraham said to the chief-captain: "Greetings, most honored warrior, bright as the sun and most beautiful above all the sons of men; you are welcome; therefore, I implore your presence, tell me from where the youth of your age has come; teach me, your suppliant, from where and from what army and from what journey your beauty has come here." ⁵The chief-captain said, "I, O righteous Abraham, come from the great city. I have been sent by the great King to take the place of a good friend of His, for the King has summoned him." ⁶And Abraham said, "Come, my Lord, go with me as far as my field." The chief-captain said, "I come"; and going into the field of the plowing, they sat down beside the company. ⁷And Abraham said to his servants, the sons of Masek, "Go to the herd of horses, and bring two horses, quiet, and gentle, and tame, so that I and this stranger may sit thereon." ⁸But the chief-captain said, "No, my Lord Abraham, let them not bring horses, for I abstain from ever sitting on any four-footed beast. Is my king not rich in much merchandise, having power over both men and all kinds of cattle? ⁹But I abstain from ever sitting on any four-footed beast. Let us go, then, O righteous soul, walking lightly until we reach your house." ¹⁰And Abraham said, "Amen, be it so."

CHAPTER 3

¹And as they went on from the field toward his house, beside that way there stood a cypress tree, and by the command of the LORD the tree cried out with a human voice, saying, "HOLY, HOLY, HOLY is the LORD God that calls Himself to those that love Him"; but Abraham hid the mystery, thinking that the chief-captain had not heard the voice of the tree. ²And coming near to the house they sat down in the court, and Isaac, seeing the face of the messenger, said to his mother Sarah, "My lady mother, behold, the man sitting with my father Abraham is not a son of the race of those that dwell on the earth." ³And Isaac ran, and saluted him, and fell at the feet of the incorporeal, and the incorporeal blessed him and said, "The LORD God will grant you His promise that He made to your father Abraham and to his seed, and will also grant you the precious prayer of your father and your mother." ⁴Abraham said to his son Isaac, "My son Isaac, draw water from the well, and bring it me in the vessel, that we may wash the feet of this stranger, for he is tired, having come to us from off a long journey." ⁵And Isaac ran to the well and drew water in the vessel and brought it to them, and Abraham went up and washed the feet of the chief captain Michael, and the heart of Abraham was moved, and he wept over the stranger. ⁶And Isaac, seeing his father weeping, wept also, and the chief captain, seeing them weeping, also wept with them, and the tears of the chief captain fell on the vessel into the water of the basin and became precious stones. ⁷And Abraham seeing the marvel, and being astonished, took the stones secretly, and hid the mystery, keeping it by himself in his heart.

CHAPTER 4

¹And Abraham said to his son Isaac, "Go, my beloved son, into the inner chamber of the house and beautify it. Spread two couches for us there—one for me and one for this man that is guest with us this day. ²Prepare a seat, and a candlestick, and a table for us there with abundance of every good thing. ³Beautify the chamber, my son, and spread under us linen and purple and fine linen. Burn every precious and excellent incense there, and bring sweet-smelling plants from the garden and fill our house with them. ⁴Kindle seven lamps full of oil, so that we may rejoice, for this man that is our guest this day is more glorious than kings or rulers, and his appearance surpasses all the sons of men." ⁵And Isaac prepared all things well, and Abraham taking the chief-messenger Michael, went into the chamber, and they both sat down on the couches, and between them he placed a table with abundance of every good thing. ⁶Then the chief-captain arose and went out, as if by constraint of his belly to make issue of water, and ascended to Heaven in the twinkling of an eye, and stood before the LORD, and said to Him: "LORD and Master, let Your power know that I am unable to remind that righteous man of his death, for I have not seen on the earth a man like him, pitiful, hospitable, righteous, truthful, devout, refraining from every evil deed. ⁷And now know, Lord, that I cannot remind him of his death." ⁸And the LORD said, "Go down, chief-captain Michael, to my friend Abraham, and whatever he says to you, that do also, and whatever he eats, eat also with him. ⁹And I will send My Holy Spirit on his son Isaac, and will put the remembrance of his death into the heart of Isaac, so that even he in a dream may see the death of his father, and Isaac will relate the dream, and you will interpret it, and he himself will know his end." ¹⁰And the chief-captain said, "Lord, all the heavenly spirits are incorporeal, and neither eat nor drink, and this man has set before me a table with abundance of all good things earthly and corruptible. ¹¹Now, Lord, what will I do? How will I escape him, sitting at one table with him?" ¹²The LORD said, "Go down to him, and take no thought for this, for when you sit down with him, I will send on you a devouring spirit, and it will consume out of your hands and through your mouth all that is on the table. ¹³Rejoice together with him in everything, only you will interpret well the things of the vision, that Abraham may know

TESTAMENT OF ABRAHAM

the sickle of death and the uncertain end of life, and may make disposal of all his possessions, for I have blessed him above the sand of the sea and as the stars of the heavens."

CHAPTER 5

¹Then the chief captain went down to the house of Abraham, and sat down with him at the table, and Isaac served them. ²And when the supper was ended, Abraham prayed after his custom, and the chief-captain prayed together with him, and each lay down to sleep on his couch. ³And Isaac said to his father, "Father, I too would fain sleep with you in this chamber, that I also may hear your discourse, for I love to hear the excellence of the conversation of this virtuous man." ⁴Abraham said, "No, my son, but go to your own chamber and sleep on your own couch, lest we be troublesome to this man." ⁵Then Isaac, having received the prayer from them, and having blessed them, went to his own chamber and lay down on his couch. ⁶But the LORD cast the thought of death into the heart of Isaac as in a dream, and about the third hour of the night Isaac awoke and rose up from his couch, and came running to the chamber where his father was sleeping together with the chief-messenger. ⁷Isaac, therefore, on reaching the door cried out, saying, "My father Abraham, arise and open to me quickly, that I may enter and hang on your neck, and embrace you before they take you away from me." ⁸Abraham therefore arose and opened to him, and Isaac entered and hung on his neck, and began to weep with a loud voice. ⁹Abraham therefore being moved at heart, also wept with a loud voice, and the chief-captain, seeing them weeping, wept also. ¹⁰Sarah being in her room, heard their weeping, and came running to them, and found them embracing and weeping. ¹¹And Sarah said with weeping, "My Lord Abraham, what is this that you weep? Tell me, my Lord, has this brother that has been entertained by us this day brought you tidings of Lot, your brother's son, that he is dead? Is it for this that you grieve thus?" ¹²The chief-captain answered and said to her, "No, my sister Sarah, it is not as you say, but your son Isaac, it seems to me, beheld a dream, and came to us weeping, and we, seeing him, were moved in our hearts and wept."

CHAPTER 6

¹Then Sarah, hearing the excellence of the conversation of the chief-captain, immediately knew that it was a messenger of the LORD that spoke. ²Sarah therefore signified to Abraham to come out toward the door, and said to him, "My Lord Abraham, do you know who this man is?" ³Abraham said, "I do not know." Sarah said, "You know, my Lord, the three men from Heaven that were entertained by us in our tent beside the oak of Mamre, when you killed the kid without blemish, and set a table before them. ⁴After the flesh had been eaten, the kid rose again, and sucked its mother with great joy. Do you not know, my Lord Abraham, that by promise they gave to us Isaac as the fruit of the womb? This is one of these three holy men." ⁵Abraham said, "O Sarah, in this you speak the truth. Glory and praise from our God and the Father. ⁶For late in the evening when I washed his feet in the basin I said in my heart, These are the feet of one of the three men that I washed then; and his tears that fell into the basin then became precious stones." ⁷And shaking them out from his lap he gave them to Sarah, saying, "If you do not believe me, look now at these." ⁸And Sarah receiving them, bowed down and saluted, and said, "Glory be to God that shows us wonderful things. ⁹And now know, my Lord Abraham, that there is among us the revelation of something, whether it be evil or good!"

CHAPTER 7

¹And Abraham left Sarah, and went into the chamber, and said to Isaac, "Come here, my beloved son, tell me the truth, what it was you saw and what befell you that you came so hastily to us." ²And Isaac answering began to say, "I saw, my Lord, in this night the sun and the moon above my head, surrounding me with its rays and giving me light. ³As I gazed at this and rejoiced, I saw the Heaven opened, and a man bearing light descend from it, shining more than seven suns. ⁴And this man like the sun came and took away the sun from my head, and went up into the heavens from where he came, but I was greatly grieved that he took away the sun from me. ⁵After a little while, as I was still sorrowing and sorely troubled, I saw this man come forth from Heaven a second time, and he also took away the moon from me, from off my head, ⁶and I wept greatly and called on that man of light, and said, Do not, my Lord, take away my glory from me; pity me and hear me, and if you take away the sun from me, then leave the moon to me. ⁷He said, Permit them to be taken up to the King above, for He wishes them there. And he took them away from me, but he left the rays on me." ⁸The chief-captain said, "Hear, O righteous Abraham; the sun which your son saw is you his father, and the moon likewise is Sarah his mother. ⁹The man bearing light who descended from Heaven, this is the one sent from God who is to take your righteous soul from you. ¹⁰And now know, O most honored Abraham, that at this time you will leave this worldly life, and remove to God." ¹¹Abraham said to the chief captain, "O strangest of marvels! And now are you he that will take my soul from me?" ¹²The chief-captain said to him, "I am the chief-captain Michael, that stands before the LORD, and I was sent to you to remind you of your death, and then I will depart to Him as I was commanded." ¹³Abraham said, "Now I know that you are a messenger of the LORD, and were sent to take my soul, but I will not go with you; but do whatever you are commanded."

CHAPTER 8

¹The chief-captain, hearing these words, immediately vanished, and ascending into Heaven stood before God, and told all that he had seen in the house of Abraham; ²and the chief-captain said this also to his Lord, "Thus says Your friend Abraham, I will not go with you, but do whatever you are commanded; and now, O LORD Almighty, does Your glory and immortal kingdom order anything?" ³God said to the chief-captain Michael, "Go to My friend Abraham yet once again, and speak to him thus, Thus says the LORD your God, He that brought you into the land of promise, that blessed you above the sand of the sea and above the stars of the heavens, that opened the womb of barrenness of Sarah, and granted you Isaac as the fruit of the womb in old age: ⁴Truly I say to you that blessing I will bless you, and multiplying I will multiply your seed, and I will give you all that you will ask from Me, for I am the LORD your God, and besides Me there is no other. ⁵Tell me why you have rebelled against Me, and why there is grief in you, and why you rebelled against My chief-messenger Michael? ⁶Do you not know that all who have come from Adam and Eve have died, and that none of the prophets has escaped death? ⁷None of those that rule as kings is immortal; none of your forefathers has escaped the mystery of death. ⁸They have all died, they have all departed into Hades, they are all gathered by the sickle of death. But on you I have not sent death, I have not suffered any deadly disease to come on you, I have not permitted the sickle of death to meet you, I have not allowed the nets of Hades to enfold you, I have never wished you to meet with any evil. ⁹But for good comfort I have sent my chief-captain Michael to you, that you may know your departure from the world, and set your house in order, and all that belongs to you, and bless your beloved son Isaac. ¹⁰And now know that I have done this not wishing to grieve you. ¹¹Why then have you said to my chief-captain, I will not go with you? Why have you spoken thus? ¹²Do you not know that if I give leave to death and he comes on you, then I should see whether you would come or not?"

CHAPTER 9

¹And the chief-captain, receiving the exhortations of the LORD, went down to Abraham, and seeing him the righteous one, fell on his face to the ground as one dead, and the chief-captain told him all that he had heard from the Most High. ²Then the holy and just Abraham, rising with many tears, fell at the feet of the incorporeal, and implored him, saying, "I implore you, chief-captain of the hosts above, since you have wholly deigned to come yourself to me a sinner and in all things your unworthy servant, I implore you even now, O chief-captain, to carry my word yet again to the Most High, and you will say to Him: ³Thus says your servant Abraham, Lord, Lord, in every work and word which I have asked of You You have heard me, and have fulfilled all my counsel. ⁴Now, Lord, I do not resist Your power, for I too know that I am not immortal but mortal. ⁵Since, therefore, all things yield to Your command, and fear and tremble at the face of Your power, I also fear, but I ask one request of You, and now, Lord

and Master, hear my prayer, for while still in this body I desire to see all the inhabited earth, and all the creations which You established by one word, and when I see these, then if I will depart from life I will be without sorrow." ⁶So the chief-captain went back again, and stood before God, and told him all, saying, "Thus says Your friend Abraham, I desired to behold all the earth in my lifetime before I died. ⁷And the Most High hearing this, again commanded the chief-captain Michael, and said to him, Take a cloud of light, and the messengers that have power over the chariots, and go down, take the righteous Abraham on a chariot of the cherubim, and exalt him into the air of Heaven that he may behold all the earth."

CHAPTER 10

¹And the chief-messenger Michael went down and took Abraham on a chariot of the cherubim, and exalted him into the air of Heaven, and led him on the cloud together with sixty messengers, and Abraham ascended on the chariot over all the earth. ²And Abraham saw the world as it was in that day, some plowing, others driving wagons, in one place men herding flocks, and in another watching them by night, and dancing and playing and harping, in another place men striving and contending at law, elsewhere men weeping and having the dead in remembrance. ³He also saw the newly-wedded received with honor, and in a word he saw all things that are done in the world, both good and bad. ⁴Abraham therefore, passing over them, saw men bearing swords, wielding in their hands sharpened swords, and Abraham asked the chief-captain, "Who are these?" ⁵The chief-captain said, "These are thieves, who intend to commit murder, and to steal, and burn, and destroy." ⁶Abraham said, "Lord, Lord, hear my voice, and command that wild beasts may come out of the wood and devour them." ⁷And even as he spoke there came wild beasts out of the wood and devoured them. ⁸And he saw in another place a man with a woman committing fornication with each other, and said, "Lord, Lord, command that the earth may open and swallow them," and immediately the earth was cleft and swallowed them. ⁹And he saw in another place men digging through a house, and carrying away other men's possessions, and he said, "Lord, Lord, command that fire may come down from Heaven and consume them." ¹⁰And even as he spoke, fire came down from Heaven and consumed them. ¹¹And immediately there came a voice from Heaven to the chief-captain, saying thus, "O chief-captain Michael, command the chariot to stop, and turn Abraham away that he may not see all the earth, for if he beholds all that live in wickedness, he will destroy all creation. ¹²For behold, Abraham has not sinned, and has no pity on sinners, but I have made the world, and do not desire to destroy any one of them, but wait for the death of the sinner, until he [may] be converted and live. ¹³But take Abraham up to the first gate of Heaven, that he may see there the judgments and repayments, and regret the souls of the sinners that he has destroyed."

CHAPTER 11

¹So Michael turned the chariot and brought Abraham to the east, to the first gate of Heaven; and Abraham saw two ways, the one narrow and contracted, the other broad and spacious, and there he saw two gates, the one broad on the broad way, and the other narrow on the narrow way. ²And outside the two gates there he saw a man sitting on a gilded throne, and the appearance of that man was terrible, as of the LORD. And they saw many souls driven by messengers and led in through the broad gate, and other souls, few in number, that were taken by the messengers through the narrow gate. ³And when the wonderful one who sat on the golden throne saw few entering through the narrow gate, and many entering through the broad one, immediately that wonderful one tore the hairs of his head and the sides of his beard, and threw himself on the ground from his throne, weeping and lamenting. ⁴But when he saw many souls entering through the narrow gate, then he arose from the ground and sat on his throne in great joy, rejoicing and exulting. ⁵And Abraham asked the chief-captain, "My Lord chief-captain, who is this most marvelous man, adorned with such glory, and sometimes he weeps and laments, and sometimes he rejoices and exults?" ⁶The incorporeal one said, "This is the first-created Adam who is in such glory, and he looks on the world because all are born from him, and when he sees many souls going through the narrow gate, then he arises and sits on his throne rejoicing and exulting in joy, because this narrow gate is that of the just that leads to life, and they that enter through it go into Paradise. For this, then, the first-created Adam rejoices, because he sees the souls being saved. ⁷But when he sees many souls entering through the broad gate, then he pulls out the hairs of his head, and casts himself on the ground weeping and lamenting bitterly, for the broad gate is that of sinners, which leads to destruction and continuous punishment. ⁸And for this the first-formed Adam falls from his throne weeping and lamenting for the destruction of sinners, for they are many that are lost, and they are few that are saved, for in seven thousand there is scarcely found one soul saved, being righteous and undefiled."

CHAPTER 12

¹While he was yet saying these things to me, behold two messengers, fiery in aspect, and pitiless in mind, and severe in look, and they drove on thousands of souls, pitilessly lashing them with fiery thongs. ²The messenger laid hold of one soul, and they drove all the souls in at the broad gate to destruction. ³So we also went along with the messengers, and came within that broad gate, and between the two gates stood a throne terrible of aspect, of terrible crystal, gleaming as fire, and on it sat a wondrous man bright as the sun, like to the Son of God. ⁴Before him stood a table like crystal, all of gold and fine linen, and on the table there was lying a scroll, the thickness of it six cubits, and the breadth of it ten cubits, and on the right and left of it stood two messengers holding paper, and ink, and pen. ⁵Before the table sat a messenger of light, holding in his hand a balance, and on his left sat a messenger all fiery, pitiless, and severe, holding in his hand a trumpet, having within it all-consuming fire with which to try the sinners. ⁶The wondrous man who sat on the throne himself judged and sentenced the souls, and the two messengers on the right and on the left wrote down, the one on the right the righteousness and the one on the left the wickedness. ⁷The one before the table, who held the balance, weighed the souls, and the fiery messenger, who held the fire, tried the souls. ⁸And Abraham asked the chief-captain Michael, "What is this that we behold?" ⁹And the chief-captain said, "These things that you see, holy Abraham, are the judgment and repayment." ¹⁰And behold, the messenger holding the soul in his hand, and he brought it before the judge, and the judge said to one of the messengers that served him, "Open this scroll, and find me the sins of this soul." ¹¹And opening the scroll he found its sins and its righteousness equally balanced, and he neither gave it to the tormentors, nor to those that were saved, but set it in the midst.

CHAPTER 13

¹And Abraham said, "My Lord chief-captain, who is this most wondrous judge? And who are the messengers that write down? And who is the messenger like the sun, holding the balance? And who is the fiery messenger holding the fire?" ²The chief-captain said, "Do you see, most holy Abraham, the terrible man sitting on the throne? ³This is the son of the first-created Adam, who is called Abel, whom the wicked Cain killed, and he sits thus to judge all creation, and examines righteous men and sinners. ⁴For God has said, I will not judge you, but every man born of man will be judged. ⁵Therefore He has given to him judgment, to judge the world until His great and glorious coming, and then, O righteous Abraham, is the perfect judgment and repayment, continuous and unchangeable, which no one can alter. ⁶For every man has come from the first-created, and therefore they are first judged here by his son, and at the second coming they will be judged by the twelve tribes of Israel, every breath and every creature. ⁷But the third time they will be judged by the LORD God of all, and then, indeed, the end of that judgment is near, and the sentence terrible, and there is none to deliver. ⁸And now by three tribunals the judgment of the world and the repayment is made, and for this reason a matter is not finally confirmed by one or two witnesses, but by three witnesses will everything be established. ⁹The two messengers on the right hand and on the left, these are they that write down the sins and the righteousness, the one on the right hand writes down the righteousness, and the one on the left the sins.

¹⁰The messenger like the sun, holding the balance in his hand, is the chief-messenger Dokiel, the just weigher, and he weighs the righteousnesses and sins with the righteousness of God. ¹¹The fiery and pitiless messenger, holding the fire in his hand, is the chief-messenger Puruel, who has power over fire, and tries the works of men through fire, and if the fire consumes the work of any man, the messenger of judgment immediately seizes him, and carries him away to the place of sinners, a most bitter place of punishment. ¹²But if the fire approves the work of anyone, and does not seize on it, that man is justified, and the messenger of righteousness takes him and carries him up to be saved in the lot of the just. ¹³And thus, most righteous Abraham, all things in all men are tried by fire and the balance."

CHAPTER 14

¹And Abraham said to the chief-captain, "My Lord the chief-captain, the soul which the messenger held in his hand, why was it adjudged to be set in the midst?" ²The chief-captain said, "Listen, righteous Abraham: because the judge found its sins and its righteousnesses equal, he neither committed it to judgment nor to be saved, until the Judge of all will come." ³Abraham said to the chief-captain, "And what yet is wanting for the soul to be saved?" ⁴The chief-captain said, "If it obtains one righteousness above its sins, it enters into salvation." ⁵Abraham said to the chief-captain, "Come here, chief-captain Michael, let us make prayer for this soul, and see whether God will hear us." ⁶The chief-captain said, "Amen, be it so"; and they made prayer and entreaty for the soul, and God heard them, and when they rose up from their prayer they did not see the soul standing there. ⁷And Abraham said to the messenger, "Where is the soul that you held in the midst?" ⁸And the messenger answered, "It has been saved by your righteous prayer, and behold a messenger of light has taken it and carried it up into Paradise." Abraham said, "I glorify the Name of God, the Most High, and His immeasurable mercy." ⁹And Abraham said to the chief-captain, "I implore you, chief-messenger, listen to my prayer, and let us yet call on the LORD, and supplicate His compassion, and entreat His mercy for the souls of the sinners whom I formerly, in my anger, cursed and destroyed, whom the earth devoured, and the wild beasts tore in pieces, and the fire consumed through my words. ¹⁰Now I know that I have sinned before the LORD our God. Come then, O Michael, chief-captain of the hosts above, come, let us call on God with tears that He may forgive me my sin, and grant them to me." ¹¹And the chief-captain heard him, and they made entreaty before the LORD, and when they had called on Him for a long space, ¹²there came a voice from Heaven, saying, "Abraham, Abraham, I have listened to your voice and your prayer, and forgive you your sin, and those whom you think that I destroyed I have called up and brought them into life by My exceeding kindness, because for a season I have repaid them in judgment, and those whom I destroy living on earth, I will not repay in death."

CHAPTER 15

¹And the voice of the LORD also said to the chief-captain Michael, "Michael, My servant, turn Abraham back to his house, for behold his end has come near, and the measure of his life is fulfilled, that he may set all things in order, and then take him and bring him to Me." ²So the chief-captain, turning the chariot and the cloud, brought Abraham to his house, and going into his chamber he sat on his couch. ³And his wife Sarah came and embraced the feet of the incorporeal, and spoke humbly, saying, "I give you thanks, my Lord, that you have brought my Lord Abraham, for behold, we thought he had been taken up from us." ⁴And his son Isaac also came and fell on his neck, and in the same way all his menservants and maidservants surrounded Abraham and embraced him, glorifying God. ⁵And the incorporeal one said to them, "Listen, righteous Abraham. Behold your wife Sarah, behold also your beloved son Isaac, behold also all your menservants and maidservants around you. ⁶Make disposition of all that you have, for the day has come near in which you will depart from the body and go to the LORD once for all." ⁷Abraham said, "Has the LORD said it, or do you say this of yourself?" The chief-captain answered, "Listen, righteous Abraham. ⁸The LORD has commanded, and I tell it to you." Abraham said, "I will not go with you." ⁹The chief-captain, hearing these words, immediately went forth from the presence of Abraham, and went up into the heavens, and stood before God the Most High, and said, "LORD Almighty, behold I have listened to Your friend Abraham in all he has said to You, and have fulfilled his requests. ¹⁰I have shown to him Your power, and all the earth and sea that is under Heaven. I have shown to him judgment and repayment by means of cloud and chariots, and again he says, I will not go with you." ¹¹And the Most High said to the messenger, "Does My friend Abraham say thus again, I will not go with you?" ¹²The chief-messenger said, "LORD Almighty, he says thus, and I refrain from laying hands on him, because from the beginning he is Your friend, and has done all things pleasing in Your sight. ¹³There is no man like him on earth, not even Job the wondrous man, and therefore I refrain from laying hands on him. Command, therefore, Immortal King, what will be done."

CHAPTER 16

¹Then the Most High said, "Call to me here Death that is called the shameless countenance and the pitiless look." ²And Michael the incorporeal went and said to Death, "Come here; the Lord of creation, the immortal King, calls you." ³And Death, hearing this, shivered and trembled, being possessed with great terror, and coming with great fear it stood before the invisible Father, shivering, groaning, and trembling, awaiting the command of the LORD. ⁴Therefore the invisible God said to Death, "Come here, you bitter and fierce name of the world, hide your fierceness, cover your corruption, and cast away your bitterness from you, and put on your beauty and all your glory, and go down to My friend Abraham, and take him and bring him to Me. ⁵But now also I tell you not to terrify him, but bring him with fair speech, for he is My own friend." ⁶Having heard this, Death went out from the presence of the Most High, and put on a robe of great brightness, and made his appearance like the sun, and became fair and beautiful above the sons of men, assuming the form of a chief-messenger, having his cheeks flaming with fire, and he departed to Abraham. ⁷Now the righteous Abraham went out of his chamber, and sat under the trees of Mamre, holding his chin in his hand, and awaiting the coming of the chief-messenger Michael. ⁸And behold, a smell of sweet fragrance came to him, and a flashing of light, and Abraham turned and saw Death coming toward him in great glory and beauty. ⁹And Abraham arose and went to meet him, thinking that it was the chief-captain of God, and Death beholding him saluted him, saying, "Rejoice, precious Abraham, righteous soul, true friend of the Most High God, and companion of the holy messengers." ¹⁰Abraham said to Death, "Greetings you of appearance and form like the sun, most glorious helper, bringer of light, wondrous man, from where does your glory come to us, and who are you, and from where do you come?" ¹¹Then Death said, "Most righteous Abraham, behold, I tell you the truth: I am the bitter lot of death." ¹²Abraham said to him, "No, but you are the comeliness of the world, you are the glory and beauty of messengers and men, you are fairer in form than every other, and you say, I am the bitter lot of death, and not rather, I am fairer than every good thing." ¹³Death said, "I tell you the truth. What the LORD has named me, that also I tell you." ¹⁴Abraham said, "Why have you come here?" Death said, "I have come for your holy soul." ¹⁵Then Abraham said, "I know what you mean, but I will not go with you"; and Death was silent and did not answer him a word.

CHAPTER 17

¹Then Abraham arose, and went into his house, and Death also accompanied him there. And Abraham went up into his chamber, and Death went up with him. ²And Abraham lay down on his couch, and Death came and sat by his feet. Then Abraham said, "Depart, depart from me, for I desire to rest on my couch." Death said, "I will not depart until I take your spirit from you." ³Abraham said to him, "By the immortal God I charge you to tell me the truth. Are you death?" Death said to him, "I am Death. I am the destroyer of the world." ⁴Abraham said, "I implore you, since you are Death, tell me if you come thus to all in such fairness, and glory, and beauty?" ⁵Death said, "No, my Lord Abraham, for your righteousnesses, and the boundless sea of your hospitality, and the greatness of your

love toward God has become a crown on my head, and in beauty and great peace and gentleness I approach the righteous, but to sinners I come in great corruption, and fierceness, and the greatest bitterness, and with fierce and pitiless look." ⁶Abraham said, "I implore you, listen to me, and show me your fierceness and all your corruption and bitterness." ⁷And Death said, "You cannot behold my fierceness, most righteous Abraham." ⁸Abraham said, "Yes, I will be able to behold all your fierceness by means of the Name of the living God, for the might of my God that is in Heaven is with me." ⁹Then Death put off all his comeliness and beauty, and all his glory and the form like the sun with which he was clothed, and put on himself a tyrant's robe, and made his appearance gloomy and fiercer than all kind of wild beasts, and more unclean than all uncleanness. ¹⁰And he showed to Abraham seven fiery heads of serpents and fourteen faces, [one] of flaming fire and of great fierceness, and a face of darkness, and a most gloomy face of a viper, and a face of a most terrible precipice, and a face fiercer than an asp, and a face of a terrible lion, and a face of a cerastes and basilisk. ¹¹He showed him also a face of a fiery scimitar, and a sword-bearing face, and a face of lightning, lightening terribly, and a noise of dreadful thunder. ¹²He also showed him another face of a fierce stormy sea, and a fierce rushing river, and a terrible three-headed serpent, and a cup mingled with poisons, and in short, he showed to him great fierceness and unendurable bitterness, and every mortal disease as of the odor of death. ¹³And from the great bitterness and fierceness there died servants and maidservants in number about seven thousand, and the righteous Abraham came into indifference of death so that his spirit failed him.

CHAPTER 18
¹And the all-holy Abraham, seeing these things thus, said to Death, "I implore you, all-destroying Death, hide your fierceness, and put on your beauty and the shape which you had before." ²And immediately Death hid his fierceness, and put on his beauty which he had before. ³And Abraham said to Death, "Why have you done this, that you have slain all my servants and maidservants? Has God sent you here for this end this day?" ⁴Death said, "No, my Lord Abraham, it is not as you say, but on your account I was sent here." ⁵Abraham said to Death, "How then have these died? Has the LORD not spoken it?" Death said, "Believe, most righteous Abraham, that this is also wonderful, that you also were not taken away with them. ⁶Nevertheless I tell you the truth, for if the right hand of God had not been with you at that time, you also would have had to depart from this life." ⁷The righteous Abraham said, "Now I know that I have come into indifference of death, so that my spirit fails, but I implore you, all-destroying Death, since my servants have died before their time, come, let us pray to the LORD our God that He may hear us and raise up those who died by your fierceness before their time." ⁸And Death said, "Amen, be it so." ⁹Therefore Abraham arose and fell on the face of the ground in prayer, and Death together with him, and the LORD sent a spirit of life on those that were dead and they were made alive again. ¹⁰Then the righteous Abraham gave glory to God.

CHAPTER 19
¹And going up into his chamber he lay down, and Death came and stood before him. And Abraham said to him, "Depart from me, for I desire to rest, because my spirit is in indifference." Death said, "I will not depart from you until I take your soul." ²And Abraham, with an austere countenance and angry look, said to Death, "Who has ordered you to say this? ³You say these words of yourself boastfully, and I will not go with you until the chief-captain Michael comes to me, and I will go with him. ⁴But this I also tell you, if you desire that I will accompany you, explain to me all your changes, the seven fiery heads of serpents and what the face of the precipice is, and what the sharp sword, and what the loud-roaring river, and what the tempestuous sea that rages so fiercely. ⁵Teach me also the unendurable thunder, and the terrible lightning, and the evil-smelling cup mingled with poisons. Teach me concerning all these." ⁶And Death answered, "Listen, righteous Abraham. For seven ages I destroy the world and lead all down to Hades, kings and rulers, rich and poor, slaves and free men, I convoy to the bottom of Hades, and for this I showed you the seven heads of serpents. ⁷The face of fire I showed you because many die consumed by fire, and behold death through a face of fire. ⁸The face of the precipice I showed you, because many men die descending from the tops of trees or terrible precipices and losing their life, and see death in the shape of a terrible precipice. ⁹The face of the sword I showed you because many are slain in wars by the sword, and see death as a sword. ¹⁰The face of the great rushing river I showed you because many are drowned and perish snatched away by the crossing of many waters and carried off by great rivers, and see death before their time. ¹¹The face of the angry raging sea I showed you because many in the sea falling into great surges and becoming shipwrecked are swallowed up and behold death as the sea. ¹²The unendurable thunder and the terrible lightning I showed you because many men in the moment of anger meet with unendurable thunder and terrible lightning coming to seize on men, and see death thus. ¹³I showed you also the poisonous wild beasts, asps and basilisks, leopards and lions and lions' whelps, bears and vipers, and in short, the face of every wild beast I showed you, most righteous one, because many men are destroyed by wild beasts, and others by poisonous snakes—serpents, and asps, and cerastes, and basilisks, and vipers—breathe out their life and die. ¹⁴I also showed you the destroying cups mingled with poison, because many men, being given poison to drink by other men, immediately depart unexpectedly."

CHAPTER 20
¹Abraham said, "I implore you, is there also an unexpected death? Tell me." ²Death said, "Truly, truly, I tell you in the truth of God that there are seventy-two deaths. One is the just death, buying its fixed time, and many men in one hour enter into death being given over to the grave. ³Behold, I have told you all that you have asked, now I tell you, most righteous Abraham, to dismiss all counsel, and cease from asking anything once for all, and come, go with me, as the God and judge of all has commanded me." ⁴Abraham said to Death, "Depart from me yet a little while, that I may rest on my couch, for I am very faint at heart, for since I have seen you with my eyes my strength has failed me, all the limbs of my flesh seem to me a weight as of lead, and my spirit is exceedingly distressed. ⁵Depart for a little while; for I have said I cannot bear to see your shape." ⁶Then his son Isaac came and fell on his breast weeping, and his wife Sarah came and embraced his feet, lamenting bitterly. ⁷There also came his menservants and maidservants and they surrounded his couch, lamenting greatly. ⁸And Abraham came into indifference of death, and Death said to Abraham, "Come, take my right hand, and may cheerfulness, and life, and strength come to you." ⁹For Death deceived Abraham, and he took his right hand, and immediately his soul adhered to the hand of Death. ¹⁰And immediately the chief-messenger Michael came with a multitude of messengers and took up his precious soul in his hands in a divinely woven linen cloth, ¹¹and they tended the body of the just Abraham with divine ointments and perfumes until the third day after his death, and buried him in the land of promise, the oak of Mamre, but the messengers received his precious soul, and ascended into Heaven, singing the hymn of "Thrice Holy" to the LORD, the God of all, and they set it there to worship the God and Father. ¹²And after great praise and glory had been given to the LORD, and Abraham bowed down to worship, there came the undefiled voice of the God and Father, saying thus: "Take, therefore, My friend Abraham into Paradise, where the dwelling places of my righteous ones are, and the abodes of my saints Isaac and Jacob in his bosom, where there is no trouble, nor grief, nor sighing, ¹³but peace, and rejoicing, and life unending." [[¹³And let us, too, my beloved brothers, imitate the hospitality of the patriarch Abraham, and attain to his virtuous way of life, that we may be thought worthy of the continuous life, glorifying the Father, Son, and Holy Spirit—to whom be glory and power forever. Amen.]]

TESTAMENT OF ISAAC

Likely from the 2nd century, the Testament of Isaac begins with Isaac being told of his impending death by an angel, and his message to his son in response. Isaac foretells both the 12 tribes of Israel and Christ.

THIS IS THE GOING FORTH FROM THE BODY OF ISAAC THE PATRIARCH. HE DIED ON THE TWENTY-FOURTH OF MESORE IN THE PEACE OF GOD. AMEN.

CHAPTER 1

¹Now the patriarch Isaac writes his testament and addresses his words of instruction to his son Jacob and to all those gathered around him. ²The blessings of the patriarch will be on those who come after us, even those who listen to these words, to these words of instruction and these medicines of life, so that the grace of God may be with all those who believe. ³This is the end of obedience, as it is written: You have heard a word, let it abide with you—which means that a man should strive patiently with what he hears. ⁴God gives grace to those who believe; he who believes the words of God and of His saints will be an inheritor of the Kingdom of God. ⁵God has been with the generations gone by, which have passed away, because of their innocence and their faith toward God. He will also be with the generations to come.

CHAPTER 2

¹Now it came to pass, when the time had come for the Patriarch Isaac to go forth from the body, God sent to him the messenger of his father Abraham at dawn on the twenty-second of Mesore. ²He said to him, "Greetings, son of promise!" Now it was the daily custom of the righteous old man Isaac to converse with the messengers. ³He lifted his face up to the face of the messenger: he saw him assuming the likeness of his father Abraham; and he opened his mouth and raised his voice and cried out in great joy, "I have seen your face like someone who has seen the face of God." ⁴The messenger said to him, "Listen, my beloved Isaac: I have been sent for you by God to take you to the heavens and set you beside your father Abraham, so that you can see all the saints; for your father is expecting you and is coming for you himself. ⁵Behold, a throne has been set up for you close to your father Abraham, and your lot and your beloved son Jacob's lot will surpass that of all others in the whole of God's creation; that is why you have been given forevermore the name of Patriarch and Father of the World." ⁶But the God-loving old man Isaac said to the messenger, "I am astonished by you, for you are my father." ⁷The messenger answered, "My beloved Isaac, I am the messenger that ministers to your father Abraham. But rejoice now, for I am to take you out of sorrow into gladness, out of suffering to rest forever. ⁸I am to transport you from prison to a place where you can range at will—to a place of joy and gladness; I am to take you to where there is light, and merriment, and rejoicing, and abundance that never fails. ⁹So then, draw up your testament and a statement for your household, for I am to translate you to rest for all eternity. ¹⁰Blessed is your father who begot you; blessed are you also; blessed is your son Jacob; and blessed are your descendants that will come after you."

CHAPTER 3

¹Now Jacob heard them talking together, but he said nothing. Our father Isaac said to the messenger with a heavy heart, "What will I do about the light of my eyes, my beloved son Jacob? ²For I am afraid of what Esau might do to him—you know the situation." ³The messenger said to him, "My beloved Isaac, if all the nations on earth were gathered together, they would not be able to bring these blessings pronounced over Jacob to nothing. ⁴When you blessed him, the Father, and the Son, and the Holy Spirit blessed him; and Michael, and Gabriel, and all the messengers, and all the heavenly ones, and the spirits of all the righteous, and your father Abraham all answered, Amen. ⁵Therefore, the sword will not touch his body, but he will be held in high honor and grow great and spread far and wide, and twelve thrones will spring from him." ⁶Our father Isaac said to the messenger, "You have given me much comfort, but do not let Jacob know in case he is distressed." ⁷The messenger said to him, "My beloved Isaac, blessed is every righteous man who goes forth from the body; blessed are they when they meet with God. ⁸Woe, woe, woe—three times woe—to the sinner, because he has been born into this world; great sufferings will come to him. ⁹Isaac, beloved of God, give these instructions, therefore, to your sons, and the instructions your father has given you. ¹⁰Hide nothing from Jacob, so that he can write them as instructions for the generations that will come after you, and those who love God may live their lives in accordance with them. ¹¹And take care that I am able to fetch you with joy, without delay. The peace of my Lord that He has given me, I give to you, as I go to Him who sent me."

CHAPTER 4

¹And when the messenger had said this, he rose from the bed on which Isaac was sleeping. He went back to the worlds on high while our father Isaac watched him go, astonished at the vision he had seen. ²And he said, "I will not see daylight before I am sent for." And while he was thinking this, behold, Jacob got up and came to the door of the room. ³The messenger had cast a sleep over him so that he should not hear them; and he got up and ran to where his father slept and said to him, "My father, whom have you been talking to?" ⁴Our father Isaac said to him, "You have heard, my son: your aged father has been sent for to be taken from you," and Jacob put his arms around his father's neck and wept, saying, "Ah me! My strength has left me! Today you have made me an orphan, my father." ⁵Our father Isaac embraced his son Jacob and wept; and both wept together until they could weep no more. ⁶And Jacob said, "Take me with you, father Isaac." But Isaac replied, "I would not have it so, my son; wait until you are sent for, my loved one. I remember on the day when the whole earth was shaken from end to end talking to my lord and father Abraham, and I had no strength to do anything. ⁷What God has ordained, He has ordained for each one by sure authority; His ordinances are immutable. ⁸But I know, and I am glad that I am to go to God, and I am strengthened by a guiding spirit; for this is a way that no one can escape. ⁹Listen, my son. Where is the first creation of the hands of God—our father Adam and our mother Eve? Where is Abel, and after him Mahalalel, and Jared, and our father Enoch, and Methuselah, and our father Noah, and his sons Shem, Ham, and Japheth? ¹⁰After these Arphaxad, and Cainan, and Shelah, and Eber, and Reu, and Serug, and Nahor, and Terah, and my blessed father Abraham, and his brother Lot? ¹¹All these experienced death except the perfect one, our father Enoch. ¹²After these, forty-two generations more will pass until Christ comes, born of a pure virgin called Mary. ¹³He will spend thirty years preaching in the world. At the end of all this, He will choose twelve men and reveal to them His mysteries and teach them about the archetype of His body and His true blood by means of bread and wine: ¹⁴and the bread will become the body of God and the wine will become the blood of God. ¹⁵And then He will ascend the tree of the Cross and die for the whole creation, and rise on the third day and despoil Hades, and deliver all mankind from the enemy. ¹⁶The generations to come will be saved by His body and by His blood until the end of time. ¹⁷The sacrifices of Christians will not cease until the end of time, whether offered secretly or openly; ¹⁸and the Antichrist will not appear so long as they offer up their sacrifice. ¹⁹Blessed is every man who performs that service and believes in it, because the archetypal service is in the heavens; and they will celebrate with the Son of God in His kingdom."

CHAPTER 5

¹While the God-loving old man, our father Isaac, was saying this, all his household gathered around him and wept. ²His son told all his relations, and they came to him in tears. ³Now our father Isaac had made for himself a bedroom in his house; and when his sight began to fail, he withdrew into it and remained there for one hundred years, fasting daily until evening, and offering for himself and his household a young animal for their soul. ⁴And he spent half the night in prayer and

praise of God. ⁵Thus he lived an ascetic life for one hundred years. And he kept three periods of forty days as fasts each year, neither drinking wine nor eating fruit nor sleeping on his bed. ⁶And he prayed and gave thanks to God continually.

CHAPTER 6

¹Now when it became generally known that the man of God had regained his sight, people gathered to him from everywhere, listening to his words of life; for they realized that [the] Holy Spirit of God was speaking in him. ²The great ones who came said to him, "You can now see clearly enough: how come it [is] that after your sight had failed you have now regained it?" ³The God-loving old man smiled and said to them, "My sons and brothers, the God of my father Abraham has brought this about to comfort me in my old age." ⁴But the priest of God said to him, "Tell me what I ought to do, my father Isaac." ⁵Our father Isaac said to him, "Keep your body holy, for the temple of God is set in it. Do not engage in controversy with other men in case an angry word escapes your mouth. Be on your guard against evil-speaking, against vainglory, and against uttering any thoughtless word; and see that your hands do not reach out after what is not yours. ⁶Do not offer a sacrifice with a blemish in it; and wash yourself with water when you approach the altar. Do not mix the thoughts of the world with the thoughts of God when you stand before Him. ⁷Do your utmost to be at peace with everyone. When you stand before God and offer your sacrifice—when you come to offer it on the altar— ⁸you should recite privately one hundred prayers to God and make this confession to God, saying, Oh God, the inexplicable, the unfathomable, the unattainable, the pure treasure, purify me in love, for I am flesh and blood and I run defiled to You, that You may purify me. ⁹I come burdened, and I ask that You may lighten my burden. A fire will burn wood, and Your mercy will take away my iniquities. Forgive me—I that am a sinner; I forgive the whole creation that You have made, I have no complaint against anyone: ¹⁰I am at peace with all that is made in Your image. ¹¹I am unmoved by all the evil reasonings that have been brought before me. I am Your servant and the son of Your maidservant: I am the one who sins, You are the one who forgives. ¹²Forgive me and enable me to stand in Your holy place. Let my sacrifice be acceptable before You. ¹³Do not reject me because of my sins, but receive me to You, in spite of my many sins, like a sheep that has gone astray. ¹⁴God who has been with our father Adam, and Abel, and Noah, and our father Abraham, and his son Isaac, who has been with Jacob, be with me also, and receive my sacrifice from my hand. ¹⁵As you recite all this, take your sacrifice and offer it; and strive heavenwards because of the sacrifice of God, so that you do not displease Him. For the work of the priest is no small thing."

CHAPTER 7

¹Every priest today, and until the end of time, must be temperate as regards his food, and drink, and sleep; neither should he talk about events connected with this world, nor listen to anyone who is talking about them. ²Rather should he spend his whole life occupied with prayer, and vigils, and recitation until our God sends for him in peace. ³Every man on earth, be he priest or monk—for after a long time they will love the life of holy retreat—must renounce the world and all its evil cares and join in the holy service the messengers render in purity to God. ⁴And they will be honored before God and His messengers because of their holy sacrifices and their angelic service, which is like the archetype that is rendered in the heavens. ⁵And the messengers will be their friends, because of their perfect faith and their purity; and great is their honor before God. ⁶In a word, whether great or small, sinlessness is required of us. ⁷The chief sins worthy of conversion are these: You will not kill with the sword; You will not kill with the tongue either; ⁸You will not commit fornication with your body; You will not commit fornication with your thoughts; You will not go in to the young to defile them; ⁹You will not be envious; You will not be angry until the sun has set; ¹⁰You will not be proud in disposition; You will not rejoice over your neighbour's fall; You will not slander; ¹¹You will not look at a woman with a lustful eye; and, Do not readily listen to slander. ¹²We need to beware of these things, and of others like them, until each one of us is secure from the wrath that will be revealed from Heaven."

CHAPTER 8

¹Now when the people gathered about him heard him, they cried out aloud, saying, "This is appropriate and right. Amen." But the God-loving old man was silent: he drew up his blanket [and] he covered his face. ²And the people and the priest were silent, so that he could rest himself a little while. ³But the messenger of his father Abraham came to him and took him up into the heavens. He saw terrors and tumults spread abroad on this side and on that; and it was a terror and a tumult fearful to behold. ⁴Some had the face of a camel, others had the face of a lion; some had the face of a dog, others had but one eye and had tongs in their hands, three ells long, all of iron. ⁵I looked, and behold, a man was brought, and those who brought him went with him. When they reached the beasts, those who went with him withdrew to one side. The lion advanced toward him, tore him apart into little pieces, and swallowed him; ⁶it then vomited him up, and he became like himself again; and the next beast treated him in just the same way. ⁷In short, they passed him on from one to the other; each one would tear him into pieces, swallow him, and then vomit him up; and he would become like himself again. ⁸I said to the messenger, "What sin has this man committed, my lord, that all this is done to him?" The messenger said to me, "This man you are looking at now had a quarrel with his neighbour, and he died without their being reconciled. ⁹See, he has been handed over to five chief tormentors: they spend a year tormenting him for every hour he spent quarreling with his neighbour." ¹⁰The messenger also said to me, "My beloved Isaac, do you think these are the only ones? Believe me Isaac, beloved of God, there are six hundred thousand tormentors. ¹¹They spend a year tormenting a man for every hour that he spends sinning—if he did not convert, that is, before he went forth from the body."

CHAPTER 9

¹He led me on and brought me to a fiery river, the waters of which were an ell high, and its noise like the noise of Heaven's thunder. ²And I saw a host of souls submerged in it; and those who were in that river cried out and wept aloud, and there was a great commotion and much groaning. ³But it is a discerning fire that does not touch the righteous, yet burns up sinners and boils them in the stench that surrounds them. ⁴I also saw the pit of the abyss, the smoke of which went up in clouds; I saw men sunk in it grinding their teeth, crying out and wailing, and each one was groaning. ⁵The messenger said to me, "Look and see these others too." And when I had looked at them the messenger said to me, "These are those who have committed the sin of Sodom; these are indeed in great distress." I also saw pits full of worms that do not sleep; I saw Abdemerouchos who is in charge of the punishments, made all of fire, threatening the tormentors in Gehenna, and saying, "Beat them until they know that God is." I saw a house built of fiery stone, and there were grown men underneath it, crying out and wailing. The messenger said to me, "Look with your eyes and contemplate the punishments." I said to the messenger, "My eyes could not endure it; for how long must these punishments go on?" He said to me, "Until the merciful God has pity."

CHAPTER 10

¹After this the messenger took me up into the heavens; I saw my father Abraham, and I made obeisance to him. ²He saluted me, with all the saints, and the saints honored me because of my father; they walked with me and took me to my [heavenly] Father—I worshiped Him with all the saints. ³Songs of praise rang out: "YOU ARE HOLY, YOU ARE HOLY, YOU ARE HOLY. King, LORD of Hosts, the heavens and the earth are full of Your holy glory." ⁴The LORD said to my father from the holy place, "[It] is good that you have come, Abraham, you righteous root and faithful saint: it is good that you have come to our city. Whatever you may want to ask now, make your requests in the name of your beloved son Isaac, and they will be yours indeed." ⁵My father Abraham said, "Yours is the power, O LORD Almighty." The LORD said to Abraham, "As for all those who are given the name of my beloved Isaac, let each one of them copy out his testament and honor it, and feed a poor man with bread in the name of my beloved Isaac on the day of

TESTAMENT OF ISAAC

his holy commemoration; I will grant them to you as sons in My kingdom." ⁶Abraham said, "My almighty Lord, if a man cannot copy out his testament, can You not in Your mercy accept him, for You are merciful and compassionate?" ⁷The LORD said to Abraham, "Let him feed a poor man with bread, and I will give him to you as a gift and as a son in My Kingdom, and he will come with you to the first hour of the thousand years." ⁸Abraham said, "Suppose he is poor and has no means of getting bread?" ⁹The LORD said, "Let him spend the night of my beloved Isaac's commemoration without sleep, and I will give him to you as a gift and an inheritor in My Kingdom." ¹⁰My father Abraham said, "Suppose he is weak and has no strength, can You not in Your mercy accept him in love?" ¹¹The LORD said to him, "Let him offer up a little incense in the name of your beloved son Isaac, and I will give him to you as a son in My Kingdom. ¹²If he has no means of getting incense, let him seek out a copy of his testament and read it on my beloved Isaac's day. ¹³If he cannot read it, let him go and listen to others who can. If he is unable to do any of these things, let him go into his house and say one hundred prayers, and I will give him to you as a son in My Kingdom. ¹⁴But the most essential thing of all is that he should offer a sacrifice in my beloved Isaac's name, for his body was offered as a sacrifice. ¹⁵Yet not only will I give you everyone called by my beloved Isaac's name as a son in My Kingdom, [but] I will also give you everyone who does one of the things I have mentioned. ¹⁶And I will give you everyone who concerns himself about Isaac's life and his testament, or does any compassionate act, such as giving someone a cup of water to drink, or who copies out his testament with his own hand, and those who read it with all their heart in faith, believing everything that I have said. ¹⁷My power and the power of My beloved Son and the Holy Spirit will be with them, and I will give them to you as sons in My Kingdom. Peace to all of you, all My saints."

CHAPTER 11

¹Now when He had said this, songs of praise rang out: "YOU ARE HOLY, YOU ARE HOLY, YOU ARE HOLY. King, LORD of Hosts, the heavens and the earth are full of Your holy glory." ²The Father said to Michael from the holy place, "Michael, My steward, go quickly and gather together the messengers and all the saints, so that they may come and meet My beloved Isaac." ³And Michael sounded the trumpet at once. All the saints gathered with the messengers and came to the couch of our father Isaac. ⁴The LORD mounted His chariot, and the seraphim were in front of Him with the messengers. And when they came to our father Isaac's couch, our father Isaac beheld our Lord's face immediately turned toward him full of joy. ⁵He cried out, "It is good that You have come, my Lord, and Your great chief-messenger Michael! It is good that you have come, my father Abraham, and all the saints."

CHAPTER 12

¹Now when he had said this, Jacob embraced his father; he kissed his mouth and wept. Our father Isaac fixed his eyes on him and motioned to him to be silent. ²Our father Isaac said to the LORD, "Remember my beloved Jacob." The LORD said to him, "My power will be with him; and when the time comes and I become man and die and rise from the dead on the third day, I will put your name in everyone's mind, and they will invoke you as their father." ³Isaac said to Jacob, "My beloved son, this is the last commandment I give you today: keep a sharp eye on yourself; do not dishonor the image of God; for what you do to the image of man, you do to the image of God, and God will do it to you, too, in the place where you will meet Him. This is the beginning and the end." ⁴Now when he had said this, our Lord brought his soul out of his body, and it was white as snow. ⁵He greeted it [and] set it on the chariot with Him; He took it up into the heavens, with the seraphim making music before Him, and all the messengers and the saints. ⁶He freely granted him the good things of His Kingdom forever, and all the requests our father Abraham had asked of the LORD He freely granted him as a covenant forever.

CHAPTER 13

¹This is the going forth from the body of our father Isaac, the patriarch, on the twenty-fourth of the month Mesore. ²And the day on which his father Abraham offered him as a sacrifice is the eighteenth of Mechir. ³The heavens and the earth were full of the soothing fragrance of our father Isaac, like choice silver: this is the sacrifice of our father Isaac the patriarch. ⁴When Abraham offered him as a sacrifice to God, the soothing fragrance of Isaac's sacrifice went up into the heavens. ⁵Blessed is every man who performs an act of mercy in the name of these patriarchs, for they will be their sons in the kingdom of the heavens. ⁶For our Lord has made a covenant with them forever, that everyone who performs an act of mercy on the day of their commemoration will be given to them as a son in the kingdom of the heavens forever. ⁷And they will come to the first hour of the thousand years, in accordance with the promise of our Lord, even our God and our Savior Jesus Christ, ⁸through whom every glory is due to Him, and His good Father, and the Holy Spirit, the giver of life to all creation and one in being with the Father and the Son, now and always, forever and ever. Amen.

TESTAMENT OF JACOB

The Testament of Jacob is the tale of Jacob's visitation by the archangel Michael who tells him of his impending death. Jacob is then taken on a visit to Heaven, where he sees the torment of the sinful dead, and then meets his deceased grandfather Abraham. In this Testament it is the angels that Jacob meets who deliver most of the sermonizing material. It was probably written in the 2nd or 3rd century AD.

CHAPTER 1

¹In the Name of the Father, the Son, and the Holy Spirit—the one God. ²We begin, with the help of God Most High and through His intercession, to write the account of the life of our father, the patriarch Jacob, son of the patriarch Isaac, on the twenty-eighth day of the month of Mesore. ³May the blessing of his prayer guard and protect us from the temptations of the unyielding adversary. Amen! Amen! Amen! ⁴He said, "Come, listen, my beloved ones and my brothers who love the LORD, to what has been received." ⁵Now when the time of our father Jacob, father of fathers, son of Isaac, son of Abraham, approached and drew near for him to go forth from his body, this faithful one was advanced in years and distinction. ⁶So the LORD sent Michael to him, the chief of the messengers, who said to him, "O Israel, my beloved, of noble lineage, write down your spoken legacy and your instruction for your household and give them a covenant; also concern yourself with the proper ordering of your household, for the time has drawn near for you to go to your fathers to rejoice with them forever." ⁷So when our father Jacob, the faithful one, heard this from the messenger, he answered and said, as was his custom every day to speak in this manner with the messengers, ⁸"Let the will of the LORD be done." And God pronounced a blessing on our father Jacob. ⁹Jacob had a secluded place which he would enter to offer his prayers before the LORD in the night and in the day. ¹⁰The messengers would visit him and guard him and strengthen him in all things. ¹¹God blessed him and multiplied his people in the land of Egypt at the time when he went down to the land of Egypt to meet his son Joseph. ¹²His eyes had become dull from weeping, but when he went down to Egypt he saw clearly when he beheld his son. ¹³So Jacob-Israel bowed with his face to the ground, then fell on the neck of his son Joseph and kissed him, while weeping and saying, "I can die now, my son, because I have seen your face once more in my lifetime; O my beloved son."

CHAPTER 2

¹Joseph continued to rule over all Egypt, while Jacob stayed in the land of Goshen for

TESTAMENT OF JACOB

seventeen years and became very old, so that his lifespan was completed. ²He continually kept all the commandments and feared the LORD. ³His eyes grew dim and his lifetime was so nearly finished that he could not see a single person because of his advanced age and decline. ⁴Then he lifted his eyes toward the light of Isaac, but he was afraid and became disturbed. ⁵So the messenger said to him, "Do not fear, O Jacob; ⁶I am the messenger who has been walking with you and guarding you from your infancy. ⁷I announced that you would receive the blessing of your father and of Rebekah, your mother. ⁸I am the one who is with you, O Israel, in all your acts and in everything which you have witnessed. ⁹I saved you from Laban when he was endangering you and pursuing you. ¹⁰At that time I gave you all his possessions and blessed you, your wives, your children, and your flocks. ¹¹I am the one who saved you from the hand of Esau. ¹²I am the one who accompanied you to the land of Egypt, O Israel, and a very great people was given to you. ¹³Blessed is your father Abraham, for he has become the friend of God—may He be exalted—because of his generosity and love of strangers. ¹⁴Blessed is your father Isaac who begot you, for he was a perfect sacrifice, acceptable to God. ¹⁵Blessed are you also, O Jacob, for you have seen God face to face. ¹⁶You saw the messenger of God—may He be exalted—and you saw the ladder standing firm on the ground with its top in the heavens. ¹⁷Then you beheld the LORD sitting at its top with a power which no one could describe. ¹⁸You spoke out and said, This is the house of God and this is the gate of Heaven. ¹⁹Blessed are you, for you have come near to God and He is strong among mankind, so now do not be troubled, O chosen one of God. ²⁰Blessed are you, O Israel, and blessed is all your progeny. ²¹For all of you will be called The Patriarchs to the end of the age and of the epochs; you are the people and the lineage of the servants of God. ²²Blessed is the nation which will strive for your purity and will see your good works. Blessed is the man who will remember you on the day of your noble festival. ²³Blessed is the one who will perform acts of mercy in honor of your several names, and will give someone a cup of water to drink, or will come with an offering to the sanctuary, or will take in strangers, or visit the sick and console their children, or will clothe a naked one in honor of your several names. ²⁴Such a one will neither lack any of the good things of this world, nor life everlasting in the world to come. ²⁵Moreover, whoever will have caused the stories of your several lives and sufferings to be written at his own expense, or will have written them by his own hand, or will have read them soberly, or will hear them in faith, or will remember your deeds—such persons will have their sins forgiven and their trespasses pardoned, and they will go on account of you and your progeny into the kingdom of the heavens. ²⁶And now rise up, Jacob, for you will be translated from hardship and pain of heart to continuous rest, and you will enter into the repose which will not pass away, into mercy, continuous light, and spiritual joy. ²⁷So now make your statement to your household, and peace be on you, for I am about to go to Him who sent me."

CHAPTER 3

¹So when the messenger had made this statement to our father Jacob, he ascended from him into Heaven, as Jacob bid him farewell. ²Those who were around Jacob heard him as he thanked God and glorified Him with praise. ³And all the members of his household, great and small, gathered around him, weeping over him, deeply grieving and saying, "You are going away and leaving us as orphans." ⁴And they kept on saying to him, "O our beloved father, what will we do, for we are in a strange land?" ⁵So Jacob said to them, "Do not fear; God Himself appeared to me in Upper Mesopotamia and said to me: I am the God of your fathers; do not fear, for I am with you forever and with your descendants who will come after you. ⁶This land in which you are I am about to give to you and to your descendants after you forever. ⁷And do not be afraid to go down to Egypt. ⁸I will make a great people for you and your descendants will increase and multiply forever. ⁹Joseph will put his hand on your eyes and your people will multiply in the land of Egypt. ¹⁰Afterward they will come to this place and will be without care. I will do good to them for your sake, though for the time being they will be displaced from here."

CHAPTER 4

¹After this, the time for Jacob-Israel to leave his body had arrived. ²So he summoned Joseph and said to him, "If indeed you have found grace, place your blessed hand under my side and swear an oath before the LORD that you will place my body in the tomb of my fathers." ³Then Joseph said to him, "I will do exactly what you command me, O beloved of God." ⁴But he said to Joseph, "I want you to swear to me." ⁵So Joseph swore to Jacob, his father, to the effect that he would carry his body to the tomb of his fathers, and Jacob accepted the oath of his son. ⁶Afterward, this report reached Joseph: "Your father has become uneasy." ⁷So he took his two sons, Ephraim and Manasseh, and went before his father Jacob. ⁸Joseph said to him, "These are my sons whom God has given me in the land of Egypt to come after me." ⁹Israel said, "Bring them closer to me here." ¹⁰For the eyes of Israel had become dim from his advanced age so that he could not see. ¹¹So Joseph brought his sons closer and Jacob kissed them. Then Joseph commanded them, namely Ephraim and Manasseh, to bow down before Jacob to the ground. ¹²Joseph took Manasseh and put him at Israel's right hand and Ephraim at his left hand. ¹³But Israel reversed his hands and let his right hand rest on the head of Ephraim and his left hand on the head of Manasseh. ¹⁴He blessed them and gave them back to their father and said, "May the God under whose authority my fathers, Abraham and Isaac, served in reverence, the God who has strengthened me from my youth up to the present time when the messenger has saved me from all my afflictions, may he bless these boys, Manasseh and Ephraim. ¹⁵May my name be on them, also the names of my holy fathers, Abraham and Isaac." ¹⁶After this, Israel said to Joseph, "I will die, and all of you will return to the land of your fathers and God will be with you. ¹⁷And you have personally received a mighty favor, greater than that of your brothers, for I have taken this arrow with my bow and my sword from the Amorites."

CHAPTER 5

¹Then Jacob sent for all his children and said to them, "Gather around me that I may inform you of everything which will come on you and what will overtake each one of you in the last days." ²So they gathered around Israel from the eldest to the youngest of them. ³Then Jacob-Israel spoke up and said to his sons, "Listen, O sons of Jacob, listen to your father Israel, from Reuben my firstborn to Benjamin." ⁴Then he told them what would come on the twelve children, calling each one of them and his tribe by name; ⁵and he blessed them with the celestial blessing. ⁶After this they were silent for a short time in order that he might rest. So the heavens rejoiced that he could observe the places of repose. ⁷And behold, there approached numerous tormentors differing in their aspects. They were prepared to torment the sinners, who are these: adulterers, male and female; those lusting after males; the vicious who degrade the semen given by God; ⁸the astrologers and the sorcerers; the evildoers and the worshipers of idols who hold onto abominations; and the slanderers who pass judgment with two tongues. ⁹And as to all these sinners, their punishment is the fire which will not be extinguished and the outer darkness where there is weeping and gnashing of teeth.

CHAPTER 6

¹And when the days of their mourning were finished, Pharaoh was still weeping over Jacob because of his regard for Joseph. ²Then Joseph addressed the nobles of Pharaoh and said to them, "Since I have found favor with you, will you speak on my behalf to Pharaoh the king, and say to him that Jacob made me take an oath that when he went out from his body I would bury his body in the tomb of my fathers in the land of Canaan, in that very place?" ³So Pharaoh said to Joseph, "Go in peace and bury your father in accordance with the oath which he required of you. ⁴And take chariots and horses with you, the best of my kingdom and from my own household as you desire." ⁵So Joseph worshiped God in the presence of Pharaoh, went forth from him, and set out to bury his father. ⁶And there set out with him the slaves of Pharaoh, the elders of Egypt, all the household of Joseph, and his brothers and all Israel. ⁷They all went up with him into the chariots, and the entourage moved along like a great army. ⁸They descended into the land of

Canaan to the riverbank across the Jordan and they mourned for him in that place with very great grief indeed. ⁹They maintained that great grief for him for seven days. ¹⁰So when the inhabitants of Dan heard about the mourning in their land, they said, "This great mourning is that of the Egyptians." ¹¹To this day [[they call that place "the Mourning of the Egyptians"]]. ¹²Then Israel was carried forward and was buried in the land of Canaan in the second tomb. ¹³This is the one which Abraham had bought with authorization for burials from Ephron opposite Mature. ¹⁴After that, Joseph returned to the land of Egypt with his brothers and all the entourage of Pharaoh. ¹⁵And Joseph lived after the death of his father many years. ¹⁶He continued to rule over Egypt, though Jacob had died and was left behind with his own people.

CHAPTER 7

¹This is what we have transmitted: We have described the demise of and the mourning for the father of fathers, Jacob-Israel, to the extent of our ability to do this; ²also as it is written in the spiritual scrolls of God and as we have found it in the ancient treasury of knowledge of our fathers, the holy, pure apostles. ³And if you wish to know the life history and get new knowledge of the father of fathers, Jacob, then take a father who is attested in the Old Testament. ⁴Moses is the one who wrote it, the first of the prophets, the author of the Law. Read from it and enlighten your insights. ⁵You will find this and more in it, written for your sake. ⁶You will find that God and His messengers were their friends while they were in their bodies, and that God kept on speaking to them many times in various passages from the Scroll. ⁷Also He says in many passages with regard to the patriarch Jacob, the father of fathers, in the Scroll, thus, "My son, I will bless your descendants like the stars of the heavens." ⁸And our father Jacob would speak to his son Joseph and say to him, "My God appeared to me in the land of Canaan at Luz and blessed me and said to me, I will bless you and multiply you and make you a mighty people. ⁹They will go out [to war] like the other nations of this earth and your descendants will increase forever." ¹⁰This is what we have heard, O my brothers and my loved ones, from our fathers, the patriarchs. ¹¹And it is incumbent on us that we have zeal for their deeds, their purity, their faith, their love of mankind, and their acceptance of strangers; ¹²in order that we may lay claim to be their sons in the kingdom of the heavens, so that they will intercede for us before God that we may be saved from the torture of Gehenna. ¹³These are the ones whom the Arabs have designated as the holy fathers. ¹⁴Jacob instructed his sons with regard to punishment, and he would call them the sword of the LORD, which is the river of fire, prepared with its waves to engulf the evildoers and the impure. ¹⁵These are the things the power of which the father of fathers, Jacob, expounded and taught to all his sons that the wise ones might hear and pursue righteousness in mutual love with mercy and compassion. ¹⁶For mercy saves people from penalties and mercy overcomes a multitude of wrongs. Truly, one who shows mercy to the poor, that one makes a loan to God. ¹⁷So now, my beloved sons, do not slacken from prayer and fasting ever at any time, and by the life of the religion you will drive away the demons. ¹⁸O my dear son, avoid the evil ways of the world, which are anger and depravity and all vicious deeds. ¹⁹And beware of injustice and blasphemy and abduction. ²⁰For the unjust will not inherit the Kingdom of God, nor will the adulterers, nor the accursed, nor those who commit outrages and have sexual intercourse with males, nor the gluttons, nor the worshipers of idols, nor those who utter imprecations, nor those who pollute themselves outside of pure marriage; and others whom we have not presented or even mentioned will not come near the Kingdom of God. ²¹O my sons, honor the saints, for they are the ones who will intercede for you. ²²O my sons, be generous to strangers and you will be given exactly what was given to the great Abraham, the father of fathers, and to our father Isaac, his son. ²³O my sons, do for the poor what will increase compassion for them here and now, so that God will give you the bread of life forever in the Kingdom of God. ²⁴For to the one who has given a poor person bread in this world God will give a portion from the Tree of Life. ²⁵Clothe the poor person who is naked on the earth, so that God may clothe you with the apparel of glory in the kingdom of the heavens, and you will be the sons of our holy fathers, Abraham, Isaac, and Jacob in Heaven forever. ²⁶Be concerned with the reading of the word of God in His scrolls here below, and remember the saints who have written of their lives, their sufferings, and their prostrations in prayer. ²⁷In the future, it will not be prevented that they should be inscribed in the Scroll of Life in the kingdom of the heavens. ²⁸And you will be counted among the saints, those who pleased God in their lifetime and will rejoice with the messengers in the land of continuous life.

CHAPTER 8

¹You will honor the memory of our fathers, the patriarchs, at this time each year and on this same day, which is the twenty-eighth of the month of Mesore. ²This is what we have found written in the ancient documents of our fathers, the saints who were pleasing to God. ³Because of their intercession and their prayer, we will have all things, namely a share and a place in the kingdom of the heavens which belongs to our Lord and our God and our Master and our Savior, Jesus the Messiah. ⁴He is the one whom we ask to forgive us for our mistakes and our errors and to overlook our misdeeds. ⁵May He be kind to us on the day of His judgment and let us hear the voice filled with joy, kindness, and gladness, saying, "Come to Me, O blessed ones of My Father, inherit the kingdom which was yours from before the creation of the world." ⁶And may we be worthy to receive His divine secrets, which are the means to the pardon of our sins. ⁷May He help us toward the salvation of our souls, and may He ward off from us the blows of the wicked enemy. ⁸May He let us stand at His right hand on the great and terrible day for the intercession of the mistress of intercessions, the source of purity, generosity, and blessings, the mother of salvation, and for the intercession of all the martyrs, saints, doers of pleasing deeds, and everyone who has pleased the LORD with his pious deeds and his good will. ⁹Amen! Amen! Amen! And praise to God always, forever, [and] perpetually.

LADDER OF JACOB

The Ladder of Jacob, composed in the 2nd century AD at the latest, has been preserved only in Slavonic, which is itself clearly a translation from a now lost Greek version. The book is an expansion of the biblical account of Jacob's dream found in Genesis 28:11–19. Chapter 7 (7–8 here) is thought by some to be a later Christian development of the text.

CHAPTER 1

[[¹Now Jacob went to his uncle Laban, and he found a place and fell asleep there, laying his head on a stone, for the sun was set: and there he saw a vision.]] ²And behold, a ladder was set up on the earth, whose top reached to Heaven. ³And the top of the ladder was a face as of a man, hewn out of fire. ⁴Now it had twelve steps up to the top of the ladder, and on each step up to the top were two human faces on the right and on the left—twenty-four faces seen to their breast, on the ladder. ⁵But the middle face was higher than them all, which I saw made of fire, to the shoulder and the arm, very terribly, more than the twenty-four faces. ⁶And as I looked, behold, the messengers of God ascending and descending thereon, but the LORD was set above it, ⁷and He called me, saying, "Jacob, Jacob." And I said, "Here I am, Lord"; ⁸And He said to me, "The land whereon you sleep I will give to you and to your seed after you: and I will multiply your seed as the stars of the heavens and as the sand of the sea; through your seed all the earth will be blessed, and they that dwell thereon, to the last times, the years of the end. ⁹My blessing with which I have blessed you will

LADDER OF JACOB

pour out from you to the last generation. All in the east and the west will be full of your seed."

CHAPTER 2

¹And when I heard it from above, fear and trembling fell on me, and I rose up from my dream. ²And while the Voice of God was yet in my ears, I said, "How dreadful is this place! This is none other than the house of God, and this is the gate of Heaven." ³And I set up the stone that was under my head for a pillar, and poured oil on the top of it, and I called the name of that place the house of God. ⁴[[And I prayed to God and said,]] "LORD God of Adam—Yours—and LORD God of Abraham and my father Isaac, and of all whose ways are right before You, You that sit mighty on the cherubim and on the throne of the majesty, of fire and full of eyes, as I saw in my dream; ⁵that holds the cherubim with four faces, that bears the seraphim full of eyes, that bears the whole world under His arm, and is borne of none. ⁶You have established the Heaven for the glory of Your Name. You have spread out on the clouds of the heavens the heaven that flies [[or rests]] under You, that under it You may move the sun and hide it in the night, lest it be held for God. ⁷You have ordained the way for the moon and the stars, and You make her to wax and wane, but for the stars, You have commanded them to pass over, lest these also should be supposed gods. ⁸Before the face of Your majesty the six-winged seraphim fear, and hide their feet and their face with their wings, and with the others they fly, and sing: ⁹… Highest, with twelve faces, many-named, fiery, lightning-formed, Holy One! HOLY, HOLY, HOLY, YAH THE LORD, YAH'EL, SABAKDOS, CHABOD, SABAOTH, OMLELECH, ELABER, AME, S'ME BARECH, PERPETUAL KING, [who is] strong, mighty, very great, long-suffering. ¹⁰[The] Blessed One that fills the heavens, and earth, and the sea, and the abyss, and all ages with Your glory. ¹¹Hear my song with which I have praised You, and grant me my petition for which I pray to You, and show me the interpretation of my dream. ¹²For You are strong, and mighty, and glorious, a holy God, the Lord of me and my fathers."

CHAPTER 3

¹And while I yet spoke my prayer, there appeared a voice before my face, saying, "Sarekl, prince of them that rejoice, you that are over visions, go make Jacob to understand the interpretation of the dream which he saw, and show him all things, whatever he saw, but first bless him." ²And the chief-messenger Sarekl came to me, and I saw: it was a face … terrible. ³But I did not fear before his look, for the face which I had seen in my dream … was more than this, and I did not fear the face of a messenger. ⁴And the messenger said to me, "What is your name?" And I said, "Jacob." [He said to me,] "Your name will no longer be called Jacob, but your name will be like my name, Israel." ⁵And when I came from Fandana, in Syria, to meet my brother Esau, he came to me and blessed me, and called my name Israel, and did not tell me his name until I adjured him, and then he told me: "Because you were …"

CHAPTER 4

¹But this he said to me: "The ladder which you saw, which had twelve steps having two human faces which changed their appearance—now this ladder is this age, and the twelve steps are the times of this age, and the twenty-four faces are the kings of the lawless heathen of this age. ²Under these kings [[your children's children and the line]] of your sons will be tried: they will rise up against the lawlessness of your descendants and will lay this place waste through four descents [because] of the sins of your descendants, ³and of the substance of the forefathers this palace will be built in the temple of the Name of your God and your fathers; ⁴but through the wrath of your descendants it will be desolate until the fourth descent of this age; for you saw four visions [[or faces]]."

CHAPTER 5

¹"The first that stumbles on the steps … messengers ascending and descending and faces in the midst of the steps: ²the Most High will raise up an heir of the descendants of your brother Esau, and all the lords of the nations of the earth will accept it, who have done evil against your seed, and will be given into his hand, and he will be hardly borne by them. ³But he begins to rule them with violence and to reign over them, and they cannot resist him, until the day when his decree goes forth against them to serve the idols … ⁴… and to all them that appear in such a cause, and so many [[to the Most High out of your race, and]] so many to Thalkonagargael."

CHAPTER 6

¹"And know, O Jacob, that your seed will be strangers in a strange land, and men will mistreat them with bondage and lay blows on them daily, but the LORD will judge the people whom they serve. ²When a king arises and fights, then there will be to that place … then your seed, even Israel, will go forth out of the bondage of the heathen who ruled over them with violence, and will be set free from all reproach of their enemies. ³For this king is the head of every revenge and retribution of them that make attacks on you, Israel. ⁴And [at] the end of the age—for the miserable will rise and cry, and the LORD hears them, and will be softened, and the mighty lets Himself pity their sufferings, because the messengers and chief-messengers pour out their prayers for the saving of your race. ⁵Then their women will bear much fruit, and then the LORD will fight for your race."

CHAPTER 7

[[¹"But whereas you saw messengers descending and ascending on the ladder, in the last times there will be a Man from the Most High, and He will desire to join the upper with the lower. ²Before His coming, your sons and your daughters will prophesy of Him, and your young men will see visions of Him. ³For there will be such signs as these at the time of His coming: a tree felled by the axe will drop blood; boys of three months old will speak rationally; a child in its mother's womb will proclaim His way; a young man will be as an old man. ⁴And then comes the Expected One, whose path will be perceived by no man. ⁵Then the earth will rejoice, because it has received the glory of Heaven. That which was above will be below. ⁶And a royal Root of your seed will grow up; and He will increase and destroy the power of the evil one, but He Himself will be a Savior of the heathen, and the rest of them that are weary, and a cloud which shades the whole world from the heat, ⁷for otherwise that which is disordered could not be put in order, if He did not come: otherwise, that which is below could not be joined to that which is above."

CHAPTER 8

¹"Now at His coming images of brass, and stone, and all graven things will utter their voice for three days long. ²And they announce to the wise men and let them know what will befall on earth, and by the star they will know the way to Him, when they see Him on earth whom the messengers do not see above. ³Then the Almighty will be found in a body on the earth, and encompassed by the arms of a mortal, and He renews the state of man and restores [Adam and] Eve that died through the fruit of the tree. ⁴Then the deceit of the godless one will be overcome, and all idols fall on their faces, for they will be put to shame by one who is adorned with honor, because they made lying inventions. ⁵From then on, they will not have power to rule or to give prophecies, for their honor will be taken from them, and they will remain without glory. ⁶For He that has come takes the power and might from them and repays to Abraham the truth [[or righteousness]] which He promised him. ⁷Then He rounds off all that is sharp, and He makes every rough thing smooth, and He casts all unrighteousness into the depths of the sea: and He does wonders in Heaven and on the earth. ⁸And He will be wounded in the midst of the house of the beloved. But when He is wounded, then also the saving and the end of all corruption draws near. ⁹For they that have wounded Him will themselves receive a wound which will not be healed for them forever. ¹⁰But all creatures will worship the Wounded One, and many will hope on Him, and everywhere, and among all the nations, He will be known. But they that have known His Name will not be put to shame. And His own might and His years will not fail forever."]]

JOSEPH AND ASENATH

Joseph and Asenath is an embellished account of Joseph's relationship with Asenath, the daughter of the Egyptian priest of Heliopolis. Joseph's marriage to Asenath, given only a brief mention in Genesis 41:45–50 and 46:20, is herein turned into a sweeping narrative describing Asenath's conversion to faith in YHWH, her subsequent marriage to Joseph, the birth of Ephraim and Manasseh, and a fanciful plot by Pharaoh's son, along with Dan and Gad, to kill Joseph. The story is thought to have been written sometime between 200 BC and AD 200, either as a Jewish midrash with later Christian interpolations, or as a Judeo-Christian work from the onset.

CHAPTER 1

¹In the first year of plenty, in the second month, on the fifth of the month, Pharaoh sent Joseph to go around all the land of Egypt; and in the fourth month of the first year, on the eighteenth of the month, Joseph came to the borders of Heliopolis, and he was gathering the corn of that country as the sand of the sea. ²And there was a certain man in that city, Pentephres by name, who was a priest of Heliopolis and a satrap of Pharaoh, and chief of all Pharaoh's satraps and princes; and this man was exceedingly rich and very sage and gentle, and he was also a counselor of Pharaoh, because he was prudent beyond all Pharaoh's princes. ³And he had a virgin daughter, by name Asenath, of eighteen years, tall and lovely, and exceedingly beautiful to behold—beyond every virgin on the earth. ⁴Now Asenath herself bore no likeness to the daughters of the Egyptians, but was in all things like the daughters of the Hebrews, being tall as Sarah, and lovely as Rebecca, and beautiful as Rachel; ⁵and the fame of her beauty spread abroad into all that land and to the ends of the world, so that by reason of this all the sons of the princes and the satraps desired to woo her, moreover, and the sons of the kings also—all young men and mighty—and there was great strife among them because of her, and they strove to fight against one another. ⁶And Pharaoh's firstborn son also heard about her, and he continued entreating his father to give her to him to be [his] wife and saying to him: "Give me, father, Asenath, the daughter of Pentephres, the first man of Heliopolis, to be [my] wife." ⁷And his father Pharaoh said to him, "Therefore, do you on your part seek a wife lower than yourself when you are king of all this land? ⁸But rather, behold, the daughter of Joacim, the king of Moab, is betrothed to you, and she herself is a queen and exceedingly beautiful to behold. Take this one then to yourself to be [your] wife."

CHAPTER 2

¹But Asenath set at nothing and scorned every man, being boastful and haughty, and a man had never seen her, inasmuch as Pentephres had in his house an adjoining tower, great and exceedingly high, and above the tower was a loft containing ten chambers. ²And the first chamber was great, and very lovely, and paved with purple stones, and the walls thereof were faced with precious and multicolored stones, and also the roof of that chamber was of gold. ³And within that chamber gods of the Egyptians, whereof was no number, gold and silver, were fixed, and Asenath worshiped all of those, and she feared them, and she performed sacrifices to them every day. ⁴And the second chamber also contained all of Asenath's adornments and chests, and there was gold in it, and much silver and limitless gold-woven raiment, and choice stones of great price, and fine garments of linen, and all the adornment of her virginity was there. ⁵And the third chamber was Asenath's storehouse, containing all the good things of the earth. ⁶And the remaining seven chambers the seven virgins who ministered to Asenath occupied, each one having one chamber, for they were of the same age, born on the same night with Asenath, and she loved them much; ⁷and they were also exceedingly beautiful as the stars of heaven, and a man or male child never conversed with them. ⁸Now Asenath's great chamber where her virginity was fostered had three windows; and the first window was very large, looking over the court to the east; ⁹and the second looked toward the south, and the third looked over the street. ¹⁰And a golden bedstead stood in the chamber looking toward the east; and the bed was laid with purple stuff interwoven with gold, the bed being woven of scarlet and crimson stuff and fine linen. ¹¹On this bed Asenath slept alone, and never had man or other woman sat thereon. ¹²And there was also a great court adjoining the house all round, and an exceedingly high wall around the court built of great rectangular stones; and there were also four gates in the court overlaid with iron, and these were each kept by eighteen strong young men, armed; ¹³and there were also planted along the wall fair trees of all kinds and all bearing fruit, their fruit being ripe, for it was the season of harvest; ¹⁴and there was also a rich fountain of water springing from the right of the same court; and beneath the fountain was a great cistern receiving the water of that fountain, from where there went, as it were, a stream through the midst of the court and it watered all the trees of that court.

CHAPTER 3

¹And it came to pass in the first year of the seven years of plenty, in the fourth month, on the twenty-eighth of the month, that Joseph came to the borders of Heliopolis collecting the corn of that district. ²And when Joseph drew near to that city, he sent twelve men before him to Pentephres, the priest of Heliopolis, saying, "I will come in to you today, because it is the time of noon and of the midday meal, and there is great heat of the sun, and that I may cool myself under the roof of your house." ³And Pentephres, when he heard these things, rejoiced with exceedingly great joy, and said, "Blessed be the LORD God of Joseph, because my lord Joseph has thought me worthy." ⁴And Pentephres called the overseer of his house and said to him, "Hurry and make my house ready, and prepare a great dinner, because Joseph, the mighty one of God, comes to us today." ⁵And when Asenath heard that her father and mother had come from the possession of their inheritance, she rejoiced greatly and said, "I will go and see my father and mother, because they have come from the possession of our inheritance." (For it was the season of harvest). ⁶And Asenath hastened into her chamber where her robes lay, and put on a fine linen robe made of crimson stuff and interwoven with gold, and girded herself with a golden girdle, and [placed] bracelets around her hands; ⁷and around her feet she put golden buskins, and around her neck she cast an ornament of great price and precious stones, which were embellished on all sides, also having the names of the gods of the Egyptians everywhere engraved on them, both on the bracelets and the stones; ⁸and she also put a tiara on her head, and bound a diadem around her temples, and covered her head with a mantle.

CHAPTER 4

¹And thereon she hurried and went down the stairs from her loft, and came to her father and mother, and kissed them. ²And Pentephres and his wife rejoiced over their daughter Asenath with exceedingly great joy, for they beheld her adorned and embellished as the bride of God; ³and they brought forth all the good things which they had brought from the possession of their inheritance and gave them to their daughter; ⁴and Asenath rejoiced over all the good things, over the late summer fruit, and the grapes, and the dates, and over the doves, and over the mulberries and the figs, because they were all fair and pleasant to taste. ⁵And Pentephres said to his daughter Asenath, "Child." And she said, "Here I am, my lord." ⁶And he said to her, "Sit down between us, and I will speak my words to you." ⁷She sat down between her father and her mother, and her father Pentephres took hold of her right hand with his right hand, and kissed it tenderly, and said, "Dearest child." ⁸And she said to him, "Here I am, my lord father." And Pentephres said to her, "Behold, Joseph, the mighty one of God, comes to us today, and this man is ruler of all the land of Egypt; ⁹and King Pharaoh appointed him ruler of all our land and king, and he himself gives corn to all this country, and saves it from the coming famine; ¹⁰and this Joseph is a man that worships God, and [is as] discreet and a virgin as you are

today, and a man mighty in wisdom and knowledge, and the Spirit of God is on him, and the grace of the LORD is in him. ¹¹Come, dearest child, and I will give you over to him to be [his] wife, and you will be to him for a bride, and he himself will be your bridegroom forever." ¹²And when Asenath heard these words from her father, a great sweat was poured out on her over her face, and she grew angry with great anger, and she looked suspiciously with her eyes at her father, ¹³and said, "Therefore, my lord father, [why] do you speak these words? Do you wish to give me over as a captive to an alien, and a fugitive, and one that has been sold? Is this not the son of the shepherd from the land of Canaan? And he himself has been left behind by him. ¹⁴Is this not he who lay with his mistress, and his lord cast him into the prison of darkness, and Pharaoh brought him out from the prison inasmuch as he interpreted his dream, as the older women of the Egyptians also interpret? ¹⁵But rather, I will be married to the king's firstborn son, because he himself is king of all the land." ¹⁶When he heard these things Pentephres was ashamed to speak further to his daughter Asenath about Joseph, for she answered him with boastfulness and anger.

CHAPTER 5

¹And behold, a young man of Pentephres' servants sprang in, and he says to him, "Behold, Joseph stands before the doors of our court." ²And when Asenath heard these words, she fled from the face of her father and mother, and went up into the loft, and she came into her chamber, and stood at the great window looking east to see Joseph coming into her father's house. ³And Pentephres came out with his wife, and all their relatives, and their servants, to meet Joseph; ⁴and when the gates of the court that looked east were opened, Joseph came in, seated in the second chariot of Pharaoh; ⁵and there were yoked four horses white like snow with golden bits, and the chariot was fashioned entirely of pure gold. ⁶And Joseph was clad in a tunic white and rare, and the robe that was thrown around him was purple, made of fine linen interwoven with gold, and a golden wreath was on his head, and around his wreath were twelve choice stones, and above the stones twelve golden rays, and in his right hand a royal staff, which had an olive branch outstretched, and there was abundance of fruit thereon. ⁷When, then, Joseph had come into the court and the doors thereof had been shut, and every strange man and woman remained outside the court, for the guards of the gates drew to and closed the doors, Pentephres came with his wife and all their relatives, except their daughter Asenath, and they paid homage to Joseph on their faces on the earth; ⁸and Joseph descended from his chariot and greeted them with his hand.

CHAPTER 6

¹And when Asenath saw Joseph she was sorely struck in the soul, and her heart was crushed, and her knees were loosed, and her whole body trembled, and she feared with great fear, ²and then she groaned and said in her heart: "Oh miserable me! Where now will I, the wretched one, go away? Or where will I be hidden from his face? Or how will Joseph, the son of God, see me, for on my part I have spoken evil things about him? Oh miserable me! ³Where will I go away and be hidden, because he himself sees every hiding place, and knows all things, and no hidden thing escapes him by reason of the great light that is in him? ⁴And now may the God of Joseph be gracious to me because in ignorance I have spoken wicked words against him. ⁵What now will I, the wretched one, follow? Have I not said, Joseph comes, the son of the shepherd, from the land of Canaan? ⁶Now he has therefore come to us in his chariot as the sun from heaven, and he entered our house today, and he shines into it like light on the earth. ⁷But I am foolish and bold, because I scorned him, and spoke evil words about him, and did not know that Joseph is a son of God. ⁸For who among men will ever beget such beauty, or what womb of woman will give birth to such light? ⁹I am wretched and foolish, because I have spoken evil words to my father. ¹⁰Now therefore, let my father give me to Joseph for a handmaid and a bondwoman rather, and I will be in bondage to him forever."

CHAPTER 7

¹And Joseph came into the house of Pentephres and sat on a chair. ²And they washed his feet, and set a table before him separately, for Joseph did not eat with the Egyptians, since this was an abomination to him. ³And Joseph looked up and saw Asenath peeping out, and he says to Pentephres: "Who is that woman who is standing in the loft by the window? Let her go away from this house." ⁴For Joseph feared, saying, "Lest she herself also annoy me," for all the wives and daughters of the princes and the satraps of all the land of Egypt used to annoy him in order that they might lie with him; ⁵but many wives and daughters of the Egyptians also, as many as beheld Joseph, were distressed on account of his beauty; ⁶and the envoys whom the women sent to him with gold, and silver, and precious gifts Joseph sent back with threatening and insult, saying, "I will not sin in the sight of the LORD God and the face of my father Israel." ⁷For Joseph always had God before his eyes and always remembered the injunctions of his father; ⁸for Jacob often spoke and admonished his son Joseph and all his sons: "Keep yourselves, children, securely from a strange woman so as not to have fellowship with her, for fellowship with her is ruin and destruction." ⁹Therefore Joseph said, "Let that woman depart from this house." ¹⁰And Pentephres said to him, "My lord, that woman whom you have seen standing in the loft is not a stranger, but is our daughter, one who hates every man, and no other man has ever seen her except you only today; ¹¹and if you wish, lord, she will come and speak to you, for that daughter of ours is as your sister." ¹²And Joseph rejoiced with exceedingly great joy, for Pentephres said, "She is a virgin hating every man." ¹³And Joseph said to Pentephres and his wife, "If she is your daughter, and is a virgin, let her come, for she is my sister, and I love her from today as my sister."

CHAPTER 8

¹Then her mother went up into the loft and brought Asenath to Joseph, and Pentephres said to her, "Kiss your brother, because he is also a virgin even as you [are] today and hates every strange woman even as you hate every strange man." ²And Asenath said to Joseph, "Greetings, lord, blessed of God Most High." ³And Joseph said to her, "God who quickens all things will bless you, girl." ⁴Then Pentephres says to his daughter Asenath, "Come and kiss your brother." ⁴When Asenath then came up to kiss Joseph, Joseph stretched forth his right hand, and laid it on her chest between her two breasts (for her breasts were already standing forth like lovely apples), ⁵and Joseph said, "It is not fitting for a man that worships God, who blesses the living God with his mouth, and eats the blessed bread of life, and drinks the blessed cup of immortality, and is anointed with the blessed unction of incorruption, to kiss a strange woman who blesses dead and deaf idols with her mouth, and eats the bread of strangling from their table, and drinks the cup of deceit from their libation, and is anointed with the unction of destruction; ⁶but the man that worships God will kiss his mother, and the sister who is born of his mother, and the sister who is born of his tribe, and the wife who shares his couch, who bless the living God with their mouth. ⁷Likewise also, it is not fitting for a woman that worships God to kiss a strange man, for this is an abomination in the sight of the LORD God." ⁸And when Asenath heard these words from Joseph, she was sorely distressed and groaned; ⁹and as she was looking steadfastly at Joseph with her eyes open, they were filled with tears. ¹⁰And Joseph, when he saw her weeping, pitied her exceedingly, for he was mild, and merciful, and one who feared the LORD. ¹¹Then he lifted up his right hand above her head and said, "LORD God of my father Israel, the Most High and the mighty God, who quickened all things and called from the darkness to the light, and from error to truth, and from death to life, ¹²bless this virgin also, and quicken her, and renew her with Your Holy Spirit, and let her eat the bread of Your life and drink the cup of Your blessing, and number her with Your people whom You chose before all things were made, ¹³and let her enter into Your rest which You prepared for Your elect, and let her live in Your continuous life forever."

CHAPTER 9

¹And Asenath rejoiced over the blessing of Joseph with exceedingly great joy. ²Then she hurried and came up into her loft by herself, and fell on her bed in infirmity, for there was in her joy, and sorrow, and great fear; ³and a continuous sweat was poured over her when

she heard these words from Joseph, and when he spoke to her in the Name of God Most High. ⁴Then she wept with a great and bitter weeping, and she turned in penitence from her gods whom she was accustomed to worship, and the idols which she spurned, and waited for evening to come. ⁵But Joseph ate and drank; and he told his menservants to yoke the horses to their chariots, and to go around all the land. ⁶And Pentephres said to Joseph, "Let my lord lodge here today, and in the morning you will go your way." ⁷And Joseph said, "But rather, I will go away today, for this is the day on which God began to make all His created things, and on the eighth day I also return to you and will lodge here."

CHAPTER 10

¹And when Joseph had left the house, Pentephres also and all his relatives departed to their inheritance, and Asenath was left alone with the seven virgins, listless and weeping until the sun set; and she neither ate bread nor drank water, but while all slept, she herself alone was awake, and weeping, and frequently beating her breast with her hand. ²And after these things Asenath rose from her bed, and quietly went down the stairs from the loft, and on coming to the gateway, found the doorkeeper sleeping with her children; ³and she hurried and took down from the door the leather cover of the curtain, and filled it with cinders, and carried it up to the loft, and laid it on the floor. ⁴And thereon she shut the door securely, and fastened it with the iron bolt from the side, and groaned with great groaning together with much and very great weeping. ⁵But the virgin whom Asenath loved above all the virgins, having heard her groaning, hurried and came to the door after also awaking the other virgins and found it shut. ⁶And when she had listened to the groaning and the weeping of Asenath, she said to her [while] standing outside, "What is it, my mistress? And are you therefore sad? And what is it that troubles you? Open to us and let us see you." ⁷And Asenath said to her, being shut inside, "Great and grievous pain has attacked my head, and I am resting in my bed, and I am not able to rise and open to you, for I am weak in all my limbs. ⁸Therefore, each of you go to her chamber and sleep, and let me be still." ⁹And when the virgins had departed, each to her own chamber, Asenath rose, and opened the door of her bedroom quietly, and went away into her second chamber where the chests of her adornment were, and she opened her coffer, and took a black and somber tunic which she had put on and mourned in when her firstborn brother died. ¹⁰Having taken, then, this tunic, she carried it into her chamber, and again shut the door securely, and put the bolt through from the side. ¹¹Then, therefore, Asenath took off her royal robe, and put on the mourning tunic, and loosed her golden girdle, and girded herself with a rope, and put off the tiara, that is the turban, from her head, likewise also the diadem, and the chains from her hands and her feet were also all laid on the floor. ¹²Then she takes her choice robe, and the golden girdle, and the turban, and her diadem, and she cast them through the window that looked toward the north, to the poor. ¹³And thereon she took all her gods that were in her chamber, the gods of gold and of silver whereof there was no number, and broke them up into fragments, and cast them through the window to poor men and beggars. ¹⁴And again Asenath took her royal dinner, and the fatlings, and the fish, and heifer's flesh, and all the sacrifices of her gods, and the vessels of the wine of libation, and cast all of them through the window that looked north as food for the dogs. ¹⁵And after these things she took the leather cover containing the cinders and poured them on the floor; and thereon she took sackcloth and girded her loins; and she also loosed the net of the hair of her head and sprinkled ashes over her head. ¹⁶And she also strewed cinders on the floor, and fell on the cinders, and kept beating her breast constantly with her hands and weeping all night with groaning until the morning. ¹⁷And when Asenath arose in the morning and saw, and behold, the cinders were beneath her as clay from her tears, she again fell on her face on the cinders until the sun set. ¹⁸Thus Asenath did for seven days, not tasting anything whatsoever.

CHAPTER 11

¹And on the eighth day, when the dawn came, and the birds were already chirping, and the dogs barking at the passers by, Asenath lifted up her head a little from the floor and the cinders whereon she was seated, for she was exceedingly weary and had lost the power of her limbs from her great humiliation; ²for Asenath had grown weary and faint and her strength was failing, and thereon she turned toward the wall, sitting under the window that looked east; ³and she laid her head on her bosom, wrapping the fingers of her hands over her right knee; ⁴and her mouth was shut, and she did not open it during the seven days and during the seven nights of her humiliation. ⁵And she said in her heart, not opening her mouth: "What will I do—I, the lowly one—or where will I go? And with whom again will I find refuge hereafter? Or to whom will I speak—the virgin that is an orphan, and desolate, and abandoned by all, and hated? ⁶Everyone has now come to hate me, and among these even my father and my mother, for I spurned the gods with loathing, and made away with them, and have given them to the poor to be destroyed by men. ⁷For my father and my mother said, Asenath is not our daughter, but all my relatives have also come to hate me, and all men, for I have given their gods to destruction. ⁸And I have hated every man and all who wooed me, and now in this humiliation of mine I have been hated by all and they rejoice over my tribulation. ⁹But the Lord and God of the mighty Joseph hates all who worship the idols, for He is a zealous God and terrible, as I have heard, against all who worship strange gods; ¹⁰from which He has hated me also, because I worshiped dead and deaf idols and blessed them. ¹¹But now I have shunned their sacrifice, and my mouth has become estranged from their table, and I have no courage to call on the LORD God of Heaven—the Most High and powerful one of the mighty Joseph—for my mouth is polluted from the sacrifices of the idols. ¹²But I have heard many saying that the God of the Hebrews is a true God, and a living God, and a merciful God, and compassionate, and long-suffering, and full of mercy, and gentle, and one who does not reckon the sin of a man who is humble, and especially of one who sins in ignorance, and does not convict of lawlessnesses in the time of the affliction of a man that is afflicted; ¹³accordingly, I also, the humble one, will be bold, and will turn to Him, and seek refuge with Him, and confess all my sins to Him, and pour out my petition before Him, and He will have mercy on my misery. ¹⁴For who knows if He will see this humiliation of mine and the desolation of my soul and pity me, and will also see the orphanhood of my wretchedness and [my] virginity and defend me. ¹⁵For, as I hear, He is Himself a Father of orphans, and a consolation of the afflicted, and a helper of the persecuted. ¹⁶But in any case, I also, the humble one, will be bold and will cry to Him." ¹⁷Then Asenath rose up from the wall where she was sitting, and raised herself on her knees toward the east, and directed her eyes toward Heaven, and opened her mouth, and said to God:

CHAPTER 12

¹"LORD God of the righteous, || Who created the ages and gives life to all things, || Who gave the breath of life to all Your creation, || Who brought the invisible things out into the light, ²Who made all things and made manifest things that did not appear, || Who lifted up the heaven and founded the earth on the waters, || Who fixed the great stones on the abyss of the water, || Which will not be submerged but are to the end doing Your will, ³For You, LORD, said the word and all things came into being, || And Your word, LORD, is the life of all Your creatures— ⁴To You I flee for refuge, O LORD my God; From henceforth I will cry to You, LORD, || And to You I will confess my sins; ⁵To you I will pour out my petition, Master, || And to You I will reveal my lawlessnesses. ⁶Spare me, LORD, spare, || For I committed many sins against You, || I did lawlessness and ungodliness, || I have spoken things not to be uttered, || And wicked in Your sight; ⁷My mouth, LORD, has been polluted from the sacrifices of the idols of the Egyptians, || And from the table of their gods: ⁸I sinned, LORD, I sinned in Your sight, || Both in knowledge and in ignorance I did ungodliness || In that I worshiped dead and deaf idols, || And I am not worthy to open my mouth to You, LORD— ⁹I, the miserable Asenath, daughter of Pentephres the priest, || The virgin and queen who was once proud and haughty || And one that prospered in my father's riches above all men, ¹⁰But now an orphan, and desolate, and abandoned by all men. ¹¹To You I flee, LORD, || And to You I offer my petition, || And to You I

will cry. Deliver me from them that pursue me, Master, || Before I am taken by them; ¹²For as an infant in fear of some one flees to his father and mother, || And his father stretches out his hands and catches him up against his breast, || So you, LORD, stretch out Your undefiled and terrible hands on me || Like a child-loving father, || And catch me out of the hand of the transcendent enemy. ¹³For behold, the ancient, and savage, and cruel lion pursues me, || For he is father of the gods of the Egyptians, || And the gods of the idol-maniacs are his children, || And I have come to hate them, || And I made away with them, || Because they are a lion's children; ¹⁴And I cast all the gods of the Egyptians from me || And did away [with] them, || And the lion, or their father the Devil, || In wrath against me is trying to swallow me up. ¹⁵But You, LORD, deliver me from his hands, || And I will be rescued from his mouth, || Lest he tears me apart || And casts me into the flame of fire, || And the fire casts me into a storm, || And the storm prevails over me in darkness || And casts me into the depth of the sea, || And the great beast who is from everlasting swallows me up, || And I perish forever. ¹⁶Deliver me, LORD, before all these things come on me; Deliver me, Master, the desolate and defenseless, || For my father and my mother have denied me || And said, Asenath is not our daughter, || Because I broke their gods in pieces and made away with them, || As having wholly hated them. ¹⁷And now I am an orphan and desolate, || And I have no other hope except You, LORD, || Nor another refuge except Your mercy—You friend of men, ¹⁸Because You alone are Father of the orphans, || And champion of the persecuted, || And helper of the afflicted. ¹⁹Have mercy on me, LORD, || And keep me pure and virgin, the forsaken and orphan, || For You alone, LORD, || Are a sweet, and good, and gentle Father. ²⁰For what father is [as] sweet and good as You, LORD? ²¹For behold, all the houses of my father Pentephres, || Which he has given to me for an inheritance, || Are for a moment and [are] vanishing; But the houses of Your inheritance, LORD, || Are incorruptible and perpetual."

CHAPTER 13

¹"Visit, LORD, my humiliation, || And have mercy on my orphanhood, || And pity me, the afflicted. ²For behold, I, Master, fled from all || And sought refuge with You, || The only friend of men. ³Behold, I left all the good things of the earth || And sought refuge with You. LORD—in sackcloth and ashes, naked and solitary. ⁴Behold, now I put off my royal robe of fine linen || And of crimson stuff interwoven with gold || And have put on a black tunic of mourning. ⁵Behold, I have loosed my golden girdle, || And cast it from me, || And girded myself with rope and sackcloth. ⁶Behold, I have cast my diadem and my turban from my head || And I have sprinkled myself with cinders. ⁷Behold, the floor of my chamber that was paved with multicolored and purple stones, || Which was formerly moistened with ointments || And was dried with bright linen cloths, || Is now moistened with my tears || And has been dishonored in that it is strewn with ashes. ⁸Behold, my Lord, from the cinders and my tears || Much clay has been formed in my chamber as on a broad road. ⁹Behold, my Lord, my royal dinner || And the meats I have given to the dogs. ¹⁰Behold, I have also, Master, been fasting seven days and seven nights || And neither ate bread nor drank water, ¹¹And my mouth is [as] dry as a wheel || And my tongue [is] as a horn, || And my lips [are] as a potsherd, || And my face has shrunk, || And my eyes have failed from shedding tears. ¹²But You, LORD my God, deliver me from my many ignorances, || And forgive me for that, being a virgin and unknowing, || I have gone astray. ¹³Behold, now all the gods whom I worshiped before in ignorance || I have now known to have been deaf and dead idols, || And I broke them in pieces || And gave them to be trampled on by all men, || And the thieves spoiled them, || Who were [only] gold and silver; ¹⁴And with You I sought refuge, LORD God, || The only compassionate one and friend of men. ¹⁵Forgive me, LORD, for I committed many sins against You in ignorance, || And have spoken blasphemous words against my lord Joseph, || And did not know—I, the miserable—That he is Your son. ¹⁶LORD, since the wicked men urged by envy said to me, || Joseph is a son of a shepherd from the land of Canaan, || Therefore I, the miserable one, have believed them and gone astray, || And I set him at nothing, || And have spoken wicked things about him, || Not knowing that he is Your son. ¹⁷For who among men begot or will ever beget such beauty? Or who else is such as he, wise and mighty, as the all-beautiful Joseph? ¹⁸But to You, LORD, I commit him, || Because for my part I love him more than my soul. ¹⁹Keep him safe in the wisdom of Your grace, || And commit me to him for a handmaid and a bondwoman, || That I may wash his feet, and make his bed, || And minister to him, and serve him, ²⁰And I will be a bondwoman to him for [all] the times of my life."

CHAPTER 14

¹And when Asenath had ceased making confession to the LORD, behold, the morning star also arose out of the heaven in the east; ²and Asenath saw it, and rejoiced, and said, "Has the LORD God then heard my prayer? For this star is a messenger and herald of the light of the great day." ³And behold, close by the morning star the heaven was rent and a great and ineffable light appeared. ⁴And when she saw it Asenath fell on her face on the cinders, and immediately there came to her a man from Heaven, sending forth rays of light, and stood above her head. ⁵And as she lay on her face, the divine messenger said to her, "Asenath, stand up." ⁶And she said, "Who is he that called me, for the door of my chamber is shut and the tower is high, and how then has he come into my chamber? ⁷And he called her again a second time, saying, "Asenath, Asenath." And she said, "Here I am, lord, tell me who you are." ⁸And he said, "I am the chief captain of the LORD God and commander of all the host of the Most High: stand up and stand on your feet, that I may speak my words to you." ⁹And she lifted up her face and saw, and behold, a man in all things like to Joseph, in robe, and wreath, and royal staff, except that his face was as lightning, and his eyes as the light of the sun, and the hairs of his head as the flame of fire of a burning torch, and his hands and his feet like iron shining from fire, for sparks, as it were, proceeded both from his hands and from his feet. ¹⁰Seeing these things, Asenath feared and fell on her face, unable even to stand on her feet, for she became greatly afraid and all her limbs trembled. ¹¹And the man said to her, "Be of good cheer, Asenath, and do not fear; but stand up and stand on your feet, that I may speak my words to you." ¹²Then Asenath stood up and stood on her feet, and the messenger said to her, "Go without impediment into your second chamber, and lay aside the black tunic wherein you are clad, and cast off the sackcloth from your loins, and shake out the cinders from your head, and wash your face and your hands with pure water, and put on a white untouched robe, and gird your loins with the bright girdle of virginity—the double one—and come to me again, and I will speak to you the words that are sent to you from the LORD." ¹³Then Asenath hurried and went into her second chamber wherein were the chests of her adorning, and opened her coffer, and took a white, fine, untouched robe, and put it on, having first put off the black robe, and also ungirded the rope and the sackcloth from her loins, and girded herself in a bright, double girdle of her virginity—one girdle around her loins and another girdle around her breast. ¹⁴And she also shook out the cinders from her head, and washed her hands and face with pure water, and she took a most beautiful and fine mantle and veiled her head.

CHAPTER 15

¹And thereon she came to the divine chief captain and stood before him, and the messenger of the LORD says to her, "Now take the mantle from your head, for you are a pure virgin today, and your head is as of a young man." ²And Asenath took it from her head. ³And again the divine messenger says to her, "Be of good cheer, Asenath, the virgin and pure, for behold, the LORD God heard all the words of your confession and your prayer, ⁴and He has also seen the humiliation and affliction of the seven days of your abstinence, for from your tears much clay has been formed before your face on these cinders. ⁵Accordingly, be of good cheer, Asenath, the virgin and pure, for behold, your name has been written in the Scroll of Life and will not be blotted out forever; ⁶but from this day [forward] you will be renewed, and refashioned, and re-quickened, ⁷and you will eat the blessed bread of life, and drink a cup filled with immortality, and be anointed with the blessed unction of incorruption. ⁸Be of good cheer, Asenath, the virgin and pure, behold, the LORD God has given you to Joseph

for a bride today, and he himself will be your bridegroom forever. ⁹And henceforth you will no longer be called Asenath, but your name will be City of Refuge, for in you many nations will seek refuge and they will lodge under your wings, and many nations will find shelter by your means, and on your walls they who cleave to God Most High through penitence will be kept secure; ¹⁰for Penitence is a daughter of the Most High, and she herself entreats God Most High for you every hour and for all that convert, since He is father of Penitence, and she herself is the completion and overseer of all virgins, loving you exceedingly and imploring the Most High for you every hour, ¹¹and for all who convert she will provide a place of rest in the heavens, and she renews everyone who has converted. ¹²And Penitence is exceedingly lovely, a virgin pure, and gentle, and mild; and therefore God Most High loves her, and all the messengers revere her, and I love her exceedingly, for she herself is also my sister, and as she loves you virgins, I also love you. ¹³And behold, for my part I go to Joseph and will speak to him all these words concerning you, and he will come to you today, and see you, and rejoice over you, and love you, and be your bridegroom, and you will be his beloved bride forever. ¹⁴Accordingly, hear me, Asenath, and put on a wedding robe, the ancient and first robe that is yet laid up in your chamber from of old, and also put all your choice adornments around you, and adorn yourself as a good bride and make yourself ready to meet him; ¹⁵for behold, he himself comes to you today and will see you and rejoice." ¹⁶And when the messenger of the LORD, in the shape of a man, had finished speaking these words to Asenath, she rejoiced with great joy over all the things that were spoken by him, and fell on her face on the earth, and paid homage before his feet, ¹⁷and said to him, "Blessed is the LORD your God who sent you to deliver me from the darkness and to bring me from the foundations of the abyss itself into the light, and blessed is your name forever. ¹⁸If I have found grace, my lord, in your sight, and will know that you will perform all the words which you have said to me so that they are accomplished, let your handmaid speak to you." ¹⁹And the messenger says to her, "Speak on." ²⁰And she said, "Please, lord, sit down on this bed [for] a little while, because this bed is pure and undefiled, for another man or other woman never sat on it, ²¹and I will set a table and bread before you, and you will eat, and I will also bring you wine, aged and good, the aroma of it will reach to heaven, and you will drink thereof and afterward will depart on your way." ²²And he says to her, "Hurry and bring it quickly."

CHAPTER 16

¹And Asenath hurried and set an empty table before him; and as she was starting to fetch bread, the divine messenger says to her, "Bring me a honeycomb also." ²And she stood still, and was perplexed, and grieved because she did not have a bee's comb in her storehouse. ³And the divine messenger says to her, "You therefore stand still?" ⁴And she said, "My lord, I will send a boy to the suburb, because the possession of our inheritance is near, and he will come and bring one quickly from there, and I will set it before you." ⁵The divine messenger says to her, "Enter your storehouse and you will find a bee's comb lying on the table; take it up and bring it here." ⁶And she said, "Lord, there is no bee's comb in my storehouse." And he said, "Go and you will find [one]." ⁷And Asenath entered her storehouse and found a honeycomb lying on the table; and the comb was great and white like snow and full of honey, and that honey was as the dew of heaven, and the aroma of it [was] as the aroma of life. ⁸Then Asenath wondered and said in herself: "Is this comb from the mouth of this man himself?" And Asenath took that comb, and brought it, and set it forth on the table, ⁹and the messenger said to her, "Why is it that you said, There is no honeycomb in my house, and behold, you have brought it to me?" ¹⁰And she said, "Lord, I have never put a honeycomb in my house, but as you said so, it has been made. Did this come forth from your mouth? For the aroma of it is as the aroma of ointment." ¹¹And the man smiled at the woman's understanding. ¹²Then he calls her to himself, and when she came, he stretched out his right hand and took hold of her head, and when he shook her head with his right hand, Asenath feared the messenger's hand greatly, for sparks proceeded from his hands after the manner of red-hot iron, and accordingly, she was gazing with much fear and trembling at the messenger's hand the whole time. ¹³And he smiled and said, "Blessed are you, Asenath, because the ineffable mysteries of God have been revealed to you; and blessed are all who cleave to the LORD God in penitence, because they will eat of this comb, ¹⁴for this comb is the Spirit of life, and the bees of the paradise of delight have made this from the dew of the roses of life that are in the paradise of God and [from] every flower, ¹⁵and the messengers, and all the elect of God, and all the sons of the Most High eat of it, and whosoever will eat of it will not die forever." ¹⁶Then the divine messenger stretched out his right hand and took a small piece from the comb and ate, and with his own hand placed what was left in Asenath's mouth and said to her, "Eat," and she ate. ¹⁷And the messenger says to her, "Behold, now you have eaten the bread of life, and have drunk the cup of immortality, and been anointed with the unction of incorruption; ¹⁸behold, now today your flesh produces flowers of life from the fountain of the Most High, and your bones will be made fat like the cedars of the paradise of delight of God, and unwearying powers will maintain you; ¹⁹accordingly, your youth will not see old age, nor will your beauty fail forever, but you will be as a walled mother-city of all." ²⁰And the messenger incited the comb, and many bees arose from the cells of that comb, and the cells were numberless—myriads of myriads and thousands of thousands. ²¹And the bees were also white like snow, and their wings as purple and crimson stuff and as scarlet; and they also had sharp stings and injured no man. ²²Then all those bees encircled Asenath from feet to head, and other great bees like their queens arose from the cells, and they circled around on her face and on her lips, and made a comb on her mouth and on her lips like the comb that lay before the messenger; ²³and all those bees ate from the comb that was on Asenath's mouth. And the messenger said to the bees, "Go now to your place." ²⁴Then all the bees rose, and flew, and departed to Heaven; but as many as wished to injure Asenath all fell on the earth and died. ²⁵And thereon the messenger stretched his staff over the dead bees and said to them, "Rise and depart, you also, into your place." ²⁶Then all the dead bees rose, and departed into the court that adjoined Asenath's house, and took up their lodging on the fruit-bearing trees.

CHAPTER 17

¹And the messenger saith to Asenath, "Have you seen this thing?" And she said, "Yes, my lord, I have seen all these things." ²The divine messenger says to her, "So all my words will be, as many as I have spoken to you today." ³Then the messenger of the LORD stretched forth his right hand for the third time and touched the side of the comb, and immediately fire came up from the table and devoured the comb, but it did not injure the table a bit. ⁴And when much fragrance had come forth from the burning of the comb and filled the chamber, Asenath said to the divine messenger, "Lord, I have seven virgins who were brought up with me from my youth and were born on one night with me, who wait on me, and I love all of them as my sisters. I will call them, and you will bless them too, even as you blessed me." ⁵And the messenger said to her, "Call them." Then Asenath called the seven virgins and set them before the messenger, ⁶and the messenger said to them, "The LORD God Most High will bless you, and you will be [pillars] of refuge of seven cities, and all the elect of that city who dwell together will [rest on you] forever." ⁷And after these things the divine messenger says to Asenath, "Take away this table." ⁸And when Asenath turned to remove the table, he immediately departed from her eyes, and Asenath saw as it were a chariot with four horses that were going eastward to Heaven, ⁹and the chariot was as a flame of fire, and the horses as lightning, and the messenger was standing above that chariot. ¹⁰Then Asenath said, "Silly and foolish am I, the lowly one, for I have spoken as that a man came into my chamber from Heaven! ¹¹I did not know that God came into it; and behold, now he goes back to Heaven, to his place." ¹²And she said in herself: "Be gracious, LORD, to Your bondmaid, and spare your handmaid, because, for my part, I have spoken rash things before You in ignorance."

CHAPTER 18

¹And while Asenath was yet speaking these words to herself, behold, a young man, one of

the servants of Joseph, came, saying, "Joseph, the mighty man of God, comes to you today." ²And immediately Asenath called the overseer of her house and said to him, "Hurry and prepare my house and make a good dinner ready, for Joseph, the mighty man of God, comes to us today." ³And when the overseer of the house saw her (for her face had shrunk from the seven days' affliction, and weeping, and abstinence) he sorrowed and wept; ⁴and he took hold of her right hand, and kissed it tenderly, and said, "What afflicts you, my lady, that your face is thus shrunken?" ⁵And she said, "I have had great pain about my head, and sleep departed from my eyes." ⁶Then the overseer of the house went away and prepared the house and the dinner. ⁷And Asenath remembered the messenger's words and his injunctions, and hurried and entered her second chamber where the chests of her adornments were, and opened her great coffer, and brought out her first robe, like lightning to behold, and put it on; ⁸and she also girded herself with a bright and royal girdle that was of gold and precious stones, and on her hands she put golden bracelets, and on her feet golden buskins, and a precious ornament around her neck, and she put a golden wreath around her head; ⁹and on the wreath as on its front was a great sapphire stone, and around the great stone [were] six stones of great price, and with a very marvelous mantle she veiled her head. ¹⁰And when Asenath remembered the words of the overseer of her house, for he said to her that her face had shrunk, she sorrowed exceedingly, and groaned, and said, "Woe is me, the lowly one, since my face is shrunken. ¹¹Joseph will see me thus and I will be set at nothing by him." ¹²And she says to her handmaid, "Bring me pure water from the fountain." ¹³And when she had brought it, she poured it out into the basin, and bending down to wash her face, she sees her own face shining like the sun, and her eyes as the morning star when it rises, and her cheeks as a star of heaven, and her lips as red roses; ¹⁴the hairs of her head were as the vine that blooms among his fruits in the paradise of God, her neck as an all-variegated cypress. ¹⁵And Asenath, when she saw these things, marveled in herself at the sight, and rejoiced with exceedingly great joy, and did not wash her face, for she said, "Lest I wash off this great and attractive beauty." ¹⁶The overseer of her house then came back to tell her, "All things are done that you commanded"; ¹⁷and when he beheld her, he feared greatly and was seized with trembling for a long time, and he fell at her feet and began to say, "What is this, my mistress? What is this beauty that surrounds you that is great and marvelous? ¹⁸Has the LORD God of Heaven chosen you as a bride for His son Joseph?"

CHAPTER 19

¹And while they were yet speaking these things, a boy came, saying to Asenath, "Behold, Joseph stands before the doors of our court." ²Then Asenath hurried and went down the stairs from her loft with the seven virgins to meet Joseph and stood in the porch of her house. ³And Joseph, having come into the court, the gates were shut, and all strangers remained outside. ⁴And Asenath came out from the porch to meet Joseph, and when he saw her, he marveled at her beauty, and said to her, "Who are you, girl? Tell me quickly." ⁵And she says to him, "I, lord, am your handmaid Asenath; I have cast all the idols away from me and they perished. ⁶And a man came to me today from Heaven and has given me bread of life and I ate, and I drank a blessed cup, ⁷and he said to me, I have given you for a bride to Joseph, and he himself will be your bridegroom forever; ⁸and your name will not be called Asenath, but it will be called City of Refuge, and the LORD God will reign over many nations, and through you they will seek refuge with God Most High. ⁹And the man said, I will also go to Joseph that I may speak into his ears these words concerning you. And now you know, lord, if that man has come to you and if he has spoken to you concerning me." ¹⁰Then Joseph says to Asenath, "Blessed are you, woman, of God Most High, and blessed is your name forever, for the LORD God has laid the foundations of your walls, and the sons of the living God will dwell in your city of refuge, and the LORD God will reign over them forever. ¹¹For that man came from Heaven to me today and said these words to me concerning you. ¹²And now come here to me, you virgin and pure—and [why] do you therefore stand far off?" ¹³Then Joseph stretched out his hands and embraced Asenath, and Asenath Joseph, and they kissed one another for a long time, and both lived again in their spirit. ¹⁴And Joseph kissed Asenath and gave her the Spirit of life, then the second time he gave her the Spirit of wisdom, and the third time he kissed her tenderly and gave her the Spirit of truth.

CHAPTER 20

¹And when they had embraced around one another for a long time and intertwined the chains of their hands, Asenath said to Joseph, "Come here, lord, and enter our house, for on my part I have prepared our house and a great dinner." ²And she took hold of his right hand, and led him into her house, and seated him on the chair of her father Pentephres; and she brought water to wash his feet. ³And Joseph said, "Let one of the virgins come and wash my feet." ⁴And Asenath said to him, "No, lord, for henceforth you are my lord and I am your handmaid. ⁵And do you therefore seek this— that another virgin should wash your feet? ⁶For your feet are my feet, and your hands my hands, and your soul my soul, and another will not wash your feet." ⁷And she constrained him and washed his feet. ⁸Then Joseph took hold of her right hand and kissed her tenderly and Asenath kissed his head tenderly, and thereon he seated her at his right hand. ⁹Her father, and mother, and all her relatives then came from the possession of their inheritance, and they saw her sitting with Joseph and clad in a wedding garment. ¹⁰And they marveled at her beauty and rejoiced and glorified God who quickens the dead. ¹¹And after these things they ate and drank; and all having made cheer, Pentephres said to Joseph, "Tomorrow I will call all the princes and satraps of all the land of Egypt, and will make a wedding for you, and you will take my daughter Asenath to be [your] wife." ¹²But Joseph said, "Tomorrow I go to Pharaoh the king, for he himself is my father and appointed me ruler over all this land, and I will speak to him concerning Asenath, and he will give her to me to be [my] wife." ¹³And Pentephres said to him, "Go in peace."

CHAPTER 21

¹And Joseph stayed with Pentephres that day, and he did not go in to Asenath, for he was accustomed to say: "It is not fitting for a man who worships God to sleep with his wife before his marriage." ²And Joseph rose early, and departed to Pharaoh, and said to him, "Give me Asenath, daughter of Pentephres, priest of Heliopolis, to be [my] wife." ³And Pharaoh rejoiced with great joy, and he says to Joseph, "Behold, has this one not been betrothed to you to be [your] wife from eternity? ⁴Accordingly, let her be your wife henceforth and to time continuous." ⁴Then Pharaoh sent and called Pentephres, and Pentephres brought Asenath and set her before Pharaoh; ⁵and when Pharaoh saw her he marveled at her beauty and said, "The LORD God of Joseph will bless you, child, and this beauty of yours will remain forever, for the LORD God of Joseph chose you as a bride for him, for Joseph is as the son of the Most High, and you will be called his bride henceforth and forever." ⁶And after these things Pharaoh took Joseph and Asenath and set golden wreaths on their heads, which were in his house from of old and from ancient times, and Pharaoh set Asenath at Joseph's right hand. ⁷And Pharaoh put his hands on their heads and said, "The LORD God Most High will bless you and will multiply, and magnify, and glorify you to time continuous." ⁸Then Pharaoh turned them around to face one another and brought them mouth to mouth, and they kissed one another. ⁹And Pharaoh made a wedding for Joseph, and a great dinner, and much drinking during seven days, ¹⁰and he called together all the rulers of Egypt and all the kings of the nations, having made proclamation in the land of Egypt, saying, "Every man who will do work during the seven days of the wedding of Joseph and Asenath will surely die." ¹¹And while the wedding was going on, and when the dinner was ended, Joseph went in to Asenath, and Asenath conceived by Joseph and bore Manasseh and his brother Ephraim in Joseph's house.

CHAPTER 22

¹And when the seven years of plenty had passed, the seven years of famine began to come. ²And when Jacob heard about his son Joseph, he came into Egypt with all his relatives in the second year of the famine, in the second month, on the twenty-first of the

month, and settled in Goshen. ³And Asenath said to Joseph, "I will go and see your father, for your father Israel is as my father and God." ⁴And Joseph said to her, "You will go with me and see my father." ⁵And Joseph and Asenath came to Jacob in the land of Goshen, and Joseph's brothers met them and paid homage to them on their faces on the earth. ⁶Then both went in to Jacob; and Jacob was sitting on his bed, and he himself was an old man in a robust old age. ⁷And when Asenath saw him, she marveled at his beauty, for Jacob was exceedingly beautiful to behold and his old age as the youth of a handsome man, ⁸and all his head was white like snow, and the hairs of his head were all close and exceedingly thick, and his beard [was] white, reaching to his breast, his eyes cheerful and glittering, his sinews, and his shoulders, and his arms as of a messenger, his thighs, and his calves, and his feet as of a giant. ⁹Then Asenath, when she saw him thus, marveled, and fell down, and paid homage on her face on the earth. ¹⁰And Jacob said to Joseph, "Is this my daughter-in-law, your wife? She will be blessed of God Most High." ¹¹Then Jacob called Asenath to himself, and blessed her, and kissed her tenderly; ¹²and Asenath stretched out her hands, and took hold of Jacob's neck, and hung on to his neck, and kissed him tenderly. ¹³And after these things they ate and drank. ¹⁴And thereon both Joseph and Asenath went to their house; and Simeon and Levi, the sons of Leah, alone conducted them forth, but the sons of Bilhah and Zilpah, the handmaids of Leah and Rachel, did not join in conducting them forth, for they envied and detested them. ¹⁵And Levi was at Asenath's right and Simeon at her left. ¹⁶And Asenath took hold of Levi's hand, for she loved him exceedingly above all of Joseph's brothers and as a prophet, and a worshiper of God, and one who feared the LORD. ¹⁷For he was an understanding man and a prophet of the Most High, and he himself saw letters written in Heaven, and read them, and revealed them to Asenath in secret; ¹⁸for Levi himself also loved Asenath much and saw the place of her rest in the highest.

CHAPTER 23

¹And it came to pass as Joseph and Asenath were passing by, when they were going to Jacob, Pharaoh's firstborn son saw them from the wall, and when he saw Asenath, he became crazed with her by reason of her surpassing beauty. ²Then Pharaoh's son sent messengers, and called Simeon and Levi to himself; ³and when they came and stood before him, Pharaoh's firstborn son says to them, "I for my part know that you are today mighty men above all men on the earth, and with these right hands of yours the city of the Shechemites was overthrown, and with your two swords thirty thousand warriors were cut down. ⁴And I today will take you to myself as companions and give you much gold, and silver, and menservants, and handmaids, and houses, and great inheritances, and you contend on my side and do me kindness; ⁵for I received great injury from your brother Joseph, since he himself took Asenath to be [his] wife, and this woman was betrothed to me from of old. ⁶And now come with me, and I will fight against Joseph to slay him with my sword, and I will take Asenath to be [my] wife, and you will be to me as brothers and faithful friends. ⁷But if you will not listen to my words, I will slay you with my sword." ⁸And when he had said these things, he drew out his sword and showed it to them. ⁹And Simeon was a bold and daring man, and he thought to lay his right hand on the hilt of his sword, and draw it from the sheath thereof, and smite Pharaoh's son, for he had spoken hard words to them. ¹⁰Levi then saw the thought of his heart, because he was a prophet, and he trod with his foot on Simeon's right foot and pressed it, signaling to him to cease from his wrath. ¹¹And Levi was quietly saying to Simeon, "Are you therefore angry against this man? We are men who worship God, and it is not fitting for us to render evil for evil." ¹²Then Levi said to Pharaoh's son openly, with mildness of heart, "Does our lord therefore speak these words? We are men who worship God, and our father is a friend of God Most High, and our brother is as a son of God. ¹³And how will we do this wicked thing, to sin in the sight of our God and of our father Israel and in the sight ot our brother Joseph? ¹⁴And now hear my words: it is not fitting for a man who worships God to harm any man in any way; and if anyone wishes to harm a man who worships God, that man who worships God does not avenge himself on him, for there is no sword in his hands. ¹⁵And you must beware of speaking anymore of these words about our brother Joseph. ¹⁶But if you continue in your evil counsel, behold, our swords are drawn against you." ¹⁷Then Simeon and Levi drew their swords from their sheaths and said, "Do you now see these swords? ¹⁸With these two swords the LORD punished the injury of the Shechemites, by which they did injury to the sons of Israel through our sister Dinah, whom Shechem the son of Hamor defiled." ¹⁹And Pharaoh's son, when he saw the swords drawn, feared exceedingly and trembled all over his body, for they glittered like a flame of fire, and his eyes became dim, and he fell on his face on the earth beneath their feet. ²⁰Then Levi stretched out his right hand and took hold of him, saying, "Stand up and do not fear, only beware of speaking any evil word anymore concerning our brother Joseph." ²¹And so both Simeon and Levi went out from before his face.

CHAPTER 24

¹Pharaoh's son then continued to be full of fear and grief for he feared Joseph's brothers, and again he was exceedingly crazed by reason of Asenath's beauty, and he grieved greatly. ²Then his menservants say in his ear: "Behold, the sons of Bilhah and the sons of Zilpah, the handmaids of Leah and Rachel, Jacob's wives, are at great enmity against Joseph and Asenath and hate them; these will be to you in all things according to your will." ³Therefore Pharaoh's son immediately sent messengers and called them, and they came to him at the first hour of the night, and they stood in his presence, ⁴and he says to them, "I have learned from many that you are mighty men." ⁵And Dan and Gad, the elder brothers, said to him, "Let my lord now speak to his menservants what he wishes [so] that your menservants may hear and we may do according to your will." ⁶Then Pharaoh's son rejoiced with exceedingly great joy and said to his menservants, "Withdraw now for a short space from me, for I have secret speech to hold with these men." And they all withdrew. ⁷Then Pharaoh's son lied, and he says to them, "Behold, now blessing and death are before your faces: you therefore take the blessing rather than the death, because you are mighty men and will not die as women; but be brave and avenge yourselves on your enemies. ⁸For I have heard your brother Joseph saying to Pharaoh, my father: "Dan, and Gad, and Naphtali, and Asher are not my brothers, but children of my father's handmaids: I therefore wait for my father's death and will blot them out from the earth and all their issue, lest they should inherit with us, because they are children of handmaids. ⁹For these also sold me to the Ishmaelites, and I will render to them again according to their injury which they wickedly committed against me; only my father will die. ¹⁰And my father Pharaoh commended him for these things and said to him, "You have spoken well, child. ¹¹Accordingly, take mighty men from me and proceed against them according to what they worked against you, and I will be a helper to you." ¹²And when Dan and Gad heard these things from Pharaoh's son they were very troubled, and exceedingly grieved, ¹³and they said to him, "Please, lord, help us; for henceforth we are your slaves and bondmen and will die with you." ¹⁴And Pharaoh's son said, "I will be a helper to you if you will also listen to my words." ¹⁵And they said to him, "Command us what you wish and we will do according to your will." ¹⁶And Pharaoh's son says to them, "I will slay my father Pharaoh this night, for Pharaoh is as Joseph's father and said to him that he would help against you; ¹⁷and you slay Joseph, and I will take Asenath to myself to be [my] wife, and you will be my brothers and fellow-heirs of all my possessions. Only do this thing." ¹⁸And Dan and Gad said to him, "We are your menservants today and will do all [the] things that you have commanded us. ¹⁹And we have heard Joseph saying to Asenath, Go tomorrow to the possession of our inheritance, for it is the season of the vintage; and he sent six hundred mighty men to war with her and fifty forerunners. ²⁰Now therefore, hear us and we will speak to our lord." And they spoke to him all their secret words. ²¹Then Pharaoh's son gave the four brothers five hundred men each and appointed them their chiefs and leaders. ²²And Dan and Gad said to him, "We are your menservants today and will do all the things that you have commanded us, and we will set forth by night, and lie in wait in the ravine, and hide ourselves in the thicket of the reeds; ²³and

you take with yourself fifty bowmen on horses and go a long way before us, and Asenath will come and fall into our hands, and we will cut down the men that are with her, and she herself will flee before [us] with her chariot and fall into your hands, and you will do to her as your soul desires; ²⁴and after these things we will also slay Joseph while he is grieving for Asenath; ²⁵we will also likewise slay his children before his eyes." ²⁶Pharaoh's firstborn son then, when he heard these things, rejoiced exceedingly, and he sent them forth and two thousand fighting men with them. ²⁷And when they came to the ravine, they hid themselves in the thicket of the reeds, and they divided into four companies, and took up their station on the far side of the ravine as in the front part—five hundred men on this side of the road and on that; ²⁸and on the near side of the ravine likewise the rest remained, and they themselves also took up their station in the thicket ot the reeds—five hundred men on this side and on that of the road; and between them was a broad and wide road.

CHAPTER 25

¹Then Pharaoh's son rose up the same night and came to his father's bed-chamber to slay him with the sword. ²His father's guards thereon hindered him from coming in to his father and said to him, "What do you command, lord?" ³And Pharaoh's son said to them, "I wish to see my father, for I am going to gather the vintage of my newly planted vineyard." ⁴And the guards said to him, "Your father suffers pain, and lies awake the whole night, and now rests, and he said to us that no one was to come in to him, Not even if it is my firstborn son." ⁵And he on hearing these things went away in wrath and immediately took mounted bowmen, fifty in number, and went away before them as Dan and Gad had said to him. ⁶And the younger brothers, Naphtali and Asher, spoke to their elder brothers Dan and Gad, saying, "Therefore do you on your part again work wickedness against your father Israel and against your brother Joseph? ⁷And God preserves him as the apple of an eye. Behold, did you not once sell Joseph? And he is king today of all the land of Egypt and food-giver. ⁸Now therefore, if you again wish to work wickedness against him, he will cry to the Most High, and He will send fire from Heaven and it will devour you, and the messengers of God will fight against you." ⁹Then the elder brothers were moved to anger against them and said, "And will we die as women? Far be it." ¹⁰And they went out to meet Joseph and Asenath.

CHAPTER 26

¹And Asenath rose in the morning and said to Joseph, "I am going to the possession of our inheritance as you have said; but my soul exceedingly fears for you are parting from me." ²And Joseph said to her, "Be of good cheer and do not be afraid, but rather go away rejoicing, in dread of no man whatsoever, for the LORD is with you and He Himself will preserve you as the apple of an eye from every evil. ³And I will set forth for my giving of food and will give to all the men in the city, and no man will perish of hunger in the land of Egypt." ⁴Then Asenath departed on her way, and Joseph for his giving of food. ⁵And when Asenath reached the place of the ravine with the six hundred men, suddenly they who were with Pharaoh's son came forth from their ambush and joined battle with those who were with Asenath, and cut them all down with their swords, and all her forerunners they slew, but Asenath fled with her chariot. ⁶Then Levi, the son of Leah, knew all these things by the Spirit as a prophet and told his brothers of Asenath's danger, and immediately each of them took his sword on his thigh, and their shields on their arms, and the spears in their right hands, and pursued after Asenath with great speed. ⁷And as Asenath was fleeing before, behold, Pharaoh's son met her and fifty horsemen with him: ⁸and Asenath, when she saw him, was seized with very great fear and was trembling, and she called on the Name of the LORD her God.

CHAPTER 27

¹And Benjamin was sitting with her on the chariot on the right side; and Benjamin was a strong young man of about nineteen years, and on him was ineffable beauty and might as of a lion's whelp, and he was also one who feared God exceedingly. ²Then Benjamin leapt down from the chariot, and took a round stone from the ravine, and filled his hand, and hurled [it] at Pharaoh's son, and struck his left temple, and wounded him with a grievous wound, and he fell from his horse on the earth half-dead. ³And thereon Benjamin, having run up onto a rock, says to Asenath's charioteer: "Give me stones from the ravine." ⁴And he gave him fifty stones. And Benjamin hurled the stones and slew the fifty men who were with Pharaoh's son, all the stones sinking in through their temples. ⁵Then the sons of Leah, Reuben and Simeon, Levi and Judah, Issachar and Zebulun, pursued after the men who had lain in wait against Asenath, and fell on them stealthily, and cut them all down; and the six men slew two thousand and seventy-six men. ⁶And the sons of Bilhah and Zilpah fled from their face and said, "We have perished at the hands of our brothers, and Pharaoh's son has also died by the hand of the young man Benjamin, and all who were with him perished by the hand of the boy Benjamin. ⁷Accordingly, therefore, come let us slay Asenath and Benjamin and flee to the thicket of these reeds." ⁸And they came against Asenath, holding their swords drawn, covered with blood. ⁹And when Asenath saw them, she feared greatly and said, "LORD God, who quickened me and delivered me from the idols and the corruption of death, even as You said to me that my soul will live forever, now also deliver me from these wicked men." ¹⁰And the LORD God heard Asenath's voice, and immediately the swords of the adversaries fell from their hands on the earth and were turned into ashes.

CHAPTER 28

¹And the sons of Bilhah and Zilpah, when they saw the strange miracle that had been worked, feared and said, "The LORD fights against us on Asenath's behalf." ²Then they fell on their faces on the earth, and paid homage to Asenath, and said, "Have mercy on us, your bondmen, for you are our mistress and queen. ³We wickedly committed evil deeds against you and against our brother Joseph, but the LORD repaid us according to our works. ⁴Therefore we your bondmen beg you: have mercy on us, the lowly and miserable, and deliver us from the hands of our brothers, for they will make themselves avengers of the injury done to you and their swords are against us. ⁵Accordingly, be gracious to your bondmen, mistress, before them." ⁶And Asenath said to them, "Be of good cheer and do not be afraid of your brothers, for they themselves are men who worship God and fear the LORD; ⁷but go into the thicket of these reeds until I will appease them on your behalf and stay their wrath on account of the great crimes which you on your part have dared to commit against them. ⁸But may the LORD see and judge between me and you." ⁹Then Dan and Gad fled into the thicket of the reeds; and their brothers, Leah's sons, came running like stags with great haste against them. ¹⁰And Asenath stepped down from the chariot that was her cover and gave them her right hand with tears, ¹¹and they themselves fell down and paid homage to her on the earth and wept with a loud voice; ¹²and they continued asking for their brothers, the sons of the handmaids, to put them to death. ¹³And Asenath said to them, "Please spare your brothers, and do not render to them evil for evil. ¹⁴For the LORD saved me from them and shattered their daggers and swords from out of their hands, and behold, they have melted and were burned to ashes on the earth like wax from before fire, and this is sufficient for us that the LORD fights for us against them. ¹⁵Accordingly, spare your brothers, for they are your brothers and the blood of your father Israel." ¹⁶And Simeon said to her, "Does our mistress therefore speak good words on behalf of her enemies? ¹⁷No, but rather we will cut them down limb from limb with our swords, for they devised evil things concerning our brother Joseph and our father Israel and against you, our mistress, today." ¹⁸Then Asenath stretched out her right hand, and touched Simeon's beard, and kissed him tenderly, and said, "In no way, brother, render evil for evil to your neighbor, for the LORD will avenge this injury. ¹⁹They themselves, you know, are your brothers and the offspring of your father Israel, and they fled far from your face. Accordingly, grant them pardon." ²⁰Then Levi came up to her and kissed her right hand tenderly, for he knew that she was pleased to save the men from their brothers' anger that they should not slay them. ²¹And they themselves were near at hand in the thicket of the reed-bed: and their brother Levi, knowing this, did not declare it to his brothers, for he

feared lest in their anger they should cut their brothers down.

CHAPTER 29

¹And Pharaoh's son rose from the earth, and sat up, and spat blood from his mouth, for the blood was running down from his temple into his mouth. ²And Benjamin ran up to him, and took his sword, and drew it from Pharaoh's son's sheath (for Benjamin was not wearing a sword on his thigh), and wished to strike Pharaoh's son on the breast. ³Then Levi ran up to him, and took hold of his hand, and said, "In no way, brother, do [this], for it is not fitting for a man who worships God to render evil for evil, nor to trample on one who has fallen, nor utterly to crush his enemy even to death. ⁴And now put back the sword into his place, and come and help me, and let us heal him of this wound; and if he lives, he will be our friend and his father Pharaoh will be our father." ⁵Then Levi raised Pharaoh's son from the earth, and washed away the blood from his face, and tied a bandage over his wound, and set him on his horse, and led him to his father Pharaoh, relating to him all the things that had happened and befallen. ⁶And Pharaoh arose from his throne, and paid homage to Levi on the earth, and blessed him. ⁷Then when the third day had passed, Pharaoh's son died from the stone with which he was wounded by Benjamin. ⁸And Pharaoh mourned for his firstborn son exceedingly, from which grief Pharaoh fell sick and died at one hundred and nine years, and he left his diadem to the all-beautiful Joseph. ⁹And Joseph reigned alone in Egypt forty-eight years; and after these things Joseph gave back the diadem to Pharaoh's younger child, who was at the breast when the old man Pharaoh died. ¹⁰And Joseph was then on as father of Pharaoh's younger child in Egypt until his death, glorifying and praising God.

TESTAMENT OF JOB

The Testament of Job is a book likely written in the 1st century BC or the 1st century AD (thus part of a tradition often called "intertestamental literature" by Christian scholars). The earliest surviving manuscript is in Coptic of the 5th century; other early surviving manuscripts are in Greek and Old Slavonic. Similar to other apocryphal testaments, it is an account of the last events and words of the protagonist (here, Job).

CHAPTER 1

¹On the day he became sick and knew that he would have to leave his bodily abode, he called his seven sons and his three daughters together and spoke to them as follows: ²Form a circle around me, children, and hear, and I will relate to you what the LORD did for me and all that happened to me. ³For I am your father Job. ⁴Know then, my children, that you are the generation of a chosen one and take heed of your noble birth. ⁵For I am of the sons of Esau. My brother is Nahor, and your mother is Dinah. I have become your father by her. ⁶For my first wife died with my other ten children in bitter death. ⁷Hear now, children, and I will reveal to you what happened to me. ⁸I was a very rich man living in the east, in the land of Uz, and before the LORD had named me Job, I was called Jobab. ⁹The beginning of my trial was thus: near my house there was the idol of one worshiped by the people; and I saw burnt-offerings constantly brought to him as a god. ¹⁰Then I pondered and said to myself, "Is this he who made the heavens and earth, the sea, and all of us? How will I know the truth?" ¹¹And in that night as I lay asleep, a voice came and called: "Jobab! Jobab! Rise up, and I will tell you who is the One whom you wish to know. ¹²This, however, to whom the people bring burnt-offerings and libations, is not God, but this is the power and work of the Seducer by which he deceives the people." ¹³And when I heard this, I fell on the earth and I prostrated myself, saying, ¹⁴"O my Lord, who speaks for the salvation of my soul—please, if this is the idol of Satan, please, let me go on and destroy it and purify this spot. ¹⁵For there is none that can forbid me doing this, as I am the king of this land, so that those that live in it will no longer be led astray." ¹⁶And the voice that spoke out of the flame answered to me: "You can purify this spot. ¹⁷But behold, I announce to you what the LORD ordered me to tell you, for I am the chief-messenger of the God." ¹⁸And I said, "Whatever will be told to His servant, I will hear." ¹⁹And the chief-messenger said to me, "Thus speaks the LORD: If you undertake to destroy and take away the image of Satan, he will set himself with wrath to wage war against you, and he will display all his malice against you. ²⁰He will bring on you many severe plagues and take from you all that you have. ²¹He will take away your children and will inflict many calamities on you. ²²Then you must wrestle like an athlete and resist pain, [being] sure of your reward, [and] overcome trials and afflictions. ²³But when you endure, I will make your name renowned throughout all generations of the earth until the [very] end of the world. ²⁴And I will restore you to all that you had, and the double part of what you will lose will be given to you in order that you may know that God does not consider the person but gives to each who deserves the good. ²⁵And also to you will it be given, and you will put on a crown of amaranth. ²⁶And at the resurrection you will awaken for continuous life. Then you will know that the LORD is just, and true, and mighty." ²⁷Immediately, my children, I replied: "I will from love of God endure all that will come on me until death, and I will not shrink back." ²⁸Then the messenger put his seal on me and left me.

CHAPTER 2

¹After this I rose up in the night and took fifty slaves and went to the temple of the idol and destroyed it to the ground. ²And so I went back to my house and gave orders that the door should he firmly locked, saying to my doorkeepers: ³"If somebody will ask for me, bring no report to me, but tell him: He investigates urgent affairs. He is inside." ⁴Then Satan disguised himself as a beggar and knocked heavily at the door, saying to the doorkeeper: ⁵"Report to Job and say that I desire to meet him," ⁶and the doorkeeper came in and told me that, but heard from me that I was studying. ⁷The evil one, having failed in this, went away and took on his shoulder an old, torn basket and went in and spoke to the doorkeeper, saying, "Tell Job: Give me bread from your hands that I may eat." ⁸And when I heard this, I gave her burnt bread to give it to him, and I made known to him: "Do not expect to eat of my bread, for it is forbidden to you." ⁹But the doorkeeper, being ashamed to hand him the burnt and ashy bread, as she did not know that it was Satan, took of her own fine bread and gave it to him. ¹⁰But he took it, and knowing what occurred, said to the maiden, "Go on, bad servant, and bring me the bread that was given you to hand to me." ¹¹And the servant cried and spoke in grief: "You speak the truth, saying that I am a bad servant, because I have not done as I was instructed by my master." ¹²And he turned back and brought him the burnt bread and said to him, "Thus says my lord: You will not eat of my bread anymore, for it is forbidden to you. ¹³And he gave me this in order that the charge may not be brought against me that I did not give to the enemy who asked." ¹⁴And when Satan heard this, he sent the servant back to me, saying, "As you see this bread all burnt, so I will soon burn your body to make it like this." ¹⁵And I replied, "Do what you desire to do and accomplish whatever you plot. For I am ready to endure whatever you bring on me." ¹⁶And when the Devil heard this, he left me, and walking up to under the [highest] Heaven, he took from the LORD the oath that he might have power over all my possessions. ¹⁷And after having taken the power, he went and instantly took away all my wealth.

TESTAMENT OF JOB

CHAPTER 3
¹For I had one hundred and thirty thousand sheep, and of these I separated seven thousand for the clothing of orphans, and widows, and of needy and sick ones. ²I had a herd of eight hundred dogs who watched my sheep, and besides these two hundred to watch my house. ³And I had nine mills working for the whole city and ships to carry goods, and I sent them into every city, and into the villages to the feeble, and sick, and to those that were unfortunate. ⁴And I had three hundred and forty thousand nomadic donkeys, and of these I set aside five hundred, and the offspring of these I order to be sold and the proceeds to be given to the poor and the needy. ⁵For from all the lands the poor came to meet me. ⁶For the four doors of my house were opened, each, being in charge of a watchman who had to see whether there were any people coming, asking [for] alms, and whether they would see me sitting at one of the doors so that they could leave through the other and take whatever they needed. ⁷I also had thirty immovable tables set at all hours for the strangers alone, and I also had twelve tables spread for the widows. ⁸And if anyone came asking for alms, he found food on my table to take all he needed, and I turned nobody away to leave my door with an empty stomach. ⁹I also had three thousand five hundred yokes of oxen, and I selected of these five hundred and had them tend to the plowing. ¹⁰And with these I had done all the work in each field by those who would take it in charge, and I laid aside the income of their crops for the poor on their table. ¹¹I also had fifty bakeries from which I sent [the bread] to the table for the poor. ¹²And I had slaves selected for their service. ¹³There were also some strangers who saw my good will; they wished to serve as waiters themselves. ¹⁴Others, being in distress and unable to obtain a living, came with the request, saying, ¹⁵"Please, since we can also fill this office of servants and have no possession, have pity on us and advance money to us in order that we may go into the great cities and sell merchandise. ¹⁶And the surplus of our profit we may give as help to the poor, and then we will return to you your own [money]." ¹⁷And when I heard this, I was glad that they should take this altogether from me for the farming of charity for the poor. ¹⁸And I gave them what they wanted with a willing heart, and I accepted their written bond, but would not take any other security from them except the written document. ¹⁹And they went abroad and gave to the poor as far as they were successful. ²⁰Frequently, however, some of their goods were lost on the road or on the sea, or they would be robbed of them. ²¹Then they would come and say, "Please act generously toward us in order that we may see how we can restore to you your own." ²²And when I heard this, I had sympathy with them, and handed their bond to them, and often, having read it before them, tore it up and released them of their debt, saying to them, ²³"What I have consecrated for the benefit of the poor, I will not take from you." ²⁴And so I accepted nothing from my debtor. ²⁵And when a man with cheerful heart came to me, saying, "I am not in need to be compelled to be a paid worker for the poor, ²⁶but I wish to serve the needy at your table," and he consented to work, and he ate his share, ²⁷so I gave him his wages nevertheless, and I went home rejoicing. ²⁸And when he did not wish to take it, I forced him to do so, saying, "I know that you are a laboring man who looks for and waits for his wages, and you must take it." ²⁹I never deferred paying the wages of the hireling or any other, nor kept back in my house for a single evening his hire that was due to him. ³⁰Those that milked the cows and the ewes signaled to the passers by that they should take their share. ³¹For the milk flowed in such plenty that it curdled into butter on the hills and by the roadside; and by the rocks and the hills the cattle lay which had given birth to their offspring. ³²For my servants grew weary keeping the meat of the widows and the poor and dividing it into small pieces. ³³For they would curse and say, "Oh that we had of his flesh that we could be satisfied," although I was very kind to them. ³⁴I also had six harps, [and six slaves to play the harps,] and also a cithara, [and] a decachord, and I struck it during the day. ³⁵And I took the cithara, and the widows responded after their meals. ³⁶And with the musical instrument I reminded them of God, that they should give praise to the LORD. ³⁷And when my maidservants would murmur, then I took the musical instruments and played as much as they would have done for their wages, and gave them respite from their labor and sighs.

CHAPTER 4
¹And my children, after having taken charge of the service, took their meals each day along with their three sisters beginning with the older brother, and made a feast. ²And I rose in the morning and offered fifty rams and nineteen sheep as a sin-offering for them, and what remained as a residue was consecrated to the poor. ³And I said to them, "Take these as residue and pray for my children. ⁴Perhaps my sons have sinned before the LORD, speaking in haughtiness of spirit: We are children of this rich man. All these goods are ours; why should we be servants of the poor? ⁵And speaking thus in a haughty spirit they may have provoked the anger of God, for overbearing pride is an abomination before the LORD." ⁶So I brought oxen as offerings to the priest at the altar, saying, "May my children never think evil toward God in their hearts." ⁷While I lived in this manner, the Seducer could not bear to see the good [I did], and he demanded the warfare of God against me. ⁸And he came on me cruelly. ⁹First he burned up the large number of sheep, then the camels, then he burned up the cattle and all my herds; or they were captured not only by enemies but also by such as had received benefits from me. ¹⁰And the shepherds came and announced that to me. ¹¹But when I heard it, I gave praise to God and did not blaspheme. ¹²And when the Seducer learned of my fortitude, he plotted new things against me. ¹³He disguised himself as [the] king of Persia and besieged my city, and after he had led off all that were therein, he spoke to them in malice, saying in boastful language, ¹⁴"This man Job, who has obtained all the goods of the earth and left nothing for others, has destroyed and torn down the temple of god. ¹⁵Therefore I will repay to him what he has done to the house of the great god. ¹⁶Now come with me and we will pillage all that is left in his house." ¹⁷And they answered and said to him: "He has seven sons and three daughters. ¹⁸Take heed lest they flee into other lands and they may become our tyrants and then come over us with force and kill us." ¹⁹And he said, "Do not be afraid at all. I have destroyed his flocks and his wealth by fire, and I have captured the rest, and behold, I will kill his children." ²⁰And having spoken thus, he went and threw the house on my children and killed them. ²¹And my fellow-citizens, seeing that what was said by him had become true, came and pursued me, and robbed me of all that was in my house. ²²And I saw with mine own eyes the pillage of my house, and men without culture and without honor sat at my table and on my couches, and I could not remonstrate against them. ²³For I was exhausted like a woman with her loins let loose from multitude of pains, remembering chiefly that this warfare had been predicted to me by the LORD through His messenger. ²⁴And I became like one who, when seeing the rough sea and the adverse winds, while the lading of the vessel in mid-ocean is too heavy, casts the burden into the sea, saying, ²⁵"I wish to destroy all this only in order to come safely into the city so that I may take as profit the rescued ship and the best of my things." ²⁶Thus I managed my own affairs. ²⁷But there came another messenger and announced to me the ruin of my own children, and I was shaken with terror. ²⁸And I tore my clothes and said, "The LORD has given, the LORD has taken. As it has deemed best to the LORD, thus it has come to be. May the Name of the LORD be blessed."

CHAPTER 5
¹And when Satan saw that he could put me to despair, he went and asked of the LORD [for] my body in order to inflict plague on me, for the evil one could not bear my patience. ²Then the LORD delivered me into his hands to use my body as he wanted, but He gave him no power over my soul. ³And he came to me as I was sitting on my throne, still mourning over my children. ⁴And he resembled a great hurricane and turned over my throne and threw me on the ground. ⁵And I continued lying on the floor for three hours, and he struck me with a hard plague from the top of my head to the toes of my feet. ⁶And I left the city in great terror and woe and sat down on a dunghill, my body being worm-eaten. ⁷And I wet the earth with the moistness of my sore body, for matter flowed off my body, and many worms covered it. ⁸And when a single worm crept off my body, I put it back, saying,

"Remain on the spot where you have been placed until He who has sent you will order you elsewhere." ⁹Thus I endured for several years, sitting on a dunghill outside of the city while being plague-stricken. ¹⁰And I saw with my own eyes my longed-for children [carried by messengers to Heaven], ¹¹and my humbled wife who had been brought to her bridal chamber in such great luxuriousness and with spearmen as bodyguards. I saw her do a water-carrier's work like a slave in the house of a common man in order to win some bread and bring it to me. ¹²And in my sore affliction I said, "Oh that these braggart city rulers whom I should not have thought to be equal with my shepherd dogs should now employ my wife as servant!" ¹³And after this I took courage again. ¹⁴Yet afterward they withheld even the bread that she should only have her own nourishment. ¹⁵But she took it and divided it between herself and me, saying woefully, "Woe to me! Very soon he may no longer have bread to eat, and he cannot go to the market to ask [for] bread from the bread-sellers in order to bring it to me that he may eat." ¹⁶And when Satan learned this, he took the guise of a bread-seller, and it was as if by chance that my wife met him and asked him for bread thinking that it was that sort of man. ¹⁷But Satan said to her, "Give me the value, and then take what you wish." ¹⁸Immediately she answered, saying, "Where will I get money? Do you not know what misfortune happened to me? If you have pity, show it to me; if not, you will see." ¹⁹And he replied, saying, "If you did not deserve this misfortune, you would not have suffered all this. ²⁰Now, if there is no silver piece in your hand, give me the hair of your head and take three loaves of bread for it, so that you may live on these for three days." ²¹Then she said to herself: "What is the hair of my head in comparison with my starving husband?" ²²And so after having pondered over the matter, she said to him, "Rise and cut off my hair." ²³Then he took a pair of scissors and took off the hair of her head in the presence of all, and gave her three loaves of bread. ²⁴Then she took them and brought them to me. And Satan went behind her on the road, hiding himself as he walked and troubling her heart greatly.

CHAPTER 6

¹And immediately my wife came near me, and crying aloud and weeping she said, "Job! Job! How long will you sit on the dunghill outside of the city, still pondering for a while and expecting to obtain your hoped-for salvation? ²And I have been wandering from place to place, roaming around as a hired servant; behold, the memory has already died away from earth. ³And my sons and the daughters that I carried on my bosom and the labors and pains that I sustained have been for nothing. ⁴And you sit in the fetid state of soreness and worms, passing the nights in the cold air. ⁵And I have undergone all trials, and troubles, and pains day and night, until I succeeded in bringing bread to you. ⁶For your surplus of bread is no longer allowed to me; and as I can scarcely take my own food and divide it between us, I pondered in my heart that it was not right that you should be in pain and hunger for bread. ⁷And so I ventured to go to the market without bashfulness, and when the bread-seller told me: Give me money, and you will have bread; I disclosed to him our state of distress. ⁸Then I heard him say: If you have no money, hand me the hair of your head, and take three loaves of bread in order that you may live on these for three days. ⁹And I yielded to the wrong and said to him: Rise and cut off my hair! And he rose and in disgrace cut off with the scissors the hair of my head on the marketplace while the crowd stood by and wondered. ¹⁰Who would then not be astonished, saying, Is this Sitis, the wife of Job, who had fourteen curtains to cover her inner sitting room, and doors within doors so that he was greatly honored who would be brought near her? And now behold, she barters off her hair for bread! ¹¹Who had camels laden with goods, and they were brought into remote lands to the poor, and now she sells her hair for bread! ¹²Behold her who had seven tables immovably set in her house at which each poor man and each stranger ate, and now she sells her hair for bread! ¹³Behold her who had the basin with which to wash her feet made of gold and silver, and now she walks on the ground and [[sells her hair for bread!]] ¹⁴Behold her who had her garments made of byssus interwoven with gold, and now she exchanges her hair for bread! ¹⁵Behold her who had couches of gold and of silver, and now she sells her hair for bread! ¹⁶In short then, Job, after the many things that have been said to me, I now say in one word to you: ¹⁷since the feebleness of my heart has crushed my bones, rise then and take these loaves of bread and enjoy them, and then speak some word against the LORD and die! ¹⁸For I too would exchange the torpor of death for the sustenance of my body." ¹⁹But I replied to her, "Behold, I have been plague-stricken for these seven years, and I have withstood the worms of my body, and I was not weighed down in my soul by all these pains. ²⁰And as to the word which you say: Speak some word against God and die; together with you I will sustain the evil which you see, and let us endure the ruin of all that we have. ²¹Yet you desire that we should say some word against God and that He should be exchanged for the great Pluto. ²²Why do you not remember those great goods which we possessed? If these goods come from the lands of the LORD, should we not also endure evils and be high-minded in everything until the LORD will have mercy again and show pity to us? ²³Do you not see the Seducer stand behind you and confound your thoughts in order that you should deceive me?" ²⁴And he turned to Satan and said, "Why do you not come openly to me? Stop hiding yourself you wretched one! ²⁵Does the lion show his strength in the weasel cage? Or does the bird fly in the basket? I now tell you: go away and wage your war against me." ²⁶Then he went off from behind my wife and placed himself before me, crying, and he said, "Behold, Job, I yield and give way to you who are but flesh while I am a spirit. ²⁷You are plague-stricken, but I am in great trouble. ²⁸For I am like a wrestler contesting with a wrestler who has, in single-handed combat, torn down his antagonist and covered him with dust and broken every limb of his, whereas the other one who lies beneath, having displayed his bravery, gives forth sounds of triumph testifying to his own superior excellence. ²⁹Thus you, O Job, are beneath and stricken with plague and pain, and yet you have carried the victory in the wrestling-match with me, and behold, I yield to you." Then he left me embarrassed. ³⁰Now my children, you must also show a firm heart in all the evil that happens to you, for firmness of heart is greater than all things.

CHAPTER 7

¹At this time the kings heard what had happened to me and they rose and came to me—each from his land—to visit me and to comfort me. ²And when they came near me, they cried with a loud voice and each tore his clothes. ³And after they had prostrated themselves, touching the earth with their heads, they sat down next to me for seven days and seven nights, and none spoke a word. ⁴They were four in number: Eliphaz, the king of Teman, and Bildad, and Zophar, and Elihu. ⁵And when they had taken their seat, they conversed about what had happened to me. ⁶Now when they had come to me for the first time and I had shown them my precious stones, they were astonished and said, ⁷"If of us three kings all our possessions would be brought together into one, it would not come up to the precious stones of Jobab's kingdom. For you are of greater nobility than all the people of the east." ⁸And when, therefore, they now came to the land of Uz to visit me, they asked in the city: "Where is Jobab, the ruler of this whole land?" ⁹And they told them concerning me: "He sits on the dunghill outside of the city, for he has not entered the city for seven years." ¹⁰And then they again inquired concerning my possessions, and there was revealed to them all what happened to me. ¹¹And when they had learned this, they went out of the city with the inhabitants, and my fellow-citizens pointed me out to them. ¹²But these remonstrated and said, "Surely this is not Jobab." ¹³And while they hesitated, Eliphaz, the King of Teman, said, "Come, let us step near and see." ¹⁴And when they came near, I remembered them, and I wept very much when I learned the purpose of their journey. ¹⁵And I threw earth on my head, and while shaking my head I revealed to them that I was [Job]. ¹⁶And when they saw me shake my head, they threw themselves down on the ground, all overcome with emotion. ¹⁷And while their hosts were standing around, I saw the three kings lie on the ground for three hours like dead. ¹⁸Then they rose and said to each other, "We cannot believe that this is Jobab." ¹⁹And finally, after they had inquired after everything concerning

me and searched for my flocks and other possessions for seven days, they said, ²⁰"Do we not know how many goods were sent by him to the cities and the villages around to be given to the poor, aside from all that was given away by him within his own house? How then could he have fallen into such a state of perdition and misery?" ²¹And after the seven days Elihu said to the kings, "Come, let us step near and examine him accurately, whether he is truly Jobab or not." ²²And they, being not four stadia distant from his fetid body, rose and stepped near, carrying perfume in their hands, while their soldiers went with them and threw fragrant incense around them so that they could come near me. ²³And after they had thus passed three hours, covering the way with aroma, they drew near. ²⁴And Eliphaz began and said, "Are you, indeed, Job, our fellow-king? Are you the one who owned the great glory? ²⁵Are you he who once shone like the sun of day on the whole earth? Are you he who once resembled the moon and the stars, radiant throughout the night?" ²⁶And I answered him and said, "I am," and thereon all wept and lamented, and they sang a royal song of lamentation, their whole army joining them in a chorus. ²⁷And again Eliphaz said to me, "Are you he who had ordered seven thousand sheep to be given for the clothing of the poor? Where then has the glory of your throne gone? ²⁸Are you he who had ordered three thousand cattle to do the plowing of the field for the poor? Where then has your glory gone? ²⁹Are you he who had golden couches, and now you sit on a dunghill? [[Where then has your glory gone?]] ³⁰Are you he who had sixty tables set for the poor? Are you he who had censers for the fine perfume made of precious stones, and now you are in a fetid state? Where then has your glory gone? ³¹Are you he who had golden candelabras set on silver stands, and now must you long for the natural gleam of the moon? [[Where then has your glory gone?]] ³²Are you the one who had ointment made of the spices of frankincense, and now you are in a state of repulsiveness? [[Where then has your glory gone?]] ³³Are you he who laughed the wrongdoers and sinners to scorn and now you have become a laughingstock to all? [[Where then has your glory gone?]] ³⁴And when Eliphaz had cried and lamented for a long time, while all the others joined him, so that the commotion was very great, I said to them, ³⁵"Be silent and I will show you my throne, and the glory of its splendor: my glory will be everlasting. ³⁶The whole world will perish, and its glory will vanish, and all those who hold fast to it will remain beneath, but my throne is in the upper world and its glory and splendor will be to the right of the Savior in the heavens. ³⁷My throne exists in the life of the holy ones and its glory in the imperishable world. ³⁸For rivers will be dried up and their arrogance will go down to the depth of the abyss, but the streams of my land in which my throne is erected will not dry up but will remain unbroken in strength. ³⁹The kings perish, and the rulers vanish, and their glory and pride are as the shadow in a looking-glass, but my kingdom lasts forever and ever, and its glory and beauty are in the chariot of my Father."

CHAPTER 8

¹When I spoke thus to them, Eliphaz became angry and said to the other friends, "For what purpose is it that we have come here with our hosts to comfort him? ⁹Behold, he scolds us. Therefore, let us return to our countries. ²This man sits here in misery, worm-eaten amidst an unbearable state of putrefaction, and yet he challenges its saving: Kingdoms will perish and their rulers, but my kingdom, he says, will last forever." ³Eliphaz then rose in great commotion, and turning away from them in great fury, said, "I go on. We have indeed come to comfort him, but he declares war to us in view of our armies." ⁴But then Bildad seized him by the hand and said, "One ought not to speak thus to an afflicted man, and especially to one stricken down with so many plagues. ⁵Behold, we, being in good health, dared not approach him on account of the offensive odor, except with the help of plenty of fragrant aroma. But you, Eliphaz, are forgetful of all this. ⁶Let me speak plainly. Let us be magnanimous and learn what the cause is. Must he, in remembering his former days of happiness, not become mad in his mind? ⁷Who should not be altogether perplexed seeing himself thus lapse into misfortune and plagues? But let me step near him that I may find by what cause he is thus." ⁸And Bildad rose and approached me, saying, "Are you Job?" And he said, "Is your heart still in good keeping?" ⁹And I said, "I did not hold fast to the earthly things, since the earth, with all that inhabit it, is unstable. But my heart holds fast to Heaven, because there is no trouble in Heaven." ¹⁰Then Bildad rejoined and said, "We know that the earth is unstable, for it changes according to season. At times it is in a state of peace, and at times it is in a state of war. But of Heaven we hear that it is perfectly steady. ¹¹But are you truly in a state of calmness? Therefore let me ask and speak, and when you answer me to my first word, I will have a second question to ask, and if again you answer in well-set words, it will be manifest that your heart has not been unbalanced." ¹²And he said, "On what do you set your hope?" And I said, "On the living God." ¹³And he said to me, "Who deprived you of all you possessed, and who inflicted you with these plagues?" And I said, "God." ¹⁴And he said, "If you still place your hope on God, how can He do wrong in judgment, having brought on you these plagues and misfortunes, and having taken from you all your possessions? ¹⁵And since He has taken these, it is clear that He has given you nothing. No king will disgrace his soldier who has served him well as bodyguard." ¹⁶[[And I answered, saying,]] "Who understands the depths of the LORD and of His wisdom to be able to accuse God of injustice?" ¹⁷[And Bildad said,] "Answer me, O Job, to this. Again, I say to you: if you are in a state of calm reason, teach me if you have wisdom: ¹⁸why do we see the sun rise in the east and set in the west? And again, when rising in the morning we find him rise in the east. Tell me your thought about this." ¹⁹Then I said, "Why will I betray the mighty mysteries of God? And should my mouth stumble in revealing things belonging to the Master? Never! ²⁰Who are we that we should pry into matters concerning the upper world while we are only of flesh, no, earth and ashes! ²¹In order that you know that my heart is sound, hear what I ask you: ²²through the stomach comes food, and water you drink through the mouth, and then it flows through the same throat, and when the two go down to become excrement, they again part; who effects this separation?" ²³And Bildad said, "I do not know." And I rejoined and said to him, "If you do not even understand the exits of the body, how can you understand the celestial circuits?" ²⁴Then Zophar rejoined and said, "We do not inquire after our own affairs, but we desire to know whether you are in a sound state, and behold, we see that your reason has not been shaken. ²⁵What now do you wish that we should do for you? Behold, we have come here and brought the physicians of three kings, and if you wish, you may be cured by them." ²⁶But I answered and said, "My cure and my restoration come from God, the Maker of physicians."

CHAPTER 9

¹And when I spoke thus to them, behold, there my wife Sitis came running, dressed in rags from the service of the master by whom she was employed as slave though she had been forbidden to leave, lest the kings, on seeing her, might take her as captive. ²And when she came, she threw herself prostrate to their feet, crying and saying, "Remember, Eliphaz and you other friends, what I once was with you, and how I have changed, how I am now dressed to meet you." ³Then the kings broke forth in great weeping, and, being in double perplexity, they kept silent. But Eliphaz took his purple mantle and cast it around her to wrap her up with it. ⁴But she asked him, saying, "I ask as a favor of you, my lords, that you order your soldiers that they should dig among the ruins of our house which fell on my children, so that their bones could be brought in a perfect state to the tombs. ⁵For as we have, owing to our misfortune, no power at all, and so we may at least see their bones. ⁶For I have, like a brute, the motherly feeling of wild beasts that my ten children should have perished on one day and I could not give a decent burial to one of them." ⁷And the kings gave order that the ruins of my house should be dug up. But I prohibited it, saying, ⁸"Do not go to the trouble in vain; for my children will not be found, for they are in the keeping of their Maker and Ruler." ⁹And the kings answered and said, "Who will deny that he is out of his mind and raves? ¹⁰For while we desire to bring the bones of his children back, he forbids us to do so, saying, They have been taken and placed [in] the keeping of their Maker. Therefore, prove the truth to us." ¹¹But I said to them, "Raise me that I may stand up," and they lifted me, holding up my arms from both sides.

¹²And I stood upright, and first pronounced the praise of God and after the prayer I said to them: "Look with your eyes to the east." ¹³And they looked and saw my children with crowns near the glory of the King, the Ruler of Heaven. ¹⁴And when my wife Sitis saw this, she fell to the ground and prostrated [herself] before God, saying, "Now I know that my memory remains with the LORD." ¹⁵And after she had spoken this, and the evening came, she went to the city, back to the master whom she served as slave, and lay herself down at the manger of the cattle and died there from exhaustion. ¹⁶And when her despotic master searched for her and did not find her, he came to the fold of his herds, and there he saw her stretched out on the manger dead, while all the animals around were crying about her. ¹⁷And all who saw her wept and lamented, and the cry extended throughout the whole city. ¹⁸And the people brought her down and wrapped her up and buried her by the house which had fallen on her children. ¹⁹And the poor of the city made a great mourning for her and said, "Behold this Sitis whose like in nobility and in glory is not found in any woman. Aah! She was not found worthy of a proper tomb!" ²⁰The dirge for her you will find in the record.

CHAPTER 10

¹But Eliphaz and those that were with him were astonished at these things, and they sat down with me and replying to me, spoke in boastful words concerning me for twenty-seven days. ²They repeated it again and again that I suffered deservedly thus for having committed many sins, and that there was no hope left for me, but I retorted to these men in zest of contention myself. ³And they rose in anger, ready to part in wrathful spirit. But Elihu conjured them to stay yet a little while until he would have shown them what it was. ⁴"For," he said, "you passed so many days allowing Job to boast that he is just. But I will no longer permit it. ⁵For from the beginning I continued crying over him, remembering his former happiness. But now he speaks boastfully, and in overbearing pride he says that he has his throne in the heavens. ⁶Therefore, hear me, and I will tell you what the cause of his destiny is." ⁷Then, imbued with the spirit of Satan, Elihu spoke hard words which are written down in the records left of Elihu. ⁸And after he had ended, God appeared to me in a storm and in clouds, and spoke, blaming Elihu and showing me that he who had spoken was not a man, but a wild beast. ⁹And when God had finished speaking to me, the LORD spoke to Eliphaz: "You and your friends have sinned in that you have not spoken the truth concerning My servant Job. ¹⁰Therefore rise up and make him bring a sin-offering for you in order that your sins may be forgiven; for were it not for him, I would have destroyed you." ¹¹And so they brought to me all that belonged to a sacrifice, and I took it and brought a sin-offering for them, and the LORD received it favorably and forgave them their wrong. ¹²Then when Eliphaz, Bildad, and Zophar saw that God had graciously pardoned their sin through His servant Job, but that He did not stoop to pardon Elihu, then Eliphaz began to sing a hymn while the others responded, their soldiers also joining while standing by the altar. ¹³And Eliphaz spoke thus: "The sin is removed, and our injustice gone, ¹⁴But Elihu, the evil one, will have no remembrance among the living; His luminary is extinguished and has lost its light. ¹⁵The glory of his lamp will announce itself for him, || For he is the son of darkness, and not of light. ¹⁶The doorkeepers of the place of darkness || Will give him their glory and beauty as share. His kingdom has vanished, his throne has decayed, || And the honor of his stature is in Hades. ¹⁷For he has loved the beauty of the serpent and the scales of the dragon—His gall and his venom belong to the Northern One. ¹⁸For he did not own himself to the LORD nor did he fear Him, || But he hated those whom He has chosen. ¹⁹Thus God forgot him, and the holy ones forsook him, || His wrath and anger will be to him desolation, || And he will have no mercy in his heart nor peace, || Because he had the venom of an adder on his tongue. ²⁰The LORD is righteous, and His judgments are true. With Him there is no preference of person, || For He judges all alike. ²¹Behold, the LORD comes! Behold, the holy ones have been prepared! The crowns and the prizes of the victors precede them! ²²Let the saints rejoice, and let their hearts exult in gladness, || For they will receive the glory which is in store for them. Chorus: ²³Our sins are forgiven, our injustice has been cleansed, || But Elihu has no remembrance among the living." ²⁴After Eliphaz had finished the hymn, we rose and went back to the city, each to the house where they lived. ²⁵And the people made a feast for me in gratitude and delight of God, and all my friends came back to me. ²⁶And all those who had seen me in my former state of happiness, asked me, saying, "What are those three ones among us here?"

CHAPTER 11

¹But I, being desirous to take up my work of benevolence for the poor again, asked them, saying, ²"Give me each a lamb for the clothing of the poor in their state of nakedness, and four drachmas of silver or gold." ³Then the LORD blessed all that was left to me, and after a few days I became rich again in merchandise, in flocks and all things which I had lost, and I received all in double number again. ⁴Then I also took your mother as wife and became the father of you ten in place of the ten children that had died. ⁵And now, my children, let me admonish you: "Behold, I die. You will take my place. ⁶Only do not forsake the LORD. Be charitable toward the poor; Do not disregard the feeble. Do not take wives from strangers to yourselves. ⁷Behold, my children, I will divide what I possess among you, so that each may have control over his own and have full power to do good with his share." ⁸And after he had spoken thus, he brought all his goods and divided them among his seven sons, but he gave nothing of his goods to his daughters. ⁹Then they said to their father, "Our lord and father! Are we not also your children? Why, then, do you not also give us a share of your possessions?" ¹⁰Then Job said to his daughters, "Do not become angry my daughters. I have not forgotten you. Behold, I have preserved for you a possession better than that which your brothers have taken." ¹¹And he called his daughter, whose name was Day, and said to her, "Take this double ring used as a key, and go to the treasure-house, and bring me the golden casket, that I may give you your possession." ¹²And she went and brought it to him, and he opened it and took out three-stringed girdles about the appearance of which no man can speak. ¹³For they were not earthly work, but celestial sparks of light flashed through them like the rays of the sun. ¹⁴And he gave one string to each of his daughters and said, "Put these as girdles around you in order that all the days of your life they may encircle you and endow you with every good thing." ¹⁵And the other daughter, whose name was Kassiah, said, "Is this the possession of which you say it is better than that of our brothers? Now how can we live on this?" ¹⁶And their father said to them, "Not only do you have here [what is] sufficient to live on, but these bring you into a better world to live in—in the heavens. ¹⁷Or do you not know, my children, the value of these things here? Hear then! When the LORD had deemed me worthy to have compassion on me and to take the plagues and the worms off my body, He called me and handed these three strings to me. ¹⁸And He said to me, Rise and gird up your loins like a man. I will demand of you and you will declare it to Me. ¹⁹And I took them and girt them around my loins, and immediately the worms left my body, and likewise the plagues, and my whole body took new strength through the LORD, and thus I passed on, as though I had never suffered. ²⁰But I also forgot the pains in my heart. Then the LORD spoke to me in His great power and showed to me all that was and will be. ²¹Now then, my children, in keeping these, you will not have the enemy plotting against you nor [evil] intentions in your mind because this is a charm from the LORD. ²²Rise then and gird these around you before I die in order that you may see the messengers come at my parting so that you may behold, with wonder, the powers of God." ²³Then the one whose name was Day rose and girt herself; and immediately she departed her body as her father had said, and she put on another heart, as if she never cared for earthly things. ²⁴And she sang angelic hymns in the voice of messengers, and she chanted forth the angelic praise of God while dancing. ²⁵Then the other daughter, Kassia by name, put on the girdle, and her heart was transformed, so that she no longer wished for worldly things. ²⁶And her mouth assumed the dialect of the heavenly rulers and she sang the doxology of the work of the High Place, and if anyone wishes to know the work of the heavens, he may take an insight into the hymns of Kassia. ²⁷Then the other daughter, by the name of Amalthea's

Horn, girt herself and her mouth spoke in the language of those on high; for her heart was transformed, being lifted above the worldly things. ²⁸She spoke in the dialect of the cherubim, singing the praise of the Ruler of the cosmic powers and extolling their [[*or* His]] glory. ²⁹And he who desires to follow the vestiges of the "Glory of the Father" will find them written down in the Prayers of Amalthea's Horn.

CHAPTER 12

¹After these three had finished singing hymns, I, Nahor, brother of Job, sat down next to him as he lay down. ²And I heard the marvelous things of the three daughters of my brother, one always succeeding the other amidst awful silence. ³And I wrote down this scroll containing the hymns, except the hymns and signs of the [holy] word, for these were the great things of God. ⁴And Job lay down from sickness on his couch, yet without pain and suffering, because his pain did not take strong hold of him on account of the charm of the girdle which he had wound around himself. ⁵But after three days Job saw the holy messengers come for his soul, and instantly he rose and took the cithara and gave it to his daughter Day, ⁶and he gave a censer to Kassia, and he gave a timbrel to Amalthea's Horn in order that they might bless the holy messengers who came for his soul. ⁷And they took these, and sang, and played on the psaltery, and praised and glorified God in the holy dialect. ⁸And after this He came—He who sits on the great chariot—and kissed Job, while his three daughters looked on, but the others did not see it. ⁹And He took the soul of Job and He soared upward, taking her [(the soul)] by the arm and carrying her on the chariot, and He went toward the east. ¹⁰His body, however, was brought to the grave while the three daughters marched ahead, having put on their girdles and singing hymns in praise of God. ¹¹Then Nahor, his brother, and his seven sons, with the rest of the people and the poor, the orphans and the feeble ones, held a great mourning over him, saying, ¹²"Woe to us! For today the strength of the feeble, the light of the blind, the father of the orphans has been taken from us! ¹³The receiver of strangers has been taken—the leader of the erring, the cover of the naked, the shield of the widows. Who should not mourn for the man of God?" ¹⁴And as they were mourning in this and in that form, they would not permit him to be put into the grave. ¹⁵After three days, however, he was finally put into the grave, like one in sweet slumber, and he received the name of the beautiful who will remain renowned throughout all generations of the world. ¹⁶He left seven sons and three daughters, and there were no daughters found on earth as fair as the daughters of Job. ¹⁷The name of Job was formerly Jobab, and he was called Job by the LORD. ¹⁸He had lived eighty-five years before his plague, and after the plague he took the double share of all; hence he also doubled his years, which were one hundred seventy years. Thus, he lived two hundred fifty-five years altogether, ¹⁹and he saw sons of his sons to the fourth generation. It is written that he will rise up with those whom the LORD will reawaken. To our Lord be glory. Amen.

TESTAMENT OF MOSES

The Testament of Moses, also called the Assumption of Moses, is thought to have been composed in the 1st century BC or 1st century AD, in Hebrew or a similar Semitic language, and then translated into Koine. The surviving manuscript is actually a 6th century Latin translation of the Greek. There is speculation that a missing portion of the work includes the dispute between Michael and Satan over the body of Moses, which is also found in Jude 1:9. The book is backward and forward-looking, and apocalyptic in nature, dealing with Moses' handoff to Joshua prior to death.

CHAPTER 1

¹And it came to pass in the one hundred and twentieth year of the life of Moses, ²that is, the two thousand five hundredth year from the creation of the world, ⁶that he called Joshua the son of Nun to himself, a man approved of the LORD, ⁷that he might be the minister of the people and of the Dwelling Place of the testimony with all its holy things, ⁸and that he might bring the people into the land given to their fathers, ⁹that it should be given to them according to the covenant and the oath, which he spoke in the Dwelling Place to give [it] by Joshua, saying these words to Joshua: ¹⁰"Be strong and of good courage, according to your might so as to do what has been commanded that you may be blameless to God"— ¹¹so says the Lord of the world. ¹²For He has created the world on behalf of His people. ¹³But He was not pleased to manifest this purpose of creation from the foundation of the world, in order that the nations might thereby be convicted, indeed, [that] by [their] arguments they might convict one another to their own humiliation. ¹⁴Accordingly, He designed and devised me, and He prepared me before the foundation of the world, that I should be the mediator of His covenant. ¹⁵And now I declare to you that the time of the years of my life is fulfilled and I am passing away to sleep with my fathers even in the presence of all the people. ¹⁶Now receive this writing that you may know how to preserve the scrolls which I will deliver to you, ¹⁷and you will set these in order, and anoint them with oil of cedar, and put them away in earthen vessels in the place which He made from the beginning of the creation of the world, ¹⁸that His Name should be called on until the day of conversion in the visitation with which the LORD will visit them in the consummation of the end of the days.

CHAPTER 2

¹And now they will go by means of you into the land which He determined and promised to give to their fathers, ²in which you will bless, and give to them individually, and confirm to them their inheritance in me, and establish the kingdom for them, and appoint prefectures for them according to the good pleasure of their Lord, in judgment and righteousness. ³And in the sixth year after they enter into the land, that thereafter they will be ruled by chiefs and kings for eighteen years, and for nineteen years the ten tribes will be apostates. ⁴And the twelve tribes will go down and transfer the Dwelling Place of the testimony. Then the God of Heaven will make the court of His Dwelling Place and the tower of His sanctuary, and the two holy tribes will be established [there], ⁵but the ten tribes will establish kingdoms for themselves according to their own ordinances. ⁶And they will offer sacrifices throughout twenty years, ⁷and seven will entrench the walls, and I will protect nine, but [four] will transgress the covenant of the LORD and profane the oath which the LORD made with them. ⁸And they will sacrifice their sons to strange gods, and they will set up idols in the sanctuary, to worship them. ⁹And in the house of the LORD they will work impiety and engrave every [form] of beast—many abominations.

CHAPTER 3

¹And in those days a king from the east will come against them and cover their land with [his] cavalry. ²And he will burn their colony with fire, together with the holy temple of the LORD, and he will carry away all the holy vessels. ³And he will cast forth all the people, and he will take them to the land of his nativity, yes, he will take the two tribes with him. ⁴Then the two tribes will call on the ten tribes and will be indignant as a lioness on the dusty plains, being hungry and thirsty. ⁵And they will cry aloud: "Righteous and holy is the LORD, for, inasmuch as you have sinned, we too, in like manner, have been carried away with you, together with our children." ⁶Then the ten tribes will mourn on hearing the reproaches of the two tribes, ⁷and they will say, "What have we done to you, brothers? Surely this tribulation has not come on all the house of Israel?" ⁸And all the tribes will mourn, crying to Heaven and saying, ⁹"God of Abraham, God of Isaac, and God of Jacob, remember Your covenant which You made with them, and the oath which You swore to them by Yourself, that their seed should never

TESTAMENT OF MOSES

fail in the land which You have given them." ¹⁰Then they will remember me, saying, in that day, tribe to tribe and each man to his neighbour: ¹¹"Is this not that which Moses declared to us then in prophecies, who suffered many things in Egypt, and in the Red Sea, and in the wilderness for forty years, ¹²and assuredly called the heavens and earth to witness against us, that we should not transgress His commandments, in the which he was a mediator to us? ¹³Behold these things have befallen us after his death according to his words and according to his declaration, as he declared to us at that time—yes, behold, these have taken place even to our being carried away captive into the country of the east, ¹⁴who will also be in bondage for about seventy-seven years."

CHAPTER 4

¹Then there will enter one who is over them, and he will spread forth his hands, and kneel on his knees, and pray on their behalf, saying, ²"Lord of all, King on the lofty throne, who rules the world, and willed that this people should be Your chosen people: then You willed that You should be called their God, according to the covenant which You made with their fathers, ³and yet they have gone into captivity with their wives and their children into another land, and around the gates of strange peoples, and where there is great vanity. ⁴Regard and have compassion on them, O Lord of Heaven." ⁵Then God will remember them on account of the covenant which He made with their fathers, and He will also manifest His compassion in those times. ⁶And He will put it into the mind of a king to have compassion on them, and he will send them off to their land and country. ⁷Then some portions of the tribes will go up, and they will come to their appointed place, and they will entrench the place, restoring [it]. ⁸And the two tribes will continue in their prescribed faith, sad and lamenting because they will not be able to offer sacrifices to the Lord of their fathers. ⁹And the ten tribes will increase and multiply among the nations during the time of their captivity.

CHAPTER 5

¹And when the times of discipline draw near and vengeance arises through the kings who share in their guilt and punish them, ²they themselves will also be divided as to the truth. ³For what reason it has come to pass: "They will turn aside from righteousness and approach iniquity, and they will defile the house of their worship with pollutions," and "they will go whoring after strange gods." ⁴For they will not follow the truth of God, but some will pollute the altar with the very gifts which they offer to the Lord, who are not priests but slaves, sons of slaves. ⁵And many will respect rich persons in those times, and will receive gifts, and wrest judgment [on receiving presents]. ⁶And on this account the colony and the borders of their habitation will be filled with lawless deeds and iniquities: they will forsake the Lord; they will be impious judges; they will be ready to judge for money as each may wish.

CHAPTER 6

¹Then kings will be raised up to them bearing rule, and they will call themselves high priests of God; they will assuredly work iniquity in the Holy of Holies. ²And an insolent king will succeed them who will not be of the race of the priests, a man bold and shameless, and he will judge them as they will deserve. ³And he will cut off their chief men with the sword, and will destroy [them] in secret places, so that no one may know where their bodies are. ⁴He will slay the old and the young, and he will not spare. ⁵Then the fear of him will be bitter to them in their land. ⁶And he will execute judgments on them as the Egyptians executed on them for thirty-four years, and he will punish them. ⁷And he will beget children, who succeeding him will rule for shorter periods. ⁸Into their parts cohorts and a powerful king of the west will come, who will conquer them; ⁹and he will take them captive, and burn a part of their temple with fire, [and] will crucify some around their colony.

CHAPTER 7

¹And when this is done the times will be ended, in a moment the [second] course will be [ended], the four hours will come. ²They will be forced … ³And, in the time of these, scornful and impious men will rule, saying that they are just. ⁴And these will conceal the wrath of their minds, being treacherous men, self-pleasers, impostors in all their own affairs, and lovers of banquets at every hour of the day, gluttons, gourmands … ⁵… ⁶devourers of the goods of the poor, saying that they do so on the ground of their justice, but [in reality] to destroy them, complainers, deceitful, concealing themselves lest they should be recognized, impious, filled with lawlessness and iniquity from sunrise to sunset, ⁸saying, "We will have feastings and luxury, eating and drinking, yes, we will drink our fill, we will be as princes." ⁹And though their hands and their minds touch unclean things, yet their mouth will speak great things, and they will furthermore say, ¹⁰"Do not touch me lest you should pollute me in the place where I stand."

CHAPTER 8

¹And there will come on them a second visitation and wrath, such as has not befallen them from the beginning until that time, in which He will stir up against them a king of the kings of the earth and one that rules with great power, who will crucify those who confess to their circumcision: ²and he will torture those who conceal [it] and deliver them up to be bound and led into prison. ³And their wives will be given to the gods among the nations, and their young sons will be operated on by the physicians in order to bring forward their foreskin. ⁴And others among them will be punished by tortures, and fire, and sword, and they will be forced to bear their idols in public, [which are as] polluted as the [shrines] that contain them. ⁵And they will likewise be forced by those who torture them to enter their inmost sanctuary, and they will be forced by goads to blaspheme the Name with insolence, [and] finally, after these things, the laws and what they had above their altar [as well].

CHAPTER 9

¹Then in that day there will be a man of the tribe of Levi, whose name will be Taxo, who having seven sons will speak to them exhorting [them]: ²"Observe, my sons; behold, a second ruthless [and] unclean visitation has come on the people, and a punishment merciless and far exceeding the first. ³For what nation, or what region, or what people of those who are impious toward the Lord, who have done many abominations, have suffered calamities as great as have befallen us? ⁴Now therefore, my sons, hear me; for observe and know that neither [our] fathers nor their forefathers tempted God, so as to transgress His commands. ⁵And you know that this is our strength, and thus we will do. ⁶Let us fast for the space of three days, and on the fourth let us go into a cave which is in the field, and let us die rather than transgress the commands of the Lord of lords, the God of our fathers. ⁷For if we do this and die, our blood will be avenged before the Lord."

CHAPTER 10

¹And then His kingdom will appear throughout all His creation, || And then Satan will no longer be, || And sorrow will depart with him. ²Then the hands of the messenger will be filled, || And he will be appointed chief, || And he will immediately avenge them of their enemies. ³For the heavenly One will arise from His royal throne, || And He will go forth from His holy habitation, || And His wrath will burn on account of His sons. ⁴And the earth will tremble: It will be shaken to its confines, || And the high mountains will be made low, || And the hills will be shaken and fall. ⁵And the horns of the sun will be broken, || And he will be turned into darkness; And the moon will not give her light, || And will be turned wholly into blood; And the circle of the stars will be disturbed. ⁶And the sea will retire into the abyss, || And the fountains of waters will fail, || And the rivers will dry up. ⁷For the Most High will arise, the Perpetual God alone, || And He will appear to punish the nations, || And He will destroy all their idols. ⁸Then you, O Israel, will be happy, || And you will mount up on the neck [and wings] of the eagle, || And [the days of your mourning] will be ended. ⁹And God will exalt you, || And He will cause you to approach to the heaven of the stars, || And He will establish your habitation among them. ¹⁰And you will look from on high and will see your enemies in Gehenna, || And you will recognize them and rejoice, || And you will give thanks and confess your Creator. ¹¹And you, Joshua [the son of] Nun, must keep these words and this scroll, ¹²for from my death—[my] assumption—until His advent there will be two hundred fifty times. ¹³And this is their

TESTAMENT OF MOSES

course which they will pursue until they are consummated. ¹⁴And I will go to sleep with my fathers. ¹⁵For what reason, Joshua—you, [son of] Nun—be of good courage; God has chosen [you] to be my successor in the same covenant.

CHAPTER 11

¹And when Joshua had heard the words of Moses that were written in his writing, as well as all that he had previously said, he tore his clothes and cast himself at Moses' feet. ²And Moses comforted him and wept with him. ³And Joshua answered him and said, ⁴"Why do you comfort me, lord Moses? And how will I be comforted in regard to that which you have spoken—the bitter word which has gone forth from your mouth, which is full of tears and lamentation, in that you depart from this people? ⁵And now what place will receive you? ⁶Or what will be the sign that marks [your] grave? ⁷Or who will dare to move your body from there as a man from place to place? ⁸For when they die, all men have their graves on earth according to their age, but your grave is from the rising to the setting sun, and from the south to the confines of the north: all the world is your grave. ⁹My lord, you are departing, and who will feed this people? ¹⁰Or who is there that will have compassion on them, and who will be their guide by the way? ¹¹Or who will pray for them, not omitting a single day, in order that I may lead them into the land of [their] forefathers? ¹²Therefore, how am I to control this people as a father [his] only son, or as a mistress [her] virgin daughter, who is being prepared to be handed over to the husband she will revere, while she guards her person from the sun, and [takes care] that her feet are not unshod for running on the ground? ¹³And how will I supply them with food and drink according to the pleasure of their will? ¹⁴For of them there will be six hundred thousand men, for these have multiplied to this degree through your prayers, [my] lord Moses. ¹⁵And what wisdom or understanding do I have that I should judge or answer by word in the house of the LORD? ¹⁶And the kings of the Amorites will also be emboldened to attack us then; [and] believing that there is no longer among them the sacred spirit who was worthy of the LORD, manifold and incomprehensible, the lord of the word, who was faithful in all things, God's chief prophet throughout the earth, the most perfect teacher in the world, that he is no longer among them, they will say, Let us go against them. ¹⁷If the enemy has but once worked impiously against their Lord, they have no advocate to offer prayers on their behalf to the LORD, as Moses the great messenger did, who every hour day and night had his knees fixed to the earth, praying to and looking for help from Him that rules all the world with compassion and righteousness, calling to mind the covenant of the fathers, and propitiating the LORD with the oath. ¹⁸For they will say, He is not with them; therefore, let us go and destroy them from off the face of the earth. ¹⁹What then will become of this people, my lord Moses?"

CHAPTER 12

¹And when Joshua had finished [these] words, he again cast himself at the feet of Moses. ²And Moses took his hand and raised him into the seat before him, and answered and said to him, ³"Joshua, do not despise yourself, but set your mind at ease, and listen to my words. ⁴All the nations which are in the earth God has created as He has us; He has foreseen [both] them and us from the beginning of the creation of the earth to the end of the age, and nothing has been neglected by Him even to the least thing, but He has foreseen all things and caused all to come forth. ⁵All things which are to be in this earth the LORD has foreseen, and behold, they are brought forward [into the light]…⁶…[[The LORD]] has appointed me on their behalf to pray for their sins and make intercession for them. ⁷For [it was] not because of any virtue or strength of mine, but in His compassion and longsuffering was He pleased to call me. ⁸For I say to you, Joshua: it is not on account of the godliness of this people that you will root out the nations. ⁹The lights of the heavens [and] the foundations of the earth have been made and approved by God and are under the signet ring of His right hand. ¹⁰Therefore, those who do and fulfill the commandments of God will increase and be prospered, ¹¹but those who sin and set the commandments at nothing will be without the blessings previously mentioned, and they will be punished by the nations with many torments. ¹²But to wholly root out and destroy them is not permitted. ¹³For God, who has foreseen all things forever, will go forth; and His covenant has been established and the oath which…"

TESTAMENT OF SOLOMON

The Testament of Solomon is the account of his receiving a ring of great power from the archangel Michael that enables him to systematically overcome and enslave a series of demons. He then forces these demons to help build the First Temple in Jerusalem. It is thought by most that the text was developed and organized in the medieval period, but at least some of the core material likely dates from the 1st century AD or earlier because of early citations and even an early reference to the title.

[THE] TESTAMENT OF SOLOMON, SON OF DAVID, WHO WAS KING IN JERUSALEM, AND [WHO] MASTERED AND CONTROLLED ALL SPIRITS OF THE AIR, ON THE EARTH, AND UNDER THE EARTH. BY MEANS OF THEM HE ALSO WORKED ALL THE TRANSCENDENT WORKS OF THE TEMPLE, ALSO TELLING OF THE AUTHORITIES THEY WIELD AGAINST MEN, AND BY WHAT MESSENGERS THESE DEMONS ARE BROUGHT TO NOTHING. OF THE SAGE SOLOMON. BLESSED ARE YOU, O LORD GOD, WHO GAVE SOLOMON SUCH AUTHORITY. GLORY TO YOU AND MIGHT TO THE AGES! AMEN.

CHAPTER 1

¹And behold, when the temple of the city of Jerusalem was being built and the craftsmen were working there, the demon Ornias came among them toward sunset; ²and he took away half of the pay of the chief-deviser's little boy, as well as half his food. He also continued to suck the thumb of his right hand every day. ³And the child grew thin, although he was very much loved by the king. ⁴So King Solomon called the boy one day, and questioned him, saying, "Do I not love you more than all the artisans who are working in the temple of God? ⁵Do I not give you double wages and a double supply of food? How is it that day by day and hour by hour you grow thinner?" ⁶But the child said to the king, "Please, O king. Listen to what has befallen all that your child has. After we are all released from our work on the temple of God, after sunset, when I lie down to rest, one of the evil demons comes and takes away from me one half of my pay and one half of my food. ⁷Then he also takes hold of my right hand and sucks my thumb. And behold, my soul is oppressed, and so my body waxes thinner every day."

CHAPTER 2

¹Now when I, Solomon, heard this, I entered the temple of God, and prayed with all my soul, night and day, that the demon might be delivered into my hands, and that I might gain authority over him. ²And it came about through my prayer that grace was given to me from the LORD of Hosts by His chief-messenger Michael. ³[He brought me] a little ring, having a seal consisting of an engraved stone, and said to me, "Take, O Solomon—king, son of David—the gift which the LORD God, the Highest of Hosts, has sent you. With it you will lock up all demons of the earth, [both] male and female; and with their help you will build up Jerusalem. ⁴[But] you [must] wear this seal of God. And this engraving of the seal

of the ring sent to you is a Pentalpha." ⁵And I, Solomon, was overjoyed, and praised and glorified the God of the heavens and earth. And on the next day I called the boy, and gave him the ring, ⁶and said to him, "take this, and at the hour in which the demon will come to you, throw this ring at the chest of the demon, and say to him: In the Name of God, King Solomon calls you here. ⁷And then come running to me, without having any misgivings or fear in respect of anything you may hear on the part of the demon."

CHAPTER 3

¹So the child took the ring and went off; and behold, at the customary hour Ornias, the fierce demon, came like a burning fire to take the pay from the child. ²But the child, according to the instructions received from the king, threw the ring at the chest of the demon, and said, "King Solomon calls you here." ³And then he went off running to the king. But the demon cried out aloud, saying, "Child, why have you done this to me? Take the ring off me, and I will render the gold of the earth to you. Only take this off me, and refrain from leading me away to Solomon." ⁴But the child said to the demon, "As the LORD God of Israel lives, I will not allow you [this], so come here." ⁵And the child came running, rejoicing, to the king, and said, "I have brought the demon, O king, as you commanded me, O my master. ⁶And behold, he stands before the gates of the court of your palace, crying out, and supplicating with a loud voice, offering me the silver and gold of the earth if I will only bring him to you."

CHAPTER 4

¹And when Solomon heard this, he rose up from his throne, and went outside into the vestibule of the court of his palace; ²and there he saw the demon, shuddering and trembling. ³And he said to him, "Who are you?" And the demon answered: "I am called Ornias." ⁴And Solomon said to him, "Tell me, O demon, to which of the twelve signs you are subject." And he answered: "To the Water-pourer [[or Aquarius]]. And those who are consumed with desire for the noble virgins on earth ... these I strangle. ⁵But in case there is no disposition to sleep, I am changed into three forms. Whenever men come to be enamored with women, I transform myself into a beautiful female; and I take hold of the men in their sleep and play with them. ⁶And after a while I take to my wings again and hasten to the heavenly regions. ⁷I also appear as a lion, and I am commanded by all the demons. I am an offspring of the chief-messenger Uriel, the power of God."

CHAPTER 5

¹I, Solomon, having heard the name of the chief-messenger, prayed and glorified God, the Lord of the heavens and earth. ²And I sealed the demon and set him to work at stone-cutting, so that he might cut the stones in the temple, which, lying along the shore, had been brought by the Sea of Arabia. ³But he, fearful of the iron, continued and said to me, "Please, King Solomon, let me go free, and I will bring you all the demons." ⁴And as he was not willing to be subject to me, I pleaded [with] the chief-messenger Uriel to come and assist me; and I immediately beheld the chief-messenger Uriel coming down to me from the heavens.

CHAPTER 6

¹And the messenger commanded the whales of the sea to come out of the abyss. And he cast his destiny on the ground, and that [destiny] made the great demon subject [to him]. ²And he commanded the great demon and bold Ornias to cut stones at the temple. ³And accordingly I, Solomon, glorified the God of Heaven and Maker of the earth. ⁴And he commanded Ornias to come with his destiny, and gave him the seal, saying, "Away with you, and bring the prince of all the demons here to me."

CHAPTER 7

¹So Ornias took the finger-ring, and went off to Beelzebul, who has kingship over the demons. He said to him, "Here! Solomon calls you." ²But Beelzebul, having heard, said to him, "Tell me, who is this Solomon of whom you speak to me?" Then Ornias threw the ring at the chest of Beelzebul, saying, "Solomon the king calls you." ³But Beelzebul cried aloud with a mighty voice, and shot out a great burning flame of fire; and he arose, and followed Ornias, and came to Solomon. ⁴And when I saw the prince of demons, I glorified the LORD God, Maker of the heavens and earth, and I said, "Blessed are You, LORD God Almighty, who has given wisdom to Your servant Solomon, the assessor of the wise, and has subjected all the power of the Devil to me." ⁵And I questioned him, and said, "Who are you?" The demon replied: "I am Beelzebul, the exarch of the demons. And all the demons have their chief seats close to me. ⁶And it is I who make the apparition of each demon manifest." ⁷And he promised to bring all the unclean spirits to me in bonds. And I again glorified the God of the heavens and earth, as I always give thanks to Him.

CHAPTER 8

¹I then asked of the demon if there were females among them. And when he told me that there were, I said that I desired to see them. ²So Beelzebul went off at high speed, and brought to me Onoskelis, who had a very pretty shape, and the skin of a lovely woman; and she tossed her head. ³And when she had come, I said to her, "Tell me, who are you?" But she said to me, "I am called Onoskelis, a spirit worked ... lurking on the earth. ⁴There is a golden cave where I lie. But I have a place that always shifts. At one time I strangle men with a noose; at another, I creep up from the nature to the arms. ⁵But my most frequent dwelling-places are the precipices, caves, [and] ravines. Oftentimes, however, I consort with men in the semblance of a woman, and above all with those of a dark skin. ⁶For they share my star with me, since it is they who privily or openly worship my star, without knowing that they harm themselves, and but whet my appetite for further mischief. ⁷For they wish to provide money by means of memory, but I supply a little to those who worship me fairly." ⁸And I, Solomon, questioned her about her birth, and she replied: "I was born of an untimely voice, the so-called echo of a man's filth dropped in a wood." ⁹And I said to her, "Under what star do you pass?" And she answered me: "Under the star of the full moon, for the reason that the moon travels over most things." ¹⁰Then I said to her, "And what messenger is it that frustrates you?" And she said to me, "He that in you [[or through you]] is reigning." ¹¹And I thought that she mocked me, and I commanded a soldier to strike her, but she cried aloud and said, "I am [subjected] to you, O king, by the wisdom of God given to you, and by the messenger Joel." ¹²So I commanded her to spin the hemp for the ropes used in the building of the house of God; and accordingly, when I had sealed and bound her, she was so overcome and brought to nothing as to stand night and day spinning the hemp.

CHAPTER 9

¹And I immediately commanded another demon to be led to me; and instantly the demon Asmodeus approached me, bound, and I asked him, "Who are you?" ²But he shot a glance of anger and rage at me, and said, "And who are you?" And I said to him, "Thus punished as you are, [this is how] you answer me?" ³But he, with rage, said to me, "But how will I answer you, for you are a son of man, whereas I was born of a messenger's seed by a daughter of man, so that no word of our heavenly kind addressed to the earth-born can be overconfident. ⁴For what reason also my star is bright in the sky, and some men call it the Wagon [[or Ursa Major]], and some the Dragon's Child. I keep near to this star. ⁵So do not ask me many things; for your kingdom also after a short time is to be disrupted, and your glory is but for a season. ⁶And your tyranny over us will be short; and then we will have free range over mankind again, so as that they will revere us as if we were gods, not knowing, men that they are, the names of the messengers set over us." ⁷And I, Solomon, on hearing this, bound him more carefully, and ordered him to be flogged with thongs of ox-hide, and to humbly tell me what was his name and what [was] his business. ⁸And he answered me thus: "I am called Asmodeus among mortals, and my business is to plot against the newly wedded, so that they may not know one another. ⁹And I utterly sever them by many calamities, and I waste away the beauty of virgin women, and estrange their hearts." And I said to him, "Is this your only business?" ¹⁰And he answered me: "I transport men into fits of madness and desire, when they have wives of their own, so that they leave them, and go off by night and day to others that belong to other men, with the result that they commit sin, and fall into murderous deeds." ¹¹And I adjured him by the

TESTAMENT OF SOLOMON

Name of the LORD of Hosts, saying, "Fear God, Asmodeus, and tell me by what messenger you are frustrated." ¹²But he said, "By Raphael, the chief-messenger that stands before the throne of God. But the liver and gall of a fish put me to flight, when smoked over ashes of the tamarisk." ¹³I asked him again, and said, "Do not hide anything from me. For I am Solomon, son of David, King of Israel. Tell me the name of the fish which you revere." ¹⁴And he answered: "It is the Glanos by name, and is found in the rivers of Assyria, for what reason it is that I roam around in those parts." ¹⁵And I said to him, "Do you have nothing else [to say] concerning yourself, Asmodeus?" ¹⁶And he answered: "The power of God knows, which has bound me with the indissoluble bonds of that one's seal, that whatever I have told you is true. Please, King Solomon, do not condemn me to [go into] water." ¹⁷But I smiled, and said to him, "As the LORD God of my fathers lives, I will lay iron on you to wear. But you will also make the clay for the entire construction of the temple, treading it down with your feet." ¹⁸And I ordered them to give him ten water-jars to carry water in. And the demon groaned terribly and did the work I ordered him to do. ¹⁹And I did this because that fierce demon Asmodeus even knew the future. And I, Solomon, glorified God, who gave wisdom to me, His servant Solomon. ²⁰And I hung the liver of the fish and its gall on the spike of a reed and burned it over Asmodeus because of his being so strong, and his unbearable malice was thus frustrated.

CHAPTER 10

¹And I summoned Beelzebul, the prince of demons, to stand before me again, and I sat him down on a raised seat of honor and said to him, "Why are you alone, prince of the demons?" ²And he said to me, "Because I alone am left of the messengers of Heaven that came down. For I was first messenger in the first heaven being entitled Beelzebul. And now I control all those who are bound in Tartarus. ³But I too have a child, and he haunts the Red Sea. And on any suitable occasion he comes up to me again, being subject to me, and reveals to me what he has done, and I support him." ⁴I, Solomon, said to him, "Beelzebul, what is your employment?" ⁵And he answered me: "I destroy kings. I ally myself with foreign tyrants. And my own demons I set on to men, in order that the latter may believe in them and be lost. ⁶And the chosen servants of God, priests and faithful men, I excite to desires for wicked sins, and evil heresies, and lawless deeds; and they obey me, and I bear them on to destruction. ⁷And I inspire men with envy, and murder, and for wars, and sodomy, and other evil things. And I will destroy the world." ⁸So I said to him, "Bring to me your child, who is, as you say, in the Red Sea." ⁹But he said to me, "I will not bring him to you, but another demon called Ephippas will come to me. I will bind him, and he will bring him up to me from the deep." ¹⁰And I said to him, "How does your son come to be in the depth of the sea, and what is his name?" ¹¹And he answered me: "Do not ask me, for you cannot learn from me. However, he will come to you by any command, and will tell you openly." ¹²I said to him, "Tell me by what messenger you are frustrated." ¹³And he answered: "By the holy and precious Name of the Almighty God, called by the Hebrews by a row of numbers, of which the sum is six hundred forty-four, and among the Greeks it is Emmanuel. And if one of the Romans adjures me by the great name of the power Eleéth, I disappear at once." ¹⁴I, Solomon, was astounded when I heard this; and I ordered him to saw up Theban marbles. And when he began to saw the marbles, the other demons cried out with a loud voice, howling because of their king, Beelzebul. ¹⁵But I, Solomon, questioned him, saying, "If you would gain a respite, discourse to me about the things in Heaven." ¹⁶And Beelzebul said, "Hear, O king, if you burn gum, and incense, and bulb of the sea, with nard and saffron, and light seven lamps in an earthquake, you will firmly fix your house. ¹⁷And if, being pure, you light them at dawn in the sun gleaming, then you will see the heavenly dragons, how they wind themselves along and drag the chariot of the sun." ¹⁸And I, Solomon, having heard this, rebuked him, and said, "Silence for this moment, and continue to saw the marbles as I commanded you."

CHAPTER 11

¹And I, Solomon, praised God, and commanded another demon to present himself to me, ²and one came before me who carried his face high up in the air, but the rest of the spirit curled away like a snail. ³And it broke through the few soldiers, and also raised a terrible dust on the ground, and carried it upwards, and then hurled it back again to frighten us, and asked what questions I could ask as a rule. ⁴And I stood up, and spat on the ground in that spot, and sealed [it] with the ring of God. And immediately the dust-wind stopped. ⁵Then I asked him, saying, "Who are you, O wind?" Then he once more shook up a dust, and answered me: "What would you have [of me], King Solomon?" ⁶I answered him: "Tell me what you are called, and I would will to ask you a question. But so far I give thanks to God who has made me wise to answer their evil plots." ⁷But [the demon] answered me: "I am the spirit of the ashes (Tephras)." ⁸And I said to him, "What is your pursuit?" And he said, "I bring darkness on men, and set fire to fields, and I bring homesteads to nothing. But I am most busy in summer. ⁹However, when I get an opportunity, I creep into corners of the wall, by night and day. For I am offspring of the great one, and nothing less." ¹⁰Accordingly I said to him, "Under what star do you lie?" And he answered: "In the very tip of the moon's horn, when it is found in the south. My star is there. ¹¹For I have been commanded to restrain the convulsions of the tertian fever; and this is why many men pray for the tertian fever using these three names: Bultala, Thallal, Melchal. And I heal them." ¹²And I said to him, "I am Solomon; when therefore you would do harm, by whose aid do you do it?" But he said to me, "By the messenger's, by whom also the third day's fever is lulled to rest." ¹³So I questioned him, and said, "And by what name?" And he answered: "That of the chief-messenger Azael." ¹⁴And I summoned the chief-messenger Azael, and set a seal on the demon, and commanded him to seize great stones and toss them up to the workmen on the higher parts of the temple. ¹⁵And, being compelled, the demon began to do what he was commanded to do.

CHAPTER 12

¹And I again glorified God who gave me this authority and ordered another demon to come before me, ²and seven spirits came, females, bound and woven together—lovely in appearance and beautiful. ³And I, Solomon, seeing them, questioned them and said, "Who are you?" ⁴But they, with one accord, said with one voice: "We are of the thirty-three elements of the cosmic ruler of the darkness." ⁵And the first said, "I am Deception." The second said, "I am Strife." The third: "I am Klothod, which is Battle." The fourth: "I am Jealousy." The fifth: "I am Power." The sixth: "I am Error." ⁶The seventh: "I am the worst of all, and our stars are in Heaven. Seven stars humble in sheen, and all together. And we are called, as it were, goddesses. ⁷We change our place—all and together, and together we live, sometimes in Lydia, sometimes in Olympus, sometimes in a great mountain." ⁸So I, Solomon, questioned them one by one, beginning with the first, and going down to the seventh. ⁹The first said, "I am Deception, I deceive and weave snares here and there. I whet and excite heresies. But I have a messenger who frustrates me, Lamechalal." ¹⁰Likewise also the second said, "I am Strife, strife of strifes. I bring timbers, stones, hangers—my weapons on the spot. But I have a messenger who frustrates me, Baruchiachel." ¹¹Likewise also the third said, "I am called Klothod, which is Battle, and I cause the well-behaved to scatter and fall foul of one another. And why do I say so much? I have a messenger that frustrates me: Marmarath." ¹²Likewise also the fourth said, "I cause men to forget their sobriety and moderation. I part them and split them into parties; for Strife follows me hand in hand. I tear the husband from the sharer of his bed, and children from parents, and brothers from sisters. But why tell so much to my disdain? I have a messenger that frustrates me, the great Balthial." ¹³Likewise also the fifth said, "I am Power. By power I raise up tyrants and tear down kings. I furnish power to all rebels. I have a messenger that frustrates me, Asteraôth." ¹⁴Likewise also the sixth said, "I am Error, O King Solomon. And I will make you to err, as I have before made you to err, when I caused you to slay your own brother. I will lead you into error, so as to pry into graves, and teach them that dig; and I lead errant souls away from all piety, and many other evil traits are mine. But I have a messenger that frustrates me, Uriel." ¹⁵Likewise also the

seventh said, "I am the worst, and I make you worse off than you were, because I will impose the bonds of Artemis. But the locust will set me free, for by means thereof it is fated that you will achieve my desire … For if one were wise, he would not turn his steps toward me." ¹⁶So I, Solomon, having heard and wondered, sealed them with my ring; and since they were so considerable, I commanded them to dig the foundations of the temple of God. ¹⁷For the length of it was two hundred fifty cubits. And I commanded them to be industrious, and with one murmur of joint protest they began to perform the tasks enjoined.

CHAPTER 13

¹But I, Solomon, glorified the LORD, and commanded another demon to come before me, ²and a demon having all the limbs of a man was brought to me, but without a head. ³And I, seeing him, said to him, "Tell me, who are you?" And he answered: "I am a demon." So I said to him, "Which?" ⁴And he answered me: "I am called Envy. For I delight to devour heads, being desirous to secure a head for myself, but I do not eat enough, but am anxious to have such a head as you have." ⁵I, Solomon, on hearing this, sealed him, stretching out my hand against his chest, ⁶whereon the demon leapt up, and threw himself down, and gave a groan, saying, "Woe is me! Where have I come to? O traitor Ornias, I cannot see!" ⁷So I said to him, "I am Solomon. Tell me then how you manage to see." ⁸And he answered me: "By means of my feelings." ⁹I then, Solomon, having heard his voice come up to me, asked him how he managed to speak. And he answered me: "I, O King Solomon, am wholly voice, for I have inherited the voices of many men. For in the case of all men who are called dumb, it is I who smashed their heads when they were children and had reached their eighth day. ¹⁰Then when a child is crying in the night, I become a spirit, and glide by means of his voice … ¹¹In the crossways I also have many services to render, and my encounter is fraught with harm. ¹²For in an instant I grasp a man's head, and with my hands, as with a sword, I cut it off, and put it on myself. ¹³And in this way, by means of the fire which is in me, it is swallowed up through my neck. It is I that send grave and incurable mutilations on men's feet, and inflict sores." ¹⁴And I, Solomon, on hearing this, said to him, "Tell me how you discharge forth the fire? Out of what sources do you emit it?" ¹⁵And the spirit said to me, "From the Daystar. For here that Elburion, to whom men offer prayers and kindle lights, has not yet been found. And his name is invoked by the seven demons before me. And he cherishes them." ¹⁶But I said to him, "Tell me his name." But he answered: "I cannot tell you. For if I tell his name, I render myself incurable. But he will come in response to his name." ¹⁷And on hearing this, I, Solomon, said to him, "Tell me then by what messenger you are frustrated." ¹⁸And he answered: "By the fiery flash of lightning." ¹⁹And I bowed myself before the LORD God of Israel, and commanded him to remain in the keeping of Beelzebul until I should come.

CHAPTER 14

¹Then I ordered another demon to come before me, and a hound came into my presence having a very large shape, and it spoke with a loud voice, and said, "Greetings, lord, King Solomon!" ²And I, Solomon, was astounded. I said to it, "Who are you, O hound?" And it answered: "I do indeed seem to be a hound to you, but before you were, O King Solomon, I was a man that worked many unholy deeds on earth. ³I was surpassingly educated in letters, and was so mighty that I could hold the stars of the heavens back. ⁴And I prepared many divine works. For I do harm to men who follow after our star and turn them … ⁵And I seize the frenzied men by the larynx, and so destroy them." ⁶And I, Solomon, said to him, "What is your name?" And he answered: "Staff" (Rabdos). ⁷And I said to him, "What is your employment? And what results can you achieve?" ⁸And he replied, "Give me your man, and I will lead him away into a mountainous spot, and will show him a green stone tossed to and fro, with which you may adorn the temple of the LORD God." ⁹And I, Solomon, on hearing this, ordered my servant to set off with him, and to take the finger-ring bearing the seal of God with him. ¹⁰And I said to him, "Whoever will show you the green stone, seal him with this finger-ring, and mark the spot with care, and bring me the demon here." ¹¹And the demon showed him the green stone, and he sealed it, and brought the demon to me. ¹²And I, Solomon, decided to confine with my seal on my right hand the two—the headless demon [and] likewise the hound that was so huge; he should be bound as well. ¹³And I commanded the hound to keep the fiery spirit safe so that lamps, as it were, might cast their light through its maw on the artisans at work by day and night. ¹⁴And I, Solomon, took from the mine of that stone two hundred shekels for the supports of the table of incense, which was similar in appearance. ¹⁵And I, Solomon, glorified the LORD God, and then closed around the treasure of that stone. ¹⁶And again I ordered the demons to cut marble for the construction of the house of God. ¹⁷And I, Solomon, prayed to the LORD, and asked the hound, saying, "By what messenger are you frustrated?" And the demon replied, "By the great Brieus."

CHAPTER 15

¹And I praised the LORD God of the heavens and earth and commanded another demon to come forward to me, and one in the form of a roaring lion came before me. ²And he stood and answered me, saying, "O king, in the form which I have, I am a spirit quite incapable of being perceived. ³I leap on all men who lie prostrate with sickness, coming stealthily along; and I render the man weak, so that his habit of body is enfeebled. But I also have another glory, O king: ⁴I cast out demons, and I have legions under my control. And I am capable of being received in my dwelling-places, along with all the demons belonging to the legions under me." ⁵But I, Solomon, on hearing this, asked him: "What is your name?" But he answered: "Lion-bearer, Rath in kind." ⁶And I said to him, "How are you to be frustrated along with your legions? What messenger is it that frustrates you?" ⁷And he answered: "If I tell you my name, I do not only bind myself, but also the legions of demons under me." ⁸So I said to him, "I adjure you in the Name of the God of Hosts to tell me by what name you are frustrated along with your host." ⁹And the spirit answered me: "THE GREAT AMONG MEN, who is to suffer many things at the hands of men, whose name is the figure six hundred forty-four, which is Emmanuel; it is He who has bound us, and who will then come and plunge us from the steep under water. He is spread abroad in the three letters which bring Him down." ¹⁰And I, Solomon, on hearing this, glorified God, and condemned his legion to carry wood from the thicket. ¹¹And I condemned the lion-shaped one himself to saw up the wood small with his teeth, for burning in the unquenchable furnace for the temple of God.

CHAPTER 16

¹And I worshiped the LORD God of Israel and commanded another demon to come forward, and a dragon came before me, three-headed, of fearful aspect. ²And I questioned him: "Who are you?" And he answered me: "I am a caltrop-like spirit, whose activity [is] in three lines. ³But I blind children in women's wombs and twirl their ears around. And I make them deaf and mute. ⁴And I have again in my third head means of slipping in. And I strike men in the limbless part of the body, and cause them to fall down, and foam, and grind their teeth. ⁵But I have my own way of being frustrated, Jerusalem being signified in writing, to the place called [PLACE] OF [THE] SKULL." ⁶For there is appointed beforehand the Messenger of the great counsel, and now He will openly dwell on the Cross. He frustrates me, and I am subject to Him. ⁷But in the place where you sit, O King Solomon, stands a column in the air, of purple … The demon called Ephippas has brought [it] up from the Red Sea, from inner Arabia. ⁸It is he that will be shut up in a skin-bottle and brought before you. ⁹But at the entrance of the temple, which you have begun to build, O King Solomon, lies much stored gold, which you can dig up and carry off." ¹⁰And I, Solomon, sent my servant, and found it to be as the demon told me. And I sealed him with my ring and praised the LORD God." ¹¹So I said to him, "What are you called?" And the demon said, "I am the crest of dragons." And I commanded him to make bricks in the temple. He had human hands.

CHAPTER 17

¹And I adored the LORD God of Israel and commanded another demon to present himself, and a spirit in woman's form came before me that had a head without any limbs, and her hair was dishevelled. ²And I said to

her, "Who are you?" But she answered: "No, who are you? And why do you want to hear concerning me? But, as you would learn, here I stand bound before your face. ³Go then into your royal storehouses and wash your hands. Then sit down again before your tribunal, and ask me questions, and you will learn, O king, who I am." ⁴And I, Solomon, did as she enjoined me, and restrained myself because of the wisdom dwelling in me, in order that I might hear of her deeds, and reprehend them, and manifest them to men. ⁵And I sat down, and said to the demon, "What are you?" And she said, "I am called Obizuth among men; and I do not sleep by night, but go my rounds over all the world, and visit women in childbirth. ⁶And divining the hour, I take my stand; and if I am lucky, I strangle the child. But if not, I retire to another place. For I cannot retire unsuccessfully for a single night. ⁷For I am a fierce spirit, of myriad names and many shapes. And now here, now there I roam. And to westward parts I go my rounds. ⁸But as it now is, though you have sealed me around with the ring of God, you have done nothing. I am not standing before you, and you will not be able to command me. ⁹For I have no work other than the destruction of children, and the making their ears to be deaf, and the working of evil to their eyes, and the binding their mouths with a bond, and the ruin of their minds, and paining of their bodies." ¹⁰When I, Solomon, heard this, I marveled at her appearance, for I beheld all her body to be in darkness. ¹¹But her glance was altogether bright and greenish, and her hair was tossed wildly like a dragon's; and the whole of her limbs were invisible. ¹²And her voice was very clear as it came to me. And I cunningly said, "Tell me by what messenger you are frustrated, O evil spirit?" ¹³But she answered me: "By the messenger of God called Afarôt, which is interpreted Raphael, by whom I am frustrated now and for all time. ¹⁴His name, if any man knows it, and writes the same on a woman in childbirth, then I will not be able to enter her. Of this name the number is six thousand four hundred and one." ¹⁵And I, Solomon, having heard this, and having glorified the LORD, ordered her hair to be bound, and that she should be hung up in front of the temple of God, that all the sons of Israel, as they passed, might see it, and glorify the LORD God of Israel, who had given me this authority, with wisdom and power from God, by means of this signet.

CHAPTER 18

¹And I again ordered another demon to come before me, and this came, rolling itself along—one in appearance like to a dragon, but having the face and hands of a man. ²And all its limbs, except the feet, were those of a dragon; and it had wings on its back. ³And when I beheld it, I was astonished, and said, "Who are you, demon, and what are you called? And from where have you come? Tell me." ⁴And the spirit answered and said, "This is the first time I have stood before you, O King Solomon. I am a spirit made into a god among men, but now brought to nothing by the ring and wisdom given to you by God. ⁵Now I am the so-called winged dragon, and I do not chamber with many women, but only with a few that are of fair shape, which possess the name of Xuli, of this star. ⁶And I pair with them in the guise of a spirit winged in form, committing sodomy. ⁷And she on whom I have leapt goes heavy with child, and that which is born of her becomes desire. ⁸But since such offspring cannot be carried by men, the woman in question breaks wind. Such is my role. ⁹Suppose then that I alone am satisfied, and all the other demons molested and disturbed by you will speak the whole truth. ¹⁰But those composed of fire will cause the material of the logs which is to be collected by them for the building in the temple to be burned up by fire." ¹¹And as the demon said this, I saw the spirit going forth from his mouth, and it consumed the wood of the frankincense-tree, and it burned up all the logs which we had placed in the temple of God. ¹²And I, Solomon, saw what the spirit had done, and I marveled. ¹³And, having glorified God, I asked the dragon-shaped demon, and said, "Tell me, by what messenger are you frustrated?" ¹⁴And he answered: "By the great messenger who has his seat in the second heaven, which is called in Hebrew Bazazeth." And I, Solomon, having heard this, and having invoked his messenger, condemned him to saw up marbles for the building of the temple of God.

CHAPTER 19

¹And I praised God and commanded another demon to come before me, ²and another spirit came before my face, as it were a woman in the form she had. But on her shoulders she had two other heads with hands. ³And I asked her, and said, "Tell me, who are you?" And she said to me, "I am Enêpsigos, who also have a myriad of names." ⁴And I said to her, "By what messenger are you frustrated?" But she said to me, "What do you seek, what do you ask? I undergo changes, I am called like the goddess. And I change again, and pass into possession of another shape. ⁵And do not be desirous, therefore, to know all that concerns me. But since you are before me for this much, listen. I have my abode in the moon, and for that reason I possess three forms. ⁶At times I am magically invoked by the wise as Kronos. ⁷At other times, in connection with those who bring me down, I come down and appear in another shape. ⁸The measure of the element is inexplicable and undefinable, and not to be frustrated. I then, changing into these three forms, come down and become such as you see me; but I am frustrated by the messenger Rathanael, who sits in the third heaven. ⁹This then is why I speak to you. That temple cannot contain me." ¹⁰Therefore I, Solomon, prayed to my God, and I invoked the messenger of whom Enépsigos spoke to me, and used my seal. ¹¹And I sealed her with a triple chain, and [placed] the fastening of the chain beneath her. ¹²I used the seal of God, and the spirit prophesied to me, saying, "This is what you, King Solomon, do to us. But after a time, your kingdom will be broken, and again in season this temple will be split apart; and all Jerusalem will be undone by the King of the Persians, and Medes, and Chaldaeans. ¹³And the vessels of this temple, which you make, will be put to servile uses of the gods; and along with them all the jars, in which you shut us up, will be broken by the hands of men. ¹⁴And then we will go forth in great power here and there, and be disseminated all over the world. ¹⁵And we will lead the inhabited world astray for a long season, until the Son of God is stretched on the Cross. ¹⁶For never before does a king arise like Him—one frustrating us all, whose mother will not have contact with man. ¹⁷Who else can receive such authority over spirits, except He, whom the first Devil will seek to tempt, but will not prevail over? The number of His Name is six thousand four hundred forty-two, which is Emmanuel. ¹⁸For what reason, O King Solomon, your time is evil, and your years short and evil, and your kingdom will be given to your servant." ¹⁹And I, Solomon, having heard this, glorified God. And though I marveled at the apology of the demons, I did not credit it until it came true. ²⁰And I did not believe their words, but when they were realized, then I understood, and at my death I wrote this Testament to the sons of Israel, and gave it to them, so that they might know the powers of the demons and their shapes, and the names of their messengers, by which these messengers are frustrated. ²¹And I glorified the LORD God of Israel and commanded the spirits to be bound with indissoluble bonds.

CHAPTER 20

¹And having praised God, I commanded another spirit to come before me, and another demon came before my face, having the shape of a horse in front, but [that] of a fish in back. ²And he had a mighty voice, and said to me, "O King Solomon, I am a fierce spirit of the sea, and I am greedy for gold and silver. ³I am such a spirit as rounds itself and comes over the expanses of the water of the sea, and I trip up the men who sail thereon. ⁴For I round myself into a wave, and transform myself, and then throw myself on ships and come right in on them. ⁵And that is my business, and my way of getting hold of money and men. For I take the men, and whirl them around with myself, and hurl the men out of the sea. ⁶For I am not covetous of men's bodies, but cast them up out of the sea so far. ⁷But since Beelzebul, ruler of the spirits of air and of those under the earth, and lord of earthly ones, has a joint kingship with us in respect of the deeds of each one of us, I therefore went up from the sea, to get a certain outlook in his company. ⁸But I also have another character and role. I transform myself into waves and come up from the sea. ⁹And I show myself to men, so that those on earth call me Kunospaston, because I assume the human form. ¹⁰And my name is a true one. For by my passage up into men, I send forth a certain nausea. ¹¹I came then to take counsel with the prince

Beelzebul, and he bound me and delivered me into your hands. ¹²And I am here before you because of this seal, and you now torment me. ¹³Behold now, in two or three days the spirit that [now] converses with you will fail, because I will have no water." ¹⁴And I said to him, "Tell me by what messenger you are frustrated." And he answered: "By Lameth." And I glorified God. ¹⁵I commanded the spirit to be thrown into a vial along with ten jugs of seawater of two measures each. ¹⁶And I sealed them around, above the marbles, and asphalt, and pitch in the mouth of the vessel. And having sealed it with my ring, I ordered it to be deposited in the temple of God.

CHAPTER 21

¹And I ordered another spirit to come before me, ²and another enslaved spirit came before my face, having the obscure form of a man, with gleaming eyes, and bearing a blade in his hand. ³And I asked: "Who are you?" But he answered: "I am a lascivious spirit, engendered of a giant man who dies in the massacre in the time of the giants." ⁴I said to him, "Tell me what you are employed in on earth, and where you have your dwelling." ⁵And he said, "My dwelling is in fruitful places, but my procedure is this: I seat myself beside the men who pass along among the tombs, and in untimely season I assume the form of the dead; ⁶and if I catch anyone, I immediately destroy him with my sword. But if I cannot destroy him, I cause him to be possessed with a demon, and to devour his own flesh, and the hair to fall off his chin." ⁷But I said to him, "Be then in fear of the God of Heaven and of earth, and tell me by which messenger you are frustrated." ⁸And he answered: "He destroys me who is to become Savior, a Man whose figure, if anyone will write it on his forehead, he will defeat me, and I will quickly retreat in fear. ⁹And, indeed, if anyone writes this sign on him, I will be in fear." And I, Solomon, on hearing this, and having glorified the LORD God, shut this demon up like the rest.

CHAPTER 22

¹And I commanded another demon to come before me, and thirty-six spirits came before my face, their heads shapeless like dogs, but in themselves they were human in form, with faces of donkeys, faces of oxen, and faces of birds. ²And I, Solomon, on hearing and seeing them, wondered, and I asked them and said, "Who are you?" ³But they, of one accord with one voice, said, "We are the thirty-six elements, the world-rulers of this darkness. ⁴But, O King Solomon, you will not wrong us nor imprison us, nor lay command on us; but since the LORD God has given you authority over every spirit, in the air, and on the earth, and under the earth, therefore we also present ourselves before you like the other spirits, from ram and bull, from both twin and crab, lion and virgin, scales and scorpion, archer, goat-horned, water-pourer, and fish." ⁵Then I, Solomon, invoked the Name of the LORD of Hosts, and questioned each in turn as to what was its character. ⁶And I commanded each one to come forward and tell of its actions. ⁷Then the first one came forward, and said, "I am the first decan of the ecliptic, and I am called the ram, and with me are these two." ⁸So I put the question to them: "Who are you called?" The first said, "I, O lord, am called Ruax, and I cause the heads of men to be idle, and I pillage their brows. But let me only hear the words, Michael, imprison Ruax, and I immediately retreat." ⁹And the second said, "I am called Barsafael, and I cause those who are subject to my hour to feel the pain of migraine. If only I hear the words, Gabriel, imprison Barsafael, I immediately retreat." ¹⁰The third said, "I am called Arôtosael. I do harm to eyes, and grievously injure them. Only let me hear the words, Uriel, imprison Arôtosael, I immediately retreat." ¹¹The fifth said, "I am called Iudal, and I bring about a block in the ears and deafness of hearing. If I hear, Uruel Iudal, I immediately retreat." ¹²The sixth said, "I am called Sphendonaêl. I cause tumors of the parotid gland, and inflammations of the tonsils, and tetanic recurvation. If I hear, Sabrael, imprison Sphendonaêl, I immediately retreat." ¹³And the seventh said, "I am called Sphandôr, and I weaken the strength of the shoulders, and cause them to tremble; and I paralyze the nerves of the hands, and I break and bruise the bones of the neck. And I suck out the marrow. But if I hear the words, Araêl, imprison Sphandôr, I immediately retreat." ¹⁴And the eighth said, "I am called Belbel. I distort the hearts and minds of men. If I hear the words, Araêl, imprison Belbel, I immediately retreat." ¹⁵And the ninth said, "I am called Kurtaêl. I send colics in the bowels. I induce pains. If I hear the words, Iaôth, imprison Kurtaêl, I immediately retreat." ¹⁶The tenth said, "I am called Metathiax. I cause the reins to ache. If I hear the words, Adônaêl, imprison Metathiax, I immediately retreat." ¹⁷The eleventh said, "I am called Katanikotaêl. I create strife and wrongs in men's homes and send on them hard temper. If anyone would be at peace in his home, let him write on seven leaves of laurel the name of the messenger that frustrates me, along with these names: Iae, Ieô, sons of hosts, in the Name of the great God let him shut up Katanikotaêl. Then let him wash the laurel-leaves in water, and sprinkle his house with the water, from within to the outside. And I immediately retreat." ¹⁸The twelfth said, "I am called Saphathoraél, and I inspire partisanship in men, and delight in causing them to stumble. If anyone will write on paper these names of messengers, Iacô, Iealô, Iôelet, Sabaôth, Ithoth, Bae, and having folded it up, wear it around his neck or against his ear, I immediately retreat and dissipate the drunken fit." ¹⁹The thirteenth said, "I am called Bobêl, and I cause nervous sickness by my assaults. If I hear the name of the great Adonaêl, imprison Bothothêl, I immediately retreat." ²⁰The fourteenth said, "I am called Kumeatêl, and I inflict shivering fits and torpor. If only I hear the words: Zôrôel, imprison Kumentaêl, I immediately retreat." ²¹The fifteenth said, "I am called Roêlêd. I cause cold, and frost, and pain in the stomach. Let me only hear the words: Lax, do not remain, do not be warmed, for Solomon is fairer than eleven fathers, I [immediately] retreat." ²²The sixteenth said, "I am called Atrax. I inflict on men fevers, irremediable and harmful. If you would imprison me, chop up coriander and smear it on the lips, reciting the following charm: The fever which is from dirt—I exorcise you by the throne of the Most High God, retreat from dirt and retreat from the creature fashioned by God. And I immediately retreat." ²³The seventeenth said, "I am called Ieropaêl. On the stomach of men I sit, and cause convulsions in the bath and in the road; and wherever I am found, or find a man, I throw him down. But if anyone will say to the afflicted, into their ear, these names three times over, into the right ear: Ludarizê, Sabunê, Denôê, I immediately retreat." ²⁴The eighteenth said, "I am called Buldumêch. I separate wife from husband and bring about a grudge between them. If anyone writes down the names of your sires, Solomon, on paper and places it in the ante-chamber of his house, I retreat there. And the legend written will be as follows: The God of Abram, and the God of Isaac, and the God of Jacob commands you—retreat from this house in peace. And I immediately retreat." ²⁵The nineteenth said, "I am called Naôth, and I take my seat on the knees of men. If anyone writes on paper: Phnunoboêol, depart Nathath, and you do not touch the neck, I immediately retreat." ²⁶The twentieth said, "I am called Marderô. I send on men incurable fever. If anyone writes on the page of a scroll: Sphênêr, Raphael, retreat, do not drag me around, do not flay me, and ties it around his neck, I immediately retreat." ²⁷The twenty-first said, "I am called Alath, and I cause coughing and hard-breathing in children. If anyone writes on paper: Rorêx, pursue Alath, and fastens it around his neck, I immediately retreat." ²⁸The twenty-third said, "I am called Nefthada. I cause the reins to ache, and I bring about dysuria. If anyone writes on a plate of tin the words: Lathôth, Uruêl, Nephthada, and fastens it around the loins, I immediately retreat." ²⁹The twenty-fourth said, "I am called Akton. I cause ribs and lumbar muscles to ache. If one engraves on copper material, taken from a ship which has missed its anchorage, this: Marmaraôth, Sabaôth, pursue Akton, and fastens it round the loin, I immediately retreat." ³⁰The twenty-fifth said, "I am called Anatreth, and I tear burnings and fevers into the entrails. But if I hear: Arara, Charara, I immediately retreat." ³¹The twenty-sixth said, "I am called Enenuth. I steal away men's minds, and change their hearts, and make a man toothless. If one writes: Allazoôl, pursue Enenuth, and ties the paper around him, I immediately retreat." ³²The twenty-seventh said, "I am called Phêth. I make men consumptive and cause hemorrhaging. If one exorcises me in wine, sweet-smelling and unmixed by the eleventh age, and says: I exorcise you by the eleventh age to stop, I demand, Phêth (Axiôphêth), then gives it to the patient to drink, I then

immediately retreat." ³³The twenty-eighth said, "I am called Harpax, and I send sleeplessness on men. If one writes Kokphnêdismos, and binds it around the temples, I immediately retreat." ³⁴The twenty-ninth said, "I am called Anostêr. I engender uterine mania and pains in the bladder. If one powders into pure oil three seeds of laurel and smears it on, saying, I exorcise you, Anostêr, stop by Marmaraô, I immediately retreat." ³⁵The thirtieth said, "I am called Alleborith. If in eating fish one has swallowed a bone, then he must take a bone from the fish and cough, and I immediately retreat." ³⁶The thirty-first said, "I am called Hephesimireth, and cause lingering disease. If you throw salt, rubbed in the hand, into oil and smear it on the patient, saying, Seraphim, cherubim, help me! I immediately retreat." ³⁷The thirty-second said, "I am called Ichthion. I paralyze muscles and contuse them. If I hear Adonaêth, help! I immediately retreat." ³⁸The thirty-third said, "I am called Agchoniôn. I lie among swaddling-clothes and in the precipice. And if anyone writes on fig-leaves Lycurgos, taking away one letter at a time, and writes it reversing the letters, I immediately retreat—Lycurgos, ycurgos, curgos, urgos, gos, os." ³⁹The thirty-fourth said, "I am called Autothith. I cause grudges and fighting. Therefore, I am frustrated by Alpha and Omega, if written down." ⁴⁰The thirty-fifth said, "I am called Phthenoth. I cast an evil eye on every man. Therefore, the eye, much suffering, if it is drawn, frustrates me." ⁴¹The thirty-sixth said, "I am called Bianakith. I have a grudge against the body. I lay waste houses, I cause flesh to decay, and all else that is similar. If a man writes on the front-door of his house: Mêltô, Ardu, Anaath, I flee from that place."

CHAPTER 23

¹And I, Solomon, when I heard this, glorified the God of the heavens and earth. And I commanded them to fetch water in the temple of God. ²And I furthermore prayed to the LORD God to cause the demons outside, that hamper humanity, to be bound and made to approach the temple of God. ³I condemned some of these demons to do the heavy work of the construction of the temple of God. ⁴Others I shut up in prisons. Others I ordered to wrestle with fire in [the making of] gold and silver, sitting down by lead and spoon, ⁵and to make places ready for the other demons in which they should be confined. ⁶And I, Solomon, had much quiet in all the earth, and spent my life in profound peace, honored by all men and by all under Heaven. ⁷And I built the entire temple of the LORD God. And my kingdom was prosperous, and my army was with me. ⁸And for the rest, the city of Jerusalem had repose, rejoicing and delighted. ⁸And all the kings of the earth came to me from the ends of the earth to behold the temple which I built to the LORD God. ⁹And having heard of the wisdom given to me, they paid homage to me in the temple, bringing gold, and silver, and many and various precious stones, and bronze, and iron, and lead, and cedar logs. ¹⁰And woods did not decay [that] they brought me for the equipment of the temple of God. ¹¹And among them the queen of the south, being a witch, also came in great concern and bowed low to the earth before me. ¹²And having heard my wisdom, she glorified the God of Israel, and she made formal trial of all my wisdom, of all love in which I instructed her, according to the wisdom imparted to me. And all the sons of Israel glorified God.

CHAPTER 24

¹And behold, in those days one of the workmen of ripe old age threw himself down before me, and said, "King Solomon, pity me, because I am old." ²So I commanded him to stand up, and said, "Tell me, old man, all you will." ³And he answered: "I implore you king, I have an only-born son, and he insults and beats me openly, and plucks out the hair of my head, and threatens me with a painful death. Therefore, I implore you: avenge me." ⁴And I, Solomon, on hearing this, felt compunction as I looked at his old age; and I commanded the child to be brought to me. ⁵And when he was brought, I questioned him whether it was true. And the youth said, "I was not so filled with madness as to strike my father with my hand. Be kind to me, O king. ⁶For I have not dared to commit such impiety, poor wretch that I am." ⁷But I, Solomon, on hearing this from the youth, exhorted the old man to reflect on the matter, and accept his son's apology. ⁸However, he would not, but said he would rather let him die. And as the old man would not yield, I was about to pronounce sentence on the youth, when I saw the demon Ornias laughing. ⁹I was very angry at the demon's laughing in my presence; and I ordered my men to remove the other parties and bring Ornias forward before my tribunal. ¹⁰And when he was brought before me, I said to him, "Accursed one, why did you look at me and laugh?" ¹¹And the demon answered: "Please, king, it was not because of you I laughed, but because of this ill-fated old man and the wretched youth—his son. ¹²For after three days his son will die untimely; and behold, the old man desires to unfairly make away with him." ¹³But I, Solomon, having heard this, said to the demon, "Is that which you speak true?" And he answered: "It is true, O king." ¹⁴And I, on hearing that, commanded them to remove the demon, and that they should bring the old man with his son before me again. ¹⁵I commanded them to make friends with one another again, and I supplied them with food. ¹⁶And then I told the old man after three days to bring his son to me again here; "and," I said, "I will attend to him." And they saluted me and went their way. ¹⁷And when they were gone, I ordered Ornias to be brought forward, and said to him, "Tell me how you know this"; and he answered: "We demons ascend into the expanse of Heaven, and fly around among the stars. And we hear the sentences which go forth on the souls of men, and immediately we come, and whether by force of influence, or by fire, or by sword, or by some accident, we veil our act of destruction; ¹⁹and if a man does not die by some untimely disaster or by violence, then we demons transform ourselves in such a way as to appear to men and be worshiped in our human nature." ²⁰I therefore, having heard this, glorified the LORD God, and I questioned the demon again, saying, "Tell me how you can ascend into Heaven, being demons, and intermingle amidst the stars and holy messengers." ²¹And he answered: "Just as things are fulfilled in Heaven, so also on earth the types of all of them. ²²For there are principalities, authorities, world-rulers, and we demons fly around in the air; and we hear the voices of the heavenly beings, and survey all the powers. ²³And as having no ground on which to descend and rest, we lose strength and fall off like leaves from trees. ²⁴And men seeing us imagine that the stars are falling from [the] sky. ²⁵But it is not really so, O king; but we fall because of our weakness, and because we have nothing anywhere to lay hold of; and so we suddenly fall down like lightnings in the depth of night. ²⁶And we set cities in flames and the fields [on] fire. For the stars have firm foundations in the heavens like the sun and the moon." ²⁷And I, Solomon, having heard this, ordered the demon to be guarded for five days. ²⁸And after the five days I recalled the old man and was about to question him, but he came to me in grief and with dark countenance. ²⁹And I said to him, "Tell me, old man, where is your son? And what does this [gloomy] appearance mean?" ³⁰And he answered: "Behold, I have become childless and sit by my son's grave in despair. For it is already two days that he is dead." But I, Solomon, on hearing that, and knowing that the demon Ornias had told me the truth, glorified the God of Israel.

CHAPTER 25

¹And the queen of the south saw all this, and marveled, glorifying the God of Israel; and she beheld the temple of the LORD being built. ²And she gave a siklos of gold and one hundred myriads of silver and choice bronze, and she went into the temple. ³And [she beheld] the altar of incense and the brazen supports of this altar, and the gems of the lamps flashing forth of different colors, and of the lampstand of stone, and of emerald, and hyacinth, and sapphire; ⁴and she beheld the vessels of gold, and silver, and bronze, and wood, and the folds of skins dyed red with madder. ⁵And she saw the bases of the pillars of the temple of the LORD. All were of one gold … ⁶… apart from the demons whom I condemned to labor. And there was peace in the circle of my kingdom and over all the earth.

CHAPTER 26

¹And it came to pass, when I was in my kingdom, the king of the Arabians, Adares, sent me a letter, and the writing of the letter was written as follows: ²"To King Solomon, greetings! Behold, we have heard, and it has been heard to all the ends of the earth,

concerning the wisdom given in you, and that you are a man merciful from the LORD. ³And understanding has been granted to you over all the spirits of the air, and on earth, and under the earth. ⁴Now indeed, there is present in the land of Arabia a spirit of the following kind: at early dawn there begins to blow a certain wind until the third hour. ⁵And its blast is harsh and terrible, and it slays man and beast. And no spirit can live on earth against this demon. ⁶Please then, forasmuch as the spirit is a wind, contrive something according to the wisdom given in you by the LORD your God, and deign to send a man [who is] able to capture it. ⁷And behold, King Solomon, I, and my people, and all my land will serve you to death. ⁸And all Arabia will be at peace with you, if you will perform this act of righteousness for us. ⁹For what reason, please do not despise our humble prayer, and do not permit the territory subordinated to your authority to be utterly brought to nothing. ¹⁰Because we are suppliants—both I, and my people, and all my land. ¹¹Farewell to my lord. All health [be to you]!" ¹²And I, Solomon, read this letter; and I folded it up and gave it to my people, and said to them, "After seven days you will remind me of this letter." ¹³And Jerusalem was built, and the temple was being completed. And there was a stone, the end stone of the corner lying there—great, chosen out, one which I desired to lay in the head of the corner of the completion of the temple. ¹⁴And all the workmen, and all the demons helping them, came to the same place to bring up the stone and lay it on the pinnacle of the holy temple, and were not strong enough to stir it and lay it on the corner allotted to it. ¹⁵For that stone was exceedingly great and useful for the corner of the temple. ¹⁶And after seven days, being reminded of the letter of Adares, king of Arabia, I called my servant and said to him, "Order your camel and take a leather flask for yourself, and also take this seal. ¹⁷And go away into Arabia to the place in which the evil spirit blows; and take the flask there, and the signet-ring in front of the mouth of the flask, and [hold them] toward the blast of the spirit. ¹⁸And when the flask is blown out, you will understand that the demon is [in it]. ¹⁹Then quickly tie up the mouth of the flask, and seal it securely with the seal-ring, and lay it carefully on the camel, and bring it to me here. ²⁰And if on the way it offers you gold, or silver, or treasure in return for letting it go, see that you are not persuaded. But arrange [it] without using an oath to release it. ²¹And then if it points out to the places where gold or silver are, mark the places and seal them with this seal. And bring the demon to me. And now depart, and farewell." ²²Then the youth did as was commanded him. And he ordered his camel, and laid a flask on it, and set off into Arabia. ²³And the men of that region would not believe that he would be able to catch the evil spirit. ²⁴And when it was dawn, the servant stood before the spirit's blast, and laid the flask on the ground, and the finger-ring on the mouth of the flask. ²⁵And the demon blew through the middle of the finger-ring into the mouth of the flask, and going in, blew out the flask. ²⁶But the man promptly stood up to it and drew the mouth of the flask tight with his hand in the Name of the LORD God of Hosts. ²⁷And the demon remained within the flask. And after that, the youth remained in that land three days to make trial. ²⁸And the spirit no longer blew against that city. And all the Arabs knew that he had safely shut the spirit in. ²⁹Then the youth fastened the flask on the camel, and the Arabs sent him forth on his way with much honor and precious gifts, praising and magnifying the God of Israel. ³⁰But the youth brought in the bag and laid it in the middle of the temple. And on the next day, I, King Solomon, went into the temple of God and sat in deep distress regarding the stone of the end of the corner. ³¹And when I entered the temple, the flask stood up and walked around some seven steps and then fell on its mouth and paid homage to me. ³²And I marveled that even along with the bottle the demon still had power and could walk around; and I commanded it to stand up. ³³And the flask stood up and stood on its feet all blown out. And I questioned him, saying, "Tell me, who are you?" ³⁴And the spirit within said, "I am the demon called Ephippas, that is in Arabia." ³⁵And I said to him, "Is this your name?" And he answered: "Yes; wheresoever I will, I descend, and set fire, and do [it] to death." ³⁶And I said to him, "By what messenger are you frustrated?" And he answered: "By the only-ruling God that even has authority over me to be heard— ³⁷He that is to be born of a virgin and crucified by the Jews on a cross, whom the messengers and chief-messengers worship. ³⁸He frustrates me and weakens me of my great strength, which has been given to me by my father the Devil." ³⁹And I said to him, "What can you do?" And he answered: "I am able to remove mountains, to overthrow the oaths of kings. I wither trees and make their leaves to fall off." ⁴⁰And I said to him, "Can you raise this stone, and lay it for the beginning of this corner which exists in the fair plan of the temple?" ⁴¹And he said, "Not only raise this, O king, but also, with the help of the demon who presides over the Red Sea, I will bring up the pillar of air, and will stand it where you will in Jerusalem." ⁴²Saying this, I laid stress on him, and the flask became as if depleted of air. And I placed it under the stone, and [the spirit] girded himself up, and lifted it up [to the] top of the flask. ⁴³And the flask went up the steps, carrying the stone, and laid it down at the end of the entrance of the temple. ⁴⁴And I, Solomon, beholding the stone raised aloft and placed on a foundation, said, "Truly the Writing is fulfilled, which says: The stone which the builders rejected on trial, that same has become the head of the corner. ⁴⁵For this is not mine to grant, but God's, that the demon should be strong enough to lift up such a great stone and deposit it in the place I wished." ⁴⁶And Ephippas led the demon of the Red Sea with the column. And they both took the column and raised it aloft from the earth. ⁴⁷And I outwitted these two spirits, so that they could not shake the entire earth in a moment of time. ⁴⁸And then I sealed around on this side and that with my ring, and said, "Watch." ⁴⁹And the spirits have remained upholding it until this day, for proof of the wisdom given to me. And there the pillar was hanging of enormous size, in midair, supported by the winds. ⁵⁰And thus the spirits appeared underneath, like air, supporting it. And if one looks fixedly, the pillar is a little oblique, being supported by the spirits; and it is so today.

CHAPTER 27

¹And I, Solomon, questioned the other spirit which came up with the pillar from the depth of the Red Sea. ²And I said to him, "Who are you, and what calls you? And what is your business? For I hear many things about you." ³And the demon answered: "I, O King Solomon, am called Abezithibod. I am a descendant of the chief-messenger. ⁴When once I sat in the first heaven, of which the name is Ameleouth, I was then a fierce and winged spirit, and with a single wing I was plotting against every spirit under Heaven. ⁵I was present when Moses went in before Pharaoh, king of Egypt, and I hardened his heart. ⁶I am he whom Jannes and Jambres invoked, striving with Moses in Egypt. I am he who fought against Moses with wonders with signs." ⁷I therefore said to him, "How were you found in the Red Sea?" ⁸And he answered: "In the exodus of the sons of Israel I hardened the heart of Pharaoh. ⁹And I excited his heart and that of his ministers. And I caused them to pursue after the sons of Israel. ¹⁰And Pharaoh followed with [me] and all the Egyptians. Then I was present there, and we followed together. ¹¹And we all came up on the Red Sea. And it came to pass when the sons of Israel had crossed over, the water returned and hid all the host of the Egyptians and all their might. ¹²And I remained in the sea, being kept under this pillar. But when Ephippas came, being sent by you, shut up in the vessel of a flask, he fetched me up to you." ¹³I, therefore, Solomon, having heard this, glorified God and adjured the demons not to disobey me, but to remain supporting the pillar. ¹⁴And they both swore, saying, "[As] the LORD your God lives, we will not let go of this pillar until the world's end. But on whatever day this stone falls, then will be the end of the world."

CHAPTER 28

¹And I, Solomon, glorified God, and adorned the temple of the LORD with all pleasant appearance. ²And I was glad in spirit in my kingdom, and there was peace in my days. And I took wives of my own from every land, who were numberless. ³And I marched against the Jebusites, and there I saw a Jebusite man's daughter, and fell violently in love with her, and desired to take her to be [my] wife along with my other wives. ⁴And I said to their priests, "Give me the Shunammite to be [my] wife." ⁵But the priests of Moloch said to me, "If you love this maiden, go in and worship our gods, the great god Remphan and the god called Moloch." ⁶I, therefore, was

in fear of the glory of God, and did not follow to worship. ⁷And I said to them, "I will not worship a strange god. What is this proposal, that you compel me to do so much?" But they said, "… by our fathers." ⁸And when I answered that I would on no account worship strange gods, they told the maiden not to sleep with me until I complied and sacrificed to the gods. ⁹I then was moved, but crafty Eros brought and laid by her five grasshoppers for me, saying, "Take these grasshoppers, and crush them together in the name of the god Moloch; and then I will sleep with you." ¹⁰And I actually did this. And at once the Spirit of God departed from me, and I became weak as well as foolish in my words. ¹¹And after that I was obliged by her to build a temple of idols to Ba'al, and to Rapha, and to Moloch, and to the other idols. ¹²I then, wretch that I am, followed her advice, and the glory of God yet departed from me, and my spirit was darkened, and I became the sport of idols and demons. ¹³For this reason I wrote out this Testament, that you who get possession of it may pity, and attend to the last things, and not to the first, ¹⁴so that you may find grace forever and ever. Amen.

PSALMS OF SOLOMON

The apocryphal psalms attributed to Solomon were likely written in the 1st or 2nd centuries BC. While they do not belong to any current canon, they have been found in copies of the Peshitta and Septuagint.

PSALM 1

¹I cried to the LORD when I was in distress, || To God when sinners assailed. ²Suddenly the alarm of war was heard before me; [I said], "He will listen to me, for I am full of righteousness." ³I thought in my heart that I was full of righteousness, || Because I was well off and had become rich in children. ⁴Their wealth spread to the whole earth, || And their glory to the end of the earth. ⁵They were exalted to the stars; They said they would never fall. ⁶But they became insolent in their prosperity, || And they were without understanding, ⁷Their sins were in secret, || And even I had no knowledge [of them]. ⁸Their transgressions [went] beyond those of the heathen before them; They utterly polluted the holy things of the LORD.

PSALM 2

¹A PSALM OF SOLOMON. CONCERNING JERUSALEM. When the sinner waxed proud, with a battering-ram he cast down fortified walls, || And You did not restrain [him]. ²Alien nations ascended Your altar, || They trampled [it] proudly with their sandals, ³Because the sons of Jerusalem had defiled the holy things of the LORD, || [And] had profaned with iniquities the offerings of God. ⁴Therefore He said, "Cast them far from Me"; ⁵It was set at nothing before God, || It was utterly dishonored; ⁶The sons and the daughters were in grievous captivity, || Their neck [was] sealed, [it was] branded among the nations. ⁷He has done to them according to their sins, || For He has left them in the hands of them that prevailed. ⁸He has turned His face away from pitying them— Young, and old, and their children together; ⁹For they had done evil, one and all, in not listening. ¹⁰And the heavens were angry, || And the earth abhorred them; ¹¹For no man on it had done what they did, ¹²And the earth recognized all Your righteous judgments, O God. ¹³They set the sons of Jerusalem to be mocked at in return for [the] harlots in her; Every wayfarer entered in in the full light of day. ¹⁴They made a mockery with their transgressions, as they themselves were frequent to do; In the full light of day they revealed their iniquities. ¹⁵And the daughters of Jerusalem were defiled in accordance with Your judgment, || Because they had defiled themselves with unnatural intercourse. I am pained in my bowels and my inward parts for these things. ¹⁶And yet, I will justify You, O God, in uprightness of heart, || For in Your judgments is Your righteousness [displayed], O God. ¹⁷For You have rendered to the sinners according to their deeds, || Yes, according to their sins, which were very wicked. ¹⁸You have uncovered their sins, that Your judgment might be manifest; ¹⁹You have wiped out their memorial from the earth. God is a righteous judge, || And He is no respecter of persons. ²⁰For the nations reproached Jerusalem, trampling it down; Her beauty was dragged down from the throne of glory. ²¹She girded on sackcloth instead of beautiful raiment, || A rope [was] around her head instead of a crown. ²²She put off the glorious diadem which God had set on her, || In dishonor her beauty was cast on the ground. ²³And I saw and entreated the LORD and said, || "Long enough, O LORD, has Your hand been heavy on Israel in bringing the nations on [them]. ²⁴For they have made sport unsparingly in wrath and fierce anger; ²⁵And they will make an utter end, unless You, O LORD, rebuke them in Your wrath. ²⁶For they have not done it in zeal, but in lust of soul, || Pouring out their wrath on us with a view to plunder. ²⁷Do not delay, O God, to repay them on [their] heads, || To turn the pride of the dragon into dishonor." ²⁸And I did not have long to wait before God showed me the insolent one || Slain on the mountains of Egypt, || Esteemed of less account than the least on land and sea; ²⁹His body, [too,] borne here and there on the billows with much insolence, || With none to bury [him], because He had rejected him with dishonor. ³⁰He did not consider that he was man, || And did not consider the latter end; ³¹He said, "I will be lord of land and sea"; And he did not recognize that it is God who is great, || Mighty in His great strength. ³²He is King over the heavens, || And judges kings and kingdoms, ³³Who sets me up in glory, || And brings down the proud to continuous destruction in dishonor, || Because they did not know Him. ³⁴And now behold, you princes of the earth, || The judgment of the LORD, || For [He is] a great and righteous King, || Judging [all] that is under Heaven. ³⁵Bless God, you that fear the LORD with wisdom, || For the mercy of the LORD will be on them that fear Him, in the Judgment, ³⁶So that He will distinguish between the righteous and the sinner, || [And] repay the sinners forever according to their deeds, ³⁷And have mercy on the righteous, [delivering him] from the affliction of the sinner, || And repaying the sinner for what he has done to the righteous. ³⁸For the LORD is good to them that call on Him in patience, || Doing according to His mercy to His pious ones, || Establishing [them] at all times before Him in strength. ³⁹Blessed is the LORD forever before His servants.

PSALM 3

¹A PSALM OF SOLOMON. CONCERNING THE RIGHTEOUS. Why do you sleep, O my soul, || And do not bless the LORD? ²Sing a new song, || To God who is worthy to be praised. Sing and be wakeful against His awaking, || For a psalm [sung] to God from a glad heart is good. ³The righteous remember the LORD at all times, || With thanksgiving and declaration of the righteousness of the LORD's judgments. ⁴The righteous does not despise the disciplining of the LORD; His will is always before the LORD. ⁵The righteous stumbles and holds the LORD righteous: He falls and looks out for what God will do to him; ⁶He seeks out from where his deliverance will come. ⁷The steadfastness of the righteous is from God their deliverer; There does not lodge in the house of the righteous sin on sin. ⁸The righteous continually searches his house, || To utterly remove [all] iniquity [done] by him in error. ⁹He makes atonement for [sins of] ignorance by fasting and afflicting his soul, || ¹⁰And the LORD counts guiltless every pious man and his house. ¹¹The sinner stumbles and curses his life, || The day when he was begotten, and his mother's travail. ¹²He adds sins to sins, while he lives; He falls—truly grievous is his fall— and rises no longer. ¹³The destruction of the sinner is forever, || And he will not be remembered when the righteous is visited. ¹⁴This is the portion of sinners forever. ¹⁵But they that fear the LORD will rise to continuous life, || And their life [will be] in the light of the LORD, and will come to an end no more.

PSALM 4

¹A CONVERSATION OF SOLOMON WITH THE MEN-PLEASERS. Why do you sit, O profane [man], in the council of the pious, || Seeing that your heart is far removed from the LORD, || Provoking the God of Israel with

transgressions? ²Extravagant in speech, extravagant in outward seeming beyond all [men], || Is he that is severe of speech in condemning sinners in judgment. ³And his hand is first on him as [though he acted] in zeal, || And [yet] he is himself guilty in respect of manifold sins and of wantonness. ⁴His eyes are on every woman without distinction; His tongue lies when he makes contract with an oath. ⁵By night and in secret he sins as though unseen, || With his eyes he talks to every woman of evil compacts. ⁶He is swift to enter every house with cheerfulness as though guileless. ⁷Let God remove those that live in hypocrisy in the company of the pious, || [Even] the life of such a one with corruption of his flesh and destitution. ⁸Let God reveal the deeds of the men-pleasers, || The deeds of such a one with laughter and derision; ⁹That the pious may count righteous the judgment of their God, || When sinners are removed from before the righteous, ¹⁰[Even the] man-pleaser who utters law guilefully. ¹¹And their eyes [are fixed] on any man's house that is [still] secure, || That they may, like [the] Serpent, destroy the wisdom of… with words of transgressors, ¹²His words are deceitful that [he] may accomplish [his] wicked desire. ¹³He never ceases from scattering [families] as though [they were] orphans, || Yes, he lays waste a house on account of [his] lawless desire. ¹⁴He deceives with words, [saying,] "There is none that sees, or judges." ¹⁵He fills one [house] with lawlessness, || And [then] his eyes [are fixed] on the next house, || To destroy it with words that give wing to [desire]. [Yet] with all these his soul, like Sheol, is not satisfied. ¹⁶Let his portion, O LORD, be dishonored before You; Let him go forth groaning and come home cursed. ¹⁷Let his life be [spent] in anguish, and destitution, and want, O LORD; Let his sleep be [beset] with pains and his awaking with perplexities. ¹⁸Let sleep be withdrawn from his eyelids at night; Let him fail dishonorably in every work of his hands. ¹⁹Let him come home empty-handed to his house, || And his house be void of everything with which he could satisfy his appetite. ²⁰[Let] his old age [be spent] in childless loneliness until his removal. ²¹Let the flesh of the men-pleasers be torn by wild beasts, || And [let] the bones of the lawless [lie] dishonored in the sight of the sun. ²²Let ravens peck out the eyes of the hypocrites. ²³For they have laid waste many houses of men, in dishonor, || And scattered [them] in [their] lust; ²⁴And they have not remembered God, || Nor feared God in all these things; ²⁵But they have provoked God's anger and vexed Him. May He remove them from off the earth, || Because with deceit they deceived the souls of the flawless. ²⁶Blessed are they that fear the LORD in their flawlessness; ²⁷The LORD will deliver them from guileful men and sinners, || And deliver us from every stumbling-block of the lawless [men]. ²⁸Let God destroy them that insolently work all unrighteousness, || For a great and mighty judge is the LORD our God in righteousness. ²⁹Let Your mercy, O LORD, be on all them that love You.

PSALMS OF SOLOMON

PSALM 5

¹A PSALM OF SOLOMON. O LORD God, I will praise Your Name with joy, || In the midst of them that know Your righteous judgments. ²For You are good and merciful, the refuge of the poor; ³When I cry to You, do not silently disregard me. ⁴For no man takes spoil from a mighty man. ⁵Who, then, can take anything of all that You have made, except You Yourself give? ⁶For man and his portion [lie] before You in the balance; He cannot add to, so as to enlarge, what has been prescribed by You. ⁷O God, when we are in distress, we call on You for help, || And You do not turn back our petition, for You are our God. ⁸Do not cause Your hand to be heavy on us, || Lest through necessity we sin. ⁹Even though You do not restore us, we will not keep away; But we will come to You. ¹⁰For if I hunger, I will cry to You, O God; And You will give to me. ¹¹You nourish birds and fish, || In that You give rain to the plains that green grass may spring up, || To prepare fodder in the plain for every living thing; ¹²And if they hunger, they lift up their face to You. ¹³You nourish kings, and rulers, and peoples, O God; And who is the help of the poor and needy, if not You, O LORD? ¹⁴And You will listen—for who is good and gentle but You— Making glad the soul of the humble by opening Your hand in mercy. ¹⁵Man's goodness is [bestowed] grudgingly and … And if he repeats [it] without murmuring, even that is marvelous. ¹⁶But Your gift is great in goodness and wealth, || And he whose hope is [set] on You will have no lack of gifts. ¹⁷Your mercy is on the whole earth, O LORD, in goodness. ¹⁸Happy is he whom God remembers in [granting to him] a due sufficiency; ¹⁹If a man abounds over much, he sins. ²⁰Sufficient are moderate means with righteousness, || And hereby the blessing of the LORD [becomes] abundance with righteousness. ²¹They that fear the LORD rejoice in good [gifts], || And Your goodness is on Israel in Your kingdom. Blessed is the glory of the LORD, for He is our King.

PSALM 6

¹IN HOPE. OF SOLOMON. Happy is the man whose heart is fixed to call on the Name of the LORD; ²When he remembers the Name of the LORD, he will be saved. ³His ways are made even by the LORD, || And the works of his hands are preserved by the LORD his God. ⁴At what he sees in his bad dreams, his soul will not be troubled; ⁵When he passes through rivers and the tossing of the seas, he will not be dismayed. ⁶He arises from his sleep, and blesses the Name of the LORD: ⁷When his heart is at peace, he sings to the Name of his God, || And he entreats the LORD for all his house. ⁸And the LORD hears the prayer of everyone that fears God, || And the LORD accomplishes every request of the soul that hopes for Him. ⁹Blessed is the LORD, who shows mercy to those who love Him in sincerity.

PSALM 7

¹OF SOLOMON. OF TURNING. Do not make Your dwelling far from us, O God; Lest they assail us that hate us without cause. ²For You have rejected them, O God; Do not let their foot trample on Your holy inheritance. ³Discipline us Yourself in Your good pleasure; But do not give [us] up to the nations; ⁴For, if You send pestilence, || You Yourself give it charge concerning us; For You are merciful, || And will not be angry to the point of consuming us. ⁵While Your Name dwells in our midst, we will find mercy; ⁶And the nations will not prevail against us. For You are our shield, || ⁷And when we call on You, You listen to us; ⁸For You will pity the seed of Israel forever || And You will not reject [them], || But we [will be] under Your yoke forever, || And [under] the rod of Your disciplining. ⁹You will establish us in the time that You help us, || Showing mercy to the house of Jacob on the day wherein You promised [to help them].

PSALM 8

¹OF SOLOMON. OF THE CHIEF MUSICIAN. My ear has heard distress and the sound of war; The sound of a trumpet announcing slaughter and calamity, ²The sound of many people as of an exceedingly high wind, || As a tempest with mighty fire sweeping through the Negeb. ³And I said in my heart, "Surely God judges us"; ⁴I hear a sound [moving] toward Jerusalem, the holy city. ⁵My loins were broken at what I heard, my knees tottered: ⁶My heart was afraid, my bones were dismayed like flax. ⁷I said, "They establish their ways in righteousness." I thought on the judgments of God since the creation of the heavens and earth; I held God righteous in His judgments which have been from of old. ⁸God laid bare their sins in the full light of day; All the earth came to know the righteous judgments of God. ⁹In secret places underground their iniquities [were committed] to provoke [Him] to anger, ¹⁰They worked confusion, son with mother and father with daughter; ¹¹They committed adultery, every man with his neighbor's wife. They concluded covenants with one another with an oath touching these things; ¹²They plundered the sanctuary of God, as though there was no avenger. ¹³They trod the altar of the LORD, [coming straight] from all manner of uncleanness; And with menstrual blood they defiled the sacrifices, as [though these were] common flesh. ¹⁴They left no sin undone, wherein they did not surpass the heathen. ¹⁵Therefore God mingled for them a spirit of wandering; And gave them a cup of undiluted wine to drink, that they might become drunken. ¹⁶He brought him that is from the end of the earth, that strikes mightily; ¹⁷He decreed war against Jerusalem, and against her land. ¹⁸The princes of the land went to meet him with joy; They said to him, "Blessed is your way! Come, enter in with peace." ¹⁹They made the rough ways even, before his entering in; They opened the gates to Jerusalem, they crowned its walls. ²⁰As a father [enters] the house of his sons, [so] he entered [Jerusalem] in peace; He established his feet [there] in great safety. ²¹He captured her fortresses and the wall of Jerusalem; ²²For God Himself led him in safety, while they

wandered. ²³He destroyed their princes and everyone wise in counsel; He poured out the blood of the inhabitants of Jerusalem like the water of uncleanness. ²⁴He led away their sons and daughters, whom they had begotten in defilement. ²⁵They did according to their uncleanness, even as their fathers [had done]: ²⁶They defiled Jerusalem and the things that had been hallowed to the Name of God. ²⁷[But] God has shown Himself righteous in His judgments on the nations of the earth; ²⁸And the pious [servants] of God are like innocent lambs in their midst. ²⁹Worthy to be praised is the LORD that judges the whole earth in His righteousness. ³⁰Behold, now, O God, You have shown us Your judgment in Your righteousness; ³¹Our eyes have seen Your judgments, O God. We have justified Your Name that is honored forever; ³²For You are the God of righteousness, judging Israel with disciplining. ³³Turn, O God, Your mercy on us, and have pity on us; ³⁴Gather together the dispersed of Israel, with mercy and goodness; ³⁵For Your faithfulness is with us. And [though] we have stiffened our neck, yet You are our chastener; ³⁶Do not overlook us, O our God, lest the nations swallow us up, as though there were none to deliver. ³⁷But You are our God from the beginning, || And on You is our hope [set], O LORD; ³⁸And we will not depart from You, || For Your judgments on us are good. ³⁹Ours and our children's be Your good pleasure forever; O LORD our Savior, we will never more be moved. ⁴⁰The LORD is worthy to be praised for His judgments with the mouth of His pious ones; And blessed is Israel of the LORD forever.

PSALM 9

¹OF SOLOMON. FOR REBUKE. When Israel was led away captive into a strange land, || When they fell away from the LORD who redeemed them, ²They were cast away from the inheritance, which the LORD had given them. Among every nation [were] the dispersed of Israel according to the word of God, ³That You might be justified, O God, in Your righteousness by reason of our transgressions: ⁴For You are a just judge over all the peoples of the earth. ⁵For from Your knowledge none that does unjustly is hidden, ⁶And the righteous deeds of Your pious ones [are] before You, O LORD, || Where, then, can a man hide himself from Your knowledge, O God? ⁷Our works are subject to our own choice and power || To do right or wrong in the works of our hands; ⁸And in Your righteousness You visitest the sons of men. ⁹He that does righteousness lays up life for himself with the LORD; And he that does wrongly forfeits his life to destruction; ¹⁰For the judgments of the LORD are [given] in righteousness to [every] man and [his] house. To whom are You good, O God, except to them that call on the LORD? ¹²He cleanses a soul from sins when it makes confession, when it makes acknowledgement; ¹³For shame is on us and on our faces on account of all these things. ¹⁴And to whom does He forgive sins, except to them that have sinned? ¹⁵You bless the righteous, and do not reprove them for the sins that they have committed; And Your goodness is on them that sin, when they convert. ¹⁶And now, You are our God, and we the people whom You have loved: Behold and show pity, O God of Israel, for we are Yours; And do not remove Your mercy from us, lest they assail us. ¹⁷For You chose the seed of Abraham before all the nations, || And set Your Name on us, O LORD, ¹⁸And You will not reject [us] forever. You made a covenant with our fathers concerning us; ¹⁹And we hope in You, when our soul turns [to You]. May the mercy of the LORD be on the house of Israel forever and ever.

PSALM 10

¹A HYMN OF SOLOMON. Happy is the man whom the LORD remembers with reproving, || And whom He restrains from the way of evil with strokes, || That he may be cleansed from sin, that it may not be multiplied. ²He that makes his back ready for strokes will be cleansed, || For the LORD is good to them that endure disciplining. ³For He makes straight the ways of the righteous, || And does not pervert [them] by His disciplining. ⁴And the mercy of the LORD [is] on them that love Him in truth, || And the LORD remembers His servants in mercy. ⁵For the testimony [is] in the law of the perpetual covenant, || The testimony of the LORD [is] on the ways of men in [His] visitation. ⁶Just and kind is our LORD in His judgments forever, || And Israel will praise the Name of the LORD in gladness. ⁷And the pious will give thanks in the assembly of the people; And God will have mercy on the poor in the gladness of Israel; ⁸For God is good and merciful forever, || And the assemblies of Israel will glorify the Name of the LORD. May the salvation of the LORD be on the house of Israel to everlasting gladness!

PSALM 11

¹OF SOLOMON. TO EXPECTATION. Blow on the trumpet in Zion to summon [the] saints, ²Cause the voice of him that brings good tidings to be heard in Jerusalem; For God has had pity on Israel in visiting them. ³Stand on the height, O Jerusalem, and behold your children, || From the East and the West, gathered together by the LORD; ⁴From the North they come in the gladness of their God, || From the isles far off God has gathered them. ⁵He has abased high mountains into a plain for them; ⁶The hills fled at their entrance. The woods gave them shelter as they passed by; ⁷Every sweet-smelling tree God caused to spring up for them, || That Israel might pass by in the visitation of the glory of their God. ⁸Put on, O Jerusalem, your glorious garments; Make your holy robe ready; For God has spoken good concerning Israel, forever and ever. ⁹Let the LORD do what He has spoken concerning Israel and Jerusalem; Let the LORD raise up Israel by His glorious Name. May the mercy of the LORD be on Israel forever and ever.

PSALM 12

¹OF SOLOMON. AGAINST THE TONGUE OF TRANSGRESSORS. O LORD, deliver my soul from [the] lawless and wicked man, || From the tongue that is lawless and slanderous, and speaks lies and deceit. ²Manifoldly twisted are the words of the tongue of the wicked man, || Even as among a people a fire that burns up their beauty. ³So he delights to fill houses with a lying tongue, || To cut down the trees of gladness which sets transgressors on fire, ⁴To involve households in warfare by means of slanderous lips. May God remove far from the innocent the lips of transgressors by [bringing them to] want || And may the bones of slanderers be scattered [far] away from them that fear the LORD! ⁵In flaming fire, make the slanderous tongue perish [far] away from the pious! ⁶May the LORD preserve the quiet soul that hates the unrighteous; And may the LORD establish the man that follows peace at home. ⁷May the salvation of the LORD be on His servant Israel forever; And let the sinners perish together at the presence of the LORD; But let the LORD's pious ones inherit the promises of the LORD.

PSALM 13

¹A PSALM OF SOLOMON. Comfort for the righteous. The right hand of the LORD has covered me; The right hand of the LORD has spared us. ²The arm of the LORD has saved us from the sword that passed through, || From famine and the death of sinners. ³Ghastly beasts ran on them: They tore their flesh with their teeth, || And crushed their bones with their molars, || But the LORD delivered us from all these things. ⁴The righteous was troubled on account of his errors, || Lest he should be taken away along with the sinners; ⁵For the overthrow of the sinner is terrible; But not one of all these things touches the righteous. For not alike are the disciplining of the righteous [for sins done] in ignorance, || And the overthrow of the sinners. ⁷The righteous is disciplined secretly, || Lest the sinner rejoice over the righteous. ⁸For He corrects the righteous as a beloved son, || And his discipline is as that of a firstborn. ⁹For the LORD spares His pious ones, || And blots out their errors by His disciplining. For the life of the righteous will be forever, ¹⁰But sinners will be taken away into destruction, || And their memorial will be found no longer. ¹¹But the mercy of the LORD is on the pious, || And His mercy on them that fear Him.

PSALM 14

¹A HYMN OF SOLOMON. Faithful is the LORD to them that love Him in truth, || To them that endure His disciplining, || To them that walk in the righteousness of His commandments, || In the law which He commanded us that we might live. ²The pious of the LORD will live by it forever; The Paradise of the LORD, the trees of life, are His pious ones. ³Their planting is rooted forever; They will not be plucked up all the days of Heaven. For the portion and the inheritance of God is Israel. ⁴But not so are the sinners and transgressors, || Who love [the

brief] day [spent] in companionship with their sin; Their delight is in fleeting corruption, ⁵And they do not remember God. For the ways of men are known before Him at all times, || And He knows the secrets of the heart before they come to pass. ⁶Therefore their inheritance is Sheol and darkness and destruction, || And they will not be found in the day when the righteous obtain mercy; ⁷But the pious of the LORD will inherit life in gladness.

PSALM 15

¹A PSALM OF SOLOMON. WITH A SONG. When I was in distress, I called on the Name of the LORD, || I hoped for the help of the God of Jacob and was saved; ²For the hope and refuge of the poor are You, O God. ³For who, O God, is strong except to give thanks to You in truth? ⁴And wherein is a man powerful except in giving thanks to Your Name ⁵A new psalm with song in gladness of heart, || The fruit of the lips with the well-tuned instrument of the tongue, || The first-fruits of the lips from a pious and righteous heart— ⁶He that offers these things will never be shaken by evil; The flame of fire and the wrath against the unrighteous will not touch him ⁷When it goes forth from the face of the LORD against sinners, || To destroy all the substance of sinners, ⁸For the mark of God is on the righteous that they may be saved. Famine, and sword, and pestilence [will be] far from the righteous, ⁹For they will flee away from the pious as men pursued in war; But they will pursue sinners and overtake [them], || And they that do lawlessness will not escape the judgment of God; As by enemies experienced [in war], they will be overtaken, ¹⁰For the mark of destruction is on their forehead. ¹¹And the inheritance of sinners is destruction and darkness, || And their iniquities will pursue them to Sheol beneath. ¹²Their inheritance will not be found of their children, ¹³For sins will lay waste the houses of sinners. And sinners will perish forever in the day of the LORD's judgment ¹⁴When God visits the earth with His judgment. ¹⁵But they that fear the LORD will find mercy therein, || And will live by the compassion of their God; But sinners will perish forever.

PSALM 16

¹A HYMN OF SOLOMON. FOR HELP TO THE PIOUS. When my soul slumbered, [being far] from the LORD, || I had all but slipped down to the pit || When [I was] far from God; ²My soul had been well nearly poured out to death—Near to the gates of Sheol with the sinner ³When my soul departed from the LORD God of Israel—Had the LORD not helped me with His everlasting mercy. ⁴He pricked me as a horse is pricked, that I might serve Him; My Savior and helper at all times saved me. ⁵I will give thanks to You, O God, for You have helped me to [my] salvation, || And have not counted me with sinners to [my] destruction. ⁶Do not remove Your mercy from me, O God, || Nor Your memorial from my heart until I die. ⁷Rule me, O God, [keeping me back] from wicked sin, || And from every wicked woman that causes the simple to stumble. ⁸And do not let the beauty of a lawless woman deceive me, || Nor anyone that is subject to unprofitable sin. ⁹Establish the works of my hands before You, || And preserve my goings in the remembrance of You. ¹⁰Protect my tongue and my lips with words of truth; Put anger and unreasoning wrath far from me. ¹¹Remove murmuring and impatience in affliction far from me || When, if I sin, You discipline me that I may return [to You]. ¹²But support my soul with goodwill and cheerfulness; When You strengthen my soul, what is given [to me] will be sufficient for me. ¹³For if You do not give strength, || Who can endure discipline with poverty? ¹⁴When a man is rebuked by means of his corruption, || Your testing [of him] is in his flesh and in the affliction of poverty. ¹⁵If the righteous endures in all these [trials], he will receive mercy from the LORD.

PSALM 17

¹A PSALM OF SOLOMON. WITH SONG. OF THE KING. O LORD, You are our King forever and ever, || For our soul glories in You, O God. ²How long are the days of man's life on the earth? As are his days, so is the hope [set] on him. ³But we hope in God, our deliverer; For the might of our God is forever with mercy, ⁴And the kingdom of our God is forever over the nations in judgment. ⁵You, O LORD, chose David [to be] king over Israel, || And swore to him touching his seed that never should his kingdom fail before You. ⁶But, for our sins, sinners rose up against us; They assailed us and thrust us out; What You had not promised to them, they took away [from us] with violence. ⁷They did not glorify Your honorable Name at all; They set a [worldly] monarchy in place of [that which was] their excellency; ⁸They laid waste the throne of David in tumultuous arrogance. But You, O God, cast them down and removed their seed from the earth, ⁹In that there rose up against them a man that was alien to our race. ¹⁰According to their sins You repaid them, O God, || So that it befell them according to their deeds. ¹¹God showed them no pity; He sought out their seed and does not let one of them go free. ¹²Faithful is the LORD in all His judgments || Which He does on the earth. ¹³The lawless one laid waste our land so that none inhabited it, || They destroyed young and old and their children together. ¹⁴In the heat of His anger He sent them away, even to the west, || And [He exposed] the rulers of the land unsparingly to derision. ¹⁵Being an alien the enemy acted proudly, || And his heart was alien from our God. ¹⁶And all things, [whatever he did in] Jerusalem, || As also the nations [in the cities to their gods]. ¹⁷And the children of the covenant in the midst of the mingled peoples [surpassed them in evil]. There was not among them one that worked in the midst of Jerusalem mercy and truth. ¹⁸They that loved the synagogues of the pious fled from them, || As sparrows that fly from their nest. ¹⁹They wandered in deserts that their lives might be saved from harm, || And precious in the eyes of them that lived abroad was any that escaped alive from them. ²⁰They were scattered over the whole earth by lawless [men]. ²¹For the heavens withheld the rain from dropping on the earth, || Springs were stopped perennially out of the deeps [that ran down] from lofty mountains; For there was none among them that worked righteousness and justice; From the chief of them to the least [of them]—all were sinful; ²²The king was a transgressor, and the judge disobedient, and the people sinful. ²³Behold, O LORD, and raise up to them their king, the Son of David, || At the time in which You see, O God, that He may reign over Your servant Israel; ²⁴And gird Him with strength, that He may shatter unrighteous rulers, ²⁵And that He may purge Jerusalem from nations that trample [her] down to destruction. ²⁶Wisely, righteously, He will thrust out sinners from [the] inheritance, || [And] will destroy the pride of the sinner as a potter's vessel. With a rod of iron, He will break in pieces all their substance; ²⁷He will destroy the godless nations with the word of His mouth; At His rebuke nations will flee before Him, || And He will reprove sinners for the thoughts of their heart. ²⁸And He will gather together a holy people, whom He will lead in righteousness, || And He will judge the tribes of the people that has been sanctified by the LORD His God. ²⁹And He will not permit unrighteousness to lodge any more in their midst, || Nor will there dwell with them any man that knows wickedness, ³⁰For He will know them, that they are all sons of their God. And He shall divide them according to their tribes on the land, ³¹And neither sojourner nor alien will sojourn with them any more. He will judge peoples and nations in the wisdom of His righteousness. Selah. ³²And He will have the heathen nations to serve Him under His yoke; And He will glorify the LORD in a place to be seen of all the earth; ³³And He will purge Jerusalem, making it holy as of old: ³⁴So that nations will come from the ends of the earth to see His glory, || Bringing as gifts her sons who had fainted, ³⁵And to see the glory of the LORD, with which God has glorified her. And He [will be] a righteous King, taught of God, over them, ³⁶And there will be no unrighteousness in His days in their midst, || For all will be holy and their King the anointed of the LORD. ³⁷For He will not put His trust in horse, and rider, and bow, || Nor will He multiply for Himself gold and silver for war, || Nor will He gather confidence from a multitude for the day of battle. ³⁸The LORD Himself is His King, the hope of him that is mighty through [his] hope in God. All nations [will be] in fear before Him, ³⁹For He will strike the earth with the word of His mouth forever. ⁴⁰He will bless the people of the LORD with wisdom and gladness, ⁴¹And He Himself [will be] pure from sin, so that He may rule a great people. He will rebuke rulers and remove sinners by the might of His word; ⁴²And [relying] on His God, throughout His days He will not stumble; For God will make Him mighty by means of [His] Holy Spirit, || And wise by means of the spirit of understanding, with strength and righteousness. ⁴³And the blessing of the LORD [will be] with Him; He will

be strong and not stumble; ⁴⁴His hope [will be] in the LORD: who then can prevail against Him? [He will be] mighty in His works, and strong in the fear of God; ⁴⁵[He will be] shepherding the flock of the LORD faithfully and righteously, || And will permit none among them to stumble in their pasture. ⁴⁶He will lead them all correctly, || And there will be no pride among them that any among them should be oppressed. ⁴⁷This [will be] the majesty of the King of Israel whom God knows; He will raise Him up over the house of Israel to correct him. ⁴⁸His words [will be] more refined than costly gold, the choicest; In the assemblies He will judge the peoples, the tribes of the sanctified. ⁴⁹His words [will be] like the words of the holy ones in the midst of sanctified peoples. ⁵⁰Blessed are they that will be in those days, || In that they will see the good fortune of Israel which God will bring to pass in the gathering together of the tribes. ⁵¹May the LORD hasten His mercy on Israel! May He deliver us from the uncleanness of unholy enemies! The LORD Himself is our King forever and ever.

PSALM 18

¹A PSALM OF SOLOMON. AGAIN OF THE ANOINTED OF THE LORD. LORD, Your mercy is over the works of Your hands forever; Your goodness is over Israel with a rich gift. ²Your eyes look on them, so that none of them suffers want; ³Your ears listen to the hopeful prayer of the poor. Your judgments [are executed] on the whole earth in mercy; ⁴And Your love [is] toward the seed of Abraham, the sons of Israel. Your discipline is on us as [on] a firstborn, only-begotten son, ⁵To turn back the obedient soul from folly [that is worked] in ignorance. ⁶May God cleanse Israel against the day of mercy and blessing, || Against the day of choice when He brings back His anointed. ⁷Blessed will they be that will be in those days, || In that they will see the goodness of the LORD which He will perform for the generation that is to come, ⁸Under the rod of disciplining of the LORD's anointed in the fear of his God, || In the spirit of wisdom and righteousness and strength; ⁹That he may direct [every} man in the works of righteousness by the fear of God, || That he may establish them all before the LORD— ¹⁰A good generation [living] in the fear of God in the days of mercy. Selah. ¹¹Great is our God and glorious, dwelling in the highest, ¹²Who has established the lights [of Heaven] in [their] courses for determining seasons from year to year, || And they have not turned aside from the way which He appointed them; ¹³In the fear of God [they pursue] their path every day, || From the day God created them and forevermore. ¹⁴And they have not erred since the day He created them. Since the generations of old they have not withdrawn from their path, || Unless God commanded them [to do so] by the command of His servants.

LIVES OF THE PROPHETS

Lives of the Prophets is a record of the lives and deaths of the significant Old Testament-era prophets. At least some of the material is very ancient, from the 1st century AD or earlier. The Apostle Paul may have been familiar with some of these accounts as reflected in the Pauline epistles.

THE NAMES OF THE PROPHETS, AND FROM WHERE THEY WERE, WHERE THEY DIED, AND HOW AND WHERE THEY WERE BURIED.

ISAIAH

¹He was of Jerusalem. He met his death at the hands of Manasseh, sawn in two, and was buried below the fountain of Rogel, hard by the conduit of the waters which Hezekiah spoiled [for the enemy] by blocking their course. ²For the prophet's sake God worked the miracle of Siloah; for before his death, in fainting condition he prayed for water, and it was sent to him from this source. Hence it was called Siloah, which means "sent." ³Also in the time of Hezekiah, before the king made the pools and the reservoirs, at the prayer of Isaiah a little water came forth here, lest the city, at that time besieged by the nations, should be destroyed through lack of water. ⁴For the enemies were seeking a drinking place, and as they surrounded the city, they encamped near Siloah. If then the Hebrews came to the pool, water flowed forth; if the nations came, there was none. Hence even to the present day the water issues suddenly, to keep the miracle in mind. ⁵Because this was worked through the prayer of Isaiah, the people in remembrance buried his body near the spot, with care and high honor, in order that through his prayers, even after his death, they might continue to have the benefit of the water. Indeed, a revelation had been given to them concerning him. ⁶His tomb, however, is near the Tomb of the Kings, behind the Tomb of the Priests on the side toward the south. ⁷Solomon constructed the tombs, which had been designed by David, on the east of Zion, where there is an entering road from Gibeon—the town twenty stadia distant from the city. He made a winding construction, its location unsuspected; even to the present day it is unknown to most of the priests, and wholly unknown to the people. ⁸There the king kept the gold and the spices from Ethiopia. ⁹When Hezekiah showed to the nations the secret of David and Solomon, and defiled the bones of his ancestors, therefore God laid on him the curse, that his descendants should be in servitude to their enemies; and God made him to be childless, from that day.

JEREMIAH

¹He was of Anathoth, and he died in Taphnes in Egypt, stoned to death by the Jews. ²He is buried in the place where Pharaoh's palace stood; for the Egyptians held him in honor, because of the benefit which they had received through him. ³For at his prayer, the serpents which the Egyptians call "ephoth" departed from them; ⁴and even at the present day the faithful servants of God pray on that spot, and taking of the dust of the place they heal the bites of serpents. ⁵We have been told by the children of Antigonus and Ptolemy, aged men, that Alexander the Macedonian, when he stood at the place where the prophet was buried, and learned of the wonders which he had worked, carried away his bones to Alexandria, placing them around with due ceremony; ⁶immediately the whole race of poisonous serpents was driven out of the land. With like purpose he had introduced into Egypt the so-called "serpent fighters." ⁷Jeremiah also gave a sign to the priests of Egypt, that their idols would be shaken and their gods made with hands would all collapse, when there should arrive in Egypt a virgin bearing a Child of divine appearance. ⁸For what reason even to the present time they honor a virgin mother, and placing a baby in a manger they bow down to it. When Ptolemy the king sought the reason for this, they said to him, "It is a mystery handed down from our fathers, a sign delivered to them by a holy prophet, and we are awaiting its fulfillment." ⁹This prophet, before the destruction of the temple, took possession of the Ark of the Law and the things within it, and caused them to be swallowed up in a rocky cliff, and he said to those who were present, ¹⁰"The LORD departed from Sinai into Heaven, and He will again come with might; and this will be for you the sign of His appearance: when all the nations worship a piece of wood." ¹¹He also said, "No one will bring forth this Ark but Aaron, and the tablets within it no one of the priests or prophets will unfold but Moses the chosen one of God." ¹²And in the resurrection the Ark will rise first, and come forth from the rock, and will be placed on Mount Sinai; and all the saints will be assembled to it there, awaiting the LORD and fleeing from the enemy wishing to destroy them. ¹³He sealed in the rock with his finger the Name of God, and the

writing was as though carved with iron. A cloud then covered the Name; and no one knows the place, nor can the writing be read, to the present day and even to the end. ¹⁴The rock is in the wilderness where the Ark was at first, between the two mountains on which Moses and Aaron are buried, and by night there is a cloud as it were of fire, according to the primal ordinance that the glory of God should never cease from His law. ¹⁵And God gave the favor of completing this wonder to Jeremiah, so that he might be the associate of Moses, and they are together to this day.

EZEKIEL

¹He was from the district of Sarira, of the priests; and he died in the land of Chaldea, in the time of the captivity, after uttering many prophecies to those who were in Judea. ²He was slain by the leader of the Israelite exiles, who had been rebuked by him for his worship of idols; ³and they buried him in the field of Nahor, in the tomb of Shem and Arphaxad, the ancestors of Abraham. ⁴The tomb is a double cave, according to whose plan Abraham also made the tomb of Sarah in Hebron. ⁵It is called "double" because it has a winding [stairway] and there is an upper chamber hidden from the main floor, hung in the rock above the ground-level. ⁶This prophet gave a sign to the people, that they should pay attention to the River Chebar; ⁷when its waters should fail, they were to expect "the sickle of desolation to the ends of the earth"; when it should overflow, the return to Jerusalem. ⁸While the saint was dwelling there, many kept coming to him; ⁹and on one occasion, when a throng had assembled to him, the Chaldeans feared an uprising and came on them to destroy them. ¹⁰He made the water cease its flow, so that they could flee to the other side, but when the enemy ventured to pursue, they were drowned. ¹¹Through his prayer he provided for them ample sustenance in fish which came of their own accord to be caught. Many who were at the point of death he cheered with the news of life coming to them from God. ¹²When the people were being destroyed by the enemy, he went to the hostile captains and so terrified them with marvels which he worked that they ceased. ¹³It was then that he said to the people, "Are we indeed perishing? Is our hope at an end?" And by the vision of the dry bones he persuaded them that there is hope for Israel both now and in the time to come. ¹⁴While he was there, he showed to the people of Israel what was being done in Jerusalem and in the temple. ¹⁵He himself was borne away there, and came to Jerusalem, for a rebuke to the faithless. ¹⁶Also after the manner of Moses he foresaw the fashion of the temple, with its walls and its broad surroundings, as Daniel also declared that it should be built. ¹⁷He pronounced judgment in Babylon on the tribes of Dan and Gad, because they dealt wickedly against the LORD, ¹⁸persecuting those who were keeping the law; and he worked on them this grievous wonder, that their children and all their cattle should be killed by serpents. ¹⁹He also foretold, that because of their sin Israel would not return to its land but would remain in Media, until the end of this evildoing. ²⁰One of their number was the man who slew Ezekiel, for they opposed him all the days of his life.

DANIEL

¹He was of the tribe of Judah, of a prominent family in the service of the king; but in his childhood he was carried away from Judea to the land of Chaldea. ²He was born in Upper Beth-Horon. In his manhood he was chaste, so that the Jews thought he [was] a eunuch. ³He mourned greatly over the city, and in fasting abstained from every sort of delicious food. He was lean and haggard in the eyes of men, but beautiful in the grace of the Most High. ⁴He made great supplication in behalf of Nebuchadnezzar, whose son Belshazzar implored him for aid at the time when the king became a beast of the field, lest he should perish. ⁵For his head and foreparts were those of an ox, his legs and hinder parts those of a lion. ⁶The meaning of this marvel was revealed to the prophet: the king became a beast because of his self-indulgence and his stubbornness. ⁷It is the manner of tyrants that in their youth they come under the yoke of Satan; in their latter years they become wild beasts, snatching, destroying, striking, and slaying. ⁸The prophet knew by divine revelation that the king was eating grass like an ox, and that it became for him the food of a human being. ⁹Therefore it was that Nebuchadnezzar himself, recovering human reason when digestion was completed, used to weep and implore the LORD, praying forty times each day and night. ¹⁰Then the mind of a dumb animal would [again] take possession of him and he would forget that he had been a human being. ¹¹His tongue had lost the power of speech; when he understood his condition he wept, and his eyes were like raw flesh from his weeping. ¹²There were many who went out from the city to see him; Daniel alone had no wish to see him, but during all the time of his transformation he was in prayer for him. ¹³He declared that the king would be restored to human form, but they did not believe him. ¹⁴Daniel caused the seven years to become seven months. ¹⁵The mystery of the seven times was fulfilled on the king, for in seven months he was restored, and in the [remaining] six years and five months he was doing penance to the LORD and confessing his wickedness. When his sin had been forgiven, the kingdom was given back to him. ¹⁶He ate neither bread nor flesh in the time of his conversion, for Daniel had bid him to eat pulse and greens while appeasing the LORD. ¹⁷The king named the prophet Belshazzar because he wished to make him a joint heir with his children, ¹⁸but the holy man said, "Far be it from me to forsake the heritage of my fathers and join in the inheritances of the uncircumcised." ¹⁹He also did for the other Persian kings many wonderful things which were not written down. ²⁰He died there, and was buried with great honor, by himself, in the royal grave. ²¹He appointed a sign in the mountains which are above Babylon: WHEN THE MOUNTAIN ON THE NORTH WILL SMOKE, THE END OF BABYLON WILL COME; WHEN IT WILL BURN AS WITH FIRE, THE END OF ALL THE EARTH WILL BE AT HAND. IF THE MOUNTAIN ON THE SOUTH WILL FLOW WITH WATER, ISRAEL WILL RETURN TO ITS LAND; IF IT WILL RUN BLOOD, IT PORTENDS A SLAUGHTER BROUGHT BY SATAN ON ALL THE EARTH. ²²And the holy prophet slept in peace.

HOSEA

¹He was from Belemoth, of the tribe of Issachar, and he was buried in peace, in his own land. ²He gave a sign that the LORD would come to the earth when the oak tree which is in Shiloh should of its own accord be divided and become twelve oaks.

MICAH

¹He was of the tribe of Ephraim. Having given much trouble to King Ahab, he was killed, thrown from a cliff, by Ahab's son Joram, because he rebuked him for the wickedness of his fathers. ²He was given solitary burial in his own land, near the burying place of the giants.

AMOS

¹He was from Tekoa. Amaziah [the priest of Bethel] had often beaten him, and at last Amaziah's son killed him with a cudgel, striking him on the temple. ²While still living he made his way to his land, and after some days died and was buried there.

JOEL

¹He was from the territory of Reuben, of the field of Beth-Meon. He died in peace and was buried there.

OBADIAH

¹He was from the region of Shechem, of the field of Beth-Hakkerem. ²He was a pupil of Elijah, and having done much in his service he was saved from death by him. ³He was that third captain of fifty whom Elijah spared, and went down with him to Ahaziah. ⁴Afterward, leaving the service of the king he became a prophet, and on his death he was buried with his fathers.

JONAH

¹He was from the district of Kiriath-Maon, near the nation city of Azotus on the sea. ²After he had been cast on shore by the whale and had made his journey to Nineveh, on his return he did not stay in his own land, but took his mother and settled in Tyre, a country of foreign peoples. ³For he said, "In this way I will take away my reproach, that I prophesied falsely against the great city Nineveh." ⁴Elijah was at that time rebuking the house of Ahab, and having called a famine on the land he fled. Coming to the region of Tyre he found the widow and her son, for he himself could not lodge with the uncircumcised. ⁵He brought her a blessing; and when her child died, God raised him from the dead through Elijah, for he wished to show him that it is not possible to flee from God. ⁶After the famine was over, Jonah came into

LIVES OF THE PROPHETS

the land of Judea. On the way there his mother died, and he buried her beside the oak of Deborah. ⁷Thereafter having settled in the land of Seir, he died there and was buried in the tomb of the Kenizzite, the first who became judge in the days when there was no king. ⁸He gave a sign to Jerusalem and to all the land: When they should see a stone crying aloud in distress, the end would be at hand; and when they should see all the nations gathered in Jerusalem, the city would be razed to its foundations.

NAHUM

¹He was of Elkosh, on the other side of the mountains toward Beth-Gabrin, of the tribe of Simeon. ²This prophet after the time of Jonah gave a sign to Nineveh, that it would be destroyed by fresh waters and by underground fire; and indeed, this came to pass. ³For the lake which surrounded the city overwhelmed it in an earthquake, and fire coming from the desert burned its upper portion. ⁴He died in peace and was buried in his land.

HABAKKUK

¹He was from the tribe of Simeon, of the field of Beth-Zechariah. ²Before the captivity he had a vision of the destruction of Jerusalem, and he grieved exceedingly. ³When Nebuchadnezzar came against Jerusalem, he fled to Ostracina [in Egypt], and then sojourned in the land of Ishmael. ⁴When the Chaldeans returned [to their country], and all those who were left in Jerusalem went down to Egypt, he settled again in his own land. ⁵He was accustomed to carry food to the reapers of the harvest in his field; ⁶and one day, as he received the food, he announced to his family: "I am off for a far country, but will return immediately; if I should delay, carry out the food to the reapers." ⁷Finding himself immediately in Babylon, and having given Daniel his meal, he stood by the reapers as they ate; and he told no one what had happened. ⁸He had knowledge that the people would soon come back from Babylon. ⁹Two years before the return he died and was buried alone in his own field. ¹⁰He gave a sign to the people in Judea, that they would see in the temple a light shining, and thus they would know the glory of the sanctuary. ¹¹Concerning the end of the temple, he foretold that it would be brought to pass by a western nation. ¹²Then, he said, the veil of the inner sanctuary will be torn to pieces, and the capitals of the two pillars will be taken away, ¹³and no one will know where they are; but they will be carried away by messengers into the wilderness where in the beginning the Tent of Witness was pitched. ¹⁴In the end, the presence of the LORD will be made known by them, for they will give light to those who are pursued by the Serpent in darkness as at the beginning.

ZEPHANIAH

¹He was of the tribe of Simeon, of the field of Sabaratha. ²He prophesied concerning the city, also concerning the end of the nations and the confounding of the wicked. ³When he died, he was buried in his own field.

HAGGAI

¹Probably as a youth he came from Babylon to Jerusalem, and he had prophesied publicly in regard to the return of the people. ²He witnessed the building of the temple in part. On his death he was buried near the tomb of the priests, honored as though one of their number.

ZECHARIAH SON OF IDDO

¹He came from Chaldea when already advanced in age. While there, he often prophesied to the people, and did wonders in proof of his authority. ²He foretold to Jozadak that he would beget a son who would serve as priest in Jerusalem; ³he also congratulated Shealtiel on the birth of a son and gave him the name Zerubbabel. ⁴In the time of Cyrus he gave the king a sign of victory and foretold the service which he was destined to perform for Jerusalem, and he praised him greatly. ⁵His prophecies uttered in Jerusalem had to do with the end of the nations, with Israel and the temple, with the laziness of prophets and priests, and with a double judgment. ⁶After reaching great age he was taken sick, and dying, was buried beside Haggai.

MALACHI

¹He was born in Sopha, after the return from the exile. ²Even in his boyhood he lived a blameless life, and since all the people paid him honor for his piety and his mildness, they called him "Malachi"; he was also fair to look on. ³Moreover, whatever things he uttered in prophecy were repeated on that same day by a messenger of God who appeared, as had happened in the days when there was no king in Israel, as is written in the scroll of Judges. ⁴While yet in his youth, he was joined to his fathers in his own field.

NATHAN

¹He, David's prophet, was from Gibeon, of a Hivite clan, and it was he who taught the king the Law of the LORD. ²He foresaw David's sin with Bathsheba, and set out in haste to warn him, but Belial thwarted his attempt. He found the naked body of a man who had been slain lying by the road; ³and while he was detained by this duty, he knew that in that night the king had committed the sin; ⁴so he turned back to Gibeon in sorrow. Then when David caused the death of Bathsheba's husband, the LORD sent Nathan to convict him. ⁵He lived to an advanced old age, and when he died, he was buried in his own land.

AHIJAH

¹He was from Shiloh, the city of Eli, where the Dwelling Place stood in days of old. ²He declared of Solomon that he would provoke the LORD to anger. ³He also rebuked Jeroboam, because he dealt treacherously with the LORD, and he had a vision of two bullocks trampling on the people and charging on the priests. ⁴He foretold to Solomon that his wives would bring disgrace on him and all his house. ⁵On his death he was buried beside the oak of Shiloh.

JOED

¹He was of the district of Samarim. He was that prophet whom the lion attacked and slew, when he had rebuked Jeroboam concerning the bullocks— ²he who was buried in Bethel beside the false prophet who led him astray.

AZARIAH

¹He was from Subatha, the prophet who turned away from Judah the captivity that befell Israel. ²His burial was in his own field.

ZECHARIAH SON OF JEHOIADA

¹He was of Jerusalem, the son of Jehoiada the priest, the prophet whom Joash king of Judah slew beside the altar, whose blood the house of David shed within the sanctuary, in the court. The priests buried him beside his father. ²From that time on there were portentous appearances in the temple, and the priests could see no vision of messengers of God, nor give forth oracles from the inner sanctuary; nor were they able to inquire with the ephod, nor to give answer to the people by Lights and Perfections, as in former time.

ELIJAH

¹He was a Tishbite, from the land of the Arabs, of the family of Aaron, residing in Gilead because Tishbi had been assigned to the priests. ²At the time of his birth his father, Shobach, saw how certain men of shining white appearance addressed the baby, and that they wrapped him in swaddling clothes of fire and gave him a flame of fire to eat. ³When he went and reported this in Jerusalem, the oracle gave answer: "Do not fear; for his dwelling will be light, and his word revelation, and he will judge Israel with sword and with fire."

ELISHA

¹He was from Abel-Meholah, of the territory of Reuben. ²When he was born in Gilgal, a marvelous thing happened: the golden calf bellowed so loudly that the shrill sound was heard in Jerusalem; ³and the priest announced by Lights and Perfections that a prophet had been born to Israel who should destroy their graven and molten idols. ⁴On his death he was buried in Samaria.

WORDS OF GAD THE SEER

The Words of Gad the Seer is a record missing from the biblical canon but mentioned in 1 Chronicles 29:29. Gad was a prophet who operated contemporaneously with King David and the prophet Nathan (1 Sam. 22:5). The translation here provided is from a likely pseudepigraphic book by the same title, extant in the form of a manuscript from the Cochin Jews of India. While the extant manuscript shows features of medieval Kabbalistic thought, recent scholarship suggests the work, in its primal form, originated in the 1st or 2nd century AD, perhaps based on even older material; and the work is clearly Messianic in nature, pointing to the person and work of Christ, even His substitutionary sacrifice and reign (Ch. 1). Chapter 2 is an excoriating rebuke of the replacement theology and self-righteousness of Rome. The rest of the book is a collection of narratives involving King David and his son Solomon. There are also several psalms.

CHAPTER 1

¹In the thirty-first year of King David's reign in Jerusalem, which is the thirty-eighth year of David's reign, the word of the LORD came to Gad the Seer in the month of Iyar, near the stream of the Kidron Valley, saying, ²"Thus says the LORD: Go, be courageous, and stand in the midst of the stream, and cry with a great voice: Tarry and hasten, tarry and hasten, tarry and hasten! For there is still a vision for the son of Jesse. ³And during the cry, face the Eastern Gate on the east side of the city, and stretch forth your hands toward heaven." ⁴And I did exactly what I had been commanded to do. ⁵And it came to pass when I finished crying out, I opened my eyes and saw a yoke of oxen, led by a donkey and a camel, coming up from the Brook of Kidron, the donkey on the right side of the yoke and the camel on the left. ⁶And a great voice like the roll of thunder was following them, crying with a bitter voice: ⁷"Seer, seer, seer! These are four mixtures that confuse the people of the LORD. ⁸For the impure and the pure have been mixed, and then impurity took control over purity; a mixture from Seir [(Edom)] to rule over them, ⁹to increase power over, and betray, a righteous doer, ¹⁰to destroy holiness, to crown wickedness, to set up impure matters in the guise of purity." ¹¹And after the voice, a great shaking occurred that shook over the impurity and blew the donkey and the camel into the moon with a stormy wind. ¹²And the moon was opened and looked like a bow, a semicircle, and both her points reached toward the ground. ¹³And behold, the sun came out of heaven in the shape of a man, with a crown on his head, carrying a Lamb over his right shoulder, despised and rejected. ¹⁴And on the crown on his head three shepherds are seen, shackled with twelve shackles, ¹⁵and these shackles were of gold, plated with silver. And the voice of the Lamb was heard, great and dreadful like the voice of a lion roaring over his prey: "Woe to Me! Woe to Me! Woe to Me! My image has been diminished, || My refuge has been lost, || My lot and destiny has turned Me over to My spoilers, || And I was defiled until evening by the touch of impurity." ¹⁶And it came to pass when the voice of the Lamb ceased speaking, behold, a Man dressed in linen came with three vine-branches and twelve palms in His hand. ¹⁷And He took the Lamb from the hand of the sun and put the crown on His head, and the vine-branches and palms on His heart. ¹⁸And the Man, dressed in linen, cried like a ram's horn, saying, "What are you doing here, impurity, and how did you get here, impurity, ¹⁹that you have carved yourself a place to combine impurity with My covenant that I have set with the vine-branches and palms?" ²⁰And I heard the Lamb's Shepherd saying, "There is a place with Me for the pure, but not for the impure, for I am a holy God, and I do not want the impure, I only want the pure; ²¹even though I created them both, and My eyes are equally on them both. ²²But there is an advantage to the abundance of purity over the abundance of impurity, just like there is an advantage of a man over a shadow. ²³For the shadow does not exist without man, and only by the man's existence is the shadow given to the tired and exhausted; this applies in the same way to the pure and impure. ²⁴For all gates of intelligence are turned around since the death of the eight branches of the vine. ²⁵As is found in words of righteousness in the true scroll, but because of the wanderings of the sheep, their rest, and divisions, ²⁶intelligence is stopped up until I do greatly in keeping grace." ²⁷I saw that impurity was driven from the moon and was given over to a consuming wrath, ground into fine dust, and blown away by the daily wind. ²⁸And the day burns as a furnace to remove impurity and to erase the transgressions. ²⁹And the Lamb was put on the moon forever and ever. ³⁰And the Lamb took from the pure the impurity that had been mixed with them and brought it as a peace-offering sacrifice on the altar before God Almighty, zealous LORD of Hosts. ³¹And I heard those singing the song of the Lamb, saying, ³²"I will give thanks to You, O LORD, || For though You were angry with me, You forgave. ³³For the LORD is my strength and song, || And He has become my Redeemer. ³⁴I will sing to the LORD, || For He is highly exalted; He had thrown the horse and his rider into the Sea of Reeds. ³⁵Arise, intelligence; Arise, power; Arise, kingship; ³⁶Arise, majesty and glory; Arise help of the LORD. ³⁷For God has saved one who had taken away || And obliterated the impurity from the earth. ³⁸He fought my fight || And brought into the light my righteousness by His help. ³⁹My help comes from the Lord || Who made heaven and earth. ⁴⁰Truly, who is like You, || Glorious in holiness, but not in impurity? ⁴¹For You are great over all; Raised over all; You spoke and acted. ⁴²For You declared the end from the beginning, || And You sealed everything by Your words || And turned my heart and convicted me. ⁴³For Your seal is on me, my Lord, || And these are three vine-branches and twelve palms that are on my heart. ⁴⁴You glorified me, || You erased the vanity of fearing man, || And You gave me a pure heart forever. ⁴⁵For that I will praise You at all times, || And thank You among the nations, || For You have greatly redeemed me for my king || And showed favor to the Chosen One, David's seed, || Forever and ever." ⁴⁶And I heard a voice crying from Heaven, saying, ⁴⁷"You are My Son, You are My firstborn, You are My first-fruits. ⁴⁸Have I not brought You up from the Brook of Egypt wholeheartedly to be My daily delight? ⁴⁹But You have given My gifts and dressed up the impure with the pure, and that is why all these things have happened to You. ⁵⁰And who is like to You among all the creatures on earth? For they lived in Your shadow and by Your wounds they were healed. ⁵¹For consider well that which is before You. ⁵²Because You have fulfilled the words of the Shepherd all the days You have been in the sun and You did not leave them; therefore, all this honor will be Yours." ⁵³And I, Gad, son of Ahimelech of the Jabez family, of the tribe of Judah, son of Israel, was amazed by the vision and could not settle my spirit. ⁵⁴And the One dressed in linen came down to me and touched me, saying, "Write these words and seal them with the seal of truth, for YHWH is My Name, and with My Name you will bless the whole house of Israel, for they are of a true seed. ⁵⁵In a little while you will go, and be quietly gathered to your fathers, but at the end of days you will see with your own eyes all these things, not as a vision, but in reality. ⁵⁶For in those days they will not be called Jacob, but Israel; for no iniquity will be found in their remnant, for they will entirely belong to the LORD. ⁵⁷And these words will restore your life and spirit. And this will be the sign to you: when you enter the town, you will find My servant David while he is reading these words from the Scroll of [the] Covenant: ⁵⁸And yet for all that, when they are in the land of their enemies, I will not reject them, neither will I abhor them, to utterly destroy them, and to break My covenant with them; for I am the LORD their God. ⁵⁹And you will tell him about the scene you have just seen; and when he sees you, he will be glad in his heart." ⁶⁰And it came to pass, when I came to the house of David, the man of God, I found him as the One dressed in linen had said, and I told him of all

my visions. ⁶¹Then David spoke the words of this song to the LORD, saying, "I love You, O LORD, my strength." ⁶²And to me he said, "The LORD has blessed you and has not removed His covenant from you, for He is true, and His word is true, and His seal is true."

CHAPTER 2

¹After these true things, I had a vision from God, saying, ²"Set your face eastward, northward, southward, and westward. ³And whistle with your mouth as a bird whistles to its young, and say, Four corners of the earth, listen to the word of the LORD! ⁴Thus says the LORD, who sits and dwells over the cherubim: Give, give, give, take out, take out, take out My seed that I have sown in you, for the time for the seed has come. ⁵For yet a little while I will collect My seed on My threshing-floor. ⁶And the threshing-floor will be holy; an impure seed will not be found there. ⁷Prior to those days My seed was mixed with lentils, and barley, and fitches, beans, and gourds. ⁸And in the end of days the sower will be true, and the seed will be true, and from the seed all the land will be blessed. ⁹Be joyful and glad, remnant of Judah and rejected of Israel, for salvation is with the LORD. ¹⁰As you will be a curse and blasphemy to all the families of the earth, so you will be a blessing and grace forever. ¹¹At that time no cursed or unholy people will be found among you, ¹²for everyone will join you in the covenant, the Law, testimonies, statutes, and ordinances. ¹³And you and they will have one God, one covenant, one law, one language, for all will speak in the language of Hebrew, the holy language. ¹⁴Blessed are you, O Israel, who is like to you? A people saved by the LORD, for He will go before you to fight your wars with your enemies. ¹⁵Woe to you, O Edom, that sits in the land of Kittim in the north of the sea. ¹⁶For your destroyers will emerge from a terrible nation. They will not even leave you a remnant. ¹⁷For you have said: I sit on high, and I alone have a covenant with the God of gods, for the LORD chose me instead of His holy people, for He abhorred them. ¹⁸And His former people, despised and rejected, did not truly know the LORD because they did not know His image [(the Son)]. ¹⁹We are truly wise and intelligent; we know the LORD and His law, we know His image and presence. ²⁰But thus says the LORD: Because you rose up in pride to brag about the God of gods, know that you will perish in your conceitedness. ²¹For why would you put confidence in man, whose life is like a vapor, which begins in the morning, and is gone by noon-day, placing him to sit beside Me. ²²For it is not you whom I knew formerly, and where is the bill of divorce of My people, that you said would be a prey; show it to Me! ²³Your corpses will fall among My people. ²⁴O zealous LORD, come out; come out of Your place and smite Edom; consume them. ²⁵Come to Zerephath, come to Sepharad, come to Ashkenaz, come to Garmania; they will come and fall in the lowest pit, in destruction, and in the shadow of death, for your mouth will fail you, and no one will help you. ²⁶At the end of days Michael the great prince will stand up in war like a whirlwind against Samael the prince of this world to put him under his feet, in the wind of the LORD, and it will be eaten up; for the LORD has spoken it. ²⁷At the end of days the robbed will overcome the robber, and the weak, the strong, truly and in righteousness. ²⁸Your God is your Savior, O Israel; with Him you will be saved, for He is a merciful God. He will not abandon you, ²⁹for you will keep on doing all that I commanded you in the Law of My servant Moses."

CHAPTER 3

¹When the feast of Passover came, on the fifteenth of the first month, a Moabite shepherd came to David and talked with him, saying, "My lord the king, you have known that I, your servant, have been loyal to Israel from my youth, and now take me away from dwelling among uncircumcised people and circumcise the flesh of my foreskin to take away my reproach, so that I can sit among your people." ²And David said, "The LORD does not want your people, and He commanded: An Ammonite or a Moabite will not enter into the assembly of the LORD forever. And we cannot seek your peace nor your prosperity, but how can I help you today?" ³The servant answered, "Is it not true that Ruth was of our people, and you are one of her children and descendants, and the LORD has chosen you and your descendants forever?" ⁴Then he said, "You have given a convincing argument. Stand here with me to ask from the mouth of my Lord." ⁵And David asked the LORD about the statement of the Moabite servant. ⁶And David said, "O LORD, LORD of Hosts, teach me wondrous things out of Your law so that I may know how to rule for this servant, and what should be done with him." ⁷And the LORD said to Nathan the prophet, "Go to My servant David and tell him the message that I tell you." ⁸And Nathan went to David, to his chambers, saying, "This is what the LORD of Hosts says: I have heard your prayer, so tell the Moabite: You are a Moabite man, not a Moabite woman, for I never said, a Moabite woman, and, an Ammonite woman, because their women and daughters belong to the LORD; however, you are cursed by the LORD, and forbidden to enter the LORD's assembly." ⁹When the Moabite heard the message of the LORD, he cried out and exclaimed: "I am forbidden from entering the assembly of the LORD!" ¹⁰And the king took him and appointed him a shepherd among David's shepherds, and he was there until the third year of the reign of King Solomon, then he died. ¹¹And he had a daughter whose name was Sephirah; she had a beautiful form and was very fair to look on. King Solomon took her to be his concubine, and she found grace and favor in his sight more than all the other concubines, and she became the chief of the concubines' residence. ¹²And this became the statute in Israel forever.

CHAPTER 4

¹In those days a man from Beth-Lehem, the city of David, went to Jerusalem to pay the vow which he had vowed to the LORD. His name was Zabad the Parhi, and he was of the family of the Perezites. ²Zabad's father was very sick, even to the point of death, so Zabad vowed: "When the LORD heals my father of his sickness, I will weigh out two talents of silver and give them to the House of the LORD, into the hand of King David." ³And it came to pass, when he was at the house of the shepherds along the way, he lost the pouch with the money in it and he was upset. ⁴He came to the city of Jerusalem, into the inner city, and he wrote on all the gates these words: ⁵"ANYONE WHO FINDS A LOST POUCH WITH TWO TALENTS OF SILVER AND BRINGS IT TO ME I WILL GIVE HIM A TALENT OF SILVER AS A REWARD." ⁶After a while, a man from the tribe of Dan came and had in his hand the pouch with the silver talents that he found along the way and he gave it to the owner of the pouch. ⁷And the Danite said to Zabad, "Give me the talent of silver as you promised." ⁸And Zabad said, "No, there were actually three talents in my pouch, and you have already stolen one talent; I mistakenly wrote down the wrong number." ⁹So both of them came and stood before the king. ¹⁰And the king said to Zabad, "Swear to me by the LORD that you truly had three talents of silver in your pouch." And Zabad swore to him by the LORD. ¹¹And the king continued, saying to the Danite, "Swear to me by the LORD that you only found two talents of silver in the pouch." And he swore to him by the LORD. ¹²And David said to Zabad, "Give the pouch with the talents back to the Danite, because this is his money that the LORD has given to him by chance. ¹³Now, go and write on the city gates: WHOEVER FINDS THE POUCH WITH THREE TALENTS SHOULD BRING IT TO ME, because this is not your pouch." ¹⁴And David took the pouch with the talents of silver from the hand of Zabad and gave it to the Danite. ¹⁵And the Danite bowed his head, and prostrated himself to the earth, and said, "Long live my lord, King David, forever." ¹⁶And all Israel heard of this judgment, and they marveled over David and were overjoyed, because they saw that he was full of the wisdom of God.

CHAPTER 5

¹All the Philistines assembled themselves together to fight against Israel. There were so many multitudes of Philistines that they could not be numbered. ²And David was greatly distressed because he was afraid of the Philistines. ³And the LORD said to Gad, "Go and tell My servant David: Do not be worried about these uncircumcised Philistines, because tomorrow I will give them, and those other oppressors with them, into your hand." ⁴And David said to Gad, "I am not worthy of all the mercies that the LORD has shown to me, but blessed be the Name of the LORD forever and ever." ⁵That night a fire-messenger came from Heaven with his drawn sword in his hand ⁶and he attacked the camp of the uncircumcised. It was such a great slaughter that none of them were left alive. ⁷And it came to pass the next morning, they came to David, saying, "Behold, all the Philistines have been

killed by someone who rose up against them; not a single one of them was left alive." ⁸And David raised his voice and said, "Now I know that nothing can hinder the Lord. He can save us from many or few, and His salvation can be in a blink of an eye." ⁹And he said, "Blessed are You, O Lord, who has been taking revenge for us on our enemies." ¹⁰And he set up a pillar and called it the "Pillar of Revenge" to this day.

CHAPTER 6

¹The Lord said to Gad, "Go tell My servant David, ²Thus says the Lord: Do not let the mighty man glory in his might. ³But let him that glories glory in this, that My help is with him. ⁴Then you should go and not fear, for the Lord is with you." ⁵And Gad came and told David what the Lord had said. ⁶And David said to Gad, "I have known the help of the Lord from my youth. ⁷For who struck down the lion and the bear? Who destroyed the Philistines? Who destroyed my enemies? Was it not by the help of God?" ⁸And when the Lord heard that, He was very pleased with David's heart. ⁹And He said, "Because David has acknowledged My help instead of his own glory, My help will dwell in the house of David forever." ¹⁰And Gad told David what the Lord said. ¹¹And David bowed down before the Lord and said, "Blessed be the Lord, for I have found favor in His eyes."

CHAPTER 7

¹And again the anger of the Lord was kindled against Israel ²and He moved Satan against David, saying, "Go, number Israel and Judah," to bring them the evil He spoke through Samuel the seer. ³And the king said to Joab the captain and to the princes of the people: "Go now through all the tribes of Israel, from Dan even to Beersheba, and number the people, and bring me word [so] that I may know the sum of them." ⁴And Joab said to the king, "May the Lord add to the people howsoever many they may be, a hundredfold, and may the eyes of the Lord our God watch over them; but, my lord the king, are they not all my lord's servants? Why does my lord require this thing? And why should it be a cause of trespass to Israel? For the Lord has said: Which cannot be numbered for the multitude." ⁵Notwithstanding, the king's word prevailed against Joab and against the captains of the host. And Joab and the captains of the host went from the presence of the king to number the people of Israel. ⁶And they passed over the Jordan, and camped in Aroer, south of the town in the middle of the river of Gad, and toward Jazer. ⁷And they came to Gilead, and then to the land of the Hittites, to Kadesh, and they came to Dan and Enan, and around to Zidon. ⁸And they came to the stronghold of Tyre, and to all the cities of the Hivites and the Canaanites. And they went out to the south of Judah, to Beersheba. ⁹So when they had gone through all the land, they came to Jerusalem at the end of nine months and twenty days. But Joab did not number Levi and Benjamin, for the king's word was abominable to Joab. ¹⁰And Joab gave up the sum of the number of the people to David. And all they of Israel were eight hundred thousand valiant men and three hundred thousand men that drew a sword, and in Judah there were four hundred and seventy thousand valiant men and thirty thousand men that drew a sword. ¹¹And the Lord God was displeased with this act of Israel, and He sent Gad the seer to David, saying, ¹²"Thus said the Lord: I am the King of Israel, and I am their Portion; I am their Avenger, I am their Fortress and Might; and you know that it is not with a sword or a spear that I will save, and not with a man of valiance that draws a sword, for this is the portion of the heathens that stand on their might and many warriors. ¹³But you are not like that, for I am a lone warrior and there is no one with Me. Why would you do this evil to number your people? For that, I will strike Israel, so that you will know that I am the Lord in the midst of the earth." ¹⁴And David's heart was grieved after that. And David said to the Lord, "I have sinned greatly in what I have done; but now, O Lord, I beg You, take away the iniquity of Your servant, for I have acted very foolishly." ¹⁵And David rose up in the morning, and the word of the Lord had already come to Gad the prophet, David's seer, saying, ¹⁶"Go and say to David: Thus says the Lord: I offer you three things—choose one of them [so] that I may do it to you." ¹⁷So Gad came to David and told him, and said to him, "Will four years of famine come to the land of Israel and three years in the land of Judah? Or will you flee three months before your adversaries while they pursue you, while the sword of your enemies overtakes you? Or will there be three days of the sword of the Lord, which is pestilence, in your land, and the messenger of the Lord destroying throughout all the land of Israel? Now advise yourself, and decide what answer I will return to Him who sent me." ¹⁸And David said to Gad, "I am in a great strait; let me fall, and let us fall now, into the hand of the Lord, for His mercies are great; and let me not fall into the hand of man." ¹⁹So the Lord sent a pestilence on Israel, from the morning even to the time appointed; and there died of the people from Dan even to Beersheba seventy thousand men. ²⁰And God sent a messenger to Jerusalem to destroy it; and as he was destroying it, the Lord beheld, and He relented Himself of the calamity, and said to the messenger that was destroying the people: "It is enough; now stay your hand." And the messenger of the Lord was standing by the threshing-floor of Ornan the Jebusite. ²¹And David lifted up his eyes and saw the messenger of the Lord standing between the heaven and the earth, having a drawn sword in his hand stretched out over Jerusalem. And David and the elders, who were clothed in sackcloth, fell on their faces. ²²And David said to God, "Is it not I that commanded the people to be numbered? Even I it is that have sinned and acted wickedly; but these sheep, what have they done? O Lord my God, let Your hand be against me and against my father's house, but not against Your people, that they should be plagued. Will not the Judge of all the earth do justice?" ²³And the Lord said, "They incited Satan against you to number them, saying thus: We will be like all the nations; but I am a God of justice; may I return their high heart into their own bosoms. ²⁴For a broken or a contrite heart I will not despise forever." ²⁵And the messenger of the Lord told Gad to tell David that David should go up and rear an altar to the Lord on the threshing-floor of Ornan the Jebusite. ²⁶And David went up according to the words of Gad which he spoke in the Name of the Lord. ²⁷And Ornan was looking, and he saw the king and his four sons with him. Now Ornan was threshing wheat. ²⁸And Ornan looked and saw David, and he went out of the threshing-floor, and bowed down to David with his face to the ground. ²⁹Then David said to Ornan, "Sell me the place of this threshing-floor, that I may build an altar therein to the Lord; you will sell it to me for the full price, that the plague may be stayed from the people." ³⁰And Ornan said to David, "Take it, and let my lord the king do that which is good in his eyes; behold, I also give the oxen for burnt-offering, and the threshing instruments for wood, and the wheat for the meal-offering; I give it all." ³¹And King David said to Ornan, "No, but I will truly buy it for the full price; for I will not take that which is yours for the Lord, nor offer a burnt-offering without paying for it." ³²So David gave Ornan six hundred shekels of gold for the place, and for the cattle fifty shekels of silver, by weight. ³³And David built an altar there to the Lord, and offered burnt-offerings and peace-offerings, and called on the Lord; and He answered him from Heaven by fire on the altar of burnt-offering. ³⁴And the Lord commanded the messenger, and he put his sword back into the sheath thereof, and the plague was stayed from Israel. ³⁵At that time, when David saw that the Lord had answered him in the threshing-floor of Ornan the Jebusite, and He did not despise him, then he sacrificed there to the Lord for the rest of his life. ³⁶For David would no longer go and sacrifice to the Lord in the high place at Gibeon, where there was an altar to the Lord and [the] Dwelling Place which Moses made, for he was terrified and weakened because of the sword of the messenger of the Lord that he had seen.

CHAPTER 8

¹The Lord appeared to David when he was old and said to him, "Behold, I am with you, and I am your God, and behold, My covenant is with you; do not be afraid, nor discouraged, because your God is your helper." ²And David bowed down to the Lord and rejoiced in his heart. ³And the Lord said, "Speak these words in My Name to the people and make sure they understand and obey so that they will live. If they do, I will no longer be angry with them." ⁴And the Lord put His words in his mouth. ⁵Then David assembled all Israel in Jerusalem, and he made a pulpit of wood for himself, and he stood on it and addressed all the people. He opened his mouth and said, ⁶"Hear, O Israel,

your God and my God is one, the only one, and unique; there is no one like His individuality. He is hidden from everyone. He always has been and always will be. He fills His creation, but His creation does not fill Him. He sees everything, but is not seen. He knows the future and reveals it to mankind, for He is the everlasting God, and there is no end to His presence, power, and truth—whole worlds are full of His glory. ⁷He gave each person free choice: if one person wants to do good, he will be helped, but if a person wants to do evil, he will find a way. ⁸As for us, we will worship our God who is our King, our Lord, and our Savior, with love and awe. For your wisdom begins with the fear of the LORD, and if you truly understand Him, you will depart from evil. ⁹Remember and obey the Law of Moses, the man of God, so that you will live a blessed life all of your days. ¹⁰Ask your fathers, and they will teach you; ask your elders, and they will instruct you. ¹¹Do not just listen to the Law, but be strong and valiant to obey all of it. ¹²Hearing is like the seed, but a deed shows that the seed has taken root in you. It then becomes a tree of belief which produces the fruit of true righteousness. ¹³What becomes of a smelly rotten seed if no root will come out of it? ¹⁴So hurry; be quick to hear and act. For if you are a true seed, if you have belief and righteousness, then the LORD will bless you all with peace. ¹⁵Live in peace with each other. Love the deeds and those created in the image of the LORD like your own selves, ¹⁶because it is a sign that you love the Creator if you love His creation. ¹⁷You cannot take hold of the one but withdraw your hand from the other. Love the LORD and also man so that it will be well with you all the days of your life." ¹⁸David raised his voice, and lifted his hands toward Heaven, and said, "LORD, O God, the God of the spirits of all flesh, God, merciful and gracious, guard Israel forever. ¹⁹Save Your people, and bless Your inheritance, and tend to them, and uphold them forever." ²⁰And all the people called out: "Amen! Amen!" ²¹And David sent the people away and they went home peacefully.

CHAPTER 9

¹Hiram king of Tyre sent messengers to David, saying, ²"I know that the LORD your God is the one true God, so now deal with me as a true brother and teach me the Law of your God, for I will worship Him all the days of my life." ³Then the messengers came to David with an offering in their hands for the LORD and for David. They told him everything that Hiram had said and presented him with the offerings. ⁴And David replied to Hiram, ⁵"Go and tell my brother Hiram: This is what your brother David says: Reverence the LORD, creator of heaven and fire, the sea and the earth, the wet and the dry, the heat and the cold, the mineral and the vegetation, the living and the speaking, ⁶the planets, the Pleiades and Orion, the sun and the moon, the substantial and the spiritual, the wandering stars, the senses, and everything. ⁷These were all created without a blemish by God Almighty, whose Name is YHWH. ⁸If you do this and observe the commandments that were ordered to the children of your father Noah, then God will bless you all the days of your life. ⁹We are both His allies; but we are different from you by the Law of truth, sealed by the seal of [the] Almighty, called children of the true God. ¹⁰We must therefore obey the whole Law that the Name commands of us, saying, And you will be to Me a kingdom of priests, and a holy nation. These are the words which you will speak to the children of Israel. ¹¹But He has not dealt the same way with any other nation as He has with us. He did not choose us for any other reason than the great love that He has for us." ¹²The messengers then returned to Hiram, their king, and told him everything that King David had told them. ¹³And Hiram rejoiced with all his heart, and called all his princes and servants, and said to them, ¹⁴"Tyrians and Sidonians, listen carefully to what I am about to tell you: ¹⁵have reverence and respect for God Almighty, who is the God of Israel. He made everything by speaking and by the breath of His mouth; and who will tell Him what He can do? For He is one. ¹⁶Repeat after me: Blessed is the LORD God of Israel who chooses His people, and blessed is His servant David, king of His people, and blessed is Israel whom the LORD has chosen to be His inheritance. ¹⁷We would be blessed to simply be the servants of the children of Israel who are called children of the LORD their God." ¹⁸And all his princes and his servants replied: "Amen! May it be so." ¹⁹And Hiram lifted up his voice and said, "I have seen, but not now, || I have beheld, but not near: There will step forth a sun from David, || And a moon will rise out of the house of Judah, || And He will smite all the children of Ham || And break down all the children of Japheth, || And He will possess all the kingdoms of the world. And who is like the LORD, God above all gods? ²⁰And who is like Israel, a people above the nations? May our end be like theirs." ²¹When the LORD heard what Hiram had said, He was very pleased with him. ²²And the LORD said to Gad, the seer of David, ²³"Go to My servant and tell him the message that I gave you." ²⁴And Gad, the one in whose hand was the word of the LORD, came to David, and said, "Thus says the LORD God of Hosts: I have heard what Hiram, king of Tyre, has said and what his princes and servants have said, and I am very pleased. ²⁵Therefore I will give him and his people a heart of wisdom and understanding to prepare My house where I will put My Name, and that will cause his kingdom to grow, for I have chosen them and will not reject them." ²⁶And David said to Gad, "Now I know that the LORD our God rewards all His creatures and all the works He has created with goodness, because He is a God of mercy who dwells on high and looks after the lowly, and whoever is banished will not remain an outcast from Him. Blessed be the LORD forever. Amen and amen! ²⁷For as the heaven is high above the earth, so great is His mercy toward them that fear Him and toward His works. ²⁸Bless the LORD, all you His works, in all His places of His dominion. Bless the LORD, O my soul. Hallelujah!"

CHAPTER 10

¹At that time David wrote this psalm of praise: "I will exalt You, my God, O King; And I will bless Your Name forever and ever. ²Every day I will bless You, || And I will praise Your Name forever and ever. ³Great is the LORD, and greatly to be praised; And His greatness is unsearchable. ⁴Generation after generation will praise Your works, || And will declare Your mighty acts. ⁵The glorious splendor of Your majesty, || And Your wondrous works I will declare. ⁶And men will speak of the might of Your awesome works; And I will declare Your greatness. ⁷They will abundantly express the memory of Your goodness, || And they will sing of Your righteousness. ⁸The LORD is gracious and full of compassion, || Slow to anger, and great in mercy. ⁹The LORD is good to all, || And His tender mercies are over all His works. ¹⁰All Your works will thank You, O LORD; And Your saints bless You. ¹¹They will speak of the glory of Your kingdom, || And talk of Your power, ¹²To make known to the sons of men His mighty acts, || And the glorious majesty of His kingdom. ¹³Your kingdom is an everlasting kingdom, || And Your dominion endures through all generations. [[or All Your enemies have fallen, O LORD, || And all of their might has come to nothing.]] ¹⁴The LORD sustains all those who fall, || And raises up all those who are bowed down. ¹⁵The eyes of all wait on You; And You give them their food in due season. ¹⁶You open Your hands, || And satisfy the desire of every living thing with favor. ¹⁷The LORD is righteous in all His ways, || And holy in all His works. ¹⁸The LORD is near to all who call on Him, || To all that call on Him in truth. ¹⁹He will grant the desire of them that fear Him, || And He will also hear their prayer and save them. ²⁰The LORD preserves all of them that love Him, || But all the wicked He will destroy. ²¹My mouth will speak the praise of the LORD, || And let all flesh bless His holy Name forever and ever."

CHAPTER 11

¹THE PSALM OF DAVID PRAISING THE LORD ON THE DAY WHEN ELHANAN THE SON OF JAIR SLEW LAHMI THE BROTHER OF GOLIATH THE GITTITE, AND JONATHAN THE SON OF SHIMEA KILLED A MAN OF GREAT STATURE, saying, "Blessed be the LORD my rock, || Who instructs my hands for war, || And my fingers for battle. ²My mercy and my fortress; My high tower and my deliverer; My protector and He in whom I take refuge, || Who subdues peoples under me. ³LORD, what is man, that You take knowledge of him? Or the son of man, that You make account of him? ⁴Man is like to a breath: His days are as a shadow that passes away. ⁵O LORD, bow Your heavens and come down: Touch the mountains so that they smoke. ⁶Send lightning, and scatter them: Shoot out Your arrows, and destroy them. ⁷Send forth Your hand from above—deliver me, || And deliver me out of many waters, || Out of the hand of foreigners ⁸Whose mouths speak falsehood, || And whose right hand is a right hand of lying. ⁹O God, I will sing to You a new song: I will sing praise to You on a psaltery of ten strings,

¹⁰ Who gives salvation to kings, || Who rescues Your servant David from an evil sword. ¹¹ Rescue me and deliver me from the hand of foreigners || Whose mouths speak lies, || And whose right hand is a right hand of falsehood; ¹² May our children be as plants grown up in their youth; May our daughters be cornerstones hewn like the form of the temple. ¹³ May our garners be full, affording all manner of store; May our sheep increase by thousands || And myriads in our markets. ¹⁴ May our oxen be strong to labor; No breaking in, nor going out, || Nor complaining in our streets. ¹⁵ Happy is the people that is in such a case. Happy is the people whose God is the LORD. ¹⁶ Happy is he who waits until there will be good to all Israel forever."

CHAPTER 12

¹ David addressed the LORD and all of Israel shortly before his death. David said, ²"Our blessed God, who is great, the only one, guileless, just, ³avenger and benefactor of the miserable, beloved, our Father, God Almighty. ⁴ Holy One, have mercy on the vine, Your good inheritance. ⁵ Answer us this very day as we call on You. ⁶ My Lord, hear my prayer and supplication, for You hear prayers of all people; ⁷ listen and accept the cry of Your people, ⁸ for they are Your flock and Your inheritance. ⁹ Send Your light and truth to help them. ¹⁰ Give them one heart to worship You, one shoulder [to serve] as one body, so they will be one in Your hand. ¹¹ And do not lose any of them, for Your Name is to be one, as our fathers and mothers are one. ¹² For, hear, O Israel, the LORD is our God, the LORD is one. ¹³ Do not turn to the idols, for they are false and will completely pass away. ¹⁴ Cling only to your God, for only He can be your avenger and fortress; ¹⁵ only He can defeat your spiritual enemies and physical enemies and put them under your feet; ¹⁶ only He can bring you into the New Jerusalem of the future, ¹⁷ where you will see Him face to face, and be in the presence of the living God that is seen face to face. And you are one people; if you grow in belief, you will be filled with gates of intelligence. ¹⁸ Blessed is the eye that has seen all these things. ¹⁹ But if you grow in unbelief, you will reach gates of impurity. ²⁰ So then cleanse and purify yourself before the LORD, your King, and it will be well with you all the days of your life." ²¹ And David died in the afternoon on the Sabbath day, in the fortieth year of his reign over Judah and Israel. ²² He was seventy years old when he died, and he was buried with great honor in the City of David. ²³ And the rest of the deeds of King David, during his mighty reign and the events that befell him, Israel, and all the kingdoms of the countries, behold, they are written in the Scroll of Samuel the Seer and in the Scroll of Nathan the Prophet.

CHAPTER 13

¹ Solomon was able to strengthen his kingdom, because the LORD his God was with him, and greatly magnified him. ² Later, David's daughter, Tamar, sister of Absalom, fled to the house of the king of Geshur, and she spent a year and eight months in her mother's home, which is in the king's palace. ³ And King Solomon did not know that she left, because she went secretly, and she concealed her going not only from the king, but all the people as well. ⁴ And King Solomon said, "I will pay a reward of royal clothes plus fifty shekels of gold to whoever finds Tamar, the sister of my father, and brings her to me." ⁵ And the king's servants searched for her throughout all the land of Israel, but they could not find her. ⁶ And she was hiding at her mother's home in Geshur, at her grandfather's palace. ⁷ And there was a friend of the king, whose name was Pirshaz, and he lusted after the young woman very much, for she was very beautiful and attractive to look on. ⁸ In those days the king of Geshur went to see King Solomon, as all the kings of the land are required to do. ⁹ King Solomon asked him, saying, "Is it well with you?" And he said, "It is well." ¹⁰ And he said, "Is it well with Maachah [(Tamar's mother)] in your house?" And he said, "It is well." And then King Solomon cunningly asked, "Is it well with my sister Tamar?" And he lied to him, saying, "I do not know, for I have never met her." ¹¹ And it came to pass when the king of Geshur was in Jerusalem, his friend, Pirshaz, came to Tamar's room, saying to her, "Lie with me." ¹² But Tamar refused him, saying, "Let us not, my lord; do not do this indecent thing to me, because I am a king's daughter." ¹³ However, he would not listen to her, because he was burning with lust. ¹⁴ And Tamar knew she was no match for this man, so she cunningly said, "My lord, listen to the words of your maidservant. ¹⁵ Behold, I play the harp beautifully. First, lie down at my knees and listen to my song. ¹⁶ And after I play the song of my heart, then I will do all your heart's desire." And Pirshaz listened to Tamar, and he lay in her bosom. ¹⁷ And as Tamar took the harp and began to play beautifully, she said in her heart: "LORD, King of my father David, Your servant, ¹⁸ send Your light and truth to hold me, and do not allow this wicked, uncircumcised, impure man to have his way with me. ¹⁹ For You know what is in my heart, so do not let this daughter of Your servant David sin. ²⁰ My Father, my Father, my Father, remember the disgrace of Your servant David, my father, and your daughter's disgrace. ²¹ I go before God Almighty's throne of glory, and ask mercy for myself, to the God of Hosts, to help me by His help. ²² For He does not want wicked men to triumph, and His desire is to help those who have been robbed to overcome the strong. ²³ I implore You, O LORD, save me now. I implore You, O LORD, let me prosper. ²⁴ I call on You this day because I am frightened; please answer me, and do not let this impure man cause me to lose holy seed by this impure act, for You are a holy God, and I trust You." ²⁵ And the LORD heard the voice of David's daughter, and God caused Pirshaz to fall into a deep sleep. He fell asleep on her bosom while she was playing the relaxing sounds of the harp. ²⁶ And when Tamar saw that he had fallen asleep, she unsheathed the sword that was girded around his waist. ²⁷ And she said, "LORD of Hosts, remember my father David, and sustain me with Your strength like You did my father. ²⁸ Help me as You helped [Jael], the wife of Heber the Kenite, to rid sins and sinners from the earth, so all will know that You are the only LORD." ²⁹ And she took the sword and ran it through Pirshaz's heart, and Pirshaz fell to the ground dead. ³⁰ And Tamar saw that Pirshaz was dead, and she cried with a loud voice: "May all Your enemies and the enemies of Your people perish this way, O LORD. ³¹ And now I have seen that You have heard my voice because of my father. You have intervened to not allow his daughter to be disgraced by this impure man. ³² Blessed are You from everlasting to everlasting. Amen." ³³ At the time of the noon meal, Pirshaz's servants came to call their master to the king's table. ³⁴ When they came to the inner-chamber, they found Tamar with his bloody sword in her hand standing over the dead body of their master Pirshaz. ³⁵ And they turned trembling to one another, saying, "What happened?" And they took Tamar into custody and brought her to the king's ministers. ³⁶ And the king's servants said to Tamar, "What have you done? You have killed the king's friend. You know that our master, the king, will consider this a disgrace." ³⁷ And Tamar said, "Should one deal with a king's daughter like a harlot? His blood is on his own head, and I will be seen as guiltless and pure in the king's eyes." ³⁸ And they took Tamar and put her in the hands of the warden of the prison. ³⁹ And they sent a letter to their king who was still in Jerusalem, by the hands of the couriers, that Tamar, the king's granddaughter, had killed his friend Pirshaz, and that Tamar was sent to prison until the time the king returned. ⁴⁰ And the couriers came to Jerusalem and King Solomon's guards stopped them. And he asked them, "Where are you from?" ⁴¹ And they said, "We come from Geshur to bring letters to our master the king." ⁴² And the guards seized them and brought them to King Solomon. ⁴³ And King Solomon said, "You came here to spy out the land. Give me your king's letters and I will see if you are sinning against me or not." ⁴⁴ And King Solomon took the letters and gave them to the sons of Shisha, the king's scribes, to read. ⁴⁵ And they read through them and found where Tamar had killed Pirshaz and that she was in prison. ⁴⁶ And King Solomon called Ahishar, who was head of the household, and said, "Put these uncircumcised men in jail and bring the king of Geshur to me." ⁴⁷ And he did exactly as he had been commanded. And the king of Geshur was brought before King Solomon and he bowed his head toward the ground. ⁴⁸ And King Solomon said, "Why have you deceived me, lying, while my sister Tamar was with you? You told me that you had never met her in your entire life. ⁴⁹ As the LORD lives, who has redeemed my father David out of all evil, you will die this very day." ⁵⁰ And King Solomon called Benaiah, the son of Jehoiada, and said to him, "Go, and execute the king of Geshur and his couriers." And he executed them, and they

all died, because they had lied to King Solomon. ⁵¹And they buried them in a cave right before the Fish Gate. ⁵²This is why the name of the cave right before the Fish Gate is called Cave of the Uncircumcised Ones to this day. ⁵³And Solomon sent Benaiah, the son of Jehoiada, and ten thousand valiant men of Judah with him, and he said to them, ⁵⁴"Go to Geshur and bring back Tamar, my father's daughter, with you, and destroy the royal palace, but be careful not to harm Tamar's mother, for she was King David's wife." ⁵⁵And they went and did all that King Solomon had commanded, and they brought Tamar before King Solomon. ⁵⁶And Tamar bowed down to the ground, before the king, and said, "Let my lord the king, my brother, live forever." ⁵⁷And King Solomon asked her: "Why did you flee to Geshur?" ⁵⁸And she answered, "I was living in my brother Absalom's home, disgraced because of what my brother Amnon had done to me, and I decided to go to my mother's house so I would not be disgraced in the eyes of the princes there. ⁵⁹And King Solomon asked her: "Why did you kill Pirshaz?" And she answered, "This is what that uncircumcised one did to me, and this is what I did to him in revenge." ⁶⁰And King Solomon said, "The LORD has truly blessed you with discretion. You were wise, and acted, and you were victorious." ⁶¹Then King Solomon spoke openly to all of his servants, saying, "Has anyone found such a charming and heroic woman?" And he said, "Daughter, God is gracious to you. ⁶²From this day forward you will not be called my sister, but my daughter, because you were extremely wise." ⁶³And King Solomon gave his daughter Tamar to Abinadab's son to be his wife, and she found grace in her husband's eyes, and he loved her very much. ⁶⁴He was an officer over all the region of Dor. ⁶⁵And King Solomon renamed his daughter Tamar Taphath, for stacte, the first of the incense, and this was her name the rest of her life.

CHAPTER 14

¹And it came to pass on the first day of the seventh month, at the beginning of the year, in the four hundred and seventy-eighth year after the children of Israel came out of the land of Egypt, in the second year of King Solomon's reign over Israel, I had a vision from the LORD when I was on the Spring of Gihon. ²And I raised my eyes, and behold, the heavens rolled back like a scroll, and I saw the glory of the LORD sitting on an extremely high throne. ³And here is the appearance of the throne: twelve stairs led up to the throne—six of gold and six of silver—and there was a square back to the throne, like a sapphire stone. ⁴And at its right side were three chairs and at its left side were four chairs near the throne, like the seven that see the King's face, covered with gold, and silver, and precious stones. ⁵And the glory of the LORD had the appearance like that of the rainbow, His covenant. ⁶And the host of Heaven were standing before Him on His right hand and on His left, and Satan was standing by them, but behind them. ⁷And then a Man dressed in linen brought before the glory of the LORD three scrolls that contained the records of every man. ⁸And He read the first scroll and it contained the just deeds of His people, and the LORD said, "These are granted continuous life." ⁹And Satan said, "Who are these guilty people?" And the Man dressed in linen cried to Satan like a ram's horn, saying, "Silence! This day is holy to our Lord." ¹⁰And He read the second scroll, and it contained the unintentional sins of His people, and the LORD said, "Put that scroll aside, but save it until one-third of the month passes by, to see what they will do." ¹¹And He read the third scroll, and it contained the wicked deeds of His people. ¹²And the LORD said to Satan, "These are your share. Take them and do what you want with them." ¹³And Satan took the wicked to a wasteland to destroy them there. ¹⁴And the Man dressed in linen cried like a ram's horn, saying, ¹⁵"Blessed are the people who know the joyful shout, O LORD, who walk in the light of Your countenance." ¹⁶And I heard the voice of the host of Heaven rejoicing and saying, "Master of Justice, the LORD of Hosts, the whole heaven and earth is full of Your glory." ¹⁷And I was shocked by the vision since I did not know what the LORD had done for me. ¹⁸Then one of the cherubs flew up to me and he put an olive leaf on my mouth, and said, "Behold, this has touched your mouth, and your iniquity is taken away, and your sin forgiven. ¹⁹And this law that you have seen is a statute for Israel, and a law to the God of Abraham, and peace to your father Isaac. ²⁰And the LORD will bless your people in the trial with everlasting peace." ²¹And I said, "Amen. May the LORD our God do this for us forever and ever." ²²And the messenger answered, "Amen and Amen."

ASCENSION OF ISAIAH

The Ascension of Isaiah was probably composed sometime in the 1st or 2nd centuries AD and consists of three key parts: "The Martyrdom of Isaiah" (chs. 1–5), "The Testament of Hezekiah" (an insertion in chs. 3-4), and "The Vision of Isaiah" (chs. 6–11). The text revolves around an account of Isaiah's martyrdom in which he was sawn in two. It also includes prophetic material and a "vision" in which Isaiah is transported through the seven dimensions (or *levels*) of the heavens.

CHAPTER 1

¹And it came to pass in the twenty-sixth year of the reign of Hezekiah, king of Judah, that he called his son Manasseh. Now he was his only one. ²And he called him into the presence of Isaiah, the son of the prophet Amoz, and into the presence of Josab, the son of Isaiah, in order to deliver the words of righteousness to him which the king himself had seen, ³and of the continuous judgments and torments of Gehenna, and of the prince of this world, and of his messengers, and his authorities and his powers. ⁴And the words of the faith of the Beloved which he himself had seen in the fifteenth year of his reign during his sickness. ⁵And he delivered the written words to him which Samnas the scribe had written, and also those which Isaiah, the son of Amoz, had given to him, and also to the prophets, that they might write and store up with him what he himself had seen in the king's house regarding the judgment of the messengers, and the destruction of this world, and regarding the garments of the saints and their going forth, and regarding their transformation and the persecution and ascension of the Beloved. ⁶In the twentieth year of the reign of Hezekiah, Isaiah had seen the words of this prophecy and had delivered them to his son Josab. And while he gave commands, Josab, the son of Isaiah, [was] standing by. ⁷Isaiah said to Hezekiah the king—but not only in the presence of Manasseh did he say to him—"As the LORD lives, and the Spirit which speaks in me lives, all these commands and these words will be made of no effect by your son Manasseh, and through the agency of his hands I will depart amid the torture of my body. ⁸And Sammael Malchira will serve Manasseh, and execute all his desire, and he will become a follower of Belial rather than of me: ⁹and he will cause many in Jerusalem and in Judea to abandon the true faith, and Belial will dwell in Manasseh, and by his hands I will be sawn apart." ¹⁰And when Hezekiah heard these words he wept very bitterly, and tore his garments, and placed earth on his head, and fell on his face. ¹¹And Isaiah said to him, "The counsel of Sammael against Manasseh is consummated: nothing will avail you." ¹²And on that day, Hezekiah resolved in his heart to slay his son Manasseh. ¹³And Isaiah said to Hezekiah, "The Beloved has made your design of no effect, and the purpose of your heart will not be accomplished, for with this calling I have been called and I will inherit the heritage of the Beloved."

CHAPTER 2

¹And it came to pass after that Hezekiah died and Manasseh became king, [and] that he did not remember the commands of his father Hezekiah, but forgot them, and Sammael abode in Manasseh and clung fast to him. ²And Manasseh forsook the service of the God of his father, and he served Satan, and his messengers, and his powers. ³And he turned aside the house of his father, which had been

before the face of Hezekiah [from] the words of wisdom and from the service of God. ⁴And Manasseh turned aside his heart to serve Belial; for the messenger of lawlessness, who is the ruler of this world, is Belial, whose name is Mantanbuchus, and he delighted in Jerusalem because of Manasseh, and he made him strong in apostatizing [Israel] and in the lawlessness which were spread abroad in Jerusalem. ⁵And witchcraft and magic increased, and divination, and portending, and fornication, [[and adultery]], and the persecution of the righteous by Manasseh, [and Belchira,] and Tobia the Canaanite, and John of Anathoth, and by [Zadok] the chief of the works. ⁶And the rest of the acts, behold they are written in the scroll of the Kings of Judah and Israel. ⁷And when Isaiah, the son of Amoz, saw the lawlessness which was being perpetrated in Jerusalem and the worship of Satan and his wantonness, he withdrew from Jerusalem and settled in Beth-Lehem of Judah. ⁸And there also there was much lawlessness; and withdrawing from Beth-Lehem, he settled on a mountain in a desert place. ⁹And Micaiah the prophet, and the aged Ananias, and Joel and Habakkuk, and his son Josab, and many of the faithful who believed in the ascension into Heaven, withdrew and settled on the mountain. ¹⁰They were all clothed with garments of hair, and they were all prophets. And they had nothing with them but were naked, and they all lamented with a great lamentation because of the going astray of Israel. ¹¹And these eat nothing save wild herbs which they gathered on the mountains, and having cooked them, they lived thereon together with the prophet Isaiah. And they spent two years of days on the mountains and hills. ¹²And after this, while they were in the desert, there was a certain man in Samaria named Belchira, of the family of Zedekiah, the son of Chenaan, a false prophet, whose dwelling was in Beth-Lehem. Now Hezekiah the son of Chanani, who was the brother of his father, and in the days of Ahab, king of Israel, had been the teacher of the four hundred prophets of Ba'al, had himself smitten and reproved Micaiah, the son of Amada the prophet. ¹³And he, Micaiah, had been reproved by Ahab and cast into prison. [And he was] with Zedekiah the prophet: they were with Ahaziah, the son of Ahab, king in Samaria. ¹⁴And Elijah the prophet of Tebon of Gilead was reproving Ahaziah and Samaria, and prophesied regarding Ahaziah that he should die on his bed of sickness, and that Samaria should be delivered into the hand of Leba Nasr because he had slain the prophets of God. ¹⁵And [this was] when the false prophets, who were with Ahaziah, the son of Ahab, and their teacher Jalerjas of Mount Joel, had heard. ¹⁶Now he was a brother of Zedekiah when they persuaded Ahaziah, the king of Aguaron, and [slew] Micaiah.

CHAPTER 3

¹And Belchira recognized and saw the place of Isaiah and the prophets who were with him, for he dwelt in the region of Beth-Lehem and was an adherent of Manasseh. And he prophesied falsely in Jerusalem, and many belonging to Jerusalem were confederate with him, and he was a Samaritan. ²And it came to pass when Alagar Zagar, king of Assyria, had come and [made them] captive, and led them away to the mountains of the Medes and the rivers of Tazon; ³This [Belchira], while still a youth, had escaped and come to Jerusalem in the days of Hezekiah king of Judah, but he did not walk in the ways of his father of Samaria; for he feared Hezekiah. ⁴And he was found in the days of Hezekiah speaking words of lawlessness in Jerusalem. ⁵And the servants of Hezekiah accused him, and he made his escape to the region of Beth-Lehem. And they persuaded… ⁶And Belchira accused Isaiah and the prophets who were with him, saying, "Isaiah and those who are with him prophesy against Jerusalem and against the cities of Judah that they will be laid waste, and [[against the children of Judah, and]] Benjamin also, that they will go into captivity, and also against you, O lord the king, that you will go [bound] with hooks and iron chains, ⁷but they prophesy falsely against Israel and Judah. ⁸And Isaiah himself has said, I see more than Moses the prophet. ⁹But Moses said, No man can see God and live; and Isaiah has said, I have seen God and behold I live. ¹⁰Know, therefore, O king, that he is lying. And he has also called Jerusalem Sodom, and he has declared the princes of Judah and Jerusalem to be the people of Gomorrah." And he brought many accusations against Isaiah and the prophets before Manasseh. ¹¹But Belial dwelt in the heart of Manasseh, and in the heart of the princes of Judah and Benjamin, and of the eunuchs, and of the counselors of the king. ¹²And the words of Belchira pleased him, and he sent for and seized Isaiah. ¹³For Belial was in great wrath against Isaiah by reason of the vision, and because of the exposure with which he had exposed Sammael, and because through him the going forth of the Beloved from the seventh heaven had been made known, and His transformation and His descent and the likeness into which He should be transformed—the likeness of man, and the persecution with which He should be persecuted, and the torturers with which the sons of Israel should torture Him, and the coming of His twelve disciples, and the teaching, and that He should before the Sabbath be crucified on the tree, and should be crucified together with wicked men, and that He should be buried in the grave, ¹⁴and the twelve who were with Him should be offended because of Him, and the watch of those who watched the grave, ¹⁵and the descent of the messenger of the Christian Assembly, which is in the heavens, whom He will summon in the last days. ¹⁶And that [Gabriel], the messenger of the Holy Spirit, and Michael, the chief of the holy messengers, on the third day will open the grave: ¹⁷and the Beloved sitting on their shoulders will come forth and send out His twelve disciples; ¹⁸and they will teach all the nations and every tongue of the resurrection of the Beloved, and those who believe in His cross will be saved, and in His ascension into the seventh heaven from where He came, ¹⁹and that many who believe in Him will speak through the Holy Spirit, ²⁰and many signs and wonders will be worked in those days. ²¹And afterward, on the eve of His approach, His disciples will forsake the teachings of the Twelve Apostles, and their faith, and their love, and their purity. ²²And there will be much contention on the eve of [His advent and] His approach. ²³And in those days, many will love office, though devoid of wisdom. ²⁴And there will be many lawless elders, and shepherds dealing wrongly by their own sheep, and they will ravage [them], owing to their not having holy shepherds. ²⁵And many will change the honor of the garments of the saints for the garments of the covetous, and there will be much respect of persons in those days and lovers of the honor of this world. ²⁶And there will be much slander and vainglory at the approach of the LORD, and the Holy Spirit will withdraw from [the] many. ²⁷And there will not be in those days many prophets, nor those who speak trustworthy words, save one here and there in various places, ²⁸on account of the spirit of error, and fornication, and of vainglory, and of covetousness, which will be in those who will be called servants of that One and in those who will receive that One. ²⁹And there will be great hatred in the shepherds and elders toward each other. ³⁰For there will be great jealousy in the last days; for everyone will say what is pleasing in his own eyes. ³¹And they will make of no effect the prophecy of the prophets which were before me, and they will also make these visions of mine of no effect, in order to speak after the impulse of their own hearts.

CHAPTER 4

¹And now Hezekiah and my son Josab, these are the days of the completion of the world. ²After it is consummated, the great ruler Belial, the king of this world, will descend, who has ruled it since it came into being; yes, he will descend from his expanse in the likeness of a man, a lawless king, the slayer of his mother: who himself [is even] this king. ³He will persecute the plant which the Twelve Apostles of the Beloved have planted. Of the Twelve, one will be delivered into his hands. ⁴This ruler, in the form of that king, will come, and there will come with him all the powers of this world, and they will listen to him in all that he desires. ⁵And at his word the sun will rise at night and he will make the moon to appear at the sixth hour. ⁶And all that he has desired he will do in the world: he will do and speak like the Beloved and he will say, "I am God and before me there has been none." ⁷And all the people in the world will believe in him. ⁸And they will sacrifice to him and they will serve him, saying, "This is God and besides Him there is no other." ⁹And the greater number of those who will have been associated together in order to receive the Beloved, he will turn

aside after him. ¹⁰And there will be the power of his miracles in every city and region. ¹¹And he will set up his image before him in every city. ¹²And he will bear sway three years and seven months and twenty-seven days. ¹³And many believers and saints will have seen Him for whom they were hoping, who was crucified—the Lord Jesus Christ. [[After that, I, Isaiah, had seen Him who was crucified and ascended,]] and those also who were believers in Him—of these few in those days will be left as His servants, while they flee from desert to desert, awaiting the coming of the Beloved. ¹⁴And after [one thousand] three hundred and thirty-two days the LORD will come with His messengers and with the armies of the holy ones from the seventh heaven with the glory of the seventh heaven, and He will drag Belial into Gehenna and also his armies. ¹⁵And He will give rest of the godly whom He will find in the body in this world— [[and the sun wil be ashamed]]— ¹⁶and to all who because of [their] faith in Him have execrated Belial and his kings. But the saints will come with the LORD with their garments which are [now] stored up on high in the seventh heaven: they will come with the LORD, whose spirits are clothed, they will descend and be present in the world, and He will strengthen those who have been found in the body, together with the saints, in the garments of the saints, and the LORD will minister to those who have kept watch in this world. ¹⁷And afterward they will turn themselves upward in their garments, and their body will be left in the world. ¹⁸Then the voice of the Beloved will in wrath rebuke the things of Heaven, and the things of earth, and the mountains, and the hills, and the cities, and the desert, and the forests, and the messenger of the sun and that of the moon, and all things wherein Belial manifested himself and acted openly in this world, and there will be [[a resurrection and]] a judgment in their midst in those days, and the Beloved will cause fire to go forth from Him, and it will consume all the godless, and they will be as though they had not been created. ¹⁹And the rest of the words of the vision is written in the vision of Babylon. ²⁰And the rest of the vision regarding the LORD, behold, it is written in three parables according to my words which are written in the scroll which I publicly prophesied. ²¹And the descent of the Beloved into Sheol, behold, it is written in the section, where the LORD says, "Behold, My Son will understand." And all these things, behold, they are written in the parables [[or Psalms]] of David, the son of Jesse, and in the Proverbs of his son Solomon, and in the words of Korah, and Ethan the Israelite, and in the words of Asaph, and also in the rest of the Psalms which the messenger of the Spirit inspired— ²²[namely,] in those which do not have the name written, and in the words of my father Amoz, and of Hosea the prophet, and of Micah, and Joel, and Nahum, and Jonah, and Obadiah, and Habakkuk, and Haggai, and Malachi, and in the words of Joseph the Just, and in the words of Daniel.

CHAPTER 5

¹On account of these visions, therefore, Belial was angry with Isaiah, and he dwelt in the heart of Manasseh, and he sawed him apart with a wooden saw. ²And when Isaiah was being sawn apart, Belchira stood up, accusing him, and all the false prophets stood up, laughing and rejoicing because of Isaiah. ³And Belchira, with the aid of Mechembechus, stood up before Isaiah, [laughing] deriding; ⁴and Belchira said to Isaiah, "Say, I have lied in all that I have spoken, and likewise the ways of Manasseh are good and right. ⁵And the ways also of Belchira and of his associates are good." ⁶And this he said to him when he began to be sawn apart. ⁷But Isaiah was [entranced] in a vision of the LORD, and though his eyes were open, he [did not] see them. ⁸And Belchira spoke thus to Isaiah: "Say what I say to you and I will turn their hearts, and I will compel Manasseh, and the princes of Judah, and the people, and all Jerusalem to give reverence to you." ⁹And Isaiah answered and said, "So far as I have utterance: Damned and accursed are you, and all your powers, and all your house. ¹⁰For you cannot take [from me] anything except the skin of my body." ¹¹And they seized and sawed apart Isaiah, the son of Amoz, with a wooden saw. ¹²And Manasseh, and Belchira, and the false prophets, and the princes, and the people all stood looking on. ¹³And to the prophets who were with him he said before he had been sawn apart, "Go to the region of Tyre and Sidon; for God has only mingled the cup for me." ¹⁴And when Isaiah was being sawn apart, he neither cried aloud nor wept, but his lips spoke with the Holy Spirit until he was sawn in half. ¹⁵Belial did this to Isaiah through Belchira and Manasseh; for Sammael was very wrathful against Isaiah from the days of Hezekiah, king of Judah, on account of the things which he had seen regarding the Beloved. ¹⁶And on account of the destruction of Sammael, which he had seen through the LORD while his father Hezekiah was still king. And he did according to the will of Satan.

CHAPTER 6

¹THE VISION WHICH ISAIAH THE SON OF AMOZ SAW: In the twentieth year of the reign of Hezekiah, king of Judah, Isaiah the son of Amoz, and Josab the son of Isaiah, came to Hezekiah to Jerusalem from Galgala. ²And [having entered,] he sat down on the couch of the king, and they brought him a seat, but he would not sit [thereon]. ³And when Isaiah began to speak the words of faith and truth with King Hezekiah, all the princes of Israel were seated—and the eunuchs and the counselors of the king. And there were forty prophets and sons of the prophets there: they had come from the villages and from the mountains and the plains when they had heard that Isaiah was coming from Galgala to Hezekiah. ⁴And they had come to salute him and to hear his words, ⁵and that he might place his hands on them, and that they might prophesy and that he might hear their prophecy: and they were all before Isaiah. ⁶And when Isaiah was speaking the words of truth and faith to Hezekiah, they all heard a door which one had opened and the voice of the Holy Spirit. ⁷And the king summoned all the prophets and all the people who were found there, and they came, and Macaiah, and the aged Ananias, and Joel, and Josab sat on his right hand [[and on the left]]. ⁸And it came to pass when they had all heard the voice of the Holy Spirit, they all worshiped on their knees, and glorified the God of truth, the Most High who is in the upper world and who sits on high—the Holy One— and who rests among His holy ones. ⁹And they gave glory to Him who had thus bestowed a door in an alien world [and] had bestowed [it] on a man. ¹⁰And as he was speaking in the Holy Spirit in the hearing of all, he became silent, and his mind was taken up from him and he did not see the men that stood before him, ¹¹though his eyes were indeed open. Moreover, his lips were silent and the mind in his body was taken up from him. ¹²But his breath was in him, for he was seeing a vision. ¹³And the messenger who was sent to make him see was not of this expanse, nor was he of the messengers of glory of this world, but he had come from the seventh heaven. ¹⁴And the people who stood near did [not] think, but the circle of the prophets [did], that the holy Isaiah had been taken up. ¹⁵And the vision which the holy Isaiah saw was not from this world, but from the world which is hidden from the flesh. ¹⁶And after Isaiah had seen this vision, he narrated it to Hezekiah, and to his son Josab, and to the other prophets who had come. ¹⁷But the leaders, and the eunuchs, and the people did not hear, but only Samna the scribe, and Ijoaqem, and Asaph the recorder; for these were also doers of righteousness, and the sweet smell of the Spirit was on them. But the people had not heard, for Micaiah and his son Josab had caused them to go forth when the wisdom of this world had been taken from him and he became as one dead.

CHAPTER 7

¹And the vision which Isaiah saw, he told to Hezekiah, and his son Josab, and Micaiah, and the rest of the prophets, [and] said: ²At this moment, when I prophesied according to the [words] heard which you heard, I saw a glorious messenger not like to the glory of the messengers which I used to always see, but possessing such glory and position that I cannot describe the glory of that messenger. ³And having seized me by my hand he raised me on high, and I said to him, "Who are you, and what is your name, and to where are you raising me on high?" For strength was given me to speak with him. ⁴And he said to me, "When I have raised you on high and made you see the vision, on account of which I have been sent, then you will understand who I am, but you do not know my name, ⁵because you will return into this body of yours; but to where I am raising you on high, you will see; for this purpose I have been sent." ⁶And I rejoiced because he spoke courteously to me. ⁷And he said to me, "Have you rejoiced because I have spoken courteously to you?" And he said, "And you will see how [one]

greater than I am will also speak courteously and peaceably with you. ⁸And His Father who is greater you will also see; for this purpose I have been sent from the seventh heaven in order to explain all these things to you." ⁹And we ascended to the expanse, he and I, and there I saw Sammael and his hosts, and there was great fighting therein and the messengers of Satan were envying one another. ¹⁰And as above so on the earth also; for the likeness of that which is in the expanse is here on the earth. ¹¹And I said to the messenger [who was with me], "[[What is this war and]] what is this envying?" ¹²And he said to me, "So has it been since this world was made until now, and this war [will continue] until He, whom you will see will come and destroy him." ¹³And afterward he caused me to ascend [to that which is] above the expanse, which is the [first] heaven. ¹⁴And there I saw a throne in the midst, and on his right and on his left were messengers. ¹⁵And [those on the left were] not like to the messengers who stood on the right, but those who stood on the right had the greater glory, and they all praised with one voice, and there was a throne in the midst; and those who were on the left gave praise after them, but their voice was not such as the voice of those on the right, nor their praise like the praise of those. ¹⁶And I asked the messenger who conducted me, and I said to him, "To whom is this praise sent?" ¹⁷And he said to me, "[It is sent] to the praise of [Him who sits in] the seventh heaven: to Him who rests in the holy world, and to His Beloved, from where I have been sent to you." ¹⁸And again, he made me to ascend to the second heaven. Now the height of that heaven is the same as from the heaven to the earth. ¹⁹And [I saw there, as] in the first heaven, messengers on the right and on the left, and a throne in the midst, and the praise of the messengers in the second heaven; and he who sat on the throne in the second heaven was more glorious than all [the rest]. ²⁰And there was great glory in the second heaven, and the praise also was not like the praise of those who were in the first heaven. ²¹And I fell on my face to worship him, but the messenger who conducted me did not permit me, but said to me, "Worship neither throne nor messenger which belongs to the six heavens—for this reason I was sent to conduct you until I tell you in the seventh heaven. ²²For above all the heavens and their messengers your throne has been placed, and your garments and your crown which you will see." ²³And I rejoiced with great joy, that those who love the Most High and His Beloved will afterward ascend there by the messenger of the Holy Spirit. ²⁴And he raised me to the third heaven, and in like manner I saw those on the right and on the left, and there was a throne there in the midst; but the memorial of this world is there unheard of. ²⁵And I said to the messenger who was with me—for the glory of my appearance was undergoing transformation as I ascended to each heaven in turn—"Nothing of the vanity of that world is here named." ²⁶And he answered me, and said to me, "Nothing is named on account of its weakness, and nothing is hidden there of what is done." ²⁷And I wished to learn how it is known, and he answered me, saying, "When I have raised you to the seventh heaven from where I was sent, to that which is above these, then you will know that there is nothing hidden from the thrones and from those who dwell in the heavens and from the messengers." And the praise with which they praised and [the] glory of him who sat on the throne was great, and the glory of the messengers on the right hand and on the left was beyond that of the heaven which was below them. ²⁸And again he raised me to the fourth heaven, and the height from the third to the height from the third to the fourth heaven was greater than from the earth to the expanse. ²⁹And there I again saw those who were on the right hand and those who were on the left, and him who sat on the throne was in the midst, and there also they were praising. ³⁰And the praise and glory of the messengers on the right was greater than that of those on the left. ³¹And again the glory of him who sat on the throne was greater than that of the messengers on the right, and their glory was beyond that of those who were below. ³²And he raised me to the fifth heaven. ³³And again I saw those on the right hand and on the left, and him who sat on the throne possessing greater glory that those of the fourth heaven. ³⁴And the glory of those on the right hand was greater than that of those on the left [from the third to the fourth]. ³⁵And the glory of him who was on the throne was greater than that of the messengers on the right hand. ³⁶And their praise was more glorious than that of the fourth heaven. ³⁷And I praised Him who is not named, and the Only-begotten who dwells in the heavens, whose Name is not known to any flesh, who has bestowed such glory on the several heavens, and who makes great the glory of the messengers, and more excellent the glory of Him who sits on the throne.

CHAPTER 8

¹And again he raised me into the air of the sixth heaven, and I saw such glory as I had not seen in the five heavens. ²For I saw messengers possessing great glory. ³And the praise there was holy and wonderful. ⁴And I said to the messenger who conducted me, "What is this which I see, my Lord?" ⁵And he said, "I am not your lord, but your fellow servant." ⁶And again I asked him, and I said to him, "Why are there not angelic fellow servants [on the left]?" ⁷And he said, "From the sixth heaven there are no longer messengers on the left, nor a throne set in the midst, but [they are directed] by the power of the seventh heaven, where dwells He that is not named and the Chosen One, whose Name has not been made known, and none of the heavens can learn His Name, ⁸for it is He alone to whose voice all the heavens and thrones give answer. I have therefore been empowered and sent to raise you here that you may see this glory, ⁹and that you may see the Lord of all those heavens and these thrones, ¹⁰undergoing [successive] transformation until He resembles your form and likeness. ¹¹I indeed say to you, Isaiah, no man about to return into a body of that world has ascended or seen what you see or perceived what you have perceived and what you will see. ¹²For it has been permitted to you in the lot of the LORD to come here. [[And from there comes the power of the sixth heaven and of the air]]." ¹³And I magnified my Lord with praise, in that through His lot I should come here. ¹⁴And he said, "Hear, furthermore, therefore, this also from your fellow servant: when from the body by the will of God you have ascended here, then you will receive the garment which you see, and likewise other numbered garments laid up you will see. ¹⁵And then you will become equal to the messengers of the seventh heaven." ¹⁶And he raised me up into the sixth heaven, and there were no [messengers] on the left, nor a throne in the midst, but all had one appearance and their [power of] praise was equal. ¹⁷And [power] was given to me also, and I also praised along with them and that messenger also, and our praise was like theirs. ¹⁸And there they all named the primal Father and His Beloved, the Christ, and the Holy Spirit, all with one voice. ¹⁹And [their voice] was not like the voice of the messengers in the five heavens, ²⁰but the voice was different there, and there was much light there. ²¹And then, when I was in the sixth heaven, I thought the light which I had seen in the five heavens to be but darkness. ²²And I rejoiced and praised Him who has bestowed such lights on those who wait for His promise. ²³And I implored the messenger who conducted me that I should no longer return to the carnal world. ²⁴I indeed say to you, Hezekiah, and my son Josab, and Michaiah, that there is much darkness here. ²⁵And the messenger who conducted me discovered what I thought and said, "If you rejoice in this light, how much more will you rejoice when you see the light in the seventh heaven where the LORD and His Beloved are, [[from where I have been sent, who is to be called Son in this world. ²⁶It has not been manifested [when] He will be in the corruptible world]] and the garments, and the thrones, and the crowns which are laid up for the righteous, for those who trust in that Lord who will descend in your form. For the light which is there is great and wonderful. ²⁷And as concerning your not returning into the body, your days are not yet fulfilled for coming here." ²⁸And when I heard, I was troubled, and he said, "Do not be troubled."

CHAPTER 9

¹And he took me into the air of the seventh heaven, and moreover I heard a voice, saying, "How far will he ascend that dwells in the flesh?" And I feared and trembled. ²And when I trembled, behold, I heard from there another voice being sent forth, and saying, "It is permitted to the holy Isaiah to ascend here; for here is his garment." ³And I asked the messenger who was with me and said, "Who is he who forbade me and who is he who

permitted me to ascend?" ⁴And he said to me, "He who forbade you is he who is over the praise-giving of the sixth heaven. ⁵And He who permitted you, this is your LORD God, the Lord Christ, who will be called Jesus in the world, but His Name you cannot hear until you have ascended out of your body." ⁶And he raised me up into the seventh heaven, and I saw there a wonderful light and innumerable messengers. ⁷And there I saw the holy Abel and all the righteous. ⁸And there I saw Enoch and all who were with him, stripped of the garments of the flesh, ⁹and I saw them in their garments of the upper world, and they were like messengers, standing there in great glory. ¹⁰But they did not sit on their thrones, nor were their crowns of glory on them. ¹¹And I asked the messenger who was with me: "How is it that they have received the garments, but do not have the thrones and the crowns?" ¹²And he said to me, "They do not receive crowns and thrones of glory until the Beloved will descend in the form in which you will see Him descend into the world in the last days—the LORD, who will be called Christ. ¹³Nevertheless, they see and know whose thrones will be, and whose the crowns when He has descended and been made in your form, and they will think that He is flesh and is a man. ¹⁴And the god of that world will stretch forth his hand against the Son, and they will crucify Him on a tree, and will slay Him not knowing who He is. ¹⁵And thus His descent, as you will see, will be hidden even from the heavens, so that it will not be known who He is. ¹⁶And when He has plundered the messenger of death, He will ascend on the third day. ¹⁷And then many of the righteous will ascend with Him, whose spirits do not receive their garments until the Lord Christ ascends and they ascend with Him. ¹⁸Then they will indeed receive their [garments, and] thrones, and crowns when He has ascended into the seventh heaven." ¹⁹And I said to him that which I had asked him in the third heaven: ²⁰"Show me how everything which is done in that world is made known here." ²¹And while I was still speaking with him, behold, one of the messengers who stood near, more glorious than the glory of that messenger who had raised me up from the world, ²²showed me a scroll, and he opened it, and the scroll was written, but not as a scroll of this world. And he gave [it] to me and I read it, and behold, the deeds of the sons of Israel were written therein, and the deeds of those whom I [do not] know, my son Josab. ²³And I said, "In truth, there is nothing hidden in the seventh heaven, which is done in this world." ²⁴And I saw there many garments laid up, and many thrones and many crowns. ²⁵And I said to the messenger, "Whose are these garments, and thrones, and crowns?" ²⁶And he said to me, "Many from that world will receive these garments, believing in the words of that One who will be named as I told you, and they will observe those things, and believe in them, and believe in His Cross; these are laid up for them." ²⁷And I saw a certain One standing, whose glory surpassed that of all, and His glory was great and wonderful. ²⁸And after I had seen Him, all the righteous whom I had seen and also the messengers whom I had seen came to Him. And Adam, and Abel, and Seth, and all the righteous first drew near and worshiped Him, and they all praised Him with one voice, and I myself also gave praise with them, and my giving of praise was as theirs. ²⁹And then all the messengers drew near and worshiped and gave praise. ³⁰And I was transformed and became like a messenger. ³¹And thereon the messenger who conducted me said to me, "Worship this One," and I worshiped and praised. ³²And the messenger said to me, "This is the Lord of all the praise-givings which you have seen." ³³And while he was still speaking, I saw another glorious One who was like Him, and the righteous drew near and worshiped and praised, and I praised together with them. But my glory was not transformed into accordance with their form. ³⁴And thereon the messengers drew near and worshiped Him. ³⁵And I saw the LORD and the second messenger, and they were standing. ³⁶And the second whom I saw was on the left of my Lord. And I asked, "Who is this?" and he said to me, "Worship Him, for He is the Messenger—the Holy Spirit, who speaks in you and the rest of the righteous." ³⁷And I saw the great glory, the eyes of my spirit being open, and I could not thereon see, nor yet could the messenger who was with me, nor all the messengers whom I had seen worshiping my Lord. ³⁸But I saw the righteous beholding with great power the glory of that One. ³⁹And my Lord drew near to me and the Messenger—the Spirit—and He said, "See how it is given to you to see God, and on your account, power is given to the messenger who is with you." ⁴⁰And I saw how my Lord and the Messenger—the Spirit—worshiped, and they both together praised God. ⁴¹And thereon all the righteous drew near and worshiped. ⁴²And the messengers drew near and worshiped, and all the messengers praised.

CHAPTER 10

¹And thereon I heard the voices and the giving of praise, which I had heard in each of the six heavens, ascending and being heard there: ²and all were being sent up to that glorious One whose glory I could not behold. ³And I myself was hearing and beholding the praise [which was given] to Him. ⁴And the LORD and the Messenger—the Spirit—were beholding all and hearing all. ⁵And all the praises which are sent up from the six heavens are not only heard, but seen. ⁶And I heard the messenger who conducted me and he said, "This is the Most High of the high ones, dwelling in the holy world, and resting in His holy ones, who will be called by the Holy Spirit through the lips of the righteous the Father of the Lord." ⁷And I heard the voice of the Most High, the Father of my Lord, saying to my Lord Christ who will be called Jesus: ⁸"Go forth and descend through all the heavens, and You will descend to the expanse and that world; You will descend to the messenger in Sheol, but You will not go to Haguel. ⁹And You will become like to the likeness of all who are in the five heavens. ¹⁰And You will be careful to become like the form of the messengers of the expanse [[and the messengers who are also in Sheol]]. ¹¹And none of the messengers of that world will know that You are with Me of the seven heavens and of their messengers. ¹²And they will not know that You are with Me, until I have called with a loud voice [to] the heavens, and their messengers and their lights—to the sixth heaven, in order that You may judge and destroy the princes, and messengers, and gods of that world, and the world that is dominated by them, ¹³for they have denied Me and said, We are alone and there is none besides us. ¹⁴And afterward from the messengers of death You will ascend to Your place. And You will not be transformed in each Heaven, but You will ascend in glory and sit on My right hand. ¹⁵And thereon the princes and powers of that world will worship You." ¹⁶I heard the Great Glory giving these commands to my Lord. ¹⁷And so I saw my Lord go forth from the seventh heaven into the sixth heaven. ¹⁸And the messenger who conducted me said to me, "Understand, Isaiah, and see [how] the transformation and descent of the LORD will appear." ¹⁹And I saw, and when the messengers saw Him, thereon those in the sixth heaven praised and lauded Him; for He had not been transformed after the shape of the messengers there, and they praised Him, and I also praised with them. ²⁰And I saw when He descended into the fifth heaven, that in the fifth heaven He made Himself like to the form of the messengers there, and they did not praise Him [nor worship Him], for His form was like to theirs. ²¹And then He descended into the fourth heaven and made Himself like to the form of the messengers there. ²²And when they saw Him, they did not praise or laud Him, for His form was like to their form. ²³And again I saw when He descended into the third heaven, and He made Himself like to the form of the messengers in the third heaven. ²⁴And those who kept the gate of the [third] heaven demanded the password, and the LORD gave [it] to them in order that He should not be recognized. And when they saw Him, they did not praise or laud Him, for His form was like to their form. ²⁵And again I saw when He descended into the second heaven, and again He gave the password there; and those who kept the gate proceeded to demand the LORD to give [it]. ²⁶And I saw when He made Himself like to the form of the messengers in the second heaven, and they saw Him, and they did not praise Him, for His form was like to their form. ²⁷And again I saw when He descended into the first heaven, and there also He gave the password to those who kept the gate, and He made Himself like to the form of the messengers who were on the left of that throne, and they neither praised nor lauded Him, for His form was like to their form. ²⁸But as for me, no one asked me on account of the messenger who conducted me. ²⁹And again He descended into the expanse where the ruler of this world dwells, and He gave the

ASCENSION OF ISAIAH

password to those on the left, and His form was like theirs, and they did not praise Him there; but they were envying one another and fighting, for here there is a power of evil and envying about trifles. ³⁰And I saw when He descended and made Himself like to the messengers of the air, and He was like one of them. ³¹And He gave no password, for one was plundering and doing violence to another.

CHAPTER 11

¹After this I saw, and the messenger who spoke with me, who conducted me, said to me, "Understand, Isaiah, son of Amoz, for I have been sent from God for this purpose." ²And I indeed saw a woman of the family of the prophet David, named Mary, and Virgin, and she was espoused to a man named Joseph, a carpenter, and he was also of the seed and family of the righteous David of Beth-Lehem [in] Judah. ³And he came into his lot. And when she was espoused, she was found with child, and Joseph the carpenter was desirous to put her away. ⁴But the messenger of the Spirit appeared in this world, and after that Joseph did not put her away, but kept Mary and did not reveal this matter to anyone. ⁵And he did not approach Mary, but kept her as a holy virgin, though with child. ⁶And he did not live with her for two months. ⁷And after two months of days while Joseph was in his house, and Mary his wife, but both alone, ⁸it came to pass that when they were alone that Mary immediately looked with her eyes and saw a small baby, and she was astonished. ⁹And after she had been astonished, her womb was found as formerly before she had conceived. ¹⁰And when her husband Joseph said to her, "What has astonished you?" his eyes were opened and he saw the Infant and praised God, because God had come into his portion. ¹¹And a voice came to them: "Tell this vision to no one." ¹²And the story regarding the Infant was spread widely in Beth-Lehem. ¹³Some said, "The Virgin Mary has borne a child before she was married two months." ¹⁴And many said, "She has not borne a child, nor has a midwife gone up [to her], nor have we heard the cries of [labor] pains." And they were all blinded respecting Him and they all knew regarding Him, though they did not know where He was from. ¹⁵And they took Him and went to Nazareth in Galilee. ¹⁶And I saw, O Hezekiah and my son Josab, and I declare to the other prophets who are also standing by, that [this] has escaped all the heavens, and all the princes, and all the gods of this world. ¹⁷And I saw: in Nazareth He sucked the breast as a baby and as is customary in order that He might not be recognized. ¹⁸And when He had grown up, He worked great signs and wonders in the land of Israel and of Jerusalem. ¹⁹And after this the adversary envied Him and roused the sons of Israel against Him, not knowing who He was, and they delivered Him to the king, and crucified Him, and He descended to the messenger [of Sheol]. ²⁰I indeed saw Him being crucified on a tree in Jerusalem: ²¹and likewise after the third day rise again and remain [forty] days. ²²And the messenger who conducted me said, "Understand, Isaiah": and I saw when He sent out the Twelve Apostles and ascended. ²³And I saw Him, and He was in the expanse, but He had not changed Himself into their form, and all the messengers of the expanse and the adversaries saw Him, and they worshiped. ²⁴And there was much sorrow there, while they said, "How did our Lord descend in our midst, and we did not perceive the glory which we see has been on Him from the sixth heaven?" ²⁵And He ascended into the second heaven, and He did not transform Himself, but all the messengers who were on the right, and on the left, and the throne in the midst ²⁶both worshiped Him and praised Him and said, "How did our Lord escape us while descending, and we did not perceive [it]?" ²⁷And in like manner He ascended into the third heaven, and they praised and said in like manner. ²⁸And in the fourth heaven and also in the fifth they said precisely after the same manner. ²⁹But there was one glory, and from it He did not change Himself. ³⁰And I saw when He ascended into the sixth heaven, and they worshiped and glorified Him. ³¹But in all the heavens the praise increased. ³²And I saw how He ascended into the seventh heaven, and all the righteous and all the messengers praised Him. And then I saw Him sit down on the right hand of that Great Glory whose glory I told you that I could not behold. ³³And also the Messenger—the Holy Spirit—I saw sitting on the left hand. ³⁴And this messenger said to me, "Isaiah, son of Amoz, it is enough for you; for you have seen what no child of flesh has seen. ³⁵And you will return into your garment [of flesh] until your days are completed. Then you will come here." ³⁶Isaiah saw these things and told [it] to all that stood before him, and they praised. And he spoke to Hezekiah the king and said, "I have spoken these things; ³⁷both the end of this world ³⁸and all this vision will be consummated in the last generations." ³⁹And Isaiah made him swear that he would not tell [it] to the people of Israel, nor give these words to any man to transcribe. ⁴⁰… such things you will read. And watch in the Holy Spirit in order they you may receive your garments, and thrones, and crowns of glory, which are laid up in the seventh heaven. ⁴¹On account of these visions and prophecies Sammael, Satan, sawed apart Isaiah the son of Amoz, the prophet, by the hand of Manasseh. ⁴²And Hezekiah delivered all these things to Manasseh in the twenty-sixth year. ⁴³But Manasseh did not remember them nor place these things in his heart, but becoming the servant of Satan, he was destroyed. HERE ENDS THE VISION OF ISAIAH THE PROPHET WITH HIS ASCENSION.

2 BARUCH

2 Baruch is a Jewish text, likely pseudepigraphical, thought to have been written in the 1st or 2nd century AD. It is also known as the Syriac Apocalypse of Baruch (used to distinguish it from the Greek Apocalypse of Baruch—3 Baruch). The Apocalypse proper occupies the first 77 chapters of the book. Chapters 78–87 are usually referred to as the "Letter of Baruch to the Nine and a Half Tribes."

CHAPTER 1

¹And it came to pass in the twenty-fifth year of Jehoiachin, king of Judah, that the word of the LORD came to Baruch, the son of Neriah, and said to him: ²"Have you seen all that this people are doing to Me, that the evils which these two tribes which remained have done are greater than [those of] the ten tribes which were carried away captive? ³For the former tribes were forced by their kings to commit sin, but these two of themselves have been forcing and compelling their kings to commit sin. ⁴For this reason, behold, I bring calamity on this city and on its inhabitants, and it will be removed from before Me for a time, and I will scatter this people among the nations that they may do good to the nations. And My people will be disciplined, and the time will come when they will seek for the prosperity of their times."

CHAPTER 2

¹"For I have said these things to you that you may bid Jeremiah, and all those that are like you, to retire from this city. ²For your works are to this city as a firm pillar, || And your prayers as a strong wall."

CHAPTER 3

¹And I said, "O LORD, my Lord, have I come into the world for this purpose that I might see the calamities of my mother? No, my Lord. ²If I have found grace in Your sight, first take my spirit that I may go to my fathers and not behold the destruction of my mother. For two things vehemently constrain me: for I cannot resist You, and my soul, moreover, cannot behold the calamities of my mother. ⁴But one thing I will say in Your presence, O LORD. ⁵What, therefore, will there be after these things? For if You destroy Your city, and deliver up Your land to those that hate us, how will the name of Israel be remembered again? ⁶Or how will one speak of Your praises? Or to whom will that which is in Your law be explained? Or will the world return to its nature of former times, and the age revert to primeval silence? And will the multitude of

2 BARUCH

souls be taken away, and the nature of man not again be named? And where is all that which You said regarding us?"

CHAPTER 4
¹And the LORD said to me: "This city will be delivered up for a time, || And the people will be disciplined during a time, || And the world will not be given over to oblivion." [[²"Do you think that this is that city of which I said, On the palms of My hands I have graven you? ³This building now built in your midst is not that which is revealed with Me, that which [was] prepared beforehand here from the time when I took counsel to make Paradise, and showed Adam before he sinned, but when he transgressed the commandment it was removed from him, as also Paradise. ⁴And after these things I showed it to My servant Abraham by night among the portions of the victims. ⁵And again I also showed it to Moses on Mount Sinai when I showed to the likeness of the Dwelling Place and all its vessels. ⁶And now, behold, it is preserved with Me, as Paradise. ⁷Go, therefore, and do as I command you."]]

CHAPTER 5
¹And I answered and said, "So then I am destined to grieve for Zion, || For Your enemies will come to this place and pollute Your sanctuary, || And lead Your inheritance into captivity, || And make themselves masters of those whom You have loved, || And they will depart again to the place of their idols, || And will boast before them: And what will You do for Your great Name?" ²And the LORD said to me: "My Name and My glory are to all eternity; And My judgment will maintain its right in its own time. ³And you will see with your eyes || That the enemy will not overthrow Zion, || Nor will they burn Jerusalem, || But be the ministers of the Judge for the time. ⁴But you go and do whatever I have said to you." ⁵And I went and took Jeremiah, and Adu, and Seriah, and Jabish, and Gedaliah, and all the honorable men of the people, and I led them to the Valley of Kidron, and I narrated to them all that had been said to me. ⁶And they lifted up their voice, and they all wept. ⁷And we sat there and fasted until the evening.

CHAPTER 6
¹And it came to pass on the next day that, behold, the army of the Chaldees surrounded the city, and at the time of the evening, I, Baruch, left the people, and I went forth and stood by the oak. ²And I was grieving over Zion and lamenting over the captivity which had come on the people. ³And behold, suddenly a strong spirit raised me, and bore me aloft over the wall of Jerusalem. ⁴And I beheld, and behold, four messengers standing at the four corners of the city, each of them holding a torch of fire in his hands. ⁵And another messenger began to descend from Heaven, and said to them, "Hold your lamps, and do not light them until I tell you. ⁶For I am first sent to speak a word to the earth, and to place in it what the LORD the Most High has commanded me." ⁷And I saw him descend into the Holy of Holies, and take from there the veil, and holy Ark, and the propitiatory covering, and the two tablets, and the holy raiment of the priests, and the altar of incense, and the forty-eight precious stones with which the priest was adorned, and all the holy vessels of the Dwelling Place. ⁸And he spoke to the earth with a loud voice: "Earth, earth, earth! Hear the word of the mighty God, || And receive what I commit to you, || And guard them until the last times, || So that, when you are ordered, you may restore them, || So that strangers may not get possession of them. ⁹For the time comes when Jerusalem will also be delivered for a time, || Until it is said that it is again restored forever." ¹⁰And the earth opened its mouth and swallowed them up.

CHAPTER 7
¹And after these things I heard that messenger saying to those messengers who held the lamps: "Destroy, therefore, and overthrow its wall to its foundations, lest the enemy should boast and say, || We have overthrown the wall of Zion, || And we have burned the place of the mighty God." ²And they have seized the place where I had been standing before.

CHAPTER 8
¹Now the messengers did as he had commanded them, and when they had broken up the corners of the walls, a voice was heard from the interior of the temple, after the wall had fallen, saying, ²"Enter, you enemies, || And come, you adversaries; For He who kept the house has forsaken [it]." ³And I, Baruch, departed. ⁴And it came to pass after these things that the army of the Chaldees entered and seized the house, and all that was around it. And they led the people away captive and slew some of them, and bound Zedekiah the king, and sent him to the king of Babylon.

CHAPTER 9
¹And I, Baruch, came, and Jeremiah, whose heart was found pure from sins, who had not been captured in the seizure of the city. ²And we tore our garments, we wept, and mourned, and fasted seven days.

CHAPTER 10
¹And it came to pass after seven days, that the word of God came to me, and said to me: ²"Tell Jeremiah to go and support the captivity of the people to Babylon. ³But remain here amid the desolation of Zion, and I will show to you after these days what will befall at the end of days." ⁴And I spoke to Jeremiah as the LORD commanded me. ⁵And he, indeed, departed with the people, but I, Baruch, returned and sat before the gates of the temple, and I lamented with the following lamentation over Zion and said, ⁶"Blessed is he who was not born, || Or he, who having been born, has died. ⁷But as for us who live, woe to us, || Because we see the afflictions of Zion, || And what has befallen Jerusalem. ⁸I will call the Sirens from the sea, || And you Lilin, come from the desert, || And you Shedim and dragons from the forests: Awake and gird up your loins to mourning, || And take up the dirges with me, || And make lamentation with me. ⁹You farmers, do not sow again; And, O earth, why do you give your harvest fruits? Keep within you the sweets of your sustenance. ¹⁰And you, vine, why further do you give your wine? For an offering will not be made again from there in Zion, || Nor will first-fruits be offered again. ¹¹And you, O heavens, withhold your dew, || And do not open the treasuries of rain; ¹²And you, O sun, withhold the light of your rays; And you, O moon, extinguish the multitude of your light. For why should light rise again || Where the light of Zion is darkened? ¹³And you—you bridegrooms—do not enter in, || And do not let the brides adorn themselves with garlands; And, you women, do not pray that you may bear. ¹⁴For the barren will above all rejoice, || And those who have no sons will be glad, || And those who have sons will have anguish. ¹⁵For why should they bear in pain, || Only to bury in grief? ¹⁶Or why, again, should mankind have sons? Or why should the seed of their kind be named again, || Where this mother is desolate, || And her sons are led into captivity? ¹⁷From this time forward, do not speak of beauty, || And do not discourse of gracefulness. ¹⁸Moreover, you priests, take the keys of the sanctuary, || And cast them into the height of Heaven, || And give them to the LORD and say, || Guard Your house Yourself, || For behold, we are found false stewards. ¹⁹And you—you virgins who weave fine linen || And silk with gold of Ophir—Take all [these] things with haste || And cast [them] into the fire, || That it may bear them to Him who made them, || And the flame send them to Him who created them, || Lest the enemy get possession of them."

CHAPTER 11
¹Moreover, I, Baruch, say this against you, Babylon: "If you had prospered, || And Zion had dwelt in her glory, || Yet the grief to us had been great || That you should be equal to Zion. ²But now, behold, the grief is infinite, || And the lamentation measureless, || For behold, you are prospered || And Zion desolate. ³Who will be judge regarding these things? Or to whom will we complain regarding that which has befallen us? O LORD, how have You borne [it]? ⁴Our fathers went to rest without grief, || And behold, the righteous sleep in the earth in tranquility; ⁵For they did not know this anguish, || Nor yet had they heard of that which had befallen us. ⁶Would that you had ears, O earth, || And that you had a heart, O dust, || That you might go and announce in Sheol, || And say to the dead: ⁷Blessed are you more than we who live."

CHAPTER 12
¹"But I will say this as I think, || And speak against you—the land that is prospering. ²The noonday does not always burn, || Nor do the rays of the sun constantly give light. ³And do not expect to rejoice, || Nor condemn greatly. ⁴For assuredly in its season the [divine] wrath

will be awakened against you, || Which is now restrained by long-suffering as it were by a rein." ⁵And when I had said these things, I fasted seven days.

CHAPTER 13

¹And it came to pass after these things that I, Baruch, was standing on Mount Zion, and behold, a voice came forth from the height and said to me: ²"Stand on your feet, Baruch, and hear the word of the mighty God. ³Because you have been astonished at what has befallen Zion, you will therefore be assuredly preserved to the consummation of the times, that you may be for a testimony. ⁴So that, if ever those prosperous cities say: ⁵Why has the mighty God brought this retribution on us? Say to them, You and those like you will have seen this evil and retribution which is coming on you and on your people in its [appointed] time that the nations may be thoroughly smitten. ⁶And then they will be in anguish. ⁷And if they say at that time: ⁸For how long? You will say to them: You who have drunk the strained wine, || Drink also of its dregs—The judgment of the Lofty One || Who has no respect of persons; ⁹On this account He formerly had no mercy on His own sons, || But afflicted them as His enemies, because they sinned, ¹⁰Then, therefore, they were disciplined || That they might be sanctified. ¹¹But now, you peoples and nations, you are guilty || Because you have always trodden down the earth, || And used the creation unrighteously. ¹²For I have always benefited you. And you have always been ungrateful for the beneficence."

CHAPTER 14

¹And I answered and said, "Behold, You have shown me the methods of the times, and that which will be. And You have said to me that the retribution which was spoken of by You will be endured by the nations. ²And now I know that those who have sinned are many, and they have lived…and departed from the world, but that few nations will be left in those times to whom…the words [which] You said. ³And what advantage [is there] in this or what worse than [these?] ⁴But I will again speak in Your presence: ⁵What have they profited who had knowledge before You and have not walked in vanity as the rest of the nations, and have not said to the dead, Give us life, but always feared You, and have not left Your ways? ⁶And behold, they have been carried off, nor on their account have You had mercy on Zion. ⁷And if others did evil, it was due to Zion that on account of the works of those who worked good works she should be forgiven and should not be overwhelmed on account of the works of those who worked unrighteousness. ⁸But who, O LORD, my Lord, will comprehend Your judgment, || Or who will search out the profoundness of Your way? Or who will think out the weight of Your path? ⁹Or who will be able to think out Your incomprehensible counsel? Or who of those that are born has ever found || The beginning or end of Your wisdom? ¹⁰For we have all been made like a breath. ¹¹For as the breath ascends involuntarily, and again dies, so it is with the nature of men, who do not depart according to their own will, and do not know what will befall them in the end. ¹²For the righteous justly hope for the end, and without fear depart from this habitation, because they have with You a store of works preserved in treasuries. ¹³On this account also, these without fear leave this world, and trusting with joy they hope to receive the world which You have promised them. ¹⁴But as for us—woe to us, who are also now shamefully entreated, and at that time look forward [only] to calamities. ¹⁵But You know accurately what You have done by means of Your servants; for we are not able to understand that which is good as You are, our Creator. ¹⁶But again I will speak in Your presence, O LORD, my Lord. ¹⁷When of old there was no world with its inhabitants, You devised and spoke with a word, and immediately the works of creation stood before You. ¹⁸And You said that You would make for Your world man as the administrator of Your works, that it might be known that he was by no means made on account of the world, but the world on account of him. ¹⁹And now I see that as for the world which was made on account of us, behold, it abides; but we, on account of whom it was made, depart."

CHAPTER 15

¹And the LORD answered and said to me: "You are rightly astonished regarding the departure of man, but you have not judged well regarding the calamities which befall those who sin. ²And as regards what you have said, that the righteous are carried off and the impious are prospered, ³and as regards what you have said, Man does not know Your judgment—on this account hear, and I will speak to you, and listen, and I will cause you to hear My words. ⁵Man would not rightly have understood My judgment, unless he had accepted the law, and I had instructed him in understanding. ⁶But now, because he transgressed willfully, yes, just on this ground that he knows, he will be tormented. ⁷And as regards what you said touching the righteous, that on account of them this world has come, so also again, that which is to come will come on their account. ⁸For this world is to them a strife and a labor with much trouble; and that accordingly which is to come—a crown with great glory."

CHAPTER 16

¹And I answered and said, ²"LORD, my Lord, behold, the years of this time are few and evil, and who is able in his short time to acquire that which is measureless?"

CHAPTER 17

¹And the LORD answered and said to me: "With the Most High account is not taken of time nor of a few years. ²For what did it profit Adam that he lived nine hundred and thirty years and transgressed that which he was commanded? Therefore, the multitude of time that he lived did not profit him, but brought death and cut off the years of those who were born from him, wherein Moses suffered loss in that he lived only one hundred and twenty years, and inasmuch as he was subject to Him who formed him, brought the law to the seed of Jacob, and lighted a lamp for the nation of Israel?"

CHAPTER 18

¹And I answered and said, "He that lighted has taken from the light, and there are but few that have imitated him. ²But those many whom he has lighted have taken from the darkness of Adam and have not rejoiced in the light of the lamp."

CHAPTER 19

¹And He answered and said to me: "For what reason at that time he appointed for them a covenant and said, Behold, I have placed before you life and death, || And he called the heavens and earth to witness against them. ²For he knew that his time was but short, || But that the heavens and earth always endure. ³But after his death they sinned and transgressed, || Though they knew that they had the law reproving [them], || And the light in which nothing could err, || Also the spheres which testify, and Me. ⁴Now regarding everything that is, it is I that judge, but do not take counsel in your soul regarding these things, nor afflict yourself because of those which have been. ⁵For now it is the consummation of time that should be considered, whether of business, or of prosperity, or of shame, and not the beginning thereof. ⁶Because if a man is prospered in his beginnings and shamefully entreated in his old age, he forgets all the prosperity that he had. ⁷And again, if a man is shamefully entreated in his beginnings, and at his end is prospered, he does not remember again his evil entreatment. ⁸And again listen: though each one were prospered all that time—all the time from the day on which death was decreed against those who transgress—and in his end was destroyed, everything would have been in vain."

CHAPTER 20

¹"Therefore, behold! The days come, || And the times will hasten more than the former, || And the seasons will speed by more than those that are past, || And the years will pass more quickly than the present [years]. ²Therefore I have now taken Zion away, || That I may the more speedily visit the world in its season. ³Now therefore, hold fast in your heart everything that I command you, || And seal it in the recesses of your mind. ⁴And then I will show you the judgment of My might, || And My ways which are unsearchable. ⁵Go therefore and sanctify yourself seven days, and eat no bread, nor drink water, nor speak to anyone. ⁶And afterward come to that place and I will reveal Myself to you, and speak true things with you, and I will give you

commandment regarding the method of the times; for they are coming and do not tarry."

CHAPTER 21

¹And I went there and sat in the Valley of Kidron in a cave of the earth, and I sanctified my soul there, and I ate no bread, yet I was not hungry, and I drank no water, yet I did not thirst, and I was there until the seventh day, as He had commanded me. ²And afterward I came to that place where He had spoken with me. ³And it came to pass at sunset that my soul took much thought, and I began to speak in the presence of the Mighty One, and said, ⁴"O You that have made the earth, hear me, that have fixed the expanse by the word, and have made firm the height of the Heaven by the Spirit, that have called from the beginning of the world that which did not yet exist, and they obey You. ⁵You that have commanded the air by Your nod and have seen those things which are to be as those things which You are doing. ⁶You that rule with great thought the hosts that stand before You; also the countless holy beings, which You made from the beginning, of flame and fire, which stand around Your throne, You rule with indignation. ⁷To You only does this belong that You should immediately do whatever You wish. ⁸[You] who cause the drops of rain to rain by number on the earth, and alone knows the consummation of the times before they come, have respect to my prayer. ⁹For You alone are able to sustain all who are, and those who have passed away, and those who are to be, those who sin, and those who are righteous (as living and being past finding out). ¹⁰For You alone live [as] immortal and past finding out, and know the number of mankind. ¹¹And if in time many have sinned, yet others—not a few—have been righteous. ¹²You know where You preserve the end of those who have sinned, or the consummation of those who have been righteous. ¹³For if there were this life only, which belongs to all men, nothing could be more bitter than this. ¹⁴For of what profit is strength that turns to sickness, ‖ Or fullness of food that turns to famine, ‖ Or beauty that turns to ugliness. ¹⁵For the nature of man is always changeable. ¹⁶For what we were formerly now we no longer are and what we now are we will not afterward remain. ¹⁷For if a consummation had not been prepared for all, in vain would have been their beginning. But regarding everything that comes from You, You inform me, and regarding everything about which I ask You, You enlighten me. ¹⁹How long will that which is corruptible remain, and how long will the time of mortals be prospered, and until what time will those who transgress in the world be polluted with much wickedness? ²⁰Therefore command in mercy and accomplish all that You said You would bring, that Your might may be made known to those who think that Your long-suffering is weakness. ²¹And show to those who do not know, that everything that has befallen us and our city until now has been according to the long-suffering of Your power, because on account of Your Name You have called us a beloved people. ²²Therefore, henceforth, bring mortality to an end. ²³And reprove the messenger of death accordingly, and let Your glory appear, and let the might of Your beauty be known, and let Sheol be sealed so that from this time forward it may not receive the dead, and let the treasuries of souls restore those which are enclosed in them. ²⁴For there have been many years like those that are desolate from the days of Abraham, and Isaac, and Jacob, and of all those who are like them, who sleep in the earth, on whose account You said that You had created the world. ²⁵And now quickly show Your glory, and do not defer what has been promised by You." ²⁶And [when] I had completed the words of this prayer I was greatly weakened.

CHAPTER 22

¹And it came to pass after these things that, behold, the heavens were opened, and I saw, and power was given to me, and a voice was heard from on high, and it said to me: ²"Baruch, Baruch, why are you troubled? ³He who travels by a road but does not complete it, or who departs by sea but does not arrive at the port, can he be comforted? ⁴Or he who promises to give a present to another, but does not fulfill it, is it not robbery? ⁵Or he who sows the earth, but does not reap its fruit in its season, does he not lose everything? ⁶Or he who plants a plant unless it grows until the time suitable to it, does he who planted it expect to receive fruit from it? ⁷Or a woman who has conceived, if she brings forth untimely, does she not assuredly slay her infant? ⁸Or he who builds a house, if he does not roof it and complete it, can it be called a house? Tell Me that first."

CHAPTER 23

¹And I answered and said, "Not so, O LORD, my Lord." ²And He answered and said to me, "Why are you therefore troubled about that which you do not know, and why are you ill at ease about things in which you are ignorant? ³For as you have not forgotten the people who now are and those who have passed away, so I remember those who are appointed to come. ⁴Because when Adam sinned and death was decreed against those who should be born, then the multitude of those who should be born was numbered, and for that number a place was prepared where the living might dwell and the dead might be guarded. Therefore, before the number previously mentioned is fulfilled, the creature will not live again [[for My Spirit is the creator of life]], and Sheol will receive the dead. ⁶And again it is given to you to hear what things are to come after these times. ⁷For My redemption has truly drawn near and is not far distant as before."

CHAPTER 24

¹"For behold! The days come and the scrolls will be opened in which are written the sins of all those who have sinned, and again also the treasuries in which the righteousness of all those who have been righteous in creation is gathered. ²For it will come to pass at that time that you will see—and the many that are with you—the long-suffering of the Most High, which has been throughout all generations, who has been long-suffering toward all who are born, [both] those who sin and [those who] are righteous." ³And I answered and said, "But, behold! O LORD, no one knows the number of those things which have passed nor yet of those things which are to come. ⁴For I indeed know that which has befallen us, but I do not know what will happen to our enemies, and when You will visit Your works."

CHAPTER 25

¹And He answered and said to me: "You, too, will be preserved until that time until that sign which the Most High will work for the inhabitants of the earth in the end of days. ²This will therefore be the sign: ³when a stupor will seize the inhabitants of the earth, and they will fall into many tribulations, and again when they will fall into great torments. And it will come to pass when they say in their thoughts by reason of their much tribulation: The Mighty One no longer remembers the earth—yes, it will come to pass when they abandon hope, that the time will then awake."

CHAPTER 26

¹And I answered and said, "Will that tribulation which is to come continue [for] a long time, and will that necessarily comprise many years?"

CHAPTER 27

¹And He answered and said to me: "That time is divided into twelve parts, and each one of them is reserved for that which is appointed for it. ²In the first part there will be the beginning of commotions. ³And in the second part [there will be] slayings of the great ones. ⁴And in the third part the fall of many by death. ⁵And in the fourth part the sending of the sword. ⁶And in the fifth part famine and the withholding of rain. ⁷And in the sixth part earthquakes and terrors. ⁸[And in the seventh part] … ⁹And in the eighth part a multitude of specters and attacks of the Shedim. ¹⁰And in the ninth part the fall of fire. ¹¹And in the tenth part plunder and much oppression. ¹²And in the eleventh part wickedness and unchastity. ¹³And in the twelfth part confusion from the mingling together of all those things previously mentioned. ¹⁴For these parts of that time are reserved and will be mingled with one another and minister to one another. ¹⁵For some will leave out some of their own, and receive [in its stead] from others, and some complete their own and that of others, so that those may not understand who are on the earth in those days that this is the consummation of the times."

CHAPTER 28

¹"Nevertheless, whoever understands will then be wise. ²For the measure and reckoning of that time are two parts a week of seven weeks." ³And I answered and said, "It is good

for a man to come and behold, but it is better that he should not come lest he fall. ⁴[[But I will say this also: ⁵Will He who is incorruptible despise those things which are corruptible, and whatever befalls in the case of those things which are corruptible, so that He might look only to those things which are not corruptible?]] ⁶But if, O LORD, those things will assuredly come to pass which You have foretold to me, so also show this to me if indeed I have found grace in Your sight. ⁷Is it in one place or in one of the parts of the earth that those things have come to pass, or will the whole earth experience [them]?"

CHAPTER 29

¹And He answered and said to me: "Whatever will then befall [will befall] the whole earth; therefore, all who live will experience [them]. ²For at that time I will only protect those who are found in those same days in this land. ³And it will come to pass when all is accomplished that was to come to pass in those parts, that the Messiah will then begin to be revealed. ⁴And Behemoth will be revealed from his place and Leviathan will ascend from the sea—those two great monsters which I created on the fifth day of creation, and will have kept until that time; and then they will be for food for all that are left. ⁵The earth will also yield its fruit ten-thousandfold, and on each vine there will be one thousand branches, and each branch will produce one thousand clusters, and each cluster produce one thousand grapes, and each grape produce a cor of wine. ⁶And those who have hungered will rejoice: moreover also, they will behold marvels every day. ⁷For winds will go forth from before Me to bring every morning the fragrance of aromatic fruits, and at the close of the day clouds distilling the dew of health. ⁸And it will come to pass at that same time that the treasury of manna will again descend from on high, and they will eat of it in those years, because these are they who have come to the consummation of time."

CHAPTER 30

¹"And it will come to pass after these things, when the time of the advent of the Messiah is fulfilled, that He will return in glory. ²Then all who have fallen asleep in hope of Him will rise again. And it will come to pass at that time that the treasuries will be opened in which is preserved the number of the souls of the righteous, and they will come forth, and a multitude of souls will be seen together in one assemblage of one thought, and the first will rejoice and the last will not be grieved. ³For they know that the time has come of which it is said that it is the consummation of the times. ⁴But the souls of the wicked, when they behold all these things, will then waste away more. ⁵For they will know that their torment has come, and their perdition has arrived."

CHAPTER 31

¹And it came to pass after these things that I went to the people and said to them: "Assemble to me all your elders and I will speak words to them." ²And they all assembled in the Valley of the Kidron. ³And I answered and said to them: "Hear, O Israel, and I will speak to you, || And give ear, O seed of Jacob, and I will instruct you. ⁴Do not forget Zion, || But hold in remembrance the anguish of Jerusalem. ⁵For behold, the days come || When everything that is will become the prey of corruption || And be as though it had not been."

CHAPTER 32

¹"But as for you, if you prepare your hearts so as to sow in them the fruits of the law, it will protect you in that time in which the Mighty One is to shake the whole creation. ²[[Because after a short time the building of Zion will be shaken in order that it may be built again. But that building will not remain, but will again after a time be rooted out, and will remain desolate until the time. ⁴And afterward it must be renewed in glory and perfected forevermore.]] ⁵Therefore we should not be distressed so much over the calamity which has now come as over that which is still to be. ⁶For there will be a greater trial than these two tribulations when the Mighty One will renew His creation. ⁷And now do not draw near to me for a few days, nor seek me until I come to you." ⁸And it came to pass when I had spoken all these words to them, that I, Baruch, went my way, and when the people saw me setting out, they lifted up their voice and lamented and said, ⁹"To where are you departing from us, Baruch, and are you forsaking us as a father who forsakes his orphan children, and departs from them?"

CHAPTER 33

¹"Are these the commands which your companion, Jeremiah the prophet, commanded you, and said to you: Look to this people until I go and make ready the rest of the brothers in Babylon against whom has gone forth the sentence that they should be led into captivity? And now if you also forsake us, it were good for us all to die before you, then that you should withdraw from us."

CHAPTER 34

¹And I answered and said to the people: "Far be it from me to forsake you or to withdraw from you, ²but I will only go to the Holy of Holies to inquire of the Mighty One concerning you and concerning Zion, if in some respect I should receive more illumination: and after these things I will return to you."

CHAPTER 35

¹And I, Baruch, went to the holy place, and sat down on the ruins and wept, and said, ²"O that my eyes were springs, || And my eyelids a fount of tears. ³For how will I lament for Zion, || And how will I mourn for Jerusalem? ⁴Because in that place where I am now prostrate, || Of old the high priest offered holy sacrifices, || And placed an incense of fragrant odors thereon. ⁵But now our glorying has been made into dust, || And the desire of our soul into sand."

CHAPTER 36

¹And when I had said these things, I fell asleep there, and I saw a vision in the night. ²And behold, a forest of trees planted on the plain, and lofty and rugged rocky mountains surrounded it, and that forest occupied much space. ³And behold, over against it arose a vine, and from under it there went forth a fountain peacefully. ⁴Now that fountain came to the forest and was [stirred] into great waves, and those waves submerged that forest, and suddenly they rooted out the greater part of that forest and overthrew all the mountains which were around it. ⁵And the height of the forest began to be made low, and the top of the mountains was made low, and that fountain prevailed greatly, so that it left nothing of that great forest save one cedar only. ⁶Also, when it had cast it down and had destroyed and rooted out the greater part of that forest, so that nothing was left of it, nor could its place be recognized, then that vine began to come with the fountain in peace and great tranquility, and it came to a place which was not far from that cedar, and they brought the cedar which had been cast down to it. ⁷And I beheld, and behold, that vine opened its mouth and spoke and said to that cedar: "Are you not that cedar which was left of the forest of wickedness, and by whose means wickedness persisted, and was worked all those years, and never for good? ⁸And you kept conquering that which was not yours, and to that which was yours you never showed compassion, and you kept extending your power over those who were far from you, and those who drew near you, you held fast in the toils of your wickedness, and you always uplifted yourself as one that could not be rooted out! ⁹But now your time has sped, and your hour has come. ¹⁰Do you also therefore depart, O cedar, after the forest, which departed before you, and become dust with it, and let your ashes be mingled together? ¹¹And now recline in anguish and rest in torment until your last time comes, in which you will come again, and be tormented still more."

CHAPTER 37

¹And after these things I saw that cedar burning, and the vine growing, itself and all around it, the plain full of unfading flowers. ²And I indeed awoke and arose.

CHAPTER 38

¹And I prayed and said, "O LORD, my Lord, You always enlighten those who are led by understanding. ²Your law is life, and Your wisdom is right guidance. ³Therefore make known to me the interpretation of this vision. ⁴For You know that my soul has always walked in Your law, and from my [earliest] days I did not depart from Your wisdom."

CHAPTER 39

¹And He answered and said to me: "Baruch, this is the interpretation of the vision which you have seen. ²As you have seen the great forest, which lofty and rugged mountains surrounded, this is the word. ³Behold! The days come, and this kingdom will be destroyed which once destroyed Zion, and it will be subjected to that which comes after it. ⁴Moreover, that also again after a time will be destroyed, and another, a third, will arise, and that also will have dominion for its time, and will be destroyed. ⁵And after these things a fourth kingdom will arise, whose power will be harsh and evil far beyond those which were before it, and it will rule many times as the forests on the plain, and it will hold fast for times, and will exalt itself more than the cedars of Lebanon. ⁶And by it the truth will be hidden, and all those who are polluted with iniquity will flee to it, as evil beasts flee and creep into the forest. ⁷And it will come to pass when the time of its consummation—that it should fall—has approached, then the principate of My Messiah will be revealed, which is like the fountain and the vine, and when it is revealed it will root out the multitude of its host. ⁸And as touching that which you have seen, the lofty cedar, which was left of that forest, and the fact that the vine spoke those words with it which you heard, this is the word."

CHAPTER 40

¹"The last leader of that time will be left alive, when the multitude of his hosts will be put to the sword, and he will be bound, and they will take him up to Mount Zion, and My Messiah will convict him of all his impieties, and will gather and set before him all the works of his hosts. ²And afterward he will put him to death, and protect the rest of My people which will be found in the place which I have chosen. ³And His principate will stand forever, until the world of corruption is at an end, and until the times previously mentioned are fulfilled. ⁴This is your vision, and this is its interpretation."

CHAPTER 41

¹And I answered and said, "For whom and for how many will these things be? Or who will be worthy to live at that time? ²For I will speak before You everything that I think, and I will ask of You regarding those things which I meditate. ³For behold, I see many of Your people who have withdrawn from Your covenant, and cast from themselves the yoke of Your law. ⁴But others again I have seen who have forsaken their vanity and fled for refuge beneath Your wings. ⁵What therefore will be to them? Or how will the last time receive them? ⁶Or perhaps the time of these will assuredly be weighed, and as the beam inclines will they be judged accordingly?"

CHAPTER 42

¹And He answered and said to me: "I will also show these things to you. ²As for what you said—To whom will these things be, and how many [will they be]? To those who have believed there will be the good which was spoken of formerly, and to those who despise there will be the contrary of these things. ³And as for what you said regarding those who have drawn near and those who have withdrawn this in the word. ⁴As for those who were before subject, and afterward withdrew and mingled themselves with the seed of mingled peoples, the time of these was the former, and was accounted as something exalted. ⁵And as for those who before did not know but afterward knew life, and mingled [only] with the seed of the people which had separated itself, the time of these [is] the latter, and is accounted as something exalted. ⁶And time will succeed to time and season to season, and one will receive from another, and then with a view to the consummation, everything will be compared according to the measure of the times and the hours of the seasons. ⁷For corruption will take those that belong to it, and life those that belong to it. ⁸And the dust will be called, and there will be said to it: Give back that which is not yours and raise up all that you have kept until its time."

CHAPTER 43

¹"But you, Baruch, direct your heart to that which has been said to you, || And understand those things which have been shown to you; For there are many continuous consolations for you. ²For you will depart from this place, || And you will pass from the regions which are now seen by you, || And you will forget whatever is corruptible, || And will not again recall those things which happen among mortals. ³Therefore go and command your people, and come to this place, and afterward fast seven days, and then I will come to you and speak with you."

CHAPTER 44

¹And I, Baruch, went from there, and came to my people, and I called my firstborn son and [the Gedaliahs] my friends, and seven of the elders of the people, and I said to them: "Behold, I go to my fathers || According to the way of all the earth. ³But do not withdraw from the way of the law, || But guard and admonish the people which remain, || Lest they withdraw from the commandments of the Mighty One. ⁴For you see that He whom we serve is just, || And our Creator is no respecter of persons. ⁵And see what has befallen Zion, || And what has happened to Jerusalem. ⁶For the judgment of the Mighty One will [thereby] be made known, || And His ways, which, though past finding out, are right. ⁷For if you endure and persevere in His fear, || And do not forget His law, || The times will change over you for good, || And you will see the consolation of Zion. ⁸Because whatever is now is nothing, || But that which will be is very great. ⁹For everything that is corruptible will pass away, || And everything that dies will depart, || And all the present time will be forgotten, || Nor will there be any remembrance of the present time, which is defiled with evils. ¹⁰For that which runs now runs to vanity, || And that which prospers will quickly fall and be humiliated. ¹¹For that which is to be will be the object of desire, || And for that which comes afterward will we hope; For it is a time that does not pass away, ¹²And the hour comes which abides forever. And the new world [comes] which does not turn to corruption those who depart to its blessedness, || And has no mercy on those who depart to torment, || And does not lead to perdition those who live in it. ¹³For these are they who will inherit that time which has been spoken of, || And theirs is the inheritance of the promised time. ¹⁴These are they who have acquired for themselves treasures of wisdom, || And with them are found stores of understanding, || And they have not withdrawn from mercy, || And they have preserved the truth of the law. ¹⁵For the world to come will be given to them, || But the dwelling of the rest, who are many, will be in the fire."

CHAPTER 45

¹"Therefore, so far as you are able, instruct the people, for that labor is ours. ²For if you teach them, you will restore them."

CHAPTER 46

¹And my son and the elders of the people answered and said to me: "Has the Mighty One humiliated us to such a degree || As to take you from us quickly? ²And we will truly be in darkness, || And there will be no light to the people who are left, ³For where again will we seek the law, || Or who will distinguish between death and life for us?" ⁴And I said to them, "I cannot resist the throne of the Mighty One; Nevertheless, there will not be wanting to Israel a wise man || Nor a son of the law to the race of Jacob. ⁵But only prepare your hearts, that you may obey the law, || And be subject to those who in fear are wise and understanding; And prepare your souls that you may not depart from them. ⁶For if you do these things, || Good tidings will come to you, [[|| Which I before told you of; Nor will you fall into the torment, of which I testified to you before." ⁷(But with regard to the word that I was to have taken, I did not make [it] known to them or to my son.)]]

CHAPTER 47

¹And when I had gone forth and dismissed them, I went there and said to them: "Behold! I go to Hebron; for the Mighty One has sent me there." ²And I came to that place where the word had been spoken to me, and I sat there, and fasted seven days.

CHAPTER 48

¹And it came to pass after the seventh day, that I prayed before the Mighty One and said, ²"O my Lord, You summon the advent of the times, || And they stand before You; You cause the power of the ages to pass away, || And they do not resist You; You arrange the method of the seasons, || And they obey You. ³You alone know the duration of the generations, || And You do not reveal Your mysteries to many.

⁴You make known the multitude of the fire, || And You weigh the lightness of the wind. ⁵You explore the limit of the heights, || And You scrutinize the depths of the darkness. ⁶You care for the number which pass away that they may be preserved, || And You prepare an abode for those that are to be. ⁷You remember the beginning which You have made, || And the destruction that is to be, You do not forget. ⁸With nods of fear and indignation You command the flames, || And they change into spirits, || And with a word You give life to that which was not, || And with mighty power You hold that which has not yet come. ⁹You instruct created things in Your understanding, || And You make wise the spheres so as to minister in their orders. ¹⁰Innumerable armies stand before You || And minister in their orders quietly at Your nod. ¹¹Hear Your servant || And give ear to my petition. ¹²For in a short time are we born, || And in a short time we return. ¹³But with You hours are as an age, || And days as generations. ¹⁴Therefore, do not be angry with man, for he is nothing; ¹⁵And do not take account of our works; For what are we? For behold, by Your gift we come into the world, || And we do not depart of our own will. ¹⁶For we did not say to our parents, Beget us, || Nor did we send to Sheol and say, Receive us. ¹⁷What therefore is our strength that we should bear Your wrath, || Or what are we that we should endure Your judgment? ¹⁸Protect us in Your compassions, || And help us in Your mercy. ¹⁹Behold the little ones that are subject to You, || And save all that draw near to You: And do not destroy the hope of our people, || And do not cut short the times of our aid. ²⁰For this is the nation which You have chosen, || And these are the people to whom You find no equal. ²¹But now I will speak before You, || And I will say as my heart thinks. ²²We trust in You, for behold, Your law is with us, || And we know that we will not fall so long as we keep Your statutes. ²³[[We are blessed for all time at all events in this—That we have not mingled with the nations.]] ²⁴For we are all one celebrated people, || Who have received one law from One: And the law which is among us will aid us, || And the surpassing wisdom which is in us will help us." ²⁵And when I had prayed and said these things, I was greatly weakened. ²⁶And He answered and said to me: "You have prayed simply, O Baruch, || And all your words have been heard. ²⁷But My judgment exacts its own || And My law exacts its rights. ²⁸For from your words I will answer you, || And from your prayer I will speak to you. ²⁹For this is as follows: he that is corrupted is not at all; he has both worked iniquity so far as deceit could do anything, and has not remembered My goodness, nor accepted My long-suffering. ³⁰Therefore, you will surely be taken up, as I before told you. ³¹For that time will arise which brings affliction; for it will come and pass by with quick vehemence, and it will be turbulent, coming in the heat of indignation. ³²And it will come to pass in those days that all the inhabitants of the earth will be moved against one another, because they do not know that My judgment has drawn near. ³³For there will not be found many wise at that time, || And the intelligent will be but a few: Moreover, even those who know will most of all be silent. ³⁴And there will be many rumors and tidings—not a few, || And the doing of illusions will be manifest, || And promises—not a few—will be recounted, || Some of them [will prove] idle, || And some of them will be confirmed. ³⁵And honor will be turned into shame, || And strength humiliated into contempt, || And integrity destroyed, || And beauty will become ugliness. ³⁶And many will say to many at that time: Where has the multitude of intelligence hidden itself, || And to where has the multitude of wisdom removed itself? ³⁷And while they are meditating on these things, || Then envy will arise in those who had not thought anything of themselves || And passion will seize him that is peaceful, || And many will be stirred up in anger to injure many, || And they will rouse up armies in order to shed blood, || And in the end they will perish together with them. ³⁸And it will come to pass at the same time, || That a change of times will manifestly appeal to every man, || Because in all those times they polluted themselves || And they practiced oppression, || And every man walked in his own works, || And did not remember the Law of the Mighty One. ³⁹Therefore a fire will consume their thoughts, || And in flame the meditations of their reins will be tried; For the Judge will come and will not tarry. ⁴⁰Because each of the inhabitants of the earth knew when he was transgressing. But they did not know My Law by reason of their pride. ⁴¹But many will then assuredly weep, || Yes, over the living more than over the dead." ⁴²And I answered and said, "O Adam, what have you done to all those who are born from you? And what will be said to the first Eve who listened to the serpent? ⁴³For all this multitude are going to corruption, || Nor is there any numbering of those whom the fire devours. ⁴⁴But again I will speak in Your presence. ⁴⁵You, O LORD, my Lord, know what is in Your creature. ⁴⁶For You commanded the ancient dust to produce Adam, and You know the number of those who are born from him, and how far they have sinned before You, who have existed and not confessed You as their Creator. ⁴⁷And as regards all these their end will convict them, and Your law which they have transgressed will repay them on Your day." ⁴⁸[["But now let us dismiss the wicked and inquire about the righteous. ⁴⁹And I will recount their blessedness and not be silent in celebrating their glory, which is reserved for them. ⁵⁰For assuredly as in a short time in this transitory world in which you live you have endured much labor, so in that world to which there is no end, you will receive great light."]]

CHAPTER 49

¹"Nevertheless, I will again ask from You, O Mighty One, yes, I will ask You who made all things. ²In what shape will those live who live in Your day? Or how will the splendor of those who [are] after that time continue? ³Will they then resume this form of the present, || And put on these entangling members, || Which are now involved in evils, || And in which evils are consummated, || Or will You perhaps change these things which have been in the world || As also the world?"

CHAPTER 50

¹And He answered and said to me: "Hear, Baruch, this word, and write in the remembrance of your heart all that you will learn. ²For the earth will then assuredly restore the dead, [[which it now receives, in order to preserve them.]] It will make no change in their form, but as it has received, so will it restore them, and as I delivered them to it, so also will it raise them. ³For then it will be necessary to show the living that the dead have come to life again, and that those who had departed have returned [again]. ⁴And it will come to pass, when they have individually recognized those whom they now know, then judgment will grow strong, and those things which before were spoken of will come."

CHAPTER 51

¹"And it will come to pass, when that appointed day has gone by, that then will the aspect of those who are condemned be afterward changed, and the glory of those who are justified. ²For the aspect of those who now act wickedly will become worse than it is, as they will suffer torment. ³Also, the glory of those who have now been justified in My law, who have had understanding in their life, and who have planted in their heart the root of wisdom, then their splendor will be glorified in changes, and the form of their face will be turned into the light of their beauty, that they may be able to acquire and receive the world which does not die, which is then promised to them. ⁴For over this, above all, those who come will then lament that they rejected My law and stopped their ears that they might not hear wisdom or receive understanding. ⁵When, therefore, they see those over whom they are now exalted, [but] who will then be exalted and glorified more than they, they will respectively be transformed, the latter into the splendor of messengers, and the former will yet more waste away in wonder at the visions and in the beholding of the forms. ⁶For they will first behold and afterward depart to be tormented. ⁷But those who have been saved by their works, || And to whom the law has now been a hope, || And understanding an expectation, || And wisdom a confidence, || Will wondrously appear in their time. ⁸For they will behold the world which is now invisible to them, || And they will behold the time which is now hidden from them: ⁹And time will no longer age them. ¹⁰For they will dwell in the heights of that world, || And they will be made like to the messengers, || And be made equal to the stars, || And they will be changed into every form they desire, || From beauty into loveliness, || And from light into the splendor of glory. ¹¹For there will be spread before them the extents of Paradise, || And there will be shown to them the beauty of

the majesty of the living creatures which are beneath the throne, || And all the armies of the messengers, who are now held fast by My word, || Lest they should appear, and are held fast by a command, that they may stand in their places until their advent comes. ¹²Moreover, there will then be excellency in the righteous surpassing that in the messengers. ¹³For the first will receive the last, those whom they were expecting, || And the last, those of whom they used to hear that they had passed away. ¹⁴For they have been delivered from this world of tribulation, || And laid down the burden of anguish. ¹⁵For what then have men lost their life, || And for what have those who were on the earth exchanged their soul? ¹⁶For then they did not choose for themselves this time, || Which, beyond the reach of anguish, could not pass away, || But they chose for themselves that time, || Whose issues are full of lamentations and evils, || And they denied the world which does not age those who come to it, || And they rejected the time of glory, || So that they will not come to the honor of which I told you before."

CHAPTER 52

¹And I answered and said, "How can we forget those for whom woe is then reserved? ²And why therefore do we again mourn for those who die? Or why do we weep for those who depart to Sheol? ³Let lamentations be reserved for the beginning of that coming torment, || And let tears be laid up for the advent of the destruction of that time. ⁴[[But even in the face of these things I will speak. ⁵And as for the righteous, what will they do now? ⁶Rejoice in the suffering which you now suffer; For why do you look for the decline of your enemies? ⁷Make ready your soul for that which is reserved for you, || And prepare your souls for the reward which is laid up for you."]]

CHAPTER 53

¹And when I had said these things, I fell asleep there, and I saw a vision, and behold, a cloud was ascending from a very great sea, and I kept gazing on it, and behold, it was full of white and black waters, and there were many colors in those same waters, and as it were the likeness of great lightning was seen at its summit. ²And I saw the cloud passing swiftly in quick courses, and it covered all the earth. ³And it came to pass after these things that that cloud began to pour on the earth the waters that were in it. ⁴And I saw that there was not one and the same likeness in the waters which descended from it. ⁵For in the first beginning they were black and many, and afterward I saw that the waters became bright, but they were not many, and after these things again I saw black [waters], and after these things again bright, and again black and again bright. ⁶Now this was done twelve times, but the black were always more numerous than the bright. ⁷And it came to pass at the end of the cloud, that behold, it rained black waters, and they were darker than had been all those waters that were before, and fire was mingled with them, and where those waters descended, they worked devastation and destruction. ⁸And after these things I saw how that lightning which I had seen on the summit of the cloud, seized hold of it and hurled it to the earth. ⁹Now that lightning shone exceedingly, so as to illuminate the whole earth, and it healed those regions where the last waters had descended and worked devastation. ¹⁰And it took hold of the whole earth and had dominion over it. ¹¹And I saw after these things, and behold, twelve rivers were ascending from the sea, and they began to surround that lightning and to become subject to it. ¹²And by reason of my fear I awoke.

CHAPTER 54

¹And I implored the Mighty One, and said, "You alone, O LORD, know of the former times—the deep things of the world, || And the things which befall in their times You bring about by Your word, || And against the works of the inhabitants of the earth You hasten the beginnings of the times, || And You alone know the end of the seasons. ²[You] for whom nothing is too hard, || But who does everything easily by a nod: ³[You] to whom the depths come as the heights, || And whose word the beginnings of the ages serve: ⁴[You] who reveal to those who fear You what is prepared for them, || That from then on they may be comforted. ⁵You show great acts to those who do not know; You break up the enclosure of those who are ignorant, || And light up what is dark, || And reveal what is hidden to the pure, || [[Who in faith have submitted themselves to You and Your law.]] ⁶You have shown this vision to Your servant; Also reveal its interpretation to me. ⁷For I know that as regards those things wherein I implored You, I have received a response, || And as regards what I implored, You revealed to me with what voice I should praise You, || And from what members I should cause praises and hallelujahs to ascend to You. ⁸For if my members were mouths, || And the hairs of my head voices, || Even so I could not give You the reward of praise, || Nor laud You as is befitting, || Nor could I recount Your praise, || Nor tell the glory of Your beauty. ⁹For what am I among men, || Or why am I reckoned among those who are more excellent than I, || That I have heard all these marvelous things from the Most High, || And numberless promises from Him who created me? ¹⁰Blessed is my mother among those that bear, || And praised among women is she that bore me. ¹¹For I will not be silent in praising the Mighty One, || And with the voice of praise I will recount His marvelous deeds. ¹²For who does like to Your marvelous deeds, O God, || Or who comprehends Your deep thought of life? ¹³For with Your counsel You govern all the creatures which Your right hand has created, || And You have established every fountain of light beside You, || And You have prepared the treasures of wisdom beneath Your throne. ¹⁴And justly do they perish who have not loved Your law, || And the torment of judgment will await those who have not submitted themselves to Your power. ¹⁵For though Adam first sinned || And brought untimely death on all, || Yet of those who were born from him || Each one of them has prepared for his own soul torment to come, || And again each one of them has chosen for himself glories to come. ¹⁶[[For assuredly he who believes will receive reward. ¹⁷But now, as for you, you wicked that now are, || Turn to destruction, because you will be speedily visited, in that formerly you rejected the understanding of the Most High. ¹⁸For His works have not taught you, || Nor has the skill of His creation—which is at all times—persuaded you.]] ¹⁹Adam is therefore not the cause, save only of his own soul, || But each of us has been the Adam of his own soul. ²⁰But You, O LORD, expound to me regarding those things which You have revealed to me, || And inform me regarding that which I implored You. ²¹For at the consummation of the world vengeance will be taken on those who have done wickedness according to their wickedness, || And You will glorify the faithful according to their faithfulness. ²²For those who are among Your own You rule, || And those who sin You blot out from among Your own."

CHAPTER 55

¹And it came to pass when I had finished speaking the words of this prayer, that I sat there under a tree, that I might rest in the shade of the branches. ²And I wondered and was astonished, and pondered in my thoughts regarding the multitude of goodness which sinners who are on the earth have rejected, and regarding the great torment which they have despised, though they knew that they should be tormented because of the sin they had committed. And when I was pondering on these things and the like, behold, the messenger Ramiel who presides over true visions was sent to me, and he said to me: ⁴"Why does your heart trouble you, Baruch, || And why does your thought disturb you? ⁵For if owing to the report which you have only heard of judgment you are so moved, || What [will you be] when you will see it manifestly with your eyes? ⁶And if with the expectation with which you do expect the day of the Mighty One you are so overcome, || What [will you be] when you will come to its advent? ⁷And, if at the word of the announcement of the torment of those who have done foolishly you are so wholly distraught, || How much more when the event will reveal marvelous things? ⁸And if you have heard tidings of the good and evil things which are then coming and are grieved, || What—when you will behold what the majesty will reveal, || Which will convict these and cause those to rejoice?"

CHAPTER 56

¹"Nevertheless, because you have implored the Most High to reveal to you the interpretation of the vision which you have seen, I have been sent to tell you. ²And the Mighty One has assuredly made known to you

the methods of the times that have passed, and of those that are destined to pass in His world from the beginning of its creation even to its consummation, of those things which [are] deceit and of those which [are] in truth. ³For as you saw a great cloud which ascended from the sea, and went and covered the earth, this is the duration of the age which the Mighty One made when he took counsel to make the world. ⁴And it came to pass when the word had gone forth from His presence, that the duration of the world had come into being in a small degree, and was established according to the multitude of the intelligence of Him who sent it. ⁵And as you previously saw on the summit of the cloud black waters which descended previously on the earth, this is the transgression with which Adam the first man transgressed. ⁶For [since] when he transgressed || Untimely death came into being, || Grief was named || And anguish was prepared, || And pain was created, || And trouble consummated, || And disease began to be established, || And Sheol kept demanding that it should be renewed in blood, || And the begetting of children was brought about, || And the passion of parents produced, || And the greatness of humanity was humiliated, || And goodness languished. ⁷What therefore can be blacker or darker than these things? ⁸This is the beginning of the black waters which you have seen. ⁹And from these black [waters] again were black derived, and the darkness of darkness was produced. ¹⁰For he became a danger to his own soul: even to the messengers. ¹¹For moreover, at that time when he was created, they enjoyed liberty. ¹²And he became a danger; some of them descended and mingled with the women. ¹³And then those who did so were tormented in chains. ¹⁴But the rest of the multitude of the messengers, of which there is [no] number, restrained themselves. ¹⁵And those who dwelt on the earth perished together [with them] through the waters of the Flood. ¹⁶These are the black first waters."

CHAPTER 57

¹"And after these [waters] you saw bright waters: this is the fount of Abraham, also his generations and advent of his son, and of his son's son, and of those like them. ²Because at that time the unwritten law was named among them, || And the works of the commandments were then fulfilled, || And belief in the coming judgment was then generated, || And hope of the world that was to be renewed was then built up, || And the promise of the life that should come hereafter was implanted. ³These are the bright waters, which you have seen."

CHAPTER 58

¹"And the black third waters which you have seen, these are the mingling of all sins, which the nations afterward worked after the death of those righteous men, and the wickedness of the land of Egypt, wherein they did wickedly in the service with which they made their sons to serve. ²Nevertheless, these also perished at last."

CHAPTER 59

¹"And the bright fourth waters which you have seen are the advent of Moses, and Aaron, and Miriam, and Joshua the son of Nun, and Caleb, and of all those like them. ²For at that time the lamp of the perpetual law shone on all those who sat in darkness, which announced to them that believe the promise of their reward, and to them that deny, the torment of fire which is reserved for them. ³But also the heavens at that time were shaken from their place, and those who were under the throne of the Mighty One were perturbed, when He was taking Moses to Himself. ⁴For He showed him many admonitions together with the principles of the law and the consummation of the times, as also to you, and likewise the pattern of Zion and its measures, in the pattern of which the sanctuary of the present time was to be made. ⁵But then He also showed to him the measures of the fire, also the depths of the abyss, and the weight of the winds, and the number of the drops of rain; ⁶and the suppression of anger, and the multitude of long-suffering, and the truth of judgment; ⁷and the root of wisdom, and the riches of understanding, and the fount of knowledge; ⁸and the height of the air, and the greatness of Paradise, and the consummation of the ages, and the beginning of the Day of Judgment; ⁹and the number of the offerings, and the earths which have not yet come; ¹⁰and the mouth of Gehenna, and the station of vengeance, and the place of faith, and the region of hope; ¹¹and the likeness of future torment, and the multitude of innumerable messengers, and the flaming hosts, and the splendor of the lightnings, and the voice of the thunders, and the orders of the chiefs of the messengers, and the treasuries of light, and the changes of the times, and the investigations of the law. ¹²These are the bright fourth waters which you have seen."

CHAPTER 60

¹"And the black fifth waters which you have seen raining are the works which the Amorites worked, and the spells of their incantations which they worked, and the wickedness of their mysteries, and the mingling of their pollution. ²But even Israel was then polluted by sins in the days of the judges, though they saw many signs which were from Him who made them."

CHAPTER 61

¹"And the bright sixth waters which you saw, this is the time in which David and Solomon were born. ²And there was at that time the building of Zion, || And the dedication of the sanctuary, || And the shedding of much blood of the nations that sinned then, || And many offerings which were offered then in the dedication of the sanctuary. ³And peace and tranquility existed at that time, || ⁴And wisdom was heard in the assembly; And the riches of understanding were magnified in the congregations, || ⁵And the holy festivals were fulfilled in blessedness and in much joy. ⁶And the judgment of the rulers was then seen to be without guile, || And the righteousness of the precepts of the Mighty One was accomplished with truth. ⁷And the land [which] was then beloved by the LORD, || And because its inhabitants did not sin, it was glorified beyond all lands, || And the city Zion ruled then over all lands and regions. ⁸These are the bright waters which you have seen."

CHAPTER 62

¹"And the black seventh waters which you have seen, this is the perversion [brought about] by the counsel of Jeroboam, who took counsel to make two calves of gold; ²and all the iniquities which kings who were after him iniquitously worked. ³And the curse of Jezebel and the worship of idols which Israel practiced at that time. ⁴And the withholding of rain, and the famines which occurred until women ate the fruit of their wombs. ⁵And the time of their captivity which came on the nine and a half tribes, because they were in many sins. ⁶And Shalmanezzar king of Assyria came and led them away captive. ⁷But regarding the nations, it is tedious to tell how they always worked impiety and wickedness, and never worked righteousness. ⁸These are the black seventh waters which you have seen."

CHAPTER 63

¹"And the bright eighth waters which you have seen, this is the rectitude and uprightness of Hezekiah king of Judah, and the grace [of God] which came on him ²when Sennacherib was stirred up in order that he might perish, and his wrath troubled him in order that he might thereby perish, for the multitude also of the nations which were with him. ³When, moreover, Hezekiah the king heard those things which the king of Assyria was devising, to come and seize him and destroy his people—the two and a half tribes which remained—moreover, that he wished to overthrow Zion also, Hezekiah then trusted in his works, and had hope in his righteousness, and spoke with the Mighty One and said, ⁴'For behold, Sennacherib is prepared to destroy us, and he will be boastful and uplifted when he has destroyed Zion.' ⁵And the Mighty One heard him, for Hezekiah was wise, and He had respect to his prayer, because he was righteous. ⁶And thereon the Mighty One commanded His messenger Ramiel who speaks with you. ⁷And I went forth and destroyed their multitude, the number of whose chiefs alone was one hundred and eighty-five thousand, and each one of them had an equal number [at his command]. ⁸And at that time I burned their bodies within, but their raiment and arms I preserved outwardly, in order that the still more wonderful deeds of the Mighty One might appear, and that His Name might thereby be spoken of throughout the whole earth. ⁹And Zion was saved and Jerusalem delivered: Israel was also freed from

tribulation. ¹⁰And all those who were in the holy land rejoiced, and the Name of the Mighty One was glorified so that it was spoken of. ¹¹These are the bright waters which you have seen."

CHAPTER 64

¹"And the black ninth waters which you have seen, this is all the wickedness which was in the days of Manasseh the son of Hezekiah. ²For he worked much impiety, and he slew the righteous, and he wrested judgment, and he shed the blood of the innocent, and he violently polluted wedded women, and he overturned the altars, and destroyed their offerings, and drove forth their priests lest they should minister in the sanctuary. ³And he made an image with five faces: four of them looked to the four winds, and the fifth on the summit of the image as an adversary of the zeal of the Mighty One. ⁴And then wrath went forth from the presence of the Mighty One to the intent that Zion should be rooted out, as also it befell in your days. But also, against the two and a half tribes went forth a decree that they should also be led away captive, as you have now seen. ⁵And the impiety of Manasseh increased to such a degree that it removed the praise of the Most High from the sanctuary. ⁷On this account Manasseh was at that time named the impious, and finally his abode was in the fire. ⁸For though his prayer was heard with the Most High, finally, when he was cast into the brazen horse and the brazen horse was melted, it served as a sign to him for the hour. ⁹For he had not lived perfectly, for he was not worthy—but that from then on he might know by whom finally he should be tormented. ¹⁰For he who is able to benefit is also able to torment."

CHAPTER 65

¹"Thus, moreover, Manasseh acted impiously, and thought that in his time the Mighty One would not inquire into these things. ²These are the black ninth waters which you have seen."

CHAPTER 66

¹"And the bright tenth waters which you have seen: this is the purity of the generations of Josiah king of Judah, who was the only one at the time who submitted himself to the Mighty One with all his heart and with all his soul. ²And he cleansed the land from idols, and hallowed all the vessels which had been polluted, and restored the offerings to the altar, and raised the horn of the holy, and exalted the righteous, and honored all that were wise in understanding, and brought back the priests to their ministry, and destroyed and removed the magicians, and enchanters, and necromancers from the land. ³And not only did he slay the impious that were living, but they also took from the graves the bones of the dead and burned them with fire. ⁴[[And the festivals and the Sabbaths he established in their sanctity]], and their polluted ones he burned in the fire, and the lying prophets which deceived the people,

2 BARUCH

these he also burned in the fire, and the people who listened to them when they were living, he cast them into the Brook of Kidron, and heaped stones on them. ⁵And he was zealous with zeal for the Mighty One with all his soul, and he alone was firm in the law at that time, so that he left none that was uncircumcised, or that worked impiety in all the land, all the days of his life. ⁶Therefore he will receive a continuous reward, and he will be glorified with the Mighty One beyond many at a later time. ⁷For on his account and on account of those who are like him were the honorable glories, of which you were told before, created and prepared. These are the bright waters which you have seen."

CHAPTER 67

¹"And the black eleventh waters which you have seen: this is the calamity which is now befalling Zion. ²Do you think that there is no anguish to the messengers in the presence of the Mighty One, that Zion was so delivered up, and that, behold, the nations boast in their hearts, and assemble before their idols and say, She is trodden down who oftentimes trod down, and she has been reduced to servitude who reduced [other nations to servitude]? ³Do you think that in these things the Most High rejoices, or that His Name is glorified? ⁴[[But how will it serve toward His righteous judgment?]] ⁵Yet after these things the dispersed among the nations will be taken hold of by tribulation, and in shame they will dwell in every place. ⁶Because so far as Zion is delivered up and Jerusalem laid waste, idols will prosper in the cities of the nations, and the vapor of the smoke of the incense of the righteousness which is by the law is extinguished in Zion; and in the region of Zion in every place, behold, there is the smoke of impiety. ⁷But the king of Babylon will arise who has now destroyed Zion, and he will boast over the people, and he will speak great things in his heart in the presence of the Most High. ⁸But he will also fall at last. These are the black waters."

CHAPTER 68

¹"And the bright twelfth waters which you have seen: this is the word. For after these things, a time will come when your people will fall into distress, so that they will all run the risk of perishing together. ³Nevertheless, they will be saved, and their enemies will fall in their presence. ⁴And they will have in [due] time much joy. ⁵And at that time, after a short interval, Zion will again be rebuilt, and its offerings will again be restored, and the priests will return to their ministry, and also the nations will come to glorify it. ⁶Nevertheless, not fully as in the beginning. ⁷But it will come to pass after these things that there will be the fall of many nations. ⁸These are the bright waters which you have seen."

CHAPTER 69

¹"For the last waters which you have seen which were darker than all that were before them, those which were after the twelfth number, which were collected together, belong to the whole world. ²For the Most High made division from the beginning, because He alone knows what will befall. ³For as to the enormities and the impieties which should be worked before Him, He foresaw six kinds of them. ⁴And of the good works of the righteous which should be accomplished before Him, He foresaw six kinds of them, beyond those which He should work at the consummation of the age. ⁵On his account there were not black waters with black, nor bright with bright; for it is the consummation."

CHAPTER 70

¹"Therefore hear the interpretation of the last black waters which are to come: this [is] the word. ²Behold! The days come, and it will be when the time of the age has ripened, || And the harvest of its evil and good seeds has come, || That the Mighty One will bring on the earth and its inhabitants and on its rulers || Perturbation of spirit and stupor of heart. ³And they will hate one another, || And provoke one another to fight, || And the mean will rule over the honorable, || And those of low degree will be extolled above the famous. ⁴And the many will be delivered into the hands of the few, || And those who were nothing will rule over the strong, || And the poor will have abundance beyond the rich, || And the impious will exalt themselves above the heroic. ⁵And the wise will be silent, || And the foolish will speak, || Neither will the thought of men be then confirmed, || Nor the counsel of the mighty, || Nor will the hope of those who hope be confirmed. ⁶And when those things which were predicted have come to pass, || Then confusion will fall on all men, || And some of them will fall in battle, || And some of them will perish in anguish, || ⁷And some of them will be destroyed by their own. Then the peoples of the Most High, whom He has prepared before, || Will come and make war with the leaders that will then be left. ⁸And it will come to pass that whoever gets safe out of the war will die in the earthquake, || And whoever gets safe out of the earthquake will be burned by the fire, || And whoever gets safe out of the fire will be destroyed by famine. ⁹[[And it will come to pass that whoever of the victors and the vanquished gets safe out of and escapes all these things previously mentioned will be delivered into the hands of My servant Messiah.]] ¹⁰For all the earth will devour its inhabitants."

CHAPTER 71

¹"And the holy land will have mercy on its own, and it will protect its inhabitants at that time. ²This is the vision which you have seen, and this is the interpretation. ³For I have come to tell you these things, because your prayer has been heard with the Most High."

CHAPTER 72

¹"Now also hear regarding the bright lightning which is to come at the consummation after these black [waters]: this is the word. ²After

the signs have come of which you were told before, when the nations become turbulent, and the time of My Messiah is come, He will both summon all the nations, and some of them He will spare, and some of them He will slay. ³Therefore these things will come on the nations which are to be spared by Him. ⁴Every nation which does not know Israel and has not trodden down the seed of Jacob, will indeed be spared. ⁵And this because some out of every nation will be subjected to your people. ⁶But all those who have ruled over you, or have known you, will be given up to the sword."

CHAPTER 73

¹"And it will come to pass, when He has brought low everything that is in the world, || And has sat down in peace for the age on the throne of His kingdom, || That joy will then be revealed, || And rest will appear. ²And then healing will descend in dew, || And disease will withdraw, || And anxiety, and anguish, and lamentation will pass from among men, || And gladness will proceed through the whole earth. ³And no one will die untimely again, || Nor will any adversity suddenly befall. ⁴And judgments, and abusive talk, and contentions, and revenges, || And blood, and passions, and envy, and hatred, || And whatever things are like these will go into condemnation when they are removed. ⁵For it is these very things which have filled this world with evils, || And on account of these the life of man has been greatly troubled. ⁶And wild beasts will come from the forest and minister to men || And asps and dragons will come forth from their holes to submit themselves to a little child. ⁷And women will no longer then have pain when they bear, || Nor will they suffer torment when they yield the fruit of the womb."

CHAPTER 74

¹"And it will come to pass in those days that the reapers will not grow weary, || Nor those that build be toil-worn; For the works will of themselves speedily advance || Together with those who do them in much tranquility. ²For that time is the consummation of that which is corruptible, || And the beginning of that which is not corruptible. ³Therefore those things which were predicted will belong to it: Therefore, it is far away from evils, and near to those things which do not die. ⁴This is the bright lightning which came after the last dark waters."

CHAPTER 75

¹And I answered and said, "Who can understand, O LORD, Your goodness? For it is incomprehensible. ²Or who can search into Your compassions, || Which are infinite? ³Or who can comprehend Your intelligence? ⁴Or who is able to recount the thoughts of Your mind? ⁵Or who of those who are born can hope to come to those things, || Unless he is one to whom You are merciful and gracious? ⁶Because, assuredly, if You did not have compassion on man, || Those who are under Your right hand, || They could not come to those things, || But those who are in the numbers named can be called. ⁷But if, indeed, we who exist know why we have come, || And submit ourselves to Him who brought us out of Egypt, || We will come again and remember those things which have passed, || And will rejoice regarding that which has been. ⁸But if now we do not know why we have come, || And do not recognize the principate of Him who brought us up out of Egypt, || We will come again and seek after those things which have been now, || And be grieved with pain because of those things which have befallen."

CHAPTER 76

¹And He answered and said to me: "[[Inasmuch as the revelation of this vision has been interpreted to you as you requested]], hear the word of the Most High that you may know what is to befall you after these things. ²For you will surely depart from this earth, nevertheless not to death, but you will be preserved to the consummation of the times. ³Therefore go up to the top of that mountain, and there will pass before you all the regions of that land, and the figure of the inhabited world, and the top of the mountains, and the depth of the valleys, and the depths of the seas, and the number of the rivers, that you may see what you are leaving, and to where you are going. ⁴Now this will befall after forty days. Therefore, go now during these days and instruct the people so far as you are able, that they may learn so as not to die at the last time, but may learn in order that they may live at the last times."

CHAPTER 77

¹And I, Baruch, went there and came to the people, and assembled them together from the greatest to the least, and said to them: ²"Hear, you sons of Israel, behold how many you are who remain of the twelve tribes of Israel. ³For to you and to your fathers the LORD gave a law more excellent than to all peoples. ⁴And because your brothers transgressed the commandments of the Most High, || He brought vengeance on you and on them, || And He did not spare the former, || And the latter He also gave into captivity: And He did not leave a residue of them, ⁵But behold! You are here with me. ⁶If, therefore, you direct your ways correctly, || You also will not depart as your brothers departed, || But they will come to you. ⁷For He is merciful whom you worship, || And He is gracious in whom you hope, || And He is true, so that He will do good and not evil. ⁸Have you not seen here what has befallen Zion? ⁹Or do you perhaps think that the place had sinned, || And that on this account it was overthrown? Or that the land had worked foolishness, || And that therefore it was delivered up? ¹⁰And do you not know that on account of you who sinned, || That which did not sin was overthrown, || And, on account of those who worked wickedly, || That which did not work foolishness was delivered up to enemies?" ¹¹And the whole people answered and said to me: "So far as we can recall the good things which the Mighty One has done to us, we do recall them; and those things which we do not remember He in His mercy knows. ¹²Nevertheless, do this for us your people: also write to our brothers in Babylon a letter of doctrine and a scroll of hope, that you may confirm them also before you depart from us. ¹³For the shepherds of Israel have perished, || And the lamps which gave light are extinguished, || And the fountains have withheld their stream from which we used to drink. ¹⁴And we are left in the darkness, || And amid the trees of the forest, || And the thirst of the wilderness." ¹⁵And I answered and said to them: "Shepherds, and lamps, and fountains come from the law: And though we depart, yet the law abides. ¹⁶If, therefore, you have respect to the law, || And are intent on wisdom, || A lamp will not be wanting, || And a shepherd will not fail, || And a fountain will not dry up. ¹⁷Nevertheless, as you said to me, I will also write to your brothers in Babylon, and I will send by means of men, and I will write in like manner to the nine and a half tribes, and send by means of a bird." ¹⁸And it came to pass on the twenty-first day in the eighth month that I, Baruch, came and sat down under the oak under the shadow of the branches, and no man was with me, but I was alone. ¹⁹And I wrote these two letters: one I sent by an eagle to the nine and a half tribes; and the other I sent to those that were at Babylon by means of three men. ²⁰And I called the eagle and spoke these words to it: ²¹"The Most High has made you that you should be higher than all birds. ²²And now go and do not tarry in [any] place, nor enter a nest, nor settle on any tree, until you have passed over the breadth of the many waters of the Euphrates River, and have gone to the people that dwell there, and cast down this letter to them. ²³Remember, moreover, that, at the time of the Flood, Noah received from a dove the fruit of the olive, when he sent it forth from the Ark. ²⁴Yes, also the ravens ministered to Elijah, bearing him food, as they had been commanded. ²⁵Solomon also, in the time of his kingdom, wherever he wished to send or seek for anything, commanded a bird, and it obeyed him as he commanded it. ²⁶And now, do not let it weary you, and do not turn to the right hand nor the left, but fly and go by a direct way, that you may preserve the command of the Mighty One, according as I spoke to you."

THE EPISTLE OF BARUCH, THE SON OF NERIAH, WHICH HE WROTE TO THE NINE AND A HALF TRIBES

CHAPTER 78

¹These are the words of that letter which Baruch the son of Neriah sent to the nine and a half tribes, which were across the River Euphrates, in which these things were written. ²Thus says Baruch the son of Neriah to the brothers carried into captivity: "Mercy and peace." I bear in mind, my brothers, the love of Him who created us, who loved us from of old, and never hated us, but above all educated us. ³And truly I know, that behold, all

2 BARUCH

of us—the twelve tribes—are bound by one bond, inasmuch as we are born from one father. ⁴For what reason I have been more careful to leave you the words of this letter before I die, that you may be comforted regarding the calamities which have come on you, and that you may also be grieved regarding the evil that has befallen your brothers; and again, also, that you may justify His judgment which ⁵He has decreed against you that you should be carried away captive—for what you have suffered is disproportioned to what you have done—in order that, at the last times, you may be found worthy of your fathers. ⁶Therefore, if you consider that you have now suffered those things for your good, that you may not finally be condemned and tormented, then you will receive continuous hope; if above all you destroy from your heart vain error, on account of which you departed hence. ⁷For if you so do these things, He will continually remember you, He who always promised on our behalf to those who were more excellent than we, that He will never forget or forsake us, but with much mercy will again gather together those who were dispersed.

CHAPTER 79
¹Now, my brothers, first learn what befell Zion: how that Nebuchadnezzar king of Babylon came up against us. ²For we have sinned against Him who made us, and we have not kept the commandments which He commanded us, yet He has not disciplined us as we deserved. ³For what befell you we also suffer in a preeminent degree, for it befell us also.

CHAPTER 80
¹And now, my brothers, I make known to you that when the enemy had surrounded the city, the messengers of the Most High were sent, and they overthrew the fortifications of the strong wall, and they destroyed the firm iron corners, which could not be rooted out. ²Nevertheless, they hid all the vessels of the sanctuary, lest the enemy should get possession of them. ³And when they had done these things, they delivered thereon to the enemy the overthrown wall, and the plundered house, and the burnt temple, and the people who were overcome because they were delivered up, lest the enemy should boast and say: "Thus by force we have been able to lay waste even the house of the Most High in war." They have also bound your brothers and led [them] away to Babylon, and have caused them to dwell there. ⁵But we have been left here, being very few. ⁶This is the tribulation about which I wrote to you. ⁷For assuredly I know that [the consolation of] the inhabitants of Zion consoles you; so far as you knew that it was prospered, [your consolation] was greater than the tribulation which you endured in having to depart from it.

CHAPTER 81
¹But regarding consolation, hear the word. ²For I was mourning regarding Zion, and I prayed for mercy from the Most High, and I said, ³"How long will these things endure for us? And will these calamities always come on us?" ⁴And the Mighty One did according to the multitude of His mercies, || And the Most High according to the greatness of His compassion, || And He revealed to me the word, that I might receive consolation, || And He showed me visions that I should not again endure anguish, || And He made known to me the mystery of the times, || And He showed me the advent of the hours.

CHAPTER 82
¹Therefore, my brothers, I have written to you that you may comfort yourselves regarding the multitude of your tribulations. ²For know that our Maker will assuredly avenge us on all our enemies, according to all that they have done to us, also that the consummation which the Most High will make is very near, and His mercy that is coming, and the consummation of His judgment, is by no means far off. ³For behold, we see now the multitude of the prosperity of the nations, || Though they act impiously, || But they will be like a vapor: ⁴And we behold the multitude of their power, || Though they do wickedly, || But they will be made like to a drop: ⁵And we see the firmness of their might, || Though they resist the Mighty One every hour, || But they will be accounted as spittle. ⁶And we consider the glory of their greatness, || Though they do not keep the statutes of the Most High, || But they will pass away as smoke. ⁷And we meditate on the beauty of their gracefulness, || Though they have to do with pollutions, || But as grass that withers, they will fade away. ⁸And we consider the strength of their cruelty, || Though they do not remember the end, || But as a wave that passes, they will be broken. ⁹And we remark [regarding] the boastfulness of their might, || Though they deny the beneficence of God, who gave [it] to them, || But they will pass away as a passing cloud.

CHAPTER 83
¹For the Most High will assuredly hasten His times, || And He will assuredly bring on His hours. ²And He will assuredly judge those who are in His world, || And will visit in truth all things by means of all their hidden works. ³And He will assuredly examine the secret thoughts, || And that which is laid up in the secret chambers of all the members of mail, || And will make manifest in the presence of all with reproof. ⁴Let none therefore of these present things ascend into your hearts, but above all let us be expectant, because that which is promised to us will come. ⁵And let us not now look to the delights of the nations in the present, but let us remember what has been promised to us in the end. ⁶For the ends of the times, and of the seasons, and whatever is with them will assuredly pass by together. ⁷Moreover, the consummation of the age will then show the great might of its ruler, when all things come to judgment. ⁸Therefore, prepare your hearts for that which before you believed, lest you come to be in bondage in both worlds, so that you be led away captive here and be tormented there. ⁹For that which exists now, or which has passed away, or which is to come, in all these things, neither is the evil fully evil, nor again the good fully good. ¹⁰For all healthinesses of this time are turning into diseases, ¹¹And all might of this time is turning into weakness, || And all the force of this time is turning into impotence, ¹²And every energy of youth is turning into old age and consummation. And every beauty of gracefulness of this time is turning faded and hateful, ¹³And every proud dominion of the present is turning into humiliation and shame, ¹⁴And every praise of the glory of this time is turning into the shame of silence, || And every vain splendor and insolence of this time is turning into voiceless ruin. ¹⁵And every delight and joy of this time is turning to worms and corruption, ¹⁶And every clamor of the pride of this time is turning into dust and stillness. ¹⁷And every possession of riches of this time is being turned into Sheol alone, ¹⁸And all the plunder of passion of this time is turning into involuntary death, || And every passion of the lusts of this time is turning into a judgment of torment. ¹⁹And every artifice and craftiness of this time is turning into a proof of the truth, || ²⁰And every sweetness of ointments of this time is turning into judgment and condemnation, ²¹And every love of lying is turning to insult through truth. [[²²Since therefore all these things are done now, does anyone think that they will not be avenged? But the consummation of all things will come to the truth.]]

CHAPTER 84
¹Behold! I have therefore made known to you [these things] while I live, for I have said [it] that you should learn the things that are excellent; for the Mighty One has commanded me to instruct you: and I will set before you some of the commandments of His judgment before I die. ²Remember that formerly Moses assuredly called the heavens and earth to witness against you and said, "If you transgress the law you will be dispersed, but if you keep it you will be kept." ³And other things he also used to say to you when you, the twelve tribes, were together in the desert. ⁴And after his death you cast them away from you. On this account there came on you what had been predicted. ⁵And now Moses used to tell you before they befell you, and behold, they have befallen you, for you have forsaken the law. ⁶Behold, I also say to you after you have suffered, that if you obey those things which have been said to you, you will receive from the Mighty One whatever has been laid up and reserved for you. ⁷Moreover, let this letter be for a testimony between me and you, that you may remember the commandments of the Mighty One, and that there may also be a defense for me in the presence of Him who sent me. ⁸And remember the law and Zion, and the holy land and your brothers, and the

covenant of your fathers, and do not forget the festivals and the Sabbaths. And deliver this letter and the traditions of the law to your sons after you, as your fathers also delivered [them] to you. ¹⁰And at all times make request perseveringly and pray diligently with your whole heart that the Mighty One may be reconciled to you, and that He may not reckon the multitude of your sins, but remember the rectitude of your fathers. ¹¹For if He does not judge us according to the multitude of His mercies, woe to all of us who are born.

CHAPTER 85

¹Know, moreover, that in former times and in the generations of old our fathers had helpers, righteous men and holy prophets, [but] no longer. ²We were in our own land, [[and they helped us when we sinned]], and they prayed for us to Him who made us, because they trusted in their works, and the Mighty One heard their prayer and was gracious to us. ³But now the righteous have been gathered and the prophets have fallen asleep, and we have also gone forth from the land, and Zion has been taken from us, and we have nothing now except the Mighty One and His law. ⁴If, therefore, we direct and dispose our hearts, we will receive everything that we lost, and much better things than we lost by many times. ⁵For what we have lost was to corruption, and what we will receive will not be corruptible. [[⁶Moreover, I also have written thus to our brothers to Babylon, that I also may attest to them those very things.]] ⁷And let all those things previously mentioned always be before your eyes, because we are still in the spirit and the power of our liberty. ⁸Again, moreover, the Most High is also long-suffering toward us here, and He has shown to us that which is to be, and has not concealed from us what will befall in the end. ⁹Therefore, before judgment exacts its own, and truth that which is its due, let us prepare our soul that we may enter into possession of, and not be taken possession of, and that we may hope and not be put to shame, and that we may rest with our fathers and not be tormented with our enemies. ¹⁰And the strength of the creation is already exhausted, and the advent of the times is very short, yes, they have passed by; and the pitcher is near to the cistern, and the ship to the port, and the course of the journey to the city, and life to consummation. ¹¹And again prepare your souls, so that when you sail and ascend from the ship you may have rest and not be condemned when you depart. ¹²For behold, when the Most High will bring to pass all these things, there will not again be there an opportunity for returning, nor a limit to the times, nor adjournment to the hours, nor change of ways, nor place for prayer, nor sending of petitions, nor receiving of knowledge, nor giving of love, nor place of conversion, nor supplication for offenses, nor intercession of the fathers, nor prayer of the prophets, nor help of the righteous. ¹³There, there, is the sentence of corruption, the way of fire, and the path which brings to Gehenna. ¹⁴On this account there is one law by one, one age and an end for all who are in it. ¹⁵Then He will preserve those to whom He finds He may be gracious, and at the same time destroy those who are polluted with sins.

CHAPTER 86

¹When you therefore receive this—my letter—read it in your congregations with care. ²And meditate thereon, above all on the days of your fasts. ³And bear me in mind by means of this letter, as I also bear you in mind in it, and always farewell.

CHAPTER 87

¹And it came to pass when I had ended all the words of this letter, and had written it sedulously to its close, ²that I folded it, and sealed it carefully, and bound it to the neck of the eagle, and dismissed and sent it. Here ends the Scroll of Baruch, the son of Neriah.

3 BARUCH

3 Baruch, or the Greek Apocalypse of Baruch, is a visionary, likely pseudepigraphic text written some time between the fall of Jerusalem in AD 70 and the 3rd century. Scholars disagree as to Jewish or Christian authorship, or even if a clear distinction can be made in this era. It is self-attributed to Jeremiah's scribe, Baruch ben Neriah, and does not form part of any biblical canon. It is extant in certain Greek and Old Slavonic manuscripts.

A NARRATIVE AND REVELATION OF BARUCH, CONCERNING THOSE INEFFABLE THINGS WHICH HE SAW BY COMMAND OF GOD. BLESS YOU, O LORD. A REVELATION OF BARUCH, WHO STOOD ON THE RIVER GEL WEEPING OVER THE CAPTIVITY OF JERUSALEM, WHEN ABIMELECH WAS ALSO HELD BY THE HAND OF GOD, AT THE FARM OF AGRIPPA. AND HE WAS SITTING THUS AT THE BEAUTIFUL GATES, WHERE THE HOLY OF HOLIES LAY.

CHAPTER 1

¹Truly I, Baruch, was weeping in my mind and sorrowing on account of the people, and that Nebuchadnezzar the king was permitted by God to destroy His city, saying, ²"Lord, why did You set Your vineyard on fire, and lay it waste? Why did You do this? And why, Lord, did You not repay us with another discipline, but delivered us to nations such as these, so that they reproach us and say, Where is their God?" ³And behold, as I was weeping and saying such things, I saw a messenger of the LORD coming and saying to me, "Understand, O man, greatly beloved, and do not trouble yourself so greatly concerning the salvation of Jerusalem, for thus says the LORD God, the Almighty. ⁴For He sent me before you, to make known and to show to you all [the things] of God. ⁵For your prayer was heard before Him, and entered into the ears of the LORD God." ⁶And when he had said these things to me, I was silent. ⁷And the messenger said to me, "Cease to provoke God, and I will show you other mysteries, greater than these." And I Baruch said, "As the LORD God lives, if you will show me, and I hear a word of yours, I will not continue to speak any longer. ⁸God will add to my judgment in the Day of Judgment, if I speak hereafter." And the messenger of the powers said to me, "Come, and I will show you the mysteries of God."

CHAPTER 2

¹And he took me and led me where the expanse has been set fast, and where there was a river which no one can cross, nor any strange breeze of all those which God created. ²And he took me and led me to the first heaven and showed me a door of great size. ³And he said to me, "Let us enter through it," and we entered as though borne on wings, a distance of about thirty days' journey. And he showed me a plain within the heaven; and there were men dwelling thereon, with the faces of oxen, and the horns of stags, and the feet of goats, and the haunches of lambs. ⁴And I, Baruch, asked the messenger, "Make known to me, please, what is the thickness of the heaven in which we journeyed, or what is its extent, or what is the plain, in order that I may also tell the sons of men?" ⁵And the messenger whose name is Phamael said to me, "This door which you see is the door of Heaven, and as great as is the distance from earth to Heaven, so great also is its thickness; and again as great as is the distance [[from north to south, so great]] is the length of the plain which you saw." ⁶And again the messenger of the powers said to me, "Come, and I will show you greater mysteries." ⁷But I said, "Please show me what these men are." And he said to me, "These are they who built the tower of strife against God, and the LORD banished them."

CHAPTER 3

¹And the messenger of the LORD took me and led me to [the] second heaven. ²And he also showed me a door there like the first and said, "Let us enter through it." ³And we entered, being borne on wings a distance of about sixty days' journey. ⁴And he also showed me a plain there, and it was full of men, whose appearance was like that of dogs, and whose feet were like those of stags. ⁵And I asked the messenger: "Please, Lord, tell me who these are." ⁶And he said, "These are they who gave counsel to build the tower, for they whom you

see drove forth multitudes of both men and women to make bricks; among whom, a woman making bricks was not allowed to be released in the hour of child-birth, but brought forth while she was making bricks, and carried her child in her apron, and continued to make bricks. ⁷And the LORD appeared to them and confused their speech, when they had built the tower to the height of four hundred and sixty-three cubits. ⁸And they took a gimlet, and sought to pierce the heaven, saying, Let us see [whether] the heaven is made of clay, or of brass, or of iron. ⁹When God saw this, He did not permit them, but struck them with blindness and confusion of speech, and rendered them as you see."

CHAPTER 4

¹And I, Baruch, said, "Behold, Lord, you showed me great and wonderful things; and now show me all things for the sake of the LORD." ²And the messenger said to me, "Come, let us proceed." ³[And I proceeded] with the messenger from that place about one hundred and eighty-five days' journey. ⁴And he showed me a plain and a serpent, which appeared to be two hundred plethra in length. And he showed me Hades, and its appearance was dark and abominable. ⁵And I said, "Who is this dragon, and who is this monster around him?" ⁶And the messenger said, "The dragon is he who eats the bodies of those who spend their life wickedly, and he is nourished by them. And this is Hades, which itself also closely resembles him, in that it also drinks about a cubit from the sea, which does not sink at all." ⁷Baruch said, "And how?" And the messenger said, "Listen, the LORD God made three hundred and sixty rivers, of which the chief of all are Alphias, Abyrus, and the Gericus; and because of these the sea does not sink." ⁸And I said, "Please show me which is the tree which led Adam astray." And the messenger said to me, "It is the vine, which the messenger Sammael planted, at which the LORD God was angry, and He cursed him and his plant, while also on this account He did not permit Adam to touch it, and therefore the Devil being envious deceived him through his vine." [[⁹And I, Baruch, said, "Since also the vine has been the cause of such great evil, and is under judgment of the curse of God, and was the destruction of the first created, how is it now so useful?" And the messenger said, "You ask correctly. ¹⁰When God caused the Flood on earth, and destroyed all flesh, and four hundred and nine thousand giants, and the water rose fifteen cubits above the highest mountains, then the water entered into Paradise and destroyed every flower; but it wholly removed the shoot of the vine outside the bounds and cast it outside. ¹¹And when the earth appeared out of the water, and Noah came out of the Ark, he began to plant of the plants which he found. But he also found the shoot of the vine; and he took it, and was reasoning in himself, What then is it? ¹²And I came and spoke to him the things concerning it. And he said, Will I plant it, or what will I do? ¹³Since Adam was destroyed because of it, let me not also meet with the anger of God because of it. ¹⁴And saying these things he prayed that God would reveal to him what he should do concerning it. ¹⁵And when he had completed the prayer which lasted forty days, and having implored many things and wept, he said, Lord, I entreat You to reveal to me what I will do concerning this plant. But God sent His messenger Sarasael, and said to him, Arise, Noah, and plant the shoot of the vine, for thus says the LORD: Its bitterness will be changed into sweetness, and its curse will become a blessing, and that which is produced from it will become the blood of God; and as through it the human race obtained condemnation, so again through Jesus Christ, the Immanuel, they will receive in Him the upward calling, and the entry into Paradise.]] ¹⁶Know therefore, O Baruch, that as Adam through this very tree obtained condemnation, and was divested of the glory of God, so also the men who now drink insatiably the wine which is begotten of it, transgress worse than Adam, and are far from the glory of God, and are surrendering themselves to the continuous fire. ¹⁷For [no] good comes through it. For those who drink it to excess do these things: neither does a brother pity his brother, nor a father his son, nor children their parents, but from the drinking of wine come all evils, such as murders, adulteries, fornications, perjuries, thefts, and such like. And nothing good is established by it."

CHAPTER 5

¹And I, Baruch, said to the messenger, "Let me ask you one thing, Lord. ²Since you said to me that the dragon drinks one cubit out of the sea, say to me also, how great is his belly?" ³And the messenger said, "His belly is Hades; and as far as a plummet is thrown [by] three hundred men, so great is his belly. Come, then, that I may show you also greater works than these."

CHAPTER 6

¹And he took me and led me where the sun goes forth; ²and he showed me a chariot and four, under which burned a fire, and in the chariot was sitting a man, wearing a crown of fire, [and] the chariot [was] drawn by forty messengers. ³And behold, a bird circling before the sun, about nine cubits away. ⁴And I said to the messenger, "What is this bird?" And he said to me, "This is the guardian of the earth." ⁵And I said, "Lord, how is he the guardian of the earth? Teach me." ⁶And the messenger said to me, "This bird flies alongside of the sun, and expanding his wings, receives its fiery rays. For if he were not receiving them, the human race would not be preserved, nor any other living creature. ⁷But God appointed this bird to that." And he expanded his wings, and I saw on his right wing very large letters, as large as the space of a threshing-floor, the size of about four thousand modii; and the letters were of gold. ⁸And the messenger said to me, "Read them." ⁹And I read, and they ran thus: NEITHER EARTH NOR HEAVEN BRING ME FORTH, BUT WINGS OF FIRE BRING ME FORTH. ¹⁰And I said, "Lord, what is this bird, and what is his name?" ¹¹And the messenger said to me, "His name is called Phoenix." [And I said,] "And what does he eat? And he said to me, "The manna of Heaven and the dew of earth." ¹²And I said, "Does the bird excrete?" And he said to me, "He excretes a worm, and the excrement of the worm is cinnamon, which kings and princes use. ¹³But wait and you will see the glory of God." And while he was conversing with me, there was as a thunderclap, and the place was shaken on which we were standing. ¹⁴And I asked the messenger, "My Lord, what is this sound?" And the messenger said to me, "Even now the messengers are opening the three hundred and sixty-five gates of Heaven, and the light is being separated from the darkness." ¹⁵And a voice came which said, "Light giver, give to the world radiance." ¹⁶And when I heard the noise of the bird, I said, "Lord, what is this noise?" ¹⁷And he said, "This is the bird who awakens from slumber the cocks on earth. For as men do through the mouth, so also does the cock signify to those in the world, in his own speech. For the sun is made ready by the messengers, and the cock crows."

CHAPTER 7

¹And I said, "And where does the sun begin its labors, after the cock crows?" ²And the messenger said to me, "Listen, Baruch: all things, whatever I showed you, are in the first and second heaven, and in the third heaven the sun passes through and gives light to the world. But wait, and you will see the glory of God." ³And while I was conversing with him, I saw the bird, and he appeared in front, and grew less and less, and at length returned to his full size. ⁴And behind him I saw the shining sun, and the messengers which draw it, and a crown on its head, the sight of which we were not able to gaze on and behold. ⁵And as soon as the sun shone, the phoenix also stretched out his wings. ⁶But I, when I beheld such great glory, was brought low with great fear, and I fled and hid in the wings of the messenger. ⁷And the messenger said to me, "Do not fear, Baruch, but wait and you will also see their setting."

CHAPTER 8

¹And he took me and led me toward the west; and when the time of the setting came, I again saw the bird coming before it, and as soon as it came, I saw the messengers, and they lifted the crown from its head. ²But the bird stood exhausted and with wings contracted. ³And beholding these things, I said, "Lord, why did they lift the crown from the head of the sun, and why is the bird so exhausted?" ⁴And the messenger said to me, "The crown of the sun, when it has run through the day, four messengers take it, and bear it up to Heaven, and renew it, because it and its rays have been defiled on earth; moreover, it is so renewed each day." ⁵And I Baruch said, "Lord, and why are its beams defiled on earth?" ⁶And the

messenger said to me, "Because it beholds the lawlessness and unrighteousness of men, namely fornications, adulteries, thefts, extortions, idolatries, drunkenness, murders, strife, jealousies, evil-speakings, murmurings, whisperings, and such like [these], which are not well-pleasing to God. On account of these things is it defiled, and therefore is it renewed. ⁷But you ask concerning the bird, how it is exhausted: because by restraining the rays of the sun through the fire and burning heat of the whole day, it is exhausted thereby. ⁸For, as we said before, unless his wings were screening the rays of the sun, no living creature would be preserved."

CHAPTER 9

¹And they having retired, the night also fell, and at the same time the chariot of the moon came, along with the stars. ²And I, Baruch, said, "Lord, show me it also, I implore of you, how it goes forth, where it departs, and in what form it moves along." ³And the messenger said, "Wait and you will also see it shortly." And on the next day I also saw it in the form of a woman, and [she was] sitting on a wheeled chariot. And before it there were oxen and lambs in the chariot, and a multitude of messengers in like manner. ⁴And I said, "Lord, what are the oxen and the lambs?" ⁵And he said to me, "They are also messengers." And again I asked, "Why is it that it at one time increases, but at another time decreases?" ⁶And [he said to me], "Listen, O Baruch: this which you see had been written by God beautiful as no other. ⁷And at the transgression of the first Adam, it was near to Sammael when he took the serpent as a garment. ⁸And it did not hide itself but increased, and God was angry with it, and afflicted it, and shortened its days." ⁹And I said, "And how does it not also shine always, but only in the night?" ¹⁰And the messenger said, "Listen: as in the presence of a king, the courtiers cannot speak freely, so the moon and the stars cannot shine in the presence of the sun; for the stars are always suspended, but they are screened by the sun, and the moon, although it is uninjured, is consumed by the heat of the sun."

CHAPTER 10

¹And when I had learned all these things from the chief-messenger, he took [me] and led me into [the] fourth heaven. ²And I saw a monotonous plain, and in the middle of it a pool of water. ³And there were multitudes of birds in it of all kinds, but not like those here on earth. ⁴But I saw a crane as great as great oxen; and all the birds were great beyond those in the world. ⁵And I asked the messenger, "What is the plain, and what the pool, and what the multitudes of birds around it?" ⁶And the messenger said, "Listen, Baruch: the plain which contains the pool in it and other wonders is the place where the souls of the righteous come, when they hold converse, living together in choirs. ⁷But the water is that which the clouds receive, and rain on the earth, and the fruits increase." ⁸And I said again to the messenger of the LORD, "But [what] are these birds?" And he said to me, "They are those which continually sing praise to the LORD." ⁹And I said, "Lord, and how do men say that the water which descends in rain is from the sea?" ¹⁰And the messenger said, "The water which descends in rain—this is also from the sea, and from the waters on earth; but that which stimulates the fruits is [only] from the latter source. ¹¹Know therefore, henceforth, that from this source is what is called the dew of Heaven."

CHAPTER 11

¹And the messenger took me and led me from there to [the] fifth heaven. And the gate was closed. ²And I said, "Lord, is this gateway not open that we may enter?" And the messenger said to me, "We cannot enter until Michael comes, who holds the keys of the Kingdom of Heaven; but wait and you will see the glory of God." ³And there was a great sound, as thunder. And I said, "Lord, what is this sound?" ⁴And he said to me, "Even now Michael, the commander of the messengers, comes down to receive the prayers of men." ⁵And behold a voice came, "Let the gates be opened." ⁶And they opened them, and there was a roar as of thunder. ⁷And Michael came, and the messenger who was with me came face to face with him and said, "Greetings, my commander, and that of all our order." ⁸And the commander Michael said, "Greetings you also, our brother, and the interpreter of the revelations to those who pass through life virtuously." And having saluted one another thus, they stood still. ⁹And I saw the commander Michael say, "Greetings you also, our brother, and the interpreter of the revelations to those who pass through life virtuously." ¹⁰And having saluted one another thus, they stood still. And I saw the commander Michael, holding an exceedingly great vessel; its depth was as great as the distance from Heaven to earth, and its breadth as great as the distance from north to south. ¹¹And I said, "Lord, what is that which Michael the chief-messenger is holding?" ¹²And he said to me, "This is where the merits of the righteous enter, and such good works as they do, which are escorted before the heavenly God."

CHAPTER 12

¹And as I was conversing with them, behold, messengers came bearing baskets full of flowers. ²And they gave them to Michael. And I asked the messenger, "Lord, who are these, and what are the things brought here from beside them?" ³And he said to me, "These are messengers [who] are over the righteous." ⁴And the chief-messenger took the baskets and cast them into the vessel. ⁵And the messenger said to me, "These flowers are the merits of the righteous." ⁶And I saw other messengers bearing baskets which were [neither] empty nor full. ⁷And they began to lament, and did not venture to draw near, because they did not have the prizes complete. ⁸And Michael cried and said, "Come here, also, you messengers; bring what you have brought." And Michael was exceedingly grieved, and the messenger who was with me, because they did not fill the vessel.

CHAPTER 13

¹And then other messengers came in like manner, weeping and lamenting, and saying with fear, "Behold, how we are over-clouded, O Lord, for we were delivered to evil men, and we wish to depart from them." ²And Michael said, "You cannot depart from them, in order that the enemy may not prevail to the end; but say to me what you ask." ³And they said, "Please, Michael our commander, transfer us from them, for we cannot abide with wicked and foolish men, for there is nothing good in them, but every kind of unrighteousness and greed. ⁴For we do not behold them entering [[into [the] assembly at all, nor among spiritual fathers, nor]] into any good work. ⁵But where there is murder, there also are they in the midst, and where are fornications, adulteries, thefts, slanders, perjuries, jealousies, drunkenness, strife, envy, murmurings, whispering, idolatry, divination, and such like [these], then are they workers of such works, and of others worse. ⁶For what reason we entreat that we may depart from them." ⁷And Michael said to the messengers, "Wait until I learn from the LORD what will come to pass."

CHAPTER 14

¹And in that very hour Michael departed, and the doors were closed. ²And there was a sound like thunder. And I asked the messenger, "What is the sound?" ³And he said to me, "Michael is even now presenting the merits of men to God."

CHAPTER 15

¹And in that very hour Michael descended, and the gate was opened; and he brought oil. ²And as for the messengers which brought the baskets which were full, he filled them with oil, saying, "Take it away, reward our friends a hundredfold, and those who have laboriously worked good works. For those who sowed virtuously, also reap virtuously." ³And he also said to those bringing the half-empty baskets, "Come here you also; take away the reward according as you brought, and deliver it to the sons of men." [[⁴Then he also said to those who brought the full and to those who brought the half-empty baskets: "Go and bless our friends, and say to them that thus says the LORD, You are faithful over a few things, I will set you over many things; enter into the joy of your Lord."]]

CHAPTER 16

¹And turning, he also said to those who brought nothing: "Thus says the LORD, Do not be sad of countenance, and do not weep, nor leave the sons of men alone. ²But since they angered Me in their works, go and make them envious and angry and provoked against a people that is no people, a people that has no

understanding. ³Further, besides these, send forth the caterpillar and the unwinged locust, and the mildew, and the common locust, [and] hail with lightnings and anger, and punish them severely with the sword and with death, and their children with demons. ⁴For they did not listen to My voice, nor did they observe My commandments, nor do them, but were despisers of My commandments, and insolent toward the priests who proclaimed My words to them."

CHAPTER 17

¹And while he yet spoke, the door was closed, and we withdrew. ²And the messenger took me and restored me to the place where I was at the beginning. ³And having come to myself, I gave glory to God, who counted me worthy of such honor. ⁴For what reason you also, brothers, who obtained such a revelation, yourselves also glorify God, so that He also may glorify you, now and ever, and to all eternity. Amen.

4 BARUCH

4 Baruch, also called the Paralipomena of Jeremiah (meaning "things left out of Jeremiah"), appears as the title in several Ancient Greek manuscripts of the work. It is part of a larger Ethiopian Orthodox book that includes Lamentations and additions to Lamentations. 4 Baruch is usually dated to the first half of the 2nd century AD.

CHAPTER 1

¹It came to pass whenever the sons of Israel were taken captive by the king of the Chaldeans, that God spoke to Jeremiah, saying, "Jeremiah, my chosen one, arise and depart from this city, you and Baruch, since I am going to destroy it because of the multitude of the sins of those who dwell in it. ²For your prayers are like a solid pillar in its midst, and like an impenetrable wall surrounding it. ³Now then, arise and depart before the host of the Chaldeans surrounds it." ⁴And Jeremiah answered, saying, "I implore You, Lord, permit me, Your servant, to speak in Your presence." ⁵And the LORD said to him: "Speak, My chosen one Jeremiah." ⁶And Jeremiah spoke, saying, "LORD Almighty, would You deliver the chosen city into the hands of the Chaldeans, so that the king with the multitude of his people might boast and say: I have prevailed over the holy city of God? ⁷No, my Lord, but if it is Your will, let it be destroyed by Your hands." ⁹"For neither the king nor his host will be able to enter it unless I first open its gates. ¹⁰Arise, then, and go to Baruch, and tell him these words. ¹¹And when you have arisen at the sixth hour of the night, go out on the city walls and I will show you that unless I first destroy the city, they cannot enter it." ¹²When the LORD had said this, He departed from Jeremiah.

CHAPTER 2

¹And Jeremiah ran and told these things to Baruch; and as they went into the temple of God, Jeremiah tore his garments and put dust on his head and entered the holy place of God. ²And when Baruch saw him with dust sprinkled on his head and his garments torn, he cried out in a loud voice, saying, "Father Jeremiah, what are you doing? What sin has the people committed?" ³For whenever the people sinned, Jeremiah would sprinkle dust on his head and would pray for the people until their sin was forgiven. ⁴So Baruch asked him, saying, "Father, what is this?" ⁵And Jeremiah said to him: "Refrain from rending your garments—rather, let us tear our hearts! And let us not draw water for the trough, but let us weep and fill them with tears! For the LORD will not have mercy on this people." ⁶And Baruch said, "Father Jeremiah, what has happened?" ⁷And Jeremiah said, "God is delivering the city into the hands of the king of the Chaldeans, to take the people captive into Babylon." ⁸And when Baruch heard these things, he also tore his garments and said, "Father Jeremiah, who has made this known to you?" ⁹And Jeremiah said to him: "Stay with me awhile, until the sixth hour of the night, so that you may know that this word is true." ¹⁰Therefore they both remained near the altar, weeping, and their garments were torn.

CHAPTER 3

¹And when the hour of the night arrived, as the LORD had told Jeremiah they came up together on the walls of the city, Jeremiah and Baruch. ²And behold, there came a sound of trumpets; and messengers emerged from Heaven holding torches in their hands, and they set them on the walls of the city. ³And when Jeremiah and Baruch saw them, they wept, saying, "Now we know that the word is true!" ⁴And Jeremiah implored the messengers, saying, "I implore you, do not destroy the city yet, until I say something to the LORD." ⁵And the LORD spoke to the messengers, saying, "Do not destroy the city until I speak to My chosen one, Jeremiah." ⁶Then Jeremiah spoke, saying, "I beg You, Lord, bid me to speak in Your presence." ⁷And the LORD said, "Speak, My chosen one Jeremiah." ⁸And Jeremiah said, "Behold, Lord, now we know that You are delivering the city into the hands of its enemies, and they will take the people away to Babylon. What do You want me to do with the holy vessels of the temple service?" ¹⁰And the LORD said to him: "Take them and consign them to the earth, saying, Hear, Earth, the voice of Your Creator who formed you in the abundance of waters, who sealed you with seven seals for seven epochs, and after this you will receive your ornaments— ¹¹guard the vessels of the temple service until the gathering of the beloved!" ¹²And Jeremiah spoke, saying, "I implore You, Lord, show me what I should do for Abimelech the Ethiopian, for he has done many kindnesses to Your servant Jeremiah. ¹³For he pulled me out of the miry pit; and I do not wish that he should see the destruction and desolation of this city, but that You should be merciful to him and that he should not be grieved." ¹⁴And the LORD said to Jeremiah: "Send him to the vineyard of Agrippa, and I will hide him in the shadow of the mountain until I cause the people to return to the city. ¹⁵And you, Jeremiah, go with your people into Babylon and stay with them, preaching to them, until I cause them to return to the city. ¹⁶But leave Baruch here until I speak with him." ¹⁷When He had said these things, the LORD ascended from Jeremiah into Heaven. ¹⁸But Jeremiah and Baruch entered the holy place, and taking the vessels of the temple service, they consigned them to the earth as the LORD had told them. ¹⁹And immediately the earth swallowed them. ²⁰And they both sat down and wept. ²¹And when morning came, Jeremiah sent Abimelech, saying, "Take a basket and go to the estate of Agrippa by the mountain road, and bring back some figs to give to the sick among the people; for the favor of the LORD is on you and His glory is on your head." ²²And when he had said this, Jeremiah sent him away; and Abimelech went as he told him.

CHAPTER 4

¹And when morning came, behold, the host of the Chaldeans surrounded the city. ²And the great messenger trumpeted, saying, "Enter the city, host of the Chaldeans; for behold, the gate is opened for you. ³Therefore let the king enter, with his multitudes, and let him take all the people captive." ⁴But taking the keys of the temple, Jeremiah went outside the city and threw them away in the presence of the sun, saying, "I say to you, Sun, take the keys of the temple of God and guard them until the day in which the LORD asks you for them. ⁵For we have not been found worthy to keep them, for we have become unfaithful guardians." ⁶While Jeremiah was still weeping for the people, they brought him out with the people and dragged them into Babylon. ⁷But Baruch put dust on his head and sat and wailed this lamentation, saying, "Why has Jerusalem been devastated? Because of the sins of the beloved people || She was delivered into the hands of enemies || Because of our sins and those of the people. ⁸But do not let the lawless ones boast and say: We were strong enough to take the city of God by our might; But it was delivered to you because of our sins. ⁹And God will pity us and cause us || To return to our city, || But you will not survive! ¹⁰Blessed are our fathers, Abraham, Isaac and Jacob, || For they departed from this world || And did not see the destruction of this city." ¹¹When he had

said this, Baruch departed from the city, weeping and saying, "Grieving because of you, Jerusalem, I went out from you." ¹²And he remained sitting in a tomb, while the messengers came to him and explained to him everything that the LORD revealed to him through them.

CHAPTER 5

¹But Abimelech took the figs in the burning heat; and coming on a tree, he sat under its shade to rest a bit. ²And leaning his head on the basket of figs, he fell asleep and slept for sixty-six years; and he was not awakened from his slumber. ³And afterward, when he awoke from his sleep, he said, "I slept sweetly for a little while, but my head is heavy because I did not get enough sleep." ⁴Then he uncovered the basket of figs and found them dripping milk. ⁵And he said, "I would like to sleep a little longer, because my head is heavy. But I am afraid that I might fall asleep and be late in awakening and my father Jeremiah would think badly of me; for if he were not in a hurry, he would not have sent me today at daybreak. ⁶So I will get up, and proceed in the burning heat; for isn't there heat, isn't there toil every day?" ⁷So he got up and took the basket of figs and placed it on his shoulders, and he entered into Jerusalem and did not recognize it—neither his own house, nor the place—nor did he find his own family or any of his acquaintances. ⁸And he said, "The LORD be blessed, for a great trance has come over me today! ⁹This is not the city Jerusalem—and I have lost my way because I came by the mountain road when I arose from my sleep; and since my head was heavy because I did not get enough sleep, I lost my way. ¹⁰It will seem incredible to Jeremiah that I lost my way!" ¹¹And he departed from the city; and as he searched he saw the landmarks of the city, and he said, "Indeed, this is the city; I lost my way." ¹²And again he returned to the city and searched, and found no one of his own people; and he said, "The LORD be blessed, for a great trance has come over me!" ¹³And again he departed from the city, and he stayed there grieving, not knowing where he should go. ¹⁴And he put down the basket, saying, "I will sit here until the LORD takes this trance from me." ¹⁵And as he sat, he saw an old man coming from the field; and Abimelech said to him: "I say to you, old man, what city is this?" ¹⁶And he said to him: "It is Jerusalem." ¹⁷And Abimelech said to him: "Where is Jeremiah the priest, and Baruch the secretary, and all the people of this city, for I could not find them?" ¹⁸And the old man said to him: "Are you not from this city, seeing that you remember Jeremiah today, because you are asking about him after such a long time? ¹⁹For Jeremiah is in Babylon with the people; for they were taken captive by King Nebuchadnezzar, and Jeremiah is with them to preach the good news to them and to teach them the word." ²⁰As soon as Abimelech heard this from the old man, he said, "If you were not an old man, and if it were not for the fact that it is not lawful for a man to scold one older than himself, I would laugh at you and say that you are out of your mind—since you say that the people have been taken captive into Babylon. ²¹Even if the heavenly torrents had descended on them, there has not yet been time for them to go into Babylon! ²²For how much time has passed since my father Jeremiah sent me to the estate of Agrippa to bring a few figs, so that I might give them to the sick among the people? ²³And I went and got them, and when I came to a certain tree in the burning heat, I sat to rest a little; and I leaned my head on the basket and fell asleep. ²⁴And when I awoke, I uncovered the basket of figs, supposing that I was late; and I found the figs dripping milk, just as I had collected them. ²⁵But you claim that the people have been taken captive into Babylon. ²⁶But that you might know, take the figs and see!" ²⁷And he uncovered the basket of figs for the old man, and he saw them dripping milk. ²⁸And when the old man saw them, he said, "O my son, you are a righteous man, and God did not want you to see the desolation of the city, so He brought this trance on you. ²⁹For behold it is sixty-six years today since the people were taken captive into Babylon. ³⁰But that you might learn, my son, that what I tell you is true—look into the field and see that the ripening of the crops has not appeared. ³¹And notice that the figs are not in season, and be enlightened." ³²Then Abimelech cried out in a loud voice, saying, "I bless You, God of the heavens and earth, the Rest of the souls of the righteous in every place!" ³³Then he said to the old man: "What month is this?" ³⁴And he said, "Nisan," which is Abib. ³⁵And taking some of [the] figs, he gave them to the old man and said to him: "May God illuminate your way to the city above—Jerusalem."

CHAPTER 6

¹After this, Abimelech went out of the city and prayed to the LORD. ²And behold, a messenger of the LORD came and took him by the right hand and brought him back to where Baruch was sitting, and he found him in a tomb. ³And when they saw each other, they both wept and kissed each other. ⁴But when Baruch looked up, he saw with his own eyes the figs that were covered in Abimelech's basket. ⁵And lifting his eyes to Heaven, he prayed, saying, ⁶"You are the God who gives a reward to those who love You. Prepare yourself, my heart, and rejoice and be glad while you are in your dwelling place, saying to your fleshly house, Your grief has been changed to joy; for the Sufficient One is coming and will deliver you in your dwelling place—for there is no sin in you. ⁷Revive in your dwelling place, in your virginal faith, and believe that you will live! ⁸Look at this basket of figs—for behold, they are sixty-six years old and have not become shrivelled or rotten, but they are dripping milk. ⁹So it will be with you, my flesh, if you do what is commanded of you by the messenger of righteousness. ¹⁰He who preserved the basket of figs, the same will again preserve you by his power." ¹¹When Baruch had said this, he said to Abimelech: "Stand up and let us pray that the LORD may make known to us how we will be able to send to Jeremiah in Babylon the report about the shelter provided for you on the way." ¹²And Baruch prayed, saying, "LORD God, our strength is the chosen light which comes forth from Your mouth. ¹³We implore and beg of Your goodness—You whose great Name no one is able to know—hear the voice of Your servants and let knowledge come into our hearts. ¹⁴What will we do, and how will we send this report to Jeremiah in Babylon?" ¹⁵And while Baruch was still praying, behold a messenger of the LORD came and said all these words to Baruch: "Agent of the light, do not be anxious about how you will send to Jeremiah; for an eagle is coming to you at the hour of light tomorrow, and you will direct him to Jeremiah. ¹⁶Therefore, write in a letter: Say to the sons of Israel: Let the stranger who comes among you be set apart and let fifteen days go by; and after this I will lead you into your city, says the LORD. ¹⁷He who is not separated from Babylon will not enter into the city; and I will punish them by keeping them from being received back by the Babylonians, says the LORD." ¹⁸And when the messenger had said this, he departed from Baruch. ¹⁹And Baruch sent to the market of the nations and got papyrus and ink and wrote a letter as follows: Baruch, the servant of God, writes to Jeremiah in the captivity of Babylon: ²⁰Greetings! Rejoice, for God has not allowed us to depart from this body grieving for the city which was laid waste and outraged. ²¹For what reason the LORD has had compassion on our tears, and has remembered the covenant which He established with our fathers Abraham, Isaac, and Jacob. ²²And he sent His messenger to me, and he told me these words which I send to you. ²³These, then, are the words which the LORD, the God of Israel, spoke, who led us out of Egypt, out of the great furnace: Because you did not keep My ordinances, but your heart was lifted up, and you were haughty before Me, in anger and wrath I delivered you to the furnace in Babylon. ²⁴If, therefore, says the LORD, you listen to My voice, from the mouth of Jeremiah My servant, I will bring the one who listens up from Babylon; but the one who does not listen will become a stranger to Jerusalem and to Babylon. ²⁵And you will test them by means of the water of the Jordan; whoever does not listen will be exposed—this is the sign of the great seal.

CHAPTER 7

¹And Baruch got up and departed from the tomb and found the eagle sitting outside the tomb. ²And the eagle said to him in a human voice: "Greetings, Baruch, steward of the faith." ³And Baruch said to him: "You who speak are chosen from among all the birds of Heaven, for this is clear from the gleam of your eyes; tell me, then, what are you doing here?" ⁴And the eagle said to him: "I was sent here so that you might send whatever message you want through me." ⁵And Baruch said to him: "Can you carry this message to Jeremiah in Babylon?" ⁶And the eagle said to him: "Indeed, it was for this reason I was sent." ⁷And Baruch

took the letter, and fifteen figs from Abimelech's basket, and tied them to the eagle's neck and said to him: "I say to you, king of the birds, go in peace with good health and carry the message for me. ⁸Do not be like the raven which Noah sent out and which never came back to him in the Ark; but be like the dove which, the third time, brought a report to the righteous one. ⁹So you also, take this good message to Jeremiah and to those in bondage with him, that it may be well with you. Take this papyrus to the people and to the chosen one of God. ¹⁰Even if all the birds of Heaven surround you and want to fight with you, struggle—the LORD will give you strength. ¹¹And do not turn aside to the right or to the left, but straight as a speeding arrow, go in the power of God, and the glory of the LORD will be with you the entire way." ¹²Then the eagle took flight and went away to Babylon, having the letter tied to his neck; and when he arrived, he rested on a post outside the city in a desert place. ¹³And he kept silent until Jeremiah came along, for he and some of the people were coming out to bury a corpse outside the city. ¹⁴For Jeremiah had petitioned King Nebuchadnezzar, saying, "Give me a place where I may bury those of my people who have died"; and the king gave it to him. ¹⁵And as they were coming out with the body, and weeping, they came to where the eagle was. ¹⁶And the eagle cried out in a loud voice, saying, "I say to you, Jeremiah the chosen one of God, go and gather together the people and come here so that they may hear a letter which I have brought to you from Baruch and Abimelech." ¹⁷And when Jeremiah heard this, he glorified God; and he went and gathered together the people along with their wives and children, and he came to where the eagle was. ¹⁸And the eagle came down on the corpse, and it revived. ¹⁹Now this took place so that they might believe. ²⁰And all the people were astounded at what had happened, and said, "This is the God who appeared to our fathers in the wilderness through Moses, and now he has appeared to us through the eagle." ²¹And the eagle said, "I say to you, Jeremiah, come, untie this letter and read it to the people"—so he untied the letter and read it to the people. ²²And when the people heard it, they wept and put dust on their heads, and they said to Jeremiah: "Deliver us and tell us what to do that we may once again enter our city." ²³And Jeremiah answered and said to them: "Do whatever you heard from the letter, and the LORD will lead us into our city." ²⁴And Jeremiah wrote a letter to Baruch, saying thus: My beloved son, do not be negligent in your prayers, imploring God on our behalf, that He might direct our way until we come out of the jurisdiction of this lawless king. ²⁵For you have been found righteous before God, and He did not let you come here, lest you see the affliction which has come on the people at the hands of the Babylonians. ²⁶For it is like a father with an only son, who is given over for punishment; and those who see his father and console him cover his face, lest he see how his son is being punished, and be even more ravaged by grief. ²⁷For thus God took pity on you and did not let you enter Babylon lest you see the affliction of the people. ²⁸For since we came here, grief has not left us, for sixty-six years today. ²⁹For many times when I went out I found some of the people hung up by King Nebuchadnezzar, crying and saying, "Have mercy on us, God-Zar!" ³⁰When I heard this, I grieved and cried with double mourning, not only because they were hung up, but because they were calling on a foreign god, saying, "Have mercy on us." ³¹But I remembered days of festivity which we celebrated in Jerusalem before our captivity; and when I remembered, I groaned, and returned to my house wailing and weeping. ³²Now, then, pray in the place where you are—you and Abimelech—for this people, that they may listen to my voice and to the decrees of my mouth, so that we may depart from here. ³³For I tell you that the entire time that we have spent here they have kept us in subjection, saying, "Recite for us a song from the songs of Zion—the song of your God." ³⁴And we reply to them: "How will we sing for you since we are in a foreign land?" ³⁵And after this, Jeremiah tied the letter to the eagle's neck, saying, "Go in peace, and may the LORD watch over both of us." ³⁶And the eagle took flight and came to Jerusalem and gave the letter to Baruch; and when he had untied it he read it and kissed it and wept when he heard about the distresses and afflictions of the people. ³⁷But Jeremiah took the figs and distributed them to the sick among the people, and he kept teaching them to abstain from the pollutions of the nations of Babylon.

CHAPTER 8

¹And the day came in which the LORD brought the people out of Babylon. ²And the LORD said to Jeremiah: "Rise up—you and the people—and come to the Jordan and say to the people: Let anyone who desires the LORD forsake the works of Babylon. ³As for the men who took wives from them and the women who took husbands from them—those who listen to you will cross over, and you take them into Jerusalem; but those who do not listen to you, do not lead them there." ⁴And Jeremiah spoke these words to the people, and they arose and came to the Jordan to cross over. ⁵As he told them the words that the LORD had spoken to him, half of those who had taken spouses from them did not wish to listen to Jeremiah, but said to him: "We will never forsake our wives, but we will bring them back with us into our city." ⁶So they crossed the Jordan and came to Jerusalem. ⁷And Jeremiah and Baruch and Abimelech stood up and said, "No man joined with Babylonians will enter this city!" ⁸And they said to one another: "Let us arise and return to Babylon—to our place." And they departed. ⁹But while they were coming to Babylon, the Babylonians came out to meet them, saying, "You will not enter our city, for you hated us and you left us secretly; therefore you cannot come in with us. ¹⁰For we have taken a solemn oath together in the name of our god to receive neither you nor your children, since you left us secretly." ¹¹And when they heard this, they returned and came to a desert place some distance from Jerusalem and built a city for themselves and named it Samaria. ¹²And Jeremiah sent to them, saying, "Convert, for the messenger of righteousness is coming and will lead you to your exalted place."

CHAPTER 9

¹Now those who were with Jeremiah were rejoicing and offering sacrifices on behalf of the people for nine days. ²But on the tenth, Jeremiah alone offered sacrifice. ³And he prayed a prayer, saying, "HOLY, HOLY, HOLY, Fragrant Aroma of the living trees, True Light that enlightens me until I ascend to You; ⁴For Your mercy, I beg You—for the sweet voice of the two seraphim, I beg—for another fragrant aroma. ⁵And may Michael, chief-messenger of righteousness, who opens the gates to the righteous, be my guardian until he causes the righteous to enter. ⁶I beg You, almighty Lord of all creation, unbegotten and incomprehensible, in whom all judgment was hidden before these things came into existence." ⁷When Jeremiah had said this, and while he was standing near the altar with Baruch and Abimelech, he became as one whose soul had departed. ⁸And Baruch and Abimelech were weeping and crying out in a loud voice: "Woe to us! For our father Jeremiah has left us—the priest of God has departed!" ⁹And all the people heard their weeping, and they all ran to them and saw Jeremiah lying on the ground as if dead. ¹⁰And they tore their garments and put dust on their heads and wept bitterly. ¹¹And after this they prepared to bury him. ¹²And behold, there came a voice, saying, "Do not bury the one who yet lives, for his soul is returning to his body!" ¹³And when they heard the voice they did not bury him, but stayed around his dwelling place for three days, saying, "When will he arise?" ¹⁴And after three days his soul came back into his body and he raised his voice in the midst of them all and said, "Glorify God with one voice! All of you glorify God and the Son of God who awakens us—Messiah Jesus—the Light of all the ages, the inextinguishable Lamp, the Life of faith. ¹⁵But after these times there will be four hundred seventy-seven years more, and He comes to earth. ¹⁶And the Tree of Life planted in the midst of paradise will cause all the unfruitful trees to bear fruit, and will grow and sprout forth. ¹⁷And the trees that had sprouted and became haughty, and said, We have supplied our power to the air, He will cause them to wither, with the grandeur of their branches, and He will cause them to be judged—that firmly rooted tree! ¹⁸And what is crimson will become white as wool—the snow will be blackened—the sweet waters will become salty, and the salty sweet, in the intense light of the joy of God. ¹⁹And He will bless the isles so that they become fruitful by the word of the mouth of His Messiah. ²⁰For He will come, and He will go out and choose for Himself twelve apostles to proclaim the news among the nations—He whom I have seen adorned by

His Father and coming into the world on the Mount of Olives—and He will fill the hungry souls." ²¹When Jeremiah was saying this concerning the Son of God—that He is coming into the world—the people became very angry and said, "This is a repetition of the words spoken by Isaiah son of Amos, when he said, I saw God and the Son of God. ²²Come, then, and let us not kill him by the same sort of death with which we killed Isaiah, but let us stone him with stones." ²³And Baruch and Abimelech were greatly grieved because they wanted to hear in full the mysteries that he had seen. ²⁴But Jeremiah said to them: "Be silent and do not weep, for they cannot kill me until I describe for you everything I saw." ²⁵And he said to them: "Bring a stone here to me." ²⁶And he set it up and said, "Light of the ages, make this stone to become like me in appearance, until I have described to Baruch and Abimelech everything I saw." ²⁷Then the stone, by God's command, took on the appearance of Jeremiah. ²⁸And they were stoning the stone, supposing that it was Jeremiah! ²⁹But Jeremiah delivered to Baruch and to Abimelech all the mysteries he had seen, and immediately he stood in the midst of the people desiring to complete his ministry. ³⁰Then the stone cried out, saying, "O foolish sons of Israel, why do you stone me, supposing that I am Jeremiah? Behold, Jeremiah is standing in your midst!" ³¹And when they saw him, immediately they rushed on him with many stones, and his ministry was fulfilled. ³²And when Baruch and Abimelech came, they buried him, and taking the stone they placed it on his tomb and inscribed it thus: This is the stone that was the ally of Jeremiah.

APOCRYPHON OF JANNES AND JAMBRES

The Apocryphon of Jannes and Jambres, also known as the Book of Jannes and Jambres, is a likely pseudepigraphal work composed in the 1st or 2nd-century AD, narrating the undertakings of the two legendary magicians in Pharaoh's court who opposed Moses and Aaron. Only scattered fragments survive.

FRAGMENT 1

¹And [Jannes] said, "Jambres, [[I deliver to you]] a document; keep it secret and [[do not come out]] on the day on which [Pharaoh] and the nobles come out [against] the people … with them, [[but feign sickness and save your own]] soul [[from death]] and from [[the destruction of the Egyptians which the God]] of the heavens [[will carry out according to His word on behalf of the children of the Hebrews whom the Egyptians caused to die in the river. ²And when the]] time of [my] death [comes], go to our mother every day and send me letters, and when [[three years are completed]], tell her, The king [commanded] him [to remain] for another [[three years, so that our]] mother [will not] go [[to Memphis and find out that I have]] died. ³… say, He is [impure] and cannot [be seen until] he is purified." ⁴And sending word [from Memphis], he convened [all] the [nobles] of Egypt [and said to] them, "[[I am giving my]] daughter to [my] brother in marriage, and I am celebrating for seven days. ⁵And you will rejoice together with us, dear brothers. After the days, I depart from you [[to Hades." ⁶And after celebrating for]] the seven [[days of the wedding, Jannes instructed his]] brother [[regarding his]] children [[and regarding his wife]] and mother [[not to neglect her,]] nor [[to abandon]] her [[for one hour lest she be pained, but to go to her every day. ⁷And when he had]] completed [his speech], ambassadors were present [from Pharaoh], saying, "Come quickly, [and oppose] Moses the Hebrew, [[for he is]] making [[signs]] so that everyone is amazed." ⁸Jannes, [[having come]] to Pharaoh, opposed Moses and his [[brother]] Aaron, doing as many things as they [had done]. ⁹But [as] his death neared, tormented by a grievous sore in his bottom and not finding a remedy, he sent word to Pharaoh, saying, "This is God's miracle that is operating for them. Therefore, I, wishing to oppose the [[God]], depart to death." ¹⁰Jannes called his brother again [and] pleaded with him concerning his mother, not to distress her: "But remember that she took a risk in life in giving birth to us. Do not then be preoccupied concerning money [and] forget our mother. Get ready …" ¹¹… [And Jannes] questioned [Jambres]: "Which hour is the setting of [the] star?" And he replied, [["The last." ¹²And]] [Jannes] said, "Indeed, such is the hour of corrupt and deceitful hearts, which do not remember the hour of death." ¹³And [Jannes] said to him, "Come out, and see how great [a portion] is remaining of the day." And [Jambres] said to him, "None." ¹⁴And Jannes said, "Indeed, so great is the [day] of every woman who will turn away from the bed of her own husband and have intercourse with another, Jambres [my] brother."

FRAGMENT 2

¹Jambres opened the magical books of his brother Jannes, and did necromancy, and brought up from Hades the shade of his brother. ²The soul of Jannes answered him, saying, "I, your brother, did not die unjustly, but in truth, justly, and judgment will go against me, for I was wiser than all wise magicians, and I withstood the two brothers, Moses and Aaron, who did great signs and wonders: therefore, I died and was brought down from among men into Hades, where there is great burning, and the pit of perdition, from where there is no coming up. ³And now, my brother Jambres, take heed to yourself in your lifetime to do good to your sons and your friends, for in Hades there is nothing of good, but sadness and darkness; and when you will have died and will be in Hades among the dead, your dwelling-place and your abode will be twenty [[or two]] cubits broad and four cubits long."

FRAGMENT 3

¹"Where are Amān and Bārān, the giants who devoured men like locusts and wild animals, and cattle, and birds? ²They drank blood and defiled the East, because they could not be satisfied. ³However, their father Bapares, lifting a stone of one thousand talents, threw it by his own strength into the height of [the] heavens. ⁴And midday descended, and he ran that same day two hundred fifty thousand stadia and returned before the sun set. ⁵And where is he? Did he not die? Even he, and his wife, and his children died! Where is Aqāmās, whose eyes were huge? Did he not, while they were sleeping, raise up mountains with his belly? ⁶And since the dust storm was drawn out, he placed his eyes in a bowl, in four thousand two hundred pieces, but it did not concern him, for his eyes were heavy. And did not even he die? ⁷Where is the great Aklu the Gigantic? When walking, from the weight of his steps, twenty cubits [of earth] clung to his feet. ⁸And when, therefore, it happened one time [that] he drank water from the river, it decreased the water [by] five cubits. Did not even he die? ⁹Where is the great Akaryās the Gigantic, who walked in the depths of the Bantes Sea, and the water [merely] reached up to his breasts? ¹⁰This one [had] footsteps of five hundred thousand cubits, and, because of his wife's adultery, he killed giants. [And] this one killed … the Gigantic and cast his body into the Great Sea. But afterward, even he died! ¹¹Where is Yotāmār, son of Māriket, who in his intelligence understood the hours and minutes of the day and of the night, and the months of the years, and the signs provided? And he investigated much. Did not even he die? ¹²Where is Ayās, the great and mighty, the marvelous, the Gigantic, who left the eastern frontier running and …?"

APOCRYPHON OF EZEKIEL

The Apocryphon of Ezekiel, also called 2 Ezekiel, was likely composed in the 1st century BC or 1st century AD, with later Christian interpolations. It is quoted in a number of early works. Fragment 1 comes from the Dead Sea Scrolls and was quoted in the letter of Bar-Naba and the Revelation of Peter. Fragment 2 is identified from a quotation of the Apocryphon found in 1 Clement chapter 8. Fragment 3 was identified with Ezekiel by Tertullian. Fragment 4 was attributed to Jesus by Justin Martyr, and sourced from the Apocryphon by other early writers. Fragment 5 is found in the writings of Clement of Alexandria, among others. Fragment 6 was attributed to Ezekiel by Epiphanius but is dissimilar to the other fragments.

FRAGMENT 1

¹THESE ARE THE WORDS OF EZEKIEL. And the word of the LORD came to me, saying, "Son of man, prophesy and say, Behold, the day of the destruction of the nations is coming; ²… Egypt, and there will be anguish in Put, and a sword in Egypt… will shake, Cush and Put, and the mighty ones of Arabia, also some of the children of the covenant, and Arabia will fall at the gates of Egypt. ³And… will perish… by the sword of Egypt… will be devastated… you will not die… ⁴For I am the LORD, who redeems My people, giving the covenant to them." ⁵And I said, "O LORD, I have seen many from Israel who have loved Your Name and walked in the ways of righteousness. ⁶So, when will these things come to pass? And how will they be rewarded for their piety?" ⁷And the LORD said to me, "I will make it manifest… the sons of Israel to see, and they will know that I am the LORD." ⁸And He said, "Son of man, prophesy over these bones, and speak to the bone, and let them be joined bone to its bone, and joint to its joint." And it was so. ⁹And He said a second time, "Prophesy, and let sinews come on them and let skin cover them." And it was so. ¹⁰And He said, "Again, prophesy to the four winds of the heavens, and let them blow on the slain." And it was so. ¹¹And a great multitude of men came to life. And they blessed the LORD of Hosts who had given life to them. ¹²And I said, "O LORD, when will these things be completed?" And the LORD said to me, "… and after many days, a piece of wood falls down and rises again [[and when blood drips from a tree]]." ¹³… and … LORD. And all the people arose and stood on their feet to give thanks… and to praise the LORD of Hosts. ¹⁴And I also spoke with them… And the LORD said to me, "Son of man, say to them… in their graves they will lie until… from your tombs and from the earth… that the yoke of Egypt… land, and they will know that I am the LORD." ¹⁵And He said to me, "Look, son of man, at the land of Israel." And I said, "I have seen, O LORD, and behold it is a wasteland. When will You gather them together?" ¹⁶And the LORD said, "A son of Belial is planning to oppress My people, but I will not permit him. His dominion will not persist; and from the impure, no seed will survive, nor will new wine come from the caper bush, nor will a hornet make honey … and I will slay the wicked in Memphis. ¹⁷But I will bring My sons out of Memphis, and I will turn toward their remnant. As they will say, There was peace and quiet, they will say, The land will be as it was in the days of … old. Therefore, I will arouse wrath on them from the four winds of the heavens… like a devouring fire as… and he will show no mercy on the poor, but he will bring them to Babel." ¹⁸And Babel is but a cup in the hand of the LORD, in her time He will cast her away … in Babel and it will be … a dwelling place for demons … desolation and … will pasture … to Babel … instead of my grief make my soul rejoice. ¹⁹And the days will hasten quickly until men say, "Are not the days hastening so that the sons of Israel might take possession?" ²⁰And the LORD said to me, "I will not turn your face away, Ezekiel. Behold, I am cutting short the days and the years … a few, just [as] you said to Me … For the mouth of the LORD has spoken these things. ²¹… And My people will be … with a cheerful heart and with a willing soul … and hide a little while … and from the breaches …" ²²… the vision which Ezekiel saw … the brightness of the chariot, and the four living creatures, a living creature … and as they moved they did not turn back. ²³Every living creature moved on two wheels, and its two legs … on … in one there was breath. ²⁴And their faces were one beside the other. And the appearance of the faces: one of a lion, one of an eagle, one of a calf, and one of a man. ²⁵And the hand of a man was joined to the backs of the living creatures and attached to their wings … and the wheels … wheel joined to wheel when they moved, and from both sides of the wheels were streams of fire, ²⁶and in the midst of the coals were living creatures like flaming coals… and the wheels, the living creatures and the wheels. ²⁷Now there was … over their heads an expanse, like an awesome gleam of crystal. And a voice came from above the expanse…

FRAGMENT 2

¹Convert, house of Israel, from your lawless ways. ²I say to you—My people—even if the list of your sins stretches from Heaven to earth, and if they are as black as they can be, and you turn to Me, and with all of your heart say, "Father," I will forgive you, and look on you as holy.

FRAGMENT 3

¹Look at the cow, she has calved, and yet she is pregnant…

FRAGMENT 4

¹In this manner, our Lord Jesus Christ also said, "It is what I have seen you doing that I will judge you for."

FRAGMENT 5

¹"And I will bind up the lame persons, and I will heal the sick, and I will bring back the wandering. ²And I will feed them on My holy mountain, and I will be their Shepherd, and I will be closer to them than a garment is to their skin. ³They will call Me, and I will say, Behold, here I am. And if they cross, they will not slip," says the LORD.

FRAGMENT 6

[[¹A certain king had everyone in his kingdom drafted, and had no civilians with an exception of two: one lame and one blind, and each one lived by himself in his own home. ²And when the king was preparing a wedding feast for his own son, he invited everyone in his kingdom, but he despised the two civilians, the lame man and the blind man. ³And they were indignant within themselves and resolved to carry out a plot against the king. Now the king had a garden. ⁴And the blind man addressed the lame man from a distance, saying, "How much would our crumb of bread have been among the crowds who were invited to the celebration? So come on, let us retaliate [against] him for what he did to us!" "How?" asked the other. ⁵And [the blind man] said, "Let us go into his garden, and there, ruin the other things in the garden." But [the lame man] said, "But how can I, for I am lame and unable to crawl?" ⁶And the blind man said, "Am I able to do anything myself, since I am unable to see where I am going? But let us use trickery." ⁷Plucking the nearby grass and braiding a rope, [the lame man] threw [it] to the blind man, and said, "Grab [it], and come here to me by rope." ⁸And he did as he had urged. When he neared, [the lame man] said, "Come here. You be [my] feet and carry me, and I will be your eyes, guiding you from on top to the right and to the left." ⁹So by doing this, they went down into the garden. And whether they did any damage or not, nevertheless their footprints were visible in the garden. ¹⁰Now when the celebrants dispersed from the wedding feast, going down into the garden, they were surprised to find the footprints in the garden. ¹¹So they reported these things to the king, saying, "Everyone in your kingdom is a soldier and no one is a civilian. So why are there civilian footprints in the garden?" ¹²And [the king] was astounded. So he summoned the lame man and the blind man. ¹³And he asked the blind man, "Did you not come down into the garden?" But [the blind man] replied, "Who—me, lord? You see my handicap, you know that I cannot see where I walk." ¹⁴Then approaching the lame man, [the king] also asked him, "Did you come down into my garden?" ¹⁵And answering, he said, "O lord, do you wish to embitter my soul over my handicap?" ¹⁶And finally the judgment was delayed. What then did the righteous judge do? ¹⁷Realizing in what manner the two had joined together, he put the lame man on the blind man and examined them both under the lash. ¹⁸And they were unable to deny [it]. They each convicted the other. ¹⁹The lame man, on the one hand, said to the blind man, "Did you not pick me up and carry me?" ²⁰And the blind man said to the lame man, "Did you yourself not become my eyes?"]]

EPISTLE OF ARISTEAS

The Letter of Aristeas to Philocrates, herein called the Epistle of Aristeas, is a Hellenistic work from the 3rd or early 2nd century BC, thought by some biblical scholars to be pseudepigraphical. Josephus ascribes it to Aristeas of Marmora and suggests it was written to a certain Philocrates. The letter describes the Greek translation of the Hebrew Bible by seventy-two interpreters sent into Egypt from Jerusalem at the request of the librarian of Alexandria, resulting in the Septuagint translation (LXX). Some have argued that its story of the creation of the Greek translation of the Hebrew Bible is fictitious, although its ancient date provides an important counterargument. The letter is a vital resource for understanding the Hellenistic Judaism of Jesus' day and is the earliest text to mention the Great Library of Alexandria, which has been lost to history.

CHAPTER 1

¹Since I have collected material for a memorable history of my visit to Eleazar the chief priest of the Jews, and because you, Philocrates, as you lose no opportunity of reminding me, have set great store on receiving an account of the motives and object of my mission, I have attempted to draw up a clear exposition of the matter for you, for I perceive that you possess a natural love of learning, a quality which is the highest possession of man—to be constantly attempting "to add to his stock of knowledge and acquirements" whether through the study of history or by actually participating in the events themselves. ²It is by this means, by taking up into itself the noblest elements, that the soul is established in purity, and having fixed its aim on piety, the noblest goal of all, it uses this as its infallible guide and so acquires a definite purpose. ³It was my devotion to the pursuit of religious knowledge that led me to undertake the embassy to the man I have mentioned, who was held in the highest esteem by his own citizens and by others both for his virtue and his majesty and who had in his possession documents of the highest value to the Jews in his own country and in foreign lands for the interpretation of the Divine Law, for their laws are written on leather parchments in Jewish characters. ⁴I then undertook this embassy with enthusiasm, having first of all found an opportunity of pleading with the king on behalf of the Jewish captives who had been transported from Judea to Egypt by the king's father, when he first obtained possession of this city and conquered the land of Egypt. ⁵It is worthwhile that I should also tell you this story, since I am convinced that you, with your disposition toward holiness and your sympathy with men who are living in accordance with the holy Law, will all the more readily listen to the account which I purpose to set forth, since you yourself have lately come to us from the island and are anxious to hear everything that tends to build up the soul. ⁶On a former occasion I also sent you a record of the facts which I thought [were] worth relating about the Jewish race—the record which I had obtained from the most learned chief priests of the most learned land of Egypt. ⁷As you are so eager to acquire the knowledge of those things which can benefit the mind, I feel it incumbent on me to impart to you all the information in my power. I should feel the same duty toward all who possessed the same disposition, but I feel it especially toward you since you have aspirations which are so noble, and since you are not only my brother in character no less than in blood but are one with me as well in the pursuit of goodness. ⁸For neither the pleasure derived from gold nor any other of the possessions which are prized by shallow minds confers the same benefit as the pursuit of culture and the study which we expend in securing it. ⁹But that I may not weary you by a too lengthy introduction, I will proceed at once to the substance of my narrative.

CHAPTER 2

¹Demetrius of Phalerum, the president of the king's library, received vast sums of money for the purpose of collecting together, as far as he possibly could, all the scrolls in the world. ²By means of purchase and transcription, he carried out, to the best of his ability, the purpose of the king. ³On one occasion when I was present, he was asked, "How many thousand scrolls are there in the library?" ⁴And he replied, "More than two hundred thousand, O king, and I will make endeavour in the immediate future to gather together the remainder also, so that the total of five hundred thousand may be reached. I am told that the laws of the Jews are worth transcribing and deserve a place in your library." ⁵"What is to prevent you from doing this?" replied the king. "Everything that is necessary has been placed at your disposal." ⁶"They need to be translated," answered Demetrius, "for in the country of the Jews they use a peculiar alphabet (just as the Egyptians, too, have a special form of letters) and speak a peculiar dialect. They are supposed to use the Syriac tongue, but this is not the case; their language is quite different." ⁷And when the king understood all the facts of the case, he ordered a letter to be written to the Jewish chief priest that his purpose (which has already been described) might be accomplished.

CHAPTER 3

¹Thinking that the time had come to press the demand which I had often laid before Sosibius of Tarentum and Andreas, the chief of the bodyguard, for the emancipation of the Jews who had been transported from Judea by the king's father— ²for when by a combination of good fortune and courage he had brought his attack on the whole district of Coele-Syria and Phoenicia to a successful resolution, in the process of terrorizing the country into subjection, he transported some of his adversaries and others he reduced to captivity. ³The number of those whom he transported from the country of the Jews to Egypt amounted to no less than one hundred thousand. ⁴Of these he armed thirty thousand chosen men and settled them in garrisons in the country districts. ⁵(And even before this time large numbers of Jews had come into Egypt with the Persian, and in an earlier period still others had been sent to Egypt to help Psammetichus in his campaign against the king of the Ethiopians. But these were nothing like so numerous as the captives whom Ptolemy the son of Lagus transported.) ⁶As I have already stated, Ptolemy chose out the best of these, the men who were in the prime of life and distinguished for their courage, and armed them, but the great mass of the others, those who were too old or too young for this purpose, and the women too, he reduced to slavery—not that he wished to do this of his own free will, but he was compelled by his soldiers who claimed them as a reward for the services which they had rendered in war. ⁷Having, as has already been stated, obtained an opportunity for securing their emancipation, I addressed the king with the following arguments: ⁸"Let us not be so unreasonable as to allow our deeds to give the lie to our words. Since the Law which we wish not only to transcribe but also to translate belongs to the whole Jewish race, what

justification will we be able to find for our embassy while such vast numbers of them remain in a state of slavery in your kingdom? ⁹In the perfection and wealth of your clemency, release those who are held in such miserable bondage, since as I have been at pains to discover, the God who gave them their law is the God who maintains your kingdom. ¹⁰They worship the same God—the Lord and Creator of the universe, as all other men, as we ourselves, O king, though we call Him by different names, such as Zeus or Dis. ¹¹This name was very appropriately bestowed on Him by our first ancestors in order to signify that He, through whom all things are endowed with life and come into being, is necessarily the Ruler and Lord of the universe. ¹²Set all mankind an example of magnanimity by releasing those who are held in bondage." ¹³After a brief interval, while I was offering up an earnest prayer to God that He would so dispose the mind of the king that all the captives might be set at liberty (for the human race, being the creation of God, is swayed and influenced by Him), therefore with many manifold prayers I called on Him who rules the heart that the king might be constrained to grant my request. ¹⁴For I had great hopes with regard to the salvation of the men since I was assured that God would grant a fulfillment of my prayer, for when men from pure motives plan some action in the interest of righteousness and the performance of noble deeds, Almighty God brings their efforts and purposes to a successful issue. ¹⁵The king raised his head, and looking up at me with a cheerful countenance, asked, "How many thousands do you think they will number?" Andreas, who was standing near, replied, "A little more than one hundred thousand." ¹⁶"It is a small boon indeed," said the king, "that Aristeas asks of us!" ¹⁷Then Sosibius and some others who were present said, "Yes, but it will be a fit tribute to your magnanimity for you to offer the liberation of these men as an act of devotion to the supreme God. ¹⁸You have been greatly honored by Almighty God and exalted above all your forefathers in glory and it is only fitting that you should render to Him the greatest thank offering in your power." ¹⁹Extremely pleased with these arguments, he gave orders that an addition should be made to the wages of the soldiers by the amount of the redemption money that twenty drachmas should be paid to the owners for every slave, that a public order should be issued, and that registers of the captives should be attached to it. ²⁰He showed the greatest enthusiasm in the business, for it was God who had brought our purpose to fulfillment in its entirety and constrained him to redeem not only those who had come into Egypt with the army of his father but any who had come before that time or had been subsequently brought into the kingdom. ²¹It was pointed out to him that the ransom money would exceed four hundred talents.

CHAPTER 4

¹I think it will be useful to insert a copy of the decree, for in this way the magnanimity of the king, who was empowered by God to save such vast multitudes, will be made clearer and more manifest. ²The decree of the king ran as follows: "All who served in the army of our father in the campaign against Syria and Phoenicia and in the attack on the country of the Jews, and became possessed of Jewish captives, and brought them back to the city of Alexandria and the land of Egypt or sold them to others—and in the same way any captives who were in our land before that time or were brought here afterward—all who possess such captives are required to set them at liberty at once, receiving twenty drachmas per head as ransom money. ³The soldiers will receive this money as a gift added to their wages, the others from the king's treasury. ⁴We think that it was against our father's will and against all propriety that they should have been made captives and that the devastation of their land and the transportation of the Jews to Egypt was an act of military wantonness. ⁵The spoil which fell to the soldiers on the field of battle was all the plunder which they should have claimed. To reduce the people to slavery in addition was an act of absolute injustice. ⁶Therefore since it is acknowledged that we are accustomed to render justice to all men and especially to those who are unfairly in a condition of servitude, and since we strive to deal fairly with all men according to the demands of justice and piety, we have decreed, in reference to the persons of the Jews who are in any condition of bondage in any part of our dominion, that those who possess them will receive the stipulated sum of money and set them at liberty and that no man will show any tardiness in discharging his obligations. ⁷Within three days after the publication of this decree, they must make lists of slaves for the officers appointed to carry out our will, and immediately produce the persons of the captives. ⁸For we consider that it will be advantageous to us and to our affairs that the matter should be brought to a conclusion. ⁹Anyone who likes may give information about any who disobey the decree on condition that if the man is proved guilty, he will become his slave; his property, however, will be handed over to the royal treasury."

CHAPTER 5

¹When the decree was brought to be read over to the king for his approval, it contained all the other provisions except the phrase "any captives who were in the land before that time or were brought here afterward," and in his magnanimity and the largeness of his heart the king inserted this clause and gave orders that the grant of money required for the redemption should be deposited in full with the paymasters of the forces and the royal bankers, and so the matter was decided and the decree ratified within seven days. ²The grant for the redemption amounted to more than six hundred and sixty talents; for many infants at the breast were emancipated together with their mothers. ³When the question was raised whether the sum of twenty talents was to be paid for these, the king ordered that it should be done, and thus he carried out his decision in the most comprehensive way. ⁴When this had been done, he ordered Demetrius to draw up a memorial with regard to the transcription of the Jewish scrolls, for all affairs of state used to be carried out by means of decrees and with the most painstaking accuracy by these Egyptian kings, and nothing was done in a careless or haphazard fashion. ⁵And so I have inserted copies of the memorial and the letters, the number of the presents sent, and the nature of each, since every one of them excelled in magnificence and technical skill. The following is a copy of the memorial:

CHAPTER 6

¹"Since you have given me instructions, O king, that the scrolls which are needed to complete your library should be collected together, and that those which are defective should be repaired, I have devoted myself with the utmost care to the fulfillment of your wishes, and I now have the following proposal to lay before you: ²the scrolls of the Law of the Jews (with several others) are absent from the library. They are written in the Hebrew characters and language and have been carelessly interpreted, and do not represent the original text as I am informed by those who know; for they have never had a king's care to protect them. ³It is necessary that these should be made accurate for your library since the law which they contain, in as much as it is of divine origin, is full of wisdom and free from all blemish. ⁴For this reason, literary men, and poets, and the mass of historical writers have held aloof from referring to these scrolls and the men who have lived and are living in accordance with them, because their conception of life is so sacred and religious, as Hecataeus of Abdera says. ⁵If it pleases you, O king, a letter will be written to the chief priest in Jerusalem, asking him to send six elders out of every tribe—men who have lived the noblest life and are most skilled in their law—that we may find out the points in which the majority of them are in agreement, and so having obtained an accurate translation, may place it in a conspicuous place in a manner worthy of the work itself and your purpose. ⁶May continual prosperity be yours!"

CHAPTER 7

¹When this memorial had been presented, the king ordered a letter to be written to Eleazar on the matter, giving also an account of the emancipation of the Jewish captives. ²And he gave fifty talents weight of gold, and seventy talents of silver, and a large quantity of precious stones to make bowls, and vials, and a table, and libation cups. ³He also gave orders to those who had the custody of his coffers to allow the craftsmen to make a selection of any materials they might require for the purpose, and that one hundred talents in money should

EPISTLE OF ARISTEAS

be sent to provide sacrifices for the temple and for other needs. ⁴I will give you a full account of the workmanship after I have set copies of the letters before you. ⁵The letter of the king ran as follows: "King Ptolemy sends greeting and salutation to the chief priest Eleazar. ⁶Since there are many Jews settled in our realm who were carried off from Jerusalem by the Persians at the time of their power and many more who came with my father into Egypt as captives, large numbers of these he placed in the army and paid them higher wages than usual, and when he had proved the loyalty of their leaders, he built fortresses and placed them in their charge that the native Egyptians might be intimidated by them. ⁷And I, when I ascended the throne, adopted a kindly attitude toward all my subjects, and more particularly to those who were citizens of yours—I have set at liberty more than one hundred thousand captives, paying their owners the appropriate market price for them, and if ever evil has been done to your people through the passions of the mob, I have made them reparation. ⁸The motive which prompted my action has been the desire to act piously and render to the supreme God a thank offering for maintaining my kingdom in peace and great glory in all the world. ⁹Moreover, those of your people who were in the prime of life I have drafted into my army, and those who were fit to be attached to my person and worthy of the confidence of the court, I have established in official positions. ¹⁰Now since I am anxious to show my gratitude to these men, and to the Jews throughout the world, and to the generations yet to come, I have determined that your law will be translated from the Hebrew tongue, which is in use among you, into the Greek language, that these scrolls may be added to the other royal scrolls in my library. ¹¹It will be a kindness on your part and a regard for my zeal if you will select six elders from each of your tribes, men of noble life and skilled in your law and able to interpret it, that in questions of dispute we may be able to discover the verdict in which the majority agree, for the investigation is of the highest possible importance. ¹²I hope to win great renown by the accomplishment of this work. ¹³I have sent Andreas, the chief of my bodyguard, and Aristeas—men whom I hold in high esteem—to lay the matter before you and present you with one hundred talents of silver, the first-fruits of my offering for the temple and the sacrifices and other religious rites. ¹⁴If you will write to me concerning your wishes in these matters, you will confer a great favor on me and afford me a new pledge of friendship, for all your wishes will be carried out as speedily as possible. Farewell."

CHAPTER 8

¹To this letter Eleazar replied appropriately as follows: "Eleazar the chief priest sends greetings to King Ptolemy, his true friend. My highest wishes are for your welfare and the welfare of Queen Arsinoe, your sister, and your children. ²I also am well. I have received your letter and am greatly rejoiced by your purpose and your noble counsel. ³I summoned together the whole people and read it to them that they might know of your devotion to our God. ⁴I also showed them the cups which you sent, twenty of gold and thirty of silver, the five bowls, and the table of dedication, and the one hundred talents of silver for the offering of the sacrifices and providing the things of which the temple stands in need. ⁵These gifts were brought to me by Andreas, one of your most honored servants, and by Aristeas, both good men and true, distinguished by their learning, and worthy in every way to be the representatives of your high principles and righteous purposes. ⁶These men imparted your message to me and received an answer from me in agreement with your letter. I will consent to everything which is advantageous to you even though your request is very unusual. ⁷For you have bestowed on our citizens great and never to be forgotten benefits in many. ⁸Therefore I immediately offered sacrifices on behalf of you, your sister, your children, and your friends, and all the people prayed that your plans might continually prosper, and that Almighty God might preserve your kingdom in peace with honor, and that the translation of the holy Law might prove advantageous to you and be carried out successfully. ⁹In the presence of all the people I selected six elders from each tribe, good men and true, and I have sent them to you with a copy of our law. ¹⁰It will be a kindness, O righteous king, if you will give instruction that as soon as the translation of the Law is completed, the men will be restored to us again in safety. Farewell."

CHAPTER 9

¹The following are the names of the elders. Of the first tribe: Joseph, Hezekiah, Zechariah, John, Hezekiah, Elisha. ²Of the second tribe: Judas, Simon, Samuel, Adaeus, Mattathias, Eschlemias. ³Of the third tribe: Nehemiah, Joseph, Theodosius, Baseas, Ornias, Dakis. ⁴Of the fourth tribe: Jonathan, Abraeus, Elisha, Ananias, Chabrias. ⁵Of the fifth tribe: Isaac, Jacob, Jesus, Sabbataeus, Simon, Levi. ⁶Of the sixth tribe: Judas, Joseph, Simon, Zacharias, Samuel, Selemias. ⁷Of the seventh tribe: Sabbataeus, Zedekiah, Jacob, Isaac, Jesias, Natthaeus. ⁸Of the eighth tribe: Theodosius, Jason, Jesus, Theodotus, John, Jonathan. ⁹Of the ninth tribe: Theophilus, Abraham, Arsamos, Jason, Endemias, Daniel. ¹⁰Of the tenth tribe: Jeremiah, Eleazar, Zechariah, Baneas, Elisha, Dathaeus. ¹¹Of the eleventh tribe: Samuel, Joseph, Judas, Jonathes, Chabu, Dositheus. ¹²Of the twelfth tribe: Isaelus, John, Theodosius, Arsamos, Abietes, Ezekiel. ¹³They were seventy-two in all. Such was the answer which Eleazar and his friends gave to the king's letter.

CHAPTER 10

¹I will now proceed to redeem my promise and give a description of the works of art. ²They were wrought with exceptional skill, for the king spared no expense and personally superintended the workmen individually. ³They could not therefore skimp any part of the work or finish it off negligently. ⁴First of all, I will give you a description of the table. The king was anxious that this piece of work should be of exceptionally large dimensions, and he caused inquiries to be made of the Jews in the locality with regard to the size of the table already in the temple at Jerusalem. ⁵And when they described the measurements, he proceeded to ask whether he might make a larger structure. ⁶And some of the priests and the other Jews replied that there was nothing to prevent him. ⁷And he said that he was anxious to make it five times the size, but he hesitated lest it should prove useless for the temple services. ⁸He was desirous that his gift should not merely be stationed in the temple, for it would afford him much greater pleasure if the men whose duty it was to offer the fitting sacrifices were able to do so appropriately on the table which he had made. ⁹He did not suppose that it was owing to lack of gold that the former table had been made of small size, but there seems to have been, he said, some reason why it was made of this dimension. ¹⁰For had the order been given, there would have been no lack of means. Therefore, we must not transgress or go beyond the proper measure. ¹¹At the same time, he ordered them to press into service all the manifold forms of art, for he was a man of the loftiest conceptions, and nature had endowed him with a keen imagination which enabled him to picture the appearance which would be presented by the finished work. ¹²He also gave orders that where there were no instructions laid down in the Jewish Writings, everything should be made as beautiful as possible. When such instructions were laid down, they were to be carried out to the letter.

CHAPTER 11

¹They made the table two cubits long, one cubit broad, one and a half cubits high, fashioning it of pure solid gold. ²What I am describing was not thin gold laid over another foundation, but the whole structure was of massive gold welded together. ³And they made a border of a hand's breadth around it. And there was a wreath of wave-work, engraved in relief in the form of ropes marvelously wrought on its three sides. ⁴For it was triangular in shape and the style of the work was exactly the same on each of the sides, so that whichever side they were turned, they presented the same appearance. ⁵Of the two sides under the border, the one which sloped down to the table was a very beautiful piece of work, but it was the outer side which attracted the gaze of the spectator. ⁶Now the upper edge of the two sides, being elevated, was sharp since, as we have said, the rim was three-sided from whatever point of view one approached it. ⁷And there were layers of precious stones on it in the midst of the embossed cord-work, and they were interwoven with one another by an inimitable artistic device. ⁸For the sake of security they

were all fixed by golden needles which were inserted in perforations in the stones. ⁹At the sides they were clamped together by fastenings to hold them firm. ¹⁰On the part of the border around the table which slanted upwards and met the eyes, there was wrought a pattern of eggs in precious stones, elaborately engraved by a continuous piece of fluted relief-work, closely connected together around the whole table. ¹¹And under the stones which had been arranged to represent eggs, the artists made a crown containing all kinds of fruits, having at its top clusters of grapes and ears of corn, dates also and apples, and pomegranates and the like, conspicuously arranged. ¹²These fruits were wrought out of precious stones, of the same color as the fruits themselves, and they fastened them edgewise around all the sides of the table with a band of gold. ¹³And after the crown of fruit had been put on, underneath there was inserted another pattern of eggs in precious stones, and other fluting and embossed work, that both sides of the table might be used according to the wishes of the owners, and for this reason the wave-work and the border were extended down to the feet of the table. ¹⁴They made and fastened under the whole width of the table a massive plate four fingers thick, that the feet might be inserted into it, and clamped fast with linchpins which fitted into sockets under the border, so that which ever side of the table people preferred might be used. ¹⁵Thus it became manifestly clear that the work was intended to be used either way. ¹⁶On the table itself they engraved Meander, having precious stones standing out in the middle of it— rubies, and emeralds, and an onyx too, and many other kinds of stones which excel in beauty. ¹⁷And next to the Meander there was placed a wonderful piece of network, which made the center of the table appear like a rhomboid in shape, and on it a crystal and amber, as it is called, had been wrought, which produced an incomparable impression on the beholders. ¹⁸They made the feet of the table with heads like lilies, so that they seemed to be like lilies bending down beneath the table, and the parts which were visible represented leaves which stood upright. ¹⁹The basis of the foot on the ground consisted of a ruby and measured a hand's breadth high all around. It had the appearance of a shoe and was eight fingers broad. The whole expanse of the foot rested on it. ²⁰And they made the foot appear like ivy growing out of the stone, interwoven with akanthus and surrounded with a vine which encircled it with clusters of grapes, which were worked in stones, up to the top of the foot. ²¹All the four feet were made in the same style, and everything was wrought and fitted so skillfully, and such remarkable skill and knowledge were expended on making it true to nature, that when the air was stirred by a breath of wind, movement was imparted to the leaves, and everything was fashioned to correspond with the actual reality which it represented. ²²And they made the top of the table in three parts like a triptychon, and they were so fitted and dovetailed together with spigots along the whole breadth of the work, that the meeting of the joints could not be seen or even discovered. ²³The thickness of the table was not less than half a cubit, so that the whole work must have cost many talents. For since the king did not wish to add to its size, he expended on the details the same sum of money which would have been required if the table could have been of larger dimensions. ²⁴And everything was completed in accordance with his plan in a most wonderful and remarkable way, with inimitable art and incomparable beauty.

CHAPTER 12

¹Of the mixing bowls, two were wrought [in gold], and from the base to the middle were engraved with relief work in the pattern of scales, and between the scales precious stones were inserted with great artistic skill. ²Then there was a Meander one cubit in height, with its surface wrought out of precious stones of many colors, displaying great artistic effort and beauty. ³On this there was a mosaic, worked in the form of a rhombus, having a net-like appearance and reaching right up to the brim. ⁴In the middle, small shields which were made of different precious stones, placed alternately and varying in kind, not less than four fingers broad, enhanced the beauty of their appearance. ⁵On the top of the brim there was an ornament of lilies in bloom, and intertwining clusters of grapes were engraven all around. Such then was the construction of the golden bowls, and they held more than two firkins each. ⁶The silver bowls had a smooth surface and were wonderfully made as if they were intended for looking-glasses, so that everything which was brought near to them was reflected even more clearly than in mirrors. ⁷But it is impossible to describe the real impression which these works of art produced on the mind when they were finished, for when these vessels had been completed and placed side by side, first a silver bowl, and then a golden, then another silver, and then another golden, the appearance they presented is altogether indescribable, and those who came to see them were not able to tear themselves from the brilliant sight and entrancing spectacle. ⁸The impressions produced by the spectacle were various in kind. When men looked at the golden vessels, and their minds made a complete survey of each detail of workmanship, their souls were thrilled with wonder. ⁹Again, when a man wished to direct his gaze to the silver vessels as they stood before him, everything seemed to flash with light around the place where he was standing and afforded a still greater delight to the onlookers, so that it is really impossible to describe the artistic beauty of the works. ¹⁰The golden vials they engraved in the center with vine wreaths. And around the rims they wove a wreath of ivy, and myrtle, and olive in relief work and inserted precious stones in it. ¹¹The other parts of the relief work they wrought in different patterns, since they made it a point of honor to complete everything in a way worthy of the majesty of the king. ¹²In a word it may be said that neither in the king's treasury nor in any other were there any works which equalled these in costliness or in artistic skill, for the king spent no little thought on them, for he loved to gain glory for the excellence of his designs. ¹³For oftentimes he would neglect his official business and spend his time with the artists in his anxiety that they should complete everything in a manner worthy of the place to which the gifts were to be sent. ¹⁴So everything was carried out on a grand scale, in a manner worthy of the king who sent the gifts and of the chief priest who was the ruler of the land. ¹⁵There was no stint of precious stones, for not less than five thousand were used and they were all of large size. ¹⁶The most exceptional artistic skill was employed, so that the cost of the stones and the workmanship was five times as much as that of the gold.

CHAPTER 13

¹I have given you this description of the presents because I thought it was necessary. ²The next point in the narrative is an account of our journey to Eleazar, but I will first of all give you a description of the whole country. ³When we arrived in the land of the Jews, we saw the city situated in the middle of the whole of Judea on the top of a mountain of considerable altitude. ⁴On the summit the temple had been built in all its splendor. It was surrounded by three walls more than seventy cubits high and in length and breadth corresponding to the structure of the edifice. ⁵All the buildings were characterized by a magnificence and costliness quite unprecedented. It was obvious that no expense had been spared on the door and the fastenings, which connected it with the doorposts, and the stability of the lintel. ⁶The style of the curtain too was thoroughly in proportion to that of the entrance. ⁷Its fabric owing to the draught of wind was in perpetual motion, and as this motion was communicated from the bottom and the curtain bulged out to its highest extent, it afforded a pleasant spectacle from which a man could scarcely tear himself away. ⁸The construction of the altar was in keeping with the place itself and with the burnt-offerings which were consumed by fire on it, and the approach to it was on a similar scale. ⁹There was a gradual slope up to it, conveniently arranged for the purpose of decency, and the ministering priests were robed in linen garments down to their ankles. ¹⁰The temple faces the east, and its back is toward the west. ¹¹The whole of the floor is paved with stones and slopes down to the appointed places, that water may be conveyed to wash away the blood from the sacrifices, for many thousand beasts are sacrificed there on the feast days. ¹²And there is an inexhaustible supply of water, because an abundant natural spring gushes up from within the temple area. ¹³There are moreover wonderful and indescribable cisterns underground, as they

pointed out to me, at a distance of five furlongs all around the site of the temple, and each of them has countless pipes so that the different streams converge together. ¹⁴And all these were fastened with lead at the bottom and at the sidewalls, and over them a great quantity of plaster had been spread, and every part of the work had been most carefully carried out. ¹⁵There are many openings for water at the base of the altar which are invisible to all except to those who are engaged in the ministration, so that all the blood of the sacrifices which is collected in great quantities is washed away in the twinkling of an eye. ¹⁶Such is my opinion with regard to the character of the reservoirs and I will now show you how it was confirmed. ¹⁷They led me more than four furlongs outside the city and commanded me to peer down toward a certain spot and listen to the noise that was made by the meeting of the waters, so that the great size of the reservoirs became manifest to me, as has already been pointed out.

CHAPTER 14

¹The ministration of the priests is in every way unsurpassed both for its physical endurance and for its orderly and silent service. ²For they all work spontaneously, though it entails much painful exertion, and each one has a special task allotted to him. ³The service is carried on without interruption—some provide the wood, others the oil, others the fine wheat flour, others the spices; others again bring the pieces of flesh for the burnt-offering, exhibiting a wonderful degree of strength. ⁴For they take up the limbs of a calf with both hands, each of them weighing more than two talents, and throw them with each hand in a wonderful way onto the high place of the altar and never miss placing them on the proper spot. ⁵In the same way the pieces of the sheep and also of the goats are wonderful both for their weight and their fatness. ⁶For those whose business it is always select the beasts which are without blemish and especially fat, and thus the sacrifice which I have described is carried out. ⁷There is a special place set apart for them to rest in where those who are relieved from duty sit. When this takes place, those who have already rested and are ready to assume their duties rise up spontaneously since there is no one to give orders with regard to the arrangement of the sacrifices. ⁸The most complete silence reigns so that one might imagine that there was not a single person present, though there are actually seven hundred men engaged in the work, besides the vast number of those who are occupied in bringing up the sacrifices. ⁹Everything is carried out with reverence and in a way worthy of the great God.

CHAPTER 15

¹We were greatly astonished when we saw Eleazar engaged in the ministration, at the mode of his dress and the majesty of his appearance, which was revealed in the robe which he wore and the precious stones on his person. ²There were golden bells on the garment which reached down to his feet, giving forth a peculiar kind of melody, and on both sides of them there were pomegranates with variegated flowers of a wonderful hue. ³He was girded with a girdle of conspicuous beauty, woven in the most beautiful colors. ⁴On his breast he wore the oracle of God, as it is called, on which twelve stones, of different kinds, were inset, fastened together with gold, containing the names of the leaders of the tribes according to their original order, each one flashing forth in an indescribable way its own particular color. ⁵On his head he wore a tiara, as it is called, and on this in the middle of his forehead an inimitable turban, the royal diadem full of glory with the Name of God inscribed in sacred letters on a plate of gold ... having been judged worthy to wear these emblems in the ministrations. ⁶Their appearance created such awe and confusion of mind as to make one feel that one had come into the presence of a man who belonged to a different world. ⁷I am convinced that anyone who takes part in the spectacle which I have described will be filled with astonishment and indescribable wonder and be profoundly affected in his mind at the thought of the sanctity which is attached to each detail of the service.

CHAPTER 16

¹But in order that we might gain complete information, we ascended to the summit of the neighboring citadel and looked around us. ²It is situated in a very lofty spot, and is fortified with many towers, which have been built up to the very top of immense stones, with the object, as we were informed, of guarding the temple precincts, so that if there were an attack, or an insurrection, or an onslaught of the enemy, no one would be able to force an entrance within the walls that surround the temple. ³On the towers of the citadel engines of war were placed and different kinds of machines, and the position was much higher than the circle of walls which I have mentioned. ⁴The towers were also guarded by most trusty men who had given the utmost proof of their loyalty to their country. ⁵These men were never allowed to leave the citadel, except on feast days and then only in detachments; nor did they permit any stranger to enter it. ⁶They were also very careful when any command came from the chief officer to admit any visitors to inspect the place, as our own experience taught us. ⁷They were very reluctant to admit us—although we were only two unarmed men—to view the offering of the sacrifices. ⁸And they asserted that they were bound by an oath when the trust was committed to them, for they had all sworn and were bound to carry out the oath sacredly to the letter, that although they were five hundred in number, they would not permit more than five men to enter at one time. ⁹The citadel was the special protection of the temple and its founder had fortified it so strongly that it might efficiently protect it.

CHAPTER 17

¹The size of the city is of moderate dimensions. It is about forty furlongs in circumference, as far as one could conjecture. It has its towers arranged in the shape of a theater, with thoroughfares leading between them. ²Now the crossroads of the lower towers are visible, but those of the upper towers are more frequented. For the ground ascends, since the city is built on a mountain. ³There are also steps which lead up to the crossroads, and some people are always going up, and others down, and they keep as far apart from each other as possible on the road because of those who are bound by the rules of purity, lest they should touch anything which is unlawful. ⁴It was not without reason that the original founders of the city built it in due proportions, for they possessed clear insight with regard to what was required. ⁵For the country is extensive and beautiful. Some parts of it are level, especially the districts which belong to Samaria, as it is called, and which border on the land of the Idumeans, other parts are mountainous, especially [those which are contiguous to the land of Judea]. ⁶The people are therefore bound to devote themselves to agriculture and the cultivation of the soil that by this means they may have a plentiful supply of crops. ⁷In this way cultivation of every kind is carried on and an abundant harvest reaped in the whole of the aforementioned land. ⁸The cities which are large and enjoy a corresponding prosperity are well-populated, but they neglect the country districts, since all men are inclined to a life of enjoyment, for everyone has a natural tendency toward the pursuit of pleasure. ⁹The same thing happened in Alexandria, which excels all cities in size and prosperity. ¹⁰Country people by migrating from the rural districts and settling in the city brought agriculture into disrepute: and so to prevent them from settling in the city, the king issued orders that they should not stay in it for more than twenty days. ¹¹And in the same way he gave the judges written instructions, that if it was necessary to issue a summons against anyone who lived in the country, the case must be settled within five days. ¹²And since he considered the matter one of great importance, he appointed also legal officers for every district with their assistants, that the farmers and their advocates might not in the interests of business empty the granaries of the city—I mean of the produce of husbandry. ¹³I have permitted this digression because it was Eleazar who pointed out with great clearness the points which have been mentioned. ¹⁴For great is the energy which they expend on the tillage of the soil. For the land is thickly planted with multitudes of olive trees, with crops of corn and pulse, with vines too, and there is abundance of honey. ¹⁵Other kinds of fruit trees and dates do not count compared with these. ¹⁶There are cattle of all kinds in great quantities and a rich pasturage for them. ¹⁷Therefore, they rightly recognize that the country districts need a large population, and the relations between the city

and the villages are properly regulated. ¹⁸A great quantity of spices, and precious stones, and gold is brought into the country by the Arabs. ¹⁹For the country is well adapted not only for agriculture but also for commerce, and the city is rich in the arts and lacks none of the merchandise which is brought across the sea. ²⁰It also possesses suitable and commodious harbors at Ashkelon, Joppa, and Gaza, as well as at Ptolemais which was founded by the king and holds a central position compared with the other places named, being not far distant from any of them. ²¹The country produces everything in abundance, since it is well-watered in all directions and well-protected from storms. ²²The Jordan River, as it is called, which never runs dry, flows through the land. ²³Originally [the country] contained not less than sixty million acres—although afterward the neighboring peoples made incursions against it—and six hundred thousand men were settled on it in farms of a hundred acres each. ²⁴Like the Nile, the river rises in [the] time of harvest and irrigates a large portion of the land. Near the district belonging to the people of Ptolemais it issues into another river and this flows out into the sea. ²⁵Other mountain torrents, as they are called, flow down into the plain and encompass the parts around Gaza and the district of Ashdod. ²⁶The country is encircled by a natural fence and is very difficult to attack and cannot be assailed by large forces, owing to the narrow passes, with their overhanging precipices and deep ravines, and the rugged character of the mountainous regions which surround all the land. ²⁷We were told that from the neighboring mountains of Arabia copper and iron were formerly obtained. ²⁸This was stopped, however, at the time of the Persian rule, since the authorities of the time spread abroad a false report that the working of the mines was useless and expensive in order to prevent their country from being destroyed by the mining in these districts and possibly taken away from them owing to the Persian rule, since by the assistance of this false report they found an excuse for entering the district.

CHAPTER 18

¹I have now, my dear brother Philocrates, given you all the essential information on this subject in brief form. I will describe the work of translation in the sequel. ²The chief priest selected men of the finest character and the highest culture, such as one would expect from their noble parentage. ³They were men who had not only acquired proficiency in Jewish literature but had studied most carefully that of the Greeks as well. ⁴They were therefore especially qualified for serving on embassies and they undertook this duty whenever it was necessary. ⁵They possessed a great facility for conferences and the discussion of problems connected with the Law. ⁶They espoused the middle course—and this is always the best course to pursue. They renounced the rough and uncouth manner, but they were altogether above pride and never assumed an air of superiority over others, and in conversation they were ready to listen and give an appropriate answer to every question. ⁷And all of them carefully observed this rule and were anxious above everything else to excel each other in its observance and all of them were worthy of their leader and of his virtue. ⁸And one could observe how they loved Eleazar by their unwillingness to be torn away from him and how he loved them. ⁹For besides the letter which he wrote to the king concerning their safe return, he also earnestly sought Andreas to work for the same end and urged me, too, to assist to the best of my ability; ¹⁰and although we promised to give our best attention to the matter, he said that he was still greatly distressed, for he knew that the king out of the goodness of his nature considered it his highest privilege, whenever he heard of a man who was superior to his fellows in culture and wisdom, to summon him to his court. ¹¹For I have heard of a fine saying of his to the effect that by securing just and prudent men around his person he would secure the greatest protection for his kingdom, since such friends would unreservedly give him the most beneficial advice. ¹²And the men who were now being sent to him by Eleazar undoubtedly possessed these qualities. ¹³And he frequently asserted on oath that he would never let the men go if it were merely some private interest of his own that constituted the impelling motive—but it was for the common advantage of all the citizens that he was sending them. ¹⁴"For," he explained, "the good life consists in the keeping of the enactments of the Law, and this end is achieved much more by hearing than by reading." ¹⁵From this and other similar statements it was clear what his feelings toward them were.

CHAPTER 19

¹It is worthwhile to briefly mention the information which he gave in reply to our questions. ²For I suppose that most people feel a curiosity with regard to some of the enactments in the Law, especially those about meats, and drinks, and animals recognized as unclean. ³When we asked why, since there is but one form of creation, some animals are regarded as unclean for eating, and others unclean even to the touch (for though the Law is scrupulous on most points, it is especially scrupulous on such matters as these) he began his reply as follows: "You observe," he said, "what an effect our modes of life and our associations produce on us; ⁴by associating with the bad, men catch their depravities and become miserable throughout their life, but if they live with the wise and prudent, they find the means of escaping from ignorance and amending their lives. ⁵Our lawgiver first of all laid down the principles of piety and righteousness and inculcated them point by point, not merely by prohibitions, but [also] by the use of examples as well, demonstrating the injurious effects of sin and the punishments inflicted by God on the guilty. ⁶For he proved first of all that there is only one God and that His power is manifested throughout the universe, since every place is filled with His sovereignty and none of the things which are wrought in secret by men on the earth escapes His knowledge. ⁷For all that a man does and all that is to come to pass in the future are manifest to Him. ⁸Working out these truths carefully and having made them plain he showed that even if a man should think of doing evil—to say nothing of actually effecting it—he would not escape detection, for he made it clear that the power of God pervaded the whole of the Law. ⁹Beginning from this starting point he went on to show that all mankind, except ourselves, believe in the existence of many gods, though they themselves are much more powerful than the beings whom they vainly worship. ¹⁰For when they have made statues of stone and wood, they say that they are the images of those who have invented something useful for life and they worship them, although they have clear proof that they possess no feeling. ¹¹For it would be utterly foolish to suppose that anyone became a god in virtue of his inventions. ¹²For the inventors simply took certain objects already created and by combining them together, showed that they possessed a fresh utility: they did not themselves create the substance of the thing, and so it is a vain and foolish thing for people to make gods of men like themselves. ¹³For in our times there are many who are much more inventive and much more learned than the men of former days who have been deified, and yet they would never come to worship them. ¹⁴The makers and authors of these myths think that they are the wisest of the Greeks. ¹⁵Why do we need to speak of other infatuated people, Egyptians and the like, who place their reliance on wild beasts, and most kinds of creeping things, and cattle, and worship them, and offer sacrifices to them both while living and when dead?"

CHAPTER 20

¹"Now our lawgiver, being a wise man and especially endowed by God to understand all things, took a comprehensive view of each particular detail, and fenced us around with impregnable ramparts and walls of iron, that we might not mingle at all with any of the other nations, but remain pure in body and soul, free from all vain imaginations, worshiping the one Almighty God above the whole creation. ²Hence the leading Egyptian priests, having looked carefully into many matters, and being cognizant with [our] affairs, call us Men of God. This is a title which does not belong to the rest of mankind but only to those who worship the true God. ³The rest are men not of God but of meats, and drinks, and clothing, for their whole disposition leads them to find solace in these things. ⁴Among our people such things are reckoned of no account, but throughout their whole life their main consideration is the sovereignty of God. ⁵Therefore, lest we should be corrupted by any abomination, or our lives be perverted by evil communications, he

hedged us around on all sides by rules of purity, affecting alike what we eat, or drink, or touch, or hear, or see. ⁶For though, speaking generally, all things are alike in their natural constitution, since they are all governed by one and the same power, yet there is a deep reason in each individual case why we abstain from the use of certain things and enjoy the common use of others. ⁷For the sake of illustration I will run over one or two points and explain them to you, for you must not fall into the degrading idea that it was out of regard to mice, and weasels, and other such things that Moses drew up his laws with such exceeding care. ⁸All these ordinances were made for the sake of righteousness to aid the quest for virtue and the perfecting of character. ⁹For all the birds that we use are tame and distinguished by their cleanliness, feeding on various kinds of grain and pulse, such as for instance pigeons, turtle-doves, locusts, partridges, geese also, and all other birds of this class. ¹⁰But the birds which are forbidden you will find to be wild and carnivorous, tyrannizing over the others by the strength which they possess, and cruelly obtaining food by preying on the tame birds enumerated above, and not only this, but they seize lambs and kids, and also injure human beings, whether dead or alive, ¹¹and so by naming them unclean, he gave a sign by means of them that those for whom the legislation was ordained must practice righteousness in their hearts and not tyrannize over anyone in reliance on their own strength, nor rob them of anything, but steer their course of life in accordance with justice, just as the tame birds, already mentioned, consume the different kinds of pulse that grow on the earth and do not tyrannize to the destruction of their own kind. ¹²Our legislator therefore taught us that it is by such methods as these that indications are given to the wise, that they must be just, and effect nothing by violence, and refrain from tyrannizing over others in reliance on their own strength. ¹³For since it is considered unseemly even to touch such unclean animals as have been mentioned, on account of their particular habits, ought we not to take every precaution lest our own characters should be destroyed to the same extent? ¹⁴Therefore, all the rules which he has laid down with regard to what is permitted in the case of these birds and other animals, he has enacted with the object of teaching us a moral lesson. ¹⁵For the division of the hoof and the separation of the claws are intended to teach us that we must discriminate between our individual actions with a view to the practice of virtue. ¹⁶For the strength of our whole body and its activity depend on our shoulders and limbs. Therefore, he compels us to recognize that we must perform all our actions with discrimination according to the standard of righteousness—more especially because we have been distinctly separated from the rest of mankind. ¹⁷For most other men defile themselves by promiscuous intercourse, thereby working great iniquity, and whole countries and cities pride themselves on such vices. ¹⁸For they not only have intercourse with men, but they defile their own mothers and even their daughters. But we have been kept separate from such sins. ¹⁹And the people who have been separated in the aforementioned way are also characterized by the lawgiver as possessing the gift of memory. ²⁰For all animals which are cloven-footed and chew the cud represent to the initiated the symbol of memory. For the act of chewing the cud is nothing else than the reminiscence of life and existence. ²¹For life is accustomed to being sustained by means of food, therefore he also exhorts us in the Writing in these words: You will surely remember the LORD that wrought in you those great and wonderful things. ²²For when they are properly conceived, they are manifestly great and glorious: first the construction of the body, and the disposition of the food, and the separation of each individual limb, and, far more, the organization of the senses, the operation and invisible movement of the mind, the rapidity of its particular actions, and its discovery of the arts, display an infinite resourcefulness. ²³Therefore, he exhorts us to remember that the aforementioned parts are kept together by the divine power with consummate skill. ²⁴For he has marked out every time and place that we may continually remember the God who rules and preserves [us]. ²⁵For in the matter of meats and drinks he commands us first of all [to] offer part as a sacrifice and then forthwith enjoy our meal. ²⁶Moreover, on our garments he has given us a symbol of remembrance, and in like manner he has ordered us to put the divine oracles on our gates and doors as a remembrance of God. ²⁷And on our hands, too, he expressly orders the symbol to be fastened, clearly showing that we ought to perform every act in righteousness, remembering [our own creation], and above all, the fear of God. ²⁸He also commands men, when lying down to sleep and rising up again, to meditate on the works of God, not only in word, but by distinctly observing the change and impression produced on them, when they are going to sleep, and also their waking, how divine and incomprehensible the change from one of these states to the other is. ²⁹The excellency of the analogy in regard to discrimination and memory has now been pointed out to you, according to our interpretation of the cloven hoof and the chewing of the cud. ³⁰For our laws have not been drawn up at random or in accordance with the first casual thought that occurred to the mind, but with a view to truth and the indication of right reason. ³¹For by means of the directions which he gives with regard to meats, and drinks, and particular cases of touching, he commands us neither to do nor listen to anything, thoughtlessly, nor to resort to injustice by the abuse of the power of reason. ³²In the case of the wild animals, too, the same principle may be discovered, for the character of the weasel, and of mice, and such animals as these, which are expressly mentioned, is destructive. ³³Mice defile and damage everything, not only for their own food but even to the extent of rendering absolutely useless to man whatever it falls in their way to damage. ³⁴The weasel class, too, is peculiar: for besides what has been said, it has a characteristic which is defiling: it conceives through the ears and brings forth through the mouth. ³⁵And it is for this reason that a like practice is declared unclean in men. ³⁶For by embodying in speech all that they receive through the ears, they involve others in evils and work no ordinary impurity, being themselves altogether defiled by the pollution of impiety. ³⁷And your king, as we are informed, does quite right in destroying such men." ³⁸Then I said, "I suppose you mean the informers, for he constantly exposes them to tortures and to painful forms of death." ³⁹"Yes," he replied, "these are the men I mean, for to watch for men's destruction is an unholy thing. And our law forbids us to injure anyone either by word or deed. ⁴⁰My brief account of these matters ought to have convinced you that all our regulations have been drawn up with a view to righteousness, and that nothing has been enacted in the Writing thoughtlessly or without due reason, but its purpose is to enable us throughout our whole life and in all our actions to practice righteousness before all men, being mindful of Almighty God. ⁴¹And so concerning meats and things unclean, creeping things, and wild beasts, the whole system aims at righteousness and righteous relationships between man and man."

CHAPTER 21

¹He seemed to me to have made a good defense on all the points, for in reference also to the calves, and rams, and goats which are offered, he said that it was necessary to take them from the herds and flocks, and sacrifice tame animals and offer nothing wild, that the offerers of the sacrifices might understand the symbolic meaning of the lawgiver and not be under the influence of an arrogant self-consciousness. ²For he who offers a sacrifice also makes an offering of his own soul in all its moods. ³I think that these particulars with regard to our discussion are worth narrating, and on account of the sanctity and natural meaning of the Law I have been induced to explain them to you clearly, Philocrates, because of your own devotion to learning.

CHAPTER 22

¹And Eleazar, after offering the sacrifice, and selecting the envoys, and preparing many gifts for the king, despatched us on our journey in great security. ²And when we reached Alexandria, the king was at once informed of our arrival. On our admission to the palace, Andreas and I warmly greeted the king and handed over to him the letter written by Eleazar. ³The king was very anxious to meet the envoys and gave orders that all the other officials should be dismissed and the envoys summoned to his presence at once. ⁴Now this excited general surprise, for it is customary for those who come to seek an

audience with the king on matters of importance to be admitted to his presence on the fifth day, while envoys from kings or very important cities with difficulty secure admission to the court in thirty days—[5] but he counted these men worthy of greater honor since he held their master in such high esteem, and so he immediately dismissed those whose presence he regarded as superfluous and continued walking around until they came in and he was able to welcome them. [6] When they entered with the gifts which had been sent with them and the valuable parchments on which the Law was inscribed in gold in Jewish characters, for the parchment was wonderfully prepared and the connection between the pages had been so effected as to be invisible, the king, as soon as he saw them, began to ask them about the scrolls. [7] And when they had taken the rolls out of their coverings and unfolded the pages, the king stood still for a long time and then paying homage seven times, he said: "I thank you, my friends, and I thank him that sent you still more, and most of all God, whose oracles these are." [8] And when all the envoys and also the others who were present shouted out at one time and with one voice: "God save the king!" he burst into tears of joy. [9] For his exaltation of soul and the sense of the overwhelming honor which had been paid him compelled him to weep over his good fortune. [10] He commanded them to put the rolls back in their places, and then after saluting the men, said, "It was right, men of God, that I should first of all pay my reverence to the scrolls for the sake of which I summoned you here and then, [and] when I had done that, to extend the right hand of friendship to you. It was for this reason that I did this first. [11] I have decreed that this day on which you arrived will be kept as a great day, and it will be celebrated annually throughout my lifetime. [12] It so happens that it is the anniversary of my naval victory over Antigonus. Therefore, I will be glad to feast with you today. [13] Everything that you may have occasion to use," he said, "will be prepared [for you] in a suitable manner—and for me also with you." [14] After they had expressed their delight, he gave orders that the best quarters near the citadel should be assigned to them, and that preparations should be made for the banquet. [15] And Nicanor summoned the lord high steward, Dorotheus, who was the special officer appointed to look after the Jews, and commanded him to make the necessary preparation for each one. [16] For this arrangement had been made by the king and it is an arrangement which you see maintained today. For as many cities [as] have [special] customs in the matter of drinking, eating, and reclining, have special officers appointed to look after their requirements. [17] And whenever they come to visit the kings, preparations are made in accordance with their own customs, in order that there may be no discomfort to disturb the enjoyment of their visit. The same precaution was taken in the case of the Jewish envoys. [18] Now Dorotheus, who was the patron appointed to look after Jewish guests, was a very conscientious man. [19] All the stores which were under his control and set apart for the reception of such guests he brought out for the feast. [20] He arranged the seats in two rows in accordance with the king's instructions, for he had ordered him to make half the men sit at his right hand and the rest behind him in order that he might not withhold from them the highest possible honor. [21] When they had taken their seats, he instructed Dorotheus to carry out everything in accordance with the customs which were in use among his Jewish guests. [22] Therefore, he dispensed with the services of the sacred heralds, and the sacrificing priests, and the others who were accustomed to offer the prayers, and called on one of our number, Eleazar, the oldest of the Jewish priests, to offer prayer instead. [23] And he rose up and made a remarkable prayer: "May Almighty God enrich you, O king, with all the good things which He has made, and may He grant you, and your wife, and your children, and your comrades the continual possession of them as long as you live." [24] At these words a loud and joyous applause broke out which lasted for a considerable time, and then they turned to the enjoyment of the banquet which had been prepared. [25] All the arrangements for service at table were carried out in accordance with the injunction of Dorotheus. [26] Among the attendants were the royal pages and others who held places of honor at the king's court.

CHAPTER 23

[1] Taking an opportunity afforded by a pause in the banquet, the king asked the envoy who sat in the seat of honor (for they were arranged according to seniority) how he could keep his kingdom unimpaired to the end. [2] After pondering for a moment, he replied, "You could best establish its security if you were to imitate the unceasing kindness of God. For if you exhibit clemency and inflict mild punishments on those who deserve them in accordance with their deservings, you will turn them from evil and lead them to conversion." [3] The king praised the answer and then asked the next man how he could do everything for the best in all his actions. [4] And he replied, "If a man maintains a just bearing toward all, he will always act rightly on every occasion, remembering that every thought is known to God. If you take the fear of God as your starting point, you will never miss the goal." [5] The king complimented this man, too, on his answer and asked another how he could have friends like-minded with himself. [6] He replied, "If they see you studying the interests of the multitudes over whom you rule; you will do well to observe how God bestows His benefits on the human race, providing health, and food, and all other things for them in due season." [7] After expressing his agreement with the reply, the king asked the next guest how in giving audiences and passing judgments he could gain the praise even of those who failed to win their suit. [8] And he said, "If you are fair in speech to all alike and never act insolently nor tyrannically in your treatment of offenders. And you will do this if you watch the method by which God acts. [9] The petitions of the worthy are always fulfilled, while those who fail to obtain an answer to their prayers are informed by means of dreams or events of what was harmful in their requests and that God does not strike them according to their sins or the greatness of His strength, but acts with forbearance toward them." [10] The king praised the man warmly for his answer and asked the next in order how he could be invincible in military affairs. [11] And he replied, "If he did not entirely trust in his multitudes or his warlike forces, but continually called on God to bring his enterprises to a successful issue, while he himself discharged all his duties in the spirit of justice." [12] Welcoming this answer, he asked another how he might become an object of dread to his enemies. [13] And he replied, "If while maintaining a vast supply of arms and forces he remembered that these things were powerless to achieve a permanent and conclusive result. [14] For even God instills fear into the minds of men by granting reprieves and making merely a display of the greatness of His power." [15] This man the king praised and then said to the next, "What is the highest good in life?" [16] And he answered, "To know that God is Lord of the universe, and that in our finest achievements it is not we who attain success but God who by His power brings all things to fulfillment and leads us to the goal." [17] The king exclaimed that the man had answered well and then asked the next how he could keep all his possessions intact and finally hand them down to his successors in the same condition. [18] And he answered, "By praying constantly to God that you may be inspired with high motives in all your undertakings and by warning your descendants not to be dazzled by fame or wealth, for it is God who bestows all these gifts, and men never win the supremacy by themselves." [19] The king expressed his agreement with the answer and inquired of the next guest how he could bear with composure whatever befell him. [20] And he said, "If you have a firm grasp of the thought that all men are appointed by God to share the greatest evil as well as the greatest good, since it is impossible for one who is a man to be exempt from these. [21] But God, to whom we always ought to pray, inspires us with courage to endure." [22] Delighted with the man's reply, the king said that all their answers had been good. "I will put a question to one other," he added, "and then I will stop for the present [so] that we may turn our attention to the enjoyment of the feast and spend a pleasant time." [23] Thereon he asked the man, "What is the true aim of courage?" And he answered, "If a right plan is carried out in the hour of danger in accordance with the original intention. For all things are accomplished by God to your advantage, O king, since your purpose is good." [24] When all had signified by their

applause their agreement with the answer, the king said to the philosophers (for not a few of them were present), "It is my opinion that these men excel in virtue and possess extraordinary knowledge, since on the spur of the moment they have given fitting answers to these questions which I have put to them, and have all made God the starting point of their words." ²⁵And Menedemus, the philosopher of Eretria, said, "True, O king, for since the universe is managed by providence and since we rightly perceive that man is the creation of God, it follows that all power and beauty of speech proceed from God." ²⁶When the king had nodded his assent to this sentiment, the speaking ceased and they proceeded to enjoy themselves. When evening came on, the banquet ended.

CHAPTER 24

¹On the following day they sat down to table again and continued the banquet according to the same arrangements. ²When the king thought that a fitting opportunity had arrived to put inquiries to his guests, he proceeded to ask further questions of the men who sat next in order to those who had given answers on the previous day. ³He began to open the conversation with the eleventh man, for there were ten who had been asked questions on the former occasion. ⁴When silence was established, he asked how he could continue to be rich. ⁵After a brief reflection, the man who had been asked the question replied, "If he did nothing unworthy of his position, never acted licentiously, never lavished expense on empty and vain pursuits, but by acts of benevolence made all his subjects well-disposed toward himself. ⁶For it is God who is the author of all good things and man needs to obey Him." ⁷The king bestowed praise on him and then asked another how he could maintain the truth. ⁸In reply to the question he said, "By recognizing that a lie brings great disgrace on all men, and more especially on kings. For since they have the power to do whatever they wish, why should they resort to lies? ⁹In addition to this, you must always remember, O king, that God is a lover of the truth." ¹⁰The king received the answer with great delight, and looking at another, said, "What is the teaching of wisdom?" ¹¹And the other replied, "As you wish that no evil should befall you, but to be a partaker of all good things, so you should act on the same principle toward your subjects and offenders, and you should mildly admonish the noble and good, for God draws all men to Himself by His kindness." ¹²The king praised him and asked the next in order how he could be the friend of men. ¹³And he replied, "By observing that the human race increases and is born with much trouble and great suffering: therefore, you must not lightly punish or inflict torments on them, since you know that the life of men is made up of pains and penalties. ¹⁴For if you understood everything you would be filled with pity, for God is also pitiful." ¹⁵The king received the answer with approval and inquired of the next, "What is the most essential qualification for ruling?" ¹⁶"To keep oneself," he answered, "free from bribery and to practice sobriety during the greater part of one's life, to honor righteousness above all things, and to make friends of men of this type. For God, too, is a lover of justice." ¹⁷Having signified his approval, the king said to another, "What is the true mark of piety?" ¹⁸And he replied, "To perceive that God constantly works in the universe and knows all things, and no man who acts unjustly and works wickedness can escape His notice. ¹⁹As God is the benefactor of the whole world, so you, too, must imitate Him and be void of offense." ²⁰The king signified his agreement and said to another, "What is the essence of kingship?" ²¹And he replied, "To rule oneself well and not to be led astray by wealth or fame to unrestrained or unseemly desires; this is the true way of ruling if you reason the matter well out. ²²For all that you really need is yours, and God is free from need and benevolent with all. ²³Let your thoughts be such as suit a man, and do not desire many things, but only such as are necessary for ruling." ²⁴The king praised him and asked another man how his deliberations might be for the best. ²⁵And he replied, "If he constantly set justice before him in everything and thought that injustice was equivalent to deprivation of life, for God always promises the highest blessings to the just." ²⁶Having praised him, the king asked the next how he could be free from disturbing thoughts in his sleep. ²⁷And he replied, "You have asked me a question which is very difficult to answer, for we cannot bring our true selves into play during the hours of sleep, but are held fast in these by imaginations that cannot be controlled by reason. ²⁸For our souls possess the feeling that they actually see the things that enter into our consciousness during sleep, but we make a mistake if we suppose that we are actually sailing on the sea in boats, or flying through the air, or traveling to other regions, or anything else of the kind, and yet we actually do imagine such things to be taking place. ²⁹So far as it is possible for me to decide, I have reached the following conclusion: you must in every possible way, O king, govern your words and actions by the rule of piety [so] that you may have the consciousness that you are maintaining virtue and that you never choose to gratify yourself at the expense of reason, and never by abusing your power do injury to righteousness. ³⁰For the mind mostly busies itself in sleep with the same things with which it occupies itself when awake. ³¹And he who has all his thoughts and actions set toward the noblest ends establishes himself in righteousness both when he is awake and when he is asleep. ³²You must therefore be steadfast in the constant discipline of self." ³³The king bestowed praise on the man and said to another, "Since you are the tenth to answer, when you have spoken, we will devote ourselves to the banquet." ³⁴And then he put [forward] the question, "How can I avoid doing anything unworthy of myself?" ³⁵And he replied, "Always look to your own fame and your own supreme position, that you may speak and think only such things as are consistent with it, knowing that all your subjects think and talk about you. ³⁶For you must not appear to be worse than the actors, who study the role carefully, which it is necessary for them to play, and shape all their actions in accordance with it. ³⁷You are not acting a part, but are really a king, since God has bestowed on you a royal authority in keeping with your character." ³⁸When the king had applauded loud and long in the most gracious way, the guests were urged to seek repose, so when the conversation ceased, they devoted themselves to the next course of the feast.

CHAPTER 25

¹On the following day, the same arrangement was observed, and when the king found an opportunity of putting questions to the men, he questioned the first of those who had been left over for the next interrogation, "What is the highest form of government?" ²And he replied, "To rule oneself and not to be carried away by impulses. For all men possess a certain natural bent of mind. ³It is probable that most men have an inclination toward food, and drink, and pleasure, and kings a bent toward the acquisition of territory and great renown, but it is good that there should be moderation in all things. ⁴What God gives, you may take and keep, but never yearn for things that are beyond your reach." ⁵Pleased with these words, the king asked the next how he could be free from envy. ⁶And he, after a brief pause, replied, "If you consider first of all that it is God who bestows on all kings glory and great wealth and no one is king by his own power. All men wish to share this glory but cannot, since it is the gift of God." ⁷The king praised the man in a long speech and then asked another how he could despise his enemies. ⁸And he replied, "If you show kindness to all men and win their friendship, you need to fear no one. To be popular with all men is the best of good gifts to receive from God." ⁹Having praised this answer, the king ordered the next man to reply to the question how he could maintain his great renown. ¹⁰And he replied that "If you are generous and big-hearted in bestowing kindness and acts of grace on others, you will never lose your renown, but if you wish the aforementioned graces to continue [as] yours, you must continually call on God." ¹¹The king expressed his approval and asked the next, "To whom ought a man show liberality?" ¹²And he replied, "All men acknowledge that we ought to show liberality to those who are well-disposed toward us, but I think that we ought to show the same keen spirit of generosity to those who are opposed to us that by this means we may win them over to the right and to what is advantageous to ourselves. ¹³But we must pray to God that this may be accomplished, for He rules the minds of all men." ¹⁴Having expressed his agreement with the answer, the king asked the sixth to reply to the question, "To whom ought we to exhibit

gratitude?" ¹⁵And he replied, "To our parents continually, for God has given us a most important commandment with regard to the honor due to parents. ¹⁶In the next place He reckons the attitude of friend toward friend for He speaks of a friend which is as your own soul. You do well in trying to bring all men into friendship with yourself." ¹⁷The king spoke kindly to him and then asked the next, "What is it that resembles beauty in value?" ¹⁸And he said, "Piety, for it is the preeminent form of beauty, and its power lies in love, which is the gift of God. This you have already acquired and with it all the blessings of life." ¹⁹The king applauded the answer in the most gracious way and asked another how, if he were to fail, he could regain his reputation again to the same degree. ²⁰And he said, "It is not possible for you to fail, for you have sown in all men the seeds of gratitude which produce a harvest of goodwill, and this is mightier than the strongest weapons and guarantees the greatest security. ²¹But if any man fails, he must never again do those things which caused his failure, but he must form friendships and act justly, for it is the gift of God to be able to do good actions and not the contrary." ²²Delighted with these words, the king asked another how he could be free from grief. ²³And he replied, "If he never injured anyone, but did good to everybody and followed the pathway of righteousness, for its fruits bring freedom from grief. But we must pray to God that unexpected evils such as death, or disease, or pain, or anything of this kind may not come on us and injure us. ²⁴But since you are devoted to piety, no such misfortune will ever come on you." ²⁵The king bestowed great praise on him and asked the tenth, "What is the highest form of glory?" ²⁶And he said, "To honor God, and this is done not with gifts and sacrifices but with purity of soul and holy conviction, since all things are fashioned and governed by God in accordance with His will. ²⁷Of this purpose you are in constant possession as all men can see from your achievements in the past and in the present." ²⁸With a loud voice the king greeted them all and spoke kindly to them, and all those who were present expressed their approval, especially the philosophers. ²⁹For they were far superior to them both in conduct and in argument, since they always made God their starting point. ³⁰After this, the king, to show his good pleasure, proceeded to drink the health of his guests.

CHAPTER 26

¹On the following day the same arrangements were made for the banquet, and the king, as soon as an opportunity occurred, began to put questions to the men who sat next to those who had already responded, and he said to the first, "Is wisdom capable of being taught?" ²And he said, "The soul is so constituted that it is able by the divine power to receive all the good and reject the contrary." ³The king expressed approval and asked the next man, "What is it that is most beneficial to health?" ⁴And he said, "Temperance, and it is not possible to acquire this unless God creates a disposition toward it." ⁵The king spoke kindly to the man and said to another, "How can a man worthily pay the debt of gratitude to his parents?" ⁶And he said, "By never causing them pain, and this is not possible unless God disposes the mind to the pursuit of the noblest ends." ⁷The king expressed agreement and asked the next how he could become an eager listener. ⁸And he said, "By remembering that all knowledge is useful, because it enables you by the help of God in a time of emergency to select some of the things which you have learned and apply them to the crisis which confronts you. And so the efforts of men are fulfilled by the assistance of God." ⁹The king praised him and asked the next how he could avoid doing anything contrary to law. ¹⁰And he said, "If you recognize that it is God who has put the thoughts into the hearts of the lawgivers that the lives of men might be preserved, you will follow them." ¹¹The king acknowledged the man's answer and said to another, "What is the advantage of kinship?" ¹²And he replied, "If we consider that we ourselves are afflicted by the misfortunes which fall on our relatives and if their sufferings become our own—then the strength of kinship is apparent at once, for it is only when such feeling is shown that we will win honor and esteem in their eyes. ¹³For help, when it is linked with kindness, is of itself a bond which is altogether indissoluble. And in the day of their prosperity, we must not crave their possessions, but must pray [for] God to bestow all manner of good on them." ¹⁴And having accorded to him the same praise as to the rest, the king asked another how he could attain freedom from fear. ¹⁵And he said, "When the mind is conscious that it has wrought no evil and when God directs it to all noble counsels." ¹⁶The king expressed his approval and asked another how he could always maintain a right judgment. ¹⁷And he replied, "If he constantly set the misfortunes which befall men before his eyes and recognized that it is God who takes away prosperity from some and brings others to great honor and glory." ¹⁸The king gave a kindly reception to the man and asked the next to answer the question how he could avoid a life of ease and pleasure. ¹⁹And he replied, "If he continually remembered that he was the ruler of a great empire and the lord of vast multitudes, and that his mind should not be occupied with other things, but he should always be considering how he could best promote their welfare. ²⁰He must also pray to God that no duty might be neglected." ²¹Having bestowed praise on him, the king asked the tenth how he could recognize those who were dealing treacherously with him. ²²And he replied to the question, "If he observed whether the bearing of those around him was natural and whether they maintained the proper rule of precedence at receptions and councils, and in their general intercourse, never going beyond the bounds of propriety in congratulations or in other matters of conduct. ²³But God will incline your mind, O king, to all that is noble." ²⁴When the king had expressed his loud approval and praised them all individually (amid the plaudits of all who were present), they turned to the enjoyment of the feast.

CHAPTER 27

¹And on the next day, when the opportunity offered, the king asked the next man, "What is the greatest form of neglect?" ²And he replied, "If a man does not care for his children and devote every effort to their education. ³For we always pray to God not so much for ourselves as for our children that every blessing may be theirs. ⁴Our desire that our children may possess self-control is only realized by the power of God." ⁵The king said that he had spoken well and then asked another how he could be patriotic. ⁶"By keeping before your mind," he replied, "the thought that it is good to live and die in one's own country. Residence abroad brings contempt on the poor and shame on the rich as though they had been banished for a crime. ⁷If you bestow benefits on all, as you continually do, God will give you favor with all and you will be accounted patriotic." ⁸After listening to this man, the king asked the next in order how he could live amicably with his wife. ⁹And he answered, "By recognizing that womankind are by nature headstrong and energetic in the pursuit of their own desires, and subject to sudden changes of opinion through fallacious reasoning, and their nature is essentially weak. ¹⁰It is necessary to deal wisely with them and not to provoke strife. ¹¹For the successful conduct of life the pilot must know the goal toward which he ought to direct his course. ¹²It is only by calling on the help of God that men can steer a true course of life at all times." ¹³The king expressed his agreement and asked the next how he could be free from error. ¹⁴And he replied, "If you always act with deliberation and never give credence to slanders, but prove for yourself the things that are said to you, and decide by your own judgment the requests which are made to you, and carry out everything in the light of your judgment, you will be free from error, O king. ¹⁵But the knowledge and practice of these things is the work of the divine power." ¹⁶Delighted with these words, the king asked another how he could be free from wrath. ¹⁷And he said in reply to the question, "If he recognized that he had power over all even to inflict death on them, if he gave way to wrath, and that it would be useless and pitiful if he, just because he was lord, deprived many of life. ¹⁸What need was there for wrath when all men were in subjection and no one was hostile to him? ¹⁹It is necessary to recognize that God rules the whole world in the spirit of kindness and without wrath at all, and you," he said, "O king, must of necessity copy His example." ²⁰The king said that he had answered well and then inquired of the next man, "What is good counsel?" ²¹"To act well at all times and with due reflection," he explained, "comparing what is advantageous to our own policy with the injurious effects

that would result from the adoption of the opposite view, in order that by weighing every point we may be well-advised and our purpose may be accomplished. ²²And most important of all, by the power of God every plan of yours will find fulfillment because you practice piety." ²³The king said that this man had answered well, and asked another, "What is philosophy?" ²⁴And he explained, "To deliberate well in reference to any question that emerges and never to be carried away by impulses, but to ponder over the injuries that result from the passions, and to act rightly as the circumstances demand, practicing moderation. ²⁵But we must pray to God to instill into our mind a regard for these things." ²⁶The king signified his consent and asked another how he could meet with recognition when traveling abroad. ²⁷"By being fair to all men," he replied, "and by appearing to be inferior rather than superior to those among whom he was traveling. ²⁸For it is a recognized principle that God by His very nature accepts the humble. And the human race loves those who are willing to be in subjection to them." ²⁹Having expressed his approval at this reply, the king asked another how he could build in such a way that his structures would endure after him. ³⁰And he replied to the question, "If his creations were on a great and noble scale, so that the beholders would spare them for their beauty, and if he never dismissed any of those who wrought such works and never compelled others to minister to his needs without wages. ³¹For observing how God provides for the human race, granting them health, and mental capacity, and all other gifts, he himself should follow His example by rendering a recompense to men for their arduous toil. ³²For it is the deeds that are wrought in righteousness that abide continually." ³²The king said that this man had also answered well and asked the tenth, "What is the fruit of wisdom?" ³³And he replied, "That a man should be conscious in himself that he has wrought no evil and that he should live his life in the truth, since it is from these, O mighty king, that the greatest joy, and steadfastness of soul, and strong faith in God accrue to you if you rule your realm in piety." ³⁴And when they heard the answer, they all shouted with loud acclaim, and afterward the king in the fullness of his joy began to drink their healths.

CHAPTER 28

¹And on the next day the banquet followed the same course as on previous occasions, and when the opportunity presented itself, the king proceeded to put questions to the remaining guests, and he said to the first, "How can a man keep himself from pride?" ²And he replied, "If he maintains equality and remembers on all occasions that he is a man ruling over men. And God brings the proud to nothing, and exalts the meek and humble." ³The king spoke kindly to him and asked the next, "Whom should a man select as his counselors?" ⁴And he replied, "Those who have been tested in many affairs and maintain unmingled goodwill toward him and partake of his own disposition. ⁵And God manifests Himself to those who are worthy that these ends may be attained." ⁶The king praised him and asked another, "What is the most necessary possession for a king?" ⁷"The friendship and love of his subjects," he replied, "for it is through this that the bond of goodwill is rendered indissoluble. ⁸And it is God who ensures that this may come to pass in accordance with your wish." ⁹The king praised him and inquired of another, "What is the goal of speech?" ¹⁰And he replied, "To convince your opponent by showing him his mistakes in a well-ordered array of arguments, for in this way you will win your hearer, not by opposing him, but by bestowing praise on him with a view to persuading him. ¹¹And it is by the power of God that persuasion is accomplished." ¹²The king said that he had given a good answer and asked another how he could live amicably with the many different races who formed the population of his kingdom. ¹³"By acting the proper part toward each," he replied, "and taking righteousness as your guide, as you are now doing with the help of the insight which God bestows on you." ¹⁴The king was delighted by this reply, and asked another, "Under what circumstances should a man suffer grief?" ¹⁵"In the misfortunes that befall our friends," he replied, "when we see that they are protracted and irremediable. ¹⁶Reason does not allow us to grieve for those who are dead and set free from evil, but all men do grieve over them because they think only of themselves and their own advantage. ¹⁷It is by the power of God alone that we can escape all evil." ¹⁸The king said that he had given a fitting answer, and asked another, "How is reputation lost?" ¹⁹And he replied, "When pride and unbounded self-confidence hold sway, dishonor and loss of reputation are engendered. ²⁰For God is the Lord of all reputation and bestows it where He will." ²¹The king gave his confirmation to the answer, and asked the next man, "To whom should men entrust themselves?" ²²"To those," he replied, "who serve you from goodwill and not from fear or self-interest, thinking only of their own gain. ²³For the one is the sign of love, the other the mark of ill-will and time-serving. ²⁴For the man who is always watching for his own gain is a traitor at heart, but you possess the affection of all your subjects by the help of the good counsel which God bestows on you." ²⁵The king said that he had answered wisely, and asked another, "What is it that keeps a kingdom safe?" ²⁶And he replied to the question, "Care and forethought that no evil may be wrought by those who are placed in a position of authority over the people, and this you always do by the help of God who inspires you with grave judgment." ²⁷The king spoke words of encouragement to him, and asked another, "What is it that maintains gratitude and honor?" ²⁸And he replied, "Virtue, for it is the creator of good deeds, and by it evil is destroyed, even as you exhibit nobility of character toward all by the gift which God bestows on you." ²⁹The king graciously acknowledged the answer and asked the eleventh (since there were two more than seventy) how he could maintain tranquility of soul in time of war. ³⁰And he replied, "By remembering that he had done no evil to any of his subjects, and that all would fight for him in return for the benefits which they had received, knowing that even if they lose their lives, you will care for those dependent on them. ³¹For you never fail to make reparation to any—such is the kindheartedness with which God has inspired you." ³²The king loudly applauded them all, and spoke very kindly to them, and then drank a long draught to the health of each, giving himself up to enjoyment, and lavishing the most generous and joyous friendship on his guests.

CHAPTER 29

¹On the seventh day much more extensive preparations were made, and many others were present from the different cities (among them a large number of ambassadors). ²When an opportunity occurred, the king asked the first of those who had not yet been questioned how he could avoid being deceived by fallacious reasoning. ³And he replied, "By carefully noticing the speaker, the thing spoken, and the subject under discussion, and by putting the same questions again after an interval in different forms. ⁴But to possess an alert mind and to be able to form a sound judgment in every case is one of the good gifts of God, and you possess it, O king." ⁵The king loudly applauded the answer and asked another, "Why is it that the majority of men never become virtuous?" ⁶"Because," he replied, "all men are by nature intemperate and inclined to pleasure. Hence, injustice springs up and a flood of avarice. ⁷The habit of virtue is a hindrance to those who are devoted to a life of pleasure because it enjoins on them the preference of temperance and righteousness. For it is God who is the master of these things." ⁸The king said that he had answered well, and asked, "What should kings obey?" ⁹And he said, "The laws, in order that by righteous enactments they may restore the lives of men. ¹⁰Even as you by such conduct in obedience to the divine command have laid up in store for yourself a perpetual memorial." ¹¹The king said that this man had also spoken well, and asked the next, "Whom should we appoint as governors?" ¹²And he replied, "All who hate wickedness, and imitating your own conduct, act righteously that they may constantly maintain a good reputation. ¹³For this is what you do, O mighty king," he said, "and it is God who has bestowed on you the crown of righteousness." ¹⁴The king loudly acclaimed the answer and then, looking at the next man, said, "Whom should we appoint as officers over the forces?" ¹⁵And he explained, "Those who excel in courage and righteousness and those who are more anxious about the safety of their men than to gain a victory by risking their lives through rashness. ¹⁶For as God acts well toward all men, so you also in imitation of Him are the

benefactor of all your subjects." ¹⁷The king said that he had given a good answer and asked another, "What man is worthy of admiration?" ¹⁸And he replied, "The man who is furnished with reputation, and wealth, and power, and possesses a soul equal to it all. ¹⁹You yourself show by your actions that you are most worthy of admiration through the help of God who makes you care for these things." ²⁰The king expressed his approval and said to another, "To what affairs should kings devote most time?" ²¹And he replied, "To reading and the study of the records of official journeys, which are written in reference to the various kingdoms, with a view to the reformation and preservation of the subjects. ²²And it is by such activity that you have attained to a glory which has never been approached by others, through the help of God who fulfils all your desires." ²³The king spoke enthusiastically to the man and asked another how a man should occupy himself during his hours of relaxation and recreation. ²⁴And he replied, "To watch those plays which can be acted with propriety and to set before one's eyes scenes taken from life and enacted with dignity and decency are profitable and appropriate. ²⁵For there is some edification to be found even in these amusements, for often some desirable lesson is taught by the most insignificant affairs of life. ²⁶But by practicing the utmost propriety in all your actions, you have shown that you are a philosopher and are honored by God on account of your virtue." ²⁷The king, pleased with the words which had just been spoken, said to the ninth man, "How should a man conduct himself at banquets?" ²⁸And he replied, "You should summon to your side men of learning and those who are able to give you useful hints with regard to the affairs of your kingdom and the lives of your subjects (for you could not find any theme more suitable or more educational than this) since such men are dear to God because they have trained their minds to contemplate the noblest themes—as you indeed are doing yourself, since all your actions are directed by God." ²⁹Delighted with the reply, the king inquired of the next man, "What is best for the people—that a private citizen should be made king over them or a member of the royal family?" ³⁰And he replied, "He who is best by nature, for kings who come of royal lineage are often harsh and severe toward their subjects. ³¹And still more is this the case with some of those who have risen from the ranks of private citizens, who after having experienced evil and borne their share of poverty, when they rule over multitudes turn out to be crueler than the godless tyrants. ³²But, as I have said, a good nature which has been properly trained is capable of ruling, and you are a great king, not so much because you excel in the glory of your rule and your wealth, but rather because you have surpassed all men in clemency and philanthropy, thanks to God who has endowed you with these qualities." ³³The king spent some time in praising this man and then asked the last of all, "What is the greatest achievement in ruling an empire?" ³⁴And he replied, "That the subjects should continually dwell in a state of peace, and that justice should be speedily administered in cases of dispute. ³⁵These results are achieved through the influence of the ruler, when he is a man who hates evil, and loves the good, and devotes his energies to saving the lives of men, just as you consider injustice the worst form of evil and by your just administration have fashioned for yourself an undying reputation, since God bestows on you a mind which is pure and untainted by any evil." ³⁶And when he ceased, loud and joyful applause broke out for some considerable time. ³⁷When it stopped, the king took a cup and gave a toast in honor of all his guests and the words which they had uttered. ³⁸Then in conclusion he said, "I have derived the greatest benefit from your presence. I have profited much by the wise teaching which you have given me in reference to the art of ruling." ³⁹Then he ordered that three talents of silver should be presented to each of them and appointed one of his slaves to deliver over the money. ⁴⁰All at once shouted their approval, and the banquet became a scene of joy while the king gave himself up to a continuous round of festivity.

CHAPTER 30

¹I have written at length and must crave your pardon, Philocrates. ²I was astonished beyond measure at the men and the way in which on the spur of the moment they gave answers which really needed a long time to devise. ³For though the questioner had given great thought to each particular question, those who replied one after the other had their answers to the questions ready at once and so they seemed to me, and to all who were present, and especially to the philosophers, to be worthy of admiration. ⁴And I suppose that the thing will seem incredible to those who will read my narrative in the future. ⁵But it is unseemly to misrepresent facts which are recorded in the public archives. And it would not be right for me to transgress in such a matter as this. ⁶I tell the story just as it happened, conscientiously avoiding any error. ⁷I was so impressed by the force of their utterances that I made an effort to consult those whose business it was to make a record of all that happened at the royal audiences and banquets. ⁸For it is the custom, as you know, from the moment the king begins to transact business until the time when he retires to rest, for a record to be taken of all his sayings and doings—a most excellent and useful arrangement. ⁹For on the following day the minutes of the doings and sayings of the previous day are read over before business commences, and if there has been any irregularity, the matter is at once set right. ¹⁰I obtained therefore, as has been said, accurate information from the public records, and I have set forth the facts in proper order since I know how eager you are to obtain useful information.

CHAPTER 31

¹Three days later Demetrius took the men, and passing along the seawall, seven stadia long, to the island, crossed the bridge and made for the northern districts of Pharos. ²There he assembled them in a house which had been built on the seashore, of great beauty and in a secluded situation, and invited them to carry out the work of translation since everything that they needed for the purpose was placed at their disposal. ³So they set to work comparing their several results and making them agree, and whatever they agreed on was suitably copied out under the direction of Demetrius. ⁴And the session lasted until the ninth hour; after this they were set free to minister to their physical needs. ⁵Everything they wanted was furnished for them on a lavish scale. In addition to this, Dorotheus made the same preparations for them daily as were made for the king himself—for thus he had been commanded by the king. ⁶In the early morning they appeared daily at the court, and after saluting the king, went back to their own place. ⁷And as is the custom of all the Jews, they washed their hands in the sea, and prayed to God, and then devoted themselves to reading and translating the particular passage on which they were engaged. ⁸And I put the question to them why it was that they washed their hands before they prayed. ⁹And they explained that it was a token that they had done no evil (for every form of activity is wrought by means of the hands) since in their noble and holy way they regard everything as a symbol of righteousness and truth.

CHAPTER 32

¹As I have already said, they met together daily in the place which was delightful for its quiet and its brightness and applied themselves to their task. ²And it so happened that the work of translation was completed in seventy-two days, just as if this had been arranged of set purpose. ³When the work was completed, Demetrius collected together the Jewish population in the place where the translation had been made and read it over to all in the presence of the translators, who also met with a great reception from the people because of the great benefits which they had conferred on them. ⁴They also bestowed warm praise on Demetrius and urged him to have the whole Law transcribed and present a copy to their leaders. ⁵After the scrolls had been read, the priests, and the elders of the translators, and the Jewish community, and the leaders of the people stood up and said that since so excellent, and sacred, and accurate a translation had been made, it was only right that it should remain as it was, and no alteration should be made in it. ⁶And when the whole company expressed their approval, they commanded them [to] pronounce a curse in accordance with their custom on anyone who should make any alteration either by adding anything or changing in any way any of the words which had been written or making any omission. ⁷This was a very wise

precaution to ensure that the scroll might be preserved for all the future time unchanged. ⁸When the matter was reported to the king, he rejoiced greatly, for he felt that the design which he had formed had been safely carried out. ⁹The whole scroll was read over to him and he was greatly astonished at the Spirit of the lawgiver. ¹⁰And he said to Demetrius, "How is it that none of the historians or the poets have ever thought it worth their while to allude to such a wonderful achievement?" ¹¹And he replied, "Because the Law is sacred and of divine origin. And some of those who formed the intention of dealing with it have been smitten by God and therefore desisted from their purpose." ¹²He said that he had heard from Theopompus that he had been driven out of his mind for more than thirty days because he intended to insert in his history some of the incidents from the earlier and somewhat unreliable translations of the Law. ¹³When he had recovered a little, he sought God to make it clear to him why the misfortune had befallen him. ¹⁴And it was revealed to him in a dream, that from idle curiosity he was wishing to communicate sacred truths to common men, and that if he desisted, he would recover his health. ¹⁵I have heard, too, from the lips of Theodektes, one of the tragic poets, that when he was about to adapt some of the incidents recorded in the scroll for one of his plays, he was affected with a cataract in both his eyes. ¹⁶And when he perceived the reason why the misfortune had befallen him, he prayed to God for many days and was afterward restored. ¹⁷And after the king, as I have already said, had received the explanation of Demetrius on this point, he paid homage, and ordered that great care should be taken of the scrolls, and that they should be sacredly guarded. ¹⁸And he urged the translators to visit him frequently after their return to Judea, for it was only right, he said, that he should now send them home. ¹⁹But when they came back, he would treat them as friends, as was right, and they would receive rich presents from him. ²⁰He ordered preparations to be made for them to return home and treated them most lavishly. ²¹He presented each one of them with three robes of the finest sort, two talents of gold, a sideboard weighing one talent, [and] all the furniture for three couches. ²²And with the escort he sent Eleazar ten couches with silver legs and all the necessary equipment, a sideboard worth thirty talents, ten robes, purple, and a magnificent crown, and one hundred pieces of the finest woven linen, also bowls and dishes, and two golden beakers to be dedicated to God. ²³He also urged him in a letter that if any of the men preferred to come back to him, not to hinder them, for he counted it a great privilege to enjoy the society of such learned men, and he would rather lavish his wealth on them than on vanities. ²⁴And now Philocrates, you have the complete story in accordance with my promise. ²⁵I think that you find greater pleasure in these matters than in the writings of the mythologists, for you are devoted to the study of those things which can benefit the soul and spend much time on it. ²⁶I will attempt to narrate whatever other events are worth recording, that by perusing them you may secure the highest reward for your zeal.

DIDACHE

Didache, which means "Teaching," is a very early Christian treatise purporting to have been written by the Twelve Apostles per the opening line. It is thought to have been written between AD 50 and 150. The document covers basic Christian principles of godly living, conversion, and ritual.

THE LORD'S TEACHING TO THE HEATHEN BY THE TWELVE APOSTLES.

CHAPTER 1
¹There are two Ways, one of Life and one of Death, and there is a great difference between the two Ways. ²The Way of Life is this: "First, you will love the God who made you, secondly, your neighbor as yourself; and whatever you would not have done to yourself, do not do to another." ³Now, the teaching of these words is this: "Bless those that curse you, and pray for your enemies, and fast for those that persecute you. For what credit is it to you if you love those that love you? Do not even the heathen do the same?" But, for your part, "love those that hate you," and you will have no enemy. ⁴"Abstain from carnal and bodily lusts." "If any man strikes you on the right cheek, turn to him the other cheek also," and you will be perfect. "If any man impresses you to go with him one mile, go with him two. If any man takes your coat, give him your shirt also. If any man will take from you what is yours, do not refuse it"—not even if you can. ⁵Give to everyone that asks you, and do not refuse, for the Father's will is that we give to all from the gifts we have received. Blessed is he that gives according to the mandate; for he is innocent. Woe to him who receives; for if any man receive alms under pressure of need he is innocent; but he who receives it without need will be tried as to why he took and for what, and being in prison, he will be examined as to his deeds, and "he will not come out from there until he pays the last penny." ⁶But concerning this it was also said, "Let your alms sweat into your hands until you know to whom you are giving."

CHAPTER 2
¹But the second command of the teaching is this: ²"You will not murder; you will not commit adultery"; you will not commit sodomy; you will not commit fornication; you will not steal; you will not use magic; you will not use love potions; you will not procure abortion, nor commit infanticide; "you will not covet your neighbor's goods"; ³you will not commit perjury, "you will not bear false witness"; you will not speak evil; you will not bear malice. ⁴You will not be double-minded nor double-tongued, for to be double-tongued is the snare of death. ⁵Your speech will not be false, nor vain, but completed in action. ⁶You will not be covetous nor extortionate, nor a hypocrite, nor malignant, nor proud; you will make no evil plan against your neighbor. ⁷You will hate no man; but some you will reprove, and for some you will pray, and some you will love more than your own life.

CHAPTER 3
¹My child, flee from every evil man and from all like him. ²Do not be proud, for pride leads to murder, nor jealous, nor contentious, nor passionate, for from all these murders are engendered. ³My child, do not be lustful, for lust leads to fornication, nor a speaker of base words, nor a lifter up of the eyes, for from all these is adultery engendered. ⁴My child, do not regard omens, for this leads to idolatry; neither be an enchanter, nor an astrologer, nor a magician, neither wish to see these things, for from them all is idolatry engendered. ⁵My child, do not be a liar, for lying leads to theft, nor a lover of money, nor vainglorious, for from all these things are thefts engendered. ⁶My child, do not be a grumbler, for this leads to blasphemy, nor stubborn, nor a thinker of evil, for from all these are blasphemies engendered, ⁷but be "meek, for the meek will inherit the earth"; ⁸be long-suffering, and merciful, and guileless, and quiet, and good, and always fearing the words which you have heard. ⁹You will not exalt yourself, nor let your soul be presumptuous. Your soul will not consort with the lofty, but you will walk with righteous and humble men. ¹⁰Receive the accidents that befall you as good, knowing that nothing happens without God.

CHAPTER 4
¹My child, you will remember, day and night, him who speaks the word of God to you, and you will honor him as the LORD, for where the LORD's nature is spoken of, there He is present. ²And you will seek daily the presence of the holy ones, that you may find rest in their words. ³You will not desire a schism, but will

DIDACHE

reconcile those that strive. You will give righteous judgment; you will favor no man's person in reproving transgression. ⁴You will not be of two minds whether it will be or not. ⁵Do not be one who stretches out his hands to receive, but shuts them when it comes to giving. ⁶Of whatever you have gained by your hands you will give a ransom for your sins. ⁷You will not hesitate to give, nor will you grumble when you give, for you will know who the good Paymaster of the reward is. ⁸You will not turn the needy away, but will share everything with your brother, and will not say that it is your own, for if you are sharers in the imperishable, how much more in the things which perish? ⁹You will not withhold your hand from your son or from your daughter, but you will teach them the fear of God from their youth up. ¹⁰You will not command in your bitterness your slave or your handmaid, who hope in the same God, lest they cease to fear the God who is over you both; for He does not come to call men with respect of persons, but those whom the Spirit has prepared. ¹¹But you who are slaves, be subject to your master, as to God's representative, in reverence and fear. ¹²You will hate all hypocrisy, and everything that is not pleasing to the LORD. ¹³You will not forsake the commands of the LORD, but you will keep what you received, "adding nothing to it and taking nothing away." ¹⁴In the congregation you will confess your transgressions, and you will not go yourself to prayer with an evil conscience. This is the Way of Life.

CHAPTER 5

¹But the Way of Death is this: first of all, it is wicked and full of cursing, murders, adulteries, lusts, fornications, thefts, idolatries, witchcrafts, charms, robberies, false witness, hypocrisies, a double heart, fraud, pride, malice, stubbornness, covetousness, foul speech, jealousy, impudence, haughtiness, boastfulness. ²Persecutors of the good, haters of truth, lovers of lies, not knowing the reward of righteousness, not cleaving to the good nor to righteous judgment, spending wakeful nights not for good but for wickedness, from whom meekness and patience is far, lovers of vanity, following after reward, unmerciful to the poor, not working for him who is oppressed with toil, without knowledge of Him who made them, murderers of children, corrupters of God's creatures, turning away the needy, oppressing the distressed, advocates of the rich, unjust judges of the poor, altogether sinful; may you be delivered, my children, from all these.

CHAPTER 6

¹See "that no one make you to err" from this Way of the teaching, for he teaches you without God. ²For if you can bear the whole yoke of the LORD, you will be perfect, but if you cannot, do what you can. ³And concerning food, bear what you can, but keep strictly from that which is offered to idols, for it is the worship of dead gods.

CHAPTER 7

¹Concerning immersion, immerse thus: having first rehearsed all these things, "immerse in the Name of the Father, and of the Son, and of the Holy Spirit," in running water; ²but if you have no running water, immerse in other water, and if you cannot in cold, then in warm. ³But if you have neither, pour water three times on the head "in the Name of the Father, Son, and Holy Spirit." ⁴And before the immersion let the immerser and him who is to be immersed fast, and any others who are able. And you will bid him who is to be immersed to fast one or two days before.

CHAPTER 8

¹Do not let your fasts be with the hypocrites, for they fast on Mondays and Thursdays, but you fast on Wednesdays and Fridays. ²And do not pray as the hypocrites, but as the LORD commanded in His good news, pray thus: "Our Father who is in Heaven, hallowed be Your Name, Your Kingdom come, Your will be done, as in Heaven so also on earth; give us today our daily bread, and forgive us our debt as we forgive our debtors, and do not lead us into trial, but deliver us from the evil [one], for Yours is the power and the glory for all time." ³Pray thus three times a day.

CHAPTER 9

¹And concerning the Thanksgiving, hold Thanksgiving thus: ²first concerning the cup: "We give thanks to You, our Father, for the Holy Vine of Your child David, which You made known to us through Your Child Jesus. To You be glory for all time." ³And concerning the broken bread: "We give You thanks, our Father, for the life and knowledge which You made known to us through Your Child Jesus. To You be glory for all time. ⁴As this broken bread was scattered on the mountains, but was brought together and became one, so let Your Assembly be gathered together from the ends of the earth into Your Kingdom, for Yours is the glory and the power through Jesus Christ for all time." ⁵But let none eat or drink of Your Thanksgiving except those who have been immersed in the LORD's Name. For concerning this also the LORD said, "Do not give that which is holy to the dogs."

CHAPTER 10

¹But after you are satisfied with food, thus give thanks: ²"We give thanks to You, O Holy Father, for Your Holy Name which You made to dwell in our hearts, and for the knowledge, and faith, and immortality which You made known to us through Your Child Jesus. To You be glory for all time. ³You, LORD Almighty, created all things for Your Name's sake, and gave food and drink to men for their enjoyment, that they might give thanks to You, but You have blessed us with spiritual food and drink and continuous light through Your Child. ⁴Above all we give thanks to You for that You are mighty. To You be glory for all time. ⁵Remember, LORD, Your Assembly, to deliver it from all evil and to make it perfect in Your love, and gather it together in its holiness from the four winds to Your Kingdom which You have prepared for it. For Yours is the power and the glory for all time. ⁶Let grace come and let this world pass away. Hosanna to the God of David. If any man is holy, let him come! If any man is not, let him convert: Maranatha! Amen!" ⁷But permit the prophets to hold Thanksgiving as they will.

CHAPTER 11

¹Whoever then comes and teaches you all these things previously mentioned, receive him. ²But if the teacher himself is perverted and teaches another doctrine to destroy these things, do not listen to him, but if his teaching is for the increase of righteousness and knowledge of the LORD, receive him as the LORD. ³And concerning the apostles and prophets, act thus according to the ordinance of the good news. ⁴Let every apostle who comes to you be received as the LORD, ⁵but do not let him stay more than one day, or if need be a second as well; but if he stays three days, he is a false prophet. ⁶And when an apostle goes forth let him accept nothing but bread until he reaches his night's lodging; but if he asks for money, he is a false prophet. ⁷Do not test or examine any prophet who is speaking in [the] Spirit, "for every sin will be forgiven, but this sin will not be forgiven." ⁸But not everyone who speaks in a spirit is a prophet, except [if] he has the behavior of the LORD. From his behavior, then, the false prophet and the true prophet will be known. ⁹And no prophet who orders a meal in [the] Spirit will eat of it: otherwise, he is a false prophet. ¹⁰And every prophet who teaches the truth, if he does not do what he teaches, is a false prophet. ¹¹But no prophet who has been tried and is genuine, though he enacts a worldly mystery of the Assembly, if he does not teach others to do what he does himself, will be judged by you; for he has his judgment with God, for so also did the prophets of old. ¹²But whoever will say in a spirit "Give me money, or something else," you will not listen to him; but if he tells you to give on behalf of others in want, let none judge him.

CHAPTER 12

¹Let everyone who "comes in the Name of the LORD" be received; but when you have tested him you will know him, for you will have understanding of true and false. ²If he who comes is a traveler, help him as much as you can, but he will not remain with you more than two days, or, if need be, three. ³And if he wishes to settle among you and has a craft, let him work for his bread. ⁴But if he has no craft provide for him according to your understanding, so that no man will live among you in idleness because he is a Christian. ⁵But if he will not do so, he is making traffic of Christ; beware of such.

CHAPTER 13

¹But every true prophet who wishes to settle among you is "worthy of his food." ²Likewise, a true teacher is himself worthy, like the workman, of his food. ³Therefore you will take

DIDACHE

the first-fruit of the produce of the winepress and of the threshing-floor, and of oxen and sheep, and will give them as the first-fruits to the prophets, for they are your chief priests. ⁴But if you do not have a prophet, give to the poor. ⁵If you make bread, take the first-fruits, and give it according to the command. ⁶Likewise, when you open a jar of wine or oil, give the first-fruits to the prophets. ⁷Of money also and clothes, and of all your possessions, take the first-fruits, as it seems best to you, and give according to the command.

CHAPTER 14

¹On the LORD'S Day come together, break bread, and hold Thanksgiving, after confessing your transgressions that your offering may be pure; ²but let none who has a quarrel with his fellow join in your meeting until they are reconciled, that your sacrifice is not defiled. ³For this is that which was spoken by the LORD, "In every place and time offer Me a pure sacrifice, for I am a great King," says the LORD, "and My Name is wonderful among the heathen."

CHAPTER 15

¹Therefore, appoint for yourselves overseers and servants worthy of the LORD—meek men, and not lovers of money, and truthful and approved, for they also minister to you the ministry of the prophets and teachers. ²Therefore do not despise them, for they are your honorable men together with the prophets and teachers. ³And do not reprove one another in wrath, but in peace as you find in the good news, and let none speak with any who has done a wrong to his neighbor, nor let him hear a word from you until he converts. ⁴But perform your prayers, and kindness, and all your acts as you find in the good news of our Lord.

CHAPTER 16

¹"Watch" over your life; do not "let your lamps" be quenched; and do not "let your loins" be ungirded; but be "ready," for you have not known "the hour in which our Lord comes." ²But be frequently gathered together seeking the things which are profitable for your souls, for the whole time of your faith will not profit you except you be found perfect at the last time; ³for in the last days the false prophets and the corrupters will be multiplied, and the sheep will be turned into wolves, and love will change to hate; ⁴for as lawlessness increases they will hate one another, and persecute, and betray, and then the deceiver of the world will appear as a son of God, and he will do signs and wonders, and the earth will be given over into his hands, and he will commit iniquities which have never been since the world began. ⁵Then the creation of mankind will come to the fiery trial and "many will be offended" and be lost, but "they who endure" in their faith "will be saved" by the curse itself. ⁶And "then will appear the signs" of the truth. First, the sign spread out in [the] sky, then the sign of the sound of the trumpet, and thirdly the resurrection of the dead: ⁷but not of all the dead, but as it was said, "The LORD will come and all His holy ones with Him." ⁸Then the world will "see the LORD coming on the clouds of Heaven."

EPISTLES OF KING ABGAR AND JESUS

According to Eusebius in his Ecclesiastical History, King Abgar V of Edessa, after hearing about the active ministry of Jesus, purportedly wrote a letter to Him requesting that He come and heal him, to which Jesus replied in kind. Whether real or forgeries, these letters were at one point housed at the Church of St. Mary of Blachernae in Constantinople and later at the Church of the Virgin of the Pharos. They were written probably no later than the 3rd century if forgeries, and between AD 30–33 if authentic.

EPISTLE OF KING ABGAR TO JESUS

A COPY OF A LETTER WRITTEN BY ABGARUS THE TOPARCH TO JESUS AND SENT TO HIM BY MEANS OF ANANIAS THE RUNNER, TO JERUSALEM.

CHAPTER 1

¹"Abgarus Uchama the toparch to Jesus the Good Savior that has appeared in the parts of Jerusalem: Greetings! ²I have heard concerning You and Your cures, that they are done by You without drugs or herbs: for, as the report goes, You make blind men to see again, lame to walk, and cleanse lepers, and cast out unclean spirits and devils, and those that are afflicted with long sickness You heal, and raise the dead. ³And having heard all this about You, I had determined one of two things: either that You are God, having come down from Heaven, and so do these things; or [that You] are a Son of God that does these things. ⁴Therefore, I have now written and entreated You to trouble Yourself to come to me and heal the affliction which I have. ⁵For indeed, I have heard that the Jews even murmur against You and wish to do You harm. ⁶And I have a very small city, but lovely, which is sufficient for us both."

EPISTLE OF JESUS TO KING ABGAR

THE ANSWER, WRITTEN BY JESUS, SENT BY ANANIAS THE RUNNER TO ABGARUS THE TOPARCH.

CHAPTER 2

¹"Blessed are you that have believed in Me, having not seen Me. ²For it is written concerning Me that they that have seen Me will not believe in Me, and that they that have not seen Me will believe and live. ³But concerning that which you have written to Me, to come to you—it is necessary that I fulfill all things for which I was sent here, and after fulfilling them, should then be taken up to Him that sent Me. ⁴And when I am taken up, I will send you one of My disciples to heal your affliction and give life to you and them that are with you."

EPISTLE OF THE APOSTLES

The Epistula Apostolorum ("Epistle of the Apostles") is presented as a letter from the eleven remaining apostles describing events, dialogue, and predictions from the life of Jesus. It is widely regarded as pseudepigraphal and was likely composed in the early- or mid-2nd century AD.

CHAPTER 1

THE BOOK WHICH JESUS CHRIST REVEALED TO HIS DISCIPLES: and how Jesus Christ revealed the book for the company of the apostles, the disciples of Jesus Christ, even the book which is for all men. Simon and Cerinthus, the false apostles, concerning whom it is written that no man will cleave to them, for there is in them deceit with which they bring men to

EPISTLE OF THE APOSTLES

destruction. [This has been written] so that you may not flinch nor be troubled, and not depart from the word of the good news which you have heard. As we heard it, we keep it in remembrance and have written it for the whole world. We commend [to] you our sons and our daughters in joy [[in the grace of God]], in the Name of God the Father, the Lord of the world, and of Jesus Christ. Let grace be multiplied on you.

CHAPTER 2

We—John, Thomas, Peter, Andrew, James, Philip, Batholomew, Matthew, Nathanael, Judas the Zealot [(Simon)], and Cephas—write to the assemblies of the east and the west, of the north and the south, declaring and imparting to you that which concerns our Lord Jesus Christ: we write according as we have seen, and heard, and touched Him, after He was risen from the dead: and how that He revealed to us things mighty, and wonderful, and true.

CHAPTER 3

This know we: that our Lord and Redeemer Jesus Christ is God, the Son of God, who was sent of God the Lord of the whole world, the Maker and Creator of it, who is named by all names, and high above all powers, Lord of lords, King of kings, Ruler of rulers, the heavenly one, that sits above the cherubim and seraphim at the right hand of the throne of the Father; who by His word made the heavens, and formed the earth and that which is in it, and set bounds to the sea that it should not pass; the deeps also and fountains, that they should spring forth and flow over the earth; the day and the night, the sun and the moon, He established, and the stars in the sky; that separated the light from the darkness; that called forth Hades, and in the twinkling of an eye ordained the rain of the winter, the snow [(cloud)], the hail, and the ice, and the days in their several seasons; that makes the earth to quake and again establishes it; that created man in His own image, after His likeness, and by the fathers of old and the prophets is it declared [[or and spoke in allegories with the fathers of old and the prophets in truth]], of whom the apostles preached, and whom the disciples touched. In God, the Lord, the Son of God, do we believe, that He is the word become flesh: that of Mary the holy virgin He took a body, begotten of the Holy Spirit, not of the will [(lust)] of the flesh, but by the will of God; that He was wrapped in swaddling clothes in Beth-Lehem and made manifest, and grew up and came to ripe age, when also we beheld it.

CHAPTER 4

This our Lord Jesus Christ did, who was sent by Joseph and Mary His mother to be taught. [And] when he that taught Him said to Him, "Say, Alpha," then He answered and said: "Tell Me first what is Beta." [[or "Tell Me first what is Alpha, and then I will tell you what is Beta."]] This thing which then came to pass is true and factual.

CHAPTER 5

1. Thereafter there was a marriage in Cana of Galilee; and they urged Him with His mother and His brothers, and He changed water into wine. He raised the dead, He caused the lame to walk; him whose hand was withered He caused to stretch it out, and the woman which had suffered an issue of blood twelve years touched the hem of His garment and was healed in the same hour. And when we marveled at the miracle which was done, He said: "Who touched Me?" Then we said: "Lord, the pressing in of men has touched You." But He answered and said to us: "I perceive that power has gone out of Me." Promptly that woman came before Him, and she answered and said to Him: "Lord, I touched You." And He answered and said to her: "Go, your faith has made you whole." Thereafter He made the deaf to hear and the blind to see; out of them that were possessed He cast out the unclean spirits, and cleansed the lepers. The spirit which dwelt in a man, whereof the name was Legion, cried out against Jesus, saying, "Before the time of our destruction has come, you have come to drive us out." But the Lord Jesus rebuked him, saying, "Go out of this man and do him no harm." And he entered into the swine and drowned them in the water, and they were choked.

2. Thereafter He walked on the sea, and the winds blew, and He cried out against them, and the waves of the sea were calmed. And when we His disciples had no money, we asked Him: "What will we do because of the tax-gatherer?" And He answered and told us: "Let one of you cast a hook into the deep, and take out a fish, and he will find a penny therein; give that to the tax-gatherer for Me and you." And later, when we had no bread, but only five loaves and two fishes, He commanded the people to sit them down, and the number of them was five thousand, besides children and women. We set pieces of bread before them, and they ate and were filled, and there remained [food] left over, and we filled twelve baskets full of the fragments, asking one another and saying, "What do these five loaves mean?" They are the symbol of our faith in the Lord of the Christians, even in the Father, the LORD Almighty, and in Jesus Christ our Redeemer, in the Holy Spirit the Comforter, in the holy Assembly, and in the forgiveness of sins.

CHAPTER 6

These things our Lord and Savior revealed to us and taught us. And we do even as He, that you may become partakers in the grace of our Lord, and in our ministry and our giving of thanks, and think on continuous life. Be steadfast and do not waver in the knowledge and confidence of our Lord Jesus Christ, and He will have mercy on you and save you forever—world without end.

CHAPTER 7

Cerinthus and Simon have come to go to and fro in the world, but they are enemies of our Lord Jesus Christ, for they pervert the word and the true thing, even [faith in] Jesus Christ. Keep yourselves therefore far from them, for death is in them, and great pollution and corruption, even in these on whom will come judgment and the end and continuous destruction.

CHAPTER 8

Therefore, we have not shrunk from writing to you concerning the testimony of Christ our Savior, of what He did, when we followed with Him, how He enlightened our understanding …

CHAPTER 9

Concerning whom we testify that the LORD is He who was crucified by Pontius Pilate and [Herod] Archelaus between the two thieves, [[and with them He was taken down from the tree of the Cross]] and was buried in a place which is called the "Place of a Skull." And there went three women: Mary, she that was a relative to Martha, and Mary Magdalene [[or Sarrha, Martha, and Mary]], and took ointments to pour on the body, weeping and mourning over that which had come to pass. And when they drew near to the tomb, they looked in and did not find the body [[or they found the stone rolled away and the entrance opened]].

CHAPTER 10

And as they mourned and wept, the LORD showed Himself to them and said to them: "For whom do you weep? Weep no more. I am He whom you seek. But let one of you go to your brothers and say: Come, the Master is risen from the dead." Martha [[or Mary]] came and told us. We said to her: "What have we to do with you, woman? He that is dead and buried—is it possible that He should live?" And we did not believe her that the Savior had risen from the dead. Then she returned to the LORD and said to Him: "None of them have believed me, that you live." He said: "Let another of you go to them and tell them again." Mary [[or Sarrha]] came and told us again, and we did not believe her; and she returned to the LORD and she also told Him.

CHAPTER 11

Then the LORD said to Mary and her sisters: "Let us go to them." And He came and found us within, [[sitting veiled,]] and called us out; but we thought that it was a phantom and did not believe that it was the LORD. Then He said to us: "Come, do not fear. I am your master, even He, O Peter, whom you denied thrice; and do you now deny again?" And we came to Him, doubting in our hearts whether it was He. Then He said to us: "Therefore, do you still doubt and are unbelieving? I am He that spoke to you of My flesh, and My death, and My resurrection. But that you may know that I am He: you, Peter, put your finger into the print of the nails in My hands; and you also, Thomas, put your finger into the wound of the spear in My side; but you, Andrew, look on My feet and see whether they press the earth; for it is written in the prophet: A phantom of a devil makes no footprint on the earth."

CHAPTER 12

And we touched Him, that we might learn [the] truth of whether He were risen in the flesh; and we fell on our faces [and worshiped Him], confessing our sin, that we had been unbelieving. Then our Lord and Savior said to us: "Rise up, and I will reveal to you that which is above the heavens and in the [highest] Heaven, and your rest which is in the kingdom of the heavens. For My Father has given Me power to take you up there, and them also that believe on Me.

CHAPTER 13

Now that which He revealed to us is this, which He spoke: "It came to pass when I was about to come here from the Father of all things, and passed through the heavens, that then I put on the wisdom of the Father, and I put on the power of His might. I was in Heaven, and I passed by the chief-messengers and the messengers in their likeness, as if I were one of them, among the princedoms and powers. I passed through them because I possessed the wisdom of Him that had sent Me. Now the chief captain of the messengers, Michael, as well as Gabriel, and Uriel, and Raphael followed me to the fifth expanse [(heaven)], for they thought in their heart that I was one of them; such power was given Me from My Father. And on that day, I adorned the chief-messengers with a wonderful voice [[or I made them quake—amazed them]], so that they should go to the altar of the Father and serve and fulfill the ministry until I should return to Him. And so I worked the likeness by My wisdom; for I became all things in all, that I might praise the dispensation of the Father and fulfill the glory of Him that sent Me and return to Him."

CHAPTER 14

"For you know that the messenger Gabriel brought the message to Mary." And we answered: "Yes, Lord." He answered and said to us: "Do you not remember, then, that I said to you a little while ago: I became a messenger among the messengers, and I became all things in all?" We said to Him: "Yes, Lord." Then He answered and said to us: "On that day whereon I took the form of the messenger Gabriel, I appeared to Mary and spoke with her. Her heart accepted Me, and she believed [[and laughed]], and I formed Myself and entered into her body. I became flesh, for I alone was a minister to Myself in that which concerned Mary in the appearance of the shape of a messenger, for so I needed to do. Thereafter I returned to My Father."

CHAPTER 15

1. "But commemorate My death. Now when the Passover comes, one of you will be cast into prison for My Name's sake; and He will be in grief and sorrow, because you keep the Passover while he is in prison and separated from you, for he will be sorrowful because he does not keep Passover with you. And I will send My power in the form of My messenger Gabriel, and the doors of the prison will open. And he will come forth and come to you and keep the night-watch with you until the cock crows. And when you have accomplished the memorial which is made of Me, and the love [feast], he will again be cast into prison for a testimony, until he will come out from there and preach that which I have delivered to you."
2. And we said to Him: "Lord, is it then necessary that we should again take the cup and drink?" [[or "Lord, did You not Yourself fulfill the drinking of the Passover?"]] He said to us: "Yes, it is necessary, until the day when I come again with them that have been put to death for My sake."

CHAPTER 16

Then we said to Him: "Lord, that which You have revealed to us is great. Will You come in the power of any creature or in an appearance of any kind?" [[or In what power or form will You come?"]] He answered and said to us: "Truly I say to you, I will come like the sun when it is risen, and My brightness will be seven times the brightness thereof! The wings of the clouds will bear Me in brightness, and the sign of the Cross will go before Me, and I will come on earth to judge the quick and the dead."

CHAPTER 17

1. We said to Him: "Lord, after how many years will this come to pass?" He said to us: "When the hundredth part and the twentieth part is fulfilled, between the Pentecost and the Celebration of Unleavened Bread, then will the coming of My Father be."
2. We said to Him: "Now you say to us: I will come; and how [then] do you say: He that sent Me is He that will come?" Then He said to us: I am wholly in the Father and My Father is in Me." Then we said to Him: "Will you indeed forsake us until Your coming? Where can we find a master?" But He answered and said to us: "Do you not know, then, that just as until now I have been here, so also was I there with Him that sent Me?" And we said to Him: "Lord, is it then possible that You should be both here and there?" But He answered us: "I am wholly in the Father and the Father in Me ... I am of His resemblance and form, of His power and completeness, and of His light. I am His complete Word."

CHAPTER 18

But it came to pass after He was crucified, and dead, and arisen again, when the work was fulfilled which was accomplished in the flesh, and He was crucified, and the ascension was coming to pass at the end of the days, then He said thus: "The whole fulfillment of everything you will see after the redemption which has come to pass by Me, and you will see Me—how I go up to My Father which is in Heaven. But behold, now, I give to you a new commandment: Love one another and ... obey one another, that peace may always rule among you. Love your enemies, and what you do not wish that man do to you, that do to no man."

CHAPTER 19

1. "And preach this also, and teach them that believe on Me, and preach the kingdom of the heavens of My Father, and how My Father has given Me the power, that you may bring near the children of My heavenly Father. Preach, and they will obtain faith, that you may be they for whom it is ordained that they will bring His children to Heaven."
2. And we said to Him: "Lord, to You it is possible to accomplish whatever You tell us; but how will we be able to do it?" He said to us: Truly I say to you, preach and proclaim as I command you, for I will be with you, for it is My good pleasure to be with you, that you may be heirs with Me in the kingdom of the heavens, even the kingdom of Him that sent Me. Truly I say to you, you will be My brothers and My friends, for My Father has found pleasure in you: and so also will they be that believe on Me by your means. Truly I say to you, such and so great joy has My Father prepared for you that the messengers and the powers desired and do desire to see it and look on it; but it is not given to them to behold the glory of My Father." We said to Him: "Lord, what is this of which You speak to us?"
3. ... He answered us: "You will behold a light [[which shines more brightly than [any] light and is more perfect than perfection. And the Son will become perfect through the Father who is Light, for the Father is perfect which brings to pass death and resurrection, and you will see a perfection more perfect than the perfect. And I am wholly at the right hand of the Father, even in Him that makes perfect.]]"
4. And we said to Him: "Lord, in all things You have become salvation and life to us, for that You make known such a hope to us." And He said to us: "Be of good courage and rest in Me. Truly I say to you, your rest will be above, in the place where is neither eating, nor drinking, nor care, nor sorrow, nor passing away of them that are therein: for you will have no part in [[the things of earth]], but you will be received in the eternality of My Father. Like as I am in Him, so will you also be in Me."
5. Again, we said to Him: "In what form? In the fashion of messengers, or in flesh?" And He answered and said to us: "Behold, I have put on your flesh, wherein I was born and crucified, and am risen again through My Father which is in Heaven, that the prophecy of David the prophet might be fulfilled, in regard of that which was declared concerning Me and My death and resurrection, saying:
6. LORD, they are increased that fight with me, || And many are they that are risen up against me. Many there be that say to my soul: There is no help for him in his God. But You, O LORD, are my defender, || You are my worship, and the lifter up of my head. I called on the LORD with my voice and he heard me

[out of the high place of His temple]. I laid down and slept, || And rose up again: for You, O LORD, are my defender. I will not be afraid of myriads of people, || That have set themselves against me all around. Rise, O LORD, and help me, O my God! For You have stricken down all them that without cause are my enemies. You have broken the teeth of the ungodly. Salvation belongs to the LORD, || And His good pleasure is on His people.

7. If, therefore, all the words which were spoken by the prophets have been fulfilled in Me, how much more will that which I say to you come to pass indeed, that He which sent Me may be glorified by you and by them that believe on Me?"

CHAPTER 20

And when He had said this to us, we said to Him: "In all things have You had mercy on us and saved us, and have revealed all things to us; but yet we would ask of you something else if You allow us." And He said to us: "I know that you pay heed, and that your heart is well-pleased when you hear Me: now concerning that which you desire, I will speak good words to you."

CHAPTER 21

1. "For truly I say to you: Just as My Father has raised Me from the dead, so will you also rise [[in the flesh]] and be taken up into the highest Heaven, to the place whereof I have told you from the beginning, to the place which He who sent Me has prepared for you. And so will I accomplish all dispensations, even I who am unbegotten and yet begotten of mankind, who am without flesh and yet have borne flesh: for to that end I have come, that you might rise from the dead in your flesh, in the second birth, even a vesture that will not decay, together with all them that hope and believe in Him that sent Me: for so is the will of My Father, that I should give to you, and to them whom it pleases Me, the hope of the kingdom."

2. Then we said to Him: "Great is that which You permit us to hope and tell us." And He answered and said: "Do you believe that everything that I tell you will come to pass?" We answered and said: "Yes, Lord." He said to us: "Truly I say to you, that I have obtained the whole power of My Father, that I may bring back into light them that dwell in darkness, them that are in corruption into incorruption, them that are in death into life, and that I may free them that are in chains. For that which is impossible with men, is possible with the Father. I am the hope of them that despair, the helper of them that have no savior, the wealth of the poor, the health of the sick, and the resurrection of the dead."

CHAPTER 22

When He had thus spoken, we said to Him: "Lord, is it true that the flesh will be judged together with the soul and the spirit, and that the one part will rest in Heaven and the other part be punished continuously yet living?" And He said to us: "How long will you inquire and doubt?"

CHAPTER 23

Again we said to Him: "Lord, there is necessity on us to inquire of You—because You have commanded us to preach—that we ourselves may learn assuredly from You and be profitable preachers, and that they which are instructed by us may believe in You. Therefore, we must necessarily inquire of You."

CHAPTER 24

He answered us and said: "Truly I say to you, the resurrection of the flesh will come to pass with the soul therein and the spirit." And we said to Him: "Lord, is it then possible that that which is dissolved and brought to nothing should become whole? And we ask you not as unbelieving, neither as if it were impossible to You; but truly we believe that that which You say will come to pass." And He was angry with us and said: "O you of little faith! How long will you ask questions? But what you will, tell it to Me, and I Myself will tell you without grudging: only keep My commandments and do that which I command you, and do not turn your face away from any man, because I do not turn My face away from you; but without shrinking back and fear, and without respect of persons, minister in the way that is direct, and narrow, and strait. So will My Father Himself rejoice over you."

CHAPTER 25

Again, we said to Him: "Lord, we are already ashamed that we often question You and burden You." And He answered and said to us: "I know that in faith and with your whole heart you question Me; therefore, I rejoice over you, for truly I say to you: I rejoice, and My Father that is in Me, because you question Me; and your shamelessness is to Me rejoicing and to you it gives life." And when He had so spoken to us, we were glad that we had questioned Him, and we said to Him: "Lord, in all things You make us alive and have mercy on us. Will You now declare to us that which we will ask You?" Then He said to us: "Is it the flesh that passes away, or is it the spirit?" We said to Him: "The flesh is it that passes away." Then He said to us: "That which has fallen will rise again, and that which was lost will be found, and that which was weak will recover, that in these things that are so created the glory of My Father may be revealed. As He has done to Me, so will I do to all that believe in Me."

CHAPTER 26

"Truly I say to you: the flesh will arise, and the soul, alive, that their defense may come to pass on that day in regard to that which they have done, whether it was good or evil: that there may be a choosing-out of the faithful who have kept the commandments of My Father that sent Me; and so will the judgment be accomplished with strictness. For My Father said to Me: My Son, in the day of judgment You will have no respect for the rich, neither pity for the poor, but according to the sins of every man will You deliver him to continuous torment. But to My beloved that have done the commandments of My Father that sent Me, I will give the rest of life in the kingdom of My Father which is in Heaven, and they will behold that which He has given Me. And He has given Me authority to do that which I will, and to give that which I have promised and determined to give and grant to them."

CHAPTER 27

[["For to that end I went down to the place of Lazarus, and preached to the righteous and the prophets, that they might come out of the rest which is below and come up into that which is above; and I poured out on them with My right hand the water of life, and forgiveness, and salvation from all evil, as I have done to you and to them that believe on Me. But if any man believes on Me and does not do My commandments, although he has confessed My Name, he has no profit therefrom but runs a vain race: for such will find themselves in perdition and destruction, because they have despised My commandments."]]

CHAPTER 28

"But so much the more have I redeemed you, the children of light, from all evil and from the authority of the [heavenly] rulers, and everyone that believes on Me by your means. For that which I have promised to you I will give to them also, that they may come out of the prison-house and the chains of the rulers." We answered and said: "Lord, You have given to us the rest of life and have given us … by wonders, to the confirmation of faith: will You now preach the same to us, seeing that You have preached it to the [[righteous]] and the prophets?" Then He said to us: "Truly I say to you, all that have believed on Me and that believe in Him that sent Me will I take up into the heavens, to the place which My Father has prepared for the chosen, and I will give you the kingdom, the chosen kingdom, in rest, and continuous life."

CHAPTER 29

1. "But all they that have offended against My commandments and have taught other doctrine, [perverting] the Writing and adding thereto, striving after their own glory, and that teach with other words them that believe on Me in uprightness, if they make them fall thereby, will receive continuous punishment." We said to Him: "Lord, will there then be teaching by others, diverse from that which You have spoken to us?" He said to us: "It must necessarily be, that the evil and the good may be made manifest; and the judgment will be manifest on them that do these things, and according to their works will they be judged and will be delivered to death."

2. Again, we said to Him: "Lord, blessed are we in that we see You and hear You declaring such things, for our eyes have

behold these great wonders that You have done." He answered and said to us: "Yes, rather blessed are they that have not seen and yet have believed, for they will be called children of the kingdom, and they will be perfect among the perfect, and I will be to them life in the kingdom of My Father."
3. Again, we said to Him: "Lord, how will men be able to believe that You will depart and leave us; for You say to us: There will come a day and an hour when I will ascend to My Father?"

CHAPTER 30

But He said to us: "Go and preach to the twelve tribes, and preach also to the heathen, and to all the land of Israel from the east to the west and from the south to the north, and many will believe on the Son of God." But we said to Him: "Lord, who will believe us or listen to us, or [[how will we be able]] to teach the powers, and signs, and wonders which You have done?" Then He answered and said to us: "Go and preach the mercifulness of My Father, and that which He has done through Me will I Myself do through you, for I am in you, and I will give you My peace, and I will give you [the] power of My Spirit, that you may prophesy to them to continuous life. And I will also give My power to the others, that they may teach the remnant of the peoples…"

CHAPTER 31

1. "And behold, a man will meet you, whose name is Saul, which being interpreted is Paul: he is a Jew, circumcised according to the Law, and he will receive My voice from Heaven with fear, and terror, and trembling. And his eyes will be blinded, and by your hands by the sign of the Cross they will be protected [[or healed]]. Do to him all that I have done to you. Deliver it [[the good news]] to the other. And at the same time, that man will open his eyes and praise the LORD, even My Father which is in Heaven. He will obtain power among the people and will preach and instruct; and many that hear him will obtain glory and be redeemed. But thereafter men will be angry with him and deliver him into the hands of his enemies, and he will bear witness before kings that are mortal, and his end will be that he will turn to Me, whereas he persecuted Me at the first. He will preach, and teach, and abide with the chosen, as a chosen vessel and a wall that will not be overthrown, yes, the last of the last will become a preacher to the nations, made perfect by the will of My Father. Just as you have learned from the Writing that your fathers the prophets spoke of Me, and in Me it is indeed fulfilled."
2. And He said to us: "Be also therefore guides to them; and all things that I said to you, and that you write concerning Me, [declare it to them,] that I am the Word of the Father and that the Father is in Me. Such also will you be to that man, as suits you. Instruct him and bring to his mind that which is spoken of Me in the Writing and is fulfilled, and thereafter he will become the [messenger of] salvation to the nations."

CHAPTER 32

And we asked Him: "Lord, is there for us and for them [[the nations)]] the exact same expectation of the inheritance?" He answered and said to us: "Are then the fingers of the hand like to each other, or the ears of corn in the field, or do all fruit-trees bear the same fruit? Does not everyone bear fruit according to its nature?" And we said to Him: "Lord, will You again speak to us in parables?" Then He said to us: "Do not lament. Truly I say to you, you are My brothers, and My companions in the kingdom of the heavens to My Father, for so is His good pleasure. Truly I say to you, to them also whom you teach and who believe on Me I will give that expectation."

CHAPTER 33

And we asked Him again: "When will we meet with that man, and when will You depart to Your Father and our God and Lord?" He answered and said to us: "That man will come out of the land of Cilicia to Damascus of Syria, to root up the assembly which you must found there. It is I that speak through you; and he will come quickly: and he will become strong in the faith, that the word of the prophet may be fulfilled, which says: Behold, out of Syria I will begin to call together a new Jerusalem, and Zion will I subdue to Myself, and it will be taken, and the place which is childless will be called the son and daughter of My Father, and My bride. For so has it pleased Him that sent Me. But I will turn that man back, so that he does not accomplish his evil desire, and the praise of My Father will be perfected in him, and after I go home and abide with My Father, I will speak to Him from Heaven, and all things will be accomplished which I have told you before concerning him."

CHAPTER 34

1. And we said to Him again: "Lord, so many great things You have told us and revealed to us as never yet were spoken, and in everything You have given us rest and been gracious to us. After Your resurrection You revealed to us all things that we might indeed be saved; but You said to us only: There will be signs and strange appearances in the sky and on earth before the end of the world comes. Tell us now, how will we perceive it?" And He answered us: "I will teach it to you; and not that which will befall you only, but them also whom you will teach and who will believe, as well as them who will hear that man and believe on Me. In those years and days will it come to pass."
2. And we said again to Him: "Lord, what will come to pass?" And He said to us: "Then they that believe, and they that do not believe, will see a trumpet in the heavens, a vision of great stars which will be seen in the day, wonderful sights in the sky reaching down to the earth, stars which fall on the earth like fire, and a great and mighty hail of fire; the sun and the moon fighting with one another, a continual rolling and noise of thunders and lightnings, thunder and earthquake; cities falling and men perishing in their overthrow, a continual dearth for lack of rain, a terrible pestilence and great mortality, mighty and untimely, so that they that die lack burial: and the bearing forth of brothers, and sisters, and relatives will be on one bier. The relative will show no favor to his relative, nor any man to his neighbor. And they that were overthrown will rise up and behold them that overthrew them, that they lack burial, for the pestilence will be full of hatred, and pain, and envy: and men will take from one and give to another. And thereafter will it wax yet worse than before."

CHAPTER 35

1. "Then will My Father be angry at the wickedness of men, for many are their transgressions, and the abomination of their uncleanness weighs heavy on them in the corruption of their life."
2. And we asked Him: "What of them that trust in You?" He answered and said to us: "You are yet slow of heart; and how long? Truly I say to you, as the prophet David spoke of Me and of My people, so will it be for them also that believe on Me. But they that are deceivers in the world and enemies of righteousness, on them will come the fulfillment of the prophecy of David, who said: Their feet are swift to shed blood, || Their tongue utters slander, || Adders' poison is under their lips. I behold you companying with thieves, || And partaking with adulterers, || You continue speaking against your brother || And put stumbling-blocks before your own mother's son. What do you think, || That I will be like to you? Behold now how the prophet of God has spoken of all, that all things may be fulfilled which he said formerly."

CHAPTER 36

1. And again, we said to Him: "Lord, will the nations not then say, Where is their God?" And He answered and said to us: "Thereby will the chosen be known, that they, being plagued with such afflictions, come forth." We said: "Will then their departure out of the world be by a pestilence which gives them pain?" He answered us: "No, but if they suffer such affliction, it will be a proving of them, whether they have faith, and remember these sayings of Mine, and fulfill My commandments. These will arise, and short will be their expectation, that He may be glorified that sent Me, and I with Him. For He has sent Me to you to tell you these things; and that you may impart them to Israel and the nations and they may hear, and they also be redeemed and believe on Me and escape the woe of the destruction. But whoever escapes from the destruction of death, him will they take and hold him fast in the prison-house in torments like the torments of a thief."
2. And we said to Him: "Lord, will they that believe be treated like the unbelievers, and will You punish them that have escaped from the pestilence?" And He said to us: "If they that feign belief in My Name deal like the sinners, then they have done as though they had not believed." And we said again to Him:

"Lord, have they on whom this lot has fallen no life?" He answered and said to us: "Whoever has accomplished the praise of My Father, he will abide in the resting-place of My Father."

CHAPTER 37

Then we said to Him: "Lord, teach us what will come to pass thereafter?" And He answered us: "In those years and days will war be kindled on war; the four ends of the earth will be in commotion and fight against each other. Thereafter will be quakings of clouds [[*or* clouds of locusts]], darkness, and scarcity, and persecutions of them that believe on Me and against the chosen. Thereon will come doubt, and strife, and transgressions against one another. And there will be many that believe on My Name and yet follow after evil and spread vain doctrine. And men will follow after them and their riches, and be subject to their pride, and lust for drink, and bribery, and there will be respect of persons among them."

CHAPTER 38

1. "But they that desire to behold the face of God, and do not respect the persons of the rich sinners, and are not ashamed before the people that lead them astray, but rebuke them, they will be crowned by the Father. And they will also be saved that rebuke their neighbors, for they are sons of wisdom and of faith. But if they do not become children of wisdom, whoever hates his brother, and persecutes him, and shows him no favor, him will God despise and reject.

2. But they that walk in truth and in the knowledge of the faith, and have love toward Me—for they have endured insult—they will be praised for that they walk in poverty and endure them that hate them and put them to shame. Men have stripped them naked, for they despised them because they continued in hunger and thirst, but after they have endured patiently, they will have the blessedness of Heaven, and they will be with Me forever. But woe to them that walk in pride and boasting, for their end is perdition."

CHAPTER 39

1. And we said to Him: "Lord, is this your purpose, that you leave us, to come on them?" He answered and said to us: "After what manner will the judgment be? Whether righteous or unrighteous?"

2. We said to Him: "Lord, in that day they will say to You: You have not distinguished between righteousness and unrighteousness, between the light and the darkness, and evil and good." Then He said: "I will answer them and say: To Adam power was given to choose one of the two: he chose the light and laid his hand thereon, but the darkness he left behind him and cast away from him. Therefore, all men have power to believe in the light which is life, and which is the Father that has sent Me. And everyone that believes and does the works of the light will live in them; but if there is anyone that confesses that he belongs to the light, and does the works of darkness, such a one has no defense to utter, neither can he lift up his face to look on the Son of God, which Son I am. For I will say to him: As you sought, so have you found, and as you asked, so have you received. Therefore, do you condemn Me, O man? Therefore, have you departed from Me and denied Me? And therefore, have you confessed Me and yet denied Me? Does not every man have power to live and to die? Whoever then has kept My commandments will be a son of the light, that is, of the Father that is in Me. But because of them that corrupt My words I have come down from Heaven. I am the Word: I became flesh, and I wearied Myself and taught, saying: The burdened will be saved, and they that have gone astray will go astray forever. They will be chastised and tormented in their flesh and in their soul."

CHAPTER 40

1. And we said to Him: "O Lord, we are truly sorrowful for their sake." And He said to us: "You do rightly, for the righteous are sorry for the sinners, and pray for them, making prayer to My Father." Again, we said to Him: "Lord, is there none that makes intercession to You?" And He said to us: "Yes, and I will listen to the prayer of the righteous which they make for them."

2. When He had so spoken to us, we said to Him: "Lord, in all things you have taught us, and had mercy on us, and saved us, that we might preach to them that are worthy to be saved, and that we might obtain a recompense with You."

CHAPTER 41

He answered and said to us: "Go and preach, and you will be laborers, and fathers, and ministers." We said to Him: "You are He that will preach by us." Then He answered us, saying: "Are you not all fathers or all masters?" We said to Him: "Lord, You are He that said to us: Call no man your father on earth, for one is your Father, which is in Heaven, and your master. Therefore, do you now say to us: You will be fathers of many children, and servants and masters?" He answered and said to us: "You have spoken correctly. For truly I say to you: whosoever will hear you and believe on Me, will receive of you the light of the seal through Me, and immersion through Me; you will be fathers, and servants, and masters."

CHAPTER 42

1. But we said to Him: "Lord, how may it be that every one of us should be these three?" He said to us: "Truly I say to you: you will be called fathers, because with praiseworthy heart and in love you have revealed to them the things of the kingdom of the heavens. And you will be called servants, because they will receive the immersion of life and the forgiveness of their sins at My hand through you. And you will be called masters, because you have given them the word without grudging, and have admonished them, and when you admonished them, they converted themselves. You were not afraid of their riches, nor ashamed before their face, but you kept the commandments of My Father and fulfilled them. And you will have a great reward with My Father which is in Heaven, and they will have forgiveness of sins and continuous life, and be partakers in the kingdom of the heavens.

2. And we said to Him: "Lord, even if every one of us had ten thousand tongues to speak also, we could not thank You, for that You promise such things to us." Then He answered us, saying, "Only do that which I say to you, even as I Myself have also done it."

CHAPTER 43

1. "And you will be like the wise virgins which watched and did not sleep but went forth to the lord into the bridechamber; but the foolish virgins were not able to watch, but slumbered." And we said to Him: "Lord, who are the wise and who are the foolish?" He said to us: "Five wise and five foolish; for these are they of whom the prophet has spoken: Sons of God are they. Hear now their names."

2. But we wept and were troubled for them that slumbered. He said to us: "The five wise are Faith, and Love, and Grace, and Peace, and Hope. Now they of the faithful which possess these will be guides to them that have believed on Me and on Him that sent Me. For I am the Lord, and I am the bridegroom whom they have received, and they have entered into the house of the bridegroom and have laid down with Me in the bridal chamber rejoicing. But the five foolish, when they had slept and had awaked, came to the door of the bridal chamber and knocked, for the doors were shut. Then they wept and lamented that no man opened to them."

3. We said to Him: "Lord, and their wise sisters that were within in the bridegroom's house, did they continue without opening to them, and did they not sorrow for their sakes nor entreat the bridegroom to open to them?" He answered us, saying, "They were not yet able to obtain favor for them." We said to Him: "Lord, on what day will they enter in for their sisters' sake?" Then He said to us: "He that is shut out, is shut out." And we said to Him: "Lord, is this word [determined]? Who then are the foolish?" He said to us: "Hear their names. They are Knowledge, Understanding, Obedience, Patience, and Compassion. These are they that slumbered in them that have believed and confessed Me but have not fulfilled My commandments."

CHAPTER 44

"On account of them that have slumbered, they will remain outside the kingdom and the fold of the Shepherd and His sheep. But whoever will abide outside the sheepfold, him will the wolves devour, and he will be … and die in much affliction; in him will be no rest nor endurance, and although he is fiercely punished, and torn in pieces, and devoured in long and evil torment, yet he will not be able to obtain death quickly."

CHAPTER 45

And we said to Him: "Lord, well have You revealed all this to us." Then He answered us, saying, "Do you not understand these words?" We said to Him: "Yes, Lord. By five will men enter into Your kingdom [[and by five will men remain outside]]: notwithstanding, they that watched were with You the LORD and Bridegroom, even though they did not rejoice because of them that slumbered." He said to us: "They will indeed rejoice that they have entered in with the Bridegroom, the LORD; and they are sorrowful because of them that slumbered, for they are their sisters. For all ten are daughters of God, even the Father." Then we said to Him: "Lord, is it then for You to show them favor on account of their sisters?" He said to us: "[[It is not Mine,]] but His that sent Me, and I am consenting with Him."

CHAPTER 46

"But be upright, and preach rightly, and teach, and do not be abashed by any man and fear not any man, and especially the rich, for they do not do My commandments, but boast themselves in their riches." And we said to Him: "Lord, tell us if it is the rich only." He answered, saying to us: "If any man who is not rich and possesses a small livelihood gives to the poor and needy, men will call him a benefactor."

CHAPTER 47

"But if any man falls under the load of sin that he has committed, then will his neighbor correct him because of the good that he has done to his neighbor. And if his neighbor corrects him and he returns, he will be saved, and he that corrected him will receive a reward and live forever. For a needy man, if he sees him that has done him good sin, and does not correct him, will be judged with severe judgment. Now if a blind man leads a blind, they both fall into a ditch: and whoever respects persons for their sake, will be as the two, as the prophet has said: Woe to them that respect persons and justify the ungodly for reward, even they whose God is their belly. Behold that judgment will be their portion. For truly I say to you: On that day I will have neither respect for the rich nor pity for the poor."

CHAPTER 48

"If you behold a sinner, admonish him between him and you: [[if he hears you, you have gained your brother,]] and if he does not hear you, then take with you another, as many as three, and instruct your brother; again, if he does not hear you, let him be to you … as a heathen man or a tax collector."

CHAPTER 49

1. "If you hear anything against your brother, give it no credence; do not slander, and do not delight in hearing slander. For thus it is written: Do not permit your ear to receive anything against your brother; but if you see anything, correct him, rebuke him, and convert him."
2. And we said to Him: "Lord, You have in all things taught us and warned us. But, Lord, concerning the believers, even them to whom it belongs to believe in the preaching of Your Name: is it determined that among them also there will be doubt and division, jealousy, confusion, hatred, and envy? For You say: They will find fault with one another, and respect the person of them that sins, and hate them that rebuke them." And He answered and said to us: "How then will the judgment come about, that the corn should be gathered into the garner and the chaff thereof cast into the fire?"

CHAPTER 50

1. "They that hate such things, and love Me, and rebuke them that do not fulfill My commandments, will be hated, and persecuted, and despised, and mocked. Men will of purpose speak of them that which is not true and will band themselves together against them that love Me. But these will rebuke them, that they may be saved. But them that will rebuke, and chasten, and warn them, they will hate them, and thrust them aside, and despise them, and hold themselves far from them that wish them good. But they that endure such things will be like to the martyrs with the Father, because they have striven for righteousness, and have not striven for corruption."
2. And we asked Him: "Lord, will such things be among us?" And He answered us: "Do not be afraid; it will not be in many, but in a few." We said to Him: "Yet tell us, in what manner it will come to pass." And He said to us: "There will come forth another doctrine, and a confusion, and because they will strive after their own advancement, they will bring forth an unprofitable doctrine. And therein will be a deadly corruption, and they will teach it, and will turn away them that believe on Me from My commandments and cut them off from continuous life. But woe to them that falsify this word and commandment of Mine, and draw away them that listen to them from the life of the doctrine, and separate themselves from the commandment of life: for together with them they will come into continuous judgment."

CHAPTER 51

And when He had said this, and had finished His discourse with us, He said to us again: "Behold, on the third day and at the third hour will He come which has sent Me, that I may depart with Him. And as He so spoke, there was thunder, and lightning, and an earthquake, and the heavens split apart, and there appeared a radiant cloud which bore Him up. And there came voices of many messengers, rejoicing and singing praises, and saying: "Gather us, O Priest, to the light of the majesty." And when they drew near to the expanse, we heard His voice saying to us: "Depart from here in peace."

APOSTOLIC CHURCH ORDER

Not to be confused with the Apostolic Constitutions or their appended Apostolic Canons, the Apostolic Church Order is a 3rd century pseudo-Apostolic collection of moral and hierarchical rules and instructions that served as a law-code for the Egyptian, Ethiopian, and Arabian churches, and rivaled in authority the Didache, under which name it sometimes went.

GREETING, SONS AND DAUGHTERS, IN THE NAME OF THE LORD JESUS CHRIST. JOHN, AND MATTHEW, AND PETER, AND ANDREW, AND PHILIP, AND SIMON, AND JAMES, AND NATHANAEL, AND THOMAS, AND CEPHAS, AND BARTHOLOMEW, AND JUDAS OF JAMES.

CHAPTER 1

¹Since we have assembled at a command of our Lord Jesus Christ the Savior, according as He appointed previously the [injunction]: ²"You are to assign districts to determine the numbers of places, the dignities of overseers, the seats of elders, the attendance of servants, the office of readers, the blamelessness of widows," and whatever is necessary for founding an assembly, ³in order that, knowing the type of the heavenly [order], they may keep themselves from every fault, knowing that they must give an account at the Great Day of Judgment for the things which they heard and did not keep—and as He commanded us to send forth the words into all the world.

CHAPTER 2

¹Therefore, it seemed good to us, for a reminding of the brotherhood and a warning to each, ²as the Lord revealed it according to the will of God through the Holy Spirit, remembering the word to command it to you.

CHAPTER 3

¹John said: "My brothers, knowing that we will give an account for the things assigned to us, let us each not regard the person of anyone, ²but if anyone thinks it fitting to dispute, let him dispute." ³Now it seemed good to all that John should speak first.

CHAPTER 4

¹John said: "There are two ways: one of life and one of death, but there is a great

APOSTOLIC CHURCH ORDER

difference between the two ways; ²for the way of life is this: first, you will love the God who made you with all your heart, and you will glorify Him that ransomed you from death, which is [the] first commandment. ³Secondly, you will love your neighbor as yourself, which is [the] second commandment: on which hang all the Law and the Prophets."

CHAPTER 5
¹Matthew said: "All things, whatsoever you will not have done to you, you will not do to another. ²Now of these words, proclaim the teaching, brother Peter."

CHAPTER 6
¹Peter said: "You will not kill; you will not commit adultery; ²you will not commit fornication; you will not corrupt a youth; ³you will not steal; ⁴you will not be a sorcerer; ⁵you will not use enchantments; ⁶you will not slay a child by abortion, nor kill what is born; ⁷you will not covet anything that is your neighbor's; ⁸you will not bear false witness; you will not speak evil; ⁹you will not bear malice; ¹⁰you will not be split-souled, nor double-tongued, for a snare of death is duplicity of tongue. ¹¹Your speech will not be empty, nor false; you will not be covetous, nor rapacious, nor a hypocrite, nor malicious, or haughty, nor take evil counsel against your neighbor; ¹²you will not hate any man, but some you will reprove, and some you will pity; and for some you will pray, and some you will love more than your own soul."

CHAPTER 7
¹Andrew said: "My child, flee from all evil, and from everything like it. ²Do not be inclined to anger, for anger leads to murder; for wrath is a male demon. ³Do not become a zealot, nor contentious, nor passionate; for murder is prompted from these things."

CHAPTER 8
¹Philip said: "My child, do not be lustful; for lust leads to fornication and draws men to herself. ²For lust is a female demon, and the one ruins with anger, the other with lust, those that receive them. ³Now [the] way of an evil spirit is the sin of the soul; and if it has only a narrow entrance within him, it widens the way and leads that soul to all bad things and does not permit the man to look clearly and see the truth. ⁴Let your wrath be restrained, and after a short interval, bridle and check it, so that it may not hurl you into evil deeds. For wrath and evil desire, if they are allowed to remain long, become demons by reinforcement. ⁵And whenever man yields himself to them, they swell up in his soul, and grow larger, and lead him into unrighteous deeds, and deride him, and rejoice at the destruction of men."

CHAPTER 9
¹Simon said: "Child, do not be foul-mouthed, nor lofty-eyed; ²for from these things come adulteries."

CHAPTER 10
¹James said: "Child, do not be an omen-watcher, since it leads to idolatry, nor a charmer, nor an astrologer, nor a purifier, nor be willing to look on nor hear these things; ²for idolatries are begotten from all these."

CHAPTER 11
¹Nathaniel said: "Child, do not be a liar, since lying leads to theft, nor greedy, nor vainglorious; for thefts are begotten from all these things." ²[Judas said:] Child, do not be a murmurer, since it leads to blasphemy, nor self-willed, nor evil-minded; for blasphemies are begotten from all these things. ³But be meek, since the meek will inherit the Kingdom of Heaven. ⁴Be long-suffering, merciful, peace-making, pure in heart from every evil, guileless and gentle, good, and keeping and trembling at the words which you have heard; ⁵you will not exalt yourself, nor permit over-boldness to your soul, nor cleave with your soul to [the] great, but with [the] righteous and lowly you will consort. ⁶The events that befall you you will accept as good, knowing that without God nothing occurs."

CHAPTER 12
¹Thomas said: "Child, him that speaks to you the word of God, and becomes to you an author of life, and has given you the seal in the Lord, you will love as the apple of your eye, and you will remember him night and day; ²you will honor him as the Lord; for where that which pertains to the Lord is spoken, there is the Lord. ³And you will seek out his face daily and the rest of the holy ones, so that you may be refreshed by their words: for by cleaving to holy ones you will be sanctified. ⁴You will honor him, as far as you are able, from your sweat and from the labor of your hands. ⁵For if the Lord through him saw suitable that spiritual food, and drink, and eternal life be given you, you ought much more the perishable and transient food, for the laborer is worthy of his hire, and a threshing ox you will not muzzle, and no one plants a vine and does not eat its fruit."

CHAPTER 13
¹Cephas said: "You will not make divisions, but will make peace between those who contend; you will judge justly; you will not respect persons in reproving for a transgression. ²For wealth does not avail with the Lord; for dignity does not predispose, nor beauty aid, but there is equality of all before Him. ³In your prayer you will not hesitate, whether it will be or not; do not be [one who] for receiving stretches out the hands, but for giving draws them in. ⁴If you have [anything] by your hands, you will give ransom for your sins; you will not hesitate to give, nor when giving will you murmur, for you will know who is the good dispenser of the reward. ⁵You will not turn away from a needy one, but you will share in all things with your brother and will not say they are your own, for if you are partners in that which is imperishable, how much more in the corruptible things."

EPISTLE OF BARNABAS

The Epistle of Barnabas, in reality more a treatise than a letter, is preserved completely in the Codex Sinaiticus, where it is located at the end of the New Testament. It is traditionally thought Barnabas from the Acts of the Apostles penned the document, while others ascribe it to a "Barnabas of Alexandria," or some other unidentified early writer.

CHAPTER 1
¹Greetings, sons and daughters, in the Name of the LORD who loved us, in peace. ²Exceedingly and abundantly I rejoice over your blessed and glorious spirit for the greatness and richness of God's ordinances toward you—so innate a grace of the gift of the Spirit you have received. ³For what reason I congratulate myself the more in my hope of salvation, because I truly see in you that the Spirit has been poured out on you from the LORD, who is rich in His bounty, so that the sight of you, for which I longed, amazed me. ⁴Being persuaded then of this, and being conscious that since I spoke among you I have much understanding because the LORD has traveled with me in the way of righteousness, I am above all constrained to this, to love you above my own life, because great faith and love dwell in you in the "hope of His life." ⁵I have therefore reckoned that, if I make it my care in your behalf to communicate somewhat of that which I received, it will bring me the reward of having ministered to such spirits, and I hasten to send you a short letter in order that your knowledge may be perfected along with your faith. ⁶There are then three doctrines of the LORD: "the hope of life" is the beginning and end of our faith; and righteousness is the beginning and end of judgment; love of joy and of gladness is the testimony of the works of righteousness. ⁷For the LORD made known to us through the prophets, things past and things present, and has given us the first-fruits

of the taste of things to come; and when we see these things coming to pass one by one, as He said, we should make a richer and deeper offering for fear of Him. ⁸But I will show you a few things, not as a teacher but as one of yourselves, in which you will rejoice at this present time.

CHAPTER 2

¹Seeing then that the days are evil, and that the worker of evil is himself in power, we should give heed to ourselves, and seek out the ordinances of the LORD. ²Fear then, and patience, are the helpers of our faith, and long-suffering and continence are our allies. ³While then these things remain in holiness toward the LORD, wisdom, prudence, understanding, and knowledge rejoice with them. ⁴For He has made plain to us through all the prophets that He needs neither sacrifices, nor burnt-offerings, nor oblations, saying in one place, ⁵"What is the multitude of your sacrifices to Me? Says the LORD. I am full of burnt-offerings, and do not desire the fat of lambs and the blood of bulls and goats, not even when you come to appear before Me. For who has required these things at your hands? From now on you will tread My court no longer. If you bring flour, it is vain. Incense is an abomination to Me. I cannot endure your new moons and Sabbaths." ⁶These things, then, He abolished in order that the new law of our Lord Jesus Christ, which is without the yoke of necessity, might have its oblation not made by man. ⁷And again He says to them, "Did I command your fathers when they came out of the land of Egypt to offer Me burnt-offerings and sacrifices? ⁸No, but rather I commanded them this: Let none of you cherish any evil in his heart against his neighbor, and do not love a false oath." ⁹We should then understand, if we are not foolish, the loving intention of our Father, for He speaks to us, wishing that we should not err like them, but seek how we may make our offering to Him. ¹⁰To us then He speaks thus: "Sacrifice for the LORD is a broken heart, a smell of sweet savor to the LORD is a heart that glorifies Him that made it." We should, therefore, brothers, carefully inquire concerning our salvation, in order that the evil one may not achieve a deceitful entry into us and hurl us away from our life.

CHAPTER 3

¹To them He says then again concerning these things, "Why do you fast for Me—says the LORD—so that your voice is heard this day with a cry? This is not the fast which I chose—says the LORD—not a man humbling his soul; ²nor though you bend your neck as a hoop, and put on sackcloth, and make your bed of ashes, not even so will you call it an acceptable fast." ³But to us He says, "Behold this is the fast which I chose," says the LORD, "loose every bond of wickedness, set loose the fastenings of harsh agreements, send away the bruised in forgiveness, and tear up every unjust contract; give your bread to the hungry, and if you see a naked man clothe him; bring the homeless into your house, and if you see a humble man, do not despise him—neither you nor any of the household of your seed. ⁴Then your light will break forth as the dawn, and your robes will rise quickly, and your righteousness will go before you, and the glory of God will surround you." ⁵"Then you will cry and God will hear you; while you are still speaking He will say, Behold, I am here; if you put away from you bondage, and violence, and the word of murmuring, and give your bread to the poor with a cheerful heart, and pity the soul that is abased." ⁶So then, brothers, the long-suffering One foresaw that the people whom He prepared in His beloved should believe in guilelessness, and made all things plain to us beforehand that we should not be shipwrecked by conversion to their law.

CHAPTER 4

¹We should, then, inquire earnestly into the things which now are, and to seek out those which are able to deliver us. Let us then utterly flee from all the works of lawlessness, lest the works of lawlessness overcome us, and let us hate the error of this present time, that we may be loved in that which is to come. ²Let us give no freedom to our souls to have power to walk with sinners and wicked men, lest we be made like to them. ³The final stumbling block is at hand of which it was written, as Enoch says, "For to this end the LORD has cut short the times and the days, that His beloved should hurry and come to His inheritance." ⁴And the prophet also says thus: "Ten kingdoms will reign on the earth and there will rise up after them a little king, who will subdue three of the kings under one." ⁵Daniel says likewise concerning the same: "And I beheld the fourth beast, wicked, and powerful, and fiercer than all the beasts of the sea, and that ten horns sprang from it, and out of them a little outgrown horn, and that it subdued under one three of the great horns." ⁶You should then understand. And this I also ask you, as being one of yourselves, and especially as loving you all above my own life; take heed to yourselves now, and do not be made like to some, heaping up your sins and saying that the covenant is both theirs and ours. ⁷It is ours, but in this way they finally lost it when Moses had just received it, for the Writing says: "And Moses was in the mount fasting forty days and forty nights, and he received the covenant from the LORD, tablets of stone written with the finger of the hand of the LORD." ⁸But they turned to idols and lost it. For thus says the LORD: "Moses, Moses, go down quickly, for your people, whom you brought forth out of the land of Egypt, have broken the Law." And Moses understood and cast the two tablets out of his hands, and their covenant was broken, in order that the covenant of Jesus the Beloved should be sealed in our hearts in hope of His faith. ⁹(And though I wish to write much, I hasten to write in devotion to you, not as a teacher, but as it suits one who loves to leave out nothing of that which we have.) For what reason let us pay heed in the last days, for the whole time of our life and faith will profit us nothing, unless we resist, as suits the sons of God in this present evil time, against the offenses which are to come, that the dark one may have no opportunity of entry. ¹⁰Let us flee from all vanity; let us utterly hate the deeds of the path of wickedness. Do not, by retiring apart, live alone as if you were already made righteous, but come together and seek out the common good. ¹¹For the Writing says: "Woe to them who are prudent for themselves and understanding in their own sight." Let us be spiritual; let us be a temple consecrated to God; so far as lies in us, let us "exercise ourselves in the fear" of God, and let us strive to keep His commands in order that we may rejoice in His ordinances. ¹²The LORD will judge the world "without respect of persons." Each will receive according to his deeds. If he is good his righteousness will lead him; if he is evil the reward of iniquity is before him. ¹³Let us never rest as though we were called, and slumber in our sins, lest the wicked ruler gain power over us and thrust us out from the Kingdom of the LORD. ¹⁴And consider this also, my brothers, when you see that after such great signs and wonders were worked in Israel, they were even then finally abandoned; let us take heed lest, as it was written, we are found [as] "many called but few chosen."

CHAPTER 5

¹For it was for this reason that the LORD endured to deliver up His flesh to corruption, that we should be sanctified by the forgiveness of sin, that is, by His sprinkled blood. ²For the Writing concerning Him relates partly to Israel, partly to us, and it speaks thus: "He was wounded for our transgressions and bruised for our iniquities, by His stripes we were healed. He was brought as a sheep to the slaughter, and as a lamb silent before its shearer." ³Therefore we should give great thanks to the LORD that He has given us knowledge of the past, and wisdom for the present, and that we are not without understanding for the future. ⁴And the Writing says, "Not unjustly are the nets spread out for the birds." This means that a man deserves to perish who has a knowledge of the way of righteousness, but turns aside into the way of darkness. ⁵Moreover, my brothers, if the LORD endured to suffer for our life, though He is the Lord of all the world, to whom God said before the foundation of the world, "Let us make man in our image and likeness," how, then, did He endure to suffer at the hand of man? ⁶Learn [this]: the prophets who received grace from Him prophesied of Him, and He, in order that He "might destroy death," and show forth the resurrection from the dead, because He must necessarily be made "manifest in the flesh," endured ⁷in order to fulfill the promise made to the fathers, and Himself prepare for Himself the new people and show while He was on earth that He Himself will raise the dead and judge the risen. ⁸Furthermore, while teaching Israel and doing such great signs and wonders, He preached to them and loved them greatly; ⁹but when He chose out His own apostles who were to preach His good news, He chose those

who were iniquitous above all sin to show that "He came not to call the righteous but sinners": then He manifested Himself as God's Son. ¹⁰For if He had not come in the flesh, men could in no way have been saved by beholding Him, seeing that they do not have the power when they look at the sun to gaze straight at its rays, though it is destined to perish, and is the work of His hands. ¹¹So then the Son of God came in the flesh for this reason, that He might complete the total of the sins of those who persecuted His prophets to death. ¹²For this reason He endured. For God says of the discipline of His flesh that it is from them: "When they will strike their Shepherd, then the sheep of the flock will be destroyed." ¹³And He was willing to suffer thus, for it was necessary that He should suffer on a tree, for the prophet says of Him, "Spare My soul from the sword," and "Nail My flesh, for the synagogues of the wicked have risen against Me." ¹⁴And again he says: "Behold, I have given My back to scourges, and My cheeks to strokes, and I have set My face as a solid rock."

CHAPTER 6

¹Therefore, when He made the command what does He say? "Who is he that comes into court with Me? Let him oppose Me; or, who is he that seeks justice against Me? Let him draw near to the LORD's servant. ²Woe to you, for you will all wax old as a garment and the moth will eat you up." And again, the prophet says that He was placed as a strong stone for crushing, "Behold, I will place for the foundations of Zion a precious stone, chosen out, a chief cornerstone, honorable." ³Then what does he say? "And he that hopes on it will live continuously." Is then our hope on a stone? God forbid. But he means that the LORD placed His flesh in strength. For he says, "And he placed me as a solid rock." ⁴And again the prophet says, "The stone which the builders rejected, this has become the head of the corner," and again he says, "This is the great and wonderful day which the LORD made." ⁵I write to you more simply that you may understand: I am devoted to your love. ⁶What then does the prophet say again? "The synagogue of the sinners surrounded Me, they surrounded Me as bees around the honeycomb," and "They cast lots for My clothing." ⁷Therefore, since He was destined to be manifest and to suffer in the flesh, His passion was foretold. For the prophet says concerning Israel, "Woe to their soul, for they have plotted an evil plot against themselves, saying, Let us bind the Just One, for He is unprofitable to us." ⁸What does the other prophet, Moses, say to them? "Behold, thus says the LORD God, enter into the good land which the LORD swore that He would give to Abraham, Isaac, and Jacob, and inherit it, a land flowing with milk and honey." ⁹But learn what knowledge says. Hope, it says, on that Jesus who will be manifested to you in the flesh. For man is earth which suffers, for the creation of Adam was from the face of the earth. ¹⁰What then is the meaning of "into the good land, a land flowing with milk and honey"? Blessed is our Lord, brothers, who has placed in us wisdom and understanding of His secrets. For the prophet speaks an allegory of the LORD: "Who will understand except he who is wise, and learned, and a lover of his Lord?" ¹¹Since then He made us new by the forgiveness of sins, He made us another type, that we should have the soul of children, as though He were creating us afresh. ¹²For it is concerning us that the Writing says that He says to the Son, "Let Us make man after Our image and likeness, and let them rule the beasts of the earth, and the birds of the heavens, and the fishes of the sea." And the LORD said, when He saw our fair creation, "Increase, and multiply, and fill the earth"; these things were spoken to the Son. ¹³Again I will show you how He speaks to us. In the last days He made a second creation; and the LORD says, "See, I make the last things as the first." To this, then, the prophet referred when he proclaimed, "Enter into a land flowing with milk and honey, and rule over it." ¹⁴See then, we have been created afresh, as He says again in another prophet, "See," says the LORD, "I will take out from them" (that is those whom the Spirit of the LORD foresaw) "the hearts of stone and I will put in hearts of flesh." Because He Himself was going to be manifest in the flesh and to dwell among us. ¹⁵For, my brothers, the habitation of our hearts is a shrine holy to the LORD. ¹⁶For the LORD says again, "And with which will I appear before the LORD My God and be glorified?" He says, "I will confess to You in the assembly of My brothers, and will sing to You in the midst of the assembly of holy ones." We then are they whom He brought into the good land. ¹⁷What then is the milk and the honey? Because a child is first nourished with honey, and afterward with milk. Thus, therefore we also, being nourished on the faith of the promise and by the word, will live and possess the earth. ¹⁸And we have said above, "And let them increase, and multiply, and rule over the fishes." Who then is it who is now able to rule over beasts, or fishes, or the birds of the heavens? For we should understand that to rule implies authority, so that one may give commands and have domination. ¹⁹If, then, this does not happen at present, He has told us the time when it will—when we ourselves have also been made perfect as heirs of the covenant of the LORD.

CHAPTER 7

¹Therefore understand, children of gladness, that the good Lord made all things plain beforehand to us, that we should know Him to whom we should give thanks and praise for everything. ²If then the Son of God, though He was the LORD and was "destined to judge the living and the dead," suffered in order that His wounding might make us alive, let us believe that the Son of God could not suffer except for our sakes. ³But moreover, when He was crucified "He was given vinegar and gall to drink." Listen how the priests of the temple foretold this. The command was written: "Whoever does not keep the fast will die the death," and the LORD commanded this because He Himself was going to offer the vessel of the Spirit as a sacrifice for our sins, in order that the type established in Isaac, who was offered on the altar, might be fulfilled. ⁴What then does He say in the Prophet[s]? "And let them eat of the goat which is offered in the fast for all their sins." Attend carefully, "and let all the priests alone eat the entrails unwashed with vinegar." ⁵Why? Because you are going "to give to Me gall and vinegar to drink" when I am on the point of offering My flesh for My new people, therefore you alone will eat, while the people fast and mourn in sackcloth and ashes, to show that He must suffer for them. ⁶Note what was commanded: "Take two goats, attractive and alike, and offer them, and let the priest take the one as a burnt-offering for sins." ⁷But what are they to do with the other? "The other," He says, "is accursed." Notice how the type of Jesus is manifested: ⁸"And you all spit on it, and goad it, and bind the scarlet wool around its head, and so let it be cast into the desert." And when it is so done, he who takes the goat into the wilderness drives it forth, and takes away the wool, and puts it on a shrub which is called Rachel, of which we are accustomed to eat the shoots when we find them in the country: thus of Rachel alone is the fruit sweet. ⁹What does this mean? Listen: "the first goat is for the altar, but the other is accursed," and note that the one that is accursed is crowned, because then "they will see Him" on that day with the long scarlet robe "down to the feet" on His body, and they will say, "Is this not He whom we once crucified, and rejected, and pierced, and spat on? Of a truth it was He who then said that He was the Son of God." ¹⁰But how is He like to the goat? For this reason: "the goats will be alike, beautiful, and a pair," in order that when they see Him come at that time they may be astonished at the likeness of the goat. See then the type of Jesus destined to suffer. ¹¹But why is it that they put the wool in the middle of the thorns? It is a type of Jesus placed in the Assembly, because whoever wishes to take away the scarlet wool must suffer much because the thorns are terrible, and he can gain it only through pain. Thus He says, "those who will see Me, and attain to My Kingdom, must lay hold of Me through pain and suffering."

CHAPTER 8

¹But what do you think that it means, that the commandment has been given to Israel that the men in whom sin is complete offer a heifer, and slay it, and burn it, and that boys then take the ashes, and put them into vessels, and bind scarlet wool on sticks (see again the type of the Cross and the scarlet wool) and hyssop, and that the boys all sprinkle the people thus, one by one, in order that they all be purified from their sins? ²Observe how plainly He speaks to you: the calf is Jesus; the sinful men offering it are those who brought Him to be slain. Then there are no longer men, no longer the glory of sinners. ³The boys who sprinkle are they who preached to us the forgiveness of sins, and the purification of the heart, to

whom He gave the power of the good news to preach, and there are twelve as a testimony to the tribes, because there are twelve tribes of Israel. ⁴But why are there three boys who sprinkle? As a testimony to Abraham, Isaac, and Jacob, for these are great before God. ⁵And why was the wool put on the wood? Because the Kingdom of Jesus is on the wood, and because those who hope on Him will live forever. ⁶But why are the wool and the hyssop together? Because in His Kingdom there will be evil and foul days, in which we will be saved, for he also who has pain in his flesh is cured by the foulness of the hyssop. ⁷And for this reason, the things which were thus done are plain to us, but obscure to them, because they did not hear the voice of [the] LORD.

CHAPTER 9

¹For He speaks again concerning the ears, how He circumcised our hearts; for the LORD says in the Prophet[s]: "In the hearing of the ear they obey Me." And again He says, "They who are far off will hear clearly, they will know the things that I have done," and "Circumcise your hearts, says the LORD." ²And again He says, "Hear, O Israel, thus says the LORD your God," and again the Spirit of the LORD prophesies, "Who is he that will live continuously? Let him hear the voice of My servant." ³And again He says, "Hear, O Heaven, and give ear, O earth, for the LORD has spoken these things for a testimony." And again He says, "Hear the word of the LORD, you rulers of this people." And again He says, "Hear, O children, a voice of one crying in the wilderness." So then, He circumcised our hearing in order that we should hear the word and believe. ⁴But moreover, the circumcision in which they trusted has been abolished. For He declared that circumcision was not of the flesh, but they erred because an evil messenger was misleading them. ⁵He says to them, "Thus says the LORD your God" (here I find a command), "Do not sow among thorns; be circumcised to your Lord." And what does He say? "Circumcise the hardness of your heart, and do not stiffen your neck." Receive it again: "Behold, says the LORD, all the heathen are uncircumcised in the foreskin, but this people is uncircumcised in heart." ⁶But will you say [that] the people has surely received circumcision as a seal? Yes, but every Syrian, and Arab, and all priests of the idols have been circumcised; are then these also within their covenant? Indeed, even the Egyptians belong to the circumcision. ⁷Learn fully then, children of love, concerning all things, for Abraham, who first circumcised, did so looking forward in the Spirit to Jesus, and had received the doctrines of three letters. ⁸For it says, "And Abraham circumcised from his household eighteen men and three hundred." What then was the knowledge that was given to him? Notice that he first mentions the eighteen, and after a pause the three hundred. The eighteen is I [(ten)] and H [(eight)]—you have Jesus— and because the Cross was destined to have grace in the T, he says, "and three hundred." So he indicates Jesus in the two letters and the Cross in the other. ⁹He knows this who placed the gift of His teaching in our hearts. No one has heard a more excellent lesson from me, but I know that you are worthy.

CHAPTER 10

¹Now, in that Moses said, "You will not eat swine, nor an eagle, nor a hawk, nor a crow, nor any fish which has no scales on itself," he included three doctrines in his understanding. ²Moreover, He says to them in Deuteronomy, "And I will make a covenant of My ordinances with this people." So then the ordinance of God is not abstinence from eating, but Moses spoke in the Spirit. ³He mentioned the swine for this reason: you will not consort; He means with men who are like swine; that is to say, when they have plenty, they forget the LORD, but when they are in want, they recognize the LORD, just as the swine when it eats does not know its master, but when it is hungry it cries out, and after receiving food is again silent. ⁴"Neither will you eat the eagle, nor the hawk, nor the kite, nor the crow." You will not, He means, join yourself or make yourself like to such men, as do not know how to gain their food by their labor and sweat, but plunder other people's property in their iniquity, and lay wait for it, though they seem to walk in innocence, and look around to see whom they may plunder in their covetousness, just as these birds alone provide no food for themselves, but sit idle, and seek how they may devour the flesh of others, and become pernicious in their iniquity. ⁵"You will not eat," He says, "the eel, nor the mollusk, nor the cuttlefish." You will not, he means, consort with or become like such men who are utterly ungodly and who are already condemned to death, just as these fish alone are accursed, and float in the deep water, not swimming like the others, but living on the ground at the bottom of the sea. ⁶Moreover, "You will not," he says, "eat the hare." Why? "You will not be a corrupter of boys, nor like such." Because the hare multiplies, year by year, the places of its conception; for as many years as it lives so many it has. ⁷Moreover, "You will not eat the hyena." He means, "You will not be an adulterer, nor a corrupter, nor be like to them that are such." Why? Because that animal annually changes its sex, and is at one time male, and at another female. ⁸Moreover, he has rightly detested the weasel. For he means, "You will not be like to those whom we hear of as committing wickedness with the mouth, on account of their uncleanness; nor will you be joined to those impure women who commit iniquity with the mouth." For this animal conceives by the mouth." ⁹Moses received three doctrines concerning food and thus spoke of them in the Spirit; but they received them as really referring to food, owing to the lust of their flesh. ¹⁰But David received knowledge concerning the same three doctrines, and says: "Blessed is the man who has not gone in the counsel of the ungodly" as the fishes go in darkness in the deep waters, "and has not stood in the way of sinners" like those who seem to fear the LORD, but sin like the swine, "and has not sat in the seat of the scorners" like the birds who sit and wait for their prey. Grasp fully the doctrines concerning food. ¹¹Moses says again, "Eat of every animal that is cloven-hoofed and ruminant." What does he mean? That he who receives food knows Him who feeds him, and rests on Him and seems to rejoice. He spoke well with regard to the command. What then does He mean? Consort with those who fear the LORD, with those who meditate in their heart on the meaning of the word which they have received, with those who speak of and observe the ordinances of the LORD, with those who know that meditation is a work of gladness, and who ruminate on the word of the LORD. But what does "the cloven-hoofed" mean? That the righteous [man] both walks in this world and looks forward to the holy age. See how well Moses legislated. ¹²But how was it possible for them to understand or comprehend these things? But we, having a righteous understanding of them, announce the commands as the LORD wished. For this reason, He circumcised our hearing and our hearts that we should comprehend these things.

CHAPTER 11

¹But let us inquire if the LORD took pains to foretell the water of immersion and the Cross. Concerning the water, it has been written with regard to Israel that they will not receive the immersion that brings the forgiveness of sins, but will build for themselves. ²For the prophet says, "Be astonished O Heaven, and let the earth tremble the more at this, that this people has committed two evils: they have deserted Me, the spring of life, and they have dug for themselves a cistern of death. ³Is My holy mountain, Sinai, a desert rock? For you will be as the fledgling birds, fluttering about when they are taken away from the nest." ⁴And again the prophet says, "I will go before you and I will make mountains level, and I will break gates of brass, and I will shatter bars of iron, and I will give you treasures of darkness, secret, invisible, that they may know that I am the LORD God." ⁵And, "You will dwell in a lofty cave of a strong rock." And, "His water is sure; you will see the King in His glory, and your soul will meditate on the fear of the LORD." ⁶And again He says in another prophet, "And he who does these things will be as the tree, which is planted at the partings of the waters, which will give its fruit in its season, and its leaf will not fade, and all things, whatever he does, will prosper. ⁷It is not so with the wicked, it is not so; but they are even as the chaff which the wind drives away from the face of the earth. Therefore, the wicked will not rise up in judgment, nor sinners in the counsel of the righteous, for the LORD knows the way of the righteous, and the way of the ungodly will perish." ⁸Mark how He described the water and the Cross together. For He means this: blessed are those who hoped on the Cross and descended into the water. For He speaks of their reward "in his season"; "at that time," He says, "I will repay." But now when He says,

"Their leaves will not fade," He means that every word which will come forth from your mouth in faith and love, will be for conversion and hope for many. ⁹And again another prophet says, "And the land of Jacob was praised above every land." He means to say that He is glorifying the vessel of His Spirit. ¹⁰What does He say next? "And there was a river flowing on the right hand, and beautiful trees grew out of it, and whoever will eat of them will live continuously." ¹¹He means to say that we go down into the water full of sins and foulness, and we come up bearing the fruit of fear in our hearts, and having hope on Jesus in the Spirit. "And whoever will eat of them will live continuously." He means that whoever hears and believes these things spoken will live continuously.

CHAPTER 12

¹Similarly, again, He describes the Cross in another prophet, who says, "And when will all these things be accomplished? Says the LORD. When the tree will fall and rise, and when blood will flow from the tree." Here again you have a reference to the Cross, and to Him who should be crucified. ²And He says again to Moses, when Israel was assailed by strangers, and in order to remind those who were assailed that they were delivered to death by reason of their sins—the Spirit speaks to the heart of Moses to make a representation of the Cross, and of Him who should suffer, because, he says, unless they put their trust in Him, they will suffer war continuously. Therefore, Moses placed one shield on another in the midst of the fight, and standing there, raised above them all, kept stretching out his hands, and so Israel again began to be victorious: then, whenever he let them drop, they began to perish. ³Why? That they may know that they cannot be saved if they do not hope on Him. ⁴And again He says in another prophet, "I stretched out My hands the whole day to a disobedient people and one that refuses My righteous way." ⁵Again Moses makes a representation of Jesus, showing that He must suffer, and will Himself give life, though they will believe that He has been put to death, by the sign given when Israel was falling (for the LORD made every serpent bite them, and they were perishing, for the fall took place in Eve through the serpent), in order to convince them that they will be delivered over to the affliction of death because of their transgression. ⁶Moreover, though Moses commanded them: "You will have neither graven nor molten image for your God," yet he makes one himself to show a type of Jesus. Therefore, Moses makes a graven serpent, and places it in honor and calls the people by a proclamation. ⁷So they came together and implored Moses that he would offer prayer on their behalf for their healing. But Moses said to them, "Whenever one of you," he said, "is bitten, let him come to the serpent that is placed on the tree, and let him hope, in faith that it, though dead, is able to give life, and he will immediately be saved." And they did so. In this also you have again the glory of Jesus, for all things are in Him and for Him. ⁸Again, why does Moses say to Jesus [(Joshua)], the son of Nun, when he gives him, prophet as he is, this name, that the whole people should listen to him alone? Because the Father was revealing everything concerning His Son Jesus. ⁹Moses therefore says to Jesus, the son of Nun, after giving him this name, when he sent him to spy out the land, "Take a scroll in your hands and write what the LORD says, that the Son of God will tear up the whole house of Amalek by the roots in the last day." ¹⁰See again Jesus, not as Son of Man, but as Son of God, but manifested in a type in the flesh. Therefore, since they are going to say that the Christ is David's son, David himself prophesies, fearing and understanding the error of the sinners, "The LORD said to my Lord, Sit on My right hand until I make Your enemies Your footstool." ¹¹And again Isaiah speaks thus, "The LORD said to Christ my Lord, whose right hand I held, that the nations should obey before Him, and I will shatter the strength of kings." See how "David calls Him Lord" and does not say "son."

CHAPTER 13

¹Now let us see whether this people or the former people is the heir, and whether the covenant is for us or for them. ²Hear then what the Writing says concerning the people: "And Isaac prayed concerning his wife Rebecca, because she was barren, and she conceived. Then Rebecca went forth to inquire of the LORD and the LORD said to her: Two nations are in your womb, and two peoples in your belly, and one people will overcome a people, and the greater will serve the less." ³You should understand who Isaac is and who Rebecca is, and of whom He has shown that this people is greater than that people. ⁴And in another prophecy, Jacob speaks more plainly to his son Joseph, saying, "Behold, the LORD has not deprived me of your presence; bring me your sons, that I may bless them." ⁵And he brought Ephraim and Manasseh, and wished that Manasseh should be blessed, because he was the elder; for Joseph brought him to the right hand of his father Jacob. But Jacob saw in the Spirit a type of the people of the future. And what does He say? "And Jacob crossed his hands and placed his right hand on the head of Ephraim, the second and younger son, and blessed him; and Joseph said to Jacob, Change your right hand to the head of Manasseh, for he is my firstborn son. And Jacob said to Joseph, I know it, my child, I know it; but the greater will serve the less, and this one will indeed be blessed." ⁶See who it is of whom He ordained that this people is the first and heir of the covenant. ⁷If then, besides this, He also remembered it in the case of Abraham, we reach the perfection of our knowledge. What then does He say to Abraham, when he alone was faithful, and it was counted to him for righteousness? "Behold, I have made you, Abraham, the father of the nations who believe in God in uncircumcision."

CHAPTER 14

¹So it is. But let us see whether the covenant which He swore to the fathers to give to the people—whether He has given it. He has given it. But they were not worthy to receive it because of their sins. ²For the prophet says, "And Moses was fasting on Mount Sinai, to receive the covenant of the LORD for the people, forty days and forty nights. And Moses received from the LORD the two tablets, written by the finger of the hand of the LORD in the Spirit"; and Moses took them, and carried them down to give them to the people. ³And the LORD said to Moses, "Moses, Moses, go down quickly, for your people whom you brought out of the land of Egypt have broken the Law. And Moses perceived that they had again made themselves molten images, and he cast them out of his hands, and the tablets of the covenant of the LORD were broken." ⁴Moses received it, but they were not worthy. But learn how we received it. Moses received it when he was a servant, but the LORD Himself gave it to us, as the people of the inheritance, by suffering for our sakes. ⁵And it was made manifest both that the tale of their sins should be completed in their sins, and that we through Jesus, the Lord who inherits the covenant, should receive it, for He was prepared for this purpose, that when He appeared He might redeem our hearts from darkness, which were already paid over to death, and given over to the iniquity of error, and by His word might make a covenant with us. ⁶For it is written that the Father prescribes on Him that He should redeem us from darkness and prepare a holy people for Himself. ⁷The prophet therefore says, "I, the LORD your God, called you in righteousness, and I will hold your hands, and I will give you strength, and I have given you for a covenant of the people, for a light to the nations, to open the eyes of the blind, and to bring forth from their chains those that are bound and those that sit in darkness out of the prison-house." We know then from where we have been redeemed. ⁸Again the prophet says, "Behold, I have made you a light for the nations, to be for salvation to the ends of the earth, thus says the LORD, the God who redeemed you." ⁹And again the prophet says, "The Spirit of the LORD is on Me, because He anointed Me to preach the good news of grace to the humble; He sent Me to heal the brokenhearted, to proclaim delivery to the captives, and sight to the blind, to announce a year acceptable to the LORD, and a day of repayment, to comfort all who mourn."

CHAPTER 15

¹Furthermore, it was written concerning the Sabbath in the ten words which He spoke on Mount Sinai face to face with Moses: "Sanctify also the Sabbath of the LORD with pure hands and a pure heart." ²And in another place He says, "If My sons keep the Sabbath, then I will bestow My mercy on them." ³He speaks of the Sabbath at the beginning of the Creation, "And God made in six days the works of His hands and on the seventh day He made an end, and

rested in it and sanctified it." ⁴Notice, children, what is the meaning of "He made an end in six days"? He means this: that the LORD will make an end of everything in six thousand years, for a day with Him means one thousand years. And He Himself is my witness when He says, "Behold, the Day of the LORD will be as one thousand years." So then, children, in six days (that is, in six thousand years) everything will be completed. ⁵"And He rested on the seventh day." This means, when His Son comes, He will destroy the time of the wicked one, and will judge the godless, and will change the sun, and the moon, and the stars, and then He will truly rest on the seventh day. ⁶Furthermore He says, "You will sanctify it with clean hands and a pure heart." If, then, anyone has at present the power to keep holy the day which God made holy, by being pure in heart, we are altogether deceived. ⁷See that we will indeed keep it holy at that time, when we enjoy true rest, when we will be able to do so because we have been made righteous ourselves and have received the promise, when there is no more sin, but all things have been made new by the LORD: then we will be able to keep it holy because we ourselves have first been made holy. ⁸Furthermore He says to them, "Your new moons and the Sabbaths I cannot bear with." Do you see what He means? "The present Sabbaths are not acceptable to Me, but that which I have made, in which I will give rest to all things and make the beginning of an eighth day, that is the beginning of another world." ⁹For what reason we also celebrate with gladness the eighth day in which Jesus also rose from the dead, and was made manifest, and ascended into Heaven.

CHAPTER 16

¹I will also speak with you concerning the temple and show how the wretched men erred by putting their hope on the building, and not on the God who made them, and is the true house of God. ²For they consecrated him in the temple almost like the heathen. But learn how the LORD speaks, in bringing it to nothing, "Who has measured the Heaven with a span, or the earth with his outstretched hand? Have not I? Says the LORD. Heaven is My throne, and the earth is My footstool, what house will you build for Me, or what is the place of My rest?" You know that their hope was vain. ³Furthermore, He says again, "Behold, they who destroyed this temple will themselves build it." ⁴That is happening now. For owing to the war, it was destroyed by the enemy; at present, even the servants of the enemy will build it up again. ⁵Again, it was made manifest that the city, and the temple, and the people of Israel were to be delivered up. For the Writing says: "And it will come to pass in the last days that the LORD will deliver the sheep of His pasture, and the sheepfold, and their tower to destruction." And it took place according to what the LORD said. ⁶But let us inquire if a temple of God exists. Yes, it exists, where He Himself said that He makes and perfects it. For it is written: "And it will come to pass when the week is ended that a temple of God will be built gloriously in the Name of the LORD." ⁷I find then that a temple exists. Learn then how it will be built in the Name of the LORD. Before we believed in God the habitation of our heart was corrupt and weak, like a temple really built with hands, because it was full of idolatry, and was the house of demons through doing things which were contrary to God. ⁸"But it will be built in the Name of the LORD." Now give heed, in order that the temple of the LORD may be built gloriously. Learn in what way. When we received the forgiveness of sins, and put our hope on the Name, we became new, being created again from the beginning; for what reason God truly dwells in us, in the habitation which we are. ⁹How? His word of faith, the calling of His promise, the wisdom of the ordinances, the commands of the teaching, Himself prophesying in us, Himself dwelling in us, by opening the door of the temple (that is the mouth) to us, giving conversion to us, and thus He leads us, who have been enslaved to death into the incorruptible temple. ¹⁰For he who desires to be saved does not look at the man, but at Him who dwells and speaks in him, and is amazed at Him, for he has never either heard him speak such words with his mouth, nor has he himself ever desired to hear them. This is a spiritual temple being built for the LORD.

CHAPTER 17

¹So far as possibility and simplicity allow an explanation to be given to you, my soul hopes that none of the things which are necessary for salvation have been omitted, according to my desire. ²For if I write to you concerning things present or things to come, you will not understand because they are hid in allegories. This then suffices.

CHAPTER 18

¹Now let us pass on to another lesson and teaching. There are two ways of teaching and power: one of light and one of darkness. And there is a great difference between the two ways. For light-bringing messengers of God are set over the one, but messengers of Satan over the other. ²And the one is Lord from age and to age, and the other is the ruler of the present time of iniquity.

CHAPTER 19

¹The way of light is this: if any man desires to journey to the appointed place, let him be zealous in his works. Therefore the knowledge given to us of this kind that we may walk in it is as follows: ²you will love your Maker, you will fear your Creator, you will glorify Him who redeemed you from death, you will be simple in heart, and rich in [the] Spirit; you will not join yourself to those who walk in the way of death, you will hate all that is not pleasing to God, you will hate all hypocrisy; you will not desert the commands of the LORD. ³You will not exalt yourself, but will be humble-minded in all things; you will not take glory to yourself. You will form no evil plan against your neighbor, you will not let your soul be divisive. ⁴You will not commit fornication, you will not commit adultery, you will not commit sodomy. You will not let the word of God depart from you among the impurity of any men. You will not respect persons in the reproving of transgression. You will be meek, you will be quiet, you will fear the words which you have heard. You will not bear malice against your brother. ⁵You will not be in two minds whether it will be or not. "You will not take the Name of the LORD in vain." You will love your neighbor more than your own life. You will not procure abortion, you will not commit infanticide. You will not withhold your hand from your son or from your daughter, but will teach them the fear of God from their youth up. ⁶You will not covet your neighbor's goods, you will not be greedy. You will not be joined in soul with the haughty, but will converse with humble and righteous men. You will receive the trials that befall you as good, knowing that nothing happens without God. ⁷You will not be double-minded or talkative. You will obey your masters as a type of God in modesty and fear; you will not command in bitterness your slave or handmaid who hope on the same God, lest they cease to fear the God who is over you both; for He did not come to call men with respect of persons, but those whom the Spirit prepared. ⁸You will share all things with your neighbor and will not say that they are your own property; for if you are sharers in that which is incorruptible, how much more in that which is corruptible? You will not be forward to speak, for the mouth is a snare of death. So far as you can, you will keep your soul pure. ⁹Do not be one who stretches out the hands to take and shuts them when it comes to giving. You will love "as the apple of your eye" all who speak the word of the LORD to you. ¹⁰You will remember the Day of Judgment day and night, and you will seek each day the society of the holy ones, either laboring by speech, and going out to exhort, and striving to save souls by the word, or working with your hands for the ransom of your sins. ¹¹You will not hesitate to give, and when you give you will not grumble, but you will know who the good paymaster of the reward is. "You will keep the precepts" which you have received, "adding nothing and taking nothing away." You will utterly hate evil. "You will give righteous judgment." ¹²You will not cause quarrels, but will bring together and reconcile those that strive. You will confess your sins. You will not go yourself to prayer with an evil conscience. This is the way of light.

CHAPTER 20

¹But the way of the dark one is crooked and full of cursing, for it is the way of continuous death with punishment, and in it are the things that destroy their soul: idolatry, divisiveness, arrogance of power, hypocrisy, double-heartedness, adultery, murder, robbery, pride, transgression, fraud, malice, self-sufficiency, enchantments, magic, covetousness, the lack of the fear of God; ²persecutors of the good, haters of the truth,

EPISTLE OF BARNABAS

lovers of lies, not knowing the reward of righteousness, who "do not cleave to the good," nor to righteous judgment, who do not attend to the cause of the widow and orphan, spending wakeful nights not in the fear of God, but in the pursuit of vice, from whom meekness and patience are far and distant, "loving vanity, seeking rewards," without pity for the poor, not working for him who is oppressed with toil, prone to evil speaking, without knowledge of their Maker, murderers of children, corrupters of God's creation, turning away the needy, oppressing the afflicted, advocates of the rich, unjust judges of the poor, altogether sinful.

CHAPTER 21

[1] It is therefore good that he who has learned the ordinances of the LORD—as many as have been written—should walk in them. For he who does these things will be glorified in the Kingdom of God, and he who chooses the others will perish with his works. For this reason, there is a resurrection; for this reason, there is a repayment. [2] I implore those who are in high positions: if you will receive any counsel of my goodwill, have among yourselves those to whom you may do good; do not fail. [3] The day is at hand when all things will perish with the evil one; "The LORD and His reward is at hand." [4] I implore you again and again: be good lawgivers to each other, remain faithful counselors of each other, remove all hypocrisy from yourselves. [5] Now may God, who is the Lord over all the world, give you wisdom, understanding, prudence, knowledge of His ordinances, patience. [6] And be taught of God, seeking out what the LORD requires from you, and see that you be found faithful in the Day of Judgment. [7] If there is any memory of good, meditate on these things and remember me, that my desire and my watchfulness may find some good end. I implore you, asking it of your favor. [8] While the fair vessel is with you, do not fail in any of them, but seek these things diligently, and fulfill every command; for these things are worthy. [9] For what reason I was the more zealous to write to you of my ability, to give you gladness. May you gain salvation, children of love and peace. The Lord of glory and of all grace be with your spirit.

EPISTLE TO THE LAODICEANS

A purported epistle from the apostle Paul to the Laodiceans is mentioned in Colossians 4:16, although the original document has never been found. Some scholars argue that the apostle was not referencing a lost epistle, but rather a generally-circulated one, such as his epistle to the Ephesians. In any case, the pseudepigraphic letter here presented is from a 4th-century Latin text, which possibly stemmed from a Greek original. This Latin text is first witnessed in Codex Fuldensis, and it was included in Latin Bibles in the medieval period.

CHAPTER 1

[1] Paul, an apostle not of men nor by man, but by Jesus Christ, to the brothers that are at Laodicea: [2] Grace to you and peace from God the Father and the Lord Jesus Christ. [3] I give thanks to Christ in all my prayers, because you continue in Him and persevere in His works, looking for the promise at the Day of Judgment. [4] Neither do the vain murmurings of some upset you, which creep in, that they may turn you away from the truth of the good news which is preached by me. [5] And now God will cause that they that are of me will continue ministering to the increase of the truth of the good news, and accomplishing goodness, and the work of salvation, even continuous life. [6] And now my bonds are seen by all men, which I suffer in Christ, wherein I rejoice and am glad. [7] And to me, this is for everlasting salvation, which also is brought about by your prayers, and the ministry of the Holy Spirit, whether by life or by death. [8] For truly to me, life is in Christ, and to die is joy. [9] And He will also work His mercy in you, so that you may have the same love, and be of one mind. [10] Therefore, dearly beloved, as you have heard in my presence, so hold fast and work in the fear of God, and it will be to you for continuous life. [11] For it is God who works in you. [12] And do without a second thought whatever you do. [13] And [as] for the rest, dearly beloved, rejoice in Christ, and beware of them that are soiled with greed. [14] Let all your petitions be made openly before God and be steadfast in the mind of Christ. [15] And whatever things are sound, and true, and sober, and just, and to be loved: do [them]. [16] And what you have heard and received, hold fast in your heart. [17] And peace will be to you. [18] The saints salute you. [19] The grace of the Lord Jesus be with your spirit. [20] And cause this letter to be read to them of Colossae, and the letter of the Colossians to be read to you.

CORRESPONDENCE OF PAUL AND SENECA

The Correspondence of Paul and Seneca, otherwise known as the Letters of Paul and Seneca, is a collection of 14 letters purporting to be between Paul the Apostle and Seneca the Younger. They were allegedly authored from AD 58–64 during the reign of Roman Emperor Nero, but were most likely written in the middle of the fourth century. Until the Renaissance, the epistles were seen as genuine, but scholars began to critically examine them in the 15th century, and today they are widely regarded as forgeries.

FIRST EPISTLE OF SENECA TO PAUL

Seneca to Paul: Greetings. I believe, Paul, that you have been informed of the talk which I had yesterday with my Lucilius regarding the hidden writings and other things; for certain partakers in your teaching were with me. For we had retired to the gardens of Sallust, where, because of us, those whom I speak of, going in another direction, saw and joined us. We certainly wished for your presence, and I would have you know it. We were greatly refreshed by the reading of your book, by which I mean some of the many letters which you have addressed to some city or capital of a province, and which ingrain the moral life with admirable precepts. These thoughts, I take it, are not uttered by you but through you, but surely sometimes both by you and through you: for such is the greatness of them and they are imbued with such nobility, that I think whole ages of men could hardly suffice for the instilling and perfecting of them. I desire your good health, brother.

FIRST EPISTLE OF PAUL TO SENECA

Paul to Seneca: Greetings. I received your letter yesterday with delight and should have been able to answer it at once, had I had by me the youth I meant to send to you. For you know when, and by whom, and at what moment, and to whom things should be given and entrusted. Therefore, I plead that you will not think [of] yourself [as] neglected, when I am respecting the dignity of your person. Now in that you somewhere write that you are pleased with my letter, I think myself happy [to be] in the high regard of such a man: for you would not say it—you, a critic, a sophist, the teacher of a great prince, and indeed of all—unless you spoke truth. I trust you may long remain in [good] health.

CORRESPONDENCE OF PAUL AND SENECA

SECOND EPISTLE OF SENECA TO PAUL

Seneca to Paul: Greetings. I have arranged some writings in a volume and given them their proper divisions: I am also resolved to read them to Caesar, if only fortune be kind, that he may bring a fresh ear to the hearing. Perhaps you, too, will be there. If not, I will at another time set a day for you, so that we may look over the work together: indeed, I could not produce this writing to him, without first conferring with you, if only that could be done without risk, so that you may know that you are not being neglected. Farewell, dearest Paul.

SECOND EPISTLE OF PAUL TO SENECA

Paul to Annaeus Seneca: Greetings. Whenever I hear your letters read, I think of you as present and imagine nothing else but that you are always with us. As soon, then, as you begin to come, we will see each other at close quarters. I desire your good health.

THIRD EPISTLE OF SENECA TO PAUL

Seneca to Paul: Greetings. We are greatly pained by your retirement. What is it? What reasons keep you away? If it be the anger of the lady [[Poppaea]], because you have left the old rite and sect, and have converted others, there will be a possibility of pleading with her, so that she may consider it as done on due reflection and not lightly.

THIRD EPISTLE OF PAUL TO SENECA

Paul to Seneca and Lucilius: Greetings. Of the subject on which you have written I must not speak with pen and ink, of which the former marks out and draws somewhat, and the latter shows it clearly, especially as I know that among you—that is, in your homes and in you—there are those who understand me. Honor is to be paid to all, and so much the more because men grasp at opportunities of being offended. If we are patient with them, we will certainly overcome them at every point, provided they are men who can be sorry for their actions. Farewell.

FOURTH EPISTLE OF SENECA TO PAUL

Annaeus Seneca to Paul and Theophilus: Greetings. I profess myself satisfied with the reading of your letters which you sent to the Galatians, Corinthians, and Achaeans; and may we so live together as you show yourself to be inspired with the divine frenzy. For it is the Holy Spirit who is in you and high above you which expresses these exalted and lovely thoughts. I would therefore have you [be] careful regarding other points, so that the polish of the style may not be lacking to the majesty of the thought. And, brother, not to conceal anything from you, and have it on my conscience, I confess to you that the Augustus was moved by your views. When I read to him the beginning of the power that is in you, his words were these: that he could wonder that a man not regularly educated could think thus. I replied that the gods often speak by the mouths of the simple, not of those who try deceitfully to show what they can do by their learning. And when I cited him the example of Vatienus the rustic, to whom two men appeared in the territory of Reate, who afterwards were recognized as Castor and Pollux, he appeared fully convinced. Farewell.

FOURTH EPISTLE OF PAUL TO SENECA

Paul to Seneca: Greetings. Although I am aware that Caesar, even if he sometimes lapses, is a lover of our wonders, you will permit yourself to be not wounded, but admonished. For I think that you took a very serious step in bringing to his notice a matter foreign to his religion and training. For since he is a worshiper of the gods of the nations, I do not see why you thought you would wish him to know this matter, unless I am to think that you did it out of excessive attachment to me. I beg you not to do so in future. For you must be careful not to offend the empress in your love for me: yet her anger will not hurt us if it lasts, nor do good if it does not. As a queen, she will not be angry; as a woman, she will be offended. Farewell.

FIFTH EPISTLE OF SENECA TO PAUL

Seneca to Paul: Greetings. I know that you are not so much disturbed on your own account by my letter to you on the showing of your letters to Caesar, as by the nature of things, which so calls away the minds of men from all right learning and conduct—so that I am not surprised, for I have learned this for certain by many examples. Let us then act differently, and if in the past anything has been done carelessly, you will forgive it. I have sent you a book regarding [the] elegance of expression. Farewell, dearest Paul.

FIFTH EPISTLE OF PAUL TO SENECA

To Seneca, [from] Paul: Greetings. Whenever I write to you and do not place my name after yours, I do an egregious thing and one unbefitting my persuasion [(faith)]. For I ought, as I have often declared, to be all things to all men, and to observe in your person that which the Roman law has granted to the honor of the senate, and choose the last place in writing a letter, not striving to do as I please in a confused and disgraceful way. Farewell, most devoted of masters. GIVEN ON THE FIFTH OF THE KALENDS OF JULY; NERO THE FOURTH TIME, AND MESSALA, CONSULS.

SIXTH EPISTLE OF SENECA TO PAUL

Seneca to Paul: Greetings. Hail, my dearest Paul. If you, so great a man, so beloved in all ways, be—I say not joined—but intimately associated with me and my name, it will indeed be well with your Seneca. Since, then, you are the pinnacle and highest peak of all people, would you not have me glad that I am so near you as to be counted a second self of yours? Do not, then, think that you are unworthy to be named first on the heading of letters, lest you make me think you are testing me rather than playing with me—especially as you know yourself to be a Roman citizen. For the rank that is mine, I wish it were yours, and yours I wish were mine. Farewell, dearest Paul. GIVEN ON THE 10TH OF THE KALENDS OF APRIL; APRONIANUS AND CAPITO, CONSULS.

SEVENTH EPISTLE OF SENECA TO PAUL

Seneca to Paul: Greetings. Hail, my dearest Paul. Do you not think that I am in sadness and grief, that your innocent people are so often condemned to suffer? And next, that all the people think you [are] so callous and so prone to crime, that you are supposed to be the authors of every misfortune in the city? Yet let us endure it patiently and content ourselves with what fortune brings, until supreme happiness puts an end to our troubles. Former ages had to bear the Macedonian, Philip's son, and, after Darius, Dionysius, and our own times endured Gaius Caesar: to all of whom their will was law. The source of the many fires which Rome suffers is plain. But if humble men could speak out what the reason is, and if it were possible to speak without risk in this dark time, all would be plain to all. Christians and Jews are commonly executed as contrivers of the fire. Whoever the criminal is, whose pleasure is that of a butcher, and who veils himself with a lie, he is reserved for his due season: and as the best of men is sacrificed, the one for the many, so he, vowed to death for all, will be burned with fire. One hundred and thirty-two houses and four blocks have been burned in six days; the seventh brought a pause. I pray you may be well, brother. GIVEN THE FIFTH OF THE KALENDS OF APRIL; FRUGI AND BASSUS, CONSULS.

EIGHTH EPISTLE OF SENECA TO PAUL

Seneca to Paul: Greetings. Much in every part of your works is enclosed in allegory and enigma, and therefore the great force that is given you of matter and talent should be beautified—I do not say with elegance of words, but with a certain care. Nor should you fear what I remember you have often said; that many who affect such things subvert the thought and emasculate the strength of the matter. But I wish you would yield to me and humor the genius of Latin, and give beauty to your noble words, so that the great gift that has been granted [to] you may be worthily treated by you. Farewell. GIVEN ON THE DAY BEFORE THE NONES OF JUNE; LEO AND SABINUS, CONSULS.

SIXTH EPISTLE OF PAUL TO SENECA

Paul to Seneca: Greetings. To your meditations have been revealed those things which the Godhead has granted to few. With confidence, therefore, I sow in a field already fertile a most prolific seed—not such matter as is liable to corruption, but the abiding Word, an emanation from God who grows and abides forever. This wisdom of yours has attained [so], and you will see that it is unfailing—so as to judge that the laws of heathens and Israelites are to be shunned. You may become a new author, by showing forth with the graces of rhetoric the unblameable wisdom of Jesus Christ, which you, having well nearly attained it, will instill into the temporal monarch, his servants, and his intimate friends; yet the persuading of them will be a hard and difficult task, for many of them will hardly incline to your admonitions. Yet the word of God, if it be instilled into them, will be a vital gain, producing a new man, incorrupt, and an everlasting soul that will hasten from here to God. Farewell, Seneca, most dear to me. GIVEN ON THE KALENDS OF AUGUST; LEO AND SABINUS, CONSULS.

TRADITIONS OF MATTHIAS

Likely written in the 2nd century, the Traditions of Matthias, possibly identical with a lost Gospel of Matthias, is a text ascribed to the apostle Matthias. It is almost entirely missing except for these brief snippets. It was quoted by Clement of Alexandria.

FRAGMENT 1
¹Wonder at what is present.

FRAGMENT 2
¹… to fight with the flesh and misuse it, without yielding to it through undisciplined pleasure, so to increase the soul through faith and knowledge …

FRAGMENT 3
¹We must fight against the flesh and treat it with contempt, never yielding to it for pleasure's sake, but must nourish the soul through faith and knowledge.

FRAGMENT 4
¹If the neighbor of a chosen one sins, the chosen one sins. ²For if he had conducted himself as the word dictates, the neighbor would have been in awe of his life so that he would not have sinned.

EPISTLE OF LENTULUS

The Epistle of Lentulus is a letter of unknown, likely pseudepigraphic origin, purporting to be written by a Roman official in Judea to the Roman Senate. The author describes the appearance of Christ in great detail. It was translated into Latin from a Greek original in the 13th or 14th century, but the antiquity of the Greek is much debated. Scholar Friedrich Münter thought the description might have first been penned in the very late 3rd century.

CHAPTER 1
¹Lentulus, the Governor of the Jerusalemites, to the Roman Senate and People: Greetings. ²There has appeared in our times, and there still lives, a Man of great power [(virtue)] called Jesus Christ. ³The people call Him the Prophet of Truth; His disciples, Son of God. ⁴He raises the dead and heals infirmities. ⁵He is a Man of average size; He has a venerable aspect, and His beholders can both fear and love Him. ⁶His hair is of the color of the ripe hazelnut, straight down to the ears; but below the ears, wavy and curled, with a bluish and bright reflection, flowing over His shoulders. ⁷It is parted in two on the top of the head, after the pattern of the Nazarenes. ⁸His brow is smooth and very cheerful, with a face without wrinkle or spot, embellished by a slightly reddish complexion. ⁹His nose and mouth are faultless. ¹⁰His beard is abundant, of the color of His hair, not long, but divided at the chin. ¹¹His aspect is simple and mature, His eyes are blue-gray and bright. ¹²He is terrible in His rebukes, sweet and amiable in His admonitions, cheerful without loss of seriousness. ¹³He was never known to laugh, but often to weep. ¹⁴His stature is straight, His hands and arms beautiful to behold. ¹⁵His conversation is serious, infrequent, and modest. ¹⁶He is the most beautiful among the children of men. Farewell.

1 CLEMENT

Though the author of the First Epistle of Clement is anonymous, it was thought to have been written by Clement of Rome (possibly consecrated by the Apostle Peter) and is highly regarded, at one point even considered for inclusion in the New Testament canon. Internal evidence places the date of composition around the end of the 1st century, although some even suspect before AD 70.

THE ASSEMBLY OF GOD WHICH SOJOURNS AT ROME, TO THE ASSEMBLY OF GOD WHICH SOJOURNS AT CORINTH, TO THEM THAT ARE CALLED AND SANCTIFIED IN THE WILL OF GOD THROUGH OUR LORD JESUS CHRIST: GRACE AND PEACE BE MULTIPLIED TO YOU FROM ALMIGHTY GOD THROUGH JESUS CHRIST.

CHAPTER 1
¹On account of the sudden and repeated calamities and misfortunes, brothers, that have come on us, we suppose that we have the more slowly given heed to the things that are disputed among you, beloved, and to the foul and unholy sedition, alien and foreign to the chosen ones of God, which a few headstrong and self-willed persons have kindled to such a degree of madness, that your venerable and famous name, worthy to be loved of all men, is greatly blasphemed. ²For who that has tarried among you has not approved your most virtuous and firm faith, has not admired your sober and seemly piety in Christ, has not proclaimed your splendid disposition of

hospitality, has not deemed blessed your perfect and unerring knowledge? ³For you did all things without respect of persons, and walked in the laws of God, submitting yourselves to them that have the rule over you, and giving the due honor to the elders that are among you. Young men you prescribed to think such things as are sober and grave. Women you exhorted to perform all things in a blameless, and honorable, and pure conscience, loving dutifully their own husbands; and you taught them to manage the affairs of their houses with gravity, keeping in the rule of obedience, being temperate in all things.

CHAPTER 2

¹And you were all humble, boasting of nothing, submitting yourselves rather than subjecting others, more gladly giving than receiving, content with the provision that God had given you; and attending diligently to His words, you received them into your very hearts, and His sufferings were before your eyes. ²Thus a deep and rich peace was given to all, and an insatiable longing for doing good, and a plentiful outpouring of the Holy Spirit was on all of you. ³And you, being filled with a holy desire, with excellent zeal and pious confidence, stretched out your arms to Almighty God, imploring Him to be merciful to you, if you had in anything unwillingly done wrong. ⁴You contended day and night for the whole brotherhood, that in His mercy and good pleasure the number of His chosen ones might be saved. ⁵You were simple and sincere, without malice toward one another: ⁶all sedition and all schism were abominable to you. You grieved over the transgressions of your neighbor, judging his shortcomings your own. ⁷You did not relent of any well-doing, "being ready to every good work"; ⁸and being adorned with a very virtuous and holy habit of life, you did all things in His fear. The commands and ordinances of the LORD were written on the breadth of your heart.

CHAPTER 3

¹All honor and enlargement were given to you, and then was fulfilled that which is written: "The beloved ate and drank, and was enlarged and grew fat and kicked." ²From this came emulation and envy, strife and sedition, persecution and disorder, war and captivity. ³Thus the mean men were lifted up against the honorable; those of no regard against those of good regard; the foolish against the wise; the young against the elder. ⁴Through this, justice and peace are far off, because each of you leaves off the fear of God and is dimsighted in his faith, nor walks in the laws of His commands, nor behaves as becomes a citizen of Christ; but each walks according to his own evil lusts, having taken up unjust and unholy envy, by which death also entered into the world.

CHAPTER 4

¹For it is thus written: "And it came to pass after certain days, that Cain brought of the fruits of the ground a sacrifice to God, and Abel brought also of the firstlings of the sheep and of their fat. ²And God had respect to Abel and to his gifts; but to Cain and his gifts he had no regard. ³And Cain was grieved greatly, and his countenance fell. ⁴And God said to Cain, Why are you very sorrowful, and why has your countenance fallen? If you have rightly offered, but have not rightly divided, have you not sinned? ⁵Hold your peace; your gift returns to you, and you will be master over it. ⁶And Cain said to Abel, Let us pass over into the field. And it came to pass while they were in the field, Cain rose up against his brother Abel and slew him." ⁷You see, brothers, jealousy and envy worked the slaughter of a brother. ⁸Through envy our father Jacob fled from the face of his brother Esau. ⁹Envy caused Joseph to be persecuted to death, and to enter into bondage. ¹⁰Envy compelled Moses to flee from the face of Pharaoh, king of Egypt, because he heard his countryman say, "Who made you a judge or a decider over us? Will you kill me, as you did the Egyptian yesterday?" ¹¹Through envy Aaron and Miriam pitched their tents outside the camp. ¹²Envy brought down Dathan and Abiram alive to the grave, because they contended against Moses, the servant of God. ¹³Through envy David suffered jealousy not only of foreigners, but was also persecuted by Saul, king of Israel.

CHAPTER 5

¹But let us pass from ancient examples and come to those who have in the times nearest to us wrestled for the faith. ²Let us take the noble examples of our own generation. Through jealousy and envy the greatest and most just pillars of the Assembly were persecuted, and even came to death. ³Let us place before our eyes the good apostles. ⁴Peter, through unjust envy, endured not one or two but many labors, and at last, having delivered his testimony, departed to the place of glory due to him. ⁵Through envy Paul, too, showed by example the prize that is given to patience: ⁶seven times was he cast into chains; he was banished; he was stoned; having become a herald, both in the east and in the west, he obtained the noble renown due to his faith; ⁷and having preached righteousness to the whole world, and having come to the extremity of the west, and having borne witness before rulers, he departed at length out of the world, and went to the holy place, having become the greatest example of patience.

CHAPTER 6

¹To these men, who walked in holiness, there was gathered a great multitude of the chosen ones, who, having suffered, through envy, many insults and tortures, became a most excellent example among us. ²Through envy women were persecuted, even the Danaides and Dircae, who, after enduring dreadful and unholy insults, attained to the sure course of the faith; and they who were weak in body received a noble reward. ³Envy has estranged the minds of wives from their husbands, and changed the saying of our father Adam: "This is now bone of my bone, and flesh of my flesh." ⁴Envy and strife have overthrown mighty cities and rooted out great nations.

CHAPTER 7

¹These things we urge you, beloved, not only by way of admonition to you, but as also putting ourselves in mind. For we are in the same arena, and the same contest is imposed on us. ²For what reason, let us leave empty and vain thoughts, and come to the glorious and venerable rule of our holy calling. ³Let us consider what is good, and pleasing, and acceptable before Him who made us. ⁴Let us look steadfastly to the blood of Christ and see how precious in the sight of God His blood is, which, having been poured out for our salvation, brought to the whole world the grace of conversion. ⁵Let us go back to all generations and learn that in every generation God has granted a place for conversion to such as wished to return to Him. ⁶Noah preached conversion, and as many as listened to him were saved. ⁷Jonah prophesied destruction to the Ninevites, and they, converting from their sins, appeased God through prayer, and, though alien from God, obtained salvation.

CHAPTER 8

¹The ministers of the grace of God spoke by the Holy Spirit concerning conversion; ²and the Lord of all, Himself spoke concerning conversion with an oath: "As I live, says the LORD, I do not desire the death of a sinner, as I desire his conversion"; adding to that an excellent saying: ³"Convert, O house of Israel, from your iniquity: Say to the sons of My people, Though your sins reach from earth to Heaven, and though they are redder than scarlet, and blacker than sackcloth, and you turn to Me with your whole heart and say, My Father, I will listen to you as to a holy people." ⁴And in another place He speaks in this way: "Wash, and be clean; take away the wickedness from your souls from before My eyes; cease from your evil deeds, learn to do well; seek judgment; deliver him that is oppressed; give judgment for the orphan, and justify the widow; and come and let us reason together," He says, "and though your sins be as purple, I will make them white as snow; and though they are as scarlet, I will make them white as wool. And if you are willing and listen to Me, you will eat the good things of the earth; but if you are not willing, and do not listen, the sword will devour you; for the mouth of the LORD has said this." ⁵Desiring, therefore, that all His beloved ones should partake of conversion, He has confirmed it by His almighty will.

CHAPTER 9

¹For what reason, let us submit ourselves to His excellent and glorious will, and, becoming suppliants of His mercy and goodness, let us fall before Him and go ourselves to His mercies, having laid aside the vain toil, and the

strife, and the jealousy that leads to death. ²Let us look steadfastly at those that have ministered with perfectness to His excellent glory. ³Let us take as example Enoch, who, having been found just by reason of obedience, was translated, and his death was not found. ⁴Noah, having been found faithful, preached, by his ministry, regeneration to the world, and by him God preserved the animals that entered with one consent into the Ark.

CHAPTER 10

¹Abraham, who was called the friend, was found faithful, inasmuch as he became obedient to the words of God. ²This man, by obedience, went out from his land and his countrymen, and the house of his father, that, by leaving a scant land, and weak countrymen, and a small house, he might inherit the promises of God. ³For He says to him, "Go out from your land, and your countrymen, and the house of your father, to the land that I will show you, and I will make you a great nation, and bless you, and magnify your name, and you will be blessed; and I will bless them that bless you, and curse them that curse you, and in you all the tribes of the earth will be blessed." ⁴And again, when he separated from Lot, God said to him, "Lift up your eyes, and look from the place where you are now to the north and to the south, and to the east and to the sea; for all the land which you see, I will give it to you and to your seed for all time, ⁵and I will make your seed as the dust of the earth: if any man can number the dust of the earth, your seed will also be numbered." ⁶And again He says, "God brought forth Abraham, and said to him: Look up to Heaven and number the stars, if you are able to number them, so will your seed be. And Abraham believed God, and it was counted to him for righteousness." ⁷Through faith and hospitality a son was given to him in old age, and through obedience he offered him a sacrifice to God on one of the mountains that he showed him.

CHAPTER 11

¹By hospitality and goodness Lot was saved out of Sodom when the whole region around was judged with fire and brimstone; the LORD making it manifest that He does not leave them that hope on Him, but appoints to punishment and torment them that turn in another way. ²For his wife, who went out together with him, being of another mind, and not being in concord with him, was on that account placed as a sign, so that she became a pillar of salt even to this day; that it might be known to all that the double-minded, and they who doubt concerning the power of God, are for a judgment and a sign to all generations.

CHAPTER 12

¹Through faith and hospitality the harlot Rahab was saved; ²for when spies were sent to Jericho by Jesus [(Joshua)], the son of Nun, the king of the land knew that they had come to spy out his country, and sent out men to apprehend them that they might be taken and put to death. ³But the hospitable Rahab having received them, hid them in an upper story under the stalks of flax. ⁴Therefore, when the men from the king came on her, and said, "There came to you men who are spies of this land of ours; bring them out, for the king so commands it"; she answered, "The two men whom you are seeking entered in to me, but they departed quickly and are on their way"; but she did not show the men to them. ⁵And she said to the men, "I know for certain that the LORD your God has given over this city to you; for the fear and trembling of you has fallen on them that inhabit it. Therefore, when it has happened to you to take it, save me and the house of my father." ⁶And they say to her, "So will it be, even as you have spoken to us. Therefore, when you have perceived that we are coming, you will gather together all your household under your roof, and they will be saved; but as many as will be found outside the house will be destroyed." ⁷And they proceeded further to give her a sign, that she should hang scarlet from her house, making it manifest beforehand that through the blood of the LORD there will be redemption to all who believe and hope on God. ⁸Behold, beloved, how there was not only faith, but prophecy in the woman.

CHAPTER 13

¹Let us therefore, brothers, be humble, laying aside all boasting and pride, and folly and wrath, and let us do that which is written; for the Holy Spirit says, "Do not let the wise boast in his wisdom, nor the strong in his strength, nor the rich in his riches; but let him that boasts make his boast in the LORD, even by seeking Him and doing judgment and justice." Let us especially remember the words of our Lord Jesus Christ which He spoke when teaching gentleness and long-suffering, for He spoke thus: ²"Show mercy, that you may obtain mercy; forgive, that it may be forgiven to you; as you do, so will it be done to you; as you give, so will it be given to you; as you judge, so will you be judged; as you are kindly affectioned, so will kindness be showed to you; with whatsoever measure you measure, with the same will it be measured to you." ³With this command and with these exhortations let us strengthen ourselves, that we may walk obedient to His holy words with all humility. For the Holy Writing says, ⁴"On whom will I have respect but on him that is meek and quiet, and that trembles at My words?"

CHAPTER 14

¹It is therefore appropriate and right, men and brothers, that we should be obedient to God rather than follow them that in pride and disorderliness are leaders of detestable sedition. ²For we will incur no slight harm, but rather a great danger, if we rashly give ourselves up to the wills of men who launch out into strife and sedition so as to estrange us from that which is good. ³Let us, therefore, show kindness toward them according to the mercy and sweetness of Him that made us. ⁴For it is written: "The men of kindness will inherit the land. The innocent will be left on it; but they that are lawless will be destroyed out of it." ⁵And again it says, "I saw the unrighteous man exalted on high and lifted up like the cedars of Lebanon. And I passed by, and behold, he was not; I sought his place and did not find it. Keep innocence, and regard righteousness; for there is a remnant that remains to the man of peace."

CHAPTER 15

¹Let us therefore cleave to them who live in peace and godliness, not to them who hypocritically profess to desire peace. ²For He says in a certain place, "This people honors Me with their lips, but their heart is far from Me." ³And again, "They blessed with their mouth, but they cursed with their heart. ⁴And again it says, "They loved Him with their mouth, and with their tongue they lied against Him. For their heart was not right with Him, nor were they faithful in His covenant. ⁵Let the crafty lips be put to silence, and may the LORD destroy all the deceitful lips, even the haughty tongue, they who said, Let us magnify our tongue, our lips are our own; who is master over us?" ⁶"On account of the misery of the poor, and on account of the groaning of the needy, I will now arise, says the LORD; I will set him in safety, I will deal confidently with him."

CHAPTER 16

¹For Christ belongs to them that are humble, not to them that exalt themselves over His flock. ²Our Lord Jesus Christ, who is the scepter of the majesty of God, did not come in the arrogance of boasting and pride, though He was able to do so; but in humility, even as the Holy Spirit spoke concerning Him. ³For it says, "LORD, who has believed our report, and to whom has the arm of the LORD been revealed? Like a child we have delivered our message before Him; He is as a root in a thirsty land. There is no form nor glory in Him, and we beheld Him, and He had neither form nor comeliness, but His form was despised, lacking comeliness, beyond the form of the sons of men. He was a man stricken and in toil, knowing how to bear infirmity, for His face was turned away; it was dishonored and held in no reputation. ⁴He bears our sins and suffers pain on our account, and we esteemed Him as one in toil, stricken, and afflicted. ⁵He was wounded for our sins, and for our transgressions He suffered infirmity; the discipline of our peace was on Him, and by His stripes we were healed. ⁶All we, like sheep, have gone astray, everyone has erred in his own way, ⁷and the LORD has given Him up for our sins; and He, through affliction, does not open His mouth. He was led like a sheep to the slaughter, and as a lamb before its shearers is silent, so He does not open His mouth. ⁸In His humiliation His judgment was taken away, and who will declare His generation? For His life is taken from the earth; ⁹for the iniquity of My people He has come to death. ¹⁰And I will give the wicked in return for His burial, and the rich for His death, for He did not sin,

neither was guile found in His mouth: and the LORD wills to purify from Him [with] stripes. ¹¹If You make an offering for sin Your soul will prolong its days. ¹²And the LORD wills to take away from the travail of His soul, to show Him light and to form Him by knowledge, to justify the righteous man who serves many well; and He will bear their sins Himself. ¹³For what reason He will receive the inheritance of many, and will divide the spoils of the strong, because His soul was delivered up to death, and He was numbered among the transgressors, ¹⁴and He bore the sins of many, and was given up for their sins." ¹⁵And again He says, "I am a worm and no man—a reproach of men and despised of the people; ¹⁶all they who saw Me mocked Me, they spoke with their lips, they shook the head; He hoped in God, let Him deliver Him, let Him save Him, because He desires Him." ¹⁷See, beloved, what is the example that has been given to us; for if the LORD so humbled Himself, what will we do who have, through His mercy, come under the yoke of His grace?

CHAPTER 17

¹Let us also be imitators of them who went around in goatskins and sheepskins, preaching the coming of Christ; we mean Elijah, and Elisha, and Ezekiel the prophets, and beside them those who have obtained a good report. ²Abraham obtained an exceedingly good report, and was called the friend of God, and says, looking steadfastly to the glory of God in humility, "I am but earth and ashes." ³And, moreover, concerning Job, it is thus written: "Job was a just man and blameless, truthful, one that feared God and abstained from all evil." ⁴But he himself, accusing himself, says, "No one is pure from pollution, though his life is but for one day." ⁵Moses was called faithful in all his house, and by his ministry God judged His people Israel by stripes and punishment. But he, though he was greatly glorified, did not speak haughtily, but said, when the oracle was given to him out of the bush, "Who am I that You send me? I am weak of voice and slow of tongue." ⁶And again he says, "I am but as the smoke from a pot."

CHAPTER 18

¹But what will we say of David, who obtained a good report; to whom God said, "I have found a man after My own heart, David, the son of Jesse; I have anointed him with My continuous mercy. ²But he himself says to God, "Have mercy on me, O God, according to Your great mercy, according to the multitude of Your compassion do away with my iniquity; ³wash me thoroughly from my iniquity, and cleanse me from my sin. For I know my iniquity, and my sin is ever before me. ⁴Against You only have I sinned, and done this evil in Your sight, that You might be justified in Your words, and overcome when You are judged. ⁵Behold, I was fashioned in wickedness, and in sin my mother conceived me. ⁶Behold, You have loved truth; You have shown me the secret and hidden things of Your wisdom. ⁷You will sprinkle me with hyssop, and I will be clean. You will wash me, and I will be whiter than snow. ⁸You will make me to hear of joy and gladness; the bones that have been humiliated will rejoice. ⁹Turn away Your face from my sins and blot out all my misdeeds. ¹⁰Create in me a new heart, O LORD, and renew a right spirit within me. ¹¹Do not cast me away from Your presence, and do not take Your Holy Spirit from me. ¹²Give me the joy of Your salvation again, and establish me with Your guiding Spirit. ¹³I will teach sinners Your ways; the ungodly will be converted to You. ¹⁴Deliver me from blood-guiltiness, O God, You God of my salvation; ¹⁵my tongue will rejoice in Your righteousness. O LORD, You will open my mouth, and my lips will show forth Your praise. ¹⁶For if You had desired sacrifice, I would have given it; in whole burnt-offerings You will not delight. ¹⁷The sacrifice of God is a broken spirit; a broken and a contrite heart God will not despise."

CHAPTER 19

¹The humility of men so many in number and so great, and who have obtained such a good report, and their subjection through obedience, has made not only us but the generations before us better, namely, those who in fear and truth have received His oracles. ²Since, therefore, we have become the partakers in many great and glorious actions, let us finally return to that goal of peace that was given us from the beginning; let us look steadfastly to the Father and Creator of the whole world, and let us cleave to the glorious and excellent gifts and benefits of His peace. ³Let us behold Him in spirit and look with the eyes of the soul to His long-suffering will. Let us consider how gentle He is toward all His creation.

CHAPTER 20

¹The heavens, being put in motion by His appointment, are subject to Him in peace; ²night and day they accomplish the course ordered by Him, in nothing hindering one another. ³The sun, and the moon, and the dances of the stars according to His appointment, in harmony and without any violation of order, roll on the courses appointed to them. ⁴The fruitful earth brings forth in due season, according to His will, abundant nourishment for men and beasts; doubting nothing, nor changing in anything from the things that are decreed by Him. ⁵The unsearchable things of the abyss, and the secret ordinances of the lower parts of the earth, are held together by the same command. ⁶The hollow of the vast sea, gathered together by His hand into its reservoirs, does not transgress the bounds placed around it; but even as He has appointed to it, so it does; ⁷for He said, "You will come thus far, and your waves will be broken within you." ⁸The ocean, impassable to men, and the worlds that are beyond it, are governed by the same commands of their Master. ⁹The seasons of spring and summer, autumn and winter, in peace succeed one another. ¹⁰The fixed stations of the winds, each in their due time, perform their services without offense. The ever-flowing fountains, made for enjoyment and health, offer their breasts without fail to sustain the lives of men. Even the smallest of animals come together in peace and harmony. ¹¹All these things the great Maker and Master of all things has appointed to be in peace and harmony, doing good to all things, but more especially to us, who have fled for refuge to His mercies, through our Lord Jesus Christ, ¹²to whom be glory and majesty forever and ever. Amen.

CHAPTER 21

¹Beware, beloved, lest His many blessings come to be a condemnation to all of us, unless, walking worthily of Him, we do what is honorable and well pleasing before Him with oneness of mind. ²For He says in a certain place, "The Spirit of the LORD is a candle, searching out the secret places of the heart." ³Let us see how near He is at hand, and how none of our thoughts and reasonings escape Him. ⁴It is right, therefore, that we should not desert from His will. ⁵Let us offend against men who are foolish, and senseless, and puffed up in the pride of their own speech, rather than against God. ⁶Let us have respect to our Lord Jesus Christ, whose blood was given for us. Let us revere them that are over us. Let us honor our elders. Let us instruct the young in the discipline of the fear of God. Let us direct our wives to that which is good; ⁷let them show forth the lovely habit of chastity and exhibit the pure disposition of meekness. Let them make manifest by their conversation the government of their tongues; let them show love, not according to partiality, but equally to all that fear the LORD in holiness. ⁸Let your children be partakers of the discipline of Christ; let them learn how much humility avails before God; what power a pure love has with God; how His fear is honorable and great, preserving all who, with a pure mind, walk in holiness before Him. ⁹For He is a searcher out of thoughts and counsels, His breath is in us, and when He wills He will take it away.

CHAPTER 22

¹The faith which is in Christ assures all these things. For He Himself, through the Holy Spirit, thus calls to us: "Come, you children, listen to Me, I will teach you the fear of the LORD. ²What man is he that wishes for life and would gladly see good days? ³Keep your tongue from evil, and your lips that they speak no guile. ⁴Turn away from evil and do good; ⁵seek peace and pursue it. ⁶The eyes of the LORD are over the just, and His ears are open to their prayer. But the face of the LORD is against them that do evil, to destroy their memorial out of the land. ⁷The righteous cried, and the LORD heard him, and delivered him out of all his troubles." ⁸"Many are the afflictions of the sinner, but they that hope in the LORD, mercy will surround them."

CHAPTER 23

¹The Father whose mercies are over all things, who loves to do good, has yearnings of compassion for them that fear Him, and with gentleness and kindness bestows His favor on them that come to Him with a pure mind. ²For what reason let us not be double-minded, nor let our hearts form vain imaginations concerning His excellent and glorious gifts. ³Do not let that Writing be applicable to us which says, "Wretched are the double-minded, even they that doubt in their heart and say, We have heard these things in the time of our fathers; and behold, we have grown old, and none of them has happened to us." ⁴O foolish ones! Compare yourselves to a tree. Take, for example, the vine: first it sheds its leaves, then comes the bud, then the leaf, then the flower, after that the unripe grape, then the ripe grape. See how in a short time the fruit of the tree attains to maturity. ⁵Of a truth, quickly and suddenly will His will be fulfilled; the Writing also bearing witness that He will come quickly, and will not tarry; and the LORD will come suddenly into His temple, even the Holy One, whom you expect.

CHAPTER 24

¹Let us consider, beloved, how the Master shows to us continually the resurrection that is about to be, of which He has made our Lord Jesus Christ the first-fruit, having raised Him from the dead. ²Let us look, beloved, at the resurrection that is always taking place—³day and night show the resurrection to us; the night is lulled to rest, the day arises; the day departs, the night comes on. ⁴Let us consider the fruits, in what way a grain of corn is sown. ⁵The sower goes forth and casts it into the ground, and when the seeds are cast into the ground, they that fell into the ground dry and naked are dissolved; then after their dissolution, the mighty power of the providence of the LORD raises them up, and from one seed many grow up and bring forth fruits.

CHAPTER 25

¹Let us consider the wonderful sign that happens in the region of the east, even about Arabia. ²There is a bird which is called the phoenix. This, being the only one of its kind, lives for five hundred years. And when the time of its death draws near, it makes for itself a nest of frankincense, and myrrh, and the other perfumes, into which, when its time is fulfilled, it enters, and then dies. ³But as its flesh rots, a certain worm is produced, which being nourished by the moisture of the dead animal, puts forth feathers. Then, when it has become strong, it takes the nest wherein are the bones of its ancestor, and bearing them, it flies from the region of Arabia to that of Egypt, to the city which is called Heliopolis; ⁴there, in daytime, in the sight of all, it flies up, and places them on the altar of the sun, and having done so, returns back. ⁵The priests, therefore, look into the registers of the times, and find that it has come at the completion of the five-hundredth year.

CHAPTER 26

¹Will we then think it great and wonderful, if the Maker of all things will make a resurrection of those who, in the confidence of a good faith, have piously seized Him, when even by means of a bird He shows the greatness of His promises? ²For He says in a certain place, "And You will raise me up, and I will give thanks to You"; and again: "I slumbered and slept; I rose up because You are with me. ³And again Job says, "You will raise up this flesh of mine, which has suffered all these things."

CHAPTER 27

¹In this hope, therefore, let our souls be bound to Him who is faithful in His promises and just in His judgments. ²He who has commanded men not to lie, much more will He not lie, for nothing is impossible with God, except to lie. ³Let our faith, therefore, be kindled in Him afresh within us, and let us consider that all things are near to Him. ⁴By the word of His majesty He constituted all things, and by a word He is able to destroy them. ⁵"Who will say to Him, What have You done? Or who will resist the might of His strength?" He will do all things when He wills and as He wills, and none of the things decreed by Him will pass away. ⁶All things are before Him, and nothing has escaped His counsel, ⁷seeing that "the heavens declare the glory of God, and the expanse shows the work of His hands: day to day utters speech, and night to night proclaims knowledge; and there is no speech nor language where their voices are not heard."

CHAPTER 28

¹Therefore, since all things are seen and heard by Him, let us fear Him and abandon the filthy desires for evil deeds, that we may be sheltered by His mercy from the judgments to come. ²For, to where can any of us fly from His mighty hand, and what world will receive any of them that desert from Him? ³For the Writing says in a certain place: "To where will I go, and where will I conceal myself from Your face? If I ascend into Heaven, You are there; if I depart into the uttermost parts of the earth, Your right hand is there; if I will make my bed in the abyss, Your Spirit is there." ⁴To where then will we depart, and where will we fly from Him that embraces all things?

CHAPTER 29

¹Therefore, let us approach Him with holiness of spirit, lifting pure and undefiled hands to Him; loving the kind and compassionate Father who has made us a part of His chosen ones. ²For it is thus written: "When the Most High divided the nations, when He dispersed the sons of Adam, He settled the boundaries of the nations according to the number of the messengers of God. The portion of the LORD was His people Jacob." ³Israel was the measurement of His inheritance. And in another place it says, "Behold, the LORD takes to Himself a nation from the midst of the nations, even as a man takes the first-fruits of his threshingfloor; and there will go forth from that nation the Holy of Holies."

CHAPTER 30

¹Since, therefore, we are a portion of the Holy One, let us do all such things as pertain to holiness, avoiding evil-speaking, foul and impure embraces, drunkenness, disorderliness, abominable desires, detestable adultery, execrable pride; ²"for God," it says, "resists the proud, but gives grace to the humble." ³Let us cleave, therefore, to them to whom grace has been given from God. Let us clothe ourselves with concord, being humble, temperate, keeping ourselves far from all whispering and evil-speaking, justified by our deeds, and not by our words. ⁴For it says, "He who says many things will, in return, hear many things. Does he that is eloquent think himself to be just? ⁵Does he that is born of woman and lives but for a short time think himself to be blessed? Do not be abundant in speech." ⁶Let our praise be in God, and not for ourselves, for God hates the self-praisers. ⁷Let the testimony of right actions be given us from others, even as it was given to our fathers who were just. ⁸Audacity, self-will, and boldness belong to them who are accursed of God; but moderation, humility, and meekness, to them that are blessed of God.

CHAPTER 31

¹Therefore, let us cleave to His blessing, and let us see what the ways of blessing are. Let us consult the records of the things that happened from the beginning. ²On what account was our father Abraham blessed? Was it not that he worked righteousness and truth through faith? ³Isaac, with confidence, knowing the future, willingly became a sacrifice. ⁴Jacob, with humility, flying from his brother, went out from his own land and journeyed to Laban and served as a slave, and there were given to him the twelve tribes of Israel.

CHAPTER 32

¹If anyone will consider these things with sincerity and one by one, he will recognize the magnificence of the gifts that were given by him. ²For from Jacob came the priests and all the Levites that serve the altar of God. From him came our Lord Jesus Christ according to the flesh; from him came the kings, and rulers, and governors of the tribe of Judah; and the remainder of his tribes are of no small glory, since God has promised, "Your seed will be as the stars of the heavens." ³Therefore, all these have been glorified and magnified, not through themselves, or through their works, or through the righteousness that they have done, but through His will. ⁴And we who through His will have been called in Christ Jesus are justified, not by ourselves, or through our wisdom, or understanding, or godliness, or the works that we have done in holiness of heart, but by faith, by which all men from the beginning have been justified

by Almighty God, to whom be glory through the ages of the ages. Amen.

CHAPTER 33

¹What, then, will we do, brothers? Will we cease from well-doing, and abandon charity? May the Master never allow that this should happen to us! But let us rather with diligence and zeal hasten to fulfill every good work. ²For the Maker and Lord of all things rejoices in His works. ³By His supreme power He founded the heavens, and by His incomprehensible understanding He ordered them. He separated the earth from the water that surrounded it, and fixed it on the firm foundation of His own will. The animals which inhabit therein He commanded to be by His ordinance. Having made beforehand the sea and the animals that are therein, He shut them in by His own power. ⁴Man, the most excellent of all animals, infinite in faculty, He moulded with His holy and faultless hands, in the impress of His likeness. ⁵For thus says God: "Let Us make man in Our own image, and after Our own likeness. And God made man. He made them male and female." ⁶Therefore, when He had finished all things, He praised and blessed them, and said, "Be fruitful, and multiply." ⁷Let us see, therefore, how all the just have been adorned with good works. Yes, the LORD Himself rejoiced when He had adorned Himself with His works. ⁸Having, therefore, this example, let us come in without shrinking to His will; let us work with all our strength the work of righteousness.

CHAPTER 34

¹The good workman boldly receives the bread of his labor, but the slothful and remiss does not look his employer in the face. ²It is therefore right that we should be zealous in well-doing, for from Him are all things; ³for He tells us beforehand: "Behold, the LORD comes, and His reward is before His face, to give to everyone according to his work." ⁴He exhorts us, therefore, with this reward in view, to strive with our whole heart not to be slothful or remiss toward every good work. ⁵Let our glorying and our confidence be in Him; let us submit ourselves to His will; let us consider the whole multitude of His messengers, how they stand by and serve His will. ⁶For the Writing says, "Ten thousand times ten thousand stood beside Him, and thousands of thousands served Him; and they cried, HOLY, HOLY, HOLY, LORD of Hosts! All creation is full of His glory." ⁷And let us, being gathered together in harmony and a good conscience, cry earnestly, as it were with one mouth, to Him, that we may become partakers of His great and glorious promises; ⁸for He says, "Eye has not seen, and ear has not heard, neither has there entered into the heart of man, what things He has prepared for them that wait for Him."

CHAPTER 35

¹Behold, beloved, how blessed and wonderful are the gifts of God— ²life in immortality, cheerfulness in righteousness, truth in liberty, faith in confidence, temperance in sanctification; and all these things have already come within our cognizance. ³What therefore are the things that are prepared for them that abide in patience? The Maker and Father of the worlds, the All-Holy One, He knows how many and how beautiful they are. ⁴Let us, therefore, strive to be found in the number of them that await Him, that we may partake of the promised gifts. ⁵And how will this be, beloved? If our mind is established by faith toward God; if we seek out what is pleasant and acceptable in His sight; if we perform such things as harmonize with His blameless will, and follow in the way of truth, casting from us all unrighteousness and lawlessness, covetousness, strife, malice and fraud, whispering and evil-speaking, hatred of God, pride and insolence, vainglory and intractableness. ⁶For they who do these things are hateful to God, and not only they who do them, but also they who have pleasure in them that do them. ⁷For the Writing says: "But to the sinner God has said, Why do you speak of My ordinances, and take My covenant in your mouth? ⁸But you have hated instruction and have cast My words behind you. When you saw a thief you went with him and have cast in your portion with the adulterers; your mouth has abounded with evil, and your tongue has contrived deceit. You sat and spoke against your brother and have slandered the son of your mother. ⁹You have done this, and I kept silence. You thought, O wicked one, that I was like to you; ¹⁰but I will convict you and will set yourself before you. ¹¹Consider this, you who forget God, lest He seize you as a lion, and there is none to save you. ¹²The sacrifice of praise will honor Me; and there is the way by which I will show him the salvation of God."

CHAPTER 36

¹This is the way, beloved, in which we found our salvation—even Jesus Christ, the Chief Priest of our oblations, the champion and defender of our weakness. ²Through Him we look steadfastly to the heights of the heavens; through Him we behold, as in a glass, the immaculate and lofty countenance of God the Father; through Him the eyes of our heart were opened; through Him our foolish and darkened understanding springs up again to His marvelous light; through Him the LORD has willed us to taste of immortal knowledge, "who, being the brightness of His glory, is so far better than the messengers, as He has, by inheritance, obtained a more excellent Name than they." ³For it is thus written: "Who makes His messengers spirits, || His ministers a flame of fire." ⁴But of His Son the LORD has thus said, "You are My Son, today have I begotten You. Ask of Me, and I will give You the heathen for Your inheritance, || And the uttermost parts of the world for Your possession." ⁵And, again, He says to Him: "Sit on My right hand || Until I make Your enemies Your footstool." ⁶Who then are the enemies? Even the wicked, and they who resist the will of God.

CHAPTER 37

¹Let us, therefore, men and brothers, carry on our warfare with all earnestness in His faultless ordinances. ²Let us consider those who fight under our rulers, how orderly, and obediently, and submissively they perform what is commanded them. ³All are not prefects, or commanders of thousands, or commanders of hundreds, or commanders of fifties, or such-like; but each in his own rank performs what has been ordered by the king or the commanders. ⁴The great cannot exist without the small, nor the small without the great. There is a certain mixture in all things, and from there arises their use. ⁵Let us take, for example, our body: the head is nothing without the feet, nor the feet without the head. The smallest members of the body are necessary and useful to the whole body, and all unite and work with harmonious obedience for the preservation of the whole body.

CHAPTER 38

¹Therefore, let our whole body be saved in Christ Jesus, and let each be subject to his neighbor according to the gift which he has received. ²Do not let the strong man despise the weak; and let the weak pay regard to the strong. Let him that is rich minister to him that is poor. Let him that is poor praise God that He has given to him one by whom his want may be supplied. Let the wise show his wisdom, not in words, but in good deeds; let him that is humble not bear witness to himself, but leave another to bear witness to him. Let him that is pure in the flesh not boast of it, knowing that it is another that gives him the power of continence. ³Let us consider, brothers, of what matter we are made, of what sort and who we are that have come into the world, as it were out of the tomb and darkness. He that made and fashioned us has brought us into this world, having prepared beforehand His benefactions, even before we were born. ⁴Therefore, having all these things from Him, we should in all respects give thanks to Him, to whom be glory through the ages of the ages. Amen.

CHAPTER 39

¹The senseless and unwise, the foolish and unruly, make a mockery of us, wishing to exalt themselves in their own imagination. ²For what can a mortal do? Or what strength has he that is born of earth? ³For it is written: "There was no form before my eyes, only I heard a breath and a voice. ⁴For what? Will a mortal be pure before the LORD? Or is a man blameless from his works? Seeing that He puts no trust in His servants, and even beholds iniquity in His messengers; ⁵yes, the Heaven is not pure in His sight. Away, you who dwell in houses of clay, of whom are we also even of the same clay. He has smitten them even as it were a moth, and in a single day they are no more. Because they could not help themselves, they perished: ⁶He blew among them, and they died, because they had no wisdom. ⁷Call, now, and see if there is anyone that will obey you, if

you will behold any of the holy messengers. For anger destroys the fool, and envy puts him to death that is gone out of the way. ⁸I have beheld the foolish casting forth roots, but immediately his habitation was eaten up. ⁹Let his sons be far from safety, let them be mocked at the gates of their inferiors, and there will be none to deliver them. For that which had been prepared for them the just will eat, and they will not be delivered out of their troubles."

CHAPTER 40

¹Therefore, since these things have been made manifest before to us, and since we have looked into the depths of the divine knowledge, we should do everything in order, whatever the LORD has commanded us to do at the appointed seasons, and to perform the offerings and services. ²He has not commanded these to be done at random or in disorder, but at fixed times and seasons. ³But when and by whom He wishes them to be fulfilled He Himself has decided by His supreme will, that all things, being done piously, according to His good pleasure, might be acceptable to His will. ⁴Therefore, they who at the appointed seasons make their offerings are acceptable and blessed; for while following the laws of the Master they do not completely sin. ⁵For to the Chief Priest were assigned special services, and to the priests a special place has been appointed; and on the Levites special duties are imposed. But he that is a layman is bound by the ordinances of laymen.

CHAPTER 41

¹Let each of you, brothers, in his own order, give thanks to God, continuing in a good conscience, not transgressing the fixed rule of his ministry, with all gravity. ²Not in every place, brothers, are sacrifices offered continually, either in answer to prayer, or concerning sin and neglect, but in Jerusalem only; and even there the offering is not made in every place, but before the temple in the court of the altar, after that which is offered has been diligently examined by the chief priest and the appointed ministers. ³They, therefore, who do anything contrary to that which is according to His will have death for their punishment. ⁴You see, brothers, by as much as we have been thought worthy of greater knowledge, by so much the more are we exposed to danger.

CHAPTER 42

¹The apostles received the good news for us from our Lord Jesus Christ; our Lord Jesus Christ received it from God. ²Christ, therefore, was sent out from God, and the apostles from Christ; and both these things were done in good order, according to the will of God. ³They, therefore, having received the promises, having been fully persuaded by the resurrection of our Lord Jesus Christ, and having been confirmed by the word of God, with the full persuasion of the Holy Spirit, went forth preaching the good tidings that the Kingdom of God was at hand. ⁴Preaching, therefore, through the countries and cities, they appointed their first-fruits to be overseers and servants over such as should believe, after they had proved them in the Spirit. ⁵And this they did in no new way, for in truth it had in long past time been written concerning overseers and servants; for the Writing, in a certain place, says in this way: "I will establish their overseers in righteousness, and their servants in faith."

CHAPTER 43

¹And wherein is it wonderful, if they who, in Christ, were entrusted by God with this work appointed the previously mentioned officers? Since even the blessed Moses, the faithful servant in all his house, signified in the sacred scrolls all the things that were commanded to him, whom also the prophets have followed, bearing witness together to the laws which were appointed by him. ²For he, when a strife arose concerning the priesthood, and when the tribes contended which of them should be adorned with that glorious name, commanded the twelve chiefs of the tribes to bring to him rods, each inscribed with the name of a tribe; and when he had taken them, he bound them together, and sealed them with the seals of the heads of the tribes, and laid them up on the table of God, in the Dwelling Place of the testimony. ³And when he had closed the Dwelling Place, he sealed the keys, and likewise the rods, ⁴and said to them, "Men and brothers, of whatever tribe the rod will bud, this has God chosen to be His priest, and to serve Him." ⁵And when morning had come, he called together all Israel, even six hundred thousand men, and showed to the heads of the tribes the seals, and opened the Dwelling Place of the testimony and brought forth the rods, and the rod of Aaron was found not only to have budded, but also bearing fruit. ⁶What do you think, beloved? Did Moses not know beforehand that this was about to happen? Most assuredly he knew it, but, that there might be no disorder in Israel, he did thus that the Name of the true and only God might be glorified, to whom be glory through the ages of the ages. Amen.

CHAPTER 44

¹Our apostles, too, by the instruction of our Lord Jesus Christ, knew that strife would arise concerning the dignity of an overseer; ²and on this account, having received perfect foreknowledge, they appointed the above-mentioned as overseers and servants: and then gave a rule of succession, in order that, when they had fallen asleep, other men, who had been approved, might succeed to their ministry. ³Those who were thus appointed by them, or afterward by other men of good regard, with the consent of the whole Assembly, who have blamelessly ministered to the flock of Christ with humility, quietly, and without illiberality, and who for a long time have obtained a good report from all, these, we think, have been unjustly deposed from the ministry. ⁴For it will be no small sin in us if we depose from the office of overseer those who blamelessly and piously have made the offerings. ⁵Happy are the elders who finished their course before and died in mature age after they had borne fruit; for they do not fear lest anyone should remove them from the place appointed for them. ⁶For we see that you have removed some men of honest conversation from the ministry, which had been blamelessly and honorably performed by them.

CHAPTER 45

¹You are contentious, brothers, and are zealous concerning things that do not pertain to salvation. ²Look diligently into the Writings, which are the true sayings of the Holy Spirit. ³You know how that nothing unjust or corrupt has been written in them; for you will not find in them the just expelled by holy men. ⁴The just were persecuted, but it was by the lawless; they were thrown into prison, but it was by the unholy; they were stoned, but it was by sinners; they were slain, but it was by wicked men, even by those who had taken up an unjust envy against them. ⁵They, therefore, when they suffered all these things, suffered them with a good report. ⁶For what will we say, brothers? Was it by those that feared God that Daniel was cast into the den of lions? ⁷Was it by those who practiced the magnificent and glorious worship of the Most High that Hananiah, Azariah, and Mishael were shut up in the fiery furnace? Let us not suppose that such was the case. Who, then, were the men who did these things? Abominable men and full of all wickedness were inflamed to such a degree of wrath that they cast into tortures those who, with a holy and blameless purpose, served God, not knowing that the Most High is a champion and defender of those who with a pure conscience serve His most excellent Name, to whom be glory through the ages of the ages. Amen. ⁸But they, abiding steadfastly in their confidence, have inherited honor and glory, and have both been exalted and made beautiful by God, in the memory that is made of them through the ages of the ages. Amen.

CHAPTER 46

¹We should also cleave to such examples, brothers. ²For it is written: "Cleave to them that are holy, for they that cleave to them will be made holy." ³And again, in another place it says, "With the guiltless man you will be guiltless, and with the excellent you will be excellent, and with him that is crooked you will be perverse." ⁴Therefore, let us cleave to the guiltless and the just, for they are the chosen ones of God. ⁵Why are there strivings, and anger, and division, and war among you? ⁶Do we not have one God and one Christ? Is the Spirit of grace, which was poured out on us, not one? Is our calling in Christ not one? ⁷Why do we tear apart and split apart the members of Christ, and make sedition against our body, and come to such a degree of madness that we forget we are members of one another? Remember the words of our

Lord Jesus, ⁸for He said, "Woe to that man; it were good for him if he had never been born, rather than that he should cause one of My chosen ones to offend. It were better for him that a millstone were tied around him, and that he were cast into the sea, rather than that he should cause one of My little ones to offend. ⁹This schism of yours has perverted many, [and] has cast many into despondency, many into doubt, [and] all of us into grief, and, as yet, your sedition remains.

CHAPTER 47

¹Take into your hands the letter of the blessed apostle Paul. ²What did he first write to you in the beginning of his good news? ³Of a truth, he warned you spiritually, in a letter, concerning himself, and concerning Cephas and Apollos, because even then there were factions among you; ⁴but the faction of that time brought less sin on you; for you inclined to apostles of good regard, and to a man approved among them. ⁵But now consider who they are that have perverted you and have diminished the glory of your famous brotherly love. ⁶It is disgraceful, brothers, yes, very disgraceful, and unworthy of the conduct which is in Christ, that it should be reported that the most firm and ancient assembly of the Corinthians has, on account of one or two persons, made sedition against its elders. ⁷And this report did not only come to us, but also to the nations, who do not go with us, so that you heap blasphemies on the Name of the LORD through your folly, and in addition cause danger to yourselves.

CHAPTER 48

¹Therefore, let us remove this thing as quickly as possible, and let us fall before the feet of the Master, and implore Him with tears, that He will have mercy and be reconciled to us, and restore us again to the grave and pure conversation of brotherly love. ²For this is a gate of righteousness opened to life, as it is written: "Open to me the gates of righteousness; I will go in to them, and give thanks to the LORD: ³this is the gate of the LORD; the righteous will enter thereby." ⁴Now, since many gates have been opened, the gate of righteousness is that which is in Christ. Happy are all they that enter therein, and who keep their path straight in holiness and righteousness, quietly performing all their duties. ⁵If a man is faithful, if he is mighty to expound knowledge, if he is wise in the interpretation of words, if he is pure in his deeds, ⁶by so much the more should he be humble, and by as much as he seems to be greater, by so much the more should he seek the common advantage of all, and not of himself alone.

CHAPTER 49

¹Let him that has the love which is in Christ keep the commands of Christ. ²Who can describe sufficiently the bond of the love of God? ³Who is sufficient to speak as he should of the excellence of its beauty? ⁴The height to which love leads up is unspeakable. ⁵Love joins us to God; love hides a multitude of sins; love bears all things; is long suffering in all things. In love there is nothing illiberal, nothing haughty. Love has no schism; love does not make sedition; love does all things in harmony; in love all the chosen ones of God have been made perfect. Without love nothing is acceptable to God. ⁶In love, our Master has taken us to Himself. Through the love that He has for us, Jesus Christ our Lord has given His blood for us, by the will of God, His flesh for our flesh, His soul for our soul.

CHAPTER 50

¹You see, brothers, how great and wonderful a thing love is, and how there is no describing its perfection. ²Who is sufficient to be found in it, except those whom God will have deemed worthy? Therefore, let us pray and ask from His mercy that we may live in love, without human partiality, blameless. ³All the generations from Adam, even to this day, have gone by, but they who have been made perfect in love according to the grace of God, inhabit the abode of the pious and will be made manifest in the visitation of the Kingdom of Christ. ⁴For it is written: "Enter into the secret chambers but a little while, until My anger and wrath have passed, and I will remember the good day, and will raise you up from your tombs." ⁵Blessed are we, beloved, if we do the commands of God in the harmony of love, so that through love our sins may be forgiven us. ⁶For it is written: "Blessed are they whose iniquities are forgiven, and whose sins are covered. Blessed is the man to whom the LORD does not impute sin, and in whose mouth there is no guile." ⁷This blessedness comes to them who are chosen by God, through Jesus Christ our Lord, to whom be glory through the ages of the ages. Amen.

CHAPTER 51

¹Therefore, whatever errors we have committed through the assaults of the adversary, let us ask pardon for these; and they who have been leaders of the sedition and division should consider the common ground of our hope. ²For they who have their conversation in fear and love wish that they themselves, rather than their neighbors, should fall into suffering; and would rather that they should undergo condemnation themselves, than that the harmony which has been honorably and justly handed down to us should do so. ³For it is better that a man should make confession concerning his sins, than that he should harden his heart, even as the heart of them was hardened who made sedition against Moses, the servant of God—[they] whose condemnation was manifest; ⁴for they went down alive into Hades, and death swallowed them up. ⁵Pharaoh and his army, and all the leaders of Egypt, their chariots and their riders, through no other cause were sunk in the Red Sea, and perished there, than through the hardening of their foolish hearts, after that the signs and wonders happened in Egypt through the hand of Moses, the servant of God.

CHAPTER 52

¹The Lord of all things, brothers, is in need of nothing; neither does He require anything of anyone, except to confess to Him. ²For the chosen one, David, says, "I will confess to the LORD, and that will please Him more than a young calf that puts forth horns and hooves. Let the poor behold and rejoice at that." ³And again he says, "Offer to the LORD the sacrifice of praise: pay your vows to the Most High. And call on Me in the day of your affliction, and I will deliver you, and you will glorify Me. ⁴For the sacrifice to God is a broken spirit."

CHAPTER 53

¹You know, beloved, and know well, the Holy Writings, and have looked into the oracles of God; therefore, call these things to remembrance. ²For, when Moses had gone up into the mount, and had tarried there forty days and forty nights in fasting and humiliation, the LORD said to Him, "Moses, Moses, come down quickly from here, for your people, whom you brought out of the land of Egypt, have worked iniquity. They have quickly gone astray out of the way that you command them and have made molten images for themselves." ³And the LORD said to him, "I have spoken to you once and twice, saying, I have beheld this people, and behold, it is a stiff-necked people. Leave Me alone, that I may destroy them, and I will wipe out their name from under Heaven, and make of you a nation great and wonderful, and far more numerous than they." ⁴And Moses said, "Be it far from You, O LORD. Forgive this people their sin, or also wipe my name out of the Scroll of the Living." ⁵Oh, the great love! Oh, the unsurpassable perfection! The servant is bold toward the LORD: he asks forgiveness for the people or demands otherwise that he himself should be destroyed together with them.

CHAPTER 54

¹Who among you is noble? Who is compassionate? Who is filled with love? ²Let him speak in this way: "If through me sedition and strife arise, I will depart, I will go away to wherever you will, and I will do that which is commanded by the majority, only let the flock of Christ be at peace together with the appointed elders." ³He who does this will gain for himself great glory in the LORD, and every place will receive him, "for the earth is the LORD's, and the fullness thereof." ⁴These things they have done who are citizens of the Kingdom of God, which does not need to be converted of, and these things they will yet do.

CHAPTER 55

¹But, to bring forward examples from the nations, also many kings and leaders, when a time of pestilence had arisen, being warned by oracles, gave themselves to death, that they might deliver their citizens by their blood. Many went out from their own cities, that there might no longer be sedition therein. ²We

know that many among us gave themselves up to bonds, that they might deliver others. Many have given themselves up to slavery, and, having received their own price, have with that fed others. ³Many women, waxing strong through the grace of God, have performed many manly deeds. ⁴The blessed Judith, when the city was besieged, asked of the elders that she should be permitted to go forth into the camp of the aliens. ⁵She therefore delivered herself to danger and went out through love of her country and of her people, who were besieged. And the LORD delivered Holofernes into the hands of a woman. ⁶To no smaller danger did Esther, being perfect in faith, expose herself, that she might deliver the twelve tribes of Israel who were about to perish. For by fasting and humiliation she implored the Master, who overlooks all things, the God of Ages, who, seeing the humiliation of her soul, delivered the people for whose sake she put herself in danger.

CHAPTER 56

¹Therefore, let us pray for those who have fallen into any transgression, that moderation and humility may be given to them, to the end that they should submit themselves, I do not say to us, but to the will of God; for so they will obtain a fruitful and perfect remembrance and compassion before God and His holy ones. ²Let us accept, brothers, that discipline at which no one needs to be offended. The admonition which we make toward one another is exceedingly good and useful, for it joins us to the will of God. ³For thus speaks the holy word: "The LORD has disciplined me with disciplines, but He has not given me over to death." ⁴"For whom the LORD loves He disciplines, and scourges every son whom He receives." ⁵"The righteous will discipline me in pity and will rebuke me, but do not let the oil of sinners anoint my head." ⁶And again it says: "Blessed is the man whom the LORD has rebuked; do not refuse the admonition of the Almighty, for He makes you to grieve, and again He restores you; ⁷He has smitten, and His hands have healed you; ⁸six times will He deliver you from calamity, and the seventh time evil will not touch you. ⁹In the time of famine He will deliver you from death, in war He will redeem you from the hand of iron. ¹⁰From the scourge of the tongue He will hide you, and you will not be afraid when evils approach. ¹¹The unjust and the sinner you will laugh to scorn; ¹²and of the wild beasts you will not be afraid, for the wild beasts will be at peace with you. ¹³Then you will know that your house will be at peace; the habitation of your dwelling place will not fail. ¹⁴You will know that your seed is abundant, your children like all the herb of the field. ¹⁵You will come to your tomb like a ripe ear of corn reaped in due season, like the heap of a threshing-floor that is gathered at its proper time." ¹⁶You see, beloved, that there is a protection for them that are disciplined by the Master, for God chastens us because He is good, to the end that we should be admonished by His holy discipline.

CHAPTER 57

¹Therefore, you that have laid the foundation of the sedition: submit yourselves to the elders, and be disciplined to conversion, bending the knees of your hearts. ²Learn to submit yourselves, laying aside the vain and haughty self-will of your tongues; for it is better that you should be small and approved in the flock of Christ, rather than that, seeming to be superior to others, you should be cast out of His hope. ³For thus says the most excellent Wisdom: "Behold, I will send on you the language of My Spirit; I will teach you My word. ⁴Since I called and you did not listen, and prolonged My words, and you did not attend [to them], but made My counsels of no effect, and were not obedient to My reproofs, therefore I will laugh at your destruction, I will exult when desolation comes on you; when perturbation has suddenly come on you, and ruin is at hand like a whirlwind, when tribulation and oppression comes on you. ⁵For the time will come when you will call on Me, and I will not listen to you; the wicked will seek Me, and will not find Me. They hated wisdom and did not choose the fear of the LORD; they were not willing to attend to My counsels, they mocked at My rebukes. ⁶For what reason they will eat the fruits of their own way; they will be filled with their own unrighteousness. ⁷For because they wronged the innocent they will be slain, and judgment will destroy the unrighteous; but he who listens to Me will abide, trusting in hope, and will rest securely from all evil."

CHAPTER 58

¹Let us, therefore, submit to His all-holy and glorious Name, and escape the threats that have been before spoken by Wisdom against the disobedient, that we may abide trusting in the most holy Name of His greatness. ²Accept this advice of ours, and it will not be regretted by you. For as God lives, and as the Lord Jesus Christ lives, and the Holy Spirit—the confidence and hope of the chosen ones—He who observes in humility with earnest obedience, and not complaining, the ordinances and commands given by God, he will be reckoned and counted in the number of them that are saved by Jesus Christ, through whom is the glory to Him through the ages of the ages. Amen.

CHAPTER 59

¹But if some should be disobedient to the things spoken by Him through us, let them know that they will entangle themselves in no small transgression and danger, ²but that we will be guiltless of this sin; and we will ask, making our prayer and supplication with earnestness, that the Maker of all things may keep uninjured in all the world the number of those that have been numbered as His chosen ones, through His beloved Son, Jesus Christ, through whom He has called us from darkness to light, and from ignorance to a knowledge of the glory of His Name. ³That we may hope in Your Name, which is the first of all things, open the eyes of our heart to know You, who are alone highest among the highest, holy among the holy, who puts down the haughtiness of the proud, who scatters the reasonings of the nations, who exalts the humble on high, and lowers the lofty, who makes rich and makes poor, who kills and makes to live, the only benefactor of spirits, and God of all flesh, who looks into the abysses, who beholds the works of men, who is the helper of those in danger, the Savior of those who have lost hope, who is the maker and overseer of every soul, who makes the nations to multiply on earth, and out of all has chosen those that love You through Your beloved Son Jesus Christ, through whom You have taught us, have sanctified us, have honored us. ⁴We ask You, Lord, to be our helper and assister; save those of us who are in affliction, have compassion on the humble, raise the fallen, appear to those who are in need, heal the sinners, convert those of Your people who are wandering from the way, feed the hungry, ransom our prisoners, raise up the sick, encourage the feeble-hearted, let all the nations know that You are God alone and Jesus Christ Your Son, and that we are Your people and the sheep of Your pasture.

CHAPTER 60

¹You have made manifest the perpetual constitution of the world by the things that happen. You, Lord, who are faithful in all generations, have founded the world. You who are just in Your judgments, who are wonderful in strength and greatness; You who are wise in creating and prudent in establishing the things that are made; You that are good in the things that are seen and faithful among them that trust on You, merciful and compassionate, forgive us our transgressions and unrighteousnesses, our sins and our negligences. ²Do not take into account every sin of Your servants and handmaids, but purify us with the purification of Your truth, and make straight our steps in holiness, and righteousness, and singleness of heart, that we may so walk and do such things as are right and well pleasing before You, and before our rulers. ³Yes, Lord, cause Your face to appear to us in peace to our good, that we may be sheltered by Your mighty hand, and preserved from all sin by Your lofty arm, and deliver us from those that hate us unjustly. ⁴Give unity and peace both to us and to all that dwell on the earth, as You gave to our fathers when they called on You with faith and truth, so that we should become obedient to Your all-powerful and most excellent Name, and to those who rule and govern us on the earth.

CHAPTER 61

¹You, Lord, have given the authority of the Kingdom to them through Your almighty and unspeakable power, so that we, knowing the estimation and honor given to them by You, might submit ourselves to them, in no way opposing Your will; to whom give, O Lord,

1 CLEMENT

health, peace, concord, stability, so that they may discharge the rule given to them by You without offense; ²for You, heavenly Lord, perpetual King, give to the sons of men glory, and honor, and authority over the things that are on the earth. You, Lord, direct their counsel according to what is good and pleasing before You, that, fulfilling with peace, and meekness, and piety the authority given to them by You, they may obtain mercy from You. ³You who alone are able to do these and greater good things among us, to You do we give thanks through the Chief Priest and protector of our souls, Jesus Christ, through whom to You be the glory and majesty, now and to all generations, through the ages of the ages. Amen.

CHAPTER 62

¹Concerning the things that pertain to our religion, and the things that are most useful to a virtuous life, for those who are willing to live piously and righteously, we have sufficiently charged you, men and brothers. ²For we have handled every argument concerning faith and conversion, and genuine love and temperance, and moderation and patience, reminding you that you must, by righteousness, and truth, and long-suffering, approve yourselves with piety to Almighty God, being of one mind, without malice, in love and peace with earnest obedience, even as our fathers, who were previously mentioned, approved themselves with humility both with regard to God the Father and Creator, and to all men. ³And these things we have so much the more gladly put you in mind of, inasmuch as we knew plainly that we wrote to men who are faithful and of high regard, and who have looked into the oracles of the instruction of God.

CHAPTER 63

¹It is right, therefore, that those who have attended to so great and so many examples should submit their necks, and fill the place of obedience, so that being at peace from the vain sedition we may attain, without any blame, to the end set before us in truth. ²For you will afford us joy and rejoicing if, becoming obedient to the things that have been written by us, you put an end, by the suggestion of the Holy Spirit, to the unlawful wrath of your discord, according to the supplication which we have made concerning peace and unity in this letter. ³But we have also sent men to you who are faithful and prudent, who from youth up to old age have behaved blamelessly among us, who also will be witnesses between yourselves and us; ⁴and this we have done that you may know that our whole thought has been and is this: that you may speedily be at peace among yourselves.

CHAPTER 64

¹Finally, may my God, who overlooks all things, who is the Master of spirits and Lord of all flesh, who has chosen our Lord Jesus Christ, and us through Him to be a peculiar people, give to every soul that is called after His glorious and holy Name, faith, fear, peace, patience, long-suffering, continence, purity, sobriety, to the well-pleasing of His Name, through our Chief Priest and protector, Jesus Christ, through whom be ascribed to Him glory and greatness, strength and honor, both now and through the ages of the ages. Amen.

CHAPTER 65

¹See that you quickly send back to us in peace and with joy Claudius Ephebus and Valerius Bito, together also with Fortunatus, who were sent to you from us, that they may the more quickly bring us news of your peace and order, which we pray for and desire, so that we may the sooner have joy concerning your good order. ²The grace of our Lord Jesus Christ be with you, and with all who everywhere are called of God through Him, to whom through Him be glory, honor, might, majesty, and continuous dominion, through the ages of the ages. Amen.

2 CLEMENT

Like 1 Clement, the Second Epistle of Clement has an anonymous author and is ascribed to Clement of Rome by tradition, but unlike 1 Clement, the ascription of 2 Clement to Clement of Rome is more dubious. It was considered for canonization early on and is in fact included in some Coptic Bibles. It was likely written in the late 1st century or early 2nd century.

CHAPTER 1

¹Brothers, we should so think of our Lord Jesus Christ as of God, as of the Judge of quick and dead, and we should not think lightly concerning our salvation; ²for if we think little concerning Him, we also expect that we will receive little; and if we listen to it as though it were a small thing, we err, not knowing from where we are called, nor by whom, nor to what place, nor what great things Jesus Christ has endured to suffer on our behalf. ³What repayment, therefore, will we give to Him, or what fruit worthy of that which He has given to us? How many things that help to holiness has He given to us? ⁴For He has given us the light, He has called us sons as though He were our father, He has saved us when we were ready to perish. ⁵What praise, therefore, will we give to Him, or what repayment of reward for the things that we have received? ⁶For we were maimed in our understanding, worshiping stocks and stones, and gold, and silver, and iron, the work of men, and our whole life was nothing but death. We, therefore, who were surrounded with darkness, and who had our sight filled with such gloom, have recovered our sight, having, according to His will, laid aside the cloud that was around us. ⁷For He has had compassion on us, and, pitying us, has saved us, having beheld in us much wandering and destruction, when we had no hope of salvation except that which is from Him. ⁸For He has called us when as yet we were not, and has willed us to be when we were nothing.

CHAPTER 2

¹"Rejoice, you barren that do not bear; break forth and shout, you that do not travail, for the desolate has many more children than she that has a husband." In that He said, "Rejoice, you barren that do not bear," He has spoken of us, for our assembly was barren before that children were given to her. ²But in that He said, "Shout, you that do not travail," He means that we should offer our prayers to God with simplicity, that we do not faint like women in travail. ³But in that He said, "The children of the desolate are many more than they of her that has a husband," He means that our people seemed to be deserted of God, and now, after that we have believed, we have become more in number than they which seemed to have God. ⁴And another Writing says, "I did not come to call the righteous but sinners." ⁵He means this, that it is necessary to save them that are perishing. ⁶For this is great and wonderful—not to establish the things that are standing, but the things that are falling; ⁷thus Christ willed to save the things that were perishing, and He saved many, having come and called us who were already perishing.

CHAPTER 3

¹Therefore, since He has showed such compassion to us—first, that He has caused that we who live should not sacrifice to gods that are dead, neither worship them, but know through Him the Father of truth—what is this knowledge of Him except the not denying Him through whom we know Him? ²For He Himself says, "Whoever has confessed Me before men, I will confess Him before My Father." ³This, therefore, is our reward if we confess Him through whom we have been saved. ⁴But whereby will we confess Him? Even by doing what He commands, and not disobeying His commands, and honoring Him not only with our lips but with our whole heart and whole understanding. ⁵For He says in Isaiah, "This people honors Me with their lips, but their heart is far from Me."

CHAPTER 4

¹Therefore, let us not only call Him Lord, for that will not save us. ²For He says, "It is not everyone that says to Me, Lord, Lord, that will be saved, but he that does righteousness." ³For what reason, brothers, let us confess Him in

our deeds, by loving one another, by not committing adultery, and not speaking ill of each other, neither being envious, but by being continent, compassionate, kind. We should also sympathize with one another, and to abstain from covetousness; it is by these works that we acknowledge Him, and not by the contrary; ⁴and we should not fear men but rather God. ⁵For what reason, if we do these things, the LORD has said, "Though you have been gathered together with Me in My bosom and do not do My commands, I will cast you from Me, and I will say to you, Depart from Me; I do not know from where you are, you workers of iniquity."

CHAPTER 5

¹For what reason, brothers, having left our sojourning in this world, let us do the will of Him who called us, and let us not fear to depart from this world. ²For the LORD says, "You will be as lambs in the midst of wolves." ³But Peter answered and says to Him, "What, then, if the wolves tear the sheep?" ⁴Jesus says to Peter, "Do not let the lambs after that they are dead fear the wolves; and do not fear them that kill you but can do nothing more to you, but fear Him who, after you are dead, has authority over body and soul, even to cast them into the Gehenna of fire." ⁵And you know, brothers, that the sojourning of our flesh in this world is but short and for a little while, but the promise of Christ is great and wonderful, even the rest of the kingdom which is to come, and of continuous life. ⁶What, therefore, will we do that we may attain to them, except to lead a holy and just life, and to deem the things of this world to be alien to us, and not to desire them? ⁷For while we desire to obtain these things, we fall from the right way.

CHAPTER 6

¹For the LORD says, "No servant can serve two masters." If, therefore, we wish to serve both God and wealth, it is inexpedient for us; ²for what advantage is it if a man gains the whole world, but loses his soul? ³Now this life and the life to come are two enemies. ⁴This life preaches adultery, corruption, covetousness, and deceit; but the life that is to come renounces these things. ⁵We cannot, therefore, be friends to both; it is necessary for us then to renounce the one and to use the other. ⁶Therefore, let us consider that it is better to hate the things that are here, as being small, and short-lived, and corruptible, but to love the things that are there, as being good and incorruptible. ⁷If, therefore, we do the will of Christ, we will find rest; but if not, nothing will deliver us from continuous punishment, if we do not obey His commands. ⁸For the Writing says in Ezekiel: "If Noah, and Job, and Daniel should rise up, they will not deliver their children in the captivity." ⁹If, therefore, such righteous men as these cannot by their righteousness deliver their children, with what confidence will we, if we do not keep our immersion pure and undefiled, come to the Kingdom of God? Or who will be our advocate unless we are found having the works that are holy and just?

CHAPTER 7

¹For what reason, my brothers, let us strive, knowing that the contest is at hand. We know, too, that many put in for corruptible contests, but all are not crowned, but they only who have labored much and fought a good fight. ²Therefore, let us contend that we may all be crowned. ³Let us run in the straight course, in the incorruptible contest; and let us be many that put into it; and let us so contend that we may also be crowned. And if we cannot all be crowned, let us at least come near to the crown. ⁴It is necessary for us to know that he who contends in a corruptible contest, if he is found acting unfairly is flogged, and taken away, and cast out of the course. ⁵What do you think? What will he suffer that acts unfairly in an incorruptible contest? ⁶For of them who have not kept their seal he says, "Their worm will not die, and their fire will not be quenched, and they will be for a spectacle to all flesh."

CHAPTER 8

¹Therefore, while we are on the earth, let us convert. ²For we are as clay in the hands of the workman. In like manner as the potter, if while he is making a vessel, it turns wrongly in his hands, or is crushed, can mould it again, but if he has once cast it into the fiery furnace he can no longer amend it; so let us, so long as we are in this world, convert with all our hearts of the wickedness that we have committed in the flesh, that we may be saved of the LORD while as yet we have time for conversion. ³For after we have departed out of this world, we are no longer able there to confess or convert. ⁴For what reason, brothers, if we have done the will of the Father, and preserved our flesh pure, and kept the commands of the LORD, we will receive continuous life. ⁵For the LORD says in the Gospel, "If you have not kept that which is little, who will give you that which is great? For I say to you, he that is faithful in that which is least is also faithful in much." ⁶Does he not, therefore, say this, "Keep your flesh pure and your seal unspotted, that you may inherit continuous life?"

CHAPTER 9

¹And do not let any one of you say that this flesh of ours is not judged nor raised again. ²Consider this: in what were you saved, in what did you recover your sight, if not in this flesh? ³We should, therefore, guard our flesh as the temple of God; ⁴for in the same manner as you were called in the flesh, in the flesh you will also come. ⁵There is one Christ, our Lord who saved us, who being spirit at the first, was made flesh, and thus called us. So we will also receive the reward in this flesh. ⁶Therefore, let us love one another, that we may all come to the Kingdom of God. ⁷While we have opportunity to be healed, let us give ourselves up to God who heals, giving a repayment to Him. ⁸And of what kind? Conversion from a sincere heart. ⁹For He foreknows all things and knows the things that are in our hearts. ¹⁰Therefore, let us give Him praise, not from the mouth alone, but also from the heart, that He may receive us as sons. ¹¹For of a truth the LORD has said, "My brothers are they who do the will of My Father."

CHAPTER 10

¹For what reason, my brothers, let us do the will of the Father who has called us, that we may live; and let us rather pursue virtue, and abandon vice which leads us into sins, and let us fly from ungodliness lest evil seize us; for if we are zealous to do good, peace will pursue us. ²For this reason it is not possible that a man should find peace. ³For they introduce the fear of men, choosing rather the present enjoyment that is here than the future promise. ⁴For they are ignorant of how great a torment the enjoyment of this world brings, and what delight the future promise has. ⁵And if they themselves alone did these things, it would be endurable; but now they continue to instruct innocent souls in evil, not knowing that they will have a twofold condemnation—both themselves and they that listen to them.

CHAPTER 11

¹Therefore, let us serve God with a pure heart, and we will be righteous; but if we do not serve Him, because we do not believe the promise of God, we will be wretched. ²For the prophetic word says, "Wretched are the double-minded who doubt in their heart, and say, We have heard these things of old, even in the time of our fathers, but we have seen none of them, though we expect them from day to day. ³You fools, compare yourselves to a tree; take for an example the vine: in the first place it sheds its leaves, then there comes a shoot, after that the unripe grape, then the mature cluster. ⁴In like manner My people, in time past, has had disorder and trouble, but afterward it will receive the things that are good." ⁵For what reason, my brothers, let us not be double-minded, but let us abide in hope, that we may obtain our reward. ⁶Faithful is He that has promised that He will give to each the repayment of his works. ⁷If, therefore, we do righteousness before God, we will enter into His Kingdom, and receive the promises which "ear has not heard nor eye seen, neither have entered into the heart of man."

CHAPTER 12

¹Let us, therefore, in love and righteousness expect the Kingdom of God every hour, since we do not know the day of the appearing of God. ²For the LORD Himself, when He was asked by a certain man when His Kingdom should come, replied, "When two will be one, and that which is without as that which is within, and the male with the female neither male nor female." ³Now two are one when we speak the truth to one another, and there is, without hypocrisy, one soul in two bodies. ⁴And by that which is without being as that which is within, He means this: He calls the

soul that which is within, and the body that which is without; in like manner, therefore, as your body is visible, let your soul be made manifest by good deeds. ⁵And by the male with the female neither male nor female, He means this: When a brother seeing a sister does not in any way regard her as a female, nor does she regard him as a male; ⁶"when you do these things," He says, "the Kingdom of My Father will come."

CHAPTER 13

¹My brothers, therefore let us convert immediately; let us be sober and followers of what is good, for we are burdened with much folly and wickedness. Let us wipe out from among us our former sins and convert sincerely and be saved. And let us not be pleasers of men, nor let us wish to please one another alone, but let us also please them that are outside by our righteous conduct, that the Name may not be blasphemed on our account. ²For the LORD says, "My Name is continually blasphemed among all the nations"; and again, "Why is My Name blasphemed, whereby it is blasphemed? In that you do not do the things that I will." ³For the nations, when they hear from our mouth the oracles of God, admire them as beautiful and weighty; but afterward perceiving our deeds, that they are not worthy of the words that we say, they turn thereafter to blasphemy, saying that the matter is but fable and deceit. ⁴For when they hear from us that God says, "There is no thanks for you if you love them that love you, but there is thanks for you if you love your enemies and them that hate you"; when they hear these things, they wonder at the excess of the goodness. But when they see that we do not only not love those that hate us, but do not even love those that love us, they turn us to ridicule, and the Name is blasphemed.

CHAPTER 14

¹For what reason, my brothers, by doing the will of our Father, God, we will be of the first, the spiritual Assembly, which was founded before the sun and moon were made; but if we do not do the will of the LORD, we will be of the Writing that says, "My house has become a den of thieves." Therefore, let us choose to be of the Assembly of life that we may be saved. ²But I do not think that you are ignorant that the living Assembly is the body of Christ. For the Writing says: "God made man, male and female." Now, the male signifies Christ, the female the Assembly. You also know that both the Scrolls and the apostles say that the Assembly is not new, but was from the beginning; for it was of a spiritual kind, as was also our Jesus, but was made manifest in the last days that it might save us. ³But the Assembly, though spiritual, was manifested in the flesh of Christ, showing to us that if anyone keep it in his flesh, and does not corrupt it, he will receive it in the Holy Spirit; for this flesh is the counterpart of the Spirit; no one, therefore, who corrupts the copy will receive the original in exchange. He therefore means this, my brothers: "Keep the flesh pure, that you may partake of the Spirit." ⁴But if we say that the flesh is the Assembly, and the spirit, Christ, he then who does injury to the flesh does injury to the Assembly. Such a one therefore will not partake of the spirit, which is Christ. ⁵Such life and immortality is this flesh able to partake of by the union of the Holy Spirit with it. Nor can any say or declare what the LORD has prepared for His chosen ones.

CHAPTER 15

¹Now, I do not think that I have given advice of little importance concerning temperance, which, if a man practices, he will not regret it, but will save both himself and me who advise him. For it is no small service to convert a wandering and perishing soul to salvation. ²For we are able to give this repayment in return to God who created us, if he who speaks and hears both speaks and hears with faith and love. ³Therefore, let us remain with righteousness and holiness in the things in which we have believed, that we may with boldness ask of God, who says, "While you are still speaking, I will say, Behold, I am here." ⁴For this saying is the token of a great promise. For the LORD says of Himself that He is more ready to give than him that asks. ⁵Therefore, since we partake in so much goodness, let us not grudge ourselves the attaining of so many good things; for by so much as His words bring pleasure to those who do them, by so much do they bring condemnation to those who disobey them.

CHAPTER 16

¹For what reason, brothers, since we have received no small opportunity for conversion, let us, while we have time, turn to the God who has called us, while we still have one who will receive us. ²For if we bid farewell to the luxuries of this world and conquer our soul so that we do not fulfill evil lusts, we will partake of the mercy of Jesus. ³But know that the Day of Judgment is already coming as a burning furnace, and certain of the heavens will be melted, and the whole earth will be as lead melting on the fire; and then both the secret and open deeds of men will be made manifest. ⁴Therefore, kindness is good, as showing conversion from sin; better is fasting than prayer, and kindness than both; for love covers a multitude of sins, and prayer that goes forth from a good conscience saves from death. Happy is everyone who is found full of these things, for kindness becomes a lightening of sin.

CHAPTER 17

¹Therefore, let us convert with our whole heart lest any of us perish by the way. For if we have received commands and make this our business—to tear men away from idols and instruct them—how much more should a soul not perish that has already come to a knowledge of God? ²Therefore, let us endeavor to elevate with regard to what is good them that are weak, to the end that we may all be saved; and let us convert one another and reprove one another. ³And let us not seem to attend and believe now only, while we are being admonished by the elders, but also when we have departed to our homes, let us remember the commands of the LORD; and let us not, on the other hand, be drawn aside by the lusts of the world, but let us endeavor, by coming more frequently, to make progress in the commands of the LORD, to the end that we all being of one mind may be gathered together to life. ⁴For the LORD has said, "I come to gather together all the nations, tribes, and tongues." And He says this of the day of His appearing, when He will come and repay each of us according to his works. ⁵And the unbelieving will behold His glory and strength, and will be astonished when they see the kingdom of the world in the hands of Jesus, and will say, "Woe to us, for You were and we did not know it, and did not believe, nor did we obey the elders who preached to us concerning our salvation." And their worm will not die, nor their fire be quenched, and they will be for a spectacle to all flesh. ⁶He speaks of that Day of Judgment when they will see punished those among us who have lived ungodly and set at nothing the commands of Jesus Christ. ⁷But the just, who have done well, and have abided the tests, and have hated the luxuries of the soul, when they behold those who have missed the way and have denied Jesus either by words or deeds, how they are punished with dreadful tortures in unquenchable fire, will give glory to their God, saying that there will be a hope for him who has served God with his whole heart.

CHAPTER 18

¹Therefore, let us be of those who give thanks, of those who have served God, and not of the ungodly who are judged. ²For I myself, being in all respects a sinner, and not having yet escaped temptation, but being still in the midst of the snares of the Devil, yet endeavor to follow after righteousness, that I may be able, at any rate, to be near it, fearing the judgment to come.

CHAPTER 19

¹For what reason, my brothers and sisters, after the reading of the words of the God of truth, I also read an exhortation to you, to the end that you should attend to what has been written, that you may both save yourselves and him who preaches among you; for I ask of you, as my reward, that you should convert with your whole heart, gaining for yourselves salvation and life. For by so doing, we will offer an aim to all the young, who are willing to labor cheerfully for the worship and goodness of God. ²And do not let those of us who are unlearned be vexed or offended when one exhorts us and turns us from sin to righteousness. For we at times when doing what is wrong, do not know it, from the doubt and unbelief that is in our hearts, and are blinded in our understanding by vain lusts. ³Therefore, let us practice righteousness, that we may be saved at the last. Blessed are they who obey these commands, for if for a short

time they suffer in the world that now is, they will gather hereafter the immortal fruit of the resurrection. ⁴Therefore, do not let the pious man be vexed if he is afflicted in the times that now are—a blessed time awaits him. He will live above again with the fathers and will rejoice without sorrow continuously.

CHAPTER 20
¹And do not let even that trouble your mind, that we see the unjust prosperous and the servants of God in misery. ²Let us have faith, my brothers and sisters. We are making trial of the living God and contending in the present life that we may be crowned in the life to come. ³For none of the just receive a speedy reward, but wait for it. ⁴For if God gave speedily the reward of the righteous, we should immediately practice gain and not godliness; for we should seem to be righteous, not on account of what is pious, but on account of what is profitable. And on this account the divine judgment has overtaken a spirit that is not righteous, and has burdened it with chains. ⁵Now to the only God, the invisible, the Father of truth, who has sent to us the Savior and leader of immortality, through whom He has made known to us the truth and the heavenly life—to Him be the glory through the ages of the ages. Amen.

SEVEN EPISTLES OF IGNATIUS

Ignatius, the overseer of Antioch, and fellow disciple with Polycarp of John the Apostle, penned seven letters while en route to his martyrdom in Rome. These letters are generally well-attested and are considered part of the Apostolic Fathers. Ignatius is believed to have died in approximately AD 108 or 140.

TO THE EPHESIANS

IGNATIUS, WHO IS ALSO THEOPHORUS, TO HER WHICH HAS BEEN BLESSED IN GREATNESS THROUGH THE ABUNDANCE OF GOD THE FATHER; WHICH HAS BEEN FOREORDAINED BEFORE THE AGES TO BE FOREVER ABIDING AND UNCHANGEABLE GLORY, UNITED AND CHOSEN IN A TRUE PASSION, BY THE WILL OF THE FATHER AND OF JESUS CHRIST OUR GOD; EVEN TO THE ASSEMBLY WHICH IS IN EPHESUS [OF ASIA], WORTHY OF ALL COMMENDATIONS: ABUNDANT GREETINGS IN CHRIST JESUS AND IN BLAMELESS JOY.

CHAPTER 1
¹While I welcomed in God [your] well-beloved name, which you bear by natural right by faith and love in Christ Jesus our Savior—being imitators of God, and having your hearts kindled in the blood of God, you have perfectly fulfilled your congenial work— ²for when you heard that I was on my way from Syria, in bonds for the sake of the common Name and hope, and was hoping through your prayers to succeed in fighting with wild beasts in Rome, that by so succeeding I might have power to be a disciple, you were eager to visit me— ³seeing then that in God's Name I have received your whole multitude in the person of Onesimus, whose love passes utterance and who is moreover your overseer [in the flesh]—and I pray that you may love him according to Jesus Christ and that you all may be like him; for blessed is He that granted to you according to your deserving to have such an overseer.

CHAPTER 2
¹But as touching my fellow-servant Burrhus, who by the will of God is your blessed servant in all things, I pray that he may remain with me to the honor of yourselves and of your overseer. Yes, and Crocus also, who is worthy of God and of you, whom I received as an example of the love which you bear me, has relieved me in all ways—even so may the Father of Jesus Christ refresh him—together with Onesimus, and Burrhus, and Euplus, and Fronto; in whom I saw you all with the eyes of love. ²May I always have your joy, if [it] so be I am worthy of it. It is therefore appropriate for you in every way to glorify Jesus Christ who glorified you; that being perfectly joined together in one submission, submitting yourselves to your overseer and eldership, you may be sanctified in all things.

CHAPTER 3
¹I do not command you, as though I were someone. For even though I am in bonds for the Name's sake, I am not yet perfected in Jesus Christ. [For] now I am beginning to be a disciple; and I speak to you as to my schoolmates. For I should be trained by you for the contest in faith, in admonition, in endurance, in long-suffering. ²But, since love does not permit me to be silent concerning you, therefore I was forward to exhort you, that you run in harmony with the mind of God; for Jesus Christ also, our inseparable life, is the mind of the Father, even as the overseers that are settled in the farthest parts of the earth are in the mind of Jesus Christ.

CHAPTER 4
¹So then it is appropriate for you to run in harmony with the mind of the overseer; which thing also you do. For your honorable eldership, which is worthy of God, is attuned to the overseer, even as its strings to a lyre. Therefore, in your concord and harmonious love, Jesus Christ is sung. ²And you, each and all, form yourselves into a chorus, that being harmonious in concord and taking the key note of God you may in unison sing with one voice through Jesus Christ to the Father, that He may both hear you and acknowledge you by your good deeds to be members of His Son. It is therefore profitable for you to be in blameless unity, that you may also be partakers of God always.

CHAPTER 5
¹For if I in a short time had such converse with your overseer, which was not after the manner of men but in the Spirit, how much more do I congratulate you who are closely joined with him as the Assembly is with Jesus Christ and as Jesus Christ is with the Father, that all things may be harmonious in unity. ²Let no man be deceived: if anyone is not within the precinct of the altar, he lacks the bread [of God]. For, if the prayer of one and another has such great force, how much more that of the overseer and of the whole Assembly. ³Therefore, whoever does not come to the congregation thereby shows his pride and has separated himself; for it is written: "God resists the proud." Let us therefore be careful not to resist the overseer, that by our submission we may give ourselves to God.

CHAPTER 6
¹And in proportion as a man sees that his overseer is silent, let him fear him the more. For everyone whom the Master of the household sends to be steward over His own house, we should so receive as Him that sent him. Therefore, we should plainly regard the overseer as the LORD Himself. ²Now Onesimus of his own accord highly praises your orderly conduct in God, for that you all live according to truth, and that no heresy has a home among you: no, you do not so much as listen to anyone, if he speaks of anything else save concerning Jesus Christ in truth.

CHAPTER 7
¹For some are accustomed of malicious guile to carry about the Name, while they do certain other things unworthy of God. You should shun these men as wild beasts, for they are mad dogs, biting by stealth; against whom you should be on your guard, for they are hard to heal. ²There is only one Physician—of flesh and of spirit, generate and ingenerate, God in man, true Life in death, Son of Mary and Son of God, first passible and then impassible—Jesus Christ our Lord.

CHAPTER 8

¹Therefore, let no one deceive you, as indeed you are not deceived, seeing that you belong wholly to God. For when no lust is established in you, which has power to torment you, then truly you live after God. I devote myself for you, and I dedicate myself as an offering for the assembly of you Ephesians which is famous to all the ages. ²They that are of the flesh cannot do the things of the Spirit, neither can they that are of the Spirit do the things of the flesh; even as faith cannot do the things of unfaithfulness, neither unfaithfulness the things of faith. No, even those things which you do after the flesh are spiritual; for you do all things in Jesus Christ.

CHAPTER 9

¹But I have learned that certain persons passed through you from over there, bringing evil doctrine; whom you did not permit to sow seed in you, for you stopped your ears, so that you might not receive the seed sown by them. For you are stones of a temple, which were prepared beforehand for a building of God the Father, being hoisted up to the heights through the engine of Jesus Christ, which is the Cross, and using the Holy Spirit for a rope, while your faith is your windlass, and love is the way that leads up to God. ²So then you are all companions in the way, carrying your God and your shrine, your Christ and your holy things, being arrayed from head to foot in the commands of Jesus Christ. And I too, taking part in the festivity, am permitted by letter to bear you company and to rejoice with you, that you do not set your love on anything after the common life of men, but only on God.

CHAPTER 10

¹And also, pray without ceasing for the rest of mankind (for there is in them a hope of conversion), that they may find God. Therefore, permit them to take lessons at least from your works. ²Against their outbursts of wrath be meek; against their proud words be humble; against their railings set your prayers; against their errors be steadfast in the faith; against their fierceness be gentle. And do not be zealous to imitate them by requital. ³Let us show ourselves their brothers by our forbearance; but let us be zealous to be imitators of the LORD, vying with each other who will suffer the greater wrong, who will be defrauded, who will be set at nothing; that no herb of the Devil be found in you, but in all purity and temperance abide in Christ Jesus, with your flesh and with your spirit.

CHAPTER 11

¹These are the last times. From now on let us have reverence; let us fear the long-suffering of God, lest it turn into a judgment against us. For either let us fear the wrath which is to come or let us love the grace which now is—the one or the other; provided only that we be found in Christ Jesus to true life. ²Let nothing glitter in your eyes apart from Him, in whom I carry about my bonds, my spiritual pearls in which I would gladly rise again through your prayer, of which may it be my lot to be always a partaker, that I may be found in the company of those Christians of Ephesus who moreover were ever of one mind with the apostles in the power of Jesus Christ.

CHAPTER 12

¹I know who I am and to whom I write. I am a convict, you have received mercy: I am in peril, you are established. ²You are the highroad of those that are on their way to die to God. You are associates in the mysteries with Paul, who was sanctified, who obtained a good report, who is worthy of all commendations; in whose footsteps I would gladly be found treading when I will attain to God, who in every letter makes mention of you in Christ Jesus.

CHAPTER 13

¹Therefore, do your diligence to meet together more frequently for thanksgiving to God and for His glory. For when you meet together frequently, the powers of Satan are cast down; and his mischief comes to nothing in the concord of your faith. ²There is nothing better than peace, in which all warfare of things in Heaven and things on earth is abolished.

CHAPTER 14

¹None of these things is hidden from you if you are perfect in your faith and love toward Jesus Christ, for these are the beginning and end of life—faith is the beginning and love is the end—and the two being found in unity are God, while all things else follow in their train to true nobility. ²No man professing faith sins, and no man possessing love hates. The tree is manifest from its fruit; so they that profess to be Christ's will be seen through their actions. For the work is not a thing of profession now, but is seen then when one is found in the power of faith to the end.

CHAPTER 15

¹It is better to keep silence and to be, than to talk and not to be. It is a fine thing to teach, if the speaker practices [what he teaches]. Now there is one Teacher who spoke, and it came to pass: yes, and even the things which He has done in silence are worthy of the Father. ²He that truly possesses the word of Jesus is also able to listen to His silence, that he may be perfect; that through his speech he may act and through his silence he may be known. ³Nothing is hidden from the LORD, but even our secrets are near to Him. Let us therefore do all things as knowing that He dwells in us, to the end that we may be His temples and He Himself may be in us as our God. This is so, and it will also be made clear in our sight from the love which we rightly bear toward Him.

CHAPTER 16

¹Do not be deceived, my brothers. Corrupters of houses will not inherit the Kingdom of God. ²If then they which do these things after the flesh are put to death, how much more if a man through evil doctrine corrupts the faith of God for which Jesus Christ was crucified. Such a man, having defiled himself, will go into the unquenchable fire; and in like manner also will he that listens to him.

CHAPTER 17

¹For this reason the LORD received ointment on His head, that He might breathe incorruption on the Assembly. Do not be anointed with the ill odor of the teaching of the prince of this world, lest he lead you captive and rob you of the life which is set before you. ²And for what reason do we not all walk prudently, receiving the knowledge of God, which is Jesus Christ? Why should we perish in our folly, not knowing the gift of grace which the LORD has truly sent?

CHAPTER 18

¹My spirit is made an outcast for the Cross, which is a stumbling-block to them that are unbelievers, but to us—salvation and continuous life. Where is the wise? Where is the disputer? Where is the boasting of them that are called prudent? ²For our God, Jesus the Christ, was conceived in the womb by Mary according to a dispensation, of the seed of David but also of the Holy Spirit; and He was born and was immersed that by His passion He might cleanse water.

CHAPTER 19

¹And hidden from the prince of this world were the virginity of Mary, and her childbearing, and likewise also the death of the LORD—three mysteries to be cried aloud—the which were worked in the silence of God. ²How then were they made manifest to the ages? A star shone forth in the Heaven [[or sky]] above all the stars; and its light was unutterable, and its strangeness caused amazement; and all the rest of the constellations with the sun and moon formed themselves into a chorus around the star, but the star itself far outshone them all; and there was perplexity to know where this strange appearance came from which was so unlike them. ³From that time forward every sorcery and every spell was dissolved, the ignorance of wickedness vanished away, [and] the ancient kingdom was pulled down when God appeared in the likeness of man to newness of continuous life; and that which had been perfected in the counsels of God began to take effect. There all things were perturbed, because the abolishing of death was taken in hand.

CHAPTER 20

¹If Jesus Christ should count me worthy through your prayer, and it should be the Divine will, in my second tract, which I intend to write to you, I will further set before you the dispensation of which I have begun to speak, relating to the new man Jesus Christ, which consists in faith toward Him and in love toward Him, in His passion and resurrection, ²especially if the LORD should reveal anything to me. Assemble yourselves together in common, each of you separately, man by man, in grace, in one faith and one Jesus Christ, who

after the flesh was of David's race, who is Son of Man and Son of God, to the end that you may obey the overseer and eldership without distraction of mind, breaking one bread, which is the medicine of immortality and the antidote that we should not die but live forever in Jesus Christ.

CHAPTER 21

¹I am devoted to you and to those whom for the honor of God you sent to Smyrna, from where I also write to you with thanksgiving to the LORD, having love for Polycarp as I have for you also. Remember me, even as I would that Jesus Christ may also remember you. ²Pray for the assembly which is in Syria, from where I am led a prisoner to Rome—I who am the very last of the faithful there, according as I was counted worthy to be found to the honor of God. Farewell in God the Father and in Jesus Christ our common hope.

TO THE MAGNESIANS

IGNATIUS, WHO IS ALSO THEOPHORUS, TO HER WHICH HAS BEEN BLESSED THROUGH THE GRACE OF GOD THE FATHER IN CHRIST JESUS OUR SAVIOR, IN WHOM I SALUTE THE ASSEMBLY WHICH IS IN MAGNESIA ON THE MAEANDER, AND I WISH HER ABUNDANT GREETINGS IN GOD THE FATHER AND IN JESUS CHRIST.

CHAPTER 1

¹When I learned of the exceeding good order of your love in the ways of God, I was delighted, and I determined to address you in the faith of Jesus Christ. ²For being counted worthy to bear a most godly name, which I carry around in these bonds, I sing the praise of the assemblies; and I pray that there may be in them union of the flesh and of the spirit which are Jesus Christ's, our never-failing life—a union of faith and of love which is preferred before all things, and, what is more than all—a union with Jesus and with the Father, in whom, if we patiently endure all, despite the prince of this world, and escape from that, we will attain to God.

CHAPTER 2

¹Forasmuch then as I was permitted to see you in the person of Damas, your godly overseer, and your worthy elders Bassus and Apollonius, and my fellow-servant, the servant Zotion, of whom I would gladly have joy, for that he is subject to the overseer as to the grace of God and to the eldership as to the law of Jesus Christ:

CHAPTER 3

¹Yes, and it is appropriate for you also not to presume on the youth of your overseer, but according to the power of God the Father to render to him all reverence, even as I have learned that the holy elders have also not taken advantage of his outwardly youthful estate, but give place to him as to one prudent in God; yet not to him, but to the Father of Jesus Christ, even to the Overseer of all. ²For the honor, therefore, of Him that desired you, it is suitable that you should be obedient without deception. For a man does not so much deceive this overseer who is seen, as cheat that Other who is invisible; and in such a case he must reckon not with flesh but with God who knows the hidden things.

CHAPTER 4

¹It is therefore appropriate that we not only be called Christians, but also be such, even as some persons have the overseer's name on their lips, but in everything act apart from him. Such men appear to me not to keep a good conscience, forasmuch as they do not assemble themselves together lawfully according to command.

CHAPTER 5

¹Seeing, then, that all things have an end, these two are set together before us: life and death; and each man will go to his own place. ²For just as there are two coinages—the one of God and the other of the world, so also each of them has its proper stamp impressed on it—the unbelievers the stamp of this world, but the faithful in love the stamp of God the Father through Jesus Christ, through whom, unless of our own free choice we accept to die into His passion, His life is not in us.

CHAPTER 6

¹Seeing, then, that in the previously mentioned persons I beheld your whole people in faith and embraced them, I advise you: be zealous to do all things in godly concord—the overseer presiding after the likeness of God and the elders after the likeness of the council of the apostles, with the servants also who are most dear to me, having been entrusted with the office of servant of Jesus Christ, who was with the Father before the worlds and appeared at the end of time. ²Therefore, you should all study conformity to God and pay reverence to one another; and let no man regard his neighbor after the flesh, but always love one another in Jesus Christ. Let there be nothing among you which will have power to divide you, but be united with the overseer and with them that preside over you as an example and a lesson of incorruptibility.

CHAPTER 7

¹Therefore, as the LORD did nothing without the Father, either by Himself or by the apostles, so neither do you do anything without the overseer and the elders. And do not attempt to think anything right for yourselves apart from others, but let there be one prayer in common, one supplication, one mind, one hope, in love and in joy unblameable, which is Jesus Christ, than whom there is nothing better. ²Hasten for all of you to come together, as to one temple, even God; as to one altar, even to one Jesus Christ, who came forth from One Father and is with One and departed to One.

CHAPTER 8

¹Do not be seduced by strange doctrines nor by antiquated fables, which are profitless. For if even to this day we live after the manner of Judaism, we avow that we have not received grace: ²for the divine prophets lived after Christ Jesus. For this reason, they were also persecuted, being inspired by His grace to the end that they which are disobedient might be fully persuaded that there is one God who manifested Himself through His Son Jesus Christ, who is His Word that proceeded from silence, who in all things was well-pleasing to Him that sent Him.

CHAPTER 9

¹If then those who had walked in ancient practices attained to newness of hope, no longer observing Sabbaths but fashioning their lives after the LORD's Day, on which our life also arose through Him and through His death which some men deny—a mystery whereby we attained to belief, and for this reason we endure patiently, that we may be found disciples of Jesus Christ our only teacher— ²if this be so, how will we be able to live apart from Him? Seeing that even the prophets, being His disciples, were expecting Him as their teacher through the Spirit. And for this reason, He whom they rightly awaited, when He came, raised them from the dead.

CHAPTER 10

¹Therefore, let us not be insensible to His goodness. For if He should imitate us according to our deeds, we are lost. For this reason, seeing that we have become His disciples, let us learn to live as befits Christianity. For whoever is called by another name besides this, is not of God. ²Therefore, put away the vile leaven which has waxed stale and sour, and go yourselves to the new leaven, which is Jesus Christ. Be salted in Him, that none among you grow putrid, seeing that by your savor you will be proved. ³It is monstrous to talk of Jesus Christ and to practice Judaism. For Christianity did not believe in Judaism, but Judaism in Christianity, wherein every tongue believed and was gathered together to God.

CHAPTER 11

¹Now these things I say, my dearly beloved, not because I have learned that any of you are so minded; but as being less than any of you, I would have you be on your guard early, that you do not fall into the snares of vain doctrine; but be fully persuaded concerning the birth, and the passion, and the resurrection, which took place in the time of the governorship of Pontius Pilate; for these things were truly and certainly done by Jesus Christ our hope; from which hope may it not befall any of you to be turned aside.

CHAPTER 12

¹Let me have your joy in all things, if I am worthy. For even though I am in bonds, yet I am not comparable to one of you who are at liberty. I know that you are not puffed up; for you have Jesus Christ in yourselves. And, when I praise you, I know that you only feel

the more shame; as it is written: "The righteous man is a self-accuser."

CHAPTER 13

¹Therefore, do your diligence that you may be confirmed in the ordinances of the Lord and of the apostles, that you may prosper in all things—whatever you do in flesh and spirit—by faith and by love, in the Son, and Father, and in the Spirit, in the beginning and in the end, with your revered overseer, and with the fitly-wreathed spiritual circlet of your eldership, and with the servants who walk after God. ²Be obedient to the overseer and to one another, as Jesus Christ was to the Father, and as the apostles were to Christ and to the Father, that there may be union both of flesh and of spirit.

CHAPTER 14

¹Knowing that you are full of God, I have exhorted you briefly. Remember me in your prayers, that I may attain to God; and also remember the assembly which is in Syria, of which I am not worthy to be called a member. For I have need of your united prayer and love in God, that it may be granted to the assembly which is in Syria to be refreshed by the dew of your fervent supplication.

CHAPTER 15

¹The Ephesians from Smyrna salute you, from where also I write to you. They are here with me for the glory of God, as you also are; and they have comforted me in all things, together with Polycarp, overseer of the Smyrnaeans. Yes, and all the other assemblies salute you in the honor of Jesus Christ. Farewell in godly concord, and may you possess a steadfast spirit, which is Jesus Christ.

TO THE TRALLIANS

IGNATIUS, WHO IS ALSO THEOPHORUS, TO HER THAT IS BELOVED BY GOD THE FATHER OF JESUS CHRIST; TO THE HOLY ASSEMBLY WHICH IS IN TRALLES OF ASIA, CHOSEN AND WORTHY OF GOD, HAVING PEACE IN FLESH AND SPIRIT THROUGH THE PASSION OF JESUS CHRIST, WHO IS OUR HOPE THROUGH OUR RESURRECTION TO HIM; WHICH ASSEMBLY I ALSO SALUTE IN THE DIVINE ABUNDANCE AFTER THE APOSTOLIC FASHION, AND I WISH HER ABUNDANT GREETINGS.

CHAPTER 1

¹I have learned that you have a mind unblameable and steadfast in patience, not from habit, but by nature, according as your overseer Polybius informed me, who by the will of God and of Jesus Christ visited me in Smyrna; and so greatly did he rejoice with me in my bonds in Christ Jesus, that in him I beheld the whole multitude of you. ²Having therefore received your godly benevolence at his hands, I gave glory, forasmuch as I had found you to be imitators of God, even as I had learned.

CHAPTER 2

¹For when you are obedient to the overseer as to Jesus Christ, it is evident to me that you are living not after men but after Jesus Christ, who died for us, that believing on His death you might escape death. ²It is therefore necessary, even as your custom is, that you should do nothing without the overseer; but also be obedient to the eldership, as to the apostles of Jesus Christ our hope; for if we live in Him, we will also be found in Him. ³And those likewise who are servants of the mysteries of Jesus Christ must please all men in all ways. For they are not servants of meats and drinks but servants of the Assembly of God. It is therefore right that they should beware of blame as of fire.

CHAPTER 3

¹In like manner let all men respect the servants as Jesus Christ, even as they should respect the overseer as being a type of the Father and the elders as the council of God and as the college of apostles. Apart from these there is not even the name of an assembly. ²And I am persuaded that you are so minded as touching these matters; for I received the example of your love, and I have it with me, in the person of your overseer, whose very demeanor is a great lesson, while his gentleness is power—a man to whom I think even the godless pay reverence. ³Seeing that I love you I thus spare you, though I might write more sharply on his behalf, but I did not think myself competent for this, that being a convict I should order you as though I were an apostle.

CHAPTER 4

¹I have many deep thoughts in God, but I take the measure of myself, lest I perish in my boasting. For now I should be the more afraid and not to give heed to those that would puff me up; for they that say these things to me are a scourge to me. ²For though I desire to suffer, yet I do not know whether I am worthy; for the envy of the Devil is indeed unseen by many, but against me it wages the fiercer war. So then, I crave gentleness, whereby the prince of this world is brought to nothing.

CHAPTER 5

¹Am I not able to write to you of heavenly things? But I fear lest I should cause you harm, being babies. So bear with me, lest not being able to take them in, you should be choked. ²For I myself also, although I am in bonds, can comprehend heavenly things, and the arrays of the messengers, and the musterings of the principalities—things visible and things invisible—I myself am not yet by reason of this a disciple. For we lack many things, that God may not be lacking to us.

CHAPTER 6

¹Therefore I exhort you—yet not I, but the love of Jesus Christ—take only Christian food, and abstain from strange herbage, which is heresy: ²for these men even mingle poison with Jesus Christ, imposing on others by a show of honesty, like persons administering a deadly drug with honeyed wine, so that one who does not know it, fearing nothing, drinks in death with a destructive delight.

CHAPTER 7

¹Therefore, be on your guard against such men. And this will surely be, if you are not puffed up and if you are inseparable from Jesus Christ, and from the overseer, and from the ordinances of the apostles. ²He that is within the sanctuary is clean; but he that is outside the sanctuary is not clean, that is, he that does anything without the overseer, and eldership, and servants; this man is not clean in his conscience.

CHAPTER 8

¹Indeed, not that I have known of any such thing among you, but I keep watch over you early, as my beloved, for I foresee the snares of the Devil. Therefore, arm yourselves with gentleness and recover yourselves in faith, which is the flesh of the Lord, and in love which is the blood of Jesus Christ. ²Let none of you bear a grudge against his neighbor. Give no occasion to the nations, lest by reason of a few foolish men the godly multitude is blasphemed; for, "Woe to him through whom My Name is vainly blasphemed before any."

CHAPTER 9

¹Therefore, be deaf when any man speaks to you apart from Jesus Christ, who was of the race of David, who was the Son of Mary, who was truly born, and ate, and drank, was truly persecuted under Pontius Pilate, [and] was truly crucified and died in the sight of those in Heaven, and those on earth, and those under the earth; ²who moreover was truly raised from the dead, His Father having raised Him, who in like fashion will so raise us also who believe on Him—His Father, I say, will raise us—in Christ Jesus, apart from whom we do not have true life.

CHAPTER 10

¹But if it were as certain persons who are godless—that is, unbelievers—say, that He suffered only in semblance, being themselves mere semblance, why am I in bonds? And why do I also desire to fight with wild beasts? So I die in vain. Truly then I lie against the Lord.

CHAPTER 11

¹Therefore, shun those vile offshoots that gender a deadly fruit, of which if a man taste, immediately he dies. For these men are not the Father's planting, for if they had been, they would have been seen to be branches of the Cross, and their fruit imperishable—the Cross whereby He through His passion invites us, being His members. Now it cannot be that a head should be found without members, seeing that God promises union, and this union is Himself.

CHAPTER 12

¹I salute you from Smyrna, together with the assemblies of God that are present with me; men who refreshed me in all ways both in flesh and in spirit. ²My bonds exhort you, which for Jesus Christ's sake I bear about, entreating that I may attain to God; abide in your concord and in prayer with one another. For it is appropriate for you separately, and more especially the elders, to cheer the soul of your overseer to the honor of the Father [and to the honor] of Jesus Christ and of the apostles. ³I pray that you may listen to me in love, lest I be for a testimony against you by having so written. And also pray for me who has need of your love in the mercy of God, that I may be granted the lot which I am eager to attain, to the end that I am not found reprobate.

CHAPTER 13

¹The love of the Smyrnaeans and Ephesians salutes you. Remember in your prayers the assembly which is in Syria, of which I am not worthy to be called a member, being the very last of them. ²Farewell in Jesus Christ, submitting yourselves to the overseer as to the command, and likewise also to the eldership; and each of you separately must love one another with an undivided heart. ³My spirit is offered up for you, not only now, but also when I will attain to God. For I am still in peril; but the Father is faithful in Jesus Christ to fulfill my petition and yours. May we be found unblameable in Him.

TO THE ROMANS

IGNATIUS, WHO IS ALSO THEOPHORUS, TO HER THAT HAS FOUND MERCY IN THE BOUNTIFULNESS OF THE FATHER MOST HIGH AND OF JESUS CHRIST HIS ONLY SON; TO THE ASSEMBLY THAT IS BELOVED AND ENLIGHTENED THROUGH THE WILL OF HIM WHO WILLED ALL THINGS THAT ARE, BY FAITH AND LOVE TOWARD JESUS CHRIST OUR GOD; EVEN TO HER THAT HAS THE PRESIDENCY IN THE COUNTRY OF THE REGION OF THE ROMANS, BEING WORTHY OF GOD, WORTHY OF HONOR, WORTHY OF COMMENDATIONS, WORTHY OF PRAISE, WORTHY OF SUCCESS, WORTHY IN PURITY, AND HAVING THE PRESIDENCY OF LOVE, WALKING IN THE LAW OF CHRIST AND BEARING THE FATHER'S NAME; WHICH ASSEMBLY I ALSO SALUTE IN THE NAME OF JESUS CHRIST THE SON OF THE FATHER; TO THEM THAT IN FLESH AND SPIRIT ARE UNITED TO HIS EVERY COMMAND, BEING FILLED WITH THE GRACE OF GOD WITHOUT WAVERING, AND FILTERED CLEAR FROM EVERY FOREIGN STAIN; ABUNDANT GREETINGS IN JESUS CHRIST OUR GOD IN BLAMELESSNESS.

CHAPTER 1

¹In answer to my prayer to God it has been granted to me to see your godly faces, so that I have obtained even more than I asked; for wearing bonds in Christ Jesus I hope to salute you, if it be the Divine will that I should be counted worthy to reach to the end; ²for the beginning is truly well ordered, if [it] so be I will attain to the goal, that I may receive my inheritance without hindrance. For I dread your very love, lest it do me an injury; for it is easy for you to do what you will, but for me it is difficult to attain to God, unless you will spare me.

CHAPTER 2

¹For I would not have you to be men-pleasers but to please God, as indeed you do please Him. For neither will I myself ever find an opportunity such as this to attain to God, nor can you, if you are silent, win the credit of any nobler work. For, if you are silent and leave me alone, I am a word of God; but if you desire my flesh, then I will be again a mere cry. ²Grant me nothing more than that I am poured out [as] a libation to God, while there is still an altar ready, that forming yourselves into a chorus in love you may sing to the Father in Jesus Christ, for that God has granted that the overseer from Syria should be found in the west, having summoned him from the east. It is good to set from the world to God, that I may rise to Him.

CHAPTER 3

¹You never grudged anyone; you were the instructors of others. And my desire is that those lessons will hold good which as teachers you prescribe. ²Only pray that I may have power inwardly and outwardly, so that I may not only say it but also desire it; that I may not only be called a Christian, but also be found one. For if I will be found so, then I can also be called one, and be faithful then, when I am no longer visible to the world. ³Nothing visible is good. For our God Jesus Christ, being in the Father, is the more plainly visible. The work is not of persuasiveness, but Christianity is a thing of might, whenever it is hated by the world.

CHAPTER 4

¹I write to all the assemblies, and I bid all men know, that of my own free will I die for God, unless you should hinder me. I exhort you, do not be an unseasonable kindness to me. Let me be given to the wild beasts, for through them I can attain to God. I am God's wheat, and I am ground by the teeth of wild beasts that I may be found pure bread [of Christ]. ²Rather entice the wild beasts, that they may become my tomb and may leave no part of my body behind, so that I may not, when I have fallen asleep, be burdensome to anyone. Then I will truly be a disciple of Jesus Christ, when the world will not so much as see my body. Supplicate the LORD for me, that through these instruments I may be found a sacrifice to God. ³I do not command you, as Peter and Paul did. They were apostles, I am a convict; they were free, but I am a slave to this very hour. Yet if I will suffer, then I am a freedman of Jesus Christ, and I will rise free in Him. Now I am learning in my bonds to put away every desire.

CHAPTER 5

¹From Syria even to Rome I fight with wild beasts, by land and sea, by night and by day, being bound amidst ten leopards, even a company of soldiers, who only wax worse when they are kindly treated. However, through their wrongdoings I become more completely a disciple; yet am I not hereby justified. ²May I have joy of the beasts that have been prepared for me; and I pray that I may find them prompt; no, I will entice them that they may devour me promptly, not as they have done to some, refusing to touch them through fear. Yes, though of themselves they should not be willing while I am ready, I myself will force them to it. ³Bear with me. I know what is expedient for me. Now am I beginning to be a disciple. May nothing of things visible and things invisible envy me, that I may attain to Jesus Christ. Come fire, and cross, and grapplings with wild beasts, wrenching of bones, hacking of limbs, crushings of my whole body, come cruel tortures of the Devil to assail me. Only be it mine to attain to Jesus Christ.

CHAPTER 6

¹The farthest bounds of the universe will profit me nothing, neither the kingdoms of this world. It is good for me to die for Jesus Christ rather than to reign over the farthest bounds of the earth. I seek Him who died on our behalf; I desire Him who rose again for our sake. The pangs of a new birth are on me. ²Bear with me, brothers. Do not hinder me from living; do not desire my death. Do not bestow on the world one who desires to be God's, neither allure him with material things. Permit me to receive the pure light. When I have come there, then I will be a man. ³Permit me to be an imitator of the passion of my God. If any man has Him within himself, let him understand what I desire, and let him have fellow-feeling with me, for he knows the things which constrict me.

CHAPTER 7

¹The prince of this world would gladly tear me in pieces and corrupt my mind toward God. Therefore, do not let any of you who are near aid him. Rather, stand on my side, that is on God's side. Do not speak of Jesus Christ and in addition desire the world. ²Do not let envy have a home in you. Even though I myself, when I am with you, should implore you, do not obey me, but rather give credence to these things which I write to you. I write to you in the midst of life yet lusting after death. My lust has been crucified, and there is no fire of material longing in me, but only water living [[and speaking]] in me, saying within me, "Come to the Father." ³I have no delight in the food of corruption or in the delights of this life. I desire the bread of God, which is the flesh of Christ who was of the seed of David; and I desire His blood for a drink, which is love incorruptible.

CHAPTER 8

¹I no longer desire to live after the manner of men; and this will be, if you desire it. Desire that you yourselves may also be desired. ²In a brief letter I implore you; believe me. And Jesus Christ will make these things manifest to

you, that I speak the truth—Jesus Christ, the unerring mouth in whom the Father has spoken. ³Entreat [Him] for me, that I may attain [what I desire]. I do not write to you after the flesh, but after the mind of God. If I will suffer, it was your desire; if I will be rejected, it was your hatred.

CHAPTER 9

¹Remember in your prayers the assembly which is in Syria, which has God for its shepherd in my stead. Jesus Christ alone will be its overseer—He and your love. ²But for myself I am ashamed to be called one of them; for neither am I worthy, being the very last of them and an untimely birth, but I have found mercy that I should be someone, if [it] so be [that] I will attain to God. ³My spirit salutes you, and the love of the assemblies which received me in the Name of Jesus Christ, not as a mere wayfarer; for even those assemblies which did not lie on my route after the flesh went before me from city to city.

CHAPTER 10

¹Now I write these things to you from Smyrna by the hand of the Ephesians who are worthy of all commendations. And Crocus also, a name very dear to me, is with me, with many others besides. ²As touching those who went before me from Syria to Rome to the glory of God, I believe that you have received instructions; whom also apprise that I am near; for they are all worthy of God and of you, and it is appropriate for you to refresh them in all things. ³These things I write to you on the ninth before the Calends of September. Farewell to the end in the patient waiting for Jesus Christ.

TO THE PHILADELPHIANS

IGNATIUS, WHO IS ALSO THEOPHORUS, TO THE ASSEMBLY OF GOD THE FATHER AND OF JESUS CHRIST, WHICH IS IN PHILADELPHIA OF ASIA, WHICH HAS FOUND MERCY AND IS FIRMLY ESTABLISHED IN THE CONCORD OF GOD AND REJOICES IN THE PASSION OF OUR LORD AND IN HIS RESURRECTION WITHOUT WAVERING, BEING FULLY ASSURED IN ALL MERCY; WHICH ASSEMBLY I SALUTE IN THE BLOOD OF JESUS CHRIST, THAT IS CONTINUOUS AND ABIDING JOY; MORE ESPECIALLY IF THEY ARE AT ONE WITH THE OVERSEER AND THE ELDERS WHO ARE WITH HIM, AND WITH THE SERVANTS THAT HAVE BEEN APPOINTED ACCORDING TO THE MIND OF JESUS CHRIST, WHOM AFTER HIS OWN WILL HE CONFIRMED AND ESTABLISHED BY HIS HOLY SPIRIT.

CHAPTER 1

¹I have found your overseer to hold the ministry which pertains to the common [good], not of himself or through men, nor yet for vain glory, but in the love of God the Father and the Lord Jesus Christ. And I am amazed at his forbearance, whose silence is more powerful than others' speech. ²For he is attuned in harmony with the commands, as a lyre with its strings. For what reason my soul blesses his godly mind, for I have found that it is virtuous and perfect—even the composed and calm temper which he has, while living in all godly forbearance.

CHAPTER 2

¹Therefore, as children of the light and truth, shun division and wrong doctrines; and where the shepherd is, follow there as sheep. ²For many deceptive wolves with destructive delights lead captive the runners in God's race; but, where you are at one, they will find no place.

CHAPTER 3

¹Abstain from noxious herbs, which are not the farming of Jesus Christ, because they are not the planting of the Father. Not that I have found division among you, but filtering. ²For as many as are of God and of Jesus Christ, they are with the overseer; and as many as will convert and enter into the unity of the Assembly, these also will be of God, that they may be living after Jesus Christ. ³Do not be deceived, my brothers. If any man follows one that makes a schism, he does not inherit the Kingdom of God. If any man walks in strange doctrine, he has no fellowship with the passion.

CHAPTER 4

¹Therefore, be careful to observe one thanksgiving (for there is one flesh of our Lord Jesus Christ and one cup to union in His blood; there is one altar, as there is one overseer, together with the eldership and the servants—my fellow-servants), that whatever you do, you may do it after God.

CHAPTER 5

¹My brothers, my heart overflows altogether in love toward you; and rejoicing above measure I watch over your safety; yet not I, but Jesus Christ, wearing whose bonds I am the more afraid, because I am not yet perfected. But your prayer will make me perfect [to God], that I may attain to the inheritance wherein I have found mercy, taking refuge in the good news as the flesh of Jesus and in the apostles as the eldership of the Assembly. ²Yes, and we love the prophets also, because they too pointed to the good news in their preaching and set their hope on Him and awaited Him; in whom also having faith, they were saved in the unity of Jesus Christ, being worthy of all love and admiration as holy men, approved of Jesus Christ and numbered together in the good news of our common hope.

CHAPTER 6

¹But if anyone presents Judaism to you, do not hear him; for it is better to hear Christianity from a man who is circumcised than Judaism from one uncircumcised. But if either the one or the other does not speak concerning Jesus Christ, I look on them as tombstones and graves of the dead, whereon are inscribed only the names of men. ²Therefore, shun the wicked arts and plottings of the prince of this world, lest by chance you are crushed by his devices, and grow weak in your love. But assemble all yourselves together with undivided heart. ³And I give thanks to my God, that I have a good conscience in my dealings with you, and no man can boast, either in secret or openly, that I was burdensome to anyone in small things or in great. Yes, and for all among whom I spoke, it is my prayer that they may not turn it into a testimony against themselves.

CHAPTER 7

¹For even though certain persons desired to deceive me after the flesh, yet the Spirit is not deceived, being from God; for He knows from where He comes and where He goes, and He searches out the hidden things. I cried out when I was among you; I spoke with a loud voice, with God's own voice, "Give heed to the overseer, and the eldership, and servants." ²However, there were those who suspected me of saying this, because I knew beforehand of the division of certain persons. But He in whom I am bound is my witness that I did not learn it from flesh of man; it was the preaching of the Spirit who spoke concerning this: "Do nothing without the overseer; keep your flesh as a temple of God; cherish union; shun divisions; be imitators of Jesus Christ, as He Himself also was of His Father."

CHAPTER 8

¹Therefore, I did my own part, as a man composed to union. But where there is division and anger, there God does not abide. Now the LORD forgives all men when they convert, if converting they return to the unity of God and to the council of the overseer. I have faith in the grace of Jesus Christ, who will strike off every chain from you; ²and I entreat you to do nothing in a spirit of factiousness, but after the teaching of Christ. For I heard certain persons saying, "If I do not find it in the charters, I do not believe it in the good news." And when I said to them, "It is written," they answered me, "That is the question." But as for me, my charter is Jesus Christ, the inviolable charter is His cross, and His death, and His resurrection, and faith through Him, wherein I desire to be justified through your prayers.

CHAPTER 9

¹The priests likewise were good, but better is the Chief Priest to whom is committed the Holy of Holies; for to Him alone are committed the hidden things of God, He Himself being the door of the Father, through which Abraham, and Isaac, and Jacob enter in, and the prophets, and the apostles, and the whole Assembly; all these things combine in the unity of God. ²But the good news has a singular preeminence in the advent of the Savior, even our Lord Jesus Christ, and His passion and resurrection. For the beloved prophets in their preaching pointed to Him; but the good news is the completion of immortality. All things together are good, if you believe through love.

CHAPTER 10

¹Seeing that in answer to your prayer and to the tender sympathy which you have in Christ Jesus, it has been reported to me that the assembly which is in Antioch of Syria has peace, it is appropriate for you, as an assembly of God, to appoint a servant to go there as God's ambassador, that he may congratulate them when they are assembled together, and may glorify the Name. ²Blessed in Jesus Christ is he that will be counted worthy of such a service; and you yourselves will be glorified. Now if you desire it, it is not impossible for you to do this for the Name of God, even as the assemblies which are nearest have sent overseers, and others elders and servants.

CHAPTER 11

¹But as touching Philo the servant from Cilicia, a man of good report, who now also ministers to me in the word of God, together with Rhaius Agathopus, a chosen one who follows me from Syria, having bid farewell to this present life, these also bear witness to you—and I myself thank God on your behalf, because you received them, as I trust the LORD will receive you. But may those who treated them with dishonor be redeemed through the grace of Jesus Christ. ²The love of the brothers which are in Troas salutes you; from where I also write to you by the hand of Burrhus, who was sent with me by the Ephesians and Smyrnaeans as a mark of honor. The LORD will honor them, even Jesus Christ, on whom their hope is set in flesh, and soul, and spirit, by faith, by love, by concord. Farewell in Christ Jesus our common hope.

TO THE SMYRNAEANS

IGNATIUS, WHO IS ALSO THEOPHORUS, TO THE ASSEMBLY OF GOD THE FATHER AND OF JESUS CHRIST THE BELOVED, WHICH HAS BEEN MERCIFULLY ENDOWED WITH EVERY GRACE, BEING FILLED WITH FAITH AND LOVE, AND LACKING IN NO GRACE, MOST WORTHY AND BEARING HOLY TREASURES; TO THE ASSEMBLY WHICH IS IN SMYRNA OF ASIA, IN A BLAMELESS SPIRIT AND IN THE WORD OF GOD: ABUNDANT GREETINGS.

CHAPTER 1

¹I give glory to Jesus Christ, the God who bestowed such wisdom on you; for I have perceived that you are established in immovable faith, being as it were nailed on the Cross of the Lord Jesus Christ, in flesh and in spirit, and firmly grounded in love in the blood of Christ, fully persuaded as touching our Lord that He is truly of the race of David according to the flesh, but Son of God by the Divine will and power, truly born of a virgin and immersed by John that all righteousness might be fulfilled by Him, ²truly nailed up in the flesh for our sakes under Pontius Pilate and Herod the tetrarch (of which fruit we are—that is, of His most blessed passion), that He might set up an ensign to all the ages through His resurrection, for His holy ones and faithful people, whether among Jews or among nations, in one body of His Assembly.

CHAPTER 2

¹For He suffered all these things for our sakes, that we might be saved; and He truly suffered, as He also truly raised Himself; not as certain unbelievers say, that He suffered in semblance [only], being themselves mere semblance. And according as their opinions are, so will it happen to them, for they are without body and demon-like.

CHAPTER 3

¹For I know and believe that He was in the flesh even after the resurrection; ²and when He came to Peter and his company, He said to them, "Lay hold and handle Me, and see that I am not a bodiless spirit." And immediately they touched Him, and they believed, being joined to His flesh and His blood. For what reason they also despised death, no, they were found superior to death. ³And after His resurrection, He ate with them and drank with them as one in the flesh, though spiritually He was united with the Father.

CHAPTER 4

¹But these things I warn you, dearly beloved, knowing that you yourselves are so minded. However, I watch over you early to protect you from wild beasts in human form—men whom not only you should not receive, but, if it were possible, not so much as meet [them]; only pray for them, if by chance they may convert. This is indeed difficult, but Jesus Christ, our true life, has power over it. ²For if these things were done by our Lord in semblance, then I am also a prisoner in semblance. And why then have I delivered myself over to death, to fire, to sword, to wild beasts? But near to the sword, near to God; in company with wild beasts, in company with God. Only let it be in the Name of Jesus Christ, so that we may suffer together with Him. I endure all things, seeing that He Himself, who is perfect Man, enables me.

CHAPTER 5

¹But certain persons ignorantly deny Him, or rather have been denied by Him, being advocates of death rather than of the truth; and they have not been persuaded by the prophecies, nor by the Law of Moses, no, nor even to this very hour by the good news, nor by the sufferings of each of us separately; ²for they are of the same mind also concerning us. For what profit is it [to me] if a man praises me, but blasphemes my Lord, not confessing that He was a bearer of flesh? Yet he that does not affirm this, does thereby deny Him altogether, being himself a bearer of a corpse. ³But their names, being unbelievers, I have not thought fit to record in writing; no, far be it from me even to remember them, until they convert and return to the passion, which is our resurrection.

CHAPTER 6

¹Let no man be deceived. Even the heavenly beings, and the glory of the messengers, and the rulers visible and invisible, if they do not believe in the blood of Christ, judgment awaits them also. He that receives let him receive. Do not let office puff up any man; for faith and love are all in all, and nothing is preferred before them. ²But mark those who hold strange doctrine touching the grace of Jesus Christ which came to us, how that they are contrary to the mind of God. They have no care for love, none for the widow, none for the orphan, none for the afflicted, none for the prisoner, none for the hungry or thirsty. They abstain from thanksgiving and prayer, because they do not allow that the thanksgiving is the flesh of our Savior Jesus Christ, which flesh suffered for our sins, and which the Father of His goodness raised up.

CHAPTER 7

¹Therefore, they that deny the good gift of God perish by their questionings. But it would be expedient for them to have love, that they may also rise again. ²It is therefore appropriate that you should abstain from such, and not speak of them either privately or in public, but should give heed to the prophets, and especially to the good news, wherein the passion is shown to us and the resurrection is accomplished.

CHAPTER 8

¹[But] shun divisions, as the beginning of evils. All of you must follow your overseer, as Jesus Christ followed the Father, and the eldership as the apostles; and pay respect to the servants, as to God's command. Let no man do anything of things pertaining to the Assembly apart from the overseer. Let that be held a valid thanksgiving which is under the overseer or one to whom he will have committed it. ²Wherever the overseer will appear, let the people be there, even as where Jesus may be, there is the Universal Assembly. It is not lawful apart from the overseer either to immerse or to hold a love-feast; but whatever he will approve, this is also well-pleasing to God, that everything which you do may be sure and valid.

CHAPTER 9

¹It is reasonable, from now on, that we wake to soberness, while we have time to convert and turn to God. It is good to recognize God and the overseer. He that honors the overseer is honored of God; he that does anything without the knowledge of the overseer renders service to the Devil. ²Therefore, may all things abound to you in grace, for you are worthy. You refreshed me in all things, and Jesus Christ will refresh you. In my absence and in my presence, you cherished me. May God reward you, for whose sake if you endure all things, you will attain to Him.

CHAPTER 10

¹Philo and Rhaius Agathopus, who followed me in the cause of God, you did well to receive

as ministers of God—who also give thanks to the LORD for you, because you refreshed them in every way. Nothing will be lost to you. ²My spirit is devoted for you, as are my bonds also, which you did not despise, neither were ashamed of them. Nor will He, who is perfect faithfulness, be ashamed of you, even Jesus Christ.

CHAPTER 11
¹Your prayer sped forth to the assembly which is in Antioch of Syria, from where, coming [as] a prisoner in most godly bonds, I salute all men, though I am not worthy to belong to it, being the very last of them. By the Divine will this was granted to me—not of my own complicity, but by God's grace, which I pray may be given to me perfectly, that through your prayers I may attain to God. ²Therefore, that your work may be perfected both on earth and in Heaven, it is suitable that your assembly should appoint, for the honor of God, an ambassador of God that he may go as far as Syria and congratulate them because they are at peace, and have recovered their proper stature, and their proper bulk has been restored to them. ³It seemed to me, therefore, a fitting thing that you should send one of your own people with a letter, that he might join with them in giving glory for the calm which by God's will had overtaken them, and because they were already reaching a haven through your prayers. Seeing you are perfect, let your counsels also be perfect; for if you desire to do well, God is ready to grant the means.

CHAPTER 12
¹The love of the brothers which are in Troas salutes you, from where I also write to you by the hand of Burrhus, whom you sent with me jointly with the Ephesians, your brothers. He has refreshed me in all ways. And I wish that all imitated him, for he is an example of the ministry of God. The Divine grace will repay him in all things. ²I salute your godly overseer, and your venerable eldership, [and] my fellow-servants the servants, and all of you separately and in a body, in the Name of Jesus Christ, and in His flesh and blood, in His passion and resurrection, which was both carnal and spiritual, in the unity of God and of yourselves. Grace to you, mercy, peace, patience, always.

CHAPTER 13
¹I salute the households of my brothers with their wives and children, and the virgins who are called widows. I bid you farewell in the power of the Father. Philo, who is with me, salutes you. ²I salute the household of Gavia, and I pray that she may be grounded in faith and love, both of flesh and of spirit. I salute Alce, a name very dear to me, and the incomparable Daphnus, and Eutecnus, and all by name. Farewell in the grace of God.

SEVEN EPISTLES OF IGNATIUS

TO POLYCARP

IGNATIUS, WHO IS ALSO THEOPHORUS, TO POLYCARP WHO IS OVERSEER OF THE ASSEMBLY OF THE SMYRNAEANS, OR RATHER, WHO HAS FOR HIS OVERSEER GOD THE FATHER AND JESUS CHRIST: ABUNDANT GREETINGS.

CHAPTER 1
¹Welcoming your godly mind which is grounded as it were on an immovable rock, I give exceeding glory that it has been granted to me to see your blameless face, of which I would gladly have joy in God. ²I exhort you in the grace with which you are clothed to press forward in your course and to exhort all men that they may be saved. Vindicate your office in all diligence of flesh and of spirit. Have a care for union, more than which there is nothing better. Bear all men, as the LORD also bears you. Permit all men in love, as you do also. ³Give yourself to unceasing prayers. Ask for larger wisdom than you have. Be watchful and keep your spirit from slumbering. Speak to each man separately after the manner of God. Bear the ailments of all, as a perfect athlete. Where there is more toil, there is much gain.

CHAPTER 2
¹If you love good scholars, this is not worthy of thanks in you. Rather, bring the more pernicious to submission by gentleness. All wounds are not healed by the same salve. Lessen sharp pains by poultices. ²Be prudent as the serpent in all things and always guileless as the dove. Therefore, you are made of flesh and spirit, that you may humor the things which appear before your eyes; and as for the invisible things, pray that they may be revealed to you, that you may be lacking in nothing, but may abound in every spiritual gift. ³The season requires you, as pilots require winds or as a storm-tossed mariner a haven, that it may attain to God. Be sober, as God's athlete. The prize is incorruption and continuous life, concerning which you are also persuaded. In all things I am devoted to you—myself and my bonds which you cherished.

CHAPTER 3
¹Do not let those that seem to be plausible and yet teach strange doctrine dismay you. Stand firm, as an anvil when it is smitten. It is the part of a great athlete to receive blows and be victorious. But we must especially endure all things for God's sake, that He may also endure us. ²Be more diligent than you are. Mark the seasons. Await Him that is above every season—the Perpetual, the Invisible, who became visible for our sake; the Impalpable, the Impassible, who suffered for our sake, who endured in all ways for our sake.

CHAPTER 4
¹Do not let widows be neglected. After the LORD, be their protector. Let nothing be done without your consent; neither do anything without the consent of God, as indeed you do not. Be steadfast. ²Let meetings be held more frequently. Seek out all men by name. ³Do not despise slaves, whether men or women. Yet do not let these be puffed up, but rather let them serve the more faithfully to the glory of God, that they may obtain a better freedom from God. Do not let them desire to be set free at the public cost, lest they are found slaves of lust.

CHAPTER 5
¹Flee evil arts, or rather, hold discourse about these. Tell my sisters to love the LORD and to be content with their husbands in flesh and in spirit. In like manner also, charge my brothers in the Name of Jesus Christ to love their wives, as the LORD loved the Assembly. ²If anyone is able to abide in chastity to the honor of the flesh of the LORD, let him so abide without boasting. If he boasts, he is lost; and if it is known beyond the overseer, he is polluted. It is appropriate for men and women too, when they marry, to unite themselves with the consent of the overseer, that the marriage may be after the LORD and not after lust. Let all things be done to the honor of God.

CHAPTER 6
¹Give heed to the overseer, that God may also give heed to you. I am devoted to those who are subject to the overseer, the elders, [and] the servants. May it be granted to me to have my portion with them in the presence of God. Toil together with one another, struggle together, run together, suffer together, lie down together, rise up together, as God's stewards, and assessors, and ministers. ²Please the Captain in whose army you serve, from whom you will also receive your pay. Let none of you be found a deserter. Let your immersion abide with you as your shield, your faith as your helmet, your love as your spear, your patience as your body armor. Let your works be your deposits, that you may receive your assets due to you. Therefore, be long-suffering with one another in gentleness, as God is with you. May I have your joy always.

CHAPTER 7
¹Seeing that the assembly which is in Antioch of Syria has peace, as it has been reported to me, through your prayers, I myself have also been the more comforted since God has banished my care, if [it] so be [that] I may attain to God through suffering, that I may be found a disciple through your intercession. ²It is appropriate for you, most blessed Polycarp, to call together a godly council and to choose some one among you who is very dear to you and zealous also, who will be fit to bear the name of God's courier—to appoint him, I say, that he may go to Syria and glorify your zealous love to the glory of God. ³A Christian has no authority over himself, but gives his time to God. This is God's work, and yours also, when you will complete it; for I trust in the Divine grace, that you are ready for an act of well-doing which is [to] meet for God. Knowing the fervor of your sincerity, I have exhorted you in a short letter.

CHAPTER 8

¹Since I have not been able to write to all the assemblies, by reason of my sailing suddenly from Troas to Neapolis, as the Divine will prescribes, you will write to the assemblies in front, as one possessing the mind of God, to the intent that they may also do this same thing—let those who are able send messengers, and the rest letters by the persons who are sent by you, that you may be glorified by an ever memorable deed—for this is worthy of you. ²I salute all by name, and especially the wife of Epitropus with her whole household and her children's. I salute my beloved Attalus. I salute him that will be appointed to go to Syria. Grace will be with him always, and with Polycarp who sends him. ³I bid you farewell always in our God Jesus Christ, in whom you abide in the unity and supervision of God. I salute Alce, a name very dear to me. Farewell in the LORD.

EPISTLE OF POLYCARP TO THE PHILIPPIANS

Polycarp, overseer of Smyrna and a disciple of John the Apostle, was martyred for his faith in about AD 155 at the age of 86 or 87. His letter to the Philippians is a central and well-attested document among early Christian writings and forms part of what is popularly called the *Apostolic Fathers*.

POLYCARP AND THE ELDERS WITH HIM TO THE ASSEMBLY OF GOD SOJOURNING IN PHILIPPI; MERCY AND PEACE FROM GOD ALMIGHTY AND JESUS CHRIST OUR SAVIOR BE MULTIPLIED TO YOU.

CHAPTER 1

¹I greatly rejoice with you in our Lord Jesus Christ that you have followed the pattern of true love, and have helped on their way, as opportunity was given you, those who were bound in chains, which become the holy ones, and are the diadems of those who have been truly chosen by God and our Lord. ²I also rejoice that your firmly rooted faith, which was famous in past years, still flourishes and bears fruit to our Lord Jesus Christ, who endured for our sins, even to the suffering of death, "whom God raised up, having loosed the pangs of Hades, ³in whom, though you did not see Him, you believed in unspeakable and glorified joy"—into which joy many desire to come, knowing that "by grace you are saved, not by works" but by the will of God through Jesus Christ.

CHAPTER 2

¹"For what reason, girding up your loins, serve God in fear" and truth, putting aside empty vanity and vulgar error, "believing on Him who raised up our Lord Jesus Christ from the dead and gave Him glory," and a throne on His right hand, "to whom are subject all things in the heavens and earth," whom all breath serves, who is coming as "the Judge of the living and of the dead," whose blood God will require from them who disobey Him. ²Now "He who raised Him" from the dead "will also raise us up" if we do His will, and walk in His commands, and love the things which He loved, refraining from all unrighteousness, covetousness, love of money, evil speaking, false witness, "not rendering evil for evil, or railing for railing," or blow for blow, or curse for curse, ³but remembering what the LORD taught when He said, "Do not judge so that you are not judged, forgive and it will be forgiven to you, be merciful that you may obtain mercy, with what measure you mete, it will be measured to you again," and "Blessed are the poor, and they who are persecuted for righteousness' sake, for theirs is the Kingdom of God."

CHAPTER 3

¹These things, brothers, I write to you concerning righteousness, not at my own instance, but because you first invited me. ²For neither am I, nor is any other like me, able to follow the wisdom of the blessed and glorious Paul, who when he was among you in the presence of the men of that time accurately and steadfastly taught the word of truth, and also when he was absent wrote letters to you, from the study of which you will be able to build yourselves up into the faith given to you, ³"which is the mother of us all" when faith follows, and love of God, and Christ, and neighbor goes before. For if one is in this company, he has fulfilled the command of righteousness, for he who has love is far from all sin.

CHAPTER 4

¹"But the beginning of all evils is the love of money." Knowing therefore that "we brought nothing into the world and we can take nothing out of it," let us arm ourselves with the armor of righteousness, and let us first of all teach ourselves to walk in the command of the LORD; ²next teach our wives to remain in the faith given to them, and in love and purity, tenderly loving their husbands in all truth, and loving all others equally in all chastity, and to educate their children in the fear of God. ³Let us teach the widows to be discreet in the faith of the LORD, praying ceaselessly for all men, being far from all slander, evil speaking, false witness, love of money, and all evil, knowing that they are the altar of God, and that all offerings are tested, and that nothing escapes Him of reasonings or thoughts, or of "the secret things of the heart."

CHAPTER 5

¹Knowing then that "God is not mocked," we should walk worthily of His command and glory. ²Likewise must the servants be blameless before His righteousness, as the servants of God and Christ and not of man, not slanderers, not double-tongued, not lovers of money, [but] temperate in all things, compassionate, careful, walking according to the truth of the LORD, who was the "servant of all." For if we please Him in this present world, we will receive from Him that which is to come, even as He promised us to raise us from the dead, and that if we are worthy citizens of His community, "we will also reign with Him," if we have but faith. ³Likewise also, let the younger men be blameless in all things, caring, above all, for purity, and curbing themselves from all evil; for it is good to be cut off from the lust of the things in the world, because "every lust wars against the Spirit, and neither fornicators, nor the effeminate, nor sodomites will inherit the Kingdom of God," nor they who do iniquitous things. For what reason it is necessary to refrain from all these things, and to be subject to the elders and servants as to God and Christ. The virgins must walk with a blameless and pure conscience.

CHAPTER 6

¹And let the elders also be compassionate, merciful to all, bringing back those that have wandered, caring for all the weak, neglecting neither widow, nor orphan, nor poor, but "always providing for that which is good before God and man," refraining from all wrath, respect of persons, [and] unjust judgment, [and] being far from all love of money, not quickly believing evil of any, not hasty in judgment, knowing that "we all owe the debt of sin." ²If then we pray to the LORD to forgive us, we also should forgive, for we stand before the eyes of the LORD and of God, and "we must all appear before the judgment seat of Christ, and each must give an account of himself." ³So then "let us serve Him with fear and all reverence," as He Himself commanded us, and as did the apostles, who brought us the good news, and the prophets who foretold the coming of our Lord. Let us be zealous for good, refraining from offense, and from the false brothers, and from those who bear the Name of the LORD in hypocrisy, who deceive empty-minded men.

CHAPTER 7

¹"For everyone who does not confess that Jesus Christ has come in the flesh is an antichrist"; and whoever does not confess the testimony of the Cross is of the Devil; and whoever perverts the oracles of the LORD for his own lusts, and says that there is neither

EPISTLE OF POLYCARP TO THE PHILIPPIANS

resurrection nor judgment—this man is the firstborn of Satan. ²For what reason, leaving the foolishness of the crowd, and their false teaching, let us turn back to the word which was delivered to us in the beginning, "watching to prayer" and persevering in fasting, imploring the all-seeing God in our supplications "to lead us not into temptation," even as the LORD said, "The spirit is forward, but the flesh weak."

CHAPTER 8
¹Let us then persevere unceasingly in our hope, and in the pledge of our righteousness, that is in Christ Jesus, "who bore our sins in His own body on the tree, who did no sin, neither was guile found in His mouth," but for our sakes, that we might live in Him, He endured all things. ²Let us then be imitators of His endurance, and if we suffer for His Name's sake, let us glorify Him. For this is the example which He gave us in Himself, and this is what we have believed.

CHAPTER 9
¹Now I implore you all to obey the word of righteousness, and to endure with all the endurance which you also saw before your eyes, not only in the blessed Ignatius, and Zosimus, and Rufus, but also in others among yourselves, and in Paul himself, and in the other apostles; ²being persuaded that all of these "did not run in vain," but in faith and righteousness, and that they are with the LORD in the "place which is their due," with whom they also suffered. For they did not "love this present world" but Him who died on our behalf, and was raised by God for our sakes.

CHAPTER 10
¹Therefore, stand firm in these things and follow the example of the LORD, "firm and unchangeable in faith, loving the brotherhood, affectionate to one another," joined together in the truth, preempting one another in the gentleness of the LORD, despising no man. ²When you can do good, do not defer it, "for kindness sets free from death; let all be subject to one another, having your conversation blameless among the nations," that you may receive praise "for your good works" and that the LORD not be blasphemed in you. ³"But woe to him through whom the Name of the LORD is blasphemed." Therefore, teach sobriety to all and show it forth in your own lives.

CHAPTER 11
¹I am deeply sorry for Valens, who was once made an elder among you, that he so little understands the place which was given to him. I advise, therefore, that you keep from greed, and be pure and truthful. Keep yourselves from all evil. ²For how may he who cannot attain self-control in these matters prescribe it on another? If any man does not abstain from greed he will be defiled by idolatry and will be judged as if he were among the nations who "do not know the judgment of God." Or do we "not know that the holy ones will judge the world?" as Paul teaches. ³But I have neither perceived nor heard any such thing among you, among whom the blessed Paul labored, who are praised in the beginning of his Letter. For concerning you he boasts in all the assemblies who then alone had known the LORD, for we had not yet known Him. ⁴Therefore, brothers, I am deeply sorry for him [(Valens)] and for his wife, and "may the LORD grant them true conversion." Therefore, be also moderate in this matter yourselves, and "do not regard such men as enemies," but call them back as fallible and straying members, that you may make whole the body of you all. For in doing this you edify yourselves.

CHAPTER 12
¹For I am confident that you are well versed in the Writings, and from you nothing is hidden; but to me this is not granted. Only, as it is said in these Writings, "Be angry and do not sin," and "Do not let the sun go down on your wrath." Blessed is the man who remembers this, and I believe that it is so with you. ²Now may God and the Father of our Lord Jesus Christ, and the "perpetual Priest" Himself—Jesus Christ, the Son of God—build you up in faith and truth, and in all gentleness, and without wrath, and in patience, and in long-suffering, and endurance, and purity, and may He give you lot and part with His holy ones, and to us with you, and to all under Heaven who will believe in our Lord and God Jesus Christ and in His "Father who raised Him from the dead." ³"Pray for all the holy ones. Pray also for the emperors," and for potentates, and princes, and for "those who persecute you and hate you," and for "the enemies of the Cross" that "your fruit may be manifest among all men, that you may be perfected" in Him.

CHAPTER 13
¹Both you and Ignatius wrote to me that if anyone was going to Syria he should also take your letters. I will do this if I have a convenient opportunity—either myself or the man whom I am sending as a representative for you and me. ²We send you, as you asked, the letters of Ignatius, which were sent to us by him, and others which we had by us. These are appended to this letter, and you will be able to benefit greatly from them. For they contain faith, patience, and all the edification which pertains to our LORD. Let us know anything further which you have heard about Ignatius himself and those who are with him.

CHAPTER 14
¹I have written this to you by Crescens, whom I commended to you when I was present, and now commend again. For he has behaved blamelessly among us, and I believe that he will do the same with you. His sister will be commended to you when she comes to you. Farewell in the Lord Jesus Christ in grace, with all who are yours. Amen.

MARTYRDOM OF POLYCARP

Written as a letter from the church in Smyrna to the church in Philomelium, this is a vivid account of the martyrdom of Polycarp at the hands of the Romans. One of the most famous calls to Christian courage in the face of great persecution is found in this account: "Be strong … play the man!" (v. 9:1). An alternative conclusion found in the Moscow Codex (Ch. 23) was later added to address the heretical Marcionites, but is not included here.

THE ASSEMBLY OF GOD WHICH SOJOURNS IN SMYRNA, TO THE ASSEMBLY OF GOD WHICH SOJOURNS IN PHILOMELIUM, AND TO ALL THE SOJOURNINGS OF THE HOLY UNIVERSAL ASSEMBLY IN EVERY PLACE. "MERCY, PEACE, AND LOVE" OF GOD THE FATHER AND OUR LORD JESUS CHRIST BE MULTIPLIED.

CHAPTER 1
¹We write to you, brothers, the story of the martyrs and of the blessed Polycarp, who put an end to the persecution by his martyrdom as though adding the seal. For one might almost say that all that had gone before happened in order that the LORD might show to us from above a martyrdom in accordance with the good news. ²For he waited to be betrayed as also the LORD had done, that we too might become his imitators, "not thinking of ourselves alone, but also of our neighbors." For it is the mark of true and steadfast love not to wish that oneself may be saved alone, but all the brothers also.

CHAPTER 2
¹Blessed then and noble are all the martyrdoms which took place according to the will of God, for we must be very careful to assign the power over all to God. ²For who would not admire their nobility, and patience, and love of their Master? For some were torn by scourging until the mechanism of their flesh was seen even to the lower veins and arteries, and they endured so that even the bystanders pitied them and mourned. And some even reached such a pitch of nobility

that none of them groaned or wailed, showing to all of us that at that hour of their torture the noble martyrs of Christ were absent from the flesh, or rather that the LORD was standing by and talking with them. ³And paying heed to the grace of Christ they despised worldly tortures, by a single hour purchasing continuous life. And the fire of their cruel torturers had no heat for them, for they set before their eyes an escape from the fire which is continuous and is never quenched, and with the eyes of their heart they looked up to the good things which are preserved for those who have endured, "which neither ear has heard nor eye has seen, nor has it entered into the heart of man," but it was shown by the LORD to them who were no longer men but already messengers. ⁴And in the same way also, those who were condemned to the beasts endured terrible torment, being stretched on sharp shells and buffeted with other kinds of various torments, that if it were possible, the tyrant might bring them to a denial by continuous torture. For the Devil used many schemes against them.

CHAPTER 3

¹But thanks be to God, for he had no power over any. For the most noble Germanicus encouraged their fears by the endurance which was in him, and he fought gloriously with the wild beasts. For when the proconsul wished to persuade him and commanded him to have pity on his youth, he violently dragged the beast toward himself, wishing to be released more quickly from their unrighteous and lawless life. ²So after this, all the crowd, wondering at the nobility of the God-loving and God-fearing people of the Christians, cried out: "Away with the atheists! Let Polycarp be searched for."

CHAPTER 4

¹But one, named Quintus, a Phrygian having lately come from Phrygia, when he saw the wild beasts, played the coward. Now it was he who had forced himself and some others to come forward of their own accord. Him the proconsul persuaded with many entreaties to take the oath and offer sacrifice. For this reason, therefore, brothers, we do not commend those who give themselves up, since the good news does not give this teaching.

CHAPTER 5

¹But the most wonderful Polycarp, when he first heard it, was not disturbed, but wished to remain in the city; but the majority persuaded him to go away quietly, and he went out quietly to a farm, not far distant from the city, and stayed with a few friends, doing nothing but pray night and day for all, and for the assemblies throughout the world, as was his custom. ²And while he was praying, he fell into a trance three days before he was arrested and saw the pillow under his head burning with fire, and he turned and said to those who were with him: "I must be burned alive."

CHAPTER 6

¹And when the searching for him persisted he went to another farm; and those who were searching for him came up at once, and when they did not find him, they arrested young slaves, and one of them confessed under torture. ²For it was indeed impossible for him to remain hidden, since those who betrayed him were of his own house, and the police captain who had been allotted the very name, being called Herod, hastened to bring him to the arena that he might fulfill his appointed lot by becoming a partaker of Christ, while they who betrayed him should undergo the same punishment as Judas.

CHAPTER 7

¹Taking the slave then, police and cavalry went out on Friday about dinnertime, with their usual arms, as if they were advancing against a robber. And late in the evening they came up together against him and found him lying in an upper room. And he might have departed to another place, but would not, saying, "May the will of God be done." ²So when he heard that they had arrived he went down and talked with them, while those who were present wondered at his age and courage, and why there was so much haste for the arrest of an old man of such a kind. Therefore, he ordered food and drink to be set before them at that hour, whatever they should wish, and he asked them to give him an hour to pray without hindrance. ³To this they assented, and he stood and prayed—thus filled with the grace of God—so that for two hours he could not be silent, and those who listened were astounded, and many regretted that they had come against such a venerable old man.

CHAPTER 8

¹Now when he had at last finished his prayer, after remembering all who had ever even come his way, both small and great, high and low, and the whole Universal Assembly throughout the world, the hour came for departure, and they set him on a donkey, and led him into the city, on a great Sabbath day. ²And the police captain Herod and his father Niketas met him and removed him into their carriage, and sat by his side trying to persuade him, and saying, "But what harm is it to say, Lord Caesar, and to offer sacrifice, and so forth, and to be saved?" But he at first did not answer them, but when they continued he said, "I am not going to do what you counsel me." ³And they gave up the attempt to persuade him, and began to speak fiercely to him, and turned him out in such a hurry that in getting down from the carriage he scraped his shin; and without turning around, as though he had suffered nothing, he walked on promptly and quickly, and was taken to the arena, while the uproar in the arena was so great that no one could even be heard.

CHAPTER 9

¹Now when Polycarp entered into the arena there came a voice from Heaven: "Be strong, Polycarp, and play the man!" And no one saw the speaker, but our friends who were there heard the voice. And next he was brought forward, and there was a great uproar of those who heard that Polycarp had been arrested. ²Therefore, when he was brought forward the proconsul asked him if he was Polycarp, and when he admitted it he tried to persuade him to deny [it], saying, "Respect your age," and so forth, as they are accustomed to say: "Swear by the genius of Caesar, convert, say: Away with the Atheists"; but Polycarp, with a stern countenance looked on all the crowd of lawless heathen in the arena, and waving his hand at them, he groaned and looked up to Heaven and said, "Away with the Atheists." ³But when the proconsul pressed him and said, "Take the oath and I let you go; revile Christ," Polycarp said, "For eighty-six years I have been His servant, and He has done me no wrong, and how can I blaspheme my King who saved me?"

CHAPTER 10

¹But when he persisted again, and said, "Swear by the genius of Caesar," he answered him: "If you vainly suppose that I will swear by the genius of Caesar, as you say, and pretend that you are ignorant of who I am, listen plainly: I am a Christian. And if you wish to learn the doctrine of Christianity fix a day and listen." ²The proconsul said, "Persuade the people." And Polycarp said, "I have thought it worthy to give you an account, for we have been taught to render honor [to authorities] as is suitable, if it does not hurt us, to princes and authorities appointed by God. But as for those, I do not count them worthy that a defense should be made to them."

CHAPTER 11

¹And the proconsul said, "I have wild beasts. I will deliver you to them, unless you convert." And he said, "Call for them, for conversion from better to worse is not allowed us; but it is good to change from evil to righteousness." ²And again he said to him, "I will cause you to be consumed by fire, if you despise the beasts, unless you convert." But Polycarp said, "You threaten with the fire that burns for a time, and is quickly quenched, for you do not know the fire which awaits the wicked in the judgment to come and in continuous punishment. But why are you waiting? Come, do what you will."

CHAPTER 12

¹And with these and many other words he was filled with courage and joy, and his face was full of grace so that it not only did not fall with trouble at the things said to him, but that the proconsul, on the other hand, was astounded and sent his herald into the midst of the arena to announce three times: "Polycarp has confessed that he is a Christian." ²When this had been said by the herald, all the multitude of heathen and Jews living in Smyrna cried out with uncontrollable wrath and a loud shout: "This is the teacher of Asia,

the father of the Christians, the destroyer of our gods, who teaches many neither to offer sacrifice nor to worship." And when they said this, they cried out and asked Philip the Asiarch to let loose a lion on Polycarp. But he said he could not legally do this, since he had closed the games. ³Then they found it good to cry out with one mind that he should burn Polycarp alive, for the vision which had appeared to him on his pillow must be fulfilled, when he saw it burning, while he was praying, and he turned and said prophetically to those of the faithful who were with him, "I must be burned alive."

CHAPTER 13
¹These things then happened with such great speed—quicker than it takes to tell—and the crowd came together immediately, and prepared wood and bundles from the workshops and baths, and the Jews were extremely zealous, as is their custom, in assisting at this. ²Now when the fire was ready, he took off all his clothes, and loosened his girdle, and also tried to take off his shoes, though he did not do this before, because each of the faithful was always zealous, which of them might the more quickly touch his flesh. For he had been treated with all respect because of his noble life, even before his martyrdom. ³Therefore, he was immediately fastened to the instruments which had been prepared for the fire, but when they were going to nail him as well, he said, "Leave me thus, for He who gives me power to endure the fire, will grant me to remain in the flames unmoved even without the security you will give by the nails."

CHAPTER 14
¹So they did not nail him, but bound him, and he put his hands behind him and was bound as a noble ram out of a great flock, for an oblation, a whole burnt-offering made ready and acceptable to God; and he looked up to Heaven and said, "O LORD God Almighty, Father of Your beloved and blessed Child, Jesus Christ, through whom we have received full knowledge of You—the God of Messengers, and powers, and of all creation, and of the whole family of the righteous who live before You— ²I bless You, that You have granted me this day and hour, that I may share, among the number of the martyrs, in the cup of Your Christ, for the resurrection to continuous life, both of soul and body in the immortality of the Holy Spirit. And may I, today, be received among them before You, as a rich and acceptable sacrifice, as You—the God who does not lie and is truth—have prepared beforehand, and shown forth, and fulfilled. ³For this reason I also praise You for all things, I bless You, I glorify You through the continuous and heavenly Chief Priest, Jesus Christ, Your beloved Child, through whom be glory to You with Him and the Holy Spirit, both now and for the ages that are to come, Amen."

CHAPTER 15
¹Now when he had uttered his Amen and finished his prayer, the men in charge of the fire lit it, and a great flame blazed up and we, to whom it was given to see, saw a marvel. And we have been preserved to report to others what befell. ²For the fire made the likeness of a room, like the sail of a vessel filled with wind, and surrounded the body of the martyr as with a wall, and he was not within it as burning flesh, but as bread that is being baked, or as gold and silver being refined in a furnace. And we perceived such a fragrant smell as the scent of incense or other costly spices.

CHAPTER 16
¹At length the lawless men, seeing that his body could not be consumed by the fire, commanded an executioner to go up and pierce him with a dagger, and when he did this, there came out a dove, and [very] much blood, so that the fire was quenched, and all the crowd marveled that there was such a difference between the unbelievers and the chosen ones. ²And of the chosen ones was he indeed one, the wonderful martyr, Polycarp, who in our days was an apostolic and prophetic teacher, overseer of the Universal Assembly in Smyrna. For every word which he uttered from his mouth was both fulfilled and will be fulfilled.

CHAPTER 17
¹But the jealous and envious evil one who resists the family of the righteous, when he saw the greatness of his martyrdom, and his blameless career from the beginning, and that he was crowned with the crown of immortality, and had carried off the unspeakable prize, took care that not even his poor body should be taken away by us, though many desired to do so, and to have fellowship with his holy flesh. ²Therefore, he put forward Niketas, the father of Herod, and the brother of Alce, to ask the governor not to give his body, "Lest," he said, "they leave the crucified one and begin to worship this man." And they said this owing to the suggestions and pressure of the Jews, who also watched when we were going to take it from the fire, for they do not know that we will never be able either to abandon Christ, who suffered for the salvation of those who are being saved in the whole world—the innocent in place of sinners—or to worship any other. ³For we worship Him as the Son of God, but we love the martyrs as disciples and imitators of the LORD; and rightly, because of their unsurpassable affection toward their own King and Teacher. God grant that we too may be their companions and fellow-disciples.

CHAPTER 18
¹Therefore, when the centurion saw the strife caused by the Jews, he put the body in the midst of the fire and burned it. ²Thus afterward we took up his bones—more precious than precious stones, and finer than gold—and put them where it was suitable. ³There the LORD will permit us to come together according to our power in gladness and joy, and celebrate the anniversary of his martyrdom, both in memory of those who have already contested, and for the practice and training of those whose fate it will be.

CHAPTER 19
¹Such was the lot of the blessed Polycarp, who—though he was, together with those from Philadelphia, the twelfth martyr in Smyrna—is alone especially remembered by all, so that he is spoken of in every place, even by the heathen. He was not only a famous teacher, but also a notable martyr, whose martyrdom all desire to imitate, for it followed the good news of Christ. ²By his endurance he overcame the unrighteous ruler, and thus gained the crown of immortality, and he is glorifying God and the almighty Father, rejoicing with the apostles and all the righteous, and he is blessing our Lord Jesus Christ, the Savior of our souls, and Governor of our bodies, and the Shepherd of the Universal Assembly throughout the world.

CHAPTER 20
¹You, indeed, asked that the events should be explained to you at length, but we have for the present explained them in summary by our brother Marcion; therefore, when you have heard these things, send the letter to the brothers further on, that they also may glorify the LORD, who takes His chosen ones from His own servants. ²And to Him who is able to bring us all, in His grace and bounty, to His heavenly Kingdom by His only begotten Child, Jesus Christ, be glory, honor, might, and majesty for all time. Greet all the holy ones. Those who are with us, and Evarestus, who wrote the letter, with his whole house, greet you.

CHAPTER 21
¹Now the blessed Polycarp was martyred on the second day of the first half of the month of Xanthicus, the seventh day before the Calends of March, a great Sabbath, at the eighth hour. And he was arrested by Herod, when Philip of Tralles was chief priest, when Statius Quadratus was proconsul, but Jesus Christ was reigning for all time, to whom be glory, honor, majesty, and a continuous throne, from generation to generation, Amen.

CHAPTER 22
¹We bid you farewell, brothers, who walk according to the good news in the word of Jesus Christ (with whom be glory to God and the Father, and the Holy Spirit), for the salvation of the holy chosen ones, even as the blessed Polycarp suffered martyrdom, in whose footsteps may it be granted us to be found in the Kingdom of Jesus Christ. ²Gaius copied this from the writing of Irenaeus, a disciple of Polycarp, and he lived with Irenaeus, and I, Socrates, wrote it out in Corinth, from the copies of Gaius. Grace be with you all. ³And I, again, Pionius, wrote it out from the former writings, after searching for

it, because the blessed Polycarp showed it to me in a vision, as I will explain in what follows, and I gathered it together when it was almost worn out by age, that the Lord Jesus Christ may also gather me together with His chosen ones into His heavenly Kingdom, to whom be glory with the Father and the Holy Spirit, forever and ever, Amen.

EPISTLE OF MATHETES TO DIOGNETUS

The Epistle to Diognetus is one of the early Christian apologetics and is counted among the works of the Apostolic Fathers. The actual author and recipient are unknown, and it is believed to have been composed as early as AD 130 or as late as AD 200. Some scholars dispute the inclusion of chapters 11 and 12.

CHAPTER 1

[1] Since I see, most excellent Diognetus, that you are exceedingly anxious to understand the religion of the Christians, and that your inquiries respecting them are distinctly and carefully made, as to what God they trust and how they worship Him, that they all disregard the world and despise death, and take no account of those who are regarded as gods by the Greeks, neither observe the superstition of the Jews, and as to the nature of the affection which they entertain to one another, and of this new development or interest, which has entered into men's lives now and not before: I gladly welcome this zeal in you, and I ask of God, who supplies both the speaking and the hearing to us, that it may be granted to myself to speak in such a way that you may be made better by the hearing, and to you—that you may so listen that I, the speaker, may not be disappointed.

CHAPTER 2

[1] Come then, clear yourself of all the preconceptions which occupy your mind, and throw off the habit which leads you astray, and become a new man, as it were, from the beginning, as one who would listen to a new story, even as you yourself confessed. Do not see with only your eyes, but with your intellect also, of what substance or of what form they happen to be whom you call and regard as gods. [2] Is not one of them stone, like that which we tread under foot, and another bronze, no better than the vessels which are forged for our use, and another wood, which has already become rotten, and another silver, which needs a man to guard it lest it be stolen, and another iron, which is corroded with rust, and another earthenware, not a bit more pleasant than that which is supplied for the most dishonorable service? [3] Are not all these of perishable matter? Are they not forged by iron and fire? Did not the sculptor make one, and the brass-founder another, and the silversmith another, and the potter another? Before they were moulded into this shape by the crafts of these several craftsmen, was it not possible for each one of them to have been changed in form and made to resemble these several utensils? Might the vessels which are now made out of the same material, if they met with the same craftsmen, not be made like to such as these? [4] Could these things which are now worshiped by you, by human hands, not be made vessels again like the rest? Are they not all deaf and blind, are they not lifeless, senseless, motionless? Do they not all rot and decay? [5] These things you call gods, to these you are slaves, these you worship; and you end by becoming altogether like to them. [6] Therefore, you hate the Christians, because they do not consider these to be gods. [7] For do you yourselves, who now regard and worship them, not much rather despise them? Do you not much rather mock and insult them, worshiping those that are of stone and earthenware unguarded, but shutting up those that are of silver and gold by night, and setting guards over them by day, to prevent their being stolen? [8] And as for the honors which you think to offer to them, if they are sensible of them, you rather punish them thereby, whereas, if they are insensible, you reproach them by propitiating them with the blood and fat of victims. [9] Let one of yourselves undergo this treatment; let him submit to these things being done to him. No, not so much as a single individual will willingly submit to such punishment, for he has sensibility and reason; but a stone submits, because it is insensible. Therefore, you convict his sensibility. [10] Well, I could say much more concerning the Christians not being enslaved to such gods as these; but if anyone thinks what has been said insufficient, I hold it redundant to say more.

CHAPTER 3

[1] In the next place, I imagine that you are chiefly anxious to hear about their not practicing their religion in the same way as the Jews. [2] The Jews then, so far as they abstain from the mode of worship described above, do well in claiming to give reverence to one God of the universe and to regard Him as Master; but so far as they offer Him this worship in methods similar to those already mentioned, they are altogether at fault. [3] For whereas the Greeks, by offering these things to senseless and deaf images, make an exhibition of stupidity, the Jews, considering that they are presenting them to God as if He were in need of them, should in all reason count it folly and not religious worship. [4] For He that made the heavens, and the earth, and all things that are therein, and furnishes us all with what we need, cannot Himself need any of these things which He Himself supplies to them that imagine they are giving them to Him. [5] But those who think to perform sacrifices to Him with blood, and fat, and whole burnt-offerings, and to honor Him with such honors, seem to me in no way different from those who show the same respect toward deaf images; for the one class thinks fit to make offerings to things unable to participate in the honor, the other class to One who is in need of nothing.

CHAPTER 4

[1] But again their qualms concerning meats, and their superstition relating to the Sabbath, and the vanity of their circumcision, and the deception of their fasting and new moons—I do [not] suppose you need to learn from me—are ridiculous and unworthy of any consideration. [2] For of the things created by God for the use of man to receive some as created well, but to decline others as useless and superfluous, is this not impious? [3] And again to lie against God, as if He forbade us to do any good thing on the Sabbath day, is this not profane? [4] Again, to vaunt the mutilation of the flesh as a token of [divine] selection as though for this reason they were particularly beloved by God, is this not ridiculous? [5] And to watch the stars and the moon, and to keep the observance of months and of days, and to distinguish the arrangements of God and the changes of the seasons according to their own impulses, making some into festivals and others into times of mourning, who would regard this as an exhibition of godliness and not much more of folly? [6] That the Christians are therefore right in holding aloof from the common silliness and error of the Jews and from their excessive fussiness and pride, I consider that you have been sufficiently instructed; but as regards the mystery of their own religion, do not expect that you can be instructed by man.

CHAPTER 5

[1] For Christians are not distinguished from the rest of mankind either in locality, or in speech, or in customs. [2] For they do not dwell somewhere in cities of their own, neither do they use some different language, nor practice an extraordinary kind of life. [3] Nor again do they possess any invention discovered by any intelligence or study of ingenious men, nor are they masters of any human dogma as some are. [4] But while they dwell in cities of Greeks and barbarians as the lot of each is cast, and follow the native customs in dress, and food, and the other arrangements of life, yet the constitution of their own citizenship, which they set forth, is marvelous, and confessedly contradicts expectation. [5] They dwell in their own countries, but only as sojourners; they bear their share in all things as citizens, and they endure all hardships as strangers. Every foreign country is a fatherland to them, and every fatherland is foreign. [6] They marry like

all other men and they beget children; but they do not cast away their offspring. ⁷They have their meals in common, but not their wives. ⁸They find themselves in the flesh, and yet they do not live after the flesh. ⁹Their existence is on earth, but their citizenship is in Heaven. ¹⁰They obey the established laws, and they surpass the laws in their own lives. ¹¹They love all men, and they are persecuted by all. ¹²They are ignored, and yet they are condemned. They are put to death, and yet they are endued with life. ¹³They are in destitution, and yet they make many rich. They are in want of all things, and yet they abound in all things. ¹⁴They are dishonored, and yet they are glorified in their dishonor. They are evil spoken of, and yet they are vindicated. ¹⁵They are reviled, and they bless; they are insulted, and they respect. ¹⁶Doing good, they are punished as evildoers; being punished they rejoice, as if they were thereby restored by life. ¹⁷War is waged against them as aliens by the Jews, and persecution is carried on against them by the Greeks, and yet those that hate them cannot tell the reason of their hostility.

CHAPTER 6

¹In a word, what the soul is in a body, this the Christians are in the world. ²The soul is spread through all the members of the body, and Christians through the various cities of the world. ³The soul has its abode in the body, and yet it is not of the body. So Christians have their abode in the world, and yet they are not of the world. ⁴The soul which is invisible is guarded in the body which is visible; so Christians are recognized as being in the world, and yet their religion remains invisible. ⁵The flesh hates the soul and wages war with it, though it receives no wrong, because it is forbidden to indulge in pleasures; so the world hates Christians, though it receives no wrong from them, because they set themselves against its pleasures. ⁶The soul loves the flesh which hates it, and the members; so Christians love those that hate them. ⁷The soul is enclosed in the body, and yet itself holds the body together; so Christians are kept in the world as in a prison-house, and yet they themselves hold the world together. ⁸The soul, though itself immortal, dwells in a mortal dwelling place; so Christians sojourn amidst perishable things, while they look for the imperishability which is in the heavens. ⁹The soul, when ill-treated in the matter of meats and drinks, is improved; and so Christians, when punished, increase more and more daily. ¹⁰So great is the office for which God has appointed them, and which it is not lawful for them to decline.

CHAPTER 7

¹For it is no earthly discovery, as I said, which was committed to them, neither do they care to guard so carefully any mortal invention, nor have they entrusted to them the dispensation of human mysteries. ²But truly the almighty Creator of the universe, the invisible God Himself, from Heaven planted among men the truth and the holy teaching which surpasses the perception of man, and fixed it firmly in their hearts, not as any man might imagine, by sending [to mankind] a lieutenant, or messenger, or ruler, or one of those that direct the affairs of earth, or one of those who have been entrusted with the dispensations in Heaven, but the very Craftsman and Creator of the universe Himself, by whom He made the heavens, by whom He enclosed the sea in its proper bounds, whose mysteries all the elements faithfully observe, from whom [the sun] has received even the measure of the courses of the day to keep them, whom the moon obeys as He bids her shine by night, whom the stars obey as they follow the course of the moon, by whom all things are ordered, and bounded, and placed in subjection—the heavens and the things that are in the heavens, the earth and the things that are in the earth, the sea and the things that are in the sea, fire, air, abyss, the things that are in the heights, the things that are in the depths, the things that are between the two. Him He sent to them. ³Do you think He was sent as any man might suppose, to establish a sovereignty, to inspire fear and terror? ⁴Not so. But in gentleness [and] meekness He has sent Him, as a king might send his son who is a king. He sent Him as sending God; He sent Him as [a man] to men; He sent Him as Savior, as using persuasion, not force; for force is no attribute of God. ⁵He sent Him as summoning, not as persecuting; He sent Him as loving, not as judging. ⁶For He will send Him in judgment, and who will endure His presence? ⁷[Do you not see] them thrown to wild beasts so that they may deny the LORD, and yet not overcome? ⁸Do you not see that the more of them are punished, just so many others abound? ⁹These do not look like the works of a man; they are the power of God; they are proofs of His presence.

CHAPTER 8

¹For what man at all had any knowledge what God was before He came? ²Or do you accept the empty and nonsensical statements of those pretentious philosophers, of whom some said that God was fire (they call that God, whereto they themselves will go), and others water, and others some other of the elements which were created by God? ³And yet if any of these statements is worthy of acceptance, any one other created thing might just as well be made out to be God. ⁴No, all this is the quackery and deceit of the magicians; ⁵and no man has either seen or recognized Him, but He revealed Himself. ⁶And He revealed [Himself] by faith, whereby alone it is given to see God. ⁷For God, the Master and Creator of the universe, who made all things and arranged them in order, was found to be not only friendly to men, but also long-suffering. ⁸And such indeed He always was, and is, and will be: kind, and good, and dispassionate, and true, and He alone is good. ⁹And having conceived a great and unutterable plan, He communicated it to His Son alone. ¹⁰For so long as He kept and guarded His wise design as a mystery, He seemed to neglect us and to be careless about us. ¹¹But when He revealed it through His beloved Son and manifested the purpose which He had prepared from the beginning, He gave us all these gifts at once, participation in His benefits, and sight and understanding of [mysteries] which none of us ever would have expected.

CHAPTER 9

¹Having thus already planned everything in His mind with His Son, He permitted us during the former time to be borne along by disorderly impulses as we desired, led astray by pleasures and lusts, not at all because He took delight in our sins, but because He bore with us, not because He approved of the past season of iniquity, but because He was creating the present season of righteousness, that, being convicted in the past time by our own deeds as unworthy of life, we might now be made deserving by the goodness of God, and having made clear our inability to enter into the Kingdom of God of ourselves, might be enabled by the ability of God. ²And when our iniquity had been fully accomplished, and it had been made perfectly manifest that punishment and death were expected as its repayment, and the season came which God had ordained, when from now on He should manifest His goodness and power (O the exceedingly great kindness and love of God), He did not hate us, neither rejected us, nor bore us malice, but was long-suffering and patient, and in pity for us took our sins on Himself, and Himself parted with His own Son as a ransom for us—the holy for the lawless, the guileless for the evil, the just for the unjust, the incorruptible for the corruptible, the immortal for the mortal. ³For what else but His righteousness would have covered our sins? ⁴In whom was it possible for us lawless and ungodly men to have been justified, save only in the Son of God? ⁵O the sweet exchange, O the inscrutable creation, O the unexpected benefits, that the iniquity of many should be concealed in one righteous Man, and the righteousness of [the] One should justify many that are iniquitous! ⁶Having then in the former time demonstrated the inability of our nature to obtain life, and having now revealed a Savior able to save even creatures which have no ability, He willed that for both reasons we should believe in His goodness and should regard Him as nurse, father, teacher, counselor, physician, mind, light, honor, glory, strength, and life.

CHAPTER 10

¹This faith, if you also desire, first apprehend full knowledge of the Father. ²For God loved men for whose sake He made the world, to whom He subjected all things that are in the earth, to whom He gave reason and mind, whom alone He permitted to look up to Heaven, whom He created after His own image, to whom He sent His only begotten Son, to whom He promised the Kingdom, which is in Heaven, and will give it to those that have loved Him. ³And when you have

attained to this full knowledge, with what joy do you think that you will be filled, or how will you love Him that so loved you before? ⁴And loving Him you will be an imitator of His goodness. And do not marvel that a man can be an imitator of God. He can, if God wills it. ⁵For happiness does not consist in lordship over one's neighbors, nor in desiring to have more than weaker men, nor in possessing wealth and using force to inferiors; neither can anyone imitate God in these matters; no, these lie outside His greatness. ⁶But whoever takes on himself the burden of his neighbor, whoever desires to benefit one that is worse off in that in which he himself is superior, whoever by supplying to those that are in want possessions which he received from God becomes [like] God to those who receive them from him—he is an imitator of God. ⁷Then, though you are placed on earth, you will behold that God lives in Heaven; then you will begin to declare the mysteries of God; then you will both love and admire those that are punished because they will not deny God; then you will condemn the deceit and error of the world when you will perceive the true life which is in Heaven, when you will despise the apparent death which is here on earth, when you will fear the real death, which is reserved for those that will be condemned to the continuous fire that will punish those delivered over to it to the end. ⁸Then you will admire those who endure for righteousness' sake the fire that is for a season, and will count them blessed when you perceive that fire …

CHAPTER 11

¹Mine are no strange discourses, nor perverse questionings, but having been a disciple of apostles I come forward as a teacher of the nations, ministering worthily to them, as they present themselves disciples of the truth, the lessons which have been handed down. ²For who that has been rightly taught and has entered into friendship with the Word does not seek to learn distinctly the lessons revealed openly by the Word to the disciples; to whom the Word appeared and declared them, speaking plainly, not perceived by the unbelieving, but relating them to disciples who being reckoned faithful by Him were taught the mysteries of the Father? ³For this reason He sent forth the Word, that He might appear to the world, who being dishonored by the people, and preached by the apostles, was believed in by the nations. ⁴This Word, who was from the beginning, who appeared as new and yet was proved to be old, and is engendered always young in the hearts of holy ones, ⁵He, I say, who is continuous, who today was accounted [the] Son, through whom the Assembly is enriched, and grace is unfolded and multiplied among the holy ones—grace which confers understanding, which reveals secrets, which announces seasons, which rejoices over the faithful, which is bestowed on those who seek her, even those by whom the pledges of faith are not broken, nor the boundaries of the fathers overstepped. ⁶After which the fear of the law is sung, and the grace of the prophets is recognized, and the faith of the Gospels is established, and the apostles' tradition is preserved, and the joy of the Assembly exults. ⁷If you do not grieve this grace, you will understand the discourses which the Word holds by the mouth of those whom He desires when He wishes. ⁸For in all things, that by the will of the commanding Word we were moved to utter with many pains, we become sharers with you, through love of the things revealed to us.

CHAPTER 12

¹Confronted with these truths and listening to them with attention, you will know how much God bestows on those that love [Him] rightly, who become a paradise of delight, a tree bearing all manner of fruits and flourishing, growing up in themselves and adorned with various fruits. ²For in this garden a Tree of Knowledge and a Tree of Life have been planted; yet the Tree of Knowledge does not kill, but disobedience kills; ³for the Writings state clearly how God from the beginning planted a Tree [[of Knowledge and a Tree]] of Life in the midst of Paradise, revealing life through knowledge; and because our first parents did not use it genuinely, they were made naked by the deceit of the serpent. ⁴For neither is there life without knowledge, nor sound knowledge without true life; therefore the one [tree] is planted near the other. ⁵Discerning the force of this and blaming the knowledge which is exercised apart from the truth of the injunction which leads to life, the apostle says, "Knowledge puffs up, but love builds up." ⁶For the man who supposes that he knows anything without the true knowledge, which is testified by the life, is ignorant; he is deceived by the serpent, because he did not love life; whereas he who with fear recognizes and desires life plants in hope, expecting fruit. ⁷Let your heart be knowledge, and your life true reason, properly comprehended. ⁸Of which, if you bear the tree and pluck the fruit, you will ever gather the harvest which God looks for, which serpent does not touch, nor deceit infect, neither is Eve corrupted, but is believed on as a virgin, ⁹and salvation is set forth, and the apostles are filled with understanding, and the Passover of the LORD goes forward, and the congregations are gathered together, and [all things] are arranged in order, and as He teaches the holy ones, the Word is gladdened, through whom the Father is glorified, to whom be glory forever and ever. Amen.

THE SHEPHERD OF HERMAS

This work, composed as early as the late 1st century AD, but more likely in the mid 2nd century, was highly regarded and even considered canonical by some sources such as Irenaeus. It is found in the Codex Sinaiticus and takes its name from a messenger appearing as a shepherd in order to deliver twelve commands to Hermas. It is thought the shepherd may represent Jesus as the Good Shepherd. Those who believe The Shepherd of Hermas was written in the 1st century associate it with the Hermas mentioned in Romans 16:14, while the majority believe the "Hermas" in question is none other than the brother of Pius I, who would have thus written in the mid 2nd century. Besides the possibly late date of composition, also weighing heavily against its canonicity is the message of impossible moral perfectionism outside the mainstream of Christian thought, and the fact it lacks the essential message of Christ's atoning sacrifice besides a passing mention in Similitude 5. It also, while not Gnostic, arguably presents a Christology that differs from that found in the Bible—although this is not entirely clear given the work is largely an allegory. It consists of five *visions*, twelve *commands*, and ten *similitudes*.

SECTION 1:

VISIONS

VISION 1

¹He who had brought me up, sold me to one Rhode in Rome. Many years after this I recognized her, and I began to love her as a sister. Sometime after, I saw her bathe in the river Tiber; and I gave her my hand and drew her out of the river. ²The sight of her beauty made me think with myself, "I would be a happy man if I could only get a wife as attractive and good as she is." This was the only thought that passed through me: this and nothing more. ³A short time after this, as I was walking on my road to the villages, and magnifying the creatures of God, and thinking how magnificent, and beautiful, and powerful they are, I fell asleep. ⁴And the Spirit carried

me away, and took me through a pathless place, through which a man could not travel, for it was situated in the midst of rocks; it was rugged and impassible on account of water. ⁵Having passed over this river, I came to a plain. I then bent down on my knees and began to pray to the LORD and to confess my sins. And as I prayed, the heavens were opened, and I see the woman whom I had desired saluting me from the sky, and saying, "Greetings, Hermas!" ⁶And looking up to her, I said, "Lady, what are you doing here?" And she answered me, "I have been taken up here to accuse you of your sins before the LORD." "Lady," I said, "are you to be the subject of my accusation?" ⁷"No," she said; "but hear the words which I am going to speak to you. God, who dwells in the heavens, and made out of nothing the things that exist, and multiplied and increased them on account of His holy Assembly, is angry with you for having sinned against me." ⁸I answered her, "Lady, have I sinned against you? How? Or when did I speak an unseemly word to you? Did I not always think of you as a lady? Did I not always respect you as a sister? Why do you falsely accuse me of this wickedness and impurity?" ⁹With a smile she replied to me, "The desire of wickedness arose within your heart. Is it not your opinion that a righteous man commits sin when an evil desire arises in his heart? There is sin in such a case, and the sin is great," she said; ¹⁰"for the thoughts of a righteous man should be righteous. For by thinking righteously his character is established in the heavens, and he has the LORD merciful to him in every business. But those who entertain wicked thoughts in their minds are bringing on themselves death and captivity; and especially is this the case with those who set their affections on this world, and glory in their riches, and do not look forward to the blessings of the life to come. ¹¹For their regrets will be many; for they have no hope, but have despaired of themselves and their life. But pray to God, and He will heal your sins, and the sins of your whole house, and of all the holy ones." ¹²After she had spoken these words, the heavens were shut. I was overwhelmed with sorrow and fear, and said to myself, "If this sin is assigned to me, how can I be saved, or how will I propitiate God in regard to my sins, which are of the grossest character? With what words will I ask the LORD to be merciful to me? ¹³While I was thinking over these things, and discussing them in my mind, I saw opposite to me a chair, white, made of white wool, of great size. And there came up an old woman, arrayed in a splendid robe, and with a scroll in her hand; ¹⁴and she sat down alone, and saluted me, "Greetings, Hermas!" And in sadness and tears I said to her, "Lady, greetings!" ¹⁵And she said to me, "Why are you downcast, Hermas? For you were accustomed to be patient and temperate, and always smiling. Why are you so gloomy, and not cheerful?" ¹⁶I answered her and said, "O Lady, I have been reproached by a very good woman, who says that I sinned against her." ¹⁷And she said, "Far be such a deed from a servant of God. But perhaps a desire after her has arisen within your heart. Such a wish, in the case of the servants of God, produces sin. For it is a wicked and horrible wish in an all-chaste and already well-tried spirit to desire an evil deed; ¹⁸and especially for Hermas to do so, who keeps himself from all wicked desire, and is full of all simplicity, and of great guilelessness. ¹⁹"But God is not angry with you on account of this, but that you may convert [those of] your house, which have committed iniquity against the Lord, and against you, their parents. And although you love your sons, yet you did not warn your house, but permitted them to be terribly corrupted. ²⁰On this account the LORD is angry with you, but He will heal all the evils which have been done in your house. For, on account of their sins and iniquities, you have been destroyed by the affairs of this world. ²¹But now the mercy of the LORD has taken pity on you and your house, and will strengthen you, and establish you in His glory. Only, do not be easy-minded, but be of good courage and comfort your house. For as a smith hammers out his work, and accomplishes whatever he wishes, so will righteous daily speech overcome all iniquity. ²²Therefore, do not cease to admonish your sons; for I know that, if they will convert with all their heart, they will be enrolled in the scrolls of [the] living with the holy ones." ²³Having ended these words, she said to me, "Do you wish to hear me read?" I say to her, "Lady, I do." "Listen then and give ear to the glories of God." ²⁴And then I heard from her, magnificently and admirably, things which my memory could not retain. For all the words were terrible, such as man could not endure. ²⁵The last words, however, I did remember; for they were useful to us, and gentle. ²⁶"Behold, the God of powers, who by His invisible strong power and great wisdom has created the world, and by His glorious counsel has surrounded His creation with beauty, and by His strong word has fixed the heavens and laid the foundations of the earth on the waters, and by His own wisdom and providence has created His holy Assembly, which He has blessed, ²⁷behold, He removes the heavens and the mountains, the hills and the seas, and all things become plain to His chosen ones, that He may bestow on them the blessing which He has promised them, with much glory and joy, if only they will keep the commandments of God which they have received in great faith." ²⁸When she had ended her reading, she rose from the chair, and four young men came and carried off the chair and went away to the east. ²⁹And she called me to herself and touched my breast, and said to me, "Have you been pleased with my reading?" And I say to her, "Lady, the last words please me, but the first are cruel and harsh." ³⁰Then she said to me, "The last are for the righteous; the first are for heathens and apostates." ³¹And while she spoke to me, two men appeared and raised her on their shoulders, and they went to where the chair was in the east. ³²She departed with joyful countenance; and as she went, she said to me, "Behave like a man, Hermas."

VISION 2

¹As I was going to the country about the same time as on the previous year, in my walk I recalled to memory the vision of that year. And again, the Spirit carried me away, and took me to the same place where I had been the year before. ²On coming to that place, I bowed my knees and began to pray to the LORD, and to glorify His Name, because He had deemed me worthy, and had made known to me my former sins. ³On rising from prayer, I see opposite me that old woman, whom I had seen the year before, walking and reading some scroll. And she says to me, "Can you carry a report of these things to the chosen ones of God?" ⁴I say to her, "Lady, so much I cannot retain in my memory, but give me the scroll and I will transcribe it." "Take it," she says, "and you will give it back to me." ⁵Thereupon I took it, and going away into a certain part of the country, I transcribed the whole of it letter by letter; but the syllables of it I did not catch. ⁶No sooner, however, had I finished the writing of the scroll, than all of a sudden it was snatched from my hands; but who the person was that snatched it, I did not see. Fifteen days after, when I had fasted and prayed much to the Lord, the knowledge of the writing was revealed to me. ⁷Now the writing was to this effect: "Your seed, O Hermas, has sinned against God, and they have blasphemed against the LORD, and in their great wickedness they have betrayed their parents. And they passed as traitors of their parents, and by their treachery they did not reap profit. ⁸And even now they have added to their sins lusts and iniquitous pollutions, and thus their iniquities have been filled up. ⁹But make known these words to all your children, and to your wife, who is to be your sister. For she does not restrain her tongue, with which she commits iniquity; but, on hearing these words, she will control herself, and will obtain mercy. ¹⁰For after you have made known to them these words which my Lord has commanded me to reveal to you, then they will be forgiven all the sins which in former times they committed, and forgiveness will be granted to all the holy ones who have sinned even to the present day, if they convert with all their heart, and drive all doubts from their minds. ¹¹For the LORD has sworn by His glory, in regard to His chosen ones, that if any one of them sin after a certain day which has been fixed, he will not be saved. For the conversion of the righteous has limits. Filled up are the days of conversion to all the holy ones; but to the heathen, conversion will be possible even to the last day. ¹²You will tell, therefore, those who preside over the Assembly, to direct their ways in righteousness, that they may receive in full the promises with great glory. ¹³Stand steadfast, therefore, you who work righteousness, and do not doubt, that your passage may be with the holy messengers. ¹⁴Happy are you who endure the great tribulation that is coming on,

THE SHEPHERD OF HERMAS

and happy are they who will not deny their own life. For the LORD has sworn by His Son, that those who denied their Lord have abandoned their life in despair, for even now these are to deny Him in the days that are coming. To those who denied in earlier times, God became gracious, on account of His exceedingly tender mercy. ¹⁵But as for you, Hermas, do not remember the wrongs done to you by your children, nor neglect your sister, that they may be cleansed from their former sins. For they will be instructed with righteous instruction, if you do not remember the wrongs they have done to you. For the remembrance of wrongs works death. ¹⁶And you, Henna, have endured great personal tribulations on account of the transgressions of your house, because you did not attend to them, but were careless and engaged in your wicked transactions. ¹⁷But you are saved, because you did not depart from the living God, and on account of your simplicity and great self-control. These have saved you, if you remain steadfast. And they will save all who act in the same manner, and walk in guilelessness and simplicity. ¹⁸Those who possess such virtues will wax strong against every form of wickedness, and will abide to continuous life. Blessed are all they who practice righteousness, for they will never be destroyed. ¹⁹Now you will tell Maximus: Behold, tribulation is coming. If it seems good to you, deny again. The LORD is near to them who return to Him, as it is written in Eldad and Medad, who prophesied to the people in the wilderness." ²⁰Now a revelation was given to me, my brothers, while I slept, by a young man of handsome appearance, who said to me, "Who do you think that old woman is from whom you received the scroll?" ²¹And I said, "The Sibyl." "You are mistaken," he says; "it is not the Sibyl." "Who is it then?" I say. And he said, "It is the Assembly." And I said to him, "Why then is she an old woman? ²²Because," he said, "she was created first of all. On this account is she old. And for her sake was the world made." ²³After that I saw a vision in my house, and that old woman came and asked me if I had yet given the scroll to the elders. And I said that I had not. ²⁴And then she said, "You have done well for I have some words to add. But when I finish all the words, all the chosen ones will then become acquainted with them through you. ²⁵You will therefore write two scrolls, and you will send the one to Clemens and the other to Grapte. And Clemens will send his to foreign countries, for permission has been granted to him to do so. And Grapte will admonish the widows and the orphans. ²⁶But you will read the words in this city, along with the elders who preside over the Assembly.

VISION 3

¹The vision which I saw, my brothers, was of the following nature. ²Having fasted frequently, and having prayed to the LORD that He would show me the revelation which He promised to show me through that old woman, the same night that old woman appeared to me, and said to me, "Since you are so anxious and eager to know all things, go into the part of the country where you tarry; and about the fifth hour I will appear to you, and show you all that you ought to see." ³I asked her, saying "Lady, into what part of the country am I to go?" And she said, "Into any part you wish." Then I chose a spot which was suitable, and retired. ⁴Before, however, I began to speak and to mention the place, she said to me, "I will come where you wish." Accordingly, I went to the country, and counted the hours, and reached the place where I had promised to meet her. ⁵And I see an ivory seat already placed, and on it a linen cushion, and above the linen cushion was spread a covering of fine linen. Seeing these laid out, and yet no one in the place, I began to feel awe, and as it were a trembling seized hold of me, and my hair stood on end, and as it were a horror came on me when I saw that I was all alone. ⁶But on coming back to myself and calling to mind the glory of God, I took courage, bent my knees, and again confessed my sins to God as I had done before. ⁷Immediately the old woman approached, accompanied by six young men whom I had also seen before; and she stood behind me, and listened to me, as I prayed and confessed my sins to the LORD. ⁸And touching me she said, "Hermas, cease praying continually for your sins; pray for righteousness, that you may have a portion of it immediately in your house." ⁹On this, she took me up by the hand, and brought me to the seat, and said to the young men, "Go and build." ¹⁰When the young men had gone and we were alone, she said to me, "Sit here." I say to her, "Lady, permit my elders to be seated first." "Do what I bid you," she said; "sit down." ¹¹When I would have sat down on her right, she did not permit me, but with her hand beckoned to me to sit down on the left. ¹²While I was thinking about this, and feeling vexed that she did not let me sit on the right, she said, "Are you vexed, Hermas? The place to the right is for others who have already pleased God and have suffered for His Name's sake; and you have yet much to accomplish before you can sit with them. But abide as you now do in your simplicity, and you will sit with them, and with all who do their deeds and bear what they have borne." ¹³"What have they borne?" I said. "Listen," she said: "scourges, prisons, great tribulations, crosses, wild beasts, for God's Name's sake. On this account is assigned to them the division of sanctification on the right hand, and to everyone who will suffer for God's Name: to the rest is assigned the division on the left. ¹⁴But both for those who sit on the right, and those who sit on the left, there are the same gifts and promises; only those sit on the right, and have some glory. ¹⁵You then are eager to sit on the right with them, but your shortcomings are many. But you will be cleansed from your shortcomings; and all who are not given to doubts will be cleansed from all their iniquities up until this day." ¹⁶Saying this, she wished to go away. But falling down at her feet, I begged her by the LORD that she would show me the vision which she had promised to show me. And then she again took hold of me by the hand, and raised me, and made me sit on the seat to the left; ¹⁷and lifting up a splendid rod, she said to me, "Do you see something great?" And I say, "Lady, I see nothing." She said to me, "Behold, do you not see opposite to you a great tower, built on the waters, of splendid square stones?" ¹⁸For the tower was built square by those six young men who had come with her. But myriads of men were carrying stones to it, some dragging them from the depths, others removing them from the land, and they handed them to these six young men. ¹⁹They were taking them and building; and those of the stones that were dragged out of the depths, they placed in the building just as they were: for they were polished and fitted exactly into the other stones and became so united one with another that the lines of juncture could not be perceived. And in this way the building of the tower looked as if it were made out of one stone. ²⁰Those stones, however, which were taken from the earth suffered a different fate; for the young men rejected some of them, some they fitted into the building, and some they cut down, and cast far away from the tower. ²¹Many other stones, however, lay around the tower, and the young men did not use them in building; for some of them were rough, others had cracks in them, others had been made too short, and others were white and round, but did not fit into the building of the tower. ²²Moreover, I saw other stones thrown far away from the tower, and falling into the public road; yet they did not remain on the road, but were rolled into a pathless place. And I saw others falling into the fire and burning, others falling close to the water, and yet not capable of being rolled into the water, though they wished to be rolled down, and to enter the water. ²³On showing me these visions, she wished to retire. I said to her, "What is the use of my having seen all this, while I do not know what it means?" She said to me, "You are a cunning fellow, wishing to know everything that relates to the tower." "Even so, O Lady," I said, "that I may tell it to my brothers, that, hearing this, they may know the LORD in much glory." ²⁴And she said, "Many will indeed hear, and hearing, some will be glad, and some will weep. But even these, if they hear and convert, will also rejoice. ²⁵Hear, then, the allegories of the tower; for I will reveal all to you, and give me no more trouble in regard to revelation: for these revelations have an end, for they have been completed. But you will not cease praying for revelations, for you are shameless. ²⁶The tower which you see building is myself, the Assembly, who has appeared to you now and on the former occasion. Ask, then, whatever you like in regard to the tower, and I will reveal it to you, that you may rejoice with the holy ones." ²⁷I said to her, "Lady, since you have granted to reveal all to me this once, reveal it." She said to me, "Whatever ought to be revealed, will be revealed; only let your

heart be with God, and do not doubt whatever you will see." ²⁸I asked her, "Why was the tower built on the waters, O Lady?" She answered, "I told you before, and you still inquire carefully: therefore, inquiring, you will find the truth. ²⁹Hear then why the tower is built on the waters. It is because your life has been, and will be, saved through water. For the tower was founder on the word of the almighty and glorious Name and it is kept together by the invisible power of the LORD." ³⁰In reply I said to her, "This is magnificent and marvelous. But who are the six young men who are engaged in building?" And she said, "These are the holy messengers of God, who were first created, and to whom the LORD handed over His whole creation, that they might increase, and build up, and rule over the whole creation. By these the building of the tower will be finished." ³¹"But who are the other persons who are engaged in carrying the stones?" "These are also holy messengers of the LORD, but the former six are more excellent than these. The building of the tower will be finished, and all will rejoice together around the tower, and they will glorify God, because the tower is finished." ³²I asked her, saying, "Lady, I should like to know what became of the stones, and what was meant by the various kinds of stones?" ³³In reply she said to me, "Not because you are more deserving than all others that this revelation should be made to you—for there are others before you, and better than you, to whom these visions should have been revealed—but that the Name of God may be glorified, has the revelation been made to you, and it will be made on account of the doubtful who ponder in their hearts whether these things will be or not. ³⁴Tell them that all these things are true, and that none of them is beyond the truth. All of them are firm and sure, and established on a strong foundation. ³⁵Hear now with regard to the stones which are in the building. Those square white stones, which fitted exactly into each other, are apostles, overseers, teachers, and servants, who have lived in godly purity, and have acted as overseers, and teachers, and servants chastely and reverently to the chosen ones of God. ³⁶Some of them have fallen asleep, and some still remain alive. And they have always agreed with each other, and been at peace among themselves, and listened to each other. On account of this, they join exactly into the building of the tower." ³⁷"But who are the stones that were dragged from the depths, and which were laid into the building and fitted in with the rest of the stones previously placed in the tower?" "They are those who suffered for the LORD's sake." ³⁸"But I wish to know, O Lady, who are the other stones which were carried from the land." "Those," she said, "which go into the building without being polished, are those whom God has approved of, for they walked in the straight ways of the LORD and practiced His commandments." ³⁹"But who are those who are in the act of being brought and placed in the building?" "They are those who are young in faith and are faithful. But they are admonished by the messengers to do good, for no iniquity has been found in them." ⁴⁰"Who then are those whom they rejected and cast away?" "These are they who have sinned and wish to convert. On this account they have not been thrown far from the tower, because they will yet be useful in the building, if they convert. ⁴¹Those then who are to convert, if they do convert, will be strong in faith, if they now convert while the tower is building. For if the building is finished, there will not be more room for anyone, but he will be rejected. This privilege, however, will belong only to him who has now been placed near the tower. ⁴²As to those who were cut down and thrown far away from the tower, do you wish to know who they are? They are the sons of iniquity, and they believed in hypocrisy, and wickedness did not depart from them. For this reason, they are not saved, since they cannot be used in the building on account of their iniquities. ⁴³Therefore, they have been cut off and cast far away on account of the anger of the LORD, for they have roused Him to anger. ⁴⁴But I will explain to you the other stones which you saw lying in great numbers, and not going into the building. Those which are rough are those who have known the truth and not remained in it, nor have they been joined to the holy ones. On this account they are unfit for use." ⁴⁵"Who are those that have rents?" "These are they who are at discord in their hearts with one another, and are not at peace among themselves: they indeed keep peace before each other, but when they separate from one another, their wicked thoughts remain in their hearts. These, then, are the rents which are in the stones. ⁴⁶But those which are shortened are those who have indeed believed, and have the larger share of righteousness; yet they have also a considerable share of iniquity, and therefore they are shortened and not whole." ⁴⁷"But who are these, Lady, that are white and round, and yet do not fit into the building of the tower?" She answered and said, "How long will you be foolish and stupid, and continue to put every kind of question and understand nothing? These are those who indeed have faith, but they also have the riches of this world. ⁴⁸Therefore, when tribulation comes, on account of their riches and business they deny the LORD." I answered and said to her, "When, then, will they be useful for the building, Lady?" ⁴⁹"When the riches that now seduce them have been circumscribed, then they will be of use to God. For as a round stone cannot become square unless portions are cut off and cast away, so also those who are rich in this world cannot be useful to the LORD unless their riches are cut down. ⁵⁰Learn this first from your own case. When you were rich, you were useless; but now you are useful and fit for life. Be useful to God; for you also will be used as one of these stones. ⁵¹Now the other stones which you saw cast far away from the tower, and falling on the public road and rolling from it into pathless places, are those who have indeed believed, but through doubt have abandoned the true road. Thinking, then, that they could find a better [way], they wander and become wretched, and enter on pathless places. ⁵²But those which fell into the fire and were burned are those who have departed forever from the living God; nor does the thought of conversion ever come into their hearts, on account of their devotion to their lusts and to the crimes which they committed. ⁵³Do you wish to know who are the others which fell near the waters, but could not be rolled into them? These are they who have heard the word and wish to be immersed in the Name of the LORD, but when the chastity demanded by the truth comes into their recollection, they draw back, and again walk after their own wicked desires." ⁵⁴She finished her exposition of the tower. But I, shameless as I yet was, asked her, "Is conversion possible for all those stones which have been cast away and did not fit into the building of the tower, and will they yet have a place in this tower?" ⁵⁵"Conversion," she said, "is yet possible, but in this tower they cannot find a suitable place. But in another and much inferior place they will be laid, and that, too, only when they have been tortured and completed the days of their sins. ⁵⁶And on this account, they will be transferred, because they have partaken of the righteous Word. And only then will they be removed from their punishments when the thought of converting of the evil deeds which they have done has come into their hearts. But if it does not come into their hearts, they will not be saved, on account of the hardness of their heart." ⁵⁷When then I ceased asking in regard to all these matters, she said to me, "Do you wish to see anything else?" And as I was extremely eager to see something more, my countenance beamed with joy. ⁵⁸She looked toward me with a smile, and said, "Do you see seven women around the tower?" "I do, Lady," I said. ⁵⁹"This tower," she said, "is supported by them according to the precept of the LORD. Now listen to their functions. The first of them, who is clasping her hands, is called Faith. Through her the chosen ones of God are saved. ⁶⁰Another, who has her garments tucked up and acts with vigor, is called Self-restraint. She is the daughter of Faith. Whoever then follows her will become happy in his life, because he will restrain himself from all evil works, believing that, if he restrains himself from all evil desire, he will inherit continuous life." ⁶¹"But the others," I said, "O Lady, who are they?" And she said to me, "They are daughters of each other. One of them is called Simplicity, another Guilelessness, another Chastity, another Intelligence, another Love. ⁶²When then you do all the works of their mother, you will be able to live." ⁶³"I should like to know," I said, "O Lady, what power each one of them possesses." ⁶⁴"Hear," she said, "what power they have. Their powers are regulated by each other, and follow each other in the order of their birth. For from Faith arises Self-restraint; from Self-restraint, Simplicity; from Simplicity, Guilelessness; from Guilelessness, Chastity; from Chastity, Intelligence; and from

THE SHEPHERD OF HERMAS

Intelligence, Love. ⁶⁵The deeds, then, of these are pure, and chaste, and divine. Whoever devotes himself to these, and is able to hold fast by their works, will have his dwelling in the tower with the holy ones of God." ⁶⁶Then I asked her in regard to the ages, if now there is the conclusion. She cried out with a loud voice, "Foolish man! Do you not see the tower yet building? When the tower is finished and built, then comes the end; and I assure you it will soon be finished. ⁶⁷Ask me no more questions. Let you and all the holy ones be content with what I have called to your remembrance, and with my renewal of your spirits. But observe that it is not for your own sake only that these revelations have been made to you, but they have been given you that you may show them to all. ⁶⁸For after three days—this you will take care to remember—I command you to speak all the words which I am to say to you into the ears of the holy ones, that hearing them and doing them, they may be cleansed from their iniquities, and you along with them. ⁶⁹Give ear to me, O sons: I have brought you up in much simplicity, and guilelessness, and chastity, on account of the mercy of the LORD, who has dropped His righteousness down on you, that you may be made righteous and holy from all your iniquity and depravity; but you do not wish to rest from your iniquity. ⁷⁰Now, therefore, listen to me, and be at peace one with another, and visit each other, and bear each other's burdens, and do not partake of God's creatures alone, but give abundantly of them to the needy. ⁷¹For some through the abundance of their food produce weakness in their flesh, and thus corrupt their flesh; while the flesh of others who have no food is corrupted, because they have not sufficient nourishment. And on this account their bodies waste away. ⁷²This intemperance in eating is thus injurious to you who have abundance and do not distribute among those who are needy. Give heed to the judgment that is to come. ⁷³You, therefore, who are high in position, seek out the hungry as long as the tower is not yet finished; for after the tower is finished, you will wish to do good, but will find no opportunity. ⁷⁴Give heed, therefore, you who glory in your wealth, lest those who are needy should groan, and their groans should ascend to the LORD, and you are shut out with all your goods beyond the gate of the tower. ⁷⁵Therefore, I now say to you who preside over the Assembly and love the first seats: do not be like to drug-mixers. For the drug-mixers carry their drugs in boxes, but you carry your drug and poison in your heart. ⁷⁶You are hardened, and do not wish to cleanse your hearts, and to add unity of aim to purity of heart, that you may have mercy from the great King. Take heed, therefore, children, that these dissensions of yours do not deprive you of your life. ⁷⁷How will you instruct the chosen ones of the LORD if you yourselves have no instruction? Instruct each other therefore, and be at peace among yourselves, that I also, standing joyful before your Father, may give an account of you all to your Lord."

⁷⁸On her ceasing to speak to me, those six young men who were engaged in building came and conveyed her to the tower, and another four lifted up the seat and carried it also to the tower. The faces of these last I did not see, for they were turned away from me. ⁷⁹And as she was going, I asked her to reveal to me the meaning of the three forms in which she appeared to me. ⁸⁰In reply she said to me: "With regard to them, you must ask another to reveal their meaning to you." ⁸¹For she had appeared to me, brothers, in the first vision the previous year under the form of an exceedingly old woman, sitting in a chair. ⁸²In the second vision her face was youthful, but her skin and hair indicated age, and she stood while she spoke to me. She was also more joyful than on the first occasion. ⁸³But in the third vision she was entirely youthful and exquisitely beautiful, except only that she had the hair of an old woman; but her face beamed with joy, and she sat on a seat. ⁸⁴Now I was exceedingly sad in regard to these appearances, for I longed much to know what the visions meant. Then I see the old woman in a vision of the night saying to me: "Every prayer should be accompanied with humility: fast, therefore, and you will obtain from the LORD what you beg." I therefore fasted for one day. ⁸⁵That very night there appeared to me a young man, who said, "Why do you frequently ask revelations in prayer? Take heed lest by asking many things you injure your flesh; be content with these revelations. Will you be able to see greater revelations than those which you have seen?" ⁸⁶I answered and said to him, "Lord, one thing only I ask, that in regard to these three forms the revelation may be rendered complete." ⁸⁷He answered me, "How long are you senseless? But your doubts make you senseless, because you do not have your hearts turned toward the LORD." ⁸⁸But I answered and said to him, "From you, lord, we will learn these things more accurately." ⁸⁹"Hear then," he said, "with regard to the three forms, concerning which you are inquiring. Why in the first vision did she appear to you as an old woman seated on a chair? ⁹⁰Because your spirit is now old and withered up, and has lost its power in consequence of your infirmities and doubts. For, like elderly men who have no hope of renewing their strength, and expect nothing but their last sleep, so you, weakened by worldly occupations, have given yourselves up to sloth, and have not cast your cares on the LORD. Your spirit is therefore broken, and you have grown old in your sorrows." ⁹¹"I should like then to know, lord, why she sat on a chair?" He answered, "Because every weak person sits on a chair on account of his weakness, that his weakness may be sustained. Behold, you have the form of the first vision. ⁹²Now in the second vision you saw her standing with a youthful countenance, and more joyful than before; still she had the skin and hair of an aged woman. Hear," he said, "this allegory also. ⁹³When one becomes somewhat old, he despairs of himself on account of his weakness and poverty, and looks forward to nothing but the last day of his life. ⁹⁴Then suddenly an inheritance is left him: and hearing of this, he rises up, and becoming exceedingly joyful, he puts on strength. And now he no longer reclines, but stands up; and his spirit, already destroyed by his previous actions, is renewed, and he no longer sits, but acts with vigor. ⁹⁵So it happened with you on hearing the revelation which God gave you. For the LORD had compassion on you, and renewed your spirit, and you laid aside your infirmities. ⁹⁶Vigor arose within you, and you grew strong in faith; and the LORD, seeing your strength, rejoiced. On this account He showed you the building of the tower; and He will show you other things, if you continue at peace with each other with all your heart. ⁹⁷Now, in the third vision, you saw her still younger, and she was noble and joyful, and her shape was beautiful. ⁹⁸For, just as when some good news comes suddenly to one who is sad, immediately he forgets his former sorrows, and looks for nothing else than the good news which he has heard, and for the future is made strong for good, and his spirit is renewed on account of the joy which he has received; so you also have received the renewal of your spirits by seeing these good things. ⁹⁹As to your seeing her sitting on a seat, that means that her position is one of strength, for a seat has four feet and stands firmly. For the world is also kept together by means of four elements. Therefore, those who convert completely and with the whole heart, will become young and firmly established. ¹⁰⁰You now have the revelation completely given to you. Make no further demands for revelations. If anything ought to be revealed, it will be revealed to you."

VISION 4

¹Twenty days after the former vision I saw another vision, brothers—a representation of the tribulation that is to come. ²I was going to a country house along the Campanian road. Now the house lay about ten furlongs from the public road. The district is one rarely traversed. ³And as I walked alone, I prayed [for] the LORD to complete the revelations which He had made to me through His holy Assembly, that He might strengthen me, and give conversion to all His servants who were going astray, that His great and glorious Name might be glorified because He granted to show me His marvels. ⁴And while I was glorifying Him and giving Him thanks, a voice, as it were, answered me, "Do not doubt, Hermas;" ⁵and I began to think within myself, and to say, "What reason have I to doubt—I who have been established by the LORD, and who have seen such glorious sights?" ⁶I advanced a little, brothers, and behold, I see dust rising even to the heavens. I began to say to myself, "Are cattle approaching and raising the dust?" ⁷It was about a furlong's distance from me. And behold, I see the dust rising more and more, so that I imagined that it was something sent from God. But the sun now shone out a little, and behold, I see a mighty beast like a whale, and out of its mouth fiery

locusts proceeded. ⁸But the size of that beast was about a hundred feet, and it had a head like an urn. I began to weep, and to call on the LORD to rescue me from it. Then I remembered the word which I had heard, "Do not doubt, O Hermas." ⁹Clothed, therefore, my brothers, with faith in the LORD, and remembering the great things which He had taught me, I boldly faced the beast. Now that beast came on with such noise and force, that it could itself have destroyed a city. ¹⁰I came near it, and the monstrous beast stretched itself out on the ground, and showed nothing but its tongue, and did not stir at all until I had passed by it. Now the beast had four colors on its head: black, then fiery and bloody, then golden, and lastly white. ¹¹Now after I had passed by the wild beast, and had moved forward about thirty feet, behold, a virgin meets me, adorned as if she were proceeding from the bridal chamber, clothed entirely in white, and with white sandals, and veiled up to her forehead, and her head was covered by a hood. And she had white hair. ¹²I knew from my former visions that this was the Assembly, and I became more joyful. ¹³She saluted me, and said, "Greetings, O man!" And I returned her salutation, and said, "Lady, greetings!" ¹⁴And she answered, and said to me, "Has nothing crossed your path?" I say, "I was met by a beast of such size that it could destroy peoples, but through the power of the LORD and His great mercy I escaped from it." ¹⁵"Well did you escape from it," she says, "because you cast your care on God, and opened your heart to the LORD, believing that you can be saved by no other than by His great and glorious Name. ¹⁶On this account the LORD has sent His messenger, who has rule over the beasts, and whose name is Thegri, and has shut up its mouth, so that it cannot tear you. ¹⁷You have escaped from great tribulation on account of your faith, and because you did not doubt in the presence of such a beast. ¹⁸Therefore, go and tell the chosen ones of the LORD His mighty deeds, and say to them that this beast is a type of the great tribulation that is coming. If then you prepare yourselves, and convert with all your heart, and turn to the LORD, it will be possible for you to escape it, if your heart is pure and spotless, and you spend the rest of the days of your life in serving the LORD blamelessly. ¹⁹Cast your cares on the LORD, and He will direct them. Trust the Lord, you who doubt, for He is all-powerful, and can turn His anger away from you, and send scourges on the doubters. ²⁰Woe to those who hear these words and despise them: it would be better for them not to have been born." ²¹I asked her about the four colors which the beast had on his head. And she answered, and said to me, "Again you are inquisitive in regard to such matters." "Yea, Lady," I said, "make known to me what they are." ²²"Listen," she said: "the black is the world in which we dwell, and the fiery and bloody points out that the world must perish through blood and fire, and the golden part are you who have escaped from this world. ²³For as gold is tested by fire, and thus becomes useful, so are you tested who dwell in it. Those, therefore, who continue steadfast, and are put through the fire, will be purified by means of it. For as gold casts away its dross, so also will you cast away all sadness and trouble, and will be made pure so as to fit into the building of the tower. ²⁴But the white part is the age that is to come, in which the chosen ones of God will dwell, since those selected by God to continuous life will be spotless and pure. ²⁵Therefore, do not cease speaking these things into the ears of the holy ones. This then is the type of the great tribulation that is to come. If you wish it, it will be nothing. Remember those things which were written down before." ²⁶And saying this, she departed. But I did not see into what place she retired. There was a noise, however, and I turned around in alarm, thinking that that beast was coming.

VISION 5

¹After I had been praying at home, and had sat down on my couch, there entered a Man of glorious aspect, dressed like a shepherd, with a white goat's skin, a wallet on his shoulders, and a rod in His hand, and He saluted me. I returned His salutation. ²And immediately He sat down beside me, and said to me, "I have been sent by a most venerable messenger to dwell with you the remaining days of your life." ³And I thought that He had come to tempt me, and I said to Him, "Who are You? For I know Him to whom I have been entrusted." He said to me, "Do you not know Me?" "No," I said. "I," he said, "am that Shepherd to whom you have been entrusted." ⁴And as He was speaking, His figure was changed; and then I knew that it was He to whom I had been entrusted. And immediately I became confused, and fear took hold of me, and I was overpowered with deep sorrow that I had answered Him so wickedly and foolishly. ⁵But He answered, and said to me, "Do not be confounded, but receive strength from the commandments which I am going to give you. For I have been sent," He said, "to show you again all the things which you saw before, especially those of them which are useful to you. ⁶First of all, then, write down My commandments and similitudes, and you will write the other things as I will show you. ⁷For this purpose," He said, "I command you to write down the commandments and similitudes first, that you may read them easily, and be able to keep them." ⁸Accordingly, I wrote down the commandments and similitudes, exactly as He had ordered me. If then, when you have heard these, you keep them and walk in them, and practice them with pure minds, you will receive from the LORD all that He has promised to you. ⁹But if, after you have heard them, you do not convert, but continue to add to your sins, then you will receive from the LORD the opposite things. ¹⁰All these words did the Shepherd, even the Messenger of conversion, command me to write.

SECTION 2:

COMMANDMENTS

COMMANDMENT 1

¹First of all, believe that there is one God who created and finished all things, and made all things out of nothing. He alone is able to contain the whole, but Himself cannot be contained. ²Therefore, have faith in Him, and fear Him; and fearing Him, exercise self-control. ³Keep these commands, and you will cast away all wickedness from yourself, and put on the strength of righteousness, and live to God, if you keep this commandment.

COMMANDMENT 2

¹He said to me, "Be simple and guileless, and you will be as the children who do not know the wickedness that ruins the life of men. ²First, then, speak evil of no one, nor listen with pleasure to anyone who speaks evil of another. But if you listen, you will partake of the sin of him who speaks evil, if you believe the slander which you hear; for believing it, you will also have something to say against your brother. ³Thus, then, will you be guilty of the sin of him who slanders. For slander is evil and an unsteady demon. It never abides in peace, but always remains in discord. Keep yourself from it, and you will always be at peace with all. ⁴Put on a holiness in which there is no wicked cause of offense, but all deeds that are composed and joyful. ⁵Practice goodness; and from the rewards of your labors, which God gives you, give to all the needy in simplicity, not hesitating as to whom you are to give or not to give. Give to all, for God wishes His gifts to be shared among all. ⁶They who receive, will render an account to God why and for what they have received. For the afflicted who receive will not be condemned, but they who receive on false pretenses will suffer punishment. He, then, who gives is guiltless. ⁷For as he received from the LORD, so has he accomplished his service in simplicity, not hesitating as to whom he should give and to whom he should not give. This service, then, if accomplished in simplicity, is glorious with God. He, therefore, who thus ministers in simplicity, will live to God. ⁸Therefore, keep these commandments, as I have given them to you, that your conversion and the conversion of your house may be found in simplicity, and your heart may be pure and stainless."

COMMANDMENT 3

¹Again, He said to me, "Love the truth, and let nothing but truth proceed from your mouth, that the spirit which God has placed in your flesh may be found truthful before all men; and the LORD, who dwells in you, will be glorified, because the LORD is truthful in every word, and in Him is no falsehood. ²Therefore, they who lie deny the LORD, and rob Him, not giving back to Him the deposit which they have received. For they received from Him a spirit free from falsehood. If they give Him

back this spirit untruthful, they pollute the commandment of the LORD, and become robbers." ³On hearing these words, I wept most violently. When He saw me weeping, He said to me, "Why do you weep?" And I said, "Because, Lord, I do not know if I can be saved." ⁴"Why?" He said. And I said, "Because, Lord, I never spoke a true word in my life, but have ever spoken cunningly to all, and have affirmed a lie for the truth to all; and no one ever contradicted me, but credit was given to my word. How then can I live, since I have acted thus?" ⁵And He said to me, "Your feelings are indeed right and sound, for you ought as a servant of God to have walked in truth, and not to have joined an evil conscience with the spirit of truth, nor to have caused sadness to the holy and true Spirit." ⁶And I said to Him, "Never, Lord, did I listen to these words with so much attention." ⁷And He said to me, "Now you hear them, and keep them, that even the falsehoods which you formerly told in your transactions may come to be believed through the truthfulness of your present statements. For even they can become worthy of credit. ⁸If you keep these precepts, and from this time forward you speak nothing but the truth, it will be possible for you to obtain life. ⁹And whosoever will hear this commandment, and depart from that great wickedness—falsehood, will live to God."

COMMANDMENT 4

¹"I charge you," He said, "to guard your chastity, and let no thought enter your heart of another man's wife, or of fornication, or of similar iniquities; for by doing this you commit a great sin. ²But if you always remember your own wife, you will never sin. For if this thought enters your heart, then you will sin; and if, in like manner, you think other wicked thoughts, you commit sin. ³For this thought is a great sin in a servant of God. But if anyone commits this wicked deed, he works death for himself. ⁴Attend, therefore, and refrain from this thought; for where purity dwells, there iniquity ought not to enter the heart of a righteous man." ⁵I said to Him, "Lord, permit me to ask you a few questions." "Ask on," He said. ⁶And I said to Him, "Lord, if anyone has a wife who trusts in the LORD, and if he detects her in adultery, does the man sin if he continues to live with her?" ⁷And He said to me, "As long as he remains ignorant of her sin, the husband commits no transgression in living with her. But if the husband knows that his wife has gone astray, and if the woman does not convert, but persists in her fornication, and yet the husband continues to live with her, he is also guilty of her crime, and a sharer in her adultery." ⁸And I said to Him, "What then, Lord, is the husband to do, if his wife continues in her vicious practices?" ⁹And He said, "The husband should put her away, and remain by himself. But if he puts his wife away and marries another, he also commits adultery." ¹⁰And I said to Him, "What if the woman put away should convert, and wish to return to her husband: will she not be taken back by her husband?" ¹¹And He said to me, "Assuredly. If the husband does not take her back, he sins, and brings a great sin on himself; for he ought to take back the sinner who has converted. But not frequently. For there is but one conversion to the servants of God. ¹²In case, therefore, that the divorced wife may convert, the husband ought to not marry another when his wife has been put away. In this matter man and woman are to be treated exactly in the same way. ¹³Moreover, adultery is committed not only by those who pollute their flesh, but by those who imitate the heathen in their actions. Therefore, if anyone persists in such deeds, and does not convert, withdraw from him, and cease to live with him. Otherwise you are a sharer in his sin. ¹⁴Therefore the injunction has been laid on you, that you should remain by yourselves, both man and woman, for in such persons conversion can take place. ¹⁵But I do not," He said, "give opportunity for the doing of these deeds, but that he who has sinned may sin no more. But with regard to his previous transgressions, there is One who is able to provide a cure; for it is He, indeed, who has power over all." ¹⁶I asked Him again, and said, "Since the LORD has granted to always dwell with me, hear me while I utter a few words; for I understand nothing, and my heart has been hardened by my previous mode of life. ¹⁷Give me understanding, for I am exceedingly dull, and I understand absolutely nothing." And He answered and said to me, "I am set over conversion, and I give understanding to all who convert. ¹⁸Do you not think," he said, "that it is great wisdom to convert? For conversion is great wisdom. For he who has sinned understands that he acted wickedly in the sight of the LORD, and remembers the actions he has done, and he converts, and no longer acts wickedly, but does good liberally, and humbles and torments his soul because he has sinned. You see, therefore, that conversion is great wisdom." ¹⁹And I said to Him, "It is for this reason, Lord, that I inquire carefully into all things, especially because I am a sinner; that I may know what works I should do, that I may live: for my sins are many and various." ²⁰And He said to me, "You will live if you keep My commandments, and walk in them; and whosoever will hear and keep these commandments, will live to God." ²¹And I said to Him, "I should like to continue my questions." "Speak on," He said. And I said, "I heard, Lord, some teachers maintain that there is no other conversion than that which takes place, when we descended into the water and received remission of our former sins." ²²He said to me, "That was sound doctrine which you heard; for that is really the case. For he who has received remission of his sins ought not to sin anymore, but to live in purity. ²³Since, however, you inquire diligently into all things, I will also point this out to you, not as giving occasion for error to those who are to believe, or have lately believed, in the LORD. ²⁴For those who have now believed, and those who are to believe, have no conversion for their sins; but they have remission of their previous sins. For to those who have been called before these days, the LORD has set conversion. ²⁵For the LORD, knowing the heart, and foreknowing all things, knew the weakness of men and the manifold wiles of the Devil, that he would inflict some evil on the servants of God, and would act wickedly toward them. ²⁶The LORD, therefore, being merciful, has had mercy on the work of His hand, and has set conversion for them; and He has entrusted to me power over this conversion. ²⁷And therefore, I say to you, that if anyone is tempted by the Devil, and sins after that great and holy calling, in which the LORD has called His people to continuous life, he has opportunity to convert but once. ²⁸But if he should sin frequently after this, and then convert, to such a man his conversion will be of no avail; for he will live with difficulty." ²⁹And I said, "Lord, I feel that life has come back to me in listening attentively to these commandments; for I know that I will be saved, if in [the] future I sin no more." And He said, "You will be saved, you and all who keep these commandments." ³⁰And again I asked Him, saying, "Lord, since you have been so patient in listening to me, will you show me this also?" "Speak," He said. And I said, "If a wife or husband dies, and the widower or widow marries, does he or she commit sin?" ³¹"There is no sin in marrying again," He said; "but if they remain unmarried, they gain greater honor and glory with the LORD; but if they marry, they do not sin. Therefore, guard your chastity and purity, and you will live to God. ³²What commandments I now give you, and what I am to give, keep from henceforth, yea, from the very day when you were entrusted to Me, and I will dwell in your house. And your former sins will be forgiven, if you keep My commandments. ³³And all will be forgiven who keep these commandments of Mine and walk in this chastity."

COMMANDMENT 5

¹"Be patient," He said, "and of good understanding, and you will rule over every wicked work, and you will work all righteousness. For if you are patient, the Holy Spirit that dwells in you will be pure. ²He will not be darkened by any evil spirit, but, dwelling in a broad region, He will rejoice and be glad; and with the vessel in which He dwells He will serve God in gladness, having great peace within Himself. ³But if any outburst of anger takes place, immediately the Holy Spirit, who is tender, is troubled, not having a pure place, and He seeks to depart. For He is choked by the vile spirit, and cannot attend on the LORD as He wishes, for anger pollutes Him. ⁴For the LORD dwells in long-suffering, but the Devil in anger. ⁵The two spirits, then, when dwelling in the same habitation, are at discord with each other, and are troublesome to that man in whom they dwell. ⁶For if an exceedingly small piece of wormwood is taken and put into a jar of honey, is the honey not entirely destroyed, and does the exceedingly small piece of wormwood not entirely take away the sweetness of the honey, so that it no longer

affords any gratification to its owner, but has become bitter, and lost its use? ⁷But if the wormwood is not put into the honey, then the honey remains sweet, and is of use to its owner. ⁸You see, then, that patience is sweeter than honey, and useful to God, and the LORD dwells in it. But anger is bitter and useless. ⁹Now, if anger is mingled with patience, the patience is polluted, and its prayer is not then useful to God." ¹⁰"I should like, Lord," I said, "to know the power of anger, that I may guard myself against it." ¹¹And He said, "If you do not guard yourself against it, you and your house lose all hope of salvation. Guard yourself, therefore, against it. For I am with you, and all will depart from it who convert with their whole heart. ¹²For I will be with them, and I will save them all. For all are justified by the most holy Messenger. ¹³"Hear now," He said, "how wicked is the action of anger, and in what way it overthrows the servants of God by its action, and turns them from righteousness. But it does not turn away those who are full of faith, nor does it act on them, for the power of the LORD is with them. ¹⁴It is the thoughtless and doubting that it turns away. For as soon as it sees such men standing steadfast, it throws itself into their hearts, and for nothing at all the man or woman becomes embittered on account of occurrences in their daily life, as for instance on account of their food, or some superfluous word that has been uttered, or on account of some friend, or some gift or debt, or some such senseless affair. ¹⁵For all these things are foolish and empty and unprofitable to the servants of God. ¹⁶But patience is great, and mighty, and strong, and calm in the midst of great enlargement, joyful, rejoicing, free from care, glorifying God at all times, having no bitterness in her, and abiding continually meek and quiet. ¹⁷Now this patience dwells with those who have complete faith. But anger is foolish, and fickle, and senseless. ¹⁸Now, of folly is begotten bitterness, and of bitterness anger, and of anger frenzy. This frenzy, the product of so many evils, ends in great and incurable sin. ¹⁹For when all these spirits dwell in one vessel in which the Holy Spirit also dwells, the vessel cannot contain them, but overflows. The tender Spirit, then, not being accustomed to dwell with the wicked spirit, nor with hardness, withdraws from such a man, and seeks to dwell with meekness and peacefulness. ²⁰Then, when He withdraws from the man in whom He dwelt, the man is emptied of the righteous Spirit; and being henceforward filled with evil spirits, He is in a state of anarchy in every action, being dragged here and there by the evil spirits, and there is a complete darkness in his mind as to everything good. ²¹This, then, is what happens to all the angry. Therefore, depart from that most wicked spirit—anger, and put on patience, and resist anger and bitterness, and you will be found in company with the purity which is loved by the LORD. ²²Take care, then, that you do not neglect by any chance this commandment: for if you obey this commandment, you will be able to keep all the other commandments which I am to give you. ²³Be strong, then, in these commandments, and put on power, and let all put on power, as many as wish to walk in them."

COMMANDMENT 6

¹"I gave you," He said, "directions in the first commandment to attend to faith, and fear, and self-restraint." "Even so, Lord," I said. ²And He said, "Now I wish to show you the powers of these, that you may know what power each possesses. For their powers are double, and have relation alike to the righteous and the unrighteous. ³Therefore, trust the righteous, but put no trust in the unrighteous. For the path of righteousness is straight, but that of unrighteousness is crooked. ⁴But walk in the straight and even way, and do not mind the crooked. For the crooked path has no roads, but has many pathless places and stumbling-blocks in it, and it is rough and thorny. It is injurious to those who walk therein. ⁵But they who walk in the straight road walk evenly without stumbling, because it is neither rough nor thorny. You see, then, that it is better to walk in this road." ⁶"I wish to go by this road," I said. "You will go by it," He said; "and whoever turns to the LORD with all his heart will walk in it." ⁷"Hear now," He said, "in regard to faith. There are two messengers with a man—one of righteousness, and the other of iniquity." And I said to Him, "How, Lord, am I to know the powers of these, for both messengers dwell with me?" ⁸"Hear," He said, "and understand them. The messenger of righteousness is gentle and modest, meek and peaceful. Therefore, when he ascends into your heart, immediately he talks to you of righteousness, purity, chastity, contentment, and of every righteous deed and glorious virtue. ⁹When all these ascend into your heart, know that the messenger of righteousness is with you. These are the deeds of the messenger of righteousness. Trust him, then, and his works. ¹⁰Look now at the works of the messenger of iniquity. First, he is wrathful, and bitter, and foolish, and his works are evil, and ruin the servants of God. When, then, he ascends into your heart, know him by his works." ¹¹And I said to Him, "How, Lord, I will perceive him—I do not know." "Hear and understand" He said. ¹²"When anger comes on you, or harshness, know that he is in you; and you will know this to be the case also, when you are attacked by a longing after many transactions, and the richest delicacies, and drunken revels, and various luxuries, and things improper, and by a hankering after women, and by overreaching, and pride, and blustering, and by whatever is like to these. ¹³When these ascend into your heart, know that the messenger of iniquity is in you. Now that you know his works, depart from him, and in no respect trust him, because his deeds are evil, and unprofitable to the servants of God. ¹⁴These, then, are the actions of both messengers. Understand them and trust the messenger of righteousness; but depart from the messenger of iniquity, because his instruction is bad in every deed. ¹⁵For though a man be most faithful, and the thought of this messenger ascend into his heart, that man or woman must sin. ¹⁶On the other hand, be a man or woman ever so bad, yet, if the works of the messenger of righteousness ascend into his or her heart, he or she must do something good. ¹⁷You see, therefore, that it is good to follow the messenger of righteousness, but to bid farewell to the messenger of iniquity. ¹⁸This commandment exhibits the deeds of faith, that you may trust the works of the messenger of righteousness, and doing them you may live to God. But believe the works of the messenger of iniquity are hard. If you refuse to do them, you will live to God."

COMMANDMENT 7

¹"Fear," He said, "the LORD, and keep His commandments. For if you keep the commandments of God, you will be powerful in every action, and every one of your actions will be incomparable. ²For, fearing the LORD, you will do all things well. This is the fear which you ought to have, that you may be saved. ³But do not fear the Devil; for, fearing the LORD, you will have dominion over the Devil, for there is no power in him. ⁴But he in whom there is no power ought on no account to be an object of fear; but He in whom there is glorious power is truly to be feared. For every one that has power ought to be feared; but he who has no power is despised by all. ⁵Therefore, fear the deeds of the Devil, since they are wicked. For, fearing the LORD, you will not do these deeds, but will refrain from them. ⁶For fears are of two kinds: for if you do not wish to do that which is evil, fear the LORD, and you will not do it; but, again, if you wish to do that which is good, fear the LORD, and you will do it. Therefore, the fear of the LORD is strong, and great, and glorious. ⁷Fear, then, the LORD, and you will live to Him, and as many as fear Him and keep His commandments will live to God." ⁸"Why," I said, "Lord, did You say in regard to those that keep His commandments, that they will live to God?" "Because," He says, "all creation fears the LORD, but all creation does not keep His commandments. ⁹They only who fear the LORD and keep His commandments have life with God; but as to those who do not keep His commandments, there is no life in them."

COMMANDMENT 8

¹"I told you," He said, "that the creatures of God are double, for restraint is also double; for in some cases restraint has to be exercised in others [where] there is no need of restraint." ²"Make known to me, Lord," I say, "in what cases restraint has to be exercised, and in what cases it does not." ³"Restrain yourself in regard to evil, and do not do it; but exercise no restraint in regard to good, but do it. For if you exercise restraint in the doing of good, you will commit a great sin; but if you exercise restraint, so as not to do that which is evil, you are practicing great righteousness. ⁴Restrain yourself, therefore, from all iniquity, and do that which is good." ⁵"What, Lord," I say, "are the evil deeds from which we must restrain

ourselves?" ⁶"Hear," He says: "from adultery and fornication, from unlawful reveling, from wicked luxury, from indulgence in many kinds of food and the extravagance of riches, and from boastfulness, and haughtiness, and insolence, and lies, and backbiting, and hypocrisy, from the remembrance of wrong, and from all slander. ⁷These are the deeds that are most wicked in the life of men. From all these deeds, therefore, the servant of God must restrain himself. ⁸For he who does not restrain himself from these, cannot live to God. Listen, then, to the deeds that accompany these." ⁹"Are there, Lord," I said, "any other evil deeds?" "There are," He says; "and many of them, too, from which the servant of God must restrain himself—theft, lying, robbery, false witness, overreaching, wicked lust, deceit, vainglory, boastfulness, and all other vices like to these." ¹⁰"Do you not think that these are really wicked?" "Exceedingly wicked in the servants of God. From all of these the servant of God must restrain himself. ¹¹Restrain yourself, then, from all these, that you may live to God, and you will be enrolled among those who restrain themselves in regard to these matters. These, then, are the things from which you must restrain yourself. ¹²But listen," He says, "to the things in regard to which you do not have to exercise self-restraint, but which you ought to do. ¹³Do not restrain yourself in regard to that which is good, but do it." "And tell me, Lord," I say, "the nature of the good deeds, that I may walk in them and wait on them, so that doing them I can be saved." ¹⁴"Listen," He says, "to the good deeds which you ought to do, and in regard to which there is no self-restraint requisite. First of all there is faith, then fear of the LORD, love, concord, words of righteousness, truth, patience. ¹⁵Than these, nothing is better in the life of men. If anyone attends to these, and does not restrain himself from them, he is blessed in his life. ¹⁶Then there are the following attendant on these: helping widows, looking after orphans and the needy, rescuing the servants of God from necessities, the being hospitable—for in hospitality doing good finds a field—never opposing anyone, the being quiet, having fewer needs than all men, reverencing the aged, practicing righteousness, watching the brotherhood, bearing insolence, being long-suffering, encouraging those who are sick in soul, not casting those who have fallen into sin from the faith, but turning them back and restoring them to peace of mind, admonishing sinners, not oppressing debtors and the needy, and if there are any other actions like these. ¹⁷Do these seem to you good?" He says. "For what, Lord," I say, "is better than these?" "Walk then in them," He says, "and do not restrain yourself from them, and you will live to God. ¹⁸Therefore, keep this commandment. If you do good, and do not restrain yourself from it, you will live to God. All who act thus will live to God. ¹⁹And, again, if you refuse to do evil, and restrain yourself from it, you will live to God. And all will live to God who keep these commandments and walk in them."

COMMANDMENT 9

¹He says to me, "Put away doubting from you and do not hesitate to ask of the LORD, saying to yourself, How can I ask of the LORD and receive from Him, seeing I have sinned so much against Him? ²Do not thus reason with yourself, but with all your heart turn to the LORD and ask of Him without doubting, and you will know the multitude of His tender mercies; that He will never leave you, but fulfill the request of your soul. ³For He is not like men, who remember evils done against them; but He Himself does not remember evils and has compassion on His own creature. ⁴Therefore, cleanse your heart from all the vanities of this world, and from the words already mentioned, and ask of the LORD and you will receive all, and in none of your requests will you be denied which you make to the LORD without doubting. But if you doubt in your heart, you will receive none of your requests. ⁵For those who doubt regarding God are double-souled, and do not obtain one of their requests. But those who are perfect in faith ask everything, trusting in the LORD; and they obtain, because they ask nothing doubting, and not being double-souled. ⁶For every double-souled man, even if he converts, will be saved with difficulty. Cleanse your heart, therefore, from all doubt, and put on faith, because it is strong, and trust God that you will obtain from Him all that you ask. ⁷And if at any time, after you have asked of the LORD, you are slower in obtaining your request [than you expected], do not doubt because you have not soon obtained the request of your soul; for invariably it is on account of some temptation or some sin of which you are ignorant that you are slower in obtaining your request. ⁸Therefore, do not cease to make the request of your soul, and you will obtain it. But if you grow weary and waver in your request, blame yourself, and not Him who does not give to you. ⁹Consider this doubting state of mind, for it is wicked and senseless, and turns many away entirely from the faith, even though they might be very strong. ¹⁰For this doubting is the daughter of the Devil, and acts exceedingly wickedly to the servants of God. ¹¹Despise, then, doubting, and gain the mastery over it in everything; clothing yourself with faith, which is strong and powerful. For faith promises all things, perfects all things; but doubt having no thorough faith in itself, fails in every work which it undertakes. ¹²You see, then," He says, "that faith is from above—from the LORD—and has great power; but doubt is an earthly spirit, coming from the Devil, and has no power. ¹³Serve, then, that which has power, namely faith, and keep away from doubt, which has no power, and you will live to God. And all will live to God whose minds have been set on these things."

COMMANDMENT 10

¹"Remove from yourself," He says, "grief; for she is the sister of doubt and anger." "How, Lord," I say, "is she the sister of these? For anger, doubt, and grief seem to be quite different from each other." ²"You are senseless, O man. Do you not perceive that grief is more wicked than all the spirits, and most terrible to the servants of God, and more than all other spirits destroys man and crushes out the Holy Spirit, and yet, on the other hand, she saves him?" ³"I am senseless, Lord," I say, "and do not understand these allegories. For how she can crush out, and on the other hand save, I do not perceive." ⁴"Listen," He says. "Those who have never searched for the truth, nor investigated the nature of the Divinity, but have simply believed, when they devote themselves to and become mixed up with business, and wealth, and heathen friendships, and many other actions of this world, do not perceive the allegories of Divinity; ⁵for their minds are darkened by these actions, and they are corrupted and become dried up. Even as beautiful vines, when they are neglected, are withered up by thorns and various plants, so men who have believed, and have afterward fallen away into many of those actions above mentioned, go astray in their minds, and lose all understanding in regard to righteousness; ⁶for if they hear of righteousness, their minds are occupied with their business, and they give no heed at all. ⁷Those, on the other hand, who have the fear of God, and search after [the] Godhead and truth, and have their hearts turned to the LORD, quickly perceive and understand what is said to them, because they have the fear of the LORD in them. ⁸For where the LORD dwells, there is much understanding. Cleave, then, to the LORD, and you will understand and perceive all things. ⁹"Hear, then," He says, "foolish man, how grief crushes out the Holy Spirit, and on the other hand saves. When the doubting man attempts any deed, and fails in it on account of his doubt, this grief enters into the man, and grieves the Holy Spirit, and crushes Him out. ¹⁰Then, on the other hand, when anger attaches itself to a man in regard to any matter, and he is embittered, then grief enters into the heart of the man who was irritated, and he is grieved at the deed which he did, and converts that he has wrought a wicked deed. ¹¹This grief, then, appears to be accompanied by salvation, because the man, after having done a wicked deed, converted. Both actions grieve the Spirit: doubt, because it did not accomplish its object; and anger grieves the Spirit, because it did what was wicked. ¹²Both these are grievous to the Holy Spirit—doubt and anger. Therefore, remove grief from yourself, and do not crush the Holy Spirit which dwells in you, lest He entreat God against you, and He withdraw from you. ¹³For the Spirit of God which has been granted to us to dwell in this body does not endure grief nor trouble. ¹⁴Therefore, put on cheerfulness, which is always agreeable and acceptable to God, and rejoice in it. For every cheerful man does what is good, and minds what is good, and despises grief; but the sorrowful man always acts wickedly. ¹⁵First, he acts wickedly because he grieves the Holy Spirit, which was given to man—a cheerful Spirit. ¹⁶Secondly, grieving

the Holy Spirit, he works iniquity, neither entreating the LORD nor confessing to Him. For the entreaty of the sorrowful man has no power to ascend to the altar of God." ¹⁷"Why," I say, "does the entreaty of the grieved man not ascend to the altar?" "Because," He says, "grief sits in his heart. Grief, then, mingled with his entreaty, does not permit the entreaty to ascend pure to the altar of God. ¹⁸For as vinegar and wine, when mixed in the same vessel, do not give the same pleasure [as wine alone gives], so grief mixed with the Holy Spirit does not produce the same entreaty [as would be produced by the Holy Spirit alone]. ¹⁹Cleanse yourself from this wicked grief, and you will live to God; and all will live to God who drive away grief from themselves, and put on all cheerfulness."

COMMANDMENT 11

¹He pointed out to me some men sitting on a seat, and one man sitting on a chair. And He says to me, "Do you see the persons sitting on the seat?" "I do, Lord," I said. "These," He says, "are the faithful, and he who sits on the chair is a false prophet, ruining the minds of the servants of God. It is the doubters, not the faithful, that he ruins. ²These doubters then go to him as to a soothsayer, and inquire of him what will happen to them; and he, the false prophet, not having the power of a Divine Spirit in him, answers them according to their inquiries, and according to their wicked desires, and fills their souls with expectations, according to their own wishes. ³For being himself empty, he gives empty answers to empty inquirers; for every answer is made to the emptiness of man. Some true words he does occasionally utter; for the Devil fills him with his own spirit, in the hope that he may be able to overcome some of the righteous. ⁴As many, then, as are strong in the faith of the LORD, and are clothed with truth, have no connection with such spirits, but keep away from them; but as many as are of doubtful minds and frequently convert, take themselves to soothsaying, even as the heathen, and bring greater sin on themselves by their idolatry. ⁵For he who inquires of a false prophet in regard to any action is an idolater, and devoid of the truth, and foolish. For no spirit given by God requires to be asked; but such a spirit having the power of Divinity speaks all things of itself, for it proceeds from above from the power of the Divine Spirit. ⁶But the spirit which is asked and speaks according to the desires of men is earthly, light, and powerless, and it is altogether silent if it is not questioned." ⁷"How then, Lord," I say, "will a man know which of them is the prophet, and which the false prophet?" ⁸"I will tell you," He says, "about both the prophets, and then you can try the true and the false prophet according to My directions. ⁹Try the man who has the Divine Spirit by his life. First, he who has the Divine Spirit proceeding from above is meek, and peaceable, and humble, and refrains from all iniquity and the vain desire of this world, and contents himself with fewer wants than those of other men, and when asked he makes no reply; ¹⁰nor does he speak privately, nor when man wishes the spirit to speak does the Holy Spirit speak, but it speaks only when God wishes it to speak. ¹¹When, then, a man having the Divine Spirit comes into an assembly of righteous men who have faith in the Divine Spirit, and this assembly of men offers up prayer to God, then the messenger of the prophetic Spirit, who is destined for him, fills the man; and the man being filled with the Holy Spirit, speaks to the multitude as the LORD wishes. ¹²Thus, then, will the Spirit of Divinity become manifest. Whatever power therefore comes from the Spirit of Divinity belongs to the LORD. ¹³Hear, then," He says, "in regard to the spirit which is earthly, and empty, and powerless, and foolish. First, the man who seems to have the Spirit, [but does not,] exalts himself, and wishes to have the first seat, and is bold, and impudent, and talkative, and lives in the midst of many luxuries and many other delusions, and takes rewards for his prophecy; and if he does not receive rewards, he does not prophesy. ¹⁴Can, then, the Divine Spirit take rewards and prophesy? It is not possible that the prophet of God should do this, but prophets of this character are possessed by an earthly spirit. ¹⁵Then it never approaches an assembly of righteous men, but shuns them. And it associates with doubters and the vain, and prophesies to them in a corner, and deceives them, speaking to them, according to their desires, mere empty words: for they are empty to whom it gives its answers. ¹⁶For the empty vessel, when placed along with the empty, is not crashed, but they correspond to each other. ¹⁷When, therefore, it comes into an assembly of righteous men who have a Spirit of Divinity, and they offer up prayer, that man is made empty, and the earthly spirit flees from him through fear, and that man is made dumb, and is entirely crashed, being unable to speak. ¹⁸For if you closely pack a storehouse with wine or oil, and put an empty jar in the midst of the vessels of wine or oil, you will find that jar empty as when you placed it, if you should wish to clear the storehouse. ¹⁹So also the empty prophets, when they come to the spirits of the righteous, are found [on leaving] to be such as they were when they came. ²⁰This, then, is the mode of life of both prophets. Try by his deeds and his life the man who says that he is inspired. ²¹But as for you, trust the Spirit which comes from God, and has power; but the spirit which is earthly and empty do not trust at all, for there is no power in it: it comes from the Devil. ²²Hear, then, the allegory which I am to tell you. Take a stone, and throw it to the sky, and see if you can touch it. Or again, take a squirt of water and squirt into the sky, and see if you can penetrate the sky." ²³"How, Lord," I say, "can these things take place? For both of them are impossible." "As these things," He says, "are impossible, so also are the earthly spirits powerless and weak. ²⁴But look, on the other hand, at the power which comes from above. Hail is of the size of a very small grain, yet when it falls on a man's head how much annoyance it gives him! ²⁵Or again, take the drop which falls from a pitcher to the ground, and yet it hollows a stone. You see, then, that the smallest things coming from above have great power when they fall on the earth. ²⁶Thus is the Divine Spirit, which comes from above, also powerful. Trust, then, that Spirit, but have nothing to do with the other."

COMMANDMENT 12

¹He says to me, "Put away from yourself all wicked desire, and clothe yourself with good and chaste desire; for clothed with this desire you will hate wicked desire, and will rein yourself in even as you wish. ²For wicked desire is wild and is tamed with difficulty. For it is terrible and consumes men exceedingly by its wildness. Especially is the servant of God terribly consumed by it, if he falls into it and is devoid of understanding. ³Moreover, it consumes all such as do not have on them the garment of good desire, but are entangled and mixed up with this world. These it delivers up to death." ⁴"What then, Lord," I say, "are the deeds of wicked desire which deliver men over to death? Make them known to me, and I will refrain from them." ⁵"Listen, then, to the works in which evil desire slays the servants of God." "Foremost of all is the desire after another's wife or husband, and after extravagance, and many useless delicacies and drinks, and many other foolish luxuries; for all luxury is foolish and empty in the servants of God. ⁶These, then, are the evil desires which slay the servants of God. For this evil desire is the daughter of the Devil. You must refrain from evil desires, that by refraining you may live to God. ⁷But as many as are mastered by them, and do not resist them, will perish at last, for these desires are fatal. ⁸Put on, then, the desire of righteousness; and arming yourself with the fear of the LORD, resist them. For the fear of the LORD dwells in good desire. ⁹But if evil desire sees you armed with the fear of God, and resisting it, it will flee far from you, and it will no longer appear to you, for it fears your armor. ¹⁰Go, then, adorned with the crown which you have gained for victory over it, to the desire of righteousness, and, delivering up to it the prize which you have received, serve it even as it wishes. ¹¹If you serve good desire, and be subject to it, you will gain the mastery over evil desire, and make it subject to you even as you wish." ¹²"I should like to [know] how," I say, "in what way I ought to serve good desire." ¹³"Hear," He says: "You will practice righteousness and virtue, truth and the fear of the LORD, faith and meekness, and whatever excellencies are like to these. Practicing these, you will be a well-pleasing servant of God, and you will live to Him; and everyone who will serve good desire, will live to God." ¹⁴He concluded the twelve commandments, and said to me, "You now have these commandments. Walk in them and exhort your hearers that their conversion may be pure during the remainder of their life. ¹⁵Carefully fulfill this ministry which I now

entrust to you, and you will accomplish much. For you will find favor among those who are to convert, and they will give heed to your words; for I will be with you, and will compel them to obey you." [16] I say to Him, "Lord, these commandments are great, and good, and glorious, and fitted to gladden the heart of the man who can perform them. [17] But I do not know if these commandments can be kept by man, because they are exceedingly hard." [18] He answered and said to me, "If you lay it down as certain that they can be kept, then you will easily keep them, and they will not be hard. But if you come to imagine that they cannot be kept by man, then you will not keep them. [19] Now I say to you, if you do not keep them, but neglect them, you will not be saved, nor your children, nor your house, since you have already determined for yourself that these commandments cannot be kept by man." [20] He said these things to me in tones of the deepest anger, so that I was confounded and exceedingly afraid of Him, for His figure was altered so that a man could not endure His anger. [21] But seeing me altogether agitated and confused, He began to speak to me in more gentle tones; and He said: "O feel, senseless and doubting, do you not perceive how great is the glory of God, and how strong and marvelous, in that He created the world for the sake of man, and subjected all creation to him, and gave him power to rule over everything under heaven? [22] If, then, man is lord of the creatures of God, and rules over all, is he not able to be lord also of these commandments? For," He says, "the man who has the LORD in his heart can also be lord of all, and of every one of these commandments. [23] But to those who have the LORD only on their lips, but their hearts hardened, and who are far from the LORD, the commandments are hard and difficult. [24] Put, therefore—you who are empty and fickle in your faith—the LORD in your heart, and you will know that there is nothing easier or sweeter, or more manageable, than these commandments. [25] Return, you who walk in the commandments of the Devil, in hard, and bitter, and wild licentiousness, and do not fear the Devil; [26] for there is no power in him against you, for I will be with you, the Messenger of conversion, who am Lord over him. The Devil has fear only, but his fear has no strength. Do not fear him, then, and he will flee from you." [27] I say to Him, "Lord, listen to me for a moment." "Say what you wish," He says. "Man, Lord," I say, "is eager to keep the commandments of God, and there is no one who does not ask of the LORD that strength may be given him for these commandments, and that he may be subject to them; but the Devil is hard, and holds sway over them." [28] "He cannot," He says, "hold sway over the servants of God, who with all their heart place their hopes in Him. The Devil can wrestle against these, [but] he cannot overthrow them. [29] If, then, you resist him, he will be conquered, and flee in disgrace from you. As many, therefore," He says, "as are empty, fear the Devil, as possessing power. [30] When a man has filled very suitable jars with good wine, and a few among those jars are left empty, then he comes to the jars, and does not look at the full jars, for he knows that they are full; but he looks at the empty, being afraid lest they have become sour. For empty jars quickly become sour, and the goodness of the wine is gone. [31] So also, the Devil goes to all the servants of God to try them. As many, then, as are full in the faith, resist him strongly, and he withdraws from them, having no way by which he might enter them. He goes, then, to the empty, and finding a way of entrance into them, he produces in them whatever he wishes, and they become his servants. [32] But I, the Messenger of conversion, say to you: do not fear the Devil; for I was sent," He says, "to be with you who convert with all your heart, and to make you strong in faith. [33] Trust God, then, you who on account of your sins have despaired of life, and who add to your sins and weigh down your life; for if you return to the LORD with all your heart, and practice righteousness the rest of your days, and serve Him according to His will, He will heal your former sins, and you will have power to hold sway over the works of the Devil. [34] But as to the threats of the Devil, do not fear them at all, for he is powerless as the sinews of a dead man. [35] Give ear to Me, then, and fear Him who has all power, both to save and destroy, and keep His commandments, and you will live to God." [36] I say to Him, "Lord, I am now made strong in all the ordinances of the LORD, because You are with me; and I know that You will crush all the power of the Devil, and we will have rule over him, and will prevail against all his works. [37] And I hope, Lord, to be able to keep all these commandments which You have enjoined on me, the LORD strengthening me." [38] "You will keep them," He says, "if your heart is pure toward the LORD; and all will keep them who cleanse their hearts from the vain desires of this world, and they will live to God."

SECTION 3:

SIMILITUDES

SIMILITUDE 1

[1] He says to me, "You know that you who are the servants of God dwell in a strange land; for your city is far away from this one. [2] If then," He continues, "you know your city in which you are to dwell, why do you here provide lands, and make expensive preparations, and accumulate dwellings and useless buildings? He who makes such preparations for this city cannot return again to his own. [3] Oh foolish, and unstable, and miserable man! Do you not understand that all these things belong to another, and are under the power of another? [4] For the lord of this city will say, I do not wish you to dwell in my city; but depart from this city, because you do not obey my laws. [5] You, therefore, although having fields and houses, and many other things, when cast out by him, what will you do with your land, and house, and other possessions which you have gathered to yourself? [6] For the lord of this country justly says to you, Either obey my laws or depart from my dominion. What, then, do you intend to do, having a law in your own city, on account of your lands, and the rest of your possessions? [7] You will altogether deny your law, and walk according to the law of this city. See lest it be to your hurt to deny your law; for if you will desire to return to your city, you will not be received, because you have denied the law of your city, but will be excluded from it. [8] Have a care, therefore, as one living in a foreign land: make no further preparations for yourself than such merely as may be sufficient; and be ready, when the master of this city will come to cast you out for disobeying his law, to leave his city, and to depart to your own, and to obey your own law without being exposed to annoyance, but in great joy. [9] Have a care, then, you who serve the LORD, and have Him in your heart, that you work the works of God, remembering His commandments and promises which He promised, and believe that He will bring them to pass if His commandments are observed. [10] Instead of lands, therefore, buy afflicted souls, according as each one is able, and visit widows and orphans, and do not overlook them; and spend your wealth and all your preparations, which you received from the LORD, on such lands and houses. [11] For to this end the Master made you rich, that you might perform these services to Him; and it is much better to purchase such lands, and possessions, and houses, as you will find in your own city, when you come to reside in it. [12] This is a noble and sacred expenditure, attended neither with sorrow nor fear, but with joy. [13] Do not practice the expenditure of the heathen, for it is injurious to you who are the servants of God; but practice an expenditure of your own, in which you can rejoice; [14] and do not corrupt nor touch what is another's, nor covet it, for it is an evil thing to covet the goods of other men; but work your own work, and you will be saved."

SIMILITUDE 2

[1] As I was walking in the field, and observing an elm and vine, and determining in my own mind respecting them and their fruits, the Shepherd appears to me, and says, "What is it that you are thinking about the elm and vine?" [2] "I am considering," I reply, "that they suit each other exceedingly well." [3] "These two trees," he continues, "are intended as an example for the servants of God." [4] "I would like to know," I said, "the example which these trees You say, are intended to teach." [5] "Do you see," He says, "the elm and the vine?" "I see them Lord," I replied. "This vine," He continued, "produces fruit, and the elm is an unfruitful tree; but unless the vine be trained on the elm, it cannot bear much fruit when extended at length on the ground; and the fruit which it bears is rotten, because the plant is not suspended on the elm. [6] Therefore, when the vine is cast on the elm, it yields fruit both from itself and from the elm. You see, moreover, that the elm also produces much fruit, not less than the vine,

but even more; because," He continued, "the vine, when suspended on the elm, yields much fruit, and good; but when thrown on the ground, what it produces is small and rotten. ⁷This similitude, therefore, is for the servants of God—for the poor man and for the rich." "How so, Lord?" I said; "explain the matter to me." ⁸"Listen," He said: "The rich man has much wealth, but is poor in matters relating to the LORD, because he is distracted about his riches; and he offers very few confessions and intercessions to the LORD, and those which he offers are small and weak, and have no power above. ⁹But when the rich man refreshes the poor, and assists him in his necessities, believing that what he does to the poor man will be able to find its reward with God—because the poor man is rich in intercession and confession, and his intercession has great power with God—then the rich man helps the poor in all things without hesitation; ¹⁰and the poor man, being helped by the rich, intercedes for him, giving thanks to God for him who bestows gifts on him. ¹¹And he still continues to interest himself zealously for the poor man, that his wants may be constantly supplied. For he knows that the intercession of the poor man is acceptable and influential with God. Both, accordingly, accomplish their work. ¹²The poor man makes intercession; a work in which he is rich, which he received from the LORD, and with which he recompenses the master who helps him. ¹³And the rich man, in like manner, unhesitatingly bestows on the poor man the riches which he received from the LORD. And this is a great work, and acceptable before God, because he understands the object of his wealth, and has given to the poor of the gifts of the LORD, and rightly discharged his service to Him. ¹⁴Among men, however, the elm does not appear to produce fruit, and they do not know nor understand that if a drought comes, the elm, which contains water, nourishes the vine; and the vine, having an unfailing supply of water, yields double fruit both for itself and for the elm. ¹⁵So also poor men interceding with the LORD on behalf of the rich, increase their riches; and the rich, again, aiding the poor in their necessities, satisfy their souls. Both, therefore, are partners in the righteous work. ¹⁶He who does these things will not be deserted by God, but will be enrolled in the scrolls of the living. ¹⁷Blessed are they who have riches, and who understand that they are from the LORD. [[For they who are of that mind will be able to do some good.]]"

SIMILITUDE 3

¹He showed me many trees having no leaves, but withered, as it seemed to me; for all were alike. And He said to me, "Do you see those trees?" "I see, Lord," I replied, "that all are alike, and withered." ²He answered me, and said, "These trees which you see are those who dwell in this world." ³"Why, then, Lord," I said, "are they withered, as it were, and alike?" "Because," He said, "neither are the righteous manifest in this life, nor sinners, but they are alike; for this life is a winter to the righteous, and they do not manifest themselves, because they dwell with sinners: ⁴for as in winter trees that have cast their leaves are alike, and it is not seen which are dead and which are living, so in this world neither do the righteous show themselves, nor sinners, but all are alike one to another."

SIMILITUDE 4

¹He showed me again many trees, some budding, and others withered. And He said to me, "Do you see these trees?" "I see, Lord," I replied, "some putting forth buds, and others withered." ²"Those," He said, "which are budding are the righteous who are to live in the world to come; for the coming world is the summer of the righteous, but the winter of sinners. ³When, therefore, the mercy of the LORD shines forth, then they will be made manifest who are the servants of God, and all men will be made manifest. ⁴For as in summer the fruits of each individual tree appear, and it is ascertained of what sort they are, so also the fruits of the righteous will be manifest, and all who have been fruitful in that world will be made known. ⁵But the heathen and sinners, like the withered trees which you saw, will be found to be those who have been withered and unfruitful in that world, and will be burnt as wood, and made manifest, because their actions were evil during their lives. ⁶For the sinners will be consumed because they sinned and did not convert, and the heathen will be burned because they did not know Him who created them. ⁷Therefore, bear fruit, that in that summer your fruit may be known. ⁸And refrain from much business, and you will never sin: for they who are occupied with much business also commit many sins, being distracted with their affairs, and not at all serving their Lord. ⁹How, then," He continued, "can such a one ask and obtain anything from the LORD, if he does not serve Him? ¹⁰They who serve Him will obtain their requests, but they who do not serve Him will receive nothing. ¹¹And in the performance even of a single action a man can serve the LORD; for his mind will not be perverted from the LORD, but he will serve Him, having a pure mind. ¹²If, therefore, you do these things, you will be able to bear fruit for the life to come. And everyone who will do these things will bear fruit."

SIMILITUDE 5

¹While fasting and sitting on a certain mountain, and giving thanks to the LORD for all His dealings with me, I see the Shepherd sitting down beside me, and saying, "Why have you come here early in the morning?" ²"Because, Lord," I answered, "I have a station." "What is a station?" He asked. "I am fasting, Lord," I replied. "What is this fasting," He continued, "which you are observing?" "As I have been accustomed, Lord," I reply, "so I fast." ³"You do not know," He says, "how to fast to the LORD: this useless fasting which you observe to Him is of no value." "Why, Lord," I answered, "do you say this?" ⁴"I say to you," He continued, "that the fasting which you think you observe is not a fasting. But I will teach you what is a full and acceptable fasting to the LORD. ⁵Listen," He continued: "God does not desire such an empty fasting, for fasting to God in this way you will do nothing for a righteous life; ⁶but offer to God a fasting of the following kind: do no evil in your life and serve the LORD with a pure heart; keep His commandments, walking in His precepts, and let no evil desire arise in your heart; and believe in God. ⁷If you do these things, and fear Him, and abstain from every evil thing, you will live to God; and if you do these things, you will keep a great fast, and one acceptable before God. ⁸Hear the similitude which I am about to narrate to you relative to fasting. ⁹A certain man had a field and many slaves, and he planted a certain part of the field with a vineyard, and selecting a faithful, and beloved, and much valued slave, he called him to himself, and said, Take this vineyard which I have planted, and stake it until I come, and do nothing else to the vineyard; and attend to this order of mine, and you will receive your freedom from me. ¹⁰And the master of the slave departed to a foreign country. And when he was gone, the slave took and staked the vineyard; and when he had finished the staking of the vines, he saw that the vineyard was full of weeds. ¹¹He then reflected, saying, I have kept this order of my master: I will dig up the rest of this vineyard, and it will be more beautiful when dug up; and being free of weeds, it will yield more fruit, not being choked by them. ¹²Therefore, he took and dug up the vineyard, and rooted out all the weeds that were in it. And that vineyard became very beautiful and fruitful, having no weeds to choke it. ¹³And after a certain time the master of the slave and of the field returned and entered into the vineyard. And seeing that the vines were suitably supported on stakes, and the ground, moreover, dug up, and all the weeds rooted out, and the vines fruitful, he was greatly pleased with the work of his slave. ¹⁴And calling his beloved son who was his heir, and his friends who were his counselors, he told them what orders he had given his slave, and what he had found performed. And they rejoiced along with the slave at the testimony which his master bore to him. ¹⁵And he said to them, I promised this slave freedom if he obeyed the command which I gave him; and he has kept my command, and has also done a good work to the vineyard, and has pleased me exceedingly. ¹⁶In return, therefore, for the work which he has done, I wish to make him co-heir with my son, because, having good thoughts, he did not neglect them, but carried them out. ¹⁷With this resolution of the master, his son and friends were well pleased. ¹⁸After a few days the master made a feast and sent to his slave many dishes from his table. And the slave receiving the dishes that were sent him from his master, took of them what was sufficient for himself, and distributed the rest among his fellow-slaves. ¹⁹And his fellow-slaves rejoiced to receive the dishes, and began to pray for him, that he might find still greater favor with his master for having so treated them. His master heard all these

things that were done and was again greatly pleased with his conduct. ²⁰And the master again calling together his friends and his son, reported to them the slave's proceeding with regard to the dishes which he had sent him. ²¹And they were still more satisfied that the slave should become co-heir with his son." ²²I said to Him, "Lord, I do not see the meaning of these similitudes, nor am I able to comprehend them, unless You explain them to me." ²³"I will explain them all to you," He said, "and whatever I will mention in the course of our conversations I will show you. ²⁴[[Keep the commandments of the LORD, and you will be approved, and inscribed among the number of those who observe His commands.]] ²⁵And if you do any good beyond what is commanded by God, you will gain for yourself more abundant glory, and will be more honored by God than you would otherwise be. ²⁶If, therefore, in keeping the commandments of God, you do, in addition, these services, you will have joy if you observe them according to My command." ²⁷I said to Him, "Lord, whatever You enjoin on me I will observe, for I know that You are with me." ²⁸"I will be with you," He replied, "because you have such a desire for doing good; and I will be with all those," He added, "who have such a desire. ²⁹This fasting," He continued, "is very good, provided the commandments of the LORD are observed. Thus, then, will you observe the fasting which you intend to keep. ³⁰First of all, be on your guard against every evil word, and every evil desire, and purify your heart from all the vanities of this world. If you guard against these things, your fasting will be perfect. ³¹And you will also do as follows: having fulfilled what is written, in the day on which you fast you will taste nothing but bread and water; and having reckoned up the price of the dishes of that day which you intended to have eaten, you will give it to a widow, or an orphan, or to some person in want, and thus you will exhibit humility of mind, so that he who has received benefit from your humility may fill his own soul, and pray for you to the LORD. ³²If you observe fasting, as I have commanded you, your sacrifice will be acceptable to God, and this fasting will be written down; and the service thus performed is noble, and sacred, and acceptable to the LORD. ³³These things, therefore, you will thus observe with your children, and all your house, and in observing them you will be blessed; and as many as hear these words and observe them will be blessed; and whatever they ask of the LORD they will receive." ³⁴I pleaded with Him much that he would explain to me the similitude of the field, and of the master of the vineyard, and of the slave who staked the vineyard, and of the sakes, and of the weeds that were plucked out of the vineyard, and of the son, and of the friends who were fellow-counselors, for I knew that all these things were a kind of allegory. ³⁵And He answered me, and said, "You are exceedingly persistent with your questions. You ought not," He continued, "to ask any questions at all; for if it is needful to explain anything, it will be made known to you." ³⁶I said to Him "Lord, whatever You show me, and do not explain, I will have seen to no purpose, not understanding its meaning. In like manner also, if You speak allegories to me, and do not unfold them, I will have heard Your words in vain." ³⁷And He answered me again, saying, "Everyone who is the servant of God, and has his Lord in his heart, asks of Him understanding, and receives it, and opens up every allegory; and the words of the LORD become known to him which are spoken in allegories; ³⁸but those who are weak and slothful in prayer, hesitate to ask anything from the LORD; but the LORD is full of compassion, and gives without fail to all who ask Him. ³⁹But you, having been strengthened by the holy Messenger, and having obtained from Him such intercession, and not being slothful, why do you not ask of the LORD understanding, and receive it from Him?" ⁴⁰I said to Him, "Lord, having You with me, I am necessitated to ask questions of You, for You show me all things, and converse with me; but if I were to see or hear these things without You, I would then ask the LORD to explain them." ⁴¹"I said to you a little while ago," He answered, "that you were cunning and obstinate in asking explanations of the allegories; but since you are so persistent, I will unfold to you the meaning of the similitudes of the field, and of all the others that follow, that you may make them known to everyone. ⁴²Hear now," He said, "and understand them. The field is this world; and the Lord of the field is He who created, and perfected, and strengthened all things; [[and the son is the Holy Spirit;]] and the slave is the Son of God; ⁴³and the vines are this people, whom He Himself planted; and the stakes are the holy messengers of the LORD, who keep His people together; and the weeds that were plucked out of the vineyard are the iniquities of God's servants; ⁴⁴and the dishes which He sent Him from His table are the commandments which He gave His people through His Son; and the friends and fellow-counselors are the holy messengers who were first created; and the Master's absence from home is the time that remains until His appearing." ⁴⁵I said to Him, "Lord, all these are great, and marvelous, and glorious things. Could I, therefore," I continued, "understand them? No, nor could any other man, even if exceedingly wise. ⁴⁶Moreover," I added, "explain to me what I am about to ask you." "Say what you wish," He replied. "Why, Lord," I asked, "is the Son of God in the allegory in the form of a slave?" ⁴⁷"Hear," He answered: "the Son of God is not in the form of a slave, but in great power and might." "How so, Lord?" I said; "I do not understand." ⁴⁸"Because," He answered, "God planted the vineyard, that is to say, He created the people, and gave them to His Son; and the Son appointed His messengers over them to keep them; ⁴⁹and He Himself purged away their sins, having suffered many trials and undergone many labors, for no one is able to dig without labor and toil. ⁵⁰He Himself, then, having purged away the sins of the people, showed them the paths of life by giving them the law which He received from His Father. ⁵¹[[You see," He said, "that He is the Lord of the people, having received all authority from His Father.]] And why the LORD took His Son as counselor, and the glorious messengers, regarding the heirship of the slave, listen. ⁵²The holy, pre-existent Spirit, that created every creature, God made to dwell in flesh, which He chose. This flesh, accordingly, in which the Holy Spirit dwelt, was nobly subject to that Spirit, walking religiously and chastely, in no respect defiling the Spirit; ⁵³and accordingly, after living excellently and purely, and after laboring and cooperating with the Spirit, and having in everything acted vigorously and courageously along with the Holy Spirit, He assumed it as a partner with it. ⁵⁴For this conduct of the flesh pleased Him, because it was not defiled on the earth while having the Holy Spirit. Therefore, He took as fellow-counselors His Son and the glorious messengers, in order that this flesh, which had been subject to the body without a fault, might have some place of tabernacle, and that it might not appear that the reward [[of its servitude had been lost]], ⁵⁵for the flesh that has been found without spot or defilement, in which the Holy Spirit dwelt, [[will receive a reward]]. You have now the explanation of this allegory also." ⁵⁶"I rejoice, Lord," I said, "to hear this explanation." "Hear," again He replied: "Keep this flesh pure and stainless, that the Spirit which inhabits it may bear witness to it, and your flesh may be justified. ⁵⁷See that the thought never arises in your mind that this flesh of yours is corruptible, and you misuse it by any act of defilement. ⁵⁸If you defile your flesh, you will also defile the Holy Spirit; and if you defile your flesh [and spirit], you will not live." ⁵⁹"And if anyone, Lord," I said, "has been ignorant until now, before he heard these words, how can such a man be saved who has defiled his flesh?" ⁶⁰"Respecting former sins of ignorance," He said, "God alone is able to heal them, for to Him belongs all power. ⁶¹[[But be on your guard now, and the all-powerful and compassionate God will heal former transgressions]], if for the time to come you do not defile your body nor your spirit; for both are common, and cannot be defiled, the one without the other: therefore, keep both pure, and you will live to God."

SIMILITUDE 6

¹Sitting in my house, and glorifying the LORD for all that I had seen, and reflecting on the commandments, that they are excellent, and powerful, and glorious, and able to save a man's soul, I said within myself, "I will be blessed if I walk in these commandments, and everyone who walks in them will be blessed." ²While I was saying these words to myself, I suddenly see Him sitting beside me, and hear Him thus speak: "Why are you in doubt about the commandments which I gave you? They are excellent: have no doubt about them at all, but put on faith in the LORD, and you will walk in them, for I will strengthen you in them.

³These commandments are beneficial to those who intend to convert: for if they do not walk in them, their conversion is in vain. You, therefore, who convert, cast away the wickedness of this world which wears you out; and by putting on all the virtues of a holy life, you will be able to keep these commandments, and will no longer add to the number of your sins. ⁴Therefore, walk in these commandments of Mine, and you will live to God. All these things have been spoken to you by Me." ⁵And after He had uttered these words, He said to me, "Let us go into the fields, and I will show you the shepherds of the flocks." "Let us go, Lord," I replied. ⁶And we came to a certain plain, and He showed me a young man, a shepherd, clothed in a suit of garments of a yellow color: and he was herding very many sheep, and these sheep were feeding luxuriously, as it were, and riotously, and merrily skipping here and there. ⁷The shepherd himself was merry, because of his flock; and the appearance of the shepherd was joyous, and he was running about among his flock. [[And other sheep I saw rioting and luxuriating in one place, but not, however, leaping about.]] ⁸And He said to me, "Do you see this shepherd?" "I see him, Lord," I said. "This," He answered, "is the messenger of luxury and deceit: he wears out the souls of the servants of God, and perverts them from the truth, deceiving them with wicked desires, through which they will perish; ⁹for they forget the commandments of the living God, and walk in deceits and empty luxuries; and they are ruined by the messenger, some being brought to death, others to corruption." ¹⁰I said to Him, "Lord, I do not know the meaning of these words: To death, and to corruption." ¹¹"Listen," He said. "The sheep which you saw merry and leaping about, are those which have torn themselves away from God forever, and have delivered themselves over to luxuries and deceits [[of this world. Among them there is no return to life through conversion, because they have added to their other sins, and blasphemed the Name of the LORD. Such men, therefore, are appointed to death. ¹²And the sheep which you saw not leaping, but feeding in one place, are they who have delivered themselves over to luxury and deceit]], but have committed no blasphemy against the LORD. ¹³These have been perverted from the truth: among them there is the hope of conversion, by which it is possible to live. Corruption, then, has a hope of a kind of renewal, but death has continuous ruin." ¹⁴Again, I went forward a little way, and He showed me a tall shepherd, somewhat savage in his appearance, clothed in a white goatskin, and having a wallet on his shoulders, and a very hard staff with branches, and a large whip. ¹⁵And he had a very sour look, so that I was afraid of him, so forbidding was his aspect. This shepherd, accordingly, was receiving the sheep from the young shepherd, those [that were rioting and luxuriating, but not leaping]; ¹⁶and he cast them into a precipitous place, full of thistles and thorns, so that it was impossible to extricate the sheep from the thorns and thistles; but they were completely entangled among them. ¹⁷These, accordingly, thus entangled, pastured among the thorns and thistles, and were exceedingly miserable, being beaten by him; and he drove them here and there, and gave them no rest; and, altogether, these sheep were in a wretched plight. ¹⁸Seeing them, therefore, so beaten and so badly used, I was grieved for them, because they were so tormented, and had no rest at all. And I said to the Shepherd who talked with me, "Lord, who is this shepherd, who is so pitiless and severe, and so completely devoid of compassion for these sheep?" ¹⁹"This," He replied, "is the messenger of punishment; and he belongs to the just messengers, and is appointed to punish. He accordingly takes those who wander away from God, and who have walked in the desires and deceits of this world, and disciplines them as they deserve with terrible and diverse punishments." ²⁰"I would know, Lord," I said, "Of what nature are these diverse tortures and punishments?" "Hear," He said, ²¹"The various tortures and punishments. The tortures are such as occur during life. For some are punished with losses, others with want, others with sicknesses of various kinds, and others with all kinds of disorder and confusion; others are insulted by unworthy persons, and exposed to suffering in many other ways: ²²for many, becoming unstable in their plans, try many things, and none of them at all succeed, and they say they are not prosperous in their undertakings; and it does not occur to their minds that they have done evil deeds, but they blame the LORD. ²³Therefore, when they have been afflicted with all kinds of affliction, then they are delivered to Me for good training, and they are made strong in the faith of the LORD; ²⁴and for the rest of the days of their life they are subject to the LORD with pure hearts, and are successful in all their undertakings, obtaining from the LORD everything they ask; and then they glorify the LORD, that they were delivered to Me, and no longer suffer any evil." ²⁵I said to Him, "Lord, explain this to me also." "What is it you ask?" He said. "Whether, Lord," I continued, "they who indulge in luxury, and who are deceived, are tortured for the same period of time that they have indulged in luxury and deceit?" ²⁶He said to me, "They are tortured in the same manner." [["They are tormented much less, Lord," I replied;]] "for those who are so luxurious and who forget God ought to be tortured sevenfold." ²⁷He said to me, "You are foolish, and do not understand the power of torment." "Why, Lord," I said, "if I had understood it, I would not have asked You to show me." ²⁸"Hear," He said, "the power of both. The time of luxury and deceit is one hour; but the hour of torment is equivalent to thirty days. ²⁹If, accordingly, a man indulges in luxury for one day, and is deceived and is tortured for one day, the day of his torture is equivalent to a whole year. For all the days of luxury, therefore, there are as many years of torture to be undergone. ³⁰You see, then," He continued, "that the time of luxury and deceit is very short, but that of punishment and torture long." ³¹"Still," I said, "I do not quite understand about the time of deceit, and luxury, and torture; explain it to me more clearly." ³²He answered, and said to me, "Your folly is persistent; and you do not wish to purify your heart and serve God. Have a care," He added, "lest the time be fulfilled, and you are found foolish. ³³Hear now," He added, "as you desire, that you may understand these things. He who indulges in luxury, and is deceived for one day, and who does what he wishes, is clothed with much foolishness, and does not understand the act which he does until the next day; for he forgets what he did the day before. ³⁴For luxury and deceit have no memories, on account of the folly with which they are clothed; but when punishment and torture cleave to a man for one day, he is punished and tortured for a year; for punishment and torture have powerful memories. ³⁵While tortured and punished, therefore, for a whole year, he remembers at last his luxury and deceit, and knows that on their account he suffers evil. ³⁶Every man, therefore, who is luxurious and deceived is thus tormented, because, although having life, they have given themselves over to death." ³⁷"What kinds of luxury, Lord," I asked, "are hurtful?" "Every act of a man which he performs with pleasure," He replied, "is an act of luxury; for the sharp-tempered man, when gratifying his tendency, indulges in luxury; ³⁸and the adulterer, and the drunkard, and the back-biter, and the liar, and the covetous man, and the thief, and he who does things like these, gratifies his peculiar propensity, and in so doing indulges in luxury. All these acts of luxury are hurtful to the servants of God. ³⁹On account of these deceits, therefore, do they suffer, who are punished and tortured. And there are also acts of luxury which save men; ⁴⁰for many who do good indulge in luxury, being carried away by their own pleasure: this luxury, however, is beneficial to the servants of God, and gains life for such a man; ⁴¹but the injurious acts of luxury before enumerated bring tortures and punishment on them; and if they continue in them and do not convert, they bring death on themselves."

SIMILITUDE 7

¹After a few days I saw Him in the same plain where I had also seen the shepherds; and He said to me, "What do you wish with Me?" I said to Him, "Lord, that you would order the shepherd who punishes to depart out of my house, because he afflicts me exceedingly." ²"It is necessary," He replied, "that you are afflicted; for thus," He continued, "did the glorious messenger command concerning you, as he wishes you to be tried." "What have I done which is so bad, Lord," I replied, "that I should be delivered over to this messenger?" ³"Listen," he said: "Your sins are many, but not so great as to require that you are delivered over to this messenger; but your household has committed great iniquities and sins, and the glorious messenger has been incensed at them on account of their deeds; ⁴and for this

reason, he commanded you to be afflicted for a certain time, that they also might convert, and purify themselves from every desire of this world. Therefore, when they convert and are purified, then the messenger of punishment will depart." ⁵I said to Him, "Lord, if they have done such things as to incense the glorious messenger against them, yet what have I done?" ⁶He replied, "They cannot be afflicted at all, unless you, the head of the house, are afflicted: for when you are afflicted, of necessity they also suffer affliction; but if you are in comfort, they can feel no affliction." ⁷"Well, Lord," I said, "they have converted with their whole heart." "I know, too," He answered, "that they have converted with their whole heart: do you think, however, that the sins of those who convert are remitted? ⁸Not altogether, but he who converts must torture his own soul, and be exceedingly humble in all his conduct, and be afflicted with many kinds of affliction; ⁹and if he endures the afflictions that come on him, He who created all things, and endued them with power, will assuredly have compassion, and will heal him; ¹⁰and He will do this when He sees the heart of every penitent pure from every evil thing: and it is profitable for you and for your house to suffer affliction now. ¹¹But why should I say much to you? You must be afflicted, as that messenger of the LORD commanded who delivered you to Me. ¹²And for this give thanks to the LORD, because He has deemed you worthy of showing you beforehand this affliction, that, knowing it before it comes, you may be able to bear it with courage." ¹³I said to Him, "Lord, be with me, and I will be able to bear all affliction." "I will be with you," He said, "and I will ask the messenger of punishment to afflict you more lightly; ¹⁴nevertheless, you will be afflicted for a short time, and again you will be re-established in your house. ¹⁵Only, remain humble, and serve the LORD in all purity of heart—you, and your children, and your house—and walk in My commands which I enjoin on you, and your conversion will be deep and pure; ¹⁶and if you observe these things with your household, every affliction will depart from you. And affliction," He added, "will depart from all who walk in these commandments of Mine."

SIMILITUDE 8

¹He showed me a large willow tree overshadowing plains and mountains, and under the shade of this willow had assembled all those who were called by the Name of the LORD. ²And a glorious messenger of the LORD, who was very tall, was standing beside the willow, having a large pruning-knife, and he was cutting little twigs from the willow and distributing them among the people that were overshadowed by the willow; and the twigs which he gave them were small, about a cubit, as it were, in length. ³And after they had all received the twigs, the messenger laid down the pruning-knife, and that tree was sound, as I had seen it at first. ⁴And I marveled within myself, saying, "How is the tree sound, after so many branches have been cut off?" And the Shepherd said to me, "Do not be surprised if the tree remains sound after so many branches were lopped off; [but wait,] and when you will have seen everything, then it will be explained to you what it means." ⁵The messenger who had distributed the branches among the people again asked them from them, and in the order in which they had received them were they summoned to him, and each one of them returned his branch. ⁶And the messenger of the LORD took and looked at them. From some he received the branches withered and moth-eaten; those who returned branches in that state the messenger of the LORD ordered to stand apart. ⁷Others, again, returned them withered, but not moth-eaten; and these he ordered to stand apart. And others returned them half-withered, and these stood apart; and others returned their branches half-withered and having cracks in them, and these stood apart. ⁸[[And others returned their branches green and having cracks in them; and these stood apart.]] And others returned their branches, one-half withered and the other green; and these stood apart. And others brought their branches two-thirds green and the remaining third withered; and these stood apart. ⁹And others returned them two-thirds withered and one-third green; and these stood apart. And others returned their branches nearly all green, the smallest part only, the top, being withered, but they had cracks in them; and these stood apart. ¹⁰And of others very little was green, but the remaining parts withered; and these stood apart. And others came bringing their branches green, as they had received them from the messenger. ¹¹And the majority of the crowd returned branches of that kind, and with these the messenger was exceedingly pleased; and these stood apart. [[And others returned their branches green and having offshoots; and these stood apart, and with these the messenger was exceedingly delighted.]] ¹²And others returned their branches green and with offshoots, and the offshoots had some fruit, as it were; and those men whose branches were found to be of that kind were exceedingly joyful. ¹³And the messenger was exultant because of them; and the Shepherd also rejoiced greatly because of them. ¹⁴And the messenger of the LORD ordered crowns to be brought; and there were brought crowns, formed, as it were, of palms; and he crowned the men who had returned the branches which had offshoots and some fruit, and sent them away into the tower. ¹⁵And he also sent the others into the tower, those, namely, who had returned branches that were green and had offshoots but no fruit, having given them seals. And all who went into the tower had the same clothing—white as snow. ¹⁶And those who returned their branches green, as they had received them, he set free, giving them clothing and seals. ¹⁷Now after the messenger had finished these things, he said to the Shepherd, "I am going away, and you will send these away within the walls, according as each one is worthy to have his dwelling. ¹⁸And examine their branches carefully, and so dismiss them; but examine them with care. See that no one escapes [from] you," he added; "and if any escapes [from] you, I will try them at the altar." ¹⁹Having said these words to the Shepherd, he departed. And after the messenger had departed, the Shepherd said to me, "Let us take the branches of all these and plant them, and see if any of them will live." ²⁰I said to Him, "Lord, how can these withered branches live?" He answered, and said, "This tree is a willow, and of a kind that is very tenacious of life. If, therefore, the branches are planted, and receive a little moisture, many of them will live. ²¹And now let us try and pour waters on them; and if any of them live I will rejoice with them, and if they do not, I at least will not be found neglectful." ²²And the Shepherd ordered me call them as each one was placed. And they came, rank by rank, and gave their branches to the Shepherd. And the Shepherd received the branches and planted them in rows; and after He had planted them, He poured much water on them, so that the branches could not be seen for the water; ²³and after the branches had drunk it in, He said to me, "Let us go, and return after a few days, and inspect all the branches; for He who created this tree wishes all those to live who received branches from it. ²⁴And I also hope that the greater part of these branches which received moisture and drank of the water will live." ²⁵I said to Him, "Lord, explain to me what this tree means, for I am perplexed about it, because, after so many branches have been cut off, it continues sound, and nothing appears to have been cut away from it. By this, now, I am perplexed." ²⁶"Listen," He said: "This great tree that casts its shadow over plains, and mountains, and all the earth, is the law of God that was given to the whole world; and this law is the Son of God, proclaimed to the ends of the earth; and the people who are under its shadow are they who have heard the proclamation, and have believed on Him. ²⁷And the great and glorious messenger Michael is he who has authority over this people, and governs them; for this is he who gave them the law into the hearts of believers: he accordingly superintends them to whom he gave it, to see if they have kept the same. ²⁸And you see the branches of each one, for the branches are the law you see, accordingly, many branches that have been rendered useless, and you will know them all—those who have not kept the law; and you will see the dwelling of each one." ²⁹I said to Him, "Lord, why did he dismiss some into the tower, and leave others to you?" "All," he answered, "who transgressed the law which they received from him, he left under my power for conversion; but all who have satisfied the law, and kept it, he retains under his own authority." ³⁰"Who, then," I continued, "are they who were crowned, and who go to the tower?" "These are they who have suffered on account of the law; but the others, and they who returned their branches green, and with offshoots, but without fruit, are they who have been afflicted on account of the law,

but who have not suffered nor denied their law; and they who returned their branches green as they had received them, are the venerable, and the just, and they who have walked carefully in a pure heart, and have kept the commandments of the LORD. ³¹And the rest you will know when I have examined those branches which have been planted and watered." ³²And after a few days we came to the place, and the Shepherd sat down in the messenger's place, and I stood beside Him. And He said to me, "Gird yourself with pure, undressed linen made of sackcloth;" and seeing me girded, and ready to minister to Him, "Summon," He said, "the men to whom belong the branches that were planted, according to the order in which each one gave them in." ³³So I went away to the plain, and summoned them all, and they all stood in their ranks. He said to them, "Let each one pull out his own branch, and bring it to Me." ³⁴The first to give in were those who had them withered and cut; and because they were found to be thus withered and cut, He commanded them to stand apart. And next they gave them in who had them withered, but not cut. ³⁵And some of them gave in their branches green, and some withered and eaten as by a moth. Those that gave them in green, accordingly, He ordered to stand apart; and those who gave them in dry and cut, He ordered to stand along with the first. ³⁶Next, they gave them in who had them half-withered and cracked; and many of them gave them in green and without crocks; and some green and with offshoots and fruits on the offshoots, such as they had who went, after being crowned, into the tower. ³⁷And some handed them in withered and eaten, and some withered and uneaten; and some as they were, half withered and cracked. And He commanded them each one to stand apart, some toward their own rows, and others apart from them. ³⁸Then they gave in their branches who had them green, but cracked: all these gave them in green, and stood in their own row. ³⁹And the Shepherd was pleased with these, because they were all changed, and had lost their cracks. And they also gave them in who had them half-green and half-withered: of some, accordingly, the branches were found completely green; of others, half-withered; of others, withered and eaten; of others, green, and having offshoots. ⁴⁰All these were sent away, each to his own row. [[Next, they gave in who had them two parts green and one-third withered. Many of them gave them half-withered; and others withered and rotten; and others half-withered and cracked, and a few green. These all stood in their own row.]] ⁴¹And they gave them in who had them green, but to a very slight extent withered and cracked. Of these, some gave them in green, and others green and with offshoots. And these also went away to their own row. ⁴²Next, they gave them who had a very small part green and the other parts withered. Of these the branches were found for the most part green and having offshoots, and fruit on the offshoots, and others altogether green. ⁴³With these branches the Shepherd was exceedingly pleased, because they were found in this state. And these went away, each to his own row. ⁴⁴After the Shepherd had examined the branches of them all, He said to me, "I told you that this tree was tenacious of life. You see," He continued, "how many converted and were saved." ⁴⁵"I see, Lord," I replied. "That you may behold," He added, "the great mercy of the LORD, that it is great and glorious, and that He has given His Spirit to those who are worthy of conversion." ⁴⁶"Why then, Lord," I said, "did these not all convert?" He answered, "To them whose heart He saw would become pure, and obedient to Him, He gave power to convert with the whole heart. ⁴⁷But to them whose deceit and wickedness He perceived, and saw that they intended to convert hypocritically, He did not grant conversion, lest they should again profane His Name." ⁴⁸I said to Him, "Lord, show me now, with respect to those who gave in the branches, of what sort they are, and their abode, in order that they hearing it who believed, and received the seal, and broke it, and did not keep it whole, may, on coming to a knowledge of their deeds, convert, and receive from You a seal, and may glorify the LORD because He had compassion on them, and sent You to renew their spirits." ⁴⁹"Listen," He said: "they whose branches were found withered and moth-eaten are the apostates and traitors of the Assembly, who have blasphemed the LORD in their sins, and have, moreover, been ashamed of the Name of the LORD by which they were called. These, therefore, at the end were lost to God. ⁵⁰And you see that not a single one of them converted, although they heard the words which I spoke to them, which I enjoined on you. ⁵¹From such life departed, and they who gave them in withered and undecayed, these also were near to them; for they were hypocrites, and introducers of strange doctrines, and subverters of the servants of God, especially of those who had sinned, not allowing them to convert, but persuading them by foolish doctrines. ⁵²These, accordingly, have a hope of conversion. And you see that many of them have also converted since I spoke to them, and they will still convert. ⁵³But all who will not convert have lost their lives; and as many of them as converted became good, and their dwelling was appointed within the first walls; and some of them even ascended into the tower. ⁵⁴You see, then," He said, "that conversion involves life to sinners, but non-conversion death. ⁵⁵And as many as gave in the branches half-withered and cracked, hear about them also. They whose branches were half-withered to the same extent are the wavering; for they neither live, nor are they dead. And they who have them half-withered and cracked are both waverers and slanderers, [[railing against the absent,]] and never at peace with one another, but always at variance. ⁵⁶And yet to these also," he continued, "conversion is possible. You see," He said, "that some of them have converted, and there is still remaining in them," he continued, "a hope of conversion. ⁵⁷And as many of them," He added, "as have converted, will have their dwelling in the tower. And those of them who have been slower in converting will dwell within the walls. ⁵⁸And as many as do not convert at all, but abide in their deeds, will utterly perish. ⁵⁹And they who gave in their branches green and cracked were always faithful and good, though emulating each other about the foremost places, and about fame: now all these are foolish, in indulging in such a rivalry. ⁶⁰Yet they also, being naturally good, on hearing My commandments, purified themselves, and soon converted. Their dwelling, accordingly, was in the tower. But if anyone relapses into strife, he will be cast out of the tower, and will lose his life. ⁶¹Life is the possession of all who keep the commandments of the LORD; but in the commandments there is no rivalry in regard to the first places, or glory of any kind, but in regard to patience and personal humility. ⁶²Among such persons, then, is the life of the LORD, but among the quarrelsome and transgressors—death. ⁶³And they who gave in their branches half-green and half-withered, are those who are immersed in business, and do not cleave to the holy ones. For this reason, the one half of them is living, and the other half dead. ⁶⁴Many, accordingly, who heard My commands converted, and those at least who converted had their dwelling in the tower. But some of them at last fell away: these, accordingly, do not have conversion, for on account of their business they blasphemed the LORD, and denied Him. ⁶⁵They therefore lost their lives through the wickedness which they committed. And many of them doubted. These still have conversion in their power, if they convert speedily; and their abode will be in the tower. ⁶⁶But if they are slower in converting, they will dwell within the walls; and if they do not convert, they too have lost their lives. ⁶⁷And they who gave in their branches two-thirds withered and one-third green, are those who have denied [the LORD] in various ways. Many, however, converted, but some of them hesitated and were in doubt. These, then, have conversion within their reach, if they convert quickly, and do not remain in their pleasures; but if they abide in their deeds, these, too, work to themselves death. ⁶⁸And they who returned their branches two-thirds withered and one-third green, are those that were indeed faithful; but after acquiring wealth, and becoming distinguished among the heathen, they clothed themselves with great pride, and became lofty-minded, and deserted the truth, and did not cleave to the righteous, but lived with the heathen, and this way of life became more agreeable to them. ⁶⁹They did not, however, depart from God, but remained in the faith, although not working the works of faith. Many of them accordingly converted, and their dwelling was in the tower. ⁷⁰And others continuing to live until the end with the heathen, and being corrupted by their vain glories, [[departed from God, serving the works and deeds of the heathen.]] These were reckoned with the heathen. ⁷¹But others of them hesitated, not hoping to be saved on account of the deeds which they had done; while others were in doubt and caused divisions among themselves. ⁷²To those, therefore, who were in doubt on account of their deeds, conversion is still open; but their conversion ought to be speedy, that their dwelling may be in the tower. ⁷³And to those who do not convert, but abide in their pleasures, death is near. ⁷⁴And they who give in their branches green, but having the tips withered and cracked, these were always good, and faithful, and distinguished before God; but they sinned a very little through indulging small desires, and finding little faults with one another. ⁷⁵But on hearing my words the greater part of them quickly converted, and their dwelling was on the tower. Yet some of them were in doubt; and certain of them who were in doubt wrought greater dissension. ⁷⁶Among these, therefore, is hope of conversion, because they were always good; and with difficulty will any one of them perish. ⁷⁷And they who gave up their branches withered, but having a very small part green, are those who believed only, yet continue working the works of iniquity. ⁷⁸They never, however, departed from God, but gladly bore His Name, and joyfully received His servants into their houses. Having accordingly heard of this conversion, they unhesitatingly converted, and practice all virtue and righteousness; and some of them even [[suffered, being willingly put to death]], knowing their deeds which they had done. Of all these, therefore, the dwelling will be in the tower." ⁷⁹And after He had finished the explanations of all the branches, He said to me, "Go and tell them to everyone, that they may convert, and they will live to God. ⁸⁰Because the LORD, having had compassion on all men, has sent Me to give conversion, although some are not worthy of it on account of their works; but the LORD, being long-suffering, desires those who were called by His Son to be saved." ⁸¹I said to Him, "Lord, I hope that all who have heard them will convert; for I am persuaded that each one, on coming to a knowledge of his own works, and fearing the LORD, will convert." ⁸²He answered me, and said, "All who with their whole heart will purify themselves from their wickedness before enumerated, and will add no more to their sins, will receive healing from the LORD for their former transgressions, if they do not hesitate at these commandments; and they will live to God. ⁸³But you: walk in My commandments, and live." Having shown me these things, and spoken all these words, He said to me, "And the rest I will show you after a few days."

SIMILITUDE 9

¹After I had written down the commandments and similitudes of the Shepherd, the Messenger of conversion, He came to me and said, "I wish to explain to you what the Holy Spirit that spoke with you in the form of the Assembly showed you, for that Spirit is the Son of God. ²For, as you were somewhat weak in the flesh, it was not explained to you by the messenger. ³When, however, you were strengthened by the Spirit, and your strength was increased, so that you were able to see the messenger also, then accordingly was the building of the tower shown you by the Assembly. ⁴In a noble and solemn manner you saw everything as if shown you by a virgin; but now you see [them] through the same Spirit as if shown by a messenger. ⁵You must, however, learn everything from Me with greater accuracy. For I was sent for this purpose by the glorious messenger to dwell in your house, that you might see all things with power, entertaining no fear, even as it was before." ⁶And He led me away into Arcadia, to a round hill; and He placed me on the top of the hill, and showed me a large plain, and around the plain—twelve mountains, all having different forms. ⁷The first was black as soot; and the second bare, without grass; and the third full of thorns and thistles; and the fourth with grass half-withered, the upper parts of the plants green, and the parts about the roots withered; and some of the grasses, when the sun scorched them, became withered. ⁸And the fifth mountain had green grass, and was ragged. And the sixth mountain was quite full of clefts, some small and others large; and the clefts were grassy, but the plants were not very vigorous, but rather, as it were, decayed. ⁹The seventh mountain, again, had cheerful pastures, and the whole mountain was blooming, and every kind of cattle and birds were feeding on that mountain; and the more the cattle and the birds ate, the more the grass of that mountain flourished. ¹⁰And the eighth mountain was full of fountains, and every kind of the LORD's creatures drank of the fountains of that mountain. ¹¹But the ninth mountain [[had no water at all, and was wholly a desert, and had within it deadly serpents, which destroy men. And the tenth mountain]] had very large trees, and was completely shaded, and under the shadow of the trees sheep lay resting and ruminating. ¹²And the eleventh mountain was very thickly wooded, and those trees were productive, being adorned with various sons of fruits, so that anyone seeing them would desire to eat of their fruits. ¹³The twelfth mountain, again, was wholly white, and its aspect was cheerful, and the mountain in itself was very beautiful. ¹⁴And in the middle of the plain He showed me a large white rock that had arisen out of the plain. And the rock was more lofty than the mountains, rectangular in shape, so as to be capable of containing the whole world: ¹⁵and that rock was old, having a gate cut out of it; and the cutting out of the gate seemed to me as if recently done. And the gate glittered to such a degree under the sunbeams, that I marveled at the splendor of the gate; ¹⁶and around the gate were standing twelve virgins. The four who stood at the corners seemed to me more distinguished than the others—they were all, however, distinguished—and they were standing at the four parts of the gate; two virgins between each part. ¹⁷And they were clothed with linen tunics, and gracefully girded, having their right shoulders exposed, as if about to bear some burden. Thus they stood ready; for they were exceedingly cheerful and eager. ¹⁸After I had seen these things, I marveled in myself, because I was beholding great and glorious sights. And again, I was perplexed about the virgins, because, although so delicate, they were standing courageously, as if about to carry the whole heavens. ¹⁹And the Shepherd said to me, "Why are you reasoning in yourself, and perplexing your mind, and distressing yourself? For the things which you cannot understand, do not attempt to comprehend, as if you were wise; but ask the LORD, that you may receive understanding and know them. ²⁰You cannot see what is behind you, but you see what is before. Whatever, then, you cannot see, leave alone, and do not torment yourself about it: but what you see, make yourself master of it, and do not waste your labor about other things; and I will explain to you everything that I show you. Therefore, look on the things that remain." ²¹I saw six men come, tall, and distinguished, and similar in appearance, and they summoned a multitude of men. ²²And they who came were also tall men, and handsome, and powerful; and the six men commanded them to build a tower above the rock. ²³And the noise of those men who came to build the tower was great, as they ran here and there around the gate. ²⁴And the virgins who stood around the gate told the men to hasten to build the tower. Now the virgins had spread out their hands, as if about to receive something from the men. ²⁵And the six men commanded stones to ascend out of a certain pit, and to go to the building of the tower. And there went up ten shining rectangular stones, not hewn in a quarry. ²⁶And the six men called the virgins, and ordered them to carry all the stones that were intended for the building, and to pass through the gate, and give them to the men who were about to build the tower. ²⁷And the virgins put on each other the ten first stones which had ascended from the pit, and carried them together, each stone by itself. And as they stood together around the gate, those who seemed to be strong carried them, and they stooped down under the corners of the stone; and the others stooped down under the sides of the stones. ²⁸And in this way they carried all the stones. And they carried them through the gate as they were commanded, and gave them to the men for the tower; and they took the stones and proceeded with the building. ²⁹Now the tower was built on the great rock, and above the gate. Those ten stones were prepared as the foundation for the building of the tower. And the rock and gate were the support of the whole of the tower. ³⁰And after the ten stones, twenty[-five] other [stones] came up out of the pit, and these were fired into the building of the tower, being carried by the virgins as before. ³¹And after these ascended thirty-five. And these in like manner were fitted into the tower. And after these,

forty other stones came up; and all these were cast into the building of the tower, [[and there were four rows in the foundation of the tower,]] and they ceased ascending from the pit. And the builders also ceased for a little while. ³²And again, the six men commanded the multitude of the crowd to bear stones from the mountains for the building of the tower. They were accordingly brought from all the mountains of various colors, and being hewn by the men, were given to the virgins; ³³and the virgins carried them through the gate and gave them for the building of the tower. And when the stones of various colors were placed in the building, they all became white alike, and lost their different colors. ³⁴And certain stones were given by the men for the building, and these did not become shining; but as they were placed, such also were they found to remain: for they were not given by the virgins, nor carried through the gate. ³⁵These stones, therefore, were not in keeping with the others in the building of the tower. And the six men, seeing these unsuitable stones in the building, commanded them to be taken away, and to be carried away down to their own place from where they had been taken; ³⁶[[and being removed one by one, they were laid aside; and]] they say to the men who brought the stones, "Do not bring any stones at all for the building, but lay them down beside the tower, that the virgins may carry them through the gate, and may give them for the building. ³⁷For unless," they said, "they are carried through the gate by the hands of the virgins, they cannot change their colors: do not toil, therefore," they said, "for no purpose." ³⁸And on that day the building was finished, but the tower was not completed; for additional building was again about to be added, and there was a cessation in the building. ³⁹And the six men commanded all the builders to withdraw a little distance, and to rest, but enjoined the virgins not to withdraw from the tower; and it seemed to me that the virgins had been left to guard the tower. ⁴⁰Now after all had withdrawn, and were resting themselves, I said to the Shepherd, "What is the reason that the building of the tower was not finished?" ⁴¹"The tower," He answered, "cannot be finished just yet, until the Lord of it comes and examines the building, in order that, if any of the stones are found to be decayed, He may change them: for the tower is built according to His pleasure." ⁴²"I would like to know, Lord," I said, "what is the meaning of the building of this tower, and what [of] the rock and gate, and the mountains, and [the] meaning of the virgins, and the stones that ascended from the pit, and were not hewn, but came as they were to the building. ⁴³Why, in the first place, were ten stones placed in the foundation, then twenty-five, then thirty-five, then forty? ⁴⁴And I also wish to know about the stones that went to the building, and were again taken out and returned to their own place? On all these points put my mind at rest, Lord, and explain them to me." ⁴⁵"If you are not found to be curious about trifles," He replied, "you will know everything. For after a few days [[we will come here, and you will see the other things that happen to this tower, and will know accurately all the similitudes." ⁴⁶After a few days]] we came to the place where we sat down. And He said to me, "Let us go to the tower; for the Master of the tower is coming to examine it." ⁴⁷And we came to the tower, and there was no one at all near it, save the virgins only. And the Shepherd asked the virgins if perhaps the Master of the tower had come; and they replied that He was about to come to examine the building. ⁴⁸And behold, after a little while I see an array of many men coming, and in the midst of them one Man of so remarkable a size as to overtop the tower. ⁴⁹And the six men who had worked on the building were with Him, and many other honorable men were around Him. And the virgins who kept the tower ran forward and kissed Him, and began to walk near Him around the tower. ⁵⁰And that Man examined the building carefully, feeling every stone separately; and holding a rod in His hand, He struck every stone in the building three times. ⁵¹And when He struck them, some of them became black as soot, and some appeared as if covered with scabs, and some cracked, and some mutilated, and some neither white nor black, and some rough and not in keeping with the other stones, and some having very many stains: such were the varieties of decayed stones that were found in the building. ⁵²He ordered all these to be taken out of the tower, and to be laid down beside it, and other stones to be brought and put in their stead. [[And the builders asked Him from what mountain He wished them to be brought and put in their place.]] ⁵³And He did not command them to be brought from the mountains, [[but He ordered them be brought from a certain plain which was near at hand.]] ⁵⁴And the plain was dug up, and shining rectangular stones were found, and some also of a round shape; and all the stones which were in that plain were brought, and carried through the gate by the virgins. ⁵⁵And the rectangular stones were hewn and put in place of those that were taken away; but the rounded stones were not put into the building, because they were hard to hew, and appeared to field slowly to the chisel; they were deposited, however, beside the tower, as if intended to be hewn and used in the building, for they were exceedingly brilliant. ⁵⁶The glorious Man, the Lord of the whole tower, having accordingly finished these alterations, called the Shepherd to Himself, and delivered to Him all the stones that were lying beside the tower, that had been rejected from the building, and said to Him, "Carefully clean all these stones, and put aside such for the building of the tower as may harmonize with the others; and those that do not, throw [them] far away from the tower." ⁵⁷[[Having given these orders to the Shepherd, He departed from the tower]] with all those with whom He had come. ⁵⁸Now the virgins were standing around the tower, keeping it. ⁵⁹I said again to the Shepherd, "Can these stones return to the building of the tower, after being rejected?" He answered me, and said, "Do you see these stones?" "I see them, Lord," I replied. "The greater part of these stones," He said, "I will hew, and put into the building, and they will harmonize with the others." ⁶⁰"How, Lord," I said, "can they, after being cut all over, fill up the same space?" He answered, "Those that will be found small will be thrown into the middle of the building, and those that are larger will be placed on the outside, and they will hold them together." ⁶¹Having spoken these words, He said to me, "Let us go, and after two days let us come and clean these stones, and cast them into the building; for all things around the tower must be cleaned, lest the Master comes suddenly and finds the places around the tower dirty, and is displeased, and these stones are not returned for the building of the tower, and I also will seem to be neglectful toward the Master." ⁶²And after two days we came to the tower, and He said to me, "Let us examine all the stones, and ascertain those which may return to the building." I said to Him, "Lord, let us examine them!" ⁶³And beginning, we first examined the black stones: and such as they had been taken out of the building, were they found to remain; and the Shepherd ordered them to be removed out of the tower, and to be placed apart. ⁶⁴Next, He examined those that had scabs; and He took and hewed many of these and commanded the virgins to take them up and cast them into the building. And the virgins lifted them up and put them in the middle of the building of the tower. ⁶⁵And the rest He ordered to be laid down beside the black ones; for these, too, were found to be black. ⁶⁶He next examined those that had cracks; and He hewed many of these, and commanded them to be carried by the virgins to the building: and they were placed on the outside, because they were found to be sounder than the others; but the rest, on account of the multitude of the cracks, could not be hewn, and for this reason, therefore, they were rejected from the building of the tower. ⁶⁷He next examined the chipped stones, and many among these were found to be black, and some to have great crocks. And these He also commanded to be laid down along with those which had been rejected. ⁶⁸But the remainder, after being cleaned and hewn, He commanded to be placed in the building. And the virgins took them up and fitted them into the middle of the building of the tower, for they were somewhat weak. ⁶⁹He next examined those that were half white and half black, and many of them were found to be black. And He commanded these also to be taken away along with those which had been rejected. ⁷⁰And the rest were all taken away by the virgins; for, being white, they were fitted by the virgins themselves into the building. ⁷¹And they were placed on the outside, because they were found to be sound, so as to be able to support those which were placed in the middle, for no part of them was chipped at all. ⁷²He next examined those that were rough and hard; and a few of them were rejected because they could not be hewn, as they were found exceedingly hard. ⁷³But the rest of them were hewn, and carried by the virgins, and fitted into the middle of the building of the tower; for they were somewhat weak. ⁷⁴He next examined those that had stains; and of these a very few were black, and were thrown aside with the others; but the greater part were found to be bright, and these were fitted by the virgins into the building, but on account of their strength were placed on the outside. ⁷⁵He next came to examine the white and rounded stones, and said to me, "What are we to do with these stones?" "How do I know, Lord?" I replied. ⁷⁶"Have you no intentions regarding them?" "Lord," I answered, "I am not acquainted with this art, neither am I a stone-cutter, nor can I tell." "Do you not see," He said, "that they are exceedingly round? And if I wish to make them rectangular, a large portion of them must be cut away; for some of them must of necessity be put into the building." ⁷⁷"If therefore," I said, "they must, why do You torment Yourself, and not at once choose for the building those which you prefer, and fit them into it?" ⁷⁸He selected the larger ones among them, and the shining ones, and hewed them; and the virgins carried and fitted them into the outside parts of the building. And the rest which remained over were hauled away, and laid down on the plain from which they were brought. ⁷⁹They were not, however, rejected, "because," He said, "there remains yet a little addition to be built to the tower. ⁸⁰And the Lord of this tower wishes all the stones to be fitted into the building, because they are exceedingly bright." ⁸¹And twelve women were called, very beautiful in form, clothed in black, and with disheveled hair. And these women seemed to me to be fierce. But the Shepherd commanded them to lift the stones that were rejected from the building, and to carry them away to the mountains from which they had been brought. ⁸²And they were merry, and hauled away all the stones, and put them in the place from where they had been taken. ⁸³Now after all the stones were removed, and there was no longer a single one lying around the tower, He said, "Let us go around the tower and see, lest there be any defect in it." ⁸⁴So I went around the tower along with Him. And the Shepherd, seeing that the tower was beautifully built, rejoiced exceedingly; for the tower was built in such a way, that, on seeing it, I coveted the building of it, for it was constructed as if built of one stone, without a single joining. ⁸⁵And the stone seemed as if hewn out of the rock; having to me the appearance of a monolith. ⁸⁶And as I walked along with Him, I was full of joy, beholding so many excellent things. ⁸⁷And the Shepherd said to me, "Go and bring unslaked lime and fine-baked clay, that I may fill up the forms of the stones that were taken and thrown into the building; for everything about the tower must be smooth." ⁸⁸And I did as He commanded me and brought it to Him. "Assist Me," He said, "and the work will soon be finished." ⁸⁹He accordingly filled up the forms of the stones that were returned to the building, and commanded the places around the tower to be swept and to be cleaned; ⁹⁰and the virgins took brooms and swept the place, and carried all the dirt out of the tower, and brought water, and the ground around the tower became cheerful and very beautiful. ⁹¹The Shepherd says to me, "Everything has been cleared away; if the Lord of the tower comes to inspect it, He can have no fault to find with us." Having spoken these words, He wished to depart; but I laid hold of Him by the wallet, and began to adjure Him by the LORD that He would explain what He had showed me. ⁹²He said to me, "I must rest a little, and then I will explain to you everything; wait for Me here until I return." I said to Him, "Lord, what can I do here alone?" "You are not alone," He said, "for these virgins are with you." "Give me in charge to them, then," I replied. ⁹³The Shepherd called them to him, and said to them, "I entrust him to you until I come," and went away. ⁹⁴And I was alone with the virgins; and they were rather merry, but were friendly to me, especially the four more distinguished of them. ⁹⁵The virgins said to me, "The Shepherd does not come here today." "What, then," I said, "am I to do?" They replied, "Wait for Him until He comes; and if He comes, He will converse with you, and if He does not come, you will remain here with us until He does come." ⁹⁶I said to them, "I will wait for Him until it is late; and if He does not arrive, I will go away into the house, and come back early in the morning." ⁹⁷And they answered and said to me, "You were entrusted to us; you cannot go away from us." "Where, then," I said, "am I to remain?" "You will sleep with us," they replied, "as a brother, and not as a husband: for you are our brother, and for the time to come we intend to abide with you, for we love you exceedingly!" ⁹⁸But I was ashamed to remain with them. And she who seemed to be the first among them began to kiss me. [And the others seeing her kissing me, began to kiss me also], and to lead me round the tower, and to play with me. ⁹⁹And I, too, became like a young man, and began to play with them: for some of them formed a chorus, and others danced, and others sang; and I, keeping silence, walked with them around the tower, and was merry with them. ¹⁰⁰And when it grew late I wished to go into the house; and they would not let me, but detained me. So I remained with them during the night, and slept beside the tower. ¹⁰¹Now the virgins spread their linen tunics on the ground and made me lie down in the midst of them; and they did nothing at all but pray; and I without ceasing prayed with them, and not less than they. ¹⁰²And the virgins rejoiced because I thus prayed. And I remained there with the virgins until the next day at the second hour. ¹⁰³Then the Shepherd returned, and said to the virgins, "Did you offer him any insult?" "Ask him," they said. ¹⁰⁴I said to Him, "Lord, I was delighted that I remained with them." "On what," He asked, "did you dine?" "I dined, Lord," I replied, "on the words of the LORD the whole night." "Did they receive you well?" He inquired. "Yes, Lord," I answered. ¹⁰⁵"Now," He said, "what do you wish to hear first?" "I wish to hear in the order," I said, "in which You showed me from the beginning. I beg of You, Lord, that as I will ask You, so also You will give me the explanation." ¹⁰⁶"As you wish," He replied, "so also will I explain to you, and will conceal nothing at all from you." ¹⁰⁷"First of all, Lord," I said, "explain this to me: what is the meaning of the rock and the gate?" "This rock," He answered, "and this gate are the Son of God." ¹⁰⁸"How, Lord?" I said; "the rock is old, and the gate is new." "Listen," He said, "and understand, O ignorant man. The Son of God is older than all His creatures, so that He was a fellow-counselor with the Father in His work of creation: for this reason He is old." ¹⁰⁹"And why is the gate new, Lord?" I said. "Because," He answered, "He became manifest in the last days of the dispensation: for this reason the gate was made new, that they who are to be saved by it might enter into the Kingdom of God. ¹¹⁰Did you see," He said, "that those stones which came in through the gate were used for the building of the tower, and that those which did not come, were again thrown back to their own place?" "I saw, Lord," I replied. ¹¹¹"In like manner," He continued, "no one will enter into the Kingdom of God unless he receives His holy Name. For if you desire to enter into a city, and that city is surrounded by a wall, and has but one gate, can you enter into that city save through the gate which it has?" ¹¹²"Why, how can it be otherwise, Lord?" I said. "If, then, you cannot enter into the city except through its gate, so, in like manner, a man cannot otherwise enter into the Kingdom of God than by the Name of His beloved Son. ¹¹³You saw," He added, "the multitude who were building the tower?" "I saw them, Lord," I said. "Those," He said, "are all glorious messengers, and by them accordingly is the LORD surrounded. And the gate is the Son of God. This is the one entrance to the LORD. In no other way, then, will anyone enter in to Him except through His Son. ¹¹⁴Did you see," He continued, "the six men, and the tall and glorious Man in the midst of them, who walked around the tower, and rejected the stones from the building?" "I saw Him, Lord," I answered. ¹¹⁵"The glorious Man," He said, "is the Son of God, and those six glorious messengers are those who support Him on the right hand and on the left. None of these glorious messengers," He continued, "will enter in to God apart from Him. Whosoever does not receive His Name, will not enter into the Kingdom of God." ¹¹⁶"And the tower," I asked, "what does it mean?" "This tower," He replied, "is the Assembly." ¹¹⁷"And these virgins, who are they?" "They are holy spirits, and men cannot otherwise be found in the Kingdom of God unless these have put their clothing on them: for if you receive the Name only, and do not receive from them the clothing, they are of no advantage to you. ¹¹⁸For these virgins are the powers of the Son of God. If you bear His Name but do not possess His power, it will be in vain that you bear His Name. ¹¹⁹Those stones," He continued, "which you saw rejected, bore His Name, but did not put on the clothing of the virgins." ¹²⁰"Of what

THE SHEPHERD OF HERMAS

nature is their clothing, Lord?" I asked. "Their very names," He said, "are their clothing. Everyone who bears the Name of the Son of God, ought to bear the names of these also; for the Son Himself bears the names of these virgins. [121] As many stones," He continued, "as you saw [come into the building of the tower through the hands] of these virgins, and remaining, have been clothed with their strength. [122] For this reason, you see that the tower became of one stone with the rock. So also, they who have believed on the LORD through His Son, and are clothed with these spirits, will become one spirit, one body, and the color of their garments will be one. And the dwelling of such as bear the names of the virgins is in the tower." [123] "Those stones, Lord, that were rejected," I inquired, "on what account were they rejected? For they passed through the gate, and were placed by the hands of the virgins in the building of the tower." [124] "Since you take an interest in everything," He replied, "and examine minutely, hear about the stones that were rejected. [125] These all," He said, "received the Name of God, and they also received the strength of these virgins. Having received, then, these spirits, they were made strong, and were with the servants of God; and theirs was one spirit, and one body, and one clothing. For they were of the same mind, and wrought righteousness. [126] After a certain time, however, they were persuaded by the women whom you saw clothed in black, and having their shoulders exposed and their hair disheveled, and beautiful in appearance. [127] Having seen these women, they desired to have them, and clothed themselves with their strength, and put off the strength of the virgins. These, accordingly, were rejected from the house of God, and were given over to these women. [128] But they who were not deceived by the beauty of these women remained in the house of God. You have," He said, "the explanation of those who were rejected." [129] "What, then, Lord," I said, "if these men, being such as they are, convert and put away their desires after these women, and again return to the virgins, and walk in their strength and in their works, will they not enter into the house of God?" [130] "They will enter in," He said, "if they put away the works of these women, and put on again the strength of the virgins, and walk in their works. For on this account there was a cessation in the building, in order that, if these convert, they may depart into the building of the tower. [131] But if they do not convert, then others will come in their place, and these at the end will be cast out." For all these things I gave thanks to the LORD, because He had pity on all that call on His Name; and sent the Messenger of conversion to us who sinned against Him and renewed our spirit; and when we were already destroyed, and had no hope of life, He restored us to newness of life. [132] "Now, Lord," I continued, "show me why the tower was not built on the ground, but on the rock and on the gate." [133] "Are you still," He said, "without sense and understanding?" "I must, Lord," I said, "ask you of all things, because I am wholly unable to understand them; for all these things are great and glorious, and difficult for man to understand." [134] "Listen," He said: "the Name of the Son of God is great, and cannot be contained, and supports the whole world. If, then, the whole creation is supported by the Son of God, what do you think of those who are called by Him, and bear the Name of the Son of God, and walk in His commandments? [135] Do you see what kind of persons He supports? Those who bear His Name with their whole heart. He Himself, accordingly, became a foundation to them, and supports them with joy, because they are not ashamed to bear His Name." [136] "Explain to me, Lord," I said, "the names of these virgins, and of those women who were clothed in black raiment." [137] "Hear," He said, "the names of the stronger virgins who stood at the corners. The first is Faith, the second Continence, the third Power, the fourth Patience. [138] And the others standing in the midst of these have the following names: Simplicity, Innocence, Purity, Cheerfulness, Truth, Understanding, Harmony, Love. [138] He who bears these names and that of the Son of God will be able to enter into the Kingdom of God." [139] "Hear, also," He continued, "the names of the women who had the black garments; and of these, four are stronger than the rest. The first is Unbelief; the second, Incontinence; the third, Disobedience; the fourth, Deceit. [140] And their followers are called Sorrow, Wickedness, Wantonness, Anger, Falsehood, Folly, Backbiting, Hatred. The servant of God who bears these names will see, indeed, the Kingdom of God, but will not enter into it." [141] "And the stones, Lord," I said, "which were taken out of the pit and fitted into the building: what are they?" [142] "The first—" He said, "the ten, [namely, that were placed as a foundation,] are the first generation, and the twenty-five the second generation, of righteous men; and the thirty-five are the prophets of God and His ministers; and the forty are the apostles and teachers of the preaching of the Son of God." [143] "Why, then, Lord," I asked, "did the virgins also carry these stones through the gate, and give them for the building of the tower?" [144] "Because," He answered, "these were the first who bore these spirits, and they never departed from each other, neither the spirits from the men nor the men from the spirits, but the spirits remained with them until their falling asleep. And unless they had had these spirits with them, they would not have been of use for the building of this tower." [145] "Explain to me a little further, Lord," I said. "What is it that you desire?" He asked. "Why, Lord," I said, "did these stones ascend out of the pit, and be applied to the building of the tower, after having borne these spirits?" [146] "They were obliged," He answered, "to ascend through water in order that they might be made alive; for, unless they laid aside the deadness of their life, they could not in any other way enter into the Kingdom of God. Accordingly, those also who fell asleep received the seal of the Son of God. [147] For," he continued, "before a man bears the Name of the Son of God, he is dead; but when he receives the seal he lays aside his deadness, and obtains life. [148] The seal, then, is the water: they descend into the water dead, and they arise alive. And to them, accordingly, was this seal preached, and they made use of it that they might enter into the Kingdom of God." [149] "Why, Lord," I asked, "did the forty stones also ascend with them out of the pit, having already received the seal?" [150] "Because," He said, "these apostles and teachers who preached the Name of the Son of God, after falling asleep in the power and faith of the Son of God, preached it not only to those who were asleep, but themselves also gave them the seal of the preaching. [151] Accordingly, they descended with them into the water, and again ascended. [[But these descended alive and rose up again alive; whereas they who had previously fallen asleep descended dead, but rose up again alive.]] [152] By these, then, were they quickened and made to know the Name of the Son of God. For this reason, they also ascended with them, and were fitted along with them into the building of the tower, and, untouched by the chisel, were built in along with them. [153] For they slept in righteousness and in great purity, but only—they did not have this seal. Accordingly, you have the explanation of these also." [154] "I understand, Lord," I replied. "Now, Lord," I continued, "explain to me, with respect to the mountains, why their forms are various and diverse." [155] "Listen," He said: "these mountains are the twelve tribes, which inhabit the whole world. The Son of God, accordingly, was preached to them by the apostles." [156] "But why are the mountains of various kinds, some having one form, and others another? Explain that to me, Lord." [157] "Listen," He answered: "these twelve tribes that inhabit the whole world are twelve nations. And they vary in prudence and understanding. [158] As numerous, then, as are the varieties of the mountains which you saw, are also the diversities of mind and understanding among these nations. And I will explain to you the actions of each one." [159] "First, Lord," I said, "explain this: why, when the mountains are so diverse, their stones, when placed in the building, became one color, also shining like those that had ascended out of the pit." [160] "Because," He said, "all the nations that dwell under Heaven were called by hearing and believing on the Name of the Son of God. [161] Having, therefore, received the seal, they had one understanding and one mind; and their faith became one, and their love one, and with the Name they also bore the spirits of the virgins. [162] On this account the building of the tower became of one color, bright as the sun. But after they had entered into the same place, and became one body, certain of these defiled themselves, and were expelled from the race of the righteous, and again became what they were before, or rather worse." [163] "How, Lord," I said, "did they become worse, after having known God?" "He that does not know God," He answered, "and practices evil, receives a certain discipline for his wickedness; but he that has known God ought to not do evil any longer, but to do good. ¹⁶⁴If, accordingly, when he ought to do good, he does evil, does he not appear to do greater evil than he who does not know God? ¹⁶⁵For this reason, they who have not known God and do evil are condemned to death; but they who have known God, and have seen His mighty works, and still continue in evil, will be punished doubly, and will die forever. ¹⁶⁶In this way, then, the Assembly of God will be purified. For as you saw the stones rejected from the tower, and delivered to the evil spirits, and cast out from there, so [[they will also be cast out, and]] there will be one body of the purified; as the tower also became, as it were, of one stone after its purification. ¹⁶⁷In like manner also, it will be with the Assembly of God, after it has been purified, and has rejected the wicked, and the hypocrites, and the blasphemers, and the waverers, and those who commit wickedness of different kinds. ¹⁶⁸After these have been cast away, the Assembly of God will be one body, of one mind, of one understanding, of one faith, of one love. And then the Son of God will be exceedingly glad, and will rejoice over them, because He has received His people pure." ¹⁶⁹"All these things, Lord," I said, "are great and glorious. "Moreover, Lord," I said, "explain to me the power and the actions of each one of the mountains, that every soul, trusting in the LORD, and hearing it, may glorify His great, and marvelous, and glorious Name." ¹⁷⁰"Hear," He said, "the diversity of the mountains and of the twelve nations. ¹⁷¹From the first mountain, which was black, they that believed are the following: apostates and blasphemers against the LORD, and betrayers of the servants of God. ¹⁷²To these conversion is not open; but death lies before them, and on this account they are also black, for their race is a lawless one. ¹⁷³And from the second mountain, which was bare, they who believed are the following: hypocrites and teachers of wickedness. And these, accordingly, are like the former, not having any fruits of righteousness; for as their mountain was destitute of fruit, so also such men indeed have a name, but are empty of faith, and there is no fruit of truth in them. ¹⁷⁴They indeed have conversion in their power, if they convert quickly; but if they are slow in so doing, they will die along with the former." ¹⁷⁵"Why, Lord," I said, "do these have conversion, but the former do not? For their actions are nearly the same." ¹⁷⁶"On this account," He said, "these have conversion, because they did not blaspheme their Lord, nor become betrayers of the servants of God; but on account of their desire of possessions they became hypocritical, and each one taught according to the desires of men that were sinners. ¹⁷⁷But they will suffer a certain punishment; and conversion is before them, because they were not blasphemers or traitors. ¹⁷⁸And from the third mountain, which had thorns and thistles, they who believed are the following: some of them are rich, and others immersed in much business. The thistles are the rich, and the thorns are they who are immersed in much business. ¹⁷⁹Those cleave to the servants of God, but wander away, being choked by their business transactions; and the rich cleave with difficulty to the servants of God, fearing lest these should ask something of them. ¹⁸⁰Such persons, accordingly, will have difficulty in entering the Kingdom of God. For as it is disagreeable to walk among thistles with naked feet, so also it is hard for such to enter the Kingdom of God. ¹⁸¹But to all these conversion—and that speedily—is open, in order that what they did not do in former times they may make up for in these days, and do some good, and they will live to God. But if they abide in their deeds, they will be delivered to those women who will put them to death. ¹⁸²And from the fourth mountain, which had much grass—the upper parts of the plants green, and the parts about the roots withered, and some also scorched by the sun—they who believed are the following: ¹⁸³the doubtful, and they who have the LORD on their lips, but do not have Him in their heart. On this account their foundations are withered and have no strength; and their words alone live, while their works are dead. Such persons are [neither alive nor] dead. ¹⁸⁴They resemble, therefore, the waverers: for the wavering are neither withered nor green, being neither living nor dead. For as their blades, on seeing the sun, were withered, so also the wavering, when they hear of affliction, on account of their fear, worship idols, and are ashamed of the Name of their Lord. ¹⁸⁵Such, then, are neither alive nor dead. But these also may yet live, if they convert quickly; and if they do not convert, they are already delivered to the women, who take away their life. ¹⁸⁶And from the fifth mountain, which had green grass, and was rugged, they who believed are the following: believers, indeed, but slow to learn, and obstinate, and pleasing themselves, wishing to know everything, and knowing nothing at all. ¹⁸⁷On account of this obstinacy of theirs, understanding departed from them, and foolish senselessness entered into them. And they praise themselves as having wisdom, and desire to become teachers, although destitute of sense. ¹⁸⁸On account, therefore, of this loftiness of mind, many became vain, exalting themselves: for self-will and empty confidence is a great demon. Of these, accordingly, many were rejected, but some converted and believed, and subjected themselves to those that had understanding, knowing their own foolishness. ¹⁸⁹And to the rest of this class conversion is open; for they were not wicked, but rather foolish, and without understanding. Therefore, if these convert, they will live to God; but if they do not convert, they will have their dwelling with the women who wrought wickedness among them. ¹⁹⁰And those from the sixth mountain, which had clefts large and small, and decayed grass in the clefts, who believed, were the following: they who occupy the small clefts are those who bring charges against one another, and by reason of their slanders have decayed in the faith. ¹⁹¹Many of them, however, converted; and the rest will also convert when they hear My commandments, for their slanders are small, and they will quickly convert. ¹⁹²But they who occupy the large clefts are persistent in their slanders, and vindictive in their anger against each other. ¹⁹³These, therefore, were thrown away from the tower, and rejected from having a part in its building. Such persons, accordingly, will have difficulty in living. ¹⁹⁴If our God and Lord, who rules over all things, and has power over all His creation, does not remember evil against those who confess their sins, but is merciful, [how] does man, who is corruptible and full of sins, remember evil against a fellow-man, as if he were able to destroy or to save him? ¹⁹⁵I, the Messenger of conversion, say to you: as many of you as are of this way of thinking, lay it aside, and convert, and the LORD will heal your former sins if you purify yourselves from this demon; but if not, you will be delivered over to him for death. ¹⁹⁶And those who believed from the seventh mountain, on which the grass was green and flourishing, and the whole of the mountain fertile, and every kind of cattle and the birds of [the] sky were feeding on the grass on this mountain, and the grass on which they pastured became more abundant, were the following: ¹⁹⁷they were always simple, and harmless, and blessed, bringing no charges against one another, but always rejoicing greatly because of the servants of God, and being clothed with the Holy Spirit of these virgins, and always having pity on every man, and giving aid from their own labor to every man, without reproach and without hesitation. ¹⁹⁸The LORD, therefore, seeing their simplicity and all their meekness, multiplied them amid the labors of their hands, and gave them grace in all their doings. ¹⁹⁹And I, the Messenger of conversion, say to you who are such: continue to be such as these, and your seed will never be blotted out; for the LORD has made trial of you, and inscribed you in the number of us, and the whole of your seed will dwell with the Son of God; for you have received of His Spirit. ²⁰⁰And they who believed from the eighth mountain, where the many fountains were, and where all the creatures of God drank of the fountains, were the following: ²⁰¹apostles and teachers who preached to the whole world, and who taught solemnly and purely the word of the LORD, and did not fall into evil desires at all, but always walked in righteousness and truth, according as they had received the Holy Spirit. Therefore, such persons will enter in with the messengers. ²⁰²And they who believed from the ninth mountain, which was deserted, and had in it creeping things and wild beasts which destroy men, were the following: ²⁰³they who had the stains as servants, who discharged their duty ill, and who plundered widows and orphans of their livelihood, and gained possessions for themselves from the ministry, which they had received. ²⁰⁴Therefore, if they remain under the dominion of the same desire, they are dead, and there is no hope of life for them; but if they convert, and finish their ministry in a holy manner, they will be able to live. ²⁰⁵And they who were covered with scabs are those who have denied their Lord, and have not returned to Him again; but becoming withered and desert-like, and not cleaving to the servants of God, but living in solitude, they destroy their own souls. ²⁰⁶For as a vine, when left within an enclosure, and meeting with neglect, is destroyed, and is made desolate by the weeds, and in time grows wild, and is no longer of any use to its master, so also are such men—as have given themselves up and become useless to their Lord—from having contracted savage habits. ²⁰⁷Therefore, these men have conversion in their power, unless they are found to have denied from the heart; but if anyone is found to have denied from the heart, I do not know if he may live. ²⁰⁸And I say this not for these present days, in order that anyone who has denied may obtain conversion, for It is impossible for him to be saved who now intends to deny his Lord; but to those who denied Him long ago, conversion seems to be possible. ²⁰⁹Therefore, if anyone intends to convert, let him do so quickly, before the tower is completed; for if not, he will be utterly destroyed by the women. ²¹⁰And the chipped stones are the deceitful and the slanderers; and the wild beasts, which you saw on the ninth mountain, are the same. ²¹⁰For as wild beasts destroy and kill a man by their poison, so also do the words of such men destroy and ruin a man. These, accordingly, are mutilated in their faith, on account of the deeds which they have done in themselves; yet some converted, and were saved. ²¹¹And the rest, who are of such a character, can be saved if they convert; but if they do not convert, they will perish with those women, whose strength they have assumed. ²¹²And from the tenth mountain, where trees were which overshadowed certain sheep, they who believed were the following: overseers given to hospitality, who always gladly received into their houses the servants of God, without dissimulation. ²¹³And the overseers never failed to protect, by their service, the widows, and those who were in want, and always maintained a holy conversation. ²¹⁴All these, accordingly, will be protected by the LORD forever. They who do these things are honorable before God, and their place is already with the messengers, if they remain serving God to the end. ²¹⁵And from the eleventh mountain, where trees were full of fruits, adorned with fruits of various kinds, they who believed were the following: they who suffered for the Name of the Son of God, and who also suffered cheerfully with their whole heart, and laid down their lives." ²¹⁶"Why, then, Lord," I said, "do all these trees bear fruit, and some of them—fairer than the rest?" ²¹⁷"Listen," He said: "all who once suffered for the Name of the LORD are honorable before God; and of all these the sins were remitted, because they suffered for the Name of the Son of God. And why their fruits are of various kinds, and some of them superior, listen. ²¹⁸All," He continued, "who were brought before the authorities and were examined, and did not deny, but suffered cheerfully—these are held in greater honor with God, and of these the fruit is superior; ²¹⁹but all who were cowards, and in doubt, and who reasoned in their hearts whether they would deny or confess, and yet suffered, of these the fruit is less, because that suggestion came into their hearts; for that suggestion—that a servant should deny his Lord—is evil. ²²⁰Have a care, therefore, you who are planning such things, lest that suggestion remain in your hearts, and you perish to God. ²²¹And you who suffer for His Name ought to glorify God, because He deemed you worthy to bear His Name, that all your sins might be healed. [[Therefore, rather deem yourselves happy]], and think that you have done a great thing, if any of you suffer on account of God. ²²²The LORD bestows life on you, and you do not understand, for your sins were heavy; but if you had not suffered for the Name of the LORD, you would have died to God on account of your sins. ²²³These things I say to you who are hesitating about denying or confessing: acknowledge that you have the LORD, lest, denying Him, you are delivered up to prison. ²²⁴If the heathen punishes their slaves when one of them denies his master, what do you think your Lord will do, who has authority over all men? Put away these counsels out of your hearts, that you may continually live to God. ²²⁵And they who believed from the twelfth mountain, which was white, are the following: they are as infant children, in whose hearts no evil originates; nor did they know what wickedness is, but always remained as children. ²²⁶Such accordingly, without doubt, dwell in the Kingdom of God, because they defiled the commandments of God in nothing; but they remained like children all the days of their life in the same mind. ²²⁷All of you, then, who will remain steadfast, and be as children, without doing evil, will be more honored than all who have been previously mentioned; for all infants are honorable before God, and are the first persons with Him. ²²⁸Blessed, then, are you who put away wickedness from yourselves, and put on innocence. You will live to God as the first of all." ²²⁹After He had finished the similitudes of the mountains, I said to Him, "Lord, now explain to me about the stones that were taken out of the plain, and put into the building instead of the stones that were taken out of the tower; and about the round stones that were put into the building; and those that still remain round." ²³⁰"Hear," He answered, "about all these also. The stones taken out of the plain and put into the building of the tower instead of those that were rejected, are the roots of this white mountain. ²³¹Therefore, when they who believed from the white mountain were all found guileless, the Lord of the tower commanded those from the roots of this mountain to be cast into the building of the tower; ²³²for He knew that if these stones were to go to the building of the tower, they would remain bright, and not one of them would become black. ²³³But if He had so resolved with respect to the other mountains, it would have been necessary for Him to visit that tower again, and to cleanse it. ²³⁴Now all these persons were found white who believed, and who will yet believe, for they are of the same race. This is a happy race, because it is innocent. Hear now, further, about these round and shining stones. ²³⁵All these are also from the white mountain. Hear, moreover, why they were found round: because their riches had obscured and darkened them a little from the truth, although they never departed from God; nor did any evil word proceed out of their mouth, but all justice, virtue, and truth. ²³⁶When the LORD, therefore, saw the mind of these persons, that they were born good, and could be good, He ordered their riches to be cut down, not to be taken away forever, that they might be able to do some good with what was left them; and they will live to God, because they are of a good race. ²³⁷Therefore, they were rounded a little by the chisel, and put in the building of the tower. ²³⁸But the other round stones, which had not yet been adapted to the building of the tower, and had not yet received the seal, were for this reason put back into their place, because they are exceedingly round. ²³⁹Now this age must be cut down in these things, and in the vanities of their riches, and then they will meet in the Kingdom of God; for they must of necessity enter into the Kingdom of God, because the LORD has blessed this innocent race. ²⁴⁰Of this race, therefore, no one will perish; for although any of them might be tempted by the most wicked devil, and commit sin, he will quickly return to his Lord. ²⁴¹I deem you happy, I, who am the Messenger of conversion, whoever of you are innocent as children, because your part is good, and honorable before God. ²⁴²Moreover, I say to you all, who have received the seal of the Son of God, be clothed with simplicity, and do not be mindful of offenses, nor remain in wickedness. ²⁴³Therefore, lay aside the recollection of your offenses and bitternesses, and you will be formed in one spirit. ²⁴⁴And heal and take away from you those wicked schisms, that if the Lord of the flocks comes, He may rejoice concerning you. And He will rejoice if He finds all things sound, and none of you will perish. ²⁴⁵But if He finds any one of these sheep strayed, woe to the shepherds! And if the shepherds themselves have strayed, what answer will they give Him for their flocks? ²⁴⁶Will they perhaps say that they were harassed by their flocks? They will not be believed, for the thing is incredible that a shepherd could suffer from his flock; rather, he will be punished on account of his falsehood. ²⁴⁷And I myself am a shepherd, and I am under a most stringent necessity of rendering an account of you. ²⁴⁸Therefore heal yourselves while the tower is still building. The LORD dwells in men that love peace, because He loved peace; but from the contentious and the utterly wicked He is far distant. ²⁴⁹Restore to Him, therefore, a spirit as sound as you received it. ²⁵⁰For when you have given a new garment to a fuller, and desire to receive it back whole at the end, if, then, the fuller returns a torn garment to you, will you take it from him, and not rather be angry, and abuse him, saying, I gave you a garment that was whole: why have you rent it, and made it useless, so that it can be of no use on account of the rent which you have made in it? [251] Would you not say all this to the fuller about the rent which you found in your garment? Therefore, if you grieve about your garment, and complain because you have not received it whole, what do you think the LORD will do to you, who gave you a sound spirit, which you have rendered altogether useless, so that it can be of no service to its possessor? [252] For its use began to be unprofitable, seeing it was corrupted by you. Therefore, will the LORD, because of this conduct of yours regarding His Spirit, not act in the same way, and deliver you over to death? [253] Assuredly, I say, He will do the same to all those whom He will find retaining a recollection of offenses. [254] Do not trample His mercy under foot, He says, but rather honor Him, because He is so patient with your sins, and is not as you are. Convert, for it is useful to you. [255] All these things which are written above, I, the Shepherd, the Messenger of conversion, have showed and spoken to the servants of God. [256] Therefore, if you believe, and listen to My words, and walk in them, and amend your ways, you will have it in your power to live: but if you remain in wickedness, and in the recollection of offenses, no sinner of that class will live to God. [257] All these words which I had to say have been spoken to you." The Shepherd said to me, "Have you asked Me everything?" And I replied, "Yes, Lord." [258] "Why did you not ask Me about the shape of the stones that were put into the building, that I might explain to you why we filled up the shapes?" And I said, "I forgot, Lord." [259] "Hear now, then," He said, "about this also. These are they who have now heard My commandments and converted with their whole hearts. [260] And when the LORD saw that their conversion was good and pure, and that they were able to remain in it, He ordered their former sins to be blotted out. For these shapes were their sins, and they were leveled down, that they might not appear."

SIMILITUDE 10

[1] After I had fully written down this scroll, that messenger who had delivered me to the Shepherd came into the house in which I was, and sat down on a couch, and the Shepherd stood on his right hand. [2] He then called me, and spoke to me as follows: "I have delivered you and your house to the Shepherd, that you may be protected by Him." "Yes, Lord," I said. [3] "If you wish, therefore, to be protected," he said, "from all annoyance, and from all harsh treatment, and to have success in every good work and word, and to possess all the virtues of righteousness, walk in these commandments which He has given you, and you will be able to subdue all wickedness. [4] For if you keep those commandments, every desire and pleasure of the world will be subject to you, and success will attend to you in every good work. [5] Take to yourself His experience and moderation, and say to all that He is in great honor and dignity with God, and that He is a president with great power, and mighty in His office. [6] To Him alone throughout the whole world is the power of conversion assigned. Does He seem to you to be powerful? [7] But you despise His experience, and the moderation which He exercises toward you." [8] I said to him, "Ask Him, lord, whether from the time that He has entered my house I have done anything improper, or have offended Him in any respect." [9] He answered, "I also know that you neither have done nor will do anything improper, and therefore I speak these words to you, that you may persevere. For He had a good report of you to me, and you will say these words to others, that they also who have either converted or will still convert may entertain the same feelings with you, and He may report well of these to me, and I to the LORD." [10] And I said, "Lord, I make known to every man the great works of God: and I hope that all those who love them, and have sinned before, on hearing these words, may convert, and receive life again." [11] "Therefore, continue in this ministry, and finish it. And all who follow out His commands will have life, and great honor with the LORD. [12] But those who do not keep His commandments, flee from His life, and despise Him. But He has His own honor with the LORD. [13] All, therefore, who will despise Him, and not follow His commands, deliver themselves to death, and every one of them will be guilty of his own blood. [14] But I enjoin you, that you obey His commands, and you will have a cure for your former sins. [15] Moreover, I sent you these virgins, that they may dwell with you. For I saw that they were courteous to you. You will therefore have them as assistants, that you may be the better able to keep His commands: for it is impossible that these commandments can be observed without these virgins. [16] I see, moreover, that they abide with you willingly; but I will also instruct them not to depart at all from your house: only, keep your house pure, as they will delight to dwell in a pure abode. [17] For they are pure, and chaste, and industrious, and have all influence with the LORD. Therefore, if they find your house to be pure, they will remain with you; but if any defilement, even a little, befalls it, they will immediately withdraw from your house. For these virgins do not like any defilement at all." [18] I said to him, "I hope, lord, that I will please them, so that they may always be willing to inhabit my house. And as He to whom you entrusted me has no complaint against me, so neither will they have." [19] He said to the Shepherd, "I see that the servant of God wishes to live, and to keep these commandments, and will place these virgins in a pure habitation." [20] When he had spoken these words, he again delivered me to the Shepherd, and called those virgins, and said to them, "Since I see that you are willing to dwell in his house, I commend him and his house to You, asking that You do not withdraw from it at all." And the virgins heard these words with pleasure. [21] The messenger then said to me, "Conduct yourself courageously in this service, and make known to everyone the great things of God, and you will have favor in this ministry. [22] Whoever, therefore, will walk in these commandments, will have life, and will be happy in his life; but whosoever will neglect them will not have life, and will be unhappy in this life. Enjoin all, who are able to act rightly, not to cease well-doing; for, to practice good works is useful to them. [23] And I say that every man ought to be saved from inconveniences. For both he who is in want, and he who suffers inconveniences in his daily life, is in great torture and necessity. Whoever, therefore, rescues a soul of this kind from necessity, will gain for himself great joy. [24] For he who is harassed by inconveniences of this kind, suffers equal torture with him who is in chains. [25] Moreover many, on account of calamities of this sort, when they could not endure them, hasten their own deaths. Whoever, then, knows a calamity of this kind afflicting a man, and does not save him, commits a great sin, and becomes guilty of his blood. [26] Therefore, do good works, you who have received good from the LORD, lest, while you delay to do them, the building of the tower is finished, and you are rejected from the edifice: there is now no other tower being built. [27] For on your account the work of building was suspended. Unless, then, you make haste to do rightly, the tower will be completed, and you will be excluded." [28] After he had spoken with me, he rose up from the couch, and taking the Shepherd and the virgins, he departed. But he said to me that he would send the Shepherd and the virgins back to my dwelling. Amen.

ODES OF PEACE

The Odes of Peace, more commonly known as the Odes of Solomon, are a collection of early Christian poems, in the form of odes, that were likely composed in the late 1st century AD or early 2nd century. They are known from early citations and various extant copies. The elaborate and beautiful language reflects the deity of Christ and exhibits a primordial Trinitarianism. While later Gnostic works cite the Odes, the Odes themselves are not Gnostic, and reflect, rather, a more orthodox view of the early Christian faith heavily influenced by wisdom literature. Ode 2 is not extant.

ODE 1

¹The LORD is on my head like a crown, || And I will not be without Him. ²They wove for me a crown of truth, || And it caused Your branches to bud in me. ³For it is not like a withered crown which does not bud, || But You live on my head, || And You have blossomed on my head. ⁴Your fruits are full-grown and perfect, || They are full of Your salvation.

ODE 3

¹… I put on. ²And His members are with Him. And I stand on them, || And He loves me: ³For I should not have known love, || If the LORD had not loved me. ⁴For who is able to distinguish love except the one that is loved? ⁵I love the Beloved and my soul loves Him: ⁶And where His rest is, || There I am also; ⁷And I will be no stranger, for with the LORD Most High and Merciful there is no grudging. ⁸I have been united to Him, || For the lover has found the Beloved, ⁹And because I will love Him that is the Son, || I will become a son; ¹⁰For he that is joined to Him that is immortal, || Will also himself become immortal; ¹¹And he who has pleasure in the Living One, || Will become living. ¹²This is the Spirit of the LORD, || Which does not lie, || Which teaches the sons of men to know His ways. ¹³Be wise and understanding and vigilant. Hallelujah!

ODE 4

¹No man, O my God, changes Your holy place; ²And it is not [possible] that he should change it and put it in another place, || Because he has no power over it, ³For You have designed Your sanctuary before You made [other] places: ⁴That which is the elder will not be altered by those that are younger than itself. ⁵You have given Your heart, O LORD, to Your believers: You will never fail, || Nor be without fruits, ⁶For one hour of Your faith is days and years. ⁷For who is there [that] put on Your grace, and is hurt? ⁸For Your seal is known, || And Your creatures know it, || And Your [heavenly] hosts possess it, || And the chosen chief-messengers are clad with it. ⁹You have given us Your fellowship. It was not that You were in need of us, || But that we are in need of You; ¹⁰Distill Your dews on us and open Your rich fountains that pour forth to us milk and honey, ¹¹For there is no relenting with You that You should relent of anything that You have promised. ¹²And the end was revealed before You, || For what You gave, You gave freely, ¹³So that You may not draw them back and take them again, ¹⁴For all was revealed before You as God, || And ordered from the beginning before You; And You, O God, have made all things. Hallelujah!

ODE 5

¹I will give thanks to You, O LORD, || Because I love You; ²O Most High, You will not forsake me for You are my hope: ³Freely I have received Your grace, || I will live thereby: ⁴My persecutors will come and not see me: ⁵A cloud of darkness will fall on their eyes; And an air of thick gloom will darken them: ⁶And they will have no light to see; They may not take hold on me. ⁷Let their counsel become thick darkness, || And what they have cunningly devised, || Let it return on their own heads, ⁸For they have devised a counsel and it did not succeed; ⁹For my hope is on the LORD and I will not fear, || And because the LORD is my salvation, || I will not fear; And He is a garland on my head and I will not be moved; Even if everything should be shaken, || I stand firm; ¹¹And if all things visible should perish, || I will not die, || Because the LORD is with me and I am with Him. Hallelujah!

ODE 6

¹As the hand moves over the harp, || And the strings speak, ²So speaks in my members the Spirit of the LORD, || And I speak by His love. ³For it destroys what is foreign and everything that is bitter: ⁴For thus it was from the beginning and will be to the end, || That nothing should be His adversary, || And nothing should stand up against Him. ⁵The LORD has multiplied the knowledge of Himself, || And is zealous that these things should be known, || Which by His grace have been given to us. ⁶And the praise of His Name He gave us: Our spirits praise His holy Spirit. ⁷For there went forth a stream that became a river great and broad; ⁸For it flooded and broke up everything and it brought [water] to the temple; ⁹And the restrainers of the children of men were not able to restrain it, || Nor the arts of those whose business it is to restrain waters; ¹⁰For it spread over the face of the whole earth, || And filled everything: And all the thirsty on earth were given to drink of it; ¹¹And thirst was relieved and quenched, || For from the Most High the drink was given. ¹²Blessed then are the ministers of that drink who are entrusted with that water ¹³They have assuaged the dry lips, || And the will that had fainted they have raised up; ¹⁴And souls that were near departing they have caught back from death; ¹⁵And limbs that had fallen they straightened and set up. ¹⁶They gave strength for their feebleness and light to their eyes, ¹⁷For everyone knew them in the LORD, || And they lived by the water of life forever. Hallelujah!

ODE 7

¹As the impulse of anger against evil, || So is the impulse of joy over what is lovely, || And brings in of its fruits without restraint: ²My joy is the LORD and my impulse is toward Him; This path of mine is excellent, ³For I have a helper—the LORD. ⁴He has caused me to know Himself, || Without grudging, by His simplicity: His kindness has humbled His greatness. ⁵He became like me, || In order that I might receive Him; He was reckoned like myself in order that I might put Him on; ⁷And I did not tremble when I saw Him, || Because He was gracious to me. ⁸He became like my nature that I might learn Him, || And like my form, that I might not turn back from Him. ⁹The Father of knowledge is the word of knowledge: ¹⁰He who created wisdom is wiser than His works; ¹¹And He who created me when I was yet not knew what I should do when I came into being, ¹²For what reason He pitied me in His abundant grace, || And granted me to ask from Him and to receive from His sacrifice, ¹³Because it is He that is incorruptible—The fullness of the ages and their Father. ¹⁴He has given Him to be seen of them that are His, || In order that they may recognize Him that made them, || And that they might not suppose that they came of themselves; ¹⁵For He has appointed knowledge as its way, || Has widened it and extended it, || And brought to all perfection, ¹⁶And set over it the traces of His light, || And I walked therein from the beginning even to the end. ¹⁷For by Him it was worked, || And He was resting in the Son, || And for its salvation He will take hold of everything. ¹⁸And the Most High will be known in His holy ones, || To announce to those that have songs of the coming of the LORD: ¹⁹That they may go forth to meet Him, || And may sing to Him with joy and with the harp of many tones. ²⁰The seers will come before Him and they will be seen before Him, ²¹And they will praise the LORD for His love, || Because He is near and beholds. ²²And hatred will be taken from the earth, || And along with jealousy it will be drowned: ²³For ignorance has been destroyed, || Because the knowledge of the LORD has arrived. ²⁴They who make songs will sing the grace of the LORD Most High; ²⁵And they will bring their songs, || And their heart will be like the day, || And like the excellent beauty of the LORD their pleasant song; ²⁶And there will neither be anything that breathes without knowledge nor any that is dumb, ²⁷For He has given a mouth to His creation, || To open the voice of the mouth toward Him, || To praise Him, ²⁸Confess His power, || And show forth His grace. Hallelujah!

ODES OF PEACE

ODE 8

¹Open, open your hearts to the exultation of the LORD, ²And let your love be multiplied from the heart and even to the lips, ³To bring forth living [and] holy fruit to the LORD, || And to talk with watchfulness in His light. ⁴Rise up, and stand erect, || You who once were brought low: ⁵Tell forth, you who were in silence, || That your mouth has been opened. ⁶You, therefore, that were despised, be lifted up from now on, || Because your righteousness has been exalted. ⁷For the right hand of the LORD is with you, || And He is your helper; ⁸And peace was prepared for you, || Before your war ever was. ⁹Hear the word of truth, || And receive the knowledge of the Most High. ¹⁰Your flesh has not known what I am saying to you: Neither have your hearts known what I am showing to you. ¹¹Keep My secret, || You who are kept by it. ¹²Keep My faith, || You who are kept by it. ¹³And understand My knowledge, || You who know Me in truth, ¹⁴Love Me with affection, || You who love! ¹⁵For I do not turn away My face from them that are Mine; ¹⁶For I know them and before they came into being I took knowledge of them, || And on their faces I set My seal, ¹⁷I fashioned their members, || [And] I prepared My own breasts for them, || That they might drink My holy milk and live thereby. ¹⁸I took pleasure in them and am not ashamed of them, ¹⁹For they are My workmanship and the strength of My thoughts. ²⁰Who then will rise up against My handiwork, || Or who is there that is not subject to them? ²¹I willed and fashioned mind and heart: And they are Mine, and by My own right hand I set My chosen ones, ²²And My righteousness goes before them and they will not be deprived of My Name, || For it is with them. ²³Ask, and abound, and abide in the love of the LORD, ²⁴You beloved ones in the Beloved—Those who are kept in Him that lives, ²⁵And they that are saved in Him that was saved— ²⁶And you will be found incorruptible in all ages through the Name of your Father. Hallelujah!

ODE 9

¹Open your ears and I will speak to you. Give me your souls that I may also give you my soul, ²The word of the LORD and His good pleasures, || The holy thought which He has devised concerning His Messiah. ³For in the will of the LORD is your salvation, || And His thought is everlasting life; And your end is immortality. ⁴Be enriched in God the Father, || And receive the thought of the Most High. ⁵Be strong and be redeemed by His grace. ⁶For I announce peace to you, || To you His holy ones, ⁷That none of those who hear may fall in war, || And that those again who have known Him may not perish, || And that those who receive may not be ashamed. ⁸Truth is an everlasting crown forever. Blessed are they who set it on their heads: ⁹It is a stone of great price; And there have been wars on account of the crown. ¹⁰And righteousness has taken it and has given it to you. ¹¹Put on the crown in the true covenant of the LORD. ¹²And all those who have conquered will be written in His scroll. ¹³For their scroll is victory which is yours. And she [(Victory)] sees you before her and wills that you will be saved. Hallelujah!

ODE 10

¹The LORD has directed My mouth by His word, || And He has opened My heart by His light, || And He has caused His deathless life to dwell in Me, ²And He gave Me that I might speak the fruit of peace: ³To convert the souls of them who are willing to come to Him, || And to lead captive a good captivity for freedom. ⁴I was strengthened and made mighty and took the world captive; ⁵And it became to Me for the praise of the Most High, || And of God My Father. ⁶And the nations were gathered together who were scattered abroad. ⁷And I was unpolluted by My love for them, || Because they confessed Me in high places: And the traces of the light were set on their heart, ⁸And they walked in My life and were saved and became My people forever and ever. Hallelujah!

ODE 11

¹My heart was split, || And its flower appeared; And grace sprang up in it: And it brought forth fruit to the LORD, ²For the Most High cleaved my heart by His Holy Spirit and searched my affection toward Him: And filled me with His love. ³And His opening of me became my salvation; And I ran in His way in His peace even in the way of truth: ⁴from the beginning and even to the end I acquired His knowledge, ⁵And I was established on the rock of truth, || Where He had set me up; ⁶And speaking waters touched my lips from the fountain of the LORD plenteously, ⁷And I drank and was inebriated with the living water that does not die; ⁸And my inebriation was not one without knowledge, || But I forsook vanity and turned to my God, the Most High, ⁹And I was enriched by His bounty, || And I forsook the folly which is diffused over the earth; And I stripped it off and cast it from me: ¹⁰And the LORD renewed me in His raiment, || And possessed me by His light, || And from above He gave me rest in incorruption; ¹¹And I became like the land which blossoms and rejoices in its fruits: ¹²And the LORD was like the sun shining on the face of the land; ¹³He lightened my eyes and my face received the dew—The pleasant fragrance of the LORD; ¹⁴And He carried me to His Paradise, || Where the abundance of the pleasure of the LORD is; ¹⁵And I worshiped the LORD on account of His glory; And I said, "Blessed, O LORD, are they who are planted in Your land, || And those who have a place in Your Paradise; ¹⁶And they grow by the fruits of the trees. And they have changed from darkness to light. ¹⁷Behold! All Your servants are fair, who do good works, || And turn away from wickedness to the pleasantness that is Yours: ¹⁸And they have turned back the bitterness of the trees from them, || When they were planted in Your land; ¹⁹And everything became like a relic of Yourself, || And memorial forever of Your faithful works. ²⁰For there is abundant room in Your Paradise, || And nothing is useless therein; ²¹But everything is filled with fruit; Glory be to You, O God, the Delight of Paradise forever. Hallelujah!"

ODE 12

¹He has filled me with words of truth, || That I may speak the same; ²And like the flow of waters flows truth from my mouth, || And my lips show forth His fruit. ³And He has caused His knowledge to abound in me, || Because the mouth of the LORD is the true Word, || And the door of His light; ⁴And the Most High has given Him to His generations, || Which are the interpreters of His own beauty, || And the repeaters of His praise, || And the confessors of His counsel, || And the heralds of His thought, || And the chasteners of His servants. ⁵For the swiftness of the Word is inexpressible, || And like His expression is His swiftness and force; ⁶And His course knows no limit. He never fails, but He stands sure, || And He does not know descent nor the way of it. ⁷For as His work is, so is His end, || For He is light and the dawning of thought; ⁸And by Him the worlds talk to one another; And in the Word there were those that were silent; ⁹And from Him came love and concord; And they spoke to one another whatever was theirs; And they were penetrated by the Word; ¹⁰And they knew Him who made them, || Because they were in concord; For the mouth of the Most High spoke to them; And His explanation ran by means of Him. ¹¹For the dwelling-place of the Word is man, || And His truth is love. ¹²Blessed are they who by means thereof have understood everything, || And have known the LORD in His truth. Hallelujah!

ODE 13

¹Behold! The LORD is our mirror: Open the eyes and see them in Him, || And learn the manner of your face, ²And tell forth praise to His Spirit, || And wipe off the filth from your face, || And love His holiness, || And clothe yourselves with it, ³And be without stain at all times before Him. Hallelujah!

ODE 14

¹As the eyes of a son to his father, || So are my eyes, O LORD, at all times toward You. ²For with You are my consolations and my delight. ³Do not turn Your mercies away from me, O LORD: And do not take Your kindness from me. ⁴Stretch out to me, O LORD, at all times Your right hand, || And be my guide even to the end, || According to Your good pleasure. ⁵Let me be well-pleasing before You, || Because of Your glory and because of Your Name. ⁶Let me be preserved from evil, || And let Your meekness, O LORD, || Abide with me, and the fruits of Your love. ⁷Teach me the psalms of Your truth, || That I may bring forth fruit in You, ⁸And open to me the harp of Your Holy Spirit, || That with all His notes I may praise You, O LORD. ⁹And according to the multitude of Your tender mercies, || So You will give to me; And hasten to grant our petitions; And You are able for all our needs. Hallelujah!

ODES OF PEACE

ODE 15

¹As the sun is the joy to them that seek for its daybreak, || So my joy is the LORD, ²Because He is my Sun, and His rays have lifted me up, and His light has dispelled all darkness from my face. In Him I have acquired eyes and have seen His holy day: ⁴Ears have become mine and I have heard His truth. ⁵The thought of knowledge has been mine, || And I have been delighted through Him. ⁶I have left the way of error, || And have walked toward Him, || And have received salvation from Him without grudging. ⁷And according to His bounty He has given to me, || And according to His excellent beauty He has made me. ⁸I have put on incorruption through His Name, || And have put off corruption by His grace. ⁹Death has been destroyed before my face, || And Sheol has been abolished by my word; ¹⁰And there has gone up deathless life in the LORD's land, ¹¹And it has been made known to His faithful ones, || And has been given without limit to all those that trust in Him. Hallelujah!

ODE 16

¹As the work of the farmer is the plowshare, || And the work of the helmsman is the guidance of the ship, ²So also my work, my craft, is the psalm of the LORD, ³Because His love has nourished my heart, || And even to my lips He poured out His fruits. ⁴For my love is the LORD, || And I will therefore sing to Him: ⁵For I am made strong in His praise, || And I have faith in Him. ⁶I will open my mouth and His Spirit will utter in me || The glory of the LORD and His beauty, || The work of His hands and the operation of His fingers, ⁷The multitude of His mercies and the strength of His word. ⁸For the Word of the LORD searches out all things, || Both the invisible and that which reveals His thought, ⁹For the eye sees His works and the ear hears His thought. ¹⁰He spread out the earth and settled the waters in the sea; ¹¹He measured the heavens and fixed the stars; And He established the creation and set it up; ¹²And He rested from His works. ¹³Thus created things run in their courses, || And do their works: ¹⁴And they do not know how to stand and be idle; And His heavenly hosts are subject to His Word. ¹⁵The treasure-chamber of the light is the sun, || And the treasury of the darkness is the night; ¹⁶And He made the sun for the day that it may be bright, || But night brings darkness over the face of the land; ¹⁷And their cycles, one after another, speak the beauty of God. ¹⁸And there is nothing that is without the LORD, For He was before anything came into being, ¹⁹And the worlds were made by His word, || And by the thought of His heart. Glory and honor to His Name. Hallelujah!

ODE 17

¹I was crowned by My God—My crown is living; ²And I was justified in My Lord—My incorruptible salvation is He. ³I was loosed from vanity, || And I was not condemned; ⁴The choking bonds were cut off by her hands. I received the face and the fashion of a new person, || And I walked in it and was delivered. ⁵And the thought of truth led me on; And I walked after it and did not wander. ⁶And all that have seen Me were amazed: And I was regarded by them as a strange person. ⁷And He who knew and brought Me up is the Most High in all His perfection. And He glorified Me by His kindness, || And raised My thoughts to the height of His truth. ⁸And from there He gave Me the way of His precepts, || And I opened the doors that were closed, ⁹And broke in pieces the bars of iron, || But my iron melted and dissolved before Me; ¹⁰Nothing appeared closed to Me, || Because I was the door of everything. ¹¹And I went over to all My bound ones to loose them, || That I might not leave any man bound or binding. ¹²And I imparted My knowledge without grudging, || And My prayer was in My love; ¹³And I sowed My fruits in hearts, || And transformed them into Myself; And they received My blessing and lived; ¹⁴And they were gathered to Me and were saved, || Because they were to Me as My own members, and I was their Head. Glory to You, our Head, the Lord Messiah. Hallelujah!

ODE 18

¹My heart was lifted up in the love of the Most High and was enlarged, || That I might praise Him for His Name's sake. ²My members were strengthened that they might not fall from His strength. ³Sicknesses departed from my body, || And it stood to the LORD by His will, || For His kingdom is true. ⁴O LORD, for the sake of them that are deficient, do not remove Your word from me! ⁵Neither for the sake of their works do You restrain from me Your perfection! ⁶Do not let the luminary be conquered by the darkness, || Nor let truth flee away from falsehood. ⁷You will appoint me to victory; Your right hand is our salvation. And You will receive men from all quarters. ⁸And You will preserve whosoever is held in evils: ⁹You are my God. Falsehood and death are not in Your mouth, ¹⁰For Your will is perfection, || And You do not know vanity, ¹¹Nor does it know You. ¹²And You do not know error, ¹³Neither does it know You. ¹⁴And ignorance appeared like a blind man, || And like the foam of the sea, ¹⁵And they supposed of that vain thing that it was something great; ¹⁶And they, too, came in likeness of it and became vain; And those have understood who have known and meditated; ¹⁷And they have not been corrupt in their imagination, || For such were in the mind of the LORD; ¹⁸And they mocked at them that were walking in error; ¹⁹And they spoke truth from the inspiration which the Most High breathed into them. Praise and great honor to His Name. Hallelujah!

ODE 19

¹A cup of milk was offered to me, || And I drank it in the sweetness of the delight of the LORD. ²The Son is the cup and He who was milked is the Father: ³And the Holy Spirit milked Him, || Because His breasts were full, || And it was necessary for Him that His milk should be sufficiently released; ⁴And the Holy Spirit opened His bosom and mingled the milk from the two breasts of the Father and gave the mixture to the world without their knowing: ⁵And they who receive in its fullness are the ones on the right hand. ⁶The Spirit opened the womb of the virgin and she received conception and brought forth; And the virgin became a mother with many mercies; ⁷And she travailed and brought forth a Son without incurring pain; ⁸And because she was not sufficiently prepared, || And she had not sought a midwife (for He brought her to bear) she brought forth, || As if she were a man, of her own will; ⁹And she brought Him forth openly, || And acquired Him with great dignity, ¹⁰And loved Him in His swaddling clothes and guarded Him kindly, || And showed Him in Majesty. Hallelujah!

ODE 20

¹I am a priest of the LORD, || And to Him I do priestly service: And to Him I offer the sacrifice of His thought. ²For His thought is not like the thought of the world nor the thought of the flesh, || Nor like them that serve carnally. ³The sacrifice of the LORD is righteousness, || And purity of heart and lips. ⁴Present your reins before Him blamelessly, || And do not let your heart do violence to heart, || Nor your soul to soul. ⁵You will not acquire a stranger by the price of your silver, || Neither will you seek to devour your neighbor, ⁶Neither will you deprive him of the covering of his nakedness. ⁷But put on the grace of the LORD without limit; And come into His Paradise and make a garland from its tree; ⁸And put it on your head and be glad; And recline on His rest, || And glory will go before you, ⁹And you will receive of His kindness and of His grace; And you will be flourishing in truth in the praise of His holiness. Praise and honor be to His Name. Hallelujah!

ODE 21

¹I lifted up my arms to the Most High, || Even to the grace of the LORD, || Because He had cast off my bonds from me, || And my Helper had lifted me up to His grace and to His salvation. ²And I put off darkness and clothed myself with light, ³And my soul acquired a body free from sorrow, or affliction, or pains. ⁴And increasingly helpful to me was the thought of the LORD, || And His fellowship in incorruption: ⁵And I was lifted up in His light; And I served before Him, ⁶And I became near to Him, || Praising and confessing Him; ⁷My heart ran over and was found in my mouth, || And it arose on my lips, || And the exultation of the LORD increased on my face, || And His praise likewise. Hallelujah!

ODE 22

¹He who brought Me down from on high, || Also brought Me up from the regions below; ²And He who gathers together the things that are in between is He who also cast Me down; ³He who scattered My enemies and My adversaries had existed from ancient [times]. ⁴He who gave Me authority over bonds that I might loose them, ⁵He that overthrew the dragon with seven heads by My hands, || And set Me over his roots that I might destroy his seed—⁶You were there and helped Me, || And

ODES OF PEACE

in every place Your Name was a rampart to Me. ⁷Your right hand destroyed his wicked poison; And Your hand leveled the way for those who believe in You. ⁸And You chose them from the graves and separated them from the dead. ⁹You took dead bones and covered them with bodies. ¹⁰They were motionless, || And You gave them energy for life. ¹¹Your way and Your face were without corruption; You brought Your world to corruption, || That everything might be dissolved, and then renewed, ¹²And that the foundation for everything might be Your rock: And on it You built Your Kingdom; And it became the dwelling-place of the holy ones. Hallelujah!

ODE 23

¹Joy is of the holy ones! And who will put it on, but they alone? ²Grace is of the chosen ones! And who will receive it except those who trust in it from the beginning? ³Love is of the chosen ones! And who will put it on except those who have possessed it from the beginning? ⁴Walk in the knowledge of the Most High without grudging: To His exultation and to the perfection of His knowledge. ⁵And His thought was like a letter; His will descended from on high, || And it was sent like an arrow which is violently [shot] from the bow: ⁶And many hands rushed to the letter to seize it and to take and read it, ⁷And it escaped their fingers, and they were frightened at it and at the seal that was on it, ⁸Because it was not permitted to them to loose its seal, || For the power that was over the seal was greater than they. ⁹But those who saw it went after the letter that they might know where it would descend, || And who should read it and who should hear it. ¹⁰But a wheel received it and came over it. ¹¹And there was with it a sign of the Kingdom and of the government, ¹²And everything which tried to move the wheel it mowed and cut down. ¹³And it gathered the multitude of adversaries, || And bridged the rivers and crossed over, and rooted up many forests and made a broad path. ¹⁴The head went down to the feet, for the wheel ran down to the feet, || And that which was a sign on it. ¹⁵The letter was one of command, || For there were included in it all districts; ¹⁶And there was seen at its head, || The Head which was revealed— even the Son of Truth from the Most High Father, ¹⁷And He inherited and took possession of everything. And the thought of many was brought to nothing. ¹⁸And all the apostates hastened and fled away. And those who persecuted and were enraged became extinct, ¹⁹And the letter was a great volume, || Which was wholly written by the finger of God: ²⁰And the Name of the Father was on it, and of the Son and of the Holy Spirit, || To rule forever and ever. Hallelujah!

ODE 24

¹The Dove fluttered over the Messiah, || Because He was her head; And she sang over Him and her voice was heard, ²And the inhabitants were afraid, and the sojourners were moved, ³The birds dropped their wings, and all creeping things died in their holes; And the abysses were opened which had been hidden, || And they cried to the LORD like women in travail: ⁴And no food was given to them, || Because it did not belong to them; ⁵And they sealed up the abysses with the seal of the LORD, || And they perished in the thought [of] those that had existed from ancient times, ⁶For they were corrupt from the beginning; And the end of their corruption was life: ⁷And each of them that was imperfect perished, || For it was not possible to give them a word that they might remain, ⁸And the LORD destroyed the imaginations of all them that did not have the truth with them. ⁹For they who were lifted up in their hearts were deficient in wisdom, and so they were rejected, || Because the truth was not with them. ¹⁰For the LORD disclosed His way and spread His grace abroad: And those who understood it know His holiness. Hallelujah!

ODE 25

¹I was rescued from my bonds and to You, my God, I fled, ²For You are the right hand of my salvation and my helper. ³You have restrained those that rise up against me, ⁴And I will see him no longer, || Because Your face was with me, || Which saved me by Your grace. ⁵But I was despised and rejected in the eyes of many, || And I was like lead in their eyes, ⁶And strength was mine from Yourself and [Your] help. ⁷You set a lamp at my right hand and at my left, || And in me there will be nothing that is not bright. ⁸And I was clothed with the covering of Your Spirit, || And You removed my raiment of skin from me; ⁹For Your right hand lifted me up and removed sickness from me, ¹⁰And I became mighty in the truth, || And holy by Your righteousness; And all my adversaries were afraid of me. ¹¹And I became admirable by the Name of the LORD, || And I was justified by His gentleness, || And His rest is forever and ever. Hallelujah!

ODE 26

¹I poured out praise to the LORD, for I am His: ²And I will speak His holy song for my heart is with Him. ³For His harp is in my hands, || And the odes of His rest will not be silent. ⁴I will cry to Him from my whole heart; I will praise and exalt Him with all my members. ⁵For from the east and even to the west is His praise; ⁶And from the south and even to the north is the confession of Him; ⁷And from the top of the hills to their utmost bound is His perfection. ⁸Who can write the psalms of the LORD, || Or who read them? ⁹Or who can train his soul for life that his soul may be saved? ¹⁰Or who can press on the Most High, || So that with His mouth He may speak? ¹¹Who is able to interpret the wonders of the LORD? ¹²For he who could interpret would be dissolved and would become that which is interpreted. ¹³For it suffices to know and to rest, || For in rest the singers stand, ¹⁴Like a river which has an abundant fountain, || And flows to the help of them that seek it. Hallelujah!

ODE 27

¹I stretched out my hands and sanctified my Lord, ²For the extension of my hands is His sign: ³And my expansion is the upright tree [[*or* cross]].

ODE 28

¹As the wings of doves over their nestlings, || And the mouth of their nestlings toward their mouths, ²So are also the wings of the Spirit over my heart. ³My heart is delighted and exults || Like the baby who exults in the womb of his mother. ⁴I believed, therefore I was at rest, || For He in whom I have believed is faithful. ⁵He has richly blessed me, and my head is with Him, || And the sword will not divide me from Him, || Nor the scimitar, ⁶For I am ready before destruction comes; And I have been set on His immortal pinions. ⁷And He showed me His sign: [Poured] forth and given me to drink, || And from that life is the spirit within me and it cannot die, for it lives. ⁸They who saw me marveled at me, || Because I was persecuted, || And they supposed that I was swallowed up, || For I seemed to them as one of the lost; ⁹And my oppression became my salvation; And I was their reprobation because there was no seal in me. ¹⁰I was hated because I did good to every man, ¹¹And they came around me like mad dogs || Who ignorantly attack their masters, ¹²For their thought is corrupt and their understanding perverted. ¹³But I was carrying water in my right hand and their bitterness I endured by my sweetness: ¹⁴And I did not perish, || For I was not their brother nor was my birth like theirs. ¹⁵And they sought for my death and did not find it, || For I was older than the memorial of them; ¹⁶And vainly did they make attack on me, || And those who, without reward, came after me: ¹⁷They sought to destroy the memorial of Him who was before them. ¹⁸For the thought of the Most High cannot be anticipated; And His heart is superior to all wisdom. Hallelujah!

ODE 29

¹The LORD is my hope: In Him I will not be confounded. ²For according to His praise He made me, || And according to His goodness even so He gave to me, ³And according to His mercies He exalted me, || And according to His excellent beauty He set me on high, ⁴And brought me up out of the depths of Sheol, || And from the mouth of death He drew me. ⁵And You laid my enemies low, || And He justified me by His grace. ⁶For I believed in the LORD's Messiah: And it appeared to me that He is the LORD. ⁷And He showed me His sign, || And He led me by His light, || And gave me the rod of His power ⁸That I might subdue the imaginations of the peoples, || And the power of the men of might, to bring them low, ⁹To make war by His word, || And to take victory by His power. ¹⁰And the LORD overthrew my enemy by His word: And he became like the stubble which the wind carries away; ¹¹And I gave praise to the Most High because He exalted me—His servant and the son of His handmaid. Hallelujah!

ODES OF PEACE

ODE 30

¹Fill waters for yourselves from the living fountain of the LORD, || For it is opened to you: ²And come all you thirsty and take the drink; And rest by the fountain of the LORD. ³For it is fair and pure and gives rest to the soul. Its waters are much more pleasant than honey; ⁴And the honeycomb of bees is not to be compared with it. ⁵For it flows forth from the lips of the LORD, || And from the heart of the LORD is its name. ⁶And it came infinitely and invisibly: And until it was set in the midst, they did not know it. ⁷Blessed are they who have drunk from that and have found rest thereby. Hallelujah!

ODE 31

¹The abysses were dissolved before the LORD, || And darkness was destroyed by His appearance. ²Error went astray and perished at His hand, || And folly found no path to walk in, || And was submerged by the truth of the LORD. ³He opened His mouth and spoke grace and joy: And He spoke a new song of praise to His Name. ⁴And He lifted up His voice to the Most High, || And offered the sons that were with Him. ⁵And His face was justified, || For thus His holy Father had given to Him. ⁶Come forth, you that have been afflicted, and receive joy, || And possess your souls by His grace; And take immortal life to yourself. ⁷And they made Me a debtor when I rose up—Me who had been a debtor: And they divided My spoil, || Though nothing was due to them. ⁸But I endured, and held My peace, and was silent as if not moved by them. ⁹But I stood unshaken like a firm rock which is beaten by the waves and endures. ¹⁰And I bore their bitterness for humility's sake, ¹¹In order that I might redeem My people and inherit it, || And that I might not make void My promises || To the fathers to whom I promised the salvation of their seed. Hallelujah!

ODE 32

¹To the blessed there is joy from their hearts, || And light from Him that dwells in them, ²And words from the Truth, who was self-existent; For He is strengthened by the holy power of the Most High: And He is unmoved forever and ever. Hallelujah!

ODE 33

¹Again Grace ran and renounced the corruptor, || And came down on him to bring him to nothing— ²And he who caused destruction [and] perdition from before him, || And devastated all his order. ³And he stood on a lofty summit || And uttered his voice from one end of the earth to the other, ⁴And drew to himself all those who obeyed him, || For he did not appear as [the] evil one. ⁵But there stood a perfect virgin who was proclaiming, and calling, and saying, ⁶"O you sons of men, return! And you daughters of men, come! ⁷And forsake the ways of that corruptor and draw near to me, || And I will enter into you, || And will bring you forth from perdition, ⁸And make yourself wise in the ways of truth, || That you are not destroyed nor perish. ⁹Hear me and be redeemed! For I am telling of the Grace of God among you": And by My means you will be redeemed and become blessed. ¹⁰I am your Judge; And they who have put Me on will not be injured, || But they will possess the new world that is incorruptible. ¹¹My chosen ones walk in Me, || And I will make known My ways to them that seek Me, || And I will make them trust in My Name. Hallelujah!

ODE 34

¹No way is hard where there is a simple heart, ²Nor is there any wound where the thoughts are upright, ³Nor is there any storm in the depth of the illuminated thought. ⁴Where one is surrounded on every side by beauty, || There is nothing that is divided. ⁵The likeness of what is below is that which is above, || For everything is above. What is below is nothing but the imagination of those that are without knowledge. ⁶Grace has been revealed for your salvation. Believe, and live, and be saved. Hallelujah!

ODE 35

¹In quietness He distilled the dew of the LORD on me, ²And He caused the cloud of peace to rise over my head, || Which guarded me continually; ³It was to me for salvation: Everything was shaken, and they were frightened; ⁴And there came forth from them smoke and judgment; And I was keeping quiet in the order of the LORD. ⁵He was more than a shelter to me and more than a foundation. ⁶And I was carried like a child by its mother: And He gave me milk, || The dew of the LORD, ⁷And I grew great by His bounty, || And rested in His perfection, ⁸And I spread out my hands in the lifting up of my soul: And I was made right with the Most High, || And I was redeemed with Him. Hallelujah!

ODE 36

¹I rested in the Spirit of the LORD, || And the Spirit raised Me on high, ²And made Me stand on My feet in the height of the LORD, || Before His perfection and His glory, || While I was praising Him by the composition of His songs. ³The Spirit brought Me forth before the face of the LORD, || And, although [the] Son of Man, || I was [also] named the Illuminate, the Son of God, ⁴While I was praised among the praising ones, || And I was great among the mighty ones. ⁵For according to the greatness of the Most High, || So He made Me; And like His own newness He renewed Me, || And He anointed Me from His own perfection. ⁶And I became one of His neighbors; And My mouth was opened like a cloud of dew, ⁷And my heart poured out as it were a gushing stream of righteousness, ⁸And my access to Him was in peace. And I was established by the Spirit of His government. Hallelujah!

ODE 37

¹I stretched out my hands to my Lord, || And to the Most High I raised my voice: ²And I spoke with the lips of my heart, || And He heard me when my voice reached Him; ³His answer came to me and gave me the fruits of my labors; ⁴And it gave me rest by the grace of the LORD. Hallelujah!

ODE 38

¹I went up to the light of Truth as if into a chariot: ²And the Truth took me and led me, || And carried me across pits and ravines; And from the rocks and the waves He preserved me. ³And He became to me a haven of salvation, || And He set me on the arms of immortal life; ⁴And He went with me and made me rest, || And did not permit me to wander because He was and is the Truth. ⁵And I ran no risk, || Because I walked with Him; ⁶And I did not err in anything because I obeyed the Truth. ⁷For error flees away from Him and does not meet Him, || But the Truth proceeds in the right path. ⁸And whatever I did not know, He made clear to me, || All the poisons of error, || And the plagues of death which they think to be sweetness. ⁹And I saw the destroying of the destroyer, || When the bride who is corrupted is adorned: And the bridegroom who corrupts and is corrupted. ¹⁰And I asked the Truth, "Who are these?" And He said to me, "This is the deceiver and the error: ¹¹And they are alike in the beloved and in his bride; And they lead astray and corrupt the whole world. ¹²And they invite many to the banquet, ¹³And give them to drink of the wine of their intoxication, || And remove their wisdom and knowledge, || And so they make them without intelligence; ¹⁴And then they leave them; And then these go about like madmen corrupting: Seeing that they are without heart, || Nor do they seek for it." ¹⁵And I was made wise so as not to fall into the hands of the deceiver; And I congratulated myself because the Truth went with me, ¹⁶And I was established, and lived, and was redeemed, ¹⁷And my foundations were laid on the hand of the LORD, || Because He established me. ¹⁸For He set the root, and watered it, and fixed it, and blessed it; And its fruits are forever. ¹⁹It struck deep, and sprung up, and spread out, and was full and enlarged. ²⁰And the LORD alone was glorified in His planting and in His farming || By His care and by the blessing of His lips, ²¹By the beautiful planting of His right hand, || And by the discovery of His planting, || And by the thought of His mind. Hallelujah!

ODE 39

¹Great rivers are the power of the LORD: ²And they carry headlong those who despise Him, || And entangle their paths; ³And they sweep away their fords, || And catch their bodies, and destroy their lives. ⁴For they are swifter than lightning and more rapid, || And those who cross them in faith are not moved; ⁵And those who walk on them without blemish will not be afraid. ⁶For the sign in them is the LORD; And the sign is the way of those who cross in the Name of the LORD; ⁷Therefore put on the Name of the Most High, || And know Him and you will cross without danger, || For the rivers will be subject to you. ⁸The LORD has bridged them by His word; And He walked and crossed them on foot: ⁹And His footsteps stand firm on the water, || And are not injured;

ODES OF PEACE

They are as firm as a tree that is truly set up. **¹⁰**And the waves were lifted up on this side and on that, || But the footsteps of our Lord Messiah stand firm, and are not obliterated, and are not defaced. **¹¹**And a way has been appointed for those who cross after Him, and for those who adhere to the course of faith in Him and worship His Name. Hallelujah!

ODE 40

¹As the honey distills from the comb of the bees, **²**And the milk flows from the woman that loves her children; **³**So also is my hope on You, my God. **⁴**As the fountain gushes out its water, **⁵**So my heart gushes out the praise of the LORD, and my lips utter praise to Him, || And my tongue His psalms, **⁶**And my face exults with His gladness, and my spirit exults in His love, and my soul shines in Him. **⁷**And reverence confides in Him, || And redemption stands assured in Him. **⁸**And His inheritance is immortal life, || And those who participate in it are incorruptible. Hallelujah!

ODE 41

¹All the LORD's children will praise Him, || And will collect the truth of His faith. **²**And His children will be known to Him. Therefore, we will sing in His love. **³**We live in the LORD by His grace, || And we receive life in His Messiah. **⁴**For a great day has shined on us: And marvelous is He who has given us of His glory. **⁵**Therefore, let all of us unite together in the Name of the LORD, || And let us honor Him in His goodness, **⁶**And let our faces shine in His light, || And let our hearts meditate in His love by night and by day. **⁷**Let us exult with the joy of the LORD. **⁸**All those that see me will be astonished, || For I am from another race; **⁹**For the Father of truth remembered me—He who possessed me from the beginning. **¹⁰**For His bounty begot me, || And the thought of His heart. **¹¹**And His Word is with us in all our ways— **¹²**The Savior who makes alive and does not reject our souls; **¹³**The Man who was humbled, || And exalted by His own righteousness. **¹⁴**The Son of the Most High appeared in the perfection of His Father, **¹⁵**And light dawned from the Word that was before time in Him. **¹⁶**The Messiah is truly one; And He was known before the foundation of the world, **¹⁷**That He might save souls forever by the truth of His Name: A new song arises from those who love Him. Hallelujah!

ODE 42

¹I stretched out my hands and approached my Lord, **²**For the stretching of my hands is His sign. **³**My expansion is the outspread tree [[or cross]], which was set up on the way of the Righteous One. **⁴**And I became of no account to those who did not take hold of Me and I will be with those who love Me. **⁵**All my persecutors are dead; And they sought after Me who hoped in Me, || Because I was alive. **⁶**And I rose up and am with them; And I will speak by their mouths, **⁷**For they have despised those who persecuted them. **⁸**And I lifted up over them the yoke of My love. **⁹**Like the arm of the bridegroom over the bride, **¹⁰**So was My yoke over those that know Me; **¹¹**And as the couch that is spread in the house of the bridegroom and bride, **¹²**So is My love over those that believe in Me. **¹³**And I was not rejected though I was reckoned to be so. **¹⁴**I did not perish [forever], || Though they devised it against Me. **¹⁵**Sheol saw Me and was made miserable: **¹⁶**Death cast Me up and many along with Me. **¹⁷**I had gall and bitterness, || And I went down with him to the utmost of his depth: **¹⁸**And the feet and the head he let go, || For they were not able to endure My face. **¹⁹**And I made a congregation of living men among his dead men, || And I spoke with them by living lips, **²⁰**Because My word will not be void. **²¹**And those who had died ran toward Me, || And they cried and said, "Son of God, have pity on us, || And do with us according to Your kindness. **²²**And bring us out from the bonds of darkness, || And open to us the door by which we will come out to You. **²³**For we see that our death has not touched You. **²⁴**Let us also be redeemed with You, || For You are our Redeemer." **²⁵**And I heard their voice, || And I sealed My Name on their heads; **²⁶**For they are free men, and they are Mine. Hallelujah!

EXPOSITION OF THE ORACLES OF THE LORD

Presented here is a translation of what remains of a five-volume work by Papias of Hierapolis, who may have had access to eyewitness disciples and those who knew the Apostles of the Lord. It is thought that these volumes were composed sometime around AD 100. Irenaeus says of him: "Now testimony is borne to these things in writing by Papias, an ancient man, who was a hearer of John, and a friend of Polycarp, in the fourth of his books; for five books were composed by him."

FRAGMENT 1

¹But I will not be unwilling to put down, along with my interpretations, **²**whatever instructions I received with care at any time from the elders, **³**and stored up with care in my memory, assuring you at the same time of their truth. **⁴**For I did not, like the multitude, take pleasure in those who spoke much, **⁵**but in those who taught the truth; **⁶**nor in those who related strange commands, **⁷**but in those who rehearsed the commands given by the LORD to faith, and proceeding from truth itself. **⁸**If then, anyone who had attended on the elders came, **⁹**I asked minutely after their sayings—what Andrew or Peter said, or what was said by Philip, or by Thomas, or by James, or by John, or by Matthew, or by any other of the LORD's disciples: **¹⁰**which things Aristion and the elder John, the disciples of the LORD, say. **¹¹**For I imagined that what was to be gotten from scrolls was not so profitable to me as what came from the living and abiding voice.

FRAGMENT 2

¹[The early Christians] called those who practiced a godly guilelessness, "children."

FRAGMENT 3

¹Judas walked about in this world a sad example of impiety; **²**for his body having swollen to such an extent that he could not pass where a chariot could pass easily, **³**he was crushed by the chariot, so that his bowels gushed out.

FRAGMENT 4

¹[The LORD taught]: "The days will come in which vines will grow, having each ten thousand branches, and in each branch ten thousand twigs, and in each true twig ten thousand shoots, **²**and in each of the shoots ten thousand clusters, and on each of the clusters ten thousand grapes, **³**and every grape when pressed will give twenty-five metretes of wine. **⁴**And when any one of the holy ones will lay hold of a cluster, another will cry out, I am a better cluster, take me; bless the LORD through me." **⁵**In like manner, [He said] that "a grain of wheat would produce ten thousand ears, and that every ear would have ten thousand grains, **⁶**and every grain would yield ten pounds of clear, pure, fine flour; **⁷**and that apples, and seeds, and grass would produce in similar proportions; **⁸**and that all animals, feeding then only on the productions of the earth, **⁹**would become peaceable and harmonious, and be in perfect subjection to man." **¹⁰**… "Now these things are credible to believers." **¹¹**And Judas the traitor, not believing, and asking, "How will such growths be accomplished by the LORD?" **¹²**The LORD said, "They will see who will come to them."

FRAGMENT 5

¹As the elders say, then those who are deemed worthy of an abode in Heaven will go there, **²**others will enjoy the delights of Paradise, **³**and others will possess the splendor of the city; **⁴**for everywhere the Savior will be seen, according as they will be worthy who see Him. **⁵**But that there is this distinction between the habitation of those who produce a hundredfold, and that of those who produce sixty-fold, and that of those who produce thirty-fold; ⁶for the first will be taken up into the heavens, the second class will dwell in Paradise, and the last will inhabit the city; ⁷and that on this account the LORD said, "In My Father's house are many rooms." ⁸For all things belong to God, who supplies all with a suitable dwelling-place, ⁹even as His word says, that a share is given to all by the Father, according as each one is or will be worthy. ¹⁰And this is the couch in which they will recline who feast, being invited to the wedding. ¹¹The elders, the disciples of the apostles, say that this is the gradation and arrangement of those who are saved, ¹²and that they advance through steps of this nature; ¹³and that, moreover, they ascend through the Spirit to the Son, and through the Son to the Father; ¹⁴and that in due time the Son will yield up His work to the Father, ¹⁵even as it is said by the apostle, "For He must reign until He has put all enemies under His feet. ¹⁶The last enemy that will be destroyed is death." For in the times of the kingdom the just man who is on the earth will forget to die. ¹⁷"But when He says all things are put under Him, it is manifest that He is excepted which did put all things under Him. ¹⁸And when all things will be subdued to Him, then will the Son also Himself be subject to Him that put all things under Him, that God may be all in all."

FRAGMENT 6

¹And the elder said this. ²Mark having become the interpreter of Peter, wrote down accurately whatever he remembered. ³It was not, however, in exact order that he related the sayings or deeds of Christ. ⁴For he neither heard the LORD nor accompanied Him. ⁵But afterward, as I said, he accompanied Peter, who accommodated his instructions to the necessities [of his hearers], ⁶but with no intention of giving a regular narrative of the LORD's sayings. ⁷For what reason Mark made no mistake in thus writing some things as he remembered them. ⁸For of one thing he took special care, not to omit anything he had heard, and not to put anything fictitious into the statements. ⁹… Matthew put together the oracles [of the LORD] in the Hebrew language, ¹⁰and each one interpreted them as best he could.

FRAGMENT 7

¹To some of them [(messengers)] He gave dominion over the arrangement of the world, and He commissioned them to exercise their dominion well, ²but it happened that their arrangement came to nothing.

APOLOGY OF ARISTIDES

The Apology of Aristides the Philosopher is the earliest complete apologetic still extant. It was written sometime between AD 117 and 138 and set the stage for all Christian apologetics to come. It may have even been the basis for a portion of the Apostles' Creed.

ALL-POWERFUL CAESAR TITUS HADRIANUS ANTONINUS, VENERABLE AND MERCIFUL, FROM MARCIANUS ARISTIDES, AN ATHENIAN PHILOSOPHER:

CHAPTER 1

¹I, O King, by the grace of God came into this world; ²and when I had considered the heavens, and the earth, and the seas, and had surveyed the sun and the rest of creation, ³I marveled at the beauty of the world. ⁴And I perceived that the world and all that is therein are moved by the power of another; ⁵and I understood that He who moves them is God, who is hidden in them, and veiled by them. ⁶And it is manifest that that which causes motion is more powerful than that which is moved. ⁷But that I should make search concerning this same Mover of all, as to what is His nature (for it seems to me, He is indeed unsearchable in His nature), ⁸and that I should argue as to the constancy of His government, so as to grasp it fully—this is a vain effort for me; ⁹for it is not possible that a man should fully comprehend it. ¹⁰I say, however, concerning this Mover of the world, that He is God of all, ¹¹who made all things for the sake of mankind. ¹²And it seems to me that this is reasonable, that one should fear God and should not oppress man. ¹³I say, then, that God is not born, not made, an ever-abiding nature without beginning and without end, immortal, perfect, and incomprehensible. ¹⁴Now when I say that He is "perfect," this means that there is not in Him any defect, ¹⁵and He is not in need of anything but all things are in need of Him. ¹⁶And when I say that He is "without beginning," this means that everything which has beginning has also an end, and that which has an end may be brought to an end. ¹⁷He has no name, for everything which has a name is related to things created. ¹⁸He has no form, nor yet any union of members; for whatever possesses these is related to things fashioned. ¹⁹He is neither male nor female. ²⁰The heavens do not limit Him, but the heavens and all things, visible and invisible, receive their bounds from Him. ²¹He has no adversary, for there exists not any stronger than He. ²²Wrath and indignation He does not possess, for there is nothing which is able to stand against Him. ²³Ignorance and forgetfulness are not in His nature, for He is altogether wisdom and understanding; ²⁴and in Him stands fast all that exists. ²⁵He requires not sacrifice and libation, nor even one of things visible; ²⁶He requires not anything from any, but all living creatures stand in need of Him.

CHAPTER 2

¹Since, then, we have addressed you concerning God, so far as our discourse can bear on Him, ²let us now come to the race of men, that we may know which of them participate in the truth of which we have spoken, and which of them go astray from it. ³This is clear to you, O King, that there are four classes of men in this world: Barbarians and Greeks, Jews and Christians. ⁴The Barbarians, indeed, trace the origin of their kind of religion from Kronos and from Rhea and their other gods; ⁵the Greeks, however, from Helenos, who is said to be sprung from Zeus. ⁶And by Helenos there were born Aiolos and Xuthos; ⁷and there were others descended from Inachos and Phoroneus, ⁸and lastly from the Egyptian Danaos and from Kadmos and from Dionysos. ⁹The Jews, again, trace the origin of their race from Abraham, who begot Isaac, of whom was born Jacob. ¹⁰And he begot twelve sons who migrated from Syria to Egypt; ¹¹and there they were called the nation of the Hebrews, by him who made their laws; ¹²and at length they were named Jews. ¹³The Christians, then, trace the beginning of their religion from Jesus the Messiah; ¹⁴and He is named the Son of God Most High. ¹⁵And it is said that God came down from Heaven, ¹⁶and from a Hebrew virgin assumed and clothed Himself with flesh; ¹⁷and the Son of God lived in a daughter of man. ¹⁸This is taught in the Gospel, as it is called, which a short time was preached among them; ¹⁹and you also if you will read therein, may perceive the power which belongs to it. ²⁰This Jesus, then, was born of the race of the Hebrews; ²¹and He had twelve disciples in order that the purpose of His incarnation might in time be accomplished. ²²But He Himself was pierced by the Jews, and He died and was buried; ²³and they say that after three days He rose and [later] ascended to Heaven. ²⁴Thereon these twelve disciples went forth throughout the known parts of the world and kept showing His greatness with all modesty and uprightness. ²⁵And hence also those of the present day who believe that preaching are called Christians, and they have become famous. ²⁶So then there are, as I said above, four classes of men: Barbarians and Greeks, Jews and Christians. ²⁷Moreover the wind is obedient to God, and fire to the messengers; the waters also to the demons and the earth to the sons of men.

CHAPTER 3

¹Let us begin, then, with the Barbarians, and go on to the rest of the nations one after another, ²that we may see which of them hold the truth as to God and which of them hold error. ³The Barbarians, then, as they did not apprehend God, went astray among the elements, ⁴and began to worship things created instead of their Creator; ⁵and for this end they made images and shut them up in shrines, and behold, they worship them, ⁶guarding them the while with much care, lest their gods be stolen by robbers. ⁷And the Barbarians did not observe that that which acts as guard is greater than that which is guarded, ⁸and that everyone who creates is greater than that which is created. ⁹If it be, then, that their gods are too feeble to see to their own safety, how will they take thought for the safety of men? ¹⁰Great then is the error into which the Barbarians wandered in worshiping lifeless images which can do nothing to help them. ¹¹And I am led to wonder, O King, at their philosophers, how that even they went astray, and gave the name of gods to images which were made in honor of the elements; ¹²and that their sages did not perceive that the elements are also dissoluble and perishable. ¹³For if a small part of an element is dissolved or destroyed, the whole of it may be dissolved and destroyed. ¹⁴If then the elements themselves are dissolved and destroyed and forced to be subject to another that is more stubborn than they, ¹⁵and if they are not in their nature gods, why, indeed, do they call the images which are made in their honor, God? ¹⁶Great, then, is the error which the philosophers among them have brought on their followers.

CHAPTER 4

¹Let us turn now, O King, to the elements in themselves, ²that we may make clear in regard to them, that they are not gods, but a created thing, liable to ruin and change, which is of the same nature as man; ³whereas God is imperishable and unvarying, and invisible, while yet He sees, and overrules, and transforms all things. ⁴Those then who believe concerning the earth that it is a god have until now deceived themselves, ⁵since it is furrowed and set with plants and trenched; ⁶and it takes in the filthy refuse of men and beasts and cattle. ⁷And at times it becomes unfruitful, for if it be burned to ashes it becomes devoid of life, ⁸for nothing germinates from an earthen jar. ⁹And besides if water be collected on it, it is dissolved together with its products. ¹⁰And behold, it is trodden under foot of men and beast, and receives the blood of the slain; ¹¹and it is dug open, and filled with the dead, and becomes a tomb for corpses. ¹²But it is impossible that a nature, which is holy and worthy and blessed and immortal, should allow of any one of these things. ¹³And hence it appears to us that the earth is not a god but a creation of God.

CHAPTER 5

¹In the same way, again, those erred who believed the waters to be gods. ²For the waters were created for the use of man, and are put under his rule in many ways. ³For they suffer change and admit impurity, and are destroyed and lose their nature while they are boiled into many substances. ⁴And they take colors which do not belong to them; ⁵they are also congealed by frost and are mingled and permeated with the filth of men and beasts, and with the blood of the slain. ⁶And being checked by skilled workmen through the restraint of aqueducts, they flow and are diverted against their inclination, ⁷and come into gardens and other places in order that they may be collected and issue forth as a means of fertility for man, ⁸and that they may cleanse away every impurity and fulfill the service man requires from them. ⁹For what reason it is impossible that the waters should be a god, but they are a work of God and a part of the world. ¹⁰In like manner also they who believed that fire is a god erred to no slight extent. ¹¹For it, too, was created for the service of men, and is subject to them in many ways: in the preparation of meats, and as a means of casting metals, and for other ends of which your Majesty is aware. ¹²At the same time it is quenched and extinguished in many ways. ¹³Again they also erred who believed the motion of the winds to be a god. ¹⁴For it is well known to us that those winds are under the dominion of another, ¹⁵at times their motion increases, and at times it fails and ceases at the command of Him who controls them. ¹⁶For they were created by God for the sake of men, in order to supply the necessity of trees and fruits and seeds; ¹⁷and to bring over the sea ships which transport for men necessities and goods from places where they are found to places where they are not found; ¹⁸and to govern the quarters of the world. ¹⁹And as for itself, at times it increases and again abates; ²⁰and in one place brings help and in another causes disaster at the bidding of Him who rules it. ²¹And mankind is also able by known means to confine and keep it in check in order that it may fulfill for them the service they require from it. ²²And of itself it does not have any authority at all. ²³And hence it is impossible that the winds should be called gods, but rather a thing made by God.

CHAPTER 6

¹So also, they erred who believed that the sun is a god. ²For we see that it is moved by the compulsion of another, and revolves and makes its journey, ³and proceeds from sign to sign, rising and setting every day, so as to give warmth for the growth of plants and trees, ⁴and to bring forth into the air with which it [(sunlight)] is mingled every growing thing which is on the earth. ⁵And to it there belongs by comparison a part in common with the rest of the stars in its course; ⁶and though it is one in its nature it is associated with many parts for the supply of the needs of men; ⁷and that not according to its own will but rather according to the will of Him who rules it. ⁸And hence it is impossible that the sun should be a god, but the work of God; ⁹and in like manner also the moon and the stars.

CHAPTER 7

¹And those who believed of the men of the past, that some of them were gods, they too were much mistaken. ²For as you yourself allow, O King, man is constituted of the four elements, and of a soul and a spirit (and hence he is called a microcosm), ³and without any one of these parts he could not consist. ⁴He has a beginning and an end, and he is born and dies. ⁵But God, as I said, has none of these things in His nature, but is uncreated and imperishable. ⁶And hence it is not possible that we should set up man to be of the nature of God— ⁷man, to whom at times when he looks for joy, there comes trouble, and when he looks for laughter there comes to him weeping, ⁸who is wrathful and covetous and envious, with other defects as well. ⁹And he is destroyed in many ways by the elements and also by the animals. ¹⁰And hence, O King, we are bound to recognize the error of the Barbarians, ¹¹that thereby, since they did not find traces of the true God, they fell aside from the truth, and went after the desire of their imagination, ¹²serving the perishable elements and lifeless images, and through their error not apprehending what the true God is.

CHAPTER 8

¹Let us turn further to the Greeks also, that we may know what opinion they hold as to the true God. ²The Greeks, then, because they are more subtle than the Barbarians, have gone further astray than the Barbarians; ³inasmuch as they have introduced many fictitious gods, and have set up some of them as males and some as females; ⁴and in that some of their gods were found who were adulterers, and did murder, and were deluded, and envious, and wrathful and passionate, and parricides, and thieves, and robbers. ⁵And some of them, they say, were crippled and limped, and some were sorcerers, and some actually went mad, and some played on lyres, and some were given to roaming on the hills, and some even died, and some were struck dead by lightning, and some were made servants even to men, and some escaped by flight, and some were kidnapped by men, and some, indeed, were lamented and deplored by men. ⁶And some, they say, went down to Sheol, and some were grievously wounded, and some transformed themselves into the likeness of animals to seduce the race of mortal women, and some polluted themselves by lying with males. ⁷And some, they say, were wedded to their mothers and their sisters and their daughters. ⁸And they say of their gods that they committed adultery with the daughters of men; ⁹and of these there was born a certain race which also was mortal. ¹⁰And they say that some of the females disputed about beauty and appeared before men for judgment. ¹¹Thus, O King, have the Greeks put forward foulness, and absurdity, and folly about their gods and

about themselves, in that they have called those that are of such a nature gods, who are not gods. ¹²And hence mankind has received incitements to commit adultery and fornication, and to steal and to practice all that is offensive and hated and abhorred. ¹³For if they who are called their gods practiced all these things which are written above, how much more should men practice them— ¹⁴men, who believe that their gods themselves practiced them. ¹⁵And owing to the foulness of this error there have happened to mankind harassing wars, and great famines, and bitter captivity, and complete desolation. ¹⁶And behold, it was by reason of this alone that they suffered and that all these things came on them; ¹⁷and while they endured those things they did not perceive in their mind that for their error those things came on them.

CHAPTER 9

¹Let us proceed further to their account of their gods that we may carefully demonstrate all that is said above. ²First of all, the Greeks bring forward as a god Kronos, that is to say Chiun [(Saturn)]. ³And his worshipers sacrifice their children to him, and they burn some of them alive in his honor. ⁴And they say that he took to himself among his wives Rhea, and begot many children by her. ⁵By her too he begot Dios, who is called Zeus. ⁶And at length he [(Kronos)] went mad, and through fear of an oracle that had been made known to him, he began to devour his sons. ⁷And from him Zeus was stolen away without his knowledge; ⁸and at length Zeus bound him, and mutilated the signs of his manhood, and flung them into the sea. ⁹And hence, as they say in a fable, there was engendered Aphrodite, who is called Astarte. ¹⁰And he [(Zeus)] cast out Kronos bound into darkness. ¹¹Great then is the error and ignominy which the Greeks have brought forward about the first of their gods, ¹²in that they have said all this about him, O King. ¹³It is impossible that a god should be bound or mutilated; and if it be otherwise, he is indeed miserable. ¹⁴And after Kronos they bring forward another god Zeus. ¹⁵And they say of him that he assumed the sovereignty and was king over all the gods. ¹⁶And they say that he changed himself into a beast and other shapes in order to seduce mortal women, and to raise up by them children for himself. ¹⁷Once, they say, he changed himself into a bull through love of Europe and Pasiphae. ¹⁸And again he changed himself into the likeness of gold through love of Danae, and to a swan through love of Leda, and to a man through love of Antiope, and to lightning through love of Luna, ¹⁹and so by these he begot many children. ²⁰For by Antiope, they say, that he begot Zethus and Amphion, and by Luna Dionysos, by Alcmena Hercules, ²¹and by Leto, Apollo and Artemis, and by Danae Perseus, and by Leda, Castor and Polydeuces, and Helene and Paludus, ²²and by Mnemosyne he begot nine daughters whom they styled the Muses, ²³and by Europe, Minos and Rhadamanthos and Sarpedon. ²⁴And lastly, he changed himself into the likeness of an eagle through his passion for Ganydemos [(Ganymede)] the shepherd. ²⁵By reason of these tales, O King, much evil has arisen among men, who to this day are imitators of their gods, ²⁶and practice adultery and defile themselves with their mothers and their sisters, ²⁷and by lying with males, ²⁸and some make bold to slay even their parents. ²⁹For if he who is said to be the chief and king of their gods does these things, how much more should his worshipers imitate him? ³⁰And great is the folly which the Greeks have brought forward in their narrative concerning him. ³¹For it is impossible that a god should practice adultery or fornication or come near to lie with males or kill his parents; ³²and if it be otherwise, he is much worse than a destructive demon.

CHAPTER 10

¹Again they bring forward as another god Hephaistos. ²And they say of him, that he is lame, and a cap is set on his head, and he holds in his hands firetongs and a hammer; ³and he follows the craft of iron working, that thereby he may procure the necessities of his livelihood. ⁴Is then this god so very needy? ⁵But it cannot be that a god should be needy or lame, else he is very worthless. ⁶And further they bring in another god and call him Hermes. ⁷And they say that he is a thief, a lover of wealth, and greedy for gain, and a magician, and mutilated, and an athlete, and an interpreter of language. ⁸But it is impossible that a god should be a magician, or greedy, or maimed, or craving for what is not his, or an athlete. ⁹And if it be otherwise, he is found to be useless. ¹⁰And after him they bring forward as another god Asclepius. ¹¹And they say that he is a physician and prepares drugs and plaster that he may supply the necessities of his livelihood. ¹²Is then this god in want? ¹³And at length he was struck with lightning by Dios on account of Tyndareos of Lacedaemon, and so he died. ¹⁴If then Asclepius were a god, and, when he was struck with lightning, was unable to help himself, how should he be able to give help to others? ¹⁵But that a divine nature should be in want or be destroyed by lightning is impossible. ¹⁶And again they bring forward another as a god, and they call him Ares. ¹⁷And they say that he is a warrior, and jealous, and covets sheep and things which are not his. ¹⁸And he makes gain by his arms. ¹⁹And they say that at length he committed adultery with Aphrodite, and was caught by the little boy Eros and by Hephaistos the husband of Aphrodite. ²⁰But it is impossible that a god should be a warrior or bound or an adulterer. ²¹And again they say of Dionysos that he, indeed, is a god, who arranges carousals by night, and teaches drunkenness, and carries off women who do not belong to him. ²²And at length, they say, he went mad and dismissed his handmaidens and fled into the desert; and during his madness he ate serpents. ²³And at last he was killed by Titanos. ²⁴If then Dionysos were a god, and when he was being killed was unable to help himself, how is it possible that he should help others? ²⁵Herakles next they bring forward and say that he is a god, who hates detestable things, a tyrant, and warrior and a destroyer of plagues. ²⁶And of him also they say that at length he became mad and killed his own children, and cast himself into a fire and died. ²⁷If then Herakles is a god, and in all these calamities was unable to rescue himself, how should others ask help from him? ²⁸But it is impossible that a god should be mad, or drunken, or a slayer of his children, or consumed by fire.

CHAPTER 11

¹And after him they bring forward another god and call him Apollo. ²And they say that he is jealous and inconstant, and at times he holds the bow and quiver, and again the lyre and plectron. ³And he utters oracles for men that he may receive rewards from them. ⁴Is then this god in need of rewards? ⁵But it is an insult that all these things should be found with a god. ⁶And after him they bring forward as a goddess Artemis, the sister of Apollo; ⁷and they say that she was a huntress and that she herself used to carry a bow and bolts, and to roam about on the mountains, leading the hounds to hunt stags or wild bears of the field. ⁸But it is disgraceful that a virgin maid should roam alone on the hills or hunt in the chase for animals. ⁹For what reason it is impossible that Artemis should be a goddess. ¹⁰Again they say of Aphrodite that she indeed is a goddess. ¹¹And at times she dwells with their gods, but at other times she is a neighbor to men. ¹²And once she had Ares as a lover, and again Adonis who is Tammuz. ¹³Once also, Aphrodite was wailing and weeping for the death of Tammuz, and they say that she went down to Sheol that she might redeem Adonis from Persephone, who is the daughter of Sheol [(Hades)]. ¹⁴If then Aphrodite is a goddess and was unable to help her lover at his death, how will she find it possible to help others? ¹⁵And this cannot be listened to, that a divine nature should come to weeping and wailing and adultery. ¹⁶And again they say of Tammuz that he is a god. ¹⁷And he is, indeed, a hunter and an adulterer. ¹⁸And they say that he was killed by a wound from a wild boar, without being able to help himself. ¹⁹And if he could not help himself, how can he take thought for the human race? ²⁰But that a god should be an adulterer or a hunter or should die by violence is impossible. ²¹Again they say of Rhea that she is the mother of their gods. ²²And they say that she had once a lover Atys, and that she used to delight in depraved men. ²³And at last she raised a lamentation and mourned for Atys her lover. ²⁴If then the mother of their gods was unable to help her lover and deliver him from death, how can she help others? ²⁵So it is disgraceful that a goddess should lament and weep and take delight in depraved men. ²⁶Again they introduce Kore and say that she is a goddess, and she was stolen away by Pluto, and could not help herself. ²⁷If then she is a goddess and was unable to help herself how will she find means to help others? ²⁸For a god who is stolen away is very powerless. ²⁹All this,

then, O King, have the Greeks brought forward concerning their gods, ³⁰and they have invented and declared it concerning them. ³¹And hence all men received an impulse to work all profanity and all defilements; and hereby the whole earth was corrupted.

CHAPTER 12

¹The Egyptians, moreover, because they are more base and stupid than every people that is on the earth, have themselves erred more than all. ²For the deities [[or religion]] of the Barbarians and the Greeks did not suffice for them, but they introduced some also of the nature of the animals, and said thereof that they were gods, ³and likewise of creeping things which are found on the dry land and in the waters. ⁴And of plants and herbs they said that some of them were gods. ⁵And they were corrupted by every kind of delusion and defilement more than every people that is on the earth. ⁶For from ancient times they worshiped Isis, and they say that she is a goddess whose husband was Osiris her brother. ⁷And when Osiris was killed by Typhon his brother, Isis fled with Horos her son to Byblos in Syria, and was there for a certain time until her son was grown. ⁸And he contended with Typhon his uncle, and killed him. ⁹And then Isis returned and went around with Horos her son and sought for the dead body of Osiris her lord, bitterly lamenting his death. ¹⁰If then Isis be a goddess, and could not help Osiris her brother and lord, how can she help another? ¹¹But it is impossible that a divine nature should be afraid, and flee for safety, or should weep and wail; or else it is very miserable. ¹²And of Osiris also they say that he is a serviceable god. ¹³And he was killed by Typhon and was unable to help himself. ¹⁴But it is well known that this cannot be asserted of divinity. ¹⁵And further, they say of his brother Typhon that he is a god, who killed his brother and was killed by his brother's son and by his bride, being unable to help himself. ¹⁶And how, pray, is he a god who does not save himself? ¹⁷As the Egyptians, then, were more stupid than the rest of the nations, these and such like gods did not suffice for them. ¹⁸No, but they even apply the name of gods to animals in which there is no soul at all. ¹⁹For some of them worship the sheep and others the calf; ²⁰and some the pig and others the shad fish; ²¹and some the crocodile, and the hawk, and the fish, and the ibis, and the vulture, and the eagle, and the raven. ²²Some of them worship the cat, and others the turbot-fish, some the dog, some the adder, and some the asp, and others the lion; ²³and others the garlic, and onions, and thorns, ²⁴and others the tiger and other such things. ²⁵And the poor creatures do not see that all these things are nothing, ²⁶although they daily witness their gods being eaten and consumed by men and also by their fellows; ²⁷while some of them are cremated, and some die and decay and become dust, without their observing that they perish in many ways. ²⁸So the Egyptians have not observed that such things which are not equal to their own deliverance, are not gods. ²⁹And if, indeed, they are weak in the case of their own deliverance, from where have they power to help in the case of deliverance of their worshipers? ³⁰Great then is the error into which the Egyptians wandered—greater, indeed, than that of any people which is on the face of the earth.

CHAPTER 13

¹But it is a marvel, O King, with regard to the Greeks, who surpass all other peoples in their manner of life and reasoning, how they have gone astray after dead idols and lifeless images. ²And yet they see their gods in the hands of their craftsmen being sawn out, and planed and docked, and hacked short, and charred, and ornamented, and being altered by them in every kind of way. ³And when they grow old, and are worn away through lapse of time, and when they are molten and crushed to powder, how, I wonder, did they not perceive concerning them, that they are not gods? ⁴And as for those who did not find deliverance for themselves, how can they serve the distress of men? ⁵But even the writers and philosophers among them have wrongly alleged that the gods are such as are made in honor of God Almighty. ⁶And they err in seeking to liken [them] to God whom man has not at any time seen nor can see to what He is like. ⁷Herein too [they err] in asserting of deity that any such thing as deficiency can be present to it; ⁸as when they say that He receives sacrifice and requires burnt-offering and libation and immolations of men, and temples. ⁹But God is not in need, and none of these things is necessary to Him; ¹⁰and it is clear that men err in these things they imagine. ¹¹Further their writers and their philosophers represent and declare that the nature of all their gods is one. ¹²And they have not apprehended God our Lord who while He is one, is in all. They err therefore. ¹³For if the body of a man while it is many in its parts is not in dread, one member of another, but, since it is a united body, wholly agrees with itself; even so also God is one in His nature. ¹⁴A single essence is proper to Him, since He is uniform in His nature and His essence; ¹⁵and He is not afraid of Himself. ¹⁶If then the nature of the gods is one, it is not proper that a god should either pursue or slay or harm a god. ¹⁷If then gods be pursued and wounded by gods, and some be kidnapped, and some struck dead by lightning, it is obvious that the nature of their gods is not one. ¹⁸And hence it is known, O King, that it is a mistake when they reckon and bring the natures of their gods under a single nature. ¹⁹If then it becomes us to admire a god which is seen and does not see, ²⁰how much more praiseworthy is it that one should believe in a nature which is invisible and all-seeing? ²¹And if further it is fitting that one should approve the handiworks of a craftsman, how much more is it fitting that one should glorify the Creator of the craftsman? ²²For behold, when the Greeks made laws, they did not perceive that by their laws they condemn their gods. ²³For if their laws are righteous, their gods are unrighteous, since they transgressed the law in killing one another, and practicing sorcery, and committing adultery, and in robbing and stealing, and in lying with males, and by their other practices as well. ²⁴For if their gods were right in doing all these things as they are described, then the laws of the Greeks are unrighteous in not being made according to the will of their gods. ²⁵And in that case the whole world is gone astray. ²⁶For the narratives about their gods are some of them myths, and some of them nature-poems, and some of them hymns and elegies. ²⁷The hymns indeed and elegies are empty words and noise. ²⁸But these nature-poems, even if they are made as they say, still those are not gods who do such things and suffer and endure such things. ²⁹And those myths are shallow tales with no depth whatever in them.

CHAPTER 14

¹Let us come now, O King, to the history of the Jews also, and see what opinion they have as to God. ²The Jews then say that God is one, the Creator of all, and omnipotent; ³and that it is not right that any other should be worshiped except this God alone. ⁴And herein they appear to approach the truth more than all the nations, especially in that they worship God and not His works. ⁵And they imitate God by the philanthropy which prevails among them; ⁶for they have compassion on the poor, and they release the captives, and bury the dead, and do such things as these, which are acceptable before God and well-pleasing also to men, ⁷which they have received from their forefathers. ⁸Nevertheless, they too erred from true knowledge. ⁹And in their imagination, they conceive that it is God they serve; ¹⁰whereas by their mode of observance it is to the messengers and not to God that their service is rendered— ¹¹as when they celebrate Sabbaths and the beginning of the months, and feasts of unleavened bread, and a great fast; ¹²and fasting, and circumcision, and the purification of meats, which things, however, they do not observe perfectly.

CHAPTER 15

¹But the Christians, O King, while they went around and made search, have found the truth; ²and as we learned from their writings, they have come nearer to truth and genuine knowledge than the rest of the nations. ³For they know and trust in God, the Creator of Heaven and of earth, in whom and from whom are all things, to whom there is no other god as companion, ⁴from whom they received commands which they engraved on their minds and observe in hope and expectation of the world which is to come. ⁵For what reason they do not commit adultery nor fornication, nor bear false witness, nor embezzle what is held in pledge, nor covet what is not theirs. ⁶They honor father and mother, and show kindness to those near to them; and whenever they are judges, they judge uprightly. ⁷They do not worship idols in the image of man; ⁸and whatever they would

not that others should do to them, they do not do to others; ⁹and of the food which is consecrated to idols they do not eat, for they are pure. ¹⁰And their oppressors they comfort and make them their friends; they do good to their enemies; ¹¹and their women, O King, are pure as virgins, and their daughters are modest; ¹²and their men keep themselves from every unlawful union and from all uncleanness, in the hope of a reward to come in the other world. ¹³Further, if one or other of them have bondmen and bondwomen, or children, through love toward them they persuade them to become Christians, ¹⁴and when they have done so, they call them brothers without distinction. ¹⁵They do not worship strange gods, and they go their way in all modesty and cheerfulness. ¹⁶Falsehood is not found among them; and they love one another, and from widows they do not turn away their esteem; ¹⁷and they deliver the orphan from him who treats him harshly. ¹⁸And he who has, gives to him who does not have, without boasting. ¹⁹And when they see a stranger, they take him into their homes and rejoice over him as a very brother; ²⁰for they do not call them brothers after the flesh, but brothers after the spirit and in God. ²¹And whenever one of their poor passes from the world, each one of them according to his ability gives heed to him and carefully sees to his burial. ²²And if they hear that one of their number is imprisoned or afflicted on account of the name of their Messiah, all of them anxiously minister to his necessity, and if it is possible to redeem him they set him free. ²³And if there is among them any that is poor and needy, and if they have no spare food, they fast two or three days in order to supply to the needy their lack of food. ²⁴They observe the precepts of their Messiah with much care, living justly and soberly as the LORD their God commanded them. ²⁵Every morning and every hour they give thanks and praise to God for His loving-kindnesses toward them; ²⁶and for their food and their drink they offer thanksgiving to Him. ²⁷And if any righteous man among them passes from the world, they rejoice and offer thanks to God; and they escort his body as if he were setting out from one place to another near. ²⁸And when a child has been born to one of them, they give thanks to God; ²⁹and if moreover it happens to die in childhood, they give thanks to God the more, as for one who has passed through the world without sins. ³⁰And further if they see that any one of them dies in his ungodliness or in his sins, for him they grieve bitterly, and sorrow as for one who goes to meet his doom.

CHAPTER 16

¹Such, O King, is the command of the law of the Christians, and such is their manner of life. ²As men who know God, they ask from Him petitions which are fitting for Him to grant and for them to receive. ³And thus they employ their whole lifetime. ⁴And since they know the loving-kindnesses of God toward them, behold, for their sake the glorious things which are in the world flow forth to view. ⁵And truly, they are those who found the truth when they went around and made search for it; ⁶and from what we considered, we learned that they alone come near to a knowledge of the truth. ⁷And they do not proclaim in the ears of the multitude the kind deeds they do, but are careful that no one should notice them; ⁸and they conceal their giving just as he who finds a treasure and conceals it. ⁹And they strive to be righteous as those who expect to behold their Messiah, and to receive from Him with great glory the promises made concerning them. ¹⁰And as for their words and their precepts, O King, and their glorying in their worship, and the hope of earning according to the work of each one of them their reward which they look for in another world, you may learn about these from their writings. ¹¹It is enough for us to have shortly informed your Majesty concerning the conduct and the truth of the Christians. ¹²For great indeed, and wonderful, is their doctrine to him who will search into it and reflect on it. ¹³And truly, this is a new people, and there is a divine admixture in the midst of them. ¹⁴Take, then, their writings, and read therein, and behold, you will find that I have not put forth these things on my own authority, nor spoken thus as their advocate; ¹⁵but since I read in their writings I was fully assured of these things as also of things which are to come. ¹⁶And for this reason I was constrained to declare the truth to such as care for it and seek the world to come. ¹⁷And to me there is no doubt but that the earth abides through the supplication of the Christians. ¹⁸But the rest of the nations err and cause error in wallowing before the elements of the world, since beyond these their mental vision will not pass. ¹⁹And they search about as if in darkness because they will not recognize the truth; ²⁰and like drunken men they reel and jostle one another and fall.

CHAPTER 17

¹Thus far, O King, I have spoken; ²for concerning that which remains, as is said above, there are found in their other writings things which are hard to utter and difficult for one to narrate, ³which are not only spoken in words but also worked out in deeds. ⁴Now the Greeks, O King, as they follow base practices in intercourse with males, and a mother and a sister and a daughter, impute their monstrous impurity in turn to the Christians. ⁵But the Christians are just and good, and the truth is set before their eyes, and their spirit is long-suffering; ⁶and, therefore, though they know the error of these [(the Greeks)], and are persecuted by them, they bear and endure it; ⁷and for the most part they have compassion on them, as men who are destitute of knowledge. ⁸And on their side, they offer prayer that these may convert from their error; ⁹and when it happens that one of them has converted, he is ashamed before the Christians of the works which were done by him; ¹⁰and he makes confession to God, saying, "I did these things in ignorance." ¹¹And he purifies his heart, and his sins are forgiven him, ¹²because he committed them in ignorance in the former time, when he used to blaspheme and speak evil of the true knowledge of the Christians. ¹³And assuredly the race of the Christians is more blessed than all the men who are on the face of the earth. ¹⁴From now on let the tongues of those who utter vanity and harass the Christians be silent; ¹⁵and hereafter let them speak the truth. ¹⁶For it is of serious consequence to them that they should worship the true God rather than worship a senseless sound. ¹⁷And truly whatever is spoken in the mouth of the Christians is of God; and their doctrine is the gateway of light. ¹⁸For what reason let all who are without the knowledge of God draw near to that; ¹⁹and they will receive incorruptible words, which are from all time and forever. ²⁰So they will appear before the awful judgment which through Jesus the Messiah is destined to come on the whole human race.

APOLOGY FOR CHRISTIANITY

This very brief fragment is all that remains of an apologetic discourse by Quadratus, who, like Aristides, addressed Hadrian, and was thus penned mere decades after John's Revelation.

FRAGMENT 1

¹But the works of our Savior were always present, for they were genuine: ²those that were healed, and those that were raised from the dead, who were seen not only when they were healed and when they were raised, but were also always present; ³and not merely while the Savior was on earth, but also after His death, they were alive for quite a while, so that some of them lived even to our day.

INFANCY GOSPEL OF JAMES

Ascribed to James, the half-brother of Jesus, this likely pseudepigraphic text was probably written in the early- or mid-2nd century. This may be the oldest infancy gospel ever written.

CHAPTER 1

¹In the records of the twelve tribes of Israel was Joachim, an exceedingly rich man; and he brought his offerings double, saying, "There will be from my surplus to all the people, and there will be the offering for my forgiveness to the LORD for a propitiation for me." ²For the great day of the LORD was at hand, and the sons of Israel were bringing their offerings. And there stood near him Rubim, saying, "It is not fitting for you first to bring your offerings, because you have not made seed in Israel." ³And Joachim was exceedingly grieved and went away to the registers of the twelve tribes of the people, saying, "I will see the registers of the twelve tribes of Israel, as to whether I alone have not made seed in Israel. ⁴And he searched and found that all the righteous had raised up seed in Israel. ⁵And he called to mind the patriarch Abraham, that in the last day God gave him a son [named] Isaac. ⁶And Joachim was exceedingly grieved and did not come into the presence of his wife, ⁷but he retired to the desert, and there pitched his tent, and fasted forty days and forty nights, saying in himself: "I will not go down either for food or for drink until the LORD my God will look on me, and prayer will be my food and drink."

CHAPTER 2

¹And his wife Anna mourned in two mournings, and lamented in two lamentations, saying, "I will lament my widowhood; I will lament my childlessness." ²And the great day of the LORD was at hand; and her maidservant Judith said, "How long do you humiliate your soul? Behold, the great day of the LORD is at hand, and it is unlawful for you to mourn. ³But take this headband, which the woman that made it gave to me; for it is not proper that I should wear it, because I am a maidservant, and it has a royal appearance." ⁴And Anna said, "Depart from me, for I have not done such things, and the LORD has brought me very low. ⁵I fear that some wicked person has given it to you, and you have come to make me a sharer in your sin." ⁶And Judith said, "Why should I curse you, seeing that the LORD has shut your womb, so as not to give you fruit in Israel?" ⁷And Anna was exceedingly grieved, and took off her garments of mourning, and cleaned her head, and put on her wedding garments, and about the ninth hour, she went down to the garden to walk. ⁸And she saw a laurel, and sat under it, and prayed to the LORD, saying, "O God of our fathers, bless me and hear my prayer, as You blessed the womb of Sarah, and gave her a son—Isaac."

CHAPTER 3

¹And gazing toward the sky, she saw a sparrow's nest in the laurel, and made a lamentation in herself, saying, "Aah! Who begot me? And what womb produced me? ²Because I have become a curse in the presence of the sons of Israel, and I have been reproached, and they have driven me in derision out of the temple of the LORD. ³Aah! To what have I been likened? I am not like the birds of the sky, because even the birds of the sky are productive before You, O LORD. ⁴Aah! To what have I been likened? I am not like the beasts of the earth, because even the beasts of the earth are productive before You, O LORD. ⁵Aah! To what have I been likened? I am not like these waters, because even these waters are productive before You, O LORD. ⁶Aah! To what have I been likened? I am not like this earth, because even the earth brings forth its fruits in season and blesses You, O LORD."

CHAPTER 4

¹And behold, a messenger of the LORD stood by, saying, "Anna, Anna, the LORD has heard your prayer, and you will conceive and will bring forth; and your seed will be spoken of in all the world." ²And Anna said, "As the LORD my God lives, if I beget either male or female, I will bring it as a gift to the LORD my God; and it will minister to Him in holy things all the days of its life." ³And behold, two messengers came, saying to her: "Behold, your husband Joachim is coming with his flocks." ⁴For a messenger of the LORD went down to him, saying, "Joachim, Joachim, the LORD God has heard your prayer. Go down from here; for behold, your wife Anna will conceive." ⁵And Joachim went down and called his shepherds, saying, "Bring me here ten she-lambs without spot or blemish, and they will be for the LORD my God; and bring me twelve tender calves, and they will be for the priests and the elders; and one hundred goats for all the people." ⁶And behold, Joachim came with his flocks; and Anna stood by the gate, and saw Joachim coming, and she ran and hung on his neck, saying, "Now I know that the LORD God has blessed me exceedingly; for behold, the widow [is] no longer a widow, and I the childless will conceive." ⁷And Joachim rested the first day in his house.

CHAPTER 5

¹And on the following day he brought his offerings, saying in himself: "If the LORD God has been rendered gracious to me, the plate on the priest's forehead will make it manifest to me." ²And Joachim brought his offerings and observed attentively the priest's plate when he went up to the altar of the LORD, and he saw no sin in himself. ³And Joachim said, "Now I know that the LORD has been gracious to me and has remitted all my sins." ⁴And he went down from the temple of the LORD justified and departed to his own house. ⁵And her months were fulfilled, and in the ninth month Anna brought forth. ⁶And she said to the midwife: "What have I brought forth?" And she said, "A girl." And Anna said, "My soul has been magnified this day." And she laid her down. ⁷And the days having been fulfilled, Anna was purified, and gave the breast to the child, and called her name Mary.

CHAPTER 6

¹And the child grew strong day by day; and when she was six months old, her mother set her on the ground to try whether she could stand, and she walked seven steps and came into her bosom; ²and she snatched her up, saying, "As the LORD my God lives, you will not walk on this earth until I bring you into the temple of the LORD." ³And she made a sanctuary in her bed-chamber and allowed nothing common or unclean to pass through her. ⁴And she called the undefiled daughters of the Hebrews, and they led her astray. ⁵And when she was a year old, Joachim made a great feast, and invited the priests, and the scribes, and the elders, and all the people of Israel. ⁶And Joachim brought the child to the priests; and they blessed her, saying, "O God of our fathers, bless this child, and give her an everlasting name to be named in all generations." ⁷And all the people said: "So be it, so be it, amen." ⁸And he brought her to the chief priests; and they blessed her, saying, "O God Most High, look on this child, and bless her with the utmost blessing, which will be forever." ⁹And her mother snatched her up, and took her into the sanctuary of her bed-chamber, and gave her the breast. ¹⁰And Anna made a song to the LORD God, saying, "I will sing a song to the LORD my God, for He has looked on me and has taken away the reproach of my enemies; and the LORD has given the fruit of His righteousness, singular in its kind, and richly endowed before Him. ¹¹Who will tell the sons of Rubim that Anna gives suck? Hear, hear, you twelve tribes of Israel, that Anna gives suck." ¹²And she laid her to rest in the bed-chamber of her sanctuary and went out and ministered to them. ¹³And when the supper was ended, they went down rejoicing and glorifying the God of Israel.

CHAPTER 7

¹And her months were added to the child. ²And the child was two years old, and Joachim said: "Let us take her up to the temple of the LORD, so that we may pay the vow that we have vowed, lest perhaps the LORD sends to us, and our offering is not received." ³And Anna said: "Let us wait for the third year, in order that the child may not seek for father or mother." And Joachim said: "So let us wait." ⁴And the child was three years old, and Joachim said: "Invite the daughters of the Hebrews that are undefiled, and let them each take a lamp, and let them stand with the lamps burning, so that the child may not turn back, and her heart be captivated from the temple

of the LORD." ⁵And they did so until they went up into the temple of the LORD. ⁶And the priest received her, and kissed her, and blessed her, saying, "The LORD has magnified your name in all generations. In you, on the last of the days, the LORD will manifest His redemption to the sons of Israel." ⁷And he set her down on the third step of the altar, and the LORD God sent grace on her; and she danced with her feet, and all the house of Israel loved her.

CHAPTER 8

¹And her parents went down marveling and praising the LORD God, because the child had not turned back. ²And Mary was in the temple of the LORD as if she were a dove that dwelt there, and she received food from the hand of a messenger. ³And when she was twelve years old, a council of the priests was held, saying, "Behold, Mary has reached the age of twelve years in the temple of the LORD. ⁴What then will we do with her, lest perhaps she defiles the sanctuary of the LORD?" ⁵And they said to the chief priest: "You stand by the altar of the LORD; go in and pray concerning her; and whatever the LORD will manifest to you, that also will we do." ⁶And the chief priest went in, taking the robe with the twelve bells into the Holy of Holies; and he prayed concerning her. ⁷And behold, a messenger of the LORD stood by him, saying to him: "Zacharias, Zacharias! Go out and assemble the widowers of the people and let them each bring his rod; and to whomsoever the LORD will show a sign, his wife will she be. ⁸And the heralds went out through all the circuit of Judea, and the trumpet of the LORD sounded, and all ran.

CHAPTER 9

¹And Joseph, throwing away his axe, went out to meet them; and when they had assembled, they went away to the high priest, taking with them their rods. ²And he, taking the rods of all of them, entered into the temple and prayed; and having ended his prayer, he took the rods, and came out, and gave them to them: ³but there was no sign in them, and Joseph took his rod last; and behold, a dove came out of the rod, and flew on Joseph's head. ⁴And the priest said to Joseph, "You have been chosen by lot to take into your keeping the virgin of the LORD." ⁵But Joseph refused, saying, "I have children, and I am an old man, and she is a young girl. I am afraid lest I become a laughingstock to the sons of Israel." ⁶And the priest said to Joseph: "Fear the LORD your God, and remember what the LORD did to Dathan, and Abiram, and Korah; how the earth opened, and they were swallowed up on account of their contradiction. ⁷And now fear, O Joseph, lest the same things happen in your house. And Joseph was afraid and took her into his keeping." ⁸And Joseph said to Mary: "Behold, I have received you from the temple of the LORD; and now I leave you in my house, and go away to build my buildings, and I will come to you. The LORD will protect you."

CHAPTER 10

¹And there was a council of the priests, saying, "Let us make a veil for the temple of the LORD." ²And the priest said, "Call to me the undefiled virgins of the family of David." ³And the officers went away, and sought, and found seven virgins. ⁴And the priest remembered the child Mary, that she was of the family of David, and undefiled before God. And the officers went away and brought her. ⁵And they brought them into the temple of the LORD. And the priest said, "Choose for me by lot who will spin the gold, and the white, and the fine linen, and the silk, and the blue, and the scarlet, and the true purple." ⁶And the true purple and the scarlet fell to the lot of Mary, and she took them, and went away to her house. ⁷And at that time, Zacharias was mute, and Samuel was in his place until the time that Zacharias spoke. And Mary took the scarlet and spun it.

CHAPTER 11

¹And she took the pitcher and went out to fill it with water. ²And behold, a voice, saying, "Hail, you who have received grace! The LORD is with you; blessed are you among women!" ³And she looked around, on the right hand and on the left, to see from where this voice came. ⁴And she went away, trembling, to her house, and put down the pitcher; and taking the purple, she sat down on her seat and drew it out. ⁵And behold, a messenger of the LORD stood before her, saying, "Do not fear, Mary; for you have found grace before the Lord of all, and you will conceive, according to His word." ⁶And she hearing, reasoned with herself, saying, "Will I conceive by the LORD, the living God? And will I bring forth as every woman brings forth?" ⁷And the messenger of the LORD said: "Not so, Mary; for the power of the LORD will overshadow you: therefore also, that holy thing which will be born of you will be called the Son of the Highest. ⁸And you will call His Name Jesus, for He will save His people from their sins." ⁹And Mary said, "Behold, the servant of the LORD before His face: let it be to me according to your word."

CHAPTER 12

¹And she made the purple and the scarlet and took them to the priest. ²And the priest blessed her, and said: "Mary, the LORD God has magnified your name, and you will be blessed in all the generations of the earth." ³And Mary, with great joy, went away to her relative Elizabeth and knocked at the door. ⁴And when Elizabeth heard her, she threw away the scarlet, and ran to the door, and opened it; and seeing Mary, she blessed her, and said: "From where is this to me, that the mother of my Lord should come to me? For behold, that which is in me leaped and blessed you." ⁵But Mary had forgotten the mysteries of which the chief-messenger Gabriel had spoken, and gazed up into the sky, and said: "Who am I, O LORD, that all the generations of the earth should bless me?" ⁶And she remained three months with Elizabeth; and day by day she grew larger. ⁷And Mary being afraid, went away to her own house, and hid herself from the sons of Israel. ⁸And she was sixteen years old when these mysteries happened.

CHAPTER 13

¹And she was in her sixth month; and behold, Joseph came back from his building, and, entering into his house, he discovered that she was heavy with child. ²And he struck his face, and threw himself on the ground on the sackcloth, and wept bitterly, saying, "With what face will I look on the LORD my God? And what prayer will I make about this maiden? ³Because I received her [as] a virgin out of the temple of the LORD, and I have not watched over her. ⁴Who is it that has hunted me down? Who has done this evil thing in my house, and defiled the virgin? ⁵Has the history of Adam not been repeated in me? For just as Adam was in the hour of his singing praise, and the serpent came, and found Eve alone, and completely deceived her, so it has happened to me also." ⁶And Joseph stood up from the sackcloth, and called Mary, and said to her: "O you who have been cared for by God, why have you done this and forgotten the LORD your God? ⁷Why have you brought low your soul—you that were brought up in the Holy of Holies, and that received food from the hand of a messenger?" ⁸And she wept bitterly, saying, "I am innocent, and have known no man." ⁹And Joseph said to her: "From where then is that which is in your womb?" ¹⁰And she said, "As the LORD my God lives, I do not know from where it is to me."

CHAPTER 14

¹And Joseph was greatly afraid, and retired from her, and considered what he should do in regard to her. ²And Joseph said: "If I conceal her sin, I find myself fighting against the Law of the LORD; ³and if I expose her to the sons of Israel, I am afraid lest that which is in her be from a messenger, and I will be found giving up innocent blood to the doom of death. ⁴What then will I do with her? I will put her away from me secretly." ⁵And night came on him; and behold, a messenger of the LORD appears to him in a dream, saying, "Do not be afraid regarding this maiden, for that which is in her is of the Holy Spirit; ⁶and she will bring forth a Son, and you will call His Name Jesus, for He will save His people from their sins. ⁷And Joseph arose from sleep, and glorified the God of Israel, who had given him this grace; and he kept her.

CHAPTER 15

¹And Annas the scribe came to him and said: "Why have you not appeared in our assembly?" ²And Joseph said to him: "Because I was weary from my journey, and rested the first day." And he turned and saw that Mary was with child. ³And he ran away to the priest and said to him: "Joseph, whom you vouched for, has committed a grievous crime." ⁴And the priest said, "How so?" And he said, "He has defiled the virgin whom he received out of the temple of the LORD, and has married her by stealth, and has not revealed it to the sons of Israel." ⁵And the priest answering, said: "Has

Joseph done this?" ⁶Then Annas the scribe said, "Send officers, and you will find the virgin with child." ⁷And the officers went away and found it as he had said; and they brought her along with Joseph to the tribunal. ⁸And the priest said, "Mary, why have you done this? ⁹And why have you brought your soul low and forgotten the LORD your God—you that were reared in the Holy of Holies, and that received food from the hand of a messenger, and heard the hymns, and danced before Him, why have you done this?" ¹⁰And she wept bitterly, saying, "As the LORD my God lives, I am pure before Him, and do not know a man." ¹¹And the priest said to Joseph: "Why have you done this?" And Joseph said, "As the LORD lives, I am pure concerning her." ¹²Then the priest said, "Do not bear false witness, but speak the truth. You have married her by stealth, and have not revealed it to the sons of Israel, and have not bowed your head under the strong hand, so that your seed might be blessed." ¹³And Joseph was silent.

CHAPTER 16

¹And the priest said, "Give up the virgin whom you received out of the temple of the LORD." ²And Joseph burst into tears. And the priest said, "I will give you to drink of the water of the ordeal of the LORD, and He will make manifest your sins in your eyes." ³And the priest took the water, and gave [it to] Joseph to drink, and sent him away to the hill-country; and he returned unhurt. ⁴And he also gave to Mary to drink, and sent her away to the hill-country; and she returned unhurt. ⁵And all the people marveled that sin did not appear in them. ⁶And the priest said, "If the LORD God has not made manifest your sins, neither do I judge you." And he sent them away. ⁷And Joseph took Mary and went away to his own house, rejoicing and glorifying the God of Israel.

CHAPTER 17

¹And there was an order from Emperor Augustus, that all in Beth-Lehem of Judea should be enrolled. ²And Joseph said, "I will enroll my sons, but what will I do with this maiden? How will I enroll her? As my wife? I am ashamed. ³As my daughter then? But all the sons of Israel know that she is not my daughter. ⁴The day of the LORD will itself bring it to pass as the LORD wills." ⁵And he saddled the donkey and set her on it; and his son led it, and Joseph followed. ⁶And when they had come within three miles, Joseph turned and saw her sorrowful; and he said to himself: "Likely that which is in her distresses her." ⁷And again, Joseph turned and saw her laughing. And he said to her: "Mary, how is it that I see in your face at one time laughter, at another sorrow?" ⁸And Mary said to Joseph, "Because I see two peoples with my eyes: the one weeping and lamenting, and the other rejoicing and exulting." ⁹And they came into the middle of the road, and Mary said to him: "Take me down from off the donkey, for that which is in me presses to come forth." ¹⁰And he took her down from off the donkey and said to her: "To where will I lead you and cover your disgrace? For the place is a desert."

CHAPTER 18

¹And he found a cave there and led her into it; and leaving his two sons beside her, he went out to seek a midwife in the district of Beth-Lehem. ²And I, Joseph, was walking, and was not walking; and I looked up into the sky and saw the sky astonished; and I looked up to the pole of the heavens, and saw it standing, and the birds of the air keeping still. ³And I looked down on the earth, and saw a trough lying, and workers reclining: and their hands were in the trough. ⁴And those that were eating did not eat, and those that were rising did not carry it up, and those that were conveying anything to their mouths did not convey it; but the faces of all were looking upward. ⁵And I saw the sheep walking, and the sheep stood still; and the shepherd raised his hand to strike them, and his hand remained up. ⁶And I looked on the current of the river, and I saw the mouths of the kids resting on the water and not drinking, and all things in a moment were driven from their course.

CHAPTER 19

¹And I saw a woman coming down from the hill-country, and she said to me: "O man, where are you going?" ²And I said: "I am seeking a Hebrew midwife." ³And she answered and said to me: "Are you of Israel?" And I said to her, "Yes." ⁴And she said, "And who is it that is bringing forth in the cave?" And I said, "A woman betrothed to me." ⁵And she said to me: "Is she not your wife?" And I said to her: "It is Mary that was reared in the temple of the LORD, and I obtained her by lot as my wife. And yet she is not my wife, but has conceived from the Holy Spirit." ⁶And the midwife said to him: "Is this true?" And Joseph said to her: "Come and see." And the midwife went away with him. ⁷And they stood in the place of the cave; and behold, a luminous cloud overshadowed the cave. ⁸And the midwife said, "My soul has been magnified this day, because my eyes have seen strange things—because salvation has been brought forth to Israel." ⁹And immediately the cloud disappeared out of the cave, and a great light shone in the cave, so that the eyes could not endure it. ¹⁰And in a short time that light gradually decreased, until the infant appeared, and went and took the breast from His mother Mary. ¹¹And the midwife cried out and said: "This is a great day to me, because I have seen this strange sight!" ¹²And the midwife went forth out of the cave, and Salome met her. And she said to her: "Salome, Salome, I have a strange sight to relate to you: a virgin has brought forth—a thing which her nature does not [naturally] permit." ¹³Then Salome said, "As the LORD my God lives, unless I thrust in my finger, and search the parts, I will not believe that a virgin has brought forth."

CHAPTER 20

¹And the midwife went in and said to Mary: "Show yourself, for no small controversy has arisen concerning you." ²And Salome put in her finger, and cried out, and said: "Woe is me for my iniquity and my unbelief, because I have tempted the living God; and behold, my hand is dropping off as if burned with fire." ³And she bent her knees before the LORD, saying, "O God of my fathers, remember that I am the seed of Abraham, and Isaac, and Jacob; do not make a show of me to the sons of Israel, but restore me to the poor; ⁴for You know, O LORD, that in Your Name I have performed my services, and that I have received my reward at Your hand." ⁵And behold, a messenger of the LORD stood by her, saying to her: "Salome, Salome, the LORD has heard you. Put your hand to the infant, and carry it, and you will have safety and joy." ⁶And Salome went and carried it, saying, "I will worship Him, because a great King has been born to Israel." ⁷And behold, Salome was immediately cured, and she went forth out of the cave justified. ⁸And behold, a voice [was heard], saying, "Salome, Salome, do not tell the strange things you have seen, until the Child has come into Jerusalem."

CHAPTER 21

¹And behold, Joseph was ready to go into Judea. And there was a great commotion in Beth-Lehem of Judea, for magi came, saying, "Where is He that is born King of the Jews? For we have seen His star in the east and have come to worship Him." ²And when Herod heard [this], he was greatly troubled, and he sent officers to the magi. ³And he sent for the priests, and examined them, saying, "How is it written concerning the Christ? Where is He to be born?" ⁴And they said, "In Beth-Lehem of Judea, for so it is written." And he sent them away. ⁵And he examined the magi, saying to them: "What sign have you seen in reference to the King that has been born?" ⁶And the magi said, "We have seen a star of great size shining among these stars, and obscuring their light, so that the stars did not appear; and we thus knew that a King has been born to Israel, and we have come to worship Him." ⁷And Herod said, "Go and seek Him; and if you find Him, let me know, in order that I may also go and worship Him." And the magi went out. ⁸And behold, the star which they had seen in the east went before them until they came to the cave, and it stood over the top of the cave. ⁹And the magi saw the Infant with His mother Mary; and they brought forth from their bag gold, and frankincense, and myrrh. ¹⁰And having been warned by the messenger not to go into Judea, they went into their own country by another road.

CHAPTER 22

¹And when Herod knew that he had been mocked by the magi, in a rage he sent murderers, saying to them: "Slay the children from two years old and under." ²And Mary, having heard that the children were being killed, was afraid, and took the Infant and swaddled Him, and put Him into an ox-stall.

INFANCY GOSPEL OF JAMES

³And Elizabeth, having heard that they were searching for John, took him, and went up into the hill-country, and kept looking where to conceal him. And there was no place of concealment. ⁴And Elizabeth, groaning with a loud voice, says: "O mountain of God, receive mother and child!" ⁵And immediately the mountain was cleft and received her. And a light shone around them, for a messenger of the LORD was with them, watching over them.

CHAPTER 23

¹And Herod searched for John, and sent officers to Zacharias, saying, "Where have you hid your son?" ²And he, answering, said to them: "I am the servant of God in holy things, and I sit constantly in the temple of the LORD: I do not know where my son is." ³And the officers went away and reported all these things to Herod. ⁴And Herod was enraged and said, "His son is destined to be king over Israel." ⁵And he sent to him again, saying, "Tell the truth; where is your son? For you know that your life is in my hand." ⁶And Zacharias said, "I am God's martyr, if you shed my blood; for the LORD will receive my spirit, because you shed innocent blood at the vestibule of the temple of the LORD." ⁷And Zacharias was murdered about daybreak. And the sons of Israel did not know that he had been murdered.

CHAPTER 24

¹But at the hour of the salutation, the priests went away, and Zacharias did not come forth to meet them with a blessing, according to his custom. ²And the priests stood waiting for Zacharias to salute him at the prayer, and to glorify the Most High. And he, still delaying, they were all afraid. ³But one of them ventured to go in, and he saw clotted blood beside the altar; and he heard a voice, saying, "Zacharias has been murdered, and his blood will not be wiped up until his avenger comes." ⁴And hearing this saying, he was afraid and went out and told it to the priests. ⁵And they ventured in and saw what had happened; and the latticework of the temple made a wailing noise, and they tore their clothes from the top even to the bottom. ⁶And they did not find his body, but they found his blood turned into stone. ⁷And they were afraid and went out and reported to the people that Zacharias had been murdered. ⁸And all the tribes of the people heard, and mourned, and lamented for him three days and three nights. ⁹And after the three days, the priests consulted as to whom they should put in his place; and the lot fell on Simeon. ¹⁰For it was he who had been warned by the Holy Spirit that he should not see death until he should see the Christ in the flesh. ¹¹And I, James, that wrote this history in Jerusalem, a commotion having arisen when Herod died, withdrew myself to the wilderness until the commotion in Jerusalem ceased, glorifying the LORD God, who had given me the gift and the wisdom to write this history. ¹²And grace will be with them that fear our Lord Jesus Christ, to whom be glory to ages of ages. Amen.

INFANCY GOSPEL OF THOMAS

While the earliest complete manuscript of this work is found in the Codex Sabaiticus from the 11th century, early writers quoted from it, and the scholarly consensus is that it was written in the mid- to late- 2nd century, not long after the Infancy Gospel of James.

CHAPTER 1

¹I, Thomas, an Israelite, write you this account, that all the brothers from among the heathen may know the miracles of our Lord Jesus Christ in His infancy, which He did after His birth in our country. ²The beginning of it is as follows:

CHAPTER 2

¹This child Jesus, when [He was] five years old, was playing in the ford of a mountain stream; and He collected the flowing waters into pools, and made them clear immediately, and by a mere word He made them obey Him. ²And having made some soft clay, He fashioned out of it twelve sparrows. And it was the Sabbath when He did these things. ³And there were also many other children playing with Him. ⁴And a certain Jew, seeing what Jesus was doing, playing on the Sabbath, went off immediately, and said to His father Joseph: "Behold, your Son is at the stream, and has taken clay, and made twelve birds from it, and has profaned the Sabbath." ⁵And Joseph, coming to the place and seeing, cried out to Him, saying, "Why do You do on the Sabbath what it is not lawful to do?" ⁶And Jesus clapped His hands, and cried out to the sparrows, and said to them: "Off you go!" And the sparrows flew and went off crying. ⁷And the Jews seeing this, were amazed, and they went away and reported to their chief men what they had seen Jesus doing.

CHAPTER 3

¹And the son of Annas the scribe was standing there with Joseph; and he took a willow branch and let out the waters which Jesus had collected. ²And Jesus, seeing what was done, was angry, and said to him: "O wicked, impious, and foolish! What harm did the pools and the waters do to you? ³Behold, even now you will be dried up like a tree, and you will not bring forth either leaves, or root, or fruit." ⁴And immediately that boy was completely dried up. And Jesus departed and went to Joseph's house. ⁵But the parents of the boy that had been dried up took him up, lamenting his youth, and brought him to Joseph, and reproached him because, they said, "You have such a Child doing such things."

CHAPTER 4

¹After that, He was again passing through the village; and a boy ran up against Him and struck His shoulder. ²And Jesus was angry and said to him: "You will not go back the way you came." And immediately he fell down dead. ³And some who saw what had taken place said: "From where was this Child begotten, that every word of His is certainly accomplished?" ⁴And the parents of the dead boy went away to Joseph, and blamed him, saying, "Since you have such a Child, it is impossible for you to live with us in the village; or else teach Him to bless, and not to curse, for He is killing our children."

CHAPTER 5

¹And Joseph called the Child apart, and admonished Him, saying, "Why do You do such things, and these people suffer, and hate us, and persecute us?" ²And Jesus said: "I know that these words of yours are not your own; nevertheless, for your sake I will be silent; but they will bear their punishment." ³And immediately those that accused Him were struck blind. ⁴And those who saw it were very afraid and in great perplexity and said about Him: "Every word which He spoke, whether good or bad, was an act, and became a wonder." ⁵And when they saw that Jesus had done such a thing, Joseph rose and took hold of His ear and pulled it hard. ⁶And the Child was very angry and said to him: "It is enough for you to seek, and not to find; and you have most certainly not done wisely. ⁷Do you not know that I am yours? Do not trouble Me."

CHAPTER 6

¹And a certain teacher, Zaccheus by name, was standing in a certain place, and heard Jesus thus speaking to His father; and he wondered exceedingly, that, being a Child, He should speak in such a way. ²And a few days thereafter he came to Joseph and said to him: "You have a sensible child, and He has some mind. Give Him to me, then, that He may learn letters; and I will teach Him along with the letters all knowledge—both how to address all the elders, and to honor them as forefathers and fathers, and how to love those of His own age." ³And He said to him all the letters from the Alpha even to the Omega, clearly and with great precision. ⁴And He looked on the teacher Zaccheus and said to him: "You who are ignorant of the nature of the Alpha, how can you teach others the Beta? You hypocrite! First, if you know. teach the Alpha, and then we will believe you about the Beta." ⁵Then He began to question the teacher about the first letter, and he was not able to answer Him. ⁶And in the hearing of many, the Child says to Zaccheus: "Hear, O teacher, the

order of the first letter, and notice here how it has lines and a middle stroke crossing those which you see common—[lines] brought together—the highest part supporting them, and again bringing them under one head; with three points of intersection; of the same kind; principal and subordinate; of equal length. You have the lines of the Alpha.

CHAPTER 7

[1] And when the teacher Zaccheus heard the Child speaking thus and such great allegories of the first letter, he was at a great loss about such a narrative, and about His teaching. [2] And He said to those that were present: "Aah! I, wretch that I am, am at a loss, bringing shame on myself by having dragged this Child here. Take him away, then, I beg you, brother Joseph. [3] I cannot endure the sternness of His look; I cannot make out His meaning at all. That Child does not belong to this earth; He can tame even fire. [4] Assuredly He was born before the creation of the world. What sort of a belly bore Him, what sort of a womb nourished Him, I do not know. Aah! My friend, He has carried me away; I cannot get at His meaning: thrice wretched that I am, I have deceived myself. [5] I made a struggle to have a scholar, and I was found to have a teacher. [6] My mind is filled with shame, my friends, because I, an old man, have been conquered by a Child. [7] There is nothing for me but despondency and death on account of this boy, for I am not able at this hour to look Him in the face; [8] and when everybody says that I have been beaten by a little child, what can I say? And how can I give an account of the lines of the first letter that He spoke about? [9] I do not know, O my friends, for I can make neither beginning nor end of Him. [10] Therefore, I beg you, brother Joseph, take Him home. What great thing He is, either God or messenger, or what I am to say, I do not know."

CHAPTER 8

[1] And when the Jews were encouraging Zaccheus, the Child laughed aloud and said: "Now let your learning bring forth fruit, and let the blind in heart see. I am here from above, that I may curse them, and call them to the things that are above, as He that sent Me on your account has commanded Me." [2] And when the Child ceased speaking, immediately all were made whole who had fallen under His curse. [3] And no one after that dared to make Him angry, lest He should curse him, and he should be maimed.

CHAPTER 9

[1] And some days later, Jesus was playing in an upper room of a certain house, and one of the children that were playing with Him fell down from the house and was killed. [2] And, when the other children saw this, they ran away, and Jesus alone stood still. [3] And the parents of the dead child coming, reproached … and they threatened Him. [4] And Jesus leaped down from the roof, and stood beside the body of the child, and cried with a loud voice, and said: "Zeno!"—for that was his name—"stand up, and tell Me: did I throw you down?" [5] And he immediately stood up and said: "Certainly not, my Lord; you did not throw me down, but have raised me up." And those that saw this were struck with astonishment. [6] And the Child's parents glorified God on account of the miracle that had happened and adored Jesus.

CHAPTER 10

[1] A few days later, a young man was splitting wood in the corner, and the axe came down and cut the sole of his foot in two, and he died from loss of blood. [2] And there was a great commotion, and people ran together, and the Child Jesus ran there too. [3] And He pressed through the crowd, and laid hold of the young man's wounded foot, and he was cured immediately. And He said to the young man: "Rise up now, split the wood, and remember Me." [4] And the crowd seeing what had happened, adored the Child, saying, "Truly the Spirit of God dwells in this Child."

CHAPTER 11

[1] And when He was six years old, His mother gave Him a pitcher and sent Him to draw water and bring it into the house. [2] But He struck against someone in the crowd, and the pitcher was broken. [3] And Jesus unfolded the cloak which He had on, and filled it with water, and carried it to His mother. [4] And His mother, seeing the miracle that had happened, kissed Him, and kept within herself the mysteries which she had seen Him doing.

CHAPTER 12

[1] And again, in seed-time, the Child went out with His father to sow corn in their land. [2] And while His father was sowing, the Child Jesus also sowed one grain of corn. And when He had reaped it, and threshed it, He made a hundred kors; and calling all the poor of the village to the threshing-floor, He gave them the corn, and Joseph took away what was left of the corn. [3] And He was eight years old when He did this miracle.

CHAPTER 13

[1] And His father was a carpenter, and at that time made plows and yokes. [2] And a certain rich man ordered him to make him a couch. And one of what is called the crosspieces being too short, they did not know what to do. [3] The Child Jesus said to His father Joseph: "Put down the two pieces of wood, and make them even in the middle." And Joseph did as the Child said to him. [4] And Jesus stood at the other end, and took hold of the shorter piece of wood, and stretched it, and made it equal to the other. [5] And His father Joseph saw it, and wondered, and embraced the Child, and blessed Him, saying, "Blessed am I, because God has given me this Child."

CHAPTER 14

[1] And Joseph, seeing that the Child was vigorous in mind and body, again resolved that He should not remain ignorant of the letters, and took Him away, and handed Him over to another teacher. [2] And the teacher said to Joseph: "I will first teach Him the Greek letters, and then the Hebrew." For the teacher was aware of the trial that had been made of the Child and was afraid of Him. [3] Nevertheless, he wrote out the alphabet, and gave Him all his attention for a long time, and He made him no answer. [4] And Jesus said to him: "If you are really a teacher, and are well acquainted with the letters, tell me the power of the Alpha, and I will tell you the power of the Beta." [5] And the teacher was enraged at this and struck Him on the head. [6] And the Child, being in pain, cursed him; and he immediately collapsed and fell to the ground on his face. [7] And the Child returned to Joseph's house; and Joseph was grieved, and he gave orders to His mother, saying, "Do not let Him go outside of the door, because those that make Him angry die."

CHAPTER 15

[1] And after some time, another master again, a genuine friend of Joseph, said to him: "Bring the Child to my school; perhaps I will be able to flatter Him into learning His letters." [2] And Joseph said: "If you have the courage, brother, take Him with you." [3] And he took Him with him in fear and great agony; but the Child went along pleasantly. [4] And going boldly into the school, He found a book lying on the reading-desk; and taking it, He did not read the letters that were in it, but opening His mouth, He spoke by the Holy Spirit, and taught the Law to those that were standing around. [5] And a great crowd, having come together, stood by and heard Him, and wondered at the ripeness of His teaching, and the readiness of His words, and that He, a child as He was, spoke in such a way. [6] And Joseph, hearing of it, was afraid, and ran to the school, in doubt lest His master too should be without experience. [7] And the master said to Joseph: "Know, brother, that I have taken the Child as a scholar, and He is full of much grace and wisdom; but I implore you, brother: take Him home." [8] And when the Child heard this, He laughed at him directly, and said: "Since you have spoken correctly, and witnessed correctly, for your sake he also that was struck down will be cured." And immediately the other master was cured. [9] And Joseph took the Child and went away home.

CHAPTER 16

[1] And Joseph sent his son James to tie up wood and bring it home, and the Child Jesus also followed him. [2] And when James was gathering the bundles, a viper bit James' hand. [3] And when he was racked with pain, and at the point of death, Jesus came near and blew on the bite; and the pain ceased directly, and the beast burst, and instantly James remained safe and sound.

CHAPTER 17

[1] And after this, the infant of one of Joseph's neighbors fell sick and died, and its mother wept grievously. [2] And Jesus heard that there was great lamentation and commotion, and ran in haste, and found the child dead, and

touched his breast, and said: "I say to you, child, be not dead, but live, and be with your mother." And it immediately looked up and laughed. ³And He said to the woman: "Take it, and give it milk, and remember Me." ⁴And seeing this, the crowd that was standing by wondered, and said: "Truly this Child was either God or a messenger of God, for every word of His is a certain fact." ⁵And Jesus went out from there, playing with the other children.

CHAPTER 18

¹And some time later, there occurred a great commotion while a house was being built, and Jesus stood up and went away to the place. ²And seeing a man lying dead, He took him by the hand, and said: "Man, I say to you: arise, and go on with your work." And he immediately rose up and adored Him. ³And seeing this, the crowd wondered, and said: "This Child is from Heaven, for He has saved many souls from death, and He continues to save throughout all His life."

CHAPTER 19

¹And when He was twelve years old, His parents went as usual to Jerusalem to the Celebration of the Passover with their fellow-travelers. ²And after the Passover, they were coming home again. And while they were coming home, the Child Jesus went back to Jerusalem. ³And His parents thought that He was in the company. And having gone one day's journey, they sought for Him among their relations; and not finding Him, they were in great grief and turned back to the city seeking for Him. ⁴And after the third day, they found Him in the temple, sitting in the midst of the teachers, both hearing the Law and asking them questions. ⁵And they were all attending to Him, and wondering that He, being a child, was shutting the mouths of the elders and teachers of the people, explaining the main points of the Law and the allegories of the Prophets. ⁶And His mother Mary coming up, said to Him: "Why have You done this to us, Child? Behold, we have been seeking for You in great trouble." ⁷And Jesus said to them: "Why do you seek Me? Do you not know that I must be about My Father's business?" ⁸And the scribes and the Pharisees said: "Are you the mother of this Child?" And she said: "I am." ⁹And they said to her: "Blessed are you among women, for God has blessed the Fruit of your womb; for such glory, and such virtue and wisdom, we have neither seen nor heard ever." ¹⁰And Jesus rose up, and followed His mother, and was subject to His parents. And His mother observed all these things that had happened. ¹¹And Jesus advanced in wisdom, and stature, and grace. To Whom be glory forever and ever. Amen.

ARABIC INFANCY GOSPEL

The Arabic Infancy Gospel, stemming from an older work written in Syriac entitled History of the Virgin, might have been translated from the Syriac as early as the 6th century. It is based heavily on the Infancy Gospel of Thomas.

IN THE NAME OF THE FATHER, AND THE SON, AND THE HOLY SPIRIT: ONE GOD.

WITH THE HELP AND FAVOR OF THE MOST HIGH, WE BEGIN TO WRITE A BOOK OF THE MIRACLES OF OUR LORD, AND MASTER, AND SAVIOR JESUS CHRIST, WHICH IS CALLED THE GOSPEL OF THE INFANCY: IN THE PEACE OF THE LORD. AMEN.

CHAPTER 1

¹We find what follows in the book of Joseph the chief priest, who lived in the time of Christ. Some say that he is Caiaphas. ²He has said that Jesus spoke, and, indeed, when He was lying in His cradle said to His mother Mary: "I am Jesus, the Son of God, the Word, whom you have brought forth, as the messenger Gabriel announced to you; and My Father has sent Me for the salvation of the world."

CHAPTER 2

¹In the three hundred and ninth year of the era of Alexander, Augustus put forth an edict that every man should be enrolled in his native place. ²Joseph therefore arose, and taking his spouse Mary, went away to Jerusalem, and came to Beth-Lehem, to be enrolled along with his family in his native city. ³And having come to a cave, Mary told Joseph that the time of the birth was at hand, and that she could not go into the city; "but," she said, "let us go into this cave." This took place at sunset. ⁴And Joseph went out in haste to go for a woman [(midwife)] to be near her. ⁵When, therefore, he was busy with that, he saw an old Hebrew woman belonging to Jerusalem, and said: "Come here, my good woman, and go into this cave, in which there is a woman near her time."

CHAPTER 3

¹Therefore, after sunset, the old woman, and Joseph with her, came to the cave, and they both went in. ²And behold, it was filled with lights more beautiful than the gleaming of lamps and candles, and more splendid than the light of the sun. ³The Child, wrapped in swaddling clothes, was suckling the breast of the Lady Mary, His mother, being placed in a stall. And when both were wondering at this light, the old woman asks the Lady Mary: "Are you the mother of this Child?" ⁴And when the Lady Mary gave her assent, she says: "You are not at all like the daughters of Eve." ⁵The Lady Mary said: "As my Son has no equal among children, so His mother has no equal among women." ⁶The old woman replied: "My mistress, I came to obtain payment; I have been for a long time affected with palsy." ⁷Our mistress the Lady Mary said to her: "Place your hands on the Child." ⁸And the old woman did so and was immediately cured. ⁹Then she went forth, saying, "Henceforth, I will be the attendant and servant of this Child all the days of my life."

CHAPTER 4

¹Then came shepherds; and when they had lit a fire, and were rejoicing greatly, there appeared to them the hosts of Heaven praising and celebrating God Most High. ²And while the shepherds were doing the same, the cave was at that time made like a temple of the upper world, since both heavenly and earthly voices glorified and magnified God on account of the birth of the Lord Christ. ³And when that old Hebrew woman saw the manifestation of those miracles, she thanked God, saying, "I give You thanks, O God, the God of Israel, because my eyes have seen the birth of the Savior of the world."

CHAPTER 5

¹And the time of circumcision, that is, the eighth day, being at hand, the Child was to be circumcised according to the Law. ²Therefore, they circumcised Him in the cave. ³And the old Hebrew woman took the piece of skin; but some say that she took the umbilical cord and laid it in a jar of old oil of nard. ⁴And she had a son, a dealer in ointments, and she gave it to him, saying, "See that you do not sell this jar of ointment of nard, even if three hundred denarii should be offered you for it." ⁵And this is that jar which Mary the sinner bought and poured on the head and feet of our Lord Jesus Christ, which thereafter she wiped with the hair of her head. ⁶Ten days after, they took Him to Jerusalem; and on the fortieth day after His birth, they carried Him into the temple, and set Him before the LORD, and offered sacrifices for Him, according to the commandment of the Law of Moses, which is: "Every male that opens the womb will be called the holy of God."

CHAPTER 6

¹Then old Simeon saw Him shining like a pillar of light, when the Lady Mary, His virgin mother, rejoicing over Him, was carrying Him in her arms. ²And messengers, praising Him, stood around Him in a circle, like bodyguards standing by a king. ³Simeon therefore went up in haste to the Lady Mary, and, with hands stretched out before her, said to the Lord Christ: "Now, O my Lord, let Your servant depart in peace, according to Your word; ⁴for my eyes have seen Your compassion, which You have prepared for the salvation of all

peoples, a light to all nations, and glory to Your people Israel." ⁵Hanna also, a prophetess, was present, and came up, giving thanks to God, and calling the Lady Mary blessed.

CHAPTER 7

¹And it came to pass, when the Lord Jesus was born at Beth-Lehem of Judea, in the time of King Herod, behold, magi came from the east to Jerusalem, as Zoroaster had predicted; ²and there were gifts with them: gold, and frankincense, and myrrh. And they adored Him and presented their gifts to Him. ³Then the Lady Mary took one of the swaddling-bands, and, on account of the smallness of her means, gave it to them; and they received it from her with the greatest marks of honor. ⁴And in the same hour, there appeared to them a messenger in the form of that star which had formerly guided them on their journey; and they went away, following the guidance of its light, until they arrived in their own country.

CHAPTER 8

¹And their kings and chief men came together to them, asking what they had seen or done, how they had gone and come back, what they had brought with them. And they showed them that swaddling cloth which the Lady Mary had given them. ²Therefore, they celebrated a feast, and, according to their custom, lit a fire and worshiped it, and threw that swaddling cloth into it; and the fire laid hold of it, and enveloped it. ³And when the fire had gone out, they took out the swaddling cloth exactly as it had been before, just as if the fire had not touched it. ⁴Therefore, they began to kiss it, and to put it on their heads and their eyes, saying, "This is truly the truth without doubt. Assuredly it is a great thing that the fire was not able to burn or destroy it." ⁵Then they took it, and with the greatest honor laid it up among their treasures.

CHAPTER 9

¹And when Herod saw that the magi had left him and not come back to him, he summoned the priests and the wise men, and he said to them: "Show me where Christ is to be born." ²And when they answered, "In Beth-Lehem of Judea," he began to think of putting the Lord Jesus Christ to death. ³Then a messenger of the LORD appeared to Joseph in his sleep and said: "Rise, take the Boy and His mother, and go away into Egypt." ⁴He rose, therefore, toward [the] cockcrow, and set out.

CHAPTER 10

¹While he is reflecting on how he is to set about his journey, morning came on him after he had gone a very short way. ²And now he was approaching a great city, in which there was an idol, to which the other idols and gods of the Egyptians offered gifts and vows. And there stood before this idol a priest ministering to him, who, as often as Satan spoke from that idol, reported it to the inhabitants of Egypt and its territories. ³This priest had a son, three years old, beset by several demons; and he made many speeches and utterances; and when the demons seized him, he tore his clothes, and remained naked, and threw stones at the people. ⁴And there was a hospital in that city dedicated to that idol. And when Joseph and the Lady Mary had come to the city, and had turned aside into that hospital, the citizens were very greatly afraid; and all the chief men and the priests of the idols came together to that idol and said to it: "What agitation and commotion is this that has arisen in our land?" ⁵The idol answered them: "God has come here in secret, who is God indeed; nor is any god besides Him worthy of divine worship, because He is truly the Son of God. ⁶And when this land became aware of His presence, it trembled at His arrival and was moved and shaken; and we are exceedingly afraid from the greatness of His power." ⁷And in the same hour, that idol fell down; and at its fall all—inhabitants of Egypt and others—fled together.

CHAPTER 11

¹And the son of the priest, his usual disease having come on him, entered the hospital, and there came Joseph and the Lady Mary, from whom all others had fled. ²The Lady Mary had washed the cloths of the Lord Christ and had spread them over some wood. That demoniac boy, therefore, came and took one of the cloths and put it on his head. ³Then the demons, fleeing in the shape of ravens and serpents, began to go forth out of his mouth. ⁴The boy, being immediately healed at the command of the Lord Christ, began to praise God, and then to give thanks to the LORD who had healed him. ⁵And when his father saw him restored to health, "My son," he said, "what has happened to you? And by what means have you been healed?" ⁶The son answered: "When the demons had thrown me on the ground, I went into the hospital, and there I found a dignified woman with a boy, whose newly-washed cloths she had thrown on some wood: one of these I picked up and placed on my head, and the demons left me and fled." ⁷At this the father greatly rejoiced and said: "My son, it is possible that this Boy is the Son of the living God who created the heavens and the earth, for when He came over to us, the idol was broken, and all the gods fell, and perished by the power of His magnificence."

CHAPTER 12

¹Here was fulfilled the prophecy which says, "Out of Egypt I called My Son." ²Joseph indeed, and Mary, when they heard that that idol had fallen down and perished, trembled and were afraid. ³Then they said: "When we were in the land of Israel, Herod thought to put Jesus to death, and on that account slew all the children of Beth-Lehem and its confines; and there is no doubt that the Egyptians, as soon as they have heard that this idol has been broken, will burn us with fire."

CHAPTER 13

¹Going out from there, they came to a place where there were robbers who had plundered several men of their baggage and clothes and had bound them. ²Then the robbers heard a great noise, like the noise of a magnificent king going out of his city with his army, and his chariots, and his drums; and at this the robbers were terrified and left all their plunder. ³And their captives rose up, untied each other's bonds, recovered their baggage, and went away. ⁴And when they saw Joseph and Mary coming up to the place, they said to them: "Where is that King, at the hearing of the magnificent sound of whose approach the robbers have left us, so that we have escaped safe?" ⁵Joseph answered them: "He will come behind us."

CHAPTER 14

¹Thereafter they came into another city, where there was a demoniac woman whom Satan, accursed and rebellious, had beset, when on one occasion she had gone out by night for water. ²She could neither bear clothes, nor live in a house; and as often as they tied her up with chains and thongs, she broke them and fled naked into waste places; ³and, standing in crossroads and cemeteries, she kept throwing stones at people and brought very heavy calamities on her friends. ⁴And when the Lady Mary saw her, she pitied her; and on this, Satan immediately left her and fled away in the form of a young man, saying, "Woe to me from you, Mary, and from your Son!" ⁵So that woman was cured of her torment, and being restored to her senses, she blushed on account of her nakedness; and shunning the sight of men, went home to her friends. ⁶And after she put on her clothes, she gave an account of the matter to her father and her friends; ⁷and as they were the chief men of the city, they received the Lady Mary and Joseph with the greatest honor and hospitality.

CHAPTER 15

¹On the day after, being supplied by them with provision for their journey, they went away, and on the evening of that day, arrived at another town, in which they were celebrating a marriage; ²but, by the arts of accursed Satan and the work of enchanters, the bride had become mute and could not speak a word. ³And after the Lady Mary entered the town, carrying her Son, the Lord Christ, that mute bride saw her, and stretched out her hands toward the Lord Christ, and drew Him to her, and took Him into her arms, and held Him close and kissed Him, and leaned over Him, moving His body back and forth. ⁴Immediately, the knot of her tongue was loosened, and her ears were opened; and she gave thanks and praise to God, because He had restored her to health. ⁵And that night the inhabitants of that town exulted with joy and thought that God and His messengers had come down to them.

CHAPTER 16

¹They remained there [for] three days, being held in great honor, and living splendidly. ²Thereafter, being supplied by them with

provision for their journey, they went away and came to another city, in which, because it was very populous, they thought of passing the night. ³And there was in that city an excellent woman: and once, when she had gone to the river to bathe, behold, accursed Satan, in the form of a serpent, had leapt on her and twisted himself around her belly; and as often as night came on, he tyrannically tormented her. ⁴This woman, seeing the mistress, the Lady Mary, and the Child, the Lord Christ, in her bosom, was struck with a longing for Him, and said to the mistress, the Lady Mary: "O mistress, give me this Child, that I may carry Him and kiss Him." ⁵She therefore gave Him to the woman; and when He was brought to her, Satan let her go, and fled, and left her, nor did the woman ever see him after that day. ⁶Therefore, all who were present praised God Most High, and that woman bestowed on them abundant gifts.

CHAPTER 17

¹On the day after, the same woman took scented water to wash the Lord Jesus; and after she had washed Him, she took the water with which she had done it and poured part of it on a girl who was living there, whose body was white with leprosy, and washed her with it. ²And as soon as this was done, the girl was cleansed from her leprosy. And the townspeople said: "There is no doubt that Joseph, and Mary, and that Boy are gods, not men." ³And when they were getting ready to go away from them, the girl who had labored under the leprosy came up to them and asked them to let her go with them.

CHAPTER 18

¹When they had given her permission, she went with them. And afterward they came to a city, in which was the castle of a most illustrious prince, who kept a house for the entertainment of strangers. ²They turned into this place; and the girl went away to the prince's wife; and she found her weeping and sorrowful, and she asked why she was weeping. "Do not be surprised," she said, "at my tears; for I am overwhelmed by a great affliction, which as yet I have not endured to tell to anyone." ³"Perhaps," said the girl, "if you reveal it and disclose it to me, I may have a remedy for it." ⁴"Hide this secret, then," replied the princess, "and tell it to no one. I was married to this prince, who is a king and ruler over many cities, and I lived long with him, but he had no son by me. ⁵And when I finally produced him a son, he was leprous; and as soon as he saw him, he turned away with loathing, and said to me: Either kill him, or give him to the nurse to be brought up in some place from which we will never hear of him again. ⁶After this I can have nothing to do with you, and I will never see you again. ⁷On this account I do not know what to do, and I am overwhelmed with grief. Oh, my son! Oh, my husband!" ⁸"Did I not say so?" Said the girl. "I have found a cure for your disease, and I will tell it you. For I too was a leper; but I was cleansed by God, who is Jesus, the son of the Lady Mary." ⁹And the woman, asking her where this God was whom she had spoken of—"Here with you," said the girl; "He is living in the same house." ¹⁰"But how is this possible?" She said. "Where is He?" "There," said the girl, "are Joseph and Mary; and the Child who is with them is called Jesus; and it is He who cured me of my disease and my torment." ¹¹"But by what means," she said, "were you cured of your leprosy? Will you not tell me that?" ¹²"Why not?" Said the girl. "I got from His mother the water in which He had been washed and poured it over myself; and so I was cleansed from my leprosy." ¹³Then the princess rose up and invited them to avail themselves of her hospitality. ¹⁴And she prepared a splendid banquet for Joseph in a great assembly of the men of the place. ¹⁵And on the following day, she took scented water with which to wash the Lord Jesus, and thereafter poured the same water over her son, whom she had taken with her; and her son was immediately cleansed from his leprosy. ¹⁶Therefore, singing thanks and praises to God, she said: "Blessed is the mother who bore You, O Jesus; do You so cleanse those who share the same nature with You with the water in which Your body has been washed?" ¹⁷Additionally, she bestowed great gifts on the mistress, the Lady Mary, and sent her away with great honor.

CHAPTER 19

¹Coming thereafter to another city, they desired to spend the night in it. ²They turned aside, therefore, to the house of a man newly married, but who, under the influence of witchcraft, was not able to enjoy his wife; ³and when they had spent that night with him, his bond was loosed. ⁴And at daybreak, when they were girding themselves for their journey, the bridegroom would not let them go and prepared for them a great banquet.

CHAPTER 20

¹They set out, therefore, on the following day; and as they came near another city, they saw three women weeping as they came out of a cemetery. ²And when the Lady Mary beheld them, she said to the girl who accompanied her: "Ask them what is the matter with them, or what calamity has befallen them." ³And to the girl's questions they made no reply, but asked in their turn: "Where are you coming from, and where are you going? For the day is already past, and night is coming on quickly." ⁴"We are travelers," said the girl, "and are seeking a house of entertainment in which we may pass the night." ⁵They said: "Go with us and spend the night with us." ⁶They followed them, therefore, and were brought into a new house with splendid decorations and furniture. ⁷Now it was winter; and the girl, going into the chamber of these women, found them again weeping and lamenting. ⁸There stood beside them a mule, covered with housings of cloth of gold, and sesame was put before him; and the women were kissing him and giving him food. ⁹And the girl said: "What is all the excitement, my ladies, concerning this mule?" ¹⁰They answered her with tears and said: "This mule, which you see, was our brother, born of the same mother with ourselves. ¹¹And when our father died and left us great wealth, and this only brother, we did our best to get him married, and were preparing his nuptials for him, after the manner of men. ¹²But some women, moved by mutual jealousy, bewitched him unknown to us; and one night, a little before daybreak, when the door of our house was shut, we saw that this brother of ours had been turned into a mule, as you now behold him. ¹³And we are sorrowful, as you see, having no father to comfort us: there is no wise man, or magician, or enchanter in the world that we have overlooked to send for; but nothing has done us any good. ¹⁴And as often as our hearts are overwhelmed with grief, we rise and go away with our mother here, and weep at our father's grave, and come back again."

CHAPTER 21

¹And when the girl heard these things, "Be of good courage," she said, "and do not weep: for the cure of your calamity is near; yes, it is beside you, and in the middle of your own house. ²For I was also a leper; but when I saw that woman, and along with her that young Child, whose Name is Jesus, I sprinkled my body with the water with which His mother had washed Him, and I was cured. And I know that He can cure your affliction also. ³But rise, go to my mistress Mary; bring her into your house, and tell her your secret; and implore and supplicate her to have pity on you." ⁴After the woman had heard the girl's words, they went in haste to the Lady Mary, and brought her into their chamber, and sat down before her weeping, and saying, "O our mistress, Lady Mary, have pity on your handmaidens; for no one older than ourselves, and no head of the family, is left—neither father nor brother—to live with us; ⁵but this mule which you see was our brother, and women have made him such as you see by witchcraft. ⁶We beg you, therefore, to have pity on us." Then, grieving at their lot, the Lady Mary took up the Lord Jesus and put Him on the mule's back; ⁷and she wept as well as the women, and she said to Jesus Christ: "Oh, my Son! Heal this mule by Your mighty power and make him a man endowed with reason as he was before." ⁸And when these words were uttered by the Lady Mary, his form was changed, and the mule became a young man, free from every defect. ⁹Then he, and his mother, and his sisters adored the Lady Mary, and lifted the Boy above their heads, and began to kiss Him, saying, "Blessed is she that bore You, O Jesus, O Savior of the world; blessed are the eyes which enjoy the ecstasy of seeing You."

CHAPTER 22

¹Moreover, both [of] the sisters said to their mother: "Our brother indeed, by the aid of the Lord Jesus Christ, and by the beneficial intervention of this girl, who pointed out to us Mary and her Son, has been raised to human form. ²Now, indeed, since our brother is

unmarried, it would do very well for us to give him as his wife this girl, their servant." ³And having asked the Lady Mary and obtained her consent, they made a splendid wedding for the girl; and their sorrow being changed into joy, and the beating of their breasts into dancing, they began to be glad, to rejoice, to exult, and sing—adorned, on account of their great joy, in most splendid and gorgeous attire. ⁴Then they began to recite songs and praises, and to say: "O Jesus, Son of David, who turns sorrow into gladness and lamentations into joy!" ⁵And Joseph and Mary remained there ten days. Thereafter they set out, treated with great honors by these people, who bade them farewell, and from bidding them farewell, returned weeping—especially the girl.

CHAPTER 23

¹And turning away from this place, they came to a desert; and hearing that it was infested by robbers, Joseph and the Lady Mary resolved to cross this region by night. ²But as they go along, behold, they see two robbers lying in the way, and along with them a great number of robbers, who were their associates, sleeping. ³Now those two robbers, into whose hands they had fallen, were Titus and Dumachus. ⁴Titus therefore said to Dumachus: "I implore you to let these persons go freely, and so that our comrades may not see them." ⁵And as Dumachus refused, Titus said to him again: "Take to yourself forty drachmas from me, and hold this as a pledge." ⁶At the same time, he held out to him the belt which he had around his waist, to keep him from opening his mouth or speaking. ⁷And the Lady Mary, seeing that the robber had done them a kindness, said to him: "The LORD God will sustain you by His right hand, and will grant you forgiveness of your sins." ⁸And the Lord Jesus answered and said to His mother: "Thirty years from now, O My mother, the Jews will crucify Me at Jerusalem, and these two robbers will be raised on the Cross along with Me: Titus on my right hand and Dumachus on my left; and after that day, Titus will go before Me into Paradise." ⁹And she said: "God keep this from You, my Son." ¹⁰And they went from there toward a city of idols, which, as they came near it, was changed into sandhills.

CHAPTER 24

¹From here they turned aside to that sycamore which is now called Matarea, and the Lord Jesus brought forth in Matarea a fountain in which the Lady Mary washed His shirt. ²And from the sweat of the Lord Jesus which she sprinkled there, balsam was produced in that region.

CHAPTER 25

¹From there they came down to Memphis, and saw Pharaoh, and remained three years in Egypt; ²and the Lord Jesus did in Egypt very many miracles which are recorded neither in the Gospel of the Infancy nor in the perfect Gospel.

CHAPTER 26

¹And at the end of the three years, He came back out of Egypt and returned. ²And when they had arrived at Judea, Joseph was afraid to enter it; but hearing that Herod was dead, and that his son Archelaus had succeeded him, he was afraid indeed, but he went into Judea. ³And a messenger of the LORD appeared to him and said: "O Joseph, go into the city of Nazareth and abide there." ⁴[It is] wonderful indeed that the Lord of the world should be thus born and carried around through the world!

CHAPTER 27

¹Thereafter, going into the city of Beth-Lehem, they saw there manifold and severe diseases infesting the eyes of the children, who were dying in consequence. ²And a woman was there with a sick son, whom, now very near death, she brought to the Lady Mary, who saw him as she was washing Jesus Christ. ³Then the woman said to her: "O my Lady Mary, look on this son of mine, who is laboring under a severe disease." ⁴And the Lady Mary listened to her and said: "Take a little of that water in which I have washed my Son and sprinkle him with it." ⁵She therefore took a little of the water, as the Lady Mary had told her, and sprinkled it over her son. ⁶And when this was done, his illness abated; and after sleeping a little, he rose up from sleep safe and sound. ⁷His mother, rejoicing at this, again took him to the Lady Mary. And she said to her: "Give thanks to God, because He has healed this son of yours."

CHAPTER 28

¹There was in the same place another woman, a neighbor of her whose son had recently been restored to health. ²And as her son was laboring under the same disease, and his eyes were now almost blinded, she wept night and day. ³And the mother of the child that had been cured said to her: "Why do you not take your son to the Lady Mary, as I did with mine when he was nearly dead? ⁴And he got well with that water with which the body of her Son Jesus had been washed." ⁵And when the woman heard this from her, she too went and got some of the same water, and washed her son with it, and his body and his eyes were instantly made well. ⁶Her also, when she had brought her son to her, and disclosed to her all that had happened, the Lady Mary ordered to give thanks to God for her son's restoration to health, and to tell nobody of this matter.

CHAPTER 29

¹There were in the same city two women, wives of one man, each having a son ill with a fever. ²The one was called Mary, and her son's name was Cleopas. She rose and took up her son, and went to the Lady Mary, the mother of Jesus, and offering her a beautiful mantle, said: "O my Lady Mary, accept this mantle, and give me one small bandage for it." ³Mary did so, and the mother of Cleopas went away, and made a shirt of it, and put it on her son. So he was cured of his disease; but the son of her rival died. ⁴Hence there sprung up hatred between them; and as they did the housework, and as it was the turn of Mary the mother of Cleopas, she heated the oven to bake bread; ⁵and going away to bring the lump that she had kneaded, she left her son Cleopas beside the oven. ⁶Her rival seeing him alone—and the oven was very hot with the fire blazing under it—seized him, and threw him into the oven, and herself fled away. ⁷Mary, coming back and seeing her son Cleopas lying in the oven laughing, and the oven quite cold, as if no fire had ever come near it, knew that her rival had thrown him into the fire. ⁸She drew him out, therefore, and took him to the Lady Mary, and told her of what had happened to him. ⁹And she said: "Keep silence, and tell nobody of the affair; for I am afraid for you if you divulge it." ¹⁰After this, her rival went to the well to draw water; and seeing Cleopas playing beside the well, and nobody near, she seized him and threw him into the well, and went home herself. ¹¹And some men who had gone to the well for water saw the boy sitting on the surface of the water; and so, they went down and drew him out. ¹²And they were seized with a great admiration of that boy and praised God. ¹³Then his mother came, and took him up, and went weeping to the Lady Mary, and said: "O my lady, see what my rival has done to my son, and how she has thrown him into the well; she will be sure to destroy him some day or another." ¹⁴The Lady Mary said to her: "God will avenge you on her." ¹⁵Thereafter, when her rival went to the well to draw water, her feet got entangled in the rope, and she fell into the well. ¹⁶Some men came to draw her out, but they found her skull fractured and her bones broken. ¹⁷Thus, she died a miserable death, and in her came to pass that saying: "They have dug a well deep, but have fallen into the pit which they had prepared."

CHAPTER 30

¹Another woman there had twin sons who had fallen into disease, and one of them died, and the other was at his last breath. ²And his mother, weeping, lifted him up, and took him to the Lady Mary, and said: "O my lady, aid me and help me. ³For I had two sons, and I have just buried the one, and the other is at the point of death. See how I am going to entreat and pray to God." ⁴And she began to say: "O LORD, You are compassionate, and merciful, and full of affection. You gave me two sons, of whom You have taken away the one: at least leave this one to me." ⁵Therefore, the Lady Mary, seeing the fervor of her weeping, had compassion on her and said: "Put your son in my Son's bed and cover him with His clothes." ⁶And when she had put him in the bed in which Christ was lying, he had already closed his eyes in death; ⁷but as soon as the smell of the clothes of the Lord Jesus Christ reached the boy, he opened his eyes, and, calling on his mother with a loud voice, he asked for bread, and took it, and consumed it. ⁸Then his mother said: "O Lady Mary, now I know that the power of God dwells in you, so that your Son heals those that partake of the same

nature with Himself, as soon as they have touched His clothes." ⁹This boy that was healed is he who in the Gospel is called Bartholomew.

CHAPTER 31

¹Moreover, there was a leprous woman there, and she went to the Lady Mary, the mother of Jesus, and said: "My lady, help me." ²And the Lady Mary answered: "What help do you seek? Is it gold or silver? Or is it that your body be made clean from the leprosy?" ³And that woman asked: "Who can grant me this?" ⁴And the Lady Mary said to her: "Wait a little, until I will have washed my Son Jesus and put Him to bed." ⁵The woman waited, as Mary had told her; and when she had put Jesus to bed, she held out to the woman the water in which she had washed His body and said: "Take a little of this water and pour it over your body." ⁶And as soon as she had done so, she was cleansed and gave praise and thanks to God.

CHAPTER 32

¹Therefore, after staying with her [for] three days, she went away; and coming to a city, she saw there one of the chief men, who had married the daughter of another of the chief men. ²But when he saw the woman, he beheld between her eyes the mark of leprosy in the shape of a star; and so the marriage was dissolved and became null and void. ³And when that woman saw them in this condition, weeping and overwhelmed with sorrow, she asked the cause of their grief. ⁴But they said: "Do not inquire into our condition, for to no one living can we tell our grief, and to none but ourselves can we disclose it." ⁵She urged them, however, and implored them to entrust it to her, saying that she would perhaps be able to tell them of a remedy. ⁶And when they showed her the girl, and the sign of leprosy which appeared between her eyes, as soon as she saw it, the woman said: "I also, whom you see here, labored under the same disease, when, on some business which happened to come in my way, I went to Beth-Lehem. ⁷There going into a cave, I saw a woman named Mary, whose Son was He who was named Jesus; ⁸and when she saw that I was a leper, she took pity on me and handed me the water with which she had washed her Son's body. With it I sprinkled my body and came out clean." ⁹Then the woman said to her: "Will you not, O lady, rise and go with us, and show us the Lady Mary?" ¹⁰And she assented; and they rose and went to the Lady Mary, carrying splendid gifts with them. ¹¹And when they had gone in and presented the gifts to her, they showed her the leprous girl whom they had brought. ¹²The Lady Mary therefore said: "May the compassion of the Lord Jesus Christ descend on you"; ¹³and also handing to them a little of the water in which she had washed the body of Jesus Christ, she ordered the wretched woman to be bathed in it. ¹⁴And when this had been done, she was immediately cured; and they, and all standing by, praised God. ¹⁵Therefore, they returned joyfully to their own city, praising the Lord for what He had done. ¹⁶And when the chief heard that his wife had been cured, he took her home, and made a second marriage, and gave thanks to God for the recovery of his wife's health.

CHAPTER 33

¹There was also a young woman afflicted by Satan there; for that accursed wretch repeatedly appeared to her in the form of a huge dragon and prepared to swallow her. ²He also sucked out all her blood, so that she was left like a corpse. ³As often as he came near her, she, with her hands clasped over her head, cried out and said: "Woe, woe to me! For nobody is near to free me from that accursed dragon." ⁴And her father and mother, and all who were around her or saw her, lamented her lot; ⁵and men stood around her in a crowd, and all wept and lamented, especially when she wept and said: "Oh, my brothers and friends, is there no one to free me from that murderer?" ⁶And the daughter of the chief who had been healed of her leprosy, hearing the girl's voice, went up to the roof of her castle, and saw her with her hands clasped over her head weeping, and all the crowds standing around her weeping as well. ⁷She therefore asked the demoniac's husband whether his wife's mother was alive. ⁸And when he answered that both her parents were living, she said: "Send for her mother to come to me." ⁹And when she saw that he had sent for her, and she had come, she said: "Is that distracted girl your daughter?" ¹⁰"Yes, O lady," said that sorrowful and weeping woman, "she is my daughter." ¹¹The chief's daughter answered: "Keep my secret, for I confess to you that I was formerly a leper; but now the Lady Mary, the mother of Jesus Christ, has healed me. ¹²But if you wish your daughter to be healed, take her to Beth-Lehem, and seek Mary the mother of Jesus, and believe that your daughter will be healed; I indeed believe that you will come back with joy, with your daughter healed." ¹³As soon as the woman heard the words of the chief's daughter, she led her daughter away in haste; and going to the place indicated, she went to the Lady Mary and revealed to her the state of her daughter. ¹⁴And the Lady Mary, hearing her words, gave her a little of the water in which she had washed the body of her Son Jesus and ordered her to pour it on the body of her daughter. ¹⁵She also gave her from the clothes of the Lord Jesus a swaddling cloth, saying, "Take this cloth and show it to your enemy as often as you will see him." ¹⁶And she saluted them and sent them away.

CHAPTER 34

¹When, therefore, they had gone away from her, and returned to their own district, and the time was at hand at which Satan was accustomed to attack her, at this very time that accursed one appeared to her in the shape of a huge dragon, and the girl was afraid at the sight of him. ²And her mother said to her: "Do not fear, my daughter; allow him to come near you, and then show him the cloth which the Lady Mary has given us, and let us see what will happen." ³Satan, therefore, having come near in the likeness of a terrible dragon, the body of the girl shuddered for fear of him; but as soon as she took out the cloth, and placed it on her head, and covered her eyes with it, flames and live coals began to dart forth from it, and to be cast on the dragon. ⁴O the great miracle which was done as soon as the dragon saw the cloth of the Lord Jesus, from which the fire darted, and was cast on his head and eyes! ⁵He cried out with a loud voice: "What have I to do with you, O Jesus, Son of Mary? To where will I fly from You?" ⁶And with great fear, he turned his back and departed from the girl, and never again did he appear to her. ⁷And the girl now had rest from him and gave praise and thanks to God, and along with her all who were present at that miracle.

CHAPTER 35

¹Another woman was living in the same place, whose son was tormented by Satan. ²He, Judas by name, as often as Satan seized him, used to bite all who came near him; and if he found no one near him, he used to bite his own hands and other limbs. ³The mother of this wretched creature, then, hearing the fame of the Lady Mary and her Son Jesus, rose up and brought her son Judas with her to the Lady Mary. ⁴In the meantime, James and Joses had taken the Child, the Lord Jesus, with them to play with the other children; and they had gone out of the house and sat down, and the Lord Jesus with them. ⁵And the demoniac Judas came up and sat down at Jesus' right hand: then, being attacked by Satan in the same manner as usual, he wished to bite the Lord Jesus, but was not able; ⁶nevertheless, he struck Jesus on the right side, whereon He began to weep. ⁷And immediately Satan went forth out of that boy, fleeing like a mad dog. ⁸And this boy who struck Jesus, and out of whom Satan went forth in the shape of a dog, was Judas Iscariot, who betrayed Him to the Jews; and that same side on which Judas struck Him, the Jews transfixed with a lance.

CHAPTER 36

¹Now, when the Lord Jesus had completed seven years from His birth, on a certain day He was occupied with boys of His own age. ²For they were playing among clay, from which they were making images of donkeys, oxen, birds, and other animals; and each one boasting of his skill, was praising his own work. ³Then the Lord Jesus said to the boys: "The images that I have made I will order to walk." ⁴The boys then asked Him if He was the Son of the Creator; and the Lord Jesus commanded them to walk. ⁵And they immediately began to leap; and then, when He had given them permission, they again stood still. ⁶And He had made figures of birds and sparrows, which flew when He told them to fly, and stood still when He told them to stand, and ate and drank when He handed them food and drink. ⁷After the boys had gone away and told this to their parents, their fathers said

to them: "My sons, be careful not to keep company with Him again, for He is a wizard: flee from Him, therefore, and avoid Him, and do not play with Him again after this."

CHAPTER 37

¹On a certain day, the Lord Jesus, running around and playing with the boys, passed the shop of a dyer, whose name was Salem; and he had many pieces of cloth in his shop which he was to dye. ²The Lord Jesus then, going into his shop, took up all the pieces of cloth and threw them into a tub full of indigo. ³And when Salem came and saw his cloths destroyed, he began to cry out with a loud voice, and to reproach Jesus, saying, "Why have You done this to me, O Son of Mary? You have disgraced me before all my townsmen: for, seeing that everyone desired the color that suited himself, You have indeed come and destroyed them all." ⁴The Lord Jesus answered: "I will change for you the color of any piece of cloth which you will wish to be changed." ⁵And immediately He began to take the pieces of cloth out of the tub, each of them of that color which the dyer wished, until He had taken them all out. ⁶When the Jews saw this miracle and prodigy, they praised God.

CHAPTER 38

¹And Joseph used to go around through the whole city and take the Lord Jesus with him, when people sent for him in the way of his trade to make for them doors, and milk-pails, and beds, and chests; and the Lord Jesus was with him wherever he went. ²As often, therefore, as Joseph had to make anything a cubit or a span longer or shorter, wider or narrower, the Lord Jesus stretched His hand toward it; and as soon as He did so, it became such as Joseph wished. ³Nor was it necessary for him to make anything with his own hand, for Joseph was not very skillful in carpentry.

CHAPTER 39

¹Now, on a certain day, the king of Jerusalem sent for him and said: "I wish you, Joseph, to make for me a throne to fit that place in which I usually sit." ²Joseph obeyed, and began the work immediately, and remained in the palace [for] two years, until he finished the work of that throne. ³And when he had it carried to its place, he perceived that each side lacked two spans of the prescribed measure. ⁴And the king, seeing this, was angry with Joseph; and Joseph, being in great fear of the king, spent the night without supper, nor did he taste anything at all. ⁵Then, being asked by the Lord Jesus why he was afraid, Joseph said: "Because I have spoiled all the work that I have spent two years at." ⁶And the Lord Jesus said to him: "Do not fear, and do not lose heart; but take hold of one side of the throne; I will take the other; and we will make it right." ⁷And Joseph, having done as the Lord Jesus had said, and each having drawn by his own side, the throne was made right and brought to the exact measure of the place. ⁸And those that stood by and saw this miracle were struck with astonishment and praised God. ⁹And the woods used in that throne were of those which are celebrated in the time of Solomon the son of David; that is, woods of manifold and various kinds.

CHAPTER 40

¹On another day, the Lord Jesus went out into the road, and saw the boys that had come together to play, and followed them; but the boys hid themselves from Him. ²The Lord Jesus, therefore, having come to the door of a certain house and seen some women standing there, asked them where the boys had gone; ³and when they answered that there was no one there, He said again: "Who are these whom you see in the furnace?" They replied that they were kids of three years old. ⁴And the Lord Jesus cried out and said: "Come out here, O kids, to your Shepherd." Then the boys, in the form of kids, came out and began to dance around Him; ⁵and the women, seeing this, were very greatly astonished, and were seized with trembling, and quickly supplicated and adored the Lord Jesus, saying, "O our Lord Jesus, Son of Mary, You are certainly that good Shepherd of Israel; have mercy on Your handmaidens who stand before You, and who have never doubted: for You have come, O our Lord, to heal, and not to destroy." ⁶And when the Lord Jesus answered that the sons of Israel were like the Ethiopians among the nations, the women said: "You, O Lord, know all things, nor is anything hid from You; now indeed, we beg You, and ask You of Your affection to restore these boys, Your servants, to their former condition." ⁷The Lord Jesus therefore said: "Come, boys, let us go and play." And immediately, while these women were standing by, the kids were changed into boys.

CHAPTER 41

¹Now in the month Adar, Jesus, after the manner of a king, assembled the boys together. They spread their clothes on the ground, and He sat down on them. ²Then they placed a crown made of flowers on His head, and, like chamber-servants, stood in His presence, on the right and on the left, as if He were a king. ³And whoever passed by that way was forcibly dragged by the boys, saying, "Come here and adore the King; then go your way."

CHAPTER 42

¹In the meantime, while these things were going on, some men came up carrying a boy. ²For this boy had gone into the mountain with those of his own age to seek wood, and there he found a partridge's nest; ³and when he stretched out his hand to take the eggs from it, a venomous serpent bit him from the middle of the nest, so that he called out for help. ⁴His comrades accordingly went to him with haste and found him lying on the ground like one dead. Then his relatives came and took him up to carry him back to the city. ⁵And after they had come to that place where the Lord Jesus was sitting like a king, and the rest of the boys standing around Him like His servants, the boys went hastily forward to meet him who had been bitten by the serpent and said to his relatives: "Come and salute the King." ⁶But when they were unwilling to go, on account of the sorrow in which they were, the boys dragged them by force against their will. ⁷And when they had come up to the Lord Jesus, He asked them why they were carrying the boy. ⁸And when they answered that a serpent had bitten him, the Lord Jesus said to the boys: "Let us go and kill that serpent." ⁹And the parents of the boy asked permission to go away, because their son was in the agony of death; but the boys answered them, saying, "Did you not hear the King saying: Let us go kill the serpent? And will you not obey Him?" ¹⁰And so, against their will, the bed was carried back. ¹¹And when they came to the nest, the Lord Jesus said to the boys: "Is this the serpent's place?" They said that it was; ¹²and the serpent, at the call of the LORD, came forth without delay and submitted itself to Him. And He said to it: "Go away and suck out all the poison which you have infused into this boy." ¹³And so, the serpent crawled to the boy and sucked out all its poison. Then the Lord Jesus cursed it, and immediately on this being done, it burst apart; ¹⁴and the Lord Jesus stroked the boy with his hand, and he was healed. And he began to weep; but Jesus said: "Do not weep, for by and by you will be My disciple." ¹⁵And this is Simon the Zealot, of whom mention is made in the Gospel.

CHAPTER 43

¹On another day, Joseph sent his son James to gather wood, and the Lord Jesus went with him as his companion. ²And when they had come to the place where the wood was, and James had begun to gather it, behold, a venomous viper bit his hand, so that he began to cry out and weep. ³The Lord Jesus then, seeing him in this condition, went up to him and blew on the place where the viper had bitten him; and this being done, he was immediately healed.

CHAPTER 44

¹One day, when the Lord Jesus was again with the boys playing on the roof of a house, one of the boys fell down from above, and immediately died. ²And the rest of the boys fled in all directions, and the Lord Jesus was left alone on the roof. ³And the relatives of the boy came up and said to the Lord Jesus: "It was You who threw our son headlong from the roof." ⁴And when He denied it, they cried out, saying, "Our son is dead, and here is He who has killed him!" ⁵And the Lord Jesus said to them: "Do not bring an evil report against Me; but if you do not believe Me, come and let us ask the boy himself, so that he may bring the truth to light." ⁶Then the Lord Jesus went down, and standing over the dead body, said with a loud voice: "Zeno! Zeno! Who threw you down from the roof?" ⁷Then the dead boy answered and said: "My Lord, it was not You who threw me down, but such a one cast me down from it." ⁸And when the LORD commanded those who were standing by to

attend to His words, all who were present praised God for this miracle.

CHAPTER 45

¹One time the Lady Mary had ordered the Lord Jesus to go and bring her water from the well. ²And when He had gone to get the water, the pitcher, already full, was knocked against something and was broken. ³And the Lord Jesus stretched out His handkerchief, and collected the water, and carried it to His mother; and she was astonished at it. ⁴And she hid and preserved in her heart all that she saw.

CHAPTER 46

¹Again, on another day, the Lord Jesus was with the boys at a stream of water, and they had again made little fish-ponds. ²And the Lord Jesus had made twelve sparrows and had arranged them around His fish-pond, three on each side. And it was the Sabbath day. ³Therefore, a Jew, the son of Hanan, coming up, and seeing them thus engaged, said in anger and great indignation: "Do you make figures of clay on the Sabbath day?" ⁴And he quickly ran and destroyed their fish-ponds. ⁵But when the Lord Jesus clapped His hands over the sparrows which He had made, they flew away chirping. ⁶Then the son of Hanan came up to the fish-pond of Jesus also, and kicked it with his shoes, and the water of it vanished away. ⁷And the Lord Jesus said to him: "As that water has vanished away, so your life will likewise vanish away." And immediately that boy dried up.

CHAPTER 47

¹At another time, when the Lord Jesus was returning home with Joseph in the evening, He met a boy, who ran up against Him with so much force that He fell. ²And the Lord Jesus said to him: "As you have thrown me down, so you will fall and not rise again." And that same hour the boy fell down and died.

CHAPTER 48

¹There was, moreover, at Jerusalem, a certain man named Zaccheus, who taught boys. He said to Joseph: "Why, O Joseph, do you not bring Jesus to me to learn His letters?" Joseph agreed to do so and reported the matter to the Lady Mary. ²They therefore took Him to the master; and he, as soon as he saw Him, wrote out the alphabet for Him, and told Him to say Aleph. And when He had said Aleph, the master ordered Him to pronounce Beth. ³And the Lord Jesus said to him: "Tell me first the meaning of the letter Aleph, and then I will pronounce Beth." ⁴And when the master threatened to flog Him, the Lord Jesus explained to him the meanings of the letters Aleph and Beth; ⁵also which figures of the letter were straight, which crooked, which drawn round into a spiral, which marked with points, which without them, why one letter went before another; ⁶and many other things He began to recount and to elucidate which the master himself had never either heard or read in any book. ⁷The Lord Jesus, moreover, said to the master: "Listen, and I will say them to you." And He began clearly and distinctly to repeat Aleph, Beth, Gimel, Daleth, [and] on to Taw. ⁸And the master was astonished and said: "I think that this boy was born before Noah." ⁹And turning to Joseph, he said: "You have brought to me to be taught a Boy more learned than all the masters." Also, to the Lady Mary he said: "This Son of yours has no need of instruction."

CHAPTER 49

¹Thereafter they took Him to another and a more learned master, who, when he saw Him, said: "Say Aleph." ²And when He had said Aleph, the master ordered him to pronounce Beth. ³And the Lord Jesus answered him and said: "First tell me the meaning of the letter Aleph, and then I will pronounce Beth." ⁴And when the master hereon raised his hand and flogged Him, immediately his hand dried up, and he died. ⁵Then Joseph said to the Lady Mary: "From this time we will not let Him go out of the house, since everyone who opposes Him is struck dead."

CHAPTER 50

¹And when He was twelve years old, they took Him to Jerusalem to the feast. ²And when the feast was finished, they indeed returned; but the Lord Jesus remained in the temple among the teachers, and elders, and learned men of the sons of Israel, to whom He put various questions on the sciences and gave answers in His turn. ³For He said to them: "Whose Son is the Christ?" They answered Him: "The Son of David." ⁴"Why then," He said, "does He in the Spirit call him his Lord, when he says, The LORD said to my Lord, Sit at My right hand, that I may put Your enemies under Your footsteps?" ⁵Again the chief of the teachers said to Him: "Have You read the scrolls?" ⁶"Both the scrolls," said the Lord Jesus, "and the things contained in the scrolls." ⁷And He explained the scrolls, and the Law, and the precepts, and the statutes, and the mysteries, which are contained in the scrolls of the prophets—things which the understanding of no creature attains to. ⁸That teacher therefore said: "I until now have neither attained to nor heard of such knowledge: who, please, do you think that Boy will be?"

CHAPTER 51

¹And a philosopher who was present there, a skillful astronomer, asked the Lord Jesus whether He had studied astronomy. ²And the Lord Jesus answered him and explained the number of the spheres, and of the heavenly bodies, their natures and operations; ²their opposition; their aspect—triangular, square, and sextile; their course—direct and retrograde; the twenty-fourths, and sixtieths of twenty-fourths; and other things beyond the reach of reason.

CHAPTER 52

¹There was also among those philosophers one very skilled in treating of natural science, and he asked the Lord Jesus whether He had studied medicine. ²And He, in reply, explained to him physics and metaphysics, hyperphysics and hypophysics, the powers likewise and humors of the body, and the effects of the same; ³also the number of members and bones, of veins, arteries, and nerves; ⁴also the effect of heat and dryness, of cold and moisture, and what these give rise to; ⁵what was the operation of the soul on the body, and its perceptions and powers; ⁶what was the operation of the faculty of speech, of anger, of desire; ⁷lastly, their conjunction and disjunction, and other things beyond the reach of any created intellect. ⁸Then that philosopher rose up, and adored the Lord Jesus, and said: "O Lord, from this time I will be Your disciple and slave."

CHAPTER 53

¹While they were speaking to each other of these and other things, the Lady Mary came, after having gone around seeking Him for three days along with Joseph. ²She, therefore, seeing Him sitting among the teachers asking them questions, and answering in His turn, said to Him: "My Son, why have You treated us this way? Behold, Your father and I have sought You with great trouble." ³But He said: "Why do you seek Me? Do you not know that I ought to occupy Myself in My Father's house?" ⁴But they did not understand the words that He spoke to them. ⁵Then those teachers asked Mary whether He was her Son; and when she signified that He was, they said: "Blessed are you, O Mary, who has brought forth such a Son." ⁶And returning with them to Nazareth, He obeyed them in all things. And His mother kept all these words of His in her heart. ⁷And the Lord Jesus advanced in stature, and in wisdom, and in favor with God and man.

CHAPTER 54

¹And from this day on He began to hide His miracles, and mysteries, and secrets, and to give attention to the Law, ²until He completed His thirtieth year, when His Father publicly declared Him at the Jordan by this voice sent down from Heaven: "This is My beloved Son, in whom I am well pleased"—the Holy Spirit being present in the form of a white dove.

CHAPTER 55

¹This is He whom we adore with supplications, who has given us being and life, and who has brought us from our mothers' wombs; ²who for our sakes assumed a human body and redeemed us, so that He might embrace us in eternal compassion and show to us His mercy according to His liberality, and beneficence, and generosity, and benevolence. ³To Him is glory, and beneficence, and power, and dominion from this time forth forevermore. Amen.

HERE ENDS THE WHOLE GOSPEL OF THE INFANCY, WITH THE AID OF GOD MOST HIGH, ACCORDING TO WHAT WE HAVE FOUND IN THE ORIGINAL.

GOSPEL OF THE NATIVITY OF MARY

Originating as part of the Gospel of Pseudo-Matthew, around the 9th century it began to be regarded as an independent work. As the name implies, it details the nativity of Mary, the mother of Jesus.

CHAPTER 1

¹The blessed and glorious Mary, ever-virgin, sprung from the royal lineage and family of David, and born in the city of Nazareth, was brought up at Jerusalem in the temple of the LORD. Her father was called Joachim and her mother Anna. ²Her father's house was of Galilee and the city of Nazareth, and her mother's race was of Beth-Lehem. ³Their life was simple and upright before the LORD, and pious and blameless before men. ⁴For they divided all their substance into three parts: one part they gave to the temple and the servants of the temple, another they devoted to strangers and the poor, the third they reserved for the use of their family and for themselves. ⁵Thus, these persons, dear to God, and good to men, passed about twenty years in chaste matrimony at home without producing children. ⁶But they vowed that if God should perhaps give them offspring, they would yield it to the service of the LORD; for which reason they were accustomed to frequent the temple of the LORD at every festival in the year.

CHAPTER 2

¹Now it came to pass that the Celebration of Dedication drew near; therefore, Joachim also with some of his relatives went up to Jerusalem. ²Now at that time, Issachar was chief priest there. ³And when among his other fellow townsmen he also saw Joachim with his offering, he despised him and spurned his gifts, asking why he who was childless should presume to stand among those who had children, saying that his gifts could not at all seem worthy to God, seeing that He had judged him unworthy of offspring, when the Writing says that everyone is accursed who has not begotten male or female in Israel. ⁴He therefore said that he must first be released from this curse by having offspring, and then finally he was to come before the LORD with his offerings. ⁵Joachim being covered with much shame by this reproach cast on him, withdrew to the shepherds who were with the flocks in their pastures, for he would not return home, lest he should be stigmatized with the same reproach by his kinsmen, who were also present and heard this from the priest.

CHAPTER 3

¹But when he had been there some time, on a certain day when he was alone, the messenger of the LORD stood by him with a very great light. ²He being troubled at the sight of him, the messenger who appeared to him relieved his fear, saying, "Do not fear, Joachim, nor be troubled at the sight of me; for I am a messenger of the LORD, sent by Him to you to tell you that your prayers are heard, and that your alms have come up in His sight. ³For He has truly seen your shame and heard the reproach of barrenness not rightly cast on you. ⁴For God is the avenger of sin, not of nature, and therefore when He makes anyone childless, He does it for this reason: that He may the more wonderfully offer relief, and that that which is born may be known not to be of lust but of the divine gift. ⁵For was not Sarah the first mother of your race unfruitful until her eightieth year? ⁶And yet in the last period of old age she bore Isaac, to whom was promised the blessing of all nations. ⁷Rachel also, so pleasant to the LORD and so loved by holy Jacob, was long barren, and yet bore Joseph—not only lord of Egypt, but the deliverer of many nations who were about to perish of hunger. ⁸Who among the princes was stronger than Samson, or holier than Samuel? ⁹And yet both of them had barren mothers. If then reason does not persuade you by my words, believe in fact that conceptions long delayed and barren births are accustomed to be more wonderful. ¹⁰Therefore, your wife Anna will bear you a daughter, and you will call her name Mary; she will be, as you have vowed, consecrated to the LORD from her infancy, and will be filled with the Holy Spirit even from her mother's womb. ¹¹She will neither eat nor drink anything impure, nor will her conversation be among public crowds out of doors, but in the temple of the LORD, so that nothing evil may be said or so much as suspected of her. ¹²Therefore, with advancing age, as she will be marvelously born of one barren, so she who is incomparably a virgin will conceive the Son of the Most High who will be called Jesus, and according to the etymology of His Name will be the Savior of all nations. ¹³And this will be to you a sign of what I announce: when you come to the Golden Gate at Jerusalem, you will have your wife Anna there to meet you, who now being anxious through the delay of your return, will then rejoice in seeing you." ¹⁴This said, the messenger departed from him.

CHAPTER 4

¹Then he appeared to his wife Anna, saying, "Do not fear, Anna, nor think it is an apparition which you see. ²For I am that messenger which has offered your prayers and alms in the sight of God, and am now sent to you to announce that a daughter will be born to you, who will be called Mary and be blessed above all women. ³She, being full of the grace of the LORD from her very birth, will remain in the house of her parents the three years of her suckling. ⁴Afterward, being given up to the service of the LORD, she will not leave the temple until her years of understanding; ⁵there in short, serving God night and day in fastings and prayers, she will abstain from everything unclean, she will never know man, but alone, without example, without spot, without corruption, without intercourse with man, as a virgin will conceive a Son, and as a handmaid [will conceive] the LORD who by grace, and Name, and work will be the Savior of the world. ⁶Therefore, go up to Jerusalem, and when you come to the gate, which is called Golden, because it is gilded, there for a sign will you meet your husband for whose safety and welfare you are anxious. ⁷Therefore, when these things happen thus, know that what I tell you will be without doubt accomplished."

CHAPTER 5

¹Therefore, according to the precept of the messenger, both of them leaving the places in which they were, went up to Jerusalem; ²and when they had come to the place indicated by the angelic prediction, there they met together. ³Then rejoicing at the sight of one another, and certainly sure of the promised offspring, they gave due thanks to the LORD, the exalter of the humble. ⁴Therefore, having adored the LORD, they returned home sure of the divine promise; and they waited cheerfully. ⁵Therefore, Anna conceived and bore a daughter, and according to the messenger's command, her parents called her name Mary.

CHAPTER 6

¹And when the course of three years had elapsed, and the time for weaning was accomplished, they brought the virgin to the temple of the LORD with their offerings. ²Now there were around the temple, according to the fifteen psalms of degrees, fifteen steps to go up: for since the temple was set on a mount, the altar of burnt offering, which was outside, could not be approached except by steps. ³On one of these, therefore, her parents set the blessed little virgin Mary. ⁴And while they took off the garments which they had worn on the journey, and arrayed themselves according to custom, in vesture more bright and clean, the virgin of the LORD went up all the steps in order, without the hand of anyone to lead and lift her, so that, in this case, you might suppose she came nothing short of perfect age. ⁵Already then, the LORD worked something great in the infancy of His virgin and showed beforehand, by the indication of this miracle, how great she should be. ⁶Therefore, when the sacrifice was accomplished, according to the custom of the Law, and their vow performed, they left the virgin with other virgins within the precincts of the temple to be brought up there; but they themselves returned home.

CHAPTER 7

¹Now the virgin of the LORD, with advancing age, also made progress in virtue; and, according to the psalmist, her father and

mother left her, but the LORD took her up. ²For she was daily attended by messengers, and daily she enjoyed the divine vision, which kept her from all evil, and caused her to abound in all good. ³She came, therefore, to her fourteenth year, and not only could they devise against her no evil, nor anything worthy of blame, but all good men who knew her judged her life and conversation worthy of admiration. ⁴Then the chief priest publicly announced that the virgins who were publicly placed in the temple, and had arrived at this time of life, should return home and seek to be married, according to the custom of the nation, and the maturity of their age. ⁵But when the others had promptly obeyed this command, Mary alone, the virgin of the LORD, answered that she could not do this, saying that her parents had given her up to the service of the LORD; ⁶and that, moreover, she had herself vowed her virginity to the LORD and would never violate it by any carnal association with man. ⁷Now the chief priest, being perplexed in mind, because he did not think the vow should be broken against the Writing, which says, "Vow and pay," neither dared introduce a custom unusual with the nation: ⁸so he gave an order that at the impending festival all the chief men of Jerusalem and the neighboring places should attend, with whose counsel he might know what was to be done in such a doubtful a matter. ⁹When this took place, it pleased them all alike, that the LORD should be consulted in this affair. ¹⁰And while they all bowed down in prayer, the chief priest went to consult God, according to custom; ¹¹nor was there any delay, for in the hearing of all, there came a voice from the oracle and the place of the propitiatory covering, that, according to the prophecy of Isaiah, inquiry must be made, to whom that virgin ought to be commended and espoused. ¹²For it is clear that Isaiah says, "A rod will go forth from the root of Jesse, || And a flower will arise from his root, || And the Spirit of the LORD will rest on Him, || A Spirit of wisdom and understanding, || A Spirit of counsel and might, || A Spirit of knowledge and piety, || And the Spirit of the fear of the LORD will fill him." ¹³According to this prophecy, therefore, he foretold that all of the house and family of David who were suitable to be married, but were not married, should bring their rods to the altar; ¹⁴and he whose rod, after it was brought, should produce a flower, while on its top the Spirit of the LORD sat in the form of a dove, it was he to whom the virgin ought to be commended and espoused.

CHAPTER 8

¹Now among others was Joseph, an aged man of the house and family of David; but when all of them brought their rods in order, he alone withdrew his. ²Therefore, when nothing appeared agreeable to the divine voice, the chief priest thought that God should be consulted again; ³and He answered that of those who were designated, he alone to whom He must espouse the virgin had not brought his rod. ⁴Joseph therefore was betrayed, for when he brought his rod, and a dove came from Heaven and sat on the top of it, it was plainly apparent to all that the virgin was to be espoused to him. ⁵When, therefore, the betrothal had been celebrated in the customary manner, he retired to the city of Beth-Lehem to set his house in order, and to procure what was required by his marriage. ⁶But Mary, the virgin of the LORD, with seven other virgins of similar age, and brought up with her, which she had received from the priest, returned to the house of her parents in Galilee.

CHAPTER 9

¹Now in those days, namely, at the time when she first came into Galilee, the messenger Gabriel was sent to her from God, and made known to her the LORD's conception, and explained to her the method or order of the conception. ²At last, having entered to her, he filled the chamber where she resided with an immense light, and saluting her most courteously, he said, "Hail, Mary! Most agreeable virgin of the LORD! Virgin, full of grace, the LORD is with you; blessed are you before all women; blessed are you before all men previously born." ³But the virgin, who already well knew the countenances of messengers, and was not unused to heavenly light, was neither terrified by the angelic vision, nor dazed by the greatness of the light, but was troubled at his word alone and began to think what that salutation, so unusual, could be, or what it portended, or what end it would have. ⁴But the messenger, divinely inspired, counteracting this thought, said: "Do not fear, Mary, as though I meant something contrary to your chastity by this salutation; for you have found grace with the LORD, because you have chosen chastity; therefore, you will conceive without sin, as a virgin, and will bear a Son. ⁵He will be great, for He will rule from sea to sea, and from the river to the ends of the world; and He will be called the Son of the Most High, for He who is born humble on earth, reigns exalted in Heaven: ⁶and the LORD God will give to Him the seat of His father David, and He will reign in the house of Jacob forever, and of His kingdom there will be no end, since He is Himself King of kings, and Lord of lords, and His throne [is] forever and ever." ⁷The virgin, not incredulous at these words of the messenger, but only wishing to know, answered, "How can this be? For since according to my vow I never knew man, how can I bring forth without human seed?" ⁸To this the messenger replied, "Do not think, Mary, that you will conceive in human manner, for without intercourse with man, as a virgin, you will conceive, as a virgin you will bring forth, as a virgin you will nourish; ⁹for the Holy Spirit will come on you, and the power of the Most High will overshadow you, contrary to all fire of lust; therefore, what is born of you will be alone holy, because alone conceived and born without sin, and will be called the Son of God." ¹⁰Then Mary, with outspread hands and eyes lifted up to Heaven, said, "Behold, the handmaid of the LORD, for I am unworthy of the name of lady; let it be to me according to your word." ¹¹It would perhaps be long and tedious to some, if we wished to insert, in this little work, all that we read preceded or followed the LORD's nativity; ¹²therefore, omitting those things which are more fully written in the Gospel, we come to the narration of those things which are less detailed.

CHAPTER 10

¹Joseph, therefore, having come from Judea into Galilee, intended to take as a wife the virgin who was espoused to him, for three months had now elapsed, and the fourth approached from the time when she had been espoused to him. ²Meanwhile, her pregnancy began to gradually show itself, and it could not be hidden from Joseph, for entering freely to the virgin in the manner of a spouse, and talking familiarly with her, he perceived her to be with child. ³Therefore, he began to be disturbed and troubled in mind, because he did not know what it was best for him to do, for he neither wished to expose her, because he was a just man, nor to defame her by a suspicion of unchastity, because he was a pious man. ⁴Therefore, he thought to dissolve his marriage privately, and to put her away secretly. ⁵But while he thought thus, behold, the messenger of the LORD appeared to him in a dream, saying, "Joseph, son of David, do not fear: that is, cherish no suspicion of unchastity against the virgin, nor think anything bad, nor fear to take her for a wife, for that which she has conceived and now vexes your mind, is not the work of man, but of the Holy Spirit. ⁶For she alone, of all, as a virgin, will bear the Son of God; and you will call His Name Jesus, that is, a Savior, for He will save His people from their sins." ⁷Therefore, Joseph, according to the command of the messenger, took the virgin for a wife, yet did not know her, but kept her carefully under his protection in chastity. ⁸And now the ninth month from her conception drew near, when Joseph, having taken his wife, with what else was necessary, went to the city of Beth-Lehem, where he was from. ⁹And it came to pass while they were there, her days were accomplished that she should bring forth, and she brought forth her firstborn Son, as the holy evangelists have taught, our Lord Jesus Christ, who, with the Father and the Holy Spirit, lives and reigns—God—forever and ever.

HISTORY OF JOSEPH THE CARPENTER

This work, probably written in the 6th or 7th century, is written as a recounting of the life of Joseph by his Son Jesus while Jesus was on the Mount of Olives. It contains a number of ancient Church traditions. Uniquely, the work claims that Joseph lived to the age of 111.

IN THE NAME OF GOD, OF ONE ESSENCE AND THREE PERSONS.

THE HISTORY OF THE DEATH OF OUR FATHER, THE HOLY OLD MAN, JOSEPH THE CARPENTER.

MAY HIS BLESSINGS AND PRAYERS PRESERVE US ALL, O BROTHERS. AMEN!

HIS WHOLE LIFE WAS ONE HUNDRED AND ELEVEN YEARS, AND HIS DEPARTURE FROM THIS WORLD HAPPENED ON THE TWENTY-SIXTH OF THE MONTH ABIB, WHICH ANSWERS TO THE MONTH AB. MAY HIS PRAYER PRESERVE US! AMEN. AND INDEED, IT WAS OUR LORD JESUS CHRIST HIMSELF WHO RELATED THIS HISTORY TO HIS HOLY DISCIPLES ON THE MOUNT OF OLIVES, AND ALL JOSEPH'S LABOR, AND THE END OF HIS DAYS. AND THE HOLY APOSTLES HAVE PRESERVED THIS CONVERSATION AND HAVE LEFT IT WRITTEN DOWN IN THE LIBRARY AT JERUSALEM. MAY THEIR PRAYERS PRESERVE US! AMEN.

CHAPTER 1

1 It happened one day, when the Savior, our Master, God, and Savior Jesus Christ, was sitting along with His disciples, and they were all assembled on the Mount of Olives, that He said to them: "O My brothers and friends, sons of the Father who has chosen you from all men, you know that I have often told you that I must be crucified, and must die for the salvation of Adam and his posterity, and that I will rise from the dead. 2 Now I will commit to you the doctrine of the sacred good news formerly announced to you, that you may declare it throughout the whole world. And I will endow you with power from on high and fill you with the Holy Spirit. 3 And you will declare to all nations conversion and forgiveness of sins. For a single cup of water, if a man will find it in the world to come, is greater and better than all the wealth of this whole world. And as much ground as one foot can occupy in the house of My Father, is greater and more excellent than all the riches of the earth. 4 Yes, a single hour in the joyful dwelling of the pious is more blessed and more precious than one thousand years among sinners: inasmuch as their weeping and lamentation will not come to an end, and their tears will not cease, nor will they find for themselves consolation and repose at any time forever. 5 And now, O My honored members, go declare to all nations, tell them, and say to them: "Truly the Savior diligently inquires into the inheritance which is due, and is the administrator of justice. 6 And the messengers will cast down their enemies and will fight for them in the day of conflict. And He will examine every single foolish and idle word which men speak, and they will give an account of it. For as no one will escape death, so also the works of every man will be laid open on the day of judgment, whether they have been good or evil." 7 Tell them also this word which I have said to you today: "Do not let the strong man glory in his strength, nor the rich man in his riches; but let him who wishes to glory, glory in the LORD."

CHAPTER 2

1 There was a man whose name was Joseph, sprung from a family of Beth-Lehem, a town of Judah, and the city of King David. 2 This same man, being well furnished with wisdom and learning, was made a priest in the temple of the LORD. He was, besides, skillful in his trade, which was that of a carpenter; and after the manner of all men, he married a wife. 3 Moreover, he begot for himself sons and daughters: four sons, namely, and two daughters. Now these are their names: Judas, Justus, James, and Simon. 4 The names of the two daughters were Assia and Lydia. Eventually the wife of righteous Joseph, a woman intent on the divine glory in all her works, departed this life. 5 But Joseph, that righteous man, My father after the flesh, and the spouse of My mother Mary, went away with his sons to his trade, practicing the art of a carpenter.

CHAPTER 3

1 Now when righteous Joseph became a widower, My mother Mary—blessed, holy, and pure—was already twelve years old. 2 For her parents offered her in the temple when she was three years of age, and she remained in the temple of the LORD nine years. 3 Then when the priests saw that the virgin, holy and God-fearing, was growing up, they spoke to each other, saying, "Let us search for a man, righteous and pious, to whom Mary may be entrusted until the time of her marriage; 4 lest, if she remain in the temple, it happen to her as is customary to happen to women, and lest on that account we sin, and God be angry with us.

CHAPTER 4

1 Therefore, they immediately sent for and assembled twelve old men of the tribe of Judah. 2 And they wrote down the names of the twelve tribes of Israel. And the lot fell on the pious old man, righteous Joseph. 3 Then the priests answered and said to My blessed mother: "Go with Joseph and be with him until the time of your marriage." 4 Therefore, righteous Joseph received My mother and led her away to his own house. And Mary found James the Lesser in his father's house, broken-hearted and sad on account of the loss of his mother, and she brought him up. 5 Hence Mary was called the mother of James. 6 Thereafter, Joseph left her at home and went away to the shop where he worked at his trade as a carpenter. 7 And after the holy virgin had spent two years in his house, her age was exactly fourteen years, including the time at which he received her.

CHAPTER 5

1 And I chose her of My own will, with the concurrence of My Father, and the counsel of the Holy Spirit. And I was made flesh of her, by a mystery which transcends the grasp of created reason. 2 And three months after her conception, the righteous man Joseph returned from the place where he worked at his trade; and when he found My virgin mother pregnant, he was greatly perplexed and thought of sending her away secretly. 3 But from fear, and sorrow, and the anguish of his heart, he could endure neither to eat nor drink that day.

CHAPTER 6

1 But at midday there appeared to him in a dream the prince of the messengers, the holy Gabriel, furnished with a command from My Father; and he said to him: "Joseph, son of David, do not fear to take Mary as your wife, for she has conceived of the Holy Spirit; 2 and she will bring forth a Son, whose Name will be called Jesus. It is He who will rule all nations with a rod of iron." 3 Having thus spoken, the messenger departed from him. And Joseph rose from his sleep and did as the messenger of the LORD had said to him; and Mary abode with him.

CHAPTER 7

1 Sometime after that, there came forth an order from Augustus Cæsar the king, that all the habitable world should be enrolled—each man in his own city. 2 Therefore, the old man, righteous Joseph, rose up and took the virgin Mary and came to Beth-Lehem, because the time of her bringing forth was at hand. 3 Joseph then inscribed his name in the list, for Joseph the son of David, whose spouse Mary was, was of the tribe of Judah. 4 And indeed Mary, My mother, brought Me forth in Beth-Lehem, in a cave near the tomb of Rachel the wife of the patriarch Jacob, the mother of Joseph and Benjamin.

CHAPTER 8

1 But Satan went and told this to Herod the Great, the father of Archelaus. 2 And it was this same Herod who ordered My friend and relative John to be beheaded. 3 Accordingly, he searched for Me diligently, thinking that My kingdom was to be of this world. But Joseph, that pious old man, was warned of this by a dream. 4 Therefore, he rose and took My mother Mary, and I lay in her bosom. Salome was also their fellow-traveler. 5 Having therefore set out from home, he retired into Egypt, and remained there the span of one whole year, until the hatred of Herod passed away.

CHAPTER 9

¹Now Herod died by the worst form of death, atoning for the shedding of the blood of the children whom he wickedly cut off, though there was no sin in them. ²And that impious tyrant Herod being dead, they returned into the land of Israel and lived in a city of Galilee which is called Nazareth. ³And Joseph, going back to his trade as a carpenter, earned his living by the work of his hands; for, as the Law of Moses had commanded, he never sought to live for nothing by another's labor.

CHAPTER 10

¹Finally, by increasing years, the old man arrived at a very advanced age. He did not, however, labor under any bodily weakness, nor had his sight failed, nor had any tooth perished from his mouth. ²In mind also, for the whole time of his life, he never wandered; but like a boy, he always displayed youthful vigor in his business, and his limbs remained unimpaired and free from all pain. ³His life, then, in all, amounted to one hundred and eleven years—his old age being prolonged to the utmost limit.

CHAPTER 11

¹Now Justus and Simeon, the elder sons of Joseph, were married and had families of their own. Both the daughters were likewise married and lived in their own houses. ²So there remained in Joseph's house, Judas and James the Lesser, and My virgin mother. ³Moreover, I dwelt along with them, not otherwise than if I had been one of his sons. But I passed all My life without fault. ⁴I called Mary My mother, and Joseph father, and I obeyed them in all that they said; nor did I ever contend against them, but complied with their commands, as other men whom earth produces are accustomed to do; nor did I at any time arouse their anger, or give any word or answer in opposition to them. ⁵On the contrary, I cherished them with great love, like the pupil of My eye.

CHAPTER 12

¹It came to pass, after these things, that the death of that old man, the pious Joseph, and his departure from this world, were approaching, as happens to other men who owe their origin to this earth. ²And as his body was on the verge of dissolution, a messenger of the LORD informed him that his death was now close at hand. ³Therefore, fear and great perplexity came on him. ⁴So he rose up and went to Jerusalem; and going into the temple of the LORD, he poured out his prayers there before the sanctuary, and he said:

CHAPTER 13

¹"O God! Author of all consolation, God of all compassion, and Lord of the whole human race; God of my soul, body, and spirit; with supplications I honor you, O LORD and my God. ²If my days are now ended, and the time draws near when I must leave this world, send me, I beg You, the great Michael, the prince of Your holy messengers: ³let him remain with me, that my wretched soul may depart from this afflicted body without trouble, without terror and impatience. ⁴For great fear and intense sadness take hold of all bodies on the day of their death, whether it be man or woman, beast wild or tame, or whatever creeps on the ground or flies in the air. In the end, all creatures under [the] sky in whom is the breath of life are struck with horror, and their souls depart from their bodies with strong fear and great depression. ⁵Now therefore, O LORD and my God, let Your holy messenger be present with his help to my soul and body, until they will be severed from each other. ⁶And do not let the face of the messenger, appointed my guardian from the day of my birth, be turned away from me; but may he be the companion of my journey even until he brings me to You: ⁷let his countenance be pleasant and cheerful to me, and let him accompany me in peace. ⁸And do not let demons of frightful appearance come near me in the way in which I am to go, until I come to You in bliss. ⁹And do not let the doorkeepers hinder my soul from entering paradise. ¹⁰And do not uncover my sins and expose me to condemnation before Your terrible tribunal. ¹¹Do not let the lions rush in on me; nor let the waves of the sea of fire overwhelm my soul—for this must every soul pass through—before I have seen the glory of Your Godhead. ¹²O God, most righteous Judge, who in justice and equity will judge mankind, and will render to each one according to his works, O LORD and my God, I beg You: ¹³be present to me in Your compassion and enlighten my path that I may come to You; for You are a fountain overflowing with all good things, and with glory forevermore. Amen."

CHAPTER 14

¹It came to pass thereafter, when he returned to his own house in the city of Nazareth, that he was seized by disease, and had to remain in his bed. ²And it was at this time that he died, according to the destiny of all mankind. For this disease was very heavy on him, and he had never been ill, as he now was, from the day of his birth. ³And thus, it assuredly pleased Christ to order the destiny of righteous Joseph. ⁴He lived forty years unmarried; thereafter his wife remained under his care [for] forty-nine years and then died. ⁵And a year after her death, my mother, the blessed Mary, was entrusted to him by the priests, that he should keep her until the time of her marriage. ⁶She spent two years in his house; and in the third year of her stay with Joseph, in the fifteenth year of her age, she brought Me forth on earth by a mystery which no creature can penetrate or understand, except Myself, and My Father, and the Holy Spirit, constituting one essence with Myself.

CHAPTER 15

¹The whole age of My father, therefore, that righteous old man, was one hundred and eleven years, My Father in Heaven having so decreed. ²And the day on which his soul left his body was the twenty-sixth of the month Abib. ³For now, the fine gold began to lose its splendor, and the silver to be worn down by use—I mean his understanding and his wisdom. ⁴He also loathed food and drink and lost all his skill in his trade of carpentry, nor did he pay attention to it anymore. ⁵It came to pass, then, in the early dawn of the twenty-sixth day of Abib, that Joseph, that righteous old man, lying in his bed, was giving up his restless soul. ⁶Therefore, he opened his mouth with many sighs and struck his hands against one another, and with a loud voice cried out and spoke after the following manner:

CHAPTER 16

¹"Woe to the day on which I was born into the world! Woe to the womb which bore me! ²Woe to the bowels which admitted me! Woe to the breasts which suckled me! ³Woe to the feet on which I sat and rested! Woe to the hands which carried me and reared me until I grew up! ⁴For I was conceived in iniquity, and in sins my mother desired me. ⁵Woe to my tongue and my lips, which have brought forth and spoken vanity, slander, falsehood, ignorance, derision, idle tales, craft, and hypocrisy! ⁶Woe to my eyes, which have looked on scandalous things! Woe to my ears, which have delighted in the words of slanderers! ⁷Woe to my hands, which have seized what did not of right belong to them! Woe to my belly and my bowels, which have lusted after food unlawful to be eaten! ⁸Woe to my throat, which like a fire has consumed all that it found! Woe to my feet, which have too often walked in ways displeasing to God! ⁹Woe to my body! And woe to my miserable soul, which has already turned aside from God its Maker! ¹⁰What will I do when I arrive at that place where I must stand before the most righteous Judge, and when He will call me to account for the works which I have heaped up in my youth? Woe to every man dying in his sins! ¹¹Assuredly that same dreadful hour, which came on my father Jacob, when his soul was flying forth from his body, is now, behold, near at hand for me. ¹²Oh, how wretched I am this day and worthy of lamentation! But God alone is the disposer of my soul and body; He also will deal with them after His own good pleasure."

CHAPTER 17

¹These are the words spoken by Joseph, that righteous old man. ²And I, going in beside him, found his soul exceedingly troubled, for he was placed in great perplexity. ³And I said to him: "Hail, My father Joseph, you righteous man; how is it with you?" ⁴And he answered me: "All hail! My well-beloved Son. Indeed, the agony and fear of death have already surrounded me; but as soon as I heard Your voice, my soul was at rest. ⁵O Jesus of Nazareth! Jesus, my Savior! Jesus, the deliverer of my soul! Jesus, my protector! ⁶Jesus! O sweetest Name in my mouth, and in the mouth of all those that love it! O eye which sees, and ear which hears, hear me! ⁷I am Your servant; this day I most humbly honor You, and before Your face I pour out my tears. You

are altogether my God; ⁸You are my Lord, as the messenger has told me times without number, and especially on that day when my soul was driven around with perverse thoughts about the pure and blessed Mary, who was carrying You in her womb, and whom I was thinking of secretly sending away. ⁹And while I was thus meditating, behold, there appeared to me in my rest messengers of the LORD, saying to me in a wonderful mystery: ¹⁰O Joseph, you son of David, do not fear to take Mary as your wife; and do not grieve your soul, nor speak improper words of her conception, because she is with child of the Holy Spirit, and will bring forth a Son, whose Name will be called Jesus, for He will save His people from their sins. ¹¹Do not for this reason wish me evil, O LORD! For I was ignorant of the mystery of Your birth. ¹²I call to mind also, my Lord, that day when the boy died of the bite of the serpent. ¹³And his relations wished to deliver You to Herod, saying that You had killed him; but You raised him from the dead and restored him to them. ¹⁴Then I went up to You, and took hold of Your hand, saying, My son, take care of Yourself. ¹⁵But You said to me in reply: Are you not My father after the flesh? I will teach you who I am. ¹⁶Now therefore, O LORD and my God, do not be angry with me, or condemn me on account of that hour. ¹⁷I am Your servant, and the son of Your handmaiden; but You are my Lord, my God and Savior, most certainly the Son of God."

CHAPTER 18

¹When My father Joseph had thus spoken, he was unable to weep [any]more. And I saw that death now had dominion over him. ²And my mother, undefiled virgin, rose and came to me, saying, "O my beloved Son, this pious old man Joseph is now dying." ³And I answered: "Oh, My dearest mother, assuredly on all creatures produced in this world the same necessity of death lies; for death holds sway over the whole human race. ⁴Even you, O My virgin mother, must look for the same end of life as other mortals. ⁵And yet your death, as also the death of this pious man, is not death, but life enduring to eternity. ⁶No, [even] more—even I must die, as concerns the body which I have received from you. ⁷But rise, O My venerable mother, and go in to Joseph, that blessed old man, in order that you may see what will happen as his soul ascends from his body."

CHAPTER 19

¹My undefiled mother Mary, therefore, went and entered the place where Joseph was. And I was sitting at his feet looking at him, for the signs of death already appeared in his countenance. ²And that blessed old man raised his head and kept his eyes fixed on My face; but he had no power of speaking to Me, on account of the agonies of death, which held him in their grasp. ³But he kept fetching many sighs. And I held his hands for a whole hour; and he turned his face to Me and made signs for Me not to leave him. ⁴Thereafter, I put My hand on his breast, and perceived his soul now near his throat, preparing to depart from its receptacle.

CHAPTER 20

¹And when My virgin mother saw Me touching his body, she also touched his feet. ²And finding them already dead and destitute of heat, she said to Me: "O my beloved Son, assuredly his feet are already beginning to stiffen, and they are as cold as snow." ³Accordingly, she summoned his sons and daughters and said to them: "Come, as many as there are of you, and go to your father, for he is now assuredly at the very point of death." ⁴And Assia, his daughter, answered and said, "Woe is me, O my brothers! This is certainly the same disease that my beloved mother died of." ⁵And she lamented and shed tears; and all Joseph's other children mourned along with her. ⁶I also, and My mother Mary, wept along with them.

CHAPTER 21

¹And turning My eyes toward the region of the south, I saw Death already approaching, and all Gehenna with him, closely attended by his army and his escorts; and their clothes, their faces, and their mouths poured forth flames. ²And when My father Joseph saw them coming straight to him, his eyes dissolved in tears, and at the same time he groaned after a strange manner. ³Accordingly, when I saw the vehemence of his sighs, I drove back Death and all the host of servants which accompanied him. And I called on My good Father, saying:

CHAPTER 22

¹"O Father of all mercy, eye which see, and ear which hear, listen to My prayers and supplications in behalf of the old man Joseph; ²and send Michael, the prince of Your messengers, and Gabriel, the herald of light, and all the light of Your messengers, and let their whole array walk with the soul of My father Joseph, until they will have conducted it to You. ³This is the hour in which My father has need of compassion. And I say to You, that all the saints, yes, as many men as are born in the world, whether they are just or whether they are perverse, must necessarily taste death."

CHAPTER 23

¹Therefore, Michael and Gabriel came to the soul of My father Joseph, and took it, and wrapped it in a shining wrapper. ²Thus, he committed his spirit into the hands of My good Father, and He bestowed on him peace. ³But as of yet, none of his children knew that he had fallen asleep. ⁴And the messengers preserved his soul from the demons of darkness which were in the way and praised God even until they conducted it into the dwelling-place of the pious.

CHAPTER 24

¹Now his body was lying prostrate and bloodless; therefore, I reached forth My hand, and put right his eyes, and shut his mouth, and said to the virgin Mary: "O My mother, where is the skill which he showed in all the time that he lived in this world? ²Behold, it has perished, as if it had never existed." And when his children heard Me speaking with My mother, the pure virgin, they knew that he had already breathed his last, and they shed tears and lamented. ³But I said to them: "Assuredly, the death of your father is not death, but life everlasting, for he has been freed from the troubles of this life, and has passed to perpetual and everlasting rest." ⁴When they heard these words, they tore their clothes and wept.

CHAPTER 25

¹And indeed, the inhabitants of Nazareth and of Galilee, having heard of their lamentation, flocked to them and wept from the third hour even to the ninth. ²And at the ninth hour, they all went together to Joseph's bed. ³And they lifted his body, after they had anointed it with costly ointments. ⁴But I entreated My Father in the prayer of the celestials—that same prayer which with My own hand I made before I was carried in the womb of the virgin Mary, My mother. ⁵And as soon as I had finished it and pronounced the amen, a great multitude of messengers came up; ⁶and I ordered two of them to stretch out their shining garments, and to wrap in them the body of Joseph, the blessed old man.

CHAPTER 26

¹And I spoke to Joseph and said, "The smell or corruption of death will not have dominion over you, nor will a worm ever come forth from your body. ²Not a single limb of it will be broken, nor will any hair on your head be changed. ³Nothing of your body will perish, O My father Joseph, but it will remain entire and uncorrupted even until the banquet of the one thousand years. ⁴And whosoever will make an offering on the day of your remembrance, him I will bless and reward in the congregation of the virgins; ⁵and whosoever will give food to the wretched, the poor, the widows, and orphans from the work of his hands, on the day on which your memory will be celebrated, and in your name, will not be in need of good things all the days of his life. ⁶And whosoever will have given a cup of water, or of wine, to drink to the widow or orphan in your name, I will give him to you, that you may go in with him to the banquet of the one thousand years. ⁷And every man who will present an offering on the day of your commemoration I will bless and reward in the assembly of the virgins: for one I will render to him thirty, sixty, and one hundred. ⁸And whosoever will write the history of your life, of your labor, and your departure from this world, and this narrative that has issued from My mouth, him I will commit to your keeping as long as he will have to do with this life. ⁹And when his soul departs from the body, and when he must leave this world, I will burn the book of his sins, nor will I torment him with any punishment in the day of judgment; ¹⁰but he will cross the sea of flames and will go

through it without trouble or pain. ⁱⁱAnd on every poor man who can give none of those things which I have mentioned, this is incumbent: if a son is born to him, he will call his name Joseph. ¹²So, there will not take place in that house either poverty or any sudden death forever.

CHAPTER 27

¹Thereafter, the chief men of the city came together to the place where the body of the blessed old man Joseph had been laid, bringing with them burial-clothes; ²and they wished to wrap it up in them after the manner in which the Jews are accustomed to arrange their dead bodies. ³And they perceived that he kept his shroud fast, for it adhered to the body in such a way, that when they wished to take it off, it was found to be like iron—impossible to be moved or loosened. ⁴Nor could they find any ends in that piece of linen, which struck them with the greatest astonishment. ⁵Finally, they carried him out to a place where there was a cave, and opened the gate, so that they might bury his body beside the bodies of his fathers. ⁶Then there came into My mind the day on which he walked with Me into Egypt, and that extreme trouble which he endured on My account. ⁷Accordingly, I grieved his death for a long time; and lying on his body, I said:

CHAPTER 28

¹"O Death! Who makes all knowledge to vanish away, and raises so many tears and lamentations, surely it is God My Father Himself who has granted you this power. ²For men die for the transgression of Adam and his wife Eve, and Death does not spare so much as one. ³Nevertheless, nothing happens to anyone, or is brought on him, without the command of My Father. ⁴There have certainly been men who have prolonged their life even to nine hundred years; but [still] they died. ⁵Yes, although some of them have lived longer, they have, notwithstanding, succumbed to the same fate; nor has any one of them ever said: I have not tasted death. ⁶For the LORD never sends the same punishment more than once, since it has pleased My Father to bring it on men. ⁷And at the very moment when it, going forth, beholds the command descending to it from Heaven, it says: I will go forth against that man, and will greatly move him. ⁸Then, without delay, it makes an onset on the soul, and obtains the mastery of it, doing with it whatever it will. ⁹For, because Adam did not do the will of My Father, but transgressed His command, the wrath of My Father was kindled against him, and He doomed him to death; and thus it was that death came into the world. ¹⁰But if Adam had observed My Father's precepts, death would never have fallen to his lot. ¹¹Do you think that I can ask My good Father to send Me a chariot of fire, which may take up the body of My father Joseph and convey it to the place of rest, in order that it may dwell with the spirits? ¹²But on account of the transgression of Adam, that trouble and violence of death has descended on all the human race. ¹³And it is for this reason that I must die according to the flesh, for My work which I have created, so that they may obtain grace."

CHAPTER 29

¹Having thus spoken, I embraced the body of My father Joseph and wept over it; ²and they opened the door of the tomb, and placed his body in it, near the body of his father Jacob. ³And at the time when he fell asleep, he had fulfilled one hundred and eleven years. ⁴Never did a tooth in his mouth hurt him, nor was his eyesight rendered less sharp, nor his body bent, nor his strength impaired; ⁵but he worked at his trade as a carpenter to the very last day of his life; and that was the twenty-sixth [day] of the month Abib.

CHAPTER 30

¹And we apostles, when we heard these things from our Savior, rose up joyfully, and prostrated ourselves in honor of Him, and said: "O our Savior, show us Your grace. ²Now we have indeed heard the word of life: nevertheless, we wonder, O our Savior, at the fate of Enoch and Elijah, inasmuch as they did not have to undergo death. ³For truly they dwell in the habitation of the righteous even to the present day, nor have their bodies seen corruption. ⁴Yet that old man Joseph the carpenter was, nevertheless, Your father after the flesh. ⁵And You have ordered us to go into all the world and preach the holy good news; and You have said: Relate to them the death of My father Joseph and celebrate him with annual solemnity a festival and sacred day. ⁶And whosoever will take anything away from this narrative, or add anything to it, commits sin. ⁷We wonder especially that Joseph, even from that day on which You were born in Beth-Lehem, called You his Son after the flesh. ⁸Therefore, then, did You not make him immortal as well as them, and You say that he was righteous and chosen?"

CHAPTER 31

¹And our Savior answered and said: "Indeed, the prophecy of My Father on Adam, for his disobedience, has now been fulfilled. ²And all things are arranged according to the will and pleasure of My Father. ³For if a man rejects the command of God and follows the works of the Devil by committing sin, his life is prolonged; for he is preserved in order that he may perhaps convert and reflect that he must be delivered into the hands of death. ⁴But if anyone has been zealous for good works, his life is also prolonged, that, as the fame of his old age increases, upright men may imitate him. ⁵But when you see a man whose mind is prone to anger, assuredly his days are shortened; for it is these that are taken away in the flower of their age. ⁶Every prophecy, therefore, which My Father has pronounced concerning the sons of men, must be fulfilled in every particular. ⁷But with reference to Enoch and Elijah, and how they remain alive to this day, keeping the same bodies with which they were born; and as for what concerns My father Joseph, who has not been allowed as well as they to remain in the body: ⁸indeed, though a man lives in the world many myriads of years, nevertheless at some time or other he is compelled to exchange life for death. ⁹And I say to you, O My brothers, that they also—Enoch and Elijah—must toward the end of time return into the world and die: in the day, namely, of commotion, of terror, of perplexity, and affliction. ¹⁰For the Antichrist will slay four bodies, and will pour out their blood like water, because of the reproach to which they will expose him, and the ignominy with which they, in their lifetime, will brand him when they reveal his impiety."

CHAPTER 32

¹And we said: "O our Lord, our God and Savior, who are those four whom You have said the Antichrist will cut off from the reproach they bring on him?" ²The LORD answered: "They are Enoch, Elijah, Schila, and Tabitha." When we heard this from our Savior, we rejoiced and exulted; ³and we offered all glory and thanksgiving to the LORD God, and our Savior Jesus Christ. ⁴It is He to whom is due glory, honor, dignity, dominion, power, and praise, as well as to the good Father with Him, and to the Holy Spirit that gives life, henceforth and in all time forevermore. Amen.

LIFE OF JOHN THE BAPTIST

Rare among books of its time, the Life of John the Baptist can allegedly be pinpointed to an exact year: AD 390. Supposedly written by Serapion, Bishop of Thmuis, this work harmonizes details of John the Baptist's life from the Gospels and adds a great number of details; especially regarding John's confrontation with Herod and Herodias.

IN THE NAME OF THE FATHER, THE SON, AND THE HOLY SPIRIT: ONE GOD. ASKING FOR GOD'S AID AND HOPEFUL FOR HIS SUPPORT FOR THIS ENDEAVOR, WE WRITE HERE THE HISTORY OF HOLY JOHN THE IMMERSER, THE SON OF ZECHARIAH. MAY HE INTERCEDE ON OUR BEHALF. AMEN.

CHAPTER 1

¹During the reign of King Herod of Judea, there was among the people of Israel a prophet, an old man named Zechariah, who was a Levite

priest from the tribe of Judah. He had a God-loving wife called Elizabeth who was a descendant of Aaron from the tribe of Levi. ²She had no children, and both she and her husband were getting along in years. They were righteous before God, living blamelessly according to all the commandments and regulations of the LORD. ³Zechariah was constantly officiating in the temple. When his turn came to offer incense to the LORD, he entered the temple at the time of the offering as usual. ⁴Suddenly a messenger of the LORD appeared to him, standing on the right side of the altar. When Zechariah saw him, he was terrified and startled, but the messenger said to him, "Rejoice and do not be afraid, Zechariah, because God has heard your prayers. ⁵Your wife Elizabeth will bear you a son who will be named John, and he will cause you great delight and joy. ⁶He will be great in the sight of the LORD; he will not drink wine or strong drink, and he will be filled with the Holy Spirit even in his mother's womb. He will turn many of the people of Israel to the LORD their God. With the spirit and strength of Elijah, he will go before Him to prepare the people for the LORD." ⁷When he heard these words, Zechariah was astonished and doubtful since he was [already] old and did not have any children. He did not remember Abraham, the greatest among the patriarchs, to whom God gave Isaac, although he had already passed the age of one hundred. Nor did Zechariah remember Sarah, Abraham's wife, who was childless just like him. ⁸Zechariah said to the messenger, "How will this happen? I am old and my wife is getting along in years." ⁹The messenger replied, "I am Gabriel, the messenger. I was sent to speak to you and bring you this good news. Because you did not believe my words, from now on you will be mute and unable to speak until the day these things occur, which will come in due time." ¹⁰And with this, the messenger disappeared. ¹¹Meanwhile, the people who were waiting outside for Zechariah were starting to wonder at his delay in the temple. When he finally came out, he could not speak to them, and they realized he had seen a vision in the temple and could only gesture at them. When his time of service had ended, he went home. ¹²Elizabeth already knew of all that had transpired. ¹³At that time, Elizabeth conceived, and she remained in seclusion until the fifth month because she was ashamed. She was afraid to be seen as an old woman with her belly growing and milk dripping from her breasts. So, she spent her days alone in a small room in her house with everything she needed there with her. ¹⁴Zechariah also lived like this, and there was a locked door separating the two of them. For some time, both were completely cut off from the world.

CHAPTER 2

¹When Elizabeth reached the sixth month, the messenger Gabriel was sent by God to a town in Galilee called Nazareth, to the betrothed of a man named Joseph, of the house of David. This virgin's name was Mary. ²When the messenger came to her, he said, "Rejoice, Mary, for you have found favor with God. You will conceive and bear a Son, and you will name Him Jesus. He will be great and He will be called the Son of the Most High." ³Mary said to the messenger, "How can this be, since I am a virgin?" The messenger replied, "The Holy Spirit will come on you, and the power of the Most High will overshadow you; therefore the Child to be born of you will be holy; He will be called the Son of God. ⁴And [even] now, your relative Elizabeth has also conceived a son, even though she is advanced in years. This is the sixth month for her who was said to be barren. For nothing will be impossible with God." ⁵Mary let go of all her doubts and said to the commander of messengers, "I am the servant of the LORD; let it be with me according to your word." The messenger then said farewell and departed from her. ⁶But Mary was still astonished at hearing about Elizabeth's pregnancy and said to herself, "Your deeds are truly great and wonderful, O omnipotent God, for You have brought forth offspring from an old barren woman. ⁷I will now go and will not stop until I meet her and see the great miracle God has performed in our times: a virgin giving birth and an old woman giving suck." ⁸At that time, Mary set out and hurried to a Judean town in the hill country. ⁹She entered the house of Zechariah, and she greeted Elizabeth, who came out to meet her with delight and joy and greeted Mary with the words, "Blessed are you among women, and blessed is the Fruit of your womb." ¹⁰The pure [and] holy virgin kissed the Word's true turtledove, and the Word immersed John while he was still in his mother's womb. David appeared between them and said, "Mercy and justice have met, and righteousness and peace have embraced." And John moved in his mother's womb as if he wanted to come out to see his Lord. ¹¹After they finished greeting each other, the virgin stayed with Elizabeth for three months until Elizabeth was about to give birth, at which time she left and went home. ¹²When the chaste Elizabeth gave birth, there was great delight and joy in her house. ¹³After eight days, they were going to circumcise him and name him Zechariah. But his mother said, "No; he is to be called John." They said to her, "None of your relatives bears this name." She said to them, "Ask his father what his name should be." He asked for a writing tablet and wrote, "His name is John." ¹⁴Immediately after he finished writing, his mouth was opened and his tongue freed, praising God who gave him this great blessing. And he proclaimed prophecies concerning his son John the Immerser, since he was aware of the gift God bestowed on him.

CHAPTER 3

¹John grew into a beautiful child, and his mother suckled him until he was two years old. The grace of God was in his face, and he grew healthy and strong with the help of the Holy Spirit. ²When Jesus was born in Beth-Lehem of Judea, wise men came from the East, saying, "Where is the Child who has been born King of the Jews? For we observed His star in the East and have come to worship Him." ³When Herod heard this, he was frightened because of what he heard from the wise men about this King of the Jews, and he immediately wanted to kill Him. ⁴A messenger of the LORD appeared to Joseph and said to him, "Get up, take the Infant and his mother, go to Egypt, and remain there until I tell you." ⁵Herod searched for the Master in order to kill Him, but did not find Him, so he started killing all the children in Beth-Lehem. ⁶Elizabeth feared that her son might be killed as well, so she took him and went to see Zechariah in the temple, and she said to him, "My lord, come, let us go with our son John to some other land, lest Herod the unbeliever kills him because of Jesus the Christ. Mary and Joseph have already left for Egypt. Come, before they kill our son John and turn our joy into grief." ⁷Zechariah responded, "I cannot leave the service of the temple of the LORD and go to a foreign country where they worship idols." ⁸She said to him, "What should I do to save my little boy?" ⁹The old man replied, "Rise and go to the wilderness near Ein Kerem, and if it pleases God, you will save your son. If they come looking for him, they will shed my blood instead of his." ¹⁰When the time came, [the boy] wept greatly that they had to be separated from each other. Zechariah held the boy to his chest, kissed him, and said, "Poor me, poor John, my son, the treasure of my old days, for they are keeping me from your grace-filled face." ¹¹He then took him to the temple and blessed him, asking God to save him. Suddenly Gabriel, commander of the messengers, came down to him from Heaven, holding a scapular and a leather belt, and said, "Zechariah, take these and put them on your son. God sent them from Heaven—this scapular that belonged to Elijah and this belt worn by Elisha." ¹²Holy Zechariah took them from the messenger and prayed over them before putting them on his son, attaching them to his clothing which was made of camel's hair. ¹³He brought him to his mother and said to her, "Take him and go with him to the wilderness, for the hand of the LORD is with him. I have learned from God that he will live in the wilderness until the day he shows himself to Israel." ¹⁴The blessed Elizabeth took him with tears in her eyes, and Zechariah was crying as well when he said, "I know I will never see both of you again while we all live. So, go with God's peace and may He guide you." ¹⁵And so Elizabeth walked away with her son; and they went to Ein Kerem where she stayed with him.

CHAPTER 4

¹When King Herod sent his soldiers to Jerusalem to kill her children, they began killing them as soon as they arrived and did not stop until the evening. ²This was on the seventh day of the month Thoth (that is the month Elul). ³As they were about to return to their king, suddenly Satan came to them and said, "Why did you leave the son of Zechariah

without killing him? He is hiding with his father in the temple. Do not let him get away; kill him, lest the king will be angry with you. Go to him, and if he tries to hide his son from you, kill him instead." ⁴The soldiers did as Satan taught them and went to the temple early in the morning. They found Zechariah serving the LORD and they said to him, "Where is your son whom you have hidden from us?" He said to them, "There is no child here with me." They said, "But you do have a child, and you have hidden him from the king's command." He replied, "You fools whose king drinks blood like lionesses, how long will you continue to shed the blood of innocents?" They said to him, "Bring out your son so that we can kill him, or we will kill you in his place." The prophet answered, "My son left for the wilderness, and I do not know where he is."

CHAPTER 5

¹When Zechariah said goodbye to Elizabeth and his son John, he blessed him and made him a priest. Then he handed him to his mother, and she said to him, "Pray over me, my holy father, so that my journey in the wilderness is easy." He said to her, "May he who gave us a child in our old age guide your path with him." ²So she took him and went to the wilderness where no one else lived. ³O blessed Elizabeth, your story is truly wondrous and righteous, for you did not ask another adult to accompany you, although you did not know where to go or where to find shelter. You did not worry about having bread or little water for the child to drink. You did not say to his father Zechariah, "To whom are you sending me in the wilderness?" ⁴There were no monasteries in the wilderness at that time, or any communities of monks, so you could not say, "I will go and stay with them together with my son." ⁵Tell me, blessed Elizabeth, what did you rely on, for the evangelist testifies that you grew old without having children, yet now you have been giving suck to this child for three years. ⁶Listen to the answer the blessed Elizabeth gave. She said, "Why are you astonished that I would go alone into the wilderness? I am not afraid of anything, because I have one of God's relatives in my arms; and Gabriel travels with me and paves the way before me." ⁷She said, "I rely on the kiss I received from Mary, mother of the LORD, because as I greeted her, the baby in my womb leaped with delight and joy and I heard both of them kissing each other in our wombs." ⁸And Elizabeth said, "I went and dressed my son in a garment made of camel hair and a leather belt, so that the mountains in the holy wilderness may become inhabited, communities of monks grow and multiply, and offerings be made in them in the Name of the LORD. ⁹So if God sustained Hagar and her son Ishmael, who were slaves, as they wandered through the desert, how can He not be bound by a rule He Himself established?"

CHAPTER 6

¹We have described to you [the] virtues of holy Elizabeth; let us now return to holy Zechariah, the holy martyr, and explain to you his many virtues. ²Me, I wish to recount your true story, but I am afraid that I will only hear your reproach, just like the happy Elizabeth did. ³I am in awe of you, pious Zechariah! When Herod's soldiers came to you asking, "Where is your little boy, the son whom you had at an advanced age?" You did not deny him, nor did you say, "I do not know him"; you said, "His mother took him to the wilderness." ⁴And when Zechariah said this about his son to the soldiers, they killed him inside the temple. The priests shrouded his body, and they placed it next to the body of his father Berechiah in a hidden tomb out of fear of the wicked. ⁵But his blood boiled on the ground and continued to do so for fifty years until Titus Vespasian, the king of Rome, destroyed Jerusalem and killed the Israelite priests for the blood of Zechariah as the LORD ordered him.

CHAPTER 7

¹As for blessed John, he wandered in the wilderness together with his mother. God prepared locusts and wild honey for him to eat in accordance with the instructions Elizabeth received not to let anything unclean enter his mouth. ²After five years, the blessed, and pious, [and] venerable Elizabeth died. Holy John sat down to cry over her because he did not know how to shroud her or how to bury her, as he was only seven years and six months old. Herod also died the same day blessed Elizabeth passed away. ³Lord Jesus, whose eyes see heaven and earth, saw His relative John sitting next to his mother crying. He also started crying and cried for a long time, but no one knew why. ⁴When Jesus' mother saw him crying, she said to him, "My son, what happened? Why are You crying? Did Joseph or somebody else make You upset?" ⁵The mouth filled with life said to her, "No, mother, it is your relative, the venerable Elizabeth. She left my beloved John [as] an orphan, and he is now crying over her body which is lying in the mountains." ⁶When the virgin heard this, she started crying for her relative, but Jesus said, "Do not cry, My virgin mother, for you will see her with your own eyes this very hour." And as He was talking to His mother, suddenly a cloud filled with light appeared and landed between them. ⁷Jesus said, "Get Salome; we will take her with us," and they mounted the cloud, and it flew with them to the wilderness near Ein Kerem, to the place where the body of blessed Elizabeth was together with holy John. ⁸The Savior said to the cloud, "Set us down here," and immediately the cloud stopped and descended to earth. The sound it made reached the ears of blessed John who became afraid, left the body of his mother, and ran. ⁹Immediately, a voice reached him which said, "Do not be scared, John, My beloved. It is Me, Jesus your Lord, Jesus your relative. I have come to you with My beloved mother to fulfill the command of your blessed mother Elizabeth, because she is a relative of My mother." When he heard this, the blessed John turned back and the Christ and His mother both kissed him. ¹⁰The Savior said to His virgin mother, "You and Salome, come and wash her body." So they washed the body of blessed Elizabeth in the spring from which she and her son used to draw water. The pure virgin Mary held the Blessed One, cried with Him, and cursed Herod for the many evils he had committed. ¹¹Suddenly, Michael and Gabriel came down from Heaven and dug a grave. The Savior said to them, "Go and bring the soul of Zechariah and the soul of Simeon the priest so that they will chant hymns while you bury her body." Michael brought the souls of Zechariah and Simeon, and they buried Elizabeth's body and sang over it for a long time while Jesus' mother and Salome cried. ¹²The priests then made a sign of the Cross and prayed over her three times before laying her to rest. Then they sealed the grave with the sign of the Cross and went back to where they came from in peace. ¹³Jesus and His mother then sat down next to the blessed John and consoled him for seven days because of his mother. They also taught him how to get by in the desert. ¹⁴And the blessed Elizabeth passed away on the fifteenth day of the month Mechir [(Shevat)]. ¹⁵Jesus said to His mother, "Come, let us go to a place where I can complete My mission." But the virgin cried because John was all alone and still a small child. And Mary said, "Son, let us take him with us, he is an orphan and has no one." Jesus said to her, "This is not the will of My Father in Heaven. He will stay in the wilderness until the day he shows himself to Israel. ¹⁶Instead of wild beasts, he will find a wilderness filled with multitudes of messengers and prophets. I have ordered Gabriel, the commander of messengers, to watch over him and give him the power of Heaven. I will also make the water in this spring sweet as his mother's milk. ¹⁷Who was it who watched over him since he was a small child? Was it not Me, because I love him, o mother, more than the world itself? Zechariah loved him as well, and I had him come and ask about him, for his body is buried in the ground, but his soul lives on. His mother Elizabeth will come see him regularly to take care of him and comfort him as if she had not died at all. ¹⁸She truly is blessed, o mother, because she bore My beloved. Her mouth will never succumb to rot because she kissed the pure lips. Her tongue will not fall apart in the ground because she spoke a prophecy concerning you which said: And blessed is she who believed that there would be a fulfillment of what was spoken to her by the LORD. Her insides will not putrefy in the ground, but her body will remain free of decay just like her soul. And my beloved John will persevere as he gazes on her and he will be comforted." ¹⁹This is what the Christ said to His mother while John was in the desert. ²⁰They mounted the cloud while John was looking at them crying. Mary cried with him and said, "O poor John, you will be all alone in the wilderness! Where is your father Zechariah? Where is your mother Elizabeth? Let them come and cry with me today." ²¹Jesus said to her, "Do not

cry for John, mother, because I will not forget him." And as He said this, the cloud lifted them up and flew with them until they arrived in Nazareth where He lived to become fully human in all things except for sin.

CHAPTER 8

¹While holy John lived in the desert, God and His messengers were with him. He led a strict ascetic life in great devotion, did not eat anything but grass and wild honey, and prayed and fasted constantly, waiting for the salvation of Israel. ²In the second year of his reign, King Herod the Younger, who ruled over the province of Judea, took the wife of his brother for his own. He did not do so openly, but found opportunity to send for her and usher her into his private chambers filled with filth where the two of them perpetrated their perversions. ³At that time, in the desert Gabriel, the commander of messengers, taught John the son of Zechariah to say, "O king, you must not take the wife of your brother while he is alive." He kept repeating this in a loud voice as the messenger taught him in the wilderness. ⁴At night, people could hear his voice, and Herodias would light a lamp and search her rooms believing there was somebody there with the two of them. But she could never find anyone and only heard the voice. ⁵Both of them were distraught over this, and she said to Herod, "Go and send your soldiers to the wilderness near Ein Kerem to kill John because this is his voice." But God was with him, and He delivered him from their hands. ⁶When she learned this, she could not find any rest in what she was doing. The wicked one then said to her, "If we hear this voice again, I will summon the magicians and order them to capture and kill him in secret." But the voice did not stop. ⁷The wicked Herodias said to Herod, "Who is this John who wanders around in the wilderness and the desert and whose body is not worthy of wearing the clothes of people, but has to dress in camel's hair? Who is he to rebuke the king of a province and the ruler of a region?" ⁸Herodias then pressed on and said to Herod, "Whatever you want to do, do it openly and do not think anyone in this province will blame you if you do it except for John. And if we find an opportunity, we will get rid of him." This is how this adulteress wooed the heart of Herod to commit this sin and seduced him until he sent his brother to his death and married her openly. ⁹And John remained in the desert and continued to rebuke Herod until he was thirty years old.

CHAPTER 9

¹As for Jesus, He grew in wisdom, stature, and grace with God and people. He did not show any signs of His divine nature, but acted humbly toward all. ²When He reached the age of twelve, He began to rebuke the Jews and the teachers who led people astray. ³In the fifteenth year of the reign of Emperor Tiberius, who ruled after Augustus, when Herod was the tetrarch of Galilee and Annas and Caiaphas were high priests, in that year, the word of God came down to John son of Zechariah in the wilderness. He came to the lands around the Jordan River, preaching, "Convert, for the kingdom of the heavens has come near." ⁴People from all over Judea and Jerusalem came to him and let themselves be immersed by him, confessing their sins. ⁵At that time, the Savior came down from Galilee to the Jordan River to see him and said to him, "Immerse Me." When John saw God standing before him asking to be immersed, he became very afraid and said to Him, "He who led the children of Israel through the Red Sea and gave them sweet water to drink from solid rock, He is now standing before His servant who himself needs to be immersed by His divine hand and says to him, Immerse Me." ⁶And with this, John began to turn away from Him. But Jesus said to him, "Stay, this is how we must finish it now." ⁷The two of them went down into the water and holy John immersed Him with these words: "I immerse the one who was sent by the Father to fulfill a great mystery." At that moment, the heavens opened, and the Holy Spirit descended on Him in the form of a dove which came face to face with John. Then the voice of the Father rang, "This is My beloved Son with whom I am well pleased; obey Him." ⁸The Savior climbed out of the water and went straight to the desert. Holy John stayed near the Jordan River and continued to immerse everyone who came to him.

CHAPTER 10

¹At that time, Herod rebelled against his brother Philip and slandered him to the emperor, saying to him, "My king, the one whom you appointed over the province of Trachonitis, that is Philip, plundered your province and said, I will not pay tribute to the king ever again because I am a king as well." ²The emperor was filled with rage and ordered Herod to take Philip's province, and all his property, and his house from him without any pity, even for his soul. ³Herod did as the king ordered and stole the province that belonged to his brother Philip, as well as his house and everything that he had, and assumed power over all that Philip had ruled. ⁴Philip had a wife whose name was Herodias, and she had a daughter with Philip whose name was Arcostariana. Only the mother was more perverted than the daughter. ⁵When Philip became poorer than anyone else, Herodias hated him very much, and she said to him, "I will not stay with you any longer. I will be with Herod the king, your master who does not lack in security, because he is better than you." ⁶And she immediately wrote a letter to Herod: "Herodias writes to Herod. Now you rule over all of Syria and all the inhabited world, yet you still have not taken me for your wife, even though I am very beautiful and better than all the women of Judea. ⁷I also have a daughter whose beauty and stature cannot be matched in all of the inhabited world. I wish to be your wife because I have come to hate your brother very much and because I am loyal to your kingdom." ⁸When these crafty words reached the ear of the wicked king, he liked what he had heard and arranged for her and her daughter to be taken from Philip's house. ⁹When Philip saw his wife taken from him by force, he said to his daughter: "Stay with your father, even though your mother is taken from me." The little whore said to him: "I will not stay with you, but I will accompany my mother wherever she goes." ¹⁰So they were both taken and brought to Herod who was greatly pleased with them because he was a whoremonger. And they performed deeds of Satanic trickery, and the perverted Herod whored with both of them day after day. ¹¹News of this reached holy John the Immerser from her husband Philip. People considered John a prophet, and he was greatly respected by everyone because he preached to people proclaiming, "Bear fruit worthy of conversion, for every tree that does not bear fruit will be cut down and thrown into the fire." ¹²When John heard this from Philip, he was saddened by their damnation—that is, of Herod and Herodias—and he immediately wrote to them the following: "John the son of Zechariah, called the Immerser, says to you: Herod, you may not marry the wife of your brother while he is still alive." ¹³When Herod heard this, he was afraid and disturbed. He went to see Herodias and said to her, "Herodias, what are we going to do? The news of our sin has reached John, and now he has rebuked us. We are doomed, because our sins have increased greatly and reached the ears of the prophets." ¹⁴The wicked woman said to him, "Calm yourself, my king. Who is this John, who wears camel's hair, to contradict a mighty king like you? He surely deserves to have his tongue pulled out." ¹⁵He said to her, "So what are we going to do? I cannot bear the rebuke of someone as mighty as him." ¹⁶She answered, "Have him brought here and kill him, then we can continue to give pleasure to each other." And she did unspeakable things to him and performed acts of devious perversion. So Satan turned his heart against John and he had him arrested and thrown into a prison. ¹⁷Herodias then had him brought to her, and she said to him, "What is your problem with me, you chaste man? Do you want to keep me and the king apart? I conjure you by the God of your fathers not to trouble me like this ever again. And I promise you, if you stop talking about me and stop making your accusations, I will release you from this prison right away and shower you with riches and honors." ¹⁸Holy John said to her, "I am telling you, Herodias, you should not be with Herod while Philip is alive." ¹⁹When the wicked woman heard this, she became angry and said to him, "I will kill you dead. I will put the hair from your head into the pillow I lie on with Herod every night and I will bury your head where I wash myself every time I sleep with him." ²⁰John said to her, "You will kill me, since God wills it, but you will not lay eyes on my head. It will stay with me after my death, and it will proclaim your humiliation and your

shame to all the world. You will suffer for my unjust murder because your ruin is near." ²¹ She said to his guards, "Take him and throw him in prison in chains. And if he escapes, you will pay with your lives." The guards took him and put him in prison.

CHAPTER 11

¹ Herodias tried to get Herod to kill him, but he said to her, "I cannot kill him just like that. The people will rise up against me, chase me out, and bring accusations against me with the king who will then take my kingdom from me like he did with my brother Philip." And he said to her, "Show me a better way to kill him." ² She said to him, "I will tell you something and when you hear it, you will find a way to kill him." He said to her, "Tell me." ³ She said to him, "Well, king's envoys are staying with you, so go and prepare a feast for them and invite all the high officials as well, since your birthday is near. Once everyone is happy, and they all start getting drunk with wine, I will send in my daughter dressed in her best clothes to dance before you, my king, with her beautiful face. ⁴ When she does that, tell her: Ask for whatever you wish; and you will swear to her by the king's life: Whatever you wish for, I will give it to you. She will then ask for the head of John, and you will have found a way to take his head." ⁵ This is how Herod was tricked by the reasoning of the adulteress, and he began to fulfill her wish because he loved her for her ruthlessness and her devilish cunningness. ⁶ That very day, he prepared a feast and the king's envoys were sitting right next to him. When they started to get drunk, the cursed Uxatriana entered the room wearing necklaces of gold and silver, perfumes, and many jewels, and she presented herself to all assembled. She danced in devilish ecstasy, and Satan filled their hearts with evil and lust through her evil trickery, so they all were enthralled with her. ⁷ Herod was proud of her and said to her, "If you ask for whatever you want, by the life of Emperor Tiberius, I will give it to you, even if it were half of my kingdom and my possessions." She said to him what her mother had taught her: "What I want here is the head of John the Immerser on a platter." ⁸ He was greatly saddened because he swore on the king's life, and it was clear to his dinner companions that he could not break the oath. And so, he ordered the executioner to go to the prison and take his head on a platter—this was the second day of the month of Thoth (Elul)—and they brought it to Herod. Herod gave it to the girl, and the girl gave it to her mother.

CHAPTER 12

¹ Before the king's men came with the executioner to take his head, John said to his disciples, "Look, the king has sent for my head. The king's men went out with unsheathed swords in their hands, carrying lanterns, and torches, and weapons. What is happening now will also happen on the night the Christ will be betrayed. ² As for me, they will take my head and present it on a platter. As for the Christ, He will be nailed to a cross, so that He will purify all with His pure blood. ³ As for me, I will go to where I am going; but woe to the king who ordered my head to be cut off, for many calamities will befall him, and the people of Israel will be scattered because of him. ⁴ As for you, do not be afraid, for no one will be able to harm you." ⁵ He then opened his mouth, and praised God, and glorified Him for His incomprehensible gifts, saying, "I bless You and praise You, invisible Father, visible Son, and consoling Holy Spirit."

CHAPTER 13

¹ Now let us return to the head of the blessed John. ² When his head was brought to Herodias, the eyes of holy John were open, and his eyes heard as well as they did when he was still alive. ³ The whore then spoke before the head, seething with anger, "Here is the eye that was not ashamed to look into the eyes of the king and answer him. I will pluck you out with my own hand and put you on a platter. I will pull out the tongue that used to say to the king, You are not permitted to take Herodias, the wife of your brother. And I will take the hair from your head and your beard and sweep it under the feet of my bed." She said this without any shame or hesitation, and with her outstretched hand she tried to grab John's head and do with it as she said. ⁴ Suddenly, the head of the blessed John let the locks of its hair loose from the plate, spread them, and flew to the center of the room in front of the king and his high officials. At that very moment, the roof of the building opened, and John's head flew high in the air. ⁵ As for Herodias, her eyes were pulled out from her head and fell on the ground. Her room collapsed on top of her, the ground opened its mouth, and its throat swallowed her, and then she sank to the depths of Hell, still alive. ⁶ Herodias' daughter went mad and broke all the vessels that were there at the feast. ⁷ In her madness, she went to a frozen lake and danced on it. The LORD ordered the ice under her to break, and the lake swallowed her. ⁸ Soldiers tried to pull her out and could not, because the LORD did not want her to be rescued. Finally, they cut off her head using the sword with which holy John was killed. At that very moment, a whale appeared and threw her out of the lake, dead. May God have no mercy on her! ⁹ Immediately after that, Herod suffered a stroke in front of his dinner companions. ¹⁰ When his aide saw these great miracles, he quickly went to the prison, took the body of John, and handed it over to his disciples. They took it and buried it in the city of Sebaste next to the body of the prophet Elisha. ¹¹ His head, however, flew over Jerusalem and preached to the city for three years, saying, "Herod, you may not marry the wife of your brother while he is still alive." ¹² Once three years of preaching over Jerusalem had passed, it left for the whole world to shout and announce Herod's scandalous actions, with the words "Herod, you may not marry the wife of your brother while he is still alive" until fifteen years since his murder had passed. ¹³ When fifteen years had passed, it stopped preaching and came to rest in the city of Homs. The faithful in that city took it and buried it with a great ceremony. ¹⁴ Sometime after that, an assembly was built over it which to this day is still standing in Homs. The head of holy John the Immerser was buried there fifteen years after the resurrection of our Lord and Savior, and it is still there.

CHAPTER 14

¹ After four hundred years had passed, during which the body of the holy one whose feast we are celebrating today (that is, John the Immerser) was buried in Sebaste, at that time there was an infidel king by the name of Julian who reigned over Syria. ² He was a Christian at the beginning of his reign, but after some time, Satan filled his heart, and he abandoned the faith of our Lord and Savior and worshiped fire. At that time, he ordered that pagan temples and sanctuaries where idols would be worshiped should be built everywhere. ³ He also ordered that a pagan temple be built in Sebaste where the body of John was, but he could not build it or worship idols there because of the bodies. ⁴ They gathered and informed him that bodies of holy men were buried there and prevented them from building the pagan temple. He said to them, "Go burn them down and build the temple." So they set the place on fire, but the fire would not come near the coffins of the prophets. ⁵ Many treasures were found there, including a vessel above the coffins which contained a leather belt, a garment made of camel's hair, and a scapular with two leather belts. ⁶ The faithful present there immediately understood that these coffins were those of John the Immerser and Elisha the prophet. They wanted to take them from that place, but they were not able to do so because they were afraid of the wicked king. ⁷ Then God brought him down with a death more wretched than anyone had ever endured. ⁸ After his death, righteous men gathered, took the coffins, and went with them to the sea, planning to take them to Alexandria to the holy father Athanasius, because they said that at that time, there was no one in the whole world who was worthy of taking possession of them except Anba Athanasius, the patriarch in Alexandria. ⁹ When they came to the seashore and found a ship sailing for Alexandria, they boarded and brought the coffins with them. They sailed on the sea until they dropped anchor in the port of Alexandria, and when they landed, they could not reveal their purpose to anyone, because [their] time was short. ¹⁰ So they went to the patriarch and told him of everything that had happened and how they were moved by the Holy Spirit to bring the coffins to him. ¹¹ The patriarch was overjoyed to have them and venerated them greatly. He went out to the ship with his brother at night, and took the remains in a kerchief, and brought them to his living quarters in the cathedral in secret. ¹² This holy

LIFE OF JOHN THE BAPTIST

father wished to build a chapel for them, but could not because of the trouble at the time caused by the wicked.

CHAPTER 15

¹The bodies remained hidden in the well where Anba Athanasius placed them until the day the holy father passed away. ²After his death, he was succeeded by Anba Peter who was followed on the patriarchal see by Anba Timothy who appointed me, your unworthy father Serapion, to this office, even though I do not deserve it. When he passed away, he was succeeded by Anba Theophilus who is now sitting on the patriarchal see. ³During his time, God's grace and faith manifested themselves and were strengthened by the pious Theodosius, and God through His love united the king and the patriarch. They opened the doors of pagan temples, which stored many treasures, notably the great pagan temple in Alexandria which opened before them. Inside, they found much gold and great amounts of silver. ⁴The pious Theodosius honored the patriarch by appointing him to oversee all the treasures; and he said to him, "Anba Theophilus, take this and use it to build assemblies from here to Aswan, for the greater glory of God and His holy ones." And indeed, the patriarch began to build assemblies. ⁵The first one to be built was an assembly dedicated to John the Immerser in Alexandria, which he adorned and made a beautiful church because he wished to place the body of John there. ⁶When he completed it, he wanted to consecrate it, and he wrote to all the overseers who were under his jurisdiction to gather and witness the consecration of the assembly he had built. I, the unworthy, also received the invitation and went with all the overseers to the Pope, Anba Theophilus. ⁷When the news reached him that all the overseers had come to the city, Theophilus was pleased with us like someone who has found many riches. He went out to meet us, together with many of those who were in the city, and led us into the city where we stayed with him for some time. ⁸After that, he began to consecrate the assembly, and he took us to see it, and we found it to be a wonderful building. ⁹And he said to us, "This is the place where Athanasius wanted to build it, but time was not in his favor." ¹⁰Anba Theophilus then said, "I was walking with them when I was just an acolyte, and I attended to him. When we came to this place, he said to me: My son Theophilus, when you find an opportunity, build an assembly here dedicated to John the Immerser and place his bones in it. ¹¹After I had built this place, I remembered the words of this man of God, Anba Athanasius, especially when I remembered that my father Athanasius was like David the prophet who wanted to build a temple to the LORD, but he was not allowed to because of wars he fought. The LORD said to him: David, you will not be the one who builds My temple, but the one who comes out of your loins will; and this was Solomon. ¹²Therefore, when I ceased waging wars on idolaters, I became worthy of building this assembly, which is dedicated to John the Immerser, the morning star." ¹³When the second day of the month Payni came, he took us to the place where the body was hidden. We did not know exactly where it was, but after a prayer, God showed it to us. ¹⁴When he brought it out, he called to him all the inhabitants of the town. They gathered around him with many lanterns and lamps so that the night shone like day. ¹⁵He let overseers carry the coffins on their heads, and the patriarch walked before them with servants singing hymns until we came with them to the assembly with a great ceremony. ¹⁶The patriarch took the coffins, embraced them, and let all the people be blessed by the holy bodies. Then he put the coffins in the chapel on a chair at the side of the altar and prepared the consecration for that very day. ¹⁷He consecrated the chapel, we said mass, and all of us received communion from the patriarch. This was the second day of the month Payni. ¹⁸After this, the patriarch said goodbye to us, and we left the city—each of us going to his own country in God's peace. Amen. ¹⁹The body of holy John the Immerser performed miracles, proofs, and healings among the Christian people, as witnessed by many wondrous stories. ²⁰Praise, and glory, and power are due to You—Father, Son, and Holy Spirit—one in nature, now, always, and forever and ever. Amen. Praise to God always. Amen.

GOSPEL OF PETER

An early (2nd century) and likely docetic pseudepigraphic gospel, the Gospel of Peter is explicitly ascribed to the apostle Peter. It recounts the crucifixion, resurrection, and ascension of Christ, exonerating Pilate for all wrongdoing.

CHAPTER 1

¹But of the Jews, none washed his hands, neither Herod nor any one of his judges. And when they had refused to wash them, Pilate rose up. ²And then Herod the king commands that the Lord be taken, saying to them, "Whatsoever things I commanded you to do to Him, do."

CHAPTER 2

¹And there was standing there Joseph, the friend of Pilate and of the Lord; and, knowing that they were about to crucify Him, he came to Pilate and asked [for] the body of the Lord for burial. ²And Pilate sent to Herod and asked [for] His body. ³And Herod said, "Brother Pilate, even if no one had asked for Him, we purposed to bury Him, especially as the Sabbath draws near: for it is written in the Law that the sun may not set on one that has been put to death."

CHAPTER 3

¹And he delivered Him to the people on the day before the Unleavened Bread, their feast. ²And they took the Lord and pushed Him as they ran, and said, "Let us drag away the Son of God, having obtained power over Him." ³And they clothed Him with purple, and set Him on the seat of judgment, saying, "Judge righteously, O King of Israel!" ⁴And one of them brought a crown of thorns and put it on the head of the Lord. ⁵And others stood and spat in His eyes, and others struck His cheeks: others pricked Him with a reed; and some scourged Him, saying, "With this honor let us honor the Son of God."

CHAPTER 4

¹And they brought two criminals, and they crucified the Lord between them. [[²But He held His peace, as though having no pain.]] ³And when they had raised the cross, they wrote the title: "This is the King of Israel." ⁴And having set His garments in front of Him, they parted them among them, and cast lots for them. ⁵And one of those criminals reproached them, saying, "We, for the evils that we have done, have suffered thus, but this Man, who has become the Savior of men, what wrong has He done to you?" ⁶And they, being angered at Him, commanded that His legs should not be broken, that He might die in torment.

CHAPTER 5

¹And it was noon, and darkness came over all Judea: and they were troubled and distressed, lest the sun should have set while He was still alive: [for] it is written for them that the sun should not set on him that has been put to death. ²And one of them said, "Give Him gall with vinegar to drink." ³And they mixed and gave Him to drink, and fulfilled all things, and accomplished their sins against their own head. ⁴And many went around with lamps, supposing that it was night, and fell down. ⁵And the Lord cried out, saying, "My Power, My Power, why have You forsaken Me?" ⁶And when He had said it, He was taken up. ⁷And in that hour the veil of the temple of Jerusalem was torn in two.

CHAPTER 6

¹And then they drew out the nails from the hands of the Lord, and laid Him on the earth, and the whole earth quaked, and great fear arose. ²Then the sun shone, and it was found the ninth hour: and the Jews rejoiced and gave His body to Joseph that he might bury it, since he had seen what good things He had done.

GOSPEL OF PETER

³And he took the Lord, and washed Him, and rolled Him in a linen cloth, and brought Him into his own tomb, which was called the Garden of Joseph.

CHAPTER 7
¹Then the Jews, and the elders, and the priests, perceiving what evil they had done to themselves, began to lament and to say, "Woe for our sins! The judgment has drawn near—and the end of Jerusalem!" ²And I with my companions was grieved; and being wounded in mind, we hid ourselves, for we were being sought for by them as criminals, and as wishing to set fire to the temple. ³And on all these things we fasted and sat mourning and weeping night and day until the Sabbath.

CHAPTER 8
¹But the scribes, and Pharisees, and elders, being gathered together with one another, when they heard that all the people murmured and beat their breasts, saying, "If by His death these most mighty signs have come to pass, see how righteous He is!" ²The elders were afraid and came to Pilate, pleading with him and saying, "Give us soldiers, so that we may guard His tomb for three days, lest His disciples come and steal Him away, and the people suppose that He is risen from the dead and do us evil." ³And Pilate gave them Petronius the centurion with soldiers to guard the tomb. ⁴And with them came elders and scribes to the tomb, and having rolled a great stone together with the centurion and the soldiers, they all together who were there set it at the door of the tomb; and they affixed seven seals, and they pitched a tent there and guarded it. ⁵And early in the morning as the Sabbath was drawing near, there came a multitude from Jerusalem and the surrounding region, that they might see the tomb that was sealed.

CHAPTER 9
¹And in the night in which the LORD's Day was drawing near, as the soldiers kept guard two by two in a watch, there was a great voice from Heaven; and they saw the heavens opened, and two men descend from there with great light and approach the tomb. ²And that stone which was put at the door rolled on its own and made way in part; and the tomb was opened, and both [of] the young men entered in.

CHAPTER 10
¹Therefore, when those soldiers saw it, they awakened the centurion and the elders, for they too were hard by keeping guard. ²And, as they declared what things they had seen, again they see three men come forth from the tomb, and two of them supporting one, and a cross following them: ³and of the two, the head reached toward the sky, but the head of Him that was led by them overpassed the heavens. ⁴And they heard a voice from the heavens, saying, "You have preached to them that sleep." And a response was heard from the cross, "Yes."

CHAPTER 11
¹Therefore, they considered with one another whether to go away and show these things to Pilate. ²And while they yet thought thereon, the heavens again are seen to open, and a certain man to descend and enter into the tomb. ³When the centurion and they that were with him saw these things, they hastened in the night to Pilate, leaving the tomb which they were watching, and declared all things which they had seen, being greatly distressed and saying, "Truly He was the Son of God." ⁴Pilate answered and said, "I am pure from the blood of the Son of God: but it was you who determined this." ⁵Then they all drew near, and implored him, and entreated him to command the centurion and the soldiers to say nothing of the things which they had seen: "For it is better," they say, "for us to be guilty of the greatest sin before God, and not to fall into the hands of the people of the Jews and to be stoned." ⁶Therefore, Pilate commanded the centurion and the soldiers to say nothing.

CHAPTER 12
¹And at dawn on the LORD's Day, Mary Magdalene, a disciple of the Lord, fearing because of the Jews, since they were burning with wrath, had not done at the Lord's tomb the things which women are accustomed to do for those that die and for those that are beloved by them—she took her friends with her and came to the tomb where He was laid. ²And they feared lest the Jews should see them, and they said, "Although on that day on which He was crucified we could not weep and lament, yet now let us do these things at His tomb. ³But who will roll away for us the stone that was laid at the door of the tomb, so that we may enter in and sit by Him and do the things that are due? ⁴For the stone was great, and we fear lest someone may see us. ⁵And if we cannot, yet if we but set at the door the things which we bring for a memorial of Him, we will weep and lament, until we come to our home."

CHAPTER 13
¹And they went and found the tomb opened; and coming near, they looked in there, and they see there a certain young man sitting in the midst of the tomb, beautiful and clothed in an exceedingly bright robe, ²who said to them, "Why then have you come? Whom do you seek? Him that was crucified? He is risen and gone. ³But if you do not believe, look in and see the place where He lay, that He is not [here], for He is risen and gone to the place from where He was sent." ⁴Then the women feared and fled.

CHAPTER 14
¹Now it was the last day of the Unleavened Bread, and many were going forth, returning to their homes, as the feast had ended. ²But we, the twelve disciples of the Lord, wept and were grieved: ³and each one, being grieved for that which had come to pass, departed to his home. ⁴But I, Simon Peter, and Andrew my brother took our nets and went to the sea; and there was with us Levi the son of Alphaeus, whom the Lord …

GOSPEL OF THOMAS

The Gospel of Thomas is perhaps the most famous of the apocryphal Gospels. The extant version presents as a lengthy list of 114 "sayings" of Christ and bears a striking resemblance in places to the gnostic heresies. However, some scholars argue that the work is not explicitly gnostic or otherwise conveys a sort of primordial Gnosticism. While many scholars have argued for an early date for its composition in the 1st century AD, an increasing number of researchers have proposed a later date on the preponderance of evidence, perhaps in the mid-2nd century. Renowned biblical scholar Dr. Craig A. Evans notes that "[o]ver half of the New Testament writings are quoted, paralleled, or alluded to in Thomas … [unlike any other] Christian writing prior to AD 150." As such, it was unlikely to have been written before or during the completion of the New Testament.

THESE ARE THE HIDDEN SAYINGS THAT THE LIVING JESUS SPOKE, AND DIDYMOS JUDAS THOMAS WROTE DOWN.

SAYING 1
And he said, "Whoever discovers the meaning of these sayings will not taste death."

SAYING 2
Jesus said, "Whoever seeks should not stop until they find. When they find, they will be disturbed. When they are disturbed, they will be … amazed and reign over all."

SAYING 3
Jesus said, "If your leaders tell you, Behold, the kingdom is in Heaven, then the birds of heaven will precede you. If they tell you, It is in the sea, then the fish will precede you. Rather, the kingdom is within you and outside of you. When you know yourselves, then you will be known, and you will realize that you are the

children of the living Father. But if you do not know yourselves, then you live in poverty, and you are the poverty."

SAYING 4
Jesus said, "The older person will not hesitate to ask a little seven-day-old child about the place of life, and they will live, because many who are first will be last, and they will become one."

SAYING 5
Jesus said, "Know what is in front of your face, and what is hidden from you will be revealed to you, because there is nothing hidden that will not be revealed."

SAYING 6
His disciples said to him, "Do you want us to fast? And how should we pray? Should we make donations? And what food should we avoid?" Jesus said, "Do not lie, and do not do what you hate, because everything is revealed in the sight of Heaven; for there is nothing hidden that will not be revealed, and nothing covered up that will stay secret."

SAYING 7
Jesus said, "Blessed is the lion that is eaten by a human and then becomes human, but how awful for the human who is eaten by a lion, and the lion becomes human."

SAYING 8
He said, "The human being is like a wise fisher who cast a net into the sea and drew it up from the sea full of little fish. Among them, the wise fisher found a fine large fish and cast all the little fish back down into the sea, easily choosing the large fish. Anyone who has ears to hear should hear!"

SAYING 9
Jesus said, "Behold, a sower went out, took a handful of seeds, and scattered them. Some fell on the roadside; the birds came and gathered them. Others fell on the rock; they did not take root in the soil and ears of grain did not rise toward the sky. Yet others fell on thorns; they choked the seeds and worms ate them. Finally, others fell on good soil; it produced fruit up toward the sky, some sixty times as much and some one hundred and twenty."

SAYING 10
Jesus said, "I have cast fire on the world, and behold, I am watching over it until it blazes."

SAYING 11
Jesus said, "This heaven will disappear, and the one above it will disappear too. Those who are dead are not alive, and those who are living will not die. In the days when you ate what was dead, you made it alive. When you are in the light, what will you do? On the day when you were one, you became divided. But when you become divided, what will you do?"

SAYING 12
The disciples said to Jesus, "We know you are going to leave us. Who will lead us then?" Jesus said to them, "Wherever you are, you will go to James the Just, for whom heaven and earth came into being."

SAYING 13
Jesus said to his disciples, "If you were to compare Me to someone, who would you say I am like?" Simon Peter said to Him, "You are like a just messenger." Matthew said to Him, "You are like a wise philosopher." Thomas said to Him, "Teacher, I am completely unable to say whom You are like." Jesus said, "I am not your teacher. Because you have drunk, you have become intoxicated by the bubbling spring I have measured out." He took him aside and told him three things. When Thomas returned to his companions, they asked, "What did Jesus say to you?" Thomas said to them, "If I tell you one of the things He said to me, you will pick up stones and cast them at me, and fire will come out of the stones and burn you up."

SAYING 14
Jesus said to them, "If you fast, you will bring guilt on yourselves; and if you pray, you will be condemned; and if you make donations, you will harm your spirits. If they welcome you when you enter any land and go around in the countryside, heal those who are sick among them and eat whatever they give you, because it is not what goes into your mouth that will defile you. What comes out of your mouth is what will defile you."

SAYING 15
Jesus said, "When you see the one who was not born of a woman, fall down on your face and worship that Person. That is your Father."

SAYING 16
Jesus said, "Maybe people think that I have come to cast peace on the world, and they do not know that I have come to cast divisions on the earth: fire, sword, and war. Where there are five in a house, there will be three against two and two against three, father against son and son against father. They will stand up and be one."

SAYING 17
Jesus said, "I will give you what no eye has ever seen, no ear has ever heard, no hand has ever touched, and no human mind has ever thought."

SAYING 18
The disciples said to Jesus, "Tell us about our end. How will it come?" Jesus said, "Have you discovered the beginning so that you can look for the end? Because the end will be where the beginning is. Blessed is the one who will stand up in the beginning. They will know the end and will not taste death."

SAYING 19
Jesus said, "Blessed is the One who came into being before coming into being. If you become My disciples and listen to My message, these stones will become your servants; because there are five trees in Paradise which do not change in summer or winter, and their leaves do not fall. Whoever knows them will not taste death."

SAYING 20
The disciples asked Jesus, "Tell us, what can the kingdom of the heavens be compared to?" He said to them, "It can be compared to a mustard seed. Though it is the smallest of all the seeds, when it falls on tilled soil it makes a plant so large that it shelters the birds of the sky."

SAYING 21
Mary said to Jesus, "Whom are Your disciples like?" He said, "They are like little children living in a field which is not theirs. When the owners of the field come, they will say, Give our field back to us. They will strip naked in front of them to let them have it and give them their field. So I say that if the owner of the house realizes the bandit is coming, they will watch out beforehand and will not let the bandit break into the house of their domain and steal their possessions. You, then, watch out for the world! Prepare to defend yourself so that the bandits do not attack you, because what you are expecting will come. May there be a wise person among you! When the fruit ripened, the reaper came quickly, sickle in hand, and harvested it. Anyone who has ears to hear should hear!"

SAYING 22
Jesus saw some little children nursing. He said to His disciples, "These nursing children can be compared to those who enter the kingdom." They said to Him, "Then will we enter the kingdom as little children?" Jesus said to them, "When you make the two into one, and make the inner like the outer and the outer like the inner, and the upper like the lower, and so make the male and the female a single one so that the male will not be male nor the female female; when you make eyes in the place of an eye, a hand in the place of a hand, a foot in the place of a foot, and an image in the place of an image; then you will enter [the kingdom]."

SAYING 23
Jesus said, "I will choose you—one out of a thousand and two out of ten thousand—and they will stand as a single one."

SAYING 24
His disciples said, "Show us the place where You are, because we need to look for it." He said to them, "Anyone who has ears to hear should hear! Light exists within a person of light, and they light up the whole world. If they do not shine, there is darkness."

GOSPEL OF THOMAS

SAYING 25
Jesus said, "Love your brother as your own soul. Protect them like the pupil of your eye."

SAYING 26
Jesus said, "You see the speck that is in your brother's eye, but you do not see the beam in your own eye. When you get the beam out of your own eye, then you will be able to see clearly to get the speck out of your brother's eye."

SAYING 27
"If you do not fast from the world, you will not find the kingdom. If you do not make the Sabbath into a Sabbath, you will not see the Father."

SAYING 28
Jesus said, "I stood in the middle of the world and appeared to them in the flesh. I found them all drunk; I did not find any of them thirsty. My soul ached for the children of humanity, because they were blind in their hearts and could not see. They came into the world empty and planned on leaving the world empty. Meanwhile, they are drunk. When they shake off their wine, then they will change."

SAYING 29
Jesus said, "If the flesh came into existence because of spirit, that is amazing. If spirit came into existence because of the body, that is really amazing! But I am amazed at how [such] great wealth has been placed in this poverty."

SAYING 30
Jesus said, "Where there are three deities, they are divine. Where there are two or one, I am with them."

SAYING 31
Jesus said, "No prophet is welcome in their own village. No doctor heals those who know them."

SAYING 32
Jesus said, "A city built and fortified on a high mountain cannot fall, nor can it be hidden."

SAYING 33
Jesus said, "What you hear with one ear, listen to with both, then proclaim from your rooftops. No one lights a lamp and puts it under a basket or in a hidden place. Rather, they put it on the stand so that everyone who comes and goes can see its light."

SAYING 34
Jesus said, "If someone who is blind leads someone else who is blind, both of them fall into a pit."

SAYING 35
Jesus said, "No one can break into the house of the strong and take it by force without tying the hands of the strong. Then they can plunder the house."

SAYING 36
Jesus said, "Do not be anxious from morning to evening or from evening to morning about what you will wear."

SAYING 37
His disciples said, "When will You appear to us? When will we see You?" Jesus said, "When you strip naked without being ashamed, and throw your clothes on the ground, and stomp on them as little children would, then [you will] see the Son of the Living One and will not be afraid."

SAYING 38
Jesus said, "Often you have wanted to hear this message that I am telling you, and you do not have anyone else from whom to hear it. There will be days when you will look for Me, but you will not be able to find Me."

SAYING 39
Jesus said, "The Pharisees and the scholars have taken the keys of knowledge and hidden them. They have not entered and have not let others enter who wanted to. So be wise as serpents and innocent as doves."

SAYING 40
Jesus said, "A grapevine has been planted outside of the Father. Since it is malnourished, it will be pulled up by its root and destroyed."

SAYING 41
Jesus said, "Whoever has something in hand will be given more, but whoever does not have anything will lose even what little they do have."

SAYING 42
Jesus said, "Become passersby."

SAYING 43
His disciples said to him, "Who are You to say these things to us?" [He replied,] "You do not realize who I am from what I say to you, but you have become like those Judeans who either love the tree but hate its fruit, or love the fruit but hate the tree."

SAYING 44
Jesus said, "Whoever blasphemes the Father will be forgiven, and whoever blasphemes the Son will be forgiven, but whoever blasphemes the Holy Spirit will not be forgiven, neither on earth nor in Heaven."

SAYING 45
Jesus said, "Grapes are not harvested from thorns, nor are figs gathered from thistles, because they do not produce fruit. [A good person] brings good things out of their treasure, and an [evil] person brings evil things out of their evil treasure. They say evil things because their heart is full of evil."

SAYING 46
Jesus said, "From Adam to John the Immerser, no one has been born who is so much greater than John the Immerser that they should not avert their eyes. But I say that whoever among you will become a little child will know the kingdom and become greater than John."

SAYING 47
Jesus said, "It is not possible for anyone to mount two horses or stretch two bows, and it is not possible for a servant to follow two leaders, because they will respect one and despise the other. No one drinks old wine and immediately wants to drink new wine. And new wine is not put in old wineskins, because they would burst. Nor is old wine put in new wineskins, because it would spoil. A new patch of cloth is not sewn onto an old coat, because it would tear apart."

SAYING 48
Jesus said, "If two make peace with each other in a single house, they will say to the mountain, Go away, and it will."

SAYING 49
Jesus said, "Blessed are those who are one—those who are chosen—because you will find the kingdom. You have come from there and will return there."

SAYING 50
Jesus said, "If they ask you, Where do you come from? tell them: We have come from the light, the place where light came into being by itself, [established] itself, and appeared in their image. If they ask you, Is it you? then say, We are its children, and we are chosen by our living Father. If they ask you, What is the sign of your Father in you? then say, It is movement and rest."

SAYING 51
His disciples said to Him, "When will the dead have rest, and when will the new world come?" He said to them, "What you are looking for has already come, but you do not know it."

SAYING 52
His disciples said to Him, "Twenty-four prophets have spoken in Israel, and they all spoke of You." He said to them, "You have ignored the Living One right in front of you, and you have talked about those who are dead."

SAYING 53
His disciples said to Him, "Is circumcision useful, or not?" He said to them, "If it were useful, parents would have children who are born circumcised. But the true circumcision in spirit has become profitable in every way."

SAYING 54
Jesus said, "Blessed are those who are poor, for yours is the kingdom of the heavens."

SAYING 55
Jesus said, "Whoever does not hate their father and mother cannot become My disciple, and whoever does not hate their

brothers and sisters and take up their cross like I do is not worthy of Me."

SAYING 56
Jesus said, "Whoever has known the world has found a corpse. Whoever has found a corpse, of them the world is not worthy."

SAYING 57
Jesus said, "My Father's kingdom can be compared to someone who had [good] seed. Their enemy came by night and sowed weeds among the good seed. The person did not let anyone pull out the weeds; so that you do not pull out the wheat along with the weeds—they said to them—On the day of the harvest, the weeds will be obvious; then they will be pulled out and burned."

SAYING 58
Jesus said, "Blessed is the person who has gone to a lot of trouble. They have found life."

SAYING 59
Jesus said, "Look for the Living One while you are still alive. If you die and then try to look for Him, you will not be able to."

SAYING 60
They saw a Samaritan carrying a lamb to Judea. He said to His disciples, "What do you think he is going to do with that lamb?" They said to Him, "He is going to kill it and eat it." He said to them, "While it is living, he will not eat it, but only after he kills it and it becomes a corpse." They said, "He cannot do it any other way." He said to them, "You, too, look for a resting place, so that you will not become a corpse and be eaten."

SAYING 61
Jesus said, "Two will rest on a couch: one will die, the other will live." Salome said, "Who are You, Lord, to climb onto my couch and eat off my table as if You are from someone?" Jesus said to her, "I am the One who exists in equality. Some of what belongs to My Father was given to Me." "I am Your disciple," [she said]. "So I am telling you, if someone is equal, they will be full of light; but if they are divided, they will be full of darkness."

SAYING 62
Jesus said, "I tell My mysteries to [those who are worthy of My] mysteries. Do not let your left hand know what your right hand is doing."

SAYING 63
Jesus said, "There was a rich man who had much money. He said, I will use my money to sow, reap, plant, and fill my barns with fruit, so that I will not need anything. That is what he was thinking to himself, but he died that very night. Anyone who has ears to hear should hear!"

SAYING 64
Jesus said, "Someone was planning on having guests. When dinner was ready, they sent their servant to call the visitors. The servant went to the first and said, My master invites you. They said, Some merchants owe me money; they are coming tonight; I need to go and give them instructions—excuse me from the dinner. The servant went to another one and said, My master invites you. They said, I have just bought a house and am needed for the day; I will not have time. The servant went to another one and said, My master invites you. They said, My friend is getting married, and I am going to make dinner; I cannot come—excuse me from the dinner. The servant went to another one and said, My master invites you. They said, I have just bought a farm and am going to collect the rent; I cannot come—excuse me. The servant went back and told the master, The ones you have invited to the dinner have excused themselves. The master said to their servant, Go out to the roads and bring whomever you find so that they can have dinner. Buyers and merchants will not [enter] the places of My Father."

SAYING 65
He said, "A [creditor] owned a vineyard. He leased it out to some sharecroppers to work it so he could collect its fruit. He sent his servant so that the sharecroppers could give him the fruit of the vineyard. They seized his servant, beat him, and nearly killed him. The servant went back and told his master. His master said, Perhaps he just did not know them. He sent another servant, but the tenants beat that one too. Then the master sent his son, thinking, Maybe they will show some respect to my son. Because they knew that he was the heir of the vineyard, the sharecroppers seized and killed him. Anyone who has ears to hear should hear!"

SAYING 66
Jesus said, "Show me the stone the builders rejected; that is the cornerstone."

SAYING 67
Jesus said, "Whoever knows everything, but is personally lacking, lacks everything."

SAYING 68
Jesus said, "Blessed are you when you are hated and persecuted, and no place will be found where you have been persecuted."

SAYING 69
Jesus said, "Blessed are those who have been persecuted in their own hearts. They have truly known the Father. Blessed are those who are hungry, so that their stomachs may be filled."

SAYING 70
Jesus said, "If you give birth to what is within you, what you have within you will save you. If you do not have that within [you], what you do not have within you [will] kill you."

SAYING 71
Jesus said, "I will destroy [this] house, and no one will be able to build it…"

SAYING 72
[A man said to Him,] "Tell my brothers to divide our inheritance with me." He said to him, "Who made me a divider?" He turned to His disciples and said to them, "Am I really a divider?"

SAYING 73
Jesus said, "The harvest really is plentiful, but the workers are few. So, pray that the Lord will send workers to the harvest."

SAYING 74
He said, "Lord, many are gathered around the well, but there is nothing to drink."

SAYING 75
Jesus said, "Many are waiting at the door, but those who are one will enter the bridal chamber."

SAYING 76
Jesus said, "The Father's kingdom can be compared to a merchant with merchandise who found a pearl. The merchant was wise; they sold their merchandise and bought that single pearl for themselves. You, too, look for the treasure that does not perish but endures, where no moths come to eat, and no worms destroy."

SAYING 77
Jesus said, "I am the light that is over all. I am the All. The All has come from Me and unfolds toward Me. Split a log; I am there. Lift the stone, and you will find Me there."

SAYING 78
Jesus said, "What did you go out into the desert to see? A reed shaken by the wind? A [[person]] wearing fancy clothes, [[like your]] rulers and powerful people? They [wear] fancy [[clothes]], but cannot know the truth."

SAYING 79
A woman in the crowd said to Him, "Blessed is the womb that bore You, and the breasts that nourished You." He said to [[her]], "Blessed are those who have listened to the message of the Father and kept it, because there will be days when you will say, Blessed is the womb that did not conceive and the breasts that have not given milk."

SAYING 80
Jesus said, "Whoever has known the world has found the body; but whoever has found the body, of them the world is not worthy."

SAYING 81
Jesus said, "Whoever has become rich should become a ruler, and whoever has power should renounce it."

SAYING 82
Jesus said, "Whoever is near Me is near the fire, and whoever is far from Me is far from the kingdom."

GOSPEL OF THOMAS

SAYING 83
Jesus said, "Images are revealed to people, but the light within them is hidden in the image of the Father's light. He will be revealed, but His image will be hidden by His light."

SAYING 84
Jesus said, "When you see your likeness, you rejoice. But when you see your images that came into being before you did—which do not die and are not revealed—how much you will have to bear!"

SAYING 85
Jesus said, "Adam came into being from a great power and great wealth, but he did not become worthy of you. If he had been worthy, [[he would not have tasted]] death."

SAYING 86
Jesus said, "[[The foxes have dens,]] and the birds have nests, but the Son of Man has nowhere to lay His head and rest."

SAYING 87
Jesus said, "How miserable is the body that depends on a body, and how miserable is the soul that depends on both."

SAYING 88
Jesus said, "The messengers and the prophets will come to you and give you what belongs to you. You will give them what you have and ask yourselves, When will they come and take what is theirs?"

SAYING 89
Jesus said, "Why do you wash the outside of the cup? Do you not know that whoever created the inside created the outside too?"

SAYING 90
Jesus said, "Come to Me, because My yoke is easy and My requirements are light. You will be refreshed."

SAYING 91
They said to Him, "Tell us who You are so that we may trust You." He said to them, "You read the face of the sky and the earth, but you do not know the One right in front of you, and you do not know how to read the present moment."

SAYING 92
Jesus said, "Look and you will find. I did not answer your questions before. Now I want to give you answers, but you are not looking for them."

SAYING 93
"Do not give what is holy to the dogs, or else it might be thrown on the dung heap. Do not throw pearls to the pigs, or else they might…"

SAYING 94
Jesus [[said]], "Whoever looks will find, [[and whoever knocks,]] it will be opened for them."

SAYING 95
[[Jesus said]], "If you have money, do not lend it at interest. Instead, give [[it to]] someone from whom you will not get it back."

SAYING 96
Jesus [[said]], "The Father's kingdom can be compared to a woman who took a little yeast and [[hid]] it in flour. She made it into large loaves of bread. Anyone who has ears to hear should hear!"

SAYING 97
Jesus said, "The Father's kingdom can be compared to a woman carrying a jar of flour. While she was walking down a long road, the jar's handle broke and the flour spilled out behind her on the road. She did not know it, and did not realize there was a problem until she got home, put down the jar, and found it empty."

SAYING 98
Jesus said, "The Father's kingdom can be compared to a man who wanted to kill someone powerful. He drew his sword in his house and drove it into the wall to figure out whether his hand was strong enough. Then he killed the powerful one."

SAYING 99
The disciples said to Him, "Your brothers and mother are standing outside." He said to them, "The people here who do the will of My Father are My brothers and mother; they are the ones who will enter My Father's kingdom."

SAYING 100
They showed Jesus a gold coin and said to Him, "Those who belong to Caesar demand tribute from us." He said to them, "Give to Caesar what belongs to Caesar, give to God what belongs to God, and give to Me what belongs to Me."

SAYING 101
"Whoever does not hate their [[father]] and mother as I do cannot become My [[disciple]], and whoever [[does not]] love their [[father]] and mother as I do cannot become My [[disciple]]. For My mother…, but [[My]] true [[Mother]] gave Me Life."

SAYING 102
Jesus said, "How awful for the Pharisees who are like a dog sleeping in a feeding trough for cattle, because the dog does not eat and [[does not let]] the cattle eat either."

SAYING 103
Jesus said, "Blessed is the one who knows where the bandits are going to enter. [[They can]] get up to assemble their defenses and be prepared to defend themselves before they arrive."

SAYING 104
They said to [[Jesus]], "Come, let us pray and fast today." Jesus said, "What have I done wrong? Have I failed? Rather, when the groom leaves the bridal chamber, then people should fast and pray."

SAYING 105
Jesus said, "Whoever knows their father and mother will be called a bastard."

SAYING 106
Jesus said, "When you make the two into one, you will become [true] children of man, and if you say, Mountain, move, it will go."

SAYING 107
Jesus said, "The kingdom can be compared to a shepherd who had one hundred sheep. The largest one strayed. He left the ninety-nine and looked for that one until he found it. Having gone through the trouble, he said to the sheep: I love you more than the ninety-nine."

SAYING 108
Jesus said, "Whoever drinks from My mouth will become like Me, and I Myself will become like them; then, what is hidden will be revealed to them."

SAYING 109
Jesus said, "The kingdom can be compared to someone who had a treasure [hidden] in their field. [They] did not know about it. After they died, they left it to their son. The son did not know it either. He took the field and sold it. The buyer plowed the field, [found] the treasure, and began to loan money at interest to whomever they wanted."

SAYING 110
Jesus said, "Whoever has found the world and become rich should renounce the world."

SAYING 111
Jesus said, "The heavens and the earth will roll up in front of you, and whoever lives from the Living One will not see death." Does not Jesus say, "Whoever finds themselves, of them the world is not worthy"?

SAYING 112
Jesus said, "How awful for the flesh that depends on the soul. How awful for the soul that depends on the flesh."

SAYING 113
His disciples said to Him, "When will the kingdom come?" [He replied,] "It will not come by looking for it. They will not say, Look over here, or, Look over there! Rather, the Father's kingdom is already spread out over the earth, and people do not see it."

SAYING 114
Simon Peter said to them, "Mary should leave us, because women are not worthy of life." Jesus said, "Behold, am I to make her a man? So that she may become a living spirit too, she is equal to you men, because every woman who makes herself manly will enter the kingdom of the heavens."

GOSPEL OF THE TWELVE HOLY APOSTLES

Written in Syriac, the Gospel of the Twelve Holy Apostles survives in the incomplete codex Harvard Syriac 93, and by palaeography, J. Rendel Harris dates it to the middle of the 8th century. It is followed by three brief apocalypses that are connected in the narrative. It begins with widely-known details from the canonical gospels, leading up to Christ's resurrection and ascension, and is followed by an apostolic prayer, requesting that the LORD reveal the end of time.

THE GOSPEL OF THE TWELVE HOLY APOSTLES TOGETHER WITH THE REVELATIONS OF EACH ONE OF THEM; DONE FROM HEBREW INTO GREEK AND FROM GREEK INTO SYRIAC.

CHAPTER 1

¹The beginning of the good news of Jesus the Christ, the Son of the living God, according as it is said by the Holy Spirit: "I send a messenger before His face, who will prepare His way." ²It came to pass in the three hundred and ninth year of Alexander the son of Philip the Macedonian, in the reign of Tiberius Caesar, in the government of Herod the ruler of the Jews, that the messenger Gabriel, the chief of the messengers, by the command of God went down to Nazareth, to a virgin called Mary, of the tribe of Judah, the son of Israel, her who was betrothed to Joseph the Just, ³and he appeared to her and said, "Behold, there arises from you the One that spoke with our fathers, and He will be a Savior to Israel; and they who do not confess Him will perish, for His authority is in the lofty heights, and His kingdom does not pass away." ⁴Then Mary was disturbed at this word, and was exceedingly terrified, and Mary answered and said, "And how is it possible that this thing should be as you have said, since a man is not known to me, and you announce a Son to me?" ⁵And the messenger said to her, "Truly, for thus the God of greatness wills it, there comes immediately the Holy Spirit, and the Lord dwells in you." ⁶And Mary knelt and worshiped God, and said, "My Lord, may it be to me according to Your word." ⁷And Mary bore a Son in Beth-Lehem of Judah, and His Name was called Jesus the Savior, and the Ruler, and the God who is over all: ⁸according as the Holy Spirit spoke by the mouth of David the prophet: "And He has put all things under His feet: all sheep and oxen, also the beast of the field, and the birds that are in the sky, and the fish of the sea, which pass through the paths of the seas": and there has been made subject to Him, to this Jesus, all that is in Heaven and all that is in the earth. ⁹And after a short time, eight months, He fled from Herod into Egypt, in order that all things that were written might be fulfilled; ¹⁰and after the death of Herod, there appeared a messenger to Joseph, and he brought the Boy back to the land of Israel; and He grew and attained to full stature, according as it is written by the four truthful evangelists; and this is the preaching of the Holy Gospel.

CHAPTER 2

¹And He worked in the world great works of power, and abundant marvels without number; a multitude of which the scribes of the Holy Gospel have left [on record]. ²He healed the sick; He cleansed the lepers; He raised the dead; He opened [the eyes of] the blind; He strengthened the paralytics; He satisfied the hungry; and He worked miracles. ³And He chose for Himself true disciples and twelve apostles, that they might be with Him, whose names are as follows: ⁴Simeon, who is called Kepha, is from the tribe of Reuben; ⁵James and John, the sons of Zebedee, are from the tribe of Issachar; ⁶and Andrew from the tribe of Zebulon; ⁷and Philip from the tribe of Joseph; ⁸and Bartholomew from the tribe of Simeon; ⁹and Matthew from the tribe of Naphtali; ¹⁰and Thomas from the tribe of Benjamin; ¹¹and James the son of Alphaeus from the tribe of Levi; ¹²and Thaddaeus from the tribe of Judah; ¹³and Simeon the Canaanite from the tribe of Asher; ¹⁴and Judas (he that betrayed Him) from the tribe of Gad. ¹⁵These twelve are His disciples to whom He promised twelve thrones that they may judge Israel. ¹⁶And it came to pass that when our Lord did all these wonders, and taught the word of God in the synagogues, and in the cities, and in the streets, it was evil in the eyes of the elders and the scribes of the people; ¹⁷and they stirred up against Him the judges and those that were possessed of authority, until they brought against Him accusations and testimonies through their envy, in order that they might destroy Him, according as all [His] life is written in the Holy Gospel of the four truthful evangelists. ¹⁸And our Lord commanded them and said to them that they should go out and evangelize in the four quarters of the world; ¹⁹and we carried out the preaching, behold, from the ends of the earth to the ends of the same.

CHAPTER 3

¹But after this, the Jews made a plot against Him—the chief priests, and the elders, and the scribes of the people—with one of His disciples, him that is called Iscariot, ²and he took money for His price, and delivered Him up to them, and they delivered Him to the judges, and they judged Him and crucified Him, and He died and was buried, and the third day He rose, according as it is written, and [as] He said to His disciples when He was with them, before He was betrayed. ³But Judas, after the death of the Righteous One, was separated and inherited bitter death by miserable strangling, according to the mystery which our Lord revealed to Simeon Kepha, and to those holy women who were ministering to them before His death. ⁴They, when He rose, announced it to the apostles, and the disciples went according to the message which they had received from our Lord, when He was with them, and there they saw Him. ⁵And there was among them one who doubted concerning the resurrection. ⁶And the eleven apostles brought in, instead of Judas, Matthias; and he stands in his place, and he was with them, and like to them, an apostle. ⁷And He appeared to the eleven when they were reclining to eat, while full of anxieties about stumbling; and He reproached them for their unbelief and reproved them for their hardness of heart; ⁸and He immediately commanded the preachers of the truth, and the proclaimers of the veracity, that they should go out into the four quarters [of the world], and preach the good news, and immerse, ⁹and say: "The Kingdom of Heaven has come near to you." And whosoever believes and hears will live forever. ¹⁰And He said to them, "In My Name they will cast out devils, they will speak with new tongues, which they have not known, nor understood, and in My Name if they will drink any deadly poison, it will not hurt them." ¹¹But Jesus, after these words which His disciples heard from Him, they say to Him, "Behold, You go away from us and ascend to Him that sent You, and there is given to You all power, both in Heaven and on earth, and You have commanded us that we should preach with new tongues." ¹²And after this, [they prayed] the following prayer. And they said, "We implore You, our Lord and God, not to deprive us of Your grace, but establish us in Your grace and enrich us in knowledge that comes from You, and cause Your Holy Spirit to dwell in us; ¹³and give us the mercies and compassion that come from Yourself; and perfect with us the gift that is from Yourself; ¹⁴and with those that call truly on Your Name, let no error come near us; and do not let the Devil strike us with his destroying arrows; ¹⁵and do not let us taste of the poison of the cruel serpent, for this was the cause of the fall of our father Adam. ¹⁶But be to us the Head and the Overseer, and the Lord and the Director, and the Liberator and the Savior; and in all that is given to us from You, in gratitude to You let it be made perfect with us until the end of the world. ¹⁷Yes, our Lord, enrich us according to Your promises, so that we may speak with new tongues, by the Spirit that is from You; ¹⁸and let us know what is the end of the world: because we stand in the midst of offenses and scandals of the world; ¹⁹reveal and interpret to us, our Lord, what is the manner of Your coming, and what is the end, and what offenses exist in the world; ²⁰for behold, You are taken up from us, and what we will say we do not know." ²¹And Jesus rebuked them and said, "Why is all this little faith yours? Behold, I have given you My promises, and have fulfilled to you your petitions: ²²and you will speak with various tongues, and nothing will be hidden from you: ²³and I have put the Holy Spirit in you, and I

have fixed My truth in your hearts for profit, and for salvation, and for the invitation to the Kingdom of Heaven of such as read, and hear, and do your words. ²⁴It is not as with other evangelists who talk of what they have seen and repeat what they have heard, ²⁵but you will speak by the Spirit of My Father, of those things that are and of those that are to come. ²⁶And those who believe and do will see new life in the kingdom of My Father in Heaven."

CHAPTER 4

¹And our Lord was immediately taken up from His twelve [apostles], and their minds were fervent [and were inflamed] like a fire that burns; ²and there was given to each one of them a tongue and grace, and Simeon spoke with them in Hebrew, and James in Latin, and John in Greek, and Andrew in Palestinian, and Philip in Egyptian, and Bartholomew in Elamite, and Matthew in Parthian, and Thomas in Indian, and James the son of Alpheus in the tongue of Mesopotamia, which is beyond the river, and Thaddaeus in African, and Simeon the Canaanite in Median, and Matthias in the Persian tongue. ³And they understood what they were saying, each man [understanding] the tongue of his fellow. ⁴And all those who heard them, were astonished and perplexed, and they said, "How have these barbarous and contemptible people suddenly become wise, and speakers of intricate things, and revealers of secrets? ⁵Who has given them this, and how have they been instructed? For behold, we hear them speaking with new tongues in which they were not born, and preaching conversion, and inviting men to the Kingdom of God! ⁶Were they not born among us, and did they not grow up with us? ⁷And they were feeble of understanding, and now we hear from them secret things and revelations such as the tongues of men cannot tell. ⁸This cannot be without the finger of God, which has enriched them!" ⁹And after they had taught and admonished the people according as they were commanded by our Lord, [they gathered] in the upper room where they had been with Jesus, and they bowed down and worshiped God: ¹⁰and all of them requested as with one soul that they might be made perfect—each one in the tongue of his fellow and of his discourse; ¹¹and that after this, with one accord and agreement, they might ask from God this gift which was promised to them; and that there might be a revelation to them concerning the end; ¹²and Simeon Kepha and the eleven disciples bowed down before God in the same upper room, and they prayed and requested from God and said the following prayer: ¹³"Lord God the Mighty, the Father and Sender of our Lord Jesus Christ, whom You sent as Your only Son, to set us free from evil and from error and to instruct us in the way of life: ¹⁴we call on You, Lord, and we seek from You that we may be found worthy of the gifts which the holy mouth of our Lord promised to us; ¹⁵and let us not be deprived of the grace and the mercies which by His promise have descended on us; ¹⁶but grant us, Lord, and count us worthy that all of us with one soul and with one mind may see Your revelation—that great and marvelous revelation by which You are to reveal to us concerning things created— ¹⁷and that we may understand the times before Your coming again, and how they pass away and are no more, and who are the rulers of those [times], and their lives; ¹⁸and what men are to see the end; and who is he that is to come as Your adversary and to contend with the truth; and whether all men err from You and cleave to error. ¹⁹Yes, our God, we plead: reveal to us in mercies and grace and show us, our Lord, give us our requests, for the knowledge and the advantage of those who read and understand; ²⁰for behold, according to Your word we have hated the world and all that is therein, and we have left fathers and race and have cleaved to You, who are the Savior of our race, and the Beginning, and the End, and the Guide, and the Governor of our life: ²¹Your mercies are over the good and over the evil; and You live and make to live; and You have authority over the exit of all of us. ²²Reveal grace to us, show us good, be propitious to Your servants, Merciful One; and give us in your holy Name to trample on the head of the bitter serpent, Your enemy." ²³And when they had finished their prayer, suddenly [the Lord] flashed lightning over them from Heaven; ²⁴and [the earth] was filled with a great light, such as men had never seen before, and like it can never be again, except that light in which our Lord is to be revealed. ²⁵And the light tarried over them for three hours, that day being the Friday; ²⁶and a mighty voice was heard from within the light which said, "Blessed and blessing is He that came and that comes in the Name of the Lord; blessed is the mystery of Salvation." ²⁷Thus they heard until that light faded from the upper room; ²⁸and suddenly a voice sounded out to them and they heard it saying, "Go forth to the mountain, to the place in which Moses and Elijah appeared to you, and there it will be spoken to you in spirit concerning the world and the end, and concerning the Kingdom of God, and all of you will speak of it in the tongues of the holy fathers." ²⁹And when the voice was silent, they fell on their faces from their fear [for] a great and long span; ³⁰and with the tears from their eyes, all the upper room was full of water; ³¹and Simeon Kepha and his eleven companions rose up, being bound and called by the Holy Spirit, and they went to where Jesus had directed them, and they were there fasting and praying [for] seven days, ³²and suddenly there were set before them [tables] full of all good things— excellent things, from where they came only our Lord knows, things from which He Himself was nourished; ³³and the next day, just as on the first day, He flashed light over them, and made them fervent in spirit and in truth, ³⁴and a voice came to them and said, "Speak out, speak out!" ³⁵And they began to glorify God and extol, and praise, and exalt our Lord, asking from Him that the gift might be completed [which He had promised].

REVELATION OF SIMEON KEPHA

CHAPTER 1

¹And Simeon was moved by the Spirit of God: and his appearance and his body were enlarged, and he glorified [God]; ²and he wept and said, "How great are Your works, O Lord, and all of them You have worked in wisdom. ³For behold, I see the hosts of God which are one thousand thousands—yes, tens of thousands without number—standing in Heaven, and glorifying the lofty throne of the Godhead, exalted above all. ⁴And there was sent to me the great messenger Michael to be a reminder to me, and I received the Spirit in abundance; ⁵and I saw the time that is to be after us, full of offenses, and evils, and sins, and lying: and the men in that [time] will be crafty, perverse and depraved, men that do not know God, and do not understand the truth; ⁶but a few of them will understand their God, because of His works which they behold daily, those which are established in Heaven, and those which are brought forth on earth; ⁷and they know the Lord, as if they did not discern Him; for this name only is called on them that are believers. ⁸And after a time, they will seek to perform miracles in the Name of our Lord Jesus, and they will not be able, because of their little faith; ⁹and they call and are not heard, because they do not call on Him with all their hearts. ¹⁰But those who are separated from them, few in number, ask and are heard because their hearts speak the truth, and know God, and understand His beloved Son, and do not deny the Spirit. ¹¹And in this way, they perform signs and great works of power; and these also in their wealth and in their faith are not allowed to live, for there will rise up against them bribed judges and also bribed deniers [of the faith]; ¹²and for the Name of our Lord they will be judged and beaten; and they will kill them by bitter and various deaths: ¹³and also, after they are killed, they will perform by their death great works of power; ¹⁴and after these things will have happened, the faith will fail from the earth and orthodoxy will come to an end: ¹⁵and those who are named as being immersed in our Lord, and as confessing His Name, will be more miserable than all men; and they will trample on the faith, and talk perversely, and they will divide our Lord; ¹⁶and in that time there will be reckoned many teachers, as the Spirit of the Father does not speak in them, and they will divide our Lord; ¹⁷and the father of lies and the calumniator, that is, Satan, will enter into them and disturb their minds; and their faith will fail, and it will come to pass that when they rise up and tear it, ¹⁸and when every man in his place will say that, I am superior in the fear of God, and I confess Him more correctly, that they will seek our Lord and will not find Him, and they will call to Him and He will not answer them. ¹⁹And the Lord will deliver them to evils, and to misery, and to wrath, and to plunder, and to tribute, ²⁰until they will ask death for themselves and will not find a savior,

and they will be enraged and blaspheme against God, ²¹and they will say, Because we have the superior knowledge of God, on this account the more have evils tracked our steps; ²²[but] the few who will be scattered in the countries, who confess the Son in the way that is right for them to do, of these the Lord will supply their needs; ²³but those who do not believe in Him, and who are called immersed people, will commend the heathen, ²⁴and they will envy them and will say, Why are these things so, and why has it been given to us in this way? ²⁵And even those who preach among them, on whom the Name of the Lord was called, in the headship over their brothers and in the offices of the Assembly, will be disturbers, and self-exalting persons, and haters one of another; ²⁶lovers of money and destroyers of order, and who do not keep the commandments: ²⁷but they will not love their flocks, and in their days men will appear as sheep who are ravenous wolves, ²⁸and they will eat up the labor of the orphans, and the sustenance of the widows, and every ruler will pervert justice, and their eyes will be blinded by bribery, and they will love glory, ²⁹and because of all these evils that are performed by them, they will call on the Lord, ³⁰and there will be none to answer them, and there will be no Savior for them, because evils are multiplied on the earth, and they have corrupted their ways before the Father in Heaven; ³¹and the destroyer will deliver them up to devastation, and to misery, and to necessity, and there will rise up against them wasps in the morning and in the evening, and they will oppress them; ³²and men will see their sons, and their daughters, and their wives, and their revenues made a prey by their enemies; ³³and there will be none that speaks and none that answers, because the Holy One wills it, and the Lofty One talks with them; ³⁴and from before Him judgment will go forth, and they will bring on them all these evils, and they will descend on them, until they will return and become one true flock and one holy Assembly, ³⁵and they will confess our Lord according as we received from Him, and according as we believed in the Son, the Life-giver and Savior of the world; ³⁶and after this will be a flock, and an assembly, and an immersion, true and one: ³⁷and it will come to pass in that day that everyone that will call on the Name of the Lord will be saved, ³⁸and whosoever worships the Paraclete will be delivered."

REVELATION OF JAMES THE APOSTLE

CHAPTER 1

¹And the messenger departed from Simeon and drew near to James; and he was shaken by the Spirit of God, and he wept, and wailed, ²and said, "Oh, our Lord Jesus! For the desolation that I see in this holy city: for behold, after a certain time the temple will be laid waste, the house of the Lord, the great and renowned; and the city [of] Jerusalem will be laid waste; ³and it will be disturbed and will become a place of pollution; and it will be delivered up to a people that does not know God and does not understand the truth because of the wickedness of them that dwell therein; ⁴in that they have blasphemed the Name of our Lord Jesus, and have crucified and killed Him." ⁵And again the apostle James was astonished and said, "Behold, I see that there comes against her a man renowned in name and fearsome in appearance, and he will devastate, and eradicate, and destroy them that dwell therein; ⁶and there will be in it much famine and wrath; and the God of Heaven will be angry with them; and the eyes of their hearts will be darkened, and they will not see the sun; ⁷and they will not understand the marvels of the Lord, because they have not known His Son, and because of their lack of intelligence they will perish; ⁸and He will banish them that dwell in her, and will kill and will destroy, and there will not be found in her any except them that wail and that weep; ⁹and after all these things have happened to the city of the Lord, there will come forth a man who oppresses them by war against his enemies, and in that war he will die; ¹⁰and there will be in authority over her another man, and he will set up his edicts and will settle her, and there will be built in her sanctuaries to the Lord, consecrated and renowned, and they will come from the ends of the earth and from its bounds; ¹¹and of all them that hear the Name of the Lord and know His praises, men will worship the Lord the Holy One there, and they will offer there vows, and aromas, and sacrifices, and libations, ¹²and the Lord will set up therein a sign that overcomes the evil of the wicked, and no man will grudge thereat nor be evil affected: ¹³for there will be therein another house of worship, because peace is decreed to her by the Holy One of Israel; ¹⁴and a great and renowned house will be built in her at great cost, with gold of Ophir and beryls of Havilah, ¹⁵and its name will go forth and be renowned, more than all those houses in the earth: ¹⁶and they will say that never before it [was there such], and never after will it be so. ¹⁷And that king who began to build it will die on the completion of his building: ¹⁸and one from his seed will rise up in his place, and will burden the chief men with many ills; ¹⁹and he will have great and vigorous rule, and the earth will be governed in his days in great peace, ²⁰because from God it has been so spoken concerning him and concerning his people by the mouth of the prophet Daniel: ²¹and it will come to pass that whosoever will call on the Name of the Lord He will save."

REVELATION OF JOHN THE LITTLE

THE BROTHER OF JAMES, AND THESE TWO ARE THE SONS OF ZEBEDEE.

CHAPTER 1

¹And there was suddenly a great earthquake, and John the brother of James, and the initiate of our Lord, fell on his face on the earth, and with a great trembling he worshiped God, the Lord of all; ²and our Lord sent to him a man in white raiment, and mounted on a horse of fire, and his appearance was like the flashing of fire; and he touched him, and set him up, ³and said to him, "John, behold you have been set by our Lord to preach the good news of salvation, along with the three that perform the truth; but you also will not be deprived of this gift; ⁴for there has been given to you the Spirit, that you should receive it in double measure: ⁵because more than your first companions you have known the mysteries of our Savior": ⁶and John was moved by the Holy Spirit, and was made fervent, and said, "Behold, I see Heaven opened and holy ones who are in the lofty heights, in appearance like lightning, glorifying God, the maker of all. ⁷And I beheld, and a messenger approached me, one of those that are near to Him; ⁸and he brought me scrolls written with the finger of truth, and inscribed in them times and generations, and the iniquities and sins of men, and the miseries that are to come on the earth; and I arose as if dazed. ⁹And there was an exceedingly dreadful voice which said, Let the mysteries be revealed that are hidden from the beginning, in soul and in spirit. ¹⁰And the messenger of God who was sent to me touched me and said to me, Open your mouth and receive; ¹¹and I opened my mouth, and I beheld, and he put therein something like beryls and white like snow: and its taste was very sweet, and I ate it. ¹²And he said to me, Behold, it is the day of salvation, and the hour of deliverance! ¹³Speak, for the Lord has pleasure in you! Speak, man, to whom has been given power over the mysteries of God! ¹⁴Speak without fear, for it is the will of God that the secret things should be expounded to you! ¹⁵And I beheld that there was written on the scrolls what men are to suffer in the last times: ¹⁶and when I saw all these things that are past, I was not willing to speak concerning them, but only that I should expound those things that are to come; ¹⁷and there was a voice which spoke in me, Woe, woe to the sons of men who are left to the generations [and] to the times that are to come! ¹⁸For there will rise up the kings of the north, and they will become strong and will shake the whole world, ¹⁹and there will be among them a man who subdues all the peoples by the marvelous sign which appeared to him in the sky, and he will be prosperous, and it will go well with him; ²⁰and after him will rise up kings of the Romans—insolent, evil, idol-worshiping, godless; accusers, and plotters, and accepters of persons; and all the people of the Romans will fall into fornication and adultery, and they will love bribery and lasciviousness through the abundance of wine that they drink; ²¹and while their power is over all the world, because of their evil sins and blasphemies against God, the Lord will send wrath on them from Heaven, ²²and Persia will become strong against them and will drive away and expel this kingdom from the world, because it has done evil exceedingly, ²³and kings will rise up among them—great and renowned, and lovers of money—and they will take away

government from the earth: ²⁴and there will be one of them who because of his love of money will destroy many men, until commerce and trade will perish from off the whole earth, and by the son of his own body, he will die; ²⁵and all the silver and gold that he has collected will not save him; ²⁶and after this, Persia will rule for a short time, and it also will be delivered over to Media; ²⁷because of their evil sins the God of Heaven will abolish their rule and will destroy their kingdom; and they will perish and cease to be. ²⁸But there will be deniers of the truth, and men that do not know God, and that do corruptly in their lasciviousness, those who provoke God, ²⁹and then suddenly will be fulfilled the prophecy of Daniel, the pure and the desired, which he spoke, that God will send forth a mighty wind, the Southern one; ³⁰and there will come forth from it a people of deformed aspect, and their appearance and manners like those of women; ³¹and there will rise up from among them a warrior, and one whom they call a prophet, and they will be brought into his hands those like to whom there has not been any in the world, neither does there exist their like; ³²and each one that hears will shake his head, and will deride him, and say, Why does he speak thus? And God sees it and regards it not. ³³And the South will do prosperously, and by the hoofs of the horses of his armies they will trample down Persia, and subdue it, and devastate Rome; ³⁴and there will not be found any that stands before them, because it has been ordained for them by the Holy One of Heaven; ³⁵and it will come to pass that every kingdom, or people, or place that hears the report of them will be afraid, and will tremble, and will be terrified at the report of this people, until it will subdue and bring under its hands the whole earth; ³⁶and twelve renowned kings will rise up from that people according as it is written in the Law when God talked with Abraham and said to him: Behold! Concerning your son Ishmael, I have heard you, and twelve princes will he beget along with many other princesses; ³⁷and he, even he, is the people of the land of the South. ³⁸He will lead captive a great captivity among all the peoples of the earth, and they will spoil a great spoil, and all the ends of the earth will do service, and there will be made subject to him many lordships; ³⁹and his hand will be over all, and also those that are under his hand he will oppress with much tribute: ⁴⁰and he will oppress, and kill, and destroy the [rulers of the] ends [of the earth]. ⁴¹And he will impose a tribute on [the earth], such as was never heard of, until a man will come out from his house and will find [there] four collectors who collect tribute; ⁴²and men will sell their sons and daughters because of their need: and they will hate their lives and will wail and weep, ⁴³and there is no voice nor discourse except, Woe! Woe! ⁴⁴And they will be covetous with a hateful greed; and they will be converted like bridegrooms and like brides, but will dread some retribution from them, because he that has will be reckoned in their days as though he had not, and he that builds and he that sells as one that gets no gain; ⁴⁵and there will prosper with them all those who take refuge with them, and they will enslave to them men renowned in race, ⁴⁶and there will be hypocrites among them and men who do not know God, and regard not men, except prodigals, fornicators, and men wicked and vengeful. ⁴⁷But woe, woe to the children of men in that time; and they will rule in a cave for one great week and the half of a great week; ⁴⁸and every king who will arise from among them will strengthen, and be made strong, and will be more vigorous than his fellow; ⁴⁹and they will gather together the gold of the earth; and they will descend and lay them up in the earth treasures which came forth from there, because their kingdom and authority is from God; ⁵⁰and it will come to pass after the week and the half of a week, the earth will be moved concerning them, ⁵¹and God will require the sins of creation at their hands, and the South wind will subside, and God will bring their covenant with them to nothing; ⁵²and they will tremble and be frightened at every report that is brought to them; and the hands of all flesh will be on them, according as it was said by the hand of Moses the servant of the Lord; ⁵³and in the end of their times, they will do evil to all flesh that is under their power, and they will oppress, and enslave, and ravage, and men will see necessity and great affliction: ⁵⁴and three and four of them will be associated in pollution. ⁵⁵And there is no one that speaks and no one that hears, except only one that says, Woe! Woe! What is come to pass in our generation? ⁵⁶And they will commend the dead of antiquity, and will ask for death for themselves, and there is none that redeems and none that replies: ⁵⁷but so much the more will they afflict all of those who confess our Lord Christ, because they will hate to the very end the Name of the Lord, and will bring to nothing His covenant; ⁵⁸and truth will not be found among them, but only villainy will they love and sin will they have an affection for. ⁵⁹And whatever is hateful in the eyes of the Lord—that they will do; and they will be called a corrupt people; ⁶⁰and after these things, the Lord will be enraged against them, as he was against Rome, and against Media and Persia; ⁶¹and immediately there will come on them the end, and suddenly the time [comes]; ⁶²and at last, in the completion of the week and a half, God will stir up desolation against them; ⁶³and a messenger of wrath will descend and will kindle calamity among them and in their midst; ⁶⁴and they will be lifted up against one another, and they will make and become two parties, and each party will seek to call himself king, and there will be war between them, and there will be many murders by them and among them, ⁶⁵and much blood will be shed among them at the fountain of waters which is in the place which was spoken of beforehand in the book of the Sibyl. ⁶⁶And when the man of the North will hear this report, he will not be frightened, and he will say, By my might and by my arm I have overcome. ⁶⁷Then he will associate with him all the peoples of the earth, and he will go forth against him, ⁶⁸and they will destroy and devastate his armies and lead captive their sons, and their daughters, and their wives, and there will fall on them a bitter marriage and misery; ⁶⁹and the Lord will cause the spirit of the South to return to his place from where he came forth, and will bring to nothing his name and his fame; ⁷⁰and it will come to pass that when they will enter again the place from where they came out, the enemy will not pursue them there, ⁷¹and they will not fear hunger, and they will not tremble, and it will come to pass in that day that their reliance [will be] on silver, which they have gotten by wrongdoing, and by plunder, which they have hidden in the place named Diglath, ⁷²and they will return and settle in the land from where they came out; ⁷³and God will stir up for them there calamitous times and times of plagues, and without war they will be laid waste, ⁷⁴and to all generations of the world there will not be among them any that holds a weapon and stands up in battle which the Father commanded concerning them from Heaven." ⁷⁵[And when] John had spoken these words, and visions, and revelations in truth, the messenger that spoke to him departed from him, ⁷⁶and a voice said, "Permit your companions, so that they may talk with you."

FRAGMENTARY GOSPELS

This section includes Gospels that are highly fragmentary.

Gospel of the Hebrews: a lost Jewish–Christian gospel containing traditions of Jesus' preexistence, incarnation, baptism, and temptation, along with some of His sayings. It is one of the earliest apocryphal gospels, probably composed in the early-2nd century.

Gospel of the Nazarenes: While some conflate this gospel with that of the Hebrews, the scholarly consensus now regards it as independent. While an exact date of composition is not known, it predates AD 200.

Gospel of the Egyptians: Not to be confused with the overtly gnostic Coptic Gospel of the Egyptians, the [Greek] Gospel of the Egyptians is an early pseudepigraphic gospel from the 2nd century. It survives only in brief quotations from early writers.

The Oxyrhynchus Gospel: The Oxyrhynchus 840 and 1224 fragments stem from an ancient Gospel (or Gospels) that were composed as early as the second half of the 1st century

The Unknown Gospel: These two fragments belong to an unknown Gospel—called "Egerton"—that was probably composed in the middle of the 2nd century at the latest.

GOSPEL OF THE HEBREWS

FRAGMENT 1
¹When Christ desired to come on the earth to men, the good Father summoned a mighty power in Heaven, which was called Michael, and entrusted Christ to the care thereof. ²And the power came into the world, and it was called Mary, and Christ was in her womb seven months.

FRAGMENT 2
¹And it came to pass when the Lord had come up out of the water, the whole fount of the Holy Spirit descended on Him, and rested on Him, and said to Him: "My Son, in all the prophets I was waiting for You, that You should come, and I might rest in You. ²For You are My rest; You are My first-begotten Son who reigns forever."

FRAGMENT 3
¹Even so did My mother, the Holy Spirit, take Me by one of My hairs and carry Me away on to the great mountain Tabor.

FRAGMENT 4
¹He that marvels will reign, and he that has reigned will rest.

FRAGMENT 5
¹And never be joyful, except when you behold your brother with love.

FRAGMENT 6
¹He that has grieved the spirit of his brother.

FRAGMENT 7
¹And when the Lord had given the linen cloth to the servant of the priest, He went to James and appeared to him. ²For James had sworn that he would not eat bread from that hour in which he had drunk the cup of the Lord until he should see Him risen from among them that sleep. ³And shortly thereafter, the Lord said: "Bring a table and bread!" ⁴And immediately it was added: He took the bread, blessed it and broke it, and gave it to James the Just, and said to him: "My brother, eat your bread, for the Son of Man has risen from among them that sleep."

GOSPEL OF THE NAZARENES

¹"Out of Egypt I called My Son." ²… "He will be called a Nazarene." ²… See, the Lord's mother and His brothers were saying to Him, "John the Immerser is immersing for removing sins; let's go and get immersed by him too." ³He said to them: "How have I sinned, so that I need him to immerse Me? Unless maybe what I've just said is [a sin of] ignorance." ⁴… to Jerusalem. ⁵… "Give us today our bread for tomorrow." ⁶… "If you are in My bosom, and you do not do the will of My Father in Heaven, I will cast you away from My bosom." ⁷… "wiser than serpents," … "plunder" … "I thank you" … "I was a mason seeking a living with my hands. ⁸I beg you, Jesus, to give me back my health, so I don't have to beg for food in shame." ⁹… "corban" … "son of John!" ¹⁰… "If your brother," He says, "sins verbally against you, and gives you satisfaction, receive him seven times in a day." ¹¹His disciple Simon said to Him, "Seven times in a day?" The Lord answered him, saying, "I say again to you, up to seventy times seven. ¹²For even in the prophets, even after the Holy Spirit anointed them, sinful speech turned up." ¹³… The other of the rich men said to Him, "Master, what good thing will I do and live?" He said to him: "Man, perform the Law and the Prophets." ¹⁴He answered Him, "I have performed them." He said to him: "Go, sell all that you have and divide it to the poor, and come, follow Me." But the rich man began to scratch his head, and it displeased him. ¹⁵And the Lord said to him: "How can you say, I have performed the Law and the Prophets? Seeing that it is written in the Law: You will love your neighbor as yourself; and look, many of your brothers, sons of Abraham, are covered with dung, dying for hunger, and your house is full of many goods, and there goes out from there nothing at all to them." ¹⁶And He turned and said to His disciple Simon, sitting by Him, "Simon, son of John, it is easier for a camel to enter through the eye of a needle than a rich man into the kingdom of the heavens." ¹⁷… "son of Joiada" … "squandered the substance with harlots and flute-women…prison"…he denied, and swore, and cursed himself … the son of their teacher, condemned for sedition and murder … a massive lintel of the temple broke and split apart … And he gave them armed men to sit right in front of the cave and guard it day and night. ¹⁸… "I will select to Myself these things: very, very, excellent are those whom My Father, who is in Heaven, has given to Me."

GOSPEL OF THE EGYPTIANS

FRAGMENT 1
¹[Salome said to Him,] "Until when will men continue to die?" [He replied,] "So long as women bear children." ²… [And she said,] "Have I done well, then, in not bearing children?" [He replied,] "Eat every plant, but that which has bitterness do not eat."

FRAGMENT 2
¹"When you have trampled on the garment of shame, and when the two become one, and the male with the female is neither male nor female…"

FRAGMENT 3
¹"I came to destroy the works of the female."

THE OXYRHYNCHUS GOSPEL

FRAGMENT 1
¹"… before he does wrong makes all manner of subtle excuse. ²But give heed lest you also suffer the same things as they; ³for the evildoers among men do not receive their reward among the living only, ⁴but also await punishment and much torment." ⁵And He took them and brought them into the very place of purification, and was walking in the temple. ⁶And a certain Pharisee, a chief priest, whose name was Levi, met them and said to the Savior, "Who gave You leave to walk in this place of purification and to see these holy vessels, ⁷when You have not washed nor yet have Your disciples bathed their feet? ⁸But You have walked in this temple defiled, which is a pure place, ⁹wherein no other man walks except he has washed himself and changed his garments, neither does he venture to see these holy vessels." ¹⁰And the Savior immediately stood still with His disciples and answered him, "Are you then, being here in the temple, clean?" ¹¹He says to Him, "I am clean; for I washed in the pool of David, and having descended by one staircase I ascended by another, ¹²and I put on white and clean garments, and then I came and looked on these holy vessels." ¹³The Savior answered and said to him, "Woe you blind, who see not. ¹⁴You have washed in these running waters wherein dogs and swine have been cast night

FRAGMENTARY GOSPELS

and day, ¹⁵and have cleansed and wiped the outside skin which also the harlots and flute-girls anoint and wash and wipe and beautify for the lust of men; ¹⁶but within they are full of scorpions and all wickedness. ¹⁷But My disciples and I, who you say have not bathed, have been dipped in the waters of continuous life which come from… ¹⁸but woe to the…"

FRAGMENT 2

¹"It weighed me down." ²Then Jesus approached in a vision and said, "Why are you discouraged? For not… you, but the …" ³."… You said, although You are not answering. ⁴What then did You renounce? What is the new doctrine that they say You teach, ⁵or what is the new immersion that You proclaim? ⁶Answer and …" ⁷When the scribes and Pharisees and priests saw Him, they were angry that He was reclining in the midst of sinners. ⁸But when Jesus heard, He said, "Those who are healthy have no need of a physician…" ⁹"… and pray for your enemies. For the one who is not against you is for you. ¹⁰The one who is far away today, tomorrow will be near you and in…" ¹¹"… the adversary…"

THE UNKNOWN GOSPEL

FRAGMENT 1

¹… [And Jesus said] to the lawyers, "[Punish] every wrongdoer and transgressor, and not Me"; ²… And turning to the rulers of the people He spoke this, saying, ³"Search the Writings, in which you think that you have life; ⁴these are they which bear witness of Me. ⁵Do not think that I came to accuse you to My Father; there is one that accuses you, even Moses, on whom you have set your hope." ⁶And when they said, "We know well that God spoke to Moses, but as for You, we do not know from where You are," ⁷Jesus answered and said to them, "Now is your unbelief accused …" ⁸[They gave counsel to] the multitude to [gather] stones together and stone Him. ⁹And the rulers sought to lay their hands on Him that they might take Him and [hand Him over] to the multitude; ¹⁰and they could not take Him, because the hour of His betrayal was not yet come. ¹¹But He Himself, even the LORD, going out through the midst of them, departed from them. ¹²And behold, there comes to Him a leper and says, "Master Jesus, journeying with lepers and eating with them in the inn I myself also became a leper. ¹³If, therefore, you will, I am made clean." ¹⁴The LORD then said to him, "I will; be made clean." ¹⁵And immediately the leprosy departed from him. ¹⁶[And the LORD said to him], "Go, [show yourself] to the [priests]…"

FRAGMENT 2

¹… coming to Him began to tempt Him with a question, saying, "Master Jesus, we know that You have come from God, for the things which You testify above all the prophets. ²Tell us therefore: Is it lawful [to render] to kings that which pertains to their rule? ³[Will we render to them], or not?" ⁴But Jesus, knowing their thought, being moved with indignation, said to them, "Why do you call Me Master with your mouth, when you do not hear what I say? ⁵Well did Isaiah prophesy of you, saying, This people honors Me with their lips, but their heart is far from Me. ⁶In vain do they worship Me, [teaching as their doctrines the] precepts [of men] …" ⁷"… shut up … in … place … its weight unweighed?" ⁸And when they were perplexed at His strange question, Jesus, as He walked, stood still on the edge of the River Jordan, ⁹and stretching forth His right hand, He [filled it with water] and sprinkled it on the … ¹⁰And then… water that had been sprinkled … before them and sent forth fruit…

ACTS OF PILATE

Also known as the Gospel of Nicodemus, the Acts of Pilate consists of three parts: a retelling of the trial, crucifixion, and subsequent resurrection of Christ, a fanciful story of Christ's descent into Hades, and an occasionally appended pseudepigraphal letter from Pontius Pilate to Emperor Claudius. It is found primarily in Greek and Latin with the Latin recensions perhaps offering a more antique text. It is, in its most primordial form, likely a 4th-century work, although the appended letter may date to the 2nd century.

THE PASSION AND RESURRECTION

[[I, ANANIAS, THE PROTECTOR, OF PRAETORIAN RANK, EDUCATED IN THE LAW, RECOGNIZED FROM THE DIVINE WRITINGS OUR LORD JESUS CHRIST, AND CAME NEAR TO HIM BY FAITH, AND WAS ACCOUNTED WORTHY OF HOLY IMMERSION: AND I SOUGHT OUT THE MEMORIALS THAT WERE MADE AT THAT SEASON IN THE TIME OF OUR MASTER JESUS CHRIST, WHICH THE JEWS DEPOSITED WITH PONTIUS PILATE, AND FOUND THE MEMORIALS IN HEBREW, AND BY THE GOOD PLEASURE OF GOD, I TRANSLATED THEM INTO GREEK FOR THE INFORMING OF ALL OF THEM THAT CALL ON THE NAME OF OUR LORD JESUS CHRIST: IN THE REIGN OF OUR LORD FLAVIUS THEODOSIUS, IN THE SEVENTEENTH YEAR, AND OF FLAVIUS VALENTINIANUS THE SIXTH, IN THE NINTH INDICTION. ALL YOU, THEREFORE, THAT READ THIS AND TRANSLATE IT INTO OTHER BOOKS, REMEMBER ME AND PRAY FOR ME THAT GOD WILL BE GRACIOUS TO ME AND BE MERCIFUL TO MY SINS WHICH I HAVE SINNED AGAINST HIM. PEACE BE TO THEM THAT READ AND HEAR THESE THINGS, AND TO THEIR SERVANTS. AMEN.

IN THE FIFTEENTH YEAR OF THE GOVERNANCE OF TIBERIUS CAESAR, EMPEROR OF THE ROMANS, AND OF HEROD, KING OF GALILEE, IN THE NINETEENTH YEAR OF HIS RULE, ON THE EIGHTH OF THE CALENDS OF APRIL, WHICH IS THE TWENTY-FIFTH OF MARCH, IN THE CONSULATE OF RUFUS AND RUBELLIO, IN THE FOURTH YEAR OF THE TWO HUNDRED AND SECOND OLYMPIAD, JOSEPH WHO IS CAIAPHAS BEING CHIEF PRIEST OF THE JEWS: THESE ARE THE THINGS WHICH AFTER THE CROSS AND PASSION OF THE LORD, NICODEMUS RECORDED AND DELIVERED TO THE CHIEF PRIEST AND THE REST OF THE JEWS: AND THE SAME NICODEMUS SET THEM FORTH IN HEBREW.]]

CHAPTER 1

1. For the chief priests and scribes assembled in council, even Annas, and Caiaphas, and Somne, and Dothaim, and Gamaliel, Judas, Levi, and Nepthalim, Alexander, and Jairus, and the rest of the Jews, and came to Pilate accusing Jesus for many deeds, saying, "We know this Man, that He is the Son of Joseph the carpenter, begotten of Mary, and He says that He is the Son of God and a King; moreover, He pollutes the Sabbaths, and He would destroy the Law of our fathers." Pilate says: "And what things are they that He does and would destroy the Law?" The Jews say: "We have a law that we should not heal any man on the Sabbath, but this Man of His evil deeds has healed the lame and the bent, the withered and the blind, and the paralytic, the dumb, and them that were possessed, on the Sabbath day!" Pilate says to them: "By what evil deeds?" They say to him: "He is a sorcerer, and by Beelzebul, the prince of the devils, he casts out devils, and they are all subject to Him." Pilate says to them: "This is not to cast out devils by an unclean spirit, but by the god Asclepius."

2. The Jews say to Pilate: "We implore your majesty that He appear before your judgment-seat and be heard." And Pilate called them to him and said: "Tell me, how can I that am a governor examine a king?" They say to him: "We do not say that He is a king, but He says it of Himself." And Pilate called the messenger and said to him: "Let Jesus be brought here, but with gentleness." And the messenger went forth, and when he perceived Jesus, he worshiped Him, and took the kerchief that was on his hand and spread it on the earth, and says to Him: "Lord, walk hereon and enter in, for the governor calls You." And when the Jews saw what the messenger had done, they cried out against Pilate, saying, "Why did you not summon Him by a herald to enter in, but by a messenger? For the messenger, when he saw Him, worshiped Him, and spread out his kerchief on the ground, and has made Him walk on it like a king!"

869

3. Then Pilate called for the messenger and said to him: "Why have you done this, and have spread your kerchief on the ground, and made Jesus to walk on it?" The messenger says to him: "Lord governor, when you sent me to Jerusalem to Alexander, I saw Jesus sitting on a donkey, and the children of the Hebrews held branches in their hands and cried out, and others spread their garments beneath Him, saying, "Save now, You that are in the highest! Blessed is He that comes in the Name of the LORD."

4. The Jews cried out and said to the messenger: "The children of the Hebrews cried out in Hebrew: why then have you done it in Greek?" The messenger says to them: "I did ask one of the Jews and said: What is it that they cry out in Hebrew? And he interpreted it to me." Pilate says to them: "And what did they cry in Hebrew?" The Jews say to him: "Hosanna, membrome! Barouchamma Adonai!" Pilate says to them: "And the Hosanna and the rest, how is it interpreted?" The Jews say to him: "Save now, You that are in the highest! Blessed is He that comes in the Name of the LORD!" Pilate says to them: "If you yourselves bear witness of the words which were said of the children, wherein has the messenger sinned?" And they held their peace. The governor says to the messenger: "Go forth and bring Him in after whatever manner you will." And the messenger went forth, and did after the former manner, and said to Jesus: "Lord, enter in: the governor calls you."

5. Now when Jesus entered in, and the ensigns were holding the standards, the images of the standards bowed and paid homage to Jesus. And when the Jews saw the carriage of the standards, how they bowed themselves and paid homage to Jesus, they cried out above measure against the ensigns. But Pilate said to the Jews: "Do not marvel that the images bowed themselves and paid homage to Jesus." The Jews say to Pilate: "We saw how the ensigns made them to bow and pay homage to Him." And the governor called for the ensigns and says to them: "Why did you do so?" They say to Pilate: "We are Greeks and servers of temples, and how could we pay Him homage? For indeed, while we held the images, they bowed of themselves and paid homage to Him."

6. Then Pilate says to the rulers of the synagogue and the elders of the people: "Choose out able and strong men and let them hold the standards, and let us see if they bow of themselves." And the elders of the Jews took twelve men, strong and able, and made them to hold the standards by sixes, and they were set before the judgment-seat of the governor; and Pilate said to the messenger: "Take Him out of the Praetorium and bring Him in again after whatever manner you will." And Jesus went out of the Praetorium—He and the messenger. And Pilate called to himself those that previously held the image and said to them: "I have sworn by the safety of Caesar that if the standards do not bow when Jesus enters in, I will cut off your heads." And the governor commanded Jesus to enter in the second time. And the messenger did after the former manner and pressed Jesus greatly that He would walk on his kerchief; and He walked on it and entered in. And when He had entered, the standards bowed themselves again and paid homage to Jesus.

CHAPTER 2

1. Now when Pilate saw it, he was afraid and sought to rise up from the judgment-seat. And while he yet thought to rise up, his wife sent to him, saying, "Have nothing to do with this just Man, for I have suffered many things because of Him by night." And Pilate called to him all the Jews, and he said to them: "Do you know that my wife fears God and rather favors the customs of the Jews, with you?" They say to him: "Yes, we know it." Pilate says to them: "Behold, my wife has sent to me, saying, Have nothing to do with this just Man, for I have suffered many things because of Him by night." But the Jews answered and said to Pilate: "Did we not say to you that He is a sorcerer? Behold, He has sent a vision of a dream to your wife."

2. And Pilate called Jesus to him and said to Him: "What is it that these witness against You? Do You say nothing?" But Jesus said: "If they had not had power, they would have spoken nothing; for every man has power over his own mouth, to speak good or evil: they will see to it."

3. The elders of the Jews answered and said to Jesus: "What will we see? Firstly, that You were born of fornication; secondly, that Your birth in Beth-Lehem was the cause of the slaying of children; thirdly, that Your father Joseph and Your mother Mary fled into Egypt because they had no confidence before the people."

4. Then certain of them that stood by, devout men of the Jews, said: "We do not say that He came of fornication, but we know that Joseph was betrothed to Mary, and He was not born of fornication." Pilate says to those Jews which said that He came of fornication: "This claim of yours is not true, for there were espousals, as these also say which are of your nation." Annas and Caiaphas say to Pilate: "The whole multitude of us cry out that He was born of fornication, and we are not believed: but these are proselytes and disciples of His." And Pilate called Annas and Caiaphas to him and said to them: "What are proselytes?" They say to him: "They were born children of Greeks, and they have now become Jews." Then they which said that He was not born of fornication, even Lazarus, Asterius, Antonius, Jacob, Amnes, Zenas, Samuel, Isaac, Phinehas, Crispus, Agrippa, and Judas, said: "We were not born proselytes, but we are children of Jews, and we speak the truth; for we were truly present at the espousals of Joseph and Mary."

5. And Pilate called to him those twelve men which said that He was not born of fornication and says to them: "I adjure you by the safety of Caesar, are these things true which you have said—that He was not born of fornication?" They say to Pilate: "We have a law that we must not swear, because it is sin; but let them swear by the safety of Caesar that it is not as we have said, and we will be guilty of death." Pilate says to Annas and Caiaphas: "Do you answer nothing to these things?" Annas and Caiaphas say to Pilate: "These twelve men are believed which say that He was not born of fornication, but the whole multitude of us cry out that He was born of fornication, and is a sorcerer, and says that He is the Son of God and a King, and we are not believed."

6. And Pilate commanded the whole multitude to go out, excepting the twelve men which said that He was not born of fornication; and he commanded Jesus to be set apart; and Pilate says to them: "For what reason do they desire to put Him to death?" They say to Pilate: "They have jealousy, because He heals on the Sabbath day." Pilate says: "For a good work do they desire to put Him to death?" They say to him: "Yes."

CHAPTER 3

1. And Pilate was filled with indignation, and went forth outside the Praetorium, and says to them: "I call the sun to witness that I find no fault in this Man." The Jews answered and said to the governor: "If this Man were not a wrongdoer we would not have delivered Him to you." And Pilate said: "You take Him [then] and judge Him according to your law." The Jews said to Pilate: "It is not lawful for us to put any man to death." Pilate said: "Has God forbidden you to slay, and allowed me?"

2. And Pilate went in again into the Praetorium, and called Jesus apart, and said to him: "Are You the King of the Jews?" Jesus answered and said to Pilate: "Did you say this thing of yourself, or did others tell it to you of Me?" Pilate answered Jesus: "Am I also a Jew? Your own nation and the chief priests have delivered You to me: what have You done?" Jesus answered: "My kingdom is not of this world; for if My kingdom were of this world, My servants would have striven that I should not be delivered to the Jews; but now My kingdom is not from here." Pilate said to Him: "Are You a king then?" Jesus answered him: "You say that I am a King—for this reason I was born and have come, that everyone that is of the truth should hear My voice." Pilate says to Him: "What is truth?" Jesus says to him: "Truth is of Heaven." Pilate says: "Is there not truth on earth?" Jesus says to Pilate: "You see how they which speak the truth are condemned by them that have authority on earth."

CHAPTER 4

1. And Pilate left Jesus in the Praetorium, and went forth to the Jews, and said to them: "I find no fault in Him." The Jews say to him: "This Man said: I am able to destroy this temple and in three days to build it up." Pilate says: "What temple?" The Jews say: "That which Solomon built in forty-six years, but which this Man says He will destroy

and build it in three days." Pilate says to them: "I am guiltless of the blood of this just Man: you see to it." The Jews say: "His blood be on us and on our children."

2. And Pilate called the elders, and the priests, and Levites to him and said to them secretly: "Do not do this, for there is nothing worthy of death whereof you have accused Him, for your accusation is concerning healing and profaning of the Sabbath." The elders, and the priests, and Levites say: "If a man blasphemes against Caesar, is he worthy of death or no?" Pilate says: "He is worthy of death." The Jews say to Pilate: "If a man is worthy of death if he blasphemes against Caesar, [how much more since] this man has blasphemed against God."

3. Then the governor commanded all the Jews to go out from the Praetorium, and he called Jesus to him and says to Him: "What will I do with You?" Jesus says to Pilate: "Do as it has been given you." Pilate says: "How has it been given?" Jesus says: "Moses and the prophets foretold concerning My death and rising again." Now the Jews inquired by stealth and heard, and they say to Pilate: "What more do you need to hear of this blasphemy?" Pilate says to the Jews: "If this word is of blasphemy, you take Him for His blasphemy, and bring Him into your synagogue, and judge Him according to your law." The Jews say to Pilate: "It is contained in our law, that if a man sins against a man, he is worthy to receive forty stripes save one, but He that blasphemes against God, that he should be stoned with stoning."

4. Pilate says to them: "Take Him and avenge yourselves on Him in whatever manner you will." The Jews say to Pilate: "We will that He be crucified." Pilate says: "He does not deserve to be crucified."

5. Now as the governor looked around on the multitude of the Jews which stood by, he beheld many of the Jews weeping, and he said: "Not all the multitude desires that He should be put to death." The elder of the Jews said: "To this end have the whole multitude of us come here, that He should be put to death." Pilate says to the Jews: "Why should He die?" The Jews said: "Because He called Himself the Son of God, and a King."

CHAPTER 5

1. But a certain man, Nicodemus, a Jew, came and stood before the governor and said: "I beg you, pious lord, allow me to speak a few words." Pilate says: "Speak." Nicodemus says: "I said to the elders, and the priests, and Levites, and to all the multitude of the Jews in the synagogue: Why do you contend with this Man? This Man does many wonderful signs, which no man has done, neither will do: leave Him alone and do not plot any evil against Him. If the signs which He does are of God, they will stand, but if they are of men, they will come to nothing. For truly Moses, when he was sent from God into Egypt, did many signs, which God commanded him to do before Pharaoh, king of Egypt; and there were there certain men, servants of Pharaoh, Jannes and Jambres, and they also did many signs of them which Moses did, and the Egyptians held them as gods, even Jannes and Jambres; and whereas the signs which they did were not of God, they perished and those also that believed on them. And now let this Man go, for He is not worthy of death."

2. The Jews say to Nicodemus: "You became His disciple and speak on His behalf." Nicodemus says to them: "Has the governor also become His disciple, that He speaks on His behalf? Did Caesar not appoint him to this dignity?" And the Jews were raging and gnashing their teeth against Nicodemus. Pilate says to them: "Why gnash your teeth against him, when you have heard the truth?" The Jews say to Nicodemus: "May you receive His truth and His portion." Nicodemus says: "Amen! Amen! May I receive it as you have said."

CHAPTER 6

1. Now one of the Jews came forward and pressed the governor that he might speak a word. The governor says: "If you will say anything, speak." And the Jew said: "Thirty-eight years I lay on a bed in suffering of pains, and at the coming of Jesus many that were possessed and laid with various diseases were healed by Him, and certain young men took pity on me, and carried me with my bed, and brought me to Him; and when Jesus saw me, He had compassion, and spoke a word to me: Take up your bed and walk. And I took up my bed and walked." The Jews say to Pilate: "Ask of him what day it was whereon he was healed?" Pilate said to him that was healed of his sickness: "Tell me truly: what day was it whereon He healed you?" He that was healed says: "On the Sabbath." The Jews say: "Did we not inform you so, that on the Sabbath He heals and casts out devils?"

2. And another Jew came forward and said: "I was born blind: I heard words but I saw no man's face; and as Jesus passed by, I cried with a loud voice: Have mercy on me, O Son of David! And He took pity on me and put His hands on my eyes, and I received sight immediately."

3. And another Jew came forward and said: "I was bowed, and He made me straight with a word." And another said: "I was a leper, and He healed me with a word."

CHAPTER 7

And a certain woman named Veronica [[or Bernice]], crying out from afar, said: "I had an issue of blood and touched the hem of His garment, and the flowing of my blood was stopped which I had [for] twelve years." The Jews say: "We have a law that a woman will not come to give testimony."

CHAPTER 8

And certain others, even a multitude both of men and women cried out, saying, "This Man is a prophet and the devils are subject to Him." Pilate says to them which said, "The devils are subject to Him": "Why were your teachers not also subject to Him?" They say to Pilate: "We do not know." Others also said: "He raised up Lazarus, who was dead, out of his tomb after four days." And the governor was afraid and said to all the multitude of the Jews: "Why will you shed innocent blood?"

CHAPTER 9

1. And he called to himself Nicodemus and those twelve men which said that He was not born of fornication, and he said to them: "What will I do, for a sedition rises among the people?" They say to him: "We do not know; let them see to it." Again, Pilate called for all the multitude of the Jews and says: "You know that you have a custom that at the Celebration of Unleavened Bread I should release a prisoner to you. Now I have a prisoner under condemnation in the prison, a murderer, Barabbas by name, and also this Jesus who stands before you, in whom I find no fault: "Whom would you have me release to you?" But they cried out: "Barabbas!" Pilate says: "What will I do then with Jesus who is called Christ?" The Jews say: "Let Him be crucified!" But certain of the Jews answered: "You are not a friend of Caesar's if you let this Man go, for He called Himself the Son of God and a King: you will therefore have Him for king, and not Caesar."

2. And Pilate was angry and said to the Jews: "Your nation is always seditious and you rebel against your benefactors." The Jews say: "Against what benefactors?" Pilate says: "According as I have heard, your God brought you out of Egypt, out of hard bondage, and led you safe through the sea as by dry land, and in the wilderness He nourished you with manna, and gave you quails, and gave you water to drink out of a rock, and gave to you a law. And in all these things you provoked your God to anger, and sought out a molten calf, and angered your God, and He sought to slay you: and Moses made supplication for you, and you were not put to death. And now you accuse me that I hate the emperor."

3. And he rose up from the judgment-seat and sought to go forth. And the Jews cried out, saying, "We know our king: even Caesar and not Jesus! For indeed, the wise men brought gifts from the east to Him as to a king, and when Herod heard from the wise men that a king was born, he sought to slay Him, and when His father Joseph knew that, he took Him and His mother and they fled into Egypt. And when Herod heard it, he destroyed the children of the Hebrews that were born in Beth-Lehem."

4. And when Pilate heard these words, he was afraid. And Pilate silenced the multitude, because they still cried out, and he said to them: "So, then, this is He whom Herod sought?" The Jews say: "Yes, this is He." And Pilate took water and washed his hands before the sun, saying, "I am innocent of the blood of this just Man: see to it." Again, the Jews cried out: "His blood be on us and on our children."

5. Then Pilate commanded the veil to be drawn before the judgment-seat whereon he sat, and he says to Jesus: "Your nation has

accused You as being a king: therefore, I have decreed that You should first be scourged according to the law of the pious emperors, and thereafter hanged on the cross in the garden wherein You were taken: and let Dysmas and Gestas, the two criminals, be crucified with You."

CHAPTER 10

1. And Jesus went forth out of the Praetorium, and the two criminals with Him. And when they had come to the place, they stripped Him of His garments, and girded Him with a linen cloth, and put a crown of thorns around His head: likewise, they also hung up the two criminals. But Jesus said: "Father forgive them, for they do not know what they do." And the soldiers divided His garments among them.

2. And the people stood looking on Him, and the chief priests and the rulers with them derided Him, saying, "He saved others, let Him [then] save Himself if He is the Son of God." And the soldiers also mocked Him, coming and offering Him vinegar with gall; and they said: "If you are the King of the Jews, save Yourself."

3. And Pilate, after the sentencing, commanded His accusation to be written for a title in letters of Greek, and Latin, and Hebrew according to the saying of the Jews: that He was the King of the Jews.

4. And one of the criminals that were hanged [(Gestas)] spoke to Him, saying, "If You are the Christ, save Yourself, and us." But Dysmas answering rebuked him, saying, "Do you not at all fear God, seeing that you are in the same condemnation? And we indeed justly, for we receive the due reward for our deeds; but this Man has done nothing wrong." And he said to Jesus: "Remember me, Lord, in Your kingdom." And Jesus said to him: "Truly, truly, I say to you, that today you will be with Me in Paradise."

CHAPTER 11

1. And it was about the sixth hour, and there was darkness over the land until the ninth hour, for the sun was darkened: and the veil of the temple was torn apart in the middle. And Jesus called with a loud voice and said: "Father, baddach ephkid rouel!" Which is interpreted: "Into your hands I commit My spirit!" And having thus spoken, He gave up the spirit. And when the centurion saw what was done, he glorified God, saying, "This Man was righteous." And all the multitudes that had come to the sight, when they beheld what was done, struck their breasts and returned.

2. But the centurion reported to the governor the things that had come to pass: and when the governor and his wife heard, they were greatly worried, and neither ate nor drank that day. And Pilate sent for the Jews and said to them: "Did you see that which came to pass?" But they said: "There was an eclipse of the sun after the accustomed sort."

3. And His acquaintance had stood far off, and the women which came with Him from Galilee, beholding these things. But a certain man named Joseph, being a counselor, of the city of Arimathea, who also himself looked for the Kingdom of God, this man went to Pilate and begged for the body of Jesus. And he took it down, and wrapped it in a clean linen cloth, and laid it in a hewn tomb wherein a man was never yet laid.

CHAPTER 12

1. Now when the Jews heard that Joseph had begged for the body of Jesus, they sought for him, and for the twelve men which said that Jesus was not born of fornication, and for Nicodemus and many others which had come forth before Pilate and declared His good works. But they all hid themselves, and Nicodemus alone was seen by them, for he was a ruler of the Jews. And Nicodemus said to them: "How did you come into the synagogue?" The Jews say to him: "How did you come into the synagogue? For you are united with Him, and His portion will be with you in the life to come." Nicodemus says: "Amen! Amen!" Likewise, Joseph also came forth and said to them: "Why is it that you are agitated against me, because I begged for the body of Jesus? Behold, I have laid it in my new tomb, having wrapped it in clean linen, and I rolled a stone over the door of the cave. And you have not dealt well with the Just One, for you did not convert when you had crucified Him, but you also pierced Him with a spear."

2. But the Jews took hold on Joseph and commanded him to be put in safeguard until the first day of the week; and they said to him: "Know that the time does not allow us to do anything against you, because the Sabbath dawns: but know that you will not obtain burial, but we will give your flesh to the birds of the sky." Joseph says to them: "This is the word of Goliath, the boastful, which reproached the living God and the holy David. For God said by the prophet: Vengeance is Mine, and I will repay, says the LORD. And now, behold, one that was uncircumcised, but circumcised in heart, took water and washed his hands before the sun, saying, I am innocent of the blood of this just person: see to it. And you answered Pilate and said: His blood be on us and on our children. And now I fear lest the wrath of the LORD come on you and on your children, as you have said." But when the Jews heard these words, they grew bitter in soul, and caught hold of Joseph, and took him, and shut him up in a house wherein was no window, and guards were set at the door; and they sealed the door of the place where Joseph was shut up.

3. And on the Sabbath day, the rulers of the synagogue, and the priests, and the Levites made an ordinance that all men should appear in the synagogue on the first day of the week. And all the multitude rose up early and took council in the synagogue by what death they should kill him. And when the council was set, they commanded him to be brought with great dishonor. And when they had opened the door, they did not find him. And all the people were beside themselves and amazed, because they found the seals closed, and Caiaphas had the key. And they did not dare any longer to lay hands on them that had spoken in behalf of Jesus before Pilate.

CHAPTER 13

1. And while they yet sat in the synagogue and marveled because of Joseph, there came certain of the guard which the Jews had asked of Pilate to keep the tomb of Jesus, lest perhaps His disciples should come and steal Him away. And they spoke and declared to the rulers of the synagogue and the priests and the Levites that which had come to pass: how there was a great earthquake, and we saw a messenger descend from Heaven, and he rolled away the stone from the mouth of the cave and sat on it. And he shined like snow and like lightning, and we were severely afraid and lay as dead men. And we heard the voice of the messenger speaking with the women which waited at the tomb, saying, "Do not fear, for I know that you seek Jesus who was crucified. He is not here: He is risen, [just] as He said. Come, see the place where the LORD lay, and go quickly and say to His disciples that He is risen from the dead, and is in Galilee."

2. The Jews say: "With what women did He speak?" They of the guard say: "We do not know who they were." The Jews say: "At what hour was it?" They of the guard say: "At midnight." The Jews say: "And why did you not take the women?" They of the guard say: "We had become as dead men through fear, and we did not look to see the light of the day; how then could we take them?" The Jews say: "As the LORD lives, we do not believe you." They of the guard say to the Jews: "So many signs you saw in that Man, and you did not believe; how then should you believe us? Truly you swore correctly, As the LORD lives, for He lives indeed." Again, they of the guard say: "We have heard that you shut up [the man] that begged for the body of Jesus, and that you sealed the door; and when you had opened it you did not find him. Therefore, give [over] Joseph, and we will give you Jesus." The Jews say: "Joseph has departed to his own city." They of the guard say to the Jews: "Jesus also is risen, as we have heard from the messenger, and He is in Galilee."

3. And when the Jews heard these words, they were severely afraid, saying, "Take heed lest this report be heard and all men incline to Jesus." And the Jews took counsel, and laid down much money, and gave it to the soldiers, saying, "Say: While we slept, His disciples came by night and stole Him away. And if this comes to the governor's hearing, we will persuade him and secure you." And they took the money and did as they were instructed. [[And this report of theirs was published abroad among all men.]]

CHAPTER 14

1. Now a certain priest named Phinehas, and Addas a teacher, and Aggaeus a Levite, came down from Galilee to Jerusalem and told the rulers of the synagogue and the priests and the Levites, saying, "We saw Jesus

and His disciples sitting on the mountain which is called Mamilch, and He said to His disciples: Go into all the world and preach to every creature: he that believes and is immersed will be saved, but he that disbelieves will be condemned. [[And these signs will follow them that believe: in My Name they will cast out devils, they will speak with new tongues, they will take up serpents, and if they drink any deadly thing it will not hurt them; they will lay hands on the sick, and they will recover.]] And while Jesus yet spoke to His disciples, we saw Him taken up into Heaven."

2. The elders, and the priests, and Levites say: "Give glory to the God of Israel and make confession to Him: did you indeed hear and see those things which you have told us?" They that told them say: "As the LORD God of our fathers Abraham, Isaac, and Jacob lives, we did [indeed] hear these things, and we saw Him taken up into Heaven." The elders, and the priests, and the Levites say to them: "Did you come for this end, that you might tell us [this], or did you come to pay your vows to God?" And they say: "To pay our vows to God." The elders, and the chief priests, and the Levites say to them: "If you came to pay your vows to God, to what purpose is this idle tale which you have babbled before all the people?" Phinehas the priest, and Addas the teacher, and Aggaeus the Levite say to the rulers of the synagogue, and priests, and Levites: "If these words which you have spoken and seen are sin, behold, we are before you: do to us as seems good in your eyes." And they took the Scroll of the Law and adjured them that they should no longer tell any man these words, and they gave them to eat and to drink, and put them out of the city; moreover, they gave them money, and three men to go with them, and they set them on their way as far as Galilee, and they departed in peace.

3. Now when these men had departed into Galilee, the chief priests, and the rulers of the synagogue, and the elders gathered together in the synagogue, and shut the gate, and lamented with a great lamentation, saying, "What is this sign which has come to pass in Israel?" But Annas and Caiaphas said: "Why are you troubled? Why do you weep? Do you not know that His disciples gave much gold to them that kept the tomb and taught them to say that a messenger came down and rolled away the stone from the door of the tomb?" But the priests and the elders said: "[If] it be so, that His disciples did steal away His body, but how has His soul entered into His body, and how does He reside in Galilee?" But they could not answer these things, and hardly in the end said: "It is not lawful for us to believe the uncircumcised. Should we believe the soldiers, that a messenger came down from Heaven and rolled away the stone from the door of the tomb? But in reality, His disciples gave … tomb. Do you not know that it is not lawful for Jews to believe any word of the uncircumcised, knowing that they who received much good from us have spoken according as we taught them?"

CHAPTER 15

1. And Nicodemus rose up and stood before the council, saying, "You speak well. Do you not know, O people of the LORD, the men that came down out of Galilee, that they fear God and are men of substance, hating covetousness, men of peace? And they have told you with an oath, saying, We saw Jesus on Mount Mamilch with His disciples and that He taught them all things that you heard of them; and they say, We saw Him taken up into Heaven. And no man asked them in what manner He was taken up. For just as the scroll of the Holy Writings has taught us that Elijah also was taken up into Heaven, and Elisha cried out with a loud voice, and Elijah cast his hairy cloak on Elisha, and Elisha cast the cloak on [the] Jordan, and passed over, and went to Jericho. And the sons of the prophets met him and said: Elisha, where is your lord Elijah? And he said that he was taken up into Heaven. And they said to Elisha: Has a spirit not caught him up and cast him on one of the mountains? But let us take our servants with us and seek after him. And they persuaded Elisha, and he went with them, and they sought him [for] three days and did not find him; and they knew that he had been taken up. And now listen to me, and let us send into all the mountains of Israel and see whether the Christ was not taken up by a spirit and cast on one of the mountains." And this saying pleased them all: and they sent into all the mountains, and sought Jesus, and did not find Him. But they found Joseph in Arimathea, and no man dared lay hands on him.

2. And they told the elders, and the priests, and the Levites, saying, "We went about throughout all the coasts of Israel, and we did not find Jesus; but Joseph we found in Arimathea." And when they heard of Joseph, they rejoiced and gave glory to the God of Israel. And the rulers of the synagogue, and the priests, and the Levites took counsel [regarding] how they should meet with Joseph, and they took a volume of paper and wrote to Joseph these words: "Peace be to you. We know that we have sinned against God and against you, and we have prayed to the God of Israel that you should agree to come to your fathers and to your children, for we are all troubled, because when we opened the door we did not find you; and we know that we devised an evil counsel against you, but the LORD helped you. And the LORD Himself made of no effect our counsel against you, O father Joseph—you that are honorable among all the people."

3. And they chose out of all Israel seven men that were friends of Joseph, whom Joseph also himself accounted his friends, and the rulers of the synagogue, and the priests, and the Levites said to them: "See: if he receives our letter and reads it, know that he will come with you to us: but if he does not read it, know that he is displeased with us, and salute him in peace and return to us." And they blessed the men and let them go. And the men came to Joseph, and paid him respect, and said to him: "Peace be to you." And he said: "Peace be to you and to all the people of Israel." And they gave him the scroll of the letter, and Joseph received it, and read it, and embraced the letter, and blessed God, and said: "Blessed be the LORD God, who has redeemed Israel from shedding innocent blood; and blessed be the LORD, who sent His messenger and sheltered me under his wings." And he kissed them and set a table before them, and they ate, and drank, and lay there.

4. And they rose up early and prayed; and Joseph saddled his female donkey and went with the men, and they came to the holy city, even Jerusalem. And all the people came to meet Joseph and cried: "Peace be to your entering in!" And he said to all the people: "Peace be to you"; and all the people kissed him. And the people prayed with Joseph, and they were astonished at the sight of him. And Nicodemus received him into his house, and made a great feast, and called Annas and Caiaphas, and the elders, and the priests, and the Levites to his house. And they celebrated, eating and drinking with Joseph. And when they had sung a hymn, every man went to his house. But Joseph abode in the house of Nicodemus.

5. And the next day, which was the Preparation, the rulers of the synagogue, and the priests, and the Levites rose up early and came to the house of Nicodemus, and Nicodemus met them and said: "Peace be to you." And they said: "Peace be to you, and to Joseph, and to all your house, and to all the house of Joseph." And he brought them into his house. And the whole council was set, and Joseph sat between Annas and Caiaphas, and no man dared speak a word to him. And Joseph said: "Why is it that you have called me?" And they beckoned to Nicodemus that he should speak to Joseph. And Nicodemus opened his mouth and said to Joseph: "Father, you know that the respected doctors, and the priests, and the Levites seek to learn a matter from you." And Joseph said: "Inquire." And Annas and Caiaphas took the Scroll of the Law and adjured Joseph, saying, "Give glory to the God of Israel and make confession to Him: [[for Achar, when he was adjured by the prophet Joshua, did not deny himself, but declared to him all things and did not hide a word from him: therefore, you also must not hide from us so much as a word." And Joseph [said]: "I will not hide one word from you."]] And they said to him: "We were greatly distressed because you begged for the body of Jesus, and wrapped it in a clean linen cloth, and laid Him in a tomb. And for this reason, we put you in safeguard in a house wherein there was no window, and we put keys and seals on the doors, and guards did keep the place wherein you were shut up. And on the first day of the week, we opened it and did not find you, and we were deeply troubled, and amazement fell on all the people of the LORD until yesterday. Now, therefore, declare to us what happened to you."

6. And Joseph said: "On the Day of Preparation, about the tenth hour, you did shut me up, and I remained there the whole

Sabbath. And at midnight, as I stood and prayed, the house wherein you shut me up was taken up by the four corners, and I saw as it were a flashing of light in my eyes, and being filled with fear, I fell to the earth. And One took me by the hand and removed me from the place whereon I had fallen; and moisture of water was shed on me from my head to my feet, and an aroma of ointment came around my nostrils. And He wiped my face, and kissed me, and said to me: Do not fear, Joseph: open your eyes and see who it is that speaks with you. And I looked up and saw Jesus, and I trembled and supposed that it was a spirit: and I said the commandments; and He said them with me. And you are not ignorant that a spirit, if it meets any man and hears the commandments, immediately flees. And when I perceived that He said them with me, I said to Him: Rabbi Elijah? And He said to me: I am not Elijah. And I said to Him: Who are You, Lord? And He said to me: I am Jesus, whose body you begged for from Pilate, and clothed Me in clean linen, and covered My face with a napkin, and laid Me in your new cave, and rolled a great stone on the door of the cave. And I said to Him that spoke with me: Show me the place where I laid You. And He brought me and showed me the place where I laid Him, and the linen cloth lay therein, and the napkin that was on His face. And I knew that it was Jesus. And He took me by the hand and set me in the midst of my house, the doors being shut, and laid me on my bed and said to me: Peace be to you. And He kissed me and said to me: Until forty days are ended, do not go out of your house: for behold, I go to My brothers—into Galilee."

CHAPTER 16

1. And when the rulers of the synagogue, and the priests, and the Levites heard these words of Joseph, they became as dead men and fell to the ground, and they fasted until the ninth hour. And Nicodemus and Joseph comforted Annas, and Caiaphas, and the priests, and the Levites, saying, "Rise up, and stand on your feet, and taste bread, and strengthen your souls, for tomorrow is the Sabbath of the LORD." And they rose up, and prayed to God, and ate, and drank, and departed—every man to his house.

2. And on the Sabbath, the teachers, and the priests, and Levites sat and questioned one another and said: "What is this wrath that has come on us? For we know His father and His mother." Levi the teacher says: "I know that His parents feared God and did not hold back their vows, and they paid tithes three times a year. And when Jesus was born, His parents brought Him up to this place and gave sacrifices and burnt-offerings to God. And the great teacher Simeon took Him into his arms and said: Now let Your servant, LORD, depart in peace, for my eyes have seen Your salvation which You have prepared before the face of all peoples: a light to lighten the nations and the glory of Your people Israel. And Simeon blessed them and said to His mother Mary: I give you good tidings concerning this Child. And Mary said: Good, my lord? And Simeon said to her: Good. Behold, He is set for the fall and rising again of many in Israel, and for a sign spoken against: and a sword will pierce through your own heart also, so that the thoughts of many hearts may be revealed."

3. They say to Levi the teacher: "How do you know these things?" Levi says to them: "Do you not know that from Him I learned the Law?" The council says to him: "We would see your father." And they sent after his father, and asked of him, and he said to them: "Why did you not believe my son? The blessed and righteous Simeon, he did teach him the Law." The council says: "Rabbi Levi, is the word true which you have spoken?" And he said: "It is true." Then the rulers of the synagogue, and the priests, and the Levites said among themselves: "Come, let us send into Galilee to the three men which came and told us of His teaching and His being taken up, and let them tell us how they saw Him taken up." And this word pleased them all, and they sent the three men which before had gone with them into Galilee and said to them: "Say to Rabbi Addas, and Rabbi Phinehas, and Rabbi Aggaeus: Peace be to you and to all that are with you. Inasmuch as great questioning has arisen in the council, we have sent to you to call you to this holy place of Jerusalem."

4. And the men went into Galilee, and found them sitting and meditating on the Law, and saluted them in peace. And the men that were in Galilee said to them that had come to them: "Peace be on all Israel." And they said: "Peace be to you." Again, they said to them: "Why have you come?" And they that were sent said: "The council calls you to the holy city [of] Jerusalem." And when the men heard that they were requested by the council, they prayed to God, and sat down to eat with the men, and ate and drank, and rose up and came in peace to Jerusalem.

5. And the next day, the council was set in the synagogue, and they examined them, saying, "Did you indeed see Jesus sitting on Mount Mamilch, as He taught His eleven disciples, and saw Him taken up?" And the men answered them and said: "Even as we saw Him taken up, even so did we tell it to you."

6. Annas says: "Set them apart from one another, and let us see if their word agrees." And they set them apart from one another, and they call Addas first and say to him: "How did you see Jesus taken up?" Addas says: "While He yet sat on Mount Mamilch and taught His disciples, we saw a cloud that overshadowed Him and His disciples: and the cloud carried Him up into Heaven, and His disciples were lying on their faces on the earth." And they called Phinehas the priest, and questioned him also, saying, "How did you see Jesus taken up?" And he spoke in like manner. And again, they asked Aggaeus, and he also spoke in like manner. And the council said: "It is contained in the Law of Moses: At the mouth of two or three will every word be established." Abuthem the teacher says: "It is written in the Law: Enoch walked with God and is not, because God took him." Jairus the teacher said: "Also, we have heard of the death of the holy Moses and have not seen him; for it is written in the Law of the LORD: And Moses died at the mouth of the LORD, and no man knew of his tomb to this day." And Rabbi Levi said: "Why was it that Rabbi Symeon said when he saw Jesus: Behold, this Child is set for the fall and rising again of many in Israel and for a sign spoken against?" And Rabbi Isaac said: "It is written in the Law: Behold, I send My messenger before your face, which will go before you to keep you in every good way, for My Name is named thereon."

7. Then Annas and Caiaphas said: "You have said those things which are written in the Law of Moses well, that no man saw the death of Enoch, and no man has named the death of Moses. But Jesus spoke before Pilate, and we know that we saw Him receive strikes and spittings on His face, and that the soldiers put a crown of thorns on Him, and that He was scourged and received condemnation from Pilate, and that He was crucified at the Place of a Skull, and two thieves with Him, and that they gave Him vinegar to drink with gall, and that Longinus the soldier pierced His side with a spear, and that Joseph, our honorable father, begged for His body, and that, as he says, He rose again, and as the three teachers say: We saw Him taken up into Heaven, and that Rabbi Levi spoke and testified to the things which were spoken by Rabbi Simeon, and that he said: Behold, this Child is set for the fall and rising again of many in Israel, and for a sign spoken against." And all the teachers said to all the people of the LORD: "If this has come to pass from the LORD, and it is marvelous in our eyes, you will surely know, O house of Jacob, that it is written: Cursed is everyone that hangs on a tree. And another Writing teaches: The gods which did not make the heavens and the earth will perish." And the priests and the Levites said to one another: "If His memorial endures until the Sommos, which is called the Jubilee, know that He will prevail forever and raise up for Himself a new people." Then the rulers of the synagogue, and the priests, and the Levites admonished all Israel, saying, "Cursed is that man who will worship that which man's hand has made, and cursed is the man who will worship creatures beside the Creator." And all the people said: "Amen! Amen!"

8. And all the people sang a hymn to the LORD and said: "Blessed be the LORD who has given rest to the people of Israel || According to all that He spoke. Not one word has fallen to the ground of all His good sayings || Which He spoke to His servant Moses. The LORD our God be with us as He was with our fathers: Let Him not forsake us. And let Him not destroy us from turning our heart toward Him, || From walking in all His ways and keeping His statutes || And His judgments which He commanded our fathers. And the LORD will be King over all the earth in that day. And there will be one Lord and His Name one, || Even the LORD our King: He will save us.

There is none like to you, O LORD. Great are You, O LORD, || And great is Your Name. Heal us, O LORD, by Your power, || And we will be healed: Save us, LORD, and we will be saved, || For we are Your portion and Your inheritance. And the LORD will not forsake His people || For His great Name's sake, || For the LORD has begun to make us to be His people." And when they had all sung this hymn, they departed—each man to his house—glorifying God. [[For His is the glory, world without end. Amen.]]

THE DESCENT INTO HADES

CHAPTER 1

1. And Joseph arose and said to Annas and Caiaphas: "Truly and rightly do you marvel because you have heard that Jesus has been seen alive after death, and that He has ascended into Heaven. Nevertheless, it is more marvelous that He did not rise alone from the dead, but raised up alive many other dead out of their tombs, and they have been seen by many in Jerusalem. And now listen to me; for we all know the blessed Simeon, the chief priest which received the Child Jesus in his hands in the temple. And this Simeon had two sons, brothers in blood, and we all were at their falling-asleep and at their burial. Therefore, go and look on their tombs: for they are open, because they have risen; and behold, they are in the city of Arimathea dwelling together in prayer. And indeed, men hear them crying out, yet they speak with no man, but are silent as dead men. But come, let us go to them and with all honor and gentleness, bring them to us, and if we adjure them, perhaps they will tell us concerning the mystery of their rising again."

2. When they heard these things, they all rejoiced. And Annas and Caiaphas, Nicodemus, and Joseph, and Gamaliel went and did not find them in their tomb, but they went to the city of Arimathea and found them there, kneeling on their knees and giving themselves to prayer. And they kissed them, and with all reverence and in the fear of God, they brought them to Jerusalem into the synagogue. And they shut the doors, and took the Law of the LORD, and put it into their hands, and adjured them by the God Adonai and the God of Israel which spoke to our fathers by the prophets, saying, "Do you believe that it is Jesus which raised you from the dead? Tell us how you have arisen from the dead."

3. And when Karinus and Leucius heard this adjuration, they trembled in their body and groaned, being troubled in heart. And looking up together toward the sky, they made the Sign of the Cross with their fingers on their tongues, and both of them immediately spoke, saying, "Give each of us a volume of paper, and let us write that which we have seen and heard." And they gave them to them, and each of them sat down and wrote, saying:

ACTS OF PILATE

CHAPTER 2

1. O Lord Jesus Christ, the life and resurrection of the dead, allow us to speak of the mysteries of Your majesty which you performed after Your death on the Cross, inasmuch as we have been adjured by Your Name. For You commanded us, Your servants, to tell no man the secrets of Your divine majesty which You worked in Hades. Now when we were set together with all our fathers in the deep, in obscurity of darkness, suddenly there came a golden heat of the sun and a purple and royal light shining on us. And immediately, the father of the whole race of men, together with all the patriarchs and prophets, rejoiced, saying, "This Light is the beginning of everlasting light which promised to send to us His coeternal Light." And Isaiah cried out and said: "This is the Light of the Father, even the Son of God, according as I prophesied when I lived on the earth: The land of Zebulon and the land of Naphtali || Beyond [the] Jordan, Galilee of the nations: The people that walked in darkness have seen a great light, || And they that dwell in the land of the shadow of death, || On them did the light shine. And now it has come and shone on us that sit in death."

2. And as we all rejoiced in the light which shined on us, there came to us our father Simeon, and he rejoicing said to us: "Glorify the Lord Jesus Christ, the Son of God; for I received Him in my hands in the temple when He was born a Child, and being moved by the Holy Spirit, I made confession and said to Him: Now my eyes have seen Your salvation, which You have prepared before the face of all people—a light to lighten the nations, and to be the glory of Your people Israel." And when they heard these things, the whole multitude of the holy ones rejoiced yet more.

3. And after that, there came one as it were a dweller in the wilderness, and he was inquired of by all: "Who are you?" And he answered them and said: "I am John, the voice and the prophet of the Most High, which came before the face of His advent to prepare His ways, to give knowledge of salvation to His people, for the forgiveness of their sins. And when I saw Him coming to me, being moved by the Holy Spirit, I said: Behold, the Lamb of God! Behold, Him that takes away the sins of the world! And I immersed Him in the Jordan River, and saw the Holy Spirit descending on Him in the likeness of a dove, and heard a voice out of Heaven, saying, This is My beloved Son, in whom I am well pleased. And now I have come before His face and come down to declare to you that He is at hand to visit us, even the Dayspring, the Son of God, coming from on high to us that sit in darkness and in the shadow of death."

CHAPTER 3

And when father Adam that was first created heard this, even that Jesus was immersed in [the] Jordan, he cried out to his son Seth, saying, "Declare to your sons the patriarchs and the prophets all that you heard from Michael the chief-messenger, when I sent you to the gates of Paradise that you might plead for God to send you His messenger to give you the oil of the Tree of Mercy to anoint my body when I was sick." Then Seth drew near to the holy patriarchs and prophets, and he said: "When I, Seth, was praying at the gates of Paradise, behold, Michael the messenger of the LORD appeared to me, saying, I am sent to you from the LORD: it is I that am set over the body of man. And I say to you, Seth, do not trouble yourself with tears, praying and pleading for the oil of the Tree of Mercy, that you may anoint your father Adam for the pain of his body: for you will not be able to receive it, except in the last days and times—except when five thousand and five hundred years are accomplished: then the most beloved Son of God will come on the earth to raise up the body of Adam and the bodies of the dead, and He will come and be immersed in [the] Jordan. And when He has come forth out of the water of [the] Jordan, then He will anoint with the oil of mercy all that believe on Him, and that oil of mercy will be to all generations of them that will be born of water and of the Holy Spirit, to life eternal. Then the most beloved Son of God, even Christ Jesus, will come down on the earth and will bring in our father Adam into Paradise, to the Tree of Mercy." And when they heard all these things from Seth, all the patriarchs and prophets rejoiced with a great rejoicing.

CHAPTER 4

1. And while all the holy ones were rejoicing, behold, Satan, the prince and chief of death, said to Hades: "Make yourself ready to receive Jesus, who boasts of Himself that He is the Son of God, whereas He is a Man that fears death and says: My soul is sorrowful even to death. And He has been my great enemy, doing me great harm, and many that I had made blind, lame, dumb, leprous, and possessed He has healed with a word: and some whom I have brought to you dead, He has taken them away from you."

2. Hades answered and said to Satan the prince: "Who is He that is so mighty, if He is a Man that fears death? For all the mighty ones of the earth are held in subjection by my power, even they whom you have brought me subdued by your power. If, then, you are mighty, what manner of Man is this Jesus who, though He fears death, resists your power? If He is so mighty in His Manhood, truly I say to you [that] He is almighty in His Godhead, and no man can withstand His power. And when He says that He fears death, He would ensnare you, and woe will be to you for everlasting ages." But Satan, the prince of Tartarus, said: "Why do you doubt and fear to receive this Jesus, which is your adversary and mine? For I tempted Him, and I have stirred up my ancient people of the Jews with envy and wrath against Him. I have sharpened a spear to thrust Him through. I have mingled gall and vinegar to give Him to drink, and I have prepared a cross to crucify Him and nails to pierce Him: and His death is near at hand, that

I may bring Him to you to be subject to you and me."

3. Hades answered and said: "You have told me that it is He that has taken away dead men from me. For there are many which while they lived on the earth have taken dead men from me, yet not by their own power but by prayer to God, and their almighty God has taken them from me. Who is this Jesus which by His own word, without prayer, has drawn dead men from me? Perhaps it is He which by the word of His command restored to life Lazarus, who was four days dead, and stank, and was corrupt—whom I held here dead." Satan, the prince of death, answered and said: "It is that same Jesus." When Hades heard that, he said to him: "I adjure you by your strength and my own that you do not bring Him to me. For at that time I, when I heard the command of His word, quaked and was overwhelmed with fear, and all my servants with me were troubled. Neither could we keep Lazarus, but he, like an eagle, shaking himself, leaped forth with all agility and swiftness, and departed from us, and the earth also which held the dead body of Lazarus immediately gave him up alive. Therefore, I now know that that Man which was able to do these things is a God strong in command and mighty in manhood, and that He is the Savior of mankind. And if you bring Him to me, He will set free all that are here shut up in the hard prison and bound in the chains of their sins that cannot be broken, and will bring them to the life of His Godhead forever."

CHAPTER 5

1. And as Satan the prince, and Hades, spoke thus together, suddenly there came a voice as of thunder and a spiritual cry: "Remove, O princes, your gates, || And be lifted up, you everlasting doors, || And the King of Glory will come in!" When Hades heard that, he said to Satan the prince: "Depart from me and go out of my abode. If you are a mighty man of war, fight against the King of Glory. But what have you to do with him?" And Hades cast Satan forth out of his dwelling. Then Hades said to his wicked servants: "Shut the hard gates of brass, and put the bars of iron on them, and resist firmly, lest we that hold captivity be taken captive."

2. But when all the multitude of the holy ones heard it, they spoke with a voice of rebuking to Hades: "Open your gates, that the King of Glory may come in!" And David cried out, saying, "Did I not, when I was alive on earth, foretell to you: Let them give thanks to the LORD, || Even His mercies and His wonders to the children of men; Who has broken the gates of brass and split the bars of iron in pieces? He has taken them out of the way of their iniquity." And thereafter, in like manner Isaiah said: "Did I not, when I was alive on earth, foretell to you: The dead will arise, || And they that are in the tombs will rise again, || And they that are in the earth will rejoice, || For the dew which comes of the LORD is their healing? And again, I said: O death, where is your sting? O Hades, where is your victory?"

3. When they heard that from Isaiah, all the holy ones said to Hades: "Open your gates! Now you will be conquered, and weak, and without strength." And there came a great voice as of thunder, saying, "Remove, O princes, your gates, || And be lifted up, you doors of Hades, || And the King of Glory will come in." And when Hades saw that they so cried out twice, he said, as if he did not know it: "Who is the King of Glory?" And David answered Hades and said: "The words of this cry do I know, for by His Spirit I prophesied the same; and now I say to you that which I said before: The LORD strong and mighty, || The LORD mighty in battle, || He is the King of Glory. And: The LORD looked down from Heaven that He might hear the groanings of them that are in chains and deliver the children of them that have been slain. And now, O you most foul and stinking Hades, open your gates, so that the King of Glory may come in." And as David spoke thus to Hades, the Lord of majesty appeared in the form of a Man, and descended the eternal darkness, and broke the bonds that could not be loosed: and the support of His everlasting might visited us that sat in the deep darkness of our transgressions and in the shadow of death of our sins.

CHAPTER 6

1. When Hades, and death, and their wicked servants saw that, they were stricken with fear—they and their cruel officers—at the sight of the brightness of such a great light in their own realm, seeing Christ suddenly in their abode, and they cried out, saying, "We are conquered by You! Who are You that is sent by the LORD for our confusion? Who are You that without all damage of corruption, and with the signs of Your majesty unblemished, does in wrath condemn our power? Who are You that is so great and so small, both humble and exalted, both soldier and commander, a marvelous warrior in the shape of a bondsman, and a King of Glory dead and living, whom the Cross bore slain on it? You that lay dead in the tomb have come down to us living; and at Your death all creation quaked and all the stars were shaken; and You have become free among the dead and routed our legions. Who are You that set free the prisoners that are held bound by original sin and restored them into their former liberty? Who are You that shed Your divine and bright light on them that were blinded with the darkness of their sins?" After the same manner, all the legions of devils were stricken with [the] same fear and cried out all together in the terror of their confusion, saying, "Where are You from, Jesus—a Man so mighty and bright in majesty, so excellent, without spot and clean from sin? For that world of earth which has always been subject to us until now, and paid tribute to our profit, has never sent to us a dead man like You, nor ever dispatched such a gift to Hades. Who then are You that so fearlessly enters our borders, and not only does not fear our torments, but also attempts to carry away all

men out of our bonds? Perhaps You are that Jesus, of whom Satan our prince said that by Your death of the Cross You should receive the dominion of the whole world."

2. Then the King of Glory in His majesty trampled on death, and laid hold on Satan the prince, and delivered him to the power of Hades, and drew Adam to Him—to His own brightness.

CHAPTER 7

Then Hades, receiving Satan the prince, with severe reproach said to him: "O prince of perdition and chief of destruction, Beelzebub, the scorn of the messengers and spitting of the righteous, why would you do this? You would crucify the King of Glory, and at His demise promised us great spoils from His death: like a fool you did not know what you did. For behold, this Jesus now puts to flight by the brightness of His majesty all the darkness of death, and has broken the strong depths of the prisons, and let out the prisoners, and loosed them that were bound. And all that were sighing in our torments rejoice against us, and at their prayers our dominions are vanquished and our realms conquered, and now no nation of men fears us anymore. And beside this, the dead which were never accustomed to be proud, triumph over us, and the captives which never could be joyful, threaten us. O prince Satan, father of all the wicked, and ungodly, and renegades, why would you do this? They that from the beginning until now have despaired of life and salvation—now none of their customary roarings are heard, neither do any groan from them ring out in our ears, nor is there any sign of tears on the face of any of them. O prince Satan, holder of the keys of Hades—those riches of yours which you had gained by the Tree of Transgression and the losing of Paradise—you have lost by the tree of the Cross, and all your gladness has perished. When you hung Christ Jesus the King of Glory, you worked against yourself and against me. Henceforth, you will know what eternal torments and infinite pains you are to suffer in my keeping forever. O prince Satan, author of death and head of all pride, you should have first sought out [some] matter of evil in this Jesus! Why did you undertake, without cause, to crucify Him unjustly, against whom you found no blame, and to bring into our realm the innocent and righteous One, and to lose the guilty, and the ungodly, and unrighteous of the whole world?" And when Hades had spoken thus to Satan the prince, then the King of Glory said to Hades: "Satan the prince will be in your power throughout all ages in the place of Adam and his children, even those that are My righteous ones."

CHAPTER 8

1. And the LORD stretching forth His hand, said: "Come to Me, all you holy ones of Mine which bear My image and My likeness—You that by the tree, and the Devil, and death were condemned. Behold! Now the Devil and death are condemned by the tree." And all the holy ones were immediately gathered together in one under the hand of the LORD. And the LORD holding the right hand of Adam, said to him: "Peace be to you with all your children that are My righteous ones." But Adam, casting himself at the knees of the LORD, prayed to Him with tears and pleadings, and said with a loud voice: "I will magnify You, O LORD, for You have set me up and not made my foes to triumph over me: O LORD my God, I cried to You and You have healed me; LORD, You have brought my soul out of Hades, You have delivered me from them that go down to the pit. Sing praises to the LORD all you holy ones of His, and give thanks to Him for the remembrance of His holiness! For there is wrath in His indignation and life is in His good pleasure!" In like manner, all the holy ones of God kneeled and cast themselves at the feet of the LORD, saying with one accord: "You have come, O Redeemer of the world! That which You foretold by the Law and by Your prophets, that have You accomplished in deed. You have redeemed the living by Your cross, and by the death of the Cross You have come down to us, so that You might save us out of Hades and death through Your majesty. O LORD, just as You have set the Name of Your glory in the heavens and set up Your cross for a sign of redemption on the earth, so, LORD, set up the sign of the victory of your cross in Hades, so that death may have no more dominion."

2. And the LORD stretched forth His hand and made the Sign of the Cross over Adam and over all His holy ones, and He took the right hand of Adam and went up out of Hades, and all the holy ones followed Him. Then holy David cried aloud and said: "Sing to the LORD a new song, || For He has done marvelous things. His right hand has worked salvation for Him and His holy arm. The LORD has made known His saving health, || Before the face of all nations He has revealed His righteousness." And the whole multitude of the holy ones answered, saying, "Such honor have all His holy ones. Amen! Hallelujah!"

3. And thereafter, Habakkuk the prophet cried out and said: "You went forth for the salvation of Your people to set free Your chosen." And all the holy ones answered, saying, "Blessed is He that comes in the Name of the LORD! God is the LORD and has shown us light. Amen! Hallelujah!" Likewise after that, the prophet Micah also cried, saying, "What God is like You, O LORD, taking away iniquity and removing sins? And now You withhold Your wrath for a testimony that You are merciful of free will, and You turn away and have mercy on us; You forgive all our iniquities and have sunk all our sins in the depths of the sea, as You swore to our fathers in the days of old." And all the holy ones answered, saying, "This is our God forever and ever; He will be our guide, world without end. Amen! Hallelujah!" And so spoke all the prophets, making mention of holy words out of their praises, and all the holy ones followed the LORD, crying: "Amen! Hallelujah!"

CHAPTER 9

But the LORD, holding the hand of Adam, delivered him to Michael the chief-messenger, and all the holy ones followed Michael the chief-messenger, and he brought them all into the glory and beauty of Paradise. And there met with them two men, ancients in days, and when they were asked by the holy ones: "Who are you that have not yet been dead in Hades with us and are set in Paradise in the body?" Then one of them answering, said: "I am Enoch, who was translated here by the word of the LORD, and this that is with me is Elijah the Tishbite, who was taken up in a chariot of fire: and up to this day we have not tasted death, but we are received until the coming of Antichrist, to fight against him with signs and wonders of God, and to be slain by Him in Jerusalem, and after three and a half days to be taken up alive again on the clouds."

CHAPTER 10

1. And as Enoch and Elijah spoke thus with the holy ones, behold, there came another man of vile attire, bearing on his shoulders the Sign of the Cross; whom when they beheld, all the holy ones said to him: "Who are you? For your appearance is as of a robber; and why is it that you bear a sign on your shoulders?" And he answered them and said: "You have rightly spoken, for I was a robber, doing all manner of evil on the earth. And the Jews crucified me with Jesus, and I beheld the wonders in the creation which came to pass through the Cross of Jesus when He was crucified, and I believed that He was the Maker of all creatures and the Almighty King, and I begged Him, saying, Remember me, Lord, when you come into Your kingdom. And He immediately received my prayer and said to me: Truly, I say to you: this day you will be with me in Paradise. And He gave me the Sign of the Cross, saying, Bear this and go to Paradise, and if the messenger that keeps Paradise does not allow you to enter in, show him the Sign of the Cross; and you will say to him: Jesus Christ, the Son of God, who now is crucified, has sent me.

2. And when I had done so, I spoke all these things to the messenger that keeps Paradise; and when he heard this from me, he immediately opened the door, and brought me in, and set me at the right hand of Paradise, saying, Behold now, tarry a little [while], and Adam the father of all mankind will enter in with all his children that are holy and righteous, after the triumph and glory of the ascending up of Christ the Lord that is crucified." When they heard all these words of the robber, all the holy patriarchs and prophets said with one voice: "Blessed is the LORD Almighty, the Father of eternal good things, the Father of mercies—You that have given such grace to Your sinners and have brought them again into the beauty of Paradise and into Your good pastures: for this is the most holy life of the Spirit. Amen. Amen."

CHAPTER 11

1. These are the divine and holy mysteries which we saw and heard, even I, Karinus, and Leucius: but we were not allowed to relate further the rest of the mysteries of God, according as Michael the chief-messenger strictly charged us, saying, "You will go with your brothers to Jerusalem and remain in prayer, crying out and glorifying the resurrection of the Lord Jesus Christ, who has raised you from the dead together with Him: and you will not be speaking with any man, but sit as mute men, until the hour comes when the LORD Himself allows you to declare the mysteries of His Godhead." But to us, Michael the chief-messenger gave command that we should go over [the] Jordan to a place rich and fertile, where there are many which rose again together with us for a testimony of the resurrection of Christ the Lord. For only three days were allowed to us who rose from the dead, to keep the Passover of the LORD in Jerusalem with our relatives that are living for a testimony of the resurrection of Christ the Lord: and we were immersed in the holy river of Jordan and received white robes, every one of us. And after the three days, when we had kept the Passover of the LORD, all of them were caught up in the clouds which had risen again with us, and were taken over [the] Jordan, and were no longer seen by any man. But to us it was said that we should remain in the city of Arimathea and continue in prayer.

2. These are all [the] things which the LORD commanded us to declare to you: give praise and thanksgiving to Him, and convert, so that He may have mercy on you. Peace be to you from the same Lord Jesus Christ which is the Savior of us all. Amen.

3. And when they had finished writing all things in the several volumes of paper, they arose; and Karinus gave that which he had written into the hands of Annas, and Caiaphas, and Gamaliel; likewise, Leucius gave that which he had written into the hands of Nicodemus and Joseph. And suddenly they were transfigured, and became exceedingly white, and were no longer seen. But their writings were found to be the same, neither more nor less by one letter.

4. And when all the synagogue of the Jews heard all these marvelous sayings of Karinus and Leucius, they said to one another: "All these things were certainly worked by the LORD; and blessed be the LORD, world without end. Amen." And they went out, all of them, in great trouble of mind, striking their breasts with fear and trembling, and departed—every man to his own home.

5. And all these things which were spoken by the Jews in their synagogue, Joseph and Nicodemus immediately declared to the governor. And Pilate himself wrote all the things that were done and said concerning Jesus by the Jews and laid up all the words in the public books of his Praetorium.

ACTS OF PILATE

CHAPTER 12

[[1. After these things, Pilate entered into the temple of the Jews and gathered together all the chiefs of the priests, and the grammarians, and scribes, and doctors of the Law, and went in with them into the holy place of the temple and commanded all the doors to be shut, and said to them: "We have heard that you have in this temple a certain great Bible; therefore, I ask you that it be presented before us." And when that great Bible adorned with gold and precious jewels was brought by four ministers, Pilate said to them all: "I adjure you by the God of your fathers which commanded you to build this temple in the place of His sanctuary, that you do not hide the truth from me. You know all the things that are written in this Bible; but tell me now if you have found in the Writings that this Jesus whom you have crucified is the Son of God which should come for the salvation of mankind, and in what year of the times He must come. Declare to me whether you crucified Him in ignorance or knowingly."

2. And Annas and Caiaphas, when they were thus adjured, commanded all the rest that were with them to go out of the temple; and they themselves shut all the doors of the temple and of the sanctuary, and they said to Pilate: "You have adjured us, O excellent judge, by the building of this temple to make manifest to you the truth and reason. After we had crucified Jesus, not knowing that He was the Son of God, but supposing that by some chance He did His wondrous works, we made a great assembly in this temple; and as we conferred with one another concerning the signs of the mighty works which Jesus had done, we found many witnesses of our own nation who said that they had seen Jesus alive after His Passion, and that He had passed into the height of Heaven. Moreover, we saw two witnesses whom Jesus raised from the dead, who declared to us many marvelous things which Jesus did among the dead, which things we have in writing in our hands. Now our custom is that every year before our assembly we open this Holy Bible and inquire of the testimony of God. And we have found in the first book of the Seventy how Michael the messenger spoke to the third son of Adam the first man concerning the five thousand and five hundred years, wherein should come the most beloved Son of God, even Christ: and furthermore, we have thought that perhaps this same was the God of Israel which said to Moses: Make an ark for the covenant, two and a half cubits in length, and one and a half cubits in breadth, and one and a half cubits in height. For by those five and a half cubits we have understood and known the fashion of the Ark of the Old Covenant, for that in five and a half thousand years Jesus Christ should come in the ark of His body: and we have found that He is the God of Israel, even the Son of God. For after His Passion, we the chiefs of the priests, because we marveled at the signs which came to pass on His account, opened the Bible, and searched out all the generations to the generation of Joseph, and Mary the mother of Christ, taking her to be the seed of David: and we found that from the day when God made the heavens, and the earth, and the first man, from that time to the Flood are two thousand two hundred and twelve years; and from the Flood to the building of the tower five hundred and thirty-one years; and from the building of the tower to Abraham six hundred and six years; and from Abraham to the coming of the children of Israel out of Egypt four hundred and seventy years; and from the going of the children of Israel out of Egypt to the building of the temple five hundred and eleven years; and from the building of the temple to the destruction of the same temple four hundred and sixty-four years: so far we found in the Scroll of Ezra; and inquiring from the burning of the temple to the coming of Christ and his birth we found it to be six hundred and eighty-six years, which together were five thousand and five hundred years, just as we found it written in the Bible that Michael the chief-messenger declared before to Seth, the third son of Adam, that after five and a half thousand years Christ the Son of God should come. Until now have we told no man, lest there should be a schism in our synagogues; and now, O excellent judge, you have adjured us by this Holy Bible of the testimonies of God, and we declare it to you: and we also have adjured you by your life and health that you do not declare these words to any man in Jerusalem." And Pilate, when he heard these words of Annas and Caiaphas, laid them all up among the acts of the Lord and Savior in the public books of his Praetorium and wrote a letter to Claudius, the king of the city of Rome, saying:]]

EPISTLE OF PILATE TO CLAUDIUS

CHAPTER 1

¹Pontius Pilate to Claudius: Greetings. ²Recently a matter occurred which I myself brought to light: for the Jews through envy have punished themselves and their posterity with fearful judgments of their own responsibility; ³for whereas their fathers had promises that their God would send them His Holy One out of Heaven who should rightly be called their King, and promised that He would send Him on earth by a virgin; ⁴He, then, came when I was governor of Judea, and they beheld Him enlightening the blind, cleansing lepers, healing the palsied, driving devils out of men, raising the dead, rebuking the winds, walking on the waves of the sea [with] dry feet, and doing many other wonders, and all the people of the Jews calling Him the Son of God: ⁵the chief priests therefore, moved with envy against Him, took Him, and delivered Him to me, and brought against Him one false accusation after another, saying that He was a sorcerer and did things contrary to their law. ⁶But I, believing that these things were so, having scourged Him, delivered Him to their will: and they crucified Him, and when He was buried, they set guards over Him. ⁷But while my soldiers watched Him, He rose again on the third day: yet so much was the malice of the Jews kindled that they gave money to the soldiers, saying, "Say that His disciples stole His body away." ⁸But they, though they took the money, were not able to keep silence concerning that which had come to pass, for they also have testified that they saw Him arisen, and that they received money from the Jews. ⁹And I have reported these things to your mightiness for this reason, lest some other should lie to you, and you should deem right to believe the false tales of the Jews.

NARRATIVE OF JOSEPH OF ARIMATHEA

The Narrative of Joseph of Arimathea is a medieval apocryphal text told from Joseph's perspective, a wealthy and righteous man who secretly supported Jesus. It focuses heavily on the two robbers crucified with Jesus, particularly Demas, an invented name for the thief who was promised Paradise.

CHAPTER 1

¹I am Joseph of Arimathea, who begged from Pilate for the body of the Lord Jesus for burial, and who for this reason was kept bound in prison by the murderous and God-fighting Jews, who also, keeping to the Law, have by Moses himself become partakers in tribulation and having provoked their Lawgiver to anger, and not knowing that He was God, crucified Him and made Him manifest to those that knew God. ²In those days in which they condemned the Son of God to be crucified, seven days before Christ suffered, two condemned robbers were sent from Jericho to the procurator Pilate; ³and their case was as follows: the first, his name Gestas, put travelers to death, murdering them with the sword, and others he exposed naked. And he hung up women by the heels, head down, and cut off their breasts, and drank the blood of infants' limbs, never having known God, not obeying the laws, being violent from the beginning, and doing such deeds. ⁴And the case of the other was as follows: he was called Demas, and was by birth a Galilean, and kept an inn. He made attacks on the rich, but was good to the poor—a thief like Tobit, for he buried the bodies of the poor. ⁵And he set his hand to robbing the multitude of the Jews, and stole the Law itself in Jerusalem, and stripped

naked the daughter of Caiaphas, who was priestess of the sanctuary, and took away from its place the mysterious deposit itself placed there by Solomon. Such were his doings. ⁶And Jesus was also taken on the third day before the Passover, in the evening. ⁷And to Caiaphas and the multitude of the Jews it was not a Passover, but it was a great mourning to them, on account of the plundering of the sanctuary by the robber. ⁸And they summoned Judas Iscariot and spoke to him, for he was son of the brother of Caiaphas the priest. He was not a disciple before the face of Jesus; but all the multitude of the Jews craftily supported him, so that he might follow Jesus, not that he might be obedient to the miracles done by Him, nor that he might confess Him, but that he might betray Him to them, wishing to catch up some lying word of Him, giving him gifts for such brave, honest conduct to the amount of a half-shekel of gold each day. ⁹And he did this for two years with Jesus, as one of His disciples called John says. ¹⁰And on the third day, before Jesus was laid hold of, Judas says to the Jews: "Come, let us hold a council; for perhaps it was not the robber that stole the Law, but Jesus Himself, and I accuse Him." ¹¹And when these words had been spoken, Nicodemus, who kept the keys of the sanctuary, came in to us, and said to all: "Do not do such a deed." For Nicodemus was true, more than all the multitude of the Jews. ¹²And the daughter of Caiaphas, Sarah by name, cried out and said: "He Himself said before all against this holy place, I am able to destroy this temple, and in three days to raise it." ¹³The Jews say to her: "You have credit with all of us." For they regarded her as a prophetess. And assuredly, after the council had been held, Jesus was arrested.

CHAPTER 2

¹And on the following day, the fourth day of the week, they brought Him at the ninth hour into the hall of Caiaphas. ²And Annas and Caiaphas say to Him: "Tell us, why have You stolen our law and renounced the ordinances of Moses and the prophets?" ³And Jesus answered nothing. ⁴And again a second time, the multitude also being present, they say to Him: "The sanctuary which Solomon built in forty-six years, why do You wish to destroy in one moment?" ⁵And to these things Jesus answered nothing. For the sanctuary of the synagogue had been plundered by the robber. ⁶And the evening of the fourth day having ended, all the multitude sought to burn the daughter of Caiaphas on account of the loss of the Law, for they did not know how they were to keep the Passover. ⁷And she said to them: "Wait, my children, and let us destroy this Jesus, and the Law will be found, and the holy feast will be fully accomplished." ⁸And secretly Annas and Caiaphas gave considerable money to Judas Iscariot, saying, "Say what you said to us before, I know that the Law has been stolen by Jesus, that the accusation may be turned against Him, and not against this maiden, who is free from blame." ⁹And Judas having received this command, said to them: "Do not let all the multitude know that I have been instructed by you to do this against Jesus; but release Jesus, and I [will] persuade the multitude that it is so." And they craftily released Jesus. ¹⁰And Judas, going into the sanctuary at the dawn of the fifth day, says to all the people: "What will you give me, and I will give up to you the overthrower of the Law, and the plunderer of the prophets?" ¹¹The Jews say to him: "If you will give Him up to us, we will give you thirty pieces of gold." ¹²And the people did not know that Judas was speaking about Jesus, for many of them confessed that He was the Son of God. And Judas received the thirty pieces of gold. ¹³And going out at the fourth hour, and at the fifth, he finds Jesus walking in the street. ¹⁴And as evening was coming on, Judas says to the Jews: "Give me the aid of soldiers with swords and staffs, and I will give Him up to you." ¹⁵They therefore gave him officers for the purpose of seizing Him. ¹⁶And as they were going along, Judas says to them: "Lay hold of the Man whom I will kiss, for He has stolen the Law and the Prophets." ¹⁷Going up to Jesus, therefore, he kissed Him, saying, "Hail, Rabbi!" It being the evening of the fifth day. ¹⁸And having laid hold of Him, they gave Him up to Caiaphas and the chief priests, Judas saying: "This is He who stole the Law and the Prophets." ¹⁹And the Jews gave Jesus an unjust trial, saying, "Why have You done these things?" And He answered nothing. ²⁰And Nicodemus and I, Joseph, seeing the seat of the plagues, stood off from them, not wishing to perish along with the counsel of the ungodly.

CHAPTER 3

¹Therefore, having done many dreadful things against Jesus that night, they gave Him up to Pilate the procurator at the dawn of the Preparation, so that he might crucify Him; and for this purpose they all came together. ²After a trial, therefore, Pilate the procurator ordered Him to be nailed to the cross, along with the two robbers. And they were nailed up along with Jesus: Gestas on the left, and Demas on the right. ³And he that was on the left began to cry out, saying to Jesus: "See how many evil deeds I have done in the earth; and if I had known that You were the King, I should have cut You off also. And why do You call yourself [the] Son of God, and cannot help Yourself in necessity? ⁴How can you provide it to another one praying for help? If You are the Christ, come down from the cross, so that I may believe in you. But now I see You perishing along with me, not like a man, but like a wild beast." ⁵And many other things he began to say against Jesus, blaspheming and gnashing his teeth against Him. For the robber was taken alive in the snare of the Devil. ⁶But the robber on the right hand, whose name was Demas, seeing the Godlike grace of Jesus, thus cried out: "I know You, Jesus Christ, that You are the Son of God. I see You, Christ, adored by myriads of myriads of messengers. ⁷Pardon me [of] my sins which I have done. Do not, in my trial, make the stars come against me, or the moon, when You will judge all the world; because in the night I have accomplished my wicked purposes. ⁸Do not urge the sun, which is now darkened on account of You, to tell the evils of my heart, for I can give You no gift for the forgiveness of my sins. Already death is coming on me because of my sins; but Yours is the propitiation. ⁹Deliver me, O Lord of all, from Your fearful judgment. Do not give the enemy power to swallow me up, and to become heir of my soul, as of that of him who is hanging on the left; for I see how the Devil joyfully takes his soul, and his body disappears. ¹⁰Do not even order me to go away into the portion of the Jews; for I see Moses and the patriarchs in great weeping, and the Devil rejoicing over them. ¹¹Before, then, O Lord, my spirit departs, order my sins to be washed away, and remember me—the sinner in Your kingdom—when on the great [and] most lofty throne You will judge the twelve tribes of Israel. For You have prepared great punishment for Your world on account of Yourself." ¹²And the robber having thus spoken, Jesus says to him: "Truly, truly, I say to you, Demas, that today you will be with Me in Paradise. ¹³And the sons of the kingdom, the children of Abraham, and Isaac, and Jacob, and Moses, will be cast out into outer darkness; there will be weeping and gnashing of teeth. And you alone will dwell in Paradise until My second appearing, when I am to judge those who do not confess My Name." ¹⁴And He said to the robber: "Go away, and tell the cherubim and the powers, that turn the flaming sword, that guard Paradise from the time that Adam, the first created, was in Paradise, and sinned, and did not keep My commandments, and I cast him out from there. ¹⁵And none of the first will see Paradise until I am to come the second time to judge living and dead." ¹⁶And He wrote thus: "Jesus Christ, the Son of God, who has come down from the heights of the heavens, who has come forth out of the bosom of the invisible Father without being separated from Him, and who has come down into the world to be made flesh, and to be nailed to a cross, in order that I might save Adam, whom I fashioned, to my chief-messenger powers, the gatekeepers of Paradise, to the officers of My Father: I will and order that he who has been crucified along with me should go in, should receive forgiveness of sins through Me, and that he, having put on an incorruptible body, should go into Paradise and dwell where no one has ever been able to dwell." ¹⁷And behold, after He had said this, Jesus gave up the spirit, on the Day of Preparation, at the ninth hour. And there was darkness over all the earth; and from a great earthquake that happened, the sanctuary fell down, and the wing of the temple.

CHAPTER 4

¹And I, Joseph, begged for the body of Jesus and put it in a new tomb where no one had been put. And of the robber on the right, the body was not found; but of him on the left, as the form of a dragon, so was his body. ²And

NARRATIVE OF JOSEPH OF ARIMATHEA

after I had begged for the body of Jesus to bury, the Jews, carried away by hatred and rage, shut me up in prison, where evildoers were kept under restraint. ³And this happened to me on the evening of the Sabbath, whereby our nation transgressed the Law. And behold, that same nation of ours endured fearful tribulations on the Sabbath. ⁴And now, on the evening of the first [day] of the week, at the fifth hour of the night, Jesus comes to me in the prison, along with the robber who had been crucified with Him on the right, whom He sent into Paradise. ⁵And there was a great light in the building. And the house was hung up by the four corners, and the place was opened, and I came out. ⁶Then I first recognized Jesus, and again the robber, bringing a letter to Jesus. ⁷And as we were going into Galilee, there shone a great light, which the creation did not produce. And there was also with the robber a great fragrance out of Paradise. ⁸And Jesus, having sat down in a certain place, thus read: "We, the cherubim and the six-winged, who have been ordered by Your Godhead to watch the garden of Paradise, make the following statement through the robber who was crucified along with You, by Your arrangement: ⁹When we saw the print of the nails of the robber crucified along with You, and the shining light of the letter of Your Godhead, the fire was indeed extinguished, not being able to bear the splendor of the print; and we crouched down, being in great fear. ¹⁰For we heard that the Maker of heaven and earth, and of the whole creation, had come down from on high to dwell in the lower parts of the earth, on account of Adam, the first created. ¹¹And when we beheld the undefiled cross shining like lightning from the robber, gleaming with sevenfold the light of the sun, trembling fell on us. ¹²We felt a violent shaking of the world below; and with a loud voice, the ministers of Hades said, along with us: HOLY, HOLY, HOLY, is He who in the beginning was in the highest. ¹³And the powers sent up a cry: O LORD, You have been made manifest in Heaven and in earth, bringing joy to the world; and, a greater gift than this, You have freed Your own image from death by the invisible purpose of the ages."

CHAPTER 5

¹After I had beheld these things, as I was going into Galilee with Jesus and the robber, Jesus was transfigured, and was not as [He was] formerly, before He was crucified, but was altogether light; and messengers always ministered to Him, and Jesus spoke with them. ²And I remained with Him three days. And none of His disciples was with Him, except the robber alone. ³And in the middle of the Celebration of Unleavened Bread, His disciple John comes, and we no longer beheld the robber as to what took place. ⁴And John asked Jesus: "Who is this, that You have not made me to be seen by him?" ⁵But Jesus answered him nothing. ⁶And falling down before Him, he said: "Lord, I know that You have loved me from the beginning, and why do You not reveal to me that man?" ⁷Jesus says to him: "Why do you seek what is hidden? Are you still without understanding? Do you not perceive the fragrance of Paradise filling the place? Do you not know who it is? The robber on the cross has become an heir of Paradise. Truly, truly, I say to you, that it will belong to him alone until the Great Day will come." ⁸And John said: "Make me worthy to behold him." ⁹And while John was yet speaking, the robber suddenly appeared; and John, struck with astonishment, fell to the earth. ¹⁰And the robber was not in his first form, as before John came; but he was like a king in great power, having on him the cross. ¹¹And the voice of a great multitude was sent forth: "You have come to the place prepared for you in Paradise. We have been commanded by Him that has sent you, to serve you until the Great Day." ¹²And after this voice, both the robber and I, Joseph, vanished, and I was found in my own house; and I no longer saw Jesus. ¹³And I, having seen these things, have written them down, in order that all may believe in the crucified Jesus Christ our Lord, and may no longer obey the Law of Moses, but may believe in the signs and wonders that have happened through Him, and in order that we who have believed may inherit eternal life, and be found in the kingdom of the heavens. For to Him are due glory, strength, praise, and majesty forever and ever. Amen.

CORRESPONDENCE OF PILATE

This section includes likely pseudepigraphal letters to and from Pontius Pilate. It includes letters, probably quite late, purportedly from Herod to Pilate and Pilate to Herod. More significantly, the Report of Pontius Pilate, also called the Anaphora Pilati, is a likely pseudepigraphal letter from Pilate to Tiberius which describes Jesus' execution and the aftermath. It may originate from the 4th century.

EPISTLE OF HEROD TO PILATE

CHAPTER 1

¹Herod to Pontius Pilate, the governor of Jerusalem: Peace. ²I am in great anxiety. I write these things to you, so that when you have heard them you may be grieved for me. ³For as my daughter Herodias, who is dear to me, was playing on a pool of water which had ice on it, it broke under her, and her whole body went down, and her head was cut off and remained on the surface of the ice. ⁴And behold, her mother is holding her head on her knees in her lap, and my whole house is in great sorrow. ⁵For I, when I heard of the Man Jesus, wished to come to you, so that I might see Him alone and hear His word, whether it was like that of the sons of men. ⁶And it is certain that because of the many evil things which were done by me to John the Baptist, and because I mocked the Christ, behold, I receive the reward of righteousness, for I have shed much blood of others' children on the earth. ⁷Therefore, the judgments of God are righteous; for every man receives according to his thought. ⁸But since you were worthy to see that God-Man, therefore it suits you to pray for me. ⁹My son Azbonius is also in the agony of the hour of death. ¹⁰And I am also in affliction and great trial, because I have [severe] swelling; and I am in great distress, because I persecuted the introducer of immersion by water, which was John. ¹¹Therefore, my brother, the judgments of God are righteous. ¹²And my wife, again, through all her grief for her daughter, has become blind in her left eye, because we desired to blind the Eye of righteousness. ¹³"There is no peace for the evildoers," says the LORD. ¹⁴For already great affliction comes on the priests and on the writers of the Law; because they delivered to you the Just One. ¹⁵For this is the consummation of the world, that they consented that the nations should become heirs. ¹⁶For the children of light will be cast out, for they have not observed the things which were preached concerning the LORD, and concerning His Son. ¹⁷Therefore, gird up your loins and receive righteousness—you with your wife remembering Jesus night and day; and the kingdom will belong to you nations, for we, the [chosen] people, have mocked the Righteous One. ¹⁸Now if there is place for our request, O Pilate, because we were at one time in power, bury my household carefully; for it is right that we should be buried by you, rather than by the priests, whom, after a short time, as the Writings say, at the coming of Jesus Christ, vengeance will overtake. ¹⁹Farewell, with your wife Procla. ²⁰I send you the earrings of my daughter and my own ring, so that they may be to you a memorial of my death. ²¹For worms already begin to issue from my body, and behold, I am receiving temporal judgment, and I am afraid of the judgment to come. ²²For in both we stand before the works of the living God; but this judgment, which is temporal, is for a time, while that to come is judgment forever. End of the letter to Pilate, the governor.

CORRESPONDENCE OF PILATE

EPISTLE OF PILATE TO HEROD

CHAPTER 1

¹Pilate to Herod the Tetrarch: Peace. Know and see, that in the day when you delivered Jesus to me, I took pity on myself, and testified by washing my hands [that I was innocent] concerning Him who rose from the grave after three days, and had performed your pleasure in Him, for you desired me to be associated with you in His crucifixion. ²But I now learn from the executioners and from the soldiers who watched His tomb that He rose from the dead. ³And I have especially confirmed what was told to me, that He appeared bodily in Galilee, in the same form, and with the same voice, and with the same doctrine, and with the same disciples, not having changed in anything, but preaching with boldness His resurrection, and an everlasting kingdom. ⁴And behold, heaven and earth rejoice; and behold, my wife Procla is believing in the visions which appeared to her, when you sent that I should deliver Jesus to the people of Israel, because of the hostility they had. ⁵Now when my wife Procla heard that Jesus had risen, and had appeared in Galilee, she took with her Longinus the centurion and twelve soldiers, the same that had watched at the tomb, and went to greet the face of Christ, as if to a great spectacle, and saw Him with His disciples. ⁶Now while they were standing, and wondering, and gazing at Him, He looked at them and said to them, "What is it? Do you believe in Me? Procla, know that in the covenant which God gave to the fathers, it is said that everyone who had perished should live by means of My death, which you have seen. ⁷And now you see that I live, whom you crucified. And I suffered many things, until I was laid in the tomb. ⁸But now, hear Me, and believe in My Father—God who is in Me. For I loosed the cords of death and broke the gates of Hades; and My coming will be hereafter." ⁹And when my wife Procla and the Romans heard these things, they came and told me, weeping; for they were also against Him when they devised the evils which they had done to Him. So that I was also on the couch of my bed in affliction, and put on a garment of mourning, and took to myself fifty Romans with my wife and went into Galilee. ¹⁰And when I was going in the way, I testified these things: that Herod did these things by me, that he took counsel with me, and constrained me to arm my hands against Him, and to judge Him that judges all, and to scourge the Just One, Lord of the just. ¹¹And when we drew near to Him, O Herod, a great voice was heard from Heaven, and dreadful thunder, and the earth trembled, and gave forth a sweet smell, like to which was never perceived even in the temple of Jerusalem. ¹²Now while I stood in the way, our Lord saw me as He stood and talked with His disciples. ¹³But I prayed in my heart, for I knew that it was He whom you delivered to me, that He was Lord of created things and Creator of all. ¹⁴But we, when we saw Him, all of us fell on our faces before His feet. ¹⁵And I said with a loud voice, "I have sinned, O Lord, in that I sat and judged You who avenges everyone in truth. And behold, I know that You are God, the Son of God, and I beheld Your humanity and not Your divinity. ¹⁶But Herod, with the children of Israel, constrained me to do evil to You. Therefore, have pity on me, O God of Israel!" ¹⁷And my wife, in great anguish, said, "God of heaven and of earth, God of Israel, do not reward me according to the deeds of Pontius Pilate, nor according to the will of the children of Israel, nor according to the thought of the sons of the priests; but remember my husband in Your glory!" ¹⁸Now our Lord drew near and raised up me, and my wife, and the Romans; and I looked at Him and saw there were on Him the scars of His cross. ¹⁹And He said, "That which all the righteous fathers hoped to receive and did not see—in your time the Lord of Time, the Son of Man, the Son of the Most High, who is forever, arose from the dead and is glorified on high by all that He created and established forever and ever." End of the Letter of Pilate to Herod.

ANAPHORA PILATI

CHAPTER 1

¹Pontius Pilate to Tiberius Caesar: Greetings. ²Regarding Jesus Christ, whom I fully made known to you in my last [report], a bitter punishment has at length been inflicted by the will of the people, although I was unwilling and apprehensive. In good truth, no age ever had or will have a man so good and strict. ³But the people made a wonderful effort, and all their scribes, chiefs, and elders agreed to crucify this Ambassador of truth, their own prophets, like the sibyls with us, advising the contrary; ⁴and when He was hanged, supernatural signs appeared; and in the judgment of philosophers, menaced the whole world with ruin. ⁵His disciples flourish, not denying their Master by their behavior and temperance of life; indeed, in His Name they are most benevolent. ⁶Had I not feared a sedition might arise among the people, who were almost furious, perhaps this Man would have yet been living with us. ⁷Although, being rather compelled by fidelity to your dignity, than led by my own inclination, I did not strive with all my might to prevent the sale and suffering of righteous blood, guiltless of every accusation, unjustly, indeed, through the maliciousness of men, and yet, as the Writings interpret, to their own destruction. ⁸Farewell. THE 5TH OF THE CALENDS OF APRIL.

PARADOSIS PILATI

The Paradosis Pilati ("The Handing Over of Pilate") is an account of Pilate being brought to Rome for judgment. While the earliest extant manuscripts are from the 12th century, it is speculated to date from the 4th or 5th centuries.

CHAPTER 1

¹And the writings having come to the city of the Romans, and having been read to Caesar, with not a few standing by, all were astounded, because through the wickedness of Pilate the darkness and the earthquake had come over the whole world. ²And Caesar, filled with rage, sent soldiers and ordered them to bring Pilate [as] a prisoner. ³And when he was brought to the city of the Romans, Caesar, hearing that Pilate had arrived, sat in the temple of the gods, in the presence of all the senate, and with all the army, and all the multitude of his power; and he ordered Pilate to stand forward. ⁴And Caesar says to him: "Why have you, O most impious [man], dared to do such things, having seen such great miracles in that Man? By daring to do an evil deed, you have destroyed the whole world." ⁵And Pilate said: "O almighty king, I am innocent of these things; but the multitude of the Jews are violent and guilty." ⁶And Caesar said: "And who are they?" Pilate says: "Herod, Archelaus, Philip, Annas and Caiaphas, and all the multitude of the Jews." ⁷Caesar says: "For what reason did you follow their counsel?" And Pilate says: "Their nation is rebellious and insubordinate, not submitting themselves to your power." ⁸And Caesar said: "When they delivered Him to you, you should have made Him secure and sent Him to me, and not have obeyed them in crucifying such a Man, righteous as He was, and One that did such good miracles, as you have said in your report. For from such miracles Jesus was obviously the Christ, the King of the Jews." ⁹And as Caesar was thus speaking, when he named the Name of Christ, all the multitude of the gods fell down collectively and became as dust, where Caesar was sitting with the senate. ¹⁰And the people standing beside Caesar all began to tremble on account of the speaking of the word and the fall of their gods; ¹¹and being seized with terror, they all went away, each to his own house, wondering at what had happened. And Caesar ordered Pilate to be kept in security, in order that he might know the truth about Jesus. ¹²And on the following day, Caesar, sitting in the Capitol with all the senate, tried again to question Pilate. ¹³And Caesar says: "Tell the truth, O most impious [man], because through your

impious action which you have perpetrated against Jesus, even here the doing of your wicked deeds has been shown by the gods having been cast down. Say, then, who He is that has been crucified; because even His Name has destroyed all the gods." [14] Pilate said: "And indeed, the records of Him are true; for assuredly I myself was persuaded from His works that He was greater than all the gods whom we worship." [15] And Caesar said: "For what reason, then, did you bring against Him such audacity and such doings, if you were not ignorant of Him, and altogether devising trouble against my kingdom?" [16] Pilate said: "On account of the wickedness and rebellion of the lawless and ungodly Jews, I did this." [17] And Caesar, being filled with rage, held a council with all his senate and his power, and ordered a decree to be written against the Jews as follows: "To Licianus, the governor of the chief places of the East: Greetings. The reckless deed which has been done at the present time by the inhabitants of Jerusalem, and the cities of the Jews surrounding [it], and their wicked action, has come to my knowledge, that they have forced Pilate to crucify a certain God named Jesus, and on account of this great fault of theirs the world has been darkened and dragged to destruction. [18] Therefore speedily, with a multitude of soldiers, go to them there, and make them prisoners, in accordance with this decree. Be obedient, and take action against them, and scatter them, and make them slaves among all the nations; and having driven them out of the whole of Judea, make them the smallest of nations, so that it may not any longer be seen at all, because they are full of wickedness. [19] And this decree having come into the region of the East, Licianus, obeying from fear of the decree, seized all the nation of the Jews; and those that were left in Judea he scattered among the nations and sold for slaves, so that it was known to Caesar that these things had been done by Licianus against the Jews in the region of the East; and it pleased him. [20] And again, Caesar set himself to question Pilate; and he orders a captain named Albius to cut off Pilate's head, saying, "Just as he laid hands on the just Man named Christ, in like manner he will also fall and not find safety." [21] And Pilate, going away to the place, prayed in silence, saying, "Lord, do not destroy me along with the wicked Hebrews, because I would not have laid hands on You, except for the nation of the lawless Jews, because they were exciting rebellion against me. [22] But You know that I did it in ignorance. Do not then destroy me for this sin of mine, but do not remember evil against me, O Lord, and against Your servant Procla, who is standing with me in this hour of my death, whom You appointed to prophesy that You should be nailed to the Cross. [23] Do not condemn her also in my sin; but pardon us, and make us to be numbered in the portion of Your righteous." [24] And behold, when Pilate had finished his prayer, there came a voice out of Heaven, saying, "All the generations and families of the nations will count you blessed, because under you have been fulfilled all those things said about Me by the prophets; [25] and you yourself will be seen as My witness at My second appearing when I will judge the twelve tribes of Israel and those that have not owned My Name. [26] And the prefect struck off the head of Pilate; and behold, a messenger of the LORD received it. And his wife Procla, seeing the messenger coming and receiving his head, being filled with joy herself also, immediately gave up the spirit and was buried along with her husband.

VINDICTA SALVATORIS

Vindicta Salvatoris (The Vengeance of the Savior) is a virulently anti-Jewish work, likely written in Latin in the 8th century. It is often included with the Acts of Pilate (Gospel of Nicodemus). The theology reflects medieval Roman Catholic and anti-Semitic sentiments and supersessionism. Differing from the Bible, which places the blame for Jesus' death on Herod, Pontius Pilate, the Gentiles, and the Jews together (Acts 4:27)—a plan foreordained by God Himself for the salvation of all sinners who turn to God in faith (Acts 4:28; Jn. 3:14-18; 1 Jn. 2:2)—Vindicta Salvatoris places the blame collectively on the Jews and has been historically used to justify attacks on the Jewish people. It also contains numerous historical issues, compressing hundreds of years of history into a short span of time, including the reigns of Herod Archelaus, Tiberius Caesar, and Vespasian, as well as the conversion of the emperors to Christianity, which did not actually occur until the 4th century.

CHAPTER 1

[1] In the days of Emperor Tiberius Caesar, when Herod was tetrarch, Christ was delivered under Pontius Pilate by the Jews and revealed by Tiberius. [2] In those days Titus was a prince under Tiberius in the region of Aquitania, in a city of Libiae [[or Albi]] which is called Burdigala. [3] And Titus had a sore in his right nostril, on account of a cancer, and he had his face torn even to the eye. [4] There went forth a certain man from Judea, by name Nathan the son of Nahum; for he was an Ishmaelite who went from land to land, and from sea to sea, and in all the ends of the earth. [5] Now Nathan was sent from Judea to Emperor Tiberius, to carry their treaty to the city of Rome. And Tiberius was ill, and full of ulcers and fevers, and had nine kinds of leprosy. [6] And Nathan wished to go to the city of Rome, but the north wind blew, and hindered his sailing, and carried him down to the harbor of a city of Libiae. [7] Now Titus, seeing the ship coming, knew that it was from Judea; and they all wondered, and said that they had never seen any vessel so coming from that quarter. [8] And Titus ordered the captain to come to him and asked him who he was. And he said: "I am Nathan the son of Nahum, of the race of the Ishmaelites, and I am a subject of Pontius Pilate in Judea. And I have been sent to go to Tiberius, the Roman emperor, to carry a treaty from Judea. And a strong wind came down on the sea and has brought me to a country that I do not know." [9] And Titus says: "If you could at any time find anything, either of cosmetics or herbs, which could cure the wound that I have in my face, as you see, so that I should become whole and regain my former health, I should bestow on you many good things." [10] And Nathan said to him: "I do not know, nor have I ever known, of such things as you speak to me about. But for all that, if you had been in Jerusalem some time ago, there you would have found a choice Prophet, whose Name was Immanuel, for He will save His people from their sins. [11] And He, as His first miracle in Cana of Galilee, made wine from water; and by His word He cleansed lepers, He opened the eyes of one born blind, He healed paralytics, He made demons flee, He raised up three dead; [12] a woman caught in adultery, and condemned by the Jews to be stoned, He set free; [13] and another woman, named Veronica, who suffered twelve years from an issue of blood, and came up to Him behind, and touched the fringe of His garment, He healed; [14] and with five loaves and two fishes He satisfied five thousand men, to say nothing of little ones and women, and there remained of the fragments twelve baskets. [15] All these things, and many others, were accomplished before His passion. After His resurrection, we saw Him in the flesh as He had been before." [16] And Titus said to Him: "How did He rise again from the dead, seeing that He was dead?" [17] And Nathan answered and said: "He was clearly dead, and hung up on the cross, and again taken down from the cross, and for three days He lay in the tomb: thereafter He rose again from the dead, and went down to Hades, and freed the patriarchs, and the prophets, and the whole human race; [18] thereafter He appeared to His disciples and ate with them; thereafter they saw Him going up into heaven. [19] And so it is the truth—all this that I tell you, for I saw it with my own eyes, and all the house of Israel." [20] And Titus said in his own words: "Woe to you, O Emperor Tiberius, full of ulcers, and enveloped in leprosy, because such a scandal has been committed in your kingdom; because you have made such laws in Judea, in the land of the birth of our Lord Jesus Christ, and they have seized the King, and put to

death the Ruler of the peoples; ²¹ and they have not made Him come to us to cure you of your leprosy and cleanse me from my sickness: on which account, if they had been before my face, with my own hands I should have slain the carcasses of those Jews and hung them up on the cruel tree, because they have destroyed my Lord, and my eyes have not been worthy to see His face." ²² And when he had thus spoken, immediately the wound fell from the face of Titus, and his flesh and his face were restored to health. ²³ And all the sick who were in the same place were made whole in that hour. ²⁴ And Titus cried out, and all the rest with him, in a loud voice, saying, "My King and my God, because I have never seen You, and You have made me whole, command me to go with the ship over the waters to the land of Your birth, to take vengeance on Your enemies; and help me, O LORD, so that I may be able to destroy them and avenge Your death: deliver them, LORD, into my hand." ²⁵ And having thus spoken, he ordered that he should be immersed. And he called Nathan to him, and he said to him: "How have you seen those immersed who believe in Christ? Come to me and immerse me in the Name of the Father, and of the Son, and of the Holy Spirit. Amen. ²⁶ For I also firmly believe in the Lord Jesus Christ with all my heart and with all my soul; because nowhere in the whole world is there another who has created me and made me whole from my wounds." ²⁷ And having thus spoken, he sent messengers to Vespasian to come with all haste with his bravest men, so prepared as if for war. ²⁸ Then Vespasian brought with him five thousand armed men, and they went to meet Titus. ²⁹ And when they had come to the city of Libiae, he said to Titus: "Why is it that you have made me come here?" ³⁰ And he said: "Know that Jesus has come into this world, and has been born in Judea, in a place which is called Beth-Lehem, and has been given up by the Jews, and scourged, and crucified on Mount Calvary, and has risen again from the dead on the third day. ³¹ And His disciples have seen Him in the same flesh in which He was born, and He has shown Himself to His disciples, and they have believed in Him. And we indeed wish to become His disciples. ³² Now, let us go and destroy His enemies from the earth, so that they may now know that there is none like the LORD our God on the face of the earth."

CHAPTER 2

¹ With this plan, then, they went forth from the city of Libiae which is called Burdigala, and went on board a ship, and proceeded to Jerusalem, and surrounded the kingdom of the Jews, and began to send them to destruction. ² And when the kings of the Jews heard of their doings, and the wasting of their land, fear came on them, and they were in great perplexity. ³ Then Archelaus was perplexed in his words, and said to his son: "My son, take my kingdom and judge it; and take counsel with the other kings who are in the land of Judah, so that you may be able to escape from our enemies." ⁴ And having said this, he unsheathed his sword and leaned on it; and turned his sword, which was very sharp, and thrust it into his breast, and died. ⁵ And his son allied himself with the other kings who were under him, and they took counsel among themselves, and went into Jerusalem with their chief men who were in their counsel, and they stood in the same place seven years. ⁶ And Titus and Vespasian took counsel to surround their city. And they did so. ⁷ And the seven years being fulfilled, there was a very severe famine, and for lack of bread they began to eat earth. ⁸ Then all the soldiers who were of the four kings took counsel among themselves and said: "Now we are sure to die: what will God do to us? Or of what good is our life to us, because the Romans have come to take our place and nation? It is better for us to kill each other, than that the Romans should say that they have slain us and gained the victory over us." ⁹ And they drew their swords, and struck themselves, and died, to the number of twelve thousand men among them. ¹⁰ Then there was a great stench in that city from the corpses of those dead men. And their kings feared with a very great fear even to death; and they could not bear the stench of them, nor bury them, nor throw them forth out of the city. ¹¹ And they said to each other: "What will we do? We indeed gave Christ up to death, and now we have given ourselves up to death. Let us bow our heads and give up the keys of the city to the Romans, because God has already given us up to death." ¹² And they immediately went up on the walls of the city, and everyone cried out with a loud voice, saying, "Titus and Vespasian: take the keys of the city, which have been given to you by Messiah, who is called Christ." ¹³ Then they gave themselves up into the hands of Titus and Vespasian and said: "Judge us, seeing that we ought to die, because we judged Christ; and He was given up without cause." ¹⁴ Titus and Vespasian seized them, and some they stoned, and some they hanged on a tree, feet up and head down, and struck them through with lances; ¹⁵ and others they gave up to be sold, and others they divided among themselves, and made four parts of them, just as they had done of the garments of the LORD. ¹⁶ And they said: "They sold Christ for thirty pieces of silver, and we will sell thirty of them for one denarius." And so they did. And having done so, they seized all the lands of Judea and Jerusalem.

CHAPTER 3

¹ Then they made a search for the face or portrait of Jesus, how they might find it, and they found a woman named Veronica who had it. ² Then they seized Pilate and sent him to prison, to be guarded by four quaternions of soldiers at the door of the prison. ³ Then they immediately sent their messengers to Tiberius, the emperor of the city of Rome, that he should send Velosianus to them. ⁴ And he said to him: "Take all that is necessary for you in the sea, and go down into Judea, and seek out one of the disciples of Him who is called Christ and Lord, that he may come to me, and in the Name of his God cure me of the leprosy and the diseases by which I am daily exceedingly burdened, and of my wounds, because I am in [great] discomfort. ⁵ And send against the kings of the Jews, who are subject to my authority, your forces and terrible siege engines, because they have put to death Jesus Christ our Lord, and condemn them to death. ⁶ And if you will there find a man as may be able to free me from this sickness of mine, I will believe in Christ the Son of God, and will immerse myself in His Name." ⁷ And Velosianus said: "My lord emperor, if I find such a man as may be able to help and free us, what reward will I promise him?" ⁸ Tiberius said to him: "The half of my kingdom, without fail, to be in his hand." ⁹ Then Velosianus immediately went forth, and went on board the ship, and hoisted the sail in the vessel, and went on sailing through the sea. And he sailed [for] one year and seven days, after which he arrived at Jerusalem. ¹⁰ And immediately he ordered some of the Jews to come to his power and began to carefully ask what the acts of Christ were. ¹¹ Then Joseph, of the city of Arimathea, and Nicodemus, came at the same time. And Nicodemus said: "I saw Him, and I indeed know that He is the Savior of the world." ¹² And Joseph said to him: "And I took Him down from the cross and laid Him in a new tomb, which had been cut out of the rock. And the Jews kept me shut up on the Day of Preparation, at evening; ¹³ and while I was standing in prayer on the Sabbath day, the house was hung up by the four corners, and I saw the Lord Jesus Christ like a gleam of light, and for fear I fell to the ground. ¹⁴ And He said to me, Look on me, for I am Jesus, whose body you buried in your tomb. And I said to Him, Show me the tomb where I laid You. And Jesus, holding my hand in His right hand, led me to the place where I buried Him." ¹⁵ And the woman named Veronica also came and said to him: "And I touched in the crowd the fringe of His garment, because for twelve years I had suffered from an issue of blood; and He immediately healed me." ¹⁶ Then Velosianus said to Pilate: "You, Pilate—impious and cruel! Why have you slain the Son of God?" And Pilate answered: "His own nation, and the chief priests Annas and Caiaphas, gave Him to me." ¹⁷ Velosianus said: "Impious and cruel! You are worthy of death and cruel punishment." And he sent him back to prison. ¹⁸ And Velosianus at last sought for the face or the countenance of the LORD. And all who were in that same place said: "It is the woman called Veronica who has the portrait of the LORD in her house." ¹⁹ And immediately he ordered her to be brought before his power. And he said to her: "Do you have the portrait of the LORD in your house?" But she said, "No." ²⁰ Then Velosianus ordered her to be tortured until she should give up the portrait of the LORD. And she was forced to say: "I have it in clean linen, my lord, and I adore it daily." Velosianus said: "Show it to me." Then she showed the portrait of the LORD. ²¹ When Velosianus saw it, he prostrated himself on the ground; and with a ready heart and true

faith, he took hold of it, and wrapped it in a golden cloth, and placed it in a casket, and sealed it with his ring. ²²And he swore with an oath and said: "As the LORD God lives, and by the health of Caesar, no man will see it on the face of the earth any longer until I see the face of my lord Tiberius." ²³And when he had thus spoken, the princes, who were the chief men of Judea, seized Pilate to take him to a seaport. And he took the portrait of the LORD, with all His disciples, and all in his pay, and they went on board the ship the same day. ²⁴Then the woman Veronica, for the love of Christ, left all that she possessed and followed Velosianus. And Velosianus said to her: "What do you wish, woman, or what do you seek?" ²⁵And she answered: "I am seeking the portrait of our Lord Jesus Christ, who enlightened me, not for my own merits, but through His own holy affection. ²⁶Give the portrait of my Lord Jesus Christ back to me; for because of this I die with a righteous longing. ²⁷But if you do not give it back to me, I will not leave it until I see where you will put it, because I, most miserable woman that I am, will serve Him all the days of my life; because I believe that He, my Redeemer, lives forever." ²⁸Then Velosianus ordered the woman Veronica to be taken down with him into the ship. ²⁹And the sails being hoisted, they began to go in the vessel in the Name of the LORD, and they sailed through the sea. ³⁰But Titus, along with Vespasian, went up into Judea, avenging all nations on their land. ³¹At the end of one year, Velosianus came to the city of Rome, brought his vessel into the river, which is called the Tiber, and entered the city which is called Rome. ³²And he sent his messenger to his lord Tiberius, the emperor, in the Lateran, concerning his prosperous arrival. ³³Then Emperor Tiberius, when he heard the message of Velosianus, rejoiced greatly and ordered him to come before his face. ³⁴And when he had come, he called him, saying, "Velosianus, how have you come, and what have you seen in the region of Judea regarding Christ the Lord and His disciples? Tell me, I beg you, that He is going to cure me of my sickness, so that I may be cleansed from that leprosy which I have over my body at once, and I give up my whole kingdom into your power and His." ³⁵And Velosianus said: "My lord emperor, I found your servants Titus and Vespasian in Judea fearing the LORD, and they were cleansed from all their ulcers and sufferings. ³⁶And I found that all the kings and rulers of Judea have been hanged by Titus; Annas and Caiaphas have been stoned; Archelaus has killed himself with his own lance; and I have sent Pilate to Damascus in bonds and kept him in prison under safe keeping. ³⁷But I have also found out about Jesus, whom the Jews most wickedly attacked with swords, and staffs, and weapons; and they crucified Him who ought to have freed and enlightened us, and to have come to us, and they hung Him on a tree. ³⁸And Joseph came from Arimathea, and Nicodemus with him, bringing a mixture of myrrh and aloes, about a hundred pounds, to anoint the body of Jesus; and they took Him down from the cross and laid Him in a new tomb. ³⁹And on the third day, He most assuredly rose again from the dead and showed Himself to His disciples in the same flesh in which He had been born. Finally, after forty days, they saw Him going up into Heaven. ⁴⁰Indeed, Jesus did many other miracles before His passion and after: first, from water He made wine; He raised the dead; He cleansed lepers; He made the blind see; He cured paralytics; He put demons to flight; He made the deaf hear [and] the mute speak; ⁴¹Lazarus, when four days dead, He raised from the tomb; the woman Veronica, who suffered from an issue of blood [for] twelve years and touched the fringe of His garment, He made whole. ⁴²Then it pleased the LORD in the heavens that the Son of God, who, sent into this world as the first-created, had died on earth, should send His messenger; and He commanded Titus and Vespasian, whom I knew in that place where your throne is. ⁴³And it pleased God Almighty that they went into Judea and Jerusalem, and seized your subjects, and put them under that sentence, as it were, in the same manner as they did when your subjects seized Jesus and bound Him. ⁴⁴And afterward, Vespasian said: What will we do about those who will remain? Titus answered: They hung our Lord on a green tree and struck Him with a lance; now let us hang them on a dry tree and pierce their bodies through and through with the lance. And they did so. ⁴⁵And Vespasian said: What about those who are left? Titus answered: They seized the tunic of our Lord Jesus Christ and made four parts from it; now let us seize them and divide them into four parts—to you one, to me one, to your men another, and to my servants the fourth part. And they did so. ⁴⁶And Vespasian said: But what will we do about those who are left? Titus answered him: The Jews sold our Lord for thirty pieces of silver: now let us sell thirty of them for one piece of silver. And they did so. ⁴⁷And they seized Pilate and gave him up to me, and I put him in prison, to be guarded by four quaternions of soldiers in Damascus. ⁴⁸Then they made a search with great diligence to seek [for] the portrait of the LORD; and they found a woman named Veronica who had the portrait of the LORD. ⁴⁹Then Emperor Tiberius said to Velosianus: "How do you have it?" And he answered: "I have it in a clean golden cloth, rolled up in a shawl." ⁵⁰And Emperor Tiberius said: "Bring it to me and spread it before my face, so that I, falling to the ground and bending my knees, may adore it on the ground." ⁵¹Then Velosianus spread out his shawl with the golden cloth on which the portrait of the LORD had been imprinted; and Emperor Tiberius saw it. And he immediately adored the image of the LORD with a pure heart, and his flesh was cleansed as the flesh of a little child. ⁵²And all the blind, the lepers, the lame, the mute, the deaf, and those possessed by various diseases, who were present there, were healed, and cured, and cleansed. ⁵³And Emperor Tiberius bowed his head and bent his knees, considering that saying: "Blessed is the womb which bore You, and the breasts which You have sucked"; ⁵⁴and he groaned to the LORD, saying with tears: "God of heaven and earth, do not permit me to sin, but confirm my soul and my body, and place me in Your kingdom, because in Your Name do I trust forever: free me from all evils, as You freed the three children from the furnace of blazing fire." ⁵⁵Then Emperor Tiberius said to Velosianus: "Velosianus, have you seen any of those men who saw Christ?" Velosianus answered: "I have." ⁵⁶He said: "Did you ask how they immerse those who believed in Christ?" Velosianus said: "My lord, we have here one of the disciples of Christ Himself." ⁵⁷Then he ordered Nathan to be summoned to come to him. ⁵⁸Nathan therefore came and immersed him in the Name of the Father, and of the Son, and of the Holy Spirit. Amen. ⁵⁹Immediately Emperor Tiberius, made whole from all his diseases, ascended his throne and said: "Blessed are You, O LORD God Almighty, and worthy to be praised, who has freed me from the snare of death and cleansed me from all my iniquities; because I have greatly sinned before You, O LORD my God, and I am not worthy to see Your face." ⁶⁰And then Emperor Tiberius was instructed in all the articles of the faith—fully, and with strong faith. ⁶¹May that same God Almighty, who is King of Kings and Lord of Lords, Himself shield us in His faith, and defend us, and deliver us from all danger and evil, and stoop to bring us to life everlasting, when this life, which is temporary, will fail; who is blessed forever and ever. Amen.

MORS PILATI

The Mors Pilati, otherwise known as The Death of Pilate, Who Condemned Jesus, is a late medieval work. The narrative offers a far less ancient and alternative explanation for the death of Pontius Pilate.

CHAPTER 1

¹And when Tiberius Caesar, the emperor of the Romans, was laboring under a grievous disease, and understanding that there was at Jerusalem a certain Physician, Jesus by Name, who by a single word cured all sicknesses, he, not knowing that the Jews and Pilate had put Him to death, ordered a certain friend of his named Volusianus: ²"Go as quickly as possible across the seas; and you will tell Pilate, my

MORS PILATI

servant and friend, to send me this Physician, so that He may restore me to my former health." ³And this Volusianus, having heard the emperor's command, immediately departed and came to Pilate as he had been commanded. ⁴And he related to the same Pilate what had been entrusted to him by Tiberius Caesar, saying, "Tiberius Caesar, the emperor of the Romans, your master, having heard that in this city there is a Physician who by His word alone heals sicknesses, begs you earnestly to send Him to him for the curing of his sickness." ⁵Pilate, hearing this, was very greatly afraid, knowing that through envy he had caused Him to be put to death. ⁶Pilate answered the same messenger thus, saying, "This Man was a criminal, and a Man who drew to Himself all the people; so a council of the wise men of the city was held, and I caused Him to be crucified." ⁷And this messenger returning to his inn, met a certain woman named Veronica, who had been a friend of Jesus; and he said: "O woman, a certain Physician who was in this city, who cured the sick by a word alone, why have the Jews put Him to death?" ⁸And she began to weep, saying, "Oh my lord, my God and my Lord, whom Pilate for envy delivered, condemned, and ordered to be crucified." ⁹Then he, being exceedingly grieved, said: "I am vehemently grieved that I am unable to accomplish that for which my lord had sent me." ¹⁰And Veronica said to him: "When my Lord was going around preaching, and I, much against my will, was deprived of His presence, I wished [for] His picture to be painted for me, in order that, while I was deprived of His presence, the figure of His picture might at least provide me consolation. ¹¹And when I was carrying the canvas to the painter to be painted, my Lord met me and asked where I was going. ¹²And when I had disclosed to Him the cause of my journey, He asked for the cloth from me and gave it back to me impressed with the image of His noble face. ¹³Therefore, if your lord will devoutly gaze on His face, he will immediately obtain the benefit of health." ¹⁴And he said to her: "Is a picture of such a sort obtainable by gold or silver?" ¹⁵She said to him: "No; but by the pious influence of devotion. I will therefore set out with you, and carry the picture to be seen by Caesar, and come back again." ¹⁶Therefore, Volusianus came with Veronica to Rome and said to Tiberius the emperor: "Jesus, whom you have been longing for, Pilate and the Jews have delivered to an unjust death, and have through envy affixed to the scaffold of the cross. ¹⁷There has therefore come with me a certain matron, bringing a picture of Jesus Himself; and if you will devoutly look on it, you will immediately obtain the benefit of your health." ¹⁸Caesar therefore ordered the way to be strewn with silk cloths, and the picture to be presented to him; and as soon as he had looked on it, he regained his former health. ¹⁹Pontius Pilate, therefore, by the command of Caesar, is taken and brought through to Rome. ²⁰Caesar, hearing that Pilate had arrived at Rome, was filled with exceeding fury against him and caused him to be brought to him. ²¹But Pilate brought down with him the seamless tunic of Jesus; and he wore it on him in the presence of the emperor. ²²And as soon as the emperor saw him, he laid aside all his anger, and immediately rose up to meet him. Nor was he able to speak harshly to him in anything; and he who seemed so terrible and fierce in his absence, now in his presence is somehow found to be mild. ²³And when he had sent him away, he immediately blazed out against him terribly, crying out that he was a wretch, inasmuch as he had not at all shown him the fury of his heart. ²⁴And he immediately made him be called back, swearing and declaring that he was the son of death, and that it was infamous that he should live on the earth. ²⁵And as soon as he saw him, he immediately saluted him and threw away all the ferocity of his mind. ²⁶Everyone marveled; and he himself wondered why he should thus blaze out against Pilate when he was absent, and that while he was present he could say nothing to him sternly. ²⁷Then, by a divine impulse, or perhaps by the advice of some Christian, he caused him to be stripped of that tunic, and immediately resumed his former ferocity of mind against him. ²⁸And when at this the emperor wondered very greatly, it was told to him that that tunic had belonged to the Lord Jesus. ²⁹Then the emperor ordered him to be kept in prison, until he should deliberate in a council of the wise men what ought to be done with him. ³⁰And a few days later, sentence was therefore passed on Pilate, that he should be condemned to the most disgraceful death. Pilate, hearing this, killed himself with his own knife, and by such a death ended his life. ³¹When Caesar knew of the death of Pilate, he said: "Truly he has died by a most disgraceful death, whom his own hand has not spared." ³²He is therefore bound to a great mass and sunk into the Tiber River. But malignant and filthy spirits in his malignant and filthy body, all rejoicing together, kept moving themselves in the waters, and in a terrible manner brought lightnings and tempests, thunders and hailstorms, in the air, so that all men were kept in horrible fear. ³³Therefore, the Romans, drawing him out of the Tiber River, carried him down to Vienna in derision and sunk him in the Rhone River. For Vienna is called, as it were, Via Gehennae, "The Way of Gehenna," because it was then a place of cursing. ³⁴But evil spirits were present there, working the same things in the same place. Those men therefore, not enduring such a visitation of demons, removed from themselves that vessel of blight and sent him to be buried in the territory of Losania. ³⁵And they, seeing that they were troubled by the aforementioned visitations, removed him from themselves and sunk him in a certain pit surrounded by mountains, where to this day, according to the account of some, certain diabolical machinations are said to bubble up.

ACTS OF PAUL

Scholars dispute whether the Acts of Paul was entirely the work of a single author, or possibly a collection of disparate acts and legends of the apostle. A number of these works have been transmitted separately, including the Acts of Paul and Thecla (The Second Act), 3 Corinthians (The Seventh Act), and the Martyrdom of Paul. It was composed in Greek, most likely in the 2nd century. In typical apocryphal fashion, the author(s) at points promote some alternative, hyper-legalistic soteriology—in the case of the Acts of Paul and Thecla, abstinence as a path to salvation. Some of the Acts are highly fragmentary.

THE FIRST ACT

1. … Paul went into [the house] at the place where the [dead boy Barnabas] was. But Phila, the wife of Panchares, was very angry and said to her husband in [great anger]: "Husband, you have gone … the wild beasts, you have not begotten … your son … where is mine?" … "[he has not] desired food … to bury him." But [Panchares] stood in the sight of all and made his prayer at the ninth hour, until the people of the city came to carry the boy out. When he had prayed, Paul [came] and saw … and of Jesus Christ … the boy … the prayer. … multitude … eight days … they thought that he raised up the [boy]. But when Paul had remained … They asked him … the men listened to him … they sent for Panchares … and cried out, saying, "We believe, Panchares, … but save the city from … many things," which they said. Panchares said to them: "You judge whether your good deeds … is not possible … but to [testify] … God who has … His Son according to … salvation, and I also believe that, my brothers, there is no other God, except Jesus Christ, the Son of the Blessed, to whom is glory forever. Amen." But when they saw that he would not turn to them, they pursued Paul, and caught him, and brought him back into the city, mistreating him, and cast stones at him, and thrust him out of their city and out of their country. But Panchares would not return evil for evil: he shut the door of his house and went in with his wife … fasting … But when it was evening, Paul came to him and said: "… God has … Jesus Christ."

THE SECOND ACT
(ACTS OF PAUL AND THECLA)

1. When Paul went up to Iconium after he fled from Antioch, there journeyed with him Demas and Hermogenes the coppersmith, which were full of hypocrisy, and they flattered Paul as though they loved him. But Paul, looking only to the goodness of Christ, did them no evil, but loved them well, so that he attempted to make sweet to them all the oracles of the LORD, and of the teaching and the interpretation [of the good news], and of the birth and resurrection of the Beloved, and related to them word by word all the great works of Christ, how they were revealed to him, [[[and] how that Christ was born of Mary the virgin, and of the seed of David]].

2. And a certain man named Onesiphorus, when he heard that Paul had come to Iconium, went out with his children Simmias, and Zeno, and his wife Lectra to meet him, so that he might receive him into his house, for Titus had told him what manner of man Paul was in appearance; for he had not seen him in the flesh, but only in the spirit.

3. And he went by the king's highway that leads to Lystra and stood expecting him, and looked on them that came, according to the description of Titus. And he saw Paul coming, a man of short stature, thin-haired on the head, crooked in the legs, of good state of body, with eyebrows joining, and nose somewhat hooked, full of grace: for sometimes he appeared like a man, and sometimes he had the face of a messenger.

4. And when Paul saw Onesiphorus, he smiled, and Onesiphorus said: "Hail, you servant of the blessed God!" And he said: "Grace be with you and with your house." But Demas and Hermogenes were envious and stirred up their hypocrisy yet more, so that Demas said: "Are we not servants of the Blessed, that you did not salute us so?" And Onesiphorus said: "I do not see in you any fruit of righteousness, but if you be such, also come into my house and refresh yourselves."

5. And when Paul entered into the house of Onesiphorus, there was great joy, and bowing of knees, and breaking of bread, and the word of God concerning continence and the resurrection; for Paul said: "Blessed are the pure in heart, for they will see God. Blessed are they that keep the flesh chaste, for they will become the temple of God. Blessed are they that abstain, for to them will God speak. Blessed are they that have renounced this world, for they will be well-pleasing to God. Blessed are they that possess their wives as though they did not have them, for they will inherit God. Blessed are they that have the fear of God, for they will become messengers of God.

6. Blessed are they that tremble at the oracles of God, for they will be comforted. Blessed are they that receive [the] wisdom of Jesus Christ, for they will be called sons of the Most High. Blessed are they that have kept their immersion pure, for they will rest with the Father and with the Son. Blessed are they that have come to the understanding of Jesus Christ, for they will be in light. Blessed are they that for love of God have departed from the fashion of this world, for they will judge messengers, and will be blessed at the right hand of the Father. Blessed are the merciful, for they will obtain mercy and will not see the bitter Day of Judgment. Blessed are the bodies of the virgins, for they will be well-pleasing to God and will not lose the reward of their continence, for the word of the Father will be to them a work of salvation in the day of His Son, and they will have rest world without end.

7. And as Paul was saying these things in the midst of the assembly in the house of Onesiphorus, a certain virgin, Thecla, whose mother was Theocleia, who was betrothed to a husband, Thamyris, sat at the window nearby and listened night and day to the word concerning chastity which was spoken by Paul: and she did not stir from the window, but was led onward by faith, rejoicing exceedingly: and further, when she saw many women and virgins entering in to Paul, she also earnestly desired to be accounted worthy to stand before Paul's face and to hear the word of Christ; for she had not yet seen the appearance of Paul, but only heard his speech.

8. Now as she did not move from the window, her mother sent to Thamyris, and he came with great joy as if he were already to take her for a wife. Thamyris therefore said to Theocleia: "Where is my Thecla?" And Theocleia said: "I have a new tale to tell you, Thamyris: for three days and three nights Thecla does not arise from the window, neither to eat nor to drink, but looking earnestly as it were on a joyful spectacle, she so attends to a stranger who teaches deceitful and various words, that I marvel how the great modesty of the maiden is so greatly reduced.

9. O Thamyris, this man upsets the [whole] city of the Iconians, and your Thecla also, for all the women and the young men go in to him and are taught by him. You must, he says, fear only one God and live chastely. And my daughter, too, like a spider at the window, bound by his words, is held by a new desire and a fearful passion: for she hangs on the things that he speaks, and the maiden is captured. But go to her and speak to her; for she is betrothed to you."

10. And Thamyris went to her, both loving her and fearing because of her disturbance, and said: "Thecla, my betrothed, why do you sit thus? And what passion is it that holds you in amazement; turn to your Thamyris and be ashamed." And her mother also said the same: "Thecla, why do you sit thus, looking downward, and answering nothing, but as one stricken?" And they wept grievously, Thamyris because he failed of a wife, and Theocleia of a child, and the maidservants of a mistress; there was, therefore, great confusion of mourning in the house. And while all this was so, Thecla did not turn away, but paid heed to the speech of Paul.

11. But Thamyris leapt up, and went forth into the street, and watched them that went in to Paul and came out. And he saw two men striving bitterly with one another and said to them: "You men, tell me who you are, and who is he that is within with you, that makes the souls of young men and maidens to err, deceiving them that there may be no marriages but they should live as they are. I therefore promise to give you much money if you will tell me of him: for I am a chief of the city."

12. And Demas and Hermogenes said to him: "Who this man is, we do not know; but he defrauds the young men of wives and the maidens of husbands, saying, You have no resurrection otherwise, except you continue chaste and do not defile the flesh, but keep it pure."

13. And Thamyris said to them: "Come, you men, into my house and refresh yourselves with me." And they went to a costly banquet with much wine, and great wealth, and a brilliant table. And Thamyris made them drink, for he loved Thecla and desired to take her for a wife: and at the dinner Thamyris said: "Tell me, you men, what is his teaching, so that I also may know it: for I am not a little afflicted concerning Thecla because she so loves the stranger, and I am defrauded of my marriage."

14. And Demas and Hermogenes said: "Bring him before Castelius the governor as one that persuades the multitudes with the new doctrine of the Christians; and so he will destroy him and you will have your wife Thecla. And we will teach you of that resurrection which he asserts, that it has already come to pass in the children which we have, and we rise again when we have come to the knowledge of the true God."

15. But when Thamyris heard this from them, he was filled with envy and wrath, and rose up early, and went to the house of Onesiphorus with the rulers, and officers, and a great crowd with staffs, saying to Paul: "You have destroyed the city of the Iconians and her that was espoused to me, so that she will not have me: let us go to Castelius the governor." And all the multitude said: "Away with the wizard, for he has corrupted all our wives." And the multitude rose up together against him.

16. And Thamyris, standing before the judgment-seat, cried aloud and said: "O proconsul, this is the man—we do not know where he is from, who does not allow maidens to marry: let him declare before you why he teaches such things." And Demas and Hermogenes said to Thamyris: "Say that he is a Christian, and so will you destroy him." But the governor kept his mind steadfast and called Paul, saying to him: "Who are you, and what do you teach? For it is no light accusation that these bring against you."

17. And Paul lifted up his voice and said: "If I am this day examined [regarding] what I teach, listen, O proconsul: the living God, the God of vengeance, the jealous God, the God that has need of nothing, but desires the salvation of men, has sent me, so that I may sever them from corruption, and uncleanness, and all pleasure and death, so that they may sin no more. Therefore, God has sent His own Child, whom I preach and teach that men should have hope in Him who alone has had compassion on the world that was in error; that men may no longer be under judgment, but have faith, and the fear of God, and the knowledge of sobriety, and the love of truth. If then I teach the things that have been revealed to me from God, what wrong do I do, O proconsul?" And the governor, having heard that, commanded Paul to be bound and taken away to prison until he should have leisure to hear him more carefully.

18. But Thecla at night took off her bracelets and gave them to the doorkeeper, and when the door was opened for her, she went into the prison and gave the jailer a mirror of silver, and so went in to Paul, and sat by his feet, and heard the wonderful works of God. And Paul did not fear at all, but walked in the confidence of God: and her faith was also increased as she kissed his chains.

19. Now when Thecla was sought by her own people and by Thamyris, she was looked for through the streets as one lost; and one of the fellow-servants of the doorkeeper said that she went out by night. And they examined the doorkeeper, and he told them that she had gone to the stranger to the prison; and they went as he told them and found her, as it were, bound with him in affection. And they went forth from there, and gathered the multitude to them, and showed it to the governor.

20. And he commanded Paul to be brought to the judgment-seat; but Thecla rolled herself on the place where Paul taught when he sat in the prison. And the governor commanded her to also be brought to the judgment-seat, and she went exulting with joy. And when Paul was brought the second time, the people cried out more vehemently: "He is a sorcerer! Away with him!" But the governor heard Paul gladly concerning the holy works of Christ: and he took counsel, and called Thecla, and said: "Why will you not marry Thamyris, according to the law of the Iconians?" But she stood looking earnestly on Paul, and when she did not answer, her mother Theocleia cried out, saying, "Burn the lawless one! Burn her that is no bride in the midst of the theater, so that all the women which have been taught by this man may be frightened."

21. And the governor was greatly moved: and he scourged Paul and sent him out of the city, but he condemned Thecla to be burned. And immediately, the governor arose and went to the theater: and all the multitude went forth to the dreadful spectacle. But Thecla, as the lamb in the wilderness looks around for the shepherd, so sought for Paul: and she looked on the multitude and saw the Lord sitting, like to Paul, and said: "As if I were not able to endure, Paul has come to look on me." And she earnestly paid heed to Him: but He departed into the heavens.

22. Now the boys and the maidens brought wood and hay to burn Thecla: and when she was brought in naked, the governor wept and marveled at the power that was in her. And they laid the wood, and the executioner ordered her to mount on the pyre: and she, making the Sign of the Cross, went up on the wood. And they lighted it, and though a great fire blazed forth, the fire took no hold on her, for God had compassion on her and caused a sound under the earth, and a cloud overshadowed her above, full of rain and hail, and all the vessel [of it] was poured out so that many were in peril of death, and the fire was quenched, and Thecla was preserved.

23. Now Paul was fasting with Onesiphorus, and his wife, and their children in an open tomb on the way whereby they go from Iconium to Daphne. And when many days passed, as they fasted, the boys said to Paul: "We are hungry." And they did not have enough to buy bread, for Onesiphorus had left the goods of this world and followed Paul with all his house. But Paul took off his upper garment and said: "Go, child, buy several loaves and bring them." And as the boy was buying, he saw his neighbor Thecla, and was astonished, and said: "Thecla, where are you going?" And she said: "I seek Paul, [for] I was preserved from the fire." And the boy said: "Come, I will bring you to him, for he mourns for you, and prays and fasts now these six days."

24. And when she came to the tomb to Paul, who had bowed his knees and was praying and saying: "O Father of Christ, do not let the fire take hold on Thecla, but spare her, for she is Yours," she, standing behind him, cried out: "O Father that made heaven and earth, the Father of Your beloved Child Jesus Christ, I bless You for that You have preserved me from the fire, so that I might see Paul." And Paul arose, and saw her, and said: "O God, the knower of hearts, the Father of our Lord Jesus Christ, I bless You that You have quickly accomplished that which I asked of You and have listened to me."

25. And there was much love within the tomb, for Paul rejoiced, and Onesiphorus, and all of them. And they had five loaves, and herbs, and water, and they rejoiced for the holy works of Christ. And Thecla said to Paul: "I will cut my hair [all] around and follow you wherever you go." But he said: "The time is repulsive and you are lovely: beware lest another temptation take you, worse than the first, and you do not endure it but play the coward." And Thecla said: "Only give me the seal in Christ, and temptation will not touch me." And Paul said: "Have patience, Thecla, and you will receive the water."

26. And Paul sent Onesiphorus away with all his house to Iconium, and so took Thecla and entered into Antioch: and as they entered in, a certain Syriarch, Alexander by name, saw Thecla, and was enamored with her, and would have bribed Paul with money and gifts. But Paul said: "I do not know the woman of whom you speak, neither is she mine." But as he was of great power, he himself embraced her in the highway; and she did not endure it, but sought after Paul and cried out bitterly, saying, "Do not force the stranger, do not force the handmaid of God. I am among the first of the Iconians, and because I would not marry Thamyris, I am cast out of the city." And she caught at Alexander, and tore his cloak, and took the wreath from his head, and made him a laughingstock.

27. But he, both loving her and being ashamed of what had happened to him, brought her before the governor; and when she confessed that she had done this, he condemned her to the beasts. But the women were greatly amazed and cried out at the judgment-seat: "An evil judgment! An impious judgment!" And Thecla asked of the governor that she might remain a virgin until she should fight the beasts; and a certain rich queen, Tryphaena by name, whose daughter had died, took her into her keeping, and had her for a consolation.

28. Now when the beasts were led in procession, they bound her to a fierce lioness, and Queen Tryphaena followed after her: but the lioness, when Thecla was set on her, licked her feet, and all the people marveled. Now the title of her accusation was: "GUILTY OF SACRILEGE." And the women with their children cried out from above: "O God, an impious judgment comes to pass in this city." And after the procession, Tryphaena took her again, for her daughter Falconilla, which was dead, had said to her in a dream: "Mother, you will take in my stead Thecla, the stranger that is desolate, so that she may pray for me and I be translated into the place of the righteous."

29. Therefore, when Tryphaena received her after the procession, she both lamented her because she was to fight the beasts the next day, and also loved her closely as her own daughter Falconilla; and she said: "Thecla, my second child, come, pray for my child that she may live forever; for I have seen this in a dream." And she without delay lifted up her voice and said: "O my God, Son of the Most High that are in Heaven, grant to her according to her desire, that her daughter Falconilla may live forever." And after she had said this, Tryphaena lamented her, considering that such great beauty was to be cast to the beasts.

30. And when it was dawn, Alexander came to take her (for it was he that was giving the games), saying, "The governor is set and the people trouble us: give me her that is to fight the beasts, so that I may take her away." But Tryphaena cried aloud so that he fled away, saying, "A second mourning for my Falconilla comes about in my house, and there is none to help, neither child, for she is dead, nor relative, for I am a widow. O God of my child Thecla, help Thecla!"

31. And the governor sent soldiers to fetch Thecla: and Tryphaena did not leave her, but took her hand herself and led her up, saying, "I brought my daughter Falconilla to the tomb; but you, Thecla, do I bring to fight the beasts." And Thecla wept bitterly and groaned to the LORD, saying, "LORD God in whom I believe, with whom I have taken refuge, that saved me from the fire, reward Tryphaena who has had pity on your handmaid and has kept me pure."

32. There was therefore a tumult, and a voice of the beasts, and shouting of the people, and of the women which sat together, some saying: "Bring in the sacrilegious one!" And the women saying: "Away with the city for this unlawful deed! Away with all of us, you proconsul! It is a bitter sight, an evil judgment!"

33. But Thecla, being taken out of the hand of Tryphaena, was stripped and a girdle was put on her, and she was cast into the stadium: and lions and bears were set against her. And a fierce lioness running to her, lay down at her feet, and the press of women cried aloud. And a bear ran on her; but the lioness ran and met him, and tore the bear in half. And again, a lion, trained against men, which was Alexander's, ran on her, and the lioness wrestled with him and was slain along with him. And the women lamented yet more, seeing that the lioness also that aided her was dead.

34. Then they put in many beasts, while she stood, and stretched out her hands, and prayed. And when she had ended her prayer, she turned and saw a great tank full of water and said: "Now is it time that I should wash myself." And she cast herself in, saying, "In the Name of Jesus Christ do I immerse myself on the last day." And all the women saw it, and all the people wept, saying, "Do not cast yourself into the water," so that even the governor wept that such great beauty should be devoured by seals. So, then, she cast herself into the water in the Name of Jesus Christ; and the seals, seeing the light of a flash of fire, floated dead on the top of the water. And there was around her a cloud of fire, so that neither did the beasts touch her, nor was she seen to be naked.

35. Now the women, when other more fearful beasts were put in, shrieked aloud, and some cast leaves, and others nard, others cassia, and some balsam, so that there was a multitude of odors; and all the beasts that were struck thereby were held as it were in sleep and did not touch her, so that Alexander said to the governor: "I have some exceedingly frightening bulls; let us bind the criminal to them." And the governor frowning, allowed it, saying, "Do what you will." And they bound her by the feet between the bulls and put hot irons under their bellies, so that they might be the more enraged and kill her. They then leaped forward; but the flame that burned around her, burned through the ropes, and she was as one not bound.

36. But Tryphaena, standing by the arena, fainted at the entry, so that her handmaids said: "Queen Tryphaena is dead!" And the governor stopped [the games] and all the city was frightened, and Alexander falling at the governor's feet said: "Have mercy on me and on the city, and let the condemned go, lest the city perish with her; for if Caesar hears this, perhaps he will destroy us and the city, because his relative, Queen Tryphaena, has died at the entry."

37. And the governor called Thecla from among the beasts and said to her: "Who are you? And what do you have surrounding you that not [even] one of the beasts has touched you?" But she said: "I am the handmaid of the living God; and what I have around me: it is that I have believed on His Son in whom God is well pleased; for whose sake not one of the beasts has touched me. For He alone is the goal [[*or* way]] of salvation and the substance of immortal life; for to them that are tossed around, He is a refuge, to the oppressed relief, to the despairing shelter, and in a word—whosoever does not believe on Him, will not live, but die everlastingly."

38. And when the governor heard this, he commanded garments to be brought and said: "Put on these garments." And she said: "He that clad me when I was naked among the beasts, the same in the Day of Judgment will clothe me with salvation." And she took the garments and put them on. And the governor immediately issued out an act, saying, "I release to you Thecla, the godly, the servant of God." And all the women cried out with a loud voice, and as with one mouth gave praise to God, saying, "One is the God who has preserved Thecla," so that with their voice all the city shook.

39. And Tryphaena, when she was told the good news, met her with many people, and embraced Thecla, and said: "Now do I believe that the dead are raised up; now do I believe that my child lives! Come inside, and I will make you heir of all my substance." Therefore, Thecla went in with her and rested in her house [for] eight days, teaching her the word of God, so that the greater part of the maidservants also believed, and there was great joy in the house.

40. But Thecla yearned after Paul and sought him, sending around in all places; and it was told to her that he was at Myra. And she took young men and maids, and girded herself, and sewed her mantle into a cloak after the fashion of a man, and departed into Myra, and found Paul speaking the word of God, and went to him. But when he saw her and the people that were with her, he was amazed, thinking in himself: "Has some other temptation come on her?" But she perceived it and said to him: "I have received the washing, O Paul; for He that has worked together with you in the good news has also worked with me for my immersing."

41. And Paul took her by the hand, and brought her into the house of Hermias, and heard all things from her; so that Paul marveled greatly, and they that heard were confirmed and prayed for Tryphaena. And Thecla arose and said to Paul: "I go to Iconium." And Paul said: "Go and teach the word of God." Now Tryphaena had sent her much apparel and gold, so that she left [it] with Paul for the ministry of the poor.

42. But she herself departed to Iconium. And she entered into the house of Onesiphorus, and fell down on the floor where Paul had sat, and taught the oracles of God, and wept, saying, "O God of myself and of this house, where the light shone on me—Jesus Christ, the Son of God, my Helper in prison, my Helper before the governors, my Helper in the fire, my Helper among the beasts: You are God, and to You be the glory forever. Amen."

43. And she found Thamyris dead, but her mother living. And she saw her mother and said to her: "Theocleia, my mother, can you believe that the LORD lives in the heavens? For whether you desire money, the LORD will give it to you through me: or your child, behold, I am here before you." And when she had so testified, she departed to Seleucia, and after she had enlightened many with the word of God, she slept a good sleep.

THE THIRD ACT

1. When Paul was teaching the word of God in Myra, there was a man there, Hermocrates by name, who had [severe] swelling, and he put himself forward in the sight of all and said to Paul: "Nothing is impossible with God, but especially with Him whom you preach; for when He came, He healed many, even that God whose servant you are. Behold, I, and my wife, and my children, we cast ourselves at your feet, so that I may also believe as you have believed on the living God."

2. Paul said to him: "I will not restore you for reward, but through the Name of Jesus Christ you will become whole in the presence of all these." And he touched his body, drawing his hand downwards: and his belly opened, and much water ran from him, and … he fell down like a dead man, so that some said: "It is better for him to die than to continue in pain." But when Paul had quieted the people, he took his hand, and raised him up, and asked him, saying, "Hermocrates, what do you desire?" And he said: "[That] I would eat." And he took a loaf and gave him to eat. And in that hour, he was [made] whole and received the grace of the seal in the LORD—he and his wife.

3. But his son Hermippus was angry with Paul, and he sought for a set time wherein to rise up with them of his own age and destroy him. For he wished that his father should not be healed but should die, so that he might soon be master of his goods. But Dion, his younger son, heard Paul gladly.

4. Now all they that were with [Hermippus] took counsel to fight against Paul, so that Hermippus … and sought to kill him … Dion fell down and died: but Hermippus watered Dion with his tears.

5. But Hermocrates mourned grievously, for he loved Dion more than his other son. [Yet] he sat at Paul's feet and forgot that Dion was dead. But when Dion was dead, his mother Nympha tore her clothes, and went to Paul, and set herself before the face of her husband Hermocrates and of Paul. And when Paul saw her, he was frightened and said: "Why are you thus, Nympha?" But she said to him: "Dion is dead"; and the whole multitude wept when they beheld her. And Paul looked on the people that mourned and sent young men, saying to them: "Go and bring me him here." And they went: but Hermippus caught hold of the body [of Dion] in the street and cried out…

6. …the word in him. But a messenger of the LORD had said to him in the night: "Paul, today you have a great conflict against your body, but God, the Father of His Son Jesus Christ, will protect you." When Paul had arisen, he went to his brothers, and remained [[sorrowful]], saying, "What does this vision mean?" And while Paul thought on this, he saw Hermippus coming, having a sword drawn in his hand, and with him many other young men with staffs. And Paul said to them: "I am not a robber, neither a murderer. The God of all things, the Father of Christ, will turn your hands backward, and your sword into its sheath, and your strength into weakness: for I am a servant of God, [though I am] alone, and a stranger, and small, and of no reputation among the nations. But You, O God, look down on their counsel and do not allow me to be brought to nothing by them."

7. And when Hermippus ran on Paul with his sword drawn, he [immediately] ceased to see, so that he cried out aloud, saying, "My dear comrades, do not forget your friend Hermippus. For I have sinned, O Paul; I have pursued after innocent blood. Learn, you foolish and you of understanding, that this world is nothing, gold is nothing, all money is nothing: I that gorged myself with all manner of goods am now a beggar and beggar of you all! Listen to me, all you my companions, and everyone that dwells in Myra. I have mocked at a man who has saved my father. I have mocked at a man who has raised up my brother … I have mocked at a man who … without doing me any evil. But plead with him: behold, he has saved my father and raised up my brother; he is therefore able to save me also." But Paul stood there weeping both before God, for that He heard him quickly, and before man, for that the proud was brought low. And he turned himself and went up…

8. But the young men took [hold of] the feet, and bore Hermippus, and brought him to the place where Paul was, and laid him before the door, and went to their house. And when they were gone, a great multitude came to the house of Hermocrates; and another great multitude entered in, to see whether Hermippus was shut up there. And Hermippus begged everyone that went in, that they would plead with Paul, with him. But they that went in saw Hermocrates and Nympha, how they rejoiced greatly at the raising up of Dion, and distributed victuals and money to the widows for his recovery. And they beheld their son Hermippus in the state of this second affliction, and how he took hold on the feet of everyone, and on the feet of his parents also, and begged them, as one of the strangers, that he might be healed.

9. And his parents were troubled and lamented to everyone that came in, so that some said: "Why do these weep? For Dion has arisen." But Hermocrates possessed goods … and brought the value of the goods, and took it and distributed it. And Hermocrates, troubled in mind and desiring that they might be satisfied, said: "Brothers, let us leave the food … and occupy ourselves … Hermocrates." And immediately Nympha cried out in great affliction to Paul … they said: "Nympha, Hermocrates calls on God … that Hermippus may see and cease to grieve, for he has resisted Christ and his minister." But they and Paul prayed to God. And when Hermippus recovered his sight, he turned himself to his mother Nympha and said to her: "Paul came to me and laid his hand on me while I wept, and in that hour I saw all things clearly." And she took his hand and led him to the widows and Paul. But while Paul wept bitterly, Hermippus gave thanks, saying to them: "Everyone that believes will…"

10. …concord and peace … Amen. And when Paul had confirmed the brothers that were in Myra, he departed to Sidon.

THE FOURTH ACT

1. Now when Paul had departed from Myra and would go to Sidon, there was great sadness of the brothers that were in Pisidia and Pamphylia, because they yearned after his word and his holy appearance in Christ; so that some from Perga followed Paul, namely Thrasymachus and Cleon with their wives Aline and Chrysa, Cleon's wife. And on the way they nourished Paul: and they were eating their bread under a tree. And as he was about to say, "Amen," there came … "… table of devils … he dies therefore, but everyone that believes on Jesus Christ who has saved us from all defilement, and all uncleanness, and all evil thoughts, he will be manifest."

2. And they drew near to the table … stood … a mighty idol. And an old man … stood up among them, saying to them: "You men, wait a little and see what befalls the priests which would draw near to our gods: for truly when our fellow-citizen Charinus listened and would … against the gods, he and his father died. And thereon also died Xanthus, Chrysa, and [[Hermocrates]], sick with swelling, and his wife Nympha."

3. "…after the manner of strange men. Why do you presume to do that which is not right? Or have you not heard of that which came to pass, which God brought on Sodom and Gomorrah, because they robbed … after the manner of strangers and of women? God did not … them but cast them down into Hades. Now therefore, we are not men of this fashion that you say, nor such as you think, but we are preachers of the living God and His Beloved. But that you may not marvel, understand … the miracles which bear witness for us." But they did not listen to him, but took the men and put them into the temple of Apollo, to keep them until the next day, whereon they assembled the whole city. And many and costly were the victuals which they gave them.

4. But Paul, who was fasting now the third day, testified all night long, being troubled, and struck his face and said: "O God, look down on their threatenings, and do not allow us to slide, and do not let our adversaries cast us down, but save us and bring down quickly Your righteousness on us." And as Paul cast himself down, with the brothers, Thrasymachus and Cleon, then the temple fell … so that they that belonged to the temple and the magistrates that were set over it … others of them in the … for [[the one part]] fell down … fell down … all around, in the midst of the two parts. And they went in and beheld what had happened, and marveled that … in their … and that the … rejoiced over the falling of the temple. And they cried out, saying, "Truly these are the works of the men of a mighty God!" And they departed and proclaimed in the city: "Apollo the god of the Sidonians has fallen—and half of his temple." And all the dwellers in the city ran to the temple and saw Paul and them that were with him, how they wept at this temptation, that they were made a spectacle for all men. But the multitude cried out: "Bring them into the theater." And the magistrates came to fetch them; and they groaned bitterly with one soul.

5. "… through me. Consider … Egyptians … and they…" … But the multitude … and followed after Paul, crying: "Praise be to the God … who has sent Paul … that we should not … of death." But Theudes … and prayed at Paul's feet and embraced his feet, that he should give him the seal in the LORD. But he commanded them to go to Tyre … in health, and they put Paul [[in a ship]] and went with him.

THE FIFTH ACT

1. Now when Paul was entered to Tyre, there came a multitude of Jews … in to him. These … and they heard the mighty works … They marveled … Amphion … saying … in … Chrysippus … devil with him … many … When Paul came … he said: "He … God and will not be an evil spirit … in Amphion … through the evil spirit … without anyone's having …" … she said to him: "Save me so that I do not die." And while the multitude … then arose the other evil spirit … And the devils immediately fled away. And when the multitude saw this, by the power of God, they praised Him who had given such power to Paul.

2. And there was there one by name … who had a son born to him who was mute.
3. "… I preach the good news of the Savior … Son of God."
4. "… for that which we say comes to pass immediately. Behold, we will bring him here to you, so that he may … you, to hear the truth of your …
5. "… On God whose desire has come to pass in him, this is the wise man … the Father and He has sent Jesus Christ."
6. "… turned toward the east. Moses … in Syria … in Cyrene …"
7. "Again, I say to you … I, that do the works … that a man is not justified by the Law, but that he is justified by the works of righteousness, and he … liberty … and the yoke … all flesh … and everyone confess that Jesus Christ is the glory of the Father."
8. "… is not water in him, but … being water, I am not hungry but I am thirsty; I am not … but not to … to permit them, to be [[devoured]] by wild beasts, not to be able … from the earth, but not to allow them to be burnt by fire, are these things of the present age testified, he which was a persecutor …"
9. "… the Law of God which is called … who walks here before them, has he not followed us throughout all the cities?" "… And when … he turned himself toward the east after this … such words, neither does he preach as you preach them, O Paul, that you may not …"
10. "You are in the presence of Jerusalem, but I trust in the LORD that you will …"
11. "For since the day when … persecuted the apostles which were … out of Jerusalem, I hid myself, so that I might have comfort, and we nourish them which stand, through the word according to the promise of His grace. I have fallen into many troubles and have subjected myself to the Law, as for your sakes. But I thought by night and by day in my trouble on Jesus Christ, waiting for Him as a lamb … when they crucified Him, He did not … did not resist … was not troubled."
12. But … was troubled because of the questioning that had come on Peter … and he cried out, saying, "Truly, God is one, and there is no God beside Him: one also is Jesus Christ, His Son, whom we … this, whom You preach, did we crucify, whom … expect in great glory, but you say that He is God and Judge of the living and the dead, the King of the ages, for in the … form of man."

THE SIXTH ACT

1. "For since … the mine, there has not … nothing good has happened to my house." And he advised that the men which were to throw Frontina down, should also throw Paul down with her, alive. Now Paul knew these things, but he worked fasting, in great cheerfulness, for two days with the prisoners. They commanded that on the third day the men … should bring forth Frontina: and the whole city followed after her. And Firmilla and Longinus lamented, and the soldiers … But the prisoners carried the bier. And when Paul saw the great mourning with the daughter and eight … Paul alive with the daughter. But when Paul had taken the daughter in his arms, he groaned to the Lord Jesus Christ because of the sorrow of Firmilla and cast himself on his knees in the mire … praying for Frontina with her in united prayer. In that hour Frontina arose. And the whole multitude was afraid and fled. Paul took the hand of the daughter and led her through the city to the house of Longinus, and the whole multitude said with one voice: "God is one, who has made heaven and earth, who has granted the life of the daughter in the presence of Paul. …" … a loaf. And he gave thanks to him. … to Philippi.

THE SEVENTH ACT
(3 CORINTHIANS)

[THEY] PRAYED THAT A MESSENGER BE SENT TO PHILIPPI. FOR THE CORINTHIANS WERE IN GREAT TROUBLE CONCERNING PAUL, THAT HE WOULD DEPART OUT OF THE WORLD BEFORE IT WAS TIME. FOR THERE WERE CERTAIN MEN WHO CAME TO CORINTH, SIMON AND CLEOBIUS, SAYING [THAT] THERE IS NO RESURRECTION OF THE FLESH, BUT THAT OF THE SPIRIT ONLY; AND THAT THE BODY OF MAN IS NOT THE CREATION OF GOD; AND ALSO CONCERNING THE WORLD, THAT GOD DID NOT CREATE IT, AND THAT GOD DOES NOT KNOW THE WORLD, AND THAT JESUS CHRIST WAS NOT CRUCIFIED, BUT IT WAS [ONLY] AN APPEARANCE, AND THAT LIE, [SAYING HE] WAS NOT BORN OF MARY, NOR OF THE SEED OF DAVID. AND IN A WORD, THERE WERE MANY THINGS WHICH THEY HAD TAUGHT IN CORINTH, DECEIVING MANY OTHER MEN, [AND DECEIVING] THEMSELVES. WHEN THEREFORE THE CORINTHIANS HEARD THAT PAUL WAS AT PHILIPPI, THEY SENT A LETTER TO PAUL, TO MACEDONIA, BY THE DEACONS THREPTUS AND EUTYCHUS. AND THE LETTER WAS AFTER THIS MANNER:

CHAPTER 1

[1]Stephanus and the elders that are with him, even Daphnus, and Eubulus, and Theophilus, and Zenon, to Paul their perpetual brother: Greetings in the LORD. [2]There have come to Corinth two men, Simon and Cleobius, which are overthrowing the faith of many with evil words, [3]which you [must] prove and examine: [4]for we have never heard such words from you nor from the other apostles: [5]but all that we have received from you or from them, that do we hold fast. [6]Since therefore the LORD has had mercy on us, that while you are still in the flesh we may hear these things again from you; [7]if it be possible, either come to us or write to us. [8]For we believe, according as it has been revealed to Theonoe, that the LORD has delivered you out of the hand of the lawless one. [9]Now the things which these men say and teach are these: [10]They say that we must not use the prophets, [11]and that God is not almighty, [12]and that there will be no resurrection of the flesh, [13]and that man was not made by God, [14]and that Christ has not come in the flesh, neither was born of Mary, [15]and that the world is not of God, but of the messengers. [16]Therefore, brother, please use all diligence to come to us, that the assembly of the Corinthians may remain without offense, and the madness of these men may be made plain. Farewell—always in the LORD.

CHAPTER 2

[1]The deacons Threptus and Eutychus brought the letter to Philippi, [2]so that Paul received it, being in bonds because of Stratonice the wife of Apollophanes, and he forgot his bonds, and was severely afflicted, [3]and cried out, saying, "It were better for me to die and to be with the LORD, than to continue in the flesh and to hear such things and the calamities of false doctrine, so that trouble comes on trouble. [4]And over and above this so great affliction I am in bonds and behold these evils whereby the devices of Satan are accomplished." [5]Paul therefore, in great affliction, wrote a letter, answering thus:

CHAPTER 3

[1]Paul, a prisoner of Jesus Christ, to the brothers which are in Corinth: Greetings. [2]Being in the midst of many tribulations, I do not marvel if the teachings of the evil one run abroad apace. [3]For my Lord Jesus Christ will hasten His coming and will set at nothing them that falsify His words. [4]For I delivered to you in the beginning the things which I received of the holy apostles which were before me, who were at all times with Jesus Christ: [5]namely, that our Lord Jesus Christ was born of Mary which is of the seed of David according to the flesh, the Holy Spirit being sent forth from Heaven from the Father to her by the messenger Gabriel, [6]that He might come down into this world and redeem all flesh by His flesh, and raise us up from the dead in the flesh, like as He has shown to us in Himself for an example. [7]And because man was formed by His Father, [8]therefore he was sought when he was lost, that he might be restored by adoption. [9]For to this end God Almighty, who made the heavens and earth, first sent the prophets to the Jews, that they might be drawn away from their sins. [10]For He designed to save the house of Israel: therefore, He conferred a portion of the Spirit of Christ on the prophets and sent them to the Jews first, and they proclaimed the true worship of God for a long space of time. [11]But the prince of iniquity, desiring to be God, laid hands on them and slew them, and bound all flesh by evil lusts [[and the end of the world by judgment drew near]]. [12]But God Almighty, who is righteous, would not cast away His own creation, but had compassion on them from Heaven, [13]and sent His Spirit into Mary in Galilee, [[[14]who believed with all her heart and received the Holy Spirit in her womb, that Jesus might come into the world,]] [15]that by that flesh whereby that wicked one had brought in death, by the same he should be shown to be overcome. [16]For by His own body Jesus Christ saved all flesh [[and restored it to life]], [17]that He might show forth the temple of righteousness in His body. [18]In whom we are

saved [[*or* in whom, if we believe, we are set free]]. ¹⁹Therefore, they are not children of righteousness but children of wrath, who reject the wisdom of God, saying that the heavens and the earth and all that are in them are not the work of God. ²⁰Therefore, they are children of wrath, for they are cursed, following the teaching of the serpent, ²¹whom you drive out from you and flee from their doctrine. [[²²for you are not children of disobedience, but of the well-beloved Assembly. ²³Therefore is the time of the resurrection proclaimed to all.]] ²⁴And as for that which they say—that there is no resurrection of the flesh—they indeed will have no resurrection to life, but to judgment, ²⁵because they do not believe in Him that is risen from the dead, not believing nor understanding, ²⁶for they do not know, O Corinthians, the seeds of wheat or of other seeds, how they are cast bare into the earth and are corrupted and rise again by the will of God with bodies, and clothed. ²⁷And not only that [body] which is cast in rises again, but manifold more blessing itself. ²⁸And if we must not take an example from seeds only, but from more noble bodies, ²⁹you know how Jonah the son of Amathi, when he would not preach to them of Nineveh, but fled, was swallowed by the sea-monster; ³⁰and after three days and three nights God heard the prayer of Jonah out of the lowest [part of] Hades, and no part of him was consumed, not even a hair nor an eyelash. ³¹How much more, O you of little faith, will He raise up you that have believed in Christ Jesus, like as He Himself arose. ³²Likewise also, a dead man was cast on the bones of the prophet Elisha by the sons of Israel, and he arose—both body, and soul, and bones, and spirit; how much more will you which have been cast on the body, and bones, and Spirit of the LORD [[*or* how much more, O you of little faith, will you which have been cast on Him]] arise again in that day having your flesh whole, even as He arose? [[³³Likewise also, concerning the prophet Elijah, he raised up the widow's son from death: how much more will the Lord Jesus raise you up from death at the sound of the trumpet, in the twinkling of an eye? For He has showed us an example in His own body.]] ³⁴If then, you receive any other doctrine, God will be witness against you; and let no man trouble me, ³⁵for I bear these bonds that I may win Christ, and I therefore bear His marks in my body that I may attain to the resurrection of the dead. ³⁶And whoever receives the rule which He has received by the blessed prophets and the holy good news, will receive a repayment from the LORD, and when he rises from the dead will obtain continuous life. ³⁷But whoever transgresses these things, with him is the fire, and with them that walk in like manner [[*or* with them that go before in the same way, who are men without God]], ³⁸which are a generation of vipers, ³⁹whom you reject in the power of the LORD, ⁴⁰and peace, grace, and love will be with you.

ACTS OF PAUL

THE EIGHTH ACT

[None of The Eighth Acts remains, but its basic premise can be reconstructed from the later Acts of Titus and quotes from Hippolytus. The interpolation below comes from the Acts of Titus.]

1. They departed from Crete and came to Asia: and at Ephesus twelve thousand believed at the teaching of the holy Paul: there he also fought with beasts, being thrown to a lion....

THE NINTH ACT

1. "The grace of the LORD will walk with me until I have fulfilled all the dispensations which will come on me with patience." But they were sorrowful and fasted. And Cleobius was in the Spirit and said to them: "Brothers, the LORD will allow Paul to fulfill every dispensation and thereafter will allow him to go up to Jerusalem. But thereafter will be ... in much instruction, and knowledge, and sowing of the word, so that men will envy him, and so he will depart out of this world." But when Paul and the brothers heard this, they lifted up their voices, saying,...
2. But the Spirit came on Myrte so that she said to them: "Brothers ... and look on this sign, that you ... For Paul the servant of the LORD will save many in Rome, so that of them will be no number, and he will manifest himself more than all the faithful. Thereafter will ... of the Lord Jesus Christ come ... a great grace is ... at Rome." And this is the manner wherein the Spirit spoke to Myrte. And everyone took the bread, and they were in joy, according to the custom of the fast, through... and the Psalms of David and ... he rejoiced.
3. to Rome ... the brothers ... grieved ... took the bread ... praised the LORD ... were very sorrowful. "... the LORD ... risen ... Jesus," Paul said to him.... they greeted.

THE MARTYRDOM OF PAUL

1. Now there were awaiting Paul at Rome Luke from Galatia and Titus from Dalmatia: whom when Paul saw, he was glad and hired a granary outside Rome, wherein with the brothers he taught the word of truth, and he became noised abroad and many souls were added to the LORD, so that there was a rumor throughout all Rome, and many people came to him from the household of Caesar, believing, and there was great joy. And a certain Patroclus, a cupbearer of Caesar, came in the evening to the granary, and not being able because of the pressing [crowd] to enter in to Paul, he sat in a high window and listened to him teaching the word of God. But whereas the evil Devil envied the love of the brothers, Patroclus fell down from the window and died, and it was immediately told to Nero. But Paul, perceiving it by the Spirit said: "Men and brothers, the evil one has gained an opportunity to tempt you: go out of the house and you will find a young man fallen from the height and now ready to give up the spirit; take him up and bring him here to me." And they went and brought him; and when the people saw it, they were troubled. But Paul said: "Now, brothers, let your faith appear; all of you come and let us weep to our Lord Jesus Christ, so that this young man may live and we continue in quietness." And when all had lamented, the young man received his spirit again, and they set him on a beast and sent him back alive, together with the rest that were of Caesar's household.
2. But Nero, when he heard of the death of Patroclus, was severely grieved, and when he came in from the bath, he commanded another to be set over the wine. But his servants told him, saying, "Caesar, Patroclus lives and stands at the table." And Caesar, hearing that Patroclus lived, was frightened and would not go in. But when he went in, he saw Patroclus, and was beside himself, and said: "Patroclus, you live?" And he said: "I live, Caesar." And he said: "Who is he that made you to live?" And the young man, full of the mind of faith, said: "Christ Jesus, the King of the ages." And Caesar was troubled and said: "Will He, then, be King of the ages and overthrow all kingdoms?" Patroclus says to him: "Yes, he overthrows all kingdoms, and He alone will be forever, and there will be no kingdom that will escape Him." And he struck him on the face and said: "Patroclus, are you also a soldier of that King?" And he said: "Yes, lord Caesar, for He raised me when I was dead." And Barsabas Justus of the broad feet, and Urion the Cappadocian, and Festus the Galatian, Caesar's chief men, said: "We are also soldiers of the King of the ages." And he shut them up in prison, having grievously tormented them, whom he loved much, and commanded the soldiers of the Great King to be sought out, and he set forth a decree to this effect: that all that were found to be Christians and soldiers of Christ should be slain.
3. And among many others, Paul was also brought, bound: to whom all his fellow-prisoners gave heed; so that Caesar perceived that he was over the camp. And he said to him: "You that are the Great King's man, but my prisoner, how did you think you would come by stealth into the government of the Romans and levy soldiers out of my province?" But Paul, filled with the Holy Spirit, said before them all: "O Caesar, not only out of your province do we levy soldiers, but out of the whole world. For so has it been ordained to us, that no man should be refused who wishes to serve my King—even if it is also you to serve Him. It is not wealth nor the splendor that is now in this life that will save you; but if you submit and pray to Him, you will be saved; for one day, He will fight against the [whole] world with fire." And when Caesar heard that, he commanded all the prisoners to be burned with fire, but Paul to be beheaded after the law of the Romans. But Paul did not keep silent

concerning the word, but communicated with Longus the prefect and Cestus the centurion. Therefore, Nero went on in Rome, slaying many Christians without a hearing, by the working of the evil one, so that the Romans stood before the palace and cried, "Enough, Caesar! For the men are our own! You destroy the strength of the Romans!" Then at that, he was persuaded and ceased, and he commanded that no man should touch any Christian, until he should learn thoroughly concerning them.

4. Then Paul was brought to him after the decree; and he abode by his word that he should be beheaded. And Paul said: "Caesar, it is not for a short time that I live for my King; and if you behead me, this I will do: I will arise and show myself to you that I am not dead but live for my Lord Jesus Christ, who comes to judge the world." But Longus and Cestus said to Paul: "Where do you have this King, that you believe in Him and will not change your mind, even to death?" And Paul communicated to them the word and said: "You men that are in this ignorance and error, change your mind and be saved from the fire that comes on all the world: for we do not serve, as you suppose, a king that comes from the earth, but from Heaven—the living God, who because of the iniquities that are done in this world, comes as a Judge; and blessed is that man who will believe in Him and will live forever when He comes to burn the world and purge it thoroughly." Then they, begging him, said: "We beg you, help us, and we will let you go." But he answered and said: "I am not a deserter of Christ, but a lawful soldier of the living God: if I had known that I should die, O Longus and Cestus, I would have done it, but seeing that I live to God and love myself, I go to the LORD, to come with Him in the glory of His Father." They say to him: "How then will we live when you are beheaded?"

5. And while they yet spoke thus, Nero sent one Parthenius and Pheres to see if Paul were already beheaded; and they found him still alive. And he called them to him and said: "Believe on the living God, who raises me and all them that believe on Him from the dead." And they said: "We go now to Nero; but when you die and rise again, then we will believe on your God." And as Longus and Cestus pleaded with him yet more concerning salvation, he says to them: "Come quickly to my grave in the morning and you will find two men praying, Titus and Luke. They will give you the seal in the LORD." Then Paul stood with his face toward the east, and lifted up his hands toward [the] sky, and prayed a long time, and in his prayer he conversed in the Hebrew tongue with the fathers, and then stretched forth his neck without speaking. And when the executioner struck off his head, milk spurted on the cloak of the soldier. And the soldier and all that were there present when they saw it marveled and glorified God who had given such glory to Paul: and they went and told Caesar what was done.

6. And when he heard it, while he marveled long and was in perplexity, Paul came around the ninth hour, when many philosophers and the centurion were standing with Caesar, and stood before them all and said: "Caesar, behold, I, Paul, the soldier of God, am not dead, but live in my God. But many calamities will happen to you and great punishment, you wretched man, because you have unjustly shed the blood of the righteous, not many days from now." And having said this, Paul departed from him. But Nero, hearing it and being greatly troubled, commanded the prisoners to be freed—and Patroclus also, and Barsabas, and them that were with him.

7. And as Paul charged them, Longus and Cestus the centurion went early in the morning and approached with fear to the grave of Paul. And when they had come there, they saw two men praying, and Paul between them, so that they, beholding the wondrous marvel, were amazed, but Titus and Luke being stricken with the fear of man when they saw Longus and Cestus coming toward them, turned to flee. But they pursued after them, saying, "We pursue you not for death but for life, so that you may give it to us, as Paul promised us, whom we saw just now standing between you and praying." And when they heard that, Titus and Luke rejoiced and gave them the seal in the LORD, glorifying the God and Father of our Lord Jesus Christ. To whom be glory, world without end. Amen.

ACTS OF PETER

Written in Greek, probably by a resident of Asia Minor, not later than AD 200. The author has read the Acts of John very carefully and modeled his language on them. One of the earliest of the apocryphal acts of the apostles, the Acts of Peter reports a contest between Simon Magus and the apostle Peter in Rome and concludes with Peter's martyrdom. The version here is from Latin, the most expansive extant manuscript. The Acts of Peter is undoubtedly pseudepigraphal, as evidenced by the language and style of Paul (Ch. 2), unlike any of his canonical epistles or recorded words in the Acts of the Apostles. This apocryphal work also promotes a sort of sinless perfectionism disparate from the genuine Pauline teaching of sola fide.

CHAPTER 1

¹At the time when Paul was sojourning in Rome and confirming many in the faith, it also came to pass that one, by name Candida, the wife of Quartus that was over the prisons, heard Paul and paid heed to his words and believed. ²And when she had instructed her husband, and he also believed, Quartus allowed Paul to go wherever he would, away from the city: to whom Paul said: "If it is the will of God, He will reveal it to me." ³And after Paul had fasted three days and asked of the LORD that which should be profitable for him, he saw a vision, even the LORD saying to him: "Arise, Paul, and become a physician in your body to them that are in Spain." ⁴He, therefore, having related to the brothers what God had commanded, doubting nothing, prepared himself to set forth from the city. ⁵But when Paul was about to depart, there was great weeping throughout all the brotherhood, because they thought that they should see Paul no more, so that they even tore their clothes. ⁶For they had in mind also how Paul had oftentimes contended with the doctors of the Jews and confuted them, saying, "Christ, on whom your fathers laid hands, abolished their Sabbaths, and fasts, and holy days, and circumcision, and the doctrines of men and the rest of the traditions He has abolished." ⁷But the brothers lamented [and adjured] Paul by the coming of our Lord Jesus Christ, that he should not be absent more than a year, saying, "We know your love for your brothers; do not forget us when you have come there, neither begin to forsake us, as little children without a mother." ⁸And when they begged him long with tears, there came a sound from Heaven and a great voice, saying, "Paul the servant of God is chosen to minister all the days of his life: by the hands of Nero, the ungodly and wicked man, he will be perfected before your eyes." ⁹And a very great fear fell on the brothers because of the voice which came from Heaven: and they were confirmed yet more in the faith.

CHAPTER 2

¹Now they brought to Paul bread and water for the sacrifice, so that he might make prayer and distribute it to everyone. ²Among whom it happened that a woman named Rufina desired, she also, to receive communion at the hands of Paul: to whom Paul, filled with the Spirit of God, said as she drew near: "Rufina, you do not come worthily to the altar of God, arising from beside one that is not your husband but an adulterer, and attempt to receive the communion of God. ³For behold, Satan will trouble your heart and cast you down in the sight of all them that believe in the LORD, so that they which see and believe may know that they have believed in the living God, the searcher of hearts. ⁴But if you convert from your act, He is faithful, and is able to blot out your sin, and set you free from this sin: but if you do not convert, while you are yet in the body, devouring fire and outer darkness will receive you forever." ⁵And immediately Rufina fell down, being stricken with palsy from her head to the nails of her feet, and she had no power to speak, for her tongue was

bound. ⁶And when both they that believed [in the faith] and the neophytes saw it, they beat their breasts, remembering their old sins, and mourned and said: "We do not know if God will forgive the former sins which we have committed." ⁷Then Paul called for silence and said: "Men and brothers, which have now begun to believe on Christ, if you do not continue in your former works of the tradition of your fathers, and keep yourselves from all guile, and wrath, and fierceness, and adultery, and defilement, and from pride, and envy, and contempt, and enmity, Jesus the living God will forgive you of what you did in ignorance. ⁸Therefore, you servants of God, arm yourselves—each one in your inner man—with peace, patience, gentleness, faith, charity, knowledge, wisdom, love of the brothers, hospitality, mercy, abstinence, chastity, kindness, justice: then you will have for your guide everlastingly the First-Begotten of all creation, and will have strength in peace with our Lord." ⁹And when they had heard these things from Paul, they begged him to pray for them. ¹⁰And Paul lifted up his voice and said: "O eternal God, God of the heavens, God of unspeakable majesty, who has established all things by Your word, who has bound on all the world the chain of Your grace, Father of Your holy Son Jesus Christ, we together pray through Your Son Jesus Christ: strengthen the souls which were unbelieving before, but are now faithful. ¹¹Once I was a blasphemer, now I am blasphemed; once I was a persecutor, now I suffer persecution of others; once I was the enemy of Christ, now I pray that I may be His friend: for I trust in His promise and in His mercy; I account myself faithful and that I have received forgiveness of my former sins. ¹²Therefore, I exhort you also, brothers, to believe in the LORD, the Father Almighty, and to put all your trust in our Lord Jesus Christ, His Son, believing in Him, and no man will be able to uproot you from His promise. ¹³Therefore, bow your knees together and commend me to the LORD, who am about to set forth to another nation, that His grace may go before me and dispose my journey well, that He may receive His holy and believing vessels, that they, giving thanks for my preaching of the word of the LORD, may be well-grounded in the faith." ¹⁴But the brothers wept long and prayed to the LORD with Paul, saying, "Lord Jesus Christ, be with Paul and restore him to us whole: for we know our weakness which is in us even to this day."

CHAPTER 3

¹And a great multitude of women were kneeling, and praying, and imploring Paul; and they kissed his feet and accompanied him to the harbor. ²But Dionysius and Balbus, of Asia, knights of Rome, and illustrious men, and a senator by name Demetrius, abode by Paul on his right hand and said: "Paul, I would desire to leave the city if I were not a magistrate, so that I might not depart from you." ³Also from Caesar's house Cleobius, and Iphitus, and Lysimachus, and Aristaeus, and two matrons, Berenice and Philostrate, with Narcissus the elder, accompanied him to the harbor: but whereas a storm of the sea came on, [Narcissus] sent the brothers back to Rome, that if any would, he might come down and hear Paul until he set sail: and hearing that, the brothers went up to the city. ⁴And when they told the brothers that had remained in the city, and the report was spread abroad, some on beasts, and some on foot, and others by way of the Tiber came down to the harbor, and were confirmed in the faith for three days, and on the fourth day until the fifth hour, praying together with Paul, and making the offering: ⁵and they put everything that was necessary on the ship, and delivered him two young men, believers, to sail with him, and bade him farewell in the LORD, and returned to Rome.

CHAPTER 4

¹Now after a few days, there was a great commotion in the midst of the Assembly, for some said that they had seen wonderful works done by a certain man whose name was Simon, and that he was at Aricia, and they added further that he said he was a great power of God and without God he did nothing. ²"Is this not the Christ? But we believe in Him whom Paul preached to us; for by Him we have seen the dead raised, and men delivered from various sicknesses: but this man seeks contention, we know it, for there is no small stirring made among us. ³Perhaps he also will now enter into Rome; for yesterday they pressed him with great acclamations, saying to him: You are God in Italy, you are the savior of the Romans: hurry quickly to Rome. ⁴But he spoke to the people with a shrill voice, saying, Tomorrow, about the seventh hour, you will see me fly over the gate of the city in the form wherein you now see me speaking to you. ⁵Therefore, brothers, if it seems good to you, let us go and await carefully the issue of the matter." ⁶They all therefore ran together and came to the gate. And when it was the seventh hour, behold, dust was suddenly seen in the sky far off, like a smoke shining with rays stretching far from it. And when he drew near to the gate, suddenly he was not seen: and thereafter he appeared, standing in the midst of the people; whom they all worshiped, and took knowledge that he was the same one that was seen by them the day before. ⁷And the brothers were not a little offended among themselves, seeing, moreover, that Paul was not at Rome, neither Timotheus nor Barnabas, for they had been sent into Macedonia by Paul, and that there was no man to comfort us, to speak nothing of them that had but just become catechumens. ⁸And as Simon exalted himself yet more by the works which he did, and many of them daily called Paul a sorcerer, and others a deceiver, of such a great multitude that had been established in the faith, all fell away except Narcissus the elder, and two women in the lodging of the Bithynians, and four that could no longer go out of their house, but were shut up [day and night]: ⁹these gave themselves to prayer, pleading with the LORD that Paul might return quickly, or some other that should visit His servants, because the Devil had made them fall by his wickedness.

CHAPTER 5

¹And as they prayed and fasted, God was already teaching Peter at Jerusalem of that which should come to pass. ²For whereas the twelve years which the Lord Christ had instructed him were fulfilled, He showed him a vision after this manner, saying to him: "Peter, that Simon the sorcerer whom you cast out of Judea, convicting him, has again come before you at Rome. And that you will know shortly: for all that believed in Me, Satan has made to fall by his craft and working: whose power Simon approves himself to be. ³But do not delay: set forth the next day, and there you will find a ship ready, setting sail for Italy, and within a few days I will show you My grace which has in it no grudging." ⁴Peter then, admonished by the vision, related it to the brothers without delay, saying, "It is necessary for me to go up to Rome to fight with the enemy and adversary of the LORD and of our brothers." ⁵And he went down to Caesarea and embarked quickly in the ship, whereof the ladder was already drawn up, not taking any provision with him. ⁶But the governor of the ship, whose name was Theon, looked on Peter and said: "Whatsoever we have, all is yours. For what good are we, if we take in a man like to ourselves who is in an uncertain situation and do not share all that we have with you? But only let us have a prosperous voyage." ⁷But Peter, giving him thanks for that which he offered, himself fasted while he was in the ship, sorrowful in mind and again consoling himself because God accounted him worthy to be a minister in His service. ⁸And after a few days, the governor of the ship rose up at the hour of his dinner and asked Peter to eat with him, and he said to him: "O you, whoever you are, I do not know you, but as I reckon, I take you for a servant of God. ⁹For as I was steering my ship at midnight, I perceived the voice of a man from Heaven saying to me: Theon, Theon! And twice it called me by my name and said to me: Among them that sail with you, let Peter be greatly honored by you, for by him will you and the rest be preserved safe without any harm from such a course as you do not hope for." ¹⁰And Peter believed that God would grant to show His providence on the sea to them that were in the ship, and thenceforth Peter began to declare to Theon the mighty works of God, and how the LORD had chosen him from among the apostles, and for what business he sailed to Italy: ¹¹and daily he communicated to him the word of God. And considering him, he perceived by his walk that he was of one mind in the faith and a worthy minister. ¹²Now when there was a calm on the ship in the Adriatic, Theon showed it to Peter, saying to him: "If you will account me worthy, whom you may immerse with the seal of the LORD, you have an opportunity." ¹³For all that were in the ship had fallen asleep, being drunken. ¹⁴And Peter went down by a rope and immersed Theon in

the Name of the Father, and the Son, and the Holy Spirit: and he came up out of the water rejoicing with great joy, and Peter also was glad because God had accounted Theon worthy of His Name. ¹⁵And it came to pass when Theon was immersed, there appeared in the same place a youth shining and beautiful, saying to them: "Peace be to you." ¹⁶And immediately Peter and Theon went up and entered into the cabin; and Peter took bread and gave thanks to the LORD who had accounted him worthy of His holy ministry, and for that the youth had appeared to them, saying, "Peace be to you." ¹⁷And he said: "You are alone the Holy One; it is You that have appeared to us, O God Jesus Christ, and in Your Name this man has now been washed and sealed with Your holy seal. Therefore, in Your Name I impart to him Your communion, so that he may be Your perfect servant without blame forever." ¹⁸And as they feasted and rejoiced in the LORD, suddenly there came a wind, not vehement but moderate, at the ship's prow, and it did not cease for six days and as many nights, until they came to Puteoli.

CHAPTER 6

¹And when they had arrived at Puteoli, Theon leapt out of the ship and went to the inn where he was accustomed to lodge, to prepare to receive Peter. ²Now he with whom he lodged was one by name Ariston, which always feared the LORD, and because of the Name, Theon entrusted himself with him. ³And when he had come to the inn and saw Ariston, Theon said to him: "God who has accounted you worthy to serve Him has communicated His grace to me also by His holy servant Peter, who has now sailed with me from Judea, being commanded by our Lord to come to Italy." ⁴And when he heard that, Ariston fell on Theon's neck, and embraced him, and begged him to bring him to the ship and show him Peter. ⁵For Ariston said that since Paul set forth to Spain, there was no man of the brothers with whom he could refresh himself, and, moreover, "a certain Jew had broken into the city, named Simon, and with his charms of sorcery and his wickedness he has made all the brotherhood fall away this way and that, so that I also fled from Rome, expecting the coming of Peter, for Paul had told us of him, and I also have seen many things in a vision. ⁶Now, therefore, I believe in my Lord that He will build His ministry up again, for all this deceit will be rooted out from among His servants. For our Lord Jesus Christ is faithful, who is able to restore our minds." ⁷And when Theon heard these things from Ariston, who wept, his spirit was raised yet more, and he was strengthened [even] more, because he perceived that he had believed on the living God. ⁸But when they came together to the ship, Peter looked on them and smiled, being filled with the Spirit; so that Ariston, falling on his face at Peter's feet, said thus: "Brother and lord, that has part in the holy mysteries and shows the right way which is in the Lord Jesus Christ our God, who by you has shown to us His coming: we have lost all them whom Paul had delivered to us, by the working of Satan; ⁹but now I trust in the LORD who has commanded you to come to us, sending you as His messenger, that He has accounted us worthy to see His great and wonderful works by your means. ¹⁰I therefore beg you: hurry to the city; for I left the brothers which have stumbled, whom I saw fall into the temptation of the Devil, and fled here, saying to them: Brothers, stand fast in the faith, for it is of necessity that within these two months the mercy of our Lord will bring His servant to you. ¹¹For I had seen a vision, even Paul, saying to me: Ariston, flee out of the city. And when I heard it, I believed without delay and went forth in the LORD, although I had a weakness in my flesh, and came here; ¹²and day after day I stood on the seashore asking the sailors: Has Peter sailed with you? But now through the abundance of the grace of God I implore you: let us go up to Rome without delay, lest the teaching of this wicked man prevails yet further." ¹³And as Ariston said this with tears, Peter gave him his hand and raised him up from the earth, and Peter also groaning, said with tears: "He which tempts all the world by his messengers has prevented us; but He that has power to save His servants from all temptations will quench his deceits and put him beneath the feet of them that have believed in Christ whom we preach." ¹⁴And as they entered in at the gate, Theon implored Peter, saying, "You did not refresh yourself on any day in such a great voyage: and now before such a difficult journey will you immediately set out from the ship? Tarry and refresh yourself, and so will you set forth, for from here to Rome on a pavement of flint I fear lest you be hurt by the shaking." ¹⁵But Peter answered and said to them: "What if it comes to pass that a millstone were hung on me, and likewise on the enemy of our Lord, even as my Lord said to us of any that offended one of the brothers, and I were drowned in the sea? ¹⁶But it might not be only a millstone, but that which is far worse, even that I, which am the enemy of this persecutor of His servants, should die far off from them that have believed on the Lord Jesus Christ." ¹⁷And by no exhortation could Theon prevail to persuade him to tarry there even one day. But Theon himself delivered all that was in the ship to be sold for the price which he thought good, and he followed Peter to Rome, whom Ariston brought to the abode of Narcissus the elder.

CHAPTER 7

¹Now the report was announced throughout the city to the brothers that were dispersed, because of Simon, that he might show him to be a deceiver and a persecutor of good men. ²All the multitude therefore ran together to see the apostle of the LORD cling to Christ. ³And on the first day of the week, when the multitude was assembled to see Peter, Peter began to say with a loud voice: "You men here present that trust in Christ, you that for a short span have suffered temptation, learn for what reason God sent His Son into the world, and why He made Him to be born of the virgin Mary; for would He have done so if not to obtain us some grace or dispensation? ⁴Even because He would take away all offense, and all ignorance, and all the scheming of the Devil—his attempts and his strength with which he prevailed in times past, before our God shined forth in the world. ⁵And whereas men through ignorance fell into death by many diverse sicknesses, Almighty God, moved with compassion, sent His Son into the world. With whom I was; and He walked on the water, whereof I myself remain a witness, and testify that He then worked in the world by signs and wonders, all of which He did." ⁶I confess, dearly-beloved brothers, that I was with Him: yet I denied Him, even our Lord Jesus Christ, and not only once, but three times; for there were evil dogs that had come around me as they did to the LORD's prophets. ⁷And the LORD did not impute it to me, but turned to me and had compassion on the weakness of my flesh, so that afterward I bitterly wept and lamented the weakness of my faith, because I was fooled by the Devil and did not keep in mind the word of my Lord. ⁸And now I say to you, O men and brothers, which are gathered together in the Name of Jesus Christ: against you also has the deceiver Satan aimed his arrows, that you might depart out of the Way. ⁹But do not faint, brothers, neither let your spirit fall, but be strong, and persevere, and do not doubt, for if Satan caused me to stumble, whom the LORD held in great honor, so that I denied the Light of my hope, and if he overthrew me and persuaded me to flee as if I had put my trust in a man, what do you think he will do to you which are but young in the faith? ¹⁰Did you suppose that he would not turn you away to make you enemies of the Kingdom of God and cast you down into perdition by a new deceit? ¹¹For whomsoever he casts out from the hope of our Lord Jesus Christ, he is a son of perdition forever. ¹²Turn yourselves, therefore, brothers, chosen of the LORD, and be strong in God Almighty, the Father of our Lord Jesus Christ, whom no man has seen at any time, neither can see, except he who has believed in Him. And be aware from where this temptation has come on you. ¹³For it is not merely by words that I would convince you that this is Christ whom I preach, but also by deeds and exceedingly great works of power I exhort you by the faith that is in Christ Jesus, that none of you look for any other except Him that was despised and mocked by the Jews, even this Nazarene who was crucified, and died, and the third day rose again."

CHAPTER 8

¹And the brothers converted and implored Peter to fight against Simon, [[who said that he was the Power of God and lodged in the house of Marcellus a senator, whom he had convinced by his charms,]] saying, "Believe us, brother Peter: there was no man among men so wise as this Marcellus. All the widows that trusted in Christ had recourse to him; all the fatherless were fed by him; and what more,

brother? All the poor called Marcellus their supporter, and his house was called the house of the strangers and of the poor, ²and the emperor said to him: I will keep you out of every office, lest you plunder the provinces to give gifts to the Christians. ³And Marcellus answered: All my goods are also yours. And Caesar said to him: They would be mine if you kept them for me; but now they are not mine, for you give them to whomever you will, and I do not know to what vile persons. ⁴Having this, then, before our eyes, brother Peter, we report it to you, how the great mercy of this man is turned to blasphemy; for if he had not turned, neither should we have departed from the holy faith of God our Lord. ⁵And now does this Marcellus in anger convert him of his good deeds, saying, All this substance I have spent in all this time, vainly believing that I gave it for the knowledge of God! ⁶So that if any stranger comes to the door of his house, he strikes him with a staff and commands him be beaten, saying, If only I had not spent so much money on these impostors: and yet more does he say, blaspheming. ⁷But if there abide in you any mercy of our Lord and anything of the goodness of His commandments, aid the error of this man who has done so many charitable deeds for the servants of God." ⁸And Peter, when he perceived this, was stricken with sharp affliction and said: "O the manifold arts and temptations of the Devil! O the plots and schemes of the wicked! ⁹He that nourishes up for himself a mighty fire in the day of wrath—the destruction of simple men, the ravenous wolf, the devourer and scatterer of eternal life! ¹⁰You ensnared the first man in lust and bound him with your old iniquity and with the chain of the flesh: you are wholly the exceedingly bitter fruit of the Tree of Bitterness, who sends diverse lusts on men. ¹⁰You compelled Judas, my fellow disciple and fellow apostle, to do wickedly and deliver up our Lord Jesus Christ, who will therefore punish you. ¹¹You hardened the heart of Herod and inflamed Pharaoh and compelled him to fight against Moses the holy servant of God; you gave boldness to Caiaphas, that he should deliver our Lord Jesus Christ to the unrighteous multitude; ¹²and even until now, you shoot at innocent souls with your poisonous arrows. ¹³You wicked one! Enemy of all men! Be accursed from the Assembly of Him, the Son of the holy God omnipotent; and as a brand cast out of the fire, you will be quenched by the servants of our Lord Jesus Christ. ¹⁴On you let your blackness be turned and on your children, an evil seed; on you be turned your wickedness and your threatenings; on you and your messengers be your temptations—you beginning of malice and bottomless pit of darkness! ¹⁵Let your darkness that you have be with you and with your vessels which you own! ¹⁶Depart from them that will believe in God, depart from the servants of Christ and from them that desire to be His soldiers. ¹⁷Keep to yourself your garments of darkness! Without cause, you knock at other men's doors, which are not yours but of Christ Jesus that keeps them. For you, ravenous wolf, would carry off the sheep that are not yours but of Christ Jesus, who keeps them with all care and diligence.

CHAPTER 9

¹As Peter thus spoke with great sorrow of mind, many were added to them that believed on the LORD. But the brothers pleaded with Peter to join battle with Simon and not allow him to distress the people any longer. ²And without delay, Peter went quickly out of the synagogue and went to the house of Marcellus, where Simon lodged: and many people followed him. ³And when he came to the door, he called the porter and said to him: "Go, say to Simon: Peter, because of whom you fled out of Judea, waits for you at the door." ⁴The porter answered and said to Peter: "Sir, whether you are Peter, I do not know: but I have a command; for he had knowledge that you entered into the city yesterday, and he said to me: Whether it is by day or by night, at whatever hour he comes, say that I am not inside." ⁵And Peter said to the young man: "You have spoken well in reporting that which he compelled you to say." ⁶And Peter turned to the people that followed him and said: "You will now see a great and marvelous wonder." ⁷And Peter, seeing a great dog bound with a strong chain, went to him and untied him, and when he was untied, the dog received a man's voice and said to Peter: "What do you command me to do—you servant of the unspeakable and living God?" ⁸Peter said to him: "Go in and say to Simon in the midst of his company: Peter says to you, Come forth outside, for your sake I have come to Rome—you wicked one and deceiver of simple souls." ⁹And immediately the dog ran and entered in, and rushed into the midst of them that were with Simon, and lifted up his front feet, and in a loud voice said: "You Simon, Peter the servant of Christ who stands at the door says to you: Come forth outside, for your sake I have come to Rome—you most wicked one and deceiver of simple souls." ¹⁰And when Simon heard it, and beheld the incredible sight, he lost the words with which he was deceiving them that stood by, and all of them were amazed.

CHAPTER 10

¹But when Marcellus saw it, he went out to the door, and cast himself at Peter's feet, and said: "Peter, I embrace your feet—you holy servant of the holy God; ²I have sinned greatly: but do not exact my sins, if there is in you the true faith of Christ, whom you preach, if you remember His commandments, to hate no man, to be unkind to no man, as I learned from your fellow apostle Paul; ³do not keep in mind my faults, but pray for me to the LORD, the holy Son of God whom I have provoked to wrath—for I have persecuted His servants—that I may not be delivered with the sins of Simon to eternal fire, who so persuaded me, that I set up a statue to him with this inscription: TO SIMON, THE NEW GOD. ⁴If I knew, O Peter, that you could be won with money, I would give you all my substance: yes, I would give it and despise it, so that I might gain my soul. ⁵If I had sons, I would account them as nothing, if only I might believe in the living God. ⁶But I confess that he would not have deceived me except that he said that he was the Power of God; ⁷yet I will tell you, O most gentle Peter: I was not worthy to hear you—you servant of God—neither was I established in the faith of God which is in Christ; therefore, I was made to stumble. ⁸I plead with you, therefore: do not take poorly that which I am about to say, that Christ our Lord whom you preach in truth said to your fellow apostles in your presence: If you have faith as a grain of mustard seed, you will say to this mountain: Remove yourself, and immediately it will remove itself. ⁹But this Simon said that you, Peter, were without faith when you doubted in the waters. ¹⁰And I have heard that Christ said this also: They that are with Me have not understood Me. ¹¹If, then, you on whom He laid His hands, whom He also chose, doubted, I, therefore, having this witness, convert and take refuge in your prayers. ¹²Receive my soul, which has fallen away from our Lord and from His promise. But I believe that He will have mercy on me who converts. For the Almighty is faithful to forgive me of my sins." ¹³But Peter said with a loud voice: "To You, our Lord, be glory and splendor, O God Almighty, Father of our Lord Jesus Christ. To You be praise, and glory, and honor, world without end. Amen. ¹⁴Because You have now fully strengthened and established us in You in the sight of all, holy Lord, confirm Marcellus, and send Your peace on him and on his house this day: ¹⁵and whatsoever is lost or out of the way, You alone can turn them all again; we implore You, Lord, Shepherd of the sheep that once were scattered, but now will be gathered as one by You. ¹⁶So also receive Marcellus as one of your lambs and no longer permit him to go astray in error or ignorance. Yes, Lord, receive him who with anguish and tears begs You."

CHAPTER 11

¹And as Peter spoke thus and embraced Marcellus, Peter turned himself to the multitude that stood by him and saw someone there that laughed, in whom was a very evil spirit. ²And Peter said to him: "Whosoever you are that laughed, show yourself openly to all that are present." ³And hearing this, the young man ran into the court of the house, and cried out with a loud voice, and dashed himself against the wall, and said: "Peter, there is a great contention between Simon and the dog whom you sent; for Simon says to the dog: Say that I am not here. To whom the dog says more than you charged him; and when he has accomplished the mystery which you commanded him, he will die at your feet." ⁴But Peter said: "And you also, devil, whosoever you are, in the Name of our Lord Jesus Christ, go out of that young man and do not harm him at all: show yourself to all that stand here." ⁵When the young man heard it, he ran forth and caught hold of a great statue of marble which was set in the court of

the house, and broke it in pieces with his feet. Now it was a statue of Caesar. ⁶Which Marcellus, beholding, struck his forehead and said to Peter: "A great crime has been committed; for if this is made known to Caesar by some busybody, he will afflict us with severe punishments." ⁷And Peter said to him: "I see you not the same as you were a little while ago, for you said that you were ready to spend all your substance to save your soul. But if you indeed convert, believing in Christ with your whole heart, take in your hands of the water that runs down, and pray to the LORD, and in His Name sprinkle it on the broken pieces of the statue, and it will be whole as it was before." ⁸And Marcellus, doubting nothing, but believing with his whole heart, before he took the water, lifted up his hands and said: "I believe in You, O Lord Jesus Christ: for I am now proved by Your apostle Peter, whether I believe correctly in Your holy Name. ⁹Therefore, I take water in my hands, and in Your Name I sprinkle these stones, so that the statue may become whole as it was before. If, therefore, Lord, it is Your will that I continue in the body and suffer nothing at Caesar's hand, let this stone be whole as it was before." ¹⁰And he sprinkled the water on the stones, and the statue became whole, at which Peter exulted that Marcellus had not doubted in asking of the LORD, ¹¹and Marcellus was exalted in spirit that such a sign was first worked by his hands; and he therefore believed with his whole heart in the Name of Jesus Christ the Son of God, by whom all things impossible are made possible.

CHAPTER 12

¹But inside the house, Simon said this to the dog: "Tell Peter that I am not inside," whom the dog answered in the presence of Marcellus: "You exceedingly wicked and shameless one—enemy of all that live and believe on Christ Jesus, here is a dumb animal sent to you, which has received a human voice to confound you and show you to be a deceiver and a liar. ²Have you taken thought [for] so long, to say at last: Tell him that I am not inside? Are you not ashamed to utter your feeble and useless words against Peter, the minister and apostle of Christ, as if you could hide from him that has commanded me to speak against you to your face: and that not for your sake but for theirs whom you were deceiving and sending to destruction? ³Therefore, you will be cursed—you enemy and corrupter of the way of the truth of Christ, who will prove by fire that does not die and in outer darkness, your iniquities that you have committed." ⁴And having said this, the dog went forth, and the people followed him, leaving Simon alone. ⁵And the dog came to Peter as he sat with the multitude that had come to see Peter's face, and the dog related what he had done to Simon. ⁶And thus spoke the dog to the messenger and apostle of the true God: "Peter, you will have a great contest with the enemy of Christ and his servants, and many that have been deceived by him you will turn to the faith; therefore, you will receive from God the reward of your work." ⁷And when the dog had said this, he fell down at the apostle Peter's feet and gave up the spirit. ⁸And when the great multitude saw with amazement the dog speaking, they began then, some to throw themselves down at Peter's feet, and some said: "Show us another sign, so that we may believe in you as the minister of the living God, for Simon also did many signs in our presence and therefore we followed him."

CHAPTER 13

¹And Peter turned and saw a herring hung in a window, and he took it and said to the people: "If you now see this swimming in the water like a fish, will you be able to believe in Him whom I preach?" ²And they said with one voice: "Truly, we will believe you." ³Then he said (now there was a bath for swimming at hand): "In Your Name, O Jesus Christ! Forasmuch as it is not believed in until now, in the sight of all these: live and swim like a fish." And he cast the herring into the bath, and it lived and began to swim. ⁴And all the people saw the fish swimming, and it did not do so at that hour only, lest it should be said that it was a delusion, but he made it to swim for a long time, so that they brought many people from all quarters and showed them the herring that was made a living fish, so that certain of the people even cast bread to it; and they saw that it was whole. ⁵And seeing this, many followed Peter and believed in the LORD. ⁶And they assembled themselves day and night to the house of Narcissus the elder. And Peter discoursed to them of the writings of the Prophets and of those things which our Lord Jesus Christ had worked both in word and in deeds.

CHAPTER 14

¹But Marcellus was confirmed daily by the signs which he saw worked by Peter through the grace of Jesus Christ which He granted to him. ²And Marcellus ran on Simon as he sat in his house in the dining chamber, and cursed him, and said to him: "You most adverse and toxic of men, corrupter of my soul and my house, who would have made me fall away from my Lord and Savior Christ!" ³And laying hands on him, he commanded him to be thrust out of his house. ⁴And the servants having received such permission, covered him with reproaches; some struck his face, others beat him with sticks, others cast stones, others emptied out vessels full of filth on his head, even those who on his account had fled from their master and been a long time chained; ⁵and others of their fellow servants of whom he had spoken evil to their master reproached him, saying to him: "Now by the will of God who has had mercy on us and on our master, we repay you with a suitable reward." ⁶And Simon, shrewdly beaten and cast out of the house, ran to the house where Peter lodged, even the house of Narcissus, and standing at the gate cried out: "Behold, here I am—Simon: come down, Peter, and I will convict you that you have believed on a Man who is [merely] a Jew and a carpenter's Son."

CHAPTER 15

¹And when it was told Peter that Simon had said this, Peter sent a woman to him, who had a sucking child, saying to her: "Go down quickly, and you will find one that seeks me. For there is no need that you answer him at all, but keep silence and hear what the child whom you hold will say to him." The woman therefore went down. ²Now the child whom she suckled was seven months old; and it received a man's voice and said to Simon: "O you despised of God and men, and destruction of truth, and evil seed of all corruption, O unprofitable fruit by nature! ³But only for a short and little season will you be seen, and thereafter eternal punishment is laid up for you—you son of a shameless father, that never put forth your roots for good but for poison, faithless generation void of all hope! ⁴You were not confounded when a dog reproved you; I, a child, am compelled by God to speak, and not even now are you ashamed. ⁵But even against your will, on the Sabbath day that comes, another will bring you into the forum of Julius, so that it may be shown what manner of man you are. ⁶Therefore, depart from the gate wherein the feet of the holy walk; for you will no longer corrupt the innocent souls whom you turned out of the Way and make sad; in Christ, therefore, will be shown your evil nature, and your schemes will be cut in pieces. ⁷And now I speak this last word to you: Jesus Christ says to you: Be stricken mute in My Name and depart out of Rome until the Sabbath that comes." ⁸And he immediately became mute, and his speech was bound; and he went out of Rome until the Sabbath and abode in a stable. ⁹But the woman returned with the child to Peter and told him and the rest of the brothers what the child had said to Simon: and they magnified the LORD who had shown these things to men.

CHAPTER 16

¹Now when the night fell, Peter, while yet waking, beheld Jesus clad in a garment of [incredible] brightness, smiling and saying to him: "Many people of the brotherhood have already returned through Me and through the signs which you have worked in My Name. ²But you will have a contest of the faith on the Sabbath that comes, and many more of the nations and of the Jews will be converted in My Name—to Me who was reproached, and mocked, and spat on. ³For I will be present with you when you ask for signs and wonders, and you will convert many: but you will have Simon opposing you by the works of his father; yet all his works will be shown to be charms and schemes of sorcery. ⁴But do not slack now, and whomsoever I will send to you, you will establish in My Name." ⁵And when it was light, he told the brothers how the LORD had appeared to him and what He had commanded him:

CHAPTER 17

¹"But believe me, men and brothers, [that] I drove this Simon out of Judea where he did many evils with his magical charms, lodging in Judea with a certain woman Eubula, who was of honorable estate in this world, having a [large] store of gold and pearls of no small price. ²Here Simon entered in by stealth with two others like himself, and none of the household saw these two, but Simon only, and by means of a spell they took away all the woman's gold and disappeared. ³But Eubula, when she found what was done, began to torture her household, saying, You have taken an opportunity by this man of God and spoiled me, when you saw him entering in to me to honor a mere woman; but his name is as the Name of the LORD. ⁴As I fasted for three days and prayed that this matter should be made plain, I saw in a vision Italicus and Antulus, whom I had instructed in the Name of the LORD, and a boy naked and chained giving me a wheat loaf and saying to me: Peter, endure yet two days and you will see the mighty works of God. ⁵As for all that is lost out of the house of Eubula, Simon has used magical arts and has caused a delusion, and with two others has stolen it away: whom you will see on the third day at the ninth hour, at the gate which leads to Neapolis, selling to a goldsmith by name Agrippinus, a young satyr [made] of gold of two pound weight, having a precious stone in it. ⁶But for you there is no need that you touch it, lest you be defiled; but let there be with you some of the matron's servants, and you will show them the shop of the goldsmith and depart from them. ⁷For by reason of this matter, many will believe on the Name of the LORD, and all that which these men by their plots and wickedness have oftentimes stolen will be openly shown. ⁸When I heard that, I went to Eubula and found her sitting with her clothes torn and her hair disheveled, mourning; to whom I said: Eubula, rise up from your mourning, and compose your face, and order your hair, and put on suitable clothing, and pray to the Lord Jesus Christ that judges every soul: for He is the invisible Son of God, by whom you must be saved, if only you convert with your whole heart from your former sins: and receive power from Him, ⁹for behold, by me the LORD says to you: You will find everything whatsoever you have lost. And after you have received them, take care that He find you, so that you may renounce this present world and seek for everlasting refreshment. ¹⁰Therefore, listen to this: let certain of your people keep watch at the gate that leads to Neapolis on the day after tomorrow, at about the ninth hour, and they will see two young men having a young satyr of gold, of two pound weight, set with gems, as a vision has shown me: which thing they will offer for sale to one Agrippinus of the household of godliness and of the faith which is in the Lord Jesus Christ: ¹¹by whom it will be shown to you that you should believe in the living God and not on Simon the magician, the unstable devil, who has desired that you should remain in sorrow, and your innocent household be tormented; ¹²who by fair words and speech alone has deceived you, and with his mouth only spoke of godliness, whereas he is wholly possessed of ungodliness. ¹³For when you thought to keep [the] holy day, and set up your idol, and veiled it, and set out all your ornaments on a table, he brought in two young men whom no man of yours saw, by a magic charm, and they stole your ornaments away and were no longer seen. ¹⁴But his plot has had no success, for my God has manifested it to me, to the end [that] you should not be deceived, neither perish in Hades, for those ungodly sins which you have committed contrary to God, who is full of all truth, and the righteous Judge of [both] living and dead; ¹⁵and there is no other hope of life to men except through Him, by whom those things which you have lost are recovered to you: and now you [also] gain your own soul. ¹⁶But she cast herself down before my feet, saying, O man, who you are I do not know; but him I received as a servant of God, and whatsoever he asked of me to give it to the poor, I gave much by his hands, and besides that, I gave much to him. What harm did I do him, that he should plot all this against my house? ¹⁷To whom Peter said: There is no faith to be put in words, but in acts and deeds: but we must go on with what we have begun. ¹⁸So I left her, and went with two stewards of Eubula, and came to Agrippinus, and said to him: See that you take note of these men; for tomorrow two young men will come to you, desiring to sell you a young satyr of gold set with jewels, which belongs to the mistress of these: and you will take it as it were to look on it, and praise the work of the craftsman, and then when these come in, God will bring the rest for evidence. ¹⁹And on the next day, the stewards of the matron came about the ninth hour, and also those young men, willing to sell to Agrippinus the young satyr of gold. ²⁰And they, being immediately taken, it was reported to the matron, and she in distress of mind came to the deputy, and with a loud voice declared all that had happened to her. ²¹And when Pompeius the deputy beheld her in distress of mind, who never had come forth abroad, he immediately rose up from the judgment-seat, and went to the praetorium, and commanded those men to be brought and tortured; ²²and while they were being tormented, they confessed that they did it in the service of Simon, who, they said, persuaded us with money to do it. ²³And being tortured a long time, they confessed that all that Eubula had lost was laid up under the earth in a cave on the other side of the gate, and many other things in addition. ²⁴And when Pompeius heard this, he rose up to go to the gate, with those two men, each of them bound with two chains. ²⁵And behold, Simon came in at the gate, seeking them because they tarried a long [time]. ²⁶And he sees a great multitude coming, and those two bound with chains; and he himself understood, and fled, and no longer appeared in Judea to this day. ²⁷But Eubula, when she had recovered all her goods, gave them for the service of the poor, and believed on the Lord Jesus Christ, and was comforted; and despised and renounced this world, and gave to the widows and fatherless, and clothed the poor. ²⁸And after a long time, she received her rest. ²⁹Now these things, dearly beloved brothers, were done in Judea, whereby he that is called the messenger of Satan was driven out from there."

CHAPTER 18

¹"Brothers, dearest and most beloved, let us fast together and pray to the LORD. For He that drove him out from there is also able to root him out of this place: ²and let Him grant to us power to withstand him and his magical charms, and to prove that he is the messenger of Satan. ³For on the Sabbath our Lord will bring him, though he would not [go himself], to the forum of Julius. ⁴Let us therefore bow our knees to Christ, who hears us, although we do not cry; it is He that sees us, though He is not seen with these eyes, yet He is in us: if we will, He will not forsake us. ⁵Let us therefore purify our souls from every evil temptation, and God will not depart from us. Yes, if we merely wink with our eyes, He is present with us."

CHAPTER 19

¹Now after these things were spoken by Peter, Marcellus also came in and said: "Peter, I have cleansed my whole house from [all] traces of Simon for you, and completely done away with even his wicked dust. ²For I took water and called on the holy Name of Jesus Christ, together with my other servants which belong to Him, and sprinkled all my house, and all the dining chambers, and all the porticoes, even to the outer gate, ³and said: I know that You, Lord Jesus Christ, are pure and untouched by any uncleanness: so let my enemy and adversary be driven out from before Your face. ⁴And now, you blessed one, I have commanded the widows and old women to assemble to you in my house which is purified, so that they may pray with us. And each one will receive a piece of gold in the name of the ministry, so that they may indeed be called servants of Christ. ⁵And everything else is now prepared for the service. ⁶I beg you, therefore, O blessed Peter: consent to their request, so that you also pay honor to their prayers in my stead; let us then go and also take Narcissus, and whichever of the brothers are here." ⁷So then Peter consented to his simplicity, to fulfill his desire, and went forth with him and the rest of the brothers.

CHAPTER 20

¹But Peter entered in, and beheld one of the aged women, a widow that was blind, and her daughter giving her her hand and leading her into Marcellus' house; ²and Peter said to her: "Come here, mother: from this day forward Jesus gives you His right hand, by whom we have inapproachable light which no darkness hides; who says to you through me: Open your eyes and see, and walk by yourself." ³And immediately the widow saw Peter laying his

hand on her. ⁴And Peter entered into the dining-hall and saw that the Gospel was being read, and he rolled up the book and said: "You men that believe and hope in Christ, learn in what manner the Holy Writing of our Lord ought to be declared: whereof we by His grace wrote that which we could receive, though yet it appears to you feeble, yet according to our power, even that which can be endured to be carried by human flesh. ⁵Therefore, we ought to first know the will and the goodness of God, how that when error was spread abroad everywhere, and many thousands of men were being cast down into perdition, God was moved by His mercy to show Himself in another form and in the likeness of man, concerning which neither the Jews nor we were able to be enlightened worthily. ⁶For every one of us, according as he could contain the sight, saw, as he was able. ⁷Now I will expound to you that which was newly read to you. ⁸Our Lord, willing that I should behold His majesty at the holy mountain—I, when I saw the brightness of His light with the sons of Zebedee, fell as one dead, and shut my eyes, and heard such a voice from Him as I am not able to describe, and thought myself to be blinded by His brightness. ⁹And when I recovered a little, I said within myself: Perhaps my Lord has brought me here so that He might blind me. And I said: If this is also Your will, Lord, I do not resist. ¹⁰And He gave me His hand and raised me up; and when I arose, I saw Him again in such a form as I was able to take in. ¹¹As, therefore, the merciful God, dearly beloved brothers, carried our weaknesses and bore our sins (as the prophet says: He bears our sins and suffers for us; but we esteemed Him to be in affliction and stricken with plagues), for He is in the Father and the Father in Him—He also is Himself the fulness of all majesty, who has shown to us all His good things: ¹²He ate and drank for our sakes, Himself being neither hungry nor thirsty; He carried and bore reproaches for our sakes, He died and rose again because of us; who both defended me when I sinned and comforted me by His greatness, and will comfort you also so that you may love Him: ¹³this God who is great and small, fair and foul, young and old, seen in time and to eternity invisible, whom the hand of man has not held, yet is held by His servants; whom no flesh has seen, yet now sees; who is the word proclaimed by the prophets and now appearing; ¹⁴not subject to suffering, but having now made trial of suffering for our sake; never punished, yet now punished; ¹⁵who was before the world and has been comprehended in time—the great beginning of all principality, yet delivered over to princes; beautiful, but among us lowly; seen of all yet foreseeing all. ¹⁶This Jesus you have, brothers, [is] the Door, the Light, the Way, the Bread, the Water, the Life, the Resurrection, the Refreshment, the Pearl, the Treasure, the Seed, the Harvest, the Mustard Seed, the Vine, the Plow, the Grace, the Faith, the Word: ¹⁷He is all things, and there is no other greater than Him. To Him be praise, world without end. Amen."

CHAPTER 21

¹And when the ninth hour had fully come, they rose up to make prayer. And behold, certain widows, of the aged, unknown to Peter, which sat there, being blind and not believing, cried out, saying to Peter: "We sit together here, O Peter, hoping and believing in Christ Jesus: as therefore you have made one of us to see, we beg you, lord Peter, grant to us also His mercy and pity." ²But Peter said to them: "If the faith that is in Christ is in you, if it is firm in you, then perceive in your mind that which you do not see with your eyes, and though your ears are closed, yet let them be open in your mind within you. ³These eyes will again be shut, seeing nothing but men, and oxen, and dumb beasts, and stones, and sticks; but not every eye sees Jesus Christ. ⁴Yet now, Lord, let Your sweet and holy Name aid these persons; touch their eyes, for You are able that these may see with their eyes." ⁵And when everyone had prayed, the hall wherein they were shone as when there is lightning, even with such a light as comes in the clouds, yet not such a light as that of the daytime, but unspeakable, invisible, such as no man can describe, ⁶even such that we were beside ourselves with bewilderment, calling on the LORD and saying: "Have mercy, Lord, on us Your servants: what we are able to bear, that, Lord, give us; for this we can neither see nor endure." ⁷And as we lay there, only those widows stood up which were blind; and the bright light which appeared to us entered into their eyes and made them to see. ⁸To whom Peter said: "Tell us what you saw." And they said: "We saw an old man of such beauty as we are not able to declare to you"; ⁹but others said: "We saw a young man"; and others: "We saw a boy touching our eyes delicately, and so were our eyes opened." ¹⁰Peter therefore magnified the LORD, saying, "You alone are the LORD God, and of what lips do we have to give You due praise? And how can we give You thanks according to Your mercy? ¹¹Therefore, brothers, as I told you but a little while before, God that is constant is greater than our thoughts, even as we have learned of these aged widows, how they beheld the LORD in various forms."

CHAPTER 22

¹And having exhorted them all to understand the LORD with their whole heart, he began together with Marcellus and the rest of the brothers to minister to the virgins of the LORD, and to rest until the morning. ²To whom Marcellus said: "You holy and inviolate virgins of the LORD, listen: you have a place to abide in, for these things that are called mine, whose are they except yours? ³Do not depart from here, but refresh yourselves: for on the Sabbath which comes, even tomorrow, Simon has a controversy with Peter the holy one of God, for as the LORD has always been with him, behold, will Christ the Lord now stand for him as His apostle. ⁴For Peter has continued tasting nothing, but fasting yet [another] day, so that he may overcome the wicked adversary and persecutor of the LORD's truth. ⁵For behold, my young men have come announcing that they have seen scaffolds being set up in the forum, and many people saying: Tomorrow at daybreak two Jews are to contend here concerning the teaching of God. Now therefore, let us watch until the morning, praying and pleading with our Lord Jesus Christ to hear our prayers on behalf of Peter." ⁶And Marcellus turned to sleep for a short span, and he awoke and said to Peter: "O Peter, you apostle of Christ, let us go boldly to that which lies before us. ⁷For just now, when I turned myself to sleep for a while, I beheld you sitting in a high place and before you a great multitude, and a woman exceedingly foul, in sight like an Ethiopian, not an Egyptian, but altogether black and filthy, clothed in rags, and with an iron collar around her neck and chains on her hands and feet, dancing. ⁸And when you saw me, you said to me with a loud voice: Marcellus! The whole power of Simon and of his god is this woman that dances; behead her. ⁹And I said to you: Brother Peter, I am a senator of a high race, and I have never defiled my hands, neither killed so much as a sparrow at any time. ¹⁰And you hearing it began to cry out yet more: Come, our true sword, Jesus Christ, and not only cut off the head of this devil, but hew all her limbs in pieces in the sight of all these whom I have approved in Your service. ¹¹And immediately, one like to you, O Peter, having a sword, hewed her in pieces: so that I looked earnestly on you both, both on you and on him that cut in pieces that devil, and marveled greatly to see how similar you were. ¹²And I awakened and have told to you these signs of Christ." ¹³And when Peter heard it, he was [all] the more filled with courage that Marcellus had seen these things, knowing that the LORD always cares for His own. And being joyful and refreshed by these words, he rose up to go to the forum.

CHAPTER 23

¹Now the brothers were gathered together, and all that were in Rome, and each one took places for a piece of gold: there came together also the senators, and the prefects, and those in authority. ²And Peter came and stood in the midst, and all cried out: "Show us, O Peter, who is your God and what is His greatness which has given you confidence. Do not resent the Romans; they are lovers of the gods. ³We have had proof of Simon, let us have it of you; convince us, both of you, whom we should truly believe." ⁴And as they said these things, Simon also came in, and standing with a troubled mind at Peter's side, at first he looked at him. ⁵And after long silence, Peter said: "You men of Rome, be true judges toward us, for I say that I have believed on the living and true God; and I promise to give you proofs of Him, which are known to me, as many among you also can bear witness. ⁶For you see that this man is now rebuked and silent, knowing that I drove him out of Judea because of the deceits

ACTS OF PETER

which he practiced on Eubula, an honorable and simple woman, by his magical arts; ⁷and being driven out from there, he has come here, thinking to escape notice among you; and behold, he stands face to face with me. ⁸Say now, Simon, did you not at Jerusalem fall at my feet and Paul's, when you saw the healings that were worked by our hands, and say: I beg you to take from me a payment—as much as you will—so that I may be able to lay hands on men and do such mighty works? ⁹And we, when we heard it, cursed you, saying: Do you think to tempt us as if we desired to possess money? And now, do you not fear at all? ¹⁰My name is Peter, because the Lord Christ approved to call me prepared for all things: for I trust in the living God by whom I will put down your sorceries. ¹¹Now let Him do in your presence the wonders which He did in times past: and what I have now said of Him, will you not believe it?" ¹²But Simon said: "You presume to speak of Jesus of Nazareth, the Son of a carpenter, and a carpenter Himself, whose birth is recorded in Judea. Hear, Peter: the Romans have understanding: they are no fools." ¹³And he turned to the people and said: "You men of Rome, is God born? Is He crucified? He that has a master is no God." ¹⁴And when he so spoke, many said: "You speak well, Simon."

CHAPTER 24

¹But Peter said: "A curse on your words against Christ! Do you presume to speak this? ²Whereas the prophet says of Him: Who will declare His generation? And another prophet says: And we saw Him, and He had no beauty nor attractiveness. And: In the last times a Child is born of the Holy Spirit: His mother does not know a man, neither does any man say that he is His father. ³And again he says: She has brought forth and not brought forth. And again: Is it a small thing for you to weary men? Behold, a virgin will conceive in the womb. ⁴And another prophet says, honoring the Father: Neither did we hear her voice, neither did a midwife come in. Another prophet says: Not born of the womb of a woman, but from a heavenly place He came down. ⁵And: A stone was cut out without hands and struck all the kingdoms. ⁶And: The stone which the builders rejected, the same has become the head of the corner; and he calls Him a precious, chosen stone. ⁷And again, a prophet says concerning Him: And behold, I saw one like the Son of Man coming on a cloud. ⁸And what more? O you men of Rome, if you knew the Writings of the prophets, I would expound everything to you: by which writings it was necessary that this should be spoken in a mystery, and that the Kingdom of God should be perfected. But these things will be opened to you hereafter. ⁹Now I turn to you, Simon: do one thing of those with which you previously deceived them, and I will bring it to nothing through my Lord Jesus Christ." ¹⁰And Simon plucked up his boldness and said: "If the prefect allows it, prepare yourselves and do not delay for my sake."

CHAPTER 25

¹But the prefect desired to show patience to both, so that he might not appear to do anything unjustly. ²And the prefect put forward one of his servants and said thus to Simon: "Take this man and deliver him to death." And to Peter he said: "And you revive him." ³And to the people the prefect said: "It is now for you to judge which of these two is acceptable to God: he that kills or he that makes alive." ⁴And immediately Simon spoke in the ear of the young man and made him speechless, and he died. ⁵And as there began to be a murmuring among the people, one of the widows who were nourished in Marcellus' house, standing behind the multitude, cried out: "O Peter, servant of God, my son is dead, the only one that I had!" ⁶And the people made space for her and led her to Peter: and she cast herself down at his feet, saying, "I only had [this] one son, which with his hands, furnished me with nourishment: he raised me up, he carried me: now that he is dead, who will reach out a hand to me?" ⁷To whom Peter said: "Go, with these for a witness, and bring your son here, so that they may see and be able to believe that by the power of God he is raised, and that this man [(Simon)] may behold it and fail." ⁸And Peter said to the young men: "We have need of some young men, and, moreover, of such as will believe." ⁹And immediately, thirty young men arose, which were prepared to carry her to her son that was dead. ¹⁰And whereas the widow had barely recovered herself, the young men picked her up; ¹¹and she was crying out and saying: "Behold, my son, the servant of Christ has sent to you"—tearing her hair and her face. ¹²Now the young men which had come examined the young man's nostrils to see whether he was indeed dead; ¹³and seeing that he was truly dead, they had compassion on the old woman and said: "If you so will, mother, and have confidence in the God of Peter, we will pick him up and carry him there, so that he may raise him up and restore him to you."

CHAPTER 26

¹And as they said these things, the prefect, looking earnestly on Peter, said: "What do you say, Peter? Behold, my young man is dead, who is also dear to the emperor, and I did not spare him, although I had with me other young men; ²but I rather desired to make a trial of you and of the God whom you preach, whether you be true, and therefore I would have this young man die." ³And Peter said: "God is not tempted nor proved, O Agrippa, but if He is loved and implored, He hears them that are worthy. But since now my God and Lord Jesus Christ is tempted among you, who has done such great signs and wonders by my hands to turn you from your sins— ⁴now also in the sight of all may You, LORD, at my word, by Your power raise him up whom Simon has slain by touching him." ⁵And Peter said to the master of the young man: "Go, take hold of his right hand, and you will have him alive and walking with you." ⁶And Agrippa the prefect ran, and went to the young man, and took his hand, and raised him up. And all the multitude seeing it cried: "There is one God! One is the God of Peter!"

CHAPTER 27

¹In the meanwhile, the widow's son was also brought on a bed by the young men, and the people made way for them and brought them to Peter. ²And Peter lifted up his eyes toward the sky, and stretched forth his hands, and said: "O holy Father of Your Son Jesus Christ, who have granted us Your power, so that we may, through You, ask and obtain, and despise all that is in the world, and follow You alone, who are seen by few and would be known of many: ³shine around us, LORD; enlighten us, appear, raise up the son of this aged widow, who cannot help herself without her son. ⁴And I, repeating the word of Christ my Lord, say to you: Young man, arise and walk with your mother so long as you can do her good; and thereafter you will serve me after a higher sort, ministering in the lot of a servant of the overseer." ⁵And immediately the dead man rose up, and the multitudes saw it and marveled, and the people cried out: "You are God the Savior—You, the God of Peter, the invisible God, the Savior." ⁶And they spoke among themselves, indeed marveling at the power of a man that called on his Lord with a word; and they received it to sanctification.

CHAPTER 28

¹The fame of it therefore being spread throughout the city, there came the mother of a certain senator, and she cast herself into the midst of the people and fell at Peter's feet, saying, "I have learned from my people that you are a servant of the merciful God and impart His grace to all those that desire this light. ²Therefore, impart the light to my son, for I know that you resent no one; do not turn away from a matron that begs you." ³To whom Peter said: "Will you believe on my God, by whom your son will be raised?" ⁴And the mother said with a loud voice, weeping, "I believe, O Peter, I believe!" And all the people cried out: "Grant the mother her son." ⁵But Peter said: "Let him be brought here before all these." ⁶And Peter turned himself to the people and said: "You men of Rome, I am also one of yourselves, and bear a man's body, and am a sinner, but have obtained mercy: therefore, do not look on me as though I, by mine own power, did that which I do, but by the power of my Lord Jesus Christ, who is the Judge of [the] living and dead. ⁷In Him do I believe, and by Him am I sent and have confidence when I call on Him to raise the dead. ⁸Therefore, you also go, O woman, and cause your son to be brought here and to rise again." ⁹And the woman passed through the midst of the people and went into the street, running with great joy, and believing in her mind. ¹⁰She came to her house, and by means of her young men, she picked him up and came to the forum. ¹¹Now she instructed the young men to put caps on their heads, and to walk before the bier, and all that she had

ACTS OF PETER

determined to burn on the body of her son to be carried before his bier; ¹²and when Peter saw it, he had compassion on the dead body and on her. ¹³And she came to the multitude, while all lamented her; and a great crowd of senators and matrons followed after, to behold the wonderful works of God: for this Nicostratus which was dead was exceedingly noble and beloved by the senate. ¹⁴And they brought him and set him down before Peter. ¹⁵And Peter called for silence, and with a loud voice said: "You men of Rome, let there now be a just judgment between me and Simon; and judge which of the two of us believes in the living God: he or I. ¹⁶Let him raise up the body that lies here, and believe in him as the messenger of God. ¹⁷But if he is not able, and I call on my God and restore the son alive to his mother, then believe that this man is a sorcerer and a deceiver, which is entertained among you." ¹⁸And when they all heard these things, they thought that it was right which Peter had spoken, and they encouraged Simon, saying, "Now, if there is anything in you, show it openly! Either overcome, or you will be overcome! Why do you stand still? Come, begin!" ¹⁹But Simon, when he saw them all insistent with him, stood silent; and thereafter, when he saw the people silent and looking on him, Simon cried out, saying, "You men of Rome, if you behold the dead man arise, will you cast Peter out of the city?" ²⁰And all the people said: "We will not only cast him out, but that very instant we will burn him with fire." ²¹Then Simon went to the head of the dead man, and stooped down, and three times raised himself up, and showed the people that [the dead man] lifted his head and moved it, and opened his eyes, and bowed himself a little to Simon. ²²And immediately they began to ask for wood and torches, with which to burn Peter. ²³But Peter receiving strength from Christ, lifted up his voice and said to them that cried out against him: "Now I see, you people of Rome, that you are—I must not say—fools and vain, as long as your eyes, and your ears, and your hearts are blinded. How long will your understanding be darkened? ²⁴Do you not see that you are bewitched, supposing that a dead man is raised, who has not lifted himself up? ²⁵It would have satisfied me, you men of Rome, to hold my peace and die without speaking, and to leave you among the deceits of this world; but I have the punishment of unquenchable fire before my eyes. ²⁶If it therefore seems good to you, let the dead man speak, let him arise if he lives, let him free his jaw that is bound with his hands, let him call on his mother, let him say to you that cry out: Why do you cry? Let him beckon to us with his hand. ²⁷If now you would see that he is dead, and yourselves bewitched, let this man depart from the bier, who has persuaded you to depart from Christ, and you will see that the dead man is such as you saw him brought here." ²⁸But Agrippa the prefect no longer had patience, but thrust Simon away with his own hands, and again the dead man lay as he was before. ²⁹And the people were enraged, and turned away from the sorcery of Simon, and began to cry out: "Listen, O Caesar! If the dead [man] does not rise now, let Simon burn instead of Peter, for he has truly blinded us." ³⁰But Peter stretched forth his hand and said: "O men of Rome, have patience! I do not say to you that if the young man is raised, Simon will burn; for if I say it, you will do it." ³¹The people cried out: "Against your will, Peter, we will do it!" To whom Peter said: "If you continue in this mind, the young man will not arise: for we do not know to render evil for evil, but we have learned to love our enemies and pray for our persecutors. ³²For if even this man can convert, it were better; for God will not remember evil. ³³Let him come, therefore, into the light of Christ; but if he cannot, let him possess the part of his father the Devil, but do not let your hands be defiled." ³⁴And when he had thus spoken to the people, he went to the young man, and before he raised him, he said to his mother: "These young men whom you have set free in the honor of your son, can yet serve their God when he lives, being free; for I know that the soul of some is hurt if they will see your son arise and know that these will yet be in bondage: but let them all continue free and receive their sustenance as they did before, for your son is about to rise again; and let them be with him." ³⁵And Peter looked long on her, to see her thoughts. ³⁶And the mother of the young man said: "What else can I do? Therefore, before the prefect I say: Whatsoever I intended to burn on the body of my son, let them possess it." ³⁷And Peter said: "Let the residue be distributed to the widows." ³⁸Then Peter rejoiced in soul and said in the Spirit: "O Lord, You are merciful! Jesus Christ, show Yourself to Your Peter who calls on You, just as You have always shown him mercy and loving-kindness: ³⁹and in the presence of all these which have obtained freedom, so that these may become Your servants, let Nicostratus now arise." ⁴⁰And Peter touched the young man's side and said: "Arise." And the young man arose, and took off his grave clothes, and sat up, and freed his jaw, and asked for different clothing; ⁴¹and he came down from the bier and said to Peter: "Please, O man of God, let us go to our Lord Christ whom I saw speaking with me; who also showed me to you and said to you: Bring him here to Me, for he is Mine." ⁴²And when Peter heard this from the young man, he was strengthened even more in soul by the help of the LORD; ⁴³and Peter said to the people: "You men of Rome, it is thus that the dead are raised up, thus do they converse, thus do they arise and walk, and live as long a time as God wills. ⁴⁴Now therefore, you that have come together to the sight: turn from these evil ways of yours, and from all your gods that are made with hands, and from all uncleanness and lust, [and] receive fellowship with Christ, believing, so that you may obtain everlasting life."

CHAPTER 29

¹And in the same hour, they worshiped him as a god, falling down at his feet, and the sick whom they had at home, so that he might heal them. ²But the prefect, seeing that such a great multitude waited on Peter, signified to Peter that he should withdraw himself: ³and Peter told the people to come to Marcellus' house. But the mother of the young man begged Peter to set foot in her house. ⁴Yet Peter had appointed to be with Marcellus on the LORD's Day, to see the widows even as Marcellus had promised, to minister to them with his own hands. ⁵Therefore, the young man who had risen again said: "I do not depart from Peter." And his mother, glad and rejoicing, went to her own house. ⁶And on the next day after the Sabbath, she came to Marcellus' house bringing to Peter two thousand pieces of gold and saying to Peter: "Divide these among the virgins of Christ which serve Him." ⁷But the young man who had risen from the dead, when he saw that he had given nothing to any man, went home, and opened the press, and himself offered four thousand pieces of gold, saying to Peter: "Behold, I who was raised also offer a double offering, and myself also from this day forward as a speaking sacrifice to God."

CHAPTER 30

¹Now on the LORD's Day, as Peter discoursed to the brothers and exhorted them toward the faith of Christ, there being present many of the senate and many knights, and rich women, and matrons, and being confirmed in the faith, one woman that was there, exceedingly rich, who was surnamed Chryse because every vessel of hers was of gold—for from her birth she never used a vessel of silver or glass, but golden ones only—said to Peter: "Peter, you servant of God, He whom you call God appeared to me in a dream and said: Chryse, carry to My minister Peter ten thousand pieces of gold; for you owe them to him. ²I have therefore brought them, fearing lest some harm should be done to me by Him who appeared to me, who also departed to Heaven." ³And saying this, she laid down the money and departed. ⁴And Peter seeing it, glorified the LORD, because they that were in need should be refreshed. ⁵Therefore, certain of them that were there said to him: "Peter, have you not done wrong to receive the money from her? For she is spoken of poorly throughout all Rome for fornication, and because she does not keep to one husband; yes, she even has to do with the young men of her house. ⁶Do not therefore be a partner with the table of Chryse, but let that which came from her be returned to her." ⁷But Peter, hearing it, laughed and said to the brothers: "What this woman is in the rest of her way of life, I do not know, but in that I have received this money, I did not do it foolishly; for she paid it as a debtor to Christ, and she gives it to the servants of Christ: for He Himself has provided for them."

CHAPTER 31

¹And they also brought to him the sick on the Sabbath, begging that they might recover from their diseases. ²And many were healed that were sick of palsy, and gout, and tertian

and quartan fevers—and of every disease of the body they were healed, believing in the Name of Jesus Christ, and very many were added every day to the grace of the LORD. ³But Simon the magician, after a few days were past, promised the multitude to convict Peter that he did not believe in the true God, but was deceived. ⁴And when he did many lying wonders, they that were firm in the faith derided him. ⁵For in dining chambers he made certain spirits enter in, which were only an apparition, and not existing in reality. ⁶And what more should I say? Although he had oftentimes been convicted of sorcery, he made lame men seem whole for a short span, and blind likewise, and once he appeared to make many dead to live and move, as he did with Nicostratus. ⁷But Peter followed him throughout and always convicted him to the beholders: ⁸and when he now made a sorry figure, and was derided by the people of Rome and disbelieved because he never succeeded in the things which he promised to perform, being in such a plight at last, he said to them: "Men of Rome, you now think that Peter has prevailed over me, as more powerful, and you pay more heed to him: you are deceived. ⁹For tomorrow I will forsake you—godless and impious as you are—and fly up to God whose power I am, though I have become weak. ¹⁰Whereas, then, you have fallen, I am he that stands, and I will go up to my father and say to him: Me also, even your son that stands, have they desired to pull down; but I did not consent to them, and have returned back to myself."

CHAPTER 32

¹And the next day, a great multitude had already assembled at the Sacred Way to watch him flying. ²And Peter came to the place to see the sight, so that he might convict him in this also; for when Simon entered into Rome, he amazed the multitudes by flying: ³but Peter who convicted him was not yet living at Rome, which city he thus deceived by illusion, so that some were carried away [in amazement] by him. ⁴So then this man, standing on a high place, beheld Peter and began to say: "Peter, at this time when I am going up before all these people who behold me, I say to you: If your God is able, whom the Jews put to death, and stoned you that were chosen by Him, let Him show that faith in Him is faith in God, and let it appear at this time, if it is worthy of God. ⁵For I, ascending up, will myself show who I am to all this multitude." ⁶And behold, when he was lifted up on high, and all beheld him raised up above all Rome, and the temples thereof, and the mountains, the faithful looked toward Peter. ⁷And Peter, seeing the strangeness of the sight, cried to the Lord Jesus Christ: "If you allow this man to accomplish that which he has set about, now will all of them who have believed on You be offended, and the signs and wonders which You have given them through me will not be believed: ⁸hasten Your grace, O Lord, and let him fall from the height and be disabled; and let him not die, but be brought to nothing, and break his leg in three places." ⁹And he fell from the height and broke his leg in three places. ¹⁰Then every man cast stones at him and went away home, and thenceforth they believed Peter. ¹¹But one of the friends of Simon quickly came out of the way, Gemellus by name, of whom Simon had received much money, having a Greek woman for a wife, and saw that he had broken his leg, and said: "O Simon, if the Power of God is broken to pieces, will not that god whose power you are, himself be blinded?" ¹²Gemellus therefore also ran and followed Peter, saying to him: "I also would be of them that believe on Christ." And Peter said: "Is there anyone that resents it, my brother? Come and sit with us." ¹³But in his affliction, Simon found some to carry him by night on a bed from Rome to Aricia; and he abode there awhile and was brought from there to Terracina, to one Castor that was banished from Rome on an accusation of sorcery. ¹⁴And there he was severely cut [[by two physicians]], and so Simon, the messenger of Satan, came to his end.

THE MARTYRDOM OF PETER

CHAPTER 33

¹Now Peter was in Rome rejoicing in the LORD with the brothers and giving thanks night and day for the multitude which were brought daily to the holy Name by the grace of the LORD. ²And there were also gathered to Peter the concubines of Agrippa the prefect, being four: Agrippina, and Nicaria, and Euphemia, and Doris; ³and they, hearing the word concerning chastity and all the oracles of the LORD, were stricken in their souls, and agreeing together to remain pure from the bed of Agrippa, they were provoked by him. ⁴Now as Agrippa was perplexed and grieved concerning them—and he loved them greatly—he observed, and sent men stealthily to see where they went, and found that they went to Peter. ⁵Therefore, he said to them when they returned: "That Christian has taught you to have no dealings with me: know that I will both destroy you, and burn him alive." ⁶They then endured to suffer every manner of evil at Agrippa's hand, if only they might not suffer the passion of love, being strengthened by the might of Jesus.

CHAPTER 34

¹And a certain woman who was exceedingly beautiful, the wife of Albinus, Caesar's friend, by name Xanthippe, came, she also, to Peter, with the rest of the matrons, and withdrew herself, she also, from Albinus. ²He therefore, being mad, and loving Xanthippe, and marveling that she would not sleep even on the same bed with him, raged like a wild beast and would have dispatched Peter; for he knew that he was the cause of her separating from his bed. ³Many other women also, loving the word of chastity, separated themselves from their husbands, because they desired them to worship God in sobriety and cleanness. ⁴And whereas there was great trouble in Rome, Albinus made known his state to Agrippa, saying to him: "Either avenge me of Peter, who has withdrawn my wife, or I will avenge myself." ⁵And Agrippa said: "I have suffered the same at his hand, for he has withdrawn my concubines." ⁶And Albinus said to him: "Why then do you tarry, Agrippa? Let us find him and put him to death for [being] a dealer in curious arts, so that we may have our wives again, and avenge them also which are not able to put him to death, whose wives he has also parted from them."

CHAPTER 35

¹And as they considered these things, Xanthippe took knowledge of the counsel of her husband with Agrippa, and she sent and showed Peter, so that he might depart from Rome. ²And the rest of the brothers, together with Marcellus, begged him to depart. But Peter said to them: "Will we be runaways, brothers?" ³And they said to him: "No, but that you may yet be able to serve the LORD." ⁴And he obeyed the brothers' voice and went forth alone, saying, "Let none of you come forth with me, but I will go forth alone, having changed the fashion of my apparel." ⁵And as he went forth from the city, he saw the LORD entering into Rome. ⁶And when he saw Him, he said: "Lord, why do You come here?" And the LORD said to him: "I go into Rome to be crucified." ⁷And Peter said to Him: "Lord, are You [being] crucified again?" He said to him: "Yes, Peter, I am [being] crucified again." ⁸And Peter came to himself; and having beheld the LORD ascending up into Heaven, he returned to Rome, rejoicing and glorifying the LORD, because He said: "I am being crucified"—which was about to happen to Peter.

CHAPTER 36

¹Therefore, he went up again to the brothers and told them that which had been seen by him: and they lamented in soul, weeping and saying: "We beg you, Peter, consider us who are young." ²And Peter said to them: "If it is the LORD's will, it comes to pass, even if we do not will it; ³but as for you, the LORD is able to establish you in His faith, and He will found you therein and make you spread abroad, whom He Himself has planted, so that you also may plant others through Him. ⁴But I, as long as the LORD wills that I be in the flesh, do not resist; and again, if He takes me, to Him I rejoice and am glad." ⁵And while Peter thus spoke, and all the brothers wept, behold, four soldiers took him and led him to Agrippa. ⁶And he in his madness commanded him to be crucified on an accusation of godlessness. ⁷The whole multitude of the brothers therefore ran together, both of rich and poor, orphans and widows, weak and strong, desiring to see and to rescue Peter, while the people shouted with one voice, and would not be silenced: "What wrong has Peter done, O Agrippa? Wherein has he hurt you? Tell the Romans!" ⁸And others said: "We fear if this man dies, his Lord will destroy us all." ⁹And when Peter came to the place, he quieted the people and said: "You men that are soldiers of

Christ! You men that hope in Christ! Remember the signs and wonders which you have seen worked through me; remember the compassion of God, how many cures He has worked for you. ¹⁰Wait for Him that comes and will reward every man according to his doings. ¹¹And now, do not be bitter against Agrippa, for he is the minister of his father's working. And this comes to pass at all events, for the LORD has manifested to me that which happens. ¹²But why should I delay and not draw near to the cross?"

CHAPTER 37

¹And having approached, and standing by the cross, he began to say: "O name of the cross, you hidden mystery! O grace ineffable, that is pronounced in the name of the cross! O nature of man, that cannot be separated from God! O unspeakable and inseparable love, that cannot be shown forth by unclean lips! ²I seize you now—I that am at the end of my delivery here. ³I will declare to you what you are: I will not keep silent regarding the mystery of the cross which before was shut and hidden from my soul. ⁴Do not let the cross be to you which hope in Christ, this which appears: for it is another thing, different from that which appears, even this passion which is according to that of Christ. ⁵And now above all, because you that can hear are able to hear it from me, that am at the last and final hour of my life, listen: separate your souls from everything that is of the senses, from everything that appears and does not exist in reality. ⁶Blind these eyes of yours, close these ears of yours, put away your doings that are seen, and you will perceive that which concerns Christ, and the whole mystery of your salvation: and let this much be said to you that hear, as if it had not been spoken. ⁷But now it is time for you, Peter, to deliver up your body to them that take it. Receive it then, you to whom it belongs. ⁸I implore you the executioners, crucify me this way: with the head downward and not otherwise: and the reason why, I will tell to them that hear."

CHAPTER 38

¹And when they had hung him up after the manner he desired, he again began to say: "You men to whom it belongs to hear, listen to that which I will declare to you at this particular time as I hang here. ²Learn the mystery of all nature, and the beginning of all things—what it was. ³For the first man, whose race I bear in my appearance, fell head downward, and showed forth a manner of birth such as was not until now: for it was dead, having no motion. ⁴He, then, being pulled down—who also cast his first state down on the earth—established this whole disposition of all things, being hung up [as] an image of the creation wherein he made the things of the right hand into left hand and the left hand into right hand, and changed about all the marks of their nature, so that he thought those things that were not fair to be fair, and those that were in truth evil, to be good. ⁵Concerning which the LORD says in a mystery: Unless you make the things of the right hand as those of the left, and those of the left as those of the right, and those that are above as those below, and those that are behind as those that are before, you will not have knowledge of the kingdom. ⁶Therefore, I have declared this thought to you; and the figure wherein you now see me hanging is the representation of that man that first came to birth. ⁷You therefore, my beloved, and you that hear me and that will hear, ought to cease from your former error and return back again. ⁸For it is right to mount on the Cross of Christ, who is the Word stretched out, the One and Only, of whom the Spirit says: For what else is Christ, but the Word, the Sound of God? ⁹So that the Word is the upright beam whereon I am crucified. ¹⁰And the Sound is that which crosses it—the nature of man. ¹¹And the nail which holds the cross-tree to the upright in the midst thereof is the conversion of man."

CHAPTER 39

¹"Now whereas You have made known and revealed these things to me, O Word of life, called now by me the Tree of Life, I give You thanks, not with these lips that are nailed to the cross, nor with this tongue by which truth and falsehood issue forth, nor with this word which comes forth by means of art whose nature is material, ²but with that voice I give You thanks, O King, which is perceived in silence, which is not heard openly, which does not proceed forth by organs of the body, which does not go into ears of flesh, which is not heard by corruptible substance, which does not exist in the world, neither is sent forth on earth, nor written in books, which is owned by one and not by another: ³but with this, O Jesus Christ, I give You thanks, with the silence of a voice, with which the Spirit that is in me loves You, speaks to You, sees You, and pleads with You. You are perceived by the Spirit only; ⁴You are to me father—You my mother, You my brother, You my friend, You my bondsman, You my steward: You are the All and the All is in You; and You are, and there is nothing else that is except You alone. ⁵Therefore, to Him you must also flee, brothers, and if you learn that in Him alone you exist, you will obtain those things whereof He says to you: which neither eye has seen nor ear heard, neither have they entered into the heart of man. ⁶We ask, therefore, for that which You have promised to give to us, O You undefiled Jesus. ⁷We praise You; we give You thanks and confess to You, glorifying You, even we men that are still without strength, for You are God alone, and none other: to whom be glory now and to all ages. Amen."

CHAPTER 40

¹And when the multitude that stood by pronounced the "Amen" with a great sound, together with the "Amen" Peter gave up his spirit to the LORD. ²And Marcellus, not asking leave of any—for it was not possible when he saw that Peter had given up the spirit—took him down from the cross with his own hands and washed him in milk and wine; ³and he cut in fine [pieces] seven minae of mastic, and of myrrh, and aloes, and Indian leaf another fifty; and he embalmed his body, and filled a coffin of marble of great price with Attic honey, and laid it in his own tomb. ⁴But Peter appeared by night to Marcellus and said: "Marcellus, have you heard that the LORD says: Let the dead be buried by their own dead?" ⁵And when Marcellus said, "Yes," Peter said to him: "That, then, which you have spent on the dead, you have lost, for you being alive have like a dead man cared for the dead." ⁶And Marcellus awoke and told the brothers of the appearing of Peter: and he was with them that had been established in the faith of Christ by Peter, also being established himself still more until the coming of Paul to Rome.

CHAPTER 41

¹But Nero, learning thereafter that Peter had departed out of this life, blamed the prefect Agrippa, because he had been put to death without his knowledge; ²for he desired to punish him more severely and with greater torment, because Peter had made disciples of certain of them that served him, and had caused them to depart from him, so that he was very wrathful and for a long season did not speak to Agrippa: ³for he sought to destroy all of them that had been made disciples by Peter. ⁴And he beheld by night one that scourged him and said to him: "Nero, you cannot now persecute nor destroy the servants of Christ: therefore, refrain your hands from them." ⁵And so Nero, being greatly frightened by such a vision, abstained from harming the disciples at that time when Peter also departed this life. ⁶And thenceforth the brothers were rejoicing with one mind and exulting in the LORD, glorifying the God and [[Father]] of our Lord Jesus Christ with the Holy Spirit, to whom be glory, world without end. Amen.

ACTS OF JOHN

Translated here from extant versions in Greek and Latin, the Acts of John is a collection of stories and ancient legends about the apostle by that name. The collection is pseudepigraphal and was likely composed in the 2nd century, and the first section, chapters 1-17, is missing. The content of 56-57 is unclear. It is generally divided into three sections (18-86, 87-105, and 106-115), with the final section relating John's death. It is likely that some of these sections were independent works. It contains primordial hallmarks of both Docetism and Gnosticism.

CHAPTER 18

¹Now John was hastening to Ephesus, moved there by a vision. ²Therefore Damonicus, and his relative Aristodemus, and a certain very rich man Cleobius, and the wife of Marcellus, hardly prevailed to keep him for one day in Miletus, reclining themselves with him. ³And when very early in the morning they had set forth, and already about four miles of the journey were accomplished, a voice came from Heaven in the hearing of all of us, saying, "John, you are about to give glory to your Lord in Ephesus, whereof you will know—you and all the brothers that are with you, and certain of them that are there, which will believe by your means." ⁴John therefore pondered, rejoicing in himself, what it should be that should happen to him at Ephesus, and said: "Lord, behold, I go according to Your will: let that be done which You desire."

CHAPTER 19

¹And as we drew near to the city, Lycomedes the praetor of the Ephesians, a man of great wealth, met us, and falling at John's feet, he pleaded with him, saying, "Is your name John? The God whom you preach has sent you to do good to my wife, who has been stricken with palsy now these seven days and lies incurable. ²But glorify your God by healing her, and have compassion on us. ³For as I was considering within myself what decision to take in this matter, One stood by me and said: Lycomedes, cease from this thought which wars against you, for it is evil: do not submit yourself to it. ⁴For I have compassion on My handmaid Cleopatra, and have sent from Miletus a man named John who will raise her up and restore her to you whole. ⁵Therefore, do not tarry—you servant of the God who has manifested Himself to me, but hurry to my wife who has nothing more than breath." ⁶And John went from the gate immediately, with the brothers that were with him and Lycomedes, to his house. ⁷But Cleobius said to his young men: "Go to my relative Callippus and receive from him comfortable entertainment—for I have come here with his son—so that we may find all things decent."

CHAPTER 20

¹Now when Lycomedes came with John into the house wherein his wife lay, he caught hold again of his feet and said: "See, lord, the withering of the beauty, see the youth, see the renowned flower of my poor wife, at which all of Ephesus was accustomed to marvel: ²wretched me, I have suffered envy, I have been humbled, the eye of my enemies has stricken me: I have never wronged anyone, although I might have injured many, for I looked before to this very thing, and took care, lest I should see any evil or any such misfortune as this. ³What profit, then, has Cleopatra from my anxiety? What have I gained by being known as a pious man until this day? Indeed, I suffer more than the impious, in that I see you, Cleopatra, lying in such a plight. ⁴The sun in his course will no longer see me conversing with you: I will go before you, Cleopatra, and rid myself of life: I will not spare my own safety though it is still young. ⁵I will defend myself before Justice, so that I have rightly deserted, for I may indict her as judging unrighteously. ⁶I will be avenged on her when I come before her as a spirit of life. ⁷I will say to her: You forced me to leave the light when you robbed me of Cleopatra; you caused me to become a corpse when you sent me this misfortune; you compelled me to insult Providence, by cutting off my joy in life."

CHAPTER 21

¹And with yet more words, Lycomedes, addressing Cleopatra, came near to the bed, and cried aloud, and lamented: ²but John pulled him away and said: "Cease from these lamentations and from your unsuitable words: you must not disobey Him that appeared to you, for know that you will receive your consort again. ³Therefore, stand with us that have come here on her account and pray to the God whom you saw manifesting Himself to you in dreams. ⁴What, then, is it, Lycomedes? Awake—you also—and open your soul. ⁵Cast off the heavy sleep from yourself: plead with the Lord, beg Him for your wife, and He will raise her up." ⁶But he fell on the floor and lamented, fainting, [[and died]]. ⁷Therefore, John said with tears: "Oh, for the fresh betrayal of my vision! For the new temptation that is prepared for me! For the new scheme of him who plots against me! ⁸The voice from Heaven that was carried to me in the way, has it devised this for me? Was it this that it foreshowed to me should come to pass here, betraying me to this great multitude of the citizens because of Lycomedes? ⁹The man lies without breath, and I know well that they will not allow me to go out of the house alive. ¹⁰Why do You tarry, Lord? Why have You shut off from us Your good promise? ¹¹Do not, I beg You, Lord, give him a reason to exult who rejoices in the suffering of others; do not give a reason to dance [to the one] who always derides us; but let Your holy Name and Your mercy make haste. Raise up these two dead [ones] whose death is against me."

CHAPTER 22

¹And even as John thus cried out, the city of the Ephesians ran together to the house of Lycomedes, hearing that he was dead. ²And John, beholding the great multitude that had come, said to the Lord: "Now is the time of refreshment and of confidence toward You, O Christ; now is the time for us who are sick to have the help that is from You [alone], O Physician who heals freely; keep my entering in here safe from derision. ³I beg You, Jesus, help this great multitude, so that it may come to You who are Lord of all things: ⁴behold the affliction, behold them that lie here. ⁵Prepare, even from them that are assembled for that end, holy vessels for Your service, when they behold Your gift. ⁶For You Yourself have said, O Christ, Ask, and it will be given to you. We therefore ask of You, O King, not gold, not silver, not substance, not possessions, nor anything of what is on earth and perishes, but two souls, ⁷by whom You will convert them that are here to Your way, to Your teaching, to Your liberty, to Your most excellent [[or unfailing]] promise: ⁸for when they perceive Your power in that those that have died are raised, they will be saved—some of them. ⁹You Yourself, therefore, give them hope in You: and so I go to Cleopatra and say: Arise, in the Name of Jesus Christ."

CHAPTER 23

¹And he came to her, and touched her face, and said: "Cleopatra, He says—whom every ruler fears, and every creature and every power, the abyss and all darkness, and unsmiling death, and the height of Heaven, and the circles of Hades, [[and the resurrection of the dead, and the sight of the blind,]] and the whole power of the prince of this world, and the pride of the ruler—Arise! ²And do not be an excuse to many that do not desire to believe, or an affliction to souls that are able to hope and to be saved." ³And Cleopatra immediately cried with a loud voice: "I arise, Master: save Your handmaid!" ⁴Now when she had arisen seven days, the city of the Ephesians was moved at the unexpected sight. ⁵And Cleopatra asked concerning her husband Lycomedes, but John said to her: "Cleopatra, if you keep your soul unmoved and steadfast, you will immediately have your husband Lycomedes standing here beside you, if at least you are not disturbed nor moved at that which has happened, having believed on my God, who by my means will grant him to you alive. ⁶Therefore, come with me into your other bedchamber, and you will behold him, a dead corpse indeed, but raised again by the power of my God."

CHAPTER 24

¹And Cleopatra, going with John into her bedchamber, and seeing Lycomedes dead for her sake, had no power to speak, and ground her teeth, and bit her tongue, and closed her eyes, raining down tears: and with composure she gave heed to the apostle. ²But John had compassion on Cleopatra when he saw that she neither raged nor was beside herself, ³and he called on the perfect and humble mercy, saying, "Lord Jesus Christ, You see the pressure of sorrow, You see the need; You see Cleopatra shrieking her soul out in silence, for she constrains within her the frenzy that cannot be endured; ⁴and I know that for Lycomedes' sake she will also die on his body." ⁵And she quietly said to John: "That I have in mind, master, and nothing else." ⁶And the apostle went to the couch whereon Lycomedes lay, and taking Cleopatra's hand he said: "Cleopatra, because of the multitude that is present, and your relatives that have come in, with strong crying, say to your husband: Arise and glorify the Name of God, for He gives back the dead to the dead." ⁷And she went to her husband and said to him, according as she was taught, and immediately raised him up. ⁸And he, when he arose, fell on the floor and kissed John's feet, but he raised him, saying, "O man, do not kiss my feet, but [rather] the feet of God by whose power you have both arisen."

CHAPTER 25

¹But Lycomedes said to John: "I implore and adjure you by the God in whose Name you have raised us, to abide with us, together with all those that are with you." ²Likewise, Cleopatra also caught his feet and said the same. ³And John said to them: "For tomorrow I will be with you." And they said to him again: "We will have no hope in your God, but will have been raised with no purpose, if you do not abide with us." ⁴And Cleobius, with Aristodemus, and Damonicus were touched in the soul and said to John: "Let us abide with them, so that they continue without offense toward the LORD." ⁵So he continued there with the brothers.

CHAPTER 26

¹Therefore, a gathering of a great multitude came together on John's account; ²and as he discoursed to them that were there, Lycomedes, who had a friend who was a skillful painter, went hastily to him and said to him: "You see me in a great hurry to come to you: come quickly to my house and paint the man whom I show you without his knowing it." ³And the painter, giving someone the necessary implements and colors, said to Lycomedes: "Show him to me, and as for the rest, have no anxiety." ⁴And Lycomedes pointed out John to the painter, and brought him near him, and shut him up in a room from which the apostle of Christ could be seen. ⁵And Lycomedes was with the blessed man, feasting on the faith and the knowledge of our God, and rejoiced yet more in the thought that he should possess him in a portrait.

CHAPTER 27

¹The painter, then, on the first day, made an outline of him and went away. ²And on the next [day], he painted him in with his colors and so delivered the portrait to Lycomedes to his great joy. ³And he took it, and set it up in his own bedchamber, and hung it with garlands, so that later John, when he perceived it, said to him: "My beloved child, what is it that you always do when you come in from the bath into your bedchamber alone? ⁴Do I not pray with you and the rest of the brothers? Or is there something you are hiding from us?" ⁵And as he said this and talked jestingly with him, he went into the bedchamber and saw the portrait of an old man crowned with garlands, and lamps and altars set before it. ⁶And he called him and said: "Lycomedes, what do you intend by this matter of the portrait? Can it be one of your gods that is painted here? For I see that you are still living in heathen fashion." ⁷And Lycomedes answered him: "My only God is He who raised me up from death with my wife: but if, next to that God, it is right that the men who have helped us should be called gods—it is you, father, whom I have had painted in that portrait, whom I crown, and love, and revere as having become my good guide."

CHAPTER 28

¹And John, who had never at any time seen his own face, said to him: "You mock me, child: am I like that in form—your Lord? How can you persuade me that the portrait is like me?" ²And Lycomedes brought him a mirror. And when he had seen himself in the mirror and looked earnestly at the portrait, he said: "As the Lord Jesus Christ lives, the portrait is like me, yet not like me, child, but like my fleshly image; ³for if this painter, who has imitated this face of mine, desires to draw me in a portrait, he will be at a loss—the colors that are now given to you, and boards, and plaster, and glue, and the position of my shape, and old age, and youth, and all things that are seen with the eye."

CHAPTER 29

¹"But you become a good painter for me, Lycomedes. ²You have colors which He gives you through me, who paints all of us for Himself, even Jesus, who knows the shapes, and appearances, and postures, and dispositions, and types of our souls. ³And the colors with which I command you to paint are these: faith in God, knowledge, godly fear, friendship, thanksgiving, meekness, kindness, brotherly love, purity, simplicity, tranquility, fearlessness, grieflessness, sobriety, ⁴and the whole band of colors that paints the likeness of your soul, and even now raises up your members that were cast down, and levels them that were lifted up, and tends your bruises, and heals your wounds, and orders your hair that was disarranged, and washes your face, and corrects your eyes, and purges your bowels, and empties your belly, and cuts off that which is beneath it; ⁵and in a word, when the whole company and mingling of such colors has come together into your soul, it will present it to our Lord Jesus Christ undaunted, whole, and with firm shape. ⁶But this that you have now done is childish and imperfect: you have drawn a dead likeness of the dead."

CHAPTER 30

¹And he commanded Verus, the brother that ministered to him, to gather the aged women that were in all Ephesus, and made ready—he, and Cleopatra, and Lycomedes—all things for the care of them. ²Verus, then, came to John, saying, "Of the aged women that are here over sixty years old, I have only found four sound in body, and of the rest some … and some palsied, and others sick." ³And when he heard that, John kept silent for a long time, and [then] rubbed his face and said: "O the slackness of them that dwell in Ephesus! O the state of dissolution, and the weakness toward God! O Devil, that have so long mocked the faithful in Ephesus! ⁴Jesus, who gives me grace and the gift to have my confidence in Him, says to me in silence: Send after the old women that are sick and come with them into the theater, and through Me, heal them: for there are some of them that will come to this spectacle whom by these healings I will convert and make them useful for some end."

CHAPTER 31

¹Now when all the multitude had come together to Lycomedes, he dismissed them on John's behalf, saying, "Come to the theater tomorrow, as many as desire to see the power of God." ²And the multitude, the next day, while it was yet night, came to the theater, so that the proconsul also heard of it, and hurried, and took his seat with all the people. ³And a certain praetor, Andronicus, who was the [most] prominent of the Ephesians at that time, spread it around that John had promised impossible and incredible things: ⁴"But if," he said, "he is able to do any such thing as I hear, let him come into the public theater, when it is open, naked, and holding nothing in his hands—neither let him name that magical Name which I have heard him utter."

CHAPTER 32

¹John, therefore, having heard this and being moved by these words, commanded the aged women to be brought into the theater; ²and when they were all brought into the midst, some of them on beds and others lying in a deep sleep, and all the city had run together, and a great silence was made, John opened his mouth and began to say:

CHAPTER 33

¹"You men of Ephesus, first of all, learn why I am visiting in your city, or what this great confidence is which I have toward you, so that it may become manifest to this general assembly and to all of you. ²I have been sent, then, on a mission which is not of man's ordering, and not on any vain journey; neither am I a merchant that makes bargains or exchanges; ³but Jesus Christ whom I preach,

being compassionate and kind, desires by my means to convert all of you who are held in unbelief and sold to evil lusts, and to deliver you from error; ⁴and by His power I will confound even the unbelief of your praetor, by raising up them that lie before you, whom you all behold, in what plight and in what sicknesses they are. ⁵And to do this, to confound Andronicus, is not possible for me if they perish: therefore they will be healed."

CHAPTER 34

¹"But this first I have desired to sow in your ears, even that you should take care for your souls—on which account I have come to you—and not expect that this time will be forever, for it is but a moment, and not lay up treasures on the earth where all things fade away. ²Neither think that when you have obtained children you can rest on them, and try not for their sakes to defraud and overreach. ³Neither, you poor, be bothered if you do not have resources to minister to pleasures; for men of wealth, when they are diseased, call you blessed. ⁴Neither, you rich, rejoice that you have much money, for by possessing these things, you provide for yourselves grief that you cannot be rid of when you lose them; and besides, while it is with you, you are afraid lest someone attacks you on account of it."

CHAPTER 35

¹"You also that are puffed up because of the attractiveness of your body, and have good looks, will see the end of the promise thereof in the grave; ²and you that rejoice in adultery, know that both law and nature avenge it on you, and before these, conscience; ³and you, adulteress, that are an adversary of the law, do not understand where you will come in the end. ⁴And you that do not share with the needy, but have money stored up, when you depart out of this body and have need of some mercy when you burn in fire, will have no one to pity you; ⁵and you, the wrathful and passionate, know that your conversation is like the brute beasts; ⁶and you, drunkard and quarreler, learn that you lose your senses by being enslaved to a shameful and dirty desire."

CHAPTER 36

¹"You that rejoice in gold and delight yourself with ivory and jewels, when night falls, can you behold what you love? ²You that are vanquished by luxurious attire, and then leave life, will those things profit you in the place where you go? ³And let the murderer know that the deserved punishment is laid up for him twofold after his departure from here. ⁴Likewise, also you poisoner, sorcerer, robber, defrauder, sodomite, thief, and as many as are of that band, you will come at last, as your works lead you, to unquenchable fire, and utter darkness, and the pit of punishment, and eternal threatenings. ⁵Therefore, you men of Ephesus, turn yourselves back, knowing this also: that kings, rulers, tyrants, boasters, and they that have conquered in wars, stripped of all things when they depart from here, suffer pain, lodged in continuous misery."

CHAPTER 37

¹And having said this, John, by the power of God, healed all the diseases. … ²Now the brothers from Miletus said to John: "We have continued a long time at Ephesus; if it seems good to you, let us also go to Smyrna; ³for we already hear that the mighty works of God have reached it also." ⁴And Andronicus said to them: "Whenever the teacher wills, then let us go." ⁵But John said: "Let us first go to the temple of Artemis, for perhaps there also, if we show ourselves, the servants of the LORD will be found."

CHAPTER 38

¹After two days, then, was the birthday of the idol temple. ²John therefore, when all were dressed in white, alone put on black attire and went up into the temple. ³And they took him and attempted to kill him. ⁴But John said: "You are mad to set on me—a man that is the servant of the only God." And he got himself up on a high pedestal and said to them:

CHAPTER 39

¹"You run the risk, men of Ephesus, of being like in character to the sea: every river that flows in and every spring that runs down, and the rains, and waves that press on each other, and torrents full of rocks are made salt together by the bitter promise that is therein. ²So you also, remaining unchanged to this day toward true godliness, have become corrupted by your ancient rites of worship. ³How many wonders and healings of diseases have you seen worked through me? And yet you are blinded in your hearts and cannot recover sight. ⁴What is it, then, O men of Ephesus? I have ventured now and even come up into this idol temple of yours. I will convict you of being most godless, and dead from the understanding of mankind. ⁵Behold, I stand here: you all say that you have a goddess, even Artemis: pray then to her that I alone may die; or else I alone, if you are not able to do this, will call on my own God, and for your unbelief, I will cause every one of you to die."

CHAPTER 40

¹But they who had previously made a trial of him and had seen dead men raised up, cried out: "Do not slay us so, we beg you, John. We know that you can do it." ²And John said to them: "If then you do not desire to die, let that which you worship be confounded, and therefore it is confounded, so that you may also depart from your ancient error. ³For it is now time that you are either converted by my God, or I myself die by your goddess; for I will pray in your presence and implore my God that mercy be shown to you."

CHAPTER 41

¹And having so spoken, he prayed thus: "O God who is God above all that are called gods, that until this day have been set at nothing in the city of the Ephesians; ²who put into my mind to come into this place, whereof I never thought; ³who convicts every manner of worship by turning men to You; ⁴at whose Name every idol flees and every evil spirit and every unclean power; ⁵now also by the flight of the evil spirit here at Your Name, even of him that deceives this great multitude, show Your mercy in this place, for they have been made to err."

CHAPTER 42

¹And as John spoke these things, the altar of Artemis was immediately divided into many pieces, and all the things that were dedicated in the temple fell and were torn apart, and likewise of the images of the gods—more than seven. ²And half of the temple fell down, so that the priest was slain at one blow by the falling of the [[roof]]. ³The multitude of the Ephesians therefore cried out: "One is the God of John! One is the God that has pity on us, for You alone are God! ⁴Now we are turned to You, beholding Your marvelous works! Have mercy on us, O God, according to Your will, and save us from our great error!" ⁵And some of them, lying on their faces, made supplication, and some kneeled and pleaded, and some tore their clothes and wept, and others tried to escape.

CHAPTER 43

¹But John spread forth his hands, and being uplifted in soul, said to the LORD: "Glory be to You, my Jesus, the only God of truth, because You gain Your servants by manifold plans." ²And having so spoken, he said to the people: "Rise up from the floor, you men of Ephesus, and pray to my God, and recognize the invisible power that comes to manifestation, and the wonderful works which are worked before your eyes. ³Artemis should have helped herself: her servant should have been helped by her and not have died. ⁴Where is the power of the evil spirit? Where are her sacrifices? Where her birthdays? Where her festivals? Where are the garlands? Where is all that sorcery and the witchcraft that is sister to that?"

CHAPTER 44

¹But the people, rising up from off the floor, went hastily and cast down the rest of the idol temple, crying, "We only know John's God, and hereafter do we worship Him, since He has had mercy on us!" ²And as John came down from there, many people took hold of him, saying, "Help us, O John! Assist us who perish in vain! You see our purpose: you see the multitude following you and hanging on you in hope toward your God. ³We have seen the way wherein we went astray when we lost Him; we have seen our gods that were set up in vain; we have seen the great and shameful derision that has come to them: ⁴but permit us, we pray, to come to your house and to be aided without hindrance. Receive us that are in bewilderment."

CHAPTER 45

¹And John said to them: "Men [of Ephesus], believe that for your sakes I have remained in Ephesus, and have put off my journey to Smyrna and to the rest of the cities, that there also the servants of Christ may turn to Him. ²But since I am not yet perfectly assured concerning you, I have continued praying to my God and pleading with Him that I should then depart from Ephesus when I have confirmed you in the faith: ³and whereas I see that this has come to pass and yet more is being fulfilled, I will not leave you until I have weaned you like children from the nurse's milk and have set you on a firm rock."

CHAPTER 46

¹Therefore, John remained with them, receiving them in the house of Andronicus. ²And one of them that were gathered laid down the dead body of the priest of Artemis before the door [of the temple], for he was his relative, and came in quickly with the rest, saying nothing of it. ³John, therefore, after the discourse to the brothers, and the prayer, and the thanksgiving, and the laying of hands on every one of the congregation, said by the Spirit: "There is one here who moved by faith in God has laid down the priest of Artemis before the gate and has come in, ⁴and in the yearning of his soul, taking care first for himself, has thought this in himself: It is better for me to take thought for the living than for my relative that is dead: for I know that if I turn to the LORD and save my own soul, John will not deny to raise up the dead also." ⁵And John, arising from his place, went to that into which that relative of the priest who had so thought had entered, and took him by the hand, and said: "Did you have this thought when you came to me, my child?" ⁶And he, taken with trembling and fright, said: "Yes, lord," and cast himself at his feet. ⁷And John said: "Our Lord is Jesus Christ, who will show His power in your dead relative by raising him up."

CHAPTER 47

¹And he made the young man rise, and took his hand, and said: "It is no great matter for a man that is a master of great mysteries to continue wearying himself over small things: or what great thing is it to rid men of diseases of the body?" ²And still holding the young man by the hand, he said: "I say to you, child, go and raise the dead yourself, saying nothing but this only: John the servant of God says to you, Arise." ³And the young man went to his relative and said this only—and many people were with him—and entered in to John, bringing him alive. ⁴And John, when he saw him that was raised, said: "Now that you are raised, you do not truly live, neither are you a partaker or heir of the true life: will you belong to Him by whose Name and power you were raised? ⁵And now believe, and you will live throughout all ages." ⁶And he immediately believed on the Lord Jesus and thereafter clung to John.

CHAPTER 48

¹Now on the next day, John, having seen in a dream that he must walk three miles outside the gates, did not neglect it, but rose up early and set out on the way, together with the brothers. ²And a certain countryman who was admonished by his father not to take for himself the wife of a fellow laborer of his who threatened to kill him—this young man would not endure the admonition of his father, but kicked him and left him without speech [(dead)]. ³And John, seeing what had happened, said to the LORD: "LORD, was it on this account that You commanded me to come out here today?"

CHAPTER 49

¹But the young man, beholding the violence of death, and looking to be taken, drew out the sickle that was in his girdle and started to run to his own abode; ²and John met him and said: "Stand still—you most shameless devil—and tell me where you run bearing a sickle that thirsts for blood." ³And the young man was troubled, and cast the iron on the ground, and said to him: "I have done a wretched and barbarous deed and I know it, and so I determined to do an evil still worse and more cruel, even to kill myself at once. ⁴For because my father was always curbing me to sobriety, so that I should live without adultery, and chastely, I could not endure him to scold me, and I kicked him and slew him, ⁵and when I saw what was done, I was hurrying to the woman for whose sake I became my father's murderer, with intent to kill her and her husband, and myself last of all: for I could not bear to be seen by the husband of the woman and undergo the judgment of death."

CHAPTER 50

¹And John said to him: "So that I may not, by going away and leaving you in danger, give room to him who desires to laugh and sport with you: come with me and show me your father, where he lies. ²And if I raise him up for you, will you hereafter abstain from the woman that has become a snare to you?" ³And the young man said: "If you raise up for me my father himself alive, and if I see him whole and continuing in life, I will hereafter abstain from her."

CHAPTER 51

¹And while he was speaking, they came to the place where the old man lay dead, and many bystanders were standing near to it. ²And John said to the youth: "You wretched man, did you not even spare the old age of your father?" ³And he, weeping and tearing his hair, said that he converted from it; ⁴and John, the servant of the LORD, said: "You showed me that I was to set forth for this place; You knew that this would come to pass, from whom nothing can be hidden of things done in life, who give me power to work every cure and healing by Your will: ⁵now also give me this old man alive, for You see that his murderer has become his own judge: and spare him, You only LORD, that did not spare his father [who] counseled him for the best."

CHAPTER 52

¹And with these words, he came near to the old man and said: "My Lord will not be weak to spread out His kind pity and His humble mercy even to you: therefore, rise up and give glory to God for the work that has come to pass at this time." And the old man said: "I arise, Lord." ²And he rose, and sat up, and said: "I was released from a terrible life and had to bear the insults of my son, dreadful and many, and his desire for natural affection, and to what end have you called me back, O man of the living God?" ³[And John answered him:] "If you are raised only for the same end, it were better for you to die; but raise yourself to better things." ⁴And he took him and led him into the city, preaching to him the grace of God, so that before he entered the gate, the old man believed.

CHAPTER 53

¹But the young man, when he beheld the unexpected raising of his father, and the saving of himself, took a sickle and mutilated himself, and ran to the house wherein he had his adulteress, and reproached her, saying, "For your sake I became the murderer of my father, and of you two, and of myself: ²there you have that which is alike guilty for everything. For God has had mercy on me, so that I should know His power."

CHAPTER 54

¹And he came back and told John in the presence of the brothers what he had done. ²But John said to him: "He that put it into your heart, young man, to kill your father and become the adulterer of another man's wife, the same made you think it a good deed to also take away the unruly members. ³But you should have done away, not with the place of sin, but the thought which through those members showed itself harmful: for it is not the instruments that are injurious, but the unseen springs by which every shameful emotion is stirred and comes to light. ⁴Therefore convert, my child, of this fault, and having learned the tricks of Satan, you will have God to help you in all the necessities of your soul." ⁵And the young man kept silent and attended, having converted from his former sins, so that he should obtain pardon from the goodness of God: and he did not separate from John.

CHAPTER 55

¹When, then, these things had been done by him in the city of the Ephesians, those of Smyrna sent to him, saying, "We hear that the God whom you preach is not envious, and has charged you not to show partiality by abiding in one place. ²Since, then, you are a preacher of such a God, come to Smyrna and to the other cities, so that we may come to know your God, and having known Him, may have our hope in Him." [[³Now one day, as John was seated, a partridge flew by and came and played in the

dust before him; and John looked on it and wondered. ⁴And a certain priest came, who was one of his hearers, and came to John, and saw the partridge playing in the dust before him, and was offended in himself, and said: "Can such and so great a man take pleasure in a partridge playing in the dust?" ⁵But John, perceiving in the Spirit his thought, said to him: "It were better for you also, my child, to look at a partridge playing in the dust and not to defile yourself with shameful and profane practices; ⁶for he who awaits the conversion and reformation of all men has brought you here on this account, for I have no need of a partridge playing in the dust. For the partridge is your own soul." ⁷Then the elder, hearing this and seeing that he was not hidden, but that the apostle of Christ had told him all that was in his heart, fell on his face on the earth and cried aloud, saying, "Now I know that God dwells in you, O blessed John! For he that tempts you tempts Him who cannot be tempted." And he implored him to pray for him. ⁸And he instructed him, and delivered him the rules, and let him go to his house, glorifying God who is over all.]]

FROM LAODICEA TO EPHESUS THE SECOND TIME.

CHAPTER 58

¹Now when a long time had passed, and none of the brothers had been at any time grieved by John, they were then grieved because he had said: "Brothers, it is now time for me to go to Ephesus, [[for so have I agreed with them that dwell there,]] lest they become slack, now for a long time having no man to confirm them. ²But all of you must have your minds steadfast toward God, who never forsakes us." ³But when they heard this from him, the brothers lamented because they were to be parted from him. ⁴And John said: "Even if I am parted from you, yet Christ is always with you: whom if you love purely, you will have His fellowship without reproach, for if He is loved, He anticipates them that love Him."

CHAPTER 59

¹And having so spoken, and bidden farewell to them, and left much money with the brothers for distribution, he went forth to Ephesus, while all the brothers lamented and groaned. ²And there accompanied him, of Ephesus, both Andronicus, and Drusiana, and Lycomedes, and Cleobius, and their families. ³And Aristobula also followed him, who had heard that her husband Tertullus had died on the way, and Aristippus with Xenophon, and the harlot that was celibate, and many others, whom he exhorted at all times to cleave to the Lord, and they would no longer be parted from Him.

CHAPTER 60

¹Now on the first day, we arrived at a deserted inn, and when we were at a loss for a bed for John, we witnessed a strange matter: ²there was one bedstead lying somewhere there without coverings, whereon we spread the cloaks which we were wearing, and we implored him to lie down on it and rest, while the rest of us all slept on the floor. ³But he, when he lay down, was troubled by the bugs, and as they continued to become yet more troublesome to him, when it was now about the middle of the night, in the hearing of all of us, he said to them: "I say to you, O bugs, behave yourselves—one and all—and leave your abode for this night, and remain quiet in one place, and keep your distance from the servants of God." ⁴And as we laughed and went on talking for some time, John talked himself to sleep; and we, talking low, gave him no disturbance.

CHAPTER 61

¹But when the day was now dawning, I arose first, and with me Verus and Andronicus, and we saw at the door of the house which we had taken, a great number of bugs standing, and while we wondered at the great sight of them, and all the brothers were roused up because of them, John continued sleeping. ²And when he was awakened, we declared to him what we had seen. ³And he sat up on the bed, and looked at them, and said: "Since you have behaved yourselves well in listening to my rebuke, come to your place." ⁴And when he had said this and risen from the bed, the bugs running from the door, hurried to the bed, and climbed up by the legs thereof, and disappeared into the joints. ⁵And John said again: "This creature listened to the voice of a man, and abode by itself, and was quiet, and did not trespass; but we which hear the voice and commandments of God disobey and are flippant—and for how long?"

CHAPTER 62

¹After these things, we came to Ephesus: and the brothers there, who had for a long time known that John was coming, ran together to the house of Andronicus (where he also came to lodge), handling his feet, and laying his hands on their own faces, and kissing them; ²and many rejoiced even to touch his garment, and were healed by touching the clothes of the holy apostle.

CHAPTER 63

¹And whereas there was great love and joy unsurpassed among the brothers, a certain one, a messenger of Satan, became enamored by Drusiana, though he saw and knew that she was the wife of Andronicus. ²To whom many said: "It is not possible for you to obtain that woman, seeing that for a long time she has even separated herself from her husband for godliness' sake. ³Are you only ignorant that Andronicus, not being aforetime that which he now is, a God-fearing man, shut her up in a tomb, saying, Either I must have you as the wife whom I had before, or you will die. ⁴And she chose rather to die than to do that filth. ⁵If, then, she would not consent, for godliness' sake, to cohabit with her lord and husband, but even persuaded him to be of the same mind as herself, will she consent to you desiring to be her seducer? ⁶Depart from this madness which has no rest in you: give up this deed which you cannot bring to accomplishment."

CHAPTER 64

¹But his familiar friends, saying these things to him, did not convince him, but with shamelessness he courted her with messages; and when he learned the insults and disgraces which she returned, he spent his life in melancholy. ²And after two days, Drusiana took to her bed from heaviness, and was in a fever and said: "If only I had not now come home to my native place—I that have become an offense to a man ignorant of godliness! ³For if it were one who was filled with the word of God, he would not have reached such a degree of madness. ⁴But now, LORD, since I have become the cause of a blow to a soul devoid of knowledge, set me free from this chain and remove me to You quickly." ⁵And in the presence of John, who knew nothing at all of such a matter, Drusiana departed out of life not wholly happy—yes, even troubled because of the spiritual hurt of the man.

CHAPTER 65

¹But Andronicus, grieved with a secret grief, mourned in his soul and wept openly, so that John checked him often and said to him: "On a better hope has Drusiana departed from this unrighteous life." ²And Andronicus answered him: "Yes, I am persuaded of it, O John, and I do not doubt at all in regard to trust in my God: but this very thing do I hold fast: that she departed out of life pure."

CHAPTER 66

¹And when she was carried forth, John took hold of Andronicus, and now that he knew the cause, he mourned more than Andronicus. ²And he kept silent, considering the provocation of the adversary, and for a span [of time], sat still. ³Then, the brothers being gathered there to hear what word he would speak of her who had departed, he began to say:

CHAPTER 67

¹"When the captain that voyages, together with them that sail with him, and the ship herself, arrives in a calm and stormless harbor, then let him say that he is safe. ²And the farmer that has committed the seed to the earth and greatly toiled in the care and protection of it, let him then take rest from his labors, when he lays up the seed with manifold increase in his barns. ³Let him that undertakes to run in the course, then exult when he carries home the prize. ⁴Let him that inscribes his name for boxing, then boast of himself when he receives the crowns: and so in succession is it with all contests and crafts, when they do not fail in the end, but show themselves to be like that which they promised."

CHAPTER 68

¹"And thus, I also think it is with the faith which each one of us practices, that it is then discerned whether it is indeed true, when it

continues like itself even until the end of life. ²For many obstacles fall into the way and prepare trouble for the minds of men: care, children, parents, glory, poverty, flattery, prime of life, beauty, conceit, lust, wealth, anger, uplifting, slackness, envy, jealousy, neglect, fear, insolence, love, deceit, money, pretense, and other such obstacles—as many as there are in this life: ³as also the captain sailing a prosperous course is opposed by the onset of contrary winds, and a great storm, and mighty waves out of calm, and the farmer by untimely winter, and blight, and creeping things rising out of the earth; ⁴and they that strive in the games just do not win, and they that exercise crafts are hindered by the various difficulties of them."

CHAPTER 69

¹"But before all things, it is necessary that the believer should look before at his ending and understand it in what manner it will come on him, whether it will be vigorous, and sober, and without any obstacle, or disturbed, and clinging to the things that are here, and bound down by desires. ²So is it right that a body should be praised as lovely when it is completely stripped, and a general as great when he has accomplished every promise of the war, and a physician as excellent when he has succeeded in every cure, and a soul as full of faith and worthy of God when it has paid its promise in full: ³not that soul which began well and was dissolved into all the things of this life and fell away, nor that which is numb, having made an effort to attain to better things, and then is weighed down by temporal things, ⁴nor that which has longed after the things of time more than those of eternity, nor that which exchanges those that do not endure, nor that which has honored the works of dishonor that deserve shame, ⁵nor that which taketh pledges of Satan, nor that which has received the serpent into its own house, nor that which suffers reproach for God's sake and then is [not] ashamed, nor that which with the mouth says yes, but indeed does not approve itself: ⁶but that which has not prevailed to be made weak by foul pleasure, not to be overcome by flippancy, not to be caught by the bait of love of money, not to be betrayed by vigor of body or wrath."

CHAPTER 70

¹And as John was discoursing yet further to the brothers that they should despise temporal things in respect for the eternal, he that was enamored with Drusiana, being inflamed with a horrible lust and possession of the many-shaped Satan, bribed the steward of Andronicus who was a lover of money with a great sum: ²and he opened the tomb and gave him opportunity to inflict the forbidden thing on the dead body. ³Not having succeeded with her when [she was] alive, he was still persistent after her death to her body, and said: "If you would not have [anything] to do with me while you lived, I will outrage your corpse now that you are dead." ⁴With this [vile] scheme, and having managed for himself the wicked act by means of the abominable steward, he rushed with him to the tomb; they opened the door and began to strip the grave-clothes from the corpse, saying, "What have you profited, poor Drusiana? Could you not have done this in life, which perhaps would not have grieved you, had you done it willingly?"

CHAPTER 71

¹And as these men were speaking thus, and only the accustomed undergarment now remained on her body, a strange spectacle was seen, such as they deserve to suffer who do such deeds: a serpent appeared from some quarter, and dealt the steward a single bite, and slew him: ²but it did not strike the young man, but coiled around his feet, hissing terribly, and when he fell, mounted on his body and sat on him.

CHAPTER 72

¹Now on the next day John came, accompanied by Andronicus and the brothers, to the tomb at dawn, it being now the third day from Drusiana's death, so that we might break bread there. ²And first, when they set out, the keys were sought for and could not be found; but John said to Andronicus: "It is quite right that they should be lost, for Drusiana is not in the tomb; nevertheless, let us go, so that you may not be neglectful, and the doors will be opened of themselves, even as the Lord has done many such things for us."

CHAPTER 73

¹And when we were at the place, at the commandment of the master, the doors were opened, and we saw by the tomb of Drusiana a beautiful youth, smiling: and John, when he saw him, cried out and said: "Have you come before us here too, beautiful one? And for what reason?" ²And we heard a voice saying to him: "For Drusiana's sake, whom you are to raise up—for I was within a moment of finding her—and for his sake that lies dead beside her tomb." ³And when the beautiful one had said this to John, he went up into the heavens in the sight of us all. ⁴And John, turning to the other side of the tomb, saw a young man—even Callimachus, one of the chiefs of the Ephesians—and a huge serpent sleeping over him, and the steward of Andronicus, Fortunatus by name, lying dead. ⁵And at the sight of the two, he stood perplexed, saying to the brothers: "What does such a sight mean? Why has the Lord not declared to me what was done here—He who has never neglected me?"

CHAPTER 74

¹And Andronicus, seeing those corpses, leapt up and went to Drusiana's tomb, and seeing her lying in her undergarment only, said to John: "I understand what has happened, you blessed servant of God, John. ²This Callimachus was enamored with my sister; and because he never won her, though he often attempted it, he has bribed this accursed steward of mine with a great sum, perhaps scheming, as now we may see, to fulfill by his means the tragedy of his conspiracy; ³for indeed, Callimachus vowed this to many, saying, If she will not consent to me when living, she will be outraged when dead. ⁴And it may be, master, that the beautiful one knew it and did not allow her body to be insulted, and therefore these have died who made that attempt. ⁵And can it be that the voice that said to you, Raise up Drusiana, foreshowed this? Because she departed out of this life in sorrow of mind. ⁶But I believe him that said that this is one of the men that have gone astray; for you were commanded to raise him up: for as to the other, I know that he is unworthy of salvation. ⁷But this one thing I beg of you: raise Callimachus up first, and he will confess to us what has come about."

CHAPTER 75

¹And John, looking on the body, said to the venomous beast: "Get away from him that is to be a servant of Jesus Christ"; ²and he stood up and prayed over him thus: "O God, whose Name is glorified by us, as of right; O God who subdue every harmful force; O God whose will is accomplished, who always hears us: now also let Your gift be accomplished in this young man; ³and if there is any dispensation to be worked through him, manifest it to us when he is raised up." ³And immediately the young man rose up, and for a whole hour kept silent.

CHAPTER 76

¹But when he came to his right senses, John asked of him about his entry into the tomb, what it meant, and learning from him that which Andronicus had told him, namely, that he was enamored with Drusiana, John inquired of him again if he had fulfilled his foul intent—to insult a body full of holiness. ²And he answered him: "How could I accomplish it when this fearful beast struck down Fortunatus at a blow in my sight: and rightly, since he encouraged my frenzy, when I was already cured of that unreasonable and horrible madness? ³But it stopped me with fright and brought me to that plight in which you saw me before I arose. ⁴And another thing yet more wondrous I will tell you, which yet went near to slay and was within a moment of making me a corpse: ⁵when my soul was stirred up with folly and the uncontrollable malady was troubling me, and I had now torn away the grave-clothes in which she was clad, and I had then come out of the grave and laid them as you see, I went again to my unholy work; ⁶and I saw a beautiful youth covering her with his mantle, and from his eyes sparks of light came forth to her eyes; and he uttered words to me, saying, "Callimachus, die that you may live." ⁷Now who he was, I did not know, O servant of God; but that now you have appeared here, I recognize that he was a messenger of God—that I know well; ⁸and this I surely know: that it is a true God that is proclaimed by you, and I am persuaded of it. ⁹But I beg you: do not be slack to deliver me

from this calamity and this fearful crime, and to present me to your God as a man deceived with a shameful and foul deceit. ¹⁰Therefore, begging for help from you, I take hold of your feet. I would become one of them that hope in Christ, that the voice may prove true which said to me, Die that you may live; ¹¹and that voice has also fulfilled its effect, for he is dead—that faithless, disorderly, godless one—and I have been raised by you: I who will be faithful, God-fearing, knowing the truth, which I plead with you may be shown to me by you."

CHAPTER 77

¹And John, filled with great gladness and perceiving the whole spectacle of the salvation of man, said: "What Your power is, Lord Jesus Christ, I do not know, bewildered as I am at Your great compassion and boundless long-suffering. ²O what a greatness that came down into bondage! O unspeakable liberty brought into slavery by us! O incomprehensible glory that has come to us! ³You that have kept the dead tabernacle safe from insult; that have redeemed the man that stained himself with blood and punished the soul of him that would defile the corruptible body; Father that have had pity and compassion on the man that did not care for You; ⁴We glorify You, and praise, and bless, and thank Your great goodness and long-suffering, O holy Jesus, for You alone are God, and no one else: whose is the might that cannot be conspired against, now and world without end. Amen.

CHAPTER 78

¹And when he had said this, John took Callimachus and kissed him, saying, "Glory be to our God, my child, who has had mercy on you and made me worthy to glorify His power— ²and you also by a good course to depart from that abominable madness and drunkenness of yours—and has called you to His own rest and to renewing of life."

CHAPTER 79

¹But Andronicus, beholding the dead Callimachus raised, pleaded with John, with the brothers, to raise Drusiana up also, saying, "O John, let Drusiana arise and spend happily that short span [of life] which she gave up through grief concerning Callimachus, when she thought she had become a stumbling block to him: ²and when the LORD will, He will take her again to Himself." ³And without delay, John went to her tomb, and took her hand, and said: "I call on You who are the only God—the greater than great, the unutterable, the incomprehensible: ⁴to whom every power of principalities is subjected; to whom all authority bows; before whom all pride falls down and keeps silent; whom devils hearing of tremble; whom all creation perceiving keeps its bounds. ⁵Let Your Name be glorified by us and raise up Drusiana, so that Callimachus may yet be [even] more confirmed to You who dispense that which to men is without a way and impossible, but to You only possible, even salvation and resurrection; ⁶and so that Drusiana may now come forth in peace, not having even the least hindrance, now that the young man has turned to You, in her course toward You."

CHAPTER 80

¹And after these words, John said to Drusiana: "Drusiana, arise." And she arose and came out of the tomb; ²and when she saw herself in her undergarment only, she was perplexed at the thing and learned everything accurately from Andronicus while John lay on his face; ³and Callimachus, with a loud voice and tears, glorified God, and she also rejoiced, glorifying Him in like manner.

CHAPTER 81

¹And when she had clothed herself, she turned and saw Fortunatus lying, and said to John: "Father, let this man also rise, even if he did attempt to become my betrayer." ²But Callimachus, when he heard her say that, said: "Do not, I beg you, Drusiana, for the voice which I heard took no thought of him, but declared concerning you only, and I saw and believed: ³for if he had been good, perhaps God would have had mercy on him also and would have raised him by means of the blessed John"; ⁴he therefore knew that the man had come to a bad end. ⁵And John said to him: "We have not learned, my child, to render evil for evil, for God, though we have done much bad and no good toward Him, has not given retribution to us, but conversion; ⁶and though we were ignorant of His Name, He did not neglect us but had mercy on us, ⁷and when we blasphemed Him, He did not punish, but pitied us, ⁸and when we disbelieved Him, He bore us no grudge, ⁹and when we persecuted His brothers, He did not repay us evil, but put into our minds conversion and abstinence from evil, and exhorted us to come to Him, as He has you also, my son Callimachus; ¹⁰and not remembering your former evil, He has made you His servant, waiting on His mercy. ¹¹Therefore, if you do not allow me to raise up Fortunatus, it is for Drusiana to do so."

CHAPTER 82

¹And she, not delaying, went with rejoicing of spirit and soul to the body of Fortunatus and said: "Jesus Christ, God of the ages, God of truth, who have granted me to see wonders and signs, and given to me to become a partaker of Your Name; ²who breathed Yourself into me with Your many-shaped countenance, and had mercy on me in many ways; ³who protected me by Your great goodness when I was oppressed by Andronicus (who was formerly my husband); ⁴who gave me Your servant Andronicus to be my brother; ⁵who have kept me, Your handmaid, pure to this day; ⁶who raised me up by Your servant John, and when I was raised, showed me him that was made to stumble free from stumbling; ⁷who have given me perfect rest in You, and lightened me from the secret madness; whom I have loved and affectioned: please, O Christ, do not refuse Your Drusiana that asks You to raise up Fortunatus, even though he attempted to become my betrayer."

CHAPTER 83

¹And taking the hand of the dead man, she said: "Rise up, Fortunatus, in the Name of our Lord Jesus Christ." ²And Fortunatus arose, and when he saw John in the tomb, and Andronicus, and Drusiana raised from the dead, and Callimachus a believer, and the rest of the brothers glorifying God, he said: "O to what the powers of these clever men have attained! I did not want to be raised, but would rather die, so as not to see them." ³And with these words, he fled and went out of the tomb.

CHAPTER 84

¹And John, when he saw the unchanged mind of Fortunatus, said: "O nature that is not changed for the better! O fountain of the soul that abides in foulness! O essence of corruption full of darkness! O death exulting in them that are yours! O fruitless tree full of fire! O tree that bear coals for fruit! O matter that dwell with the madness of matter and neighbor of unbelief! ²You have proved who you are, and you are always convicted with your children. ³And you do not know how to praise the better things, for you do not have them. ⁴Therefore, such as is your way, such also is your root and your nature. ⁵Be destroyed from among them that trust in the LORD: from their thoughts, from their mind, from their souls, from their bodies, from their acts, their life, their conversation, from their business, their occupations, their counsel, from the resurrection to God, from their sweet savor wherein you will share, from their faith, their prayers, from the holy bath, from the thanksgiving, from the food of the flesh, from drink, from clothing, from love, from care, from abstinence, from righteousness: ⁶from all these, you most unholy Satan, enemy of God, will Jesus Christ our God and of all that are like you and have your character, make you to perish."

CHAPTER 85

¹And having said this, John prayed, and took bread, and carried it into the tomb to break it; and he said: "We glorify Your Name, which converts us from error and ruthless deceit; ²we glorify You who have shown before our eyes that which we have seen; ³we bear witness to Your loving-kindness which appears in various ways; ⁴we praise Your merciful Name, O Lord—who have convicted them that are convicted by You; ⁵we give thanks to You, O Lord Jesus Christ, that we are persuaded of Your [[divinity]] which is unchanging; ⁶we give thanks to You who took on our nature so that we should be saved; ⁷we give thanks to You who have given us this assurance, for You are alone, both now and ever. ⁸We, Your servants, give You thanks, O Holy One, who are assembled with intent and are gathered out of the world."

CHAPTER 86

¹And having so prayed and given glory to God, he went out of the tomb after imparting to all the brothers of the communion of the LORD. ²And when he had come to Andronicus' house, he said to the brothers: "Brothers, [the] Spirit within me has divined that Fortunatus is about to die of poisoning from the bite of the serpent; but let someone go quickly and learn if it indeed is so." ³And one of the young men ran and found him dead and the poisoning spreading over him, and it had reached his heart; ⁴and he came and told John that he had been dead [for] three hours. And John said: "You have your child, O Devil."

CHAPTER 87

¹Those that were present inquired of the cause, and were especially perplexed, because Drusiana had said: "The LORD appeared to me in the tomb in the likeness of John, and in that of a youth." ²Forasmuch, therefore, as they were perplexed and were, in a way, not yet established in the faith, so as to endure it steadfastly, John said:

CHAPTER 88

¹"Men and brothers, you have suffered nothing strange or incredible as concerning your perception of the issue, inasmuch as we also, whom He chose for Himself to be apostles, were tried in many ways: ²I, indeed, am neither able to set forth to you nor to write the things which I both saw and heard: and now is it necessary that I should fit them for your hearing; ³and according as each of you is able to contain it, I will impart to you those things whereof you are able to become hearers, so that you may see the glory that is around Him who was and is, both now and forever. ⁴For when He had chosen Peter and Andrew, which were brothers, He comes to me and my brother James, saying, I have need of you; come to Me. ⁵And my brother, hearing that, said: John, what might this child have that is on the seashore and called us? And I said: What child? And he said to me again: He who beckons to us. ⁶And I answered: Because of our long watch we have kept at sea, you do not see correctly, my brother James; but do you not see the man that stands there—lovely, and fair, and of a cheerful countenance? ⁷But he said to me: I do not see Him, brother; but let us go forth and we will see what He might have."

CHAPTER 89

¹"And so, when we had brought the ship to land, we saw Him also helping along with us to settle the ship; ²and when we departed from that place, intending to follow Him, again He was seen by me as having a rather bald [head], but the beard [was] thick and flowing, ³but to James, [He was] as a youth whose beard had newly come. ⁴We were therefore perplexed, both of us, as to what that which we had seen should mean. ⁵And after that, as we followed Him, both of us were little by little perplexed as we considered the matter. ⁶Yet to me there then appeared this yet more wonderful thing: for I would try to see Him privately, and I never at any time saw His eyes closing, but only open. ⁷And oftentimes He would appear to me as a small man and unattractive, and then again as one reaching to the sky. ⁸Also, there was another marvel in Him: when I sat down to eat, He would take me on His own breast; and sometimes His breast was felt by me to be smooth and tender, and sometimes hard like stones, so that I was perplexed in myself and said: Why is this so to me? And as I considered this, He …"

CHAPTER 90

¹"And at another time, He takes me, and James, and Peter with Him to the mountain where He was accustomed to pray, and we saw in Him a light such as it is not possible for a man that uses corruptible speech to describe what it was like. ²Again, in like manner, he brings the three of us up into the mountain, saying, Come with Me. And we went again: and we saw Him at a distance praying. ³I, therefore, because He loved me, drew near to Him gently, as though He could not see me, and stood looking on His back: ⁴and I saw that He was not in any way clothed with garments, but was seen by us naked, and not in any way as a man, and that his feet were whiter than any snow, so that the earth there was lit up by His feet, and that His head touched the sky, so that I was afraid and cried out, ⁵and He, turning around, appeared as a man of small stature, and caught hold of my beard, and pulled it, and said to me: John, do not be faithless but believing, and not curious. And I said to Him: But what have I done, Lord? ⁶And I say to you, brothers, I suffered such a great pain in that place where He took hold of my beard for thirty days, that I said to Him: Lord, if Your [mere] twitch when You were sporting [with me] has given me such great pain, what were it if You had given me a beating? ⁷And He said to me: Let it be, henceforth, not to tempt Him who cannot be tempted."

CHAPTER 91

¹"But Peter and James were angry because I spoke with the LORD and beckoned to me that I should come to them and leave the LORD alone. ²And I went, and they both said to me: He who was speaking with the LORD on the top of the mountain, who was He? For we heard both of them speaking. ³And I, having in mind His great grace, and His unity which has many faces, and His wisdom which without ceasing looks on us, said: You will learn that if you inquire of Him."

CHAPTER 92

¹"Again, once when all of us, His disciples, were at Gennesaret sleeping in one house, I alone having wrapped myself in my mantle, watched what He would do: ²and first I heard Him say: John, go to sleep. ³And I, thereon pretending to sleep, saw another like Him [sleeping], whom I also heard say to my Lord: Jesus, they whom You have chosen do not yet believe on You. ⁴And my Lord said to him: You speak correctly, for they are [mere] men."

CHAPTER 93

¹"I will also tell you of another glory, brothers: sometimes when I would lay hold of Him, I met with a material and solid body, and at other times, again, when I felt Him, the substance was immaterial and as if it did not exist at all. ²And if at any time He were requested by someone of the Pharisees and went at the request, we went with Him, and there was set before each one of us a loaf by them that had requested us, and with us He also received one; ³and His own He would bless and part it among us: and of that little bit, everyone was filled, and our own loaves were saved whole, so that they which requested Him were amazed. ⁴And oftentimes, when I walked with Him, I desired to see the print of His foot, whether it appeared on the earth; for I saw Him, as it were, lifting Himself up from the earth: and I never saw it. ⁵And these things I speak to you, brothers, for the encouragement of your faith toward Him; for we must at the present keep silent concerning His mighty and wonderful works, inasmuch as they are unspeakable and, it might be, cannot be either uttered or heard at all."

CHAPTER 94

¹"Now before He was taken by the lawless Jews, who also were governed by the lawless serpent, He gathered all of us together and said: Before I am delivered up to them, let us sing a hymn to the Father, and so go forth to that which lies before us. ²He therefore commanded us to make, as it were, a ring, holding one another's hands; and [with] Himself standing in the midst, He said: Answer Amen to Me. ³He then began to sing a hymn and to say: Glory be to You, Father. ⁴And we, going around in a circle, answered Him: Amen. Glory be to You, Word; Glory be to You, Grace. Amen. Glory be to You, Spirit; Glory be to You, Holy One; Glory be to Your glory. Amen. ⁵We praise You, O Father; We give thanks to You, O Light, wherein darkness does not dwell. Amen."

CHAPTER 95

¹"Now whereas we give thanks, I say: I would be saved, || And I would save. Amen. ²I would be loosed, || And I would loose. Amen. ³I would be wounded, || And I would wound. Amen. ⁴I would be born, || And I would bear. Amen. ⁵I would eat, || And I would be eaten. Amen. ⁶I would hear, || And I would be heard. Amen. ⁷I would be thought, || Being wholly thought. Amen. ⁸I would be washed, || And I would wash. Amen. ⁹Grace dances. I would pipe— Dance you all. Amen. ¹⁰I would mourn— Lament you all. Amen. ¹¹The number Eight sings praise with us. Amen. ¹²The number Twelve dances on high. Amen. ¹³The Whole on high has part in our dancing. Amen. ¹⁴Whoever does not dance, || Does not know what comes to pass. Amen. ¹⁵I would flee, || And I would stay. Amen. ¹⁶I would adorn, || And I would be adorned. Amen. ¹⁷I would be

united, || And I would unite. Amen. ¹⁸A house I have not, || And I have houses. Amen. ¹⁹A place I have not, || And I have places. Amen. ²⁰A temple I have not, || And I have temples. Amen. ²¹A lamp am I to you that behold me. Amen. ²²A mirror am I to you that perceive me. Amen. ²³A door am I to you that knock at me. Amen. A way am I to you a wayfarer."

CHAPTER 96

¹"Now respond to My dancing. Behold yourself in Me who speak, and seeing what I do, keep silent concerning My mysteries. ²You that dance, perceive what I do, for you is this passion of the manhood, which I am about to suffer. ³For you could not at all have understood what you suffer if I had not been sent to you, as the Word of the Father. ⁴You that saw what I suffer saw Me as suffering, and seeing it, you did not abide but were wholly moved—moved to make wise. ⁵You have Me as a bed: rest on Me. ⁶Who I am, you will know when I depart. What I now am seen to be, that I am not. You will see when you come. ⁷If you had known how to suffer, you would have been able not to suffer. ⁸Learn to suffer, and you will be able not to suffer. ⁹What you do not know, I Myself will teach you. ¹⁰I am your God, not the god of the traitor. I would keep tune with holy souls. ¹¹In Me, know the word of wisdom. Again, say with Me: Glory be to You, Father; Glory to You, Word; Glory to You, Holy Spirit. ¹²And if you would know concerning Me, what I was, know that with a word I deceived all things and I was in no way deceived. ¹³I have leaped: but understand the whole, and having understood it, say: Glory be to You, Father. Amen."

CHAPTER 97

¹"Thus, my beloved, having danced with us, the LORD went forth. ²And we as men gone astray, or dazed with sleep, fled this way and that. ³I, then, when I saw Him suffer, did not even abide by His suffering, but fled to the Mount of Olives, weeping at that which had happened. ⁴And when He was crucified on the Friday, at the sixth hour of the day, darkness came on all the earth. ⁵And my Lord, standing in the midst of the cave and illuminating it, said: John, to the multitude below in Jerusalem I am being crucified and pierced with lances and reeds, and gall and vinegar is given to Me to drink. ⁶But to you I speak, and what I speak, hear. I put it into your mind to come up into this mountain, so that you might hear those things which it is right for a disciple to learn from his Teacher, and a man from his God."

CHAPTER 98

¹"And having thus spoken, He showed me a cross of light fixed, and around the cross a great multitude, not having one form; and in it was one form and one likeness. ²And I beheld the LORD Himself above the cross, not having any shape, but only a voice: and a voice not such as was familiar to us, but one sweet, and kind, and truly of God, saying to me: John, it is necessary that one should hear these things from Me, for I have need of one that will hear. ³This cross of light is sometimes called the word by Me for your sakes, sometimes mind, sometimes Jesus, sometimes Christ, sometimes door, sometimes a way, sometimes bread, sometimes seed, sometimes resurrection, sometimes Son, sometimes Father, sometimes Spirit, sometimes life, sometimes truth, sometimes faith, sometimes grace. ⁴And by these names it is called as toward men: but that which it is in truth, as conceived of in itself and as spoken of to you, it is the marking-off of all things, and the firm uplifting of things fixed out of things unstable, and the harmony of wisdom, and indeed wisdom in harmony. ⁵There are of the right hand and the left, powers also, authorities, lordships and demons, workings, threatenings, wraths, devils, Satan, and the lower root from which the nature of the things that come into being proceeded."

CHAPTER 99

¹"This cross, then, is that which joined all things to itself by the Word and separated the things that are from those that are below, and then also, being one, streamed forth into all things. ²But this is not the cross of wood which you will see when you go down from here: neither am I he that is on the cross, whom you now do not see, but only hear his voice. ³I was reckoned to be that which I am not, not being what I was to many others: but they will call Me something else which is vile and not worthy of Me. ⁴As, then, the place of rest is neither seen nor spoken of, much more will I, the Lord thereof, be neither seen..."

CHAPTER 100

¹"Now the multitude of one aspect that is around the cross is the lower nature: and they whom you see in the cross, if they do not have one form, it is because every member of Him that came down has not yet been comprehended. ²But when the human nature is taken up, as well as the race which draws near to Me and obeys My voice, he that now hears Me will be united therewith, and will no longer be that which he now is, but above them, as I also now am. ³For as long as you do not call yourself Mine, I am not that which I am: but if you hear Me, you, hearing, will be as I am, and I will be that which I was, when I [am with] you as I am with Myself. For from Me you are that [which I am]. ⁴Therefore, do not care for the many, and them that are outside the mystery despise; for know that I am entirely with the Father, and the Father with Me."

CHAPTER 101

¹"Nothing, therefore, of the things which they will say of Me have I suffered: indeed, that suffering also which I showed to you and the rest in the dance, I will that it be called a mystery. ²For what you are, you see, for I showed it to you; but what I am I alone know, and no one else. ³Allow Me then to keep that which is Mine, and that which is yours, behold through Me, and behold Me in truth, that I am, not what I said, but what you are able to know, because you are akin to it. ⁴You hear that I suffered, yet I did not suffer; that I did not suffer, yet I did suffer; that I was pierced, yet I was not stricken; hanged, and I was not hanged; that blood flowed from Me, and it did not flow; and, in a word, what they say of Me, that did not happen to Me, but what they do not say, that I did suffer. ⁵Now what those things are, I signify to you: for I know that you will understand. ⁶Therefore, perceive in Me the praising of the Word, the piercing of the Word, the blood of the Word, the wound of the Word, the hanging up of the Word, the suffering of the Word, the nailing of the Word, the death of the Word. ⁷And so I speak, separating off the manhood. Therefore, perceive in the first place the Word; then you will perceive the LORD, and in the third place the man, and what He has suffered."

CHAPTER 102

¹"When He had spoken these things to me, and others which I do not know how to say as He would have me, He was taken up—no one of the multitudes having beheld Him. ²And when I went down, I laughed them all to scorn, inasmuch as He had told me the things which they have said concerning Him; ³holding fast this one thing in myself: that the LORD planned all things symbolically and by a dispensation toward men, for their conversion and salvation."

CHAPTER 103

¹"Having therefore beheld, brothers, the grace of the LORD and His kind affection toward us, let us worship Him as those to whom He has shown mercy, not with our fingers, nor our mouth, nor our tongue, nor with any part whatsoever of our body, but with the disposition of our soul— ²even Him who became a man apart from this body: and let us watch, because He now also keeps ward over prisons for our sake, and over tombs, in bonds and dungeons, in reproaches and insults, by sea and on dry land, in scourgings, condemnations, conspiracies, frauds, punishments, and in a word, He is with all of us, and He Himself suffers with us when we suffer, brothers. ³When He is called on by each one of us, He does not endure to shut His ears to us, but as being everywhere, He listens to all of us; and now both to me and to Drusiana—forasmuch as He is the God of them that are shut, bringing us help by His own compassion."

CHAPTER 104

¹"Therefore, beloved, also be persuaded that it is not a [mere] man whom I preach to you to worship, but God unchangeable, God invincible, God higher than all authority and all power, and older and mightier than all messengers and creatures that are named, and all aeons. ²If then you abide in Him, and are built up in Him, you will possess your soul indestructible."

CHAPTER 105

¹And when he had delivered these things to the brothers, John departed, with Andronicus, to walk. ²And Drusiana also followed far off with all the brothers, so that they might behold the acts that were done by him and hear his speech at all times in the LORD.

THE DEATH OF JOHN

CHAPTER 106

¹John therefore continued with the brothers, rejoicing in the LORD. ²And the next day, being the LORD's Day, and all the brothers being gathered together, he began to say to them: "Brothers, and fellow-servants, and coheirs, and partakers with me in the kingdom of the LORD, you know the LORD, how many mighty works He has granted to you by my means, how many wonders, healings, signs, how great [the] spiritual gifts, teachings, governings, refreshings, ministries, knowledges, glories, graces, gifts, beliefs, communions, ³all of which you have seen given to you by Him in your sight, yet not seen by these eyes nor heard by these ears. ⁴Therefore, be established in Him, remembering Him in your every deed, knowing the mystery of the dispensation which has come to pass toward men, for which reason the LORD has accomplished it. ⁵He pleads with you by me, brothers, and implores you, desiring to remain without grief, without insult, not conspired against, not disgraced: for He knows even the insult that comes through you—He knows even dishonor, He knows even conspiracy, He knows even disgrace from them that do not listen to His commandments."

CHAPTER 107

¹"Do not let then our good God be grieved—the compassionate, the merciful, the holy, the pure, the undefiled, the immaterial, the only, the one, the unchangeable, the simple, the guileless, the un-wrathful, even our God Jesus Christ, who is above every name that we can utter or conceive, and more exalted. ²Let Him rejoice with us because we walk correctly; let Him be glad because we live purely; let Him be refreshed because our conversation is sober; let Him be without care because we live moderately, let Him be pleased because we communicate with one another; let Him smile because we are pure; let Him be glad because we love Him. ³These things I now speak to you, brothers, because I am hurrying to the work set before me, and I am already being perfected by the LORD. ⁴For what else could I have to say to you? You have the pledge of our God, you have the pledge of His goodness, you have His presence that cannot be shunned. ⁵If, then, you no longer sin, He forgives you of what you did in ignorance: but if after you have known Him, and He has had mercy on you, you walk again in the same deeds, both the former will be laid to your charge, and you will also have no part nor mercy before Him."

CHAPTER 108

¹And when he had spoken this to them, he prayed thus: "O Jesus, who have woven this crown with Your weaving, who have joined together these many blossoms into the unfading flower of Your countenance, who have sown in them these words: You, the only tender of Your servants, and Physician who heal freely; ²[the] only doer of good and despiser of none, [the] only merciful and lover of men, [the] only Savior and righteous, [the] only seer of all, who are in all, and present everywhere, and containing all things, and filling all things: ³Christ Jesus, God, Lord, who with Your gifts and Your mercy shelter them that trust in You, who clearly knows the schemes and assaults of him that is everywhere our adversary, which he devises against us: You alone, O Lord, help Your servants by Your visitation. Even so, Lord."

CHAPTER 109

¹And he asked for bread and gave thanks thus: "What praise or what offering or what thanksgiving will we, breaking this bread, name except You alone, O Lord Jesus? ²We glorify Your Name that was said by the Father; we glorify Your Name that was said through the Son; ³we glorify Your entering through the Door; we glorify the resurrection shown to us by You; we glorify Your way; ⁴we glorify of You the seed, the word, the grace, the faith, the salt, the unspeakable pearl, the treasure, the plow, the net, the greatness, the diadem, Him that for us was called Son of Man, that gave to us truth, rest, knowledge, power, the commandment, the confidence, hope, love, liberty, refuge in You. ⁵For You, Lord, are alone the root of immortality, and the fount of incorruption, and the seat of the ages: called by all these names for us now, so that calling on You by them we may make known Your greatness which at the present is invisible to us, but visible only to the pure, being portrayed in Your manhood only."

CHAPTER 110

¹And he broke the bread and gave to all of us, praying over each of the brothers, so that he might be worthy of the grace of the LORD and of the most holy communion. ²And he also partook himself likewise and said: "To me also may there be a part with you," and, "Peace be with you, my beloved."

CHAPTER 111

¹After that, he said to Verus: "Take two men with you, with baskets and shovels, and follow me." And Verus without delay did as he was commanded by John, the servant of God. ²Therefore, the blessed John went out of the house and walked forth from the gates, having told the greater part to depart from him. ³And when he had come to the tomb of a certain brother of ours, he said to the young men: "Dig, my children." And they dug, and he was insistent with them even more, saying, "Let the trench be deeper." ⁴And as they dug, he spoke to them the word of God and exhorted them that had come with him out of the house, edifying and perfecting them toward the greatness of God and praying over each one of us. ⁵And when the young men had finished the trench as he desired, we knowing nothing of it, he took off his garments with which he was clothed and laid them, as it were, for a pallet in the bottom of the trench; and standing in his undergarment only, he stretched his hands upward and prayed thus:

CHAPTER 112

¹"O You that chose us out for the apostleship of the nations; O God that sent us into the world, that revealed Yourself by the Law and the Prophets, that never rested, but always from the foundation of the world saved them that were able to be saved; ²that made Yourself known through all nature, that even proclaimed Yourself among beasts; ³that made the desolate and savage soul tame and quiet, that gave Yourself to it when it was thirsty for Your words, that appeared to it in haste when it was dying, that showed Yourself to it as a law when it was sinking into lawlessness, ⁴that manifested Yourself to it when it had been vanquished by Satan, that overcame its adversary when it fled to You, that gave it Your hand and raised it up from the things of Hades, that did not leave it to walk after a bodily sort, that showed to it its own enemy, that have made for it a clear knowledge toward You: ⁵O God, Jesus, the Father of them that are above the heavens, the Lord of them that are in the heavens, the law of them that are in the other, the course of them that are in the air, the keeper of them that are on the earth, the fear of them that are under the earth, the grace of them that are Your own: receive the soul of Your John also, which it may so be is counted worthy by You."

CHAPTER 113

¹"O You who have kept me until this hour for Yourself and untouched by union with a woman: ²who when in my youth I desired to marry, appeared to me and said to me: John, I have need of you; ³who also prepared for me a sickness of the body; ⁴who when for the third time I would marry, immediately prevented me, and then at the third hour of the day, said to me on the sea: John, if you had not been Mine, I would have permitted you to marry; ⁵who for two years blinded me and granted me to mourn and plead with you; ⁶who in the third year opened the eyes of my mind and also granted me my visible eyes; ⁷who when I saw clearly, ordained that it should be grievous to me to look on a woman; ⁸who saved me from the temporal fantasy and led me to that which always endures; ⁹who rid me of the foul madness that is in the flesh; ¹⁰who took me from the bitter death and established me on You alone; ¹¹who muzzled the secret disease of my soul and cut off the open deed; ¹²who afflicted and banished him that raised tumult in me; ¹³who made my love of You spotless; ¹⁴who made my joining to you perfect and unbroken; ¹⁵who gave me undoubting faith in You; ¹⁶who ordered and made clear my inclination toward You: ¹⁷You

ACTS OF JOHN

who give to every man the due reward of his works, who put into my soul that I should have no possession except You alone, for what is more precious than You? ⁱ⁸Now therefore, O LORD, whereas I have accomplished the dispensation with which I was entrusted, account me worthy of Your rest and grant me that end in You which is unspeakable and unutterable salvation."

CHAPTER 114

¹"And as I come to You, let the fire go backward, let the darkness be overcome, let the gulf be without strength, let the furnace die out, let Gehenna be quenched; ²let messengers follow, let devils fear, let rulers be broken, let powers fall; ³let the places of the right hand stand fast, let them of the left hand not remain; ⁴let the Devil be muzzled, let Satan be derided, let his wrath be burned out, let his madness be stilled, let his vengeance be ashamed, let his assault be in pain, let his children be stricken and all his roots plucked up. ⁵And grant me to accomplish the journey to You without suffering insolence or provocation, and to receive that which You have promised to them that live purely and have loved You alone."

CHAPTER 115

¹And having sealed himself in every part, he stood and said: "You are with me, O Lord Jesus Christ"; and he laid himself down in the trench where he had strewn his garments, ²and having said to us: "Peace be with you, brothers," he gave up his spirit, rejoicing.

ACTS OF ANDREW

Some scholars speculate that the Acts of Andrew draws on the Acts of Peter and the Acts of John, which would place the composition of this work subsequent to them; albeit, this work is still regarded as quite early, probably in the mid- to late-2nd century. It is the product of the Encratites, who forbade marriage, a heresy expressly rebuked by Paul (1 Tm. 4:1–4). Some scholars also see gnostic thought in the Acts of Andrew, but this is disputed.

CHAPTER 1

¹"… is there in you altogether slackness? Are you not yet convinced in yourselves that you do not yet bear His goodness? Let us be reverent; let us rejoice with ourselves in the bountiful fellowship which comes from Him. ²Let us say to ourselves: Blessed is our race! By whom has it been loved? Blessed is our state! From whom has it obtained mercy? ³We are not cast on the ground—we that have been recognized by such a great highness; we are not the offspring of time, afterward to be dissolved by time; we are not a product of motion, made to be again destroyed by itself, nor things of earthly birth, ending again therein. ⁴We belong, then, to a greatness, to which we aspire, of which we are the property, and perhaps to a greatness that has mercy on us. ⁵We belong to the better, therefore we flee from the worse; we belong to the beautiful, for whose sake we reject the foul; to the righteous, by whom we cast away the unrighteousness; to the merciful, by whom we reject the unmerciful; to the Savior, by whom we recognize the destroyer; to the light, by whom we have cast away the darkness; to the One, by whom we have turned away from the many; to the heavenly, by whom we have learned to know the earthly; to the abiding, by whom we have seen the transitory. ⁶If we desire to offer to God, who has had mercy on us, a worthy thanksgiving, or confidence, or hymn, or boasting, what better cause do we have than that we have been recognized by Him?"

CHAPTER 2

¹And having discoursed thus to the brothers, he sent every one of them away to his house, saying to them: "Neither are you ever forsaken by me—you that are servants of Christ—because of the love that is in Him: neither again will I be forsaken by you because of His intercession." ²And each one departed to his house: and there was among them rejoicing after this sort for many days, while Aegeates did not give consideration to prosecute the accusation against the apostle. ³Every one of them then was confirmed at that time in hope toward the LORD, and they continually assembled without fear in the prison, with Maximilla, Iphidamia, and the rest, being sheltered by the protection and grace of the LORD.

CHAPTER 3

¹But one day Aegeates, as he was hearing cases, remembered the matter concerning Andrew: and as one seized with madness, he left the case which he had in hand, and rose up from the judgment-seat, and ran quickly to the praetorium, inflamed with love for Maximilla and desiring to persuade her with flatteries. ²And Maximilla was with him beforehand, coming from the prison and entering the house. And he went in and said to her:

CHAPTER 4

¹"Maximilla, your parents counted me worthy of being your consort and gave me your hand in marriage, not looking to wealth, or descent, or renown, but it may be for my good disposition of soul: ²and, that I may skip over much that I might utter in reproach of you, both of that which I have enjoyed at your parents' hands and you from me during all our life, I have come, leaving the court, to learn from you this one thing, so answer me reasonably: if you were as the wife of former days, living with me in the way we know—sleeping, conversing, bearing offspring with me—I would deal well with you in all points; ³indeed, [even] more—I would set free the stranger whom I hold in prison; but if you will not, I would do nothing harsh to you, for indeed I cannot; but him, whom you cherish more than me, I will afflict yet more. ⁴Consider, then, Maximilla, to which of the two you incline, and answer me tomorrow; for I am fully prepared for this emergency."

CHAPTER 5

¹And with these words he went out; ²but Maximilla again at the accustomed hour, with Iphidamia, went to Andrew: and putting her hands before her own eyes, and then putting them to her mouth, she began to declare to him the whole matter of the demand of Aegeates. ³And Andrew answered her: "I know, Maximilla my child, that you yourself are moved to resist the whole attraction of marital union, desiring to cease a foul and polluted way of life; ⁴and this has long been firmly held in your intention; but now you wish for the further testimony of my opinion. ⁵I testify, O Maximilla: do not do it; do not be vanquished by the threat of Aegeates; do not be overcome by his discourse; do not fear his shameful counsels; do not fall to his artful flatteries; do not consent to surrender yourself to his impure spells, but endure all his torments looking to us for a short span, and you will see him wholly numbed and withering away from you and from all that are related to you. ⁶But that which I most needed to say to you—for I do not rest until I fulfill the business which is seen, and which comes to pass in your person—has escaped me: ⁷and rightly in you do I behold Eve converting, and in myself Adam returning: for that which she suffered in ignorance, you now set right by returning; and that which the spirit suffered, which was overthrown with her and slipped away from itself, is set right in me—with you who see yourself being brought back. ⁸For you have remedied her defect by not suffering like her; and I have perfected his imperfection by taking refuge with God. ⁹That which she disobeyed you have obeyed; that to which he consented I flee from; and that which they both transgressed we have been aware of, for it is ordained that everyone should correct his own fall."

CHAPTER 6

¹"I, then, having said this as I have said it, would go on to speak as follows: Well done, O nature that is being saved, for you have been strong and have not hidden yourself [from God like Adam]! ²Well done, O soul that cries out of what you have suffered, and you return to yourself! ³Well done, O man that

ACTS OF ANDREW

understands what is yours and presses on to what is yours! ⁴Well done, you that hear what is spoken, for I see you to be greater than things that are thought or spoken! I recognize you as more powerful than the things which seemed to overpower you; as more beautiful than those which cast you down into filth, which brought you down into captivity. ⁵Perceiving then, O man, all this in yourself, that you are immaterial, holy light, akin to Him that is unborn, that you are intellectual, heavenly, translucent, pure, above the flesh, above the world, above rulers, above principalities, over whom you are in truth, then comprehend yourself in your condition and receive full knowledge and understand wherein you excel: ⁶and beholding your own face in your essence, break all bonds apart—I say not only those that are of your birth, but those that are above birth, whereof we have set forth to you the names which are exceedingly great. ⁷Earnestly desire to see Him that is revealed to you, Him who does not come into being, whom perhaps you alone will recognize with confidence."

CHAPTER 7

¹"I have spoken these things to you, Maximilla, for in their meaning the things I have spoken reach to you. ²Just as Adam died in Eve because he consented to her confession, so I now live in you who keep the LORD's commandment and establish yourself in the dignity of your being. ³But trample down the threats of Aegeates, Maximilla, knowing that we have God who has mercy on us. ⁴And do not let his noise move you, but remain celibate; and let him punish me not only with such torments as bonds, but let him cast me to the beasts or burn me with fire, and throw me from a precipice. ⁵And what do I need to say? There is only this one body; let him abuse that as he will, for it is akin to himself."

CHAPTER 8

¹"And yet again, [this] is my speech to you, Maximilla: I say to you, do not give yourself over to Aegeates [and] withstand his ambushes; for indeed, Maximilla, I have seen my Lord saying to me: Andrew, Aegeates' father the Devil will free you from this prison. ²Therefore, let it be from this time on [that you] keep yourself celibate and pure, holy, unspotted, sincere, free from adultery, not reconciled to the discourses of our enemy, unbent, unbroken, tearless, unwounded, not storm-tossed, undivided, not stumbling, without sympathy for the works of Cain. ³For if you do not give yourself up, Maximilla, to what is contrary to these, I will also rest, although I am thus forced to leave this life for your sake (that is, for my own). ⁴But if I were thrust out from here—even I, who, it may be, might avail through you to profit others that are akin to me—and if you were persuaded by the discourse of Aegeates and the flatteries of his father the serpent, so that you turned to your former works, know that on your account I should be tormented until you yourself saw that I had despised life for the sake of a soul which was not worthy."

CHAPTER 9

¹"I therefore implore the wise man that is within you that your mind continues seeing clearly. ²I implore your mind that is not seen, so that it might be preserved whole. ³I beg you: love your Jesus and do not yield to the worse. ⁴Assist me, you whom I implore as a man, so that I may become perfect. ⁵Help me also, so that you may recognize your own true nature; feel with me in my suffering, so that you may take knowledge of what I suffer and escape suffering; see that which I see, and you will be blind to what you see; see that which you should, and you will not see what you should not; ⁶listen to what I say and cast away that which you have heard."

CHAPTER 10

¹"I have spoken these things to you and to everyone who hears, if he will hear. But you, O Stratocles," he said, looking toward him, "Why are you so oppressed, with many tears and groanings to be heard far off? ²What is the lowness of spirit that is on you? Why your great pain and your great anguish? Do you take note of what is said, and why I pray for you to be disposed in mind as my child? ³Do you perceive to whom my words are spoken? Has each of them taken hold on your understanding? Have they touched your intellect? ⁴Do I have you as one that has listened to me? Do I find myself in you? Is there in you one that speaks whom I see to be my own? ⁵Does he love Him that speaks in me and desire to have fellowship with Him? Does he wish to be made one with Him? Does he hasten to become His friend? Does he yearn to be joined with Him? ⁶Does he find in Him any rest? Does he have a place to lay his head? Does nothing oppose him there—nothing that is angry with him, resists him, hates him, flees from him, is savage, avoids, turns away, starts off, is burdened, makes war, talks with others, is flattered by others, agrees with others? Does nothing else disturb him? ⁷Is there one within that is strange to me—an adversary, a breaker of peace, an enemy, a cheat, a sorcerer, a crooked dealer, unsound, guileful, a hater of men, a hater of the word, one like a tyrant, boastful, puffed up, mad, akin to the serpent, a weapon of the devil, a friend of the fire, belonging to darkness? ⁸Is there in you anyone, Stratocles, that cannot endure my saying these things? Who is it? Answer: do I talk in vain? Have I spoken in vain? Indeed, says the man in you, Stratocles, who now weeps again."

CHAPTER 11

¹And Andrew took the hand of Stratocles and said: "I have him whom I loved; I will rest on him whom I look for; for your ongoing groaning and weeping without restraint is a sign to me that I have already found rest, that I have not spoken to you these words which are akin to me, in vain."

CHAPTER 12

¹And Stratocles answered him: "Do not think, most blessed Andrew, that there is anything else that afflicts me but you, for the words that come forth from you are like arrows of fire shot against me, and every one of them reaches me and truly burns me up. ²That part of my soul which inclines to what I hear is tormented, divining the affliction that is to follow, for you yourself depart, and, I know, nobly: but hereafter when I seek your care and affection, where will I find it, or in whom? ³I have received the seeds of the words of salvation, and you were the sower: but that they should sprout up and grow needs none other but you, most blessed Andrew. ⁴And what else do I have to say to you but this? I need much mercy and help from you, to become worthy of the seed I have from you, which will not otherwise increase perpetually or grow up into the light except [if] you will it and pray for them and for the whole of me."

CHAPTER 13

¹And Andrew answered him: "This, my child, was what I beheld in you myself. And I glorify my Lord that my thought of you did not walk on the void, but knew what it said. ²But that you may know the truth: tomorrow Aegeates will deliver me up to be crucified, for Maximilla, the servant of the LORD, will enrage the enemy that is in him, to whom he belongs, by not consenting to that which is hateful to her; and by turning against me, he will think to console himself."

CHAPTER 14

¹Now while the apostle spoke these things, Maximilla was not there, for she having heard throughout the words with which he answered her, and being in part reassured by them, and of such a mind as the words pointed out, set forth not unadvisedly nor without purpose and went to the praetorium. ²And she bade farewell to all the life of the flesh, and when Aegeates brought to her the same demand which he had told her to consider, whether she would lie with him, she rejected it—and thenceforth he [fully] disposed himself to putting Andrew to death and considered to what death he should expose him. ³And when of all deaths crucifixion alone prevailed with him, he went away with his [own] kind and dined; ⁴and Maximilla, the LORD going before her in the likeness of Andrew, came back to the prison with Iphidamia; and there being a great gathering of the brothers therein, she found Andrew discoursing thus:

CHAPTER 15

¹"I, brothers, was sent forth by the LORD as an apostle to these regions whereof my Lord thought me worthy, not to teach any man, but to remind every man that is akin to such words that they live in evils which are temporal, delighting in their damaging delusions: ²from which I have always exhorted you also to depart, and encouraged you to press toward things that endure, and to

flee from everything that is transitory—for you see that none of you stands, but that all things, even to the customs of men, are easily changeable. ³And this happens because the soul is untrained, and errs toward nature, and holds pledges to its error. ⁴I therefore account them blessed who have become obedient to the word preached and thereby see the mysteries of their own nature; for whose sake all things have been built up."

CHAPTER 16

¹"Therefore, I command you, beloved children: build yourselves firmly on the foundation that has been laid for you, which is unshaken, and against which no evil-minded [person] can conspire. ²Be then rooted on this foundation; be established, remembering what you have seen and all that has come to pass while I walked with you all. ³You have seen works worked through me which you have no power to disbelieve, and such signs come to pass as perhaps even dumb nature will proclaim aloud; ⁴I have delivered you words which I pray may so be received by you as the words themselves would have it. ⁵Be established then, beloved, on all that you have seen, and heard, and partaken of. ⁶And God on whom you have believed will have mercy on you and present you to Himself, giving you rest throughout all ages."

CHAPTER 17

¹"Now as for that which is to happen to me, do not let it really trouble you as some strange spectacle, that the servant of God to whom God Himself has granted much in deeds and words, should by an evil man be driven out of this temporal life: ²for not only to me will this come to pass, but to all of them that have loved and believed on Him and confessed Him. ³The Devil that is utterly shameless, will arm his own children against them, so that they may consent to him; and he will not have his desire. ⁴And why he attempts this, I will tell you. From the beginning of all things, and if I may say so, since He that has no beginning came down to be under his rule, the enemy that is a foe to peace drives away from [God] such a one as does not indeed belong to Him, but is someone of the weaker sort and not fully enlightened, nor yet able to recognize himself. ⁵And because he does not know Him, he must therefore be fought against by him [(the Devil)]. ⁶For he, thinking that he possesses him and is his master forever, opposes him so much, that he makes their enmity to be a kind of friendship: for suggesting to him his own thoughts, he often portrays them as pleasurable and deceptive, by which he thinks to prevail over him. ⁷He was not, then, openly shown to be an enemy, for he feigned a friendship that was worthy of him."

CHAPTER 18

¹"And this his work he carried on so long that he [(man)] forgot to recognize it, but he [(the Devil)] knew it himself: that is, he, because of his gifts. ²But when the mystery of grace was illuminated, and the counsel of rest manifested, and the light of the Word shown, and the race of them that were saved was proved, warring against many pleasures, the enemy himself despised, and himself, through the goodness of Him that had mercy on us, derided because of his own gifts, by which he had thought to triumph over man—he began to plot against us with hatred and enmity and assaults; ³and he has determined this: not to cease from us until he thinks to separate us [from God]. ⁴For before, our enemy was without care, and offered us a feigned friendship which was worthy of him, and was able not to fear that we, deceived by him, should depart from him. ⁵But when the light of dispensation was kindled … it exposed that part of his nature which was hidden and which thought to escape notice, and made it confess what it is. ⁶Knowing therefore, brothers, that which will be, let us be vigilant, not discontented, not making a proud figure, not carrying on our souls marks of him which are not our own, but wholly lifted upward by the whole word, let us all gladly await the end, and take our flight away from him, so that he may be henceforth shown as he is, who our nature to …"

THE MARTYRDOM OF ANDREW

1. And after he had thus discoursed throughout the night to the brothers, and prayed with them, and committed them to the LORD, early in the morning, Aegeates the proconsul sent for the apostle Andrew out of the prison and said to him: "The end of your judgment is at hand—you stranger, enemy of this present life, and foe of all my house! Why have you thought it good to intrude into places that are not yours, and to corrupt my wife who was previously obedient to me? Why have you done this against me and against all Achaia? Therefore, you will receive from me a gift in repayment of that you have worked against me."

2. And he commanded him to be scourged by seven men and afterward to be crucified; and charged the executioners that his legs should be left unpierced, and so he should be hung up, thinking by this means to torment him [all] the more.

3. Now the report was announced throughout all Patras that the stranger, the righteous man, the servant of Christ whom Aegeates held prisoner, was being crucified, having done nothing wrong; and they ran together with one accord to the sight, being angry with the proconsul because of his impious judgment.

4. And as the executioners led him to the place to fulfill that which was commanded them, Stratocles heard what had come to pass, and ran quickly, and overtook them, and beheld the blessed Andrew being violently dragged by the executioners like a criminal. And he did not spare them, but beating every one of them severely and tearing their coats from top to bottom, he pulled Andrew away from them, saying, "You may thank the blessed man who has instructed me and taught me to refrain from extremity of wrath, for otherwise I would have showed you what Stratocles is able to do, and what is the power of the foul Aegeates. For we have learned to endure that which others inflict on us." And he took the hand of the apostle and went with him to the place by the seashore where he was to be crucified.

5. But the soldiers who had received him from the proconsul left him with Stratocles, and returned and told Aegeates, saying, "As we went with Andrew, Stratocles prevented us, and tore our coats, and pulled him away from us, and took him with him, and behold, here we are as you see." And Aegeates answered them: "Put on other garments and go and fulfill that which I commanded you [to do] with the condemned man; but do not be seen by Stratocles, neither answer him again if he asks anything of you; for I know the rashness of his soul, what it is, and if he were provoked he would not even spare me." And they did as Aegeates said to them.

6. But as Stratocles went with the apostle to the place appointed, Andrew perceived that he was angry with Aegeates and was reviling him in a low voice, and he said to him: "My child Stratocles, I would have you from now on keep your soul unmoved and remove this temper from yourself, and neither be inwardly disposed thus toward the things that seem hard to you, nor be inflamed outwardly: for it suits the servant of Jesus to be worthy of Jesus. And I will say another thing to you and to the brothers that walk with me: that the man that is against us, when he dares anything against us and finds not one to consent to him, is stricken, and beaten, and completely deadened because he has not accomplished that which he undertook; let us therefore, little children, always have Him before our eyes, lest if we fall asleep, He slaughter us like an adversary."

7. And as he spoke this and yet more to Stratocles and them that were with him, they came to the place where he was to be crucified; and [seeing the cross set up at the edge of the sand by the seashore,] he left them all, and went to the cross, and spoke to it:

8. "Hail, O Cross! Yes, be glad indeed! I know well that you will be at rest from now on—you that have for a long time been wearied, being set up and awaiting me. I come to you whom I know to belong to me. I come to you that have yearned after me. I know your mystery, for which you have been erected: for you are planted in the world to establish the things that are unstable; and one part of you stretches up toward Heaven, so that you may signify the heavenly Word; and another part of you is spread out to the right hand and the left, so that it might cause the envious and adverse power of the evil one to flee and gather into one the things that are scattered abroad; and another part of you is planted in the earth and securely set in the depth, so that you may join the things that are in the earth and that are under the earth to the heavenly things.

ACTS OF ANDREW

9. O Cross, contrivance of the salvation of the Most High! O Cross, trophy of the victory [of Christ] over [His] enemies! O Cross, planted on the earth and having your fruit in the heavens! O name of the Cross, filled with all things.

10. Well done, O Cross, that have bound the movement of the world! Well done, O shape of understanding, that have shaped the shapeless! Well done, O unseen punishment, that severely punishes the substance of the knowledge that many gods have and drives out from among mankind him that devised it! Well done, you that clothed yourself with the LORD, and bore the thief as a fruit, and called the apostle to conversion, and did not refuse to accept us!

11. But how long will I delay, speaking thus, and not embrace the Cross, that by the Cross I might be made alive, and by the Cross [win] the common death of all and depart out of life?

12. Come here, you ministers of joy to me—you servants of Aegeates—accomplish the desire of us both, and bind the lamb to the wood of suffering, the man to the Maker, the soul to the Savior."

13. And the blessed Andrew, having thus spoken, standing on the earth, looked earnestly on the cross, and directed the brothers that the executioners should come and do that which was commanded them; for they stood far off.

14. And they came and bound his hands and his feet and did not nail them, for they had such a charge from Aegeates; for he wished to afflict him by hanging him up, and so that in the night he might be devoured alive by dogs. And they left him hanging and departed from him.

15. And when the multitudes that stood by (of them that had been made disciples in Christ by him) saw that they had done to him none of the things accustomed with them that are crucified, they hoped to hear something again from him. For as he hung, he moved his head and smiled. And Stratocles asked him, saying, "Why do you smile, O servant of God? Your laughter makes us mourn and weep because we are bereaved of you." And the blessed Andrew answered him: "Will I not laugh, my son Stratocles, at the vain assault of Aegeates, whereby he thinks to punish us? We are strangers to him and his conspiracies. He has no [ears] to hear; for if he had, he would have heard that the man of Jesus cannot be punished, because he is henceforth known by Him."

16. And thereafter he spoke to them all in common, for the heathen also had come together, being angry at the unjust judgment of Aegeates.

17. "You men that are present here—and women and children, old and young, bond and free, and all that will hear: take no heed of the vain deceit of this present life, but rather heed us who hang here for the LORD's sake and are about to depart out of this body; and renounce all the lusts of the world, and scorn the worship of the abominable idols, and run to the true worshiping of our God who does not lie, and make yourselves a temple pure and ready to receive the Word."

18. And the multitudes, hearing the things which he spoke, did not depart from the place; and Andrew continued speaking yet more to them, for a day and a night. And on the following day, beholding his endurance, and constancy of soul, and wisdom of spirit, and strength of mind, they were angry, and hastened with one accord to Aegeates, to the judgment-seat where he sat, and cried out against him, saying, "What is this judgment of yours, O proconsul? You have misjudged! You have condemned unjustly! Your court is against [the] law! What evil has this man done? Wherein has he offended? The city is troubled: you harm us all! Do not destroy Caesar's city! Give us the righteous man! Restore us the holy man! Do not slay a man dear to God! Do not destroy a man gentle and pious! Behold, he has hung for two days and yet lives, and has tasted nothing, and yet refreshes all of us with his words; and behold, we believe in the God whom he preaches. Take down the righteous man, and we will all become philosophers; untie the pure man, and all of Patras will be at peace; set free the wise man, and all of Achaia will be set free by him!"

19. But at first, when Aegeates would not hear them, but beckoned with the hand to the people that they should depart, they were filled with rage and were at the point to do him violence, being about two thousand in number.

20. And when the proconsul saw them to be nearly mad, he feared lest there should be an uprising against him, and rose up from the judgment-seat, and went with them, promising to release Andrew. And some went on ahead, and they signified to the apostle and to the rest of the people that were there why the proconsul was coming. And all the multitude of the disciples rejoiced together with Maximilla, and Iphidamia, and Stratocles.

21. But when Andrew heard it, he began to say: "O the dullness, and disobedience, and simplicity of them whom I have taught! How much have I spoken, and even to this day I have not persuaded them to flee from the love of earthly things! But they are yet bound to them, and continue in them, and will not depart from them. What does this affection, and love, and sympathy with the flesh mean? How long will you heed worldly and temporal things? How long will you not understand the things that are above us, and not press on to overtake them? From now on, leave me to be put to death in the manner which you behold, and let no man by any means free me from these bonds, for so it is appointed to me to depart out of the body and be present with the LORD, with whom I am also crucified. And this will be accomplished."

22. And he turned to Aegeates and said with a loud voice: "Why have you come, Aegeates, that are an alien to me? What will you dare anew, what plan, or what attempt? Will you tell us that you have converted and have come to free us? Indeed, not if you convert, indeed, Aegeates, will I now consent to you—not [even] if you promise me all your wealth will I depart from myself; not if you say that you are mine will I trust you. And do you, proconsul, free him that is bound? Him that has been set free? That has been recognized by his countrymen? That has obtained mercy and is beloved by him? Do you free him that is alien to you? The stranger? That only appears to you? I have one with whom I will be forever, with whom I will converse for numberless ages. To Him I go; to Him I hasten, who also made you known to me, who said to me: Understand that Aegeates and his gifts; do not let that fearful one frighten you, nor think that he holds you who are Mine. He is your enemy; he is pestilent, a deceiver, a corrupter, a madman, a sorcerer, a cheat, a murderer, wrathful, without compassion. Therefore, depart from me, you worker of all iniquity!"

23. And the proconsul, hearing this, stood speechless and was, as it were, beside himself; but as all the city made an uproar that he should free Andrew, he drew near to the cross to free him and take him down. But the blessed Andrew cried out with a loud voice: "LORD, do not permit Your Andrew, who has been bound on Your cross, to be freed again; do not give me, that am atop Your mystery, to the shameless Devil; O Jesus Christ, do not let Your adversary free him who is hung on Your grace; O Father, do not let this little one humble him that has known Your greatness any longer. But you, Jesus Christ, whom I have seen, whom I hold, whom I love, in whom I am and will be: receive me in peace into Your everlasting tabernacles, so that by my going out, there may be an entering in to You of many that are like me, and that they may rest in Your majesty." And having so spoken, and yet glorifying the LORD even more, he gave up the spirit, while we all wept and lamented at our parting from him.

24. And after the death of the blessed Andrew, Maximilla together with Stratocles, caring nothing for them that stood by, drew near and herself freed his body; and when it was evening, she paid it the customary care and buried it [[near the seashore]]. And she continued separate from Aegeates because of his brutal soul and his wicked manner of life: and she led a reverential and quiet life, filled with the love of Christ, among the brothers. Aegeates still solicited [her] much and promised that she should have rule over his affairs; but being unable to persuade her, he arose in the dead of night, and unknown to them of his house, cast himself down from a great height and perished.

25. But Stratocles, who was his brother after the flesh, would not touch any of the things that were left of his possessions, for the wretched man died without offspring, but said: "Let your goods go with you, Aegeates. For of these things we have no need, for they are polluted; but as for me, let Christ be my friend and I His servant, and all my wealth I offer to Him in whom I have believed, and I pray that by worthily hearing of the blessed teaching of the apostle, I may appear a partaker with him in the ageless and unending kingdom." And so, the uproar of the people ceased, and all were glad at the amazing, and untimely, and sudden fall of the impious and lawless Aegeates.

ACTS OF THOMAS

Containing many hallmarks of gnostic and Encratite thought, the Acts of Thomas may nevertheless contain some very early traditions pertaining to the apostle, including his mission to India. It is among the very longest of the apocryphal Acts and was likely composed in the 3rd century. It is divided into thirteen "acts," followed by the apostle's martyrdom. It also contains an independent work, the Hymn of the Soul (vv. 108–113). The authors (whose Acts were occasionally unconnected) had a strong ideological and sectarian determination that celibacy was to be universal among Christians, although this certainly fell outside of orthodoxy, reflecting the works' heretical underpinnings.

THE FIRST ACT

WHEN HE WENT INTO INDIA WITH ABBANES THE MERCHANT.

1. At that time, all of us apostles were at Jerusalem, Simon who is called Peter and his brother Andrew, James the son of Zebedee and his brother John, Philip and Bartholomew, Thomas and Matthew the tax collector, James the son of Alphaeus and Simon the Canaanite, and Judas the brother of James: and we divided the regions of the world, so that every one of us should go to the region that fell to him and to the nation to which the LORD sent him. According to lot, therefore, India fell to Judas Thomas, which is also the twin: but he would not go, saying that by reason of the weakness of the flesh he could not travel, and "I am a Hebrew man; how can I go among the Indians and preach the truth?" And as he thus reasoned and spoke, the Savior appeared to him by night and says to him: "Do not fear, Thomas, go to India and preach the word there, for My grace is with you." But he would not obey, saying, "Where You would send me, send me, but elsewhere, for I will not go to the Indians."
2. And while he thus spoke and thought, it so happened that there was a certain merchant there having come from India whose name was Abbanes, sent from King Gondophares, and having a command from him to buy a carpenter and bring him to him. Now the LORD, seeing him walking in the marketplace at noon, said to him: "Would you buy a carpenter?" And he said to Him: "Yes." And the LORD said to him: "I have a slave that is a carpenter, and I desire to sell him." And saying this, He showed him Thomas far off, and agreed with him for three litrae of silver unstamped, and wrote a deed of sale, saying, "I, Jesus, the Son of Joseph the carpenter, acknowledge that I have sold my slave, Judas by name, to you Abbanes, a merchant of Gondophares, king of the Indians." And when the deed was finished, the Savior took Judas Thomas and led him away to Abbanes the merchant, and when Abbanes saw him, he said to him: "Is this your Master?" And the apostle said: "Yes, he is my Lord." And he said: "I have bought you from Him." And Your apostle held his peace.
3. And on the following day, the apostle arose early, and having prayed and pleaded with the LORD, he said: "I will go where You will, Lord Jesus: Your will be done." And he departed to Abbanes the merchant, taking with him nothing at all except his price alone. For the LORD had given it to him, saying, "Let your price also be with you, together with My grace, wherever you go." And the apostle found Abbanes carrying his baggage on board the ship, so he also began to carry it aboard with him. And when they had embarked in the ship and were set down, Abbanes questioned the apostle, saying, "What craftsmanship do you know?" And he said: "With wood I can make plows, and yokes, and augers [[*or* ox-goads]], and boats, and oars for boats, and masts, and pulleys; and with stone, pillars, and temples, and courthouses for kings." And Abbanes the merchant said to him: "Indeed, it is of just such a workman that we have need." They then began to sail homeward; and they had a favorable wind and sailed prosperously until they reached Andrapolis, a royal city.
4. And they left the ship and entered into the city, and behold, there were noises of flutes and water-organs, and trumpets sounded around them; and the apostle inquired, saying, "What is this festival that is in this city?" And they that were there said to him: "You also have the gods brought to cause celebration in this city. For the king has an only daughter, and now he gives her in marriage to a husband: this rejoicing, therefore, and assembly of the wedding today is the festival which you have seen. And the king has sent heralds to proclaim everywhere that everyone should come to the marriage, rich and poor, bond and free, strangers and citizens: and if any refuse and do not come to the marriage, he will answer for it to the king." And hearing that, Abbanes said to the apostle: "Let us also go, lest we offend the king, especially seeing [that] we are strangers." And he said: "Let us go." And after they had put up in the inn and rested a short span, they went to the marriage; and the apostle seeing them all reclining, laid himself, he also, in the midst, and everyone looked on him, as on a stranger and one having come from a foreign land: but Abbanes the merchant, being his master, laid himself in another place.
5. And as they dined and drank, the apostle tasted nothing; so they that were around him said to him: "Why have you come here, neither eating nor drinking?" But he answered them, saying, "I have come here for something greater than the food or the drink, and that I may fulfill the king's will. For the heralds proclaim the king's message, and whoever does not listen to the heralds will be subject to the king's judgment." So when they had dined and drank, and garlands and unguents were brought to them, every man took of the unguent, and one anointed his face, and another his beard, and another other parts of his body; but the apostle anointed the top of his head, and smeared a little on his nostrils, and dropped it into his ears, and touched his teeth with it, and carefully anointed the parts around his heart: and the wreath that was brought to him, woven of myrtle and other flowers, he took, and set it on his head, and took a branch of calamus and held it in his hand. Now the flute-girl, holding her flute in her hand, went around to them all and played, but when she came to the place where the apostle was, she stood over him and played at his head for a long span: now this flute-girl was a Hebrew by race.
6. And as the apostle continued looking on the ground, one of the cupbearers stretched forth his hand and gave him a blow; and the apostle lifted up his eyes, and looked on him that struck him, and said: "My God will forgive you in the life to come [for] this iniquity, but in this world you will show forth His wonders and even now will I behold this hand that has struck me dragged off by dogs." And having said this, he began to sing and to utter this song: "The damsel is the daughter of light, || In whom consists and dwells the proud brightness of kings, || And the sight of her is delightful—She shines with beauty and cheer. Her garments are like the flowers of spring, || And from them a waft of fragrance is carried; And in the crown of her head the king is established || Who with his immortal food nourishes them that are founded on him; And in her head is set truth, || And with her feet she shows forth joy. And her mouth is opened, || And it suits her well: Thirty-two are they that sing praises to her. Her tongue is like the curtain of the door, || Which waves back and forth for them that enter in; Her neck is set in the fashion of steps which the first maker has worked, || And her two hands signify and show, || Proclaiming the dance of the blessed ages, || And her fingers point out the gates of the city. Her chamber is bright with light and breathes forth the odor of balsam and all spices, || And gives out a sweet smell of myrrh and Indian leaf, || And within are myrtles strewn on the floor, || And of all manner of

fragrant flowers, || And the doorposts are adorned with the freed.

7. And surrounding her, her groomsmen keep her, || The number of whom is seven, whom she herself has chosen. And her bridesmaids are seven, || And they dance before her. And twelve in number are they that serve before her and are subject to her, || Which have their aim and their look toward the bridegroom, || So that by the sight of him they may be enlightened; And forever will they be with her in that eternal joy, || And will be at that marriage to which the princes are gathered together, || And will attend at that banquet to which the eternal ones are accounted worthy, || And will put on royal raiment and be clad in bright robes; And they will both be in joy and exultation and will glorify the Father of all, || Whose proud light they have received, || And are enlightened by the sight of their Lord; Whose immortal food they have received, that has no failing, || And have drunk of the wine that gives then neither thirst nor desire. And they have glorified and praised with the living Spirit, || The Father of truth and the mother of wisdom."

8. And when he had sung and ended this song, all that were present there gazed on him; and he kept silent, and they saw that his likeness was changed, but that which was spoken by him they did not understand, forasmuch as he was a Hebrew and that which he spoke was spoken in the Hebrew tongue. But the flute-girl alone heard all of it, for she was a Hebrew by race, and she went away from him and played to the rest, but for the most part she gazed and looked on him, for she loved him well, as a man of her own nation; moreover, he was lovely to look on beyond all that were there. And when the flute-girl had played to them all and ended, she sat down near him, gazing and looking earnestly on him. But he looked on no man at all, neither took heed of any but only kept his eyes looking toward the ground, awaiting the time when he might depart from there. But the cupbearer that had hit him went down to the well to draw water; and there happened to be a lion there, and it slew him and left him lying in that place, having torn his limbs in pieces, and immediately dogs seized his members, and among them one black dog holding his right hand in his mouth carried it into the place of the banquet.

9. And when they saw it, everyone was amazed and inquired which of them it was that was missing. And when it became clear that it was the hand of the cupbearer which had struck the apostle, the flute-girl broke her flute, and cast it away, and went and sat down at the apostle's feet, saying, "This is either a god or an apostle of God, for I heard him say in the Hebrew tongue: I will now see the hand that has struck me dragged off by dogs, which thing you also have now beheld; for just as he said, so has it come to pass." And some believed her, and some did not. But when the king heard of it, he came and said to the apostle: "Rise up, and come with me, and pray for my daughter, for she is my only-begotten, and today I give her in marriage." But the apostle was not willing to go with him, for the LORD was not yet revealed to him in that place. But the king led him away against his will to the bridechamber, so that he might pray for them.

10. And the apostle stood, and he began to pray and to speak thus: "My Lord and my God, that travel with Your servants, that guide and correct them that believe in You, the refuge and rest of the oppressed, the hope of the poor and ransomer of captives, the physician of the souls that lie sick and Savior of all creation, that give life to the world and strengthen souls: you know things to come, and by our means accomplish them; You, LORD, are He that reveals hidden mysteries and makes manifest words that are secret; You, LORD, are the planter of the good tree, and from Your hands are all good works produced; You, LORD, are He that are in all things and pass through all, and are set in all Your works and manifested in the working of them all. Jesus Christ, Son of compassion and perfect Savior, Christ, Son of the living God, the fearless power that have overthrown the enemy, and the voice that was heard by the rulers, and made all their powers to quake, the ambassador that was sent from the height and came down even to Hades, who opened the doors and brought up from there them that for many ages were shut up in the treasury of darkness, and showed them the way that leads up to the height: l plead with You, Lord Jesus, and offer to You supplication for these young persons, so that You would do for them the things that will help them and be expedient and profitable for them." And he laid his hands on them and said: "The LORD will be with you"; and he left them in that place and departed.

11. And the king desired the groomsmen to depart out of the bridechamber; and when everyone had gone out and the doors were shut, the bridegroom lifted up the curtain of the bridechamber to fetch the bride to him. And he saw the Lord Jesus bearing the likeness of Judas Thomas and speaking with the bride—even of him that just now had blessed them and gone out from them, the apostle; and he says to Him: "Did You not go out in the sight of all? How then are You found here?" But the LORD said to him: "I am not Judas, who is also called Thomas, but I am his brother." And the LORD sat down on the bed and instructed them to also sit on chairs, and He began to say to them:

12. "Remember, My children, what My brother spoke to you and what he delivered before you; and know this: that if you abstain from this filthy intercourse, you become holy temples—pure, having quit impulses and pains, seen and unseen—and you will acquire no cares of life or of children, whose end is destruction; and if you indeed get many children, for their sakes you become greedy and covetous, stripping orphans and plundering widows, and by so doing subject yourselves to grievous punishments. For the greater part of children become useless, oppressed by devils, some openly and some invisibly, for they become either crazed, or half withered, or blind, or deaf, or mute, or paralytic, or foolish; and if they are sound, again they will be vain, doing useless or abominable acts, for they will be caught either in adultery, or murder, or theft, or fornication, and by all these you will be afflicted. But if you are persuaded and keep your souls pure before God, there will come to you living children whom these blemishes cannot touch, and you will be without care, leading a peaceful life without grief or anxiety, looking to receive that incorruptible and true marriage, and you will be therein groomsmen entering into that bridechamber which is full of immortality and light."

13. And when the young people heard these things, they believed the LORD, and gave themselves up to Him, and abstained from filthy desire, and continued so, passing the night in that place. And the LORD departed from before them, saying thus: "The grace of the LORD will be with you." And when the morning had come, the king came to meet them, and furnished a table, and brought it in before the bridegroom and the bride. And he found them sitting next to each other, and he found the face of the bride unveiled, and the bridegroom was joyful. And the mother came to the bride and said: "Why do you sit so, child, and are not ashamed, but are as if you had lived with your husband a long time?" And her father said: "Because of your great love toward your husband, do you not even veil yourself?"

14. And the bride answered and said: "Truly, father, I am greatly in love, and I pray to my Lord that the love which I have perceived this night may abide with me, and I will ask for that husband of whom I have learned today: and therefore I will no longer veil myself, because the veil of shame is removed from me; and therefore I am no longer ashamed or embarrassed, because the deed of shame and confusion has departed far from me; and that I am not confounded, it is because my astonishment has not continued with me; and that I am in cheerfulness and joy, it is because the day of my joy has not been troubled; and that I have set at nothing this husband and this marriage that passes away from before my eyes, it is because I am joined in another marriage; and that I have had no intercourse with a husband that is temporal, whereof the end is with carnality and bitterness of soul, it is because I am yoked to a true husband.

15. And while the bride was saying yet more than this, the bridegroom answered and said: "I give You thanks, O LORD, that have been proclaimed by the stranger and found in us; who have removed me far from corruption and sown life in me; who have rid me of this disease that is hard to be healed and cured and abides forever, and have implanted sober health in me; who have shown me Yourself and revealed to me all my [true] state in which I am; who have redeemed me from falling and led me to that which is better, and set me free from temporal things and made me worthy of those that are immortal and everlasting; that have made Yourself lowly even down to me and my smallness, so that You might present me to Your greatness and unite me to Yourself; who have not withheld Your own bowels from me who was ready to perish, but have shown me how to seek myself and know who I was, and who and in what manner I now am, so that I may again become that which I was: whom I did not know, but You Yourself sought me out: of whom I was not aware, but You Yourself have taken me to You: whom I have perceived, and now am not able to be unmindful of Him: whose love burns within me, and I cannot speak it as is fitting, but that which I am able to say of it is little, and paltry, and not suitably proportioned to His glory: yet He does not blame me who presumes to say to Him even that which I do not know, for it is because of His love that I say even this much."

16. Now when the king heard these things from the bridegroom and the bride, he tore his clothes and said to them that stood by him: "Go forth quickly, and go around the whole city, and take and bring me that man that is a sorcerer, who by misfortune came to this city; for with my own hands I brought him into this house, and I told him to pray over this ill-fated daughter of mine; and whoever finds and brings him to me, I will give him whatsoever he asks of me." Therefore, they went out and went around seeking him and did not find him, for he had set sail. They also went to the inn where he had lodged and found the flute-girl there, weeping and afflicted because he had not taken her with him. And when they told her the matter that had happened with the young people, she was exceedingly glad at hearing it, and put away her grief, and said: "Now I have also found rest here." And she rose up and went to them, and was with them a long time, until they had also instructed the king. And many of the brothers also gathered there until they heard the report of the apostle, that he had come to the cities of India and was teaching there: and they departed and joined themselves to him.

THE SECOND ACT

CONCERNING HIS COMING TO KING GONDOPHARES.

17. Now when the apostle had come into the cities of India with Abbanes the merchant, Abbanes went to salute King Gondophares and reported to him of the carpenter whom he had brought with him. And the king was glad and commanded him to come in to him. So, when he had come in, the king said to him: "What craft do you understand?" The apostle said to him: "The craft of carpentry and of construction." The king says to him: "What craftsmanship, then, do you know in wood, and what in stone?" The apostle says: "In wood: plows, yokes, goads, pulleys, and boats, and oars, and masts; and in stone: pillars, temples, and courthouses for kings." And the king said: "Can you build me a palace?" And he answered: "Yes, I can both build and furnish it; for to this end I have come, to build and to do the work of a carpenter."

18. And the king took him, and went out of the city gates, and began to speak with him on the way concerning the building of the courthouse, and of the foundations, how they should be laid, until they came to the place wherein he desired that the building should be; and he said: "I desire that the building should be here." And the apostle said: "Indeed, for this place is suitable for the building." But the place was wooded, and there was much water there. So the king said: "Begin to build." But he said: "I cannot begin to build now in this season." And the king said: "When can you begin?" And he said: "I will begin in the month Dius and finish in Xanthicus." But the king marveled and said: "Every building is built in summer, and can you in this very winter build and make ready a palace?" And the apostle said: "Thus it must be, and it is not possible otherwise." And the king said: "If, then, this seems good to you, draw me a plan, how the work will be, because I will return here after some long period of time." And the apostle took a reed and drew, measuring the place; and he set the doors toward the sunrising to look toward the light, and the windows toward the west, toward the breezes, and the bakehouse he appointed to be toward the south, and the aqueduct for the service toward the north. And the king saw it and said to the apostle: "You are truly a craftsman, and it is beneath you to be a servant of kings." And he left much money with him and departed from him.

19. And from time to time, he sent money, and provision, and food for him and the rest of the workmen. But Thomas, receiving it all, dispensed it, going around the surrounding cities and villages, distributing and giving alms to the poor and afflicted, and relieving them, saying, "The king knows how to obtain repayment fit for kings, but at this time it is necessary that the poor should have refreshment." After these things, the king sent an ambassador to the apostle and wrote thus: "Signify to me what you have done, or what I will send you, or of what you have need." And the apostle sent to him, saying, "The palace is built and only the roof remains." And the king, hearing it, sent him gold and silver again, and wrote to him: "Let the palace be roofed, if it is done." And the apostle said to the LORD: "I thank You, O LORD, in all things, that You died for a short span, so that I might live forever in You, and that You have sold me that by me You might set many free." And he did not cease to teach and to refresh the afflicted, saying, "The LORD has dispensed this to you, and He gives to every man his food, for He is the nourisher of orphans and steward of the widows, and to all that are afflicted He is relief and rest."

20. Now when the king came to the city, he inquired of his friends concerning the palace which Judas that is called Thomas was building for him. And they told him: "Neither has he built a palace nor done anything else of what he promised to perform, but he goes around the cities and countries, and whatsoever he has he gives to the poor, and teaches of a new God, and heals the sick, and drives out devils, and does many other wonderful things; and we think him to be a sorcerer. Yet his compassions and his cures which are done of him freely, and moreover the simplicity and kindness of him and his faith, do declare that he is a righteous man or an apostle of the new God whom he preaches; for he continually fasts and prays, and eats bread only, with salt, and his drink is water, and he wears only one garment in fair weather and in winter alike, and receives nothing from any man, and whatever he has he gives to others." And when the king heard that, he rubbed his face with his hands and shook his head for a long time.

21. And he sent for the merchant who had brought him, and for the apostle, and said to him: "Have you built me the palace?" And he said: "Yes." And the king said: "When, then, will we go and see it?" But he answered him and said: "You cannot see it now, but when you depart this life, then you will see it." And the king was exceedingly angry, and he commanded both the merchant and Judas which is called Thomas to be put in bonds and cast into prison until he should inquire and learn to whom the king's money had been given, and so destroy both him and the merchant. And the apostle went to the prison rejoicing and said to the merchant: "Fear nothing; only believe in the God that is preached by me, and you will indeed be set free from this world, but from the world to come you will receive life." And the king contemplated with what death he should destroy them. And when he had determined to flay them alive and burn them with fire, in the same night the king's brother Gad fell sick, and by reason of his unease and the deceit which the king had suffered, he was greatly oppressed; and he sent for the king and said to him: "O king, my brother, I commit my house and my children to you, for I am displeased by reason of the provocation that has happened to you, and behold, I die; and if you do not visit with vengeance on the head of that sorcerer, you will give my soul no rest in Hades." And the king said to his brother: "All night long, I have considered how I should put him to death and this has seemed good to me: to flay him and burn him with fire—both him and the merchant which brought him."

22. And as they talked together, the soul of his brother Gad departed. And the king mourned severely for Gad, for he loved him greatly, and commanded that he should be buried in royal and precious apparel. Now after this, messengers took the soul of the king's brother Gad and carried it up into Heaven, showing to him the places and dwellings that were there, and inquired of him: "In which place would you dwell?" And when they drew near to the building of Thomas the apostle, which he had built for the

king, Gad saw it and said to the messengers: "I beg you, my lords, allow me to dwell in one of the lowest rooms of these." And they said to him: "You cannot dwell in this building." And he said: "Why?" And they say to him: "This is that palace which that Christian built for your brother." And he said: "I beg you, my lords, allow me to go to my brother, so that I may buy this palace from him, for my brother does not know of what sort it is, and he will sell it to me."

23. Then the messengers let the soul of Gad go. And as they were putting his grave clothes on him, his soul entered into him, and he said to them that stood around him: "Call my brother to me, so that I may ask one petition of him." Therefore, they immediately told the king, saying, "Your brother is revived." And the king ran forth with a great company, and came to his brother, and entered in, and stood by his bed as one amazed, not being able to speak to him. And his brother said: "I know and am persuaded, my brother, that if any man had asked you for half of your kingdom, you would have given it to him for my sake; therefore, I beg of you to grant me one favor which I ask of you: that you would sell me that which I ask of you." And the king answered and said: "And what is it which you ask me to sell you?" And he said: "Convince me by an oath that you will grant it to me." And the king swore to him: "One of my possessions, whatsoever you will ask for, I will give you." And he says to him: "Sell me that palace which you have in the heavens?" And the king said: "Where should I have a palace in the heavens?" And he said: "Even that which that Christian built for you which is now in the prison, whom the merchant brought to you, having purchased him from one Jesus—I mean that Hebrew slave whom you desired to punish as having suffered deceit at his hand: at which I was grieved and died, and am now revived."

24. Then the king, considering the matter, understood it [to be] those eternal benefits which should come to him and which concerned him, and he said: "I cannot sell you that palace, but I pray to enter into it, and dwell therein, and to be accounted worthy of the inhabitants of it, but if you indeed desire to buy such a palace, behold, the man lives and will build you one better than it." And immediately he sent and brought out of prison the apostle and the merchant that was shut up with him, saying, "I plead with you, as a man that pleads with the minister of God, that you would pray for me and beg Him whose minister you are to forgive me and overlook that which I have done to you or thought to do, and that I may become a worthy inhabitant of that dwelling for which I took no pains, but you have built it for me, laboring alone—the grace of your God working with you, and that I also may become a servant and serve this God whom you preach." And his brother also fell down before the apostle and said: "I implore and supplicate you before your God that I may become worthy of His ministry and service, and that it may fall to me to be worthy of the things that were shown to me by His messengers."

25. And the apostle, filled with joy, said: "I praise You, O Lord Jesus, that You have revealed Your truth in these men, for You alone are the God of truth, and no one else, and You are He that knows all things that are unknown to most; You, LORD, are He that in all things shows compassion and spares men. For men by reason of the error that is in them have overlooked You, but You have not overlooked them. And now at my supplication and request, receive the king and his brother and join them to Your fold, cleansing them with Your washing and anointing them with Your oil from the error that engulfs them; and also keep them from the wolves, bearing them into Your meadows. And give them drink out of Your immortal fountain which is neither fouled nor dries up; for they plead with and supplicate You and desire to become Your servants and ministers, and for this they are content even to be persecuted by Your enemies, and for Your sake to be hated by them and to be mocked and to die, just as You, for our sake, suffered all these things, so that You might preserve us—You that are Lord and truly the Good Shepherd. And grant them to have confidence in You alone, and the help that comes from You and the hope of their salvation which they look for from You alone; and that they may be grounded in Your mysteries, and receive the perfect good of Your graces and gifts, and flourish in Your ministry, and come to perfection in Your Father."

26. Being therefore completely set on the apostle, both King Gondophares and his brother Gad followed him and did not depart from him at all, and they also relieved them that had need, giving to all and refreshing all. And they pleaded with him that they also might henceforth receive the seal of the Word, saying to him: "Seeing that our souls are at leisure and eager toward God, give us the seal; for we have heard you say that the God whom you preach knows His own sheep by His seal." And the apostle said to them: "I also rejoice and implore you to receive this seal, and to partake with me in this thanksgiving and blessing of the LORD, and to be made perfect therein. For this is the Lord and God of all, even Jesus Christ whom I preach, and He is the father of truth, in whom I have taught you to believe." And he commanded them to bring oil, so that they might receive the seal by the oil. Therefore, they brought the oil and lit many lamps, for it was night.

27. And the apostle arose and sealed them. And the LORD was revealed to them by a voice, saying, "Peace be to you, brothers." And they heard His voice only, but they did not see His likeness, for they had not yet received the added sealing of the seal [[or had not been immersed]]. And the apostle took the oil, and poured it on their heads, and anointed and christened them, and began to say: "Come, you holy Name of the Christ that is above every name. Come, you power of the Most High, and the compassion that is perfect. Come, gift of the Most High. Come, compassionate mother. Come, communion of the male. Come, she that reveals the hidden mysteries. Come, mother of the seven houses, that your rest may be in the eighth house. Come, elder of the five members—mind, thought, reflection, consideration, reason; communicate with these young men. Come, Holy Spirit, and cleanse their reins and their heart, and give them the added seal, in the Name of the Father, and Son, and Holy Spirit." And when they were sealed, there appeared to them a youth holding a lighted torch, so that their lamps became dim at the approach of the light thereof. And he went forth and was no longer seen by them. And the apostle said to the LORD: "Your light, O LORD, is not to be contained by us, and we are not able to bear it, for it is too great for our sight." And when the dawn came and it was morning, he broke bread and made them partakers of the communion of the Christ. And they were glad and rejoiced. And many others also, believing, were added to them and came into the refuge of the Savior.

28. And the apostle did not cease to preach and to say to them: "You men and women, boys and girls, young men and maidens, strong men and aged, whether bond or free, abstain from fornication, and covetousness, and the service of the belly: for under these three heads all iniquity comes about. For fornication blinds the mind, and darkens the eyes of the soul, and is an impediment to the life of the body, turning the whole man to weakness and casting the whole body into sickness. And greed puts the soul into fear and shame; being within the body, it seizes on the goods of others and is frightened unless it restores other men's goods to their owner; it is put to shame. And the service of the belly casts the soul into thoughts, and cares, and worries, taking thought lest it comes to be in need and have need of those things that are far from it. If, then, you are rid of these, you become free of care, and grief, and fear, and that abides with you which was said by the Savior: Take no thought for tomorrow, for tomorrow will take thought for the things of itself. Remember also that word of Him of whom I spoke: Look at the ravens and see the birds of the sky, that they neither sow, nor reap, nor gather into barns, and God dispenses to them; how much more to you, O you of little faith? But look for His coming, and have your hope in Him, and believe on His Name. For He is the Judge of [the] living and dead, and He gives to everyone according to their deeds, and at His coming and His latter appearing, no man has any word of excuse when he is to be judged by Him, as though He had not heard. For His heralds proclaim in the four quarters of the world. Convert, therefore, and believe the promise, and receive the yoke of meekness and the light burden, so that you may live and not die. These things get, these keep. Come forth from the darkness, so that the light may receive you! Come to Him who is indeed good,

so that you may receive grace from Him and implant His sign in your souls."

29. And when he had thus spoken, some of them that stood by said: "It is time for the creditor to receive the debt." And he said to them: "He that is lord of the debt always desires to receive more; but let us give him that which is due." And he blessed them, and took bread, and oil, and herbs, and salt, and blessed and gave to them; but he himself continued his fast, for the LORD's Day was approaching. And when night fell, and he slept, the LORD came and stood at his head, saying, "Thomas, rise early, and having blessed them all, after the prayer and the ministry, go by the eastern road two miles and there I will show you My glory; for by your going many will take refuge with Me, and you will bring to light the nature and power of the enemy." And he rose up from sleep and said to the brothers that were with him: "Children, the LORD will accomplish something through me today, but let us pray and plead with Him that we may have no impediment toward Him, but that as at all times, so now also, it may be done according to His desire and will by us." And having said this, he laid his hands on them, and blessed them, and broke the bread of the communion, and gave it to them, saying, "This communion will be to you for compassion and mercy, and not for judgment and retribution." And they said Amen.

THE THIRD ACT

CONCERNING THE SERVANT.

30. And the apostle went forth to go where the LORD had commanded him; and when he was near to the second milestone and had turned slightly out of the way, he saw the body of an attractive youth lying and said: "LORD, is it for this that You have brought me forth, to come here that I might see this temptation? Your will therefore be done as You desire." And he began to pray and to say: "O LORD, the Judge of [the] living and dead, of the living that stand by and the dead that lie here, and Master and Father of all things; and Father not only of the souls that are in bodies, but [also] of them that have gone forth from them, for also of the souls that are in corrupted [bodies], You are Lord and Judge; come at this hour wherein I call on You and show forth Your glory on him that lies here." And he turned himself to them that followed him and said: "This thing has not come to pass without cause, but the enemy has effected it and brought it about so that he may assault us thereby; and you see that he has not made use of another sort, nor worked through any other creature except that which is his subject."

31. And when he had said this, a great [[or black]] serpent [[or dragon]] came out of a hole, beating with his head and shaking his tail on the ground, and with a loud voice, said to the apostle: "I will tell you the cause for which I slew this man, since you have come here for that end, to rebuke my works." And the apostle said: "Yes, speak." And the serpent [replied]: "There is a certain beautiful woman in this village next to us; and as she passed by me, I saw her and was enamored with her, and I followed her and kept watch over her; and I found this youth kissing her, and he had intercourse with her and did other shameful acts with her; and for me it was easy to declare them before you, for I know that you are the twin brother of the Christ and always abolish our nature, but because I would not frighten her, I did not slay him at that time, but waited for him until he passed by in the evening and struck and slew him, and especially because he attempted to do this on the LORD's Day." And the apostle inquired of him, saying, "Tell me of what seed and of what race you are."

32. And he said to him: "I am a reptile of the reptile nature and noxious son of the noxious father: of him that hurt and struck the four brothers which stood upright; I am son to him that sits on a throne over all the earth, that receives back his own from them that borrow; I am son to him that girds around the sphere; and I am family to him that is outside the ocean, whose tail is set in his own mouth; I am he that entered through the barrier into paradise and spoke with Eve the things which my father commanded me to speak to her; I am he that kindled and inflamed Cain to kill his own brother, and on my account thorns and thistles grew up in the earth; I am he that cast down the messengers from above and bound them in lusts after women, that children born of earth might come from them, and I might work my will in them; I am he that hardened Pharaoh's heart, so that he should slay the children of Israel and enslave them with the yoke of cruelty; I am he that caused the multitude to err in the wilderness when they made the calf; I am he that inflamed Herod and enkindled Caiaphas to false accusation of a lie before Pilate, for this was fitting to me; I am he that stirred up Judas and bribed him to deliver up the Christ; I am he that inhabits and holds the deep of Tartarus, but the Son of God has wronged me, against my will, and taken them that were His own from me; I am family to him that is to come from the east, to whom also power is given to do what he will on the earth."

33. And when that serpent had spoken these things in the hearing of all the people, the apostle lifted up his voice on high and said: "Cease from now on, O most shameless one, and be put to confusion and die wholly, for the end of your destruction has come, and do not dare to tell of what you have done by them that have become subject to you. And I charge you in the Name of that Jesus who until now contends with you for the men that are His own, that you suck out your venom which you have put into this man, and draw it forth, and take it from him." But the serpent said: "The end of our time has not yet come as you have said. Why do you compel me to take back that which I have put into this man, and to die before my time? For my own father, when he will draw forth and suck out that which he has cast into the creation, [only] then will his end come." And the apostle said to him: "Show, then, now the nature of your father." And the serpent came near and set his mouth on the wound of the young man and sucked forth the gall out of it. And little by little the color of the young man which was as purple, became white, but the serpent swelled up. And when the serpent had drawn up all the gall into himself, the young man leapt up and stood, and ran and fell at the apostle's feet; but the serpent being swelled up, burst and died, and his venom and gall were shed forth; and in the place where his venom was shed, there came a great gulf, and that serpent was swallowed up therein. And the apostle said to the king and his brother: "Take workmen and fill up that place, and lay foundations and build houses on them, so that it may be a dwelling-place for strangers."

34. But the youth said to the apostle with many tears: "How have I sinned against you? For you are a man that has two forms, and wheresoever you will, there you are found, and are restrained by no man, as I behold. For I saw that Man that stood by you and said to you: I have many wonders to show forth by your means, and I have great works to accomplish by you, for which you will receive a reward; and you will make many to live, and they will be in rest in light eternal as children of God. You then—He says, speaking to you of me—resurrect this youth that has been stricken by the enemy and be his overseer at all times. Well, therefore, have you come here, and well will you depart again to Him, and yet He never will leave you at any time. But I have become without care or reproach; and He has enlightened me from the care of the night, and I am at rest from the toil of the day; and I am set free from him that provoked me to do this, sinning against Him that taught me to do contrary to this; and I have lost him that is the relation of the night that compelled me to sin by his own deeds, and have found him that is of the light, and is my family. I have lost him that darkens and blinds his own subjects, so that they may not know what they do and, being ashamed at their own works, may depart from him, and their works come to an end; and I have found Him whose works are light and His deeds truth, which if a man does, he does not convert from them. And I have left him with whom lying abides, and before whom darkness goes as a veil, and behind him follows shame, shameless in indolence; and I have found Him that shows me fair things, so that I may take hold on them—even the Son of truth that is related to concord, who scatters away the mist, and enlightens His own creation, and heals the wounds thereof, and overthrows the enemies thereof. But I beg you, O man of God: cause me to behold Him again, and to see Him that has now become hidden from me, so that I may also hear His voice, which I am not able to express the wonder of, for it does not belong to the nature of this bodily organ."

35. And the apostle answered him, saying, "If you depart from these things whereof you have received knowledge, as you have said, and if you know who it is that has worked this in you, and learn and become a hearer of Him whom now in your fervent love you seek, you will both see Him and be with Him forever, and in His rest you will rest, and you will be in His joy. But if you be loosely disposed toward Him, and turn again to your former deeds, and leave that beauty and that bright countenance which was now shown to you, and forget the shining of His light which you now desire, not only will you be bereaved of this life, but also of that which is to come, and you will depart to him whom you said you had lost, and will no longer behold Him whom you said you had found."

36. And when the apostle had said this, he went into the city, holding the hand of that youth and saying to him: "These things which you have seen, my child, are but a few of the many which God has, for He does not give us good news concerning these things that are seen, but greater things than these does He promise us; but as long as we are in the body, we are not able to speak and show forth those which He will give to our souls. If we say that He gives us light, it is this which is seen, and we have it; and if we say it of wealth, which is and appears in the world, we name it, and we do not need it, for it has been said: Hardly will a rich man enter into the kingdom of the heavens; and if we speak of apparel of clothing with which they that are luxurious in this life are adorned, it is named, and it has been said: They that wear soft clothing are in the houses of kings; and if of costly banquets, concerning these we have received a commandment to beware of them, not to be weighed down with reveling, and drunkenness, and [the] cares of this life—speaking of things that are—and it has been said: Take no thought for your life, what you will eat or what you will drink, neither for your body, what you will put on, for the soul is more than food and the body than clothing; and of rest, if we speak of this temporal rest, a judgment is appointed for this also. But we speak of the world which is above: of God and messengers, of watchers and holy ones, of the immortal food and the drink of the true vine, of clothing that endures and does not grow old, of things which eye has not seen nor ear heard, neither have they entered into the heart of sinful men—the things which God has prepared for them that love Him. Of these things do we converse and of these do we bring good news. Therefore, you must also believe on Him, so that you may live; and put your trust in Him, and you will not die. For He is not persuaded with gifts, that you should offer them to Him, neither is He in need of sacrifices, that you should sacrifice to Him. But look to Him, and He will not overlook you; and turn to Him, and He will not forsake you. For His exquisiteness and His beauty will make you completely desirous to love Him; and indeed, He does not permit you to turn yourself away."

37. And when the apostle had said these things to that youth, a great multitude joined themselves to them. And the apostle looked and saw them raising themselves up high, so that they might see him, and they were going up into high places; and the apostle said to them: "You men that have come to the assembly of Christ, and would believe on Jesus, take example hereby, and see that if you are not lifted up, you cannot see me who am short, and are not able to spy me out who am similar to you. If, then, you cannot see me who am like you unless you lift yourselves up a little bit from the earth, how can you see Him that dwells in the height and is now found in the depth, unless you first lift yourselves up out of your former conversation, and your unprofitable deeds, and your desires that do not abide, and the wealth that is left here, and the possession of earth that grows old, and the clothing that corrupts, and the beauty that waxes old and vanishes away, and yet more—out of the whole body wherein all these things are stored up, and which grows old and becomes dust, returning to its own nature? For it is the body which maintains all these things. But rather believe on our Lord Jesus Christ, whom we preach, so that your hope may be in Him, and in Him you may have life, world without end, so that He may become your fellow traveler in this land of error and may be to you a harbor in this troublesome sea. And He will be to you a fountain springing up in this thirsty land, and a chamber filled with food in this place of them that hunger, and a rest to your souls—yes, and a physician for your bodies."

38. Then the multitude of them that were gathered together, hearing these things, wept and said to the apostle: "O man of God, the God whom you preach, we dare not say that we are His, for the works which we have done are alien to Him and not pleasing to Him; but if He will have compassion on us, and pity us, and save us, overlooking our former deeds, and will set us free from the evils which we committed, being in error, and not impute them to us nor make remembrance of our former sins, we will become His servants and will accomplish His will to the end." And the apostle answered them and said: "He does not reckon [them] against you, neither takes account of the sins which you committed, being in error, but overlooks your transgressions which you have done in ignorance."

THE FOURTH ACT

CONCERNING THE COLT.

39. And while the apostle yet stood in the highway and spoke with the multitude, a donkey's colt came and stood before him, [[and Judas said: "It is not without the direction of God that this colt has come here. But to you I say, O colt, that by the grace of our Lord there will be given to you speech before these multitudes who are standing here; and say whatever you will, so that they may believe in the God of truth whom we preach." And the mouth of the colt was opened, and it spoke by the power of our Lord,]] and said: "You twin of Christ, apostle of the Most High, and initiate in the hidden word of Christ, who receive His secret oracles, fellow worker with the Son of God, who being free, have become a bondman, and being sold, have brought many into liberty. You family of the great race that has condemned the enemy and redeemed His own, that have become a cause of life to man in the land of the Indians; for you have come [[against your will]] to men that were in error, and by your appearing and your divine words, they are now turning to the God of truth who sent you: mount and sit on me and rest yourself until you enter into the city." And the apostle answered and said: "O Jesus Christ, who understand the perfect mercy! O tranquility and quiet, that now are spoken of by brute beasts! O hidden rest, that are manifested by your working, Savior of us and nourisher, keeping us and resting in alien bodies! O Savior of our souls! Spring that is sweet and unfailing; fountain secure, and clear, and never polluted; defender and helper in the fight of Your own servants, turning away and scaring the enemy from us, that fight in many battles for us and make us conquerors in all; our true and undefeated champion; our holy and victorious captain, glorious and giving to Your own a joy that never passes away, and a relief wherein no one is afflicting; good shepherd that give Yourself for Your own sheep, and have vanquished the wolf, and redeemed Your own lambs, and led them into a good pasture: we glorify and praise You, and Your invisible Father, and Your Holy Spirit [and] the mother of all creation."

40. And when the apostle had said these things, the whole multitude that were there looked on him, expecting to hear what he would answer to the colt. And the apostle stood a long time, as it were, astonished, and looked up into the sky, and said to the colt: "Of whom are you and to whom do you belong? For marvelous are the things that are shown forth by your mouth, and amazing and such as are hidden from the many." And the colt answered and said: "I am of that stock that served Balaam, and also your Lord and teacher sat on one that related to me by race. And I have also now been sent to give you rest by your sitting on me: and [so that] I may receive faith, and to me may be added that portion which I will now receive by your service with which I serve you; and when I have ministered to you, it will be taken from me." And the apostle said to him: "He is able who granted you this gift, to cause it to be fulfilled to the end in you and in them that belong to you by race: for as to this mystery I am weak and powerless." And he would not sit on him. But the colt pleaded and implored him that he might be blessed by him by ministering to him. Then the apostle mounted him and sat on him; and they followed him, some going before and some following after, and all of them ran, desiring to see the end, and how he would dismiss the colt.

41. But when he came near to the city gates, he dismounted from him, saying, "Depart, and be kept safe wherever you go." And the colt immediately fell to the ground at the apostle's feet and died. And all of them that were present were sorry and said to the apostle: "Bring him to life and raise him up." But he answered and said to them: "I am indeed able to raise him by the Name of Jesus Christ: but this is by all means expedient; for He that gave him speech that he might talk was able to cause that he should not die; and I do not raise him, not as being unable, but because this is that which is expedient and profitable for him." And he instructed them that were present to dig a trench and bury his body, and they did as they were commanded.

THE FIFTH ACT

CONCERNING THE DEVIL THAT TOOK UP HIS ABODE IN THE WOMAN.

42. And the apostle entered into the city, and the whole multitude followed him. And he thought to go to the parents of the young man whom he had made alive when he was slain by the serpent, for they earnestly pleaded with him to come to them and enter into their house. But a very beautiful woman suddenly uttered an exceedingly loud cry, saying, "O apostle of the new God that has come into India, and servant of that holy and only good God; for by you is He preached—the Savior of the souls that come to Him, and by you are healed the bodies of them that are tormented by the enemy, and you are he that has become a cause of life to all that turn to Him: command me to be brought before you, so that I may tell you what has happened to me, and perhaps I may have hope from you, and these that stand by you may be more confident in the God whom you preach. For I am not a little tormented by the adversary after this five years' time: at first, I was sitting in quiet, and peace surrounded me on every side, and I had no care for anything, for I took no thought for any other.

43. And it came to pass one day that as I came out from the bath there met me a man troubled and disturbed, and his voice and speech seemed to me exceedingly faint and dim; and he stood before me and said: you and I will be one in love, and we will have intercourse together as a man with his wife; and I answered and said to him: I never did this with my betrothed, for I refused to marry, and how will I yield myself to you that would have intercourse with me in an adulterous way? And having said this, I passed on, and I said to my handmaid that was with me: Did you see that youth and his shamelessness, how boldly he spoke with me, and had no shame? But she said to me: I saw an old man speaking to you. And when I was in my house and had dined, my heart suggested to me some suspicion, and especially because he was seen by me in two forms; and having this in my mind, I fell asleep. Therefore, he came in that night and was joined to me in his foul intercourse. And when it was day, I saw him and fled from him, and on the night following that, he came and abused me; and now as you see me, I have spent five years being troubled by him, and he has not departed from me. But I know and am persuaded that both devils, and spirits, and destroyers are subject to you and are filled with trembling at your prayers: therefore, pray for me and drive away from me the devil that always troubles me, so that I also may be set free, and be gathered to the nature that is mine from the beginning, and receive the grace that has been given to my kindred."

44. And the apostle said: "O evil that cannot be restrained! O shamelessness of the enemy! O envious one that is never at rest! O hideous one that subdues the lovely! O you of many forms! As he wills, [so] he appears, but his essence cannot be changed. O the crafty and faithless one! O the bitter tree whose fruits are like him! O the devil that overcomes them that are alien to him! O the deceit that uses impudence! O the wickedness that creeps like a serpent, and that is of his kind!" And when the apostle said this, the malicious one came and stood before him, no man seeing him except the woman and the apostle, and with an exceedingly loud voice said in the hearing of all:

45. "What have we to do with you—you apostle of the Most High! What have we to do with you—you servant of Jesus Christ? What have we to do with you—you counselor of the holy Son of God? Why will you destroy us, whereas our time has not yet come? Why will you take away our power? For to this hour we had hope and time remaining to us. What do we have to do with you? You have power over your own, and we over ours. Why will you act tyrannously against us, when you yourself teach others not to act tyrannously? Why do you crave other men's goods and not satisfy yourself with your own? Why are you made like the Son of God, who has done us wrong? For you resemble Him altogether as if you were born from Him. For we thought [we] had brought Him under the yoke just as we have the rest, but He turned and made us subject to Him, for we did not know Him; but He deceived us with His form of unattractiveness, and His poverty, and His neediness: for seeing Him to be such, we thought that He was [merely] a man wearing flesh and did not know that it is He that gives life to men. And He gave us power over our own, and that we should not in this present time leave them but have our walk in them: but you would get more than your due and that which was given to you, and afflict us altogether."

46. And having said this, the devil wept, saying, "I leave you, my fairest companion, whom long ago I found and rested in you; I forsake you, my sure sister, my beloved in whom I was well pleased. What I will do I do not know, or on whom I will call that he may hear me and help me. I know what I will do: I will depart to some place where the report of this man has not been heard, and perhaps I will call you, my beloved, by another name." And he lifted up his voice and said: "Abide in peace, for you have taken refuge with one greater than I, but I will depart and seek for one like you, and if I do not find her, I will return to you again: for I know that while you are near to this man, you have a refuge in him, but when he departs, you will be such as you were before he appeared, and you will forget him, and I will have opportunity and confidence: but now I fear the Name of Him that has saved you." And having said this, the devil vanished out of sight; but when he departed, fire and smoke were seen there: and all that stood there were astonished.

47. And the apostle seeing it, said to them: "This devil has shown nothing that is alien or strange to him, but his own nature, wherein he will also be consumed, for truly the fire will utterly destroy him and the smoke of it will be scattered abroad." And he began to say: "Jesus, the hidden mystery that has been revealed to us: You are He that have shown to us many mysteries; You that called me apart from all my fellows and spoke to me three words with which I am inflamed and am not able to speak them to others. Jesus, Man that was slain, dead, [and] buried! Jesus, God of God, Savior that resurrects the dead and heals the sick! Jesus, that were in need, that saves as one that has no need, that caught the fish for breakfast and dinner and made all satisfied with a little bread. Jesus, that rested from the weariness of journeying like a man and walked on the waves like a God.

48. Jesus Most High, voice arising from perfect mercy, Savior of all, the right hand of the light, overthrowing the evil one in his own nature, and gathering all his nature into one place; You of many forms, that are only-begotten, firstborn of many brothers, God of the Most High God, Man despised until now. Jesus Christ, that does not neglect us when we call on You, that has become [the] cause of life to all mankind, that for us was judged and shut up in prison, and freed all that are in bonds, that was called a deceiver and [yet] redeemed Your own from error: I beg You for these that stand here and believe on You, for they beg to obtain Your gifts, having good hope in Your help, and having their refuge in Your greatness; they hold their hearing ready to listen to the words that are spoken by us. Let Your peace come, and tabernacle in them, and renew them from their former deeds, and let them put off the old man with his deeds and put on the new that is now proclaimed to them by me."

49. And he laid his hands on them and blessed them, saying, "The grace of our Lord Jesus Christ will be on you forever." And they said, "Amen." And the woman pleaded with him, saying, "O apostle of the Most High, give me the seal, so that enemy does not return to me again." Then he caused her to come near to him, and laid his hands on her, and sealed her in the Name of the Father, and the Son, and the Holy Spirit; and many others were also sealed with her. And the apostle commanded his minister to set forth a table; and he set forth a stool which they found there, and spread a linen cloth on it, and set on [it] the bread of blessing; and the apostle stood by it and said: "Jesus, that have accounted us worthy to partake of the communion of Your holy body and blood, behold, we are bold to draw near to Your communion and to call on Your holy Name: come and communicate to us."

50. And he began to say: "Come, O perfect compassion! Come, O communion of the male! Come, she that knows the mysteries of Him that is chosen! Come, she that has part in all the battles of the noble champion! Come, the silence that reveals the great things of the whole greatness! Come, she that manifests the hidden things and makes the unspeakable things plain—the holy dove that carries the young twin! Come, the hidden mother! Come, she that is manifest in her deeds and gives joy and rest to them that are joined to her! Come and communicate with us in this thanksgiving which we celebrate in Your Name and in the love-feast wherein we are gathered together at Your calling." And having said this, he marked out the cross on the bread, and broke it, and began to distribute it. And first he gave to the woman, saying, "This will be to you for remission of sins and eternal transgressions." And after her, he also gave to all the others which had received the seal [[and said to them: "Let this thanksgiving be to you for life and rest, and not for judgment and vengeance." And they said, "Amen."]]

THE SIXTH ACT

CONCERNING THE YOUTH THAT MURDERED THE WOMAN.

51. Now there was a certain youth who had worked an abominable deed, and he came near and received communion with his mouth: but his two hands withered up, so that he could no longer put them to his own mouth. And they that were there saw him and told the apostle what had happened; and the apostle called him and said to him: "Tell me, my child, and do not be ashamed: what was it that you did and came here? For the communion of the LORD has convicted you. For this gift which passes among many, rather heals them that with faith and love draw near to it, but it has [caused] you to wither away; and that which has come to pass has not happened without some effectual cause." And the youth, being convicted by the communion of the LORD, came and fell at the apostle's feet and pleaded with him, saying, "I have done an evil deed, yet I thought to do something good. I was enamored with a woman who dwells at an inn outside the city, and she also loved me; and when I heard of you and believed that you proclaim [the] living God, I came and received from you the seal with the rest; for you said: Whosoever will partake in the polluted union, and especially in adultery, he will not have life with the God whom I preach. Therefore, whereas I loved her much, I implored her and would have persuaded her to become my companion in chastity and pure conversation, which you also teach: but she would not. When, therefore, she did not consent, I took a sword and slew her: for I could not endure to see her commit adultery with another man."

52. When the apostle heard this he said: "O insane union, how you cause ruin to shamelessness! O unrestrained lust, how you have stirred up this man to do this! O work of the serpent, how you are enraged against your own!" And the apostle commanded water to be brought to him in a basin; and when the water was brought, he said: "Come, you waters from the living waters that were sent to us, the true from the true, the rest that was sent to us from the rest, the power of salvation that comes from that power which conquers all things and subdues them to its own will: come and dwell in these waters, so that the gift of the Holy Spirit may be perfectly consummated in them." And he said to the youth: "Go, wash your hands in these waters." And when he had washed, they were restored; and the apostle said to him: "Do you believe that our Lord Jesus Christ is able to do all things?" And he said: "Although I am the least, I still believe. But I committed this deed thinking that I was doing something good, for I pleaded with her as I told you, but she would not obey me, to keep herself celibate."

53. And the apostle said to him: "Come, let us go to the inn where you committed this deed." And the youth went before the apostle in the way, and when they came to the inn, they found her lying dead. And when the apostle saw her, he was sorry, for she was a lovely girl. And he commanded her to be brought into the midst of the inn: and they laid her on a bed, and brought her forth, and set her down in the midst of the court of the inn. And the apostle laid his hand on her and began to say: "Jesus, who always show Yourself to us, for this is Your will: that we should seek You at all times; and You Yourself have given us this power: to ask and to receive, and have not only permitted this, but have taught us to pray; who are not seen with our bodily eyes, but are never hidden from the eyes of our soul, and in Your aspect are concealed, but in Your works are manifested to us; and in Your many acts we have known You as far as we are able, and You Yourself have given us Your gifts without measure, saying, Ask and it will be given to you, seek and you will find, knock and it will be opened to you: we therefore plead with You, having the fear of our sins; and we ask of You, not riches, not gold, not silver, not possessions, not anything else of the things which come from the earth and return again to the earth; but this we ask from You and plead for: that in Your holy Name You would raise up the woman that lies here, by Your power, to the glory and faith of them that stand by."

54. And he said to the youth, having sealed him: "Go, and take hold on her hand, and say to her: I with my hands slew you with iron, and with my hands in the faith of Jesus I raise you up." So, the youth went to her and stood by her, saying, "I have believed in You, Christ Jesus." And he looked to Judas Thomas, the apostle, and said to him: "Pray for me that my Lord may come to my help, whom I also call on." And he laid his hand on her hand and said: "Come, Lord Jesus Christ: grant life to her and to me the earnest of faith in You." And immediately, as he drew her hand, she sprang up and sat up, looking on the great company that stood by. And she saw the apostle also standing next to her; and leaving the bed, she leapt forth, and fell at his feet, and caught hold on his garment, saying, "I beg you, my lord: where is that other [one] that was with you, who did not leave me to remain in that fearful and cruel place, but delivered me to you, saying, Take this woman, so that she may be made perfect, and hereafter be gathered into her place?"

55. And the apostle said to her: "Relate to us where you have been." And she answered: "Do you who was with me and to whom I was delivered desire to hear?" And she began to say: "A man took me who was detestable to look on—altogether dark and his attire exceedingly foul; and he took me away to a place wherein were many chasms, and a great stench and revolting odor issued from there. And he caused me to look into every pit, and I saw in the [first] pit flaming fire, and wheels of fire ran around there, and souls were hung on those wheels, and were dashed against each other; and very great crying and howling was there, and there was no one to deliver. And that man said to me: These souls are of your tribe, and when the number of their days is accomplished, they are delivered to torment and affliction, and then others are brought in in their stead, and likewise these into another place. These are they that have reversed the intercourse of male and female. [[And I looked and saw infants heaped on one another and struggling with each other as they lay on them. And he answered and said to me: These are the children of those others, and therefore they are set here for a testimony against them.]]

56. And he took me to another pit, and I stooped, and looked, and saw mire and worms welling up, and souls wallowing there, and a great gnashing of teeth was heard there from them. And that man said to me: These are the souls of women which abandoned their husbands, and committed adultery with others, and are brought into this torment. He showed me another pit to which I stooped, and looked, and saw souls hanging: some by the tongue, some by the hair, some by the hands, and some head downward by the feet, and tormented with smoke and brimstone; concerning whom that man that was with me answered me: The souls which are hung by the tongue are slanderers, that uttered lying and shameful words, and were not ashamed; and they that are hung by the hair are shameless ones which had no modesty and went around in the world bareheaded; and they that are hung by the hands, these are they that took away and stole other men's goods,

ACTS OF THOMAS

and never gave anything to the needy nor helped the afflicted, but did so, desiring to take all, and had no thought at all for justice or of the law; and they that hang upside down by the feet, these are they that lightly and readily ran in evil ways and disorderly paths, not visiting the sick nor escorting them that depart this life, and therefore each and every soul receives that which was done by it.

57. Again he took me and showed me an exceedingly dark cave, breathing out a great stench, and many souls were looking out, desiring to get some of the air, but their keepers did not permit them to look forth. And he that was with me said: This is the prison of those souls which you saw: for when they have fulfilled their torments for that which each did, thereafter others succeed them; and there are some that are completely consumed and that are delivered over to other torments. And they that kept the souls which were in the dark cave said to the man that had taken me: Give her to us, so that we may bring her in to the rest until the time comes for her to be delivered to torment. But he answered them: I do not give her to you, for I fear him that delivered her to me, for I was not charged to leave her here, but I take her back with me until I will receive an order concerning her. And he took me and brought me to another place wherein men were being sharply tormented. And he that was like you took me and delivered me to you, saying thus to you: Take her, for she is one of the sheep that have gone astray. And I was taken by you, and now I am before you. I therefore beg and supplicate you that I may not depart to those places of punishment which I have seen."

58. And the apostle said: "You have heard what this woman has related: and there are not only these torments, but also others worse than these; and you, if you do not turn to this God whom I preach and abstain from your former works and the deeds which you committed without knowledge, will have your end in those torments. Therefore, believe on Christ Jesus, and He will forgive you of the sins you have previously committed, and will cleanse you from all your bodily lusts that abide on the earth, and will heal you of all your trespasses which follow you, and depart with you, and are found on you. Therefore, every one of you must put off the old man, and put on the new, and forsake your former walk and conversation; and let them that stole steal no longer, but live by laboring and working; and let the adulterous no longer fornicate, lest they deliver themselves to continuous torment; for before God, adultery is exceedingly evil beyond other sins. And put away from yourselves covetousness, and lying, and drunkenness, and slandering, and do not render evil for evil: for all these things are strange and alien to the God who is preached by me; but instead, walk in faith, and meekness, and holiness, and hope, in which God delights, so that you may become His own, expecting from Him the gifts which only a few receive."

59. Therefore, all the people believed and gave their souls obediently to the living God and Christ Jesus, rejoicing in the blessed works of the Most High and in His holy service. And they brought much money for the service of the widows, for the apostle had them gathered together in the cities, and to all of them he sent provision by his own ministers, both clothes and nourishment. And he himself did not cease preaching, and speaking to them, and showing that this is Jesus Christ whom the Writings proclaimed, who has come, and was crucified, and was raised from the dead [on] the third day. And next, he showed them plainly, beginning from the Prophets, the things concerning the Christ, that it was necessary that He should come, and that in Him should be accomplished all things that were foretold of Him. And his fame went forth into all the cities and countries, and all that had sick or them that were oppressed by unclean spirits brought them, and some they laid in the way whereby he should pass, and he healed them all by the power of the LORD. Then all that were healed by him said with one accord: "Glory be to You, Jesus, who have granted us all alike healing through Your servant and apostle Thomas. And now being whole and rejoicing, we plead with You that we may be of Your flock, and be numbered among Your sheep; therefore, receive us, LORD, and do not impute to us our transgressions and our former faults which we committed, being in ignorance."

60. And the apostle said: "Glory be to the only-begotten of the Father! Glory be to the firstborn of many brothers! Glory be to You, the defender and helper of them that come to Your refuge—that does not sleep, that awake them that are asleep, that live and give life to them that lie in death! O God Jesus Christ, Son of the living God, redeemer and helper, refuge and rest of all that are weary in Your work, giver of healing to them that for Your Name's sake bear the burden and heat of the day: we give thanks for the gifts that are given to us from You and granted to us by Your help and Your dispensation that comes to us from You.

61. Therefore, perfect these things in us to the end that we may have the boldness that is in You; look on us, because for Your sake we have forsaken our homes and our parents, and for Your sake we have gladly and willingly become strangers; look on us, LORD, for we have forsaken our own possessions for Your sake, so that we might gain You, the possession that cannot be taken away; look on us, LORD, for we have forsaken them that belong to us by race, so that we might be joined to Your family; look on us, LORD, that have forsaken our fathers, and mothers, and fosters, so that we might behold Your Father, and be satisfied with His divine food; look on us, LORD, because for Your sake we have forsaken our bodily companions and our earthly fruits, so that we might be partakers in that enduring and true fellowship, and bring forth true fruits, whose nature is from above, which no man can take from us, with whom we will abide and who will abide with us."

THE SEVENTH ACT

CONCERNING THE CAPTAIN.

62. Now while the apostle Thomas was proclaiming the word of God throughout all of India, a certain captain of the king, Misdaeus, came to him and said to him: "I have heard of you, that you take no reward from any man, but even what you have you give to them that need. For if you received rewards, I would have sent you a great sum, and would not have come myself, for the king does nothing without me; for I have much wealth and am rich—even one of the rich men of India. And I have never done wrong to any; but the contrary has happened to me. I have a wife, and I had a daughter through her, and I am well-affectioned toward her, as also nature requires, and have never made trial of another wife. Now it so happened that there was a wedding in our city, and they that made the marriage feast were well-beloved by me: they therefore came in and requested me to it, also requesting my wife and her daughter. Forasmuch then as they were my good friends, I could not refuse: I therefore sent her, though she did not desire to go, and I also sent with them many servants; so they departed, both she and her daughter, adorned with many ornaments.

63. And when it was evening, and the time had come to depart from the wedding, I sent lamps and torches to meet them: and I stood in the street to observe when she should come, and I should see her with my daughter. And as I stood, I heard a sound of lamentation. Woe for her! was heard out of every mouth. And my servants came to me with their clothes torn and told me what was done. We saw, they said, a man and a boy with him. And the man laid his hand on your wife, and the boy on your daughter, and they fled from them, and we struck them with our swords, but our swords fell to the ground. And the same hour the women fell down, gnashing their teeth and beating their heads on the earth, and seeing this, we came to tell it to you. And when I heard this from my servants, I tore my clothes and struck my face with my hands, and becoming like a madman, I ran along the street, and came and found them cast in the marketplace; and I took them and brought them to my house, and after a long span, they awoke, and stood up, and sat down.

64. I therefore began to inquire of my wife: What is it that has happened to you? And she said to me: Do you not know what you have done to me? For I pleaded with you that I might not go to the wedding, because I was not even well in my body; and as I went on the way and came near to the aqueduct wherein the water flows, I saw a dark man standing next to me, nodding at me with his head, and a boy like him standing by him; and I said to my daughter: Look at those two hideous men, whose teeth are like milk and their lips like soot. And we left them and went toward the aqueduct; and when it was sunset and we departed from the wedding, as we passed by with the young men and drew near the aqueduct, my daughter saw them first, and was frightened and fled toward me; and after her, I also beheld them coming against us: and the servants that were with us fled from them, and they struck us and cast down both me and my daughter. And when she had told me these things, the devils came on them again and threw them down: and from that hour on, they are not able to come forth, but are shut up in one room or another; and I suffer greatly on their account and am distressed, for the devils throw them down wheresoever they find them and strip them naked. I beg and supplicate you before God: help me and have pity on me, for it is now three years that a table has not been set in my house, and my wife and my daughter have not sat at a table: and especially for my unhappy daughter, who has not seen any good at all in this world."

65. And the apostle, hearing these things from the captain, was greatly grieved for him and said to him: "Do you believe that Jesus will heal them?" And the captain said: "Yes." And the apostle said: "Then commit yourself to Jesus, and He will heal them and provide them aid." And the captain said: "Show me Him, so that I may plead with Him and believe in Him." And the apostle said: "He does not appear to these bodily eyes, but is found by the eyes of the mind." The captain therefore lifted up his voice and said: "I believe You, Jesus, and plead with and supplicate You: help my little faith which I have in You." And the apostle commanded Xenophon the minister to assemble all the brothers; and when the whole multitude was gathered, the apostle stood in the midst and said:

66. "Children and brothers that have believed on the LORD: abide in this faith, preaching Jesus who was proclaimed to you by me to bring you hope in Him; and do not forsake Him, and He will not forsake you. While you sleep in this slumber that weighs down the sleepers, He, not sleeping, keeps watch over you; and when you sail, and are in peril, and none can help, He, walking on the waters, supports and aids. For I am now departing from you, and it does not appear if I will again see you according to the flesh. Therefore, do not be like the people of Israel, who losing sight of their shepherds for an hour, stumbled. But I leave to you Xenophon the deacon in my stead; for he also, like myself, proclaims Jesus: for neither am I anything, nor he, but Jesus only; for I am also a man clothed with a body, a son of man like one of you; for neither do I have riches as it is found with some, which also convict them that possess them, being wholly useless and left behind on the earth from where they also came, and they carry away with them the transgressions and blemishes of sins which fall on men by their means. And rarely are rich men found in almsgiving; but the merciful and lowly in heart—these will inherit the Kingdom of God: for it is not beauty that endures with men, for they that trust in it, when age comes on them, will suddenly be put to shame: all things therefore have their time—in their season they are loved and hated. Let your hope then be in Jesus Christ the Son of God, who is always loved and always desired; and be mindful of us, as we [are] of you, for we too, if we do not fulfill the burden of the commandments, are not worthy to be preachers of this Name, and hereafter we will pay the price of our own head."

67. And he prayed with them and continued with them a long time in prayer and supplication, and committing them to the LORD, he said: "O LORD—You that rule over every soul that is in the body; Lord, Father of the souls that have their hope in You and expect Your mercies, that redeem from error the men that are Your own, and set free from bondage and corruption Your subjects that come to Your refuge: be in the flock of Xenophon, and anoint it with holy oil, and heal it of sores, and preserve it from the ravenous wolves." And he laid his hand on them and said: "The peace of the LORD will be on you and will journey with us."

THE EIGHTH ACT

CONCERNING THE WILD DONKEYS.

68. Therefore the apostle went forth to depart on the way: and they all escorted him, weeping and adjuring him to remember them in his prayers and not to forget them. He went up then and sat on the chariot, leaving all the brothers, and the captain came and awoke the driver, saying, "I beg and pray that I may become worthy to sit beneath his feet, and I will be his driver on this way, so that he also may become my guide in that way whereby few go."

69. And when they had journeyed about two miles, the apostle requested the captain, and made him arise, and caused him to sit by him, allowing the driver to sit in his own place. And as they went along the road, it came to pass that the beasts were wearied with the great heat and could not be stirred at all. And the captain was greatly displeased, and completely cast down, and thought to run on his own feet and bring other beasts for the use of the chariot; but the apostle said: "Do not let your heart be troubled, nor frightened, but believe on Jesus Christ whom I have proclaimed to you, and you will see great wonders." And he looked and saw a herd of wild donkeys feeding by the wayside, and he said to the captain: "If you have believed on Christ Jesus, go to that herd of wild donkeys and say: Judas Thomas, the apostle of Christ the new God, says to you: Let four of you come, of whom we have need."

70. And the captain went in fear, for they were many; and as he went, they came to meet him; and when they were near, he said to them: "Judas Thomas, the apostle of the new God, commands you: Let four of you come, of whom I have need. And when the wild donkeys heard it, they ran with one accord and came to him, and when they came, they revered him. [[And Judas Thomas, the apostle of our Lord, lifted up his voice in praise and said: "Glorious are You, God of truth and Lord of all natures, for You willed with Your will, and made all Your works, and finished all Your creatures, and brought them to the rule of their nature, and laid on them all Your fear, so that they might be subject to Your command. And Your will tread the path from your secrecy to manifestation, and was caring for every soul that You made, and was spoken of by the mouth of all the prophets, in all visions, and sounds, and voices; but Israel did not obey because of their evil inclination. And You, because You are Lord of all, have a care for the creatures, so that You spread over us Your mercy in Him who came by Your will and put on the body—Your creature—which You willed and formed according to Your glorious wisdom. He whom You appointed in Your secrecy and established in Your manifestation, to Him You have given the Name of Son—He who was Your will, the power of Your thought; so that You are by various names: the Father, and the Son, and the Spirit, for the sake of the government of Your creatures, for the nourishing of all natures, and You are one in glory, and power, and will; and You are divided without being separated, and are one though divided, and all subsists in You and is subject to You, because all is Yours. And I rely on You, LORD, and by Your command have subjected these mute beasts, so that You might show Your ministering power on us and on them because it is necessary, and that Your Name might be glorified in us and in the beasts that cannot speak."]] And the apostle said to them: "Peace be to you. Yoke four of yourselves in the place of these beasts that have come to a halt." And every one of them came and pressed to be yoked: there were then four stronger than the rest, which were also yoked. And the rest, some went before and some followed. And when they had journeyed a little way, he dismissed the colts, saying, "I say to you, the inhabitants of the desert: depart to your pastures, for if I had had need of all, you would all have gone with me; but now go to your place wherein you dwell." And they departed quietly until they were no longer seen.

71. Now as the apostle, and the captain, and the driver went on, the wild donkeys drew the chariot quietly and evenly, lest they should disturb the apostle of God. And when they came near to the city gate, they turned aside and stood still before the doors of the captain's house. And the captain said: "It is not possible for me to relate what has happened, but when I see the end, I will tell it." The whole city therefore came to see the wild donkeys under the yoke; and they had also heard the report of the apostle, that he was to come and visit them. And the apostle asked the captain: "Where is your dwelling, and where do you bring us?" And he said to him: "You yourself know that we stand before the doors, and these which by Your commandment have come with you know it better than I."

72. And having said this, he came down from the chariot. The apostle therefore began to say: "Jesus Christ, that are blasphemed by the ignorance of You in this country; Jesus, the report of whom is strange in this city; Jesus, that receive all the apostles in every country and in every city, and all Yours that are worthy are glorified in You; Jesus, that took a form, and became as a man, and were seen by all of us, so that You might not separate us from Your own love: You, Lord, are He that gave Yourself for us, and with Your blood have purchased us and gained us as a possession of great price; and what have we to give You, Lord, in exchange for Your life which You gave for us? For that which we would give, You gave us: and this is so that we should plead with You and live."

73. And when he had said this, many assembled from every quarter to see the apostle of the new God. And again, the apostle said: "Why do we stand idle? Jesus, Lord, the hour has come: what will You have done? Therefore, command that that be fulfilled which needs to be done." Now the captain's wife and her daughter were severely weighed down by the devils, so that they of the house thought they would no longer arise, for they did not permit them to partake of anything, but cast them down on their beds, recognizing no man until that day when the apostle came there. And the apostle said to one of the wild donkeys that were yoked on the right hand: "Enter within the gate and stand there, and call the devils and say to them: Judas Thomas, the apostle and disciple of Jesus Christ, says to you: Come forth here, for I am sent on your account to them that pertain to you by race, to destroy you and chase you to your place, until the time of the end comes and you go down into your own deep darkness."

74. And that wild donkey went in, a great multitude being with him, and said: "I speak to you, the enemies of Jesus that is called Christ; I speak to you that shut your eyes lest you see the light; I speak to you, children of Gehenna and of destruction, of him that does not cease from evil until now, that always renews his workings and the things that suits his being; I speak to you, most shameless, that will perish by your own hands. And what I will say of your destruction and end, and what I will tell, I do not know. For there are many things and innumerable to the hearing: and greater are your doings than the torment that is reserved for you. But I speak to you, devil, and to your son that follows with you, for I am now sent against you. And why should I make many words concerning your nature and root, which yourselves know and are not ashamed? But Judas Thomas, the apostle of Christ Jesus, says to you, he that by much love and affection is sent here: Before all this multitude that stands here, come forth and tell me of what race you are."

75. And the woman immediately came forth with her daughter, both like dead persons and dishonored in aspect: and the apostle, beholding them, was grieved—especially for the girl—and says to the devils: "God forbid that for you there should be sparing or propitiation, for you do not know to spare nor to have pity; but in the Name of Jesus: depart from them and stand by their side." And when the apostle had said this, the women fell down and became as dead; for they neither had breath nor uttered speech: but the devil answered with a loud voice and said: "Have you come here again—you that deride our nature and race? Have you come again, that blot out our schemes? And as I take it, you would not allow us to be on the earth at all: but at this time you cannot accomplish this." And the apostle guessed that this devil was he that had been driven out from that other woman.

76. And the devil said: "I beg you: allow me to depart even where you will, and dwell there and take commandment from you, and I will not fear the ruler that has authority over me. For just as you have come to preach good news, so I also have come to destroy; and just as, if you do not fulfill the will of Him that sent you, He will bring punishment on your head, so I also, if I do not do the will of him that sent me, before the season and time appointed, will be sent to my own nature; and just as your Christ helps you in what you do, so also my father helps me in what I do; and just as for you He prepares vessels worthy of your inhabiting, so also for me he seeks out vessels whereby I may accomplish his deeds; and just as He nourishes and provides for His subjects, so also for me he prepares punishments and torments, with them that become my dwelling-places; and just as for a reward of your working He gives you eternal life, so also to me he gives for a reward of my works eternal destruction; and just as you are refreshed by your prayer and your good works and spiritual thanksgivings, so I also am refreshed by murders, and adulteries, and sacrifices made with wine on altars; and just as you convert men to eternal life, so I also pervert them that obey me to eternal destruction and torment: and you receive your own and I mine."

77. And when the devil had said these things and yet more, the apostle said: "Jesus commands you and your son by me to no longer enter into the habitation of man: but go forth, and depart, and dwell completely apart from the habitation of men." And the devils said to him: "You have laid a harsh commandment on us; but what will you do to them that are now concealed from you? For they that have worked all the images rejoice in them more than you: and many of them do the multitude worship and perform their will, sacrificing to them and bringing them food, by libations, and by wine and water, and offering with oblations." And the apostle said: "They will also now be abolished, with their works." And suddenly the devils vanished away, but the women lay cast on the earth as if they were dead and without speech.

78. And the wild donkeys stood together and did not separate from one another; but he to whom speech was given by the power of the LORD—while all men kept silent and looked to see what they would do—the wild donkey said to the apostle: "Why do you stand idle, O apostle of Christ the Most High, who looks that you should ask from Him the best of learning? Why then do you linger? For behold, your teacher desires to show His mighty works by your hands. Why do you stand still, O herald of the Hidden One? For your [Lord] desires to manifest His unspeakable things through you, which He reserves for them that are worthy of Him, to hear them. Why do you rest, O doer of mighty works in the Name of the LORD? For your Lord encourages you and produces boldness in you. Therefore, do not fear, for He will not forsake the soul that belongs to you by birth. Therefore, begin to call on Him and He will readily listen to you. Why do you stand marveling at all His acts and His workings? For these are small things which He has shown by your means. And what will you tell concerning His great gifts? For you will not be sufficient to declare them. And why do you marvel at His cures of the body which He works, especially when you know that healing of His which is secure and lasting, which He brings forth by His own nature? And why do you look to this temporal life, and [yet] have no thought of that which is eternal?

79. But to you, the multitudes that stand by and look to see these that are cast down raised up, I say: believe in the apostle of Jesus Christ; believe the teacher of truth; believe him that shows you the truth; believe Jesus; believe on the Christ that was born, that the born may live by His life: who was also raised up through infancy, that perfection might appear by His manhood. He taught His own disciples, for He is the teacher of the truth and makes wise men wise; who also offered the gift in the temple, so that He might show that every offering was sanctified. This is His apostle, the demonstrator of truth: this is he that performs the will of Him that sent him. But there will come false apostles and prophets of lawlessness, whose end will be according to their deeds; preaching indeed and ordaining to flee from ungodliness, but themselves at all times detected in sins, adorned indeed with sheep's clothing, but within—ravenous wolves; who do not satisfy themselves with one wife, but corrupt many women; who, saying that they despise children, destroy many children, for whom they will pay the penalty; that do not satisfy themselves with their own possessions, but desire that all useless things should minister to them only; professing to be His disciples; and with their mouth they utter one thing, but in their heart they think another; charging other men to beware of evil, but they themselves perform nothing that is good; who are considered temperate, and charge other men to abstain from fornication, theft, and covetousness, but in all these things they themselves walk secretly, teaching other men not to do them."

80. And when the wild donkey had declared all these things, all men gazed on him. And when he ceased, the apostle said: "What I will think concerning Your beauty, O Jesus, and what I will tell of You, I do not know, or rather I am not able, for I have no power to declare it, O Christ that are in rest, and only wise [one] who alone know the inside of the heart and understand the thought. Glory be to You, merciful and tranquil. Glory to You, wise Word. Glory to Your compassion that was born to us. Glory to Your mercy that was spread out over us. Glory to Your greatness that was made small for us. Glory to Your most high kingship that was humbled for us. Glory to Your might which was enfeebled for us. Glory to Your Godhead that for us was seen in [the] likeness of men. Glory to Your manhood that died for us, so that it might make us live. Glory to Your resurrection from the dead; for thereby rising, rest comes to our souls. Glory and praise to Your ascending into the heavens; for thereby You have shown us the path of the height, and promised that we will sit with You on Your right hand, and with You judge the twelve tribes of Israel. You are the heavenly Word of the Father, You are the hidden light of the understanding, shower of the way of truth, driver away of darkness, and blotter-out of error."

81. Having thus spoken, the apostle stood over the women, saying, "My Lord and my God, I am not divided from You, nor as one unbelieving do I call on You, who are always our helper, and aider, and raiser; who breath Your own power into us, and encourage us, and give confidence in love to Your own servants. I beg You: let these souls be healed, and rise up, and become such as they were before they were stricken by the devils." And when he thus spoke, the women turned and sat up. And the apostle instructed the captain that his servants should take them and bring them inside. And when they had gone in, the apostle said to the wild donkeys: "Follow me." And they went after him until he had brought them outside the gate. And when they had gone out, he said to them: "Depart in peace to your pastures." The wild donkeys therefore went away willingly; and the apostle stood and took heed to them lest they should be harmed by anyone, until they had gone far off and were no longer seen. And the apostle returned with the multitude into the house of the captain.

THE NINTH ACT

CONCERNING THE WIFE OF CHARISIUS.

82. Now it so happened that a certain woman, the wife of Charisius, that was next to the king, whose name was Mygdonia, came to see and behold the new Name, and the new God who was being proclaimed, and the new apostle who had come to visit their country: and she was carried by her own servants; and because of the great crowd and the narrow way, they were not able to bring her near to him. And she sent to her husband to send her more to minister to her; and they came and approached her, pressing on the people and beating them. And the apostle saw it and said to them: "Why do you overthrow them that come to hear the word and are eager for it? And you desire to be near me but are far off, as it was said of the multitude that came to the LORD: Having eyes you do not see, and having ears you do not hear; and He said to the multitudes: He that has ears to hear, let him hear; and: Come to Me, all you that labor and are heavy laden, and I will give you rest."

83. And looking on them that carried her, he said to them: "This blessing and this admonition which was promised to them is for you that are heavily burdened now. You are they that carry burdens grievous to be borne and are borne around by her command. And though you are men, they lay on you loads as on brute beasts, for they that have authority over you think that you are not men such as themselves, whether bond or free. For neither will possessions profit the rich, nor poverty save the poor from judgment; nor have we received a commandment which we are not able to perform, nor has He laid on us burdens grievous to be borne which we are not able to carry; nor building which men build; nor to hew stones and prepare houses, as your craftsmen do by their own knowledge. But this commandment we have received from the LORD: that that which does not please us when it is done by another, this we should not do to any other man.

84. Therefore, abstain first from adultery, for this is the beginning of all evils, and next from theft, which enticed Judas Iscariot, and brought him to hanging; [[and from covetousness,]] for as many as yield to covetousness do not see that which they do; and from boastfulness and from all corrupt deeds, especially them of the body, whereby eternal condemnation comes. For this is the chief city of all evils; and likewise, it brings them that hold their heads high to tyranny, and draws them down to the deep, and subdues them under its hands, so that they do not see what they do; therefore, the things done by them are hidden from them.

85. But become well-pleasing to God in all good things, in meekness and quietness: for these does God spare, and grants eternal life, and sets death at nothing. And in gentleness which follows on all good things, and overcomes all enemies, and alone receives the crown of victory: with gentleness, and stretching out of the hand to the poor, and supplying the want of the needy, and distributing to them that are in need, especially them that walk in holiness. For this is chosen before God and leads to eternal life: for this is before God the chief city of all good, for they that do not strive in the stadium of Christ will not obtain holiness. And holiness appeared from God, doing away with fornication, overthrowing the enemy, [being] well-pleasing to God: for she is an invincible champion, having honor from God, glorified by many; she is an ambassador of peace, announcing peace; if anyone gains her, he abides without care, pleasing the LORD, expecting the time of redemption, for she does nothing wrong, but gives life, and rest, and joy to all that gain her.

86. But meekness has overcome death and brought him under authority; meekness has enslaved the enemy; meekness is the good yoke; meekness does not fear and does not oppose the many; meekness is peace, and joy, and exaltation of rest. Therefore, abide in holiness, and receive freedom from me, and be near to meekness, for in these three heads is portrayed the Christ whom I proclaim to you. Holiness is the temple of Christ, and he that dwells in her obtains her for a habitation, because for forty days and forty nights He fasted, tasting nothing; and he that keeps her will dwell in her as on a mountain. And meekness is His boast, for He said to our fellow apostle Peter: Turn back your sword and put it again into the sheath thereof: for if I had willed to do so, could I not have brought more than twelve legions of messengers from My Father?"

87. And when the apostle had said these things in the hearing of all the multitude, they tread and pressed on one another: and the wife of Charisius, the king's relative, leapt out of her chair, and cast herself on the earth before the apostle, and caught his feet, and begged and said: "O disciple of the living God, you have come into a desert country, for we live in the desert; being like to brute beasts in our conversation, but now we will be saved by your hands; I therefore beg you: consider me, and pray for me, that the compassion of the God whom you preach may come on me, and I may become His dwelling place and be joined in prayer, and hope, and faith in Him, and I also may receive the seal and become an holy temple, and He may dwell in me."

88. And the apostle said: "I pray and plead for you all, brothers, that believe on the LORD, and for you, sisters, that hope in Christ, that in all of you the Word of God may tabernacle and have His tabernacle therein: for we have no power over them." And he began to say to the woman Mygdonia: "Rise up from the earth and compose yourself. For this attire that is put on will not profit you, nor the beauty of your body, nor your apparel, neither yet the fame of your rank, nor the authority of this world, nor the polluted intercourse with your husband will avail you if you are bereaved of the true fellowship: for the appearance of ornamenting comes to nothing, and the body waxes old and changes, and clothing wears out, and authority and lordship pass away, and the fellowship of procreation also passes away, and is, as it were, condemnation. Jesus alone abides forever, and they that hope in Him." Thus, he spoke and said to the woman: "Depart in peace, and the LORD will make you worthy of His own mysteries." But she said: "I fear to go away, lest you forsake me and depart to another nation." But the apostle said to her: "Even if I go, I will not leave you alone, but

Jesus, from His compassion, will be with you." And she fell down, and gave him reverence, and departed to her house.

89. Now Charisius, the relative of King Misdaeus, bathed himself, and returned, and laid himself down to dine. And he inquired concerning his wife, where she was; for she had not come out of her own chamber to meet him as she was accustomed. And her handmaids said to him: "She is not well." And he entered quickly into the chamber and found her lying on the bed and veiled: and he unveiled her and kissed her, saying, "Why are you sorrowful today?" And she said: "I am not well." And he said to her: "Why then did you not keep the guise of your freedom and remain in your house, but [instead] went and listened to vain speeches and looked on works of sorcery? But rise up and dine with me, for I cannot dine without you." But she said to him: "Today I decline it, for I am greatly afraid."

90. And when Charisius heard this from Mygdonia, he would not go forth to dinner, but ordered his servants to bring her [food] to dine with him [there]: then, when they brought it in, he desired her to dine with him, but she excused herself; since then she would not, he dined alone, saying to her: "On your account I refused to dine with King Misdaeus, and you—were you not willing to dine with me?" But she said: "It is because I am not well." Charisius therefore rose up as he was accustomed, and would sleep with her, but she said: "Did I not tell you that for today I refused it?"

91. When he heard that, he went to another bed and slept; and awaking out of sleep he said: "My lady Mygdonia, listen to the dream which I have seen. I saw myself recline to eat near to King Misdaeus, and a dish of all sorts was set before us; and I saw an eagle come down from the sky and carry off from before me and the king two partridges, which he set against his heart; and he came over us again and flew around above us, and the king commanded [for] a bow to be brought to him; and the eagle again caught away from before us a pigeon and a dove, and the king shot an arrow at him, and it passed through him from one side to the other and did not hurt him; and he being unscathed, rose up into his own nest. And I awoke, and I am full of fear and gravely worried, because I had tasted of the partridge, and he did not allow me to put it to my mouth again." And Mygdonia said to him: "Your dream is good, for you eat partridges every day, but this eagle had not tasted of a partridge until now."

92. And when it was morning, Charisius went and dressed himself and shod his right foot with his left shoe; and he stopped and said to Mygdonia: "What then is this matter? For look, the dream and this action of mine!" But Mygdonia said to him: "And this also is not evil, but seems to me very good; for from an unlucky act there will be a change for the better." And he washed his hands and went to salute King Misdaeus.

93. And likewise Mygdonia rose up early and went to salute Judas Thomas the apostle, and she found him discoursing with the captain and all the multitude, and he was advising them and speaking of the woman which had received the LORD in her soul, whose wife she was; and the captain said: "She is the wife of Charisius, the relative of King Misdaeus." And: "Her husband is a hard man, and in everything that he says to the king, he obeys him; and he will not allow her to continue in this mind which she has promised; for oftentimes he has praised her before the king, saying that there is none other like her in love: therefore, all things that you speak to her are strange to her." And the apostle said: "If truly and surely the LORD has risen on her soul, and she has received the seed that was cast on her, she will have no care for this temporal life, nor fear death, neither will Charisius be able to harm her at all, for greater is He whom she has received into her soul, if she has indeed received Him."

94. And Mygdonia hearing this, said to the apostle: "In truth, my lord, I have received the seed of your words, and I will bear fruit like to such seed." The apostle says: "Our souls give praise and thanks to You, O LORD, for they are Yours; our bodies give thanks to You, which You have accounted worthy to become the dwelling-place of Your heavenly gift." And he also said to them that stood by: "Blessed are the holy, whose souls have never condemned them, for they have gained them and are not divided against themselves. Blessed are the spirits of the pure, and they that have received the heavenly crown whole from the age which has been appointed them. Blessed are the bodies of the holy, for they have been made worthy to become temples of God, that Christ may dwell in them. Blessed are you, for you have power to forgive sins. Blessed are you if you do not lose that which is committed to you, but rejoicing and departing, carry it away with you. Blessed are you the holy, for to you it is given to ask and receive. Blessed are you meek, for God has counted you worthy to become heirs of the heavenly kingdom. Blessed are you meek, for you are they that have overcome the enemy. Blessed are you meek, for you will see the face of the LORD. Blessed are you that hunger for the LORD's sake, for rest is in store for you, and your souls rejoice from now on. Blessed are you that are quiet, [for you have been counted worthy] to be set free from sin [[and from the exchange of clean and unclean beasts]]." And when the apostle had said these things in the hearing of all the multitude, Mygdonia was [all] the more confirmed in the faith, and glory, and greatness of Christ.

95. But Charisius, the relative and friend of King Misdaeus, came to his breakfast and did not find his wife in the house; and he inquired of all that were in his house: "Where has your mistress gone?" And one of them answered and said: "She has gone to that stranger." And when he heard this from his servant, he was angry with the other servants because they had not immediately told him what was done; and he sat down and waited for her. And when it was evening and she had come into the house, he said to her: "Where were you?" And she answered and said: "With the physician." And he said: "Is that stranger a physician?" And she said: "Yes, he is a physician of souls, for most physicians heal bodies that are dissolved, but he [heals] souls that are not destroyed." Charisius, hearing this, was very angry in his mind with Mygdonia because of the apostle, but he answered her nothing, for he was afraid, for she was above him both in wealth and birth; but he departed to dinner, and she went into her chamber. And he said to the servants: "Call her to dinner." But she would not come.

96. And when he heard that she would not come out of her chamber, he went in and said to her: "Why will you not dine with me and perhaps not sleep with me as the custom is? Yes—concerning this I have the greater suspicion, for I have heard that that sorcerer and deceiver teaches that a man should not live with his wife, and that which nature requires, and the Godhead has ordained, he overthrows." When Charisius said these things, Mygdonia kept silent. He says to her again: "My lady and companion Mygdonia, do not be led astray by deceitful and vain words, nor by the works of sorcery which I have heard that this man performs in the Name of Father, Son, and Holy Spirit; for it was never yet heard in the world that any raised the dead, and, as I hear, it is reported of this man that he raises dead men. And for that, he neither eats nor drinks, [but] do not think that for righteousness' sake he neither eats nor drinks, but he does this because he possesses nothing, for what should he do who does not even have his daily bread? And he has one garment because he is poor, and as for his not receiving anything from anyone, [[he does so, to be sure, because he knows in himself that he does not truly heal any man.]]

97. And when Charisius said this, Mygdonia was silent as any stone, but she prayed, asking when it should be day, that she might go to the apostle of Christ. And he withdrew from her and went to dinner heavy in mind, for he thought to sleep with her according to the custom. And when he had gone out, she bowed her knees and prayed, saying, "LORD God and Master, merciful Father, Savior Christ: give me strength to overcome the shamelessness of Charisius and grant me to keep the holiness wherein You delight, so that by it I may also find eternal life." And when she had so prayed, she laid herself on her bed and veiled herself.

98. But Charisius, having dined, came on her, and she cried out, saying, "You no longer have any room by me: for my Lord Jesus is greater than you, who is with me and rests in me." And he laughed and said: "You mock well, saying this of that sorcerer, and you deride him well, who says: You have no life with God unless you purify yourselves." And when he had said this he attempted to sleep with her, but she did not endure it and cried out bitterly and said: "I call on You, Lord

Jesus: do not forsake me! For I have made my refuge with You, for I learned that You are He who seeks out them that are veiled in ignorance and saves them that are held in error. And now I implore You, whose report I have heard and believed: come to my help and save me from the shamelessness of Charisius, that his foulness may not get the upper hand over me." And she struck her hands together and fled from him naked, and as she went forth, she pulled down the curtain of the bedchamber and wrapped it around herself; and she went to her nurse and slept there with her.

99. But Charisius was in heaviness all night, and struck his face with his hands, and he intended to go that very hour and tell the king concerning the violence that was done to him, but he considered within himself, saying, "If the great heaviness which is on me compels me to go now to the king, who will bring me in to him? For I know that my abuse has overthrown me from my good looks, and my boastfulness, and majesty, and has cast me down into this vileness and separated my sister Mygdonia from me. Yes, if the king himself stood before the doors at this hour, I could not have gone out and answered him. But I will wait until dawn, and I know that whatsoever I ask of the king, he grants it to me; and I will tell him of the madness of this stranger, how that it tyrannically casts down the great and illustrious into the depth. For it is not this that grieves me, that I am deprived of her companying, but I am grieved for her, because her greatness of soul is humbled: being an honorable lady in whom none of her house ever found fault, she has fled away naked, running out of her own bedchamber, and I do not know where she has gone; and it may be that she has gone mad by the means of that sorcerer, and in her madness has gone forth into the marketplace to seek him; for there is nothing that appeals to her love except him and the things that are spoken by him."

100. And saying this, he began to lament and say: "Woe to me, O my companion, and to you also! For I am too quickly bereaved of you. Woe is me, my most dear one, for you excel all my race: neither son nor daughter have I had from you that I might find rest in them; neither have you yet dwelt with me [even] a full year, and an evil eye has caught you from me. If only the violence of death had taken you, and I should yet have reckoned myself among kings and nobles: but that I should suffer this at the hands of a stranger, and be like a slave that has run away, to my misfortune and the sorrow of my unhappy soul! Let there be no impediment for me until I destroy him and avenge this night, and may I not be well-pleasing before King Misdaeus if he does not avenge me with the head of this stranger; [[and I will also tell him]] of Siphor the captain who has been the cause of this. For by his means the stranger appeared here and lodges at his house: and there are many that go in and come out to whom he teaches a new doctrine, saying that no one can live if he does not quit all his substance and become a renouncer like himself: and he strives to make many partakers with him."

101. And as Charisius thought on these things, the day dawned; and after the night, he put on humble attire, and shod himself, and went downcast and in heaviness to salute the king. And when the king saw him, he said: "Why are you sorrowful and have come in such garb? And I see that your countenance is changed." And Charisius said to the king: "I have a new thing to tell you and a new desolation which Siphor has brought into India, even a certain Hebrew, a sorcerer, whom he has sitting in his house and who does not depart from him, and there are many that go in to him, also to whom he teaches of a new God, and lays on them new laws such as were never yet heard, saying, It is impossible for you to enter into that eternal life which I proclaim to you unless you rid yourselves of your wives, and likewise the wives of their husbands. And it so happened that my unlucky wife also went to him and became a hearer of his words, and she believed them, and in the night she abandoned me and ran to the stranger. But send for both Siphor and that sorcerer that is hidden with him and visit it on their head, lest all that are of our nation perish."

102. And when his friend Misdaeus heard this, he says to him: "Do not be grieved nor heavy, for I will send for him and avenge you, and you will have your wife again, and the others that cannot, I will avenge." And the king went forth and sat on the judgment-seat, and when he was set, he commanded Siphor the captain to be called. They therefore went to his house and found him sitting on the right hand of the apostle and Mygdonia at his feet, listening to him with all the multitude. And they that were sent from the king said to Siphor: "Do you sit here listening to vain words, while King Misdaeus in his wrath intends to destroy you because of this sorcerer and deceiver whom you have brought into your house?" And Siphor hearing it was cast down, not because of the king's threat against him, but for the apostle, because the king was disposed contrary to him. And he said to the apostle: "I am grieved concerning you, for I told you at the first that that woman is the wife of Charisius, the king's friend and relative, and he will not allow her to perform what she has promised, and all that he asks of the king he grants him." But the apostle said to Siphor: "Fear nothing, but believe in Jesus who pleads for us all, for we are gathered together to His refuge." And Siphor, hearing that, put his garment around him and went to King Misdaeus.

103. And the apostle inquired of Mygdonia: "What was the cause that your husband was angry with you and devised this against us?" And she said: "Because I did not give myself up to his corruption; for last night he desired to subdue me and subject me to that passion which he serves, and He to whom I have committed my soul delivered me out of his hands; and I fled away from him naked and slept with my nurse: but that which happened to him I do not know—why he has plotted this." The apostle says: "These things will not hurt us; but believe on Jesus, and He will overthrow the wrath of Charisius and his madness and his impulse; and He will be a companion to you in the fearful way, and He will guide you into His kingdom, and will bring you to eternal life, giving you that confidence which does not pass away nor changes."

104. Now Siphor stood before the king, and [the king] inquired of him: "Who is that sorcerer, and where [is he] from, and what does he teach whom you have lurking in your house?" And Siphor answered the king: "You are not ignorant, O king, what trouble and grief I with my friends had concerning my wife, whom you know and many others remember, and concerning my daughter, whom I value more than all my possessions, what a time and trial I suffered; for I became a laughingstock and a curse in all our country. And I heard the report of this man, and went to him, and implored him, and took him and brought him here. And as I came by the way, I saw wonderful and amazing things: and here also, many heard the wild donkey and concerning that devil whom he drove out, and he healed my wife and daughter, and now they are whole; and he asked for no reward, but requires faith and holiness, that men should become partakers with him in that which he does; and he teaches this: to worship and fear one God, the ruler of all things, and Jesus Christ His Son, that they may have eternal life. And that which he eats is bread and salt, and his drink is water from evening to evening, and he makes many prayers; and whatsoever he asks of his God, He gives him. And he teaches that this God is holy and mighty, and that Christ is living and makes alive, therefore he also charges them that are present there to come to him in holiness, and purity, and love, and faith."

105. And when King Misdaeus heard these things from Siphor, he sent many soldiers to the house of Siphor the captain, to bring Thomas the apostle and all that were found there. And they that were sent entered in and found him teaching many people; and Mygdonia sat at his feet. And when they beheld the great multitude that were around him, they feared, and departed to their king, and said: "We dared not say anything to him, for there was a great multitude around him, and Mygdonia sitting at his feet was listening to the things that were spoken by him." And when King Misdaeus and Charisius heard these things, Charisius leaped out from before the king, and drew many people with him, and said: "I will bring him, O king, and Mygdonia whose understanding he has taken away." And he came to the house of Siphor the captain, greatly disturbed, and found [Thomas] teaching; but he did not find Mygdonia, for she had withdrawn herself to her house, having learned that it had been told to her husband that she was there.

106. And Charisius said to the apostle: "Get up—you wicked one, and destroyer, and enemy of my house: for your sorcery does not harm me, for I will visit your sorcery on your [own] head." And when he said this, the apostle looked on him and said to him: "Your threatenings will return on you, for you will not harm me any bit, for greater than you, and your king, and all your army is the Lord Jesus Christ in whom I have my trust." And Charisius took a kerchief [[*or* turban]] of one of his slaves and cast it around the neck of the apostle, saying, "Drag him off and bring him away; let me see if his God is able to deliver him out of my hands." And they drug him off and led him away to King Misdaeus. And the apostle stood before the king, and the king said to him: "Tell me who you are and by what power you do these things." But the apostle kept silent. And the king commanded his officers that he should be scourged with one hundred and twenty-eight blows, and bound, and be cast into the prison; and they bound him and led him away. And the king and Charisius considered how they should put him to death, for the multitude worshipped him as a god. And they had it in mind to say: "The stranger has reviled the king and is a deceiver."

107. But the apostle went to the prison rejoicing and exulting, and he said: "I praise You, Jesus, because You have not only made me worthy of faith in You, but also to endure much for Your sake. I therefore give You thanks, LORD, that you have taken thought for me and given me patience. I thank You, LORD, that for Your sake I am called a sorcerer and a wizard. Therefore, receive me with the blessing of the poor, and of the rest of the weary, and of the blessings of them whom men hate, and persecute, and revile, and speak evil words of them. For behold, for Your sake I am hated; behold, for Your sake I am cut off from the many; and for Your sake they call me such a one as I am not."

108. And as he prayed, all the prisoners looked on him and pleaded with him to pray for them: and when he had prayed and was set down, he began to utter a psalm in this way: "When I was an infant child || In the palace of my Father || And resting in the wealth and luxury of my nurturers, || Out of the East, our native country, my Parents provisioned me and sent me. And of the wealth of those treasures of theirs they put together a load || Both great and light, so that I might carry it alone. Gold is the load, of them that are above, || And silver of the great treasures || And stones, chalcedonies from the Indians || And pearls from Kushan. And they armed me with adamant || And they put on me the garment set with gems, spangled with gold, which they had made for me because they loved me || And the robe that was yellow in hue, made for my stature. And they made a covenant with me, || And inscribed it on my understanding, so that I should not forget it, and said: If you go down into Egypt and bring back from there the one pearl, || Which is there girt around by the devouring serpent, || You will put on the garment set with gems, || And that robe whereon it rests, || And become with your Brother, that is next to Us, an heir in our kingdom.

109. And I came out of the East, by a difficult and fearful road, with two guides, || And I was untried in traveling by it. And I passed by the borders of Maishan, where the resort of the merchants of the East is, || And reached the land of the Babylonians. But when I entered into Egypt, the guides left me which had journeyed with me. And I set forth by the quickest way to the serpent, and by his hole I abode || Watching for him to slumber and sleep, so that I might take my pearl from him. And forasmuch as I was alone, I made my aspect strange and appeared as an alien to my people. And there I saw my countryman from the East—the freeborn—A young man of grace and beauty, a son of princes. He came to me and dwelt with me, || And I had him for a companion, || And made him my friend and partaker in my journey. And I charged him to beware of the Egyptians, || And of partaking of those unclean things. And I put on their raiment, lest I should seem strange, as one that had come from outside || To recover the pearl; And lest the Egyptians should awake the serpent against me. But I do not know by what occasion they learned that I was not from their country. And with guile they mingled for me a deceit, || And I tasted of their food. And I no longer knew that I was a king's son, || And I became a servant to their king. And I also forgot the pearl for which my fathers had sent me, || And by means of the heaviness of their food I fell into a deep sleep.

110. But when this befell me, my fathers were also aware of it, and grieved for me || And a proclamation was published in our kingdom, that all should meet at our doors. And then the kings of Parthia, and they that hold office, and the great ones of the East || Made a resolve concerning me, that I should not be left in Egypt, || And the princes wrote to me signifying thus: From your Father, the King of kings, and your mother that rules the East, || And your Brother that is second to us: To our son that is in Egypt, peace. Rise up and awaken out of sleep, || And listen to the words of the letter, || And remember that you are a son of kings; Behold, you have come under the yoke of bondage. Remember the pearl for which you were sent into Egypt. Remember your garment spangled with gold, || Your name is named in the scroll of life, || And with your brother whom you have received in our kingdom.

111. And the King [as ambassador] sealed it || Because of the evil ones, even the children of the Babylonians and the tyrannical demons of Labyrinthus ... || It flew and descended down by me and became all speech. And I, at the voice of it and the feeling of it, started up out of sleep, || And I took it up, and kissed it, and read it. And it was written concerning that which was recorded in my heart. And I immediately remembered that I was a son of kings, and my freedom yearned after its kind. I also remembered the pearl for which I was sent down into Egypt, || And I came with charms against the terrible serpent, || And I overcame him by naming the Name of my Father on him, || ... || And I caught away the pearl and turned back to carry it to my fathers. And I stripped off the filthy garment and left it in their land, || And directed my way immediately to the light of my fatherland in the East. And on the way, I found my letter that had awakened me, || And it, just as it had taken a voice and raised me when I slept, so also guided me with the light that came from it. For at times the royal garment of silk before my eyes, || ... || And with love leading me and drawing me onward, || I passed by Labyrinthus, and I left Babylon on my left hand, || And I came to Maishan, the great, || That lies on the shore of the sea, || ... || From the heights of Hyrcania, my parents had sent me there || By the hand of their treasurers, to whom they committed it because of their faithfulness.

112. But I did not remember the brightness of it; For I was yet a child and very young when I had left it in the palace of my Father, || But suddenly, I saw the garment made like to me as it had been in a mirror, || And I beheld on it all of myself, and I knew and saw myself through it, || That we were divided apart, being of one; and again were united in one shape. Yes, the treasurers also which brought me the garment || I beheld, that they were two, yet one shape was on both: One royal sign was set on both of them. They had money and wealth in their hands, and paid me the due price, || And the lovely garment, which was variegated with bright colors || With gold, and precious stones, and pearls of lovely hue || They were fastened above ... || And the likeness of the King of kings was everywhere in all of it. Sapphire stones were fitly set in it above.

113. And again I saw that throughout it, motions of knowledge were being sent forth, || And it was ready to utter speech. And I heard it speak: I am of him that is more valiant than all men, || For whose sake I was reared up with the Father Himself. And I also perceived His stature. And all its royal motions rested on me as it grew toward the impulse of it. And it hastened, reaching out from the hand to him that would receive it, || And me also did yearning arouse to start forth, and meet it, and receive it. And I stretched forth and received it, and adorned myself with the beauty of the colors thereof || And in my royal robe excelling in beauty, I arrayed myself wholly. And when I had put it on, I was lifted up to the place of peace and homage, || And I bowed my head and worshiped the brightness of the Father who had sent it to me, || For I had performed His commandments, || And He likewise that which He had promised, || And at the doors of His palace which was from the beginning, I mingled among, || And He rejoiced over me and received me with Him into His palace, || And all His servants praise Him with sweet voices. And He promised me that with Him I will be sent to the gates of the king, || That with my gifts and my pearl we may appear together before the king."

114. And Charisius went home glad, thinking that his wife would be with him, and that she had become such as she was before, even before she heard the divine word and believed on Jesus. And he went and found her with her hair disheveled and her clothes torn, and when he saw it, he said to her: "My lady Mygdonia, why does this cruel disease keep hold on you? And why have you done this? I am your husband from your virginity, and both the gods and the law grant me to have rule over you. What [then] is this great madness of yours, that you have become a derision in our whole nation? But put away the care that comes of that sorcerer; and I will remove his face from among us, so that you may see him no more."

115. But Mygdonia, when she heard that, gave herself up to grief, groaning and lamenting, and Charisius said again: "Have I then so greatly wronged the gods that they have afflicted me with such a disease? What is my great offense that they have cast me into such humiliation? I beg you. Mygdonia, strangle my soul no longer with the pitiful sight of you and your mean appearance, and do not afflict my heart with care for you. I am your husband Charisius, whom the whole nation honors and fears. What must I do? I do not know where to turn. What am I to think? Will I keep silent and endure? Yet who can be patient when men take his treasure? And who can endure to lose your sweet ways? And what is there for me? Your fragrance is in my nostrils, and your bright face is fixed in my eyes. They are taking away my soul, and the fair body which I rejoiced to see, they are destroying; and that sharpest of eyes, they are blinding and cutting off my right hand: my joy is turning to grief and my life to death, and the light of it is being dyed with darkness. Let no man of you my family henceforth look on me; from you no help has come to me, nor will I hereafter worship the gods of the east that have enwrapped me in such calamities, nor pray to them any longer, nor sacrifice to them, for I am bereaved of my spouse. And what else should I ask of them? For all my glory is taken away, yet I am a prince and next to the king in power; but Mygdonia has set me at nothing and taken away all these things. [[If only someone would blind one of my eyes, and that your eyes would look on me as they were accustomed.]]"

116. And while Charisius spoke thus with tears, Mygdonia sat silent and looking on the ground; and again, he came to her and said: "My lady Mygdonia, most desired of me, remember that out of all the women that are in India I chose and took you as the most beautiful, though I might have joined to myself in marriage many more beautiful: but yet I lie, Mygdonia, for by the gods it would not have been possible to find another like you in the land of India; but woe is me always, for you will not even answer me a word; but if you will, revile me, so that I might only be granted a word from you. Look at me, for I am more handsome than that sorcerer; but you are my wealth and honor, and all men know that there is none like me; and you are my race and family; and behold, he takes you away from me."

117. And when Charisius had said this, Mygdonia says to him: "He whom I love is better than you and your wealth, for your substance is of earth and returns to the earth; but He whom I love is of Heaven and will take me with Him to Heaven. Your wealth will pass away, and your beauty will vanish, and your robes, and your many works: and you will be alone, naked with your transgressions. Do not call to my remembrance your deeds, for I pray to the LORD that I may forget you, so as to no longer remember those former pleasures and the custom of the body, which will pass away as a shadow; but Jesus alone endures forever, and the souls which hope in Him. Jesus Himself will stop me from the shameful deeds which I did with you." And when Charisius heard this, he turned himself to sleep, dissolved in soul, saying to her: "Consider it by yourself all this night: and if you will be with me such as you were before, and not see that sorcerer, I will do everything according to your mind; and if you will remove your affection from him, I will take him out of the prison and let him go and depart into another country, and I will not distress you, for I know that you make much of the stranger. And not with you first did this matter come about, for he has also deceived many other women with you; and they have awoken sober and returned to themselves: do not then make nothing of my words and cause me to be a reproach among the Indians."

118. And Charisius, having thus spoken, went to sleep; but [Mygdonia] took ten denarii and went secretly to give them to the jailers, so that she might enter in to the apostle. But on the way, Judas Thomas came and met her, and she saw him and was afraid, for she thought that he was one of the rulers: for a great light went before him. And she said to herself as she fled: "I have lost you, O my unhappy soul! For you will not see Judas the apostle again among the living, and you have not yet received the holy seal." And she fled, and ran into a narrow place, and hid herself there, saying, "I would rather choose to be killed by the poorer, whom it is possible to persuade, than to fall into the hand of this mighty ruler, who will despise gifts."

THE TENTH ACT

WHEREIN MYGDONIA RECEIVES IMMERSION.

119. And while Mygdonia thought this within herself, Judas came and stood over her, and she saw him and was afraid, and fell down and became lifeless with terror. But he stood by her and took her by the hand and said to her: "Do not fear, Mygdonia: Jesus will not leave you, neither will the LORD to whom you have committed your soul overlook you. His compassionate rest will not forsake you; He that is kind will not forsake you, for His kindness' sake, nor He that is good for His goodness' sake. Rise up then from the earth—you that have become entirely above it; look on the light, for the LORD does not leave them that love Him to walk in darkness; behold Him who travels with His servants, that He is to them a defender in perils." And Mygdonia arose, and looked on him, and said: "Where did you go, my lord? And who is he that brought you out of prison to behold the sun?" Judas Thomas says to her: "My Lord Jesus is mightier than all powers and all kings and rulers."

120. And Mygdonia said: "Give me the seal of Jesus Christ and I will receive the gift at your hands before you depart out of life." And she took him with her, and entered into the court, and awoke her nurse, saying to her: "Narcia [[or Marcia]], my mother and nurse, all your service and refreshment [that] you have done for me from my childhood until my present age are vain, and for them I owe you thanks which are temporal; now do for me another favor, so that you may forever receive a reward from Him that gives great gifts." And Narcia in answer says: "What do you want, my daughter Mygdonia, and what is to be done for your pleasure? For the honors which you promised me before, the stranger has not allowed you to accomplish, and you have made me a reproach among the whole nation. And now, what is this new thing that you command me?" And Mygdonia says: "Become a partaker with me in eternal life, so that I may receive from you perfect nurturing: take bread and bring it to me, and wine mingled with water, and spare my freedom." And the nurse said: "I will bring you many loaves, and for water flagons of wine, and fulfill your desire." But she says to the nurse: "I do not desire flagons, nor the many loaves, but this only: bring wine mingled with water, and one loaf, and oil."

121. And when Narcia had brought these things, Mygdonia stood before the apostle with her head bare; and he took the oil and poured it on her head, saying, "You holy oil given to us for sanctification—secret mystery whereby the cross was shown to us: you are the straightener of the crooked limbs; you are the softener of hard things; you are it that shows the hidden treasures; you are the sprout of goodness; let your power come, let it be established on your servant Mygdonia, and heal her by this freedom." And when the oil was poured on her, he instructed her nurse to unclothe her and gird a linen cloth around her; and there was a fountain of water there on which the apostle went up and immersed Mygdonia in the Name of the Father, and the Son, and the Holy Spirit. And when she was immersed and clothed, he broke bread, and took a cup of water, and made her a partaker in the body of Christ and the cup of the Son of God, and he said: "You have received your seal: obtain for yourself eternal life." And immediately a voice was heard from above, saying, "Yes! Amen! And when Narcia heard that voice, she was amazed and pleaded with the apostle that she also might receive the seal; and the apostle gave it to her and said:

"Let the care of the Lord be around you as around the rest."

122. And having done these things, the apostle returned to the prison and found the doors open and the guards still sleeping. And Thomas said: "Who is like You, O God? You who do not withhold Your loving affection and care from any who is like You, the merciful, who have delivered Your creatures out of evil. Life that has subdued death, rest that has ended toil. Glory be to the only-begotten of the Father. Glory to the compassionate that was sent forth from His heart." And when he had said this, the guards awoke and beheld all the doors open and the prisoners asleep, and they said in themselves: "Did we not lock the doors? And how are they now open, and the prisoners within?"

123. But at dawn, Charisius went to Mygdonia and found them praying and saying: "O new God that by the stranger have come here to us, hidden God of the dwellers in India; God that have shown Your glory by Your apostle Thomas, God whose report we have heard and believed on You; God, to whom we are come to be saved; God, who for love of man and for pity came down to our smallness; God who sought us out when we did not know Him; God that dwell in the heights and from whom the depths are not hidden: turn the madness of Charisius away from us." And Charisius, hearing that, said to Mygdonia: "Rightly do you call me evil, and mad, and foul, for if I had not borne with your disobedience, and given you liberty, you would not have called on God against me and made mention of my name before God. But believe me, Mygdonia, that in that sorcerer there is no profit, and what he promises to perform he cannot: but I will perform before your sight all that I promise, so that you may believe, and bear with my words, and be to me as you were before."

124. And he came near and pleaded with her again, saying, "If you will be persuaded by me, I will henceforth have no grief. Do you remember that day when you first met me? Tell the truth: was I more beautiful to you at that time, or Jesus at this?" And Mygdonia said: "That time required its own, and this time also; that was the time of the beginning, but this of the end; that was the time of temporal life, this of eternal; that of pleasure that passes away, but this of pleasure that abides forever; that, of day and night, this of day without night. You saw that marriage that was passing, and here, but this marriage continues forever; that was a partnership of corruption, but this of eternal life; those groomsmen [and bridesmaids] were men and women of time, but these abide to the end. That marriage on earth sets up dropping dew of the love of men; that bridechamber is taken down again, but this remains forever; that bed was strewn with coverlets, but this with love and faith. You are a bridegroom that pass away and are dissolved, but Jesus is a true bridegroom, enduring forever immortal; that dowry was of money and robes that grow old, but this is of living words which never pass away."

125. And when Charisius heard these things, he went to the king and told him everything: and the king commanded Judas to be brought, so that he might judge him and destroy him. But Charisius said: "Have a little patience, O king, and first persuade the man making him afraid, that he may persuade Mygdonia to be to me as formerly." And Misdaeus sent and fetched the apostle of Christ, and all the prisoners were grieved because the apostle departed from them, for they yearned after him, saying, "Even the comfort which we had they have taken away from us."

126. And Misdaeus said to Judas: "Why do you teach this new doctrine, which both gods and men hate, and which has nothing of profit?" And Judas said: "What evil do I teach?" And Misdaeus said: "You teach, saying that men must revere the God whom you preach." Judas says: "You speak the truth, O king: I teach this. For tell me, are you not angry with your soldiers if they wait on you in filthy garments? If then you, being a king of earth and returning to earth, request your subjects to be honorable in their doings, are you angry—and you said that I teach wrongly—when I say that they who serve my King must be honorable, and pure, and free from all grief, and care of children, and unprofitable riches, and vain trouble? For you would indeed have your subjects follow your conversation and your manners, and you punish them if they despise your commandments: how much more must they that believe on Him serve my God with much reverence, and cleanness, and security, and cease from all pleasures of the body: adultery, and extravagance, and theft, and drunkenness, and self-gratification, and foul deeds?"

127. And Misdaeus, hearing these things, said: "Behold, I let you go: go then and persuade Mygdonia, the wife of Charisius, not to desire to depart from him." Judas says to him: "Do not delay if you have anything to do, for her, if she has rightly received what she has learned, neither iron, nor fire, nor anything else stronger than these will avail to harm or to root out him that is held in her soul." Misdaeus says to Judas: "Some poisons dissolve other poisons, and a theriac cures the bites of the viper; and you, if you will, can give a solvent of those diseases and make peace and concord between this couple: for by doing so, you will spare yourself, for you are not yet satiated with life; and know that if you do not persuade her, I will snatch you away from this life which is desirable to all men." And Judas said: "This life has been given as a loan, and this time is one that changes, but that life whereof I teach is incorruptible; and beauty and youth that are seen will in a little [while] cease to be." The king says to him: "I have counseled you for the best, but you know your own affairs."

128. And as the apostle went forth from before the king, Charisius came to him, and implored him, and said: "I beg you, O man: I have not sinned against you or any other at any time, nor against the gods; why have you stirred up this great calamity against me? And for what reason have you brought such disturbance on my house? And what profit do you have from it? But if you think to gain something, tell me the gain, what it is, and I will acquire it for you without labor. To what end do you make me mad and cast yourself into destruction? For if you do not persuade her, I will both dispatch you and finally take myself out of life. But if, as you say, after our departing from here there is life and death there [in the afterlife], and also condemnation, and victory, and a place of judgment, then I will also go in there to be judged with you: and if that God whom you preach is just and awards punishment justly, I know that I will gain my cause against you; for you have injured me, having suffered no wrong at my hands: for indeed, even here I am able to avenge myself on you and bring on you all that you have done to me. Therefore, be persuaded, and come home with me, and persuade Mygdonia to be with me as she was at first, before she beheld you." And Judas says to him: "Believe me, my child, that if men loved God as much as they love one another, they would ask of Him all things and receive them, and none would do them violence."

129. And as Thomas said this, they came to the house of Charisius and found Mygdonia sitting and Narcia standing by her, and her hand supporting her cheek; and she was saying: "Let the remainder of the days of my life, O mother, be cut off from me, and all the hours become as one hour, and let me depart out of life, so that I may go [all] the sooner and behold that Beautiful One, whose report I have heard, even that Living One and Giver of Life to them that believe on Him, where there is not day and night, nor light and darkness, nor good and evil, nor poor nor rich, nor male and female, nor free and bond, nor proud that subjects the humble." And as she spoke, the apostle stood by her, and she immediately rose up and paid homage to him. Then Charisius said to him: "Do you see how she fears and honors you, and all that you will instruct her [to do] she will willingly do?"

130 And as he so spoke, Judas says to Mygdonia: "My daughter Mygdonia, obey that which your brother Charisius says." And Mygdonia says: "If you were not able [to confess] the deed in word, will you [now] compel me to endure the act? For I have heard from you that this life is of no profit, and this relief is [only] for a time, and these possessions are transitory. And again, you said that whosoever renounces this life will receive the life eternal, and whosoever hates the light of day and night will behold a light that is not overtaken, that whosoever despises this money will find different and eternal money. But now you are afraid. Who that has done something and is praised for the work changes it? Immediately overthrows it from the foundation? Who digs a spring water in a thirsty land and immediately fills it in? Who finds a treasure and does not use it?" And

Charisius heard it and said: "I will not imitate you, neither will I hasten to destroy you; nor though I may do so, will I put bonds around you; but I will not allow you to speak with this sorcerer; and if you obey me—good; but if not, I know what I must do."

131. And Judas went out of Charisius' house, and departed to the house of Siphor, and lodged there with him. And Siphor said: "I will prepare a hall for Judas wherein he may teach." And he did so; and Siphor said: "I, and my wife, and daughter will from now on dwell in holiness, and in chastity, and in one affection. I beg you that we may receive the seal from you, and become worshipers of the true God, and be numbered among His sheep and lambs." And Judas said: "I am afraid to speak that which I think: yet I know something, and what I know it is not possible for me to utter."

132. And he began to say concerning immersion: "This immersion is forgiveness of sins: this again brings forth light that is shed around us; this brings to new birth the new man; this mingles the Spirit [with the body], raises up in a threefold way a new man and partaker of the forgiveness of sins. Glory be to You, Hidden One, that are communicated in immersion. Glory to You, Unseen Power, that is in immersion. Glory to You, Renewal, whereby are renewed they that are immersed and with affection take hold of You." And having said this, he poured oil over their heads and said: "Glory be to You, Love of Compassion. Glory to You, Name of Christ. Glory to You, Power established in Christ." And He commanded a vessel to be brought and immersed them in the Name of the Father, and the Son, and the Holy Spirit.

133. And when they were immersed and clothed, he set bread on the table, and blessed it, and said: "Bread of life, which who eat abide incorruptible; Bread that fills the hungry souls with the blessing thereof: You are He that grants to receive a gift, that You may become forgiveness of sins to us, and that they who eat You may become immortal: we invoke on You the Name of the Mother [(Holy Spirit)], of the unspeakable mystery of the hidden powers and authorities; we invoke on You the Name of Jesus." And he said: "Let the powers of blessing come, and be established in this bread, so that all the souls which partake of it may be washed from their sins." And he broke [the bread] and gave [it] to Siphor and his wife and daughter.

THE ELEVENTH ACT

CONCERNING THE WIFE OF MISDAEUS.

134. Now King Misdaeus, when he had let Judas go, dined, and went home, and told his wife what had happened to their relative Charisius, saying, "See what has come to pass to that unhappy man, and you yourself know, my sister Tertia, that a man has nothing better than his own wife on whom he rests; but it so happened that his wife went to that sorcerer, of whom you have heard that he has come to the land of the Indians, and fell into his charms and is separated from her own husband; and he does not know what he should do. And when I would have destroyed the wrongdoer, he would not have it. But go and counsel her to incline to her husband and forsake the vain words of the sorcerer."

135. And as soon as she arose, Tertia went to the house of Charisius, [Mygdonia's] husband, and found Mygdonia lying on the earth in humiliation, and ashes and sackcloth were spread under her, and she was praying that the LORD would forgive her for her former sins, and she might soon depart out of life. And Tertia said to her: "Mygdonia, my dear sister and companion, what is this folly? What is the disease that has overtaken you? And why do you do the deeds of madmen? Know yourself and come back to your own way; come near to your many relations, and spare your true husband Charisius, and do not do things unbefitting a free-woman." Mygdonia says to her: "O Tertia, you have not yet heard the preacher of life: not yet has he touched your ears; not yet have you tasted the medicine of life, nor are freed from corruptible mourning. You stand in the life of time, and the everlasting life and salvation you do not know, and do not perceive the incorruptible fellowship. You stand adorned in robes that grow old, and do not desire those that are eternal, and are proud of this beauty which vanishes away, and have no thought of the holiness of your soul; and you are rich with a multitude of servants, [[and have not freed your own soul from servitude,]] and pride yourself in the glory that comes of many, but do not redeem yourself from the condemnation of death."

136. And when Tertia heard this from Mygdonia, she said: "I implore you, sister: bring me to that stranger that teaches these great things, so that I may also go, and hear him, and be taught to worship the God whom he preaches, and become partaker of his prayers, and a sharer in all that you have told me of." And Mygdonia says to her: "He is in the house of Siphor the captain, for he has become the cause of life to all of them that are being saved in India." And hearing that, Tertia went quickly to Siphor's house, so that she might see the new apostle that had come there. And when she entered in, Judas said to her: "What have you come to see—a man that is a stranger, and poor, and contemptible, and needy, having neither riches nor possessions? Yet one thing I possess which neither kings nor rulers can take away, that neither perishes nor ceases, which is Jesus the Savior of all mankind, the Son of the living God, who has given life to all that believe on Him, and take refuge with Him, and are known to be of the number of His servants [[or sheep]]." To whom Tertia says: "May I become a partaker of this life which you promise that all they will receive who come together to the assembly of God?" And the apostle said: "The treasury of the holy King is opened wide, and they which worthily partake of the good things that are therein rest, and resting, reign: but first, no man comes to Him that is unclean and vile, for He knows our inmost hearts and the depths of our thought, and it is not possible for anyone to escape Him. You, then, if you truly believe in Him, will be made worthy of His mysteries; and He will magnify you, and enrich you, and make you to be an heir of His kingdom."

137. And Tertia, having heard this, returned home rejoicing and found her husband awaiting her, not having dined, and when Misdaeus saw her, he said: "Why is it that your entering in today is more beautiful? And why have you come walking, which does not suit freeborn women like you?" And Tertia says to him: "I owe you the greatest of thanks because you sent me to Mygdonia, for I went and heard of a new life, and I saw the new apostle of the God that gives life to them that believe on Him and fulfill His commandments; therefore, I myself should repay you for this favor and admonition with good advice, for you will be a great king in Heaven if you obey me, and fear the God that is preached by the stranger, and keep yourself holy to the living God. For this kingdom passes away, and your comfort will be turned into affliction: but go to that man and believe him, and you will live to the end." And when Misdaeus heard these things of his wife, he struck his face with his hands, and tore his clothes, and said: "May the soul of Charisius find no rest, for he has hurt me to the soul; and may he have no hope, for he has taken away my hope." And he went out greatly upset.

138. And he found his friend Charisius in the marketplace and said to him: "Why have you cast me into Hades to be another companion to yourself? Why have you emptied and defrauded me to gain nothing? Why have you hurt me and not profited yourself at all? Why have you slain me and not lived yourself? Why have you wronged me and not obtained justice yourself? Why did you not permit me to destroy that sorcerer before he corrupted my house with his wickedness?" And he kept hold of Charisius. And Charisius says: "Why, what has happened to you?" Misdaeus said: "He has bewitched Tertia." And both of them went to the house of Siphor the captain and found Judas sitting and teaching. And all of them that were there rose up before the king, but he did not rise. And Misdaeus perceived that it was he, and took hold of the seat, and overturned it, and took up the seat with both of his hands, and struck his head so that he wounded it, and delivered him to his soldiers, saying, "Take him away, and drag him off violently and not gently, so that his shame may be manifest to all men." And they drug him away and took him to the place where Misdaeus judged, and he stood there, held by the soldiers of Misdaeus.

THE TWELFTH ACT

CONCERNING OUAZANES [(IUZANES)], THE SON OF MISDAEUS.

139. And Iuzanes, the son of Misdaeus, came to the soldiers and said: "Give me him, so that I may speak with him until the king comes." And they gave him up, and he brought him in where the king gave judgment. And Iuzanes says: "Do you not know that I am the son of King Misdaeus, and I have power to say to the king whatever I will, and he will allow you to live? Tell me then, who is your God, and what power do you claim and glory in? For if it is some power or magic art, tell it to me and teach me, and I will let you go." Judas says to him: "You are the son of King Misdaeus who is [only] king for a time, but I am the servant of Jesus Christ the eternal King, and you have power to say to your father to save whom you will in the temporal life wherein men do not continue, which you and your father grant, but I plead with my Lord and intercede for men, and He gives them a new life which is altogether enduring. And you yourself boast of possessions, and servants, and robes, and luxury, and fornications, but I boast myself of poverty, and philosophy, and humility, and fasting, and prayer, and the fellowship of the Holy Spirit and of my brothers that are worthy of God: and I myself boast of eternal life. And you rely on a man like yourself and not able to save his own soul from judgment and death, but I rely on the living God, on the Savior of kings and princes, who is the Judge of all men. And indeed, today perhaps you are, and tomorrow are no more, but I have taken refuge with Him that abides forever and knows all our seasons and times. And if you will become the servant of this God, you will soon do so; but show that you will be a servant worthy of Him hereby: first, by holiness, which is the head of all good things, and then by fellowship with this God whom I preach, and philosophy, and simplicity, and love, and faith in Him, and unity of pure food."

140. And the young man was persuaded by the LORD and sought an opportunity for how he might let Judas escape; but while he thought thereon, the king came, and the soldiers took Judas and led him forth. And Iuzanes went forth with him and stood beside him. And when the king was set, he ordered Judas to be brought in, with his hands bound behind him; and he was brought into the midst and stood there. And the king says: "Tell me who you are and by what power you do these things." And Judas says to him: "I am a man like you, and by the power of Jesus Christ I do these things." And Misdaeus says: "Tell me the truth before I destroy you." And Judas says: "You have no power against me, as you suppose, and you will not harm me at all." And the king was angry at his words and commanded to heat iron plates and set him on them barefoot; and as the soldiers took off his shoes, he said: "The wisdom of God is better than the wisdom of men. You, Lord and King, [[take counsel against them and]] let Your goodness resist his wrath." And they brought the plates which were like fire, and set the apostle on them, and immediately water sprang up abundantly from the earth, so that the plates were swallowed up in it, and they that held him let him go and withdrew themselves.

141. And the king, seeing the abundance of water, said to Judas: "Ask your God that He deliver me from this death, so that I do not perish in the flood." And the apostle prayed and said: "You that bound this element, and gathered it into one place, and sent it forth into various lands; that brought disorder into order; that grant mighty works and great wonders by the hands of your servant Judas; that have mercy on my soul, that I may always receive Your brightness; that give wages to them that have labored; You Savior of my soul, restoring it to its own nature, so that it may have no fellowship with harmful things; that have always been the cause of life: restrain this element, so that it does not lift itself up to destroy, for there are some of them that stand here who will believe on You and live." And when he had prayed, the water was swallowed up little by little, and the place became dry. And when Misdaeus saw it, he commanded him to be taken to the prison—"Until I will consider how he must be handled."

142. And as Judas was led away to the prison, they all followed him, and the king's son Iuzanes walked at his right hand, and Siphor at the left. And he entered into the prison and sat down, and Iuzanes, and Siphor, and he persuaded his wife and his daughter to sit down, for they had also come in to hear the word of life. For they knew that Misdaeus would slay him because of the excess of his anger. And Judas began to say: "O Liberator of my soul from the bondage of the many, because I gave myself to be sold; behold, I rejoice and exult, knowing that the times are fulfilled for me to enter in and receive. Behold, I am to be set free from the cares that are on the earth; behold, I fulfill my hope and receive truth; behold, I am set free from sorrow and put on joy alone; behold, I become careless and griefless and dwell in rest; behold, I am set free from bondage and am called to liberty; behold, I have served times and seasons, and I am lifted up above times and seasons; behold, I receive my wages from my rewarder, who gives without reckoning because His wealth is sufficient for the gift; and I will not put it on again; behold, I sleep and awaken, and I will no longer go to sleep; behold, I die and live again, and I will no longer taste of death; behold, they rejoice and expect me, that I may come and be with their family and be set as a flower in their crown; behold, I reign in the kingdom whereon I set my hope, even from here; behold, the rebellious fall before me, for I have escaped them; behold, the peace has come, to where all are gathered."

143. And as the apostle spoke this, all that were there listened, supposing that in that hour he would depart out of life. And again, he said: "Believe on the Physician of all, both seen and unseen, and on the Savior of the souls that need help from Him. This is the Freeborn of kings; this [is] the Physician of His creatures; this is He that was reproached by His own slaves; this is the Father of the height, and the Lord of nature, and the Judge: He came from the greatest, the only-begotten Son of the deep; and He was called the Son of the virgin Mary, and was termed the Son of Joseph the carpenter; He whose smallness [we beheld] with the eyes of our body, but His greatness we received by faith and saw it in His works whose human body we also felt with our hands, and His aspect we saw transfigured with our eyes, but His heavenly semblance on the mountain we were not able to see; He that made the rulers stumble and assaulted death; He, the truth that does not lie, that in the end paid the tribute for Himself and His disciples; whom the prince beholding feared, and the powers that were with him were troubled; and the prince bore witness [regarding] who He was and from where [He came], and did not know the truth, because he is alien from truth; He that having authority over the world, and the pleasures therein, and the possessions and the comfort, all these things, and turns away His subjects, so that they should not use them."

144. And having fulfilled these sayings, he arose and prayed thus: "Our Father, which are in Heaven: holy is Your Name; Your kingdom come, Your will be done, as in Heaven so [also] on earth; and forgive us our debts as we have also forgiven our debtors. And lead us not into temptation, but deliver us from the evil one. My Lord and God—hope, and confidence, and teacher: you have taught me to pray this, [and] behold, I pray this prayer and fulfill Your commandment: be with me to the end; You are He that from childhood have sown life in me and kept me from corruption; You are He that have brought me to the poverty of this world and exhorted me to the true riches; You are He that have made me known to myself and showed me that I am Yours; and I have kept myself pure from woman, so that that which you require may not be found in corruption.

145. My mouth does not suffice to praise You, neither am I able to conceive the care and providence which has been around me from You, which You have had for me. For I desired to gain riches, but by a vision You showed me that they are full of loss and injury to them that gain them, and I believed what You showed [me] and continued in the poverty of the world until You, the true riches, were revealed to me, who filled both me and the rest that were worthy of You with Your own riches and set free Your own from care and anxiety. I have therefore fulfilled Your commandments, O LORD, and accomplished Your will, and become poor, and needy, and a stranger, and a bondman, and set at nothing, and a prisoner, and hungry, and thirsty, and naked, and unshod, and I have toiled for Your sake, so that my confidence might not perish, and my hope that is in You might not be confounded, and my great labor might not be in vain, and my weariness not be counted for nothing: do not let my prayers and my continual fastings perish, and my great zeal toward You; do not let my seed of wheat be changed for tares out of Your land; do not let the enemy carry it away and mingle his own tares with it, for Your land truly does not receive his tares; indeed, neither can they be laid up in Your houses.

146. I have planted Your vine in the earth; it has sent down its roots into the depth, and its growth is spread out in the height, and the fruits of it are stretched forth on the earth, and they that are worthy of You are made glad by them, whom You have also gained. The money which You have from me I laid down on the table; this, when You require it, restore to me with interest, as You have promised. With Your one mina, I have traded and made ten; You have added more to me besides what I had, as You did covenant. I have forgiven my debtor of the mina: do not require it at my hands. I was invited to the supper and I came: and I refused the land, and the yoke of oxen, and the wife, so that I might not be rejected for their sake; I was invited to the wedding, and I put on a white garment, so that I might be worthy of it and not be bound hand and foot and cast into the outer darkness. My lamp with its bright light expects the Master coming from the marriage, so that it may receive Him, and He may not see it dimmed because the oil is spent. My eyes, O Christ, look on You, and my heart exults with joy because I have fulfilled Your will and perfected Your commandments, so that I may be likened to that watchful and careful servant who in his eagerness does not neglect to keep watch. I have labored all night to keep my house from robbers, lest it be broken into.

147. I have girded my loins close with truth and bound my shoes on my feet, so that I may never see them gaping. I have put my hands to the yoked plow and have not turned backward, lest my furrows go crooked. The plowed land has become white and the harvest has come, that I may receive my wages. My garment that grows old I have worn out, and the labor that has brought me to rest I have accomplished. I have kept the first watch, and the second, and the third, so that I may behold Your face and adore Your holy brightness. I have rooted out the worst and left them desolate on earth, so that I may be filled full from Your treasures. The moist spring that was in me I have dried up, so that I may live and rest beside Your inexhaustible spring. The captive whom You committed to me I have slain, so that he which is set free in me may not fall from his confidence. Him that was inward I have made outward, and all Your fullness has been fulfilled in me. I have not returned to the things that are behind, but have gone forward to the things that are ahead, so that I may not become a reproach. I have made the dead man live, and the living one I have overcome, and that which was lacking I have filled up, so that I may receive the crown of victory, and the power of Christ may be accomplished in me. I have received reproach on earth, but give me the return and the reward in the heavens.

148. Do not let the powers and the officers perceive me, and let them not have any thought concerning me; do not let the tax collectors and exactors ply their calling on me; do not let the weak and the evil cry out against me that am valiant and humble; and when I am carried upward, do not let them rise up to stand before me, by Your power, O Jesus, which surrounds me as a crown: for they flee and hide themselves; they cannot look on You, but they suddenly fall on them that are subject to them, and the portion of the sons of the evil one itself cries out and convicts them; and it is not hidden from them, nor is their nature made known: the children of the evil one are separated off. Grant me then, LORD, that I may pass by in quietness, and joy, and peace, and pass over and stand before the Judge, and do not let the Devil look on me; let his eyes be blinded by Your light which You have made to dwell in me; muzzle his mouth, for he has found nothing against me."

149. And again, he said to them that were around him: "Believe in the Savior of them that have labored in His service, for my soul already flourishes because my time is near to receive Him; for He, being beautiful, always draws me on to speak concerning His beauty—what it is though I am not able and cannot sufficiently speak of worthily. You that are the light of my poverty, and the supplier of my defects, and nurturer of my need: be with me until I come and receive You forevermore."

THE THIRTEENTH ACT

WHEREIN IUZANES RECEIVES IMMERSION WITH THE REST.

150. And Iuzanes the youth pleaded with the apostle, saying, "I beg you, O man, apostle of God, allow me to go, and I will persuade the jailer to permit you to come home with me, that by you I may receive the seal and become your minister and a keeper of the commandments of the God whom you preach. For indeed, I formerly walked in those things which you teach, until my father compelled me and joined me to a wife by name Mnesara; for I am in my twenty-first year and have now been married seven years, and before I was joined in marriage, I knew no other woman, therefore I was also accounted useless by my father, nor have I ever had a son or daughter by this wife, and also my wife herself has lived with me in chastity all this time, and today, if she had been in health, and had listened to you, I know well that both I should have been at rest and she would have received eternal life; but she is in peril and afflicted with much illness; I will therefore persuade the keeper that he promise to come with me, for I live by myself: and you will also heal that unfortunate one." And Judas, the apostle of the Most High, hearing this, said to Iuzanes: "If you believe, you will see the marvels of God, and how He saves His servants."

151. And as they spoke thus together, Tertia, and Mygdonia, and Narcia stood at the door of the prison, and they gave the jailer three hundred sixty-three staters of silver and entered in to Judas; and they found Iuzanes, and Siphor, and his wife and daughter, and all the prisoners sitting and hearing the word. And when they stood by him, he said to them: "Who has allowed you to come to us? And who opened the sealed door to you so that you came forth?" Tertia says to him: "Did you not open the door for us and tell us to come into the prison, so that we might take our brothers that were there, and then would the LORD show forth His glory in us? And when we came near the door, I do not know how, [but] you were separated from us, and hid yourself, and came here before us, where we also heard the noise of the door when you shut us out. We therefore gave money to the keepers and came in, and behold, we are here praying that we may persuade you and let you escape until the king's wrath against you will cease." To whom Judas said: "First of all, tell us how you were locked up."

152. And she says to him: "You were with us, and never left us for one hour, and [yet] you ask how we were locked up? But if you desire to hear, hear. King Misdaeus sent for me and said to me: That sorcerer has not yet prevailed over you, for, as I hear, he bewitches men with oil, and water, and bread, and has not yet bewitched you; but obey me, for if not, I will imprison you and wear you out, and him I will destroy; for I know that if he has not yet given you oil, and water, and bread, he has not prevailed to get power over you. And I said to him: You have authority over my body, and do all that you will; but I will not let my soul perish with you. And hearing that, he locked me up in a chamber, and Charisius brought Mygdonia and shut her up with me, and you brought us out and even brought us here; but give us the seal quickly, so that the hope of Misdaeus, who counsels thus, may be cut off."

153. And when the apostle heard this, he said: "Glory be to You, O Jesus of many forms, glory to You that appear in the guise of our poor manhood; glory to You that encourage us, and make us strong, and give grace, and console, and stand by us in all perils, and strengthen our weakness." And as he thus spoke, the jailer came and said: "Put out the lamps, lest any accuse you to the king," And then they extinguished the lamps and turned to sleep; but the apostle spoke to the LORD: "It is the time now, O Jesus, for You to hurry, for behold, the children of darkness sit in their own darkness; therefore, enlighten us with the light of Your nature." And suddenly the whole prison was light as the day: and while all that were in the prison slept a deep sleep, only those that had believed in the LORD continued waking.

154. Judas therefore says to Iuzanes: "Go on ahead and make ready the things for our

ACTS OF THOMAS

need." Iuzanes therefore replies: "And who will open the doors of the prison for me? For the jailers shut them and have gone to sleep." And Judas says: "Believe in Jesus, and you will find the doors open." And when he went forth and departed from them, all the rest followed after him. And as Iuzanes had gone on ahead, his wife Mnesara met him coming to the prison. And she knew him and said: "My brother Iuzanes, is it you?" And he says, "Yes, and are you Mnesara?" And she says, "Yes." Iuzanes said to her: "To where do you walk, especially at such an untimely hour? And how were you able to rise up?" And she said: "This youth laid his hand on me and raised me up, and in a dream I say that I should go where the stranger sits and become perfectly whole." Iuzanes says to her: "What youth is with you?" And she said: "Do you not see him that is on my right hand, leading me by the hand?"

155. And while they thus spoke together, Judas, with Siphor and his wife and daughter, and Tertia, and Mygdonia, and Narcia came to Iuzanes' house. And Mnesara, the wife of Iuzanes, seeing him, paid homage and said: "Have you that saved us from the grievous disease come? You are he whom I saw in the night delivering this youth to me to bring me to the prison. But your goodness did not allow me to grow weary, but you yourself have come to me." And saying this, she turned around and saw the youth no more; and not finding him, she says to the apostle: "I am not able to walk alone, for the youth whom you gave me is not here." And Judas said: "Jesus will lead you from now on." And thereafter she came running to him. And when they entered into the house of Iuzanes, the son of King Misdaeus, though it was yet night, a great light shined and was shed around them.

156. And then Judas began to pray and to speak thus: "O companion, and defender, and hope of the weak, and confidence of the poor; refuge and lodging of the weary; voice that came forth from the height; comforter dwelling in the midst; port and harbor of them that pass through the regions of the rulers; physician that heal without payment, who among men was crucified for many; who went down into Hades with great might—the sight of whom the princes of death could not endure; and You came up with great glory; and gathering all of them that fled to You, prepared a way, and in Your footsteps they all journeyed whom You redeemed; and You brought them into Your own fold and joined them with Your sheep. Son of mercy, the Son that for love of man was sent to us from the perfect fatherland that is above, the Lord of all possessions; that serve Your servants so that they may live; that fill creation with Your own riches; the poor, that was in need and hungered [for] forty days; that satisfy thirsty souls with Your own good things: be with Iuzanes, the son of Misdaeus, and with Tertia and Mnesara, and gather them into Your fold, and mingle them with Your number; be a guide to them in the land of error; be a physician for them in the land of sickness; be a rest for them in the land of the weary; sanctify them in a polluted land; be their physician both of bodies and souls; make them holy temples for You, and let Your Holy Spirit dwell in them."

157. Having thus prayed over them, the apostle said to Mygdonia: "Unclothe your sisters." And she took off their clothes, and girded them with girdles, and brought them, but Iuzanes had first gone ahead, and they came after him; and the apostle took oil in a cup of silver and spoke thus over it: "Fruit more beautiful than all other fruits, to which none other whatsoever may be compared: altogether merciful, fervent with the force of the word, power of the tree which men putting on them overcome their adversaries, crowner of the conquerors, help and joy of the sick; that announced to men their salvation; that show light to them that are in darkness; whose leaf is bitter, but in Your most sweet fruit You are fair; that are rough to the sight but soft to the taste; seeming to be weak, but in the greatness of Your strength able to bear the power that beholds all things." Having thus said … "Jesus: let [Your] victorious might come and be established in this oil, just as it was established in the tree that was its relation, even [Your] might at that time, whereof they that crucified You could not endure the word: let the gift also come whereby breathing on [Your] enemies, You caused them to go backward and fall headlong, and let it rest on this oil, whereon we invoke Your holy Name." And having said this, he first poured it on the head of Iuzanes and then on the women's heads, saying, "In Your Name, O Jesus Christ, let it be to these souls for forgiveness of sins, and for turning back of the adversary, and for salvation of their souls." And he commanded Mygdonia to anoint them, but he himself anointed Iuzanes. And having anointed them, he led them down into the water in the Name of the Father, and the Son, and the Holy Spirit.

158. And when they had come up, he took bread and a cup, and blessed it, and said: "Your holy body which was crucified for us we eat, and Your blood that was shed for us to salvation we drink; therefore, let Your body be to us salvation and Your blood for forgiveness of sins. And for the gall which You drank for our sakes, let the gall of the Devil be removed from us; and for the vinegar which You have drunk for us, let our weakness be made strong; and for the spitting which You received for us, let us receive the dew of Your goodness; and by the reed with which they struck You for us, let us receive the perfect house; and whereas You received a crown of thorns for our sake, let us that have loved You put on a crown that does not fade away; and for the linen cloth wherein You were wrapped, let us also be girt around with Your power that is not vanquished; and for the new tomb and the burial, let us receive renewing of soul and body; and because You rose up and revived, let us revive, and live, and stand before You in righteous judgment." And he broke [the bread], and gave the communion to Iuzanes, and Tertia, and Mnesara, and the wife and daughter of Siphor, and said: "Let this communion be to you for salvation, and joy, and [the] health of your souls." And they said: "Amen." And a voice was heard, saying, "Amen! Do not fear, but only believe."

THE MARTYRDOM OF THOMAS

159. And after these things, Judas departed to be imprisoned. And Tertia, with Mygdonia, and Narcia also went to be imprisoned. And the apostle Thomas said to them—the multitude of them that had believed being present—"Daughters, and sisters, and fellow-servants which have believed in my Lord and God, ministers of my Jesus, listen to me this day: for I deliver my word to you, and I will no longer speak with you in this flesh nor in this world, for I go up to my Lord and God Jesus Christ, to Him that sold me, to that Lord that humbled Himself even to me the small and brought me up to eternal greatness, that granted to me to become His servant in truth and steadfastness: I depart to Him knowing that the time is fulfilled, and the day appointed has drawn near for me to go and receive my reward from my Lord and God; for my Reward is righteous, who knows me, how I ought to receive my reward; for He is not grudging nor envious, but is rich in His gifts; He is not a lover of sparing in what He gives, for He has confidence in His possessions which cannot fail.

160. I am not Jesus, but I am His servant; I am not Christ, but I am His minister; I am not the Son of God, but I pray to become worthy of God. Continue in the faith of Christ; continue in the hope of the Son of God; do not faint at affliction, neither be divided in mind if you see me mocked or that I am locked up in prison, for I accomplish His will. For if I had not willed to die, I know in Christ that I am able to [avoid] it: but this which is called death is not death, but a setting free from the body; therefore, I gladly receive this setting free from the body, so that I may depart and see Him that is beautiful and full of mercy, Him that is to be loved, for I have endured much toil in His service and have labored for His grace that has come on me, which does not depart from me. Do not let Satan, then, enter you by stealth and snatch away your thoughts; let there be no place in you for him, for He is mighty whom you have received. Look for the coming of Christ, for He will come and receive you, and this is He whom you will see when He comes."

161. When the apostle had ended these sayings, they went into the house, and the apostle Thomas said: "Savior that suffered many things for us, let these doors be as they were and let seals be set on them." And he left them and went to be imprisoned, and they wept and were in heaviness, for they knew that Misdaeus would slay him.

162. And the apostle found the keepers wrangling and saying: "Wherein have we sinned against this wizard? For by his magic art he has opened the doors and would have had all the prisoners escape: but let us go and report it to the king and tell him concerning his wife and his son." And as they disputed thus, Thomas held his peace. Therefore, they rose up early, and went to the king, and said to him: "Our lord and king: take away that sorcerer and cause him to be locked up somewhere else, for we are not able to hold him; for except your good fortune had kept the prison, all the condemned persons would have escaped, for now this second time we have found the doors open: and also your wife, O king, and your son, and the rest do not depart from him." And the king, hearing that, went and found the seals that were set on the doors whole; and he also took note of the doors and said to the keepers: "Why do you lie? For the seals are whole. Why did you say that Tertia and Mygdonia came to him in the prison?" And the keepers said: "We have told you the truth."

163. And Misdaeus went to the prison, and took his seat, and sent for the apostle Thomas, and had him stripped [[and girded with a girdle,]] and set him before him, and says to him: "Are you bond or free?" Thomas said: "I am the bondsman of only one, over whom you have no authority." And Misdaeus says to him: "How did you run away and come into this country?" And Thomas said: "I was sold here by my Master, so that I might save many, and by your hands depart out of this world." And Misdaeus said: "Who is your Lord? And what is His Name? And what country is He from?" And Thomas said: "My Lord is your Master, and He is Lord of heaven and earth." And Misdaeus says: "What is His Name?" Thomas says: "You cannot hear His true Name at this time, but the Name that was given to Him is Jesus Christ." And Misdaeus says to him: "I have not been hurried to destroy you, but have had long patience with you, yet you have added to your evil deeds, and your sorceries are dispersed abroad and heard of throughout the whole country; but I do this so that your sorceries may depart with you, and our land may be cleansed from them." Thomas says to him: "These sorceries depart with me when I set forth from here, and know this: that I will never forsake them that are here."

164. When the apostle had said these things, Misdaeus considered how he should put him to death, for he was afraid because of the many people that were subject to him, for many also of the nobles and of them that were in authority believed on him. He therefore took him and went forth out of the city; and armed soldiers also went with him. And the people supposed that the king desired to learn something from him, and they stood still and gave heed. And when they had walked one mile, he delivered him to four soldiers and an officer and commanded them to take him into the mountain and pierce him there with spears, and put an end to him, and return to the city again. And saying this to the soldiers, he himself also returned to the city.

165. But the men ran after Thomas, desiring to deliver him from death. And two soldiers went at the right hand of the apostle and two on his left, holding spears, and the officer held his hand and supported him. And the apostle Thomas said: "O the hidden mysteries which even until our departure are accomplished in us! O riches of His glory, who will not allow us to be swallowed up in this passion of the body! Four are they that cast me down, for of four am I made; and one is He that draws me, for of one I am, and to Him I go. And I now understand this: that my Lord and God Jesus Christ, being of one, was pierced by one, but I, which am of four, am pierced by four."

166. And having come up into the mountain to the place where he was to be slain, he said to them that held him, and to the rest: "Brothers, listen to me now at the end, for I have come to my departure out of the body. Do not let then the eyes of your heart be blinded, nor your ears be made deaf. Believe on the God whom I preach, and do not be guides to yourselves in the hardness of your heart, but walk in all your liberty, and in the glory that is toward men, and the life that is toward God."

167. And he said to Iuzanes: "You, son of King Misdaeus, but minister of our Lord Jesus Christ: give to the servants of Misdaeus their price that they may permit me to go and pray." And Iuzanes persuaded the soldiers to let him pray. And the blessed Thomas went to pray, and kneeled down, and rose up and stretched forth his hands toward the sky, and spoke thus: "My Lord and my God, and hope, and redeemer, and leader, and guide in all countries: be with all of them that serve You, and guide me this day as I come to You. Do not let any take my soul which I have committed to You. Do not let the tax collectors see me, and do not let the exactors accuse me falsely. Do not let the serpent see me, and do not let the children of the dragon hiss at me. Behold, LORD, I have accomplished Your work and perfected Your commandment. I have become a bondman; therefore, today I receive freedom. Therefore, give me this and perfect me; and I say this, not because I doubt, but so that they may hear for whom it is necessary to hear."

168. And when he had thus prayed, he said to the soldiers: "Come here and accomplish the commandments of Him that sent you." And the four came and pierced him with their spears, and he fell down and died. And all the brothers wept; and they brought beautiful robes and much fair linen and buried him in a royal tomb wherein the former kings were laid.

169. But Siphor and Iuzanes would not go down to the city, but continued sitting by him all day. And the apostle Thomas appeared to them and said: "Why do you sit here and keep watch over me? I am not here, but I have gone up and received all that I was promised. But rise up and go down from here, for after a short time you will also be gathered to me." But Misdaeus and Charisius took Mygdonia and Tertia away and afflicted them greatly, however, they never consented to their will. And the apostle appeared to them and said: "Do not be deceived: Jesus the holy, the living one, will quickly send help to you." And Misdaeus and Charisius, when they perceived that Mygdonia and Tertia did not obey them, allowed them to live according to their own desire. And the brothers gathered together and rejoiced in the grace of the Holy Spirit. Now the apostle Thomas, when he departed out of the world, made Siphor an elder and Iuzanes a minister, when he went up into the mountain to die. And the LORD worked with them, and many were added to the faith.

170. Now it came to pass after a long time that one of the children of King Misdaeus was stricken by a devil, and no man could cure him, for the devil was exceedingly fierce. And King Misdaeus took thought and said: "I will go and open the tomb, and take a bone of the apostle of God, and hang it on my son, and he will be healed." But while Misdaeus thought on this, the apostle Thomas appeared to him and said to him: "You did not believe on a living man, and will you [now] believe on the dead? Yet do not fear, for my Lord Jesus Christ has compassion on you and pities you of His goodness." And he went and opened the tomb, but did not find the apostle there, for one of the brothers had stolen him away and taken him to Mesopotamia; but from that place where the bones of the apostle had lain, Misdaeus took dust and put it around his son's neck, saying, "I believe on You, Jesus Christ, now that he has left me which troubles men and opposes them lest they should see You." And when he had hung it on his son, the young man became whole. Therefore, King Misdaeus was also gathered among the brothers and bowed his head under the hands of Siphor the priest; and Siphor said to the brothers: "Pray for King Misdaeus, that he may obtain mercy from Jesus Christ, and that he may no longer remember evil against him." Therefore, all of them, rejoicing with one accord, prayed for him; and the LORD that loves men, the King of Kings and Lord of Lords, also granted Misdaeus to have hope in Him; and he was gathered with the multitude of them that had believed in Christ, glorifying the Father, and the Son, and the Holy Spirit, whose is power and adoration, [both] now and forever, and world without end. Amen.

[[THE ACTS OF THE APOSTLE JUDAS THOMAS ARE COMPLETED, WHICH HE DID IN INDIA, FULFILLING THE COMMANDMENT OF HIM THAT SENT HIM. TO WHOM BE GLORY, WORLD WITHOUT END. AMEN.]]

ACTS OF PETER AND THE TWELVE APOSTLES

A likely 3rd century text with final redaction in the 4th century, the Acts of Peter and the Twelve Apostles was found, in fragmentary form, among the Nag Hammadi library texts. While it does not contain overtly gnostic teachings, its allegorical nature and being found among other gnostic works has led some to believe it may be gnostic in nature. The Acts are fragmentary in a number of places, including the introductory lines.

CHAPTER 1

1 … which … purpose … us … apostles … We sailed … of the body. 2 Others were not anxious in their hearts. And in our hearts, we were united. 3 We agreed to fulfill the ministry to which the LORD appointed us. And we made a covenant with each other. 4 We went down to the sea at an opportune moment, which came to us from the LORD. We found a ship moored at the shore ready to embark, and we spoke with the sailors of the ship about our coming aboard with them. 5 They showed great kindness toward us as was ordained by the LORD. And after we had embarked, we sailed a day and a night. 6 After that, a wind came up behind the ship and brought us to a small city in the midst of the sea. 7 And I, Peter, inquired about the name of this city from residents who were standing on the dock. 8 A man among them answered, saying, "The name of this city is Habitation, that is, Foundation … endurance." And the leader was among them, holding the palm branch at the edge of the dock. And after we had gone ashore with the baggage, I went into the city to seek advice about lodging. 9 A Man came out wearing a cloth bound around his waist, and a gold belt girded it. Also, a kerchief was tied over His chest, extending over His shoulders and covering His head and His hands. 10 I was staring at the Man, because He was beautiful in His form and stature. There were four parts of His body that I saw: the soles of His feet, and a portion of His chest, and the palms of His hands, and His aspect. I was able to see these things. 11 A scroll like my scrolls was in His left hand, [and] a staff of styrax wood was in His right hand. 12 His voice was resounding as He slowly spoke, crying out in the city, "Pearls! Pearls!" Indeed, I thought He was a man of that city. 13 I said to Him, "My brother and my friend!" 14 He then answered me, saying, "Rightly did you say, My brother and my friend. What is it you seek from Me?" 15 I said to him, "I ask You about lodging for me and also the brothers, because we are strangers here." 16 He said to me, "For this [very] reason I Myself have just said, My brother and My friend, because I am also a fellow stranger like you." 16 And having said these things, He cried out, "Pearls! Pearls!" 17 The rich men of that city heard His voice. They came out of their hidden storerooms, and some were looking out from the storerooms of their houses. Others looked out from their upper windows. 18 And they did not see anything [that they could gain] from Him, because there was no pouch on His back nor bundle inside His cloth and kerchief. And because of their disdain, they did not even acknowledge Him. 19 He, for His part, did not reveal Himself to them. They returned to their storerooms, saying, "This Man is mocking us."

CHAPTER 2

1 And the poor of that city heard His voice, and they came to the Man who sells this pearl. They said, "Please take the trouble to show us the pearl so that we may then see it with our [own] eyes, for we are the poor, and we do not have this … price to pay for it. But show us, so that we might say to our friends that we saw a pearl with our [own] eyes." 2 He answered, saying to them, "If it is possible, come to My city, so that I may not only show it before your [very] eyes, but give it to you for nothing." 3 And indeed, the poor of that city heard and said, "Since we are beggars, we surely know that a man does not give a pearl to a beggar, but [it is] bread and money that is usually received. 4 Now then, the kindness which we want to receive from You [is] that You would show us the pearl before our [very] eyes. And we will proudly say to our friends that we saw a pearl with our [own] eyes, because it is not found among the poor, especially such beggars [as us]." 5 He answered [and] said to them, "If it is possible, you yourselves come to My city, so that I may not only show it to you, but give it to you for nothing." The poor and the beggars rejoiced because of the Man who gives for nothing. 6 [Peter] said to the Man who sells this pearl, "I want to know Your Name and the hardships of the way to Your city, because we are strangers and servants of God. It is necessary for us to spread the word of God in every city harmoniously." 7 He answered and said, "If you seek My Name, Lithargoel is My Name, the interpretation of which is this: the light, gazelle-like stone. 8 And also, [regarding] the road to the city, which you asked Me about, I will tell you about it. No man is able to go on that road, except one who has forsaken everything that he has and has fasted daily from stage to stage. For there are many robbers and wild beasts on that road. 9 The one who carries bread with him on the road, the black dogs kill because of the bread. 10 The one who carries a costly garment of the world with him, the robbers kill because of the garment. 11 The one who carries water with him, the wolves kill because of the water, since they were thirsty for it. 12 The one who is anxious about meat and green vegetables, the lions eat because of the meat. If he evades the lions, the bulls devour him because of the green vegetables." 13 When He had said these things to me, I sighed within myself, saying, "Great hardships are on the road! If only Jesus would give us power to walk it!" 14 He looked at me since my face was sad, and I sighed. He said to me, "Why do you sigh, if you, indeed, know this Name—Jesus—and believe Him? He is [the] great power for giving strength. For I too believe in the Father who sent Him." 15 I replied, asking Him, "What is the name of the place to which you go—your city?" 16 He said to me, "This is the name of My city: Nine Gates. Let us praise God as we are mindful that the tenth is the head." After this, I went away from Him in peace.

CHAPTER 3

1 As I was about to go and call my friends, I saw waves and large high walls surrounding the bounds of the city. I marveled at the great things I saw. 2 I saw an old man sitting, and I asked him if the name of the city was really Habitation. 3 He …, "Habitation …." He said to me, "You speak the truth, for we dwell here because we endure." 4 I responded, saying, "Justly … have men named it … , because everyone who endures his trials, cities are inhabited, and a precious kingdom comes from them, because they endure in the midst of the defections and the difficulties of the storms. 5 So that in this way, the city of everyone who endures the burden of his yoke of faith will be inhabited, and he will be included in the kingdom of the heavens." 6 I hurried, and went, and called my friends, so that we might go to the city that He, Lithargoel, appointed for us. 7 In a bond of faith, we left everything as He had said [to do]. 8 We evaded the robbers, because they did not find their garments with us. 9 We evaded the wolves, because they did not find the water with us for which they thirsted. 10 We evaded the lions, because they did not find the desire for meat with us. 11 We evaded the bulls … they did not find green vegetables. 12 A great joy came on us and a peaceful carefreeness like that of our Lord. 13 We rested ourselves in front of the gate, and we talked with each other about that which is not a distraction of this world. And we continued in contemplation of the faith. 14 As we discussed the robbers on the road, whom we evaded, behold Lithargoel, having changed, came out to us. He had the appearance of a physician, since an unguent box was under His arm, and a young disciple was following Him, carrying a pouch full of medicine. We did not recognize Him. 15 Peter responded and said to Him, "We want You to do us a favor, because we are strangers: take us to the house of Lithargoel before evening comes." 16 He said, "In uprightness of heart I will show it to you. But I am amazed at how you knew this good Man. For He does not reveal Himself to every man, because He Himself is the Son of a great King. 17 Rest yourselves a little so that I may go and heal

this Man and return." He hurried and returned quickly. ¹⁸He said to Peter, "Peter!" And Peter was frightened, for how did He know that his name was Peter? ¹⁹Peter responded to the Savior, "How do You know me, for You called my name?" Lithargoel answered, "I want to ask you who gave the name Peter to you?" He said to Him, "It was Jesus Christ, the Son of the living God. He gave this name to me." ²⁰He answered and said, "It is I! Recognize Me, Peter." ²¹He loosened the garment, which clothed Him—the one into which He had changed Himself because of us—revealing to us that it was truly He. ²²We prostrated ourselves on the ground and worshiped Him (we comprised eleven disciples). He stretched forth His hand and caused us to stand. ²³We spoke humbly with Him. Our heads were bowed down in unworthiness as we said, "Whatever You wish, we will do. But give us power to do what You wish at all times." ²⁴He gave them the unguent box and the pouch that was in the hand of the young disciple. ²⁵He commanded them like this, saying, "Go into the city from which you came, which is called Habitation. Continue in endurance as you teach all those who have believed in My Name, because I have endured in [the] hardships of the faith. I will give you your reward. ²⁶To the poor of that city give what they need in order to live until I give them what is better, which I told you that I will give you for nothing." ²⁷Peter answered and said to Him, "LORD, You have taught us to forsake the world and everything in it. We have renounced them for Your sake. What we are [now] concerned with is the food for a single day. Where will we be able to find the necessities that You ask us to provide for the poor?" ²⁸The LORD answered and said, "O Peter, it was necessary that you understand the parable that I told you. Do you not understand that My Name, which you teach, surpasses all riches, and the wisdom of God surpasses gold, and silver, and precious stones?" ²⁹He gave them the pouch of medicine and said, "Heal all the sick of the city who believe in My Name." ³⁰Peter was afraid to reply to Him for the second time. He signaled to the one who was beside him, who was John: "You talk this time." ³¹John answered and said, "LORD, we are afraid to say many words before You. But it is You who asks us to practice this skill. We have not been taught to be physicians. How then will we know how to heal bodies as You have told us?" ³²He answered them, "You have spoken rightly, John, for I know that the physicians of this world heal what belongs to the world. The physicians of souls, however, heal the heart. ³³Therefore, heal the bodies first, so that through the real powers of healing for their bodies, without medicine of the world, they may believe in you, that you have power to heal the illnesses of the heart also. ³⁴However, the rich men of the city—those who did not see fit even to acknowledge Me, but who reveled in their wealth and pride—with such as these, therefore, do not dine in their houses nor be friends with them, lest their partiality influence you. ³⁵For many in the assemblies have shown partiality to the rich, because they are also sinful, and they give opportunity for others to sin. ³⁶But judge them with righteousness, so that your ministry may be glorified, and so that My Name may also be glorified in the assemblies." ³⁷The disciples answered and said, "Yes, this is truly what is right to do." ³⁸They prostrated themselves on the ground and worshiped Him. He caused them to stand and departed from them in peace. Amen.

ACTS OF PETER AND PAUL

The latest of the various apocryphal Acts included in this collection, the Acts of Peter and Paul, not to be confused with either the Acts of Peter or the Acts of Paul, contains a coherent narrative and was likely composed in the 5th century. Significantly, it reiterates the ancient traditions of Paul's death by beheading and Peter's death via crucifixion upside-down (Ch. 9). It also mentions the Vatican as the place of Peter's remains (Ch. 10).

CHAPTER 1

¹It came to pass, after Paul went out of the island [of] Gaudomeleta [(Gaulos)], that he came to Italy; and it was heard of by the Jews who were in Rome, the elder of the cities, that Paul demanded to come to Caesar. ²Having fallen, therefore, into great grief and much despondency, they said among themselves: "It does not please him that he alone has afflicted all of our brothers and parents in Judea and Samaria, and in all Palestine; and he has not been pleased with these, but, behold, he comes here also, having through imposition asked Caesar to destroy us." ³Having therefore made an assembly against Paul, and having considered many proposals, it seemed good to them to go to Nero the emperor, to ask him not to allow Paul to come to Rome. ⁴Having therefore prepared many gifts, and having carried them with them, with supplication they came before him, saying, "We beg you, O good emperor: send orders into all the governments of your worship, to the effect that Paul is not to come near these parts; ⁵because this Paul, having afflicted all the nation of our fathers, has been seeking to come here to destroy us also. And the affliction, O most worshipful emperor, which we have from Peter is enough for us." ⁶And Emperor Nero, having heard these things, answered them: "It is according to your wish. And we write to all our governments that he will not on any account come to anchor in the regions of Italy." ⁷And they also informed Simon the Magician, having sent for him, that, as has been stated, he should not come into the regions of Italy.

CHAPTER 2

¹And while they were doing this, some of those that had converted out of the nations, and that had been immersed at the preaching of Peter, sent elders to Paul with a letter to the following effect: "Paul, dear servant of our Lord Jesus Christ, and brother of Peter, the first of the apostles, we have heard from the teachers of the Jews that are in this Rome, the greatest of the cities, that they have asked Caesar to send into all his governments, in order that, wherever you may be found, you may be put to death. ²But we have believed, and do believe, that as God does not separate the two great lights which He has made, so He is not to part you from each other, that is, neither Peter from Paul, nor Paul from Peter; ³but we positively believe in our Lord Jesus Christ, into whom we have been immersed, that we have also become worthy of your teaching." ⁴And Paul, having received the two men sent with the letter on the twentieth of the month of May, became eager to go and gave thanks to the Lord and Master Jesus Christ. ⁵And having sailed from Gaudomeleta, he did not now come through Africa to the regions of Italy, but ran to Sicily, until he came to the city of Syracuse with the two men who had been sent from Rome to him. ⁶And having sailed from there, he came to Rhegium of Calabria, and from Rhegium he crossed to Mesina, and there ordained an overseer, Bacchylus by name. ⁷And when he came out of Mesina, he sailed to Didymus and remained there one night. And having sailed from there, he came to Pontiole on the second day.

CHAPTER 3

¹And Dioscorus the shipmaster, who brought him to Syracuse, sympathizing with Paul because he had delivered his son from death, having left his own ship in Syracuse, accompanied him to Pontiole. ²And some of Peter's disciples, having been found there, and having received Paul, exhorted him to stay with them. ³And he stayed one week, in hiding, because of the command of Caesar. And all the toparchs were watching to seize and kill him. ⁴But Dioscorus, the shipmaster, also being bald himself, wearing his shipmaster's attire and speaking boldly, on the first day went out into the city of Pontiole. ⁵Therefore, thinking that he was Paul, they seized him, and beheaded him, and sent his head to Caesar. ⁶Therefore, Caesar, having summoned the first men of the Jews, announced to them, saying, "Rejoice with great joy, for your enemy Paul is dead." And he showed them the head.

⁷Having therefore made great rejoicing on that day, which was the fourteenth of the month of June, each of the Jews fully believed it. ⁸And Paul, being in Pontiole, and having heard that Dioscorus had been beheaded, being grieved with great grief, gazing into the height of the heaven, said: "O LORD Almighty in Heaven, who have appeared to me in every place where I have gone on account of Your only-begotten Word, our Lord Jesus Christ: punish this city and bring out all who have believed in God and followed His word." ⁹He therefore said to them: "Follow me"; and going forth from Pontiole with those who had believed in the word of God, they came to a place called Baias; ¹⁰and looking up with their eyes, they all see that city called Pontiole sunk into the seashore about one fathom; and there it is until this day, for a remembrance, under the sea.

CHAPTER 4

¹And having gone forth from Baias, they went to Gaitas, and there he taught the word of God. ²And he stayed there three days in the house of Erasmus, whom Peter sent from Rome to teach the good news of God. ³And having come forth from Gaitas, he came to the castle called Taracinas and stayed there seven days in the house of Caesarius the minister, whom Peter had ordained by the laying on of hands. ⁴And sailing from there, he came by the river to a place called Tribus Tabernes. ⁵And those who had been saved out of the city of Pontiole (which had been swallowed up), reported to Caesar in Rome that Pontiole had been swallowed up, with all its multitude. ⁶And the emperor, being in great grief on account of the city, having summoned the chief of the Jews, said to them: "Behold, on account of what I heard from you, I have caused Paul to be beheaded, and on account of this, the city has been swallowed up." ⁷And the chief of the Jews said to Caesar: "Most worshipful emperor, did we not say to you that he troubled all the country of the East and perverted our fathers? It is therefore better, most worshipful emperor, that one city be destroyed, and not the seat of your empire; for Rome would have had to suffer this." ⁸And the emperor, having heard their words, was appeased.

CHAPTER 5

¹And Paul stayed in Tribus Tabernes four days. And departing from there, he came to Appii Forum, which is called Vicusarape; ²and having slept there that night, he saw one sitting on a golden chair, and a multitude of shadowy figures standing beside him, saying, "I have today made a son murder his father." Another said: "And I have made a house fall and kill parents with children." ³And they reported to him many evil deeds—some of one kind, some of another. ⁴And another coming, reported to him: "I have managed that the overseer Juvenalius, whom Peter ordained, should sleep with the abbess Juliana." ⁵And having heard all these things when sleeping in that Appii Forum, near Vicusarape, at once and immediately he sent to Rome one of those who had followed him from Pontiole to the overseer Juvenalius, telling him this same thing which had just been done. ⁶And on the following day, Juvenalius, running, threw himself at the feet of Peter, weeping and lamenting, and saying what had just happened; ⁷and he recounted to him the matter and said: "I believe that this is the light which you were awaiting." ⁸And Peter said to him: "How is it possible that it is he when he is dead?" And Juvenalius the overseer took to Peter him that had been sent by Paul, and he reported to him that he was alive, and on his way, and that he was at Appii Forum. ⁹And Peter thanked and glorified the God and Father of our Lord Jesus Christ. ¹⁰Then having summoned his disciples that believed, he sent them to Paul as far as Tribus Tabernes. And the distance from Rome to Tribus Tabernes is thirty-eight miles. ¹¹And Paul seeing them, having given thanks to our Lord Jesus Christ, took courage; and departing from there, they slept in the city called Aricia.

CHAPTER 6

¹And a report went around in the city of Rome that Paul the brother of Peter was coming. And those that believed in God rejoiced with great joy. ²And there was great consternation among the Jews; and having gone to Simon the Magician, they implored him, saying, "Report to the emperor that Paul is not dead, but that he is alive, and has come." ³And Simon said to the Jews: "What head is it, then, which came to Caesar from Pontiole? Was it not also bald?" ⁴And Paul, having come to Rome, great fear fell on [all] the Jews. ⁵They therefore came together to him, and exhorted him, saying, "Vindicate the faith in which you were born, for it is not right that you, being a Hebrew, and of the Hebrews, should call yourself a teacher of the nations, and vindicator of the uncircumcised; and, being yourself circumcised, that you should bring to nothing the faith of the circumcision. ⁶And when you see Peter, contend against his teaching, because he has destroyed all the bulwarks of our law; for he has prevented the keeping of Sabbaths, and new moons, and the holidays appointed by the Law." ⁷And Paul, answering, said to them: "That I am a true Jew, by this you can prove; because you have also been able to keep the Sabbath, and to observe the true circumcision; for assuredly on the day of the Sabbath God rested from all His works. ⁸We have fathers, and patriarchs, and the Law. What then does Peter preach in the kingdom of the nations? ⁹But if he will intend to bring in any new teaching, without any tumult, and envy, and trouble, send him word, that we may see, and in your presence I will convict him. ¹⁰But if his teaching is true, supported by the scroll and testimony of the Hebrews, it is right for all of us to submit to him." ¹¹Paul, saying these and similar such things, the Jews went and said to Peter: "Paul of the Hebrews has come and implores you to come to him, since those who have brought him say that he cannot meet with whomsoever he may wish until he appears before Caesar." ¹²And Peter having heard, rejoiced with great joy; and rising up, he immediately went to him. ¹³And seeing each other, they wept for joy; and long embracing one another, they dampened one another with tears.

CHAPTER 7

¹And when Paul had related to Peter the substance of all his undertakings, and how, through the disasters of the ship, he had come, Peter also told him what he had suffered from Simon the Magician and all his plots. ²And having told these things, he went away toward evening. ³And in the morning of the following day, at dawn, behold, Peter coming, finds a multitude of the Jews before Paul's door. ⁴And there was a great uproar between the Christian Jews and the nations. ⁵For, on the one hand, the Jews said: "We are a chosen race, a royal priesthood, the friends of Abraham, and Isaac, and Jacob, and all the prophets, with whom God spoke, to whom He showed His own mysteries and His great wonders. But you of the nations are no great thing in your lineage; if otherwise, you have become polluted and abominable by idols and graven images." ⁶While the Jews were saying such things, and such similar, those of the nations answered, saying, "We, when we heard the truth, immediately followed it, having abandoned our errors. ⁷But you, both knowing the mighty deeds of your fathers, and seeing the signs of the prophets, and having received the Law, and gone through the sea with dry feet, and seen your enemies sunk in its depths, and the pillar of fire by night and of cloud by day shining on you, and manna having been given to you out of Heaven, and water flowing to you out of a rock—after all these things you fashioned to yourselves the idol of a calf and worshiped the graven image. ⁸But we, having seen none of the signs, believe to be a Savior the God whom you have forsaken in unbelief." ⁹While they were contending in these and similar words, the apostle Paul said that they should not make such attacks on one other, but that they should rather give heed to this—"that God had fulfilled His promises which He swore to Abraham our father, that in his seed he should inherit all the nations, for there is no favoritism of persons with God. ¹⁰As many as have sinned in law will be judged according to law, and as many as have sinned without law will perish without law. ¹¹But we, brothers, ought to thank God that, according to His mercy, He has chosen us to be a holy people for Himself, so that in this we ought to boast, whether Jews or Greeks; for you are all one in the belief of His Name." ¹²And Paul, having thus spoken, both the Jews and those of the nations were appeased. But the rulers of the Jews attacked Peter. ¹³And Peter, when they accused him of having renounced their synagogues, said: "Hear, brothers, the Holy Spirit concerning the patriarch David, promising: Of the fruit of your womb will He set on your throne. ¹⁴Him therefore to whom the Father said, You are My Son, this day have I begotten You, the chief priests through envy

crucified; but that He might accomplish the salvation of the world, it was allowed that He should suffer all these things. ¹⁵Therefore, just as Eve was created from the side of Adam, so also from the side of Christ was the Assembly created, which has no spot nor blemish. ¹⁶In Him, therefore, God has opened an entrance to all the sons of Abraham, and Isaac, and Jacob, in order that they may be in the faith of profession toward Him and have life and salvation in His Name. ¹⁷Turn, therefore, and enter into the joy of your father Abraham, because God has fulfilled what He promised to him, from which the prophet also says, The LORD has sworn and will not relent: You are a priest forever, after the order of Melchizedek. ¹⁸For He became a priest on the Cross, when He offered the whole burnt-offering of His own body and blood as a sacrifice for the whole world." ¹⁹And Peter, saying this and such similar, the greater part of the people believed. ²⁰And it also happened that Nero's wife Libia, and the companion of Agrippa the prefect, Agrippina by name, thus believed, so that they also went away from beside their own husbands. ²¹And on account of the teaching of Paul, many, despising military life, clung to God, so that even from the emperor's [own] bedchamber some came to him, and having become Christians, were no longer willing to return to the army or the palace.

CHAPTER 8

¹Consequently, when the people were making a seditious murmuring, Simon, moved with zeal, rouses himself, and began to say many evil things about Peter, saying that he was a wizard and a cheat. ²And they believed him, wondering at his miracles, for he made a brazen serpent move itself, and stone statues to laugh and move themselves, and himself to run and suddenly to be raised into the air. ³But as a contrast to these, Peter healed the sick by a word, by praying made the blind to see, put demons to flight by a command; sometimes he even raised the dead. ⁴And he said to the people that they should not only flee from Simon's deceit, but that they should also expose him, so that they might not seem to be slaves to the Devil. ⁵And thus it happened that all pious men abhorred Simon the Magician and proclaimed him impious. ⁶But those who adhered to Simon strongly affirmed Peter to be a magician, as many of them bearing false witness as were with Simon the Magician, so that the matter even came to the ears of Nero the Caesar, and he gave an order to bring Simon the Magician before him. ⁷And he, coming in, stood before him, and suddenly began to assume different forms, so that he suddenly became a child, and after a while, an old man, and at other times a young man; ⁸for he changed himself both in face and stature into different forms, and he was in a frenzy, having the Devil as his servant. ⁹And Nero beholding this, supposed him to truly be the Son of God; but the apostle Peter showed him to be both a liar and a wizard—base, and impious, and apostate—and in all things opposed to the truth of God, and that nothing yet remained except that his wickedness, being made apparent by the command of God, might be made manifest to them all. ¹⁰Then Simon, having gone in to Nero, said: "Hear, O good emperor: I am the Son of God, having come down from Heaven. ¹¹Until now I have endured Peter only calling himself an apostle; but now he has doubled the evil, for Paul also himself teaches the same things, and having his mind turned against me, is said to preach along with him; in reference to whom, if you will not plan their destruction, it is very plain that your kingdom cannot stand." ¹²Then Nero, filled with distress, ordered to have them brought before him quickly. ¹³And on the following day, Simon the Magician, and Peter and Paul, the apostles of Christ, having come in to Nero, Simon said: "These are the disciples of the Nazarene, and it is not at all well that they should be of the people of the Jews." ¹⁴Nero replied: "What is a Nazarene?" Simon said: "There is a city of Judah which has always been opposed to us, called Nazareth, and to it the Teacher of these men belonged." ¹⁵Nero said: "God commands us to love every man; why then do you persecute them?" Simon said: "This is a race of men who have turned aside all of Judea from believing in me." ¹⁶Nero said to Peter: "Why are you thus unbelieving, according to your race?" ¹⁷Then Peter said to Simon: "You have been able to impose on all, but never on me; and those who have been deceived, God has through me recalled [them] from their error. ¹⁸And since you have learned by experience that you cannot get the better of me, I wonder with what face you boast yourself before the emperor and suppose that through your magic art you will overcome the disciples of Christ." ¹⁹Nero said: "Who is Christ?" Peter said: "He is what this Simon the Magician affirms himself to be; but this is a most wicked man, and his works are of the Devil. ²⁰But if you wish to know, O good emperor, the things that have been done in Judea concerning Christ, take the writings of Pontius Pilate sent to Claudius, and thus you will learn everything." ²¹And Nero ordered them to be brought, and to be read in their presence; and they were to the following effect: "Pontius Pilate to Claudius: Greetings. There has recently been an event which I myself was concerned with. For the Jews, through envy, have inflicted on themselves, and those coming after them, dreadful judgments. ²²Their fathers had promises that their God would send them His Holy One from Heaven, who according to reason should be called their King, and He had promised to send Him to the earth by means of a virgin. ²³He, then, when I was procurator, came into Judea. ²⁴And they saw Him making the blind see, cleansing lepers, healing paralytics, expelling demons from men, raising the dead, subduing the winds, walking on the waves of the sea, and doing many other wonders, and all the people of the Jews calling Him [the] Son of God. ²⁵Then the chief priests, moved with envy against Him, seized Him and delivered Him to me; and telling one lie after another, they said that He was a wizard and did contrary to their law. ²⁶And I, having believed that these things were so, gave Him up, after scourging Him, [according] to their will; and they crucified Him, and after He was buried set guards over Him. ²⁷But He, while my soldiers were guarding Him, rose on the third day. ²⁸And to such a degree was the wickedness of the Jews inflamed against Him, that they gave money to the soldiers, saying, Say His disciples have stolen His body. ²⁹But they, having taken the money, were not able to keep silent as to what had happened; for they have testified that they have seen Him risen, and that they have received money from the Jews. ³⁰Therefore, I have reported these things, so that no one should falsely speak otherwise, and so that you should not suppose that the falsehoods of the Jews are to be believed." ³¹And the letter having been read, Nero said: "Tell me, Peter, were all these things thus done by Him?" Peter replied: "They were. With your permission, O good emperor: for this Simon is full of lies and deceit, even if it should seem that he is what he is not—a god. ³²And in Christ there is every excellent victory through God and through man, which that incomprehensible glory assumed which through man consented to come to the assistance of men. ³³But in this Simon there are two essences: of man and of devil, who through man endeavors to ensnare men. ³⁴Simon said: "I wonder, O good emperor, that you reckon this man of any consequence—a man uneducated, a fisherman of the poorest, and endowed with power neither in word nor by rank. ³⁵But that I may not long endure him as an enemy, I will immediately order my messengers to come and avenge me on him." ³⁶Peter said: "I am not afraid of your messengers; but they will be much more afraid of me in the power and trust of my Lord Jesus Christ, whom you falsely declare yourself to be." ³⁷Nero said: "Are you not afraid, Peter, of Simon, who confirms his godhead by deeds?" ³⁸Peter said: "Godhead is in Him who searches the hidden things of the heart. Now then, tell me what I am thinking about, or what I am doing. I disclose to your servants who are here what my thought is, before he tells lies about it, in order that he may not dare to lie as to what I am thinking about." ³⁹Nero said: "Come here and tell me what you are thinking about." ⁴⁰Peter said: "Order a barley loaf to be brought, and to be given to me secretly." And when he ordered it to be brought and secretly given to Peter, Peter said: "Now tell us, Simon, what has been thought about, or what said, or what done." ⁴¹Nero said: "Do you intend me to believe that Simon does not know these things, who both raised a dead man and presented himself on the third day after he had been beheaded, and who has done whatever he said he would do?" ⁴²Peter said: "But he did not do it before me." Nero replied: "But he did all these before me. For assuredly he ordered messengers to come to him, and they came." ⁴³Peter said: "If he has done what is very great, why does he not do what is very small? Let him tell what I had in my mind, and

what I have done." Nero said: "Between you [and me], I do not know myself." ⁴⁴Simon said: "Let Peter say what I am thinking of, or what I am doing." Peter said: "What Simon has in his mind I will show that I know, by my doing what he is thinking about." ⁴⁵Simon said: "Know this, O emperor, that no one knows the thoughts of men, but God alone. Is not, therefore, Peter lying?" ⁴⁶Peter said: "You, then, who say that you are the Son of God, tell what I have in my mind; disclose, if you can, what I have just done in secret." For Peter, having blessed the barley loaf which he had received, and having broken it with his right hand and his left, had heaped it up in his sleeves. ⁴⁷Then Simon, enraged that he was not able to tell the secret of the apostle, cried out, saying, "Let great dogs come forth and devour him before Caesar!" And suddenly there appeared great dogs that rushed at Peter. ⁴⁸But Peter, stretching forth his hands to pray, showed to the dogs the loaf which he had blessed; which the dogs seeing, disappeared. ⁴⁹Then Peter said to Nero: "Behold, I have shown you that I knew what Simon was thinking of, not by words, but by deeds; for he, having promised that he would bring messengers against me, has brought dogs, in order that he might show that he did not have god-like, but rather dog-like messengers." ⁵⁰Then Nero said to Simon: "What is it, Simon? I think we have got the worst of it." ⁵¹Simon said: "This man, both in Judea and in all Palestine and Caesarea, has done the same to me; and from very often striving with me, he has learned that this is adverse to them. ⁵²This, then, he has learned how to escape from me; for the thoughts of men no one knows but God alone." ⁵³And Peter said to Simon: "You yourself surely pretend to be a god; why, then, do you not reveal the thoughts of every man?" ⁵⁴Then Nero, turning to Paul, said: "Why do you say nothing, Paul?" Paul answered and said: "Know this, O emperor: that if you permit this magician to do such things, it will bring an entrance for the greatest trouble to your country, and will bring down your empire from its position." ⁵⁵Nero said to Simon: "What do you say?" Simon said: "If I do not manifestly hold myself out to be a god, no one will bestow on me due honor." ⁵⁶Nero said: "And now, why do you delay and not show yourself to be a god, in order that these men may be punished?" ⁵⁷Simon said: "Give orders to build a lofty tower of wood for me, and I, going up on it, will call my messengers and order them to take me, in the sight of all, to my father in Heaven; and these men, not being able to do this, are put to shame as uneducated men." ⁵⁸And Nero said to Peter: "Have you heard, Peter, what has been said by Simon? From this will appear how much power either he or your God has." ⁵⁹Peter said: "O most mighty emperor, if you were willing, you might perceive that he is full of demons." Nero said: "Why do you evade me with excuses? Tomorrow will prove you." ⁶⁰Simon said: "Do you believe, O good emperor, that I who was dead, and rose again, am a magician?" ⁶¹For it had been brought about by his own cleverness that the unbelieving Simon had said to Nero: "Order me to be beheaded in a dark place, and there to be left slain; and if I do not rise on the third day, know that I am a magician; but if I rise again, know that I am the Son of God." ⁶²And Nero having ordered this, in the dark, by his magic art [Simon] managed that a ram should be beheaded. And for a long time the ram appeared to be Simon until he was beheaded. ⁶³And when he had been beheaded in the dark, he that had beheaded him, taking the head, found it to be that of a ram; but he would not say anything to the emperor, lest he should scourge him, having ordered this to be done in secret. ⁶⁴Accordingly, Simon thereafter said that he had risen on the third day, because he took away the head of the ram and the limbs, but the blood had been congealed there; ⁶⁵and on the third day, he showed himself to Nero and said: "Cause my blood that has been poured out to be wiped away, for behold, having been beheaded as I promised, I have risen again on the third day." ⁶⁶And when Nero said, "Tomorrow will prove you," turning to Paul, he says: "You, Paul, why do you say nothing? Either who taught you, or whom do you have for a master, or how have you taught in the cities, or what things have happened through your teaching? ⁶⁷For I think that you do not have any wisdom and are not able to accomplish any work of power." ⁶⁸Paul answered: "Do you suppose that I ought to speak against a desperate man, a magician, who has given his soul up to death, whose destruction and perdition will come quickly? ⁶⁹For he ought to speak [first], who pretends to be what he is not and deceives men by magic art. If you consent to hear his words, and to shield him, you will destroy your soul and your kingdom, for he is a most base man. ⁷⁰And as the Egyptians Jannes and Jambres led Pharaoh and his army astray until they were swallowed up in the sea, so also he, through the instruction of his father the Devil, persuades men to do many evils to themselves, and thus deceives many of the innocent, to the peril of your kingdom. ⁷¹But as for the word of the Devil, which I see has been poured out through this man, with groanings of my heart I am dealing with the Holy Spirit, so that it may be clearly shown what it is; for as far as he seems to raise himself toward Heaven, so far will he be sunk down into the depth of Hades, where there is weeping and gnashing of teeth. ⁷²But concerning the teaching of my Master, of which you asked me, none attain it except the pure, who allow faith to come into their heart. ⁷³For as many things as belong to peace and love, these have I taught. All around Jerusalem, and as far as Illyricum, I have fulfilled the word of peace. ⁷⁴For I have taught that they should prefer one another in honor; ⁷⁵I have taught those that are eminent and rich not to be lifted up and hope in [the] uncertainty of riches, but to place their hope in God; ⁷⁶I have taught those in a middle station to be content with food and covering; ⁷⁷I have taught the poor to rejoice in their own poverty; ⁷⁸I have taught fathers to teach their children instruction in the fear of the LORD, children to obey their parents in wholesome admonition; ⁷⁹I have taught wives to love their own husbands, and to fear them as masters, and husbands to observe fidelity to their wives; ⁸⁰I have taught masters to treat their slaves with mercy, and slaves to serve their own masters faithfully; ⁸¹I have taught the assemblies of the believers to revere one almighty, invisible, and incomprehensible God. ⁸²And this teaching has been given to me, not from men, nor through men, but through Jesus Christ, who spoke to me out of Heaven, who also has sent me to preach, saying to me, Go forth, for I will be with you; and all things, as many as you will say or do, I will make just." ⁸³Nero said: "What do you say, Peter?" He answered and said: "Everything that Paul has said is true, for when he was a persecutor of the faith of Christ, a voice called to him out of Heaven and taught him the truth; for he was not an adversary of our faith from hatred, but from ignorance. ⁸⁴For there were before us false Christs (like Simon), false apostles, and false prophets, who, contrary to the Holy Writings, set themselves to make the truth void; ⁸⁵and against these it was necessary to have in readiness this man, who from his youth up set himself to no other thing than to search out the mysteries of the divine Law, by which he might become a vindicator of truth and a persecutor of falsehood. ⁸⁶Since, then, his persecution was not on account of hatred, but on account of the vindication of the Law, the very truth out of Heaven had dealings with him, saying, I am the truth which you persecute; cease persecuting Me. ⁸⁷Therefore, when he knew that this was so, forsaking that which he was vindicating, he began to vindicate this way of Christ which he was persecuting." ⁸⁸Simon said: "O good emperor, take notice that these two have conspired against me; for I am the truth, and they intend evil against me." Peter said: "There is no truth in you, but everything you say is false." ⁸⁹Nero said: "Paul, what do you say?" Paul said: "Those things which you have heard from Peter, believe to have been spoken by me also; for we purpose the same thing, for we have the same Lord: Jesus the Christ." ⁹⁰Simon said: "Do you expect me, O good emperor, to hold an argument with these men, who have come to an agreement against me?" ⁹¹And having turned to the apostles of Christ, he said: "Listen, Peter and Paul: if I can do nothing for you here, we are going to the place where I must judge you." ⁹²Paul said: "O good emperor, see what threats he holds out against us." Peter said: "Why was it necessary to keep from laughing outright at a foolish man, made the sport of demons, so as to suppose that he cannot be made manifest?" ⁹³Simon said: "I spare you until I will receive my power." Paul said: "See if you will go out from here safe." ⁹⁴Peter said: "If you do not see, Simon, the power of our Lord Jesus Christ, you [still] will not believe yourself not to be Christ." Simon said: "Most sacred emperor, do not believe them, for they are circumcised scoundrels."

⁹⁵Paul said: "Before we knew the truth, we had the circumcision of the flesh; but when the truth appeared, in the circumcision of the heart we are both circumcised and circumcise [others]." ⁹⁶Peter said: "If circumcision is a disgrace, why have you been circumcised, Simon?" ⁹⁷Nero said: "Has, then, Simon also been circumcised?" Peter said: "For he could not have otherwise deceived souls, unless he himself pretended to be a Jew and made a show of teaching the Law of God." ⁹⁸Nero said: "Simon, you, as I see, being carried away with envy, persecute these men. For, as it seems, there is great hatred between you and their Christ; and I am afraid that you will be bested by them and involved in great evils." ⁹⁹Simon said: "You are led astray, O emperor." Nero said: "How am I led astray? What I see in you, I say. I see that you are clearly an enemy of Peter, and Paul, and their Master." ¹⁰⁰Simon said: "Christ was not Paul's master." Paul said: "Indeed [He was]; through revelation He taught me also. But tell me what I asked you: why were you circumcised?" ¹⁰¹Simon said: "Why have you asked me this?" Paul said: "We have a reason for asking you this." ¹⁰²Nero said: "Why are you afraid to answer them?" Simon said: "Listen, O emperor: at that time, circumcision was commanded by God when I received it. For this reason, I was circumcised." ¹⁰³Paul said: "Do you hear, O good emperor, what has been said by Simon? If, therefore, circumcision is a good thing, why have you, Simon, given up those who have been circumcised, and forced them, after being condemned, to be put to death?" ¹⁰⁴Nero said: "Neither about you do I perceive anything good." Peter and Paul said: "Whether this thought concerning us is good or evil has no reference to the matter; but to us it was necessary that what our Master promised should come to pass." ¹⁰⁵Nero said: "If I should not be willing?" Peter said: "Not as you will, but as He promised to us." ¹⁰⁶Simon said: "O good emperor, these men have presumed on your mercy and have bound you." ¹⁰⁷Nero said: "But neither have you yet made me sure about yourself." Simon said: "Since so many excellent deeds and signs have been shown to you by me, I wonder how you should be in doubt." ¹⁰⁸Nero said: "I neither doubt nor favor any of you; but answer me rather what I ask." ¹⁰⁹Simon said: "Henceforth, I answer you nothing." Nero said: "Seeing that you lie, therefore you say this. But if even I can do nothing to you, God, who can, will do it." Simon said: "I no longer answer you." ¹¹⁰Nero said: "Nor do I consider you to be anything, for, as I perceive, you are a liar in everything. But why do I say so much? The three of you show that your reasoning is uncertain; and thus, in all things you have made me doubt, so that I find that I can give credit to none of you." ¹¹¹Peter said: "We preach one God and Father of our Lord Jesus Christ, that has made the heavens, and the earth, and the sea, and all that is therein, who is the true King; and of His kingdom there will be no end." ¹¹²Nero said: "What king is lord?" Paul said: "The Savior of all the nations." ¹¹³Simon said: "I am he whom you speak of." Peter and Paul said: "May it never be well with you, Simon, magician, and full of bitterness." ¹¹⁴Simon said: "Listen, O Caesar Nero, that you may know that these men are liars, and that I have been sent from the heavens: tomorrow I go up into the heavens, so that I may make those who believe in me blessed, and show my wrath on those who have denied me." ¹¹⁵Peter and Paul said: "Long ago God called us to His own glory; but you, called by the Devil, hasten to punishment." Simon said: "Caesar Nero, listen to me: separate these madmen from you, in order that when I go into Heaven to my father, I may be very merciful to you." ¹¹⁶Nero said: "And how will we prove this, that you go away into Heaven?" Simon said: "Order a lofty tower to be made of wood, and of great beams, so that I may go up on it, and so that my messengers may find me in the air; for they cannot come to me on earth among the sinners." ¹¹⁷Nero said: "I will see whether you will fulfill what you say."

CHAPTER 9

¹Then Nero ordered a lofty tower to be made in the Campus Martius, and all the people and the dignities to be present at the spectacle. ²And on the following day, the whole multitude having come together, Nero ordered Peter and Paul to be present, to whom he also said: "Now the truth must be made clear." ³Peter and Paul said: "We do not expose him, but our Lord Jesus Christ, the Son of God, whom he has falsely declared himself to be." ⁴And Paul, having turned to Peter, said: "It is my part to bend the knee, and to pray to God; and yours to produce the effect, if you should see Him attempting anything, because you were first taken in hand by the LORD." And Paul, bending his knees, prayed. ⁵And Peter, looking steadfastly on Simon, said: "Accomplish what you have begun; for both your exposure and our call is at hand: for I see my Christ calling both me and Paul." ⁶Nero said: "And where will you go to against my will?" Peter said: "Wheresoever our Lord has called us." ⁷Nero said: "And who is your Lord?" Peter said: "Jesus the Christ, whom I see calling us to Himself." ⁸Nero said: "Do you also then intend to go away to Heaven?" Peter said: "If it will seem good to Him that calls us." ⁹Simon said: "In order that you may know, O emperor, that these are deceivers, as soon as I ascend into Heaven, I will send my messengers to you and will make you come to me." Nero said: "Do what you say at once." ¹⁰Then Simon went up on the tower in the face of all, and, crowned with laurels, he stretched forth his hands and began to fly. ¹¹And when Nero saw him flying, he said to Peter: "This Simon is true; but you and Paul are deceivers." To whom Peter said: "You will immediately know that we are true disciples of Christ; but that he is not Christ, but a magician, and a wrongdoer." ¹²Nero said: "Do you still persist? Behold, you see him going up into Heaven." ¹³Then Peter, looking steadfastly on Paul, said: "Paul, look up and see." And Paul, having looked up, full of tears, and seeing Simon flying, said: "Peter, why are you idle? Finish what you have begun; for our Lord Jesus Christ is already calling us." ¹⁴And Nero, hearing them, smiled a little and said: "These men see themselves bested already and have gone mad." ¹⁵Peter said: "Now you will know that we are not mad." Paul said to Peter: "Do what you will do at once." ¹⁶And Peter, looking steadfastly against Simon, said: "I adjure you—you messengers of Satan, who are carrying him into the air to deceive the hearts of the unbelievers—by the God that created all things, and by Jesus Christ, whom on the third day He raised from the dead: from this hour on, you may no longer hold him up, but must let him go." ¹⁷And immediately, being let go, he fell into a place called Sacra Via, that is, Holy Way, and was split into four parts, having perished by a terrible fate. ¹⁸Then Nero ordered Peter and Paul to be put in irons, and the body of Simon to be carefully kept three days, thinking that he would rise on the third day. ¹⁹To whom Peter said: "He will no longer rise, since he is truly dead, being condemned to everlasting punishment." ²⁰And Nero said to him: "Who commanded you to do such a dreadful deed?" Peter said: "His reflections and blasphemy against my Lord Jesus Christ have brought him into this gulf of destruction." ²¹Nero said: "I will destroy you in a terrible way." Peter said: "This is not in your power, even if it should seem good to you to destroy us; but it is necessary that what our Master promised to us should be fulfilled." ²²Then Nero, having summoned Agrippa the propraetor, said to him: "It is necessary that men introducing mischievous religious observances should die. Therefore, I order them to take iron clubs, and to be killed in the Naumachia." ²³Agrippa the propraetor said: "Most sacred emperor, what you have ordered is not fitting for these men, since Paul seems innocent beside Peter." ²⁴Nero said: "By what fate, then, will they die?" Agrippa answered and said: "As [it] seems to me, it is simply that Paul's head should be cut off, and that Peter should be raised on a cross as the cause of the murder." Nero said: "You have judged most excellently." ²⁵Then both Peter and Paul were led away from the presence of Nero. And Paul was beheaded on the Ostesian [[*or* Vostesian]] Way. ²⁶And Peter, having come to the cross, said: "Since my Lord Jesus Christ, who came down from Heaven to the earth, was raised on the Cross upright, and He has stooped down to call me to Heaven, who am of the earth, my cross ought to be fixed head down most, so as to direct my feet toward Heaven; for I am not worthy to be crucified like my Lord." ²⁷Then, having reversed the cross, they nailed his feet up. ²⁸And the multitude was assembled, reviling Caesar and wishing to kill him. ²⁹But Peter restrained them, saying, "A few days ago, being exhorted by the brothers, I was going away; and my Lord Jesus Christ met me, and having adored Him, I said, Lord, where are You going? ³⁰And He said to me, I am going to Rome to be crucified. And I said to Him, Lord, were You not crucified once for all? And the

Lord answering, said, I saw you fleeing from death, and I wish to be crucified instead of you. ³¹And I said, Lord, I go; I fulfill Your command. And He said to me, Do not fear, for I am with you. ³²On this account, then, children, do not hinder my departing; for my feet are already going on the road to Heaven. Therefore, do not grieve, but rather rejoice with me, for today I receive the fruit of my labors." ³³And thus speaking, he said: "I thank You, good Shepherd, that the sheep which You have entrusted to me, sympathize with me; I ask, then, that they may have a part with me in Your kingdom." ³⁴And having thus spoken, he gave up the spirit.

CHAPTER 10

¹And immediately there appeared men glorious and strange in appearance; and they said: "We are here on account of the holy and chief apostles from Jerusalem." ²And they, along with Marcellus—an illustrious man, who, having left Simon, had believed in Peter—took up his body secretly and put it under the terebinth near the Naumachia in the place called the Vatican. ³And the men who had said that they came from Jerusalem said to the people: "Rejoice, and be exceedingly glad, because you have been deemed worthy to have great champions. And know that Nero himself, after not many more days, will be utterly destroyed, and his kingdom will be given to another." ⁴And after these things, the people revolted against him; and when he knew of it, he fled into desert places, and through hunger and cold he gave up the spirit, and his body became food for the wild beasts. ⁵And some devout men of the regions of the East wished to carry off the relics of the holy ones, and immediately there was a great earthquake in the city; and those that dwelt in the city having become aware of it, ran and seized the men, but they fled. ⁶But the Romans having taken them, put them in a place three miles from the city, and there they were guarded [for] one year and seven months, until they had built the place in which they intended to put them. ⁷And after these things, everyone having assembled with glory and singing of praise, they put them in the place built for them. ⁸And the consummation of the holy glorious apostles Peter and Paul was on the twenty-ninth of the month of June—in Christ Jesus our Lord, to whom be glory and strength.

CHAPTER 11

¹And as Paul was being led away to be beheaded at a place about three miles from the city, he was in irons. ²And there were three soldiers guarding him who were from an eminent family. ³And when they had gone out of the gate about the length of a bowshot, there met them a God-fearing woman; and she, seeing Paul dragged along in irons, had compassion on him and wept bitterly. ⁴And the name of the woman was called Perpetua; and she was one-eyed. ⁵And Paul, seeing her weeping, says to her: "Give me your handkerchief, and when I turn back I will give it to you." ⁶And she, having taken the handkerchief, gave it to him willingly. ⁷And the soldiers laughed and said to the woman: "Why do you wish, woman, to lose your handkerchief? Do you not know that he is going away to be beheaded?" ⁸And Perpetua said to them: "I adjure you by the health of Caesar to bind his eyes with this handkerchief when you cut off his head," which was also done. ⁹And they beheaded him at the place called Aquae Salviae, near the pine tree. ¹⁰And as God had willed, before the soldiers came back, the handkerchief, having drops of blood on it, was restored to the woman. ¹¹And as she was carrying it, at once and immediately her eye was opened. ¹²And the three soldiers who had cut off the head of the holy one, Paul, when after three hours they came on the same day with the Bulla bringing it to Nero, having met Perpetua, they said to her: "What is it, woman? Behold, by your confidence you have lost your handkerchief." ¹³But she said to them: "I have both got my handkerchief, and my eye has recovered its sight. And as the LORD, the God of Paul, lives, I have also implored him that I may be deemed worthy to become the slave of his Lord." ¹⁴Then the soldiers who had the Bulla, recognizing the handkerchief and seeing that her eye had been opened, cried out with a loud voice, as if from one mouth, and said: "We too are the slaves of Paul's Master." ¹⁵Perpetua therefore having gone away, reported in the palace of Emperor Nero that the soldiers who had beheaded Paul said: "We will no longer go into the city, for we believe in Christ whom Paul preached, and we are Christians." ¹⁶Then Nero, filled with rage, ordered Perpetua, who had informed him of the soldiers, to be held fast in irons; and as for the soldiers, he ordered one to be beheaded outside of the gate about one mile from the city, another to be cut in two, and the third to be stoned. ¹⁷And Perpetua was in the prison; and in this prison there was kept Potentiana, a noble maiden, because she had said: "I forsake my parents and all the things of my father, and I wish to become a Christian." ¹⁸She therefore joined herself to Perpetua, and ascertained from her everything about Paul, and was in much anxiety about the faith in Christ. ¹⁹And the wife of Nero was Potentiana's sister; and she secretly informed her about Christ, that those who believe in Him see everlasting joy, and that everything here is temporary, but there eternal: so that she also fled out of the palace, and some of the senators' wives with her. ²⁰Then Nero, having inflicted many tortures on Perpetua, at last tied a great stone to her neck and ordered her to be thrown over a precipice. And her remains lie at the Momentan Gate. ²¹And Potentiana also underwent many torments; and at last, having made a furnace one day, they burned her.

ACTS OF ANDREW AND MATTHIAS

The Acts of Andrew and Matthias and the subsequent Acts of Peter and Andrew are heroic romances, written sometime between the 2nd and 5th centuries. Unlike the other apocryphal Acts, they appear to have no real doctrinal or theological purposes, but were merely intriguing fictional accounts of the apostles.

CHAPTER 1

¹At that time all the apostles were gathered together, and they divided the countries among themselves, casting lots, and it fell to Matthias to go to the land of the cannibals. ²Now the men of that city ate no bread nor drank wine, but ate the flesh and drank the blood of men; and every stranger who landed there they took, and put out his eyes, and gave him a magic drink which took away his understanding. ³So when Matthias arrived, he was so treated; but the drink had no effect on him, and he remained praying for help in the prison. ⁴And a light came and a Voice: "Matthias, My beloved, receive sight." And he saw. And the Voice continued: "I will not forsake you: abide twenty-seven days, and I will send Andrew to deliver you and all the rest." And the Savior went up into Heaven. ⁵Matthias remained singing praises; when the executioners came to take victims, he kept his eyes closed. ⁶They came and looked at the ticket on his hand and said: "Three more days and we will slay him," for every victim had a ticket tied on his hand to show the date when his thirty days would be fulfilled.

CHAPTER 2

¹When twenty-seven days had elapsed, the LORD appeared to Andrew in the country where he was teaching and said: "In three days Matthias is to be slain by the cannibals; go and deliver him." ²"How is it possible for me to get there in time?" "Early tomorrow, go to the shore and you will find a ship." And He left him. ³They went—Andrew and his disciples—and found a little boat and three men. The captain was the LORD, and the other two were messengers. ⁴Andrew asked where they were going. "To the land of the cannibals." "I would go there too." "Every man avoids that place; why will you go?" ⁵"I have an errand to do; and if You can, take us." He said: "Come on board." ⁶Andrew said: "I must tell You [that] we have neither money nor food." "How then do you travel?" "Our Master

forbade us to take money and provisions. If You will do us this kindness, tell us: if not, we will look for another ship." ⁷"If these are your orders, come on board and welcome, I truly desire to have disciples of Jesus on my ship." So they embarked. ⁸Jesus ordered three loaves to be brought, and Andrew summoned his disciples to partake; but they could not answer him, for they were disturbed with the sea; so Andrew explained to the captain, and He offered to set them ashore: but they refused to leave Andrew. ⁹Jesus said: "Tell your disciples some of the wonders your Master did, to encourage them, for we are going to set sail": so they did, and Jesus steered. ¹⁰And Andrew told the disciples about the stilling of the storm and prayed in himself that they might sleep: and they fell asleep. ¹¹Andrew said to Jesus: "Tell me your art, [for] I sailed the sea sixteen years, and this is the seventeenth, and I never saw such steering: the ship is as if on land." ¹²Jesus said: "I, too, have often sailed the sea and been in danger; but because you are a disciple of Jesus, the sea knows you and is still." Andrew praised God that he had met such a Man. ¹³Jesus said: "Tell me why the Jews did not believe on your Master." Andrew enumerated the miracles; "yet," he said, "the Jews did not believe." ¹⁴"Perhaps He did not do these signs before the high priests." "Yes, He did, both openly and privately, and they would not believe." ¹⁵"What were the signs He did in secret?" "O Man with the spirit of questioning, why do You tempt me thus?" "I do not tempt you, but My soul rejoices to hear of His wonderful works." ¹⁶" I will tell You, then. Once, when we the twelve went with our Lord to a heathen temple, so that He might show us the ignorance of the Devil, the high priests saw us and said: Why do you follow this Man who says He is the Son of God? Does God have a Son? Is this not Joseph and Mary's Son?—and His brothers are James and Simon. ¹⁷And our hearts were weakened, and Jesus perceived it, and took us apart into the wilderness, and did mighty signs and strengthened our faith. And we said to the priests: Come and see, for He has convinced us. ¹⁸And the priests came to the heathen temple, and Jesus showed us the form of the heavens, so that we might learn whether or not it was true. ¹⁹Thirty men of the people and four priests were with us. On the right and left of the temple, Jesus saw two sphinxes carved, and He turned to us and said: Behold the form of the Heaven: these are like the cherubim and seraphim in Heaven. ²⁰And He said to the sphinx on the right: You, likeness of that which is in Heaven, made by craftsmen, come down and convince these priests whether I am God or man. ²¹It came down, and spoke, and said: O foolish sons of Israel! This is God who made man.... Do not tell me that I am a stone image: the temples are better than your synagogue. Our priests purify themselves seven days from women, and do not approach the temple, but you come straight from defilement. ²²The temples will abolish your synagogues and become assemblies of the only-begotten Son of God. ²³The priests said: It speaks by magic, [for] you heard it say that this man spoke with Abraham. How is that possible? ²⁴... Jesus said to the sphinx: Go to the cave of Mambre and call Abraham; command him to rise with Isaac and Jacob and come to the temples of the Jebusaeans to convict the priests. ²⁵It went and called, and the twelve patriarchs rose and came out. To which of us were you sent? [The sphinx replied:] Not to you, but to the three patriarchs: go back and rest. ²⁶They went back, and the three patriarchs came and convicted the priests. Jesus [then] commanded them to return, and He sent the sphinx back to its place; but the priests did not believe. And He did many other wonders."

CHAPTER 3

¹Jesus, seeing that they were near land, leaned His head on one of the messengers and ceased speaking to Andrew: and Andrew went to sleep. ²Then Jesus commanded the messengers to take the men, and lay them outside the city of the cannibals, and return: and then they all departed to Heaven. ³Andrew awoke, and looked around him, and realized what had happened, and he roused his disciples. ⁴They told him their dream: eagles came and carried them into Paradise, and they saw the LORD on His throne, and messengers, and the three patriarchs and David singing, "and you, the twelve apostles, and twelve messengers by you, whom the LORD commanded to obey you in everything." ⁵Andrew rejoiced and prayed to the LORD to show Himself: and Jesus appeared in the form of a beautiful young child. ⁶Andrew asked forgiveness for his arrogance on the ship. Jesus reassured him, and told him what trials awaited him in the city, and encouraged him to endure them, and departed. ⁷They entered the city, unseen, and went to the prison. The seven guards fell dead at his prayer: at the Sign of the Cross the doors opened. ⁸He found Matthias, and they greeted each other. ⁹Andrew looked at the victims, who were naked and eating grass, and he struck his breast and reproached the Devil: "How long will you war with men! You caused Adam to be cast out of Paradise! You caused his bread that was on the table to be turned into stones! ¹⁰Again, you entered into the mind of the messengers, and caused them to be defiled with women, and made their savage sons the giants to devour men on the earth, so that God sent the Flood...." ¹¹Then they both prayed, and they laid their hands on the prisoners and first restored their sight and then their sense, and Andrew instructed them to go out of the city, and remain under a fig-tree, and await him: there were two hundred seventy men and forty-nine women. ¹²And Andrew commanded a cloud, and it took Matthias, and the disciples, and brothers to the mountain where Peter was teaching, and there they remained.

CHAPTER 4

¹Andrew went out, and walked in the city, and sat down by a brazen pillar with a statue on it, to see what would happen. ²The executioners came and found the prison empty and the guards dead, and they reported it to the rulers. ³They said: "Go and fetch the seven dead men for us to eat today, and assemble the old men tomorrow, and we will cast lots for seven [each] day and eat them, until we can fit out ships, and send [them], and collect people to eat." ⁴So they fetched the seven corpses; there was a furnace in the midst of the city and a great vat for the blood: they put the men on the vat. ⁵A voice came: "Andrew, look at this." Andrew prayed, and the men's swords fell, and their hands turned to stone. ⁶The rulers cried: "There are wizards in the city! Go and gather the old men, for we are hungry." They found two hundred fifteen, and lots were cast for seven. ⁷One of these said: "Take my young son and kill him instead of me." They asked leave of the rulers, and it was granted, and the old man said: "I have a daughter, take her too, and spare me." ⁸So the children were brought to the vat, begging for their lives, but there was no pity. ⁹Andrew prayed, and again the swords fell from the men's hands, and there was great alarm. ¹⁰Then the Devil came in the guise of an old man and said: "Woe to you! You will all die of hunger; but search now and look for a stranger named Andrew: he is the cause of your trouble." ¹¹Andrew was looking at the Devil, but the Devil could not see him. And Andrew said: "O Beliar, my Lord will humble you to the abyss!" ¹²The Devil said: "I hear your voice and know it; but I cannot see where you stand." Andrew said: "Are you not called Amael because you are blind?" ¹³The Devil responded: "Look for the man who spoke to me, for it is he." And they shut the gates and looked everywhere, but could not find him. ¹⁴The LORD appeared and said to Andrew: "Show yourself to them." He rose and said: "I am Andrew whom you seek." ¹⁵And they ran, and took him, and debated how to kill him: "If we cut off his head, it will not pain him enough; let us put a rope around his neck, and drag him through the streets every day until he dies, and divide his body and eat it." ¹⁶They did so, and his flesh was torn, and his blood flowed, and they cast him into prison with his hands bound behind him. ¹⁷And so they [also] did the next day, and he wept and cried to the LORD; and the Devil told the people to strike his mouth, so that he might not speak; and they bound his hands behind him and left him in the prison. ¹⁸The Devil took seven other devils, whom Andrew had driven out from places in the neighborhood, and they came to Andrew, and the Devil said: "Now we will kill you like your Master whom Herod slew." And he said: "Now my children, kill him!" ¹⁹But they saw the seal on his forehead and were afraid, and they said: "You kill him, for we cannot." ²⁰And one of them said: "If we cannot kill him, let us mock him"; and they stood before him and taunted him with his helplessness, and he wept. ²¹And a voice—the Devil's voice disguised—said: "Why do you weep?" Andrew said: "Because of our Lord's word: Have patience with them; otherwise I would have shown you..., but if the LORD grants me

a visitation in this city, I will punish you as you deserve." And they fled. ²²The next day, the people dragged him again, and he cried out to the Lord: "Here are Your words: A hair of your heads will not perish; behold, my flesh is torn from me." ²³And a Voice said in Hebrew: "My words will not pass away: look behind you." And he saw great fruit-bearing trees growing up where his flesh and blood had fallen. ²⁴And they took him back to prison and said: "Perhaps he will die tomorrow." And the Lord came and took his hand, and he rose up whole. ²⁵And there was a pillar in the prison, and on it a statue. Andrew went to it, and spread out his hands seven times, and said: "Fear the Sign of the Cross, and let this statue pour forth water as a flood. ²⁶And do not say, I am only a stone, for God made us from earth, but you are clean, and therefore God gave His people the Law on tables of stone." ²⁷And the statue poured water out of its mouth as from a canal, and it was bitter and corroded men's flesh. In the morning all the people began to flee. The water killed their cattle and their children. ²⁸Andrew said: "Let Michael wall the city around with fire." A cloud of fire came and surrounded it, and they could not escape. ²⁹The water came up to their necks and consumed their flesh. They cried and lamented until he saw their spirit was crushed, and he told the alabaster statue to cease. ³⁰And Andrew went out of the prison, the water parting before him, and the people prayed for mercy. ³¹The old man who had given up his children came and begged. But Andrew said: "I marvel at you; you and the fourteen executioners will be swallowed up and see the places of torment and of peace." ³²And he went as far as the great vat, and prayed, and the earth opened and swallowed the water, and the old man, and the executioners. And everyone feared greatly, but he consoled them. ³³Then he instructed them to bring everyone who had been killed by the water, but there were too many, so he prayed and revived them. ³⁴Then he drew out the plan for a church, and immersed them, and gave them the Lord's precepts. ³⁵And they begged him to stay with them a while; but he refused, saying, "I must first go to my disciples"; and he set forth, and they lamented grievously. ³⁶And Jesus appeared in the form of a beautiful child, and reproved him for leaving them, and told him to stay seven days; and then he should go with his disciples to the country of the barbarians, and then return and bring the men out of the abyss. And he returned and they all rejoiced greatly.

ACTS OF PETER AND ANDREW

The Acts of Peter and Andrew is a heroic romance, written sometime between the 2nd and 5th centuries, which is a sequel of sorts to the earlier Acts of Andrew and Matthias, providing entertaining, fictional adventures of the apostles; scholarship has noted no real theological imperative for the work. The extant work is fragmentary, ending abruptly.

CHAPTER 1

¹It came to pass when Andrew, the apostle of Christ, went forth from the city of the cannibals, behold, a bright cloud snatched him up and carried him away to the mountain where Peter, and Matthew, and Alexander were sitting. ²And when he saw them, they saluted him with great joy. Then Peter says to him: "What has happened to you, brother Andrew? Have you sown the word of truth in the country of the cannibals or not?" ³Andrew says to him: "Yes, father Peter, through your prayers; but the men of that city have caused me many troubles, for they dragged me through their street [for] three days, so that my blood stained the whole street." ⁴Peter says to him: "Be a man in the Lord, brother Andrew, and come here, and rest from your labor. For if the good farmer laboriously tills the ground, it will also bear fruit, and immediately all his toil will be turned into joy; but if he toils, and his land brings forth no fruit, he has double toil." ⁵And while he was thus speaking, the Lord Jesus Christ appeared to them in the form of a child and said to them: "Hail, Peter, overseer of the whole of My Assembly! Hail, Andrew! My co-heirs, be courageous, and struggle for mankind; ⁶for truly I say to you: you will endure toils in this world for mankind, but be bold. ⁷I will give you rest in one hour of repose in the kingdom of My Father. ⁸Arise, then, and go into the city of the barbarians and preach in it; and I will be with you in the wonders that will happen in it by your hands." ⁹And the Lord Jesus, after saluting them, went up into the heavens in glory.

CHAPTER 2

¹And Peter, and Andrew, and Alexander, and Rufus, and Matthias, went into the city of the barbarians. ²And after they had come near the city, Andrew answered and said to Peter: "Father Peter, must we again undergo toils in this city, as in the country of the cannibals?" ³Peter says to him: "I do not know. But behold, there is an old man before us sowing in his field: if we go up to him, let us say to him, Give us bread; and if he gives us bread, we may know that we are not to suffer in this city; but if he says to us, We have no bread, on the other hand, we will know that suffering awaits us again." ⁴And when they came up to the old man, Peter says to him: "Hail, farmer!" And the farmer says to them: "Hail you too, merchants!" Peter says to him: "Do you have bread to give to these children? For we have been in need." ⁵The old man says to them: "Wait a little, and look after the oxen, and the plow, and the land, so that I may go into the city and get loaves for you." ⁶Peter says to him: "If you provide hospitality for us, we will look after the cattle and the field." The old man says: "So be it." ⁷Peter says to him: "Are the oxen your own?" The old man says: "No; I have them on hire." Peter says to him: "Go into the city." And the old man went into the city. ⁸And Peter arose, and girded up his cloak and his undergarment, and says to Andrew: "It is not right for us to rest and be idle—especially when the old man is working for us, having left his own work." Then Peter took hold of the plow and sowed the wheat. ⁹And Andrew was behind the oxen, and he says to Peter: "Father Peter, why do you bring toil on us, especially when we already have enough work!" ¹⁰Then Andrew took the plow out of Peter's hand and sowed the wheat, saying, "O seed cast into the ground in the field of the righteous, come up, and come to the light. Let the young men of the city therefore come forth, whom I found in the pit of destruction until today; for behold, the apostles of Christ are coming into the city, pardoning the sins of those who believe in them, and healing every disease, and every sickness. ¹¹Pray for me, so that He may have mercy on me, and that I may be delivered from this difficulty." ¹²And many of the multitude believed in Christ, because of what was said; and they fell at the feet of the apostles and adored them. ¹³And they laid their hands on them. And they healed those in the city that were sick, and gave sight to the blind and hearing to the deaf, and drove out the demons. ¹⁴The whole multitude glorified the Father, and the Son, and the Holy Spirit.

CHAPTER 3

¹And there was a certain rich man in the city, Onesiphorus by name. ²He, having seen the miracles done by the apostles, says to them: "If I believe in your God, can I also do a miracle like you?" Andrew says to him: "If you will forsake all that belongs to you, and your wife and your children, as we also have done, then you will also do miracles." ³When Onesiphorus heard this, he was filled with rage, and took his scarf, and threw it over Andrew's neck, and struck him, and said to him: "You are a sorcerer! How do you force me to abandon my wife, and my children, and my goods?" ⁴Then Peter, having turned and seen him striking Andrew, says to him: "Man, stop striking Andrew immediately!" Onesiphorus says to him: "I see that you are more sensible than he. Do you then tell me to leave my wife, and my children, and my goods. What do you say?" ⁵Peter says to him: "One thing I say to you: it is easier for a camel to go through the eye of a needle, than for a rich man to go into the kingdom of the heavens." ⁶When Onesiphorus heard this, he was even more filled with rage and anger, and took his

scarf off the neck of Andrew, and threw it on the neck of Peter; and so he dragged him along, saying, "You are truly a great sorcerer—more than the other; for a camel cannot go through the eye of a needle. ⁷But if you will show me this miracle, I will believe in your God; and not only I, but also the whole city. But if not, you will be grievously punished in the midst of the city." ⁸And when Peter heard this, he was exceedingly grieved, and stood and stretched forth his hands toward the sky, and prayed, saying, "O LORD our God, listen to me at this time, for they will ensnare us from Your own words; for no prophet has [yet] spoken to set forth this explanation of his, and no patriarch that we might learn the interpretation of it; and now we seek for ourselves the explanation with boldness. ⁹Do You then, LORD, not overlook us? For You are He who is praised by the cherubim." ¹⁰And after he had said this, the Savior appeared in the form of a child, twelve years of age, wearing a linen garment; and He says to them: "Be courageous and do not tremble, My chosen disciples; for I am with you always. Let the needle and the camel be brought." And after saying this, He went up into the heavens. ¹¹And there was a certain merchant in the city who had believed in the LORD through the apostle Philip; and when he heard of this, he ran and searched for a needle with a big eye, to do a favor for the apostles. ¹²When Peter learned this, he said: "My son, do not search for a big needle; for nothing is impossible with God: rather bring us a small needle." ¹³And after the needle had been brought, and the whole multitude of the city were standing by to see, Peter looked up and saw a camel coming. And he ordered her to be brought. ¹⁴Then he fixed the needle in the ground and cried out with a loud voice, saying, "In the Name of Jesus Christ, who was crucified under Pontius Pilate: I order you, O camel, to go through the eye of the needle." ¹⁵Then the eye of the needle was opened like a gate, and the camel went through it, and the whole multitude saw it. ¹⁶Peter again says to the camel: "Go through the needle again." And the camel went a second time. ¹⁷When Onesiphorus saw this, he said to Peter: "Truly you are a great sorcerer; but I will not believe unless I send and bring a camel and a needle." ¹⁸And he called one of his servants and said to him privately: "Go and bring me here a camel and a needle; also find an unclean woman and force her to come here, for these men are sorcerers." ¹⁹And Peter, having learned the mystery through the Spirit, says to Onesiphorus: "Send and bring the camel, and the woman, and the needle." And when they brought them, Peter took the needle and fixed it in the ground. And the woman was sitting on the camel. ²⁰Then Peter says: "In the Name of our Lord Jesus Christ the crucified: I order you, O camel, to go through this needle." And immediately the eye of the needle was opened and became like a gate, and the camel went through it. ²¹Peter again says to the camel: "Go through it again, so that everyone may see the glory of our Lord Jesus Christ, in order that some may believe on Him." Then the camel went through the needle again. ²²And Onesiphorus seeing it, cried out and said: "Truly great is the God of Peter and Andrew, and from this time forth I will believe in the Name of our Lord Jesus Christ. ²³Now then, hear my words, O Peter: I have cornfields, vineyards, and fields; I also have twenty-seven pounds of gold, and fifty pounds of silver; and I have very many slaves. I give my possessions to the poor, so that I may also do one miracle like you." ²⁴And Peter was grieved, lest the powers should not work in him, seeing that he had not received the seal in Christ. ²⁵And while he was considering this, behold, a Voice out of Heaven was saying to him: "Do to him what he wishes, because I will accomplish for him what he desires." ²⁶Peter says to him: "My son, come here; do as we do." And Onesiphorus came up, and stood before the camel and the needle, and said: "In the Name…"

ACTS OF BARNABAS

A pseudepigraphal work of the 5th century designed to strengthen the claim of the Church of Cyprus to apostolic authority, the Acts of Barnabas is a relatively short work that details the travels of Barnabas and Paul from the perspective of John Mark.

CHAPTER 1

¹Since from the descent of the presence of our Savior Jesus Christ—the unwearied, and benevolent, and mighty Shepherd, and Teacher, and Physician—I beheld and saw the ineffable, and holy, and unspotted mystery of the Christians, who hold the hope in holiness, and who have been sealed; ²and since I have zealously served Him, I have deemed it necessary to give an account of the mysteries which I have heard and seen. ³I, John [Mark], accompanying the holy apostles Barnabas and Paul, being formerly a servant of Cyrillus the high priest of Jupiter, but now having received the gift of the Holy Spirit through Paul, and Barnabas, and Silas, who were worthy of the calling, and who immersed me in Iconium. ⁴After I was immersed, then, I saw a certain man standing clothed in a white garment; and he said to me: "Be of good courage, John, for your name will assuredly be changed to Mark, and your glory will be proclaimed in all the world. And the darkness in you has passed away from you, and there has been given to you understanding to know the mysteries of God." ⁵And when I saw the vision, becoming greatly terrified, I fell at the feet of Barnabas and related to him the mysteries which I had seen and heard from that man. And the apostle Paul was not nearby when I disclosed the mysteries. ⁶And Barnabas said to me: "Tell no one the miracle which you have seen. For by me also this night the LORD stood, saying, Be of good courage: for as you have given your life for My Name to death and banishment from your nation, thus you will also be made perfect. ⁷Moreover, as for the servant who is with you, also take him with yourself; for he has certain mysteries. Now then, my child, keep to yourself the things which you have seen and heard; for a time will come for you to reveal them."

CHAPTER 2

¹And I, having been instructed in these things by him, remained in Iconium many days, for there was a holy and pious man there, who also entertained us, whose house Paul had also sanctified. ²Therefore, from there we came to Seleucia, and after staying three days, sailed away to Cyprus; and I was ministering to them until we had gone around all of Cyprus. ³And setting sail from Cyprus, we landed in Perga of Pamphylia. And there I then stayed about two months, wishing to sail to the regions of the West; and the Holy Spirit did not allow me. ⁴Turning, therefore, I again sought the apostles; and having learned that they were in Antioch, I went to them. ⁵And I found Paul in bed in Antioch from the toil of the journey, who also seeing me, was exceedingly grieved on account of my delay in Pamphylia. ⁶And Barnabas coming, encouraged him and tasted bread, and he took a little of it. ⁷And they preached the word of the LORD and enlightened many of the Jews and Greeks. And I only attended to them, and was afraid to come near Paul, both because he held me as having spent too much time in Pamphylia, and because he was quite enraged against me. ⁸And I gave conversion on my knees on the earth to Paul, and he would not endure it. ⁹And when I remained for three Sabbaths in petition and prayer on my knees, I was unable to prevail on him concerning myself; for his great grievance against me was on account of my keeping several parchments in Pamphylia.

CHAPTER 3

¹And when it came to pass that they finished teaching in Antioch, on the first of the week they took counsel together to set out for the places of the East, and after that to go into Cyprus and oversee all the assemblies in which they had spoken the word of God. ²And Barnabas implored Paul to first go to Cyprus and oversee his own in his village; and Lucius implored him to take the oversight of his city of Cyrene. ³And a vision was seen by Paul in [his] sleep, that he should hasten to Jerusalem, because the brothers expected him there. But

Barnabas urged that they should go to Cyprus, and pass the winter [there], and then that they should go to Jerusalem at the feast. Great contention, therefore, arose between them. ⁴And Barnabas urged me also to accompany them, on account of my being their servant from the beginning, and on account of my having served them in all of Cyprus until they came to Perga of Pamphylia; and I had remained many days there. ⁵But Paul cried out against Barnabas, saying, "It is impossible for him to go with us." And those who were with us there urged me also to accompany them, because there was a vow on me to follow them to the end. ⁶So that Paul said to Barnabas: "If you will take John"—who is also surnamed Mark—"with you, take another road, for he will not come with us." ⁷And Barnabas coming to himself, said: "The grace of God does not desert him who has once served the good news and journeyed with us. If, therefore, this is agreeable to you, Father Paul, I will take him and go." ⁸And he said: "Go in the grace of Christ, and we in the power of the Spirit." Therefore, bending their knees, they prayed to God. ⁹And Paul, groaning aloud, wept, and in like manner also Barnabas, saying to one another: "It would have been good for us, as at first, so also at last, to work in common among men; but since it has thus seemed good to you, Father Paul, pray for me that my labor may be made perfect to commendation: for you know how I have served you also to the grace of Christ that has been given to you. ¹⁰For I go to Cyprus and hasten to be made perfect; for I know that I will no longer see your face, O Father Paul." And falling on the ground at his feet, he wept long. ¹¹And Paul said to him: "The LORD stood by me also this night, saying, Do not force Barnabas not to go to Cyprus, for there it has been prepared for him to enlighten many; and you also, in the grace that has been given to you, go to Jerusalem to worship in the holy place, and there it will be shown you where your martyrdom has been prepared." ¹²And we saluted one another, and Barnabas took me to himself.

CHAPTER 4

¹And having come down to Laodicea, we sought to cross to Cyprus; and having found a ship going to Cyprus, we embarked. ²And when we had set sail, the wind was found to be contrary. And we came to Corasium; and having gone down to the shore where there was a fountain, we rested there, showing ourselves to no one, so that no one might know that Barnabas had separated from Paul. ³And having set sail from Corasium, we came to the regions of Isauria, and from there came to a certain island called Pityusa; and a storm having come on, we remained there three days; and a certain pious man entertained us, Euphemus by name, whom Barnabas also instructed in many things in the faith, with all his house. ⁴And from there we sailed past the Aconesiae and came to the city of Anemurium; and having gone into it, we found two Greeks. ⁵And coming to us, they asked from where and who we were. And Barnabas said to them: "If you wish to know from where and who we are, throw away the clothing which you have, and I will put clothing on you which never becomes soiled; for neither is there in it anything filthy, but it is altogether splendid." ⁶And being astonished at the saying, they asked us: "What is that garment which you are going to give us?" And Barnabas said to them: "If you will confess your sins and submit yourselves to our Lord Jesus Christ, you will receive that garment which is incorruptible forever." ⁷And being pricked at heart by the Holy Spirit, they fell at his feet, begging and saying: "We beg you, father, give us that garment; for we believe in the living and true God whom you proclaim." ⁸And leading them down to the fountain, he immersed them into the Name of Father, and Son, and Holy Spirit. ⁹And they knew that they were clothed with power and a holy robe [that does not wear out]. ¹⁰And having taken one robe from me, he put it on the one; and his own robe he put on the other. And they brought money to him, and immediately Barnabas distributed it to the poor. ¹¹And the sailors were also able to gain many things from them. ¹²And they having come down to the shore, he spoke to them the word of God; and he having blessed them, we saluted them and boarded the ship. ¹³And one of them, who was named Stephanus, wished to accompany us, and Barnabas did not permit him. ¹⁴And we, having gone across, sailed down to Cyprus by night; and having come to the place called Crommyacita, we found Timon and Ariston, the temple servants, at whose house we were also entertained. ¹⁵And Timon was afflicted by much fever. And having laid our hands on him, we immediately removed his fever, having called on the Name of the Lord Jesus. ¹⁶And Barnabas had received documents from Matthew, a scroll of the word of God, and a narrative of miracles and doctrines. ¹⁷This Barnabas laid [them] on the sick in each place that we came to, and it immediately cured their sufferings.

CHAPTER 5

¹And when we had come to Lapithus, and an idol festival being celebrated in the theater, they did not allow us to go into the city, but we rested for a while at the gate. And Timon, after he rose up from his disease, came with us. ²And having gone forth from Lapithus, we traveled through the mountains and came to the city of Lampadistus, of which Timon was also a native; in addition to whom, having also found that Heracleius was there, we were entertained by him. ³He was of the city of Tamasus and had come to visit his relations; and Barnabas, looking steadfastly at him, recognized him, having met with him formerly at Citium with Paul; to whom the Holy Spirit was also given at immersion, and he changed his name to Heracleides. ⁴And having ordained him overseer over Cyprus, and having confirmed the assembly in Tamasus, we left him in the house of his brothers that dwelt there. ⁵And having crossed the mountain called Chionodes, we came to Old Paphos, and there found Rhodon, a temple servant, who also, having himself believed, accompanied us. ⁶And we met a certain Jew, by name Bar-Jesus, coming from Paphos, who also recognized Barnabas, as having formerly been with Paul. He did not wish for us to go into Paphos; but having turned away, we came to Curium. ⁷And we found that a certain abominable race was being run in the road near the city, where a multitude of naked women and men were performing the race. And there was great deception and error in that place. ⁸And Barnabas turning, rebuked it; and the western part fell, so that many were wounded, and many of them also died, and the rest fled to the temple of Apollo, which was close at hand in the city, which was called sacred. ⁹And when we came near the temple, a great multitude of Jews who were there, having been put up to it by Bar-Jesus, stood outside of the city and did not allow us to go into the city; but we spent the evening under a tree near the city and rested there.

CHAPTER 6

¹And on the following day, we came to a certain village where Aristoclianus dwelt. He, being a leper, had been cleansed in Antioch, whom Paul and Barnabas also sealed to be an overseer and sent to his village in Cyprus, because there were many Greeks there. ²And we were entertained in the cave by him in the mountain, and there we remained one day. ³And from there we came to Amathus, and there was a great multitude of Greeks in the temple in the mountain—low women and men pouring libations. ⁴There also Bar-Jesus, getting a head start on us, gained over the nation of the Jews and did not allow us to enter into the city; but a certain widow woman, eighty years old, being outside of the city, and she also not worshiping the idols, coming forward to us, took us into her house [for] one hour. ⁵And when we came out, we shook the dust off our feet near that temple where the libation of the abominable took place. ⁶And having gone out from there, we went through desert places, and Timon also accompanied us. ⁷And having come to Citium, and there also being a great uproar there in their hippodrome, having learned this, we came forth out of the city, having all shaken the dust off our feet; for no one received us, except that we rested one hour in the gate near the aqueduct.

CHAPTER 7

¹And having set sail in a ship from Citium, we came to Salamis and landed in the so-called islands, where there was a place full of idols; and high festivals and libations took place there. ²And having found Heracleides there again, we instructed him to proclaim the good news of God, and to set up assemblies and ministers in them. ³And having gone into Salamis, we came to the synagogue near the place called Biblia; and when we had gone into it, Barnabas, having unrolled the Gospel

which he had received from his fellow-laborer Matthew, began to teach the Jews. ⁴And Bar-Jesus, having arrived after two days, after not a few Jews had been instructed, was enraged and brought together all the multitude of the Jews; and they having laid hold of Barnabas, wished to hand him over to Hypatius, the governor of Salamis. ⁵And having bound him to take him away to the governor, and a pious Jebusite, a relative of Nero, having come to Cyprus, the Jews, learning this, took Barnabas by night and bound him with a rope around the neck; ⁶and having dragged him to the hippodrome from the synagogue, and having gone out of the city, standing around him, they burned him with fire, so that even his bones became ashes. ⁷And immediately that night, having taken his ashes, they cast it into a cloth; and having secured it with lead, they intended to throw it into the sea. ⁸But I, finding an opportunity in the night, and being able along with Timon and Rhodon to carry it, we came to a certain place, and having found a cave, put [his ashes] down there, where the nation of the Jebusites formerly dwelt. ⁹And having found a secret place in it, we hid [his ashes] away with the documents which he had received from Matthew. ¹⁰And it was the fourth hour of the night of the second [day] of the week. And when we were hidden in the place, the Jews made no small search after us; and having almost found us, they pursued us as far as the village of the Ledrians; and we, having also found a cave there near the village, took refuge in it, and thus escaped them. ¹¹And we were hidden in the cave [for] three days; and the Jews having gone away, we came forth and left the place by night. ¹²And taking with us Ariston and Rhodon, we came to the village of Limnes. ¹³And having come to the shore, we found an Egyptian ship; and having embarked in it, we landed at Alexandria. ¹⁴And there I remained, teaching the brothers that came the word of the LORD, enlightening them, and preaching what I had been taught by the apostles of Christ, who also immersed me into the Name of Father, and Son, and Holy Spirit; who also changed my name to Mark in the water of immersion, by which I also hope to bring many to the glory of God through His grace; because to Him is due honor and everlasting glory. Amen.

THE JOURNEYINGS AND MARTYRDOM OF THE HOLY APOSTLE BARNABAS HAVE BEEN FULFILLED THROUGH GOD.

ACTS OF XANTHIPPE, POLYXENA, AND REBECCA

The Acts of Xanthippe, Polyxena, and Rebecca is a New Testament apocryphal text, estimated to date from the 3rd or 4th century AD. Set during Nero's reign, it comprises two main stories: Xanthippe's spiritual awakening after hearing of Paul's teachings in Spain, and her sister Polyxena's adventurous quest for baptism. Polyxena faces abductions, miraculous rescues by apostles like Peter and Philip, and a lioness guiding her to baptism alongside Rebecca, a minor Jewish slave character. Reflecting Greek romance influences, the narrative emphasizes faith, chastity, and divine intervention, culminating in their return to Spain and reunion with Paul.

ACT OF XANTHIPPE

1. When the blessed Paul was at Rome through the word of the LORD, it so happened that a certain servant of a ruler of Spain came to Rome with letters from his master and heard the word of God from Paul—the truly golden and beautiful nightingale. This servant being greatly touched, and being unable to remain and be filled with the divine word because he was hastened along by the letters, returned into Spain in great grief; and being unable to show his desire to anyone, because his master was an idolater, he was always pained at heart and sighing greatly. Now this servant was honored and faithful to his masters, and as time went on, the servant fell sick and grew lean in body, which his master perceiving said to him, "What has happened to you that you have thus fallen together in countenance?" The servant said, "There is a great pain in my heart, and I can in no way find rest." His master said to him, "And what is the pain that cannot receive healing from my chief physician?" The servant said, "While I was still in Rome, this pain and its recurring mishap made itself known to me." His master said, "And do you not know of any who have fallen into this disease and been healed?" The servant said, "Yes, but where that physician [who can heal] is, I do not know, for I left him in Rome. As many as have been attended by that physician and have gone through the water in his hands, have received healing immediately." His master said, "I should not hesitate to send you yet again to Rome, if perhaps you might obtain healing."

2. And while they spoke thus, behold his mistress, Xanthippe by name, overhearing these words, and learning of the teaching of Paul, said, "What is the name of that physician, and what is the healing to ward off such a disease?" The servant said to her, "The calling on a new Name, and anointing with oil, and washing with water. By this treatment I have seen many that had incurable pains receive healing." As he said this, the images of the idols that stood in the house began to be shake and fall down. And his mistress beckoned to him, saying, "Do you see, brother, the images of the idols being shaken, how they cannot endure the power of the word?" And his master, Probus by name, arose from his midday sleep with a very gloomy countenance, for the Devil had greatly disturbed him, because the knowledge of God had come into his house. And he questioned the servant of everything in order, and the servant having been seized by sickness by the foreknowledge of God, disclosed to him the life of man, and Xanthippe was incurable in her soul concerning this teaching. So Probus was also grieved for Xanthippe, because from that time on she was wasting herself away with waking, and abstinence, and other austerities.

3. And Xanthippe going away to her couch and groaning, said, "Woe is me, wretched one, lying in darkness, that I have not learned the name of the new teacher, that I might summon his prayer to help me, and what to say I do not know. Will I call on him by the Name of his God? But I cannot say, The God that is preached by such a one. Nevertheless, I will say this by conjecture: O God, giving light in Hades, and guiding those in darkness, Lord of free men and kings, and preached by worthy servants in all the world, called on as a brother by sinful men and quick to hear, to whom not even chief-messengers can send up worthy songs of praise, who have shown to me, humble and unworthy, the always-living and abiding seed (though my ignorance does not permit me to receive it), hurry along also the things that concern me, LORD, since by Your will You have made Yourself heard by me, and in Your compassion show me the proclamation of Your herald, so that I may learn from him what is pleasing to You. Indeed, I beg You to look on my ignorance, O God, and enlighten me with the light of Your face—You that never overlook any of those that call on You in truth." Her husband Probus said to her, "Lady, why do you trouble yourself so much and not turn to sleep at all?" Xanthippe said, "I cannot sleep, for there is an incurable pain in me." Probus said to her, "And what is your pain or grief, O lady, that I am not sufficient to comfort you? All that you have wanted up to this day I have served you in, and now what is it that you have, and do not tell me?" Xanthippe says to him, "I only beg you [for] this [one] thing, my lord: permit me for a short time—and only for today—to sleep apart from you." And Probus said to her, "Be it as you will, lady; only cease your groaning."

4. Then entering into her bedchamber alone, she spoke thus with tears: "In what way, my God, I will act, or what counsel I will take, I do not know. Will I declare the thought that has come on me? I fear the madness and disorder of the city. Will I fly from this impious

city? I fear the scheme of the Devil for seizing the sheep. Will I await the mercy and swiftness of the LORD? Again, I fear the untimely snatching away of life, for the death of sinners has no warning. Will I depart and flee to Rome? I fear the length of the journey, being unable to go on foot. But while I say these things by conjecture, constrained by my desire (for I cannot speak with security), may I find pardon with You, my God, and may You fulfill my desire with an excess of right words, and think me but worthy to hear Your preacher, for to see his face, I ask a great thing. Blessed is he that is found in the company of Your preachers and is satisfied with their precious countenances. Blessed are they that are yoked under the preaching of Your commandments. Blessed are they that keep Your commandments; but where now, O LORD, are Your mercies to our fathers, so that we may also be their successors in love toward You and heirs of faith? But behold now, O LORD, I cannot find anyone that has love for You, that communing with him I might refresh my soul even a little. Therefore, hurry, O LORD, to yoke me in desire for You, and keep me under the shadow of Your wings, for You alone are God, glorified for all eternity. Amen."

5. Therefore Xanthippe, saying these words and others like them, groaned continually all through the night, and Probus heard her and was greatly distressed; and arising from his couch when the morning came, he went in to her, and seeing her eyes inflamed with tears, he said, "Why, lady, do you thus upset me, and will not tell me your pain? Tell it to me, so that I may do whatever is pleasing to you, and do not distress me with your trouble." Xanthippe says to him, "Rather be of good cheer, my lord, and do not be upset, for my trouble will not harm you, but if I have found favor before you, go forth now to the salutation, and allow me to indulge myself in it as I will, for it is not possible for man to take from me the insatiable pain." And listening to her, he immediately went out to receive the salutations of the men of the city, for he was the great man among them, and was also known to Nero, the emperor. And sitting down, great grief appeared in his countenance, and being asked the reason for his grief by the chief men of the city, he said to them that he had fallen into many unfounded charges.

6. And Xanthippe went out into the garden, so that she might wait there looking closely for certainty of her husband, and she saw the delight of the trees, and the various singing of the birds, and said, groaning, "O beauty of the world! For that which we previously thought came from itself, we now know that all things are beautifully fashioned by the Beautiful One. O power and invention of wisdom! For not only has He placed in men a thousand leagues, but also in birds he has distinguished various voices, as if from anthems and responses to receive sweet-voiced and heart-stirring hymns from His own works. O delightfulness of the air, declaring the incomparable Creator! Who will turn my sorrow into rejoicing?" And again she said, "God to whom praise is sung by all: give me peace and comfort." As she said these things, Probus also came up from the street to break his fast, and when he saw her countenance altered by tears, he began to pull out the hairs of his head, but he did not dare speak to her then, so as not to mix other trouble with her trouble. So, he went and fell on his couch, and he said, groaning, "Oh, if only I had the consolation of a child from her, but instead, I only acquire grief on grief! Two years are not yet complete since I was wedded to her, and already she contemplates divorce."

7. But Xanthippe was always keeping watch through the doors into the streets of the city; and the blessed Paul—the preacher, and teacher, and illuminator of the world—left Rome and even came into Spain by the foreknowledge of God. And coming up to the gates of the city, he stood and prayed, and crossing himself, he entered the city. When Xanthippe saw the blessed Paul walking quietly and equally, and adorned with all virtue and understanding, she was greatly delighted in him and her heart pounded continually, and possessed with an unexpected joy, she said within herself, "Why does my heart beat vehemently at the sight of this man? Why is his walk quiet and composed, as of one who expects to take in his arms one that is pursued? Why is his countenance so kind, as of one that tends the sick? Why does he look so lovingly here and there, as one who desires to assist those who are seeking to flee from the mouths of dragons? Who will tell me that this is one from the flock of preachers? If it were possible for me, I would want to touch the hem of his garments, so that I may behold his kindness and be ready to receive [the] sweet aroma (for the servant had told her this also, that the hems of his garments had the odor of precious perfumes)."

8. Now Probus heard her words, and immediately ran out by himself into the street, and laying hold of Paul's hand, said to him, "Man, who you are I do not know, but stoop to enter into my house; perhaps you may be a cause of salvation for me." Paul said to him, "It will be well with you, son, after your request!" And they went in together to Xanthippe. When Xanthippe therefore saw the great Paul, the intellectual eyes of her heart were uncovered, and she read on his forehead, having as it were golden seals, these words, "PAUL THE PREACHER OF GOD." Then exulting and rejoicing, she threw herself at his feet; and twisting her hair together, she wiped his feet, saying, "Welcome, O man of God, to us humble ones, that live as shadows among shadows. For you have looked on those who were running into Hades as into something beautiful, who addressed the crooked serpent and destroyer as provider and protector, who were running into the dark Hades as to their father—those that were fashioned with a rational nature but have become like irrational creatures. You have sought me, a lowly one, having the sun of righteousness in my heart. Now the poison is restrained now that I have seen your precious face. Now he that troubled me has flown away, when your most beautiful counsel has appeared to me. Now I will be considered worthy of conversion, when I have received the seal of the preacher of the LORD. Before now, I have deemed many blessed who met with you, but I say boldly that from this time forth, I myself will be called blessed by others, because I have touched your hem, because I have received your prayers, because I have enjoyed your sweet and soothing teaching. You have not hesitated to come to us—you that fish the dry land in your course and gather the fish that fall in your way into the net of the kingdom of the heavens."

9. The great Paul said to her, "Arise, daughter, and do not look on me as having been sought out of your ignorance by my foresight. For Christ, the provider of the world, the searcher out of sinners and the lost, who has not only called to mind those on earth, but also by His own presence has redeemed those in Hades, He Himself has pitied you and sent me here so that He might visit and pity many others together with you. For this mercy and visitation are not of us, but are His order and command, even as we have also received mercy and been saved by Him." Hearing this, Probus was astonished at their words, for he was altogether ignorant of these things. But Paul raised Xanthippe up from his feet by force, and she, running, set a new gilded chair for Paul to sit down on. The great Paul said to her, "My daughter Xanthippe, do not do this, for you have not yet agreed to the faith of Christ, but wait a while, until the LORD will set in order what is necessary." Xanthippe said to Paul, "Do you say this to try me, O preacher of God, or do you have any foreknowledge?" Paul said, "No, daughter, but the Devil, who hates the servants of God, sows wickedness in the hearts of his own servants, to oppose those that labor for Christ in preaching, for his wickedness has extended to the apostles and always against the LORD Himself. Therefore, it is fitting to approach the unbelievers gently and kindly." Xanthippe said to Paul, "I beg you, if you love your servants, pray for Probus, and let me see if he that is hated by you can work in him; let me see if he can even stand against your prayer." And Paul rejoiced exceedingly at the words of her faith and said to her, "Believe me, daughter, that by his suggestion and working I have not passed a single hour without chains and blows." Xanthippe said to him, "But you allow these things by your own free will, since you have not neglected your preaching even to [the point of] scourging, but I tell you this again, so that your bonds will be the defeat of the prompter, and your humiliation their overthrow."

10. Now the report of his presence ran through the whole city and the surrounding country, for some from that city, having been at Rome, had seen the signs and wonders that were done by the blessed Paul and came to

see if this was he. Therefore, many came into the house of Probus, and he began to be annoyed and to say, "I will not allow my house to be made an inn." Xanthippe, knowing that the face of Probus had begun to be estranged, and that he spoke thus, was greatly distressed, saying, "Oh, wretched me! We will not be thought fully worthy to keep this man in our house; for if Paul comes here, the assembly will also be held elsewhere." Then Xanthippe, considering these matters, put her hand on the foot of Paul, and taking dust, she called Probus to her, and placing her hand on the middle of his breast, [she prayed:] "O LORD my God, who have sought me out—lowly one and ignorant of You—send what is right into this heart." And Paul perceived her prayer, and made the Sign of the Cross, and for several days the people entered unhindered, and as many as had sick and those disturbed by unclean spirits brought them, and all were healed.

11. And Xanthippe said to Paul, "Teacher, my heart is greatly consumed because I have not as of yet received immersion." And after this, Probus, being moved by the Devil again, cast Paul out of the house and shut Xanthippe up in her chamber. Then one of the chief men, Philotheus by name, pleaded with the great Paul to come into his house, but the great Paul was unwilling to do so, saying, "Lest Probus trouble your house on my account." Philotheus said to him, "No, father, I am not subject to him at all, for in no other thing is he greater than me, except in rank, and that because the parents of Xanthippe are above me. But if Probus comes to me, I am above him in riches and in war." Then Paul, the great apostle of the LORD, was persuaded, and went into the house of Philotheus the ex-prefect. All this was done by the evil one, so that Xanthippe might receive holy immersion with tribulation and be fainthearted concerning the commandments of Christ.

12. Therefore, Xanthippe said to her servants with tears: "Have you learned where Paul has gone to?" They said, "Yes—to the house of Philotheus the ex-prefect"; and Xanthippe rejoiced greatly that Philotheus also believed, being able, as she said, to persuade Probus also. Then Probus called Xanthippe to dinner, and when she did not consent, Probus said, "Do not think that you will also keep away from me in bed." But when he reclined for dinner, Xanthippe, bending her knees, prayed to the LORD, saying, "Eternal and immortal God, that took dust from the ground and did not value it according to the nature of its creation, but called it the son of immortality; You who came from the heart of the Father to the heart of the earth for our sake, on whom the cherubim dare not fix their gaze, and for us was hidden in the womb, so that by taking up Your abode in a mother, You might make good the offense of Eve; You that drank gall and vinegar, and was pierced in the side by a spear, so that You might heal the wound given by the rib to Adam—for Eve, being his rib, worked a blow for Adam, and through him for all the world; You that gave imperceptible slumber to the serpent, so that he might not know Your Incarnation: remember also my groaning and tears, and grant fulfillment to my sleep, and bring sleep on Probus until I will be deemed worthy of the gift of holy immersion, for I fervently desire to obtain this—to the glory and praise of Your holy Name."

13. But Probus, while still at dinner, commanded the doors of their house to be secured by cruel and wicked soldiers, and having given these orders, he immediately fell asleep on the couch. Then the servants came and announced this to Xanthippe, so that he might be awakened, but she said, "Put out the lights, my children, and leave him thus." And during the first sleep, taking three hundred pieces of gold, she went to the doors, saying within herself, "Perhaps the porter will be persuaded by the amount of money." But he, being evil and disobedient, would not be persuaded to do this, and she, also untying her girdle, which was set with precious stones and worth two hundred pieces of gold, gave it to him and went out saying, "LORD, I win over my own slaves with money, so that Your preacher Paul may not be oppressed by Probus." And Xanthippe went on to the house of Philotheus the ex-prefect, as to a great and incredible work, running and praising God. As she therefore passed through a certain place, the demons pursued her with fiery torches and lightning, and she, turning, saw behind her this terrible sight, and being possessed with great fear said, "What has happened to you now, O wretched soul? You have been deprived of your desire. You were running to salvation, you were running to immersion, and you have fallen into the serpent and his servants, and your sins have prepared these things for you." Speaking thus, she was even fainting at heart from great despair; but the great Paul, being forewarned by God of the assault of the demons, immediately stood beside her, also being preceded by a beautiful youth. And immediately the vision of the demons disappeared, and Paul said to her, "Arise, daughter Xanthippe, and behold the LORD desired by you, by whose flame the heavens are shaken and the deep is dried up, coming to you, and pitying and saving you. Behold Him who accepts your prayers and listens immediately. See Him coming in the shape of a man and take courage against the demons." Then she, rising from the ground, said to him, "Master, why have you left me alone? Even now, be quick to seal me, so that if death overtakes me, I may depart to Him who is full of compassion and has no arrogance."

14. Therefore, the great Paul, immediately taking her hand, went into the house of Philotheus and immersed her in the Name of the Father, and of the Son, and of the Holy Spirit. Then taking bread, he also gave her communion, saying, "Let this be to you for forgiveness of sins and for a renewing of your soul." Then the blessed Xanthippe, receiving the divine grace of holy immersion, returned to her own house, rejoicing and praising the LORD. The porter, seeing her, complained loudly in violent words, so that her departure might be deemed to have been without his will if Probus should notice it; but he that gave her light along with Paul kept the whole house, together with Probus, in a deep sleep, and they did not hear his words at all. Then she went running into her bedchamber, saying, "What will I say of You, searcher out of sinners, who are most present with us in tribulations? Your goodness does these things, since for the sake of man whom You made You went down even to death, for however many times man arouses You to anger, yet You, O LORD, pour out Your mercies on him. O depth of compassion and wealth of mercy; O immeasurable goodness and incomparable kindness; O treasure of good things, and giver of mercy, and enricher of all who believe in You! If, therefore, one who loves You says, Be near me, LORD, You have already anticipated him. If he says, I give You thanks; hear my words, before they are spoken, You understand. And as for those that ask of You, You give to each after his asking. Your goodness seeks out those that do not know You, and You run to sinners. O cheerful look, filling the ways of sinners with mercy; O excellent watching and exhortation of the ignorant! Who will tell my lord Paul of the salvation that has now happened to me, so that he might come and give words of thanksgiving for me to this Protector of sinners? Come, many, and behold and know the LORD, who hates sin, but has mercy on sinners. Come, now, O Paul, preacher of God, for even with you I now sit under instruction; and give words of thanksgiving for me, for I desire to keep silent, since human reason makes me afraid, and I do not have the grace of eloquence. I desire to keep silent and [yet] am compelled to speak, for someone inflames and sweetens me within. If I say, I will shut my mouth, there is someone that murmurs within me. Will I say a great thing? Is it not that Teacher that is within Paul, without arrogance, filling the heavens, speaking within and waiting without, sitting on the throne with the Father and stretched on the Cross by man? What, therefore, I will do I do not know. My worthless mind delights me and is not unfolded to the end. You that had Your hands fixed with nails and Your side pierced with the spear—You star out of Jacob and lion's cub out of Judah; You rod out of Jesse and man and God out of Mary; You invisible God in the bosom of the Father, that cannot be looked on by cherubim and are mocked in Israel: glory be to You, who appeared on the earth and was taken by the people, hung on the tree, and by the report of the wicked, falsely said to be stolen, and that have purchased all of us together."

15. While she was still speaking this, a cross appeared on the eastern wall, and immediately there entered through it a beautiful Youth, having trembling rays [of light] around Him, and under Him an extended light, on which He also walked. And as He entered within, all the foundations of that house shook and reverberated with a great trembling. Xanthippe, seeing Him, cried out and fell to the ground as if dead; but He, being pitiful and kind, changing immediately into the shape of Paul, raised her up, saying, "Arise, Xanthippe, and do not fear, for the servants of God are thus glorified." Then Xanthippe arising, gazed on Him, and thinking He was Paul, said, "How have You come in here, preacher of God, seeing that I have given five hundred pieces of gold to the porter, and that although he is my slave, while You have no money?" The LORD said to her, "My servant Paul is richer than all wealth, for whatever treasure he acquires here, he sends it before him into the kingdom of the heavens, so that departing there, he may rest in the unending and eternal rest. This is the treasure of Paul: you and your like." Then Xanthippe, gazing on Him [and] desiring to say something, saw his face shining as the light; and being greatly amazed, and putting both of her hands over her face, she threw herself to the ground and said, "Hide Yourself, LORD, from my bodily eyes and enlighten my understanding, for I now know who You are: You are He whose precursor was the Cross, the only-begotten Son of the Father alone above, and only Son of the virgin alone below; You are He who was pierced in the hands and who tore the rocks; You are He whom none other can carry except the bosom of the Father."

16. And as she spoke this, the LORD was again hidden from her, and Xanthippe, coming to herself, said, "Woe is me, O wretched one, that no one has told me what the gratitude of slaves is toward their master. If Paul, the preacher of the LORD, were here, how could he give praise? But perhaps in the face of such favors and gifts they are silent, possessed only with tears, for it is not possible to praise anyone worthily according to his favor." Saying this, she was seized with great faintness from lack of food, for having been strongly possessed with desire for Christ, she had forgotten to take nourishment. Therefore, being greatly exhausted by abstinence, and the vision, and lack of sleep and other austerities, she was unable to rise from the ground.

17. And Probus arose from his couch with a very gloomy countenance, for in his sleep he had seen a dream and was greatly troubled concerning it. But the porter seeing him about to proceed to the marketplace, having his countenance thus troubled, was greatly afraid, "Lest," he said, "he understand what has happened, and will miserably destroy me." Probus, however, having gone forth and signified to those in the market what was suitable for the day and season, quickly returned into the house and said to his servants, "Quickly call the wise men Barandus and Gnosteas to me." When they were summoned, he said to them, "I have seen a very terrible vision, and what appeared in it is difficult for our power to interpret. However, disclose this to me, as being the most excellent [interpreters] in all the world. Explain it to me when I tell it to you." Barandus says to him, "If the vision can be interpreted by our wisdom, we will explain it to you, but if it regards the faith that is now spoken of, we cannot explain it to you, for it is of another wisdom and understanding. However, let our lord and master tell the dream, and let us see if there is any explanation for it." Probus says to Gnosteas, "Why do you say nothing?" Gnosteas said, "I have not heard the dream, and what can I say but whatever it may be, if it is by reason of Paul? Tell me now, and you will find it so." Probus said, "I thought I was standing in a certain unknown and strange country, and that an Ethiopian king sat there, who ruled over all the earth and never seemed to have any successor. Multitudes of servants stood beside him, and all [of them] hastened to destroy and had mastery far and wide. And when that Ethiopian seemed to have gained his purpose, there arose a raven, and standing above him, it croaked with a pitiful voice. And immediately there arose from the eastern parts an eagle, and it seized his kingdom, and his power was made vain, and those standing by him fled to the eagle. Then that king strove against those that fled to the eagle, but the eagle carried it up into Heaven, and behold, there came a Helper to those that fled to the eagle and left His staff to them. Then laying hold of it, they were not overcome by the violence of that king. As many as ran to those who had the staff, He washed them in pure water, and they that were washed had power over his kingdom. And by that staff, the enemies [serving] the king were put to flight, therefore capable men laying hold of the staff turned great multitudes to themselves. And that king strove against them, and had no might at all, but he hindered many from believing in Him that sent out the men into the world to bear witness, and for that reason many were grieved. Nevertheless, this one did not constrain any like the other, for He Himself was ruler of all light. This then was the end."

18. Then the wise Barandus said, "By the grace of God I will explain the things sent into the world by the LORD. The king whom you saw is the Devil, and the multitudes of his servants are the demons, and the throngs around him are they that worship the gods. Whereas he thought to have no successor, he did not look for the coming of Christ. The raven portended the weakness of his kingdom, for the raven did not remain obedient to the righteous Noah, but loved pitiful things. The eagle that arose, and took away his kingdom, and carried it up into Heaven, and that there came a protector of those that fled to the eagle, having a staff, that is the Lord Jesus Christ, who left to them His staff, that is, His precious Cross; and that He washed those that fled to Him signifies the invulnerable breastplate of immersion, and therefore they were not overcome. The capable men sent into the world with the Cross are the preachers of God, like Paul who is now with us, against whom that king has no power. This was made known to you because even on those who are hard in unbelief, God has compassion in some way. See therefore whether even you will be able to injure Paul though you desire, for the mighty power that shields him has been shown to you by the LORD. Therefore, understand what has been said to you by me, and do not serve that king of darkness, for as you saw his kingdom vanish away, so will all his servants perish with him. Therefore, come now, my lord, [and] let us go to Paul and receive immersion from him, lest Satan have mastery over us also." Probus said, "Let us first go to Xanthippe and see whether she still lives, for behold, there are twenty-nine days since she has tasted anything; for I saw her face in the evening, and it was as of one prepared to depart."

19. And as they went into the chamber, they heard her singing: "Praise the LORD, you sinners also, || Because He accepts your prayers also—Hallelujah! Praise the LORD, you that have despaired like me, || For His mercies are many—Hallelujah! Praise Him, you ungodly, || Because He was crucified for you—Hallelujah! Praise Him, you that strive for the salvation of sinners, || Because God loves you—Hallelujah! Praise Him, you that rejoice at the calling of sinners, || Because you are fellow-citizens with the holy ones—Hallelujah!" As she said these words and more than these with tears, the wise men Barandus and Gnosteas, opening the door, entered and fell at her feet, saying, "Pray for us lowly ones, O servant of Christ, that He may also bring us into your number." But she said to them, "Brothers, I am not Paul who remits sins, but neither is he far from you. Therefore, do not fall before my knees, but go to him, who is also more able to benefit you." Then they came running to the house of Philotheus to Paul and found him teaching a great multitude. And Probus also came to hear Paul, and Xanthippe entered along with him to salute him, and coming near to Paul and bending her knees, she paid him homage. Seeing this, Probus marveled that her very proud spirit had changed to such great humility, for she sat beside the feet of Paul on the ground humbly and as one of the worthless. And Probus was greatly grieved, not yet attending to the hearing of the word, but was continuously gazing and fixing his attention on Xanthippe.

20. The great Paul was teaching thus, "Let those that burn in the flesh observe lawful marriage, avoiding fornication, especially that with another's wife; and let those that are united keep to one another." Probus heard this teaching with delight and said, "O Paul, how excellently and wisely you employ this teaching. Why then has Xanthippe withdrawn from me?" And Paul said, "My son Probus, they that foresee that the works of men will be tried with fire, and that always have in their mind the certainty of death, cast out all desire that cleaves to the flesh. But woe when the desire will judge him that desired; then he will gnash his teeth to no effect and in vain, for the amendment of conversion is past." Hearing this, Probus went up into his house marveling and tasted nothing that day, but went and lay down on his bed. And about the third hour of the night, he arose and said, "Oh how wretched was the day in which I was wedded to Xanthippe! If only I had died and not seen her." Saying this, he arose and said, "I will pray to the God of Paul. Perhaps He will also do to me what is right, so that I may not become a reproach in the world, being rejected by her." And immediately, falling on the ground, he said, "O God of Paul, if, as I have heard from Xanthippe, You seek after the ignorant and turn back those that have gone astray, also do to me what is right; for You are the King of life and death, as I have heard, and have dominion over things in Heaven, and on earth, and under the earth, and over all the thoughts and desires of men, and to You alone belongs glory for all eternity. Amen."

21. Then Probus, arising from the ground, fell again on the couch; and arising early, he came to Paul, and finding him immersing many in the Name of the lifegiving Trinity, he said, "My lord Paul, if only I were worthy to receive immersion—behold the hour." Paul said to him, "Son, behold the water is ready for the cleansing of those that come to Christ." Therefore, immediately taking off his clothes, and Paul laying hold of him, he leapt into the water, saying, "Jesus Christ, Son of God, and everlasting God: let all my sins be taken away by this water." And Paul said, "We immerse you in the Name of the Father, and Son, and Holy Spirit." After this, he made him to receive the communion of Christ. Then Xanthippe, having greatly rejoiced, began in the house toward evening, together with her husband, to celebrate with all those in the house and to prepare a feast, and when they came, after lofty orders for the dinner to be magnificent, she herself went up to the chamber. And behold, on the stairs a demon coming in the likeness of one of the actors, and standing in a dark corner, was desirous to frighten and terrify Xanthippe. But she, thinking it to be the actor that she ordinarily had, said in anger, "Many times I have said to him that I no longer care for games, and he despises me as being a woman"; and immediately seizing an iron lampstand, she hurled it at his face and crushed all his features. Then the demon cried out, saying, "Violence from this destroyer! Even women have received power to strike us!" But Xanthippe was greatly afraid.

ACT OF POLYXENA

22. After dinner, Probus then went forth to hear the word, but Xanthippe, sitting in her bedchamber, was reading the Prophets, [and] her sister Polyxena was lying on the couch. Xanthippe loved Polyxena exceedingly, because she was younger than herself, and beautiful in appearance, and Probus also loved her greatly. And as Polyxena lay on the couch, she saw this dream, that a dragon, hideous in appearance, came and signaled to her to come to him, and when she did not obey him to go to him, he came running and swallowed her. From fear of this, the girl leapt up trembling, and Xanthippe, running to her, said, "What has happened to you, dearest, that you have leapt up so suddenly?" For a long time she was unable to speak; then coming to herself, she said, "Oh, my sister Xanthippe! What [great] danger or tribulation awaits me, I do not know; for I saw in my dream that a hideous dragon came and signaled to me to come to him, and, when I would not go, he came running and swallowed me, beginning at my feet. While I was terrified at this, there suddenly spoke out of the air, in the light of the sun, a beautiful Youth, whom I thought to be the brother of Paul, saying, Truly, you have no power. Who also took me by the hand and immediately drew me out of him, and immediately the dragon disappeared. And behold, His hand was full of sweet aroma as of balsam or anything else for fragrance." Xanthippe said to her, "Truly, you must be greatly troubled, my sister Polyxena, but God holds you dear, seeing that He has shown you strange and marvelous things. Therefore, arise quickly in the morning, and receive holy immersion, and ask in the immersion to be delivered from the snares of the dragon."

23. Xanthippe, having said this to Polyxena, and having made a cross of wood, went to Paul, but Polyxena remained alone in the bedchamber, her nurse having gone together with Xanthippe. And about the middle of the night, a certain man, powerful in wealth and assistance, finding the doors open and using magical arts, entered within, desiring to carry Polyxena away. Discovering this, she fled into the mill, but the magicians led by the demons found her. And she, not finding any door to escape by, said, "Aah! I am given over to this destroyer"; for she had heard that he was at enmity with her suitor, and he did this to attack and trouble him, being a man who was a robber and exceedingly cruel. Therefore, seizing her, they went out of the city, dragging her to the sea. She looked around this way and that, but there was no one to deliver her; and groaning, she said, "Oh, my sister Xanthippe, you sent seven hundred pieces of gold to Rome and buy books, that through them you might prophesy by me; for this evening you read, I looked to my right hand and beheld, but there was no one that knew me; flight perished from me, and there is no one that seeks out my soul."

24. While she said these words, those that were dragging her away walked in haste, and coming to the shore, they hired a ship and sailed for Babylonia, for he that carried her off had a brother there, a ruler of a district. But the wind blew against them, so that they could not proceed by reason of it, and as they were rowing on the sea, behold, the great apostle of the LORD, Peter, was sailing past in a ship, being urged by a dream to go to Rome, because when Paul departed for Spain, there had entered into Rome a certain deceiver and magician, Simon by name, and had broken up the assembly which Paul had established. And behold, as he journeyed he heard a voice from Heaven saying to him, "Peter, tomorrow a ship coming from Spain will meet you; therefore, arise and pray for the soul that is troubled in it." Therefore, as soon as Peter saw the ship, remembering the dream, he said, "O Jesus, that have care for the troubled, whom the tribulation of those in a strange land moves to compassion, whom the weeping of those in captivity made to come on the earth, who give us whatsoever we desire at all times, and never turn away from our request, show now also pity and assistance to the soul that is tossed around in that ship, because You, O LORD, pity those in pain at all times." The demons then, perceiving his prayer, said to the magicians, "Avoid the course of that ship, for if we meet with it, we cannot move."

25. But the loving God, taking care of Polyxena, the vessel arrived in Greece, the blessed Philip being there (having come down to the shore by a vision), and there also accompanied him great multitudes of those who were being taught by him. And behold, the vessel which Polyxena was in appeared, terribly tossed about. And the blessed Philip said, "See the vessel, on account of which we came down here, in which there is a soul in trouble." When the vessel arrived, and everyone had disembarked on the dry land, they lay as half dead, because they had been greatly tossed around in the sea. But the apostle Philip ordered Polyxena to be lifted and taken to the place where he was lodging, and the rest to be tended to. But he that had carried off Polyxena, recovering from the disorder of the sea, was desirous to take her again, for Philip, having entrusted Polyxena to one of those that were taught by him, went on his way rejoicing. But he that had her said, "She was committed to me by a holy man, and I cannot give her up to you." He, however, giving no heed to him and finding a relation of his there, a nobleman, prepared for war, gathering eight thousand men. Polyxena, knowing this, went forth by night and departed, but he that had charge of Polyxena said, "Taking the tunic of Philip, I will go forth alone to meet them"; but as he said this, it was announced to him that the maid was not there. Then he, leaving all thought of the war, ran into the bedchamber, and not finding the maid threw himself on the ground, saying, "Woe is me, wretched one, that have become an enemy of Philip! What will I answer him, when he asks [for] the maiden from me?" His servants came and said to him, "Arise, our lord, from the ground, for the forces have surrounded your house, and the maid cannot be found." He said, "Leave me thus to die on her account. Perhaps, even by this, Philip the servant of Christ may be fully satisfied, since I will be found despising his command." Then the servants, seeing that he did not listen to them, took counsel to flee from the enemies, but again after a little while, being moved by the foreknowledge of God, they said, "It is not right for our master to die. Come, let us go forth to meet them, raising the Sign of the Cross." Then, raising the precious Cross, they went forth, about thirty men, on the enemy, and slew five thousand, and the rest fled. And they returned with victory to their master, praising God and saying, "What God is so great as our God, who has not allowed His servant to be slain by the wicked?" And coming on their lord, still weeping, they said to him, "Arise, lord, and do not weep, for it is right to not be as we will, but as the Lord wills."

26. Polyxena, however, going out of the city, and not knowing by what way she should walk, found herself in desert places of the hills, and sitting down, said thus with tears, "Woe is me—outcast and captive—that I cannot find even a wild beast's den to rest in. Woe is me, left desolate, that not even Hades, that no one escapes, has devoured me. Woe is me, who at one time did not even show myself to my servants, now display myself to demons. Woe is me, that I am now made manifest to all those by whom I disdained to be seen. Woe is me, that was formerly devoted to idols; for this, now even the mercy of God has passed me in silence. Whom then will I call on to help me? The God of Paul whom I have constantly offended? But who will help me now? No one sees, or heeds, or hears my groaning. Truly I will beg Him that sees the hidden things, for who is more pitiful and compassionate than He who always keeps watch over the oppressed? But because my mouth is unclean and defiled, I do not dare ask for help from Him. If only I were as one of the wild beasts, so that I might not know what captivity is. If only I had been drowned in the sea; perhaps having received the divine immersion, I should have gone where no one is made captive. What then will I do, for death delays, and night has come on, and there is no help anywhere?" Having said this, she arose and began to walk onwards, and passing through a narrow area, she fell into very thick and large woods, and finding a hollow in a tree there, which was the den of a lioness, she sat down there, for the lioness had gone forth for her food. And sitting down, she said, "O wretched begetting, O grievous hour in which I, unhappy one, came into this world; O mother that bore me: why, foreseeing my troubles and wanderings, did you name me Polyxena? Has anyone else ever fallen into such tribulations and misfortunes? Truly, my sister Xanthippe, you read concerning me, [the] unhappy one, saying, I have suffered affliction and been utterly bowed down. You uttered these words with grief, while I lay on the couch, not contemplating all of my sorrows. On this account, I have now come into the depths of evils and pass the night in deserts like a wild beast. But the beasts live with others of their kind, while I am left solitary, as not being of one race with mankind."

27. And as she was saying these words, and more than these, the morning dawned, and the lioness came from her hunting. Polyxena, seeing the wild beast, trembled and said, "By the God of Paul: O wild beast, have compassion on me, and do not tear me apart until I receive immersion." And the wild beast, fearing the adjuration, immediately went away, and standing far off, it gazed at her. And she said, "Behold, the beast has obeyed me; I will also depart from its dwelling." And she immediately began to journey toward the east, and the beast went before her until she had come out of the wood. Then Polyxena said, "What will I give to you in return, O beast? The God of Paul will repay you [for] this kindness"; and the wild beast, hearing her prayer, immediately returned to its place. Then she, descending, found a public road, and standing on it wept, not knowing where she should go, and though many went past, she turned to none of them, but said, "Perhaps the God of Paul will remember me, and whoever will have pity on me, to him will I go."

28. As she said this, Andrew, the apostle of the Lord, also came journeying to that place, and as he drew near to Polyxena, he felt in his heart some commotion arising in himself. Therefore, standing to pray and folding his arms in the shape of the Cross, he said, "Lord Jesus Christ, partaker of light and knower of hidden things, from whom nothing on earth is hid, do to me kindness and mercy, and make clear to me this commotion in [my] heart, and calm my reason—You that always make peace with those that love peace." Then Polyxena ran to him, and Andrew, the apostle of the Lord, said to her, "Do not approach me, daughter, but tell me who and from where you are." Polyxena said, "My lord, I am a stranger here, but I see [that] your face is gracious, and your words as the words of Paul, and I suppose you to be of the same God." Andrew understood that she spoke of the apostle Paul, and he said to her, "And from where do you know of Paul?" She said, "From my own country, for I left him in Spain." Andrew said to her, "And how do you happen to be here—that country being [so] far away?" She said, "Because it was thus appointed for me and came to pass; but I beg you and fall at your feet: seal me, as Paul seals, by the immersion of regeneration, so that even I, lowly one, may be known by our God, for the kind God, seeing my tribulation and distress, sent you to pity me." Andrew, the great apostle of the Lord, said to her, "Let us go, daughter, where there is water."

ACT OF REBECCA

29. And when they had gone a short distance, they came to a well most transparent and pure. And as the blessed Andrew stood to pray beside the well, behold, a certain maiden named Rebecca, of the tribe of Israel, brought as a captive to that country, came to draw water at the well, and seeing the blessed Andrew, knew him by his appearance. For Rebecca said, "This is the appearance of a prophet, and this is one of the apostles." And bowing down to him, she said, "Have mercy on me, servant of the true God, who am captive and sold for the third time, who was once honored by prophets and am now insulted by idolaters; and recall me, lowly one—you that were sent to call back many sinners." Andrew, the apostle of Christ, said, "God will care for you also, daughter, as well as for this stranger. Therefore, receive immersion now and be as of one people, glorifying God always."

30. Therefore, the apostle prayed standing, and behold, the lioness came running and stood gazing at him. And Andrew, the apostle of the Lord, said, "What then does this beast want?" Opening her mouth, the lioness spoke with a human voice: "Andrew, apostle of Christ: the prayer of her who stands on your right hand has overtaken me. Therefore, confirm, and instruct, and admonish them in the right and true faith of Christ, for they greatly desire the Name of the Lord." And behold the wonderful humility of God, that even on irrational and untamable beasts He has poured out His mercy. Weeping, the blessed Andrew said, "What will I say or what will I speak concerning Your mercy, O God, that You thus cleave to the lowly at all times and take care of those in ignorance, being without arrogance and full of mercy?" And having completed the prayer, he immersed the maidens in the Name of the Father, Son, and Holy Spirit. Then the lioness immediately set off to the mountain, and the Apostle Andrew said to the maidens, "Be zealous, daughters, to be of good reputation before God by living well in a strange land, and do not separate from each other, and may God, who is always present to those that call on Him, keep you in holiness, driving the evil one away from you. And pray also for me." Polyxena said, "We will follow you wherever you go." The apostle Andrew said, "This was not made known to me by the Lord, daughters; therefore, remain with peace, hoping in the Lord, and He will preserve you to the end."

31. And Andrew went on his way, rejoicing and glorifying God. Then Polyxena said, "Where will we go, sister?" Rebecca said, "Let us depart to wherever you desire, lest my mistress send and separate us." Polyxena said, "Come, let us depart to the lioness in the mountain." Rebecca said, "It is indeed better for us to live with wild beasts and perish of hunger than to be compelled by Greeks and idolaters to fall into the filth of marriage." So, they began to journey, and behold, by the providence of God, they met a man driving donkeys, who seeing them said, "You are not of this country, and, as I see, you do not wear its [customary] attire. Therefore, command your servant to eat bread and receive one piece of silver, so that you may remember your servant when you buy bread." And he made haste, and took the sacks off his donkeys, and spread them on the ground, and made the maidens to sit on them, and said to them, "Seeing that the wine which your servant carries is gathered by Greeks, tell me of what faith you are, that we may thus taste of it." Polyxena said, "We, brother, taste no wine, and are of the God of Paul." The donkey-driver said, "Is this God on earth?" Polyxena said to him, "God is everywhere—both in Heaven and on earth." The donkey-driver, being desirous to learn clearly, said, "Does this Paul then have the same God that is preached by Philip?" Polyxena, learning that he was a Christian, said, "Yes, brother, this is the God of all, whom Paul and Philip preach."

32. Hearing this, the donkey-driver wept unceasingly, and Polyxena said, "Has then the providence of God overtaken you, that you weep like this?" The donkey-driver said, "If you are desirous to learn why I weep, hear the truth, for one should not hesitate to tell the things of Christ. I was a disciple of Philip, the apostle of Christ, and seeing how all his focus was toward the poor, I took all that I had and sold it. And taking the price, I bought bread and wine and divided them throughout the cities to those that had need; when therefore I had done this for some time in the neighboring city, a certain maimed person cried out, saying (though it was not himself that spoke, but Satan through his mouth), I desire nothing; I take nothing from you, because you are a Christian. Then the whole city arose against me and sought to take me, but some ran one way and some another, while I went through their midst, and no one saw me. And leaving from the city, I gave praise and glory to God that I had been thus rewarded, and I prayed to my God that I should meet someone who knew His all-holy Name, so that relating these things, I might obtain relief. For the men of this country will not hear at all concerning Christ, being full of impiety and filled with wickedness. I therefore exhort you: take one coin from me also, and if it seems good, also rest on the donkeys." Polyxena said, "May you obtain mercy from God, brother. But if you will receive a full reward, deliver us as far as the sea, so that, if God wills, we may sail for Spain."

33. The donkey-driver, as if commanded by the voice of God, eagerly receiving the maidens, went on his way rejoicing in the LORD. And he said to Polyxena, "Alter your appearance to that of a man, lest for your beauty's sake someone may snatch you away from me." And coming to an inn, they stayed there, and the next day they went forward, paying careful attention to the way. And behold, there came past a certain prefect journeying to Greece, who, seeing the maidens, ordered Polyxena to be carried off on his chariot. Then the donkey-driver followed, crying and saying, "A prefect does violence to no one! Why do you do this?" Then they beat him and drove him away.

34. And he, going on his way, lamented, saying, "Woe is me—wretched and abominable one! Woe is me, that thought to do good, but now I have caused trouble! Woe is me, that my trouble and my course were unacceptable! If only I had died before yesterday, so that I might not have met with these maidens at all. But why do you trouble me, O wretched soul? Let us go to Philip, the apostle of God. If there is no forgiveness for me, it is better for me to choose death in whatsoever fashion than to live with such evil and bitter conscience." So, he went and found Philip, the apostle of Christ, and said to him, "O disciple and preacher of Christ, thus and thus has happened to me and overtaken me. Does my soul have salvation?" Philip, the apostle of Christ, said, "Do not be distressed concerning this, my son, it is impossible for them to be dishonored, seeing that no one ever overcomes God; for this same Polyxena, when she first came from the sea, I entrusted to a certain brother, who was also greatly distressed because of her running away secretly from his house. Him also I persuaded not to grieve, for through her tribulation and wanderings, many will know God."

35. The prefect therefore carried Polyxena to the city where he stayed and ordered her to be shut up in a chamber. And one of the soldiers seized Rebecca, but the maid, secretly escaping, fled into the house of an old woman, who received the maiden kindly and implored her well. And sitting down, she wept, saying, "Oh, my sister Polyxena! I, [the] wretched one, did not think that anyone was oppressed like myself, but now I am persuaded and know that all my misfortunes and tribulations do not compare with one day of yours. And most grievous of all: behold, I have been separated from you and am again a captive, but search for me, even into the next world, my sister Polyxena." The old woman said to her, "What bothers you, daughter, that you weep so bitterly?" Rebecca said, "Allow me, mother, to be distressed and to lament the great and incurable pain of my heart." The old woman, greatly sympathizing with her, wept greatly, for the maid had told her all that had happened to her, and how through Polyxena she had believed in Christ. So too Polyxena, shut up in the chamber, said, "Woe is me—wretched one! Woe for me—miserable one! Now I clearly know how the Devil hates virginity, but O Lord Jesus Christ, God of all, since I do not dare beg You by myself, I bring to you the prayers of Your holy preacher Paul, so that You might not allow my virginity to be destroyed by anyone."

36. And as she was yet praying, the attendants came to lead her to the couch of the prefect. But Polyxena said to them, "Brothers, do not hurry to anyone's destruction, for this time will quickly pass away, and they that work together with the destroyers will perish with them. Rather, assist strangers, so that you are not found strangers to the messengers of God." The men, being shamed by these words, went to the prefect and said, "The maid, from fear, is seized with a violent fever." And the prefect said, "Leave her alone." And behold, the son of the prefect came to Polyxena by night, and she seeing him was afraid, but the youth said to her, "Do not fear, girl. I do not seek to be wedded with you as the bridegroom of destruction, for I know from your prayer that you are the bride of the God of Heaven. I know this God, who is never overcome by anyone, for a certain man of glorious countenance recently preached this God in Antioch, and a certain maid, whose name was Thecla, believing him followed him and encountered dangers on account of her beauty, of whom I have heard that she was condemned to the wild beasts. Therefore, I continually gazed on the man, and he having observed me said to me, God give regard to you, my son. Therefore, from that time on I have not gone into the sacrifices of idols by the grace of Christ, but sometimes pretending illness and sometimes involving myself in some business, my father said to me, Because you have no zeal for the sacrifices of the gods, therefore neither are you in good health, not being worthy of the gods. But I rejoiced, hearing that I was not worthy of the sacrifices to idols; and by the grace of God, you have come here as providence to me." Polyxena said, "And what is the name of that man?" The youth said, "Paul is his name." Polyxena said, "He is in my city." The youth said, "Come then, girl; put on my appearance, and go down to the shore, and wait for me there; having taken money, I will come quickly."

37. And one of the servants overhearing them, told all of this to the prefect, who being filled with great anger, condemned them to be thrown to the wild beasts. And when they were thrown into the arena, a fierce lioness was let loose on them, which ran and embraced the feet of Polyxena and licked the soles of her feet. Then the prefect and all the city, seeing this fearful and wonderful sight, gave praise and glory to the merciful God, saying, "You—and He, that is named by Polyxena—are God alone, for the gods of the heathen are the works of men's hands, unable to save or assist anyone. Let them perish now, both themselves and their makers." And the prefect, immediately taking his son and Polyxena into the palace, heard from them in order the faith and religion in Christ without omission, and he and all in the city believed, and there was great joy and giving of glory to God. And Polyxena said to the prefect, "Be of good cheer, my lord, for the man of God will quickly come, who will perfectly teach, exhort, instruct, and enlighten you in the knowledge of Christ." She, however, quickly prepared to depart into Spain.

38. And as I, Onesimus, was sailing into Spain to Paul, I received from the LORD a revelation saying to me, "Onesimus, the vessel which you are now in will land in the regions of Greece, and you will find on the shore of the harbor two maids and one youth. Assist them and take them to Paul." When we reached this place according to the command of the LORD, we found the maids, together with the youth, seeking a vessel. Therefore, when the maids saw us, they knew that we were of the hope of Christ, and Polyxena running to us said, "Truly the man of God cannot be concealed, for the grace and kindness of his countenance makes him evident." And when we sought to sail away, the sea was troubled by the providence of God. And a disciple of Paul was with us, Lucius by name, capable in word to teach the city. Therefore, we remained seven days, and God opened a great door of faith to that place, and twenty thousand believed, and there was great joy and rejoicing throughout the whole city. And when the season was favorable for us to sail, the prefect again constrained us, and we stayed another seven days, until everyone believed and rejoiced in the LORD.

39. Thus, now by the foreknowledge of Christ, the prefect sent us away with supplies for the voyage, also sending his son with us. And when we had sailed twenty days, Polyxena was greatly exhausted, and we stopped at a certain island for the sake of rest. And behold, certain fierce and hardened men, coming down to us and seeing Polyxena, prepared for battle; but by the grace of Christ, our men defended Polyxena and vanquished them, although the strangers were more numerous and more powerful. Polyxena, therefore fearing becoming a captive again, threw herself into the sea; but the captain dragged her out, having suffered no harm. Then we embarked in the vessel and fled, for the places were rough and wooded, and we were afraid to remain, and in twelve days we arrived in Spain, by the grace of God.

40. And Paul, seeing us, rejoiced greatly, and he said, "Welcome, you that have been troubled." And Polyxena, laying hold of his feet, said, "It may be that this trouble came on me because I would have blasphemed you, but now I beg and plead that I may not be delivered into such troubles and misfortunes again." And Paul said, weeping, "Thus must we be troubled, my daughter, so that we may know our defender, Jesus Christ."

41. And while we were giving the letters of the brothers to Paul, one ran and told Xanthippe of the arrival of Polyxena. And she made haste and came to us, and seeing Polyxena, was overcome by an unspeakable joy and fell to the ground; but Polyxena, embracing her and caressing her for a long time, brought her back to life. Then Xanthippe said to her, "I, my true sister Polyxena, did not go forth at all for forty days, praying much for you to the loving God, that your virginity might not be taken away." And Paul, the preacher of God, said to me, "Her virginity will not be taken away, and she will come quickly." And Probus said to me, "It was assigned to her by God to be afflicted like this. Do you see how by many methods God saves many? But now, my beloved sister, having unexpectedly seen your face, I will now willingly die."

42. Then he who had carried her away came up again and sought for Polyxena, but the great Paul persuaded him to refrain from her, and he also believed and was immersed by Paul, as also the suitor of Polyxena believed, and there was great joy in all that city of Spain for the recovery of Polyxena. From that time forward, she did not leave the blessed Paul at all because of her fear of temptations. These things then being thus, everyone rejoiced in the LORD, glorifying [the] Father, Son, and Holy Spirit—one God, to whom is glory and power, now and forever, and to all eternity. Amen.

ACTS OF PERPETUA AND FELICITAS

The Acts of Perpetua and Felicitas is an early Christian martyrdom text recounting the imprisonment and execution of Perpetua, a young noblewoman, and Felicitas, a pregnant slave, along with others in Carthage. Written partly by Perpetua herself, it details their arrest in AD 203 during Emperor Septimius Severus' persecution of Christians. Refusing to renounce their faith, they faced trials, imprisonment, and eventual death in the arena, mauled by wild beasts and executed by sword. This account offers a vivid firsthand narrative of early Christian courage and steadfastness amid Roman persecution.

PREFACE

If ancient illustrations of faith which both testify to God's grace and tend to man's edification are collected in writing, so that by the scrutiny of them, as if by the reproduction of the facts, as well God may be honored, as man may be strengthened; why should new instances not also be collected, that will be equally suitable for both purposes—if only on the ground that these modern examples will one day become ancient and available for posterity, although in their present time they are considered of less authority, by reason of the presumed veneration of antiquity? But let men look into it, if they judge the power of the Holy Spirit to be one, according to the times and seasons; since some things of later date must be regarded of more account as being nearer to the very last times, in accordance with the abundance of grace manifested in the final periods determined for the world. For "in the last days, says the LORD, || I will pour out of My Spirit on all flesh, || And their sons and their daughters will prophesy. And on My servants and My handmaidens I will pour out My Spirit, || And your young men will see visions, || And your old men will dream dreams." And thus we—who both acknowledge and revere modern visions as equally promised to us, even as we do the [ancient] prophecies, and consider the other powers of the Holy Spirit as an agency of the Assembly for which He was also sent, administering all gifts in all, even as the LORD distributed to everyone as well—necessarily collect them in writing and commemorate them in reading to God's glory, so that no weakness or despondency of faith may suppose that the divine grace dwelt only among the ancients, whether in respect of the humility that raised up martyrs, or that gave revelations; since God always carries into effect what He has promised, for a testimony to unbelievers, to believers for a benefit. And we therefore, what we have heard and handled, declare also to you, brothers and little children, so that just as you who were concerned in these matters [directly] may be reminded of them again to the glory of the LORD, so too you who know them by report may have communion with the blessed martyrs, and through them with the Lord Jesus Christ, to whom be glory and honor, forever and ever. Amen.

CHAPTER 1

1. The young catechumens, Revocatus and his fellow-servant Felicitas, Saturninus and Secundulus, were apprehended. And among them was also Vivia Perpetua, respectably born, liberally educated, a married matron, having a father, and mother, and two brothers (one of whom, like herself, was a catechumen), and a son, an infant at the breast. She herself was about twenty-two years of age. From this point onward she will herself narrate the whole course of her martyrdom, as she left it described by her own hand and with her own mind.

2. "While," she says, "we were still with the persecutors, and my father, for the sake of his affection for me, was persisting in seeking to turn me away, and to cast me down from the faith—Father, I said, do you see, let us say, this vessel lying here to be a little pitcher, or something else? And he said, I see it to be so. And I replied to him, Can it be called by any other name than what it is? And he said, No. Neither can I call myself anything other than what I am: a Christian. Then my father, provoked at this saying, threw himself on me, as if he would tear my eyes out. But he only distressed me and went away overcome by the Devil's arguments. Then, in a few days after I had been without my father, I gave thanks to the LORD; and his absence became a source of consolation to me. In that same interval of a few days, we were immersed, and to me the Spirit prescribed that in the water of immersion nothing else was to be sought for bodily endurance. After a few days, we are taken into the dungeon, and I was very greatly afraid, because I had never felt such darkness. O terrible day! O the fierce heat of the shock of the soldiers, because of the crowds! I was very unusually distressed by my anxiety for my infant. Tertius and Pomponius were present there, the blessed ministers who ministered to us, and had arranged by means of a gratuity that we might be refreshed by being sent out for a few hours into a more pleasant part of the prison. Then, going out of the dungeon, everyone attended to their own needs. I suckled my child, which was now weakened with hunger. In my anxiety for it, I addressed my mother, and comforted my brother, and commended my son to their care. I was languishing because I had seen them languishing on my account. I suffered such concern for many days, and I obtained for my infant to remain in the dungeon with me; and immediately I grew strong and was relieved from distress and anxiety concerning my infant; and the dungeon became to me as it were a palace, so that I preferred being there to being elsewhere.

3. Then my brother said to me, My dear sister, you are already in a position of great dignity, and are such that you may ask for a vision, and that it may be made known to you whether this is to result in a passion or an escape. And I, who knew that I was privileged to converse with the LORD, whose kindnesses I had found to be so great, boldly promised him, and said, I will tell you tomorrow. And I asked, and this was what was shown to me: I saw a golden ladder of marvelous height, reaching up even to the sky, and very narrow, so that persons could only ascend it one by one; and on the sides of the ladder was fixed every kind of iron weapon. There were swords, lances, hooks, [and] daggers, so that if anyone went up carelessly, or not looking upward, he would be torn to pieces, and his flesh would cleave to the iron weapons. And under the ladder itself was crouching a dragon of gigantic proportions, who lay in wait for those who ascended, and frightened them from the ascent. And Saturus went up first, who had subsequently delivered himself up freely on our account, not having been present at the time that we were taken prisoner. And he attained the top of the ladder, and turned toward me, and said to me, Perpetua, I am waiting for you; but be careful that the dragon does not bite you. And I said, In the Name of the Lord Jesus Christ, he will not hurt me. And from under the ladder itself, as if in fear of me, he slowly lifted up his head; and as I stepped on the first step, I stepped on his head. And I went up, and I saw an immense extent of garden, and in the midst of the garden a white-haired Man sitting in the dress of a shepherd, of large stature, milking sheep; and standing around were many thousand white-robed ones. And He raised His head, and looked on me, and said to me, You are welcome, daughter. And He called me, and from the cheese as He was milking, He gave me, as it were, a little cake, and I received it with folded hands; and I ate it, and all who stood around said, Amen. And at the sound of their voices, I was awakened, still tasting a sweetness which I cannot describe. And I immediately related this to my brother, and we understood that it was to be a passion, and we ceased from then on to have any hope in this world."

CHAPTER 2

1. "After a few days, a report prevailed that we should be heard. And then my father came to me from the city, worn out with anxiety. He came up to me, so that he might cast me down, saying, Have pity, my daughter, on my grey hairs. Have pity on your father—if I am worthy to be called a father by you. If with these hands I have brought you up to this flower of your age, if I have preferred you to all your brothers, do not deliver me up to the scorn of men. Have regard for your brothers; have regard for your mother and your aunt; have regard for your son, who will not be able to live after you. Lay aside your courage, and do not bring us all to destruction; for none of us will speak in freedom if you should suffer anything. My father said these things in his affection, kissing my hands and throwing himself at my feet; and with tears, he called me not Daughter, but Lady. And I grieved over the grey hairs of my father, that he alone of all my family would not rejoice over my passion. And I comforted him, saying, On that scaffold, whatever God wills will happen. Therefore, know that we are not placed in our own power, but in that of God. And he departed from me in sorrow.

2. Another day, while we were at dinner, we were suddenly taken away to be heard, and we arrived at the town-hall. At once the rumor spread through the neighborhood of the public place, and an immense number of people were gathered together. We ascend the platform. The rest were interrogated and confessed. Then they came to me, and my father immediately appeared with my boy, and withdrew me from the step, and said in a supplicating tone, Have pity on your baby. And Hilarianus the procurator, who had just received the power of life and death in the place of the proconsul Minucius Timinianus, who was deceased, said, Spare the grey hairs of your father, spare the infancy of your boy, offer sacrifice for the wellbeing of the emperors. And I replied, I will not do so. Hilarianus said, Are you a Christian? And I replied, I am a Christian. And as my father stood there to cast me down from the faith, he was ordered by Hilarianus to be thrown down, and he was beaten with rods. And my father's misfortune grieved me as if I myself had been beaten; I was so grieved for his miserable old age. The procurator then delivers judgment on all of us, and condemns us to the wild beasts, and we went down cheerfully to the dungeon. Then, because my child had been accustomed to be suckled by me, and to stay with me in the prison, I send Pomponius the minister to my father to ask for the infant, but my father would not give it to him. And even as God willed it, the child no longer desired the breast, nor did my breast cause me uneasiness, lest I should be tormented by care for my baby and by the pain of my breasts at once.

3. After a few days, while we were all praying, suddenly, in the middle of our prayer, a word came to me, and I named Dinocrates; and I was amazed that that name had never come into my mind until then, and I was grieved as I remembered his misfortune. And I immediately felt myself to be worthy, and to be called on to ask on his behalf. And I earnestly began to make supplication for him, and to cry with groaning to the LORD. Without delay, on that very night, this was shown to me in a vision: I saw Dinocrates going out from a gloomy place, where there were also several others, and he was parched and very thirsty, with a filthy countenance and pale color, and the wound on his face which he had when he died. This Dinocrates had been my brother after the flesh, seven years of age, who died miserably with disease—his face being so eaten out with cancer, that his death caused revulsion to all men. I had made my prayer for him, and between him and me there was a large interval, so that neither of us could approach the other. And moreover, in the same place where Dinocrates was, there was a pool full of water, having its edge higher than the stature of the boy; and Dinocrates raised himself up as if to drink. And I was grieved that, although that pool held water, still, on account of the height to its edge, he could not drink. And I was aroused and knew that my brother was in suffering. But I trusted that my prayer would bring help to his suffering; and I prayed for him every day until we passed over into the prison of the camp, for we were to fight in the camp-show. Then was the birthday of Geta Caesar, and I made my prayer for my brother day and night, groaning and weeping that he might be granted to me.

4. Then, on the day on which we remained in chains, this was shown to me: I saw that that place which I had formerly observed to be in gloom was now bright; and Dinocrates, with a clean, well-clothed body, was finding refreshment. And where there had been a wound, I saw a scar; and that pool which I had seen before, I now saw with its margin lowered even to the boy's navel. And someone drew water from the pool incessantly, and on its edge was a goblet filled with water; and Dinocrates drew near and began to drink from it, and the goblet did not fail. And when he was satisfied, he went away from the water to play joyfully, after the manner of children, and I awoke. Then I understood that he was translated from the place of punishment."

CHAPTER 3

1. "Again, after a few days, Pudens, a soldier, an assistant overseer of the prison, who began to hold us in high esteem, perceiving that the great power of God was in us, admitted many brothers to see us, so that both we and they might be mutually refreshed. And when the day of the exhibition drew near, my father, worn with suffering, came in to me, and began to tear out his beard, and to throw himself on the earth, and to cast himself down on his face, and to reproach his years, and to utter such words as might move all creation. I grieved for his unhappy old age.

2. The day before that on which we were to fight, I saw in a vision that the minister Pomponius came here to the gate of the prison and knocked forcefully. I went out to him and opened the gate for him; and he was clothed in a richly ornamented white robe, and he had on manifold calliculae. And he said to me, Perpetua, we are waiting for you; come! And he held his hand to me, and we began to go through rough and winding places. We had barely arrived breathless at the amphitheater, when he led me into the middle of the arena and said to me, Do not fear, I am here with you, and I am laboring with you; and he departed. And I gazed on an immense assembly in astonishment. And because I knew that I was given to the wild beasts, I marveled that the wild beasts were not let loose on me. Then a certain Egyptian came forth against me, horrible in appearance, with his backers, to fight with me. And there came to me, as my helpers and encouragers, handsome youths; and I was stripped and became [like] a man [for battle]. Then my helpers began to rub me with oil, as is the custom for contest; and I beheld that Egyptian on the other hand rolling in the dust. And a certain man came forth, of wondrous height, so that he even exceeded the top of the amphitheater; and he wore a loose tunic and a purple robe between two bands over the middle of the breast; and he had on calliculae of varied form, made of gold and silver; and he carried a rod, as if he were a trainer of gladiators, and a green branch on which were apples of gold. And he called for silence, and said, This Egyptian, if he should overcome this woman, will kill her with the sword; and if she will conquer him, she will receive this branch. Then he departed. And we drew near to one another and began to deal out blows. He sought to lay hold of my feet, while I struck at his face with my heels; and I was lifted up in the air and began thus to thrust at him as if spurning the earth. But when I saw that there was some delay, I joined my hands so as to intertwine my fingers with one another; and I took hold on his head, and he fell on his face, and I stomped on his head. And the people began to shout, and my backers to exult. And I drew near to the trainer and took the branch; and he kissed me, and said to me, Daughter, peace be with you: and I began to go gloriously to the Sanavivarian Gate. Then I awoke and perceived that I was not to fight with beasts, but against the Devil. Still, I knew that the victory was awaiting me." This, so far, I have completed several days before the exhibition; but what passed at the exhibition itself, let who will write.

CHAPTER 4

1. Moreover, the blessed Saturus also related his vision, which he himself committed to writing: "We had suffered," he says, "and we had gone forth from the flesh, and we were beginning to be carried by four messengers into the east; and their hands did not touch us. And we did not float supine, looking upward, but as if ascending a gentle slope. And being set free, we finally saw the first boundless light; and I said, Perpetua (for she was at my side), this is what the LORD promised to us; we have received the promise. And while we are carried by those same four messengers, there appears to us a vast space which was like a pleasure-garden, having rose-trees and every kind of flower. And the height of the trees was after the measure of a cypress, and their leaves were falling incessantly. Moreover, there in the pleasure-garden four other messengers appeared, brighter than the previous ones, who, when they saw us, gave us honor and said to the rest of the messengers, Here they are! Here they are! with admiration. And those four messengers who carried us, being greatly afraid, put us down; and we passed over on foot, the space of a stadium in a broad path. There we found Jocundus, and Saturninus, and Artaxius, who having suffered the same persecution, were burnt alive; and Quintus, who was also a martyr himself, had departed in the prison. And we asked them where the rest were. And the messengers said to us, Come first, enter and greet your Lord.

2. And we came near to a place, the walls of which were such as if they were built of light; and before the gate of that place stood four messengers, who clothed those who entered with white robes. And being clothed, we entered and saw the boundless light and heard the united voice of some who said without ceasing, HOLY, HOLY, HOLY! And in the midst of that place we saw, as it were, a silvery man sitting, having snow-white hair, and with a youthful appearance; and we did not see His feet. And on His right hand and on His left were twenty-four elders, and behind them a great many others were standing. We entered with great wonder and stood before the throne; and the four messengers raised us up, and we kissed Him, and He passed His hand over our face. And the rest of the elders said to us, Let us stand; and we stood and made peace. And the elders said to us, Go and play. And I said, Perpetua, you have what you wish. And she said to me, Thanks be to God, that joyous as I was in the flesh, I am now more joyous here.

3. And we went forth and saw before the entrance Optatus the overseer at the right hand, and Aspasius the elder, a teacher, at the left hand, separate and sad; and they cast themselves at our feet and said to us, Restore peace between us, because you have gone forth and have left us this way. And we said to them, Are you not our father, and you our elder, that you should throw yourselves at our feet? And we prostrated ourselves, and we embraced them; and Perpetua began to speak with them, and we drew them apart in the pleasure-garden under a rose-tree. And while we were speaking with them, the messengers said to them, Leave them alone, so that they may refresh themselves; and if you have any dissensions between you, forgive one another. And they drove them away. And they said to Optatus, Rebuke your people, because they assemble to you as if returning from the circus, and contending about sectarian matters. And then it seemed to us as if they would shut the doors. And in that place, we began to recognize many brothers, and moreover martyrs. We were all nourished with an indescribable aroma, which satisfied us. Then, I awoke joyfully."

CHAPTER 5

1. The above were the more eminent visions of the blessed martyrs Saturus and Perpetua themselves, which they themselves committed to writing. But God called Secundulus, while he was still in the prison, by an earlier exit from the world, not without favor, so as to give relief to the beasts. Nevertheless, even if his soul did not acknowledge a cause for thankfulness, assuredly his flesh did.

2. But respecting Felicitas (for to her also the LORD's favor approached in the same way), when she had already gone eight months with child (for she had been pregnant when she was apprehended), as the day of the exhibition was drawing near, she was in great grief lest on account of her pregnancy she should be delayed—because pregnant women are not allowed to be publicly punished—and lest she should shed her sacred and guiltless blood among some who had been subsequently wicked. Moreover, her fellow martyrs were also painfully saddened lest they should leave such an excellent friend, and as it were companion, alone in the path of the same hope. Therefore, joining together their united cry, they poured forth their prayer to the LORD [for] three days before the exhibition. Immediately after their prayer her pains came on her, and when, with the difficulty natural to an eight months' delivery, in the labor of bringing forth, she was sorrowing, someone of the servants of the Cataractarii said to her, "You who are in such suffering now, what will you do when you are thrown to the beasts, which you despised when you refused to sacrifice?" And she replied, "It is now that I suffer what I suffer; but then there will be Another in me, who will suffer for me, because I am also about to suffer for Him." Thus, she brought forth a little girl, which a certain sister brought up as her daughter.

3. Since then the Holy Spirit permitted, and by permitting willed, that the proceedings of that exhibition should be committed to writing, although we are unworthy to complete the description of such great glory; yet we obey, as it were, the command of the most blessed Perpetua, indeed, her sacred trust, and add one more testimony concerning her faithfulness and her loftiness of mind. While they were treated with more severity by the tribune, because, from the insinuations of certain deceitful men, he feared lest they should be withdrawn from the prison by some sort of magic incantations, Perpetua answered to his face and said, "Why do you not at least permit us to be refreshed, being as we are objectionable to the most noble Caesar, and having to fight on his birthday? Or is it not your glory if we are brought forward fatter on that occasion?" The tribune shuddered and blushed, and commanded that they should be kept with more humanity, so that permission was given to their brothers and others to go in and be refreshed with them—even the keeper of the prison now trusting them himself.

4. Moreover, on the day before, when in that last meal, which they call the free meal, they were partaking as much as they could—not of a free supper, but of a love [feast]—with

the same firmness they were uttering such words as these to the people, denouncing against them the judgment of the LORD, bearing witness to the joy of their passion, laughing at the curiosity of the people who came together; while Saturus said, "Tomorrow is not enough for you, for you to behold with pleasure that which you hate. Friends today, enemies tomorrow. Yet note our faces diligently, so that you may recognize them on the Day of Judgment." Thus, everyone departed from there astonished, and from these things many believed.

CHAPTER 6

1. The day of their victory shone forth, and they proceeded from the prison into the amphitheater, as if to an assembly, joyful and of brilliant countenances; if perhaps shrinking, it was with joy, and not with fear. Perpetua followed with placid look, and with step and gait as a matron of Christ, beloved of God; casting down the luster of her eyes from the gaze of all. Moreover, Felicitas, rejoicing that she had safely brought forth, so that she might fight with the wild beasts; from the blood and from the midwife to the gladiator, to wash after childbirth with a second immersion. And when they were brought to the gate and were constrained to put on the clothing—the men, that of the priests of Saturn, and the women, that of those who were consecrated to Ceres—that noble-minded woman resisted even to the end with endurance. For she said, "We have come this far of our own accord, for this reason, that our liberty might not be restrained. For this reason, we have yielded our minds, so that we might not do any such thing as this: we have agreed on this with you." Injustice acknowledged the justice; the tribune yielded to their being brought as simply as they were. Perpetua sang psalms, already treading underfoot the head of the Egyptian; Revocatus, and Saturninus, and Saturus uttered threats against the gazing people surrounding this martyrdom. When they came within sight of Hilarianus, by gesture and nod, they began to say to Hilarianus, "You judge us," they say, "but God will judge you." At this, the people, exasperated, demanded that they should be tormented with scourges as they passed along the rank of the venatores. And they indeed rejoiced that they should have incurred any one of their Lord's passions.

2. But He who had said, "Ask, and you will receive," gave to them when they asked, that death which each one had wished for. For when at any time they had been discoursing among themselves about their wish in respect of their martyrdom, Saturninus indeed had professed that he wished that he might be thrown to all the beasts; doubtless that he might wear a more glorious crown. Therefore, in the beginning of the exhibition he and Revocatus made trial of the leopard, and moreover on the scaffold they were harassed by the bear. Saturus, however, held nothing in greater abomination than a bear; but he imagined that he would be ended with one bite from a leopard. Therefore, when a wild boar was supplied, it was rather the huntsman who had supplied that boar who was gored by that same beast and died the day after the shows. Saturus was only drawn out; and when he had been bound on the floor near to a bear, the bear would not come forth from his den. And so Saturus for the second time is recalled unharmed.

3. Moreover, the Devil prepared a very fierce cow for the young women, provided especially for that purpose contrary to custom, also mocking their sex in that of the beasts. And so, stripped and clothed with nets, they were led forth. The populace shuddered as they saw one young woman of delicate frame, and another with breasts still dropping from her recent childbirth. So, being recalled, they are unbound. Perpetua is first led in. She was tossed and fell on her loins; and when she saw her tunic torn from her side, she drew it over her as a veil for her middle, rather mindful of her modesty than her suffering. Then she was called for again and bound up her disheveled hair; for it was not appropriate for a martyr to suffer with disheveled hair, lest she should appear to be mourning in her glory. So she rose up; and when she saw Felicitas crushed, she approached, and gave her her hand, and lifted her up. And both of them stood together; and the brutality of the populace being appeased, they were recalled to the Sanavivarian Gate. Then Perpetua was received by a certain one who was still a catechumen, Rusticus by name, who kept close to her; and she, as if aroused from sleep, so deeply had she been in the Spirit and in an ecstasy, began to look around her, and to say to the amazement of all, "I cannot tell when we are to be led out to that cow." And when she had heard what had already happened, she did not believe it until she had perceived certain signs of injury in her body and in her dress, and had recognized the catechumen. Afterward, causing that catechumen and the brother to approach, she addressed them, saying, "Stand firm in the faith, and love one another, all of you, and do not be offended at my sufferings."

4. The same Saturus at the other entrance exhorted the soldier Pudens, saying, "Assuredly I am here, just as I have promised and foretold, for up to this moment I have felt no beast. And now believe with your whole heart. Behold, I am going forth to that beast, and I will be destroyed with one bite of the leopard." And immediately, at the conclusion of the exhibition, he was thrown to the leopard; and with one bite of his he was bathed with such a quantity of blood, that the people shouted out to him as he was returning, the testimony of his second immersion, "Saved and washed! Saved and washed!" Clearly, he who had been glorified in such a spectacle was most certainly saved. Then to the soldier Pudens he said, "Farewell, and be mindful of my faith; and do not let these things disturb, but confirm you." And at the same time, he asked for a little ring from his finger and returned it to him bathed in his wound, leaving to him an inherited token and the memory of his blood. And then lifeless, he is cast down with the rest, to be slaughtered in the usual place. And when the populace called for them into the midst, that as the sword penetrated into their body, they might make their eyes partners in the murder, they rose up of their own accord and transferred themselves where the people wished; but they first kissed one another, so that they might consummate their martyrdom with the kiss of peace. The rest indeed, immoveable and silent, received the sword-thrust; much more Saturus, who also had first ascended the ladder, and first gave up his spirit, for he was also waiting for Perpetua. But Perpetua, so that she might taste some pain, being pierced between the ribs, cried out loudly, and she herself placed the wavering right hand of the youthful gladiator to her throat. Possibly such a woman could not have been slain unless she herself had willed it, because she was feared by the impure spirit. O most brave and blessed martyrs! O truly called and chosen to the glory of our Lord Jesus Christ! Whom whoever magnifies, and honors, and adores, assuredly ought to read these examples for the edification of the Assembly, not less than the ancient ones, so that new virtues may also testify that one and the same Holy Spirit is always operating even until now, and God the Father Almighty, and His Son Jesus Christ our Lord, whose is the glory and infinite power forever and ever. Amen.

REVELATION OF ABRAHAM

The Apocalypse of Abraham, called the Revelation of Abraham in the LSV—"apocalypse" meaning a "revelation," "unveiling," or, even more literally, "an uncovering"—was written fairly early in the current era, possibly between AD 70 and 150. The narrative includes a history of Abraham in his father's house and his conversion to monotheism. That section is followed by a prophetic vision and an account of his journey through the heavens.

THE SCROLL OF THE REVELATION OF ABRAHAM, THE SON OF TERAH, THE SON OF NAHOR, THE SON OF SERUG, THE SON OF REU, THE SON OF ARPHAXAD, THE SON OF SHEM, THE SON OF NOAH, THE SON OF LAMECH, THE SON OF METHUSELAH, THE SON OF ENOCH, THE SON OF JARED.

CHAPTER 1

¹On the day when I planed the gods of my father Terah and the gods of his brother Nahor, when I was searching as to who the Mighty God in truth is—I, Abraham, at the time when it fell to my lot, when I fulfilled the sacrifices of my father Terah to his gods of wood and stone, gold and silver, brass and iron; having entered into their temple for service, I found the god whose name was Merumath [which was] hewn out of stone, fallen forward at the feet of the iron god Nahon. ²And it came to pass, when I saw it, my heart was perplexed, and I considered in my mind that I should not be able to bring him back to his place, I, Abraham, alone, because he was heavy, being of a large stone, and I went forth and made it known to my father. ³And he entered with me, and when both of us moved him forward, so that we might bring him back to his place, his head fell from him while I was still holding him by the head. ⁴And it came to pass, when my father saw that the head of Merumath had fallen from him, he said to me: "Abraham!" And I said, "Here I am." ⁵And he said to me: "Bring me an axe, of the small ones, from the house." And I brought it to him. ⁶And he correctly hewed another Merumath out of another stone, without head, and the head which had been thrown down from Merumath he placed on it, and the rest of Merumath he shattered.

CHAPTER 2

¹And he made five other gods, and gave them to me [and] commanded me to sell them outside in the street of the town. ²And I saddled my father's donkey, and placed them on it, and went toward the inn to sell them. And behold, merchants from Fandana in Syria were traveling with camels going to Egypt, to trade. And I spoke with them. ³And one of their camels uttered a groan, and the donkey took fright and sprang away and upset the gods; and three of them were smashed, and two were preserved. ⁴And it came to pass, when the Syrians saw that I had gods, they said to me: "Why did you not tell us [[that you had gods? Then we would have bought them]] before the donkey heard the sound of the camel, and they would not have been lost. ⁵Give us, at any rate, the gods that remain, and we will give you the proper price for the broken gods, also for the gods that have been preserved." ⁶For I was concerned in my heart as to how I could bring to my father the purchase-price; and the three broken ones I cast into the water of the River Gur, which was at that place, and they sank into the depths, and there was nothing more of them.

CHAPTER 3

¹When I was still going on the way, my heart was perplexed within me, and my mind was distracted. ²And I said in my heart: [["What evil deed is this that my father is doing? Is he not, rather, the god of his gods, since they come into existence through his chisels and lathes, and his wisdom, and is it not rather fitting that they should worship my father, since they are his work? What is this delusion of my father in his works?]] ³Behold, Merumath fell and could not rise in his own temple, nor could I, by myself, move him until my father came, and the two of us moved him; and as we were thus too weak, his head fell from him, and he set it on another stone of another god, which he had made without head. ⁴And the other five gods were broken in pieces down from the donkey, which were able neither to help themselves, nor to hurt the donkey, because it had broken them to pieces; nor did their broken fragments come up out of the river." ⁵And I said in my heart: "If this be so, how can Merumath, my father's god, having the head of another stone, and himself being made of another stone, rescue a man, or hear a man's prayer and reward him?"

CHAPTER 4

¹And while I meditated thus, I reached my father's house; and having watered the donkey, and set out hay for it, I brought the silver and gave it into the hand of my father Terah. ²When he saw it, he was glad, [and] he said, "Blessed are you, Abraham, of my gods, because you have brought the price of the gods, so that my work was not in vain." ³And I answered and said to him: "Hear, O my father Terah! Blessed are the gods of you, for you are their god, since you have made them; for their blessing is ruination, and their power is vain; they who did not help themselves, how will they, then, help you or bless me? ⁴I have been kind to you in this affair, because by [using] my intelligence, I have brought you the money for the broken gods." ⁵And when he heard my word, he became furiously angry with me, because I had spoken hard words against his gods.

CHAPTER 5

¹I, however, having thought over my father's anger, went out; [[and after I had gone out]] my father cried, saying, "Abraham!" ²And I said, "Here I am." And he said, "Take and collect the splinters of the wood out of which I made gods of pinewood before you came; and make ready for me the food of the midday meal." ³And it came to pass, when I collected the splinters of wood, I found under them a little god which had been lying among the brushwood on my left, and on his forehead was written: GOD BARISAT. ⁴And I did not inform my father that I had found the wooden god Barisat under the chips. ⁵And it came to pass, when I had laid the splinters in the fire, in order that I might make food ready for my father—on going out to ask a question regarding the food, I placed Barisat before the kindled fire, ⁶saying threateningly to him: "Pay careful attention, Barisat, [that] the fire does not die down until I come; if, however, it dies down, blow on it that it may burn up again." ⁷And I went out and accomplished my purpose. And on returning I found Barisat fallen backwards, and his feet surrounded by fire and horribly burnt. ⁸I burst into a fit of laughter, and I said to myself: "Truly, O Barisat, you can kindle the fire and cook food!" ⁹And it came to pass, while I spoke [thus] in my laughter he was gradually burned up by the fire and reduced to ashes. And I brought the food to my father, and he ate. ¹⁰And I gave him wine and milk, and he was gladdened and blessed his god Merumath. And I said to him, "O father Terah, do not bless your god Merumath, and do not praise him, but rather praise your god Barisat because, loving you more, he has cast himself into the fire to cook your food!" ¹¹And he said to me, "And where is he now?" [And I said,] "He is burned to ashes in the violence of the fire and is reduced to dust." ¹²And he said, "Great is the power of Barisat! I make another today, and tomorrow he will prepare my food."

CHAPTER 6

¹However, when I, Abraham, heard such words from my father, I laughed in my mind and sighed in the grief and in the anger of my soul, and said, "How then can that which is made by him—manufactured statues—be a helper of my father? ²Or will the body then be subject to its soul, and the soul to the spirit, and the spirit to folly and ignorance?" ³And I said, "It is fitting to once endure evil, so I will direct my mind to what is pure and lay my thoughts open before him." ⁴[And] I answered and said, "O father Terah, whichever of these you praise as a god, you are foolish in your mind. Behold the gods of your brother Ora, which stand in the holy temple, are more worthy of honor than [these of] yours. ⁵For behold, Zucheus, the god of your brother Oron, is more worthy of honor than your god Merumath, because he is made of gold which

is highly valued by people, and when he grows old in years he will be remodeled; ⁶but if your god Merumath is changed or broken, he will not be renewed, because he is a stone; the which is also the case with the god Joavon [[who stands with Zucheus over the other gods—how much more worthy of honor is he than the god Barisat, who is made of wood, while he is forged of silver! ⁷How is he made, by adaptation of man, valuable to outward appearance! But your god Barisat, while he still was, before he had been prepared, rooted up on the earth and was great and wonderful with the glory of branches and blossom, you hewed out with the axe, and by means of your axe he has been made into a god. ⁸And behold, his fatness is already withered and perished, he is fallen from the height to the ground, he has come from great estate to littleness, and the appearance of his countenance has vanished, and he,]] ⁹Barisat himself, is burned up by fire and reduced to ashes and is no more; and you say: Today I will make another which tomorrow will make my food ready! He has perished to utter destruction!"

CHAPTER 7

¹"Behold, the fire is more worthy of honor than all things formed because even that which is not subjected is subjected to it, and things easily perishable are mocked by its flames. ²But even more worthy of honor is the water, because it conquers the fire and satisfies the earth. But even it I do not call god, because it is subjected to the earth under which the water inclines. But I call the earth much more worthy of honor, because it overpowers the nature of the water. ³Even it, however, I do not call god—it, too, is dried up by the sun, [and] is apportioned to man to be tilled. ⁴[[I call the sun more worthy of honor than the earth,]] because it with its rays illuminates the whole world and the different atmospheres. ⁵[But] even it I do not call god, because at night and by clouds its course is obscured. ⁶Nor, again, do I call the moon or the stars god, because they also in their season obscure [their] light at night. ⁷[But] hear [this], my father Terah; for I will make known to you the God who has made everything, not these we consider as gods. ⁸Who then is He, || Or what is He, who has crimsoned the heavens, and made the sun golden, || And the moon lustrous, and with it the stars; And has made the earth dry in the midst of many waters, ⁹And set you in … [[and tested me in the confusion of my thoughts]]. Yet may God reveal Himself to us through Himself!"

CHAPTER 8

¹And it came to pass while I spoke thus to my father Terah in the court of my house, there comes down the voice of a Mighty One from Heaven in a fiery rainstorm, saying and crying: "Abraham, Abraham!" ²And I said, "Here I am." And He said, "You are seeking in the understanding of Your heart the God of gods and the Creator; I am He: Go out from your father Terah, and get out from the house, that you also are not slain in the sins of your father's house." ³And I went out. And it came to pass when I went out, that before I succeeded in getting out in front of the door of the court, there came a sound of a [great] thunder and [fire] burned him, and his house, and everything, whatever was in his house, down to the ground—forty cubits.

CHAPTER 9

¹Then a voice came to me speaking twice: "Abraham, Abraham!" And I said, "Here I am!" ²And He said, "Behold, it is I; do not fear, for I am before the worlds, and a mighty God who has created the light of the world. I am a shield over you, and I am your helper. ³Go, bring Me a young heifer of three years old, and a female goat of three years old, and a ram of three years old, and a turtledove and a pigeon, and bring Me a pure sacrifice. ⁴And in this sacrifice, I will lay before you the ages [to come], and make known to you what is reserved, and you will see great things which you have not seen [until now], because you have loved to search Me out, and I have named you My friend. ⁵But abstain from every form of food that proceeds out of the fire, and from the drinking of wine, and from anointing [yourself] with oil, forty days, and then set forth for Me the sacrifice which I have commanded you, in the place which I will show you on a high mountain, ⁶and there I will show you the ages which have been created and established, made and renewed, by My Word, and I will make known to you what will come to pass in them on those who have done evil and [practiced] righteousness in the generation of men."

CHAPTER 10

¹And it came to pass, when I heard the voice of Him who spoke such words to me, [and] I looked here and there, and behold, there was no breath of a man, and my spirit was frightened, and my soul fled from me, and I became like a stone, and fell down on the earth, for I had no more strength to stand on the earth. ²And while I was still lying with my face on the earth, I heard the voice of the Holy One speaking: "Go, Yahoel, and by means of My ineffable Name raise that man for Me, and strengthen him [so that he recovers] from his trembling." ³And the messenger came, whom He had sent to me, in the likeness of a man, and grasped me by my right hand, and set me up on my feet, and said to me: "Stand up, friend of God who loves you; do not let the trembling of man seize you! ⁴For behold, I have been sent to you to strengthen you and bless you in the Name of God—who loves you—the Creator of the celestial and terrestrial. Be fearless and hasten to Him. ⁵I am called Yahoel by Him who moves that which exists with me on the seventh heaven on the expanse, a power in virtue of the ineffable Name that is dwelling in me. ⁶I am the one who has been given to restrain, according to His commandment, the threatening attack of the living creatures of the cherubim against one another, and teach those who carry Him the song of the seventh hour of the night of man. ⁷I am ordained to restrain the Leviathan, for to me are subject the attack and menace of every single reptile. [[I am he who has been commissioned to loosen Hades, to destroy him who stares at the dead.]] ⁸I am the one who was commissioned to set on fire your father's house together with him, because he displayed reverence for dead [idols]. ⁹I have been sent to bless you now, and the land which the Perpetual One, whom you have invoked, has prepared for you, and for your sake I have journeyed my way on the earth. ¹⁰Stand up, Abraham! Go without fear; be rightly glad and rejoice; and I am with you! For continuous honor has been prepared for you by the Perpetual One. ¹¹Go, fulfill the sacrifices commanded. For behold, I have been appointed to be with you and with the generation prepared [to spring] from you; and with me Michael blesses you forever. Be of good cheer, go!"

CHAPTER 11

¹And I rose up and saw him who had grasped me by my right hand and set me up on my feet: ²and the appearance of his body was like sapphire, and the look of his countenance like chrysolite, and the hair of his head like snow, and the turban on his head like the appearance of the rainbow, and the clothing of his garments like purple; and a golden scepter was in his right hand. ³And he said to me, "Abraham!" And I said, "Here I am, your servant." ⁴And he said, "Do not let my look frighten you, nor my speech, that your soul is not perturbed. ⁵Come with me and I will go with you, until the sacrifice, visible, but after the sacrifice, invisible forever. Be of good cheer, and come!"

CHAPTER 12

¹And we went, the two of us together, forty days and nights, and I ate no bread, and drank no water, because my food was to see the messenger who was with me, and his speech—that was my drink. ²And we came to the Mount of God, the glorious Horeb. And I said to the messenger: "Singer of the Perpetual One! Behold, I have no sacrifice with me, nor am I aware of a place of an altar on the mountain; how can I bring a sacrifice?" ³And he said to me, "Look around!" And I looked around, and behold, there were following us all the prescribed sacrificial [animals]—the young heifer, and the female goat, and the ram, and the turtle-dove, and the pigeon. ⁴And the messenger said to me, "Abraham!" I said, "Here I am." And he said to me, "Slaughter all of these, and divide the animals into halves, one against the other, but do not sever the birds; and give to the men, whom I will show you, standing by you, for these are the altar on the mountain, to offer a sacrifice to the Perpetual; ⁵but give the turtledove and the pigeon to me, for I will ascend on the wings of the bird, in order to show you in Heaven, and on the earth, and in the sea, and in the abyss, and in the underworld, and in the Garden of Eden, and in its rivers and in the fullness of the

whole world and its circle—you will gaze in [them] all."

CHAPTER 13

¹And I did everything according to the commandment of the messenger, and gave the messengers, who had come to us, the divided animals, but the messenger took the birds. ²And I waited for the evening sacrifice. And there flew an unclean bird down on the carcasses, and I drove it away. ³And the unclean bird spoke to me, and said, "What are you doing, Abraham, on the holy heights, where no man eats or drinks, neither is there on them food of man, but these consume everything with fire, and burn you up? ⁴Forsake the man who is with you and flee; for if you ascend to the heights, they will make an end of you." ⁵And it came to pass, when I saw the bird speak, I said to the messenger, "What is this, my lord?" And he said, "This is ungodliness, this is Azazel." ⁶And he said to it: "Disgrace on you, Azazel! For Abraham's lot is in Heaven, but yours on the earth, because you have chosen and loved this for the dwelling-[place] of your uncleanness, therefore the perpetual mighty LORD made you a dweller on the earth and through you every evil spirit of lies, and through you wrath and trials for the generations of ungodly men; ⁷for God, the Perpetual, Mighty One, has not permitted that the bodies of the righteous should be in your hand, in order that thereby the life of the righteous and the destruction of the unclean may be assured. ⁸Hear, friend, go away from me with shame. For it has not been given to you to play the tempter in regard to all the righteous. ⁹Depart from this man! You cannot lead him astray, because he is an enemy to you, and of those who follow you and love what you will. ¹⁰For behold, the vesture which in Heaven was formerly yours has been set aside for him, and the mortality which was his has been transferred to you."

CHAPTER 14

¹The messenger said to me, [["Abraham!" And I said, "Here I am, your servant." ²And he said, "Know from now on that the Perpetual One has chosen you, [He] whom you love; be of good courage and use this authority, so far as I bid you, against him who slanders truth; ³should I not be able to put him to shame who has scattered over the earth the secrets of Heaven and has rebelled against the Mighty One?]] ⁴Say to him: Be the burning coal of the furnace of the earth; go, Azazel, into the inaccessible parts of the earth; [[for your heritage is over those existing with you being born with the stars and clouds, with the men whose portion you are, and through your being exist; and your enmity is justification. ⁵On this account, by your perdition disappear from me." And I uttered the words which the messenger had taught me. And he said, "Abraham!" ⁶And I said, "Here I am, your servant."]] ⁷And the messenger said to me: "Do not answer him; for God has given him will over those who answer him." [[⁸And the messenger spoke to me a second time and said, "Now rather, however much he speaks to you, do not answer him, that his will may have no free course in you, because the Perpetual and Mighty One has given him weight and will; do not answer him." I did what was commanded me by the messenger;]] ⁹and however much he spoke to me, I answered him nothing at all.

CHAPTER 15

¹And it came to pass when the sun went down, that behold, [there was] a smoke as of a furnace. And the messengers who had the portions of the sacrifice ascended from the top of the smoking furnace. ²And the messenger took me with the right hand and set me on the right wing of the pigeon, and set himself on the left wing of the turtle-dove, which [birds] had neither been slaughtered nor divided. ³And he bore me to the borders of the flaming fire [[and we ascended as with many winds to the Heaven which was fixed on the surface. And I saw on the air]] on the height, to which we ascended a strong light, which it was impossible to describe, ⁴and behold, in this light a fiercely burning fire for people, many people of male appearance, all [constantly] changing in aspect and form, running and being transformed, and worshiping and crying with a sound of words which I did not know.

CHAPTER 16

¹And I said to the messenger, "Why have you brought me up here now, because now I cannot see, for I have already grown weak, and my spirit departs from me?" ²And he said to me, "Remain by me; do not fear! And He whom you see come straight toward us with great voice of holiness —that is the Perpetual One who loves you; but Himself you cannot see. ³But do not let your spirit grow faint [[on account of the loud crying]], for I am with you, strengthening you."

CHAPTER 17

¹And while he yet spoke, behold, fire came against us [all] around, and a voice was in the fire like a voice of many waters, like the sound of the sea in its uproar. ²And the messenger bent his head with me and worshiped. And I desired to fall down on the earth, and the high place, on which we stood, [[at one moment rose upright,]] but at another rolled downwards. ³And he said, "Only worship, Abraham, and utter the song which I have taught you"; because there was no earth to fall on. ⁴And I only worshiped and uttered the song which he had taught me. And he said, "Recite without ceasing." ⁵And I recited, and he also himself recited the song with me: "Perpetual, mighty, Holy, El, God alone—Supreme! ⁶You who are self-existent, incorruptible, spotless, || Uncreated, immaculate, immortal, || Self-complete, self-illuminating; ⁷Without father, without mother, unbegotten, || Exalted, fiery One! Lover of men, benevolent, bountiful, jealous over me and very compassionate; ⁸Eli, that is, || My God—Perpetual, mighty Holy [One] of Hosts, very glorious El, El, El, El, YAH'EL! ⁹You are He whom my soul has loved! Perpetual Protector, shining like fire, || Whose voice is like the thunder, || Whose look is like the lightning—all-seeing, || Who receives the prayers of such as honor You, [[¹⁰And turns away from the requests of such as embarrass with the embarrassment of their provocations, || Who dissolves the confusions of the world which arise from the ungodly and righteous in the corruptible age, renewing the age of the righteous!]] ¹¹You, O Light, shine before the light of the morning on Your creatures, || And in Your heavenly dwelling places there is no need of any other light than [that] of the unspeakable splendor from the lights of Your countenance. ¹²Accept my prayer [[and be well-pleased with it]], likewise also the sacrifice which You have prepared through me who sought You! Accept me favorably, and show me, and teach me, || And make known to Your servant as You have promised me!"

CHAPTER 18

¹And while I still recited the song, the mouth of the fire which was on the surface rose up on high. And I heard a voice like the roaring of the sea; nor did it cease on account of the rich abundance of the fire. ²And as the fire raised itself up, ascending into the height, I saw a throne of fire under the fire, and all-seeing ones around it, reciting the song, and under the throne four fiery living creatures singing, and their appearance was one, each one of them with four faces. ³And such was the appearance of their countenances: of a lion, of a man, of an ox, of an eagle; four heads [[were on their bodies so that the four creatures had sixteen faces]]; and each had six wings; from their shoulders, [[and their sides,]] and their loins. ⁴And with the [two] wings from their shoulders they covered their faces, and with the [two] wings which [sprang] from their loins they covered their feet, while the [two] middle wings they spread out for flying straightforward. ⁵And when they had ended the singing, they looked at one another and threatened one another. ⁶And it came to pass when the messenger who was with me saw that they were threatening each other, he left me and went running to them, and turned the countenance of each living creature from the countenance immediately confronting him, in order that they might not see their countenances threatening each other. ⁷And he taught them the song of peace which has its origin [[in the Perpetual One]]. ⁸And as I stood alone and looked, I saw behind the living creatures a chariot with fiery wheels, each wheel full of eyes [all] around; and over the wheels was a throne, which I saw, and this was covered with fire, and fire encircled it around, and behold, an indescribable fire enclosed a fiery host. ⁹And I heard its holy voice like the voice of a man.

CHAPTER 19

¹And a voice came to me out of the midst of the fire, saying, "Abraham, Abraham!" I said,

"Here I am!" ²And He said, "Consider the expanses which are under the expanse on which you are placed, and see how on no single expanse is there any other but He whom you have sought, or who has loved you." ³And while He was yet speaking [and], behold, the expanses opened, and beneath me the heavens. ⁴And I saw on the seventh heaven on which I stood a fire widely extended, and light, and dew, and a multitude of messengers, and a power of invisible glory over the living creatures which I saw; but I saw no other being there. ⁵And I looked from the mountain in which I stood [[downwards]] to the sixth heaven, and saw a multitude of messengers there, of [pure] spirit, without bodies, who carried out the commands of the fiery messengers who were on the eighth heaven, as I was standing suspended over them. ⁶And behold, on this expanse there were no other powers of [any] other form, but only messengers of [pure] spirit, like the power which I saw on the seventh heaven. ⁷And He commanded that the sixth heaven should be taken away. ⁸And I saw there, on the fifth heaven, the powers of the stars which carry out the commands laid on them, and the elements of the earth obeyed them.

CHAPTER 20

¹And the Perpetual Mighty One said to me, "Abraham, Abraham!" And I said, "Here I am." [[And He said,]] "Consider from above the stars which are beneath you, and number them [[for Me]], and make known [[to Me]] their number." ²And I said, "When can I? For I am but a man [[of dust and ashes]]." ³And He said to me, "As the number of the stars and their power, [so will] I make your seed a nation and a people, set apart for Me in My heritage with Azazel." ⁴And I said, "O Perpetual, Mighty One! Let Your servant speak before You, and do not let Your anger kindle against Your chosen one! ⁵Behold, before You led me up, Azazel raged against me. How, then, while he is not now before You, have You constituted Yourself with him?"

CHAPTER 21

¹And He said to me, "Now look beneath your feet at the heavens and understand the creation foreshadowed in this expanse, the creatures existing on it, and the age prepared according to it." ²And I saw beneath [[the surfaces of the feet, and I saw beneath]] the sixth heaven and what was therein, and then the earth and its fruits, and what moved on it and its animate beings; and the power of its men, and the ungodliness of their souls, and their righteous deeds, [[and the beginnings of their works]], and the lower regions and the perdition therein, the abyss and its torments. ³I saw there the sea and its islands, and its monsters and its fishes, and Leviathan and his dominion, and his camping-ground, and his caves, and the world which lay on him, and his movements, and the destructions of the world on his account. ⁴I saw streams there and the rising of their waters, and their windings. ⁵And I saw there the Garden of Eden and its fruits, the source of the stream issuing from it, and its trees and their bloom, and those who behaved righteously. ⁶And I saw therein their foods and blessedness. ⁷And I saw there a great multitude—men, and women, and children—[[half of them on the right side of the picture]] and half of them on the left side of the picture.

CHAPTER 22

¹And I said, "O Perpetual, Mighty One! What is this picture of the creatures?" And He said to me, "This is My will with regard to those who exist in the [divine] world-counsel, and it seemed well-pleasing before My sight, and then afterward I gave commandment to them through My Word. ²And it came to pass, whatever I had determined to be, was already planned beforehand in this [picture], and it stood before Me before it was created, as you have seen." ³And I said, "O LORD, mighty and perpetual! Who are the people in this picture on this side and on that?" ⁴And He said to me, "These which are on the left side are the multitude of the peoples which have formerly been in existence and which are destined after you, some for judgment and restoration, and others for vengeance and destruction at the end of the world. ⁵But these which are on the right side of the picture—they are the people set apart for me of the peoples with Azazel. ⁶These are they whom I have ordained to be born of you and to be called My people."

CHAPTER 23

¹"Now look again in the picture, who it is who seduced Eve and what is the fruit of the tree, [[and]] you will know what there will be, and how it will be to your seed among the people at the end of the days of the age, and so far as you cannot understand I will make known to you, for you are well-pleasing in My sight, and I will tell you what is kept in My heart." ²And I looked into the picture, and my eyes ran to the side of the Garden of Eden. ³And I saw there a man very great in height and fearful in breadth, incomparable in aspect, embracing a woman, who likewise approximated to the aspect and shape of the man. ⁴And they were standing under a tree of Eden, and the fruit of this tree was like the appearance of a bunch of grapes of the vine, and behind the tree was standing as it were a serpent in form, having hands and feet like a man's, and wings on its shoulders—six on the right side and six on the left, and they were holding the grapes of the tree in their hands, and both were eating it whom I had seen embracing. ⁵And I said, "Who are these mutually embracing, or who is this who is between them, or what is the fruit which they are eating, O Mighty Perpetual One?" ⁶And He said, "This is the human world, this is Adam, and this is their desire on the earth, [and] this is Eve; but he who is between them represents ungodliness, their beginning [on the way] to perdition, even Azazel." ⁷And I said, "O Perpetual, Mighty One! Why have You given such power to destroy the generation of men in their works on the earth?" ⁸And He said to me, "They who will [to do] evil—and how much I hated [it] in those who do it—over them I gave him power, and to be beloved of them." ⁹And I answered and said, "O Perpetual, Mighty One! Why have You willed to effect that evil should be desired in the hearts of men, since You indeed are angered over that which was willed by You, at him who is doing what is unprofitable in Your counsel?"

CHAPTER 24

¹And He said to me, "Being angered at the nations on your account, and on account of the people of your family who are [to be] separated after you, as you see in the picture the burden [of destiny] that [is laid] on them—and I will tell you what will be, and how much will be, in the last days. Now look at everything in the picture." ²And I looked and saw there what was before me in creation; I saw Adam, and Eve existing with him, and with them the cunning Adversary, ³and Cain who acted lawlessly through the Adversary, and the slaughtered Abel, [and] the destruction brought and caused on him through the lawless one. ⁴I also saw impurity there, and those who lust after it, and its pollution, and their jealousy, and the fire of their corruption in the lowest parts of the earth. ⁵I saw theft there, and those who hasten after it, and the arrangement [[of their retribution, the judgment of the Great Court]]. ⁶I saw naked men there, the foreheads against each other, and their disgrace, and their passion which [they had] against each other, and their retribution. ⁷I saw desire there, and in her hand the head of every kind of lawlessness, [[and her scorn, and her waste assigned to perdition]].

CHAPTER 25

¹I saw the likeness of the idol of jealousy there, having the likeness of woodwork such as my father was accustomed to make, and its statue was of glittering bronze; and before it a man, and he worshiped it; ²and in front of him an altar, and on it a boy slain in the presence of the idol. ³But I said to Him, "What is this idol, or what is the altar, or who are they that are sacrificed, or who is the sacrificer? ⁴Or what is the temple which I see that is beautiful in art, and its beauty [being like] the glory that lies beneath Your throne?" ⁵And He said, "Hear, Abraham. This which you see, the temple, and altar, and beauty, is My idea of the priesthood of My glorious Name, in which dwells every single prayer of man, and the rise of kings and prophets, and whatever sacrifice I ordain to be offered to Me among My people who are to come out of your generation. ⁶But the statue which you saw is My anger with which the people anger Me who are to proceed for Me from you. ⁷But the man whom you saw slaughtering—that is he who incites murderous sacrifices, of which are a witness to Me of the final judgment, even at the beginning of creation."

CHAPTER 26

¹And I said, "O Perpetual, Mighty One! Why have You established that it should be so, and then proclaim the knowledge thereof?" ²And He said to me, "Hear, Abraham; understand what I say to you, and answer Me as I question you. Why did your father Terah not listen to your voice, and [why] did he not cease from the devilish idolatry until he perished [[and]] his whole household with him?" ³And I said, "O Perpetual, [[Mighty One]]! [It was] entirely because he did not choose to listen to me; but I, too, did not follow his works." ⁴And He said [[to me]]: "Hear, Abraham. As the counsel of your father is in him, and as your counsel is in you, so also is the counsel of My will in Me ready for the coming days, before you have knowledge of these, or [can] see with your eyes what is future in them. How those of your seed will be, look in the picture."

CHAPTER 27

¹And I looked and saw: behold, the picture swayed and on its left side a heathen people emerged, and they pillaged those who were on the right side—men, and women, and children; [[some they slaughtered,]] others they retained with themselves. ²Behold, I saw them run toward them through four entrances, and they burned the temple with fire, and the holy things that were therein they plundered. ³And I said, "O Perpetual One! Behold, the people [that spring] from me, whom You have accepted, the hordes of the heathen plunder, and some they kill, while others they hold fast as aliens, and they have burned the temple with fire, and they rob the beautiful things therein. ⁴O Perpetual, Mighty One! If this be so, why have You now lacerated my heart, and why should this be so?" ⁵And He said to me, "Hear, Abraham. What you have seen will happen on account of your seed who anger Me by reason of the statue which you saw, and on account of the human slaughter in the picture, through zeal in the temple; and as you saw so will it be." ⁶And I said, "O Perpetual, Mighty One! May the works of evil [worked] in ungodliness now pass by, but [show me] rather those who fulfilled the commandments, even the works of his righteousness, ⁷for You can do this." And He said to me, "The time of the righteous meets [them] first through the holiness from kings and righteous-dealing rulers whom I at first created in order from such to rule among them. ⁸But from these issue men who care for their interests, as I have made known to you and you have seen."

CHAPTER 28

¹And I answered and said, "O Mighty, [[Perpetual One]], hallowed by Your power! Be favorable to my petition, [[for this have You brought me up here—and show me]]. ²As You have brought me up to Your height, so make [this] known to me, Your beloved one, as much as I ask—whether what I saw will happen to them for long?" ³And He showed me a multitude of His people, and said to me: "On their account through four issues, as you saw, I will be provoked by them, and in these My retribution for their deeds will be [accomplished]. ⁴But in the fourth outgoing of one hundred years and one hour of the age—the same is one hundred years—it will be in misfortune among the heathen, [[but one hour in mercy and insult, as among the heathen]]."

CHAPTER 29

¹And I said, "O Perpetual, [[Mighty One]]! And how long a time is an hour of the age?" ²And He said, "I have ordained twelve years of this ungodly age to rule among the heathen and in your seed; and until the end of the times it will be as you saw. ³And reckon, and understand, and look into the picture." ⁴And I [[looked and]] saw a Man going out from the left side of the heathen; and there went out men, and women, and children from the side of the heathen, many hosts, and worshiped Him. ⁵And while I still looked there came out from the right side [many], and some insulted that Man, while some struck Him; others, however, worshiped Him. ⁶[And] I saw how these worshiped Him, and Azazel ran and worshiped Him, and having kissed His face he turned and stood behind Him. ⁷And I said, "O Perpetual, Mighty One! Who is the Man insulted and beaten, who is worshiped by the heathen with Azazel?" ⁸And He answered and said, "Hear, Abraham! The Man whom you saw insulted and beaten and again worshiped—that is the relief [granted] by the heathen to the people who proceed from you, in the last days, in this twelfth hour of the age of ungodliness. ⁹But in the twelfth year of My final age, I will set up this Man from your generation, whom you saw from My people; all will follow this one, and such as are called by Me [will] join, [even] those who change in their counsels. ¹⁰And those whom you saw emerge from the left side of the picture—the meaning is [this]: there will be many from the heathen who set their hopes on Him; and as for those whom you saw from your seed on the right side, some insulting and striking, others worshiping Him—many of them will be offended at Him. ¹¹He, however, is testing those who have worshiped Him of your seed, in that twelfth hour of the end, with a view to shortening the age of ungodliness. ¹²Before the age of the righteous begins to grow, My judgment will come on the lawless heathen through the people of your seed who have been separated for Me. ¹³In those days I will bring on all creatures of the earth ten plagues, through misfortune and disease and sighing of the grief of their soul. ¹⁴Thus much will I bring on the generations of men that be on it on account of the provocation and the corruption of its creatures, whereby they provoke Me. ¹⁵And then will righteous men of your seed be left in the number which is kept secret by Me, hastening in the glory of My Name to the place prepared beforehand for them, which you saw devastated in the picture; ¹⁶and they will live and be established through sacrifices and gifts of righteousness and truth in the age of the righteous, and will rejoice in Me continually; ¹⁷and they will destroy those who have destroyed them, and will insult those who have insulted them; and of those who defamed them they will spit in the face, scorned by Me, while they will behold Me full of joy, rejoicing with My people, and receiving those who return to Me [[in conversion]]. ¹⁸See, Abraham, what you have seen, and [hear] what you have heard, and [[take full knowledge of]] what you have come to know. Go to your heritage, and behold, I am with you forever."

CHAPTER 30

¹But while He was still speaking, I found myself on the earth. And I said, "O Perpetual, [[Mighty One]], I am no longer in the glory in which I was [while] on high, and what my soul longed to understand in my heart I do not understand." ²And He said to me, "What is desired in your heart I will tell you, because you have sought to see the ten plagues which I have prepared for the heathen, and have prepared beforehand at the passing over of the twelfth hour of the earth. ³Hear what I divulge to you, so will it come to pass: the first [is] pain of great distress; the second, conflagration of many cities; ⁴the third, destruction and pestilence of animals; the fourth, hunger of the whole world and of its people; ⁵the fifth by destruction among its rulers, destruction by earthquake and the sword; ⁶the sixth, multiplication of hail and snow; the seventh, the wild beasts will be their grave; ⁷the eighth, hunger and pestilence will alternate with their destruction; the ninth, punishment by the sword and flight in distress; ⁸the tenth, thunder, and voices, and destructive earthquake."

CHAPTER 31

¹"And then I will sound the trumpet out of the air, and will send My Chosen One, having in Him all My power—one measure; ²and this one will summon My despised people from the nations, and I will burn with fire those who have insulted them and who have ruled among them in [this] age. ³And I will give those who have covered Me with mockery to the scorn of the coming age; and I have prepared them to be food for the fire of Hades and for ceaseless flight to and fro through the air in the underworld beneath the earth—[[the body filled with worms. ⁴For on them will they see the righteousness of the Creator—those, namely, who have chosen to do My will, and those who have openly kept My commandments, [and] they will rejoice with joy over the downfall of the men who still remain, who have followed the idols and their murders. ⁵For they will decay in the body of the evil worm Azazel, and be burned with the fire of Azazel's tongue; ⁶for I hoped that they would come to Me, and not have loved and praised the strange [god], and not have adhered to him for whom they were not allotted, but [instead] they have forsaken the mighty LORD."

CHAPTER 32

¹ "Therefore hear, O Abraham, and see; behold, your seventh generation [will] go with you, and they will go out into a strange land, and they will enslave them, ² and mistreat them as it were an hour of the age of ungodliness, but the nation whom they will serve I will judge."]]

REVELATION OF ELIJAH

The Revelation of Elijah, commonly called the Apocalypse of Elijah or Apocalypse of Elias, may have been written in the 1st or 2nd century AD, and some speculate Paul briefly quoted from the work in 1 Corinthians 2:9 and Ephesians 5:14, although the Ephesians reference is unlikely and the 1 Corinthians 2:9 reference would require the Revelation of Elijah to be pre-Pauline, which may also be unlikely. The text may, however, have a more primordial core of material, with other parts added in later, including an account of the Antichrist and the two witnesses (identified in the book as Elijah and Enoch).

CHAPTER 1

¹ The word of the LORD came to me, saying, "Son of man, say to this people, Why do you add sins to your sins, and anger the LORD God who created you?" ² Don't love the world or the things which are in the world, for the boasting of the world and its destruction belong to the Devil. ³ Remember that the Lord of glory, who created everything, had mercy on you so that He might save us from the captivity of this age. ⁴ For many times the Devil desired not to let the sun rise above the earth and not to let the earth yield fruit, since he desires to consume men like a fire which rages in stubble, and he desires to swallow them like water. ⁵ Therefore, on account of this, the God of glory had mercy on us, and He sent His Son to the world so that He might save us from the captivity. ⁶ He did not inform a messenger or a chief-messenger or any principality when He was about to come to us, but He changed Himself to be like a man when He was about to come to us so that He might save us … ⁷ Therefore, become sons to Him since He is a father to you. ⁸ Remember that He has prepared thrones and crowns for you in Heaven, saying, "Everyone who will obey Me will receive thrones and crowns among those who are Mine." ⁹ The LORD said, "I will write My Name on their forehead and I will seal their right hand, and they will not hunger or thirst. ¹⁰ Neither will the son of lawlessness prevail over them, nor will the thrones hinder them, but they will walk with the messengers up to My city." ¹¹ Now as for the sinners, they will be shamed and they will not pass by the thrones, but the thrones of death will seize them and rule over them because the messengers will not agree with them. ¹² They have alienated themselves from His dwellings. ¹³ Hear, O wise men of the land, concerning the deceivers who will multiply in the last times so that they will set down for themselves doctrines which do not belong to God, setting aside the Law of God, those who have made their belly their God, saying, "The fast does not exist, nor did God create it," making themselves strangers to the covenant of God and robbing themselves of the glorious promises. ¹⁴ Now these are not ever correctly established in the firm faith. Therefore, don't let those people lead you astray. ¹⁵ Remember that from the time when He created the heavens, the LORD created the fast for a benefit to men on account of the passions and desires which fight against you so that the evil will not inflame you. ¹⁶ "But it is a pure fast which I have created," said the LORD. ¹⁷ The one who fasts continually will not sin although jealousy and strife are within him. ¹⁸ Let the pure one fast, but whenever the one who fasts is not pure, he has angered the LORD and also the messengers. ¹⁹ And he has grieved his soul, gathering up wrath for himself for the day of wrath. ²⁰ But a pure fast is what I created, with a pure heart and pure hands. ²¹ It releases sin. It heals diseases. It casts out demons. ²² It is effective up to the throne of God for an ointment and for a release from sin by means of a pure prayer. ²³ Who among you, if he is honored in his craft, will go forth to the field without a tool in his hand? Or who will go forth to the battle to fight without a breastplate on? ²⁴ If he is found, will he not be killed because he despised the service of the king? ²⁵ Likewise, no one is able to enter the holy place if he is double-minded. ²⁶ The one who is double-minded in his prayer is darkness to himself. And even the messengers do not trust him. ²⁷ Therefore be single-minded in the LORD at all times so that you might know every moment.

CHAPTER 2

¹ Furthermore, concerning the kings of Assyria and the dissolution of the Heaven and the earth and the things beneath the earth. ² "Now therefore, they will not be overcome," says the LORD, "nor will they fear in the battle." ³ When they see [one] who rises in the north, "the king of Assyria," this king of injustice [will increase] his battles and his disturbances against Egypt. ⁴ The land will groan together because your children will be seized. ⁵ Many will desire death in those days, but death will flee from them. ⁶ And a king who will be called "the king of peace" will rise up in the west. ⁷ He will run on the sea like a roaring lion. ⁸ He will kill the king of injustice, and he will take vengeance on Egypt with battles and much bloodshed. ⁹ It will come to pass in those days that he will command [peace] and a gift in Egypt. ¹⁰ [He will give] peace to these who are holy, [saying], "The Name of [God] is one." ¹¹ [He will] give honors to the [saints and] an exalting to the places of the saints. ¹² He will give vain gifts to the house of God. ¹³ He will wander around in the cities of Egypt with guile, without their knowing. ¹⁴ He will take count of the holy places. He will weigh the idols of the heathen. He will take count of their wealth. He will establish priests for them. ¹⁵ He will command that the wise men and the great ones of the people be seized, and they will be brought to the metropolis which is by the sea, saying, "There is but one language." ¹⁶ But when you hear, "Peace and joy exist," I will … ¹⁷ Now I will tell you his signs so that you might know him. ¹⁸ For he has two sons: one on his right and one on his left. ¹⁹ The one on his right will receive a demonic face, [and] he will fight against the Name of God. ²⁰ Now four kings will descend from that king. ²¹ In his thirtieth year he will come up to Memphis, [and] he will build a temple in Memphis. ²² On that day his own son will rise up against him and kill him. ²³ The whole land will be disturbed. ²⁴ On that day he will issue an order over the whole land so that the priests of the land and all of the saints will be seized, saying, "You will repay doubly every gift and all of the good things which my father gave to you." ²⁵ He will shut up the holy places. He will take their houses. He will take their sons prisoner. ²⁶ He will give command, and sacrifices and abominations and bitter evils will be done in the land. ²⁷ He will appear before the sun and the moon. ²⁸ On that day the priests of the land will tear their clothes. ²⁹ Woe to you , O rulers of Egypt, in those days because your day has passed. ³⁰ The violence [being done to] the poor will turn against you, and your children will be seized as plunder. ³¹ In those days the cities of Egypt will groan for the voice of the one who sells and the one who buys will not be heard. The markets of the cities of Egypt will become dusty. ³² Those who are in Egypt will weep together. They will desire death, [but] death will flee and leave them. ³³ In those days, they will run up to the rocks and leap off, saying, "Fall on us." And still they will not die. ³⁴ A double affliction will multiply on the whole land. ³⁵ In those days, the king will command, and all the nursing women will be seized and brought to him bound. They will suckle serpents. And their blood will be drawn from their breasts, and it will be applied as poison to the arrows. ³⁶ On account of their distress of the cities, he will command again, and all the young boys from twelve years and under will be seized and presented in order to teach them to shoot arrows. ³⁷ The midwife who is on the earth will grieve. The woman who has given birth will lift her eyes to Heaven, saying, "Why did I sit on the birthstool, to bring forth a son to the earth?" ³⁸ The barren woman and the virgin will rejoice, saying, "It is our time to rejoice, because we have no child on the earth, but our

children are in Heaven." ³⁹In those days, three kings will arise among the Persians, and they will take captive the Jews who are in Egypt. They will bring them to Jerusalem, and they will inhabit it and dwell there. ⁴⁰Then when you hear that there is security in Jerusalem, tear you garments, O priests of the land, because the son of perdition will soon come. ⁴¹In those days, the lawless one will appear in the holy places— ⁴²In [those] days the kings of the Persians will hasten, and they will stand to fight with the kings of Assyria. Four kings will fight with three. ⁴³They will spend three years in that place until they carry off the wealth of the temple which is in that place. ⁴⁴In those days, blood will flow from Kos to Memphis. The river of Egypt will become blood, and they will not be able to drink from it for three days. ⁴⁵Woe to Egypt and those who are in it. ⁴⁶In those days a king will arise in the city which is called "The City of the Sun," and the whole land will be disturbed. He will flee to Memphis. ⁴⁷In the sixth year, the Persian kings will plot an ambush in Memphis. They will kill the Assyrian king. ⁴⁸The Persians will take vengeance on the land, and they will command to kill all the heathen and the lawless ones. They will command to build the temples of the saints. ⁴⁹They will give double gifts to the house of God. They will say, "The Name of God is one." ⁵⁰The whole land will greet the Persians. ⁵¹Even the remnant, who did not die under the afflictions, will say, "The LORD has sent us a righteous king so that the land will not become a desert." ⁵²He will command that no royal matter be presented for three years and six months. The land will be full of good in an abundant well-being. ⁵³Those who are alive will go to those who are dead, saying, "Rise up and be with us in this rest."

CHAPTER 3

¹In the fourth year of that king, the son of lawlessness will appear, saying, "I am the Christ," although he is not. Don't believe him! ²When the Christ comes, He will come in the manner of a covey of doves with the crown of doves surrounding Him. He will walk on the vaults of Heaven with the sign of the Cross leading Him. ³The whole world will behold Him like the sun which shines from the eastern horizon to the western. ⁴This is how He will come, with all His messengers surrounding Him. ⁵But the son of lawlessness will begin to stand again in the holy places. ⁶He will say to the sun, "Fall," and it will fall. He will say, "Shine," and it will do it. He will say, "Darken," and it will do it. ⁷He will say to the moon, "Become bloody," and it will do it. ⁸He will go forth with them from the sky. He will walk on the sea and the rivers as on dry land. ⁹He will cause the lame to walk. He will cause the deaf to hear. He will cause the dumb to speak. He will cause the blind to see. ¹⁰The lepers he will cleanse. The sick he will heal. The demons he will cast out. ¹¹He will multiply his signs and his wonders in the presence of everyone. ¹²He will do the works which the Christ did, except for raising the dead alone. ¹³In this you will know that he is the son of lawlessness, because he is unable to give life. ¹⁴For behold I will tell you his signs so that you might know him. ¹⁵He is a ... of a skinny-legged young man, having a tuft of gray hair at the front of his bald head. His eyebrows will reach to his ears. There is a leprous bare spot on the front of his hands. ¹⁶He will transform himself in the presence of those who see him. He will become a young child. He will become old. ¹⁷He will transform himself in every sign. But the signs of his head will not be able to change. ¹⁸Therein you will know that he is the son of lawlessness.

CHAPTER 4

¹The virgin, whose name is Tabitha, will hear that the shameless one has revealed himself in the holy places. And she will put on her garment of fine linen. ²And she will pursue him up to Judea, scolding him up to Jerusalem, saying, "O shameless one, O son of lawlessness, O you who have been hostile to all the saints." ³Then the shameless one will be angry at the virgin. He will pursue her up to the regions of the sunset. He will suck her blood in the evening. ⁴And he will cast her on the temple, and she will become a healing for the people. ⁵She will rise up at dawn. And she will live and scold him, saying, "O shameless one, you have no power against my soul or my body, because I live in the LORD always. ⁶And also my blood which you have cast on the temple has become a healing for the people." ⁷Then when Elijah and Enoch hear that the shameless one has revealed himself in the holy place, they will come down and fight with him, saying, ⁸"Are you indeed not ashamed? When you attach yourself to the saints, because you are always estranged. ⁹You have been hostile to those who belong to Heaven. You have acted against those belonging to the earth. ¹⁰You have been hostile to the thrones. You have acted against the messengers. You are always a stranger. ¹¹You have fallen from Heaven like the morning stars. You were changed, and your tribe became dark for you. ¹²But you are not ashamed, when you stand firmly against God you are a devil." ¹³The shameless one will hear and he will be angry, and he will fight with them in the marketplace of the great city. And he will spend seven days fighting with them. ¹⁴And they will spend three and one half days in the marketplace dead, while all the people see them. ¹⁵But on the fourth day they will rise up and they will scold him saying. "O shameless one, O son of lawlessness. Are you indeed not ashamed of yourself since you are leading astray the people of God for whom you did not suffer? Do you not know that we live in the LORD?" ¹⁶As the words were spoken, they prevailed over him, saying, "Furthermore, we will lay down before the flesh for the spirit, and we will kill you since you are unable to speak on that day because we are always strong in the LORD. But you are always hostile to God." ¹⁷The shameless one will hear, and he will be angry and fight them. ¹⁸And the whole city will surround them. ¹⁹On that day they will shout up to Heaven as they shine while all the people and all the world see them. ²⁰The son of lawlessness will not prevail over them. He will be angry at the land, and he will seek to sin against the people. ²¹He will pursue all of the saints. They and the priests of the land will be brought back bound. ²²He will kill them and destroy them ... them. And their eyes will be removed with iron spikes. ²³He will remove their skin from their heads. He will remove their nails one by one. He will command that vinegar and lime be put in their nose. ²⁴Now those who are unable to bear up under the tortures of that king will take gold and flee over the fords to the desert places. They will lie down as one who sleeps. ²⁵The LORD will receive their spirits and their souls to Himself. ²⁶Their flesh will petrify. No wild animals will eat them until the last Day of the Great Judgment. ²⁷And they will rise up and find a place of rest, but they will not be in the kingdom of the Christ as those who have endured because the LORD said, "I will grant to them that they sit on My right hand." ²⁸They will receive favor over others, and they will triumph over the son of lawlessness. And they will witness the dissolution of the heavens and earth. ²⁹They will receive the thrones of glory and the crowns. ³⁰The sixty righteous ones who are prepared for this hour will hear. ³¹And they will gird on the breastplate of the LORD, and they will run to Jerusalem and fight with the shameless one, saying, "All powers which the prophets have done from the beginning you have done. But you were unable to raise the dead because you have no power to give life. Therein we have known that you are the son of lawlessness." ³²He will hear, and he will be angry and command to kindle altars. ³³And the righteous ones will be bound. They will be lifted up and burned.

CHAPTER 5

¹And on that day the heart of many will harden and they will flee from him, saying, "This is not the Christ. The Christ does not kill the righteous. He does not pursue men so that He might seek them, but He persuades them with signs and wonders." ²On that day the Christ will pity those who are His own. And He will send from Heaven his sixty-four thousand messengers, each of whom has six wings. ³The sound will move the heavens and earth when they give praise and glory. ⁴Now those on whose forehead the Name of Christ is written and on whose hand is the seal—both the small and the great—will be taken up on their wings and lifted up before His wrath. ⁵Then Gabriel and Uriel will become a pillar of light leading them into the holy land. ⁶It will be granted to them to eat from the Tree of Life. They will wear white garments ... and messengers will watch over them. They will not thirst, nor will the son of lawlessness be able to prevail over them. ⁷And on that day the earth will be disturbed, and the sun will darken, and peace will be removed from the earth. ⁸The birds will fall on the earth, dead. ⁹The earth will be dry. The waters of the sea will dry up. ¹⁰The sinners will groan on the

earth, saying, "What have you done to us, O son of lawlessness, saying, I am the Christ, when you are the Devil? ¹¹You are unable to save yourself so that you might save us. You produced signs in our presence until you alienated us from the Christ who created us. Woe to us because we listened to you. ¹²Behold, now we will die in a famine. Where indeed is now the trace of a righteous one and we will worship him, or where indeed is the one who will teach us, and we will appeal to him. ¹³Now indeed we will be wrathfully destroyed because we disobeyed the LORD. ¹⁴We went to the deep places of the sea, and we did not find water. We dug in the rivers and papyrus reeds, and we did not find water." ¹⁵Then on that day, the shameless one will speak, saying, "Woe to me because my time has passed by for me while I was saying that my time would not pass by for me. ¹⁶My years became months and my days have passed away as dust passes away. Now therefore I will perish together with you. ¹⁷Now therefore run forth to the desert. Seize the robbers and kill them. ¹⁸Bring up the saints. For because of them, the earth yields fruit. For because of them the sun shines on the earth. For because of them the dew will come on the earth." ¹⁹The sinners will weep, saying, "You made us hostile to the LORD. If you are able, rise up and pursue them." ²⁰Then he will take his fiery wings and fly out after the saints. He will fight with them again. ²¹The messengers will hear and come down. They will fight with him a battle of many swords. ²²It will come to pass on that day that the LORD will hear and command the Heaven and the earth with great wrath. And they will send for fire. ²³And the fire will prevail over the earth seventy-two cubits. It will consume the sinners and the devils like stubble. ²⁴A true judgment will occur. ²⁵On that day, the mountains and the earth will utter speech. The byways will speak with one another, saying, "Have you heard today the voice of a man who walks who has not come to the judgment of the Son of the LORD?" ²⁶The sins of each one will stand against him in the place where they were committed, whether those of the day or of the night. ²⁷Those who belong to the righteous and… will see the sinners and those who persecuted them and those who handed them over to death in their torments. ²⁸Then the sinners will see the place of the righteous. ²⁹And thus grace will occur. In those days, that which the righteous will ask for many times will be given to them. ³⁰On that day, the LORD will judge the Heaven and the earth. He will judge those who transgressed in Heaven, and those who did so on earth. ³¹He will judge the shepherds of the people. He will ask about the flock of sheep, and they will be given to Him, without any deadly guile existing in them. ³²After these things, Elijah and Enoch will come down. They will lay down the flesh of the world, and they will receive their spiritual flesh. They will pursue the son of lawlessness and kill him since he is not able to speak. ³³On that day, he will dissolve in their presence like ice which was dissolved by a fire. He will perish like a serpent which has no breath in it. ³⁴They will say to him, "Your time has passed by for you. Now, therefore, those who believe you will perish." ³⁵They will be cast into the bottom of the abyss and it will be closed for them. ³⁶On that day, the Christ, the King and all His saints will come forth from Heaven. ³⁷He will burn the earth. He will spend one thousand years on it. ³⁸Because the sinners prevailed over it, He will create a new Heaven and a new earth. No deadly devil will exist in them. ³⁹He will rule with His saints, ascending and descending, while they are always with the messengers and they are with the Christ for one thousand years.

REVELATION OF ZEPHANIAH

The Apocalypse of Zephaniah (Revelation of Zephaniah in the LSV), purporting to be additional words from the Old Testament prophet, was likely written between 100 BC and the late 2nd century AD, probably in the late 1st century AD. Fragment 1 is a quotation of the text made by Clement of Alexandria. Fragment 2 is from a Coptic manuscript from the 5th century. Fragment 3, the longest, and also Coptic, was found on papyri from the 4th century.

FRAGMENT 1
¹And a spirit took me and brought me up into the fifth heaven. And I saw messengers who are called "lords." ²And the crown was set on them in the Holy Spirit, and the throne of each of them was seven times brighter than the light of the rising sun. ³And they were dwelling in the temples of salvation and singing hymns to the indescribable God.

FRAGMENT 2
¹I saw a soul which five thousand messengers punished and guarded. ²They took it to the east, and they brought it to the west. They beat its … they gave it one hundred … lashes for each one daily. ³I was afraid, and I cast myself on my face so that my joints dissolved. ⁴The messenger helped me. He said to me, "Be strong, O one who will triumph, and prevail so that you will triumph over the accuser and you will come up from Hades." ⁵And after I arose, I said, "Who is this whom they are punishing?" ⁶He said to me, "This is a soul which was found in its lawlessness." And before it attained to converting, it was visited and taken out of its body. ⁷Truly, I, Zephaniah, saw these things in my vision. ⁸And the messenger of the LORD went with me. I saw a great broad place, thousands of thousands surrounded it on its left side and myriads of myriads on its right side. The form of each one was different. ⁹Their hair was loose like that belonging to women. Their teeth were like the teeth of…

FRAGMENT 3

CHAPTER 1
¹… dead. We will bury him like any man. ²Whenever he dies, we will carry him out playing the lyre before him and chanting psalms and odes over his body.

CHAPTER 2
¹Now I went with the messenger of the LORD, and he took me over all of my city. There was nothing before my eyes. ²Then I saw two men walking together on one road. I watched them as they talked. ³And, moreover, I also saw two women grinding together at a mill. And I watched them as they talked. ⁴And I also saw two on a bed, each one of them acting for their [mutual] … on a bed. ⁵And I saw the whole inhabited world hanging like a drop of water which is suspended from a bucket when it comes up from a well. ⁶I said to the messenger of the LORD. "Then does darkness or night not exist in this place?" ⁷He said to me, "No, because darkness does not exist in that place where the righteous and the saints are, but rather they always exist in the light." ⁸And I saw all the souls of men as they existed in punishment. ⁹And I cried out to the LORD Almighty, "O God, if You remain with the saints, You [certainly] have compassion on behalf of the world and the souls which are in this punishment."

CHAPTER 3
¹The messenger of the LORD said to me, "Come, let me show you the place of righteousness." ²And he took me up on Mount Seir and he showed me three men, as two messengers walked with them rejoicing and exulting over them. ³I said to the messenger, "Of what sort are these?" ⁴He said to me, "These are the three sons of Joatham, the priest, who neither kept the commandment of their father nor observed the ordinances of the LORD." ⁵Then I saw two other messengers weeping over the three sons of Joatham, the priest. ⁶I said, "O messenger, who are these?" He said, "These are the messengers of the LORD Almighty. They write down all the good deeds of the righteous on their scrolls as they watch at the gate of Heaven. ⁷And I take them from their hands and bring them up before the LORD Almighty; He writes their name in the Scroll of the Living. ⁸Also the messengers of the accuser who is on the earth, they also write down all the sins of men on their scrolls. ⁹They also sit at the gate of Heaven. They tell the accuser and he writes them on his scroll so that he might

REVELATION OF ZEPHANIAH

accuse them when they come out of the world [and go] down there."

CHAPTER 4

¹Then I walked with the messenger of the LORD. I looked before me and I saw a place there. ²Thousands of thousands and myriads of myriads of messengers entered through it. ³Their faces were like a leopard, their tusks being outside their mouth like wild boars. ⁴Their eyes were mixed with blood. Their hair was loose like the hair of women, and fiery scourges were in their hands. ⁵When I saw them, I was afraid. I said to that messenger who walked with me, "Of what sort are these?" ⁶He said to me, "These are the servants of all creation who come to the souls of ungodly men and bring them and leave them in this place. ⁷They spend three days going around with them in the air before they bring them and cast them into their continuous punishment." ⁸I said, "I implore you, O Lord, do not give them authority to come to me." ⁹The messenger said, "Do not fear. I will not permit them to come to you because you are pure before the LORD. I will not permit them to come to you because the LORD Almighty sent me to you because [you] are pure before Him." ¹⁰Then he beckoned to them, and they withdrew themselves and they ran from me.

CHAPTER 5

¹But I went with the messenger of the LORD, and I looked in front of me and I saw gates. ²Then when I approached them, I discovered that they were bronze gates. ³The messenger touched them, and they opened before him. I entered with him and found its whole square like a beautiful city, and I walked in its midst. ⁴Then the messenger of the LORD transformed himself beside me in that place. ⁵Now I looked at them, and I discovered that they were bronze gates and bronze bolts and iron bars. ⁶Now my mouth was shut therein. I beheld the bronze gates in front of me as fire was being cast forth for about fifty stadia.

CHAPTER 6

¹Again I turned back and walked, and I saw a great sea. ²But I thought that it was a sea of water. I discovered that it was entirely a sea of flame like a slime which casts forth much flame and whose waves burn sulfur and bitumen. ³They began to approach me. ⁴Then I thought that the LORD Almighty had come to visit me. ⁵Then when I saw, I fell on my face before him in order that I might worship him. ⁶I was very much afraid, and I entreated him that he might save me from this distress. ⁷I cried out, saying, "Eloi, LORD, Adonai, of Hosts. I implore You to save me from this distress because it has befallen me." ⁸In that same instant I stood up, and I saw a great messenger before me. His hair was spread out like that of lionesses'. His teeth were outside his mouth like a bear. His hair was spread out like women's. His body was like the serpent's when he wished to swallow me. ⁹And when I saw him, I was afraid of him so that all the parts of my body were loosened, and I fell on my face. ¹⁰I was unable to stand, and I prayed before the LORD Almighty, "You will save me from this distress. You are the one who saved Israel from the hand of Pharaoh, the king of Egypt. You saved Susanna from the hand of the elders of injustice. You saved the three holy men, Shadrach, Meshach, Abednego, from the furnace of burning fire. I beg you to save me from this distress." ¹¹Then I arose and stood, and I saw a great messenger standing before me with his face shining like the rays of the sun in its glory since his face is like that which is perfected in its glory. ¹²And he was girded as if a golden girdle were on his breast. His feet were like bronze which is melted in a fire. ¹³And when I saw him, I rejoiced, for I thought that the LORD Almighty had come to visit me. ¹⁴I fell on my face, and I worshiped him. ¹⁵He said to me, "Take heed. Do not worship me. I am not the LORD Almighty, but am the great messenger, Eremiel, who is over the abyss and Hades, the one in which all of the souls are imprisoned from the end of the Flood, which came on the earth, until this day." ¹⁶Then I inquired of the messenger, "What is the place to which I have come?" He said to me, "It is Hades." ¹⁷Then I asked him, "Who is the great messenger who stands thus, whom I saw?" He said, "This is the one who accuses men in the presence of the LORD."

CHAPTER 7

¹Then I looked, and I saw him with a scroll in his hand. He began to unroll it. ²Now after he had spread it out, I read it in my [own] language. I found that all my sins which I had done were written in it, those which I had done from my youth until this day. ³They were all written on that scroll of mine without there being a false word in them. ⁴If I did not go to visit a sick man or a widow, I found it written down as a shortcoming on my manuscript. ⁵If I did not visit an orphan, it was found written down as a shortcoming on my scroll. ⁶A day on which I did not fast [or] pray in the time of prayer I found written down as a failing on my scroll. ⁷And a day when I did not turn to the sons of Israel—since it is a shortcoming—I found written down on my scroll ⁸so that I threw myself on my face and prayed before the LORD Almighty, "May Your mercy reach me and may You wipe out my scroll because Your mercy has come to be in every place and has filled every place." ⁹Then I arose and stood, and I saw a great messenger before me, saying to me, "Triumph, prevail because you have prevailed and have triumphed over the accuser, and you have come up from Hades and the abyss. You will now cross over the crossing place." ¹⁰Again he brought another scroll which was written by hand. ¹¹He began to unroll it, and I read it, and found it written in my [own] language …

CHAPTER 8

¹… They helped me and set me on that boat. ²Thousands of thousands and myriads of myriads of messengers gave praise before me. ³I, myself, put on an angelic garment. I saw all of those messengers praying. ⁴I, myself, prayed together with them. ⁵I knew their language, which they spoke with me. ⁶Now, moreover, my sons, this is the trial because it is necessary that the good and the evil be weighed in a balance.

CHAPTER 9

¹Then a great messenger came forth having a golden trumpet in his hand, and he blew it three times over my head, saying, "Be courageous! O one who has triumphed. Prevail! O one who has prevailed. For you have triumphed over the accuser, and you have escaped from the abyss and Hades. ²You will now cross over the crossing place. For your name is written in the Scroll of the Living." ³I wanted to embrace him, [but] I was unable to embrace the great messenger because his glory is great. ⁴Then he ran to all the righteous ones, namely, Abraham, and Isaac, and Jacob, and Enoch, and Elijah, and David. ⁵He spoke with them as friend to friend speaking with one another.

CHAPTER 10

¹Then the great messenger came to me with the golden trumpet in his hand, and he blew it up to Heaven. ²Heaven opened from the place where the sun rises to where it sets, from the north to the south. ³I saw the sea which I had seen at the bottom of Hades. Its waves came up to the clouds. ⁴I saw all the souls sinking in it. I saw some whose hands were bound to their neck, with their hands and feet being bound. ⁵I said, "Who are these?" He said to me, "These are the ones who were bribed and they were given gold and silver until the souls of men were led astray." ⁶And I saw others covered with mats of fire. ⁷I said, "Who are these?" He said to me, "These are the ones who give money at interest, and they receive interest for interest." ⁸And I also saw some blind ones crying out. And I was amazed when I saw all these works of God. ⁹I said, "Who are these?" He said to me, "These are catechumens who heard the word of God, but they were not perfected in the work which they heard." ¹⁰And I said to him, "Then they have no conversion here?" He said, "Yes," ¹¹I said, "How long?" He said to me, "Until the day when the LORD will judge." ¹²And I saw others with their hair on them. ¹³I said, "Then there is hair and body in this place?" ¹⁴He said, "Yes, the LORD gives body and hair to them as He desires."

CHAPTER 11

¹And I also saw multitudes. He brought them forth. ²As they looked at all of the torments, they called out, praying before the LORD Almighty, saying, "We pray to You on account of those who are in all these torments so that You might have mercy on all of them." ³And when I saw them, I said to the messenger who spoke with me, [["Who are these?"]] ⁴He said, "These who implore the LORD are Abraham, and Isaac, and Jacob. ⁵Then at a certain hour daily they come forth with the great messenger. He sounds a trumpet up to Heaven and another sounds on the earth. ⁶All

the righteous hear the sound. They come running, praying to the LORD Almighty daily on behalf of these who are in all these torments."

CHAPTER 12

¹And again the great messenger comes forth with the golden trumpet in his hand, blowing over the earth. ²They hear [it] from the place of the sunrise to the place of the sunset and from the southern regions to the northern regions. ³And again he blows [it] up to Heaven and its sound is heard. ⁴I said, "O Lord, why did you not leave me until I saw them all?" ⁵He said to me, "I have no authority to show them to you until the LORD Almighty rises up in His wrath to destroy the earth and the heavens. ⁶They will see and be disturbed, and they will all cry out, saying, All flesh which is ascribed to You we will give to You on the Day of the LORD. ⁷Who will stand in His presence when He rises in His wrath [to destroy] the earth [and the heavens]? ⁸Every tree which grows on the earth will be plucked up with its roots and fall down. And every high tower and the birds which fly will fall…"

REVELATION OF PETER

The Revelation or Apocalypse of Peter was listed in the Muratorian Canon among the two apocalypses (the other being the Revelation of John). It was also supported by Clement of Alexandria. The translation that follows comes from the Ethiopic text. A Greek fragment discovered at Akhmîm differs considerably (cf. chs. 2, 4), but seems less supported—the Ethiopic thought to be older. Two other small Greek fragments have been found (Bodleian and Rainer).

CHAPTER 1

¹THE SECOND COMING OF CHRIST AND RESURRECTION OF THE DEAD WHO DIED BECAUSE OF THEIR SINS, FOR THAT THEY DID NOT KEEP THE COMMAND OF GOD THEIR CREATOR. ²And he [(Peter)] pondered thereon, that he might perceive the mystery of the Son of God, the merciful and lover of mercy. ³And when the LORD was seated on the Mount of Olives, His disciples came to Him. ⁴And we implored and entreated Him separately and pleaded [to] Him, saying to Him, "Declare to us what are the signs of Your coming and of the end of the world, that we may perceive and mark the time of Your coming and instruct them that come after us, to whom we preach the word of Your good news, and whom we set over Your Assembly, that when they hear it they may take heed to themselves and mark the time of Your coming." ⁵And our Lord answered us, saying, "Take heed that no man deceive you, and that you not be doubters and serve other gods. Many will come in My Name, saying, I am the Christ. Do not believe them, neither draw near to them. For the coming of the Son of God will not be plain, but as the lightning that shines from the east to the west, so I will come on the clouds of Heaven with a great host in My majesty; I will come in My majesty with My cross going before My face; I will come in My majesty—shining sevenfold more than the sun—with all My holy ones, My messengers. And My Father will set a crown on My head, that I may judge the quick and the dead and reward every man according to his works. ⁶And you, take the likeness thereof from the fig tree: so soon as the shoot thereof has come forth and the twigs grown, the end of the world will come." ⁷And I, Peter, answered and said to Him, "Interpret to me concerning the fig tree, whereby we will perceive it; for throughout all its days the fig tree sends forth shoots, and every year it brings forth its fruit for its master. What, then, does the allegory of the fig tree mean? We do not know it." ⁸And the Master answered and said to me, "Do you not understand that the fig tree is the house of Israel? Even as a man that planted a fig tree in his garden, and it brought forth no fruit. And he sought the fruit thereof many years and when he did not find it, he said to the keeper of his garden: Root up this fig tree [so] that it does not make our ground to be unfruitful. And the gardener said to God: [Allow us] to rid it of weeds and dig the ground around it and water it. If then it does not bear fruit, we will immediately remove its roots out of the garden and plant another in place of it. Have you not understood that the fig tree is the house of Israel? Truly I say to you, when the twigs thereof have sprouted forth in the last days, then pretend Christs will come and awake expectation, saying, I am the Christ that has now come into the world. And when they [(Israel)] will perceive the wickedness of their deeds, they will turn away after them and deny him [whom our fathers praised], even the first Christ whom they crucified and therein sinned a great sin. But this deceiver [(the Antichrist)] is not the Christ. And when they reject him, he will slay with the sword, and there will be many martyrs. Then the twigs of the fig tree—that is, the house of Israel—will shoot forth; many will become martyrs at his hand. Enoch and Elijah will be sent to teach them that this is the deceiver which must come into the world and do signs and wonders to deceive. And therefore, they that die by his hand will be martyrs, and will be reckoned among the good and righteous martyrs who have pleased God in their life." ⁹And He showed me in His right hand the souls of all men, and on the palm of His right hand the image of that which will be accomplished at the last day: and how the righteous and the sinners will be separated, and how they do that are upright in heart, and how the evildoers will be rooted out throughout all ages. We beheld how the sinners wept in great affliction and sorrow, until all that saw it with their eyes wept, whether righteous or messengers, and He Himself also. ¹⁰And I asked Him and said to him, "Lord, permit me to speak Your word concerning the sinners: It were better for them if they had not been created." And the Savior answered and said to me, "Peter, why do you speak thus, that it were better for them to not have been created? You resist God. You would not have more compassion than He for His image, for He has created them and brought them forth out of not being. Now because you have seen the lamentation which will come on the sinners in the last days, therefore your heart is troubled; but I will show you their works, whereby they have sinned against the Most High. ¹¹Now behold what will come on them in the last days, when the Day of God and the Day of the decision of the judgment of God comes. From the east to the west all the children of men will be gathered together before My Father that lives forever. And He will command Hades to open its bars of adamant and give up all that is therein. ¹²And He will command the wild beasts and the birds to restore all the flesh that they have devoured, because He wills that men should appear; for nothing perishes before God, and nothing is impossible with Him, because all things are His. ¹³For all things come to pass on the day of decision, on the Day of Judgment, at the word of God: and as all things were done when He created the world and commanded all that is therein, and it was done—even so will it be in the last days; for all things are possible with God. And, therefore, He says in the Writing: Son of man, prophesy on the several bones and say to the bones: Bone to bone, in joints, sinew, nerves, flesh, and skin, and hair thereon, [[and soul, and spirit]]. ¹⁴And the great Uriel will give them soul and spirit at the command of God; for God has set him over the rising again of the dead at the Day of Judgment. ¹⁵Behold and consider the corns of wheat that are sown in the earth. As things dry and men sow them in the earth without soul, so they live again and bear fruit, and the earth restores them as a pledge entrusted to it. ¹⁶[[And this that dies, that is sown as seed in the earth, and will become alive and be restored to life, is man.]] ¹⁷How much more will God raise up on the Day of Decision them that believe in Him and are chosen of Him, for whose sake He made the world? And the earth will restore all things on

the Day of Decision, for it will also be judged with them, and the Heaven with it. ¹⁸And at the Day of Judgment this will come on them that have fallen away from faith in God and that have committed sin: floods of fire will be let loose, and darkness and obscurity will come up and clothe and veil the whole world, and the waters will be changed and turned into coals of fire, and all that is in them will burn, and the sea will become fire. Under the sky will be a sharp fire that cannot be quenched, and [it] flows to fulfill the judgment of wrath. And the stars will fly in pieces by flames of fire, as if they had not been created, and the powers [[or expanses]] of the heavens will pass away for lack of water and will be as though they had not been. And the lightnings of the sky will no longer be, and by their enchantment they will frighten the world [[or The sky will turn to lightning and the lightnings thereof will frighten the world. The spirits of the dead bodies will also be like to them]] and will become fire at the command of God. ¹⁹And so soon as the whole creation dissolves, the men that are in the east will flee to the west, [and those in the west] to the east; they that are in the south will flee to the north, and they that are in the [north to the] south. And in all places the wrath of a fearful fire will overtake them, and an unquenchable flame driving them will bring them to the judgment of wrath, to the stream of unquenchable fire that flows, flaming with fire, and when the waves thereof part themselves from one another, burning, there will be a great gnashing of teeth among the children of men. ²⁰Then they will all behold Me coming on a continuous cloud of brightness—and the messengers of God that are with Me. And I will sit on the throne of My glory at the right hand of My heavenly Father; and He will set a crown on My head. And when the nations behold it, they will weep, every nation apart. ²¹Then He will command them to enter into the river of fire while the works of each of them will stand before them—to every man according to his deeds. As for the chosen ones that have done good, they will come to Me and not see death by the devouring fire. But the unrighteous, the sinners, and the hypocrites will stand in the depths of darkness that will not pass away, and their discipline is the fire, and messengers bring forward their sins and prepare for them a place wherein they will be punished agelong [[everyone according to his transgression]]. ²²Uriel, the messenger of God, will bring forth the souls of those sinners who perished in the Flood, and of all that dwelt in all idols, in every molten image, in every [object of] love, and in pictures, and of those that dwelt on all hills, and in stones, and by the wayside, whom men called gods: they will burn them with them in continuous fire; and after that, all of them—with their dwelling places—are destroyed. They will be punished agelong."

CHAPTER 2

¹"Then men and women will come to the place prepared for them. By their tongues with which they have blasphemed the way of righteousness they will be hanged up. There is spread under them unquenchable fire, and they do not escape it. ²Behold, another place: therein is a pit, great and full. In it are they that have denied righteousness; and messengers of punishment punish them and there they kindle on them the fire of their torment. ³And again, behold—women: they hang them up by their neck and by their hair; they will cast them into the pit. These are they which plaited their hair, not for good [[or not to make them beautiful]] but to turn them to fornication, that they might ensnare the souls of men to perdition. And the men that lay with them in fornication will be hung by their loins in that place of fire; and they will say to one another: We did not know that we should come to continuous punishment. ⁴And the murderers and them that have made common cause with them they will cast into the fire, in a place full of venomous beasts, and they will be tormented without rest, feeling their pains; and their worms will be as many in number as a dark cloud. And the messenger Azrael will bring forth the souls of them that have been slain, and they will behold the torment of them that slew them, and say to one another: Righteousness and justice is the judgment of God. For we heard, but we did not believe, that we should come into this place of continuous judgment. ⁵And near by this flame will be a great and very deep pit, and into it flows from above all manner of torment, foulness, and issue. And women are swallowed up therein up to their necks and tormented with great pain. These are they that have caused their children to be born untimely and have corrupted the work of God that created them. Over against them will be another place where their children sit alive, and they cry to God. And lightnings go forth from those children and pierce the eyes of them that for fornication's sake have caused their destruction. ⁶Other men and women will stand above them, naked; and their children stand over against them in a place of delight, and sigh and cry to God because of their parents, saying, These are they that have despised, and cursed, and transgressed Your commands and delivered us to death: they have cursed the messenger that formed us, and have hanged us up, and withheld from us the light which You have given to all creatures. And the milk of their mothers flowing from their breasts will congeal, and from it will come beasts devouring flesh, which will come forth, and turn, and torment them agelong with their husbands, because they forsook the commands of God and slew their children. As for their children, they will be delivered to the messenger Temlakos. And they that slew them will be tormented continuously, for God wills it so. ⁷Azrael, the messenger of wrath, will bring men and women—the half of their bodies burning—and cast them into a place of darkness, even the Gehenna of men; and a spirit of wrath will punish them with all manner of torment, and a worm that does not sleep will devour their entrails: and these are the persecutors and betrayers of My righteous ones. ⁸And beside them that are there, will be other men and women, gnawing their tongues; and they will torment them with red-hot iron and burn their eyes. These are they that slander and doubt of My righteousness. Other men and women whose works were done in deceitfulness will have their lips cut off, and fire enters into their mouth and their entrails. These are the false witnesses [[or these are they that caused the martyrs to die by their lying]]. ⁹And beside them, in a place near at hand, on the stone will be a pillar of fire, and the pillar is sharper than swords. And there will be men and women clad in rags and filthy garments, and they will be cast thereon, to suffer the judgment of a torment that does not cease: these are they that trusted in their riches and despised the widows and the woman with fatherless children … before God. ¹⁰And into another place hard by, full of filth, they cast men and women up to the knees. These are they that lent money and took usury. ¹¹And other men and women cast themselves down from a high place and return again and run, and devils drive them. And they put them to the end of their wits, and they cast themselves down. And thus they do continually, and are tormented continuously. These are they which have cut their flesh as [apostles] of a man: and the women that were with them … and these are the men that defiled themselves together as women. ¹²And beside them will be a brazier, and beneath them the messenger Azrael will prepare a place of much fire: and all the idols of gold and silver, all idols, the work of men's hands, and the semblances of images of cats and lions, of creeping things and wild beasts, and the men and women that have prepared the images thereof, will be in chains of fire and will be punished because of their error before the idols, and this is their judgment forever. ¹³And beside them will be other men and women, burning in the fire of the judgment, and their torment is continuous. These are they that have forsaken the command of God and followed the persuasions of devils."

CHAPTER 3

¹"And there will be another place—very high. [[There will be a furnace and a brazier wherein fire will burn. The fire that will burn will come from one end of the brazier.]] The men and women whose feet slip will go rolling down into a place where fear is. And again, while the fire that is prepared flows, they mount up, and fall down again, and continue to roll down. Thus they will be tormented continuously. These are they that did not honor their father and mother, and of their own accord withheld themselves from them. Therefore, they will be punished continuously. ²Furthermore, the messenger Azrael will bring children and maidens to show them those that are tormented. They will be punished with pains, with hanging up, and with a multitude of wounds which flesh-devouring birds will inflict on them. These are

REVELATION OF PETER

they that boast themselves in their sins, and do not obey their parents, and do not follow the instruction of their fathers, and do not honor them that are more aged than they. ³Beside them will be girls clad in darkness for a garment and they will be severely punished, and their flesh will be torn in pieces. These are they that did not keep their virginity until they were given in marriage, and with these torments they will be punished, and will feel them. ⁴And again, other men and women, gnawing their tongues without ceasing, and being tormented with continuous fire—these are the servants which were not obedient to their masters; and this then is their continuous judgment. ⁵And hard by this place of torment will be men and women mute and blind, whose raiment is white. They will crowd on one another and fall on coals of unquenchable fire. These are they that give alms and say, We are righteous before God, whereas they have not sought after righteousness. ⁶Azrael, the messenger of God, will bring them forth out of this fire and establish a judgment of decision. This then is their judgment: a river of fire will flow and all [those in] judgment will be drawn down into the middle of the river. And Uriel will set them there. ⁷And there are wheels of fire and men and women hung thereon by the strength of the whirling thereof. And they that are in the pit will burn: now these are the sorcerers and sorceresses. Those wheels will be in a decision by fire without number. ⁸Thereafter the messengers will bring My chosen ones and righteous which are perfect in all uprightness, and bear them in their hands, and clothe them with the raiment of the life that is above. They will see their desire on them that hated them, when he punishes them, and the torment of everyone will be continuous according to his works. ⁹And all they that are in torment will say with one voice: Have mercy on us, for now we know the judgment of God, which He declared to us formerly, and we did not believe. And the messenger Tatirokos will come and punish them with yet greater torment, and say to them: Now do you convert, when it is no longer the time for conversion, and nothing of life remains. And they will say: The judgment of God is righteous, for we have heard and perceived that His judgment is good; for we are repaid according to our deeds. ¹⁰Then I will give to My chosen ones and righteous the immersion and the salvation for which they have implored Me, in the field of Acherusa [[or Elysium]]. They will adorn the portion of the righteous with flowers, and I will go ... I will rejoice with them. I will cause the peoples to enter into My continuous Kingdom and show them that continuous thing [[or life]] whereon I have made them to set their hope, even I and My Father which is in Heaven. ¹¹I have spoken this to you, Peter, and declared it to you. Therefore, go forth and go to the land [[or city]] of the west. [[And enter into the vineyard which I will tell you of, in order that by the sufferings of the Son who is without sin the deeds of corruption may be sanctified. As for you, you are chosen according to the promise which I have given you. Therefore, spread My good news throughout all the world in peace. Truly men will rejoice: My words will be the source of hope and of life, and suddenly the world will be ravished.]]"

CHAPTER 4

¹And my Lord Jesus Christ our King said to me, "Let us go to the holy mountain." And His disciples went with Him, praying. And behold, there were two men there, and we could not look on their faces, for a light came from them, shining more than the sun, and their raiment was also shining, and cannot be described, and nothing is sufficient to be compared to them in this world. And the sweetness of them ... that no mouth is able to utter the beauty of their appearance, for their aspect was astonishing and wonderful. And the other, great, I say, shines in his aspect above crystal. Like the flower of roses is the appearance of the color of his aspect and of his body. Their head was a marvel. And on his [[or their]] shoulders and on their foreheads was a crown of nard woven of fair flowers. As the rainbow in the water [[or in the time of rain]], so was their hair. And such was the comeliness of their countenance, adorned with all manner of ornament. And when we saw them all of a sudden, we marveled. And I drew near to the Lord Jesus Christ and said to Him, "O my Lord, who are these?" And He said to me, "They are Moses and Elijah." And I said to Him, "[What about] Abraham, and Isaac, and Jacob, and the rest of the righteous fathers?" And He showed us a great garden, open, full of fair trees and blessed fruits, and of the fragrance of perfumes. The fragrance thereof was pleasant and came even to us. And thereof I saw much fruit. And my Lord and God Jesus Christ said to me, "Have you seen the companies of the fathers? ²As is their rest, such also is the honor and the glory of them that are persecuted for My righteousness' sake." And I rejoiced, and believed, and understood that which is written in the scroll of my Lord Jesus Christ. And I said to Him, "O my Lord, will You that I make three shelters here, one for You, and one for Moses, and one for Elijah?" And He said to me in wrath: "Satan makes war against you and has veiled your understanding; and the good things of this world prevail against you. Your eyes, therefore, must be opened and your ears unstopped that [you may perceive] a dwelling place not made with men's hands, which My heavenly Father has made for Me and for the chosen ones." And we beheld it and were full of gladness. ³And behold, suddenly there came a voice from Heaven, saying, "This is My beloved Son in whom I am well pleased." And then came a great and exceeding white cloud over our heads and carried away our Lord, and Moses, and Elijah. And I trembled and was afraid: and we looked up and the sky opened, and we beheld men in the flesh, and they came and greeted our Lord, and Moses, and Elijah and went into another heaven. And the word of the Writing was fulfilled: "This is the generation that seeks Him and seeks the face of the God of Jacob." And great fear and commotion was there in Heaven and the messengers pressed on one another that the word of the Writing might be fulfilled which says: "Open the gates, you princes." ⁴Thereafter the sky that had been open was shut. ⁵And we prayed and went down from the mountain, glorifying God, who has written the names of the righteous in Heaven in the Scroll of Life.

REVELATION OF THOMAS

Written between the 2nd and 4th centuries, the Revelation or Apocalypse of Thomas made popular the medieval list of supposed prophetic signs called Fifteen Signs before Doomsday. These signs were widely used in millenarian circles.

CHAPTER 1

¹Hear, O Thomas, for I am the Son of God the Father, and I am the father of all spirits. ²Hear from Me the signs which will come to pass at the end of this world, when the end of the world will be fulfilled—before My chosen ones depart out of the world. ³I will tell you that which will come to pass openly to men, but when these things will be, the princes of the messengers do not know, seeing it is now hidden from before them. ⁴Then there will be in the world distributions between king and king, and in all the earth will be great famine, great pestilences, and many distresses, ⁵and the sons of men will be led captive among all nations and will fall by the edge of the sword, [[and there will be great commotion in the world]]. ⁶Then after that, when the hour of the end draws near, there will be for seven days great signs in the sky, and the powers of the heavens will be moved.

CHAPTER 2

¹Then there will be on the first day the beginning: at the third hour of the day, a great and mighty voice in the firmament of the heavens and a bloody cloud coming up [[or down]] out of the north, and great thunderings and mighty lightnings will follow it, and it will cover the whole sky, and there will be a rain of blood on all the earth. ²These are the signs of the first day. ³And on the

REVELATION OF THOMAS

second day there will be a great voice in the firmament of the heavens, and the earth will be moved out of its place, and the gates of Heaven will be opened in the firmament of the heavens toward the east, and the smoke of a great fire will break forth through the gates of Heaven and will cover all the sky until evening. ⁴In that day there will be fears and great terrors in the world. ⁵These are the signs of the second day. ⁶But on the third day, about the third hour, there will be a great voice in Heaven, and the abysses of the earth will roar from the four corners of the world; ⁷the pinnacles of the firmament of the heavens will be opened, and all the air will be filled with pillars of smoke. ⁸There will be a stench of brimstone, very evil, until the tenth hour, and men will say: "We think the time draws near in which we perish." ⁹These are the signs of the third day. ¹⁰And on the fourth day, at the first hour, from the land of the east the abyss will melt and roar. ¹¹Then all the earth will be shaken by the might of an earthquake. In that day the ornaments of the heathen will fall, and all the buildings of the earth, before the might of the earthquake. ¹²These are the signs of the fourth day. ¹³But on the fifth day, at the sixth hour, suddenly there will be a great thunder in the sky, and the powers of light and the wheel of the sun will be caught away, and there will be great darkness in the world until evening, and the air will be gloomy without sun or moon, and the stars will cease from their service. ¹⁴In that day, all nations will behold as in a mirror and will despise the life of this world. ¹⁵These are the signs of the fifth day. ¹⁶And on the sixth day, at the fourth hour, there will be a great voice in Heaven, and the firmament of the heavens will be split from the east to the west, and the messengers of the heavens will be looking forth on the earth by the openings of the heavens, and all these that are on the earth will behold the host of the messengers looking forth out of Heaven. ¹⁷Then all men will flee to the mountains, and hide themselves from the face of the righteous messengers, and say: "If only the earth would open and swallow us up!" ¹⁸And such things will come to pass as never were since this world was created.

CHAPTER 3
¹Then they will behold Me coming from above in the light of My Father with the power and honor of the holy messengers. ²Then at My coming, the fence of fire of Paradise will be done away with—because Paradise is girded around with fire. ³And this will be that perpetual fire that will consume the earth and all the elements of the world. ⁴Then the spirits and souls of all men will come forth from Paradise and will come on all the earth: and every one of them will go to his own body, where it is laid up, ⁵and every one of them will say: "Here lies my body." ⁶And when the great voice of those spirits will be heard, then there will be a great earthquake over all the world, and by the might thereof, the mountains will be split from above and the rocks from beneath. ⁷Then every spirit will return into his own vessel, and the bodies of the holy ones which have fallen asleep will arise. ⁸Then their bodies will be changed into the image, and likeness, and honor of the holy messengers, and into the power of the image of My holy Father. ⁹Then they will be clothed with the garment of eternal life, out of the cloud of light which has never been seen in this world; for that cloud comes down out of the highest realm of Heaven from the power of My Father. ¹⁰And that cloud will encompass, with the beauty thereof, all the spirits that have believed in Me. ¹¹Then they will be clothed and will be borne by the hands of the holy messengers just as I have told you before. ¹²Then they will also be lifted up into the air on a cloud of light, and will go with Me rejoicing to Heaven, and then they will continue in the light and honor of My Father. ¹³Then there will be to them great gladness with My Father and before the holy messengers. ¹⁴These are the signs of the sixth day.

CHAPTER 4
¹And on the seventh day, at the eighth hour, there will be voices in the four corners of the sky. ²And all the air will be shaken and filled with holy messengers, and they will make war among them all day long. ³And in that day, My chosen ones will be sought out by the holy messengers from the destruction of the world. ⁴Then all men will see that the hour of their destruction draws near. ⁵These are the signs of the seventh day. ⁶And when the seven days are over, on the eighth day, at the sixth hour, there will be a sweet and tender voice in Heaven from the east. ⁷Then that messenger will be revealed which has power over the holy messengers: ⁸and all the messengers will go forth with him, sitting on chariots of the clouds of My holy Father, rejoicing and running on the air beneath the heavens to deliver the chosen ones that have believed in Me. ⁹And they will rejoice that the destruction of this world has come. ¹⁰THE WORDS OF THE SAVIOR TO THOMAS ARE ENDED, CONCERNING THE END OF THIS WORLD.

REVELATION OF STEPHEN

Serving as an expansion to the biblical account of the martyr Stephen's death, the Revelation or Apocalypse of Stephen was written some time before the 6th century. The final section, on Pilate, may be a later addition.

CHAPTER 1
¹Two years after the Ascension, there was a contest concerning Jesus. Many learned men had assembled at Jerusalem from Ethiopia, the Thebaid, Alexandria, Jerusalem, Asia, Mauretania, and Babylon. ²There was a great clamor among them like thunder, lasting until the fourth hour. ³Stephen, a learned man of the tribe of Benjamin, stood on a high place and addressed the assembly. "Why this tumult?" He said, "Blessed is he who has not doubted concerning Jesus. Born of a pure virgin, He filled the world with light. ⁴By Satan's schemes, Herod slew fourteen thousand children. He spoke of the miracles of Jesus. Woe to the unbelievers when He will come as judge, with messengers, a fiery chariot, a mighty wind: ⁵the stars will fall, the heavens open, the scrolls be brought forward. ⁶The twelve messengers who are set over every soul will unveil the deeds of men. ⁷The sea will move and give up what is in it. ⁸The mountains fall, all the surface of the earth become smooth. Great winged thrones are set. ⁹The LORD, and Christ, and the Holy Spirit take Their seats. The Father commands Jesus [to] sit on His right hand."

CHAPTER 2
¹At this point the crowd cried out: "Blasphemy!" And took Stephen before Pilate. ²Pilate stood on the steps and reproached them: "You compelled me to crucify the Innocent; why rage against this man? Why gnash your teeth? Are you still [so] foolish?" ³They led Stephen away. ⁴Caiaphas ordered him to be beaten until the blood ran. ⁵And he prayed: "Do not lay this sin to their charge" We saw how messengers ministered to him. ⁶In the morning, Pilate called his wife and two children: they immersed themselves and praised God.

CHAPTER 3
¹Three thousand men now assembled and disputed with Stephen for three days and three nights. ²On the fourth day, they took counsel and sent to Caesarea of Palestine for Saul of Tarsus, who had a commission to seize [the] Christians. ³He took his place on the judgment seat and said: "I marvel that you, a wise man, and my countryman, believe all this. None of the Sanhedrin have given up the Law. ⁴I have been through all Judea, Galilee, Peraea, Damascus, and the city of the Jesitites to seek out believers." ⁵Stephen lifted up his hands and said: "Silence, persecutor! Recognize the Son of God. ⁶You make me doubt my own descent. But I see that you will long drink of the same cup as I. What you do, do quickly." ⁷Saul tore his clothes and beat Stephen. Gamaliel, Saul's teacher, sprang forth and gave Saul a strike, saying, "Did I teach you

REVELATION OF STEPHEN

such conduct? Know that what this man says is acceptable and good." ⁸Saul was yet more enraged, and he looked fiercely on him, saying, "I spare your old age, but you will reap a due reward for this." ⁹Gamaliel answered: "I ask nothing better than to suffer with Christ." ¹⁰The elders tore their clothes, cast dust on their heads, and cried: "Crucify the blasphemers!" ¹¹Saul said, "Guard them until the morning." ¹²The next day, he sat on the judgment seat and had them brought before him, and they were led away to be crucified. ¹³A messenger came and cast away. the cross, and Stephen's wounds were healed. ¹⁴Seven men came and poured molten lead into his mouth and pitch into his ears. ¹⁵They drove nails into his breast and feet, and he prayed for their forgiveness. ¹⁶Again, a messenger came down and healed him, and a great multitude believed.

CHAPTER 4

¹The next day, everyone assembled and took him out of the city to judge him. ²He ascended a stone and addressed them: "How long will you harden your hearts? The Law and the Prophets spoke of Christ. ³In the first Law, and the second, and the other scrolls it is written: When the year of the covenant comes, I will send My beloved Messenger, the good spirit of sonship, from a pure maiden, the fruit of truth, without plowshare and without seed, and an image of sowing, and the fruit will grow after the … of planting forever from the word of My covenant, and signs will come to pass. ⁴And Isaiah says: To us a Child is born. And again: Behold, a virgin will conceive. ⁵And the prophet Nathan said: I saw one, a maiden and without touch of man, and a Manchild in her arms, and that was the Lord of the earth to the end of the earth. ⁶And again, the prophet Baruch says: Christ the eternal appears as a stone from the mountain and breaks in pieces the idol temples of the … ⁷David also said: Arise, O LORD, to Your resting place. ⁸Understand then, O foolish ones, what the prophet says: In this word you will judge." ⁹And he looked up toward the sky and said: "I see Heaven opened and the Son of Man standing at the right hand of God." ¹⁰Then they laid hands on him, saying, "He blasphemes!" ¹¹Gamaliel said: "Wherein? This righteous man has seen the Son saying to the Father: Behold, the Jews rage against Me and do not cease to mistreat them that confess My Name. ¹²And the Father said: Sit on My right hand until I make Your enemies Your footstool." ¹³Then they bound Stephen and took him away to Alexander, the reader, who was a chief of the people, and of the troop in Tiberias. ¹⁴In the fourth watch of the night, a light as of lightning shone around him, and a voice said: "Be strong. You are My first martyr, and your hour is near. I will write the record of you in the scroll of everlasting life." ¹⁵The Jews took counsel and decreed that he should be stoned. ¹⁶There were with him Abibas, Nicodemus, Gamaliel, Pilate, his wife and two children, and a multitude of believers. ¹⁷Saul stood forth, and beckoned, and said: "It would have been better that this man should not be slain, because of his great wisdom: but forasmuch as he is an apostate, I condemn Stephen to be stoned." ¹⁸The people said: "He will be stoned"; but those who stood in the front rank with staffs looked on each other and did not dare lay hands on him, for he was renowned among the people. ¹⁹Saul was angry, and stripped those servants of their garments, and laid them on the table, and commanded the men to stone Stephen. ²⁰Stephen looked around and said: "Saul, Saul, that which you do to me today, that same will the Jews do to you tomorrow. And when you suffer, you will think of me." ²¹The people cast stones at him so thickly that the light of the sun was darkened. ²²Nicodemus and Gamaliel put their arms around him and shielded him, and were slain, and gave up their souls to Christ. ²³Stephen prayed, saying, "Forgive them that stone us, for by their means we trust to enter into your Kingdom." ²⁴And at the tenth hour, he gave up the spirit. ²⁵Then beautiful youths appeared, and fell on the bodies, and wept aloud: and the people beheld the souls borne up by messengers into Heaven and saw the heavens open and the hosts coming to meet the souls. ²⁶And the people mourned for three days and three nights.

CHAPTER 5

¹Pilate took the bodies and put each one into a silver coffin with his name on it, but Stephen's coffin was gilded. ²And he laid them in his secret tomb. ³But Stephen prayed [from Heaven]: "Let my body be buried in my land of Serasima in Caphargamala until the revealing, when the martyrs that follow me will be gathered together." ⁴And a messenger came and removed the bodies to that place. ⁵But Pilate rose early to burn incense before the bodies and did not find them; and he tore his clothes, saying, "Was I then not worthy to be Your servant?" ⁶On the following night, Stephen appeared and said to him: "Do not weep. I implored God to hide our bodies. ⁷In the time of our revealing, one of your seed will find us after a vision, and your desire will be fulfilled. ⁸But build a house of prayer and celebrate our feast in the month of April. After seven months you also will rest." ⁹And Pilate did so: and he died and was buried at Kapartasala; and his wife also died in peace. ¹⁰But the holy martyrs appeared to venerable and believing men three times, speaking to them and revealing divine words: for after their death, many believed.

REVELATION OF THE VIRGIN

More commonly called the Apocalypse of the Virgin, the Revelation of the Virgin is a 4th-century work, existing manuscripts conflict in regard to the protagonist: some have the apostle Paul and others, as in this collection, have Mary in the role. It is likely the Pauline apocalypse is older. The present translation comes from Ethiopic.

CHAPTER 1

¹The all-holy mother of God was about to proceed to the Mount of Olives to pray; ²and praying to the LORD our God, she said: "In the Name of the Father, and the Son, and the Holy Spirit; let the chief-messenger Gabriel descend, so that he may tell me concerning the punishments, and concerning things in Heaven, and on the earth, and under the earth." ³And as she said the word, the chief-messenger Michael descended with the messengers of the East and the West, and messengers of the South and the North, ⁴and they saluted the highly favored one and said to her: "Hail, reflection of the Father, hail dwelling of the Son, hail command of the Holy Spirit, hail firmament of the seven heavens, hail firmament of the eleven strongholds, hail devotion of the messengers, hail loftier than the prophets to the throne of God." ⁵And the holy mother of God said to the messenger: "Hail Michael, commander-in-chief, the minister of the invisible Father, ⁶hail Michael, commander-in-chief, associate of my Son, hail Michael, commander-in-chief, most dread of the six-winged, ⁷hail Michael, commander-in-chief, who rules through all things and is worthy to stand beside the throne of the LORD, ⁸hail Michael, commander-in-chief, who is about to sound the trumpet and awaken those who have been asleep for ages: ⁹hail Michael, commander-in-chief, first of all to the throne of God."

CHAPTER 2

¹And having greeted all the messengers in like manner, the highly favored one implored the commander-in-chief regarding the punishments, saying, "Tell to me all things on the earth." ²And the commander-in-chief said to her: "If you ask me, highly favored one, I will tell you." ³And the highly favored one said to him: "How many are the punishments with which the race of man is punished?" ⁴And the chief-messenger said to her: "The punishments are innumerable." ⁵And the highly favored one said to him: "Tell me the things in Heaven and on the earth."

CHAPTER 3

¹Then the commander-in-chief, Michael, commanded the Western messengers that revelation should be made, ²and Hades opened, and she saw those who were punished in Hades: ³and there lay there a multitude of men and women, and there was a great lamentation. ⁴And the highly favored one asked the commander-in-chief: "Who are these, and what is their sin?" ⁵And the commander-in-chief said: "These, all-holy, are those who did not worship the Father, and the Son, and the Holy Spirit, and for this reason, they are thus punished here."

CHAPTER 4

¹And she saw in another place a great darkness, and the all-holy said: "What is this darkness, and who are they who are being punished?" ²And the commander-in-chief said: "Many souls are lying in this darkness." ³And the all-holy one said: "Let this darkness be taken away in order that I may see this punishment also." ⁴And the commander-in-chief said to the highly favored one: "It is not possible, all-holy, that you should see this punishment also." ⁵And the messengers guarding them answered and said: "We have a command from the invisible Father that they will not see the light until your blessed Son will shine forth." ⁶And plunged into grief, the all-holy lifted up her eyes to the messengers touching the undefiled Word of the Father, and said: "In the Name of the Father, and the Son, and the Holy Spirit, let the darkness be taken away, so that I may see this punishment also." ⁷And immediately that darkness was lifted up and covered the seven heavens: and there lay a great multitude of both men and women, and there arose a great lamentation and a great cry began. ⁸And seeing them, the all-holy wept and said to them: "What are you doing, wretched ones? Who are you? And why are you found there?" ⁹And there was no voice or listening. And the messengers guarding them said: "Why do you not speak to the highly favored one?" ¹⁰And those who were under punishment said to her: "O highly favored one, from eternity we do not see the light, and we are not able to keep off that up there." ¹¹And splashing pitch flowed down on them: and seeing them, the all-holy wept. ¹²And again, those who were being punished said to her: "How do you ask concerning us, holy lady, mother of God? ¹³Your blessed Son came to the earth and did not make inquiry concerning us, neither Abraham the patriarch, nor John the Baptist, nor Moses the great prophet, nor the apostle Paul, and to us their light did not shine; ¹⁴and now, all-holy mother of God, the armor of the Christians, the bringer of great comfort on account of the Christians, why do you ask concerning us?" ¹⁵Then the all-holy mother of God said to Michael, the commander-in-chief: "What is their sin?" ¹⁶And Michael, the commander-in-chief, said: "These are they who did not believe in the Father, and the Son, and the Holy Spirit, and did not confess you to be the mother of God, and that the Lord Jesus Christ was born of you and took flesh, and for this reason they are punished there." ¹⁷And again weeping, the all-holy mother of God said to them: "Why did you err so greatly, O wretched ones? Did you not hear that the whole creation names my name?" ¹⁸And having said these words, the darkness fell over them as it was from the beginning.

CHAPTER 5

¹And the commander-in-chief said: "To where would you go, highly favored one? To the West or to the South?" And the highly favored answered: "Let us go to the South." ²And immediately there appeared the cherubim, and the seraphim, and four hundred messengers, and led out the highly favored one to the South, where the river of fire came out, ³and there lay a multitude of men and women, some up to the girdle, others up to the neck, and others up to the crown of the head: ⁴and seeing them, the all-holy mother of God cried out with a loud voice to the commander-in-chief and said: "Who are these, and what is their sin who stand in the fire up to the girdle?" ⁵And the commander-in-chief said: "These, all-holy one, are they who inherited the curse of father and mother, and for this reason they are thus punished here as accursed."

CHAPTER 6

¹And the all-holy one said: "And who are these standing in the fire up to the breasts?" ²And the commander-in-chief said: "These are whosoever cast off their wives and defiled them in adultery, and for this reason they are thus punished here."

CHAPTER 7

¹And the all-holy one said to the commander-in-chief: "Who are these standing up to the neck in the flame of the fire?" ²And the commander-in-chief said: "These, all-holy one, are whosoever ate the flesh of men." ³And the all-holy one said: "And how is it possible for one man to eat the flesh of another?" ⁴And the commander-in-chief said: "Listen, all-holy one, and I will tell you: these are they whosoever brought down their own children out of their own wombs and cast them out as food for dogs, ⁵and whosoever gave up their brothers in the presence of kings and governors—these ate the flesh of man, and for this reason they are thus punished."

CHAPTER 8

¹And the all-holy one said: "Who are these set in the fire up to the crown?" ²And the commander-in-chief said: "These, all-holy one, are whosoever lays hold of the precious Cross and [yet] swears to a lie by the power of the Cross of the LORD. ³The messengers tremble and worship with fear, and men lay hold of it, and swear to a lie, and do not know what they testify, and for this reason they are thus punished here."

CHAPTER 9

¹And in another place the all-holy one saw a man hung by the feet, and worms devoured him. ²And she asked the commander-in-chief: "Who is this and what is his sin?" ³And the commander-in-chief said: "This is he who took interest for his gold, and for this reason he is thus punished here."

CHAPTER 10

¹And she saw a woman hanging by her two ears, and all the beasts came out of her mouth and gnawed her in pieces; ²and the highly favored one asked the commander-in-chief: "Who is she, and what is her sin?" ³And the commander-in-chief said: "She is she who turned aside into strange houses and those of her neighbors and spoke evil words to cause strife, and for that reason she is thus punished here."

CHAPTER 11

¹And seeing these things, the all-holy mother of God wept and said to the commander-in-chief: "It were better for man that he had not been born." ²And the commander-in-chief said: "Truly, all-holy one, you have not seen the great punishments." ³And the all-holy one said to the commander-in-chief: "Come, Michael, great commander-in-chief, and lead me that I may see all the punishments." ⁴And the commander-in-chief said: "Where do you wish, all-holy one, that we should go?" ⁵And the highly favored one answered: "To the West"; and immediately the cherubim appeared and led the highly favored to the West.

CHAPTER 12

¹And she saw a cloud full of fire and in it there was a multitude of men and women. ²And the all-holy one said: "What was their sin?" ³And the commander-in-chief said: "These, all-holy one, are they who on the morning of the LORD's Day sleep like the dead, and for that reason they are thus punished here." ⁴And the all-holy one said: "If anyone cannot rise, what will he do?" ⁵And the commander-in-chief said: "Listen, all-holy one: if anyone's house is fastened on the four [sides] and surrounds him, and he cannot come out, he has forgiveness."

CHAPTER 13

¹And she saw in another place burning benches of fire and on them sat a multitude of men and women and burned on them. ²And the all-holy one asked: "Who are these, and what is their sin?" ³And the commander-in-chief said: "These, all-holy one, are they who do not rise up to the elder when they enter into the assembly of God, and for this reason they are thus punished here."

CHAPTER 14

¹And the all-holy one saw in another place an iron tree and it had branches of iron, and on it there hung a multitude of men and women by their tongues. ²And seeing them, the all-holy one wept and asked the commander-in-chief, saying, "Who are these, and what was their sin?" ³And the commander-in-chief said: "These are perjurers, blasphemers,

slanderers, whosoever divided brothers from brothers." ⁴And the all-holy one said: "How is it possible to divide brothers from brothers?" ⁵And the commander-in-chief said: "Listen, all-holy one, and I will tell you about this: when some from among the nations desired to be blasphemed, he will receive ceaseless retribution."

CHAPTER 15

¹And in another place the all-holy one saw a man hanging from his four extremities, and from his nails blood gushed out vehemently, and his tongue was tied in a flame of fire, and he was unable to groan and say the "LORD, have mercy." ²And when she had seen him, the all-holy one wept and herself said the "LORD, have mercy" three times; ³and after the saying of the prayer, the messenger who had authority over the scourge came and loosed the man's tongue, ⁴and the all-holy one asked the commander-in-chief: "Who is this wretched one who has this punishment?" ⁵And the commander-in-chief said: "This, all-holy one, is the steward who did not do the will of God, but ate the things of the assembly and said, He who ministers to the altar will be nourished from the altar, and for this reason he is thus punished here." ⁶And the all-holy one said: "Let it be to him according to his faith." And he tied his tongue again.

CHAPTER 16

¹And Michael, the commander-in-chief, said: "Come here, all-holy one, and I will show to you where the priests are punished." ²And the all-holy one came out and saw elders hanging by their twenty nails, and fire came out of their heads. ³And seeing them, the all-holy one asked the commander-in-chief: "Who are these, and what is their sin?" ⁴And the commander-in-chief said: "These, all-holy one, are they who stand beside the throne of God, and when they sang of the body of our Lord Jesus Christ, the pearls fell out, and the awful throne of Heaven shook, and the footstool of our Lord Jesus Christ trembled, ⁵and they did not perceive it, and for this reason they are thus punished here."

CHAPTER 17

¹And the all-holy one saw a man and a winged beast having three heads like flames of fire: the two heads were toward his eyes and the third head toward his mouth. ²And seeing him, the all-holy one asked the commander-in-chief: "Who is this, that he cannot save himself from the mouth of the dragon?" ³And the commander-in-chief said to her: "This, all-holy one, is the reader who does not practice in his own habits according to what is worthy of the holy Gospel, and for this reason he is thus punished here."

CHAPTER 18

¹And the commander-in-chief said: "Come here, all-holy one, and I will show you where the forms of the messenger and chief-messenger are punished." ²She proceeded and saw them lying in the fire and the sleepless worm gnawed them; ³and the all-holy one said: "Who are these, and what is their sin?" ⁴And the commander-in-chief said: "These, all-holy one, are they who possessed the form of the chief-messenger and apostle. ⁵Listen, all-holy one, concerning this: on earth they were called patriarchs and overseers, and they were not worthy of their name; ⁶on earth they heard, Bless [the LORD] you holy ones, and in Heaven they were not called holy ones, because they did not act as bearers of the form of the chief-messenger, and for this reason they are thus punished here."

CHAPTER 19

¹And she saw women hanging by their nails, and a flame of fire came out of their mouth and burned them: ²and all the beasts coming out of the fire gnawed them to pieces, and groaning they cried out: "Have pity on us, have pity, for we are punished worse than all those who are under punishment." ³And seeing them, the all-holy one wept and asked the commander-in-chief, Michael: "Who are these, and what is their sin?" ⁴And the commander-in-chief said: "These are the wives of elders who did not honor the elders, but after the death of the elder took husbands, and for this reason they are thus punished here."

CHAPTER 20

¹And the all-holy one also saw after the same manner a deaconess hanging from a crag and a beast with two heads devoured her breasts. ²And the all-holy one asked: "What is her sin?" ³And the commander-in-chief said: "She, all-holy one, is a chief deaconess who defiled her body in fornication, and for this reason she is thus punished here."

CHAPTER 21

¹And she saw other women hanging over the fire, and all the beasts devoured them. ²And the all-holy one asked the commander-in-chief: "Who are these, and what is their sin?" ³And he said: "These are they who did not do the will of God: lovers of money, and those who took interest on accounts, and the immodest."

CHAPTER 22

¹And when she had heard these things, the all-holy one wept and said: "Woe to sinners!" ²And the commander-in-chief said: "Why do you lament, all-holy one? Now truly you have not seen the great punishments." ³And the highly favored one said: "Come, Michael, the great commander-in-chief of the powers above, tell me how I may see all the punishments." ⁴And the commander-in-chief said: "Where do you wish that we should go, all-holy one? To the East or toward the leftward parts of Paradise?" ⁵And the all-holy one said: "To the leftward parts of Paradise."

CHAPTER 23

¹And immediately, when she had spoken, the cherubim and seraphim stood beside her and led the highly favored one out to the leftward parts of Paradise. ²And behold, there was a great river, and the appearance of the river was blacker than pitch, and in it there were a multitude of men and women: ³it boiled like a furnace of forges, and its waves were like a wild sea over the sinners; and when the waves rose, they sank the sinners ten thousand cubits, ⁴and they were unable to keep it off and say, "Have mercy on us, you just Judge," for the sleepless worm devoured them, and there was no reckoning of the number of those who devoured them. ⁵And seeing the all-holy mother of God, the messengers who punished them cried out with one voice: "Holy is God who has compassion on account of the mother of God! ⁶We give You thanks, O Son of God, that from eternity we did not see the light, and today through the mother of God we have seen the light"; ⁷and again, they shouted with one voice, saying, "Hail, highly favored mother of God! Hail, lamp of the inaccessible light! Hail to you also, Michael, the commander-in-chief— ⁸you that are ambassador from the whole creation, for we, seeing the punishment of sinners, are greatly grieved." ⁹And the all-holy one, when she saw the messengers humbled on account of the sinners, lamented and said: "Woe to sinners and their neighbors!" ¹⁰And the all-holy one said: "Let us see the sinners." ¹¹And the highly favored one, coming with the chief-messenger Michael and all the armies of the messengers, lifted up one voice, saying, "LORD have mercy." ¹²And after making the prayer earnestly, the wave of the river rested, and the fiery waves grew calm, and the sinners appeared as a grain of mustard-seed; ¹³and seeing them, the all-holy one lamented and said: "What is this river, and what are its waves?" ¹⁴And the commander-in-chief said: "This river is the outer fire, and those who are being tortured are the Jews who crucified our Lord Jesus Christ, the Son of God, and who refused holy immersion, ¹⁵and those who commit fornication and sin against the sweet and passionless perfume of marriage, and he who debauches mother and daughter, and the poisoners and those who slay with the sword, and the women who strangle their offspring." ¹⁶And the all-holy one said: "According to their faith, so be it to them." ¹⁷And immediately the waves rose over the sinners and the darkness covered them. ¹⁸And the commander-in-chief said: "Listen, you highly favored one: if anyone will be cast into this darkness, his remembrance will never be in the sight of God." ¹⁹And the all-holy mother of God said: "Woe to sinners, because the flame of the fire is everlasting."

CHAPTER 24

¹And the commander-in-chief said: "Come here, all-holy one, and I will show the lake of fire to you; and see where the race of the Christians is punished." ²And the all-holy one proceeded and saw: and some she heard, but others she did not see; ³and she asked the commander-in-chief: "Who are these, and what is their sin?" ⁴And the commander-in-chief said: "These, all-holy one, are those who were Christian, but worked the works of the

devil and wasted the time of their conversion, and for this reason they are thus punished here."

CHAPTER 25

¹And she said: "Please, I will make one request of you: let me also be punished with the Christians, because they are the children of my Son." ²And the commander-in-chief said: "Rest in Paradise, holy lady, mother of God." ³And the all-holy one said: "I beg you: move the fourteen firmaments and the seven heavens, and let us pray for the Christians that the LORD our God may listen to us and have mercy on them." ⁴And the commander-in-chief said: "As the LORD God lives, the great Name, seven times a day and seven times a night, when we lead up the hymn of the LORD, we make remembrance for the sake of sinners, and the LORD accounts us as nothing."

CHAPTER 26

¹And the all-holy one said: "I beg you, commander-in-chief: command the armies of the messengers and let them place me on the height of Heaven, and let me into the presence of the invisible Father." ²And immediately the commander-in-chief commanded, and the chariot of the cherubim and seraphim appeared, and they exalted the highly favored one to the height of Heaven and placed her in the presence of the invisible Father; ³and she stretched forth her hands to the undefiled throne of the Father and said: "Have mercy, O LORD, on the Christian sinners, for I saw them being punished, and I cannot bear their complaint. ⁴Let me go forth and be punished myself for the Christians. I do not pray, O LORD, for the unbelieving Jews, but for the Christians I plead for Your compassion." ⁵And there came a second voice from the invisible Father, saying, "How can I have mercy on them, when they did not have mercy on their own brothers?" ⁶And the all-holy one said: "LORD, have mercy on the sinners: behold the punishments, for every creature on the earth calls on my name; ⁷and when the soul comes forth out of the body, it cries, saying, Holy lady, mother of God." ⁸Then the LORD said to her: "Listen, all-holy mother of God, if anyone names and calls on your name, I will not forsake him, either in Heaven or on earth."

REVELATION OF THE VIRGIN

CHAPTER 27

¹And the all-holy one said: "Where is Moses? Where are all the prophets and fathers who never sinned? Where are you, holy Paul of God? ²Where is the holy LORD's Day, the boast of the Christians? ³Where is the power of the precious and life-giving Cross, which delivered Adam and Eve from the ancient curse?" ⁴Then Michael and all the messengers raised one voice, saying, "LORD, have mercy on the sinners." ⁵Then Moses also cried: "Have mercy, LORD, on those to whom I gave Your Law." ⁶Then John also called: "Have mercy, LORD, on those to whom I gave Your Gospel." ⁷Then Paul cried: "Have mercy, LORD, on those to whom I brought Your letters in the Assembly." ⁸And the LORD God said: "Listen, all you righteous: if according to the Law which Moses gave, and according to the Gospel which John gave, and according to the letters which Paul carried, they are thus judged." ⁹And they had nothing to say except, "Have mercy, O just Judge."

CHAPTER 28

¹And the all-holy mother of God said: "Have mercy, LORD, on the Christians, because they kept Your Law and gave heed to Your Gospel, but they were simple ones." ²Then the LORD said to her: "Listen, all-holy one: if anyone did evil to them, and they did not repay him the evil, you say well that they attended to both My Law and My Gospel; ³but if he did not do them wrong, and they repaid him evil, how may I say that these are holy men? Now they will be rewarded according to their wrongdoing." ⁴Then everyone hearing the voice of the LORD had nothing to answer; and the all-holy one, when she saw that the holy ones were at a loss, and their Lord did not hear, and His mercy was hidden from them, then the all-holy one said: "Where is Gabriel, who announced to me: Hail, you that from eternity will conceive Him who is without beginning like the Father, and now does not look on sinners? ⁵Where is the great commander-in-chief? Come here, all you holy ones whom God justified, and let us fall down in the presence of the invisible Father, in order that the LORD God may hear us and have mercy on sinners." ⁶Then Michael, the commander-in-chief, and all the holy ones fell on their faces in the presence of the invisible Father, saying, "Have mercy, LORD, on the Christian sinners."

CHAPTER 29

¹Then the LORD, seeing the prayer of the holy ones, had compassion and said: "Go down, My beloved Son, and because of the prayer of the holy ones, let Your face shine on earth to sinners." ²Then the LORD came down from His undefiled throne; and when they saw Him, those who were under punishment raised one voice, saying, "Have mercy on us, King of the ages." ³Then the Lord of all things said: "Listen, all you sinners and righteous men: I made a paradise and made man after My image, but he transgressed, and for his own sins was delivered to death; but I did not allow the works of My hands to be tyrannized over by the serpent. ⁴Therefore, I bowed the heavens, and came down, and was born of Mary, the holy undefiled mother of God, so that I might set you free: ⁵I was sin; I was nailed to the Cross to free you from the ancient curse; I asked for water and you gave Me vinegar mingled with gall; ⁶I was laid in the grave; I trampled on the enemy; I raised up My chosen ones, and even thus you would not hear Me. ⁷But now, because of the prayer of My mother Mary, because she has wept much for your sake, and because of Michael My chief-messenger, and because of the multitude of My holy ones, I grant you to have rest on the day of Pentecost to glorify the Father, and the Son, and the Holy Spirit."

CHAPTER 30

¹Then all the messengers and chief-messengers, thrones, lordships, authorities, governments, powers, and the many-eyed cherubim, and the six-winged seraphim, and all the apostles, and prophets, and martyrs, and all the holy ones raised one voice, saying, "Glory to You, O LORD! Glory to You, lover of men! Glory to You, King of the ages! Glory be to Your compassion! Glory be to Your long-suffering! ²Glory be to Your unspeakable justice of judgment, because You have been long-suffering with sinners and impious men! It is Yours to pity and to save." ³To Him be the glory and the power: to the Father, and to the Son, and to the Holy Spirit, forever and ever. Amen.

THE SIBYLLINE ORACLES

The Sibylline Oracles are a collection of 12 books and additional fragments (the fragments are placed in a 13th book in this LSV collection) purporting to be the oracular utterances of the Sibyls of old—ancient Gentile prophetesses, primarily active in ancient Greece. While the extant oracles show extensive Judeo-Christian recension and invention, and are generally considered pseudepigraphal, it should be noted that some portions may reflect the original utterances, particularly portions of Book III attributed to an Erythraean Sibyl (at least one of whom was actually from Chaldea and a daughter of the historian Berossus), as well as portions of Books IV and V. As it was widely believed by writers in the early Church (e.g., Theophilus and Athenagoras) that the Sibyls prophesied of Christ, the extant oracles demonstrate the possibility that as the time of the Messiah drew near, His coming was foretold even among those outside of the Jewish nation. The first Sibyl was active at Delphi as early as the 11th century BC, and at their most active point there may have been as many as 10: a Persian, Libyan, Delphic, Cimmerian, Erythraean, Samian, Cumaean, Hellespontine, Phrygian, Tiburtine, Hebrew, Chaldean, and Egyptian. Unlike the plain language often found in the Bible's poetry and prophecy, the oracles are often cryptic and unintelligible, requiring speculative interpretation. The books are numbered I–VIII and XI–XIV; Books IX and X are merely duplicated material from I–VIII, thus there are 12 books and not 14.

[It is assumed that this Preface was prepared by the person who collected and arranged these pseudepigraphal oracles in the order in which they have come down to us. The exact time of his writing is unknown. Alexandre (Excursus ad Sibyllina, ch. xv, pp. 421–433) argues that the Preface was probably written in the 6th century, during the reign of Justinian.]

PREFACE

1. If the labor bestowed on the reading of the writings of the Greeks brings much advantage to them that perform it, since it is able to make those who work on these things very knowledgeable, much more is it fitting that they who are possessed of good understanding devote their leisure continually to the Holy Writings, which tell about God and the things which minister profit to the soul, therefore gaining the double benefit of ability to profit both themselves and their readers. It seemed good to me, therefore, to set forth in one connected and orderly series the so-called Sibylline Oracles, which are found scattered and in a confused condition, but which are helpful to the reading and understanding of those [Holy Writings], so that being easily brought together under the eye of the readers they may bring to these [readers] by way of reward the advantage that is to be derived from them, setting forth not a few necessary and useful things, and also rendering their study more valuable and varied. For [these oracles] also speak clearly of the Father, the Son, and the Holy Spirit: the sacred and life-originating Trinity; and of the incarnate dispensation of our Lord, and God, and Savior Jesus Christ—I mean His birth from a virgin without emanation, and of the acts of healing performed by Him, as also of His life-giving passion, and of His resurrection from the dead on the third day, and of the judgment to come, and of recompense for what we all have done in this life; furthermore, [these oracles] distinctly set forth what is made known in the Mosaic writings and in the books of the prophets concerning the creation of the world, and the formation of man, and his expulsion from the Garden, and of his new formation hereafter. With regard to certain things which have [already] been or perhaps are yet to be, they prophesy in various ways; and in a word, they are able in no small measure to profit their readers.

2. Sibyl is a Latin word meaning "prophetess," or rather "soothsayer"; hence the female soothsayers were called by one name. Now Sibyls, according to many writers, have arisen in different times and places, to the number of ten. There was first the Chaldean, or rather the Persian [Sibyl], whose proper name is Sambethe. She was of the family of the most blessed Noah and is said to have foretold the exploits of Alexander of Macedon; Nicanor, who wrote the life of Alexander, mentions her. The second was the Libyan, of whom Euripides makes mention in the preface [of his play] of the Lamia. The third was the Delphian, born at Delphi, and spoken of by Chrysippus in his book on divination. The fourth was the Italian, in Cimmerium in Italy, whose son Evander founded in Rome the shrine of Pan which is called the Lupercal. The fifth was the Erythraean, who predicted the Trojan war, and of whom Apollodorus the Erythraean bears positive testimony. The sixth was the Samian, whose proper name is Phyto, of whom Eratosthenes wrote. The seventh was the Cumman, called Amalthea, also Herophile, and in some places Taraxandra. But Vergil calls the Cumaean Sibyl Deiphobe, daughter of Glaucus. The eighth was the Hellespontine, born in the village of Marpessus near the small town of Gergithion, which, according to Heraclides of Pontus, was formerly, in the time of Solon and Cyrus, within the boundaries of the Troad. The ninth was the Phrygian, and the tenth the Tiburtine, named Albunaea.

3. It is said, moreover, that the Cumaean Sibyl once brought nine books of her oracles to Tarquinius Priscus, who was at that time king of the Romans, and demanded for them three hundred pieces of gold. But having been disdainfully treated, and not even questioned as to what they were, she committed three of them to the fire. Again, in another audience with the king she brought forward the six remaining books, and still demanded the same amount. But not being deemed worthy of attention, again she burned three more. Then a third time bringing the three that were left, and asking the same price, she said that if he would not procure them, she would burn these also. Then, it is said, the king examined them and was astonished, and gave for them a hundred pieces of gold, took them in charge and made request for the others. But she declared that neither had she the like of those that were burned nor had she any such knowledge apart from inspiration, but that certain persons from various cities and countries had at times excerpted what was esteemed by them necessary and useful, and that out of these excerpts a collection ought to be made. And this [the Romans] did as quickly as possible. For that which was given from God, though truly laid up in a corner, did not escape their search. And the books of all the Sibyls were deposited in the capitol of ancient Rome. Those of the Cumaean Sibyl, however, were hidden and not made known to many, because she proclaimed more especially and distinctly things that were to happen in Italy, while the others became known to all. But those that were written by the Erythraean Sibyl have the name that was given her from the place, while the other books are without inscription to mark who is the author of each, but are without distinction [regarding authorship].

4. Now Firmianus, being an esteemed philosopher and a priest of the aforementioned capitol, having looked to the Christ, our eternal Light, set down in his own works the things spoken of by the Sibyls concerning the ineffable glory, and ably exposed the senselessness of Hellenic error. His forcible exposition is in the Italian tongue, but the Sibylline verses were published in the Greek language. And that this may not appear incredible, I will produce the testimony of the man previously mentioned, which is after this manner:

5. "Inasmuch as the Sibylline Oracles which are found in our city not only, as being very plentiful, are held in low esteem by those of the Greeks who are cognizant of them (for it is things which are rare that are held in honor), but also since not all of the verses keep to the precision of the meter, their credit is lower. But this is the fault not of the prophetess, but of the shorthand writers who could not keep up with the rush of the Sibyl's words, or who were uneducated; for her remembrance of the things she had spoken ceased with the spell of inspiration—which fact Plato also had in view when he said that [the prophets] treat correctly many and great

matters while they know nothing of the things of which they speak."

6. We will, accordingly, from those oracles which were brought to Rome by the ambassadors [of Tarquin], produce, as much as possible. Now, concerning the God who is without beginning, one declared these things:

One God, who rules alone, immense, unborn.
But God alone is one, highest of all,
Who made the heaven
and sun and stars and moon,
Fruit-bearing earth and billows of the sea.
He only is God, Maker uncontrolled;
He fixed the pattern of the human form,
And did the nature of all mortals mix
Himself, the generator of [all] life.

7. This [the Sibyl] has said either on the ground that being joined together, [husband and wife] become one flesh, or with the thought that out of the four elements which are opposite to each other, God fashioned both the world and man.

BOOK I

[Announcement, 1–5. Creation of the earth and man, 6–47. First sin and penalty, 48–81. Condition of the first race, 82–107. The second race of men, 108–129. Third and fourth races, 130–148. The race of giants, 149–153. Call and preaching of Noah, 154–243. Entrance into the Ark, and the Flood, 244–281. Abatement of the waters, 282–319. Exit from the Ark, 320–343. The sixth race and the Titans, 344–386. Prophecy of Christ, 387–468. Dispersion of the Hebrews, 469–485.]

Beginning with the generation first
Of mortal men down to the very last
I'll prophesy each thing: what once has been,
And what is now, and what will yet befall
⁵The world through the impiety of men.
First now God urges on me to relate
Truly how into being came the world.
And you, shrewd mortal,
prudently make known,
Lest ever you should my commands neglect,
¹⁰The King Most High,
who brought into existence
The whole world, saying, "Let there be,"
and there was.
For He the earth established, placing it
All around Tartarus, and He Himself
Gave the sweet light;
He raised the heaven on high,
¹⁵Spread out the gleaming sea,
and crowned the sky
With an abundance of bright-shining stars,
And decked the earth with plants,
and mingled sea
With rivers, and the air with zephyrs mixed
And watery clouds; and then, another race
²⁰Appointing, He gave fishes to the seas
And birds to the winds, and to the woods
The beasts of shaggy neck,
and snakes that crawl,
And all things which now
on the earth appear.
These by His word He made, and everything
²⁵Was speedily and with precision done;
For He was self-caused
and from heaven looked down
And finished was the world exceedingly well.
And then thereafter fashioned He again
A living product, copying a new man
³⁰From His own image, beautiful, divine,
And bade him in ambrosial Garden dwell,
That labors beautiful might be his care.
But in that fertile field of Paradise
He longed for conversation, being alone,
³⁵And prayed that he might see another form
Such as he had. And forthwith,
from man's side
Taking a bone, God Himself made fair Eve,
A wedded spouse, and in that Paradise
Gave her to dwell with him.
And, when he gazed
⁴⁰On her, suddenly filled with joy
Great admiration held his soul, he saw
A pattern so exact; and with wise words
Spontaneous flowing answered he in turn
For God had care for all things. For the mind
⁴⁵They darkened not with passion,
nor concealed
Their nakedness, but with hearts far from evil
Even like wild beasts they walked
with limbs exposed.
And afterward delivering them commands
God showed them not to touch a certain tree;
⁵⁰But the dread serpent drew them off
by guile
To go away to the fate of death
And to gain knowledge of both good and evil.
But the wife then first traitress
proved to God;
She gave, and urged the unknowing man
to sin.
⁵⁵And he, persuaded by the woman's words,
Forgot the immortal Maker utterly,
And treated plain commandments
with neglect.
Therefore, instead of good, received they evil
According to their deed. And then the leaves
⁶⁰Of the sweet fig-tree piercing
they made clothes
And put them on each other, and concealed
The sexual parts, because
they were ashamed.
But on them the Immortal set His wrath
And cast them out of the immortal land.
⁶⁵For their abiding now in mortal land
Was brought to pass, since hearing
they kept not
The word of the immortal mighty God.
And at once they, on the fruitful soil
Forthgoing, with their tears
and groans were wet;
⁷⁰And to them then the immortal God Himself
A word more excellent spoke: "Multiply,
Increase, work constantly on the earth,
That with the sweat of labor you may have
Sufficient food." Thus He spoke; and He made
⁷⁵The author of deceit to press the ground
On belly and on side, a crawling snake,
Driving him out severely; and He sent
Dire enmity between them and the one
Is on the look-out to preserve his head,
⁸⁰But man his heel; for death is neighbor near
Of evil-plotting vipers and of men.
And then indeed the race was multiplied
As the Almighty Himself gave command,
And there grew up one people on another
⁸⁵Innumerable. And houses they adorned
Of all kinds and made cities and their walls
Well and expertly; and to them was given
A day of long time for a life much-loved;
For they did not worn out with troubles die,
⁹⁰But as subdued by sleep; most happy men
Of great heart, whom the immortal Savior
loved,
The King, God. But they also did transgress,
Stricken with folly. For with impudence
They mocked their fathers
and their mothers scorned;
⁹⁵Kinsmen they knew not,
and they formed intrigues
Against their brothers.
And they were impure,
Having defiled themselves with human gore,
And they made wars. And then
on them came
The last calamity sent forth from Heaven,
¹⁰⁰Which snatched the dreadful men
away from life;
And Hades then received them; it was called
Hades since Adam, having tasted death,
Went first and earth encompassed
him around.
And therefore, all men born on the earth
¹⁰⁵Are in abodes of Hades called to go.
But even in Hades all these when they came
Had honor, since they were the earliest race.
But when Hades received these, secondly
[[Of the surviving and most righteous men]]
¹¹⁰God formed another very subtle race
That cared for lovely works, and noble toils,
Distinguished reverence and solid wisdom;
And they were trained in arts of every kind,
Finding inventions by their lack of means.
¹¹⁵And one devised to till the land with plows,
Another worked in wood, another cared
For sailing, and another watched the stars
And practiced augury with winged birds;
And use of drugs had interest for one,
¹²⁰While for another magic had a charm;
And others were in every other are
Which men care for instructed, wide awake,
Industrious, worthy of that eponym
Because they had a sleepless mind within
¹²⁵And a huge body; stout with mighty form
They were; but, notwithstanding,
down they went
Into Tartarean chamber terrible,
Kept in firm chains to pay full penalty
In Gehenna of strong, furious, quenchless fire.
¹³⁰And after these a third strong-minded race
Appeared, a race of overbearing men
And terrible, who worked among themselves
Many an evil. And fights, homicides,
And battles did continually destroy
¹³⁵Those men possessed of
overweening heart,
And from these afterward another race
Proceeded, late-completed, youngest born,
Blood-stained, perverse in counsel;
of men these
Were in the fourth race; much

of blood they spilled,
¹⁴⁰Nor feared they God nor had regard
    for men,
For maddening wrath and sore impiety
Were sent on them. And wars, homicides,
And battles sent some into Erebus,
Since they were arrogant impious men.
¹⁴⁵But the rest did the heavenly God Himself
In anger afterward change from His world,
Casting them into mighty Tartarus
Down under the foundation of the earth.
And later yet another race much worse
¹⁵⁰[[Of men He made,
    to whom no good thereafter]]
The Immortal formed, since they worked
    many evils.
For they were much more violent than those,
Giants perverse, foul language pouring out.
Single among all men, most just and true,
¹⁵⁵Was the most faithful Noah, full of care
For noblest works. And to him God Himself
From Heaven thus spoke: "Noah,
    be of good cheer
In yourself and to all the people preach
Conversion, so that they may all be saved.
¹⁶⁰But if, with shameless soul,
    they heed Me not
The whole race I will utterly destroy
With mighty floods of waters. Quickly now
An undecaying house I bid you frame
Of planks strong and impervious to the wet.
¹⁶⁵I will put understanding in your heart,
And subtle skill, and rule of measurement
And order; and for all things will I care
That you be saved, and all who dwell
    with you.
And I am He who is, and in your heart
¹⁷⁰Do you discern. I clothe Me
    with the heavens,
And cast the sea around Me, and for Me
Earth is a footstool, and the air is poured
Around My body; and on every side
Around Me runs the chorus of the stars.
¹⁷⁵Nine letters have I; of four syllables
I am; discern Me. The first three have each
Two letters, the remaining one the rest,
And five are mates; and of the entire sum,
The hundreds are twice eight
    and thrice three tens
¹⁸⁰Along with seven. Now, knowing who I am,
Do not be uninitiate in My lore."
Thus He spoke; and great trembling
    seized on him
At what he heard. And then, within his mind
Having contrived each matter, he besought
¹⁸⁵The people and began with words
    like these:
"O men insatiate, smit with madness great,
Whatever things you practiced they will not
Escape God's notice; for He knows all things,
Immortal Savior overseeing all,
¹⁹⁰Who bade me warn you, that you
    perish not.
Be sober, cut off badness, do not fight
Perforce each other with blood-guilty heart,
Nor irrigate much land with human gore.
Revere, O mortals, the supremely great
¹⁹⁵And fearless heavenly Creator—God
Imperishable—whose dwelling is the sky;
And do you all entreat Him—He is kind—

For life of cities and of all the world,
And of four-footed beasts and flying birds;
²⁰⁰Entreat Him to be gracious to all.
For when the whole unbounded world
    of men
Will be destroyed by waters loud you'll raise
A fearful cry. And suddenly for you
The air will be disordered, and from Heaven
²⁰⁵The fury of the mighty God will come
On you. And it certainly will be
That the immortal Savior against men
Will send wrath if you do not placate God
And from this time convert;
    and nothing more
²¹⁰Fretful and evil lawlessly will you
One to another do, but let there be
A guarding of one's self by holy life."
But when they heard him,
    each turned up his nose,
Calling him mad, a frenzy-stricken man.
²¹⁵And then again did Noah sound this strain:
"O men exceedingly wretched, base in heart,
Unstable, leaving modesty behind
And loving shamelessness, rapacious lords,
Fierce sinners, false, insatiate, mischievous,
²²⁰In nothing true, stealthy adulterers,
Flippant in language, pouring forth
    foul words,
The wrath of God Most High not fearing, kept
To the fifth generation to atone!
In no way do you wail, harsh men, but laugh;
²²⁵Sardonic smile will you laugh,
    when will come
That which I speak—
    God's dire incoming flood,
When Eve's polluted race, in the great earth
Blooming perennial in impervious stem,
Will, root and branch, in one night disappear,
²³⁰And cities, men and all,
    will the Earth-shaker
From the depths scatter and their walls
    destroy.
And then the whole world
    of unnumbered men
Will die. But how will I weep, how lament
In wooden house, how mingle tears
    with waves?
²³⁵For, if this water bidden of God will come,
Earth will float, hills float,
    and even sky will float;
Everything will be water, and all things
Will be destroyed by waters. And the winds
Will stand still, and a second age will come.
²⁴⁰O Phrygia, you will from the water's crest
First rise up, and you first another race
Of men will nourish, once again anew
Beginning; and you will be nurse for all."
But when now to the lawless generation
²⁴⁵He had thus vainly spoken, the Most High
Appeared, and once more cried aloud
    and said:
"The time has now come, Noah, to proclaim
Each thing, even all which I that day to you
Did promise and confirm, and to complete,
²⁵⁰Because of a people disobedient,
Throughout the boundless world
    even all the things
Which generations of a former time
Did practice, evil things innumerable.
But as for you: quickly enter with your sons

²⁵⁵And the wives. Call as many as I bid,
Of tribes of beasts and creeping things
    and birds,
And in as many as I ordain for life
Will I then put a willingness to go."
Thus He spoke; forth went [Noah] and aloud
²⁶⁰Cried out and called. And then wife,
    sons and brides,
Entered the house of wood; then also went
The other things, as many as God willed
To shut in. But when fitting bolt was put
About the lid, and in its polished place
²⁶⁵Was fitted sideways, then was brought
    to pass
At once the purpose of the God of Heaven.
And He massed clouds,
    and bid the sun's bright disk,
And moon, and stars, and circle
    of the heavens,
Obscuring all things round;
    He thundered loud,
²⁷⁰Terror of mortals, sending lightnings forth;
And all the winds together were aroused,
And all the veins of water were unloosed
By opening of great cataracts from Heaven,
And from earth's caverns
    and the tireless deep
²⁷⁵Appeared the myriad waters,
    and the whole
Illimitable earth was covered o'er.
But on the water swam that
    wondrous house;
And torn by many furious waves, and struck
By force of winds, it rushed on fearfully;
²⁸⁰But with its keel it cut the mass of foam
While the loud-babbling waters
    dashed around.
But when God flooded all the world
    with rains
Then also Noah took thought to observe
By counsels of the Immortal; for he now
²⁸⁵Had had enough of Nereus. And at once
The house he opened from the polished wall,
That crosswise was bound fast
    with skillful stays.
And looking out on the mighty mass
Of boundless waters Noah on all sides—
²⁹⁰And 'twas his fortune with his eyes to see!
Fear possessed and shook mightily his heart.
And then the air became a little calm,
Since it was weary wetting all the world
Many days; parting, then, it brought to light
²⁹⁵How pale and blood-red was
    the mighty sky
And sun's bright disk wearied; scarcely held
Noah his courage. And then forth afar
Sent he a dove alone, that he might learn
If yet firm land appeared. But with tired wing,
³⁰⁰Flying round all things, she again returned;
For not yet had the water ebbed away;
For it was deeply filling every place.
But after resting quietly for days
He sent the dove once more, to learn if yet
³⁰⁵Had ceased the many waters. And she flew
And flew on, and went o'er the earth and,
    resting
Her body lightly on the humid ground,
Again to Noah back she came and bore
An olive branch—of tidings a great sign.
³¹⁰Courage now filled them all,

and great delight,
Because they hoped to look on the land.
But then thereafter yet another bird,
Of black wing, sent he forth as hastily;
Which, trusting to its wings, flow willingly,
³¹⁵And coming to the land continued there.
And Noah knew the land was nearer now.
But when on dashing waves the craft divine
Had here and there o'er
    ocean's billows swum,
It was made fast on the narrow strand.
³²⁰There is in Phrygia on the dark mainland
A steep, tall mountain; Ararat its name,
Because on it all were to be saved
From death, and there was great desire
    of heart;
Thence streams of the great river
    Marsyas spring.
³²⁵There on a lofty peak the ark abode
When the waters ceased,
    and then again from Heaven
The voice divine of the great God this word
Proclaimed: "O Noah, guarded, faithful, just,
Come boldly forth, with your sons
    and your wife
³³⁰And the three brides, and fill you
    all the earth,
Increasing, multiplying, rendering justice
To one another through all generations,
Until to judgment every race of men
Will come; for judgment will be to all."
³³⁵Thus spoke the voice divine.
    Then from his couch
Noah, encouraged, hastened on the land,
And with him went
    his sons and wife and brides,
And creeping things, and birds
    and quadrupeds,
And all things else went from
    the wooden house
³⁴⁰Into one place. And then went Noah forth
As eighth, most just of men, when on
    the waters
He had made full twice twenty days and one
Because of counsels of the mighty God.
Then a new stock of life again arose,
³⁴⁵Golden first, which indeed was sixth,
    and best,
From the time when
    the first-formed man appeared;
Heavenly its name, because all things to God
Will be a care. O first race of sixth age!
O mighty joy which I thereafter shared,
³⁵⁰When I escaped sheer ruin, by the waves
Much tossed, with husband
    and with brothers-in-law,
Stepfather and stepmother, and with wives
Of husband's brothers suffering terribly.
Fitting things now will I sing: There will be
³⁵⁵On the fig-tree a many-colored flower,
And afterward the royal power and sway
Will Kronos have. For three kings
    of great soul,
Men most just, will distribute portions then,
And many a year rule, rendering what is just
³⁶⁰To men who care for toil and deeds of love.
And earth will glory in her many fruits
Self-growing, yielding much corn for the race.
And the foster-fathers, ageless all their days,
Will from diseases chill and dreadful be
³⁶⁵Far aloof; they will die as fallen on sleep,
And to Acheron in the abodes
Of Hades they will go away, and there
Will they have honor, since they were a race
Of blessed ones, fortunate heroes, whom
³⁷⁰The LORD of Hosts gave a noble mind,
And with whom always He
    His counsels shared.
But blessed will they be even when they go
In Hades. And then afterward again
Oppressive, strong, another second race
³⁷⁵Of earth-born men, the Titans. All excel
In figure, stature, growth; and there will be
One language, as of old from the first race
God in their breasts implanted.
    But even these,
Having a haughty heart and rushing on
³⁸⁰To ruin, will at last resolve to fight
Against the starry heavens. And then
    the stream
Of the great ocean will on them pour
Its raging waters. But the mighty LORD
Of Hosts though enraged will check
    His wrath,
³⁸⁵Because He promised that again no flood
Should be brought on men of evil soul.
But when the great high-thundering God
    will cause
The boundless swelling of
    the many waters—
With their waves here and there
    rising high—
³⁹⁰To cease from wrath, and into other depths
Of sea their measure lessen, setting bounds
By harbors and rough headlands
    round the land;
Then also will a Child of the great God
Come, clothed in flesh, to men,
    and fashioned like
³⁹⁵To mortals in the earth; and He does hear
Four vowels, and two consonants in Him
Are twice announced; the whole sum
    I will name:
For eight ones, and as many tens on these,
And yet eight hundred will reveal the name
⁴⁰⁰To men insatiate; and do you discern
In your own understanding that the Christ
Is child of the immortal God Most High.
And He will fulfill God's law, not destroy,
Bearing His very image, and all things
⁴⁰⁵Will He teach. To Him will priests convey
And offer gold, and myrrh, and frankincense;
For all these things He'll also bring to pass.
But when a voice will through the desert land
Come bearing tidings to men, and to all
⁴¹⁰Will call to make straight paths,
    and from the heart
Cast wickedness out and illuminate
With water all the bodies of mankind,
That being born again they may no more
From what is righteous go at all astray—
⁴¹⁵And one of barbarous mind,
    by dances bound,
Cutting that [voice] off will bestow reward—
Then on a sudden there will be a sign
To mortals, when, watched over,
    there will come
Out of the land of Egypt a fair stone;
⁴²⁰And on it will the Hebrew people stumble;
But by His guiding nations will be brought
Together; for the God who rules on high
They also will know through Him,
    and the way
In common light. For to chosen men
⁴²⁵Will He show life eternal, but the fire
Will be for ages on the lawless bring.
And then will He the sickly heal, and all
Who are blameworthy who will trust in Him.
And then the blind will see, the lame
    will walk,
⁴³⁰The deaf will hearken, and the dumb
    will speak.
Demons will He drive out, and of the dead
There will be an uprising; on the waves
Will He walk; also in a desert place
Will He five thousand satisfy with food
⁴³⁵From five loaves and a fish out of the sea,
And with the remnants of them, for the hope
Of peoples, will He fill twelve baskets full.
And then will Israel, drunken, not discern,
Nor will they hear, oppressed
    with feeble cares.
⁴⁴⁰But when the maddening wrath
    of the Most High
Will come on the Hebrews, and take faith
Away from them, because they slew the Son
Of the heavenly God; then also with foul lips
Will Israel give Him cuffs and spittle drugged.
⁴⁴⁵And gall for food and vinegar unmixed
For drink will they, with evil madness
    stricken
In bosom and in heart, give impiously,
Not seeing with their eyes, more blind
    than moles,
More terrible than crawling
    poisonous beasts,
⁴⁵⁰Fast bound by heavy sleep.
    But when His hands
He will spread forth and measure out
    all things,
And bear the crown of thorns,
    and they will pierce
His side with reeds,
    for which dark monstrous night
Will be for three hours in the midst of day,
⁴⁵⁵Then also will the temple of Solomon
Bring to an end a mighty sign for men,
When He will to the house of Hades go
Proclaiming resurrection to the dead.
But when in three days He will come again
⁴⁶⁰To the light, and show His form to men
And teach all things, ascending in the clouds
To the house of Heaven will He go
Leaving the world a Gospel covenant.
And in His Name will blossom a new shoot
⁴⁶⁵From nations that are guided by the law
Of the Mighty One. But also after this
There will be wise guides,
    and then afterward
There will be a cessation of the prophets.
After that, when the Hebrew people reap
⁴⁷⁰Their evil harvest, will a Roman king
Much gold and silver utterly destroy.
And afterward will other royal powers
Continuously arise as kingdoms perish,
And they will oppress mortals. But great fall
⁴⁷⁵Will be for those men, when they will begin
Unrighteous arrogance. But when the temple
Of Solomon in the holy land will fall,
Cast down by barbarous men in brazen mail,

And from the land the Hebrews
    will be driven
⁴⁸⁰Wandering and wasted, and among
    the wheat
They will much darnel mingle, there will be
Evil contention among, all mankind;
And the cities suffering outrage will bewail
Each other, in their breasts receiving wrath
⁴⁸⁵Of the great God,
    since they worked evil work.

BOOK II

[Introduction, 1-6. A time of plagues and wickedness, 7-15. The tenth race, 16-28. A time of peace, 29-36. Great sign and contest, 37-63. A chapter of proverbs, 64-188. The contest, 189-195. Woes of the last generation, 196-222. Events of the last day, 223-263. Resurrection and judgment, 264-312. Punishment of the wicked, 313-383. Blessedness of the righteous, 384-403. Some saved from the fire, 404-415. The Sibyl's wail, 416-427.]

Now while I much entreated God restrained
My wise song, also in my breast again
He put the charming voice of words divine.
In my whole body terror-stricken these
⁵I follow; for I know not what I speak,
But God impels me to proclaim each thing.
But when on earth come shocks,
    fierce thunderbolts,
Thunders and lightnings, storms,
    and evil blight,
And rage of jackals and of wolves,
    manslaughter,
¹⁰Destruction of men and of lowing cows,
Four-footed cattle and laborious mules,
And goats and sheep, then will
    the ample field
Be barren from neglect, and fruits will fail,
And there will be a selling of their freedom
¹⁵Among most men, and robbery of temples.
And then will, after these, appear of men
The tenth race,
    when the earth-shaking Lightener
Will break the zeal for idols and will shake
The people of seven-hilled Rome,
    and riches great
²⁰Will perish, burned by Vulcan's fiery flame.
And then will bloody signs
    from Heaven descend—
But yet the whole world of unnumbered men
Enraged will kill each other, and in tumult
Will God send famines, plagues,
    and thunderbolts
²⁵On men who, without justice, judge of rights.
And lack of men will be in all the world,
So that if anyone beheld a trace
Of man on earth, he would be wonderstruck.
And then will the great God
    who dwells in Heaven
³⁰Savior of pious men in all things prove.
And then will there be peace
    and wisdom deep,
And the fruit-bearing land will yield again
Abundant fruits, divided not in parts
Nor yet enslaved. And every harbor then,

³⁵And every haven, will be free to men
As formerly, and shamelessness will perish.
And then will God show mortals a great sign:
For like a lustrous crown will shine a star,
Bright, all-resplendent, from the radiant sky
⁴⁰Days not a few; and then will He display
From Heaven a crown for contest to men
Who wrestle. And then there will be again
A mighty contest of triumphal march
Into the heavenly sky, and it will be
⁴⁵For all men in the world, and have the fame
Of immortality. And every people
Will then in the immortal contests strive
For splendid victory. For no one there
Can shamelessly with silver buy a crown.
⁵⁰For to them will the pure Christ adjudge
That which is due, and crown
    the ones approved,
And give His martyrs an immortal prize
Who carry on the contest to death.
And to chaste men who run their race well
⁵⁵Will He the incorruptible reward
Of the prize give, and to all men allot
That which is due, and also to strange nations
That live a holy life and know one God.
And those who have regard for marriages
⁶⁰And keep themselves far from adulteries,
To them rich gifts, eternal hope, He'll give.
For every human soul is God's free gift,
And 'tis not right men stain it with vile deeds.
[[Do not be rich unrighteously, but lead]]
⁶⁵A life of probity. Be satisfied
With what you have and keep yourself
    from that
Which is another's. Speak not what is false,
But have a care for all things that are true.
Revere not idols vainly; but the God
⁷⁰Imperishable honor always first,
And next your parents. Render all things due,
And into unjust judgment do not come.
Do not cast out the poor unrighteously,
Nor judge by outward show; if wickedly
⁷⁵You judge, God hereafter will judge you.
Avoid false testimony; tell the truth.
Maintain your virgin purity, and guard
Love among all. Deal measures that are just;
For beautiful is measure full to all.
⁸⁰Strike not the scales one side,
    but draw them equal.
Forswear not ignorantly nor willingly;
God hates the perjured man in that he swore.
A gift proceeding out of unjust deeds
Never receive in hand. Do not steal seed;
⁸⁵Accursed through many generations he
Who took it to scattering of life.
Indulge not vile lusts, slander not, nor kill.
Give the toilworn his hire; do not afflict
The poor man. To orphans help afford
⁹⁰And to widows and the needy.
    Talk with sense;
Hold fast in heart a secret. Be unwilling
To act unjustly nor yet tolerate
Unrighteous men. Give to the poor at once
And say not, "Come tomorrow." Of your grain
⁹⁵Give to the needy with perspiring hand.
He who gives alms knows how
    to lend to God.
Mercy redeems from death
    when judgment comes.
Not sacrifice, but mercy God desires

Rather than sacrifice. The naked clothe,
¹⁰⁰Share your bread with the hungry,
    in your house
Receive the shelterless and lead the blind.
Pity the shipwrecked; for the voyage is
Uncertain. To the fallen give a hand;
And save the man that stands
    without defense.
¹⁰⁵Common to all is suffering, life's a wheel,
Riches unstable. Having wealth, reach out
To the poor your hand. Of what God
    gave to you
Bestow you also on the needy one.
Common is the whole life of mortal men;
¹¹⁰But it comes out unequal. When you see
A poor man never banter him with words,
Nor harshly accost a man
    who may be blamed.
One's life in death is proven; if one did
The unlawful or just, it will be decided
¹¹⁵When he to judgment comes. Disable not
Your mind with wine nor drink excessively.
Eat not blood, and abstain from things
Offered to idols. Gird not on the sword
For slaughter, but defense;
    and would you might
¹²⁰It neither lawlessly nor justly use:
For if you kill an enemy, your hand
You do defile. Keep from
    your neighbor's field,
Nor trespass on it; just is every landmark,
And trespass painful. Useful is possession
¹²⁵Of lawful wealth, but of unrighteous gains
'Tis worthless. Harm not any growing fruit
Of the field. And let strangers be esteemed
In equal honor with the citizens;
For much-enduring hospitality
¹³⁰Will all experience as each other's guests;
But let there not be anyone a stranger
Among you, since, you mortals, all of you
Are of one 'blood, and no land has for men
Any sure place. Wish not nor pray for wealth;
¹³⁵But pray to live from few things
    and possess
Nothing at all unjust. The love of gain
Is mother of all evil. Do not long
For gold or silver; in them there will be
A double-edged and soul-destroying iron.
¹⁴⁰A snare to men continually are gold
And silver. Gold, of evils source, of life
Destructive, troubling all things,
    would that you
Were, not to mortals such a longed-for bane!
For wars, because of you, and pillaging
¹⁴⁵And murders come, and children hate
    their sires,
And brothers and sisters
    those of their own blood.
Plot no deceit, and do not arm your heart
Against a friend. Keep not concealed within
A different thought from what
    you speak forth;
¹⁵⁰Nor, like rock-clinging polyp,
    change with place.
But with all be frank, and things from the soul
Speak you forth. Whosoever willfully
Commits a wrong, an evil man is he;
But he that does it under force, the end
¹⁵⁵I tell not; but let each man's will be right.
Pride not yourself in wisdom, power,

or wealth;
God only is the wise and mighty one
And full of riches. Do not vex your heart
With evils that are past; for what is done
[160] Can never be undone. Let not your hand
Be hasty, but ferocious passion curb;
For many times has one in striking done
Murder without design. Let suffering
Be common, neither great nor overmuch.
[165] Excessive good has not brought forth
    to men
That which is helpful. And much luxury
Leads to immoderate lusts.
    Much wealth is prowl,
And makes one grow to wanton violence.
Passionate feeling, creeping in, effects
[170] Destructive madness. Anger is a lust,
And when it is excessive it is wrath.
The zeal of good men is a noble thing,
But of the base is base. Of wicked men
The boldness is destructive, but renown
[175] Follows that of the good. To be revered
Is virtuous love, but that of Cypris works
Increase of shame. A silly man is called
Very agreeable among his fellows.
With moderation eat, drink, and converse;
[180] Of all things moderation is the best;
But trespass of its limit brings to grief.
Do not be envious, faithless, or abusive,
Or evil-minded, or a false deceiver.
Be prudent and abstain from
    shameless deeds.
[185] Do not imitate what's evil, but leave
Vengeance to justice; for persuasion is
A useful thing, but strife engenders strife.
Trust not too quickly ere you see the end.
This is the contest, these are the rewards;
[190] These are the prizes; this the gate of life
And entrance into immortality,
Which God in Heaven to most righteous men
Appointed a reward for victory;
And through this gate will gloriously pass
[195] Those who will then receive
    the victor's crown.
But when this sign will everywhere appear—
Children with gray hair on
    their temples born—
And human sufferings, famines, plagues,
    and wars,
And change of times, and many a tearful wail,
[200] Ah! Of how many parents in the lands
Will children mourn and piteously weep,
And with shrouds bury flesh
    and limbs in earth,
Mother of peoples, with the blood and dust
Themselves defiling. O you wretched men
[205] Of the last generation, evildoers,
Terrible, childish, not perceiving this,
That when the tribes of women do not bear
The harvesttime of mortal men is come.
Near is the ruin when impostors come
[210] Instead of prophets speaking on the earth.
And Beliar will come and many signs
Perform for men. And then of holy men,
Chosen and faithful, there will be confusion,
And pillaging of them and of the Hebrews.
[215] And there will be on them fearful wrath
When from the east a people of twelve tribes
Will come in search of kindred
    Hebrew people

Whom Assyrian shoot destroyed;
    and over these
Will nations perish. But they afterward
[220] Will over men exceeding mighty rule,
Chosen and faithful Hebrews, and enslave
Them as before, since their power
    ne'er will fail.
He that is highest of all, the all-surveying,
Dwelling in Heaven, will scatter sleep
    on men,
[225] Covering the eyelids o'er.
    O blessed servants
Whom when the Master comes
    He finds awake!
And they all watch at all times and expect
With sleepless eyes. For it will be at dawn
Or eve or midday; but He sure will come,
[230] And it will be as I say, it will be,
To them that sleep, that from
    the starry heavens
The stars at midday will to all appear
With the two lights as the time hastens on.
And then the Tishbite, urging from
    the Heaven
[235] His chariot celestial, and on earth
Arriving, will to all the world display
Three evil signs of life to be destroyed.
Woe for all the women in that day
Who will be found with burden in the womb!
[240] Woe for all who suckle tender babes!
Woe for all who will dwell on the waves!
Woe for women who will see that day!
For a dark mist will hide
    the boundless world,
East, west, and south, and north.
    And then will flow
[245] A mighty stream of burning fire
    from Heaven
And every place consume—earth, ocean vast,
And gleaming sea, and lakes and rivers,
    springs,
And cruel Hades and the heavenly sky.
And heavenly lights will break up into one
[250] And into outward form all-desolate.
For stars from the heavens will fall
    into all seas.
And all the souls of men will gnash their teeth
Burned both by sulfur stream
    and force of fire
In ravenous soil, and ashes hide all things.
[255] And then of the world all the elements
Will be bereft—air, earth, sea, light, sky, days,
Nights; and no longer in the air will fly
Birds without number, nor will living things
That swim the sea swim any more at all,
[260] Nor freighted vessel o'er the billows pass,
Nor cows straight-guiding plow the field,
    nor sound
Of furious winds; but He will fuse all things
Together, and will pick out what is pure.
But when the immortal God's
    eternal messengers
[265] Arakiel, Ramiel, Uriel, Samiel,
And Azael, they that know how many evils
Anyone did before, will from dark gloom
Then lead to judgment all the souls of men
Before the judgment-seat of the great God
[270] Immortal; for imperishable is
One only, Himself the Almighty, One,
Who will be judge of mortals; and to them

That dwell beneath will then
    the Heavenly One
Give souls and spirit and voice,
    and also bones
[275] Fitted with joints to all kinds of flesh,
And both the flesh and sinews, veins and skin
Around the body, and hair as before;
Divinely fashioned and with breathing
    moved
Will bodies of those on earth
    one day be raised.
[280] And then will Uriel, mighty messenger,
    break
The bolts of stern and lasting adamant
Which, monstrous, bold the brazen gates
    of Hades,
Straight cast them down,
    and to judgment lead
All forms that have endured much suffering,
[285] Chiefly the shapes of Titans born of old,
And giants, and all whom
    the flood whelmed,
And all that perished in the billowy seas,
And all that furnished banquet for the beasts
And creeping things and birds,
    these in a mass
[290] Will [Uriel] summon to the judgment-seat;
And also those whom flesh-devouring fire
Destroyed in flame, even these will he collect
And place before the judgment-seat of God.
And when the high-thundering LORD of Hosts
[295] Making an end of fate will raise the dead,
Sit on His heavenly throne, and firmly fix
The mighty pillar, then amid the clouds
Christ, who Himself is incorruptible,
Will come to the Incorruptible
[300] In glory with pure messengers, and will sit
At the right hand on the great judgment-seat
To judge the life of pious and the way
Of impious men. And Moses, the great friend
Of the Most High, will come enrobed in flesh;
[305] Also great Abraham himself will come,
Isaac and Jacob, Joshua, Daniel,
Elijah, Habakkuk and Jonah, and
Those whom the Hebrews slew.
    But He'll destroy
The Hebrews after Jeremiah, all
[310] Who are to be judged at the judgment-seat,
That worthy recompense they may receive
And pay for all each did in mortal life.
And then will all pass through
    the burning stream
Of flame unquenchable; but all the just
[315] Will be saved; and the godless furthermore
Will to all ages perish, all who did
Evils formerly, and committed murders,
And all who are accomplices therein,
Liars and thieves, and destroyers of home,
[320] Crafty and terrible, and parasites,
And marriage-breakers pouring forth
    vile words,
Dread, wanton, lawless, and idolaters;
And all who left the great immortal God,
Became blasphemers did the pious harm,
[325] Destroying faith and killing righteous men
And all that with a shamelessness deceitful
And double-faced rush in as elders
And reverend ministers, who knowingly
Give unjust judgments, yielding to
    false words

³³⁰More hurtful than the leopards
    and the wolves
And more vile; and ill that are grossly proud
And usurers, who gains on gains amass
And damage orphans and widows
    in each thing;
³³⁵The fruit of unjust deeds, and all that cast
Reproach in giving from their own hard toils;
And all that left their parents in old age,
Not paying them at all, nor offering
To parents filial duty, and all who
³⁴⁰Were disobedient and against their sires
Spoke a harsh word; and all that pledges took
And then denied them; and the servants all
Who were against their masters, and again
Those who licentiously defiled the flesh;
³⁴⁵And all who loosed the girdle of the maid
For secret intercourse, and all who caused
Abortions, and all who their offspring cast
Unlawfully away; and sorcerers
And sorceresses with them, and these wrath
³⁵⁰Of the heavenly and immortal God
    will drive
Against a pillar where will all around
In a circle flow a restless stream of fire;
And deathless messengers
    of the immortal God,
Whoever is, will bind with lasting bonds
³⁵⁵In chains of flaming fire and from above
Punish them all by scourge most terribly;
And in Gehenna, in the gloom of night,
Will they be cast 'neath many horrid beasts
Of Tartarus, where darkness is immense.
³⁶⁰But when there will be many punishments
Enforced on all who had an evil heart,
Yet afterward will there a fiery wheel
From a great river circle them around,
Because they had a care for wicked deeds.
³⁶⁵And then one here, another there, will sires,
Young children, mothers, nursing babes,
    in tears
Wail their most piteous fate. No fill of tears
Will be for them, nor piteous voice be heard
Of them that moan, one here, another there,
³⁷⁰But long worn under dark, dank Tartarus
Aloud will they cry; and they will repay
In cursed places thrice as much as all
The evil work they did, burned
    with much fire;
And all of them, consumed by raging thirst
³⁷⁵And hunger, will in anguish
    gnash their teeth
And call death beautiful, and death will flee
Away from them. For neither death nor night
Will ever give them rest. And many things
    in vain
Will they ask of the God that rules on high,
³⁸⁰And then will He His face turn openly
Away from them. For He to erring men
Gave, in seven ages for conversion, signs
By the hands of a virgin undefiled.
But the others, all to whom right
    and fair works
³⁸⁵And piety and thoughts most just
    were dear,
Will messengers, bearing through
    the burning stream,
Lead to light and life exempt from care,
Where comes the immortal way

of the great God
And fountains three—of honey, wine,
    and milk.
³⁹⁰And equal land for all, divided not
By walls or fences, more abundant fruits
Spontaneous will then bear, and the course
Of life be common and wealth
    unapportioned.
For there no longer will be poor nor rich,
³⁹⁵Tyrant nor slave, nor any great nor small,
Nor kings nor leaders; all alike in common.
No more at all will one say, "night has come,"
Nor "morrow comes,"
    nor "yesterday has been";
Nor will there many days of anxious care,
⁴⁰⁰Nor spring, nor winter,
    nor the summer-heat,
Nor autumn be [[nor marriage, nor yet death,
Nor sales, nor purchases]], nor set of sun
Nor rising; for a long day will God make.
And to the pious will the Almighty God
⁴⁰⁵Imperishable grant another thing,
When they will ask the imperishable God:
That He will suffer men from raging fire
And endless gnawing anguish be saved;
And this will He do. For hereafter He
⁴¹⁰Will pluck them from the restless flame,
    elsewhere
Remove them, and for His own people's sake
Send them to other and eternal life
With the immortals, in Elysian field,
Where move far-stretching billows
    of the lake
⁴¹⁵Of ever-flowing Acheron profound.
Ah, miserable woman that I am!
What will I be in that day? For I sinned—
Being busy foolishly about all things,
Caring for neither marriage-bond nor reason;
⁴²⁰But even in my wealthy husband's house
I shut the needy out; and formerly
I knowingly performed unlawful things.
But, Savior, though I
    shameless things performed,
Do You from my tormentors rescue me,
⁴²⁵A shameless woman. And I pray You now
Make me to rest a little from my song,
Holy Giver of manna, King of the great realm.

BOOK III

[Introduction, 1-10. Unity and power of God extolled, 11-34. Oracle against idolatry and sin, 35-64. Coming and judgment of the Great King, 55-76. Coming of Beliar, 76-90. Reign of the woman and end of the world, 90-111. All things subject to Christ, 112-116. The tower of Babel, 117-132. Kronos, Titan, and Iapetus, 132-154. Kronos, Rhea, and the Titans, 155-187. End of the Titans and rise of many kingdoms, 188-196. The Sibyl's message, 196-201. Rule of the house of Solomon, 202-207. Rule of the Hellenes, 208-212. The Western Kingdom, 213-235. The Sibyl's burden, 236-241. Woes on the Titans and on many nations, 242-260. The righteous race, 261-303. The exodus and giving of the law, 304-325. Desolation and exile, 325- 351. Restoration from exile, 352-361. The Sibyl ceases and begins again, 362-371. Woe on Babylon, 372-386. Woe on Egypt, 387-392. Woe on Gog and Magog, 393-397. Woe on Libya, 399-412. Great signs and woes on many cities, 413-433. Retributive judgment on Rome, 434-450. Doom of Smyrna, Samos, Delos, and Rome, 461-456. Peace of Asia and Europe, 457-473. The Macedonian woe, 474-482. The unnamed rulers. 483-499. The sign for Phrygia, 600-615. The fate of Ilium, 516-522. gongs of the blind old man, 523-541. Woes of Lycia, Chalcedon, Cyzicus, Byzantium, Rhodes, Lydia, Samos, Cyprus, and Trallis, 642-582. Italy's tribal wars, 683-590. Woes of Laodicea, Campania, Corsica, and Sardinia, 591-607. Woes of Mysia, Chalcedon, Galatia, Tenedos, Sicyon, and Corinth, 608-615. The Sibyl ceases and begins again, 616-619. Woes of Phoenicia, Crete, Thrace, Gog, Magog, Maurians, Ethiopians, and provinces of Asia Minor, 620-656. Oracles against Greece, 657-723. The holy race, 724-756, Egypt subdued, 766-774. Time of blessedness, 775-783. Exhortation to worship God, 184-794. Time of judgment, 795-816. The God-sent king, 817-829. Fearful time of judgment, 830-871. The Sibyl's testimony, 872-876. A Jewish millennium, 877-911. Exhortation to the Greek s, 912-928. Day of prosperity and peace, 928-947. Exhortation to serve God, 948-953. The Messianic day, 954-988. Signs of the end, 989-1003. The Sibyl's account of herself, 1004-1031.]

O You high-thundering blessed
    Heavenly One,
Who have set in their place the cherubim,
I, who have uttered what is all too true,
Entreat You, let me have a little rest;
⁵For my heart has grown weary from within.
But why again leaps my heart, and my soul
With a whip stricken from within
    constrained
To utter forth its message to all?
But yet again will I proclaim all things
¹⁰Which God commands me
    to proclaim to men.
O men, that in your image have a form
Fashioned of God, why do you vainly stray
And walk not in the straight way,
    always mindful
Of the immortal Maker? God is one,
¹⁵Sovereign, ineffable, dwelling in Heaven,
The self-existent and invisible,
Himself alone beholding everything;
Him sculptor's hand did not make,
    nor is his form
Shown by man's art from gold or ivory;
²⁰But He, eternal Lord, proclaims Himself
As one who is and was before and will be
Again hereafter. For who being mortal
Can see God with his eyes? Or who will bear
To hear the only Name of Heaven's great God,
²⁵The ruler of the world? He by His word
Created all things, even heaven and sea,
And tireless sun, and full moon

and bright stars,
And mighty mother Tethys, springs
and rivers,
Imperishable fire, and days and nights.
³⁰This is the God who formed
four-lettered Adam,
The first one formed, and filling
with his Name
East, west, and south, and north.
The same is He
Who fixed the pattern of the human form,
And made wild beasts, and creeping things,
and birds.
³⁵You do not worship, neither do you
fear God,
But vainly go astray and bow the knee
To serpents, and make offering to cats,
And idols, and stone images of men,
And sit before the doors of godless temples;
⁴⁰You guard Him who is God,
who keeps all things,
And merry with the wickedness of stones,
Forget the judgment of the immortal Savior
Who made the heavens and earth. Woe!
A race
That has delight in blood, deceitful, vile,
⁴⁵Ungodly, of false, double-tongued,
immoral men,
Adulterous, idolatrous, designing fraud,
An evil madness raving in their hearts,
For themselves plundering,
having shameless soul;
For no one who has riches will impart
⁵⁰To another, but dire wickedness will be
Among all mortals, and for sake of gain
Will many widows not at all keep faith,
But secretly love others, and the bond
Of life those who have husbands do not keep.
⁵⁵But when Rome will o'er Egypt also rule
Governing always, then will there appear
The greatest kingdom of the immortal King
Over men. And a holy Lord will come
To hold the scepter over every land
⁶⁰To all ages of fast-hastening time.
And then will come inexorable wrath
On Latin men; three will by piteous fate
Endamage Rome. And perish will all men,
With their own houses, when from Heaven
will flow
⁶⁵A fiery cataract. Ah, wretched me!
When will that day and when
will judgment come
Of the immortal God, the mighty King?
But just now, O you cities, you are built
And all adorned with temples
and race-grounds,
⁷⁰Markets, and images of wood, of gold,
Of silver and of stone, that you may come
To the bitter day. For it will come,
When there will pass among all men a stench
Of brimstone. Yet each thing will I declare,
⁷⁵In all the cities where men suffer ills.
From the Sebastenes Beliar will come
Hereafter, and the height of hills will he
Establish, and will make the sea stand still
And the great fiery sun and the bright moon
⁸⁰And he will raise the dead, and many signs
Work before men: but nothing
will be brought
By him to completion but deceit,

And many mortals will be lead astray
Hebrews both true and choice,
and lawless men
⁸⁵Besides who never gave ear to God's word.
But when the threatenings of the mighty God
Will draw near, and a flaming power
will come
By billow to the earth, it will consume
Both Beliar and all the haughty men
⁹⁰Who put their confidence in him.
And thereon
Will the whole world be governed
by the hands
Of a woman and obedient everywhere.
Then when a widow will o'er all the world
Gain the rule, and cast in the mighty sea
⁹⁵Both gold and silver, also brass and iron
Of short-lived men into the deep will cast,
Then all the elements will be bereft
Of order, when the God who dwells on high
Will roll the heavens, even as a scroll is rolled;
¹⁰⁰And to the mighty earth and sea will fall
The entire multiform sky; and there will flow
A tireless cataract of raging fire,
And it will burn the land, and burn the sea,
And heavenly sky, and night, and day,
and melt
¹⁰⁵Creation itself together and pick out
What is pure. No more laughing spheres
of light,
Nor night, nor dawn, nor many days of care,
Nor spring, nor winter, nor the summertime,
Nor autumn. And then of the mighty God
¹¹⁰The judgment midway in a mighty age
Will come, when all these things
will come to pass.
O navigable waters and each land
Of the Orient and of the Occident,
Subject will all things be to Him who comes
¹¹⁵Into the world again, and therefore He
Himself became first conscious of His power.
But when the threatenings of the mighty God
Are fulfilled, which He threatened
mortals once,
When in Assyrian land they built a tower—
¹²⁰(And they all spoke one language,
and resolved
To mount aloft into the starry heavens)—
But on the air the Immortal at once put
A mighty force; and then winds from above
Cast down the great tower
and stirred mortals up
¹²⁵To wrangling with each other
(therefore men
Gave to that city the name of Babylon);
Now when the tower fell
and the tongues of men
Turned to all sorts of sounds, promptly
all earth
Was filled with men
and kingdoms were divided;
¹³⁰And then the generation tenth appeared
Of mortal men, from the time when the Flood
Came on earlier men. And Kronos reigned,
And Titan and Iapetus; and men called them
Best offspring of Gaia and of Uranus,
¹³⁵Giving to them names both of earth
and heaven,
Since they were very first of mortal men.
So there were three divisions of the earth

According to the allotment of each man,
And each one having his own portion reigned
¹⁴⁰And fought not; for a father's oaths
were there
And equal were their portions. But the time
Complete of old age on the father came,
And he died; and the sons infringing oaths
Stirred up against each other bitter strife,
¹⁴⁵Which one should have the royal rank
and rule
Over all mortals; and against each other
Kronos and Titan fought. But Rhea and Gaia,
And Aphrodite fond of crowns, Demeter,
And Hestia and Dione of fair locks
¹⁵⁰Brought them to friendship,
and together called
All who were kings, both brothers
and near kin,
And others of the same ancestral blood,
And they judged Kronos should reign
king of all,
For he was oldest and of noblest form.
¹⁵⁵But Titan laid on Kronos mighty oaths
To rear no male posterity, that he
Himself might reign when age
and fate should come
To Kronos. And whenever Rhea bore
Beside her sat the Titans, and all males
¹⁶⁰In pieces tore, but let the females live
To be reared by the mother. But when now
At the third birth the august Rhea bore,
She brought forth Hera first;
and when they saw
A female offspring, the fierce Titan men
¹⁶⁵Took them to their dwellings.
And then thereon
Rhea a male child bore, and having bound
Three men of Crete by oath she quickly sent
Him into Phrygia to be reared apart
In secret; therefore did they name him Zeus,
¹⁷⁰For he was sent away. And thus she sent
Poseidon also secretly away.
And Pluto, third, did Rhea yet again,
Noblest of women, at Dodona bear,
Whence flows Europus' river's liquid course,
¹⁷⁵And with Peneus mixed, pours in the sea
Its water, and men call it Stygian.
But when the Titans heard
that there were sons
Kept secretly, whom Kronos and his wife
Rhea begot, then Titan sixty youths
¹⁸⁰Together gathered, and held fast in chains
Kronos and his wife Rhea, and concealed
Them in the earth and guarded them
in bonds.
And then the sons of powerful Kronos heard,
And a great war and uproar they aroused.
¹⁸⁵And this is the beginning of dire war
Among all mortals. [[For it is indeed
With mortals the prime origin of war.]]
And then did God award the Titans evil.
And all of Titans and of Kronos born
¹⁹⁰Died. But then as time rolled around
there rose
The Egyptian kingdom, then that
of the Persians
And of the Medes, and Ethiopians,
And of Assyria and Babylon,
And then that of the Macedonians,
¹⁹⁵Egyptian yet again, then that of Rome.

And then a message of the mighty God
Was set within my breast, and it bade me
Proclaim through all earth and in royal hearts
Plant things which are to be. And to my mind
²⁰⁰This God imparted first,
    how many kingdoms
Have been gathered together of mankind.
For first of all the house of Solomon
Will include horsemen of Phoenicia
And Syria, and of the islands too,
²⁰⁵And the race of Pamphylians and Persians
And Phrygians, Carians, and Mysians
And the race of the Lydians rich in gold.
And then will Hellenes, proud and impure,
Then will a Macedonian nation rule,
²¹⁰Great, shrewd, who as a fearful cloud of war
Will come to mortals. But the God of Heaven
Will utterly destroy them from the depth.
And then will be another kingdom, white
And many-headed, from the western sea,
²¹⁵Which will rule much land,
    and shake many men,
And to all kings bring terror afterward,
And out of many cities will destroy
Much gold and silver; but in the vast earth
There will again be gold, and silver too,
²²⁰And ornament.
    And they will oppress mortals;
And to those men will great disaster be,
When they begin unrighteous arrogance.
And forthwith in them there will be a force
Of wickedness, male will consort with male,
²²⁵And children they will place
    in dens of shame;
And in those days there will be among men
A great affliction, and it will disturb
All things, and break all things, and fill
    all things
With evils by a shameful covetousness,
²³⁰And by ill-gotten wealth in many lands,
But most of all in Macedonia.
And it will stir up hatred, and all guile
Will be with them even to
    the seventh kingdom,
Of which a king of Egypt will be king
²³⁵Who will be a descendant from the Greeks.
And then the nation of the mighty God
Will be again strong and they will be guides
Of life to all men. But why did God place
This also in my mind to tell: what first,
²⁴⁰And what next, and what evil last will be
On all men? Which of these will take the lead?
First on the Titans will God visit evil.
For they will pay to mighty Kronos' sons
The penal satisfaction, since they bound
²⁴⁵Both Kronos and the mother dearly loved.
Again will there be tyrants for the Greeks
And fierce kings overweening and impure,
Adulterous and altogether bad;
And for men will be no more rest from war.
²⁵⁰And the dread Phrygians will perish all,
And to Troy will evil come that day.
And to the Persians and Assyrians
Evil will straightaway come, and to all Egypt
And Libya and the Ethiopians,
²⁵⁵And to the Carians and Pamphylians—
Evil to pass from one place to another,
And to all mortals. Why now one by one
Do I speak forth? But when the first receive
Fulfillment, then promptly will come on men

²⁶⁰The second. So the very first I'll tell.
There will an evil come to pious men
Who dwell by the great temple of Solomon
And who are progeny of righteous men.
Alike of all these also I will tell
²⁶⁵The tribe and line of fathers
    and homeland—
All things with care, O mortal shrewd
    in mind.
There is a city … on the earth,
Ur of the Chaldees, whence there is a race
Of men most righteous, to whom
    both good will
²⁷⁰And noble deeds have ever been a care.
For they have no concern about the course
Of the sun's revolution, nor the moon's,
Nor wondrous things beneath the earth,
    nor depth
Of joy-imparting sea Oceanus,
²⁷⁵Nor signs of sneezing, nor the wings
    of birds,
Nor soothsayers, nor wizards,
    nor enchanters,
Nor tricks of dull words of ventriloquists,
Neither do they astrologize with skill
Of the Chaldeans, nor astronomize;
²⁸⁰Indeed, these are all deceptive, in so far
As foolish men go seeking day by day
Training their souls to no useful work;
And then did they teach miserable men
Deceptions, whence to mortals on the earth
²⁸⁵Come many evils leading them astray
From good ways and just deeds.
    But they have care
For righteousness and virtue, and not greed,
Which breeds unnumbered ills
    to mortal men,
War and unending famine. But with them
²⁹⁰Just measure, both in fields and cities, holds,
Nor steal they from each other in the night,
Nor drive off herds of cattle, sheep, and goats,
Nor neighbor remove landmarks
    of a neighbor,
Nor any man of great wealth grieve the one
²⁹⁵Less favored, nor to widows cause distress,
But rather aids them, ever helping them
With wheat and wine and oil;
    and always does
The rich man in the country send a share
At the time of the harvests to them
³⁰⁰That have not, but are needy, thus fulfilling
The saying of the mighty God, a hymn
In legal setting; for the Heavenly One
Finished the earth a common good for all.
Now when the people of twelve tribes depart
³⁰⁵From Egypt, and with leaders sent of God
Nightly pursue their way by a pillar of fire
And during all the day by one of cloud,
For them then God a leader will appoint—
A great man, Moses, whom a princess found
³¹⁰Beside a marsh, and carried off and reared
And called her son. And at the time he came
As leader for the people whom God led
From Egypt to the … Sinai mount,
His own law God delivered them
    from Heaven
³¹⁵Writing on two flat stones
    all righteous things
Which He enjoined to do; and if, perchance,
One give no heed, he must to the law

Make satisfaction, either at men's hands
Or, if men's notice he escape, he will
³²⁰By ample satisfaction he destroyed.
[[For the Heavenly finished earth
    a common good
For all, and in all hearts as best gift thought.]]
To them alone the bounteous field yields fruit
A hundredfold from one, and thus completes
³²⁵God's measure. But to them will also come
Misfortune, nor do they escape from plague.
And even you, forsaking your fair shrine,
Will flee away when it becomes your lot
To leave the holy land. And you will be
³³⁰Carried to the Assyrians, and will see
Young children and wives
    serving hostile men;
And every means of life and wealth
    will perish;
And every land will be filled up with you,
And every sea; and everyone will be
³³⁵Offended with your customs; and your land
Will all be desert; and the altar fenced
And temple of the great God and long walls
Will all fall to the ground, since in your heart
The holy law of the immortal God
³⁴⁰You did not keep, but, erring, you did serve
Unseemly images, and did not fear
The immortal Father, God of all mankind,
Nor will to honor Him; but images
Of mortals you honored; Therefore now
³⁴⁵Of time, seven decades,
    will your fruitful land
And the wonders of your temple all be waste.
But there remains for you a wonderful end
And greatest glory, as the immortal God
Granted you. But you must wait and confide
³⁵⁰In the great God's pure laws,
    when He will lift
Your wearied knee upright to the light.
And then will God from Heaven send a king
To judge each man in blood and light of fire.
There is a royal tribe, the race of which
³⁵⁵Will be unfailing; and as times revolve
This race will bear rule and begin to build
God's temple new. And all the Persian kings
Will aid with bronze and gold
    and well-worked iron.
For God Himself will give the holy dream
³⁶⁰By night. And then the temple will again
Be, as it was before …
Now when my soul had rest
    from inspired song,
And I prayed the great Father for a rest
From constraint; even in my heart again
³⁶⁵Was set a message of the mighty God
And He bade me proclaim
    through all the earth
And plant in royal minds things yet to be.
And in my mind God put this first to say
How many lamentable sufferings
³⁷⁰The Immortal purposed on Babylon
Because she His great temple had destroyed.
Woe, woe for you! O Babylon,
And for the offspring of the Assyrian men!
Through all the earth the rush of sinful men
³⁷⁵Will some time come, and shout
    of mortal men
And stroke of the great God,
    who inspires songs,
Will ruin every land. For high in air to you

THE SIBYLLINE ORACLES

O Babylon, will it come from above,
And out of Heaven from holy ones to you
³⁸⁰Will it come down, and the soul
    in your children
Will the Eternal utterly destroy.
And then will you be, as you were before,
As one not born; and then will you be filled
Again with blood, as you yourself before
³⁸⁵Did shed that of good, just, and holy men,
Whose blood yet cries out
    to the lofty Heaven.
To you, O Egypt, will a great blow come
And dreadful, to your homes,
    which you did hope
Might never fall on you. For through
    your midst
³⁹⁰A sword will pass, and scattering and death
And famine will prevail until of kings
The seventh generation, and then cease.
Woe for you, O land of Gog and Magog
In the midst of the rivers of Ethiopia!
³⁹⁵What pouring out of blood will you receive,
And house of judgment among men be called,
And your land of much dew
    will drink black blood!
Woe for you, O Libya, and woe,
Both sea and land! O daughters of the west,
⁴⁰⁰So will you come to a bitter day.
And you will come pursued
    by grievous strife,
Dreadful and grievous; there will be again
A dreadful judgment, and you all will come
By force to destruction, for you tore
⁴⁰⁵In pieces the great house of the Immortal,
And with iron teeth you chewed it dreadfully.
Therefore will you then look on your land
Full of the dead, some of them fallen by war
And by the demon of all violence,
⁴¹⁰Famine and plague, and some
    by barbarous foes.
And all your land will be a wilderness,
And desolations will your cities be.
And in the west there will a star shine forth
Which they will call a comet, sign to men
⁴¹⁵Of the sword and of famine and of death,
And murder of great leaders and chief men.
And yet again there will be among men
Greatest signs; for deep-eddying Tanais
Will leave Maeotis' lake, and there will be
⁴²⁰Down the deep stream a fruitful,
    furrow's track,
And the vast flow will hold a neck of land.
And there are hollow chasms
    and yawning pits;
And many cities, men and all, will fall:—
In Asia—Iassus, Cebren, Pandonia,
⁴²⁵Colophon, Ephesus, Nicaea, Antioch,
Syagra, Sinope, Smyrna, Myrina,
Most happy Gaza, Hierapolis,
Astypalaia; and in Europe—Tanagra,
Clitor, Basilis, Meropeia, Antigone,
⁴³⁰Magnessa, Mykene, Oiantheia.
Know then that the destructive race of Egypt
Is near destruction, and the past year then
Is better for the Alexandrians.
As much of tribute as Rome received
⁴³⁵Of Asia, even thrice as many goods
Will Asia back again from Rome receive,
And her destructive outrage pay her back.
As many as from Asia ever served
A house of the Italians, twenty times
⁴⁴⁰As many Italians will in Asia serve
In poverty, and numerous debts incur.
O virgin, soft rich child of Latin Rome,
Oft at your much-remembered
    marriage feasts
Drunken with wine, now will you be a slave
⁴⁴⁵And wedded in no honorable way.
And oft will mistress shear your pretty hair,
And wreaking satisfaction cast you down
From sky to earth, and from the earth again
Raise you to sky, for mortals of low rank
⁴⁵⁰And of unrighteous life are held fast bound.
And of avenging Smyrna overthrown
There will be no thought, but by evil plans
And wickedness of them that have command
Will Samos be sand, Delos will be dull,
⁴⁵⁵And Rome a room; but the decrees of God
Will all of them be perfectly fulfilled.
And a calm peace to Asian land will go.
And Europe will be happy then, well fed,
Pure air, full of years, strong, and undisturbed
⁴⁶⁰By wintry storms and hail, bearing,
    all things,
Even birds and creeping things
    and beasts of earth.
O happy on earth will that man be
Or woman; what a home unspeakable
Of happy ones! For from the starry heavens
⁴⁶⁵Will all good order come on mankind,
And justice, and the prudent unity
Which of all things is excellent for men,
And kindness, confidence, and love of guests;
But far from them will lawlessness depart,
⁴⁷⁰Blame, envy, wrath, and folly; poverty
Will flee away from men, and force will flee,
And murder, baneful strifes and bitter feuds,
And theft, and every evil in those days.
But Macedonia will to Asia bear
⁴⁷⁵A grievous suffering, and the greatest sore
To Europe will spring up from Cronian stock,
A family of bastards and of slaves.
And she will tame fenced city Babylon,
And of each land the sun looks down on
⁴⁸⁰Call herself mistress,
    and then come to nothing
By ruinous misfortunes, having fame
In later generations distant far.
And sometime into Asia's prosperous land
Will come a man unheard of, shoulder-clad
⁴⁸⁵With purple robe, fierce, unjust, fiery;
And this man he who wields the thunderbolt
Roused forward; and all Asia will sustain
An evil yoke, and her soil wet with rain
Will drink much murder. But even so
    will Hades
⁴⁹⁰Destroy the unknown king;
    and that man's offspring
Will forthwith perish by the race of those
Whose offspring he himself
    would gladly destroy;
Producing one root which the bane of men
Will cut from ten horns, and plant
    by their side
⁴⁹⁵Another plant. A father purple-clad
Will cut a warlike father off, and Ares,
Baneful and hostile, by a grandson's hand
Will himself perish; and then will the horn
Planted beside them forthwith bear the rule.
⁵⁰⁰And to life-sustaining Phrygia
At once will there a certain token be,
When Rhea's blood-stained race,
    in the great earth
Blooming perennial in impervious roots,
Will, root and branch, in one night disappear
⁵⁰⁵With a city, men and all, of the Earth-shaker
Poseidon; which place they will
    sometime call
Dorylaeum, of dark ancient Phrygia,
Much-bewailed. Therefore will that time
    be called
Earth-shaker; dens of earth will he break up
⁵¹⁰And walls demolish. And not signs of good
But a beginning of evil will be made;
The baneful violence of general war
You'll have, sons of Aeneas, Dative blood
Of Ilus from the soil. But afterward
⁵¹⁵A spoil will you become for greedy men.
O Ilium, I pity you; for there will bloom
In Sparta an Erinys very fair,
Ever-famed, noblest scion, and will leave
On Asia and Europe a wide-spreading wave;
⁵²⁰But to you most of all she'll bear and cause
Wailings and toils and groans;
    but there will be
Undying fame with those who are to come.
And there will be an aged mortal then,
False writer and of doubtful native land;
⁵²⁵And in his eyes the light will fade away;
Large mind and verses measured
    with great skill
Will he have and be blended with two names,
Will call himself a Chian and will write
Of Ilium, not truthfully, indeed,
⁵³⁰But skillfully; for of my verse and meters
He will be master; for he first my books
Will open with his hands; but he himself
Will much embellish helmed chiefs of war,
Hector of Priam and Achilles, son
⁵³⁵Of Peleus, and the others who have care
For warlike deeds. And also by their side
Will he make gods stand, empty-headed men,
False-writing every way. And it will be
Glory the rather, widely spread, for them
⁵⁴⁰To die at Ilium; but he himself
Will also works of recompense receive.
Also to Lycia will a Locrian race
Cause many evils. And you, Chalcedon,
Holding by lot a strait of narrow sea,
⁵⁴⁵Will an Aetolian youth sometime despoil.
Cyzicus, also your vast wealth the sea
Will break off. And, Byzantium of Ares,
You sometime will by Asia be laid waste,
And also groans and blood immeasurable
⁵⁵⁰Will you receive. And Cragus, lofty mount
Of Lycia, from your peaks
    by yawning chasms
Of opened rock will babbling water flow,
Until even Patara's oracles will cease.
O Cyzicus, that dwell by Propontis
⁵⁵⁵The wine-producing, round you Rhyndacus
Will crash the crested billow.
    And you, Rhodes,
Daughter of day, will long be unenslaved,
And great will be your happiness hereafter,
And on the sea your power will be supreme.
⁵⁶⁰But afterward a spoil will you become
For greedy men, and put on your neck
By beauty and by wealth a fearful yoke.
A Lydian earthquake will again despoil

THE SIBYLLINE ORACLES

The power of Persia, and most horribly
⁵⁶⁵Will the people of Europe
    and Asia suffer pain.
And Sidon's hurtful king with battle-din
Dreadful will work a mournful overthrow
To the seafaring Samians. On the soil
Will slain men's dark blood babble to the sea;
⁵⁷⁰And wives together with the noble brides
Will their outrageous insolence lament,
Some for their bridegrooms,
    some for fallen sons.
O sign of Cyprus, may an earthquake waste
Your phalanxes away, and many souls
⁵⁷⁵With one accord will Hades bold in charge.
And Trallis near by Ephesus, and walls
Well made, and very precious wealth of men
Will be dissolved by earthquake; and the land
Will burst out with hot water; and the earth
⁵⁸⁰Will swallow down those who are
    by the fire
And stench of brimstone heavily oppressed.
And Samos will in time build royal houses.
But to you, Italy, no foreign war
Will come, but lamentable tribal blood
⁵⁸⁵Not easily exhausted, much renowned,
Will make you, impudent one, desolate.
And you yourself beside hot ashes stretched,
As you in your own heart did not foresee,
Will slay yourself. And you will not of men
⁵⁹⁰Be mother, but a nurse of beasts of prey.
But when from Italy will come a man,
A spoiler, then, Laodicea, you,
Beautiful city of the Carians
By Lycus' wondrous water, falling prone,
⁵⁹⁵Will weep in silence for your boastful sire.
Thracian Crobyzi will rise up on Haemus.
Chatter of teeth to the Campanians comes
Because of wasting famine; Corsica
Weeps her old father, and Sardinia
⁶⁰⁰Will by great storms of winter
    and the strokes
of a holy God sink down in ocean depths,
Great wonder to them of the sea.
Woe, woe, how many virgin maids
Will Hades wed, and of as many youths
⁶⁰⁵Will the deep take without funeral rites!
Woe, woe, the helpless little ones
And the vast riches swimming in the sea!
O happy land of Mysians, suddenly
A royal race will be formed. Truly now
⁶¹⁰Not for a long time will Chalcedon be.
And there will be a very bitter grief
To the Galatians. And to Tenedos
Will there a last but greatest evil come.
And Sicyon, with strong yells,
    and Corinth, you
⁶¹⁵Will boast o'er all,
    but flute will sound like strain.
Now, when my soul had rest
    from inspired song,
Even again within my heart was set
A message of the mighty God, and He
Commanded me to prophesy on earth.
⁶²⁰Woe, woe to the race of Phoenician men
And women, and all cities by the sea;
Not one of you will in the common light
Abide before the shining of the sun,
Nor of life will there any longer be
⁶²⁵Number and tribe, because of unjust speech
And lawless life impure which they lived,

Opening a mouth impure, and fearful words
Deceitful and unrighteous forth,
And stood against the God, the King,
⁶³⁰And opened loathsome mouth deceitfully;
Therefore may He subdue them terribly
By strokes o'er all the earth, and bitter fate
Will God send on them burning
    from the ground
Cities, and of the cities the foundations.
⁶³⁵Woe, woe to you, O Crete! To you will come
A very painful stroke, and terribly
Will the Eternal sack you; and again
Will every land behold you black with smoke,
Fire ne'er will leave you,
    but you will be burned.
⁶⁴⁰Woe, woe to you, O Thrace!
    So will you come
Beneath a servile yoke, when the Galatians
United with the sons of Dardanus
Rush on to ravage Hellas, yours will be
The evil; and to a foreign land
⁶⁴⁵Much will you give, not anything receive.
Woe to you, Gog and Magog, and to all,
One after another, Mardians and Daians;
How many evils fate will bring on you!
Woe also to the soil of Lycia,
⁶⁵⁰And those of Mysia and Phrygia.
And many nations of Pamphylians,
And Lydians, Carians, Cappadocians,
And Ethiopian and Arabian men
Of a strange tongue will fall. How now may I
⁶⁵⁵Of each speak fitly? For on all the nations
Which dwell on earth the Highest
    will send dire plague.
When now again a barbarous nation comes
Against the Greeks it will slay many heads
Of chosen men; and they will tear in pieces
⁶⁶⁰Many fat flocks of sheep of men, and herds
Of horses and of mules and lowing cows;
And well-made houses will they burn
    with fire
Lawlessly; and to a foreign land
Will they by force lead many slaves away,
⁶⁶⁵And children, and deep-girded women soft
From bridal chambers creeping on before
With delicate feet; and they will be bound fast
With chains by their foes of foreign tongue,
Suffering all fearful outrage; and to them
⁶⁷⁰There will not be one to supply the toil
Of battle and come to their help in life.
And they will see their goods
    and all their wealth
Enrich the enemy; and there will be
A trembling of the knees. And there will fly
⁶⁷⁵A hundred, and one will destroy them all;
And five will rout a mighty company;
But they, among themselves
    mixed shamefully,
Will by war and dire tumult bring delight
To enemies, but sorrow to the Greeks.
⁶⁸⁰And then on all Hellas there will be
A servile yoke; and war and pestilence
Together will on all mortals come.
And God will make the mighty heavens
    on high
Like brass and over all the earth a drought,
⁶⁸⁵And earth itself like iron. And thereon
Will mortals all lament the barrenness
And lack of cultivation; and on earth
Will He set, who created heaven and earth,

A much-distressing fire; and of all men
⁶⁹⁰The third part only will thereafter be.
O Greece, why have you trusted mortal men
As leaders, who cannot escape from death?
And therefore bring you your foolish gifts
To the dead and sacrifice to idols?
⁶⁹⁵Who put the error in your heart to do
These things and leave the face
    of God the mighty?
Honor the All-Father's Name, and let it not
Escape you. It is now a thousand years,
Yes, and five hundred more,
    since haughty kings
⁷⁰⁰Ruled o'er the Greeks,
    who first to mortal men
Introduced evils, setting up for worship
Images many of gods that are dead,
Because of which
    you were taught foolish thoughts.
But when the anger of the mighty God
⁷⁰⁵Will come on you, then you'll recognize
The face of God the mighty. And all souls
Of men, with mighty groaning lifting up
Their hands to the broad heavens, will begin
To call the great King helper, and to seek
⁷¹⁰The rescuer from great wrath who is to be.
But come and learn this
    and store in your hearts,
What troubles in the rolling years will come.
And what as whole burnt-offering
    Hellas brought
Of cows and bellowing bulls to the temple
⁷¹⁵Of the great God, she from ill-sounding war
And fear and pestilence will flee away
And from the servile yoke escape again.
But until that time there will be a race
Of godless men, even when that fated day
⁷²⁰Will reach its end. For offering to God
You should not make till all things
    come to pass,
Which God alone will purpose not in vain
To be all fulfilled; and strong force will urge.
And there will be again a holy race
⁷²⁵Of godly men who, keeping to the counsels
And mind of the Most High, will honor much
The great God's temple with drink-offerings,
Burnt-offerings, and holy hecatombs,
With sacrifices of fat bulls, choice rams,
⁷³⁰Firstlings of sheep and the fat thighs
    of lambs,
Sacredly offering whole burnt-offerings
On the great altar. And in righteousness,
Having obtained the Law of the Most High,
Blessed will they dwell in cities
    and rich fields.
⁷³⁵And prophets will be set on high for them
By the Immortal, bringing great delight
To all mortals. For to them alone
The mighty God His gracious counsel gave
And faith and noblest thought
    within their hearts;
⁷⁴⁰They have not by vain things
    been led astray,
Nor pay they honor to the works of men
Made of gold, brass, silver, and ivory,
Nor statues of dead gods of wood and stone
[[Besmeared clay, figures of
    the painter's art]],
⁷⁴⁵And all that empty-minded mortals will;
But they lift up their pure arms to Heaven,

Rise from the couch at daybreak,
    always hands
With water cleanse, and honor only Him
Who is immortal and who ever rules,
750 And then their parents; and above all men
Do they respect the lawful marriage-bed;
And they have not base intercourse
    with boys,
As do Phoenicians, Latins, and Egyptians
And spacious Greece, and nations
    many more
755 Of Persians and Galatians and all Asia,
Transgressing the immortal God's pure law
Which they were under. Therefore,
    on all men
Will the Immortal put bane, famine, pains,
Groans, war, and pestilence
    and mournful woes;
760 Because they would not honor piously
The immortal Sire of all men, but revered
And worshiped idols made with hands,
    which things
Mortals themselves will cast down
    and for shame
Conceal in clefts of rocks, when a young king,
765 The seventh of Egypt, will rule his own land,
Reckoned from the dominion of the Greeks,
Which countless Macedonian men will rule;
And there will come from Asia a great king,
A fiery eagle, who with foot and horse
770 Will cover all the land, cut up all things,
And fill all things with evils; he will cast
The Egyptian kingdom down; and taking off
All its possessions carry them away
Over the spacious surface of the sea.
775 And then will they before, the mighty God,
The King immortal, bend the fair white knee
On the much-nourishing earth;
    and all the works
Made with hands will fall by a flame of fire.
And then will God bestow great joy on men;
780 For land and trees
    and countless flocks of sheep
Their genuine fruit to men will offer—wine,
And the sweet honey, and white milk,
    and wheat,
Which is for mortals of all things the best.
But you, O mortal full of various wiles,
785 Do not delay and loiter, but indeed you,
Tossed to and fro, turn and propitiate God.
Offer to God your hecatombs of bulls
And firstling lambs and goats,
    as times revolve.
But Him propitiate, the immortal God,
790 If perhaps He show mercy. For He is
The only God, and other there is none.
And honor justice and oppress no man.
For these things the Immortal does enjoin
On miserable men. But you must heed
795 The cause of the wrath of the mighty God,
When on all mortals there will come
    the height
Of pestilence and conquered they will meet
A fearful judgment, and king will seize king
And wrest his land away, and nations bring
800 Ruin on nations and lords plunder tribes,
And chiefs all flee into another land,
And the land change its men, and foreign rule
Ravage all Hellas and drain the rich land.
Of its wealth, and to strife among themselves

805 Because of gold and silver they will come—
The love of gain an evil shepherdess
Will be for cities—in a foreign land.
And they will all be without burial,
And vultures and wild beasts of earth
    will spoil
810 Their flesh; and when these things
    are brought to pass,
Vast earth will waste the relics of the dead.
And all unsown will it be and unplowed,
Proclaiming sad the filth of men defiled
Many lengths of time in the revolving years,
815 And shields and javelins
    and all sorts of arms;
Nor will the forest wood be cut for fire.
And then will God send from the East a king,
Who will make all earth cease from evil war,
Killing some, others binding
    with strong oaths.
820 And he will not by his own counsels do
All these things, but obey the good decrees
Of God the mighty. And with
    incredible wealth,
With gold and silver and purple ornament,
The temple of the mighty God again
825 Will be weighed down;
    and the full-bearing earth
And the sea will be filled full of good things.
And kings against each other will begin
To hold ill will, in heart abetting evils.
Envy is not a good to wretched men.
830 But again kings of nations on this land
Will rush in masses, bringing on themselves
Destruction; for they'll purpose to despoil
The great God's temple and the noblest men.
What time they reach the land, polluted kings
835 Will set around the city each his throne
And have his people that do not obey God.
And then will God speak with a mighty voice
To all rude people of an empty mind,
And judgment from the mighty God
    will come
840 On them, and they all will be destroyed
By His immortal arm. And fiery swords
Will fall from the sky on earth;
    and great bright lights
Will come down flaming in the midst of men.
And in those days will earth, all-mother, reel
845 By His immortal arm, and shoals of fish
In the deep sea, and all wild, beasts of earth,
And countless tribes of winged bird, and all
The souls of men and every sea will tremble
Before the face of the Immortal One,
850 And there will be dismay.
    High mountain peaks
And monstrous hills will He asunder break,
And to all will dark Erebus appear.
And misty gorges in the lofty hills
Will be full of the dead; and rocks will stream
855 With blood and every torrent fill the plain.
And well-built walls of evil-minded men
Will all fall to the earth, since they knew not
The law nor judgment of the mighty God,
But with a senseless soul all hurried on
860 Against the temple and raised up
    their spears.
And God will judge all by war and by sword
And by fire and by overwhelming storm;
And brimstone there will be from the sky,
    and stones

And great and grievous hail;
    and death will come
865 On the quadrupeds. And then will they
Know God, the Immortal,
    who performs these things;
And wailing, and on the boundless earth
Will be at once a shout of perishing men;
And all the unholy will be bathed in blood;
870 And earth herself will also drink the blood
Of the perishing, and beasts be gorged
    with flesh.
And all these things the great eternal God
Himself bade me proclaim. And that will not
Be unaccomplished, or be unfulfilled,
875 Whatever only in my heart He placed;
For truthful is God's Spirit in the world.
But children of the mighty God will all
Again around the temple live in peace,
Rejoicing in those things which He will give
880 Who is Creator, righteous Judge and King.
For He Himself, great, present far and wide,
Will be a shelter, as on all sides round
A wall of flaming fire. And they will be
In cities and in country without war.
885 For not the hand of evil war, but rather
The Immortal will Himself be their defender
And the hand of the Holy One.
    And then will all
The islands and the cities tell how much
The immortal God loves those men;
    for all things
890 Help them in conflict and deliver them
Heaven, and divinely fashioned sun,
    and moon.
[[And in those days will earth,
    all-mother, reel.]]
Sweet word will they send
    from their mouths in hymns:
"Come, falling on the earth let us all pray
895 The immortal King, and great eternal God.
To the temple let us in procession go,
Since He alone is Lord; and let us all
Meditate on the Law of God Most High,
Which is most righteous of all [laws] on earth.
900 And from the path of the Immortal we
Have wandered and with senseless soul
    we honor
Works made by hand and wooden images
Of dead men." These things souls
    of faithful men
Will cry out: "Come, having,
    at the house of God
905 Fallen on our faces, let us with our hymns
Make joy to God the Father at our homes,
Supplied through all our land
    with arms of foes
Seven lengths of time in the revolving years;
Even shields and helmets
    and all sorts of arms,
910 And a great store of bows
    and arrows barbed";
For forest wood will not be cut for
But wretched Hellas, stop your arrogance
And be wise; and entreat the Immortal One
Magnanimous, and be on your guard.
915 Send now against this city yet again
The people inconsiderate, who have come
Out of the holy land of the mighty One.
Do not move Camarina; for 'tis better
She be unmoved; a leopard from the lair,

⁹²⁰Do not let an evil one meet with you.
But keep off, do not hold within your breast
An arrogant and overbearing soul,
Ready for mighty contest. And serve God
The mighty, that you may share those things;
⁹²⁵And when that fated day will reach its end,
[[And judgment of the immortal God
    will come
To mortals]], judgment great
    and power will come
On men. For all-mother earth will yield
To mortals best fruit boundless—
    wheat, wine, oil;
⁹³⁰Also from Heaven a delightful drink
Of honey and trees will give their fruit,
And fatted sheep and cattle there will be,
Young lambs and kids of goats;
    earth will break forth
With sweet springs of white milk;
    and of good things
⁹³⁵The cities will be full and fat the fields;
Nor sword nor uproar will be on the earth;
No more will earth groan heavily and quake;
Nor will war longer be on earth, nor drought,
Nor famine, nor the fruit-destroying hail;
⁹⁴⁰But great peace will be on all the earth,
And king to king be friend until the end
Of the age, and o'er all earth common law
Will the Immortal in the starry heavens
Perfect for men, touching whatever things
⁹⁴⁵Have been by miserable mortals done;
For He alone is God, there is no other;
And the stern rage of men He'll burn
    with fire.
But change entirely the thoughts
    in your heart,
And flee unrighteous worship; serve the One
⁹⁵⁰Who [ever] lives; guard against adultery
And deeds of lewdness;
    your own offspring rear
And do not murder; for the Immortal One
Is angry with him who in these things sins.
And then a kingdom over all mankind
⁹⁵⁵Will He raise up for ages, who once gave
Holy law to the pious, to whom
He pledged to open every land, the world
And portals of the blessed, and all joys,
And mind immortal and eternal bliss.
⁹⁶⁰And out of every land to the house
Of the great God will they bring frankincense
And gifts, and there will be no other house
To be inquired of by men yet to be,
But what God gave for faithful men to honor;
⁹⁶⁵For mortal temple of the mighty God
Will call it. And all pathways of the plain
And rough hills and high mountains
    and wild waves
Of the deep will be easy in those days
For crossing and for sailing; for all peace
⁹⁷⁰On the land of the good will come;
    and sword
Will prophets of the mighty God remove;
For they are judges and the righteous kings
Of mortals. And there will be
    righteous wealth
Among mankind; for of the mighty God
⁹⁷⁵This is the judgment and also the power.
Be of good cheer, O maiden, and be glad;
For He who made the heaven
    and earth gave you

Joy in your age. And He will dwell in you;
And yours will be immortal and wolves
⁹⁸⁰And lambs will in the mountains
    feed on grass
Together, and with kids will leopards graze;
And bears will lodge
    among the pasturing calves;
And the carnivorous lion will eat chaff
At the manger like the cow; and little children
⁹⁸⁵In bonds will lead them;
    for He will make beasts
Helpless on earth. With babes will fall asleep
Serpents, along with asps, and do no harm;
For over them will be the hand of God.
Now I tell you a sign exceedingly clear,
⁹⁹⁰That you may know
    when the end of all things
On earth will be. When in the starry heavens
Swords will by night point straight toward
    west and east,
Promptly will there be also from the heavens
A cloud of dust borne forth to all the earth,
⁹⁹⁵And the sun's brightness in the midst
    of the sky
Will be eclipsed, and the moon's beams
    appear
And come again on earth; by drops of blood
Distilling from the rocks a sign will be;
And in the cloud, you will behold a war
¹⁰⁰⁰Of foot and horse, like the chase
    of wild beasts
In the dense fog. This end of all things God
Will consummate, whose dwelling
    is in Heaven.
But all must sacrifice to the great King.
These things I show you, I who madly left
¹⁰⁰⁵The long walls of Assyrian Babylon
For Hellas to proclaim to all the wrath
Of God, fire sent…
And that I might to mortals prophesy
Of mysteries divine. And men will say
¹⁰¹⁰In Hellas that I am of foreign land,
Of Erythre born, shameless; others say
That I'm a Sibyl, born of mother Circe
And father Gnostos raving mad and false;
But at that time when all things come to pass
¹⁰¹⁵You will remember me, and no one again
Will call me mad, the great God's prophetess,
For He showed me what happened formerly
To my ancestors; what things were the first
Those God made known to me;
    and in my mind
¹⁰²⁰Did God put all things to be afterward,
That I might prophesy of things to come,
And things that were, and tell them to men.
For when the world was flooded with a flood
Of waters, and one man of good repute
¹⁰²⁵Alone was left and in a wooden house
Sailed o'er the waters with the beasts
    and birds,
In order that the world might be refilled,
I was his son's bride and was of his race
To whom the first things happened,
    and the last
¹⁰³⁰Were all made known;
    and thus from my own mouth
Let all these truthful things remain declared.

BOOK IV

[Introduction, 1-28. Blessedness of the righteous, 29-60. The Assyrian kingdom, 61-65. The Medes and Persians, 66-82. Woes on Phrygia, Asia, and Egypt, 83-100. Sicily burned by fire of Aetna, 101-104. Strife in Greece, 105-108. Triumphs of Macedon, 109-129. Triumphs of Italy, 130-168. Italy's punishment, 169-180. Woes of Antioch, Cyprus, and Caria, 181-197. Wrath in reserve for the impious, 198-209. Exhortations and threatening, 210-230. Resurrection, judgment, and reward, 231-248.]

People of boastful Asia and of Europe,
Hear how much, all too true, I am about,
Through a month many-toned,
    from my great hall
To prophesy; no oracle am I
⁵Of lying Phoebus whom vain men called god,
And further falsified by calling seer;
But of the mighty God, whom hands of men
Formed not like speechless idols carved
    of stone.
For He has not for His abode a stone
¹⁰Most dumb and toothless
    to a temple drawn,
Of immortals a dishonor very sore;
For He may not be seen from earth
    nor measured
By mortal eyes, nor formed by mortal hand;
He, looking down at once on all, is seen
¹⁵Himself by no one; His are murky night,
And day, and sun, and stars, and moon,
    and seas
With fish, and land, and rivers, and the month
Of springs perennial, creatures meant for life,
And rains at once producing fruit of field
²⁰And tree and vine and oil. This God a whip
Struck through my heart within
    to make me tell
Truly to men what things have now befallen
And how much will befall them yet again
From the first generation to the eleventh;
²⁵For He Himself by bringing them to pass
Will prove all things. But do you in all things,
O people, to the Sibyl give all ear,
Who pours from holy mouth a truthful voice.
Blessed of men will they be on the earth
³⁰As many as will love the mighty God,
Offering Him praise before they drink
    and eat;
Trusting in piety. When they behold
Temples and altars, figures of dumb stones,
[[Stone images and statues
    made with hands]]
³⁵Polluted with the blood of living things
And sacrifices of four-footed beasts,
They will reject them all; and they will look
To the great glory of one God and not
Commit presumptuous murder nor dispose
⁴⁰Of stolen gain, which things most horrid are;
Nor shameful longing for another's bed
Have they, nor vile and hateful lust of males.
Their manner, piety, and character
Will other men, that love a shameless life,

⁴⁵Not ever imitate; but, mocking them
With jest and joke like babes
    in senselessness,
They'll falsely charge to them as many deeds
Blameful and wicked as they do themselves.
For slow is the whole race of humankind
⁵⁰To believe. But when judgment of the world
And mortals comes,
    which God Himself will bring,
Judging at once the impious and the pious,
Then indeed will He send the ungodly back
To lower darkness [[and then they will know
⁵⁵How much impiety they worked]];
    but the pious
Will still remain on the fruitful land,
God giving to them breath and life and grace.
But these things all in the tenth generation
Will come to pass; and now what things
    will be
⁶⁰From the first generation, those I'll tell.
First over all mortal will Assyrians rule,
And for six generations hold the power
Of the world, from the time
    the God of Heaven
Being angry against the cities and all men
⁶⁵Sea with a bursting flood covered earth.
Them will the Medes o'erpower,
    but on the throne
For two generations only will exult;
In which times those events
    will come to pass:
Dark night will come at the mid hour of day
⁷⁰And from the heavens
    the stars and circling moon
Will disappear; and earth in tumult shaken
By a great earthquake will throw many cities
And works of men headlong;
    and from the deep
They will peer out the islands of the Sea.
⁷⁵But when the great Euphrates will
    with blood
Be surging, then will there be also set
Between the Medes and Persians
    dreadful strife
In battle; and the Medes will fall and fly
'Neath Persian spears beyond
    the mighty water
⁸⁰Of Tigris. And the Persian power will be
Greatest in all the world, and they will have
One generation of most prosperous rule.
And there will be as many evil deeds
As men will wish away—the din of war,
⁸⁵And murders, and disputes,
    and banishments,
And overthrow of towers and waste of cities,
When Hellas very glorious will sail
Over broad Hellespont, and will convey
To Phrygia sorrow and to Asia doom.
⁹⁰And to Egypt, land of many furrows,
Will sorry famine come, and barrenness
Will during twenty circling years prevail,
What time the Nile, corn-nourisher, will hide
His dark wave somewhere underneath
    the earth.
⁹⁵And there will come from Asia a great king
Bearing a spear, with ships innumerable,
And he will walk the wet paths of the deep,
And will sail after he has cut the mount
Of lofty summit; him a fugitive
¹⁰⁰From battle, fearful Asia will receive.

And Sicily the wretched will a stream
Of powerful fire set all aflame while Etna
Her flame disgorges; and in the deep chasm
Down will the mighty city Croton fall.
¹⁰⁵And strife will be in Hellas; they will rage
Against each other, cast down many cities,
And fighting make an end of many men;
But equally balanced is the strife with both.
But, when the race of mortal men will come
¹¹⁰To the tenth generation, also then
On the Persians will a servile yoke
And terror be. But when the Macedonians
Will boast the scepter there will be
    for Thebes
An evil conquest from behind, and Carians
¹¹⁵Will dwell in Tyre, and Tyrian
    be destroyed.
And Babylon, great to see but small to fight,
Will stand with walls
    that were in vain hopes built.
In Bactria Macedonians will dwell;
But those from Susa and from Bactria
¹²⁰Will all into the land of Hellas flee.
It will take place among those yet to be,
When silver-eddying Pyramus his banks
O'erpouring, to the sacred isle will come.
And Cibyra will fall and Cyzicus,
¹²⁵When, earth being shaken by earthquakes,
    cities fall.
And sand will hide all Samos under banks.
And Delos visible no more, but things
Of Delos will all be invisible.
And to Rhodes will come evil last,
    but greatest.
¹³⁰The Macedonian power will not abide;
But from the west a great Italian war
Will flourish, under which the world will bear
A servile yoke and the Italians serve.
And you, O wretched Corinth, you will look
¹³⁵Sometime on your conquest.
    And your tower,
O Carthage, will press lowly on the ground.
Wretched Laodicea, you sometime
Will earthquake lay low,
    casting headlong down,
But you, a city firmly set, again
¹⁴⁰Will stand. O Lycia Myra beautiful,
You never will the agitated earth
Set fast; but falling headlong down on earth
Will you, in manner like an alien, pray
To flee away into another land,
¹⁴⁵When sometime the dark water of the sea
With thunders and earthquakes
    will stop the din
Of Patara for its impieties.
Also for you, Armenia, there remains
A slavish fate; and there will also come
¹⁵⁰To Solyma an evil blast of war
From Italy, and God's great temple spoil.
But when these, trusting folly, will cast off
Their piety and murders consummate
Around the temple, then from Italy
¹⁵⁵A mighty king will like a runaway slave
Flee over the Euphrates' stream unseen,
Unknown, who will sometime
    dare loathsome guilt
Of matricide, and many other things,
Having confidence in his most wicked hands.
¹⁶⁰And many for the throne with blood
Rome's soil while he flees over Parthian land.

And out of Syria will come
    Rome's foremost man,
Who having burned the temple of Solyma,
And having slaughtered many of the Jews,
¹⁶⁵Will destruction on their great broad land.
And then too will an earthquake overthrow
Both Salamis and Paphos, when dark water
Will dash o'er Cyprus washed
    by many a wave.
But when from deep cleft of Italian land
¹⁷⁰Fire will come flashing forth
    in the broad heavens,
And many cities burn and men destroy,
And much black ashes will fill the great sky,
And small drops like red earth
    will fall from the sky,
Then know the anger of the God of Heaven,
¹⁷⁵For that they without reason will destroy
The nation of the pious. And then strife
Awakened of war will come to the West,
Will also come the fugitive of Rome,
Bearing a great spear, having marched across
¹⁸⁰Euphrates with his many myriads.
O wretched Antioch, they will call you
No more a city when around their spears
Because of your own follies you will fall.
And then on Scyros will a pestilence
¹⁸⁵And dreadful battle-din destruction bring.
Woe, woe! O wretched Cyprus, you
Will a broad wave of the sea cover, you
Tossed on high by the whirling
    stormy winds.
And into Asia there will come great wealth,
¹⁹⁰Which Rome herself once, plundering,
    put away
In her luxurious homes; and twice as much
And more will she to Asia render back,
And then there will be an excess of war.
And Carian cities by Maeander's waters,
¹⁹⁵Girded with towers and very beautiful,
Will by a bitter famine be destroyed,
When the Maeander his dark water hides.
But when piety will perish from mankind,
And faith and right be hidden in the world,
²⁰⁰... Fickle ... and in unholy boldness
Living will practice wanton violence,
And reckless evil deeds, and of the pious
No one will make account, but even them all
From thoughtlessness they utterly destroy
²⁰⁵In childish folly, in their violence
Exulting and in blood holding their hands;
Then surely know God is no longer mild,
But gnashing with fury and destroying all
The race of men by conflagration great.
²¹⁰Ah! Miserable mortals, change these things,
Nor lead the mighty God to wrath extreme;
But giving up your swords
    and pointed knives,
And homicides and wanton violence,
Wash your whole body in perennial streams,
²¹⁵And lifting up your hands to Heaven,
    seek pardon
For former deeds and expiate with praise
Bitter impiety; and God will give
Conversion; He will not destroy; and wrath
Will He again restrain, if in your hearts
²²⁰You all will practice honored piety.
But if, ill-disposed, you obey me not,
But with a fondness for strange lack of sense
Receive all these things with an evil ear,

There will be over all the world a fire
²²⁵And greatest omen with sword
    and with trump
At sunrise; the whole world will hear the roar
And mighty sound. And He will burn all earth,
And destroy the whole race of men, and all
The cities and the rivers and the sea;
²³⁰All things He'll burn, and it will be
    black dust.
But when now all things
    will have been reduced
To dust and ashes, and God will have calmed
The fire unspeakable which He lit up,
The bones and ashes of men God Himself
²³⁵Again will fashion, and He will again
Raise mortals up, even as they were before.
And then will be the judgment, at which God
Himself as judge will judge the world again;
And all who sinned with impious hearts,
    even them,
²⁴⁰Will He again hide under mounds of earth
[[Dark Tartarus and Stygian Gehenna]].
But all who will be pious will again
Live on the earth [[and [will inherit there]
The great immortal God's unwasting bliss,]]
²⁴⁵God giving spirit life and joy to them
[[The pious; and they all will see themselves
Beholding the sun's sweet and cheering light.
O happy on the earth will be that man.]]

BOOK V

[Introduction, 1, 2. Rome's first emperors, 2-733. Grief of the Sibyl, 74-76. Inundation of Egypt, 77-84. Oracle against Memphis, 85-100. Idolatry and woes of Egypt, 101-147. Woes on various cities of the East and of Asia Minor, 148-169. Woe on Lycia, Phrygia, and Thessaly, 110-185. The vile and fearful king, 186-209. Oracle against Rome, 210-241. Lamentation over Egypt, 242-272. Britons and Gauls, 273-280. Ethiopians and Indians perish by conflict of the stars, 281-291. Doom of Corinth, 292-308. Oracle against Rome, 309-334. The blessed Jews, 335-345. The heavenly Joshua, 346-350. Lovely Judea, 351-382. Woe on western Asia and Ephesus, 383-398. God's wrath on the wicked, 399-410. Woes on Smyrna, Cyme, Lesbos, Corcyra, Hierapolis, and Tripolis, 411-434. Doom of Miletus, 433-439. Prayer for the land of Judah, 440-446. Wretched Thrace, Hellespont, and Italy, 447-463. Divine judgment and majesty, 464-484. Wars and woes of the last time, 485 517. Appeal to the wicked city, 518-555. Messianic day, 556-580. Fall of Babylon, 581-600. Woes of Asia, Crete, Cyprus, and Phoenicia, 601-615. Vast armies in Egypt, Macedon, and Asia, 616-624. Destruction of the Thracians, 625-629. Mankind made few by woes, 630-639. Final darkness, 640-648. Ruin of Isis and Serapis, 649-660. The temple in Egypt, 661-676. Sin and doom of the Ethiopians, 677-687. Battle of the constellations, 688-711.]

But come, now, hear of me the mournful time
Of sons of Latium. And first of all,
After the kings of Egypt were destroyed
And the like earth had downwards
    borne them all,
⁵And after Pella's townsman, under whom
The whole East and the rich West
    were cast down,
whom Babylon dishonored,
    and stretched out
For Philip a dead body (not of Zeus,
Of Ammon not true things were prophesied),
¹⁰And after that one of the race and blood
Of King Assaracus, who came from Troy,
Even he who cleft the violence of fire,
And after many lords, and after men
To Ares dear, and after the young babes,
¹⁵The children of the beast
    that feeds on sheep,
The very first lord will be, who will sum
Twice ten with the first letter of his name;
In wars exceedingly mighty will he be;
And he will have the initial sign of ten;
²⁰And in like manner after him to reign
Is one who has the alphabet's first letter;
Before him Thrace and Sicily will crouch,
Then Memphis, Memphis cast headlong
    to earth
By reason of the cowardice of rulers
²⁵And of a woman unenslaved who falls
On the wave. And laws will he ordain
For peoples and put all things under him;
But after a long time will he transmit
His power to another, who will have
³⁰Three hundred for his first initial sign,
And of a river the beloved name,
And the Persians he will rule and Babylon;
And then he will strike Medians
    with his spear.
Then one will rule who has the initial sign
³⁵Of the number three. And then will be a lord
Who will for first initial have twice ten;
And he will come to Ocean's utmost water
And by Ausonia cleave the refluent tide.
And one whose mark is fifty will be lord,
⁴⁰A dreadful serpent breathing grievous war,
Who sometime stretching forth his hands
    will make
An end of his own race and stir all things,
Acting the athlete, driving chariots,
Putting to death and daring countless things;
⁴⁵And he will cleave the mountain of two seas
And sprinkle it with gore; but out of sight
Will also vanish the destructive man;
Then, making himself equal to God,
Will he return; but God
    will prove him nothing.
⁵⁰And after him will three kings be destroyed
By one another. Then a great destroyer
Of pious men will come,
    whom seven times ten
Will point out clearly. But from him a son,
Whom the first letter
    of three hundred proves,
⁵⁵Will take the power. And after him will be
A ruler, of the initial sign of four,
A life-destroyer. Then a reverend man
Of the number fifty. Next, succeeding him
Who has the first mark of the initial sign
⁶⁰Three hundred, will a Celtic mountaineer,

Into the strife of battle pressing on,
Escape not fate unseemly, but will be
Worn weary to death; him foreign dust,
But dust that of Nemea's flower has name,
⁶⁵Will hide a corpse. And after him will rule
Another man, with silver helmet decked;
And to him will be the name of a sea;
And he will be a man the best of all
And in all things discreet. And on you,
⁷⁰You best of all, above all, dark-haired one,
And on your shoots will be all these days.
After him three will rule; but the third one
Will at a late time hold the royal power.
Worn out am I, thrice-miserable one,
⁷⁵Sister of Isis, to lay up in heart
An evil message, and an inspired song
Of oracles. First Maenades will dart
Around your much-lamented temple's steps,
And you will be in evil hands that day
⁸⁰When the Nile some time
    will fill the whole land
Of Egypt even to sixteen cubits deep;
It will wash all the land, and water it
For mortals; and the pleasure of the land
Will be still and the glory of her face.
⁸⁵Memphis, you most will wail over Egypt;
For of old ruling mightily the land
You will become poor, so that out of Heaven
The Thunderer will Himself
    with great voice cry:
"O mighty Memphis, who did boast of old
⁹⁰O'er craven mortals greatly, you will wail
Full of pain and utter doom, so that you
Yourself will the eternal God perceive
Immortal in the clouds. Where among men
Is now your mighty pride? Because you did
⁹⁵Against My God-anointed children rave,
And did urge evil forward on good men,
You will for such things suffer penalty
In some like manner. No more openly
For you will there be right
    among the blessed;
¹⁰⁰Fallen from the stars,
    you will not rise to Heaven."
Now these things to Egypt God bade me
Speak out for the last time, when men will be
Utterly evil. But they labor hard,
Evil men evil things awaiting, wrath
¹⁰⁵Of the immortal Thunderer in Heaven,
Worshiping stones and beasts instead of God,
And also fearing many things besides
Which have no speech, nor mind,
    nor power to hear;
Which things it is not right for me to mention,
¹¹⁰Each one an idol, formed by mortal hands;
Of their own labors
    and presumptuous thoughts
Did men receive gods made of wood
    and stone
And brass, and gold and silver—foolish too,
Without life and dumb, molten in the fire
¹¹⁵They made them,
    vainly trusting such things...
Thmois and Xois are in sore distress,
And stricken is the hall of Heracles
And Zeus and Hermes [king]. And as for you,
O Alexandria, famed nourisher
¹²⁰[Of cities] war will not leave, nor [plague]...
For your pride you will pay as many things
As you before did. Silent will you be

THE SIBYLLINE ORACLES

A long age, and the day of your return...
No more for you will flow luxurious drink...
[125]For there will come a Persian on your dale,
And like hail will he all the land destroy,
And artful men, with blood and corpses...
By sacred altars one of barbarous mind,
Strong, full of blood and raging senselessly,
[130]With countless numbers
    rushing to destruction.
And then will you, in cities very rich,
Be very weary. Falling on the earth
All Asia will wail on account of gifts
Crowning her head with which
    she was by you
[135]Delighted. But, as he himself obtained
The Persian land by lot, he will make war
And killing every man destroy all life,
So that there will remain
    for wretched mortals
A third part. But with nimble leap will he
[140]Himself speed from the West,
    and all the land
Besiege and waste. But when he will possess
The height of power and odious reverence,
He will come, wishing to destroy the city
Even of the blessed. And a certain king
[145]Sent forth from God against him
    will destroy
All mighty kings and bravest men. And thus
Will judgment by the Immortal come to men.
Woe, woe for you, unhappy heart!
Why do you move me to declare these things,
[150]The painful rule of Egypt over many?
Go to the East, to races of the Persians
Who lack in understanding, and show them
That which is now and that which is to be.
The river of Euphrates will bring on
[155]A flood, and it will destroy the Persians,
Iberians and Babylonians
And the Massagetae that relish war
And trust in bows. All Asia fire-ablaze
Will to the isles beam brightly. Pergamos,
[160]Revered of old, will perish from its base,
And Pitane among men will appear
All-desolate. All Lesbos will sink deep
Into the deep, and thus will be destroyed.
Smyrna, whirled down her cliffs,
    will wail aloud,
[165]She that was once revered
    and given a name
Will perish utterly. Bithynians
Will over their own country, then reduced
To ashes, wail, and o'er great Syria,
And o'er Phoenicia that has many tribes.
[170]Woe, woe for you, O Lycia;
How many evils does the sea contrive
Against you, mounting up of its own will
On the painful land! And it will dash
With evil earthquake and with bitter streams
[175]On the rough Lycian land
    that once breathed perfume.
And there will be for Phrygia fearful wrath
Because of sorrow for which Rhea came,
Mother of Zeus, and there continued long.
The sea will overthrow the Centaur race
[180]And barbarous nation,
    and beneath the earth
Will tear away the Lapithaean land.
The river of deep eddies and deep flow,
Peneus, will destroy Thessalian land,
Snatching men from the earth. Eridanus
[185][Pretending once to bear the forms,
    of beasts].
Hellas thrice wretched will the poets weep,
When one from Italy will strike the neck
Of the isthmus, mighty king of mighty Rome,
A man made equal to God, whom, they say,
[190]Zeus himself and the august Hera bore—
He, courting by his voice all-musical
Applause for his sweet songs,
    will put to death
With his own wretched mother many men.
From Babylon will flee the fearful lord
[195]And shameless whom all mortals
    and best men
Abhor; for he slew many and laid hands
On the womb; against his wives he sinned
And of men stained with blood
    had he been formed.
And he will come to monarchs of the Medes
[200]And Persians, first whom he loved
    and to whom
He brought renown,
    while with those wicked men
He lurked against a nation not desired
And on the temple made by God he seized
And citizens and people going in,
[205]Of whom I justly sang the praise, he burned;
For when this man appeared
    the whole creation
Was shaken and kings perished—
    and yet power
Remained among them,
    and they quite destroyed
The mighty city and the righteous people.
[210]But when the fourth year
    a great star will shine,
Which alone will the whole earth overpower
Because of honor, which was first assigned
To lord Poseidon; then a great star will come
From the sky into the dreadful sea and burn
[215]The fathomless deep, and Babylon itself,
And the land of Italy, because, of which
There perished many holy faithful men
Among the Hebrews and a people true.
You will be among evil mortals made
[220]To suffer evils, but you will remain
All-desolate whole ages by yourself
Hating your soil; for you did have desire
For sorcery, adulteries were with you
And lawless carnal intercourse with boys,
[225]You evil city, womanish, unjust,
Ill-fated above all. Woe, woe!
You city of the Latin land, unclean
In all things, Maenad having joy in snakes,
Over your banks a widow will you sit
[230]And the Tiber River will lament for you
His consort—you who have
    a blood-stained heart
And impious soul. Did you not understand
What God can do, and what He devises?
But you said, "I'm alone, and me no one
[235]Will sack." But now will God, who ever is,
You and all yours destroy, and in that land
No longer will your ensign yet remain,
As of old, when the mighty God received
Your honors. Stay, O lawless one, alone,
[240]And mixed with burning fire, inhabit
In Hades the Tartarean lawless land.
And now again, O Egypt, I bewail
Your blind delusion; Memphis, first in toils,
You will be filled up with the dead; in you
[245]The pyramids will speak a ruthless sound.
O Python, who were justly called of old
The double city, be for ages silent,
So that you may cease from wickedness.
Reckless in evils, treasury of toils,
[250]Much-wailing Maenad, suffering, dire ills,
Much-weeping, you a widow will remain
Through all time. You did
    full of years become
While you alone were ruling o'er the world;
But when the white dress Barea
    round herself
[255]Will put on over that which is defiled,
Would that I neither were nor had been born
O Thebes, where is your great strength?
    A fierce man
Will slay the people; but you, wretched one,
Grasping your dusky dress will wail alone,
[260]And you will make atonement for all things
Which you formerly with a shameless soul
Did perpetrate. They also will behold
A mourning on account of lawless deeds.
And a mighty man of the Ethiopians
[265]Will overthrow Syene; by their might
Will swarthy Indians occupy Teucheira.
Pentapolis, a man of mighty strength
Will burn you whole. All-tearful Libya,
Who will explain your follies? And Cyrene,
[270]Of mortals, who will pitiably weep
For you? You will not even to the time
Of your destruction cease your hateful wail.
Among the Britons and among the Gauls,
Rich in gold, Ocean will be roaring loud
[275]Filled with much blood; for evil things
Did they to God's children, when a king
Of the Sidonians, a Phoenician, led
A mighty Gallic host from Syria;
And he will slaughter you, yourself, Ravenna,
[280]And to slaughter he will lead the way.
O Indians and great-hearted Ethiops,
Together fear; for when
    with these the course
Of Capricorn and Taurus in the Twins
Will wind around the middle of the heavens,
[285]Virgo then rising, and about his front
Fastening a belt the sun will lead all heaven,
There will be moving downwards
    to the earth
A mighty conflagration high in air,
And a new nature in the warlike stars,
[290]So that the whole land of the Ethiops
Will perish in the midst of fire and groans.
And weep you, Corinth, the destruction sad
Which is ill you; for when with pliant threads
The Fates three sisters, spinning will aloft
[295]Lead him who flees by guile
    against the voice
Of the isthmus, until all will look at him
Who once cut out the rock with ductile brass,
He also will destroy and strike your land,
As it has been appointed. For to him
[300]God gave strength to accomplish
    that which could
No earlier of all the kings together.
And first with sickle cleaving off the roots
From three heads he will give food in excess
To others, so that kings unclean will eat
[305]The flesh of parents. For to all men

Slaughter and terrors are laid up in store
because of the great city and just people
Saved through all time,
    whom Providence held high.
O you unstable one and ill-advised,
³¹⁰By evil fates surrounded, for mankind
Both a beginning and great end of toil—
Of suffering creation and of part
Restored again—you leader insolent
Of evils, and for men a great curse, who
³¹⁵Of mortals wished for you?
    Who has not been
Embittered from within? Cast down ill, you
A king his honored life lost. Wickedly
Have you disposed all things
    and washed away
All that is fair, and by you have been changed
³²⁰The world's fair folds.
    In strife with us perhaps
You have brought forward
    these unstable things;
And how do you say, "I will persuade you,"
And "If in anything you blame me, speak?"
There was once among men
    the sun's bright light
³²⁵The prophets' common ray
    being spread abroad;
Speech dripping honey, fair drink for all men,
Appeared and grew, and day arose on all.
Because of this, you narrowminded one—
Leader of greatest evils—both a sword
³³⁰And grief will come in that day.
    For mankind
Both a beginning and great end of toil,
Of suffering creation and of part
Restored again, hear, O you curse of men,
The bitter oracle intolerable.
³³⁵But when the Persian land will keep away
From war and plague and groaning,
    in that day
A race divine of blessed heavenly Jews
Will offer prayer, who will dwell all around
God's city in mid portions of the land,
³⁴⁰And even as far as Joppa building round
A great wall they will carry it aloft
To the gloomy clouds. No more will trump
Sound battle—din nor by a foe's mad hands
Will they be cut off; but they will set up
³⁴⁵Their trophies for an age of evil men.
And One will come again from Heaven, a Man
Preeminent, whose hands on fruitful tree
By far the noblest of the Hebrews stretched,
Who at one time did make the sun stand still
³⁵⁰When He spoke with fair word
    and holy lips,
No longer vex your soul within your breast
By reason of the sword, rich child of God,
Flower longed for by Him only, perfect light
And noble branch, a scion much beloved,
³⁵⁵Pleasant Judea, city beautiful,
Inspired by hymns. No more will
    unclean foot
Of Greeks keep revel all around your land,
Who held within their breast a lawless mind;
But you will glorious children honor much
³⁶⁰[[And be expert in songs
    and holy tongues]],
With sacrifices of all kinds and prayers
Honored of God. All who endure the toils
Of small affliction and the just will have
More that is altogether beautiful;
³⁶⁵But the wicked,
    who to Heaven sent lawless speech,
Will cease their speaking against
    one another,
And hide themselves until
    the world is changed.
And there will be a rain of gleaming fire
From the clouds; and no longer
    will mortals reap
³⁷⁰The fair corn from the earth;
    all things unsown
And unplowed, until mortal men will know
The Lord of all things, the immortal God
Always existing, and no longer revere
Mortal things—neither dogs
    nor vultures' nests,
³⁷⁵And what things Egypt taught to magnify
With dumb months and dull lips.
    But all these things
The holy land of the only pious men
Will bring forth, from
    the honey-dripping rock,
A stream and from a spring ambrosial milk
³⁸⁰Will flow for all the just; for in one God,
One Father, who alone is glorious,
Having great piety and faith they hoped.
But why does the wise mind grant me
    these things?
And now you, wretched Asia, piteously
³⁸⁵I mourn and the race of Ionians
And Carians and Lydians rich in gold.
Woe, woe for you, O Sardis; and woe
For Trallis much beloved; woe, woe,
Laodicea, city beautiful;
³⁹⁰Thus will you be by earthquakes
    overthrown
And ruined, and also be changed to dust.
And to Asia gloomy …
Artemis' temple fixed at Ephesus …
By chasms, and earthquakes
    come headlong down
³⁹⁵Sometime into the dreadful sea, as storms
Overwhelm ships. And up-turned Ephesus
Will wail aloud, lament beside her banks,
And for her temple search which is no more.
And then incensed will be God the immortal,
⁴⁰⁰Who dwells on high,
    hurl thunderbolts from Heaven
Down on the head of him that is impure.
And in the place of winter there will be
In that day summer. And to mortal men
Will then be great woe; for the Thunderer
⁴⁰⁵Will utterly destroy all shameless men,
And with His thunders
    and with lightning-flames
And blazing thunderbolts [strike]
    men of ill-will,
And thus will He destroy the impious ones,
So that there will remain on the earth
⁴¹⁰Dead bodies more in number
    than the sand.
For Smyrna also, weeping her Lycurgus,
Will come [near] to the gates of Ephesus
And she herself will perish even more.
And foolish Cyme with her inspired streams
⁴¹⁵Cast down by hands of godless men unjust
And lawless, will to Heaven not so much
As a word utter; but she will remain
Dead in Cymaean streams. And then will they
Together weep, awaiting evil things.
⁴²⁰Cyme's rough populace
    and shameless tribe,
Having a sign, will know for what they toiled.
And then, when they will have
    bewailed their land
Reduced to ashes, by Eridanus
Will Lesbos be forever overthrown.
⁴²⁵Woe, Corcyra, city beautiful,
Woe for you, cease from your revelry.
You also, Hierapolis, sole land
With riches mixed,
    what you have longed to have
You will have, even a land of many tears,
⁴³⁰Since you were angry toward a land beside
Thermodon's streams. Rock-clinging Tripolis,
Beside the waters of Maeander, you
Will by the nightly surges under shore
God's wrath and foresight utterly destroy.
⁴³⁵Take me not, willing,
    to the neighboring land
Of Phoebus; sometime will a thunderbolt
Dainty Miletus from above destroy,
Because she seized on Phoebus' crafty song
And the wise care and prudent plan of men.
⁴⁴⁰Father of all, be gracious to the land
Of Judah, well fed, fruit-abounding, great,
In order that Your judgments we may see.
For You, O God, in kindness regarded
This land first that it might appear to be
⁴⁴⁵Your gracious gift to all mortal men
And to hold fast what God put in their charge.
The works thrice wretched of the Thracians
I yearn to see, and wall between two seas
Trailed in the dust along beneath the mist,
⁴⁵⁰Even like a river for the swimming fish.
O wretched Hellespont, sometime a child
Of the Assyrians will throw a yoke
Across you; battle of the Thracians comes
And will despoil your strength.
    And there will
⁴⁵⁵Over the land of Macedonia
A king of Egypt, and a barbarous clime
Will waste the strength of captains. Lydians,
And the Galatians, and Pamphylians
With the Pisidians, all equipped for war
⁴⁶⁰Will in a mass bring evil strife to pass.
Thrice wretched Italy, then will remain
All-desolate, unwept, in blooming land
By deadly sting to perish utterly.
And sometime high in
    the broad heavens above
⁴⁶⁵Like thunder-roaring
    will God's voice be heard.
And the unwasting flames of the sun himself
Will be no more, nor will the brilliant light
Of the moon again be in the latest time,
When God will be the ruler. And dark gloom
⁴⁷⁰Will be o'er all the earth, and blinded men
And evil beasts and woe; that day will be
A long time, so that men will see that God
Himself is Lord, the overseer of all
In front of Heaven. And then will He Himself
⁴⁷⁵Not pity hostile men, who sacrifice
Their herds of lambs and sheep
    and calves and goats
And bellowing golden-horned bulls,
    offering them
To lifeless Hermae and to gods of stone.
But let the law of wisdom be your guide

And the glory of the righteous;
 lest sometime
The imperishable God incensed destroy
Each race of men and shameless tribe of life,
It does behoove them faithfully to love
The Father, the wise God who ever is.
⁴⁸⁵ In the last time, at the turning of the moon,
There will be raging through the world a war
And carried on with cunning, and in guile.
And from the limits of the earth will come
Fleeing and pondering sharp things
 in his mind,
⁴⁹⁰ A matricidal man who every land
Will overpower and over all things rule,
And see all things more wisely than all men;
And that for whose sake he himself was slain
Will he seize forthwith. And he will destroy
⁴⁹⁵ Many men and great tyrants and will burn
All of them, as none other ever did,
And he will raise up them that are afraid
For emulation's sake. And from the West
Much war will come to men,
 and blood will flow
⁵⁰⁰ Downhill till it becomes
 deep-eddying streams.
And in the plains of Macedonia
Will wrath distill and give help
 from the West,
But to the king destruction. And a wind
Of winter then will blow on the earth,
⁵⁰⁵ And the plain be filled with evil war again.
For fire will rain down from
 the heavenly plains
On mortals, and therewith blood, water, flash
Of lightning, murky darkness, night in the sky,
And waste in war and o'er the slaughter mist,
⁵¹⁰ And these together will destroy all kings
And noblest men. Thus will be made to cease
Then the destruction pitiable of war.
And no more will one fight with swords
 or iron
Or even darts, which things will not again
⁵¹⁵ Be lawful. But wise people will have peace,
Who were left, having made proof
 of wickedness,
That they might at the last be filled with joy.
You matricides, leave off your impudence
And evil-working boldness, who of old
⁵²⁰ provided lawlessly lewd couch with boys,
And placed as harlots maidens pure before
In brothels by assault and punishment
And by much-laboring indecency.
For in you mother with her child did hold
⁵²⁵ Unlawful intercourse, and daughter was
With her own father wedded as a bride;
And in you kings have their ill-fated mouth
Polluted, and in you have wicked men
Found couch with cattle.
 Be in silence hushed,
⁵³⁰ You wicked city all-bewailed, possessed
Of revelry; for by you virgin maids
Will care no longer for the fire divine
Of sacred wood that fondly nourishes;
Before you was a much-loved house of old
⁵³⁵ Extinguished, when I saw the second house
Cast headlong down and overwhelmed
 with fire
By an unholy hand, house ever flourishing,
God's watchful temple, brought forth
 of His holy ones
And being always indestructible,
⁵⁴⁰ By the soul hoped for and the body itself.
For not without the rites of burial
Will one praise God out of the unseen earth,
Nor did wise workman make a stone
 by them,
Nor had he fear of gold, cheat of the world
⁵⁴⁵ And of souls, but the mighty Father, God
Of all things God-inspired, did he revere
With holy offerings and fair hecatombs.
But now an unseen and unholy king
With multitude great
 and with men renowned
⁵⁵⁰ Rose into power and cast
 His dwelling down
And let it go unbuilt. But he himself
When he set foot on the immortal land
Destroyed the ground.
 And such a sign no longer
Was worked on men, so that it appeared
⁵⁵⁵ That others the great city should destroy.
For there came from the heavenly plains
 a Man,
One blessed, with a scepter in His hand,
Which God gave Him,
 and He ruled all things well,
And to all the good did He restore
⁵⁶⁰ The riches which the earlier men
 had seized.
And many cities with much fire He took
From their foundations, and He set on fire
The towns of mortals who before did evil,
And He did make that city, which God loved,
⁵⁶⁵ More radiant than stars and sun and moon,
And He set order, and a holy house
Incarnate made, pure, very fair, and formed
In many stadia a great and boundless tower
Touching the clouds themselves
 and seen by all,
⁵⁷⁰ So that all holy and all righteous men
Might see the glory of the eternal God,
A sight that has been longed for. Rising sun
And setting day hymned forth
 the praise of God.
For there are then no longer fearful things
⁵⁷⁵ For wretched mortals, nor adulteries
And lawless love of boys, nor homicide,
Nor tumult, but a righteous strife in all.
It is the last time of the holy ones when God
Accomplishes these things, high Thunderer,
⁵⁸⁰ Founder of temple most magnificent.
Woe, woe for you, O Babylon,
For golden throne and golden sandal famed,
Kingdom of many years and of the world
Sole ruler, who were great in ancient time
⁵⁸⁵ And city of all cities, you no longer
Will lie in golden mountains and by streams
Of the Euphrates; you will be laid low
By rout of earthquake. But the Parthians dire
Caused you to suffer all things. For hold fast
⁵⁹⁰ Your unknown speech,
 impure Chaldean race;
Do not ask nor be concerned
 how you will lead
The Persians or how you will rule the Medes;
For on account of your supremacy,
Which you had, sending hostages to Rome
⁵⁹⁵ And serving Asia, you that formerly
Did also think yourself a queen, will come
To the judgment of antagonists,
Because of whom you have suffered
 baneful things;
And you will give instead of crooked words
⁶⁰⁰ Bitter vexation to the enemies,
And in the last time will the sea be dry
And ships no longer sail to Italy,
And Asia the great then, utterly doomed, will
Be water, and then Crete will be a plain.
⁶⁰⁵ And Cyprus will endure great misery
And Paphos will bewail a dreadful fate,
So that even Salamis, great city, will
Be seen to undergo great misery;
And now the dry land will be fruitless sand
⁶¹⁰ On the shore. And locusts not a few
Will utterly destroy the Cyprian land.
Looking at Tyre, doomed mortals,
 you will weep.
Phoenicia, dreadful wrath remains for you,
Until you to a worthless ruin fall,
⁶¹⁵ So that even Sirens truly may lament.
In the fifth generation, when the ruin
Of Egypt has ceased, it will come to pass
That shameless kings will be together joined,
And races of Pamphylians will encamp
⁶²⁰ In Egypt, and in Macedonia
And in Asia and among the Libyans
Will in the dust be a world-maddening war
Exceedingly bloody, which the king of Rome
And rulers of the West will make to cease.
⁶²⁵ When wintry storm will drop down
 like the snow,
While frozen are great river and vast lakes,
Forthwith a barbarous race will make
 their way
Into the Asian land and will destroy
The race of dreadful Thracians, hard to quell.
⁶³⁰ And then will mortals feeding lawlessly
Devour their parents, being by hunger worn,
And will gulp down the entrails.
 And wild beasts
Will devour from all houses table-food,
And they and birds all mortals will devour.
⁶³⁵ The ocean with dead bodies will be filled
From the river and be red with flesh
 and blood
Of the foolish ones. Then thus a feebleness
Will be on earth, so that of men the number
May be seen and the measure of the women,
⁶⁴⁰ And the dire race will wail
 for myriad things
At last when the sun sets to rise no more,
But to remain submerged in Ocean's waves;
For it beheld the wickedness unclean
Of many mortals. And a moonless night
⁶⁴⁵ Will be a fame around the mighty heavens,
And no small mist will hide
 the world's ravines
A second time; then afterward God's light
Will guide the good men,
 who sang praise to God.
Isis, thrice wretched goddess, you alone
⁶⁵⁰ Will on the waters of the Nile remain,
A Maenad out of order on the sands
Of Acheron, and no longer will remain
Remembrance of you over all the earth.
And also you, Sarapis, who are placed
⁶⁵⁵ On many glistening stones, a ruin vast
Will you in thrice unhappy Egypt lie.
But those whom love of Egypt led to you
Will all lament you badly; but who put

Imperishable reason in their breast,
⁶⁶⁰And who praised God,
  will know you to be nothing.
And sometime will a linen-vested man,
A priest, say: "Come, let us raise up of God
A beautiful true temple; come, let us
The fearful law of our forefathers change,
⁶⁶⁵Because of which they did not understand
That they were to gods of stone and clay
Making processions and religious rites.
Let us turn our souls, giving praise to God
The imperishable, who Himself is Father,
⁶⁷⁰The everlasting One, the Lord of all,
The true One, the King, life-sustaining Father,
The mighty God existing forevermore."
And then will there a great pure temple be
In Egypt, and the people made by God
⁶⁷⁵Will into it their sacrifices bring.
And to them God will give life uncorrupted.
But when the Ethiopians, forsaking
The shameless tribes of the Triballians,
Will cultivate their Egypt, they will then
⁶⁸⁰Begin their baseness, that the later things
May all occur. For they will overthrow
The mighty temple of the Egyptian land;
And God will rain down on the earth
  dire wrath
Among them, so that all the wicked ones
⁶⁸⁵And all without sense perish. And no longer
Will there be any sparing in that land,
Because they did not keep
  that which God gave.
I saw the threatening of the shining sun
Among the stars, and in the lightning flash
⁶⁹⁰The dire wrath of the moon;
  the stars travailed
With battle; and God gave them up to light.
For long fire-flames rebelled against the sun;
Morning star [(Venus)] treading
  on Leo's back
Began the fight; and the moon's double horn
⁶⁹⁵Changed its shape;
  Capricorn struck Taurus' neck;
And Taurus took away from Capricorn
Returning day. Orion would no longer
Abide his yoke; the lot of Gemini
Did Virgo change in Aries; no longer shone
⁷⁰⁰The Pleiades; Draco disavowed his zone;
Down into Leo's girdle Pisces went.
Cancer remained not, for he feared Orion;
Scorpio down on dire Leo backwards moved;
And from the sun's flame Sirius slipped away;
⁷⁰⁵And the strength of the mighty Shining One
Aquarius kindled. Uranus himself
Was roused, until he shook the warring ones;
And being incensed
  he hurled them down on earth.
Then swiftly stricken down on the baths
⁷¹⁰Of Ocean they set all the earth on fire;
And the high heavens remained
  without a star.

BOOK VI

[Preexistence, incarnation, and immersion of the Son of God, 1-9. His teaching and His miracles, 10-25. Miseries in store for the guilty land, 26-32. The blessed Cross, 33-36.]

The great Son of the Immortal famed in song
I from the heart proclaim, to whom a throne,
To be held fast the most Father gave
Ere, He was brought forth;
  then was He raised up
⁵According to flesh given, washed,
  at the mouth
Of the Jordan River, which goes rushing on
Trailing its gleaming billows, from the fire
Escaping He first will see God's sweet Spirit
Descending with the wings of a white dove.
¹⁰And a pure flower will bloom,
  and springs be full.
And He will show the ways to men, and show
The heavenly paths, and teach all with wise
And He will come for judgment and persuade
A disobedient people while He boasts
¹⁵Descent praiseworthy from a heavenly Sire.
Billows will He tread, sickness of mankind
Will He destroy, He will raise up the dead,
And many sufferings will He drive away;
And from one scrip will be men's fill of bread,
²⁰When the house of David
  will bring forth a Child;
And in His hand the whole world,
  earth, heaven, sea.
And He will flash on the earth, as once
The two begotten from each other's ribs
Saw human form appearing. It will be
²⁵When earth will be glad in the hope of child.
But for you only, Sodomitic land,
Are evil woes laid up; for you yourself
Ill-disposed did not apprehend your God
Who mocks at mortal schemes;
  but from a thorn
³⁰Did crown Him with a crown,
  and fearful gall
Did mingle to insolence and spirit.
This will bring evil woes about for you.
O the Wood, O so blessed, on which
God was outstretched;
  the earth will not have You,
³⁵But You will look on a heavenly house,
When You, O God, will flash Your eye of fire.

BOOK VII

[Woes of Rhodes, Delos, Cyprus, and Sicily, 1-9. The Flood, 10-15. Ruin of Phrygia, Ethiopia, and Egypt, 16-28. Woe of Laodicea, 29-31. Signs and powers of Messiah, 32-49. The new shoot, 50-52. Persian wars, 53-67. Fall of Ilias, 68-72. Doom of Colophon, Thessaly, Corinth, and Tyre, 73-86. Coele-Syria accursed, 87-102. Rules for sacrifice and alms giving, 103-130. Doom of Sardinia, Mygdonia, the Celtic land, Rome, Syria, and Thebes, 131-161. The devouring fire, 162-190. Long night followed by a better time, 101-205. Confession and doom of the Sibyl, 206-221.]

O Rhodes, you are unhappy; for first you,
You will I mourn; and you will be the first
Of cities, and first will you be destroyed,
Bereft of men, but of the means of life
⁵Not wholly destitute. And you will sail,

Delos, and be unstable on the water;
Cyprus, a billow of your gleaming sea
Will sometime you destroy; you, Sicily,
The fire that burns within you will consume.
¹⁰Nor heed God's terrible and foreign water.
Noah sole fugitive from all men came.
Earth will float, hills float,
  and even sky will float,
Everything will be water and all things
Will be destroyed by waters. And the winds
¹⁵Will stand still and a second age will be.
O Phrygia, first will you flame from the crest
Of the water; and first in impiety
You will deny God Himself, courting favor
With false gods, which will utterly destroy
²⁰You, wretched one,
  while many years roll round.
The doomed Ethiopians under pain,
Suffering things lamentable, will by swords
Be stricken while they crouch on the ground.
Rich Egypt ever caring for her corn,
²⁵Which Nilus by his seven
  swimming streams
Intoxicates, will in intestine strife
Destroy; and thence men unexpectedly
Will drive out Apis, not the god for men.
Woe, woe, Laodicea! You
³⁰Not ever seeing God will lie, bold one;
And over you will dash a wave of Lycus.
He Himself who is born the mighty God,
Who will work many signs,
  will through Heaven hang
An axle in the midst, and place for men
³⁵A mighty terror to be seen on high,
Measuring a column with a mighty fire
Whose drops will slay the races of mankind
That have dared evils. But a common Lord
There will at some time be, and then will men
⁴⁰Propitiate God, but will not make an end
Of fruitless sorrows. And through
  David's house
Will all things come to pass. For God Himself
Gave Him the power and put it in His hand;
Under His feet will sleep His messengers,
⁴⁵And some will kindle fires,
  and some will make
Rivers appear, and some will rescue towns,
And some will send forth winds.
  But furthermore
A grievous life will come on many men,
Entering their souls and changing
  human hearts.
⁵⁰But when a new shoot will out of a root
Put forth eyes, the creation, which to all
Once gave abundant food…
And it will with the times be full. But when
Others will rule, a tribe of warlike Persians,
⁵⁵Bride-chambers at once will be terrible
Because of lawless deeds. For her own son
Will mother have as husband; son will be
The ruin of his mother; and with sire
Will daughter lie down and will put to sleep
⁶⁰This foreign law. But to them afterward
Will Roman Ares flash from many a spear;
And they will mix much land
  with human blood.
But then a chief of Italy will flee
From the force of the spear.
  But they will leave
⁶⁵On the land a lance inscribed with gold,

THE SIBYLLINE ORACLES

Which as the signal ensign of their rule
The foremost fighters carry constantly.
And it will be, when evil and ill-starred
Ilias will piteously complete for all
⁷⁰A tomb, not marriage,
    then will brides sorely weep,
Because they did not know God,
    but always gave
By kettle-drums and cymbals
    boisterous sound.
Consult the oracle, O Colophon;
For a great fearful fire hangs over you.
⁷⁵Ill-wedded Thessaly, the earth no longer
Will see you, nor your ashes, and alone
Escaping from the mainland you will swim;
Thus, O you wretched one, will you of war
Be melancholy refuse, having fallen
⁸⁰By swiftly flowing rivers and by swords.
And you, O wretched Corinth, will receive
Around yourself stern Ares, ill-fated one,
And you will perish on one another.
Tyre, you, unhappy, will be left alone;
⁸⁵For, made a widow by the feebleness
Of pious men, you will be brought to nothing.
Ah, Coele-Syria, of Phoenician men
The last hold, on whom the briny sea
Of Berytus disgorging is poured forth,
⁹⁰O wretched one, you did not know
    your God,
Who once in the mouth
    of Jordan washed Himself,
—And the Spirit spread His wings in flight
    toward Him—
Who before both the earth
    and starry heavens
Was, actual Word, begotten by His Father,
⁹⁵And by the Holy Spirit donning flesh
He quickly flew to His Father's house.
And for Him three towers
    did the mighty Heaven
Establish, in which dwell God's noble guides:
Hope, piety, and reverence much-desired,
¹⁰⁰Not having in gold or in silver joy,
But in the reverential acts of men—
Both sacrifices and most righteous thoughts.
And you will sacrifice to the immortal
And mighty God august, not melting grains
¹⁰⁵Of frankincense in fire, nor with the sword
Slaying the shaggy-haired lamb, but with all
Who bear your blood take wild birds,
    offer prayer,
And fixing eyes on Heaven, send them away;
And you will sprinkle water on pure fire
¹¹⁰Having cried: "As the Father did beget
You, the Word, Father, I sent forth a bird,
Swift messenger of words, with holy waters
Sprinkling Your immersion, O Word,
    through which
You did make Yourself manifest in fire."
¹¹⁵You will not shut your door,
    when there will come
A stranger to you in need to curb
His hunger which comes from his poverty,
But taking hold of that man sprinkle him
With water and pray thrice; and to your God
¹²⁰Do you thus cry: "I do not long for wealth;
A suppliant, I once publicly received
A suppliant; Father, You provider—hear."
When you have prayed you will give to him;
And the man went away thereafter . . .
¹²⁵Do not afflict me, holy fear of God
And righteous, as to birth pure, unenslaved,
Attested . . .
Do You, O Father, make my wretched heart
Stand still; to You have I looked, to You
¹³⁰The undefiled, whom hands
    did not produce.
Sardinia, weighty now, you will be changed
To ashes. You will be no more an isle,
When the tenth time will come.
    Amid the waves
Will sailors seek you when you are no more,
¹³⁵And o'er you will kingfishers wail sad dirge.
Rugged Mygdonia, beacon of the sea
Hard to get out of, ages will you boast
And to ages will be all destroyed
With a hot wind, and rave with many woes.
¹⁴⁰O Celtic land, on mountain range so great,
Beyond impassable Alp, you deep sand
Will altogether bury; you will give
Tribute no more, nor corn, nor pasturage;
And you from peoples ever far away
¹⁴⁵Will be all-desolate, and becoming thick
With chill ice, you will for an outrage pay,
Which you did not perceive, unholy one.
Stout-hearted Rome, you to Olympus will
Flash lightning after Macedonian spears;
¹⁵⁰But God will make you utterly unknown,
When you would to the eye seem to remain
Much more firm. Then to you
    such things I'll cry.
Perishing, you will then cry out and boil
In pain; a second time to you, O Rome,
¹⁵⁵Again a second time I am to speak.
And now for you, O wretched Syria,
Do I wail bitterly in pitying grief.
O Thebans ill-advised, an evil sound
Is over you while flutes speak out their tones;
¹⁶⁰For you will trumpet sound an evil noise
And you will see the entire land destroyed!
Woe, woe for you, you wretched one;
Woe, woe you evil-minded sea!
You will be wholly eaten up of fire
¹⁶⁵And people with your brine
    will you destroy.
For there will be such raging fire on earth
As flows like water, and it will destroy
The whole land. It will set the hills on fire,
Will burn the rivers, and exhaust the springs.
¹⁷⁰The world will be disordered
    while mankind
Are perishing. And then the wretched ones,
Burned badly, will look to the sky patterned
Not with stars, but with fire. Not speedily
Will they be made to perish, but dissolved
¹⁷⁵From under flesh, and burning in the spirit
For age-long years, they will know
    that God's law
Is always hard to put to test and not
To be deceived; and then earth,
    seized by force,
Daring whatever god she did admit
¹⁸⁰To her altars, cheated, turned to smoke
Through the changed air;
    and they will undergo
Much suffering who for gain will prophesy
Shameful things, nourishing the evil time.
And the Hebrews who put
    on the shaggy skins
¹⁸⁵Of sheep will prove false, in which race
Obtained no portion by inheritance,
But talking mere words over sorrows they
Are misers, who will change their course
    of life
And not mislead the just,
    who through the heart
¹⁹⁰All-faithfully propitiate their God.
But in the third lot of revolving years,
Eighth the first, will another world appear.
Night will be all . . . long and without light.
And then will pass around
    the dreadful stench
¹⁹⁵Of brimstone, messenger of homicides,
When they will be by night and hunger slain.
Then a pure mind will God beget in men,
And will the race establish, as it was
Formerly; longer will not any one
²⁰⁰Deep furrow cut with round plow,
    nor two oxen
Straight guiding dip the iron down; nor vines
Will be nor ears of corn; but all will eat
Together dewy manna with white teeth.
And then among them God will also be,
²⁰⁵And He will teach them
    as He has taught me,
The sad one. For how many evil things
I did with knowledge once, and many things
Heedless I also wickedly performed.
Countless my couches, but no marriage-bond
²¹⁰Was cared for; and I, all-unfaithful, brought
To all a savage oath. I turned away
Those in need and among the foremost went
Into like glen and minded not God's word.
Therefore, fire consumed me and will gnaw;
²¹⁵For I will not live always, but a time
Of evil will destroy me, when for me
Men will beside the margin of the sea
Construct a tomb, and will slay me
    with stones;
For lying with my father a dear son
²²⁰Did I present him. Strike me, strike me all;
For thus will I live and fix eyes on Heaven.

BOOK VIII

[Introduction, 1–4. The five monarchies, 5–21. Lust of gain, 21–46. Doom of Rome, 47–63. The gray-haired prince, 61–83. The three rulers, 84–94. Misery of Rome, 95–115. Final judgment of Rome, 116–140. Dirge over Rome, 141–173. The sixth race of Latin kings, 174–182. Appearance of the Phoenix, 183–186. Fall of Rome, 187–210. Woes of Rhodes, Thebes, Egypt, Rome, Delos, Samos, and the Persians, 211–222. The Messianic King, 223–225. The day of evil and of doom, 226–251. The Sibyl's wish, 255–260. The end of all things, 261–283. Christian acrostic concerning the last day, 284–330. Moses a type of the Messiah, 331–337. The Messianic Savior portrayed, 338–379. The Crucifixion, 380–410. Entrance into Hades and the Resurrection, 411–429. Exhortation to honor the Messianic King, 430–447. Another picture of the day of doom, 448–475. Self-declaration of the Creator through the Sibyl, 476–568. The heavenly Ruler addressed, 569–607. The incarnation of the Word, 608–641. Additional Christian precepts, 642–669.]

God's declarations of great wrath to come
In the last age on the faithless world
I make known, prophesying to all men
According to their cities. From the time
⁵When the great tower fell
    and the tongues of men
Were parted into many languages
Of mortals, first was Egypt's royal power
Established, that of Persians and of Medes,
And also of the Ethiopians,
¹⁰And of Assyria and Babylon,
Then the great pride of boasting Macedon,
Then, fifth, the famous lawless kingdom last
Of the Italians will show many evils
To all mortals and will spend the toils
¹⁵Of men of every land. And it will lead
The untamed kings of nations to the West,
Make laws for peoples and subject all things.
Late do the mills of God grind the fine flour.
Fire then will destroy all things and give back
²⁰To fine dust the heads of
    the high-leafed hills
And of all flesh. First cause of ills to all
Are covetousness and a lack of sense.
For there will be love of deceitful gold
And silver; for than these did mortals choose
²⁵Nothing greater, neither light
    of sun nor heaven,
Nor sea, nor broad-backed earth
    whence all things grow,
Nor God who does give all things, of all things
The Father, nor yet faith and piety
Chose they before them. Of impiety
³⁰A fount, and of disorder forward guide,
An instrument of wars and foe of peace
Is lack of sense, that sets at enmity
Parents and children. And along with gold
Will marriage not be honorable at all.
³⁵And the land will have its borders
    and each sea
Its watchers craftily distributed
To all those that have gold; for ages thus
Will those who purpose to possess the land
That feeds many plunder laboring men,
⁴⁰In order that, procuring larger space,
They may enslave them by a false pretense.
And if the huge earth from the starry heavens
Held not her throne far off,
    there had not been
For men an equal light, but, bought with gold,
⁴⁵It had belonged to rich men and God must
For poor men have prepared another world.
There will come to you sometime from above
A heavenly stroke deserved,
    O haughty Rome.
And you will be the first to bend your neck
⁵⁰And be razed to the ground, and you will fire
Destructive utterly consume, cast down
On your pavements, and your wealth
    will perish,
And wolves and foxes
    dwell in your foundations.
And then will you be wholly desolate,
⁵⁵As if not born. Where your Palladium then?
What god will save you,
    whether worked of gold
Or stone or brass? Or then
    where your decrees
Of senate? Where will be the race of Rhea,
Of Kronos, or of Zeus, and of all those
⁶⁰Whom you did worship, demons
    without life,
Images of the worn-out dead, whose tombs
Crete the ill-starred will hold a cause of pride,
And honor the unconscious dead
    with thrones?
But when you will have had voluptuous kings
⁶⁵Thrice five, enslaving the world
    from the east
To the west, there will then be a lord
Gray-headed, having name of the near sea,
The world inspecting with a nimble foot,
Bringing gifts, having a large amount of gold
⁷⁰And plundering hateful silver even more,
And stripping it off he will pick it up.
And he will have part in all mysteries
Of Magian shrines, display his child as god,
Abolish all things sacred, and disclose
⁷⁵The ancient mysteries of deceit to all.
Sad then the time when he himself, sad one,
Will perish. And yet will the people say:
"Your mighty strength, O city, will fall down,"
At once perceiving that the evil day
⁸⁰Is coming on. And, your most piteous fate
Foreseeing, fathers and young children then
Will mourn together;
    they "Woe! Woe!" will wail
Beside the Tiber's lamentable banks.
After him at the latest day of all
⁸⁵Will three rule, filling out a name of God
The heavenly, of whom is the power
    both now
And to all ages. One of them being old
The scepter long will wield,
    most piteous king,
Who in his houses will shut up and guard
⁹⁰All the goods of the world, in order that,
When from the utmost limits of the earth
That man, the matricidal fugitive,
Will come again, he may bestow these things
On all and furnish Asia with great wealth.
⁹⁵And then will you mourn and will put aside
The luster of the broad-striped purple robe
Of your commanders and wear
    mourning dress,
O haughty queen, offspring of Latin Rome;
The glory of that arrogance of yours
¹⁰⁰Will be for you no longer, nor will you,
Ill-fated, ever be raised up again,
But will lie prostrate. For the glory also
Of eagle-bearing legions will fall low.
Where then your power?
    What allied land will be
¹⁰⁵Subjected by your follies lawlessly?
For then in all earth will confusion be
Of mortals, when the Almighty will Himself
To the tribunal come to judge the souls
Of the living and the dead and all the world.
¹¹⁰And parents will not be to children dear
Nor children to their parents, on account
Of their impiety and their distress
Unlooked-for. Yours thenceforth
    will gnashing be
And scattering and conquest,
    and when the fall
¹¹⁵Of cities comes and yawnings of the earth.
When a dragon charged with fire
    in both his eyes
And with full belly will come on the waves
And will afflict your children, and there be
Famine and war of kinsmen, near at hand
¹²⁰Is the end of the world and the last day
And judgment of the immortal God for them
That are approved and chosen.
    And there will
Against the Romans first of all be wrath
Implacable, and there will come a time
¹²⁵Of drinking blood
    and wretched course of life.
Woe, woe for you, you reckless land—
Great barbarous nation; you did not perceive
Whence naked and unworthy you did come
To the sun's light, that to that place again
¹³⁰Naked you might withdraw and afterward
Come to judgment, as unjustly judging....
With hands gigantic coming from on high
Alone through all the world, you will abide
Under the earth. By naphtha and asphalt
¹³⁵And brimstone and much fire you utterly
Will disappear and will be burning dust
For [all] ages; and each one who sees
    will hear
From Hades a great mournful bellowing
And gnashing of teeth, and you noisily
¹⁴⁰Beating with your own hands
    your godless breast.
For all together there is equal night;
For rich and poor; and naked from the earth
Naked again to earth they haste away
And cease from life
    when they complete their time.
¹⁴⁵No slave is there, nor any lord, nor tyrant,
Nor king, nor leader having much conceit,
Nor speaker learned in law, nor magistrate
Judging for money; nor do they pour out
The blood of sacrifices in libations
¹⁵⁰On the altars; there sounds not a drum
Nor cymbal ...
Nor perforated flute that has a power
To madden mind itself, nor sound of pipe
That was the likeness of a crooked snake,
¹⁵⁵Nor trumpet, harsh-toned
    messenger of wars;
Nor those made drunken in the lawless feasts
Of revelry, nor in the choral dance;
Nor sound of harp, nor harmful instrument;
Nor strife, nor anger manifold, nor sword
¹⁶⁰Is with the dead; but an eternity
Common to all is keeper of the key
Of the great prison before
    God's judgment-seat
With images of gold and silver and stone
You are ready, that to the bitter day
¹⁶⁵You may come to see
    your first punishment,
O Rome, and gnashing of teeth. And no more
Will Syrian or Greek lay down his neck
Beneath your servile yoke, nor foreigner,
Nor other nation. Plundered you will be
¹⁷⁰And made to suffer what you did exact,
And in fear wailing you will give, until
You pay back all things; and you for the world
Will be a triumph and reproach of all.
Then will the sixth race of the Latin kings
¹⁷⁵End life at last and scepters leave behind
From the same race another king will reign,
Who will rule every land and scepters wield;

THE SIBYLLINE ORACLES

And having full power, and by the decrees
Of God most mighty, will his children rule,
¹⁸⁰And of unshaken children is his race;
For thus it is decreed while time
    moves round,
When there will be of Egypt thrice five kings.
Thereafter when the limit of the time
Of the Phoenix will come round,
    there will be a race
¹⁸⁵Of peoples come to plunder,
    tribes confused,
Enemy of the Hebrews. Then will Ares
Go plundering Ares; and he will himself
Destroy the haughty threatening
    of the Romans.
For Rome's power perished then
    while in its bloom;
¹⁹⁰An ancient queen with cities
    dwelling round,
No longer will the land of fertile Rome
Prevail, when out of Asia one will come
To rule with Ares. And when he has worked
All these things, to the city afterward
¹⁹⁵Will he come. And three times
    three hundred
And eight and forty will you make complete,
When, taking you by force, an ill-starred fate
Will come on you and complete your name.
Ah me, I the thrice wretched, will I see
²⁰⁰Sometime that day to you destructive,
    Rome,
But to all Latins most? It honors him
With counsels who goes, up on Trojan car
With hidden children from the Asian land,
Having a fiery soul. But when he will
²⁰⁵Cut through the isthmus looking wistfully,
Moving against all, passing o'er the sea,
Then will dark blood pursue
    the mighty beast.
And a dog chased the lion which destroys
The shepherds. And then will they take away
²¹⁰His scepter and to Hades he will pass.
And to Rhodes will come an evil last,
But greatest. There will also be for Thebes
An evil conquest afterward, and Egypt
Will perish by the wickedness of rulers,
²¹⁵And he who, being mortal, even so
Escaped headlong destruction afterward,
Thrice blessed was, even four times
    happy man.
And Rome will be a room, and Delos dull,
And Samos sand ...
²²⁰Later again thereafter there will come
An evil to the Persians for their pride,
And all their insolence will come to nothing.
And then a holy Lord of all the earth
Having raised up the dead
    will wield the scepter
²²⁵To all ages. Thrice then to Rome
Will the Most High bring pitiable fate
And to all men, and by their own works
They'll perish; but they would not
    be persuaded,
Which would have been
    much more to be desired.
²³⁰But when forthwith there
    will increase for ill
An evil day of famine and of plague
And of intolerable battle-din,
Even then again, the former daring lord
Will, having called the senate, counsel take
²³⁵How he will utterly destroy ...
Dry land will bloom together with the leaves
Appearing; and the heavenly expanses
Will bring to light on the solid rock
Rainstorm and flame, and much wind
    on the land,
²⁴⁰And over all the earth a multitude
Of poisonous sowings. But with
    shameless soul
Will they again act, fearing not the wrath
Of God or men, forsaking modesty,
Longing for and greedy tyrants
²⁴⁵And violent sinners, false, insatiate,
Workers of evil and in nothing true,
Destroyers of faith, on foul speech
In false words; they will have no fill of wealth;
But shamelessly will they strip off still more;
²⁵⁰Under the rule of tyrants they will perish.
The stars will all fall forward in the sea,
All one by one, yet will men see in the sky
A brilliant cornet, sign of much distress
About to come, of war and battle-strife.
²⁵⁵Let me not live when
    the glad woman reigns,
But then when heavenly grace
    will reign within,
And when the holy Child will crush
    with bonds
The mischievous destroyer of all men,
Opening the depth to view, and suddenly
²⁶⁰The wooden house
    will cover mortals round.
But when the generation tenth will be
Within the house of Hades, afterward
The mighty sway of one of female sex;
And God Himself will increase many evils
²⁶⁵When she with royal honor
    has been crowned;
And altogether then an impious age.
The sun obscurely looking shines by night;
The stars will leave the sky;
    and with much storm
A hurricane will desolate the earth;
²⁷⁰And there will be a rising of the dead;
The running of the lame will be most swift,
The deaf will bear, the blind will see,
    and those
That talk not will talk, and to all
Will life and wealth be common. And the land
²⁷⁵Alike for all, divided not by walls
Or fences, will bear more abundant fruits.
And fountains of sweet wine
    and of white milk
And honey it will give ...
And judgment of the immortal God
    [(great king)].
²⁸⁰But when God will change times ...
Winter producing summer, then will be
[All] oracles [fulfilled] ...
But when the world has perished ...
And the earth will perspire,
    when there will be
²⁸⁵The sign of judgment.
    And from Heaven will come
The King who for the ages is to be,
Present to judge all flesh
    and the whole world.
Faithful and faithless mortals will see God
The Most High with the holy ones
    at the end of time.
²⁹⁰And of men bearing flesh He judges souls
On His throne, when sometime
    the whole world
Will be a desert and a place of thorns.
And mortals will their idols cast away
And all wealth. And the searching fire
    will burn
²⁹⁵Earth, heavens, and sea;
    and it will burn the gates,
Of Hades' prison. Then will come all flesh
Of the dead to the free light of the holy ones;
But the lawless will that fire
    whirl round and round.
For ages. Howsoever much one did
³⁰⁰In secret, then will he all things declare;
For God will open dark breasts to the light.
And lamentation will there be from all
And gnashing of teeth. Brightness of the sun
Will be eclipsed and dances of the stars.
³⁰⁵He will roll up the heavens;
    and of the moon
The light will perish. And He will exalt
The valleys and destroy the heights of hills,
And height no longer will appear remaining
Among men. And the hills will with the plains
³¹⁰Be level and no more on any sea
Will there be sailing. For the earth will then
With heat be shriveled
    and the dashing streams
Will with the fountains fall.
    The trump will send
From Heaven a very lamentable sound,
³¹⁵Howling the loathsomeness
    of wretched men
And the world's woes.
    And then the yawning earth
Will show Tartarean chaos. And all kings
Will come to the judgment seat of God.
And there will out of Heaven a stream of fire
³²⁰And brimstone flow.
    But for all mortals then
Will there a sign be, a distinguished seal—
The Wood among believers, and the horn
Fondly desired, the life of pious men—
But it will be stumbling block of the world,
³²⁵Giving illumination to the chosen
By water in twelve springs;
    and there will rule
A shepherding iron rod. This One who now
Is in acrostics which give signs of God
Thus written openly, the Savior is:
³³⁰Immortal King, who suffered for our sake;
Him Moses typified when he stretched out
Holy arms, conquering Amalek by faith,
That the people might know Him
    to be chosen
And honorable before His Father God,
³³⁵The rod of David and the very stone
Which he indeed aid promise, and in which
He that believes will have eternal life.
For not in glory, but as mortal man
Will He come to creation, pitiable,
³⁴⁰Unhonored, without seemly form, to give
Hope to the pitiable; and He will give
Fair form to mortal flesh, and heavenly faith
To those without faith, and He'll give
    fair form
To the man who was fashioned from the first
³⁴⁵By the holy hands of God,

and whom by guile
The serpent led astray to the fate
Of death to go and knowledge to receive
Of good and evil, so that leaving God
He serves the ways of mortals. For at first
³⁵⁰Receiving Him as fellow-counselor
From the beginning the Almighty said:
"Let both of us, O Son, make mortal tribes—
Stamping them with the impress
    of Our image;
I now by My hands, and You by the Word
³⁵⁵In after time will for Our form provide
That We may jointly cause it to arise."
Keeping in mind this purpose He will come
To the creation, to a holy virgin
Bringing the likeness antitypical,
³⁶⁰Immersing with water by the elders' hands,
And by the Word accomplishing all things,
And healing every sickness. By His word
The winds will He make cease,
    and with His foot
Will calm the raging sea, walking thereon
³⁶⁵In peaceful faith.
    And from five loaves of bread
And a fish of the sea five thousand men
Will He fill in the desert; and then taking
All the remaining fragments for the hope
Of peoples, will He fill twelve baskets full.
³⁷⁰And the souls of the blessed He will call,
And love the pitiable, who, being mocked,
Beaten, and whipped, will evil do for good
Desiring poverty. He who perceives
All things and sees all things
    and hears all things
³⁷⁵Will search the heart and bare it
    to conviction;
For of all things is He Himself the ear
And mind and sight,
    and Word that makes forms
To whom all things submit, and He preserves
Them that are dead and every sickness heals.
³⁸⁰Into the hands of lawless men, at last,
And faithless He will come, and they will give
To God ruthless beatings with impure hands
And poisonous spittle with polluted mouths.
And He to whips will openly give then
³⁸⁵His holy back; [[for He to the world
A holy virgin will Himself commit.]]
And silent He will be when buffeted
Lest anyone should know whose Son He is
Or whence He came, that He may talk
    to the dead.
³⁹⁰And He will also wear a crown of thorns;
For of thorns is the crown an ornament
Chosen, eternal. They will pierce His side
With a reed that they may fulfill their law;
For of reeds shaken by another spirit
³⁹⁵Were nourished inclinations of the soul,
Of anger and revenge. But when these things
Will be accomplished, of the which I spoke,
Then to Him will every law be loosed
Which from the first by the decrees of men
⁴⁰⁰Was given because of disobedient people.
He'll spread His hands
    and measure all the world.
But gall for food and vinegar to drink
They gave Him; this inhospitable board
They'll show Him. But the curtain
    of the temple
⁴⁰⁵Will be asunder rent and in midday
There will be for three hours dark,
    monstrous night.
For it was no more pointed out again
How to serve secret temple and the law,
Which had been covered
    with the world's displays,
⁴¹⁰When the Eternal came Himself on earth.
And into Hades will He come announcing
Hope to all the holy ones, the end of ages
And the last day; and having fallen asleep
The third day, He will end the lot of death;
⁴¹⁵Then from the dead departing He will come
To light, the first to show forth to the chosen
Beginning of resurrection, and wash off
By means of waters of immortal spring
Their former wickedness, that, being born
⁴²⁰From above, they might be
    no more enslaved
To the unlawful customs of the world.
And first then openly to His own
Will He as Lord in flesh be visible,
As He before was, and in hands and feet
⁴²⁵Exhibit four marks fixed in His own limbs,
Denoting east and west and south and north;
For of the world so many royal powers
Will against our Exemplar consummate
The deed so lawless and condemnable.
⁴³⁰Daughter of Zion, holy one, rejoice,
Who have suffered many things;
    your King Himself
Mounted on a foal is hastening on;
Behold, meek He will come, that He may lift
Our slavish yoke, so grievous to be borne
⁴³⁵Lying on our neck, and may annul
Our godless laws and bonds compulsory.
Know indeed your God Himself,
    who is God's Son;
Him glorify and hold within your heart,
From your soul love Him and extol His Name.
⁴⁴⁰Put off your former friends
    and wash yourself
From their blood; for He is not by your songs
Nor by your prayers appeased,
    nor does He give
To perishable sacrifices heed,
Being imperishable; but present
⁴⁴⁵The holy hymn of understanding mouths
And know who this One is, and you will then
Behold the Father …
And then will all the elements of the world
Abide in solitude: air, earth, sea, light
⁴⁵⁰Of gleaming fire, and heavenly sky
    and night
And all days into one will run together
And into outward form all-desolate.
For from the sky will the stars of light all fall.
And there will fly no longer in the air
⁴⁵⁵The well-winged birds,
    nor stepping be on earth;
For wild beasts will all perish. Nor will be
Voices of men, nor of beasts, nor of birds.
The world will hear no serviceable sound,
Being disordered; but a mighty sound
⁴⁶⁰Of threatening will the deep sea
    sound aloud,
And swimming trembling creatures
    of the sea
Will all die; and no longer on the waves
Will sail the freighted ship.
    And earth will groan
Blood-stained by wars; and all the souls
    of men
⁴⁶⁵Will gnash with their teeth,
    [[of the lawless souls
Both by loud crying and by fear,]] dissolved
By thirst, by famine, and by plague and
    murders,
And they will call death beautiful and death
Will flee away from them; for death no longer
⁴⁷⁰Nor night will give them rest.
    And many things
Will they in vain ask God who rules on high,
And then will He His face turn openly
Away from them. For He to erring men
Gave in seven ages for conversion signs
⁴⁷⁵By the hands of a virgin undefiled.
All these things in my mind
    God Himself showed
And all that have been spoken by my mouth
Will He accomplish: "And I know the number
Of the sands and the measures of the sea,
⁴⁸⁰I know the inmost places of the earth
And gloomy Tartarus, I know the numbers
Of the stars, and the trees, and all the tribes
Of quadrupeds, and of the swimming things
And flying birds, and of men who are now
⁴⁸⁵And of those yet to be, and of the dead;
For I Myself the forms and mind of men
Did fashion, and right reason did I give
And knowledge taught; I who formed
    eyes and ears,
Who see and hear and every thought discern,
⁴⁹⁰And who within am conscious of all things,
I am still; and hereafter will convict
[[And punishing what any mortal did
In secret, and on God's judgment-seat
Coming and speaking to mortal men]].
⁴⁹⁵I understand the dumb man and I hear
Him that speaks not, and how great
    the whole height
From earth to heaven is, and the beginning
And end I know, who made the heavens
    and earth.
[[For all things
    have proceeded from Him, things
⁵⁰⁰From the beginning to the end He knows.]]
For I alone am God and other God
There is not. They My image formed of wood
Treat as divine, and shaping it by hand
They sing their praises over idols dumb
⁵⁰⁵With supplications and unholy rites.
Forsaking the Creator they were slaves
To lewdness. Men possessing everything
Bestow their gifts on things which cannot aid,
As if they for My honors deemed these things
⁵¹⁰All useful, with the smell of sacrifice
Filling the feast, as if for their own dead.
For they flesh and bones full of marrow burn
Offering on altars, and they pour out blood
To demons, and they kindle lights to Me
⁵¹⁵The giver of light, and as to a god
That thirsts do mortals drunken
    pour out wine
In vain to idols that can give no aid.
I have no need of your burnt offerings,
Nor your libations, nor polluted smoke,
⁵²⁰Nor blood most hateful. For in memory
Of kings and tyrants they will do these things
To dead demons, as to heavenly beings,
Performing service godless and destructive.

And godless they their images call gods,
⁵²⁵Forsaking the Creator, having faith
That from them they derive all hope and life,
Deaf and dumb, in the evil putting trust,
But they are wholly ignorant of good.
Two ways did I Myself before them set,
⁵³⁰Of life and of death, and before them set
Judgment to choose good life;
    but they themselves
Hastened to death and to eternal fire.
Man is My image, having upright reason.
For him a table pure and without blood
⁵³⁵Make ready and with good things fill it up,
And give the hungry bread, the thirsty drink,
And to the body that is naked clothes
From your own labors with unsullied hands
Providing. Recreate the afflicted man,
⁵⁴⁰And help the weary, and provide for Me,
The living One, a living sacrifice
Sowing piety, that also I to you
Sometime may give immortal fruits, and light
Eternal you will have and fadeless life
⁵⁴⁵When I will prove all by fire. For all things
I will fuse and will pick out what is pure;
Heaven will I roll up and the depths of earth
Lay open, and then will I raise the dead
Making an end of fate and sting of death,
⁵⁵⁰And afterward for judgment will I come
Judging the manner both of pious men
And impious; I will set ram close to ram,
Shepherd to shepherd, calf to calf, for test,
Close to each other; whosoever were
⁵⁵⁵Exalted, proven by trial, and who stopped
The mouth of everyone, that they themselves
Vying with them that lead a holy life
May likewise bring them into slavery,
Enjoining silence, urged by love of gain,
⁵⁶⁰Not proved before Me,
    then will all withdraw.
No longer henceforth will you grieving say,
Tomorrow will be, nor, Yesterday has been;
Not many days of care, nor spring,
    nor winter,
Nor summer then, nor autumn, nor sunset
⁵⁶⁵Nor sunrise; for a long day I will make.
And to ages there will be the light
Longed for of the great…"
[[Christ Jesus, of ages]] …
You who are self-begotten, undefiled,
⁵⁷⁰True and eternal, measuring
    by Your power
From Heaven the fiery blast,
    and with rough torch
From clashing does the scepter keep,
    and calm
The crashings of
    the heavy-sounding thunders,
And driving earth into confusion do
⁵⁷⁵Hold back the rushing noises.…
And the fire-blazing scourges You do blunt
Of lightnings, and the vast outpour of storms
And of autumnal hail, and chilling stroke
Of clouds and shock of winter. For of these
⁵⁸⁰Each one indeed is marked out
    in Your mind,
Whatever seems good to Yourself to do
Your Son nods His assent to, having been
Begotten in Your bosom before all
Creation, fellow-counselor with You,
⁵⁸⁵Former of mortals and creator of life.

Him with the first sweet utterance of mouth
You did address: "Behold, let Us make man
In a form altogether like Our own,
And let Us give him life-sustaining breath;
⁵⁹⁰Him being yet mortal all things of the world
Will serve, and to him formed out of clay
We will subject all things." And You did speak
These things by word, and all things
    came to pass
According to Your heart; and Your command
⁵⁹⁵Together all the elements obeyed,
And an eternal creature was arranged
In mortal figure, also heavens, air, fire,
And earth and water of the sea, sun, moon,
Chorus of stars, hills…
⁶⁰⁰Both night and day, sleeping
    and waking up,
Spirit and passion, soul and understanding,
Are, might and strength, and the wild tribes
Of living things both swimming things
    and birds,
And of those walking, and amphibia,
⁶⁰⁵And those that creep
    and those of double nature;
For acting in accord with His own will
Under Your leading He arranged all things.
But in the latest times the earth He passed,
And coming late from
    the virgin Mary's womb
⁶¹⁰A new light rose,
    and going forth from Heaven
Put on a mortal form.
    First then did Gabriel show
His strong pure form; and bearing
    his own news,
He next addressed the maiden with his voice:
"O virgin, in your bosom undefiled,
⁶¹⁵Receive you God."
    Thus speaking he inbreathed
God's grace on the sweet maiden; and at once
Alarm and wonder seized her as she heard,
And she stood trembling;
    and her mind was wild
With flutter of excitement while at heart
⁶²⁰She quivered at the unlooked-for things
    she heard.
But she again was gladdened and her heart
Was cheered by the voice,
    and the maiden laughed
And her cheek reddened with a sense of joy,
And spell-bound was her heart
    with sense of shame.
⁶²⁵And confidence came to her. And the Word
Flew into the womb, and in course of time
Having become flesh and endued with life
Was made a human form and came to be
A Boy distinguished by His virgin birth;
⁶³⁰For this was a great wonder to mankind,
But it was no great wonder to God
The Father, nor was it to God the Son.
And the glad earth received
    the newborn babe,
The heavenly throne laughed
    and the world rejoiced.
⁶³⁵And the prophetic new-appearing star
Was honored by the wise men, and the babe
Born was shown in a manger to them
That obeyed God, and keepers of the herds,
And goatherds and to shepherds
    of the lambs;

⁶⁴⁰And Beth-Lehem called by God
    the fatherland
Of the Word was chosen…
And in heart practice lowliness of mind
And cruel deeds hate, and your neighbor love
Wholly, even as yourself; and from your soul
⁶⁴⁵Love God and do Him service. Therefore we
Sprung from the holy race
    of the heavenly Christ
Are called of common blood, and we restrain
In worship recollection of good cheer,
And walk the paths of piety and truth.
⁶⁵⁰Not ever are we suffered to approach
The inmost sanctuary of the temples,
Nor pour libations to carved images,
Nor honor them with prayers,
    nor with the smells
Much-pleasing of flowers,
    nor with light of lamps,
⁶⁵⁵Nor yet with shining votive offerings
Adorn them, nor with smoke of frankincense
That sends forth flame of altars; nor do you,
Adding to the sacrifice of bulls
And taking pleasure in defilement send
⁶⁶⁰Blood of sheep-slaughtering outrage,
    thus to give
Ransom for penalty beneath the earth;
Nor by the smoke of flesh-consuming pyre
And odors foul pollute the light of the sky;
But joyful with pure minds and cheerful soul,
⁶⁶⁵With love abounding
    and with generous hands,
With soothing psalms and songs
    that honor God,
We are commanded to sing praise to You,
The imperishable and without deceit,
All-father God, of understanding mind…

BOOK XI

[Introduction, 1–6. From the Flood to the Tower of Babel, 7–22. Egyptian kings and judges, 23–40. The Exodus and giving of the Law, 41–47. A notable Egyptian king, 48–53. The Persian domination, 54–68. Woes of many nations, 69–89. Rule of the Indian prince, 90–105. The great Assyrian king Solomon, 106–123. Many and mighty kings, 124–136. Alexander's fierce wars, 137–143. Origin of Rome, 144–160. The fall of Ilium, 161–189. Escape of Aeneas and founding of the Latin race, 190–216. The wise old minstrel, 217–227. Wars of the nations, 228–236. The terrible invader of Greece, 237–248. Philip of Macedon, 249–259. Alexander the Conqueror, 260–298. The kings of Egypt, 299–315. Egypt an asylum for the Jews, 316–320. The eight kings and treacherous queen of Egypt, 321–344. Reign of the Roman Caesars, 345–365. Fall of Cleopatra, 366–394. Subjection of Egypt, 395–416. The Sibyl's testimony of herself, 417–429.]

O world of men wide-scattered,
    and long walls,
The cities huge and nations numberless,
Throughout the east and west
    and south and north,

THE SIBYLLINE ORACLES

Divided off by various languages
⁵And kingdoms; other things, the very worst,
Against you I am now about to speak.
For from the time when on the earlier men
The Flood came and the Almighty One
 Himself
Destroyed that race by many waters, then
¹⁰Brought He in yet another race of men
Untiring; and they, setting themselves up
Against Heaven, built to height unspeakable
A tower; and tongues of all
 were loosed again;
And on them hurled came wrath
 of God Most High,
¹⁵By which the tower unutterably great
Fell; and against each other they stirred up
An evil strife. And then of mortal men
Was the tenth race since these things
 came to pass;
And the whole earth was among foreign men
²⁰And various languages distributed,
Whose numbers I will tell and in acrostics
Of the initial letter show the name.
And first will Egypt royal power receive
Preeminent and just; and then in her
²⁵Will many-counseling men be governors;
Moreover, then a fearful man will rule,
Close-fighter very strong; and he will have
This letter of the acrostic of his name:
Sword will he stretch out against pious men.
³⁰And while this one is ruler there will be
A fearful sign in the Egyptian land,
Which, gladdening very greatly,
 will with corn
Souls perishing with famine then supply;
The law-giver, himself a prisoner,
³⁵The East and offspring of Assyrian men
Will nourish; and his name know you …
… of the measure of the number ten.
But when there will come
 from the radiant Heaven
Ten strokes of judgment on Egypt, then
⁴⁰Will I again proclaim these things to you.
Memphis, woe, woe for you! Woe,
Great royal one! The Erythraean Sea
Will your much people utterly destroy.
Then when the people of twelve tribes
 will leave
⁴⁵The fruitful land of ruin by command
Of the Immortal, the Lord God Himself
Will also give a law to mankind.
And o'er the Hebrews then a mighty king
Magnanimous will rule, and have a name
⁵⁰Derived from sandy Egypt, Theban man
Of doubtful native land; and Memphis he,
Dread serpent, will show outward signs
 of love,
And he will watch o'er many things in wars.
Now the tenth kingdom
 being twelve times complete
⁵⁵Seven besides and even
 to the tenth hundred,
Others being altogether left behind,
Then will arise the Persian sovereignty.
And then calamity will befall the Jews,
Famine and pestilence intolerable
⁶⁰They do not make escape from in that day.
But when a Persian will rule, and a son
Of his son's son will lay the scepter down,
While years roll round to five fours,
 and to these
A hundred more, and you a hundred nines
⁶⁵Will finish and all things will you repay;
And then to the Persians and the Medes
Will you be given over as a slave,
Destroyed with blows by reason
 of hard fights.
At once to Persians and Assyrians
⁷⁰And to all Egypt will an evil come,
And to Libya and the Ethiopians,
And to the Carians and Pamphylians
And to all other mortals. And he then
Will to the grandsons give the royal power,
⁷⁵Who again snatching the whole earth away
Will plunder races for their many spoils,
Not having fellow-feeling. Mournful dirges
Will the sad Persians by the Tigris wail,
And Egypt water many a land with tears.
⁸⁰And then to you, O Median land, a man
Of wealth abundant and of Indian birth
Will many evils do, till you repay
All things which you,
 possessed of shameless soul,
Have done before. Woe, woe for you,
⁸⁵You Median nation; you will afterward
Be servant to Ethiopian men
Beyond the land of Meroe; wretched you
Will from the first seven and a hundred years
Complete, and put your neck
 beneath the yoke.
⁹⁰And then an Indian of dark countenance
And gray hair and great soul will afterward
Become lord, who will many evils bring
On the East by reason of hard fights;
And he will treat you much more spitefully
⁹⁵And will destroy all your men. But when he
The twentieth and the tenth year will be king,
Among them, also seven and the tenth,
Then every nation of a royal power
Will be mad and declare their liberty,
¹⁰⁰And during three years
 leave their servile blood.
But he will come again and every nation
Of valiant men will put their neck again
Under the yoke, serve the king as before,
And of its own free will again obey.
¹⁰⁵There will be great peace
 throughout all the world.
And then o'er the Assyrians there will rule
A mighty king, a man preeminent,
And will persuade all to speak
 pleasing things,
Which God ordained according to the Law;
¹¹⁰Then all kings arrogant with pointed spears
Timid and speechless will before him quail,
And him will very powerful rulers serve
Because of counsels of the mighty God;
For he will carry all things in detail
¹¹⁵By reason, and all things will he subject,
And he the temple of the mighty God
And lovely altar will himself erect
In his might, and will hurl the idols down;
And gathering tribes together, both the race
¹²⁰Of fathers and the helpless little ones,
He will encompass the inhabitants;
His name will have two hundred
 for its number,
And of the eighteenth letter show the sign.
But when for rolling decades two and five
¹²⁵He will rule, going forward toward the end
Of his time, there will be as many kings
As there are tribes of men, as there are clans,
As there are cities, and as isles and coasts,
And fields and lands
 that bring forth pleasant fruit.
¹³⁰But one of these will be a mighty king,
A leader among men; and many kings
Of lofty spirit will submit to him,
And to his sons and grandsons opulent
Give portions on account of royal power.
¹³⁵Decades of decades, eight ones on these
Of years will they rule, and at last will end.
But when with cruel Ares there will come
A powerful wild beast, even then for you,
O queenly land, will wrath spring forth again.
¹⁴⁰Woe, woe for you, then Persian land;
What an outpouring of the blood of men
Will you receive when that
 stronger-minded man
Comes to you; then I'll shout
 these things again.
But when Italian soil will generate,
¹⁴⁵Great wonder to mortals, there will be
Moans of young children by a fountain pure,
In shady cavern offspring of wild beast
That feeds on sheep, who to manhood grown
Will on seven strong hills with reckless soul
¹⁵⁰Hurl many headlong down,
 in numbers both
Having a hundred, and their names will show
A great sign to them that are yet to be;
And they will build on the seven hills
Strong walls and wage around them
 grievous war.
¹⁵⁵And then again will there be growing up
Revolt of men around you, then great land
Of fine ears, high-souled Egypt; but again
I'll cry these things. And yet then will receive
A great stroke in your houses; and again
¹⁶⁰Will there be a revolt of your own men.
Now over you, O wretched Phrygia,
I weep in pity; for to you from Greece,
Tamer of horses, there will conquest come
And war and plague by reason of hard fights.
¹⁶⁵Ilium, I pity you; for there will come
From Sparta an Erinys to your halls
Mixed with a deadly sting; and most of all
Will she bring you toils, troubles,
 groans, and wails,
When well-skilled men the battle will begin,
¹⁷⁰By far the noblest heroes of the Greeks
Who are to Ares dear. And one of these
Will be a strong brave king; of foulest deeds
He for his brother's sake will go in quest.
And they will overthrow the famous walls
¹⁷⁵Of Phrygian Troy; when of the rolling years
Twice five will be filled with the bloody deeds
Of savage war, a wooden artifice
Will sudden cover men, and on your knees
You will receive this, not perceiving it
¹⁸⁰To be an ambush pregnant with the Greeks,
O cause of grievous woe. Woe, woe,
How much in one night Hades will receive,
And what spoils of the old man
 weeping much
Will he bear off! But with those yet to come
¹⁸⁵Will be undying fame. And the great king,
A hero sprung from Zeus, will have his name
Of the first letter of the alphabet;
Homewards will he in order go. And then

Will he fall by a treacherous woman's hand.
¹⁹⁰And there will rule a child sprung
  from the race
And the blood of Assaracus, renowned
Of heroes, both a strong and valiant man.
And he will come out of the mighty fire
Of ravaged Troy, fleeing from fatherland
¹⁹⁵By reason of the fearful toil of war;
Bearing his aged father on his shoulders
And also holding his son by the hand
He will perform a pious work of law,
Who, looking cautiously around him, cleft
²⁰⁰The onset of the fire of burning Troy,
And hurrying through the multitude in dread
He will pass over land and fearful sea.
And he will have a trisyllabic name,
For the beginning of the alphabet
²⁰⁵Points out this highest man
  as not unknown.
And then a city for the powerful Latins
He will raise up. And in his fifteenth year,
Destroyed by waters in the depths of sea,
Will he lay hold on the event of death.
²¹⁰But him though dead the nations
  of mankind
Will not forget; for his race over all
Will rule hereafter even to Euphrates
And River Tigris, throughout the middle land
Of the Assyrians, where the Parthians
²¹⁵Extended. For those who are yet to come
It will be, when all these things come to pass.
And there will be an old man, minstrel wise,
Whom all will among mortals call most wise,
By whose good understanding
  the whole world
²²⁰Will be instructed; for his chapters he
According to their power of thoughts
  will write.
And wisely will he write
  most marvelous things,
At times appropriating words of my
Measures and verses; for he will the first
²²⁵My books unfold and after these things
  bide them
And to men bring them to light no more
Until the end of baneful death and life.
But when quickly these things
  have been fulfilled
Which I spoke, yet again the Greeks will fight
²³⁰With one another; and Assyrians,
Arabians and the quiver-bearing Medes,
And Persians and Sicilians will rise up,
And Lydians, Thracians and Bithynians,
And they who dwell in the land of fair corn,
²³⁵Beside the streams of Nile; and among all
Will God the imperishable put at once
Confusion. But exceedingly terrible
Will an Assyrian base-born fiery man
Come suddenly, possessed of beastly soul,
²⁴⁰And looking cautiously around him cut
Through every isthmus, going against all,
And sailing o'er the sea. Then,
  faithless Greece,
To you will happen very many things.
Woe, woe for you, O wretched Greece,
²⁴⁵How many things you are obliged to wail!
And during seven and eighty rolling years
You will the miserable refuse be
Of fearful battle among all the tribes.
Then will a Macedonian man again

²⁵⁰Bring forth for Hellas woe and will destroy
All Thrace, and toil of Ares on the isles
And coasts and the war-loving Triballi.
He will among the foremost fighters be,
And he will share that name
  which shows the sign
²⁵⁵Of numbers ten times fifty. And short-lived
Will he be; but behind him he will leave
The greatest kingdom on
  the boundless earth.
But by base spearman he himself will fall
While thought to live in quiet as none else.
²⁶⁰And afterward will a great-hearted child
Of this one rule, beginning with his name
The alphabet; but his race will pass out.
Not of Zeus, not of Amnion will they call
This one true son, yet still a bastard son
²⁶⁵Of Kronos as they all imagine him.
And cities he of many mortal men
Will plunder; and for Europe will shoot up
The greatest sore. And also terribly
Will he abuse the city Babylon,
²⁷⁰And every land the sun looks down on,
And he alone will sail both east and west.
Woe, woe for you, O Babylon,
You will serve triumphs,
  who were called a queen;
Down on Asia Ares comes, he comes
²⁷⁵Surely and will your many children slay.
And then will you send forth your royal man
Named by the number four,
  expert with spear
Among the mighty warriors, terrible,
Shooting with bow and arrow.
  And then famine
²⁸⁰And war will hold possession of the midst
Of the Cilicians and Assyrians;
But kings of lofty spirit will embrace
The dreadful state of heart-consuming strife.
But you, fleeing, leaving the former king,
²⁸⁵Be neither willing to remain nor fear
To be unhappy; for on you will come
A dreadful lion, a flesh-eating beast,
Wild, strange to justice,
  wearing on his shoulders
A mantle. Flee the thunder-striking man.
²⁹⁰And Asia all will bear an evil yoke,
And many a murder will the wet earth drink.
But when a mighty city prosperous
Ares of Pella will in Egypt found,
And it will be named from him,
  fate and death,
²⁹⁵By his companions treacherously betrayed
For barbarous murder will destroy this man
Around the tables when he will have left
The Indians and will come to Babylon.
Thereafter other kings, in a few years,
³⁰⁰Devourers of the people, arrogant
And faithless, will rule each by his own tribe;
But a great-hearted hero, who will glean
All fenced Europe, from the time each land
Will drink the blood of all tribes, will quickly
³⁰⁵Abandon life, unloosing his own fate.
And other kings there will be, twice four men
Of his race, and the same name to them all.
And there will be a bride of Egypt then
Commanding and a noble city great
³¹⁰Of Macedonian lord, Queen Alexandria,
Famed nourisher of cities, shining fair
She alone will be the metropolis.

Let Memphis then upbraid them
  that command.
And peace will be deep
  throughout all the world;
³¹⁵Then will the land of black soil
  have more fruits.
And then there will come evil to the Jews,
Nor will they in that day make their escape
From famine and intolerable plague;
But the new world of black soil and fair corn,
³²⁰Divine land, will receive
  much-wandering men.
But marshy Egypt's eight kings will fill up
The numbers of two hundred years
  and three
And thirty. Yet will offspring perish not
Of all of them, but there will issue forth
³²⁵A female root, a bane of mortal men,
Betrayer of her kingdom. But they will
According to their evil deeds perform
Their wickedness thereafter, and one here
Another there will perish; son that wears
³³⁰The purple will cut off his warlike sire,
And he himself in turn by his own son,
And ere he will put forth another shoot—
He will cease; but a root will sprout again
Thereafter of itself; and there will be
³³⁵A race beside him growing. For a queen
There will be of the land by Nilus' streams
Which comes down through seven mouths
  into the sea,
And her name very lovely will be that
Of the number twenty; and she will demand
³⁴⁰Numberless things and gather up all goods
Of gold and silver; but from her own men
Will treachery befall her. Then again
For you, O dusky land, will there be wars
And battles and great slaughter of mankind.
³⁴⁵When many over fertile Rome will rule,
Examples not at all of happy men,
But tyrants, and there be of thousands chiefs
And of ten thousands, and the overseers
Of popular assemblies under law,
³⁵⁰Then will the mightiest Caesars
  bear the rule
Ill-fated all their days; and of these last
Will for initial have the number ten,
Last Caesar stretching on the earth his limbs,
Struck by dire Ares by a hostile man,
³⁵⁵Whom carrying in their hands the youth
  of Rome
Will bury piously, and over him
Pour out their token for his friendship's sake
Rendering a tribute to his memory.
But when you will come to an end of time
³⁶⁰And have completed
  twice three hundred years
And twice ten, from the time
  when he will rule
Who is your founder, child of the wild beast,
There will no longer a dictator be
Ruling a measured period; but a lord
³⁶⁵Will become king, man equal to the gods.
Then, Egypt, know the king
  that comes to you;
And dreadful Ares of the glittering helm
Will surely come. For there will be for you,
O widowed one, a capture afterward;
³⁷⁰For round the walls of your land
  there will be

Terrible raging mischief-working wars.
But having suffered misery in wars
You, wretched, will yourself flee from above
Those lately wounded; and then to the couch
³⁷⁵Will you come to the dreadful man himself;
The wedlock, sharing one bed, is the end.
Woe, woe for you, ill-wedded bride,
Your royal power to the Roman king
Will you give, and you will repay all things,
³⁸⁰Which you formerly did
    with masculine hands;
You will give the whole land by way of dower
As far as Libya and the dark-skinned men
To the resistless man. And you will be
No more a widow, but you will cohabit
³⁸⁵With a man-eating lion terrible,
A furious warrior. And then will you be
Unhappy and among all men unknown;
For you will leave possessed
    of shameless soul;
And you, the stately, will the encircling tomb
³⁹⁰Receive … is gone … living within …
Adapted at the summits, beautiful,
Worked curiously, and a great multitude
Will mourn you and the dreadful king
    will make
A piteous lamentation over you.
³⁹⁵And then will Egypt be the toiling slave
Who many years against the Indians bears
Her trophies; and she will serve shamefully,
And with the river, the fruit-bearing Nile,
    her tears, for having gathered wealth
⁴⁰⁰And store of all good things, a nourisher
Of cities, she will feed sheep-eating race
Of fearful men. All, to how many beasts,
O very wealthy Egypt, you will be
Booty and spoil, but giving peoples laws;
⁴⁰⁵And formerly delighting in great kings
You will to peoples be a wretched slave
On account of that people, whom of old
Piously living you led to much woe
Of toils and wailings, and did put a plow
⁴¹⁰On their neck and irrigate the fields
With mortal tears. Therefore,
    the LORD Himself,
The imperishable God who dwells in Heaven,
Will utterly destroy and send you on
To wailing; and you will make recompense
⁴¹⁵For what you did unlawfully of old,
And know at last that God's wrath
    came to you.
But I to Python and to Panopeus
Of pleasant towers will go; and then will all
Declare that I am a true prophetess—
⁴²⁰Oracle-singing, yet a messenger
With maddened soul …
And when you will come forward
    to the books
You will not tremble, and all things to come
And things that were you will know
    from our words;
⁴²⁵Then none will call
    the God-seized prophetess
An oracle-singer of necessity.
But now, Lord, end my very lovely strain,
Driving off frenzy and real voice inspired
And fearful madness,
    and give charming song.

THE SIBYLLINE ORACLES

BOOK XII

[Introduction, 1, 2. The first Caesars, 3–46. The mighty warrior, 47–61. The guileful king, 62–87. The king of wide sway, 88–100. The dreadful and contemptible king, 101–125. The three kings, 126–130. The royal destroyer of pious men, 131–153. The princes famed for filial devotion, 154–161. The peaceful king, 162–183. The venerable king, 184–189. Another warrior king, 190–204. The Celtic warrior, 205–210. The king with the name of a sea, 211–227. The three rulers, 228–242. The wise and pious king, 243–270. The king that sought to rival Hercules, 271–289. Period of Roman dominion, 290–303. The twentieth king, 303–314. The short-lived king, 315–320. The ruler from the East, 321–328. The crafty ruler from the West, 329–344. The youthful Caesar, 345–354. A time of woes, 356–368. Only those who honor God attain happiness, 369–373. The Sibyl's prayer, 374–382.]

But come now, hear of me the mournful time
Of sons of Latium; and first of all
After the kings of Egypt were destroyed,
And the like earth had downwards
    borne them all,
⁵And after Pella's townsman, under whom
The whole East and the rich West
    were cast down,
Whom Babylon dishonored,
    and stretched out
For Philip a dead body (not of Zeus,
Of Ammon not true things were prophesied),
¹⁰And after that one of the race and blood
Of King Assaracus, who came from Troy,
Even he who cleft the violence of fire,
And after many lords, and after men
To Ares dear, and after the young babes,
¹⁵The children of the beast
    that feeds on sheep,
And after the passing of six hundred years
And decades two of Rome's dictatorship,
The very first lord, from the western sea,
Will be of Rome the ruler, very strong
²⁰And warlike, the initial of whose name
Begins the letters, and fast binding you,
O you of abundant fruit, he will be full
Of man-destroying Ares; you will pay
The outrage which you, willing, did force on;
For he, great soul, will be the best in wars;
²⁵Before him Thrace and Sicily will crouch,
With Memphis, Memphis cast headlong
    to earth
By reason of the wickedness of rulers
And of a woman unenslaved who falls
Under the spear. And laws will he ordain
³⁰For peoples and put all things under him;
Having great fame, he will wield scepter long;
For no short time will he last nor will ever
Be other greater scepter-bearing king
³⁵Than this one, o'er the Romans,
    not one hour,
For God did lavish all things on him,
And also in the noble earth he showed
Great marvelous seasons, and with them
    showed signs.
But when a radiant star all like the sun
⁴⁰Will shine forth out of the sky
    in the middays,
Then will the secret Word of the Most High
Come clothed in flesh like mortals;
    but with Him
The might of Rome and of
    the illustrious Latins
Will increase. But the mighty king himself
⁴⁵Will under his appointed lot expire,
Transmitting to another royal power.
But after him a man, a warrior strong,
Wearing the purple mantle on his shoulders,
Will bear rule, and with his initial be
⁵⁰Numbers three hundred,
    and he will destroy
The Medes and arrow-hurling Parthians;
And he himself by his power will subvert
The high-gate city; and again will come
Evil to Egypt and the Assyrians,
⁵⁵And to the Colchian Heniochi,
And to those by the waters of the Rhine,
The Germans dwelling o'er the sandy shores.
And he himself will ravage afterward
The high-gate city near Eridanus
⁶⁰Which is devising evils. And then he
Will quickly fall down, struck
    by gleaming iron.
And afterward will rule another man
Weaving guile, and the initial of his name
Will show the number three;
    and he much gold
⁶⁵Will gather; and with him there will not be
Satiety of wealth, but plundering more
Recklessly he'll put all things in the earth.
But peace will come, and Ares will desist
From wars; and he will make known
    many things
⁷⁰In divination of the greatest things,
Inquiring for the sake of means of life;
Yet there will be on him the greatest sign:
From the sky down on the king
    while perishing
There will flow many little drops of blood.
⁷⁵And many lawless things will he perform,
And put around the neck of Romans pain
Trusting in divination; and the heads
Of the assembly he will also slay.
And famine will seize Cappadocians,
⁸⁰And Thracians, Macedonians, and Italians.
And Egypt will alone feed numerous tribes;
And the king himself beguiling secretly
Will craftily destroy the virgin maid;
But her the citizens in tearful grief
⁸⁵Will bury; and against the king they all
Holding wrath will abuse him craftily.
While strong Rome blossoms, the strong man
    will perish.
And again, there will rule another lord
Of the number of twice ten;
    and then will come
⁹⁰To the Sauromatians and to Thrace
And the Triballi, famed for hurling darts,
Wars and sad cares; and Roman Ares will
Tear all in pieces. And a fearful sign
Will there be when this man will rule the land
⁹⁵Of the Italians and Pannonians;
And there will be at the mid hour of day

THE SIBYLLINE ORACLES

Dark night around them
    and then from the heavens
A shower of stones; and thereon the lord
And vigorous judge of the Italians
[100] Will go in Hades' halls by his own fate.
Again, another fearful man will come
And dreadful, numbering fifty; and from all
The cities many noblest citizens
Born to wealth he will utterly destroy,
[105] A dreadful serpent breathing grievous war,
Who sometime stretching forth his hands
    will make
An end of his own race and stir all things,
Acting the athlete, driving chariots,
Putting to death and daring countless things;
[110] And he will cleave the mountain
    of two seas,
And sprinkle it with gore. And out of sight
Will also vanish the destructive man;
Then making himself equal to God
Will he return, but God
    will prove him nothing.
[115] And while he rules
    there will be peace profound
And not the fears of men; and from the ocean
Flowing, and cleaving by Ausonia,
Will come untrodden water; and around
Looking with anxious care he will appoint
[120] His very many contests for the people,
And he himself an actor will contend
With voice and cithara, and sing a song
Along with harp-string; later he will flee
And leave the royal power, and perishing
[125] Gravely will he repay the harm he worked.
After him three will rule and two of them
Will have the number seventy
    by their names,
And in addition to these will be one
Of the third letter; and one here, one there,
[130] Will perish by strong Ares' sturdy hands.
Then will a mighty ruler of men come,
Destroyer of the pious, strong-minded man,
Spear-wielding Ares,
    whom seven times the tenth
Will point out clearly; he will overthrow
[135] Phoenicia and destroy Assyria.
A sword will come on the sacred land
Of Solyma even to the utmost bend
Of the Tiberian Sea. Woe, woe,
Phoenicia, O how much will you endure,
[140] Grief-laden with your trophies
    tightly bound,
And every nation will on you tread.
Woe, woe! Over to the Assyrians
Will you come and will see
young children serve
Among unfriendly men and with the wives,
[145] And every means of life
    and wealth will perish;
For on you God's wrath causing grievous woe
Will come, because they did not keep His law,
But served all idols with unseemly arts.
And many wars and fights and homicides,
[150] Famines, and pestilences, and confusion
Of cities will be. But the reverend king
Of mighty soul will at the end of life
Himself fall by a strong necessity.
Then will two other chief men, cherishing
[155] The memory of their father, great king, rule,
And in contending warriors glory much.

And [one] of these will be a noble man
And lordly, whose name
    will three hundred hold;
Yet he will also fall by treachery,
[160] Not in the warring companies
    stretched out,
But struck in Rome's plain
    by the two-edged brass.
And after him a powerful warlike man
Of the letter four will rule the mighty realm,
Whom all men on the boundless earth
    will love,
[165] And then will there be over all the world
A rest from war. Yet all, from west to east,
Will serve him willingly, not by constraint,
And cities will be under his control
And of themselves be subject. For to him
[170] Will heavenly Hosts much glory bring,
The imperishable God who dwells on high.
And then will famine waste Pannonia
And all the Celtic land, and will destroy
One here, another there. And there will be
[175] For the Assyrians, whom Orontes leaves,
Structures and ornament
    and what may seem
Yet greater anywhere. And the great king
Will have a fondness for these and love them
Above the others far (and there are many);
[180] But he himself will in mid breast receive
A great wound, and seized at the end of life
Craftily, by a friend, in holy house
Of the great royal hall will he fall down
Wounded; and after him will be a ruler
[185] Numbering fifty, venerable man,
Who above measure will destroy from Rome
Many inhabitants and citizens;
But he will rule few; for in Hades' halls
For a former king's sake he will wounded go.
[190] But then another king, a warrior strong,
Who has three hundred for initial sign,
Will bear rule and lay waste
    the Thracians' land
Which is much varied, and he will destroy
The powerful Germans dwelling by the Rhine
[195] And the Iberians that shoot the arrow.
Moreover, there will be to the Jews
Another greatest evil, and with them
Bedewed with murder will Phoenicia drink;
And the walls of the Assyrians will fall
[200] By many warriors. And again, a man
Destroying life will waste them utterly.
And then will threatenings of the mighty God,
Earthquakes, and great plagues
    be on every land,
Untimely snow-storms, and strong
    thunderbolts.
[205] And then the great king,
    mountain-roaming Celt,
Will for the toil of Ares not escape
A fate unseemly, hastening eagerly
After the strife of battle, but worn out
Will he be; foreign dust will hide his corpse,
[210] But dust that of Nemea's flower has name.
And after him another will arise,
A silver-headed man, and of the sea
Will be his name, and of four syllables,
Ares himself first of the alphabet
[215] Presenting. Temples he will dedicate
In all the cities, watching o'er the world
By his own foot, and bringing gifts away,

Both gold and amber much will he supply
For many; and magicians' mysteries
[220] All will he from the sanctuaries keep;
And what is much more excellent for men
Will he place ... ruling ... thunderbolt;
And great peace will be when he will be lord;
And he will be a minstrel of rich voice
[225] And a participant in lawful things,
And a just minister of what is right;
But he will fall, unloosing his own fate.
After him three will rule, and the third late
Will rule, three decades keeping; yet again
[230] Of the first unit will another king
Bear the rule; and another after him
Will be commander, of tens
    numbering seven;
And their names will be honored;
    and they will
Themselves destroy men marked
    by many a spot,
[235] Britons and mighty Moors and Dacians
And the Arabians. But when the last
Of these will perish, fearful Ares then,
He that before was wounded, will again
Against the Parthians come, and utterly
[240] Will he destroy them. And then will the king
Himself fall by a treacherous wild beast
Training his hands—excuse itself of death.
And after him another man will rule,
In many wise things skilled, and he will have
[245] Himself the name of the first mighty king
Of the first unit; and he will be good
And mighty; and for the illustrious Latins
Will this strong one accomplish many things
In memory of his father; and at once
[250] Will he adorn the walls of Rome with gold
And silver and ivory; and he will go
Within the marketplaces and the temples
With a strong man. And sometime
    direst wound
Will shoot up like ears in the Roman wars;
[255] And he will sack the whole land
    of the Germans,
When a great sign of God will be displayed
From the sky, and will for the king's piety
Save men in brazen armor and distress;
For God who is in Heaven and hears all things
[260] Will wet him with unseasonable rain
When he prays. But when these things
    are fulfilled
Of which I spoke, then with the rolling years
Will also the renowned dominion cease
Of the great pious king; and at the end
[265] Of his life, having then proclaimed his son
Succeeding to the kingdom, he will die
By his own lot and leave the royal power
To the ruler with the golden hair,
Who with two tens in his name, born a king
[270] From the race of his father, will receive
Dominion. This man with superior powers
Of mind will grasp all things; and he will rival
Great-hearted overweening Hercules,
And be the best in mighty arms and have
[275] The greatest fame in chase
    and horsemanship;
But he will live in peril all alone.
And while this man is ruler there will be
A fearful sign: there will be a great mist
Then in the plain of Rome, so that a man
[280] May not discern his neighbor.

And then wars
Will come to pass along with mournful cares,
When the king himself, overly mad with love,
And weakly, will come in the marriage-bed
Shaming his youthful offspring, infamous
²⁸⁵ For inconsiderate wedding-songs impure.
And then, in helpless loneliness concealed,
The mighty baneful man held under wrath
Will in a bathhouse suffer evil plight,
Manslaying Ares bound by treacherous fate.
²⁹⁰ Know then the fatal lot of Rome is near
Because of zeal for power; and by the hands
Of Ares many in Palladian halls
Will perish. And then Rome will be bereft
And will repay all things, which she alone
²⁹⁵ Before accomplished by her many wars.
My heart laments, my heart
    within me mourns;
For from the time when your first king,
    proud Rome,
Gave good law to you and to men on earth,
And the Word of the great immortal God
³⁰⁰ Came to the earth, until
    the nineteenth reign
Will have been finished, Kronos will complete
Two hundred years, twice twenty
    and twice two,
With six months added; then
    the twentieth king,
When stricken with sharp brass
    he with the sword
³⁰⁵ Will in your houses pour out blood,
    will make
Your race a widow, having in his name
The letter which the number eighty shows,
And burdened with old age; but he will make
A widow of you in a little time,
³¹⁰ When many warriors, many overthrows,
And murders, homicides, and deadly feuds
And miseries of conquests there will be,
And in confusion many a horse and man
Will, cleft by force of hands, fall in the plain.
³¹⁵ And then another man will rule, and have
The sign of his name in the number ten;
And many sorrows will he bring to pass,
And groans, and he will plunder many men;
But he himself will be short-lived and fall
³²⁰ By mighty Ares, struck by gleaming iron.
Another, numbering fifty, then will come,
A warrior roused up by the East for rule;
A warlike Ares he will come to Thrace;
And he will flee thereafter and will come
³²⁵ Into the land of the Bithynians
And the Cilician plain; but brazen Ares
The life-destroyer will with speedy stroke
Utterly spoil him in the Assyrian fields.
And then again there will rule craftily
³³⁰ A man skilled in fraud, full of various wiles,
Roused up by the West, and his name
    will have
The number of two hundred. And again
Another sign: he will contrive a war
For royal power against Assyrian men,
³³⁵ Raise a whole army and subject all things.
And he will rule the Romans with his might;
But there is much contrivance in his heart,
Impulse of baleful Ares; serpent dire,
And violent in war, who will [then] destroy
³⁴⁰ All high-born men on the earth, and slay
The noble for their wealth, and, robber-like,

Stripping all earth while men are perishing,
He will go to the East; and all deceit
Will be to him ...
³⁴⁵ Then will a youthful Caesar reign with him,
Having the name of a potent lord
Of Macedon, by the first letter known;
Bringing in broils around him he will flee
The hard deception of the coming king
³⁵⁰ In the bosom of the army; but the one
Who rules by his barbaric usages,
A temple-guard, will perish suddenly,
Slain by strong Ares with the gleaming iron;
Him even dead will people tear in pieces.
³⁵⁵ And then the kings of Persia will rise up;
And ... Roman Ares Roman lord.
And Phrygia will with earthquakes
    groan again
Wretched. Woe, woe, Laodicea;
Woe, woe, sad Hierapolis;
³⁶⁰ For you first once the yawning earth
    received.
Of Rome ... immense Aus ...
All things as many ...
Will wail ... while men are perishing
In the hands of Ares; and the lot of men
³⁶⁵ Will be bad; but then by the eastern way
Hastening to look down on Italy,
Stripped naked he will fall by gleaming iron,
Acquiring hatred for his mother's sake.
For seasons are of all sorts; each holds back
³⁷⁰ The other ... gleaming and this
    not at once all know;
For all things will not be [the lot] of all,
But only those will be for happiness
Who honor God and shun idolatry.
And now, Lord of the world, of every realm
³⁷⁵ Unfeigned immortal King—for You did put
Into my heart the oracle divine—
Make the word now cease; for I do not know
What things I say; for You are in me He
That speaks all these things. Now let me rest
³⁸⁰ A little and put from my heart aside
The charming song; for weary is my heart
Foretelling with divine words royal power.

BOOK XIII

[Introduction, 1–8. A time of wars and woes, 9–16. Persian insurrection and the Roman soldier king, 17–28. The warrior out of Syria and his son, 29–47. Persian war and the grain-producing land of Nile, 48–65. Another song for Alexandrians announced, 66–71. Wrath on Assyrians and Aegeans, 72–78. Wretched Antioch, 79–84. Cities of Arabia admonished, 85–97. Wars and treachery, 98–106. Roman ruler from Dacia, 107–116. The Syrian robber, 117–135. The Gallic king and dreadful woes, 136–156. Wretched Syria, 157–165. Wretched Antioch, 165–171. Woes on many cities of Asia, 172–189. Murders and wars, 190–208. Allegory of the bull, dragon, stag, lion, and goat, 209–230. Prayer of the Sibyl, 231–232.]

Great word divine He bids me sing again—
The immortal holy God imperishable,
Who gives to kings their power

and takes away,
And who determined for them time
    both ways,
⁵ Both that of life and that of baneful death.
And these the heavenly God enjoins on me,
Unwilling to bring tidings to kings
Concerning royal power ...
And spear impetuous Ares; and by him
¹⁰ All perish, child and the old man who gives
To the assemblies laws; and many wars
And battles there will be, and homicides,
Famines and pestilences, earthquake-shocks
And mighty thunderbolts, and many ways
¹⁵ Of the Assyrians over all the world,
And pillaging and robbery of temples.
And then an insurrection there will be
Of the industrious Persians, and with them
Indians, Armenians, and Arabians;
²⁰ And to these again a Roman king
Insatiate in war and leading on
His spearmen against the Assyrians
Will draw near, a young Ares, and as far
As the deep-flowing silvery Euphrates
²⁵ Will warlike Ares stretch his deadly spear
Because of ...
For by his friend betrayed he will fall down
In the ranks stricken by the gleaming iron.
And at once coming out of Syria
³⁰ There will a purple-loving warrior rule,
Terror of Ares, and also his son,
A Caesar, will even all the earth oppress;
And the one name is to both of them:
On first and twentieth there are to be placed
³⁵ Five hundred. But when these in wars
    will rule,
And laws will be enacted, there will be
A little rest from war, not for a long time;
But when a wolf will to a flock of sheep
Pledge solemn oaths against
    the white-toothed dogs,
⁴⁰ Then, having misled, he will tear in pieces
The woolly sheep, and cast his oaths aside;
And then will there be an unlawful strife
Of haughty kings in wars, and Syrians
Will perish terribly, and Indians
⁴⁵ And the Armenians and Arabians,
The Persians and the Babylonians
Will one another by hard fights destroy.
But when a Roman Ares will destroy
A German Ares ruinous of life
⁵⁰ Triumphing on the ocean, then is war
Of many years for haughty Persian men,
But for them there will not be victory;
For as a fish swims not on the point
Of a high many-ridged and windy rock
⁵⁵ Precipitant, nor does a tortoise fly,
Nor does an eagle into water come,
So also are the Persians in that day
Far off from victory, while the fond nurse
Of the Italians, in the plain of Nile
⁶⁰ Reposing by the sacred water's side,
Sends forth the appointed lot
    to seven-hilled Rome.
Now these things are;
    and while the name of Rome
Will hold in numbers of revolving time,
So many years will the great noble city
⁶⁵ Of Macedon's lord, willing, deal out corn.
Another much-distressing pain I'll sing
For Alexandrians who are destroyed

By reason of the strife of shameful men.
Strong men who were formerly terrible
⁷⁰Being then impotent will pray for peace
By reason of the wickedness of chiefs.
And there will come wrath of the mighty God
On the Assyrians and a mountain stream
Will utterly destroy them, which will come
⁷⁵To Caesar's city and harm Canaanites.
The Pyramus will irrigate the city
Of Mopsus; then will the Aegaeans fall
Because of strife of very mighty men.
You, wretched Antioch, will Ares strong
⁸⁰Leave not when round you an Assyrian war
Is pressing, for a chief of men will dwell
Within your houses who will fight with all
The arrow-hurling Persians, he himself
Having obtained of Romans royal power.
⁸⁵Now, cities of Arabians, deck yourselves
With temples and with places for the race,
And with broad markets
    and with splendid wealth,
With images, gold, silver, ivory;
And you who are of all most fond of learning,
⁹⁰Bostra and Philippopolis,
    that you may come
Into great sorrow; and the laughing spheres
Of the zodiacal vault, Aries,
Taurus, and Gemini, and as many stars
Ruling hours as with them in the sky appear
⁹⁵Will benefit you not; you, wretched one,
Have trusted many when that very man
Will afterward bring near that which is yours.
And now for Alexandrians loving war
Will I sing wars most dreadful;
    and much people
¹⁰⁰Will perish while their cities are destroyed
By citizens against each other matched
And fighting for the sake of hateful strife,
And round them horrid Ares, rushing on,
Will cease from war. And then one
    of great soul
¹⁰⁵Along with his own mighty son will fall
By treachery on the older king's account.
And after him there will rule powerfully
O'er fertile Rome another great-souled lord
Versed in war, coming from the Dacians
¹¹⁰And numbering three hundred;
    he will have
Also the letter of the number four,
And many will he slay, and then the king
Will all his brothers and his friends destroy
Even while the kings are cut off, and at once
¹¹⁵Will there be fights and pillagings
    and murders
Suddenly on the older king's account.
Then, when a cunning man
    will summoned come,
A robber and a Roman not well known
From Syria appearing, he by guile
¹²⁰Into a race of Cappadocian men
Will drive through and, besieging,
    will press hard,
Insatiate of war. And then for you,
Tyana and Mazaka, there will be
A capture; you will be enslaved and put
¹²⁵On your neck again a fearful yoke.
Arid Syria will mourn for men destroyed
And then Selenian goddess will not guard
Her holy city. But when he by flight
From Syria will before the Romans come,

¹³⁰And will pass over the Euphrates' streams,
No longer like the Romans, but like fierce
Dart-shooting Persians, then, fulfilling fate,
Down will the ruler of the Italians fall
In the ranks stricken by the gleaming iron;
¹³⁵And close on him will his children perish.
But when another king of Rome will reign,
Then also to the Romans there will come
Unstable nations, on the walls of Rome
Destructive Ares with his bastard son;
¹⁴⁰Then also will be famines, pestilence,
And mighty thunderbolts, and dreadful wars,
And anarchy in cities suddenly;
And the Syrians will perish fearfully;
For there will come on them the great wrath
¹⁴⁵Of the Most High and promptly an uprising
of the industrious Persians, and mixed up
With Persians will the Syrians destroy
The Romans, but by the divine decree
They will not make a conquest of their laws.
¹⁵⁰Woe, how many with their goods will flee
From the East to men of other tongues!
Woe, the dark blood of how many men
The land will drink! For that will be a time
In which the living uttering o'er the dead
¹⁵⁵A blessing will by word of mouth
    pronounce
Death beautiful and death will flee
    from them.
And now for you, O wretched Syria,
I weep in sorrow; for to you will come
A dreadful blow from arrow-shooting men,
¹⁶⁰Which you did never think
    would come to you.
Also, the fugitive of Rome will come
Bearing a great spear, Crossing on his way
Euphrates with his many myriads,
And he will burn you, and dispose all things
¹⁶⁵In a bad way. O wretched Antioch,
And you a city they will never call,
When by your lack of prudence you will fall
Under the spears; and stripping off all things
And making naked, he will leave you thus
¹⁷⁰Coverless, homeless; and when anyone
Sees he will immediately weep for you.
And you will be, O Hierapolis,
A triumph, also you, Beroea; weep
At Chalcis over lately wounded sons.
¹⁷⁵Woe, how many by the steep high mount
Of Casius will dwell and by Amanus
How many, and how many Lycus leaves,
And Marsyas as many and Pyramus
The silver-eddying; for even to the bounds
¹⁸⁰Of Asia they will treasure up their spoils,
Make cities naked, and bear idols off
And cast down temples
    on much-nourishing earth.
And sometime to Gauls and Pannonians,
To Mysians and Bithynians there will be
¹⁸⁵Great sorrow when a warrior
    will have come.
O Lycians, Lycians, there will come a wolf
To lick your blood, when Sannians will come
With city-wasting Ares and the Carpians
Will draw near with Ausonians to fight.
¹⁹⁰And then by his own
    shameless recklessness
The bastard son will put the king to death,
And he himself for his impiety
Will promptly perish. And again will rule

After him yet another whose name shows
¹⁹⁵First letter; but he too will quickly fall
By mighty Ares, struck by gleaming iron.
And yet again the world will be confused,
Men perishing by pestilence and war.
And the Persians maddened
    by the Ausonians
²⁰⁰Will in the toil of Ares yet again
Force their way. And then there will be
    a flight
Of Romans; and thereafter there will come
The priest heard of all around, sent by
    the sun,
From Syria appearing and by guile
²⁰⁵Will he accomplish all things. And then too
The city of the sun will offer prayer;
And all around her will the Persians dare
The fearful threatenings of the Phoenicians.
But when two chiefs, men swift in war,
    will rule
²¹⁰The very mighty Romans, one of whom
Will have the number seventy, and the other
The number three, even then the stately bull,
That digs the earth with his hoofs and stirs up
The dust with his two horns, will many ills
²¹⁵On a dark-skinned reptile perpetrate—
Which draws a trail with his scales;
    and besides,
Himself will perish. And yet after him
Again will come another fair-horned stag,
Hungry on the mountains, striving hard
²²⁰To feed on the venom-shedding beasts
Then will a dread and fearful lion come,
Sent from the sun
    and breathing forth much flame.
And then too by his shameless recklessness
Will he destroy the well-horned rapid stag,
²²⁵And the mightiest venom-shedding beast
So dread, that sends forth
    many piping sounds,
And the male goat that sideways
    moves along,
And after him fame follows; he himself
Sound, unhurt, unapproachable, will rule
²³⁰The Romans, and the Persians will be weak.
But, LORD, King of the world, O God, restrain
The song of our words and give
    charming song.

BOOK XIV

[Warning against the lust of power, 1–14. The bull-destroyer, 16–22. The man known by the number one, 23–27. Two rulers of the number forty, 28–34. Young ruler of the number seventy, 115–55. Ruler of the number forty, 66–61. Wolf from the West, 62–65. Ruler known by the letter A, 66–73. Three kings of haughty soul, of the numbers one, thirty, and three hundred, 74–93. King known by the number three, 94–98. The old king of the number four, 99–101. Wars and woes on various peoples, 102–120. The venerable king of the number five, 121–134. Two kings of the numbers three hundred and three, 115–147. The king of many schemes, 148–159. King of the number three hundred, 160–172. King like a wild beast, of the number thirty, 173–188. Ruler of the number four, 189–200. A great sign from Heaven, 201–205. Ruler out of Asia, of the number fifty, 206–216. Ruler out of Egypt, 217–223. The man of potent signs and the peaceful king of the number five, 224–245. Many tyrants and the holy king known by the letter A, 246–261. Burning and restoration of Rome, 262–271. Woe for various Greeks, 272–278. The fratricide, 279–283. The fierce king of the number eighty and the terrors of his time, 284–508. Many obtain royal power, 309–312. Three kings and their destruction, 313–329. Many spearmen, 330–335. God's judgment on the shameless, 336–343. Rome's wretched plight and the last race of Latin kings, 344–358. Egypt and her prudent king, 359–375. The Alexandrians, 376–381. Fearful nameless woe, 382–398. The Sicilians, 399–406. The lion and lioness, 407–418. The dragon and the ram, 419–425. Second war in Egypt, 426–433. Destructive slaughter, 434–447. The Messianic era, 448–468.]

O men, why do you vainly think on things
Too lofty, as if you were immortal?
And you are ruling but a little time,
And over mortals all desire to reign,
⁵Not understanding that God Himself hates
The lust of rule, and most of all things hates
Insatiate kings fearful in wickedness,
And over them He stirs up what is dark;
Therefore, instead of good works
    and just thoughts,
¹⁰You all choose for your garments
    purple robes,
Desiring wretched fights and homicides!
Them God imperishable
    who dwells in Heaven
Will make short-lived, destroy them utterly,
And overthrow one here, another there.
¹⁵But when there will a bull-destroyer come
Trusting in his own might,
    thick-haired and grim,
And will destroy all, he will also tear
Shepherds in pieces, and no victory
Will be theirs unless soon, with speed of feet
²⁰Pursuing eagerly through wooded glens,
Young dogs will meet in conflict; for a dog
Pursued the lion which destroys
    the shepherds.
And then there will be a lord confident
In his might, and named with four syllables,
²⁵And shown forth clearly from
    the number one;
But him will brazen Ares quickly slay
Because of conflict with insatiate men.
Then will two other princely men bear rule,
Both of the number forty; and with them
³⁰Will great peace be in the world and to all
The people law and right; but them in turn
Will men with gleaming helmet, needing gold
And silver, impiously put to death
For these things, catching them
    by their deft plans.
³⁵And then again a dreadful lord will rule,
Young, fighting hand to hand,
    whose name will show
The number seventy, life-destroying, fierce,
Who to the army basely will betray
The people of Rome, slain by wickedness
⁴⁰Because of wrath of kings, and he will hurl
Down every city and hut of the Latins.
And Rome is no more to be seen or heard,
Such as of late another traveler saw;
For all these things will in the ashes lie,
⁴⁵Nor will there be a sparing of her works;
For vengeful He Himself
    will come from Heaven,
God the immortal from the sky will send
Lightnings and thunderbolts on mankind;
And some He will destroy
    by lightnings burned,
⁵⁰And others with His mighty thunderbolts.
And Rome's strong children
    and the famous Latins
Will then the shameless dreadful ruler slay.
Around him dead the dust will not lie light,
But he will be a sport for dogs and birds
⁵⁵And wolves, for he a martial people spoiled.
After him, numbering forty, there will rule
Another, famous Parthian-destroyer,
German-destroyer, putting down
    dread beasts
That kill men, which on the ocean's streams
⁶⁰And the Euphrates press constantly on.
And then will Rome again be as before.
But when there comes a great wolf
    in your plains,
A ruler marching onward from the West,
Then will he under powerful Ares die,
⁶⁵Being cleft asunder by the piercing brass.
And o'er the very mighty Romans then
Will there rule yet again another man
Of great heart, from Assyria brought to light,
Of the first letter, and he will himself
⁷⁰By means of wars put all things under him,
And by his armies at once power display
And lay down laws; but him will brazen Ares
Quickly destroy by treacherous
    armies falling.
After him three of haughty heart will rule,
⁷⁵One having the first number, one three tens,
And the other with three hundred
    will partake,
Cruel, who gold and silver in much fire
Will melt in statues of gods made with hands,
And to the armies they, equipped for war,
⁸⁰Will, for the sake of victory, moneys give,
Dividing many costly things and goods;
And in like manner, striving eagerly
After power, they will purge disastrously
The arrow-shooting Parthians of the deep
⁸⁵And swift Euphrates, and the hostile Medes,
And the soft-haired warlike Massagetae
And Persians also, quiver-bearing men.
But when the king will his own fate unloose,
Leaving to his sons more fit for arms
⁹⁰The royal scepter and entreating right,
Then they, forgetful of their father's words
And having their hands all prepared for war,
Will rush in conflict for the royal power.
And then another lord, of the third number,
⁹⁵Will rule alone, and stricken by a sword,
Will quickly see his fate. Then after him
Will many perish at each other's hands,
Being very valiant for the royal power.
Moreover, a great-hearted one will rule
¹⁰⁰The very mighty Romans, an old lord,
Of the number four, and manage
    all things well.
And then on Phoenicia will come war
And conflict when there will come
    nations near
Of arrow-shooting Persians; ah, how many
¹⁰⁵Will before men of barbarous speech
    fall down!
Sidon and Tripolis and Berytus
The loudly-boasting will behold each other
Amid the blood and bodies of the dead.
Wretched Laodicea, around yourself
¹¹⁰You will a great and unsuccessful war
Stir up through the impiety of men;
Ah, hapless Tyrians, you will gather in
An evil harvest; when in the daytime
The sun that lightens mortals will withdraw,
¹¹⁵And his disk not appear, and drops of blood
Thick and abundant will flow down
    from the sky
On the earth. And then the king will die,
Betrayed by his companions. After him
Will many shameless leaders still promote
¹²⁰The wicked strife and one another kill.
And then will there a reverend ruler be,
Of much skill, with a name that numbers five,
Confiding in great armies, whom mankind
Will fondly love because of royal power;
¹²⁵And having the good name he will thereto
Add by good deeds. But while he reigns
    there will
'Twixt Taurus and snow-clad Amanus be
A fearful sign. From the Cilician land
A city new and beautiful and strong
¹³⁰Will by the deep strong rivers be destroyed.
And in Propontis and in Phrygia
Will there be many earthquakes.
    And the king
Of great renown will under his own lot
By wasting deadly sickness lose his life.
¹³⁵And after him will rule two lordly kings,
One numbering three hundred,
    and one three;
And many will he utterly destroy
In defense of the seven-hill city Rome,
And for the sake of powerful sovereignty.
¹⁴⁰And then will evil to the senate come,
Nor will it from the angry king escape
While he holds wrath against it. And a sign
Will then appear to all men on earth;
And fuller will the rains be, snow and hail
¹⁴⁵Will ruin field-fruits o'er
    the boundless earth.
But they will fall in wars, slain by strong Ares
In behalf of the war for the Italians.
And then again, another king will rule,
Full of devices, gathering all the army,
¹⁵⁰And for the sake of war distributing
Money to those with brazen breastplate clad;
But thereon will Nilus, abundant in corn,
Beyond the Libyan mainland irrigate
For two years the dark soil and fruitful land
¹⁵⁵Of Egypt; but all things will famine seize
And war and robbers, murders, homicides.
And many cities will by warlike men
Be thrown down headlong
    by the army's hands;
And he, betrayed, will fall by gleaming iron.

¹⁶⁰After him one whose number
   is three hundred
Will rule the Romans, very mighty men;
He will stretch forth a life-destroying spear
Against the Armenians and the Parthians,
The Assyrians and the Persians firm in war.
¹⁶⁵And then anew will a creation be
Of splendidly built Rome
   with gold and amber
And silver and ivory in order raised;
And in her many people will abide
From all the East and from
   the prosperous West;
¹⁷⁰And the king will make other laws for her;
But then will death destructive
   and strong fate
In turn receive him in a boundless isle.
And there will rule another, of ten triads,
A man like a wild beast, fair-haired and grim,
¹⁷⁵Who will be a descendant of the Greeks.
And then a city of Molossian Phthia
Feeding much, and Larissa will be bent
Down on Peneus' overhanging brows;
And then too in horse-feeding Scythia
¹⁸⁰Will be an insurrection. And dire war
Will be hard by the waters of the lake
Maeotis, at streams by the utmost mouth
Of the fount of watery Phasis on the mead
Of asphodel; and there will many fall
¹⁸⁵By powerful warriors. Ah, how many men
Will Ares with strong brass receive!
   And then,
Having destroyed a Scythian race, the king
Will die in his own lot unloosing life.
And yet another of the number four
¹⁹⁰Will rule thereafter, openly made known
A dreadful man, whom all Armenians,
Who drink the best ice of the flowing stream
Araxes, and the Persians of great soul
Will fear in wars. And between Colchians
¹⁹⁵And very strong Pelasgi there will be
Wars, fights, and homicides.
   And those who hold
The cities of the land of Phrygia
And those of the Propontis, and make bare
From out their scabbards
   the two-edged swords,
²⁰⁰Will strike each other
   through sore impiousness.
And then will God to mortal men display
From the sky a great sign
   with the rolling years,
A bat, the portent of bad war to come.
And then the king will not escape stern fate,
²⁰⁵But die by hand, slain by the gleaming iron.
After him, numbering fifty, there will rule
Again another coming out of Asia,
A dreadful terror, fighting hand to hand;
And he will set war on Rome's stately walls,
²¹⁰And among Colchians, and Heniochi,
And the milk-drinking Agathyrsians
By Euxine Sea, at Thracia's sandy bay.
And then the king will not escape stern fate,
And they will tear in pieces his dead corpse.
²¹⁵And then, the king slain,
   man-ennobling Rome
Will be a desert, and much people perish.
And then again one terrible and dread
From mighty Egypt will rule, and destroy
Great-hearted Parthians and Medes
   and Germans,
²²⁰And Agathyrsians of the Bosporus,
Iernians, Britons, and Iberians
That bear the quiver, bent Massagetae,
And Persians thinking themselves
   more than men.
And then a famous man will look on
²²⁵All Hellas, acting as an enemy
To Scythia and windy Caucasus.
And there will be a dread sign while he rules:
Crowns altogether like the shining stars
Will from the sky in the south
   and north appear.
²³⁰And then will he impart the royal power
To his son whose initial letter heads
The alphabet, when in the halls of Hades
The manly king in his own lot will go.
But when the son of this man in the land
²³⁵Of Rome will rule, shown by
   the number one,
There will be over all the earth great peace
Much longed for, and the Latins will love him
As king because of his own father's worth;
Him, eager to go both to East and West,
²⁴⁰The Roman people will against his will
Retain at home and in command of Rome,
For among all there is a friendly heart
Felt for their royal and illustrious lord.
But baneful death will snatch him out of life,
²⁴⁵Short-lived, abandoned to his destiny.
But others afterward again will strike
Each other, powerful warriors, carrying on
An evil strife, not holding kingly power,
But being tyrants. And in all the world
²⁵⁰Will they bring many evil things to pass,
But chiefly for the Romans till the time
Of the third Dionysus, until armed
With helmet Ares will from Egypt come,
Whom they will surname Dionysus lord.
²⁵⁵But when the famous royal purple cloak
A murderous lion and murderous lioness
Will rend, together they will grasp the lungs
Of the changed kingdom; then a holy king,
Whose name has the first letter,
   pressing hard
²⁶⁰For victory, will cast down hostile chiefs
To be the food of dogs and birds of prey.
Woe for you, O city burned with fire,
O powerful Rome! How many things
   must you
Need to suffer when all these things
   come to pass!
²⁶⁵But the great far-famed king will afterward
Raise you all up again with gold and amber
And silver and ivory, and in the world
You will in your possessions foremost be,
Also in temples, marketplaces, wealth,
²⁷⁰And race-grounds; and then
   will you be again
A light for all, even as you were before.
Ah, wretched Cecropes and Cadmeans
And the Laconians, who are positioned
Around Peneus and Molossian stream
²⁷⁵Thick grown with rushes,
   Tricca and Dodona,
And high-built Ithome, Pierian ridge
Around the summit of Olympian mount,
Ossa, Larissa, and high-gate Calydon.
But when God will for mortals bring to pass
²⁸⁰A great sign, day dark twilight
   round the world,
Even then to you, O king, the end will come,
Nor is it possible that you escape
A brother's piercing dart against you hurled.
And then again will rule a life-destroyer,
²⁸⁵A fiery eagle from the royal race,
Who will of Egypt's offspring take fast hold,
Younger, but than his brother much stronger,
Who has for his first sign the number eighty.
And then the whole world
   will for honor's sake
²⁹⁰Bear in its lap the soul-distressing wrath
Of the immortal God; and there will come
On mortal men, the creatures of a day,
Famines and plagues and wars
   and homicides,
And an incessant darkness o'er the earth,
²⁹⁵Mother of peoples, and relentless wrath
From Heaven, and disorder of the times,
And earthquake shocks,
   and flaming thunderbolts,
And stones and storms of rain
   and squalid drops.
And the high summits of the Phrygian land
³⁰⁰Feel the shock, bases of the Scythian hills
Feel the shock, cities tremble, and all earth
Trembles at the cliffs of the land of Greece.
And many cities, God being very angry,
Will fall prone under burning thunderbolts,
³⁰⁵And with lamenting, and to shun the wrath
And make escape is not even possible.
And then the king will by a strong hand fall,
Struck as if he were no one by his men.
After him of the Latins many men
³¹⁰Wearing the purple mantle
   on their shoulders
Will be again raised up, who will by lot
Desire to lay hold on the royal power.
And then on the stately walls of Rome
Will be three kings, two having
   the first number,
³¹⁵And one the eponym of victory
Bearing as no one else. They will love Rome
And all the world, concerned for mortal men;
But they will not accomplish anything;
For God has not been gracious to the world
³²⁰Neither will He be gentle with mankind,
Because they have done many evil things.
Therefore, to kings will He a mean soul bring
Still worse than that of leopards
   and of wolves;
For harshly seizing them
   with their own hands,
³²⁵Like feeble women who are idly slain,
Will men in brazen breastplate utterly
Destroy the kings together
   with their scepters.
Ah, wretched lofty men of glorious Rome,
Trusting in false oaths you will be destroyed.
³³⁰And then will many masters with the spear,
Men rushing disordered [and] franticly on,
Take away offspring of the firstborn men
In their blood… Therefore thrice
Will the Most High then bring
   on dreadful doom,
³³⁵And all men with their works
   will He destroy.
But into judgment yet again will God
Cause them to come that have
   a shameless soul,

THE SIBYLLINE ORACLES

As many as determined evil things;
And they themselves are fenced in, falling one
³⁴⁰On another, and given over there
Into that condemnation of wickedness.
All one by one, yet a brilliant comet
Of much to come, of war and battle strife,
But at the time when one around the isles
³⁴⁵Will gather many oracles that speak
To strangers of fight and of battle strife,
And grievous harm of temples, he will bid
One in great haste to gather in Rome's halls
For twelve months wheat
    and barley in abundance,
³⁵⁰And this most quickly. And in
    wretched plight
The city will be those days, and promptly
Will it again be prosperous not a little;
And rest will be when that rule is destroyed.
And then the last race of the Latin kings
³⁵⁵Will be, and after it again will grow
Dominion, children and the children's race
Will be unshaken; for it will be known,
Since of a surety God Himself is King.
There is a land dear, nourisher of men,
³⁶⁰Positioned in a plain, and round it Nile
Marks off the boundary and separates
All Libya and Ethiopia.
And Syrians short-lived, one from one place,
Another from another, from that land
³⁶⁵Will snatch away all movable effects;
A great and careful lord will be their king,
Training up youth and sending off for men,
And planning something fearful about those
Most fearful, above all he will send forth
³⁷⁰A powerful helper of all Italy
The lofty-minded. And when he will come
To the dark sea of Assyria
He will despoil Phoenicians in their homes,
And fastening evil war and battle dire
³⁷⁵Will be one lord of the two lords of earth.
And now will I for Alexandrians sing
Their grievous end; woe, barbarians
Will possess sacred Egypt, land unharmed,
Unshaken, when wrath
    from the gods will come.
³⁸⁰... making winter summer,
Then will the oracles be all fulfilled.
But when three youths in
    the Olympian games
Will conquer, and you will bid
    them that know
The oracles that call on God to cleanse
³⁸⁵First by the blood of sucking quadruped,
Thrice therefore will the Most High
    then bring on
A fearful lot, and he will over all
Brandish the mournful long spear;
    then much blood
Barbarian will be poured out in the dust
³⁹⁰When the city will be plundered utterly
By inhospitable strangers. Happy he
Who is dead, also happy anyone
Who is without a child; for he who once
Was leader surnamed for them that are free,
³⁹⁵Far-famed in song, no longer in his mind
Revolving earlier plans, will place their neck
Under a servile yoke; such slavery,
Cause of much weeping, will a lord impose.
And then promptly an army of Sicilians
⁴⁰⁰Ill-fated will come, carrying dismay,

When a barbarian nation will again
Come suddenly; and the fruit, when it grows,
They from the field will sever. On them
Will God the lofty Thunderer bestow
⁴⁰⁵Evil instead of good; continually
Will stranger pluck from stranger
    hateful gold.
But now when all will look on the blood
Of the flesh-eating lion and there comes
On the body a murderous lioness,
⁴¹⁰Down from his head will be the scepter cast
Away from him. And as in friendly feast
In Egypt when the people all partake,
They perform valiant deeds,
    and one restrains
Another, and among them there is much
⁴¹⁵Shouting aloud; so also will there be
On mankind the fear of furious strife,
And many will be utterly destroyed
And others kill each other by hard fights.
And then one, covered with dark scales
    will come;
⁴²⁰Two others will come acting in concert
With one another, and with them a third—
A great ram from Cyrene, whom before
I spoke of as a fugitive in war
Beside the streams of Nile; but in no wise
⁴²⁵An unsuccessful way do all complete.
And then the lengths of the revolving years
Will be exceedingly quiet; yet again
Thereafter will a second war for them
In Egypt be stirred up, and there will be
⁴³⁰A battle on the sea, but victory
Will not be theirs. Ah, wretched ones,
    there will
A conquest of the famous city be,
And it will be a spoil of war not long.
And then men having common boundaries
⁴³⁵Of much land will flee wretched,
    and will lead
Their wretched parents. And they will again,
Having great victory, descend on a land,
And will destroy the Jews, men staunch
    in war,
Wasting by wars far as the hoary deep,
⁴⁴⁰On both sides, fighting in
    the foremost ranks
For fatherland and parents. And a race
Of trophy-bearing men will for the dead
Be reckoned. Ah, how many men will swim
Along the waves! For on the sandy beach
⁴⁴⁵Many will lie; and heads of golden hair
Will fall beneath Egyptian winged birds.
And then for the Arabians mortal blood
Will go in quest. But when wolves
    will with dogs
Pledge in a sea-girt island solemn oaths,
⁴⁵⁰Then will there be the raising of a tower,
And the city that suffered very many things
Men will inhabit. For deceitful gold
Will no more be nor silver, nor acquiring
Of the earth, nor much-laboring servitude;
⁴⁵⁵But one fast friendship and one mode of life
With cheerful soul; and all things
    will be common
And equal light among the means of life.
And wickedness will sink down
    from the earth
Into the vast sea. And then near at hand
⁴⁶⁰Has come the harvesttime of mortal men.

There is imposed a strong necessity
That these things be fulfilled. And at that time
There will not any other traveler say,
In this conjecturing, that the race of men
⁴⁶⁵Though perishable will ever cease to be.
And then a holy nation will prevail
And hold the sovereignty of all the earth
To all ages with their mighty sons.

ORACLE FRAGMENTS

[There are a number of fragments from the Sibylline Oracles that cannot be clearly placed. There may be justification for placing the first of these at the beginning of Book III.]

FRAGMENT 1

You mortal men of flesh, who are nothing,
How quickly are you puffed up, not seeing
The end of life! Do you not tremble now
And fear God—Him who watches over you,
⁵The one who is most high,
    the one who knows,
The all-observant witness of all things,
All-nourishing Creator, who has put
In all things His sweet Spirit and has made
Him leader of all mortals? God is one,
¹⁰Who rules alone, supremely great, unborn,
Almighty and invisible, Himself
Alone beholding all things, but not seen
Is He Himself by any mortal flesh.
For what flesh is there able to behold
¹⁵With eyes the heavenly and true God divine,
Who has His habitation in the sky?
Not even before the bright rays of the sun
Can men stand still, men who are
    mortal born,
Existing but as veins and flesh on bones.
²⁰Him who alone is ruler of the world,
Who alone is forever and has been
From everlasting, give reverence to Him,
The self-existent unbegotten one
Who rules all things through all time,
    dealing out
²⁵To all mortals in a common light
The judgment. And the merited reward
Of evil counseling will you receive,
For ceasing the true and eternal God
To glorify, and holy hecatombs
³⁰To offer him, you made your sacrifice
To the demons that in Hades dwell.
And you in self-conceit and madness walk,
And having left the true, straightforward path
You went away and roamed about
    through thorns
³⁵And thistles. O you foolish mortals, cease
Roving in darkness and black night obscure,
And leave the darkness of night, and lay hold
On the Light. Behold, He is clear to all
And cannot err; come, do not always chase
⁴⁰Darkness and gloom. Behold,
    the sweet-looking light
Of the sun shines with a surpassing glow.
Now, treasuring wisdom in your hearts,
    know
That God is one, who sends forth
    rains and winds,
Earthquakes and lightnings, famines,

pestilence,
⁴⁵And mournful cares, and storms of snow, and ice.
But why do I thus speak them one by one?
He guides Heaven, rules earth,
over Hades reigns.

FRAGMENT 2
Now if gods beget offspring and remain
Immortal there had been more gods
than men,
And there had never been sufficient room
For mortals to stand.

FRAGMENT 3
Now if all that is born must also perish,
It is not possible for God to be
Formed from the thighs of man
and from a womb;
But God alone is one and all-supreme,
⁵Who made Heaven and the sun
and stars and moon,
Fruit-bearing earth and billows of the sea,
And lofty hills and mouth of lasting springs.
He also brings forth great multitudes
Of creatures that amid the waters live
¹⁰Innumerable, and the creeping things
That move on earth He sustains with life,
And dappled, delicate, shrill-twittering birds,
That ply the air shrill-whirring
with their wings.
And in the glens of mountains wild be placed
¹⁵The race of beasts, and to us mortals made
All cattle subject, and the God-formed one
He constituted ruler of all things,
And to man all variegated things
Made subject, things incomprehensible.
²⁰For all these things what mortal flesh can know?
For He Himself alone, who made these things
At the beginning, knows, the incorrupt
Eternal Maker, dwelling in the Heaven,
Bringing to the good good recompense
²⁵Much more abundant, but awakening wrath
And anger for the evil and unjust,
And war and pestilence, and tearful woes.
O men, why, vainly puffed up, do you root
Yourselves out? Be ashamed to deify
³⁰Polecats and monsters. Is it not a craze
And frenzy, taking sense of mind away,
If gods steal plates and carry off earthen pots?
Instead of dwelling in the golden Heaven
In plenty, see them eaten by the moth
³⁵And woven over with thick spider-webs!
O fools, that bow to serpents, dogs, and cats,
And reverence birds and creeping beasts
of earth,
Stone images and statues made with hands,
And stone-heaps by the roads—
these you revere,
⁴⁰And also many other idle things
Which it would even be a shame to tell;
These are the baneful gods of senseless men,
And from their mouth is
deadly poison poured.
But of Him is life and eternal light
⁴⁵Imperishable, and He sheds a joy
Sweeter than honey sweet on righteous men,
And to Him only do you bow your neck,
And among pious lives incline your way.
Forsaking all these, in a spirit mad
⁵⁰With folly you did all drain off the cup
Of judgment that was filled full, very pure,
Closely pressed, weighed down,
and also unmixed.
And you will not wake from your
drunken sleep
And come to sober reason, and know God
⁵⁵To be the King who oversees all things.
Therefore, on you the flash of gleaming fire
Is coming, you will be with torches burned
The livelong day through an eternal age,
At your false useless idols feeling shame.
⁶⁰But they who fear the true eternal God
Inherit life, and they forever dwell
Alike in fertile field of Paradise,
Feasting on sweet bread
from the starry heavens.

FRAGMENT 4
Hear me, O men, the King eternal reigns.

FRAGMENT 5
He only is God, Maker uncontrolled;
He fixed the pattern of the human form,
And did the nature of all mortals mix
Himself, the generator of [all] life.

FRAGMENT 6
Whenever He will come
A smoky fire will be in mid-night dark.

FRAGMENT 7
The Erythraean Sibyl, addressing God, says:
"Why do you, O Lord, enjoin on me the necessity of prophesying, and not rather take me aloft from the earth and preserve me to the most blessed day of Your coming?

FIRST APOLOGY

Justin Martyr, one of Christianity's earliest theologians and apologists (born c. AD 90–100; died c. 165), was born into a Greek family in Flavia Neapolis, near the biblical city of Shechem. He pursued truth in the philosophical schools of Stoicism, Peripateticism, Pythagoreanism, and eventually Platonism, but found all of man's philosophies sorely lacking. Then one day, perchance he stumbled upon an old man by the seashore—a Syrian Christian—who persuaded him that supreme truth is found only in Christ, the incarnate Word, who merely 100 years earlier had died and risen again in the very region in which Justin had been born and raised. Justin placed his faith in Christ and dedicated his life to the truth. He founded a philosophical school in Rome to further the Gospel, but the stoic philosopher Crescens denounced him to the Roman authorities, and Justin and six of his friends were martyred for their faith via beheading, valiantly refusing to deny the Name of Christ. His most famous extant works are his two Apologies, the first addressed to the emperor Antoninus Pius, his sons, and the Senate; and the second to the Roman Senate alone. The First Apology was written in about AD 155.

CHAPTER 1
¹To the Emperor Titus Aelius Adrianus Antoninus Pius Augustus Caesar, and to his son Verissimus the Philosopher, and to Lucius the Philosopher, the natural son of Caesar, and the adopted son of Pius, a lover of learning, and to the sacred Senate, with the whole People of the Romans, ²I, Justin, the son of Priscus and grandson of Bacchius, natives of Flavia Neapolis in Palestine, present this address and petition on behalf of those of all nations who are unjustly hated and wantonly abused, myself being one of them.

CHAPTER 2
¹Reason directs those who are truly pious and philosophical to honor and love only what is true, declining to follow traditional opinions, if these are worthless. ²For not only does sound reason direct us to refuse the guidance of those who did or taught anything wrong, but it is incumbent on the lover of truth, by all means, and if death be threatened, even before his own life, to choose to do and say what is right. ³You then, since you are called pious and philosophers, guardians of justice and lovers of learning, give good heed, and listen to my address; and if you are indeed such, it will be manifested. ⁴For we have come, not to flatter you by this writing, nor please you by our address, but to beg that you pass judgment, after an accurate and searching investigation, not flattered by prejudice or by a desire of pleasing superstitious men, nor induced by irrational impulse or evil rumors which have long been prevalent, to give a decision which will prove to be against yourselves. ⁵For as for us, we reckon that no evil can be done to us, unless we are convicted as evildoers or are proved to be wicked men; and you, you can kill, but not [truly] hurt us.

FIRST APOLOGY

CHAPTER 3
¹But lest anyone think that this is an unreasonable and reckless utterance, we demand that the charges against the Christians be investigated, and that, if these are substantiated, they be punished as they deserve; [[or rather, indeed, we ourselves will punish them.]] ²But if no one can convict us of anything, true reason forbids you, for the sake of a wicked rumor, to wrong blameless men, and indeed rather yourselves, who think fit to direct affairs, not by judgment, but by passion. ³And every sober-minded person will declare this to be the only fair and equitable adjustment, namely, that the subjects render an unexceptional account of their own life and doctrine; and that, on the other hand, the rulers should give their decision in obedience, not to violence and tyranny, but to piety and philosophy. ⁴For thus would both rulers and ruled reap benefit. ⁵For even one of the ancients somewhere said, "Unless both rulers and ruled philosophize, it is impossible to make states blessed." It is our task, therefore, to afford to all an opportunity of inspecting our life and teachings, lest, on account of those who are accustomed to be ignorant of our affairs, we should incur the penalty due to them for mental blindness; and it is your business, when you hear us, to be found, as reason demands, good judges. ⁶For if, when you have learned the truth, you do not do what is just, you will be without excuse before God.

CHAPTER 4
¹By the mere application of a name, nothing is decided, either good or evil, apart from the actions implied in the name; and indeed, so far at least as one may judge from the name we are accused of, we are most excellent people. ²But as we do not think it just to beg to be acquitted on account of the name, if we are convicted as evildoers, so, on the other hand, if we are found to have committed no offense, either in the matter of thus naming ourselves, or of our conduct as citizens, it is your part very earnestly to guard against incurring just punishment, by unjustly punishing those who are not convicted. ³For from a name neither praise nor punishment could reasonably spring, unless something excellent or base in action is proved. ⁴And those among yourselves who are accused you do not punish before they are convicted; but in our case you receive the name as proof against us, and this although, so far as the name goes, you ought rather to punish our accusers. ⁵For we are accused of being Christians, and to hate what is excellent is unjust. ⁶Again, if any of the accused deny the name, and say that he is not a Christian, you acquit him, as having no evidence against him as a wrongdoer; but if anyone acknowledges that he is a Christian, you punish him on account of this acknowledgment. ⁷Justice requires that you inquire into the life both of him who confesses and of him who denies, that by his deeds it may be apparent what kind of man each is. ⁸For as some who have been taught by the Master, Christ, not to deny Him, give encouragement to others when they are put to the question, so in all probability do those who lead wicked lives give occasion to those who, without consideration, take on them to accuse all the Christians of impiety and wickedness. And this also is not right. ⁹For of philosophy, too, some assume the name and the garb who do nothing worthy of their profession; and you are well aware, that those of the ancients whose opinions and teachings were quite diverse, are yet all called by the one name of philosophers. ¹⁰And of these some taught atheism; and the poets who have flourished among you raise a laugh out of the uncleanness of Jupiter with his own children. ¹¹And those who now adopt such instruction are not restrained by you; but, on the contrary, you bestow prizes and honors on those who erroneously insult the gods.

CHAPTER 5
¹Why, then, should this be? In our case, who pledge ourselves to do no wickedness, nor to hold these atheistic opinions, you do not examine the charges made against us; ²but, yielding to unreasoning passion, and to the instigation of evil demons, you punish us without consideration or judgment. ³For the truth will be spoken; since of old these evil demons, effecting apparitions of themselves, both defiled women and corrupted boys, and showed such fearful sights to men, that those who did not use their reason in judging of the actions that were done, were struck with terror; ⁴and being carried away by fear, and not knowing that these were demons, they called them gods, and gave to each the name which each of the demons chose for himself. ⁵And when Socrates endeavored, by true reason and examination, to bring these things to light, and deliver men from the demons, then the demons themselves, by means of men who rejoiced in iniquity, compassed his death, as an atheist and a profane person, on the charge that he was introducing new divinities; and in our case they display a similar activity. ⁶For not only among the Greeks did reason prevail to condemn these things through Socrates, but also among the barbarians were they condemned by Reason Himself, who took shape, and became a man, and was called Jesus Christ; ⁷and in obedience to Him, we not only deny that they who did such things as these are gods, but assert that they are wicked and impious demons, whose actions will not bear comparison with those even of men desirous of virtue.

CHAPTER 6
¹Hence we are called atheists. And we confess that we are atheists, so far as gods of this sort are concerned, but not with respect to the most true God, the Father of righteousness, and temperance, and the other virtues, who is free from all impurity. ²But both Him, and the Son (who came forth from Him and taught us these things, and the host of the other good messengers who follow and are made like to Him), and the prophetic Spirit, we worship and adore, knowing them in reason and truth, and declaring without grudging to everyone who wishes to learn, as we have been taught.

CHAPTER 7
¹But someone will say, "Some have before now been arrested and convicted as evildoers." For you condemn many, many times, after inquiring into the life of each of the accused individually, but not on account of those of whom we have been speaking. ²And this we acknowledge, that as among the Greeks those who teach such theories as please themselves are all called by the one name Philosopher, though their doctrines are diverse, so also among the barbarians this name on which accusations are accumulated is the common property of those who are and those who seem wise. For all are called Christians. ³Therefore, we demand that the deeds of all those who are accused to you be judged, in order that each one who is convicted may be punished as an evildoer, and not as a Christian; ⁴and if it is clear that anyone is blameless, that he may be acquitted, since by the mere fact of his being a Christian he does no wrong. ⁵For we will not require that you punish our accusers, they being sufficiently punished by their present wickedness and ignorance of what is right.

CHAPTER 8
¹And reckon that it is for your sakes we have been saying these things; for it is in our power, when we are examined, to deny that we are Christians; but we would not live by telling a lie. ²For, driven by the desire of the continuous and pure life, we seek the abode that is with God, the Father and Creator of all, and hasten to confess our faith, persuaded and convinced as we are that they who have proved to God by their works that they followed Him, and loved to abide with Him where there is no sin to cause disturbance, can obtain these things. ³This, then, to speak shortly, is what we expect, and have learned from Christ, and teach. ⁴And Plato, in like manner, used to say that Rhadamanthus and Minos would punish the wicked who came before them; and we say that the same thing will be done, but at the hand of Christ, and on the wicked in the same bodies united again to their spirits which are now to undergo continuous punishment; and not only, as Plato said, for a period of a thousand years. ⁵And if anyone says that this is incredible or impossible, this error of ours is one which concerns ourselves only, and no other person, so long as you cannot convict us of doing any harm.

CHAPTER 9
¹And neither do we honor with many sacrifices and garlands of flowers such deities as men have formed and set in shrines and called gods; ²since we see that these are soulless and dead, and have not the form of God (for we do not consider that God has such a form as some say that they imitate to His honor), but have the names and forms of those wicked demons which have appeared.

³For why do we need to tell you who already know, into what forms the craftsmen, carving and cutting, casting and hammering, fashion the materials? ⁴And often out of vessels of dishonor, by merely changing the form, and making an image of the requisite shape, they make what they call a god; which we consider not only senseless, but to be even insulting to God, who, having ineffable glory and form, thus gets His Name attached to things that are corruptible, and require constant service. ⁵And that the artificers of these are both unreasonable, and, not to enter into particulars, are practiced in every vice, you very well know; even their own girls who work along with them they corrupt. ⁶What infatuation! That dissolute men should be said to fashion and make gods for your worship, and that you should appoint such men the guardians of the temples where they are enshrined, not recognizing that it is unlawful even to think or say that men are the guardians of gods.

CHAPTER 10

¹But we have received by tradition that God does not need the material offerings which men can give, seeing, indeed, that He Himself is the provider of all things. ²And we have been taught, and are convinced, and do believe, that He accepts those only who imitate the excellences which reside in Him: temperance, and justice, and charity, and as many virtues as are peculiar to a God who is called by no proper name. ³And we have been taught that He in the beginning did of His goodness, for man's sake, create all things out of unformed matter; ⁴and if men by their works show themselves worthy of this design of His, they are deemed worthy, and so we have received—of reigning in company with Him, being delivered from corruption and suffering. ⁵For as in the beginning He created us when we were nothing, so do we consider that, in like manner, those who choose what is pleasing to Him are, on account of their choice, deemed worthy of incorruption and of fellowship with Him. ⁶For the coming into being at first was not in our own power; and in order that we may follow those things which please Him, choosing them by means of the rational faculties He has Himself endowed us with, He both persuades us and leads us to faith. ⁷And we think it for the advantage of all men that they are not restrained from learning these things but are even urged thereto. ⁸For the restraint which human laws could not effect, the Word, inasmuch as He is divine, would have effected, had not the wicked demons, taking as their ally the lust of wickedness which is in every man, and which draws variously to all manner of vice, scattered many false and profane accusations, none of which attach to us.

CHAPTER 11

¹And when you hear that we look for a kingdom, you suppose, without making any inquiry, that we speak of a human kingdom; ²whereas we speak of that which is with God, as appears also from the confession of their faith made by those who are charged with being Christians, though they know that death is the punishment awarded to him who so confesses. ³For if we looked for a human kingdom, we should also deny our Christ, that we might not be slain; and we should strive to escape detection, that we might obtain what we expect. ⁴But since our thoughts are not fixed on the present, we are not concerned when men cut us off, since also death is a debt which must at all events be paid.

CHAPTER 12

¹And more than all other men are we your helpers and allies in promoting peace, seeing that we hold this view, that it is alike impossible for the wicked, the covetous, the conspirator, and for the virtuous, to escape the notice of God, and that each man goes to continuous punishment or salvation according to the value of his actions. ²For if all men knew this, no one would choose wickedness even for a while, knowing that he goes to the continuous punishment of fire, but would by all means restrain himself, and adorn himself with virtue, that he might obtain the good gifts of God, and escape the punishments. ³For those who, on account of the laws and punishments you impose, endeavor to escape detection when they offend (and they offend, too, under the impression that it is quite possible to escape your detection, since you are but men), those persons, if they learned and were convinced that nothing, whether actually done or only intended, can escape the knowledge of God, would by all means live decently on account of the penalties threatened, as even you yourselves will admit. ⁴But you seem to fear lest all men become righteous, and you no longer have any to punish. ⁵Such would be the concern of public executioners, but not of good princes. ⁶But, as we said before, we are persuaded that these things are prompted by evil spirits, who demand sacrifices and service even from those who live unreasonably; but as for you, we presume that you who aim at [a reputation for] piety and philosophy will do nothing unreasonable. ⁷But if you also, like the foolish, prefer custom to truth, do what you have power to do. But just so much power have rulers who esteem opinion more than truth, as robbers have in a desert. ⁸And that you will not succeed is declared by the Word, than whom, after God who begot Him, we know there is no ruler more kingly and just. ⁹For as all shrink from succeeding to the poverty or sufferings or obscurity of their fathers, so whatever the Word forbids us to choose, the sensible man will not choose. ¹⁰That all these things should come to pass, I say, our Teacher foretold—He who is both Son and Apostle of God the Father of all and the Ruler, Jesus Christ; from whom we also have the name of Christians; ¹¹from which we become more assured of all the things He taught us, since whatever He beforehand foretold should come to pass, is seen in fact coming to pass; and this is the work of God, to tell of a thing before it happens, and as it was foretold so to show it happening. ¹²It were possible to pause here and add nothing more, reckoning that we demand what is just and true; ¹³but because we are well aware that it is not easy suddenly to change a mind possessed by ignorance, we intend to add a few things, for the sake of persuading those who love the truth, knowing that it is not impossible to put ignorance to flight by presenting the truth.

CHAPTER 13

¹What sober-minded man, then, will not acknowledge that we are not atheists, worshiping as we do the Maker of this universe, and declaring, as we have been taught, that He has no need of streams of blood, and libations, and incense; ²Whom we praise to the utmost of our power by the exercise of prayer and thanksgiving for all things with which we are supplied, as we have been taught that the only honor that is worthy of Him is not to consume by fire what He has brought into being for our sustenance, but to use it for ourselves and those who need, and with gratitude to Him to offer thanks by invocations and hymns for our creation, and for all the means of health, and for the various qualities of the different kinds of things, and for the changes of the seasons; ³and to present before Him petitions for our existing again in incorruption through faith in Him. ⁴Our teacher of these things is Jesus Christ, who also was born for this purpose, and was crucified under Pontius Pilate, procurator of Judea, in the times of Tiberius Caesar; ⁵and that we reasonably worship Him, having learned that He is the Son of the true God Himself, and holding Him in the second place, and the prophetic Spirit in the third, we will prove. ⁶For they proclaim our madness to consist in this, that we give to a crucified man a place second to the unchangeable and eternal God, the Creator of all; for they do not discern the mystery that is herein, to which, as we make it plain to you, we pray you to give heed.

CHAPTER 14

¹For we forewarn you to be on your guard, lest those demons whom we have been accusing should deceive you, and quite divert you from reading and understanding what we say. ²For they strive to hold you [as] their slaves and servants; and sometimes by appearances in dreams, and sometimes by magical impositions, they subdue all who make no strong opposing effort for their own salvation. ³And thus we also, because of our persuasion by the Word, stand apart from them, and follow the only unbegotten God through His Son—we who formerly delighted in fornication, but now embrace chastity alone; ⁴we who formerly used magical arts, dedicate ourselves to the good and unbegotten God; we who valued above all things the acquisition of wealth and possessions, now bring what we have into a common stock, and communicate to everyone in need; ⁵we who

hated and destroyed one another, and on account of their different manners would not live with men of a different tribe, now, since the coming of Christ, live familiarly with them, and pray for our enemies, and endeavor to persuade those who hate us unjustly to live conformably to the good precepts of Christ, to the end that they may become partakers with us of the same joyful hope of a reward from God the ruler of all. ⁶But lest we should seem to be reasoning sophistically, we consider it right, before giving you the promised explanation, to cite a few precepts given by Christ Himself. ⁷And be it yours, as powerful rulers, to inquire whether we have been taught and teach these things accurately. Brief and concise utterances fell from Him, for He was no sophist, but His word was the power of God.

CHAPTER 15

¹Concerning chastity, He uttered such sentiments as these: "Whosoever looks on a woman to lust after her, has committed adultery with her already in his heart before God." ²And, "If your right eye offend you, cut it out; for it is better for you to enter into the kingdom of the heavens with one eye, than, having two eyes, to be cast into continuous fire." ³And, "Whosoever will marry her that is divorced from another husband, commits adultery." ⁴And, "There are some who have been made eunuchs of men, and some who were born eunuchs, and some who have made themselves eunuchs for the kingdom of the heavens' sake; but all cannot receive this saying." ⁵So that all who, by human law, are twice married, are in the eye of our Master sinners, and those who look on a woman to lust after her. ⁶For not only he who in act commits adultery is rejected by Him, but also he who desires to commit adultery: since not only our works, but also our thoughts, are open before God. ⁷And many, both men and women, who have been Christ's disciples from childhood, remain pure at the age of sixty or seventy years; and I boast that I could produce such from every race of men. ⁸For what will I say, too, of the countless multitude of those who have reformed uncontrolled habits, and learned these things? ⁹For Christ called not the just nor the chaste to conversion, but the ungodly, and the licentious, and the unjust; His words being, "I came not to call the righteous, but sinners to conversion." ¹⁰For the heavenly Father desires rather the conversion than the punishment of the sinner. ¹¹And of our love to all, He taught thus: "If you love them that love you, what new thing are you doing? For even fornicators do this. But I say to you, pray for your enemies, and love them that hate you, and bless them that curse you, and pray for them that despitefully use you." ¹²And that we should communicate to the needy, and do nothing for glory, He said, "Give to him that asks, and from him that would borrow do not turn away; for if you lend to them of whom you hope to receive, what new thing are you doing? Even the tax collectors do this. ¹³Do not lay up for yourselves treasure on earth, where moth and rust corrupt, and where robbers break through; but lay up for yourselves treasure in Heaven, where neither moth nor rust corrupt. ¹⁴For what is a man profited, if he will gain the whole world, and lose his own soul? Or what will a man give in exchange for it? Lay up treasure, therefore, in Heaven, where neither moth nor rust corrupt." ¹⁵And, "Be kind and merciful, as your Father also is kind and merciful, and makes His sun to rise on sinners, and the righteous, and the wicked. ¹⁶Take no thought of what you will eat, or what you will put on: are you not better than the birds and the beasts? And God feeds them. Take no thought, therefore, what you will eat, or what you will put on; for your heavenly Father knows that you have need of these things. ¹⁷But seek the kingdom of the heavens, and all these things will be added to you. For where his treasure is, there also is the mind of a man." ¹⁸And, "Do not do these things to be seen of men; otherwise you have no reward from your Father which is in Heaven."

CHAPTER 16

¹And concerning our being patient of injuries, and ready to serve all, and free from anger, this is what He said: "To him that strikes you on the one cheek, offer also the other; and him that takes away your cloak or coat, do not forbid [it]. ²And whosoever will be angry is in danger of the fire. And everyone that compels you to go with him a mile, follow him two. ³And let your good works shine before men, that they, seeing them, may glorify your Father which is in Heaven." ⁴For we ought not to strive; neither has He desired us to be imitators of wicked men, but He has exhorted us to lead all men, by patience and gentleness, from shame and the love of evil. ⁵And this indeed is proved in the case of many who once were of your way of thinking, but have changed their violent and tyrannical disposition, being overcome either by the constancy which they have witnessed in their neighbors' lives, or by the extraordinary forbearance they have observed in their fellow-travelers when defrauded, or by the honesty of those with whom they have transacted business. ⁶And with regard to our not swearing at all, and always speaking the truth, He enjoined as follows: "Do not swear at all; but let your yes be yes, and your no, no; for whatsoever is more than these comes from evil." ⁷And that we ought to worship God alone, He thus persuaded us: "The greatest commandment is, You will worship the LORD your God, and Him only will you serve, with all your heart, and with all your strength, the LORD God that made you." ⁸And when a certain man came to Him and said, "Good Master," He answered and said, "There is none good but God only, who made all things." ⁹And let those who are not found living as He taught, be understood to be no Christians, even though they profess with the lip the precepts of Christ; ¹⁰for not those who make profession, but those who do the works, will be saved, according to His word: "Not everyone who says to Me, Lord, Lord, will enter into the kingdom of the heavens, but he that does the will of My Father which is in Heaven. For whosoever hears Me, and does My sayings, hears Him that sent Me. ¹¹And many will say to Me, Lord, Lord, have we not eaten and drunk in Your Name, and done wonders? And then will I say to them, Depart from Me, you workers of iniquity. ¹²Then will there be wailing and gnashing of teeth, when the righteous will shine as the sun, and the wicked are sent into continuous fire. ¹³For many will come in My Name, clothed outwardly in sheep's clothing, but inwardly being ravening wolves. By their works you will know them. And every tree that does not bring forth good fruit, is cut down and cast into the fire." ¹⁴And as for those who are not living pursuant to these teachings of His, and are Christians only in name, we demand that all such be punished by you.

CHAPTER 17

¹And everywhere we, more readily than all men, endeavor to pay to those appointed by you the taxes both ordinary and extraordinary, as we have been taught by Him; ²for at that time some came to Him and asked Him if one ought to pay tribute to Caesar; and He answered, "Tell Me, whose image does the coin bear?" And they said, "Caesar's." ³And again, He answered them, "Render therefore to Caesar the things that are Caesar's, and to God the things that are God's." From which to God alone we render worship, but in other things we gladly serve you, acknowledging you as kings and rulers of men, and praying that with your kingly power you are found to also possess sound judgment. ⁴But if you pay no regard to our prayers and frank explanations, we will suffer no loss, since we believe (or rather, indeed, are persuaded) that every man will suffer punishment in continuous fire according to the merit of his deed, and will render account according to the power he has received from God, as Christ intimated when He said, "To whom God has given more, of him will more be required."

CHAPTER 18

¹For reflect on the end of each of the preceding kings, how they died the death common to all, which, if it issued in insensibility, would be a godsend to all the wicked. ²But since sensation remains to all who have ever lived, and continuous punishment is laid up [for the wicked], see that you do not neglect to be convinced, and to hold as your belief, that these things are true. ³For let even necromancy, and the divinations you practice by immaculate children, and the evoking of departed human souls, and those who are called among the magi, Dream-senders and Assistant-spirits, and all that is done by those who are skilled in such matters—let these persuade you that even after death souls are in a state of sensation; ⁴and those who are seized and cast about by the spirits of the dead, whom all call demoniacs or madmen;

and what you repute as oracles, both of Amphilochus, Dodana, Pytho, and as many other such as exist; and the opinions of your authors, Empedocles and Pythagoras, Plato and Socrates, and the pit of Homer, and the descent of Ulysses to inspect these things, and all that has been uttered of a similar kind. ⁵Such favor as you grant to these, grant also to us, who not less but more firmly than they believe in God; since we expect to receive again our own bodies, though they are dead and cast into the earth, for we maintain that with God nothing is impossible.

CHAPTER 19

¹And to any thoughtful person would anything appear more incredible, than, if we were not in the body, and someone were to say that it was possible that from a small drop of human seed bones, and sinews, and flesh be formed into a shape such as we see? ²For let this now be said hypothetically: if you yourselves were not such as you now are, and born of such parents [and causes], and one were to show you human seed and a picture of a man, and were to say with confidence that from such a substance such a being could be produced, would you believe before you saw the actual production? ³No one will dare to deny [that such a statement would surpass belief]. ⁴In the same way, then, you are now incredulous because you have never seen a dead man rise again. ⁵But as at first you would not have believed it possible that such persons could be produced from the small drop, and yet now you see them thus produced, so also judge that it is not impossible that the bodies of men, after they have been dissolved, and like seeds resolved into earth, should in God's appointed time rise again and put on incorruption. ⁶For what power worthy of God those imagine who say that each thing returns to that from which it was produced, and that beyond this not even God Himself can do anything, we are unable to conceive; ⁷but this we see clearly, that they would not have believed it possible that they could have become such and produced from such materials, as they now see both themselves and the whole world to be. ⁸And that it is better to believe even what is impossible to our own nature and to men, than to be unbelieving like the rest of the world, we have learned; ⁹for we know that our Master Jesus Christ said, "What is impossible with men is possible with God," and, "Do not fear them that kill you, and after that can do no more; but fear Him who after death is able to cast both soul and body into Gehenna." ¹⁰And Gehenna is a place where those are to be punished who have lived wickedly, and who do not believe that those things which God has taught us by Christ will come to pass.

CHAPTER 20

¹And the Sibyl and Hystaspes said that there should be a dissolution by God of corruptible things. ²And the philosophers called Stoics teach that even God Himself will be resolved into fire, and they say that the world is to be formed anew by this revolution; but we understand that God, the Creator of all things, is superior to the things that are to be changed. ³If, therefore, on some points we teach the same things as the poets and philosophers whom you honor, and on other points are fuller and more divine in our teaching, and if we alone afford proof of what we assert, why are we unjustly hated more than all others? ⁴For while we say that all things have been produced and arranged into a world by God, we will seem to utter the doctrine of Plato; ⁵and while we say that there will be a burning up of all, we will seem to utter the doctrine of the Stoics; ⁶and while we affirm that the souls of the wicked, being endowed with sensation even after death, are punished, and that those of the good being delivered from punishment spend a blessed existence, we will seem to say the same things as the poets and philosophers; ⁷and while we maintain that men ought not to worship the works of their hands, we say the very things which have been said by the comic poet Menander, and other similar writers, for they have declared that the workman is greater than the work.

CHAPTER 21

¹And when we also say that the Word, who is the first-begotten of God, was produced without sexual union, and that He, Jesus Christ, our Teacher, was crucified and died, and rose again, and ascended into Heaven, we propound nothing different from what you believe regarding those whom you esteem sons of Jupiter. ²For you know how many sons your esteemed writers ascribed to Jupiter: Mercury, the interpreting word and teacher of all; Asclepius, who, though he was a great physician, was struck by a thunderbolt, and so ascended to heaven; and Bacchus too, after he had been torn limb from limb; and Hercules, when he had committed himself to the flames to escape his toils; and the sons of Leda, and Dioscuri; and Perseus, son of Danae; and Bellerophon, who, though sprung from mortals, rose to heaven on the horse Pegasus. ³For what will I say of Ariadne, and those who, like her, have been declared to be set among the stars? ⁴And what of the emperors who die among yourselves, whom you deem worthy of deification, and in whose behalf you produce someone who swears he has seen the burning Caesar rise to heaven from the funeral pyre? ⁵And what kind of deeds are recorded of each of these reputed sons of Jupiter, it is needless to tell to those who already know. ⁶This only will be said: that they are written for the advantage and encouragement of youthful scholars; for all reckon it an honorable thing to imitate the gods. ⁷But far be such a thought concerning the gods from every well-conditioned soul, as to believe that Jupiter himself, the governor and creator of all things, was both a parricide and the son of a parricide, and that being overcome by the love of base and shameful pleasures, he came in to Ganymede and those many women whom he had violated and that his sons did like actions. ⁸But, as we said above, wicked devils perpetrated these things. ⁹And we have learned that those only are deified who have lived near to God in holiness and virtue; and we believe that those who live wickedly and do not convert are punished in continuous fire.

CHAPTER 22

¹Moreover, the Son of God called Jesus, even if only a man by ordinary generation, yet, on account of His wisdom, is worthy to be called the Son of God; for all writers call God the Father of men and gods. ²And if we assert that the Word of God was born of God in a peculiar manner, different from ordinary generation, let this, as said above, be no extraordinary thing to you, who say that Mercury is the angelic word of God. ³But if anyone objects that He was crucified, in this also He is on par with those reputed sons of Jupiter of yours, who suffered as we have now enumerated. ⁴For their sufferings at death are recorded to have been not all alike, but diverse; so that not even by the peculiarity of His sufferings does He seem to be inferior to them; ⁵but, on the contrary, as we promised in the preceding part of this discourse, we will now prove Him superior—or rather have already proved Him to be so—for the superior is revealed by His actions. ⁶And if we even affirm that He was born of a virgin, accept this in common with what you accept of Perseus. ⁷And in that we say that He made whole the lame, the paralytic, and those born blind, we seem to say what is very similar to the deeds said to have been done by Asclepius.

CHAPTER 23

¹And that this may now become evident to you—that whatever we assert in conformity with what has been taught us by Christ, and by the prophets who preceded Him, are alone true, and are older than all the writers who have existed; ²that we claim to be acknowledged, not because we say the same things as these writers said, but because we say true things; ³and that Jesus Christ is the only proper Son who has been begotten by God, being His Word and first-begotten, and power; ⁴and, becoming man according to His will, He taught us these things for the conversion and restoration of the human race; ⁵and that before He became a man among men, some, influenced by the demons before mentioned, related beforehand, through the instrumentality of the poets, those circumstances as having really happened, which, having fictitiously devised, they narrated, in the same manner as they have caused to be fabricated the scandalous reports against us of infamous and impious actions, of which there is neither witness nor proof—we will bring forward the following proof.

CHAPTER 24

¹In the first place [we furnish proof], because, though we say things similar to what the Greeks say, we alone are hated on account of

the Name of Christ, and though we do no wrong, are put to death as sinners; ²other men in other places worshiping trees, and rivers, and mice, and cats, and crocodiles, and many irrational animals. ³Nor are the same animals esteemed by all; but in one place one is worshiped, and another in another, so that all are profane in the judgment of one another, on account of their not worshiping the same objects. ⁴And this is the sole accusation you bring against us, that we do not reverence the same gods as you do, nor offer to the dead libations and the savor of fat, and crowns for their statues, and sacrifices. ⁵For you very well know that the same animals are with some esteemed gods, with others wild beasts, and with others sacrificial victims.

CHAPTER 25

¹And, secondly, because we—who, out of every race of men, used to worship Bacchus the son of Semele, and Apollo the son of Latona (who in their loves with men did such things as it is shameful even to mention), and Proserpine and Venus (who were maddened with love of Adonis, and whose mysteries also you celebrate), or Asclepius, or someone or other of those who are called gods—have now, through Jesus Christ, learned to despise these, though we are threatened with death for it, and have dedicated ourselves to the unbegotten and impassible God; ²of whom we are persuaded that never was he goaded by lust of Antiope, or such other women, or of Ganymede, nor was rescued by that hundred-handed giant whose aid was obtained through Thetis, nor was anxious on this account that her son Achilles should destroy many of the Greeks because of his concubine Briseis. ³Those who believe these things we pity, and those who invented them we know to be devils.

CHAPTER 26

¹And, thirdly, because after Christ's ascension into Heaven the devils put forward certain men who said that they themselves were gods; and they were not only not persecuted by you, but even deemed worthy of honors. ²There was a Samaritan, Simon, a native of the village called Gitto, who in the reign of Claudius Caesar, and in your royal city of Rome, did mighty acts of magic, by virtue of the art of the devils operating in him. ³He was considered a god, and as a god was honored by you with a statue, which statue was erected on the Tiber River, between the two bridges, and bore this inscription, in the language of Rome: SIMONI DEO SANCTO, TO SIMON THE HOLY GOD. ⁴And almost all the Samaritans, and a few even of other nations, worship him, and acknowledge him as the first god; and a woman, Helena, who went around with him at that time, and had formerly been a prostitute, they say is the first idea generated by him. ⁵And a man, Menander, also a Samaritan, of the town Capparetaea, a disciple of Simon, and inspired by devils, we know to have deceived many while he was in Antioch by his magical art. ⁶He persuaded those who adhered to him that they should never die, and even now there are some living who hold this opinion of his. And there is Marcion, a man of Pontus, who is even at this day alive, and teaching his disciples to believe in some other god greater than the Creator. ⁷And he, by the aid of the devils, has caused many of every nation to speak blasphemies, and to deny that God is the maker of this universe, and to assert that some other being, greater than He, has done greater works. ⁸All who take their opinions from these men, are, as we before said, called Christians; just as also those who do not agree with the philosophers in their doctrines, have yet in common with them the name of philosophers given to them. ⁹And whether they perpetrate those fabulous and shameful deeds—the upsetting of the lamp, and promiscuous intercourse, and eating human flesh—we know not; but we do know that they are neither persecuted nor put to death by you, at least on account of their opinions. ¹⁰But I have a treatise against all the heresies that have existed already composed, which, if you wish to read it, I will give you.

CHAPTER 27

¹But as for us, we have been taught that to expose newborn children is the part of wicked men; ²and this we have been taught lest we should do anyone an injury, and lest we should sin against God, first, because we see that almost all so exposed (not only the girls, but also the males) are brought up to prostitution. ³And as the ancients are said to have reared herds of oxen, or goats, or sheep, or grazing horses, so now we see you rear children only for this shameful use; ⁴and for this pollution a multitude of females and hermaphrodites, and those who commit unmentionable iniquities, are found in every nation. ⁵And you receive the hire of these, and duty and taxes from them, whom you ought to exterminate from your realm. ⁶And anyone who uses such persons, besides the godless, and infamous, and impure intercourse, may possibly be having intercourse with his own child, or relative, or brother. ⁷And there are some who prostitute even their own children and wives, and some are openly mutilated for the purpose of sodomy; ⁸and they refer these mysteries to the mother of the gods, and along with each of those whom you esteem gods there is painted a serpent, a great symbol and mystery. ⁹Indeed, the things which you do openly and with applause, as if the divine light were overturned and extinguished, these you lay to our charge; which, in truth, does no harm to us who shrink from doing any such things, but only to those who do them and bear false witness against us.

CHAPTER 28

¹For among us the prince of the wicked spirits is called the serpent, and "Satan," and the "Devil," as you can learn by looking into our writings. ²And that he would be sent into the fire with his host, and the men who follow him, and would be punished for an endless duration, Christ foretold. ³For the reason why God has delayed to do this, is His regard for the human race. For He foreknows that some are to be saved by conversion, some even that are perhaps not yet born. ⁴In the beginning He made the human race with the power of thought and of choosing the truth and doing right, so that all men are without excuse before God; for they have been born rational and contemplative. ⁵And if anyone disbelieves that God cares for these things, he will thereby either insinuate that God does not exist, or he will assert that though He exists He delights in vice, or exists like a stone, and that neither virtue nor vice are anything, but only in the opinion of men these things are reckoned good or evil. And this is the greatest profanity and wickedness.

CHAPTER 29

¹And again [we fear to expose children], lest some of them are not picked up, but die, and we become murderers. ²But whether we marry, it is only that we may bring up children; or whether we decline marriage, we live continently. ³And that you may understand that promiscuous intercourse is not one of our mysteries, one of our number a short time ago presented to Felix the governor in Alexandria a petition, craving that permission might be given to a surgeon to make him a eunuch. ⁴For the surgeons there said that they were forbidden to do this without the permission of the governor. ⁵And when Felix absolutely refused to sign such a permission, the youth remained single, and was satisfied with his own approving conscience, and the approval of those who thought as he did. ⁶And it is not out of place, we think, to mention here Antinous, who was alive but lately, and whom all were prompt, through fear, to worship as a god, though they knew both who he was and what was his origin.

CHAPTER 30

¹But lest anyone should meet us with the question, "What should prevent that He whom we call Christ, being a man born of men, performed what we call His mighty works by magical art, and by this appeared to be the Son of God?" ²We will now offer proof, not trusting mere assertions, but being of necessity persuaded by those who prophesied [of Him] before these things came to pass, for with our own eyes we behold things that have happened and are happening just as they were predicted; and this will we think appear even to you the strongest and truest evidence.

CHAPTER 31

¹There were, then, among the Jews certain men who were prophets of God, through whom the prophetic Spirit published things beforehand that were to come to pass, before they ever happened. ²And their prophecies, as they were spoken and when they were uttered, the kings who happened to be reigning among the Jews at the different times carefully preserved in their possession, when

they had been arranged in books by the prophets themselves in their own Hebrew language. ³And when Ptolemy king of Egypt formed a library, and endeavored to collect the writings of all men, he also heard of these prophets, and sent to Herod, who was at that time king of the Jews, requesting that the books of the prophets be sent to him. And Herod the king did indeed send them, written, as they were, in the aforementioned Hebrew language. ⁴And when their contents were found to be unintelligible to the Egyptians, he again sent and requested that men be commissioned to translate them into the Greek language. ⁵And when this was done, the books remained with the Egyptians, where they are until now. ⁶They are also in the possession of all Jews throughout the world; but they, though they read, do not understand what is said, but count us foes and enemies; and, like yourselves, they kill and punish us whenever they have the power, as you can well believe. ⁷For in the Jewish war which lately raged, Simon bar Kokhba, the leader of the revolt of the Jews, gave orders that Christians alone should be led to cruel punishments, unless they would deny Jesus Christ and utter blasphemy. ⁸In these books, then, of the prophets we found Jesus our Christ foretold as coming, born of a virgin, growing up to man's estate, and healing every disease and every sickness, and raising the dead, and being hated, and unrecognized, and crucified, and dying, and rising again, and ascending into Heaven, and being called the Son of God. ⁹We find it also predicted that certain persons should be sent by Him into every nation to publish these things, and that rather among the nations [than among the Jews] men should believe in Him. ¹⁰And He was predicted before He appeared, first five thousand years before, and again three thousand, then two thousand, then one thousand, and yet again eight hundred; for in the succession of generations prophet after prophet arose.

CHAPTER 32

¹Moses then, who was the first of the prophets, spoke in these very words: "The scepter will not depart from Judah, nor a lawgiver from between his feet, until He come for whom it is reserved; and He will be the desire of the nations, binding His foal to the vine, washing His robe in the blood of the grape." ²It is yours to make accurate inquiry, and ascertain up to whose time the Jews had a lawgiver and king of their own. ³Up to the time of Jesus Christ, who taught us, and interpreted the prophecies which were not yet understood, [they had a lawgiver] as was foretold by the holy and divine Spirit of prophecy through Moses, that a ruler would not fail the Jews until He should come for whom the kingdom was reserved (for Judah was the forefather of the Jews, from whom they also have their name of Jews); ⁴and after He appeared, you began to rule the Jews, and gained possession of all their territory. ⁵And the prophecy, "He will be the expectation of the nations," signified that there would be some of all nations who should look for Him to come again. ⁶And this indeed you can see for yourselves and be convinced of by fact. For of all races of men there are some who look for Him who was crucified in Judea, and after whose crucifixion the land was promptly surrendered to you as spoil of war. ⁷And the prophecy, "binding His foal to the vine, and washing His robe in the blood of the grape," was a significant symbol of the things that were to happen to Christ, and of what He was to do. ⁸For the foal of a donkey stood bound to a vine at the entrance of a village, and He ordered His acquaintances to bring it to Him then; and when it was brought, He mounted and sat on it, and entered Jerusalem, where the vast temple of the Jews was which was afterward destroyed by you. ⁹And after this He was crucified, that the rest of the prophecy might be fulfilled. ¹⁰For this washing His robe in the blood of the grape was predictive of the passion He was to endure, cleansing by His blood those who believe in Him. ¹¹For what is called by the Divine Spirit through the prophet His robe, are those men who believe in Him in whom abides the seed of God, the Word. ¹²And what is spoken of as the blood of the grape, signifies that He who should appear would have blood, though not of the seed of man, but of the power of God. ¹³And the first power after God the Father and Lord of all is the Word, who is also the Son; and of Him we will, in what follows, relate how He took flesh and became man. ¹⁴For as man did not make the blood of the vine, but God, so it was hereby intimated that the blood should not be of human seed, but of divine power, as we have said above. ¹⁵And Isaiah, another prophet, foretelling the same things in other words, spoke thus: "A star will rise out of Jacob, || And a flower will spring from the root of Jesse; And His arm will the nations trust." ¹⁶And a star of light has arisen, and a flower has sprung from the root of Jesse—this Christ. ¹⁷For by the power of God He was conceived by a virgin of the seed of Jacob, who was the father of Judah, who, as we have shown, was the father of the Jews; and Jesse was His forefather according to the oracle, and He was the son of Jacob and Judah according to lineal descent.

CHAPTER 33

¹And hear again how Isaiah in express words foretold that He should be born of a virgin; for he spoke thus: "Behold, a virgin will conceive, || And bring forth a Son, || And they will say for His Name, God with us." ²For things which were incredible and seemed impossible with men, these God predicted by the Spirit of prophecy as about to come to pass, in order that, when they came to pass, there might be no unbelief, but faith, because of their prediction. ³But lest some, not understanding the prophecy now cited, should charge us with the very things we have been laying to the charge of the poets who say that Jupiter went in to women through lust, let us try to explain the words. ⁴This, then, "Behold, a virgin will conceive," signifies that a virgin should conceive without intercourse. ⁵For if she had had intercourse with anyone whatsoever, she was no longer a virgin; but the power of God having come on the virgin, overshadowed her, and caused her while yet a virgin to conceive. ⁶And the messenger of God who was sent to the same virgin at that time brought her good news, saying, "Behold, you will conceive of the Holy Spirit, and will bear a Son, and He will be called the Son of the Highest, and you will call His Name Jesus, for He will save His people from their sins"; as they who have recorded all that concerns our Savior Jesus Christ have taught, whom we believed, since by Isaiah also, whom we have now adduced, the Spirit of prophecy declared that He should be born as we intimated before. ⁷It is wrong, therefore, to understand the Spirit and the power of God as anything else than the Word, who is also the first-begotten of God, as the aforementioned prophet Moses declared; and it was this which, when it came on the virgin and overshadowed her, caused her to conceive, not by intercourse, but by power. ⁸And the Name Jesus in the Hebrew language means "Savior" in the Greek tongue. Therefore, too, the messenger said to the virgin, "You will call His Name Jesus, for He will save His people from their sins." ⁹And that the prophets are inspired by no other than the Divine Word, even you, as I desire, will grant.

CHAPTER 34

¹And hear what part of earth He was to be born in, as another prophet, Micah, foretold. He spoke thus: "And you, Beth-Lehem, the land of Judah, are not the least among the princes of Judah; for out of you will come forth a Governor, who will feed My people." ²Now there is a village in the land of the Jews, thirty-five stadia from Jerusalem, in which Jesus Christ was born, as you can also ascertain from the registers of the taxing made under Cyrenius, your first procurator in Judea.

CHAPTER 35

¹And how Christ after He was born was to escape the notice of other men until He grew to man's estate, which also came to pass, hear what was foretold regarding this. ²There are the following predictions: "To us a Child is born, || And to us a Son is given, || And the government will be on His shoulders"; which is significant of the power of the Cross, for to it, when He was crucified, He applied His shoulders, as will be more clearly made out in the ensuing discourse. ³And again, the same prophet Isaiah, being inspired by the prophetic Spirit, said, "I have spread out My hands to a disobedient and opposing people, || To those who walk in a way that is not good. They now ask of Me judgment, || And dare to draw near to God." ⁴And again, in other words, through another prophet, He says, "They pierced My hands and My feet, || And for My vesture they cast lots." ⁵And indeed David, the king and prophet, who uttered these things, suffered none of them; but Jesus Christ stretched forth His hands, being crucified by

the Jews speaking against Him, and denying that He was the Christ. ⁶And as the prophet spoke, they tormented Him, and set Him on the judgment-seat, and said, "Judge us." ⁷And the expression, "They pierced My hands and My feet," was used in reference to the nails of the Cross which were fixed in His hands and feet. ⁸And after He was crucified, they cast lots on His vesture, and they that crucified Him parted it among them. ⁹And that these things happened, you can ascertain from the Acts of Pontius Pilate. ¹⁰And we will cite the prophetic utterances of another prophet, Zephaniah, to the effect that He was foretold expressly as to sit on the foal of a donkey and to enter Jerusalem. ¹¹The words are these: "Rejoice greatly, O daughter of Zion; Shout, O daughter of Jerusalem: Behold, your King comes to you, || Lowly, and riding on a donkey, and on a colt, the foal of a donkey."

CHAPTER 36
¹But when you hear the utterances of the prophets spoken as it were personally, you must not suppose that they are spoken by the inspired themselves, but by the Divine Word who moves them. ²For sometimes He declares things that are to come to pass, in the manner of one who foretells the future; ³sometimes He speaks as from the person of God the Lord and Father of all; sometimes as from the person of Christ; ⁴sometimes as from the person of the people answering the Lord or His Father, just as you can see even in your own writers, one man being the writer of the whole, but introducing the persons who converse. ⁵And this the Jews who possessed the books of the prophets did not understand, and therefore did not recognize Christ even when He came, but even hate us who say that He has come, and who prove that, as was predicted, He was crucified by them.

CHAPTER 37
¹And that this too may be clear to you, there were spoken from the person of the Father through Isaiah the prophet, the following words: "The ox knows his owner, || And the donkey his master's crib; But Israel does not know, || And My people have not understood. Woe, sinful nation, a people full of sins, || A wicked seed, children that are transgressors, || You have forsaken the LORD." ²And again elsewhere, when the same prophet speaks in the same manner from the person of the Father, "What is the house that you will build for Me? Says the LORD. The heavens are My throne, || And the earth is My footstool." ³And again, in another place, "Your new moons and your sabbaths My soul hates, || And the great day of the fast and of ceasing from labor I cannot endure; Nor, if you come to be seen of Me, will I hear you: Your hands are full of blood; And if you bring fine flour, incense, || It is an abomination to Me: The fat of lambs and the blood of bulls I do not desire. For who has required this at your hands? But release every bond of wickedness, || Tear asunder the tight knots of violent contracts, || Cover the homeless and naked, || Deal your bread to the hungry." ⁴What kind of things are taught through the prophets from [the person of] God, you can now perceive.

CHAPTER 38
¹And when the Spirit of prophecy speaks from the person of Christ, the utterances are of this sort: "I have spread out My hands to a disobedient and opposing people, || To those who walk in a way that is not good." ²And again: "I gave My back to the scourges, || And My cheeks to the beatings; I did not turn away My face from the shame of spittings; And the LORD was My helper: Therefore I was not confounded, || But I set My face as a firm rock, || And I knew that I should not be ashamed, || For He is near that justifies Me." ³And again, He says, "They cast lots on My vesture, || And pierced My hands and My feet. And I lay down and slept, || And rose again, because the LORD sustained Me." ⁴And again, He says, "They spoke with their lips, they wagged the head, || Saying, Let Him deliver Himself." ⁵And that all these things happened to Christ at the hands of the Jews, you can ascertain. For when He was crucified, they did shoot out the lip, and wagged their heads, saying, "Let Him who raised the dead save Himself."

CHAPTER 39
¹And when the Spirit of prophecy speaks as predicting things that are to come to pass, He speaks in this way: "For out of Zion will go forth the law, || And the word of the LORD from Jerusalem. And He will judge among the nations, || And will rebuke many people; And they will beat their swords into plowshares, || And their spears into pruning-hooks: Nation will not lift up sword against nation, || Neither will they learn war anymore." ²And that it did so come to pass, we can convince you. For from Jerusalem there went out into the world, men, twelve in number, and these illiterate, of no ability in speaking: but by the power of God they proclaimed to every race of men that they were sent by Christ to teach to all the word of God; ³and we who formerly used to murder one another do not only now refrain from making war on our enemies, but also, that we may not lie nor deceive our examiners, willingly die confessing Christ. ⁴For that saying, "The tongue has sworn but the mind is unsworn," might be imitated by us in this matter. ⁵But if the soldiers enrolled by you, and who have taken the military oath, prefer their allegiance to their own life, and parents, and country, and all kindred, though you can offer them nothing incorruptible, it were truly ridiculous if we, who earnestly long for incorruption, should not endure all things, in order to obtain what we desire from Him who is able to grant it.

CHAPTER 40
¹And hear how it was foretold concerning those who published His doctrine and proclaimed His appearance, the aforementioned prophet and king speaking thus by the Spirit of prophecy: "Day to day utters speech, || And night to night shows knowledge. There is no speech nor language where their voice is not heard. Their voice has gone out into all the earth, || And their words to the ends of the world. In the sun He has set His tabernacle, || And he as a bridegroom going out of his chamber will rejoice as a giant to run his course." ²And we have thought it right and relevant to mention some other prophetic utterances of David besides these; from which you may learn how the Spirit of prophecy exhorts men to live, and how He foretold the conspiracy which was formed against Christ by Herod the king of the Jews, and the Jews themselves, and Pilate, who was your governor among them, with his soldiers; ³and how He should be believed on by men of every race; and how God calls Him His Son, and has declared that He will subdue all His enemies under Him; and how the devils, as much as they can, strive to escape the power of God the Father and Lord of all, and the power of Christ Himself; and how God calls all to conversion before the Day of Judgment comes. ⁴These things were uttered thus: "Blessed is the man who has not walked in the counsel of the ungodly, || Nor stood in the way of sinners, || Nor sat in the seat of the scornful: But his delight is in the Law of the LORD; And in His law he will meditate day and night. ⁵And he will be like a tree planted by the rivers of waters, || Which will give his fruit in his season; And his leaf will not wither, || And whatsoever he does will prosper. ⁶The ungodly are not so, || But are like the chaff which the wind drives away from the face of the earth. ⁷Therefore, the ungodly will not stand in the judgment, || Nor sinners in the council of the righteous. For the LORD knows the way of the righteous; But the way of the ungodly will perish. ⁸Why do the heathen rage, || And the people imagine new things? The kings of the earth set themselves, || And the rulers take counsel together, || Against the LORD, and against His Anointed, saying, || Let us break Their bands apart, || And cast Their yoke from us. He that dwells in the heavens will laugh at them, || And the LORD will have them in derision. ⁹Then He will speak to them in His wrath, || And trouble them in His sore displeasure. Yet I have been set by Him a King on Zion His holy hill, || Declaring the decree of the LORD. The LORD said to Me, You are My Son, this day have I begotten You. Ask of Me, and I will give You the heathen for Your inheritance, || And the uttermost parts of the earth as Your possession. ¹⁰You will herd them with a rod of iron; As the vessels of a potter, You will dash them in pieces. Be wise now, therefore, O you kings; Be instructed, all you judges of the earth. Serve the LORD with fear, || And rejoice with trembling. ¹¹Embrace instruction, lest at any time the LORD be angry, || And you perish from the right way, || When His wrath has been suddenly kindled. Blessed are all they that put their trust in Him."

CHAPTER 41
¹And again, in another prophecy, the Spirit of prophecy, through the same David, intimated that Christ, after He had been crucified, should

reign, and spoke as follows: "Sing to the LORD, all the earth, || And day by day declare His salvation. For great is the LORD, || And greatly to be praised, || To be feared above all the gods. For all the gods of the nations are idols of devils; But God made the heavens. ²Glory and praise are before His face, || Strength and glorying are in the habitation of His holiness. Give Glory to the LORD, the Father everlasting. Receive grace, and enter His presence, || And worship in His holy courts. ³Let all the earth fear before His face; Let it be established, and not shaken. Let them rejoice among the nations. The LORD has reigned from the tree."

CHAPTER 42

¹But when the Spirit of prophecy speaks of things that are about to come to pass as if they had already taken place—as may be observed even in the passages already cited by me—that this circumstance may afford no excuse to readers [for misinterpreting them], we will make even this also quite plain. ²The things which He absolutely knows will take place, He predicts as if already they had taken place. ³And that the utterances must be thus received, you will perceive, if you give your attention to them. ⁴The words cited above, David uttered [[one thousand five hundred]] years before Christ became a man and was crucified; and no one of those who lived before Him, nor yet of His contemporaries, afforded joy to the nations by being crucified. ⁵But our Jesus Christ, being crucified and dead, rose again, and having ascended to Heaven, reigned; and by those things which were published in His Name among all nations by the apostles, there is joy afforded to those who expect the immortality promised by Him.

CHAPTER 43

¹But lest some suppose, from what has been said by us, that we say that whatever happens, happens by a fatal necessity, because it is foretold as known beforehand, this too we explain. ²We have learned from the prophets, and we hold it to be true, that punishments, and chastisements, and good rewards, are rendered according to the merit of each man's actions. ³Since if it is not so, but all things happen by fate, neither is anything at all in our own power. For if it is fated that this man is good, and this other evil, neither is the former meritorious nor the latter to be blamed. ⁴And again, unless the human race has the power of avoiding evil and choosing good by free choice, they are not accountable for their actions, of whatever kind they are. ⁵But that it is by free choice they both walk uprightly and stumble, we thus demonstrate. We see the same man making a transition to opposite things. ⁶Now, if it had been fated that he were to be either good or bad, he could never have been capable of both the opposites, nor of so many transitions. ⁷But not even would some be good and others bad, since we thus make fate the cause of evil, and exhibit her as acting in opposition to herself; or that which has been already stated would seem to be true, that neither virtue nor vice is anything, but that things are only reckoned good or evil by opinion; which, as the true word shows, is the greatest impiety and wickedness. ⁸But this we assert is inevitable fate, that they who choose the good have worthy rewards, and they who choose the opposite have their merited awards. ⁹For not like other things, as trees and quadrupeds, which cannot act by choice, did God make man: for neither would he be worthy of reward or praise did he not of himself choose the good, but were created for this end; ¹⁰nor, if he were evil, would he be worthy of punishment, not being evil of himself, but being able to be nothing else than what he was made.

CHAPTER 44

¹And the Holy Spirit of prophecy taught us this, telling us by Moses that God spoke thus to the man first created: "Behold, before your face are good and evil: choose the good." ²And again, by the other prophet Isaiah, that the following utterance was made as if from God the Father and Lord of all: "Wash yourselves, || Make yourselves clean; Put away evils from your souls; Learn to do well; Judge the orphan, || And plead for the widow; And come and let us reason together, says the LORD: And if your sins are as scarlet, || I will make them white as wool; And if they are red like as crimson, || I will make them white as snow. ³And if you are willing and obey Me, || You will eat the good of the land; But if you do not obey Me, || The sword will devour you: For the mouth of the LORD has spoken it." ⁴And that expression, "The sword will devour you," does not mean that the disobedient will be slain by the sword, but the sword of God is fire, of which they who choose to do wickedly become the fuel. ⁵Therefore, He says, "The sword will devour you: For the mouth of the LORD has spoken it." ⁶And if He had spoken concerning a sword that cuts and at once dispatches, He would not have said, "will devour." ⁷And so, too, Plato, when he says, "The blame is his who chooses, and God is blameless," took this from the prophet Moses and uttered it. For Moses is more ancient than all the Greek writers. ⁸And whatever both philosophers and poets have said concerning the immortality of the soul, or punishments after death, or contemplation of things heavenly, or doctrines of the like kind, they have received such suggestions from the prophets as have enabled them to understand and interpret these things. ⁹And hence there seem to be seeds of truth among all men; but they are charged with not accurately understanding [the truth] when they assert contradictions. ¹⁰So that what we say about future events being foretold, we do not say it as if they came about by a fatal necessity; ¹¹but God foreknowing all that will be done by all men, and it being His decree that the future actions of men will all be recompensed according to their respective value, He foretells by the Spirit of prophecy that He will bestow fitting rewards according to the merit of the actions done, always urging the human race to effort and recollection, showing that He cares and provides for men. ¹²But by the agency of the devils death has been decreed against those who read the books of Hystaspes, or of the Sibyl, or of the prophets, that through fear they may prevent men who read them from receiving the knowledge of the good, and may retain them in slavery to themselves; which, however, they could not always effect. ¹³For not only do we fearlessly read them, but, as you see, bring them for your inspection, knowing that their contents will be pleasing to all. ¹⁴And if we persuade even a few, our gain will be very great; for, as good farmers, we will receive the reward from the Master.

CHAPTER 45

¹And that God the Father of all would bring Christ to Heaven after He had raised Him from the dead, and would keep Him there until He has subdued His enemies the devils, and until the number of those who are foreknown by Him as good and virtuous is complete, on whose account He has still delayed the consummation—hear what was said by the prophet David. ²These are his words: "The LORD said to My Lord, || Sit at My right hand, || Until I make Your enemies Your footstool. The LORD will send to You the rod of power out of Jerusalem, || And rule in the midst of Your enemies. With You is the government in the day of Your power, || In the beauties of Your holy ones: From the womb of morning I have begotten You." ³That which he says, "He will send to You the rod of power out of Jerusalem," is predictive of the mighty word, which His apostles, going forth from Jerusalem, preached everywhere; and though death is decreed against those who teach or at all confess the Name of Christ, we everywhere both embrace and teach it. ⁴And if you also read these words in a hostile spirit, you can do no more, as I said before, than kill us; which indeed does no harm to us, but to you and all who unjustly hate us, and do not convert, brings continuous punishment by fire.

CHAPTER 46

¹But lest some should, without reason, and for the perversion of what we teach, maintain that we say that Christ was born one hundred and fifty years ago under Cyrenius, and subsequently, in the time of Pontius Pilate, taught what we say He taught; and should cry out against us as though all men who were born before Him were irresponsible—let us anticipate and solve the difficulty. ²We have been taught that Christ is the first-begotten of God, and we have declared above that He is the Word of whom every race of men were partakers; ³and those who lived reasonably are Christians, even though they have been thought atheists; as, among the Greeks, Socrates and Heraclitus, and men like them; and among the barbarians, Abraham, and Ananias, and Azarias, and Misael, and Elias, and many others whose actions and names we now decline to recount, because we know it would be tedious. ⁴So that even they who lived before Christ, and lived without reason, were wicked and hostile to Christ, and slew

those who lived reasonably. ⁵But who, through the power of the Word, according to the will of God the Father and Lord of all, He was born of a virgin as a man, and was named Jesus, and was crucified, and died, and rose again, and ascended into Heaven, an intelligent man will be able to comprehend from what has been already so largely said. ⁶And we, since the proof of this subject is less necessary now, will pass for the present to the proof of those things which are urgent.

CHAPTER 47

¹That the land of the Jews, then, was to be laid waste, hear what was said by the Spirit of prophecy. ²And the words were spoken as if from the person of the people wondering at what had happened. ³They are these: "Zion is a wilderness, || Jerusalem a desolation. The house of our sanctuary has become a curse, || And the glory which our fathers blessed is burned up with fire, || And all its glorious things are laid waste: And You refrain Yourself at these things, || And have held Your peace, || And have humbled us very severely." ⁴And you are convinced that Jerusalem has been laid waste, as was predicted. ⁵And concerning its desolation, and that no one should be permitted to inhabit it, there was the following prophecy by Isaiah: "Their land is desolate, || Their enemies consume it before them, || And none of them will dwell therein." ⁶And that it is guarded by you lest anyone dwell in it, and that death is decreed against a Jew apprehended entering it, you know very well.

CHAPTER 48

¹And that it was predicted that our Christ should heal all diseases and raise the dead, hear what was said. ²There are these words: "At His coming the lame will leap as a deer, || And the tongue of the stammerer will be speaking clearly: The blind will see, || And the lepers will be cleansed; And the dead will rise, and walk around." ³And that He did those things, you can learn from the Acts of Pontius Pilate. And how it was predicted by the Spirit of prophecy that He and those who hoped in Him should be slain, hear what was said by Isaiah. ⁴These are the words: "Behold now the righteous perishes, || And no man lays it to heart; And just men are taken away, || And no man considers. From the presence of wickedness is the righteous man taken, || And his burial will be in peace: He is taken from our midst."

CHAPTER 49

¹And again, how it was said by the same Isaiah, that the Gentile nations who were not looking for Him should worship Him, but the Jews who always expected Him should not recognize Him when He came. ²And the words are spoken as from the person of Christ; and they are these: "I was manifest to them that did not ask for Me; I was found by them that did not seek Me: I said, Behold Me, to a nation that did not call on My Name. ³I spread out My hands to a disobedient and opposing people, || To those who walked in a way that is not good, || But follow after their own sins—A people that provokes Me to anger to My face." ⁴For the Jews having the prophecies, and being always in expectation of the Christ to come, did not recognize Him; and not only so, but even treated Him shamefully. ⁵But the nations, who had never heard anything about Christ, until the apostles set out from Jerusalem and preached concerning Him, and gave them the prophecies, were filled with joy and faith, and cast away their idols, and dedicated themselves to the unbegotten God through Christ. ⁶And that it was foreknown that these infamous things should be uttered against those who confessed Christ, and that those who slandered Him, and said that it was well to preserve the ancient customs, should be miserable, hear what was briefly said by Isaiah; it is this: "Woe to them that call sweet bitter, || And bitter sweet."

CHAPTER 50

¹But that, having become man for our sakes, He endured to suffer and to be dishonored, and that He will come again with glory, hear the prophecies which relate to this; they are these: "Because they delivered His soul to death, || And He was numbered with the transgressors, || He has borne the sin of many, || And will make intercession for the transgressors. ²For, behold, My Servant will deal prudently, || And will be exalted, || And will be greatly extolled. As many were astonished at You, || So marred will Your form be before men, || And so hidden from them Your glory, || So will many nations wonder, || And the kings will shut their mouths at Him. ³For they to whom it was not told concerning Him, || And they who have not heard, will understand. O LORD, who has believed our report? And to whom is the arm of the LORD revealed? ⁴We have declared before Him as a child, || As a root in a dry ground. He had no form, nor glory; And we saw Him, and there was no form nor beauty, || But His form was dishonored and marred more than the sons of men. ⁵A man under the stroke, and knowing how to bear infirmity, || Because His face was turned away: He was despised, and of no reputation. ⁶It is He who bears our sins, || And is afflicted for us; Yet we considered Him stricken, beaten, and afflicted. But He was wounded for our transgressions, || He was bruised for our iniquities, || The chastisement of peace was on Him, || [And] by His stripes we are healed. ⁷All we, like sheep, have gone astray; Every man has wandered in his own way. And He delivered Him for our sins; And He did not open His mouth for all His affliction. ⁸He was brought as a sheep to the slaughter, || And as a lamb before his shearer is silent, || So He does not open His mouth. In His humiliation, His judgment was taken away." ⁹Accordingly, after He was crucified, even all His acquaintances forsook Him, having denied Him; ¹⁰and afterward, when He had risen from the dead and appeared to them, and had taught them to read the prophecies in which all these things were foretold as coming to pass, and when they had seen Him ascending into Heaven, and had believed, and had received power sent from there by Him on them, and went to every race of men, they taught these things, and were called apostles.

CHAPTER 51

¹And that the Spirit of prophecy might signify to us that He who suffers these things has an indescribable origin, and rules His enemies, He spoke thus: "His generation who will declare? Because His life is cut off from the earth: For their transgressions He comes to death. ²And I will give the wicked for His burial, || And the rich for His death; Because He did no violence, || Neither was any deceit in His mouth. And the LORD is pleased to cleanse Him from the stripe. ³If He is given for sin, || Your soul will see His seed prolonged in days. And the LORD is pleased to deliver His soul from grief, || To show Him light, and to form Him with knowledge, || To justify the righteous who richly serves many. And He will bear our iniquities. ⁴Therefore, He will inherit many, || And He will divide the spoil of the strong, || Because His soul was delivered to death, || And He was numbered with the transgressors; And He bore the sins of many, || And He was delivered up for their transgressions." ⁵Hear, too, how He was to ascend into Heaven according to prophecy. It was thus spoken: "Lift up the gates of Heaven; Be opened, that the King of glory may come in. Who is this King of glory? The LORD, strong and mighty." ⁶And how He should also come again out of Heaven with glory, hear what was spoken in reference to this by the prophet [[Jeremiah]]. His words are: "Behold, as the Son of Man He comes in the clouds of Heaven, || And His messengers with Him."

CHAPTER 52

¹Since, then, we prove that all things which have already happened had been predicted by the prophets before they came to pass, we must necessarily also believe that those things which are in like manner predicted, but are yet to come to pass, will certainly happen. ²For as the things which have already taken place came to pass when foretold, and even though unknown, so will the things that remain, even though they are unknown and disbelieved, yet come to pass. ³For the prophets have proclaimed two comings of His: the one, that which is already past, when He came as a dishonored and suffering Man; ⁴but the second, when, according to prophecy, He will come from Heaven with glory, accompanied by His angelic host, when He will also raise the bodies of all men who have lived, and will clothe those of the worthy with immortality, and will send those of the wicked, endued with continuous sensibility, into continuous fire with the wicked devils. ⁵And that these things have also been foretold as yet to be, we will prove. By Ezekiel the prophet it was said: "Joint will be joined to joint, and bone to bone, || And flesh will grow again; And every knee will bow to the LORD, || And every tongue will

confess Him." ⁶And in what kind of sensation and punishment the wicked are to be, hear from what was said in like manner with reference to this; it is as follows: "Their worm will not rest, || And their fire will not be quenched"; and then they will convert, when it does not profit them. ⁷And what the people of the Jews will say and do, when they see Him coming in glory, has been thus predicted by Zechariah the prophet: "I will command the four winds to gather the scattered children; I will command the north wind to bring them, || And the south wind, that it does not hold back. ⁸And then in Jerusalem there will be great lamentation, || Not the lamentation of mouths or of lips, || But the lamentation of the heart; And they will not rend their garments, but their hearts. ⁹Tribe by tribe they will mourn, || And then they will look on Him whom they have pierced; And they will say, Why, O LORD, have You made us to err from Your way? The glory which our fathers blessed, || Has for us been turned into shame."

CHAPTER 53

¹Though we could bring forward many other prophecies, we refrain, judging these sufficient for the persuasion of those who have ears to hear and understand; ²and considering also that those persons are able to see that we do not make mere assertions without being able to produce proof, like those fables that are told of the so-called sons of Jupiter. ³For with what reason should we believe of a crucified man that He is the first-begotten of the unbegotten God, and Himself will pass judgment on the whole human race, unless we had found testimonies concerning Him published before He came and was born as man, and unless we saw that things had happened accordingly—the devastation of the land of the Jews, and men of every race persuaded by His teaching through the apostles, and rejecting their old habits, in which, being deceived, they had their conversation; yes, seeing ourselves too, and knowing that the Christians from among the nations are both more numerous and more true than those from among the Jews and Samaritans? ⁴For all the other human races are called nations by the Spirit of prophecy; but the Jewish and Samaritan races are called the tribe of Israel, and the house of Jacob. ⁵And the prophecy in which it was predicted that there should be more believers from the nations than from the Jews and Samaritans, we will produce; it goes like this: "Rejoice, O barren, you that do not bear; Break forth and shout, you that do not travail, || Because many more are the children of the desolate || Than of her that has a husband." ⁶For all the nations were desolate of the true God, serving the works of their hands; but the Jews and Samaritans, having the word of God delivered to them by the prophets, and always expecting the Christ, did not recognize Him when He came, except only a few, of whom the Spirit of prophecy by Isaiah had predicted that they should be saved. He spoke as from their person: "Unless the LORD had left us a seed, || We should have been as Sodom and Gomorrah." ⁷For Sodom and Gomorrah are related by Moses to have been cities of ungodly men, which God burned with fire and brimstone, and overthrew, no one of their inhabitants being saved except a certain stranger, a Chaldean by birth, whose name was Lot; with whom also his daughters were rescued. ⁸And those who care may yet see their whole country desolate, and burned, and remaining barren. ⁹And to show how those from among the nations were foretold as more true and more believing, we will cite what was said by Isaiah the prophet; for he spoke as follows: "Israel is uncircumcised in heart, || But the nations are uncircumcised in the flesh." ¹⁰So many things therefore, as these, when they are seen with the eye, are enough to produce conviction and belief in those who embrace the truth, and are not bigoted in their opinions, nor are governed by their passions.

CHAPTER 54

¹But those who hand down the myths which the poets have made, adduce no proof to the youths who learn them; and we proceed to demonstrate that they have been uttered by the influence of the wicked demons, to deceive and lead astray the human race. ²For having heard it proclaimed through the prophets that the Christ was to come, and that the ungodly among men were to be punished by fire, they put forward many to be called sons of Jupiter, under the impression that they would be able to produce in men the idea that the things which were said with regard to Christ were mere marvelous tales, like the things which were said by the poets. ³And these things were said both among the Greeks and among all nations where [the demons] heard the prophets foretelling that Christ would specially be believed in; but that in hearing what was said by the prophets they did not accurately understand it, but imitated what was said of our Christ, like men who are in error, we will make plain. ⁴The prophet Moses, then, was, as we have already said, older than all writers; and by him, as we have also said before, it was thus predicted: "There will not fail a prince from Judah, || Nor a lawgiver from between his feet, || Until He come for whom it is reserved; And He will be the desire of the nations, || Binding His foal to the vine, || Washing His robe in the blood of the grape." ⁵The devils, accordingly, when they heard these prophetic words, said that Bacchus was the son of Jupiter, and gave out that he was the discoverer of the vine, and they number wine [[*or* the donkey]] among his mysteries; and they taught that, having been torn in pieces, he ascended into heaven. ⁶And because in the prophecy of Moses it had not been expressly intimated whether He who was to come was the Son of God, and whether He would, riding on the foal, remain on earth or ascend into Heaven, and because the name of foal could mean either the foal of a donkey or the foal of a horse, they, not knowing whether He who was foretold would bring the foal of a donkey or of a horse as the sign of His coming, nor whether He was the Son of God, as we said above, or of man, gave out that Bellerophon, a man born of man, himself ascended to heaven on his horse Pegasus. ⁷And when they heard it said by the other prophet Isaiah, that He should be born of a virgin, and by His own means ascend into Heaven, they pretended that Perseus was spoken of. ⁸And when they knew what was said, as has been cited above, in the prophecies written formerly, "Strong as a giant to run his course," they said that Hercules was strong, and had journeyed over the whole earth. ⁹And when, again, they learned that it had been foretold that He should heal every sickness, and raise the dead, they produced Asclepius.

CHAPTER 55

¹But in no instance, not even in any of those called sons of Jupiter, did they imitate [His] being crucified; for it was not understood by them, all the things said of it having been put symbolically. ²And this, as the prophet foretold, is the greatest symbol of His power and role; as is also proved by the things which fall under our observation. ³For consider all the things in the world, whether without this form they could be administered or have any community. ⁴For the sea is not traversed except [if] that trophy which is called a sail abides safely in the ship; and the earth is not plowed without it: diggers and mechanics do not do their work, except with tools which have this shape. ⁵And the human form differs from that of the irrational animals in nothing else than in its being erect and having the hands extended, and having on the face extending from the forehead what is called the nose, through which there is respiration for the living creature; and this shows no other form than that of the cross. ⁶And so it was said by the prophet, "The breath before our face is the Lord Christ." ⁷And the power of this form is shown by your own symbols on what are called vexilla [(banners)] and trophies, with which all your state possessions are made, using these as the insignia of your power and government, even though you do so unwittingly. ⁸And with this form you consecrate the images of your emperors when they die, and you name them gods by inscriptions. ⁹Since, therefore, we have urged you both by reason and by an evident form, and to the utmost of our ability, we know that now we are blameless even though you disbelieve; for our part is done and finished.

CHAPTER 56

¹But the evil spirits were not satisfied with saying, before Christ's appearance, that those who were said to be sons of Jupiter were born of him; ²but after He had appeared, and been born among men, and when they learned how He had been foretold by the prophets, and knew that He should be believed on and looked for by every nation, they again, as was said above, put forward other men, the Samaritans Simon and Menander, who did

many mighty works by magic, and deceived many, and still keep them deceived. ³For even among yourselves, as we said before, Simon was in the royal city Rome in the reign of Claudius Caesar, and so greatly astonished the sacred senate and people of the Romans, that he was considered a god, and honored, like the others whom you honor as gods, with a statue. ⁴Therefore, we pray that the sacred senate and your people may, along with yourselves, be arbiters of this memorial of ours, in order that if anyone is entangled by that man's doctrines, he may learn the truth, and so be able to escape error; and as for the statue, if you please, destroy it.

CHAPTER 57

¹Nor can the devils persuade men that there will be no conflagration for the punishment of the wicked, as they were unable to effect that Christ should be hidden after He came. ²But this only can they effect, that they who live irrationally, and were brought up licentiously in wicked customs, and are prejudiced in their own opinions, should kill and hate us, whom we not only do not hate, but, as is proved, pity and endeavor to lead to conversion. ³For we do not fear death, since it is acknowledged we must surely die; and there is nothing new, but all things continue the same in this administration of things; ⁴and if satiety overtakes those who enjoy even one year of these things, they ought to give heed to our doctrines, that they may live continuously free both from suffering and from need. ⁵But if they believe that there is nothing after death, but declare that those who die pass into insensibility, then they become our benefactors when they set us free from sufferings and necessities of this life, and prove themselves to be wicked, and inhuman, and bigoted. ⁶For they kill us with no intention of delivering us, but cut us off that we may be deprived of life and pleasure.

CHAPTER 58

¹And, as we said before, the devils put forward Marcion of Pontus, who is even now teaching men to deny that God is the maker of all things in the heavens and on earth, and that the Christ predicted by the prophets is His Son, and preaches another god besides the Creator of all, and likewise another son. ²And this man many have believed, as if he alone knew the truth, and laughs at us, though they have no proof of what they say, but are carried away irrationally as lambs by a wolf, and become the prey of atheistical doctrines, and of devils. ³For they who are called devils attempt nothing else than to seduce men from God who made them, and from Christ His first-begotten; ⁴and those who are unable to raise themselves above the earth they have riveted, and do now rivet, to things earthly, and to the works of their own hands; ⁵but those who devote themselves to the contemplation of divine things, they secretly beat back; and if they do not have a wise sober-mindedness, and a pure and passionless life, they drive them into godlessness.

CHAPTER 59

¹And that you may learn that it was from our teachers—we mean the account given through the prophets—that Plato borrowed his statement that God, having altered matter which was shapeless, made the world, hear the very words spoken through Moses, who, as above shown, was the first prophet, and of greater antiquity than the Greek writers; ²and through whom the Spirit of prophecy, signifying how and from what materials God at first formed the world, spoke thus: "In the beginning God created the heavens and the earth. ³And the earth was invisible and unfurnished, and darkness was on the face of the deep; and the Spirit of God moved over the waters. ⁴And God said, Let there be light; and it was so." ⁵So that both Plato and they who agree with him, and we ourselves, have learned, and you also can be convinced, that by the Word of God the whole world was made out of the substance spoken of before by Moses. ⁶And that which the poets call Erebus, we know was spoken of formerly by Moses.

CHAPTER 60

¹And the physiological discussion concerning the Son of God in the Timaeus of Plato, where he says, "He placed Him crosswise in the universe," he borrowed in like manner from Moses; ²for in the writings of Moses it is related how at that time, when the Israelites went out of Egypt and were in the wilderness, they fell in with poisonous beasts, both vipers and asps, and every kind of serpent, which slew the people; ³and that Moses, by the inspiration and influence of God, took brass, and made it into the figure of a cross, and set it in the holy tabernacle, and said to the people, "If you look to this figure, and believe, you will be saved thereby." ⁴And when this was done, it is recorded that the serpents died, and it is handed down that the people thus escaped death. ⁵Which things Plato reading, and not accurately understanding, and not apprehending that it was the figure of the cross, but taking it to be a placing crosswise, he said that the Power next to the first God was placed crosswise in the universe. ⁶And as to his speaking of a third, he did this because he read, as we said above, that which was spoken by Moses, that "the Spirit of God moved over the waters." ⁷For he gives the second place to the Word which is with God, who he said was placed crosswise in the universe; ⁸and the third place to the Spirit who was said to be borne on the water, saying, "And the third around the third." ⁹And hear how the Spirit of prophecy signified through Moses that there should be a conflagration. ¹⁰He spoke thus: "Continuous fire will descend and will devour to the pit beneath." ¹¹It is not, then, that we hold the same opinions as others, but that all speak in imitation of ours. ¹²Among us these things can be heard and learned from persons who do not even know the forms of the letters, who are uneducated and barbarous in speech, though wise and believing in mind; some, indeed, even maimed and deprived of eyesight; so that you may understand that these things are not the effect of human wisdom but are uttered by the power of God.

CHAPTER 61

¹I will also relate the manner in which we dedicated ourselves to God when we had been made new through Christ; lest, if we omit this, we seem to be unfair in the explanation we are making. ²As many as are persuaded and believe that what we teach and say is true, and [who] undertake to be able to live accordingly, are instructed to pray and to entreat God with fasting for the forgiveness of their sins that are past, [while] we are praying and fasting with them. ³Then they are brought by us where there is water and are regenerated in the same manner in which we were ourselves regenerated. ⁴For, in the Name of God, the Father and Lord of the universe, and of our Savior Jesus Christ, and of the Holy Spirit, they then receive the washing with water. ⁵For Christ also said, "Unless you are born again, you will not enter into the Kingdom of Heaven." ⁶Now, that it is impossible for those who have once been born to enter into their mothers' wombs, is manifest to all. ⁷And how those who have sinned and convert will escape their sins, is declared by Isaiah the prophet, as I wrote above; he thus speaks: "Wash yourselves, make yourselves clean; Put away the evil of your doings from your souls; Learn to do well; Judge the fatherless, || And plead for the widow: And come and let us reason together, says the LORD. ⁸And though your sins are as scarlet, || I will make them white like wool; And though they be as crimson, || I will make them white as snow. ⁹But if you refuse and rebel, || The sword will devour you: For the mouth of the LORD has spoken it." ¹⁰And for this [rite] we have learned from the apostles this reason. ¹¹Since at our birth we were born without our own knowledge or choice, by our parents coming together, and were brought up in bad habits and wicked training; in order that we may not remain the children of necessity and of ignorance, but may become the children of choice and knowledge, and may obtain in the water the forgiveness of sins formerly committed, there is pronounced over him who chooses to be born again and has converted from his sins: ¹²[first,] the Name of God the Father and Lord of the universe; he who leads to the laver the person that is to be washed calling Him by this Name alone. ¹³For no one can utter the Name of the ineffable God; and if anyone dares to say that there is a name, he raves with a hopeless madness. ¹⁴And this washing is called illumination, because they who learn these things are illuminated in their understandings; ¹⁵and [second,] in the Name of Jesus Christ, who was crucified under Pontius Pilate; ¹⁶and [third,] in the Name of the Holy Spirit; who through the prophets foretold all things about Jesus; he who is illuminated is washed.

CHAPTER 62

¹And the devils, indeed, having heard this washing published by the prophet, instigated those who enter their temples, and are about to approach them with libations and burnt-offerings, to also sprinkle themselves; ²and they cause them to also wash themselves entirely, as they depart [from the sacrifice], before they enter into the shrines in which their images are set. ³And the command, too, given by the priests to those who enter and worship in the temples, that they take off their shoes, the devils, learning what happened to the aforementioned prophet Moses, have given in imitation of these things. ⁴For at that juncture, when Moses was ordered to go down into Egypt and lead out the people of the Israelites who were there, and while he was tending the flocks of his maternal uncle in the land of Arabia, our Christ conversed with him under the appearance of fire from a bush, and said, "Take off your shoes, and draw near and hear." ⁵And he, when he had taken off his shoes and drawn near, heard that he was to go down into Egypt and lead out the people of the Israelites there; ⁶and he received mighty power from Christ, who spoke to him in the appearance of fire, and went down and led out the people, having done great and marvelous things; which, if you desire to know, you will learn them accurately from his writings.

CHAPTER 63

¹And all the Jews even now teach that the nameless God spoke to Moses; from which the Spirit of prophecy, accusing them by Isaiah the prophet mentioned above, said "The ox knows his owner, || And the donkey his master's crib; But Israel does not know Me, || And My people do not understand." ²And Jesus the Christ, because the Jews did not know what the Father was, and what the Son, in like manner, accused them; and [He] Himself said, "No one knows the Father, but the Son; nor the Son, but the Father, and they to whom the Son reveals Him." ³Now the Word of God is His Son, as we have said before. ⁴And He is called Messenger and Apostle; for He declares whatever we ought to know, and is sent forth to declare whatever is revealed; as our Lord Himself says, "He that hears Me, hears Him that sent Me." ⁵From the writings of Moses this will also be manifest; for thus it is written in them: "And the Messenger of God spoke to Moses in a flame of fire out of the bush, and said, I AM THAT I AM, the God of Abraham, the God of Isaac, the God of Jacob, the God of your fathers; go down into Egypt, and bring forth My people." ⁶And if you wish to learn what follows, you can do so from the same writings; for it is impossible to relate the whole here. ⁷But so much is written for the sake of proving that Jesus the Christ is the Son of God and His Apostle, being of old the Word, and appearing sometimes in the form of fire, and sometimes in the likeness of messengers; but now, by the will of God, having become man for the human race, He endured all the sufferings which the devils instigated the senseless Jews to inflict on Him; ⁸who, though they have it expressly affirmed in the writings of Moses, "And the Messenger of God spoke to Moses in a flame of fire in a bush, and said, I AM THAT I AM, the God of Abraham, and the God of Isaac, and the God of Jacob," ⁹yet maintain that He who said this was the Father and Creator of the universe, from which the Spirit of prophecy also rebukes them, and says, "Israel does not know Me, || My people have not understood Me." ¹⁰And again, Jesus, as we have already shown, while He was with them, said, "No one knows the Father, but the Son; nor the Son but the Father, and those to whom the Son will reveal Him." ¹¹The Jews, accordingly, being ubiquitously of [the] opinion that it was the Father of the universe who spoke to Moses, though He who spoke to him was indeed the Son of God, who is called both Messenger and Apostle, are justly charged, both by the Spirit of prophecy and by Christ Himself, with knowing neither the Father nor the Son. ¹²For they who affirm that the Son is the Father, are proved neither to have become acquainted with the Father, nor to know that the Father of the universe has a Son; who also, being the first-begotten Word of God, is even God. ¹³And of old He appeared in the shape of fire and in the likeness of a messenger to Moses and to the other prophets; ¹⁴but now in the times of your reign, having, as we said before, become Man by a virgin, according to the counsel of the Father, for the salvation of those who believe in Him, He endured both to be set at nothing and to suffer, that by dying and rising again He might conquer death. ¹⁵And that which was said out of the bush to Moses, "I AM THAT I AM, the God of Abraham, and the God of Isaac, and the God of Jacob, and the God of your fathers," this signified that they, even though dead, are yet in existence, and are men belonging to Christ Himself. ¹⁶For they were the first of all men to busy themselves in the search after God; Abraham being the father of Isaac, and Isaac of Jacob, as Moses wrote.

CHAPTER 64

¹From what has been already said, you can understand how the devils, in imitation of what was said by Moses, asserted that Proserpine was the daughter of Jupiter, and instigated the people to set up an image of her under the name of Kore at the spring-heads. ²For, as we wrote above, Moses said, "In the beginning God made the heavens and the earth. ³And the earth was without form and unfurnished: and the Spirit of God moved on the face of the waters." ⁴In imitation, therefore, of what is here said of the Spirit of God moving on the waters, they said that Proserpine was the daughter of Jupiter. ⁵And in like manner also they craftily feigned that Minerva was the daughter of Jupiter, not by sexual union, but, knowing that God conceived and made the world by the Word, they say that Minerva is the first conception, which we consider to be very absurd, bringing forward the form of the conception in a female shape. ⁶And in like manner the actions of those others who are called sons of Jupiter sufficiently condemn them.

CHAPTER 65

¹But we, after we have thus washed him who has been convinced and has assented to our teaching, bring him to the place where those who are called brothers are assembled, in order that we may offer hearty prayers in common for ourselves and for the immersed person, and for all others in every place, ²that we may be counted worthy, now that we have learned the truth, by our works also to be found good citizens and keepers of the commandments, so that we may be saved with a perpetual salvation. ³Having ended the prayers, we salute one another with a kiss. ⁴There is then brought to the president of the brothers bread and a cup of wine mixed with water; and he taking them, gives praise and glory to the Father of the universe, through the Name of the Son and of the Holy Spirit, and offers thanks at considerable length for our being counted worthy to receive these things at His hands. ⁵And when he has concluded the prayers and thanksgivings, all the people present express their assent by saying "Amen." ⁶This word "Amen" answers in the Hebrew language to "so be it." ⁷And when the president has given thanks, and all the people have expressed their assent, those who are called by us "servants" give to each of those present to partake of the bread and wine mixed with water over which the thanksgiving was pronounced, and to those who are absent they carry away a portion.

CHAPTER 66

¹And this food is called among us "Thanksgiving," of which no one is allowed to partake but the man who believes that the things which we teach are true, and who has been washed with the washing that is for the forgiveness of sins, and to regeneration, and who is so living as Christ has enjoined. ²For not as common bread and common drink do we receive these; but in like manner as Jesus Christ our Savior, having been made flesh by the Word of God, had both flesh and blood for our salvation, so likewise have we been taught that the food which is blessed by the prayer of His word, and from which our blood and flesh by transmutation are nourished, is the flesh and blood of that Jesus who was made flesh. ³For the apostles, in the memoirs composed by them, which are called Gospels, have thus delivered to us what was commanded on them, that Jesus "took bread, and when He had given thanks, said, Do this in remembrance of Me; this is My body"; ⁴and that, after the same manner, "having taken the cup and given thanks, He said, This is My blood"; and gave it to them alone. ⁵Which the wicked devils have imitated in the mysteries of Mithras, commanding the same thing to be done. ⁶For, that bread and a cup of water are placed with certain incantations in the mystic rites of one who is being initiated, you either know or can learn.

FIRST APOLOGY

CHAPTER 67

¹And afterward we continually remind each other of these things. ²And the wealthy among us help the needy; and we always keep together; and for all things with which we are supplied, we bless the Maker of all through His Son Jesus Christ, and through the Holy Spirit. ³And on the day called Sunday, all who live in cities or in the country gather together to one place, and the memoirs of the apostles or the writings of the prophets are read, as long as time permits; then, when the reader has ceased, the president verbally instructs and exhorts to the imitation of these good things. ⁴Then we all rise together and pray, and, as we said before, when our prayer is ended, bread, and wine, and water are brought, and the president in like manner offers prayers and thanksgivings, according to his ability, and the people assent, saying "Amen"; ⁵and there is a distribution to each, and a participation of that over which thanks have been given, and to those who are absent a portion is sent by the servants. ⁶And they who are well to do, and willing, give what each thinks fit; and what is collected is deposited with the president, who aids the orphans and widows and those who, through sickness or any other cause, are in need, and those who are in bonds and the strangers sojourning among us, and in a word takes care of all who are in need. ⁷But Sunday is the day on which we all hold our common assembly, because it is the first day on which God, having worked a change in the darkness and matter, made the world; and Jesus Christ our Savior on the same day rose from the dead. ⁸For He was crucified on the day before that of Saturn [(Saturday)]; ⁹and on the day after that of Saturn, which is the day of the sun, having appeared to His apostles and disciples, He taught them these things, which we have submitted to you also for your consideration.

CHAPTER 68

¹And if these things seem to you to be reasonable and true, honor them; but if they seem nonsensical, despise them as nonsense, and do not decree death against those who have done no wrong, as you would against enemies. ²For we forewarn you, that you will not escape the coming judgment of God, if you continue in your injustice; and we ourselves will invite you to do that which is pleasing to God. ³And though from the letter of the greatest and most illustrious Emperor Hadrian, your father, we could demand that you order judgment to be given as we have desired, yet we have made this appeal and explanation, not on the ground of Hadrian's decision, but because we know that what we ask is just. ⁴And we have subjoined the copy of Hadrian's letter, that you may know that we are speaking truly about this.

SECOND APOLOGY

Justin Martyr's Second Apology was written sometime shortly after the First, probably in the range of AD 155–157. It is addressed to the Roman Senate and is thought to be supplementary to his first Apology.

CHAPTER 1

¹Romans, the things which have recently happened in your city under Urbicus, and the things which are likewise being done unreasonably everywhere by the governors, have compelled me to frame this composition for your sakes, who are men of like passions, and brothers, though you do not know it, and though you are unwilling to acknowledge it on account of your glorying in what you regard as dignities. ²For everywhere, whoever is corrected by father, or neighbor, or child, or friend, or brother, or husband, or wife, for a fault, for being hard to move, for loving pleasure and being hard to urge to what is right (except those who have been persuaded that the unjust and unrestrained will be punished in continuous fire, but that the virtuous and those who lived like Christ will dwell with God in a state that is free from suffering—we mean, those who have become Christians), and the evil demons, who hate us, and who keep such men as these subject to themselves, and serving them in the capacity of judges, incite them, as rulers actuated by evil spirits, to put us to death. ³But that the cause of all that has taken place under Urbicus may become quite plain to you, I will relate what has been done.

CHAPTER 2

¹A certain woman lived with an unrestrained husband; she herself, too, having formerly been self-indulgent. ²But when she came to the knowledge of the teachings of Christ, she became sober-minded, and endeavored to persuade her husband likewise to be temperate, citing the teaching of Christ, and assuring him that there will be punishment in continuous fire inflicted on those who do not live temperately and conformably to right reason. ³But he, continuing in the same excesses, alienated his wife from him by his actions. ⁴For she, considering it wicked to live any longer as a wife with a husband who sought in every way means of indulging in pleasure contrary to the law of nature, and in violation of what is right, wished to be divorced from him. ⁵And when she was overpersuaded by her friends, who advised her still to continue with him, in the idea that sometime or other her husband might give hope of amendment, she did violence to her own feeling and remained with him. ⁶But when her husband had gone into Alexandria and was reported to be conducting himself worse than ever, she—that she might not, by continuing in matrimonial connection with him, and by sharing his table and his bed, become a partaker also in his wickednesses and impieties—gave him what you call a bill of divorce, and was separated from him. ⁷But this noble husband of hers—while he ought to have been rejoicing that those actions which formerly she unhesitatingly committed with the servants and hirelings, when she delighted in drunkenness and every vice, she had now given up, and desired that he too should give up the same—when she had gone from him without his desire, brought an accusation against her, affirming that she was a Christian. ⁸And she presented a paper to you, the emperor—a very bold address, like that of Huss to the emperor Sigismund, which crimsoned his forehead with a blush of shame—requesting that first she be permitted to arrange her affairs, and afterward to make her defense against the accusation, when her affairs were set in order. And this you granted. ⁹And her former husband, since he was now no longer able to prosecute her, directed his assaults against a man, Ptolemaeus, whom Urbicus punished, and who had been her teacher in the Christian doctrines. ¹⁰And this he did in the following way: he persuaded a centurion—who had cast Ptolemaeus into prison, and who was friendly to himself—to take Ptolemaeus and interrogate him on this sole point: whether he were a Christian. ¹¹And Ptolemaeus, being a lover of truth, and not of a deceitful or false disposition, when he confessed himself to be a Christian, was bound by the centurion, and for a long time punished in the prison; ¹²and, at last, when the man came to Urbicus, he was asked this one question only: whether he was a Christian. ¹³And again, being conscious of his duty, and the nobility of it through the teaching of Christ, he confessed his discipleship in the divine virtue. ¹⁴For he who denies anything either denies it because he condemns the thing itself, or he shrinks from confession because he is conscious of his own unworthiness or alienation from it, neither of which cases is that of the true Christian. ¹⁵And when Urbicus ordered him to be led away to punishment, one Lucius, who was also himself a Christian, seeing the unreasonable judgment that had thus been given, said to Urbicus: "What is the ground of this judgment? ¹⁶Why have you punished this man, not as an adulterer, nor fornicator, nor murderer, nor thief, nor robber, nor convicted of any crime at all, but who has only confessed that he is called by the name of Christian? ¹⁷This judgment of yours, O Urbicus, does not become the emperor Pius, nor the philosopher, the son of Caesar, nor the sacred senate." ¹⁸And he said nothing else in answer to Lucius than this: "You also seem to me to be such a one." And when Lucius answered, "Most certainly I am," he again ordered him also to be led away. ¹⁹And he professed his

thanks, knowing that he was delivered from such wicked rulers, and was going to the Father and King of the heavens. ²⁰And still a third, having come forward, was condemned to be punished.

CHAPTER 3
¹I too, therefore, expect to be plotted against and fixed to the stake, by some of those I have named, or perhaps by Crescens, that lover of bravado and boasting; for the man is not worthy of the name of philosopher who publicly bears witness against us in matters which he does not understand, saying that the Christians are atheists and impious, and doing so to win favor with the deluded mob, and to please them. ²For if he assails us without having read the teachings of Christ, he is thoroughly depraved, and far worse than the illiterate, who often refrain from discussing or bearing false witness about matters they do not understand. ³Or, if he has read them and does not understand the majesty that is in them, or, understanding it, acts thus that he may not be suspected of being such [a Christian], he is far more base and thoroughly depraved, being conquered by illiberal and unreasonable opinion and fear. ⁴For I would have you to know that I proposed to him certain questions on this subject, and interrogated him, and found most convincingly that he, in truth, knows nothing. ⁵And to prove that I speak the truth, I am ready, if these disputations have not been reported to you, to conduct them again in your presence. And this would be an act worthy of a prince. ⁶But if my questions and his answers have been made known to you, you are already aware that he is acquainted with none of our matters; or, if he is acquainted with them, but, through fear of those who might hear him, does not dare to speak out, like Socrates, he proves himself, as I said before, no philosopher, but an opinionative man; ⁷at least he does not regard that Socratic and most admirable saying: "But a man must in no way be honored before the truth." ⁸But it is impossible for a Cynic, who makes indifference his end, to know any good but indifference.

CHAPTER 4
¹But lest someone say to us, "Go then, all of you, and kill yourselves, and pass even now to God, and do not trouble us, I will tell you why we do not do so, but why, when examined, we fearlessly confess. ²We have been taught that God did not make the world aimlessly, but for the sake of the human race; ³and we have before stated that He takes pleasure in those who imitate His properties and is displeased with those that embrace what is worthless either in word or deed. ⁴If, then, we all kill ourselves we will become the cause, as far as in us lies, why no one should be born, or instructed in the divine doctrines, or even why the human race should not exist [at all]; ⁵and we will, if we so act, be ourselves acting in opposition to the will of God. ⁶But when we are examined, we make no denial, because we are not conscious of any evil, but count it impious not to speak the truth in all things, which also we know is pleasing to God, and because we are also now very desirous to deliver you from an unjust prejudice.

CHAPTER 5
¹But if this idea takes possession of someone, that if we acknowledge God as our helper, we should not, as we say, be oppressed and persecuted by the wicked; this, too, I will solve. ²God, when He had made the whole world, and subjected things earthly to man, and arranged the heavenly elements for the increase of fruits and rotation of the seasons, and appointed this divine law—for these things He evidently also made for man—committed the care of men and of all things under Heaven to messengers whom He appointed over them. ³But the messengers transgressed this appointment, and were captivated by love of women, and begot children who are those that are called demons; and besides, they afterward subdued the human race to themselves, partly by magical writings, and partly by fears and the punishments they occasioned, and partly by teaching them to offer sacrifices, and incense, and libations, of which things they stood in need after they were enslaved by lustful passions; ⁴and among men they sowed murders, wars, adulteries, intemperate deeds, and all wickedness. ⁵Which also the poets and mythologists, not knowing that it was the messengers and those demons who had been begotten by them that did these things to men, and women, and cities, and nations, which they related, ascribed them to a god himself, and to those who were accounted to be his very offspring, and to the offspring of those who were called his brothers, Neptune and Pluto, and to the children again of these offspring of theirs. ⁶For whatever name each of the messengers had given to himself and his children, by that name they called them.

CHAPTER 6
¹But to the Father of all, who is unbegotten, there is no name given. For by whatever name He is called, He has as His elder the person who gives Him the name. ²But these words Father, and God, and Creator, and LORD, and Master, are not names, but appellations derived from His good deeds and functions. ³And His Son, who alone is properly called Son, the Word who also was with Him and was begotten before the works, when at first He created and arranged all things by Him, is called Christ, in reference to His being anointed and God's ordering all things through Him; ⁴this Name itself also containing an unknown significance; as also the appellation God is not a name, but an opinion implanted in the nature of men of a thing that can hardly be explained. ⁵But Jesus, His Name as Man and Savior, also has significance. For He was made man also, as we before said, having been conceived according to the will of God the Father, for the sake of believing men, and for the destruction of the demons. And now you can learn this from what is under your own observation. ⁶For numberless demoniacs throughout the whole world, and in your city, many of our Christian men exorcising them in the Name of Jesus Christ, who was crucified under Pontius Pilate, have healed and do heal, rendering helpless and driving the possessing devils out of the men, though they could not be cured by all the other exorcists, and those who used incantations and drugs.

CHAPTER 7
¹Therefore, God delays causing the confusion and destruction of the whole world, by which the wicked messengers, and demons, and men will cease to exist, because of the seed of the Christians, who know that they are the cause of preservation in nature. ²Since, if it were not so, it would not have been possible for you to do these things, and to be impelled by evil spirits; but the fire of judgment would descend and utterly dissolve all things, even as formerly the Flood left no one but him only with his family who is by us called Noah, and by you Deucalion, from whom again such vast numbers have sprung, some of them evil and others good. ³For so we say that there will be the conflagration, but not as the Stoics, according to their doctrine of all things being changed into one another, which seems most degrading. ⁴But neither do we affirm that it is by fate that men do what they do, or suffer what they suffer, but that each man by free choice acts rightly or sins; ⁵and that it is by the influence of the wicked demons that earnest men, such as Socrates and the like, suffer persecution and are in bonds, while Sardanapalus, Epicurus, and the like, seem to be blessed in abundance and glory. ⁶The Stoics, not observing this, maintained that all things take place according to the necessity of fate. ⁷But since God in the beginning made the race of messengers and men with free-will, they will justly suffer in continuous fire the punishment of whatever sins they have committed. And this is the nature of all that is made, to be capable of vice and virtue. ⁸For neither would any of them be praiseworthy unless there were power to turn to both [virtue and vice]. ⁹And this also is shown by those men everywhere who have made laws and philosophized according to right reason, by their prescribing to do some things and refrain from others. ¹⁰Even the Stoic philosophers, in their doctrine of morals, steadily honor the same things, so that it is evident that they are not very felicitous in what they say about principles and incorporeal things. ¹¹For if they say that human actions come to pass by fate, they will maintain either that God is nothing else than the things which are ever turning, and altering, and dissolving into the same things, ¹²and will appear to have had a comprehension only of things that are destructible, and to have looked on God Himself as emerging both in part and in whole in every wickedness; or that neither vice nor

virtue is anything; which is contrary to every sound idea, reason, and sense.

CHAPTER 8

¹And those of the Stoic school—since, so far as their moral teaching went, they were admirable, as were also the poets in some particulars, on account of the seed of reason, [the Word] implanted in every race of men—were, we know, hated and put to death—Heraclitus for instance, and, among those of our own time, Musonius and others. ²For, as we intimated, the devils have always effected that all those who anyhow live a reasonable and earnest life, and shun vice, be hated. ³And it is nothing wonderful if the devils are proved to cause those to be much worse hated who live not according to a part only of the Word diffused [among men] but by the knowledge and contemplation of the whole Word, which is Christ. ⁴And they, having been shut up in continuous fire, will suffer their just punishment and penalty. ⁵For if they are even now overthrown by men through the Name of Jesus Christ, this is an intimation of the punishment in continuous fire which is to be inflicted on themselves and those who serve them. ⁶For thus did both all the prophets foretell, and our own teacher Jesus teach.

CHAPTER 9

¹And that no one may say what is said by those who are deemed philosophers, that our assertions that the wicked are punished in continuous fire are big words and hobgoblins, and that we wish men to live virtuously through fear, and not because such a life is good and pleasant; ²I will briefly reply to this, that if this is not so, God does not exist; or, if He exists, He cares not for men, and neither virtue nor vice is anything, and, as we said before, lawgivers unjustly punish those who transgress good commandments. ³But since these are not unjust, and their Father teaches them by the word to do the same things as Himself, they who agree with them are not unjust. ⁴And if one objects that the laws of men are diverse, and say that with some, one thing is considered good, another evil, while with others what seemed bad to the former is esteemed good, and what seemed good is esteemed bad, let him listen to what we say to this. ⁵We know that the wicked messengers appointed laws conformable to their own wickedness, in which the men who are like them delight; and the right Reason, when He came, proved that not all opinions nor all doctrines are good, but that some are evil, while others are good. ⁶Therefore, I will declare the same and similar things to such men as these, and, if need be, they will be spoken of more at large. But at present I return to the subject.

CHAPTER 10

¹Our doctrines, then, appear to be greater than all human teaching; because Christ, who appeared for our sakes, became the whole rational being, both body, and reason, and soul. ²For whatever either lawgivers or philosophers uttered well, they elaborated by finding and contemplating some part of the Word. But since they did not know the whole of the Word, which is Christ, they often contradicted themselves. ³And those who by human birth were more ancient than Christ, when they attempted to consider and prove things by reason, were brought before the tribunals as impious persons and busybodies. ⁴And Socrates, who was more zealous in this direction than all of them, was accused of the very same crimes as ourselves. ⁵For they said that he was introducing new divinities and did not consider those to be gods whom the state recognized. ⁶But he cast out from the state both Homer and the rest of the poets, and taught men to reject the wicked demons and those who did the things which the poets related; ⁷and he exhorted them to become acquainted with the God who was to them unknown, by means of the investigation of reason, saying, "It is neither easy to find the Father and Maker of all, nor, having found Him, is it safe to declare Him to all." But these things our Christ did through His own power. ⁸For no one trusted in Socrates so as to die for this doctrine, but in Christ, who was partially known even by Socrates (for He was and is the Word who is in every man, and who foretold the things that were to come to pass both through the prophets and in His own person when He was made of like passions, and taught these things), not only philosophers and scholars believed, but also artisans and people entirely uneducated, despising both glory, and fear, and death; since He is a power of the ineffable Father, not the mere instrument of human reason.

CHAPTER 11

¹But neither should we be put to death, nor would wicked men and devils be more powerful than we, were not death a debt due by every man that is born. Therefore, we give thanks when we pay this debt. ²And we judge it right and opportune to tell here, for the sake of Crescens and those who rave as he does, what is related by Xenophon. ³Hercules, says Xenophon, coming to a place where three ways met, found Virtue and Vice, who appeared to him in the form of women: Vice, in a luxurious dress, and with a seductive expression rendered blooming by such ornaments, and her eyes of a quickly melting tenderness, said to Hercules that if he would follow her, she would always enable him to pass his life in pleasure and adorned with the most graceful ornaments, such as were then on her own person; ⁴and Virtue, who was of squalid look and dress, said, "But if you obey me, you will adorn yourself not with ornament nor beauty that passes away and perishes, but with everlasting and precious graces." ⁵And we are persuaded that everyone who flees those things that seem to be good and follows hard after what are reckoned difficult and strange, enters into blessedness. ⁶For Vice, when by imitation of what is incorruptible (for what is really incorruptible she neither has nor can produce) she has thrown around her own actions, as a disguise, the properties of virtue, and qualities which are really excellent, leads captive earthly-minded men, attaching to Virtue her own evil properties. ⁷But those who understood the excellences which belong to that which is real, are also uncorrupt in virtue. ⁸And this every sensible person ought to think both of Christians and of the athletes, and of those who did what the poets relate of the so-called gods, concluding as much from our contempt of death, even when it could be escaped.

CHAPTER 12

¹For I myself as well, when I was delighting in the doctrines of Plato, and heard the Christians slandered, and saw them fearless of death, and of all other things which are counted fearful, perceived that it was impossible that they could be living in wickedness and pleasure. ²For what sensual or uncontrolled man, or who that counts it good to feast on human flesh, could welcome death that he might be deprived of his enjoyments, and would not rather continue always the present life, and attempt to escape the observation of the rulers; ³and much less would he denounce himself when the consequence would be death? This also the wicked demons have now caused to be done by evil men. ⁴For having put some to death on account of the accusations falsely brought against us, they also dragged to the torture our servants, either children or weak women, and by dreadful torments forced them to admit those fabulous actions which they themselves openly perpetrate; ⁵about which we are the less concerned, because none of these actions are really ours, and we have the unbegotten and ineffable God as witness both of our thoughts and deeds. ⁶For why did we not even publicly profess that these were the things which we esteemed good, and prove that these are the divine philosophy, saying that the mysteries of Saturn are performed when we slay a man, and that when we drink our fill of blood, as it is said we do, we are doing what you do before that idol you honor, and on which you sprinkle the blood not only of irrational animals, but also of men, making a libation of the blood of the slain by the hand of the most illustrious and noble man among you? ⁷And imitating Jupiter and the other gods in sodomy and shameless intercourse with woman, might we not bring as our apology the writings of Epicurus and the poets? ⁸But because we persuade men to avoid such instruction, and all who practice them and imitate such examples, as now in this discourse we have striven to persuade you, we are assailed in every kind of way. But we are not concerned, since we know that God is a just observer of all. ⁹But would that even now someone would mount a lofty platform, and shout with a loud voice: "Be ashamed, be ashamed, you who charge the guiltless with those deeds which you yourselves openly commit and ascribe things which apply to yourselves and to your gods to those who

have not even the slightest sympathy with them. Be converted; become wise."

CHAPTER 13

¹For I myself, when I discovered the wicked disguise which the evil spirits had thrown around the divine doctrines of the Christians, to turn aside others from joining them, laughed both at those who framed these falsehoods, and at the disguise itself and at popular opinion and I confess that I both boast and with all my strength strive to be found a Christian; ²not because the teachings of Plato are different from those of Christ, but because they are not in all respects similar, as neither are those of the others—Stoics, and poets, and historians. ³For each man spoke well in proportion to the share he had of the spermatic Word, seeing what was related to it. ⁴But they who contradict themselves on the more important points appear not to have possessed the heavenly wisdom, and the knowledge which cannot be spoken against. ⁵Whatever things were rightly said among all men, are the property of us Christians. ⁶For next to God, we worship and love the Word who is from the unbegotten and ineffable God, since also He became a man for our sakes, that becoming a partaker of our sufferings, He might also bring us healing. ⁷For all the writers were able to see realities darkly through the sowing of the implanted Word that was in them. ⁸For the seed and imitation impacted according to capacity is one thing, and quite another is the thing itself, of which there is the participation and imitation according to the grace which is from Him.

CHAPTER 14

¹And we therefore request you to publish this little book, appending what you think right, that our opinions may be known to others, and that these persons may have a fair chance of being freed from erroneous notions and ignorance of good, who by their own fault have become subject to punishment; ²that so these things may be published to men, because it is in the nature of man to know good and evil; ³and by their condemning us, whom they do not understand, for actions which they say are wicked, and by delighting in the gods who did such things, and even now require similar actions from men, and by inflicting on us death, or bonds, or some other such punishment, as if we were guilty of these things, they condemn themselves, so that there is no need of other judges.

CHAPTER 15

¹And I despised the wicked and deceitful doctrine of Simon of my own nation. And if you give this book your authority, we will expose him before all, so that, if possible, they may be converted. For this end alone we composed this treatise. ²And our doctrines are not shameful, according to a sober judgment, but are indeed more lofty than all human philosophy: and if not so, they are at least unlike the doctrines of the Sotadists, and Philaenidians, and Dancers, and Epicureans, and such other teachings of the poets, which all are allowed to acquaint themselves with both as acted and as written. ³And henceforth we will be silent, having done as much as we could, and having added the prayer that all men everywhere may be counted worthy of the truth. ⁴And if only you would also, in a manner fitting piety and philosophy, judge justly for your own sakes!

APOLOGY TO MARCUS AURELIUS

Melito's only mostly extant work, his Apology to Marcus Aurelius, addressed to his then contemporary Roman emperor, was written sometime in the years AD 169–170. Aurelius succeeded Antoninus Pius, co-reigning with Lucius Verus; thus, Melito's Apology comes under the very next emperor's reign after the time when Justin Martyr wrote, only 13 or so years earlier.

A DISCOURSE WHICH WAS IN THE PRESENCE OF ANTONINUS CAESAR, AND HE EXHORTED THE SAID CAESAR TO ACQUAINT HIMSELF WITH GOD AND SHOWED TO HIM THE WAY OF TRUTH. HE BEGAN TO SPEAK AS FOLLOWS:

CHAPTER 1

¹"It is not easy," said Melito, "speedily to bring into the right way the man who has a long time before been held fast by error. ²It may, however, be accomplished: for, when a man turns away ever so little from error, the mention of the truth is acceptable to him. ³For, just as when the cloud breaks ever so little there comes fair weather, even so, when a man turns toward God, the thick cloud of error which deprived him of true vision is quickly withdrawn from before him. ⁴For error, like disease and sleep, long holds fast those who come under its influence; but truth uses the word as a goad, and strikes the slumberers, and awakens them; ⁵and when they are awake, they look at the truth and also understand it: they hear and distinguish that which is from that which is not. ⁶For there are men who call iniquity righteousness: they think, for example, that it is righteousness for a man to err with the many. ⁷But I, for my part, affirm that it is not a good excuse for error that a man errs with the many. ⁸For, if one man only sins, his sin is great: how much greater will be the sin when many sin together!"

CHAPTER 2

¹"Now, the sin of which I speak is this: when a man abandons that which really exists and serves that which does not really exist. ²There is that which really exists, and it is called God. He, I say, really exists, and by His power does everything subsist. ³This being is in no sense made, nor did He ever come into being; but He has existed from eternity, and will continue to exist forever and ever. ⁴He does not change, while everything else changes. No eye can see Him, nor thought apprehend Him, nor language describe Him; and those who love Him speak of Him thus: Father, and God of Truth."

CHAPTER 3

¹"If, therefore, a man forsakes the light, and says that there is another God, it is plain from what he himself says that it is some created thing which he calls God. ²For, if a man calls fire God, it is not God, because it is fire; and, if a man calls water God, it is not God, because it is water; ³and, if he so calls this earth on which we tread, or these heavens which are seen by us, or the sun, or the moon, or some one of these stars which run their course without ceasing by Divine command, and do not speed along by their own will, neither are these gods; and, if a man calls gold and silver gods, are not these objects things which we use as we please? ⁴And, if he so calls those pieces of wood which we burn, or those stones which we break, how can these things be gods? ⁵For behold: they are for the use of man. How can they escape the commission of great sin, who in their speech change the great God into those things which, so long as they continue, continue by Divine command?"

CHAPTER 4

¹"But, notwithstanding this, I say that so long as a man does not hear, and so does not discern or understand that there is a Lord over these creatures, he is not perhaps to be blamed: because no one finds fault with a blind man though he walks ever so badly. ²For, in the same manner as the blind, so men also, when they were seeking after God, stumbled on stones and blocks of wood; ³and such of them as were rich stumbled on gold and silver, and were prevented by their stumblings from finding that which they were seeking after. ⁴But now that a voice has been heard through all the earth, declaring that there is a God of truth, and there has been given to every man an eye with which to see, those persons are without excuse who are ashamed of incurring the censure of their former companions in error, and yet desire to

walk in the right way. ⁵For those who are ashamed to be saved must necessarily perish. I therefore counsel them to open their eyes and see—for behold: light is given abundantly to us all to see thereby; ⁶and if, when light has arisen on us, anyone closes his eyes so as not to see, into the ditch he must go. ⁷But why is a man ashamed of the censure of those who have been in error along with himself? ⁸Rather does it behoove him to persuade them to follow in his steps; and, if they should not be persuaded by him, then to disengage himself from their society. ⁹For there are some men who are unable to rise from their mother earth, and therefore they also make them gods, from the earth their mother; ¹⁰and they are condemned by the judgments of truth, forasmuch as they apply the Name of Him who is unchangeable to those objects which are subject to change, and do not shrink from calling those things gods which have been made by the hands of man, and dare to make an image of God whom they have not seen."

CHAPTER 5

¹"But I have to remark further, that the Sibyl also has said concerning them that it is the images of deceased kings that they worship. ²And this is easy to understand; for behold: even now they worship and honor the images of those of Caesarean rank more than their former gods; ³for from those former gods of theirs both monetary tribute and produce accrue to Caesar, as to one who is greater than they. ⁴On this account, those who despise them, and so cause Caesar's revenue to fall short, are put to death. ⁵But to the treasury of other kings also it is appointed how much the worshipers in various places will pay, and how many vessels full of water from the sea they will supply. ⁶Such is the wickedness of the world of those who worship and fear that which has no sensation. ⁷Many of them, too, who are crafty, either for the sake of gain, or for vainglory, or for dominion over the multitude, both themselves worship, and incite those who are destitute of understanding to worship, that which has no sensation."

CHAPTER 6

¹"I will further write and show, as far as my ability goes, how and for what causes images were made to kings and tyrants, and how they came to be regarded as gods. ²The people of Argos made images to Hercules because he belonged to their city, and was strong, and by his valor slew noxious beasts, and more especially because they were afraid of him. ³For he was subject to no control and carried off the wives of many: for his lust was great, like that of Zuradi the Persian, his friend. ⁴Again, the people of Acre worshiped Dionysus, a king, because he had recently planted the vine in their country. ⁵The Egyptians worshiped Joseph the Hebrew, who was called Serapis, because he supplied them with corn during the years of famine. ⁶The Athenians worshiped Athene, the daughter of Zeus, king of the island of Crete, because she built the town of Athens, and made Ericthippus her son king there, whom she had by adultery with Hephaestus, a blacksmith, son of a wife of her father. ⁷She was, too, always courting the society of Hercules, because he was her brother on her father's side. ⁸For Zeus the king became enamored with Alcmene, the wife of Electryon, who was from Argos, and committed adultery with her, and she gave birth to Hercules. ⁹The people of Phoenicia worshiped Balthi, queen of Cyprus, because she fell in love with Tamuz, son of Cuthar king of the Phoenicians, and left her own kingdom and came and dwelt in Gebal, a fortress of the Phoenicians, and at the same time made all the Cyprians subject to King Cuthar. ¹⁰Also, before Tamuz she had fallen in love with Ares, and committed adultery with him; and Hephaestus, her husband, caught her, and his jealousy was roused against her, and he came and killed Tamuz in Mount Lebanon, as he was hunting wild boars; and from that time Balthi remained in Gebal, and she died in the city of Aphiki, where Tamuz was buried. ¹¹The Elamites worshiped Nuh, daughter of the king of Elam: when the enemy had carried her captive, her father made for her an image and a temple in Shushan, a royal residence which is in Elam. ¹²The Syrians worshiped Athi, a Hadibite, who sent the daughter of Belat, a person skilled in medicine, and she healed Simi, the daughter of Hadad king of Syria; and sometime afterward, when Hadad himself had the leprosy on him, Athi entreated Elisha the Hebrew, and he came and healed him of his leprosy. ¹³The people of Mesopotamia also worshiped Cuthbi, a Hebrew woman, because she delivered Bakru, the paternal king of Edessa, from his enemies. ¹⁴With respect to Nebo, who is worshiped in Mabug, why should I write to you? For behold: all the priests who are in Mabug know that it is the image of Orpheus, a Thracian magus. ¹⁵Hadran, again, is the image of Zaradusht, a Persian magus. For both of these magi practiced magic at a well which was in a wood in Mabug, in which was an unclean spirit, and it assaulted and disputed the passage of everyone who passed by in all that country in which the town of Mabug is situated; ¹⁶and these magi, in accordance with what was a mystery in their Magian system, bade Simi, the daughter of Hadad, to draw water from the sea and pour it into the well, so that the spirit should not come up and commit assault. ¹⁷In like manner, the rest of mankind made images to their kings and worshiped them; of which matter I will not write further."

CHAPTER 7

¹"But you, a person of liberal mind, and familiar with the truth, if you will properly consider these matters, commune with your own self; and, though they should clothe you in the garb of a woman, remember that you are a man. ²Believe in Him who is in reality God, and to Him lay open your mind, and to Him commit your soul, and He is able to give you immortal life forever, for everything is possible to Him; ³and let all other things be esteemed by you just as they are—images as images, and sculptures as sculptures; and do not let that which is only made be put by you in the place of Him who is not made, but let Him, the ever-living God, be constantly present in your mind. ⁴For your mind itself is His likeness: for it too is invisible and impalpable, and not to be represented by any form, yet by its will is the whole bodily frame moved. ⁵Know, therefore, that if you constantly serve Him who is immoveable—even He exists forever—so you also, when you will have put off this body, which is visible and corruptible, will stand before Him forever, endowed with life and knowledge, and your works will be to you wealth inexhaustible and possessions unfailing. ⁶And know that the chief of your good works is this: that you know God and serve Him. Know, too, that He asks nothing of you, [except faith]: He needs nothing."

CHAPTER 8

¹"Who is this God? He who is Himself truth, and His word truth. And what is truth? That which is not fashioned, nor made, nor represented by art: that is, which has never been brought into existence, and is on that account called truth. ²If, therefore, a man worships that which is made with hands, it is not the truth that he worships, nor yet the word of truth."

CHAPTER 9

¹"I have very much to say on this subject; but I feel ashamed for those who do not understand that they are superior to the work of their own hands, nor perceive how they give gold to the artists that they may make gods for them, and give them silver for their adornment and honor, and move their riches about from place to place, and then worship them. ²And what infamy can be greater than this, that a man should worship his riches, and forsake Him who bestowed those riches on him? ³And that he should revile man, yet worship the image of man; and slay a beast, yet worship the likeness of a beast? ⁴This also is evident, that it is the workmanship of their fellow men that they worship: for they do not worship the treasures while they are laid by in the bag, but when the artists have fashioned images out of them they worship them; ⁵neither do they worship the gold or the silver considered as property, but when the gravers have sculptured them then they worship them. ⁶Senseless man to what addition has been made to your gold, that now you worship it? If it is because it has been made to resemble a winged animal, why do you not worship the winged animal itself? ⁷And if because it has been made like a beast of prey, behold: the beast of prey itself is before you. ⁸And if it is the workmanship itself that pleases you, let the workmanship of God please you, who made all things, and in His own likeness made the workmen, who strive to do like Him, but do not resemble Him.

CHAPTER 10

¹"But perhaps you will say: How is it that God did not so make me that I should serve Him, and not images? ²In speaking thus, you are seeking to become an idle instrument, and not a living man. For God made you as perfect as it seemed good to Him. ³He has given you a mind endowed with freedom; He has set before you objects in great number, that you on your part may distinguish the nature of each thing and choose for yourself that which is good; ⁴He has set before you the heavens, and placed in them the stars; He has set before you the sun and the moon, and they too every day run their course therein; ⁵He has set before you the multitude of waters, and restrained them by His word; He has set before you the wide earth, which remains at rest, and continues before you without variation: ⁶yet, lest you should suppose that of its own nature it so continues, He makes it also to quake when He pleases; He has set before you the clouds, which by His command bring water from above and satisfy the earth—that from this you may understand that He who puts these things in motion is superior to them all, and may accept thankfully the goodness of Him who has given you a mind whereby to distinguish these things from one another."

CHAPTER 11

¹"Therefore, I counsel you to know yourself, and to know God. ²For understand how that there is within you that which is called the soul—by it the eye sees, by it the ear hears, by it the mouth speaks; and how it makes use of the whole body; and how, whenever He pleases to remove the soul from the body, this falls to decay and perishes. ³From this, therefore, which exists within yourself and is invisible, understand how God also moves the whole by His power, like the body; ⁴and that, whenever it pleases Him to withdraw His power, the whole world also, like the body, will fall to decay and perish."

CHAPTER 12

¹"But why this world was made, and why it passes away, and why the body exists, and why it falls to decay, and why it continues, you cannot know until you have raised your head from this sleep in which you are sunk, and have opened your eyes and seen that God is One, the Lord of all, and have come to serve Him with all your heart. ²Then will He grant you to know His will: for everyone that is severed from the knowledge of the living God is dead and buried even while in his body. ³Therefore, it is that you wallow on the ground before demons and shadows and ask vain petitions from that which has nothing to give. ⁴But you: stand up from among those who are lying on the earth and caressing stones, and giving their substance as food for the fire, and offering their raiment to idols; ⁵and, while they themselves are possessed of senses, are bent on serving that which has no sensation; ⁶and offer for your imperishable soul petitions for that which does not decay—to God who suffers no decay—and your freedom will be at once apparent; ⁷and be careful of it, and give thanks to God who made you and gave you the mind of the free, that you might shape your conduct even as you will. ⁸He has set before you all these things, and shows you that, if you follow after evil, you will be condemned for your evil deeds; but that, if after goodness, you will receive from Him abundant good, together with immortal life forever."

CHAPTER 13

¹"There is, therefore, nothing to hinder you from changing your evil manner of life, because you are a free man; or from seeking and finding out who is the Lord of all; ²or from serving Him with all your heart: because with Him there is no reluctance to give the knowledge of Himself to those that seek it, according to the measure of their capacity to know Him."

CHAPTER 14

¹"Let it be your first care not to deceive yourself. For, if you say of that which is not God: This is God, you deceive yourself, and sin before the God of truth. You fool! Is that a god which is bought and sold? Is that a god which is in want? Is that a god which must be watched over? ²How do you buy him as a slave, and serve him as a master? How do you ask from him, as of one that is rich, to give to you, and yourself give to him as to one that is poor? How do you expect of him that he will make you victorious in battle? ³For behold: when your enemies have conquered you, they strip him likewise."

CHAPTER 15

¹"Perhaps one who is a king may say: I cannot behave myself rightly, because I am a king; it is fitting for me to do the will of the many. ²He who speaks thus really deserves to be laughed at: for why should not the king himself lead the way to all good things, and persuade the people under his rule to behave with purity, and to know God in truth, and in his own person set before them the patterns of all things excellent—since thus it is fitting for him to do? ³For it is a shameful thing that a king, however badly he may conduct himself, should yet judge and condemn those who go awry."

CHAPTER 16

¹"My opinion is this: that in this way a kingdom may be governed in peace—when the sovereign is acquainted with the God of truth, and is withheld by fear of Him from doing wrong to those who are his subjects, and judges everything with equity, as one who knows that he himself will also be judged before God; ²while, at the same time, those who are under his rule are withheld by the fear of God from doing wrong to their sovereign, and are restrained by the same fear from doing wrong to one another. ³By this knowledge of God and fear of Him all evil may be removed from the realm. ⁴For, if the sovereign abstains from doing wrong to those who are under his rule, and they abstain from doing wrong to him and to each other, it is evident that the whole country will dwell in peace. ⁵Many blessings, too, will be enjoyed there, because amongst them all the Name of God will be glorified. For what blessing is greater than this, that a sovereign should deliver the people that are under his rule from error, and by this good deed render himself pleasing to God? ⁶For from error arise all those evils from which kingdoms suffer; but the greatest of all errors is this: when a man is ignorant of God, and in God's stead worships that which is not God."

CHAPTER 17

¹"There are, however, persons who say: It is for the honor of God that we make the image: in order, that is, that we may worship the God who is concealed from our view. ²But they are unaware that God is in every country, and in every place, and is never absent, and that there is nothing done that He does not know. Yet you, despicable man! ³Within whom He is, and without whom He is, and above whom He is, have nevertheless gone and bought yourself wood from the carpenter's, and it is carved and made into an image insulting to God. ⁴To this you offer sacrifice, and do not know that the all-seeing eye sees you, and that the word of truth reproves you, and says to you: How can the unseen God be sculptured? ⁵No, it is the likeness of yourself that you make and worship. Because the wood has been sculptured, do you not have the insight to perceive that it is still wood, or that the stone is still stone? ⁶The gold the workman also takes according to its weight in the balance. And when you have had it made into an image, why do you weigh it? Therefore, you are a lover of gold, and not a lover of God. ⁷And are you not ashamed, if perhaps it is deficient, to demand of the maker of it why he has stolen some of it? Though you have eyes, do you not see? And though you have intelligence, do you not understand? ⁸Why do you wallow on the ground, and offer supplication to things which are without sense? ⁹Fear Him who shakes the earth, and makes the heavens to revolve, and strikes the sea, and removes the mountain from its place—Him who can make Himself like a fire, and consume all things; ¹⁰and, if you are not able to clear yourself of guilt, yet add not to your sins; and, if you are not able to know God, yet do not doubt that He exists."

CHAPTER 18

¹"Again, there are persons who say: Whatsoever our fathers have bequeathed to us, that we reverence. ²Therefore, of course, it is, that those whose fathers have bequeathed them poverty strive to become rich! And those whose fathers did not instruct them, desire to be instructed, and to learn that which their fathers did not know! ³And why, indeed, do the children of the blind see, and the children of the lame walk? ⁴No, it is not well for a man to follow his predecessors, if they are those whose course was evil; but rather that

we should turn from that path of theirs, lest that which befell our predecessors should bring disaster on us also. ⁵Therefore, inquire whether your father's course was good: and, if so, you also follow in his steps; but, if your father's course was very evil, let yours be good, and so let it be with your children after you. ⁶Be grieved also for your father because his course is evil, so long as your grief may avail to help him. ⁷But, as for your children, speak to them thus: There is a God, the Father of all, who never came into being, neither was ever made, and by whose will all things subsist. ⁸He also made the luminaries, that His works may see one another; and He conceals Himself in His power from all His works: for it is not permitted to any being subject to change to see Him who changes not. ⁹But such as are mindful of His words, and are admitted into that covenant, which is unchangeable, they see God—so far as it is possible for them to see Him. ¹⁰These also will have power to escape destruction, when the flood of fire comes on all the world. ¹¹For there was once a flood and a wind, and the great men were swept away by a violent blast from the north, but the just were left, for a demonstration of the truth. ¹²Again, at another time there was a flood of water, and all men and animals perished in the multitude of waters, but the just were preserved in an ark of wood by the command of God. ¹³So also will it be at the last time: there will be a flood of fire, and the earth will be burnt up, together with its mountains; and mankind will be burnt up, along with the idols which they have made, and the carved images which they have worshiped; and the sea will be burnt up, together with its islands; ¹⁴but the righteous will be preserved from wrath, just as were their fellows of the Ark from the waters of the Flood. ¹⁵And then will those who have not known God, and those who have made them idols, bemoan themselves, when they will see those idols of theirs being burnt up, together with themselves, and nothing will be found to help them."

CHAPTER 19

¹"When you, Antoninus Caesar, will become acquainted with these things, and your children also with you, then will you bequeath to them an inheritance forever which never fades away, and you will deliver your soul, and the souls of your children also, from that which will come on the whole earth in the judgment of truth and of righteousness. ²For, according as you have acknowledged Him here, so will He acknowledge you there; and, if you account Him here superfluous, He will not account you one of those who have known Him and confessed Him. ³These may suffice your Majesty; and, if they be too many, yet deign to accept them." HERE ENDS MELITO.

FRAGMENT 1

1. "For the race of the pious is now persecuted in a way contrary to all precedent, being harassed by a new kind of edicts everywhere in Asia. For unblushing informers, and such as are greedy of other men's goods, taking occasion from the orders issued, carry on their robbery without any disguise, plundering of their property night and day those who are guilty of no wrong.

2. If these proceedings take place at your bidding, well and good. For a just sovereign will never take unjust measures; and we, on our part, gladly accept the honor of such a death. This request only do we present to you: that you would first of all examine for yourself into the behavior of these reputed agents of so much strife, and then come to a just decision as to whether they merit death and punishment or deserve to live in safety and quiet. But if, on the contrary, it will turn out that this measure, and this new sort of command, which it would be unbecoming to employ even against barbarian enemies, do not proceed from you, then all the more do we entreat you not to leave us thus exposed to the spoliation of the populace.

3. For the philosophy current with us flourished in the first instance among barbarians; and, when it afterward sprang up among the nations under your rule, during the distinguished reign of your ancestor Augustus, it proved to be a blessing of most happy omen to your empire. For from that time the Roman power has risen to greatness and splendor. To this power you have succeeded as the much desired possessor; and such will you continue, together with your son, if you protect that philosophy which has grown up with your empire, and which took its rise with Augustus; to which also your more recent ancestors paid honor, along with the other religions prevailing in the empire. A very strong proof, moreover, that it was for good that the system we profess came to prevail at the same time that the empire of such happy commencement was established, is this: that ever since the reign of Augustus nothing unexpected has happened; but, on the contrary, everything has contributed to the splendor and renown of the empire, in accordance with the devout wishes of all. Nero and Domitian alone of all the emperors, imposed on by certain calumniators, have cared to bring any impeachment against our doctrines. They, too, are the source from which it has happened that the lying slanders on those who profess them have, in consequence of the senseless habit which prevails of taking things on hearsay, flowed down to our own times. But the course which they in their ignorance pursued was set aside by your pious progenitors, who frequently and in many instances rebuked by their rescripts those who dared to set on foot any hostilities against them. It appears, for example, that your grandfather Hadrian wrote, among others, to Fundanus, the proconsul then in charge of the government of Asia. Your father, too, when you yourself were associated with him in the administration of the empire, wrote to the cities, forbidding them to take any measures adverse to us: among the rest to the people of Larissa, and of Thessalonica, and of Athens, and, in short, to all the Greeks. And as regards yourself, seeing that your sentiments respecting the Christians are not only the same as theirs, but even much more generous and wise, we are the more persuaded that you will do all that we ask of you."

FRAGMENT 2

"We are not those who pay homage to stones, that are without sensation; but of the only God, who is before all and over all, and, moreover, we are worshipers of His Christ, who is veritably God the Word existing before all time."

DISCOURSES OF MELITO

Melito, overseer of the church at Sardis, had numerous other works, but none fully extant, except perhaps his topical Peri Pascha. The present book, called in the LSV collection Discourses of Melito, contains many of the fragments from his discourses and works that are still available today. Notably, from the Book of Extracts (Ch. 6 in the present work), Melito certifiably defines the canon of the Old Testament; this, in combination with the Muratorian Canon (see Apocryphal Fragments), demonstrates quite conclusively that the present 66-book canon is essentially traceable to the 2nd century at the latest, and not post-Nicaea as many conspiracists suppose.

FROM THE DISCOURSE ON SOUL AND BODY.

CHAPTER 1

¹For this reason, the Father sent His Son from Heaven without a bodily form, that, when He should put on a body by means of the Virgin's womb, and be born man, He might save man, and gather together those members of His which death had scattered when He divided man. ²… The earth shook, and its foundations trembled; the sun fled away, and the elements turned back, and the day was changed [into night]: ³for they could not endure the sight of their Lord hanging on a tree. ⁴The [whole] creation was amazed, marveling and saying, "What new mystery, then, is this? ⁵The Judge is judged, and holds His peace; the Invisible One is seen, and is not ashamed; the Incomprehensible is laid hold on, and is not

indignant; the Illimitable is circumscribed, and does not resist; the Impossible suffers, and does not avenge; the Immortal dies, and does not answer a word; the Celestial is laid in the grave, and endures! What new mystery is this?" ⁶The [whole] creation, I say, was astonished; but, when our Lord arose from the place of the dead, and trampled death underfoot, and bound the strong one, and set man free, then the whole creation clearly saw that for man's sake the Judge was condemned, and the Invisible was seen, and the Illimitable was circumscribed, and the Impassible suffered, and the Immortal died, and the Celestial was laid in the grave. ⁷For our Lord, when He was born man, was condemned in order that He might show mercy, was bound in order that He might loose, was seized in order that He might release, suffered in order that He might feel compassion, died in order that He might give life, was laid in the grave that He might raise [from the dead].

FROM THE DISCOURSE ON THE CROSS.

CHAPTER 2

¹On these accounts He came to us; on these accounts, though He was incorporeal, He formed for Himself a body after our fashion—appearing as a sheep, yet still remaining the Shepherd; being esteemed a servant, yet not renouncing the Sonship; ²being carried in the womb of Mary, yet arrayed in the nature of His Father; treading on the earth, yet filling Heaven; ³appearing as an infant, yet not discarding the eternity of His nature; ⁴being invested with a body, yet not circumscribing the unmixed simplicity of His Godhead; ⁵being esteemed poor, yet not divested of His riches; ⁶needing sustenance inasmuch as He was man, yet not ceasing to feed the entire world inasmuch as He is God; ⁷putting on the likeness of a servant, yet not impairing the likeness of His Father. ⁸He sustained every character belonging to Him in an immutable nature: He was standing before Pilate, and at the same time was sitting with His Father; He was nailed on the tree, and yet was the Lord of all things.

FROM THE DISCOURSE ON FAITH.

CHAPTER 3

¹We have collected together extracts from the Law and the Prophets relating to those things which have been declared concerning our Lord Jesus Christ, that we may prove to your love that this Being is perfect reason, the Word of God; ²He who was begotten before the light; He who is Creator together with the Father; ³He who is the Fashioner of man; He who is all in all; He who among the patriarchs is Patriarch; He who in the law is the Law; among the priests, Chief Priest; ⁴among kings, the Ruler; among prophets, the Prophet; among the messengers, Chief-messenger; in the voice of the preacher, the Word; among spirits, the Spirit; in the Father, the Son; in God, God; King forever and ever. ⁵For this is He who was pilot to Noah; He who was guide to Abraham; He who was bound with Isaac; He who was in exile with Jacob; He who was sold with Joseph; ⁶He who was captain of the host with Moses; He who was the divider of the inheritance with Jesus the son of Nun; He who in David and the prophets announced His own sufferings; ⁷He who put on a bodily form in the Virgin; He who was born in Beth-Lehem; He who was wrapped in swaddling-clothes in the manger; ⁸He who was seen by the shepherds; He who was glorified by the messengers; He who was worshiped by the magi; ⁹He who was pointed out by John; He who gathered together the apostles; He who preached the kingdom; He who cured the lame; He who gave light to the blind; He who raised the dead; He who appeared in the temple; ¹⁰He who was not believed on by the people; He who was betrayed by Judas; He who was apprehended by the priests; He who was condemned by Pilate; ¹¹He who was pierced in the flesh; He who was hanged on the tree; He who was buried in the earth; He who rose from the place of the dead; ¹²He who appeared to the apostles; He who was carried up to Heaven; He who is seated at the right hand of the Father; ¹³He who is the repose of those that are departed; the recoverer of those that are lost; the light of those that are in darkness; the deliverer of those that are captive; the guide of those that go astray; the asylum of the afflicted; the bridegroom of the Assembly; ¹⁴the charioteer of the cherubim; the captain of the messengers; God who is from God; the Son who is from the Father; Jesus Christ the King forevermore. Amen.

CHAPTER 4

¹This is He who took a bodily form in the Virgin, and was hanged on the tree, and was buried within the earth, and did not suffer decomposition; ²He who rose from the place of the dead, and raised up men from the earth—from the grave below to the height of Heaven. ³This is the Lamb that was slain; this is the Lamb that did not open His mouth. ⁴This is He who was born of Mary, fair sheep of the fold. ⁵This is He that was taken from the flock, and was led to the slaughter, and was slain in the evening, and was buried at night; He who had no bone of His broken on the tree; He who suffered no decay within the earth; He who rose from the place of the dead, and raised up the race of Adam from the grave below: ⁶This is He who was put to death! And where was He put to death? In the midst of Jerusalem. ⁷By whom? By Israel: because He cured their lame, and cleansed their lepers, and gave light to their blind, and raised their dead! This was the cause of His death. ⁸You, O Israel, were giving commands, and He was being crucified; you were rejoicing, and He was being buried; you were reclining on a soft couch, and He was watching in the grave and the shroud. ⁹O Israel, transgressor of the Law, why have you committed this new iniquity, subjecting the LORD to new sufferings—your own Lord, Him who fashioned you, Him who made you, Him who honored you, who called you Israel? ¹¹But you have not been found to be Israel: for you have not seen God, nor understood the LORD. ¹²You have not known, O Israel, that this was the firstborn of God, who was begotten before the sun, who made the light to shine forth, who lighted up the day, who separated the darkness, who fixed the first foundations, who poised the earth, who collected the ocean, who stretched out the expanse, who adorned the world. ¹³Bitter were your nails, and sharp; bitter your tongue, which you sharpened; bitter was Judas, to whom you gave hire; bitter your false witnesses, whom you stirred up; bitter your gall, which you prepared; bitter your vinegar, which you made; bitter your hands, filled with blood. ¹⁴You slew your Lord, and He was lifted up on the tree; and an inscription was fixed above, to show who He was that was slain. ¹⁵And who was this? (That which we will not say is too shocking to hear, and that which we will say is very dreadful: nevertheless listen, and tremble.) ¹⁶It was He because of whom the earth quaked; He that hung up the earth in space was Himself hanged up; He that fixed the heavens was fixed with nails; He that bore up the earth was borne up on a tree; ¹⁷the Lord of all was subjected to humiliation in a naked body—God put to death! The King of Israel slain with Israel's right hand! ¹⁸Woe for the new wickedness of the new murder! The LORD was exposed with naked body: He was not deemed worthy even of covering; and, in order that He might not be seen, the luminaries turned away, and the day became darkened because they slew God, who hung naked on the tree. ¹⁹It was not the body of our Lord that the luminaries covered with darkness when they set, but the eyes of men. ²⁰For, because the people did not tremble, the earth quaked; because they were not frightened, the earth was frightened. ²¹You struck your Lord: you also have been stricken on the earth. ²²And you indeed lie dead; but He is risen from the place of the dead, and ascended to the height of Heaven, having suffered for the sake of those who suffer, and having been bound for the sake of Adam's race which was imprisoned, and having been judged for the sake of him who was condemned, and having been buried for the sake of him who was buried. ²³… This is He who made the heavens and the earth, and in the beginning, together with the Father, fashioned man; who was announced by means of the Law and the Prophets; who put on a bodily form in the Virgin; ²⁴who was hung on the tree; who was buried in the earth; who rose from the place of the dead, and ascended to the height of Heaven, and sits on the right hand of the Father.

CHAPTER 5

¹He that bore up the earth was borne up on a tree. ²The LORD was subjected to humiliation with naked body—God put to death—the King of Israel slain!

DISCOURSES OF MELITO

FROM THE BOOK OF EXTRACTS, SHOWING THE ACCEPTED CANON OF THE OLD TESTAMENT.

CHAPTER 6

¹Melito to his brother Onesimus: Greetings! ²As you have often, prompted by your regard for the word of God, expressed a wish to have some extracts made from the Law and the Prophets concerning the Savior, and concerning our faith in general, and have desired, moreover, to obtain an accurate account of the Ancient Books, ³as regards their number and their arrangement, I have striven to the best of my ability to perform this task: knowing full well your zeal for the faith, and your eagerness to become acquainted with the word, ⁴and especially because I am assured that, through your yearning after God, you esteem these things beyond all things else, engaged as you are in a struggle for eternal salvation. ⁵I accordingly proceeded to the East and went to the very spot where the things in question were preached and took place; ⁶and, having made myself accurately acquainted with the books of the Old Testament, I have set them down below, and herein send you the list. ⁷Their names are as follows: The five books of Moses—Genesis, Exodus, Leviticus, Numbers, Deuteronomy; Joshua, Judges, Ruth, the four books of Kings, the two of Chronicles, the book of the Psalms of David, the Proverbs of Solomon, also called the Book of Wisdom, Ecclesiastes, the Song of Songs, Job, the books of the prophets Isaiah, Jeremiah, of the twelve contained in a single book, Daniel, Ezekiel, Esdras. ⁸From these I have made my extracts, dividing them into six books.

FROM THE CATENA ON GENESIS.

CHAPTER 7

¹In place of Isaac the just, a ram appeared for slaughter, in order that Isaac might be liberated from his bonds. ²The slaughter of this animal redeemed Isaac from death. ³In like manner, the LORD, being slain, saved us; being bound, He loosed us; being sacrificed, He redeemed us … For the LORD was a lamb, like the ram which Abraham saw caught in the bush Sabec. ⁴But this bush represented the cross, and that place Jerusalem, and the lamb the LORD bound for slaughter. ⁵For as a ram He was bound—he says concerning our Lord Jesus Christ—and as a lamb He was shorn, and as a sheep He was led to the slaughter, and as a lamb He was crucified; ⁶and He carried the cross on His shoulders when He was led up to the hill to be slain, as was Isaac by his father. ⁷But Christ suffered, and Isaac did not suffer: for he was but a type of Him who should suffer. ⁸Yet, even when serving only for a type of Christ, he struck men with astonishment and fear. ⁹For a new mystery was presented to view: a son led by his father to a mountain to be slain, whose feet he bound together, and laid him on the wood of the sacrifice, preparing with care whatever was necessary to his immolation. ¹⁰Isaac on his part is silent, bound like a ram, not opening his mouth, nor uttering a sound with his voice. ¹¹For, not fearing the knife, nor quailing before the fire, nor troubled by the prospect of suffering, he sustained bravely the character of the type of the LORD. ¹²Accordingly, there lies Isaac before us, with his feet bound like a ram, his father standing by, with the knife all bare in his hand, not shrinking from shedding the blood of his son.

TWO SCHOLIA ON GENESIS 22:13.

CHAPTER 8

¹The Syriac and the Hebrew use the word "suspended," as more clearly typifying the Cross. ²The word Sabek some have rendered [forgiveness], others [upright], as if the meaning, agreeing with the popular belief, were a goat walking erect up to a bush, and there standing erect caught by his horns, so as to be a plain type of the Cross. ³For this reason, it is not translated, because the single Hebrew word signifies in other languages many things. ⁴To those, however, who ask it is proper to give an answer, and to say that Sabek denotes [lifted up].

FROM THE DISCOURSE ON THE NATURE OF CHRIST.

CHAPTER 9

¹For there is no need, to persons of intelligence, to attempt to prove, from the deeds of Christ subsequent to His immersion, that His soul and His body, His human nature like ours, were real, and no phantom of the imagination. ²For the deeds done by Christ after His immersion, and especially His miracles, gave indication and assurance to the world of the Deity hidden in His flesh. ³For, being at once both God and perfect man likewise, He gave us sure indications of His two natures: of His Deity, by His miracles during the three years that elapsed after His immersion; ⁴of His humanity, during the thirty similar periods which preceded His immersion, in which, by reason of His low estate as regards the flesh, He concealed the signs of His Deity, although He was the true God existing before all ages.

CHAPTER 10

1. The head of the LORD: His simple Divinity; because He is the Beginning and Creator of all things in Daniel.
2. The white hair of the LORD, because He is "the Ancient of Days" (as above).
3. The eyes of the LORD: the Divine inspection: because He sees all things. Like that in the apostle: "For all things are naked and open in His eyes."
4. The eyelids of the LORD: hidden spiritual mysteries in the Divine precepts. In the Psalm: "His eyelids question, that is to test the children of men."
5. The smelling of the LORD: His delight in the prayers or works of the holy ones. In Genesis: "And the LORD smelled an odor of sweetness."
6. The mouth of the LORD: His Son, or word addressed to men. In the prophet: "The mouth of the LORD has spoken"; and elsewhere: "They provoked His mouth to anger."
7. The tongue of the LORD: His Holy Spirit. In the Psalm: "My tongue is a pen."
8. The face of the LORD: His manifestation. In Exodus: "My face will go before you"; and in the prophet: "The face of the LORD divided them."
9. The word of the LORD: His Son. In the Psalm: "My heart has uttered a good word."
10. The arm of the LORD: His Son, by whom He has worked all His works. In the prophet Isaiah: "And to whom is the arm of the LORD revealed?"
11. The right hand of the LORD: that is, His Son; as also above in the Psalm: "The right hand of the LORD has done valiantly."
12. The right hand of the LORD: as in Deuteronomy: "In His right hand is a fiery law."
13. The wings of the LORD: Divine protection. In the Psalm: "In the shadow of Your wings will I hope."
14. The shoulder of the LORD: the Divine power, by which He lowers to carry the feeble. In Deuteronomy: "He took them up and put them on His shoulders."
15. The hand of the LORD: Divine operation. In the prophet: "Have not My hands made all these things?"
16. The finger of the LORD: the Holy Spirit, by whose operation the tables of the Law in Exodus are said to have been written; and in the Gospel: "If I by the finger of God cast out demons."
17. The fingers of the LORD: The lawgiver Moses, or the prophets. In the Psalm: "I will regard the heavens," that is, the books of the Law and the Prophets, "the works of Your fingers."
18. The wisdom of the LORD: His Son. In the apostle: "Christ the power of God, and the wisdom of God"; and in Solomon: "The wisdom of the LORD reaches from one end to the other mightily."
19. The womb of the LORD: the hidden recess of Deity out of which He brought forth His Son. In the Psalm: "Out of the womb, before dawn, have I borne You."
20. The feet of the LORD: His immovableness and eternity. In the Psalm: "And thick darkness was under His feet."
21. The throne of the LORD: messengers, or holy ones, or simply sovereign dominion. In the Psalm: "Your throne, O God, is forever and ever."
22. The seat [of the LORD]: the same as above, messengers or holy ones, because the LORD sits on these. In the Psalm: "The LORD sat on His holy seat."
23. The descent of the LORD: His visitation of men. As in Micah: "Behold, the LORD will come forth from His place; He will come down trampling underfoot the ends of the earth." Likewise in a bad sense. In Genesis: "The LORD came down to see the tower."
24. The ascent of the LORD: the raising up of man, who is taken from earth to Heaven.

In the Psalm: "Who ascends above the Heaven of heavens to the east."
25. The standing of the LORD: the patience of the Deity, by which He bears with sinners that they may come to conversion. As in Habakkuk: "He good and measured the earth; and in the Gospel: "Jesus stood, and bade him to be called," that is, the blind man.
26. The transition of the LORD: His assumption of our flesh, through which by His birth, His death, His resurrection, His ascent into Heaven, He made transitions, so to say. In the Song of Songs: "Behold, He comes, leaping on the mountains, bounding over the hills."
27. The going of the LORD: His coming or visitation. In the Psalm.
28. The way of the LORD: the operation of the Deity. As in Job, in speaking of the devil: "He is the beginning of the ways of the LORD."
29. Again: The ways of the LORD: His precepts. In Hosea: "For the ways of the LORD are straight, and the just will walk in them."
30. The footsteps of the LORD: the signs of His secret operations. As in the Psalm: "And Your footsteps will not be known."
31. The knowledge of the LORD: that which makes men to know Him. To Abraham He says: "Now I know that you fear the LORD"; that is, I have made you to know.
32. The ignorance of God is His disapproval. In the Gospel: "I know you not."
33. The remembrance of God: His mercy, by which He rejects and has mercy on whom He will. So in Genesis: "The LORD remembered Noah"; and in another passage: "The LORD has remembered His people."
34. The conversion of the LORD: His change of procedure. As in the book of Kings: "I have changed My mind that I have made Saul king."
35. The anger and wrath of the LORD: the vengeance of the Deity on sinners, when He bears with them with a view to punishment, does not at once judge them according to strict equity. As in the Psalm: "In His anger and in His wrath will He trouble them."
36. The sleeping of the LORD: when, in the thoughts of some, His faithfulness is not sufficiently wakeful. In the Psalm: "Awake, why do You sleep, O LORD?"
37. The watches of the LORD: in the guardianship of His chosen, He is always at hand by the presence of His Deity. In the Psalm: "Behold! He will not slumber nor sleep."
38. The sitting of the LORD: His ruling. In the Psalm: "The LORD sits on His holy seat."
39. The footstool of the LORD: man assumed by the Word; or His holy ones, as some think. In the Psalm: "Worship [at] His footstool, for it is holy."
40. The walking of the LORD: the delight of the Deity in the walks of His chosen. In the prophet: "I will walk in them and will be their Lord."
41. The trumpet of the LORD: His mighty voice. In the apostle: "At the command, and at the voice of the chief-messenger, and at the trumpet of God, will He descend from Heaven."

A PLEA FOR THE CHRISTIANS

In about AD 177, seven short years after Melito's Apology, Athenagoras of Athens likewise wrote to Emperor Marcus Aurelius, requesting justice for the Christians and defending the faith in apologetic form. Notably, although he does not use a word for "Trinity" as Theophilus would do as shortly as three years subsequent to Athenagoras' work, he aptly defends the biblical doctrine of One God in three Persons (see Ch. 10). Given that the two were contemporaries, it is evident that the doctrine of the Trinity was well established in the Church by the mid- and late-2nd century.

TO THE EMPERORS MARCUS AURELIUS ANONINUS AND LUCIUS AURELIUS COMMODUS, CONQUERORS OF ARMENIA AND SARMATIA, AND MORE THAN ALL, PHILOSOPHERS.

CHAPTER 1

1. In your empire, greatest of sovereigns, different nations have different customs and laws; and no one is hindered by law or fear of punishment from following his ancestral usages, however ridiculous these may be. A citizen of Ilium calls Hector a god, and pays divine honors to Helen, taking her for Adrasteia. The Lacedaemonian venerates Agamemnon as Zeus, and Phylonoe the daughter of Tyndarus; and the man of Tenedos worships Tennes. The Athenian sacrifices to Erechtheus as Poseidon. The Athenians also perform religious rites and celebrate mysteries in honor of Agraulus and Pandrosus, women who were deemed guilty of impiety for opening the box. In short, among every nation and people, men offer whatever sacrifices and celebrate whatever mysteries they please. The Egyptians reckon among their gods even cats, and crocodiles, and serpents, and asps, and dogs. And to all these both you and the laws give permission so to act, deeming, on the one hand, that to believe in no god at all is impious and wicked, and on the other, that it is necessary for each man to worship the gods he prefers, in order that through fear of the deity, men may be kept from wrongdoing. But why—for do not, like the multitude, be led astray by hearsay—why is a mere name odious to you?

2. Names are not deserving of hatred: it is the unjust act that calls for penalty and punishment. And accordingly, with admiration of your mildness and gentleness, and your peaceful and benevolent disposition toward every man, individuals live in the possession of equal rights; and the cities, according to their rank, share in equal honor; and the whole empire, under your intelligent sway, enjoys profound peace. But for us who are called Christians you have not in like manner cared; but although we commit no wrong—no, as will appear in the sequel of this discourse, are of all men most piously and righteously disposed toward the Deity and toward your government—you allow us to be harassed, plundered, and persecuted, the multitude making war on us for our name alone. We venture, therefore, to lay a statement of our case before you—and you will learn from this discourse that we suffer unjustly, and contrary to all law and reason—and we implore you to bestow some consideration on us also, that we may cease at length to be slaughtered at the instigation of false accusers. For the fine imposed by our persecutors does not aim merely at our property, nor their insults at our reputation, nor the damage they do us at any other of our greater interests.

3. These we hold in contempt, though to the generality they appear matters of great importance; for we have learned, not only not to return blow for blow, nor to go to court with those who plunder and rob us, but to those who strike us on one side of the face to offer the other side also, and to those who take away our coat to give likewise our cloak. But, when we have surrendered our property, they plot against our very bodies and souls, pouring on us wholesale charges of crimes of which we are guiltless even in thought, but which belong to these idle babblers themselves, and to the whole tribe of those who are like them.

CHAPTER 2

If, indeed, anyone can convict us of a crime, be it small or great, we do not ask to be excused from punishment, but are prepared to undergo the sharpest and most merciless inflictions. But if the accusation relates merely to our name—and it is undeniable, that up to the present time the stories told about us rest on nothing better than the common undiscriminating popular talk, nor has any Christian been convicted of crime—it will devolve on you, illustrious and benevolent and most learned sovereigns, to remove by law this despiteful treatment, so that, as throughout the world both individuals and cities partake of your generosity, we also may feel grateful to you, exulting that we are no longer the victims of false accusation. For it does not comport with your justice, that others when charged with crimes should not be punished until they are convicted, but that in our case the name we bear should have more force than the evidence adduced on the trial, when the judges, instead of inquiring whether the person arraigned has committed any crime, vent their insults on the name, as if that were itself a crime. But no name in and by itself is reckoned either good or bad; names appear bad or good according as the actions underlying them are bad or good. You, however, have yourselves a dear knowledge of this since you are well-instructed in philosophy and all learning. For this reason, too, those who are brought before you for trial, though they may be arraigned on the gravest charges, have no fear, because they know that you will inquire respecting their previous life, and not be influenced by names if they mean nothing, nor by the charges contained in the indictments if they should be false: they accept with equal satisfaction, as regards its fairness, the sentence whether of condemnation or acquittal. What, therefore, is conceded as the common right of all, we claim for ourselves, that we will not be hated and punished because we are called Christians (for what has the name to do with our being bad men?), but be tried on any charges which may be brought against us, and either be released on our disproving them, or punished if convicted of crime—not for the name (for no Christian is a bad man unless he falsely professes our doctrines), but for the wrong which has been done. It is thus that we see the philosophers judged. None of them before trial is deemed by the judge either good or bad on account of his science or craft, but if found guilty of wickedness he is punished, without thereby affixing any stigma on philosophy (for he is a bad man for not cultivating philosophy in a lawful manner, but science is blameless), while if he refutes the false charges he is acquitted. Let this equal justice, then, be done to us. Let the life of the accused persons be investigated, but let the name stand free from all imputation. I must at the outset of my defense entreat you, illustrious emperors, to listen to me impartially: not to be carried away by the common irrational talk and prejudge the case, but to apply your desire of knowledge and love of truth to the examination of our doctrine also. Thus, while you on your part will not err through ignorance, we also, by disproving the charges arising out of the undiscerning rumor of the multitude, will cease to be assailed.

CHAPTER 3
Three things are alleged against us: atheism, Thyestean feasts, Oedipodean intercourse. But if these charges are true, spare no class: proceed at once against our crimes; destroy us root and branch, with our wives and children, if any Christian is found to live like the brutes. And yet even the brutes do not touch the flesh of their own kind; and they pair by a law of nature, and only at the regular season, not from simple wantonness; they also recognize those from whom they receive benefits. If anyone, therefore, is more savage than the brutes, what punishment that he can endure will be deemed adequate to such offenses? But, if these things are only idle tales and empty slanders, originating in the fact that virtue is opposed by its very nature to vice, and that antitheses war against one another by a divine law (and you are yourselves witnesses that no such iniquities are committed by us, for you forbid information to be laid against us), it remains for you to make inquiry concerning our life, our opinions, our loyalty and obedience to you and your house and government, and thus at length to grant to us the same rights—we ask nothing more—as to those who persecute us. For we will then conquer them, unhesitatingly surrendering, as we now do, our very lives for the truth's sake.

CHAPTER 4
As regards, first of all, the allegation that we are atheists—for I will confront the charges one by one, that we may not be ridiculed for having no answer to give to those who make them—with reason the Athenians judged Diagoras guilty of atheism, in that he not only divulged the Orphic doctrine, and published the mysteries of Eleusis and of the Cabiri, and chopped up the wooden statue of Hercules to boil his turnips, but openly declared that there was no God at all. But to us, who distinguish God from matter, and teach that matter is one thing and God another, and that they are separated by a wide interval (for that the Deity is uncreated and eternal, to be beheld by the understanding and reason alone, while matter is created and perishable), is it not absurd to apply the name of atheism? If our sentiments were like those of Diagoras, while we have such incentives to piety—in the established order, the universal harmony, the magnitude, the color, the form, the arrangement of the world—with reason might our reputation for impiety, as well as the cause of our being thus harassed, be charged on ourselves. But, since our doctrine acknowledges one God, the Maker of this universe, who is Himself uncreated (for that which is [self-existent] does not come to be, but [only] that which is not) but has made all things by the Word which is from Him, we are treated unreasonably in both respects, in that we are both defamed and persecuted.

CHAPTER 5
1. Poets and philosophers have not been voted atheists for inquiring concerning God. Euripides, speaking of those who, according to popular preconception, are ignorantly called gods, says doubtingly: "If Zeus indeed reigns in the heavens above, || He ought not to send afflictions on the righteous." But speaking of Him who is apprehended by the understanding as matter of certain knowledge, he gives his opinion decidedly, and with intelligence, thus: "Do you see him on high who, with humid arms, || Clasps both the boundless ether and the earth? Him reckon Zeus, and him regard as god."
2. For, as to these so-called gods, he neither saw any real existences, to which a name is usually assigned, underlying them ("Zeus," for instance: "who Zeus is I do not know, but by report"), nor that any names were given to realities which actually do exist (for of what use are names to those who have no real existences underlying them?); but he saw Him by means of His works, considering with an eye to things unseen the things which are manifest in air, in ether, [and] on earth. Him therefore, from whom proceed all created things, and by whose Spirit they are governed, he concluded to be God; and Sophocles agrees with him, when he says: "There is one God—in truth there is but one, || Who made the heavens and the broad earth beneath."
3. [Euripides is speaking] of the nature of God, which fills His works with beauty, and teaching both where God must be, and that He must be One.

CHAPTER 6
1. Philolaus, too, when he says that all things are included in God as in a stronghold, teaches that He is one, and that He is superior to matter. Lysis and Opsimus thus define God: the one says that He is an ineffable number, the other that He is the excess of the greatest number beyond that which comes nearest to it. So that since ten is the greatest number according to the Pythagoreans, being the Tetractys, and containing all the arithmetic and harmonic principles, and the Nine stands next to it, God is a unit—that is, one. For the greatest number exceeds the next least by one. Then there are Plato and Aristotle—not that I am about to go through all that the philosophers have said about God, as if I wished to exhibit a complete summary of their opinions; for I know that, as you excel all men in intelligence and in the power of your rule, in the same proportion do you surpass them all in an accurate acquaintance with all learning, cultivating as you do each individual branch with more success than even those who have devoted themselves exclusively to anyone. But inasmuch as it is impossible to demonstrate without the citation of names that we are not alone in confining the notion of God to unity, I have ventured on an enumeration of opinions. Plato, then, says, "To find out the Maker and Father of this universe is difficult; and, when found, it is impossible to declare Him to all," conceiving of one uncreated and eternal God. And if he recognizes others as well, such as the sun, moon, and stars, yet he recognizes them as created: "gods, offspring of gods, of whom I am the Maker, and the Father of works which are indissoluble apart from My will; but whatever is compounded can be dissolved." If,

therefore, Plato is not an atheist for conceiving of one uncreated God, the Framer of the universe, neither are we atheists who acknowledge and firmly hold that He is God who has framed all things by the Word, and holds them in being by His Spirit. Aristotle, again, and his followers, recognizing the existence of one whom they regard as a sort of compound living entity, speak of God as consisting of soul and body, thinking His body to be the ethereal space and the planetary stars and the sphere of the fixed stars, moving in circles; but His soul, the reason which presides over the motion of the body, itself not subject to motion, but becoming the cause of motion to the other. The Stoics also, although by the appellations they employ to suit the changes of matter, which they say is permeated by the Spirit of God, they multiply the Deity in name, yet in reality they consider God to be one.

2. For, if God is an artistic fire advancing methodically to the production of the several things in the world, embracing in Himself all the seminal principles by which each thing is produced in accordance with fate, and if His Spirit pervades the whole world, then God is one according to them, being named Zeus in respect of the fervid part of matter, and Hera in respect of the air, and called by other names in respect of that particular part of matter which He pervades.

CHAPTER 7

Since, therefore, the unity of the Deity is confessed by almost all, even against their will, when they come to treat of the first principles of the universe, and we in our turn likewise assert that He who arranged this universe is God, why is it that they can say and write with impunity what they please concerning the Deity, but that against us a law lies in force, though we are able to demonstrate what we apprehend and justly believe, namely that there is one God, with proofs and reason accordant with truth? For poets and philosophers, as to other subjects so also to this, have applied themselves in the way of conjecture, moved, by reason of their affinity with the inspiration from God, each one by his own soul, to try whether he could find out and apprehend the truth; but they have not been found competent to fully apprehend it, because they thought fit to learn, not from God concerning God, but each one from himself; hence they each came to his own conclusion respecting God, and matter, and forms, and the world. But we have for witnesses of the things we apprehend and believe, prophets, men who have pronounced concerning God and the things of God, guided by the Spirit of God. And you too will admit, excelling all others as you do in intelligence and in piety toward the true God, that it would be irrational for us to cease to believe in the Spirit from God, who moved the mouths of the prophets like musical instruments, and to give heed to mere human opinions.

CHAPTER 8

As regards, then, the doctrine that there was from the beginning one God, the Maker of this universe, consider it in this way, that you may also be acquainted with the logical grounds of our faith. If there were from the beginning two or more gods, they were either in one and the same place, or each of them separately in his own. In one and the same place they could not be. For, if they are gods, they are not alike; but because they are uncreated, they are distinct: for created things are like their patterns; but the uncreated are distinct, being neither produced from anyone, nor formed after the pattern of anyone. Hand, and eye, and foot are parts of one body, making up together one man: is God in this sense one? And indeed, Socrates was compounded and divided into parts, just because he was created and perishable; but God [who] is uncreated, and impassible, and indivisible, does not, therefore, consist of parts. But if, on the contrary, each of them exists separately, since He that made the world is above the things created, and around the things He has made and set in order, where can the other or the rest be? For if the world, being made spherical, is confined within the circles of heaven, and the Creator of the world is above the things created, managing that by His providential care of these, what place is there for the second god, or for the other gods? For he is not in the world, because it belongs to the other; nor around the world, for God the Maker of the world is above it. But if he is neither in the world nor around the world (for all that surrounds it is occupied by this one), where is he? Is he above the world and [the first] God? In another world, or around another? But if he is in another or around another, then he is not around us, for he does not govern the world; nor is his power great, for he exists in a circumscribed space. But if he is neither in another world (for all things are filled by the other), nor around another (for all things are occupied by the other), he clearly does not exist at all, for there is no place in which he can be. Or what does he do, seeing [that] there is another to whom the world belongs, and he is above the Maker of the world, and yet is neither in the world nor around the world? Is there, then, some other place where he can stand? But God, and what belongs to God, are above him. And what, too, will be the place, seeing that the other fills the regions which are above the world? Perhaps he exerts a providential care? And yet, unless he does so, he has done nothing. If, then, he neither does anything nor exercises providential care, and if there is not another place in which he is, then this Being of whom we speak is the one God from the beginning, and the sole Maker of the world.

CHAPTER 9

If we satisfied ourselves with advancing such considerations as these, our doctrines might by some be looked on as human. But, since the voices of the prophets confirm our arguments—for I think that you also, with your great zeal for knowledge, and your great attainments in learning, cannot be ignorant of the writings either of Moses or of Isaiah and Jeremiah, and the other prophets, who, lifted in ecstasy above the natural operations of their minds by the impulses of the Divine Spirit, uttered the things with which they were inspired, the Spirit making use of them as a flute-player breathes into a flute—what, then, do these men say? "The LORD is our God; No other can be compared with Him." And again: "I am God, the first and the last, || And besides Me there is no God." In like manner: "Before Me there was no other God, || And after Me there will be none; I am God, and there is none besides Me." And as to His greatness: "Heaven is My throne, and the earth is the footstool of My feet: What house will you build for Me, || Or what is the place of My rest?" But I leave it to you, when you deal with the books themselves, to examine carefully the prophecies contained in them, that you may on suitable grounds defend us from the abuse cast on us.

CHAPTER 10

That we are not atheists, therefore, seeing that we acknowledge one God, uncreated, eternal, invisible, impassible, incomprehensible, limitless, who is apprehended by the understanding only and the reason, who is encompassed by light, and beauty, and spirit, and ineffable power, by whom the universe has been created through His Word, and set in order, and is kept in being—I have sufficiently demonstrated. [I say "His Word"], for we also acknowledge [the] Son of God. Nor let anyone think it ridiculous that God should have a Son. For though the poets, in their fictions, represent the gods as no better than men, our mode of thinking is not the same as theirs, concerning either God the Father or the Son. But the Son of God is the Word of the Father, in idea and in operation; for after the pattern of Him and by Him were all things made, the Father and the Son being one. And the Son being in the Father and the Father in the Son, in [the] oneness and power of [the] Spirit, the understanding and reason of the Father is the Son of God. But if, in your surpassing intelligence, it occurs to you to inquire what is meant by the Son, I will state briefly that He is the first product of the Father, not as having been brought into existence (for from the beginning, God, who is the eternal mind, had the Word in Himself, being from eternity filled with the Word), but inasmuch as He came forth to be the idea and energizing power of all material things, which lay like a nature without attributes, and an inactive earth, the grosser particles being mixed up with the lighter. The prophetic Spirit also agrees with our statements. "The LORD," He says, "made Me, the beginning of His ways to His works." The Holy Spirit Himself also, which operates in the prophets, we assert to be an [eternal] effluence of God, flowing from Him, and returning back again like a beam of the sun. Who, then, would not be astonished to hear men who speak of God the Father, and of God the Son, and of the Holy Spirit, and who declare both Their power in union and Their distinction in order, called atheists? Nor is our teaching in what relates to the divine nature confined to these points; but we recognize also a multitude of messengers and ministers, whom God the Maker and Framer of the world distributed and appointed to their individual places by His Word, to occupy themselves with the elements, and the heavens, and the world, and the things in it, and the pleasant ordering of them all.

CHAPTER 11

If I go meticulously into the particulars of our doctrine, let it not surprise you: it is so that you may not be carried away by the popular and irrational opinion, but may have the truth clearly before you. For presenting the opinions themselves to which we adhere, as being not human but uttered and taught by God, we will be able to persuade you not to think of us as atheists. What, then, are those teachings in which we are brought up? "I say to you: love your enemies; bless them that curse you; pray for them that persecute you; that you may be the sons of your Father who is in Heaven, who causes His sun to rise on the evil and the good and sends rain on the just and the unjust." Allow me here to lift up my voice boldly in loud and audible outcry, pleading as I do before philosophic princes. For who of those that reduce syllogisms, and clear up ambiguities, and explain etymologies, or of those who teach homonyms and synonyms, and predicaments and axioms, and what is the subject and what the predicate, and who promise their disciples by these and such similar instructions to make them happy: who of them have so purged their souls as, instead of hating their enemies, to love them; and, instead of speaking ill of those who have reviled them (to abstain from which is of itself an evidence of no small restraint), to bless them; and to pray for those who plot against their lives? On the contrary, they never cease with evil intent to search out skillfully the secrets of their art, and are always bent on working some harm, making the art of words and not the exhibition of deeds their business and profession. But among us you will find uneducated persons, and artisans, and old women, who, if they are unable in words to prove the benefit of our doctrine, yet by their deeds exhibit the benefit arising from their persuasion of its truth: they do not rehearse speeches, but exhibit good works; when struck, they do not strike again; when robbed, they do not go to court; they give to those that ask of them, and love their neighbors as themselves.

CHAPTER 12

Should we, then, unless we believed that a God presides over the human race, thus purge ourselves from evil? Most certainly not. But, because we are persuaded that we will give an account of everything in the present life to God, who made us and the world, we adopt a temperate, and benevolent, and generally despised method of life, believing that we will suffer no such great evil here, even should our lives be taken from us, compared with what we will there receive for our meek, and benevolent, and moderate life from the Great Judge. Plato indeed has said that Minos and Rhadamanthus will judge and punish the wicked; but we say that even if a man is Minos or Rhadamanthus himself, or their father, even he will not escape the judgment of God. Are, then, those who consider life to be comprised in this, "Let us eat and drink, for tomorrow we die," and who regard death as a deep sleep and forgetfulness ("sleep and death, twin-brothers"), to be accounted pious; while men who reckon the present life of very small worth indeed, and who are conducted to the future life by this one thing alone, that they know God and His Word, what is the oneness of the Son with the Father, what the communion of the Father with the Son, what is the Spirit, what is the unity of these three—the Spirit, the Son, the Father, and their distinction in unity—and who know that the life for which we look is far better than can be described in words, provided we arrive at it pure from all wrongdoing; who, moreover, carry our benevolence to such an extent, that we not only love our friends ("for if you love them," He says, "that love you, and lend to them that lend to you, what reward will you have?")—will we, I say, when such is our character, and when we live such a life as this, that we may escape condemnation at last, not be accounted pious? These, however, are only small matters taken from great, and a few things from many, that we may not further trespass on your patience; for those who test honey and whey, judge by a small quantity whether the whole is good.

CHAPTER 13

1. But, as most of those who charge us with atheism, and that because they have not even the vaguest conception of what God is, and are dumb and utterly unacquainted with natural and divine things, and such as measure piety by the rule of sacrifices, charge us with not acknowledging the same gods as the cities, be pleased to attend to the following considerations, O emperors, on both points. And first, as to our not sacrificing: the Framer and Father of this universe does not need blood, nor the odor of burnt-offerings, nor the fragrance of flowers and incense, forasmuch as He is Himself perfect fragrance, needing nothing either within or without; but the noblest sacrifice to Him is for us to know who stretched out and vaulted the heavens, and fixed the earth in its place like a center, who gathered the water into seas and divided the light from the darkness, who adorned the sky with stars and made the earth to bring forth seed of every kind, who made animals and fashioned man. When, holding God to be this Framer of all things, who preserves them in being and superintends them all by knowledge and administrative skill, we "lift up holy hands" to Him, what need has He further of a hecatomb? "For they, when mortals have transgressed or failed || To do rightly, by sacrifice and prayer, || Libations and burnt-offerings, may be soothed."

2. And what have I to do with burnt-offerings, which God does not stand in need of? (Although it indeed behooves us to offer a bloodless sacrifice and "the service of our reason.")

CHAPTER 14

1. Then, as to the other complaint, that we do not pray to and believe in the same gods as the cities, it is an exceedingly silly one. Why, the very men who charge us with atheism for not admitting the same gods as they acknowledge, are not agreed among themselves concerning the gods. The Athenians have set up as gods Celeus and Metanira: the Lacedaemonians Menelaus; and they offer sacrifices and hold festivals to him, while the men of Ilium cannot endure the very sound of his name and pay their adoration to Hector. The Ceans worship Aristaeus, considering him to be the same as Zeus and Apollo; the Thasians Theagenes, a man who committed murder at the Olympic games; the Samians Lysander, notwithstanding all the slaughters and all the crimes perpetrated by him; Alcman and Hesiod Medea, and the Cilicians Niobe; the Sicilians Philip the son of Butacides; the Amathusians Onesilus; the Carthaginians Hamilcar.

2. Time would fail me to enumerate the whole. When, therefore, they differ among themselves concerning their gods, why do they bring the charge against us of not agreeing with them? Then look at the practices prevailing among the Egyptians: are they not perfectly ridiculous? For in the temples at their solemn festivals they beat their breasts as for the dead, and sacrifice to the same beings as gods; and no wonder, when they look on the brutes as gods, and shave themselves when they die, and bury them in temples, and make public lamentation. If, then, we are guilty of impiety because we do not practice a piety corresponding with theirs, then all cities and all nations are guilty of impiety, for they do not all acknowledge the same gods.

CHAPTER 15

But grant that they acknowledge the same. What then? Because the multitude, who cannot distinguish between matter and God, or see how great is the interval which lies between them, pray to idols made of matter, are we therefore, who do distinguish and separate the uncreated and the created, that which is and that which is not, that which is apprehended by the understanding and that which is perceived by the senses, and who give the fitting name to each of them—are we to come and worship images? If, indeed, matter and God are the same, two names for one thing, then certainly, in not regarding stocks and stones, gold and silver, as gods, we are guilty of impiety. But if they are at the greatest extent removed from one another—

as far apart as the artist and the materials of his are—why are we called to account? For as is the potter and the clay (matter being the clay, and the artist the potter), so is God, the Framer of the world, and matter, which is subservient to Him for the purposes of His art. But as the clay cannot become vessels of itself without artistry, so neither did matter, which is capable of taking all forms, receive, apart from God the Framer, distinction, and shape, and order. And as we do not hold the pottery of more worth than him who made it, nor the vessels or glass and gold than him who worked them; but if there is anything about them elegant in art we praise the artificer, and it is he who reaps the glory of the vessels: even so with matter and God—the glory and honor of the orderly arrangement of the world belongs of right not to matter, but to God, the Framer of matter. So that, if we were to regard the various forms of matter as gods, we should seem to be without any sense of the true God, because we should be putting the things which are dissoluble and perishable on a level with that which is eternal.

CHAPTER 16

The world is beautiful without a doubt, excelling, as well in its magnitude as in the arrangement of its parts, both those in the oblique circle and those around the north, and also in its spherical form. Yet it is not this, but its Artificer, that we must worship. For when any of your subjects come to you, they do not neglect to pay their homage to you, their rulers and lords, from whom they will obtain whatever they need, and address themselves to the magnificence of your palace; but, if they happen to come on the royal residence, they bestow a passing glance of admiration on its beautiful structure: but it is to you yourselves that they show honor, as being "all in all." You sovereigns, indeed, rear and adorn your palaces for yourselves; but the world was not created because God needed it; for God is Himself everything to Himself—unapproachable light, a perfect world, spirit, power, reason. If, therefore, the world is an instrument in tune, and moving in well-measured time, I adore the Being who gave its harmony, and strikes its notes, and sings the accordant strain, and not the instrument. For at the musical contests the adjudicators do not pass by the lute-players and crown the lutes. Whether, then, as Plato says, the world is a product of divine art, I admire its beauty, and adore the Artificer; or whether it is His essence and body, as the Peripatetics affirm, we do not neglect to adore God, who is the cause of the motion of the body, and descend "to the poor and weak elements," adoring in the impassible air (as they term it), passible matter; or, if anyone apprehends the several parts of the world to be powers of God, we do not approach and do homage to the powers, but their Maker and Lord. I do not ask of matter what it has not to give, nor passing God by do I pay homage to the elements, which can do nothing more than what they were commanded; for, although they are beautiful to look on, by reason of the art of their Framer, yet they still have the nature of matter. And to this view Plato also bears testimony: "For," he says, "that which is called heavens and earth has received many blessings from the Father, but yet partakes of body; hence it cannot possibly be free from change." If, therefore, while I admire the heavens and the elements in respect of their art, I do not worship them as gods, knowing that the law of dissolution is on them, how can I call those objects gods of which I know the makers to be men? Attend, I beg, to a few words on this subject.

CHAPTER 17

An apologist must adduce more precise arguments than I have yet given, both concerning the names of the gods, to show that they are of recent origin, and concerning their images, to show that they are, so to say, but of yesterday. You yourselves, however, are thoroughly acquainted with these matters, since you are versed in all departments of knowledge, and are beyond all other men familiar with the ancients. I assert, then, that it was Orpheus, and Homer, and Hesiod who gave both genealogies and names to those whom they call gods. Such, too, is the testimony of Herodotus. "My opinion," he says, "is that Hesiod and Homer preceded me by four hundred years, and no more; and it was they who framed a theogony for the Greeks, and gave the gods their names, and assigned them their several honors and functions, and described their forms." Representations of the gods, again, were not in use at all, so long as statuary, and painting, and sculpture were unknown; nor did they become common until Saurias the Samian, and Crato the Sicyonian, and Cleanthes the Corinthian, and the Corinthian harlot appeared, when drawing in outline was invented by Saurias, who sketched a horse in the sun, and painting by Crato, who painted in oil on a whitened tablet the outlines of a man and woman; and the art of making figures in relief was invented by the harlot, who, being in love with a person, traced his shadow on a wall as he lay asleep, and her father, being delighted with the exactness of the resemblance (he was a potter), carved out the sketch and filled it up with clay: this figure is still preserved at Corinth. After these, Daedalus and Theodorus the Milesian further invented sculpture and statuary. You perceive, then, that the time since representations of form and the making of images began is so short, that we can name the artist of each particular god. The image of Artemis at Ephesus, for example, and that of Athena (or rather of Athela, for so is she named by those who speak more in the style of the mysteries; for thus was the ancient image made of the olive-tree called), and the sitting figure of the same goddess, were made by Endoeus, a pupil of Daedalus; the Pythian god was the work of Theodorus and Telecles; and the Delian god and Artemis are due to the art of Tectaeus and Angelio; Hera in Samos and in Argos came from the hands of Smilis, and the other statues were by Phidias; Aphrodite the courtesan in Cnidus is the production of Praxiteles; Asclepius in Epidaurus is the work of Phidias. In a word, of not one of these statues can it be said that it was not made by man. If, then, these are gods, why did they not exist from the beginning? Why, in reality, are they younger than those who made them? Why, in reality, for their coming into existence, did they need the aid of men and art? They are nothing but earth, and stones, and matter, and curious art.

CHAPTER 18

1. But, since it is affirmed by some that, although these are only images, yet there exist gods in honor of whom they are made; and that the supplications and sacrifices presented to the images are to be referred to the gods, and are in fact made to the gods; and that there is not any other way of coming to them, "For it is hard for man || To meet in visible presence a god"; and whereas, in proof that such is the fact, they adduce the energies possessed by certain images, let us examine into the power attached to their names. And I would implore you, greatest of emperors, before I enter on this discussion, to be indulgent to me while I bring forward true considerations; for it is not my design to show the fallacy of idols, but by disproving the slanders vented against us, to offer a reason for the course of life we follow. May you, by considering yourselves, be able to discover the heavenly kingdom also! For as all things are subservient to you, father and son, who have received the kingdom from above (for "the king's soul is in the hand of God," says the prophetic Spirit), so too the one God and the Word proceeding from. Him, the Son, apprehended by us as inseparable from Him, all things are in like manner subjected. This then especially I beg you carefully to consider. The gods, as they affirm, were not from the beginning, but every one of them has come into existence just like ourselves. And in this opinion, they all agree. Homer speaks of "Old Oceanus, the sire of gods, and Tethys"; and Orpheus (who, moreover, was the first to invent their names, and recounted their births, and narrated the exploits of each, and is believed by them to treat with greater truth than others of divine things, whom Homer himself follows in most matters, especially in reference to the gods)—he, too, has fixed their first origin to be from water: "Oceanus, the origin of all."

2. For, according to him, water was the beginning of all things, and from water mud was formed, and from both was produced an animal, a dragon with the head of a lion growing to it, and between the two heads there was the face of a god, named Heracles and Kronos. This Heracles generated an egg of enormous size, which, on becoming full, was, by the powerful friction of its generator, burst into two, the part at the top receiving the form of heaven [(Ouranos)], and the lower part that of earth [(Ge)]. The goddess Ge, moreover, came forth with a body; and Ouranos, by his union with Ge, begot females: Clotho, Lachesis, and Atropos; and males: the hundred-handed Cottys, Gyges, Briareus, and the Cyclopes Brontes, and Steropes, and Argos, whom he also bound and hurled down to Tartarus, having learned that he was to be ejected from his government by his children; whereon Ge, being enraged, brought forth the Titans.

3. "The godlike Gaia bore to Ouranos ‖ Sons who are by the name of Titans known, ‖ Because they took vengeance on Ouranos, ‖ Majestic, gleaming with his starry crown."

CHAPTER 19

Such was the beginning of the existence both of their gods and of the universe. Now what are we to make of this? For each of those things to which divinity is ascribed is conceived of as having existed from the beginning. For, if they have come into being, having previously had no existence, as those say who treat of the gods, [then] they do not exist. For, a thing is either uncreated and eternal, or created and perishable. Nor do I think one thing and the philosophers another. "What is that which always is, and has no origin; or what is that which has been originated, yet never is?" Discoursing of the intelligible and the sensible, Plato teaches that that which always is, the intelligible, is unoriginated, but that which is not, the sensible, is originated, beginning to be and ceasing to exist. In like manner, the Stoics also say that all things will be burned up and will again exist, the world receiving another beginning. But if, although there is, according to them, a twofold cause, one active and governing, namely providence, the other passive and changeable, namely matter, it is nevertheless impossible for the world, even though under the care of Providence, to remain in the same state, because it is created—how can the constitution of these gods remain, who are not self-existent, but have been originated? And in what are the gods superior to matter, since they derive their constitution from water? But not even water, according to them, is the beginning of all things. From simple and homogeneous elements what could be constituted? Moreover, matter requires an artificer, and the artificer requires matter. For how could figures be made without matter or an artificer? Neither, again, is it reasonable that matter should be older than God; for the efficient cause must of necessity exist before the things that are made.

CHAPTER 20

If the absurdity of their theology were confined to saying that the gods were created, and owed their constitution to water, since I have demonstrated that nothing is made which is not also liable to dissolution, I might proceed to the remaining charges. But, on the one hand, they have described their bodily forms: speaking of Hercules, for instance, as a god in the shape of a coiled-up dragon; of others as hundred-handed; of the daughter of Zeus, whom he begot of his mother Rhea; or of Demeter, as having two eyes in the natural order, and two in her forehead, and the face of an animal on the back part of her neck, and as also having horns, so that Rhea, frightened at her monster of a child, fled from her, and did not give her the breast, from which mystically she is called Athela, but commonly Persephone and Kore, though she is not the same as Athena, who is called Kore from the pupil of the eye; and, on the other hand, they have described their admirable achievements, as they deem them: how Kronos, for instance, mutilated his father, and hurled him down from his chariot, and how he murdered his children, and swallowed the males of them; and how Zeus bound his father, and cast him down to Tartarus, as Ouranos also did to his sons, and fought with the Titans for the government; and how he persecuted his mother Rhea when she refused to wed him, and, she becoming a she-dragon, and he himself being changed into a dragon, bound her with what is called the Herculean knot, and accomplished his purpose, of which fact the rod of Hermes is a symbol; and again, how he violated his daughter Persephone, in this case also assuming the form of a dragon, and became the father of Dionysus. In face of narrations like these, I must say at least this much: what proper or useful is there in such a history, that we must believe Kronos, Zeus, Kore, and the rest, to be gods? Is it the descriptions of their bodies? Why, what man of judgment and reflection will believe that a viper was begotten by a god (thus Orpheus: "But from the sacred womb Phanes begot ‖ Another offspring, horrible and fierce, ‖ In sight a frightful viper, on whose head ‖ Were hairs: its face was lovely; but the rest, ‖ From the neck downwards, bore the aspect dire ‖ Of a dread dragon"); or who will admit that Phanes himself, being a firstborn god (for it was he that was produced from the egg), has the body or shape of a dragon, or was swallowed by Zeus, that Zeus might be too large to be contained? For if they differ in no respect from the lowest brutes (since it is evident that the Deity must differ from the things of earth and those that are derived from matter), they are not gods. How, then, I ask, can we approach them as suppliants, when their origin resembles that of cattle, and they themselves have the form of brutes, and are hideous to behold?

CHAPTER 21

1. But should it be said that they only had fleshly forms, and possess blood and seed, and the affections of anger and sexual desire, even then we must regard such assertions as nonsensical and ridiculous; for there is neither anger, nor desire and appetite, nor procreative seed, in gods. Let them, then, have fleshly forms, but let them be superior to wrath and anger, that Athena may not be seen "burning with rage and inwardly angry with Jove"; nor Hera appear thus: "Juno's breast could not contain her rage."

2. And let them be superior to grief: "A woeful sight my eyes behold: a man I love in flight around the walls! My heart for Hector grieves." For I call even men rude and stupid who give way to anger and grief. But when the "father of men and gods" mourns for his son—"Woe, woe! That fate decrees my best beloved Sarpedon, by Patroclus' hand to fall"; and is not able while he mourns to rescue him from his peril: "The son of Jove, yet Jove did not preserve him"—who would not blame the folly of those who, with tales like these, are lovers of the gods, or rather, live without any god?

3. Let them have fleshly forms, but do not let Aphrodite be wounded by Diomedes in her body: "The haughty son of Tydeus, Diomed, ‖ Has wounded me"; or by Ares in her soul: "Me, awkward me, she scorns; and yields her charms ‖ To that fair lecher, the strong god of arms." "The weapon pierced the flesh." He who was terrible in battle, the ally of Zeus against the Titans, is shown to be weaker than Diomedes: "He raged, as Mars, when brandishing his spear." Be silenced O Homer! A god never rages. But you describe the god to me as blood-stained, and the bane of mortals: "Mars, Mars, the bane of mortals, stained with blood"; and you tell of his adultery and his bonds: "Then, nothing loth, the enamored fair he led, ‖ And sunk transported on the conscious bed—Down rushed the toils."

4. Do they not pour forth impious stuff of this sort in abundance concerning the gods? Ouranos is mutilated; Kronos is bound and thrust down to Tartarus; the Titans revolt; Styx dies in battle: yes, they even represent them as mortal; they are in love with one another; they are in love with human beings—"Aeneas, amid Ida's jutting peaks, ‖ Immortal Venus to Anchises bore."

5. Are they not in love? Do they not suffer? No, truly, they are gods, and desire cannot touch them! Even though a god may assume flesh in pursuance of a divine purpose, he is therefore the slave of desire. "For never yet did such a flood of love, ‖ For goddess or for mortal, fill my soul; Not for Ixion's beautiful wife, who bore ‖ Pirithous, sage in council as the gods; Nor the neat-footed maiden Danae, ‖ Acrisius' daughter, her who Perseus bore, ‖ The observed of all; nor noble Phoenix child; … nor for Semele; Nor for Alcmena fair; … No, nor for Ceres, golden-tressed queen; Nor for Latona bright; nor for yourself."

6. He is created, he is perishable, with no trace of a god in him. No, they are even the hired servants of men: "Admetus' halls, in which I have endured ‖ To praise the menial table, though a god." And they tend cattle: "And coming to this laud, I fed cattle, ‖ For him that was my host, and kept this house." Admetus, therefore, was superior to the god. A prophet and wise one, and who can foresee for others the things that will be, you did not divine the slaughter of your beloved, but did even kill him with your own hand, dear as he was: "And I believed Apollo's divine mouth ‖ Was full of truth, as well as prophet's art."

(Aeschylus is reproaching Apollo for being a false prophet: "The very one who slugs while at the feast, || The one who said these things, indeed! Is he || Who slew my son.")

CHAPTER 22

1. But perhaps these things are poetic oddity, and there is some natural explanation of them, such as this by Empedocles: "Let Jove be fire, and Juno source of life, || With Pluto and Nestis, who bathes with tears || The human founts."

2. If, then, Zeus is fire, and Hera the earth, and Aidoneus the air, and Nestis water, and these are elements—fire, water, air—none of them is a god, neither Zeus, nor Hera, nor Aidoneus; for from matter separated into parts by God is their constitution and origin: "Fire, water, earth, and the air's gentle height, || And harmony with these."

3. Here are things which without harmony cannot abide; which would be brought to ruin by strife. How then can anyone say that they are gods? Friendship, according to Empedocles, has an aptitude to govern; things that are compounded are governed, and that which is apt to govern has the dominion; so that if we make the power of the governed and the governing one and the same, we will be unintentionally ourselves putting perishable, and fluctuating, and changeable matter on an equality with the uncreated, and eternal, and ever self-accordant God. Zeus is, according to the Stoics, the fervid part of nature; Hera is the air—the very name, if it is joined to itself, signifying this; Poseidon is what is drunk [(water)]. But these things are by different persons explained of natural objects in different ways. Some call Zeus twofold masculine-feminine air; others the season which brings about mild weather, on which account it was that he alone escaped from Kronos. But to the Stoics it may be said, if you acknowledge one God, the supreme and uncreated and eternal One, and as many compound bodies as there are changes of matter, and say that the Spirit of God, which pervades matter, obtains according to its variations a diversity of names, the forms of matter will become the body of God; but when the elements are destroyed in the conflagration, the names will necessarily perish along with the forms, the Spirit of God alone remaining. Who, then, can believe that those bodies, of which the variation according to matter is allied to corruption, are gods? But to those who say that Kronos is time, and Rhea the earth, and that she becomes pregnant by Kronos, and brings forth, from which she is regarded as the mother of all; and that he begets and devours his offspring; and that the mutilation is the intercourse of the male with the female, which cuts off the seed and casts it into the womb, and generates a human being, who has in himself the sexual desire, which is Aphrodite; and that the madness of Kronos is the turn of season, which destroys animate and inanimate things; and that the bonds and Tartarus are time, which is changed by seasons and disappears—to such persons we say, if Kronos is time, he changes; if a season, he turns around; if darkness, or frost, or the moist part of nature, none of these is abiding; but the Deity is immortal, and immoveable, and unalterable: so that neither Kronos nor his image is God. As regards Zeus again: if he is air, born of Kronos, of which the male part is called Zeus and the female Hera (from which [are] both sister and wife), he is subject to change; if a season, he turns around: but the Deity neither changes nor shifts around. But why should I trespass on your patience by saying more, when you know so well what has been said by each of those who have resolved these things into nature, or what various writers have thought concerning nature, or what they say concerning Athena, whom they affirm to be the wisdom pervading all things; and concerning Isis, whom they call the birth of all time, from whom all have sprung, and by whom all exist; or concerning Osiris, on whose murder by Typhon his brother Isis with her son Orus sought after his limbs, and finding them honored them with a tomb, which tomb is to this day called the tomb of Osiris? For while they wander up and down around the forms of matter, they miss finding the God who can only be beheld by the reason, while they deify the elements and their individual parts, applying different names to them at different times: calling the sowing of the corn, for instance, Osiris (hence they say, that in the mysteries, on the finding of the members of his body, or the fruits, Isis is thus addressed: "We have found, we wish you joy"), the fruit of the vine Dionysus, the vine itself Semele, the heat of the sun the thunderbolt. And yet, in fact, they who refer the fables to actual gods, do anything rather than add to their divine character; for they do not perceive, that by the very defense they make for the gods, they confirm the things which are alleged concerning them. What have Europa, and the bull, and the swan, and Leda, to do with the earth and air, that the abominable intercourse of Zeus with them should be taken for the intercourse of the earth and air? But missing to discover the greatness of God, and not being able to rise on high with their reason (for they have no affinity for the heavenly place), they pine away among the forms of matter, and rooted to the earth, deify the changes of the elements: just as if anyone should put the ship he sailed in the place of the pilot. But as the ship, although equipped with everything, is of no use if it does not have a pilot, so neither are the elements, though arranged in perfect order, of any service apart from the providence of God. For the ship will not sail of itself; and the elements without their Framer will not move.

CHAPTER 23

You may say, however, since you excel all men in understanding, "How does it come to pass, then, that some of the idols manifest power, if those to whom we erect the statues are not gods?" For it is not likely that images destitute of life and motion can of themselves do anything without a mover. That in various places, cities, and nations, certain effects are brought about in the name of idols, we are far from denying. None the more, however, if some have received benefit, and others, on the contrary, suffered harm, will we deem those to be gods who have produced the effects in either case. But I have made careful inquiry, both why it is that you think the idols to have this power, and who they are that, usurping their names, produce the effects. It is necessary for me, however, in attempting to show who they are that produce the effects ascribed to the idols, and that they are not gods, to have recourse to some witnesses from among the philosophers. First Thales, as those who have accurately examined his opinions report, divides [superior beings] into God, demons, and heroes. God he recognizes as the [Supreme] Intelligence of the world; by demons he understands beings possessed of soul; and by heroes, the separated souls of men, the good being the good souls, and the bad the worthless. Plato again, while withholding his assent on other points, also divides [superior beings] into the uncreated God and those produced by the Uncreated One for the adornment of heaven, the planets, and the fixed stars, and into demons; concerning which demons, while he does not think fit to speak himself, he thinks that those ought to be listened to who have spoken about them. "To speak concerning the other demons, and to know their origin, is beyond our powers; but we ought to believe those who have spoken before, the descendants of gods, as they say—and surely they must be well acquainted with their own ancestors: it is impossible, therefore, to disbelieve the sons of gods, even though they speak without probable or convincing proofs; but as they profess to tell of their own family affairs, we are bound, in pursuance of custom, to believe them. In this way, then, let us hold and speak as they do concerning the origin of the gods themselves. Of Ge and Ouranos were born Oceanus and Tethys; and of these, Phorcus, Kronos, and Rhea, and the rest; and of Kronos and Rhea, Zeus, Hera, and all the others, who, we know, are all called their brothers; besides other descendants again of these." Did, then, he who had contemplated the eternal Intelligence and God who is apprehended by reason, and declared His attributes—His real existence, the simplicity of His nature, the good that flows forth from Him that is truth—and discoursed of primal power, and how "all things are about the King of all, and all things exist for His sake, and He is the cause of all," and about two and three, that He is "the second moving around the seconds, and the third around the thirds"—did this man think, that to learn the truth concerning those who are said to have been produced from sensible things, namely earth and heaven, was a task transcending his powers? It is not to be believed for a moment. But because he thought it impossible to believe that gods beget and are brought forth, since everything that begins to be is followed by an end, and—

for this is much more difficult—to change the views of the multitude, who receive the fables without examination, on this account it was that he declared it to be beyond his powers to know and to speak concerning the origin of the other demons, since he was unable either to admit or teach that gods were begotten. And as regards that saying of his, "The great sovereign in heaven, Zeus, driving a winged car, advances first, ordering and managing all things, and there follow him a host of gods and demons," this does not refer to the Zeus who is said to have sprung from Kronos; for here the name is given to the Maker of the universe. This is shown by Plato himself: not being able to designate Him by another title that should be suitable, he availed himself of the popular name, not as peculiar to God, but for distinctness, because it is not possible to discourse of God to all men as fully as one might; and he adds at the same time the epithet "Great," so as to distinguish the heavenly from the earthly, the uncreated from the created, who is younger than heaven and earth, and younger than the Cretans, who stole him away, that he might not be killed by his father.

CHAPTER 24

What need is there, in speaking to you who have searched into every department of knowledge, to mention the poets, or to examine opinions of another kind? Let it suffice to say this much. If the poets and philosophers did not acknowledge that there is one God, and concerning these gods were not of opinion, some that they are demons, others that they are matter, and others that they once were men, there might be some show of reason for our being harassed as we are, since we employ language which makes a distinction between God and matter, and the natures of the two. For, as we acknowledge a God, and a Son—His Logos, and a Holy Spirit, united in essence: the Father, the Son, the Spirit, because the Son is the intelligence, reason, [and] wisdom of the Father, and the Spirit an effluence, as light from fire; so we also apprehend the existence of other powers, which exercise dominion over matter, and by means of it, and one in particular, which is hostile to God: not that anything is really opposed to God, like strife to friendship, according to Empedocles, and night to day, according to the appearing and disappearing of the stars (for even if anything had placed itself in opposition to God, it would have ceased to exist, its structure being destroyed by the power and might of God), but that to the good that is in God, which belongs of necessity to Him, and coexists with Him, as color with body, without which it has no existence (not as being part of it, but as an attendant property coexisting with it, united and blended, just as it is natural for fire to be yellow and the ether dark blue)—to the good that is in God, I say, the spirit which is over matter, who was created by God; just as the other messengers were created by Him, and entrusted with the control of matter and the forms of matter, is opposed. For this is the office of the messengers—to exercise providence for God over the things created and ordered by Him, so that God may have the universal and general providence of the whole, while the particular parts are provided for by the messengers appointed over them. Just as with men, who have freedom of choice as to both virtue and vice (for you would not either honor the good or punish the bad, unless vice and virtue were in their own power; and some are diligent in the matters entrusted to them by you, and others faithless), so it is among the messengers. Some, free agents, you will observe, such as they were created by God, continued in those things for which God had made and over which He had ordained them; but some outraged both the constitution of their nature and the government entrusted to them: namely, this ruler of matter and its various forms, and others of those who were placed over this first expanse (you know that we say nothing without witnesses, but state the things which have been declared by the prophets); these fell into impure love of virgins, and were subjugated by the flesh, and he became negligent and wicked in the management of the things entrusted to him. Of these lovers of virgins, therefore, were begotten those who are called giants. And if something has been said by the poets, too, about the giants, do not be surprised at this: worldly wisdom and divine differ as much from each other as truth and plausibility: the one is of Heaven and the other of earth; and indeed, according to the prince of matter: "We know we often speak lies that look like truths."

CHAPTER 25

1. These messengers, then, who have fallen from Heaven, and haunt the air and the earth, and are no longer able to rise to heavenly things, and the souls of the giants, which are the demons who wander around the world, perform actions similar, the one (that is, the demons) to the natures they have received, the other (that is, the messengers) to the appetites they have indulged. But the prince of matter, as may be seen merely from what transpires, exercises a control and management contrary to the good that is in God: "Oftentimes this anxious thought has crossed my mind, || Whether 'tis chance or deity that rules || The small affairs of men; and, spite of hope || As well as justice, drives to exile some || Stripped of all means of life, while others still || Continue to enjoy prosperity."

2. Prosperity and adversity, contrary to hope and justice, made it impossible for Euripides to say to whom belongs the administration of earthly affairs, which is of such a kind that one might say of it: "How then, while seeing these things, can we say, There is a race of gods, or yield to laws?"

3. The same thing led Aristotle to say that the things below the heavens are not under the care of Providence, although the eternal providence of God concerns itself equally with us below: "The earth, let willingness move her or not, || Must herbs produce, and thus sustain my flocks"—and addresses itself to the deserving individually, according to truth and not according to opinion; and all other things, according to the general constitution of nature, are provided for by the law of reason. But because the demoniac movements and operations proceeding from the adverse spirit produce these disorderly attacks, and moreover move men, some in one way and some in another, as individuals and as nations, separately and in common, in accordance with the tendency of matter on the one hand, and of the affinity for divine things on the other, from within and from without—some who are of no mean reputation have therefore thought that this universe is constituted without any definite order, and is driven here and there by an irrational chance. But they do not understand, that of those things which belong to the constitution of the whole world there is nothing out of order or neglected, but that each one of them has been produced by reason, and that, therefore, they do not transgress the order prescribed to them; and that man himself, too, so far as He that made him is concerned, is well-ordered, both by his original nature, which has one common character for all, and by the constitution of his body, which does not transgress the law imposed on it, and by the termination of his life, which remains equal and common to all alike; but that, according to the character peculiar to himself and the operation of the ruling prince and of the demons, his followers, he is impelled and moved in this direction or in that, notwithstanding that all possess in common the same original constitution of mind.

CHAPTER 26

1. They who draw men to idols, then, are the aforementioned demons, who are eager for the blood of the sacrifices, and lick them; but the gods that please the multitude, and whose names are given to the images, were men, as may be learned from their history. And that it is the demons who act under their names, is proved by the nature of their operations. For some castrate, as Rhea; others wound and slaughter, as Artemis; the Tauric goddess puts all strangers to death. I pass over those who lacerate with knives and scourges of bones and will not attempt to describe all the kinds of demons; for it is not the part of a god to incite to things against nature. "But when the demon plots against a man, || He first inflicts some hurt on his mind."

2. But God, being perfectly good, is eternally doing good. That, moreover, those who exert the power are not the same as those to whom the statues are erected, very strong evidence is afforded by Troas and Parium. The one has statues of Neryllinus, a man of our own times; and Parium of Alexander and Proteus: both the tomb and the statue of Alexander are still in the forum. The other statues of Neryllinus, then, are a public ornament, if indeed a city can be adorned by

such objects as these; but one of them is supposed to utter oracles and to heal the sick, and on this account the people of the Troad offer sacrifices to this statue, and overlay it with gold, and hang chaplets on it. But of the statues of Alexander and Proteus (the latter, you are aware, threw himself into the fire near Olympia), that of Proteus is likewise said to utter oracles; and to that of Alexander— "Wretched Paris, though in form so fair, || You slave of woman"—sacrifices are offered and festivals are held at the public cost, as to a god who can hear. Is it, then, Neryllinus, and Proteus, and Alexander who exert these energies in connection with the statues, or is it the nature of the matter itself? But the matter is brass. And what can brass do of itself, which may be made again into a different form, as Amasis treated the foot pan, as told by Herodotus? And Neryllinus, and Proteus, and Alexander, what good are they to the sick? For what the image is said now to effect, it effected when Neryllinus was alive and sick.

CHAPTER 27

What then? In the first place, the irrational and fantastic movements of the soul about opinions produce a diversity of images from time to time: some they derive from matter, and some they fashion and bring forth for themselves; and this happens to a soul especially when it partakes of the material spirit and becomes mingled with it, looking not at heavenly things and their Maker, but downwards to earthly things, wholly at the earth, as being now mere flesh and blood, and no longer pure spirit. These irrational and fantastic movements of the soul, then, give birth to empty visions in the mind, by which it becomes madly set on idols. When, too, a tender and susceptible soul, which has no knowledge or experience of sounder doctrines, and is unaccustomed to contemplate truth, and to consider thoughtfully the Father and Maker of all things, gets impressed with false opinions respecting itself, then the demons who hover around matter, greedy of sacrificial odors and the blood of victims, and ever ready to lead men into error, avail themselves of these delusive movements of the souls of the multitude; and, taking possession of their thoughts, cause to flow into the mind empty visions as if coming from the idols and the statues; and when, too, a soul of itself, as being immortal, moves conformably to reason, either predicting the future or healing the present, the demons claim the glory for themselves.

CHAPTER 28

1. But it is perhaps necessary, in accordance with what has already been adduced, to say a little about their names. Herodotus, then, and Alexander the son of Philip, in his letter to his mother (and each of them is said to have conversed with the priests at Heliopolis, and Memphis, and Thebes), affirm that they learned from them that the gods had been men. Herodotus speaks thus: "Of such a nature were, they said, the beings represented by these images; they were very far indeed from being gods. However, in the times anterior to them it was otherwise; then Egypt had gods for its rulers, who dwelt on the earth with men, one being always supreme above the rest. The last of these was Horus the son of Osiris, called by the Greeks Apollo. He deposed Typhon and ruled over Egypt as its last god-king. Osiris is named Dionysus [(Bacchus)] by the Greeks. Almost all the names of the gods came into Greece from Egypt." Apollo was the son of Dionysus and Isis, as Herodotus likewise affirms: "According to the Egyptians, Apollo and Diana are the children of Bacchus and Isis; while Latona is their nurse and their preserver." These beings of heavenly origin had for their first kings: partly from ignorance of the true worship of the Deity, partly from gratitude for their government, they esteemed them as gods together with their wives. "The male cows, if clean, and the male calves are used for sacrifice by the Egyptians universally; but the females, they are not allowed to sacrifice, since they are sacred to Isis. The statue of this goddess has the form of a woman but with horns like a cow, resembling those of the Greek representations of Io." And who can be more deserving of credit in making these statements than those who in family succession, son from father, received not only the priesthood, but also the history? For it is not likely that the priests, who make it their business to commend the idols to men's reverence, would assert falsely that they were men. If Herodotus alone had said that the Egyptians spoke in their histories of the gods as of men, when he says, "What they told me concerning their religion it is not my intention to repeat, except only the names of their deities, things of very trifling importance," it would befit us not to credit even Herodotus as being a fabulist. But as Alexander and Hermes surnamed Trismegistus, who shares with them in the attribute of eternity, and innumerable others, not to name them individually, [declare the same,] no room is left even for doubt that they, being kings, were esteemed gods. That they were men, the most learned of the Egyptians also testify, who, while saying that ether, earth, sun, moon, are gods, regard the rest as mortal men, and the temples as their tombs. Apollodorus, too, asserts the same thing in his treatise concerning the gods.
2. But Herodotus calls even their sufferings mysteries: "The ceremonies at the feast of Isis in the city of Busiris have been already spoken of. It is there that the whole multitude, both of men and women, many thousands in number, beat themselves at the close of the sacrifice in honor of a god whose name a religious scruple forbids me to mention." If they are gods, they are also immortal; but if people are beaten for them, and their sufferings are mysteries, they are men, as Herodotus himself says: "Here, too, in this same precinct of Minerva at Sais, is the burial-place of one whom I think it not right to mention in such a connection. It stands behind the temple against the back wall, which it entirely covers. There are also some large stone obelisks in the enclosure, and there is a lake near, adorned with an edging of stone. In form it is circular, and in size, as it seemed to me, about equal to the lake at Delos called the Hoop. On this lake it is that the Egyptians represent by night his sufferings whose name I refrain from mentioning, and this representation they call their mysteries." And not only is the tomb of Osiris shown, but also his embalming: "When a body is brought to them, they show the bearer various models of corpses made in wood and painted so as to resemble nature. The most perfect is said to be after the manner of him whom I do not think it religious to name in connection with such a matter."

CHAPTER 29

1. But among the Greeks, also, those who are eminent in poetry and history say the same thing. Thus, of Heracles: "That lawless wretch, that man of brutal strength, || Deaf to Heaven's voice, the social rite transgressed." Such being his nature, he deservedly went mad, and he deservedly lighted the funeral pile and burned himself to death. Of Asclepius, Hesiod says: "The mighty father both of gods and men || Was filled with wrath, and from Olympus' top || With flaming thunderbolt cast down and slew || Latona's well-loved son— such was his ire."
2. And Pindar: "But even wisdom is ensnared by gain. The brilliant bribe of gold seen in the hand || Even him perverted: therefore, Kronos' son || With both hands quickly stopped his vital breath, || And by a bolt of fire ensured his doom." Either, therefore, they were gods and did not hanker after gold—"O gold, the fairest prize to mortal men, || Which neither mother equals in delight, || Nor children dear"—for the Deity is in need of nothing, and is superior to carnal desire, nor did they die; or, having been born men, they were wicked by reason of ignorance, and overcome by love of money. What more need I say, or refer to Castor, or Pollux, or Amphiaraus, who, having been born, so to speak, only the other day, men of men, are looked on as gods, when they imagine even Ino after her madness and its consequent sufferings to have become a goddess? "Sea-rovers will name her Leucothea." And her son: "August Palaemon, sailors will invoke."

CHAPTER 30

1. For if detestable and god-hated men had the reputation of being gods, and the daughter of Derceto, Semiramis, a lewd and blood-stained woman, was esteemed a Syrian goddess; and if, on account of Derceto, the Syrians worship doves and Semiramis (for, a thing impossible, a woman was changed into a dove: the story is in Ctesias), what wonder if some should be called gods by their people on the ground of their rule and sovereignty (the Sibyl, of whom Plato also makes mention, says: "It was the generation then the tenth, || Of men endowed with speech, since forth the Flood || Had burst on the men of former times, || And Kronos, Japetus, and Titan reigned, || Whom men, of Ouranos and Gaia || Proclaimed the noblest sons, and named them so, || Because of men endowed with gift of speech || They were the first"); and others for their strength, as Heracles and Perseus; and others for their art, as Asclepius? Those, therefore, to whom either the subjects gave honor or the rulers themselves [assumed it], obtained the name, some from fear, others from revenge. Thus Antinous, through the benevolence of your ancestors toward their subjects, came to be regarded as a god. But those who came after adopted the worship without examination.

2. "The Cretans always lie; for they, O king, || Have built a tomb to you who are not dead." Though you believe, O Callimachus, in the nativity of Zeus, you do not believe in his tomb; and while you think to obscure the truth, you in fact proclaim him dead, even to those who are ignorant; and if you see the cave, you call to mind the childbirth of Rhea; but when you see the coffin, you throw a shadow over his death, not considering that the unbegotten God alone is eternal. For either the tales told by the multitude and the poets about the gods are unworthy of credit, and the reverence shown them is superfluous (for those do not exist, the tales concerning whom are untrue); or if the births, the affairs, the murders, the thefts, the castrations, the thunderbolts, are true, they no longer exist, having ceased to be since they were born, having previously had no being. And on what principle must we believe some things and disbelieve others, when the poets have written their stories in order to gain greater veneration for them? For surely those through whom they have gotten to be considered gods, and who have striven to represent their deeds as worthy of reverence, cannot have invented their sufferings. That, therefore, we are not atheists, acknowledging as we do God, the Maker of this universe, and His Word, has been proved according to my ability, if not according to the importance of the subject.

CHAPTER 31

But they have further also invented stories against us of impious feasts and forbidden intercourse between the sexes, both that they may appear to themselves to have rational grounds of hatred, and because they think either by fear to lead us away from our way of life, or to render the rulers harsh and inexorable by the magnitude of the charges they bring. But they lose their labor with those who know that from of old it has been the custom, and not in our time only, for vice to make war on virtue. Thus Pythagoras, with three hundred others, was burnt to death; Heraclitus and Democritus were banished, the one from the city of the Ephesians, the other from Abdera, because he was charged with being mad; and the Athenians condemned Socrates to death. But as they were none the worse in respect of virtue because of the opinion of the multitude, so neither does the undiscriminating slander of some persons cast any shade on us as regards rectitude of life, for with God we stand in good repute. Nevertheless, I will meet these charges also, although I am well assured that by what has already been said I have cleared myself to you. For as you excel all men in intelligence, you know that those whose life is directed toward God as its rule, so that each one among us may be blameless and irreproachable before Him, will not entertain even the thought of the slightest sin. For if we believed that we should live only the present life, then we might be suspected of sinning, through being enslaved to flesh and blood, or overmastered by gain or carnal desire; but since we know that God is witness to what we think and what we say both by night and by day, and that He, being Himself light, sees all things in our heart, we are persuaded that when we are removed from the present life we will live another life, better than the present one, and heavenly, not earthly (since we will abide near God, and with God, free from all change or suffering in the soul, not as flesh, even though we will have flesh, but as heavenly spirit), or, falling with the rest, a worse one and in fire; for God has not made us as sheep or beasts of burden, a mere by-work, and that we should perish and be annihilated. On these grounds it is not likely that we should wish to do evil or deliver ourselves over to the Great Judge to be punished.

CHAPTER 32

It is, however, nothing wonderful that they should make up tales about us such as they tell of their own gods, of the incidents of whose lives they make mysteries. But it suits them, if they meant to condemn shameless and promiscuous intercourse, to hate either Zeus, who begot children of his mother Rhea and his daughter Kore, and took his own sister to wife, or Orpheus, the inventor of these tales, which made Zeus more unholy and detestable than Thyestes himself; for the latter defiled his daughter in pursuance of an oracle, and when he wanted to obtain the kingdom and avenge himself. But we are so far from practicing promiscuous intercourse, that it is not lawful among us to indulge even a lustful look. "For," He says, "he that looks on a woman to lust after her, has already committed adultery in his heart." Those, then, who are forbidden to look at anything more than that for which God formed the eyes, which were intended to be a light to us, and to whom a wanton look is adultery, the eyes being made for other purposes, and who are to be called to account for their very thoughts, how can anyone doubt that such persons practice self-control? For our account lies not with human laws, which a bad man can evade (at the outset I proved to you, sovereign lords, that our doctrine is from the teaching of God), but we have a law which makes the measure of rectitude to consist in dealing with our neighbor as ourselves. On this account, too, according to age, we recognize some as sons and daughters, others we regard as brothers and sisters, and to the more advanced in life we give the honor due to fathers and mothers. On behalf of those, then, to whom we apply the names of brothers and sisters, and other designations of relationship, we exercise the greatest care that their bodies should remain undefiled and uncorrupted; for the Word again says to us, "If anyone kisses a second time because it has given him pleasure, [he sins]"; adding, "Therefore the kiss, or rather the salutation, should be given with the greatest care, since, if there be mixed with it the least defilement of thought, it excludes us from continuous life."

CHAPTER 33

Therefore, having the hope of continuous life, we despise the things of this life, even to the pleasures of the soul, each of us reckoning her his wife whom he has married according to the laws laid down by us, and that only for the purpose of having children. For as the farmer throwing the seed into the ground awaits the harvest, not sowing more on it, so to us the procreation of children is the measure of our indulgence in appetite. No, you would find many among us, both men and women, growing old unmarried, in hope of living in closer communion with God. But if the remaining in virginity and in the state of a eunuch brings nearer to God, while the indulgence of carnal thought and desire leads away from Him, in those cases in which we shun the thoughts, much more do we reject the deeds. For we bestow our attention—not on the study of words, but on the exhibition and teaching of actions—that a person should either remain as he was born or be content with one marriage; for a second marriage is only a specious adultery. "For whosoever puts away his wife," He says, "and marries another, commits adultery"; not permitting a man to send her away whose virginity he has brought to an end, nor to marry again. For he who deprives himself of his first wife, even though she is dead, is a cloaked adulterer, resisting the hand of God, because in the beginning God made one man and one woman, and dissolving the strictest union of flesh with flesh, formed for the intercourse of the race.

CHAPTER 34

But though such is our character (Oh! Why should I speak of things unfit to be uttered?), the things said of us are an example of the proverb, "The harlot reproves the chaste." For those who have set up a market for fornication and established infamous resorts for the young for every kind of vile pleasure, who do not abstain even from males, males with males committing shocking abominations, outraging all the noblest and lovely bodies in all sorts of ways, so dishonoring the fair workmanship of God (for beauty on earth is not self-made, but sent here by the hand and will of God)—these men, I say, revile us for the very things which they are conscious of themselves, and ascribe to their own gods, boasting of them as noble deeds, and worthy of the gods. These adulterers and pederasts defame the eunuchs and the once-married (while they themselves live like fishes; for these gulp down whatever falls in their way, and the stronger chases the weaker: and, in fact, this is to feed on human flesh, to do violence in contravention of the very laws which you and your ancestors, with due care for all that is fair and right, have enacted), so that not even the governors of the provinces sent by you suffice for the hearing of the complaints against those, to whom it even is not lawful, when they are struck, not to offer themselves for more blows, nor when defamed not to bless: for it is not enough to be just (and justice is to return like for like), but it is incumbent on us to be good and patient of evil.

CHAPTER 35

What man of sound mind, therefore, will affirm, while such is our character, that we are murderers? For we cannot eat human flesh until we have killed someone. The former charge, therefore, being false, if anyone should ask them in regard to the second, whether they have seen what they assert, not one of them would be so brazen as to say that he had. And yet we have slaves, some more and some fewer, by whom we could not help being seen; but even of these, not one has been found to invent even such things against us. For when they know that we cannot endure even to see a man put to death, though justly; who of them can accuse us of murder or cannibalism? Who does not reckon among the things of greatest interest the contests of gladiators and wild beasts, especially those which are given by you? But we, deeming that to see a man put to death is much the same as killing him, have renounced such spectacles. How, then, when we do not even look on, lest we should contract guilt and pollution, can we put people to death? And when we say that those women who use drugs to bring on abortion commit murder, and will have to give an account to God for the abortion, on what principle should we commit murder? For it does not belong to the same person to regard the very child in the womb as a created being, and therefore an object of God's care, and when it has passed into life, to kill it; and not to expose an infant, because those who expose them are chargeable with child-murder, and on the other hand, when it has been reared to destroy it. But we are in all things always alike and the same, submitting ourselves to reason, and not ruling over it.

CHAPTER 36

Who, then, that believes in a resurrection, would make himself into a tomb for bodies that will rise again? For it is not the part of the same persons to believe that our bodies will rise again, and to eat them as if they would not; and to think that the earth will give back the bodies held by it, but that those which a man has entombed in himself will not be demanded back. On the contrary, it is reasonable to suppose, that those who think they will have no account to give of the present life, ill or well spent, and that there is no resurrection, but calculate on the soul perishing with the body, and being as it were quenched in it, will refrain from no deed of daring; but as for those who are persuaded that nothing will escape the scrutiny of God, but that even the body which has ministered to the irrational impulses of the soul, and to its desires, will be punished along with it, it is not likely that they will commit even the smallest sin. But if to anyone it appears sheer nonsense that the body which has rotted away, and been dissolved, and reduced to nothing, should be reconstructed, we certainly cannot with any reason be accused of wickedness with reference to those that do not believe, but only of folly; for with the opinions by which we deceive ourselves we injure no one else. But that it is not our belief alone that bodies will rise again, but that many philosophers also hold the same view, it is out of place to show just now, lest we should be thought to introduce topics irrelevant to the matter at hand, either by speaking of the intelligible and the sensible, and the nature of these respectively, or by contending that the incorporeal is older than the corporeal, and that the intelligible precedes the sensible, although we become acquainted with the latter earliest, since the corporeal is formed from the incorporeal, by the combination with it of the intelligible, and that the sensible is formed from the intelligible; for nothing hinders, according to Pythagoras and Plato, that when the dissolution of bodies takes place, they should, from the very same elements of which they were constructed at first, be constructed again. But let us defer the discourse concerning the resurrection.

CHAPTER 37

And now may you, who are entirely in everything, by nature and by education, upright, and moderate, and benevolent, and worthy of your rule, now that I have disposed of the individual accusations, and proved that we are pious, and gentle, and temperate in spirit, bend your royal head in approval. For who are more deserving to obtain the things they ask, than those who, like us, pray for your government, that you may, as is most equitable, receive the kingdom, son from father, and that your empire may receive increase and addition, all men becoming subject to your sway? And this is also for our advantage, that we may lead a peaceable and quiet life, and may ourselves readily perform all that is commanded of us.

APOLOGY TO AUTOLYCUS

The Apology to Autolycus is one of the earliest extant Christian apologetic discourses, penned by the 2nd-century overseer Theophilus of Antioch, who wrote his apology during the reign of Commodus in the second half of the century. Notably, his apology is the earliest extant work using the word "Trinity" to define the Godhead (τριάς in the Greek). He was also a clear proponent of conditionalism and utilization of the Sibylline Oracles as evidenced by various statements, quotes, and expositions within the Apology.

BOOK I

CHAPTER 1

¹A fluent tongue and an elegant style afford pleasure and such praise as vainglory delights in, to wretched men who have been corrupted in mind; ²the lover of truth does not give heed to ornamental speeches, but examines the real matter of the speech, what it is, and what kind it is. ³Since, then, my friend, you have assailed me with empty words, boasting of your gods of wood and stone, hammered and cast, carved and graven, which neither see nor hear, for they are idols, and the works of men's hands; ⁴and since, besides, you call me a Christian, as if this were a damning name to bear, I, for my part, avow that I am a Christian, and bear this name beloved of God, hoping to be serviceable to God. ⁵For it is not the case, as you suppose, that the Name of God is hard to bear; but possibly you entertain this opinion of God, because you are yourself yet unserviceable to Him.

CHAPTER 2

¹But if you say, "Show me your God," I would reply, "Show me yourself, and I will show you my God." ²Show, then, that the eyes of your soul are capable of seeing, and the ears of your heart able to hear; ³for as those who look with the eyes of the body perceive earthly objects and what concerns this life, and discriminate at the same time between things that differ, whether light or darkness, white or black, deformed or beautiful, well-proportioned and symmetrical or disproportioned and awkward, or monstrous or mutilated; ⁴and as in like manner also, by the sense of hearing,

we discriminate either sharp, or deep, or sweet sounds; so the same holds true regarding the eyes of the soul and the ears of the heart, that it is by them we are able to behold God. [5]For God is seen by those who are enabled to see Him when they have the eyes of their soul opened: for all have eyes; but in some they are overspread, and do not see the light of the sun. [6]Yet it does not follow, because the blind do not see, that the light of the sun does not shine; but let the blind blame themselves and their own eyes. [7]So you also, O man, have the eyes of your soul overspread by your sins and evil deeds. [8]As a burnished mirror, so ought man to have his soul pure. When there is rust on the mirror, it is not possible for a man's face to be seen in the mirror; so also when there is sin in a man, such a man cannot behold God. [9]Therefore, show me yourself, whether you are not an adulterer, or a fornicator, or a thief, or a robber, or a thief; [10]whether you do not corrupt boys; whether you are not insolent, or a slanderer, or passionate, or envious, or proud, or pompous; whether you are not a brawler, or covetous, or disobedient to parents; and whether you do not sell your children; [11]for to those who do these things God is not manifest, unless they have first cleansed themselves from all impurity. [12]All these things, then, involve you in darkness, as when a filmy defluxion on the eyes prevents one from beholding the light of the sun: thus also do iniquities, man, involve you in darkness, so that you cannot see God.

CHAPTER 3

[1]You will say, then, to me, "Do you, who see God, explain to me the appearance of God?" [2]Hear, O man. The appearance of God is ineffable, and indescribable, and cannot be seen by eyes of flesh. [3]For He is incomprehensible in glory, unfathomable in greatness, inconceivable in height, incomparable in power, unrivaled in wisdom, unmatched in goodness, unspeakable in kindness. [4]For if I say He is Light, I name but His own work; if I call Him Word, I name but His sovereignty; if I call Him Mind, I speak but of His wisdom; if I say He is Spirit, I speak of His breath; if I call Him Wisdom, I speak of His offspring; [5]if I call Him Strength, I speak of His sway; if I call Him Power, I am mentioning His activity; if Providence, I but mention His goodness; if I call Him Kingdom, I but mention His glory; if I call Him Lord, I mention His being judge; if I call Him Judge, I speak of Him as being just; [6]if I call Him Father, I speak of all things as being from Him; if I call Him Fire, I but mention His anger. [7]You will say, then, to me, "Is God angry?" Yes; He is angry with those who act wickedly, but He is good, and kind, and merciful, to those who love and fear Him; [8]for He is a chastener of the godly, and father of the righteous; but He is a judge and punisher of the impious.

CHAPTER 4

[1]And He is without beginning, because He is unbegotten; and He is unchangeable, because He is immortal. [2]And He is called God on account of His having placed all things on security afforded by Himself; and on account of being the Mover, for Mover means running, and moving, and being active, and nourishing, and foreseeing, and governing, and making all things alive. [3]But He is Lord, because He rules over the universe; Father, because He is before all things; Fashioner and Maker, because He is creator and maker of the universe; the Highest, because of His being above all; and Almighty, because He Himself rules and embraces all. [4]For the heights of the heavens, and the depths of the abysses, and the ends of the earth, are in His hand, and there is no place of His rest. [5]For the heavens are His work, the earth is His creation, the sea is His handiwork; man is His formation and His image; sun, moon, and stars are His elements, made for signs, and seasons, and days, and years, that they may serve and be slaves to man; [6]and all things God has made out of things that were not into things that are, in order that through His works His greatness may be known and understood.

CHAPTER 5

[1]For as the soul in man is not seen, being invisible to men, but is perceived through the motion of the body, so God cannot indeed be seen by human eyes, but is beheld and perceived through His providence and works. [2]For, in like manner, as any person, when he sees a ship on the sea rigged and in sail, and making for the harbor, will no doubt infer that there is a pilot in her who is steering her; [3]so we must perceive that God is the governor of the whole universe, though He is not visible to the eyes of the flesh, since He is incomprehensible. [4]For if a man cannot look on the sun, although it is a very small heavenly body, on account of its exceeding heat and power, how will a mortal man not be much more unable to face the glory of God, which is unutterable? [5]For as the pomegranate, with the rind containing it, has within it many cells and compartments which are separated by tissues, and has also many seeds dwelling in it, so the whole creation is contained by the Spirit of God, and the containing Spirit is, along with the creation, contained by the hand of God. [6]As, therefore, the seed of the pomegranate, dwelling inside, cannot see what is outside the rind, itself being within, so neither can man, who along with the whole creation is enclosed by the hand of God, behold God. [7]Then again, an earthly king is believed to exist, even though he is not seen by all; for he is recognized by his laws and ordinances, and authorities, and forces, and statues; and are you unwilling that God should be recognized by His works and mighty deeds?

CHAPTER 6

[1]Consider, O man, His works—the timely rotation of the seasons, and the changes of temperature; the regular march of the stars; [2]the well-ordered course of days and nights, and months, and years; the various beauty of seeds, and plants, and fruits; and the various species of quadrupeds, and birds, and reptiles, and fishes, both of the rivers and of the sea; or consider the instinct implanted in these animals to beget and rear offspring, not for their own profit, but for the use of man; [3]and the providence with which God provides nourishment for all flesh, or the subjection in which He has ordained that all things subserve mankind. Consider, too, the flowing of sweet fountains and never-failing rivers, and the seasonable supply of dews, and showers, and rains; [4]the manifold movement of the heavenly bodies, the morning star rising and heralding the approach of the perfect luminary; and the constellation of Pleiades, and Orion, and Arcturus, and the orbit of the other stars that circle through the heavens, all of which the manifold wisdom of God has called by names of their own. [5]He is God alone who made light out of darkness, and brought forth light from His treasures, and formed the chambers of the south wind, and the treasure-houses of the deep, and the bounds of the seas, and the treasuries of snows and hail-storms, collecting the waters in the storehouses of the deep, and the darkness in His treasures, and bringing forth the sweet, and desirable, and pleasant light out of His treasures; who causes the vapors to ascend from the ends of the earth: [6]He makes lightnings for the rain; who sends forth His thunder to terrify, and foretells by the lightning the peal of the thunder, that no soul may faint with the sudden shock; [7]and who so moderates the violence of the lightning as it flashes out of the sky, that it does not consume the earth; for, if the lightning were allowed all its power, it would burn up the earth; and were the thunder allowed all its power, it would overthrow all the works that are therein.

CHAPTER 7

[1]This is my God, the Lord of all, who alone stretched out the heavens, and established the breadth of the earth under it; who stirs the deep recesses of the sea, and makes its waves roar; who rules its power, and stills the tumult of its waves; who founded the earth on the waters, and gave a spirit to nourish it; [2]whose breath gives light to the whole, who, if He withdraws His breath, the whole will utterly fail. By Him you speak, O man; His breath you breathe yet Him you do not know. [3]And this is your condition, because of the blindness of your soul, and the hardness of your heart. But, if you will, you may be healed. [4]Entrust yourself to the Physician, and He will arrange the eyes of your soul and of your heart. [5]Who is the Physician? God, who heals and makes alive through His Word and Wisdom. [6]God by His own Word and Wisdom made all things; for by His Word were the heavens made, and all the host of them by the breath of His mouth. [7]Most excellent is His Wisdom. By His Wisdom God founded the earth; and by knowledge He prepared the heavens; and by understanding were the fountains of the great deep broken up, and the clouds poured out their dews. [8]If you perceive these things, O

man, living chastely, and piously, and righteously, you can see God. ⁹But before all, let faith and the fear of God have rule in your heart, and then you will understand these things. ¹⁰When you will have put off the mortal, and put on incorruption, then you will see God worthily. ¹¹For God will raise your flesh immortal with your soul; and then, having become immortal, you will see the Immortal, if now you believe in Him; and then you will know that you have spoken unjustly against Him.

CHAPTER 8

¹But you do not believe that the dead are raised. When the resurrection will take place, then you will believe, whether you want to or not; and your faith will be reckoned for unbelief, unless you believe now. ²And why do you not believe? Do you not know that faith is the leading principle in all matters? ³For what farmer can reap unless he first trusts his seed to the earth? Or who can cross the sea unless he first entrusts himself to the boat and the pilot? ⁴And what sick person can be healed unless he first trusts himself to the care of the physician? And what art or knowledge can anyone learn unless he first applies and entrusts himself to the teacher? ⁵If, then, the farmer trusts the earth, and the sailor the boat, and the sick the physician, will you not place confidence in God, even when you hold so many pledges at His hand? ⁶For first He created you out of nothing, and brought you into existence (for if your father was nothing, nor your mother, how much more were you yourself at one time not in being), and formed you out of a small and moist substance, even out of the least drop, which at one time had no being itself; and God introduced you into this life. ⁷Moreover, you believe that the images made by men are gods, and do great things; and can you not believe that the God who made you is also able to make you afterward?

CHAPTER 9

¹And, indeed, the names of those whom you say you worship, are the names of dead men. And these, too, who and what kind of men were they? ²Is not Saturn found to be a cannibal, destroying and devouring his own children? ³And if you name his son Jupiter, hear also his deeds and conduct—first, how he was suckled by a goat on Mount Ida, and having slain it, according to the myths, and flayed it, he made himself a coat of the hide. ⁴And his other deeds—his incest, and adultery, and lust—will be better recounted by Homer and the rest of the poets. ⁵Why should I further speak of his sons? How Hercules burnt himself; and about the drunk and raging Bacchus; and of Apollo fearing and fleeing from Achilles, and falling in love with Daphne, and being unaware of the fate of Hyacinthus; and of Venus wounded, and of Mars, the pest of mortals; and of the ichor flowing from the so-called gods. ⁶And these, indeed, are the milder kinds of legends; since the god who is called Osiris is found to have been torn limb from limb, whose mysteries are celebrated annually, as if he had perished, and were being found, and sought limb by limb. ⁷For neither is it known whether he perished, nor is it shown whether he is found. ⁸And why should I speak of Atys mutilated, or of Adonis wandering in the wood, and wounded by a boar while hunting; or of Asclepius struck by a thunderbolt; or of the fugitive Serapis chased from Sinope to Alexandria; or of the Scythian Diana, herself, too, a fugitive, and a murderer, and a huntress, and a passionate lover of Endymion? ⁹Now, it is not we who publish these things, but your own writers and poets.

CHAPTER 10

¹Why should I further recount the multitude of animals worshiped by the Egyptians, both reptiles, and cattle, and wild beasts, and birds, and river-fishes; and even washpots and disgraceful noises? ²But if you cite the Greeks and the other nations, they worship stones and wood, and other kinds of material substances—the images, as we have just been saying, of dead men. ³For Phidias is found in Pisa making for the Eleians the Olympian Jupiter, and at Athens the Minerva of the Acropolis. ⁴And I will inquire of you, my friend, how many Jupiters exist. For there is, firstly, Jupiter surnamed Olympian, then Jupiter Latiaris, and Jupiter Cassius, and Jupiter Tonans, and Jupiter Propator, and Jupiter Pannychius, and Jupiter Poliuchus, and Jupiter Capitolinus; ⁵and that Jupiter, the son of Saturn, who is king of the Cretans, has a tomb in Crete, but the rest, possibly, were not thought worthy of tombs. ⁶And if you speak of the mother of those who are called gods, far be it from me to utter with my lips her deeds, or the deeds of those by whom she is worshiped (for it is unlawful for us so much as to name such things), and what vast taxes and revenues she and her sons furnish to the king. ⁷For these are not gods, but idols, as we have already said, the works of men's hands and unclean demons. And such may all those become who make them and put their trust in them!

CHAPTER 11

¹Therefore, I will rather honor the king [than your gods], not, indeed, worshiping him, but praying for him. But God, the living and true God, I worship, knowing that the king is made by Him. ²You will say, then, to me, "Why do you not worship the king?" Because he is not made to be worshiped, but to be reverenced with lawful honor, for he is not a god, but a man appointed by God, not to be worshiped, but to judge justly. ³For in a kind of way his government is committed to him by God: as He will not have those called kings whom He has appointed under Himself; for king is his title, and it is not lawful for another to use it; so neither is it lawful for any to be worshiped but God only. Therefore, O man, you are wholly in error. ⁴Accordingly, honor the king, be subject to him, and pray for him with loyal mind; for if you do this, you do the will of God. For the law that is of God, says, "My son, fear the LORD and the king, and do not be disobedient to them; for they will suddenly take vengeance on their enemies."

CHAPTER 12

¹And about your laughing at me and calling me a Christian, you do not know what you are saying. ²First, because that which is anointed is sweet and serviceable, and far from contemptible. ³For what ship can be serviceable and seaworthy, unless it is first caulked [[*or* anointed]]? Or what castle or house is beautiful and serviceable when it has not been anointed? And what man, when he enters into this life or into the gymnasium, is not anointed with oil? And what work has either ornament or beauty unless it is anointed and burnished? ⁴Then the air and all that is under the sky is in a certain way anointed by light and spirit; and are you unwilling to be anointed with the oil of God? ⁵Therefore, we are called Christians on this account, because we are anointed with the oil of God.

CHAPTER 13

¹Then, as to your denying that the dead are raised—for you say, "Show me even one who has been raised from the dead, that seeing I may believe"—first, what great thing is it if you believe when you have seen the thing done? ²Then, again, you believe that Hercules, who burned himself, lives; and that Asclepius, who was struck with lightning, was raised; and do you disbelieve the things that are told you by God? ³But suppose I should show you a dead man raised and alive, even this you would disbelieve. God indeed exhibits to you many proofs that you may believe Him. ⁴For consider, if you please, the dying of seasons, and days, and nights, how these also die and rise again. And what? Is there not a resurrection going on of seeds and fruits, and this, too, for the use of men? ⁵A seed of wheat, for example, or of the other grains, when it is cast into the earth, first dies and rots away, then is raised, and becomes a stalk of grain. ⁶And the nature of trees and fruit-trees—is it not that according to the appointment of God they produce their fruits in their seasons out of what has been unseen and invisible? ⁷Moreover, sometimes also a sparrow or some of the other birds, when in drinking it has swallowed a seed of apple or fig, or something else, has come to some rocky mound or tomb, and has left the seed in its droppings, and the seed, which was once swallowed, and has passed through so great a heat, now striking root, a tree has grown up. ⁸And all these things the Wisdom of God effects, in order to manifest even by these things, that God is able to effect the general resurrection of all men. ⁹And if you would witness a more wonderful sight, which may prove a resurrection not only of earthly but of heavenly bodies, consider the resurrection of the moon, which occurs monthly; how it wanes, dies, and rises again. ¹⁰Hear further, O man, of the work of resurrection going on in yourself, even though you are unaware of it.

APOLOGY TO AUTOLYCUS

¹¹For perhaps you have sometimes fallen sick, and lost flesh, and strength, and beauty; but when you received again from God mercy and healing, you rebounded in flesh and appearance, and also recovered your strength. ¹²And as you do not know where your flesh went away and disappeared to, so neither do you know from what it grew, or from where it came again. But you will say, "From meats and drinks changed into blood." Quite so; but this, too, is the work of God, who thus operates, and not of any other.

CHAPTER 14

¹Therefore, do not be skeptical, but believe; for I myself also used to disbelieve that this would take place, but now, having taken these things into consideration, I believe. ²At the same time, I encountered the Holy Writings of the holy prophets, who also by the Spirit of God foretold the things that have already happened, just as they came to pass, and the things now occurring as they are now happening, and things future in the order in which they will be accomplished. ³Admitting, therefore, the proof which events happening as predicted afford, I do not disbelieve, but I believe, obedient to God, whom, if you please, you also should submit to, believing Him, lest if now you continue unbelieving, you be convinced hereafter, when you are tormented with continuous punishments; ⁴which punishments, when they had been foretold by the prophets, the later-born poets and philosophers stole from the Holy Writings, to make their doctrines worthy of credit. ⁵Yet these have also spoken beforehand of the punishments that are to descend on the profane and unbelieving, in order that none are left without a witness, or are able to say, "We have not heard, neither have we known." ⁶But you should also, if you please, give reverential attention to the prophetic Writings, and they will make your way plainer for escaping the continuous punishments, and obtaining the perpetual prizes of God. ⁷For He who gave the mouth for speech, and formed the ear to hear, and made the eye to see, will examine all things, and will judge righteous judgment, rendering merited awards to each. ⁸"To those who by patient continuance in well-doing seek immortality, He will give continuous life," joy, peace, rest, and abundance of good things, which "neither eye has seen, nor ear heard, nor has it entered into the heart of man to conceive." ⁹"But to the unbelieving and despisers, who do not obey the truth, but are obedient to unrighteousness," when they will have been filled with adulteries, and fornications, and filthiness, and covetousness, and unlawful idolatries, "there will be anger and wrath, tribulation and anguish," and at the end continuous fire will possess such men. ¹⁰Since you said, "Show me your God"—this is my God, and I counsel you to fear Him and to trust Him.

BOOK II

CHAPTER 1

¹When we formerly had some dialogue, my very good friend Autolycus, and when you inquired who my God was, and for a little while paid attention to my discourse, I made some explanations to you concerning my religion; ²and then having bid one another farewell, we each went with much mutual friendliness to his own house, although at first you had been somewhat hard on me. ³For you know and remember that you supposed our doctrine was foolishness. ⁴As you then afterward urged me to do, I am desirous, though not educated to the art of speaking, of more accurately demonstrating, by means of this tractate, the vain labor and empty worship in which you are held; ⁵and I wish also, from a few of your own histories which you read, and perhaps do not yet quite understand, to make the truth plain to you.

CHAPTER 2

¹And in reality, it does seem to me absurd that sculptors and carvers, or painters, or molders, should both design and paint, and carve, and mold, and prepare gods, who, when they are produced by the artificers, are reckoned of no value; ²but as soon as they are purchased by some and placed in some so-called temple, or in some house, not only do those who bought them sacrifice to them, but also those who made and sold them come with much devotion, and apparatus of sacrifice, and libations, to worship them; ³and they reckon them gods, not seeing that they are just such as when they were made by themselves, whether stone, or brass, or wood, or color, or some other material. ⁴And this is your case, too, when you read the histories and genealogies of the so-called gods. ⁵For when you read of their births, you think of them as men, but afterward you call them gods, and worship them, not reflecting nor understanding that, when born, they are exactly such beings as you read of before.

CHAPTER 3

¹And of the gods of former times, if indeed they were begotten, the generation was sufficiently prolific. ²But now, where is their generation exhibited? For if of old they begot and were begotten, it is plain that even to the present time there should be gods begotten and born; or at least if it is not so, such a race will be reckoned impotent. ³For either they have grown old, and on that account no longer beget, or they have died out and no longer exist. ⁴For if the gods were begotten, they ought to be born even until now, as men, too, are born; yes, much more numerous should the gods be than men, as the Sibyl says:

⁵For if the gods beget, and each remains
Immortal, then the race of gods must be
More numerous than mortals, and the throng
So great that mortals find no room to stand.

⁶For if the children begotten of men who are mortal and short-lived make an appearance even until now, and men have not ceased to be born, so that cities and villages are full, and even the country places are also inhabited, how ought not the gods, who, according to your poets, do not die, much rather to beget and be begotten, since you say that the gods were produced by generation? ⁷And why was the mountain, which is called Olympus, formerly inhabited by the gods, but now lies deserted? ⁸Or why did Jupiter, in days of yore, dwell on Ida, and was known to dwell there, according to Homer and other poets, but now is beyond sight? And why was he found only in one part of the earth, and not everywhere? ⁹For either he neglected the other parts or was not able to be present everywhere and provide for all. ¹⁰For if he were in an eastern place, he was not in the western; and if, on the other hand, he were present in the western parts, he was not in the eastern. ¹¹But this is the attribute of God, the Highest and Almighty, and the living God, not only to be present everywhere, but also to see all things and to hear all, and by no means to be confined in a place; ¹²for if He were, then the place containing Him would be greater than He; for that which contains is greater than that which is contained. For God is not contained but is Himself the place of all. ¹³But why has Jupiter left Ida? Was it because he died, or did that mountain no longer please him? And where has he gone? To Heaven? No. ¹⁴But you will perhaps say, "To Crete?" Yes, for there, too, his tomb is shown to this day. Again, you will say, "To Pisa," where he reflects glory on the hands of Phidias to this day. ¹⁵Let us, then, proceed to the writings of the philosophers and poets.

CHAPTER 4

¹Some of the philosophers of the Porch say that there is no God at all; or, if there is, they say that He cares for none but Himself; ²and these views the folly of Epicurus and Chrysippus has set forth at large. ³And others say that all things are produced without external agency, and that the world is uncreated, and that nature is eternal, and have dared to suggest that there is no providence of God at all, but maintain that God is only each man's conscience. ⁴And others again maintain that the spirit which pervades all things is God. ⁵But Plato and those of his school acknowledge indeed that God is uncreated, and the Father and Maker of all things; but then they maintain that matter as well as God is uncreated, and over that it is coequal with God. ⁶But if God is uncreated and matter uncreated, God is no longer, according to the Platonists, the Creator of all things, nor, so far as their opinions hold, is the monarchy of God established. ⁷And further, as God, because He is uncreated, is also unalterable; so if matter, too, were uncreated, it also would be unalterable, and equal to God; for that which is created is mutable and alterable, but that which is uncreated is immutable and unalterable. ⁸And what great thing is it if God made the world out of existent materials? For

even a human artist, when he gets material from someone, makes of it what he pleases. ⁹But the power of God is manifested in this, that out of things that are not He makes whatever He pleases; just as the bestowal of life and motion is the prerogative of no other than God alone. ¹⁰For even man indeed makes an image, but reason and breath, or feeling, he cannot give to what he has made. ¹¹But God has this property in excess of what man can do, in that He makes a work, endowed with reason, life, [and] sensation. ¹²As, therefore, in all these respects God is more powerful than man, so also in this—that out of things that are not He creates and has created things that are, and whatever He pleases, as He pleases.

CHAPTER 5

¹So that the opinion of your philosophers and authors is discordant; for while the former have propounded the foregoing opinions, the poet Homer is found explaining the origin not only of the world, but also of the gods, on quite another hypothesis. ²For he says somewhere: "Father of Gods, Oceanus, and she || Who bore the gods, their mother Tethys, too, || From whom all rivers spring, and every sea." In saying which, however, he does not present God to us. For who does not know that the ocean is water? But if water, then not God. ³God indeed, if He is the creator of all things, as He certainly is, is the creator both of the water and of the seas. ⁴And Hesiod himself also declared the origin, not only of the gods, but also of the world itself. And though he said that the world was created, he showed no inclination to tell us by whom it was created. ⁵Besides, he said that Saturn, and his sons Jupiter, Neptune, and Pluto, were gods, though we find that they are more recently born than the world. ⁶And he also relates how Saturn was assailed in war by his own son Jupiter; for he says: "His father Saturn he by might o'ercame, || And 'mong the immortals ruled with justice wise, || And honors fit distributed to each." ⁷Then he introduces in his poem the daughters of Jupiter, whom he names Muses, and as whose suppliant he appears, desiring to ascertain from them how all things were made; for he says: "Daughters of Jove, all hail! Grant me your aid || That I in numbers sweet and well-arrayed, || Of the immortal gods may sing the birth; ⁸Who of the starry heavens were born, and earth; Who, springing from the murky night at first, || Were by the briny ocean reared and nursed. ⁹Tell, too, who form to the earth first gave, || And rivers, and the boundless sea whose wave || Unwearied sinks, then rears its crest on high; And how was spread yon glittering canopy || Of glistening stars that stud the wide-spread sky. ¹⁰From where sprang the gods by whom all good is given? Tell from their hands what varied gifts there came, || Riches to some, to others wealth, or fame; How they have dwelt from the remotest time || In many-nooked Olympus' sunny clime. ¹¹These things, you Muses, say, whoever dwells || Among Olympian shades—since you can tell: From the beginning there your feet have strayed; Then tell us which of all things first was made." ¹²But how could the Muses, who are younger than the world, know these things? Or how could they relate to Hesiod [what was happening], when their father was not yet born?

CHAPTER 6

¹And in a certain way he indeed admits matter [as self-existent] and the creation of the world [without a creator], saying, "First of all things was chaos made, and next || Broad-bosomed earth's foundations firm were fixed, || Where safely the immortals dwell for sure, || Who in the snowy-peaked Olympus stay. ²Afterward gloomy Tartarus had birth || In the recesses of broad-pathwayed earth, || And Love, even among gods most beauteous still, || Who comes all-conquering, bending mind and will, || Delivering from care, and giving then || Wise counsel in the breasts of gods and men. ³From chaos Erebus and night were born, || From night and Erebus sprung air and morn. Earth in her likeness made the starry heavens, || That to all things shelter might be given, || And that the blessed gods might there repose. ⁴The lofty mountains by her power arose, || For the wood-nymphs she made the pleasant caves, || Begot the sterile sea with all his waves, || Loveless; but when by heavens her love was sought, || Then the deep-eddying ocean forth she brought." ⁵And saying this, he has not yet explained by whom all this was made. For if chaos existed in the beginning, and matter of some sort, being uncreated, was previously existing, who was it that effected the change on its condition, and gave it a different order and shape? ⁶Did matter itself alter its own form and arrange itself into a world (for Jupiter was born, not only long after matter, but long after the world and many men; and so, too, was his father Saturn), or was there some ruling power which made it; I mean, of course, God, who also fashioned it into a world? ⁷Besides, he is found in every way to talk nonsense, and to contradict himself. For when he mentions earth, and sky, and sea, he makes us to understand that from these the gods were produced; ⁸and from these again he declares that certain very dreadful men were sprung—the race of the Titans and the Cyclopes, and a crowd of giants, and of the Egyptian gods—or, rather, vain men, as Apollonides, surnamed Horapius, mentions in the book entitled Semenouthi, and in his other histories concerning the worship of the Egyptians and their kings, and the vain labors in which they engaged.

CHAPTER 7

¹Why must I recount the Greek fables—of Pluto, king of darkness, of Neptune descending beneath the sea, and embracing Melanippe and begetting a cannibal son—or the many tales your writers have woven into their tragedies concerning the sons of Jupiter, and whose pedigree they register because they were born men, and not gods? ²And the comic poet Aristophanes, in the play called The Birds, having himself undertaken to handle the subject of the Creation, said that in the beginning the world was produced from an egg, saying: "A windy egg was laid by black-winged night || At first." ³But Satyrus, also giving a history of the Alexandrine families, beginning from Philopator, who was also named Ptolemy, suggests that Bacchus was his progenitor; therefore also Ptolemy was the founder of this family. ⁴Satyrus then says that Dejanira was born of Bacchus and Althea, the daughter of Thestius; and from her and Hercules the son of Jupiter there sprang, as I suppose, Hyllus; ⁵and from him Cleodemus, and from him Aristomachus, and from him Temenus, and from him Ceisus, and from him Maron, and from him Thestrus, and from him Acous, and from him Aristomidas, and from him Caranus, and from him Coenus, and from him Tyrimmas, and from him Perdiccas, ⁶and from him Philip, and from him Aeropus, and from him Alcetas, and from him Amyntas, and from him Bocrus, and from him Meleager, and from him Arsinoë and from her and Lagus Ptolemy Soter, and from him and Arsinoe Ptolemy Euergetes, and from him and Berenicé, daughter of Maga, king of Cyrene, Ptolemy Philopator. ⁷Thus, then, stands the relationship of the Alexandrine kings to Bacchus. ⁸And therefore in the Dionysian tribe there are distinct families: the Althean from Althea, who was the wife of Dionysus and daughter of Thestius; the family of Dejanira also, from her who was the daughter of Dionysus and Althea, and wife of Hercules—from which, too, the families have their names: ⁹the family of Ariadne, from Ariadne, daughter of Minos and wife of Dionysus, a dutiful daughter, who had intercourse with Dionysus in another form; the Thestian, from Thestius, the father of Althea; the Thoantian, from Thoas, son of Dionysus; the Staphylian, from Staphylus, son of Dionysus; the Euaenian, from Eunous, son of Dionysus; the Maronian, from Maron, son of Ariadne and Dionysus—for all these are sons of Dionysus. ¹⁰And, indeed, many other names were thus originated and exist to this day: as the Heraclidae from Hercules, and the Apollonidae from Apollo, and the Poseidonii from Poseidon, and from Zeus the Dii and Diogenae.

CHAPTER 8

¹And why should I recount further the vast array of such names and genealogies? So that all the authors and poets, and those called philosophers, are wholly deceived; and so, too, are they who give heed to them. ²For they abundantly composed fables and foolish stories about their gods, and did not exhibit them as gods, but as men, and men, too, of whom some were drunken, and others fornicators and murderers. ³But also concerning the origin of the world, they uttered contradictory and absurd opinions. ⁴First, some of them, as we explained before, maintained that the world is uncreated. And those that said it was uncreated and self-producing contradicted those who proposed that it was created. ⁵For by conjecture and

human conception they spoke, and not knowing the truth. ⁶And others, again, said that there was a providence, and destroyed the positions of the former writers. ⁷Aratus, indeed, says: "From Jove begin my song; nor ever be || The name unuttered: all are full of you; The ways and haunts of men; the heavens and sea: On you our being hangs; in you we move; All are your offspring and the seed of Jove. ⁸Benevolent, he warns mankind to good, || Urges to toil and prompts the hope of food. He tells where cattle best may graze, and where || The soil, deep-furrowed, yellow grain will bear. What time the farmer should plant or sow, || 'Tis his to tell, 'tis his alone to know." ⁹Who, then, will we believe: Aratus as here quoted, or Sophocles, when he says: "And foresight of the future there is none; 'Tis best to live at random, as one can?" ¹⁰And Homer, again, does not agree with this, for he says that virtue "waxes or wanes in men as Jove decrees." ¹¹And Simonides says: "No man nor state has virtue save from God; Counsel resides in God; and wretched man || Has in himself nothing but his wretchedness." ¹²So, too, Euripides: "Apart from God, there's nothing owned by men." And Menander: "Save God alone, there's none for us provides." ¹³And Euripides again: "For when God wills to save, all things He'll bend || To serve as instruments to work His end." And Thestius: "If God design to save you, safe you are, || Though sailing in mid-ocean on a mat." ¹⁴And saying countless things of a similar kind, they contradicted themselves. At least Sophocles, who in another place denied Providence, says: "No mortal can evade the stroke of God." ¹⁵Besides, they both introduced a multitude of gods, and yet spoke of a Unity; and against those who affirmed a Providence they maintained in opposition that there was no Providence. ¹⁶Therefore, Euripides says: "We labor much and spend our strength in vain, || For empty hope, not foresight, is our guide." ¹⁷And without meaning to do so, they acknowledge that they do not know the truth, but being inspired by demons and puffed up by them, they spoke at their instance whatever they said. ¹⁸For indeed the poets—Homer, namely, and Hesiod, being, as they say, inspired by the Muses—spoke from a deceptive fancy, and not with a pure but an erring spirit. ¹⁹And this, indeed, clearly appears from the fact that even to this day the possessed are sometimes exorcised in the Name of the living and true God; ²⁰and these spirits of error themselves confess that they are demons who also formerly inspired these writers. ²¹But sometimes some of them awakened in soul, and, that they might be for a witness both to themselves and to all men, spoke things in harmony with the prophets regarding the monarchy of God, and the judgment, and similar [things].

CHAPTER 9

¹But men of God carrying in them [the] Holy Spirit and becoming prophets, being inspired and made wise by God, became God-taught, and holy, and righteous. ²Therefore, they were also deemed worthy of receiving this reward, that they should become instruments of God, and contain the Wisdom that is from Him, through which Wisdom they uttered both what regarded the creation of the world and all other things. ³For they also predicted pestilences, and famines, and wars. ⁴And there was not one or two, but many, at various times and seasons among the Hebrews; and also among the Greeks there was the Sibyl; and they all have spoken things consistent and harmonious with each other, both what happened before them and what happened in their own time, and what things are now being fulfilled in our own day: ⁵therefore we are also persuaded concerning the future things that they will come to pass, as also the first have been accomplished.

CHAPTER 10

¹And first, they taught us with one consent that God made all things out of nothing; for nothing was coequal with God: but He being His own place, and needing nothing, and existing before the ages, willed to make man by whom He might be known; for him, therefore, He prepared the world. ²For he that is created is also needy; but He that is uncreated stands in need of nothing. ³God, then, having His own Word internal within His own bowels, begot Him, emitting Him along with His own Wisdom before all things. ⁴He had this Word as a helper in the things that were created by Him, and by Him He made all things. He is called [the] governing principle, because He rules, and is Lord of all things fashioned by Him. ⁵He, then, being [the] Spirit of God, and governing principle, and Wisdom, and power of the highest, came down on the prophets, and through them spoke of the creation of the world and of all other things. ⁶For the prophets were nothing when the world came into existence, but the Wisdom of God which was in Him, and His holy Word which was always present with Him. ⁷Therefore, He speaks thus by the prophet Solomon: "When He prepared the heavens I was there, || And when He appointed the foundations of the earth I was by Him as one brought up with Him." ⁸And Moses, who lived many years before Solomon, or, rather, the Word of God by him as by an instrument, says, "In the beginning God created the heavens and the earth." ⁹First, he named the beginning, and creation, then he thus introduced God; for not lightly and on slight occasion is it right to name God. ¹⁰For the divine Wisdom foreknew that some would conjecture and name a multitude of gods that do not exist. ¹¹In order, therefore, that the living God might be known by His works, and that [it might be known that] by His Word God created the heavens and the earth, and all that is therein, he said, "In the beginning God created the heavens and the earth." ¹²Then having spoken of their creation, he explains to us: "And the earth was without form, and void, and darkness was on the face of the deep; and the Spirit of God moved on the water." ¹³This Holy Writing teaches at the outset, to show that matter, from which God made and fashioned the world, was in some manner created, being produced by God.

CHAPTER 11

¹Now, the beginning of the creation is light, since light manifests the things that are created. Therefore, it is said: "And God said, Let light be, and light was; and God saw the light, that it was good," manifestly made good for man. ²"And God divided the light from the darkness; and God called the light Day, and the darkness He called Night. And the evening and the morning were the first day. ³And God said, Let there be an expanse in the midst of the waters, and let it divide the waters from the waters: and it was so. ⁴And God made the expanse, and divided the waters which were under the expanse from the waters which were above the expanse. ⁵And God called the expanse Heavens: and God saw that it was good. And the evening and the morning were the second day. ⁶And God said, Let the water under the heavens be gathered into one place, and let the dry land appear: and it was so. ⁷And the waters were gathered together into their places, and the dry land appeared. ⁸And God called the dry land Earth, and the gathering together of the waters He called Seas: and God saw that it was good. ⁹And God said, Let the earth bring forth grass, the herb yielding seed after his kind and in his likeness, and the fruit-tree yielding fruit after his kind, whose seed is in itself, in his likeness: and it was so. ¹⁰And the earth brought forth grass, the herb yielding seed after his kind, and the fruit-tree yielding fruit, whose seed was in itself, after his kind, on the earth: and God saw that it was good. And the evening and the morning were the third day. ¹¹And God said, Let there be lights in the expanse of the heavens, to give light on earth, to divide the day from the night; and let them be for signs, and for seasons, and for days, and for years; and let them be for lights in the expanse of the heavens, to give light on the earth: and it was so. ¹²And God made two great lights; the greater light to rule the day, and the lesser light to rule the night: He made the stars also. ¹³And God set them in the expanse of the heavens to give light on the earth, and to rule over the day and over the night, and to divide the light from the darkness: and God saw that it was good. And the evening and the morning were the fourth day. ¹⁴And God said, Let the waters bring forth the creeping things that have life, and bird flying over the earth in the expanse of [the] heavens: and it was so. ¹⁵And God created great whales, and every living creature that creeps, which the waters brought forth after their kind, and every winged bird after his kind: and God saw that it was good. ¹⁶And God blessed them, saying, Increase and multiply, and fill the waters of the sea, and let bird multiply in the earth. And the evening and the morning were the fifth day. ¹⁷And God said, Let the earth bring forth the living creature after his kind, cattle, and creeping thing, and beast of the earth after his kind: and it was so. ¹⁸And God made the beasts of the earth after their

kind, and the cattle after their kind, and all the creeping things of the earth. ¹⁹And God said, Let Us make man in Our image, after Our likeness; and let them have dominion over the fish of the sea, and over the bird of the heavens, and over the cattle, and over all the earth, and over every creeping thing that creeps on the earth. ²⁰And God created man: in the image of God He created him; male and female He created them. ²¹And God blessed them, saying, Be fruitful, and multiply, and replenish the earth, and subdue it, and have dominion over the fish of the sea, and over the bird of the heavens, and over all cattle, and over all the earth, and over all the creeping things that creep on the earth. ²²And God said, Behold I have given you every herb bearing seed, which is on the face of all the earth, and every tree in which is the fruit of a tree yielding seed—to you it will be for food, and to all the beasts of the earth, and to all the birds of [the] heavens, and to every creeping thing that creeps on the earth, which has the breath of life in it; every green herb for food: and it was so. ²³And God saw everything that He had made, and behold, it was very good. And the evening and the morning were the sixth day. ²⁴And the heavens and the earth were finished, and all the host of them. And on the sixth day God finished His works which He made and rested on the seventh day from all His works which He made. ²⁵And God blessed the seventh day and sanctified it; because in it He rested from all His works which God began to create."

CHAPTER 12

¹Of this six days' work no man can give a worthy explanation and description of all its parts, not though he had ten thousand tongues and ten thousand mouths; no, though he were to live ten thousand years, sojourning in this life, not even so could he utter anything worthy of these things, on account of the exceeding greatness and riches of the wisdom of God which there is in the six days' work narrated above. ²Many writers have indeed imitated [the narration] and attempted to give an explanation of these things; yet, though from there they derived some suggestions, both concerning the creation of the world and the nature of man, they have emitted no slightest spark of truth. ³And the utterances of the philosophers, and writers, and poets have an appearance of trustworthiness, on account of the beauty of their diction; but their discourse is proved to be foolish and idle, because the multitude of their nonsensical frivolities is very great; and not a stray morsel of truth is found in them. ⁴For even if any truth seems to have been uttered by them, it has a mixture of error. ⁵And as a toxic drug, when mixed with honey or wine, or some other thing, makes the whole [mixture] harmful and profitless, so also eloquence is in their case found to be labor in vain; yes, rather an injurious thing to those who credit it. ⁶Moreover, [they spoke] concerning the seventh day, which all men acknowledge; but most do not know that what among the Hebrews is called the Sabbath, is translated into Greek the "Seventh," a name which is adopted by every nation, although they do not know the reason of the appellation. ⁷And as for what the poet Hesiod says of Erebus being produced from chaos, as well as the earth and love which lords it over his gods and men, his dictum is shown to be idle and frigid, and quite foreign to the truth. ⁸For it is not fitting that God would be conquered by pleasure, since even men of temperance abstain from all base pleasure and wicked lust.

CHAPTER 13

¹Moreover, [Hesiod's] human, and mean, and very weak conception, so far as regards God, is discovered in his beginning to relate the creation of all things from the earthly things here below. ²For man, being below, begins to build from the earth, and cannot in order make the roof, unless he has first laid the foundation. ³But the power of God is shown in this, that first of all, He creates out of nothing, according to His will, the things that are made. "For the things which are impossible with men are possible with God." ⁴Therefore, the prophet also mentioned that the creation of the heavens first of all took place, as a kind of roof, saying, "At the first God created the heavens"—that is, that by means of the first principle the heavens were made, as we have already shown. ⁵And by earth he means the ground and foundation, as by the deep he means the multitude of waters; and darkness he speaks of, on account of the heaven which God made covering the waters and the earth like a lid. ⁶And by the Spirit, which is borne above the waters, he means that which God gave for animating the creation, as he gave life to man, mixing what is fine with what is fine. ⁷For the Spirit is fine, and the water is fine, that the Spirit may nourish the water, and the water penetrating everywhere along with the Spirit, may nourish creation. ⁸For the Spirit being one, and holding the place of light, was between the water and the heaven, in order that the darkness might not in any way communicate with the heaven, which was nearer God, before God said, "Let there be light." ⁹The heaven, therefore, being like a dome-shaped covering, comprehended matter which was like a clod. ¹⁰And so another prophet, Isaiah by name, spoke in these words: "It is God who made the heavens as a vault, || And stretched them out as a tent to dwell in." ¹¹The command, then, of God, that is, His Word, shining as a lamp in an enclosed chamber, lit up all that was under [this] heaven, when He had made light apart from the world. ¹²And the light God called Day, and the darkness Night. Since man would not have been able to call the light Day, or the darkness Night, nor, indeed, to have given names to the other things, had he not received the nomenclature from God, who made the things themselves. ¹³In the very beginning, therefore, of the history and generation of the world, the Holy Writing did not speak concerning this expanse [which we see], but concerning another Heaven, which is invisible to us, after which this heaven which we see has been called sky, and to which half the water was taken up that it might serve for rains, and showers, and dews to mankind. ¹⁴And half the water was left on earth for rivers, and fountains, and seas. The water, then, covering all the earth, and especially its hollow places, God, through His Word, next caused the waters to be collected into one collection, and the dry land to become visible, which formerly had been invisible. ¹⁵The earth thus becoming visible, was yet without form. God therefore formed and adorned it with all kinds of herbs, and seeds and plants.

CHAPTER 14

¹Consider, further, their variety, and diverse beauty, and multitude, and how through them resurrection is exhibited, for a pattern of the resurrection of all men which is to be. ²For who that considers it will not marvel that a fig-tree is produced from a fig-seed, or that very huge trees grow from the other very little seeds? ³And we say that the world resembles the sea. For as the sea, if it had not had the influx and supply of the rivers and fountains to nourish it, would long since have been parched by reason of its saltiness; so also the world, if it had not had the Law of God and the prophets flowing and welling up sweetness, and compassion, and righteousness, and the doctrine of the holy commandments of God, would long before now have come to ruin, by reason of the wickedness and sin which abound in it. ⁴And as in the sea there are islands, some of them habitable, and well-watered, and fruitful, with havens and harbors in which the storm-tossed may find refuge—so God has given to the world which is driven and storm tossed by sins, assemblies (we mean [the] holy assemblies) in which survive the doctrines of the truth, as in the island-harbors of good anchorage; ⁵and into these run those who desire to be saved, being lovers of the truth, and wishing to escape the wrath and judgment of God. ⁶And as, again, there are other islands, rocky and without water, and barren, and infested by wild beasts, and uninhabitable, and serving only to injure navigators and the storm-tossed, on which ships are wrecked, and those driven among them perish—so there are doctrines of error (I mean heresies)—which destroy those who approach them. ⁷For they are not guided by the word of truth; but as pirates, when they have filled their vessels, drive them on the aforementioned places, that they may spoil them: so also it happens in the case of those who err from the truth, that they are all totally ruined by their error.

CHAPTER 15

¹On the fourth day the luminaries were made; because God, who possesses foreknowledge, knew the follies of the vain philosophers, that they were going to say that the things which grow on the earth are produced from the heavenly bodies, so as to exclude God. ²In order, therefore, that the truth might be obvious, the plants and seeds were produced

prior to the heavenly bodies, for what is posterior cannot produce that which is prior. ³And these contain the pattern and type of a great mystery. For the sun is a type of God, and the moon of man. And as the sun far surpasses the moon in power and glory, so far does God surpass man. ⁴And as the sun remains ever full, never becoming less, so does God always abide perfect, being full of all power, and understanding, and wisdom, and immortality, and all good. ⁵But the moon wanes monthly, and in a manner dies, being a type of man; then it is born again, and is crescent, for a pattern of the future resurrection. ⁶In like manner also the three days which were before the luminaries, are types of the Trinity—of God, and His Word, and His Wisdom. ⁷And the fourth is the type of man, who needs light, that so there may be God, the Word, Wisdom, man. Therefore, also on the fourth day the lights were made. ⁸The disposition of the stars, too, contains a type of the arrangement and order of the righteous and pious, and of those who keep the law and commandments of God. ⁹For the brilliant and bright stars are an imitation of the prophets, and therefore they remain fixed, not declining, nor passing from place to place. ¹⁰And those which hold the second place in brightness, are types of the people of the righteous. ¹¹And those, again, which change their position, and flee from place to place, which are also called planets, they too are a type of the men who have wandered from God, abandoning His law and commandments.

CHAPTER 16

¹On the fifth day the living creatures which proceed from the waters were produced, through which is also revealed the manifold wisdom of God in these things; for who could count their multitude and very manifold kinds? ²Moreover, the things proceeding from the waters were blessed by God, that this also might be a sign of men's being destined to receive conversion and forgiveness of sins, through the water and laver of regeneration—as many as come to the truth, and are born again, and receive blessing from God. ³But the monsters of the deep and the birds of prey are a similitude of covetous men and transgressors. ⁴For as the fish and the birds are of one nature—some indeed abide in their natural state, and do no harm to those weaker than themselves, but keep the Law of God, and eat of the seeds of the earth—others of them, again, transgress the Law of God, and eat flesh, and injure those weaker than themselves: ⁵thus, too, the righteous, keeping the law of God, bite and injure none, but live piously and righteously. ⁶But robbers, and murderers, and godless persons are like monsters of the deep, and wild beasts, and birds of prey, for they virtually devour those weaker than themselves. ⁷The race, then, of fishes and of creeping things, though partaking of God's blessing, received no very distinguishing property.

CHAPTER 17

¹And on the sixth day, God having made the quadrupeds, and wild beasts, and the land reptiles, pronounced no blessing on them, reserving His blessing for man, whom He was about to create on the sixth day. ²The quadrupeds, too, and wild beasts, were made for a type of some men, who neither know nor worship God, but mind earthly things, and do not convert. ³For those who turn from their iniquities and live righteously, in spirit fly upwards like birds, and mind the things that are above, and are well-pleasing to the will of God. ⁴But those who do not know nor worship God, are like birds which have wings, but cannot fly nor soar to the high things of God. ⁵Thus, too, though such persons are called men, yet being pressed down with sins, they mind groveling and earthly things. ⁶And the animals are named wild beasts, from their being hunted, not as if they had been made evil or venomous from the first—for nothing was made evil by God, but all things good, yes, very good—but the sin in which man was concerned brought evil on them. For when man transgressed, they also transgressed with him. ⁷For as, if the master of the house himself acts rightly, the servants also necessarily conduct themselves well; but if the master sins, the servants also sin with him; ⁸so in like manner it came to pass that in the case of man's sin, he being master, all that was subject to him sinned with him. ⁹When, therefore, man again will have made his way back to his natural condition, and no longer does evil, those will also be restored to their original gentleness.

CHAPTER 18

¹But as to what relates to the creation of man, his own creation cannot be explained by man, though it is a succinct account of it which [the] Holy Writing gives. For when God said, "Let Us make man in Our image, after Our likeness," He first intimates the dignity of man. ²For God having made all things by His Word, and having reckoned them all mere byworks, reckons the creation of man to be the only work worthy of His own hands. ³Moreover, God is found, as if needing help, to say, "Let Us make man in Our image, after Our likeness." But to no one else than to His own Word and Wisdom did He say, "Let Us make." ⁴And when He had made and blessed him, that he might increase and replenish the earth, He put all things under his dominion, and at his service; ⁵and He appointed from the beginning that he should find sustenance from the fruits of the earth, and from seeds, and herbs, and acorns, having at the same time appointed that the animals be of habits similar to man's, that they also might eat of the seeds of the earth.

CHAPTER 19

¹God having thus completed the heavens, and the earth, and the sea, and all that are in them on the sixth day, rested on the seventh day from all His works which He made. ²Then [the] Holy Writing gives a summary in these words: "This is the book of the generation of the heavens and the earth, when they were created, in the day that the LORD made the heavens and the earth, and every green thing of the field, before it was made, and every herb of the field before it grew. For God had not caused it to rain on the earth, and there was not a man to till the ground." ³By this He signifies to us that the whole earth was at that time watered by a divine fountain and had no need that man should till it; but the earth produced all things spontaneously by the command of God, that man might not be wearied by tilling it. ⁴But that the creation of man might be made plain, so that there should not seem to be an insoluble problem existing among men, since God had said, "Let Us make man"; ⁵and since His creation was not yet plainly related, [the] Writing teaches us, saying: "And a fountain went up out of the earth, and watered the face of the whole earth; and God made man of the dust of the earth, and breathed into his face the breath of life, and man became a living soul"—from which also by most persons the soul is called immortal. ⁶And after the formation of man, God chose out for him a region among the places of the East, excellent for light, brilliant with a very bright atmosphere, [abundant] in the finest plants; and in this He placed man.

CHAPTER 20

¹[The] Writing thus relates the words of the sacred history: "And God planted Paradise, eastward, in Eden; and there He put the man whom He had formed. ²And out of the ground God made every tree to grow that is pleasant to the sight, and good for food; the Tree of Life also in the midst of Paradise, and the Tree of the Knowledge of Good and Evil. ³And a river flows out of Eden, to water the garden; from there it is parted into four heads. ⁴The name of the first is Pison: that is it which surrounds the whole land of Havilah, where there is gold; and the gold of that land is good, and there is bdellium and the onyx stone. ⁵And the name of the second river is Gihon: the same is it that surrounds the whole land of Ethiopia. ⁶And the third river is Tigris: this is it which goes toward Syria. And the fourth river is Euphrates. ⁷And the LORD God took the man whom He had made and put him in the garden to till and to keep it. ⁸And God commanded Adam, saying, Of every tree that is in the garden you may freely eat; but of the Tree of the Knowledge of Good and Evil, you will not eat of it; for in the day you eat of it you will surely die. ⁹And the LORD God said, It is not good that the man should be alone; let Us make him a helper for him. And out of the ground God formed all the beasts of the field, and all the birds of heaven, and brought them to Adam. ¹⁰And whatsoever Adam called every living creature, that was the name thereof. And Adam gave names to all cattle, and to the birds of the air, and to all the beasts of the field. ¹¹But for Adam there was not found a helper for him. And God caused an ecstasy to fall on Adam, and he slept; and He took one of his ribs and closed up the flesh instead thereof. ¹²And the rib, which the LORD

God had taken from man, He made [into] a woman, and brought her to Adam. And Adam said, This is now bone of my bones, and flesh of my flesh; she will be called Woman, because she was taken out of man. ¹³Therefore, a man will leave his father and his mother, and will cleave to his wife, and the two will be one flesh. And they were both naked, Adam and his wife, and were not ashamed."

CHAPTER 21

¹"Now the serpent was more subtle than any beast of the field which the LORD God had made. ²And the serpent said to the woman, Why has God said, You will not eat of every tree of the garden? And the woman said to the serpent, We [may] eat of every tree of the garden, but of the fruit of the tree which is in the midst of the garden God has said, You will not eat of it, neither will you touch it, lest you die. ³And the serpent said to the woman, You will not surely die. For God knows that in the day you eat thereof, then your eyes will be opened, and you will be as gods, knowing good and evil. ⁴And the woman saw that the tree was good for food, and that it was pleasant to the eyes, and a tree to be desired to make one wise; and having taken of the fruit thereof, she ate, and also gave to her husband with her: and they ate. ⁵And the eyes of both of them were opened, and they knew that they were naked; and they sewed fig leaves together, and made themselves aprons. ⁶And they heard the voice of the LORD God walking in the garden in the breeze of the day, and Adam and his wife hid themselves from the presence of the LORD God among the trees of the garden. ⁷And the LORD God called to Adam, and said to him, Where are you? And he said to Him, I heard Your voice in the garden, and I was afraid, because I was naked, and I hid myself. And He said to him, Who told you that you were naked, unless you have eaten of the tree of which I commanded you that you should not eat? And Adam said, The woman whom You gave to be with me, she gave me of the tree, and I ate. ⁸And God said to the woman, What is this that you have done? And the woman said, The serpent deceived me, and I ate. ⁹And the LORD God said to the serpent, Because you have done this, you are accursed above all the beasts of the earth; on your breast and belly will you go, and dust will you eat all the days of your life: and I will put enmity between you and the woman, and between your seed and her Seed; He will bruise your head, and you will bruise His heel. ¹⁰And to the woman He said, I will greatly multiply your sorrow and your travail: in sorrow will you bring forth children; and your desire will be to your husband, and he will rule over you. ¹¹And to Adam He said, Because you have listened to the voice of your wife, and have eaten of the tree of which I commanded you, saying, You will not eat of it, cursed is the ground in your works: in sorrow will you eat of it all the days of your life; thorns and thistles will it bring forth to you; and you will eat the herb of the field. ¹²In the sweat of your face will you eat your bread, until you return to the earth; for out of it you were taken: for dust you are, and to dust you will return." ¹³Such is the account given by [the] Holy Writing of the history of man and of Paradise.

CHAPTER 22

¹You will say, then, to me: "You said that God cannot be contained in a place, and how do you now say that He walked in Paradise?" Hear what I say. ²The God and Father, indeed, of all cannot be contained, and is not found in a place, for there is no place of His rest; but His Word, through whom He made all things, being His power and His wisdom, assuming the person of the Father and Lord of all, went to the garden in the person of God, and conversed with Adam. ³For the Divine Writing itself teaches us that Adam said that he had heard the voice. But what else is this voice but the Word of God, who is also His Son? Not as the poets and writers of myths talk of the sons of gods begotten from intercourse, but as truth expounds, the Word, that always exists, residing within the heart of God. ⁴For before anything came into being He had Him as a counselor, being His own mind and thought. ⁵But before God desired to make everything that He determined, He begot this Word, uttered, the firstborn of all creation, not Himself being emptied of the Word [(Reason)], but having begotten Reason, and always conversing with His Reason. ⁶And hence the Holy Writings teach us, and all the spirit-bearing men, one of whom, John, says, "In the beginning was the Word, and the Word was with God," showing that at first God was alone, and the Word in Him. ⁷Then he says, "The Word was God; all things came into existence through Him; and apart from Him not one thing came into existence." ⁸The Word, then, being God, and being naturally produced from God, whenever the Father of the universe wills, He sends Him to any place; and He, coming, is both heard and seen, being sent by Him, and is found in a place.

CHAPTER 23

¹Man, therefore, God made on the sixth day, and made known this creation after the seventh day, when also He made Paradise, that he might be in a better and distinctly superior place. ²And that this is true, the fact itself proves. For how can one miss seeing that the pains which women suffer in childbirth, and the oblivion of their labors which they afterward enjoy, are sent in order that the word of God may be fulfilled, and that the race of men may increase and multiply? ³And do we not also see the judgment of the serpent—how hatefully he crawls on his belly and eats the dust—that we may have this, too, for evidence of the things which were formerly spoken?

CHAPTER 24

¹God, then, caused to spring out of the earth every tree that is beautiful in appearance, or good for food. ²For at first there were only those things which were produced on the third day—plants, and seeds, and herbs; but the things which were in Paradise were made of a superior loveliness and beauty, since in it the plants were said to have been planted by God. ³As to the rest of the plants, indeed, the world contained plants like them; but the two trees—the Tree of Life and the Tree of Knowledge—the rest of the earth did not possess, but only Paradise. ⁴And that Paradise is earth, and is planted on the earth, the Writing states, saying, "And the LORD God planted Paradise in Eden eastwards, and placed man there; and out of the ground the LORD God made every tree to grow that is pleasant to the sight and good for food." ⁵By the expressions, therefore, "out of the ground," and "eastwards," the Holy Writing clearly teaches us that Paradise is under this [same] heaven, under which the east and the earth are. And the Hebrew word Eden signifies delight. ⁶And it was signified that a river flowed out of Eden to water Paradise, and after that divides into four heads; of which the two called Pison and Gihon water the eastern parts, especially Gihon, which encompasses the whole land of Ethiopia, and which, they say, reappears in Egypt under the name of Nile. ⁷And the other two rivers are manifestly recognizable by us—those called Tigris and Euphrates—for these border on our own regions. ⁸And God having placed man in Paradise, as has been said, to till and keep it, commanded him to eat of all the trees—manifestly of the Tree of Life also; but only of the Tree of Knowledge He commanded him not to taste. ⁹And God transferred him from the earth, out of which he had been produced, into Paradise, giving him means of advancement, in order that, maturing and becoming perfect, and being even declared a god, he might thus ascend into Heaven in possession of immortality. ¹⁰For man had been made a middle nature, neither wholly mortal, nor altogether immortal, but capable of either; so also the place, Paradise, was made in respect of beauty intermediate between earth and Heaven. ¹¹And by the expression, "till it," no other kind of labor is implied than the observance of God's command, lest, disobeying, he should destroy himself, as indeed he did destroy himself, by sin.

CHAPTER 25

¹The Tree of Knowledge itself was good, and its fruit was good. For it was not the tree, as some think, but the disobedience, which had death in it. ²For there was nothing else in the fruit than only knowledge; but knowledge is good when one uses it discreetly. ³But Adam, being yet an infant in age, was on this account as yet unable to receive knowledge worthily. ⁴For now, also, when a child is born it is not at once able to eat bread, but is nourished first with milk, and then, with the increment of years, it advances to solid food. ⁵Thus, too, would it have been with Adam; for not as one who grudged him, as some suppose, did God command him not to eat of knowledge. But He wished also to make proof of him, whether he was submissive to His commandment. ⁶And at the same time, He wished man, infant as he

was, to remain for some time longer simple and sincere. ⁷For this is holy, not only with God, but also with men, that in simplicity and guilelessness subjection is yielded to parents. But if it is right that children are subject to parents, how much more to the God and Father of all things? ⁸Besides, it is improper that children in infancy be wise beyond their years; for as in stature one increases in an orderly progress, so also in wisdom. ⁹But as when a law has commanded abstinence from anything, and someone has not obeyed, it is obviously not the law which causes punishment, but the disobedience and transgression—for a father sometimes enjoins on his own child abstinence from certain things, and when he does not obey the paternal order, he is flogged and punished on account of the disobedience; ¹⁰and in this case the actions themselves are not the [cause of] stripes, but the disobedience procures punishment for him who disobeys—so also for the first man, disobedience procured his expulsion from Paradise. ¹¹Not, therefore, as if there were any [innate] evil in the Tree of Knowledge; but from his disobedience man drew, as from a fountain, labor, pain, grief, and at last fell prey to death.

CHAPTER 26

¹And God showed great kindness to man in this, that He did not allow him to remain in sin forever; but, as it were, by a kind of banishment, cast him out of Paradise, in order that, having by punishment expiated, within an appointed time, the sin, and having been disciplined, he should afterward be restored. ²Therefore also, when man had been formed in this world, it is mystically written in Genesis, as if he had been twice placed in Paradise, so that the one was fulfilled when he was placed there, and the second will be fulfilled after the resurrection and judgment. ³For just as a vessel, when on being fashioned it has some flaw, is remolded or remade, that it may become new and whole, so also it happens to man by death. ⁴For somehow or another he is broken apart, that he may rise in the resurrection whole—I mean spotless, and righteous, and immortal. ⁵And as to God's calling, and saying, "Where are you, Adam?" God did this, not as if ignorant of this, but being long-suffering, He gave him an opportunity of conversion and confession.

CHAPTER 27

¹But someone will say to us, "Was man made by nature mortal?" Certainly not. "Was he, then, immortal?" Neither do we affirm this. But one will say, "Was he, then, nothing?" Not even this hits the mark. ²He was by nature neither mortal nor immortal. For if He had made him immortal from the beginning, He would have made him God. Again, if He had made him mortal, God would seem to be the cause of his death. ³Neither, then, immortal nor yet mortal did He make him, but, as we have said above, capable of both, so that if he should incline to the things of immortality, keeping the commandment of God, he should receive as reward from Him immortality, and should become a god; but if, on the other hand, he should turn to the things of death, disobeying God, he should himself be the cause of death to himself. For God made man free, and with power over himself. ⁴That, then, which man brought on himself through carelessness and disobedience, this God now grants to him as a gift through His own generosity and pity, when men obey Him. ⁵For as man, disobeying, drew death on himself, so obeying the will of God, he who desires is able to procure for himself everlasting life. ⁶For God has given us a law and holy commandments; and everyone who keeps these can be saved, and, obtaining the resurrection, can inherit incorruption.

CHAPTER 28

¹And Adam having been cast out of Paradise, in this condition knew his wife Eve, whom God had formed into a wife for him out of his rib. ²And this He did, not as if He were unable to make his wife separately, but God foreknew that man would call on a number of gods. ³And having this foresight, and knowing that through the serpent error would introduce a number of gods which had no existence—for there being but one God, even then error was striving to disseminate a multitude of gods, saying, "You will be as gods"—lest, then, it should be supposed that one God made the man and another the woman, therefore He made them both; ⁴and God made the woman together with the man, not only that thus the mystery of God's sole government might be exhibited, but also that their mutual affection might be greater. Therefore, Adam said to Eve, "This is now bone of my bones, and flesh of my flesh." ⁵And besides [this], he prophesied, saying, "For this reason a man will leave his father and his mother, and will cleave to his wife, and the two will be one flesh"; which also itself has its fulfillment in ourselves. ⁶For who that marries lawfully does not despise mother and father, and his whole family connection, and all his household, cleaving to and becoming one with his own wife, fondly preferring her? ⁷So that often, for the sake of their wives, some submit even to death. This Eve, on account of her having been in the beginning deceived by the serpent, and having become the author of sin, the wicked demon, who also is called Satan, who then spoke to her through the serpent, and who works even to this day in those men that are possessed by him, invokes as Eve. ⁸And he is called demon and dragon, on account of his revolting from God. For in [the] beginning, he was a messenger. ⁹And concerning his history there is a great deal to be said; therefore, I at present omit the relation of it, for I have also given an account of him in another place.

CHAPTER 29

¹When, then, "Adam knew his wife Eve, she conceived and bore a son, whose name was Cain; and she said, I have gotten a man from God. And yet again she bore a second son, whose name was Abel, who began to be a keeper of sheep, but Cain tilled the ground." ²Their history receives a very full narration, yes, even a detailed explanation: therefore, the book itself, which is entitled "The Genesis of the World," can more accurately inform those who are anxious to learn their story. ³When, then, Satan saw Adam and his wife not only still living, but also begetting children—being carried away with spite because he had not succeeded in putting them to death—when he saw that Abel was well-pleasing to God, he worked on the heart of his brother called Cain, and caused him to kill his brother Abel. ⁴And thus, death got a beginning in this world, to find its way into every race of man, even to this day. ⁵But God, being pitiful, and wishing to afford to Cain, as to Adam, an opportunity of conversion and confession, said, "Where is your brother Abel?" But Cain answered God rebelliously, saying, "I do not know; am I my brother's keeper?" ⁶God, being thus made angry with him, said, "What have you done? The voice of your brother's blood cries to Me from the earth, which opened her mouth to receive your brother's blood from your hand. Groaning and trembling will you be on the earth." ⁷From that time the earth, through fear, no longer receives human blood, no, nor the blood of any animal; by which it appears that it is not the cause [of death], but man, who transgressed.

CHAPTER 30

¹Cain also had a son himself, whose name was Enoch; and he built a city, which he called by the name of his son, Enoch. From that time on a beginning was made of the building of cities, and this before the Flood; not as Homer falsely says: "Not yet had men built a city." ²And to Enoch was born a son, by name Irad; who begot a son called Mehujael; and Mehujael begot Methusael; and Methusael, Lamech. ³And Lamech took to him two wives, whose names were Adah and Zillah. At that time a beginning was made of polygamy, and also of music. ⁴For Lamech had three sons: Jabal, Jubal, Tubal[-Cain]. And Jabal became a keeper of cattle and dwelt in tents; but Jubal is he who made known the psaltery and the harp; and Tubal became a smith, a forger in brass and iron. ⁵So far the seed of Cain is registered; and for the rest, the seed of his line has sunk into oblivion, on account of his fratricide of his brother. ⁶And, in place of Abel, God granted to Eve to conceive and bear a son, who was called Seth, from whom the remainder of the human race proceeds until now. ⁷And to those who desire to be informed regarding all generations, it is easy to give explanations by means of the Holy Writings. ⁸For, as we have already mentioned, this subject, the order of the genealogy of man, has been partly handled by us in another discourse, in the first book of The History. ⁹And all these things the Holy Spirit teaches us, who speaks through Moses and the rest of the prophets, so that the writings which belong to us godly people are more ancient, yes, and are shown to be more truthful, than all writers and poets. ¹⁰But also, concerning music, some

have fabled that Apollo was the inventor, and others say that Orpheus discovered the art of music from the sweet voices of the birds. ¹¹Their story is shown to be empty and vain, for these inventors lived many years after the Flood. And what relates to Noah, who is called by some Deucalion, has been explained by us in the book previously mentioned, and which, if you wish it, you are at liberty to read.

CHAPTER 31

¹After the Flood there was again a beginning of cities and kings, in the following manner: The first city was Babylon, and Erech, and Accad, and Calneh, in the land of Shinar. And their king was called Nebroth [(Nimrod)]. From these came Asshur, from whom also the Assyrians receive their name. ²And Nimrod built the cities Nineveh and Rehoboth, and Calah, and Resen, between Nineveh and Calah; and Nineveh became a very great city. ³And another son of Shem, the son of Noah, by name Mitzraim, begot Ludim, and those called Anamim, and Lehabim, and Naphtuhim, and Pathrusim, and Casluhim, out of whom came Philistim. ⁴Of the three sons of Noah, however, and of their death and genealogy, we have given a succinct register in the above-mentioned book. ⁵But now we will mention the remaining facts both concerning cities and kings, and the things that happened when there was one speech and one language. Before the dividing of the languages, these aforementioned cities existed. ⁶But when men were about to be dispersed, they took counsel of their own judgment, and not at the instigation of God, to build a city, a tower whose top might reach into [the] heavens, that they might make a glorious name for themselves. ⁷Since, therefore, they had dared, contrary to the will of God, to attempt a grand work, God destroyed their city, and overthrew their tower. From that time on, He confounded the languages of men, giving to each a different dialect. ⁸And similarly the Sibyl spoke when she declared that wrath would come on the world. She says:

When are fulfilled the threats
    of the great God,
With which He threatened men,
    when formerly
In the Assyrian land they built a tower,
And all were of one speech,
    and wished to rise
Even till they climbed to the starry heavens,
⁹Then the Immortal raised a mighty wind
And laid on them strong necessity;
For when the wind threw down
    the mighty tower,
Then rose among mankind
    fierce strife and hate.
One speech was changed to many dialects,
And earth was filled with various
    tribes and kings.

¹⁰And so on. These things, then, happened in the land of the Chaldeans. ¹¹And in the land of Canaan there was a city, by name Haran. And in these days, Pharaoh, who by the Egyptians was also called Nechaoth, was [the] first king of Egypt, and thus the kings followed in succession. ¹²And in the land of Shinar, among those called Chaldeans, the first king was Arioch, and next after him Ellasar, and after him Chedorlaomer, king of Elam, and after him Tidal, king of the nations called Assyrians. ¹³And there were five other cities in the territory of Ham, the son of Noah: the first called Sodom, then Gomorrah, Admah, Zeboiim, and Balah, which was also called Zoar. ¹⁴And the names of their kings are these: Bera, king of Sodom; Birsha, king of Gomorrah; Shinab, king of Admah; Shemeber, king of Zeboiim; Bela, king of Zoar, which is also called Kephalac. ¹⁵These served Chedorlaomer, the king of the Assyrians, for twelve years, and in the thirteenth year they revolted from Chedorlaomer; and thus, it came to pass at that time that the four Assyrian kings waged war on the five kings. ¹⁶This was the first commencement of making war on the earth; and they destroyed the giants [of] Karnaim, and the strong nations that were with them in their city, and the Horites of the mountains called Seir, as far as the plain of Paran, which is by the wilderness. ¹⁷And at that time there was a righteous king called Melchizedek, in the city of Salem, which now is Jerusalem. This was the first priest of all priests of the Most High God; and from him the above-named city Hierosolyma was called Jerusalem. And from his time priests were found in all the earth. ¹⁸And after him, Abimelech reigned in Gerar; and after him another Abimelech. Then reigned Ephron, surnamed the Hittite. Such are the names of the kings that were in former times. ¹⁹And the rest of the kings of the Assyrians, during an interval of many years, have been passed over in silence unrecorded, all writers narrating the events of our recent days. ²⁰There were these kings of Assyria: Tiglath-Pileser, and after him Shalmaneser, then Sennacherib; and Adrammelech the Ethiopian, who also reigned over Egypt, was his triarch—though these things, in comparison with our books, are quite recent.

CHAPTER 32

¹Hence, therefore, may the lovers of learning and of antiquity understand the history, and see that those things are recent which are told by us apart from the holy prophets. ²For though at first there were few men in the land of Arabia and Chaldea, yet, after their languages were divided, they gradually began to multiply and spread over all the earth; and some of them tended toward the east to dwell there, and others to the parts of the great continent, and others northwards, so as to extend as far as Britain, in the Arctic regions. ³And others went to the land of Canaan, which is called Judea, and Phoenicia, and the region of Ethiopia, and Egypt, and Libya, and the country called torrid, and the parts stretching toward the west; ⁴and the rest went to places by the sea, and Pamphylia, and Asia, and Greece, and Macedonia, and also to Italy, and the whole country called Gaul, and Spain, and Germany, so that now the whole world is thus filled with inhabitants. ⁵Since then the occupation of the world by men was at first in three divisions—in the east, and south, and west—afterward, the remaining parts of the earth were inhabited, when men became very numerous. ⁶And the writers, not knowing these things, are [perhaps] presumptuous to maintain that the world is shaped like a sphere, and to compare it to a cube. ⁷But how can they say what is true regarding these things, when they do not know about the creation of the world and its population? Men gradually increasing in number and multiplying on the earth, as we have already said, the islands also of the sea and the rest of the countries were inhabited.

CHAPTER 33

¹Who, then, of those called sages, and poets, and historians, could truly tell us of these things, themselves being born much later, and introducing a multitude of gods, who were born so many years after the cities, and are more modern than kings, and nations, and wars? ²For they should have made mention of all events, even those which happened before the Flood—both of the creation of the world and the formation of man, and the whole succession of events. ³The Egyptian or Chaldean prophets, and the other writers, should have been able to tell accurately, if at least they spoke by a divine and pure spirit, and spoke truth in all that was uttered by them; and they should have announced not only things past or present, but also those that were to come on the world. ⁴And therefore, it is proved that all others have been in error, and that we Christians alone have possessed the truth, inasmuch as we are taught by the Holy Spirit, who spoke in the holy prophets, and foretold all things.

CHAPTER 34

¹And for the rest, if only in a humble spirit you would investigate divine things—I mean the things that are spoken by the prophets—in order that, by comparing what is said by us with the utterances of the others, you might be able to discover the truth. ²We have shown from their own histories which they have compiled, that the names of those who are called gods are found to be the names of men who lived among them, as we have shown above. ³And to this day their images are daily fashioned, idols, the works of men's hands. And these the mass of foolish men serve, while they reject the Maker and Fashioner of all things and the Nourisher of all breath of life, giving credit to vain doctrines through the deceitfulness of the senseless tradition received from their fathers. ⁴But God at least, the Father and Creator of the universe, did not abandon mankind, but gave a law, and sent holy prophets to declare and teach the race of men, that each one of us might awake and understand that there is one God. ⁵And they also taught us to refrain from unlawful idolatry, and adultery, and murder, fornication, theft, greed, false swearing, wrath,

CHAPTER 35

¹The Divine Law, then, not only forbids the worshiping of idols, but also of the heavenly bodies—the sun, the moon, or the other stars; yes, not heaven, nor earth, nor the sea, nor fountains, nor rivers, must be worshiped, but we must serve in holiness of heart and sincerity of purpose only the living and true God, who also is Maker of the universe. ²Therefore, the Holy Law says: "You will not commit adultery; you will not steal; you will not bear false witness; you will not desire your neighbor's wife." So also the prophets. ³Solomon indeed teaches us that we must not sin with so much as a turn of the eye, saying, "Let your eyes look right on, and let your eyelids look straight before you." ⁴And Moses, who was also himself a prophet, says, concerning the sole government of God: "Your God is He who establishes the heavens, and forms the earth, whose hands have brought forth all the host of [the] heavens; and He has not set these things before you that you should go after them." ⁵And Isaiah himself also says: "Thus says the LORD God || Who established the heavens, || And founded the earth and all that is therein, || And gives breath to the people on it, || And spirit to them that walk therein. This is the LORD your God." ⁶And again, through him He says: "I have made the earth, and man on it. I by My hand have established the heavens." ⁷And in another chapter, "This is your God, who created the ends of the earth; He does not hunger, neither is [He] weary, || And there is no searching of His understanding." ⁸So, too, Jeremiah says: "Who has made the earth by His power, || And established the world by His wisdom, || And by His discretion has stretched out the heavens, || And a mass of water in the heavens, || And He caused the clouds to ascend from the ends of the earth; He made lightnings with rain, || And brought forth winds out of His treasures." ⁹One can see how consistently and harmoniously all the prophets spoke, having given utterance through one and the same Spirit concerning the unity of God, and the creation of the world, and the formation of man. ¹⁰Moreover, they were in terrible travail, grieving the godless race of men, and they reproached those who seemed to be wise for their error and hardness of heart. ¹¹Jeremiah, indeed, said: "Every man is brutishly gone astray from the knowledge of Him; Every founder is confounded by his graven images; In vain the silversmith makes his molten images; There is no breath in them: In the day of their visitation they will perish." ¹²The same, too, David says: "They are corrupt, they have done abominable works; There is none that does good, no, not one; They have all gone aside, || They have together become profitless." ¹³So also Habakkuk: "What profits the graven image || That he has graven it a lying image? Woe to him that says to the stone, Awake, || And to the wood, Arise." Likewise spoke the other prophets of the truth. ¹⁴And why should I recount the multitude of prophets, who are numerous, and said ten thousand things consistently and harmoniously? ¹⁵For those who desire it, can, by reading what they uttered, accurately understand the truth, and no longer be carried away by opinion and profitless labor. ¹⁶These, then, whom we have already mentioned, were prophets among the Hebrews—illiterate, and shepherds, and uneducated.

CHAPTER 36

¹And the Sibyl, who was a prophetess among the Greeks and the other nations, in the beginning of her prophecy, reproaches the race of men, saying:

How are you still so quickly lifted up,
And how so thoughtless of the end of life,
You mortal men of flesh, who are nothing?
Do you not tremble, nor fear God Most High?
²Your Overseer, the Knower, Seer of all,
Who always keeps those whom
    His hand first made,
Puts His sweet Spirit into all His works,
And gives Him for a guide to mortal men.
³There is only one uncreated God,
Who reigns alone, all-powerful, very great,
From whom is nothing hid. He sees all things,
Himself unseen by any mortal eye.
Can mortal man see the immortal God,
Or fleshly eyes, which shun
    the noontide beams,
Look on Him, who dwells
    beyond the heavens?
⁴Worship Him then, the self-existent God,
The unbegotten Ruler of the world,
Who alone was from everlasting time,
And will to everlasting still abide.
⁵Of evil counsels you will reap the fruit,
Because you have not honored the true God,
Nor offered to Him sacred hecatombs.
To those who dwell in Hades you make gifts,
And to demons offer sacrifice.
⁶In madness and in pride you have
    your walk;
And leaving the right way, you wander wide,
And lose yourselves in pitfalls and in thorns.
⁷Why do you wander thus, O foolish men?
Cease your vain wanderings in the black,
    dark night;
Why follow darkness and perpetual gloom
When, see, there shines for you
    the blessed light?
⁸Behold, He is clear—in Him there is no spot.
Turn, then, from darkness,
    and behold the day;
Be wise, and treasure wisdom
    in your breasts.
⁹There is one God who sends
    the winds and rains,
The earthquakes, and the lightnings,
    and the plagues,
The famines, and the snowstorms,
    and the ice,
And all the woes that visit our sad race.
¹⁰Nor these alone, but all things else
    He gives,
Ruling omnipotent in heavens and earth,
And self-existent from eternity.

¹¹And regarding those [gods] that are said to have been born, she said:

If all things that are born must also die,
God cannot be produced by mortal man.
¹²But there is only One, the All-Supreme,
Who made the heavens,
    with all their starry host,
The sun and moon; likewise,
    the fruitful earth,
With all the waves of ocean, and the hills,
The fountains, and the ever-flowing streams;
He also made the countless multitude
Of ocean creatures, and He keeps alive
All creeping things, both of the earth and sea;
And all the tuneful choir of birds He made,
Which cleave the air with wings,
    and with shrill pipe
Trill forth at morn their tender,
    clear-voiced song.
¹³Within the deep glades of the hills,
    He placed
A savage race of beasts; and to men
He made all cattle subject, making man
The God-formed image, ruler over all,
And putting in subjection to his sway
Things many and incomprehensible.
¹⁴For who of mortals can know
    all these things?
He only knows who made them at the first,
He the Creator, incorruptible,
Who dwells in upper air eternally;
Who offers to the good most rich rewards,
And against evil and unrighteous men
Rouses revenge, and wrath, and bloody wars,
And pestilence, and many a tearful grief.
¹⁵O man exalted vainly—say why thus
Have you so utterly destroyed yourself?
Have you no shame worshiping beasts
    for gods?
And to believe the gods should steal
    your beasts,
Or that they need your vessels—is it not
Frenzy's most profitless and foolish thought?
¹⁶Instead of dwelling in the golden heavens,
You see your gods become
    the prey of worms,
And hosts of creatures filthy and unclean.
¹⁷O fools! You worship serpents, dogs,
    and cats,
Birds, and the creeping things of earth
    and sea,
Images made with hands, statues of stone,
And heaps of rubbish by the wayside placed.
¹⁸All these, and many more vain things,
    you serve,
Worshiping things disgraceful even to name:
These are the gods who lead vain men astray,
From whose mouth streams
    of deadly poison flow.
¹⁹But to Him in whom alone is life,
Life, and undying, everlasting light;
Who pours into man's cup of life a joy

Sweeter than sweetest honey to his taste—
To Him bow the head, to Him alone,
And walk in ways of everlasting peace.
²⁰Forsaking Him, you all have turned aside,
And, in your raving folly, drained the cup
Of justice quite unmixed, pure,
      mastering, strong;
And you will not again be sober men,
You will not come to a sober mind,
And know your God and King,
      who looks on all:
Therefore, on you burning fire will come,
And ages you will daily burn in flames,
Ashamed for ages of your useless gods.
²¹But those who worship the eternal God,
They will inherit everlasting life,
Inhabiting the blooming realms of bliss,
And feasting on sweet food
      from starry heaven.

²²That these things are true, and useful, and just, and profitable to all men, is obvious. Even the poets have spoken of the punishments of the wicked.

CHAPTER 37

¹And that evildoers must necessarily be punished in proportion to their deeds, has already been, as it were, oracularly uttered by some of the poets, as a witness both against themselves and against the wicked, declaring that they will be punished. ²Aeschylus said: "He who has done must also suffer." And Pindar himself said: "It is fit that suffering follow doing." ³So, too, Euripides: "The deed rejoiced you—suffering endure; The taken enemy must surely be pained." And again: "The foe's pain is the hero's wage." ⁴And similarly, Archilochus: "One thing I know, I hold it ever true, || The evildoer evil will endure." ⁵And that God sees all, and that nothing escapes His notice, but that, being long-suffering, He refrains until the time when He is to judge—concerning this, too, Dionysius said: "The eye of Justice seeing all, || Yet seems not to see." ⁶And that God's judgment is to be, and that evils will suddenly overtake the wicked—this, too, Aeschylus declared, saying, "Swift-footed is the approach of fate, || And none can justice violate, || But feels its stern hand soon or late. ⁷'Tis with you, though unheard, unseen; You draw night's curtain in between, || But even sleep affords no screen. 'Tis with you if you sleep or wake; And if abroad your way you take, || Its still, stern watch you cannot break. ⁸'Twill follow you, or cross your path; And even night no virtue has || To hide you from the Avenger's wrath. To show the ill the darkness flees; Then, if sin offers joy or ease, || Oh stop, and think that someone sees!" ⁹And may we not cite Simonides also? "To men no evil comes unheralded; But God with sudden hand transforms all things." ¹⁰Euripides again: "The wicked and proud man's prosperity || Is based on sand: his race does not abide; And time proclaims the wickedness of men." Once more Euripides: "Not without judgment is the Deity, || But sees when oaths are struck unrightneously, || And when from men unwilling they are wrung." ¹¹And Sophocles: "If ills you do, ills you also must bear." That God will make inquiry both concerning false swearing and concerning every other wickedness, they themselves have nearly predicted. ¹²And concerning the conflagration of the world, they have, willingly or unwillingly, spoken in conformity with the prophets, though they were much more recent, and stole these things from the Law and the Prophets. The poets corroborate the testimony of the prophets.

CHAPTER 38

¹But why does it matter whether they were before or after them? Certainly they did at all times utter things confirmatory of the prophets. ²Concerning the burning up of the world, Malachi the prophet foretold: "The Day of the LORD comes as a burning oven, || And will consume all the wicked." ³And Isaiah: "For the wrath of God is as a violent hailstorm, || And as a rushing mountain torrent." ⁴The Sibyl, then, and the other prophets, yes, and the poets and philosophers, have clearly taught both concerning righteousness, and judgment, and punishment; ⁵and also concerning providence, that God cares for us, not only for the living among us, but also for those that are dead: though, indeed, they said this unwillingly, for they were convinced by the truth. ⁶And among the prophets indeed, Solomon said of the dead: "There will be healing to your flesh, || And care taken of your bones." And David says the same: "The bones which You have broken will rejoice." ⁷And in agreement with these sayings was that of Timocles: "The dead are pitied by the loving God." ⁸And the writers who spoke of a multiplicity of gods came at length to the doctrine of the unity of God, and those who asserted chance spoke also of providence; ⁹and the advocates of impunity confessed there would be a judgment, and those who denied that there is a sensation after death acknowledged that there is. ¹⁰Homer, accordingly, though he had said, "Like a fleeting vision, the soul passed away," says in another place: "To Hades went the disembodied soul"; and again: "That I may quickly pass through Hades' gates, || Bury me." ¹¹And as regards the others whom you have read, I think you know with sufficient accuracy how they have expressed themselves. ¹²But all these things will everyone understand who seeks the wisdom of God and is well pleasing to Him through faith, and righteousness, and the doing of good works. ¹³For one of the prophets whom we already mentioned, Hosea by name, said, "Who is wise, and he will understand these things? Prudent, and he will know them? For the ways of the LORD are right, || And the just will walk in them; But the transgressors will fall therein." ¹⁴He, then, who is desirous of learning, should learn much. Therefore, endeavor to meet [with me] more frequently, that, by hearing the living voice, you may accurately ascertain the truth.

BOOK III

CHAPTER 1

¹Theophilus to Autolycus: Greetings! Seeing that writers are fond of composing a multitude of books for vainglory—some concerning gods, and wars, and chronology, and some, too, concerning useless legends, and other such labor in vain, in which you also have been used to employ yourself until now, and do not grudge to endure that toil; ²but though you conversed with me, are still of opinion that the word of truth is an idle tale, and suppose that our writings are recent and modern—on this account I also will not grudge the labor of compendiously setting forth to you, God helping me, the antiquity of our books, reminding you of it in few words, that you may not grudge the labor of reading it, but may recognize the folly of the other authors.

CHAPTER 2

¹For it was fitting that they who wrote should themselves have been eyewitnesses of those things concerning which they made assertions, or should accurately have ascertained them from those who had seen them; for they who write of things unascertained beat the air. ²For what did it profit Homer to have composed the Trojan War, and to have deceived many; or Hesiod, the register of the Theogony of those whom he calls gods; or Orpheus, the three hundred and sixty-five gods, whom in the end of his life he rejects, maintaining in his precepts that there is one God? ³What profit did the sphaerography of the world's circle confer on Aratus, or those who held the same doctrine as he, except glory among men? And not even that did they reap as they deserved. ⁴And what truth did they utter? Or what good did their tragedies do to Euripides and Sophocles, or the other tragedians? ⁵Or their comedies to Menander, and Aristophanes, and the other comedians? Or their histories to Herodotus and Thucydides? Or the shrines and the pillars of Hercules to Pythagoras, or the Cynic philosophy to Diogenes? ⁶What good did it do Epicurus to maintain that there is no providence; or Empedocles to teach atheism; or Socrates to swear by the dog, and the goose, and the plane-tree, and Asclepius struck by lightning, and the demons whom he invoked? ⁷And why did he willingly die? What reward, or of what kind, did he expect to receive after death? What did Plato's system of culture profit him? Or what benefit did the rest of the philosophers derive from their doctrines, not to enumerate the whole of them, since they are numerous? ⁸But these things we say, for the purpose of exhibiting their useless and godless opinions.

CHAPTER 3

¹For all these, having fallen in love with vain and empty reputation, neither themselves knew the truth, nor guided others to the truth:

for the things which they said themselves convict them of speaking inconsistently; and most of them demolished their own doctrines. ²For not only did they refute one another, but some, too, even frustrated their own teachings, so that their reputation has resulted in shame and folly, for they are condemned by men of understanding. ³For either they made assertions concerning the gods, and afterward taught that there was no god; or if they spoke even of the creation of the world, they finally said that all things were produced spontaneously. ⁴Yes, and even speaking of providence, they taught again that the world was not ruled by providence. ⁵But what? Did they not, when they essayed to write even of honorable conduct, teach the perpetration of lasciviousness, and fornication, and adultery; and did they not introduce hateful and unutterable wickedness? ⁶And they proclaim that their gods took the lead in committing unutterable acts of adultery, and in monstrous banquets. ⁷For who does not sing Saturn devouring his own children, and Jove his son gulping down Metis, and preparing for the gods a horrible feast, at which also they say that Vulcan, a lame blacksmith, did the waiting; and how Jove not only married Juno, his own sister, but also with foul mouth did abominable wickedness? ⁸And the rest of his deeds, as many as the poets sing, it is likely you are acquainted with. ⁹Why must I further recount the deeds of Neptune and Apollo, or Bacchus and Hercules, of the bosom-loving Minerva, and the shameless Venus, since in another place we have given a more accurate account of these?

CHAPTER 4

¹Nor indeed was there any necessity for my refuting these, except that I see you still in doubt about the word of the truth. For though you [are] prudent, you endure fools gladly. ²Otherwise you would not have been moved by senseless men to yield yourself to empty words, and to give credit to the prevalent rumor with which godless lips falsely accuse us, who are worshipers of God, and are called Christians, alleging that the wives of us are all held in common and made promiscuous use of; and that we even commit incest with our own sisters, and, what is most impious and barbarous of all, that we eat human flesh. ³But further, they say that our doctrine has but recently come to light, and that we have nothing to allege in proof of what we receive as truth, nor of our teaching, but that our doctrine is foolishness. ⁴I wonder, then, chiefly that you, who in other matters are studious, and a scrutinizer of all things, give but a careless hearing to us. For if it were possible for you, you would not resent spending the night in the libraries.

CHAPTER 5

¹Since, then, you have read much, what is your opinion of the precepts of Zeno, and Diogenes, and Cleanthes, which their books contain, instructing the eating of human flesh: that fathers be cooked and eaten by their own children; and that if anyone refuses or rejects a part of this infamous food, he himself be devoured who will not eat? ²An utterance even more godless than these is found—that, namely, of Diogenes, who teaches children to bring their own parents in sacrifice and devour them. ³And does not the historian Herodotus narrate that Cambyses, when he had slaughtered the children of Harpagus, cooked them also, and set them as a meal before their father? ⁴And, still further, he narrates that among the Indians the parents are eaten by their own children. ⁵Oh! The godless teaching of those who recorded, yes, rather, instructed such things! Oh! Their wickedness and godlessness! Oh! The conception of those who thus accurately philosophized and profess philosophy! ⁶For they who taught these doctrines have filled the world with iniquity.

CHAPTER 6

¹And regarding lawless conduct, those who have blindly wandered into the choir of philosophy have, almost to a man, spoken with one voice. ²Certainly Plato, to mention him first who seems to have been the most respectable philosopher among them, expressly, as it were, legislates in his first book, entitled The Republic, that the wives of all be common, using the precedent of the son of Jupiter and the lawgiver of the Cretans, in order that under this pretext there might be an abundant offspring from the best persons, and that those who were worn with toil might be comforted by such intercourse. ³And Epicurus himself, too, as well as teaching atheism, teaches along with it incest with mothers and sisters, and this in transgression of the laws which forbid it; ⁴for Solon distinctly legislated regarding this, in order that from a married parent children might lawfully spring, that they might not be born of adultery, so that no one should honor as his father him who was not his father, or dishonor him who was really his father, through ignorance that he was so. ⁵And these things the other laws of the Romans and Greeks also prohibit. ⁶Why, then, do Epicurus and the Stoics teach incest and sodomy, with which doctrines they have filled libraries, so that from boyhood this lawless intercourse is learned? ⁷And why should I further spend time on them, since even of those they call gods, they relate similar things?

CHAPTER 7

¹For after they had said that these are gods, they again made them of no account. For some said that they were composed of atoms; and others, again, that they eventuate in atoms; and they say that the gods have no more power than men. ²Plato, too, though he says these are gods, would have them composed of matter. ³And Pythagoras, after he had made such a toil and drudgery about the gods, and traveled up and down [for information], at last determines that all things are produced naturally and spontaneously, and that the gods care nothing for men. ⁴And how many atheistic opinions Clitomachus the academic introduced, [I need not recount]. ⁵And did Critias and Protagoras of Abdera not say, "For whether the gods exist, I am not able to affirm concerning them, nor to explain of what nature they are, for there are many things that would prevent me?" ⁶And to speak of the opinions of the most atheistic Euhemerus is superfluous, for having made many daring assertions concerning the gods, he at last would absolutely deny their existence and have all things to be governed by self-regulated action. ⁷And Plato, who spoke so much of the unity of God and of the soul of man, asserting that the soul is immortal, is not he himself afterward found, inconsistently with himself, to maintain that some souls pass into other men, and that others take their departure into irrational animals? ⁸How can his doctrine fail to seem dreadful and monstrous—to those at least who have any judgment—that he who was once a man will afterward be a wolf, or a dog, or a donkey, or some other irrational brute? ⁹Pythagoras, too, is found venting similar nonsense, besides his demolishing providence. ¹⁰Which of them, then, will we believe: Philemon, the comic poet, who says, "Good hope have they who praise and serve the gods"; or those whom we have mentioned—Euhemerus, and Epicurus, and Pythagoras, and the others—who deny that the gods are to be worshiped, and who abolish providence? ¹¹Concerning God and providence, Ariston said: "Be of good courage: God will still preserve || And greatly help all those who so deserve. If no promotion waits on faithful men, || Say what advantage goodness offers then. ¹²'Tis granted—yet I often see the just || Faring but ill, from ev'ry honor thrust; While they whose own advancement is their aim, || Oft in this present life have all they claim. But we must look beyond, and wait the end, || That consummation to which all things tend. ¹³'Tis not, as vain and wicked men have said, || By an unbridled destiny we're led: It is not blinded chance that rules the world, || Nor uncontrolled are all things onward hurled. ¹⁴The wicked blinds himself with this belief; But be sure, of all rewards, the chief || Is still reserved for those who holy live; And Providence to wicked men will give || Only the just reward which is their wage, || And fitting punishment for each bad deed." ¹⁵And one can see how inconsistent with each other are the things which others, and indeed almost the majority, have said about God and providence. ¹⁶For some have absolutely canceled God and providence; and others, again, have affirmed God, and have avowed that all things are governed by providence. ¹⁷The intelligent hearer and reader must therefore give meticulous attention to their expressions; as also Simylus said: "It is the custom of the poets to name by a common designation the surpassingly wicked and the excellent; we therefore must discriminate." ¹⁸As also Philemon says: "A senseless man

who sits and merely hears is a troublesome feature; for he does not blame himself, so foolish is he." [19]We must then pay attention and consider what is said, critically inquiring into what has been uttered by the philosophers and the poets.

CHAPTER 8

[1]For denying that there are gods, they again acknowledge their existence, and they said they committed grossly wicked deeds. [2]And, first, of Jove the poets erroneously sing the wicked actions. And Chrysippus, who talked a deal of nonsense, is he not found publishing that Juno had the foulest intercourse with Jupiter? [3]For why should I recount the impurities of the so-called mother of the gods, or of Jupiter Latiaris thirsting for human blood, or the castrated Attis; or of Jupiter, surnamed Tragedian, and how he defiled himself, as they say, and now is worshiped among the Romans as a god? [4]I am silent about the temples of Antinous, and of the others whom you call gods. For when related to sensible persons, they excite laughter. [5]They who elaborated such a philosophy regarding either the non-existence of God, or promiscuous intercourse and beastly concubinage, are themselves condemned by their own teachings. [6]Moreover, we find from the writings they composed that the eating of human flesh was received among them; and they record that those whom they honor as gods were the first to do these things.

CHAPTER 9

[1]Now we also confess that God exists, but that He is one, the Creator, and Maker, and Fashioner of this universe; and we know that all things are arranged by His providence, but by Him alone. [2]And we have learned a holy law; but we have as lawgiver Him who is really God, who teaches us to act righteously, and to be pious, and to do good. [3]And concerning piety He says, "You will have no other gods before Me. You will not make for yourselves any graven image, or any likeness of anything that is in [the] heavens above, or that is in the earth beneath, or that is in the water under the earth: you will not bow down yourself to them, nor serve them, for I am the LORD your God." [4]And of doing good He said: "Honor your father and your mother, that it may be well with you, and that your days may be long in the land which I the LORD God give you." [5]Again, concerning righteousness: "You will not commit adultery. You will not kill. You will not steal. You will not bear false witness against your neighbor. You will not covet your neighbor's wife, you will not covet your neighbor's house, nor his land, nor his manservant, nor his maidservant, nor his ox, nor his beast of burden, nor any of his cattle, nor anything that is your neighbor's." [6]You will not wrest the judgment of the poor in his cause. Keep far from every unjust matter. The innocent and righteous you will not slay; you will not justify the wicked; and you will not take a gift, for gifts blind the eyes of them that see and pervert righteous words." [7]Of this Divine Law, then, Moses, who was also God's servant, was made the minister both to all the world, and chiefly to the Hebrews, who were also called Jews, whom an Egyptian king had in ancient days enslaved, and who were the righteous seed of godly and holy men—Abraham, and Isaac, and Jacob. [8]God, being mindful of them, and doing marvelous and strange miracles by the hand of Moses, delivered them, and led them out of Egypt, leading them through what is called the desert; whom He also settled again in the land of Canaan, which afterward was called Judea, and gave them a law, and taught them these things. [9]Of this great and wonderful Law, which tends to all righteousness, the ten heads are such as we have already rehearsed.

CHAPTER 10

[1]Since therefore they were strangers in the land of Egypt, being by birth Hebrews from the land of Chaldea—for at that time, there being a famine, they were obliged to migrate to Egypt for the sake of buying food there, where also for a time they sojourned; [2]and these things befell them in accordance with a prediction of God—having sojourned, then, in Egypt for 430 years, when Moses was about to lead them out into the desert, God taught them by the Law, saying, "You will not afflict a stranger; for you know the heart of a stranger: for [you] yourselves were strangers in the land of Egypt."

CHAPTER 11

[1]And when the people transgressed the Law which had been given to them by God, God being good and pitiful, unwilling to destroy them, in addition to His giving them the Law, afterward also sent forth prophets to them from among their brothers, to teach and remind them of the contents of the Law, and to turn them to conversion, that they might sin no more. [2]But if they persisted in their wicked deeds, He forewarned them that they should be delivered into subjection to all the kingdoms of the earth; and that this has already happened to them is manifest. [3]Concerning conversion, then, Isaiah the prophet, generally indeed to all, but expressly to the people, says: "Seek the LORD while He may be found, || Call on Him while He is near: Let the wicked forsake his ways, || And the unrighteous man his thoughts, || And let him return to the LORD his God, || And he will find mercy, || For He will abundantly pardon." [4]And another prophet, Ezekiel, says: "If the wicked will turn || From all his sins that he has committed, || And keep all My statutes, || And does that which is right in My sight, || He will surely live, he will not die. All his transgressions that he has committed, || They will not be mentioned to him; But in his righteousness that he has done he will live: For I do not desire the death of the sinner, says the LORD, || But that he might turn from his wicked way and live." [5]Again Isaiah: "You who take deep and wicked counsel: Turn, that you may be saved." [6]And another prophet, Jeremiah: "Turn to the LORD your God, as a grape-gatherer to his basket, and you will find mercy." [7]Many therefore—yes, rather, countless—are the sayings in the Holy Writings regarding conversion, God always desiring that the race of men turn from all their sins.

CHAPTER 12

[1]Moreover, concerning the righteousness which the Law enjoined, confirmatory utterances are found both with the prophets and in the Gospels, because they all spoke inspired by one Spirit of God. [2]Isaiah accordingly spoke thus: "Put away the evil of your doings from your souls, || Learn to do well, || Seek judgment, relieve the oppressed, || Judge the fatherless, plead for the widow." [3]And again the same prophet said: "Loose every band of wickedness, || Dissolve every oppressive contract, || Let the oppressed go free, || And tear up every unrighteous bond. Deal out your bread to the hungry, || And bring the homeless poor to your home. [4]When you see the naked, cover him, || And do not hide yourself from your own flesh. Then your light will break forth as the morning, || And your health will spring forth speedily, || And your righteousness will go before you." [5]In like manner also, Jeremiah says: "Stand in the ways and see, || And ask which is the good way of the LORD your God and walk in it, || And you will find rest for your souls. Judge just judgment, || For in this is the will of the LORD your God." [6]So also says Hosea: "Keep judgment, and draw near to your God, || Who established the heavens and created the earth." [7]And another, Joel, spoke in agreement with these: "Gather the people, sanctify the congregation, || Assemble the elders, || Gather the children that are in arms, || Let the bridegroom go forth from his chamber, || And the bride out of her closet, || And pray to the LORD your God urgently || That He may have mercy on you || And blot out your sins." [8]In like manner also another, Zachariah: "Thus says the LORD Almighty: Execute true judgment, || And show mercy and compassion—every man to his brother; And do not oppress the widow, || Nor the fatherless, nor the stranger; And let none of you imagine evil against his brother in your heart, || Says the LORD Almighty."

CHAPTER 13

[1]And concerning chastity, the holy word teaches us not only not to sin in act, but not even in thought, not even in the heart to think of any evil, nor look on another man's wife with our eyes to lust after her. [2]Solomon, accordingly, who was a king and a prophet, said: "Let your eyes look right on, || And let your eyelids look straight before you: Make straight paths for your feet." [3]And the voice of the Gospel teaches still more urgently concerning chastity, saying, "Whosoever looks on a woman who is not his own wife, to lust after her, has already committed adultery with her in his heart." [4]"And he that marries," says [the Gospel], "her that is divorced from her husband, commits adultery; and

whosoever puts away his wife, except for the cause of fornication, causes her to commit adultery." ⁵Indeed, Solomon says: "Can a man take fire in his bosom, || And his clothes not be burned? Or can one walk on hot coals, || And his feet not be burned? So he that goes in to a married woman will not be innocent."

CHAPTER 14

¹And that we should be inclined toward kindness, not only toward those of our own relation, as some suppose, Isaiah the prophet said: "Say to those that hate you || And that cast you out, || You are our brothers, || That the Name of the LORD may be glorified || And be apparent in their joy." ²And the Gospel says: "Love your enemies and pray for them that despitefully use you. For if you love them who love you, what reward will you have? This the robbers and the tax collectors also do." ³And those that do good it teaches not to boast, lest they become men-pleasers. For it says: "Do not let your left hand know what your right hand does." ⁴Moreover, concerning subjection to authorities and powers, and prayer for them, the divine word gives us instructions, in order that we may lead a quiet and peaceable life. ⁵And it teaches us to render all things to all—honor to whom honor, fear to whom fear, tribute to whom tribute; to owe no man anything, but to love all.

CHAPTER 15

¹Consider, therefore, whether those who teach such things can possibly live indifferently, and be mingled in unlawful intercourse, or, most impious of all, eat human flesh, especially when we are forbidden so much as to witness shows of gladiators, lest we become partakers and abettors of murders. ²But neither may we see the other spectacles, lest our eyes and ears be defiled, participating in the utterances sung there. ³For if one should speak of cannibalism, in these spectacles the children of Thyestes and Tereus are eaten; and as for adultery, both in the case of men and of gods, whom they celebrate in elegant language for honors and prizes, this is made the subject of their dramas. ⁴But far be it from Christians to conceive any such deeds; for with them temperance dwells, self-restraint is practiced, monogamy is observed, chastity is guarded, iniquity exterminated, sin uprooted, righteousness exercised, law administered, worship performed, God acknowledged; ⁵truth governs, grace guards, peace screens them; the Holy Word guides, wisdom teaches, life directs, God reigns. ⁶Therefore, though we have much to say regarding our manner of life, and the ordinances of God, the Maker of all creation, we yet consider that we have for the present reminded you of enough to induce you to study these things, especially since you can now read [our writings] for yourself, that as you have been fond of acquiring information, you may still be studious in this direction also.

CHAPTER 16

¹But I now wish to give you a more accurate demonstration, God helping me, of the historical periods, that you may see that our doctrine is not modern nor fabulous, but more ancient and true than all poets and authors who have written in uncertainty. ²For some, maintaining that the world was uncreated, went into infinity; and others, asserting that it was created, said that one hundred fifty-three thousand [and] seventy-five years had already passed. This is stated by Apollonius the Egyptian. ³And Plato, who is esteemed to have been the wisest of the Greeks, into what nonsense did he run? ⁴For in his book entitled The Republic, we find him expressly saying: "For if things had perpetually remained in their present arrangement, when could any new thing ever be discovered? ⁵For ten thousand times ten thousand years elapsed without record, and one thousand or twice as many years have gone by since some things were discovered by Daedalus, and some by Orpheus, and some by Palamedes." ⁶And when he says that these things happened, he implies that ten thousand times ten thousand years elapsed from the Flood to Daedalus. ⁷And after he has said a great deal about the cities of the world, and the settlements, and the nations, he owns that he has said these things conjecturally. ⁸For he says, "If then, my friend, some god should promise us," "that if we attempted to make a survey of legislation," "the things now said," etcetera, which shows that he was speaking by guess; and if by guess, then what he says is not true.

CHAPTER 17

¹It was therefore right that he should rather become a scholar of God in this matter of legislation, as he himself confessed that in no other way could he gain accurate information than by God's teaching him through the Law. ²And did not the poets Homer, and Hesiod, and Orpheus profess that they themselves had been instructed by Divine Providence? ³Moreover, it is said that among your writers there were prophets and prognosticators, and that those wrote accurately who were informed by them. ⁴How much more, then, will we know the truth who are instructed by the holy prophets, who were possessed by the Holy Spirit of God! ⁵On this account all the prophets spoke harmoniously and in agreement with one another and foretold the things that would come to pass in all the world. ⁶For the very accomplishment of predicted and already consummated events should demonstrate to those who are fond of information, yes rather, who are lovers of truth, that those things are really true which they declared concerning the epochs and eras before the Flood: ⁷namely, how the years have run on since the world was created until now, so as to manifest the ridiculous mendacity of your authors, and show that their statements are not true.

CHAPTER 18

¹For Plato, as we said above, when he had demonstrated that a flood had happened, said that it extended not over the whole earth, but only over the plains, and that those who fled to the highest hills saved themselves. ²But others say that there existed Deucalion and Pyrrha, and that they were preserved in a chest; and that Deucalion, after he came out of the chest, flung stones behind him, and that men were produced from the stones; from which circumstance they say that men in the mass are named people. ³Others, again, say that Clymenus existed in a second flood. From what has already been said, it is evident that they who wrote such things and philosophized to so little purpose are miserable, and very profane and senseless persons. ⁴But Moses, our prophet and the servant of God, in giving an account of the origin of the world, related in what manner the Flood came on the earth, telling us, besides [this], how the details of the Flood came about, and relating no fable of Pyrrha nor of Deucalion or Clymenus; nor, indeed, that only the plains were submerged, and that those only who escaped to the mountains were saved.

CHAPTER 19

¹And neither does he make out that there was a second flood: on the contrary, he said that never again would there be a flood of water on the world; as neither indeed has there been, nor ever will be [again]. ²And he says that eight human beings were preserved in the Ark, in that which had been prepared by God's direction, not by Deucalion, but by Noah; which Hebrew word means rest, as we have elsewhere shown that Noah, when he announced to the men then alive that there was a flood coming, prophesied to them, saying, "Come there, God calls you to conversion." ³On this account he was fitly called Deucalion. ⁴And this Noah had three sons (as we mentioned in the second book), whose names were Shem, and Ham, and Japheth; and these had three wives, one wife each; each man and his wife. This man some have surnamed Eunuchus. ⁵All the eight persons, therefore, who were found in the Ark were preserved. ⁶And Moses showed that the Flood lasted forty days and forty nights, torrents pouring from [the] sky, and from the fountains of the deep breaking up, so that the water overtopped every high hill [by at least] fifteen cubits. ⁷And thus, the race of all the men that then were was destroyed, and only those who were protected in the Ark were saved; and these, we have already said, were eight. ⁸And of the Ark, the remains are to this day to be seen in the [[Arabian]] mountains. This, then, is the history of the Flood in summary.

CHAPTER 20

¹And Moses, becoming the leader of the Jews, as we have already stated, was expelled from the land of Egypt by the king, Pharaoh, whose name was Amasis [(Ahmose I)], and who, they say, reigned after the expulsion of the

people twenty-five years and four months, as Manetho assumes. ²And after him [reigned] Chebron, thirteen years. And after him Amenophis, twenty years seven months. And after him his sister Amessa, twenty-one years one month. ³And after her Mephres, twelve years nine months. And after him Methramuthosis, twenty years and ten months. ⁴And after him Tythmoses, nine years eight months. And after him Damphenophis, thirty years ten months. And after him Orus, thirty-five years five months. ⁵And after him his daughter, ten years three months. After her Mercheres, twelve years three months. And after him his son Armais, thirty years one month. ⁶After him Messes, son of Miammus, six years two months. After him Rameses, one year four months. After him Amenophis, nineteen years six months. ⁷After him his sons Thoessus and Rameses, ten years, who, it is said, had a large cavalry force and naval equipment. ⁸The Hebrews, indeed, after their own separate history, having at that time migrated into the land of Egypt, and been enslaved by King Tethmosis, as already said, built for him strong cities, Peitho, and Rameses, and On, which is Heliopolis; ⁹so that the Hebrews, who also are our ancestors, and from whom we have those sacred books which are older than all authors, as already said, are proved to be more ancient than the cities which were at that time renowned among the Egyptians. ¹⁰And the country was called Egypt from King Sethos. For the word Sethos, they say, is pronounced Egypt. ¹¹And Sethos had a brother, by name Armais. He is called Danaus, the same who passed from Egypt to Argos, whom the other authors mention as being of very ancient date.

CHAPTER 21

¹And Manetho, who among the Egyptians produced a great deal of nonsense, and even impiously charged Moses and the Hebrews who accompanied him with being banished from Egypt on account of leprosy, could give no accurate chronological statement. ²For when he said they were shepherds, and enemies of the Egyptians, he uttered truth indeed, because he was forced to do so. ³For our forefathers who sojourned in Egypt were truly shepherds, but not lepers. ⁴For when they came into the land called Jerusalem, where they also afterward dwelt, it is well known how their priests, in pursuance of the appointment of God, continued in the temple, and there healed every disease, so that they cured lepers and every disorder. ⁵The temple was built by Solomon, the king of Judea. ⁶And from Manetho's own statement his chronological error is manifest. (As it is also in respect of the king who expelled them, Pharaoh by name. For he no longer ruled them. For having pursued the Hebrews, he and his army were engulphed in the Red Sea. And he is in error still further, in saying that the shepherds made war against the Egyptians.) ⁷For they went out of Egypt, and thereafter dwelt in the country now called Judea, three hundred thirteen years before Danaus came to Argos. ⁸And that most people consider him older than any other of the Greeks is manifest. ⁹So Manetho has unwillingly declared to us, by his own writings, two particulars of the truth: first, avowing that they were shepherds; secondly, saying that they went out of the land of Egypt; so that even from these writings Moses and his followers are proven to be nine hundred or even one thousand years prior to the Trojan War.

CHAPTER 22

¹Then concerning the building of the temple in Judea, which Solomon the king built five hundred sixty-six years after the exodus of the Jews from Egypt, there is among the Tyrians a record how the temple was built; ²and in their archives writings have been preserved, in which the temple is proven to have existed one hundred forty-three years eight months before the Tyrians founded Carthage, and this record was made by Hiram (that is the name of the king of the Tyrians), the son of Abimalus, on account of the hereditary friendship which existed between Hiram and Solomon, and at the same time on account of the surpassing wisdom possessed by Solomon. ³For they continually engaged with each other in discussing difficult problems. And proof of this exists in their correspondence, which to this day is preserved among the Tyrians, and the writings that passed between them; ⁴as Menander the Ephesian, while narrating the history of the Tyrian kingdom, records, speaking thus: "For when Abimalus the king of the Tyrians died, his son Hiram succeeded to the kingdom. He lived fifty-three years. ⁵And Bazorus succeeded him, who lived forty-three, and reigned seventeen years. And after him followed Methuastartus, who lived fifty-four years, and reigned twelve. ⁶And after him succeeded his brother Atharymus, who lived fifty-eight years, and reigned nine. He was slain by his brother of the name of Helles, who lived fifty years, and reigned eight months. ⁷He was killed by Juthobalus, priest of Astarte, who lived forty years, and reigned twelve. He was succeeded by his son Bazorus, who lived forty-five years, and reigned seven. ⁸And to him his son Metten succeeded, who lived thirty-two years, and reigned twenty-nine. ⁹Pygmalion, son of Pygmalius, succeeded him, who lived fifty-six years, and reigned seven. And in the seventh year of his reign, his sister, fleeing to Libya, built the city which to this day is called Carthage. ¹⁰The whole period, therefore, from the reign of Hiram to the founding of Carthage, amounts to one hundred fifty-five years and eight months. ¹¹And in the twelfth year of the reign of Hiram the temple in Jerusalem was built. So the entire time from the building of the temple to the founding of Carthage was one hundred forty-three years and eight months.

CHAPTER 23

¹So then let what has been said suffice for the testimony of the Phoenicians and Egyptians, and for the account of our chronology given by the writers Manetho the Egyptian, and Menander the Ephesian, and also Josephus, who wrote [about] the Jewish war, which they waged with the Romans. ²For from these very old records, it is proven that the writings of the rest are more recent than the writings given to us through Moses—yes, and [more recent] than the subsequent prophets. ³For the last of the prophets, who was called Zechariah, was contemporary with the reign of Darius. ⁴But even the lawgivers themselves are all found to have legislated subsequently to that period. ⁵For if one were to mention Solon the Athenian, he lived in the days of the kings Cyrus and Darius, in the time of the prophet Zechariah first mentioned, who was by many years the last of the prophets. ⁶Or if you mention the lawgivers Lycurgus, or Draco, or Minos, Josephus tells us in his writings that the sacred books take precedence of them in antiquity, since even before the reign of Jupiter over the Cretans, and before the Trojan War, the writings of the Divine Law which has been given to us through Moses were in existence. ⁷And that we may give a more accurate exhibition of eras and dates, we will, God helping us, now give an account not only of the dates after the Flood, but also of those before it, so as to reckon the whole number of all the years, as far as possible, tracing up to the very beginning of the creation of the world, which Moses the servant of God recorded through the Holy Spirit. ⁸For having first spoken of what concerned the creation and genesis of the world, and of the first man, and all that happened after in the order of events, he also signified the years that elapsed before the Flood. ⁹And I pray for favor from the only God, that I may accurately speak the whole truth according to His will, that you and everyone who reads this work may be guided by His truth and favor. ¹⁰I will then begin first with the recorded genealogies, and I begin my narration with the first man.

CHAPTER 24

¹Adam lived until he begot a son, two hundred thirty years. And his son Seth, two hundred five. ²And his son Enos, one hundred ninety. And his son Cainan, one hundred seventy. ³And his son Mahalalel, one hundred sixty-five. And his son Jared, one hundred sixty-two. ⁴And his son Enoch, one hundred sixty-five. And his son Methuselah, one hundred sixty-seven. ⁵And his son Lamech, one hundred eighty-eight. ⁶And Lamech's son was Noah, of whom we have spoken above, who begot Shem when five hundred years old. ⁷During Noah's life, in his six hundredth year, the Flood came. The total number of years, therefore, until the Flood, was two thousand two hundred forty-two. ⁸And immediately after the Flood, Shem, who was one hundred years old, begot Arphaxad. And Arphaxad, when one hundred thirty-five years old, begot Salah. ⁹And Salah begot a son when one hundred thirty. And his son Eber, when one hundred thirty-four. ¹⁰And from him the Hebrews

name their race. And his son Peleg begot a son when one hundred thirty. [11]And his son Reu, when one hundred thirty-two. And his son Serug, when one hundred thirty. [12]And his son Nahor, when seventy-five. And his son Terah, when seventy. [13]And his son Abraham, our patriarch, begot Isaac when he was one hundred years old. Until Abraham, therefore, there are three thousand two hundred seventy-eight years. [14]The aforementioned Isaac lived until he begot a son, sixty years, and begot Jacob. Jacob, until the migration into Egypt, of which we have spoken above, lived one hundred thirty years. [15]And the sojourning of the Hebrews in Egypt lasted four hundred thirty years; and after their departure from the land of Egypt they spent forty years in the wilderness, as it is called. [16]All these years, therefore, amount to three thousand nine hundred thirty-eight. [17]And at that time, Moses having died, Jesus [(Joshua)] the son of Nun succeeded to his rule and governed them twenty-seven years. And after Jesus, when the people had transgressed the commandments of God, they served the king of Mesopotamia, by name Chusarathon, eight years. [18]Then, on the conversion of the people, they had judges: Gothonoel, forty years; Eglon, eighteen years; Aoth, eight years. Then having sinned, they were subdued by strangers for twenty years. [19]Then Deborah judged them forty years. Then they served the Midianites seven years. [20]Then Gideon judged them forty years; Abimelech, three years; Thola, twenty-two years; Jair, twenty-two years. Then the Philistines and Ammonites ruled them eighteen years. [21]After that, Jephthah judged them six years; Esbon, seven years; Ailon, ten years; Abdon, eight years. Then strangers ruled them forty years. [22]Then Samson judged them twenty years. Then there was peace among them for forty years. [23]Then Samera judged them one year; Eli, twenty years; Samuel, twelve years.

CHAPTER 25

[1]And after the judges they had kings, the first named Saul, who reigned twenty years; then David, our forefather, who reigned forty years. [2]Accordingly, there are to the reign of David [from Isaac] four hundred ninety-six years. And after these kings, Solomon reigned, who also, by the will of God, was the first to build the temple in Jerusalem; he reigned forty years. [3]And after him Rehoboam, seventeen years; and after him Abias, seven years; and after him Asa, forty-one years; and after him Jehoshaphat, twenty-five years; and after him Joram, eight years; and after him Ahaziah, one year; and after him Athaliah, six years; [4]and after her Josiah, forty years; and after him Amaziah, thirty-nine years; and after him Uzziah, fifty-two years; and after him Jotham, sixteen years; and after him Ahaz, seventeen years; [5]and after him Hezekiah, twenty-nine years; and after him Manasseh, fifty-five years; and after him Amon, two years; and after him Josiah, thirty-one years; and after him Jehoahaz, three months; and after him Jehoiakim, eleven years. [6]Then another Jehoiakim, three months ten days; and after him Zedekiah, eleven years. [7]And after these kings, the people, continuing in their sins, and not converting, the king of Babylon, named Nebuchadnezzar, came up into Judea, according to the prophecy of Jeremiah. [8]He transferred the people of the Jews to Babylon and destroyed the temple which Solomon had built. And in the Babylonian banishment the people passed seventy years. [9]Until the sojourning in the land of Babylon, there are therefore, in all, four thousand nine hundred fifty-four years six months and ten days. [10]And according as God had, by the prophet Jeremiah, foretold that the people should be led captive to Babylon, in like manner He signified beforehand that they should also return into their own land after seventy years. [11]These seventy years then being accomplished, Cyrus becomes king of the Persians, who, according to the prophecy of Jeremiah, issued a decree in the second year of his reign, enjoining by his edict that all Jews who were in his kingdom should return to their own country, and rebuild their temple to God, which the aforementioned king of Babylon had demolished. [12]Moreover, Cyrus, in compliance with the instructions of God, gave orders to his own bodyguards, Sabessar and Mithridates, that the vessels which had been taken out of the temple of Judea by Nebuchadnezzar should be restored, and placed again in the temple. [13]Therefore, in the second year of Darius the seventy years are fulfilled which were foretold by Jeremiah.

CHAPTER 26

[1]Hence one can see how our Holy Writings are shown to be more ancient and truer than those of the Greeks and Egyptians, or any other historians. [2]For Herodotus and Thucydides, as also Xenophon, and most other historians, began their relations from about the reign of Cyrus and Darius, not being able to speak with accuracy of prior and ancient times. [3]For what great matters did they disclose if they spoke of Darius and Cyrus, barbarian kings, or of the Greeks Zopyrus and Hippias, or of the wars of the Athenians and Lacedaemonians, or the deeds of Xerxes or of Pausanias, who ran the risk of starving to death in the temple of Minerva, or the history of Themistocles and the Peloponnesian war, or of Alcibiades and Thrasybulus? [4]For my purpose is not to furnish mere matter of much talk, but to throw light on the number of years from the foundation of the world, and to condemn the empty labor and trifling of these authors, because there have neither been twenty thousand times ten thousand years from the Flood to the present time, as Plato said, affirming that there had been so many years; [5]nor yet fifteen times ten thousand three hundred seventy-five years, as we have already mentioned Apollonius the Egyptian asserted; [6]nor is the world uncreated, nor is there a spontaneous production of all things, as Pythagoras and the rest dreamed; [7]but, being indeed created, it is also governed by the providence of God, who made all things; [8]and the whole course of time and the years are made plain to those who wish to obey the truth. [9]Lest, then, I seem to have made things plain up to the time of Cyrus, and to neglect the subsequent periods, as if through inability to exhibit them, I will endeavor, by God's help, to give an account, according to my ability, of the course of the subsequent times.

CHAPTER 27

[1]When Cyrus, then, had reigned twenty-nine years, and had been slain by Tomyris in the country of the Massagetae, this being in the sixty-second Olympiad, then the Romans began to increase in power, God strengthening them, Rome having been founded by Romulus, the reputed child of Mars and Ilia, in the seventh Olympiad, on the twenty-first day of April, the year being then reckoned as consisting of ten months. [2]Cyrus, then, having died, as we have already said, in the sixty-second Olympiad, this date falls two hundred twenty [years since] the founding of the city [of Rome], in which year also Tarquinius, surnamed Superbus, reigned over the Romans, who was the first who banished Romans and corrupted the youth, and made eunuchs of the citizens, and, moreover, first defiled virgins, and then gave them in marriage. [3]On this account he was fitly called Superbus in the Roman language, and that is translated the Proud. [4]For he first decreed that those who saluted him should have their salute acknowledged by someone else. He reigned twenty-five years. [5]After him, yearly consuls were introduced, tribunes also and magistrates for four hundred fifty-three years, whose names we consider it long and superfluous to recount. [6]For if anyone is anxious to learn them, he will ascertain them from the tables which Chryserus the nomenclator compiled: he was a freeman of Aurelius Verus, who composed a very lucid record of all things, both names and dates, from the founding of Rome to the death of his own patron, the emperor Verus. [7]The annual magistrates ruled the Romans, as we say, for four hundred fifty-three years. [8]Afterward those who are called emperors began in this order: first, Caius Julius, who reigned three years four months six days; then Augustus, fifty-six years four months one day; Tiberius, twenty-two years; then another Caius, three years eight months seven days; [9]Claudius, twenty-three years eight months twenty-four days; Nero, thirteen years six months fifty-eight days; Galba, two years seven months six days; Otho, three months five days; Vitellius, six months twenty-two days; [10]Vespasian, nine years eleven months twenty-two days; Titus, two years twenty-two days; Domitian, fifteen years five months six days; Nerva, one year four months ten days; Trajan, nineteen years six months sixteen days; [11]Hadrian, twenty years ten months twenty-eight days; Antoninus, twenty-two years seven months six days; Verus, nineteen years ten days. [12]Therefore, the time of the Caesars to the death of the emperor Verus is two hundred

APOLOGY TO AUTOLYCUS

thirty-seven years five days. ¹³From the death of Cyrus, therefore, and the reign of Tarquinius Superbus, to the death of the emperor Verus, the whole time amounts to seven hundred forty-four years.

CHAPTER 28

¹And from the foundation of the world the whole time is thus traced, so far as its main epochs are concerned. ²From the creation of the world to the Flood were two thousand two hundred forty-two years. ³And from the Flood to the time when Abraham our forefather begot a son, one thousand thirty-six years. ⁴And from Isaac, Abraham's son, to the time when the people dwelt with Moses in the desert, six hundred sixty years. ⁵And from the death of Moses and the rule of Joshua the son of Nun to the death of the patriarch David, four hundred ninety-eight years. ⁶And from the death of David and the reign of Solomon to the sojourning of the people in the land of Babylon, five hundred eighteen years six months ten days. ⁷And from the government of Cyrus to the death of Emperor Aurelius Verus, seven hundred forty-four years. ⁸All the years from the creation of the world amount to a total of five thousand six hundred ninety-eight years, and the odd months and days.

CHAPTER 29

¹These periods, then, and all the above-mentioned facts, being viewed collectively, one can see the antiquity of the prophetic writings and the divinity of our doctrine, that the doctrine is not recent, nor our tenets mythical and false, as some think, but very ancient and true. ²For Thallus mentioned Belus, king of the Assyrians, and Saturn, son of Titan, alleging that Belus with the Titans made war against Jupiter and the so-called gods in his alliance; and on this occasion he says that Gyges, being defeated, fled to Tartessus. ³At that time Gyges ruled over that country, which then was called Acte, but now is named Attica. ⁴And from what the other countries and cities derived their names, we think it unnecessary to recount, especially to you who are acquainted with history. ⁵That Moses—and not only he, but also most of the prophets who followed him—is proven to be older than all writers, and [older] than Saturn, and Belus, and the Trojan War, is manifest. ⁶For according to the history of Thallus, Belus is found to be three hundred twenty-two years prior to the Trojan War. ⁷But we have shown above that Moses lived somewhere around nine hundred or one thousand years before the sacking of Troy. ⁸And as Saturn and Belus flourished at the same time, most people do not know which is Saturn and which is Belus. ⁹Some worship Saturn, and call him Bel or Bal, especially the inhabitants of the eastern countries, for they do not know who either Saturn or Belus is. ¹⁰And among the Romans he is called Saturn, for neither do they know which of the two is more ancient—Saturn or Bel. ¹¹So far as regards the commencement of the Olympiads, they say that the observance dates from Iphitus, but according to others from Linus, who is also called Ilius. The order which the whole number of years and Olympiads holds, we have shown above. ¹²I think I have now, according to my ability, accurately discoursed both of the godlessness of your practices, and of the whole number of the epochs of history. ¹³For if even a chronological error has been committed by us of fifty, or one hundred, or even two hundred years, yet not of thousands and tens of thousands, as Plato, and Apollonius, and other unreliable authors have until now written. ¹⁴And perhaps our knowledge of the whole number of the years is not quite accurate, because the odd months and days are not set down in the sacred books. ¹⁵But so far as regards the periods we speak of, we are corroborated by Berossus, the Chaldean philosopher, who made the Greeks acquainted with the Chaldean literature, and uttered some things concerning the Flood, and many other points of history, in agreement with Moses; and with the prophets Jeremiah and Daniel also, he spoke in a measure of agreement. ¹⁶For he mentioned what happened to the Jews under the king of the Babylonians, whom he calls Abobassor, and who is called by the Hebrews Nebuchadnezzar. ¹⁷And he also spoke of the temple of Jerusalem, how it was desolated by the king of the Chaldeans, and that the foundations of the temple having been laid the second year of the reign of Cyrus, the temple was completed in the second year of the reign of Darius.

CHAPTER 30

¹But the Greeks make no mention of the histories which give the truth: first, because they themselves only recently became partakers of the knowledge of letters; and they themselves own it, alleging that letters were invented, some say among the Chaldeans, and others with the Egyptians, and others again say that they are derived from the Phoenicians. ²And secondly, because they sinned, and still sin, in not making mention of God, but of vain and useless matters. ³For thus they most heartily celebrate Homer and Hesiod, and the rest of the poets, but the glory of the incorruptible and only God they not only omit to mention, but blaspheme; yes, and they persecuted, and daily persecute, those who worship Him. ⁴And not only so, but they even bestow prizes and honors on those who in harmonious language insult God; ⁵but of those who are zealous in the pursuit of virtue and practice a holy life, some they stoned, some they put to death, and up to the present time they subject them to savage tortures. ⁶Therefore, such men have necessarily lost the wisdom of God and have not found the truth.

DISCOURSE CONCERNING HADES

Also called Against Plato on the Cause of the Universe, the Discourse to the Greeks concerning Hades is a short discourse attributed to Josephus for many centuries but actually penned by Hippolytus of Rome. This places its composition in the early 3rd century AD.

CHAPTER 1

¹Now as to Hades, wherein the souls of the righteous and unrighteous are detained, it is necessary to speak of it. Hades is a place in the world not regularly finished: a subterraneous region, wherein the light of this world does not shine; from which circumstance, that in this region the light does not shine, it cannot be but [that] there must be in it perpetual darkness. ²This region is allotted as a place of custody for souls, in which messengers are appointed as guardians to them, who distribute to them temporary punishments, agreeable to everyone's behavior and manners.

CHAPTER 2

¹In this region there is a certain place set apart, as a lake of unquenchable fire, whereinto we suppose no one has thus far been cast; but it is prepared for a day previously determined by God, in which one righteous sentence will deservedly be passed on all men; ²when the unjust, and those that have been disobedient to God, and have given honor to such idols as have been the vain operations of the hands of men as to God Himself, will be condemned to this continuous punishment, as having been the causes of defilement; while the just will obtain an incorruptible and never-fading kingdom. ³These are now indeed confined in Hades, but not in the same place wherein the unjust are confined.

CHAPTER 3

¹For there is one descent into this region, at whose gate we believe there stands a chief-messenger with a host; which gate when those pass through that are conducted down by the messengers appointed over souls, they do not go the same way; ²but the just are guided to the right hand, and are led with hymns, sung by the messengers appointed over that place, to a region of light, ³in which the just have dwelt from the beginning of the world; not constrained by necessity, but always enjoying the prospect of the good things they see, and rejoicing in the expectation of those new enjoyments which

will be peculiar to every one of them, and esteeming those things beyond what we have here; with whom there is no place of toil, no burning heat, no piercing cold, nor are any briers there; ⁴but the countenance of the fathers, and of the just, which they see, always smiles on them, while they wait for that rest and continuous new life in Heaven, which is to succeed this region. This place we call THE BOSOM OF ABRAHAM.

CHAPTER 4

¹But as to the unjust, they are dragged by force to the left hand by the messengers allotted for punishment, no longer going with goodwill, but as prisoners driven by violence; ²to whom are sent the messengers appointed over them to reproach them and threaten them with their terrible looks, and to thrust them still downwards. ³Now those messengers that are set over these souls drag them into the neighborhood of hell itself; who, when they are nearby it, continually hear the noise of it, and do not stand clear of the hot vapor itself; ⁴but when they have a near view of this spectacle, as of a terrible and exceedingly great prospect of fire, they are struck with a fearful expectation of a future judgment, and in effect punished thereby: ⁵and not only so, but where they see the place [or choir] of the fathers and of the just, even hereby are they punished; ⁶for a chaos deep and large is fixed between them; insomuch that a just man that has compassion on them cannot be admitted, nor can one that is unjust, if he were bold enough to attempt it, pass over it.

CHAPTER 5

¹This is the discourse concerning Hades, wherein the souls of all men are confined until a proper season, which God has determined, when He will make a resurrection of all men from the dead, not procuring a transmigration of souls from one body to another, but raising again those very bodies, which you Greeks, seeing to be dissolved, do not believe [in]. ²But do not learn to disbelieve it; for while you believe that the soul is created, and yet is made immortal by God, according to the doctrine of Plato, and this in time, do not be incredulous; ³but believe that God is able, when He has raised to life that body which was made as a compound of the same elements, to make it immortal; for it must never be said of God, that He is able to do some things, and unable to do others. ⁴We have therefore believed that the body will be raised again; for although it is dissolved, it has not perished; for the earth receives its remains, and preserves them; ⁵and while they are like seed, and are mixed among the more fruitful soil, they flourish, and what is sown is indeed sown [as] bare grain, but at the mighty sound of God the Creator, it will sprout up, and be raised in a clothed and glorious condition, though not before it has been dissolved, and mixed [with the earth]. ⁶So that we have not rashly believed the resurrection of the body; for although it is dissolved for a time on account of the original transgression, it exists still, and is cast into the earth as into a potter's furnace, in order to be formed again, not in order to rise again such as it was before, but in a state of purity, and so as never to be destroyed anymore. ⁷And to everybody will its own soul be restored. And when it has clothed itself with that body, it will not be subject to misery, but, being itself pure, it will continue with its pure body, and rejoice with it, with which it having walked righteously now in this world, and never having had it as a snare, it will receive it again with great gladness. ⁸But as for the unjust, they will receive their bodies not changed, not freed from diseases or distempers, nor made glorious, but with the same diseases wherein they died; and such as they were in their unbelief, the same will they be when they will be faithfully judged.

CHAPTER 6

¹For all men, the just as well as the unjust, will be brought before God the Word: for to Him has the Father committed all judgment; and He, in order to fulfill the will of His Father, will come as Judge, whom we call Christ. ²For Minos and Rhadamanthus are not the judges, as you Greeks suppose, but He whom God the Father has glorified: concerning whom we have elsewhere given a more particular account, for the sake of those who seek after truth. ³This person, exercising the righteous judgment of the Father toward all men, has prepared a just sentence for everyone, according to his works; at whose judgment-seat when all men, and messengers, and demons will stand, they will send forth one voice, and say, "Just is your judgment"; the rejoinder to which will bring a just sentence on both parties, by giving justly to those that have done well a continuous fruition; but allotting to the lovers of wicked works continuous punishment. ⁴To these belong the unquenchable fire, and that without end, and a certain fiery worm, never dying, and not destroying the body, but continuing its eruption out of the body with never-ceasing grief: neither will sleep give ease to these men, nor will the night afford them comfort; death will not free them from their punishment, nor will the interceding prayers of their kindred profit them; for the just are no longer seen by them, nor are they thought worthy of remembrance. ⁵But the just will remember only their righteous actions, whereby they have attained the heavenly kingdom, in which there is no sleep, no sorrow, no corruption, no care, no night, no day measured by time, no sun driven in his course along the circle of heaven by necessity, and measuring out the bounds and conversions of the seasons, for the better illumination of the life of men; no moon decreasing and increasing, or introducing a variety of seasons, nor will she then moisten the earth; no burning sun, no Bear turning around [the pole], no Orion to rise, no wandering of innumerable stars. ⁶The earth will not then be difficult to be passed over, nor will it be hard to find out the court of Paradise, nor will there be any fearful roaring of the sea, forbidding the passengers to walk on it; even that will be made easily passable to the just, though it will not be void of moisture. ⁷Heaven will not then be uninhabitable by men, and it will not be impossible to discover the way of ascending there. ⁸The earth will not be uncultivated, nor require too much labor of men, but will bring forth its fruits of its own accord and will be well adorned with them. ⁹There will be no more generations of wild beasts, nor will the substance of the rest of the animals shoot out anymore; for it will not produce men, but the number of the righteous will continue, and never fail, together with righteous messengers, and spirits [of God], and with his word, as a choir of righteous men and women that never grow old, and continue in an incorruptible state, singing hymns to God, who has advanced them to that happiness, by the means of a regular institution of life; ¹⁰with whom the whole creation also will lift up a perpetual hymn from corruption, to incorruption, as glorified by a splendid and pure spirit. ¹¹It will not then be restrained by a bond of necessity, but with a lively freedom will offer up a voluntary hymn, and will praise Him that made them, together with the messengers, and spirits, and men now freed from all bondage.

CHAPTER 7

¹And now, if you nations will be persuaded by these motives, and leave your vain imaginations about your pedigrees, and gaining of riches, and philosophy, and will not spend your time about subtleties of words, and thereby lead your minds into error, ²and if you will apply your ears to the hearing of the inspired prophets, the interpreters both of God and of His word, and will believe in God, you will both be partakers of these things, and obtain the good things that are to come; you will see the ascent to the immense Heaven plainly, and that kingdom which is there. ³For what God has now concealed in silence [will then be made manifest], what "neither eye has seen, nor ear has heard, nor has it entered into the heart of man, the things that God has prepared for them that love Him."

CHAPTER 8

¹"In whatsoever ways I will find you, in them I will judge you entirely": so cries the End of all things. And he who has at first lived a virtuous lift, but toward the latter end falls into vice, these labors by him before endured will be altogether vain and unprofitable, even as in a play, brought to an ill catastrophe. ²Whosoever will have lived wickedly and luxuriously may convert; however, there will be need of much time to conquer an evil habit, and even after conversion his whole life must be guarded with great care and diligence, after the manner of a body, which, after it has been a long time afflicted with a disease, requires a stricter diet and method of living; ³for though it may be possible, perhaps, to break off the chain of our irregular affections at once, yet our amendment cannot be secured without the grace of God, the prayers of good men, the

help of the brothers, and our own sincere conversion and constant care. ⁴It is a good thing not to sin at all; it is also good, having sinned, to convert; as it is best to have health always, but it is a good thing to recover from a disease. To God be glory and dominion forever and ever. Amen.

THE MURATORIAN CANON

The Muratorian Fragment, the oldest surviving list of the New Testament canon, which is thought to have been composed around AD 170, lists all of the current twenty-seven books of the New Testament, minus Hebrews, James, and both Epistles of Peter. The fragment is damaged where Matthew and Mark are listed, but their inclusion is beyond dispute. The Revelation of Peter and Wisdom are included, although Peter's Apocalypse is disputed by the author.

FRAGMENT 1

¹...at which nevertheless he was present, and so he placed [them in his narrative]. ²The third scroll of the Gospel is that according to Luke. ³Luke, the well-known physician, after the ascension of Christ, when Paul had taken with him as one zealous for the law, composed it in his own name, according to [the general] belief. ⁴Yet he himself had not seen the LORD in the flesh; and therefore, as he was able to ascertain events, so indeed he begins to tell the story from the birth of John. ⁵The fourth of the Gospels is that of John, [one] of the disciples. ⁶To his fellow disciples and overseers, who had been urging him [to write], he said, "Fast with me from today to three days, and what will be revealed to each one let us tell it to one another." ⁷In the same night it was revealed to Andrew, [one] of the apostles, that John should write down all things in his own name while all of them should review it. ⁸And so, though various elements may be taught in the individual scrolls of the Gospels, nevertheless this makes no difference to the faith of believers, ⁹since by the one sovereign Spirit all things have been declared in all [the Gospels]: ¹⁰concerning the nativity, concerning the passion, concerning the resurrection, concerning life with His disciples, and concerning His twofold coming; ¹¹the first in lowliness when He was despised, which has taken place, the second glorious in royal power, which is still in the future. ¹²What marvel is it then, if John so consistently mentions these particular points also in his Epistles, ¹³saying about himself, "What we have seen with our eyes and heard with our ears and our hands have handled, these things we have written to you"? ¹⁴For in this way he professes [himself] to be not only an eyewitness and hearer, but also a writer of all the marvelous deeds of the LORD, in their order. ¹⁵Moreover, the Acts of all the Apostles were written in one scroll. ¹⁶For "most excellent Theophilus" Luke compiled the individual events that took place in his presence— ¹⁷as he plainly shows by omitting the martyrdom of Peter as well as the departure of Paul from the city [of Rome] when he journeyed to Spain. ¹⁸As for the Epistles of Paul, they themselves make clear to those desiring to understand, which ones [they are], from what place, or for what reason they were sent. ¹⁹First of all, to the Corinthians, prohibiting their heretical schisms; ²⁰next, to the Galatians, against circumcision; ²¹then to the Romans he wrote at length, explaining the order [[or plan]] of the Writings, and also that Christ is their principle. ²²It is necessary for us to discuss these one by one, since the blessed apostle Paul himself, following the example of his predecessor John, writes by name to only seven assemblies in the following sequence: ²³To the Corinthians first, to the Ephesians second, to the Philippians third, to the Colossians fourth, to the Galatians fifth, to the Thessalonians sixth, to the Romans seventh. ²⁴It is true that he writes once more to the Corinthians and to the Thessalonians for the sake of admonition, ²⁵yet it is clearly recognizable that there is one Assembly spread throughout the whole extent of the earth. ²⁶For John also in the Revelation, though he writes to seven assemblies, nevertheless speaks to all. ²⁷[Paul also wrote] out of affection and love one to Philemon, one to Titus, and two to Timothy; ²⁸and these are held sacred in the esteem of the Assembly universal for the regulation of ecclesiastical discipline. ²⁹There is current also [an epistle] to the Laodiceans, [and] another to the Alexandrians, [both] forged in Paul's name to [further] the heresy of Marcion, ³⁰and several others which cannot be received into the Universal Assembly—for it is not fitting that gall be mixed with honey. ³¹Moreover, the epistle of Jude and two of the above-mentioned [[or bearing the name of]] John are counted [[or used]] in the universal [Assembly]; ³²and Wisdom, written by the friends of Solomon in his honor. ³³We receive only the revelations of John and Peter, though some of us are not willing that the latter be read in an assembly. ³⁴But Hermas wrote the Shepherd very recently, in our times, in the city of Rome, while overseer Pius, his brother, was occupying the chair of the assembly of the city of Rome. ³⁵And therefore it should indeed be read; but it cannot be read publicly to the people in an assembly either among the prophets, whose number is complete, or among the apostles, for it is after [their] time. ³⁶But we accept nothing whatever of Arsinous or Valentinus or Miltiades, who also composed a new scroll of psalms for Marcion, together with Basilides, the Asian founder of the Cataphrygians...

GELASIAN DECREE

The Gelasian Decree (Decretum Gelasianum in Latin) is a late 5th century decretal of Pope Gelasius I which briefly discusses Christ and the Holy Spirit and their interrelation; more significantly, it lists out the canonical books of the Holy Bible followed by a list of spurious and rejected works. It is based on a possibly older Damasine List from the 4th century.

HERE BEGINS THE COUNCIL OF ROME UNDER POPE DAMASUS "ON EXPLAINING THE FAITH."

CHAPTER 1

It was said:

1. Firstly, the seven-fold Spirit which remains in Christ should be discussed: the Spirit of wisdom: "Christ the power and wisdom of God"; the Spirit of understanding: "I will give you understanding, and I will instruct you in the way you will go"; the Spirit of counsel: "And his name is called the messenger of great counsel"; the Spirit of virtues: as above, "The power of God and the wisdom of God"; the Spirit of knowledge: "Because of the eminence of the knowledge of the apostle of Christ Jesus"; the Spirit of truth: "I am the way the life and the truth"; the Spirit of the fear of God: "The fear of the LORD is the beginning of wisdom."

2. However, the dispensation of Christ has a name of many forms:

God, who is spirit; the Word, who is God; the Son, who is only-begotten of the Father; the Man, who was born of the virgin; the Priest, who offered Himself as a sacrifice; the Shepherd, who is the guard; the Worm, who arose from the dead; the Mountain, which is strong; the Way, which is straight; the Harbor, which one may pass through into life; the Lamb, which was slain; the Stone, which is the cornerstone; the Master, who is the bringer of life; the Sun, which is the illuminator; the True, which is of the Father; the Life, which is the Creator; the Bread, which is dear; the Samaritan, who is the guard and the merciful; the Christ, who is the Anointed One; Jesus, who is the Savior; God, who is from God; the Messenger, who was sent; the Bridegroom, who is the mediator; the Vine, by whose own blood we are redeemed; the Lion, who is king; the Rock, which is the foundation; the Flower, which is chosen; the Prophet, who revealed the future.

3. For the Holy Spirit is not of the Father only or of the Son only, but of the Father and the Son; for it is written: "He who delights in the world, the Spirit of the Father is not in him"; again it is written: "However, anyone who does not have the Spirit of Christ, does not belong to Him." So, the Holy Spirit is understood to be called of the Father and the Son, [and] of whom the Son Himself in the Gospel says that the Holy Spirit "proceeds from the Father" and "He will receive from Me, and He will make known to you."

CHAPTER 2

Likewise, it was said:

Now indeed, the issue of the Divine Writings must be discussed, which the Universal Assembly receives or which it is required to avoid.

1. THIS IS THE ORDER OF THE OLD TESTAMENT:

Genesis	one book
Exodus	one book
Leviticus	one book
Numbers	one book
Deuteronomy	one book
Joshua	one book
Judges	one book
Ruth	one book
Kings	four books
Chronicles	two books
One hundred fifty Psalms	one book

Three books of Solomon:

Proverbs	one book
Ecclesiastes	one book
Song of Songs	one book
The same of Wisdom	one book
Ecclesiasticus	one book

2. LIKEWISE, THE ORDER OF THE PROPHETS:

Isaiah	one book
Jeremiah with Cinoth	one book
Ezekiel	one book
Daniel	one book
Hosea	one book
Amos	one book
Micah	one book
Joel	one book
Obadiah	one book
Jonah	one book
Nahum	one book
Habakkuk	one book
Zephaniah	one book
Haggai	one book
Zechariah	one book
Malachi	one book

3. LIKEWISE, THE ORDER OF THE HISTORIES:

Job	one book
Tobit	one book
Esdras	two books
Esther	one book
Judith	one book
Maccabees	two books

4. LIKEWISE, THE ORDER OF THE WRITINGS OF THE NEW TESTAMENT WHICH THE HOLY AND UNIVERSAL ROMAN ASSEMBLY UPHOLDS AND VENERATES:

Four books of the Gospels:

According to Mathew	one book
According to Mark	one book
According to Luke	one book
According to John	one book
Likewise, the Acts of the Apostles	one book

The letters of the apostle Paul—fourteen in number:

To the Romans	one letter
To the Corinthians	two letters
To the Ephesians	one letter
To the Thessalonians	two letters
To the Galatians	one letter
To the Philippians	one letter
To the Colossians	one letter
To Timothy	two letters
To Titus	one letter
To Philemon	one letter
To the Hebrews	one letter
Likewise, the Revelation of John	one book

Likewise, the canonical [general] letters—seven in number:

of the apostle Peter	two letters
of the apostle James	one letter
of the apostle John	one letter
of the other John the elder	two letters
of the apostle Judas the Zealot	one letter

HERE ENDS THE CANON OF THE NEW TESTAMENT.

CHAPTER 3

Likewise, it was said:

HERE BEGINS THE DECRETAL "ON BOOKS TO BE RECEIVED AND NOT TO BE RECEIVED" WHICH WAS WRITTEN BY POPE GELASIUS AND SEVENTY MOST ERUDITE OVERSEERS AT THE APOSTOLIC SEAT IN THE CITY OF ROME.

1. After all these [writings of] the prophets and the evangelical and apostolic Writings which we discussed above, on which the Universal Assembly is founded by the grace of God, we also have thought necessary to say what, although the Universal Assembly diffused throughout the world is the single bride of Christ, however, the holy Roman assembly is given first place by the rest of the assemblies without [the need for] a synodical decision, but from the voice of the LORD our Savior in the Gospel obtained primacy: "You are Peter," he said, "and on this rock I will build My Assembly and the gates of Hades will not prevail against it; and to you I give the keys of the kingdom of the heavens, and whatever you will bind on earth will also be bound in Heaven and whatever you release on earth will also be released in Heaven."

2. In addition, there is also the presence of the blessed apostle Paul, "the chosen vessel," who not in opposition, as the heresies jabber, but on the same date and the same day was crowned in glorious death with Peter in the city of Rome, suffering under Nero Caesar; and equally they made the above-mentioned holy Roman assembly special in Christ the LORD and gave preference in their presence and veneration-worthy triumph before all other cities in the whole world.

3. Therefore, first is the seat at the Roman assembly of the apostle Peter "having no spot or wrinkle or any other [defect]." However, the second place was given in the name of blessed Peter to Mark, his disciple and gospel-writer at Alexandria, and who himself wrote down the word of truth directed by Peter the apostle in Egypt and gloriously consummated [his life] in martyrdom. Indeed, the third place is held at Antioch of the most blessed and honorable apostle Peter, who lived there before he came to Rome and where first the name of the new race of the Christians was heard.

CHAPTER 4

And although "no other foundation can be established except that which has been established, Christ Jesus," however, for edification, likewise, the holy Roman assembly after the books of the Old and New Testaments which we have enumerated above according to the canon, also does not prohibit the reception of these writings:

1. The holy synod of Nicaea, of three hundred eighteen fathers chaired by Emperor Constantine the Great, at which the heretic Arius was condemned;

The holy synod of Constantinople, chaired by Theodosius the senior Augustus, at which the heretic Macedonius escaped his deserved condemnation;

The holy synod of Ephesus, at which Nestorius was condemned with the consent of the blessed Pope Caelestinus, chaired by Cyril of Alexandria in the magistrate's seat and by Arcadius the overseer sent from Italy;

The holy synod of Chalcedon, chaired by Marcian Augustus and by Anatolius, overseer of Constantinople, at which the Nestorian and Eutychian heresies together with Dioscorus and his sympathisers were condemned.

2. But also, if there are councils previously held by the holy fathers of lesser authority than those four, we have decreed [that] they must be both kept and received. Here added below is on the works of the holy fathers, which are received in the Universal Assembly:

Likewise, the works of blessed Caecilius Cyprian, the martyr and overseer of Carthage.

Likewise, the works of blessed Gregory Nanzanensis, the overseer.

Likewise, the works of blessed Basil, overseer of Cappadocia.

Likewise, the works of blessed John, overseer of Constantinople.

Likewise, the works of blessed Theophilus, overseer of Alexandria.

Likewise, the works of blessed Cyril, overseer of Alexandria.

Likewise, the works of blessed Hilary, overseer of Poitiers.

Likewise, the works of blessed Ambrosius, overseer of Milan.

Likewise, the works of blessed Augustine, overseer of Hippo.

Likewise, the works of blessed Jerome the priest.

Likewise, the works of blessed Prosper, a most religious man.

3. Likewise, the letter of blessed Pope Leo sent to Flavian, overseer of Constantinople, of which text however if any portion is disputed and it is not that anciently received by all, let it be condemnded.

Likewise, the works and every treatise of all the orthodox fathers, who deviated in nothing from the common [teaching] of the holy Roman assembly, neither separated from its faith or worship but remained in communion by the grace of God to the last day of their life, we decree are to be read.

Likewise, the decretal letters, which blessed popes gave for the consideration of various fathers at various times from the city of Rome, are to be upheld reverently.

4. Likewise, the deeds of the holy martyrs, who are glorious from the manifold tortures on the rack and their wonderful triumphs of steadfastness. Who of the universal [Christians] doubts that most of them would still be enduring in agonies with their full strength but would bear it by the grace of God and the help of everyone? But according to ancient custom, by the greatest caution, they are not read in the holy Roman assembly, because the names of those who wrote are not properly known and separate from unbelievers and idiots, or [the accounts] are thought less attached to the order of events than they should have been; for instance, the [accounts of] Cyricus and Julitta, like Georgius and the sufferings of others like these which appear to have been composed by heretics. On account of this, as it was said, so that no pretext for casual mockery can arise, they are not read in the holy Roman assembly. However, we venerate together with the aforementioned assembly all the martyrs and their glorious sufferings, which are better known to God than to men, with every devotion.

Likewise, the lives of the fathers Paul, Antony, and Hilarion, which with all the hermits described by that blessed man Jerome we receive with honor.

Likewise, the acts of blessed Silvester, overseer of the apostolic seat, although the name of him who wrote [them] is unknown, [but] we know to be read by many universal [Christians], however, in the city of Rome; and because of the ancient use of the multitude, this is imitated by the assembly.

Likewise, the writings on the finding of the Cross and certain other novel writings on the finding of the head of the blessed John the Baptist are romances and some of them are read by universal [Christians]; but when these come into the hand of universal [Christians], the saying of Paul the blessed apostle should be [considered] first: "Prove all things, hold fast to what is good."

Likewise, Rufinus, a most religious man, worked many books of ecclesiastical works, also some interpreting the Writings; but since the venerable Jerome noted that he took arbitary liberties in some of them, we think those [acceptable] which we know the aforementioned blessed Jerome thought [acceptable]; and not only those of Rufinus, but also [those] of anyone whom that man often remembered for his zeal for God and for the religion of faith criticised.

Likewise, some works of Origen, which the blessed man Jerome does not reject, we receive to be read, but we say that the rest with their author must be refused.

Likewise, the chronicle of Eusebius of Caesarea and the books of his Ecclesiastical History—however much he fell flat in the first book of his narration and [although he also] afterward wrote one book in praise and to excuse Origen the schismatic; however, on account of his narration of remarkable things, which are useful for instruction, we do not say to anyone that it must be refused.

Likewise, we praise Orosius, a most erudite man, who wrote a very necessary history for us against the lies of the pagans and and with marvelous brevity.

Likewise, the paschal work of that venerable man Sedulius, which was written in heroic verses [(hexameters)], we give preference to with manifest praise.

Likewise, the laborious work of Iuvencus we nevertheless do not spurn but are amazed by.

CHAPTER 5

The remaining writings which have been compiled or been recognized by heretics or schismatics the universal and apostolic Roman assembly does not in any way receive; of these we have thought it right to cite below a few which have been handed down and which are to be avoided by universal [Christians]:

LIKEWISE, A LIST OF APOCRYPHAL BOOKS:

Firstly, we confess that the synod of Sirmium, called together by Constantius Caesar, the son of Constantine, through the prefect Taurus is damned then, and now, and forever.

The Itinerary in the name of Peter the apostle, which is called the nine books of the holy Clement: apocryphal

The Acts in the name of the apostle Andrew: apocryphal

The Acts in the name of the apostle Thomas: apocryphal

The Acts in the name of the apostle Peter: apocryphal

The Acts in the name of the apostle Philip: apocryphal

The Gospel in the name of Matthias: apocryphal

The Gospel in the name of Barnabas: apocryphal

The Gospel in the name of James the Younger: apocryphal

The Gospel in the name of the apostle Peter: apocryphal

The Gospel in the name of Thomas which the Manichaeans use: apocryphal

The Gospels in the name of Bartholomew: apocryphal

The Gospels in the name of Andrew: apocryphal

The Gospels which Lucianus forged: apocryphal

The Gospels which Hesychius forged: apocryphal

The book on the infancy of the Savior: apocryphal

The book of the nativity of the Savior and of Mary or the midwife: apocryphal

The book which is called by the name of the Shepherd: apocryphal

All the books which Leucius the disciple of the Devil made: apocryphal

The book which is called the Foundation: apocryphal

The book which is called the Treasure: apocryphal

The book of the daughters of Adam (Leptogenesis): apocryphal

The cento on Christ put together in Virgilian verses: apocryphal

The book which is called the Acts of Thecla and Paul: apocryphal

The book which is called Nepos': apocryphal

The books of Proverbs written by heretics and prefixed with the name of holy Sixtus: apocryphal

The Revelation which is called Paul's: apocryphal

The Revelation which is called Thomas': apocryphal

The Revelation which is called Stephen's: apocryphal

The book which is called the Assumption of Holy Mary: apocryphal

The book which is called the Conversion of Adam: apocryphal

GELASIAN DECREE

The book about Og, the giant of whom the heretics assert that after the Flood he fought with the dragon: apocryphal

The book which is called the Testament of Job: apocryphal

The book which is called the Conversion of Origen: apocryphal

The book which is called the Conversion of holy Cyprian: apocryphal

The book which is called the Conversion of Jamne and Mambre: apocryphal

The book which is called the Lots of the Apostles: apocryphal

The book which is called the Grave-plate of the Apostles: apocryphal

The book which is called the Canons of the Apostles: apocryphal

The book Physiologus, written by heretics and prefixed with the name of blessed Ambrose: apocryphal

The History of Eusebius Pamphilii: apocryphal

The works of Tertullian: apocryphal

The works of Lactantius, also known as Firmianus: apocryphal

The works of Africanus: apocryphal

The works of Postumianus and Gallus: apocryphal

The works of Montanus, Priscilla, and Maximilla: apocryphal

The works of Faustus the Manichaean: apocryphal

The works of Commodian: apocrypha

The works of the other Clement, of Alexandria: apocryphal

The works of Thascius Cyprianus: apocryphal

The works of Arnobius: apocryphal

The works of Tichonius: apocryphal

The works of Cassian the Gallic priest: apocryphal

The works of Victorinus of Pettau: apocryphal

The works of Faustus of Riez in Gaul: apocryphal

The works of Frumentius Caecus: apocryphal

The cento on Christ stitched together from verses of Virgil: apocryphal

The Letter from Jesus to Abgar: apocryphal

The Letter of Abgar to Jesus: apocryphal

The Passion of Cyricus and Julitta: apocryphal

The Passion of Georgius: apocryphal

The writing which is called the Interdiction of Solomon: apocryphal

All amulets which are not compiled in the name of the messengers as they pretend but are written in the names of great demons: apocryphal

These and those similar ones, which Simon Magus, Nicolaus, Cerinthus, Marcion, Basilides, Ebion, Paul of Samosata, Photinus and Bonosus, who suffered from similar error, also Montanus with his obscene followers, Apollinaris, Valentinus the Manichaean, Faustus the African, Sabellius, Arius, Macedonius, Eunomius, Novatus, Sabbatius, Calistus, Donatus, Eustasius, Jovianus, Pelagius, Julian of Eclanum, Caelestius, Maximian, Priscillian from Spain, Nestorius of Constantinople, Maximus the Cynic, Lampetius, Dioscorus, Eutyches, Peter and the other Peter, of whom one disgraced Alexandria and the other Antioch, Acacius of Constantinople with his associates, and what also all disciples of heresy and of the heretics and schismatics, whose names we have scarcely preserved, have taught or compiled, we acknowledge is to be not merely rejected but eliminated from the whole Roman universal and apostolic Assembly and with their authors and the followers of its authors to be damned in the inextricable shackles of condemnation forever.

THE EARLIEST CREEDS

This collection includes, in approximate chronological order, 25 of the earliest Christian creeds and theological definitions, beginning with the Rule of Faith in the 2nd century (from Irenaeus' Against Heresies) and culminating with the Athanasian Creed of the 5th. Most of these creeds were developed in the context of the universal, orthodox Church in an effort to dissuade heresy and reinforce the faith that had been handed down over the centuries; in particular, the earliest creeds dealt heavily with the [historical] life of Christ, Trinitarianism, and Christology. Between Nicea (AD 325) and the Niceno-Constantinopolitan Creed (AD 381), a number of the creeds from those intervening years included here reflect the schismatic Semi-Arian position that was ultimately defeated at Constantinople.

RULE OF FAITH
(CIRCA AD 180)

The Assembly, though dispersed throughout the whole world, even to the ends of the earth, has received from the Apostles and their disciples this faith in one God, the Father Almighty, Maker of Heaven, and earth, and the sea, and all things that are in them; and in one Christ Jesus, the Son of God, who became incarnate for our salvation; and in the Holy Spirit, who proclaimed through the prophets the dispensations of God, and the advents, and the birth from a virgin, and the passion, and the resurrection from the dead, and the ascension into Heaven in the flesh of the beloved Christ Jesus, our Lord, and His [future] manifestation from Heaven in the glory of the Father "to gather all things in one," and to raise up anew all flesh of the whole human race, in order that to Christ Jesus, our Lord, and God, and Savior, and King, according to the will of the invisible Father, "every knee should bow, of things in Heaven, and things in earth, and things under the earth, and that every tongue should confess" to Him, and that He should execute just judgment toward all; that He may send "spiritual wickednesses," and the messengers who transgressed and became defectors, together with the ungodly, and unrighteous, and wicked, and profane among men, into continuous fire; but may, in the exercise of His grace, confer immortality on the righteous and holy, and those who have kept His commands, and have persevered in His love, some from the beginning, and others from their conversion, and may surround them with continuous glory.

OLD ROMAN SYMBOL
(CIRCA AD 215)

I believe in God, the Father Almighty,
and in Christ Jesus, His only Son, our Lord,
Who was born of the Holy Spirit
    and the virgin Mary,
Who under Pontius Pilate was crucified
    and buried;
on the third day He rose again from the dead,
ascended to Heaven,
sits at the right hand of the Father,
from where He will come to judge the living
    and the dead;
and in the Holy Spirit,
the holy Assembly,
the forgiveness of sins,
the resurrection of the flesh,
[[the life everlasting]].

THE EARLIEST CREEDS

CREED OF CYPRIAN OF CARTHAGE
(CIRCA AD 250)

I believe in God the Father,
in His Son Christ,
in the Holy Spirit.
I believe [in] the forgiveness of sins,
and eternal life
through the holy Assembly.

DEIR BALYZEH CREED
(3RD CENTURY AD)

I believe in God, the Father Almighty,
and in Your only begotten Son, our Lord—
our Lord Jesus Christ,
in the Holy Spirit,
in the resurrection of the flesh,
in the Holy Universal Assembly.

CREED OF ANTIOCH
(AD 325)

This faith has been set down by spiritual men; those who should not be considered as living or reasoning according to the flesh, because they have been trained by the Spirit in the Holy Writings found in God-breathed books. Our faith is as follows:

To believe in one God, Father, almighty, incomprehensible, unchangeable and unalterable, administrator and governor of all—just, good, Maker of heaven and earth, and all that is in them, the Lord of the Law, and the Prophets, and the New Testament.

And in one Lord Jesus Christ, the only-begotten Son, begotten not from nothing, but from the Father; not made, but a legitimate offspring. He was begotten inexpressibly and unutterably, because only the Father who begot and the Son who was begotten know it, "for no one knows the Father except the Son, or the Son except the Father."

He always exists and never before did He not exist, for we have been taught from the Holy Writings that He alone is God's [exact] image. He is not unbegotten, for He is clearly begotten of the Father. This status has not been placed on Him; in fact, it would be godless blasphemy to say so. But the Writings say that He is the real and truly begotten Son, so we believe Him to be unchangeable and unalterable. He has not been begotten or come into being merely by the Father's will, nor has this status been placed on Him, which would make Him appear to be from nothing. But He was begotten as was fitting for Him, not at all according to the impermissible idea that He resembles, is of similar nature to, or is associated with any of the things that came into existence through Him.

But, because this transcends all thought, conception, and expression, we simply confess that He has been begotten from the unbegotten Father: God the Word, true Light, righteousness, Jesus Christ, Lord of all and Savior. He is the image—not of the will or of anything else except the actual being of the Father. This one—the Son, God the Word—was also born in the flesh from Mary, the mother of God, and was made flesh. After suffering and dying, He rose from the dead and was taken into Heaven, and He sits at the right hand of the Majesty of the Most High. He is coming to judge the living and the dead.

Just as the Holy Writings teach us to believe in our Savior, so they also teach us to believe in one Spirit, one Universal Assembly, the resurrection of the dead, and the judgment which will pay back to each man according to what he has done in the flesh, whether good or evil.

We curse those who say or think or proclaim that the Son of God is a creation, has come into being, or was made, or was not truly begotten; or that there was a time when He did not exist (for we believe that He [always] was and that He is Light); still also those who think He is unchangeable only by His free will, as with those who think He did not exist before He was begotten, and that He is not unchanging by His nature as the Father is. He has been proclaimed as the Father's image in every respect, especially in this respect: that He does not change.

This faith was put forth, and indeed the entire holy synod consented and confessed that this is the apostolic teaching which alone is able to save.

NICENE CREED
(AD 325)

We believe in one God, the Father Almighty, Maker of all things seen and unseen.

And in one Lord, Jesus Christ the Son of God, begotten of the Father, the only-begotten, that is, of the essence of the Father—God from God, Light from Light, true God from true God, begotten, not made, of the same being as the Father, through whom all things came to be, both the things in heaven and on earth, who for us humans and for our salvation came down and was made flesh, becoming human, who suffered and rose again on the third day, ascended into Heaven, who is coming to judge the living and the dead.

And in the Holy Spirit.

The universal and apostolic Assembly condemns those who say concerning the Son of God that "there was a time when He was not," or "He did not exist before He was begotten," or "He came to be from nothing," or who claim that He is of another subsistence or essence, or a creation, or changeable, or alterable.

APOSTLES' CREED
(CIRCA AD 340)

I believe in God the Father Almighty,
    Maker of heaven and earth,

and in Jesus Christ, His only Son, our Lord,
who was conceived of the Holy Spirit
    and born of the virgin Mary,
who suffered under Pontius Pilate,
    was crucified, died, and was buried,
descended into Hades,
    rose again from the dead
    on the third day,
ascended into Heaven
    and is seated at the right hand
    of God the Father almighty,
who will come again
    to judge the living and the dead.

I believe in the Holy Spirit,
the Holy Universal Assembly,
    the communion of saints,
the forgiveness of sins,
the resurrection of the body,
and the life everlasting. Amen.

FIRST CREED OF ANTIOCH
(AD 341)

We have not been followers of Arius; indeed, how could overseers, such as we, follow an elder? Nor did we receive any other faith besides that which has been handed down from the [very] beginning. But, after taking it on ourselves to examine and verify his faith, we admitted him rather than followed him, as you will understand from our present declarations.

For we have been taught from the [very] first to believe in one God, the God of the universe, the framer and preserver of all things—both intellectual and sensible.

And in one Son of God, only-begotten, who existed before all ages, and was with the Father who had begotten Him, by whom all things were made, both visible and invisible, who in the last days according to the good pleasure of the Father came down and has taken on flesh of the virgin, and jointly fulfilled all His father's will, and suffered and rose again, and ascended into Heaven, and sits on the right hand of the Father, and will come again to judge the living and the dead, and remains King and God for all ages.

And we also believe in the Holy Spirit; and if it be necessary to add: we believe in the resurrection of the flesh and the life everlasting.

THE EARLIEST CREEDS

SECOND CREED OF ANTIOCH
(AD 341)

We believe, conformably to the evangelical and apostolic tradition, in one God, the Father Almighty, the Framer, and Maker, and Provider of the universe, from whom are all things.

And in one Lord Jesus Christ, His Son, only-begotten God, by whom are all things, who was begotten before all ages from the Father: God from God, whole from whole, sole from sole, perfect from perfect, King from King, Lord from Lord, Living Word, Living Wisdom, true Light, Way, Truth, Resurrection, Shepherd, Door, both unalterable and unchangeable; exact image of the godhead, essence, will, power and glory of the Father; the firstborn of every creature, who was in the beginning with God, God the Word, as it is written in the Gospel: "and the Word was God"; by whom all things were made and in whom all things consist; who in the last days descended from above, and was born of a virgin according to the Writings, and was made man, Mediator between God and man, and Apostle of our faith, and Prince of life, as He says, "I came down from Heaven, not to do My own will, but the will of Him that sent Me"; who suffered for us, and rose again on the third day, and ascended into Heaven, and sat down on the right hand of the Father, and is coming again with glory and power to judge the living and the dead.

And in the Holy Spirit, who is given to those who believe for comfort, and sanctification, and initiation, as also our Lord Jesus Christ commanded His disciples, saying, "Go and teach all nations, immersing them in the Name of the Father, and the Son, and the Holy Spirit"; namely of a Father who is truly Father, and a Son who is truly Son, and of the Holy Spirit who is truly Holy Spirit, the names not being given without meaning or effect, but denoting accurately the peculiar subsistence, rank, and glory of each that is named, so that they are three in subsistence, and in agreement one.

Holding then this faith—and holding it in the presence of God and Christ, from beginning to end—we curse every heretical heterodoxy. And if anyone teaches [anything] besides the sound and right faith of the Writings, that time, or season, or age, either is or has been before the generation of the Son, may he be cursed. Or if anyone says that the Son is a creature as one of the creatures, or an offspring as one of the offspring's, or a work as one of the works, and not the aforementioned articles one after another, as the Divine Writings have delivered, or if he teaches or preaches besides what we received, may he be cursed. For all that has been delivered in the Divine Writings whether by prophets or apostles, do we truly and reverently both believe and follow.

THIRD CREED OF ANTIOCH
(AD 341)

God knows, whom I invoke as a witness on my soul, that so I believe: in God the Father Almighty, the Creator and Maker of the universe, from whom are all things.

And in His only-begotten Son—Word, Power, and Wisdom—our Lord Jesus Christ, through whom are all things; who has been begotten from the Father before the ages, perfect God from perfect God, and was with God in subsistence, and in the last days descended, and was born of the virgin according to the Writings, and was made man, and suffered, and rose again from the dead, and ascended into the heavens, and sat down on the right hand of His Father, and will come again with glory and power to judge the living and the dead, and remains forever.

And in the Holy Spirit, the Comforter, the Spirit of Truth, which God also promised by His prophet to pour out on His servants, and the LORD promised to send to His disciples, which also He sent as the acts of the Apostles witness.

But if anyone teaches, or holds in his mind, anything besides this faith, may he be cursed; or with Marcellus of Ancyra, or Sabellius, or Paul of Samosata, may he be cursed—both himself and those who communicate with him.

FOURTH CREED OF ANTIOCH
(AD 341 OR 342)

We believe in one God, the Father Almighty, Creator and Maker of all things; from whom all fatherhood in heaven and on earth is named.

And in His only-begotten Son, our Lord Jesus Christ, who before all ages was begotten from the Father—God from God, Light from Light—by whom all things were made in the heavens and on the earth, visible and invisible, being Word, and Wisdom, and Power, and Life, and True Light; who in the last days was made man for us, and was born of the holy virgin; who was crucified, and died, and was buried, and rose again from the dead the third day, and was taken up into Heaven, and sat down on the right hand of the Father; and is coming at the consummation of the age to judge the living and the dead, and to render to everyone according to his works; whose kingdom endures indissolubly into the infinite ages; for He will be seated on the right hand of the Father, not only in this age but in that which is to come.

And in the Holy Spirit, that is, the Comforter; which, having promised to the Apostles, He sent forth after His ascension into Heaven, to teach and remind them of all things; through whom also will be sanctified the souls of those who sincerely believe in Him.

But those who say that the Son was from nothing, or from another subsistence and not from God, and [that] there was a time when He was not, the Universal Assembly regards as aliens.

CREED OF THE WESTERN SERDICAN COUNCIL
(AD 343)

We declare those men excommunicated from the Universal Assembly who say that Christ is God, but not the true God; that He is the Son, but not the true Son; and that He is both begotten and made; for such persons acknowledge that they understand by the term "begotten," that which has been made; and because, although the Son of God existed before all ages, they attribute to Him, who exists not in time but before all time, a beginning and an end.

Valens and Ursacius have, like two vipers brought forth by an asp, proceeded from the Arian heresy. For they boastingly declare themselves to be unquestionable Christians, and yet affirm that the Word and the Holy Spirit were both crucified and slain, and that they died and rose again; and they persistently maintain, like the heretics, that the Father, the Son, and the Holy Spirit are of diverse and distinct essences. We have been taught, and we hold the universal and apostolic tradition, and faith, and confession which teach that the Father, the Son, and the Holy Spirit have one essence, which is termed substance by the heretics. If it is asked, "What is the essence of the Son?" We confess that it is that which is acknowledged to be that of the Father alone; for the Father has never been, nor could ever be, without the Son, or the Son without the Father. It is most absurd to affirm that the Father ever existed without the Son, for that this could never be so has been testified by the Son Himself, who said, "I am in the Father, and the Father in Me," and "I and My Father are one." None of us denied that He was begotten; but we say that He was begotten before all things, whether visible or invisible; and that He is the Creator of chief-messengers and messengers, and of the world, and of the human race. It is written: "Wisdom, which is the worker of all things, taught Me," and again, "All things were made by Him."

He could not have existed forever if He had had a beginning, for the everlasting Word has no beginning, and God will never have an end. We do not say that the Father is Son, or that the Son is Father; but that the Father is Father, and the Son of the Father [is] Son. We confess that the Son is Power of the Father. We confess that the Word is Word of God the Father, and that beside Him there is no other. We believe the Word to be the true God, and Wisdom and Power. We affirm that He is truly the Son, yet not in the way in which others are said to be sons: for they are either gods by reason of their regeneration, or are called sons of God on account of their merit, and not on account of their being of one essence, as is the case with the Father and the Son. We confess an only-begotten and a firstborn; but that the Word is only-begotten, who always was and is in the Father. We use the word "firstborn" with respect to His human nature. But He is superior [to man] in the new creation [of the Resurrection], inasmuch as He is the firstborn from the dead.

We confess that God is; we confess the divinity of the Father and of the Son to be one. No one denies that the Father is greater than the Son: not on account of another essence, nor yet on account of their difference, but simply from the very Name of the father being greater than that of the Son. The words uttered by our Lord, "I and My Father are one," are by those men explained as referring to the agreement and harmony which prevail between the Father and the Son; but this is a blasphemous and perverse interpretation. We as [members of the] Universal Assembly, unanimously condemned this foolish and lamentable opinion: for just as mortal men on a difference having arisen between them quarrel and afterwards are reconciled, so do such interpreters say that disputes and dissention are liable to arise between God the Father Almighty and His Son; a supposition which is altogether absurd and unjustified. But we believe and maintain that those holy words, "I and my Father are one," point out the oneness of essence which is one and the same in the Father and in the Son.

We also believe that the Son reigns with the Father, that His reign has neither beginning nor end, and that it is not bounded by time, nor can ever cease: for that which always exists never begins to be, and can never cease.

We believe in and we receive the Holy Spirit, the Comforter, whom the LORD both promised and sent. We believe in it as sent.

It was not the Holy Spirit who suffered, but the manhood with which He clothed Himself; which he took from the virgin Mary, which being man was capable of suffering; for man is mortal, whereas God is immortal. We believe that on the third day He rose—the man in God, not God in the man; and that He brought as a gift to His Father the manhood which He had delivered from sin and corruption.

We believe that, at a proper and fixed time, He Himself will judge all men and all their deeds.

So great is the ignorance and mental darkness of those whom we have mentioned, that they are unable to see the light of truth. They cannot comprehend the meaning of the words: "that they may be one in Us." It is evident why the word "one" was used: it was because the Apostles received the Holy Spirit of God, and yet there were none amongst them who were the Spirit, neither was there anyone of them who was Word, Wisdom, Power, or Only-begotten. "As You," He said, "and I are one, that they may be one in Us," are strictly accurate: for the LORD did not say, "one in the same way that I and the Father are one," but He said, "that the disciples, being knit together and united, may be one in faith and in confession, and so in the grace and piety of God the Father, and by the indulgence and love of our Lord Jesus Christ, may be able to become one."

CREED OF THE EASTERN SERDICAN COUNCIL

(AD 343)

We believe in one God, the Father Almighty, Creator and Maker of all things, from whom all fatherhood in heaven and earth is named.

And we believe in His Only-begotten Son, our Lord Jesus Christ, who before all ages was begotten of the Father, God of God, Light of Light, through whom were made all things which are in heaven and earth, visible and invisible; who is the Word, and Wisdom, and Might, and Life, and true Light; and who in the last days for our sake was incarnate, and was born of the holy virgin, who was crucified, and died, and was buried, and rose from the dead on the third day, and was received into Heaven, and sits on the right hand of the Father, and will come to judge the living and the dead and to give to every man according to his works; whose kingdom remains without end forever and ever. For He sits on the right hand of the Father, not only in this age, but also in the age to come.

We also believe in the Holy Spirit, that is, the Comforter, whom, according to His promise, He sent to His apostles after His return into the heavens to teach them and to bring all things to their remembrance, through whom also the souls of them that believe sincerely in Him are sanctified.

But those who say that the Son of God is sprung from things non-existent or from another substance and not from God, and that there was a time or age when He was not, the Holy Universal Assembly holds them as aliens. Likewise also, those who say that there are three Gods, or that Christ is not God and that before the ages He was neither Christ nor Son of God, or that He Himself is the Father, and the Son, and the Holy Spirit, or that the Son is incapable of birth; or that the Father begat the Son without purpose or will: the Holy Universal Assembly curses.

THE LONG-LINED CREED

(AD 345)

We believe in one God, the Father Almighty, the Creator and Maker of all things, from whom all fatherhood in heaven and on earth is named.

And in His Only-begotten Son, our Lord Jesus Christ, who before all ages was begotten from the Father, God from God, Light from Light, by whom all things were made, in heaven and on the earth, visible and invisible, being Word, and Wisdom, and Power, and Life, and True Light, who in the last days was made man for us, and was born of the holy virgin, crucified, and died, and was buried, and rose again from the dead on the third day, and was taken up into Heaven, and sat down on the right hand of the Father, and is coming at the consummation of the age to judge the living and the dead, and to render to everyone according to his works; whose kingdom endured unceasingly to all the ages; for He sits on the right hand of the Father, not only in this age, but also in that which is to come.

And we believe in the Holy Spirit, that is, the Comforter, which, having promised to the Apostles, He sent forth after the ascension into Heaven, to teach and remind them of all things; through whom also will be sanctified the souls of those who sincerely believe in Him.

But those who say that the Son was from nothing, or from other subsistence and not from God; and that there was a time or age when He was not, the universal and holy Assembly regards as aliens. Likewise, those who say that there are three Gods, or that Christ is not God, or that before the ages He was neither Christ nor Son of God, or that Father, and Son, or Holy Spirit are the same, or that the Son is ingenerate, or that the Father begot the Son not by choice or will: the Holy and Universal Assembly curses.

1.   For neither is it safe to say that the Son is from nothing (since this is nowhere spoken of Him in divinely inspired Writing), nor again of any other subsistence previously existing beside the Father, but from God alone do we define Him genuinely to be generated. For the divine Word teaches that the Ingenerate and Unbegotten, the Father of Christ, is One.

2.   Nor may we, adopting the dangerous position, "There was a time when He was not," from unscriptural sources, imagine any interval of time before Him, but only the God who has generated Him apart from time; for through Him both times and ages came to be. Yet we must not consider the Son to be co-unbegotten and co-ingenerate with the Father; for no one can be properly called Father or Son of one who is co-

unbegotten and co-ingenerate with Him. But we acknowledge that the Father who alone is unbegotten and ingenerate, has generated inconceivably and incomprehensibly to all; and that the Son has been generated before ages, and in no way to be ingenerate Himself like the Father, but to have the Father who generated Him as His source; for "the head of Christ is God."

3. Nor again, in confessing three realities and three Persons—of the Father, and the Son, and the Holy Spirit—according to the Writings, do we therefore make three Gods, since we acknowledge the self-complete, and ingenerate, and unbegotten, and invisible God to be one only—the God and Father of the Only-begotten, who alone has being from Himself, and alone grants this to all others bountifully.

4. Nor again, in saying that the Father of our Lord Jesus Christ is one only God, the only ingenerate, do we therefore deny that Christ is also God before ages, as the disciples of Paul of Samosata, who say that after the incarnation He was by advance made God, from being made by nature a mere man. For we acknowledge, that though He is subordinate to His Father and God, yet, being before ages begotten of God, He is perfect God according to nature and true, and not first man and then God, but first God and then becoming man for us, and never having been deprived of being.

5. We additionally abhor and condemn those who make a pretense of saying that He is but the mere word of God and nonexistent, having His being in another— now as if pronounced, as some speak, now as mental— holding that He was not Christ, or Son of God, or mediator, or image of God before ages; but that He first became Christ and Son of God, when He took our flesh from the virgin, not quite four hundred years ago. For they will have it that then Christ began His kingdom, and that it will have an end after the consummation of all and the judgment. Such are the disciples of Marcellus and Scotinus of Galatian Ancyra, who, equally with Jews, rejected Christ's existence before ages, and His Godhead, and unending kingdom, upon pretense of supporting the divine monarchy. We, on the contrary, regard Him not as simply God's pronounced word or self, and Son of God and Christ, being and abiding with His Father before ages, and that not in foreknowledge only, and ministering to Him for the whole framing whether of things visible or invisible. For it is He to whom the Father said, "Let Us make man in Our image, after Our likeness," who also was seen in His own person by the patriarchs, gave the Law, was spoken by the prophets, and at last became man and manifested His own Father to all men, and reigns to never-ending ages. For Christ has taken no recent dignity, but we have believed Him to be perfect from the first and like in all things to the Father.

6. And those who say that the Father, and Son, and Holy Spirit are the same, and irreligiously take the three names of one and the same reality and person, we justly proscribe from the Assembly, because they suppose the illimitable and impassible Father to be also limitable and passable through His becoming man. For such are they whom Romans call Patripassians, and we Sabellians. For we acknowledge that the unchangeable Godhead and that Christ who was sent fulfilled the dispensation of the Incarnation.

7. And at the same time, those who irreverently say that the Son has been generated not by choice or will, thus encompassing God with a necessity which excludes choice and purpose, so that He begat the Son unwillingly, we account as most irreligious and alien to the Assembly; in that they have dared to define such things concerning God, beside the common notions concerning Him, so, beside the intention of divinely inspired Writing. For we, knowing that God is absolute and sovereign over Himself, have a religious judgment that He generated the Son voluntarily and freely. Yet, as we have a reverent belief in the Son's words concerning Himself, "The LORD created Me a beginning of His ways for His works," we do not understand Him to have been originated like the creatures or works which through Him came to be. For it is irreligious and alien to the ecclesiastical faith to compare the Creator with handiworks created by Him, and to think that He has the same manner of origination with the rest. For Divine Writing teaches us assuredly and truly that the Only-begotten Son was generated sole and solely. Yet, in saying that the Son is in Himself, and both lives and exists like the Father, we do not on that account separate Him from the Father, imagining place and interval between Their union in the way of bodies. For we believe that They are united with each other without mediation or distance, and that They exist inseparably. All the Father encompassing the Son, and all the Son hanging and adhering to the Father, and alone resting on the Father's breast continually. Believing then in the all-perfect Triad, the most holy, that is, in the Father, and the Son, and the Holy Spirit, and calling the Father God, and the Son God, yet we confess in them, not two Gods, but one dignity of Godhead, and one exact harmony of dominion—the Father alone being head over the whole universe wholly, and over the Son Himself, and the Son subordinated to the Father; but, excepting Him, ruling over all things after Him which through Himself have come to be, and granting the grace of the Holy Spirit unsparingly to the saints at the Father's will. For that such is the account of the Divine Monarchy toward Christ, the sacred oracles have delivered to us.

Thus much, in addition to the faith previously published in epitome, we have been compelled to draw forth at length, not in any officious display, but to clear away all unjust suspicion concerning our opinions among those who are ignorant of our affairs; and that all in the West may know, both the audacity of the slanders of the heterodox, and as to the Easterners, their ecclesiastical mind in the LORD, to which the divinely inspired Writings bear witness without violence, where men are not perverse.

CREED OF JERUSALEM
(CIRCA AD 350)

We believe in one God, the Father Almighty, Maker of heaven and earth, and of all things visible and invisible.

And in one Lord, Jesus Christ, the only-begotten Son of God, begotten of the Father before all ages, very God, by whom all things were made; who appeared in the flesh and became man [[of the virgin and the Holy Spirit]]; was crucified and was buried, rose on the third day, and ascended into Heaven, and sits on the right hand of the Father; and will come again in glory
to judge the living and the dead; of whose kingdom there will be no end.

And in one Holy Spirit, the Comforter, who spoke in the Prophets.

And in one immersion of conversion for the forgiveness of sins; and in one Holy Universal Assembly; and in the resurrection of the flesh, and in life everlasting.

FIRST CREED OF SIRMIUM
(AD 351)

We believe in one God, the Father Almighty, the Creator and Maker of all things, "from whom all fatherhood in heaven and earth is named."

And in His only-begotten Son, our Lord Jesus Christ, who before all the ages was begotten from the Father, God from God, light from light, by whom all things were made, in heaven and on the earth, visible and invisible, being Word, and Wisdom, and True Light, and Life, who in the last of days was made man for us, and was born of the holy virgin, and was crucified, and died, and was buried, and rose again from the dead the third day, and was taken up into Heaven, and sat down on the right hand of the Father, and is coming at the consummation of the age to judge the living and the dead, and to render to everyone according to his works; whose kingdom being unceasing endures to the infinite ages; for He will sit on the right hand of the Father, not only in this age, but also in that which is to come.

THE EARLIEST CREEDS

And in the Holy Spirit, that is, the Comforter; which, having promised to the Apostles to send forth after His ascension into Heaven, to teach and to remind them of all things, He did send; through whom also are sanctified the souls of those who sincerely believe in Him.

1. But those who say that the Son was from nothing or from other subsistence and not from God, and that there was a time or age when He was not, the Holy and Universal Assembly regards as aliens.

2. Again we say, whoever says that the Father and the Son are two Gods, may he be cursed.

3. And whosoever, saying that Christ is God, before ages Son of God, does not confess that He has subserved the Father for the framing of the universe, may he be cursed.

4. Whoever presumes to say that the ingenerate, or a part of Him, was born of Mary, may he be cursed.

5. Whoever says that according to foreknowledge the Son is before Mary and not that, generated from the Father before ages, He was with God, and that through Him all things were originated, may he be cursed.

6. Whoever will pretend that the essence of God is dilated or contracted, may he be cursed.

7. Whoever says that the essence of God, being dilated, made the Son, or will name the dilation of His essence Son, may he be cursed.

8. Whoever calls the Son of God the mental or pronounced Word, may he be cursed.

9. Whoever says that the Son from Mary is only man, may he be cursed.

10. Whoever, speaking of Him who is from Mary, God and man, thereby means God the Ingenerate, may he be cursed.

11. Whoever expounds, "I, God, the first and I the last, and besides Me there is no God"—which is stated for the denial of idols and of gods that are not—to the denial of the Only-begotten, before ages God, as Jews do, may he be cursed.

12. Whoever hearing "the Word was made flesh," considers that the Word has changed into flesh, or will say that He has undergone alteration by taking flesh, may he be cursed.

13. Whoever hearing the only-begotten Son of God to have been crucified, will say that His Godhead has undergone corruption, or passion, or alteration, or diminution, or destruction, may he be cursed.

14. Whoever says that "Let Us make man," was not said by the Father to the Son, but by God to Himself, may he be cursed.

15. Whoever says that Abraham saw, not the Son, but the ingenerate God or part of Him, may he be cursed.

16. Whoever says that Jacob wrestled with, not the Son as man, but the ingenerate God or part of Him, may he be cursed.

17. Whoever will explain, "The LORD rained fire from the LORD," was not the Father and the Son, and says that He rained from Himself, may he be cursed. For the Son, being LORD, rained from the Father who is LORD.

18. Whoever, hearing that the Father is LORD and the Son LORD and the Father and Son LORD, for there is LORD from LORD, says there are two Gods, may he be cursed. For we do not place the Son in the Father's order, but as subordinate to the Father; for He did not descend on Sodom without the Father's will, nor did He rain from Himself, but from the LORD, that is, the Father authorizing it. Nor is He of Himself set down on the right hand, but He hears the Father saying, "Sit on My right hand."

19. Whoever says that the Father, and the Son, and the Holy Spirit are one Person, may he be cursed.

20. Whoever, speaking of the Holy Spirit as Comforter, will mean the ingenerate God, may he be cursed.

21. Whoever denies what the LORD taught us, that the Comforter is other than the Son, for He said, "and the Father will send you another Comforter, whom I will ask," may he be cursed.

22. Whoever says that the Holy Spirit is part of the Father or of the Son, may he be cursed.

23. Whoever will say that the Father, and the Son, and the Holy Spirit are three Gods, may he be cursed.

24. Whoever says that the Son of God came to be at the will of God, as one of the works, may he be cursed.

25. Whoever says that the Son has been generated, the Father not wishing it, may he be cursed. For not by compulsion, led by physical necessity, did the Father, as He did not wish, generate the Son, but He at once willed, and, after generating Him from Himself apart from time and passion, manifested Him.

26. Whoever says that the Son is without beginning and ingenerate, as if speaking of two unbegotten and two ingenerate, and making two Gods, may he be cursed. For the Son is the head, namely the beginning of all; and God is the head, namely the beginning of Christ. And so, to one unbegotten beginning of the universe do we religiously refer all things through the Son.

27. And in accurate delineation of the idea of Christianity we say this again: whoever does not say that Christ is God, Son of God, as being before ages, and having subserved the Father in the framing of the universe, but that from the time that He was born of Mary, from there He was called Christ and Son, and took an origin of being God, may he be cursed.

SECOND CREED OF SIRMIUM
(AD 357)

It is held for certain that there is one God, the Father Almighty, as also is preached in all the world.

And His one only-begotten Son, our Lord Jesus Christ, generated from Him before the ages; and that we may not speak of two Gods, since the LORD Himself has said, "I go to My Father and your Father, and My God and your God." On this account He is God of all, as also the Apostle taught: "Is He God of the Jews only, is He not also of the nations? Yes, of the nations also; since there is one God who will justify the Circumcision from faith, and the Uncircumcision through faith." And everything else agrees and has no ambiguity.

But since many persons are disturbed by questions concerning what is called in Latin "substantia," but in Greek "ousia" (or, to put it more clearly, "co-essential," or "of the same essence") these terms should not be used at all, nor should they be expounded on in the Assembly. And here are the reasons: nothing is written about them in Holy Writing; they are beyond mankind's knowledge and understanding; and no one can declare the Son's generation, as it is written, "Who will declare His generation?" For it is clear that only the Father knows how He generated the Son, and again the Son how He has been generated by the Father. No one can question that the Father is greater, for no one can doubt that the Father is greater in honor, and dignity, and Godhead, and in the very Name of Father. The Son Himself testifies, "The Father that sent Me is greater than I." And no one is ignorant that it is universal doctrine that there are two persons—Father and Son; that the Father is greater, and the Son is subordinated to the Father together with all things which the Father has subordinated to Him; that the Father has no beginning, is invisible, and immortal, and impassible. But the Son has been generated from the Father, God from God, light from light, and His origin (as previously stated), no one knows except the Father. And that the Son Himself and our Lord and God, took flesh (that is, a body; that is, man) from the virgin Mary, as the messenger announced beforehand; and as all the

THE EARLIEST CREEDS

Writings teach, and especially the apostle himself, the doctor of the nations, Christ took on manhood from the virgin Mary, through which He has suffered.

And the whole faith is summed up and secured in this: that a Trinity should always be preserved, as we read in the Gospel, "Go and immerse all the nations in the Name of the Father, and of the Son, and of the Holy Spirit." And whole and perfect is the number of the Trinity; but the Comforter, the Holy Spirit, sent forth through the Son, came according to the promise, that He might teach and sanctify the Apostles and all believers.

FOURTH CREED OF SIRMIUM
(AD 359)

The universal faith was published in the presence of our master, the most religious and gloriously victorious Emperor, Constantius, Augustus, the eternal and august, in the consulate of the most illustrious Flavii, Eusebius, and Hypatius, in Sirmium on the eleventh of the Calends of June.

We believe in only one and true God, the Father Almighty, Creator and Framer of all things.

And in one only-begotten Son of God, who, before all ages, and before all origin, and before all conceivable time, and before all comprehensible essence, was begotten impassibly from God—through whom the ages were disposed and all things were made; and Him begotten as the only-begotten, only from the only Father, God from God. Like the Father who begot Him, according to the Writings; whose origin no one knows except the Father alone who begot Him. We know that He, the only-begotten Son of God, at the Father's command, came from the heavens for the eradication of sin, and was born of the virgin Mary, and conversed with the disciples, and fulfilled the dispensation according to the Father's will, and was crucified, and died, and descended into the parts beneath the earth, and regulated the things there, whom the gatekeepers of Hades saw and shuddered; and He rose from the dead [on] the third day, and conversed with the disciples, and fulfilled all the dispensation, and when the forty days were fulfilled, ascended into the heavens, and sits on the right hand of the Father, and is coming in the last day of the resurrection in the glory of the Father, to render to everyone according to his works.

And in the Holy Spirit, whom the only-begotten of God Himself, Jesus Christ, had promised to send to the race of men, the Comforter, as it is written, "I go to My Father, and I will ask the Father, and He will send to you another Comforter—even the Spirit of Truth. He will take of Mine and will teach and bring to your remembrance all things."

But whereas the term "essence," has been adopted by the Fathers in simplicity, and gives offense as being misconceived by the people, and is not contained in the Writings, it has seemed good to remove it, that it may never be in any case used of God again, because the Divine Writings nowhere use it of Father and Son. But we say that the Son is like the Father in all things, as also the Holy Writings say and teach.

NICENO-THRACIAN CREED
(AD 359)

We believe in only one true God, Father Almighty, of whom are all things.

And in the only-begotten Son of God, who before all ages and before every beginning was begotten of God, through whom all things were made, both visible and invisible; alone begotten, only-begotten of the Father alone, God of God; like the Father that begot Him, according to the Writings, whose generation no one knows except only the Father that begot Him. This only-begotten Son of God, sent by His Father, we know to have come down from Heaven, as it is written, for the destruction of sin and death; begotten of the Holy Spirit and the virgin Mary, as it is written, according to the flesh. Who accompanied His disciples, and when the dispensation was fulfilled, according to the Father's will, was crucified, died, and was buried, and descended to the world below, at whom Hades himself trembled. On the third day, He rose from the dead and accompanied His disciples [for] forty days. He was taken up into Heaven, and sits on the right hand of His Father, and is coming at the last day of the Resurrection, in His Father's glory, to render to everyone according to his works.

And we believe in the Holy Spirit, which the only-begotten Son of God, Jesus Christ, both God and Lord, promised to send to man, the Comforter, as it is written, the Spirit of Truth. This Spirit He Himself sent after He had ascended into Heaven and sat at the right hand of the Father, from there to come to judge both the living and the dead.

But the word "substance," which was too simply inserted by the Fathers, and, not being understood by the people, was a cause of scandal through its not being found in the Writings, it has seemed good to us to remove, and that for the future no mention whatsoever may be permitted of the "substance" of the Father and the Son. Nor must one "essence" be named in relation to the person of Father, Son, and Holy Spirit. And we call the Son like the Father, as the Holy Writings call Him and teach; but all the heresies, both those already condemned, and any, if such there may be, which have risen against the document thus put forth, let them be cursed.

NINTH CONFESSION OF SELEUCIA
(AD 359)

We do not decline to bring forward the authentic faith published at the dedication at Antioch, although our fathers certainly at the time met together for a particular subject under investigation. But since "coessential" and "like-in-essence" have troubled many persons in times past and up to this day, and since moreover some are said to have recently devised the Son's "unlikeness" to the Father, on their account we reject "coessential" and "like-in-essence," as alien to the Writings, but "unlike" we curse, and account all who profess it as aliens from the Assembly. And we distinctly confess the "likeness" of the Son to the Father, according to the apostle, who says of the Son, "Who is the image of the invisible God."

And we confess and believe in one God, the Father Almighty, the Maker of heaven and earth, of all things visible and invisible.

And we also believe in our Lord Jesus Christ, His Son, generated from Him impassibly before all the ages: God the Word, God from God, Only-begotten, Light, Life, Truth, Wisdom, Power, through whom all things were made in the heavens and on the earth, whether visible or invisible. He, as we believe, at the end of the world, for the eradication of sin, took flesh of the holy virgin, and was made man, and suffered for our sins, and rose again, and was taken up into Heaven, and sits on the right hand of the Father, and is coming again in glory to judge the living and the dead.

We also believe in the Holy Spirit, which our Savior and Lord named Comforter, having promised to send Him to the disciples after His own departure, as He did send; through whom He sanctifies those in the Assembly who believe and are immersed in the Name of Father, Son, and Holy Spirit.

But those who preach anything besides this faith, the Universal Assembly regards as aliens. And that to this faith that is equivalent which was published recently at Sirmium, under sanction of his religiousness, the emperor, is plain to all who read it.

HOMOIAN CREED
(AD 360)

We believe in one God, Father Almighty, from whom are all things.

And in the only-begotten Son of God, begotten from God before all ages and before every beginning, by whom all things were made, visible and invisible, and begotten as only-begotten, only from the Father alone, God from God, like to the Father that begot Him according to the Writings; whose origin no

THE EARLIEST CREEDS

one knows, except the Father alone who begot Him. He, as we acknowledge, the only-begotten Son of God, the Father having sent Him, came here from the heavens, as it is written, for the undoing of sin and death, and was born of the Holy Spirit, of the virgin Mary according to the flesh, as it is written, and conversed with the disciples, and having fulfilled the whole dispensation according to the Father's will, was crucified, and died, and was buried, and ascended to the parts below the earth, at whom Hades itself shuddered; who also rose from the dead on the third day, and abode with the disciples, and forty days being fulfilled, was taken up into the heavens, and sits on the right hand of the Father to come in the last day of the resurrection in the Father's glory, so that He may render to every man according to his works.

And in the Holy Spirit, whom the only-begotten Son of God Himself, Christ, our Lord and God, promised to send to the race of man, as Comforter, as it is written, the Spirit of Truth, which He sent to them when He had ascended into the heavens.

But the name of "essence," which was set down by the Fathers in simplicity, and, being unknown by the people, caused offense, because the Writings do not contain it, it has seemed good to abolish, and for the future to make no mention of it at all, since the Divine Writings have made no mention of the essence of Father and Son. For neither should "subsistence" be named concerning Father, Son, and Holy Spirit. But we say that the Son is like the Father, as the Divine Writings say and teach; and all the heresies, both those which have been already condemned, and whatever are of modern date, being contrary to this published statement, may they be cursed.

NICENO-CONSTANTINOPOLITAN CREED
(AD 381)

We believe in one God, the Father Almighty, Maker of heaven and earth, of all that is, seen and unseen.

And [we believe] in one Lord, Jesus Christ, the only-begotten Son of God, eternally begotten of the Father, Light from Light, true God from true God, begotten, not made, of one being with the Father. Through Him all things were made.

For us humans, and for our salvation, He descended from Heaven, was incarnate of the Holy Spirit and the virgin Mary, and became fully human.

For our sake He was crucified under Pontius Pilate. He suffered death and was buried.

He rose again on the third day in accordance with the Writings.

He ascended into Heaven and is seated at the right hand of the Father.

He will come again in glory to judge the living and the dead, and His kingdom will have no end.

And [we believe] in the Holy Spirit, the LORD, the giver of life, who proceeds from the Father, who in unity with the Father and the Son is worshiped and glorified, who has spoken through the prophets.

[We believe] in one holy universal and apostolic Assembly.

We acknowledge one immersion for the forgiveness of sins.

We look for the resurrection of the dead and the life of the world to come. Amen.

CREED OF THE FIRST COUNCIL OF TOLEDO
(AD 400)

1. We believe in one true God, Father, and Son, and Holy Spirit, Creator of that which is visible and invisible, through whom everything in heaven and on earth was created.

2. This one God also has one divine Name: the Trinity.

3. The Father is not the Son, but He has the Son, who is not the Father.

4. The Son is not the Father, but is by nature the Son of God.

5. Also, the Spirit is the Comforter, who is Himself neither the Father nor the Son, but proceeds from the Father.

6. Therefore, the Father is unbegotten, the Son begotten, the Comforter not begotten, but is proceeding from the Father.

7. It is the Father whose voice is heard from Heaven, saying, "This is My beloved Son, in whom I am well pleased. Listen to Him."

8. It is the Son who said, "I came forth from the Father and I came into this world from God."

9. It is the Comforter Himself about whom the Son said, "Unless I go to the Father, the Comforter will not come to you."

10. This Trinity is distinct in persons, of one substance, virtue, power, and undivided majesty, unable to be differentiated.

11. Besides Him there is no one else with a divine nature, neither messenger, nor spirit, nor anything else of excellence which one should believe to be God.

12. Therefore, this Son of God, being God, born from the Father before everything, the beginning of all, made holy the womb of the blessed virgin Mary and assumed true humanity from her without procreation through a man's seed.

13. That is, the Lord Jesus Christ.

14. His body was neither imaginary nor did it merely have form, but had [real] substance.

15. And so, He had hunger, and thirst, and suffered pain, and wept, and felt every kind of bodily hurt.

16. In the end, He was crucified, died, and was buried, and rose on the third day.

17. Afterward, He spoke with His disciples.

18. He ascended to Heaven on the fortieth day.

19. This Son of Man is also named the Son of God; however, the Son of God is God and should not be called [merely] son of man.

20. We truly believe in the resurrection of the human body.

21. However, the soul of man is not a divine substance or a part of God, but rather a creation which by divine will is imperishable.

CURSES:

1. Therefore, if anyone should say or believe that this world was not made by the omnipotent God and His instruments, let him be cursed.

2. If anyone should say or believe that God the Father is Himself the Son or the Comforter, let him be cursed.

3. If anyone should say or believe that God the Son is Himself the Father or Comforter, let him be cursed.

4. If anyone should say or believe that the Comforter, the Spirit, is either the Father or the Son, let him be cursed.

5. If anyone should say or believe that the human Jesus Christ was not assumed by the Son of God, let him be cursed.

6. If anyone should say or believe that the Son of God as God suffered, let him be cursed.

7. If anyone should say or believe that the human Jesus Christ, as a human, was incapable of suffering, let him be cursed.

THE EARLIEST CREEDS

8. If anyone should say or believe that there is one God of the Old Testament and another of the Gospel, let him be cursed.

9. If anyone should say or believe that the world was made by another god than by the one of whom it is written, "In the beginning God created the heavens and the earth," let him be cursed.

10. If anyone should say or believe that the human body will not rise after death, let him be cursed.

11. If anyone should say or believe that the human soul is a part or substance of God, let him be cursed.

12. If anyone should say or believe that there is another Writing than that which the Universal Assembly accepts or believes to be held as authoritative or has venerated, let him be cursed.

CHALCEDONIAN CREED
(AD 451)

Following, then, the holy Fathers, we all unanimously teach that our Lord Jesus Christ is to us one and the same Son, the same perfect in Godhead, the same perfect in Manhood; truly God and truly Man; the same of a rational soul and body; co-essential with the Father according to the Godhead, the same co-essential with us according to the Manhood; like us in all things, excepting sin; before the ages begotten of the Father as to the Godhead, but in the last days, the same, for us and for our salvation, [born] of the virgin Mary, mother of God, as to the Manhood; one and the same Christ, Son, Lord, only-begotten; acknowledged in two natures unconfusedly, unchangeably, indivisibly, inseparably; the difference of the natures being in no way removed because of the union, but rather the properties of each nature being preserved, and [both] concurring into one Person and one Subsistence; not as though He was parted or divided into two persons, but one and the same Son and only-begotten God, Word, Lord, Jesus Christ; even as from the beginning the prophets have taught concerning Him, and as the Lord Jesus Christ Himself has taught us, and as the Symbol of the Fathers has handed down to us.

ATHANASIAN CREED
(4TH OR 5TH CENTURY AD)

Whoever desires to be saved, before all things it is necessary that he hold the universal faith, which except everyone will have kept [it] whole and unbroken, without a doubt he will perish eternally.

Now the universal faith is that we worship one God in trinity and Trinity in unity, neither confounding the Persons nor dividing the substance. For there is one Person of the Father, another of the Son, another of the Holy Spirit. But the Godhead of the Father, of the Son, and of the Holy Spirit, is One—the glory equal, the majesty co-eternal.

Such as the Father is, such is the Son, and such is the Holy Spirit; the Father uncreated, the Son uncreated, and the Holy Spirit uncreated; the father infinite, the Son infinite, and the Holy Spirit infinite; the Father eternal, the Son eternal, and the Holy Spirit eternal. And yet not three eternals but one eternal, as also not three infinites, nor three uncreated, but one uncreated, and one infinite. So, likewise, the Father is almighty, the Son almighty, and the Holy Spirit almighty; and yet not three almighties but one almighty.

So the Father is God, the Son God, and the Holy Spirit God; and yet not three Gods but one God. So the Father is Lord, the Son Lord, and the Holy Spirit Lord; and yet not three Lords but one Lord. For just as we are compelled by Christian truth to acknowledge every Person by Himself to be both God and Lord, so are we forbidden by the universal religion to say [that] there are three Gods or three Lords.

The Father is made of none, neither created nor begotten. The Son is of the Father alone, not made nor created, but begotten. The Holy Spirit is of the Father and the Son, not made, nor created, nor begotten, but proceeding. So there is one Father not three Fathers, one Son not three Sons, and Holy Spirit not three Holy Spirits. And in this Trinity, there is nothing before or after, nothing greater or less, but the whole three Persons are co-eternal together and co-equal.

So that in all things, as is aforementioned, the Trinity in unity and the Unity in trinity is to be worshiped. He therefore who desires to be saved, let him think thus of the Trinity.

But it is necessary for eternal salvation that he also believe faithfully the Incarnation of our Lord Jesus Christ. The right faith therefore is that we believe and confess that our Lord Jesus Christ, the Son of God, is God and Man.

He is God of the substance of the Father begotten before the worlds, and He is man of the substance of His mother born in the world—perfect God [and] perfect man subsisting of a reasoning soul and human flesh; equal to the Father as touching His Godhead, inferior to the Father as touching His Manhood.

Who although He be God and Man, yet He is not two but one Christ; one however not by conversion of the Godhead in the flesh, but by taking of the Manhood in God; one altogether not by confusion of substance but by unity of Person. For as the reasoning soul and flesh is one man, so God and Man is one Christ.

Who suffered for our salvation, descended into Hades, rose again from the dead, ascended into Heaven, sits at the right hand of the Father, from where He will come to judge the living and the dead. At whose coming all men will rise again with their bodies and will give account for their own works. And they that have done good will go into eternal life, and they who indeed have done evil into eternal fire.

This is the universal faith, which except a man will have believed faithfully and firmly he cannot be saved.

KEY EXTRABIBLICAL REFERENCES

This section includes 12 monumental discoveries that provide external, secular support for the Bible, as well as the historicity of Christ and the Gospel accounts.

The Famine Stele is an inscription from the Ptolemaic period describing a seven-year famine during the reign of Djoser, a possible candidate for the pharaoh to whom Joseph reported. Some speculate Imhotep, Djoser's chancellor, was in fact Joseph.

The Admonitions of Ipuwer, from the Ipuwer Papyrus, were possibly composed in the same century as the Exodus and describe plagues across the land of Egypt and a great change of fortunes for the slaves of the land.

The Tel Dan Stele, from the 9th century BC, provides a reference to "the house of David," proving the historicity of the Israelite king by that name.

The Merneptah Stele, from the 13th century BC, references Israel during the period of the Judges.

The Mesha Stele, from the 9th century BC, repeatedly references the king of Israel, might also reference David, and utilizes a script virtually identical to Paleo-Hebrew.

The Kurkh Monoliths, also from the 9th century BC, mention both King Ahab and Israel—the only explicit mention of Israel in ancient Assyrian and Babylonian records.

Mar bar Serapion was a stoic philosopher, writing shortly after AD 73, who apparently referenced the death of Jesus.

Pliny the Younger was governor of Bithynia from AD 110–113 and wrote to the emperor Trajan regarding the burgeoning Christian religion which was rapidly spreading. Pliny's letter and Trajan's response not only provide one of the earliest secular references to Christianity, but demonstrate that the faith was both mature and widespread by the late 1st century and early 2nd century, mere years after John's Revelation.

Tacitus, a Roman senator and historian, who held strong, anti-Christian views, nevertheless confirmed both Christ's existence, His death under Pontius Pilate, and the unfair persecution and genocide of Christians in Rome at the behest of Nero, who used false charges to justify the killings. He wrote circa AD 116.

The Roman historian Seutonius, writing within about 90 years of Christ's death (circa AD 120), mentions both Christ, as the originator of the Christian sect, and Christians generally, in the context of the persecutions unleashed by both Claudius and Nero.

The Greek writer Phlegon of Tralles, writing in the mid-2nd century, references a widespread darkness that coincided chronologically with the period in which Christ was crucified. This provides possible secular support for the crucifixion darkness. He also mentions the basic Christian beliefs regarding Christ. Most of his Chronicles are no longer extant.

FAMINE STELE

YEAR EIGHTEEN OF HORUS: Neter-Khet; the King of Upper and Lower Egypt: Neter-Khet; Two-Ladies: Neter-Khet; Gold-Horus: Djoser; under the Count, Prince, Governor of the domains of the South, Chief of the Nubians in Yebu, Mesir. There was brought to him this royal decree. To inform you:

CHAPTER 1

I was in mourning on my throne, || Those of the palace were in grief, || My heart was in great affliction, || Because Hapi had failed to come in time || In a period of seven years. Grain was scant, || Kernels were dried up, || Sparse was every kind of food. || Every man robbed his twin, || Those who entered did not go. Children cried, || Youths fell, || The hearts of the old were grieving; Legs drawn up, they hugged the ground, || Their arms clasped around them. Courtiers were needy, || Temples were shut, || Shrines covered with dust, || Everyone was in distress. I directed my heart to turn to the past, || I consulted one of the staff of the Ibis, || The chief lector-priest of Imhotep, || Son of Ptah South-of-his-Wall: "In which place is Hapi born? Which is the town of the Sinuous one? Which god dwells there, so that he might join with me?" He stood: "I will go to Mansion-of-the-Net, || It is designed to support a man in his deeds; I will enter the House of Life, || Unroll the Souls of Ra, || I will be guided by them." He departed, he returned to me quickly, || He let me know the flow of Hapi, || His shores and all the things they contain. He disclosed to me the hidden wonders, || To which the ancestors had made their way, || And no king had equaled them since. He said to me: "There is a town in the midst of the deep, || Surrounded by Hapi, Yebu by name; It is first of the first, || First nome to Wawat, || Earthly elevation, celestial hill, || Seat of Ra when he prepares || To give life to every face. Its temple's name is Joy-of-life, || Twin Caverns is the water's name, || They are the breasts that nourish all. It is the house of sleep of Hapi, || He grows young in it in [his time], || [It is the place from where] he brings the flood: Bounding up he copulates, || As man copulates with woman, || Renewing his manhood with joy; Coursing twenty-eight cubits high, || He passes Sema-Behdet at seven. Khnum is the god [who rules] there, || [He is enthroned above the deep], || His sandals resting on the flood; He holds the door bolt in his hand, || Opens the gate as he wishes. He is eternal there as Shu, || Bounty-giver, Lord-of-fields, || So his name is called. He has reckoned the land of the South and the North, || To give parts to every god; It is he who governs barley, [emmer], || Birds, and fish, and all one lives on. Cord and scribal board are there, || The pole is there with its beam … || His temple opens southeastward, || Ra rises in its face every day; Its water rages on its south for an iter, || A wall against the Nubians each day. There is a mountain massif in its eastern region, || With precious stones and quarry stones of all kinds, || All the things sought for building temples || In Egypt, south and north, || And stalls for sacred animals, || And palaces for kings, || All statues too that stand in temples and in shrines."

CHAPTER 2

"Their gathered products are set before the face of Khnum and around him; likewise tall plants and flowers of all kinds that exist between Yebu and Senmut, and are there on the east and the west. There is in the midst of the river, covered by water at its annual flood, a place of relaxation for every man who works the stones on its two sides. There is in the river, in front of this town of Yebu, a central elevation of difficult body which is called Crophi. Learn the names of the gods and goddesses of the temple of Khnum: Satis, Anukis, Hapi, Shu, Geb, Nut, Osiris, Horus, Isis, Nephthys. Learn the names of the stones that are there, lying in the borderland: those that are in the east and the west, those [on the shores] of Yebu's canal, those in Yebu, those in the east and west, and those in the river: greywacke, granite, mhtbtb, r'gs, wtsy in the east; prdn in the west; tsy in the west and in the river. The names of the precious stones of the quarries that are in the upper region, some among them at a distance of four iter, are: gold, silver, copper, iron, lapis lazuli, turquoise, thnt, red jasper, k', mnw, emerald, tm-ikr. In addition, nsmt, red ochre, garnet, ibht, bks-'nh, green eye-paint, black eye-paint, carnelia, shrt, mm, and ochre are within this township." When I heard what was there, my heart was guided. Having heard of the flood, [I] opened the wrapped books, made a purification, conducted a procession of the hidden ones, [and] made a complete offering of bread, beer, oxen, and birds, and all good things for the gods and goddesses in Yebu whose names had been pronounced. As I slept in peace, I found the god standing before me. [I] propitiated him by adoring him and praying to him. He revealed himself to me with gracious countenance; he said: "I am Khnum, your maker! My arms are around you, || To steady your body, || To safeguard your limbs. I bestow on you stones on stones, || That were not previously found, || Of which no work was made, || For building temples, || Rebuilding ruins, || Inlaying statues' eyes. For I am the master who makes, || I am he who made himself, || Exalted Nun, who first came forth, || Hapi who hurries at will; Fashioner of everyone, || Guide of each man in his hour, || Tatenen, father of gods, || Great Shu, high in heaven! The shrine I dwell in has two lips, ||

KEY EXTRABIBLICAL REFERENCES

When I open up the well, || I know Hapi hugs the field, || A hug that fills each nose with life, || For when hugged, the field is reborn! I will make Hapi gush for you, || No year of lack and want anywhere, || Plants will grow weighed down by their fruit; With Renutet ordering all, || All things are supplied in millions! I will let your people fill up, || They will grasp together with you! Gone will be the years of hunger, || Ended the dearth in their bins. Egypt's people will come striding, || Shores will shine in the excellent flood, || Hearts will be happier than ever before!"

CHAPTER 3

THE DONATION. I awoke with a racing heart. Freed from fatigue, I made this decree on behalf of my father Khnum. A royal offering to Khnum, lord of the cataract region and chief of Nubia: "In return for what you have done for me, I offer you Manu as western border, Bakhu as eastern border, from Yebu to Kemsat, being twelve iter on the east and the west, consisting of fields and pastures, of the river, and of every place in these miles. All tenants who cultivate the fields, and the vivifiers who irrigate the shores and all the new lands that are in these miles, their harvests will be taken to your granary, in addition to your share which is in Yebu. All fishermen, all hunters, who catch fish and trap birds and all kinds of game, and all who trap lions in the desert—I exact from them one-tenth of the stock of all of these, and [of] all the young animals born of the females in these miles. One will give the branded animals for all burnt offerings and daily sacrifices; and one will give one-tenth of gold, ivory, ebony, carob wood, ochre, carnelian, shrt, diw-plants, nfw-plants, all kinds of timber—all the things brought by the Nubians of Khent-hen-nefer' [to] Egypt, and [by] every man who comes with arrears from them. No officials are to issue orders in these places or take anything from them, for everything is to be protected for your sanctuary. I grant you this domain with [its] stones and good soil. No person there ... anything from it. But the scribes that belong to you and the overseers of the South will dwell there as accountants, listing everything that the kiry-workers, and the smiths, and the master craftsmen, and the goldsmiths, and the ... and the Nubians, and the crew of Apiru, and all corvée labor who fashion the stones, will give of gold, silver, copper, lead, baskets of ... firewood—the things that every man who works with them will give as dues, namely one-tenth of all these. And there will be given one-tenth of the precious stones and quarrying stones that are brought from the mountain side, being the stones of the east. And there will be an overseer who measures the quantities of gold, silver, copper, and genuine precious stones—the things which the sculptors will assign to the gold house [to] fashion the sacred images and to refit the statues that were damaged, and any implements lacking there. Everything will be placed in the storehouse until one fashions anew—when one knows everything that is lacking in your temple, so that it will be as it was in the beginning." Engrave this decree on a stele of the sanctuary in writing, for it happened as stated, [and] on a tablet, so that the divine writings will be on them in the temple twice. He who spits [on it] treacherously will be handed over for punishment. The overseers of the priests and the chief of all the temple personnel will make my name abide in the temple of Khnum-Ra, lord of Yebu, ever-mighty.

ADMONITIONS OF IPUWER

CHAPTER 1

... The door[keepers] say: "Let us go and plunder." The confectioners .... The washerman refuses to carry his load .... The bird[catchers] have drawn up in line of battle .... [The inhabitants] of the Delta carry shields. The brewers ... sad. A man regards his son as his enemy. Confusion ... another. Come and conquer; judge ... what was ordained for you in the time of Horus, in the age [of the Ennead]. The virtuous man goes in mourning because of what has happened in the land ... goes ... the tribes of the desert have become Egyptians everywhere.

Indeed, the face is pale; ... what the ancestors foretold has come to [fruition] ... the land is full of confederates, and a man goes to plow with his shield.

Indeed, the meek say: "[He who is ... of] face is as a nobleman."

Indeed, [the face] is pale; the bowman is ready, wrongdoing is everywhere, and there is no man of yesterday.

Indeed, the plunderer ... everywhere, and the servant takes what he finds.

Indeed, the Nile overflows, yet none plow for it. Everyone says: "We do not know what will happen throughout the land."

Indeed, the women are barren, and none conceive. Khnum no longer fashions [men] because of the condition of the land.

CHAPTER 2

Indeed, poor men have become owners of wealth, and he who could not make sandals for himself is now a possessor of riches.

Indeed, men's slaves, their hearts are sad, and magistrates do not associate with their people when they shout.

Indeed, [hearts] are violent, pestilence is throughout the land, blood is everywhere, death is not lacking, and the mummy-cloth speaks even before one comes near it.

Indeed, many dead are buried in the river; the stream is a tomb, and the place of embalmment has become a stream.

Indeed, noblemen are in distress, while the poor man is full of joy. Every town says: "Let us suppress the powerful among us."

Indeed, men are like ibises. Squalor is throughout the land, and there are indeed none whose clothes are white in these times.

Indeed, the land turns around as does a potter's wheel; the robber is a possessor of riches and [the rich man has become] a plunderer.

Indeed, trusty servants are ... ; the poor man [complains]: "How terrible! What am I to do?"

Indeed, the river is blood, yet men drink of it. Men shrink from human beings and thirst after water.

Indeed, gates, columns, and walls are burned up, while the hall of the palace stands firm and endures.

Indeed, the ship of [the southerners] has broken up, towns are destroyed, and Upper Egypt has become an empty waste.

Indeed, crocodiles [are filled] with the fish they have taken, for men go to them of their own accord; it is the destruction of the land. Men say: "Do not walk here; behold, it is a net." Behold, men tread [the water] like fishes, and the frightened man cannot distinguish it because of terror.

Indeed, men are few, and he who places his brother in the ground is everywhere. When the wise man speaks, [he flees without delay].

Indeed, the nobleman ... through lack of recognition, and the child of his lady has become the son of his maidservant.

CHAPTER 3

Indeed, the desert is throughout the land, the nomes are laid waste, and barbarians from abroad have come to Egypt.

Indeed, men arrive ... and indeed, there are no Egyptians anywhere.

Indeed, gold and lapis lazuli, silver and turquoise, carnelian and amethyst, Ibhet-stone and ... are strung on the necks of maidservants. Good things are throughout the land, [yet] housewives say: "Oh, that we had something to eat!"

Indeed, ... noblewomen. Their bodies are in sad plight by reason of their rags, and their hearts sink when greeting [one another].

Indeed, chests of ebony are broken up, and precious ssndm-wood is cleft asunder in beds ...

Indeed, the builders [of pyramids have become] cultivators, and those who were in the sacred bark are now yoked [to it]. None indeed will sail northward to Byblos today; what will we do for cedar trees for our mummies, and with the produce of which priests are buried and with the oil of which [chiefs] are embalmed as far as Keftiu? They come no more; gold is lacking ... and materials for every kind of craft have come to an end. The ... of the palace is despoiled. How often do people of the oases come with their festival spices, mats, and skins, with fresh rdmt-plants, [and] grease of birds ... ?

Indeed, Elephantine and Thinis [are in the series] of Upper Egypt, [but] without paying taxes owing to civil strife. Lacking are grain, charcoal, irtyw-fruit, mm, 'w-wood, nwt-wood, and brushwood. The work of craftsmen and … are the profit of the palace. To what purpose is a treasury without its revenues? Happy indeed is the heart of the king when truth comes to him! And every foreign land [comes]! That is our fate and that is our happiness! What can we do about it? Everything is a ruin!

Indeed, laughter has perished and is [no longer] made; it is groaning that is throughout the land, mingled with complaints.

CHAPTER 4

Indeed, every dead person is as a nobleman. Those who were Egyptians [have become] foreigners and are thrust aside.

Indeed, hair [has fallen out] for everybody, and the man of rank can no longer be distinguished from him who is nobody.

Indeed, … because of noise; noise is not … in years of noise, and there is no end [of] noise.

Indeed, great and small [say]: "I wish I might die." Little children say: "He should not have caused [me] to live."

Indeed, the children of princes are dashed against walls, and the children of the neck are laid out on the high ground.

Indeed, those who were in the place of embalmment are laid out on the high ground, and the secrets of the embalmers are thrown down because of it.

Indeed, that has perished which yesterday has seen, and the land is left over to its weakness like the cutting of flax.

Indeed, the Delta in its entirety will not be hidden, and Lower Egypt puts trust in trodden roads. What can one do? No … exist anywhere, and men say: "Perdition to the secret place!" Behold, it is in the hands of those who do not know it like those who know it. The desert dwellers are skilled in the crafts of the Delta.

Indeed, citizens are put to the corn-rubbers, and those who used to don fine linen are beaten with …. Those who used to never see the day have gone out unhindered; those who were on their husbands' beds, let them lie on rafts. I say: "It is too heavy for me," concerning rafts bearing myrrh. Load them with vessels filled with … [Let] them know the palanquin. As for the butler: he is ruined. There are no remedies for it; noblewomen suffer like maidservants, minstrels are at the looms within the weaving-rooms, and what they sing to the Songstree-goddess is mourning. Talkers … corn-rubbers.

Indeed, all female slaves are free with their tongues, and when their mistress speaks, it is irksome to the maidservants.

Indeed, trees are felled and branches are stripped off.

CHAPTER 5

I have separated him and his household slaves, and men will say when they hear it: "Cakes are lacking for most children; there is no food … What is the taste of it like today?"

Indeed, magnates are hungry and perishing, followers are followed … because of complaints.

Indeed, the hot-tempered man says: "If I knew where God is, then I would serve Him."

Indeed, [the right] pervades the land in name, but what men do in trusting to it is wrong.

Indeed, runners are fighting over the spoil [of] the robber, and all his property is carried off.

Indeed, all animals, their hearts weep; cattle moan because of the state of the land.

Indeed, the children of princes are dashed against walls, and the children of the neck are laid out on the high ground. Khnum groans because of his weariness.

Indeed, terror kills; the frightened man opposes what is done against your enemies. Moreover, the few are pleased, while the rest are …. Is it by following the crocodile and cleaving it asunder? Is it by slaying the lion roasted on the fire? [Is it] by sprinkling for Ptah and taking … ? Why do you give to him? There is no reaching him. It is misery which you give to him.

Indeed, slaves … throughout the land, and the strong man sends to everyone; a man strikes his maternal brother. What is it that has been done? I speak to a ruined man.

Indeed, the ways are … , the roads are watched; men sit in the bushes until the ignorant traveler comes in order to plunder his burden, and what is on him is taken away. He is beaten with blows of a stick and murdered.

Indeed, that has perished which yesterday has seen, and the land is left over to its weakness like the cutting of flax, commoners coming and going in dissolution …

CHAPTER 6

If only there were an end of men, without conception, without birth! Then the land would be quiet from noise, and tumult [would] be no more.

Indeed, [men eat] pasturage and wash [it] down with water; neither fruit nor pasturage can be found [for] the birds, and … is taken away from the mouth of the pig. No face is bright which you have … for me through hunger.

Indeed, everywhere barley has perished, and men are stripped of clothes, spice, and oil; everyone says: "There is none." The storehouse is empty, and its keeper is stretched on the ground—a happy state of affairs!

Would that I had raised my voice at that moment, that it might have saved me from the pain in which I am [in].

Indeed, the private council-chamber, its writings are taken away and the mysteries which were [in it] are laid bare.

Indeed, magic spells are divulged; smw- and shnw-spells are frustrated because they are remembered by men.

Indeed, public offices are opened, and their inventories are taken away; the serf has become an owner of serfs.

Indeed, [scribes] are killed, and their writings are taken away. Woe is me because of the misery of this time!

Indeed, the writings of the scribes of the cadaster are destroyed, and the corn of Egypt is [now] common property.

Indeed, the laws of the council chamber are thrown out; indeed, men walk on them in public places, and poor men break them up in the streets.

Indeed, the poor man has attained to the state of the Nine Gods, and the former procedure of the House of the Thirty is divulged.

Indeed, the great council-chamber is a popular resort, and poor men come and go to the Great Mansions.

Indeed, the children of magnates are ejected into the streets; the wise man agrees, and the fool says "no," and it is pleasing in the sight of him who knows nothing about it.

Indeed, those who were in the place of embalmment are laid out on the high ground, and the secrets of the embalmers are thrown down because of it.

CHAPTER 7

Behold, the fire has gone up on high, and its burning goes forth against the enemies of the land.

Behold, things have been done which have not happened for a long time past; the king has been deposed by the rabble.

Behold, he who was buried as a falcon [is devoid] of biers, and what the pyramid concealed has become empty.

Behold, it has happened that the land has been deprived of the kingship by a few lawless men.

Behold, men have fallen into rebellion against the Uraeus, the … of Ra, even she who makes the Two Lands content.

Behold, the secret of the land, whose limits were unknown, is divulged, and the Residence is thrown down in a moment.

Behold, Egypt has fallen to [the] pouring of water, and he who poured water on the ground has carried off the strong man in misery.

Behold, the Serpent is taken from its hole, and the secrets of the Kings of Upper and Lower Egypt are divulged.

Behold, the Residence is afraid because of need, and [men go around] unopposed to stir up strife.

Behold, the land has tangled itself up with factions, and the coward takes the brave man's property.

Behold, the Serpent … the dead: he who could not make a sarcophagus for himself is now the possessor of a tomb.

Behold, the possessors of tombs are ejected on to the high ground, while he who

KEY EXTRABIBLICAL REFERENCES

could not make a coffin for himself is now [the possessor] of a treasury.

Behold, this has happened [to] men; he who could not build a room for himself is now a possessor of walls.

Behold, the magistrates of the land are driven out throughout the land: … are driven out from the palaces.

Behold, noblewomen are now on rafts, and magnates are in the labor establishment, while he who could not sleep even on walls is now the possessor of a bed.

Behold, the possessor of wealth now spends the night thirsty, while he who once begged [for] dregs for himself is now the possessor of overflowing bowls.

Behold, the possessors of robes are now in rags, while he who could not weave for himself is now a possessor of fine linen.

Behold, he who could not build a boat for himself is now the possessor of a fleet; their former owner looks at them, but they are not his.

Behold, he who had no shade is now the possessor of shade, while the former possessors of shade are now in the full blast of the storm.

Behold, he who was ignorant of the lyre is now the possessor of a harp, while he who never sang for himself now vaunts the Songstress-goddess.

Behold, those who possessed vessel-stands of copper … not one of the jars thereof has been adorned.

CHAPTER 8

Behold, he who slept wifeless through need [finds] riches, while he whom he never saw stands making dole.

Behold, he who had no property is now a possessor of wealth, and the magnate praises him.

Behold, the poor of the land have become rich, and the [former owner] of property is one who has nothing.

Behold, servants have become masters of butlers, and he who was once a messenger now sends someone else.

Behold, he who had no loaf is now the owner of a barn, and his storehouse is provided with the goods of another.

Behold, he whose hair has fallen out and who had no oil has now become the possessors of jars of sweet myrrh.

Behold, she who had no box is now the owner of a coffer, and she who had to look at her face in the water is now the owner of a mirror.

Behold, ….

Behold, a man is happy eating his food. Consume your goods in gladness and unhindered, for it is good for a man to eat his food; God commands it for him whom He has favored….

[[Behold, he who did not know]] his god now offers to him with incense of another [who is] not known [to him].

[[Behold,]] great ladies, once possessors of riches, now give their children for beds.

Behold, a man [to whom is given] a noble lady as wife, her father protects him, and he who has not … killing him.

Behold, the children of magistrates are … [the calves] of cattle [are given over] to the plunderers.

Behold, priests transgress with the cattle of the poor …

Behold, he who could not slaughter for himself now slaughters bulls, and he who did not know how to carve now sees …

Behold, priests transgress with geese, which are given [to] the gods instead of oxen.

Behold, maidservants … offer ducks; noblewomen ….

Behold, noblewomen flee; the overseers of … and their [children] are cast down through fear of death.

[[Behold,]] the chiefs of the land flee; there is no purpose for them because of need. The lord of …

CHAPTER 9

[[Behold,]] those who once owned beds are now on the ground, while he who once slept in squalor now lays out a skin-mat for himself.

Behold, noblewomen go hungry, while the priests are sated with what has been prepared for them.

Behold, no offices are in their right place, like a herd running at random without a herdsman.

Behold, cattle stray and there is none to collect them, but everyone fetches for himself those that are branded with his name.

Behold, a man is slain beside his brother, who runs away and abandons him to save his own skin.

Behold, he who had no yoke of oxen is now the owner of a herd, and he who could find for himself no plowman is now the owner of cattle.

Behold, he who had no grain is now the owner of granaries, and he who had to fetch loan-corn for himself is now one who issues it.

Behold, he who had no dependents is now an owner of serfs, and he who was [a magnate] now performs his own errands.

Behold, the strong men of the land, the condition of the people is not reported [to them]. Everything is ruin!

Behold, no craftsmen work, for the enemies of the land have impoverished its craftsmen.

[[Behold, he who once recorded]] the harvest now knows nothing about it, while he who never plowed [[for himself is now the owner of corn; the reaping]] takes place but is not reported. The scribe [sits in his office], but his hands [are idle] in it.

Destroyed is … in that time, and a man looks [on his friend as] an adversary. The sick man brings coolness [to what is hot] … fear …. Poor men … [the land] is not bright because of it.

CHAPTER 10

Destroyed is … their food is taken from them … [through] fear of his terror. The commoner begs … messenger, but not … time. He is captured laden with goods and [all his property] is taken away…. men pass by his door … the outside of the wall, a shed, and rooms containing falcons. It is the common man who will be vigilant, the day having dawned on him without his dreading it. Men run because of … [for] the temple of the head, strained through a woven cloth within the house. What they make are tents, just like the desert people.

Destroyed is the doing of that for which men are sent by retainers in the service of their masters; they have no readiness. Behold, they are five men, and they say: "Go on the road you know, for we have arrived."

Lower Egypt weeps; the king's storehouse is the common property of everyone, and the entire palace is without its revenues. To it belong emmer and barley, birds and fish; to it belong white cloth and fine linen, copper and oil; to it belong carpet and mat, … flowers, and wheat-sheaf, and all good revenues …. If the … it in the palace were delayed, men would be devoid [of] ….

Destroy the enemies of the august Residence, splendid of magistrates … in it like … ; indeed, the governor of the city goes unescorted.

Destroy [the enemies of the august Residence,] splendid …

[[Destroy the enemies of]] that former august Residence, manifold of laws …

[[Destroy the enemies of]] that former august [[Residence]] ….

Destroy the enemies of that former august Residence … none can stand …

Destroy the enemies of that former august Residence, manifold of offices; indeed …

Remember to immerse … him who is in pain when he is sick in his body; show respect … because of his god that he may guard the utterance … his children who are witnesses of the surging of the flood.

CHAPTER 11

Remember to … shrine, to fumigate with incense, and to offer water in a jar in the early morning.

Remember [to bring] fat r-geese, trp-geese, and ducks and to offer [the] god's offerings to the gods.

Remember to chew natron and to prepare white bread; a man [should do it] on the day of wetting the head.

Remember to erect flagstaffs and to carve offering stones—the priest cleansing the chapels, and the temple being plastered [white] like milk; to make pleasant the odor of the horizon and to provide bread-offerings.

Remember to observe regulations, to fix dates correctly, and to remove him who enters on the priestly office in impurity of body, for that is doing it wrongfully, it is destruction of the heart … the day which

KEY EXTRABIBLICAL REFERENCES

precedes eternity, the months … years are known.

Remember to slaughter oxen …

Remember to go forth purged … who calls to you; to put r-geese on the fire … to open the jar … the shore of the waters … of women … clothing … to give praise … in order to appease you.

… lack of people; come … Ra who commands … worshiping him … West until … are diminished …

Behold, why does he seek to fashion [men] … ? The frightened man is not distinguished from the violent one.

CHAPTER 12
He brings coolness on heat; men say: "He is the herdsman of mankind, and there is no evil in his heart." Though his herds are few, yet he spends a [whole] day to collect them—their hearts being on fire. If only he had perceived their nature in the first generation! Then he would have imposed obstacles, he would have stretched out his arm against them, he would have destroyed their herds and their heritage. Men desire the giving of birth, but sadness follows, with needy people on all sides. So it is, and it will not pass away while the gods who are in the midst of it exist. Seed goes forth into mortal women, but none are found on the road. Combat has gone forth, and he who should be a redresser of evils is one who commits them; neither do men act as pilot in their hour of duty. Where is he today? Is he asleep? Behold, his power is not seen. If we had been fed, I would not have found you, I would not have been summoned in vain: "Aggression against it means pain of heart" is a saying on the lips of everyone. Today he who is afraid … a myriad of people; … did not see … against the enemies of … at his outer chamber; who enter the temple … weeping for him … that one who confounds what he has said … The land has not fallen … the statues are burned and their tombs destroyed … he sees the day of …. He who could not make for himself … between sky and ground is afraid of everyone…. if he does it … what you dislike taking. Authority, knowledge, and truth are with you, yet confusion is what you set throughout the land—also the noise of tumult. Behold, one deals harm to another, for men conform to what you have commanded. If three men travel on the road, they are found to be only two, for the many kill the few.

CHAPTER 13
Does a herdsman desire death? Then may you command reply to be made, because it means that one loves [that] another detests; it means that their existences are few everywhere; it means that you have acted so as to bring those things to pass. You have told lies, and the land is a weed which destroys men, and none can count on life. All these years are strife, and a man is murdered on his housetop even though he was vigilant in his gate lodge. Is he brave and saves himself? It means he will live.

When men send a servant for humble folk, he goes on the road until he sees the flood; the road is washed out and he stands worried. What is on him is taken away; he is beaten with blows of a stick and wrongfully slain. Oh, that you could taste a little of the misery of it! Then you would say … from someone else as a wall, over and above … hot … years ….

[[It is indeed good]] when ships fare upstream … robbing them. It is indeed good ….

[[It is indeed]] good when the net is drawn in and birds are tied up ….

It is [[indeed]] good … dignities for them, and the roads are passable.

It is indeed good when the hands of men build pyramids, when ponds are dug and plantations of the trees of the gods are made.

It is indeed good when men are drunk; they drink myt and their hearts are happy.

CHAPTER 14
It is indeed good when shouting is in men's mouths, when the magnates of districts stand looking on at the shouting in their houses, clad in a cloak, cleansed in front and well-provided within.

It is indeed good when beds are prepared, and the headrests of magistrates are safely secured. Every man's need is satisfied with a couch in the shade, and a door is now shut on him who once slept in the bushes.

It is indeed good when fine linen is spread out on New Year's Day … on the bank; when fine linen is spread out, and cloaks are on the ground. The overseer of … the trees, the poor … in their midst like Asians …. Men … the state thereof; they have come to an end of themselves; none can be found to stand up and protect themselves …. Everyone fights for his sister and saves his own skin. Is it Nubians? Then will we guard ourselves; warriors are made many in order to ward off foreigners. Is it Libyans? Then we will turn away. The Medjay are pleased with Egypt.

CHAPTER 15
How does it come to pass that every man kills his brother? The troops whom we marshaled for ourselves have turned into foreigners and have taken to ravaging. What has come to pass through it is informing the Asians of the state of the land; all the desert folk are possessed with the fear of it. What the masses have tasted … without giving Egypt over [to] the sand. It is strong … speak about you after years … devastate itself, it is the threshing floor which nourishes their houses … to nourish his children … said by the troops … fish … gum, lotus leaves … excess of food.

CHAPTER 16
What Ipuwer said when he addressed the Majesty of the Lord of All: … all herds. It means that ignorance of it is what is pleasing to the heart. You have done what was good in their hearts, and you have nourished the people with it. They cover their faces through fear of the next day. That is how a man grows old before he dies, while his son is a youth of understanding; he does not open [his] mouth to speak to you, but you seize him in the doom of death … weep … go … after you, that the land may be … on every side.

CHAPTER 17
If men call to … weep … them, who break into the tombs and burn the statues … the corpses of the nobles … of directing work.

TEL DAN STELE

… and cut …
… my father went up [[against him
    when h]]e fought at …
and my father lay down,
    he went to his [[ancestors]].
And the king of Israel
entered previously in my father's land,
    [and] Hadad made me king,
And Hadad went in front of me,
    [and] I departed from the seven …
… of my kingdom,
    and I slew [[seve]]nty kin[[gs]], who
        harnessed th[[ousands of cha]]riots
and thousands of horsemen [[or horses]].
    [[I killed Jeho]]ram son [[of Ahab]],
king of Israel, and [I] killed [[Ahaz]]iah
    son of [[Jehoram]],
[[king]] of the House of David,
    and I set [[their towns into ruins
        and turned]]
their land into [[desolation]]
… other … [[and Jehu ru]]led
over Is[[rael and I laid]]
slege on …

MERNEPTAH STELE

The princes are prostrate, saying, "Peace!"
Not [even] one raises his head
    among the Nine Bows.
Desolation is for Libya;
Hatti is pacified;
Canaan is plundered with every calamity;
Ashkelon is carried away;
Gezer is seized;
Yanoam is made non-existent;
Israel is laid waste—its seed is no more;
Kharru has become a widow
    because of Egypt.
All lands, together, are pacified.
Everyone who was restless
    has been restrained.

MESHA STELE

I am Mesha, son of Chemosh-Gad, king of Moab, the Dibonite. My father reigned over Moab [for] thirty years, and I have reigned after my father. And I have built this sanctuary for Chemosh in Karchah, a sanctuary of salvation, for he saved me from all aggressors

KEY EXTRABIBLICAL REFERENCES

and made me look on all my enemies with contempt.

Omri was king of Israel and oppressed Moab during many days, and Chemosh was angry with his aggressions. His son succeeded him, and he also said, "I will oppress Moab." In my days he said, "Let us go, and I will see my desire on him and his house," and Israel said, "I will destroy it forever." Now Omri took the land of Madeba and occupied it in his day, and in the days of his son, forty years. And Chemosh had mercy on it in my time. And I built Baal-Meon and made therein the ditch, and I built Kiriathaim.

And the men of Gad dwelled in the country of Ataroth from ancient times, and the king of Israel fortified Ataroth. I assaulted the wall, and captured it, and killed all the warriors of the city for the satisfaction of Chemosh and Moab, and I removed from it all the spoil, and offered it before Chemosh in Kirjath; and I placed therein the men of Siran, and the men of Mochrath. And Chemosh said to me, "Go, take Nebo against Israel," and I went in the night, and I fought against it from the break of day until noon, and I took it; and I killed in all seven thousand men…women and maidens, for I devoted them to Ashtar-Chemosh; and I took from it the vessels of YHWH, and offered them before Chemosh.

And the king of Israel fortified Jahaz, and occupied it, when he made war against me, and Chemosh drove him out before me, and I took from Moab two hundred men in all, and placed them in Jahaz, and took it to annex it to Dibon.

I built Karchah, the wall of the forest, and the wall of the Hill. I have built its gates, and I have built its towers. I have built the palace of the king, and I made the prisons for the criminals within the wall. And there were no wells in the interior of the wall in Karchah. And I said to all the people, "Make, every man, a well in his house." And I dug the ditch for Karchah with the chosen men of Israel. I built Aroer, and I made the road across the Arnon. I built Beth-Bamoth, for it was destroyed. I built Bezer, for it was cut down by the armed men of Daybon, for all Daybon was now loyal; and I reigned from Bikran, which I added to my land. And I built Beth-Gamul, and Beth-Diblathaim … Beth-Baal-Meon, and I placed the poor people of the land there.

And as for Horonaim, the men of Edom dwelt therein, on the descent from old. And Chemosh said to me, "Go down, make war against Horonaim, and take it." And I assaulted it, and I took it, for Chemosh restored it in my days. Wherefore I made … year…and I…

KURKH MONOLITHS

610. In the year of Dâian-Assur, in the month of Airu, the fourteenth day, I departed from Nineveh, crossed the Tigris, and drew near to the cities of Giammu, [near] the Balih River. At the fearfulness of my sovereignty, the terror of my frightful weapons, they became afraid; with their own weapons his nobles killed Giammu. I entered into Kitlala and Til-sha-mâr-ahi. I had my gods brought into his palaces. In his palaces I spread a banquet. I opened his treasury. I saw his wealth. His goods, his property, I carried off and brought to my city [of] Assur. I departed from Kitlala. I drew near to Kâr-Shalmaneser. In [goat-]skin boats I crossed the Euphrates the second time, at its flood. The tribute of the kings on that side of the Euphrates—of Sangara of Carchemish, of Kundashpi of Kumuhu, of Arame son of Gûzi, of Lalli the Milidean, of Haiani son of Gahari, of Kalparoda of Hattina, of Kalparuda of Gurgum—silver, gold, lead, copper, vessels of copper, at Ina-Assur-uttir-asbat, on that side of the Euphrates, on the river Sagur, which the people of Hatti call Pitru, there I received [it]. From the Euphrates I departed, I drew near to Halman [(Aleppo)]. They were afraid to fight with [me]; they seized my feet. I received silver [and] gold as their tribute. I offered sacrifices before the god Adad of Halman. From Halman I departed. To the cities of Irhulêni, the Hamathite, I drew near. The cities of Adennu, Bargâ, Arganâ, his royal cities, I captured. His spoil, his property, the goods of his palaces, I brought out. I set fire to his palaces. I departed from Argana. I drew near to Karkar.

611. Karkar, his royal city, I destroyed, I devastated, I burned with fire. One thousand two hundred chariots, one thousand two hundred cavalry, twenty thousand soldiers, of Hadadezer of Aram; seven hundred chariots, seven hundred cavalry, ten thousand soldiers of Irhulêni of Hamath; two thousand chariots, ten thousand soldiers of Ahab the Israelite; five hundred soldiers of the Gueans; one thousand soldiers of the Musreans; ten chariots, ten thousand soldiers of the Irkanateans; two hundred soldiers of Matinuba'il the Arvadite; two hundred soldiers of the Usanateans; thirty chariots, … soldiers of Adunu-Ba'il the Shianean; one thousand camels of Gindibu' the Arabian; … soldiers [of] Ba'sa, son of Ruhubi, the Ammonite. These twelve kings he brought to his support, to provide battle and fight, they came against me. [Trusting] in the exalted might which Assur, the lord, had given [me], in the mighty weapons, which Nergal, who goes before me, had presented [to me], I battled with them. From Karkar, as far as the city of Gilzau, I routed them. Fourteen thousand of their warriors I slew with the sword. Like Adad, I rained destruction on them. I scattered their corpses far and wide, [and] filled the face of the desolate plain with their widespread armies. With [my] weapons I made their blood flow down the valleys of the land. The plain was too small to let their bodies fall; the wide countryside was expended in burying them. With their bodies I spanned the Arantu as with a bridge. In that battle I took from them their chariots, their cavalry, their horses, broken to the yoke.

MARA BAR SERAPION ON JESUS

What else can we say, when the wise are forcibly dragged off by tyrants, their wisdom is captured by insults, and their minds are oppressed and without defense? What advantage did the Athenians gain from murdering Socrates? Famine and plague came on them as a punishment for their crime. What advantage did the men of Samos gain from burning Pythagoras? In a moment their land was covered with sand. What advantage did the Jews gain from executing their wise King? It was just after that their kingdom was abolished. God justly avenged these three wise men: the Athenians died of hunger; the Samians were overwhelmed by the sea; and the Jews, desolate and driven from their own kingdom, live in complete dispersion. But Socrates is not dead, because of Plato; neither is Pythagoras, because of the statue of Juno; nor is the wise King, because of the "new law" He laid down.

PLINY THE YOUNGER ON CHRISTIANS

It is my practice, my lord, to refer to you all matters concerning which I am in doubt. For who can better give guidance to my hesitation or inform my ignorance? I have never participated in trials of Christians. Therefore, I do not know what offenses it is the practice to punish or investigate, and to what extent. And I have been not a little hesitant as to whether there should be any distinction on account of age or no difference between the very young and the more mature; whether pardon is to be granted for conversion, or, if a man has [ever] once been a Christian, it does him no good to have ceased to be one; whether the name itself, even without offenses, or only the offenses associated with the name are to be punished. Meanwhile, in the case of those who were denounced to me as Christians, I have observed the following procedure: I interrogated these as to whether they were Christians; those who confessed, I interrogated a second and a third time, threatening them with punishment; those who persisted, I ordered executed. For I had no doubt that, whatever the nature of their creed, stubbornness and unyielding obstinacy surely deserve to be punished. There were others possessed of the same folly, but because they were Roman citizens, I signed an order for them to be transferred to Rome. Soon accusations spread, as usually happens, because of the proceedings occurring, and several incidents ensued. An anonymous

KEY EXTRABIBLICAL REFERENCES

document was published containing the names of many persons. Those who denied that they were or had been Christians, when they invoked the gods in words dictated by me, offered prayer with incense and wine to your image, which I had ordered to be brought for this purpose together with statues of the gods, and moreover cursed Christ (none of which those who are really Christians, it is said, can be forced to do). I thought these should be discharged. Others named by the informer declared that they were Christians, but then denied it, asserting that they had been [before], but had [since] ceased to be, some three years before, others many years, some as much as twenty-five years. They all worshiped your image and the statues of the gods, and cursed Christ. They asserted, however, that the sum and substance of their fault or error had been that they were accustomed to meet on a fixed day before dawn and sing responsively a hymn to Christ as to a god, and to bind themselves by oath, not to some crime, but not to commit fraud, theft, or adultery, not falsify their trust, nor to refuse to return a trust when called on to do so. When this was over, it was their custom to depart and to assemble again to partake of food—but ordinary and innocent food. Even this, they affirmed, they had ceased to do after my edict by which, in accordance with your instructions, I had forbidden political associations. Accordingly, I judged it all the more necessary to find out what the truth was by torturing two female slaves who were called deaconesses. But I discovered nothing else but depraved, excessive superstition. Therefore, I postponed the investigation and hurried to consult you. For the matter seemed to me to warrant consulting you, especially because of the number involved. For many persons of every age, every rank, and also of both sexes are and will be endangered. For the contagion of this superstition has spread not only to the cities, but also to the villages and farms. But it seems possible to check and cure it. It is certainly quite clear that the temples, which had been almost deserted, have begun to be frequented, that the established religious rites, long neglected, are being resumed, and that from everywhere sacrificial animals are coming, for which until now very few purchasers could be found. Hence it is easy to imagine what a multitude of people can be reformed if an opportunity for conversion is offered.

TRAJAN'S REPLY TO PLINY

You observed proper procedure, my dear Pliny, in sifting the cases of those who had been denounced to you as Christians. For it is not possible to lay down any general rule to serve as a kind of fixed standard. They are not to be sought out; if they are denounced and proved guilty, they are to be punished, with this reservation: that whoever denies that he is a Christian and really proves it—that is, by worshiping our gods—even though he was under suspicion in the past, will obtain pardon through conversion. But anonymously posted accusations should have no place in any prosecution. For this is both a dangerous kind of precedent and out of step with the spirit of our age.

TACITUS ON CHRISTIANS

But all human efforts, all the lavish gifts of the emperor, and the propitiations of the gods, did not banish the sinister belief that the fire was the result of [Nero's own] order. Consequently, to get rid of the report, Nero fastened the guilt and inflicted the most exquisite tortures on a class hated for their abominations, called Christians by the populace. Christ, from whom the Name had its origin, suffered the extreme penalty during the reign of Tiberius at the hands of one of our procurators, Pontius Pilatus, and a most troublesome superstition, thus checked for the moment, again broke out not only in Judea, the first source of the evil, but even in Rome, where all things hideous and shameful from every part of the world find their center and become popular. Accordingly, an arrest was first made of all who pleaded guilty; then, on their information, an immense multitude was convicted, not so much of the crime of burning the city, as of hatred against mankind. Mockery of every sort was added to their deaths. Covered with the skins of beasts, they were torn by dogs and perished, or were nailed to crosses, or were doomed to the flames and burnt, to serve as a nightly illumination, when daylight had expired. Nero offered his gardens for the spectacle, and was exhibiting a show in the circus, while he mingled with the people in the dress of a charioteer or stood aloft on a car. Hence, even for criminals who deserved extreme and exemplary punishment, there arose a feeling of compassion [for the Christians]; for it was not, as it seemed, for the public good, but to satiate one man's cruelty, that they were being destroyed.

SUETONIUS ON CHRISTIANS

Since the Jews constantly made disturbances at the instigation of Christ, [Claudius] expelled them from Rome. ... During [Nero's] reign, many abuses were severely punished and put down, and no fewer new laws were made: a limit was set to expenditures; the public banquets were confined to a distribution of food; the sale of any kind of cooked items in the taverns was forbidden, with the exception of pulse and vegetables, whereas before every sort of delicacy was exposed for sale. Punishment was inflicted on the Christians, a class of men given to a new and troublesome superstition. He put an end to the diversions of the chariot drivers, who from immunity of long standing claimed the right of ranging at large and amusing themselves by cheating and robbing the people. The pantomimic actors and their partisans were banished from the city.

PHLEGON OF TRALLES

FRAGMENT 1
Jesus, while alive, was of no assistance to Himself, but that He arose after death, and exhibited the marks of His punishment, and showed how His hands had been pierced by nails.

FRAGMENT 2
In the fourth year, however, of Olympiad 202, an eclipse of the sun happened, greater and more excellent than any that had happened before it; at the sixth hour, day turned into dark night, so that the stars were seen in the sky, and an earthquake in Bithynia toppled many buildings of the city of Nicaea.

1082

With your purchase of

the *All-In-One Holy Bible with Apocrypha*,

in addition to these 300 print books, you have gained access to

THE EXPANDED DIGITAL LIBRARY

Thousands of additional Judeo-Christian books with easy navigation

STEP 1
SCAN THE QR CODE BELOW AND FOLLOW THE LINK, OR TYPE IN THE URL PROVIDED:

(https://www.lsvbible.com/p/all-in-one-holy-bible-with-apocrypha.html)

STEP 2
ENTER YOUR EXCLUSIVE ACCESS CODE (INCLUDE DASHES EXACTLY AS SHOWN BELOW):

7773-3339-9237-0731

ISSUES WITH YOUR KEY?

EMAIL COVENANTPRESS@CCC.ONE FOR ALTERNATIVE VERIFICATION

STEP 3
DOWNLOAD THE *EXPANDED DIGITAL LIBRARY* CONTENT TO ANY DEVICE

NOTE: FOR INDIVIDUAL, PERSONAL USE ONLY. LIMITED TO 5 DEVICES.

KEEP YOUR KEY IN A SAFE PLACE AND FOLLOW COVENANT PRESS FOR ADDITIONAL FUTURE CONTENT INCLUDED WITH YOUR PURCHASE.

APPENDIX
Additional writings, resources, and maps

ABOUT THE BIBLE

The Bible is a written record of God's revelations to mankind. As originally transcribed by the Spirit-led men who recorded these revelations, it is completely inerrant—a perfect record of history, science, and spiritual truth. The theme of the Bible regards the fall of human beings into spiritual death in the Garden of Eden and God's plan to redeem them through a substitutionary sacrifice. This promised "Seed," born of woman, would crush the head of the serpent—the Devil—and free those who trust in God from death and the penalty and power of sin. In the Hebrew Bible, which Christians call the *Old Testament*, the Seed is prophesied to be the Messiah, or "Anointed One" of God, who would inherit the throne of His ancestor David and save believers from their sins. In the Greek portion of the Bible, called the *New Testament*, the Messiah is revealed to be God's only begotten Son, the Lord Jesus Christ. Jesus the Messiah lived a sinless life and took upon Himself the sins of all on the Cross. He was crucified, buried in a tomb, and on the third day He came back to life. Hundreds of His disciples witnessed Him risen from the dead and many went on to give their lives in martyrdom, testifying to the truth of forgiveness of sins in Christ alone, and the promise that all who trust in Him will be resurrected to inherit eternal life in union with God. In accordance with the Scriptures, the Lord Jesus will return to earth one day to restore the Kingdom to Israel and to reign over all the nations of the world. Preceding this event, believers are promised to be transformed into immortal bodies, being taken to Heaven to escape the coming wrath.

Languages of the Bible:	Hebrew, Aramaic, and Greek	Most of the Old Testament was originally composed in Hebrew, although some scholars argue a nearly equal portion was composed in Aramaic. At minimum, large portions of Daniel and Ezra were written in Aramaic. It is thought that all of the New Testament was written in Greek with strong Hebrew and Aramaic influences.
Dates of composition:	Circa 15th century BC through the end of the 1st century AD	It is traditionally thought that Moses transcribed the first five books, called the *Torah* or *Pentateuch*. The Apostle John is believed to be the author of some of the latest books of the New Testament, including the Gospel of John and Revelation, which were written toward the end of the 1st century.
Number of canonical books:	66	There have been varying schools of thought as to what constitutes the full canon of Scripture, but among Christian scholars there is widespread consensus that the 66 books found in most versions constitute the unquestionable Protocanon. Other books, called the Deuterocanon, are sometimes included.

LANGUAGES OF THE BIBLE

HEBREW: The language of most of the Old Testament, Hebrew is a Northwest Semitic language and a regional dialect of the Canaanite languages. It was natively spoken by the ancient Israelites and remained in regular use as a first language until after AD 200 and as the liturgical language of Judaism and Samaritanism. Hebrew was revived as a spoken language in the 19th century and is the only successful largescale example of linguistic revival. It is the only Canaanite language still spoken today, and in 2018, Hebrew became the official language of Israel. The original Hebrew writings were recorded in Paleo-Hebrew (shown below), a script almost indistinguishable from Phoenician and other regional Canaanite dialects. It was slowly replaced with the better-known square script, derived from Aramaic, but found some continued usage in Judea even into the 1st century BC. A variation still lives on among the Samaritans and is found in the Samaritan Pentateuch.

Alef (1)	Beyt (2)	Gimel (3)	Dalet (4)	He (5)	Waw (6)	Zayin (7)	Chet (8)	Tet (9)	Yod (10)	Kaf (20)
Lamed (30)	Mem (40)	Nun (50)	Samekh (60)	Ayin (70)	Pe (80)	Tsade (90)	Qof (100)	Resh (200)	Shin (300)	Taw (400)

By the 5th century BC, Paleo-Hebrew script was largely replaced with the Aramaic alphabet, which evolved in the Hebrew context to eventually become the well-known square Hebrew script of the Masoretic Text of the Bible and Modern Hebrew (shown below).

Alef (1)	Beyt (2)	Gimel (3)	Dalet (4)	He (5)	Waw (6)	Zayin (7)	Chet (8)	Tet (9)	Yod (10)	Kaf (20)
Lamed (30)	Mem (40)	Nun (50)	Samekh (60)	Ayin (70)	Pe (80)	Tsade (90)	Qof (100)	Resh (200)	Shin (300)	Taw (400)

ARAMAIC: Aramaic is a Northwest Semitic language, closely related to Hebrew, that originated in the ancient region of Syria and quickly spread to Mesopotamia, the southern Levant, southeastern Anatolia, eastern Arabia, and the Sinai Peninsula, where it has been continually written and spoken in different varieties for over 3,000 years. Small portions of the Old Testament (primarily in Daniel and Ezra) were written in Imperial Aramaic, the script of which is shown below; however, the Masoretic Text of the Hebrew Bible utilizes the square Hebrew script, even in these Aramaic passages.

Alef (1)	Beyt (2)	Gimel (3)	Dalet (4)	He (5)	Waw (6)	Zayin (7)	Chet (8)	Tet (9)	Yod (10)	Kaf (20)
Lamed (30)	Mem (40)	Nun (50)	Samekh (60)	Ayin (70)	Pe (80)	Tsade (90)	Qof (100)	Resh (200)	Shin (300)	Taw (400)

GREEK: Greek is an Indo-European language, constituting an independent Hellenic branch within the Indo-European language family. It is native to Greece, Cyprus, Italy (in Calabria and Salento), southern Albania, and other regions of the Balkans, Caucasus, the Black Sea coast, Asia Minor, and the eastern Mediterranean. It has the longest documented history of any Indo-European language, spanning at least 3,400 years of written records. Its writing system is the Greek alphabet, which has been used for approximately 2,800 years. The Old Testament was translated from Hebrew to Greek in the 3rd and 2nd centuries BC, and most or all of the New Testament was originally composed in Koine Greek, the lingua franca of the Mediterranean region and common dialect of Greek written and spoken during the Hellenistic period. Like Hebrew, Greek letters signified numbers, but the numbers 6 and 90 were denoted by the obsolete letters digamma and koppa, respectively.

Αα Alpha (1)	Ββ Beta (2)	Γγ Gamma (3)	Δδ Delta (4)	Εε Epsilon (5)	Ζζ Zeta (7)	Ηη Eta (8)	Θθ Theta (9)	Ιι Iota (10)	Κκ Kappa (20)	Λλ Lambda (30)	Μμ Mu (40)
Νν Nu (50)	Ξξ Xi (60)	Οο Omicron (70)	Ππ Pi (80)	Ρρ Rho (100)	Σσς Sigma (200)	Ττ Tau (300)	Υυ Upsilon (400)	Φφ Phi (500)	Χχ Chi (600)	Ψψ Psi (700)	Ωω Omega (800)

BEFORE THERE WAS TIME

Why do things exist? Where did the universe come from? Is it just part of an endless cycle of compressions and expansions, without real cause or origin? Did it simply appear out of the void of nothingness? Is it merely one of a virtually infinite number of universes bubbling out of an all-encompassing multiverse as posited by many string theorists? And what, if anything, existed *before* the universe came into being?

Mankind has developed a myriad of theories regarding origins and who or what existed before time—if "before" can even be used to describe *a time without time*. According to the Bible, it is **God** who existed before the creation of the world:

> *"Before mountains were brought forth, || And You form the earth and the world, || Even from age to age You [are] God." (Ps. 90:2)*

And He Himself was created by no one:

> *"You [are] My witnesses, a declaration of Y<small>HWH</small>, || And My servant whom I have chosen, || So that you know and give credence to Me, || And understand that I [am] He, || Before Me there was no God formed, || And after Me there is none." (Isa. 43:10)*

And again:

> *"Thus said Y<small>HWH</small>, King of Israel, || And his Redeemer, Y<small>HWH</small> of Hosts: 'I [am] the first, and I [am] the last, || And besides Me there is no God.'" (Isa. 44:6)*

THE UNMOVED MOVER

We can plainly see that things exist, and things cannot come from true nothingness. There must be something (or *someone*) that brought visible and invisible things into existence. This is what we call **the cosmological argument**. The original and ultimate cause of all things must necessarily be transcendent and self-existent or else it would itself have been created and there would be an eternal procession of created things causing created things, which is a logical impossibility.

This bedrock truth of an "unmoved mover"—*as Aristotle coined it*—has been one of the fundamentals of philosophy, in one form or another, throughout all of human history and was promulgated not only by Judeo-Christianity and the Abrahamic traditions, but also by the ancient Greeks, Romans, and Arabs, and is even acceded to by modern scientific philosophers who posit the existence of an eternal, self-existent, all-encompassing dimension that might have given rise to our universe. Secular philosophers acknowledge the logical necessity for there to be something that is itself uncreated and ungenerated, and that this self-existent entity contains all possible information, energy, and dimension. Whether they call it "the Multiverse," "the 11th Dimension," "the 26th Dimension," or some other permutation thereof, the secular mind still chooses to regard it as unintelligent and unaware, but that is folly. The "unmoved mover" has the same attributes as the God of the Bible, but these attributes are often described using terminology more at home in metaphysics than in theology (e.g., unlimited energy vs. omnipotence; all possible information vs. omniscience; boundless infinity vs. omnipresence).

OTHER LOGICAL ARGUMENTS FOR GOD

The Ontological Argument: God is the greatest conceivable being and it is greater to exist than not to exist, thus God must necessarily exist or else He would not be the greatest conceivable being. In this way, the existence of the supreme, self-existent being can be deduced through reason and intellect alone.

The Teleological Argument: It is beyond improbable for non-life to give rise to life because of the incomprehensible complexity of living things. Considering that the universe appears perfectly and improbably tailored for the existence of life, there must necessarily be a super-intelligence that created the universe with the perfect parameters for life who then created incomprehensibly complex lifeforms.

Common rebuttals to this argument simply skirt the issue. For instance, the multiverse hypothesis proposes a virtually infinite number of universes, so that there will eventually be some small fraction that have the right parameters for life, but as explained in the previous section, the all-encompassing dimension would itself be the unmoved mover ("God" by another name). *Panspermia*, the theory that life was simply seeded on earth via extraterrestrials or inadvertently planted here by hitching a ride on space dust or an asteroid, is simply moving the goalpost. No longer does one have to explain how impossibly-complex life arose on earth—now they must explain how impossibly-complex life arose somewhere else in the universe.

Abstract Ideas and Truths: We can perceive the universality of spiritual truths such as beauty, morality, and love, and that such things cannot be adequately explained through mere natural mechanisms. The origin of these obvious, yet abstract concepts must be a being who is Himself beautiful, moral, and loving.

In conclusion, all belief systems aside from monotheism, such as atheism, polytheism, and pantheism, disregard these basic and most fundamental truths of common sense and simple logic. Given the logical necessity for the existence of God, the ultimate truth and purpose of life must be found in believing in and worshiping this transcendent God who created all things and who has chosen to reveal Himself to us through means of reason, creation, and spiritual revelation.

WHICH GOD?

Concluding that God must exist, we can discern which God must be followed and believed in. There are many religious texts that claim to reveal the true God and there are many people who have claimed to either be God or to know God, but only one text withstands all scrutiny and only one person's claim to be God passes muster.

Judeo-Christianity predates every other contemporary religion, beginning in the 20th century BC when Abram heeded God's call to migrate to Canaan. His monotheistic faith not only set the stage for the Bible to be written, but also for the coming of the *Messiah* (the Redeemer of mankind). Judaism proper—adherence to the Law of Moses—came about in the 15th century BC when the Israelites escaped Egypt and their earthly leader Moses received God's instructions (the first five books of the Bible, called the *Torah* or *Pentateuch*). All other modern religions developed later: Hinduism circa 1000–500 BC, Zoroastrianism circa 600 BC, Buddhism in the 5th century BC, Taoism in the 4th century BC, and Islam in the 6th or 7th century AD. Judeo-Christianity preceded all of these by at least 500 years.

Some might argue that Christianity was not established until AD 30 to 33 when Jesus of Nazareth was crucified, and, according to His disciples, rose from the dead and subsequently ascended into Heaven. This is why we use the term *Judeo-Christianity*. The central theme in all of the ancient Hebrew religious texts is the belief in a coming Messiah who would redeem God's people. This Anointed One (called *Christ* in Greek or *Messiah* in Hebrew) would fulfill the Law, Psalms, and Prophets, save the lost, and establish an everlasting Kingdom. The very first prophecy given in the Bible is about Him (Gen. 3:15) and the Old Testament (called the *Tanakh* in Judaism) is replete with descriptions about Him and what He would do and accomplish (e.g., Deut. 18:14–22; Job 19:25; Ps. 2; Ps. 22; Isa. 9:1–7; Is. 53; Zech. 12:10–14; 14:3–4). The Old Testament is about Christ and His people the Israelites. It is proto-Christianity in the truest sense.

The root of monotheism and religion itself is Judeo-Christianity. Common religious concepts like *God, worship, ritual, faith, forgiveness, grace*, and *redemption* all stem from the Bible and the revelations contained therein. All other religions are corrupted and twisted imitations—counterfeits of the original.

In secular circles it is common to speak collectively of books like the Bible, Koran, and Bhagavad Gita as "sacred texts" or "holy books," but the terms are inaccurate and cause confusion. By very definition the terms equate all truth claims and neglect objectivity. Each of these books contain numerous mutually exclusive tenets and statements that are presented as facts. Not all are true and not all are holy. For example, the Bible repeatedly claims that Yahweh is the **only** God (e.g., Deut. 4:35, 39; 6:4; 32:39; Isa. 43:10; 44:6, 8; 45:21; 46:9; Mk. 12:29–34; Jn. 17:3; 1 Cor. 8:4–6; Eph. 4:6; 1 Tim. 2:5; Jas. 2:19) and that Jesus is the **only** source of salvation (e.g., Ps. 2:1–12; Jn. 3:18, 36; 8:24; 14:6; Acts 4:12; 2 Thess. 1:8; 1 Tim. 2:5; 1 Jn. 5:11–13). Allah, Brahma, Zeus, and Ba'al cannot be gods, and neither can Islam, Hinduism, or the Buddha be paths to salvation if the Bible's claims are true.

A principal belief of the Judeo-Christian faith presented in the Bible is that reality itself is rooted in the self-existent God (*Yahweh/Yehovah*, whose Name means "I Am that I Am" or "The One who is, who was, and who is to come") and only God's revelations to mankind can be regarded as objective truth. From the very beginning of the Bible, we discover that the book presents the Deity as self-existent, outside of time, transcendent, and personally involved in His creation—both before and after His creative activity. Therefore, the Bible and the Noahic-Abrahamic traditions that preceded it proclaim monotheism to be objective truth. This necessarily rules out pantheism, panentheism, polytheism, animism, and deism—the bulk of all other religions.

But is the Bible's claim about the Deity correct? The cosmological, teleological, and ontological arguments—and numerous other arguments—are indisputable rationale for the existence of a transcendent, self-existent being. This scholarly and philosophical foundation is unique to monotheism among all other religions and belief systems. God is the simplest, most logical, and most rational explanation for all that we see around us.

"For the invisible things of Him from the creation of the world, by the things made being understood, are plainly seen, both His eternal power and Godhead—to their being inexcusable…" (Rm. 1:20)

*"You—you have been shown [it], to know that He, Y*HWH*, [is] God; there is none else besides Him." (Deut. 4:35)*

But how do we know the Bible itself is true? The correct answer is because the Bible is God-breathed. In its original Hebrew, Aramaic, and Greek manuscripts it is inerrant and infallible. The true God spoke true words audibly, and sometimes into the minds, of fallible human beings (cf. 2 Tim. 3:16–17 and 2 Pet. 1:20–21). But, understandably, that answer will not satisfy the skeptic. There are at least six key arguments that powerfully vouch for the Bible's unique authenticity:

1. Every claim in the Bible that can be demonstrably tested has been verified. In other words, if we presently possess some scientific know-how, archaeological discovery, or corroborating text that can directly test a specific claim from the Bible, the claim has been verified. As a matter of fact, this truth has caused a great deal of consternation for secular historians over the past several decades as discovery after discovery has proven the Bible true even after historians had said "it just can't be." Whether it be the fallen walls of Jericho, the reign of King Hezekiah, or even the existence of a Jewish temple, every bit of physical evidence that has turned up to answer the Bible's claims has proven the Bible true.

2. There are more ancient manuscripts of the Bible than any other ancient text. Furthermore, the discovery of the Dead Sea Scrolls in 1946/47 dealt a significant defeat to the theory of that generation's textual critics. They had taught that the Old Testament was composed much later than Jews and Christians believed and had undergone a significant evolution in content. Not only did the Dead Sea Scrolls disprove that claim, showing that the Old Testament we have today is equivalent to the one used by Christ and His disciples, but they also provided rock-solid evidence that numerous prophecies about Jesus Christ were written before He was born.

3. The Bible contains self-verifying mathematical and thematic codes underlying the text. In recent years scholars have discovered numerous number patterns in the text in various books, such as Genesis and the synoptic gospels, that would be impossible for humans to have developed on their own. There are similar thematic codes that testify to the Bible's divine origins.

4. Despite having been written over a period of 1,600 years by 40 different authors, the Bible forms a single metanarrative. The Bible forms a continuous story with a clear beginning, ending, climax, protagonist, antagonist and complex, repeating themes that recur in almost every book. Yet its authors' lives were separated by many centuries, occurring on three different continents, and in several different ancient cultures. This incredible collection of history, poetry, prophecy, and letters forms a single, overarching story from beginning to end. The protagonist and antagonist show up at the beginning of the story, continue their parts throughout, and reach a climactic moment, culminating with a final showdown—the final battle at the culmination of the ages. Dozens of themes, symbols, and patterns recur through the entire text, from Genesis to Revelation. No other religious text can boast of such miraculous development.

5. The Bible forms a doctrinal hologram. Typical religious texts are one or two-dimensional. If you take out a passage from the text the religious message is fundamentally altered—removing key doctrines. It is like a painting on a canvas—mar a section of the picture and you can no longer see the whole. Strangely, the Bible is different. From a doctrinal perspective it forms something analogous to a three-dimensional hologram. You can remove any piece of a hologram, move to a different viewing angle, and still see the whole. Doctrines revealed in the Bible are spread out across the entire book, like an interconnected web. This is strong evidence that the book's underlying author intended His message to get through even if someone tampered with the text. This complex web or layering is hinted at in Isaiah 28: *"...precept upon precept, line upon line, here a little, there a little."*

6. Prophecy is unique to the Bible and is its watermark of authenticity. Other religious texts contain "prophecy," but unique to the Bible are very specific prophecies that can be demonstrably proven to have been written before the events occurred. Isaiah 53 is an important example. Written some 700 years before Jesus Christ was born, it correctly prophesied that He would come from humble origins, die as a substitutionary sacrifice for our sins, be buried in a rich man's tomb, rise to life again, and be glorified. There are hundreds of other such prophecies.

WHO AND WHAT IS GOD?

Through simple deduction we have concluded that God must exist and that the God of the Bible is the true God because His revealed word is uniquely and demonstrably true. But who is He and what has He revealed about Himself?

We know that He is self-existent (Ex. 3:14; Is. 43:10), eternal (Ps. 90:2; Is. 40:28), omnipotent (Lk. 1:37; Mt. 19:26), omniscient (Ps. 147:4–5; Heb. 4:13), omnipresent (Ps. 139:7–10; Eph. 4:10), and unchanging (Mal. 3:6; Heb. 13:8; Jas. 1:17). We also know that He is good (Ps. 34:8; 145:9), His word is infallible (Mt. 5:18; 2 Tim. 3:16), and His nature is love (1 Jn. 4:8). Most importantly, we know that He is One (Deut. 6:4). These characteristics and attributes help us to understand the nature of God, but we need to know Him on a deeper level.

In Scripture we learn that though God is one being, He exists as the mutual indwelling of three divine Persons: The Father, the Son, and the Holy Spirit (Mt. 3:13–17; 28:19; Mk. 1:9–11; Lk. 1:35; 3:21–22; Jn. 1:29–34; 14:26; Acts 1:4–8; 2 Cor. 13:14; Eph. 1:3–17; 1 Pt. 1:2; Rev. 4:3, 5; 5:1–6). God is One and cannot be divided, thus these three Persons are neither *parts* nor *forms* (also called *modes* in theological lingo). They are different and distinguishable in relationship and personality, but not in being or essence.

Praise God, from whom all blessings flow;
Praise Him, all creatures here below;
Praise Him above, ye heav'nly host;
Praise Father, Son, and Holy Ghost!

Intriguingly, it would seem God has left His mark of three-in-one all over the universe. The fundamental universe consists of space, time, and substance (elementary particles of energy and matter), and each of these things is precisely three-in-one:

Space, which gives the universe structure, consists of height, width, and depth. Each dimension is necessary, or space would not exist. If there was no height, then there would be neither width nor depth. And if there was no depth, there would be neither height nor width. Each dimension gives the other two dimensions substance. A single, unitary space consists of exactly three dimensions.

Time, which produces history and change, consists of past, present, and future. Just like space, each aspect is necessary for the others. If there was never a past, then there could not be a present or future. And if there is not a future, then we would be frozen in a three-dimensional picture, like a static hologram. Time consists of a single continuum of exactly three components: past, present, and future.

Matter, which is the tangible structure of the universe, the air we breathe, the water we drink, and the flesh and bones of our bodies, takes the form of a solid, liquid, or gas. Each of the three is distinct, but each remains matter regardless of its form. H_2O's forms of water, ice, and steam are a perfect demonstration of this. Plasma is often described as a fourth fundamental state of matter, although it is always defined as *gas*, albeit ionized.

There are a great many examples of this concept of three-in-one embedded throughout the created order:

Subatomic particles of an atom: proton, neutron, and electron	**Types of elements:** metals, metalloids, and nonmetals
Elementary particles of a proton: two up quarks and one down quark	**Elementary particles of a neutron:** one up quark and two down quarks
Fundamental types of elementary particles: quarks, leptons, and bosons	**Types of strong interaction (QCD):** ±red, ±green, and ±blue
Generations of elementary particles: first, second, and third	**Modes of heat transfer:** conduction, convection, and radiation
Properties of color: hue, saturation, and brightness	**Primary colors:** RGB (additive) or CMY (subtractive)
Largescale parts of the universe: LQGs, galaxy filaments, and superclusters	**Types of galaxies:** spiral, elliptical, and irregular
Largescale parts of a galaxy: stars, dust, and free-floating gas	**Spheroids in a solar system:** stars, planets, and moons
Largescale parts of a terrestrial planet: the crust, mantle, and inner core	**Largescale parts of a gas giant:** gaseous layer, liquid layer, and inner core
Types of rock: igneous, sedimentary, and metamorphic	**Types of sedimentary rock:** clastic, chemical, and organic
Types of soil: clayey, sandy, and loamy	**The water cycle:** evaporation, condensation, and precipitation
Levels of the ocean: euphotic, dysphotic, and aphotic	**General types of clouds:** cumulus, cirrus, and stratus
Levels of the rainforest: the canopy, understory, and forest floor	**Types of organism relationships:** mutualism, commensalism, and parasitism
Components of DNA and RNA: phosphate, pentose sugar, and a nitrogenous base	**Types of plants:** mosses, grasses, and flowering plants
Organisms with cell walls: plants, fungi, and bacteria	**Types of stem cells:** totipotent, pluripotent, and multipotent
Types of muscle: cardiac, skeletal, and smooth	**Types of neurons:** sensory neurons, interneurons, and motor neurons
Types of fatty acids: saturated, monounsaturated, and polyunsaturated	**Types of hormones:** lipid-derived, amino acid-derived, and peptide
Sex hormone groups: estrogens, androgens, and progesterones	**Types of symmetry:** rotation, translation, and reflection
Fundamental types of government: monarchy, oligarchy, and democracy	**Branches of government:** executive, legislative, and judicial
Fundamental parts of written language: letters, words, and sentences	**Types of love:** erotic love, brotherly love, and sacrificial love
Parts of a human being: the body, soul, and spirit (1 Thess. 5:23; Heb. 4:12)	**Reproduction:** male, female, and offspring

Hundreds of other such examples could be easily supplied. The principle of three-in-one is everywhere and in everything. God has left His mark for everyone to see. A particularly interesting argument that Islamic scholars have used to supposedly disprove the doctrine of the Trinity is the mathematical equation 1+1+1=3. Muslim apologists argue that if you add up three parts you end up with, well, three parts, rather than one single whole. They make a good point but miss a glaring problem: God is not *parts*, He is *Persons*. You cannot divide the single being and essence of God into parts or modes. A more accurate mathematical test of God's being would be 1x1x1. And guess what that equals? **One**.

$$1^3 = 1$$

In the beginning God revealed Himself as the Father and Creator of the universe. And then, in the fullness of time, God revealed Himself as the eternal Logos, Son of the Father, who came to demonstrate the depth of God's love for fallen humanity by dying as a propitiation for our sins and rising again. Finally, when the Church was formed on Pentecost some 50 days later, God revealed Himself as the purifying and sanctifying Holy Spirit who has come to convict the world of sin and to seal all of those with faith in Jesus Christ. God has progressively revealed Himself to mankind through the dispensations of time and this God whom we believe in can be known personally and relationally. We declare of Him that there is no other and none else deserving of worship, glory, and praise. It is from Him that we have learned the way of salvation, which is found only in His Son, Jesus Christ.

The "Shield of the Trinity" or *Scutum Fidei* was a diagram developed in medieval Europe as a visual aid to explain the doctrine of the Trinity and the relationship of the Persons within the Godhead:

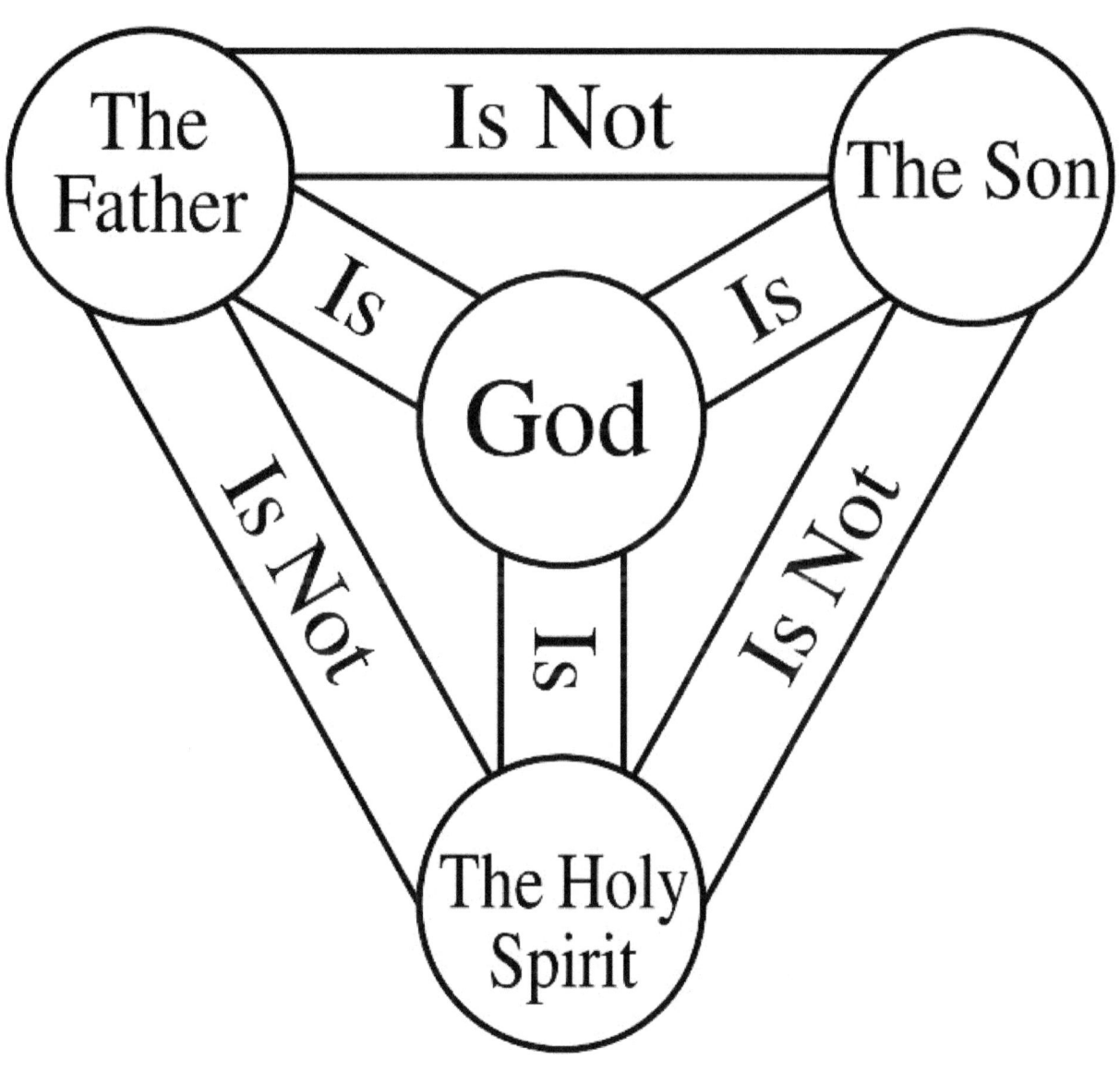

CREATION

Having established that God alone is the self-existent being who transcends space and time, who made the cosmos by His power, we move on to the question of creation itself. How and when was it made? What was it made from?

> *"And YHWH answers Job out of the whirlwind and says: 'Who [is] this—darkening counsel, || By words without knowledge? Now gird your loins as a man, || And I ask you, and you cause Me to know. Where were you when I founded the earth? Declare, if you have known understanding. Who placed its measures—if you know? Or who has stretched out a line on it? On what have its sockets been sunk? Or who has cast its cornerstone—In the singing together of [the] stars of morning, || When all [the] sons of God shout for joy?'"* (Job 38:1–7)

God Himself questions those who would question Him. In the 21st century, mankind prizes questioning authority, critiquing all truth claims, and speculating on what, other than God, might explain what we see, but God is self-evident (Ps. 10:4; 14:1; 53:1; Rom. 1:18–32; 1 Cor. 1:20) and the ultimate example of Occam's razor in action. Modern sensibilities and speculation are incompatible with the thoughts of a God who was quite literally present to see the creation of the world—who laid its foundations Himself.

Every parent is intimately acquainted with the incalcitrant stage of childhood when the wiseacre is convinced that he or she knows more than them. The parent knows with genuine certainty that the child is self-deceived. Scripture tells us that this is how we behave toward God. He is the perfect parent who actually *does* know everything, but we continually question just about everything He says. It is like an ant questioning an astrophysicist, but the gulf is infinitely greater. When we ask these important questions about the origins of the universe, we must first ask who is more trustworthy: men, or God?

From the book of Genesis, we learn that the universe had a definitive beginning and God is the one who created it. It was not formed from preexisting matter, nor is it part of God, for God did not create Himself. God alone is immortal (1 Tim. 6:16). The biblical concept of creation is what has been termed *creatio ex nihilo*, which is Latin for "creation out of nothing." Indeed, God is the only eternal and self-existent entity because He is the greatest conceivable being and the immutable, unmoved mover.

> *"In [the] beginning* **[time]** *God created the heavens* **[space]** *and the earth* **[matter]**, *and the earth was formless and void, and darkness [was] on the face of the deep, and the Spirit of God [was] fluttering on the face of the waters, and God says, "Let light be"* **[energy]**; *and light is."* (Gen. 1:1–3)

Time, space, matter, and energy all *began to exist*. God never began to exist because He has always existed.

Side note #1: when you cross-reference John 1:1 (*"in the beginning was the Word, and the Word was with God, and the Word was God"*) with Genesis 1:1–3, it is clear that all three Persons of the Godhead were intimately involved in creation. God (the Father) created the heavens and the earth (v. 1); the Holy Spirit was fluttering over the primordial sea (v. 2); and God the Son, the preincarnate *Logos* or "Word," speaks things into existence (v. 3).

Side note #2: Genesis 1 explains that the universe had a clear beginning, while other passages, such as Isaiah 65:17–19, 2 Peter 3:10–13, and Revelation 21:1–5, explain that the present creation has a definitive end—to be replaced by a permanent "new heavens and new earth."

IN SIX DAYS

We have answered how the universe was made and what it was made from, but now we move to the contentious question of *when*. Secular estimates suggest it came to be approximately 13.8 billion years ago. Many Christian scholars who adhere to a literal hermeneutic believe it is much younger and have been labeled "young earth creationists." What does the Bible say, and can it withstand any sort of scrutiny?

To adequately answer this question, we must return to the earlier question asked: *who is more trustworthy: men, or God?* Remember that the Creator Himself questions those who would presume to know more than they really do and who would think it is logical to question Him—like the ant questioning the astrophysicist, or the child questioning an adult ten times his age. *"Where were you when I founded the earth?"*

> *"... for it has been written: 'I will destroy the wisdom of the wise, and the intelligence of the intelligent I will bring to nothing'; where [is] the wise? Where the scribe? Where a disputer of this age? Did God not make foolish the wisdom of this world?"* (1 Cor. 1:19–20)

The humble heart will acknowledge that the supreme, all-knowing, all-powerful, everywhere-present, necessarily-existent being is the One to go to for the answers. He has not remained hidden, but has revealed the answers in His word, the Bible. Scientists may be brilliant, but if they are searching for the solutions to these questions with pride, they are destined to find the wrong answers (Prov. 1:7; 11:2; 16:18; 18:12; Jas. 4:6).

The Bible emphatically and repeatedly states that the universe was created **in six days** (Gen. 2:2; Ex. 20:11; 31:17). And that is not just the earth, but the heavens and the sea as well (according to those passages). There have been clever attempts to circumvent this in order to reconcile the Bible to modern, secular estimations, but they run into exegetical trouble in great abundance.

In Genesis 1–2, not only are the days of creation numbered from one to six, but the phrase *"and there is an evening, and there is a morning"* is included for each and every day. Attempting to get around the crystal clear, prima facie teaching of Scripture involves the insertion of some unmentioned, ambiguous "gap" of time before, during, or between the days of Creation, or redefining the normative meaning of "day." These allegorical hermeneutics are complicated workarounds with lots of moving parts and subjective assumptions. Rarely will two allegorists agree, since allegorism is often, by its very nature, a subjective exercise. The allegorists run headlong into the plain, normatively understood meaning of the text.

Not only does Scripture state that the universe was created in six days and that each of these days featured an evening and a morning, but Scripture subsequent to Genesis—from Exodus to the very end of the Bible—seems to treat the Genesis account as historical narrative rather than an allegorical literary feature. For instance, Jesus Himself proclaims that men and women were such since the beginning of creation (Mk. 10:6). If the universe was 13.8 billion years old, then His statement would be categorically false.

The First Day	God creates time ("in the beginning"), space ("the heavens"), matter ("the earth"), and energy ("light"). He separates the light from the darkness, creating, from the vantage point of earth, "day" and "night."
The Second Day	God creates the firmament—"sky."
The Third Day	God gathers the water under the sky and causes dry ground to appear, thus creating the land and the sea. He also creates vegetation.
The Fourth Day	God creates the sun, moon, and stars to serve as signs, to mark appointed times, and to give light on the earth.
The Fifth Day	God creates all the living creatures of the sky and sea.
The Sixth Day	God creates all the living creatures that dwell on land, including human beings, made in His image.

So how long ago did God fashion the world in six days? This question depends, at least in part, on which manuscripts of the Old Testament are authentic to the original text. The primary chronological distinctions are found in the Hebrew Masoretic Text (MT) and the Greek Septuagint (LXX). Most Bibles printed today use the MT as the basis for translation, although a sizable number use the LXX. The LXX is a translation from the 3rd and 2nd centuries BC, whereas the MT is more recent, although scholars tend to favor both as containing original readings in certain passages. The question is, which manuscript contains the correct ages found in Genesis 5 and 11? These two chapters provide a record from the first man Adam all the way to Abraham. The MT chronology tells us that the universe was created approximately 6,000 years ago, whereas the chronology presented in the LXX suggests a creation date about 1,500 years prior. Based on the biblical text, we can determine that the earth is approximately 6,000 or 7,500 years old.

YOUNG OR OLD?

Though belief in a young earth is often thought to be a peculiarity of modern biblical literalism, it was actually the default view of the Church for most of its history, as well as the default view of Judaism and much of the rest of the ancient Near East. Times have certainly changed with the advent of Darwinism, uniformitarianism, and Old Earth Creationism, but these views are recent, largely dating from the 19th century—*less than two hundred years ago*. Though these theories self-proclaim their verifiability through science, each of them has at its core two massive assumptions that make them shaky at best:

The **first assumption** is that observable phenomena are always best explained through other observable phenomena. In other words, natural things demand natural explanations. The result of this assumption is that things that have a genuinely supernatural explanation will *always* be misexplained and misidentified. To give an example: suppose the biblical account of Jesus turning water into wine at Cana is an event that actually occurred. And suppose a scientist armed with all his testing apparatus stumbled upon the jars of wine. And suppose also that this particular scientist demanded a natural explanation. What would his conclusion be? He would test the wine and tell you it came from such and such vineyard, and was some particular vintage, from some number of decades ago. His tests would prove it out, so to speak, but his conclusion would be completely false. Did his equipment lie to him? Did Jesus deceive him by creating aged wine? No, of course not. The scientist deceived himself with his assumptions, which precluded the supernatural.

The **second assumption** is that man, who was **not** present to witness the origin of many of the things he claims to understand, can reason out an explanation with the three pounds of knobby cerebrum behind his eyes. Remember what God has said: *"I will destroy the wisdom of the wise, and the intelligence of the intelligent I will bring to nothing,"* and, *"Where were you when I founded the earth?"* and also, *"A fool has said in his heart, 'There is no God...'"*

And just as the cosmological, ontological, and teleological arguments, among others, demand the existence of a supreme, all-powerful God/Being/Entity, so the secular mind, try as it might, will never be able to outmaneuver the possibility of supernatural explanations. An all-powerful God can do what to mortal man is certifiably **impossible** (Lk. 1:37; Mt. 19:26).

Many young earth creationists have oddly boxed themselves in while attempting to counter those who by very definition are boxed in by naturalistic and humanistic assumptions. Some creationists have tried to prove a young earth through natural means, using the same kinds of arguments as those who reject the supernatural. That might work in *some* instances, but not in all. In their effort to defend the truth of the Bible, have some of those who have defended the Bible's earth age inadvertently overlooked some of the simple answers?

Many creationists have sought to show that all evidence points to a young earth. They have cleverly devised alternative interpretations of starlight data, Precambrian geology, ocean salinity, radiometric dating, and the fossil record, and some of these arguments are surprisingly strong, but the million-dollar question is this: does the earth appear old because it is that old, or because God made it old to begin with? Is it heretical to think God may have created the universe a short time ago with the appearance of great age? Some would claim that if God did it that way, He would be deceptive, but was Jesus deceptive when He turned water into deliciously-aged wine? Or was Jesus deceptive in creating enough bread and fish—things that naturally take time to grow—to feed thousands? Was God deceptive in creating Adam, Eve, and the animals already grown? The Bible is full of examples of God creating things with the appearance of age, or doing things that cannot happen naturally. Creation itself was a miraculous, supernatural event, and a plain reading of the Genesis 1–2 account seems to confirm that God *did* create the universe with the appearance of age—with fully-formed earth and sea, sun, moon, and stars, sea creatures, birds, and land-dwelling animals.

Early on the sixth day, before Eve was even formed, God was already bringing fully-formed animals to Adam for him to name. Adam was *old enough* to walk, talk, and creatively name each of the different animal kinds. And later that same day he was *old enough* to declare of Eve, *"This at last! Bone of my bone, and flesh of my flesh!"* He was apparently *old enough* to marry her that same day, too (Gen. 2:23–25; cf. 3:8). Yet Adam had only existed in spacetime for less than a day.

Uniformitarians say that the universe looks old because it is old. Many creationists say the universe looks young because it is young. The Bible seems to say, quite plainly actually, that the universe looks old, at least by some measurements, because God made it old from the beginning. The Bible tells us that the universe was created some 6,000 or 7,500 years ago with the appearance of great age. That does not mean that *everything* points to an old earth in terms of appearance, but it does mean that the *appearance of age* in the universe is 1. compatible with the biblical account, 2. reconcilable with a young earth in actual age (thousands of years vs. millions of years), and 3. not an act of deception by God since the Bible plainly declares that is how He did it—the creative pattern and mechanism in Genesis 1–2 is similar to how God works miraculously and supernaturally throughout Scripture. And God will apparently create a new universe with the appearance of age in the future (Rev. 21; 2 Pt. 3:10–13).

When it comes to the young earth vs. old earth debate, it is best to step back and view the evidence collectively. And when you do, you see a picture that fits well with the biblical account of an old earth made recently, but it is a picture that is not easily explained by either of the other extremes. The table below shows evidence that points more toward a young earth (A), evidence that shows the appearance of an old earth (B), and evidence that cannot necessarily substantiate either (C).

Appears Young (A)	Appears Old (B)	Both/Either (C)
Helium diffusion from zircon[1]	Starlight[5]	Ice layers[7]
Polonium radiohalos		Radiometric dating[8]
Ocean salinity[2]		Stalactite and stalagmite formation[9]
Magnetic field decay rate[3]	Fossil accumulation[6]	Petroleum quantity and formation rate[10]
Moon drift rate[4]		Missing transitional species and fossil deposition[11]
Bent sedimentary rock layers without fracturing		Erosion

1. The rapid rate at which helium diffuses from rock, and the amount of helium remaining in ancient, Precambrian rocks like zircon, suggests that the earth is thousands, rather than billions, of years old. A number of uniformitarian rebuttals have been attempted to disprove this evidence, but they have not satisfactorily resolved the primary inconsistency with their view.

2. Calculating the rate of ocean salinity increase is another way to place a limiting factor on the earth's age. The oceans are continually becoming saltier and saltier as rivers mix in sediment from the continents, rains wash sediments into the sea, and lava deposits even more salt content into the oceans. The ocean is so salty that if you were to take a one foot by one foot by one foot box, fill it with seawater, and let all the water evaporate away, you would be left with around one quart of salt. That is *a lot* of salt! There have been several critics of using this method as a limiting factor for earth age, but the critics all have one thing in common: they have yet to discover any method that removes more salt from the oceans than the oceans take in naturally. Even natural evaporation does not remove salt from the oceans. Runoff from rain brings more salt into the sea, but evaporation does not bring any salt back to the land—evaporation only removes H_2O from the sea, not salt. And on top of that, tectonic movements only add to the salt content as well, as more and more lava flows bring salts up from the earth's crust and mantle. Using this method, we can put an upper limiting factor on the age of the earth's oceans at 62 million years—billions of years closer to the Bible's estimate than the uniformitarian estimate.

3. The earth's magnetic field decay rate is another example: the earth's magnetic field is losing more energy than it takes in—and it is losing its energy at an exponential rate. As a matter of fact, the current magnetic field was twice as strong only 1,500 years ago. This rate places an upper limit on the age of the earth of approximately 8,700 years, prior to this time the field would have been too strong to support life.

4. The moon is pulling away from the earth at a constant rate. Since this rate is constant (about 1.5 inches per year), then we can extrapolate backwards to find a point when the earth and moon were literally touching—an upper limit of about 1.5 billion years ago (only one-third of the supposed 4.5-billion-year age of the earth). The moon's proximity to the earth would have killed off all life on our planet much more recently—the moon's tidal effects grow exponentially more powerful as it gets closer to the earth. Only hundreds of millions of years ago the moon's proximity would have caused a global flood literally every day, but over the course of 6,000 years the moon has only drifted about half of a mile!

5. As of yet, no evidence conclusively shows that the speed of light (186,000 mi/s) has changed over time (i.e., *slowed down*). This means that light from distant celestial objects does *appear* to have been travelling for millions or even billions of years.

6. There are fossil beds with such large quantities of deposited organisms that it is thought unlikely that they could have all been contemporary. Proponents of a young earth tend to explain these as accumulations resulting from water currents during the Flood and also evidence for huge pre-Flood populations.

7. There are ice sheets with hundreds of thousands of layers, however, layers can be deposited many times per year. The uniformitarian view tends to view layers as representing annual accumulations, but this is not the span of time over which layers naturally form. For example, crashed aircraft from World War II have been found under 300 feet of ice, representing many hundreds of individual layers. Even secular glaciologists have abandoned the previous dogmatism, recognizing that layers can be formed much more often than annually, and the deeper one looks for ice core samples, it becomes a much more difficult and subjective exercise determining where one layer ends and the next one begins.

8. Radiometric/radioisotope dating often suggests rocks are hundreds of millions of years old, however, different tests on the same sample often result in estimates separated by *literally hundreds of millions of years*. Additionally, test results from rocks formed only decades ago often show up as being several million years old.

9. Stalactites and stalagmites are commonly said to form over hundreds of thousands of years, but under the right conditions they can actually form very rapidly—within years. In fact, they are frequently found under overpasses and bridges, and hanging from manmade concrete structures.

10. The quantity and origin of hydrocarbons is thought by many to suggest long geological ages, however, like stalactites and stalagmites, under the right conditions they have been shown to form rapidly. Also, the secular view that the bulk of petroleum has an organic origin has increasingly come under pressure as evidence shows that many deposits cannot be explained organically.

11. The original theory of evolution by natural selection predicted the discovery of a very large number of transitional species in the fossil record to account for the present variation seen. Around the time of Darwin's *On the Origin of Species*, he assumed that as science advanced we would find an "inconceivably great" number of "missing" transitional fossils and his theory would be validated, but as he grew older and few if any of the "missing links" were found, he grew increasingly disturbed by and skeptical of his own theory.

Here are the numbers: **250,000** and **0**. 250,000 is the approximate number of species we have found in the fossil record (a number which constitutes tens of millions of independent specimens). 0 is the number of transitional fossils universally agreed upon as transitional by proponents of Darwinian evolution. And one more number just for kicks: 2,000,000,000 (two billion with a 'b'). That is a *low-end estimate* of the number of species we should have found in the fossil record to accommodate the 250,000 niche species already found and catalogued. Because of this overwhelming lack of evidence for macro-evolution, paleontologists have proposed what is called *Punctuated Equilibrium*. Their theory posits that since no conclusive transitional species have been catalogued, they must have all "transitioned" really quickly over "punctuated" periods of time and not made it into the record. In other words, on the face of it the fossil record looks more like a snapshot confirming the biblical account—evidence for unique animal species and kinds, rather than a "tree of life" with abundant evidence of transitional linkage.

Even some of the classic examples of "missing links" are now understood to either be misclassified or outright frauds. An example of a misclassification would be archaeopteryx, which is now generally regarded as a regular perching bird (with some peculiar features). Examples of outright fraud would be Lucy, Nebraska man, and Piltdown man. Furthermore, soft tissues have now been found from several dinosaur species, including tyrannosaurus, triceratops, iguanodon, and gorgosaurus—animals that were supposed to have died out over 64 million years ago.

The absence of transitional fossils does not attest to the age of the earth by itself, but it does appear to poke a big hole in the predominant uniformitarian view of macro-evolution. In terms of fossil deposition itself, both sides have theories to explain what we see. Fossil accumulation quantity might favor an old earth perspective, whereas the absence of transitional species and the appearance of sudden speciation (e.g., the Cambrian explosion) and catastrophism (e.g., animals fossilized whole, fossilized while eating or in combat, polystrate fossils, etc) tend to favor the young earth view.

IS THE EARTH FLAT?

A debate that has resurfaced in a big way in recent years regards whether or not the earth is flat. While proponents of a flat earth come from a variety of religious backgrounds, many have used the Bible in an attempt to defend their view, suggesting that a literal interpretation of Scripture necessarily causes one to believe in a flat earth. However, the flat earth view is not necessary with a literal hermeneutic, nor does it withstand scientific scrutiny. Here are the reasons:

1. The Bible does not actually state that the earth is flat. This is a huge, gaping hole in the argument that a literal interpretation of Scripture necessitates a flat earth. Without such direct scriptural evidence, flat-earth proponents are left with interpreting certain figurative passages of Scripture in such a way as suits their theory. Passages that are emphasized include those that speak of the earth having four corners (e.g., Isa. 11:12; Rev. 7:1; 20:8), being set on pillars (e.g., 1 Sam. 2:8), and being unmoved (e.g., Ps. 104:5).

The problem with their view is that the Bible also speaks of the earth as **a circle** (Isa. 40:22; cf. Prov. 8:27). A circle does not have corners. And a circle is the shape that a sphere appears from any single vantage point. In addition, the biblical words for "earth" and "land" are the same. The *land* of planet earth *does* have corners, such as the extremities of continents and so forth.

In regard to the passages that speak of pillars, or the earth not being moved, we also have passages that say the earth is suspended *over nothing* (Job. 26:7) and *does move* (Isa. 24:20; Nah. 1:5; Heb. 12:25–29). Thus, we can reconcile the full counsel of Scripture in that the planet itself is not moved from its stable course and orbit, and the land of the earth is not moved from the vantage point of an earth dweller. The pillars of the earth are a figurative symbol, but if taken literally, perhaps a description of the natural structures that undergird the surface of the land since the earth is not actually hollow.

2. Other celestial objects appear to be spheres, including the sun, moon, planets, and stars. They are not just simple lights in the sky. And in fact, we can observe many of these objects rotate on their axes.

3. The earth casts a circular shadow on the moon.

4. Objects over the horizon do not suddenly pop into view but appear to emerge from below the horizon because of the earth's curvature.

5. Even with no obstacles, an observer at ground level cannot see the same distance as an observer higher than him. This is because the earth is round. If it was flat, then an observer at ground level would see the same distance as an observer who is miles up in the air.

6. The argument of a mass, coordinated deception of evidence is necessary to defend the flat earth view. There is substantial, observable proof that the earth is a sphere: circumnavigation via aircraft, circumnavigation via ship, pictures taken from thousands of satellites and spacecraft, hundreds of thousands of eyewitness testimonies, and so forth.

THE CREATION OF HEAVENLY BEINGS

Genesis clearly explains the timing of the creation of things we can see and experience from here on earth, such as the sun, moon, and stars, the land and the sea, and the flora and fauna of our planet, but what about angels and other creatures in the heavenly realms? The Bible is clear that life is not for earth alone, but it also exists in the heavens.

*"He who is sitting on the circle of the earth, || And its inhabitants [are] as grasshoppers, || He who is stretching out **the heavens** as a thin thing, || **And spreads them as a tent to dwell in.**" (Isa. 40:22)*

*"And suddenly there came with the messenger **a multitude of the heavenly host**, praising God, and saying, 'Glory in the highest to God, and on earth peace, among men—good will!'" (Lk. 2:13-14)*

When were these heavenly creatures created?

The Bible does not tell us explicitly as it does with the creation of our own world, but we can probably deduce a relatively clear answer. As has been laid out through the plain teaching of Scripture, God not only made the earth in six days, but He also made the heavens in that same period of time. The first day of creation involved the creation of time, space, matter, and energy. To be created "before" time began, so to speak, is thought to be a logical inconsistency since things happen *within* time. Creation is an *action*. Actions take time to occur. They *transpire*. In this sense, God's initial creative actions coincided with the creation of time itself.

If the heavens themselves were created *"in the beginning"* then we can conclude that those creatures who dwell in them were not created before they had a **place** to be **placed**! Genesis 1-2 and the other confirming passages (e.g., Ex. 20:11; 31:17) tell us the heavens are a created thing just as the earth is. God *alone* is eternal and transcendent to time and space. Heaven and angels are not. Created things can be *everlasting*—meaning that they can endure forever if God so chooses. But created things can never properly be *eternal*—meaning without beginning or end. God alone is eternal, so we can conclude that the heavenly beings, like angels, were created sometime during the six days of creation. And Job chapter 38 appears to tell us on which day they were created:

*"Where were you when I founded the earth?... Or who has cast its cornerstone—In the singing together of [the] **stars of morning**, || When all [the] **sons of God** shout for joy?" (Job 38:4, 6b-7)*

This account features God questioning Job about creation. God was there at creation and is the only accurate source for information about what transpired. He tells Job that when He founded the earth "stars of morning," the "sons of God," sang and shouted for joy. The luminaries of the sky—sun, moon, and stars—are inanimate objects that do not sing, so these "stars" here refer to something besides Polaris, Spica, or Sirius. The Bible routinely uses "stars" as a symbolic term for *angels* (e.g., Rev. 1:20; 12:3-4, 7-9). And the account in Job drives the point home by directly paralleling the "stars of morning" with the "sons of God" (transliterated *bene Elohim* from Hebrew), which is another term used for angels (e.g., Job 1:6; Gen. 6:4). The angels were alive and singing when the earth was created, and the earth was created on the first day according to Genesis 1. The chronology in the first verse of Genesis even accords with this view: *"In [the] beginning God created **1**. the heavens and **2**. the earth..."*

We could conjecture an order of events on the first day of creation as follows: 1. God creates time and space ("the heavens"), 2. God creates the heavenly creatures (e.g., angels), 3. God creates the earth, 4. God creates light, and 5. God separates the light from the darkness.

Alternatively, if the founding of the earth in Job 38 has the narrower meaning of the appearance of *dry land*—"earth" and "land" in Genesis 1 and Job 38 being the same word in Hebrew—then the angels may have been created on the second day of creation or on the third day of creation prior to the appearance of dry land.

In conclusion, we can determine from Scripture that the sentient *stars*—the heavenly beings—were created on the first, second, or third day of creation, whereas the inanimate stars, which serve as lights and signs for the earth, were explicitly created on the fourth day.

"For the scientist who has lived by his faith in the power of reason, the story ends like a bad dream. He has scaled the mountains of ignorance, he is about to conquer the highest peak; as he pulls himself over the final rock, he is greeted by a band of theologians who have been sitting there for centuries."
— Robert Jastrow, *God and the Astronomers*

"We need intimate knowledge of the past. Not that the past has any magic about it, but because we cannot study the future, and yet need something to set against the present, to remind us that the basic assumptions have been quite different in different periods and that much which seems certain to the uneducated is merely temporary fashion. A man who has lived in many places is not likely to be deceived by the local errors of his native village: the scholar has lived in many times and is therefore in some degree immune from the great cataract of nonsense that pours from the press and the microphone of his own age."
— C.S. Lewis, *The Weight of Glory*

"All that we call human history—money, poverty, ambition, war, prostitution, classes, empires, slavery—[is] the long terrible story of man trying to find something other than God which will make him happy."
— C.S. Lewis, *Mere Christianity*

"Remember former things of old, || For I [am] Mighty, and there is none else, || God—and there is none like Me. Declaring the latter end from the beginning, || And from of old that which has not been done, || Saying, My counsel stands, || And all My delight I do."
— THE CREATOR (Isa. 46:9–10, LSV)

GENESIS CHRONOLOGIES

Patriarch	Masoretic Text (MT)		Samaritan Pentateuch (SP)		Septuagint (LXX)	
	Begetting Age	*Lifespan*	*Begetting Age*	*Lifespan*	*Begetting Age*	*Lifespan*
Adam	130	930	130	930	230	930
Seth	105	912	105	912	205	912
Enosh	90	905	90	905	190	905
Kenan	70	910	70	910	170	910
Mahalalel	65	895	65	895	165	895
Jared	162	962	62	847	162	962
Enoch	65	365	65	365	165	365
Methuselah	187	969	67	720	167	969
Lamech	182	777	53	653	188	753
Noah	502	950	502	950	502	950
Shem	100	600	100	600	100	600
Arphaxad	35	438	135	438	135	565
Cainan[1]	-	-	-	-	130	460
Shelah[2]	30	433	130	433	130	533
Eber	34	464/404	134	404	134	504
Peleg	30	239	130	239	130	339
Reu	32	239	132	239	132	339
Serug	30	230	130	230	130	330
Nahor	29	148	79	148	79	208
Terah	70–145[3]	205	70	145	70–145	205
Abraham	100	175	100	175	100	175
From Adam to the Flood:	1,656 years		1,307 years		2,262 years	
From Adam to Abraham:	1,948–2,023 years		2,249 years		3,334–3,409 years	
Approximate age of the earth in the early 21st century AD:	~6,000 years		~6,300 years		~7,600 years	

General Note: The ages above are taken from Genesis 5, 11, and 17–21. Begetting ages and lifespans that match across chronologies are shaded. The begetting age represents when the next successive Patriarch was born (i.e., Adam's begetting age of 130 indicates that he was 130 when Seth was born).

Note 1: Cainan is not found in the MT or SP genealogies. Cainan is mentioned in most, but not all, manuscripts containing Luke 3:36. Some suppose this to be a scribal error in the transmission of Luke's Gospel.

Note 2: Shelah is also transliterated as *Salah* in some English translations.

Note 3: Terah began to have sons when he was 70 (Gen. 11:26). In Genesis 11, the Messianic lineage from Shem to Terah is clearly given, but Terah's age is only given as 70 when he began to have sons; the common assumption that Terah was 70 when Abram was born is untenable unless he had three sons the same year; rather, Abram was possibly the youngest, which explains why Haran had Lot long before Abram had children and why Acts 7:4 indicates that Abram left Haran *after* the death of his father. In truth, Terah's exact age when Abram was born is not indicated; we know only that he had three sons—Abram, Nahor, and Haran—and whomever was the eldest was born when Terah was 70. Abram could have been born when Terah was as young as 70 or as old as 145.

TIMELINE OF HISTORY

Year(s) (Approx.)	Major Historical Event(s)
5554 BC	Creation according to the LXX
4004 BC	Creation according to James Ussher's chronology
3972–3968 BC	Corrected date range of creation according to the MT
3842–3838 BC	Seth born
3737–3733 BC	Enosh born
3647–3643 BC	Kenan born
3577–3573 BC	Mahalalel born
3512–3508 BC	Jared born; the Watchers (rebel angels) descend—equivalent to the Greco-Roman "Titans"—and begin to corrupt the earth soon thereafter; Nephilim ("giants") are born, equivalent to the Greco-Roman "Gigantes" and other mythological heroes of antiquity
3350–3346 BC	Enoch born; he is taken from the earth 365 years later
3298 BC	The Great Flood according to the LXX
3285–3281 BC	Methuselah born; the longest-living Patriarch, he dies at the age of 969
3098–3094 BC	Lamech born; the grandfather of Noah, he lives to be 777
2916–2912 BC	Noah born
2316–2312 BC	The Great Flood; Assyrian, Greek, Mexican, and Chinese records corroborate a date close to these years; some believe the Durupinar Site near Üzengili in Turkey contains the authentic remains of Noah's Ark; others, citing historical sources, prefer Mt. Cudi
2314–2310 BC	Arphaxad born
2277–2273 BC	Shelah/Salah born
2249–2245 BC	Eber born (ancestor of the Hebrews)
2234 BC	Date of the founding of Babylon according to the Chaldean astronomical records received by Alexander the Great
2214–2210 BC	Peleg born ("in his days the earth was divided"); the building of the Tower of Babel and the division of language groups occurred shortly before or during his life
2200 BC	Approximate date of the building of the Tower of Babel according to Armenian records
2188 BC	Date of the founding of Egypt according to the historian Constantinus Manasses
2186–2182 BC	Reu born
2151–2147 BC	Serug born
2123–2119 BC	Nahor born
2095–2091 BC	Terah born
2089 BC	The first Greek city-state of Sicyon founded by Egialeus according to Eusebius
1950–1948 BC	Abram born
1875–1874 BC	Abram leaves Haran; by inclusive reckoning, 430 years before the Exodus (Gal. 3:17)
1850–1849 BC	Isaac born
1845–1839 BC	Isaac mocked by Ishmael, son of Hagar the Egyptian, initiating 400 years of persecution of Israel by the Egyptians, ending with the Exodus
1790–1789 BC	Jacob and Esau born
1660–1653 BC	The seven-year famine when Joseph was prime minister of Egypt; the Famine Stela near Aswan, Egypt, records Djoser and Imhotep (possibly Joseph) overseeing the land during a seven-year famine, according perfectly with the biblical record; the stela itself was written much later (perhaps around 300 BC), so shows a reinterpretation of Imhotep/Joseph as worshiping false gods, which he of course did not do
1446–1444 BC	The Exodus during the reign of Neferhotep I or Amenhotep II; the spring of 1446 BC is the most likely date; the Ipuwer Papyrus provides extra-biblical corroboration
1406–1404 BC	Entrance into the Promised Land; the Spring of 1406 BC is most likely
967 BC	Solomon's fourth year as king and the year construction began on the First Temple—480 years after the Exodus by inclusive reckoning (1 Kgs. 6:1)
722 BC	The northern kingdom (Kingdom of Israel/Samaria) conquered by the Assyrians

605 BC	Battle of Carchemish: Babylonia takes power over the ancient Near East; Egyptian and Assyrian forces defeated; the first deportation from Judea
598–597 BC	Siege of Jerusalem and second deportation of the Jews
587–586 BC	The First Temple destroyed by Babylonian forces
574 BC	Ezekiel's vision of the Millennial Temple
457 BC	First decree of Artaxerxes (decree spoken of in Daniel 9 if "70 weeks of years" are reckoned as regular, solar years)
445–444 BC	Second decree of Artaxerxes (decree spoken of in Daniel 9 if "70 weeks of years" are years of 360 days each)
164 BC	The Second Temple is recaptured by the Jewish revolt and rededicated (Hanukkah)
5–1 BC	The Messiah Jesus is born; the astronomical alignment followed by the magi from the east seemingly plays out from 3–2 BC
AD 27–30	Jesus' ministry begins
AD 30–33	Jesus is crucified as a substitutionary sacrifice for the sins of the world in fulfillment of Isaiah 53, among other prophecies, is buried in the tomb of Joseph of Arimathea, and rises from the dead on the third day in either AD 30, 31, 32, or 33, while Pontius Pilate was governor of Judea; that same year the Church is founded on Pentecost when the Holy Spirit is sent from Heaven
AD 33–34	Road to Damascus; Paul commissioned
AD 44	The apostle James beheaded by the order of King Agrippa because of his faith in the Risen Lord
AD 47–49	Paul's first missionary journey
AD 48–50	The Council of Jerusalem: the Apostles confirm that salvation is by faith alone and this same message is to be promulgated among the Jews and Gentiles (Acts 15)
AD 49–53	Paul's second missionary journey
AD 53–57	Paul's third missionary journey
AD 64–67	The apostle Paul beheaded in Rome because of his faith in the Risen Lord
AD 64–68	The apostle Peter crucified upside down in Rome because of his faith in the Risen Lord
AD 70	Jerusalem and the Second Temple are destroyed by the Roman armies under the command of Titus Vespasian; the Jews are dispersed all over the known world
AD 95	The apostle John receives the Revelation while exiled on the island of Patmos
AD 132–136	Bar Kokhba Revolt ends with Jewish defeat
AD 325	Council of Nicaea affirms the deity of Christ and the doctrine of the Trinity
AD 363	Julian, a nephew of Constantine and the last pagan Roman emperor, in an effort to oppose Christianity supported a Jewish attempt to rebuild the Temple; fireballs and an earthquake struck the area, killing some of the workmen and ending the project permanently; Julian died that same year
AD 381	Council of Constantinople affirms the Nicene Creed as the belief of the global Church
AD 1054	The Great Schism splits the institutional Church between East and West
AD 1517	The *Ninety-five Theses* and Protestant Reformation
AD 1760–1840	Industrial Revolution
AD 1859	Charles Darwin publishes *On the Origin of Species* which denies the historicity of Genesis and argues that nature, rather than God, explains the development of life
AD 1903	Heavier-than-air flight
AD 1906	Azusa Street Revival begins the modern Pentecostal movement
AD 1914–1918	World War I
AD 1939–45	World War II
AD 1945	The United Nations founded: the first proto-global government
AD 1948	Israel reestablished: "that generation will not pass away"
AD 1967	Israel recaptures Jerusalem
AD 1987	The Temple Institute founded to rebuild the Temple in Jerusalem
AD 1989	The World Wide Web invented
AD 2015	World leaders begin a process for total control and global transformation: Agenda 2030
AD 2017	A "Great Sign" in the heavens (Rev. 12:1–2; cf. Gen 1:14; Lk. 21:11, 25)
AD 2023–2026	Alien disclosure and deception underway (2 Thess. 2:7–11; Rev. 12:3–12; Gen. 6:1–4); general AI technology nears (Rev. 13:14–15); technology for the Mark of the Beast becomes prevalent and ubiquitous (Rev. 13:16–17)

TABLE OF NATIONS

Noah		
Shem (Semitic)	**Ham (African, Asian)**	**Japheth (European)**
Elam (Elamites, Persians)	**Cush (Ethiopia)**	**Gomer (Celts, Cimmerians)**
Asshur (Assyria)	Seba (Meroe)	Ashkenaz (Nysia, Phrygia)
Arphaxad (Chaldeans)	Havilah (Arabia)[1]	Riphath
Shelah	Sabtah (Sabbatha)	Togarmah (Armenia)
Eber (Hebrews)	Raamah (Persian Gulf)	**Magog (Scythians)**
Peleg	Sheba	**Madai (Medes)**
Joktan (Arabia)	Dedan	**Javan (Greeks)**
Almodad	Sabtechah	Elishah (Aeolians)
Sheleph	Nimrod	Tarshish (Tartessus)
Hazarmaveth	**Mizraim (Egypt)**	Kittim (Cyprus)
Jerah	Ludim (Nubia)	Dodanim (Trojans)
Hadoram	Anamim	**Tubal (Turks)**
Uzal	Lehabim (Libya)	**Meshech (Slavs)**
Diklah	Naphtuhitim (Napetu)	**Tiras (Thracians, Etruscans)**
Obal	Pathrusim (Pathros)	
Abimael	Casluhim (Philistia)	
Sheba	Caphtorim (Crete)	
Ophir	**Phut (Libya)**[2]	
Havilah	**Canaan**	
Jobab	Sidonites	
Lud (Lydians)	Hittites	
Aram (Syrians)	Jebusites	
Uz	Amorites	
Hul	Girgashites	
Gether	Hivites	
Mash	Arkites	
	Sinites (East Asians)[3]	
	Arvadites	
	Zemarites	
	Hamathites	

General Note: The Table of Nations above is derived from Genesis Chapter 10. The sons and grandsons of Noah are bolded. Indentation represents ancestry (e.g., Arphaxad is the son of Shem, Shelah is the son of Arphaxad, Eber is the son of Shelah, etc.).

Notes 1 and 2: A nation or people group's ancestry cannot be wholly attributed to just one of the names above; intermarriage, alliances, and physical proximity have played a monumental role in the historical development of nations and races. Joktan and Havilah, among others, were both possible ancestors of the Arab peoples. Lehabim and Phut are ancestors of the Libyans (note that Phut's nephew was the father of the Lehabim).

Note 3: There is not always agreement regarding which of the names above represents the original ancestor of the peoples of East Asia. In *The Genesis Record*, Henry Morris writes: *"The Biblical mention of a people in the Far East named 'Sinim' (Isa. 49:12), together with references in ancient secular histories to people in the Far East called 'Sinae,' at least suggests the possibility that some of Sin's descendants migrated eastward ... It is significant that the Chinese people have always been identified by the prefix 'Sino-.'"*

MAP OF ISRAEL

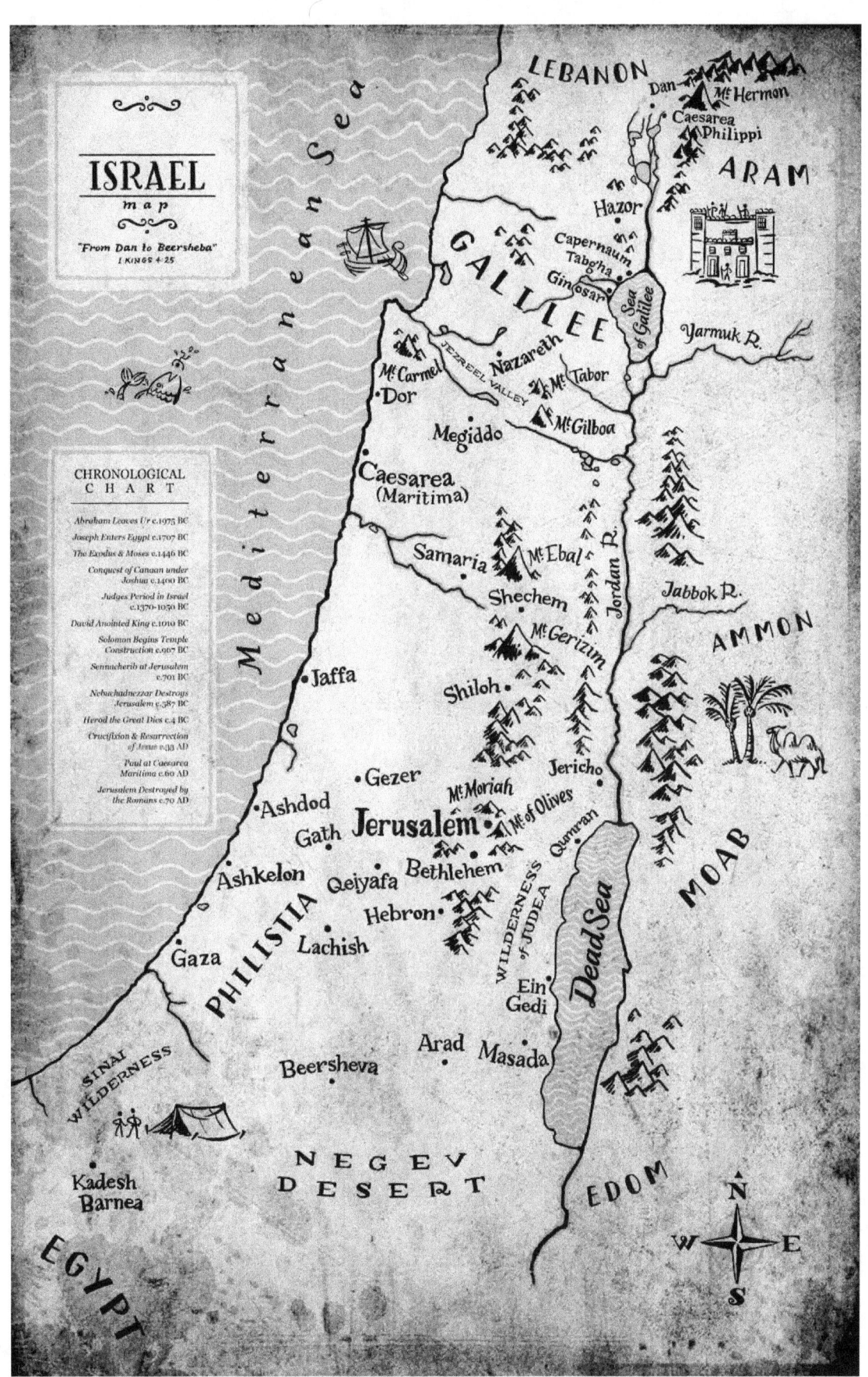

JERUSALEM IN THE 1ST CENTURY

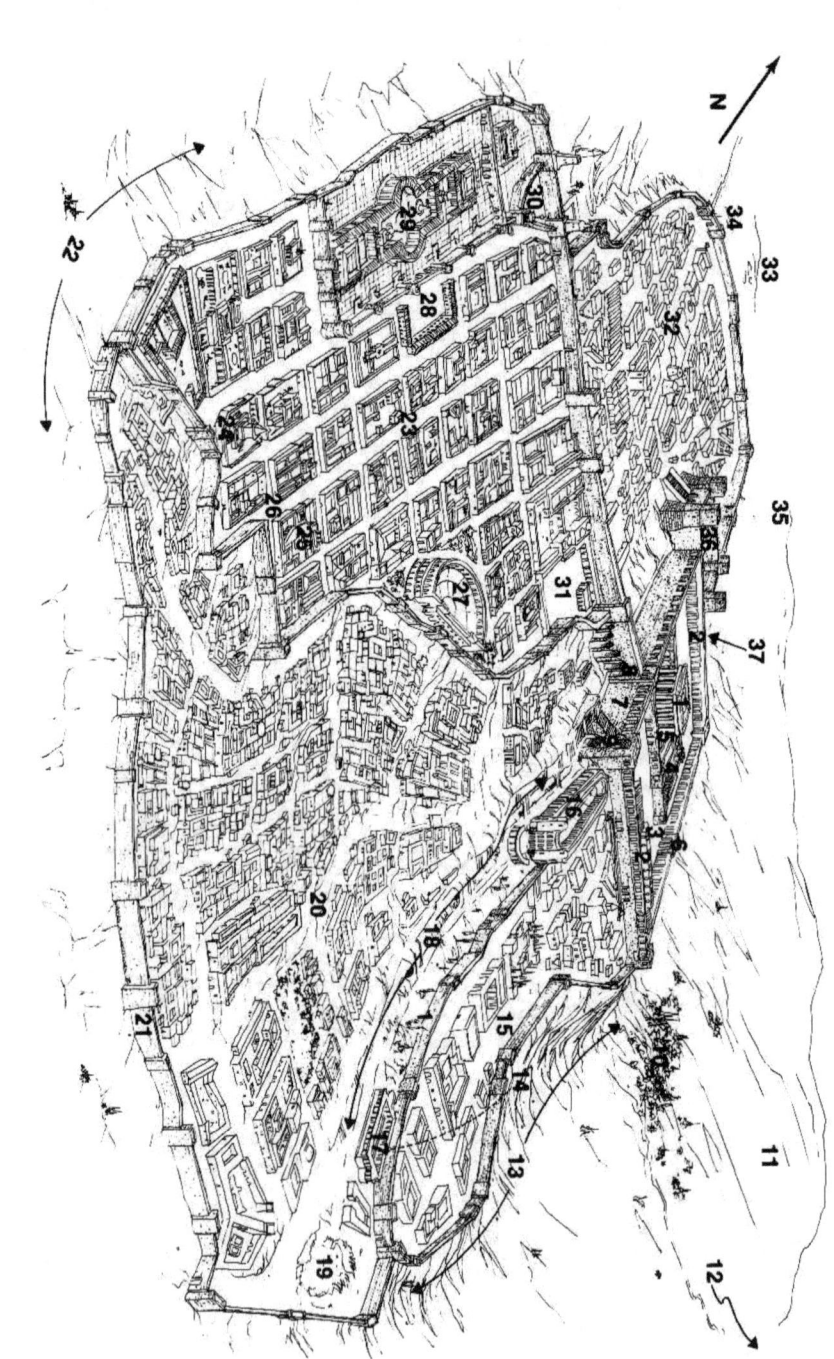

1–9. Mt. Moriah
1. Temple
2. Solomon's Porches
3. Court of the Gentiles
4. Court of the Women
5. Court of the Levites
6. Golden Gate
7. Modern Wailing Wall
8. Wilson's Arch
9. Robinson's Arch
10. Garden of Gethsemane From 14–17: Hezekiah's Tunnel
11. Mt. of Olives
12. To Bethphage
13. Kidron Valley
14. Gihon Spring
15. David's City
16. Herod's Hippodrome
17. Pool of Siloam
18. Tyropoeon Valley
19. King's Dale
20. Lower City (poor section)
21. Wall added by Agrippa
22. Hinnom Valley (Gehenna)
23. Mt. Zion and Upper City
24. David's Tomb
25. Palace of Caiaphas
26. Upper Room
27. Amphitheater
28. Market
29. Herod's Palace
30. The Citadel
31. Hasmonean Palace
32. New City
33. Golgotha (Calvary)
34. Garden Tomb
35. Mt. Scopus
36. Antonia Fortress
37. Pool of Bethesda

GLOSSARY

Aaron: The brother and spokesman of Moses, he served as the first high priest under the Levitical system.

Abel: The second son of Adam and Eve; he is considered the first prophet in the Bible (Lk. 11:51) and brought God an acceptable sacrifice that foreshadowed the death of Christ.

Abomination of Desolation: The ultimate desecration of the Temple prophesied by the prophet Daniel in Daniel 9; it was prefigured by a desecration by Antiochus IV Epiphanes.

Abraham: The descendant of Shem whom God chose to be the father of a great nation; a Chaldean by birth, he left his homeland and eventually settled in the Promised Land; it is through Abraham that the Messiah would come.

Acts of the Apostles: The second part of Luke's two-part Luke-Acts work; Acts details the initiation of the Church in Jerusalem at Pentecost when the Holy Spirit was sent to indwell believers; from there, the Church spread throughout Judea and then to the ends of the earth.

Adam: The first man; the name Adam means "man."

Age: A period of time defined by prevailing circumstances set by God, such as the age or dispensation before the Fall, the age before the Flood, the age during which the Law of Moses was in force, and the present age of the Church; a kingdom age is yet to come in which Christ will rule all nations.

Alexandrian Text: Early manuscripts of the Greek New Testament largely sourced from Egypt; they are held in high regard by reasoned eclectics.

Amos: A prophet contemporary to Isaiah and Hosea who prophesied against the northern Kingdom of Israel before its destruction at the hands of the Assyrians.

Andrew: The brother of Simon Peter and one of the Twelve.

Angel: see *Messenger*.

Antichrist: A future world ruler described in great detail by the prophet Daniel and apostles Paul and John; he was foreshadowed in world history by various rulers (Pharaoh, kings of Assyria and Babylon, Alexander the Great, Antiochus IV Epiphanes, Nero, Titus Vespasian, et al.); he will be directly empowered by Satan (see Rev. 13) to rule over the world's nations for a brief period of time preceding the Second Coming.

Ammon: One of the two sons of Lot born by his daughters; Ammon was the progenitor of the civilization by that name situated directly east of Israel.

Apocalypse: A "revealing" or "uncovering"; the Apocalypse—*Revelation*—is the last book of the New Testament, given by Jesus, delivered by an angel, and recorded by the apostle John, detailing the conclusion of history, the revealing of Christ to the world, and the future hope of the believer; an apocalypse can also refer to any of various apocalyptic works containing prophecy, symbolism, and future expectation.

Apocrypha: Meaning "secret," "concealed," or "hidden," apocryphal works are those less-known writings usually in the Judeo-Christian tradition which are generally not found in the biblical canon because of a lack of apostolic authority, universal acceptance, or scriptural compatibility.

Apostle: One sent forth to carry the message of Christ and expand the bounds of the Church into new areas.

Ark of the Covenant: The ceremonial box, covered in gold and adorned with figures of cherubim, in which were placed the Ten Commandments, among other articles; it was carried by the Israelites in battle and was housed at various locations (the Tabernacle, the Temple) before eventually disappearing from history; God's presence accompanied the Ark, and disregard for the sanctity of the Ark resulted in severe curses, including disease and death.

Ark, Noah's: The nearly 500-foot-long wooden ship that God instructed Noah to build in order for him, his family, and representative land animals from all over the earth to escape the waters of the Flood.

Atonement: "At-one-ment" is the means by which people are reconciled to God; Christ is the atoning sacrifice for sins.

Babel, Tower of: A tower that mankind intended to build in order to prevent their dispersion after the Flood (Gen. 11); the project ceased after God confused their languages; it was from this judgment that mankind spread all over the world.

Babylon: A prominent city in ancient Mesopotamia, not far from modern-day Baghdad; it served as the capital of the Neo-Babylonian Empire and was the place to which many Jews and Israelites were sent during the Exile.

Babylon, Mystery: Both a wicked city and world system in place at the time of the end that is ultimately destroyed by the Antichrist and judged by God; while historically thought to represent Rome, it is perhaps most straightforward to see it as present, unbelieving Jerusalem and the world system at large that rejects Christ.

Baptism: The act of both Jewish and Christian initiation whereby a proselyte is washed and usually immersed in water; also, the invisible baptism of the Holy Spirit, supplanting water (Acts 1:5), whereby all who believe in Jesus are regenerated and sealed (1 Cor. 12:13; Eph. 4:30).

Bartholomew: see *Nathaniel*.

Beast from the Earth: Described in Revelation 13; see *False Prophet*.

Beast from the Sea: Described in Revelation 13; see *Antichrist*.

Byzantine Text: Also called the Majority Text and closely associated with the Received Text, it is the collection of Greek manuscripts of the New Testament that are found primarily in the regions to which the Epistles were originally written; these comprise over 90 percent of extant manuscripts.

Cain: The firstborn son of Adam and Eve; he brought an unacceptable sacrifice, representing the works, efforts, and merits of man; he ultimately murdered his brother Abel.

Cherubim: Angelic beings of very high rank and power described throughout the biblical account (e.g., Gen. 3; Ex. 25–26; 36–37; Ezek. 10); they are often portrayed with four wings, possibly six, and tasked with guarding God's glory; they may be equivalent to the living creatures of Revelation 4–5; Satan is said to have originally been a cherub (Ezek. 28).

Christ: A transliteration of the Greek word for Messiah; see *Messiah*.

Church, A: Any local body of believers in the Lord Jesus Christ.

Church, The: The universal, mystical body of Christ composed of all true believers from every nation and time period.

Communion: see *Lord's Supper*.

Conversion: The act of placing one's faith in Jesus and choosing to follow Him as a disciple.

Creation: The six days during which God made the universe; also, a theological term for the whole cosmos and everything in it that God has made.

Crucifixion: The method of execution by which a criminal is hung to die on a wooden stake or cross; it was practiced by both the Assyrians and Romans.

Daniel: The prophet whose prophecies were recorded in the book of his namesake; he was thrown into a den of lions because of his fealty to God but was miraculously spared; he went on to prophesy of the sequence of future world empires culminating with the final empire of Christ.

David: The second king of Israel; while he committed many grievous sins, his faith in God was steadfast, and God thus rewarded him with an eternal dynasty; through his lineage would come the ultimate son of David—*the Christ*; he defeated Goliath in single combat, conquered Jerusalem, and penned many of the Psalms still present in modern Bibles.

Deluge: see *Flood*.

Demon: An unclean spirit; by tradition, these were the disembodied spirits of the Nephilim and distinct from Watchers and other fallen angels.

Devil: see *Satan*.

Disciple: A student or follower of Christ.

Dispersion, The: Can refer to several things: (1) the dispersal of Jews and Israelites during the Exile; (2) Jews dispersed abroad for any number of historical reasons; (3) the dispersion of Jews after the First Jewish-Roman War and the destruction of Jerusalem.

Edom: The descendants of Esau dwelling south and east of Judah; they were frequently at enmity with the Jews.

Elder: A mature male believer appointed for leadership in a local church.

Elders, The 24: A group of heavenly beings thought by most conservative scholars to represent the glorified Church in Heaven.

Enoch: The patriarch, who in the seventh generation from Adam, was removed from the earth before the Flood because of his faith.

Epistle: A letter.

Esau: The elder brother of Jacob; he was swindled out of his birthright and became a representative of those that reject God's promises rashly; he became the progenitor of the Edomites.

Essenes: One of the Jewish sects prevalent in the 1st century AD; unlike the Pharisees and Sadducees, they often dwelt away from larger society, such as in communities like Qumran; they often had strong messianic expectations and some believe many of them transitioned to Christian faith after the resurrection of Christ.

Esther: Hadassah by birth, Esther was a Jewish woman who dwelt in Susa, the capital of the ancient Medo-Persian Empire; she was chosen to be the new wife and queen of King Ahasuerus, and using her position of influence, she thwarted a plan by Haman to destroy the Jews.

Eve: The first woman, created from one of Adam's ribs.

Evil: That which is opposed to God's glory.

Exile, The: The removal of the Israelites, primarily the Jews, Levites, and Benjamites, from the land of Israel to the city and region of Babylon; the Exile lasted 70 years.

Exodus: The miraculous deliverance of the enslaved Israelites from Egyptian captivity.

Expiation: The removal of sin; Christ's atoning death removes the sins of those who place their faith in Him.

Ezekiel: An Israelite priest and prophet who prophesied in the early 6th century BC; he prophesied of the coming war of Gog and Magog (Ezek. 38–39), the mass, physical resurrection of Israelites (Ezek. 37), and the future Millennial Temple (Ezek. 40–48).

Ezra: A Jewish scribe and priest operating in the 5th century BC; he led a religious revival among the post-exilic Jews in Jerusalem.

Faith: Believing in and trusting God and His promises despite not seeing God or having those promises yet realized (Heb. 11).

False Prophet: An individual claiming to speak for God, yet who was not sent by God; the simple test of a false prophet is whether or not their prediction comes to pass; *the* False Prophet is a specific man described in Revelation 13 who leads the world to worship and submit to the Antichrist.

Flood, The: The first global cataclysm, described explicitly in Genesis 6–8, in which God destroyed all life on the face of the earth because of the pervasiveness of the corruption of sin (note: not sea life); of human beings, only Noah, his three sons, and their wives were spared by taking refuge in the Ark.

Gehenna: The place of the ultimate fiery judgment of God's enemies, prefigured by the Valley of Hinnom outside Jerusalem in which refuse was perpetually burned; it is described as a lake of fire in the Book of Revelation.

God: The supreme, self-existent, and greatest conceivable being, called *Elohim* in the Hebrew Old Testament, and *Theos* in the Greek New Testament; He is the Creator of the universe, Sustainer of all things, Redeemer of mankind, and the only One worthy of worship.

Godhead: see *Trinity*.

Goliath: A nearly 10-foot-tall Philistine giant who taunted the Israelites and was subsequently slain by the shepherd David; he was one of a number of giants who resided in Canaan many centuries after the Flood.

Good: That which is in accordance with God's nature and will.

Gospel, The: Literally "good news," it is the message that Christ has died for our sins and physically risen again (1 Cor. 15:1–4); this is the fundamental and primary message of Christianity according to the apostle Paul.

Gospels: Any of the four biographical works that describe the life and teachings of Jesus of Nazareth (Matthew, Mark, Luke, and John).

Grace: Undeserved favor, goodness, and blessing.

Great Commission: The commission given by Christ to His disciples as described in Matthew 28:19–20, commanding them to make disciples throughout the world.

Habakkuk: An Israelite prophet whose short work was likely recorded in the late-7th century BC.

Hades: The realm of the dead in which disembodied spirits are kept until judgment; the righteous were also housed here until the Gospel was realized (see Lk. 16).

Haggai: The first post-exilic prophet, he prophesied of God's command to rebuild the Temple.

Ham: One of the three sons of Noah; his descendants spread to Africa and Asia.

Heaven: Heaven can indicate several things: (1) the place where God dwells manifestly; (2) wherever God is; (3) the cosmos beyond earth (i.e., space); (4) the sky; (5) any of various heavenly realms.

Hebrew: Possibly etymologically related to *Eber*, the great-grandson of Shem and ancestor of Abraham; any of those belonging to the family and line of Abraham, Isaac, and Jacob; can also refer to the native language of Israel which has been lately revived; see *Israel*.

Holy Spirit: The third person of the Godhead; He convicts the world of sin, convicts the believer of imputed righteousness, and regenerates, seals, and guides the believer as he or she journeys through life.

Hosea: A prophet in the 8th century BC who was famously commanded by God to marry the prostitute Gomer in order to represent God's relationship with unfaithful Israel.

Immutability: The attribute of God's unchanging nature.

Imputation: The act of God whereby the sinner, despite moral and spiritual inability, is given the righteousness and moral perfection of Christ as a gift (2 Cor. 5:21; Rm. 5:15–19).

Iniquity: The premeditated and willful evil residing within the unrepentant.

Isaac: The promised son of Abraham, born in his old age; God commanded Abraham to sacrifice his son Isaac, but intervened via an angel to prevent the sacrifice; in his stead, a ram was provided, prefiguring the atoning sacrifice of Christ.

Isaiah: The first of the major prophets, Isaiah prophesied in the late-8th and early-7th centuries BC; his prophecies are profound, often future-focused, and highly messianic; he prophesied of Christ's virgin birth (Isa. 7, 9), atoning death and resurrection (Isa. 53), and the creation of a new heavens and earth (Isa. 65).

Israel: The name given by God to Jacob; the whole people Abraham, Isaac, and Jacob; the land of the Israelites, promised and secured by God, situated in western Asia, along the eastern coast of the Mediterranean Sea.

Jacob: The son of Isaac whom God renamed Israel; the descendants of Jacob are the Israelites; his twelve sons became the twelve tribes of Israel.

James the Greater: Designated "greater," not as an acclaim of greater importance, but for either greater age or stature, James the Greater was one of the Twelve and the first apostle to be martyred for his faith (in circa AD 44).

James the Lesser: One of the Twelve and possible brother of Matthew; by one tradition, he was martyred by stoning.

James, the half-brother of Jesus: He initially rejected his brother, but after the resurrection, came to faith and led the church in Jerusalem; it is said he was entrapped by legalism and opposed the Gospel, but came to repentance as recorded in Acts 15; he penned the epistle bearing his name.

Japheth: One of the three sons of Noah; his descendants primarily spread to Europe.

Jeremiah: One of the major prophets, he is known as "the weeping prophet"; he prophesied of Jerusalem's destruction.

Jerusalem: An ancient Jebusite city which became the center of Israelite governance after David conquered the city; since then, it has taken on an increasingly central role in Jewish life and biblical prophecy.

Jesus of Nazareth: A Jewish man, born in Bethlehem circa 5–1 BC, who died in Jerusalem circa AD 30–33; claiming to be fully God and fully man, His claims were validated by His powerful miracles, steadfast love, sacrificial death, and bodily resurrection from the dead; the authors of the New Testament unwaveringly held to the belief that salvation is only found in Him (Jn. 14:6; Acts 4:12).

Jew: Specifically, a person belonging to the tribe of Judah, the term is also used more broadly to refer to any Israelite or modern-day Israeli.

Joel: One of the minor prophets, he wrote as early as the 9th century BC, and his prophecy is quoted by the apostle Peter on the day of Pentecost (Acts 2).

John: One of the Twelve and the likely author of the Gospel and epistles bearing his name, as well as the Book of Revelation.

John the Baptist: The son of Zechariah and Elizabeth and cousin of Jesus; he came in the spirit and power of Elijah and prepared the way for Jesus; he was beheaded for his stalwart defense of truth.

Jonah: The Israelite prophet who tried to flee from God, but who was swallowed by a great fish and eventually obeyed God, prophesying to the people of Nineveh to repent before certain judgment.

Joshua: Joshua, son of Nun, led the Israelites into the Promised Land after the death of Moses; his leadership enabled the tribes to obtain their possessions and transitioned the Israelites into the period of the Judges.

Judas Iscariot: One of the original Twelve Apostles; he betrayed Jesus to the Jewish authorities, and despairing of what he had done while lacking true faith in Christ, he committed suicide by hanging.

Justification: To be considered or proven right; from a theological perspective, to be declared righteous by sovereign decree of God.

Lake of Fire: see *Gehenna*.

Law: Generically, a rule enacted by a sovereign that must be followed; theologically, the Law of Moses given by God at Mount Sinai; it was designed to condemn the world under sin so that sinners would be prepared to receive grace through faith in Christ (Rm. 3; Gal. 3).

Lord's Supper: The memorial meal instituted by Christ on the night before His death; Christians share bread, representing Christ's body, and wine, representing Christ's blood, to remember the sacrifice He made for sinners.

Love: Sacrificial care for another at the expense of one's own rights, dignity, and resources; the ultimate demonstration of which was the sacrificial death of Christ who died in the place of sinners.

Maccabees: A league of Jewish rebels who overthrew Seleucid rule in Judea in the 2nd century BC, founding the Hasmonean Dynasty and reigning until the mid-1st century BC; the rededication of the Temple, from which is derived the Jewish holiday of Hanukkah, occurred during their uprising.

Malachi: One of the minor prophets, although some believe Malachi was the pen name of Ezra the Scribe; he prophesied in the 5th century BC and his work concludes the Old Testament with a prophecy of the coming of John the Baptist and the incarnate Messiah (Mal. 3–4).

Man of Lawlessness: Described by the apostle Paul in 2 Thessalonians 2, a man, empowered by Satan, who is coming to deceive the inhabitants of earth; see *Antichrist*.

Mary: The mother of Jesus, the mother of God, wife of Joseph.

Mary Magdalene: The disciple of Jesus from whom He cast out seven demons; she followed Him closely and was the first to see Him risen from the dead.

Masoretic Text: The prevalent Hebrew text of the Tanakh in use by Jews today and underlying most English translations of the Old Testament.

Matthew: A former tax collector, he followed Jesus, becoming one of the Twelve; he later recorded the Gospel attributed to him.

Matthias: The apostle, chosen by lot, who replaced Judas Iscariot according to Acts 1:23–26.

Mercy: Not receiving deserved punishment or retribution.

Messenger: One sent to deliver a message; messengers in the Bible are often heavenly entities sent to deliver God's messages to mankind; the Greek word for "messenger," *angelos*, is transliterated "angel" in many translations.

Messiah: The Hebrew term for "Anointed One"; the Messiah was the long-expected Savior and King who would not only satisfy prophetic hopes pertaining to Israel, but as the Seed promised to Eve (Gen. 3:15), Gentile hopes as well.

Micah: One of the minor prophets, he prophesied during the time of the Assyrian conquest of the northern Kingdom of Israel and Sennacherib's invasion of Judah; he prophesied that Israel's future King was preexistent and to be born in Bethlehem (Mic. 5:2).

Miriam: The sister of Moses.

Moab: One of the two sons of Lot born by his daughters; Moab was the progenitor of the civilization by that name situated east of the Dead Sea, south of Ammon, and north of Edom.

Monotheism: Belief in one God.

Moses: The Hebrew who was adopted by Pharaoh's daughter after being found in a basket in the Nile River; he eventually fled to Midian, encountered God at the Burning Bush, and returned to Egypt to lead the Israelites out of slavery; he became a mediator between God and the people and led the Israelites in their wilderness wanderings.

Nahum: One of the minor prophets, he prophesied against Nineveh and Assyria in the late-7th century BC.

Nathaniel: A friend of Philip and one of the Twelve; he is the one whom Jesus saw under a fig tree while not present with him; Jesus said of him that he was "a true Israelite, in whom is nothing false"; he is often identified with Bartholomew.

Nehemiah: A biblical figure instrumental in leading the restoration effort of Jerusalem among the post-exilic Jews.

Nephilim: The offspring of the angels who sinned in Genesis 6; while the word might mean something like "fallen ones," a strong linguistic case can be made that it is best translated "giants."

New Covenant: The covenant enacted by Christ with His followers through His sacrificial death and resurrection; it is a covenant of grace rather than law.

New Testament: The 27 books, beginning with Matthew and ending with Revelation, that reveal Christ as the fulfillment of Old Testament prophecy and expectation, and the enactor of the New Covenant.

Noah: The antediluvian man who found grace in the eyes of God; he built the Ark to escape the Flood and he and his family was spared judgment, along with two of every unclean land-dwelling animal and seven of every clean animal kind.

Obadiah: One of the minor prophets; he wrote as early as the 9th century BC, making him a possible contemporary of Elijah.

Old Covenant: The Law given by God to the Israelites at Mount Sinai; see *Law*.

Old Testament: The sacred and divinely-inspired books beginning with Genesis and ending with Malachi that describe creation, the fall of mankind into sin, the establishment and development of the nation of Israel, and the messianic expectation among God's followers.

Omnipotence: The attribute of God's infinite power.

Omnipresence: The attribute of God's universal presence.

Omniscience: The attribute of God's limitless knowledge.

Overseer: From the same Greek word which is translated as "bishop," these local church leaders are identifiable with elders.

Parousia: The appearing of Christ; this can refer to both the pre-tribulational appearing of Christ for the Church, as well as the post-tribulational appearing of Christ in glory during the Second Coming.

Passover: The sacred festival generally occurring in the March to April timeframe during which the people of Israel celebrated their release from Egyptian bondage; the sacrifice of a lamb during the festival ultimately prefigured the death of Christ, who died on Passover.

Paul: A Pharisee who greatly persecuted the Church, but who came face to face with Jesus on the road to Damascus and went on to be the primary apostle to the Gentiles; much of Acts records his story and most of the New Testament epistles are his.

Pentecost: The 50th day, inclusive, after the Feast of First Fruits; 50 days after Christ's resurrection on First Fruits, the Holy Spirit was sent to indwell believers and initiate the Church.

Peter, Simon: A Galilean fisherman and brother of Andrew; he was called by Jesus and became a key leader of the Twelve; he was later martyred in Rome via crucifixion, but refusing the dignity of being crucified in the same manner as his Master, he was crucified upside down.

Pharaoh: Any of various kings of Egypt.

Pharisees: The most popular Jewish sect among the people at the time of Christ, known for high regard for Judaism and a generally literal interpretation of Scripture; they were often defined by legalism and opposed the message of grace and humility that Christ brought.

Philip: One of the Twelve, he was martyred in Hierapolis according to tradition; he features heavily in the Gospel of John.

Philistines: A possibly Minoan people who settled on the southwestern coast of Canaan during the period of the Judges; a number of giants lived among them, including Goliath and his brothers; they were the primary enemy of Israel for generations. It is thought by some linguists that the term "Palestine" is ultimately derived from Philistia.

Prophecy: The revealing of God's will, often by predicting the outcome of future events.

Propitiation: The satisfaction of God's wrath against sin; Christ's atoning death made propitiation for the sins of mankind.

Pseudepigrapha: False writings; writings attributed to an author who did not in fact write the text.

Rapture: The future removal of believers from the earth preceding the 70th Week of Daniel, as described by the apostle Paul in 1 Thessalonians 4:16–18, 1 Corinthians 15, John in Revelation 3–4, and the prophet Isaiah in Isaiah 26 and 66, among others.

Repentance: From Greek *metanoia* (lit. "after thought"; i.e., to think differently afterwards), the word is non-theological in Greek and means to change one's mind about something; in a theological context, it means to change one's mind from unbelief in Christ to belief in Christ.

Resurrection: Returning to life, bodily, after a real and complete death; according to the Apostles and hundreds of eyewitnesses, Jesus was resurrected on the third day after His crucifixion.

Righteousness: Goodness and real justification by God's perfect standard.

Ruth: The Moabite daughter-in-law of the Israelite Naomi; she eventually married Boaz, a kinsman redeemer; the marriage of Boaz, an Israelite, and Ruth, a Gentile, prefigured Christ the Jewish Redeemer in union with His primarily Gentile Church.

Sabbath: The seventh day of the week on which God ceased from His creative work; it is this day—Friday evening through Saturday evening—that the Israelites were commanded to rest from their work in remembrance.

Sadducees: A Hellenized Jewish sect often at enmity with the Pharisees; they held to a less supernatural view of Scripture and often denied the eschatological hope of resurrection; they held considerable power in Jerusalem and were frequently opposed to Jesus.

Salvation: The process by which a spiritually-dead person is forgiven of their sins through faith in Jesus Christ and thus spiritually regenerated by the Holy Spirit, adopted by God into His heavenly family, and granted everlasting life.

Samaritan Pentateuch: A Paleo-Hebrew text of the Pentateuch in use by the Samaritans.

Samuel: A prophet of God whose ministry oversaw the transition from the period of the Judges to the period of the Kings.

Satan: The prime sentient adversary of God, described in the books of Job, Isaiah, Ezekiel, and Zechariah, and frequently throughout the New Testament; he is explicitly identified with the serpent in the Garden of Eden in Revelation 12; while he is frequently described as "fallen," his final fall is still yet future when he will be cast to the earth (Rev. 12) and ultimately bound for 1,000 years and eternally judged (Rev. 20).

Saul: The first king of Israel; anointed by Samuel, he eventually transgressed a number of God's commands which led to his loss of the kingdom.

Second Coming: The return of Christ to the earth to establish supreme rulership for one thousand years in advance of a new creation; it is described in great detail in Zechariah 14 and Revelation 19–20, among other passages.

Septuagint: The Greek translation of the Old Testament Scriptures.

Seraphim: Six-winged angelic beings described by the prophet Isaiah.

Seth: The third son of Adam and Eve through whom came the lineage of Noah, his sons, and ultimately all the people of earth.

Shem: One of the three sons of Noah and the one through whom would come Abraham, Isaac, and Jacob; it is from Shem that the term Semite is derived.

Simon the Zealot: One of the Twelve; he was affiliated, likely formerly, with the Zealots.

Sin: Literally "missing the mark," sin is the corruption that entered the world through Adam's disobedience; sin is whatever does not come from faith in God (Rm. 14:23); while not all sin is equal in gravity, all sin causes death.

Sin Nature: The corrupted nature of all human beings as a result of the sin that entered the world through Adam; the sin nature predisposes human beings to sin; Christ alone was born without a sin nature as He had no earthly father, and thus did not inherit the predisposition of Adam.

Sola Fide: Faith alone; the belief that a person is justified through faith in Jesus Christ, rather than doing enough good to win God's favor.

Sola Gratia: Grace alone; the belief that a person is saved by God's unmerited grace.

Sola Scriptura: Scripture alone; the belief that doctrine and truth are established on the basis of God's revealed word alone.

Soli Deo Gloria: For the glory of God alone; the belief that all things are ultimately for God's glory, including salvation.

Solomon: The son of David and third king of Israel; under his leadership the First Temple was built in Jerusalem.

Solus Christus: In Christ alone; the belief that salvation is only found in Jesus; there are not many paths to God.

Tabernacle: The tent constructed by the Israelites after the Exodus to house the Ark and conduct the priestly services; it was carried by the Israelites during their journeys and was later replaced by the Temple in Jerusalem.

Tabernacles, Feast of: A harvest festival in the autumn in which the Jews dwell in sukkahs or tent-like booths; it was one of the three pilgrimage festivals.

Tanakh: The Jewish Bible; see *Old Testament*.

Temple: Any of several large stone structures built as a permanent house for the Ark of the Covenant, the priestly services, and the presence of God on earth; the first was built by King Solomon in Jerusalem and was destroyed in the 6th century BC; the second was built by the returning exiles and lasted until AD 70; a third temple is prophesied to be built during the Tribulation period, and a fourth, often called the Millennial Temple, will be built during the Millennial Kingdom (cf. Ezek. 40–48); the Church itself is a spiritual temple in which the presence of God resides via the indwelling Holy Spirit.

Ten Commandments: The first ten laws given by God to Moses at Mount Sinai; while these were the only laws written on tablets of stone, they were only one portion of a much larger collection of 613 laws given to the Israelites as an all-or-nothing proposition: if kept, the nation would be blessed; if not kept in their entirety, the nation would be cursed.

Thaddeus: Sometimes identified with Jude; one of the Twelve.

Thomas: One of the Twelve; he is known for his doubts regarding the resurrection of Christ, but whose faith was restored when Jesus physically appeared to him.

Timothy: An associate and student of Paul's to whom Paul wrote in 1 and 2 Timothy. He was charged with faithful church stewardship and contending for the Christian faith as a good shepherd.

Tomb: particularly in the New Testament era, these were artificial caves hewn out of rock for the entombment of corpses.

Transcendence: The attribute describing how God is not equal to or identifiable with His creation as found in beliefs like pantheism or panentheism; rather, God is beyond and superior to His creation.

Transgression: Overstepping a set boundary; breaking a law of God.

Trinity: The community of persons within the Godhead: Father, Son, and Holy Spirit (Mt. 28:19); the three persons share the one divine nature ("God") and are thus a single being and essence, yet distinct in personhood.

Watchers: The specific group of approximately 200 angels that "left their first estate" and married human women, through whom giant, hybrid offspring, called *Nephilim*, were born.

Zealots: A militant Jewish sect in the 1st century that was known for sometimes violent opposition to Rome.

Zechariah: The son of Berechiah, the son of Iddo, a prophet who prophesied in the 6th century BC; not to be confused with the Zechariah in the Gospels who was the father of John the Baptist.

Zephaniah: A prophet who prophesied in the days of Josiah, king of Judah, in the 7th century BC.

Zion: A prophetic and political term referring to Jerusalem and the land of Israel at large; it can also prophetically and symbollically refer to the heavenly city in which believers will have citizenship.

THE FAITH ONCE DELIVERED

"Beloved, using all diligence to write to you concerning our common salvation, I had necessity to write to you, exhorting [you] to fight for the faith once delivered to the holy ones…" (Jd. 1:3)

GOD AS TRINITY: The Trinity is the foundational Christian belief pertaining to God's nature (*theology*), that God is one Being (infinite, indivisible, uncreated essence) who exists in three Persons. The Persons—Father, Son, and Holy Spirit—are co-equal and co-eternal. The divine nature comes from the Father (i.e., the three Persons share in the nature of the Father), but the Father is not the Son, and the Holy Spirit is neither Father nor Son. The Son is eternally generated by the Father, and the Holy Spirit proceeds eternally from Father and Son. (*References:* Mt. 28:19; Lk. 1:35; 3:21–22; Jn. 1:1–2; 10:30; 14:16; 2 Cor. 13:14; 1 Pt. 1:2; see also Gen. 1:26; 3:22; 11:7)

JESUS CHRIST: The study of the nature of Jesus Christ (*Christology*) based on the revealed word of God, demonstrates that, according to His humanity, Christ was a descendant of King David, of the tribe of Judah, born of the virgin Mary in the town of Bethlehem, and raised in the region of Galilee, in the town of Nazareth; He lived, by all accounts, a morally-flawless and sinless life of devotion to God and sacrificial love. Moreover, He died by crucifixion at the hands of the Roman and Jewish authorities, was buried in the tomb of Joseph of Arimathea, and was resurrected from the dead on the third day (early Sunday morning, before dawn); 40 days post-resurrection, Christ ascended into Heaven. According to His divinity, Christ is the eternal Son of the Father and the incarnate Son of God. He is thus fully God and fully man, possessing both natures completely, and yet is one Person. (*References:* Isa. 7:14; 9:6; Mt. 1:23; 2:1–12; Lk. 1:35; Jn. 1:1–2, 14; 1 Cor. 15:3–4; Phil. 2:5–11; Col. 1:16–17; 2:9; Heb. 1:3; 4:15)

THE GOSPEL: The Gospel (*lit.* "Good News") is the fundamental belief in Christianity pertaining to salvation (*soteriology*), programmatically stated by the apostle Paul in 1 Corinthians 15:3–4, that (1) Christ died for our sins, (2) was buried, and (3) was physically/bodily resurrected from the dead. The Gospel message outlined and proclaimed by Paul and the other apostles rests on several key recognitions: *first*, Jesus is the Christ (the Messiah of Israel, the Chosen One of God); *second*, Christ was truly killed, and His death was substitutional (the sinless Christ died in the place of sinners, taking the punishment of death due to sinners upon Himself); *third*, Christ returned to life, not merely as an apparition or figuratively, but physically and bodily; and *fourth*, salvation is found in Christ alone. When a person places their faith in Jesus Christ, believing in the complete Gospel message, they are forgiven of all their sins, adopted as God's own child, and granted everlasting life. (*References:* Isa. 53; Lk. 24:46–47; Jn. 3:7–18; 8:24; 14:6; Acts 4:12; Rm. 3:21–24; 6:23; 10:5–13; 1 Cor. 15; Eph. 2:8–9; 1 Jn. 1:9; 3:1–3)

THE CHURCH: The Church (*lit.* "Assembly") is the universal collective of Jews and Gentiles with faith in Jesus Christ. The biblical doctrine of the Church (*ecclesiology*) details that the members of the Church come from all nations, collectively form Christ's mystical body, are called to evangelism and discipleship in the present age, baptize new converts and share the Lord's Supper (i.e., communion), and have a shared future united with Christ in the heavenly realms. The true Church is known only to God. (*References:* Mt. 28:19–20; Lk. 22:19–20; Jn. 14:1–3; Acts 20:28; 1 Cor. 12:27; Eph. 2:6; 1 Thess. 4:13–18; Rev. 5:9)

THE FUTURE: The biblical study of "last things" (*eschatology*) reveals that the earth, mankind, and the universe, now broken and corrupted by sin, will be restored, but in such a way even more glorious than the Edenic order of Genesis 1 and 2. Christ will gather His Church, taking believers to the heavenly place prepared, return to earth to judge the nations and establish His kingdom, reign for one thousand years, judge unbelievers, eradicate all sin and death, and then establish a perfect eternal order where Heaven and earth are united and God dwells intimately with His children forever. (*References:* Mt. 24–25; Jn. 14:1–3; 1 Cor. 15:50–53; 1 Thess. 4:13–18; Rev. 19–22)

FALSE TEACHINGS REJECTED BY THE CHURCH (HERESIES)

"...for I have known this, that there will enter in, after my departing, grievous wolves to you, not sparing the flock..." (Acts 20:29)

1ST AND 2ND CENTURIES

Legalism (Judaizers): The belief that circumcision and/or keeping the Law of Moses, in addition to faith in Jesus, is necessary for salvation for both Jews and Gentiles.

Antinomianism: The idea that there is no obligation to live with Christian virtue or moral responsibilities; while the historic Christian faith recognizes that believers are now free from the legal demands of the Law of Moses (the Old Covenant), there is still an important recognition that the Law reveals the heart of God, and Christians are called to live lives worthy of their salvation under the New Covenant.

Docetism: The belief of Docetism holds that Jesus Christ did not have a real physical body, but only an apparent or illusory one.

Montanism: A movement that emphasized the importance of ecstatic experiences and new prophecies not found in Scripture.

Gnosticism: A complex system of thought that teaches that the material world is evil, and that salvation can be achieved through superior knowledge (gnosis).

- **Valentinianism:** A gnostic heresy that taught that the world was created by a series of emanations from the supreme being. Valentinians believed that salvation came from knowledge of the true nature of the universe.
- **Marcionism:** A heresy that arose in the 2nd century AD. Marcionists believed that the God of the Old Testament was a different god from the God of the New Testament.
- **Sethianism:** Sethianism was a 2nd-century gnostic movement that believed in a supreme god, Sophia, the demiurge, and gnosis as the path to salvation.
- **Basilideanism:** Basilideanism was a gnostic Christian sect founded by Basilides of Alexandria. Basilidians believed that the material world was created by an evil demiurge and that the goal of salvation was to escape from this world and return to the spiritual realm.

Monarchianism: A heresy that taught that the Father, Son, and Holy Spirit were all the same unitarian being, and not distinct, co-eternal Persons. Monarchians were also known as Unitarians.

- **Modalism:** Modalism is the belief that the Father, Son, and Holy Spirit are three different modes of God, as opposed to a Trinitarian view of three distinct Persons within the Godhead.
  - **Sabellianism:** The belief that the Father, Son, and Holy Spirit are not three distinct persons, but are simply different manifestations of the same divine being.
  - **Patripassianism:** The belief that the Father and Son are not two distinct persons, and both God the Father and the Son suffered on the cross as Jesus.
- **Adoptionism:** The belief that Jesus Christ was not the Son of God from eternity, but was adopted by God at some point in His life.

Psilanthropism: The belief that Jesus is merely human and that He never became divine, or that He never existed prior to His birth.

3RD CENTURY

Novatianism: A movement that arose in response to the persecution of Christians by the Roman Empire. Novatians believed that Christians who had lapsed during the persecution could not be forgiven.

4TH CENTURY

Arianism: The belief that Jesus Christ is not fully divine, but is a created being.

Donatism: A movement that arose in North Africa in the 4th century AD. Donatists believed that the Church had become corrupt and that only the Donatists were the true Christians.

Apollinarianism: The belief that Jesus did not have a human mind or soul, but only a human body.

Tritheism: The belief that there are three gods, rather than one God in three Persons.

Collyridianism: The belief that the Trinity consists of the Father, Son, and Mary, and that the Son results from the marital union between the other two.

Binitarianism: Binitarianism is a Christian heresy that teaches that there are only two persons in the Godhead: the Father and the Son. The Holy Spirit is not considered to be a separate Person, but rather an aspect of the Son or the Father.

Subordinationism: A heresy that teaches that the Son and the Holy Spirit are not co-equal with the Father. Subordinationists believe that the Son and the Holy Spirit are ontologically subordinate to the Father.

Anomoeanism: A heresy that taught that Jesus was not fully divine, but was a created being. Anomoeans also believed that Christ could not be like God because He lacked the quality of self-existence.

Priscillianism: This heresy emerged in Spain during the 4th century and was influenced by the Gnostic-Manichaean teachings of Marcus, an Egyptian from Memphis.

5TH CENTURY

Nestorianism: The belief that Jesus Christ was two persons: the divine Son of God and the human Jesus of Nazareth. Nestorius said that the virgin Mary is not the mother of God (*Theotokos*) because she gave birth to the human part of Jesus, not the divine Son of God, and he called her *Christotokos*. Nestorianism was condemned as a heresy by the Council of Ephesus.

Pelagianism: The belief that humans can be saved by their own efforts, without the need for God's grace.

Eutychianism: The belief that Christ is in one nature and of two, with the humanity of Christ subsumed by the divinity.

Monophysitism: The belief that Christ has only one nature, which is divine.

Miaphysitism: The belief that Christ is fully divine and fully human, in one nature (*physis*).

MODERN HERESIES (18TH THROUGH 21ST CENTURIES)

Modernism: The belief that all doctrines are subject to change, and that doctrines ought to change depending on the time and location.

Mormonism: Based on the unique teachings of Joseph Smith and his Book of Mormon, proponents teach that the Bible was corrupted, that God is not one, that Jesus and the Holy Spirit are distinct beings from God the Father, that other gods exist beyond the Godhead, and that divinity is ultimately an unending procession of created beings attaining Godhood.

Jehovah's Witnesses: A nontrinitarian sect that denies both the divinity of Christ and salvation through faith alone. It is managed by the sectarian Watch Tower Society.

Universalism: The belief that most or all religions provide a legitimate path to salvation and that the various gods of the world's religions are ultimately manifestations of the supreme being or transcendent spiritual reality.

COVENANT OF THE CCC

WE BELIEVE in One God, revealed to the world as YHWH of Israel,
Uncreated, self-existent, eternal, all-powerful, and unchanging.
He knows all things and there is nowhere where He is not.
He is good, His word is inerrant, and His nature is love.

WE BELIEVE God subsists as the mutual indwelling of three persons:
The Father, the Son, and the Holy Spirit, in eternal communion.
God the Son and God the Holy Spirit come from God the Father,
And throughout eternity they have always existed with the Father.

WE BELIEVE God created time, space, matter, and all things,
Accomplishing His initial act of creation in only six days.
On the sixth day God created Man in His own image out of dust,
Adam the first male and Eve the first female.

WE BELIEVE God said the man should be joined to his wife,
And in so doing the two would become one flesh in marriage.
In diversity He created the marital union sacred, monogamous,
And dissoluble only by death or unfaithfulness.

WE BELIEVE God gave Man the choice of obedience or rebellion,
And Adam and Eve willfully rebelled by eating the forbidden fruit,
Which came from the Tree of the Knowledge of Good and Evil.
They suffered spiritual death and passed their sin nature on to us.

WE BELIEVE that God justly judged the world with a flood,
Sparing Noah and his family through whom came the nations.
And from Noah's son Shem came Abraham, Isaac, and Jacob,
And from Jacob the twelve tribes of Israel and the prophets.

WE BELIEVE that in the fullness of time God gave us His Son,
Born under the law to redeem those condemned by the law.
He was born in the town of Bethlehem to a virgin named Mary,
And in accordance with God's command was named Jesus.

WE BELIEVE Jesus was chosen before the creation of the world,
To live a sinless human life in perfect obedience to the Father,
That He might die a substitutionary death in place of sinners,
Giving forgiveness of sins and eternal life to all who trust in Him.

WE BELIEVE Jesus freely gave His life in obedience to the Father,
And at the order of Pontius Pilate was flogged and crucified.
At the ninth hour He declared His purpose in death was finished,
And He died and was buried in the tomb of Joseph of Arimathea.

WE BELIEVE that death had no power over God's perfect Son,
And on the third day He conquered death by rising to life again.
This was literal, physical, and attested to by over 500 witnesses,
And is the event that gives power and validation to our faith.

WE BELIEVE men are only reconciled to God through Jesus Christ,
And receive salvation by grace through faith apart from works.
By the Spirit all believers are baptized into one body, the Church.
Christians baptize, share communion, and love one another.

WE BELIEVE the Church is a universal priesthood of believers.
Membership is not obtained by belonging to a denomination,
But is received by trusting in Jesus for the forgiveness of sins.
The Church awaits Jesus' soon return when He will call us home.

CONVICTIONS OF THE CCC

1. THERE IS ONE GOD WHO IS ETERNAL, SELF-EXISTENT, ALL-POWERFUL, ALL-KNOWING, EVERYWHERE-PRESENT, COMPLETELY GOOD, AND NEVER CHANGING. GOD IS PERFECT IN MORAL CHARACTER AND HIS NATURE IS LOVE. GOD ALONE CAN DECLARE WHETHER CONDUCT IS RIGHT OR WRONG.

Scripture References: Deuteronomy 6:4, Isaiah 44:8, Psalm 90:2, Isaiah 40:28, Exodus 3:14, Revelation 19:6, Psalm 147:5, 1 John 3:20, Psalm 139:7–8, Jeremiah 23:24, Psalm 119:68, James 1:17, Hebrews 13:8, 1 John 4:8, Judges 21:25, Isaiah 45:19

2. GOD SUBSISTS ETERNALLY IN THREE PERSONS: THE FATHER, THE SON, AND THE HOLY SPIRIT. THESE THREE ARE NEITHER PARTS NOR MODES.

Scripture References: Matthew 28:19, Luke 1:35, 3:21–22, John 1:1–2, 10:30, 14:16, 2 Corinthians 13:14, 1 Peter 1:2; see also Genesis 1:26, 3:22, 11:7

3. THE BIBLE IS A COMPILATION OF GOD'S WORDS AND IN ITS ORIGINAL HEBREW, GREEK, AND ARAMAIC FORM IS INERRANT AND SUFFICIENT IN ITSELF FOR TEACHING CHRISTIAN BELIEF AND PRACTICE. IT SHOULD BE INTERPRETED LITERALLY, HISTORICALLY, AND AT FACE VALUE UNLESS THE TEXT ITSELF ALLOWS FOR A DIFFERENT INTERPRETATION IN A SPECIFIC PASSAGE.

Scripture References: Exodus 20:11, Matthew 5:18, 19:4–6, 24:37–39, John 10:35, Acts 1:16, Romans 15:4, 2 Timothy 3:16, 2 Peter 1:20–21, 3:15–16, 2 Thessalonians 2:14–15, Revelation 22:18–19; see also Genesis 41:25–27, Matthew 13:18–23, 13:36–43, Revelation 1:20

4. MANKIND WAS GIVEN THE FREE CHOICE TO OBEY GOD OR REBEL AGAINST HIM IN THE GARDEN OF EDEN AND FREELY CHOSE TO REBEL BY EATING THE FORBIDDEN FRUIT FROM THE TREE OF THE KNOWLEDGE OF GOOD AND EVIL. THIS CHOICE BROUGHT DEATH, SEPARATION FROM GOD, AND A SINFUL NATURE TO THE ENTIRE HUMAN RACE.

Scripture References: Genesis 2:16–17, 3, 6:5, Isaiah 59:1–2, Romans 3:23, 5:12–18, 6:23, 1 Corinthians 15:22

5. GOD PLANNED IN ADVANCE TO SEND HIS SON INTO THE WORLD TO DIE FOR THE SINS OF MANKIND. THIS PLAN INCLUDED THE COVENANT OF BLESSING WITH ABRAHAM AND THE INSTITUTION OF THE NATION OF ISRAEL AND WAS FORESHADOWED BY THE SYSTEM OF ATONING SACRIFICES IN THE LEVITICAL LAW.

Scripture References: Genesis 22:17–18, Isaiah 53, Jeremiah 1:5, Luke 24:27, John 5:39, Acts 8:30–35, Colossians 2:17, Hebrews 10:1–23, Revelation 13:8

6. GOD BECAME MAN IN THE PERSON OF JESUS CHRIST. JESUS LIVED A SINLESS AND MORALLY PERFECT LIFE. HE WAS CRUCIFIED AT THE HANDS OF THE ROMANS AND THROUGH DEATH HE ATONED FOR THE SINS OF MANKIND. HE WAS BURIED AND ON THE THIRD DAY ROSE PHYSICALLY FROM THE DEAD, CONQUERING DEATH AND SIN. SALVATION IS FOUND IN CHRIST ALONE BY GRACE ALONE THROUGH FAITH ALONE AND NOT BY WORKS.

Scripture References: Isaiah 7:14, 9:6, Matthew 1:22–23, Luke 1:35, John 1:14, Philippians 2:6–8, Colossians 1:15, 1 John 4:2, Isaiah 53:9, John 19:4, 2 Corinthians 5:21, 1 Peter 1:18–19, 2:22, Hebrews 4:15, 1 John 3:5, Mark 15:43–47, Matthew 28:1–15, Romans 6:4, 8:11, 1 Corinthians 15:1–32, 1 Peter 1:3, Ephesians 2:8–9

7. JESUS PROMISED THAT IN ACCORDANCE WITH THE SCRIPTURES HE WOULD PHYSICALLY RETURN TO EARTH TO RESCUE HIS CHURCH, PUT AN END TO SIN, AND REIGN AS KING OVER ISRAEL AND THE WHOLE EARTH. BY HIM THE LIVING AND THE DEAD WILL BE JUDGED, SOME INHERITING ETERNAL LIFE AND OTHERS RECEIVING ETERNAL PUNISHMENT. CHRISTIANS MUST BE WATCHFUL AND READY FOR THESE EVENTS.

Scripture References: Psalms 72:8–11, Daniel 2:44, 7:13–14, Ezekiel 33:1–6, Zechariah 14:1–9, Matthew 16:27, 24:37–44, 25:1–13, 25:46, Luke 12:37–40, 17:28–30, 18:8, 21:34–36, John 5:22, 14:3, Romans 2:16, 1 Corinthians 15:52, 1 Thessalonians 4:13–18, Revelation 1:7, 11:15, 20:4–6

POSITIONS OF THE CCC

All believers and associated denominations are strongly exhorted to hold fast to these positions regardless of familial, cultural, or political pressure, recognizing that believing in and practicing biblical morality is strong evidence of one's saving faith.

Abortion is without question the murder of a child made in God's image. It should not be permitted even in the case of rape or incest as the child is innocent of any perpetrator's crime. The commission of the terrible evil of rape or incest can never justify the terrible evil of murder. In exceptional cases a mother's life may be jeopardized by pregnancy and only in this exceptional case does the CCC not take an absolute position. However, the mark of a Christian is love and sacrifice and the exemplary mother will put her child's life before her own, trusting that God will be faithful in the midst of tragic circumstances.

Adultery is intrinsically evil and never permissible under any circumstances, not only the physical act of adultery (Ex. 20:14), but also adulterous thoughts (Mt. 5:27–28).

Alcohol consumption is permissible and is in fact encouraged in some Scriptures (1 Tim. 5:23; Eccl. 9:7), but moderation is necessary. Intoxication and drunkenness are not permissible (Eph. 5:18; 1 Cor. 6:10). The Christian should never drink so much that he or she loses cognitive control and the ability to maintain a Christlike demeanor (Prov. 20:1; Prov. 23:29–35).

Anti-Semitism, a form of racism, should never be found in the thoughts, words, writings, or actions of a believer. Gentile believers have not replaced Jewish believers and in fact salvation has come from the Jews. The Apostle Paul likens the entirety of the people of God to an olive tree, which is Israel. Unbelieving Jews have been cut off from the tree and believing Gentiles have been grafted in (Rom. 11:17–24), but the roots of the tree remain Jewish through Abraham, Isaac, Jacob, and the King of the Jews—Jesus. In fact, the Bible promises that one day the Jews will return to God and all Israel will be saved (Rom. 11:25–28; Isa. 45:17; Jer. 31:1). God gave to the descendants of Abraham through Isaac and Jacob a specific area of land that they still have yet to take full possession of according to the promise. Since God is the ultimate sovereign of the earth and His word is true and the land deed still stands, Christians cannot support efforts such as the two-state solution. The Bible proclaims that judgment will befall those who divide God's covenant land (Jl. 3:1–2).

Contraception is not mentioned in Scripture except in the case of Onan who sinned by preventing his wife from becoming pregnant in order to withhold from her dead husband an heir (Gen. 38:8–10). For this reason only contraception that may result in the death of an embryo or done against the will of one's spouse is forbidden. Christians should be wise about this and research diligently before engaging in intercourse with one's spouse. Drugs such as Plan B are never permissible, but even typical hormonal contraception drugs may result in abortion and their use is thus discouraged. Natural family planning is encouraged and in all cases the husband and wife should be one in heart and mind.

Divorce is inherently evil (Mk. 10:11–12), except in the case of marital unfaithfulness (Mt. 5:32). However, even in the case of adultery it is exemplary and most commendable to extend grace and forgiveness and ultimately reconcile with one's spouse recognizing that Christ died for us while we were yet sinners (Rom. 5:8) and God has reconciled us by the death of His Son (Rom. 5:10).

Embryonic stem cell research is never permissible because the embryos are in fact children in their earliest stage of development and therefore those who destroy embryos are murdering children made in the image of God. The Bible is clear that human life begins in the womb (Job 31:15; Ps. 22:10; 139:13; Jer. 1:5; Ex. 21:22–23) and science is clear that an organism's life begins at conception.

Eugenics in most forms should be understood as evil—especially historic eugenics programs that aimed at eradicating minority populations, killing the mentally handicapped, and murdering the terminally ill. Eugenics continues today in many forms including sex-selective abortions, minority-focused placement of abortion facilities, abortion of babies with trisomy disorders, and many instances of euthanasia. These are all intrinsically evil and Christians should themselves avoid these things while preaching forcefully against them.

Euthanasia, which is the intentional killing of a man or woman by both the perpetrator and the one being killed, is unquestionably murder and must not be committed or advocated by any believer.

Fornication, which is sexual activity outside of marriage, is always sinful (Mt. 15:19; 1 Cor. 6:9). God created sex to be enjoyed within the boundaries of marriage and within those boundaries there is great freedom for husband and wife. God created sex for building unity between husband and wife (Gen. 2:24; Mk. 10:8), for pleasure (1 Cor. 7:3–9; Prov. 5:18–19; Song 4:1–16), and for producing offspring (Gen. 1:28; 9:7; Mal. 2:15) and it is only in the context of marriage that these three purposes find their ultimate fulfillment. Men and women in a romantic relationship should not cohabitate before marriage, so that they avoid fornication and the appearance of evil (1 Thess. 5:22).

Gender roles are biblical and must be upheld in the Christian community. Men and women are equal before God in regard to intrinsic value and salvation (Gen. 1:27; Gal. 3:28), but nevertheless have been given by God specific callings. The man is the head of his family—not as a coercive force, but as a servant leader (1 Cor. 11:3). The man is called by God to protect and manage his family well (1 Tim. 3:4), love his wife, and even lay his life down for her (Eph. 5:25). In regard to church leadership, men are called to exercise authority over the congregation, both in teaching to the collective assembly (1 Cor. 14:34–35) and in shepherding (1 Tim. 2:8–3:13). Women are called to respect their husbands out of willful humility (1 Pet. 3:1) and to help and encourage them (Gen. 2:18). In the Christian community women are uniquely called to teach and disciple other women (Tit. 2:3–5).

Genetic manipulation of plants and animals without combining genes from different species is permissible although the Bible does not appear to speak to this issue. Wisdom should be exercised in regard to this issue. However, the creation of hybrid species is unadvisable since God created plants and animals after their own kind (Gen. 1:11, Gen. 1:24). The creation of human/animal hybrids, three-parent babies, or babies resulting from the genetic material of two men or two women are intrinsically evil acts and Christian geneticists should seriously and prayerfully consider the spiritual implications of these creations.

Homosexuality is repeatedly condemned in the Bible as a sin and an abomination (1 Tim. 1:9–10; 1 Cor. 6:9–10; Lev. 18:22; 20:13), as well as unnatural (Rom. 1:26–28). God created sexuality for the purpose of intimacy and pleasure between a husband and wife and ultimately for bringing children into the world. Christians who struggle with homosexuality should flee temptation by any means necessary and should not define themselves by their struggle (1 Cor. 6:11).

Homosexual marriage is intrinsically evil for two reasons: first, because homosexual acts are sinful and unnatural, and second, because it is diametrically opposed to God's design for marriage, which is repeatedly defined in the Bible as the union of one man and one woman (Gen. 2:24; Mt. 19:5; Mk. 10:7; Eph. 5:31).

In Vitro Fertilization is not permissible for the same reason embryonic stem cell research is not permissible: embryos are necessarily destroyed thus the act of murder is committed.

Marrying unbelievers is not permissible for the committed Christian (2 Cor. 6:14), though having already been married before coming to faith is a common occurrence. In such a case the believer must remain committed to their unbelieving spouse and through love and faithfulness attempt to win them over with the Gospel (1 Cor. 7:12–16; 1 Pet. 3:1).

Media must be monitored and controlled in the Christian life. There is no justification, artistic or otherwise, for Christians to watch or listen to sinful things for the purpose of entertainment. There is much media a believer can enjoy, but that which is full of cursing, wonton violence, or sexuality is never permissible. The martyr Telemachus stands as an eternal symbol of this truth.

Narcotic use for the express purpose of treating an injury or disease is permissible, but narcotic use for the purpose of intoxication is a great and destructive evil to oneself, to one's family, and to one's society. There is evidence that drug intoxication is partly what was intended when the Bible speaks of the sin of sorcery.

Pornography is never permissible in any form as it is a form of adultery, or in the case of the unmarried, fornication. Pornography also promotes the objectification and abuse of women and children, is by some measures more addictive than heroine, causes permanent emotional and physical desensitization, and even induces early puberty in children exposed from a young age.

Racism is not in accord with the character of Christ who has made all believers one (Gal. 3:28; Rom. 3:29) for God does not show partiality (Acts 10:34; Rom. 2:11). Believers must not favor the rich over the poor (Jas. 2:1–9), but must show equal favor to all in regard to wealth, station, fame, or race. However, culture has greatly twisted and abused the word *racism* by extending it to include areas where believers in fact should lovingly discriminate between right and wrong: regarding religion, culture, and sinful behaviors.

Slavery, including and especially sexual slavery and trafficking, is never tolerable. Modern slavery differs greatly from biblical indentured servitude, which in certain times and cultures was lawful, in that modern slavery is illegal, always abusive, and routinely violent and coercive. With more people enslaved today than at any time in history, Christians should advocate zealously for their freedom and protection.

Speech should be Christlike in every way and "seasoned with salt" (Col. 4:6). Lies, curses, crude joking, and malicious gossip should never proceed from the mouth of a believer (Mt. 12:36; Prov. 19:5; Tit. 3:2; Eph. 5:4; 1 Tim. 5:13).

Theft is an obvious and unquestionable sin and is not dependent on circumstance (Ex. 20:15). The poor may not steal from the rich even though the rich have more and the poor have less. Instead, the believer struggling with poverty should work diligently (2 Thess. 3:10), trusting in God to provide (Mt. 6:25–34), and making his or her needs known openly to the Christian community (Acts 2:44–45). Believers should not take anything unlawfully, including intellectual property, music, or media. Believers selling products or services that they know are scams or falsely advertised are committing theft as well as lying and should cease immediately (Prov. 11:1; 20:23), returning the money that was stolen.

Transgenderism is both sinful and a great deceit. Sinful in that it defies God's created order of male and female and deceitful in that it convinces a person that they can be something that they are not nor could ever be. Christians must refer to a man in masculine terms and a female in feminine terms regardless of how that person may define himself—even if this results in physical, emotional, or legal consequences for the believer. Men should strive for masculinity and women for femininity (1 Cor. 6:9; 16:13), fully embracing God's design.

The Covenant Christian Coalition is an international, evangelical, post-denominational coalition of churches still faithful to Christ and the Gospel.

You can learn more at www.ccc.one.

SOLA FIDE · SOLA GRATIA
· SOLUS CHRISTUS ·
SOLA SCRIPTURA · SOLI DEO GLORIA

www.ingramcontent.com/pod-product-compliance
Lightning Source LLC
Chambersburg PA
CBHW060408010526
44107CB00005B/625